W9-DEQ-956

CHILTON'S
CHASSIS ELECTRONICS SERVICE MANUAL

Managing Editor John H. Weise, S.A.E. □ **Assistant Managing Editor** David H. Lee, A.S.E., S.A.E.

Service Editors Lawrence C. Braun, S.A.E., A.S.C., Dennis Carroll, Nick D'Andrea,
Jack T. Kaufmann, Robert McAnally, Ron Webb
Editorial Consultants Edward K. Shea, S.A.E., Stan Stephenson

Production Manager John J. Cantwell
Manager Editing & Design Dean F. Morgantini
Art & Production Coordinator Robin S. Miller
Supervisor Mechanical Paste-up Margaret A. Stoner
Mechanical Artists Cynthia Fiore, William Gaskins

National Sales Manager Albert M. Kushnerick □ **Assistant** Jacquelyn T. Powers
Regional Sales Managers Joseph Andrews, David Flaherty, James O. Callahan

OFFICERS
President Lawrence A. Fornasieri
Vice President & General Manager John P. Kushnerick

CHILTON BOOK COMPANY Chilton Way, Radnor, Pa. 19089
Manufactured in USA ©1986 Chilton Book Company ISBN 0–8019–7726–6
Library of Congress Catalog Card No. 85–43611
234567890 543210987

GRAND ISLAND PUBLIC LIBRARY

SAFETY NOTICE

Proper service and repair procedures are vital to the safe, reliable operation of all motor vehicles, as well as the personal safety of those performing repairs. This manual outlines procedures for servicing and repairing vehicles using safe effective methods. The procedures contain many NOTES, CAUTIONS and WARNINGS which should be followed along with standard safety procedures to eliminate the possibility of personal injury or improper service which could damage the vehicle or compromise its safety.

It is important to note that repair procedures and techniques, tools and parts for servicing motor vehicles, as well as the skill and experience of the individual performing the work vary widely. It is not possible to anticipate all of the conceivable ways or conditions under which vehicles may be serviced, or to provide cautions as to all of the possible hazards that may result. Standard and accepted safety precautions and equipment should be used when handling toxic or flammable fluids, and safety goggles or other protection should be used during cutting, grinding, chiseling, prying, or any other process that can cause material removal or projectiles.

Some procedures require the use of tools specially designed for a specific purpose. Before substituting another tool or procedure, you must be completely satisfied that neither your personal safety, nor the performance of the vehicle will be endangered.

Part numbers listed in this reference are not recommendations by Chilton for any product by brand name. They are references that can be used with interchange manuals and aftermarket supplier catalogs to locate each brand supplier's discrete part number.

Although information in this manual is based on industry sources and is as complete as possible at the time of publication, the possibility exists that some car manufacturers made later changes which could not be included here. While striving for total accuracy, Chilton Book Company cannot assume responsibility for any errors, changes, or omissions that may occur in the compilation of this data.

"No part of this publication may be reproduced, transmitted or stored in any form or by any means, electronic or mechanical, including photocopy, recording or by information storage or retrieval system without prior written permission from the publisher."

INDEX

TURN SIGNAL FLASHER, HAZARD WARNING FLASHER AND FUSE BLOCK
LOCATION CHART
1982–87 American Motors

Model	Turn Signal Flasher	Hazard Warning Flasher	Fuse Block Location
Eagle	1	2	3
Concord	1	2	3
Spirit	1	2	3

1 The turn signal flasher is plugged into a connector located on the instrument panel, behind the headlamp switch.
2 The hazard flasher is plugged directly into the fuse block.
3 The fuse panel is located on the drivers side of the dash panel, adjacent to the parking brake mechanism.

TURN SIGNAL FLASHER, HAZARD WARNING FLASHER AND FUSE BLOCK
LOCATION CHART
1982–87 Chrysler Corp.

Model	Turn Signal Flasher	Hazard Warning Flasher	Fuse Block Location
FRONT WHEEL DRIVE			
Omni	1	2	3
Horizon	1	2	3
Aries	4	5	3
Dodge 400	1	6	3
Reliant	7	8	3
LeBaron	7	5	3
LeBaron GTS	7	5	9
New Yorker	7	8	3
Laser	10	11	3
Charger	1	2	3
Turismo	1	2	3
Daytona	12	13	3
Dodge 600	7	8	3
E-Class	1	14	3
Lancer	15	15	9
Caravelle	7	8	9
Ram/Van	1	16	17
Caravan	1	2	18
Voyager	1	2	18
REAR WHEEL DRIVE			
Diplomat	1	2	3
Mirada	1	2	3
Cordoba	1	2	3
Imperial	1	2	3
New Yorker	1	2	3
Gran Fury	1	2	3
Fifth Avenue	1	2	3
Newport	1	2	3
Mini Ram/Van	1	2	18

1 The turn signal flasher is plugged directly into the fuse block.
2 The hazard flasher is plugged directly into the fuse block.
3 The fuse panel is located on the drivers side of the dash panel, adjacent to the parking brake mechanism.
4 On the 1985–87 models the turn signal flasher is plugged directly into the relay module adjacent to the fuse block. The 1982–84 models are plugged directly into the fuse block.
5 On the 1982 models the hazard flasher is plugged directly into the fuse block. On the 1983–84 models the hazard flasher is taped to the main harness and on the 1985–87 models the hazard flasher is located on the relay module adjacent to the fuse block.
6 The hazard flasher on the 1983 models, is taped to the main wiring harness.
7 On the 1982–84 models the turn signal flasher is plugged directly into the fuse block. On the 1985–87 models the turn signal flasher is clipped to the instrument panel below the fuse block.

8 On the 1982, '85, '86 and '87 models the hazard flasher is plugged directly into the fuse block. On the 1983–84 models the hazard flasher is taped to the main harness.

9 The fuse block is located in the glove box on the 1985–87 models.

10 On the 1985–87 models the turn signal flasher is plugged directly into the relay module adjacent to the fuse block. The 1984 model is plugged directly into the fuse block.

11 On the 1984 model the hazard flasher is taped to the main harness and on the 1985–87 models the hazard flasher is located on the relay module adjacent to the fuse block.

12 On the 1984 model the flasher is plugged directly into the fuse block. On the 1985–87 models the flasher is clipped to the instrument panel below the fuse block.

13 On the 1984 model the hazard flasher is taped to the main harness and on the 1985–87 models the hazard flasher is plugged directly into the fuse block.

14 On the 1982 models the hazard flasher is plugged directly into the fuse block. On the 1983–84 models the hazard flasher is taped to the main harness.

15 Both flashers are plugged directly into the relay module adjacent to the fuse block.

16 The hazard warning flasher is clipped below the fuse block.

17 The fuse block is located in a small box underneath the glove box door.

18 The fuse access panel is located under the parking brake handle on the left (driver) side of the vehicle.

TURN SIGNAL FLASHER, HAZARD WARNING FLASHER AND FUSE BLOCK LOCATION CHART
1982–87 Ford Motor Co.

Model	Turn Signal Flasher	Hazard Warning Flasher	Fuse Block Location
FRONT WHEEL DRIVE			
Escort	1	4	3
Lynx	1	4	3
EXP	1	4	3
LN7	1	4	3
Tempo	1	5	3
Topaz	1	5	3
Taurus	1	2	8
Sable	1	2	8
REAR WHEEL DRIVE			
Granada	1	6	3
Cougar	1	7	3
Mustang	1	6	3
Capri	1	6	3
Zephyr	1	6	3
Fairmont Futura	1	6	3
XR-7	1	6	3
Thunderbird	1	5	3
Continental	1	5	3
Town Car	1	2	3
LTD	1	2	3
Crown Victoria	1	2	3
Grand Marquis	1	2	3
Continental Mark VI	1	5	3
Continental Mark VII	1	5	3
Marquis	1	5	3
Aerostar	1	4	9

1 The turn signal flasher is plugged directly into the fuse block.

2 The hazard flasher is plugged directly into the fuse block.

3 The fuse panel is located on the driver's side of the dash panel, adjacent to the parking brake mechanism.

4 The hazard flasher is mounted to the instrument panel and is located between the steering column and fuse block.

5 The hazard flasher is located in the rear of the fuse block.

6 The hazard relay is attached to a relay bracket located above the glove box.

7 On the 1982 model, the hazard warning flasher is attached to a relay bracket located above the glove box. On the 1983–87 models, the hazard flasher is located in the rear of the fuse block.

8 The fuse block is located in a swing down compartment located below the parking brake release handle.

9 The fuse block is located in the lower left hand side of the instrument panel behind a plastic cover, which is held in by two fasteners.

TURN SIGNAL FLASHER, HAZARD WARNING FLASHER AND FUSE BLOCK LOCATION CHART
1982–87 General Motors Corp.

Model	Turn Signal Flasher	Hazard Warning Flasher	Fuse Block Location
BUICK			
Century	3	7	6
Skylark	3	7	6
Skyhawk	3	7	5
Electra	3	2	5
Park Avenue	3	7	5
Riviera	3	2	8
Somerset Regal	3	7	5
Regal	3	2	5
La Sabre	3	7	5
CADILLAC			
DeVille	13	9	10
Fleetwood	13	9	10
Fleetwood Brougham	11	2	10
Eldorado	11	2	10
Seville	11	2	10
Cimarron	11	12	10
CHEVROLET			
Citation	3	14	6
Caprice	1	2	5
Impala	1	2	5
Malibu	1	2	5
Monte Carlo	15	7	5
El Camino	1	2	5
Chevette	16	2	5
Celebrity	3	12	6
Cavalier	3	15	5
Camaro	15	7	5
Corvette	18	18	17
Nova	19	19	20
Sprint	19	19	5
Spectrum	19	19	5
Astro	29	29	28
OLDSMOBILE			
Omega	3	7	6
98 Regency	3	9	5
Toronado	3	2	5
Firenza	3	12	5
Calais	3	12	5
Cutlass	1	2	5
Cutlass Ciera	21	7	6
Delta 88	1	2	5
Olds 98	3	9	5
Hurst Olds	1	2	5
PONTIAC			
1000	24	2	5
2000	3	12	5
6000	3	23	22
Sunbird	15	25	5
Phoenix	15	7	6
Grand Am	3	26	5
Grand Prix	1	2	5
Parisienne	1	2	5
Bonneville	1	2	5

TURN SIGNAL FLASHER, HAZARD WARNING FLASHER AND FUSE BLOCK LOCATION CHART
1982–87 General Motors Corp.

Model	Turn Signal Flasher	Hazard Warning Flasher	Fuse Block Location
Firebird	27	7	5
Trans AM	27	7	5
Fiero	3	7	5

1 The turn signal flasher is plugged directly into the fuse block.
2 The hazard flasher is plugged directly into the fuse block
3 The turn signal flasher is located under the left side of the instrument panel on or near the steering column support.
4 On the 1982–83 models the hazard flasher is plugged directly into the fuse block. On the 1984–87 models the hazard flasher is located behind the left side of the instrument panel.
5 The fuse block is located on the cowl under the left side of the instrument panel (behind the trim panel on some later models).
6 The fuse block is located on the right hand side of the instrument panel.
7 The hazard flasher is located on the right hand side of the instrument panel, on the convenience center. On some of the later models it is located on the right hand side of the steering column brace.
8 The fuse block is located on the cowl under the left side of the instrument panel. On the later models the fuse block is located in the center of the instrument panel in front of the console.
9 The hazard flasher is located on the lower steering column trim panel on the later models and plugged directly into the fuse block on the earlier models.
10 The fuse block is located to the left of the steering column and behind the instrument panel. A mini fuse block is integral with the accessory relay panel and is attached to the left side of the fuse block on all models except for Cimarron. The Cimarron model does not use the mini fuse block.
11 The turn signal flasher is located on the right of the steering column support panel.
12 The hazard flasher is located on the left hand side of the instrument panel, on the convenience center.
13 The turn signal flasher is located on the lower steering column trim panel.
14 The hazard flasher is located on the right hand side of the instrument panel, on the convenience center. On the Citation II the hazard warning flasher is located to the left of the glove box.
15 The turn signal flasher is located on the right hand side of the instrument panel, on the convenience center.
16 The turn signal flasher is located above the brake pedal on the 82–83 models and plugged directly into the fuse block on the 1984–87 models.
17 On the 1982–83 models the fuse block is located to the left of the steering column and behind the instrument panel. On the 1984–87 models the fuse block is either accessible from a swing down unit located underneath the instrument panel near the steering column or through the glove box on the right hand side.
18 On the 1982–83 models the flasher is located on the right hand side of the instrument panel, on the convenience center. On the 1984–87 models the flasher is located behind the center of the instrument panel.
19 The turn signal and hazard flashers are located on the drivers side kick panel. In order to gain access to the unit, it will be necessary to first remove certain dash padding.
20 The fuse block is located on the left side of the vehicle behind the driver's side kick panel.
21 The turn signal flasher is located under the instrument panel near the steering column support on the early models and on the late models the flasher is located in the convenience center to the right of the glove box.
22 The fuse block is located under the right side of the instrument panel on the earlier models and in the glove box on the later models.
23 On the 1982–83 models the hazard warning flasher is located in the convenience center near or on the steering column support and on the 1984–87 models the flasher is located behind glove box.
24 The turn signal flasher is located above the brake pedal on the 1982–83 models and plugged directly into the fuse block on the 1984–87 models the turn signal flasher is located under the left side of the instrument panel on or near the steering column support.
25 The hazard flasher is located on the left side of the vehicle behind the driver's side kick panel.
26 The hazard flasher is located at the front of the console.
27 The turn signal flasher is located on the right hand side of the instrument panel, on the convenience center on the earlier models and on the later models on the right of the steering column support.
28 The fuse block is either accessible from a swing down unit located underneath the instrument panel near the steering column or through the glove box on the right hand side.
29 The turn signal and hazard warning flashers are located in the convenience center to the right of the steering column.

DOMESTIC VEHICLES

CIRCUIT BREAKERS, FUSIBLE LINKS, RELAYS, SENSORS AND COMPUTER LOCATIONS

NOTE: When using this section, some of the components may not be used on a particular vehicle. This is because either the particular component in question was used on an earlier model or a later model. This section is being published from the latest information available at the time of this publication.

AMERICAN MOTORS

Circuit Breakers

EAGLE, CONCORD AND SPIRIT

POWER WINDOWS

One 30 amp breaker located in the fuse block.

POWER DOOR LOCKS

One 30 amp breaker located in the fuse block.

POWER SEATS

One 30 amp breaker located in the fuse block.

HEADLIGHTS

One 20 amp breaker located in the headlight switch.

REAR WIPER/WASHER

One 4.5 amp breaker located in the instrument panel.

TRAILER TOWING

One 10 amp breaker located in the left rear body harness.

WINSHIELD WIPER

One 8 amp breaker located in the wiper switch.

Fusible Links

EAGLE, CONCORD AND SPIRIT

RED 16 GAUGE WIRE

It is located at the battery terminal of the starter solenoid to the main wire harness and protects the head lights and heated backlight.

PINK 20 GAUGE WIRE

It is located at the battery terminal of the horn relay to the main wire harness and protects the horn circuit.

RED 18 GAUGE WIRE

It is located at the battery terminal of the starter solenoid to the main wire harness and protects the ignition/power optional engine compartment lamp and deck lid release.

RED 18 GAUGE WIRE

It is located at the battery terminal of the starter solenoid to the main wire harness and protects the power options.

RED 14 GAUGE WIRE

It is located at the alternator to battery terminal of the starter solenoid and protects the alternator output wire.

Relays, Sensors And Computer Locations

1982-83 EAGLE, SPIRIT AND CONCORD

- **Air Temperature Sensor (6 Cyl.)** — is located in the air cleaner.
- **Coolant Temperature Switch** — is located at the rear of the intake manifold.
- **Cruise Control Regulator** — is located under the instrument panel.
- **Cruise Control Speed Sensor** — is located between the upper and lower speedometer cables.
- **Differential Valve Switch** — is located in the combination valve.
- **Electronic Control Module (ECM)** — the ECM is located behind the right side kick panel in the passenger compartment.
- **Intake Manifold Heater Switch** — is located on the side of the intake manifold.
- **Knock Sensor (6 Cyl.)** — is located in the intake manifold.
- **Oil Pressure Sensor** — is located on the right side of the block near the oil filter.
- **Oxygen Sensor** — is located in the exhaust manifold.
- **Relays** — most of all the relays (fuel pump relay, power relay, etc.) are mounted on a bracket attached to the front of the shock tower on the passenger side of the engine compartment. The horn relay is located near the fuse block.
- **TAC Sensor (4 Cyl.)** — is located in the air cleaner.
- **Thermal Electric Switch (TES)** — is installed inside the air cleaner.
- **Thermal Vacuum Switch (6 Cyl.)** — is located in the air cleaner.
- **Vacuum Switch** — is located on the right side of the engine block.
- **Wide Open-Throttle Switch** — is located on the rear of the throttle body.

1984-87 EAGLE

- **4 in. Hg Vacuum Switch** — is mounted on a bracket which is attached to the inside of the right fender.
- **10 in. Hg Vacuum Switch** — is incorporated in the same bracket as the 4 in. Hg vacuum switch.
- **A/C Relay** — is located in the engine compartment.
- **All Power Accessory Circuit Breakers** — are located in the fuse block.

• **Anti-Diesel Delay Relay** – is located on the right front inner fender panel.

• **Anti-Diesel Relay** – is located on the right front inner fender panel.

• **Choke Relay** – is located on the right front inner fender panel.

• **Cruise Control Regulator** – is located under the instrument panel.

• **Cruise Control Speed Sensor** – is located between the upper and lower speedometer cables.

• **E-Cell (Emissions) Timer** – is located under the left side of the dash panel.

• **Electronic Control Module (ECM)** – the ECM is located behind the right side kick panel in the passenger compartment.

• **Fog Light Circuit Relay** – is located on the right front inner fender panel.

• **Horn Relay** – is located on the right front inner fender panel.

• **Idle Speed Control Relay** – is located in the engine comaprtment.

• **Ignition Control Module** – is located on the right front inner fender panel.

• **Intake Manifold Heater** – is located in the bottom of the intake manifold.

• **Intake Manifold Heater Relay** – is located on the right front inner fender panel.

• **Key Lights On Warning Buzzer** – is located on the right side of the fuse block.

• **Keyless Entry Reciecver** – is located in between the sun visors.

• **Keyless Entry Relays** – are located on a bracket at the lower edge of the dash to the right of the glove box.

• **Knock Sensor** – is located in the cylinder head.

• **Load Level Compressor Relay** – is located on the load level compressor bracket.

• **Manifold Absolute Pressure Sensor** – is located in the passenger compartment under the middle of the dash panel.

• **Manifold Air/Fuel Temperature Sensor** – is located in the intake manifold in front of an intake port.

• **Oil Pressure Sensor** – is located on the right side of the block.

• **Oxygen Sensor** – is located in the exhaust manifold.

• **Rear Defogger Timer/Relay** – is located in the rear defogger switch assembly.

• **Ride Height Sensor** – is located above the right rear axle housing.

• **Seat Belt Thermal Timer/Buzzer** – is located on the left side of the fuse block.

• **Throttle Position Sensor (TPS)** – this sensor is mounted on the throttle body and connected to the throttle shaft.

• **Trailer Towing Relay** – is located in the engine compartment.

• **Windshield Wiper Interval Governor** – is located under the dash panel near the wiper switch.

CHRYSLER CORPORATION

Circuit Breakers

ALL MODELS

POWER SUN ROOF

One 15 amp circuit breaker located in the left side cowl to protect the sun roof electrical system.

HEADLIGHTS

One 20 amp breaker located in the headlight switch.

WINDSHIELD WIPERS

One 10 amp breaker located in the windshield wiper switch.

REAR WIPER AND WASHER

There is a 6 amp circuit breaker located in the fuse block for the rear wiper and washer motor on all models. This breaker also protects the rear deck lid and lift gate circuit.

CONCEALED HEADLAMP DOORS

There is a circuit breaker whick is located in a relay that protects the concealed headlamp door system.

POWER SEATS AND POWER DOOR LOCKS

There is a 30 amp breaker which is located in the fuse block that protects the power seats and door locks on all models except for the Omni, Horizon, Turismo and Charger.

POWER WINDOWS

There is a 30 amp breaker which is located in the fuse block that protects the power window motors on all models except for the Omni, Horizon, Turismo and Charger.

VANITY MIRROR

One 1.5 amp circuit breaker which is located on the visor and protects the mirror circuit.

Fusible Links

ALL MODELS

Depending on the different equipment options on the vehicle, there could be several fusible links used. Before correcting any blown fusible link, try to find out what caused it and replace or repair the problem. Never replace fusible link wire with standard wire, always use wire with hypalon insulation and make sure it is the same gauge as the original wire. The wire gauge size and color for the fusible links are as follows; black is 12 gauge, red is 14 gauge, dark blue is 16 gauge, gray is 18 gauge and orange is 20 gauge. On the front wheel drive models most of the fusible links are located in front of the left side shock tower in the engine compartment. On most rear wheel drive models the fusible links are located to the rear of the left front wheel housing.

Relay, Sensors And Computer Locations

1982-83 IMPERIAL

- **Air Flow Meter** — is located on the front of the air cleaner.

- **Air Switching Timer** — is located on the right center side of the firewall.
- **Auto Calibrator** — is located on the side of the air cleaner.
- **Back-Up Indicator Relay** — is taped to the harness near the fuse block.
- **Ballast Resistor** — is located on the right side of the firewall.
- **Brake Warning Light Switch** — is located on the left side of the frame below the master cylinder.
- **Chime Module** — is located behind the glove box.
- **EFI Coolant Switch** — is located ont he upper front of the engine block.
- **EFI Down Module** — is located on the right front inner fender well.
- **EFI Throttle Sensor** — is located in the air cleaner.
- **Electronic Fuel Metering Module** — is located on the side of the air cleaner.
- **Electronic Spark Advance** — is located on the side of the air cleaner.
- **Engine Temperature Switch** — is located on the front of the intake manifold.
- **Horn Relay** — is located in the fuse block, that is located on the left side of the pedal support bracket.
- **Illuminated Entry Relay** — is located on the lower right side of the instrument cluster under the dash panel.
- **In-Tank Fuel Pump By-Pass Relay** — is located on the right front inner fender panel.
- **Intermittent Wiper Control Module** — is located behind the instrument panel at the lower left instrument cluster.
- **Knock Sensor** — is located behind the distributor.
- **Low Washer Fluid Sensor** — is located on the washer bottle at the right rear corner of the engine compartment.
- **Oil Pressure Switch** — is located at the right side of the distributor.
- **Oxygen Sensor** — is located in the rear of the left exhaust manifold.
- **Power Antenna Module** — is located behind the instrument panel at the lower left instrument cluster.
- **Power Module** — is located on the front of the throttle body.
- **Seatbelt Warning Buzzer** — is located in the fuse block, that is located on the left side of the pedal support bracket.
- **Speed Control Servo** — is located on the left rear inner fender panel.
- **Speed Switch** — is located in the speedometer cable at the left front inner fender panel.
- **Starter Relay** — is located in the upper left dash panel.
- **Stop Lamp Switch Relay** — is located on the left front inner fender well.
- **Throttle Body Switch Relay** — is located on the left front inner fender well.
- **Time Delay Relay** — is located in the fuse block, that is located on the left side of the pedal support bracket.
- **Vacuum Sensor** — is located in the center of the instrument panel.

1982-83 OMNI AND HORIZON

- **A/C Clutch Cycling Switch** — is located on the expansion valve.
- **A/C Low Pressure Switch** — is located on the expansion valve.
- **A/C Thermal Switch** — is located on the expansion valve.

- **Anti-Diesel Relay** – is located on the left front inner fender panel.
- **Audible Message Center Control** – is located under the dash above the glove box.
- **Bulkhead Disconnect** – is located at the left rear corner of the engine compartment.
- **Carburetor Switch** – is located at the end of the idle stop on the carburetor.
- **Coolant Switch** – is located on the thermostat housing.
- **Coolant Temperature Sensor (1.6L)** – is located on the thermostat housing.
- **Coolant Temperature Switch** – is located on the top left side of the 1.6L engine and on right front section of the 1.7L and 2.2L engines.
- **Cooling Fan Switch** – is located on the side of the radiator.
- **Heater Blower Motor Resistor** – is located on the heater.
- **Horn Relay** – is located on the upper right side of the fuse block.
- **Oil Pressure Switch** – is located on the left side of the 1.7L engine and on the right front side of the 1.6L and 2.2L engine.
- **Oxygen Sensor** – is located in the exhaust manifold.
- **Seatbelt Warning Buzzer** – is located on the fuse block.
- **Spark Control Computer** – is located in the left front corner of the engine compartment.
- **Spark Control Module** – is located in front of the battery.
- **Speed Control Servo** – is located on the bottom of the battery tray.
- **Starter Relay** – is located on the left front shock housing.
- **Time Delay Relay** – is taped the the harness near the fuse block.
- **Vacuum Transducer** – is located on the spark control computer.

1984-87 OMNI, HORIZON, CHARGER AND TURISMO

- **A/C Clutch Cut-Out Relay** – is located on the left inner fender panel.
- **A/C Clutch Cycling Switch** – is located on the expansion valve.
- **A/C-Heater Blower Motor Resistor** – is located on the right side of the heater box.
- **A/C Low Pressure Switch** – is located on the expansion valve.
- **A/C Thermal Switch** – is located on the expansion valve.
- **Ambient Temperature Sensor** – is located on the hood latch support strut.
- **Anti-Diesel Relay** – is located on the left front inner fender panel.
- **Audible Message Center Control** – is located under the dash above the glove box.
- **Brake Fluid Level Sensor** – is located in the master cyliner.
- **Bulkhead Disconnect** – is located at the left rear corner of the engine compartment.
- **Coolant Level Sensor** – is located in the radiator overflow bottle.
- **Coolant Switch** – is located on the thermostat housing.
- **Coolant Temperature Sensor** – is located on the thermostat housing.
- **Cooling Fan Motor Relay** – is located on the left front shock housing.
- **Cooling Fan Motor Relay** – is located on the left shock tower.
- **Cooling Fan Switch** – is located on the side of the radiator.

- **Diagnostic Connector** – is located on the right front shock tower.
- **Distance Sensor** – is located on the transaxle end of the speedometer.
- **EFI Logic Module** – is located on the right kick panel.
- **EFI Power Module** – is located in the left front corner of the engine compartment.
- **Engine Oil Level Sensor** – is located near the thermostat housing.
- **Horn Relay** – is located on the upper right side of the fuse block.
- **Illuminated Entry Relay** – is located on the lower right dash panel.
- **Intermittent Wiper Control Unit** – is located on the brake pedal support bracket.
- **Knock Sensor** – is located on the top right side of the engine.
- **Low Fuel Relay** – is located on the rear of the instrument panel.
- **Low Windshield Washer Fluid Sensor** – is located on the top of the washer bottle.
- **Manifold Absolute Pressure Sensor** – is located above the logic module on the right side kick panel.
- **Oil Pressure Switch** – is located on the lower left side of the engine block.
- **Oxygen Sensor** – is located in the exhaust manifold.
- **Rear Window Defrost Timer** – is mounted on the end of the defrost switch.
- **Rear Wiper/Washer Circuit Breaker** – is located in the fuse block.
- **Seatbelt Warning Buzzer** – is located on the fuse block.
- **Spark Control Computer** – is located in the left front corner of the engine compartment.
- **Spark Control Module** – is located in front of the battery.
- **Speed Control Servo** – is located on the bottom of the battery tray.
- **Speed Sensor** – is located on the left front inner fender panel.
- **Starter Relay** – is located on the left front shock housing.
- **Tachometer Drive Module** – Is located on the rear of the instrument cluster.
- **Throttle Position Sensor** – is located on top of the throttle body.
- **Time Delay Relay** – is taped the the harness near the fuse block.
- **Trunk/Liftgate Release Relay** – is located on the lower right instrument panel brace.
- **Vacuum Transducer** – is located on the spark control computer.

1982-87 NEW YORKER, DODGE 600, E CLASS AND CARAVELLE (1985)

- **A/C Clutch Cycling Switch (2.6L)** – is located on the expansion valve.
- **A/C Cut-Out Relay** – is located on the lower left front inner fender panel.
- **A/C-Heater Blower Resistor** – is located under the upper right side of the instrument panel.
- **A/C Low Pressure Switch** – is located on the right side of the expansion valve.
- **A/C Thermal Switch (2.2L)** – is located on the expansion valve.
- **Audible Message Center Control** – is located under the dash panel above the glove box.
- **Audible Message Vacuum Switch** – is located at the left front inner fender panel.
- **Automatic Shut Down Relay** – is located on the upper right side of the cowl.

- **Carburetor Switch (2.2L)** – is located at the end of the idle stop on the carburetor.
- **Chime Warning Module** – is located under the dash panel above the glove box.
- **Coolant Switch** – is located on the thermostat housing on the 2.2L engine and behind the distributor on the 2.6L engine.
- **Cooling Fan Motor Relay** – is located on the left front shock housing.
- **Cooling Fan Switch** – is located on the left side of the radiator.
- **Diagnostic Connector** – is located on the right side of the dash panel.
- **Distance Sensor** – is located in the speedometer cable at the left front inner fender panel.
- **EFI Logic Module** – is located at the right side of the cowl.
- **EFI Power Module** – is located in the left front section of the engine compartment.
- **Engine Oil Level Sensor** – is located near the thermostat housing.
- **Fuel Flow Sensor** – is located in the fuel line at the right front side of the carburetor.
- **Fuel Pump Relay (EFI)** – is located on the upper right kick panel.
- **Horn Relay** – is located on the bottom of the fuse block.
- **Ignition Time Delay Relay** – Is located on the bottom of the fuse block.
- **Intermittent Wiper Control Unit** – is located on the bracket on the left lower instrument panel reinforcement.
- **Knock Sensor** – is located on the rear of the intake manifold.
- **Lift Gate Release Relay** – is located on the lower right instrument panel brace.
- **Low Washer Fluid Sensor** – is located on the washer fluid bottle.
- **Manifold Absolute Pressure Sensor (2.2L EFI)** – is located on the upper right kick panel.
- **Oil Pressure Switch** – is located on the lower left side of the engine block on the 2.2L engine or near the oil filter on the 2.6L engine.
- **Oxygen Sensor (2.2L)** – is located in the exhaust manifold.
- **Power Antenna Relay** – is located on the lower right instrument panel brace.
- **Spark Control Computer** – is located near the ignition coil.
- **Spark Control Module** – is located in front of the battery.
- **Speed Control Servo** – is located at the bottom of the battery tray.
- **Speed Sensor** – is located on the left front inner fender panel on the 2.2L engine and on the right front inner fender panel on the 2.6L engine.
- **Starter Relay** – is located on the left front shock tower.
- **Vacuum Transducer (2.2L Carb.)** – is located on the spark control computer.

1982-83 MIRADA AND CORDOBA

- **All Power Accessories Circuit Breakers** – are located in the fuse block.
- **Ballast Resistor** – is located on the center of the right front inner fender panel.
- **Brake Warning Light Switch** – is located on the master cyliner.
- **Carburetor Switch (V8)** – is located on the lower right side of the carburetor.
- **Charge Temperature Switch** – is located on the intake manifold.
- **Chime Module** – is located behind the glove box.

- **Coolant Switch (6 Cyl.)** – is located on the front of the cylinder head.
- **Coolant Temperature Sensor** – is located on the front of the cylinder head on the 6 cylinder engines and on the front of the intake manifold on the V8 engines.
- **EGR Time Relay Control** – is located on the right side of the firewall.
- **EGR Vacuum Timer (6 Cyl.)** – is located on the outboard side of the right strut on the dash panel.
- **Electronic Control Unit Module** – is located on the center of the right side of the firewall.
- **Electronic Control Unit Relay** – is located on the center of the right front inner fender panel.
- **Electronic Control Unit Throttle Control** – is located on the right side of the firewall.
- **Electronic Ignition Control Unit** – is located on the right front fender side shield.
- **Engine Temperature Switch (V8)** – is located on the front of the intake manifold.
- **Electronic Throttle Control Timer** – is located on the outboard side of the right strut on the dash panel.
- **Horn Relay** – is located in the fuse block, on the left side of the brake pedal support bracket.
- **Illuminated Entry Relay** – is located on the lower right side of the instrument cluster under the dash panel.
- **Intermittent Wiper Control Module** – is located behind the instrument panel, at the lower left cluster area.
- **Knock Sensor (V8)** – is located on the intake manifold.
- **Low Washer Fluid Sesnor** – is located on the washer fluid bottle.
- **Oil Pressure Switch** – is next the oil filter on the 6 cylinder engine and on the right side of the distributor on the V8 engines.
- **Oxygen Sensor** – is located in the exhaust manifold.
- **Power Antenna Module** – is located behind the instrument panel, at the lower left cluster area.
- **Seat Belt Warning Buzzer** – is located in the fuse block, on the left side of the brake pedal support bracket.
- **Spark Control Computer (V8)** – is located on the left side of the air cleaner.
- **Speed Control Servo** – is located on the left rear inner fender panel.
- **Starter Relay** – is located in the upper left side of the firewall.
- **Throttle Control Timer (6 Cyl.)** – is located in the center of the dash panel.
- **Time Delay Relay** – is located in the fuse block, on the left side of the brake pedal support bracket.

1982-84 FIFTH AVENUE, GRAN FURY AND DIPLOMAT

- **Accessory Power Relay** – is located on the left side of the brake pedal support bracket.
- **All Power Accessories Circuit Breakers** – are located in the fuse block.
- **Brake Warning Light Switch** – is located on the master cyliner.
- **Charge Temperature Switch** – is located on the intake manifold.
- **Chime Module** – is located on the instrument panel left reinforcement bracket.
- **Coolant Temperature Sensor** – is located on or near the thermostat housing.
- **EGR Time Relay Control** – is located on the right side of the firewall.
- **EGR Vacuum Timer (6 Cyl.)** – is located on the outboard side of the right strut on the dash panel.

• **Electronic Control Unit Module** – is located on the center of the right side of the firewall.

• **Electronic Control Unit Throttle Control** – is located on the right side of the firewall.

• **Electronic Ignition Control Unit** – is located on the right front fender side shield.

• **Electronic Throttle Control Timer** – is located on the outboard side of the right strut on the dash panel.

• **Engine Temperature Switch (V8)** – is located on the front of the intake manifold.

• **Horn Relay** – is located in the fuse block, on the left side of instrument panel.

• **Ignition Ballast Resistor** – is located on the center of the right front inner fender panel.

• **Illuminated Entry Relay** – is located on the lower right side of the brake pedal support brace.

• **Intermittent Wiper Control Module** – is located behind the right side of the instrument panel.

• **Knock Sensor** – is located on the top right side of the engine.

• **Low Washer Fluid Sesnor** – is located on the washer fluid bottle.

• **Oil Pressure Switch** – is located on the lower left side of the block.

• **Oxygen Sensor** – is located in the exhaust manifold.

• **Power Antenna Module** – is located behind the instrument panel, at the lower left cluster area.

• **Seat Belt Warning Buzzer** – is located in the fuse block, on the left side of the instrument panel.

• **Spark Control Computer** – is located on the left side of the air cleaner.

• **Speed Control Servo** – is located on the left front inner fender panel.

• **Starter Relay** – is located in the upper left side of the firewall.

• **Throttle Control Timer (6 Cyl.)** – is located in the center of the dash panel.

• **Time Delay Relay** – is located in the fuse block, on the left side of the instrument panel.

1985-87 FIFTH AVENUE, GRAN FURY, NEWPORT AND DIPLOMAT

• **Accessory Power Relay** – is located on the left side of the brake pedal support bracket.

• **All Power Accessories Circuit Breakers** – are located in the fuse block.

• **Ambient Temperature Sensor** – is located under the right side of the dash panel.

• **Brake Warning Light Switch** – is located on the master cyliner.

• **Carburetor Switch (V8)** – is located on the lower right side of the carburetor.

• **Charge Temperature Switch** – is located on the intake manifold.

• **Chime Module** – is located on the instrument panel left reinforcement bracket.

• **Coolant Switch (6 Cyl.)** – is located on the front of the cylinder head.

• **Coolant Temperature Sensor** – is located on the front of the cylinder head on the 6 cylinder engines and on the front of the intake manifold on the V8 engines.

• **Engine Temperature Switch (V8)** – is located on the front of the intake manifold.

• **Horn Relay** – is located in the fuse block, on the left side of instrument panel.

• **Ignition Ballast Resistor** – is located on the center of the right front inner fender panel.

• **Illuminated Entry Relay** – is located on the lower right side of the brake pedal support brace.

• **Intermittent Wiper Control Module** – is located behind the right side of the instrument panel.

• **Knock Sensor (V8)** – is located on the intake manifold.

• **Low Washer Fluid Sesnor** – is located on the washer fluid bottle.

• **Oil Pressure Switch** – is next the oil filter on the 6 cylinder engine and on the right side of the distributor on the V8 engines.

• **Oxygen Sensor** – is located in the exhaust manifold.

• **Power Door Lock Relay** – is located on the lower right kick panel.

• **Rear Window Defrost Relay** – is located on the end of the rear window defrost switch.

• **Seat Belt Warning Buzzer** – is located in the fuse block, on the left side of the instrument panel.

• **Spark Control Computer** – is located on the left side of the air cleaner.

• **Starter Relay** – is located in the upper left side of the firewall.

• **Time Delay Relay** – is located in the fuse block, on the left side of the instrument panel.

• **Vacuum Transducer** – is located on the spark control computer.

1982-83 ARIES AND RELIANT

• **A/C Clutch Cycling Switch (2.6L)** – is located on the expansion valve.

• **A/C-Heater Blower Resistor** – is located under the upper right side of the instrument panel.

• **A/C Low Pressure Switch** – is located on the right side of the expansion valve.

• **A/C Thermal Switch (2.2L)** – is located on the expansion valve.

• **Audible Message Vacuum Switch** – is located at the left front inner fender panel.

• **Carburetor Switch (2.2L)** – is located at the end of the idle stop on the carburetor.

• **Coolant Switch** – is located on the thermostat housing on the 2.2L engine and behind the distributor on the 2.6L engine.

• **Cooling Fan Motor Relay** – is located on the left front shock housing.

• **Cooling Fan Switch** – is located on the left side of the radiator.

• **Distance Sensor** – is located in the speedometer cable at the left front inner fender panel.

• **Fuel Flow Sensor** – is located in the fuel line at the right front side of the carburetor.

• **Horn Relay** – is located on the bottom of the fuse block.

• **Intermittent Wiper Control Unit** – is located on the bracket on the left lower instrument panel reinforcement.

• **Lift Gate Release Relay** – is located on the lower right instrument panel brace.

• **Low Washer Fluid Sensor** – is located on the washer fluid bottle.

• **Oil Pressure Switch** – is located on the lower left side of the engine block on the 2.2L engine or near the oil filter on the 2.6L engine.

• **Oxygen Sensor (2.2L)** – is located in the exhaust manifold.

• **Spark Control Computer (2.2L)** – is located near the ignition coil.

• **Spark Control Module (2.2L)** – is located in front of the battery.

• **Speed Control Servo** – is located at the bottom of the battery tray.

• **Speed Control Switch** – is located at the rear of the battery.

11

- **Speed Sensor** – is located on the left front inner fender panel on the 2.2L engine and on the right front inner fender panel on the 2.6L engine.
- **Starter Relay** – is located on the left front shock tower.
- **Vacuum Transducer (2.2L Carb.)** – is located on the spark control computer.

1984-87 ARIES AND RELIANT

- **A/C Cut-Out Relay** – is located on the left front inner fender panel.
- **A/C-Heater Blower Resistor** – is located on the heater housing.
- **All Power Accessories Circuit Breakers** – are located in the fuse block.
- **Ambient Temperature Sensor** – is located on the hood latch support strut.
- **Audible Message Center Control** – is located above the glove box.
- **Brake Warning Light Switch** – is located on the master cylinder.
- **Bulkhead Disconnect** – is located at the left rear side of the engine compartment.
- **Coolant Level Sensor** – is located in the radiator overflow bottle.
- **Coolant Temperature Sensor** – is located on the thermostat housing.
- **Cooling Fan Motor Relay** – is located on the left front shock tower.
- **Distance Sensor** – is located in the speedometer cable on the left front inner fender panel.
- **Door Lock Relay** – is located under the right side of the dash panel.
- **Engine Temperature Sensor** – is located on the side of the block.
- **Fuel Flow Sensor** – is located in the fuel line at the right front side of the carburetor.
- **Horn Relay** – is located on the bottom of the fuse block.
- **Ignition Time Delay Relay** – is located above the fuse block.
- **Illuminated Entry Relay** – is located above the glove box.
- **Intermittent Wiper Control Unit** – is located on the bracket on the left lower instrument panel reinforcement.
- **Liftgate Release Relay** – is located on the lower right instrument panel brace.
- **Liftgate Release Relay (Wagon)** – is located on the right lower instrument panel reinforcement.
- **Low Washer Fluid Sensor** – is located on the washer fluid bottle.
- **Oxygen Sensor** – is located in the exhaust manifold.
- **Rear Window Defrost Timer** – is mounted on the end of the defrost switch.
- **Seat Belt Buzzer** – is located above the glove box.
- **Spark Control Computer** – is located near the ignition coil.
- **Spark Control Module** – is located in front of the battery.
- **Speed Sensor** – is located on the left inner fender panel.
- **Starter Relay** – is located on the left front shock tower.
- **Transaxle Pressure Sensor** – is located on the side of the transaxle.
- **Vacuum Transducer** – is located on the spark control computer.

1982-84 LEBARON AND DODGE 400

- **A/C Clutch Cycling Switch (2.6L)** – is located on the expansion valve.

- **A/C-Heater Blower Resistor** – is located under the upper right side of the instrument panel.
- **A/C Low Pressure Switch** – is located on the right side of the expansion valve.
- **A/C Thermal Switch (2.2L)** – is located on the expansion valve.
- **Audible Message Vacuum Switch** – is located at the left front inner fender panel.
- **Carburetor Switch (2.2L)** – is located at the end of the idle stop on the carburetor.
- **Chime Warning Module** – is located above the glove box.
- **Coolant Switch** – is located on the thermostat housing on the 2.2L engine and behind the distributor on the 2.6L engine.
- **Cooling Fan Motor Relay** – is located on the left front shock housing.
- **Cooling Fan Switch** – is located on the left side of the radiator.
- **Distance Sensor** – is located in the speedometer cable at the left front inner fender panel.
- **Fuel Flow Sensor** – is located in the fuel line at the right front side of the carburetor.
- **Horn Relay** – is located on the bottom of the fuse block.
- **Intermittent Wiper Control Unit** – is located on the bracket on the left lower instrument panel reinforcement.
- **Lift Gate Release Relay** – is located on the lower right instrument panel brace.
- **Low Washer Fluid Sensor** – is located on the washer fluid bottle.
- **Oil Pressure Switch** – is located on the lower left side of the engine block on the 2.2L engine or near the oil filter on the 2.6L engine.
- **Oxygen Sensor (2.2L)** – is located in the exhaust manifold.
- **Spark Control Computer (2.2L)** – is located near the ignition coil.
- **Spark Control Module (2.2L)** – is located in front of the battery.
- **Speed Control Servo** – is located at the bottom of the battery tray.
- **Speed Sensor** – is located on the left front inner fender panel.
- **Starter Relay** – is located on the left front shock tower.
- **Time Delay Relay** – is located on the fuse block.
- **Vacuum Transducer (2.2L Carb.)** – is located on the spark control computer.

1985-87 LANCER AND LEBARON GTS

- **A/C Clutch Cut-Out Relay** – is located on the left front inner fender panel.
- **A/C Clutch Cycling Switch** – is located on the expansion valve.
- **A/C-Heater Blower Resistor** – is located under the upper right side of the instrument panel.
- **A/C Low Pressure Switch** – is located on the right side of the expansion valve.
- **Audible Message Center Control** – is located above the glove box.
- **Audible Message Vacuum Switch** – is located at the right front inner fender panel.
- **Brake Fluid Level Sensor** – is located on the master cylinder.
- **Chime Warning Module** – is located on the back of the glove box.
- **Coolant Level Sensor** – is located in the radiator overflow bottle.
- **Coolant Temperature Sensor** – is located on the thermostat housing.
- **Cooling Fan Motor Relay** – is located on the left front shock housing.

- **Distance Sensor** – is located on the transaxle end of the speedometer cable.
- **EFI Logic Module** – is located on the right kick panel.
- **EFI Power Module** – is located in the left front corner of the engine compartment.
- **Engine Oil Level Sensor** – is located near the thermostat housing.
- **Gauge Alert Module** – is located on the back of the instrument cluster.
- **Horn Relay** – is located on the relay block.
- **Ignition Time Delay Relay** – is located on the relay block.
- **Illuminated Entry Relay** – is located on the back of the glove box assembly.
- **Intermittent Wiper Control Unit** – is located at the bottom of the steering column.
- **Knock Sensor** – is located on the top right side of the engine.
- **Low Washer Fluid Sensor** – is located on the washer fluid bottle.
- **Oil Pressure Sending Unit** – is located on the lower left side of the block.
- **Oxygen Sensor** – is located in the exhaust manifold.
- **Rear Window Defrost Timer** – is mounted on the end if the defrost switch.
- **Relay Block** – is located behind the cup holder on the right side of the dash panel.
- **Starter Relay** – is located on the left front shock tower.
- **Tachometer Drive Module** – is located on the back of the instrument cluster.

1984-87 LASER AND DAYTONA

- **A/C Clutch Cut-Out Relay** – is located on the left front inner fender panel.
- **A/C-Heater Blower Resistor** – is located on the heater housing.
- **All Power Accessories Circuit Breakers** – are located in the fuse block.
- **Audible Message Center Control** – is located above the glove box.
- **Bulkhead Disconnect** – is located at the left rear side of the engine compartment.
- **Chime Warning Module** – is located on the back of the glove box.
- **Coolant Temperature Sensor** – is located on the thermostat housing.
- **Cooling Fan Motor Relay** – is located on the left front inner fender panel.
- **EFI Logic Module** – is located on the right kick panel.
- **EFI Power Module** – is located in the left front corner of the engine compartment.
- **Engine Oil Level Sensor** – is located near the thermostat housing.
- **Engine Speed Sensor** – is located in the speedometer cable below the master cylinder.
- **Fuel Pump Relay** – is located on the right kick panel.
- **Headlight Outage Sensor** – is located on the fuse/relay block.
- **Horn Relay** – is located on the bottom of the fuse/relay block.
- **Ignition Time Delay Relay** – is located on the fuse/relay block.
- **Illuminated Entry Relay** – is located on the back of the glove box assembly.
- **Knock Sensor** – is located on the intake manifold.
- **Liftgate Release Relay** – is located at the lower right instrument panel reinforcement.
- **Low Washer Fluid Sensor** – is located on the washer fluid bottle.

- **Manifold Absolute Pressure Sensor** – is located on the right kick panel.
- **Oil Pressure Sending Unit** – is located on the engine block, below the water outlet.
- **Oxygen Sensor** – is located in the exhaust manifold.
- **Rear Window Defrost Timer** – is mounted on the end if the defrost switch.
- **Starter Relay** – is located on the left front shock tower.
- **Throttle Position Sensor** – is located on the throttle body housing.
- **Turbo Boost Vacuum Module** – is located on the right kick panel above the logic module.

1986-87 SHADOW AND SUNDANCE

- **A/C Clutch Cut-Out Relay** – is located in front of the left front shock tower, on the inner fender panel.
- **A/C-Heater Blower Resistor** – is located on the heater housing.
- **A/C Low Pressure Switch** – is located in the refrigerant line near the right front shock tower and the "H" valve.
- **All Power Accessories Circuit Breakers** – are located in the fuse block.
- **Brake Warning Switch** – is located on the left front frame rail.
- **Charge Temperature Switch (2.2L Turbo)** – is located next the the knock sensor on top of the engine block.
- **Chime Warning Module** – is located under the right side of the instrument panel, above the glove box.
- **Coolant Temperature Sending Unit** – is located in the engine block, behind the A/C compressor.
- **Coolant Temperature Sensor** – is located near the thermostat housing.
- **Cooling Fan Relay** – is located on the left front shock tower.
- **Distance Sensor** – on the engine block near the starter motor.
- **Fuse Block** – is located under the lower left side of the instrument panel.
- **Intermittent Wiper Control** – is located behind the center of the instrument panel.
- **Knock Sensor (2.2L Turbo)** – is located on the top of the engine block near the fuel rail.
- **Logic Module** – is located on the right side kick panel.
- **Low Washer Fluid Sensor** – is located in the washer fluid bottle.
- **Manifold Absolute Pressure Sensor** – is located on the right kick panel.
- **Oil Pressure Switch** – is located on the engine block behind the oil filter.
- **Oxygen Sensor** – is located in the exhaust manifold.
- **Power Module** – is located in the left front corner of the engine compartment.
- **Relay (Block) Module** – is located under the glove box access cover.
- **Spark Control Computer** – is located on the left front inner fender panel, next to the battery tray and the radiator overflow bottle.
- **Speed Control Servo** – is located under the battery tray.
- **Starter Relay** – is located on the left front shock tower.
- **Throttle Body Temperature Sensor (2.2L EFI)** – is located near the throttle body asembly.
- **Throttle Position Sensor** – is located near the throttle body.
- **Vacuum Transducer** – is located on the spark control computer.

1984-87 MINI RAM VAN, VOYAGER AND CARAVAN

• **A/C-Heater Blower Resistor** – is located on the right of the firewall.
• **A/C Relay** – is located on the left front shock tower.
• **All Power Accessories Circuit Breakers** – are located in the fuse block.
• **Audible (Chimes) Tone Generator** – is located under the instrument panel in between the radio and the steering column.
• **Bulkhead Disconnect** – is located in the left rear corner of the engine compartment.
• **Cooling Fan Motor Relay** – is located on the left front shock tower.
• **Distance Sensor** – is located on the transaxle case, near the starter.
• **Engine Speed Sensor (2.6L Calif.)** – is located in the right front corner of the engine compartment.
• **Engine Temperature Sensor (2.2L)** – is located on the thermostat housing.
• **Horn Relay** – is located on the bottom of the fuse/relay block.
• **Ignition Time Delay Relay** – is located on the fuse/relay block.

• **Illuminated Entry Relay** – is located on the back of the glove box assembly.
• **Intermittent Wiper Control Unit** – is located under the instrument panel to the right of the steering column.
• **Liftgate Release Relay** – is located below the fuse/relay block.
• **Low Fuel Relay** – is located on the rear of the instrument cluster.
• **Low Washer Fluid Sensor** – is ocated on top of the washer fluid bottle.
• **Oil Pressure Sending Unit (2.2L)** – is located on the engine block, near the thermostat housing.
• **Oil Pressure Sending Unit (2.6L)** – is located on the engine block, near the oil filter.
• **Oxygen Sensor (2.2L)** – is located on the exhaust manifold, near the exhaust pipe flange.
• **Rear Window Defrost Timer** – is mounted on the end if the defrost switch.
• **Spark Control Computer (2.2L)** – is located in the left front corner of the engine compartment.
• **Starter Relay** – is located on the left front shock tower.
• **Vacuum Transducer (2.2L Carb.)** – is located on the spark control computer.

COMPONENT LOCATIONS

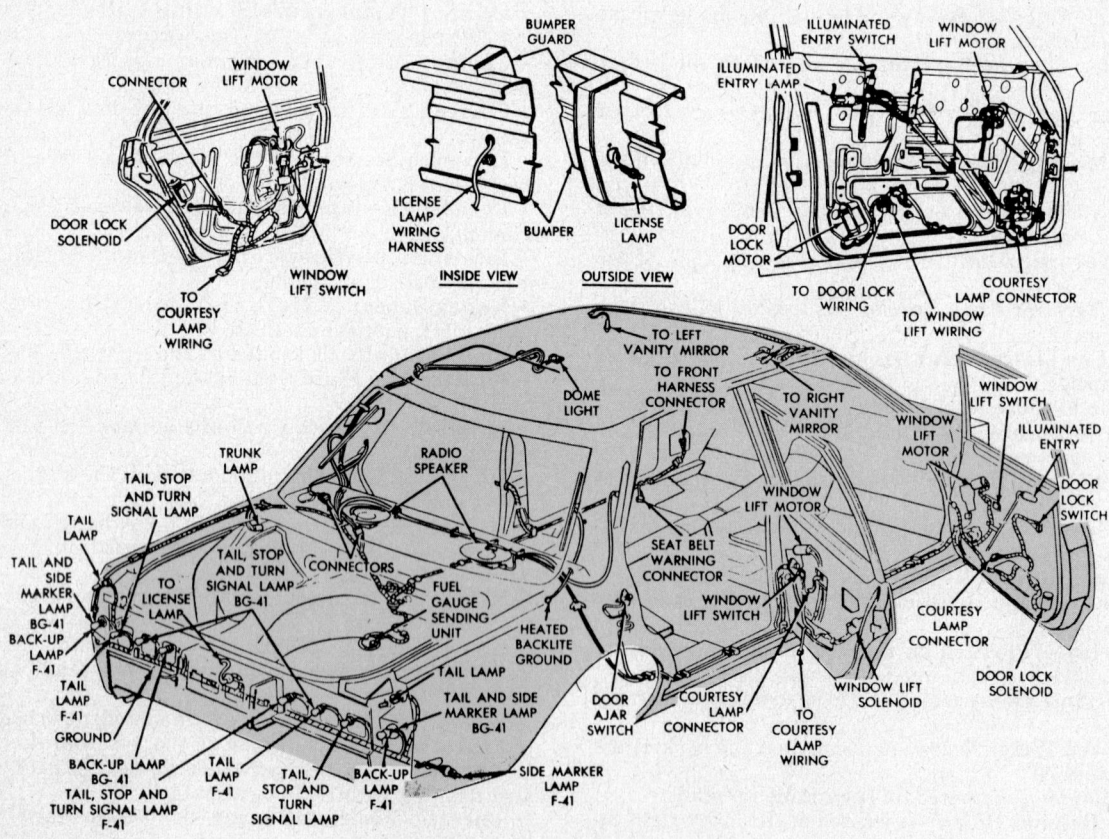

Body Compartment Electrical Component Identification (B, F, G 4 Door)

1983 rear wheel drive models

COMPONENT LOCATIONS

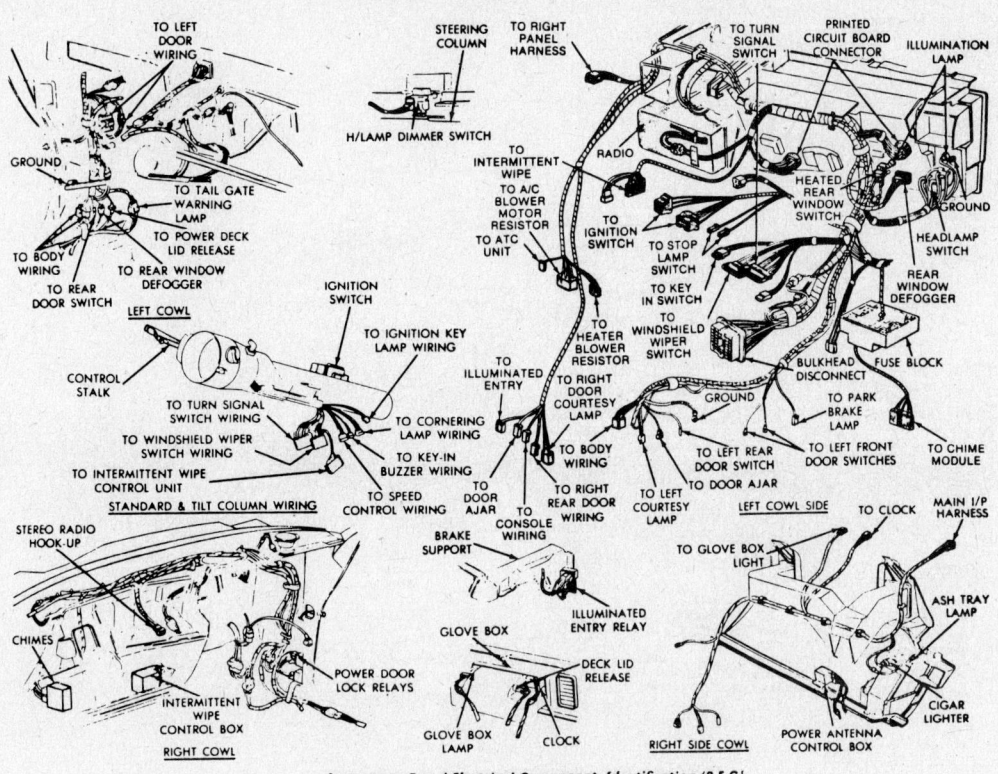

Instrument Panel Electrical Component Identification (B,F,G)

1983 rear wheel drive models

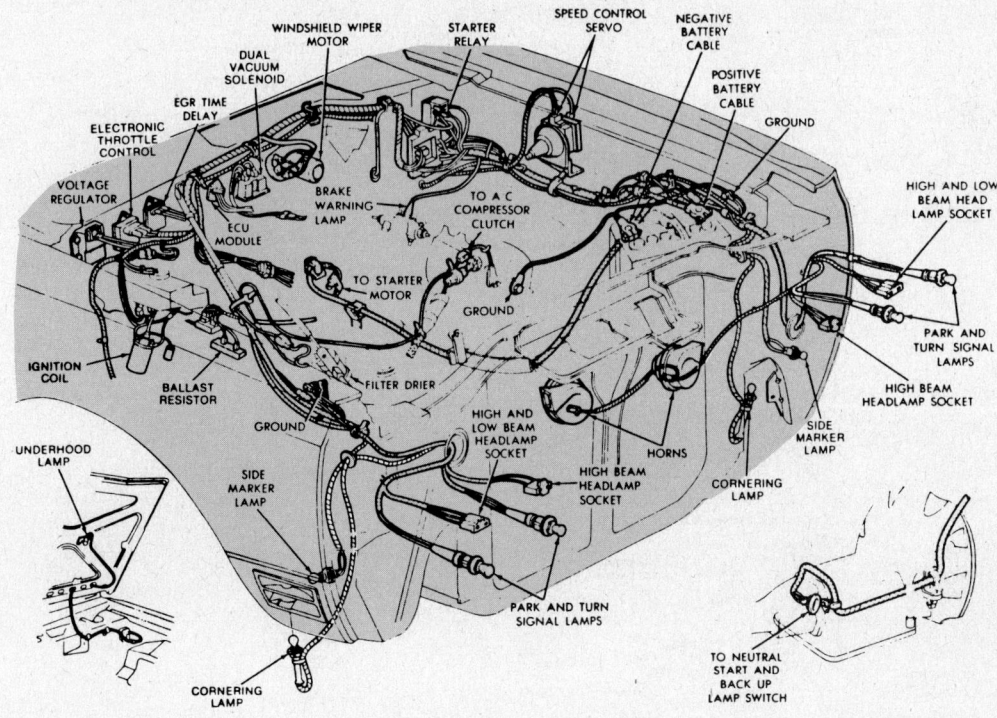

Engine Compartment Electrical Component Identification (B,F,G)

1983 rear wheel drive models

COMPONENT LOCATIONS

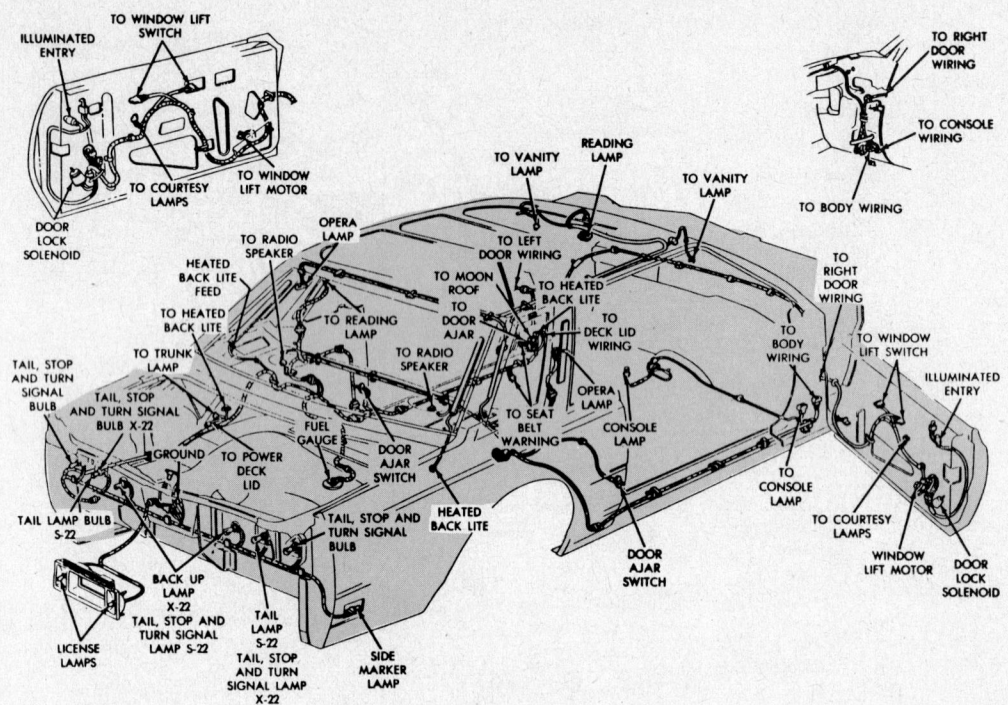

Body Compartment Electrical Component Identification (X-S)

1983 Cordoba and Mirada

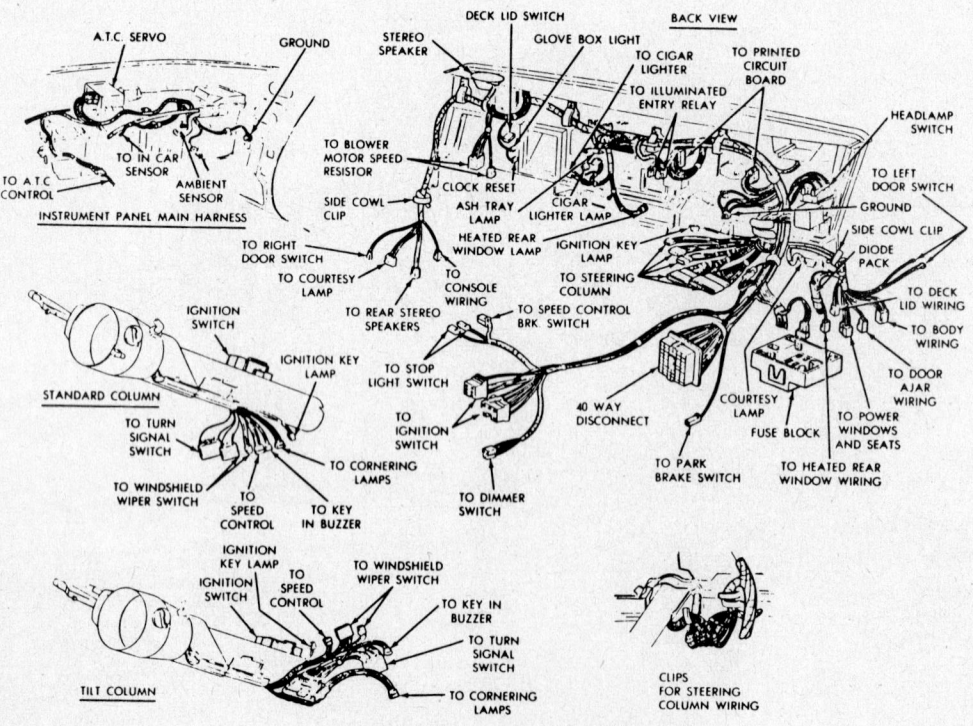

Instrument Panel Electrical Component Identification (X-S)

1983 Cordoba and Mirada

COMPONENT LOCATIONS

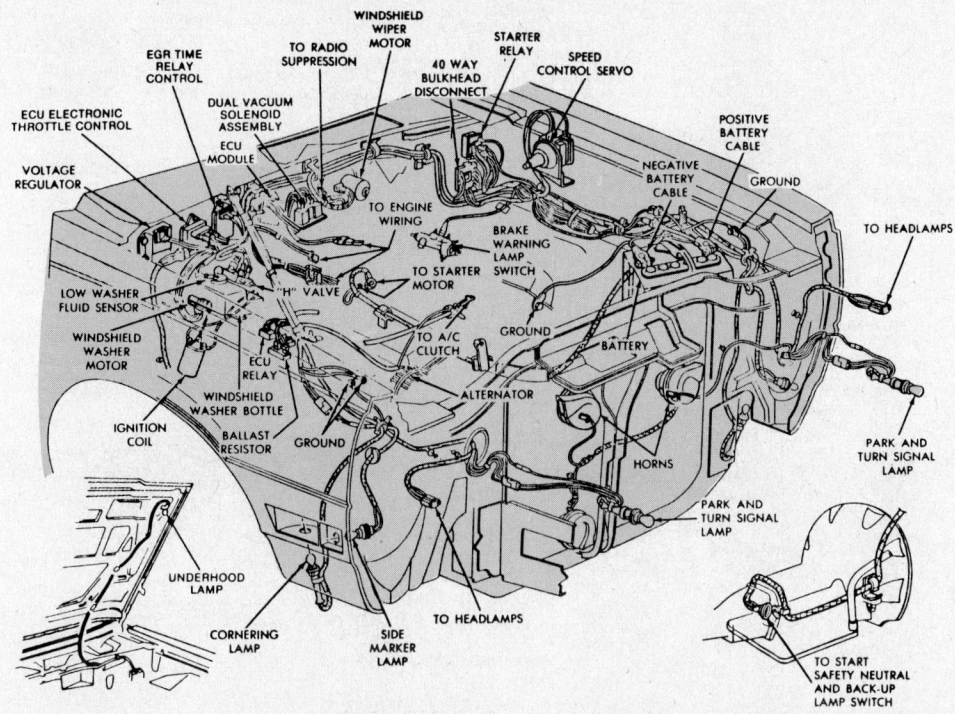

Engine Compartment Electrical Component Identification (X-S)

1983 Cordoba and Mirada

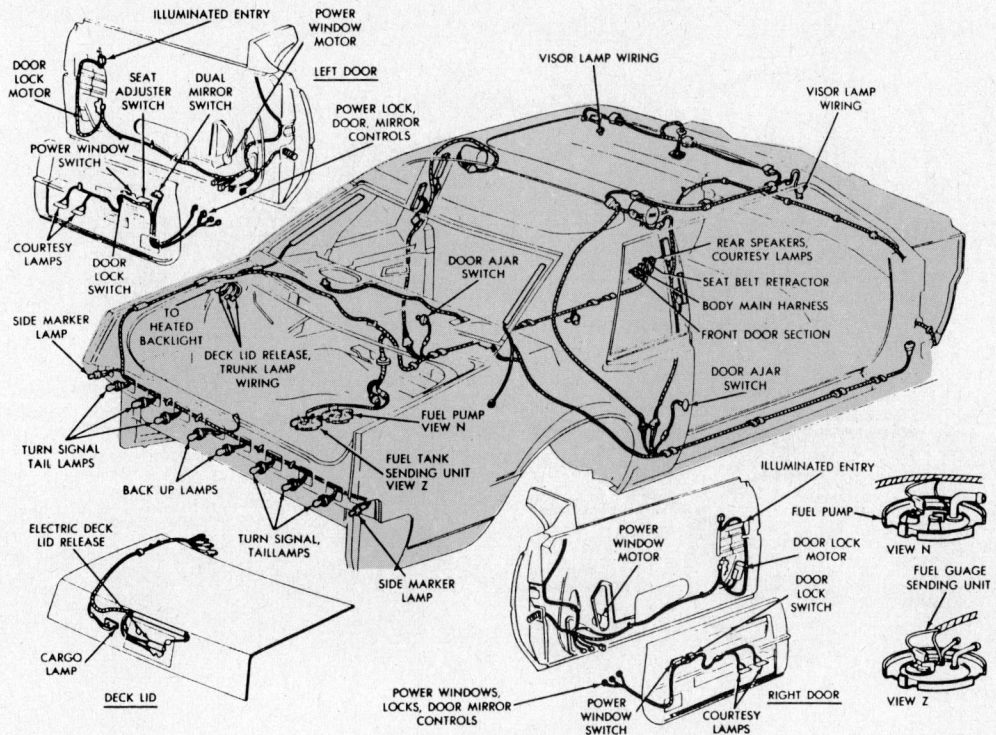

Body Compartment Electrical Component Identification (Y)

1983 Imperial

COMPONENT LOCATIONS

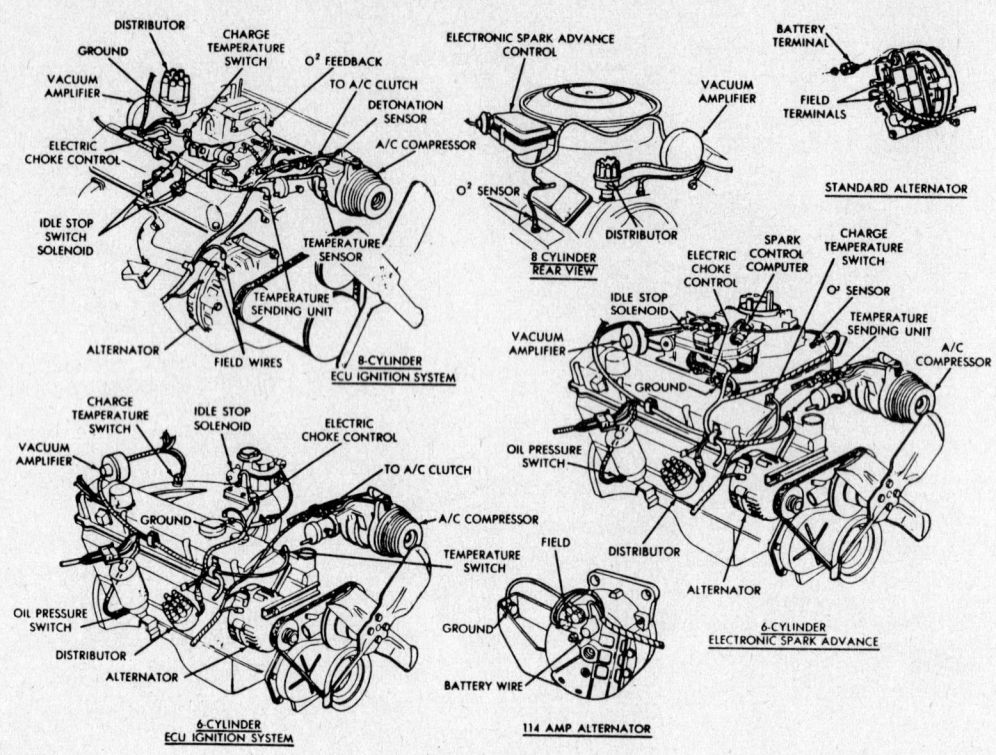

Engine Component Identification (B,F,G,S,X)

1983 rear drive models except Imperial

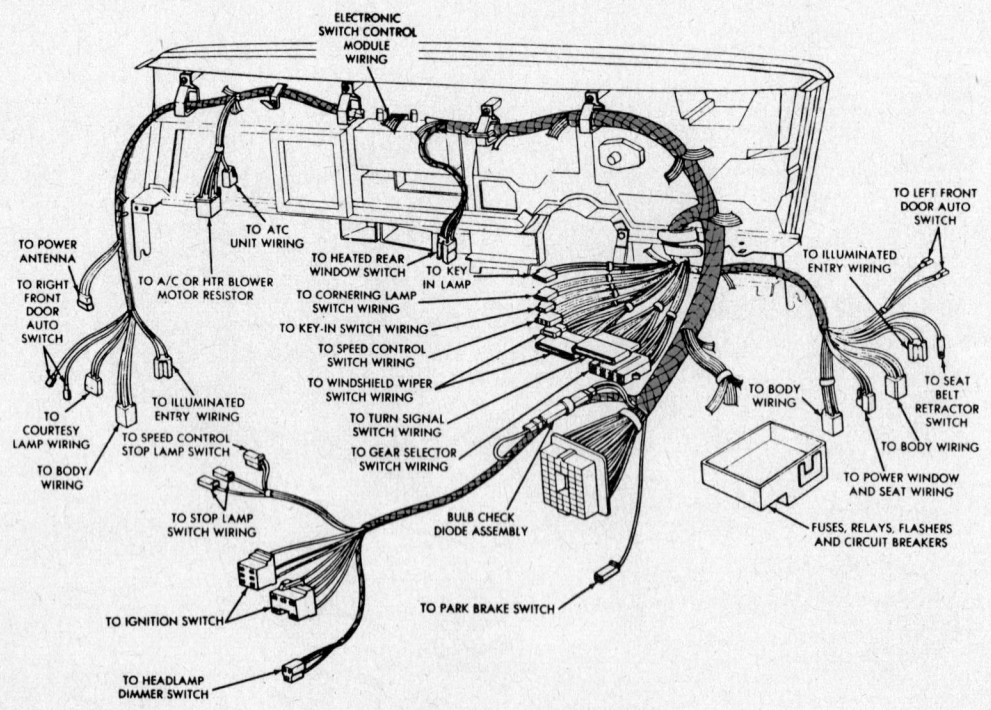

Instrument Panel Electrical Component Identification (Y)

1983 Imperial

COMPONENT LOCATIONS

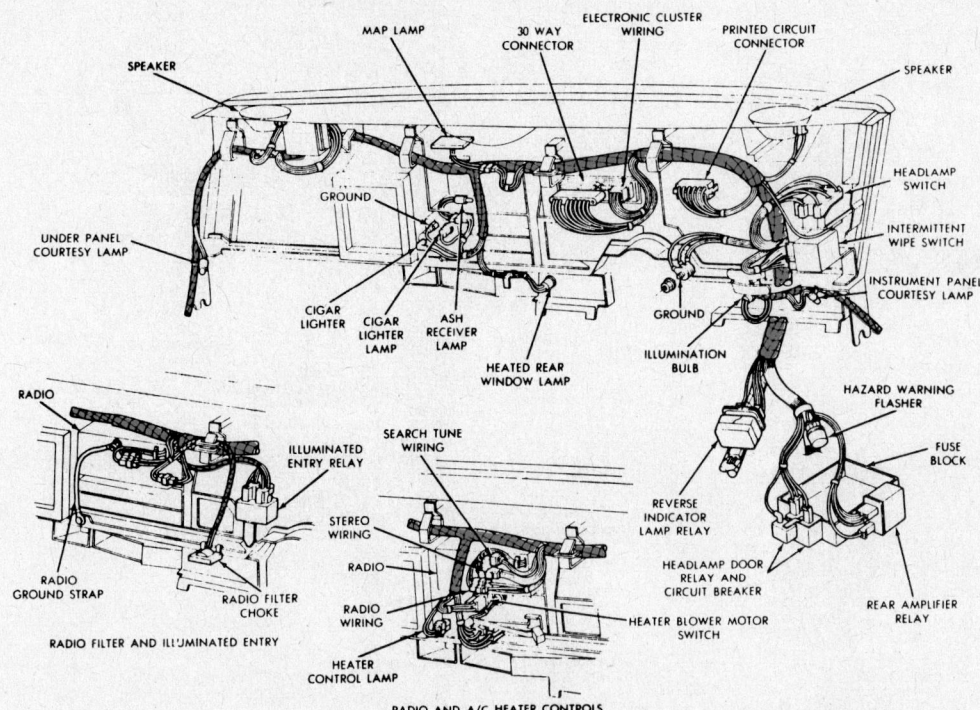

Instrument Panel Electrical Component Identification (Y)

1983 Imperial

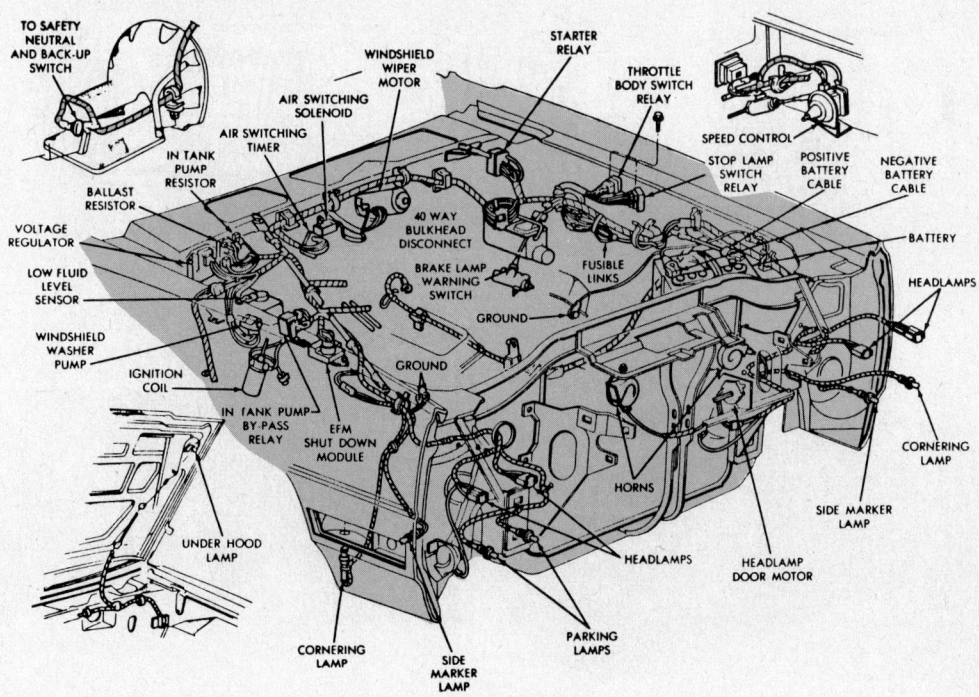

Engine Compartment Electrical Component Identification (Y)

1983 Imperial

COMPONENT LOCATIONS

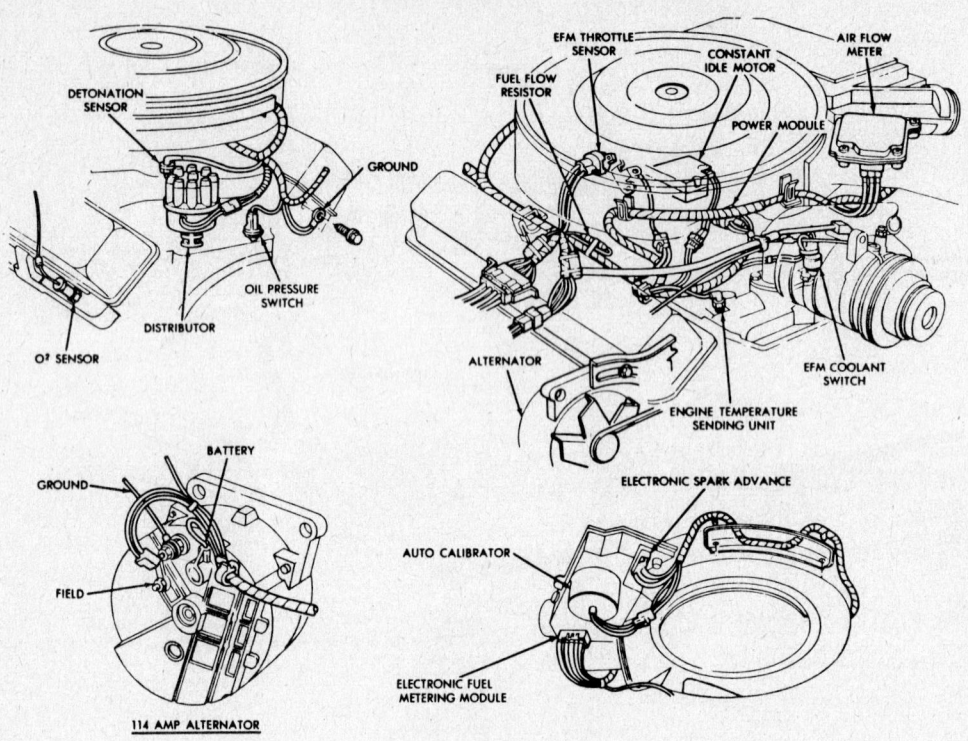

Engine Component Identification (Y)

1983 Imperial

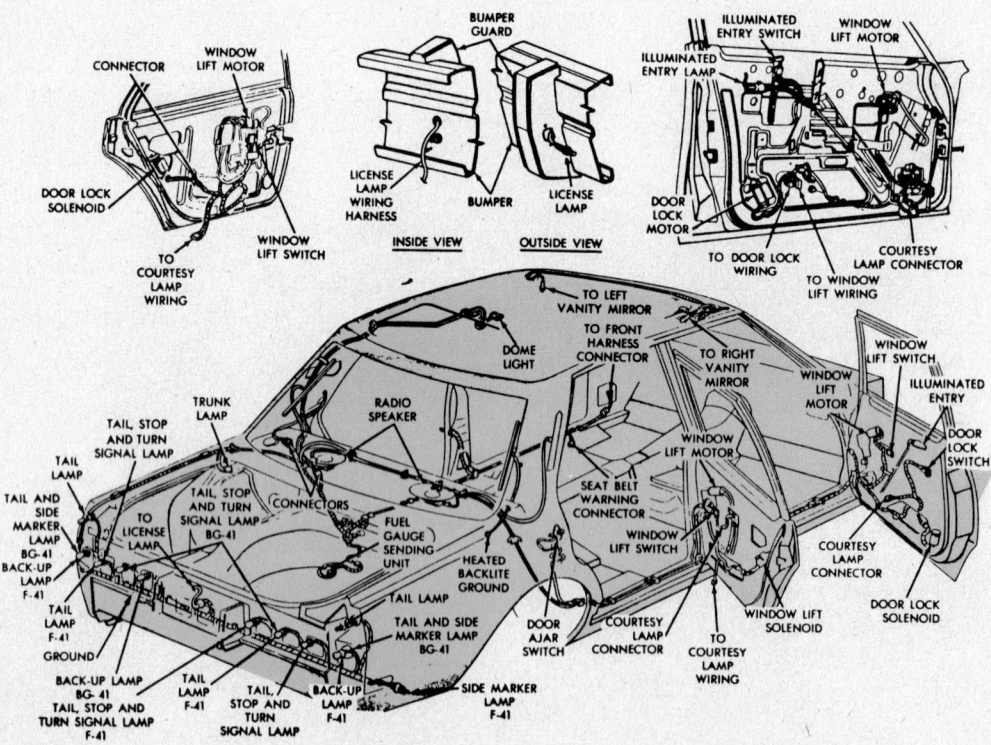

Body Compartment Electrical Component Identification M/B,F,G

1984 Fifth Avenue, Diplomat, Gran Fury and Newport

COMPONENT LOCATIONS

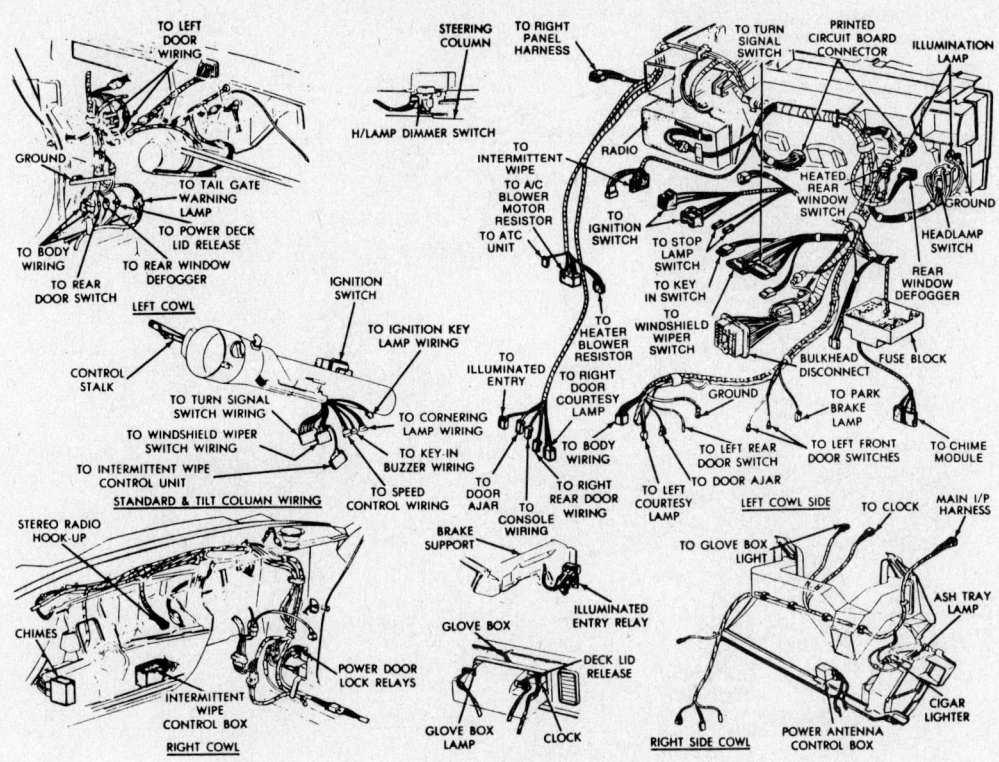

Instrument Panel Electrical Component Identification M/B,F,G

1984 Fifth Avenue, Diplomat, Gran Fury and Newport

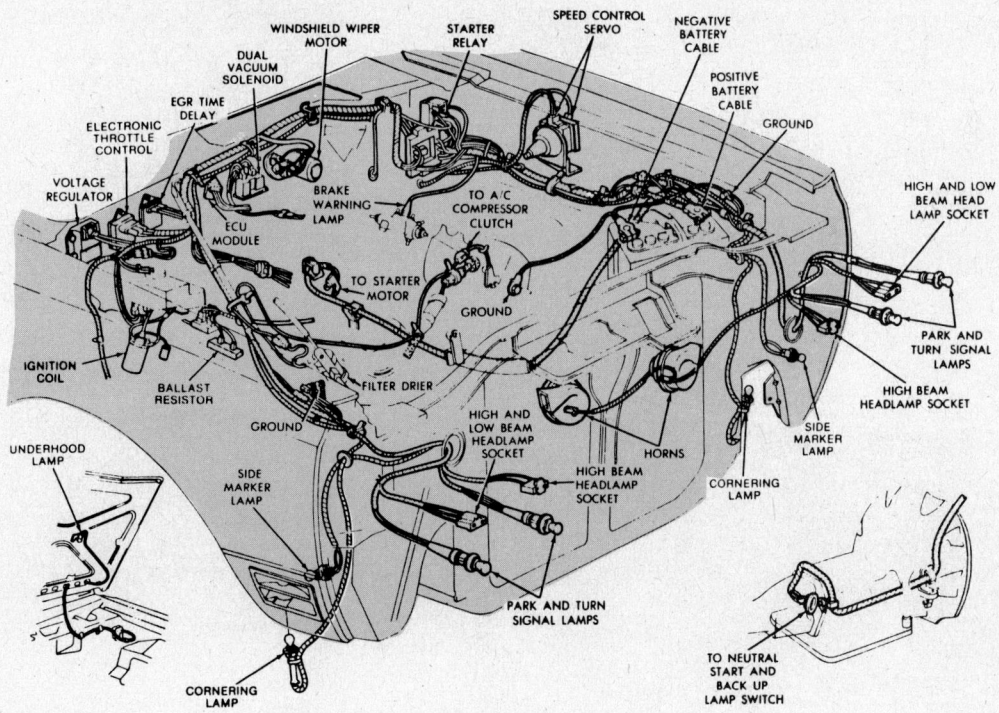

Engine Compartment Electrical Component Identification M/B,F,G

1984 Fifth Avenue, Diplomat, Gran Fury and Newport

COMPONENT LOCATIONS

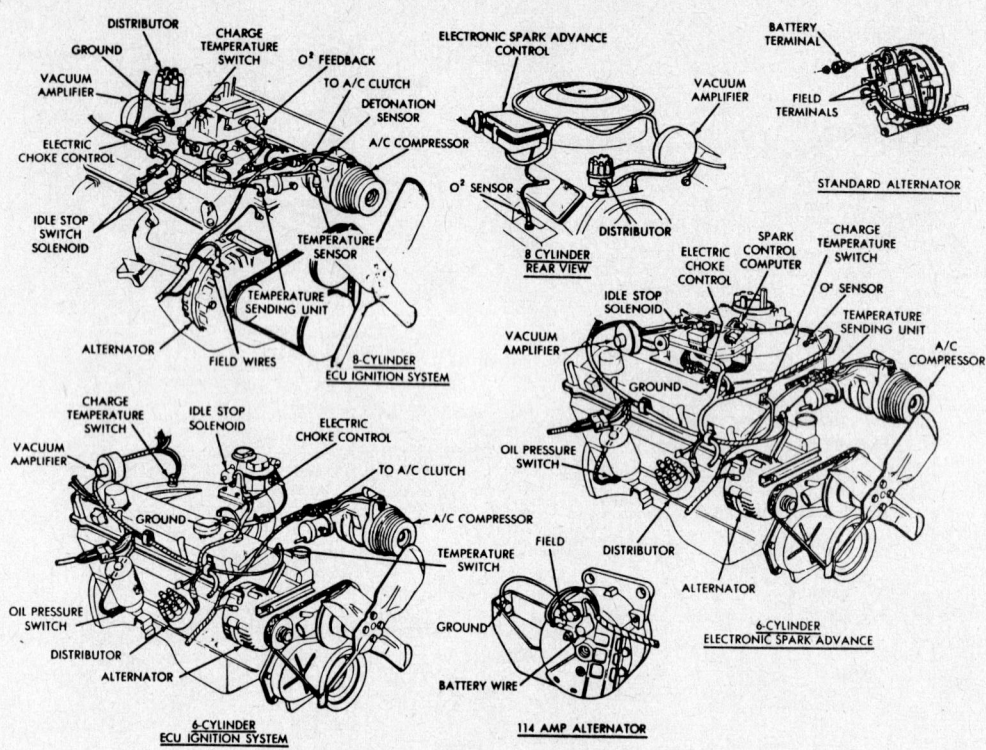

Engine Component Identification M/B,F,G

1984 Fifth Avenue, Diplomat, Gran Fury and Newport

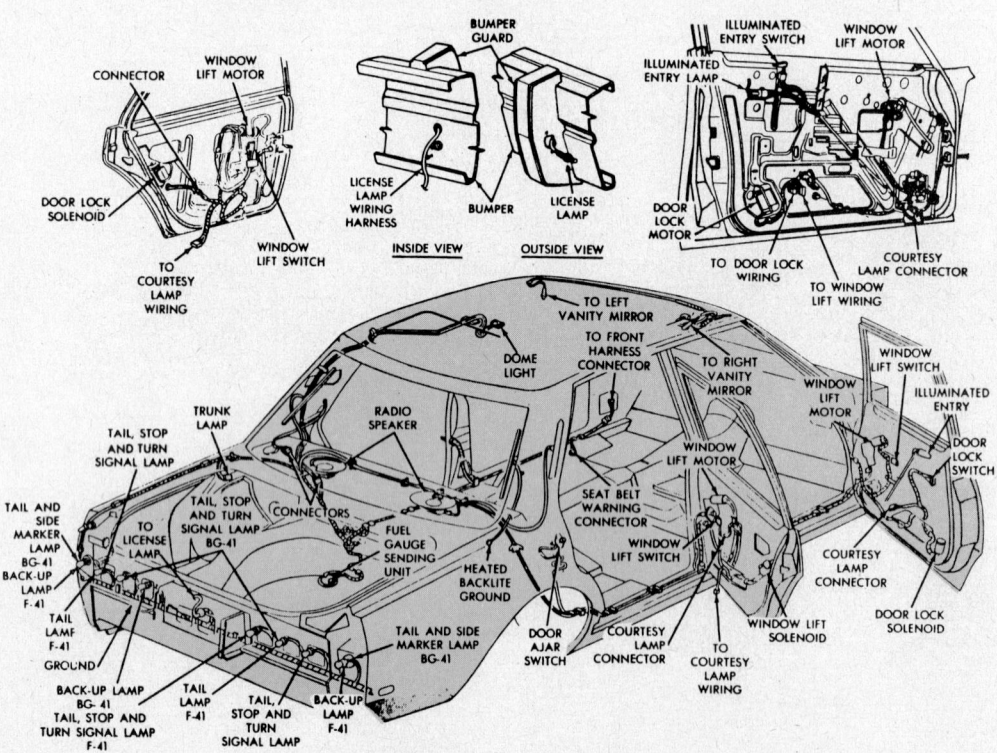

Body Compartment Wiring and Component Identification

1985-86 Fifth Avenue, Diplomat, Gran Fury and Newport

COMPONENT LOCATIONS

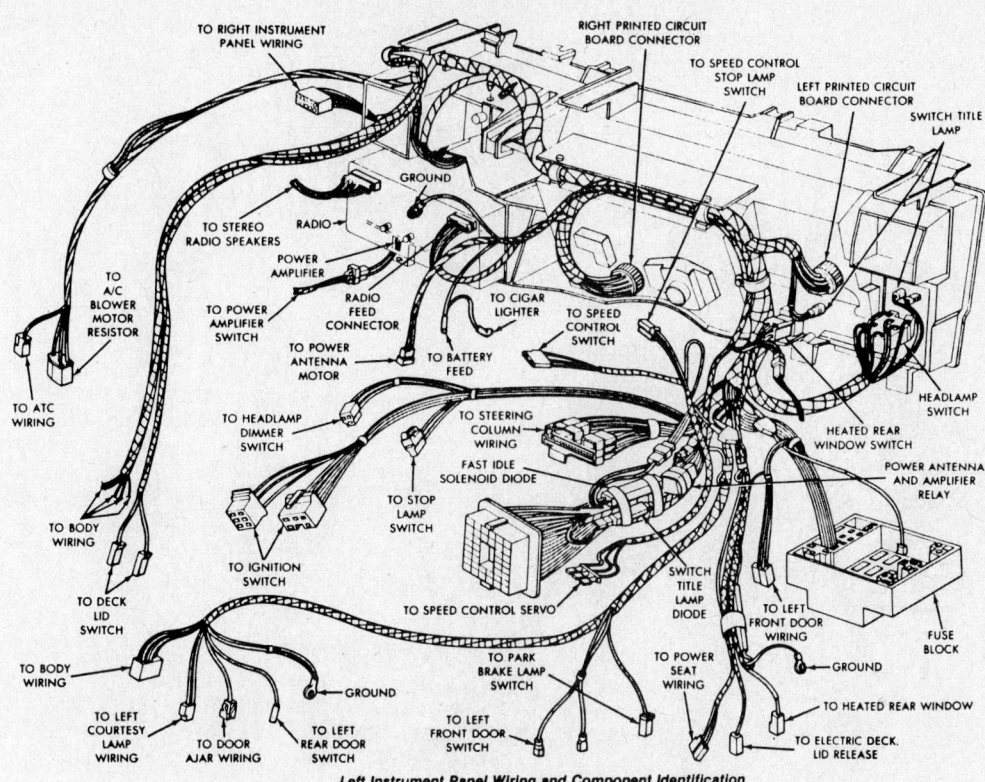

Left Instrument Panel Wiring and Component Identification

1985-86 Fifth Avenue, Diplomat, Gran Fury and Newport

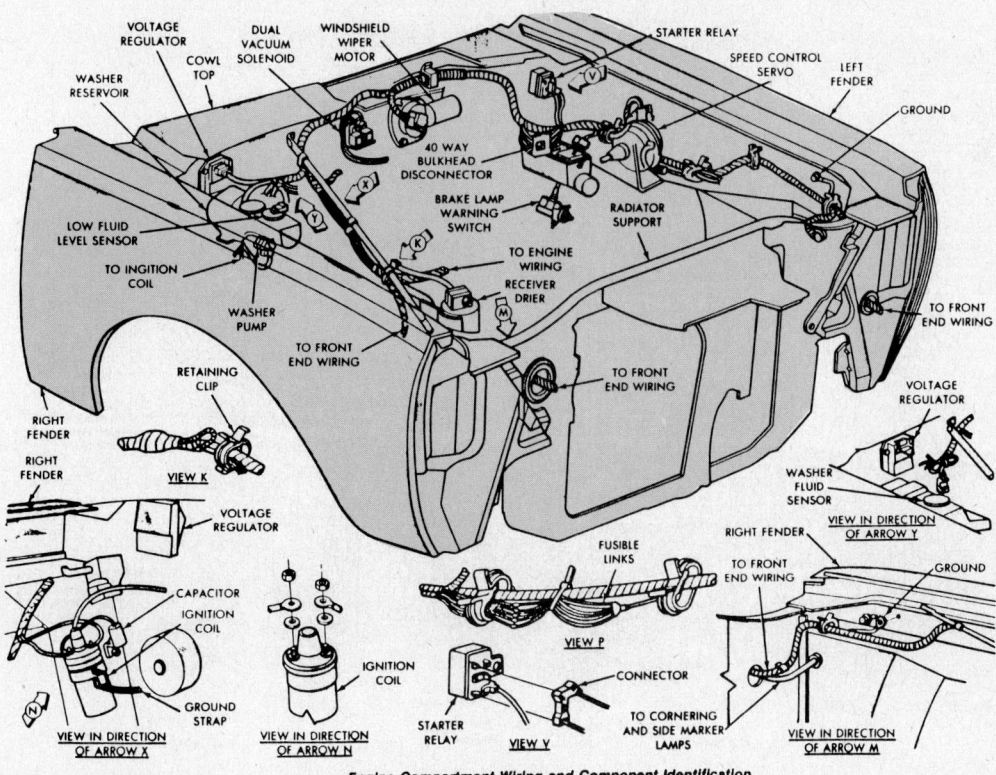

Engine Compartment Wiring and Component Identification

1985-86 Fifth Avenue, Diplomat, Gran Fury and Newport

COMPONENT LOCATIONS

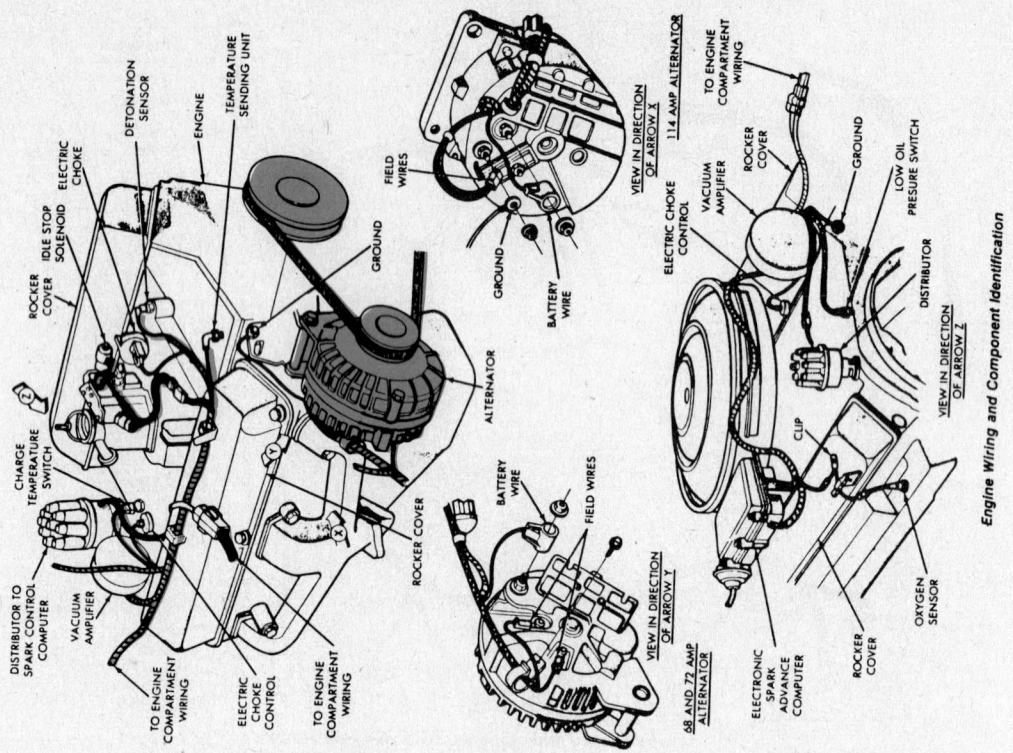

Engine Wiring and Component Identification

1985-86 Fifth Avenue, Diplomat, Gran Fury and Newport

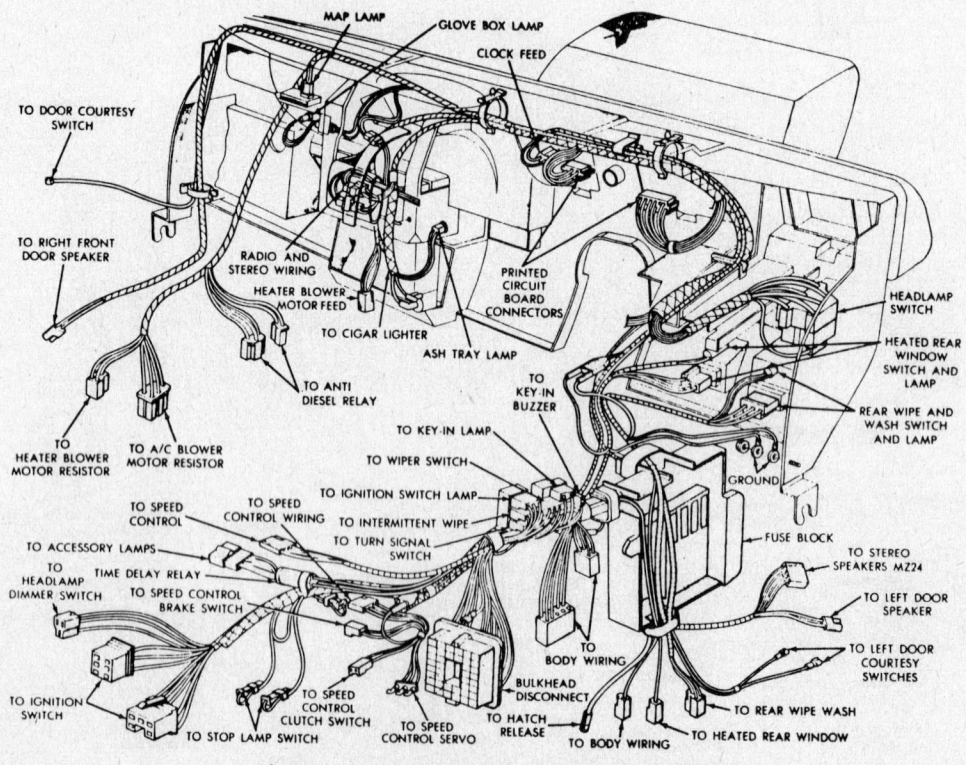

Instrument Panel Wiring and Component Identification (MZ-24-28-44)

1983 Horizon, Omni, Turismo and Charger

COMPONENT LOCATIONS

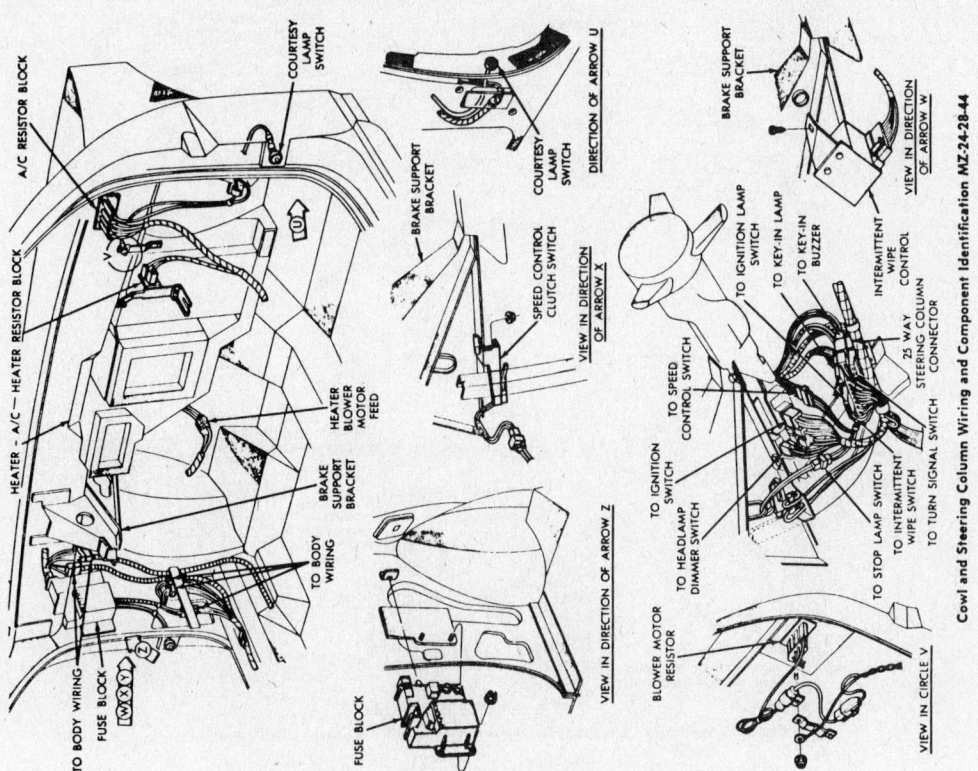

1983 Horizon, Omni, Turismo and Charger

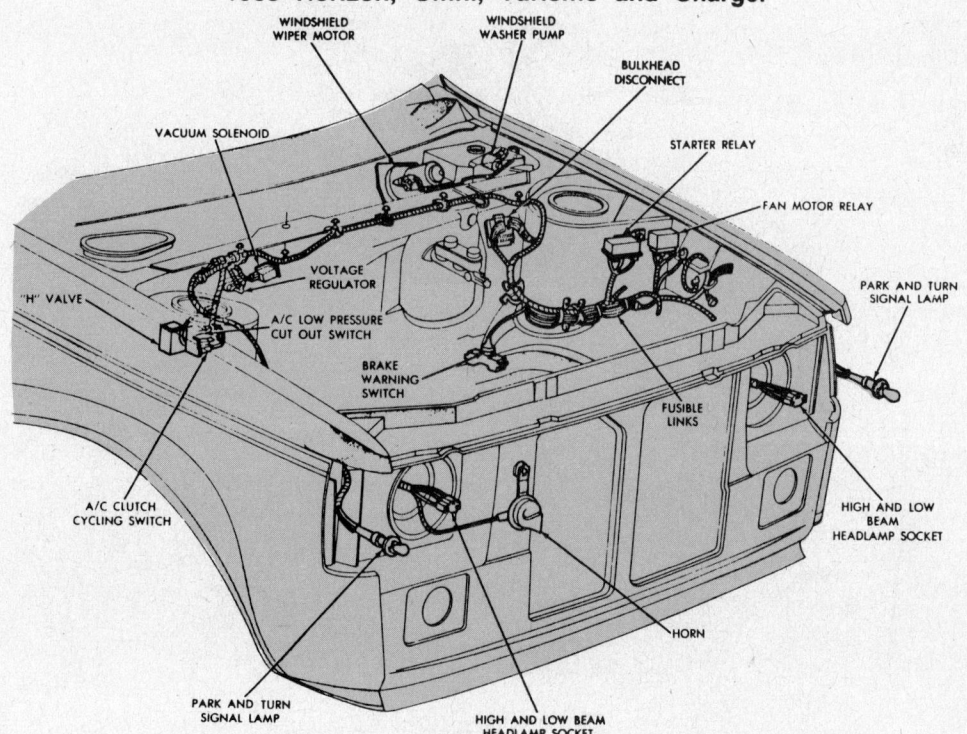

Engine Compartment Wiring and Component Identification 1.7L and 2.2L Engine MZ-24-28-44

1983 Horizon, Omni, Turismo and Charger

COMPONENT LOCATIONS

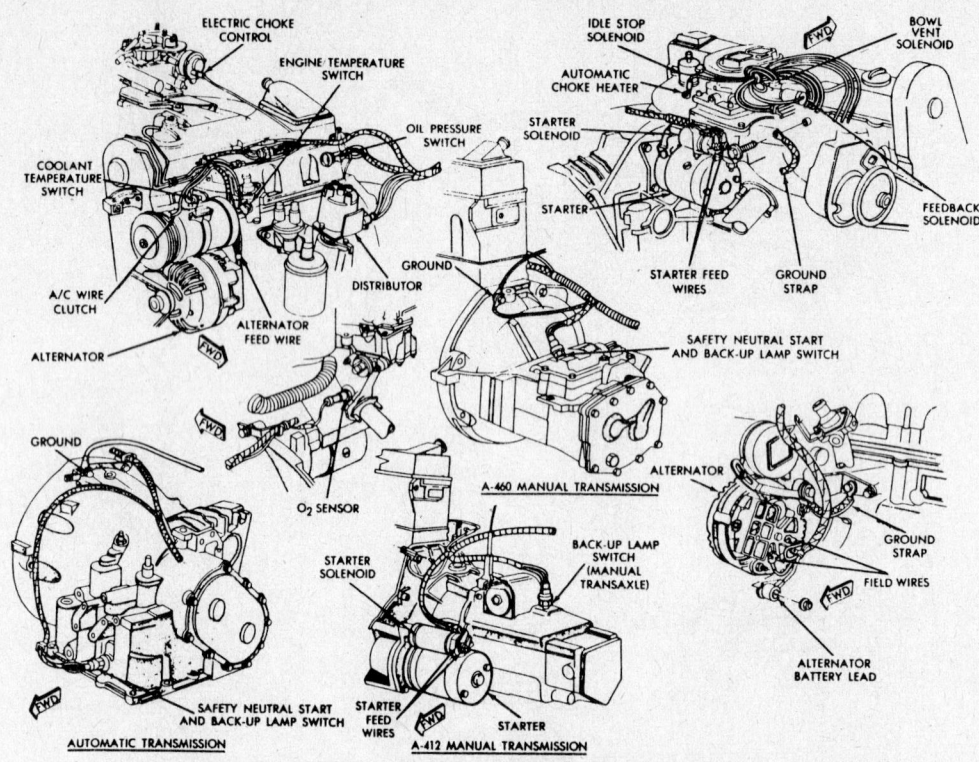

Engine Compartment Starter and Transmission Wiring and Component Identification 1.7L Engine MZ-24-28-44

1983 Horizon, Omni, Turismo and Charger

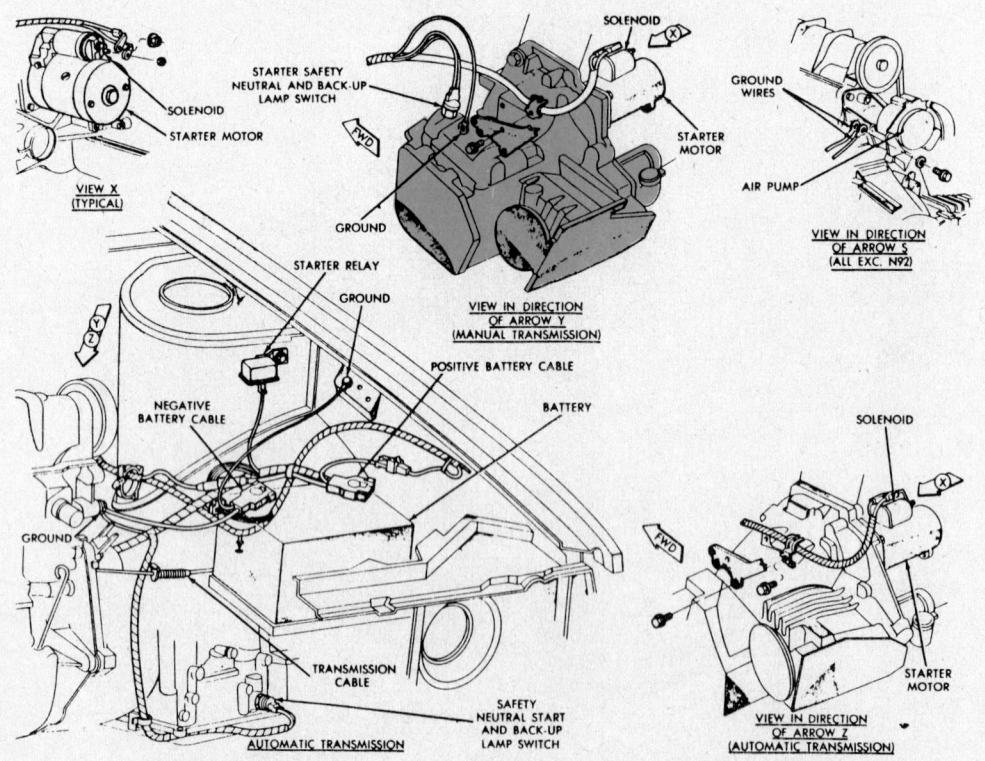

Engine Compartment—Starter and Transmission Wiring and Component Identification 2.2L Engine MZ–24-28-44

1983 Horizon, Omni, Turismo and Charger

COMPONENT LOCATIONS

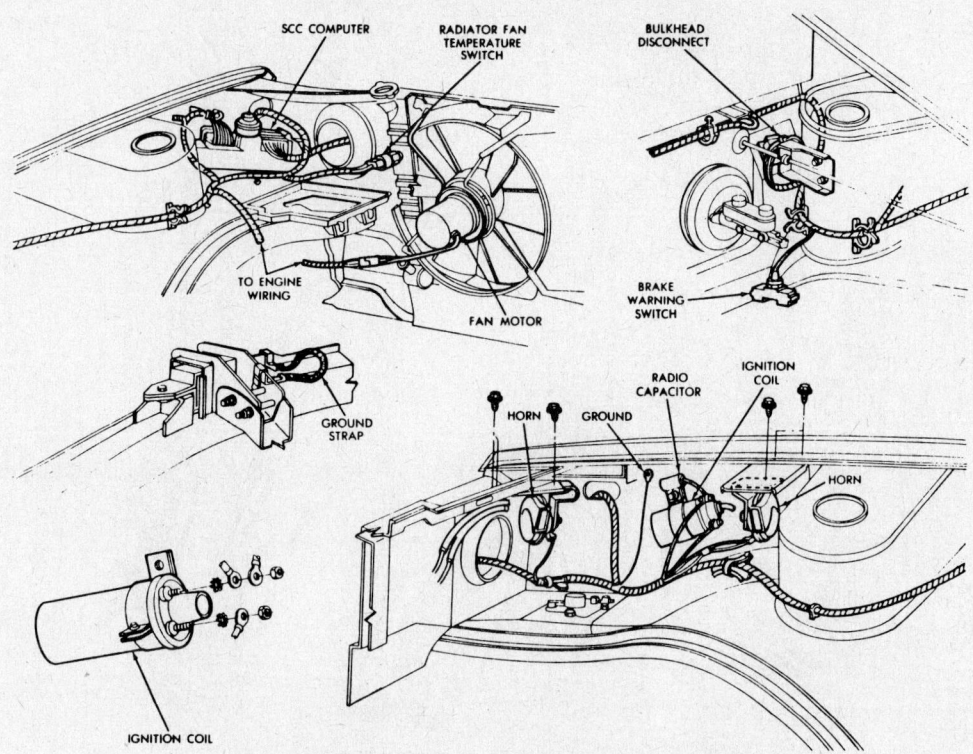

Engine Compartment Main Harness Wiring and Component Identification MZ-24-28-44

1983 Horizon, Omni, Turismo and Charger

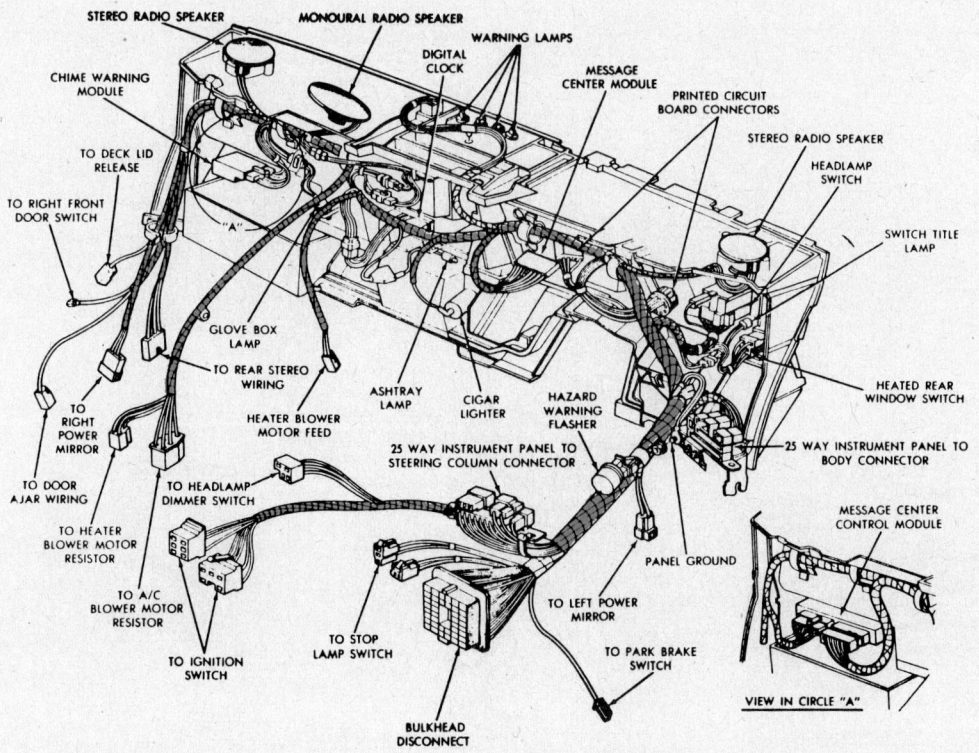

Instrument Panel Wiring and Component Identification C-V-L-J-E-T

1983 Reliant, Aries, LeBaron, 400, Caravelle, 600, E-Class and New Yorker

COMPONENT LOCATIONS

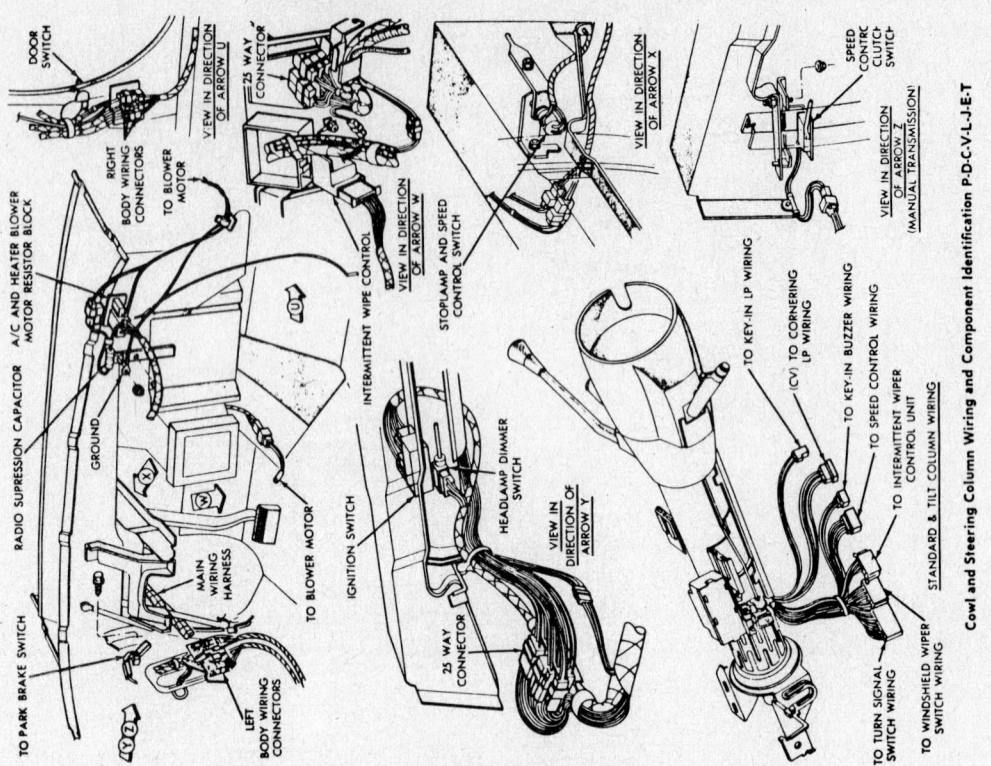

1983 Reliant, Aries, LeBaron, 400, Caravelle, 600, E-Class and New Yorker

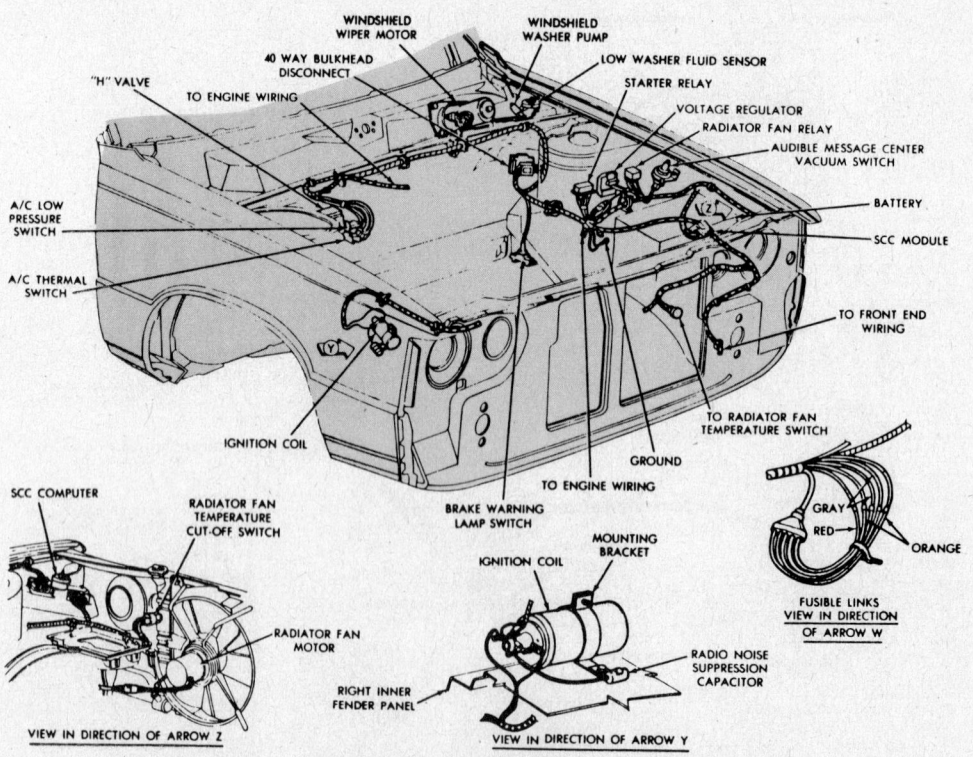

Engine Compartment Wiring and Component Identification 2.2L Engine P-D-C-V-L-J-E-T

1983 Reliant, Aries, LeBaron, 400, Caravelle, 600, E-Class and New Yorker

COMPONENT LOCATIONS

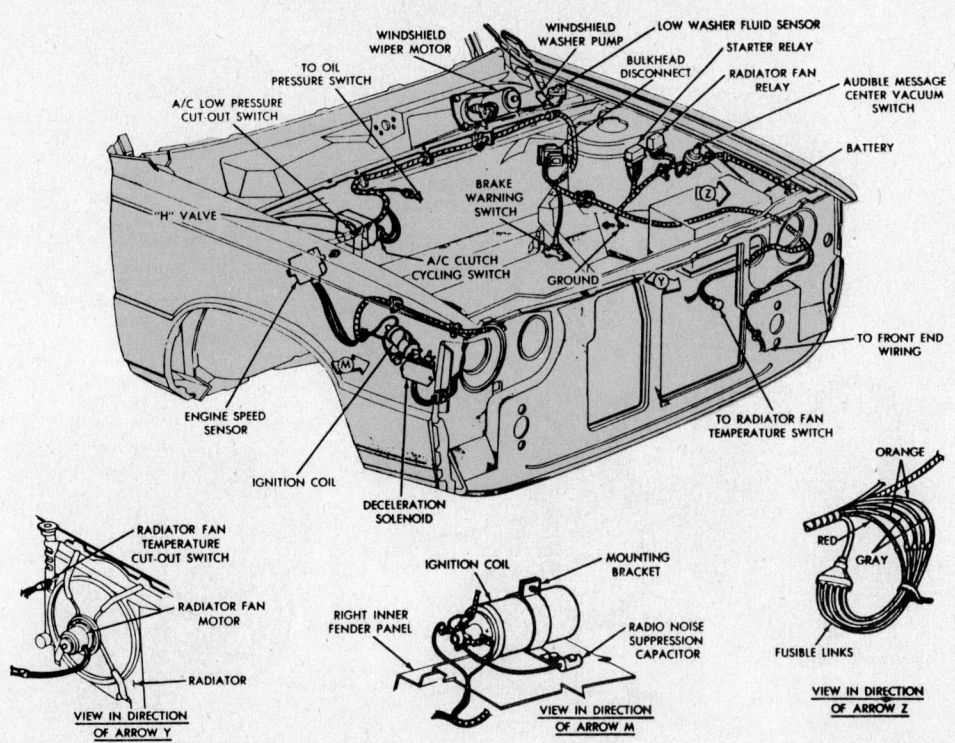

1983 Reliant, Aries, LeBaron, 400, Caravelle, 600, E-Class and New Yorker

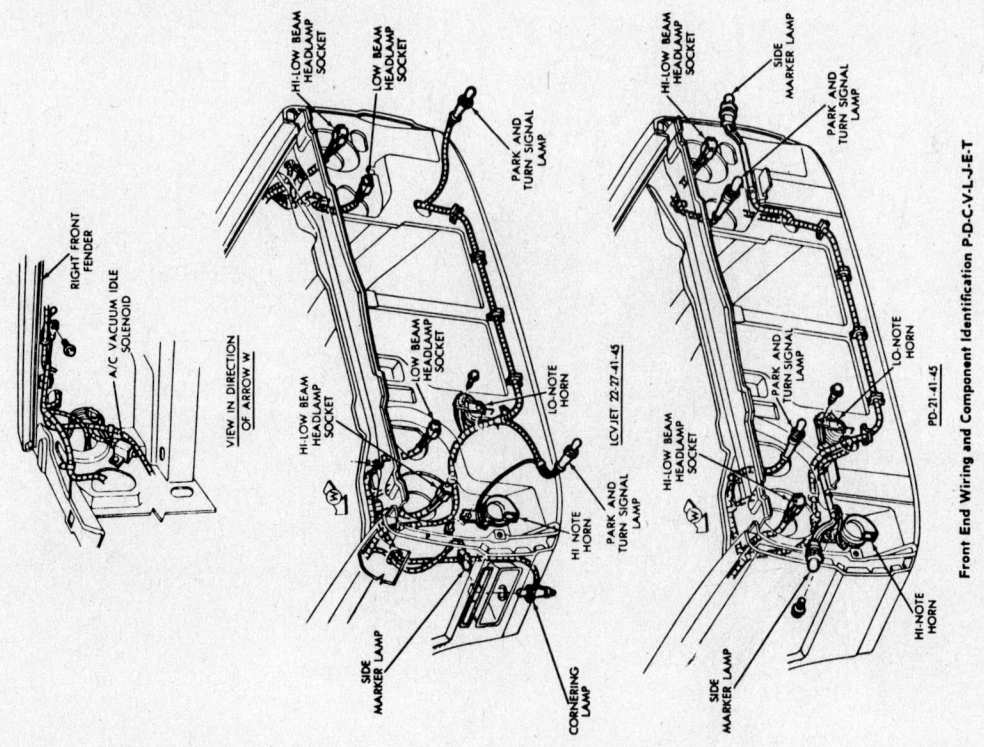

1983 Reliant, Aries, LeBaron, 400, Caravelle, 600, E-Class and New Yorker

29

COMPONENT LOCATIONS

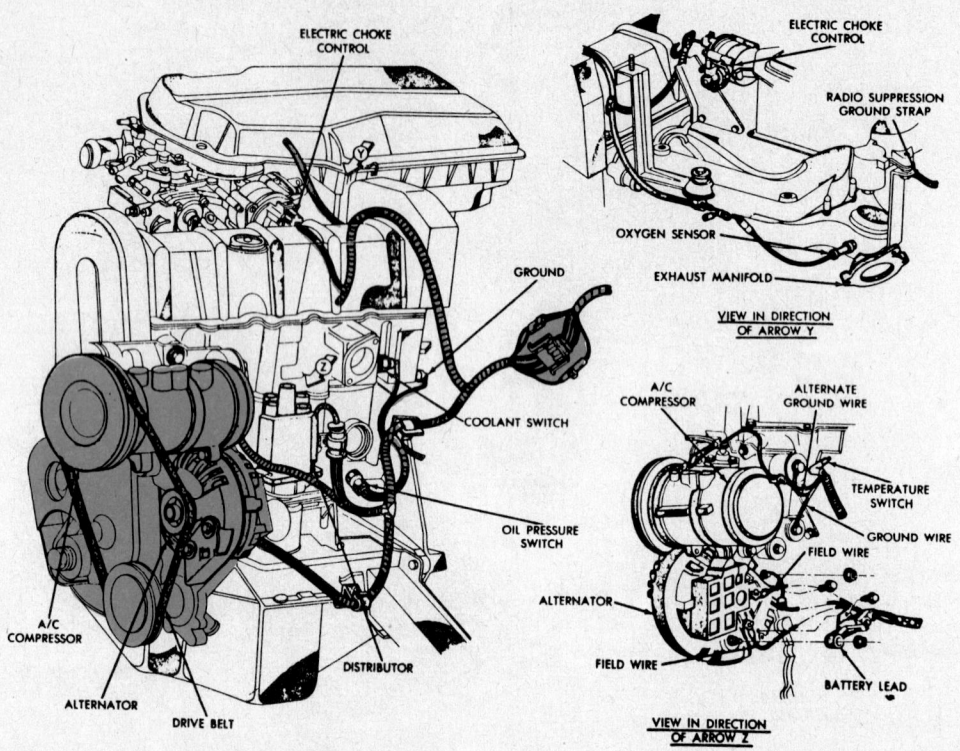

1983 Reliant, Aries, LeBaron, 400, Caravelle, 600, E-Class and New Yorker

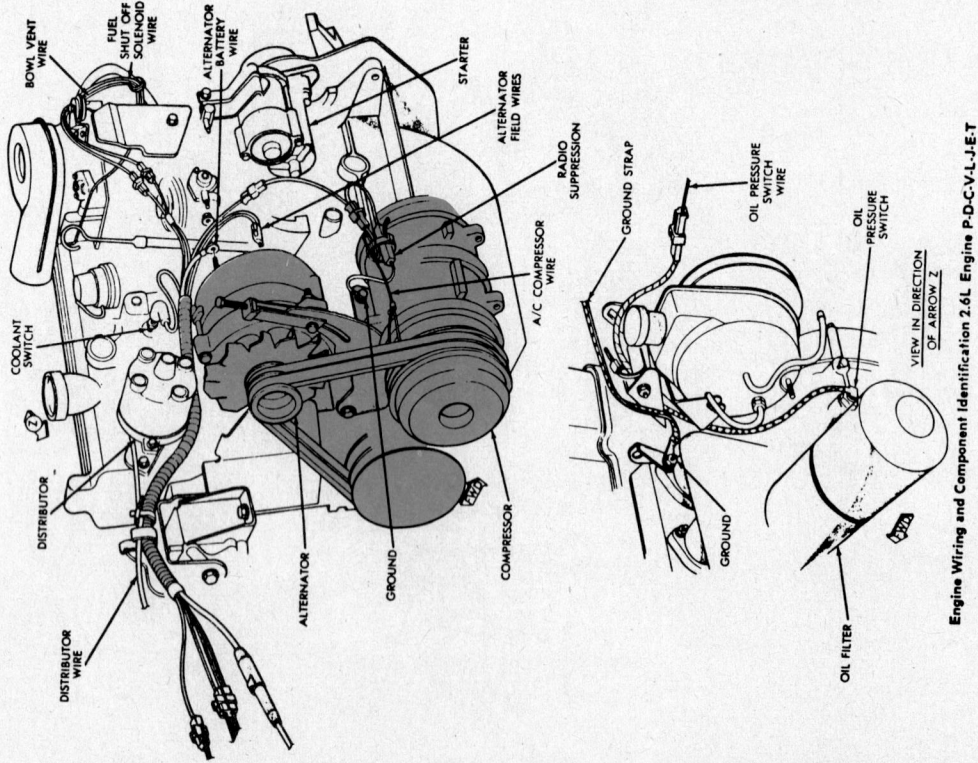

1983 Reliant, Aries, LeBaron, 400, Caravelle, 600, E-Class and New Yorker

COMPONENT LOCATIONS

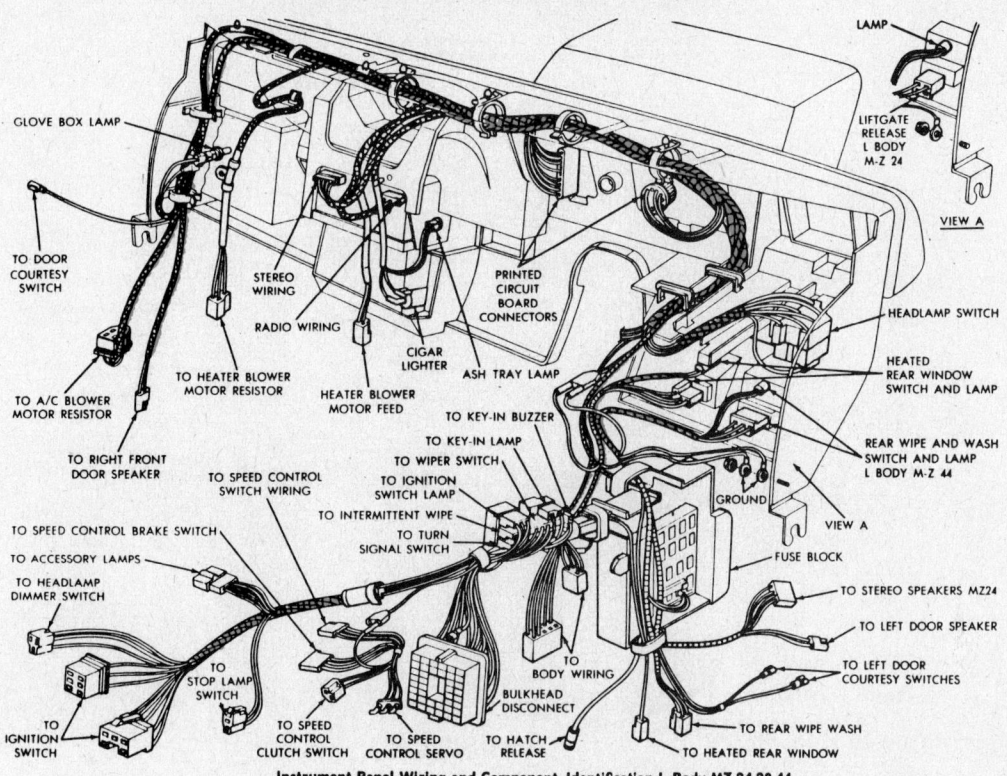

Instrument Panel Wiring and Component Identification L Body MZ-24-28-44

1984 Horizon, Omni, Turismo and Charger

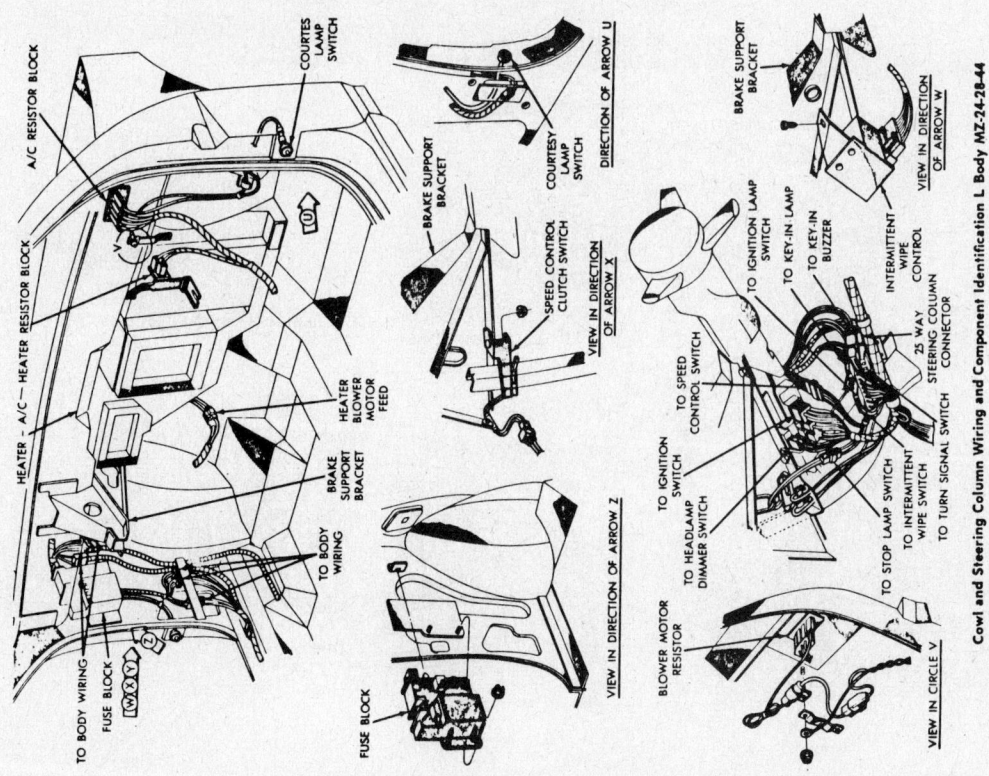

Cowl and Steering Column Wiring and Component Identification L Body MZ-24-28-44

1984 Horizon, Omni, Turismo and Charger

COMPONENT LOCATIONS

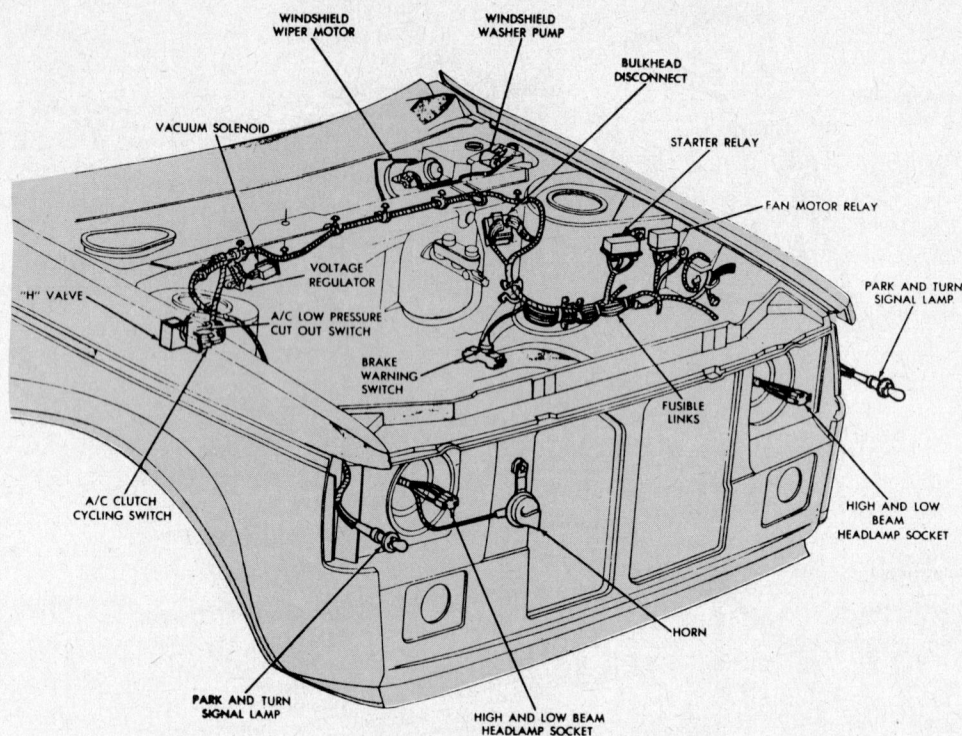

Engine Compartment Wiring and Component Identification 1.6L and 2.2L Engine L Body MZ-24-28-44

1984 Horizon, Omni, Turismo and Charger

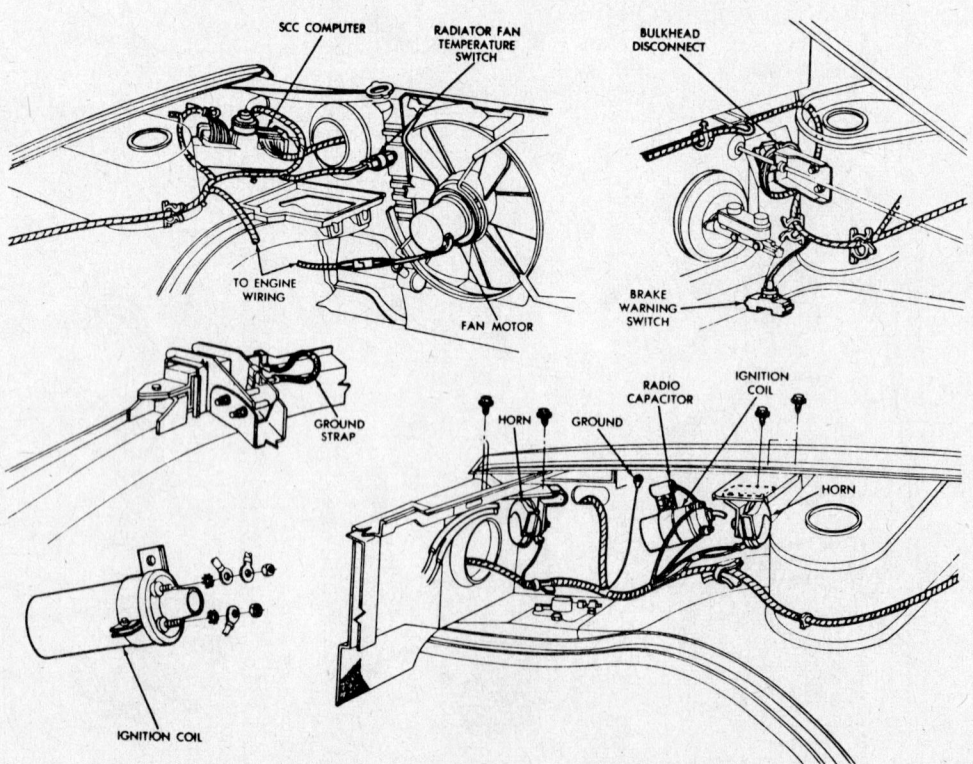

Engine Compartment Main Harness Wiring and Component Identification L Body MZ-24-28-44

1984 Horizon, Omni, Turismo and Charger

COMPONENT LOCATIONS

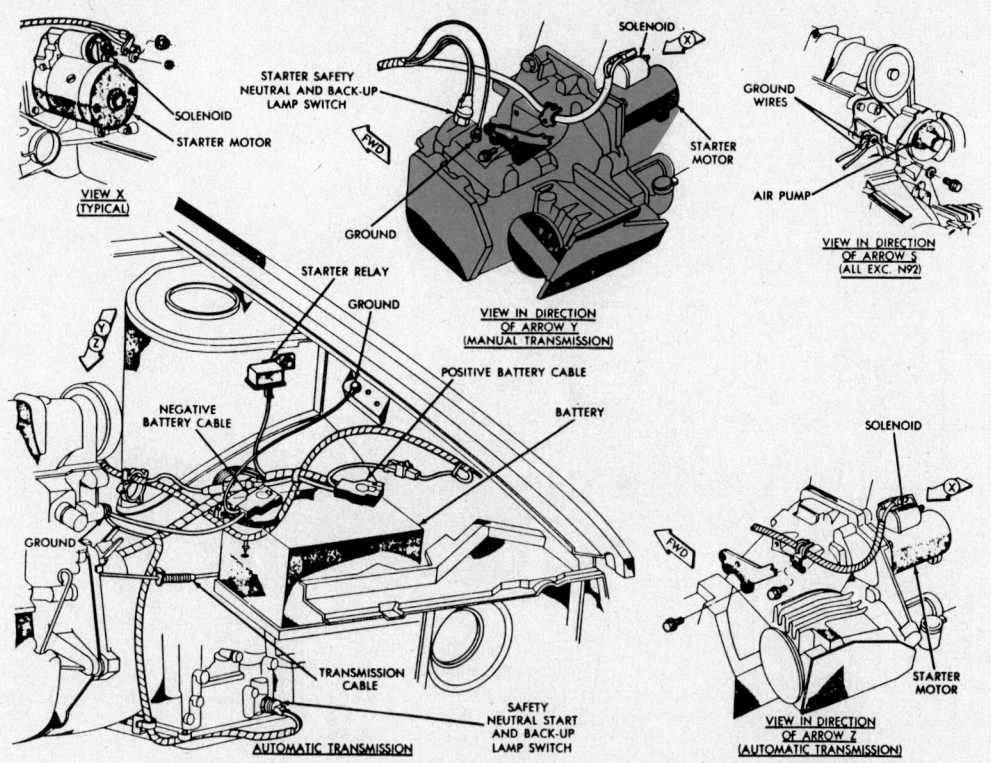

Engine Compartment—Starter and Transmission Wiring and Component Identification L Body 2.2L Engine MZ-24-28-44

1984 Horizon, Omni, Turismo and Charger

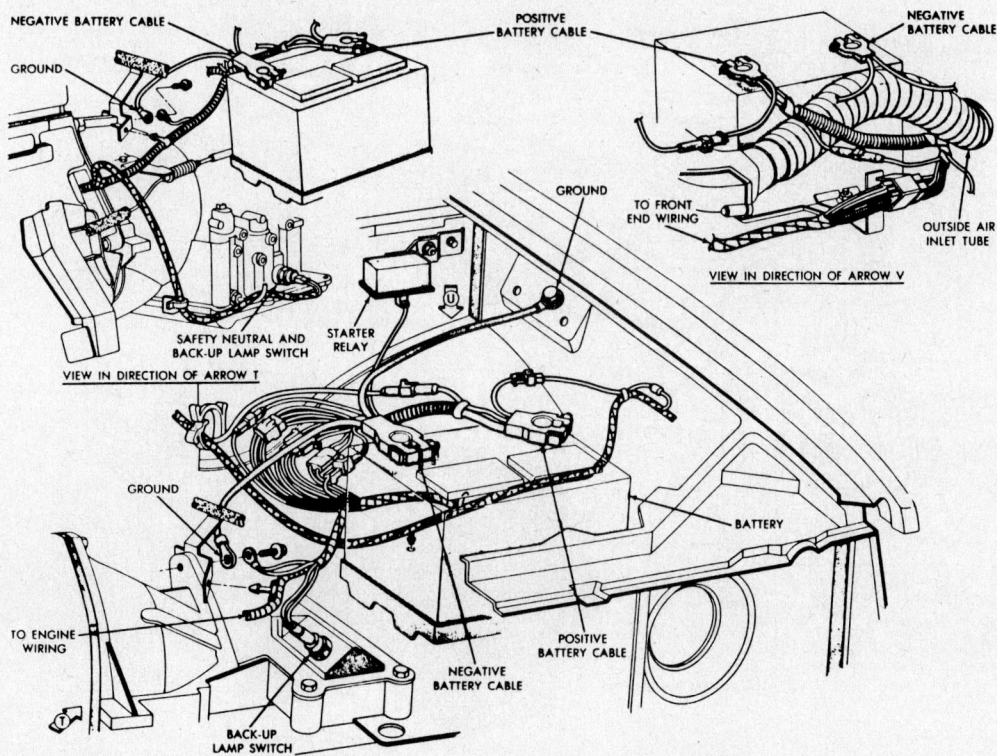

Engine Compartment Battery Cables and Transmission Switches 1.6L Engine L Body MZ-24-28-44

1984 Horizon, Omni, Turismo and Charger

COMPONENT LOCATIONS

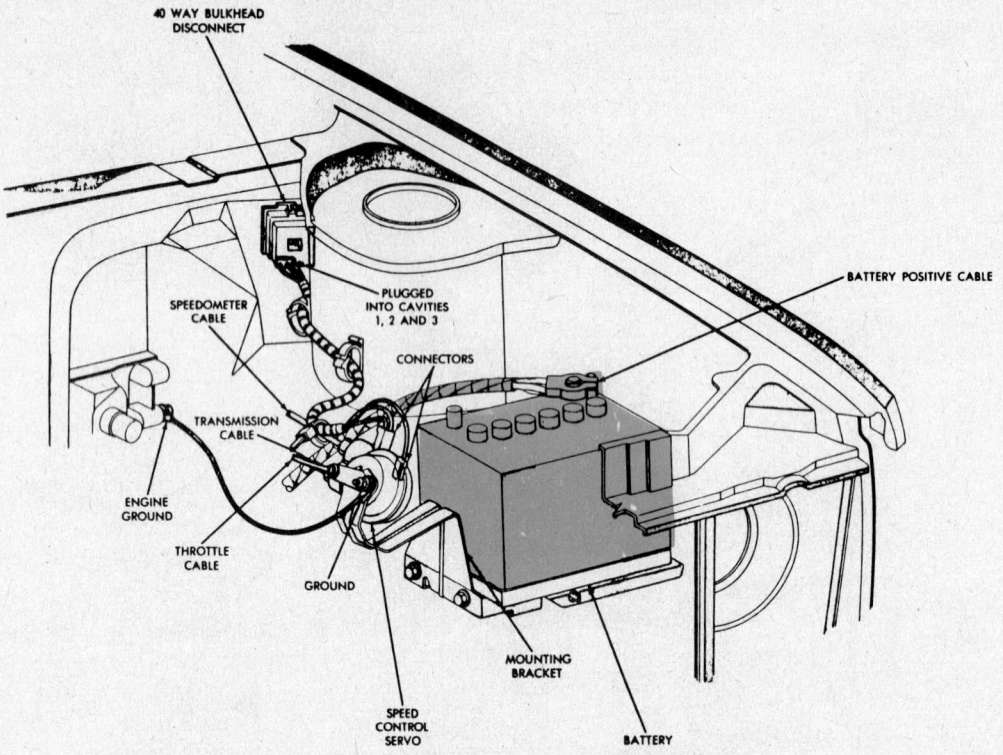

Engine Compartment Speed Control Wiring and Components L Body MZ-24-28-44

1984 Horizon, Omni, Turismo and Charger

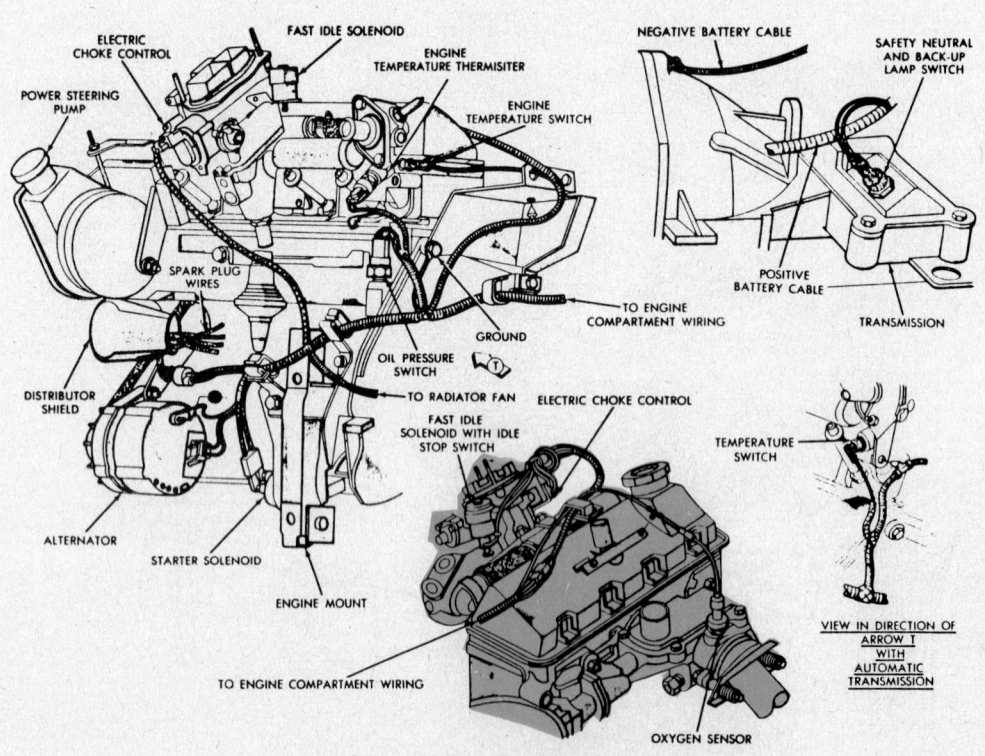

Engine Wiring and Component Identification 1.6L Engine MZ-24-28-44

1984 Horizon, Omni, Turismo and Charger

COMPONENT LOCATIONS

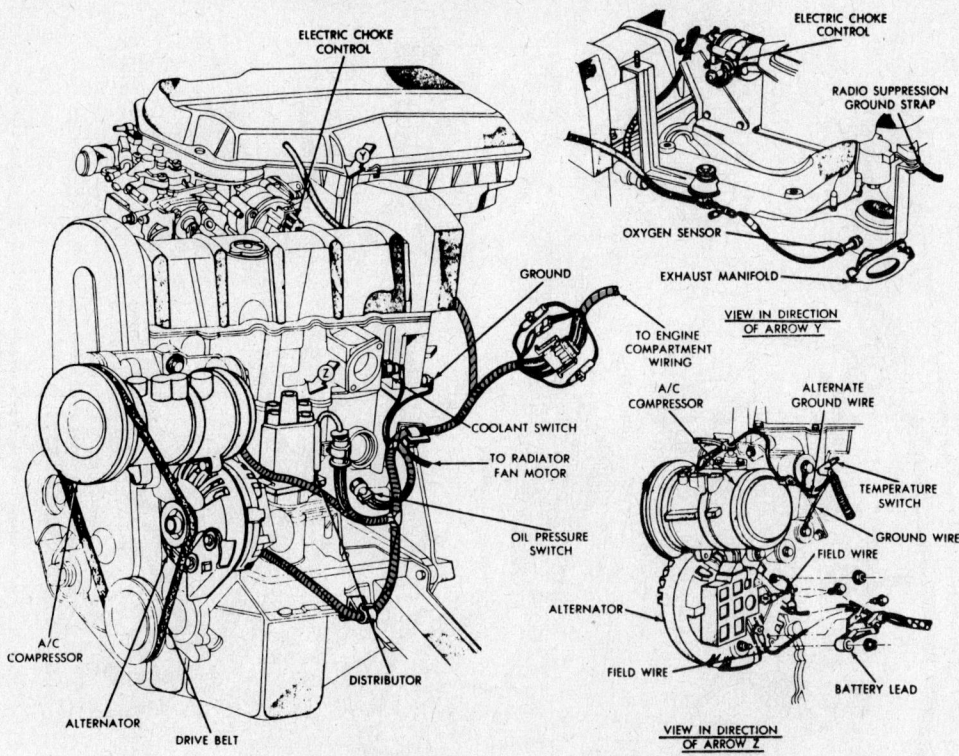

Engine Wiring and Component Identification 2.2L Engine L Body MZ-24-28-44

1984 Horizon, Omni, Turismo and Charger

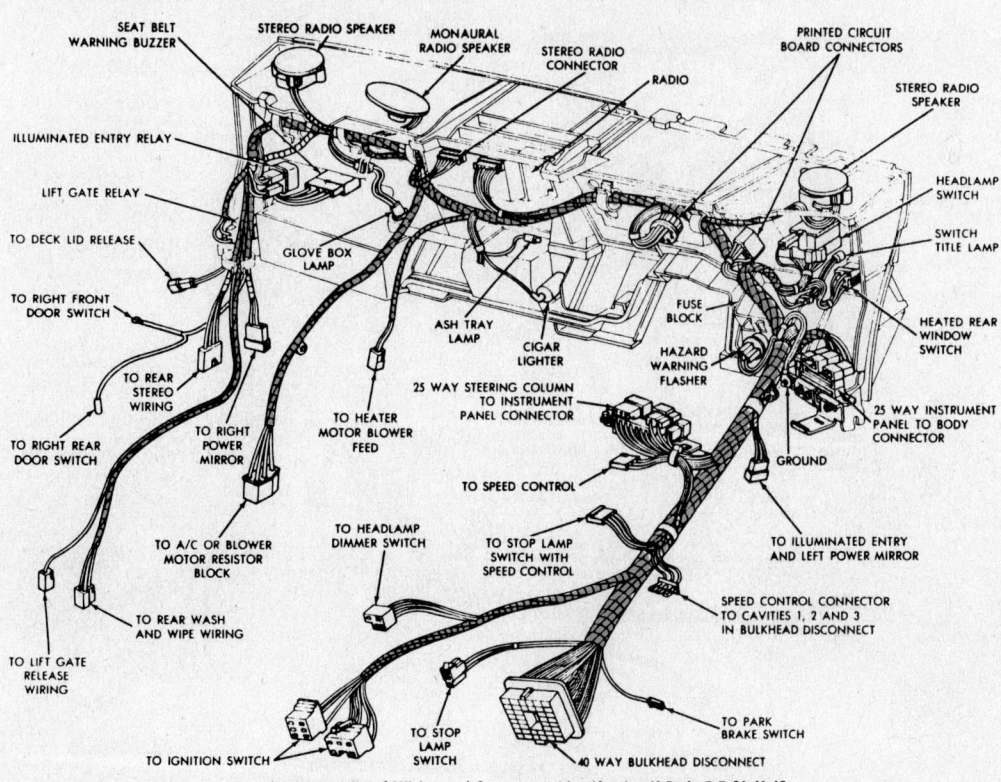

Instrument Panel Wiring and Component Identification K Body P-D-21-41-45

1984 Caravelle, 600, E-Class, New Yorker, Aries, Reliant and LeBaron

COMPONENT LOCATIONS

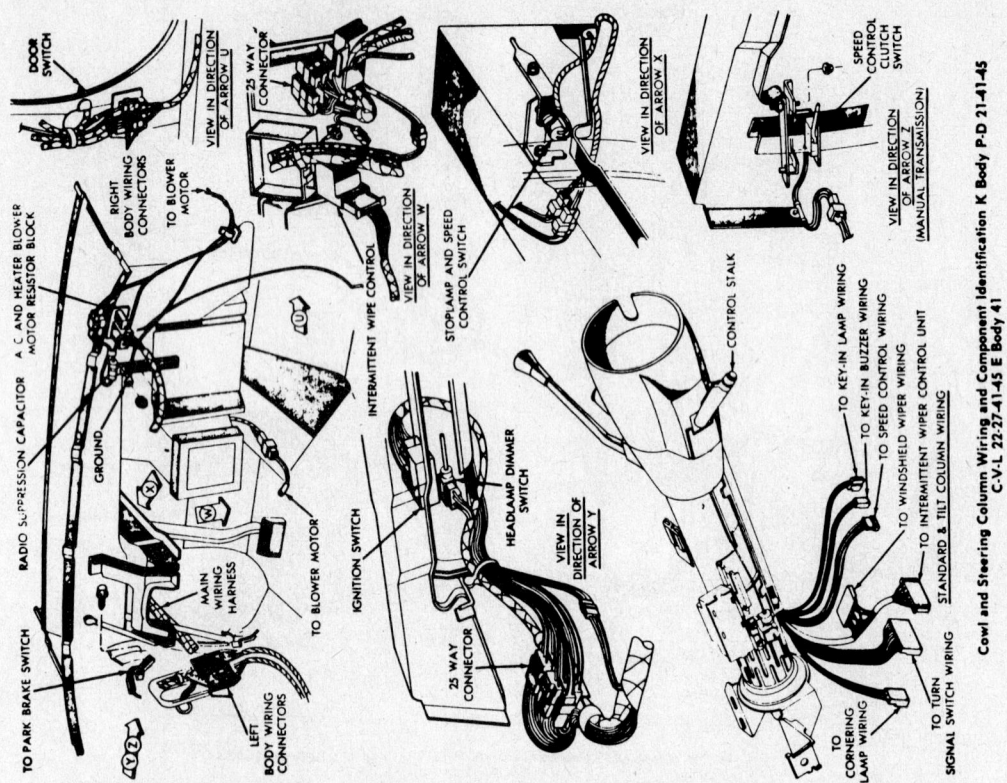

1984 Caravelle, 600, E-Class, New Yorker, Aries, Reliant and LeBaron

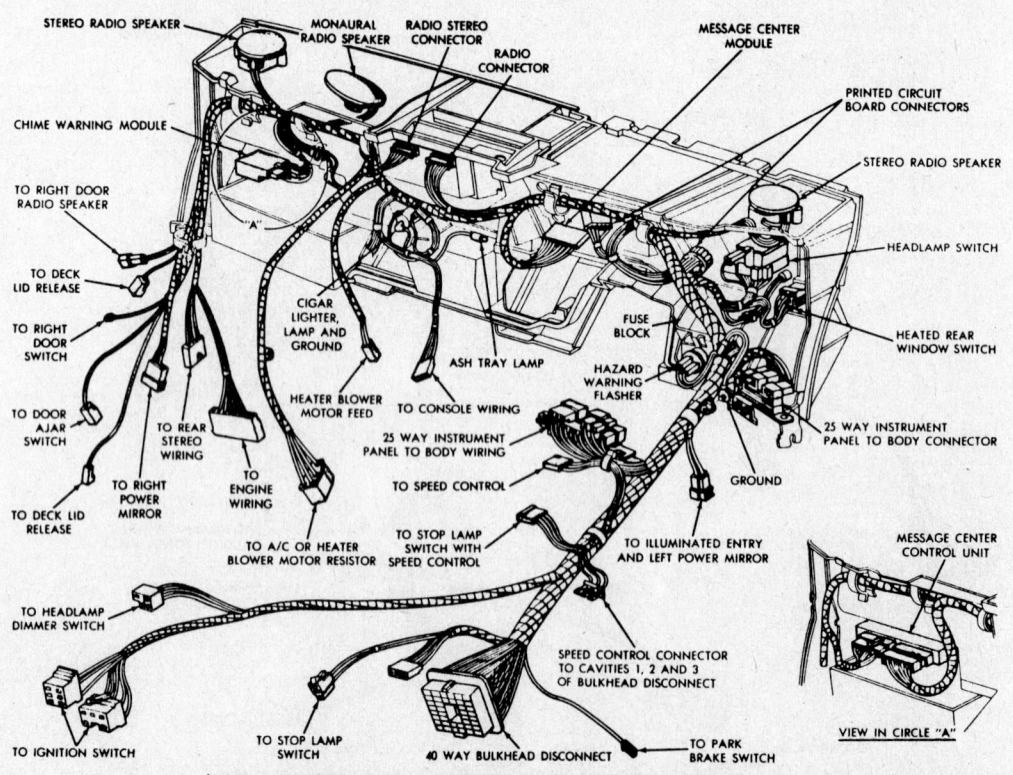

Instrument Panel Wiring and Component Identification K Body C-V-L 22-27-41-45 E Body J-E-T 41

1984 Caravelle, 600, E-Class, New Yorker, Aries, Reliant and LeBaron

COMPONENT LOCATIONS

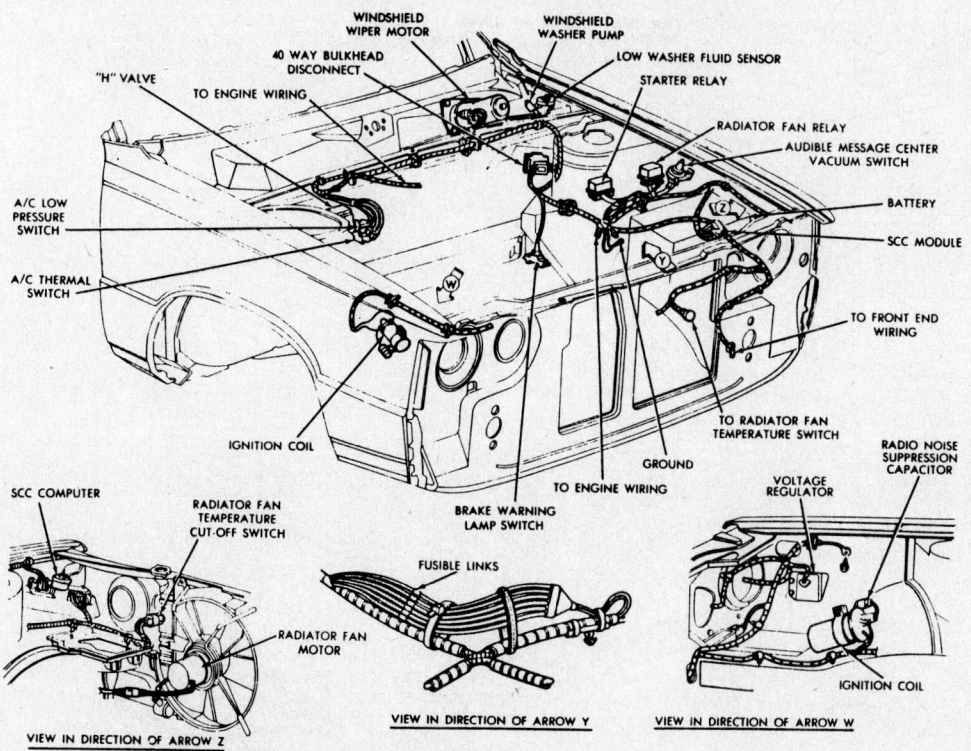

Engine Compartment Wiring and Component Identification 2.2L Engine K & E Body All

1984 Caravelle, 600, E-Class, New Yorker, Aries, Reliant and LeBaron

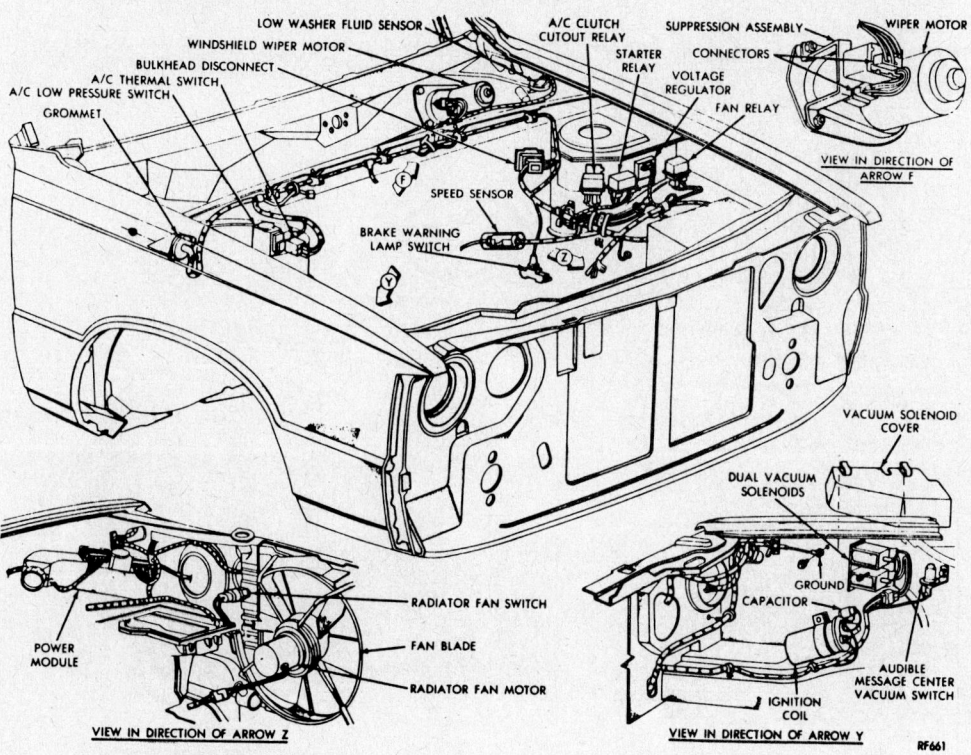

RF661

Engine Compartment Wiring and Components Identification 2.2L Engine with EFI or Turbo K Body C-V-L 22-27-41 E Body J-E-T 41

1984 Caravelle, 600, E-Class, New Yorker, Aries, Reliant and LeBaron

COMPONENT LOCATIONS

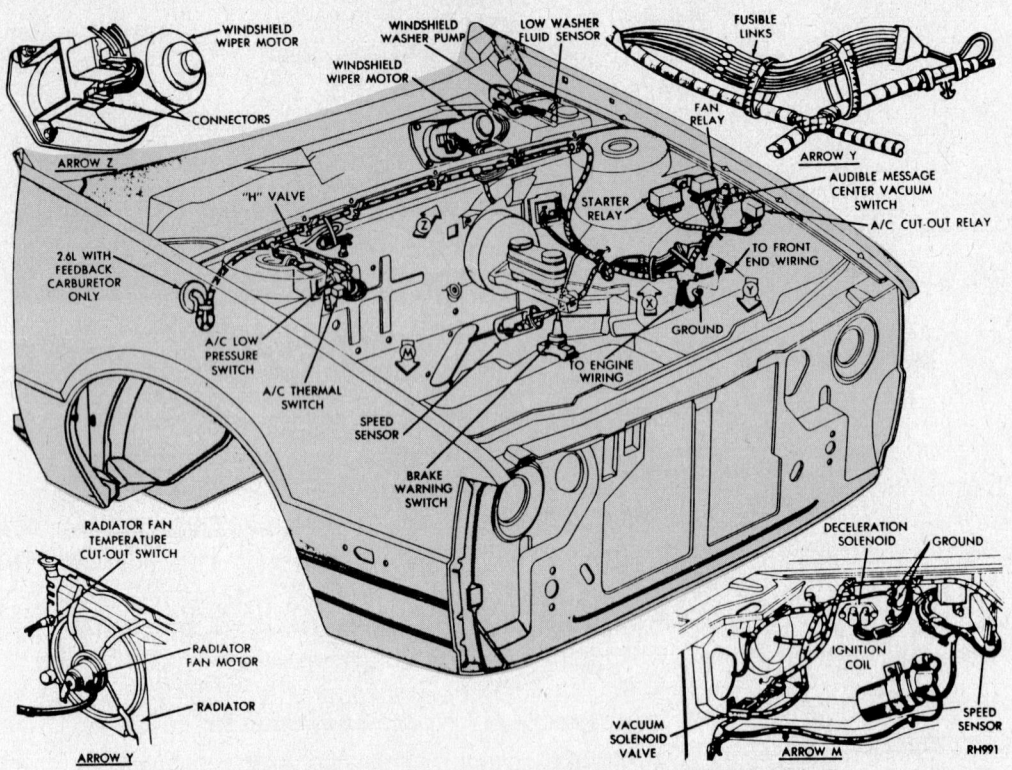

Engine Compartment Wiring and Component Identification 2.6L Engine K & E Body All

1984 Caravelle, 600, E-Class, New Yorker, Aries, Reliant and LeBaron

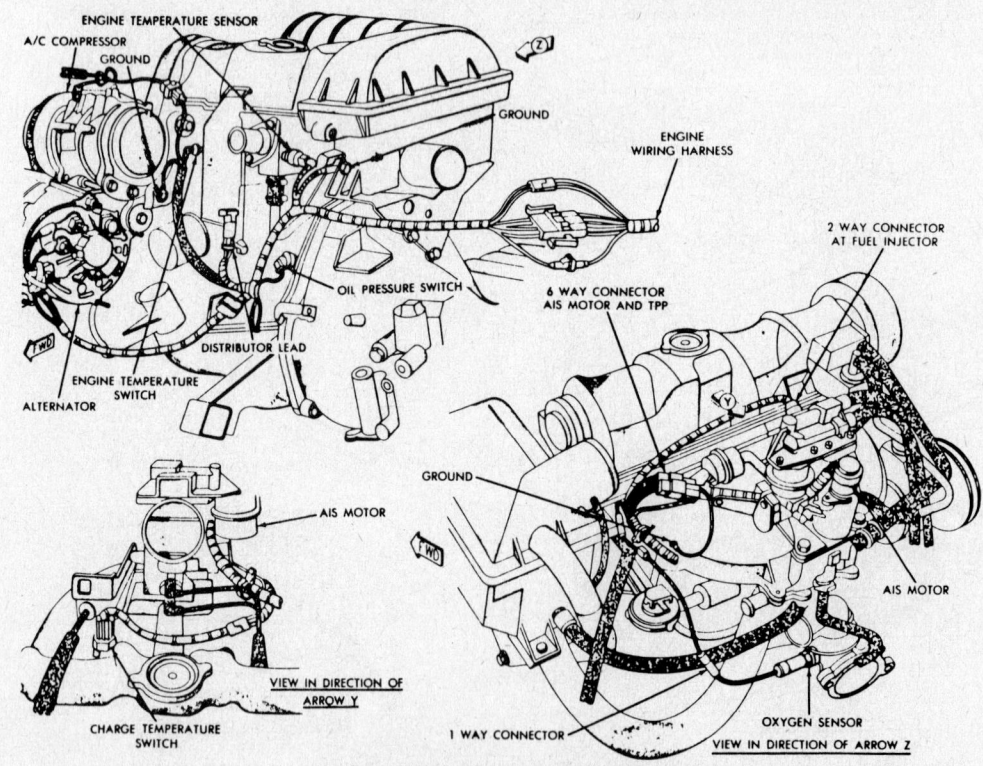

Engine Wiring and EFI Components E Body E-T 41

1984 Caravelle, 600, E-Class, New Yorker, Aries, Reliant and LeBaron

COMPONENT LOCATIONS

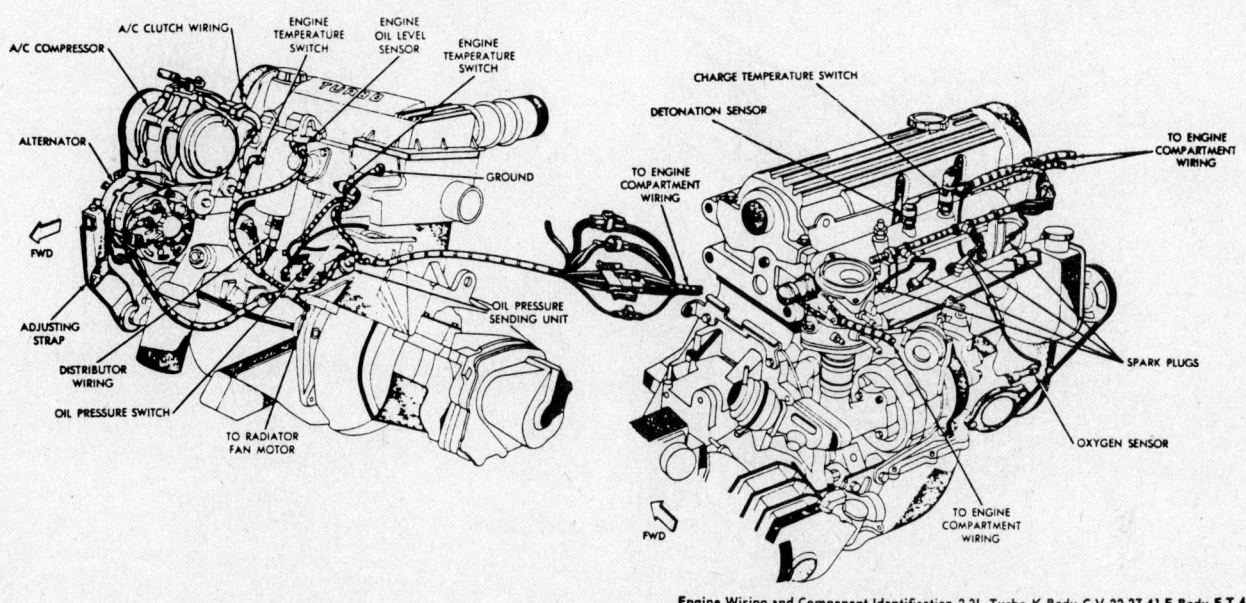

Engine Wiring and Component Identification 2.2L Turbo K Body C-V 22-27-41 E Body E-T 4

1984 Caravelle, 600, E-Class, New Yorker, Aries, Reliant and LeBaron

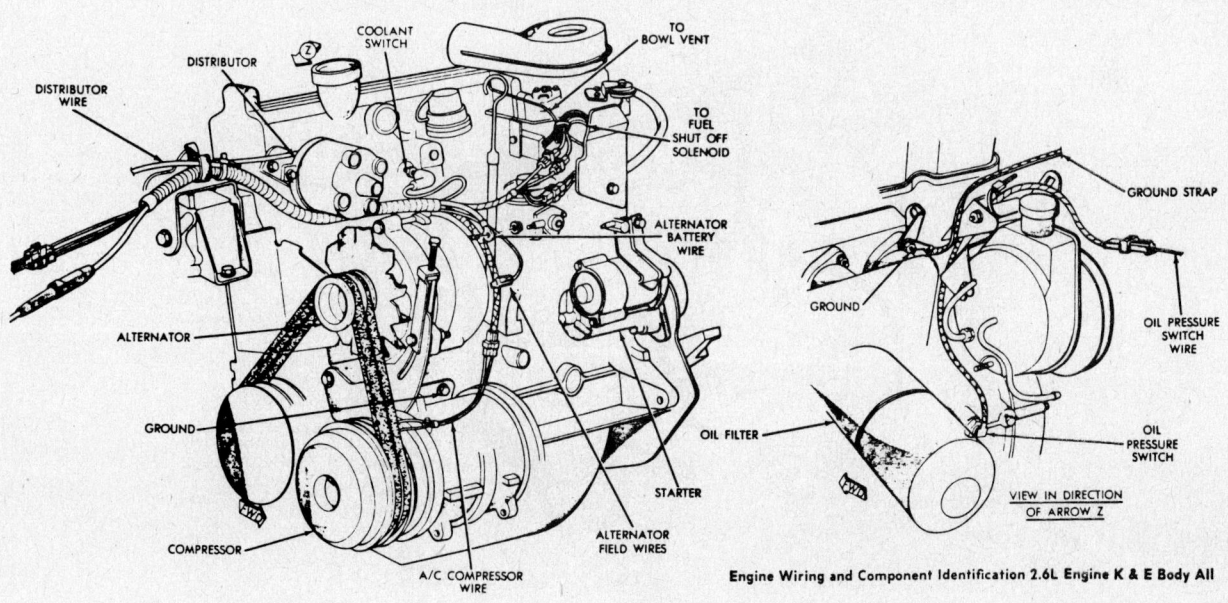

Engine Wiring and Component Identification 2.6L Engine K & E Body All

1984 Caravelle, 600, E-Class, New Yorker, Aries, Reliant and LeBaron

COMPONENT LOCATIONS

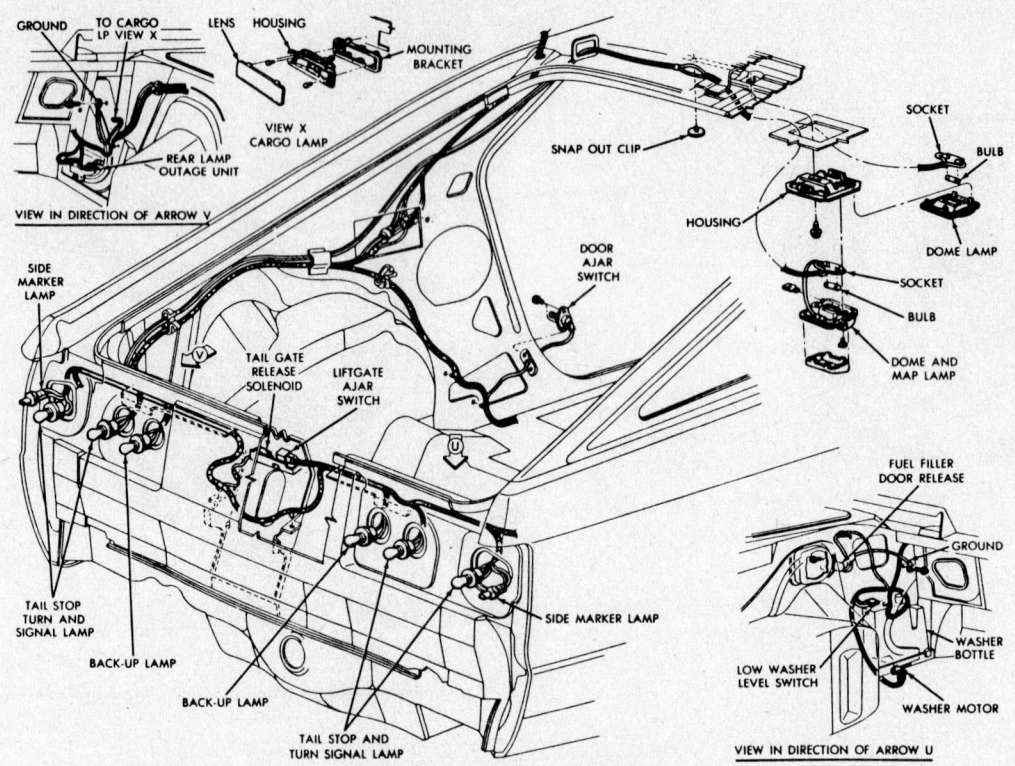

Body Wiring and Component Identification G Body All

1984 Caravelle, 600, E-Class, New Yorker, Aries, Reliant and LeBaron

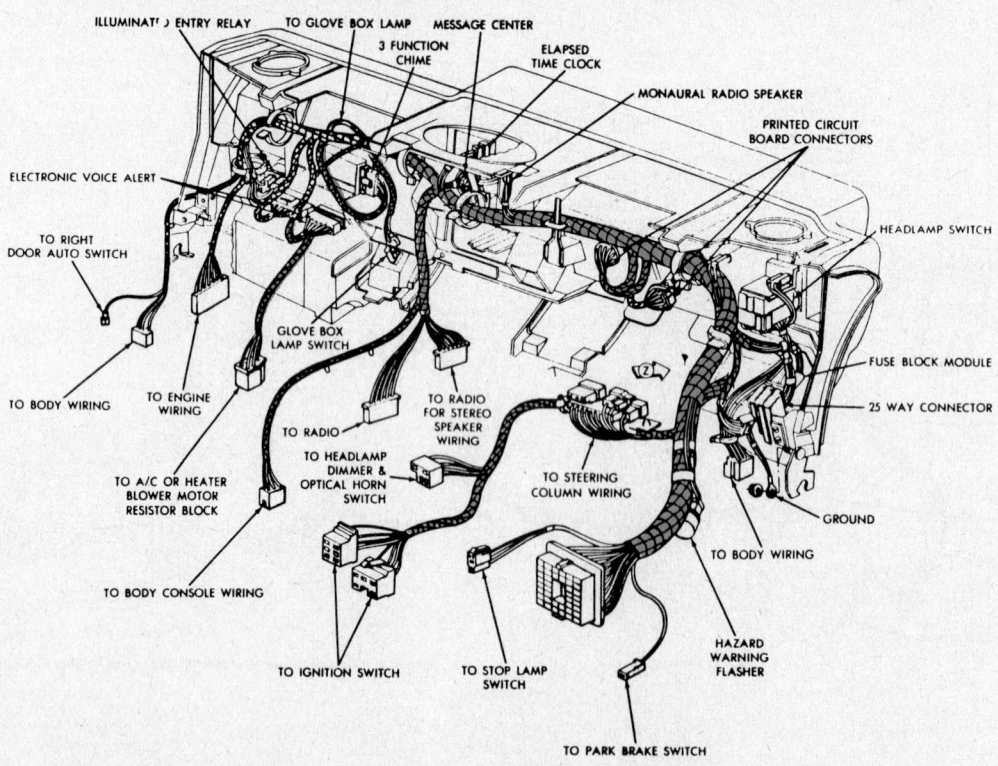

Instrument Panel Wiring and Components G Body

1984 Caravelle, 600, E-Class, New Yorker, Aries, Reliant and LeBaron

COMPONENT LOCATIONS

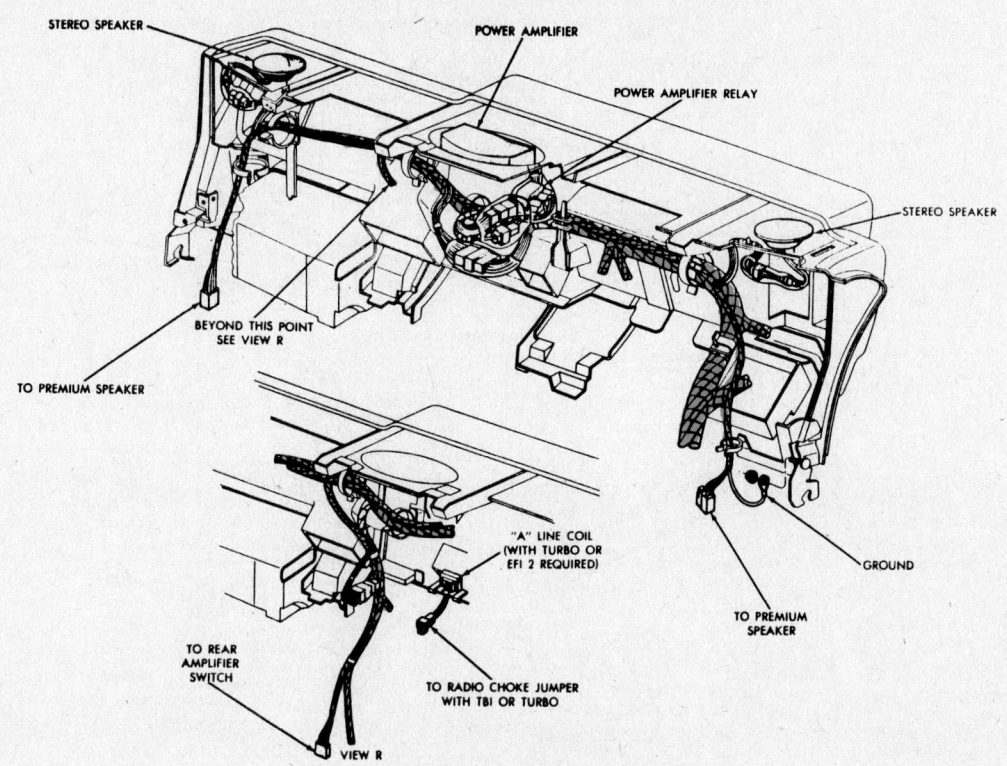

STEREO SPEAKER

POWER AMPLIFIER

POWER AMPLIFIER RELAY

STEREO SPEAKER

BEYOND THIS POINT
SEE VIEW R

TO PREMIUM SPEAKER

GROUND

"A" LINE COIL
(WITH TURBO OR
EFI 2 REQUIRED)

TO PREMIUM
SPEAKER

TO REAR
AMPLIFIER
SWITCH

TO RADIO CHOKE JUMPER
WITH TBI OR TURBO

VIEW R

Instrument Panel Premium Speakers G Body
1984 Laser and Daytona

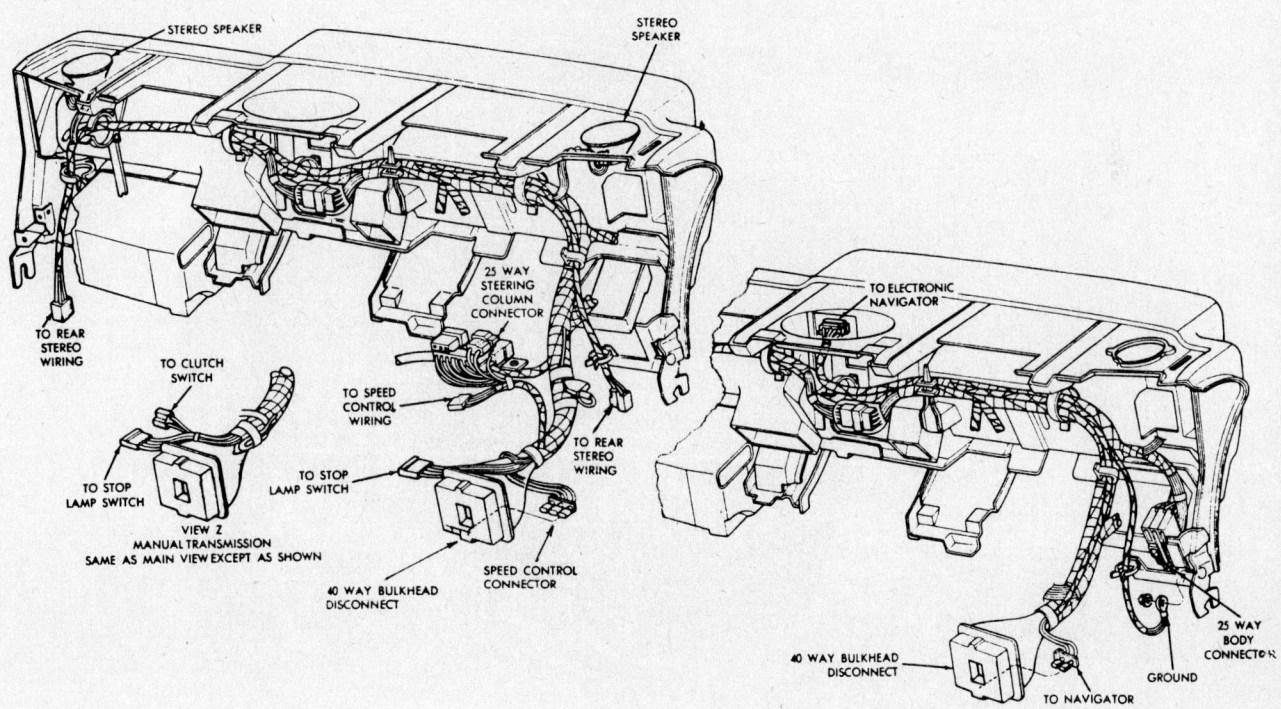

STEREO SPEAKER

STEREO
SPEAKER

25 WAY
STEERING
COLUMN
CONNECTOR

TO ELECTRONIC
NAVIGATOR

TO REAR
STEREO
WIRING

TO CLUTCH
SWITCH

TO SPEED
CONTROL
WIRING

TO REAR
STEREO
WIRING

TO STOP
LAMP SWITCH

TO STOP
LAMP SWITCH

VIEW Z
MANUAL TRANSMISSION
SAME AS MAIN VIEW EXCEPT AS SHOWN

40 WAY BULKHEAD
DISCONNECT

SPEED CONTROL
CONNECTOR

40 WAY BULKHEAD
DISCONNECT

TO NAVIGATOR

GROUND

25 WAY
BODY
CONNECTOR

Instrument Panel Wiring Speed Control, Stereo Speakers and Navigator G Body

1984 Laser and Daytona

COMPONENT LOCATIONS

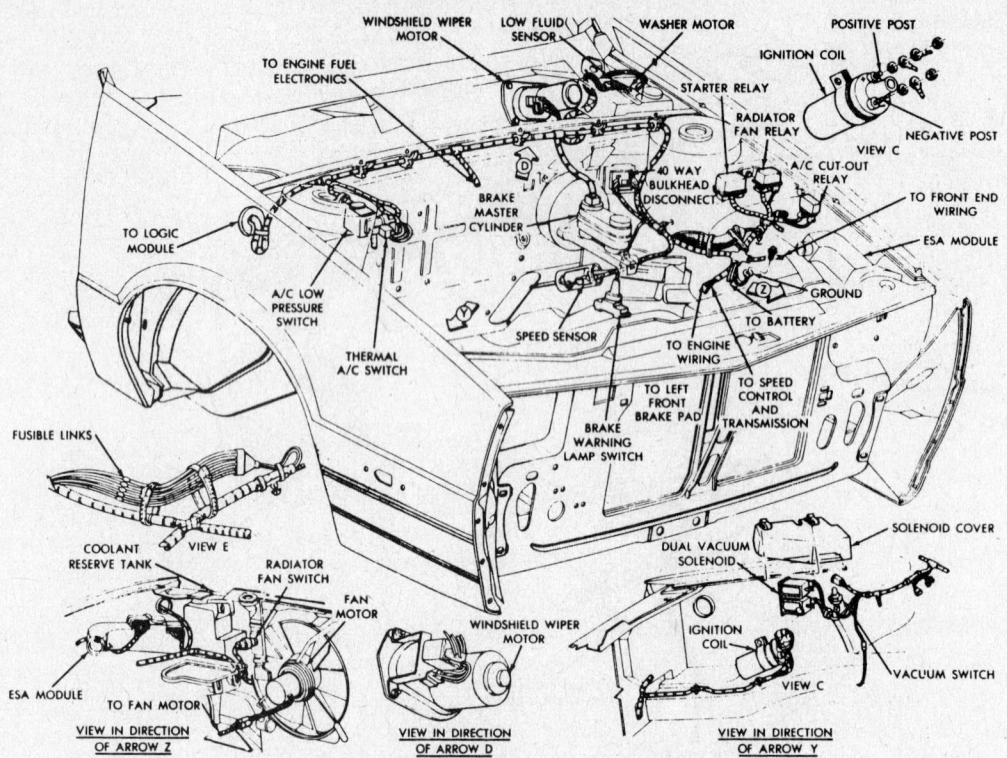

Engine Compartment Wiring and Component Identification 2.2L EFI and Turbo Engine G Body

1984 Laser and Daytona

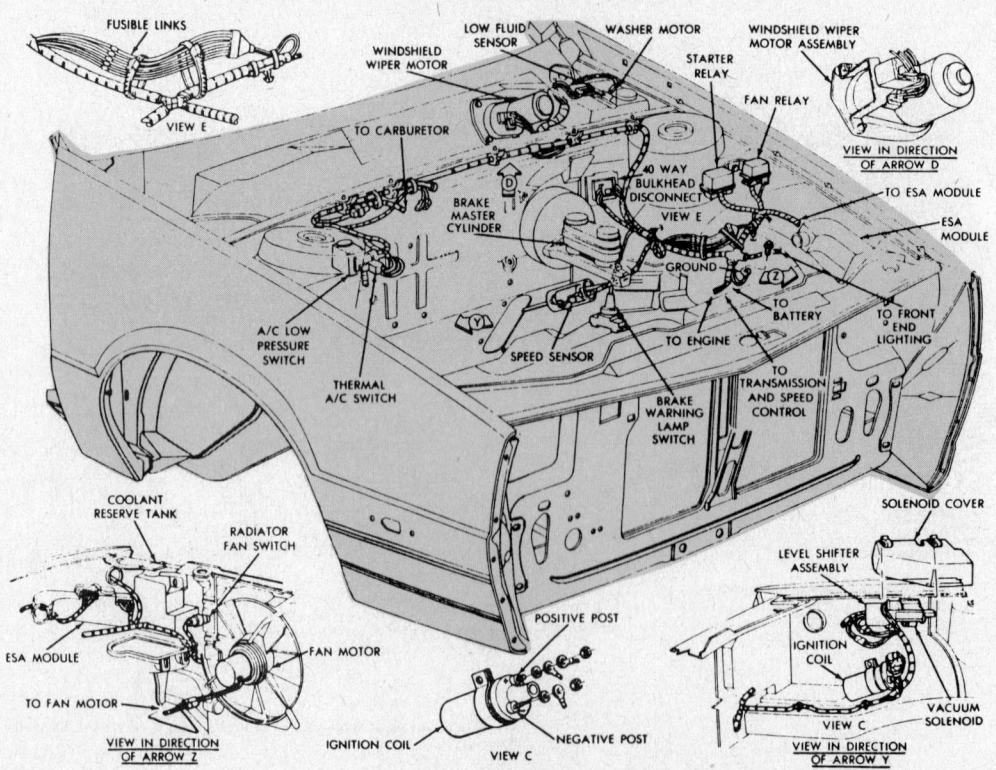

Engine Compartment Wiring and Component Identification 2.2L G Body

1984 Laser and Daytona

COMPONENT LOCATIONS

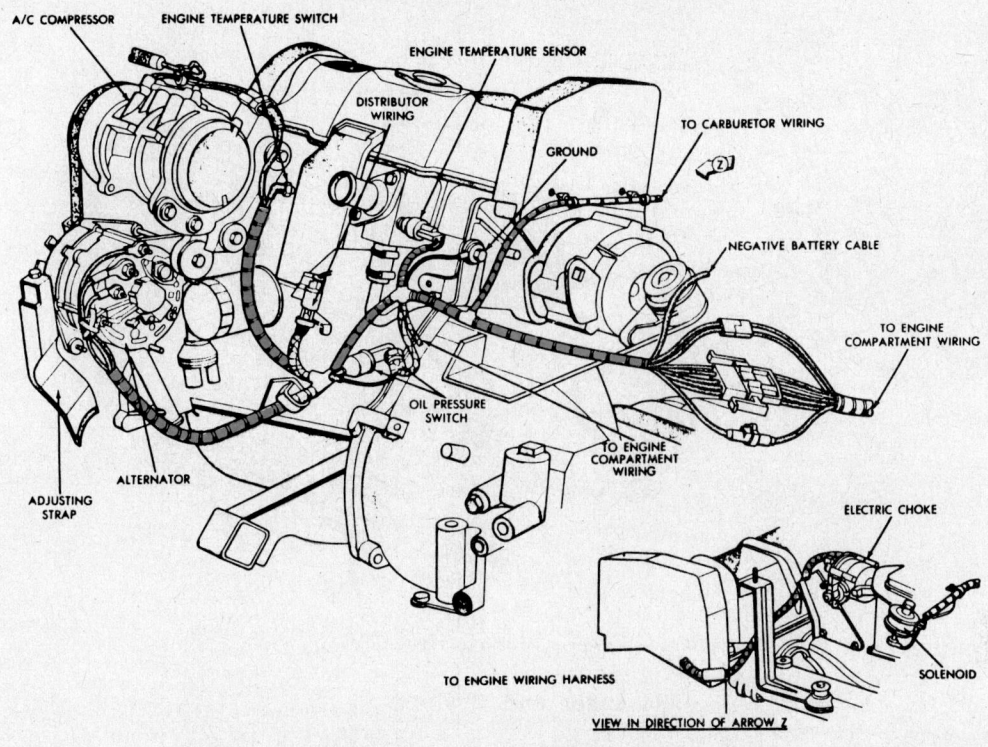

Engine Wiring and Component Identification 2.2L Engine G Body

1984 Laser and Daytona

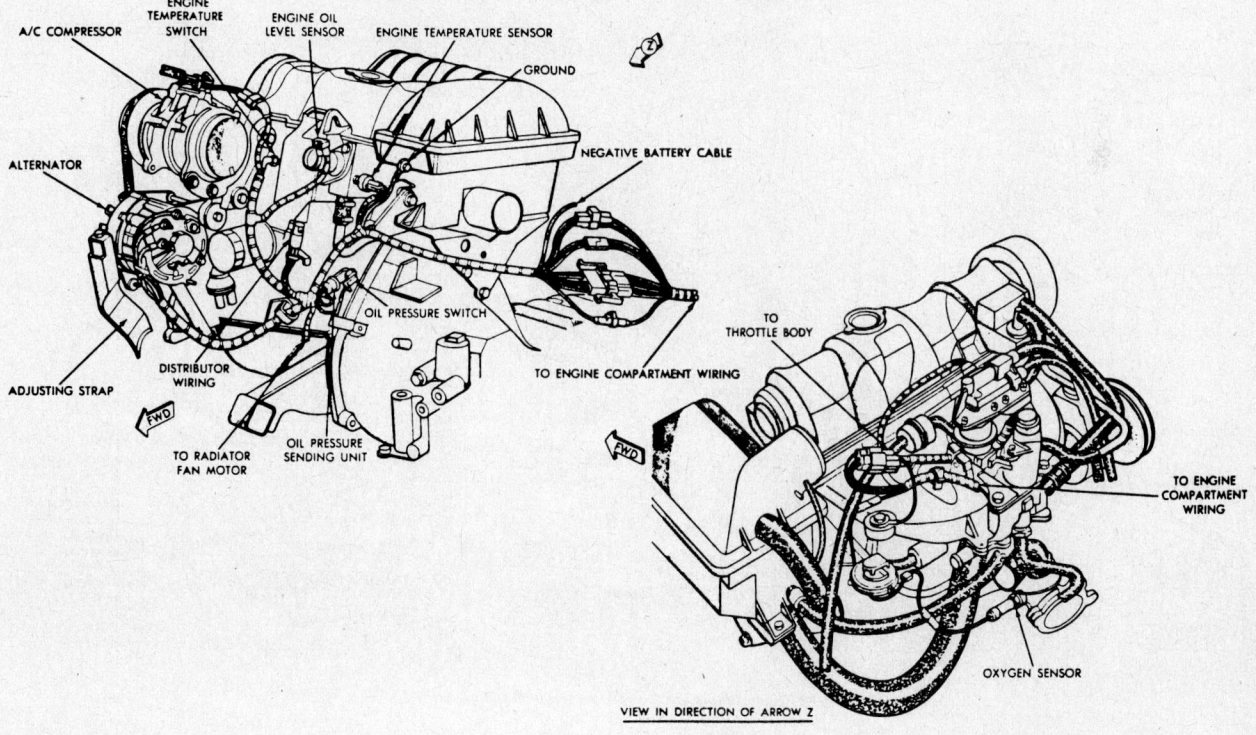

Engine Wiring and Component Identification 2.2L EFI Engine G Body

1984 Laser and Daytona

COMPONENT LOCATIONS

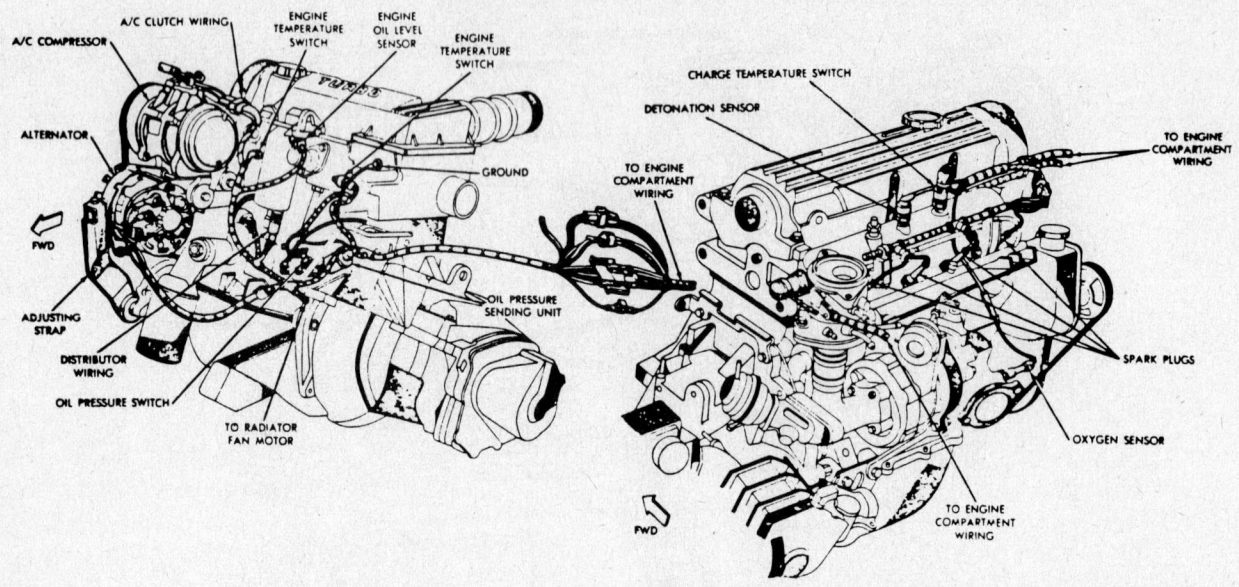

Engine Wiring and Component Identification 2.2L Turbo G Body

1984 Laser and Daytona

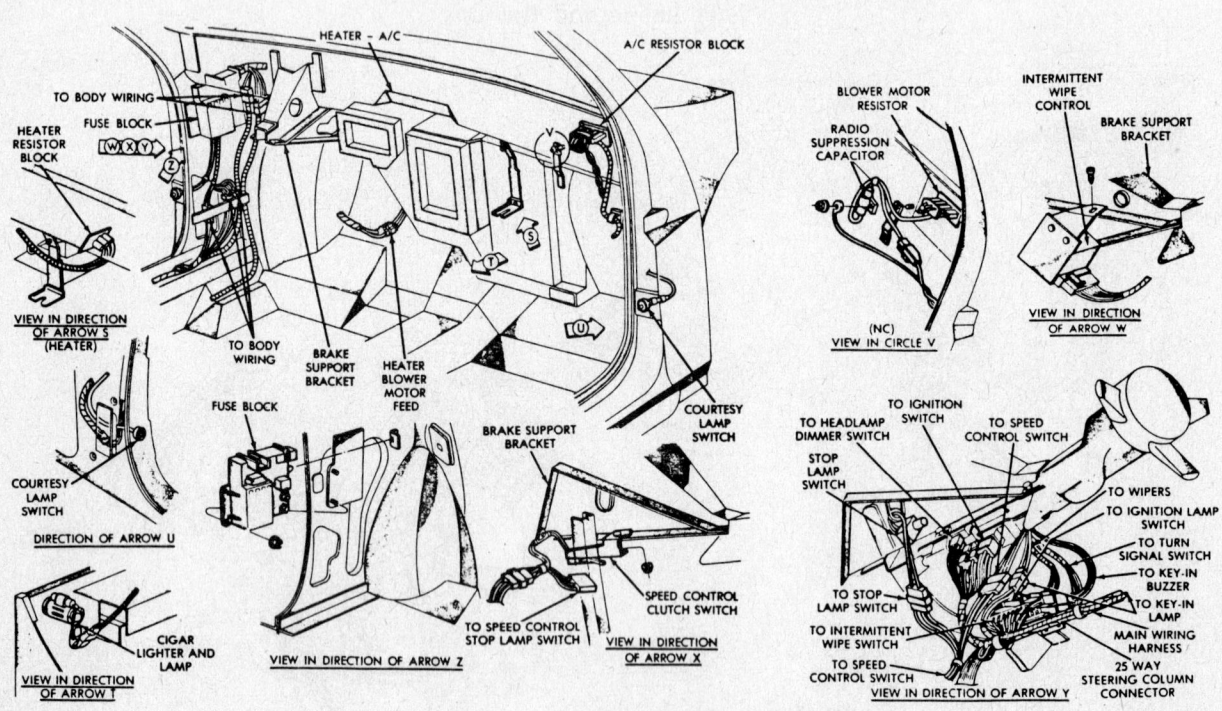

Cowl and Steering Column Wiring and Component Identification L Body M,Z,24,44

1985-86 Omni, Horizon, Charger and Turismo

COMPONENT LOCATIONS

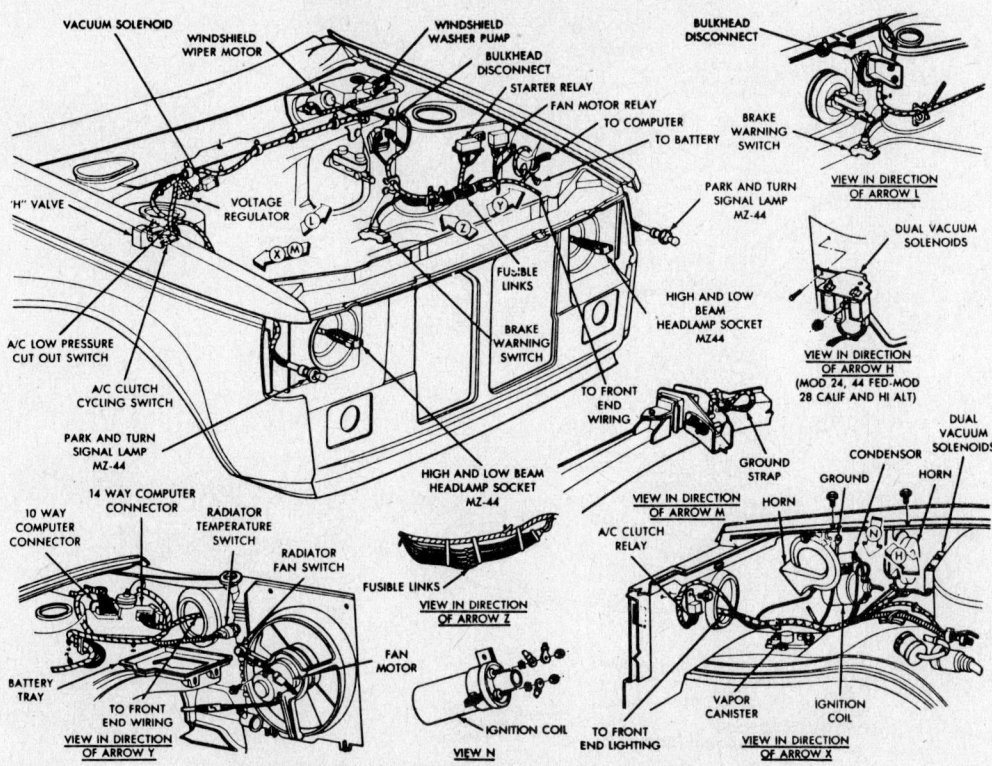

Engine Compartment Wiring and Component Identification 1.6L and 2.2L Engine L Body M,Z,24,44

1985-86 Omni, Horizon, Charger and Turismo

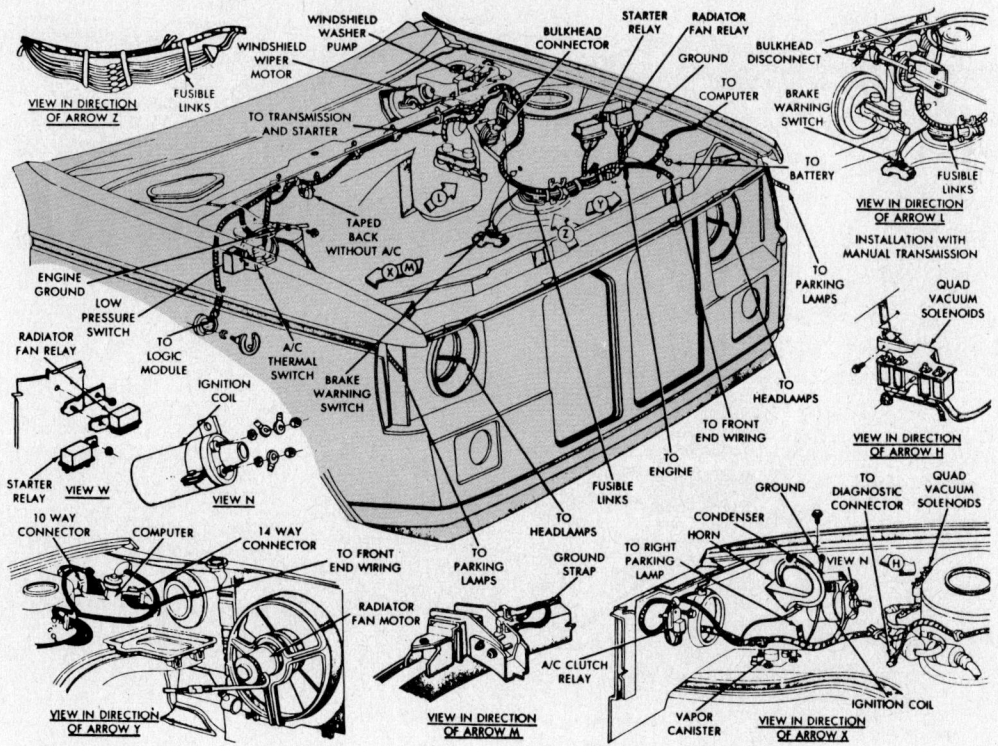

Engine Compartment Wiring and Component Identification L Body M,Z,24 2.2L Turbo

1985-86 Omni, Horizon, Charger and Turismo

COMPONENT LOCATIONS

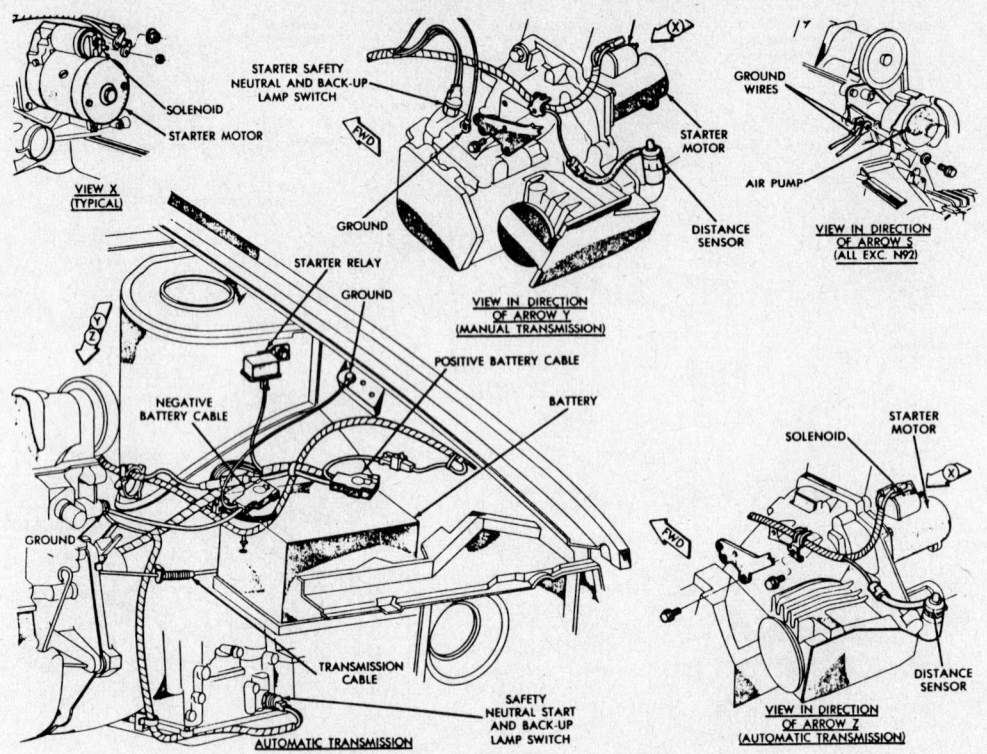

Engine Compartment, Starter and Transmission Switch Wiring and
Component Identification L Body 2.2L Engine M,Z,24,44

1985-86 Omni, Horizon, Charger and Turismo

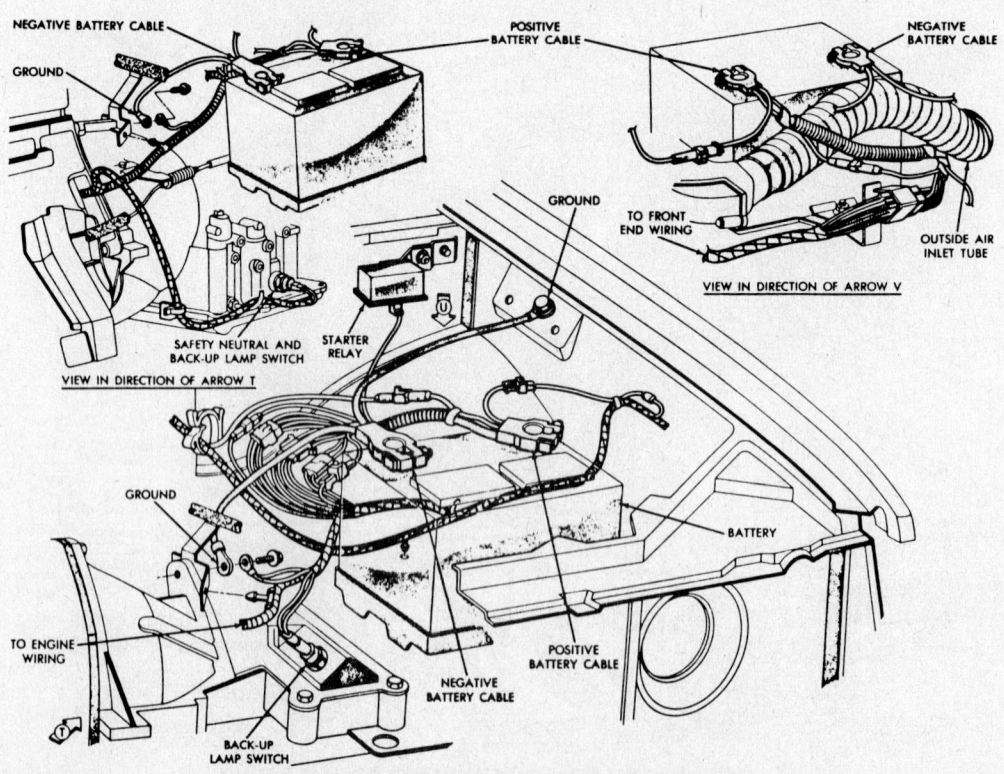

Engine Compartment Battery Cables and Transmission Switches 1.6L Engine L Body M,Z,24,44

1985-86 Omni, Horizon, Charger and Turismo

COMPONENT LOCATIONS

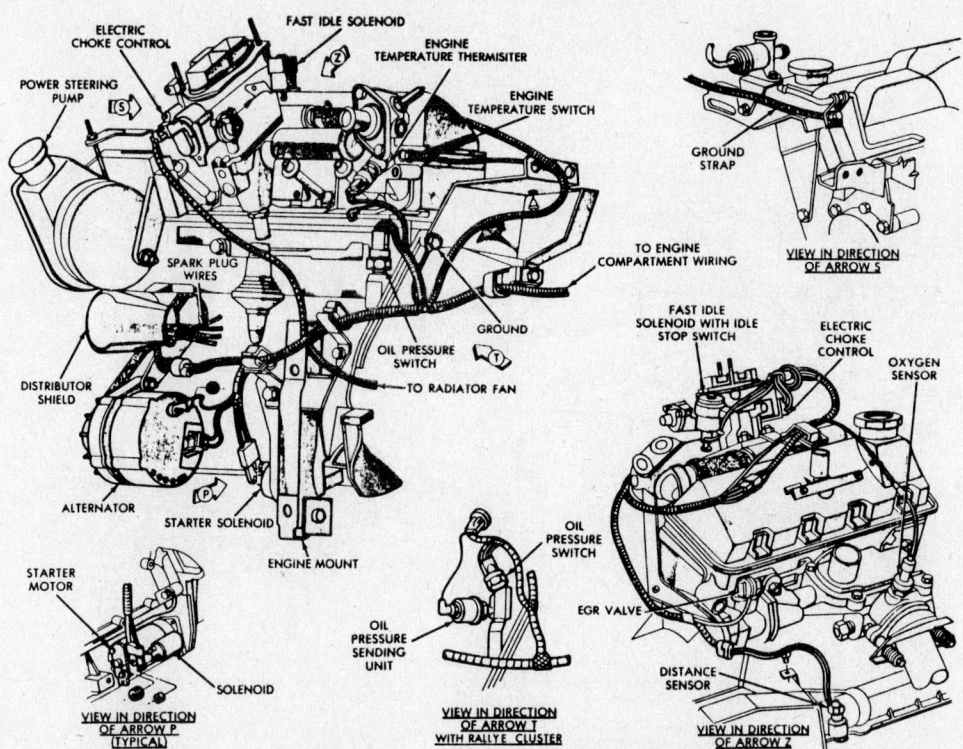

Engine Wiring and Component Identification 1.6L Engine M,Z,24,44

1985-86 Omni, Horizon, Charger and Turismo

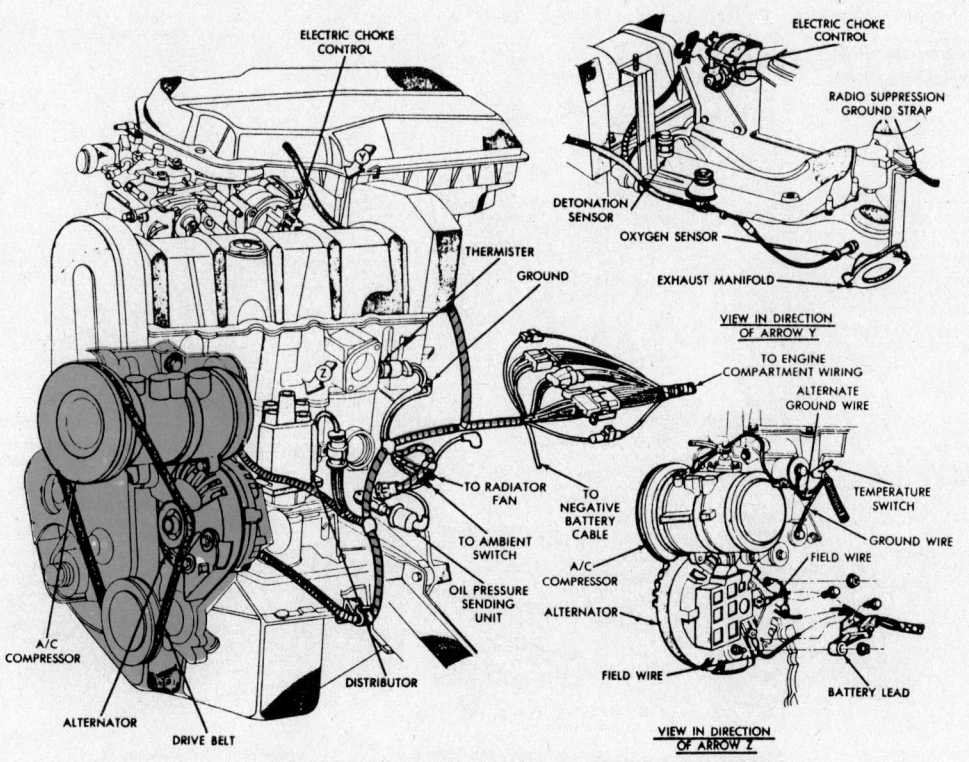

Engine Wiring and Component Identification 2.2L Engine L Body M,Z,24,44

1985-86 Omni, Horizon, Charger and Turismo

COMPONENT LOCATIONS

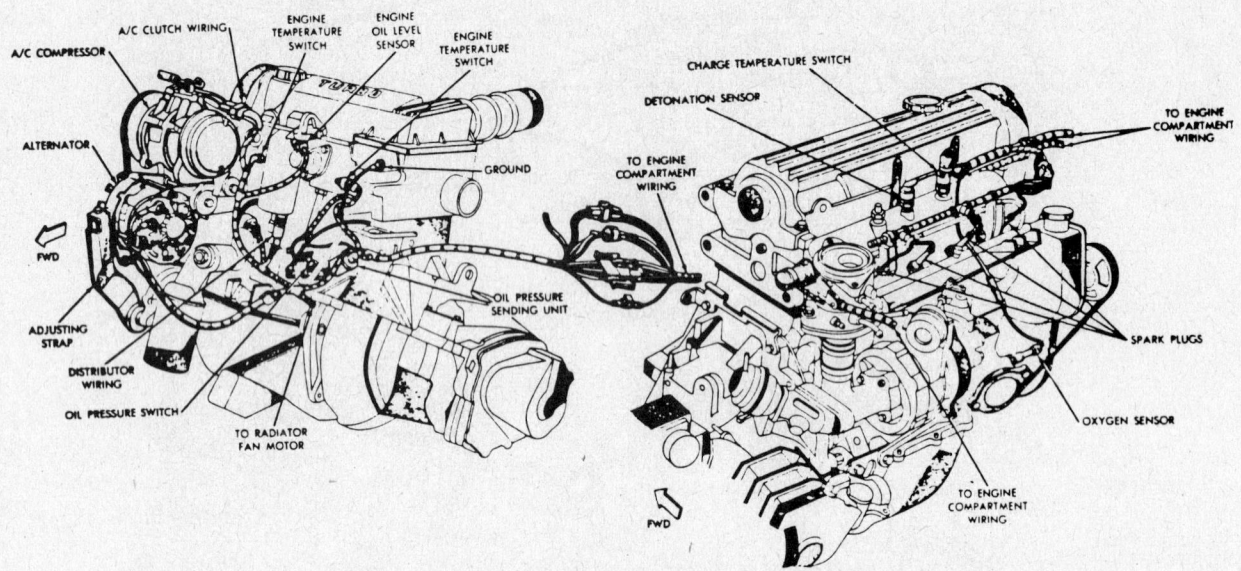

A/C COMPRESSOR

A/C CLUTCH WIRING

ENGINE TEMPERATURE SWITCH

ENGINE OIL LEVEL SENSOR

ENGINE TEMPERATURE SWITCH

ALTERNATOR

FWD

ADJUSTING STRAP

DISTRIBUTOR WIRING

OIL PRESSURE SWITCH

TO RADIATOR FAN MOTOR

GROUND

OIL PRESSURE SENDING UNIT

CHARGE TEMPERATURE SWITCH

DETONATION SENSOR

TO ENGINE COMPARTMENT WIRING

TO ENGINE COMPARTMENT WIRING

SPARK PLUGS

OXYGEN SENSOR

TO ENGINE COMPARTMENT WIRING

FWD

Engine Wiring and Component Identification 2.2L Turbo Engine L Body Z,24

1985-86 Omni, Horizon, Charger and Turismo

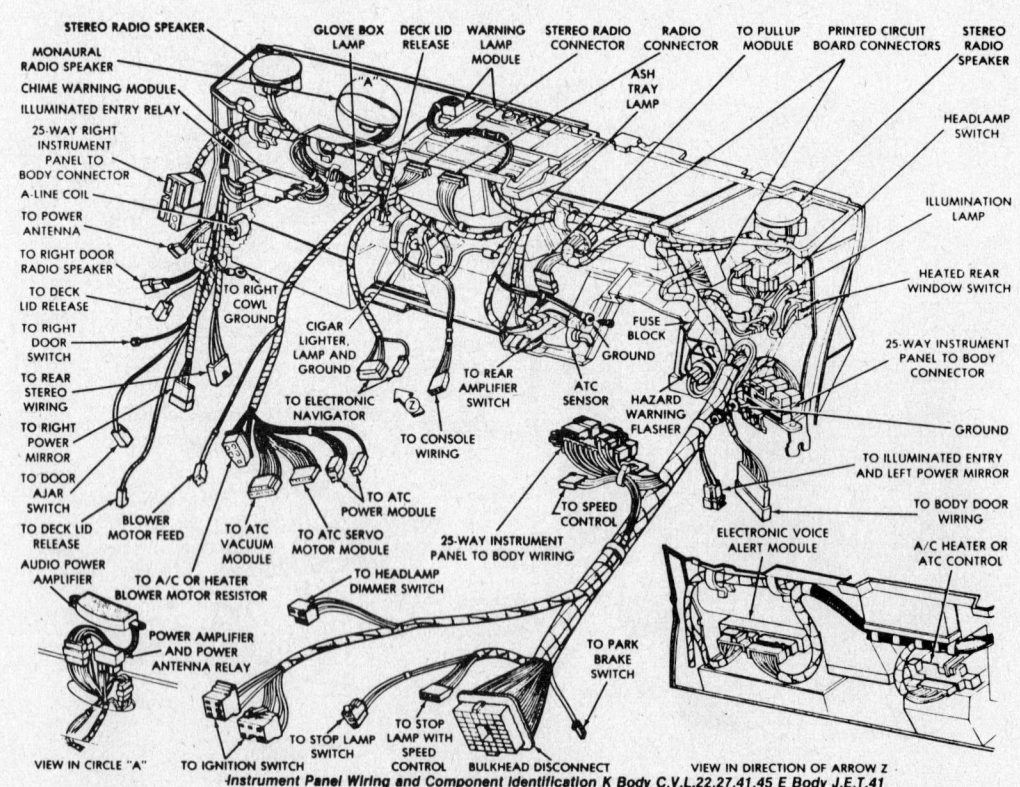

STEREO RADIO SPEAKER

MONAURAL RADIO SPEAKER

CHIME WARNING MODULE

ILLUMINATED ENTRY RELAY

25-WAY RIGHT INSTRUMENT PANEL TO BODY CONNECTOR

A-LINE COIL

TO POWER ANTENNA

TO RIGHT DOOR RADIO SPEAKER

TO DECK LID RELEASE

TO RIGHT DOOR SWITCH

TO REAR STEREO WIRING

TO RIGHT POWER MIRROR

TO DOOR AJAR SWITCH

TO DECK LID RELEASE

AUDIO POWER AMPLIFIER

POWER AMPLIFIER AND POWER ANTENNA RELAY

VIEW IN CIRCLE "A"

GLOVE BOX LAMP

DECK LID RELEASE

WARNING LAMP MODULE

STEREO RADIO CONNECTOR

RADIO CONNECTOR

TO PULLUP MODULE

PRINTED CIRCUIT BOARD CONNECTORS

STEREO RADIO SPEAKER

"A"

ASH TRAY LAMP

HEADLAMP SWITCH

ILLUMINATION LAMP

HEATED REAR WINDOW SWITCH

25-WAY INSTRUMENT PANEL TO BODY CONNECTOR

GROUND

TO ILLUMINATED ENTRY AND LEFT POWER MIRROR

TO BODY DOOR WIRING

A/C HEATER OR ATC CONTROL

TO RIGHT COWL GROUND

CIGAR LIGHTER, LAMP AND GROUND

TO ELECTRONIC NAVIGATOR

BLOWER MOTOR FEED

TO ATC VACUUM MODULE

TO ATC SERVO MOTOR MODULE

TO ATC POWER MODULE

TO REAR AMPLIFIER SWITCH

TO CONSOLE WIRING

25-WAY INSTRUMENT PANEL TO BODY WIRING

FUSE BLOCK GROUND

ATC SENSOR

HAZARD WARNING FLASHER

TO SPEED CONTROL

ELECTRONIC VOICE ALERT MODULE

TO A/C OR HEATER BLOWER MOTOR RESISTOR

TO HEADLAMP DIMMER SWITCH

TO IGNITION SWITCH

TO STOP LAMP SWITCH

TO STOP LAMP WITH SPEED CONTROL

BULKHEAD DISCONNECT

TO PARK BRAKE SWITCH

VIEW IN DIRECTION OF ARROW Z

Instrument Panel Wiring and Component Identification K Body C,V,L,22,27,41,45 E Body J,E,T,41

1985-86 Caravelle, 600, LeBaron (K), New Yorker, Aries and Reliant

COMPONENT LOCATIONS

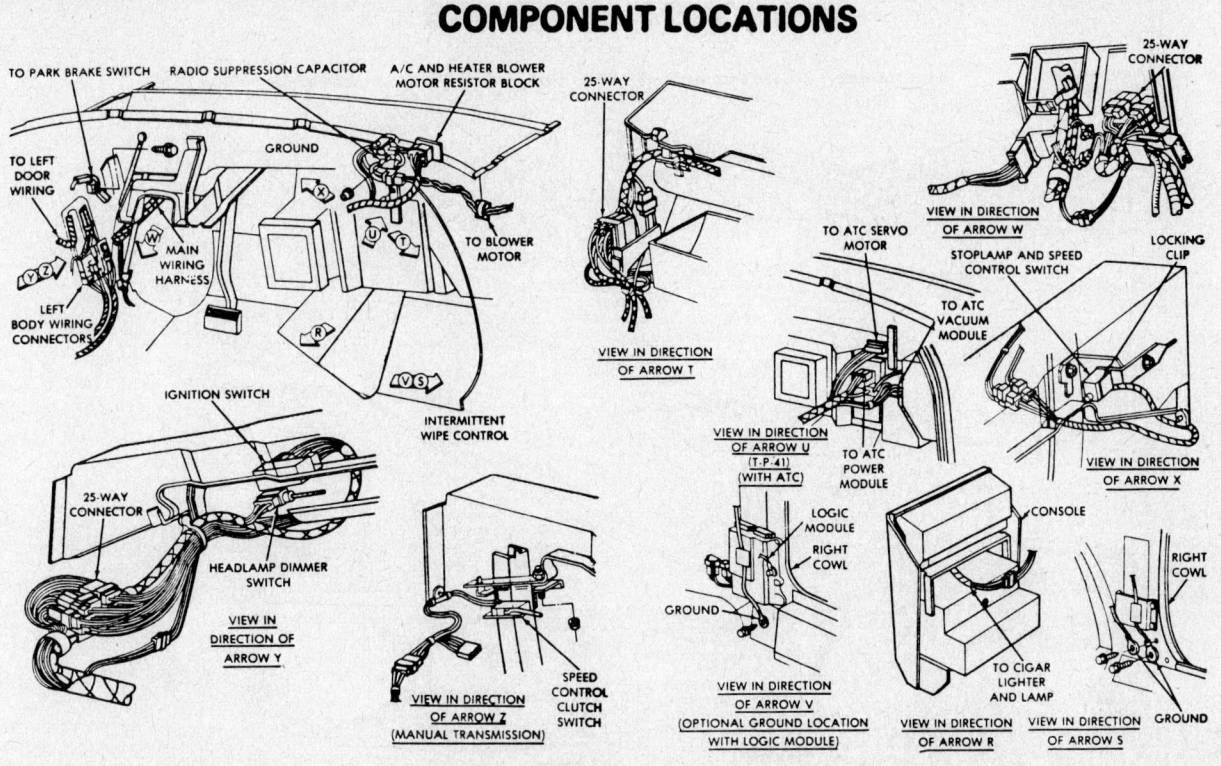

Cowl Wiring and Component Identification K & E Body All

1985-86 Caravelle, 600, LeBaron (K), New Yorker, Aries and Reliant

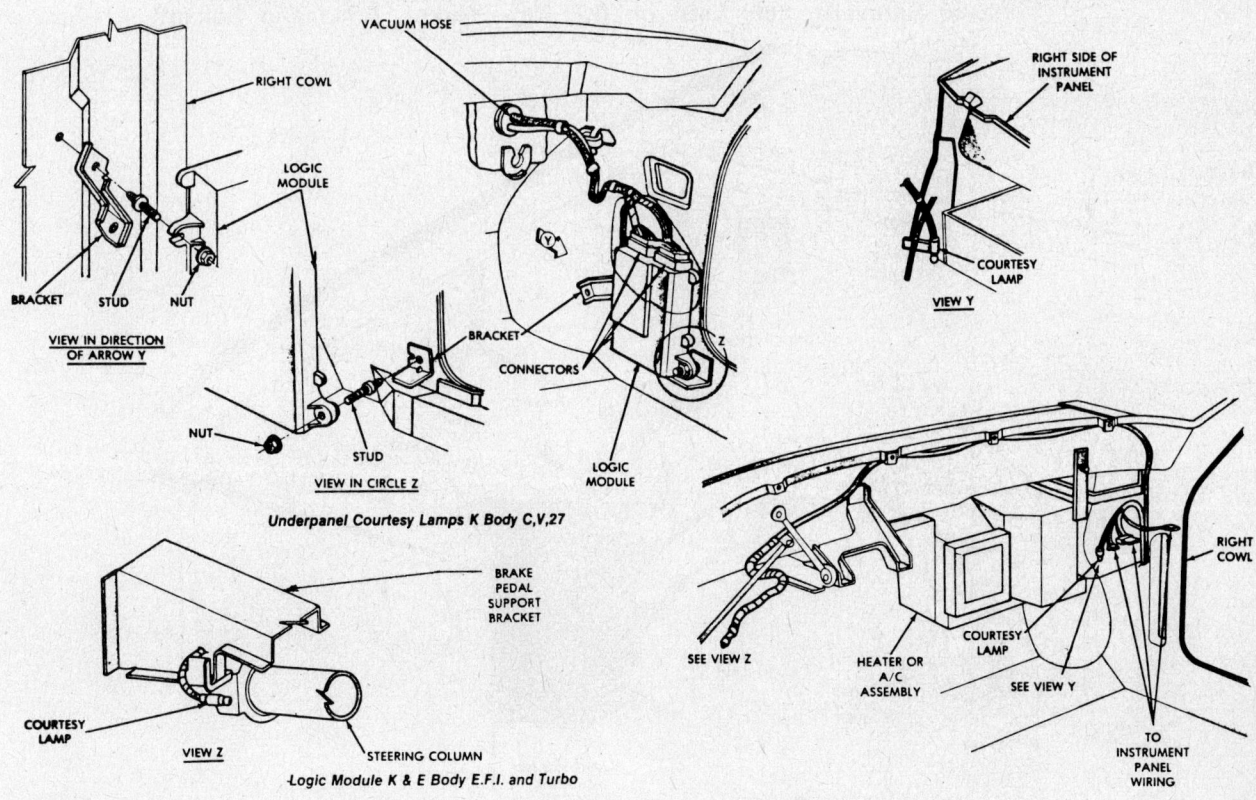

Underpanel Courtesy Lamps K Body C,V,27

Logic Module K & E Body E.F.I. and Turbo

1985-86 Caravelle, 600, LeBaron (K), New Yorker, Aries and Reliant

COMPONENT LOCATIONS

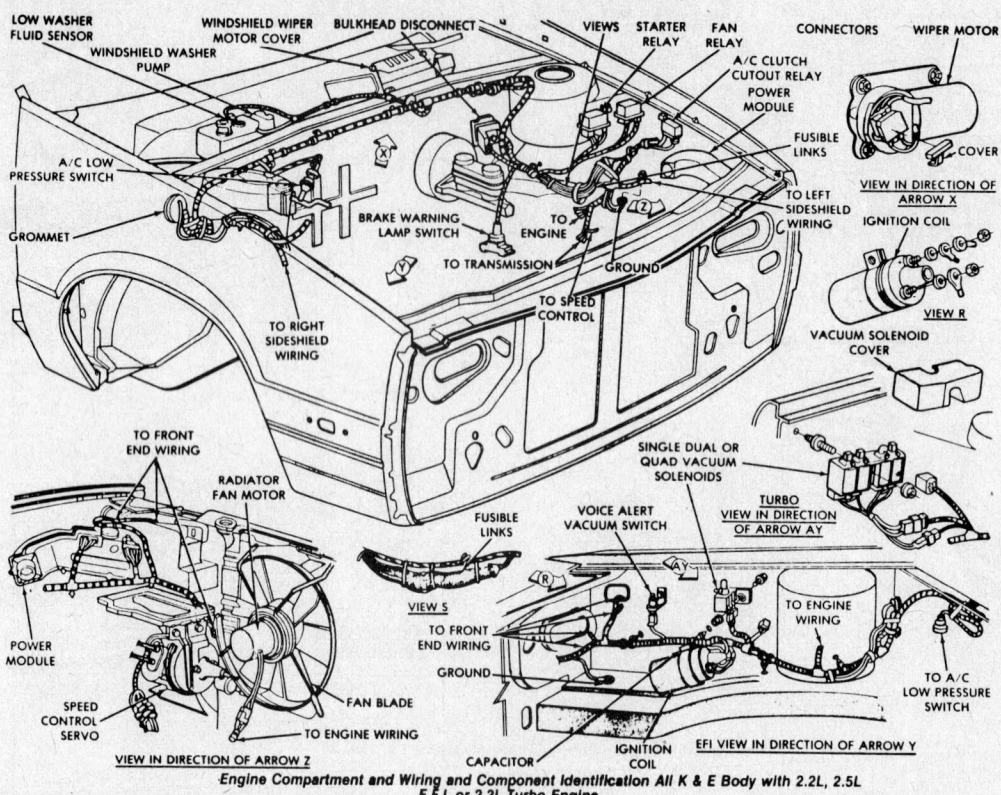

Engine Compartment and Wiring and Component Identification All K & E Body with 2.2L, 2.5L E.F.I. or 2.2L Turbo Engine

1985-86 Caravelle, 600, LeBaron (K), New Yorker, Aries and Reliant

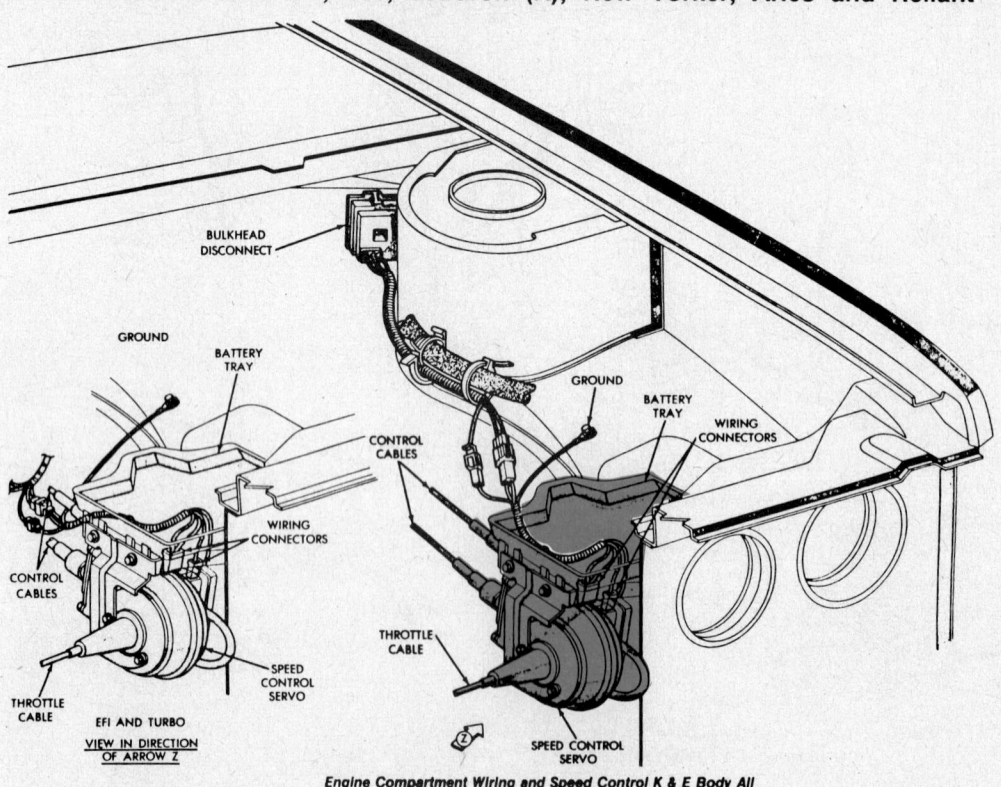

Engine Compartment Wiring and Speed Control K & E Body All

1985-86 Caravelle, 600, LeBaron (K), New Yorker, Aries and Reliant

COMPONENT LOCATIONS

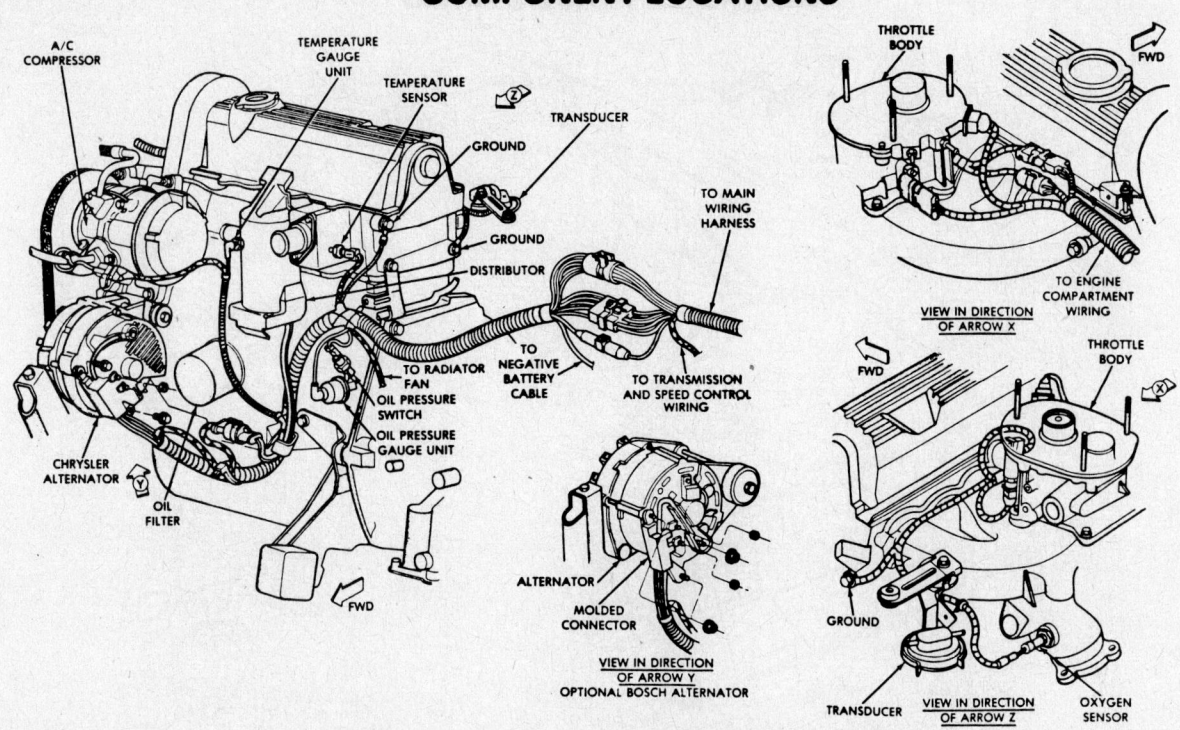

Engine Wiring and Component Identification 2.2L and 2.5L E.F.I. Engine K & E Body

1985-86 Caravelle, 600, LeBaron (K), New Yorker, Aries and Reliant

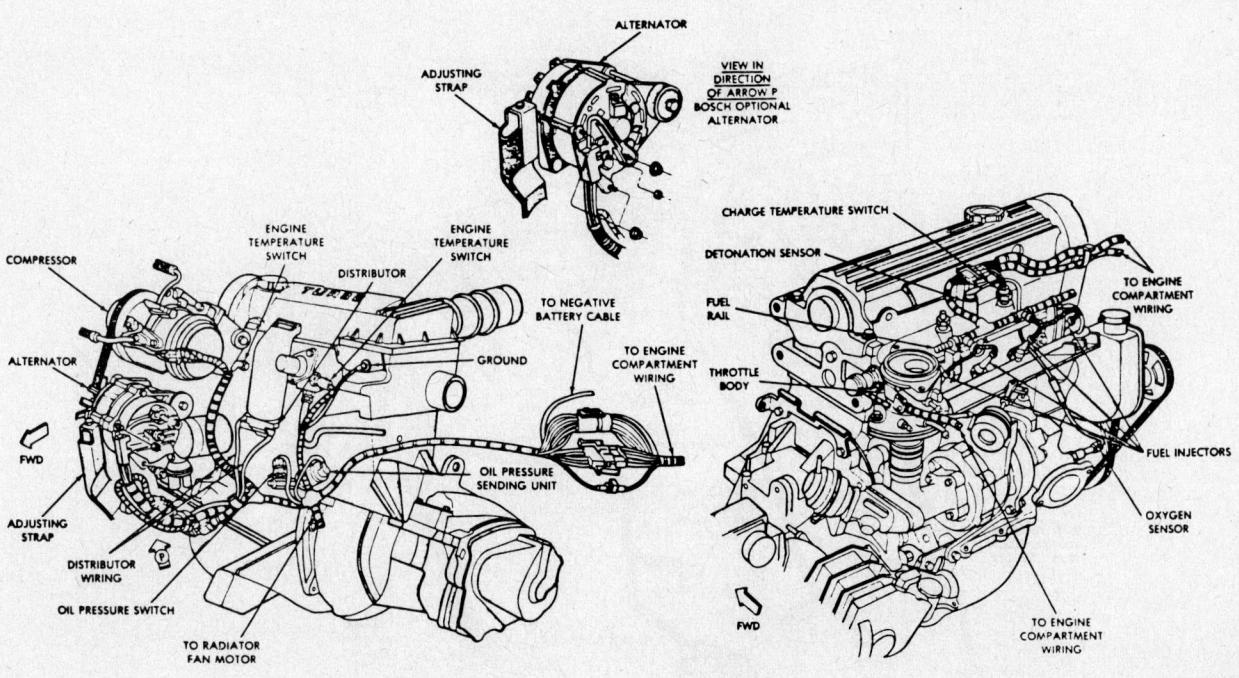

Engine Wiring and Component Identification 2.2L Turbo K & E Body C,V,L,J,E,T

1985-86 Caravelle, 600, LeBaron (K), New Yorker, Aries and Reliant

COMPONENT LOCATIONS

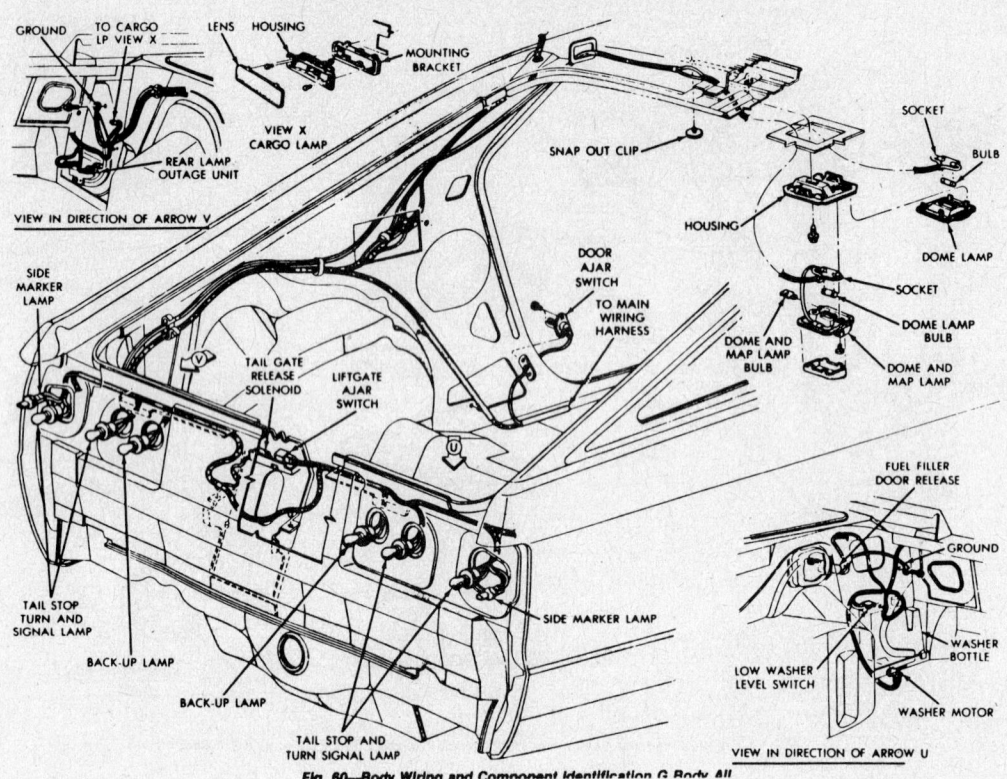

Fig. 60—Body Wiring and Component Identification G Body All

1985-85 Laser and Daytona

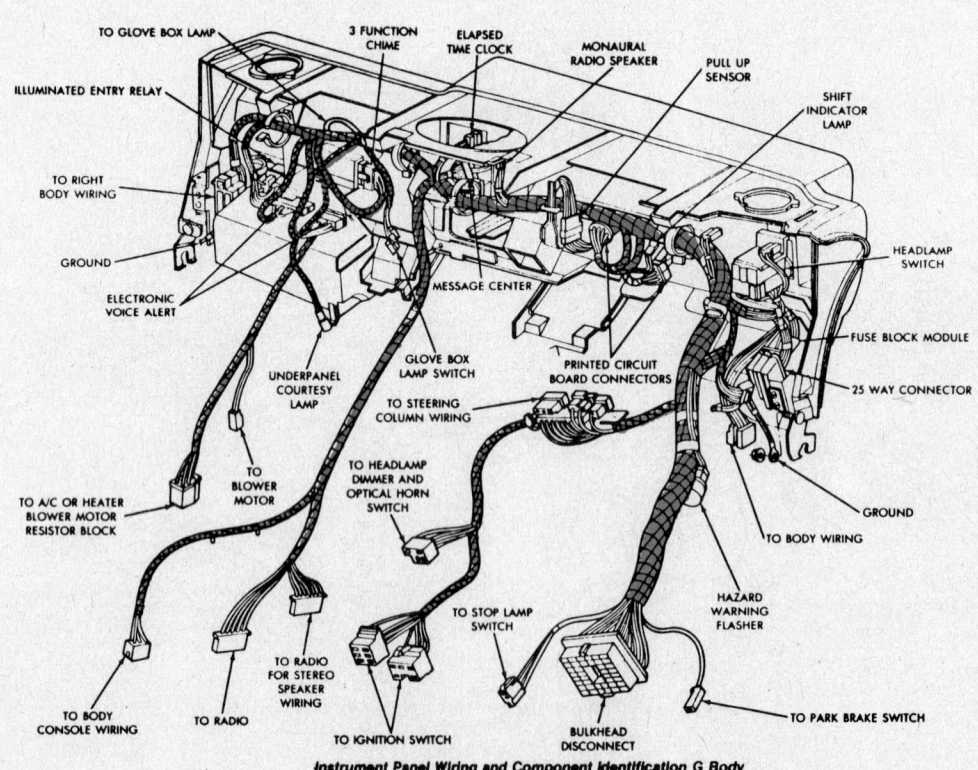

Instrument Panel Wiring and Component Identification G Body

1985-85 Laser and Daytona

COMPONENT LOCATIONS

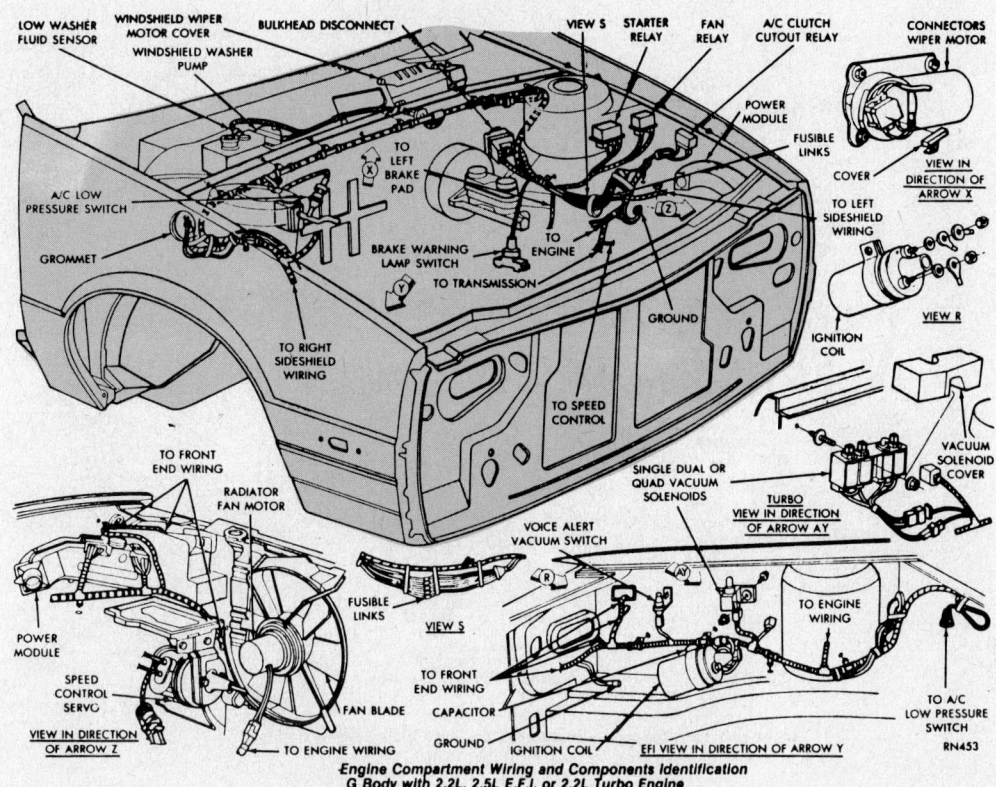

Engine Compartment Wiring and Components Identification
G Body with 2.2L, 2.5L E.F.I. or 2.2L Turbo Engine

1985-85 Laser and Daytona

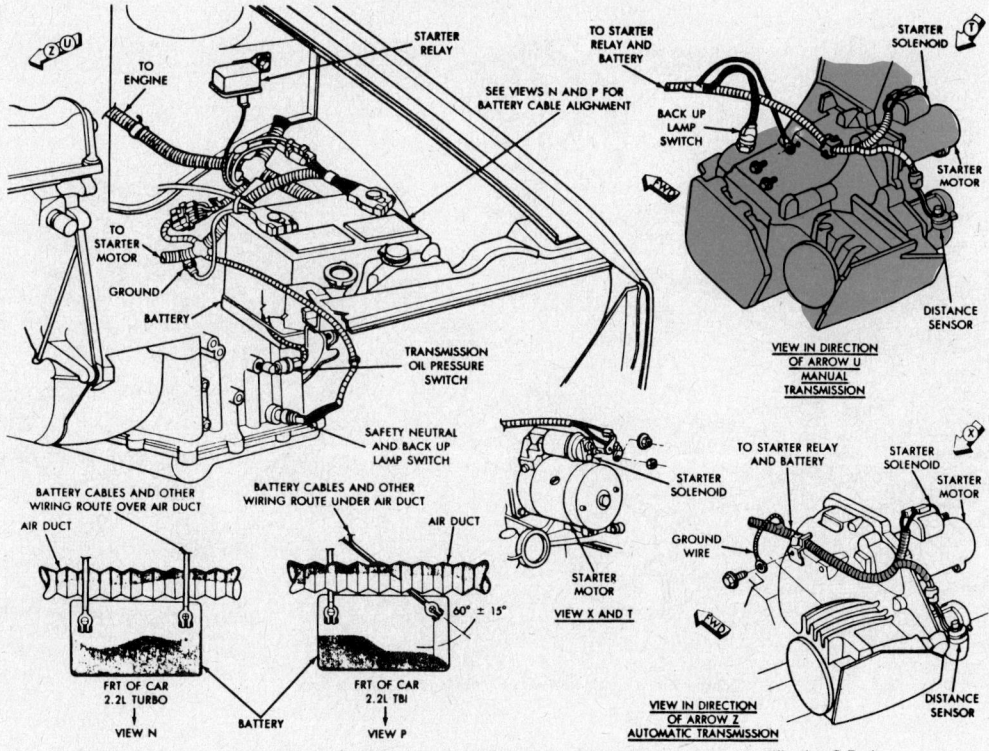

Engine Compartment Starter and Transmission Switch Wiring and Component Identification G Body

1985-85 Laser and Daytona

COMPONENT LOCATIONS

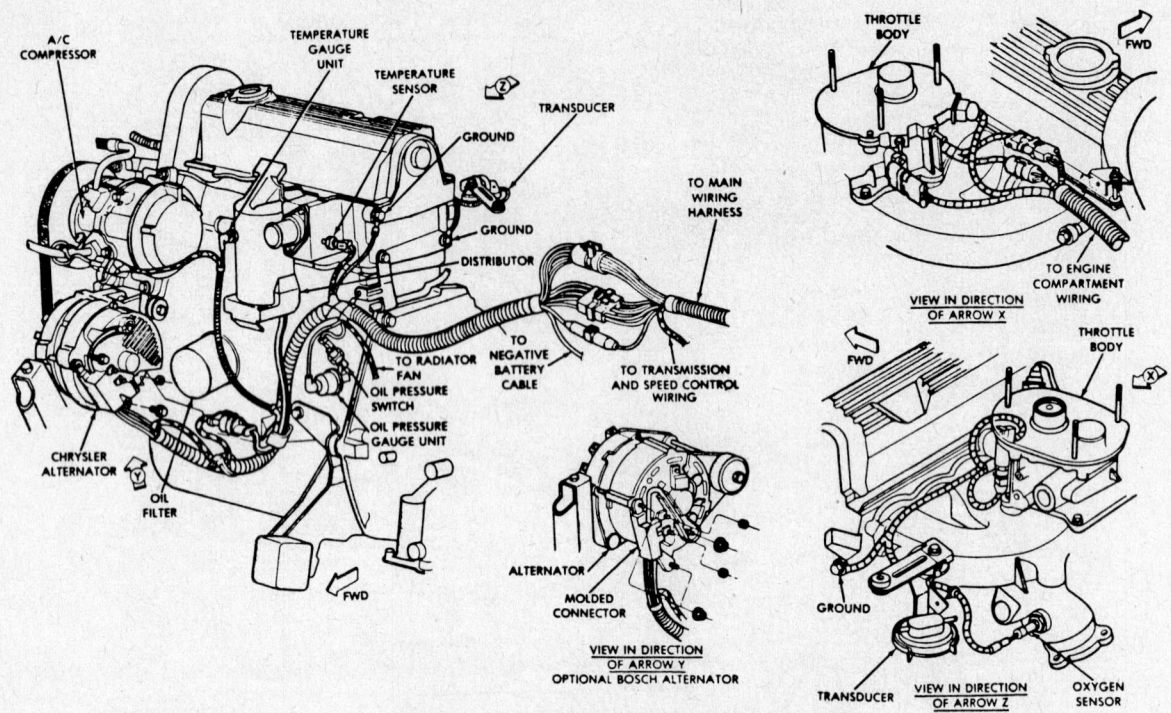

Engine Wiring and Component Identification 2.2L and 2.5L E.F.I. Engine G Body

1985-85 Laser and Daytona

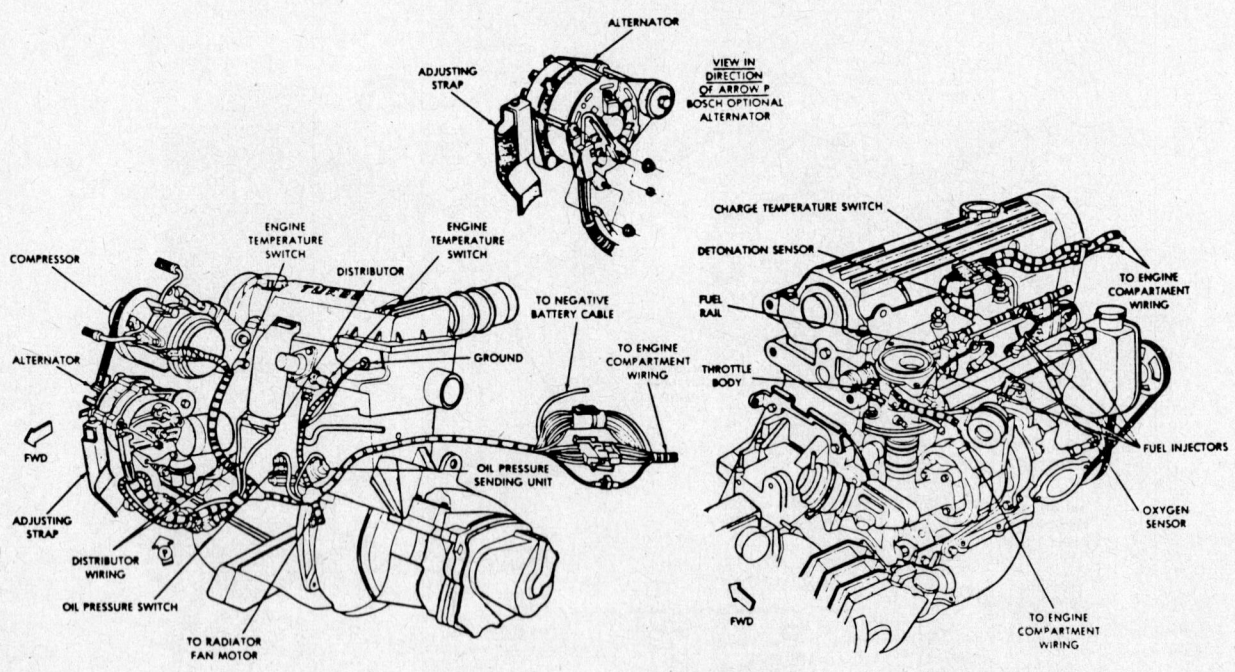

Engine Wiring and Component Identification 2.2L Turbo G Body

1985-85 Laser and Daytona

COMPONENT LOCATIONS

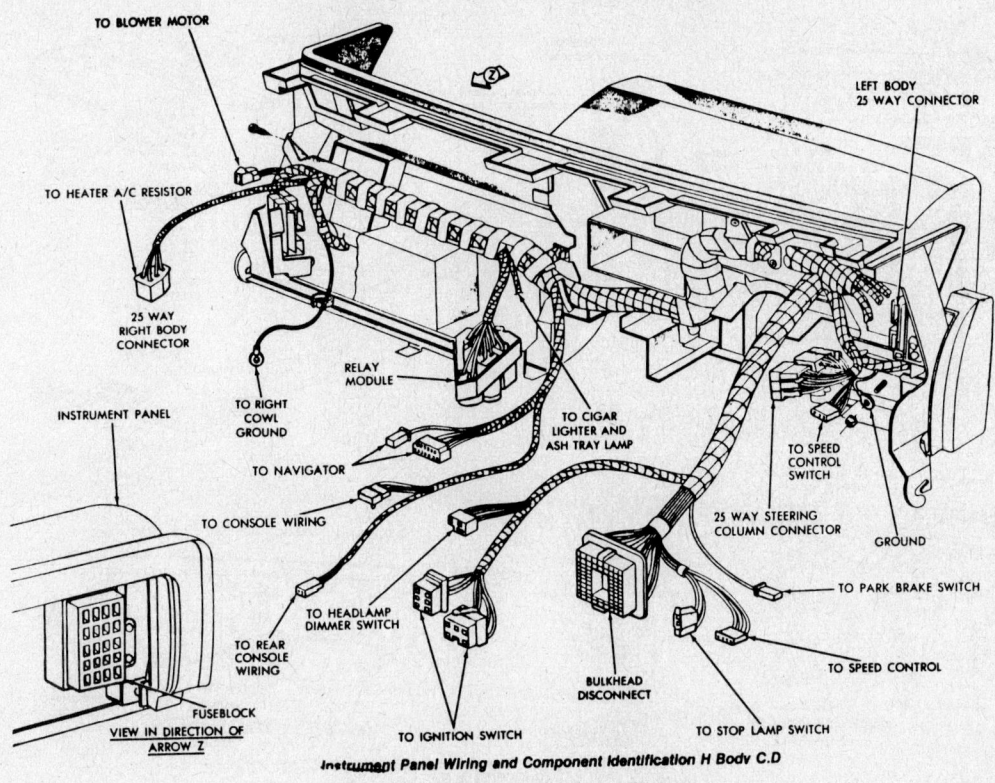

TO BLOWER MOTOR

TO HEATER A/C RESISTOR

25 WAY RIGHT BODY CONNECTOR

INSTRUMENT PANEL

TO RIGHT COWL GROUND

RELAY MODULE

TO NAVIGATOR

TO CONSOLE WIRING

TO REAR CONSOLE WIRING

TO HEADLAMP DIMMER SWITCH

FUSEBLOCK

VIEW IN DIRECTION OF ARROW Z

TO IGNITION SWITCH

BULKHEAD DISCONNECT

TO CIGAR LIGHTER AND ASH TRAY LAMP

LEFT BODY 25 WAY CONNECTOR

TO SPEED CONTROL SWITCH

25 WAY STEERING COLUMN CONNECTOR

GROUND

TO PARK BRAKE SWITCH

TO SPEED CONTROL

TO STOP LAMP SWITCH

Instrument Panel Wiring and Component Identification H Body C,D

1985-85 Lancer and LeBaron

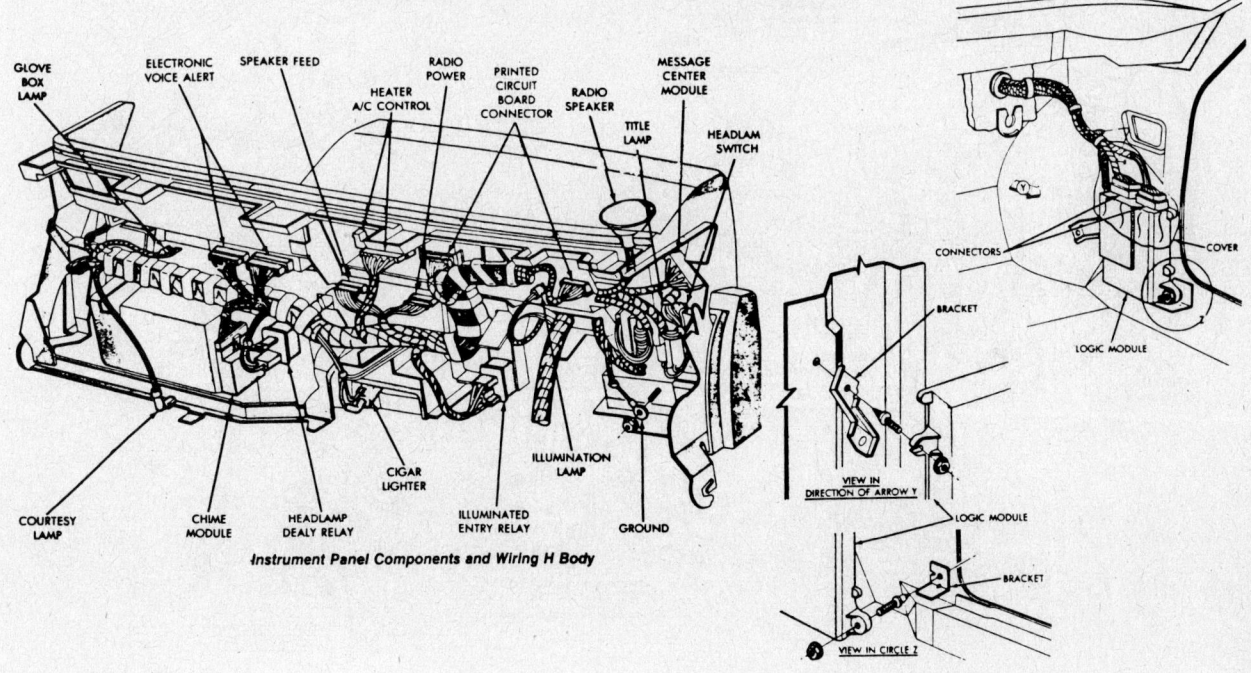

GLOVE BOX LAMP

ELECTRONIC VOICE ALERT

SPEAKER FEED

HEATER A/C CONTROL

RADIO POWER

PRINTED CIRCUIT BOARD CONNECTOR

RADIO SPEAKER

MESSAGE CENTER MODULE

TITLE LAMP

HEADLAM SWITCH

CONNECTORS

COVER

BRACKET

LOGIC MODULE

VIEW IN DIRECTION OF ARROW Y

LOGIC MODULE

BRACKET

VIEW IN CIRCLE Z

COURTESY LAMP

CHIME MODULE

HEADLAMP DEALY RELAY

CIGAR LIGHTER

ILLUMINATED ENTRY RELAY

ILLUMINATION LAMP

GROUND

Instrument Panel Components and Wiring H Body

Logic Module H Body E.F.I. and Turbo

1985-85 Lancer and LeBaron

COMPONENT LOCATIONS

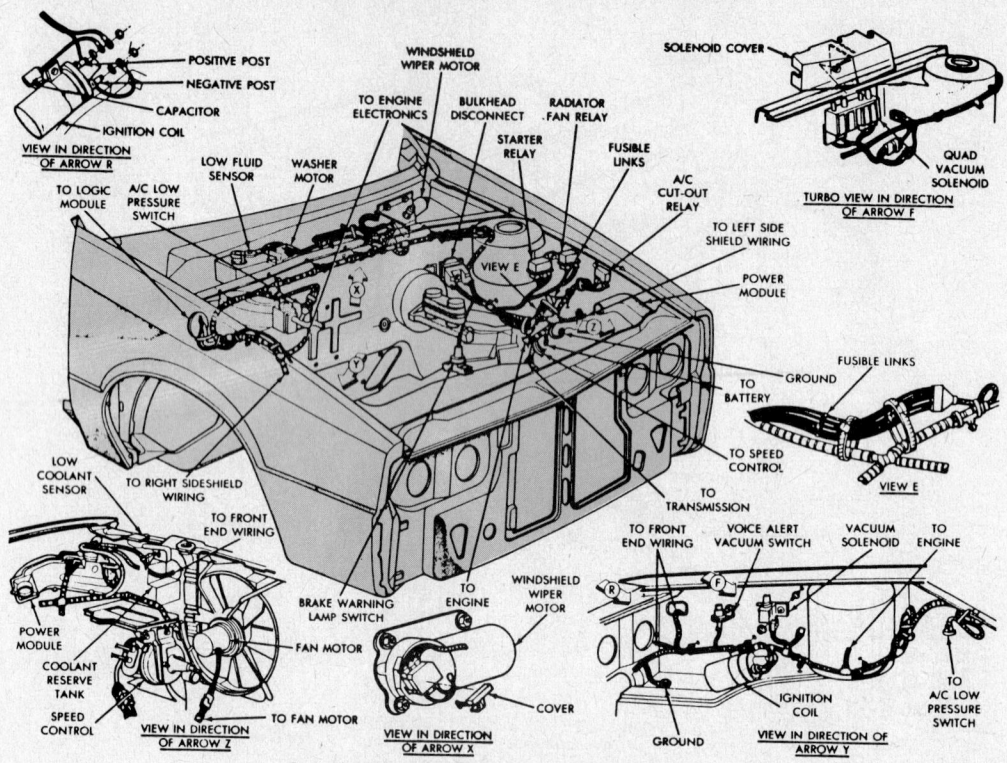

Engine Compartment Wiring and Component Identification 2.2L, 2.5L E.F.I.
and 2.2L Turbo H Body C,D

1985-85 Lancer and LeBaron

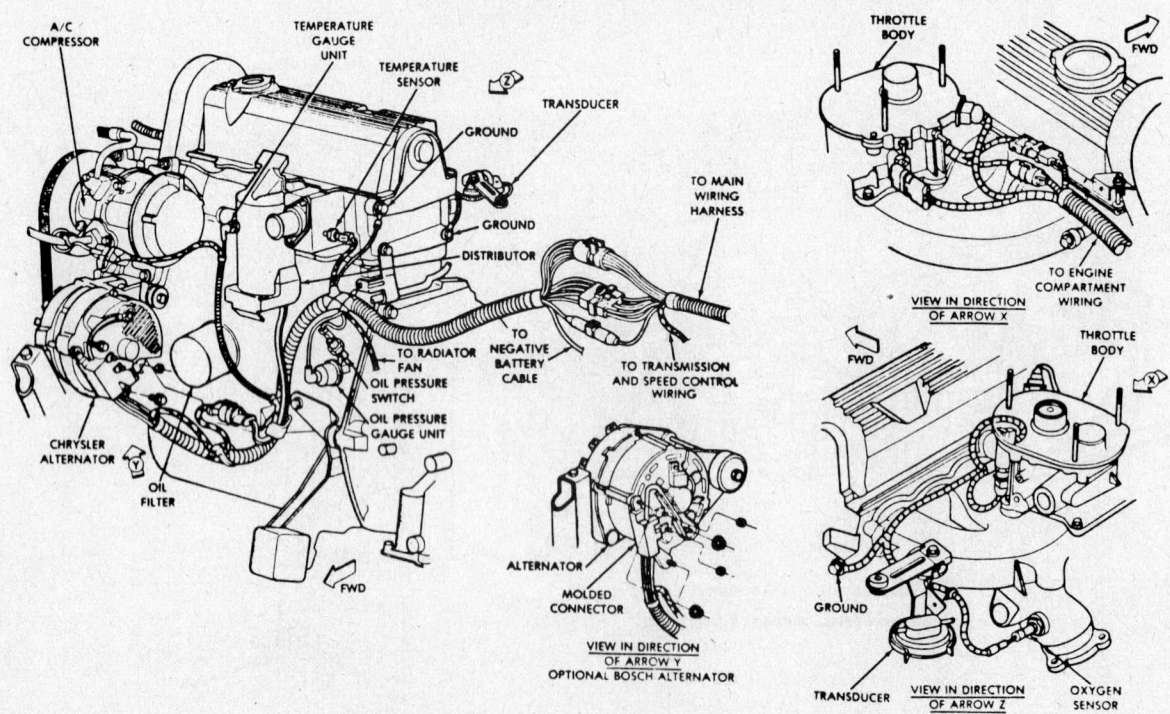

Engine Wiring and Component Identification 2.2L and 2.5L E.F.I. Engine H Body C,D

1985-85 Lancer and LeBaron

COMPONENT LOCATIONS

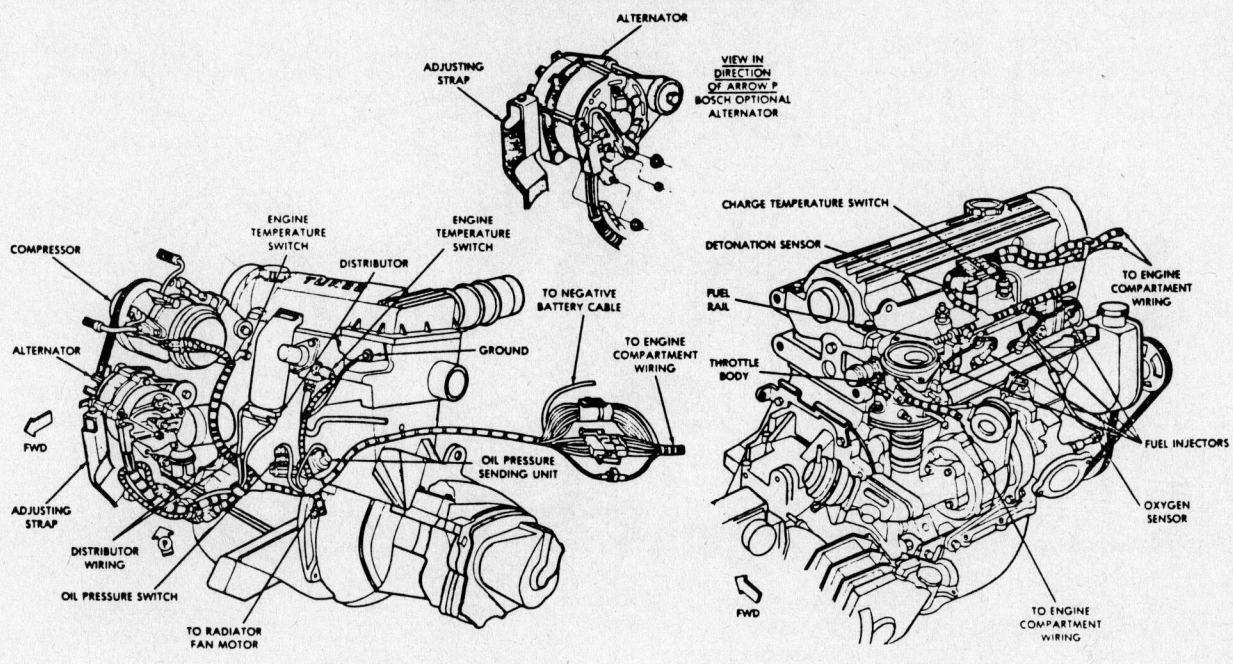

Engine Wiring and Component Identification 2.2L Turbo H Body C,D

1985-85 Lancer and LeBaron

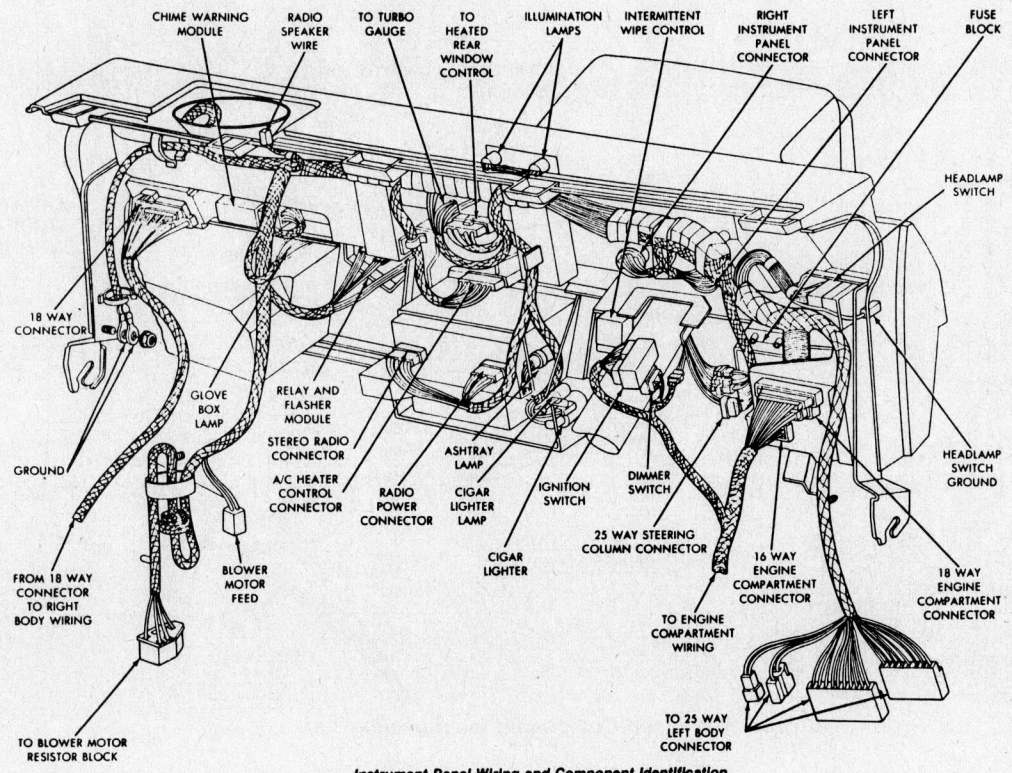

Instrument Panel Wiring and Component Identification

1987 Sundance and Shadow

COMPONENT LOCATIONS

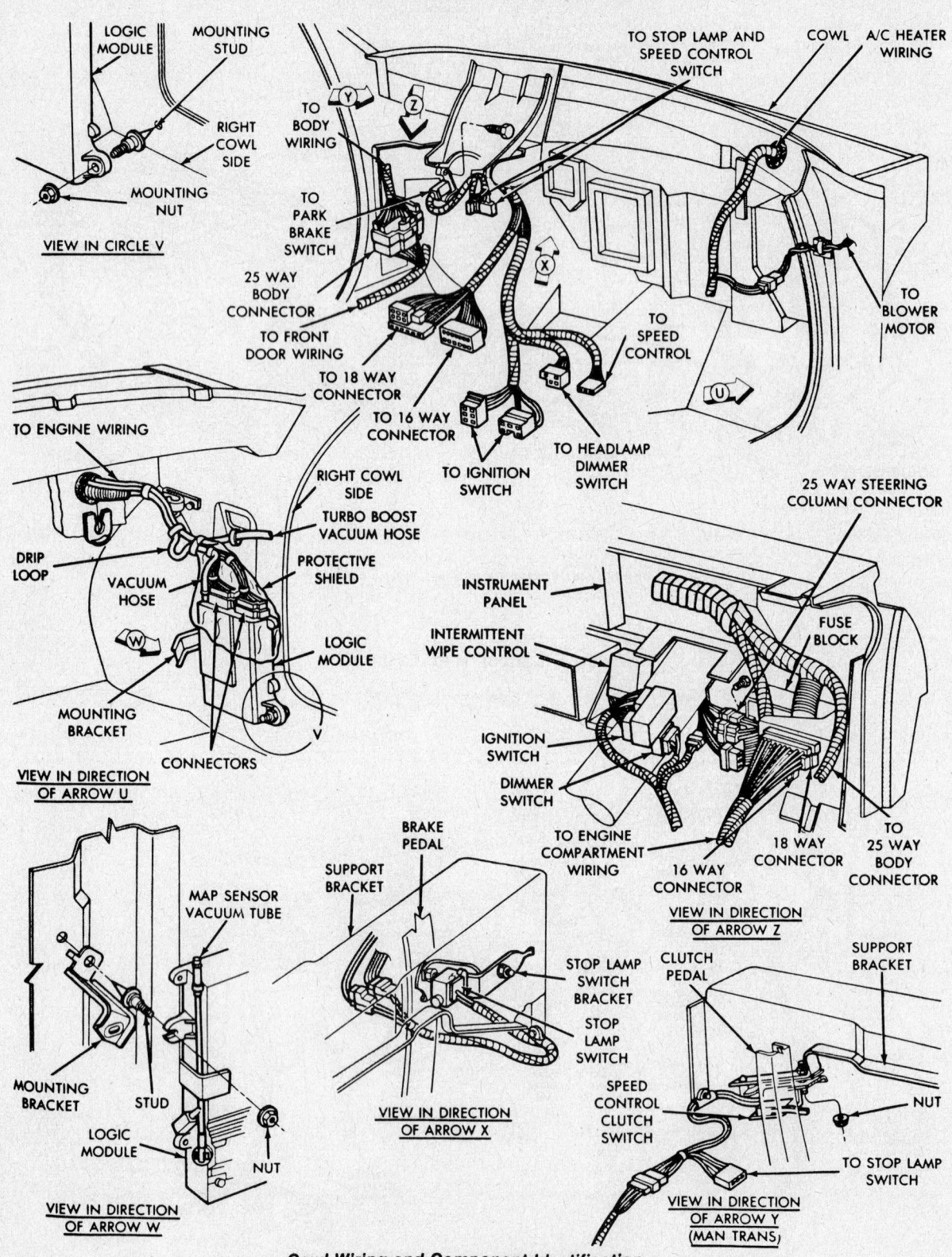

LOGIC MODULE
MOUNTING STUD
RIGHT COWL SIDE
MOUNTING NUT

VIEW IN CIRCLE V

TO STOP LAMP AND SPEED CONTROL SWITCH
COWL
A/C HEATER WIRING

TO BODY WIRING
TO PARK BRAKE SWITCH
25 WAY BODY CONNECTOR
TO FRONT DOOR WIRING
TO 18 WAY CONNECTOR
TO 16 WAY CONNECTOR
TO IGNITION SWITCH
TO HEADLAMP DIMMER SWITCH
TO SPEED CONTROL
TO BLOWER MOTOR

TO ENGINE WIRING
DRIP LOOP
VACUUM HOSE
MOUNTING BRACKET
CONNECTORS
RIGHT COWL SIDE
TURBO BOOST VACUUM HOSE
PROTECTIVE SHIELD
LOGIC MODULE

VIEW IN DIRECTION OF ARROW U

25 WAY STEERING COLUMN CONNECTOR
INSTRUMENT PANEL
INTERMITTENT WIPE CONTROL
FUSE BLOCK
IGNITION SWITCH
DIMMER SWITCH
TO ENGINE COMPARTMENT WIRING
16 WAY CONNECTOR
18 WAY CONNECTOR
TO 25 WAY BODY CONNECTOR

VIEW IN DIRECTION OF ARROW Z

MAP SENSOR VACUUM TUBE
MOUNTING BRACKET
STUD
LOGIC MODULE
NUT

VIEW IN DIRECTION OF ARROW W

SUPPORT BRACKET
BRAKE PEDAL
STOP LAMP SWITCH BRACKET
STOP LAMP SWITCH

VIEW IN DIRECTION OF ARROW X

CLUTCH PEDAL
SUPPORT BRACKET
SPEED CONTROL CLUTCH SWITCH
NUT
TO STOP LAMP SWITCH

VIEW IN DIRECTION OF ARROW Y (MAN TRANS)

Cowl Wiring and Component Identification

1987 Sundance and Shadow

COMPONENT LOCATIONS

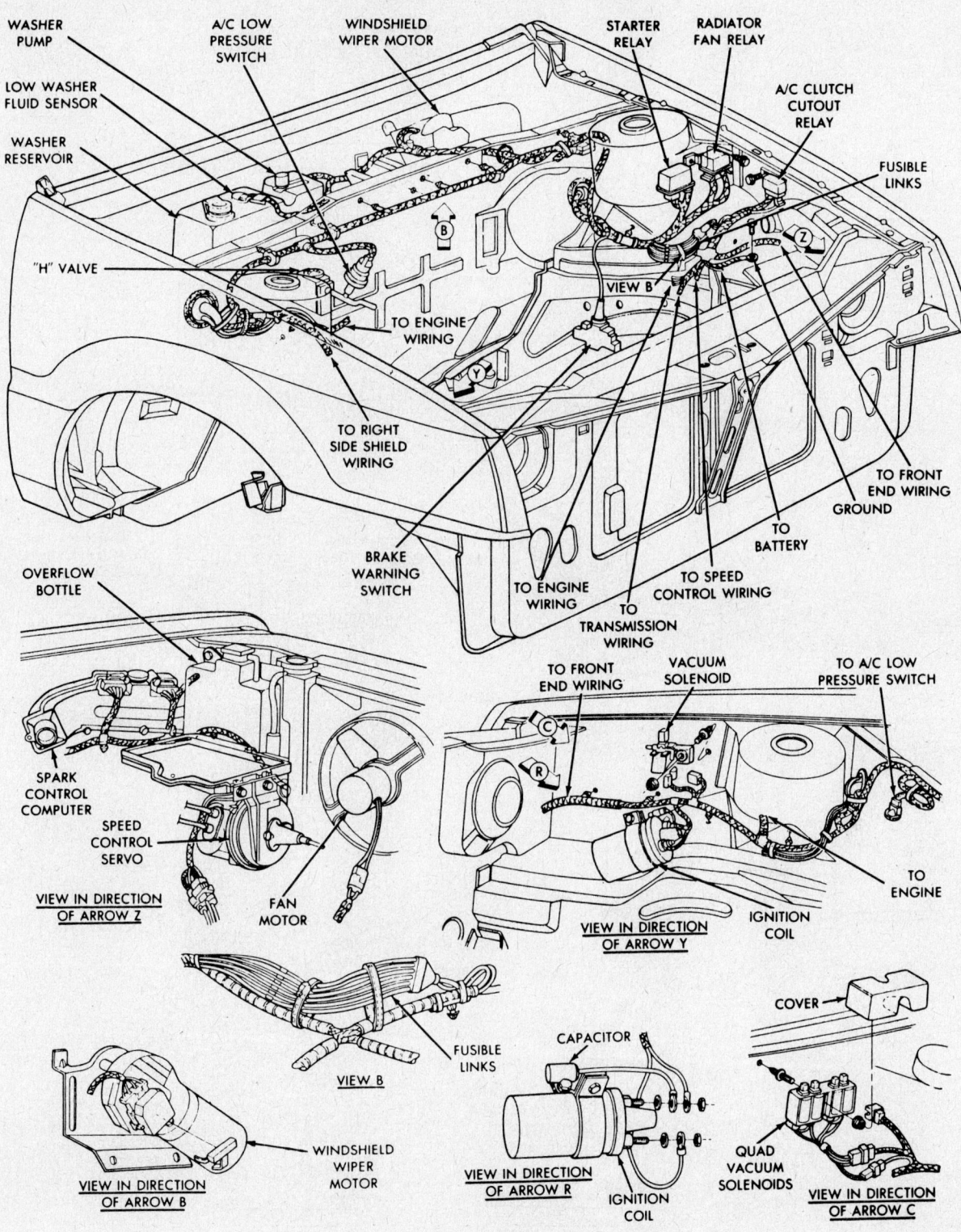

Engine Compartment Wiring and Component Identification

1987 Sundance and Shadow

COMPONENT LOCATIONS

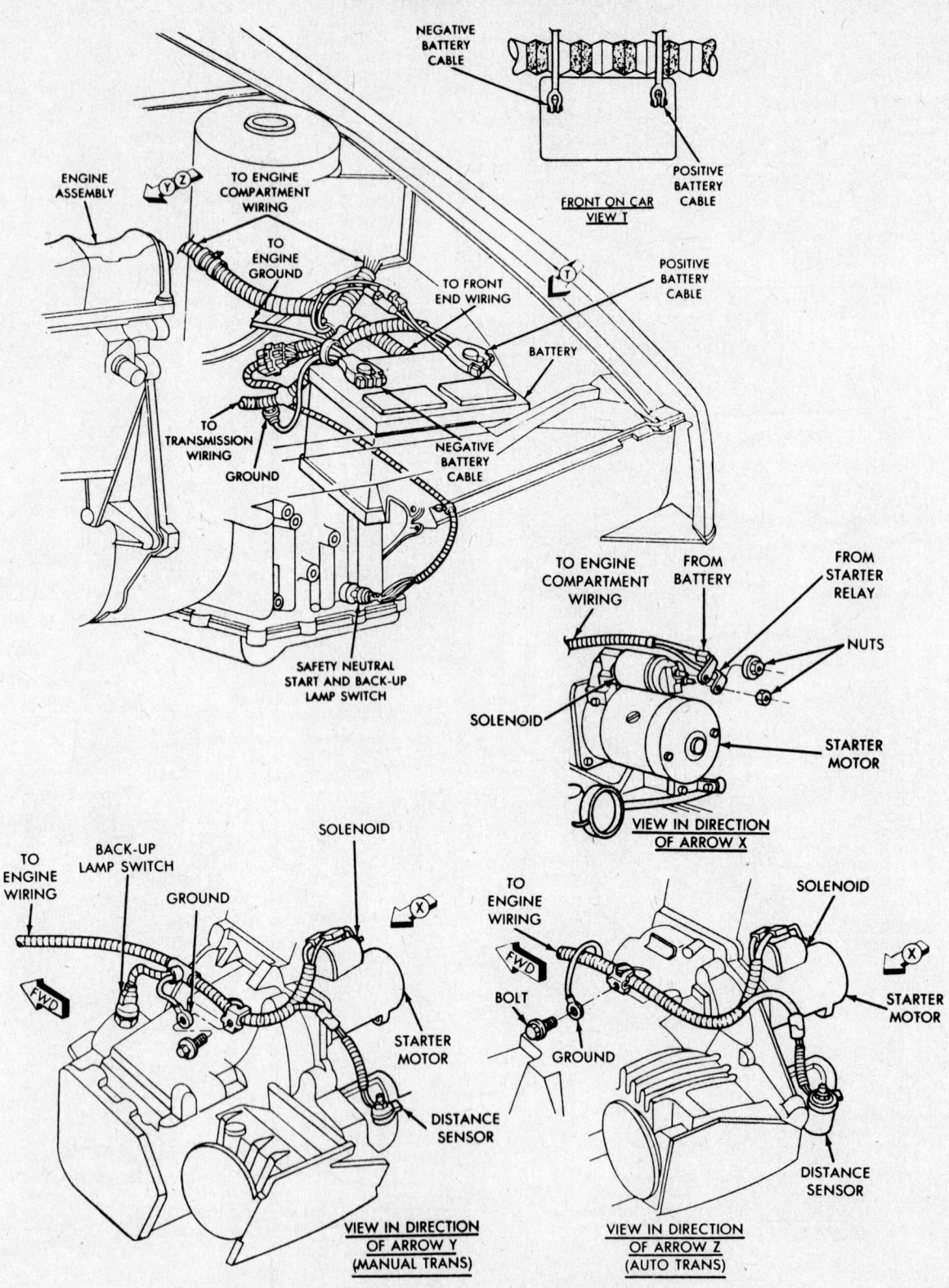

NEGATIVE BATTERY CABLE

POSITIVE BATTERY CABLE

FRONT ON CAR VIEW T

ENGINE ASSEMBLY

TO ENGINE COMPARTMENT WIRING

TO ENGINE GROUND

TO FRONT END WIRING

POSITIVE BATTERY CABLE

BATTERY

TO TRANSMISSION WIRING

GROUND

NEGATIVE BATTERY CABLE

SAFETY NEUTRAL START AND BACK-UP LAMP SWITCH

TO ENGINE COMPARTMENT WIRING

FROM BATTERY

FROM STARTER RELAY

NUTS

SOLENOID

STARTER MOTOR

VIEW IN DIRECTION OF ARROW X

TO ENGINE WIRING

BACK-UP LAMP SWITCH

SOLENOID

GROUND

STARTER MOTOR

DISTANCE SENSOR

FWD

VIEW IN DIRECTION OF ARROW Y (MANUAL TRANS)

TO ENGINE WIRING

SOLENOID

FWD

BOLT

GROUND

STARTER MOTOR

DISTANCE SENSOR

VIEW IN DIRECTION OF ARROW Z (AUTO TRANS)

Battery, Starter, Transmission Wiring, and Component Identification

1987 Sundance and Shadow

COMPONENT LOCATIONS

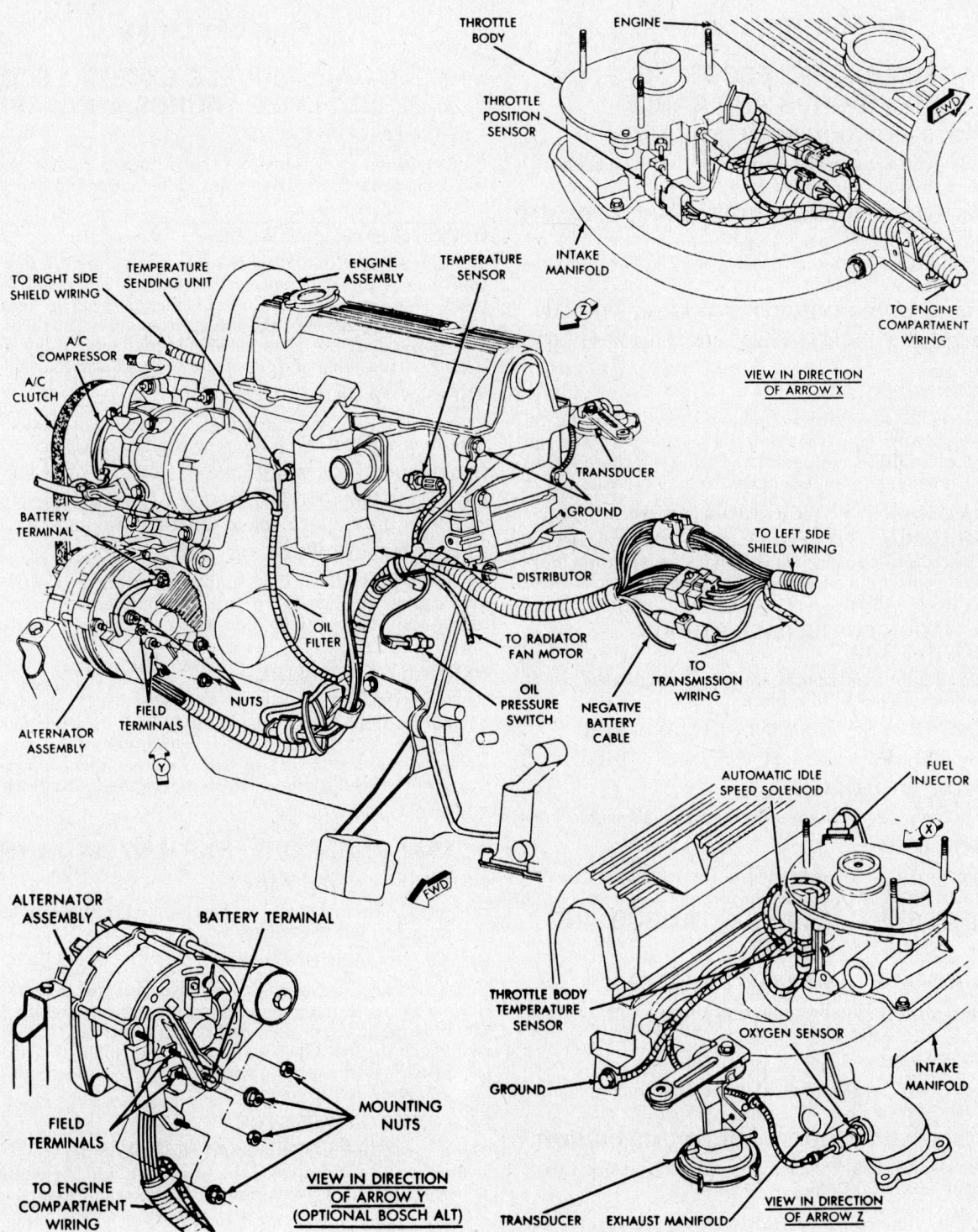

THROTTLE BODY

ENGINE

THROTTLE POSITION SENSOR

INTAKE MANIFOLD

TO ENGINE COMPARTMENT WIRING

VIEW IN DIRECTION OF ARROW X

TO RIGHT SIDE SHIELD WIRING

TEMPERATURE SENDING UNIT

ENGINE ASSEMBLY

TEMPERATURE SENSOR

A/C COMPRESSOR

A/C CLUTCH

TRANSDUCER

GROUND

BATTERY TERMINAL

DISTRIBUTOR

TO LEFT SIDE SHIELD WIRING

OIL FILTER

TO RADIATOR FAN MOTOR

TO TRANSMISSION WIRING

FIELD TERMINALS

NUTS

OIL PRESSURE SWITCH

NEGATIVE BATTERY CABLE

ALTERNATOR ASSEMBLY

ALTERNATOR ASSEMBLY

BATTERY TERMINAL

AUTOMATIC IDLE SPEED SOLENOID

FUEL INJECTOR

THROTTLE BODY TEMPERATURE SENSOR

OXYGEN SENSOR

GROUND

INTAKE MANIFOLD

FIELD TERMINALS

MOUNTING NUTS

TO ENGINE COMPARTMENT WIRING

VIEW IN DIRECTION OF ARROW Y (OPTIONAL BOSCH ALT)

TRANSDUCER

EXHAUST MANIFOLD

VIEW IN DIRECTION OF ARROW Z

Engine Wiring and Component Identification 2.2L E.F.I. Engine

1987 Sundance and Shadow

FORD MOTOR COMPANY

Circuit Breakers

ALL MODELS EXCEPT ESCORT, EXP, LN7, LYNX, TAURUS AND SABLE

HEADLIGHTS AND HIGH BEAM INDICATOR

One 18 amp circuit breaker (22 amp in the 1986-87 models) incorporated in the lighting switch.

FRONT AND REAR MARKER, SIDE PARKING, REAR AND LICENSE LAMPS

One 15 amp circuit breaker incorporated in the lighting switch.

WINDSHIELD WIPER CIRCUIT AND REAR WINDOW

One 4.5 amp circuit breaker located in the windshield wiper switch.

POWER WINDOWS

There are two 20 amp circuit breakers (except for the 82 models, they only use one) located in the starter relay and the fuse block. On the l985 Continental and Mark VII there is a 30 amp circuit breaker use inplace of the 20 amp breaker.

POWER SEATS AND POWER DOOR LOCKS

One 20 amp circuit breaker located in the fuse block is used on all models except, LTD, Marquis, Crown Victoria, Grand Marquis. These models use a 30 amp circuit breaker, which is also located in the fuse block.

STATION WAGON POWER BACK WINDOW (TAILGATE SWITCH)

One 20 amp circuit breaker (or 30 amp depending on the size of the vehicle) located in the fuse block.

INTERMITENT 2 – SPEED WINDSHIELD WIPER

One 8.25 amp circuit breaker located in the fuse block.

DOOR CIGAR LIGHTER

One 20 or 30 amp circuit breaker located in the fuse block.

LIFTGATE WIPER

One 4.5 amp circuit breaker located in the instrument panel.

ESCORT, EXP, LN7, LYNX, TAURUS AND SABLE

HEADLIGHTS AND HIGH BEAM INDICATOR

One 22 amp circuit breaker incorporated in the lighting switch.

LIFTGATE WIPER

One 4.5 amp circuit breaker located in the instrument panel to the left of the radio.

WINDSHIELD WIPER AND WASHER PUMP CIRCUIT

One 6 amp circuit breaker (8.25 amp on the Escort and Lynx) located in the in the fuse block.

NOTE: The Taurus and Sable have three circuit breakers all located in the fuse block. The 6 amp circuit breaker is used for the windshield wiper circuit and one 20 amp circuit breaker is used for the instrument illumination. There is also an in-line 30 amp circuit breaker for the power windows.

Fusible Links

1982-83 – ALL MODELS EXCEPT ESCORT, EXP, LN7, LYNX, TAURUS AND SABLE

GREEN 14 GAUGE WIRE

Protects the starter relay and the voltage regulator and is located between the starter relay, alternator and the voltage relay.

ORANGE 16 GAUGE WIRE

There are three links used to protect the starter relay, one of the links is located between the starter relay and the fuse block. There is another link that is incorporated in the wire between the starter relay and the ignition wire. The third link is incorporated in the wire between the starter relay and the trailer wiring and it also protects the trailer circuits.

YELLOW 16 GAUGE WIRE

Protects the rear window defogger and is incorporated in the wire from the battery to the rear window defogger.

BLUE 18 GAUGE WIRE

Protects the trailer wiring circuits and is incorporated in the wire from the starter relay to the trailer wiring.

RED 18 GAUGE WIRE

There are two of these links and they protect the electronic engine control module. They are incorporated in the wire between the starter relay and the electronic engine control module.

BLUE 20 GAUGE WIRE

There are three of these links used to protect the feedback carburetor control circuits. One of the links is incorporated in the wire to the choke heater, one is incorporated in the wire to the feedback carburetor control and the other links is located in the wire between the ignition switch to the feedback carburetor control.

1982-83 ESCORT, EXP, LN7 AND LYNX

GREEN 14 GAUGE WIRE

Protects the ammeter and is incorporated in the wire between the ammeter and the starter relay.

BLACK 16 GAUGE WIRE

There are two of these links used to protect the ammeter, ignition switch, alternator and voltage regulator circuits. One of the links is incorporated in the wire between the ignition switch and the fuse block to the alternator wiring junction. The other link is located in the wire between the alternator wiring junction and the fuse block.

BROWN 18 GAUGE WIRE

There is one link used to protect the cooling fan motor and is located in the wire between the alternator and the cooling fan. The other link is used to protect the electronic engine control components and is incorporated in the wire between the starter relay and the electronic engine control system.

BLUE 20 GAUGE WIRE

One link is used to protect the EFE heater and is incorporated in the wire between the EFE heater and the alternator wiring junction. Another link is used to protect the cooling fan and is

link located in the wire between the ammeter, defogger and the fuel door release. There are three links on the LTD and Marquis, two of the links are located in the wire between the battery and trailer wiring and the other link is located in the wire between the starter relay and the ignition switch.

On the Capri, Mustang and Topaz, there is three links located in the wire between the ammeter to ignition switch, fuse block and the defogger. On the Cougar, Escort, EXP, Lynx, Tempo and Thunderbird, there is one link located in the wire between the starter relay, fuse block and ignition switch.

On the Cougar, Escort, EXP, LYNX, LTD, Marquis and Thunderbird, there is one link located in the wire from the battery to the defogger. On all models except the Capri, Topaz, Continental, Mark VII ans the Cougar and Thunderbird with 3.0L and 5.0L engines, there is a link located in the wire between the starter relay and the fuse block. There is one link located in the wire between the battey to the A/C cooling fan control on the Cougar and Thunderbird with the 2.3L turbo charged engine.

RED 18 GAUGE WIRE

On the LTD and the Marquis there is one link located in the wire between the battery and the fuel pump. On the Escort, EXP and Lynx equipped with diesel engines, there is one link located in the wire between the starter relay and the A/C fan control. On the Cougar and Thunderbird (not the 2.3L engine) there are two links (one link on the Continental and Mark VII) located in the wire between starter relay and the EEC module.

BLUE 18 GAUGE WIRE

On the Lincoln Town Car, there is one link located in the wire between the starter relay to the trailer wiring. On the LTD and Marquis there are two links located in the wire between the starter relay to the EEC module and the A/C cooling fan.

BROWN 18 GAUGE WIRE

On the Tempo there is one link located in the wire between the starter relay to the defogger switch and fuel door release. On the Tempo and Topaz there is one link located in the wire running from the starter relay to EEC module, EEC relay, A/C fan control and fan temperature control. On the Escort, EXP, and Lynx there is on link located in the wire between starter relay and the A/C fan control.

On the Capri and Mustang there is one link located in the wire between the alternator, voltage regulator and A/C fan control. On the Capri, Mustang, Town Car, EFI Escort, EXP, Lynx and the Cougar and Thunderbird with the 2.3L turbo engine, there is two links located in the wire between starter relay and the EEC module.

BLUE 20 GAUGE WIRE

On the Lincoln Town Car there is one link located in the wire between the starter relay and the message center. On the Escort, EXP, Lynx with gasoline engines, there is one link in the wire between the starter relay and the EFE heater. On the Tempo and Topaz there is one link located in the wire between the ignition switch and the A/C-heater cooling fan. On the Tempo, Topaz, LTD, Marquis, Cougar and Thunderbird, there is one link located in the wire between the battery and the engine compartment light. On the Continental and Mark VII, there is one link located in the wire between the starter relay, air suspension and EEC module.

1985-87 — ALL MODELS EXCEPT TAURUS AND SABLE

GRAY 12 GAUGE

There is one link located in the wire between the trailer wire and the rear window defogger on the Cougar and Thunderbird equipped with the 3.8L and the 5.0L engines.

GREEN 14 GAUGE WIRE

On the Cougar and Thunderbird only, there is one link located in the wire from the trailer wiring to the battery charging relay. Ther is one link located in the load leveling system, on the Lincoln Town Car only. On the Escort and Lynx diesel models, there are two links (one for the Tempo and Topaz) located in the glow plug wiring to protect the glow plug control.

On the 2.3L turbocharged engine Capri, Mustang, Cougar and Thunderbird, there is a link located in the ammeter wiring to protect the ammeter. There is a link located in the wire between the battery and the charging system on all models.

ORANGE 16 GAUGE WIRE

On the Continental and Mark VII only, there are two links used to protect the ignition switch and fuse block and one link used to protect the rear window defogger.

On the Cougar and Thunderbird models equipped with the 3.0L and 5.0L engines, there is one link located in the rear defogger wiring. There are two links protecting the trailer wiring and rear window defogger option and two more links protecting the ignition switch and fuse block.

BLACK 16 GAUGE WIRE

On the Cougar and Thunderbird models equipped with the located in the wire between the ignition switch and the cooling fan. The third link is used to protect the engine compartment light and is located in the wire between the ammeter power feed and the engine compartment light.

1984

GREEN 14 GAUGE WIRE

The Escort and Lynx diesel models, have two links located in the wire between the starter relay and the glow plug control. The LTD and Marquis has one link that is located in the wire between the battery and trailer wiring. On all the other models, there is one link located in the wire between the starter relay. alternator and voltage relay.

ORANGE 16 GAUGE WIRE

On the Continental and Mark VII, there is one link located in the wire between the starter relay, ignition switch and fuse block. On the Continental, Mark VII and Cougar/Thunderbird with the 2.3L engine, there is one link located in the wire between the starter relay and the fuse block. On all other models there is a link located in the wire between the battery and the rear window defogger.

YELLOW 16 GAUGE WIRE

There a two links located in the wire between the battery and the defogger and the trailer wiring on the Lincoln Town Car.

BLACK AND ORANGE 16 GAUGE WIRE

There is one link located in the wire between the battery and the trailer wiring on the Lincoln Town Car.

BLACK 16 GAUGE WIRE

On the Tempo there is one link located in the wire between the starter relay and the anti-theft relay. On the Topaz there is one 2.3L turbocharged engine, there is one link located in the heater fan motor control wiring and another link located in the rear window defogger wiring.

On the Capri and Mustang only, there is one link used to protect the rear window defogger and the convertible top circuit. On the LTD, Marquis, Town Car, Escort, EXP and Lynx, there is one link located in the wiring for the rear window defogger. On the Tempo and Topaz, there is one link located in the wiring for the anti-theft system.

There are two links used for the optional trailer wiring on the Continental and Mark VII models equipped with the 5.0L engine and also the Town Car. On all models except for the

Continental, Mark VII and the Cougar and Thunderbird models equipped with the 3.8L and the 5.0L engines. There are two links used to protect the ignition switch and the fuse block.

RED 18 GAUGE WIRE

On the Tempo and Topaz models equipped with gasoline engines, there is one link used to protect the carburetor circuits. On the Continental and Mark VII models equipped with diesel engines, there is one link used to protect the glow plug circuit and another link used to protect the heater fan motor circuit.

On the Continental and Mark VII models equipped with gasoline engines, there is one link used to protect the trailer electric brake circuit. On the Escort, EXP and Lynx models equipped with diesel engines, there is one link located in the heater fan wiring to protect the heater fan motor circuit.

On the LTD and Marquis models equipped with the 3.8L and 5.0L engines, there is one link (there are two links used on the Cougar and Thunderbird models with the same engines) used to protect the EEC module.

BROWN 18 GAUGE WIRE

On the Tempo and Topaz there is one link used to protect the rear window defogger and the fuel door release. On the Escort, EXP, Lynx, Capri and Mustang, there is one link used to protect the heater fan motor circuit.

There is one link (two on the Capri and Mustang) used to protect the EEC module on the Town Car, Tempo, Topaz, Escort, EXP, Lynx and Cougar and Thunderbird (with the 2.3L engine).

BLUE 20 GAUGE WIRE

On the Lincoln Town Car there is one link located in the wire between the starter relay and the message center. On the Escort, EXP, Lynx with gasoline engines, there is two links in the wire between the starter relay and the EFE heater. On the Tempo and Topaz there is one link located in the wire between the ignition switch and the A/C-heater cooling fan. On the Tempo, Topaz, LTD, Marquis, Cougar, Thunderbird, Capri and Mustang, there is one link located in the wire between the battery and the engine compartment light. On the Continental and Mark VII, there is one link located in the wire between the starter relay, air suspension and EEC module.

On the Town Car, LTD and Marquis there is one link used to protect the EEC module circuit. On the Grand Marquis and the Crown Victoria, there is one link located at the top of the brake booster, which protects the EEC module circuit. On the Tempo, Topaz, Escort, EXP and Lynx models equipped with diesel engines, there is one link used to protect the vacuum pump circuit.

On the Tempo, Topaz, LTD, and Marquis, there is one link used to protect the heater fan motor circuit. On the Town Car, there are tow links used to protect the ignition system. On the Mustang and Capri, There is one link used to protect the fog ligh t circuit and one link used to protect the voltage regulator, which is located on the left hand side shock tower of the engine compartment.

On the Crown Victoria and Grand Marquis, the link located at the top of the brake booster is used to protect the electric choke circuit and the link incorporated in the fuel flow wiring assembly (which is located on the firewall) protects the MCU module and the tripminder.

1985-87 — Taurus and Sable

GREEN 14 GAUGE WIRE

This fusible link is located in the wiring going to the starter relay and it protects the starter circuit.

BLACK 16 GAUGE WIRE

This fusible link is located in the wiring going to the starter relay and it protects the rear window defrost circuit.

BLACK 16 GAUGE WIRE

This fusible link is located on the left front inner fender panel, near the voltage regulator and is used to protect the voltage regulator and alternator circuit.

BLACK 16 GAUGE WIRE

This fusible link is located in the wiring going to the starter relay and it protects the starter and alternator circuit.

BLUE 20 GAUGE WIRE

This fusible link is located on the starter relay and protects the electrical system in general.

Relays, Sensors and Computer Locations

1982-83 ESCORT, EXP, LN7 AND LYNX

- **Carburetor Float Bowl Vent Solenoid** — located at the center left hand side of the carburetor.
- **Cargo Light Relay** — located at the rear of the left hand side wheel housing.
- **Clutch Interrupt Switch** — located at the top of the clutch pedal cluster.
- **Clutch Switch** — Attached to the top of the clutch support.
- **Coolant Temperature Switch** — is located in the heater supply pipe.
- **Cooling Fan Relay** — located on the left hand side of the instrument panel.
- **Dimmer Relay** — located at the right hand side of the cowl area.
- **EFE Heater Relay** — is mounted on the left hand side fender apron.
- **EGR Control Solenoid** — located at the left hand side of the instrument panel.
- **Electric Fuel Pump** — located forward of the fuel tank on the right hans side.
- **Electric Ported Vacuum Switch** — at the rear center of the engine, above the oil filter.
- **Electronic Control Assembly (ECA)** — located at the front of the console.
- **Electronic Engine Control (EEC) Power Relay** — located at the front of the console near the Electronic Control Assembly.
- **Engine Coolant Temperature Sensor** — located at the rear of the engine to the right of the oil filter.
- **Engine Idle Air Bypass Solenoid** — located at the top left hand side of the engine.
- **Exhaust Gas Oxygen Sensor** — located in the exhaust manifold.
- **Fuel Pump Relay** — loacted at the front of the console near the ECA.
- **Graphic Display Module** — located in the front of the floor console.
- **Horn Relay** — is located behind the instrument panel on the left side of the radio.
- **Inertia Switch (Sedans)** — located at the left hand side rear quarter panel, to the rear of the wheelhouse.
- **Inertia Switch (4 door liftgate)** — loacted at the left hand side rear quarter panel, in the rear light opening.
- **Liftgate Ajar Flasher Relay** — located behind the left side of the instrument panel.
- **Low Fuel Warning Module** — attached behind upper center of the console.
- **Neutral Safety Switch** — located to the rear of the right hand side of the transmission assembly.
- **RPM Module** — is located behing the glove box.
- **RPM Sensor** — located on the fuel injection pump.

- **Speed Sensor** – is located at the left hand side of the engine assembly.
- **Starter Relay** – located on the left hand side of the fender apron in front of the shock tower.
- **Thick Film Ignition Module (TFI)** – is connected to the right hand side of the distributor.
- **Throttle Kicker Solenoid** – located at the left hand side of dash panel.
- **Throttle Position Sensor (TPS)** – located at the upper rear center of the engine.
- **Transmission Neutral Switch** – located in the transmission.
- **Vane Air Flow Meter** – located on the left hand side fender apron, near the starter relay.
- **Wide-Open Throttle A/C Cutout Switch** – is located on the lower left side of the carburetor.

1984-87 ESCORT, EXP AND LYNX

- **Altitude Solenoid** – located on the left hand side fender apron.
- **Barometric Pressure Switch** – located on the left hand side fender apron.
- **Canister Purge Control Solenoid** – located on the left hand side fender apron.
- **Carburetor Float Bowl Vent Solenoid** – located at the center left hand side of the carburetor.
- **Cargo Light Relay** – located at the rear of the left hand side wheel housing.
- **Clutch Interrupt Switch** – located at the top of the clutch pedal cluster.
- **Clutch Switch** – Attached to the top of the clutch support.
- **Coolant Temperature Switch** – is located in the heater supply pipe.
- **Cooling Fan Relay** – located on the left hand side of the instrument panel.
- **Dimmer Relay** – located at the right hand side of the cowl area.
- **EFE Heater Relay** – is mounted on the left hand side fender apron.
- **EGR Control Solenoid** – located at the left hand side feder apron.
- **Electric Fuel Pump** – located forward of the fuel tank on the right hans side.
- **Electric Ported Vacuum Switch** – at the rear center of the engine, above the oil filter.
- **Electronic Control Assembly (ECA)** – located at the front of the console.
- **Electronic Engine Control (EEC) Power Relay** – located at the left hand side of the instrument panel.
- **Engine Coolant Temperature Sensor** – located at the rear of the engine to the right of the oil filter.
- **Engine Idle Air Bypass Solenoid** – located at the top left hand side of the engine.
- **Exhaust Gas Oxygen Sensor** – located in the exhaust manifold.
- **Fuel Pump Relay** – loacted at the left hand side of the instrument panel.
- **Graphic Display Module** – located in the front of the floor console.
- **Horn Relay** – is located behind the instrument panel on the left side of the radio.
- **Idle Fuel Solenoid** – located on the lower right hand rear of carburetor.
- **Inertia Switch (Sedans)** – located at the left hand side rear quarter panel, to the rear of the wheelhouse.
- **Inertia Switch (4 door liftgate)** – loacted at the left hand side rear quarter panel, in the rear light opening.
- **Liftgate Ajar Flasher Relay** – located behind the left side of the instrument panel.

- **Low Fuel Warning Module** – attached behind upper center of the console.
- **Manifold Absolute Pressure Sensor** – is located on the left hand side fender apron.
- **Neutral Safety Switch** – located to the rear of the right hand side of the transmision assembly.
- **Power Door Lock Relay** – located in the door arm rests.
- **RPM Module** – is located behing the glove box.
- **RPM Sensor** – located on the fuel injection pump.
- **Speed Sensor** – is located on the transaxle.
- **Starter Relay** – located on the left hand side of the fender apron in front of the shock tower.
- **Thick Film Ignition Module (TFI)** – is connected to the right hand side of the distributor.
- **Throttle Kicker Solenoid** – located at the left hand side of dash panel.
- **Throttle Position Sensor (TPS)** – located at the upper rear center of the engine.
- **Transmission Neutral Switch** – located in the transmission.
- **Vane Air Flow Meter** – located on the left hand side fender apron, near the starter relay.
- **Wide-Open Throttle A/C Cutout Switch** – is located on the lower left side of the carburetor.

DIESEL MODELS

- **Diesel Control Module** – is located on the left side of the steering column support brace.
- **Dropping Resistor** – is located in the air intake at the engine manifold.
- **Fuel Filter Conditioner** – is attached to the right hand side shock tower.
- **Fuel Shut-Off Solenoid** – located at the front left hand side of the engine.
- **Glow Plugs** – located at the top of the engine.
- **Low Vacuum Warning Switch** – is located on the left hand side of the dash panel.
- **Non-Neutral Switch** – is located at the rear of the transmission.
- **Pre-Glow Relay No.1** – is located at the top center of the dash panel.
- **Pre-Glow Relay No.2** – is located at the top center of the dash panel.
- **Thermoswitch** – is located at the upper front end of the engine.
- **Water-in-Fuel Module** – is located behind the instrument panel, attached to the left side of the steering column support.
- **Water-in-Fuel Sensor** – is attached to the fuel filter conditioner.

TEMPO AND TOPAZ

- **A/C Clutch Cycling Pressure Switch** – is located at the suction accumulator.
- **After Glow Relay No.1 (Diesel)** – is located at the top center of the firewall.
- **After Glow Relay No.2 (Diesel)** – is located at the top center of the firewall.
- **Air Charge Temperature Sensor** – is located in the intake manifold air stream.
- **Anti-Diesel Solenoid** – is located on the carburetor.
- **Canister Purge Solenoid** – is located in the left rear side of the engine.
- **Carburetor Float Bowl Vent Solenoid** – is located on the right side of the carburetor.
- **Coolant Temperature Switch** – is located in the left side cylinder head.
- **Cooling Fan Controller** – is located behind the left side of the instrument panel.

- **Cooling Fan Controller Module**—is located behind the right side of the instrument panel.
- **Cooling Fan Temperature Switch**—is located in the upper left hand side of the engine near the distributor.
- **De-Icing Relay**—is located on the right side of the radiator support.
- **De-Icing Temperature Switch**—is located in the intake manifold below the carburetor.
- **Diesel Control Module (Diesel)**—is located under the left side of the instrument panel.
- **Dimmer Relay**—is located behind the left side of the instrument panel.
- **Door Lock Actuators**—are located on the door, below the handle switch.
- **Dropping Resistor (Diesel)**—is located in the air intake of the engine manifold.
- **Dual Brake Warning Switch**—is attached to the master cylinder.
- **Dual Warning Buzzer**—is located behind the center of the instrument panel, near the radio.
- **EGR Vacuum Regulator**—is located on the left side of the firewall in the engine compartment.
- **EGR Valve Position Sensor**—is located on the EGR valve, on the left side of the engine.
- **Electronic Control Assembly**—is located under the left side of the instrument panel.
- **Electronic Engine Control Power Relay**—is located behind the glove box on the right side of the instrument panel.
- **Engine Coolant Temperature Sensor**—is located in the intake water jacket in the rear of the engine.
- **Engine Speed Sensor**—is mounted on the injection pump.
- **Fuel Filler Door Release Solenoid**—is located near the fuel tank line inlet.
- **Fuel Pump Relay**—is located behind the glove box.
- **Fuel Shut-Off Solenoid (Diesel)**—is located on the injection pump.
- **Glow Plugs (Diesel)**—are located at the top of the engine.
- **Graphic Warning Module**—is located on the front console.
- **Horn Relay**—is located in the fuse block.
- **Idle Speed Control Motor**—is located on the fuel charging assembly.
- **Illuminated Entry Module**—is located on a crossmember behind the right seat.
- **Isolation Relay**—is located on the left front fender apron.
- **Lock Control Switch**—is located in the door trim panel.
- **Low Fuel Warning Module**—is located on the front console.
- **Low Vacuum Warning Switch (Diesel)**—is located on the left side of the instrument panel.
- **Manifold Absolute Pressure Sensor**—is located on the center of the firewall in the engine compartment.
- **Multi-Warning Buzzer**—is located behind the center of the instrument panel, near the radio.
- **Oxygen Sensor**—is located in the exhaust manifold towards the rear of the engine.
- **Power Steering Pressure Switch**—is located in the power steering pressure line above the steering gear.
- **Power Steering Switch**—is located at the power steering pump.
- **Power Window Relay**—is located in the fuse block.
- **Speed Control Amplifier**—is located under the left side of the instrument panel.
- **Speed Control Servo**—is located on the left front shock tower.
- **Speed Sensor**—is located at the left rear side of the transmission.
- **Starter Relay**—is located on the left front fender apron in front of the shock tower.
- **Thermoswitch (Diesel)**—is located at the upper rear end

of the engine.
- **Thick Film Ignition Module**—is attached to the right side of the carbureto.
- **Throttle Kicker Solenoid**—is located on the carburetor.
- **Throttle Position Sensor**—is located on the fule charging assembly on the right side of the engine.
- **Top Gear Switch**—is mounted to the transmission.
- **Vacuum Dump Valve**—is located at the top of the brake pedal support.
- **Water-In-Fuel Module (Diesel)**—is located in the right side cowl panel.
- **Water-In-Fuel Sensor (Diesel)**—is located in the top of the fuel filter/conditioner.
- **Wide Open Throttle Cut-Out Switch**—is located on the left side of the carburetor.

TAURUS AND SABLE

- **A/C Clutch Cycling Pressure Switch**—is located on the A/C accumulator, on the firewall.
- **Air Change Temperature Sensor**—is located on the left side of the engine.
- **Alternator Output Control Relay**—is located between the right front inner fender and the fender splash shield.
- **Ambient Temperature Sensor**—is located on the left front fender apron.
- **Autolamp Relay No.1**—is located on top of the rear shake brace, under the left side of the instrument panel.
- **Autolamp Relay No.2**—is located on top of the rear shake brace, under the left side of the instrument panel.
- **Automatic Overdrive Transaxle Speed Sensor**—is located on the left side of the radiator.
- **Canister Purge Solenoid**—is located on the left side of the radio support.
- **Cold Engine Lockout**—is located on the firewall near the windshield wiper motor.
- **Cold Engine Lock Out Sensor (3.0L engine)**—is located on the lower left hand side of the engine.
- **Dimmer Rheostat**—is located in the lower left front corner of the instrument panel.
- **Dual Brake Warning Switch**—is located on the left front fender apron.
- **EGR Vacuum Regulator Solenoid**—is located on the left front fender apron.
- **Electronic Automatic Temperature Control Unit**—is located behind the instrument panel.
- **Electronic Control Assembly**—is located under the right side of the instrument panel.
- **Engine Coolant Temperature Sensor**—is located at the top right hand side of the engine.
- **Headlamp Dimmer Relay**—is located on top of the rear shake brace, under the left side of the instrument panel.
- **Horn Relay**—is located under the left side of the instrument panel.
- **Idle Speed Controller (3.0L engine)**—is located on the left hand side of the engine.
- **Illuminated Entry Timer**—is located on a package tray behind the rear seat.
- **In-Car Temperature Sensor**—is located on the right hand top side of the instrument panel.
- **Integrated Controller**—is located on the radiator support.
- **Keyless Entry Module**—is located on a package tray behind the rear seat.
- **Knock Sensor**—is located on the right hand side of the engine.
- **Lamp Out Warning Module**—is located under the extreme right side of the instrument panel.
- **Left Hand Side Sun Sensor**—is located above the main light switch.

• **Light Sensor/Amplifier** – is located to the top underside of the left side of the instrument panel.
• **Low Oil Level Relay** – is locted under the instrument panel attached to the instrument panel brace.
• **Manifold Absolute Pressure Sensor** – is located on the right side of the firewall.
• **Oxygen Sensor** – is located in the lower front side of the engine in the exhaust pipe.
• **Power Steering Pressure Switch** – is located on the right front fender apron.
• **Power Window Safety Relay** – is located on the left side of the center instrument panel brace.
• **Pressure Feedback Electronic Sensor (3.0L engine)** – is located on the left hand side of the engine.
• **Self-Test Connector** – is located in the wiring harness behind the alternator.
• **Speed Control Servo** – is attached to the electronic control assembly.
• **Speed Control Switch** – is lopcated int he steering wheel.
• **Starter Relay** – is located on the left front fender apron in front of the shock tower.
• **Temperature Sender** – is located on the left side of the engine block.
• **Thick Film Ignition Module** – is connected to the right side of the distributor.
• **Throttle Air Bypass Valve Solenoid** – is located on the left front fender apron.
• **Throttle Position Sensor** – is located on the left hand side of the engine.
• **Trunk Release Solenoid** – is attached to the trunk latch assembly.
• **Vehicle Speed Sensor** – is located near the electronic control assembly.
• **Voice Alert Module** – is located under the left side of the instrument panel.
• **Warning Chime** – is located under the left side of the instrument panel.

1982-83 MUSTANG AND CAPRI

• **Anti-Diesel Solenoid** – is located at the top of the engine behind the carburetor.
• **Barometric Pressure Switch** – is located on the left fender apron.
• **Canister Purge Control Solenoid** – located at the left hand side of the engine near the carburetor.
• **Carburetor Float Bowl Solenoid** – is located on the carburetor.
• **Choke Relay** – is located on the right hans side fender apron near the voltage regulator.
• **Coolant Temperature Switch** – is located in the heater supply pipe.
• **Dimmer Relay** – is located behind the instrument panel, to the right of the steering column support.
• **Dual Temperature Switch** – located at the rear left hand side of the engine.
• **Electric Ported Vacuum Switch** – located at the left hand side of the engine behind the distributor.
• **Fuel Control Solenoid** – located on the carburetor.
• **Graphic Warning Module** – is located at the top center of the console.
• **Horn Relay** – is located on right side of the instrument panel.
• **Idle Tracking Switch** – located at the center rear of the carburetor.
• **Ignition Module** – is located on the left hand side fender apron.
• **Liftgate Release Solenoid** – is on the right hand side liftgate lid at the striker box.

• **Low Fuel Warning Module** – is behind the right hand side of the instrument panel above the glove box.
• **Manifold Vacuum Switch** – is located behind the left hand side shock tower.
• **MCU Resistor** – located in the wiring harness near the MCU.
• **Microprosseor Control Unit (MCU)** – located at the left hand side fender apron next to the ignition coil.
• **Oxygen Sensor** – Lower right side of the exhaust manifold.
• **Speed Sensor** – attached to the transmission
• **Starter Relay** – is located on the right hand side fender apron in front of the wheel well.
• **Thermactor Air Bypass Solenoid** – is attached to the right hand side of the dash panel.
• **Thermactor Air Diverter Solenoid** – is attached to the right hand side shock tower.
• **Thermactor Dump Control Relay** – is located under the instrument panel on the right side of the steering
• **Throttle Kicker Solenoid** – is located at the upper right hand side of the dash panel.
• **Timer Relay** – is located on the right side of the steering column support.
• **Trunk Release Solenoid** – is located at the center of the tailgate lid.
• **Upshift Module** – is located above the brake pedal.
• **Wide Open A/C Cutout Relay** – is located under the instrument panel on the left side of the steering column brace.
• **Wide Open A/C Cutout Switch** – is located on the left hand side of the carburetor.
• **Wide-Open Throttle Cutout Switch** – located on the carburetor.
• **Wide-Open Throttle Switch** – is attached to the rear of the right hand side shock tower.

1984-87 MUSTANG AND CAPRI

• **Anti-Diesel Solenoid** – is located at the top of the engine behind the carburetor.
• **Barometric Pressure Sensor** – is located on the right hand side fender apron.
• **Canister Purge Solenoid** – is on the left hand side of the engine.
• **Choke Relay** – is located on the right hand side fender apron near the voltage regulator.
• **Control Solenoid** – mounted on the rear of the carburetor.
• **Convertible Top Lower Relay** – lower left rear quarter panel.
• **Convertible Top Raise Relay** – lower left rear quarter panel.
• **Coolant Temperature Switch** – is located in the heater supply pipe.
• **Dimmer Relay** – is located behind the instrument panel, to the right of the steering column support.
• **EGR Control Solenoid** – is located on the right side fender apron.
• **EGR Valve position Sensor** – is at the top of the right front side of the engine.
• **EGR Vent Solenoid** – is located at the right front fender apron.
• **Electronic Control Assembly (ECA)** – is attached to the lower left side of the cowl.
• **Electronic Engine Control (EEC) Power Relay** – is attached to the lower right side cowl near the electronic control assembly.
• **Engine Coolant Temperature Sensor** – is at the top of the engine in front of the carburetor.
• **Exhaust Heat Control Solenoid** – is located on the right hand side of the engine compartment.

• **Exhaust Oxygen Sensor** – is located in the left rear side of the engine.
• **Fog Light Relay** – is located on the left side of the instrument panel.
• **Fuel Pump Relay** – is located under the driver's seat.
• **Fuel Relays** – is at the center of the instrument panel behind the dash panel.
• **Graphic Warning Module** – is located at the top center of the console.
• **Heated Exhaust Oxygen sensor** – is on the lower right side of the engine manifold.
• **Horn Relay** – is located on right side of the instrument panel.
• **Idle Speed Motor** – is attached to the left hand side of the carburetor.
• **Ignition Module** – is located on the left hand side fender apron.
• **Inertia Switch** – is in the floor of the trunk to the left of the tire well.
• **Knock Sensor** – is at the bottom of the left side of the engine.
• **Liftgate Release Solenoid** – is on the right hand side liftgate lid at the striker plate.
• **Low Fuel Warning Module** – is behind the right hand side of the instrument panel above the glove box.
• **Low Oil Level Relay** – is located in the center of the dash panel.
• **Manifold Charge Temperaturte Sensor** – is on the right side of the engine on the manifold.
• **Manifold Vacuum Switch** – is located behind the left hand side shock tower.
• **Speed Sensor** – attached to the transmission
• **Starter Relay** – is located on the right hand side fender apron in front of the wheel well (lefthand side on Turbo models).
• **Thermactor Air Bypass Solenoid** – is attached to the right hand side of the dash panel.
• **Thermactor Air Diverter Solenoid** – is attached to the right hand side shock tower.
• **Thermactor Air Solenoids** – is on the right side fender apron.
• **Thermactor Dump Control Relay** – is located under the instrument panel on the right side of the steering
• **Thick Film Ignition Module (TFI)** – is connected to the right side of the distributor.
• **Throttle Kicker Solenoid** – is on the right hand side of the dash panel.
• **Throttle Position Sensor Non-Turbo Models** – is attached to the right side of the carburetor.
• **Throttle Position Sensor Turbo Models** – is at the upper rear center of the engine.
• **Timer Relay** – is located on the right side of the steering column support.
• **Trunk Release Solenoid** – is located at the center of the tailgate lid.
• **Upshift Module** – is located above the brake pedal.
• **Vane Air Flow Meter** – is inside the right front fender apron.
• **Wide Open A/C Cutout Relay** – is located under the instrument panel on the left side of the steering column brace.
• **Wide Open A/C Cutout Switch** – is located on the left hand side of the carburetor.
• **Wide Open Throttle Cutout Switch** – located on the carburetor.

1982 GRANADA, COUGAR AND XR7

• **Anti-Diesel Solenoid** – is located at the top of the engine behind the carburetor.

• **Canister Purge Control Solenoid (6 cyl.)** – located at the left hand side of the valve cover.
• **Canister Purge Control Solenoid (8 cyl.)** – located at the right hand side of the valve cover.
• **Carburetor Float Bowl Solenoid** – is located on the carburetor.
• **Choke Relay** – is located on the right hand side fender apron near the voltage regulator.
• **Coolant Temperature Switch** – is located in the heater supply pipe.
• **Cornering Light Relays** – is in the center of the dash panel on the left side of the dash panel bracket.
• **De-Ice Switch/Relay** – is located on the right side of the instrument panel above the glove box.
• **Electric Ported Vacuum Switch (4 cyl.)** – located at the left hand side of the engine behind the distributor.
• **Electric Ported Vacuum Switch (8 cyl.)** – located at the top of the engine between the valve covers.
• **Graphic Warning Module** – is located at the top center of the console.
• **Horn Relay** – is located on right side of the instrument panel.
• **Idle Tracking Switch** – located at the center rear of the carburetor.
• **Ignition Module** – is located on the left hand side fender apron.
• **Low Fuel Warning Module** – is behind the right hand side of the instrument panel.
• **MCU Resistor** – located in the rear of the carburetor near the idle tracking.
• **Microprosseor Control Unit (MCU)** – located at the left hand side fender apron.
• **Oxygen Sensor** – Lower left side of the exhaust manifold.
• **Power Door Lock Relay** – is on the crossbar under the driver's seat.
• **Power Window Safety Relay** – Attached to the bottom of the shake brace.
• **Speed Sensor** – is near the left hand side of the dash panel.
• **Starter Relay** – is located on the right hand side fender apron in front of the shock tower.
• **Thermactor Air Bypass Solenoid (4 cyl.)** – is attached at the right rear side of the engine compartment.
• **Thermactor Air Bypass Solenoid (6 cyl.)** – is attached at the left hand side of the valve cover.
• **Thermactor Air Bypass Solenoid (8 cyl.)** – is located at the right rear side of the engine on top of the valve cover.
• **Thermactor Air Diverter (4 cyl.)** – is attached at the right rear side of the engine compartment.
• **Thermactor Air Diverter (6 cyl.)** – is attached at the left hand side of the valve cover.
• **Thermactor Air Diverter (8 cyl.)** – is located at the right rear side of the engine on top of the valve cover.
• **Throttle Kicker Solenoid** – is located at the left side of the engine on top of the valve cover.
• **Trunk Release Solenoid** – is located at the center of the tailgate lid.
• **Upshift Module** – is located above the brake pedal.
• **Wide-Open Throttle Vacuum Switch** – is attached to the left side fender apron.

1982-83 FAIRMONT, FUTURA AND ZEPHYR

• **Anti-Diesel Solenoid** – is located at the top of the engine behind the carburetor.
• **Canister Purge Control Solenoid** – located at the right hand side of the valve cover.
• **Carburetor Float Bowl Solenoid** – is located on the carburetor.

• **Choke Relay** — is located on the right hand side fender apron near the voltage regulator.
• **Coolant Temperature Switch** — is located in the heater supply pipe.
• **Dimmer Relay** — is located behind the instrument panel, to the right of the steering column support.
• **Dual Temperature Switch** — located at the top left hand side of the engine.
• **Electric Ported Vacuum Switch** — located at the left hand side of the engine behind the distributor.
• **Fuel Control Solenoid** — located on right front fender well.
• **Graphic Warning Module** — is located at the top center of the console.
• **Horn Relay** — is located on right side of the instrument panel.
• **Idle Tracking Switch** — located at the center rear of the carburetor.
• **Ignition Module** — is located on the left hand side fender apron.
• **Low Fuel Warning Module** — is behind the right hand side of the instrument panel above the glove box.
• **MCU Resistor** — located in the wiring harness near the MCU.
• **Microprosseor Control Unit (MCU)** — located at the left hand side fender apron next to the ignition coil.
• **Oxygen Sensor** — Lower right side of the exhaust manifold.
• **Power Door Lock Relay** — is on the crossbar under the driver's seat.
• **Power Window Safety Relay** — Attached to the bottom of the shake brace.
• **Speed Sensor** — attached to the transmission
• **Starter Relay** — is located on the right hand side fender apron in front of the wheel well.
• **Thermactor Air Bypass Solenoid** — is attached to the right hand side of the dash panel.
• **Thermactor Air Diverter Solenoid** — is attached to the right hand side shock tower.
• **Throttle Kicker Solenoid** — is located at the upper right hand side of the dash panel.
• **Timer Relay** — is located on the right side of the steering column support.
• **Trunk Release Solenoid** — is located at the center of the tailgate lid.
• **Upshift Module** — is located above the brake pedal.
• **Wide-Open Throttle Cutout Switch** — attached to the right side shock tower.
• **Wide-Open Throttle Switch** — is attached to the rear of the right hand side shock tower.

1982-83 THUNDERBIRD AND 1983 COUGAR

• **A/C Throttle Kicker Solenoid** — is located on the right side shock tower.
• **Alarm Relay** — is located in the upper right side of the trunk.
• **Anti-Theft Module** — is located in the upper right side of the trunk.
• **Auto-Lamp Relay** — is attached to the top rear of steering column support brace.
• **Barometric Pressure Sensor** — is located on the left hand side fender apron.
• **Canister Purge Solenoid** — is on the right hand top of the engine.
• **Carburetor Float Bowl Solenoid** — is located on the carburetor.

• **Chime Ignition Relay** — is attached to the top of the steering column support.
• **Coolant Temperature Switch** — is located in the heater supply pipe.
• **Cornering Light Relays** — is in the center of the dash panel on the left side of the dash panel bracket.
• **Dis-Arm Relay** — is located in the upper right side of the trunk.
• **EGR Control Solenoid** — is located on the right side shock tower.
• **EGR Valve Position Sensor** — is at the top of the right front side of the engine behind the carburetor.
• **EGR Vent Solenoid** — is located at the right side shock tower.
• **Electronic Control Assembly (ECA)** — is under theright side of the instrument panel.
• **Electronic Engine Control (EEC) Power Relay** — is under the right side of the instrument panel.
• **Engine Coolant Temperature Sensor** — is at the top of the engine on the right side of the distributor.
• **Exhaust Heat Control Solenoid** — is located on the left side shock tower.
• **Exhaust Oxygen Sensor** — is located in the right side of the exhaust manifold.
• **Fuel Pump Relay** — is located above right rear wheel well.
• **Horn Relay** — is located on right side of the instrument panel.
• **Ignition Module** — is located on the left hand side fender apron.
• **Illuminated Entry Timer** — is located on a crossmember behind the rear seat.
• **Inertia Switch** — is attached to the left rear wheel well.
• **Keyless Entry Module** — is located on a crossmember behind the rear seat.
• **Light Out Warning Module** — is located behind the extreme right side of the instrumnet panel.
• **Light Sensor/Amplifier** — is attached to the top of the underside of the instrument panel.
• **Low Fuel Warning Module** — is behind the right hand side of the instrument panel.
• **Manifold Absolute Pressure Sensor** — is on the left side fender apron.
• **Manifold Charge Temperature Sensor** — is on the rear left hand side of the engine on the manifold.
• **Power Door Lock Relay** — is on the crossbar under the passengers seat.
• **Power Window Safety Relay** — Attached to the bottom of the shake brace.
• **Speed Sensor** — is at the left side of the transmission.
• **Starter Relay** — is located on the right hand side fender apron.
• **Start Interrupt Relay** — under the left side of the instrument panel.
• **Thermactor Air Bypass Solenoid** — is attached to the right hand side of the cowl.
• **Thermactor Air Diverter Solenoid** — is attached to the upper right hand side of the cowl.
• **Throttle Kicker Solenoid** — is on the left hand side shock tower.
• **Throttle Position Sensor** — is attached to the right side of the carburetor.
• **Trigger Relay** — is located in the upper right side of the trunk.
• **Tripminder Module** — is in the center of the instrument panel, above the radio.
• **Trunk Release Solenoid** — is located at the center of the tailgate lid.
• **Voice Alert Module** — is located behind the left side of the instrument panel.

1984-87 THUNDERBIRD AND COUGAR

2.3L TURBOCHARGED ENGINE

- **A/C Cutout Relay** – is on the left front fender apron.
- **A/C Throttle Kicker Solenoid** – is located on the right side shock tower.
- **Alarm Relay** – is located in the upper right side of the trunk.
- **Ambient Temperature Sensor** – is located on the right side of the instrument panel.
- **Anti-Dieseling Time Relay** – is located on the right side front fender apron.
- **Anti-Theft Module** – is located in the upper right side of the trunk.
- **Auto-Lamp Relay No.1** – is attached to the top rear of steering column support brace.
- **Auto-Lamp Relay No.2** – is attached to the top rear of steering column support brace.
- **Barometric Pressure Sensor** – is located on the right hand side fender apron.
- **Boost Control Solenoid** – is located at the acess hole on the right side of the cowl.
- **Boost Control Switch** – is located at the acess hole on the right side of the cowl.
- **Chime Isolation Relay** – is attached to the top of the steering column support.
- **Coolant Temperature Switch** – is located in the heater supply pipe.
- **Cooling Fan Relay** – is located behind the strut tower on the right front fender apron.
- **Cornering Light Relays** – is in the center of the dash panel on the left side of the dash panel bracket.
- **Dis-Arm Relay** – is located in the upper right side of the trunk.
- **EGR Control Solenoid** – is located on the right side shock tower.
- **Electronic Control Assembly (ECA)** – is located at the acess hole on the right side of the cowl.
- **Electronic Engine Control (EEC) Power Relay** – is under the right side of the instrument panel on the cowl.
- **Engine Coolant Temperature Sensor** – is located on the front left hand side of the engine.
- **Exhaust Oxygen Sensor** – is located in the exhaust manifold.
- **Flash-to-Pass Relay** – is located behind the center of the instrument panel.
- **Fuel Flow Sensor** – is between the carburetor and right side fender apron.
- **Fuel Pump Relay** – is located above right rear wheel well.
- **Headlight Dimmer Relay** – is attached to the top rear of steering column support brace.
- **Hi-Lo Beam Relay** – is located behind the left side of the instrumnet panel.
- **Horn Relay** – is located on right side of the instrument panel.
- **Idle Speed Actuator** – is located at the upper right hand side of the engine.
- **Ignition Module** – is located on the left hand side fender apron.
- **Illuminated Entry Timer** – is located on a crossmember behind the rear seat.
- **In-Car Temperature Sensor** – is located on the right side of the instrumnet panel.
- **Inertia Switch** – is located in the trunk behind the right rear wheel.
- **Keyless Entry Module** – is located on a crossmember behind the rear seat.
- **Knock Sensor** – is located at the lower left side of the engine.

- **Light Out Warning Module** – is located behind the extreme right side of the instrumnet panel.
- **Light Sensor/Amplifier** – is attached to the top of the underside of the instrument panel.
- **Low Fuel Warning Module** – is behind the right hand side of the instrument panel.
- **Power Door Lock Relay** – is on the crossbar under the passengers seat.
- **Power Window Safety Relay** – Attached to the bottom of the shake brace.
- **Speed Sensor** – is at the left side of the transmission.
- **Start Interrupt Relay** – under the left side of the instrument panel.
- **Starter Relay** – is located on the right hand side fender apron.
- **Thick Film Ignition Module** – is attached to the right side of the distributor.
- **Throttle Position Sensor** – is located at the upper rear center of the engine.
- **Trigger Relay** – is located in the upper right side of the trunk.
- **Tripminder Module** – is in the center of the instrument panel, above the radio.
- **Trunk Release Solenoid** – is located at the center of the tailgate lid.
- **Vane Air Flow Meter** – is inside the right front fender apron.
- **Voice Alert Module** – is located behind the left side of the instrument panel.
- **Wide-Open-Throttle A/C Cutout Relay** – is located on the right front fender apron.

3.0L AND 5.0L ENGINES

- **A/C Cutout Relay** – is on the left front fender apron.
- **A/C Throttle Kicker Solenoid** – is located on the right side shock tower.
- **Alarm Relay** – is located in the upper right side of the trunk.
- **Ambient Temperature Sensor** – is located on the right side of the instrument panel.
- **Anti-Dieseling Time Relay** – is located on the right side front fender apron.
- **Anti-Theft Module** – is located in the upper right side of the trunk.
- **Auto-Lamp Relay No.1** – is attached to the top rear of steering column support brace.
- **Auto-Lamp Relay No.2** – is attached to the top rear of steering column support brace.
- **Chime Isolation Relay** – is attached to the top of the steering column support.
- **Coolant Temperature Switch** – is located in the heater supply pipe.
- **Cooling Fan Relay** – is located behind the strut tower on the right front fender apron.
- **Cornering Light Relays** – is in the center of the dash panel on the left side of the dash panel bracket.
- **Dis-Arm Relay** – is located in the upper right side of the trunk.
- **EGR Control Solenoid** – is located on the right side shock tower.
- **EGR Valve Position Sensor** – is at the top of the engine behind the carburetor.
- **EGR Vent Solenoid** – is located on the right side shock tower.
- **Electronic Control Assembly (ECA)** – is located under the right side of the instrument panel.
- **Electronic Engine Control (EEC) Power Relay** – is under the right side of the instrument panel on the cowl.
- **Engine Coolant Temperature Sensor** – is located on top of the engine, to the right of the manifold.

- **Exhaust Heat Control Solenoid** – is located on the left side shock tower.
- **Exhaust Oxygen Sensor** – is located in the right side exhaust manifold.
- **Flash-to-Pass Relay** – is located behind the center of the instrument panel.
- **Fuel Flow Sensor** – is between the carburetor and right side fender apron.
- **Fuel Pump Relay** – is located above right rear wheel well.
- **Headlight Dimmer Relay** – is attached to the top rear of steering column support brace.
- **Hi-Lo Beam Relay** – is located behind the left side of the instrument panel.
- **Horn Relay** – is located on right side of the instrument panel.
- **Idle Speed Control Motor** – is located on top of the engine.
- **Ignition Module** – is located on the left hand side fender apron.
- **Illuminated Entry Timer** – is located on a crossmember behind the rear seat.
- **In-Car Temperature Sensor** – is located on the right side of the instrunet panel.
- **Inertia Switch** – is attached to the left rear wheel well.
- **Keyless Entry Module** – is located on a crossmember behind the rear seat.
- **Light Out Warning Module** – is located behind the extreme right side of the instrumnet panel.
- **Light Sensor/Amplifier** – is attached to the top of the underside of the instrument panel.
- **Low Fuel Warning Module** – is behind the right hand side of the instrument panel.
- **Low Oil Level Relay** – is located under the left side of the instrument panel.
- **Manifold Absolute Pressure Sensor** – is located on the left front fender apron.
- **Manifold Charge Temperature Sensor** – is located on the top left hand side of the engine.
- **Power Door Lock Relay** – is on the crossbar under the passengers seat.
- **Power Window Safety Relay** – Attached to the bottom of the shake brace.
- **Speed Sensor** – is at the left side of the transmission.
- **Start Interrupt Relay** – under the left side of the instrument panel.
- **Starter Relay** – is located on the right hand side fender apron.
- **Thermactor Air Bypass Solenoid** – is attached to the upper right hand side of the cowl.
- **Thermactor Air Diverter Solenoid** – is attached to the upper right hand side of the cowl.
- **Throttle Kicker Solenoid (5.0L engine only)** – is attached on the left side shock tower.
- **Throttle Position Sensor** – is attached to the right side of the carburetor.
- **Trigger Relay** – is located in the upper right side of the trunk.
- **Tripminder Module** – is in the center of the instrument panel, above the radio.
- **Trunk Release Solenoid** – is located at the center of the tailgate lid.
- **Voice Alert Module** – is located behind the left side of the instrument panel.
- **Wide-Open-Throttle A/C Cutout Relay** – is located on the right front fender apron.

1982-83 LTD AND MARQUIS

- **A/C Throttle Kicker Solenoid** – is located at the upper right hand side of the engine cowl.

- **Anti-Diesel Solenoid** – is located at the top of the engine behind the carburetor.
- **Auto-Lamp Relay** – is attached to the top rear of steering column support brace.
- **Barometeric Pressure Switch** – is located on the left front fender apron.
- **Canister Purge Control Solenoid** – located at the right hand side of the valve cover.
- **Carburetor Float Bowl Solenoid** – is located at the front of the carburetor.
- **Choke Relay (4 cyl.)** – is located on the right hand side fender apron near the voltage regulator.
- **Coolant Temperature Switch (4 cyl.)** – is located in the lower left rear side of the engine.
- **Coolant Temperature Switch (3.3L)** – is located in the upper left rear side of the engine.
- **Coolant Temperature Sensor (3.8L V6)** – is located in the left front side of the engine.
- **Cooling Fan Temperature Switch (4 cyl.)** – is located in the center right side rear of the cylinder head in the heat pipe.
- **Cornering Light Relays** – is in the center of the dash panel on the left side of the dash panel bracket.
- **Electric Ported Vacuum Switch** – is located on the left side of the engine, behind the distributor.
- **Fuel Control Solenoid** – is located on the right side of the carburetor.
- **Fuel Flow Sensor** – located between the carburetor and the right side valve cover.
- **Headlight Dimmer Relay** – is attached to the top rear of steering column support brace.
- **Horn Relay** – is located on right side of the instrument panel.
- **Idle Tracking Switch** – located at the left side of the engine behind the carburetor.
- **Ignition Module** – is located on the left hand side of the steering column.
- **Illuminated Entry Timer (Sedan)** – is located inside the trunk, attached to the right rear quarter panel.
- **Illuminated Entry Timer (Station Wagon)** – is located below the entrance of the right rear window.
- **Light Out Warning Module** – is located behind the extreme right side of the instrumnet panel behind the glove box.
- **Light Sensor/Amplifier** – is attached to the top center of the instrument panel.
- **Low Fuel Warning Module** – is behind the right hand side of the instrument panel.
- **MCU Resistor** – located in the rear of the carburetor near the idle tracking.
- **Microprosseor Control Unit (MCU)** – located at the left hand side fender apron.
- **Oxygen Sensor** – Lower left side of the exhaust manifold.
- **Power Door Lock Relay** – is on the crossbar under the driver's seat.
- **Power Window Safety Relay** – Attached to theleft side of the instrument panel on the shake brace.
- **RPM Module** – is located above the brake pedal.
- **Speed Sensor** – is located on the left rear side of the transmission.
- **Starter Relay** – is located on the right hand side fender apron in front of the shock tower.
- **Thermactor Air Bypass Solenoid** – is attached at the right rear side of the engine compartment.
- **Thermactor Air Diverter Solenoid** – is attached to the right hand side shock tower.
- **Throttle Kicker Solenoid Valve (4 cyl.)** – is located on the right hand side of the dash panel.
- **Timer-Relay** – is located under the right side of the instrument panel.
- **Tripminder Module** – is located at the top center of the instrument panel, above the radio.

• **Trunk Release Solenoid** – is located at the center of the tailgate lid.
• **Wide-Open-Throttle A/C Cutout Relay (4 cyl.)** – is located at the carburetor.
• **Wide-Open Throttle Vacuum Switch** – is attached to the left side fender apron.

1984-87 LTD AND MARQUIS

2.3L ENGINE

• **A/C Throttle Kicker Solenoid** – is located at the upper right hand side of the engine cowl.
• **A/C Throttle Kicker Solenoid Valve** – is located on the right hand side of the engine cowl.
• **Anti-Diesel Solenoid** – is located at the top of the engine behind the carburetor.
• **Auto-Lamp Relay** – is attached to the left side of the steering column support brace.
• **Barometric Pressure Sensor** – is located on the left hand side fender apron.
• **Canister Purge Solenoid** – is on the right front side of the carburetor.
• **Choke Relay** – is located on the right hand side fender apron near the voltage regulator.
• **Coolant Temperature Sensor (3.8L V6)** – is located in the left front side of the engine.
• **Coolant Temperature Switch (4 cyl.)** – is located in the lower left rear side of the engine.
• **Cornering Light Relays** – is in the center of the dash panel on the left side of the dash panel bracket.
• **EGR Control Solenoid** – is located on the right side shock tower.
• **Electronic Control Assembly (ECA)** – is under the right side of the instrument panel on the cowl.
• **Electronic Engine Control (EEC) Power Relay** – is under the right side of the instrument panel on the cowl.
• **Engine Coolant Temperature Sensor** – is at the rear of the intake manifold.
• **Exhaust Oxygen Sensor** – is located in the right side of the exhaust manifold.
• **Feedback Carburetor Solenoid** – is attached on the carburetor.
• **Horn Relay** – is located in the center of the instrument panel.
• **Idle Speed Control Motor** – is attached to the carburetor.
• **Ignition Module** – is attached to the steering column.
• **Illuminated Entry Timer (Sedan)** – is located inside the trunk, attached to the right rear quarter panel.
• **Illuminated Entry Timer (Station Wagon)** – is located below the entrance of the right rear window.
• **Keyless Entry Module** – is located on a crossmember behind the rear seat.
• **Light Out Warning Module** – is located behind the extreme right side of the instrumnet panel behind the glove box.
• **Light Sensor/Amplifier** – is attached to the top center of the instrument panel.
• **Low Fuel Warning Module** – is behind the right hand side of the instrument panel.
• **Low Oil Level Relay** – is under the instrument panel attached to a support brace.
• **Low Oil Level Sensor** – is located in the oil pan.
• **Manifold Absolute Pressure Sensor** – is on the left side fender apron.
• **Power Door Lock Relay** – is on the crossbar under the passengers seat.
• **Power Door Unlock Relay** – is on the crossbar under the passengers seat.
• **Power Window Safety Relay** – Attached to the bottom of a shake brace under the left side of the instrument panel.

• **Speed Sensor** – is located on the left rear side of the transmission.
• **Starter Relay** – is located on the right front fender apron in front of the shock tower.
• **Thermactor Air Bypass Solenoid** – is attached to the left front fender apron.
• **Thermactor Air Diverter Solenoid** – is attached to the left front fender apron.
• **Throttle Position Sensor** – is attached to the right side of the carburetor.
• **Tripminder Module** – is located at the top center of the instrument panel.
• **Trunk Release Solenoid** – is located at the center of the trunk lid latch.
• **Voice Alert Module** – is located behind the left side of the instrument panel.
• **Warning Chime Relay** – is located under the left side of the instrument panel.
• **Wide-Open Throttle Cutout Switch** – is attached to the carburetor.

3.8L AND 5.0L ENGINES

• **A/C Throttle Kicker Solenoid** – is located at the upper right hand side of the engine cowl.
• **A/C Throttle Kicker Solenoid Valve** – is located on the right hand side of the engine cowl.
• **Air Charge Temperature Sensor** – is located on the top left hand side of the engine.
• **Anti-Diesel Solenoid** – is located at the top of the engine behind the carburetor.
• **Auto-Lamp Relay** – is attached to the left side of the steering column support brace.
• **Choke Relay** – is located on the right hand side fender apron near the voltage regulator.
• **Cornering Light Relays** – is in the center of the dash panel on the left side of the dash panel bracket.
• **EGR Control Solenoid** – is located on the left front fender apron.
• **EGR Valve Position Sensor** – is at the top of the engine behind the carburetor.
• **EGR Vent Solenoid** – is located on the left front fender apron.
• **Electronic Control Assembly (ECA)** – is located under the right side of the instrument panel cowl.
• **Electronic Engine Control (EEC) Power Relay** – is under the right side of the instrument panel on the cowl.
• **Engine Coolant Temperature Sensor** – is located on top of the engine, to the right of the distributor.
• **Exhaust Heat Control Solenoid** – is located on the left front fender apron.
• **Exhaust Oxygen Sensor** – is located in the right and left side exhaust manifolds.
• **Fuel Pump Relay** – is located above right rear wheel well.
• **Horn Relay** – is located in the center of the instrument panel.
• **Idle Speed Control Motor** – is attached to the fuel charging assembly.
• **Ignition Module** – is attached to the steering column.
• **Illuminated Entry Timer (Sedan)** – is located inside the trunk, attached to the right rear quarter panel.
• **Illuminated Entry Timer (Station Wagon)** – is located below the entrance of the right rear window.
• **Inertia Switch** – is attached to the left rear wheel well.
• **Keyless Entry Module** – is located on a crossmember behind the rear seat.
• **Light Out Warning Module** – is located behind the extreme right side of the instrumnet panel behind the glove box.
• **Light Sensor/Amplifier** – is attached to the top center of the instrument panel.
• **Low Fuel Warning Module** – is behind the right hand side of the instrument panel.

- **Low Oil Level Relay** – is under the instrument panel attached to a support brace.
- **Low Oil Level Sensor** – is located in the oil pan.
- **Manifold Absolute Pressure Sensor** – is located on the left front fender apron, near the starter relay.
- **Power Door Lock Relay** – is on the crossbar under the passengers seat.
- **Power Door Unlock Relay** – is on the crossbar under the passengers seat.
- **Power Window Safety Relay** – Attached to the bottom of a shake brace under the left side of the instrument panel.
- **Speed Sensor** – is located on the left rear side of the transmission.
- **Starter Relay** – is located on the left hand side fender apron.
- **Thermactor Air Bypass Solenoid** – is attached to the left front fender well.
- **Thermactor Air Diverter Solenoid** – is attached to the left front fender apron.
- **Throttle Position Sensor** – is attached to the right side of the fuel charging assembly.
- **Tripminder Module** – is located at the top center of the instrument panel.
- **Trunk Release Solenoid** – is located at the center of the trunk lid latch.
- **Voice Alert Module** – is located behind the left side of the instrument panel.
- **Warning Chime Relay** – is located under the left side of the instrument panel.
- **Wide Open Throttle A/C Cutout Relay** – is loctaed on the right front fender well.
- **Wide-Open Throttle Cutout Switch** – is attached to the carburetor.

1983 CROWN VICTORIA AND GRAND MARQUIS

FEEDBACK CARBURETOR CONTROLLED MODELS

- **Auto-Lamp Relay** – is attached to the left side of the steering column support brace.
- **Canister Purge Control Solenoid** – located at the right hand side of the valve cover.
- **Carburetor Actuator Stepper Motor** – is located on the right rear side of the carburetor.
- **Carburetor Float Bowl Solenoid** – is located at the front of the carburetor.
- **Coolant Hi/Lo Switch** – is located at the top front of the engine.
- **Coolant Temperature Switch** – is on the the top left hand side of the engine, near the valve cover.
- **Cornering Light Relays** – is in the center of the dash panel on the left side of the dash panel bracket.
- **De-Ice Switch/Relay** – is attached to the left side of the instrument panel.
- **Electric Ported Vacuum Switch** – is located on the right side, in front of the engine.
- **Fuel Flow Sensor** – is left of the right side valve cover, behind the distributor.
- **Horn Relay** – is located in the center of the instrument panel.
- **Ignition Module** – is located on the left front fender apron.
- **Illuminated Entry Timer** – is located under the instrument panel on the right side of the steering column.
- **Knock Sensor** – is located on the right side of the carburetor.
- **Light Sensor/Amplifier** – is attached to the top center of the instrument panel.

- **Low Fuel Warning Module** – is behind the right hand side of the instrument panel, beneath the speaker cut-out.
- **Microprosseor Control Unit (MCU)** – located at the left hand side fender apron.
- **Oxygen Sensor** – Lower right side of the exhaust manifold.
- **Power Door Lock Relay** – is inside the upper right hand cowl access hole.
- **Power Door Unlock Relay** – is inside the upper right hand cowl access hole.
- **Power Window Safety Relay** – Attached to the bottom of a shake brace under the left side of the instrument panel.
- **Speed Sensor** – is located on the left rear side of the transmission.
- **Starter Relay** – is located on the right hand side fender apron in front of the shock tower.
- **Thermactor Air Bypass Solenoid** – is attached at the right front fender apron.
- **Thermactor Air Diverter Solenoid** – is attached to the right front wheel well.
- **Thermactor Control Relay** – on the left side of the instrumnet panel attached to a shake brace.
- **Thermactor Dump Relay** – on the left side of the instrumnet panel attached to a shake brace.
- **Thermactor Dump Timer** – on the left side of the instrumnet panel attached to a shake brace.
- **Throttle Boost Solenoid** – is located on the front left side of the carburetor.
- **Throttle Kicker Control Relay** – is located on the right front fender apron.
- **Trailer Battery Charging Relay (Optional)** – is located near the left rear wheel well.
- **Trailer Exterior Lamp Relay (Optional)** – is located near the left rear wheel well.
- **Trailer Left Hand Turn Lamp Relay (Optional)** – is located near the left rear wheel well.
- **Trailer Right Hand Turn Lamp Relay (Optional)** – is located near the left rear wheel well.
- **Tripminder Module** – is located at the top center of the instrument panel above the radio.
- **Trunk Release Solenoid** – is located at the center of the trunk lid latch.

ELECTRONIC ENGINE CONTROL MODELS

- **Auto-Lamp Relay** – is attached to the left side of the steering column support brace.
- **Barometric Pressure Sensor** – is located on the right hand side fender apron.
- **Canister Purge Solenoid** – is on the right hand top of the engine.
- **Carburetor Float Bowl Solenoid** – is located on the carburetor.
- **Coolant Temperature Switch** – is on the the top left hand side of the engine, near the valve cover.
- **Cornering Light Relays** – is in the center of the dash panel on the left side of the dash panel bracket.
- **Crankshaft Position Sensor** – is at the lower right front side of the engine.
- **De-Ice Switch/Relay** – is attached to the left side of the instrument panel.
- **EGR Control Solenoid** – is located on the left side valve cover.
- **EGR Valve Position Sensor** – is at the top of the right front side of the engine behind the carburetor.
- **EGR Vent Solenoid** – is located on the left side valve cover.
- **Electronic Control Assembly (ECA)** – is under the left side of the instrument panel.
- **Electronic Engine Control (EEC) Power Relay** – is located on the left front fender apron.

- **Engine Coolant Temperature Sensor** – is at the top of the engine on the right side of the distributor.
- **Exhaust Oxygen Sensor** – is located in the right side of the exhaust manifold.
- **Fuel Flow Sensor** – is left of the right side valve cover, behind the distributor.
- **Fuel Pump Relay** – is located on the left front fender apron.
- **Horn Relay** – is located in the center of the instrument panel.
- **Ignition Module** – is located on the left front fender apron.
- **Illuminated Entry Timer** – is located under the instrument panel on the right side of the steering column.
- **Inertia Switch** – is attached to the left rear wheel well.
- **Light Sensor/Amplifier** – is attached to the top center of the instrument panel.
- **Low Fuel Warning Module** – is behind the right hand side of the instrument panel, beneath the speaker cut-out.
- **Manifold Absolute Pressure Sensor** – is on the right side fender apron.
- **Manifold Charge Temperature Sensor** – is on the rear left hand side of the engine on the manifold.
- **Message Center Module** – is under the center of the instrument panel on the center brace.
- **Power Door Lock Relay** – is inside the upper right hand cowl access hole.
- **Power Door Unlock Relay** – is inside the upper right hand cowl access hole.
- **Power Window Safety Relay** – Attached to the bottom of a shake brace under the left side of the instrument panel.
- **Speed Sensor** – is located on the left rear side of the transmission.
- **Starter Relay** – is located on the right hand side fender apron in front of the shock tower.
- **Thermactor Air Bypass Solenoid** – is attached at the right front fender apron.
- **Thermactor Air Diverter Solenoid** – is attached to the right front wheel well.
- **Throttle Kicker Solenoid** – is on the left hand side valve cover.
- **Throttle Position Sensor** – is attached to the right side of the carburetor.
- **Trailer Battery Charging Relay (Optional)** – is located near the left rear wheel well.
- **Trailer Exterior Lamp Relay (Optional)** – is located near the left rear wheel well.
- **Trailer Left Hand Turn Lamp Relay (Optional)** – is located near the left rear wheel well.
- **Trailer Right Hand Turn Lamp Relay (Optional)** – is located near the left rear wheel well.
- **Tripminder Module** – is located at the top center of the instrument panel above the radio.
- **Trunk Release Solenoid** – is located at the center of the trunk lid latch.

1984-87 CROWN VICTORIA AND GRAND MARQUIS

FEEDBACK CARBURETOR CONTROLLED MODELS

- **Auto-Lamp Relay** – is attached to the left side of steering column support brace.
- **Barometric Pressure Switch** – is on the left front fender apron.
- **Canister Purge Control Solenoid** – located at the right hand side of the valve cover.
- **Carburetor Actuator Stepper Motor** – is located on the right rear side of the carburetor.
- **Carburetor Float Bowl Solenoid** – is located at the front of the carburetor.

- **Compressor Relay (Load Leveling) Sedan** – is located on a bracket on the right rear quarter panel.
- **Compressor Relay (Load Leveling) Wagon** – is located on a bracket on the right rear quarter panel.
- **Compressor Vent Solenoid Sedan** – is located on a bracket on the right rear quarter panel.
- **Compressor Vent Solenoid Wagon** – is located on a bracket on the right rear quarter panel.
- **Cornering Light Relays** – is in the center of the dash panel on the left side of the dash panel bracket.
- **Coolant Hi/Lo Switch** – is located at the top front of the engine.
- **Coolant Temperature Switch** – is on the top left hand side of the engine, near the valve cover.
- **Electric Ported Vacuum Switch** – is located on the right side, in front of the engine.
- **Fuel Flow Sensor** – is left of the right side valve cover, behind the distributor.
- **Height Sensor** – is located under the floor, to the left of the fuel sensor.
- **Horn Relay** – is located in the center of the instrument panel.
- **Ignition Module** – is located on the left front fender apron.
- **Illuminated Entry Timer** – is located under the instrument panel on the right side of the steering column.
- **Knock Sensor** – is located on the right side of the carburetor.
- **Level Control Module (Sedan)** – is located on a bracket on the right rear quarter panel.
- **Level Control Module (Wagon)** – is located on a bracket on the right rear quarter panel.
- **Light Sensor/Amplifier** – is attached to the top center of the instrument panel.
- **Low Fuel Warning Module** – is behind the right hand side of the instrument panel, beneath the speaker cut-out.
- **Microprosseor Control Unit (MCU)** – located at the left hand side fender apron.
- **Mid-Engine Temperature Switch** – is located on the top right front side of the engine.
- **Oxygen Sensor** – Lower right side of the exhaust manifold.
- **Power Door Lock Relay** – is inside the upper right hand cowl access hole.
- **Power Door Un-Lock Relay** – is inside the upper right hand cowl access hole.
- **Power Window Safety Relay** – Attached to the bottom of a shake brace under the left side of the instrument panel.
- **Speed Sensor** – is located on the left rear side of the transmission.
- **Starter Relay** – is located on the right hand side fender apron in front of the shock tower.
- **Starter Relay Filter** – is on the upper right hand side of the cowl.
- **Thermactor Air Bypass Solenoid** – is attached at the right front fender apron.
- **Thermactor Air Diverter Solenoid** – is attached to the right front wheel well.
- **Thermactor Control Relay** – on the left side of the instrumnet panel attached to a shake brace.
- **Thermactor Dump Relay** – on the left side of the instrumnet panel attached to a shake brace.
- **Thermactor Dump Timer** – on the left side of the instrumnet panel attached to a shake brace.
- **Thick Film Ignition Module** – is attached to the distributor.
- **Throttle Boost Solenoid** – is located on the front left side of the carburetor.
- **Throttle Kicker Control Relay** – is located on the right front fender apron.
- **Throttle Kicker Solenoid** – is attached to the left side

valve cover.
- **Throttle Vaccum Sensor** – is located in the left valve cover.
- **Trailer Battery Charging Relay (Optional)** – is located near the left rear wheel well.
- **Trailer Exterior Lamp Relay (Optional)** – is located near the left rear wheel well.
- **Trailer Left Hand Turn Lamp Relay (Optional)** – is located near the left rear wheel well.
- **Trailer Right Hand Turn Lamp Relay (Optional)** – is located near the left rear wheel well.
- **Tripminder Module** – is located at the top center of the instrument panel above the radio.
- **Trunk Release Solenoid** – is located at the center of the trunk lid latch.

ELECTRONIC ENGINE CONTROLLED MODELS

- **Auto-Lamp Relay** – is attached to the left side of the steering column support brace.
- **Barometric Pressure Sensor** – is located on the right hand side fender apron.
- **Canister Purge Solenoid** – is on the right hand top of the engine.
- **Carburetor Float Bowl Solenoid** – is located on the carburetor.
- **Compressor Relay (Load Leveling) Sedan** – is located on a bracket on the right rear quarter panel.
- **Compressor Relay (Load Leveling) Wagon** – is located on a bracket on the right rear quarter panel.
- **Compressor Vent Solenoid Sedan** – is located on a bracket on the right rear quarter panel.
- **Compressor Vent Solenoid Wagon** – is located on a bracket on the right rear quarter panel.
- **Coolant Temperature Switch** – is on the the top left hand side of the engine, near the valve cover.
- **Cornering Light Relays** – is in the center of the dash panel on the left side of the dash panel bracket.
- **Crankshaft Position Sensor** – is at the lower right front side of the engine.
- **EGR Control Solenoid** – is located on the left side valve cover.
- **EGR Valve Position Sensor** – is at the top of the right front side of the engine behind the carburetor.
- **EGR Vent Solenoid** – is located on the left side valve cover.
- **Electronic Control Assembly (ECA)** – is under the left side of the instrument panel.
- **Electronic Engine Control (EEC) Power Relay** – is located on the left front fender apron.
- **Engine Coolant Temperature Sensor** – is at the top of the engine on the right side of the distributor.
- **Exhaust Oxygen Sensor** – is located in the right side of the exhaust manifold.
- **Fuel Flow Sensor** – is left of the right side valve cover, behind the distributor.
- **Fuel Pump Relay** – is located on the left front fender apron.
- **Height Sensor** – is located under the floor, to the left of the fuel sensor.
- **Horn Relay** – is located in the center of the instrument panel.
- **Ignition Module** – is located on the left front fender apron.
- **Illuminated Entry Timer** – is located under the instrument panel on the right side of the steering column.
- **Inertia Switch** – is attached to the left rear wheel well.
- **Level Control Module (Sedan)** – is located on a bracket on the right rear quarter panel.
- **Level Control Module (Wagon)** – is located on a bracket on the right rear quarter panel.

- **Light Sensor/Amplifier** – is attached to the top center of the instrument panel.
- **Low Fuel Warning Module** – is behind the right hand side of the instrument panel, beneath the speaker cut-out.
- **Manifold Absolute Pressure Sensor** – is on the right side fender apron.
- **Manifold Charge Temperature Sensor** – is on the rear left hand side of the engine on the manifold.
- **Message Center Module** – is under the center of the instrument panel on the center brace.
- **Power Door Lock Relay** – is inside the upper right hand cowl access hole.
- **Power Door Un-Lock Relay** – is inside the upper right hand cowl access hole.
- **Power Window Safety Relay** – Attached to the bottom of a shake brace under the left side of the instrument panel.
- **Speed Sensor** – is located on the left rear side of the transmission.
- **Starter Relay** – is located on the right hand side fender apron in front of the shock tower.
- **Thermactor Air Bypass Solenoid** – is attached at the right front fender apron.
- **Thermactor Air Diverter Solenoid** – is attached to the right front wheel well.
- **Thick Film Ignition Module** – is attached to the distrubutor.
- **Throttle Kicker Solenoid** – is on the left hand side valve cover.
- **Throttle Position Sensor** – is attached to the right side of the carburetor.
- **Throttle Vacuum Sensor** – is located in the left valve cover.
- **Trailer Battery Charging Relay (Optional)** – is located near the left rear wheel well.
- **Trailer Exterior Lamp Relay (Optional)** – is located near the left rear wheel well.
- **Trailer Left Hand Turn Lamp Relay (Optional)** – is located near the left rear wheel well.
- **Trailer Right Hand Turn Lamp Relay (Optional)** – is located near the left rear wheel well.
- **Tripminder Module** – is located at the top center of the instrument panel above the radio.
- **Trunk Release Solenoid** – is located at the center of the trunk lid latch.

1982-83 CONTINENTAL

- **A/C Throttle Kicker Relay** – is located on the right front fender apron.
- **Alarm Relay** – is located under the right side of the package tray in the trunk.
- **Anti-Theft Controller** – is located under the right side of the package tray in the trunk.
- **Anti-Theft Starter Interrupt Relay** – is located under the instrumnet panel on the left side support brace.
- **Anti-Theft Warning Lamp** – is in the instrument panel near the tripminder.
- **Auto-Lamp Relay** – is attached to the left side of the steering column support brace.
- **Barometric Pressure Sensor** – is located on the left hand side fender apron.
- **Central Fuel Injection (CFI) Relay** – located on the right side of the cowl.
- **Cornering Light Relays** – is in the center of the dash panel on the left side of the dash panel bracket.
- **Crankshaft Position Sensor (5.0L engine only)** – is at the lower right front side of the engine.
- **De-Ice Switch/Relay** – Is located in the center of the instrument panel.

- **Disarm Relay** – is located under the right side of the package tray in the trunk.
- **EGR Control Solenoid** – is located on the right front fender apron.
- **EGR Valve Position Sensor (5.0L engine)** – is at the top of the right front side of the engine behind the throttle body.
- **EGR Vent Solenoid** – is located on the right front fender apron.
- **Electronic Control Assembly (ECA)** – is located on the right side of the cowl.
- **Engine Coolant Temperature Sensor** – is at the top of the engine on the right side of the distributor.
- **Exhaust Heat Control Solenoid** – is mounted on the right front fender apron.
- **Exhaust Oxygen Sensor** – is located in the right side of the exhaust manifold.
- **Flash-to-Pass Relay** – is attached to the instrument panel brace.
- **Fuel Flow Sensor** – is located at the top of the engine torwards the right.
- **Fuel Pump Relay** – is located on the right hand deck-lid hinge support.
- **Hi-Lo Beam Relay** – is attached to the instrument panel brace.
- **Horn Relay** – is located in the center of the instrument panel.
- **Ignition Module** – is located on the left front fender apron.
- **Illuminated Entry Actuator** – is located under the package tray in the trunk.
- **Inertia Switch** – is located on the inboard side of the right hand deck-lid hinge support.
- **Interior Light Relay** – is in the center of the dash panel on the left side of the dash panel bracket.
- **Inverter Relay** – is located under the right side of the package tray in the trunk.
- **Keyless Entry Module** – is located under the right side of the package tray in the trunk.
- **Light Sensor/Amplifier** – is attached to the top center of the instrument panel.
- **Lights On/Key Warning Chime** – is located behind the center of the instrument panel to the left of the radio.
- **Lights Out Warning Module** – is located behind the center of the instrument panel, under the A/C control.
- **Low Fuel Warning Module** – is behind the center of the instrument panel.
- **Manifold Absolute Pressure Sensor** – is on the left side fender apron.
- **Manifold Charge Temperature Sensor (3.8L engine)** – is on the top right hand side of the engine.
- **Manifold Charge Temperature Sensor (5.0L engine)** – is on the rear left hand side of the engine on the manifold.
- **Message Center Module** – is under the center of the instrument panel on the center brace.
- **Power Window Safety Relay** – Attached to the bottom of a shake brace under the left side of the instrument panel.
- **Starter Relay** – is located on the right hand side fender apron in front of the shock tower.
- **Thermactor Air Bypass Solenoid** – is attached at the right front fender apron.
- **Thermactor Air Diverter Solenoid** – is attached to the right front wheel well.
- **Throttle Actuator Vacuum Solenoid** – is on the right front apron..
- **Throttle Position Sensor** – is attached to the right side of the throttle body.
- **Tripminder Module** – is located in the center of the instrument panel.

- **Trunk Release Solenoid** – is located at the center of the trunk lid latch.

1982-83 TOWN CAR AND MARK VI

- **Auto-Lamp Relay** – is attached to the left side of the steering column support brace.
- **Barometric Pressure Sensor** – is located on the right hand side fender apron.
- **Canister Purge Solenoid** – is on the right hand top of the engine.
- **Carburetor Float Bowl Solenoid** – is located on the carburetor.
- **Coolant Temperature Switch** – is on the the top left hand side of the engine, near the valve cover.
- **Cornering Light Relays** – is in the center of the dash panel on the left side of the dash panel bracket.
- **Crankshaft Position Sensor** – is at the lower right front side of the engine.
- **EGR Control Solenoid** – is located on the left side valve cover.
- **EGR Valve Position Sensor** – is at the top of the right front side of the engine behind the carburetor.
- **EGR Vent Solenoid** – is located on the left side valve cover.
- **Electronic Control Assembly (ECA)** – is under the left side of the instrument panel.
- **Electronic Engine Control (EEC) Power Relay** – is located on the left front fender apron.
- **Engine Coolant Temperature Sensor** – is at the top of the engine on the right side of the distributor.
- **Exhaust Oxygen Sensor** – is located in the right side of the exhaust manifold.
- **Fuel Flow Sensor** – is left of the right side valve cover, behind the distributor.
- **Fuel Pump Relay** – is located on the left front fender apron.
- **Horn Relay** – is located in the center of the instrument panel.
- **Ignition Module** – is located on the left front fender apron.
- **Illuminated Entry Timer** – is located under the instrument panel on the right side of the steering column.
- **Inertia Switch** – is attached to the left rear wheel well.
- **Light Sensor/Amplifier** – is attached to the top center of the instrument panel.
- **Low Fuel Warning Module** – is behind the right hand side of the instrument panel, beneath the speaker cut-out.
- **Manifold Absolute Pressure Sensor** – is on the right side fender apron.
- **Manifold Charge Temperature Sensor** – is on the rear left hand side of the engine on the manifold.
- **Message Center Module** – is under the center of the instrument panel on the center brace.
- **Power Door Lock Relay** – is inside the upper right hand cowl access hole.
- **Power Door Un-Lock Relay** – is inside the upper right hand cowl access hole.
- **Power Window Safety Relay** – Attached to the bottom of a shake brace under the left side of the instrument panel.
- **Speed Sensor** – is located on the left rear side of the transmission.
- **Starter Relay** – is located on the right hand side fender apron in front of the shock tower.
- **Thermactor Air Bypass Solenoid** – is attached at the right front fender apron.
- **Thermactor Air Diverter Solenoid** – is attached to the right front wheel well.

- **Thick Film Ignition Module** – is attached to the distrubutor.
- **Throttle Kicker Solenoid** – is on the left hand side valve cover.
- **Throttle Position Sensor** – is attached to the right side of the carburetor.
- **Throttle Vacuum Sensor** – is located in the left valve cover.
- **Trailer Battery Charging Relay (Optional)** – is located near the left rear wheel well.
- **Trailer Exterior Lamp Relay (Optional)** – is located near the left rear wheel well.
- **Trailer Left Hand Turn Lamp Relay (Optional)** – is located near the left rear wheel well.
- **Trailer Right Hand Turn Lamp Relay (Optional)** – is located near the left rear wheel well.
- **Tripminder Module** – is located at the top center of the instrument panel above the radio.
- **Trunk Release Solenoid** – is located at the center of the trunk lid latch.

1984-87 CONTINENTAL, MARK VII AND LINCOLN

- **A/C Cut-Out Relay** – is located on the left front fender apron.
- **Air Charge Temperature Sensor** – is on the rear left hand side of the engine on the manifold.
- **Air Spring Vent Solenoid** – is located on top of the respective air spring.
- **Air Suspension Control Module** – is attached to the left hinge support in the trunk.
- **Air Suspension Relay (Load Leveling)** – is located on the left frontr fenser apron.
- **Alarm Relay** – is located under the right side of the package tray in the trunk.
- **Ambient Temperature Sensor** – is located on the right side of the instrument panel.
- **Anti-Theft Controller** – is located under the right side of the package tray in the trunk.
- **Anti-Theft Starter Interrupt Relay** – is located under the instrumnet panel on the left side support brace.
- **Anti-Theft Warning Lamp** – is in the instrument panel near the tripminder.
- **Auto-Lamp Relay** – is attached to the left side of the steering column support brace.
- **Coolant Temperature Switch** – is on the left side of the engine.
- **Cooling Fan Relay** – is located on the right front fender apron.
- **Cornering Light Relays** – is in the center of the dash panel on the left side of the dash panel bracket.
- **Defrost Switch/Relay** – Is located in the center of the instrument panel.
- **Disarm Relay** – is located under the right side of the package tray in the trunk.
- **EGR Control Solenoid** – is located on the right front fender apron.
- **EGR Valve Position Sensor** – is at the top of the right front side of the engine behind the throttle body.
- **EGR Vent Solenoid** – is located on the right front fender apron.
- **Electronic Control Assembly (ECA)** – is located on the right side of the cowl.
- **Electronic Engine Control (EEC) Relay** – located on the right side of the cowl.
- **Engine Coolant Temperature Sensor** – is at the top of the engine on the right side of the distributor.
- **Exhaust Heat Control Solenoid** – is mounted on the right front fender apron.

- **Exhaust Oxygen Sensor** – is located in the right side of the exhaust manifold.
- **Flash-to-Pass Relay** – is attached to the instrument panel brace.
- **Fuel Flow Sensor** – is located at the top of the engine torwards the right.
- **Fuel Pump Relay** – is located on the left hand deck-lid hinge support.
- **Heated Seat Relays** – is located under the driver's or the passenger's seat.
- **Hi-Lo Beam Relay** – is attached to the instrument panel brace (above the fuse block on the Continental).
- **Horn Relay** – is located in the center of the instrument panel.
- **Ignition Module** – is attached to the distributor.
- **Illuminated Entry Actuator** – is located under the package tray in the trunk.
- **In-Car Temperature Sensor** – is located on the right side of the instrument panel.
- **Inertia Switch** – is located on the inboard side of the left hand deck-lid hinge support.
- **Interior Light Relay** – is in the center of the dash panel on the left side of the dash panel bracket.
- **Inverter Relay** – is located under the right side of the package tray in the trunk.
- **Keyless Entry Module** – is located under the right side of the package tray in the trunk.
- **Left Front Height Sensor** – is attached to the left front lower control arm.
- **Light Sensor/Amplifier** – is attached to the top center of the instrument panel.
- **Lights On/Key Warning Chime** – is located behind the center of the instrument panel to the left of the radio.
- **Lights Out Warning Module** – is located behind the center of the instrument panel, near the stering column.
- **Manifold Absolute Pressure Sensor** – is on the right side fender apron.
- **Message Center Module** – is under the center of the instrument panel on the center brace.
- **Power Antenna Relay** – is located in the right side of the trunk.
- **Power Mirror Relays** – are located in the left side of the trunk.
- **Power Window Safety Relay** – Attached to the bottom of a shake brace under the left side of the instrument panel.
- **Rear Height Sensor** – is attached to the right side of the rear axle.
- **Right Front Height Sensor** – is attached to the right front lower control arm.
- **Roof Console Indicator Module** – is located in the roof console.
- **Speed Sensor** – is located at the rear of the transmission.
- **Starter Relay** – is located on the left hand side fender apron.
- **Thermactor Air Bypass Solenoid** – is attached at the right front fender apron.
- **Thermactor Air Diverter Solenoid** – is attached to the right front wheel well.
- **Throttle Actuator Vacuum Solenoid** – is on the right front fender apron..
- **Throttle Position Sensor** – is attached to the right side of the throttle body.
- **Trailer Back-Up Lamp Relay (Optional)** – is located in the trunk near the latch bracket.
- **Trailer Battery Charging Relay (Optional)** – is located in the trunk near the latch bracket.
- **Trailer Exterior Lamp Relay (Optional)** – is located in the trunk near the latch bracket.
- **Trailer Left Hand Turn Lamp Relay (Optional)** – is located in the trunk near the latch bracket.
- **Trailer Right Hand Turn Lamp Relay (Optional)** – is

located in the trunk near the latch bracket.
- **Tripminder Module** – is located in the center of the instrument panel.
- **Trunk Release Solenoid** – is located at the center of the trunk lid latch.
- **Warning Indicator Module** – is behind the center of the instrument panel.

AEROSTAR

- **A/C-Auxilary Heater Relay** – is located on the left front fender apron.
- **A/C Charge Temperature Sensor** – is located on the left side of the engine on the manifold.
- **A/C-Heater Blower Motor Resistors** – is located on the right side of the A/C-Heater blower housing.
- **A/C-Heater In-Line Diode** – is located on the left fender apron, near the starter relay.
- **A/C Wide Open Throttle Cut-Out Relay** – is located on the left front fender apron.
- **Choke Heater Relay** – is located on the left front fender apron.
- **Coolant Temperature Sending Unit (2.3L)** – is located on the rear left side of the engine.
- **Coolant Temperature Sending Unit (2.8L)** – is located on the thermostat housing.
- **Coolant Temperature Sensor (2.8L)** – is located on the thermostat housing.
- **Door Ajar Relay** – is located on the top corner of the right cowl.
- **Door Lock/Unlock Relay** – is located on the left front fender apron.
- **Dual Warning Buzzer** – is located behind the center of the instrument panel.
- **EGR Valve Position Sensor** – is located on the EGR valve.
- **Electronic Control Assembly (ECA)** – is located on the lower right cowl.
- **Electrionic Engine Control Power Relay** – is located on the left front fender apron.

- **Engine Coolant Temperature Sensor** – is located on the left front side of the engine.
- **Fuel Flow Sensor** – is located between the carburetor and the right front fender apron.
- **Fuel Pump Relay (2.3L)** – is located on the left front fender apron.
- **Horn Relay** – is located under the instrument panel, to the right of the steering column.
- **Illuminated Entry Module** – is located on the bottom of the left door panel.
- **In-Line Circuit Breaker** – is located behind the right instrument panel pod.
- **Knock Sensor** – is located on the left rear side of the engine.
- **Manifold Absolute Pressure Sensor** – is located on the right fender apron.
- **Mileage Sensor** – is located on the right cowl.
- **Oil Pressure Sending Unit (2.3L)** – is located on the left rear side of the engine.
- **Oil Pressure Sending Unit (2.8L)** – is located on the left front side of
- **Oxygen Sensor** – is located on the exhaust manifold.
- **Remote Headphone Module** – is located on the left rear trim panel.
- **Self-Test Connectors** – are located on the left front fender apron.
- **Speed Control Amplifier** – is located under the instrument panel, to the right of the steering column.
- **Speed Control Servo** – is located on the left front fender apron.
- **Speed Sensor** – is located on the transmission extension housing.
- **Starter Relay** – is located on the left front fender apron.
- **Throttle Position Sensor** – is located on the right side of the carburetor.
- **Tripminder Module** – is located under the instrument panel, to the right of the steering column.
- **Useful Life Sensor** – is located under the instrument panel, near the bulkhead connector.
- **Wiper/Washer Interval Governor** – is located under the instrument panel, near the parking brake.

GENERAL MOTORS CORPORATION

BUICK

Circuit Breakers

Note: On all models, there is a thermo circuit breaker incorporated in the headlight switch assembly to protect the headlight circuits. Also there is a circuit breaker integral with the windshield wiper motor.

CENTURY AND SKYLARK

POWER ACCESORIES

One 30 amp circuit breaker located in the fuse block, which protects the defogger, power seats and power door locks. It also protects the theft deterrent system on the Century only.

POWER WINDOWS

One 30 amp circuit breaker located in the fuse block, which protects the power windows. It also protects the rear winshield wiper on the Century models.

1982-84 ELECTRA, LE SABRE, REGAL AND RIVIERA

POWER ACCESSORIES

One 30 amp circuit breaker located in the fuse block, which protects the defogger, power door locks and power seats on all models. It also protects the automatic door locks, power seat recliner and memory seats on all models except the Regal. The theft deterrent system on all models except the Riviera. The radio and trunk lid pull down on the Riviera only. Tailgate power windows on the Electra and Le Sabre wagons.

1985-87 ELECTRA

POWER WINDOWS

One 30 amp circuit breaker located in the fuse block, which protects the power windows and the sunroof.

POWER ACCESSORIES

One 30 amp circuit breaker located in the fuse block, which protects the automatic door locks, rear window defogger, keyless entry, power door locks, power seats and trunk lid pulldown.

1985-87 LE SABRE, REGAL AND RIVIERA

POWER ACCESSORIES

One 30 amp circuit breaker located in the fuse block, which protects the defogger, power door locks and power seats on all models. It also protects the automatic door locks, power seat recliner and memory seats on all models except the Regal. The theft deterrent system on all models except the Riviera. The radio and trunk lid pull down on the Riviera only. Tailgate power windows on the Le Sabre wagon.

SKYHAWK

POWER WIDOWS

One 35 amp circuit breaker located in the fuse block, which protects the power window system.

POWER ACCESSORIES

One 35 amp circuit breaker located in the fuse block, which protects the defogger, power door locks and power seats.

SOMERSET REGAL

POWER ACCESSORIES

One 35 amp circuit breaker is located in the fuse block, which protects the rear window defogger, radio, power seat and power door locks.

POWER WINDOWS

One 35 amp circuit breaker is located in the fuse block and it protects the power window circuit.

Fusible Links

All models are equipped with fusible links which attach to the lower ends of main feed wires and connect at the battery or starter solenoid. On the diesel models, the fusible links attach to the wiring harness and connect to the glow plug relay. On all models there are also fusible links located at the EST distributor to protect the computer command control system. The Skyhawk model has fusible links loacted in the following places; the firewall connector to protect the cooling fan, at the left front fender apron to protect the vacuum pump and in the underhood wiring to protect the underhood light. On the 1984 and later Electra, Le Sabre and Riviera models, there are two in-line (25 amp) fuses located under the left side of the instrument panel near the fuse block. These in-line fuses are used to protect the Theft Deterrent System.

Relay, Sensors And Computer Locations

CENTURY

- **A/C Compressor Control Relay (SFI)** – is located on the right side of the firewall.
- **A/C Compressor Control Relay (4 cyl.)** – is located on the right corner of the firewall.
- **A/C Coolant Fan Relay (4 cyl.)** – is located on the right side of the firewall.
- **A/C High Pressure Cut-Off Switch** – is located on the front of the engine, near the left side of the A/C compressor.
- **A/C High Pressure Switch (SFI)** – is located in the refrigerant line near the A/C compressor.
- **A/C High Pressure Switch (6 cyl.)** – is located on the right side of the engine and to the left of the A/C compressor.
- **A/C Low Pressure Cut-Off Switch** – is located on the right side of the engine and to the rear of the A/C compressor.
- **Antenna Relay** – is located under the instrument panel, behind the glove box.
- **Assembly Line Diagnostic Link** – is located in the center of the instrument panel, underneath the steering column.
- **Audio Alarm Module** – is located under the left side of the instrument panel, in the convenience center.
- **Automatic Transaxle Selector Switch** – is located on the top left hand side of the transaxle.

• **Barometeric Pressure Sensor**—is taped to the computer command control harness, behind the glove box.
• **Blower Relay**—is located on the right side of the firewall.
• **Constant Relay**—is located in front of the left front shock tower, on the fender apron.
• **Convenience Center (1982)**—is located behind the right side of the instrument panel, near the glove box.
• **Convenience Center (1983-85)**—is located behind the instrument panel, to the left of the steering column.
• **Convenience Center (1986-87)**—is located behind the right side of the instrument panel, behind the glove box.
• **Coolant Fan Delay Relay (SFI)**—is located in front of the left front shock tower, on a bracket.
• **Coolant Fan Relay**—is located in front of the left front shock tower.
• **Coolant Fan Switch (SFI)**—is located on the top right hand side of the engine and to the left of the generator.
• **Coolant Fan Switch (4 cyl.)**—is located on the top of the engine, near the distributor.
• **Coolant Temperature Fan Switch (4 cyl.)**—is located on the left front side of the engine, below the valve cover.
• **Coolant Temperature Sensor (6 cyl.)**—is located on the top of the engine above the water pump.
• **Coolant Temperature Sensor (4 cyl.)**—is located on the left side of the engine below the water cooolant outlet.
• **Cruise Control Module**—is located above the accelerator pedal, under the instrument panel.
• **Cruise Control Servo (SFI & 4 cyl.)**—is located in front of the left front shock tower, on the fender apron.
• **Cruise Control Servo (6 cyl.)**—is located on the left rear corner of the engine.
• **Door Lock Relay**—is located under the instrument panel, to the right of the glove box.
• **Early Fuel Evaporation Heater**—is located on top of the engine.
• **Early Fuel Evaporation Heater Switch**—is located on top of the engine, near the distributor.
• **EGR Solenoid Valve**—is located on a bracket, above the left side of the valve cover.
• **Electronic Control Module**—is located under the right side of the instrument panel, behind the glove box.
• **Electronic Level Control Height Sensor**—is located on the frame under the rear of the vehicle.
• **Electronic Level Control Relay**—is located on the frame behind the left rear wheel well.
• **Electronic Spark Timing Distributor (6 cyl.)**—is located on the top right side of the engine.
• **Electronic Spark Timing Distributor (4 cyl.)**—is located on the top left rear side of the engine.
• **Fuel Bowl Vent Solenoid**—is located on the top of the engine near the generator.
• **Fuel Pump Relay (4 cyl.)**—is located in the relay bracket on the right side of the firewall.
• **High Speed Coolant Fan Relay**—is located on the left front side of the engine.
• **Horn Relay**—is located under the instrument panel, in the convenience center.
• **Idle Air Control Stepper Motor**—is located behind the left side of the throttle body assembly.
• **Idle Boost Solenoid**—is located on the carburetor.
• **Light Driver Module**—is taped to the instrument panel harness, behind the glove box.
• **Low Speed Coolant Fan Relay**—is located near the battery, on the left side of the radiator shroud.
• **Manifold Air Pressure Sensor (6 cyl.)**—is located on the right side of the radiator shroud, near the blower motor.
• **Manifold Air Pressure Sensor (4 cyl.)**—is located on the top of the engine, on the right side of the air cleaner assembly.
• **Mixture Control Solenoid**—is located on the carburetor.
• **Oxygen Sensor**—is located in the exhaust manifold.

• **Power Steering Cut-Out Switch**—is located on the bottom of the steering rack.
• **Power Steering Pressure Switch**—is located on the left side of the engine above the transaxle.
• **Pressure Cycling Switch**—is located on the firewall near the accumulator.
• **Purge Solenoid Valve**—is located in the left front side of the engine compartment.
• **Rear Wiper Relay**—is located in the top center of the tailgate.
• **Sentinel Amplifier**—is located under the center of the instrument panel, behind the ashtray.
• **Sentinel Photocell**—is located on the top left side of the instrument panel, in the end of the defrost grill.
• **Starter Interrupt Relay**—is taped to the instrument panel harness, above the right side ashtray.
• **Theft Deterrent Controller**—is located under the instrument panel, below the headlight switch.
• **Theft Deterrent Relay**—is strapped to the controller, under the instrument panel.
• **Throttle Kicker Relay**—is located in the left front side of the engine compartment.
• **Throttle Kicker Solenoid Valve**—is located on the top of the engine near the carburetor.
• **Throttle Position Sensor**—is located on the front of the throttle body.
• **Vehicle Speed Sensor**—is connected to the rear center of the instrument cluster.
• **Vehicle Speed Sensor Buffer**—is located under the left side of the instrument panel, behind the instrument cluster.
• **Wiper/Washer Motor Module**—is located on the left side of the firewall.

1982-84 REGAL

• **A/C Blower Relay**—is located in the blower motor assembly.
• **A/C Cut-Out Switch**—is located on the accelerator pedal.
• **A/C-Heater Blower Resistors**—is located in the heater module in front of the blower motor.
• **A/C Presuure Cycling Switch**—is located on the top of the vacuum tank.
• **A/C Temperature Cut-Out Relay**—is located behind the right front fender apron or at the center of the firewall.
• **A/C Temperature Cut-Out Switch**—is located on the left front side of the engine near the alternator.
• **Altitude Advance Relay (1984 Diesel)**—is located on the upper center of the firewall.
• **Barometric Pressure Sensor**—is located behind the right side of the instrument panel.
• **Brake Pressure Switch**—is located on the rear base of the left front wheel well.
• **"Check Engine" Light Driver Module**—is taped to the instrument panel harness to the left of the glove box.
• **Choke Heater Relay**—is located on the left engine cowl to the right of the steering column.
• **Cold Advance Diode (1984 Diesel)**—is located in the engine harness, to the right of the master cylinder.
• **Cold Inhibit Switch (Diesel)**—is located below the right valve cover.
• **Convenience Center (1982-83)**—is located behind the instrument panel, to the left of the steering column.
• **Convenience Center (1984)**—is located behind the left side of the instrument panel, near the headlight switch.
• **Coolant Temperature Sensor**—is located on the front of ther engine behind the alternator on the V6 engines and on the top left front of the engine ong the V8. Behind the water on the diesel engine.
• **Coolant Temperature Switch**—is located on the top of the engine behind the alternator or water pump on the V6 and

diesel engine and on the left side of the engine near the exhaust manifold on the V8 engines.
- **Cruise Control Unit** — is located under the left side of the dash panel, above the accelerator pedal.
- **Defogger Timer (1982-83)** — is located under the left side of the instrument panel attached to the top of the fuse block.
- **Diesel Electronics Module** — is located behind the instrument panel to the right of the glove box behind the right kick panel.
- **Door Lock Relay** — is located on the lower right kick panel at the bottom access hole.
- **Early Fuel Evaporation (EFE) Relay** — is located on the front of the engine. On the 1984 models this relay is located at the right side of the engine compartment, above the wheel well.
- **Early Fuel Evaporation Solenoid** — is located at the top center of the right valve cover.
- **EGR Cut-Out Relay (1982-83)** — is located on the right front fender well.
- **EGR Solenoid** — is located at the top center of the right valve cover on the V6 engine and on the bracket rear of the right valve cover or top front left side on the V8 engines.
- **Electronic Control Module (ECM)** — is located on the right shroud near the lower access hole.
- **Electronic Spark Control Module (1984)** — is located above the right wheel well on the V6 engine and at the top left side of the engine on the V8 engine.
- **Engine Temperature Switch (Diesel)** — is located below the left valve cover. On the 84 models this switch is located behind the water pump.
- **Fast Idle Relay** — is located on the left side of the engine cowl.
- **Fast Idle Solenoid** — is located on the top of the engine near the front.
- **Fuel Metering Solenoid** — is located on the right side of the carburetor on the V6 engine and/or the top right side of the engine on the V8.
- **Gear Selector Switch** — is attached to the base of the steering coulmn.
- **Glow Plug Controller** — is located at the top left rear of the engine, above the glow plug relay.
- **Glow Plug Relay (Diesel)** — is located on the top of the right front fender well.
- **High Altitude Advance Solenoid (1984 Diesel)** — is located in the fuel line, near the right valve cover.
- **Horn Relay** — is located behind the left side of the instrument panel above the fuse block.
- **Ignition Key Warning Buzzer** — is located behind the left side of the dash panel.
- **Lights-On Buzzer** — is attached to the fuse block.
- **Low Altitude Advance Solenoid (1984 Diesel)** — is located above the right valve cover.
- **Low Altitude Diode (1984 Diesel)** — is located in the engine harness, to the right of the master cylinder.
- **Low Brake Vacuum Delay Module** — is taped to the instrument panel harness above the fuse block.
- **Manifold Absolute Pressure Sensor** — is located on the top right front fender well.
- **Multi-Function Chime Module** — is located behind the instrument panel to the left of the steering column at the convenience center.
- **Oil Pressure Sender/Switch** — is located on the right rear of the engine on the V6 diesel and/or the front of the engine on the other engines.
- **Oxygen Sensor** — is located in the right rear exhaust manifold on the V6 and/or below the the right valve cover on the V8.
- **Power Antenna Relay** — is located behind the right side of the glove box on 1982-83 models on the 84 models the relay is behind the center of the instrument panel to the right of the radio.

- **Power Door Lock and Power Seat Circuit Breaker** — is located in the fuse block.
- **Seat Belt Timer Buzzer** — is located behind left side of the instrument panel at the convenience center.
- **Theft Deterrent Control Unit** — is located behind the instrument panel to the left of the steering column.
- **Theft Deterrent Diode** — is taped to the instrument panel harness to the left of the steering column.
- **Theft Deterrent Relay** — is located behind the instrument panel to the left of the steering column.
- **Throttle Kicker Relay (1984)** — is located on the firewall near the brake booster.
- **Throttle Position Sensor** — is located at the front of the carburetor.
- **Tone Generator (1984)** — is located at the convenience center.
- **Torque Converter Clutch Switch** — is located on the brake pedal support.
- **Trunk Release Solenoid** — is located at the rear center of the trunk lid, just above the license plate.
- **Turbo Boost Indicator Switch** — is located above the front part of the left front fender well.
- **Vacuum Regulator Vacuum Switch (1984 Diesel)** — is located just forward of the intake manifold crossover.
- **Vacuum Sensor (on the V8)** — is connect to the right front fender well.
- **Vehicle Speed Sensor** — is located behind the speedometer.
- **Wastegate Solenoid** — is located at the rear of the left valve cover.
- **Wide Open Throttle Relay (1984)** — is located at the rear of the engine compartment.
- **Window and Sunroof Circuit Breaker** — is located under the left side of the dash panel, at the fuse block.

1985-87 REGAL

- **A/C Blower Relay** — is located on the evaporator case behind the acumulator
- **A/C Compressor Clutch Diode** — is taped to the inside compressor connector on the front of the compressor.
- **A/C Cut-Out Switch** — is located on the accelerator pedal bracket.
- **A/C Fast Idle Solenoid** — is located to the left of the carburetor on the gas engines and on the top center of the engine on the diesel models.
- **A/C-Heater Blower Resistors** — are located on the evaporator case in the engine compartment.
- **A/C Pressure Cycling Switch** — is located on the right side of the firewall on the accumulator.
- **A/C Temperature Cut-Out Relay** — is located behind the right front fender apron or at the center of the firewall.
- **Altitude Advance Relay (Diesel)** — is located on the upper center of the firewall.
- **Ambient Temperature Sensor** — is located under the right side of the dash panel, above rthe blower motor.
- **Anti-Diesel Solenoid** — is located on the left front valve cover.
- **Assembly Line Diagnostic Connector** — is located on the bootom left center of the dash panel.
- **Barometric Pressure Sensor (V6)** — is located behind the right side of the dash panel above the glove box.
- **Barometric Pressure Sensor (V8)** — is located on a braket with the ESC module.
- **Brake Accumulator Pressure Switch** — is located on the left side of the firewall, near the brake booster.
- **Brake Torque Converter Clutch Switch** — is located at the top of the brake pedal support.
- **Camshaft Sensor (Regal Turbo)** — is located at the front center of the engine.

• **Fuel Shut-Off Solenoid (Diesel)**—is located under the fuel injection pump cover.
• **Gear Selector Switch**—is attached to the base of the steering column.
• **Generator Diode**—is located taped in the harness behind the fuse block.
• **Glow Plug Controller/Relay (Diesel)**—is located on the top right (left on the Cutlass models) valve cover.
• **Glow Plug Relay (Diesel)**—is located on the top of the right front fender well.
• **Headlight Relay**—is located at the front side of the engine compartment, near the headlight.
• **Horn Relay**—is located behind the left side of the instrument panel above the fuse block.
• **Idle Stop Solenoid**—is located on the top of the engine and to the left of the carburetor.
• **Ignition Key Warning Buzzer**—is located behind the left side of the dash panel.
• **In-Car Sensor**—is located at the right side of the dash panel as part of the speaker grille assembly.
• **Low Brake Vacuum Delay Module**—is taped to the instrument panel harness, above the fuse block.
• **Manifold Absolute Pressure Sensor**—is located on the air cleaner on the 4.3L engine and at the right side of the engine compartment above the wheel well on all other engines.
• **Mass Airflow Sensor (EFI)**—is located on the air intake hose at the top left side of the engine compartment.
• **Metering Valve Sensor (Diesel)**—is located on the diesel injection pump.
• **Mixture Control Solenoid**—is located on the front or right side of the carburetor or throttle body.
• **Multi-Function Chime Module**—is located behind the instrument panel to the left of the steering column at the convenience center.
• **Oxygen Sensor**—is located in the exhaust manifold.
• **Power Accessory Circuit Breaker**—is located above the flasher relay in the fuse block.
• **Power Antenna Relay**—is located behind the center of the instrument panel to the right of the radio.
• **Power Master Brake Relay**—is located on top of the electro-hydraulic pump motor below the master cylinder.
• **Seat Belt Timer Buzzer**—is located behind left side of the instrument panel at the convenience center.
• **Theft Deterrent Controller**—is located under the left side of the dash panel, near the kick panel.
• **Theft Deterrent Diode**—is located behind the left side of the dash panel in connector " C-857".
• **Theft Deterent Relay**—is located behind the instrument panel to the left of the steering column.
• **Third and Fourth Gear Switches**—are located in the middle of the left side of the transmission.
• **Throttle Position Sensor**—is located at the front of the carburetor or on the side of the throttle body.
• **Tone Generator**—is located behind the left side of the dash panel, in the convenience center.
• **Torque Converter Clutch solenoid**—is located in the middle of the left side of the transmission.
• **Trunk Release Solenoid**—is located at the rear of the trunk lid above the liscense plate.
• **Turbo Boost Gauge Sensor**—is located on the right front inner fender above the wheelwell.
• **Turbo Boost Indicator Switch**—is located on the right front fender, above the wheel well.
• **Twilight Sentinel Amplifier**—is located under the dash panel, near the radio.
• **Twilight Sentinel Photocell**—is located at the top center of the dash panel.
• **Vacuum Sensor**—is located at the rear of the engine above the valve cover.
• **Vehicle Speed Buffer**—is located under the left side of the dash panel, to the right of the steering column.

• **Vehicle Speed Sensor**—is located behind the dash panel and to the right of the steering column.
• **Water-In-Fuel Module (Diesel)**—is located at the top rear side of the engine.
• **Window and Sun Roof Circuit Breaker**—is located in the fuse block.
• **Wiper/Washer Motor Module**—is located on the upper left corner of the firewall in the engine compartment.

1982-84 ELECTRA, PARK AVENUE AND LESABRE

• **A/C Blower Relay**—on the right side of the engine cowl, in front of the blower motor.
• **A/C Compressor Clutch Diode**—is taped to the inside compressor clutch connector.
• **A/C Compressor Cut-Out Switch**—is located below the left side of the instrument panel on the accelerator plate.
• **A/C-Heater Resistors**—is located on the right side of the engine cowl, infront of the blower motor.
• **A/C Pressure Cycling Switch**—is located on the right side of the ngine cowl, above the front relay.
• **"Check Engine " Light Driver**—is taped to the instrumnet panel harness at the left of the glove box.
• **Choke Heater Relay**—is located on the left engine cowl to the right of the steering column.
• **Convenience Center (1985)**—is located behind the left side of the instrument panel, near the headlight switch.
• **Convenience Center (1986-87)**—is located behind the left side of the instrument panel, near the radio.
• **Coolant Temperature Sending Unit**—is located at the top of the engine.
• **Coolant Temperature Sensor**—is located at the top of the engine.
• **Coolant Temperature Switch (3.8L)**—is located behind the water pump at the top of the engine.
• **Coolant Temperature Switch (4.3L)**—is located behind the A/C compressor.
• **Coolant Temperature Switch (V8)**—is located on the left side of the engine, below the exhaust manifold.
• **Crankshaft Sensor (Regal Turbo)**—is located at the front center of the engine.
• **Cruise Control Module**—is located under the left isde of the dash panel, above the accelerator pedal.
• **Defogger Timer Relay**—is located under the left side of the instrument panel attached to the top of the fuse block.
• **Detonation (Knock) Sensor (3.8L)**—is located on the top rear side of the engine.
• **Detonation (Knock) Sensor (4.3L)**—is located on the lower left side of the engine block.
• **Detonation (Knock) Sensor (V8-Gas)**—is located on the lower right side of the engine block in fron tof the starter motor.
• **Diagnostic Dwell Meter Connector**—is strapped to the wiring harness at the top right side of the engine.
• **Diesel Electronic Control Module (DEC)**—is located behind the right side kick panel.
• **Differential Pressure Sensor (Cutlass)**—is located at the right front corner of the engine compartment behind the reservoir compartment.
• **Door Lock Relay**—is located on the lower right kick panel at the bottom access hole.
• **Early Fuel Evaporation (EFE)**—is located at the top of the engine, above the water pump.
• **Early Fuel Evaporation (EFE) Relay (with gauges)**—this relay is located at the left side of the engine compartment, above the wheel well.
• **Early Fuel Evaporation (EFE) Relay (without**

gauges)—this relay is located at the right side of the engine compartment, above the wheel well.

• **EGR Temperature Switch (4.3L)**—is located on the intake manifold, in front of the distributor.

• **Electronic Control Module (ECM)**—is located behind the right kick panel.

• **Electronic Level Control Relay**—is located on the electronic level control compressor.

• **Electronic Level Control Sensor**—is located on the rear portion of the crossmember.

• **Electronic Spark Control Module (ESC)**—is located on the bracket at the top of the right front fender well.

• **Electronic Vacuum Regulator Valve Module**—is located at the top center of the right valve cover.

• **EPR Solenoid (Diesel)**—is located on the right valve cover.

• **Fuel Control In-Line Fuse**—is located on the bracket next to the ESC module, on the 4.3L V6 engine.

• **Fuel Metering Solenoid (3.8L)**—is located on the carburetor.

• **Fuel Pump Prime Connector**—is located in the wiring harness near the fuel control in-line fuse.

• **Fast Idle Relay**—is located on the same bracket as the electronic spark control module, which is located at the top of the right front fender well.

• **Fuel Pump Relay**—is located on a bracket in the right side of the engine compartment.

• **A/C Programmer Unit**—is located behind the right side of the instrument panel.

• **A/C Temperaturer Cut-Out Relay**—is located on the top center of the engine cowl.

• **A/C Temperature Cut-Out Switch**—is located on the top front of the engine near the left valve cover.

• **Barometric Pressure Sensor (V6)**—is located behind the glove box.

• **Booster Low Vacuum Switch**—is located on the power boost unit.

• **Brake Pressure Switch**—is located under the left side engine cowl, attached to the frame.

• **Brake Vacuum Relay**—is located behind the instrument panel, to the left of the sterring column.

• **Cold Inhibit Switch (Diesel)**—is located below the rear portion of the right valve cover.

• **Converter Clutch Switch (Diesel)**—is located on the brake pedal support.

• **Coolant Temperature Sender**—is located on the top left rear of the engine on the diesel models and on the front of the engine on the gas models.

• **Coolant Temperature Sensor (V6)**—is located is located on the front of the engine near the carburetor.

• **Cruise Control Throttle Servo**—is located on the top front portion of the engine.

• **Defogger Timer Relay**—is attached to the top of the fuse block.

• **Detonation (Knock) Sensor**—is located on the top left rear of the engine.

• **Diode Module (Diesel)**—is located on the top center of the engine cowl.

• **Door Lock Control Unit**—is located is attached to the upper right cowl.

• **Door Lock Relay**—is located on the upper right cowl.

• **Door Unlock Relay**—is located on the upper right cowl.

• **Early Fuel Evaporation Relay (V6)**—is located on the front top portion of the engine.

• **Early Fuel Evaporation Solenoid (V6)**—is located on the top center of the right valve cover.

• **EGR Solenoid**—is located on the top center of the right valve cover.

• **Electronic Control Module (ECM)**—is located on the right side kick panel.

• **Engine Temperature Switch (Diesel)**—is located below

the rear portion of the left valve cover.

• **Fast Idle Solenoid (Diesel)**—is located on the top center of the engine in front of the injection pump.

• **Gear Selector Switch**—is located on the lower top portion of the steering column.

• **Glow Plug Relay (Diesel)**—is located on the front of the right front wheel well.

• **Glow Plug Thermal Control Unit (Diesel)**—is located on the top of the engine, in front of the fast idle solenoid.

• **Horn Relay**—is attached to the left side of the fuse block.

• **Idle Speed Control Unit (V6)**—is located on the left side of the carburetor.

• **Ignition Key Warning Buzzer**—is attached to the left side of the fuse block.

• **Illuminated Entry Timer**—is located on the upper left shroud, near the junction block.

• **Level Control Height Sensor**—is located on the rear center part of the crossmember.

• **Level Control Relay**—is located on the left front fender well, in front of the level control compressor.

• **Light Switch/Sentinel Control**—is located under the left side of the instrument panel, near the parking brake.

• **Manifold Absolute Pressure Sensor**—is located on the top of the front wheel well.

• **Mixture Control Solenoid**—is located in the carburetor.

• **Multi-Function Chime Module**—is located is located on the left side of the fuse block.

• **Oil Pressure Switch**—is located on the lower right side of the engine on the (V6) and on the top front left side of the engine on the V8 engines.

• **Oxygen Sensor**—is located on the rear right exhaust manifold on the V6 engine and on the rear left exhaust manifold on the V8 engine.

• **Power Seat Relay**—is located under the left or right seat.

• **Seat Belt Warning Buzzer**—is attached to the left side of the fuse block.

• **Seat Belt Warning Module**—is taped to the harnes located above the fuse block.

• **Tailgate Ajar Switch**—is located inside the lower right corner of the tailgate assembly.

• **Temperature Indicator Switch**—is located on the front of the engine near the carburetor on the V6 engine and on the top left side of the engine on the V8 engines.

• **Throttle Position Sensor**—is located on the careburetor.

• **Tone Generator**—is located under the left side of the instrument panel, near the parking brake.

• **Trunk Release Solenoid**—is located on the rear center of the trunk lid.

• **Twilight Sentinel Amplifier**—is located under the left side of the instrument panel, near the parking brake.

• **Twilight Sentinel Photocell**—is located on the left side of the engine cowl.

• **Vacuum Regulator Switch (Diesel)**—is located on the top center of the engine on the fuel injection pump.

• **Vacuum Sensor**—is located on the right front wheel well.

• **Vehicle Speed Sensor (V6)**—is located behind the instrument panel above the left side of the steering column.

• **Wait Lamp Control Relay (Diesel)**—is located on the top center of the engine.

• **Wiper Motor Relay Diode**—is located in the wipwer motor connector.

1985-87 LESABRE

• **A/C Blower Relay**—is located in the engine compartment at the center of the firewall, near the blower motor.

• **A/C Compressor Clutch Diode**—is taped to the inside compressor connector on the front of the compressor.

• **A/C-Heater Blower Resistors**—is located in the engine

compartment on the right side of the firewall near the blower motor.

- **A/C Temperature Cut-Out Relay** – is located on the top right front engine cowl.
- **A/C Programmer (Tempmatic)** – is located behind the right side of the dash panel.
- **Ambient Temperature Sensor** – is located in the right air inlet, below screen.
- **Assembly Line Data Link Connector** – is located under the left side of the dash panel, to the right of the steering panel.
- **Audio Alarm Module** – is located on the left side of the fuse block.
- **Automatic Door Lock Controller** – is attached to the upper portion of the right kick panel.
- **Automatic Door Lock Diode** – is located behind the left kick panel, near the lower access hole.
- **Barometeric Pressure Sensor** – is located behind the glove box.
- **Blower and Clutch Control Module** – is located on the top of the blower housing.
- **"Check Engine" Light Driver** – is taped to the instrument panel harness, above the glove box.
- **Convenience Center** – is located behind the left side of the instrument panel, near the fuse box.
- **Coolant Temperature Sensor (3.8L)** – is located on the left front side of the engine.
- **Coolant Temperature Sensor (4.3L)** – is located on the front of the engine below the coolant outlet.
- **Coolant Temperature Sensor (5.0L & 5.7L)** – is located on the front side of the engine, on the coolant outlet.
- **Coolant Temperature Sensor (5.7L Diesel)** – is located on the left front side of the engine.
- **Cruise Control Module** – is located under the left side of the dash, to the left of the steering column.
- **Cruise Control Servo** – is located at the left front side of the engine on the gas models and above the left side valve cover on the diesel models.
- **Defogger Time Relay** – is located on the top of the fuse block.
- **Detonation (Knock) Sensor (6 cyl.)** – is located at the lower left rear side of the engine.
- **Detonation (Knock) Sensor (8 cyl.)** – is located at the right front side of the engine.
- **Diagnostic Dwell Meter Connector (Green)** – is taped the the wiring harness near the carburetor.
- **Diesel Electronic Control Module (DEC)** – is located behind the kick panel.
- **Early Fuel Evaporation Relay (3.8L)** – is located on the top right front engine cowl.
- **Electronic Control Moduel (ECM)** – is located behind the right kick panel.
- **Electronic Level Control Height Sensor** – is located on the rear center of the rear crossmember.
- **Electronic Level Control Relay** – is located on the left front fender, behind the horn.
- **Electronic Spark Control (ESC) Module** – is located on the right front side of the engine compartment.
- **Fast Idle Relay (4.3L)** – is located in the center of the firewall in the engine compartment.
- **Fuel Pump Relay (4.3L) Relay** – is located on the upper right inner fender panel.
- **Glow Plug Controller Relay (Diesel)** – is located on the top left rear of the engine.
- **Horn Relay** – is attached to the left side of the fuse block.
- **Illuminated Entry Timer** – is located behind the upper portion of the left kick panel, near the junction block.
- **In-Car Sensor** – is located in the right upper part of the dash, to the left of the right speaker.
- **Low Coolant Level Sensor** – is located in the radiator.
- **Manifold Absolute Pressure Sensor** – is located on the air cleaner.

- **Metering Valve Sensor (Diesel)** – is located on the diesel fuel injection pump.
- **Multi-Function Chime Module** – is located in the convenience center.
- **Oxygen Sensor** – is located on the exhaust manifold.
- **Power Antenna Relay** – is located on the bracket under the right side of the instrument panel, to the left of the glove box.
- **Power Door Lock Relay** – is located behind the bottom right kick panel.
- **Power Door Unlock Relay** – is located behind the upper portion of the right side kick panel.
- **Power Master Cylinder Brake In-Line Fuse** – is located under the left side of the dash panel, near the fuse block.
- **Power Master Cylinder Relay** – is located in the connector at the brake reservoir pump motor.
- **Power Seat Relay** – is located on under the right or left seat.
- **Seat Memory Module** – is located under the driver's seat.
- **Starter Interrupt Relay** – is located under the left side of the dash panel, above the steering column.
- **Theft Deterrent Controller** – is located under the left side of the dash, to the right of the steering column.
- **Theft Deterrent Diode** – is located under the left side of the dash panel, near the fuse block.
- **Theft Deterrent In-Line Fuses** – are located above the fuse block taped to the instrument panel wiring harness.
- **Theft Deterrent Relay** – is located at the right of the theft deterrent controller.
- **Throttle Position Sensor** – is located on the carburetor or throttle body.
- **Trailer Relays** – are located on the lower right corner of the fuse block.
- **Twilight Sentinel Amplifier** – is located on a bracket behind the right side of the dash panel.
- **Twilight Sentinel Control** – is located under the left side of the dash, to the right of the steering column.
- **Twilight Sentinel Photocell** – is located on the top left side of the dash panel.
- **Vacuum Sensor** – is located on the right front engine cowl.
- **Vehicle Speed sensor** – is located behind the instrument panel, is a part of the cluster.
- **Vehicle Speed Sensor Buffer** – is taper top the instrument panel wiring under the left side of the daash near the fuse block.
- **Water-In-Fuel Module (Diesel)** – is located on top of the fuel filter assembly.
- **Washer Pump Motor Diode** – is located in the washer motor connector.
- **Wide Open Throttle Relay** – is located in the engine compartment at the center of the firewall.
- **Window and Sunroof Circuit Breaker** – is located at the top right corner of the fuse block.
- **Wiper Motor Relay Diode** – is located in the wiper motor connector.

1985-87 ELECTRA AND PARK AVENUE

- **A/C Compressor Clutch Diode** – is located in the connector at the rear of the .
- **A/C Compressor Control Relay (Gas)** – is located on the right side of the firewall in the engine compartment.
- **A/C Compressor Control Relay (Diesel)** – is located behind the right side of the dash panel, to the right of the plenum.
- **A/C Constant Run Relay** – is located on the right side of the fire wall in the engine compartment.
- **A/C-Heater Blower Control Module** – is located on the right side of the firewall in the engine compartment.

- **A/C-Heater Relay** – is located on the right side of the firewall in the engine compartment.
- **A/C-Heater Resistors** – are located on the right side of the firewall in the engine compartment, in the top of the plenum.
- **Altitude Advance Relay (Diesel)** – is located on the right side of the firewall in the engine compartment.
- **Amplifier Relay** – is located under the right side of the dash panel, near the connector C201.
- **Assembly Line Diagnostic Link Connector** – is located under the left side of the dash panel, to the left of the steering column.
- **Automatic Door Lock Controller** – is located behind the right side of the dash, on connector C210.
- **Automatic Door Lock Diode** – is located behind the right side of the dash panel, near the connector C201.
- **Brake Warning System Diode** – is located in the instrument panel wiring harness under the right side of the dash panel, to the right of the plenum.
- **"Check Engine" Light Driver** – is taped to the instrument panel harness under the right side of the dash panel, to right of the plenum.
- **Cooling Fan Diode** – is taped to the harness in the connector behind the left shock tower.
- **Cooling Fan Relay** – is located on the right side of the firewall in the engine compartment.
- **Cooling Fan Resistor** – is located on the fan support frame behind the radiator.
- **Cruise Control Module** – is located above the accelerator pedal.
- **Decoder Module** – is located under the right side of the dash panel, at the top of connector C201.
- **Defogger Relay** – is located under the left side of the dash panel, to the left of the steering column.
- **Diagnostic Dwell Meter Connector** – is taped to the harness at the front of the engine, behind the valve cover.
- **Diesel Diode Module** – is located on the right side of the firewall in the engine compartment.
- **Diesel Electronic Control Module (DEC)** – is located behind the right side of the dash panel.
- **Early Fuel Evaporation (EFE) Relay (3.0L Carb.)** – is located on the right side of the firewall in the engine compartment.
- **Electrical Energy Reserve Module** – is located in front of the left front shock tower.
- **Electronic Climate Control Programmer (EEC)** – is located under the right side of the dash panel, on the right side of the plenum.
- **Electronic Control Module (ECM)** – is located behind the right side of the dash panel.
- **Electronic Level Control Diode** – is located in the instrument panel wiring harness, behind the radio.
- **Electronic Level Control Relay** – is located to the left of the level control compressor.
- **Electronic Level Control Test Connector** – is located near the top of the electronic level control compressor.
- **Electronic Spark Control Module (ECS)** – is located on the right side of the firewall in the engine compartment.
- **Electronic Tune Radio Diode** – is located in the instrument panel wiring harness, behind the radio.
- **Fan Control Relay** – is located in the wiring harness near the electronic level control compressor.
- **Fiber Optic Light Source** – are located one in each door.
- **Fuel Control Diode (Diesel)** – is located in the wiring harness at the right rear corner of the engine compartment.
- **Fuel Pump Relay (3.0L)** – is located on the right side of the firewall in the engine compartment.
- **Generator Diode** – Taped to the wiring harness at the left front wheel well.

- **Glow Plug Controller/Relay (Diesel)** – is located on the top left side of the engine, to the left of the valve cover.
- **Headlight Washer Relay** – is located on the fluid reservoir on the front of the right front shock tower.
- **High Mount Stop Light Relays** – are located on the left rear wheelwell inside the trunk.
- **High Speed Cooling Fan Relay** – is located on the firewall, behind the left shock tower.
- **Horn Relay** – is located under the left side of the dash panel, to the left of the steering column.
- **Illuminated Entry Timer** – is located behind the right side of the dash near connector C201.
- **Key Pad Module** – is located in the driver's door, near the door lock motor.
- **Keyless Entry Diode** – is located behind the right side of the dash panel, near connector C201.
- **Keyless Entry Module** – is located in the trunk, above the rear wheelwell.
- **Low Brake Vacuum Relay** – is located behind the right side of the dash near connector C201.
- **Memory Disable Relay** – is located behind the right side of the dash near connector C201.
- **Multi-Function Chime Module** – is located behind the right side of the dash trim, above the glove box.
- **Oil Light Relay (3.0L Fuel Injected)** – is located on the right side of the firewall in the engien compartment.
- **Power Antenna Relay** – is located behind the right side of the dash panel, near the connector C201.
- **Power Door Lock Relay** – is located behind the right side of the dash panel, on the top right side of connector C210.
- **Power Door Unlock Relay** – is located behind the right side of the dash panel, to the right of connector C210.
- **Power Seat Diode** – is located in the connector at the front of each seat.
- **Power Seat Memory Module** – is under the left side of the driver's seat.
- **Power Seat Recliner Capacitor** – is located in the connector at the front of each seat.
- **Power Seat Relay** – is located on the lower seat rail under the seat.
- **Power Window Circuit Breaker** – is located in the fuse block.
- **Select Switch Relay** – is located behind the right side of the dash panel, on the bottom of connector C201.
- **Starter Interupt Relay** – is located on a bracket under the left side of the dash panel, to the left of the steering column.
- **Sun Roof Module** – is located in the windshield header above the right seat.
- **TCC Pulse Relay (Diesel)** – is located on the right side of the fire wall in the engine compartment.
- **Theft Deterrent Controller** – is located under the left side of the dash panel, to the left of the steering column.
- **Theft Deterrent Diode** – Taped to the instrument panel wiring harness under the right side of the dash panel, above connector C201.
- **Theft Deterrent Relay** – is located behind a bracket under the left side of the instrument panel.
- **Torque Converter Clutch Controller** – is located on the right side of the firewall in the engine compartment.
- **Trunk Pull-Down In-Line Fuse** – near the latch at the center of the trunk lid.
- **Twilight Sentinel Amplifier** – is located under the left side of the dash panel, to the right of the steering column.
- **Twilight Sentinel Photocell** – is located on the top left side of the dash panel, below the right side speaker grille.
- **Vehicle Speed Sensor Buffer** – is located under the right side of the dash panel, on the right side of the plenum.
- **Water-In-Fuel Module (Diesel)** – is located on top of the fuel filter assembly.

1982-84 SKYLARK

- **A/C Clutch Diode** – is located inside the A/C compressor connector.
- **A/C Compressor Relay** – is located in the upper right corner of the engine cowl.
- **A/C Diode** – is located in the A/C harness, near the vacuum tank.
- **A/C-Heater Blower Resistors** – are located on the front of the plenum.
- **A/C High Speed Blower Relay** – is located on the top of the plenum, near the vacuum tank.
- **Audio/Buzzer Alarm Module** – is located on the conveience center.
- **Charging System Relay** – is taped to the instrument panel harness, above the accelerator pedal.
- **"Check Engine" Light driver** – is taped to the right side of the instrument panel harness.
- **Choke Heater Relay** – is located behind the instrument panel.
- **Convenience Center** – is located behind the right side of the instrument panel, to the left of the glove box.
- **Coolant Fan Relay** – is located on the left front wheel well.
- **Coolant Temperature Sensor** – is located on the left side of the coolant inlet on the 4 cylinder engines and on the top left front side of the engine on the V6 engines.
- **Defogger Timer/Relay** – is located above the glove box.
- **Door Lock Relay** – is located on the upper center of the right shroud.
- **Early Fuel Evaporation Heater Relay** – is located on the upper right side of the engine cowl.
- **Electronic Control Module (ECM)** – is located behind the instrument panel.
- **Fuel Pump Relay** – is located on the upper right side of the engine cowl.
- **Horn Relay** – is located in the convenience center.
- **Lights-On Buzzer** – is located behind the right side of the instrument panel, near the glove box.
- **Manifold Absolute Pressure Sensor** – is located on the right side of the air filter.
- **Oil Pressure Sender** – is located at the rear of the engine above the distributor on the 4 cylinder engines and above the oil filter on the V6 engines.
- **Oxygen Sensor** – is located in the exhaust manifold.
- **Power Accesories Circuit Breaker** – is located in the buse block.
- **Power Antenna Relay** – is located behind the right side of the instrument panel, near the glove box.
- **Power Window Circuit Breaker** – is located in the fuse block.
- **Throttle Position Sensor** – is located on the throttle body.
- **Vacuum Sensor** – is located in the upper right side of the engine cowl.
- **Vehicle Speed Sensor** – is located as part of the speedometer assembly.
- **Wiper Pulse Module** – is located behind the left side of the instrument panel.

1985-87 SKYLARK

- **A/C Clutch Diode** – is located inside the A/C compressor connector.
- **A/C Compressor Relay** – is located in the upper right corner of the firewall on the 2.5L engine and in the right side of the radiator support on the 2.8L engine.
- **A/C Diode** – is located in the A/C harness, near the vacuum tank.
- **A/C-Heater Blower Resistors** – are located on the front of the plenum.
- **A/C High Speed Blower Relay** – is located on the top of the plenum, near the vacuum tank.
- **Audio/Buzzer Alarm Module** – is located on the conveience center.
- **Barometric Pressure Sensor** – is located in the right rea corner of the engine compartment.
- **Charging System Relay** – is taped to the instrument panel harness, above the accelerator pedal.
- **"Check Engine" Light driver** – is taped to the right side of the instrument panel harness.
- **Choke Heater Relay** – is taped to the instrument panel harness, near the fuse block.
- **Convenience Center (1985)** – is located behind the right side of the instrument panel, to the left of the glove box.
- **Cooling Fan In-Line Fuse** – is located on the left front shock tower.
- **Coolant Fan Relay** – is located on the left front wheel well.
- **Coolant Temperature Sensor** – is located on the left side of the coolant inlet on the 2.5L engine and on the top left front side of the engine on the 2.8L engine.
- **Cruise Control Module** – is located under the left side of the instrument panel, above the accelerator pedal.
- **Defogger Timer/Relay** – is located above the glove box.
- **Diagnostic Dwell Meter Connector** – is located in the harness, in the right rear corner of the engine compartment.
- **Door Lock Relay** – is located on the upper center of the right shroud.
- **Early Fuel Evaporation Heater Relay** – is located on the upper right side of the engine cowl.
- **Electronic Control Module (ECM)** – is located behind the instrument panel.
- **Fuel Pump In-Line Fuse** – is located on the left front shock tower.
- **Fuel Pump Prime Connector** – is located on the rear of the engine, near the starter.
- **Fuel Pump Relay** – is located on the upper right side of the firewall on the 2.5L engine and on the left front shock tower on the 2.8L engine.
- **Horn Relay** – is located in the convenience center.
- **Lights-On Buzzer** – is located behind the right side of the instrument panel, near the glove box.
- **Manifold Absolute Pressure Sensor** – is located on the right side of the air filter.
- **Manifold Air Temperature Sensor** – is located on the air cleaner assembly.
- **Mass Airflow In-Line Fuse** – is located on the left front shock tower.
- **Mass Airflow Relay** – is located on the left front shock tower.
- **Mass Airflow Sensor** – is located in the front of the engine.
- **Oil Pressure Sender** – is located at the rear of the engine above the distributor on the 2.5L engine and above the oil filter on the 2.8L engine.
- **Oxygen Sensor** – is located in the exhaust manifold.
- **Power Accesories Circuit Breaker** – is located in the buse block.
- **Power Antenna Relay** – is located behind the right side of the instrument panel, near the glove box.
- **Power Window Circuit Breaker** – is located in the fuse block.
- **Throttle Kicker Relay** – is located in the right front cornewr of the engine compartment.
- **Throttle Position Sensor** – is located on the throttle body.
- **Vacuum Sensor** – is located in the upper right side of the firewall.

- **Vehicle Speed Sensor** – is located as part of the speedometer assembly.
- **Wiper Pulse Module** – is located behind the left side of the instrument panel.

1982-84 SKYHAWK

- **A/C Ambient Air Sensor** – is located on the engine cowl, above the power steering reservoir.
- **A/C Blower Relay** – is located on the front center of the plenum.
- **A/C Compressor Control Relay** – is located behind the right front shock tower.
- **A/C Compressor Run Relay** – is located behind the right front shock tower.
- **A/C-Heater Blower Resistors** – are located on the front left side of the plenum.
- **Blocking Diode** – is located in the instrument panel harness, near the fuse block.
- **Convenience Center** – is located below the instrument panel, near the left shroud.
- **Coolant Fan Relay** – on the left front fender in front of the shock tower.
- **Coolant Temperature Sender** – is located on the left side of the engine, near the coolant outlet.
- **Coolant Temperature Sensor** – is located on the front of the engine on the thermostat housing on the 1.8L engine and on the left side of the engine under the water outlet on the other engines.
- **Cruise Control Throttle Servo** – is located on the bracket on the left front shock tower.
- **Defogger Time Relay** – is located behind the left side of the dash panel.
- **Door Lock Relay** – is located on the upper right side of the steering column support.
- **Electronic Control Module (ECM)** – is located behind the glove box.
- **Electronic Fuel Injection Ambient Sensor** – is located on the engine cowl above the washer reservoir.
- **Fuel Pump Relay** – is located on the right engine cowl, behind the shock tower.
- **Hatch/Tailgate/Trunk Release Relay** – is taped to the wire harness, located behind the right side of the radio.
- **Horn Relay** – is located on the conveience center.
- **Idle Speed Motor** – is taped in the EFI harness. to the right of the electronic control module.
- **Manifold Absolute Presure Sensor** – is located on the right shock tower.
- **Oxygen Sensor** – is located in the exhaust manifold.
- **Power Accessories Circuit Breaker** – is located in the fuse block.
- **Power Antenna Relay** – is located behind the instrument panel, below the right side of the radio.
- **Power Window Circuit Breaker** – is located in the fuse block.
- **Throttle Position Sensor** – is located on the throttle body.
- **Torque Converter Clutch Relay (TCC)** – is located on the transmission cowling.
- **Vehicle Speed Sensor** – is located behind the instrument panel, the the right of the steering column.
- **Wiper Pulse Module** – is located below the steering column, above the trim cover.

1985-87 SKYHAWK

- **A/C Blower Relay** – is located on the front center of the plenum.

- **A/C Compressor Control Relay** – is located behind the right front shock tower.
- **A/C Compressor Run Relay** – is located behind the right front shock tower.
- **A/C-Heater Blower Resistors** – are located on the front left side of the plenum.
- **A/C In-Car Temperature Sensor** – is located on the right side of the dash, above the glove box.
- **Assembly Line Diagnostic Link** – is located behind the instrument panel, on the right side of the fuse block.
- **Blocking Diode** – is located in the instrument panel harness, near the bulkhead connector.
- **Convenience Center (1985)** – is located behind the instrument panel, to the left of the steering column.
- **Convenience Center (1986-87)** – is located behind the left side of the instrument panel, at the kick panel.
- **Coolant Fan Relay** – on the left front fender in front of the shock tower or on the firewall to the left of the brake booster.
- **Coolant Temperature Sender** – is located on the left side of the engine, near the coolant outlet.
- **Coolant Temperature Sensor** – is located on the front of the engine on the thermostat housing on the 1.8L engine and on the left side of the engine under the water outlet on the other engines.
- **Cruise Control Module (2-door)** – is located behind the instrument panel, above the left side of the steering column.
- **Cruise Control Module (4-door)** – is located behind the right side of the dash panel, above the glove box.
- **Defogger Time Relay** – is located behind the left side of the dash panel.
- **Electronic Control Module (ECM)** – is located behind the glove box.
- **Electronic Fuel Injection Ambient Sensor** – is located on the engine cowl above the washer reservoir.
- **Electronic Speed Sensor** – is located on the top right side of the transaxle.
- **Fog Lamp Relays** – are taped to the instrument panel harness, near the fog lamp switch.
- **Fuel Pump In-Line Fuse** – is located on the firewall, behind the brake booster.
- **Fuel Pump Relay** – is located on the right engine cowl, behind the shock tower or on the firewall, above the brake booster.
- **Hatch/Tailgate/Trunk Release Relay** – is taped to the wire harness, located behind the right side of the radio.
- **Horn Relay** – is located on the conveience center.
- **Knock Sensor** – is located on the right side of the starter below the starter.
- **Low Coolant Module** – is located behind the instrument panel, above the left side of the steering column.
- **Low Coolant Temperature Sensor** – is located in the engine compartment, on the right front side of the radiator.
- **Manifold Absolute Presure Sensor** – is located on the right shock tower.
- **Manifold Air Temperature Sensor** – is located on the engine, underneath or on top of the intake manifold.
- **Mass Airflow Relay** – is located on the firewall, behind the brake booster.
- **Mass Airflow Sensor** – is located on the top of the left side of the engine, behind the air cleaner.
- **Mass Airflow Sensor In-Line Fuse** – is located on the firewall, behind the brake booster.
- **Outside Air Temperature Sensor** – is located in the engine compartment, behind the right side of the grill.
- **Oxygen Sensor** – is located in the exhaust manifold.
- **Power Accessories/Convertible Top Circuit Breaker** – is located in the fuse block.
- **Power Antenna Relay** – is located behind the instrument panel, below the right side of the radio.
- **Power Door Lock Relay** – is located on the upper right

side of the steering column support.
- **Power Unit Dimmer** — is located behind the instrument panel, to the left of the steering column.
- **Power Window Circuit Breaker** — is located in the fuse block.
- **Release Relay** — is taped to the instrument panel harness, behind the radio or glove box.
- **Throttle Position Sensor** — is located on the throttle body. On the 2.8L engine it is located, behind the distributor.
- **Torque Converter Clutch Relay (TCC)** — is located on the transmission cowling.
- **Turbo Release Relay** — is located on the transaxle cowling.
- **Twilight Sentinel Amplifier** — is located behind the instrument panel, to the left of the steering column.
- **Twilight Sentinel Photocell** — is located on the dash panel, on the right side of the defrost vent.
- **Vehicle Speed Sensor** — is located behind the instrument panel, the the right of the steering column.
- **Vehicle Speed Sensor Buffer** — is located behind the instrument cluster, below the speed sensor.

1985-87 SOMERSET REGAL

- **A/C Compressor Clutch Diode** — is located in the connector at the compressor clutch.
- **A/C Compressor Control Relay (2.5L)** — is located on the relay bracket at the center of the firewall in the engine compartment.
- **A/C Cooling Fan Relay (3.0L)** — is located on the relay bracket at the center of the firewall in the engine compartment.
- **A/C Cut-Out Relay (3.0L)** — is located on the relay bracket at the center of the firewall in the engine compartment.
- **A/C-Heater Blower Motor Relay** — is located on the right side of the firewall in the engine compartment, to the left of the blower motor.
- **Audio Alarm Module** — is located on the fuse block or above the glove box.
- **Computer Control Ignition Module (3.0L)** — is located at the top right rear of the engine.
- **Coolant Temperature Sensor** — is located at the top right end of the engine (top left on the 2.5L engine).
- **Cooling Fan Relay** — is located is located on the relay bracket at the center of the firewall in the engine compartment.
- **Cooling Fan Resistor (3.0L)** — is located on the lower bracket behind the cooling fan.
- **Cruise Control Module** — is attached under the rear of the left side of the dash panel.
- **Defogger Timer Relay** — is located behind the left side f the dash panel, near the fuse block.
- **Driver Information Center Display Module** — is located in the center of the dash, below the radio.
- **Driver Information Center Lights Monitor Module** — is located below the center of the dash panel, in front of the console.
- **Dual Crank Sensor (3.0L)** — is located on the lower right front side of the engine.
- **Electronic Control Module (ECM)** — is located behind the right side kick panel.
- **Electronic Spark Control Module (3.0L)** — is located is located on the relay bracket at the center of the firewall in the engine compartment.
- **Fog Light Relay** — is located on the left front inner fender panel, in front of the shock tower.
- **Fuel Pump Relay** — is located on the relay bracket at the center of the firewall in the engine compartment.
- **Generator Diode (2.5L)** — is located in the instrument panel wiring harness, under the left side of the dash panel.

- **High Mount Stop Lamp Relays** — are located on the left rear wheelwell inside the trunk.
- **Horn Relay** — is located in the instrument panel wiring harness near the fuse block.
- **Illumination Control Relay** — is located behind the center of the instrument panel, in front of the console.
- **Knock (Detonation) Sensor (3.0L)** — is located at the top left side of the engine.
- **Manifold Absolute Pressure Sensor (2.5L)** — is located on the air cleaner assembly.
- **Manifold Absolute Pressure Sensor (3.0L)** — is located on the left side of the engine compartment, behind the radiator.
- **Manifold Airflow Sensor (3.0L)** — is located on the left side of the engine compartment, behind the radiator.
- **Oxygen Sensor** — is located in the exhaust manifold.
- **Power Accessories Circuit Breaker** — is located in the fuse block.
- **Power Antenna Relay** — is located at the right side of the trunk.
- **Power Door Lock Relay Assembly** — is located behind the right side kick panel.
- **Power Window Circuit Breaker** — is located in the fuse block.
- **Remote Dimmer Module** — is located in the instrument panel wiring harness, to the right of the radio.
- **Throttle Postion Sensor** — is located on the throttle body.
- **Vehicle Speed Sensor (ATX)** — is located at the rear of the engine, on the right end of the transaxle.
- **Vehicle Speed Sensor (MTX)** — is located at the rear of the engine, on the top of the transaxle.
- **Vehicle Speed Sensor Buffer Amplifier** — is located behind the right side of the dash panel.
- **Wiper/Washer Motor Module** — is located in the left rear corner of the engine compartment, to the right of the shock tower.

1982-84 RIVIERA

- **A/C Ambient Sensor** — is located on right engine cowl, above blower motor.
- **A/C Blower Relay** — is located on right engine cowl, near blower motor.
- **A/C Clutch Control Module** — is located on right engine cowl, left of blower motor.
- **A/C Cut-Out Relay** — is locatd on top center portion of engine cowl.
- **A/C Cut-Out Relay (Turbo)** — is located on top right front wheel well.
- **A/C-Heater Blower Resistors** — is located on top left side of blower assembly.
- **Amplifier Relay** — is located behind instrument panel, near steering column.
- **Barometric Pressure Sensor (V6)** — is located behind right side of instrument panel.
- **"Check Engine" Light Driver** — is taped to instrument panel harness, above truck switch (V6) or right side of radio (V8).
- **Convenience Center (1982)** — is located behind the left side of the instrument panel.
- **Convenience Center (1983-84)** — is located behind the instrument panel, to the left of the steering column.
- **Convertible Top Circuit Breaker** — is located behind instrument panel, left of steering column.
- **Convertible Top Relays** — are located in the trunk, behind rear seat.
- **Coolant Temperature Sensor** — Is located near coolant outlet.
- **Coolant Temperature Sensor** — Is located on front of en-

gine, above water pump (V6), top of engine behind alternator (V6 Turbo) or top of engine near front of left valve cover (V8).
- **Detonation Sensor (V6)** – is located on top of rear of engine
- **Diode Module (Diesel)** – is located on top center of engine cowl.
- **Door Lock Control Unit** – is located behind dash, above glove box.
- **Door Lock Relay** – Behind glove box.
- **Door Locks Diode** – is located on left shroud, near center access hole.
- **Door Unlock Relay** – is taped to automatic door lock control unit.
- **Dwell Meter Conector (V8)** – is located on front of engine.
- **EFE Heater Relay (V6 Turbo)** – is located on top of left wheel well
- **Electronic Vacuum Regulator Valve** – is located on rear of engine, below left valve cover (Turbo), on top center of right valve cover (V6).
- **Electronic Control Module (ECM)** – is located behind right kick panel.
- **Electronic Spark Control Unit** – is located on top of right front wheel well.
- **Fuel Pump Relay** – is located on top of right front wheel well.
- **Glow Plug Relay** – is located on top of right front wheel well.
- **Glow Plug Thermal Control Unit** – is located on top front of engine.
- **Hazard Flasher Relay** – is located on upper left corner of fuse block.
- **Horn Relay** – is located on convenience center
- **Idle Speed Control Unit** – is located behind instrument panel, near steering column
- **Idle Speed-up Relay** – is located behind instrument panel, above base of steering column.
- **Illuminated Entry Timer** – is locatedon upper left shroud, near junction block.
- **Level Control Height Sensor** – is attached to left side of rear crossmember
- **Level Control Relay** – is located on convenience center
- **Low Brake Vacuum Delay Unit** – Behind instrument panel, near steering column.
- **Manifold Absolute Pressure Sensor** – is located on top of right front wheel well.
- **Memory Seat Disable Relay** – is located under driver's seat.
- **Multi-Function Chime Module** – is located on convenience center.
- **Oxygen Sensor** – is located on rear of right (V6) or left (V8) exhaust manifold.
- **Power Acc. Circuit Breaker** – is located in fuse block.
- **Power Antenna Relay** – is located on convenience center, to left of steering column.
- **Power Seat Relay** – is located under the driver's seat.
- **Power Window Circuit Breaker** – is located in fuse block.
- **Power Window Relay (Front)** – is located on right or left shroud, near access hole.
- **Power Window Relay (Rear)** – is located below right or left rear window, behind trim panel.
- **Seat Memory Module** – is located under driver's seat.
- **Starter Interrupt Relay** – is taped to dash harness, near fuse block.
- **Stop/Turn Lift Relays** – are located in trunk, ahead of left tail lights.
- **Theft Deterrent Control Unit** – is located on accelerator pedal lever plate.
- **Theft Deterrent Diode** – is located behind instrument panel, above steering column.

- **Theft Deterrent Relay** – is attached to bottom of theft deterrent control unit.
- **Throttle Position Sensor** – is located on throttle body.
- **Time Relay Module** – is located behind instrument panel, left of steering column.
- **Twilight Sentinel Amplifier** – is located behind instrument panel, to right of glove box.
- **Twilight Sentinel Photocell** – is located on top of instrument panel, above right side of glove box.
- **Vacuum Sensor (V8)** – is located on top of right front wheel well
- **Vehicle Speed Sensor** – is located behind instrument panel, to right of steering column.
- **Wait Lamp Control Relay (Diesel)** – is located on top center of engine cowl.
- **Wiper Motor Relay Diode** – is located in wiper motor connector.

1985-87 RIVIERA

- **A/C Air Inlet Valve Actuator** – is located behind the instrument panel, on the bottom right side of the A/C Module.
- **A/C Ambient Sensor** – is located on right engine cowl, above blower motor.
- **A/C Blower Relay** – is located on right engine cowl, near blower motor.
- **A/C Clutch Control Module** – is located on right engine cowl, left of blower motor.
- **A/C Defrost Valve Actuator** – is located behind the instrument panel, on the top left side.
- **A/C-Heater Blower Control Module** – is located on right side of the firewall in the engine compartment.
- **A/C-Heater Blower Resistors** – is located on top left side of blower assembly.
- **A/C Mode Valve Actuator** – is located behind the instrument panel, on the bottom left side of the A/C Module.
- **A/C Temperature Cut-Out Relay** – is located in the engine compartment on the left side of the A/C Module.
- **A/C Temperature Cut-Out Relay (Turbo)** – is located on top right front wheel well.
- **A/C Temperature Door Actuator** – is located behind the instrument panel, on the bottom left side of the A/C Module.
- **A/C Water Diverter Valve Actuator** – is located in the engine, above the left side of the A/C module.
- **A/C Water Diverter Valve Actuator (Diesel)** – is located on the firewall, at the rear of the engine.
- **Amplifier Relay** – is located behind instrument panel, near steering column.
- **Assembly Line Diagnostic Link Connector** – is located under the instrument panel, below the steering column.
- **Barometric Pressure Sensor (V6)** – is located behind right side of instrument panel.
- **Camshaft Sensor** – is located on top of the engine.
- **"Check Engine" Light Driver** – is taped to instrument panel harness, above truck switch (V6) or right side of radio (V8).
- **Convenience Center (1985)** – is located behind the instrument panel, to the left of the steering column.
- **Convertible Top Relays** – are located in the trunk, behind rear seat.
- **Coolant Temperature Sender** – is located near coolant outlet.
- **Coolant Temperature Sensor** – is located on front of engine, above water pump (V6), top of engine behind alternator (V6 Turbo) or top of engine near front of left valve cover (V8).
- **Cruise Control Module** – is located behind the left side of the instrument panel, above the steering column.
- **Diode Module (Diesel)** – is located on top center of engine cowl.

- **Diesel Electronic Controller (DEC)** – is located behind the instrument panel near the right shroud.
- **Door Lock Control Unit** – is located behind dash, above glove box.
- **Door Lock Relay** – is located behind glove box.
- **Door Locks Diode** – is located on left shroud, near center access hole.
- **Door Unlock Relay** – is taped to automatic door lock control unit.
- **Dwell Meter Conector** – is located on front of engine.
- **EFE Heater Relay** – is located on top of left wheel well.
- **Electronic Control Module (ECM)** – is located behind right kick panel.
- **Electronic Spark Control Unit(V6)** – is located on top of the right front wheel well.
- **Electronic Spark Control Unit(V8)** – is located on top of the left front wheel well.
- **Fuel Pump Relay** – is located on top of right front wheel well.
- **Glow Plug Relay (Diesel)** – is located on top of right front wheel well.
- **Glow Plug Thermal Control Unit** – is located on top front of engine.
- **Horn Relay** – is located on convenience center
- **Idle Speed Control Unit (V6)** – is located on the left side of the carburetor.
- **Illuminated Entry Timer** – is located on upper left shroud, near junction block.
- **In-Car Sensor** – is located on the front center of the instrument panel, above the radio.
- **Knock (Detonation) Sensor (V6)** – is located on top of rear of engine
- **Level Control Height Sensor** – is attached to left side of rear crossmember
- **Level Control Relay** – is located on convenience center
- **Low Brake Vacuum Delay Unit** – is located behind instrument panel, near steering column.
- **Manifold Absolute Pressure Sensor** – is located on top of right front wheel well.
- **Manifold Vacuum Sensor (V8)** – is located on top of right front wheel well
- **Mass Airflow Sensor** – is located in the air induction duct work, near the left valve cover.
- **Memory Seat Disable Relay** – is located behind the right side of the instrument panel.
- **Multi-Function Chime Module** – is located on convenience center.

- **Oxygen Sensor** – is located on rear of right (V6) or left (V8) exhaust manifold.
- **Power Accessories Circuit Breaker** – is located in fuse block.
- **Power Antenna Relay** – is located on convenience center, to left of steering column.
- **Power Seat Relay** – is located under the driver's seat.
- **Power Window Circuit Breaker** – is located in fuse block.
- **Power Window Relay (Front)** – is located on right or left shroud, near access hole.
- **Power Window Relay (Rear)** – is located below right or left rear window, behind trim panel.
- **Seat Memory Module** – is located under driver's seat.
- **Starter Interrupt Relay** – is taped to dash harness, near fuse block.
- **Stop/Turn Lift Relays** – are located in trunk, ahead of left tail lights.
- **Tachometer Test Connector** – is taped to the harness, near the front of the left valve cover.
- **Theft Deterrent Control Unit** – is located on accelerator pedal lever plate.
- **Theft Deterrent Diode** – is located behind instrument panel harness, above fuse block.
- **Theft Deterrent Relay** – is attached to bottom of theft deterrent control unit.
- **Throttle Position Sensor** – is located on throttle body.
- **Time Relay Module** – is located behind instrument panel, left of steering column.
- **Torque Converter Clutch Connector** – is located on the left side of the transmission, below the exhaust manifold.
- **Turbo Boost Gauge Sensor** – is located on the top of the right front wheel well.
- **Twilight Sentinel Amplifier** – is located behind instrument panel, to right of the radio.
- **Twilight Sentinel Photocell** – is located on top of instrument panel, in the left speaker grille.
- **Underhood Relay Center (1986-87)** – is located on the inner left front fender panel, behind the headlights.
- **Vehicle Speed Sensor** – is located behind instrument panel, to right of steering column.
- **Wait Lamp Control Relay (Diesel)** – is located on top center of engine cowl.
- **Wiper Motor Relay Diode** – is located in wiper motor connector.

COMPONENT LOCATIONS

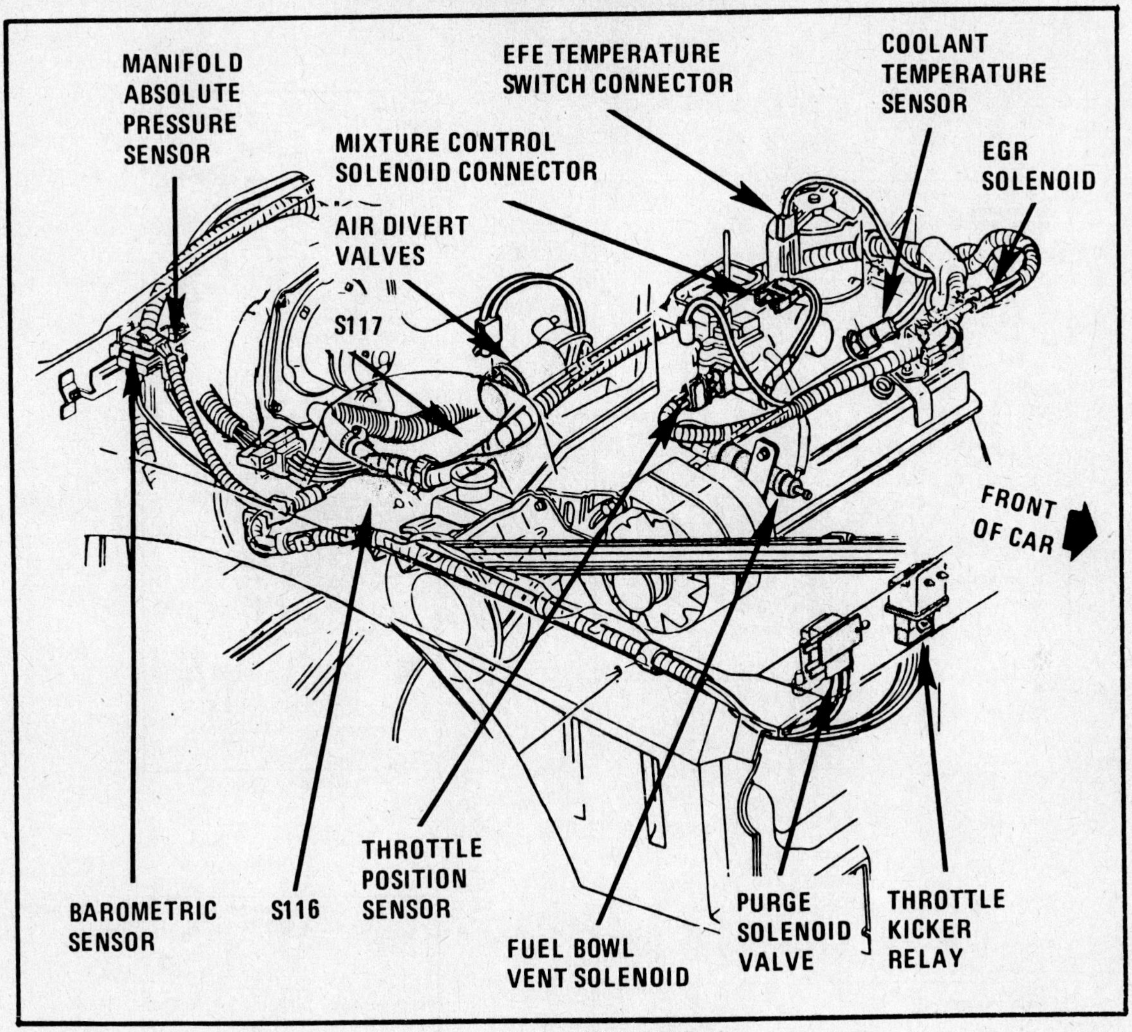

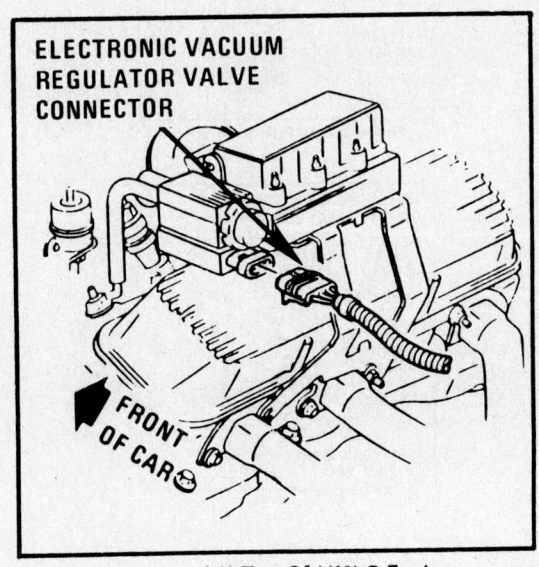

MANIFOLD ABSOLUTE PRESSURE SENSOR

EFE TEMPERATURE SWITCH CONNECTOR

COOLANT TEMPERATURE SENSOR

MIXTURE CONTROL SOLENOID CONNECTOR

EGR SOLENOID

AIR DIVERT VALVES

S117

FRONT OF CAR

BAROMETRIC SENSOR

S116

THROTTLE POSITION SENSOR

FUEL BOWL VENT SOLENOID

PURGE SOLENOID VALVE

THROTTLE KICKER RELAY

Top Of VIN X Engine

ELECTRONIC VACUUM REGULATOR VALVE CONNECTOR

FRONT OF CAR

LH Top Of VIN B Engine

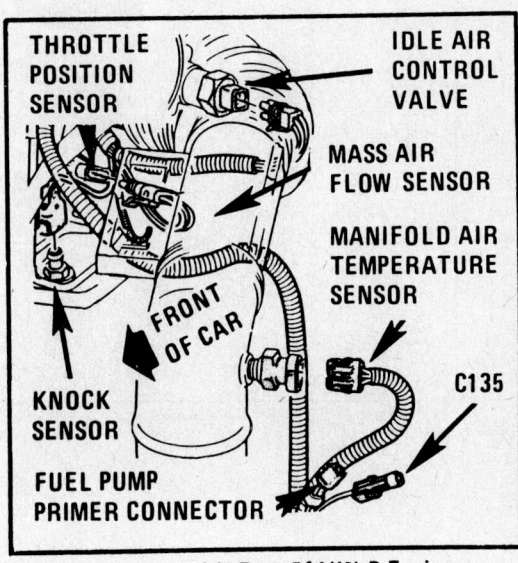

THROTTLE POSITION SENSOR

IDLE AIR CONTROL VALVE

MASS AIR FLOW SENSOR

MANIFOLD AIR TEMPERATURE SENSOR

FRONT OF CAR

C135

KNOCK SENSOR

FUEL PUMP PRIMER CONNECTOR

LH Rear Of VIN B Engine

1985-86 Buick Century

COMPONENT LOCATIONS

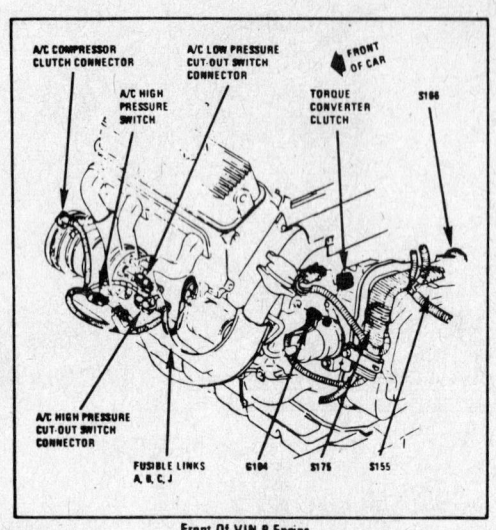

Front Of VIN B Engine

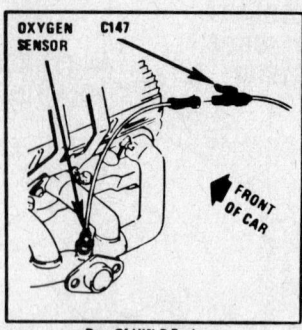

Rear Of VIN B Engine

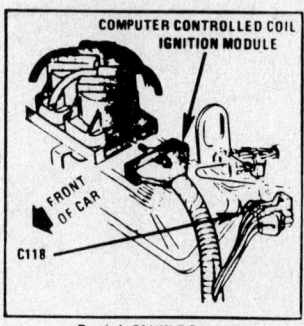

Top Left Of VIN B Engine

1985-86 Buick Century

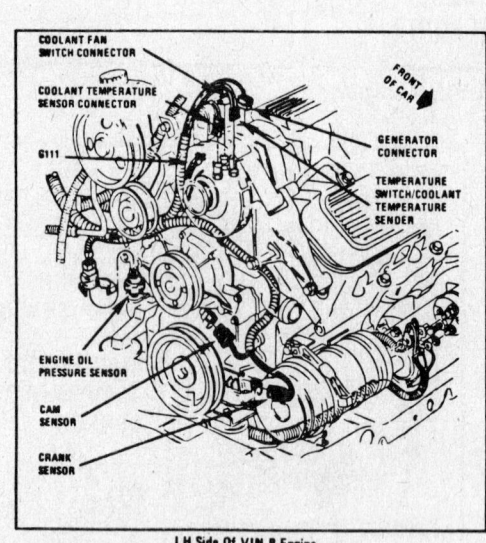

LH Side Of VIN B Engine

RH Side Of VIN B Engine Compartment

RH Front Of Dash

1985-86 Buick Century

COMPONENT LOCATIONS

LH Top Of VIN X Engine

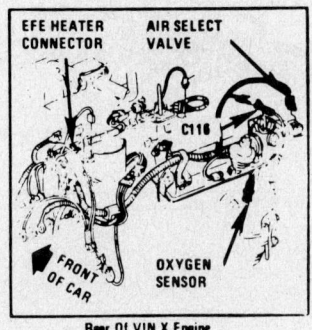

Rear Of VIN X Engine

Front Of VIN X Engine

1985-86 Buick Century

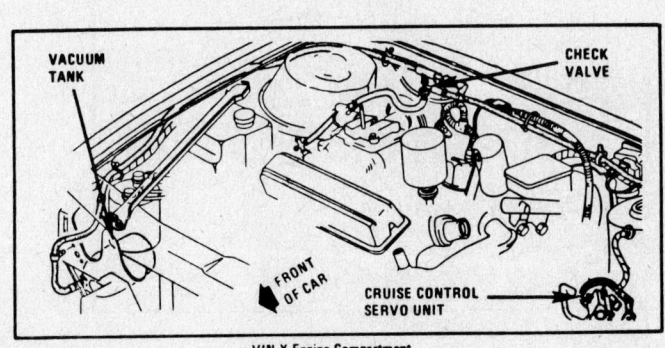

VIN X Engine Compartment

Rear Of VIN R Engine

1985-86 Buick Century

COMPONENT LOCATIONS

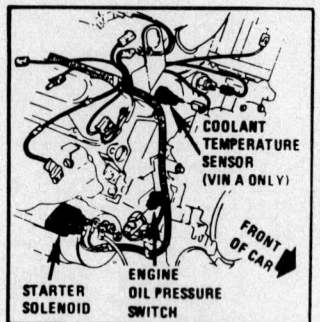

Front RH Side of VIN A Engine

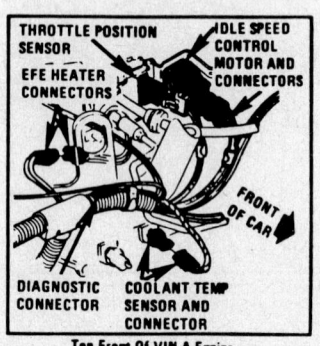

Top Front Of VIN A Engine

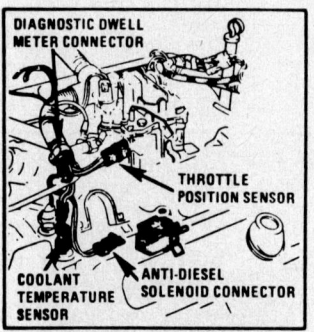

Top RH Of Engine Compartment (VIN Y)

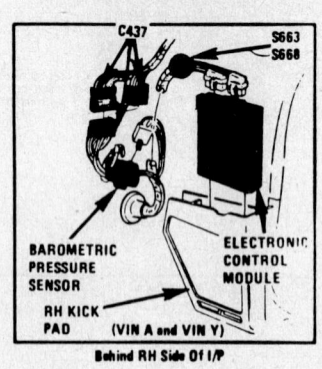

Behind RH Side Of I/P

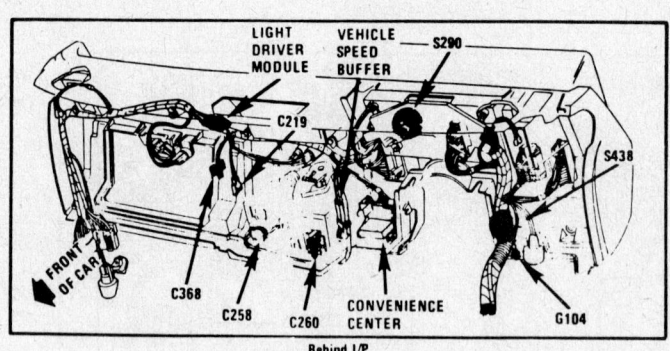

Rear Of VIN A Engine

1985-86 Buick Regal

Behind I/P

1985-86 Buick Regal

COMPONENT LOCATIONS

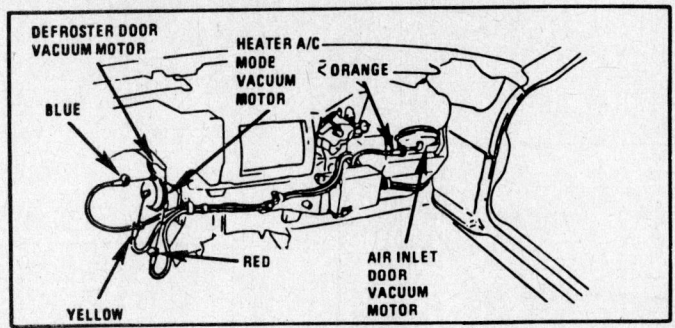

Behind I/P, (Electronic A/C)

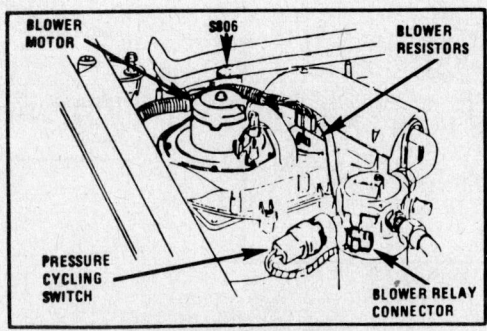

RH Front Of Dash VIN 7 Manual A/C

1985-86 Buick Regal

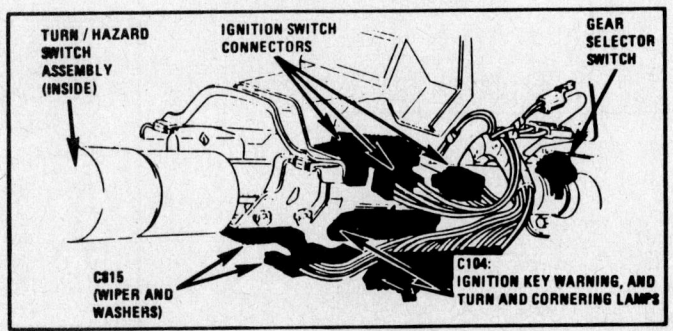

RH Side Of Steering Column

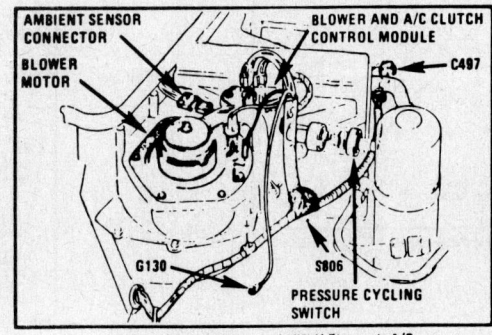

RH Front Of Dash VIN A And VIN Y Electronic A/C

1985-86 Buick Regal

COMPONENT LOCATIONS

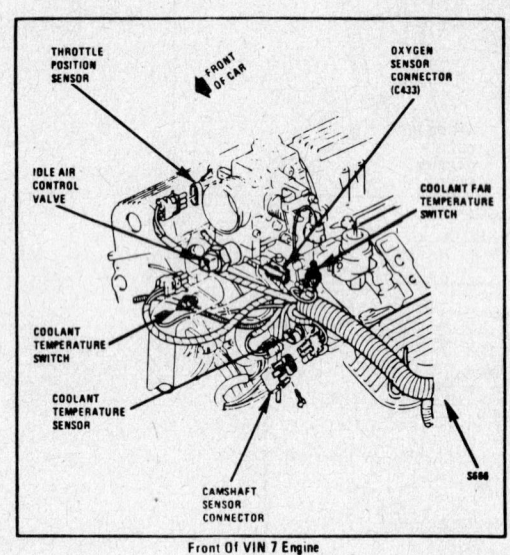

Front Of VIN 7 Engine

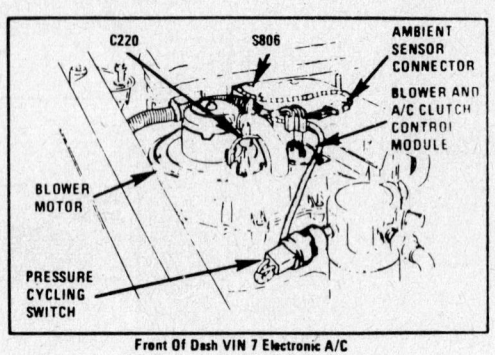

Front Of Dash VIN 7 Electronic A/C

1985-86 Buick Regal

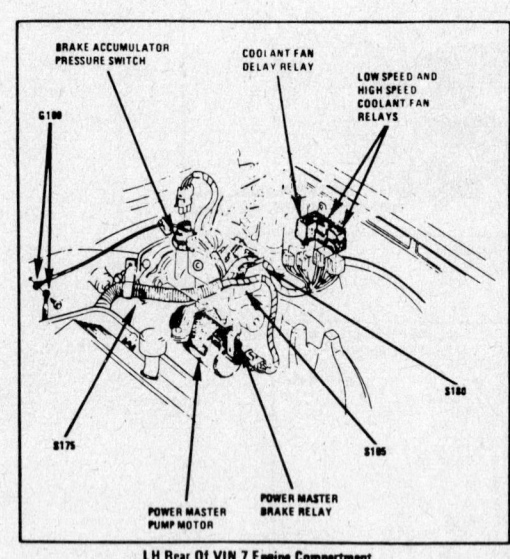

LH Rear Of VIN 7 Engine Compartment

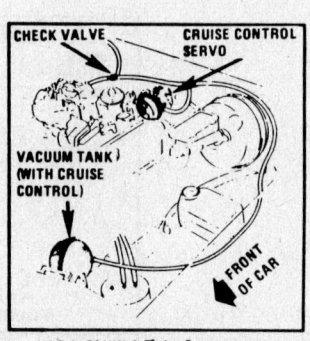

LH Side Of VIN A Engine Compartment

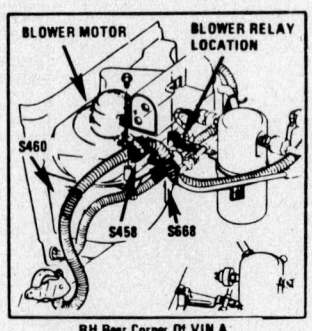

RH Rear Corner Of VIN A
Engine Compartment

1985-86 Buick Riviera

COMPONENT LOCATIONS

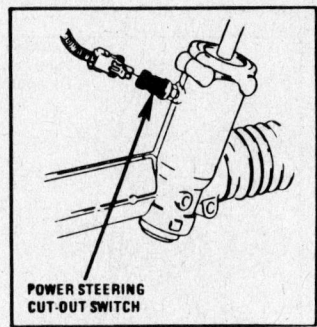

POWER STEERING
CUT-OUT SWITCH

Rear Of Engine Compartment Near
Steering Gear Assembly

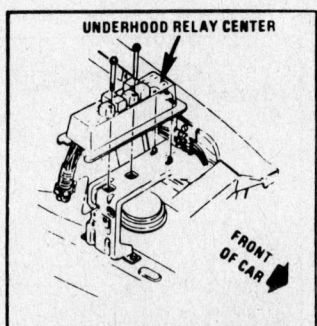

UNDERHOOD RELAY CENTER

FRONT OF CAR

LH Front Of Engine Compartment

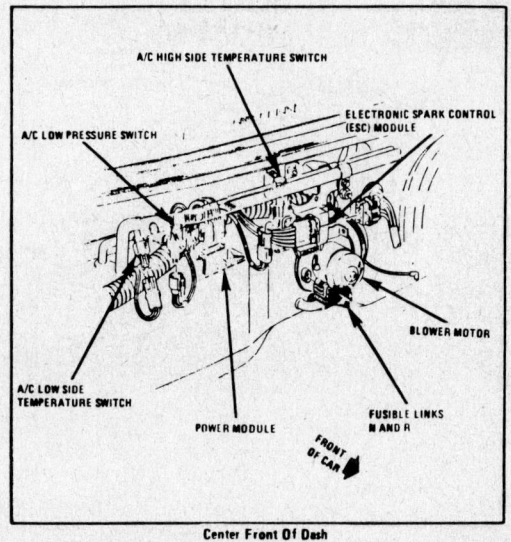

A/C HIGH SIDE TEMPERATURE SWITCH

A/C LOW PRESSURE SWITCH

ELECTRONIC SPARK CONTROL
(ESC) MODULE

A/C LOW SIDE
TEMPERATURE SWITCH

POWER MODULE

FRONT OF CAR

BLOWER MOTOR

FUSIBLE LINKS
N AND R

Center Front Of Dash

1985-86 Buick Riviera

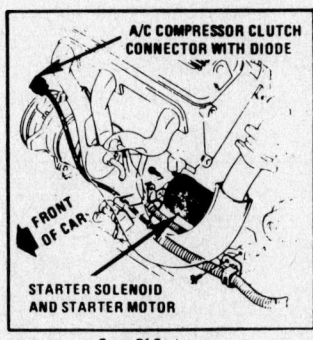

A/C COMPRESSOR CLUTCH
CONNECTOR WITH DIODE

FRONT OF CAR

STARTER SOLENOID
AND STARTER MOTOR

Front Of Engine

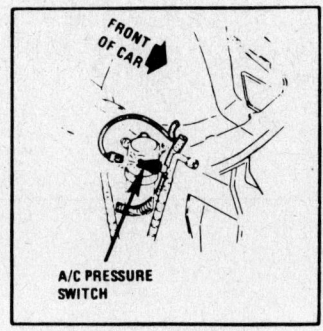

FRONT OF CAR

A/C PRESSURE
SWITCH

LH Front Corner Of Engine Compartment

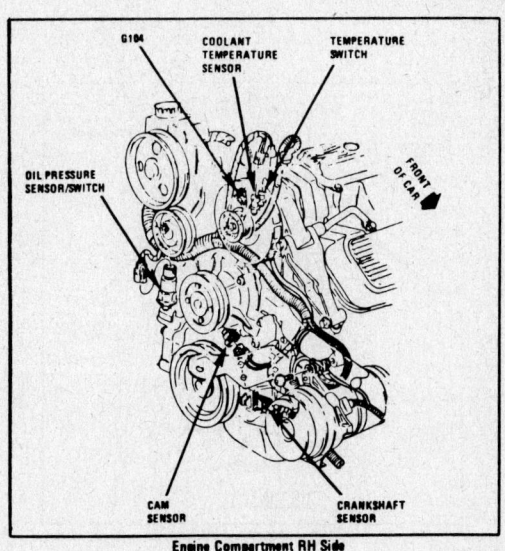

G104

COOLANT
TEMPERATURE
SENSOR

TEMPERATURE
SWITCH

OIL PRESSURE
SENSOR/SWITCH

FRONT OF CAR

CAM
SENSOR

CRANKSHAFT
SENSOR

Engine Compartment RH Side

1985-86 Buick Riviera

COMPONENT LOCATIONS

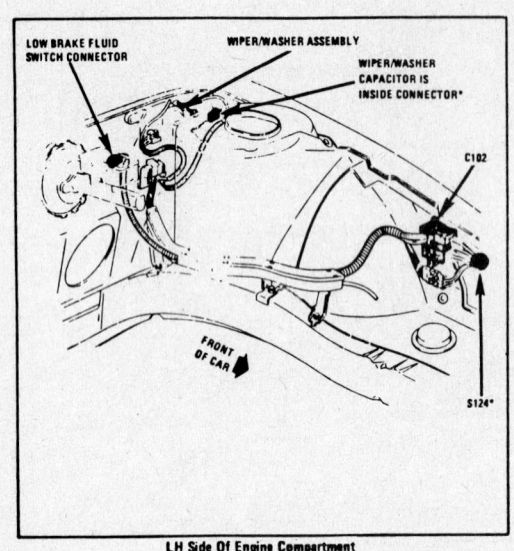

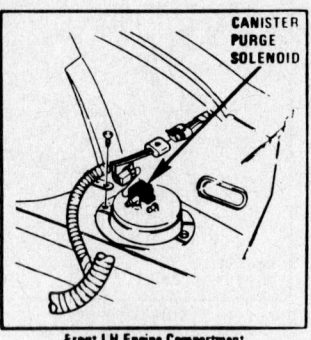

Front LH Engine Compartment

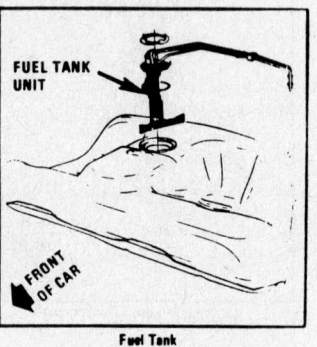

Fuel Tank

1985-86 Buick Riviera

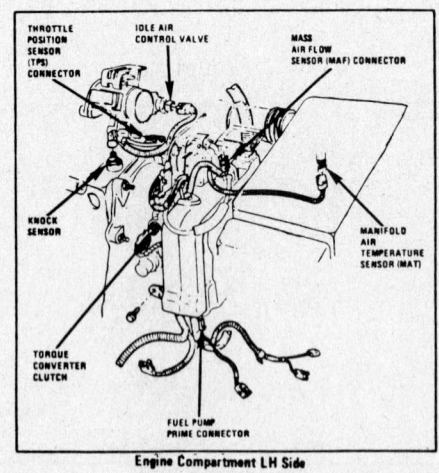

Engine Compartment LH Side

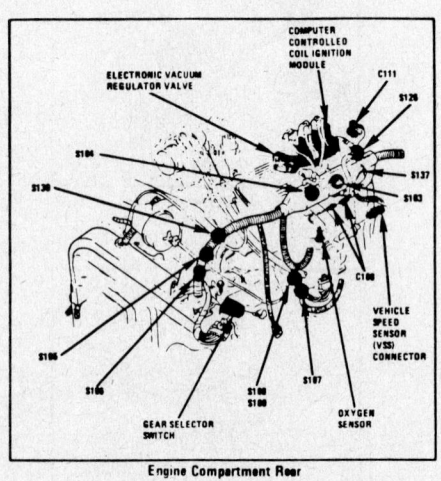

Engine Compartment Rear

1985-86 Buick Riviera

COMPONENT LOCATIONS

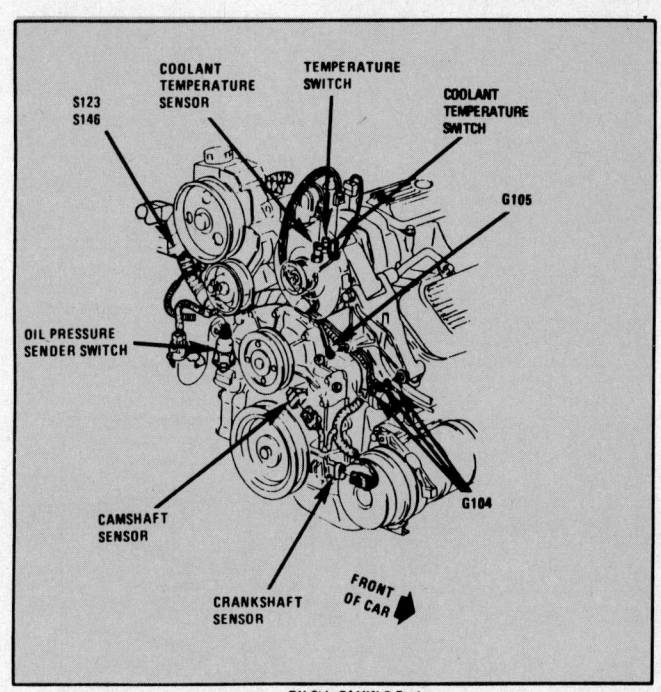

RH Side Of VIN B Engine

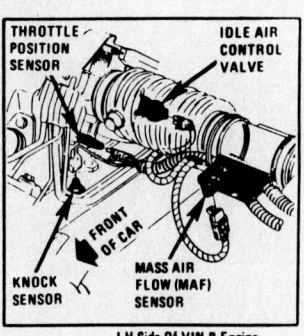

LH Side Of VIN B Engine

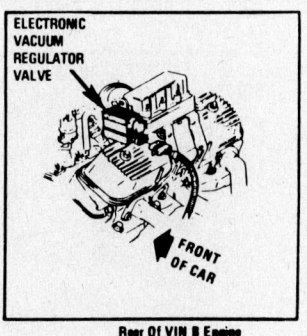

Rear Of VIN B Engine

1985-86 Buick Electra

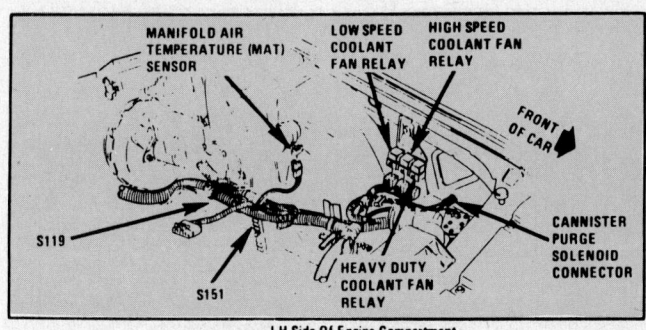

LH Side Of Engine Compartment

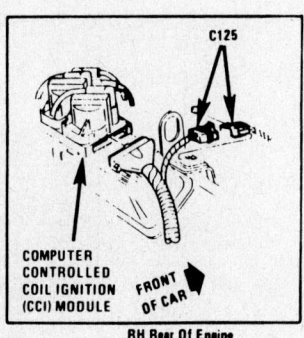

RH Rear Of Engine

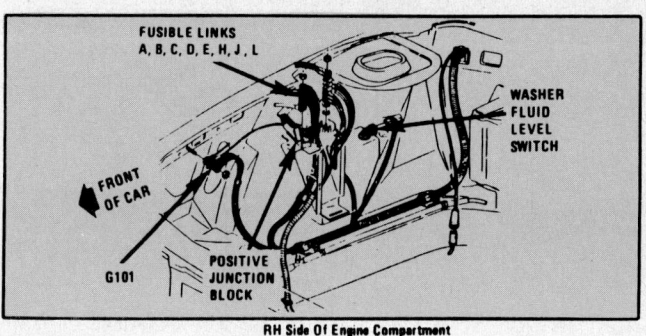

RH Side Of Engine Compartment

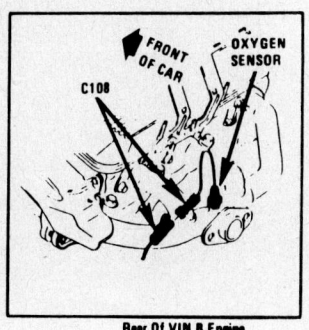

Rear Of VIN B Engine

1985-86 Buick Electra

COMPONENT LOCATIONS

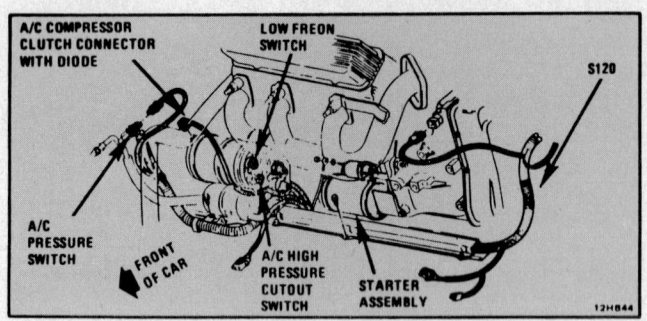

Figure A - Front Of VIN B Engine

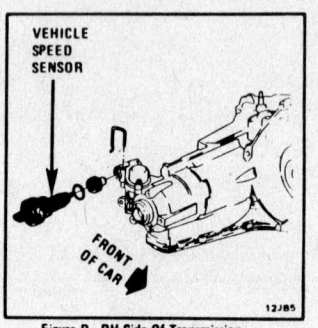

Figure C - Above Transaxle

Figure B - RH Front Of Engine Compartment

Figure D - RH Side Of Transmission

1985-86 Buick Electra

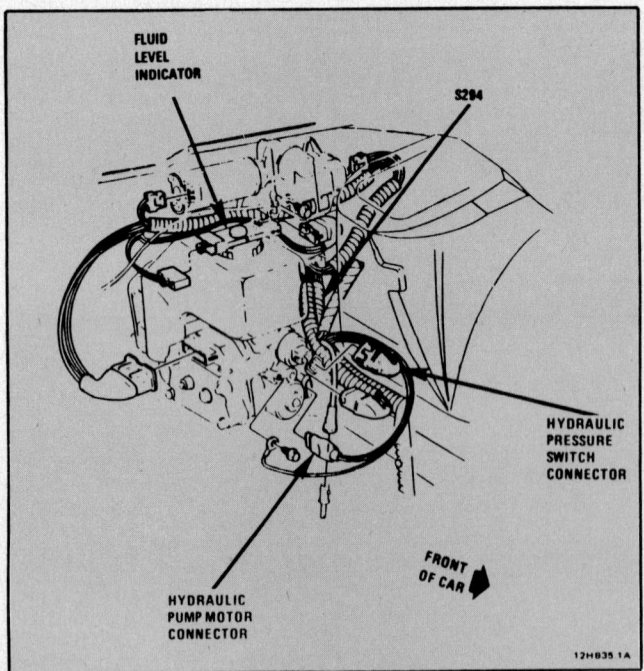

Figure A - LH Front Of Dash

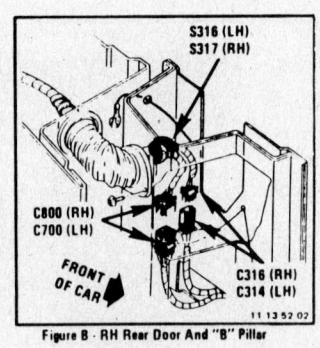

Figure B - RH Rear Door And "B" Pillar

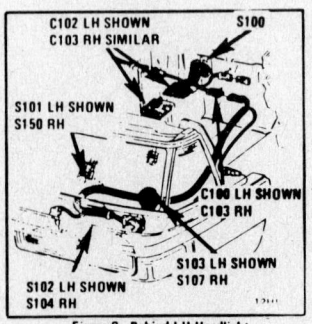

Figure C - Behind LH Headlight

1985-86 Buick Electra

COMPONENT LOCATIONS

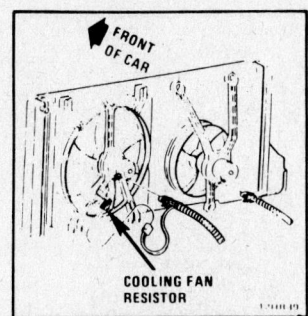

Figure A - Cooling Fans

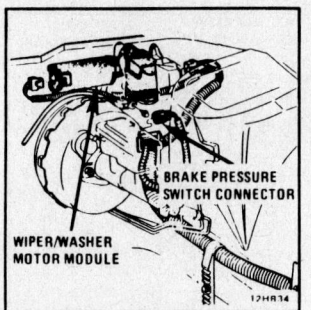

Figure C - LH Front Of Dash

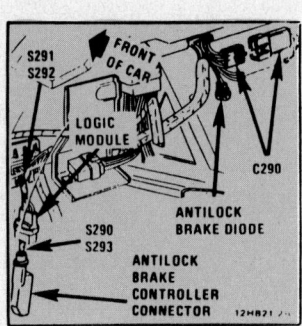

Figure E - Behind LH Side Of I/P

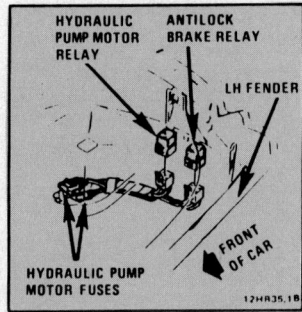

Figure B - LH Front Of Dash

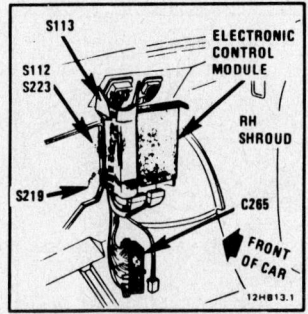

Figure D - Behind RH Side Of I/P

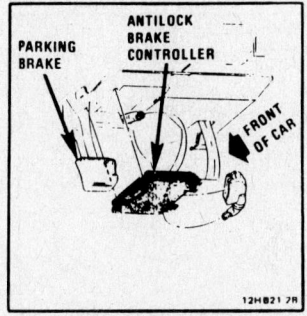

Figure F - Under LH Side Of I/P

1985-86 Buick Electra

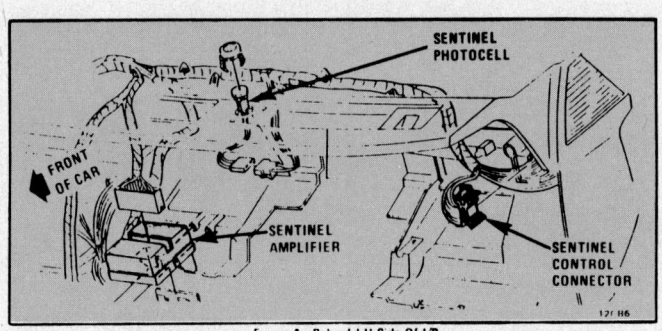

Figure A - Behind LH Side Of I/P

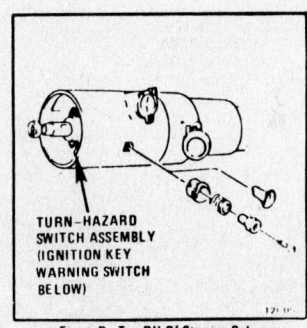

Figure D - Top RH Of Steering Column

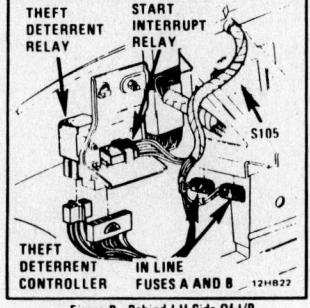

Figure B - Behind LH Side Of I/P

Figure C - LH Side Of I/P

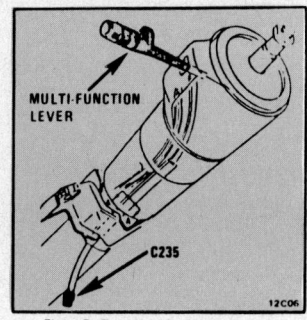

Figure E - Top LH Of Steering Column

1985-86 Buick Electra

COMPONENT LOCATIONS

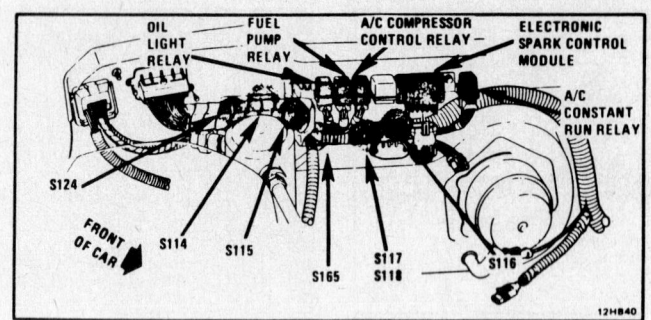

Figure A - RH Front Of Dash

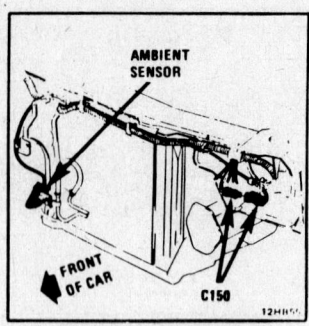

Figure D - Front Of Car, Behind Headlights

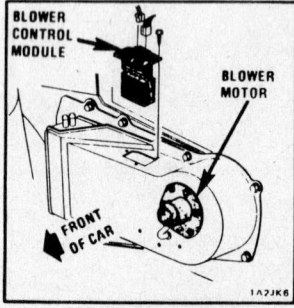

Figure B - RH Front Of Dash

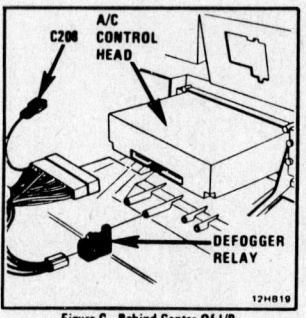

Figure C - Behind Center Of I/P

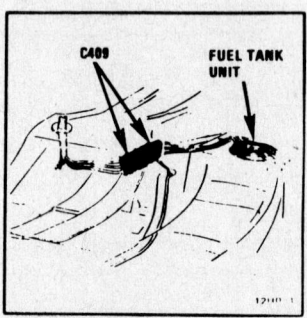

Figure E - Rear Of Car

1985-86 Buick Electra

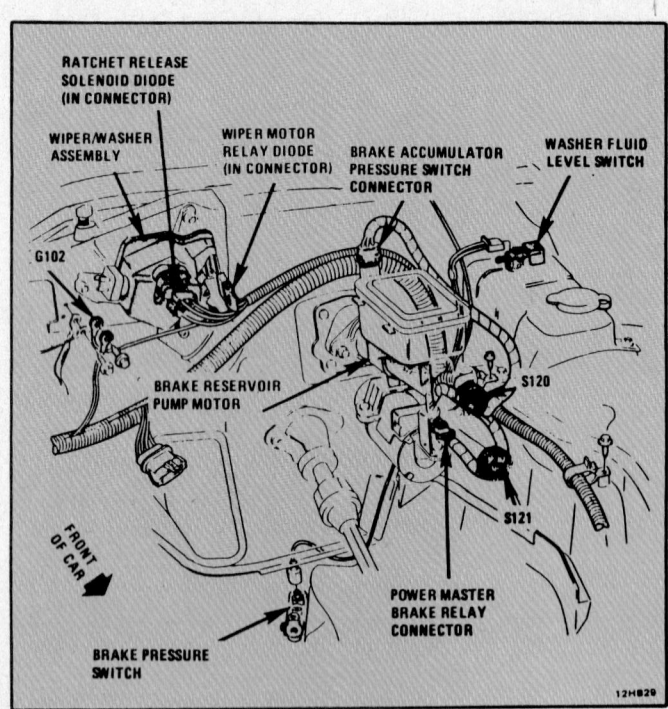

Figure A - LH Front Of Dash

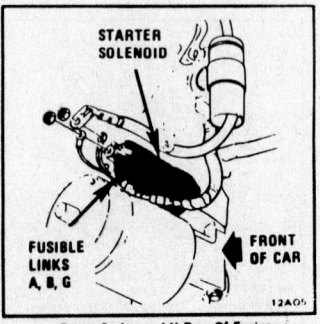

Figure B - RH Shroud

Figure C - Lower LH Rear Of Engine

1985-86 Buick Electra/LeSabre Wagon

COMPONENT LOCATIONS

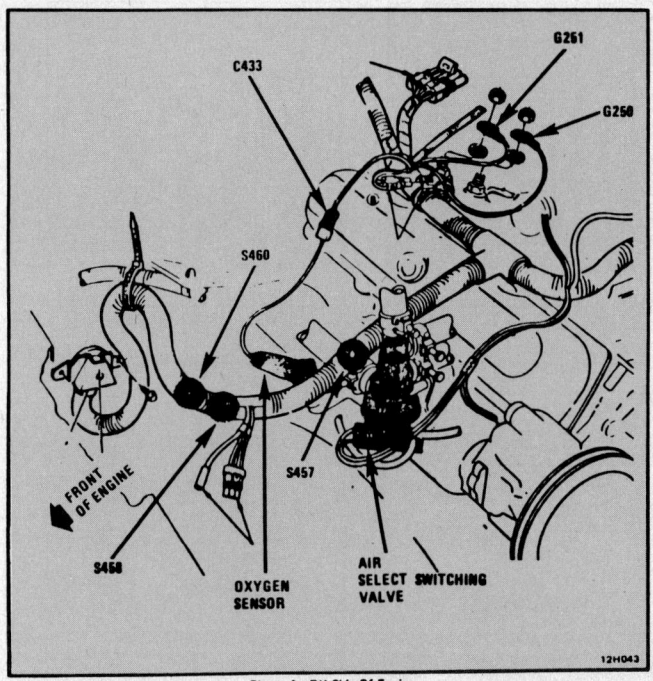

Figure A - RH Side Of Engine

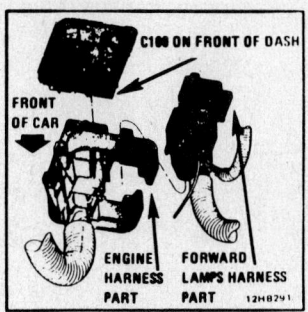

Figure B - LH Side, Front Of Dash

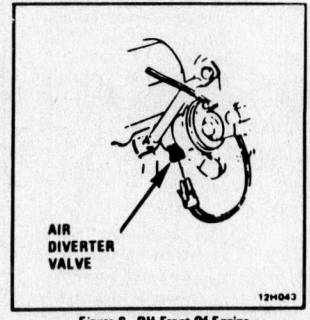

Figure C - RH Front Of Engine

1985-86 Buick Electra/LeSabre Wagon

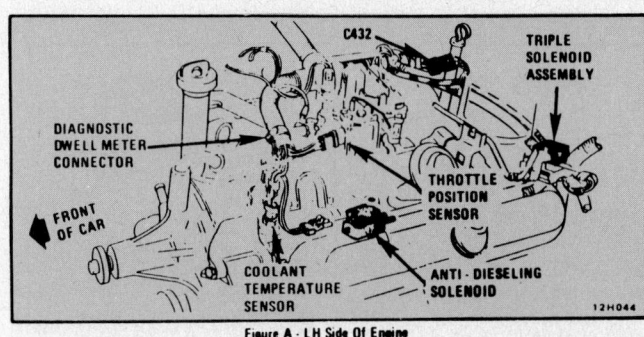

Figure A - LH Side Of Engine

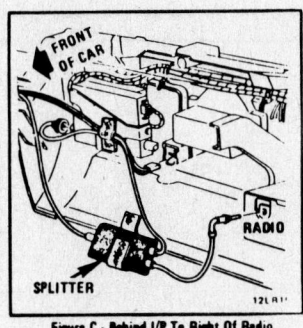

Figure C - Behind I/P To Right Of Radio

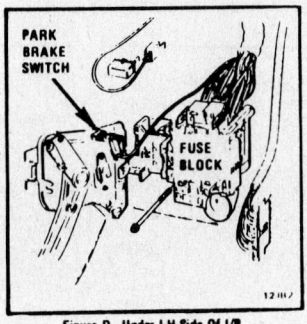

Figure B - Behind I/P

Figure D - Under LH Side Of I/P

1985-86 Buick Electra/LeSabre Wagon

COMPONENT LOCATIONS

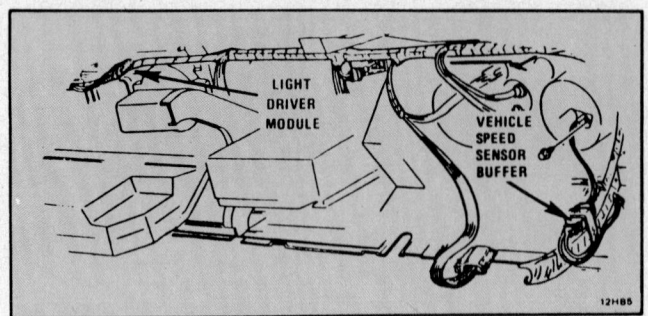

Figure A - Behind LH To Center Of I/P

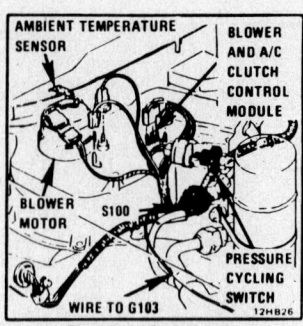

Figure D - RH Front Of Dash

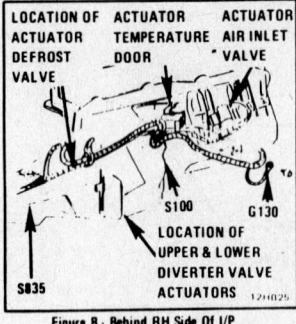

Figure B - Behind RH Side Of I/P

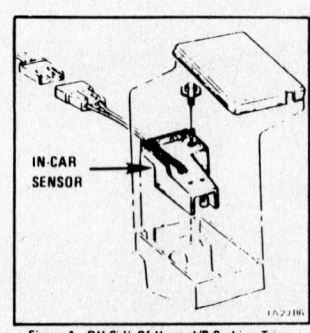

Figure A - RH Side Of Upper I/P Cushion Trim

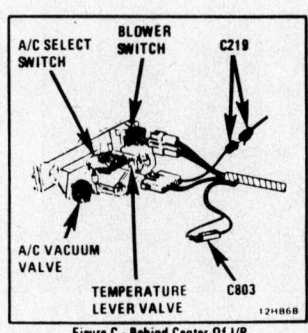

Figure C - Behind I/P

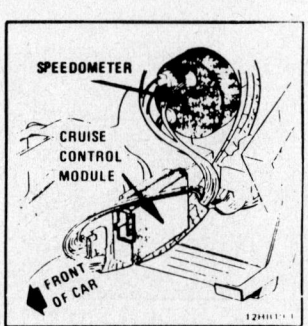

Figure E - Air Conditioning Module

1985-86 Buick Electra/LeSabre Wagon

Figure B - Engine Compartment

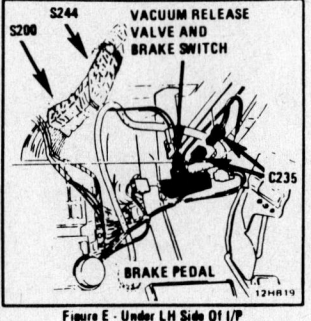

Figure E - Under LH Side Of I/P

1985-86 Buick Electra/LeSabre Wagon

Figure C - Behind Center Of I/P

Figure D - Behind LH I/P Under Speedometer

COMPONENT LOCATIONS

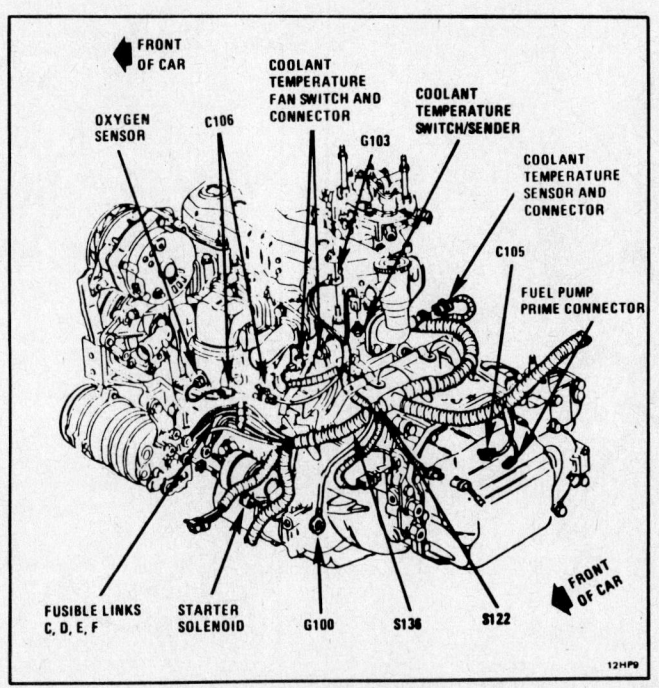

Figure A - LH Front Of VIN U Engine

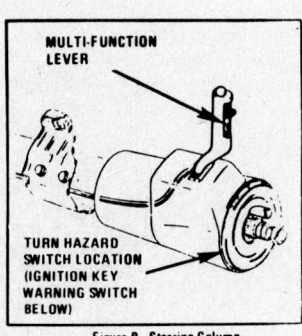

Figure B - Steering Column

1985-86 Buick Somerset/Skylark

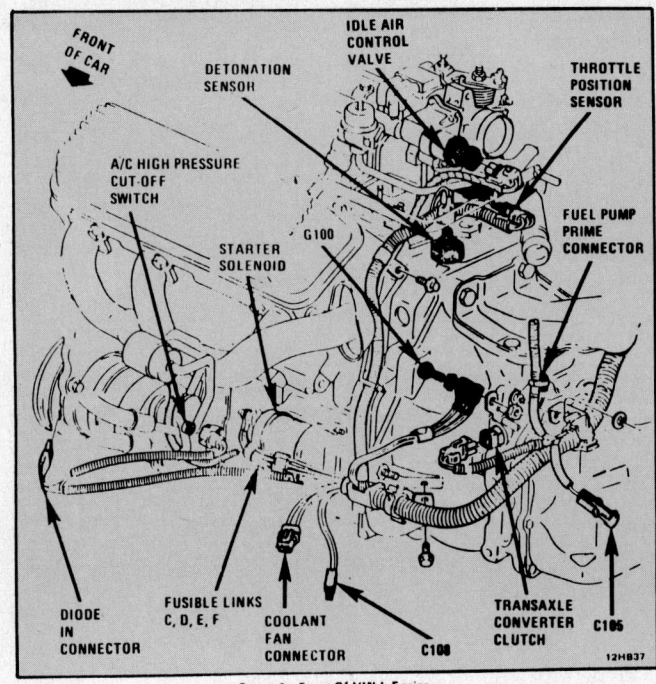

Figure A - Front Of VIN L Engine

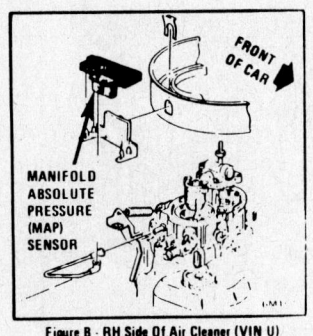

Figure B - RH Side Of Air Cleaner (VIN U)

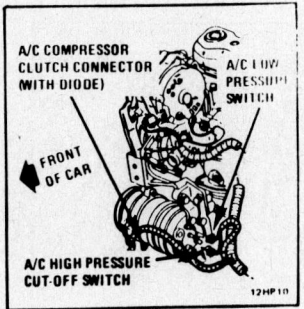

Figure C - RH Front Of VIN U Engine

1985-86 Buick Somerset/Skylark

COMPONENT LOCATIONS

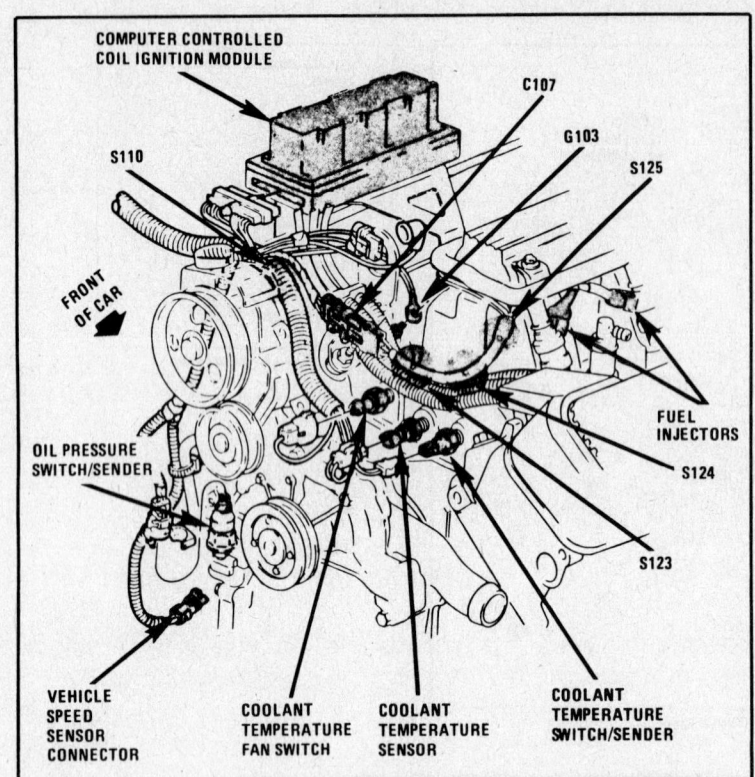

Top RH Side Of VIN L Engine

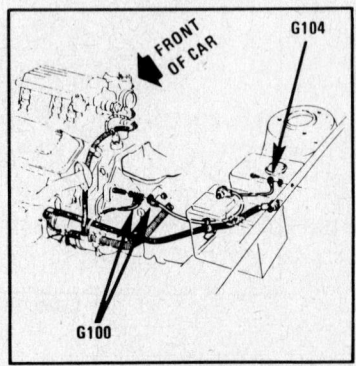

Figure B - LH Rear Corner Of VIN L Engine Compartment

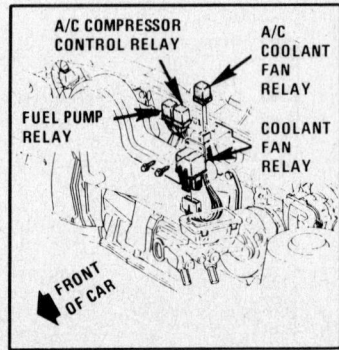

LH Front Of VIN L Engine Compartment

1985-86 Buick Somerset/Skylark

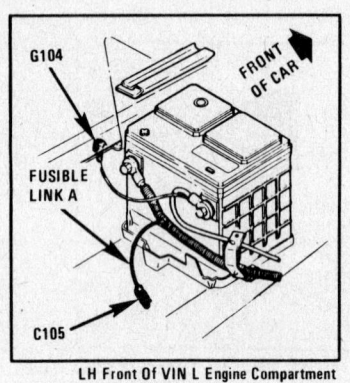

LH Front Of VIN L Engine Compartment

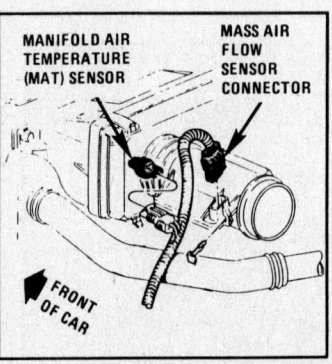

LH Front Of VIN L Engine Compartment

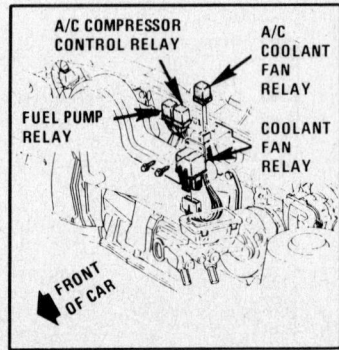

Front Of VIN U Dash

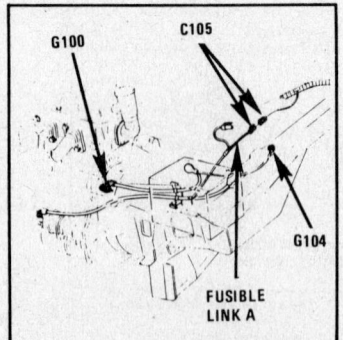

LH Front Of VIN U Engine Compartment

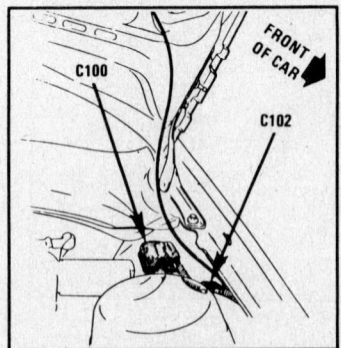

LH Front Of Dash

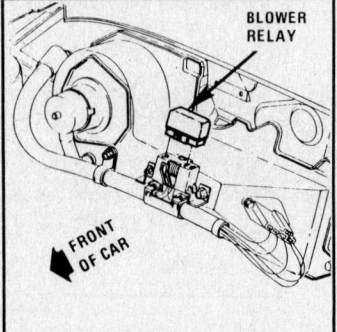

Center Front Of Dash

1985-86 Buick Somerset/Skylark

COMPONENT LOCATIONS

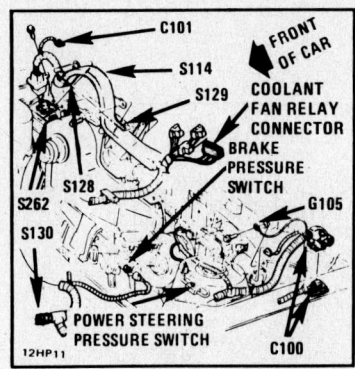

Front Of VIN U Dash

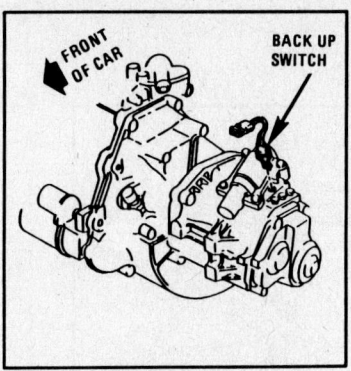

Top LH End Of Transaxle

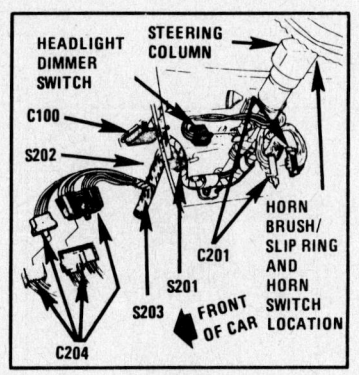

Left Of Steering Column

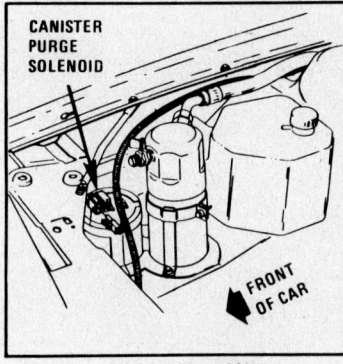

RH Front Corner Of VIN L
Engine Compartment

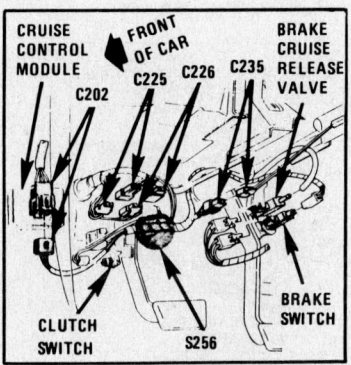

Under LH Side Of I/P

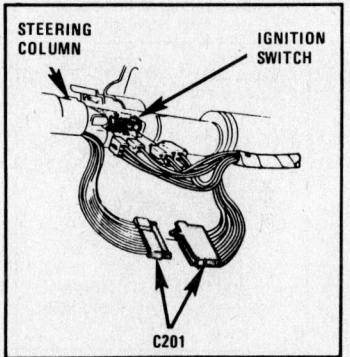

RH Side Of Steering Column

1985-86 Buick Somerset/Skylark

Behind Center Of I/P

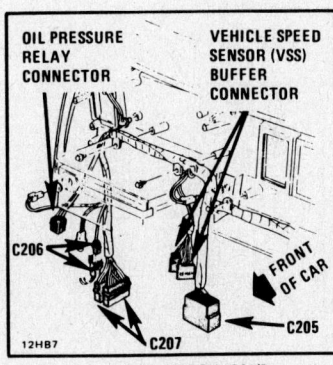

Behind RH Side Of I/P

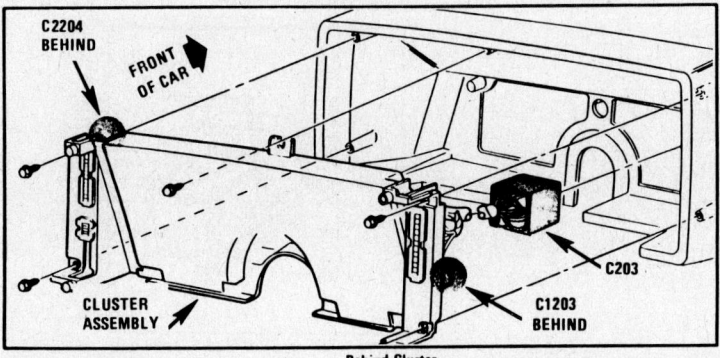

Behind Cluster

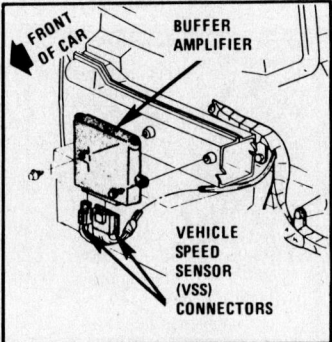

Behind RH Side Of I/P

1985-86 Buick Somerset/Skylark

COMPONENT LOCATIONS

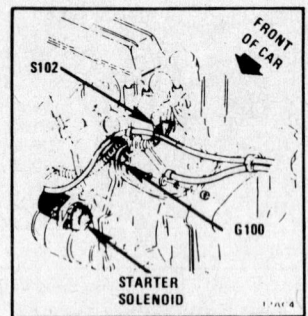

Figure A · LH Front Of VIN P Engine, Above Starter Solenoid

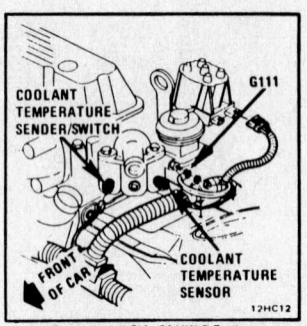

Figure C · LH Side Of VIN P Engine

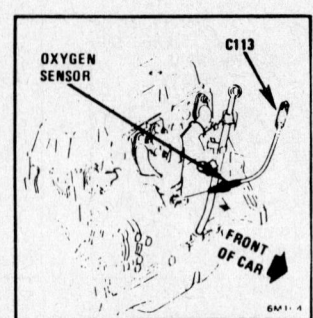

Figure E · Front of VIN P Engine

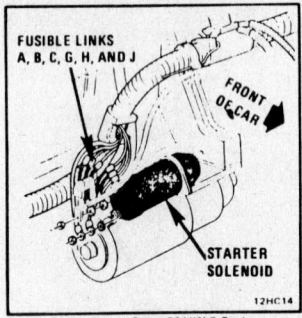

Figure B · LH Front Of VIN P Engine

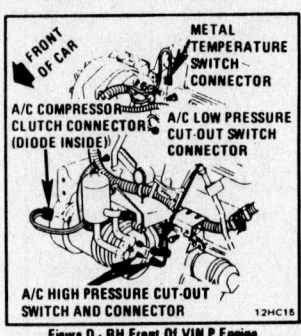

Figure D · RH Front Of VIN P Engine

1985-86 Buick Skyhawk

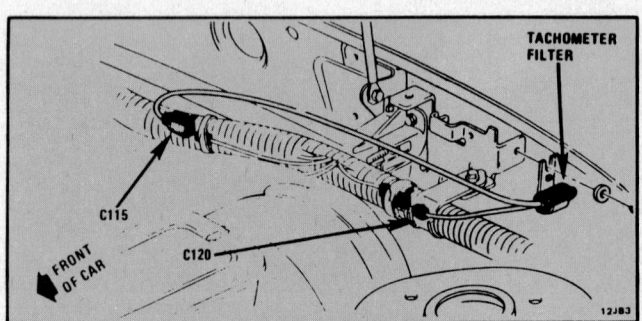

Figure A · LH Side Of VIN P Dash

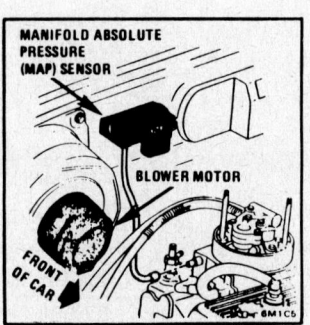

Figure D · Front Of Dash (VIN P)

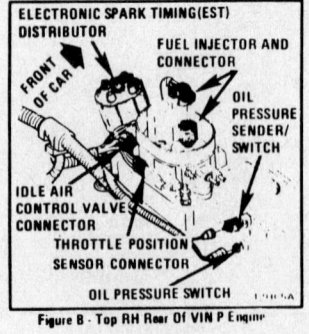

Figure B · Top RH Rear Of VIN P Engine

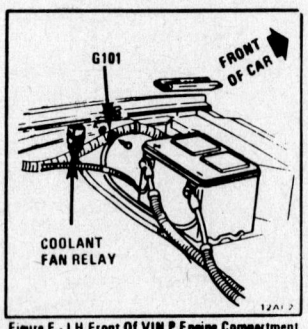

Figure E · LH Front Of VIN P Engine Compartment

1985-86 Buick Skyhawk

COMPONENT LOCATIONS

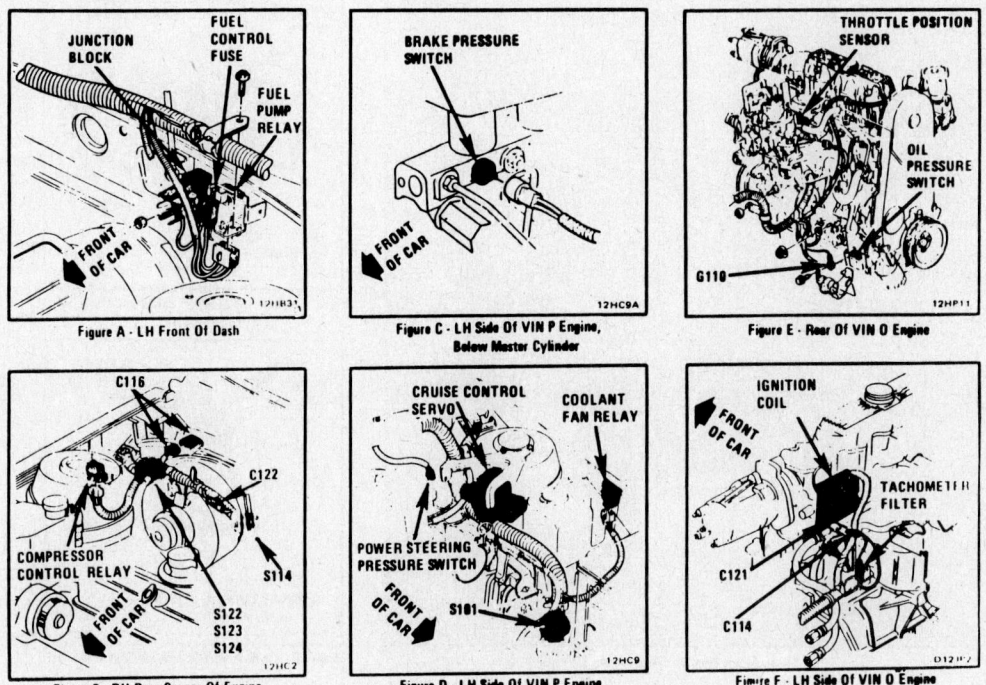

Figure A - LH Front Of Dash

Figure C - LH Side Of VIN P Engine, Below Master Cylinder

Figure E - Rear Of VIN O Engine

Figure B - RH Rear Corner Of Engine Compartment (VIN P)

Figure D - LH Side Of VIN P Engine

Figure F - LH Side Of VIN O Engine

1985-86 Buick Skyhawk

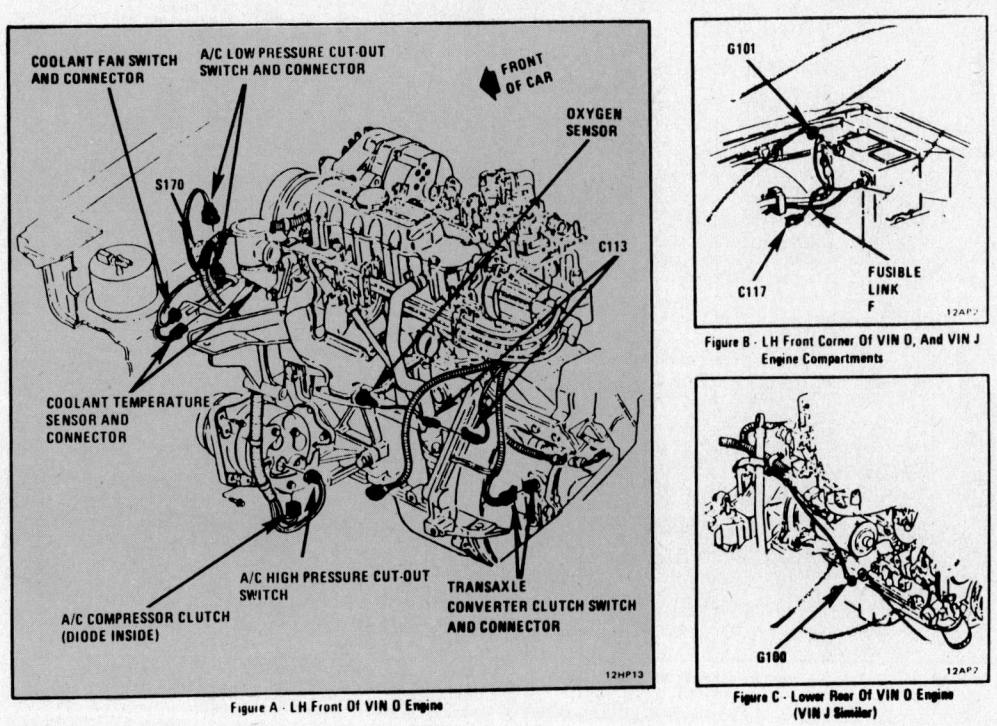

Figure A - LH Front Of VIN O Engine

Figure B - LH Front Corner Of VIN O, And VIN J Engine Compartments

Figure C - Lower Rear Of VIN O Engine (VIN J Similar)

1985-86 Buick Skyhawk

COMPONENT LOCATIONS

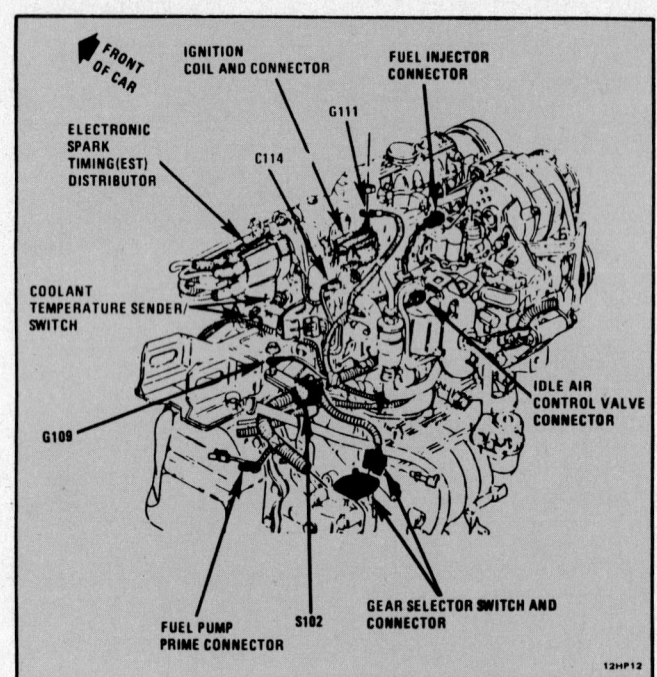

Figure A - LH Rear Of VIN O Engine

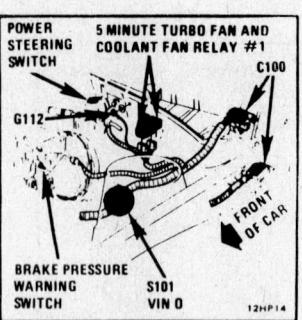

Figure B - LH Front Of Dash (VIN J Shown, VIN O Similar)

Figure C - LH Rear Of VIN J Engine (VIN O Similar)

1985-86 Buick Skyhawk

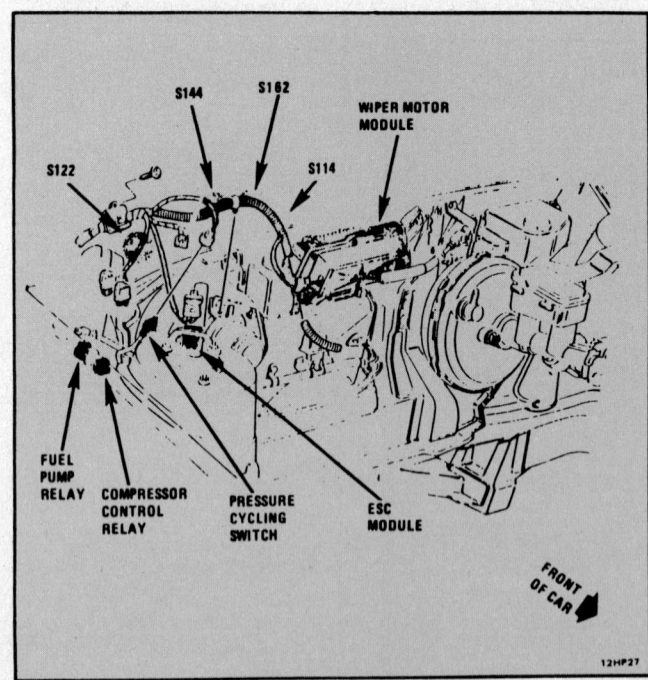

Figure A - RH Side Of Dash (VIN J)

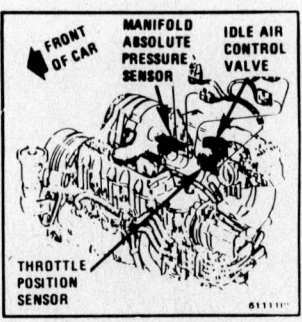

Figure B - Top Of VIN J Engine

Figure C - Top Of VIN J Engine, Rear Of Valve Cover

1985-86 Buick Skyhawk

CADILLAC

Circuit Breakers

ALL 1982-83 MODELS

REAR DEFOGGER

The circuit breaker for the rear defogger is located on the lower steering column cover reinforcement.

WINDSHIELD WIPER

This circuit breaker is integral with the windshield wiper switch.

HEADLIGHTS – TWILIGHT SENTINEL

This circuit breaker is integral with the windshield wiper switch.

IN-LINE FUSES

TRUNK LID PULL DOWN

There is one 20 amp fuse located behind the right hand fabric rear end panel, which is inside the trunk.

THEFT DETERRENT

There is a 20 amp in-line fuse used for the lights and a 25 amp in-line fuse used for the horn, which is located above the radio in the instrument panel.

VANITY MIRROR

There is a 2 amp in-line fuse which is located behind the mirror.

ALL 1984 AND LATER MODELS

POWER MIRRORS

On each power mirror motor there is a self resetting circuit breaker (except Cimarron).

WINDSHIELD WIPER

This circuit brekaer is integral with the windshield wiper switch.

HEADLIGHTS – TWILIGHT SENTINEL

This circuit breaker is integral with the windshield wiper switch.

POWER WINDOWS

On each power window motor there is a self resetting circuit breaker.

IN-LINE FUSES

TRUNK LID PULL DOWN

There is one 20 amp (yellow wire) fuse located behind the right hand fabric rear end panel, which is inside the trunk.

THEFT DETERRENT

There is a 20 amp (yellow wire) in-line fuse used for the lights and a 25 amp (white wire) in-line fuse used for the horn, which is located above the steering column.

VANITY MIRROR

There is a 2 amp in-line fuse which is located behind the mirror.

DEFOGGER

There is one 7.5 amp (brown wire) in-line fuse used for the rear defogger and mirror defogger, which is located behind the instrument panel near the fuse block.

Fusible Links

All models are equipped with fusible links which attach to the lower ends of main feed wires and connect at the battery or starter solenoid. On the diesel models, the fusible links attach to the wiring harness and connect to the glow plug relay. The fusible link wire gauge size is marked on the insulation and each link is four sizes smaller than the cable it is designed to protect. The same wire with special hypalon insulation must be used when replacing a fusible link.

Relay, Sensors And Computer Locations

1982-84 CIMARRON

- **A/C Ambient Air Sensor** – is located on the engine cowl, above the power steering reservoir.
- **A/C Blower Relay** – is located on the front center of the plenum.
- **A/C Compressor Control Relay** – is located behind the right front shock tower.
- **A/C Compressor Run Relay** – is located behind the right front shock tower.
- **A/C-Heater Blower Resistors** – are located on the front left side of the plenum.
- **Blocking Diode** – is located in the instrument panel harness, near the fuse block.
- **Coolant Fan Relay** – on the left front fender in front of the shock tower.
- **Coolant Temperature Sender** – is located on the left side of the engine, near the coolant outlet.
- **Coolant Temperature Sensor** – is located on the front of the engine on the thermostat housing on the 1.8L engine and on the left side of the engine under the water outlet on the other engines.
- **Cruise Control Throttle Servo** – is located on the bracket on the left front shock tower.
- **Door Lock Relay** – is located on the upper right side of the steering column support.
- **Defogger Time Relay** – is located behind the left side of the dash panel.
- **Electronic Control Module (ECM)** – is located behind the glove box.
- **Electronic Fuel Injection Ambient Sensor** – is located on the engine cowl above the washer reservoir.
- **Fuel Pump Relay** – is located on the right engine cowl, behind the shock tower.
- **Hatch/Tailgate/Trunk Release Relay** – is taped to the wire harness, located behind the right side of the radio.
- **Horn Relay** – is located on the conveience center.
- **Idle Speed Motor** – is taped in the EFI harness. to the right of the electronic control module.
- **Manifold Absolute Presure Sensor** – is located on the right shock tower.
- **Oxygen Sensor** – is located in the exhaust manifold.

• **Power Accessories Circuit Breaker**—is located in the fuse block.
• **Power Antenna Relay**—is located behind the instrument panel, below the right side of the radio.
• **Power Window Circuit Breaker**—is located in the fuse block.
• **Throttle Position Sensor**—is located on the throttle body.
• **Torque Converter Clutch Relay (TCC)**—is located on the transmission cowling.
• **Vehicle Speed Sensor**—is located behind the instrument panel, the the right of the steering column.
• **Wiper Pulse Module**—is located below the steering column, above the trim cover.

1985-87 CIMARRON

• **A/C Compressor Run Relay**—is located behind the right front shock tower.
• **A/C-Heater Blower Resistors**—are located on the front left side of the plenum.
• **A/C In-Car Temperature Sensor**—is located on the right side of the dash, above the glove box.
• **Assembly Line Diagnostic Link**—is located behind the instrument panel, on the right side of the fuse block.
• **Blocking Diode**—is located in the instrument panel harness, near the bulkhead connector.
• **Coolant Fan Relay**—on the left front fender in front of the shock tower or on the firewall to the left of the brake booster.
• **Coolant Temperature Sender**—is located on the left side of the engine, near the coolant outlet.
• **Coolant Temperature Sensor**—is located on the front of the engine on the thermostat housing on the 1.8L engine and on the left side of the engine under the water outlet on the other engines.
• **Cruise Control Module (2-door)**—is located behind the instrument panel, above the left side of the steering column.
• **Cruise Control Module (4-door)**—is located behind the right side of the dash panel, above the glove box.
• **Defogger Time Relay**—is located behind the left side of the dash panel.
• **Electronic Control Module (ECM)**—is located behind the glove box.
• **Electronic Fuel Injection Ambient Sensor**—is located on the engine cowl above the washer reservoir.
• **Electronic Speed Sensor**—is located on the top right side of the transaxle.
• **Fog Lamp Relays**—are taped to the instrument panel harness, near the fog lamp switch.
• **Fuel Pump In-Line Fuse**—is located on the firewall, behind the brake booster.
• **Fuel Pump Relay**—is located on the right engine cowl, behind the shock tower or on the firewall, above the brake booster.
• **Hatch/Tailgate/Trunk Release Relay**—is taped to the wire harness, located behind the right side of the radio.
• **Horn Relay**—is located on the conveience center.
• **Knock Sensor**—is located on the right side of the starter below the starter.
• **Low Coolant Module**—is located behind the instrument panel, above the left side of the steering column.
• **Low Coolant Temperature Sensor**—is located in the engine compartment, on the right front side of the radiator.
• **Mass Airflow Relay**—is located on the firewall, behind the brake booster.
• **Manifold Absolute Presure Sensor**—is located on the right shock tower.
• **Manifold Air Temperature Sensor**—is located on the engine, underneath or on top of the intake manifold.

• **Mass Airflow Sensor**—is located on the top of the left side of the engine, behind the air cleaner.
• **Mass Airflow Sensor In-Line Fuse**—is located on the firewall, behind the brake booster.
• **Outside Air Temperature Sensor**—is located inthe engine compartment, behind the right side of the grill.
• **Oxygen Sensor**—is located in the exhaust manifold.
• **Power Accessories/Convertible Top Circuit Breaker**—is located in the fuse block.
• **Power Antenna Relay**—is located behind the instrument panel, below the right side of the radio.
• **Power Door Lock Relay**—is located on the upper right side of the steering column support.
• **Power Unit Dimmer**—is located behind the instrument panel, to the left of the steering column.
• **Power Window Circuit Breaker**—is located in the fuse block.
• **Release Relay**—is taped to the instrument panel harness, behind the radio or glove box.
• **Throttle Position Sensor**—is located on the throttle body. On the 2.8L engine it is located, behind the distributor.
• **Torque Converter Clutch Relay (TCC)**—is located on the transmission cowling.
• **Turbo Release Relay**—is located on the transaxle cowling.
• **Twilight Sentinel Amplifier**—is located behind the instrument panel, to the left of the steering column.
• **Twilight Sentinel Photocell**—is located on the dash panel, on the right side of the defrost vent.
• **Vehicle Speed Sensor**—is located behind the instrument panel, the the right of the steering column.
• **Vehicle Speed Sensor Buffer**—is located behind the instrument cluster, below the speed sensor.

1982-84 DEVILLE AND FLEETWOOD

• **A/C Ambient Sensor**—is an integral part of the aspirator near the programmer.
• **A/C Compressor Cycling Switch**—is located to the left of the blower motor attached to the evaporator case.
• **A/C In-Car Sensor**—is located behind the telltale housing above the instrument panel glove box.
• **A/C Low Presure Switch**—is located at the back of the compressor attached to the front of the engine.
• **A/C Power Module (Gas)**—is located on the top left side of the blower evaporator case.
• **A/C Programmer**—is located under the instrument panel attached to the right side of the A/C—Heater assembly.
• **Barometeric Pressure Sensor**—is located under the instrument panel to the right of the air distributor.
• **Brake Vacuum Light Module**—is located behind the instrument panel to the left of the radio.
• **Brake Vacuum Switch**—is located on the brake vacuum booster.
• **Check Engine Light Module**—is attached to the harness on the opposite of the diode module.
• **Coolant Temperature Sensor**—is located on the left front of the diesel engine and on the front near the radiator inlet on the gas engine.
• **Cruise Control Brake Switch**—is attached to the brake pedal mounting bracket.
• **Cruise Control Buffer Amplifier (Gas)**—is connected to the speed sensor harness behind the instrument cluster.
• **Cruise Control Servo (Gas)**—is located on the left front inner fender well.
• **Cruise Control Speed Sensor**—is attached to the speedometer behind the instrument cluster.
• **Defogger Relay**—is located on the relay panel under the instrument panel to the left of the fuse block.

- **Diode Module (Diesel)** — is attached to the wiring harness leading to the center bulkhead connector.
- **Door Lock Relay** — is attached to the lower right shroud panel behind the kick panel.
- **Electronic Control Module (ECM)** — is located behind the instrument panel below the glove box liner.
- **Engine Metal Temperature Switch** — is located on the rear of the left cylinder head.
- **Fast Idle Switch (Diesel)** — is is located on the rear of the left cylinder head.
- **Fourth Gear Switch** — is located in the transmission to the lower left side of the engine.
- **Fuel Pump Relay (Gas)** — is located on the relay panel under the instrument panel to the left of the fuse block.
- **Glow Plug Control Switch** — is located on the right front of the intake manifold.
- **Glow Plug Relay** — is located on the right front fender well.
- **Glow Plug Temperature Switch** — is located on the rear of the left cylinder head.
- **Guidematic Power Relay** — is located under the dash panel, near the fuse block.
- **Horn Relay** — is located on the relay panel under the instrument panel to the left of the fuse block.
- **Key Warning Buzzer** — is located under the instrument panel, between the steering column and the radio.
- **Lower Control Relay** — is located on the relay panel under the instrument panel to the left of the fuse block.
- **Manifold Absolute Pressure Sensor** — is located under the instrument panel to the right of the air distributor.
- **Manifold Air Temperature Sensor** — is located on the intake manifold in front of the throttle body.
- **Oil Pressure Switch** — is located on the left front on the diesel engines and on the right front on the gas engines.
- **Outside Temperature Sensor** — is located at the rear of the radiator grille.
- **Oxygen Sensor** — is attached to the left exhaust manifold.
- **Power Antenna Relay** — is located on the relay panel under the instrument panel to the left of the fuse block.
- **Power Seat Relay** — is located under the driver's seat.
- **Seat Belt Warning Chime** — is located under the instrument panel, between the steering column and the radio.
- **Seat Belt Warning Timer** — is located under the instrument panel attached to the fuse block.
- **Starter Interupt Relay** — is taped to the wire harness, near the turn signal flasher.
- **Stop/Turn Light Relays** — is located at the left rear quarter panel.
- **Tone Generator** — is located under instrument panel between the steering column and the radio.
- **Twilight Sentinel Amplifier** — is located under the instrument panel on the relay panel mounting bracket.
- **Twilight Sentinel Photocell** — is locatwed under the left front speaker grille.

1985-87 DEVILLE AND FLEETWOOD

- **A/C Compressor Clutch Diode** — is located in the connector at the rear of the compressor.
- **A/C Compressor Control Relay (Gas)** — is located on the right side of the firewall in the engine compartment.
- **A/C Compressor Control Relay (Diesel)** — is located behind the right side of the dash panel, to the right of the plenum.
- **A/C Constant Run Relay** — is located on the right side of the fire wall in the engine compartment.
- **A/C-Heater Blower Control Module** — is located on the right side of the firewall in the engine compartment.
- **A/C-Heater Relay** — is located on the right side of the firewall in the engine compartment.
- **A/C-Heater Resistors** — are located on the right side of the firewall in the engine compartment, in the top of the plenum.
- **Altitude Advance Relay (Diesel)** — is located on the right side of the firewall in the engine compartment.
- **Amplifier Relay** — is located under the right side of the dash panel, near the connector C201.
- **Assembly Line Diagnostic Link Connector** — is located under the left side of the dash panel, to the left of the steering column.
- **Automatic Door Lock Controller** — is located behind the right side of the dash, on connector C210.
- **Automatic Door Lock Diode** — is located behind the right side of the dash panel, near the connector C201.
- **Brake Warning System Diode** — is located in the instrument panel wiring harness under the right side of the dash panel, to the right of the plenum.
- **"Check Engine" Light Driver** — is taped to the instrument panel harness under the right side of the dash panel, to right of the plenum.
- **Cooling Fan Diode** — is taped to the harnessin the connector behind the left shock tower.
- **Cooling Fan Relay** — is located on the right side of the firewall in the engine compartment.
- **Cooling Fan Resistor** — is located on the fan support frame behind the radiator.
- **Cruise Control Module** — is located above the accelerator pedal.
- **Decoder Module** — is located under the right side of the dash panel, at the top of connector C201.
- **Defogger Relay** — is located under the left side of the dash panel, to the left of the steering column.
- **Diagnostic Dwell Meter Connector** — is taped to the harness at the front of the engine, behind the valve cover.
- **Diesel Diode Module** — is located on the right side of the firewall in the engine compartment.
- **Diesel Electronic Control Module (DEC)** — is located behind the right side of the dash panel.
- **Early Fuel Evaporation (EFE) Relay** — is located on the right side of the firewall in the engine compartment.
- **Electrical Energy Reserve Module** — is located in front of the left front shock tower.
- **Electronic Climate Control Programmer (EEC)** — is located under the right side of the dash panel, on the right side of the plenum.
- **Electronic Control Module (ECM)** — is located behind the right side of the dash panel.
- **Electronic Level Control Diode** — is located in the instrument panel wiring harness, behind the radio.
- **Electronic Level Control Relay** — is located to the left of the level control compressor.
- **Electronic Level Control Test Connector** — is located near the top of the electronic level control compressor.
- **Electronic Tune Radio Diode** — is located in the instrument panel wiring harness, behind the radio.
- **Electronic Spark Control Module (ECS)** — is located on the right side of the firewall in the engine compartment.
- **Fan Control Relay** — is located in the wiring harness near the electronic level control compressor.
- **Fiber Optic Light Source** — are located one in each door.
- **Fuel Control Diode (Diesel)** — is located in the wiring harness at the right rear corner of the engine compartment.
- **Generator Diode** — Taped to the wiring harness at the left front wheel well.
- **Glow Plug Controller/Relay (Diesel)** — is located on the top left side of the engine, to the left of the valve cover.
- **Headlight Washer Relay** — is located on the fluid reservoir on the front of the right front shock tower.
- **High Mount Stop Light Relays** — are located on the left rear wheelwell inside the trunk.
- **High Speed Cooling Fan Relay** — is located on the firewall, behind the left shock tower.

- **Horn Relay** – is located under the left side of the dash panel, to the left of the steering column.
- **Illuminated Entry Timer** – is located behind the right side of the dash near connector C201.
- **Key Pad Module** – is located in the driver's door, near the door lock motor.
- **Keyless Entry Diode** – is located behind the right side of the dash panel, near connector C201.
- **Keyless Entry Module** – is located in the trunk, abovbe the rear wheelwell.
- **Low Brake Vacuum Relay** – is located behind the right side of the dash near connector C201.
- **Memory Disable Relay** – is located behind the right side of the dash near connector C201.
- **Multi-Function Chime Module** – is located behind the right side of the dash trim, above the glove box.
- **Power Antenna Relay** – is located behind the right side of the dash panel, near the connector C201.
- **Power Door Lock Relay** – is located behind the right side of the dash panel, on the top right side of connector C210.
- **Power Door Unlock Relay** – is located behind the right side of the dash panel, to the right of connector C210.
- **Power Seat Diode** – is located in the connector at the front of each seat.
- **Power Seat Memory Module** – is under the left side of the driver's seat.
- **Power Seat Recliner Capacitor** – is located in the connector at the front of each seat.
- **Power Seat Relay** – islocated on the lower seat rail under the seat.
- **Power Window Circuit Breaker** – is located in the fuse block.
- **Select Switch Relay** – is located behind the right side of the dash panel, on the bottom of connector C201.
- **Starter Interupt Relay** – is located on a bracket under the left side od the dash panel, to the left of the steering column.
- **Sun Roof Module** – is located in the windshield header above the right seat.
- **TCC Pulse Relay (Diesel)** – is located on the right side of the fire wall in the engine compartment.
- **Theft Deterrent Controller** – is located under the left side of the dash panel, to the left of the steering column.
- **Theft Deterrent Diode** – Taped to the instrument panel wiring harness under the right side of the dash panel, above connector C201.
- **Theft Deterrent Relay** – is located behind a bracket under the left side of the instrument panel.
- **Torque Converter Clutch Controller** – is located on the right side of the firewall in the engine compartment.
- **Trunk Pull-Down In-Line Fuse** – near the latch at the center of the trunk lid.
- **Twilight Sentinel Amplifier** – is located under the left side of the dash panel,to the right of the steering column.
- **Twilight Sentinel Photocell** – is located on the top left side of the dash panel, below the right side speaker grille.
- **Vehicle Speed Sensor Buffer** – is located under the right side of the dash panel, on the right side of the plenum.
- **Water-In-Fuel Module (Diesel)** – is located on top of the fuel filter assembly.

1982-84 ELDORADO AND SEVILLE

- **A/C Ambient Sensor** – is an integral part of the aspirator near the programmer.
- **A/C Compressor Cycling Switch** – is located to the left of the blower motor attached to the evaporator case.
- **A/C In-Car Sensor** – is located behind the telltale housing above the instrument panel glove box.

- **A/C Low Presure Switch** – is located at the back of the compressor attached to the front of the engine.
- **A/C Power Module (Gas)** – is located on the top of the left side of the blower evaporator case.
- **A/C Programmer Unit** – is located under the dash, attached to the right of the A/C-Heater assembly.
- **Barometeric Pressure Sensor** – is located under the instrument panel to the right of the glove box.
- **Brake Vacuum Light Module (Gas)** – is located behind the instrument panel, to the left of the radio.
- **Brake Vacuum Switch** – is located on the brake vacuum booster.
- **Convertible Top Relays** – are located in the trunk, near the top of the motor.
- **Convertible Top Time-Delay Module** – under the dash panel, near the junction block.
- **Coolant Temperature Sensor** – is located on the left front of the diesel engine and on the front near the radiator inlet on the gas engine.
- **Cruise Control Brake Switch** – is attached to the brake pedal mounting bracket.
- **Cruise Control Buffer Amplifier (Gas)** – is connected to the speed sensor harness behind the instrument cluster.
- **Cruise Control Controller (Diesel)** – is located behind the headlight switch in the instrument panel.
- **Cruise Control Servo (Gas)** – is located on the front of the engine on the diesel models and onthe left rear of the engine on the gas engines. They are attached to the power unit diaphragm.
- **Cruise Control Speed Sensor** – is attached to the speedometer behind the instrument cluster.
- **Defogger Relay** – is located on the relay panel above the lower instrument panel cover, to the left of the steering column.
- **Demand Hi-Beam Relay** – is taped to the wire harness near the fuse block.
- **Diode Module (Diesel)** – is taped to the wiring harness behind the radio.
- **Door Lock Relay** – is located on the upper right side of the cowl behind the glove box.
- **Electronic Control Module (ECM)** – is located behind the dash panel, below the glove box liner.
- **Engine Metal Temperature Switch** – is located on the rear of the left cylinder head.
- **Fast Idle Switch (Diesel)** – is is located on the rear of the left cylinder head.
- **Fourth Gear Switch** – is located in the transmission to the lower left side of the engine.
- **Fuel Pump Relay (Gas)** – is located in the relay panel above the lower instrument panel cover, to the left of the steering column.
- **Glow Plug Control Switch** – is located on the right front of the intake manifold.
- **Glow Plug Relay** – is located on the right front inner fender well.
- **Glow Plug Temperature Switch** – is located on the rear of the left cylinder head.
- **Guidematic Relay** – is located under the dash panel next to the fuse block.
- **Horn Relay** – is located on the relay panel above the lower instrument panel cover, to the left of the steering column.
- **Illuminated Entry Time Delay Relay** – is attached to the cowl above the junction block.
- **Level Control Height Sensor** – is mounted in the frame crossmember, in front of the fuel tank.
- **Level Control Relay** – is located on the relay panel above the lower instrument panel cover, to the left of the steering column.
- **Manifold Absolute Pressure Sensor** – is located under the instrument panel to the right of the air distributor.

- **Manifold Air Temperature Sensor**—is located on the intake manifold in front of the throttle body.
- **Oil Pressure Switch**—is located on the left front on the diesel engines and on the right front on the gas engines.
- **Outside Temperature Sensor**—is located at the rear of the radiator grille.
- **Oxygen Sensor**—is attached to the left exhaust manifold.
- **Power Accessories Circuit Breaker**—is located in the fuse block.
- **Power Seat Relay**—is located under the driver's seat.
- **Power Window Circuit Breaker**—is located in the fuse block.
- **Power Window Defogger Circuit Breaker**—is located in the fuse block.
- **Power Window Relay (Front)**—is located in the shroud, below the center access hole.
- **Power Window Relay (Rear)**—is located in the trunk, behind the seat.
- **Seat Belt Warning Chime**—is located under the instrument panel, to the left of the glove box liner.
- **Seat Belt Warning Timer**—is located under the instrument panel, is attached to the fuse block.
- **Starter Interupt Relay**—is located taped to the wire harness, near the turn signal flasher.
- **Stop/Turn Light Relays**—are located at the left rear quarter panel.
- **Tone Generator**—is located under instrument panel between the steering column and the radio.
- **Turn Signal Relay (1982-83 Seville)**—is attached to the rear package shelf under the speaker enclosures.
- **Twilight Sentinel Amplifier**—is located under the instrument panel on the relay panel mounting bracket.
- **Twilight Sentinel Photocell**—is located under the left front speaker grille on the diesel models and on the defroster grille on the gas models.

1985-87 ELDORADO, SEVILLE AND FLEETWOOD BROUGHAM

- **A/C Ambient Temperature Sensor (Eldorado/Seville)**—is located on the right side of the firewall, in the engine compartment.
- **A/C Ambient Temperature Sensor (Fleetwood Brougham)**—is located under left side of the dash panel, behind the glove box.
- **A/C Compressor Clutch Diode**—is located in the connector at the rear of the compressor.
- **A/C-Heater Resistors**—are located on the right side of the firewall in the engine compartment, in the top of the plenum.
- **Amplifier Relay**—is located under the instrument panel, near the fuse block.
- **Assembly Line Diagnostic Link Connector**—is located under the left side of the dash panel, near the ashtray.
- **Audio Alarm Module**—is located under the right side of the dash, to the left of the glove box (to the left of the radio on the Fleetwood Brougham).
- **Automatic Door Lock Controller**—is located behind the right side of the dash panel, near the glove box.
- **Barometeric Pressure Sensor**—is located under the instrument panel to the right of the glove box.
- **Convertible Top Relays**—are located in the trunk, near the top of the motor.
- **Convertible Top Time Delay Module**—is attached to the junction block under the left side of the dash.
- **Coolant Temperature Sensor**—is located on the top left side of the engine near the A/C compressor.
- **Cruise Control Module (Diesel)**—is located under the left side of the dash panel, to the left of the steering column.

- **Defogger Relay**—is located on the relay panel above the lower instrument panel cover, to the left of the steering column.
- **Demand Hi-Beam Relay**—is taped to the wire harness near the fuse block.
- **Diesel Electronic Control Module (DEC)**—is located behind the right side of the dash panel, near the glove box.
- **Door Lock Relay (Eldorado/Seville)**—is located on the upper right side of the cowl behind the glove box.
- **Door Lock Relay (Fleetwood Brougham)**—are located in each door.
- **Electronic Control Module (ECM)**—is located behind the right side of the dash panel, near the glove box.
- **Electronic Climate Control Power Module**—is located in the plenum on the right side of the firewall, in the engine compartment.
- **Electronic Climate Control Programmer**—is located under the right side of the dash panel, on the right side of the plenum.
- **Electronic Level Control Relay**—is located on the relay panel above the lower instrument panel cover, to the left of the steering column.
- **Electronic Level Control Test Connector(Eldorado/Seville)**—is located near of the left front wheelwell.
- **Electronic Level Control Test Connector(Fleetwood Brougham)**—is located on the left side of the firewall, to the left of the power brake unit.
- **Electronic Tune Radio Diode**—is located in the instrument panel wiring harness, behind the radio.
- **Fiber Optic Light Source**—are located one in each door.
- **Fiber Optic Light Source (Opera Lights)**—is located on the left rear wheelwell flange in the trunk.
- **Fuel Pump Relay (Gas)**—is located in the relay panel above the lower instrument panel cover, to the left of the steering column.
- **Glow Plug Controller/Relay**—is located on the top left side of the engine, to the left of the valve cover.
- **Guidematic Power Relay**—is located under the dash panel next to the fuse block.
- **Housing Pressure Cold Advance Relay**—is located on the relay panel above the lower instrument panel cover, to the left of the steering column.
- **Horn Relay**—is located on the relay panel above the lower instrument panel cover, to the left of the steering column.
- **Ignition Key Warning Module**—is located on the fuse block.
- **Illuminated Entry Timer**—is located behind the left side f the dash panel, to the left of the steering column.
- **In-Car Temperature Sensor**—is located in the right side of the dash panel, behind the trim plate.
- **Level Control Height Sensor**—is mounted on the rear crossmember.
- **Level Control Relay**—is located on the relay panel above the lower instrument panel cover, to the left of the steering column.
- **Lock Enable Relay (Eldorado/Seville)**—is located under the left side of the dash panel, above the junction block.
- **Lock Enable Relay (Fleetwood Brougham)**—is located behind the right side kick panel.
- **Manifold Absolute Pressure Sensor**—is located under the right side of instrument panel, behind the trimp panel.
- **Manifold Air Temperature Sensor**—is located on the intake manifold in front of the throttle body.
- **Outside Temperature Sensor**—is located at the rear of the radiator grille.
- **Oxygen Sensor**—is attached to the left exhaust manifold.
- **Power Antenna Relay**—is located on the relay panel above the lower instrument panel cover, to the left of the steering column.
- **Power Seat Memory Module**—is located below the driver's seat.

- **Power Seat Relay**—is located under the driver's seat.
- **Power Window Relay (Front)**—is located behind the left side kick panel, below the center access hole.
- **Power Window Relay (Rear)**—is located in the trunk, behind the seat.
- **Seat Belt Chime Module**—is located on the fuse block.
- **Seat Belt Timer**—is located on top of the fuse block.
- **Starter Interupt Relay**—is located taped to the wire harness, near the turn signal flasher.
- **Stop/Turn Light Relays**—are located in the trunk, at the left rear quarter panel.
- **Theft Deterrent Controller**—is located under the left side of the dash, near the accelerator pedal bracket.
- **Theft Deterrent Diodes**—one is taped to the wiring harness connector at the upper end of the left kick panel. The other one is taped to the wiring harness connector near the fuse block.

- **Theft Deterrent Relay**—is located under the left side of the instrument panel, on or near the theft deterrent controller.
- **Throttle Position Sensor**—is located on the top right side of the engine, near the throttle body.
- **Trunk Pull-Down In-Line Fuse**—near the latch at the center of the trunk lid.
- **Twilight Sentinel Amplifier**—is located under the left side of the dash panel, near the light switch assembly.
- **Twilight Sentinel Photocell**—is located on the top left side of the dash panel, below the left side speaker grille.
- **Vehicle Speed Sensor**—is located on the right side of the transaxle.
- **Vehicle Speed Sensor Buffer**—is located under the left side of the dash panel, near the steering column.
- **Washer Indicator Diode**—is located behind the instrument cluster on the Eldorado and Seville gas engine models.

COMPONENT LOCATIONS

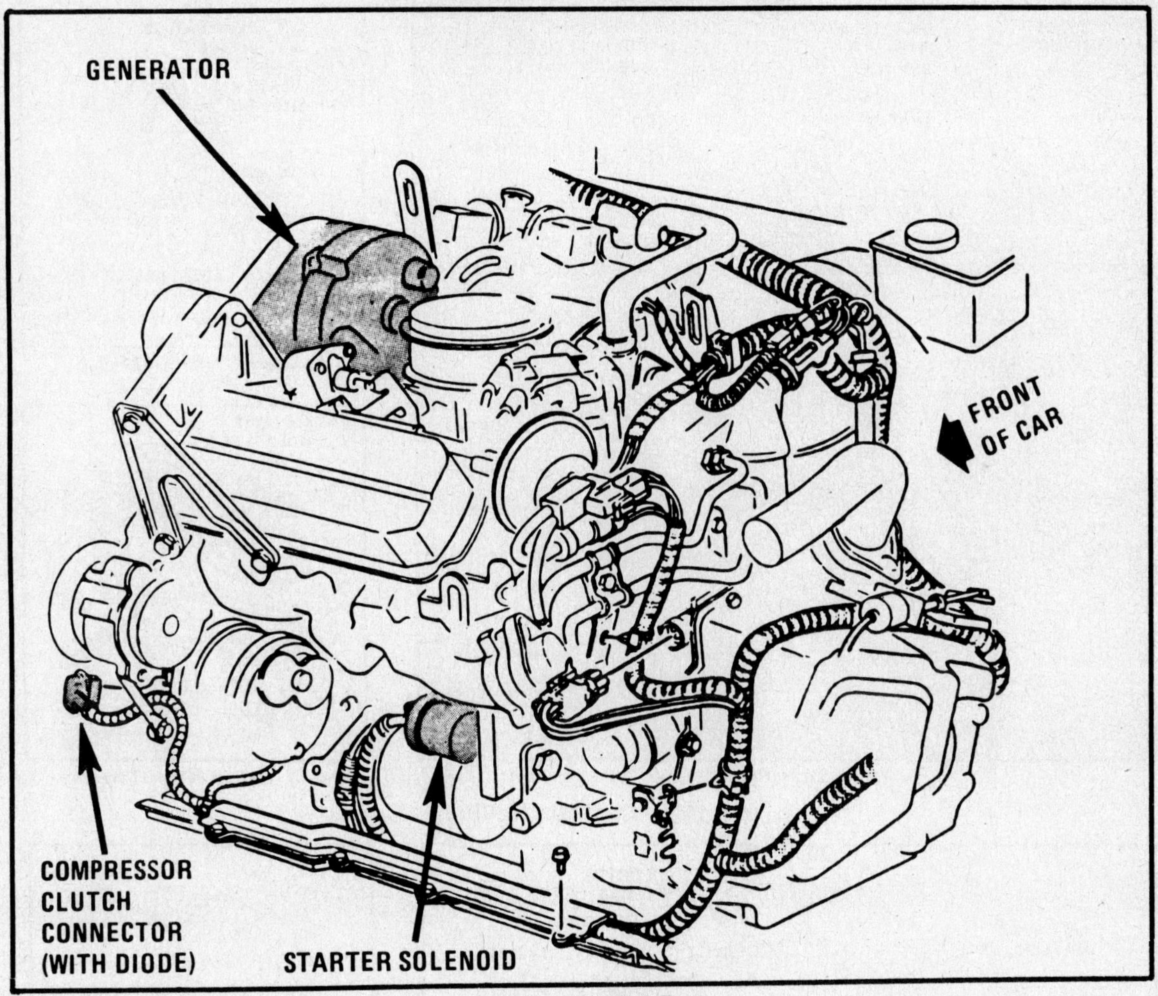

GENERATOR

FRONT OF CAR

COMPRESSOR CLUTCH CONNECTOR (WITH DIODE)

STARTER SOLENOID

Front Of VIN 8 Engine

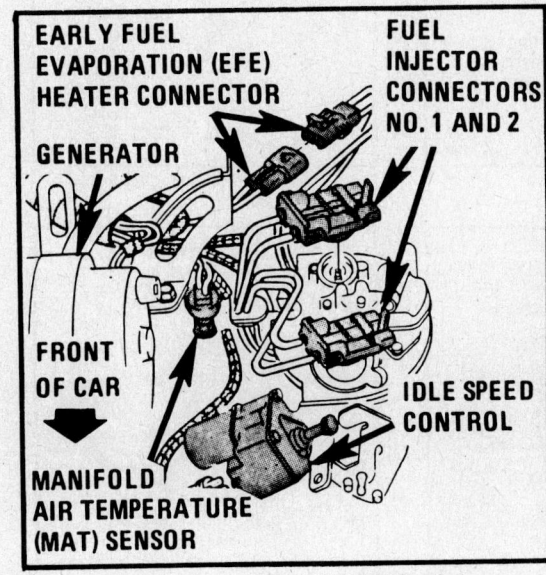

EARLY FUEL EVAPORATION (EFE) HEATER CONNECTOR

FUEL INJECTOR CONNECTORS NO. 1 AND 2

GENERATOR

FRONT OF CAR

MANIFOLD AIR TEMPERATURE (MAT) SENSOR

IDLE SPEED CONTROL

Top Of VIN 8 Engine

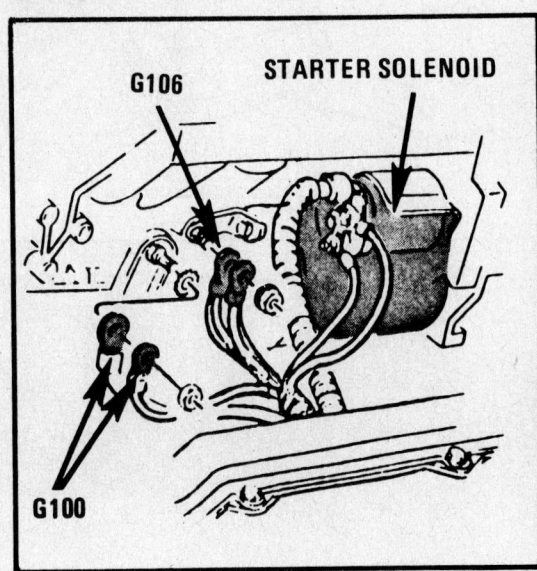

G106

STARTER SOLENOID

G100

Bottom Front Of Vin 8 Engine

1986 Cadillac DeVille

COMPONENT LOCATIONS

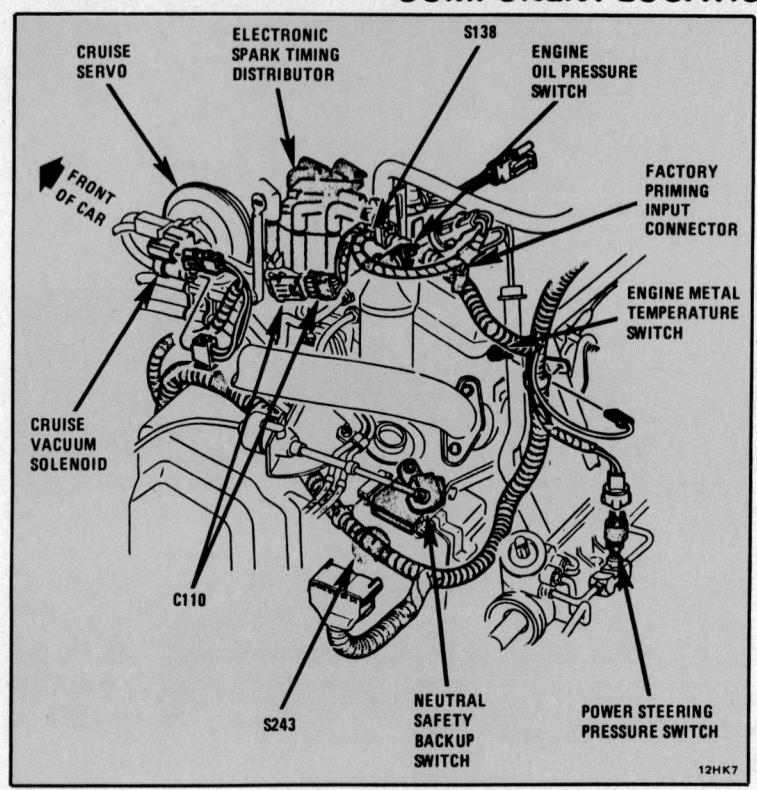

Figure A - LH Side Of VIN 8 Engine

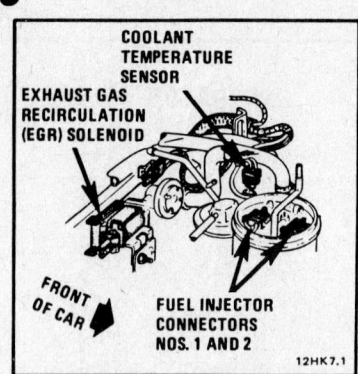

Figure B - Top Of VIN 8 Engine

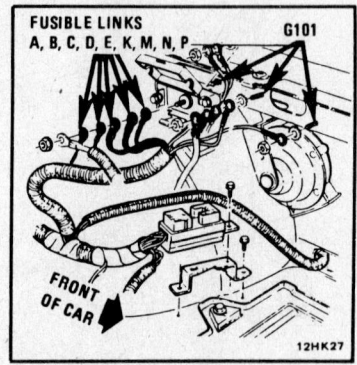

Figure C - LH Front Of Engine Compartment

1986 Cadillac DeVille

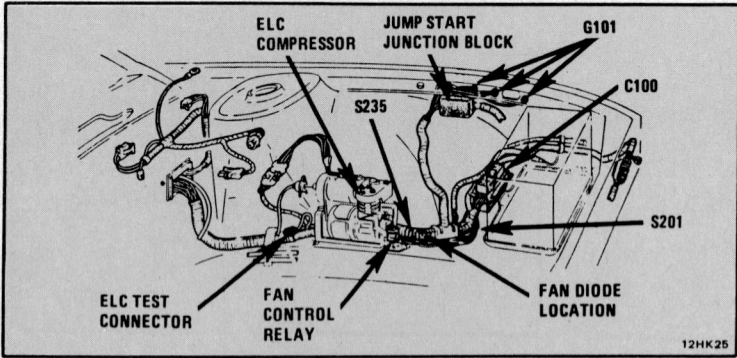

Figure A - Top Of VIN 8 Engine

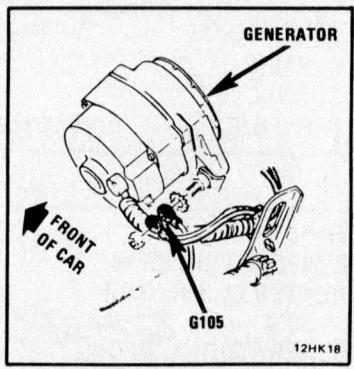

Figure C - RH Side Of VIN 8 Engine

Figure B - LH Side Of Engine Compartment

Figure D - Inside LH Front Fender

1986 Cadillac DeVille

COMPONENT LOCATIONS

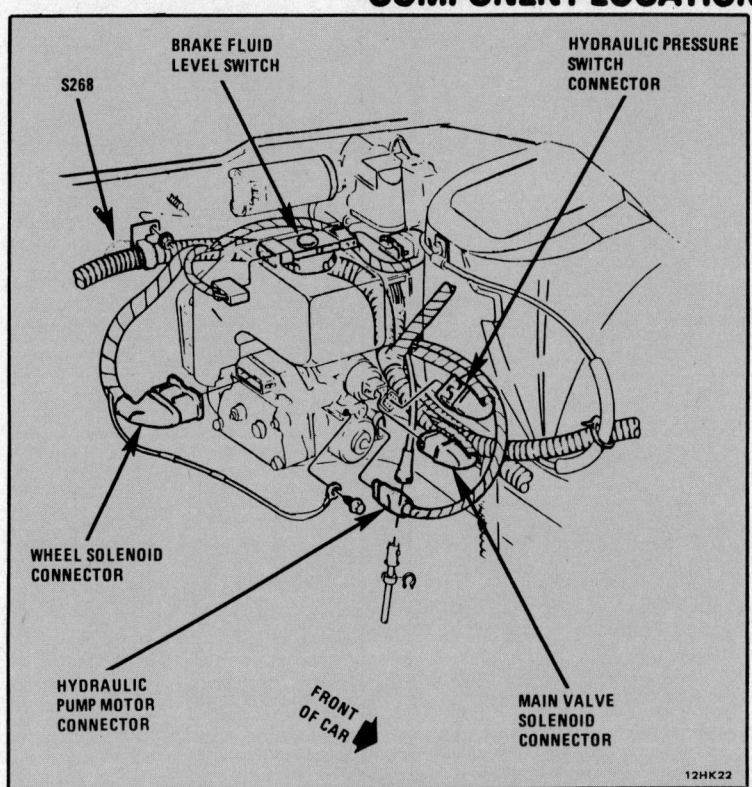

Figure A - Brake Hydraulic Unit (With Antilock Brake)

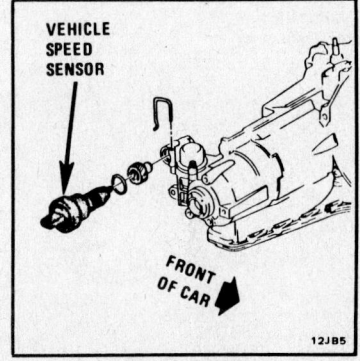

Figure B - LH Front Of Dash (Without Antilock Brake)

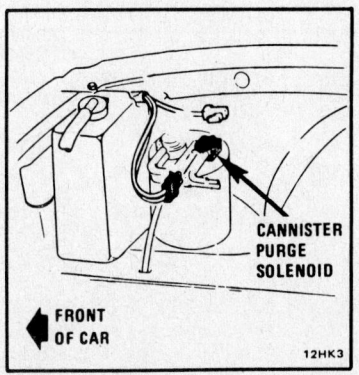

Figure C - Transaxle

1986 Cadillac DeVille

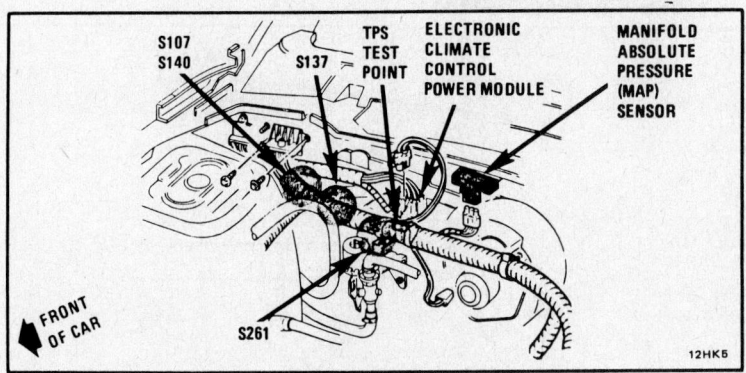

Figure A - RH Front Of Dash

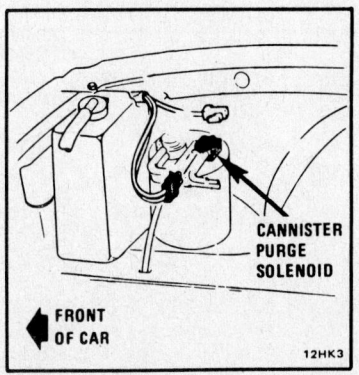

Figure D - Front RH Side Of Engine Compartment

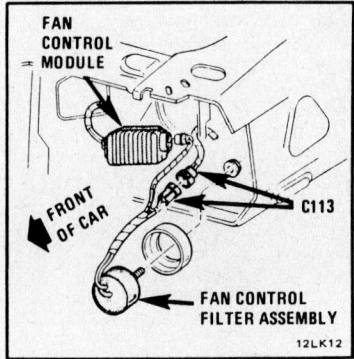

Figure B - Behind LH Headlamps

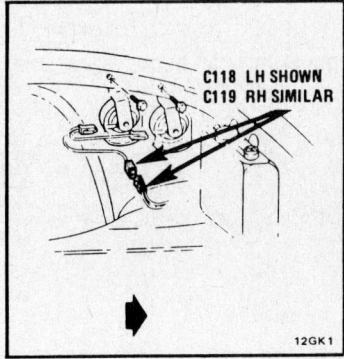

Figure C - Front LH Side Of Engine Compartment

Figure E - Above RH Rear Suspension

1986 Cadillac DeVille

COMPONENT LOCATIONS

Figure A - Behind LH Side Of I/P

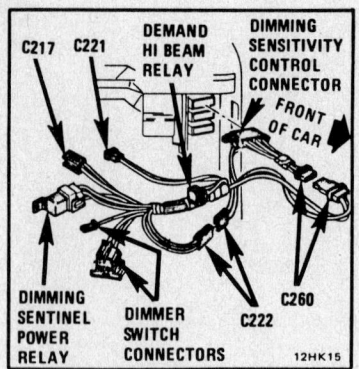

Figure D - Behind Side Of I/P

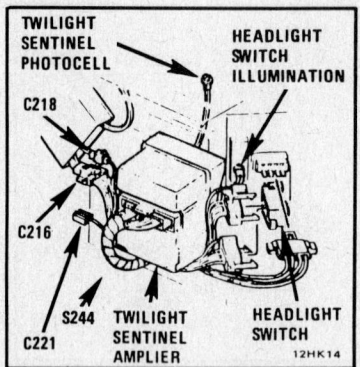

Figure B - Behind LH Side Of I/P
With Twilight Sentinel

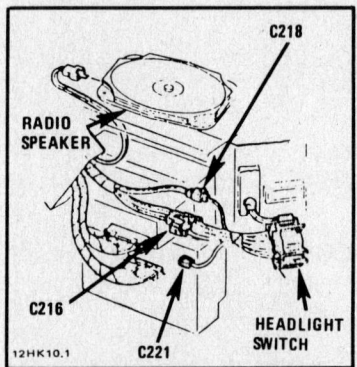

Figure C - Behind LH Side Of I/P
Without Twilight Sentinel

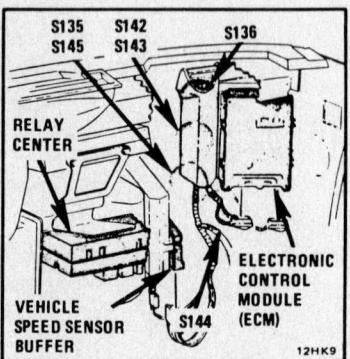

Figure E - Behind RH Side Of I/P

1986 Cadillac DeVille

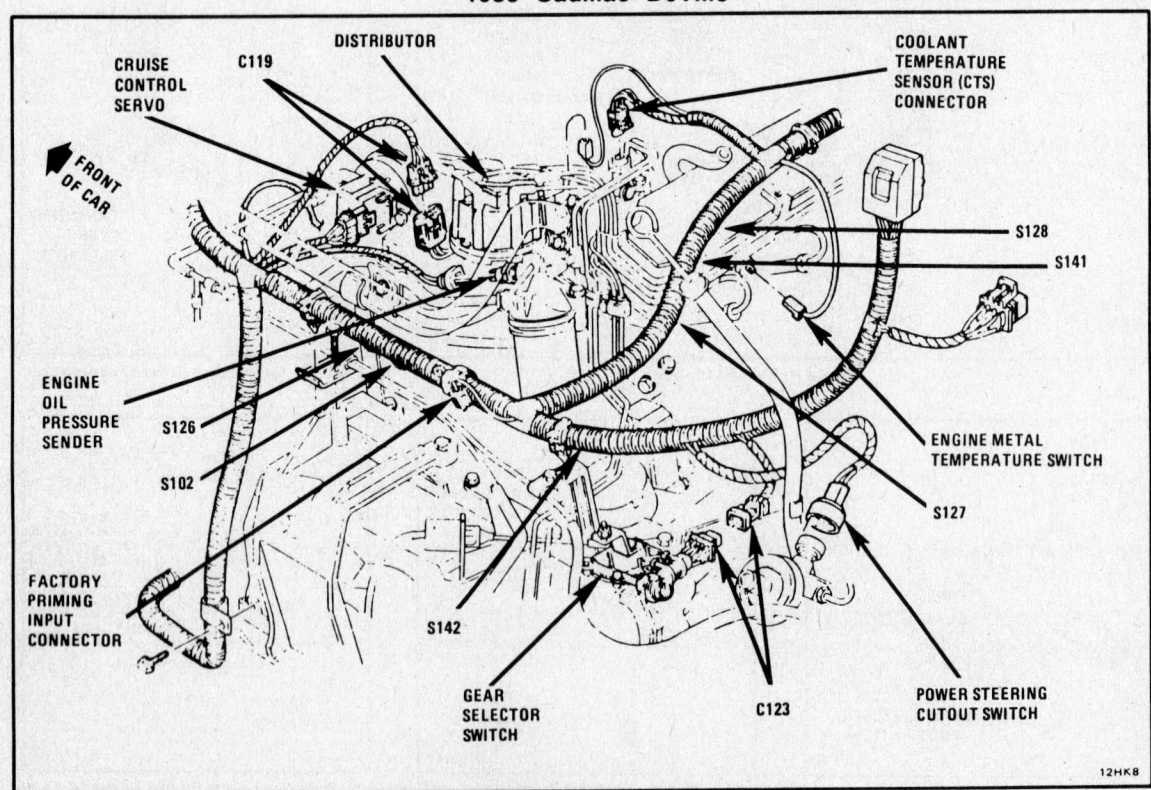

Figure A - LH Side Of Engine

1986 Cadillac Eldorado and Seville

COMPONENT LOCATIONS

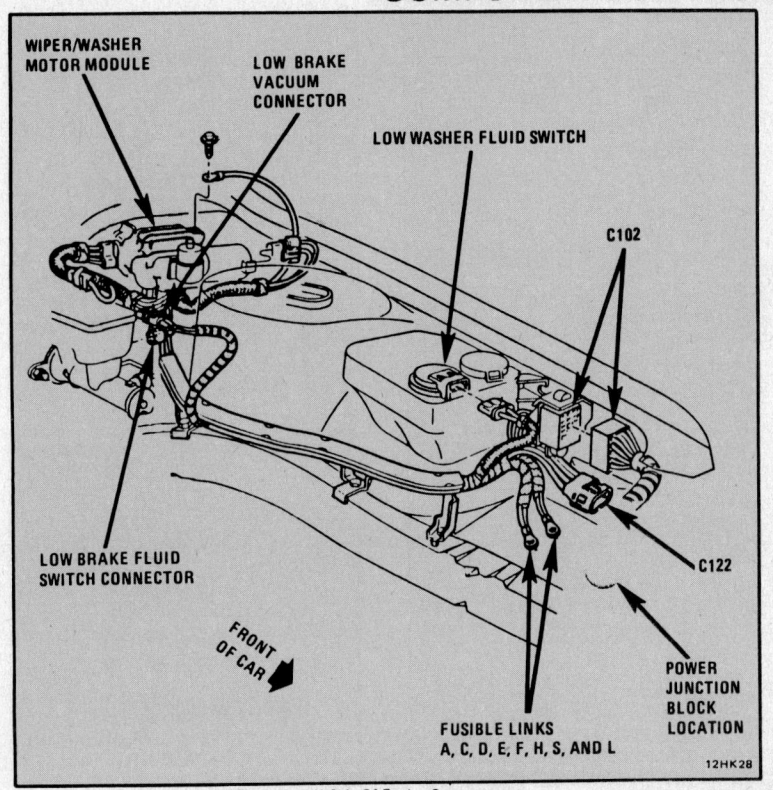

Figure A - LH Side Of Engine Compartment

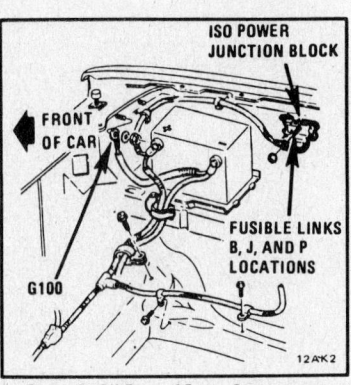

Figure B - RH Front of Engine Compartment

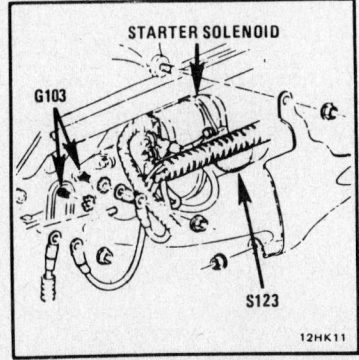

Figure C - Front Of Engine

1986 Cadillac Eldorado and Seville

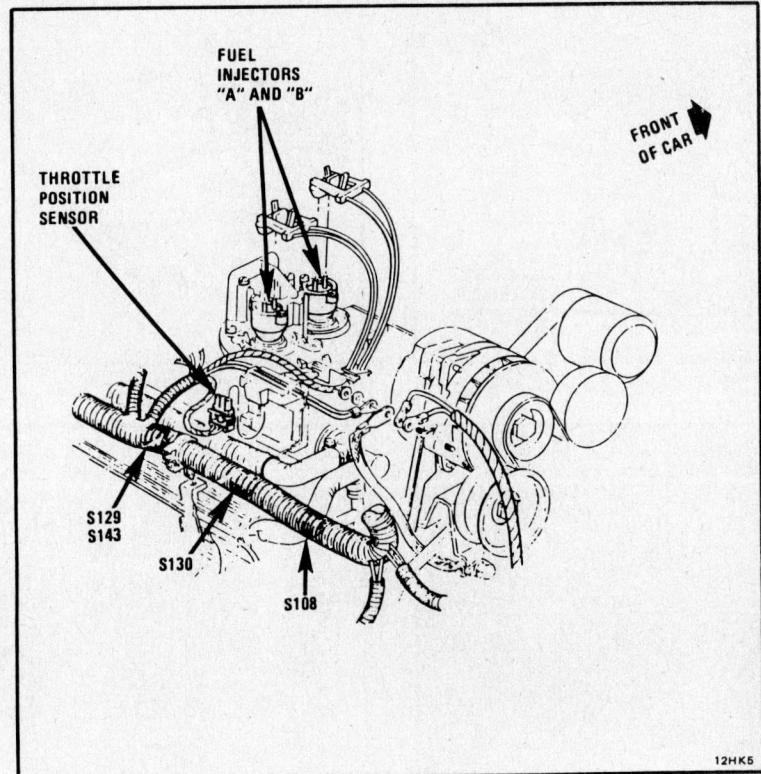

Figure A - Top RH Of Engine

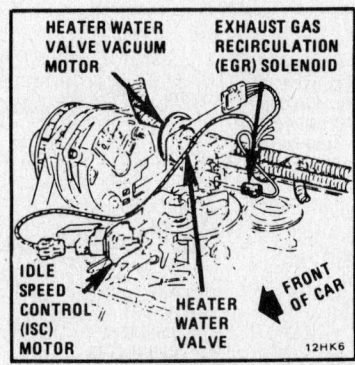

Figure B - Top RH Side Of Engine

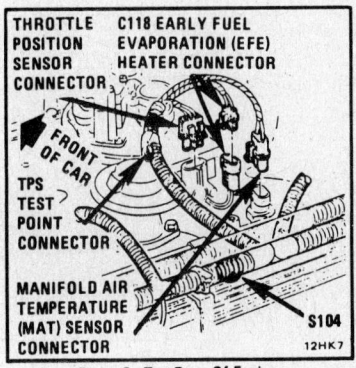

Figure C - Top Rear Of Engine

1986 Cadillac Eldorado and Seville

COMPONENT LOCATIONS

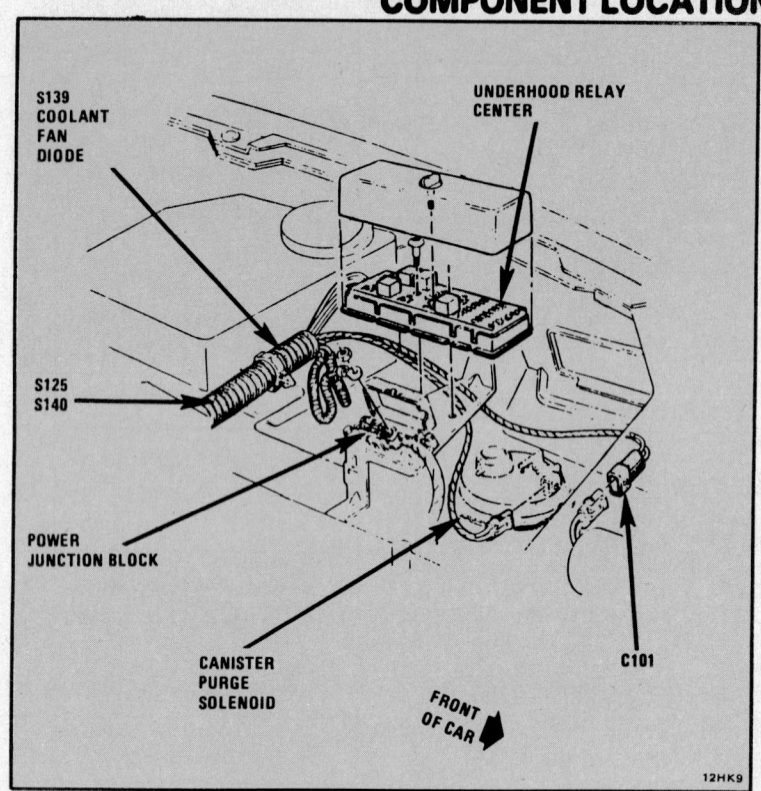

Figure A - LH Front Of Engine Compartment

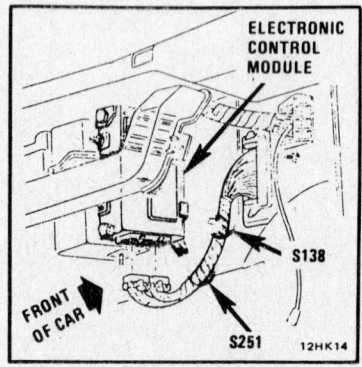

Figure B - LH Front Of Car

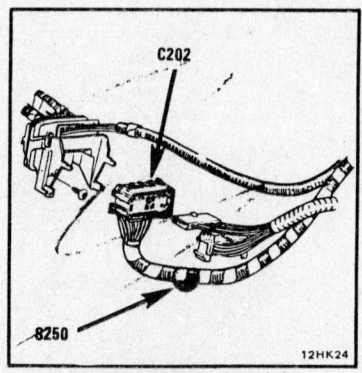

Figure C - Behind RH Side Of I/P

1986 Cadillac Eldorado and Seville

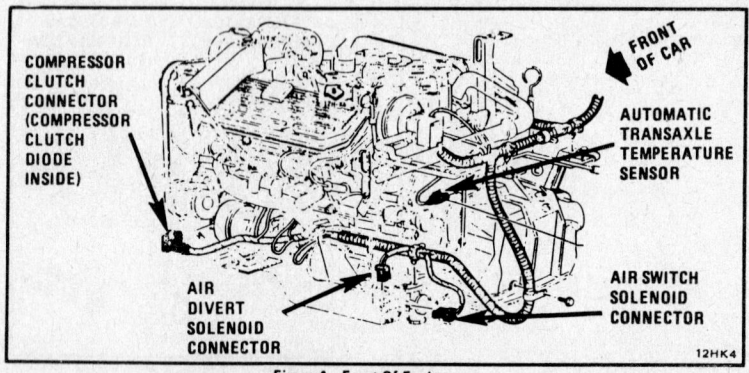

Figure A - Front Of Engine

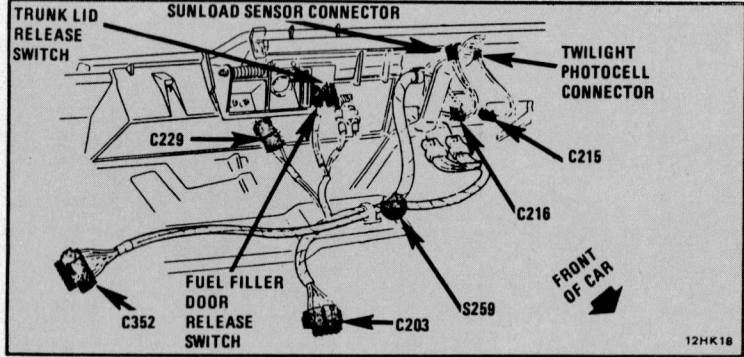

Figure B - Rear Of Center Of I/P

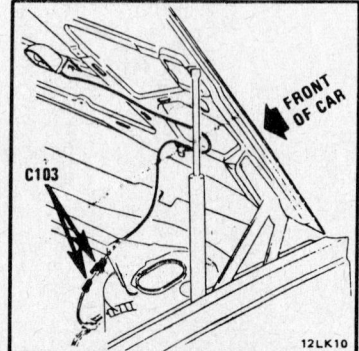

Figure C - Behind LH Side Of I/P

Figure D - LH Rear Corner Of Engine Compartment

1986 Cadillac Eldorado and Seville

COMPONENT LOCATIONS

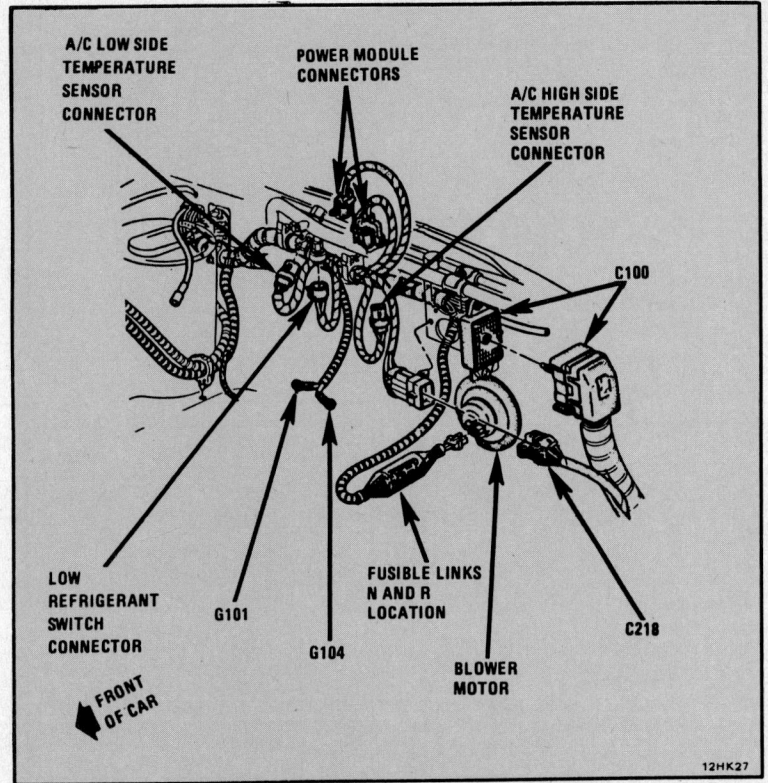

Figure A - Front Of Dash And RH Side Of Engine Compartment

12HK27

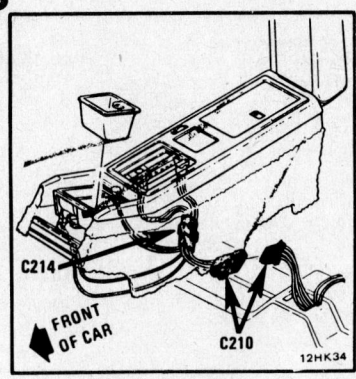

Figure B - Center Console

12HK34

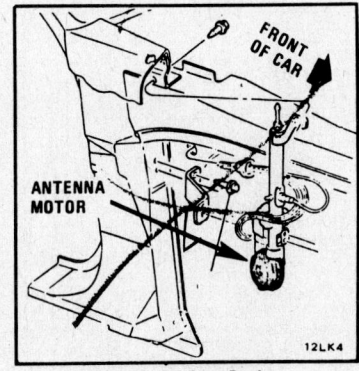

Figure C - RH Front Fender

12LK4

1986 Cadillac Eldorado and Seville

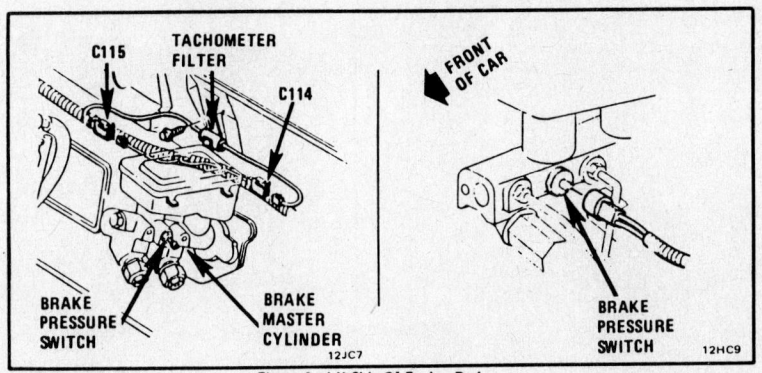

Figure A - LH Side Of Engine Dash

12JC7   12HC9

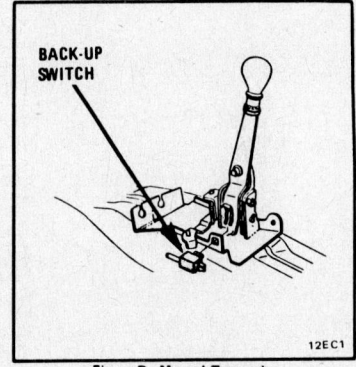

Figure D - Manual Transaxle

12EC1

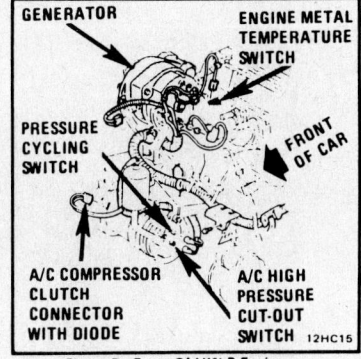

Figure B - Front Of VIN P Engine

12HC15

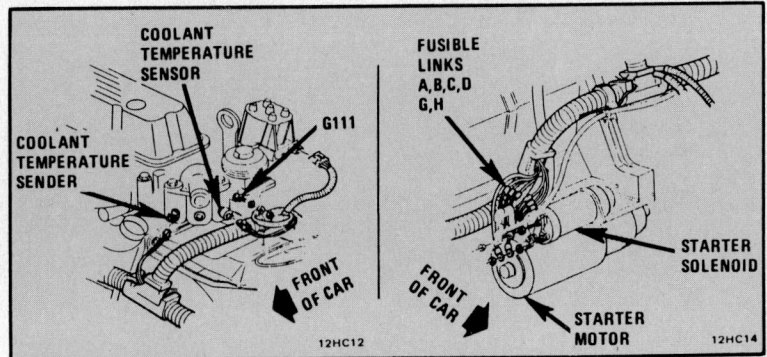

Figure C - LH End Of VIN P Engine

12HC12   12HC14

1986 Cadillac Cimarron

COMPONENT LOCATIONS

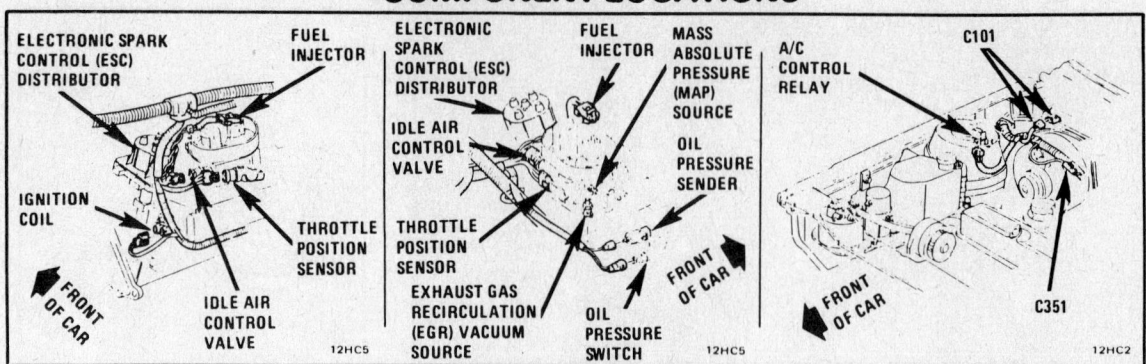

Figure A - Top Rear Of VIN P Engine

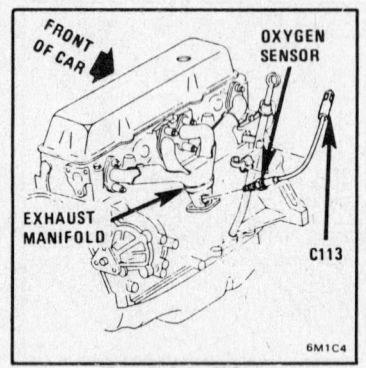

Figure B - Front Of Engine

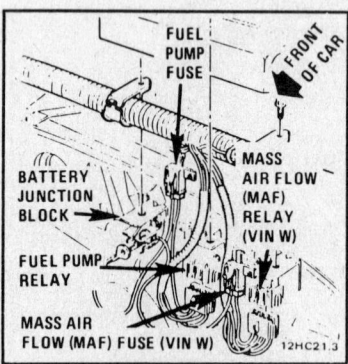

Figure C - LH Front Of Dash

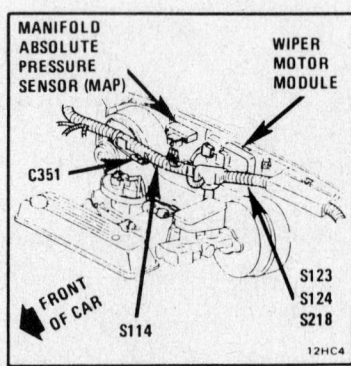

Figure D - RH Rear Corner Of Engine Compartment

1986 Cadillac Cimarron

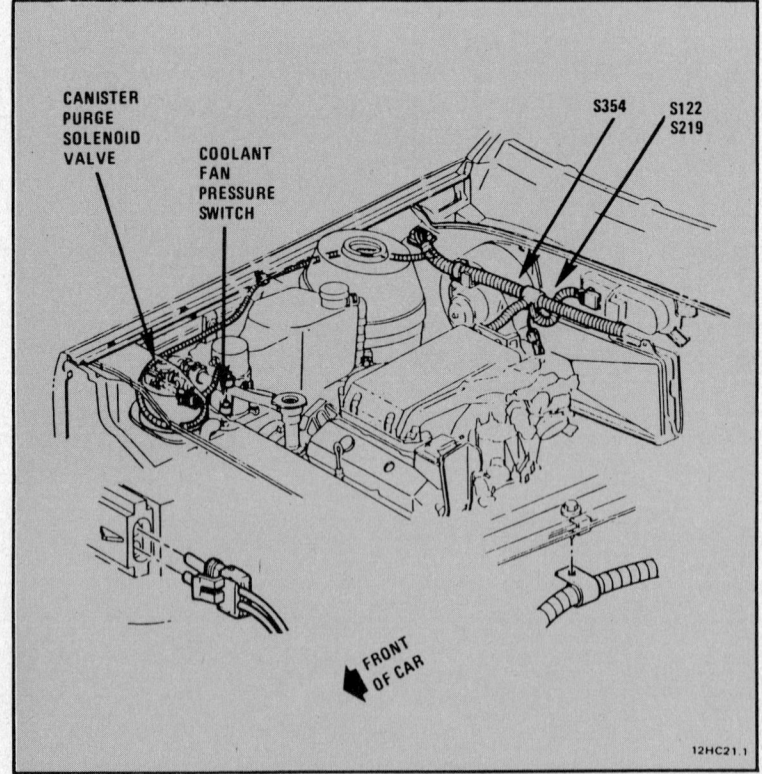

Figure A - VIN W Engine Compartment

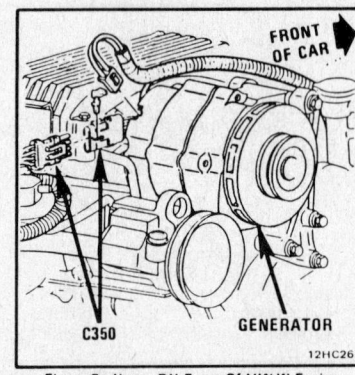

Figure B - Upper RH Front Of VIN W Engine

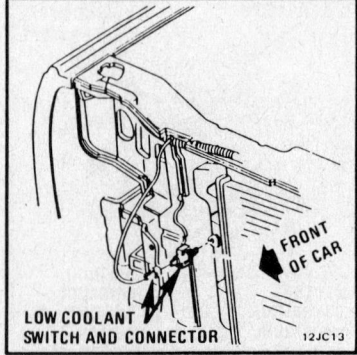

Figure C - RH Front Of Radiator Bracket (Vin W)

1986 Cadillac Cimarron

COMPONENT LOCATIONS

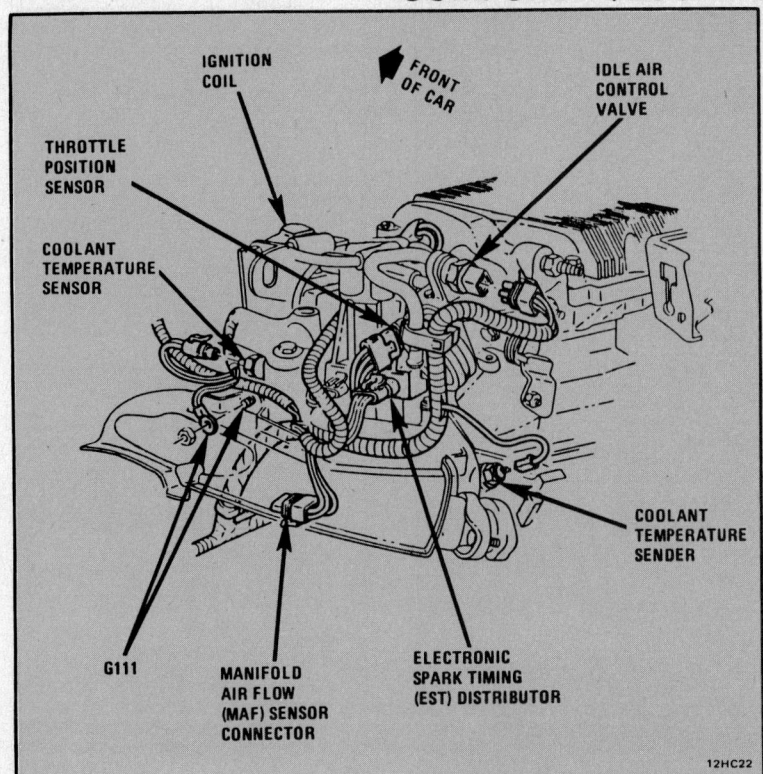

Figure A - Upper LH Rear Of VIN W Engine

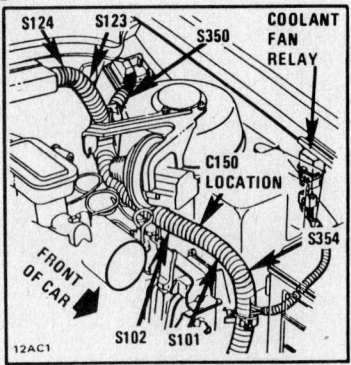

Figure B - LH Rear Corner Of Engine Compartment

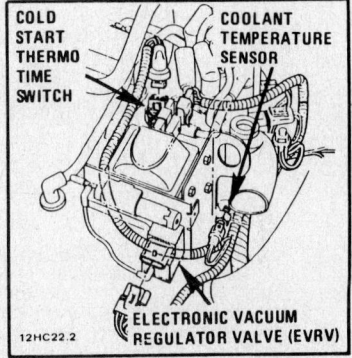

Figure C - Upper LH Front Of VIN W Engine

1986 Cadillac Cimarron

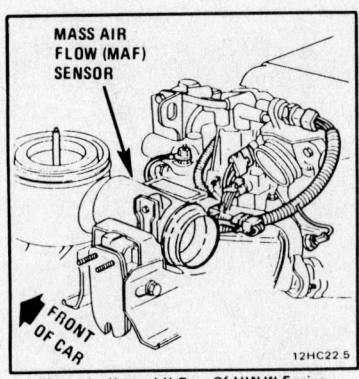

Figure A - Upper LH Rear Of VIN W Engine

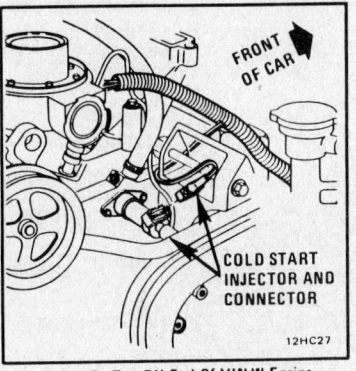

Figure C - Top RH End Of VIN W Engine

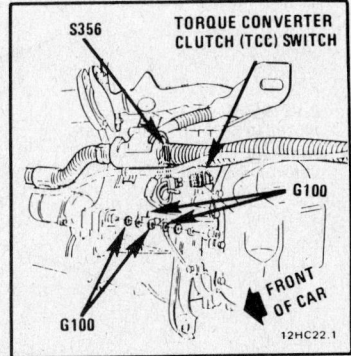

Figure E - Automatic Transaxle (3 Speed)

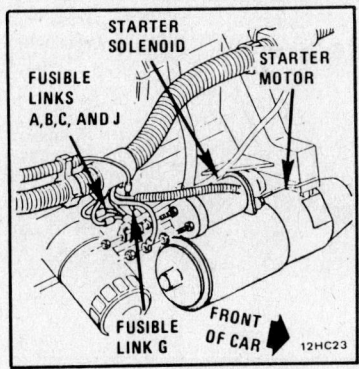

Figure B - Lower LH Front Of VIN W Engine

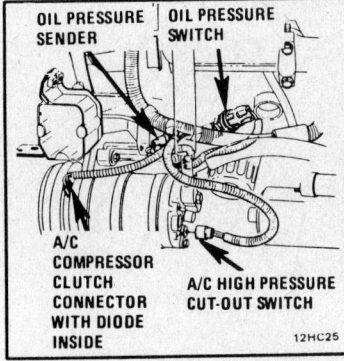

Figure D - Lower RH Front Of Vin W Engine

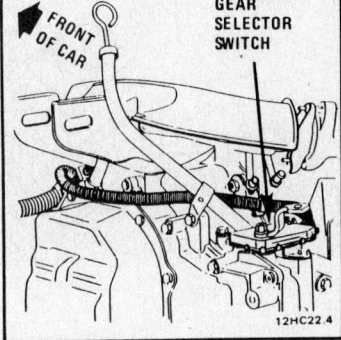

Figure F - Automatic Transaxle (3 Speed)

1986 Cadillac Cimarron

125

COMPONENT LOCATIONS

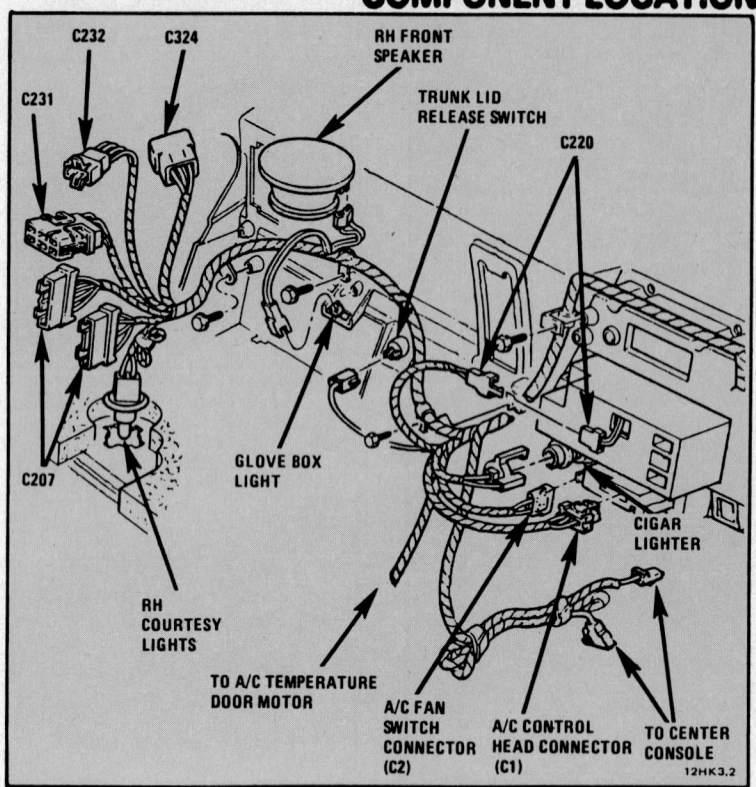

Figure A - Behind RH Side Of I/P

12HK3.2

Labels: C232, C324, C231, RH FRONT SPEAKER, TRUNK LID RELEASE SWITCH, C220, C207, GLOVE BOX LIGHT, RH COURTESY LIGHTS, TO A/C TEMPERATURE DOOR MOTOR, A/C FAN SWITCH CONNECTOR (C2), A/C CONTROL HEAD CONNECTOR (C1), TO CENTER CONSOLE, CIGAR LIGHTER

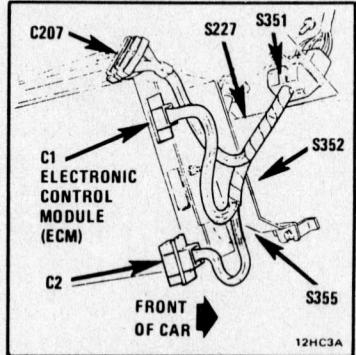

Figure B - Behind RH Side Of I/P (VIN P)

12HC3

Labels: C207, S219, C1 ELECTRONIC CONTROL MODULE (ECM), S227, C2, FRONT OF CAR

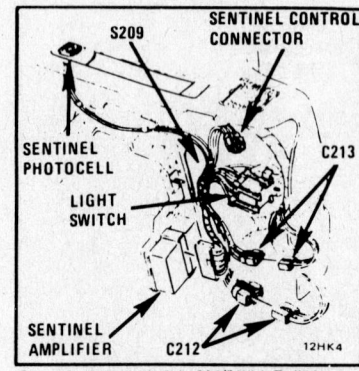

Figure C - Behind RH Side Of I/P (VIN W)

12HC3A

Labels: C207, S227, S351, C1 ELECTRONIC CONTROL MODULE (ECM), S352, C2, S355, FRONT OF CAR

1986 Cadillac Cimarron

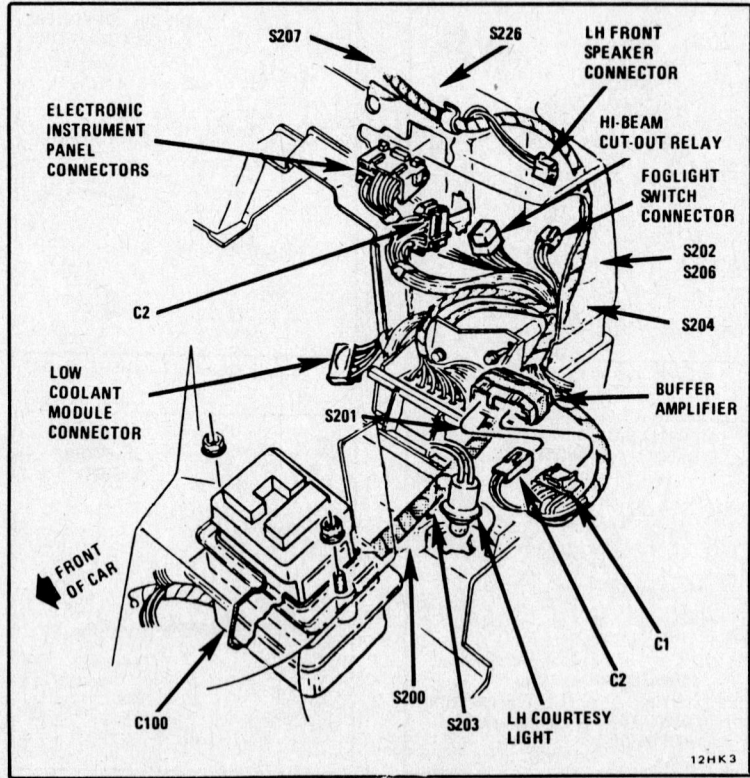

Figure A - Behind LH Side Of I/P

12HK3

Labels: S207, S226, LH FRONT SPEAKER CONNECTOR, ELECTRONIC INSTRUMENT PANEL CONNECTORS, HI-BEAM CUT-OUT RELAY, FOGLIGHT SWITCH CONNECTOR, S202, S206, C2, S204, LOW COOLANT MODULE CONNECTOR, BUFFER AMPLIFIER, S201, FRONT OF CAR, C1, C2, C100, S200, S203, LH COURTESY LIGHT

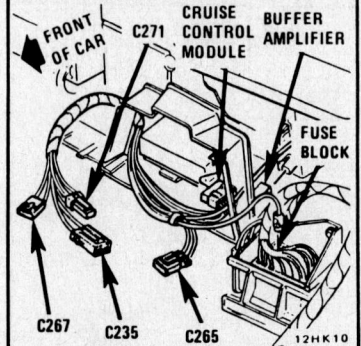

Figure B - Behind LH Side Of I/P With Twilight Sentinel, Without Twilight Sentinel Similar

12HK4

Labels: S209, SENTINEL CONTROL CONNECTOR, SENTINEL PHOTOCELL, LIGHT SWITCH, C213, SENTINEL AMPLIFIER, C212

Figure C - Behind LH Side Of I/P

12HK10

Labels: FRONT OF CAR, C271, CRUISE CONTROL MODULE, BUFFER AMPLIFIER, FUSE BLOCK, C267, C235, C265

1986 Cadillac Cimarron

CHEVROLET

Circuit Breakers

HEADLIGHTS

There is a circuit breaker incorporated in the headlight switch to protect the headlight circuit.

REAR WINDOW DEFOGGER

There is a circuit breaker located in the fuse block to protect the rear window defogger circuit on all models except the El Camino and the Chevette. The Chevette circuit breaker is located on the left side inner fender skirt.

WINDSHIELD WIPER

This circuit breaker is integral with the windshield wiper motor on all models except the Chevette and the Cavalier.

POWER ACCESSORIES

This circuit breaker is located in the fuse block on all models except the Chevette.

Fusible Links

The fusible links are used on all models and are usually located in the engine compartment. All models use fusible links attached to the starter solenoid to protect the wiring in the starter circuit. Some models may use a fusible link at the alternator and the under hood lighting wiring. The diesel models use fusible links to protect the glow plug circuits. All models(except the Chevette) equipped with Electronic Spark Timing use a fusible link at the electronic spark timing distributor.

Relay, Sensors And Computer Locations

1982-84 EL CAMINO, MALIBU AND MONTE CARLO

- **A/C Blower Relay** – is located in the blower motor assembly.
- **A/C Cut-Out Switch** – is located on the accelerator pedal.
- **A/C-Heater Blower Resistors** – is located in the heater module in front of the blower motor.
- **A/C Pressure Cycling Switch** – is located on the top of the vacuum tank.
- **A/C Temperature Cut-Out Relay** – is located behind the right front fender apron or at the center of the firewall.
- **A/C Temperature Cut-Out Switch** – is located on the left front side of the engine near the alternator.
- **Altitude Advance Relay (1984 Diesel)** – is located on the upper center of the firewall.
- **Barometric Pressure Sensor** – is located behind the right side of the instrument panel.
- **Brake Pressure Switch** – is located on the rear base of the left front wheel well.
- **"Check Engine" Light Driver Module** – is taped to the instrument panel harness to the left of the glove box.
- **Choke Heater Relay** – is located on the left engine cowl to the right of the steering column.
- **Cold Advance Diode (1984 Diesel)** – is located in the engine harness, to the right of the master cylinder.
- **Cold Inhibit Switch (Diesel)** – is located below the right valve cover.

- **Coolant Temperature Sensor** – is located on the front of ther engine behind the alternator on the V6 engines and on the top left front of the engine ong the V8. Behind the water on the diesel engine.
- **Coolant Temperature Switch** – is located on the top of the engine behind the alternator or water pump on the V6 and diesel engine and on the left side of the engine near the exhaust manifold on the V8 engines.
- **Cruise Control Unit** – is located under the left side of the dash panel, above the accelerator pedal.
- **Defogger Timer (1982-83)** – is located under the left side of the instrument panel attached to the top of the fuse block.
- **Diesel Electronics Module** – is located behind the instrument panel to the right of the glove box behind the right kick panel.
- **Door Lock Relay** – is located on the lower right kick panel at the bottom access hole.
- **Early Fuel Evaporation (EFE) Relay** – is located on the front of the engine. On the 1984 models this relay is located at the right side of the engine compartment, above the wheel well.
- **Early Fuel Evaporation Solenoid** – is located at the top center of the right valve cover.
- **EGR Cut-Out Relay (1982-83)** – is located on the right front fender well.
- **EGR Solenoid** – is located at the top center of the right valve cover on the V6 engine and on the bracket rear of the right valve cover or top front left side on the V8 engines.
- **Electronic Control Module (ECM)** – is located on the right shroud near the lower access hole.
- **Electronic Spark Control Module (1984)** – is located above the right wheel well on the V6 engine and at the top left side of the engine on the V8 engine.
- **Engine Temperature Switch (Diesel)** – is located below the left valve cover. On the 84 models this switch is located behind the water pump.
- **Fast Idle Relay** – is located on the left side of the engine cowl.
- **Fast Idle Solenoid** – is located on the top of the engine near the front.
- **Fuel Metering Solenoid** – is located on the right side of the carburetor on the V6 engine and/or the top right side of the engine on the V8.
- **Gear Selector Switch** – is attached to the base of the steering column.
- **Glow Plug Controller** – is located at the top left rear of the engine, above the glow plug relay.
- **Glow Plug Relay (Diesel)** – is located on the top of the right front fender well.
- **High Altitude Advance Solenoid (1984 Diesel)** – is located in the fuel line, near the right valve cover.
- **Horn Relay** – is located behind the left side of the instrument panel above the fuse block.
- **Ignition Key Warning Buzzer** – is located behind the left side of the dash panel.
- **Lights-On Buzzer** – is attached to the fuse block.
- **Low Altitude Advance Solenoid (1984 Diesel)** – is located above the right valve cover.
- **Low Altitude Diode (1984 Diesel)** – is located in the engine harness, to the right of the master cylinder.
- **Low Brake Vacuum Delay Module** – is taped to the instrument panel harness above the fuse block.
- **Manifold Absolute Pressure Sensor** – is located on the top right front fender well.

- **Multi-Function Chime Module** — is located behind the instrument panel to the left of the steering column at the convenience center.
- **Oil Pressure Sender/Switch** — is located on the right rear of the engine on the V6 diesel and/or the front of the engine on the other engines.
- **Oxygen Sensor** — is located in the right rear exhaust manifold on the V6 and/or below the the right valve cover on the V8.
- **Power Antenna Relay** — is located behind the right side of the glove box on 1982-83 models on the 84 models the relay is behind the center of the instrument panel to the right of the radio.
- **Power Door Lock and Power Seat Circuit Breaker** — is located in the fuse block.
- **Seat Belt Timer Buzzer** — is located behind left side of the instrument panel at the convenience center.
- **Theft Deterrent Control Unit** — is located behind the instrument panel to the left of the steering column.
- **Theft Deterrent Diode** — is taped to the instrument panel harness to the left of the steering column.
- **Theft Deterrent Relay** — is located behind the instrument panel to the left of the steering column.
- **Throttle Kicker Relay (1984)** — is located on the firewall near the brake booster.
- **Throttle Position Sensor** — is located at the front of the carburetor.
- **Tone Generator (1984)** — is located at the convenience center.
- **Torque Converter Clutch Switch** — is located on the brake pedal support.
- **Trunk Release Solenoid** — is located at the rear center of the trunk lid, just above the license plate.
- **Turbo Boost Indicator Switch** — is located above the front part of the left front fender well.
- **Vacuum Regulator Vacuum Switch (1984 Diesel)** — is located just forward of the intake manifold crossover.
- **Vacuum Sensor (on the V8)** — is connect to the right front fender well.
- **Vehicle Speed Sensor** — is located behind the speedometer.
- **Wastegate Solenoid** — is located at the rear of the left valve cover.
- **Wide Open Throttle Relay (1984)** — is located at the rear of the engine compartment.
- **Window and Sunroof Circuit Breaker** — is located under the left side of the dash panel, at the fuse block.

1985-87 EL CAMINO, MALIBU AND MONTE CARLO

- **A/C Blower Relay** — is located on the evaporator case behind the acumulator
- **A/C Compressor Clutch Diode** — is taped to the inside compressor connector on the front of the compressor.
- **A/C Cut-Out Switch** — is located on the accelerator pedal bracket.
- **A/C Fast Idle Solenoid** — is located to the left of the carburetor on the gas engines and on the top center of the engine on the diesel models.
- **A/C-Heater Blower Resistors** — are located on the evaporator case in the engine compartment.
- **A/C Pressure Cycling Switch** — is located on the right side of the firewall on the accumulator.
- **A/C Temperature Cut-Out Relay** — is located behind the right front fender apron or at the center of the firewall.
- **Altitude Advance Relay (Diesel)** — is located on the upper center of the firewall.

- **Ambient Temperature Sensor** — is located under the right side of the dash panel, above rthe blower motor.
- **Anti-Diesel Solenoid** — is located on the left front valve cover.
- **Assembly Line Diagonstic Connector** — is located on the bootom left center of the dash panel.
- **Barometric Pressor Sensor (V6)** — is located behind the right side of the dash panel above the glove box.
- **Barometric Pressor Sensor (V8)** — is located on a braket with the ESC module.
- **Brake Accumulator Pressure Switch** — is located on the left side of the firewall, near the brake booster.
- **Brake Torque Converter Clutch Switch** — is located at the top of the brake pedal support.
- **Camshaft Sensor** — is located at the front center of the engine.
- **Choke Heater Relay** — is located on the left engine cowl to the right of the steering column.
- **"Check Engine" Light Driver** — is taped to the instrumnet panel harness at the left of the glove box.
- **Coolant Temperature Sending Unit** — is located at the top of the engine.
- **Coolant Temperature Sensor** — is located at the top of the engine.
- **Coolant Temperature Switch (3.8L)** — is located behind the water pump at the top of the engine.
- **Coolant Temperature Switch (4.3L)** — is located behind the A/C compressor.
- **Coolant Temperature Switch (V8)** — is located on the left side of the engine, below the exhaust manifold.
- **Crankshaft Sensor** — is located at the front center of the engine.
- **Cruise Control Module** — is located under the left isde of the dash panel, above the accelerator pedal.
- **Defogger Timer Relay** — is located under the left side of the instrument panel attached to the top of the fuse block.
- **Detonation (Knock) Sensor (3.8L)** — is located on the top rear side of the engine.
- **Detonation (Knock) Sensor (4.3L)** — is located on the lower left side of the engine block.
- **Detonation (Knock) Sensor (V8-Gas)** — is located on the lower right side of the engine block in fron tof the starter motor.
- **Diagnostic Dwell Meter Connector** — is strapped to the wiring harness at the top right side of the engine.
- **Diesel Electronic Control Module (DEC)** — is located behind the right side kick panel.
- **Differential Pressure Sensor** — is located at the right front corner of the engine compartment behind the reservoir compartment.
- **Door Lock Relay** — is located on the lower right kick panel at the bottom access hole.
- **Early Fuel Evaporation (EFE)** — is located at the top of the engine, above the water pump.
- **Early Fuel Evaporation (EFE) Relay with (gauges)** — this relay is located at the left side of the engine compartment, above the wheel well.
- **Early Fuel Evaporation (EFE) Relay (without gauges)** — this relay is located at the right side of the engine compartment, above the wheel well.
- **EGR Temperature Switch (4.3L)** — is located on the intake manifold, in front of the distributor.
- **Electronic Control Module (ECM)** — is located behind the right kick panel.
- **Electronic Level Control Relay** — is located on the electronic level control compressor.
- **Electronic Level Control Sensor** — is located on the rear portion of the crossmember.
- **Electronic Spark Control Module (ESC)** — is located on the bracket at the top of the right front fender well.

- **Electronic Vacuum Regulator Valve Module**—is located at the top center of the right valve cover.
- **EPR Solenoid (Diesel)**—is located on the right valve cover.
- **Fast Idle Relay**—is located on the same bracket as the electronic sapark control module, which is located at the top of the right front fender well.
- **Fuel Control In-Line Fuse**—is located on the bracket next to the ESC module, on the 4.3L V6 engine.
- **Fuel Metering Solenoid (3.8L)**—is located on the carburetor.
- **Fuel Pump Prime Connector**—is located in the wiring harness near the fuel control in-line fuse.
- **Fuel Pump Relay**—is located on a bracket in the right side of the engine compartment.
- **Fuel Shut-Off Solenoid (Diesel)**—is located under the fuel injection pump cover.
- **Gear Selector Switch**—is attached to the base of the steering column.
- **Generator Diode**—is located taped in the harness behind the fuse block.
- **Glow Plug Controller/Relay (Diesel)**—is located on the top right (left on the Cutlass models) valve cover.
- **Glow Plug Relay (Diesel)**—is located on the top of the right front fender well.
- **Headlight Relay**—is located at the front side of the engine compartment, near the headlight.
- **Horn Relay**—is located behind the left side of the instrument panel above the fuse block.
- **Idle Stop Solenoid**—is located on the top of the engine and to the left of the carburetor.
- **Ignition Key Warning Buzzer**—is located behind the left side of the dash panel.
- **In-Car Sensor**—is located at the right side of the dash panel as part of the speaker grille assembly.
- **Low Brake Vacuum Delay Module**—is taped to the instrument panel harness, above the fuse block.
- **Manifold Absolute Pressure Sensor**—is located on the air cleaner on the 4.3L engine and at the right side of the engine compartment above the wheel well on all other engines.
- **Mass Airflow Sensor (EFI)**—is located on the air intake hose at the top left side of the engine compartment.
- **Metering Valve Sensor (Diesel)**—is located on the diesel injection pump.
- **Mixture Control Solenoid**—is located on the front or right side of the carburetor or throttle body.
- **Multi-Function Chime Module**—is located behind the instrument panel to the left of the steering column at the convenience center.
- **Oxygen Sensor**—is located in the exhaust manifold.
- **Power Accessory Circuit Breaker**—is located above the flasher relay in the fuse block.
- **Power Antenna Relay**—is located behind the center of the instrument panel to the right of the radio.
- **Power Master Brake Relay**—is located on top of the electro-hydraulic pump motor below the master cylinder.
- **Seat Belt Timer Buzzer**—is located behind left side of the instrument panel at the convenience center.
- **Theft Deterrent Controller**—is located under the left side of the dash panel, near the kick panel.
- **Theft Deterrent Diode**—is located behind the left side of the dash panel in connector " C-857".
- **Theft Deterrent Relay**—is located behind the instrument panel to the left of the steering column.
- **Third and Fourth Gear Switches**—are located in the middle of the left side of the transmission.
- **Throttle Position Sensor**—is located at the front of the carburetor or on the side of the throttle body.
- **Tone Generator**—is located behind the left side of the dash panel, in the convenience center.

- **Torque Converter Clutch solenoid**—is located in the middle of the left side of the transmission.
- **Trunk Release Solenoid**—is located at the rear of the trunk lid above the liscense plate.
- **Twilight Sentinel Amplifier**—is located under the dash panel, near the radio.
- **Twilight Sentinel Photocell**—is located at the top center of the dash panel.
- **Vacuum Sensor**—is located at the rear of the engine above the valve cover.
- **Vehicle Speed Buffer**—is located under the left side of the dash panel, to the right of the steering column.
- **Vehicle Speed Sensor**—is located behind the dash panel and to the right of the steering column.
- **Water-In-Fuel Module (Diesel)**—is located at the top rear side of the engine.
- **Window and Sun Roof Circuit Breaker**—is located in the fuse block.
- **Wiper/Washer Motor Module**—is located on the upper left corner of the firewall in the engine compartment.

1982-84 CAPRICE/IMPALA

- **A/C Blower Relay**—on the right side of the engine cowl, in front of the blower motor.
- **A/C Compressor Clutch Diode**—is taped to the inside compressor clutch connector.
- **A/C Compressor Cut-Out Switch**—is located below the left side of the instrument panel on the accelerator plate.
- **A/C-Heater Resistors**—is located on the right side of the engine cowl, infront of the blower motor.
- **A/C Pressure Cycling Switch**—is located on the right side of the engine cowl, above the front relay.
- **A/C Programmer Unit**—is located behind the right side of the instrument panel.
- **A/C Temperaturer Cut-Out Relay**—is located on the top center of the engine cowl.
- **A/C Temperature Cut-Out Switch**—is located on the top front of the engine near the left valve cover.
- **Barometric Pressure Sensor (V6)**—is located behind the glove box.
- **Booster Low Vacuum Switch**—is located on the power boost unit.
- **Brake Pressure Switch**—is located under the left side engine cowl, attached to the frame.
- **Cold Inhibit Switch (Diesel)**—is located below the rear portion of the right valve cover.
- **Converter Clutch Switch (Diesel)**—is located on the brake pedal support.
- **Coolant Temperature Sender**—is located on the top left rear of the engine on the diesel models and on the front of the engine on the gas models.
- **Coolant Temperature Sensor (V6)**—is located is located on the front of the engine near the carburetor.
- **Cruise Control Throttle Servo**—is located on the top front portion of the engine.
- **Defogger Timer Relay**—is attached to the top of the fuse block.
- **Detonation (Knock) Sensor**—is located on the top left rear of the engine.
- **Door Lock Control Unit**—is located is attached to the upper right cowl.
- **Door Lock Relay**—is located on the upper right cowl.
- **Door Unlock Relay**—is located on the upper right cowl.
- **Diode Module (Diesel)**—is located on the top center of the engine cowl.
- **Level Control Relay**—is located on the left front fender well, in front of the level control compressor.

- **Early Fuel Evaporation Relay (V6)** — is located on the front top portion of the engine.
- **Early Fuel Evaporation Solenoid (V6)** — is located on the top center of the right valve cover.
- **EGR Solenoid** — is located on the top center of the right valve cover.
- **Electronic Control Module (ECM)** — is located on the right side kick panel.
- **Engine Temperature Switch (Diesel)** — is located below the rear portion of the left valve cover.
- **Fast Idle Solenoid (Diesel)** — is located on the top center of the engine in front of the injection pump.
- **Gear Selector Switch** — is located on the lower top portion of the steering column.
- **Glow Plug Relay (Diesel)** — is located on the front of the right front wheel well.
- **Glow Plug Thermal Control Unit (Diesel)** — is located on the top of the engine, in front of the fast idle solenoid.
- **Horn Relay** — is attached to the left side of the fuse block.
- **Idle Speed Control Unit (V6)** — is located on the left side of the carburetor.
- **Ignition Key Warning Buzzer** — is attached to the left side of the fuse block.
- **Illuminated Entry Timer** — is located on the upper left shroud, near the junction block.
- **Level Control Height Sensor** — is located on the rear center part of the crossmember.
- **Light Switch/Sentinel Control** — is located under the left side of the instrument panel, near the parking brake.
- **Lower Brake Vacuum Relay** — is located behind the instrument panel, to the left of the sterring column.
- **Manifold Absolute Pressure Sensor** — is located on the top of the front wheel well.
- **Mixture Control Solenoid** — is located in the carburetor.
- **Multi-Function Chime Module** — is located is located on the left side of the fuse block.
- **Oil Pressure Switch** — is located on the lower right side of the engine on the (V6) and on the top front left side of the engine on the V8 engines.
- **Oxygen Sensor** — is located on the rear right exhaust manifold on the V6 engine and on the rear left exhaust manifold on the V8 engine.
- **Power Seat Relay** — is located under the left or right seat.
- **Seat Belt Warning Buzzer** — is attached to the left side of the fuse block.
- **Seat Belt Warning Module** — is taped to the harnes located above the fuse block.
- **Tailgate Ajar Switch** — is located inside the lower right corner of the tailgate assembly.
- **Temperature Indicator Switch** — is located on the front of the engine near the carburetor on the V6 engine and on the top left side of the engine on the V8 engines.
- **Throttle Position Sensor** — is located on the careburetor.
- **Tone Generator** — is located under the left side of the instrument panel, near the parking brake.
- **Trunk Release Solenoid** — is located on the rear center of the trunk lid.
- **Twilight Sentinel Amplifier** — is located under the left side of the instrument panel, near the parking brake.
- **Twilight Sentinel Photocell** — is located on the left side of the engine cowl.
- **Vacuum Regulator Switch (Diesel)** — is located on the top center of the engine on the fuel injection pump.
- **Vacuum Sensor** — is located on the right front wheel well.
- **Vehicle Speed Sensor (V6)** — is located behind the instrument panel above the left side of the steering column.
- **Wait Lamp Control Relay (Diesel)** — is located on the top center of the engine cowl.
- **Wiper Motor Relay Diode** — is located in the wipwer motor connector.

1985-87 CAPRICE/IMPALA

- **A/C Blower Relay** — is located in the engine compartment at the center of the firewall, near the blower motor.
- **A/C Compressor Clutch Diode** — is taped to the inside compressor connector on the front of the compressor.
- **A/C-Heater Blower Resistors** — is located in the engine compartment on the right side of the firewall near the blower motor.
- **A/C Programmer (Tempmatic)** — is located behind the right side of the dash panel.
- **A/C Temperature Cut-Out Relay** — is located on the top right front engine cowl.
- **Ambient Temperature Sensor** — is located in the right air inlet, below screen.
- **Assembly Line Data Link Connector** — is located under the left side of the dash panel, to the right of the steering panel.
- **Audio Alarm Module** — is located on the left side of the fuse block.
- **Automatic Door Lock Controller** — is attached to the upper portion of the right kick panel.
- **Automatic Door Lock Diode** — is located behind the left kick panel, near the lower access hole.
- **Barometeric Pressure Sensor** — is located behind the glove box.
- **Blower and Clutch Control Module** — is located on the top of the blower housing.
- **"Check Engine" Light Driver** — is taped to the instrument panel harness, above the glove box.
- **Coolant Temperature Sensor (3.8L)** — is located on the left front side of the engine.
- **Coolant Temperature Sensor (4.3L)** — is located on the front of the engine below the coolant outlet.
- **Coolant Temperature Sensor (5.0L & 5.7L)** — is located on the front side of the engine, on the coolant outlet.
- **Coolant Temperature Sensor (5.7L Diesel)** — is located on the left front side of the engine.
- **Cruise Control Module** — is located under the left side of the dash, to the left of the steering column.
- **Cruise Control Servo** — is located at the left front side of the engine on the gas models and above the left side valve cover on the diesel models.
- **Diagnostic Dwell Meter Connector (Green)** — is taped the the wiring harness near the carburetor.
- **Diesel Electronic Control Module (DEC)** — is located behind the kick panel.
- **Defogger Time Relay** — is located on the top of the fuse block.
- **Detonation (Knock) Sensor (6 cyl.)** — is located at the lower left rear side of the engine.
- **Detonation (Knock) Sensor (8 cyl.)** — is located at the right front side of the engine.
- **Early Fuel Evaporation Relay (3.8L)** — is located on the top right front engine cowl.
- **Electronic Control Module (ECM)** — is located behind the right kick panel.
- **Electronic Level Control Height Sensor** — is located on the rear center of the rear crossmember.
- **Electronic Level Control Relay** — is located on the left front fender, behind the horn.
- **Electronic Spark Control (ESC) Module** — is located on the right front side of the engine compartment.
- **Fast Idle Relay (4.3L)** — is located in the center of the firewall in the engine compartment.
- **Fuel Pump Relay (4.3L) Relay** — is located on the upper right inner fender panel.
- **Glow Plug Controller Relay (Diesel)** — is located on the top left rear of the engine.
- **Horn Relay** — is attached to the left side of the fuse block.

- **Illuminated Entry Timer** – is located behind the upper portion of the left kick panel, near the junction block.
- **In-Car Sensor** – is located in the right upper part of the dash, to the left of the right speaker.
- **Low Coolant Level Sensor** – is located in the radiator.
- **Manifold Absolute Pressure Sensor** – is located on the air cleaner.
- **Metering Valve Sensor (Diesel)** – is located on the diesel fuel injection pump.
- **Multi-Function Chime Module** – is located in the convenience center.
- **Oxygen Sensor** – is located on the exhaust manifold.
- **Power Antenna Relay** – is located on the bracket under the right side of the instrument panel, to the left of the glove box.
- **Power Door Lock Relay** – is located behind the bottom right kick panel.
- **Power Door Unlock Relay** – is located behind the upper portion of the right side kick panel.
- **Power Master Cylinder Brake In-Line Fuse** – is located under the left side of the dash panel, near the fuse block.
- **Power Master Cylinder Relay** – is located in the connector at the brake reservoir pump motor.
- **Power Seat Relay** – is located on under the right or left seat.
- **Seat Memory Module** – is located under the driver's seat.
- **Starter Interrupt Relay** – is located under the left side of the dash panel, above the steering column.
- **Trailer Relays** – are located on the lower right corner of the fuse block.
- **Theft Deterrent Controller** – is located under the left side of the dash, to the right of the steering column.
- **Theft Deterrent Diode** – is located under the left side of the dash panel, near the fuse block.
- **Theft Deterrent In-Line Fuses** – are located above the fuse block taped to the instrument panel wiring harness.
- **Theft Deterrent Relay** – is located at the right of the theft deterrent controller.
- **Throttle Position Sensor** – is located on the carburetor or throttle body.
- **Twilight Sentinel Amplifier** – is located on a bracket behind the right side of the dash panel.
- **Twilight Sentinel Control** – is located under the left side of the dash, to the right of the steering column.
- **Twilight Sentinel Photocell** – is located on the top left side of the dash panel.
- **Vacuum Sensor** – is located on the right front engine cowl.
- **Vehicle Speed Sensor** – is located behind the instrument panel, is a part of the cluster.
- **Vehicle Speed Sensor Buffer** – is taper top the instrument panel wiring under the left side of the daash near the fuse block.
- **Washer Pump Motor Diode** – is located in the washer motor connector.
- **Water-In-Fuel Module (Diesel)** – is located on top of the fuel filter assembly.
- **Wide Open Throttle Relay** – is located in the engine compartment at the center of the firewall.
- **Window and Sunroof Circuit Breaker** – is located at the top right corner of the fuse block.
- **Wiper Motor Relay Diode** – is located in the wiper motor connector.

1982-84 CITATION AND CITATION II

- **A/C Clutch Diode** – is located inside the A/C compressor connector.
- **A/C Compressor Relay** – is located in the upper right corner of the engine cowl.

- **A/C Diode** – is located in the A/C harness, near the vacuum tank.
- **A/C-Heater Blower Resistors** – are located on the front of the plenum.
- **A/C High Speed Blower Relay** – is located on the top of the plenum, near the vacuum tank.
- **Audio/Buzzer Alarm Module** – is located on the conveience center.
- **Charging System Relay** – is taped to the instrument panel harness, above the accelerator pedal.
- **"Check Engine" Light driver** – is taped to the right side of the instrument panel harness.
- **Choke Heater Relay** – is located behind the instrument panel.
- **Coolant Fan Relay** – is located on the left front wheel well.
- **Coolant Temperature Sensor** – is located on the left side of the coolant inlet on the 4 cylinder engines and on the top left front side of the engine on the V6 engines.
- **Defogger Timer/Relay** – is located above the glove box.
- **Door Lock Relay** – is located on the upper center of the right shroud.
- **Early Fuel Evaporation Heater Relay** – is located on the upper right side of the engine cowl.
- **Electronic Control Module (ECM)** – is located behind the instrument panel.
- **Fuel Pump Relay** – is located on the upper right side of the engine cowl.
- **Horn Relay** – is located in the convenience center.
- **Lights-On Buzzer** – is located behind the right side of the instrument panel, near the glove box.
- **Manifold Absolute Pressure Sensor** – is located on the right side of the air filter.
- **Oil Pressure Sender** – is located at the rear of the engine above the distributor on the 4 cylinder engines and above the oil filter on the V6 engines.
- **Oxygen Sensor** – is located in the exhaust manifold.
- **Power Accesories Circuit Breaker** – is located in the buse block.
- **Power Antenna Relay** – is located behind the right side of the instrument panel, near the glove box.
- **Power Window Circuit Breaker** – is located in the fuse block.
- **Throttle Position Sensor** – is located on the throttle body.
- **Vacuum Sensor** – is located in the upper right side of the engine cowl.
- **Vehicle Speed Sensor** – is located as part of the speedometer assembly.
- **Wiper Pulse Module** – is located behind the left side of the instrument panel.

1985-86 CITATION II

- **A/C Clutch Diode** – is located inside the A/C compressor connector.
- **A/C Compressor Relay** – is located in the upper right corner of the firewall on the 2.5L engine and in the right side of the radiator support on the 2.8L engine.
- **A/C Diode** – is located in the A/C harness, near the vacuum tank.
- **A/C-Heater Blower Resistors** – are located on the front of the plenum.
- **A/C High Speed Blower Relay** – is located on the top of the plenum, near the vacuum tank.
- **Audio/Buzzer Alarm Module** – is located on the conveience center.
- **Barometric Pressure Sensor** – is located in the right rea corner of the engine compartment.

• **Charging System Relay**—is taped to the instrument panel harness, above the accelerator pedal.
• **"Check Engine" Light driver**—is taped to the right side of the instrument panel harness.
• **Choke Heater Relay**—is taped to the instrument panel harness, near the fuse block.
• **Coolant Fan Relay**—is located on the left front wheel well.
• **Coolant Temperature Sensor**—is located on the left side of the coolant inlet on the 2.5L engine and on the top left front side of the engine on the 2.8L engine.
• **Cooling Fan In-Line Fuse**—is located on the left front shock tower.
• **Cruise Control Module**—is located under the left side of the instrument panel, above the accelerator pedal.
• **Defogger Timer/Relay**—is located above the glove box.
• **Diagnostic Dwell Meter Connector**—is located in the harness, in the right rear corner of the engine compartment.
• **Door Lock Relay**—is located on the upper center of the right shroud.
• **Early Fuel Evaporation Heater Relay**—is located on the upper right side of the engine cowl.
• **Electronic Control Module (ECM)**—is located behind the instrument panel.
• **Fuel Pump In-Line Fuse**—is located on the left front shock tower.
• **Fuel Pump Prime Connector**—is located on the rear of the engine, near the starter.
• **Fuel Pump Relay**—is located on the upper right side of the firewall on the 2.5L engine and on the left front shock tower on the 2.8L engine.
• **Horn Relay**—is located in the convenience center.
• **Lights-On Buzzer**—is located behind the right side of the instrument panel, near the glove box.
• **Manifold Absolute Pressure Sensor**—is located on the right side of the air filter.
• **Manifold Air Temperature Sensor**—is located on the air cleaner assembly.
• **Mass Airflow In-Line Fuse**—is located on the left front shock tower.
• **Mass Airflow Relay**—is located on the left front shock tower.
• **Mass Airflow Sensor**—is located in the front of the engine.
• **Oil Pressure Sender**—is located at the rear of the engine above the distributor on the 2.5L engine and above the oil filter on the 2.8L engine.
• **Oxygen Sensor**—is located in the exhaust manifold.
• **Power Accesories Circuit Breaker**—is located in the buse block.
• **Power Antenna Relay**—is located behind the right side of the instrument panel, near the glove box.
• **Power Window Circuit Breaker**—is located in the fuse block.
• **Throttle Kicker Relay**—is located in the right front cornewr of the engine compartment.
• **Throttle Position Sensor**—is located on the throttle body.
• **Vacuum Sensor**—is located in the upper right side of the firewall.
• **Vehicle Speed Sensor**—is located as part of the speedometer assembly.
• **Wiper Pulse Module**—is located behind the left side of the instrument panel.

1982-84 CAVALIER

• **A/C Ambient Air Sensor**—is located on the engine cowl, above the power steering reservoir.

• **A/C Blower Relay**—is located on the front center of the plenum.
• **A/C Compressor Control Relay**—is located behind the right front shock tower.
• **A/C Compressor Run Relay**—is located behind the right front shock tower.
• **A/C-Heater Blower Resistors**—are located on the front left side of the plenum.
• **Blocking Diode**—is located in the instrument panel harness, near the fuse block.
• **Coolant Fan Relay**—on the left front fender in front of the shock tower.
• **Coolant Temperature Sender**—is located on the left side of the engine, near the coolant outlet.
• **Coolant Temperature Sensor**—is located on the front of the engine on the thermostat housing on the 1.8L engine and on the left side of the engine under the water outlet on the other engines.
• **Cruise Control Throttle Servo**—is located on the bracket on the left front shock tower.
• **Defogger Time Relay**—is located behind the left side of the dash panel.
• **Door Lock Relay**—is located on the upper right side of the steering column support.
• **Electronic Control Module (ECM)**—is located behind the glove box.
• **Electronic Fuel Injection Ambient Sensor**—is located on the engine cowl above the washer reservoir.
• **Fuel Pump Relay**—is located on the right engine cowl, behind the shock tower.
• **Hatch/Tailgate/Trunk Release Relay**—is taped to the wire harness, located behind the right side of the radio.
• **Horn Relay**—is located on the conveience center.
• **Idle Speed Motor**—is taped in the EFI harness. to the right of the electronic control module.
• **Manifold Absolute Presure Sensor**—is located on the right shock tower.
• **Oxygen Sensor**—is located in the exhaust manifold.
• **Power Accessories Circuit Breaker**—is located in the fuse block.
• **Power Antenna Relay**—is located behind the instrument panel, below the right side of the radio.
• **Power Window Circuit Breaker**—is located in the fuse block.
• **Throttle Position Sensor**—is located on the throttle body.
• **Torque Converter Clutch Relay (TCC)**—is located on the transmission cowling.
• **Vehicle Speed Sensor**—is located behind the instrument panel, the the right of the steering column.
• **Wiper Pulse Module**—is located below the steering column, above the trim cover.

1985-87 CAVALIER

• **A/C Blower Relay**—is located on the front center of the plenum.
• **A/C Compressor Control Relay**—is located behind the right front shock tower.
• **A/C Compressor Run Relay**—is located behind the right front shock tower.
• **A/C-Heater Blower Resistors**—are located on the front left side of the plenum.
• **A/C In-Car Temperature Sensor**—is located on the right side of the dash, above the glove box.
• **Assembly Line Diagnostic Link**—is located behind the instrument panel, on the right side of the fuse block.
• **Blocking Diode**—is located in the instrument panel harness, near the bulkhead connector.

- **Coolant Fan Relay**—on the left front fender in front of the shock tower or on the firewall to the left of the brake booster.
- **Coolant Temperature Sender**—is located on the left side of the engine, near the coolant outlet.
- **Coolant Temperature Sensor**—is located on the front of the engine on the thermostat housing on the 1.8L engine and on the left side of the engine under the water outlet on the other engines.
- **Cruise Control Module (2-door)**—is located behind the instrument panel, above the left side of the steering column.
- **Cruise Control Module (4-door)**—is located behind the right side of the dash panel, above the glove box.
- **Defogger Time Relay**—is located behind the left side of the dash panel.
- **Electronic Control Module (ECM)**—is located behind the glove box.
- **Electronic Fuel Injection Ambient Sensor**—is located on the engine cowl above the washer reservoir.
- **Electronic Speed Sensor**—is located on the top right side of the transaxle.
- **Fog Lamp Relays**—are taped to the instrument panel harness, near the fog lamp switch.
- **Fuel Pump In-Line Fuse**—is located on the firewall, behind the brake booster.
- **Fuel Pump Relay**—is located on the right engine cowl, behind the shock tower or on the firewall, above the brake booster.
- **Hatch/Tailgate/Trunk Release Relay**—is taped to the wire harness, located behind the right side of the radio.
- **Horn Relay**—is located on the conveience center.
- **Knock Sensor**—is located on the right side of the starter below the starter.
- **Low Coolant Module**—is located behind the instrument panel, above the left side of the steering column.
- **Low Coolant Temperature Sensor**—is located in the engine compartment, on the right front side of the radiator.
- **Manifold Absolute Presure Sensor**—is located on the right shock tower.
- **Manifold Air Temperature Sensor**—is located on the engine, underneath or on top of the intake manifold.
- **Mass Airflow Relay**—is located on the firewall, behind the brake booster.
- **Mass Airflow Sensor**—is located on the top of the left side of the engine, behind the air cleaner.
- **Mass Airflow Sensor In-Line Fuse**—is located on the firewall, behind the brake booster.
- **Outside Air Temperature Sensor**—is located in the engine compartment, behind the right side of the grill.
- **Oxygen Sensor**—is located in the exhaust manifold.
- **Power Accessories/Convertible Top Circuit Breaker**—is located in the fuse block.
- **Power Antenna Relay**—is located behind the instrument panel, below the right side of the radio.
- **Power Door Lock Relay**—is located on the upper right side of the steering column support.
- **Power Unit Dimmer**—is located behind the instrument panel, to the left of the steering column.
- **Power Window Circuit Breaker**—is located in the fuse block.
- **Release Relay**—is taped to the instrument panel harness, behind the radio or glove box.
- **Throttle Position Sensor**—is located on the throttle body. On the 2.8L engine it is located, behind the distributor.
- **Torque Converter Clutch Relay (TCC)**—is located on the transmission cowling.
- **Turbo Release Relay**—is located on the transaxle cowling.
- **Twilight Sentinel Amplifier**—is located behind the instrument panel, to the left of the steering column.

- **Twilight Sentinel Photocell**—is located on the dash panel, on the right side of the defrost vent.
- **Vehicle Speed Sensor**—is located behind the instrument panel, the the right of the steering column.
- **Vehicle Speed Sensor Buffer**—is located behind the instrument cluster, below the speed sensor.

1982-87 CHEVETTE

- **A/C Compressor Cut-Out Switch**—is located on the accelerator pedal support.
- **A/C-Heater Blower Resistors**—are located in the engine compartment on the lower right side of the A/C-heater assembly.
- **A/C High Speed Blower Relay**—is located in the engine compartment at the center of the A/C heater assembly.
- **A/C Pressure Cycling Switch**—is located on the accumulator /drier.
- **A/C Vacuum Advance Relay**—is located on the left side of the firewall in front of the electronic speed sensor.
- **Assembly Line Diagnostic Line Connector**—is located under the right side of the dash panel.
- **Audio Alarm Module**—is located on the fuse block.
- **"Check Engine" Light Driver**—is located under the right side of the dash panel.
- **Coolant Temperature Sender (Gas)**—is located in the left center of the engine.
- **Coolant Temperature Switch (Diesel)**—is located in the left center of the engine.
- **Diagnostic Dwell Meter Connector**—is taped to the wiring harness, at the rear of the intake manifold.
- **Dropping Resistor**—is located under the glow plug relay assembly cover.
- **Early Fuel Evaporation Temperature Switch**—is located on the left side of the engine.
- **Electronic Control Module (ECM)**—is located under the center of the instrument panel.
- **Electronic Speed Sensor**—is located on the firewall near the bulkhead connector.
- **Fast Idle switch**—is located on the left front side of the engine.
- **Glow Plug Controller (Diesel)**—is located on the right side cowl panel under the instrument panel.
- **Glow Plug Controller Thermal Switch (Diesel)**—is located on the left front side of the engine.
- **Glow Plug Dropping Resistors (Diesel)**—is located on the right front fender apron.
- **Glow Plug Relays (Diesel)**—are located on the right front fender apron.
- **Horn Relay**—is located below the bulkhead connector on the firewall.
- **Key Reminder Buzzer**—is located on the instrument panel near the bulkhead connector.
- **Lamp Reminder Buzzer**—is located on the audio alarm module.
- **Low Vacuum Warning Switch (Diesel)**—is located on the left side of the engine.
- **Oil Pressure Sender (Gas)**—is located on the left front side of the engine.
- **Oil Pressure Switch (Diesel)**—is located on the lower right rear side of the engine below the starter.
- **Oxygen Sensor**—is located in the exhaust manifold.
- **Power Steering Cut-Off Relay**—is located on the left side of the firewall in front of the electronic speed sensor.
- **Rear Defogger Control Timer**—is located on the right side of the instrument panel.
- **Seat Belt Buzzer**—is located below the left side of the dash panel, in the right side of the fuse block.
- **Speed Sensor**—is located on the left side of the firewall on

the gas engines and on the right rear side of the engine on the diesel engines.
• **Throttle Position Sensor** – is located on the throttle body.
• **Torque Converter Vacuum Switch** – is located on the right front of the engine on the diesel engines and on the left side engine cowl on the gas engines.
• **Vacuum Advance Relay** – is located on the left side of the firewall near the electronic speed sensor.

1985-87 NOVA

• **A/C Condenser Fan Fusible Link** – is located in the wiring to the condenser fan near the fan shroud.
• **A/C Fan Relays** – is located in the fuse/relay block attached to the left front inner fender panel, in front of the shock tower.
• **A/C High Pressure Switch** – is located under the battery tray in the engine compartment.
• **A/C Idle Stabilizer Amplifier** – is attached to the bottom of the cooling unit under the instrument panel, behind the glove box.
• **A/C Low Pressure Switch** – is attached to the bottom of the cooling unit under the instrument panel, behind the glove box.
• **A/C Thermistor** – is attached to the cooling unit under the instrument panel, behind the glove box.
• **Air Shut-Off Valve** – is located in the vacuum line feeding the choke opener on the carburetor.
• **Auxiliary Acceleration Pump** – is located on the carburetor.
• **Charge Light Relay** – is located under the right side of the instrument panel behind the glove box.
• **Coolant Level Warning Switch** – is attached to to the front left shock tower.
• **Coolant Temperature Switches** – are located on the rear of the engine near the transaxle.
• **Cooling Fan Relay** – is located in the fuse/relay block attached to the left front inner fender panel, in front of the shock tower.
• **Cruise Control Actuator** – is mounted on the left front inner fender panel.
• **Cruise Control Computer** – is located behind the right side kick panel.
• **Defogger Relay** – is located in the fuse/relay block attached to the right side kick panel.
• **Door Lock Solenoid** – is located inside the driver's side door.
• **Emission Control Computer** – is located under the right side of the instrument panel above the glove box.
• **Headlight Relay** – is located in the fuse/relay block attached to the left front inner fender panel, in front of the shock tower.
• **Heater Relay** – is located in the fuse/relay block attached to the right side kick panel.
• **Main Relay** – is located in the fuse/relay block attached to the left front inner fender panel, in front of the shock tower.
• **Neutral Start Switch (Auto.Trans.)** – is located on the transaxle.
• **Power Circuit Breaker** – is located under the right side of the instrument panel behind the glove box.
• **Rear Door Lock Solenoid** – is located inside the left rear door.
• **Seat Belt Relay** – is located under the right side of the instrument panel above the glove box.
• **Starter Relay** – is mounted to the right front inner fender panel.
• **Tail Light Relay** – is located on the fuse/relay block which is located behind the left side kick panel.
• **Throttle Positioner** – is located on the carburetor.

• **Vacuum Switch** – is mounted to the right front inner fender panel, behind the shock tower.

1983-84 CELEBRITY

• **A/C Blower Resistors** – is located on the right side of the engine cowl.
• **A/C Compressor Relay** – is located on the upper right corner of the engine cowl.
• **A/C Delay Relay** – is located in the upper right corner of the engine cowl.
• **A/C High Pressure Cut-Out Switch** – is located on the left side of the compressor.
• **A/C Temperature Cut-Out Switch** – is located on the top of the engine near the fuel filter.
• **Audio Alarm Module** – is located behind the instrument panel, to the left of the steering column.
• **Charging System Relay** – is located behind the instrument panel, near the fuse block.
• **"Check Engine" Light Driver** – is taped to the instrument panel harness behind the glove box.
• **Choke Relay (Non EFI)** – is located on the convenience center.
• **Coolant Fan Relay** – is located on the left front wheel well on the bracket on the 4 cylinder engine and on the fender panel ahead of the left front shock tower on the V6 engine.
• **Coolant Fan Switch** – is located in front of the engine below the left side valve cover on the 4 cylinder engine and on the top of the V6 engine in front of the distributor.
• **Coolant Temperature Sensor** – is located on the left center side of the 4 cylinder engines and on the top of the V6 engine in front of the distributor.
• **Coolant Temperature Switch** – is located on the top of the engine near the fuel filter.
• **Diagnostic Dwell Meter Connector** – is located near the upper right side of the engine cowl.
• **Diesel Diode Module** – is located on the right side of the engine cowl on a bracket.
• **Early Fuel Evaporation Heater Relay** – is located on the upper right side of the engine cowl.
• **Electronic Control Module (ECM)** – is located behind the right side of the instrument panel.
• **Electronic Level Control Height Sensor** – is located on the frame under the trunk.
• **Electronic Level Control Relay** – is located on the frame behind the left rear wheel well.
• **Fuel Pump Relay** – is located on the upper right side of the engine cowl.
• **Glow Plug Relay (Diesel)** – is located behind the left battery on the wheel well.
• **Headlight-Key-Seat Buzzer** – is located on the convenience center.
• **Heater Blower Resistors** – is located on the right plenum.
• **Horn Relay** – is located on the convenience center.
• **Low Brake Vacuum Relay** – is taped to the instrument panel above the fuse block.
• **Low Brake Vacuum Switch** – is located on top of the brake booster unit.
• **Manifold Absolute Pressure Sensor** – is located in the upper right engine cowl on the 4 cylinder engines and on the behind the right front shock tower on the V6 engines.
• **Oxygen Sensor** – is located in the exhaust manifold.
• **Power Accessories Circuit Breaker** – is located in the fuse block.
• **Power Antenna Relay** – is located behind the instrument panel on the rear of the glove box.
• **Power Window Circuit Breaker** – is located in the fuse block.

- **Thermal Controller (Diesel)** – is located on the top of the engine near the fuel filter.
- **Throttle Position Sensor** – is located on the throttle body.
- **Wait Lamp Control Relay (Diesel)** – is located in the upper right corner of the engine cowl on a bracket.
- **Water-In-Fuel Sensor** – is located in the fuel tank.

1985-87 CELEBRITY

- **A/C Blower Resistors** – is located on the right side of the engine cowl.
- **A/C Compressor Relay** – is located on the upper right corner of the engine cowl.
- **A/C Delay Relay** – is located in the upper right corner of the engine cowl.
- **A/C Heater Blower Relay** – is located on the plenum, on the right side of the firewall.
- **A/C High Pressure Cut-Out Switch** – is located on the left side of the compressor.
- **A/C Temperature Cut-Out Switch** – is located on the top of the engine near the fuel filter.
- **Altitude Advance Relay** – is located on the left inner fender, in front of the shock tower.
- **Assembly Line Diagnostic Link** – is located on the bottom of the instrument oanel, near the steering column.
- **Audio Alarm Module** – is located behind the instrument panel, to the left of the steering column.
- **Barometric Pressure Sensor** – is located on the firewall, at the right side of the blower motor.
- **Buffer Amplifier** – is located behind the right side of the instrument panel, in front of the electronic control module.
- **Charging System Relay** – is located behind the instrument panel, near the fuse block.
- **"Check Engine" Light Driver** – is taped to the instrument panel harness behind the glove box.
- **Choke Relay (Non EFI)** – is located on the convenience center.
- **Constant Run Relay** – is located on the left inner fender wheel well.
- **Coolant Fan In-Line Fuse** – is located in the engine compartment in front of the left front shock tower.
- **Coolant Fan Low-Speed Relay** – is located on the left inner fender wheel well, on a bracket on the 4 cylinder engines and on the fender panel in front of the left front shock tower on the V6 models.
- **Coolant Fan Relay** – is located on the left front wheel well on the bracket on the 4 cylinder engine and on the fender panel ahead of the left front shock tower on the V6 engine.
- **Coolant Fan Switch** – is located in front of the engine below the left side valve cover on the 4 cylinder engine and on the top of the V6 engine in front of the distributor.
- **Coolant Temperature Sensor** – is located on the left center side of the 4 cylinder engines and on the top of the V6 engine in front of the distributor.
- **Coolant Temperature Switch** – is located on the top of the engine near the fuel filter.
- **Cruise Control Module** – is located behind the instrument panel, above the accelerator pedal.
- **Defogger Timer Relay** – is located behind the instrument panel, under the instrument cluster.
- **Diagnostic Dwell Meter Connector** – is located near the upper right side of the engine cowl.
- **Diesel Diode Module** – is located on the right side of the engine cowl on a bracket.
- **Diesel Electronic Controller (DEC)** – is located behind the right side of the instrument panel.
- **Diesel Generator Diode** – is located in the engine harness, to the right of the glow plug controller.

- **Early Fuel Evaporation Heater Relay** – is located on the upper right side of the engine cowl.
- **Electronic Control Module (ECM)** – is located behind the right side of the instrument panel.
- **Electronic Level Control Height Sensor** – is located on the frame under the trunk or in front of the fuel tank on the Wagon models.
- **Electronic Level Control Relay** – is located on the frame behind the left rear wheel well.
- **Fuel Pump Relay** – is located on the upper right side of the engine cowl.
- **Glow Plug Controller/Relay (Diesel)** – is located on the rear of the engine, to the left of the cylinder head.
- **Glow Plug Relay (Diesel)** – is located behind the left battery on the wheel well.
- **Headlight-Key-Seat Buzzer** – is located on the convenience center.
- **Heater Blower Resistors** – is located on the right plenum.
- **High Mount Stop Light Relays** – are located on the left rear wheel well, in the trunk.
- **Horn Relay** – is located on the convenience center.
- **Knock Sensor** – is located on the top left side of the engine, below the front of the oxygen sensor.
- **Low Brake Vacuum Relay** – is taped to the instrument panel above the fuse block.
- **Low Brake Vacuum Switch** – is located on top of the brake booster unit.
- **Manifold Absolute Pressure Sensor** – is located in the upper right engine cowl on the 4 cylinder engines and on the behind the right front shock tower on the V6 engines.
- **Manifold Air Temperature Sensor** – is located in the canister, at the front of the engine compartment.
- **Mass Airflow Relay** – is located in the engine compartment, on the front of the left shock tower.
- **Mass Air Flow Sensor In-Line Fuse** – is located in the engine compartment, on the front of the left shock tower.
- **Metering Valve Sensor (MVS)** – is located on top of the engine.
- **Oxygen Sensor** – is located in the exhaust manifold.
- **Power Accessories Circuit Breaker** – is located in the fuse block.
- **Power Antenna Relay** – is located behind the instrument panel on the rear of the glove box.
- **Power Door Lock Relay** – is located on the right shroud, to the right of the glove box.
- **Power Window Circuit Breaker** – is located in the fuse block.
- **Pulse Relay** – is located on the left inner fender, in ftont of the left front shock tower.
- **Rear Wiper Relay** – is located in the top center of the tailgate.
- **Sentinel Amplifier** – is located behind the center of the instrument panel, behind the ashtray.
- **Speed Sensor** – is located on the top right side of the transaxle.
- **Starter Interrupt Relay** – is located above the ashtray, taped to the instrument panel harness.
- **Theft Deterrent Relay** – is located behind the instrument panel, strapped to the theft deterrent controller.
- **Thermal Controller (Diesel)** – is located on the top of the engine near the fuel filter.
- **Throttle Kicker Relay** – is located on the front of the engine compartment, at the right side of the radiator support.
- **Throttle Position Sensor** – is located on the throttle body.
- **Wait Lamp Control Relay (Diesel)** – is located in the upper right corner of the engine cowl on a bracket.
- **Water-In-Fuel Sensor** – is located in the fuel tank.

1982-83 CAMARO

- **A/C Blower Resistors**—are located near the blower motor on the A/C module.
- **A/C Blower Speed High Speed Relay**—is located near the blower module on the A/C module.
- **A/C Compressor Relay**—is located on the left side engine cowl near the brake bosster.
- **A/C Pressure Cycling Switch**—is located on the accumulator/drier.
- **"Check Engine" Light Driver Module**—is taped to the instrument panel harness near the console.
- **Choke Relay**—is located in the convenience center.
- **Coolant Temperature Sensor (4 cyl. and V6)**—is located on the top left side of the engine.
- **Coolant Temperature Sensor (V8 Carb.)**—is located on the lower left side of the engine.
- **Coolant Temperature Sensor (V8 E.F.I.)**—is located on the lower right side of the engine.
- **Coolant Temperature Switch (4 cyl. and V6)**—is located on the top left side of the engine.
- **Coolant Temperature Switch (V8 Carb.)**—is located on the lower left side of the engine.
- **Coolant Temperature Switch (V8 E.F.I.)**—is located on the lower right side of the engine.
- **Cruise Control Servo**—is located on the left rear inner fenser panel.
- **Early Fuel Evaporation Relay**—is located on the upper right side of the engine cowl.
- **Electronic Control Module (ECM)**—is located behind the right side of the instrument panel.
- **Electronic Spark Control Unit**—is located on the left side of the engine cowl.
- **Fuel Pump Relay**—is located on the left side of the engine cowl.
- **Hatch Release Relay**—is located under the front part of the console.
- **Headlight Warning Buzzer**—is located in the convenience center.
- **Hood Louver Relay**—is located on the left side of the engine cowl.
- **Horn Relay**—is located in the convenience center.
- **Knock Sensor (V8)**—is located on the lower right side of the engine.
- **Manifold Absolute Pressure Sensor (4 cyl.)**—is located on the right rear of the engine.
- **Manifold Absolute Pressure Sensor (V8 E.F.I.)**—is located on the left side of the engine cowl.
- **Oxygen Sensor**—is located in the exhaust manifold/
- **Power Antenna Relay**—is located behind the right side of the instrument panel lower cover.
- **Seat Belt Warning Buzzer**—is located in the covenience center.
- **Throttle Kicker Relay (V8)**—is located on the left side of the engine cowl.
- **Vacuum Sensor**—is located on the upper left side of the engine cowl.

1984-87 CAMARO

- **A/C Blower Resistors**—are located near the blower motor on the A/C module.
- **A/C Control Module (Berlinetta)**—is located in the right side of the dash panel.
- **A/C Blower Relay Assembly (Berlinetta)**—is located under the dash in the module on the A/C plenum housing.
- **A/C Blower Speed High Speed Relay**—is located near the blower module on the A/C module.

- **A/C Compressor Diode**—is taped to the inside of the compressor clutch connector.
- **A/C Compressor Relay**—is located on the left side engine cowl near the brake bosster.
- **A/C-Heater Blower Resistors**—are located on the right side of the engine cowl.
- **A/C Pressure Cycling Switch**—is located on the accumulator/drier.
- **Assembly Line Diagnostic Link**—is located at the convenience center.
- **Barometric Pressure Sensor**—is located on the top right side of the engine cowl.
- **Beam Change Relay (Berlinetta)**—is located inside the light module.
- **Burn Off Relay**—is located behind the ECM.
- **"Check Engine" Light Driver Module**—is taped to the instrument panel harness near the console.
- **Choke Heater Relay**—is located int he convenience center.
- **Coolant Temperature Sensor (4 cyl.)**—is located on the coolant outlet on the front of the engine.
- **Coolant Temperature Sensor (V6)**—is located on the top of the engine behind the A/C cpompressor.
- **Coolant Temperature Sensor (V8)**—is located on the top front of the engine behind the alternator.
- **Coolant Temperature Switch (4 cyl.)**—is located in the rear of the engine, near the oil filler tube.
- **Coolant Temperature Switch (V6)**—is located on the top front section of the engine.
- **Coolant Temperature Switch (V8)**—is located on the left cylinder head below the valve cover.
- **Cooling Fan Relay (V6)**—is located on the left side of the firewall.
- **Cooling Fan Relay (V8)**—is located on the right side of the radiator or the left side of the firewall.
- **Courtesy Light Relay 9Berlinetta)**—is located in the light module.
- **Cruise Control Module**—is located behind the right side of the dash.
- **Cruise Control Servo**—is located on the left rear inner fenser panel.
- **Diagnostic Dwell Meter Connector (V6)**—is taped next to the ECM harness, next to the right valve cover.
- **Diagnostic Dwell Meter Connector (V8)**—is taped next to the ECM harness, behind the right shock tower.
- **Early Fuel Evaporation Relay**—is located on the upper right side of the engine cowl.
- **EGR Diagnostic Connector**—is on the top rear section of the engine.
- **Electronic Control Module (ECM)**—is located behind the right side of the instrument panel.
- **Electronic Spark Control Unit**—is located on the left side of the engine cowl.
- **Fast Idle Relay (V6)**—is located behind the right headlight on the side of the radiator.
- **Fast Idle Relay (V8)**—is located on the upper right side of the engine cowl.
- **Flasher Select Relay (Berlinetta)**—is located inside the light module.
- **Fog Light Relay**—is located on the left rear inner fender panel.
- **Fuel Pump In-Line Fuse**—is located on the right front wheel well in the engine compartment.
- **Fuel Pump Relay**—is located on the upper right side of the firewall.
- **Fuel Pump Relay**—is located on the left side of the engine cowl.
- **Generator Diode**—is located behind the left side of the dash panel.

• **Hatch Release Relay** – is located under the front part of the console.
• **Headlight Relay (Berlinetta)** – is located inside the light module.
• **Headlight Warning Buzzer** – is located in the convenience center.
• **Heater Blower Resistors** – are located on the blower motor.
• **Hood Louver Relay** – is located on the left side of the engine cowl.
• **Horn Relay** – is located in the convenience center.
• **Isolation Relay** – is located behind the right headlight.
• **Knock Sensor (V8)** – is located on the lower right side of the engine.
• **Left turn Signal Relay (Berlinetta)** – is located inside the light module.
• **Light Control Module (Berlinetta)** – is located under the right side od the dash panel next to the ECM.
• **Light Monitor Module** – is located on the upper left side of the dash panel, above the clutch pedal.
• **Low Blower Relay** – is located on the right side of the firewall, near the blower motor.
• **Manifold Absolute Pressure Sensor** – is located on the front of the air cleaner assembly.
• **Mass Air Flow Relay** – is located on the right side of the radiator support bracket.
• **Mass Air Flow Sensor (4 cyl.)** – is located on top of the air horn, at the front of the engine compartment.
• **Mass Air Flow Sensor (8 cyl.)** – is located on top of the engine.
• **Mass Air Flow Sensor In-Line Fuse (V6)** – is located in the right front corner of the engine comaprtment.
• **Mass Air Flow Sensor In-Line Fuse (V8)** – is located behind the battery, near the positive battery cable.
• **Oxygen Sensor** – is located in the exhaust manifold/
• **Park/Turn Relay (Berlinetta)** – is located inside the light module.
• **Power Accessories Circuit Breaker** – is located in the fuse block.
• **Power Antenna Relay** – is located behind the right side of the instrument panel lower cover.
• **Power Door Lock Relay** – is located behind the left kick panel in the lower opening.
• **Power Window/Rear Wiper Circuit Breaker** – is located in the fuse block.
• **Rear Defogger Timer/Relay** – is located below the right side of the dash, near the ECM.
• **Rear Hatch Release Relay** – is located under the console.
• **Right Turn Signal Relay (Berlinetta)** – is located inside the light module.
• **Seat Belt Warning Buzzer** – is located in the covenience center.
• **Speed Buffer (Berlinetta)** – is located on the left kick panel under the dash.
• **Throttle Kicker Relay (V8)** – is located on the left side of the engine cowl or the right frint inner fender panel.
• **Throttle Position Sensor (4 cyl.)** – is located on the top right side of the engine.
• **Throttle Position Sensor (V6)** – is located on the top front section of the engine.
• **Throttle Position Sensor (V8)** – is located on the top right side of the engine.
• **Vacuum Sensor** – is located on the upper left side of the engine cowl.
• **Vehicle Speed Sensor** – is located on the printed circuit at the rear of the speedometer on all models except Berlinetta. On the Berlinetta the speed sensor is located on the left side of the transmission below the shifter.

• **Wide Open Throttle Relay** – is located in the left rear corner of the engine compartment.
• **Wiper/Washer Motor Module** – is located on the upper left side of the engine cowl.

1982-84 CORVETTE

• **A/C-Heater Blower Resistors** – is located on the A/C-Heater plenum.
• **Anti-Theft Relay** – is located in the convenience center.
• **Assembly Line Diagnostic Link** – is located under the left side of the dash panel.
• **Convenience Center** – is located under the center section of the dash panel.
• **Coolant Temperature Sensor** – is located on the lower front side of the engine.
• **Cruise Control Module** – is built into the liquid crystal display instrument cluster.
• **Cruise Control Servo Assembly** – is located behind the front headlight.
• **Electronic Control Module (ECM)** – is located behind the right side of the dash panel.
• **Electronic Spark Controller** – is located on the A/C-Heater blower housing.
• **Engine Cooling Fan Relay** – is located under the brake bosster assembly.
• **Fuel Pump Relay** – is located on the left side of the firewall in the engine comaprtment.
• **Headlight Actuator Relays** – is located on the support in the front of the left front wheel well.
• **Headlight Actuators** – are located next to each headlight assembly.
• **High Speed Blower Relay** – is located on the A/C-Heater blower assembly.
• **Horn Relay** – is located in the convenience center.
• **Interior Light Timer** – is located on the instrument panel harness, behind the convenience center.
• **Isolation Relay** – is located on the support in the front of the left front wheel well.
• **Knock Sensor** – is located on the lower right center of the engine.
• **Manifold Absolute Pressure Sensor** – is located on the left side of the firewall.
• **Multi-Warning Buzzer** – is located in the covenience center.
• **Oil Pressure Sender** – is located on the top ot the engine towards the rear.
• **Oil Temperature Sensor** – is located on the lower left side of the engine.
• **Overdrive Relay** – is located on the rear of the right front fender apron.
• **Oxygen Sensor** – is located at the bottom of the left exhaust manifold.
• **Power Accessories Circuit Breaker** – is located in the fuse block.
• **Power Antenna Relay** – is located on the rear of the center console.
• **Power Door Lock Relay** – is located in the convenience center.
• **Power Window Circuit Breaker** – is located in the fuse block.
• **Rear Hatch Release Relay** – is located at the rear hatch release latch.
• **Speaker Relay** – is located behind the right side of the dash panel.
• **Speed Sensor** – is located on the left rear side of the transmission.

- **Starter Interrupt Relay**—is located in the convenience center.
- **Theft Deterrent Control Module**—is located on the the door lock pillar support.
- **Throttle Position Sensor**—is located on the throttle body.
- **Vehicle Elasped Time Sensor**—is located behind the right side of the instrument panel.

1985-87 CORVETTE

- **A/C-Heater Blower Resistors**—is located on the A/C-Heater plenum.
- **Amplifier Relay**—is located behind the center of the dash panel.
- **Anti-Theft Relay**—is located in the convenience center.
- **Assembly Line Diagnostic Link**—is located under the left side of the dash panel.
- **Audio Alarm Module**—is located in the convenience center.
- **Auxiliary Engine Cooling Fan Relay**—is located in the left rear corner of the engine compartment.
- **Burn Off Module**—is located behind the right side of the dash panel.
- **Convenience Center**—is located under the center section of the dash panel.
- **Coolant Temperature Sensor**—is located on the side of the left cylinder head.
- **Cruise Control Module**—is built into the liquid crystal display instrument cluster.
- **Cruise Control Servo Assembly**—is located behind front headlight.
- **Diode Module**—is located in the right rear corner of the vehicle.
- **ECM Coolant Temperature Sensor**—is located on the front of the engine, below the throttle body.
- **Electronic Control Module (ECM)**—is located behind the right side of the dash panel.
- **Electronic Spark Controller**—is located on the A/C-Heater blower housing.
- **Engine Cooling Fan Relay**—is located under the brake bosster assembly.
- **Fuel Pump Relay**—is located on the left side of the firewall in the engine comaprtment.
- **Headlight Actuator Relays**—is located on the support in the front of the left front wheel well.
- **Headlight Actuators**—are located next to each headlight assembly.
- **Headlight Door Motor**—is located behind the headlight assembly.
- **High Speed Blower Relay**—is located on the A/C-Heater blower assembly.
- **Horn In-Line Fuse**—is located in the convenience center.
- **Horn Relay**—is located in the convenience center.
- **Interior Light Timer**—is located on the instrument panel harness, behind the convenience center.
- **Isolation Relay**—is located on the support in the front of the left front wheel well.
- **Knock Sensor**—is located on the lower right center of the engine.
- **Manifold Absolute Pressure Sensor**—is located on the left side of the firewall.
- **Manifold Absolute Temperature Sensor**—is located on the right rear of the engine.
- **Mass Air Flow Sensor**—is located on the fron tof the engine , ahead of the throttle body.
- **Multi-Warning Buzzer**—is located in the covenience center.

- **Oil Pressure Sender**—is located on the top ot the engine towards the rear.
- **Oil Temperature Sensor**—is located on the lower left side of the engine.
- **Overdrive Relay**—is located on the rear of the right front fender apron.
- **Oxygen Sensor**—is located at the bottom of the left exhaust manifold.
- **Power Accessories Circuit Breaker**—is located in the fuse block.
- **Power Antenna Relay**—is located on the rear of the center console.
- **Power Door Lock Relay**—is located in the convience center.
- **Power Window Circuit Breaker**—is located in the fuse block.
- **Rear Hatch Release Relay**—is located at the rear hatch release latch.
- **Speaker Relay**—is located behind the right side of the dash panel.
- **Speed Sensor**—is located on the left rear side of the transmission.
- **Starter Interrupt Relay**—is located in the convenience center.
- **Theft Deterrent Control Module**—is located on the the door lock pillar support.
- **Throttle Position Sensor**—is located on the throttle body.
- **Vehicle Elasped Time Sensor**—is located behind the right side of the instrument panel.

1985-87 SPECTRUM

- **A/C Cycling Switch**—is located behind the A/C compressor on the front grille support.
- **A/C Relay**—is located under the left side of the instrument panel, near the left kick panel.
- **Air Temperature Sensor**—is located on the right side of the firewall, in the engine compartment.
- **Assembly Line Diagnostic Link**—is located under the right side of the dash panel near the kick panel.
- **"Check Engine" Lamp Driver**—is located under the right side of the dash panel near the kick panel.
- **Choke Relay**—is located on the right side of the firewall, in the engine compartment.
- **Coolant Sensor**—is located on the right side of the firewall, in the engine compartment.
- **Cooling Fan Relay**—is located on the left front inner fender panel, in front of the battery.
- **Defogger Relay**—is located behind the right side of the instrument panel.
- **Diode Box**—is located under the right side of the dash panel near the kick panel.
- **Early Fuel Evaporation Relay**—is located on the right side of the firewall, in the engine compartment.
- **Electronic Control Module (ECM)**—is located under the right side of the dash panel near the kick panel.
- **FICD Relay**—is located on the right side of the firewall, in the engine compartment.
- **Intermittent Wiping Relay**—is located under the left side of the instrument panel, near the left kick panel.
- **Oil Pressure Switch**—is located on the top front section of the engine.
- **Oxygen Sensor**—is located in the exhaust manifold.
- **Power Steering Pressure Switch**—is located on the right side of the firewall, in the engine compartment.
- **Restart Relay**—is located under the left side of the instrument panel, near the left kick panel.
- **Stop Light Relay**—is located in the rear trunk panel.

- **Thermo Unit** – is located behind the A/C Compressor.
- **Upshift Relay** – is located under the left side of the instrument panel, near the left kick panel.

1985-87 SPRINT

- **A/C Condenser Fan Relay** – is located on the left side of the firewall above the shock tower.
- **A/C High Pressure Switch** – is located on the right front inner fender panel. behind the winshield washer fluid reservoir.
- **A/C Idle-Up Assembly** – is located on top of the engine under the air cleaner assembly.
- **A/C Low Pressure Switch** – is located on the right front inner fender panel, below the winshield washer fluid reservoir.
- **A/C Magnetic Clutch Relay** – is located on the left side of the firewall above the shock tower.
- **Coolant Temperature Switch** – is located on the top of the engine, on the coolant intake pipe.
- **Electronic Control Module (ECM)** – is located under the left side of the instrument panel.
- **Fan Thermo Switch** – is located in the thermostat housing.
- **Idle Micro Switch** – is located on the carburetor.
- **Idle-Up Actuator** – is located on the carburetor.
- **Oxygen Sensor** – is located in the the exhaust manifold.
- **Thermal Switch** – is located in the intake manifold.
- **Thermo Sensor** – is located in the air cleaner assembly.
- **Vacuum Switching Valve** – is located in the center of the firewall, next to the igntion switch.
- **Wide-Open Throttle Micro Switch** – is located on the carburetor.

ASTRO

- **A/C Compressor Relay** – is located on a bracket on the right side of the engine compartment.
- **A/C-Heater Blower Motor Relay** – is located on a bracket on the right side of the engine compartment.
- **Assembly Line Diagnostic Link** – is located under the left side of the dash panel.

- **"Check Engine" Light Driver** – is located above the convenience center under the left side of the dash panel.
- **Convenience Center** – is located under the dash panel and to the left of the steering column.
- **Coolant Temperature Sending Unit (4 cyl.)** – is located on the top of the cylinder head.
- **Coolant Temperature Sending Unit (V6)** – is located on the top of the cylinder head.
- **Coolant Temperature Sensor** – is located in the thermostat housing.
- **Cruise Control Module** – is located under the dash on a bracket at the right of the steering column.
- **Diagnostic Dwell Meter Connection** – is located in the wiring harness at the right front corner of the engine.
- **Differential Pressure Sensor (V6)** – is located on the rear of the air cleaner housing.
- **Electronic Control Module (ECM)** – is located under the right side of the dash.
- **Electronic Spark Control Module (ESC)** – is located on a bracket at the right rear cylinder head or under the right side of the dash.
- **Fuel Pump Relay** – is located on a bracket on the right side of the engine compartment.
- **Fuel Pump Test Connection** – is located in the G terminal of the assembly line diagnostic link.
- **Headlight Warning Buzzer** – is located on the wiring harness behind the instrument panel.
- **Horn Relay** – is located on the convience center.
- **Knock Sensor (V6)** – is located on the lower left side of the engine block.
- **Manifold Absolute Pressure Sensor (4 cyl)** – is located on the front of the air cleaner housing.
- **Power Accesories Circuit Breaker** – is located in the fuse block.
- **Power Window Circuit Breaker** – is located in the fuse block.
- **Throttle Position Sensor (4 cyl.)** – is located on the throttle body.
- **Throttle Position Sensor (V6)** – is located in the carburetor air horn.
- **Throttle Vacuum Kicker Relay** – is located on a bracket on the right side of the engine compartment.
- **Vehicle Speed Sensor** – is located under the dash panel, besides the convenience center.

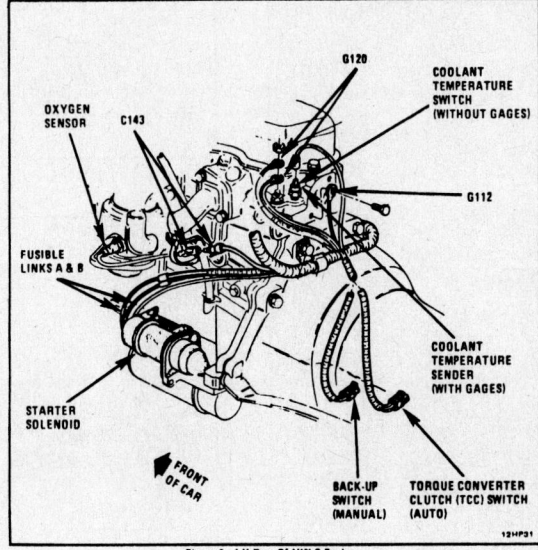

Figure A - LH Rear Of VIN 2 Engine

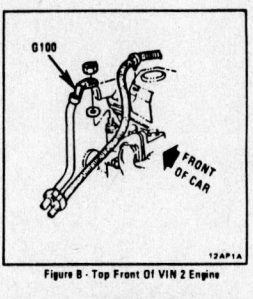

Figure B - Top Front Of VIN 2 Engine

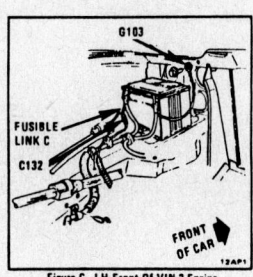

Figure C - LH Front Of VIN 2 Engine

1985-86 Chevrolet Camaro

COMPONENT LOCATIONS

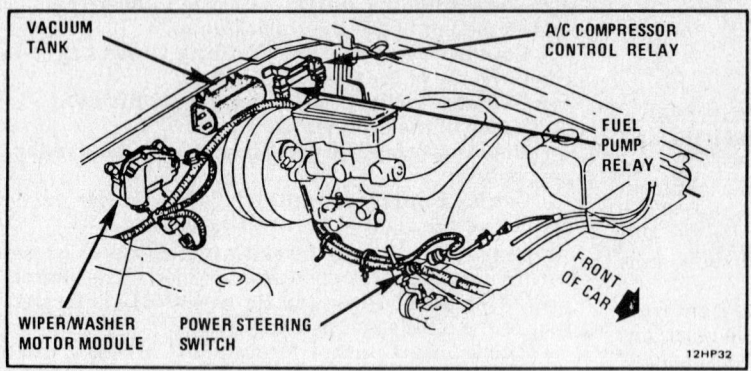

Figure A - LH Side Of VIN 2 Engine Compartment

VACUUM TANK
A/C COMPRESSOR CONTROL RELAY
FUEL PUMP RELAY
WIPER/WASHER MOTOR MODULE
POWER STEERING SWITCH
FRONT OF CAR
12HP32

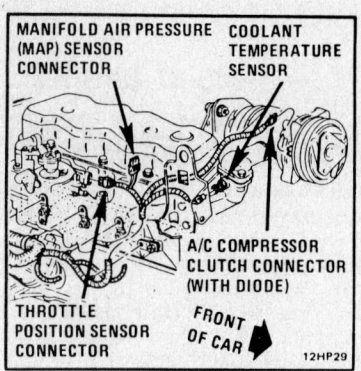

Figure C - RH Side Of VIN 2 Engine

MANIFOLD AIR PRESSURE (MAP) SENSOR CONNECTOR
COOLANT TEMPERATURE SENSOR
A/C COMPRESSOR CLUTCH CONNECTOR (WITH DIODE)
THROTTLE POSITION SENSOR CONNECTOR
FRONT OF CAR
12HP29

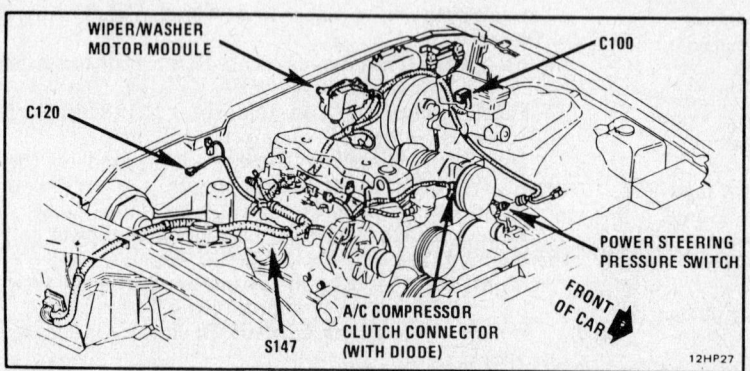

Figure B - VIN 2 Engine Compartment

WIPER/WASHER MOTOR MODULE
C100
C120
POWER STEERING PRESSURE SWITCH
S147
A/C COMPRESSOR CLUTCH CONNECTOR (WITH DIODE)
FRONT OF CAR
12HP27

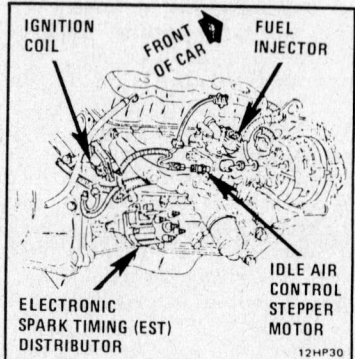

Figure D - RH Rear Of VIN 2 Engine

IGNITION COIL
FRONT OF CAR
FUEL INJECTOR
IDLE AIR CONTROL STEPPER MOTOR
ELECTRONIC SPARK TIMING (EST) DISTRIBUTOR
12HP30

1985-86 Chevrolet Camaro

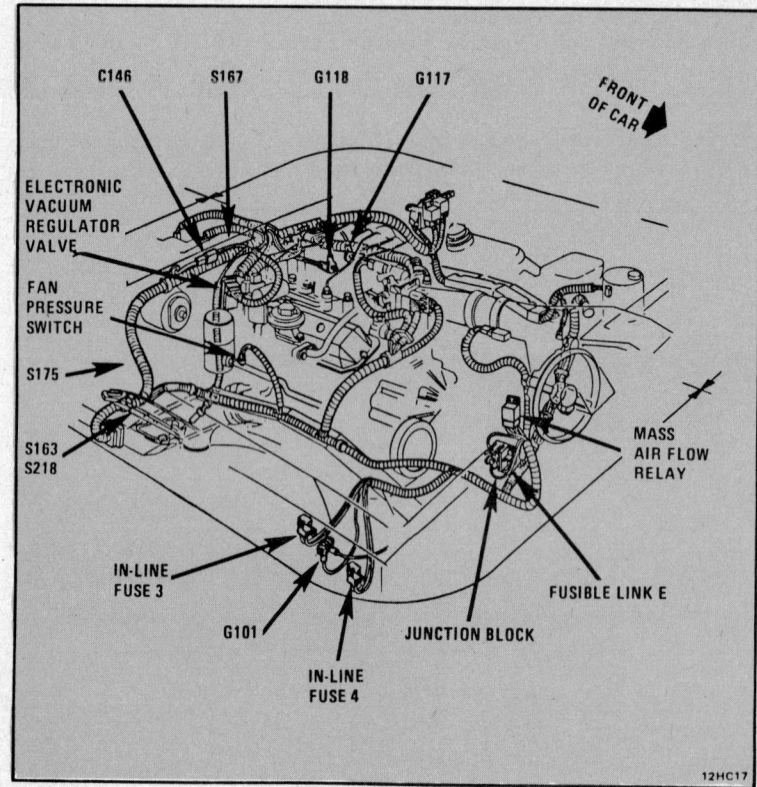

Figure A - VIN S Engine Compartment

C146
S167
G118
G117
FRONT OF CAR
ELECTRONIC VACUUM REGULATOR VALVE
FAN PRESSURE SWITCH
S175
S163
S218
IN-LINE FUSE 3
G101
IN-LINE FUSE 4
JUNCTION BLOCK
MASS AIR FLOW RELAY
FUSIBLE LINK E
12HC17

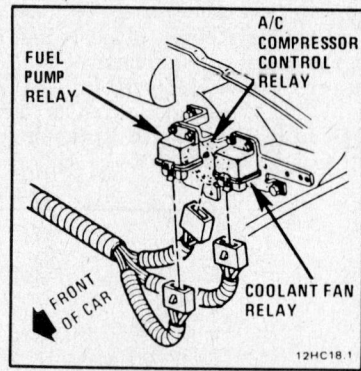

Figure B - LH Front Of Dash (VIN S)

FUEL PUMP RELAY
A/C COMPRESSOR CONTROL RELAY
FRONT OF CAR
COOLANT FAN RELAY
12HC18.1

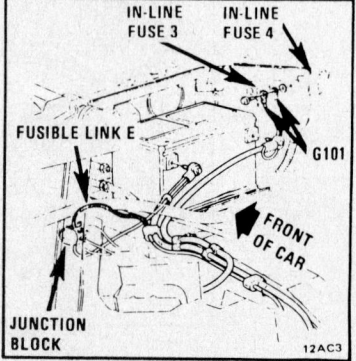

Figure C - RH Front Corner Of VIN S Engine Compartment

IN-LINE FUSE 3
IN-LINE FUSE 4
FUSIBLE LINK E
G101
JUNCTION BLOCK
FRONT OF CAR
12AC3

1985-86 Chevrolet Camaro

COMPONENT LOCATIONS

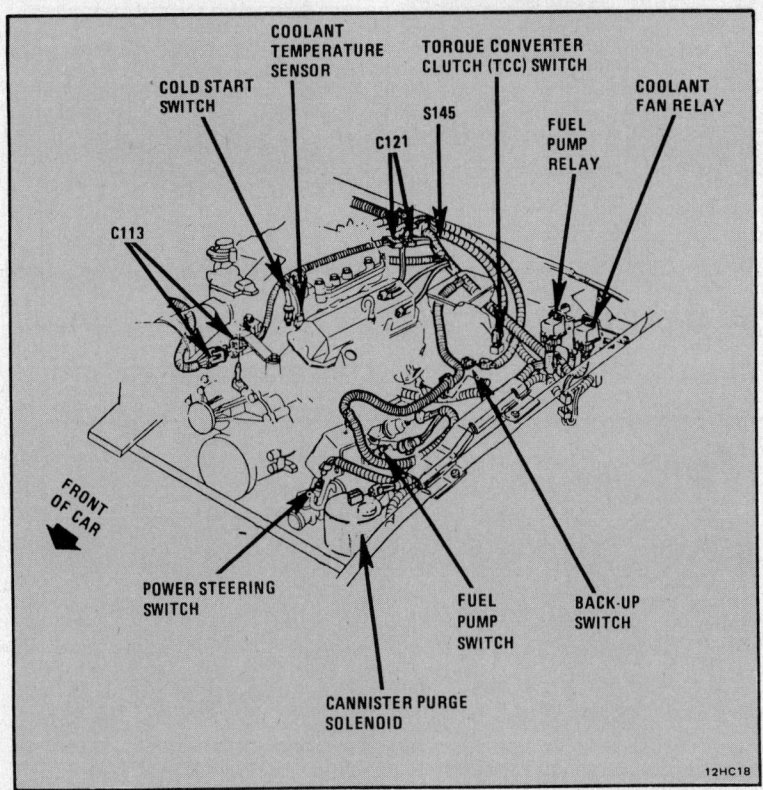

Figure A - LH Side Of VIN S Engine Compartment

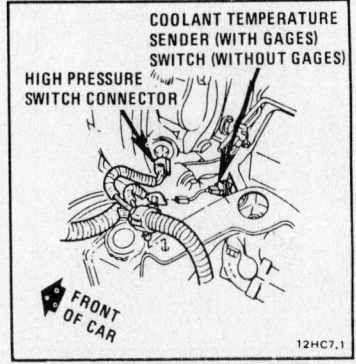

Figure B - LH Side Of VIN F Engine

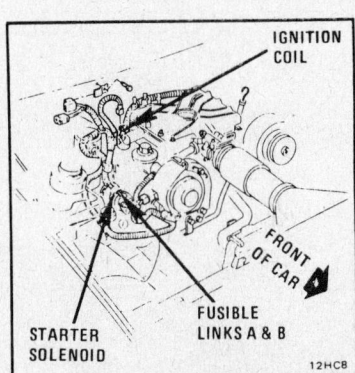

Figure C - Top LH Front Of VIN S Engine

1985-86 Chevrolet Camaro

Figure A - VIN S Engine

Figure B - RH Side Of VIN S Engine

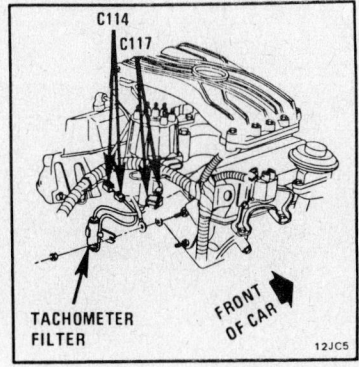

Figure C - Top Rear Of VIN S Engine (Berlinetta)

1985-86 Chevrolet Camaro

COMPONENT LOCATIONS

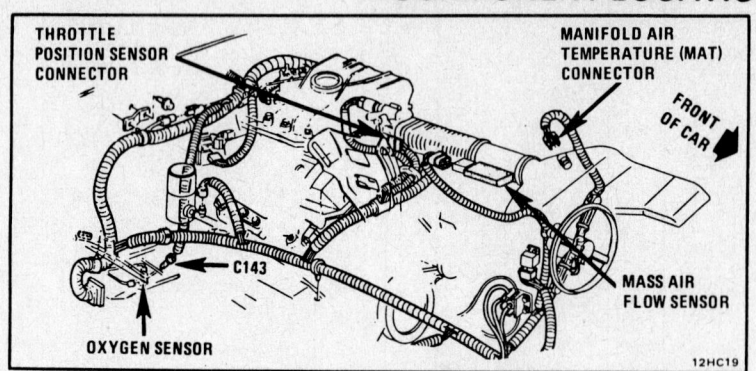

Figure A - RH Side Of VIN S Engine
12HC19

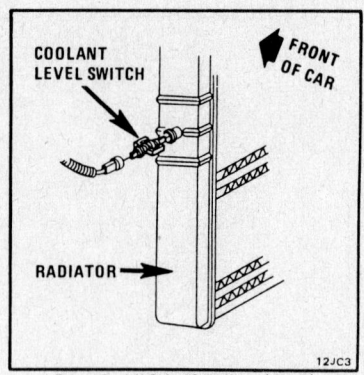

Figure D - LH Side Of Radiator (VIN S)
12JC3

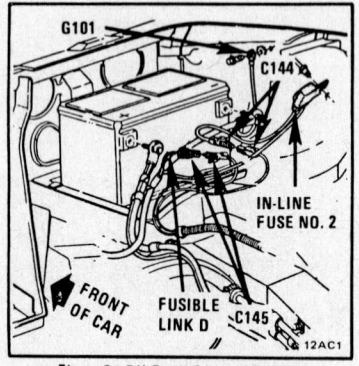

Figure B - RH Front Corner Of VIN F Engine Compartment
12AC1

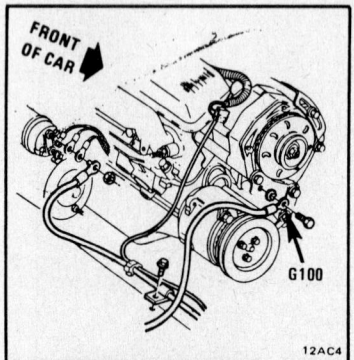

Figure C - RH Front Of VIN F Engine
12AC4

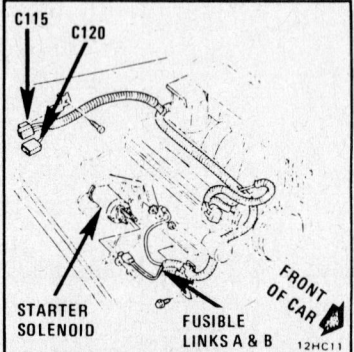

Figure E - RH Side Of VIN F Engine
12HC11

1985-86 Chevrolet Camaro

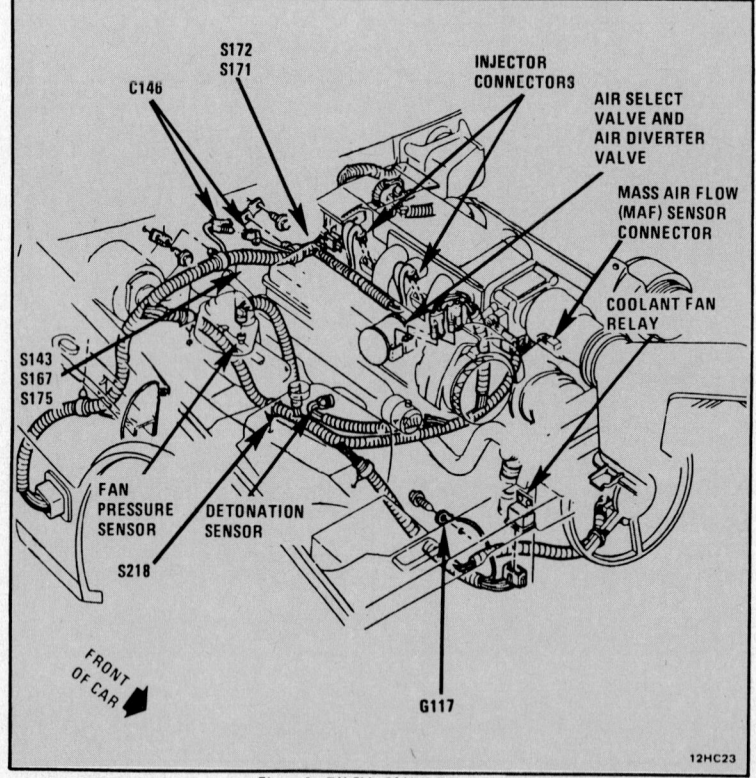

Figure A - RH Side Of VIN F Engine
12HC23

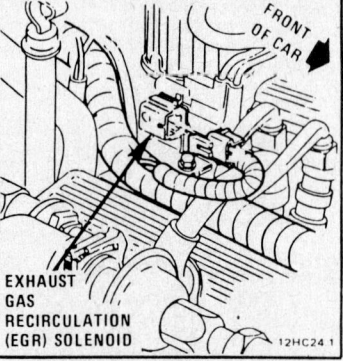

Figure B - Top RH Rear Of VIN F Engine
12HC24 1

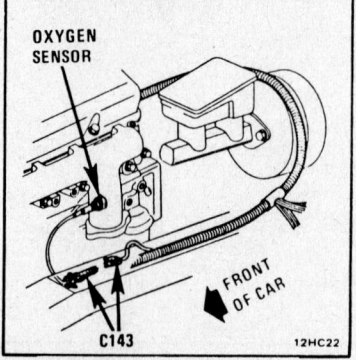

Figure C - LH Rear Of VIN F Engine
12HC22

1985-86 Chevrolet Camaro

COMPONENT LOCATIONS

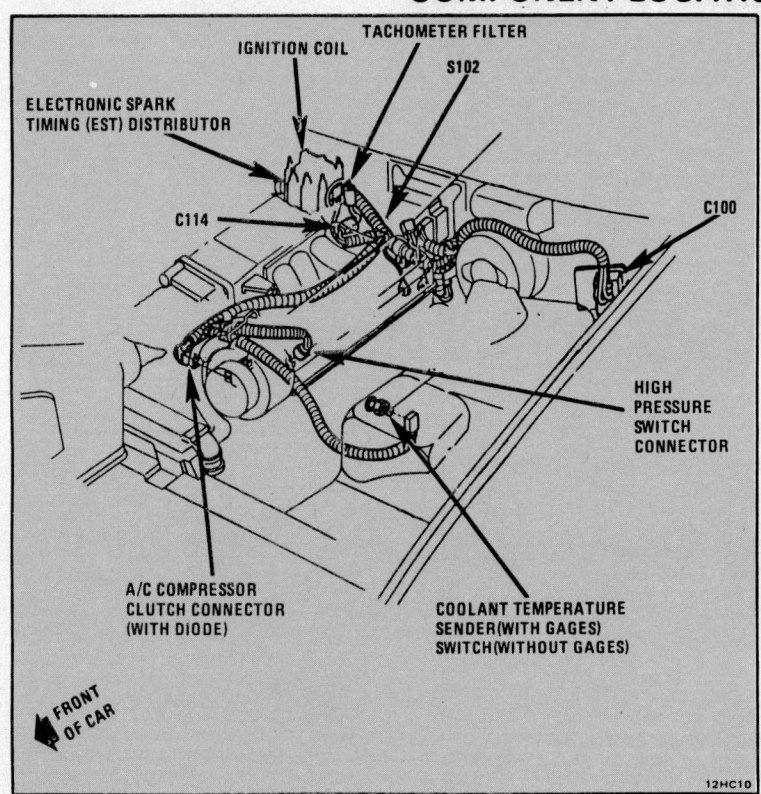

A/C COMPRESSOR CLUTCH CONNECTOR (WITH DIODE)

COOLANT TEMPERATURE SENDER(WITH GAGES) SWITCH(WITHOUT GAGES)

HIGH PRESSURE SWITCH CONNECTOR

FRONT OF CAR

Figure A - LH Side Of VIN F Engine

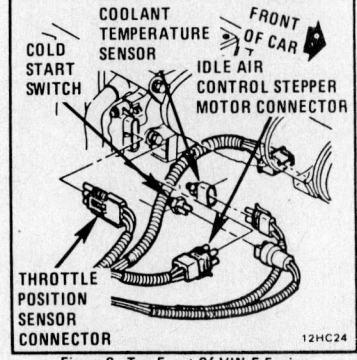

EGR VACUUM SENSOR DIAGNOSTIC CONNECTOR

FRONT OF CAR

MANIFOLD AIR TEMPERATURE (MAT) SENSOR CONNECTOR   12HC24B

Figure B - Top Rear Of VIN F Engine

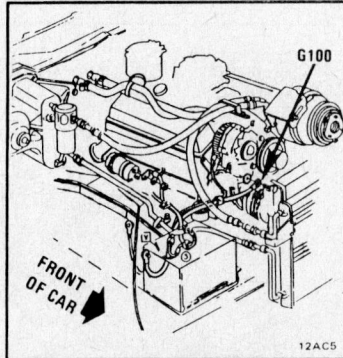

COLD START SWITCH

COOLANT TEMPERATURE SENSOR

FRONT OF CAR

IDLE AIR CONTROL STEPPER MOTOR CONNECTOR

THROTTLE POSITION SENSOR CONNECTOR   12HC24

Figure C - Top Front Of VIN F Engine

1985-86 Chevrolet Camaro

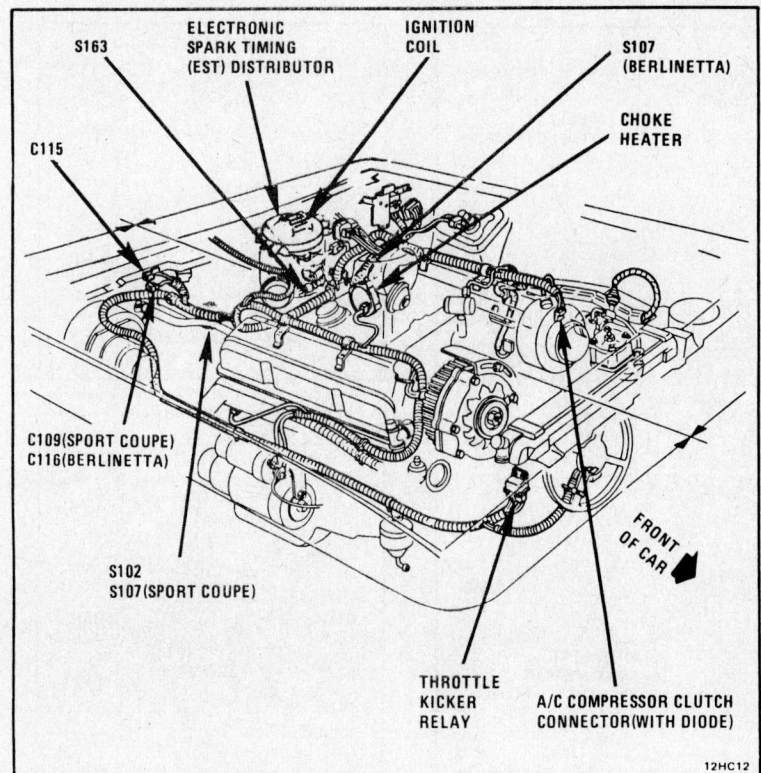

Figure A - RH Side Of VIN H Engine Compartment (VIN G Similar)

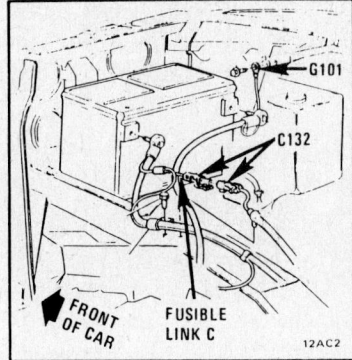

Figure B - RH Side Of VIN H & VIN G Engine (VIN F Similar)

G101

C132

FRONT OF CAR

FUSIBLE LINK C   12AC2

Figure C - RH Front Corner Of VIN H And VIN G Engine Compatment

1985-86 Chevrolet Camaro

143

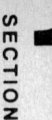

COMPONENT LOCATIONS

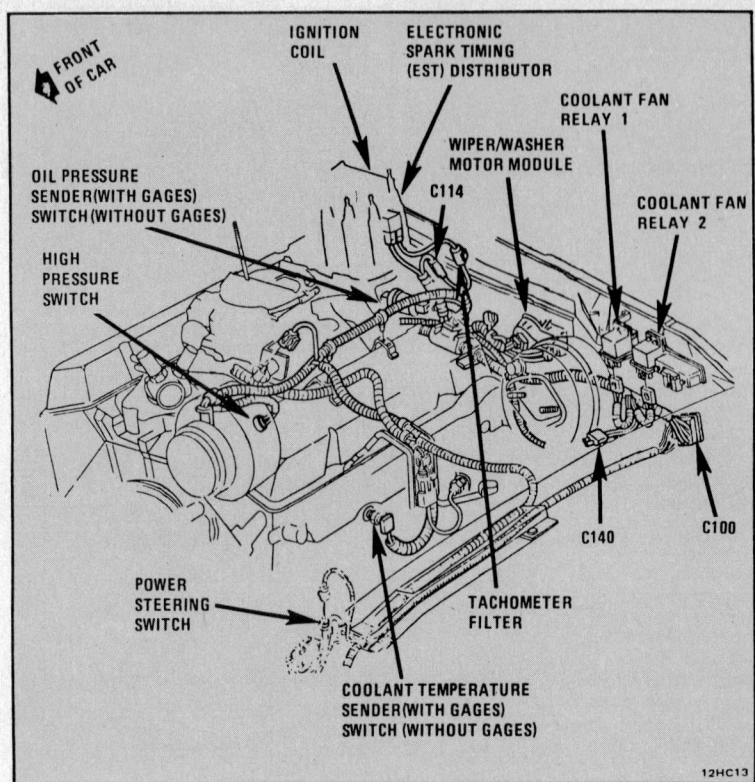

Figure A - Top Rear Of VIN H Engine(VIN G Similar)

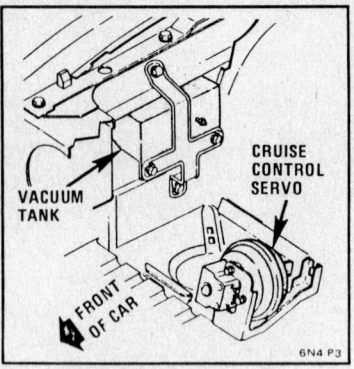

Figure B - Front RH Corner Of VIN 2 Engine Compartment

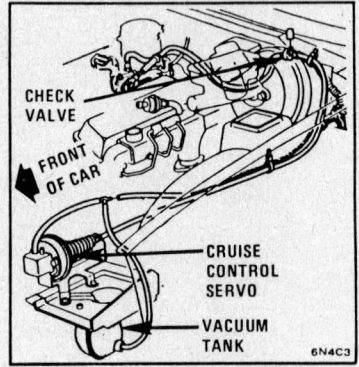

Figure C - LH Side Of Engine Compartment (Except VIN 2)

1985-86 Chevrolet Camaro

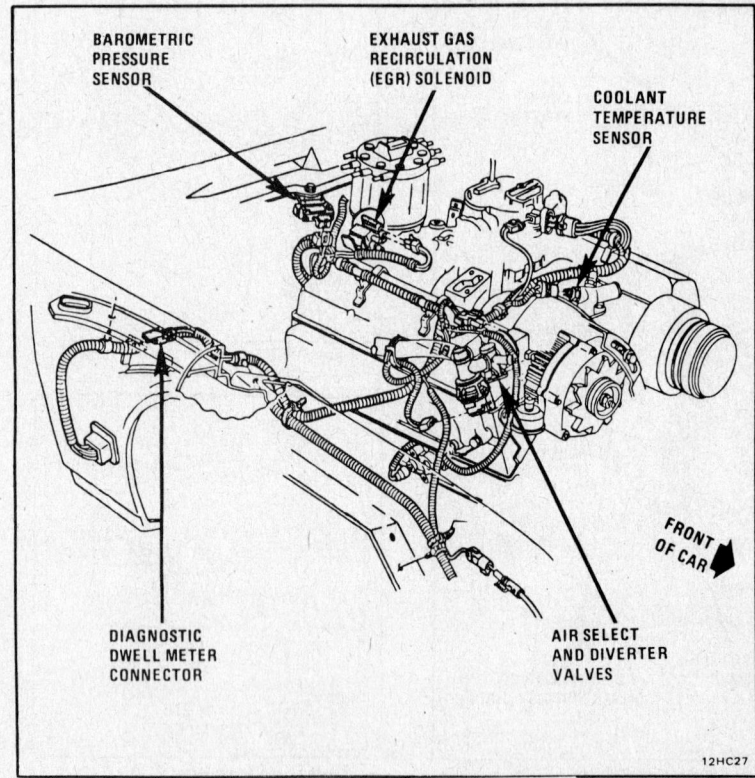

Figure A - RH Side Of VIN H Engine (VIN G Similar)

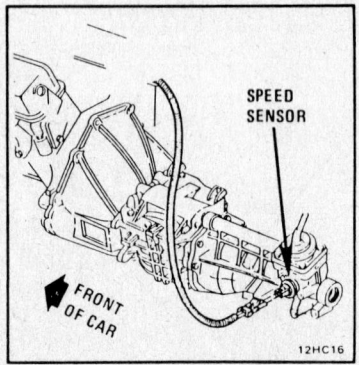

Figure B - LH Side Of Manual Transmission, (Automatic Similar)

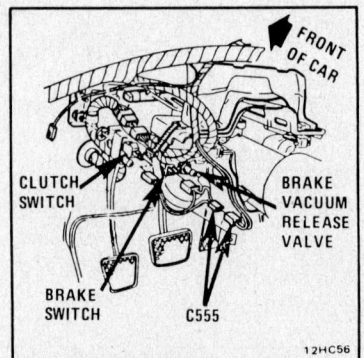

Figure C - Below LH Side Of I/P

1985-86 Chevrolet Camaro

COMPONENT LOCATIONS

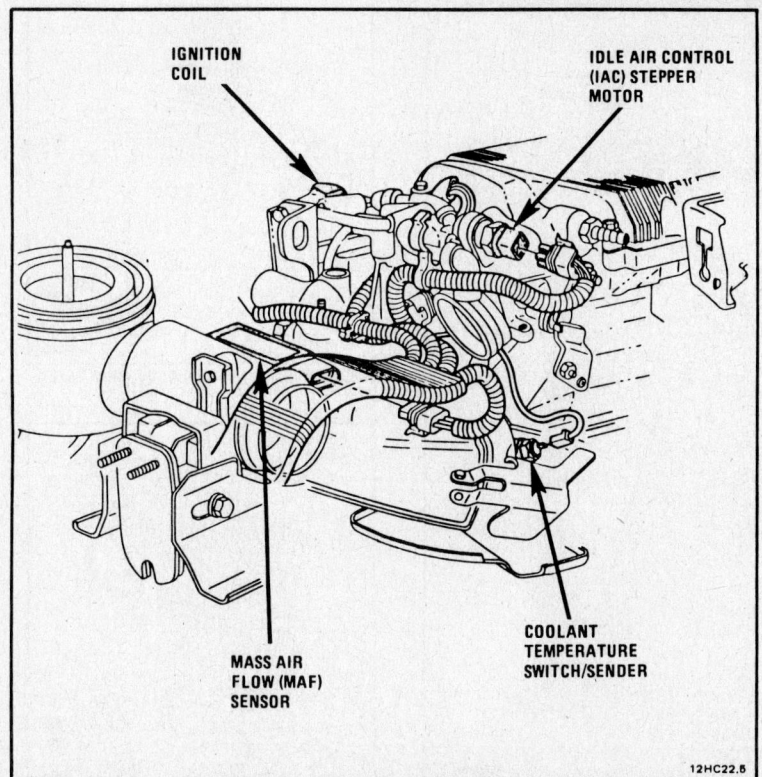

IGNITION COIL

IDLE AIR CONTROL (IAC) STEPPER MOTOR

MASS AIR FLOW (MAF) SENSOR

COOLANT TEMPERATURE SWITCH/SENDER

12HC22.5

Figure A - Top LH Side Of V6 VIN W Engine

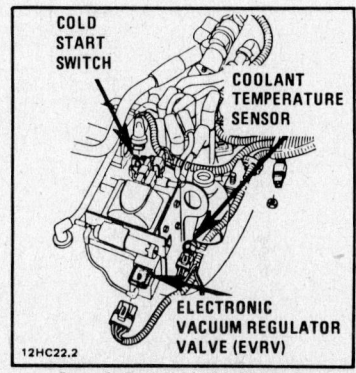

THROTTLE POSITION SENSOR

IDLE AIR CONTROL (IAC) STEPPER MOTOR

COOLANT TEMPERATURE SWITCH/SENDER CONNECTOR

ELECTRONIC SPARK TIMING (EST) DISTRIBUTOR

12HC22.6

Figure B - Left Side Of V6 VIN W Engine

COLD START SWITCH

COOLANT TEMPERATURE SENSOR

ELECTRONIC VACUUM REGULATOR VALVE (EVRV)

12HC22.2

Figure C - Top LH Of V6 VIN W Engine

1985-86 Chevrolet Cavalier

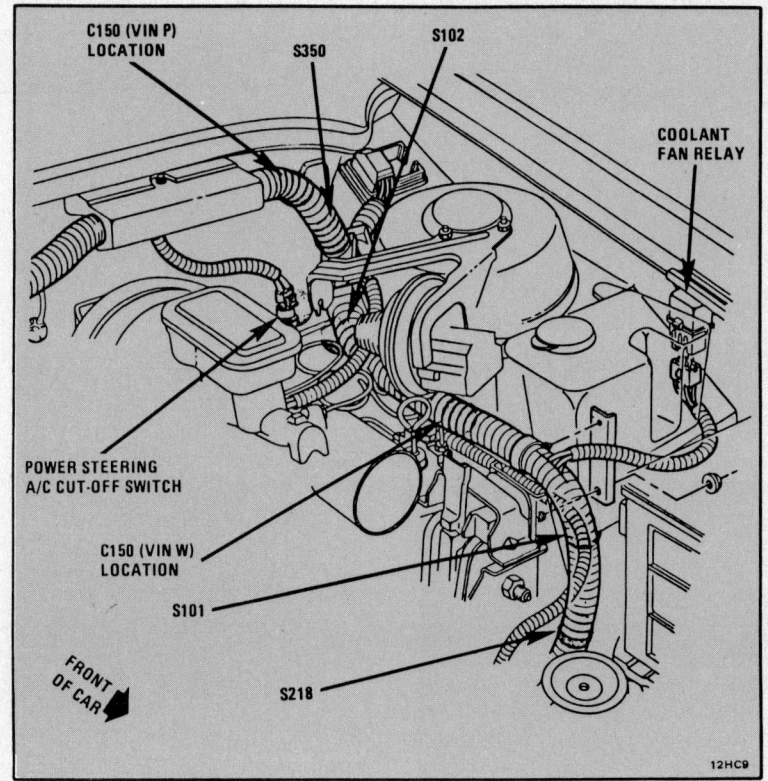

C150 (VIN P) LOCATION

S350

S102

COOLANT FAN RELAY

POWER STEERING A/C CUT-OFF SWITCH

C150 (VIN W) LOCATION

S101

S218

FRONT OF CAR

12HC9

Figure A' - LH Side Of V6 VIN W Engine Compartment (L4 VIN P Similar)

C350

12HC26

Figure B - RH Rear Of V6 VIN W Engine

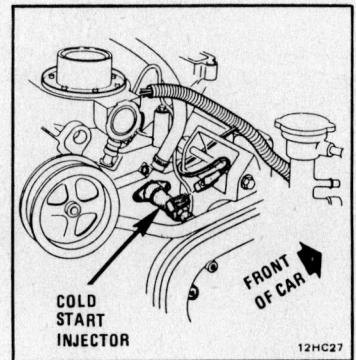

COLD START INJECTOR

FRONT OF CAR

12HC27

Figure C - Top RH Side Of V6 VIN W Engine

1985-86 Chevrolet Cavalier

COMPONENT LOCATIONS

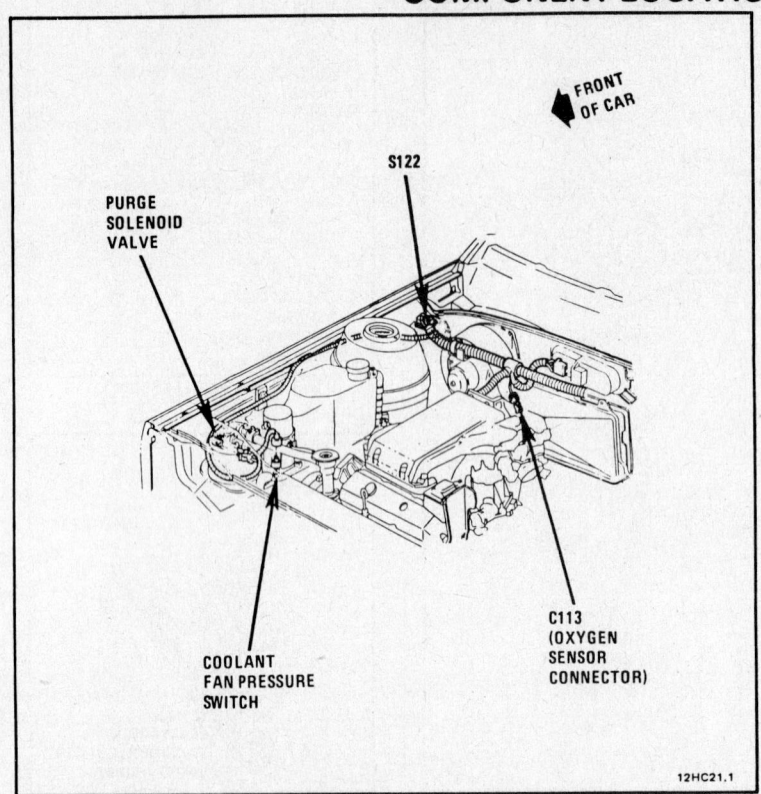

Figure A - RH Side Of V6 VIN W Engine Compartment

1985-86 Chevrolet Cavalier

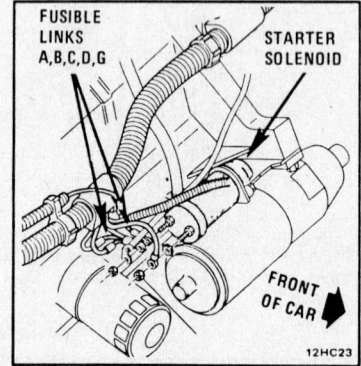

Figure B - Lower LH Front Of V6 VIN W Engine

Figure C - LH Front Of V6 VIN W Engine

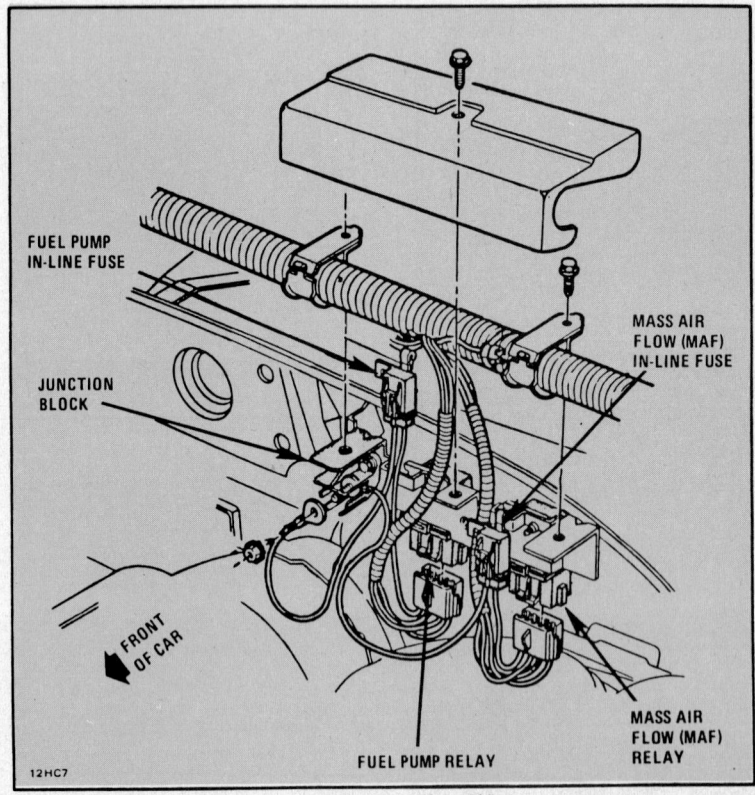

Figure A - LH Front Of Dash

1985-86 Chevrolet Cavalier

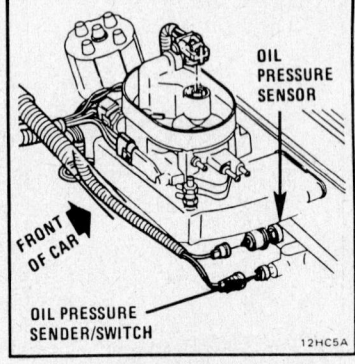

Figure B - Middle Rear Of L4 VIN P Engine

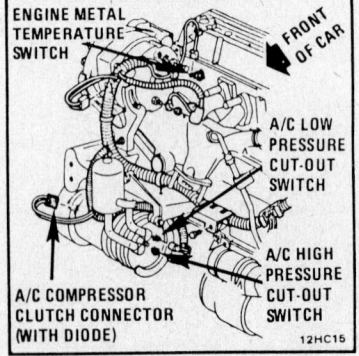

Figure C - Front Of L4 VIN P Engine

COMPONENT LOCATIONS

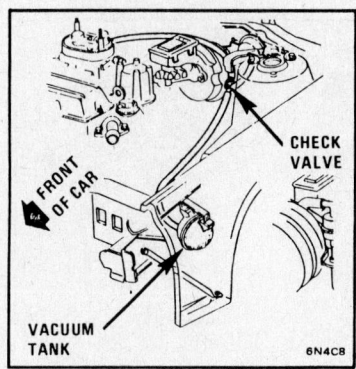

Figure A - LH Side Of L4 VIN P
Engine Compartment

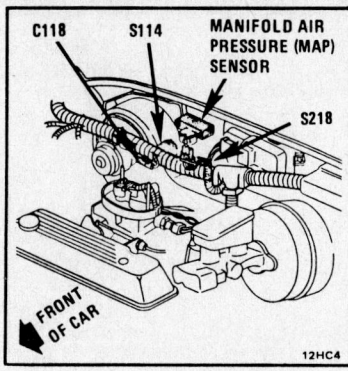

Figure C - Center Front Of L4 VIN P Dash

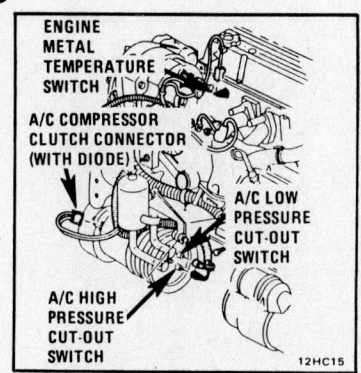

Figure E - Front Of VIN P Engine

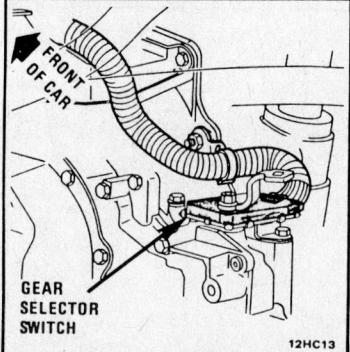

Figure B - Top Of Automatic Transaxle

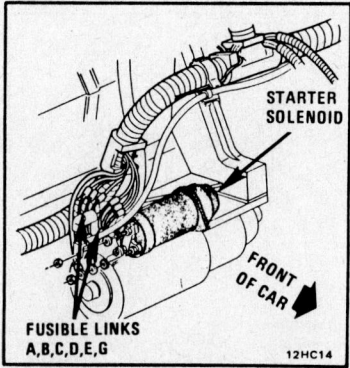

Figure D - LH Front Of L4 VIN P Engine

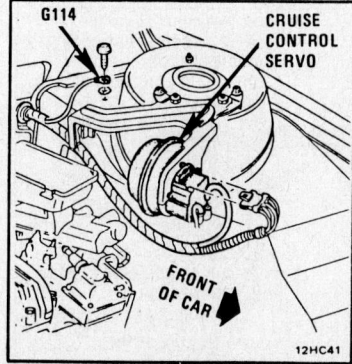

Figure F - LH Side Of V6 VIN W Compartment
(L4 VIN P Similar)

1985-86 Chevrolet Cavalier

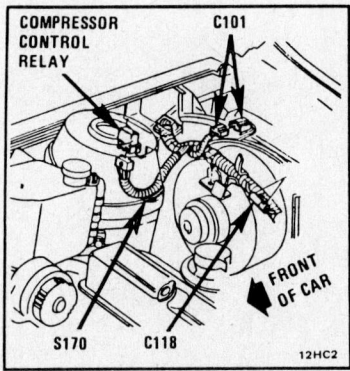

Figure A - RH Rear Corner Of L4 VIN P Engine
Compartment (V6 VIN W Similar)

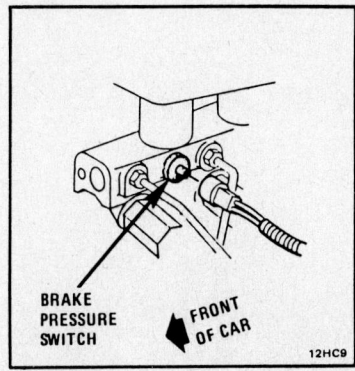

Figure C - LH Rear Corner Of Engine Compartment

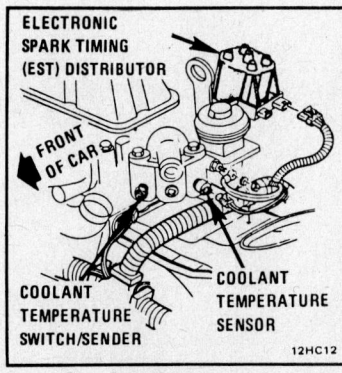

Figure E - LH Top Of L4 VIN P Engine

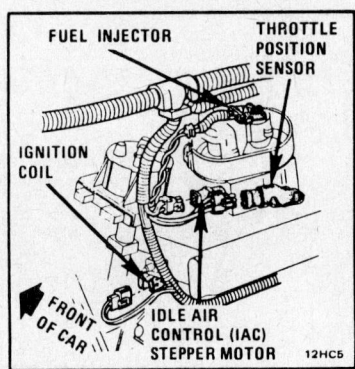

Figure B - Middle Rear Of L4 VIN P Engine

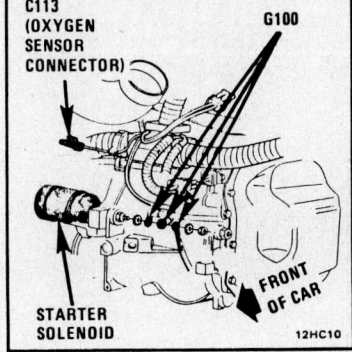

Figure D - Lower LH Front Of L4 VIN P Engine

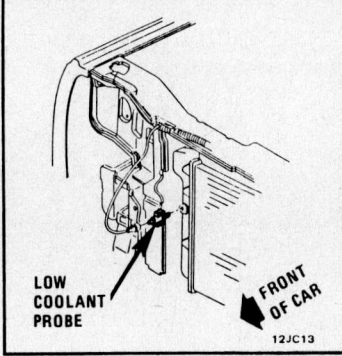

Figure F - Right Front Of Radiator

1985-86 Chevrolet Cavalier

COMPONENT LOCATIONS

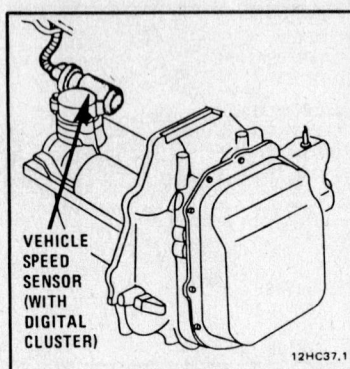

Figure A - Transaxle In Engine Compartment

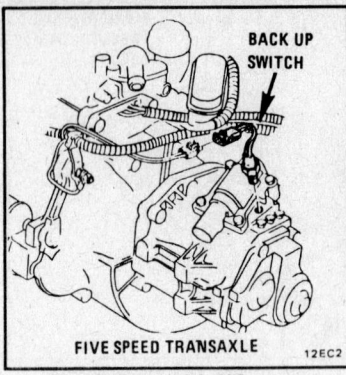

Figure C - Front LH Side Of Engine

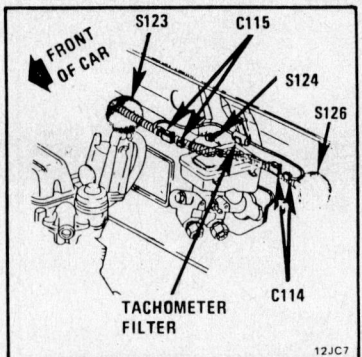

Figure E - Upper LH Side Front Of Dash

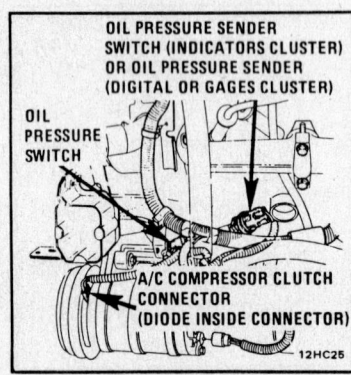

Figure B - LH Front Of V6 VIN W Engine

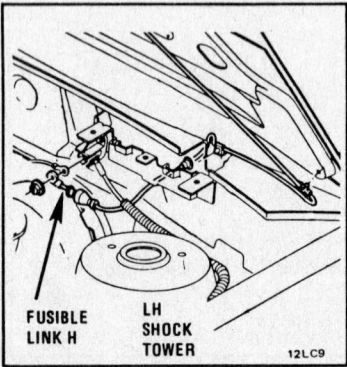

Figure D - LH Rear Corner Of Engine Compartment

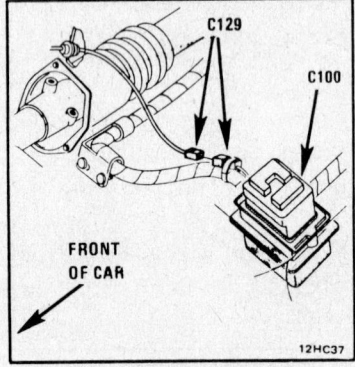

Figure F - Behind LH Side Of I/P

1985-86 Chevrolet Cavalier

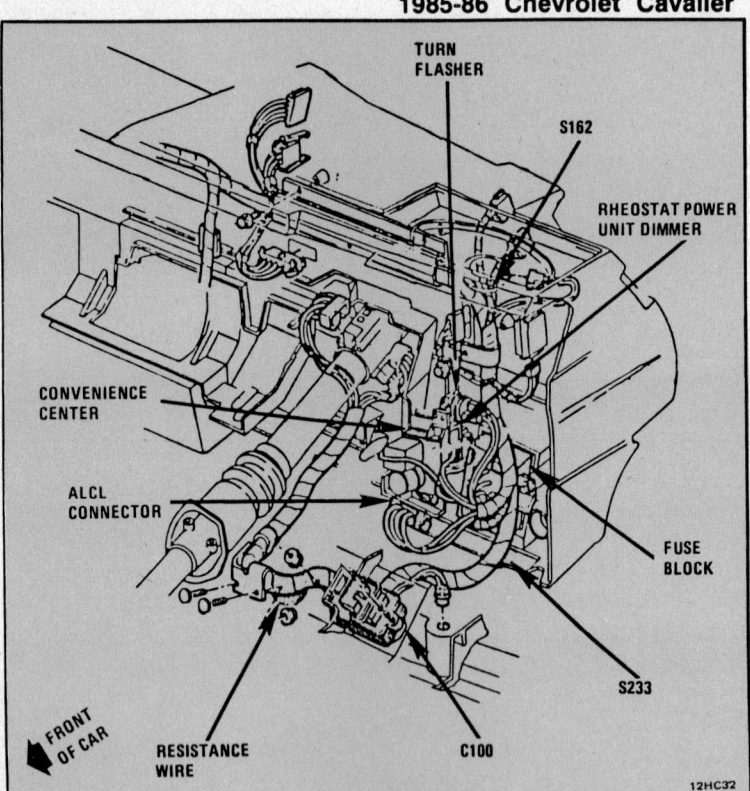

Figure A - Behind LH Side Of I/P

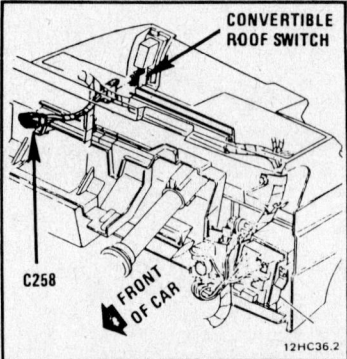

Figure B - Behind LH Side Of I/P

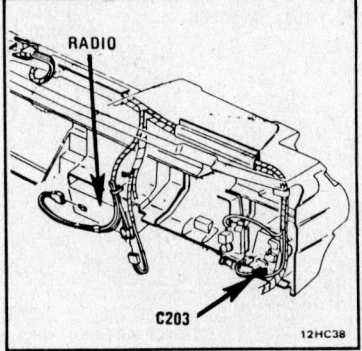

Figure C - Behind LH Side Of I/P

1985-86 Chevrolet Cavalier

COMPONENT LOCATIONS

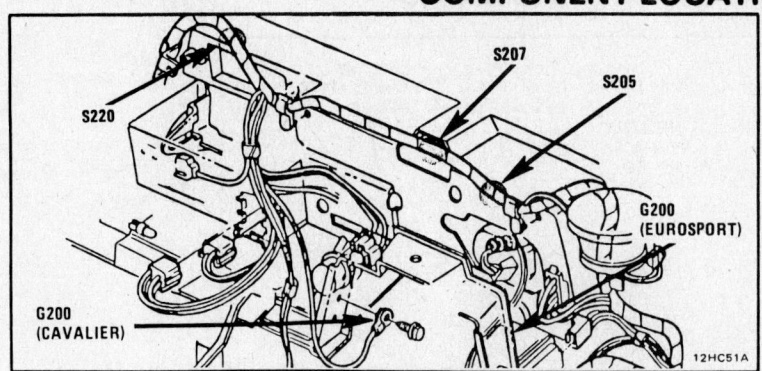

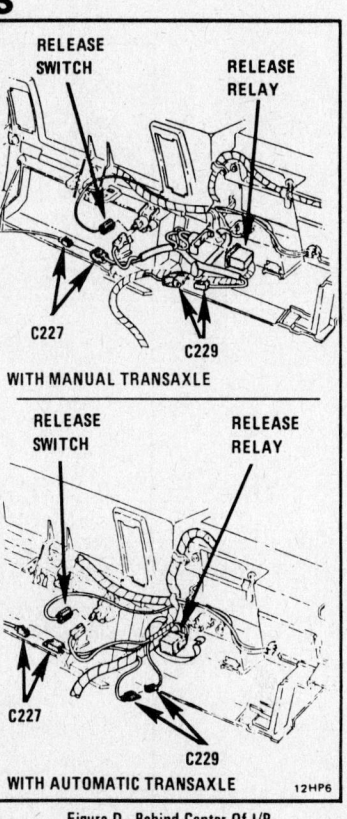

Figure A - Behind Center Of I/P

WITH MANUAL TRANSAXLE

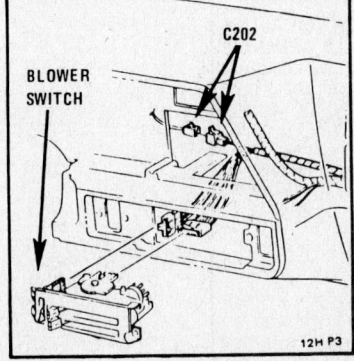

Figure B - Behind Center Of I/P

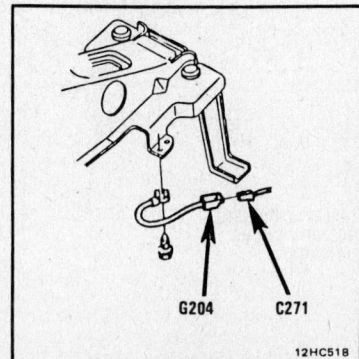

Figure C - Behind Center Of I/P

WITH AUTOMATIC TRANSAXLE

Figure D - Behind Center Of I/P

1985-86 Chevrolet Cavalier

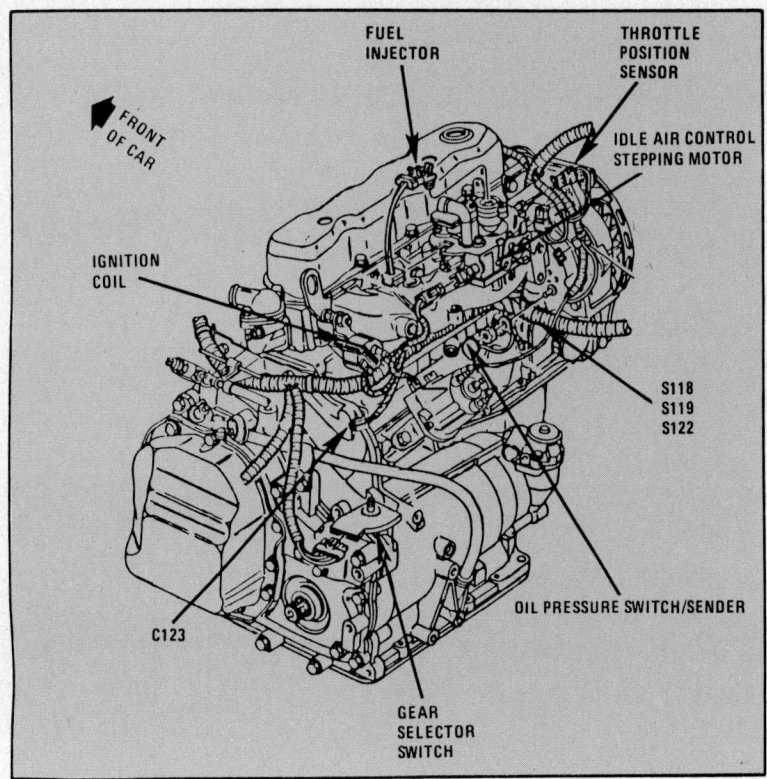

Figure 1 - Rear Side Of (VIN R) Engine

1985-86 Chevrolet Citation

COMPONENT LOCATIONS

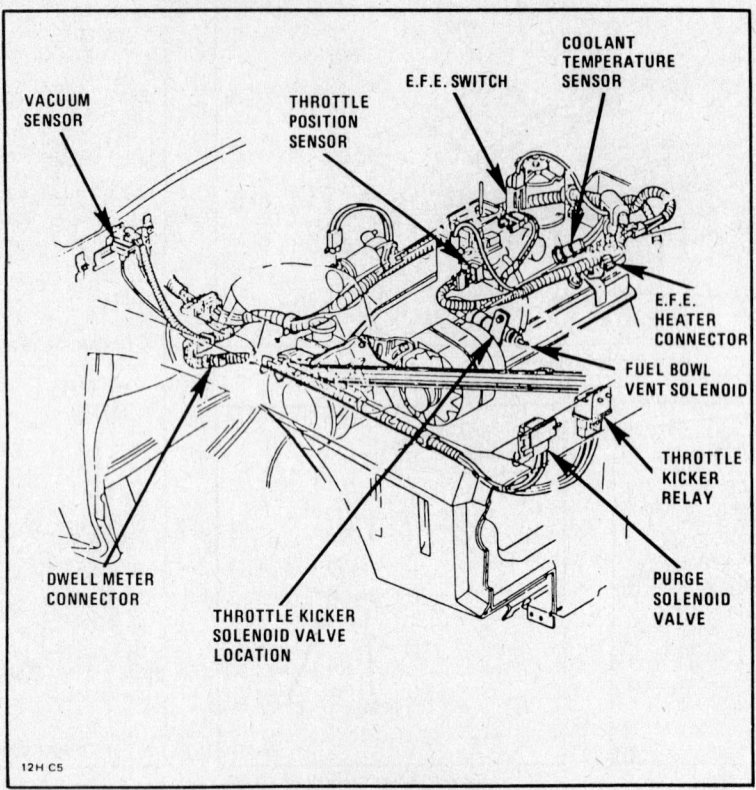

VACUUM SENSOR

THROTTLE POSITION SENSOR

E.F.E. SWITCH

COOLANT TEMPERATURE SENSOR

E.F.E. HEATER CONNECTOR

FUEL BOWL VENT SOLENOID

THROTTLE KICKER RELAY

PURGE SOLENOID VALVE

DWELL METER CONNECTOR

THROTTLE KICKER SOLENOID VALVE LOCATION

12H C5

Figure 1 - Front Engine View (V6)

1985-86 Chevrolet Citation

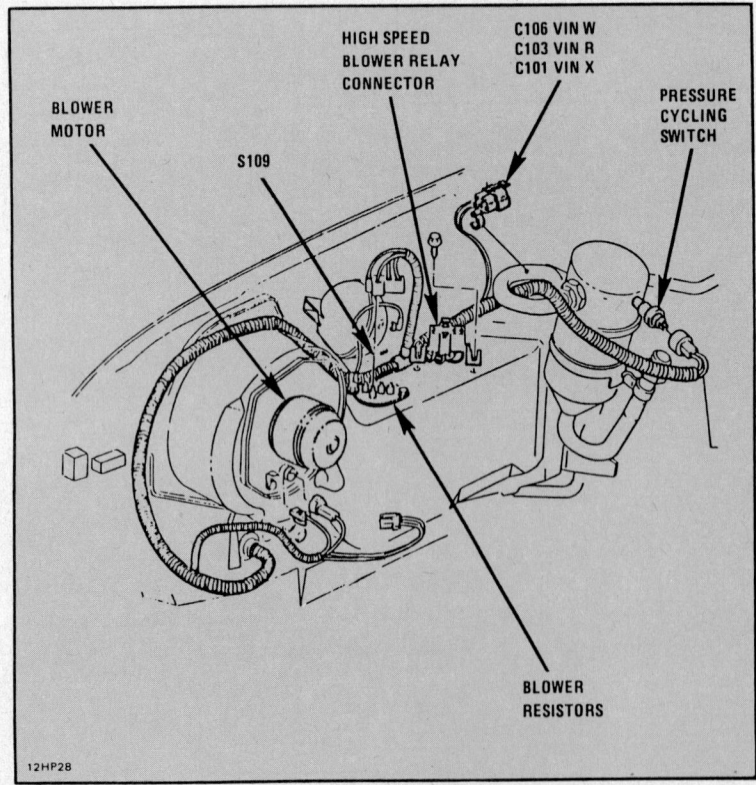

BLOWER MOTOR

S109

HIGH SPEED BLOWER RELAY CONNECTOR

C106 VIN W
C103 VIN R
C101 VIN X

PRESSURE CYCLING SWITCH

BLOWER RESISTORS

12HP28

Figure 1 - Center Of Engine Cowl

1985-86 Chevrolet Citation

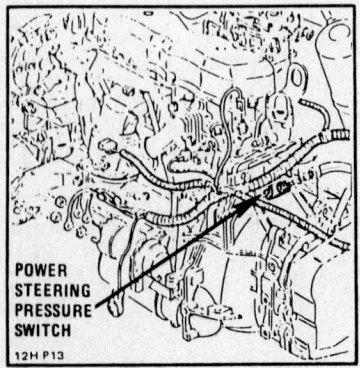

POWER STEERING PRESSURE SWITCH

12H P13

Figure 2 - Engine Compartment (VIN R)

COMPONENT LOCATIONS

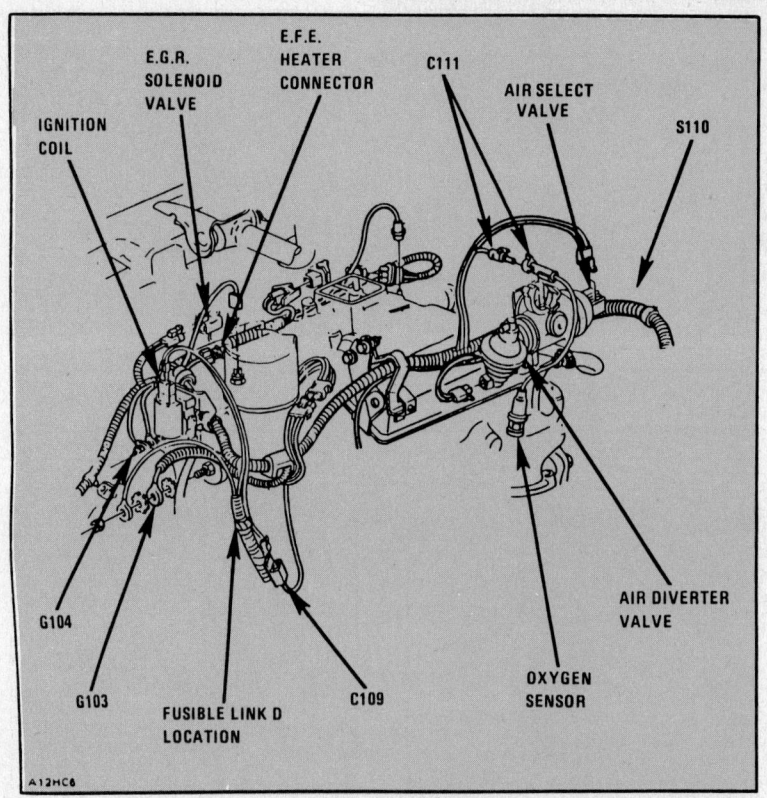

Figure 1 - LH Rear Of (V6) Engine

1985-86 Chevrolet Citation

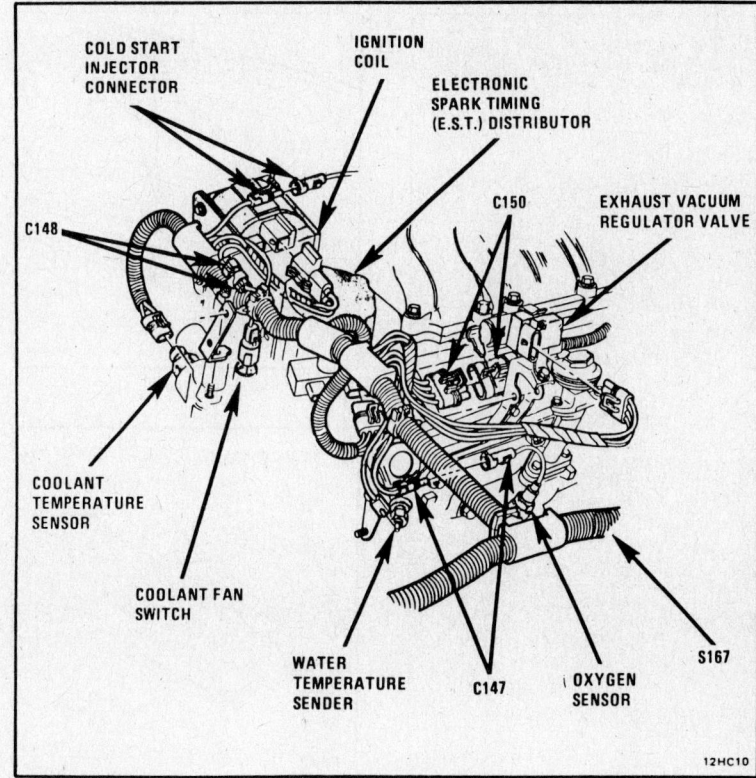

Figure A - LH Rear Of VIN W Engine

1985-86 Chevrolet Celebrity

Figure 2 - Top Of (VIN R) Engine

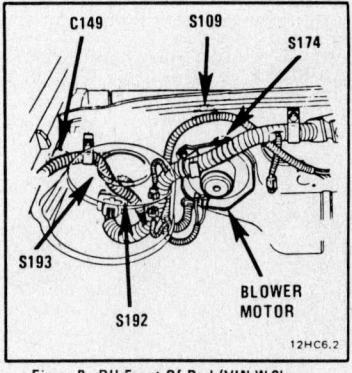

Figure B - RH Front Of Dash(VIN W Shown, Others Similar)

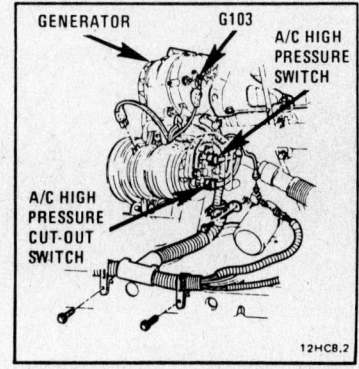

Figure C - RH Front Of VIN W Engine

COMPONENT LOCATIONS

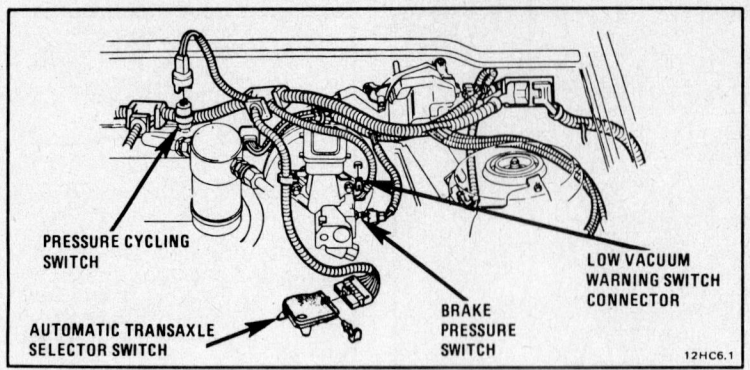

PRESSURE CYCLING SWITCH

AUTOMATIC TRANSAXLE SELECTOR SWITCH

BRAKE PRESSURE SWITCH

LOW VACUUM WARNING SWITCH CONNECTOR

12HC6.1

Figure A - LH Front Of Dash

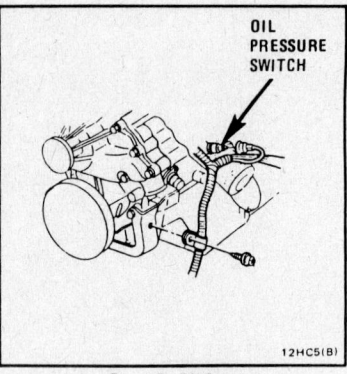

OIL PRESSURE SWITCH

12HC5(B)

Figure D - RH Front

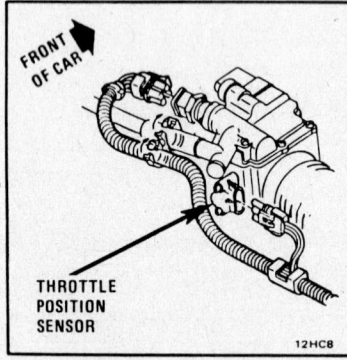

FRONT OF CAR

THROTTLE POSITION SENSOR

12HC8

Figure B - Rear Of Throttle Body

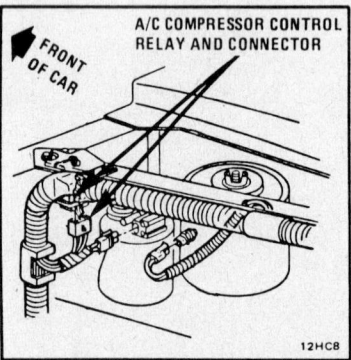

A/C COMPRESSOR CONTROL RELAY AND CONNECTOR

FRONT OF CAR

12HC8

Figure C - RH Front Of V6 Engine Compartment

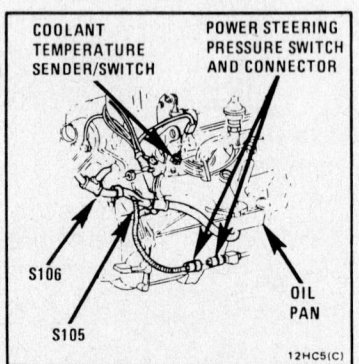

COOLANT TEMPERATURE SENDER/SWITCH

POWER STEERING PRESSURE SWITCH AND CONNECTOR

S106

S105

OIL PAN

12HC5(C)

Figure E - LH Rear Of VIN X Engine

1985-86 Chevrolet Celebrity

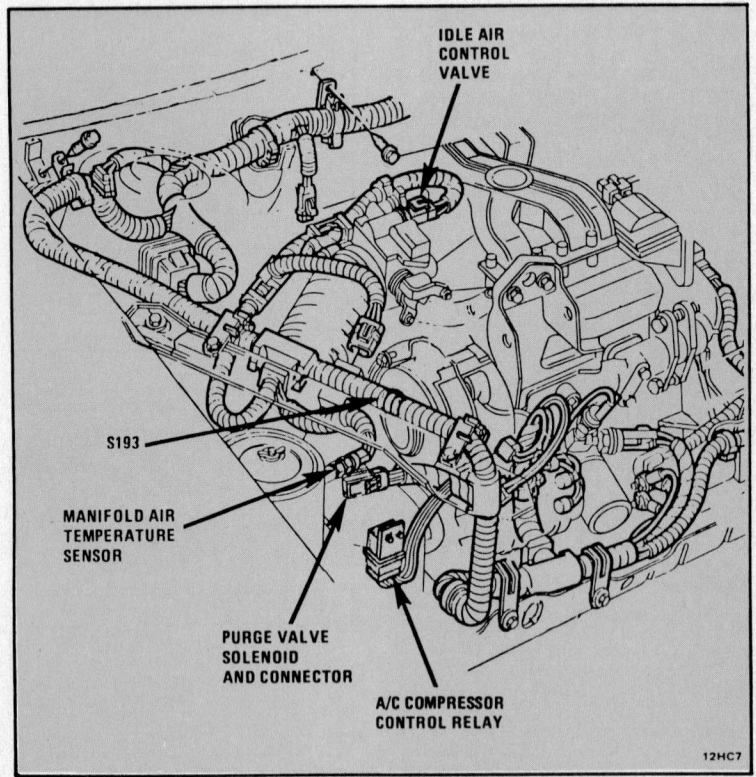

IDLE AIR CONTROL VALVE

S193

MANIFOLD AIR TEMPERATURE SENSOR

PURGE VALVE SOLENOID AND CONNECTOR

A/C COMPRESSOR CONTROL RELAY

12HC7

Figure A - Top RH Front Of VIN W Engine

1985-86 Chevrolet Celebrity

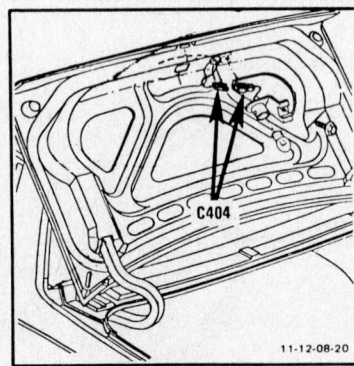

C404

11-12-08-20

Figure B - Underside Of Trunk Lid

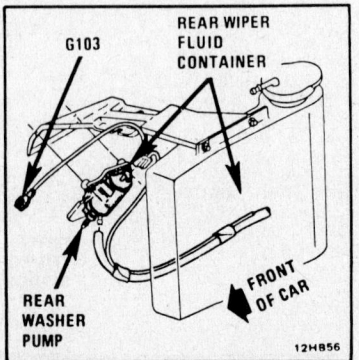

G103

REAR WIPER FLUID CONTAINER

REAR WASHER PUMP

FRONT OF CAR

12HB56

Figure C - RH Side Of VIN W Engine Compartment

COMPONENT LOCATIONS

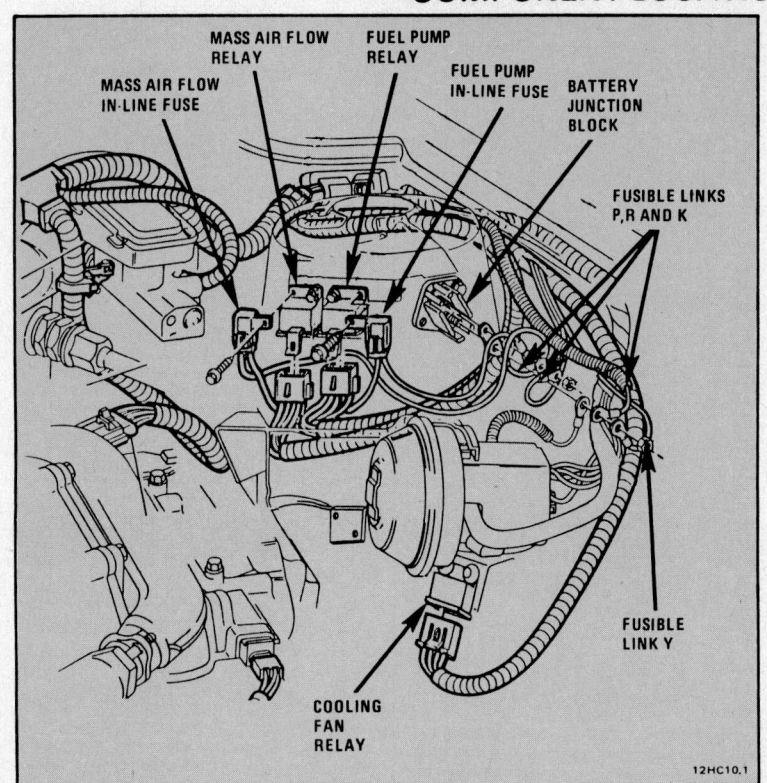

MASS AIR FLOW RELAY

FUEL PUMP RELAY

MASS AIR FLOW IN-LINE FUSE

FUEL PUMP IN-LINE FUSE

BATTERY JUNCTION BLOCK

FUSIBLE LINKS P, R AND K

FUSIBLE LINK Y

COOLING FAN RELAY

12HC10.1

Figure A - LH Shock Tower Of VIN W

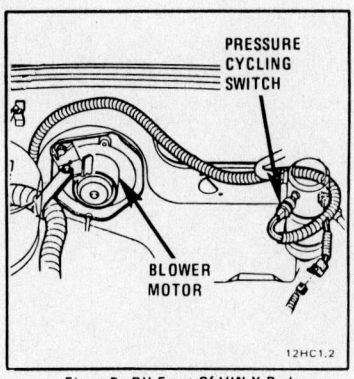

PRESSURE CYCLING SWITCH

BLOWER MOTOR

12HC1.2

Figure B - RH Front Of VIN X Dash

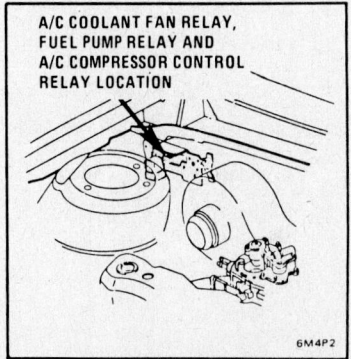

A/C COOLANT FAN RELAY, FUEL PUMP RELAY AND A/C COMPRESSOR CONTROL RELAY LOCATION

6M4P2

Figure C - RH Corner Of VIN R Dash

1985-86 Chevrolet Celebrity

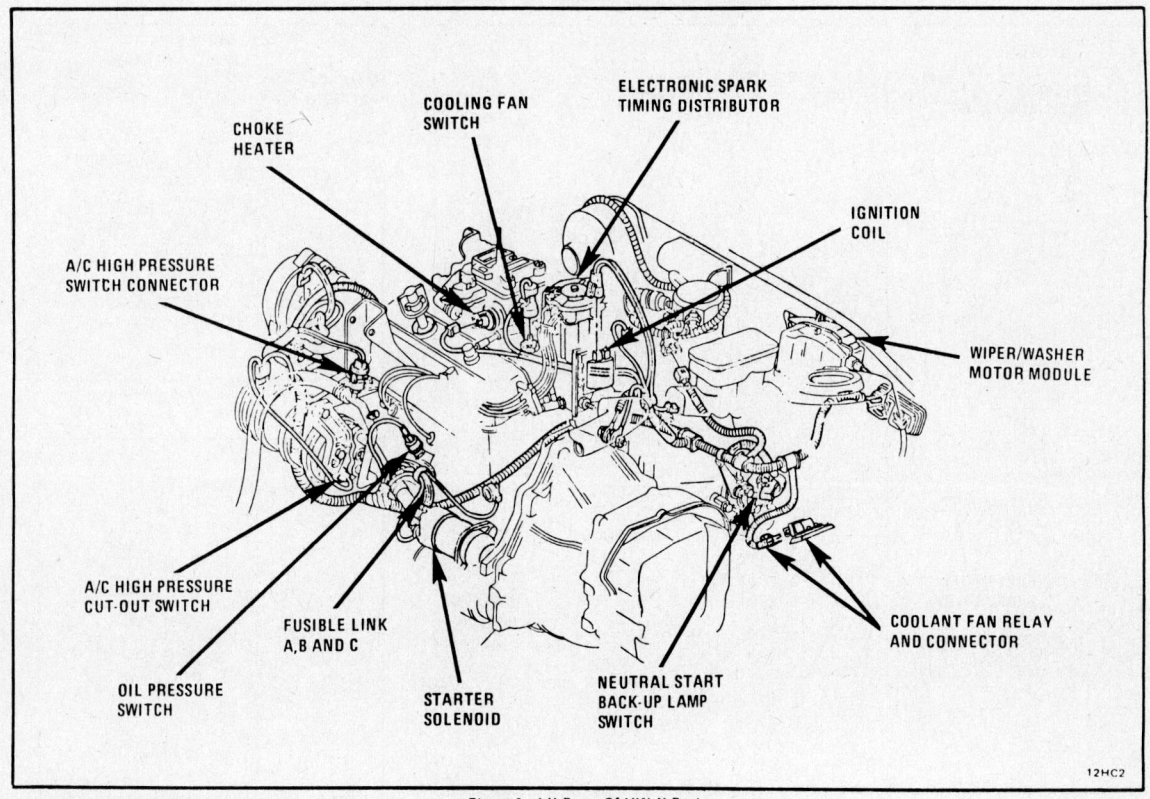

CHOKE HEATER

COOLING FAN SWITCH

ELECTRONIC SPARK TIMING DISTRIBUTOR

IGNITION COIL

A/C HIGH PRESSURE SWITCH CONNECTOR

WIPER/WASHER MOTOR MODULE

A/C HIGH PRESSURE CUT-OUT SWITCH

OIL PRESSURE SWITCH

FUSIBLE LINK A, B AND C

STARTER SOLENOID

NEUTRAL START BACK-UP LAMP SWITCH

COOLANT FAN RELAY AND CONNECTOR

12HC2

Figure A - LH Front Of VIN X Engine

1985-86 Chevrolet Celebrity

COMPONENT LOCATIONS

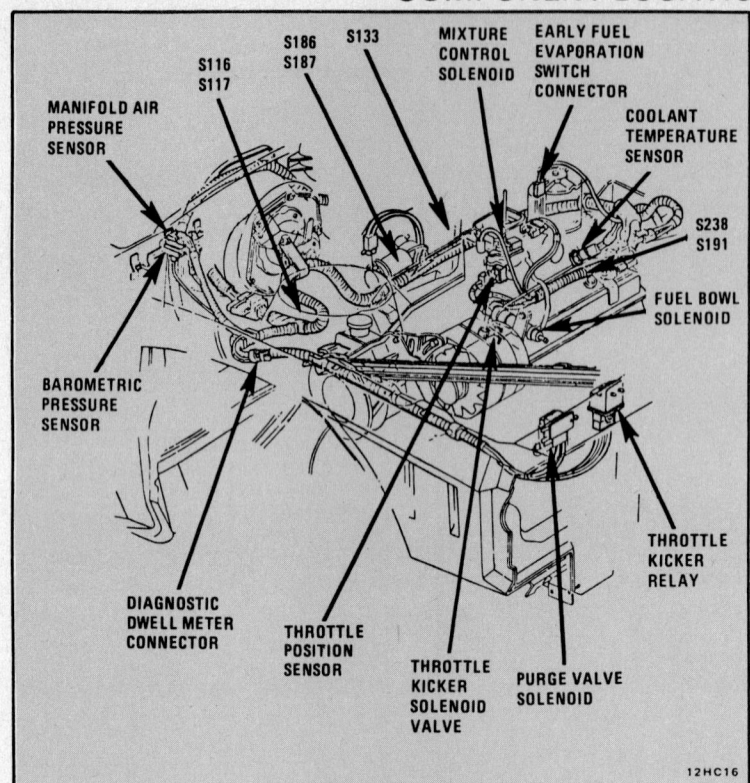

MANIFOLD AIR PRESSURE SENSOR

BAROMETRIC PRESSURE SENSOR

S116 S117

S186 S187

S133

MIXTURE CONTROL SOLENOID

EARLY FUEL EVAPORATION SWITCH CONNECTOR

COOLANT TEMPERATURE SENSOR

S238 S191

FUEL BOWL SOLENOID

THROTTLE KICKER RELAY

DIAGNOSTIC DWELL METER CONNECTOR

THROTTLE POSITION SENSOR

THROTTLE KICKER SOLENOID VALVE

PURGE VALVE SOLENOID

12HC16

Figure A - RH Side Of VIN X Engine

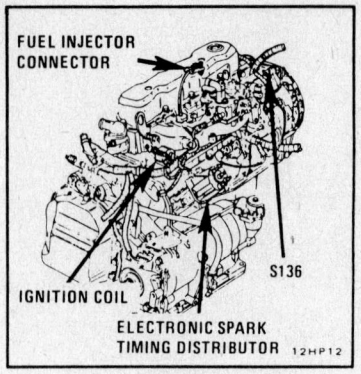

FUEL INJECTOR CONNECTOR

IGNITION COIL

S136

ELECTRONIC SPARK TIMING DISTRIBUTOR

12HP12

Figure B - LH Rear Of VIN R Engine

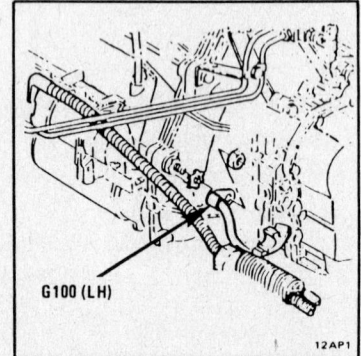

G100 (LH)

12AP1

Figure C - Lower LH Side Of VIN R Engine, Others Similar

1985-86 Chevrolet Celebrity

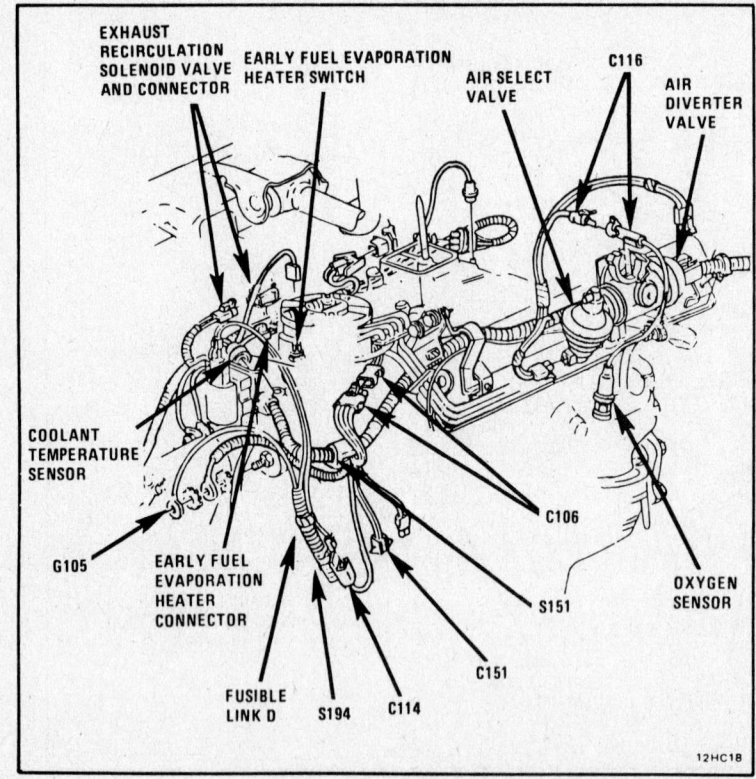

EXHAUST RECIRCULATION SOLENOID VALVE AND CONNECTOR

EARLY FUEL EVAPORATION HEATER SWITCH

AIR SELECT VALVE

C116

AIR DIVERTER VALVE

COOLANT TEMPERATURE SENSOR

G105

EARLY FUEL EVAPORATION HEATER CONNECTOR

FUSIBLE LINK D

S194

C114

C151

C106

S151

OXYGEN SENSOR

12HC18

Figure A - LH Side Of VIN X Engine

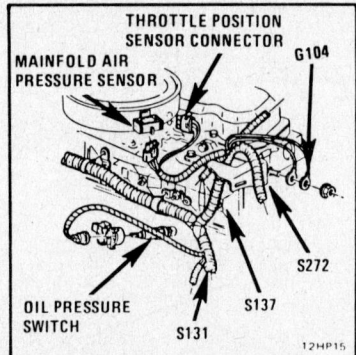

THROTTLE POSITION SENSOR CONNECTOR

MAINFOLD AIR PRESSURE SENSOR

G104

OIL PRESSURE SWITCH

S131

S137

S272

12HP15

Figure B - RH Rear Of VIN R Engine

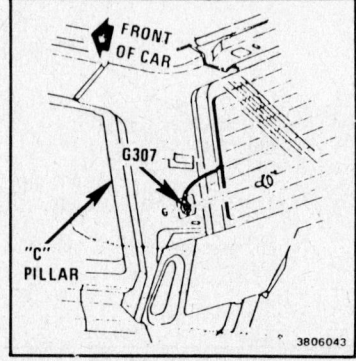

FRONT OF CAR

G307

"C" PILLAR

3806043

Figure C - RH Rear "C" Pillar

1985-86 Chevrolet Celebrity

COMPONENT LOCATIONS

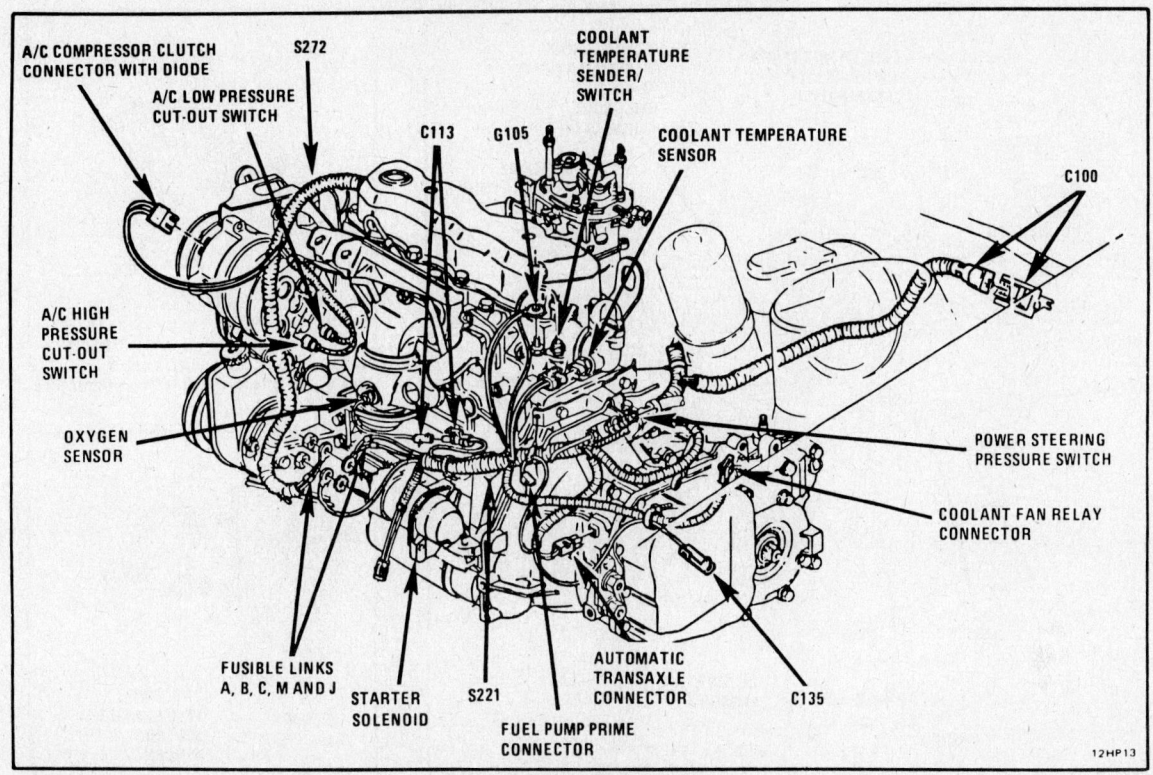

Figure A - Front Of VIN R Engine

1985-86 Chevrolet Celebrity

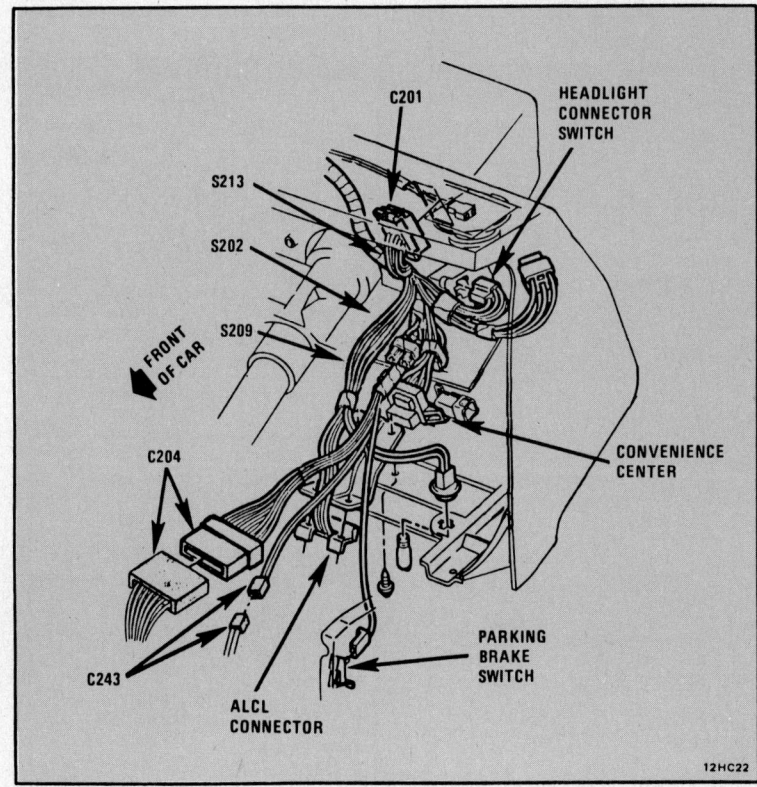

Figure A - Behind LH Side Of I/P

1985-86 Chevrolet Celebrity

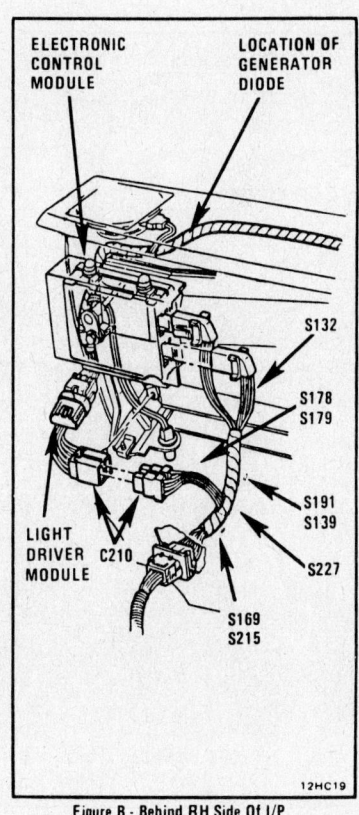

Figure B - Behind RH Side Of I/P

COMPONENT LOCATIONS

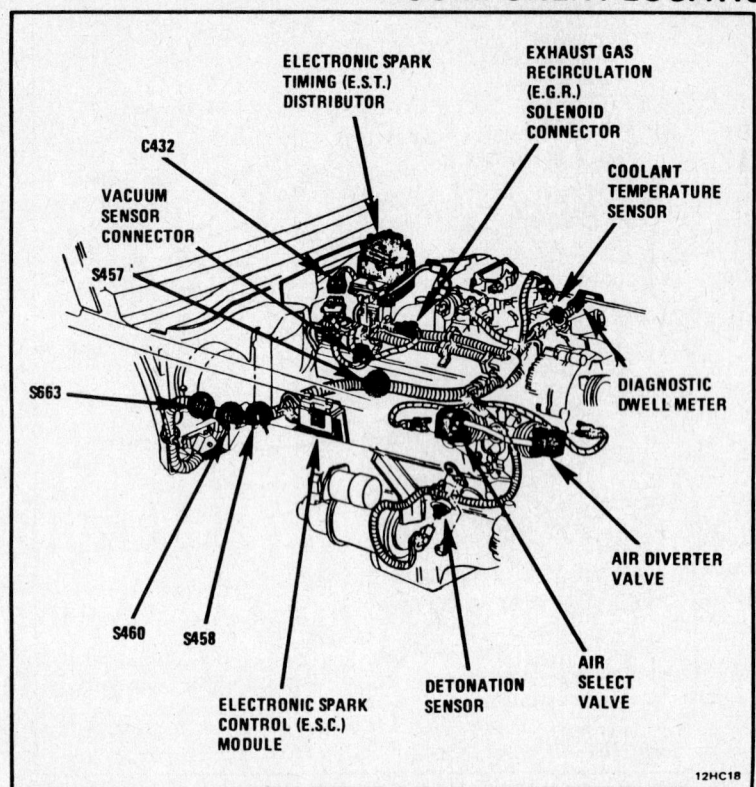

ELECTRONIC SPARK TIMING (E.S.T.) DISTRIBUTOR

EXHAUST GAS RECIRCULATION (E.G.R.) SOLENOID CONNECTOR

C432

VACUUM SENSOR CONNECTOR

COOLANT TEMPERATURE SENSOR

S457

S663

DIAGNOSTIC DWELL METER

AIR DIVERTER VALVE

S460   S458

AIR SELECT VALVE

ELECTRONIC SPARK CONTROL (E.S.C.) MODULE

DETONATION SENSOR

Figure A - RH Front Of VIN H Engine
(VIN Y Similar)

12HC18

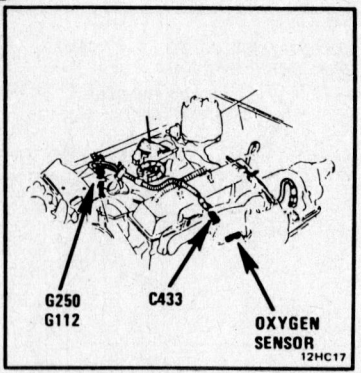

G250
G112   C433   OXYGEN SENSOR

Figure B - Top Of Engine, VIN H Shown (Other Similar)

12HC17

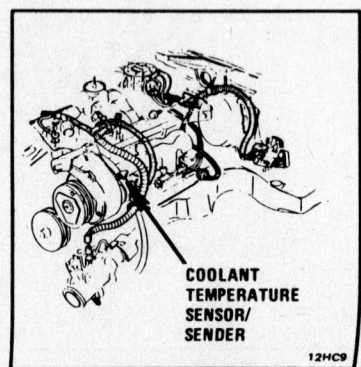

COOLANT TEMPERATURE SENSOR/ SENDER

Figure C - RH Front Of VIN H
(VIN Y Similar)

12HC9

1985-86 Chevrolet Celebrity

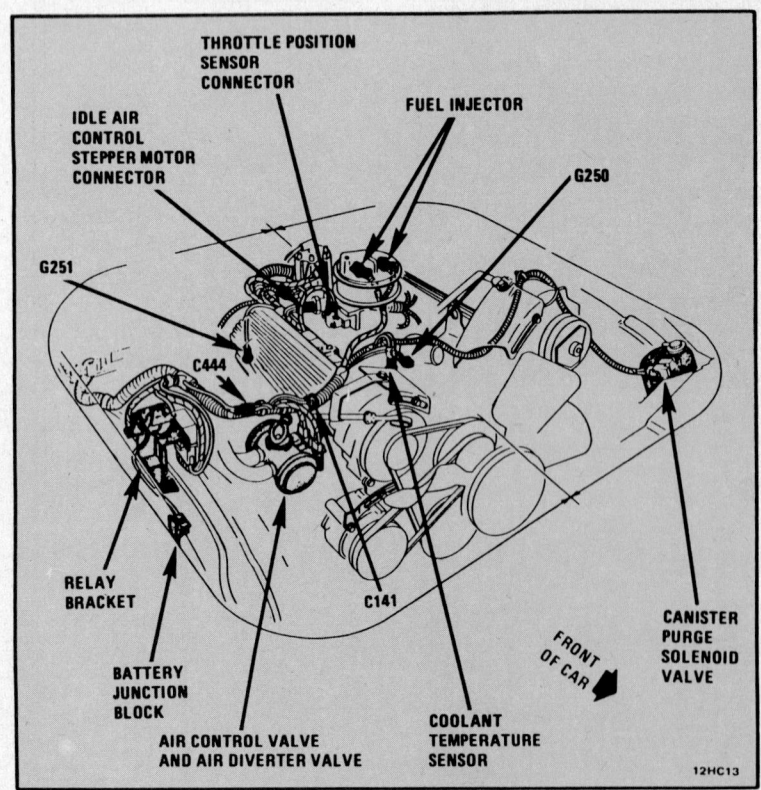

THROTTLE POSITION SENSOR CONNECTOR

FUEL INJECTOR

IDLE AIR CONTROL STEPPER MOTOR CONNECTOR

G250

G251

C444

RELAY BRACKET

BATTERY JUNCTION BLOCK

AIR CONTROL VALVE AND AIR DIVERTER VALVE

C141

COOLANT TEMPERATURE SENSOR

FRONT OF CAR

CANISTER PURGE SOLENOID VALVE

Figure A - RH Front Of VIN Z Engine

12HC13

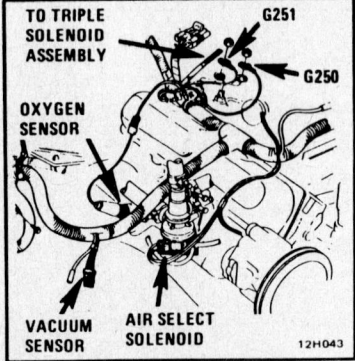

TO TRIPLE SOLENOID ASSEMBLY

G251

G250

OXYGEN SENSOR

VACUUM SENSOR

AIR SELECT SOLENOID

Figure B - RH Side Of All Engines

12H043

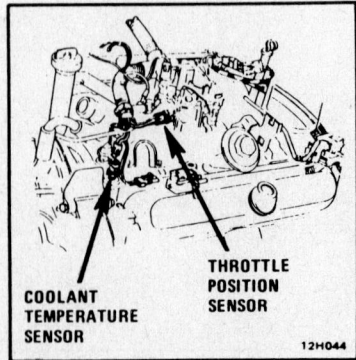

VACUUM SENSOR

AIR SELECT SOLENOID

COOLANT TEMPERATURE SENSOR

THROTTLE POSITION SENSOR

Figure C - Top LH Side Of VIN Y Engine

12H044

1985-86 Chevrolet Caprice

COMPONENT LOCATIONS

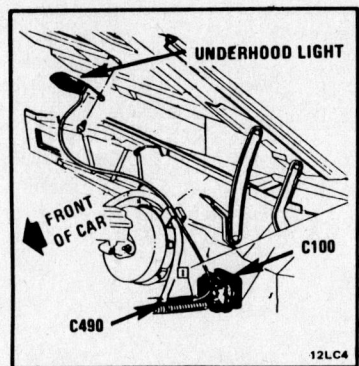

Figure A - Engine Compartment, LH Rear

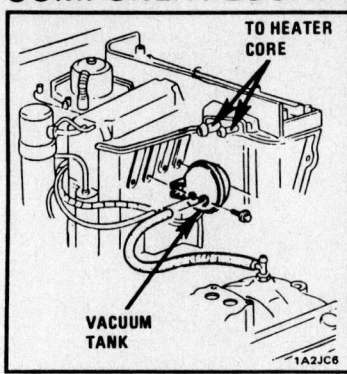

Figure C - RH Side Of Engine Dash
(VIN H Shown, Others Similar)

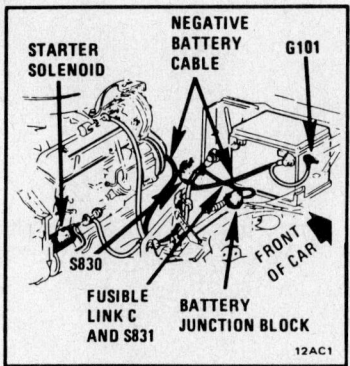

Figure E - RH Front Of VIN Z Engine Compartment
(VIN H Similar)

Figure B - Front Of VIN H Engine
(VIN Y And VIN Z Similar)

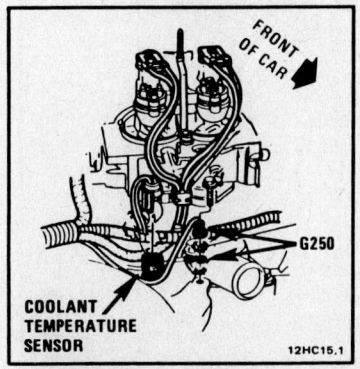

Figure D - Top Front Of VIN Z Engine

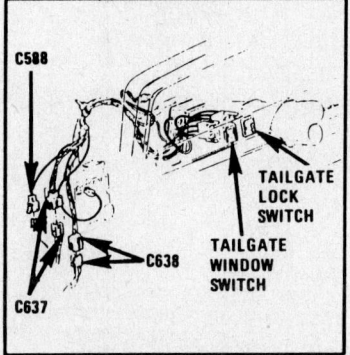

Figure F - Behind LH Side Of I/P

1985-86 Chevrolet Caprice

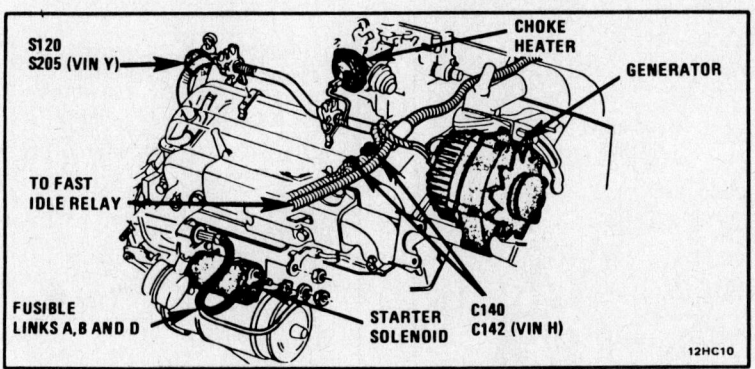

Figure A - RH Side Of VIN H And VIN Y Engine

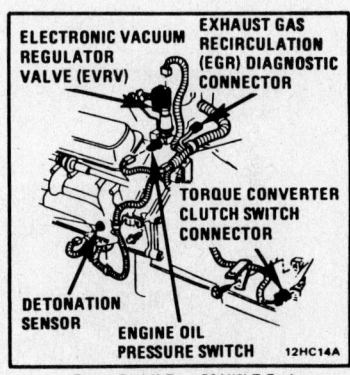

Figure D - LH Rear Of VIN Z Engine

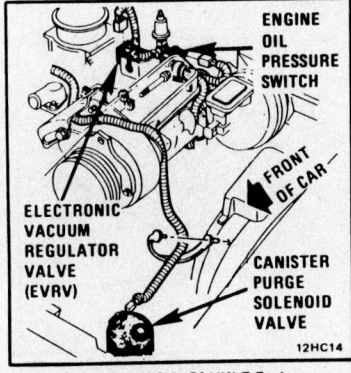

Figure B - LH Side Of VIN Z Engine

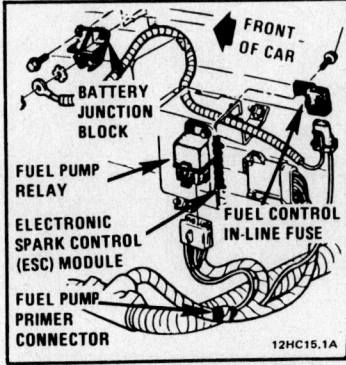

Figure C - RH Inner Fender Panel Of VIN Z

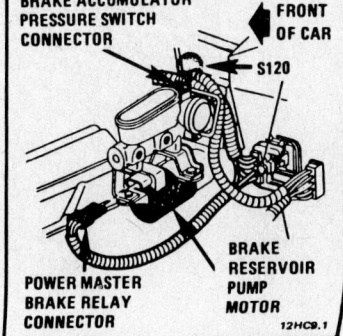

Figure E - LH Front Of Dash (VIN H And VIN Y)

1985-86 Chevrolet Caprice

157

COMPONENT LOCATIONS

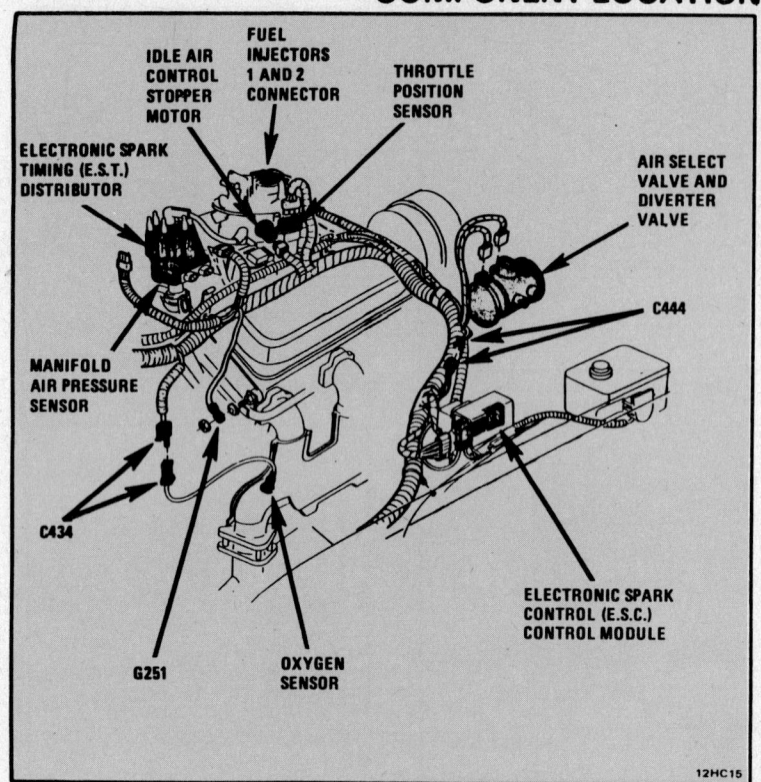

IDLE AIR CONTROL STOPPER MOTOR

FUEL INJECTORS 1 AND 2 CONNECTOR

THROTTLE POSITION SENSOR

ELECTRONIC SPARK TIMING (E.S.T.) DISTRIBUTOR

AIR SELECT VALVE AND DIVERTER VALVE

C444

MANIFOLD AIR PRESSURE SENSOR

C434

G251

OXYGEN SENSOR

ELECTRONIC SPARK CONTROL (E.S.C.) CONTROL MODULE

12HC15

Figure A - Rear RH Of VIN Z Engine (Others Similar)

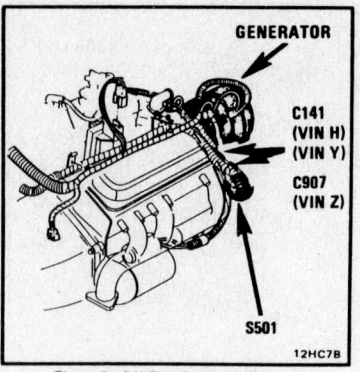

GENERATOR

C141 (VIN H) (VIN Y)

C907 (VIN Z)

S501

12HC7B

Figure B - RH Side Of VIN Z Engine

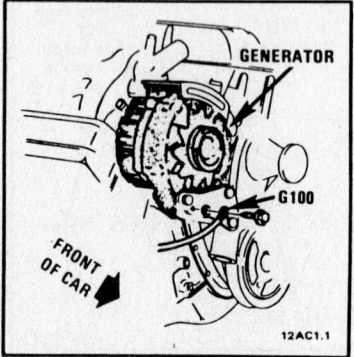

GENERATOR

G100

FRONT OF CAR

12AC1.1

Figure C - RH Front Of VIN Z Engine

1985-86 Chevrolet Monte Carlo

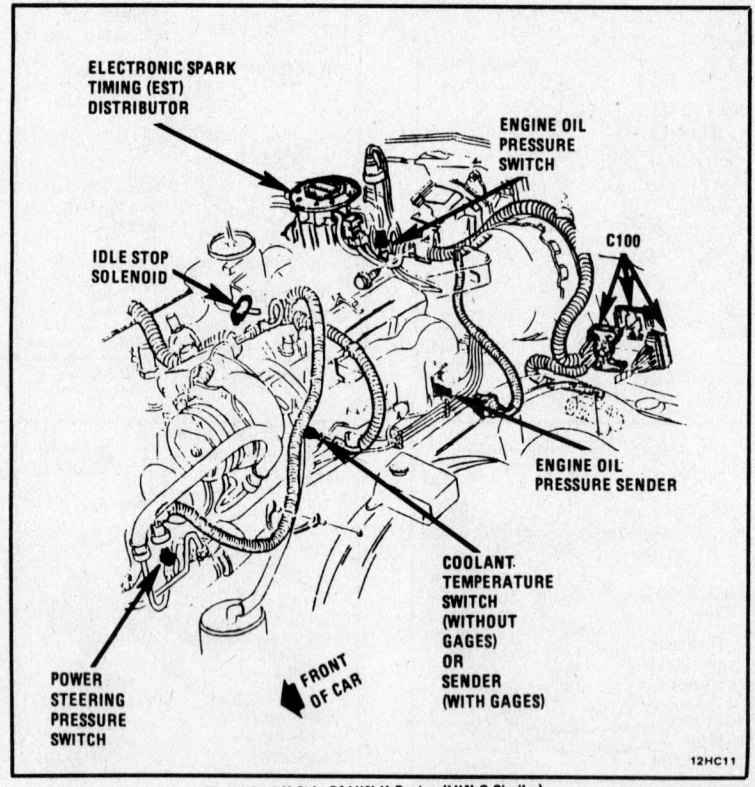

ELECTRONIC SPARK TIMING (EST) DISTRIBUTOR

ENGINE OIL PRESSURE SWITCH

C100

IDLE STOP SOLENOID

ENGINE OIL PRESSURE SENDER

COOLANT TEMPERATURE SWITCH (WITHOUT GAGES) OR SENDER (WITH GAGES)

POWER STEERING PRESSURE SWITCH

FRONT OF CAR

12HC11

Figure A - LH Side Of VIN H Engine (VIN G Similar)

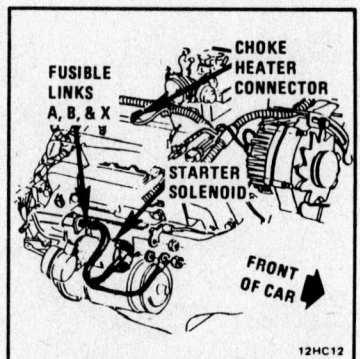

FUSIBLE LINKS A, B, & X

CHOKE HEATER CONNECTOR

STARTER SOLENOID

FRONT OF CAR

12HC12

Figure B - RH Side Of VIN H Engine (VIN G Similar)

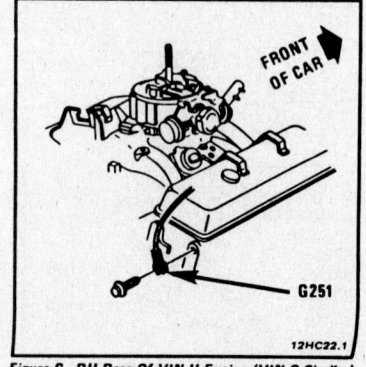

FRONT OF CAR

G251

12HC22.1

Figure C - RH Rear Of VIN H Engine (VIN G Similar)

1985-86 Chevrolet Monte Carlo

COMPONENT LOCATIONS

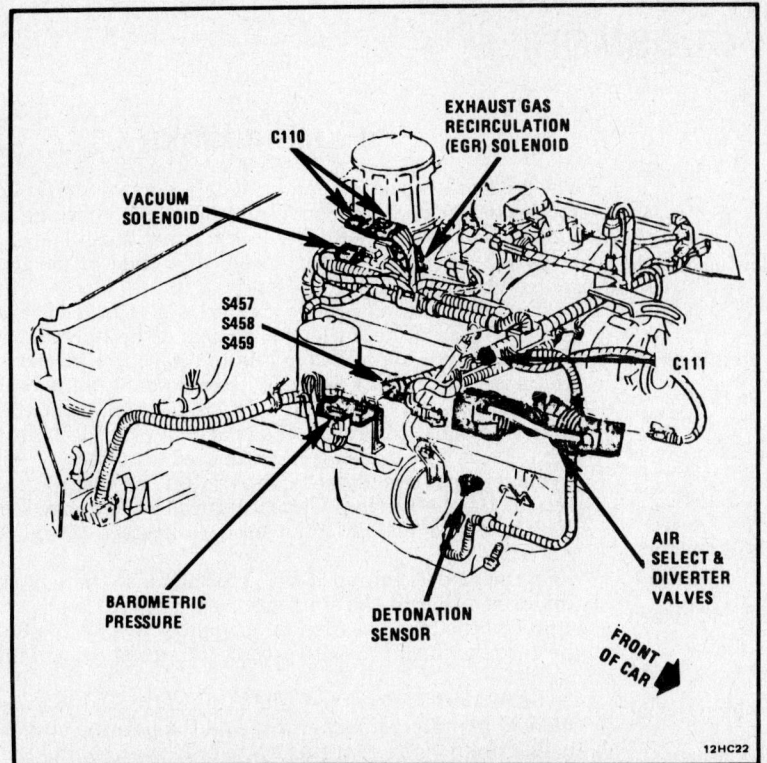

Figure A - RH Side Of VIN H Engine (VIN G Similar)

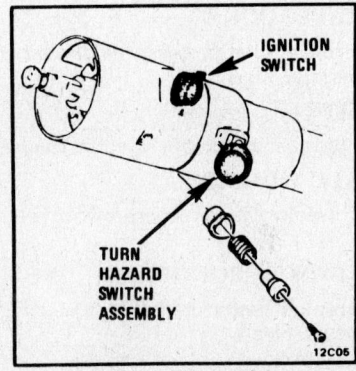

Figure B - Top Of Steering Column

Figure C - Top Of Steering Column

1985-86 Chevrolet Monte Carlo

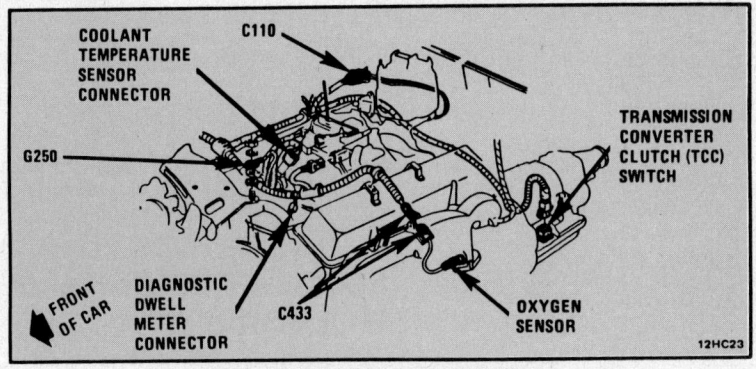

Figure A - LH Side Of VIN H Engine (VIN G Similar)

Figure D - Behind LH Side Of I/P

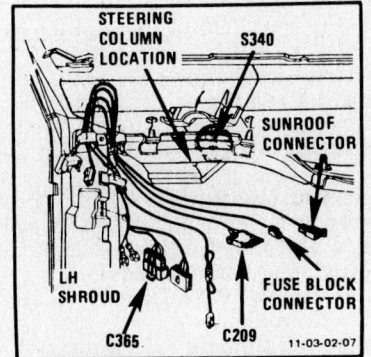

Figure B - Behind LH Side Of I/P

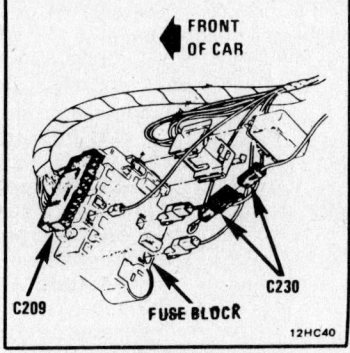

Figure C - Behind LH Side Of I/P

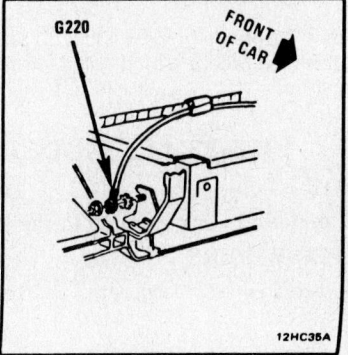

Figure E - Behind Center Of I/P

1985-86 Chevrolet Monte Carlo

OLDSMOBILE

Circuit Breaker

1982-84 ALL MODELS

POWER WINDOWS

The circuit breaker that protects the power window circuit, is located in the fuse block.

POWER SEATS

The circuit breaker that protects the power seat circuit, is located in the fuse block.

POWER DOOR LOCKS

The circuit breaker that protects the power door lock circuit, is located in the fuse block.

HEADLIGHTS

This circuit breaker is incorporated in the headlight switch.

WINDSHIELD WIPERS

This circuit breaker is incorporated in the winshield wiper motor.

REAR WINDOW DEFOGGER

The circuit breaker that protects the rear defogger circuit, is located in the fuse block.

Fusible Links

There are fusible links used on all models and are usally located as follows; There are two fusible links attached to the starter solenoid to protect the charging and the lighting circuits on all models except the V6 Toronado. There is one link at the starter to protect the Computer Command Control on the Toronado models. Thereis also a fusible link in the harness above the the alternator to protect the electronic level control on the 88 and 98 models.

On the models equipped with cooling fans , there is a fusible link used either at the starter or near the bulkhead connector to protect the fan. The Firenza models have a fusible link near the front shock tower to protect the vacuum pump. The diesel models use fusible links at each glow plug to protect the glow plug circuit.

In-Line Fuses

The 88, 98 and Toronado models use 2 25 amp in-line fuses located near the fuse block, which are used to protect the theft deterrent system.

1985-87 ALL MODELS

HEADLIGHTS

This circuit breaker is incorporated in the headlight switch.

WINDSHIELD WIPERS

This circuit breaker is incorporated in the winshield wiper motor.

POWER ACCESSORIES

This circuit breaker is located in the front of the fuse block.

Fusible Links

The 88, Cutlass and Toronado models use two fusible links attached to the starter solenoid to protect the charging and the lighting circuits. One fusible link for the charging system, located behind the alternator. Two fusible links at the glow plug controller on the diesel models.

The Calais models use two fusible links attached to the starter solenoid to protect the charging and the lighting circuits. The Calais alos use a fusible link to protect the electronic control module. This link is usaaly located behind the battery.

The Cutlass Ciera uses two fusible links attached to the starter solenoid to protect the charging and the lighting circuits. There is also one fusible link used to protect the electronic control module and another to protect the electronic fuel injection. On the Cutlass Ciera equipped with a diesel engine, there are two fusible links used to protect the glow plug controller.

On the models equipped with cooling fans , there is a fusible link used either at the starter or near the bulkhead connector to protect the fan. The Firenza models have a fusible link near the battery which is usedto protect the electronic fuel injection circuit.

The 98 models use two fusible links attached to the starter solenoid to protect the charging and the lighting circuits. One fusible link for the charging system, located behind the alternator. On the 98 models equipped with a diesel engine, there are two fusible links at the glow plug controller. There is one fusible link used for charging system which is located between the alternator and the jump start junction block. There is also a fusible link located behind the battery used for ignition system.

In-Line Fuses

The Toronado models use 2 25 amp (White) in-line fuses located near the fuse block, which are used to protect the theft deterrent system.

Relay, Sensors And Computer Locations

1982-84 CUTLASS

- **A/C Blower Relay** – is located in the blower motor assembly.
- **A/C Cut-Out Switch** – is located on the accelerator pedal.
- **A/C-Heater Blower Resistors** – is located in the heater module in front of the blower motor.
- **A/C Presuure Cycling Switch** – is located on the top of the vacuum tank.
- **A/C Temperature Cut-Out Relay** – is located behind the right front fender apron or at the center of the firewall.
- **A/C Temperature Cut-Out Switch** – is located on the left front side of the engine near the alternator.
- **Altitude Advance Relay (1984 Diesel)** – is located on the upper center of the firewall.
- **Barometric Pressure Sensor** – is located behind the right side of the instrument panel.
- **Brake Pressure Switch** – is located on the rear base of the left front wheel well.

- **"Check Engine" Light Driver Module** – is taped to the instrument panel harness to the left of the glove box.
- **Choke Heater Relay** – is located on the left engine cowl to the right of the steering column.
- **Cold Advance Diode (1984 Diesel)** – is located in the engine harness, to the right of the master cylinder.
- **Cold Inhibit Switch (Diesel)** – is located below the right valve cover.
- **Coolant Temperature Sensor** – is located on the front of ther engine behind the alternator on the V6 engines and on the top left front of the engine ong the V8. Behind the water on the diesel engine.
- **Coolant Temperature Switch** – is located on the top of the engine behind the alternator or water pump on the V6 and diesel engine and on the left side of the engine near the exhaust manifold on the V8 engines.
- **Cruise Control Unit** – is located under the left side of the dash panel, above the accelerator pedal.
- **Defogger Timer (1982-83)** – is located under the left side of the instrument panel attached to the top of the fuse block.
- **Diesel Electronics Module** – is located behind the instrument panel to the right of the glove box behind the right kick panel.
- **Door Lock Relay** – is located on the lower right kick panel at the bottom access hole.
- **Early Fuel Evaporation (EFE) Relay** – is located on the front of the engine. On the 1984 models this relay is located at the right side of the engine compartment, above the wheel well.
- **Early Fuel Evaporation Solenoid** – is located at the top center of the right valve cover.
- **EGR Cut-Out Relay (1982-83)** – is located on the right front fender well.
- **EGR Solenoid** – is located at the top center of the right valve cover on the V6 engine and on the bracket rear of the right valve cover or top front left side on the V8 engines.
- **Electronic Control Module (ECM)** – is located on the right shroud near the lower access hole.
- **Electronic Spark Control Module (1984)** – is located above the right wheel well on the V6 engine and at the top left side of the engine on the V8 engine.
- **Engine Temperature Switch (Diesel)** – is located below the left valve cover. On the 84 models this switch is located behind the water pump.
- **Fast Idle Relay** – is located on the left side of the engine cowl.
- **Fast Idle Solenoid** – is located on the top of the engine near the front.
- **Fuel Metering Solenoid** – is located on the right side of the carburetor on the V6 engine and/or the top right side of the engine on the V8.
- **Gear Selector Switch** – is attached to the base of the steering coulmn.
- **Glow Plug Controller** – is located at the top left rear of the engine, above the glow plug relay.
- **Glow Plug Relay (Diesel)** – is located on the top of the right front fender well.
- **High Altitude Advance Solenoid (1984 Diesel)** – is located in the fuel line, near the right valve cover.
- **Horn Relay** – is located behind the left side of the instrument panel above the fuse block.
- **Ignition Key Warning Buzzer** – is located behind the left side of the dash panel.
- **Lights-On Buzzer** – is attached to the fuse block.
- **Low Altitude Advance Solenoid (1984 Diesel)** – is located above the right valve cover.
- **Low Altitude Diode (1984 Diesel)** – is located in the engine harness, to the right of the master cylinder.
- **Low Brake Vacuum Delay Module** – is taped to the instrument panel harness above the fuse block.
- **Manifold Absolute Pressure Sensor** – is located on the top right front fender well.
- **Multi-Function Chime Module** – is located behind the instrument panel to the left of the steering column at the convenience center.
- **Oil Pressure Sender/Switch** – is located on the right rear of the engine on the V6 diesel and/or the front of the engine on the other engines.
- **Oxygen Sensor** – is located in the right rear exhaust manifold on the V6 and/or below the the right valve cover on the V8.
- **Power Antenna Relay** – is located behind the right side of the glove box on 1982-83 models on the 84 models the relay is behind the center of the instrument panel to the right of the radio.
- **Power Door Lock and Power Seat Circuit Breaker** – is located in the fuse block.
- **Seat Belt Timer Buzzer** – is located behind left side of the instrument panel at the convenience center.
- **Theft Deterrent Control Unit** – is located behind the instrument panel to the left of the steering column.
- **Theft Deterrent Diode** – is taped to the instrument panel harness to the left of the steering column.
- **Theft Deterrent Relay** – is located behind the instrument panel to the left of the steering column.
- **Throttle Kicker Relay (1984)** – is located on the firewall near the brake booster.
- **Throttle Position Sensor** – is located at the front of the carburetor.
- **Tone Generator (1984)** – is located at the convenience center.
- **Torque Converter Clutch Switch** – is located on the brake pedal support.
- **Trunk Release Solenoid** – is located at the rear center of the trunk lid, just above the license plate.
- **Turbo Boost Indicator Switch** – is located above the front part of the left front fender well.
- **Vacuum Regulator Vacuum Switch (1984 Diesel)** – is located just forward of the intake manifold crossover.
- **Vacuum Sensor (on the V8)** – is connect to the right front fender well.
- **Vehicle Speed Sensor** – is located behind the speedometer.
- **Wastegate Solenoid** – is located at the rear of the left valve cover.
- **Wide Open Throttle Relay (1984)** – is located at the rear of the engine compartment.
- **Window and Sunroof Circuit Breaker** – is located under the left side of the dash panel, at the fuse block.

1985-87 CUTLASS

- **A/C Blower Relay** – is located on the evaporator case behind the acumulator.
- **A/C Compressor Clutch Diode** – is taped to the inside compressor connector on the front of the compressor.
- **A/C Cut-Out Switch** – is located on the accelerator pedal bracket.
- **A/C Fast Idle Solenoid** – is located to the left of the carburetor on the gas engines and on the top center of the engine on the diesel models.
- **A/C-Heater Blower Resistors** – are located on the evaporator case in the engine compartment.
- **A/C Pressure Cycling Switch** – is located on the right side of the firewall on the accumulator.
- **A/C Temperature Cut-Out Relay** – is located behind the right front fender apron or at the center of the firewall.
- **Altitude Advance Relay (Diesel)** – is located on the upper center of the firewall.
- **Ambient Temperature Sensor** – is located under the right side of the dash panel, above rthe blower motor.

- **Anti-Diesel Solenoid** – is located on the left front valve cover.
- **Assembly Line Diagonstic Connector** – is located on the bootom left center of the dash panel.
- **Barometric Pressor Sensor (V6)** – is located behind the right side of the dash panel above the glove box.
- **Barometric Pressor Sensor (V8)** – is located on a braket with the ESC module.
- **Brake Accumulator Pressure Switch** – is located on the left side of the firewall, near the brake booster.
- **Brake Torque Converter Clutch Switch** – is located at the top of the brake pedal support.
- **Camshaft Sensor (Regal Turbo)** – is located at the front center of the engine.
- **"Check Engine" Light Driver** – is taped to the instrumnet panel harness at the left of the glove box.
- **Choke Heater Relay** – is located on the left engine cowl to the right of the steering column.
- **Coolant Temperature Sending Unit** – is located at the top of the engine.
- **Coolant Temperature Sensor** – is located at the top of the engine.
- **Coolant Temperature Switch (3.8L)** – is located behind the water pump at the top of the engine.
- **Coolant Temperature Switch (4.3L)** – is located behind the A/C compressor.
- **Coolant Temperature Switch (V8)** – is located on the left side of the engine, below the exhaust manifold.
- **Crankshaft Sensor (Regal Turbo)** – is located at the front center of the engine.
of the engine block in fron tof the starter motor.
- **Cruise Control Module** – is located under the left isde of the dash panel, above the accelerator pedal.
- **Defogger Timer Relay** – is located under the left side of the instrument panel attached to the top of the fuse block.
- **Detonation (Knock) Sensor (3.8L)** – is located on the top rear side of the engine.
- **Detonation (Knock) Sensor (4.3L)** – is located on the lower left side of the engine block.
- **Detonation (Knock) Sensor (V8-Gas)** – is located on the lower right side.
- **Diagonstic Dwell Meter Connector** – is strapped to the wiring harness at the top right side of the engine.
- **Diesel Electronic Control Module (DEC)** – is located behind the right side kick panel.
- **Differential Pressure Sensor (Cutlass)** – is located at the right front corner of the engine compartment behind the reservoir compartment.
- **Door Lock Relay** – is located on the lower right kick panel at the bottom access hole.
- **Early Fuel Evaporation (EFE)** – is located at the top of the engine, above the water pump.
- **Early Fuel Evaporation (EFE) Relay (with gauges)** – this relay is located at the left side of the engine compartment, above the wheel well.
- **Early Fuel Evaporation (EFE) Relay (without gauges)** – this relay is located at the right side of the engine compartment, above the wheel well.
- **EGR Temperature Switch (4.3L)** – is located on the intake manifold, in front of the distributor.
- **Electronic Control Module (ECM)** – is located behind the right kick panel.
- **Electronic Level Control Relay** – is located on the electronic level control compressor.
- **Electronic Level Control Sensor** – is located on the rear portion of the crossmember.
- **Electronic Spark Control Module (ESC)** – is located on the bracket at the top of the right front fender well.
- **Electronic Vacuum Regulator Valve Module** – is located at the top center of the right valve cover.

- **EPR Solenoid (Diesel)** – is located on the right valve cover.
- **Fast Idle Relay** – is located on the same bracket as the electronic sapark control module, which is located at the top of the right front fender well.
- **Fuel Control In-Line Fuse** – is located on the bracket next to the ESC module, on the 4.3L V6 engine.
- **Fuel Metering Solenoid (3.8L)** – is located on the carburetor.
- **Fuel Pump Prime Connector** – is located in the wiring harness near the fuel control in-line fuse.
- **Fuel Pump Relay** – is located on a bracket in the right side of the engine compartment.
- **Fuel Shut-Off Solenoid (Diesel)** – is located under the fuel injection pump cover.
- **Gear Selector Switch** – is attached to the base of the steering column.
- **Generator Diode** – is located taped in the harness behind the fuse block.
- **Glow Plug Controller/Relay (Diesel)** – is located on the top right (left on the Cutlass models) valve cover.
- **Glow Plug Relay (Diesel)** – is located on the top of the right front fender well.
- **Headlight Relay** – is located at the front side of the engine compartment, near the headlight.
- **Horn Relay** – is located behind the left side of the instrument panel above the fuse block.
- **Idle Stop Solenoid** – is located on the top of the engine and to the left of the carburetor.
- **Ignition Key Warning Buzzer** – is located behind the left side of the dash panel.
- **In-Car Sensor** – is located at the right side of the dash panel as part of the speaker grille assembly.
- **Low Brake Vacuum Delay Module** – is taped to the instrument panel harness, above the fuse block.
- **Manifold Absolute Pressure Sensor** – is located on the air cleaner on the 4.3L engine and at the right side of the engine compartment above the wheel well on all other engines.
- **Mass Airflow Sensor (EFI)** – is located on the air intake hose at the top left side of the engine compartment.
- **Metering Valve Sensor (Diesel)** – is located on the diesel injection pump.
- **Mixture Control Solenoid** – is located on the front or right side of the carburetor or throttle body.
- **Multi-Function Chime Module** – is located behind the instrument panel to the left of the steering column at the convenience center.
- **Oxygen Sensor** – is located in the exhaust manifold.
- **Power Accessory Circuit Breaker** – is located above the flasher relay in the fuse block.
- **Power Antenna Relay** – is located behind the center of the instrument panel to the right of the radio.
- **Power Master Brake Relay** – is located on top of the electro-hydraulic pump motor below the master cylinder.
- **Seat Belt Timer Buzzer** – is located behind left side of the instrument panel at the convenience center.
- **Theft Deterrent Controller** – is located under the left side of the dash panel, near the kick panel.
- **Theft Deterrent Diode** – is located behind the left side of the dash panel in connector "C-857".
- **Theft Deterrent Relay** – is located behind the instrument panel to the left of the steering column.
- **Third and Fourth Gear Switches** – are located in the middle of the left side of the transmission.
- **Throttle Position Sensor** – is located at the front of the carburetor or on the side of the throttle body.
- **Tone Generator** – is located behind the left side of the dash panel, in the convenience center.
- **Torque Converter Clutch solenoid** – is located in the middle of the left side of the transmission.

- **Trunk Release Solenoid** – is located at the rear of the trunk lid above the liscense plate.
- **Turbo Boost Gauge Sensor** – is located on the right front inner fender above the wheelwell.
- **Turbo Boost Indicator Switch** – is located on the right front fender , above the wheel well.
- **Twilight Sentinel Amplifier** – is located under the dash panel , near the radio.
- **Twilight Sentinel Photocell** – is located at the top center of the dash panel.
- **Vacuum Sensor** – is located at the rear of the engine above the valve cover.
- **Vehicle Speed Buffer** – is located under the left side of the dash panel, to the right of the steering column.
- **Vehicle Speed Sensor** – is located behind the dash panel and to the right of the steering column.
- **Water-In-Fuel Module (Diesel)** – is located at the top rear side of the engine.
- **Window and Sun Roof Circuit Breaker** – is located in the fuse block.
- **Wiper/Washer Motor Module** – is located on the upper left corner of the firewall in the engine compartment.

1982-84 88 AND 98 – ALL MODELS

- **A/C Blower Relay** – on the right side of the engine cowl, in front of the blower motor.
- **A/C Compressor Clutch Diode** – is taped to the inside compressor clutch connector.
- **A/C Compressor Cut-Out Switch** – is located below the left side of the instrument panel on the accelerator plate.
- **A/C-Heater Resistors** – is located on the right side of the engine cowl, infront of the blower motor.
- **A/C Pressure Cycling Switch** – is located on the right side of the ngine cowl, above the front relay.
- **A/C Programmer Unit** – is located behind the right side of the instrument panel.
- **A/C Temperature Cut-Out Relay** – is located on the top center of the engine cowl.
- **A/C Temperature Cut-Out Switch** – is located on the top front of the engine near the left valve cover.
- **Barometric Pressure Sensor (V6)** – is located behind the glove box.
- **Booster Low Vacuum Switch** – is located on the power boost unit.
- **Brake Pressure Switch** – is located under the left side engine cowl, attached to the frame.
- **Cold Inhibit Switch (Diesel)** – is located below the rear portion of the right valve cover.
- **Converter Clutch Switch (Diesel)** – is located on the brake pedal support.
- **Coolant Temperature Sender** – is located on the top left rear of the engine on the diesel models and on the front of the engine on the gas models.
- **Coolant Temperature Sensor (V6)** – is located is located on the front of the engine near the carburetor.
- **Cruise Control Throttle Servo** – is located on the top front portion of the engine.
- **Defogger Timer Relay** – is attached to the top of the fuse block.
- **Detonation (Knock) Sensor** – is located on the top left rear of the engine.
- **Diode Module (Diesel)** – is located on the top center of the engine cowl.
- **Door Lock Control Unit** – is located is attached to the upper right cowl.
- **Door Lock Relay** – is located on the upper right cowl.
- **Door Unlock Relay** – is located on the upper right cowl.

- **Early Fuel Evaporation Relay (V6)** – is located on the front top portion of the engine.
- **Early Fuel Evaporation Solenoid (V6)** – is located on the top center of the right valve cover.
- **EGR Solenoid** – is located on the top center of the right valve cover.
- **Electronic Control Module (ECM)** – is located on the right side kick panel.
- **Engine Temperature Switch (Diesel)** – is located below the rear portion of the left valve cover.
- **Fast Idle Solenoid (Diesel)** – is located on the top center of the engine in front of the injection pump.
- **Gear Selector Switch** – is located on the lower top portion of the steering column.
- **Glow Plug Relay (Diesel)** – is located on the front of the right front wheel well.
- **Glow Plug Thermal Control Unit (Diesel)** – is located on the top of the engine, in front of the fast idle solenoid.
- **Horn Relay** – is attached to the left side of the fuse block.
- **Idle Speed Control Unit (V6)** – is located on the left side of the carburetor.
- **Ignition Key Warning Buzzer** – is attached to the left side of the fuse block.
- **Illuminated Entry Timer** – is located on the upper left shroud, near the junction block.
- **Level Control Height Sensor** – is located on the rear center part of the crossmember.
- **Level Control Relay** – is located on the left front fender well, in front of the level control compressor.
- **Light Switch/Sentinel Control** – is located under the left side of the instrument panel, near the parking brake.
- **Lower Brake Vacuum Relay** – is located behind the instrument panel, to the left of the sterring column.
- **Manifold Absolute Pressure Sensor** – is located on the top of the front wheel well.
- **Mixture Control Solenoid** – is located in the carburetor.
- **Multi-Function Chime Module** – is located is located on the left side of the fuse block.
- **Oil Pressure Switch** – is located on the lower right side of the engine on the (V6) and on the top front left side of the engine on the V8 engines.
- **Oxygen Sensor** – is located on the rear right exhaust manifold on the V6 engine and on the rear left exhaust manifold on the V8 engine.
- **Power Seat Relay** – is located under the left or right seat.
- **Seat Belt Warning Buzzer** – is attached to the left side of the fuse block.
- **Seat Belt Warning Module** – is taped to the harnes located above the fuse block.
- **Tailgate Ajar Switch** – is located inside the lower right corner of the tailgate assembly.
- **Temperature Indicator Switch** – is located on the front of the engine near the carburetor on the V6 engine and on the top left side of the engine on the V8 engines.
- **Throttle Position Sensor** – is located on the careburetor.
- **Tone Generator** – is located under the left side of the instrument panel, near the parking brake.
- **Trunk Release Solenoid** – is located on the rear center of the trunk lid.
- **Twilight Sentinel Amplifier** – is located under the left side of the instrument panel, near the parking brake.
- **Twilight Sentinel Photocell** – is located on the left side of the engine cowl.
- **Vacuum Regulator Switch (Diesel)** – is located on the top center of the engine on the fuel injection pump.
- **Vacuum Sensor** – is located on the right front wheel well.
- **Vehicle Speed Sensor (V6)** – is located behind the instrument panel above the left side of the steering column.
- **Wait Lamp Control Relay (Diesel)** – is located on the top center of the engine cowl.

- **Wiper Motor Relay Diode** – is located in the wipwer motor connector.

1985-87 88 AND 98—ALL MODELS

- **A/C Blower Relay** – is located in the engine compartment at the center of the firewall, near the blower motor.
- **A/C Compressor Clutch Diode** – is taped to the inside compressor connector on the front of the compressor.
- **A/C-Heater Blower Resistors** – is located in the engine compartment on the right side of the firewall near the blower motor.
- **A/C Programmer (Tempmatic)** – is located behind the right side of the dash panel.
- **A/C Temperature Cut-Out Relay** – is located on the top right front engine cowl.
- **Ambient Temperature Sensor** – is located in the right air inlet, below screen.
- **Assembly Line Data Link Connector** – is located under the left side of the dash panel, to the right of the steering panel.
- **Audio Alarm Module** – is located on the left side of the fuse block.
- **Automatic Door Lock Controller** – is attached to the upper portion of the right kick panel.
- **Automatic Door Lock Diode** – is located behind the left kick panel, near the lower access hole.
- **Barometeric Pressure Sensor** – is located behind the glove box.
- **Blower and Clutch Control Module** – is located on the top of the blower housing.
- **"Check Engine" Light Driver** – is taped to the instrument panel harness, above the glove box.
- **Coolant Temperature Sensor (3.8L)** – is located on the left front side of the engine.
- **Coolant Temperature Sensor (4.3L)** – is located on the front of the engine below the coolant outlet.
- **Coolant Temperature Sensor (5.0L & 5.7L)** – is located on the front side of the engine, on the coolant outlet.
- **Coolant Temperature Sensor (5.7L Diesel)** – is located on the left front side of the engine.
- **Cruise Control Module** – is located under the left side of the dash, to the left of the steering column.
- **Cruise Control Servo** – is located at the left front side of the engine on the gas models and above the left side valve cover on the diesel models.
- **Defogger Time Relay** – is located on the top of the fuse block.
- **Detonation (Knock) Sensor (6 cyl.)** – is located at the lower left rear side of the engine.
- **Detonation (Knock) Sensor (8 cyl.)** – is located at the right front side of the engine.
- **Diagnostic Dwell Meter Connector (Green)** – is taped the the wiring harness near the carburetor.
- **Diesel Electronic Control Module (DEC)** – is located behind the kick panel.
- **Early Fuel Evaporation Relay (3.8L)** – is located on the top right front engine cowl.
- **Electronic Control Module (ECM)** – is located behind the right kick panel.
- **Electronic Level Control Height Sensor** – is located on the rear center of the rear crossmember.
- **Electronic Level Control Relay** – is located on the left front fender, behind the horn.
- **Electronic Spark Control (ESC) Module** – is located on the right front side of the engine compartment.
- **Fast Idle Relay (4.3L)** – is located in the center of the firewall in the engine compartment.

- **Fuel Pump Relay (4.3L) Relay** – is located on the upper right inner fender panel.
- **Glow Plug Controller Relay (Diesel)** – is located on the top left rear of the engine.
- **Horn Relay** – is attached to the left side of the fuse block.
- **Illuminated Entry Timer** – is located behind the upper portion of the left kick panel, near the junction block.
- **In-Car Sensor** – is located in the right upper part of the dash, to the left of the right speaker.
- **Low Coolant Level Sensor** – is located in the radiator.
- **Manifold Absolute Pressure Sensor** – is located on the air cleaner.
- **Metering Valve Sensor (Diesel)** – is located on the diesel fuel injection pump.
- **Multi-Function Chime Module** – is located in the convenience center.
- **Oxygen Sensor** – is located on the exhaust manifold.
- **Power Antenna Relay** – is located on the bracket under the right side of the instrument panel, to the left of the glove box.
- **Power Door Lock Relay** – is located behind the bottom right kick panel.
- **Power Door Unlock Relay** – is located behind the upper portion of the right side kick panel.
- **Power Master Cylinder Brake In-Line Fuse** – is located under the left side of the dash panel, near the fuse block.
- **Power Master Cylinder Relay** – is located in the connector at the brake reservoir pump motor.
- **Power Seat Relay** – is located on under the right or left seat.
- **Seat Memory Module** – is located under the driver's seat.
- **Starter Interrupt Relay** – is located under the left side of the dash panel, above the steering column.
- **Theft Deterrent Controller** – is located under the left side of the dash, to the right of the steering column.
- **Theft Deterrent Diode** – is located under the left side of the dash panel, near the fuse block.
- **Theft Deterrent In-Line Fuses** – are located above the fuse block taped to the instrument panel wiring harness.
- **Theft Deterrent Relay** – is located at the right of the theft deterrent controller.
- **Throttle Position Sensor** – is located on the carburetor or throttle body.
- **Trailer Relays** – are located on the lower right corner of the fuse block.
- **Twilight Sentinel Amplifier** – is located on a bracket behind the right side of the dash panel.
- **Twilight Sentinel Control** – is located under the left side of the dash, to the right of the steering column.
- **Twilight Sentinel Photocell** – is located on the top left side of the dash panel.
- **Vacuum Sensor** – is located on the right front engine cowl.
- **Vehicle Speed Sensor** – is located behind the instrument panel, is a part of the cluster.
- **Vehicle Speed Sensor Buffer** – is taper top the instrument panel wiring under the left side of the daash near the fuse block.
- **Wide Open Throttle Relay** – is located in the engine compartment at the center of the firewall.
- **Washer Pump Motor Diode** – is located in the washer motor connector.
- **Water-In-Fuel Module (Diesel)** – is located on top of the fuel filter assembly.
- **Window and Sunroof Circuit Breaker** – is located at the top right corner of the fuse block.
- **Wiper Motor Relay Diode** – is located in the wiper motor connector.

1982-84 OMEGA

- **A/C Clutch Diode** – is located inside the A/C compressor connector.
- **A/C Compressor Relay** – is located in the upper right corner of the engine cowl.
- **A/C Diode** – is located in the A/C harness, near the vacuum tank.
- **A/C-Heater Blower Resistors** – are located on the front of the plenum.
- **A/C High Speed Blower Relay** – is located on the top of the plenum, near the vacuum tank.
- **Audio/Buzzer Alarm Module** – is located on the conveience center.
- **Charging System Relay** – is taped to the instrument panel harness, above the accelerator pedal.
- **"Check Engine" Light Driver** – is taped to the right side of the instrument panel harness.
- **Choke Heater Relay** – is located behind the instrument panel.
- **Coolant Fan Relay** – is located on the left front wheel well.
- **Coolant Temperature Sensor** – is located on the left side of the coolant inlet on the 4 cylinder engines and on the top left front side of the engine on the V6 engines.
- **Defogger Timer/Relay** – is located above the glove box.
- **Door Lock Relay** – is located on the upper center of the right shroud.
- **Early Fuel Evaporation Heater Relay** – is located on the upper right side of the engine cowl.
- **Electronic Control Module (ECM)** – is located behind the instrument panel.
- **Fuel Pump Relay** – is located on the upper right side of the engine cowl.
- **Horn Relay** – is located in the convenience center.
- **Lights-On Buzzer** – is located behind the right side of the instrument panel, near the glove box.
- **Manifold Absolute Pressure Sensor** – is located on the right side of the air filter.
- **Oil Pressure Sender** – is located at the rear of the engine above the distributor on the 4 cylinder engines and above the oil filter on the V6 engines.
- **Oxygen Sensor** – is located in the exhaust manifold.
- **Power Accesories Circuit Breaker** – is located in the buse block.
- **Power Antenna Relay** – is located behind the right side of the instrument panel, near the glove box.
- **Power Window Circuit Breaker** – is located in the fuse block.
- **Throttle Position Sensor** – is located on the throttle body.
- **Vacuum Sensor** – is located in the upper right side of the engine cowl.
- **Vehicle Speed Sensor** – is located as part of the speedometer assembly.
- **Wiper Pulse Module** – is located behind the left side of the instrument panel.

1985 OMEGA

- **A/C Clutch Diode** – is located inside the A/C compressor connector.
- **A/C Compressor Relay** – is located in the upper right corner of the firewall on the 2.5L engine and in the right side of the radiator support on the 2.8L engine.
- **A/C Diode** – is located in the A/C harness, near the vacuum tank.
- **A/C-Heater Blower Resistors** – are located on the front of the plenum.
- **A/C High Speed Blower Relay** – is located on the top of the plenum, near the vacuum tank.
- **Audio/Buzzer Alarm Module** – is located on the conveience center.
- **Barometric Pressure Sensor** – is located in the right rea corner of the engine compartment.
- **Charging System Relay** – is taped to the instrument panel harness, above the accelerator pedal.
- **"Check Engine" Light Driver** – is taped to the right side of the instrument panel harness.
- **Choke Heater Relay** – is taped to the instrument panel harness, near the fuse block.
- **Coolant Fan Relay** – is located on the left front wheel well.
- **Coolant Temperature Sensor** – is located on the left side of the coolant inlet on the 2.5L engine and on the top left front side of the engine on the 2.8L engine.
- **Cooling Fan In-Line Fuse** – is located on the left front shock tower.
- **Cruise Control Module** – is located under the left side of the instrument panel, above the accelerator pedal.
- **Defogger Timer/Relay** – is located above the glove box.
- **Diagnostic Dwell Meter Connector** – is located in the harness, in the right rear corner of the engine compartment.
- **Door Lock Relay** – is located on the upper center of the right shroud.
- **Early Fuel Evaporation Heater Relay** – is located on the upper right side of the engine cowl.
- **Electronic Control Module (ECM)** – is located behind the instrument panel.
- **Fuel Pump In-Line Fuse** – is located on the left front shock tower.
- **Fuel Pump Prime Connector** – is located on the rear of the engine, near the starter.
- **Fuel Pump Relay** – is located on the upper right side of the firewall on the 2.5L engine and on the left front shock tower on the 2.8L engine.
- **Horn Relay** – is located in the convenience center.
- **Lights-On Buzzer** – is located behind the right side of the instrument panel, near the glove box.
- **Manifold Absolute Pressure Sensor** – is located on the right side of the air filter.
- **Manifold Air Temperature Sensor** – is located on the air cleaner assembly.
- **Mass AirFlow In-Line Fuse** – is located on the left front shock tower.
- **Mass Airflow Relay** – is located on the left front shock tower.
- **Mass Airflow Sensor** – is located in the front of the engine.
- **Oil Pressure Sender** – is located at the rear of the engine above the distributor on the 2.5L engine and above the oil filter on the 2.8L engine.
- **Oxygen Sensor** – is located in the exhaust manifold.
- **Power Accesories Circuit Breaker** – is located in the buse block.
- **Power Antenna Relay** – is located behind the right side of the instrument panel, near the glove box.
- **Power Window Circuit Breaker** – is located in the fuse block.
- **Throttle Kicker Relay** – is located in the right front cornewr of the engine compartment.
- **Throttle Position Sensor** – is located on the throttle body.
- **Vacuum Sensor** – is located in the upper right side of the firewall.
- **Vehicle Speed Sensor** – is located as part of the speedometer assembly.
- **Wiper Pulse Module** – is located behind the left side of the instrument panel.

1982-84 FIRENZA

- **A/C Ambient Air Sensor** — is located on the engine cowl, above the power steering reservoir.
- **A/C Blower Relay** — is located on the front center of the plenum.
- **A/C Compressor Control Relay** — is located behind the right front shock tower.
- **A/C Compressor Run Relay** — is located behind the right front shock tower.
- **A/C-Heater Blower Resistors** — are located on the front left side of the plenum.
- **Blocking Diode** — is located in the instrument panel harness, near the fuse block.
- **Coolant Fan Relay** — on the left front fender in front of the shock tower.
- **Coolant Temperature Sender** — is located on the left side of the engine, near the coolant outlet.
- **Coolant Temperature Sensor** — is located on the front of the engine on the thermostat housing on the 1.8L engine and on the left side of the engine under the water outlet on the other engines.
- **Cruise Control Throttle Servo** — is located on the bracket on the left front shock tower.
- **Defogger Time Relay** — is located behind the left side of the dash panel.
- **Door Lock Relay** — is located on the upper right side of the steering column support.
- **Electronic Control Module (ECM)** — is located behind the glove box.
- **Electronic Fuel Injection Ambient Sensor** — is located on the engine cowl above the washer reservoir.
- **Fuel Pump Relay** — is located on the right engine cowl, behind the shock tower.
- **Hatch/Tailgate/Trunk Release Relay** — is taped to the wire harness, located behind the right side of the radio.
- **Horn Relay** — is located on the conveience center.
- **Idle Speed Motor** — is taped in the EFI harness. to the right of the electronic control module.
- **Manifold Absolute Presure Sensor** — is located on the right shock tower.
- **Oxygen Sensor** — is located in the exhaust manifold.
- **Power Accessories Circuit Breaker** — is located in the fuse block.
- **Power Antenna Relay** — is located behind the instrument panel, below the right side of the radio.
- **Power Window Circuit Breaker** — is located in the fuse block.
- **Throttle Position Sensor** — is located on the throttle body.
- **Torque Converter Clutch Relay (TCC)** — is located on the transmission cowling.
- **Vehicle Speed Sensor** — is located behind the instrument panel, the the right of the steering column.
- **Wiper Pulse Module** — is located below the steering column, above the trim cover.

1985-87 FIRENZA

- **A/C Blower Relay** — is located on the front center of the plenum.
- **A/C Compressor Control Relay** — is located behind the right front shock tower.
- **A/C Compressor Run Relay** — is located behind the right front shock tower.
- **A/C-Heater Blower Resistors** — are located on the front left side of the plenum.
- **A/C In-Car Temperature Sensor** — is located on the right side of the dash, above the glove box.

- **Assembly Line Diagnostic Link** — is located behind the instrument panel, on the right side of the fuse block.
- **Blocking Diode** — is located in the instrument panel harness, near the bulkhead connector.
- **Coolant Fan Relay** — on the left front fender in front of the shock tower or on the firewall to the left of the brake booster.
- **Coolant Temperature Sender** — is located on the left side of the engine, near the coolant outlet.
- **Coolant Temperature Sensor** — is located on the front of the engine on the thermostat housing on the 1.8L engine and on the left side of the engine under the water outlet on the other engines.
- **Cruise Control Module (2-door)** — is located behind the instrument panel, above the left side of the steering column.
- **Cruise Control Module (4-door)** — is located behind the right side of the dash panel, above the glove box.
- **Defogger Time Relay** — is located behind the left side of the dash panel.
- **Electronic Control Module (ECM)** — is located behind the glove box.
- **Electronic Fuel Injection Ambient Sensor** — is located on the engine cowl above the washer reservoir.
- **Electronic Speed Sensor** — is located on the top right side of the transaxle.
- **Fog Lamp Relays** — are taped to the instrument panel harness, near the fog lamp switch.
- **Fuel Pump In-Line Fuse** — is located on the firewall, behind the brake booster.
- **Fuel Pump Relay** — is located on the right engine cowl, behind the shock tower or on the firewall, above the brake booster.
- **Hatch/Tailgate/Trunk Release Relay** — is taped to the wire harness, located behind the right side of the radio.
- **Horn Relay** — is located on the conveience center.
- **Knock Sensor** — is located on the right side of the starter below the starter.
- **Low Coolant Module** — is located behind the instrument panel, above the left side of the steering column.
- **Low Coolant Temperature Sensor** — is located in the engine compartment, on the right front side of the radiator.
- **Manifold Absolute Pressure Sensor** — is located on the right shock tower.
- **Manifold Air Temperature Sensor** — is located on the engine, underneath or on top of the intake manifold.
- **Mass Airflow Relay** — is located on the firewall, behind the brake booster.
- **Mass Airflow Sensor** — is located on the top of the left side of the engine, behind the air cleaner.
- **Mass Airflow Sensor In-Line Fuse** — is located on the firewall, behind the brake booster.
- **Outside Air Temperature Sensor** — is located inthe engine compartment, behind the right side of the grill.
- **Oxygen Sensor** — is located in the exhaust manifold.
- **Power Accessories/Convertible Top Circuit Breaker** — is located in the fuse block.
- **Power Antenna Relay** — is located behind the instrument panel, below the right side of the radio.
- **Power Door Lock Relay** — is located on the upper right side of the steering column support.
- **Power Unit Dimmer** — is located behind the instrument panel, to the left of the steering column.
- **Power Window Circuit Breaker** — is located in the fuse block.
- **Release Relay** — is taped to the instrument panel harness, behind the radio or glove box.
- **Throttle Position Sensor** — is located on the throttle body. On the 2.8L engine it is located, behind the distributor.
- **Torque Converter Clutch Relay (TCC)** — is located on the transmission cowling.
- **Turbo Release Relay** — is located on the transaxle

cowling.

- **Twilight Sentinel Amplifier** – is located behind the instrument panel, to the left of the steering column.
- **Twilight Sentinel Photocell** – is located on the dash panel, on the right side of the defrost vent.
- **Vehicle Speed Sensor** – is located behind the instrument panel, the the right of the steering column.
- **Vehicle Speed Sensor Buffer** – is located behind the instrument cluster, below the speed sensor.

1983-84 CIERA

- **A/C Blower Resistors** – is located on the right side of the engine cowl.
- **A/C Compressor Relay** – is located on the upper right corner of the engine cowl.
- **A/C Delay Relay** – is located in the upper right corner of the engine cowl.
- **A/C High Pressure Cut-Out Switch** – is located on the left side of the compressor.
- **A/C Temperature Cut-Out Switch** – is located on the top of the engine near the fuel filter.
- **Audio Alarm Module** – is located behind the instrument panel, to the left of the steering column.
- **Charging System Relay** – is located behind the instrument panel, near the fuse block.
- **"Check Engine" Light Driver** – is taped to the instrument panel harness behind the glove box.
- **Choke Relay (Non EFI)** – is located on the convenience center.
- **Coolant Fan Relay** – is located on the left front wheel well on the bracket on the 4 cylinder engine and on the fender panel ahead of the left front shock tower on the V6 engine.
- **Coolant Fan Switch** – is located in front of the engine below the left side valve cover on the 4 cylinder engine and on the top of the V6 engine in front of the distributor.
- **Coolant Temperature Sensor** – is located on the left center side of the 4 cylinder engines and on the top of the V6 engine in front of the distributor.
- **Coolant Temperature Switch** – is located on the top of the engine near the fuel filter.
- **Diagnostic Dwell Meter Connector** – is located near the upper right side of the engine cowl.
- **Diesel Diode Module** – is located on the right side of the engine cowl on a bracket.
- **Early Fuel Evaporation Heater Relay** – is located on the upper right side of the engine cowl.
- **Electronic Control Module (ECM)** – is located behind the right side of the instrument panel.
- **Electronic Level Control Height Sensor** – is located on the frame under the trunk.
- **Electronic Level Control Relay** – is located on the frame behind the left rear wheel well.
- **Fuel Pump Relay** – is located on the upper right side of the engine cowl.
- **Glow Plug Relay (Diesel)** – is located behind the left battery on the wheel well.
- **Headlight-Key-Seat Buzzer** – is located on the convenience center.
- **Heater Blower Resistors** – is located on the right plenum.
- **Horn Relay** – is located on the convenience center.
- **Low Brake Vacuum Relay** – is taped to the instrument panel above the fuse block.
- **Low Brake Vacuum Switch** – is located on top of the brake booster unit.
- **Manifold Absolute Pressure Sensor** – is located in the upper right engine cowl on the 4 cylinder engines and on the behind the right front shock tower on the V6 engines.
- **Oxygen Sensor** – is located in the exhaust manifold.

- **Power Accessories Circuit Breaker** – is located in the fuse block.
- **Power Antenna Relay** – is located behind the instrument panel on the rear of the glove box.
- **Power Window Circuit Breaker** – is located in the fuse block.
- **Thermal Controller (Diesel)** – is located on the top of the engine near the fuel filter.
- **Throttle Position Sensor** – is located on the throttle body.
- **Wait Lamp Control Relay (Diesel)** – is located in the upper right corner of the engine cowl on a bracket.
- **Water-In-Fuel Sensor** – is located in the fuel tank.

1985-87 CIERA

- **A/C Blower Resistors** – is located on the right side of the engine cowl.
- **A/C Compressor Relay** – is located on the upper right corner of the engine cowl.
- **A/C Delay Relay** – is located in the upper right corner of the engine cowl.
- **A/C Heater Blower Relay** – is located on the plenum, on the right side of the firewall.
- **A/C High Pressure Cut-Out Switch** – is located on the left side of the compressor.
- **A/C Temperature Cut-Out Switch** – is located on the top of the engine near the fuel filter.
- **Altitude Advance Relay** – is located on the left inner fender, in front of the shock tower.
- **Assembly Line Diagnostic Link** – is located on the bottom of the instrument oanel, near the steering column.
- **Audio Alarm Module** – is located behind the instrument panel, to the left of the steering column.
- **Barometric Pressure Sensor** – is located on the firewall, at the right side of the blower motor.
- **Buffer Amplifier** – is located behind the right side of the instrument panel, in front of the electronic control module.
- **Charging System Relay** – is located behind the instrument panel, near the fuse block.
- **"Check Engine" Light Driver** – is taped to the instrument panel harness behind the glove box.
- **Choke Relay (Non EFI)** – is located on the convenience center.
- **Constant Run Relay** – is located on the left inner fender wheel well.
- **Coolant Fan In-Line Fuse** – is located in the engine compartment in front of the left front shock tower.
- **Coolant Fan Low-Speed Relay** – is located on the left inner fender wheel well, on a bracket on the 4 cylinder engines and on the fender panel in front of the left front shock tower on the V6 models.
- **Coolant Fan Relay** – is located on the left front wheel well on the bracket on the 4 cylinder engine and on the fender panel ahead of the left front shock tower on the V6 engine.
- **Coolant Fan Switch** – is located in front of the engine below the left side valve cover on the 4 cylinder engine and on the top of the V6 engine in front of the distributor.
- **Coolant Temperature Sensor** – is located on the left center side of the 4 cylinder engines and on the top of the V6 engine in front of the distributor.
- **Coolant Temperature Switch** – is located on the top of the engine near the fuel filter.
- **Cruise Control Module** – is located behind the instrument panel, above the accelerator pedal.
- **Defogger Timer Relay** – is located behind the instrument panel, under the instrument cluster.
- **Diagnostic Dwell Meter Connector** – is located near the upper right side of the engine cowl.

- **Diesel Diode Module** – is located on the right side of the engine cowl on a bracket.
- **Diesel Electronic Controller (DEC)** – is located behind the right side of the instrument panel.
- **Diesel Generator Diode** – is located in the engine harness, to the right of the glow plug controller.
- **Early Fuel Evaporation Heater Relay** – is located on the upper right side of the engine cowl.
- **Electronic Control Module (ECM)** – is located behind the right side of the instrument panel.
- **Electronic Level Control Height Sensor** – is located on the frame under the trunk or in front of the fuel tank on the Wagon models.
- **Electronic Level Control Relay** – is located on the frame behind the left rear wheel well.
- **Fuel Pump Relay** – is located on the upper right side of the engine cowl.
- **Glow Plug Controller/Relay (Diesel)** – is located on the rear of the engine, to the left of the cylinder head.
- **Glow Plug Relay (Diesel)** – is located behind the left battery on the wheel well.
- **Headlight-Key-Seat Buzzer** – is located on the convenience center.
- **Heater Blower Resistors** – is located on the right plenum.
- **High Mount Stop Light Relays** – are located on the left rear wheel well, in the trunk.
- **Horn Relay** – is located on the convenience center.
- **Knock Sensor** – is located on the top left side of the engine, below the front of the oxygen sensor.
- **Low Brake Vacuum Relay** – is taped to the instrument panel above the fuse block.
- **Low Brake Vacuum Switch** – is located on top of the brake booster unit.
- **Manifold Absolute Pressure Sensor** – is located in the upper right engine cowl on the 4 cylinder engines and on the behind the right front shock tower on the V6 engines.
- **Manifold Air Temperature Sensor** – is located in the canister, at the front of the engine compartment.
- **Mass Airflow Relay** – is located in the engine compartment, on the front of the left shock tower.
- **Mass Air Flow Sensor In-Line Fuse** – is located in the engine compartment, on the front of the left shock tower.
- **Metering Valve Sensor (MVS)** – is located on top of the engine.
- **Oxygen Sensor** – is located in the exhaust manifold.
- **Power Accessories Circuit Breaker** – is located in the fuse block.
- **Power Antenna Relay** – is located behind the instrument panel on the rear of the glove box.
- **Power Door Lock Relay** – is located on the right shroud, to the right of the glove box.
- **Power Window Circuit Breaker** – is located in the fuse block.
- **Pulse Relay** – is located on the left inner fender, in ftont of the left front shock tower.
- **Rear Wiper Relay** – is located in the top center of the tailgate.
- **Sentinel Amplifier** – is located behind the center of the instrument panel, behind the ashtray.
- **Speed Sensor** – is located on the top right side of the transaxle.
- **Starter Interrupt Relay** – is located above the ashtray, taped to the instrument panel harness.
- **Theft Deterrent Relay** – is located behind the instrument panel, strapped to the theft deterrent controller.
- **Thermal Controller (Diesel)** – is located on the top of the engine near the fuel filter.
- **Throttle Kicker Relay** – is located on the front of the engine compartment, at the right side of the radiator support.

- **Throttle Position Sensor** – is located on the throttle body.
- **Wait Lamp Control Relay (Diesel)** – is located in the upper right corner of the engine cowl on a bracket.
- **Water-In-Fuel Sensor** – is located in the fuel tank.

1985-87 CALAIS

- **A/C Compressor Clutch Diode** – is located in the connector at the compressor clutch.
- **A/C Compressor Control Relay (2.5L)** – is located on the relay bracket at the center of the firewall in the engine compartment.
- **A/C Cooling Fan Relay (3.0L)** – is located on the relay bracket at the center of the firewall in the engine compartment.
- **A/C Cut-Out Relay (3.0L)** – is located on the relay bracket at the center of the firewall in the engine compartment.
- **A/C-Heater Blower Motor Relay** – is located on the right side of the firewall in the engine compartment, to the left of the blower motor.
- **Audio Alarm Module** – is located on the fuse block or above the glove box.
- **Computer Control Ignition Module (3.0L)** – is located at the top right rear of the engine.
- **Coolant Temperature Sensor** – is located at the top right end of the engine (top left on the 2.5L engine).
- **Cooling Fan Relay** – is located is located on the relay bracket at the center of the firewall in the engine compartment.
- **Cooling Fan Resistor (3.0L)** – is located on the lower bracket behind the cooling fan.
- **Cruise Control Module** – is attached under the rear of the left side of the dash panel.
- **Defogger Timer Relay** – is located behind the left side f the dash panel, near the fuse block.
- **Driver Information Center Display Module** – is located in the center of the dash, below the radio.
- **Driver Information Center Lights Monitor Module** – is located below the center of the dash panel, in front of the console.
- **Dual Crank Sensor (3.0L)** – is located on the lower right front side of the engine.
- **Electronic Control Module (ECM)** – is located behind the right side kick panel.
- **Electronic Spark Control Module (3.0L)** – is located is located on the relay bracket at the center of the firewall in the engine compartment.
- **Fog Light Relay** – is located on the left front inner fender panel, in front of the shock tower.
- **Fuel Pump Relay** – is located on the relay bracket at the center of the firewall in the engine compartment.
- **Generator Diode (2.5L)** – is located in the instrument panel wiring harness, under the left side of the dash panel.
- **High Mount Stop Lamp Relays** – are located on the left rear wheelwell inside the trunk.
- **Illumination Control Relay** – is located behind the center of the instrument panel, in front of the console.
- **Horn Relay** – is located in the instrument panel wiring harness near the fuse block.
- **Knock (Detonation) Sensor (3.0L)** – is located at the top left side of the engine.
- **Manifold Absolute Pressure Sensor (2.5L)** – is located on the air cleaner assembly.
- **Manifold Absolute Pressure Sensor (3.0L)** – is located on the left side of the engine compartment, behind the radiator.
- **Manifold Airflow Sensor (3.0L)** – is located on the left side of the engine compartment, behind the radiator.
- **Oxygen Sensor** – is located in the exhaust manifold.

- **Power Accessories Circuit Breaker** – is located in the fuse block.
- **Power Antenna Relay** – is located at the right side of the trunk.
- **Power Door Lock Relay Assembly** – is located behind the right side kick panel.
- **Power Window Circuit Breaker** – is located in the fuse block.
- **Remote Dimmer Module** – is located in the instrument panel wiring harness, to the right of the radio.
- **Throttle Postion Sensor** – is located on the throttle body.
- **Vehicle Speed Sensor (ATX)** – is located at the rear of the engine, on the right end of the transaxle.
- **Vehicle Speed Sensor (MTX)** – is located at the rear of the engine, on the top of the transaxle.
- **Vehicle Speed Sensor Buffer Amplifier** – is located behind the right side of the dash panel.
- **Wiper/Washer Motor Module** – is located in the left rear corner of the engine compartment, to the right of the shock tower.

1982-83 TORONADO

- **A/C Blower Relay** – is located near the blower motor.
- **A/C Cut-Out Relay** – is located on the top center portion of the engine cowl.
- **A/C Cut-Out Switch** – is located on the front of the engine near the left valve cover.
- **A/C-Heater Blower Resistors** – is located on the top left side of the blower assembly.
- **A/C Pressure Cycling Switch** – is connected to the top of the accumulator drier.
- **A/C Programmer** – is located inside the right section of the plenum.
- **Barometric Pressure Sensor (V6)** – is located on the right shroud near the engine cowl grommet.
- **Cold Inhibit Switch (Diesel)** – is located below the center of the right valve cover.
- **Convenience Center** – is located in the center of the instrument panel, behind the radio.
- **Coolant Temperature Sensor (V6)** – is located at the front top section of the engine behind the alternator.
- **Coolant Temperature Sensor (V8)** – is located at the top left section of the engine.
- **Coolant Temperature Switch (Diesel)** – is locatedon the top left rear section of the engine.
- **Defogger Timer Relay** – is located at the right side of the fuse block.
- **Door Lock Diode** – is located on the left shroud near the center access hole.
- **Electronic Control Module (ECM)** – is located behind the right kick panel.
- **Electronic Spark Control Unit** – is located on the top right front wheel well.
- **Engine Temperature Switch (Diesel)** – is located below the rear part of the left valve cover.
- **Glow Plug Relay (Diesel)** – is located on the top of the right front wheel well.
- **Glow Plug Thermal Control Unit (Diesel)** – is located on the top front section of the engine.
- **Horn Relay** – is taped to the instrument panel harnes to the left of the steering column or connected to the convenience center.
- **Idle Speed Control Unit (V6)** – is located on the left side of the carburetor.
- **Illluminated Entry Timer** – is located on the upper left shroud near the junction block.
- **Level Control Height Sensor** – is attached to the left side of the rear crossmember.

- **Level Control Relay** – is located under the left side of the instrument panel, above the fuse block.
- **Manifold Absolute Pressure Sensor** – is located on the top of the right front wheel well.
- **Memory Seat Disable Relay** – is located behind the right side of the instrument panel.
- **Multi-Function Chime Module** – is located in the convenience center.
- **Oil Pressure Switch (V6)** – is located below the right valve cover.
- **Oil Pressure Switch (V8)** – is located on the top left section of the engine.
- **Oxygen Sensor** – is located on the exhaust manifold behind the right valve cover on the V6 engine and on the left exhaust manifold on the V8 engine.
- **Power Door Lock Relay** – is located behind the glove box.
- **Remote Light Drive Module** – is located behind the instrument panel, above the footwell.
- **Seat Memory Module** – is located under the driver's seat.
- **Starter Interrupt Relay** – is taped to the dash harness near the fuse block.
- **Theft Deterrent Control Unit** – is attached to the accelerator pedla lever plate.
- **Theft Deterrent Relay** – is attached to the bottom of the theft deterrent control unit.
- **Theft Deterrent Diode** – is located in the instrument panel harness above the fuse block.
- **Tone Generator** – is located behind the center of the instrument panel.
- **Twilight Sentinel Amplifier** – is located behind the instrument panel to the right of the radio.
- **Twilight Sentinel Photocell** – is located on the top of the instrument panel in the left speaker grille.
- **Vacuum Sensor (V8)** – is connected to the right front wheel well.
- **Vehicle Speed Sensor** – is located behind the right side of the cluster carrier.
- **Wait Lamp Control Relay (Diesel)** – is located on the top center of the engine cowl.
- **Wiper Motor Relay Diode** – is located in the wiper motor connector.

1984-87 TORONADO

- **A/C Blower Relay** – is located near the blower motor.
- **A/C Compressor Clutch Diode** – is located on the A/C clutch connector.
- **A/C Cut-Out Relay** – is located on the top center portion of the engine cowl.
- **A/C Cut-Out Switch** – is located on the front of the engine near the left valve cover.
- **A/C-Heater Blower Resistors** – is located on the top left side of the blower assembly.
- **A/C Pressure Cycling Switch** – is connected to the top of the accumulator drier.
- **A/C Programmer** – is located inside the right section of the plenum.
- **A/C Temperature Cut-Out Relay** – is located on the top center section of the right inner fender panel.
- **Alarm Module** – is located behind the instrument panel, on the convenience center.
- **Alternator Diode** – is located in the engine harness, near the alternator.
- **Amplifier Relay** – is located behind the instrument panel, near the fuse block.
- **Antenna Relay** – is located behind the instrument panel near the courtesy light.
- **Assembly Line Diagnostic Link Connector** – is located

on the instrument panel cover, below the left side of the steering column.

- **Barometric Pressure Sensor**—is located behind the right kick panel, near the ECM.
- **"Check Engine" Light Module**—is located behind the left side instrument panel, above the passenger's kick panel.
- **Convenience Center**—is located in the center of the instrument panel, to the right of the steering column.
- **Coolant Temperature Sensor**—is located at the top left section of the engine., behind the alternator.
- **Coolant Temperature Sensor (Diesel)**—is located on the top left rear section of the engine.
- **Cruise Control Module**—is located behind the right side of the dash, mounted on the plenum.
- **Defogger Timer Relay**—is located at the right side of the fuse block.
- **Diode Module**—is located on the top center of the engine cowl.
- **Door Lock Control Unit**—is located behind the instrument panel, above the glove box.
- **Door Lock Diode**—is located on the left shroud near the center access hole.
- **Electronic Control Module (ECM)**—is located behind the right kick panel.
- **Electronic Spark Control Unit**—is located on the top right front wheel well.
- **Fiber Optic Light Source**—is located behind the instrument panel, to the left of the steering column.
- **Glow Plug Relay (Diesel)**—is located on the top of the right front wheel well.
- **Glow Plug Thermal Control Unit (Diesel)**—is located on the top front section of the engine.
- **Horn Relay**—is taped to the instrument panel harnes to the left of the steering column or connected to the convenience center.
- **Idle Speed Control Unit (V6)**—is located on the left side of the carburetor.
- **Illuminated Entry Timer**—is located on the upper left shroud near the junction block.
- **In-Car Temperature Sensor**—is located behind the right side of the dash panel, near the speaker.
- **Level Control Height Sensor**—is attached to the left side of the rear crossmember.
- **Level Control Relay**—is located under the left side of the instrument panel, above the fuse block.
- **Low Coolant Sensor**—is located on the upper right side of the radiator.

- **Manifold Absolute Pressure Sensor**—is located on the top right section of the engine near the air cleaner.
- **Memory Seat Disable Relay**—is located behind the right side of the instrument panel.
- **Multi-Function Chime Module**—is located in the convenience center.
- **Oil Pressure Switch**—is located on the top left section of the engine.
- **Outside Temperature Sensor**—is located on the center of the radiator support.
- **Oxygen Sensor**—is located at the right rear of the exhaust manifold.
- **Power Accessories Circuit Breaker**—is located in the fuse block.
- **Power Door Lock Relay**—is located behind the glove box.
- **Power Window Circuit Breaker**—is located in the fuse block.
- **Seat Memory Module**—is located under the driver's seat.
- **Starter Interrupt Relay**—is taped to the dash harness near the fuse block.
- **Theft Deterrent Control Unit**—is attached to the accelerator pedla lever plate.
- **Theft Deterrent Diode**—is located in the instrument panel harness above the fuse block.
- **Theft Deterrent Relay**—is attached to the bottom of the theft deterrent control unit.
- **Throttle Position Sensor**—is located on the left front side of the carburetor.
- **Tone Generator**—is located behind the center of the instrument panel.
- **Twilight Sentinel Amplifier**—is located behind the instrument panel to the right of the radio.
- **Twilight Sentinel Photocell**—is located on the top of the instrument panel in the left speaker grille.
- **Vacuum Sensor**—is connected to the right front wheel well.
- **Vehicle Speed Buffer**—is located on the left side of the instrument cluster.
- **Vehicle Speed Sensor**—is located behind the left side of the instrument cluster.
- **Voice/Alarm Module**—is located behind the instrument panel, below the ashtray.
- **Wait Lamp Control Relay (Diesel)**—is located on the top center of the engine cowl.
- **Wiper Motor Relay Diode**—is located in the wiper motor connector.

COMPONENT LOCATIONS

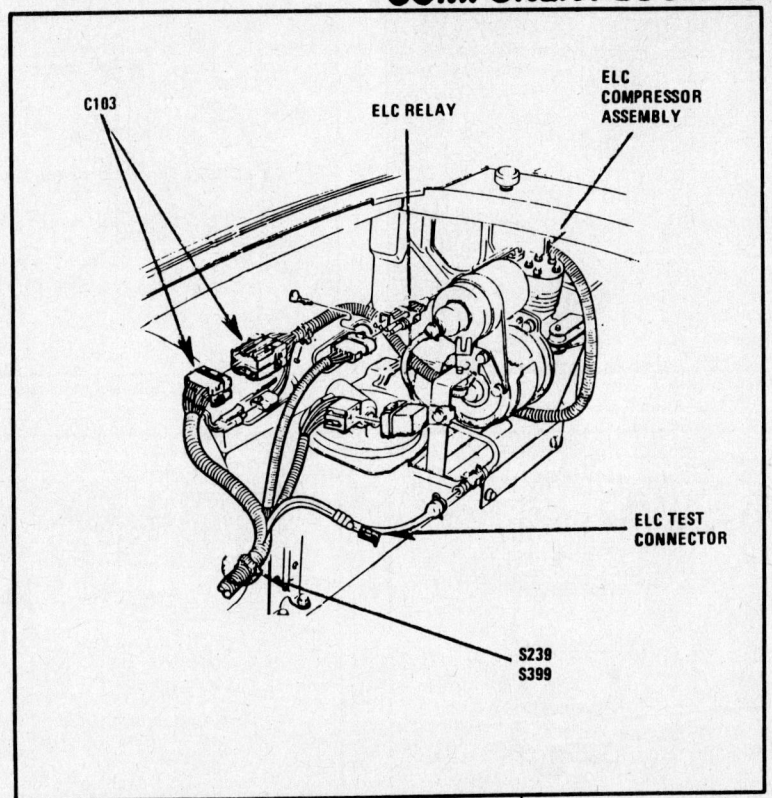

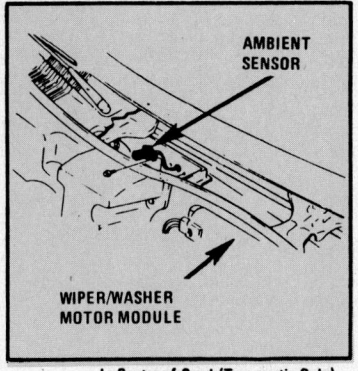

In Center of Cowl (Tempmatic Only)

LH Front Of Delta 88 Royale Engine Compartment

1985-86 Oldsmobile 98 and 88

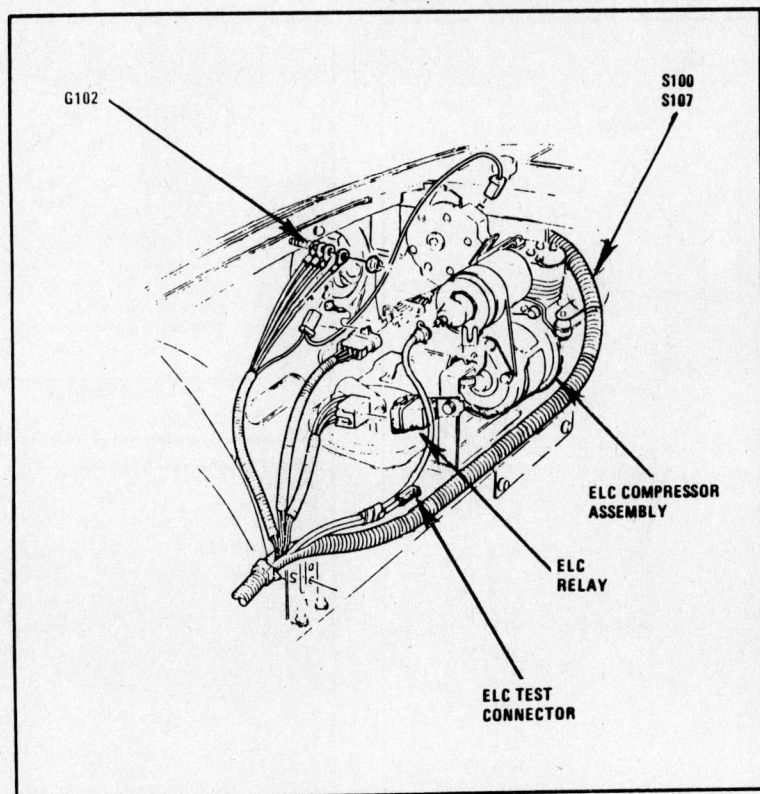

RH Front Of Engine

LH Front Of Ninety-Eight Regency Engine Compartment

1985-86 Oldsmobile 98 and 88

COMPONENT LOCATIONS

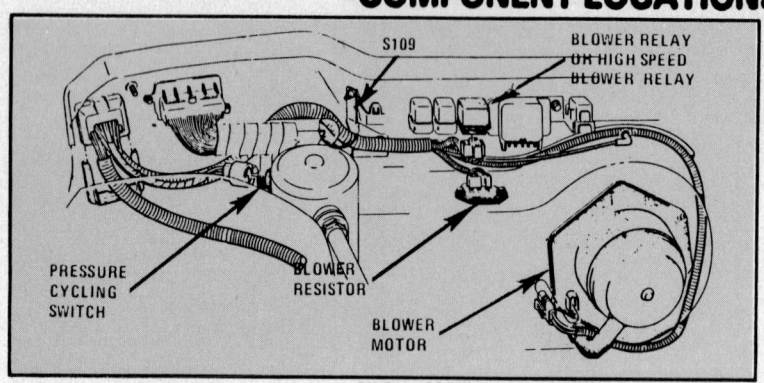

S109

BLOWER RELAY OR HIGH SPEED BLOWER RELAY

PRESSURE CYCLING SWITCH

BLOWER RESISTOR

BLOWER MOTOR

RH Front Of Dash

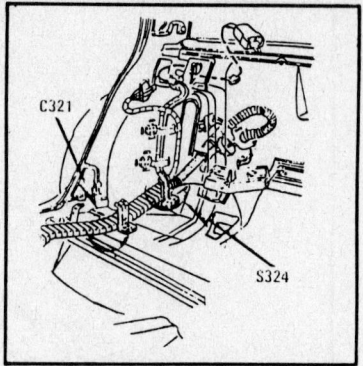

C321

S324

RH Rear Of Passenger Compartment

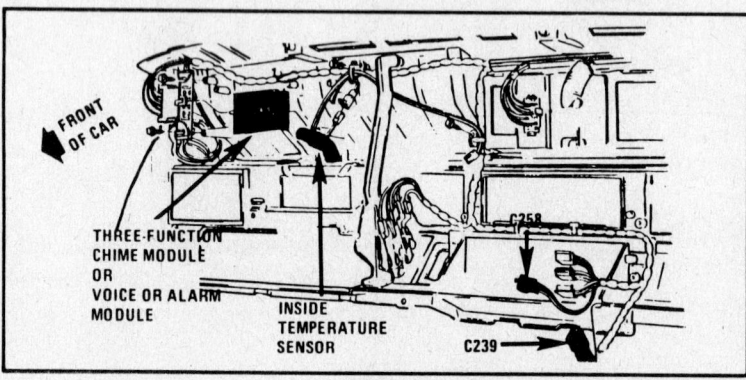

FRONT OF CAR

THREE-FUNCTION CHIME MODULE OR VOICE OR ALARM MODULE

INSIDE TEMPERATURE SENSOR

C258

C239

Behind RH Side Of I/P

IN CAR SENSOR

RH Side Of I/P

1985-86 Oldsmobile 98 and 88

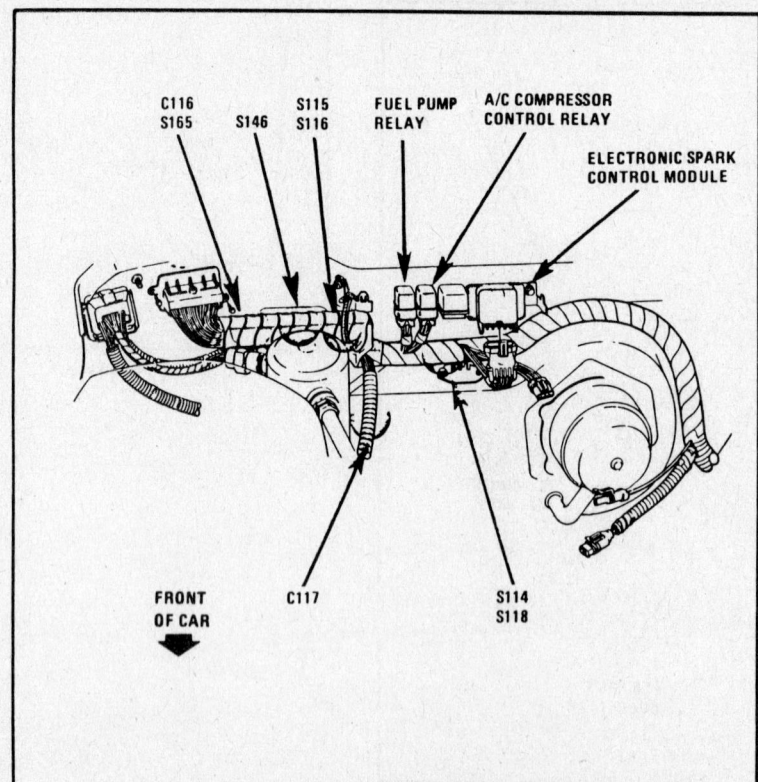

C116
S165   S146   S115
              S116   FUEL PUMP RELAY   A/C COMPRESSOR CONTROL RELAY

ELECTRONIC SPARK CONTROL MODULE

FRONT OF CAR

C117

S114
S118

Front Of Dash

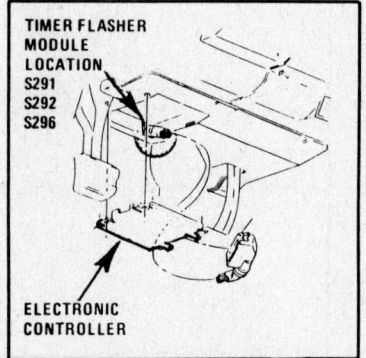

ANTILOCK BRAKE DIODE

STEERING COLUMN SUPPORT

Behind LH Side Of I/P

TIMER FLASHER MODULE LOCATION
S291
S292
S296

ELECTRONIC CONTROLLER

Below LH Side Of I/P

1985-86 Oldsmobile 98 and 88

COMPONENT LOCATIONS

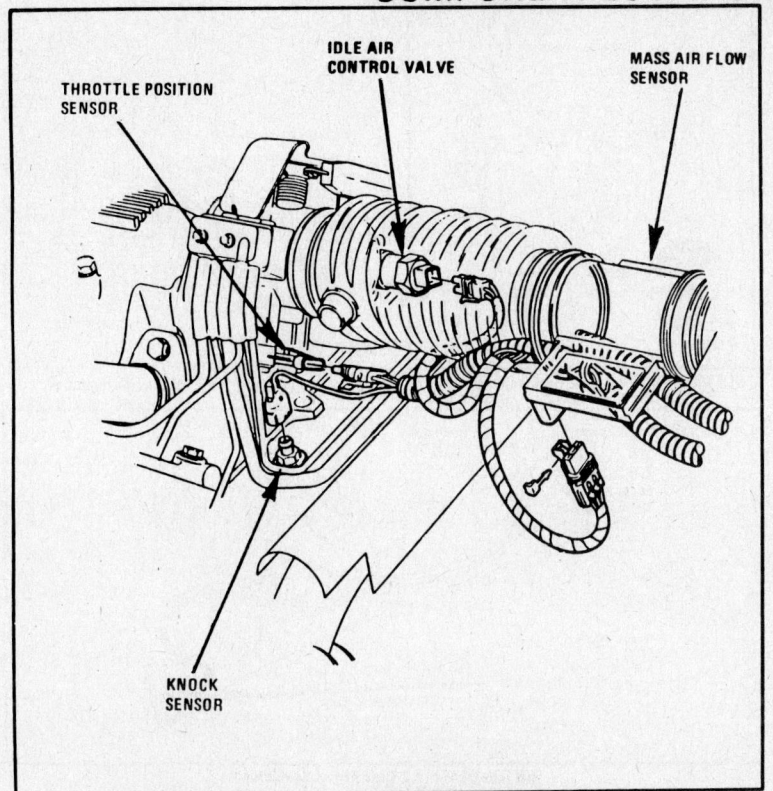

Top Of VIN B And VIN 3 Engines

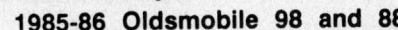

1985-86 Oldsmobile 98 and 88

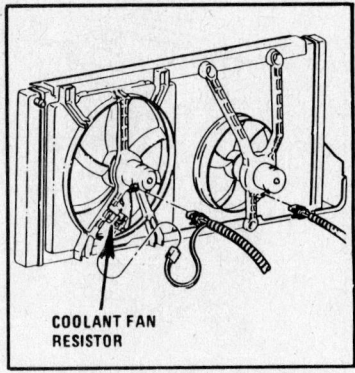

Front Of Engine Compartment

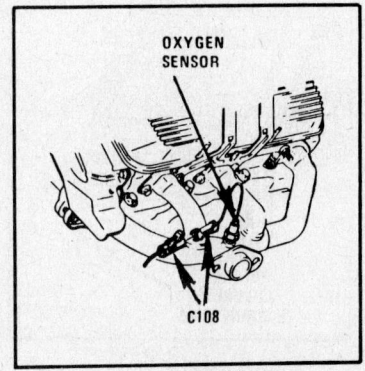

Rear Of Engine

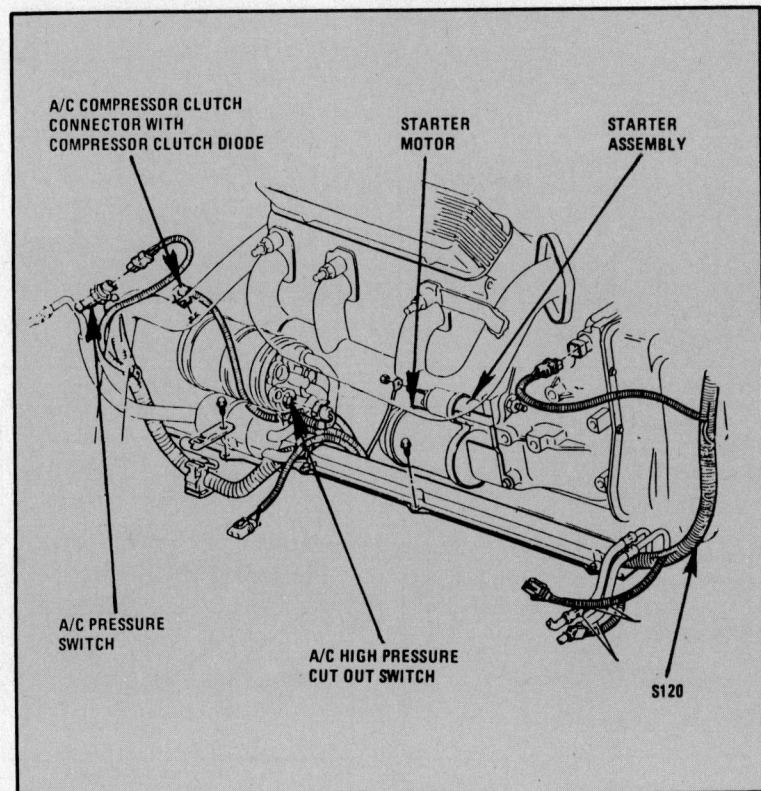

Front Of Engine

1985-86 Oldsmobile 98 and 88

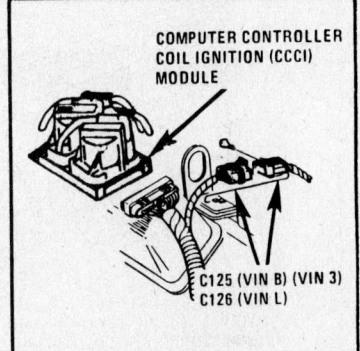

Top Rear Of Engine

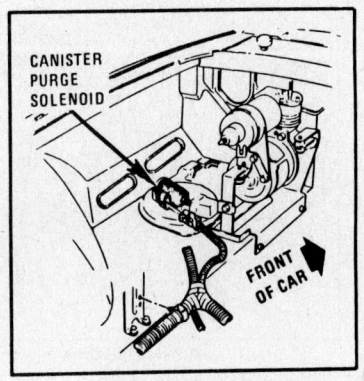

LH Front Of Engine Compartment

COMPONENT LOCATIONS

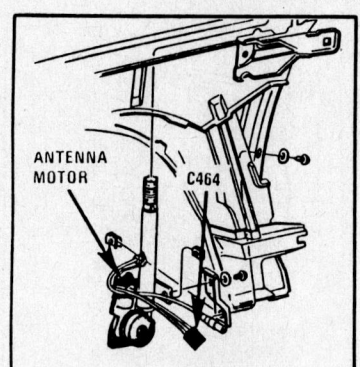

Rear Of RH Front Fender

RH Side Of VIN Y 4 Door Engine Compartment

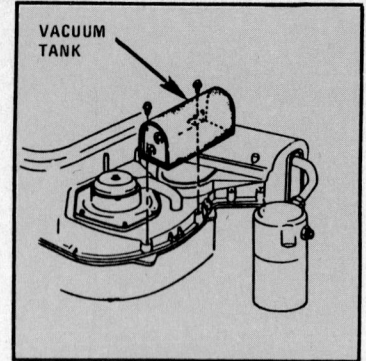

RH Rear Of Engine Compartment

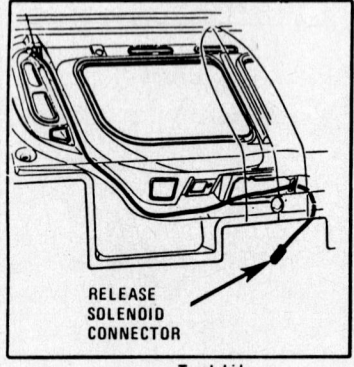

Trunk Lid

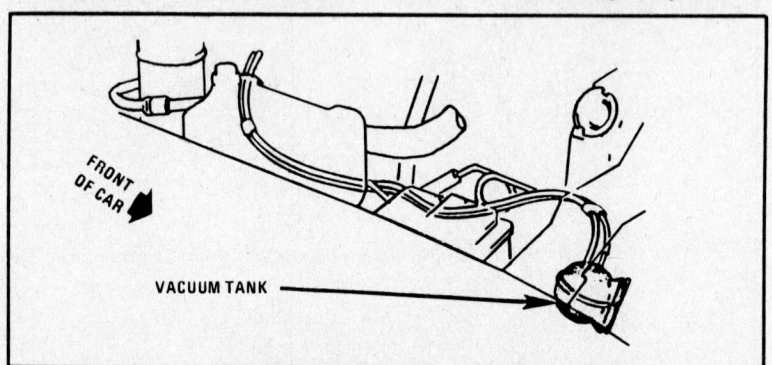

RH Side Of VIN Y 2 Door Engine Compartment

1985-86 Oldsmobile Cutlass Supreme

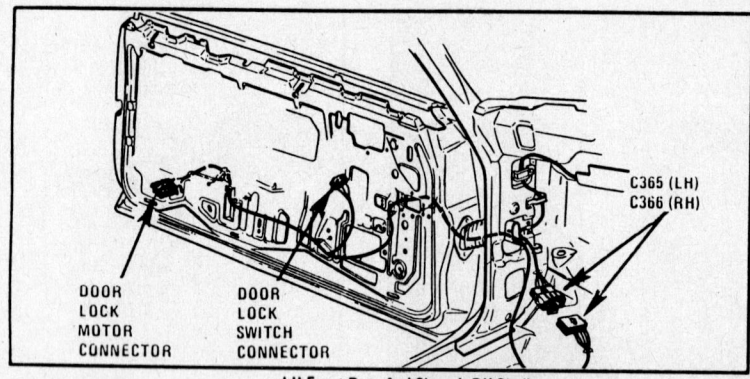

LH Front Door And Shroud, RH Similar

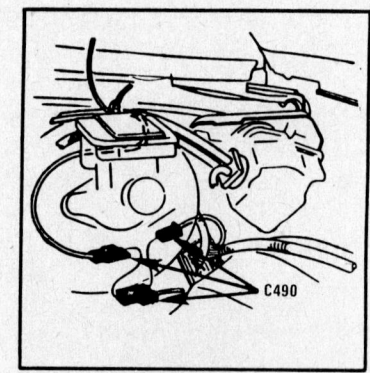

LH Front Of Dash

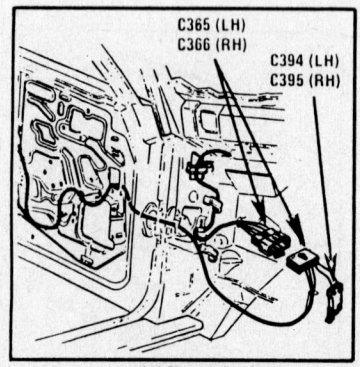

LH Shroud, RH Similar

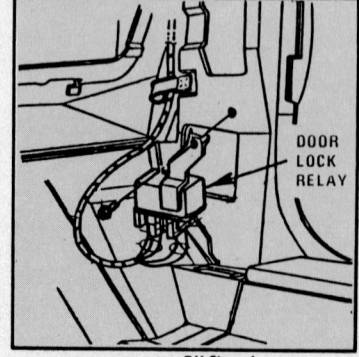

RH Shroud

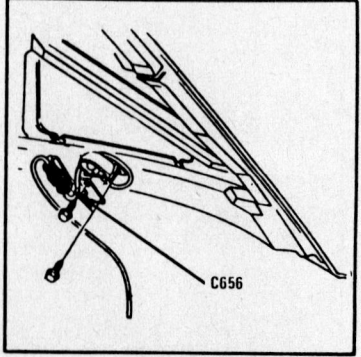

Under LH Side Of Hood

1985-86 Oldsmobile Cutlass Supreme

COMPONENT LOCATIONS

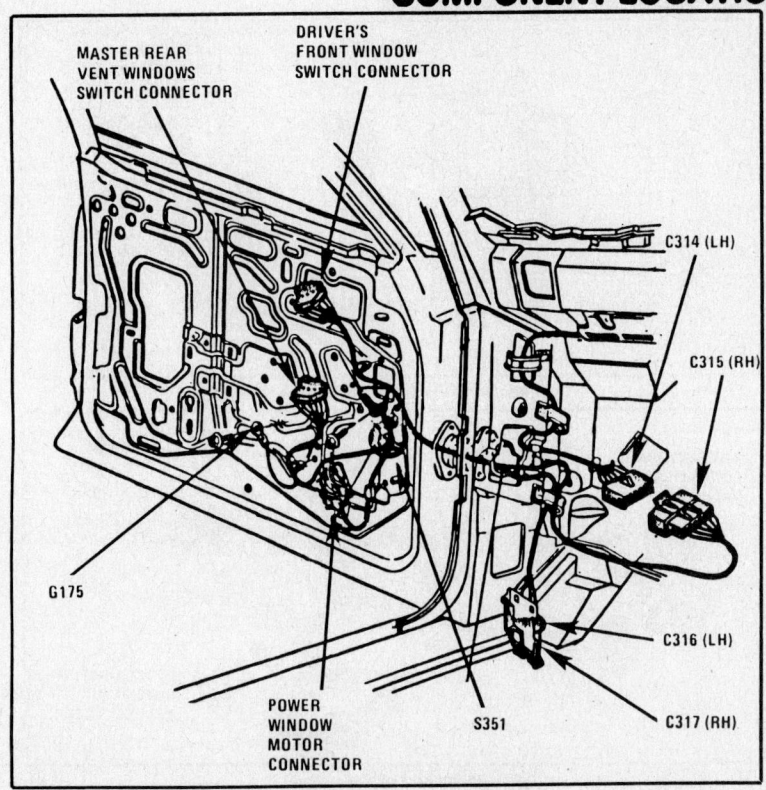

LH Front Door And Shroud (4 Door)

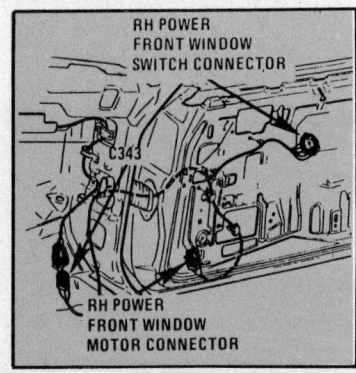

LH Front Door And Shroud (2 Door)

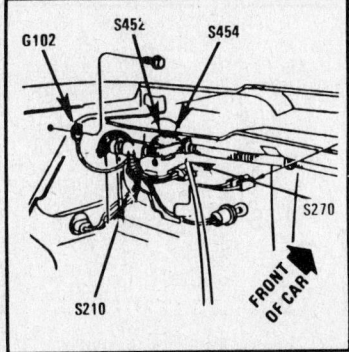

RH Front Door And Shroud

1985-86 Oldsmobile Cutlass Supreme

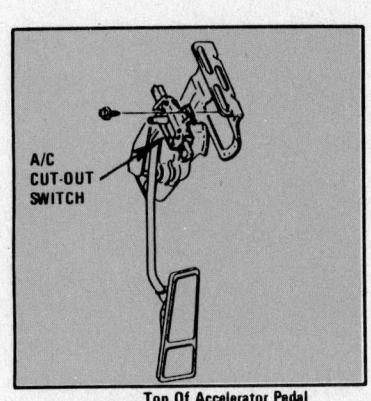

Top Of Accelerator Pedal

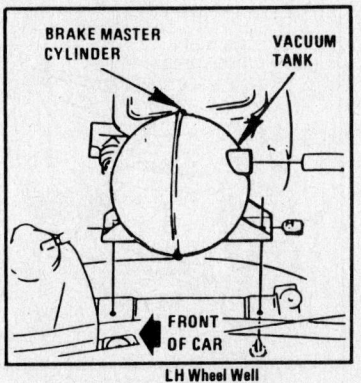

LH Wheel Well

Front LH Corner Of Engine Compartment

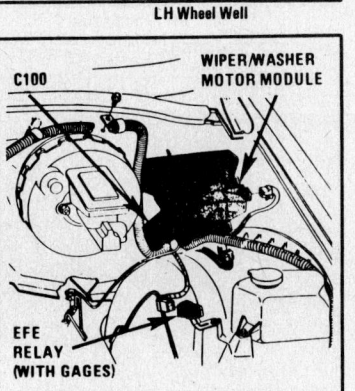

RH Front Of Dash

LH Rear Of Engine Compartment

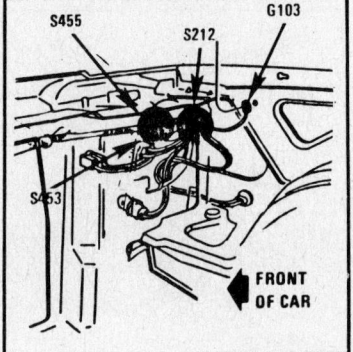

Front RH Corner Of Engine Compartment

1985-86 Oldsmobile Cutlass Supreme

COMPONENT LOCATIONS

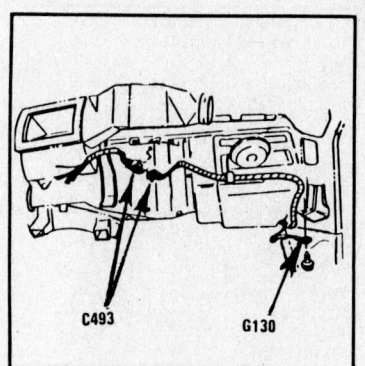

C493   G130

Under I/P, RH Side

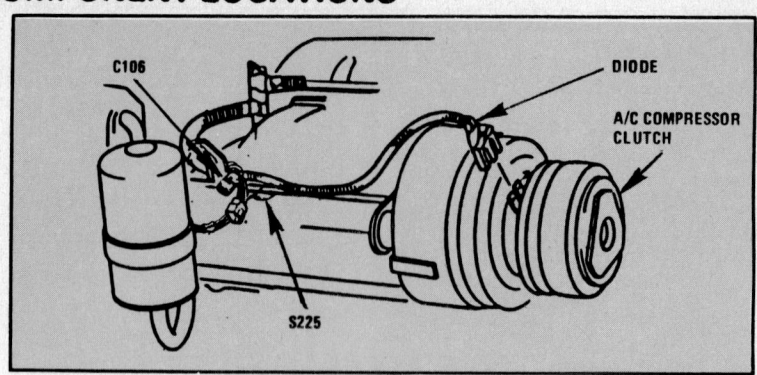

C106   DIODE

A/C COMPRESSOR CLUTCH

S225

RH Side Of VIN 9 And VIN Y Engines, VIN A Similar

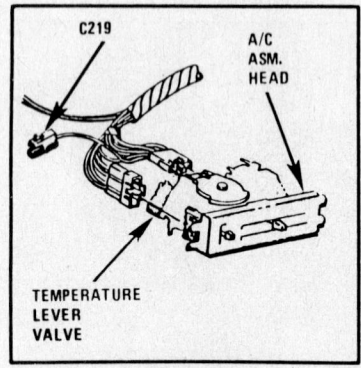

C219   A/C ASM. HEAD

TEMPERATURE LEVER VALVE

Center Of I/P

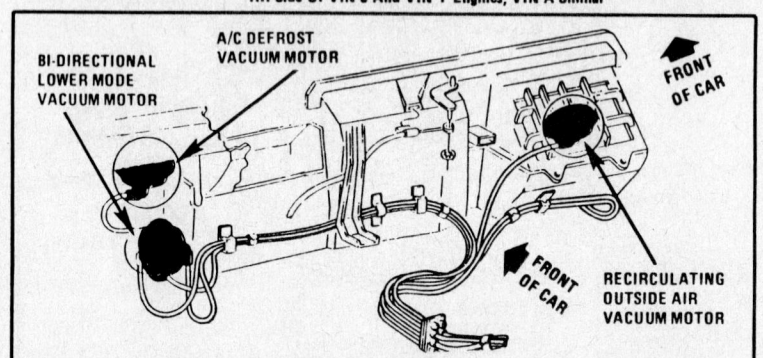

BI-DIRECTIONAL LOWER MODE VACUUM MOTOR   A/C DEFROST VACUUM MOTOR

FRONT OF CAR

FRONT OF CAR

RECIRCULATING OUTSIDE AIR VACUUM MOTOR

Behind I/P, In A/C Module

1985-86 Oldsmobile Cutlass Supreme

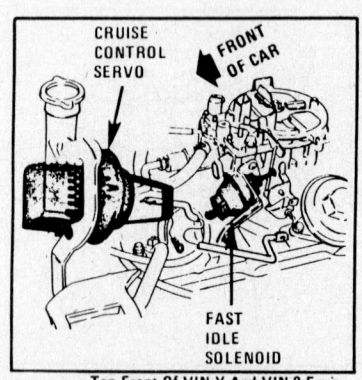

CRUISE CONTROL SERVO   FRONT OF CAR

FAST IDLE SOLENOID

Top Front Of VIN Y And VIN 9 Engine

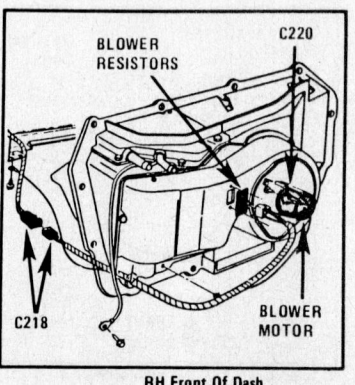

BLOWER RESISTORS   C220

C218   BLOWER MOTOR

RH Front Of Dash

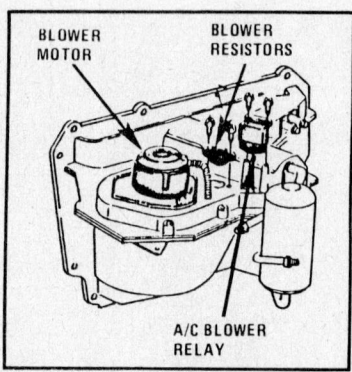

BLOWER MOTOR   BLOWER RESISTORS

A/C BLOWER RELAY

RH Front Of Dash

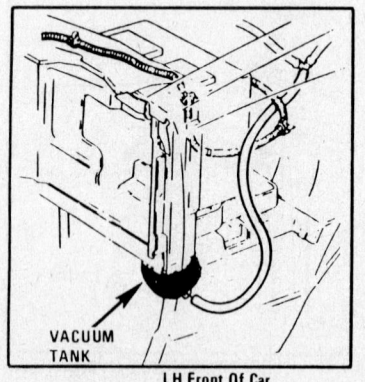

VACUUM TANK

LH Front Of Car

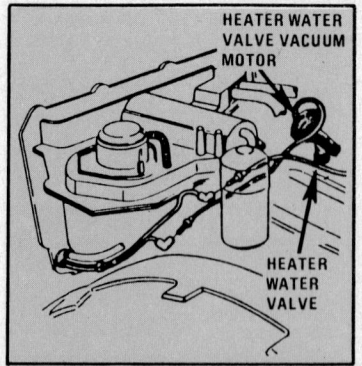

HEATER WATER VALVE VACUUM MOTOR

HEATER WATER VALVE

RH Rear Of Engine Compartment

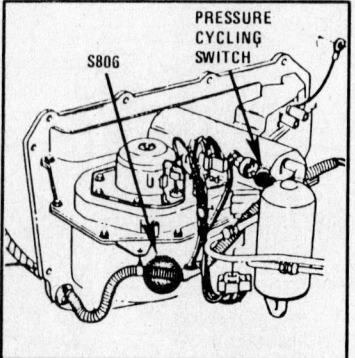

PRESSURE CYCLING SWITCH

S806

RH Front Of Dash

1985-86 Oldsmobile Cutlass Supreme

COMPONENT LOCATIONS

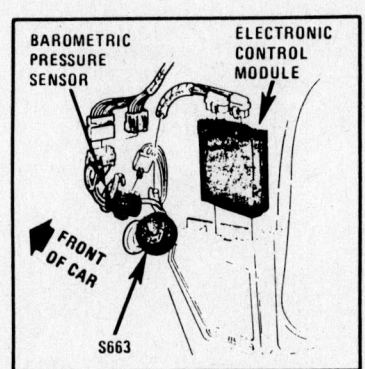

RH Shroud

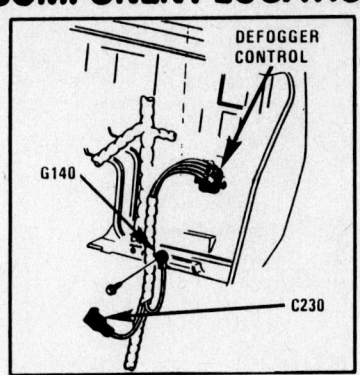

Behind LH Side Of I/P

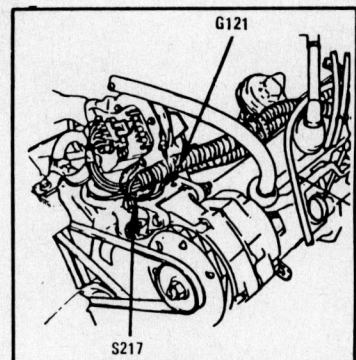

Front Of VIN 9 VIN Y Engines

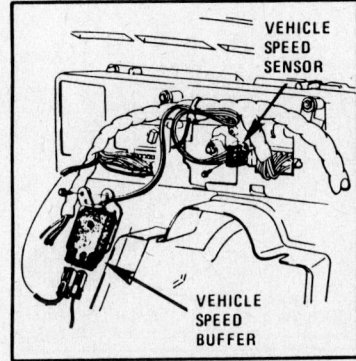

LH Side Of I/P, Behind Cluster

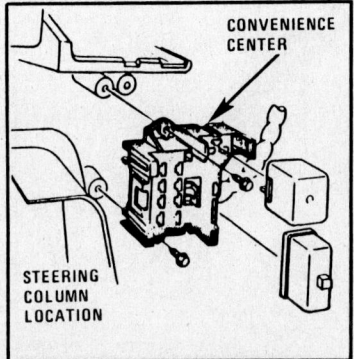

LH Side, Behind I/P

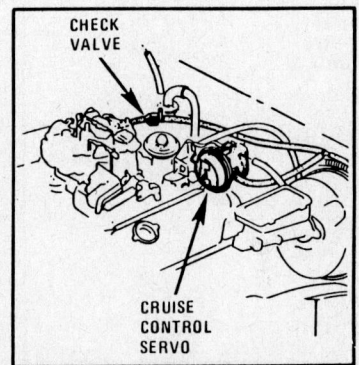

Rear Of VIN A Engine

1985-86 Oldsmobile Cutlass Supreme

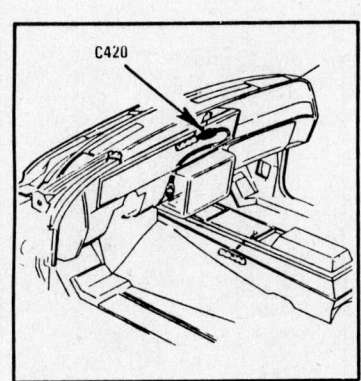

Behind Center Of I/P

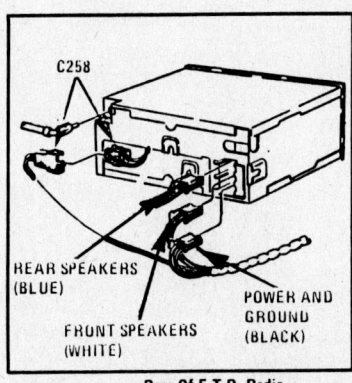

Rear Of E.T.R. Radio

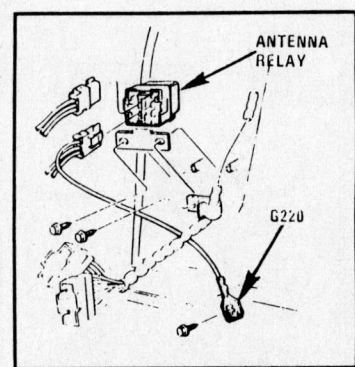

Behind RH Side Of I/P

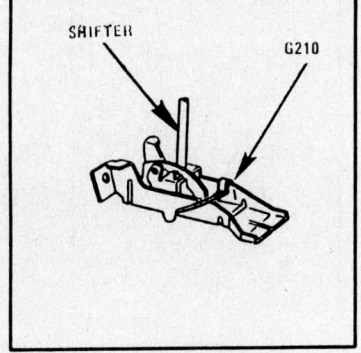

In Center Console

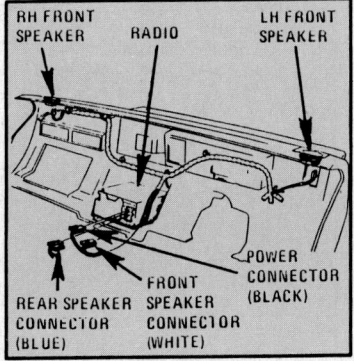

Behind I/P

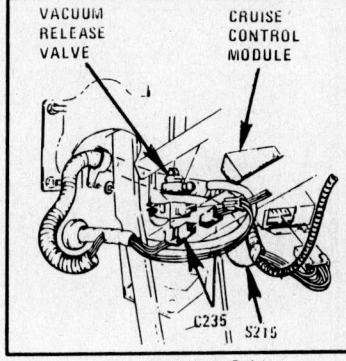

Above Brake Pedal

1985-86 Oldsmobile Cutlass Supreme

COMPONENT LOCATIONS

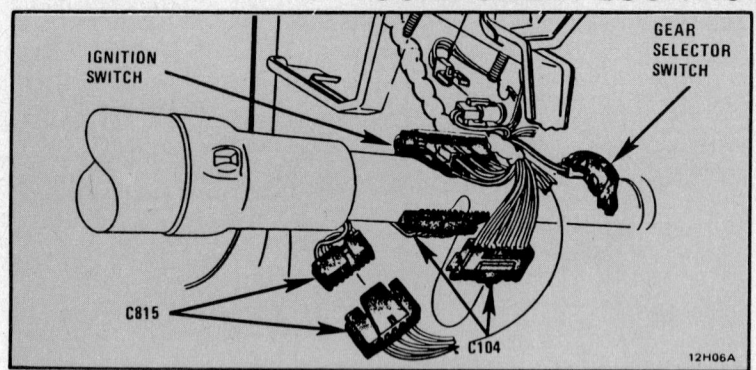

Figure A - RH Side Of Steering Column

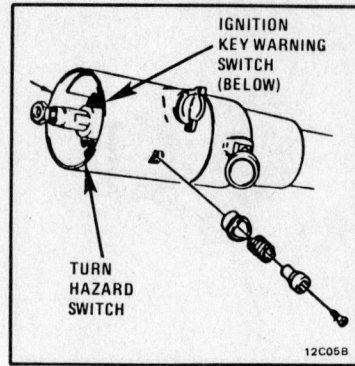

Figure D - Top RH Side Of Steering Column

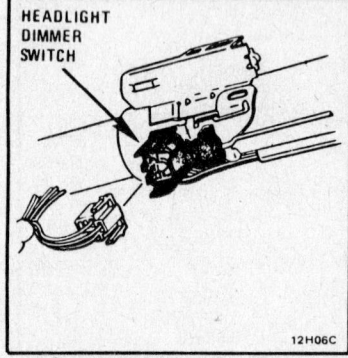

Figure B - LH Side Of Steering Column

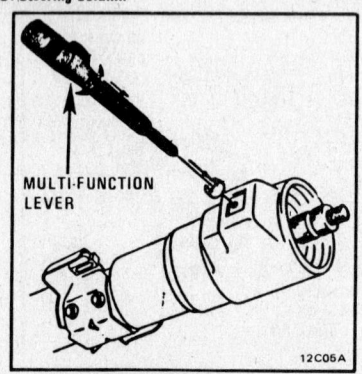

Figure C - Top LH Side Of Steering Column

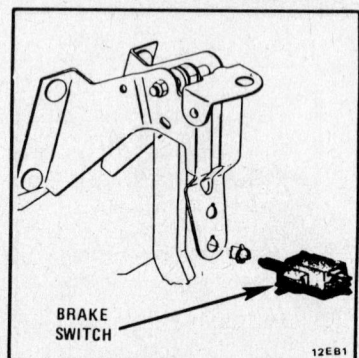

Figure E - Top Of Brake Pedal

1985-86 Oldsmobile Cutlass Supreme

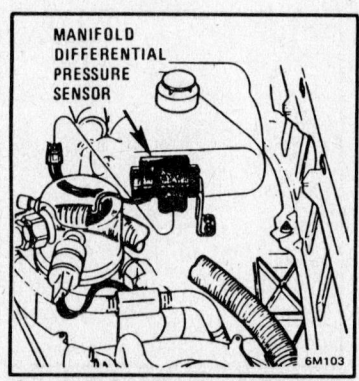

Figure A - RH Front Wheel Well, VIN 9 And VIN Y

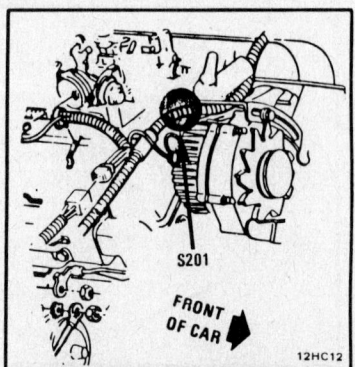

Figure E - RH Front Of Engine

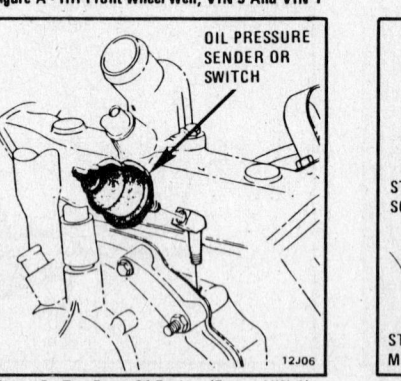

Figure B - Top Front Of Engines (Except VIN A)

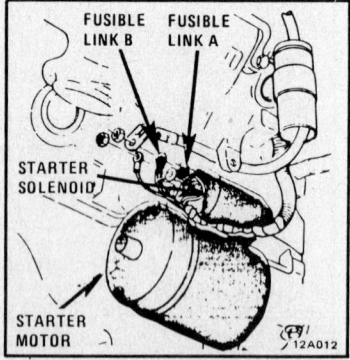

Figure D - Lower LH Side Of Engine (Except VIN A)

Figure F - LH Front Of Engine (VIN Y And VIN 9)

1985-86 Oldsmobile Cutlass Supreme

COMPONENT LOCATIONS

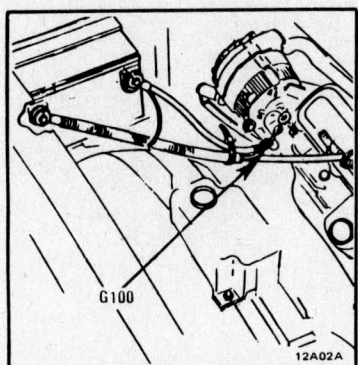

Figure A - Front LH Side Of Engine

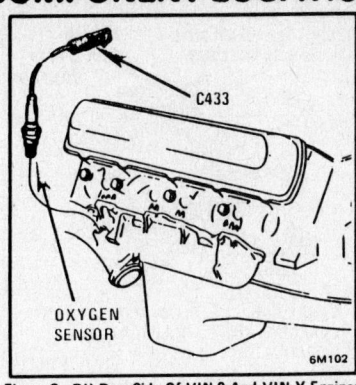

Figure C - RH Rear Side Of VIN 9 And VIN Y Engines

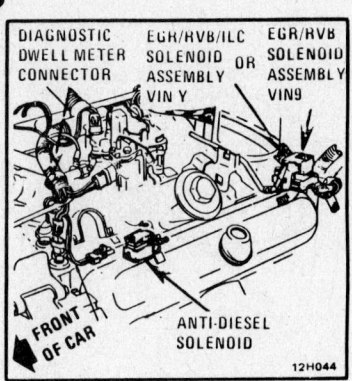

Figure E - Top Of VIN 9 And VIN Y Engines

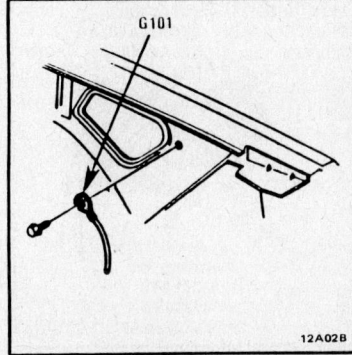

Figure B - Front Of RH Fender

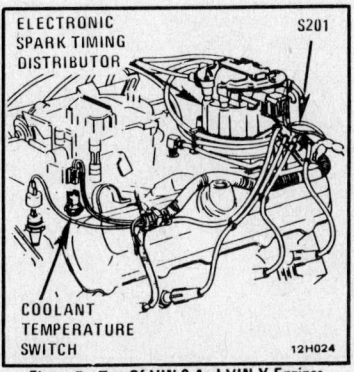

Figure D - Top Of VIN 9 And VIN Y Engines

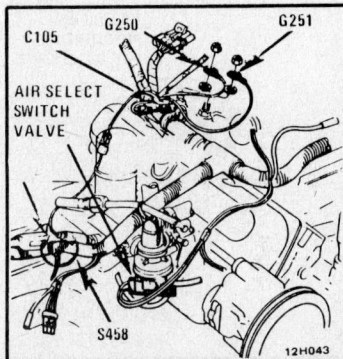

Figure F - RH Side Of VIN 9 And VIN Y Engine Compartment

1985-86 Oldsmobile Cutlass Supreme

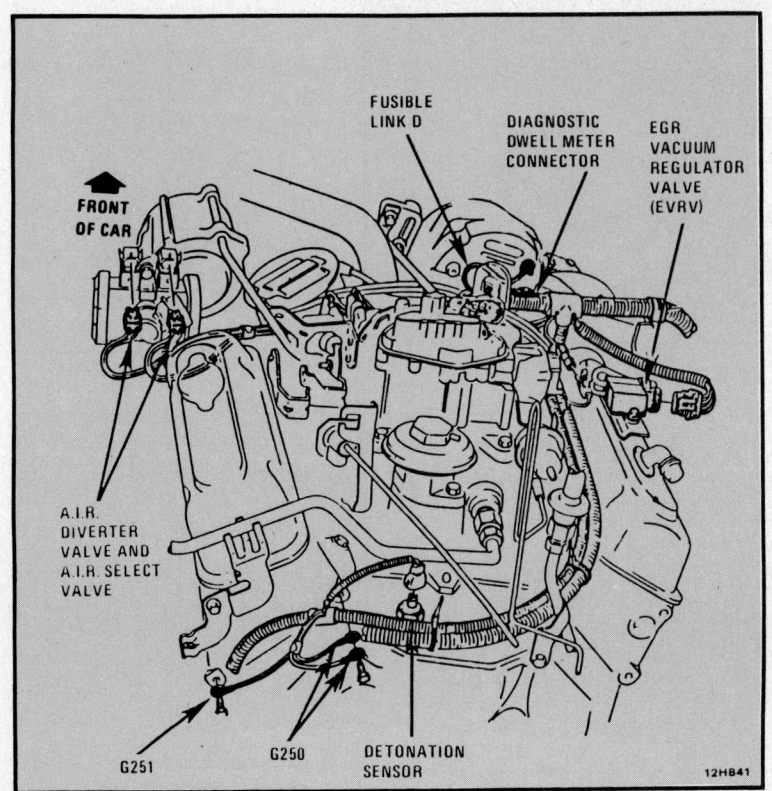

Figure A - Top Of VIN A Engine

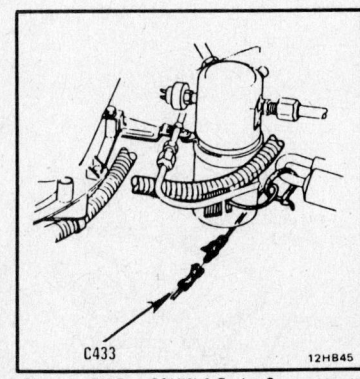

Figure B - RH Rear Of VIN A Engine Compartment

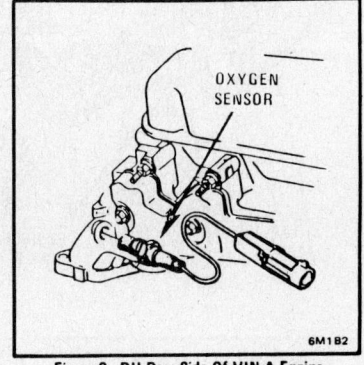

Figure C - RH Rear Side Of VIN A Engine

1985-86 Oldsmobile Cutlass Supreme

179

COMPONENT LOCATIONS

Figure A - RH Front Of Dash

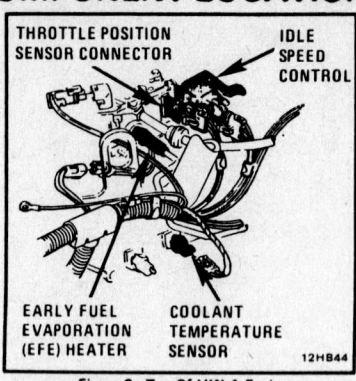

Figure C - Top Of VIN A Engine

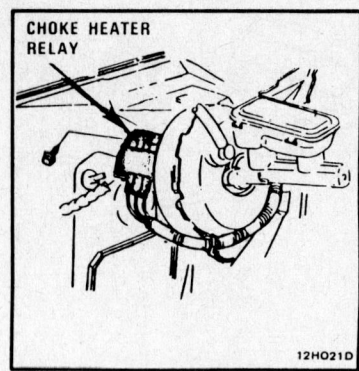

Figure E - LH Front Of Dash

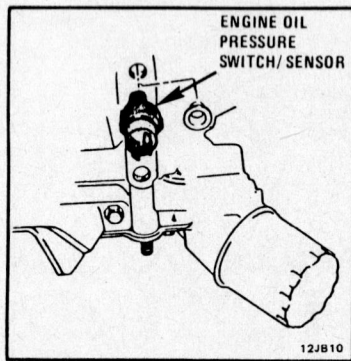

Figure B - RH Side Of VIN A Engine

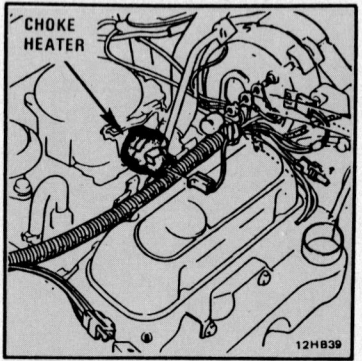

Figure D - Top Center Of VIN A Engine

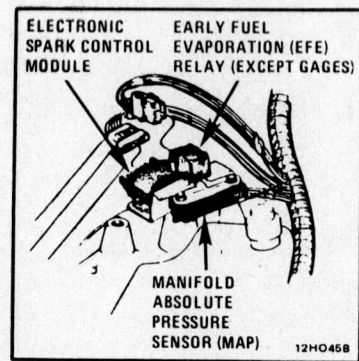

Figure F - Top Of VIN A RH Wheel Well

1985-86 Oldsmobile Cutlass Supreme

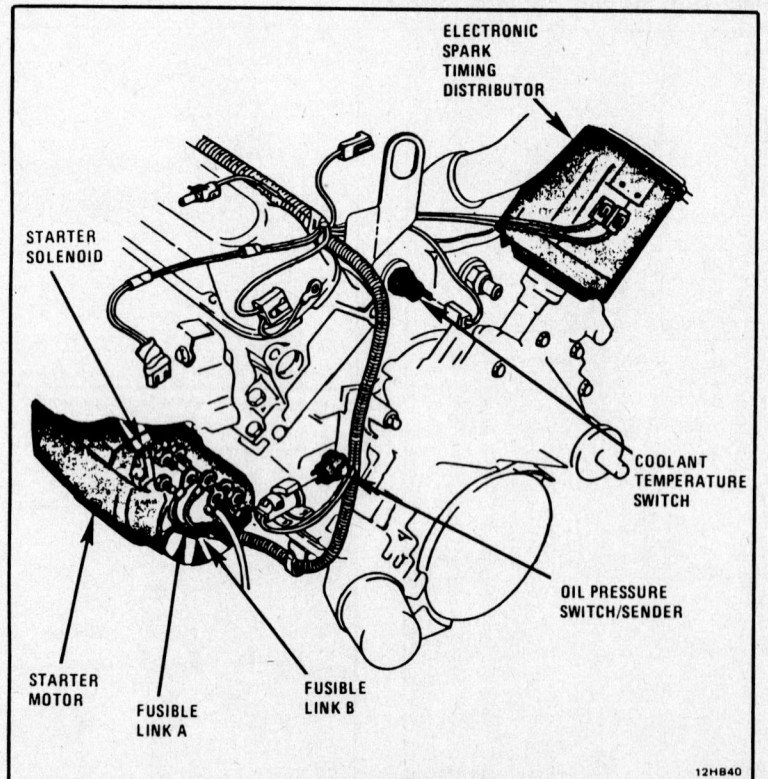

Figure A - Front RH Side Of V6 VIN A Engine

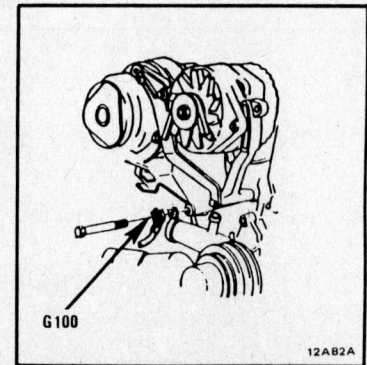

Figure B - Front Of Engine, Below Generator

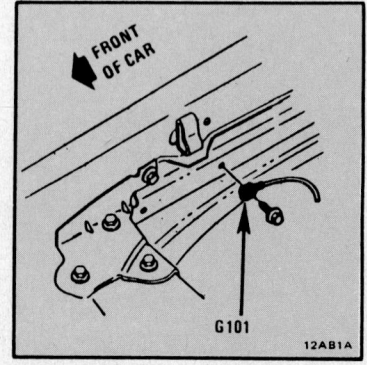

Figure C - Front Of RH Fender

1985-86 Oldsmobile Cutlass Supreme

COMPONENT LOCATIONS

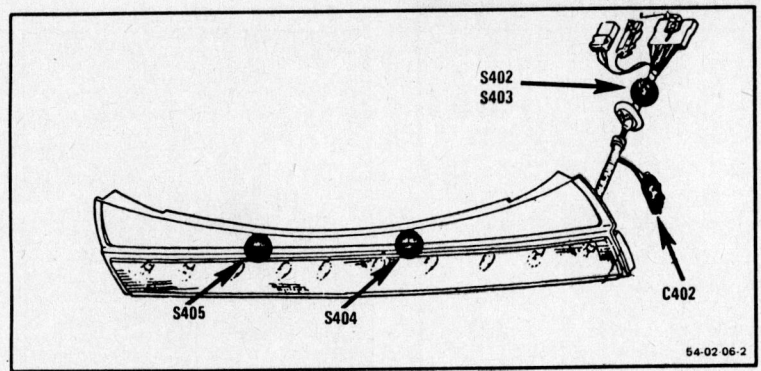

Figure A - Rear Lights Panel

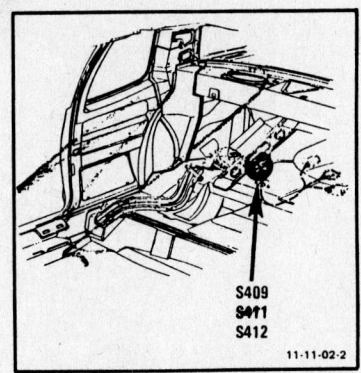

Figure C - RH Rear Of Passenger Compartment

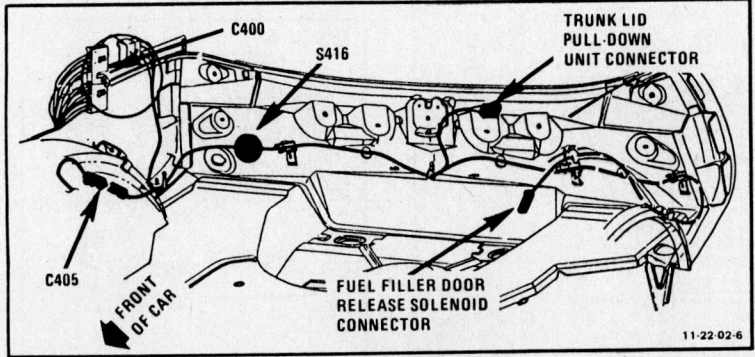

Figure B - Rear Of Trunk

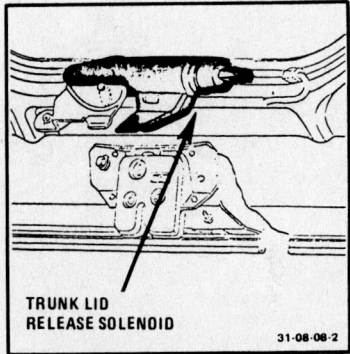

Figure D - Rear Of Trunk Lid

1985-86 Oldsmobile Tornado

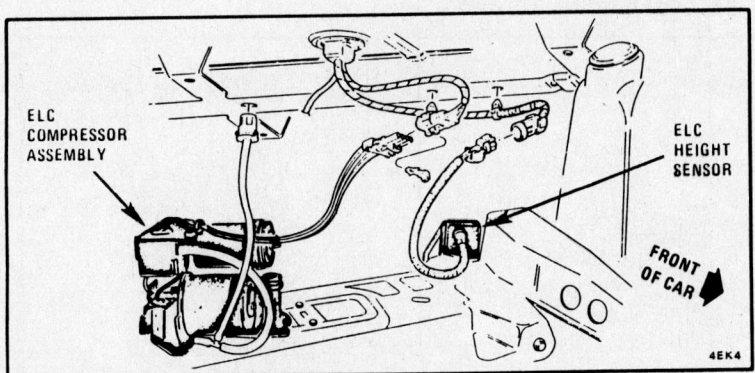

Figure A - Below Rear Of Car

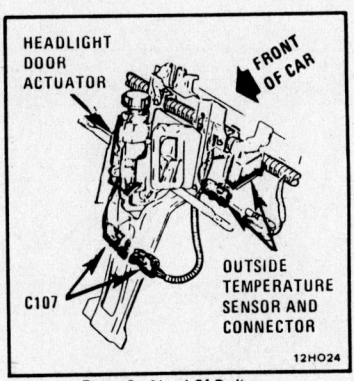

Figure C - Ahead Of Radiator

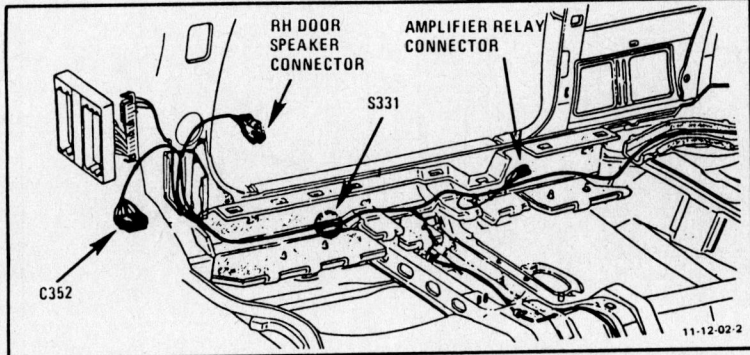

Figure B - RH Side Of Passenger Compartment

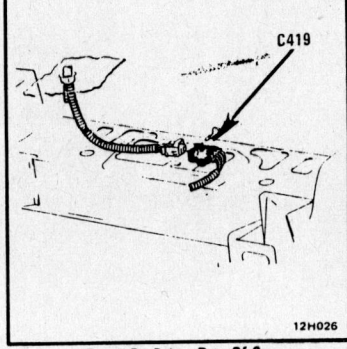

Figure D - Below Rear Of Car

1985-86 Oldsmobile Tornado

COMPONENT LOCATIONS

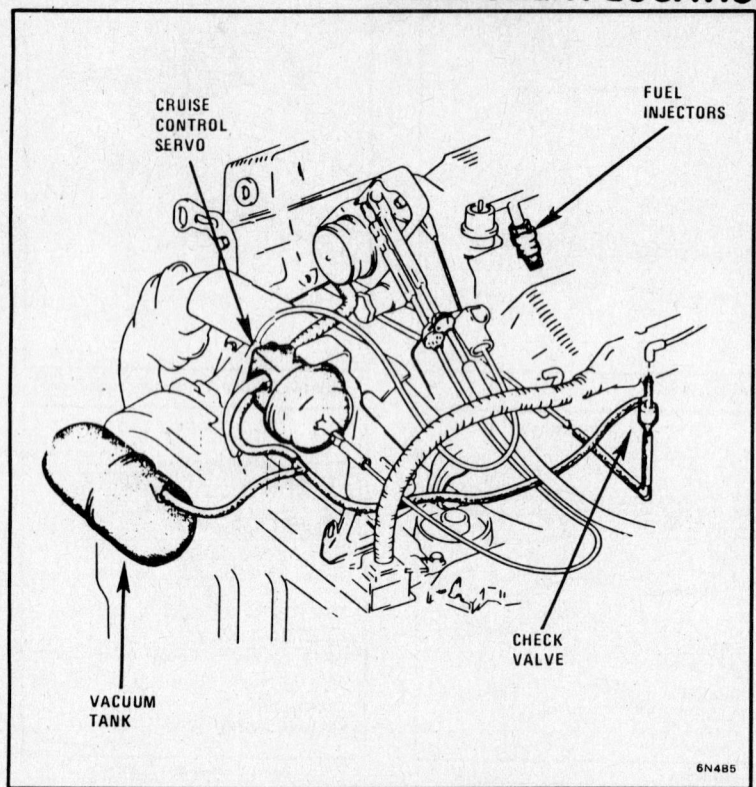

Figure A - RH Rear Of VIN B Engine

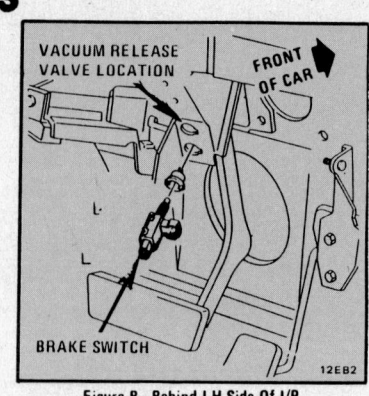

Figure B - Behind LH Side Of I/P

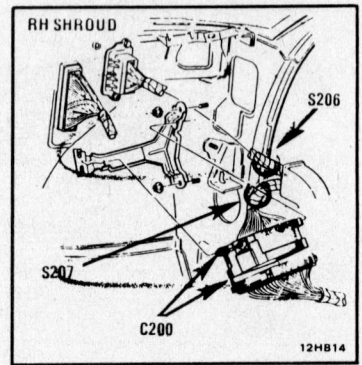

Figure C - Behind RH Side Of I/P

1985-86 Oldsmobile Tornado

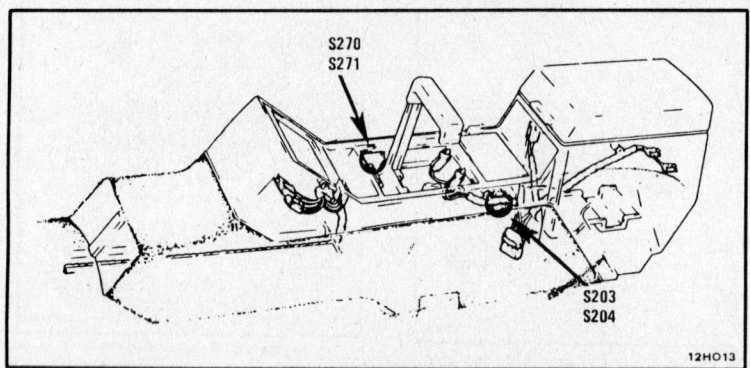

Figure A - Center Console

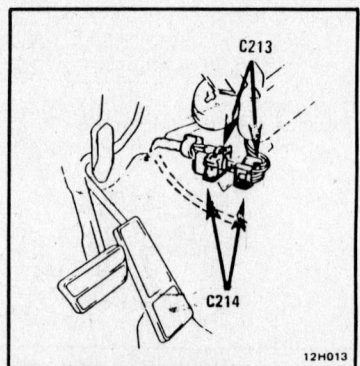

Figure C - RH Side Of Drivers Footwell

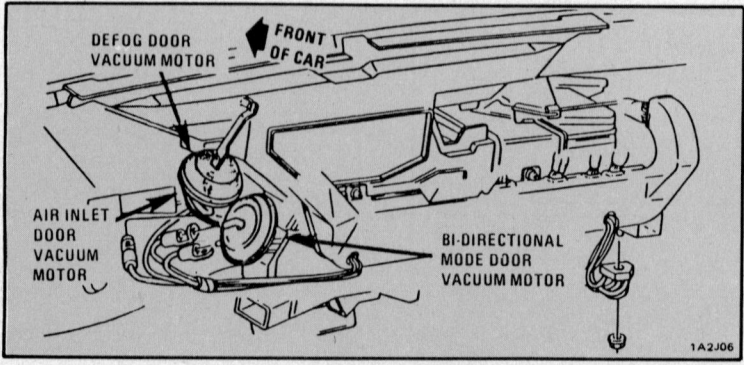

Figure B - Behind RH Side Of I/P

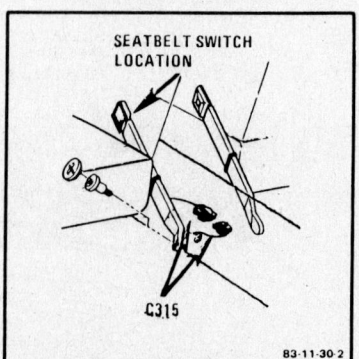

Figure D - Between Front Seats

1985-86 Oldsmobile Tornado

COMPONENT LOCATIONS

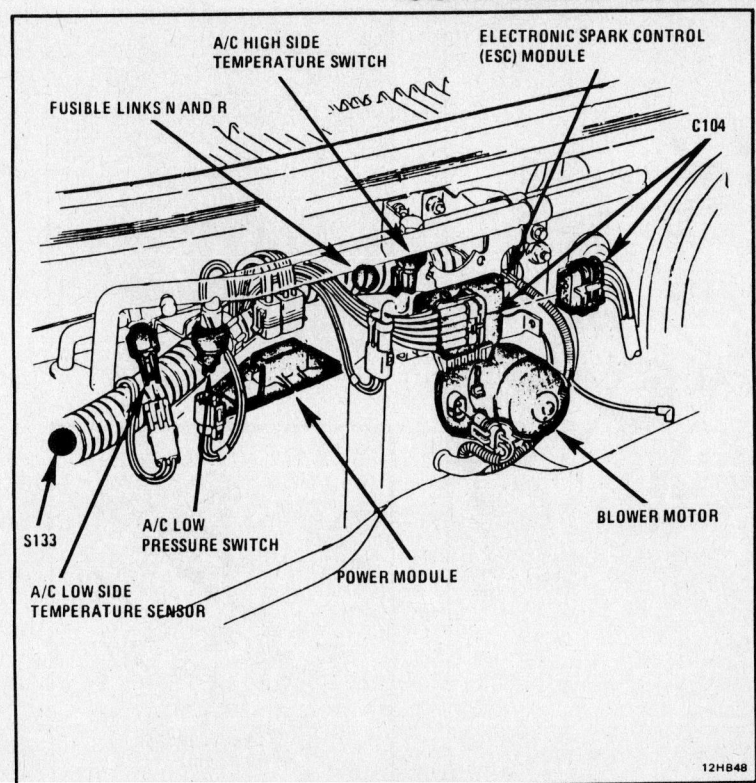

A/C HIGH SIDE TEMPERATURE SWITCH

ELECTRONIC SPARK CONTROL (ESC) MODULE

FUSIBLE LINKS N AND R

C104

S133

A/C LOW PRESSURE SWITCH

A/C LOW SIDE TEMPERATURE SENSOR

POWER MODULE

BLOWER MOTOR

12HB48

Figure A - Front Of Dash

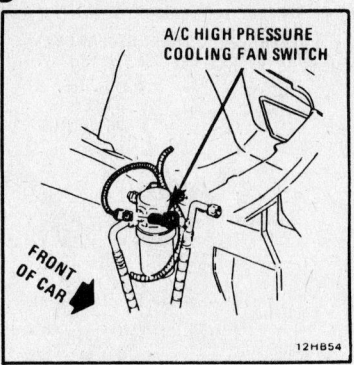

A/C HIGH PRESSURE COOLING FAN SWITCH

FRONT OF CAR

12HB54

Figure B - LH Front Of Engine Compartment

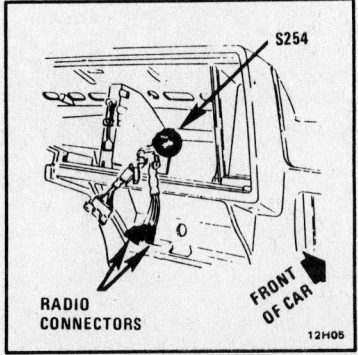

S254

RADIO CONNECTORS

FRONT OF CAR

12H05

Figure C - In Center Of I/P

1985-86 Oldsmobile Tornado

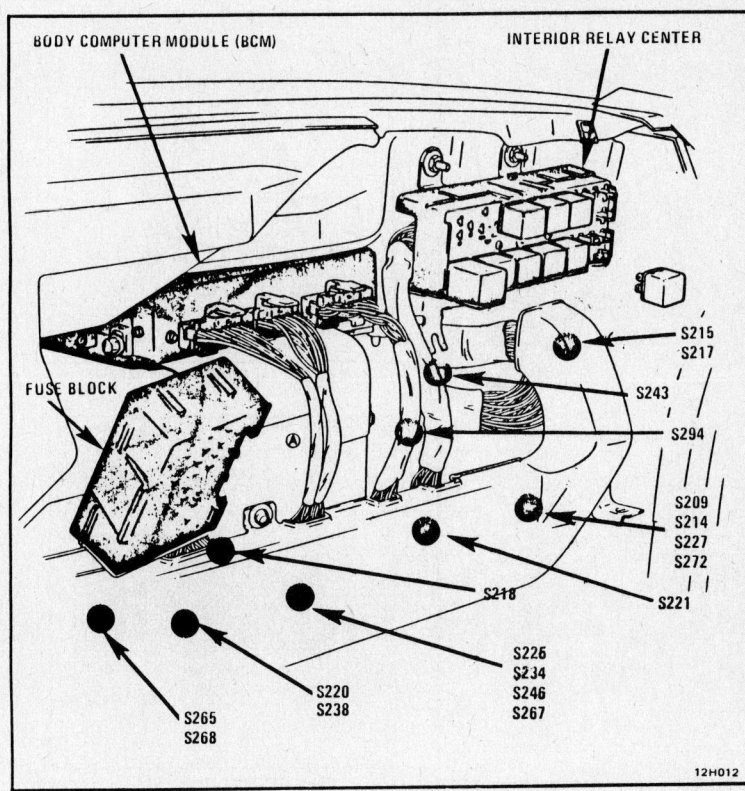

BODY COMPUTER MODULE (BCM)

INTERIOR RELAY CENTER

FUSE BLOCK

S215
S217

S243

S294

S209
S214
S227
S272

S218

S221

S226
S234
S246
S267

S220
S238

S265
S268

12H012

Figure A - Behind RH Side Of I/P

1985-86 Oldsmobile Tornado

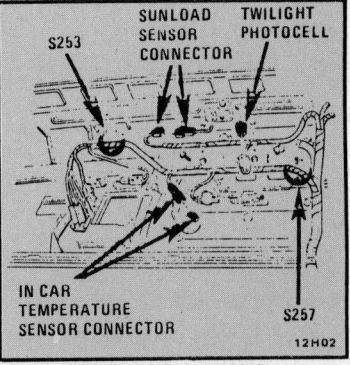

SUNLOAD SENSOR CONNECTOR

TWILIGHT PHOTOCELL

S253

IN CAR TEMPERATURE SENSOR CONNECTOR

S257

12H02

Figure B - Behind Center Of I/P

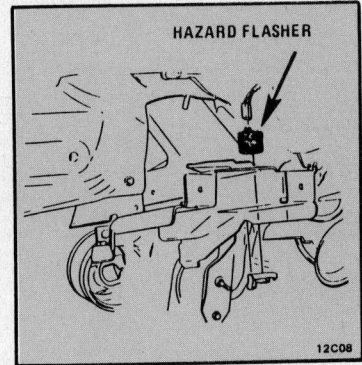

HAZARD FLASHER

12C08

Figure C - Above Steering Column

COMPONENT LOCATIONS

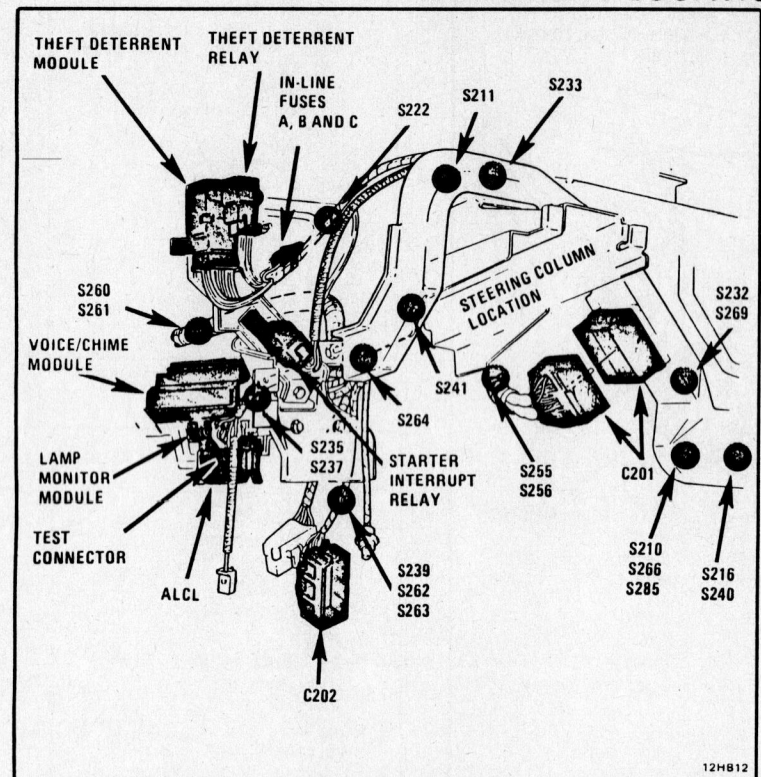

Figure A - Behind LH Side Of I/P

THEFT DETERRENT MODULE
THEFT DETERRENT RELAY
IN-LINE FUSES A, B AND C
S222
S211
S233
S260 S261
VOICE/CHIME MODULE
LAMP MONITOR MODULE
TEST CONNECTOR
ALCL
S235 S237
S241
S264
STARTER INTERRUPT RELAY
STEERING COLUMN LOCATION
S232 S269
S255 S256
C201
S210 S266 S285
S216 S240
S239 S262 S263
C202
12H812

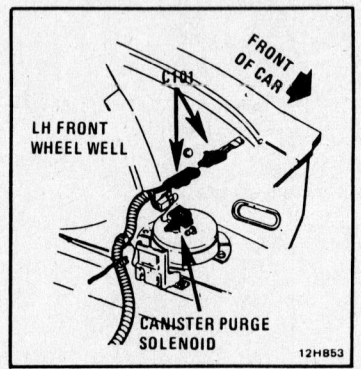

Figure B - Behind LH Side Of I/P

S252
STEERING COLUMN LOCATION
TURN FLASHER
FRONT OF CAR
12H01

1985-86 Oldsmobile Tornado

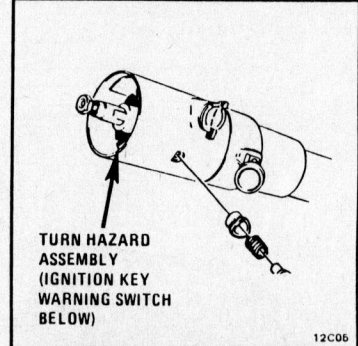

Figure C - LH Front Of Engine Compartment

C101
FRONT OF CAR
LH FRONT WHEEL WELL
CANISTER PURGE SOLENOID
12H853

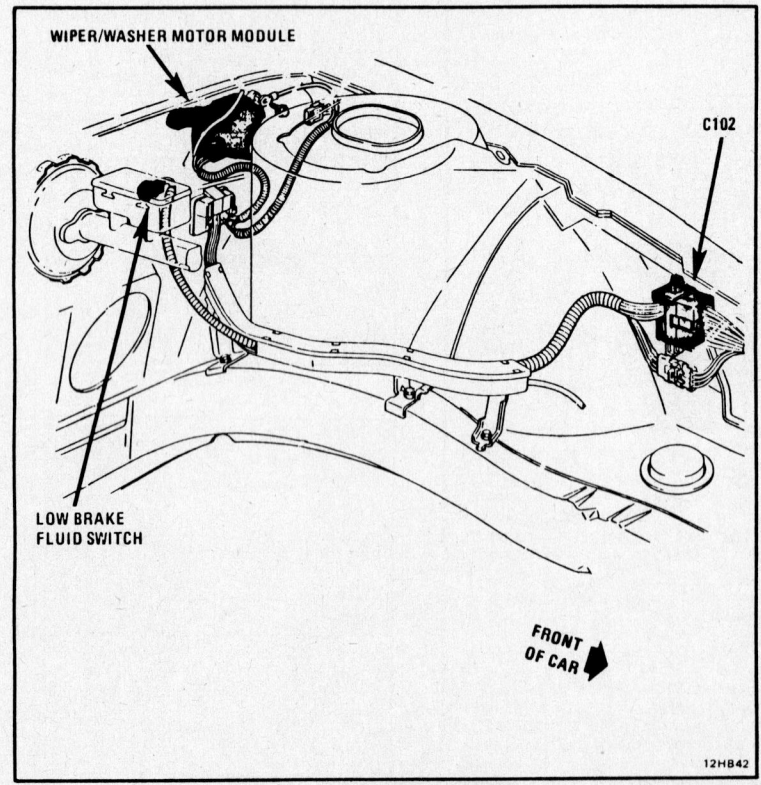

Figure A - LH Side Of Engine Compartment

WIPER/WASHER MOTOR MODULE
C102
LOW BRAKE FLUID SWITCH
FRONT OF CAR
12H842

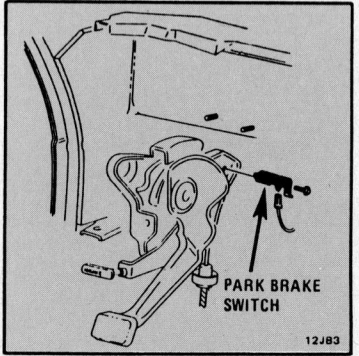

Figure B - Top RH Of Steering Column

TURN HAZARD ASSEMBLY (IGNITION KEY WARNING SWITCH BELOW)
12C06

Figure C - Behind LH Side Of I/P

PARK BRAKE SWITCH
12J83

1985-86 Oldsmobile Tornado

COMPONENT LOCATIONS

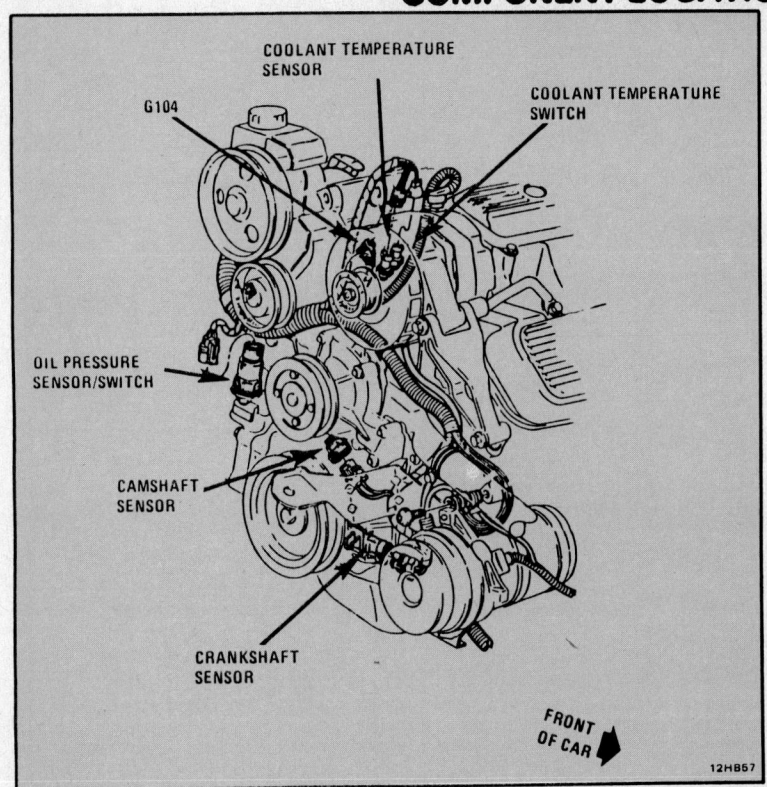

Figure A - RH Side Of VIN B Engine

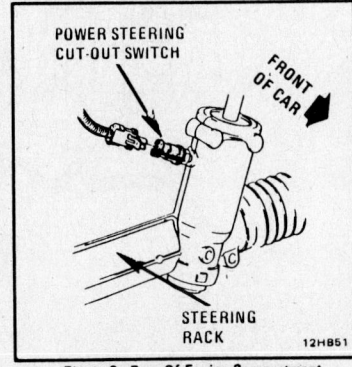

Figure B - LH Rear Of Engine Compartment

Figure C - Rear Of Engine Compartment

1985-86 Oldsmobile Tornado

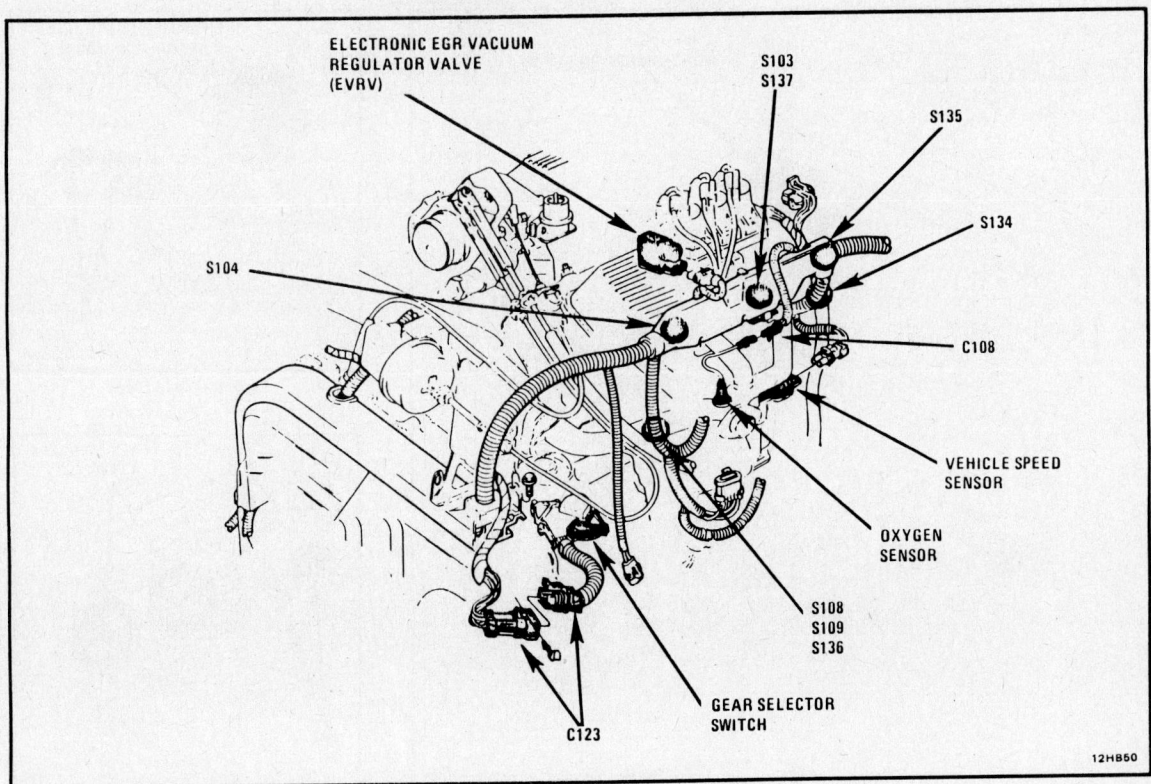

Figure A - Rear Of VIN B Engine

1985-86 Oldsmobile Tornado

COMPONENT LOCATIONS

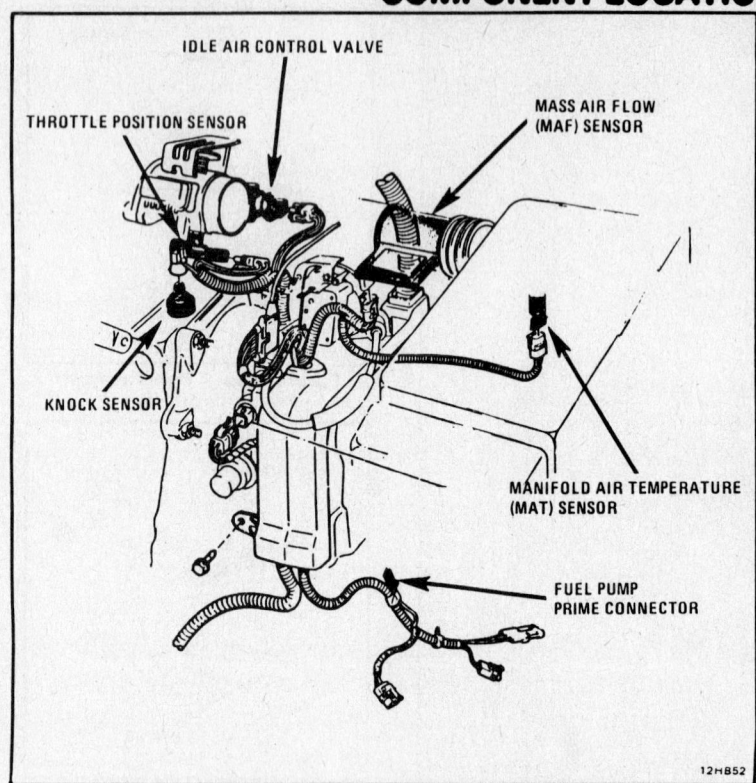

IDLE AIR CONTROL VALVE

THROTTLE POSITION SENSOR

MASS AIR FLOW (MAF) SENSOR

KNOCK SENSOR

MANIFOLD AIR TEMPERATURE (MAT) SENSOR

FUEL PUMP PRIME CONNECTOR

12H852

Figure A - LH Side Of Engine Compartment

1985-86 Oldsmobile Tornado

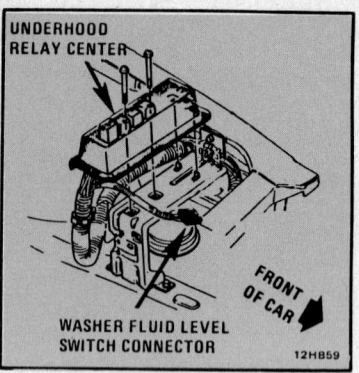

UNDERHOOD RELAY CENTER

FRONT OF CAR

WASHER FLUID LEVEL SWITCH CONNECTOR

12H859

Figure B - LH Front Of Engine Compartment

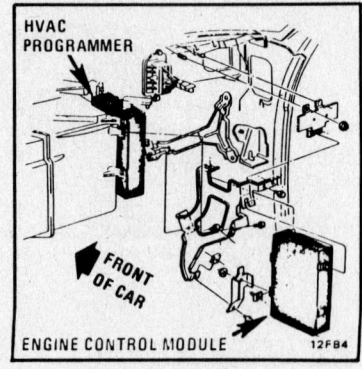

HVAC PROGRAMMER

FRONT OF CAR

ENGINE CONTROL MODULE

12F84

Figure C - Behind RH Side Of I.P

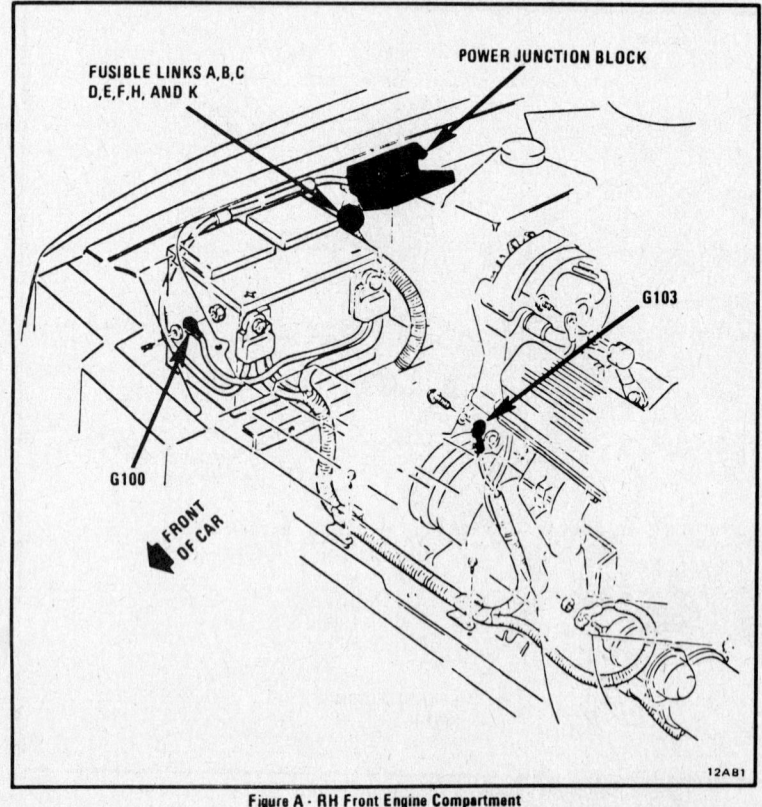

FUSIBLE LINKS A,B,C D,E,F,H, AND K

POWER JUNCTION BLOCK

G103

G100

FRONT OF CAR

12A81

Figure A - RH Front Engine Compartment

1985-86 Oldsmobile Tornado

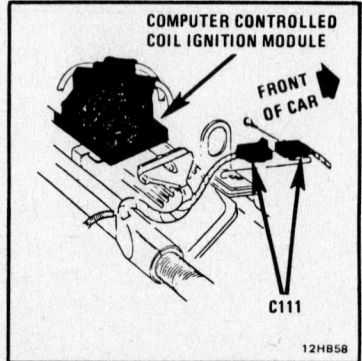

COMPUTER CONTROLLED COIL IGNITION MODULE

FRONT OF CAR

C111

12H858

Figure B - Top Of Engine

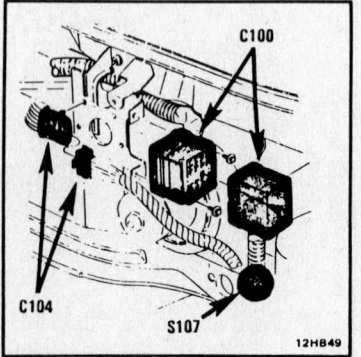

C100

C104

S107

12H849

Figure C - Center Front Of Dash

COMPONENT LOCATIONS

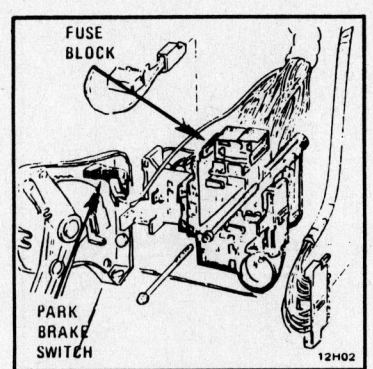

Figure A - Behind LH Side Of I/P, Near LH Shroud

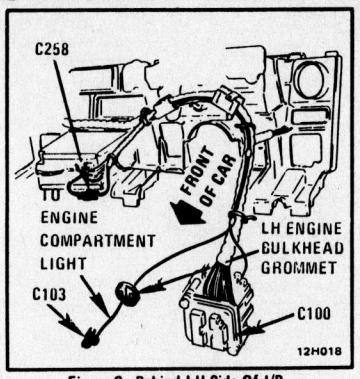

Figure C - Behind LH Side Of I/P

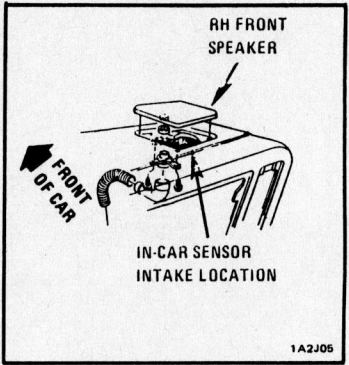

Figure E - Top RH Side Of I/P

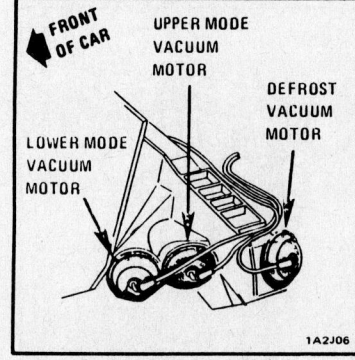

Figure B - Below Center Of I/P

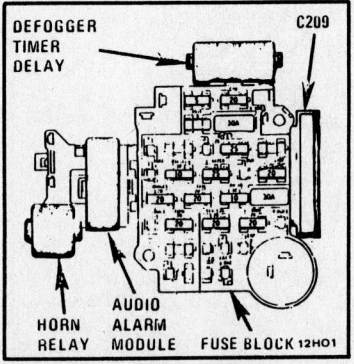

Figure D - Behind LH Side Of I/P

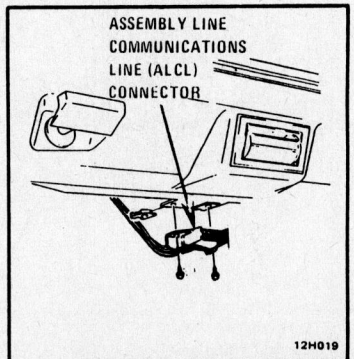

Figure F - Below LH Side Of I/P

1985-86 Oldsmobile Custom Cruiser

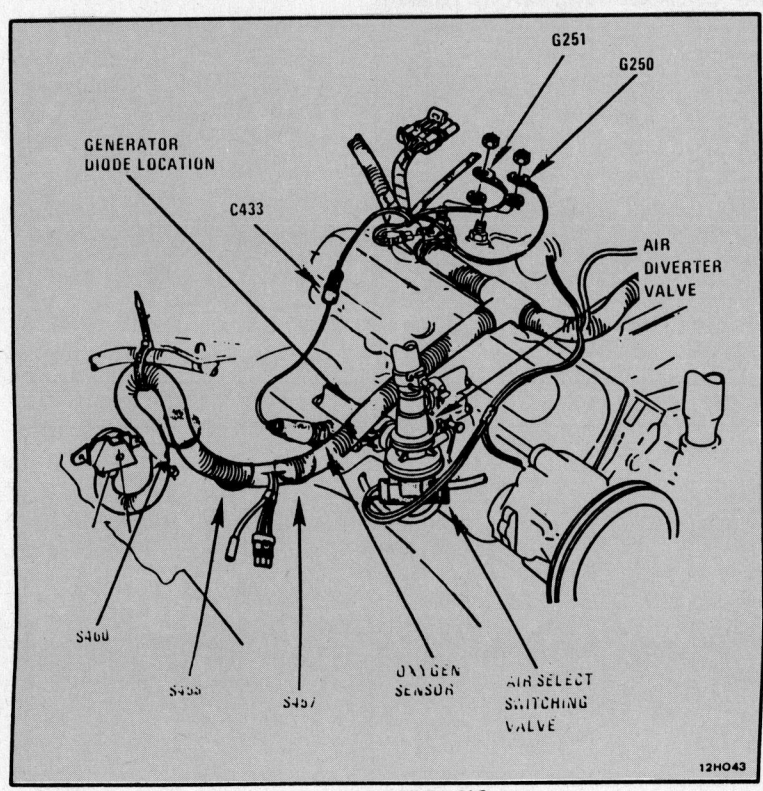

Figure A - RH Side Of Engine

Figure B - Base Of RH Shroud

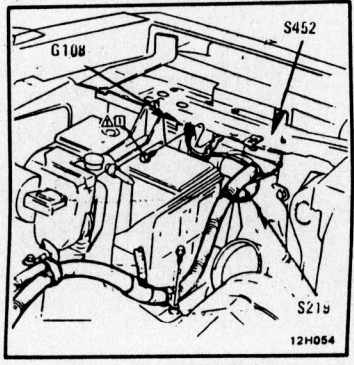

Figure C - Behind LH Headlight

1985-86 Oldsmobile Custom Cruiser

COMPONENT LOCATIONS

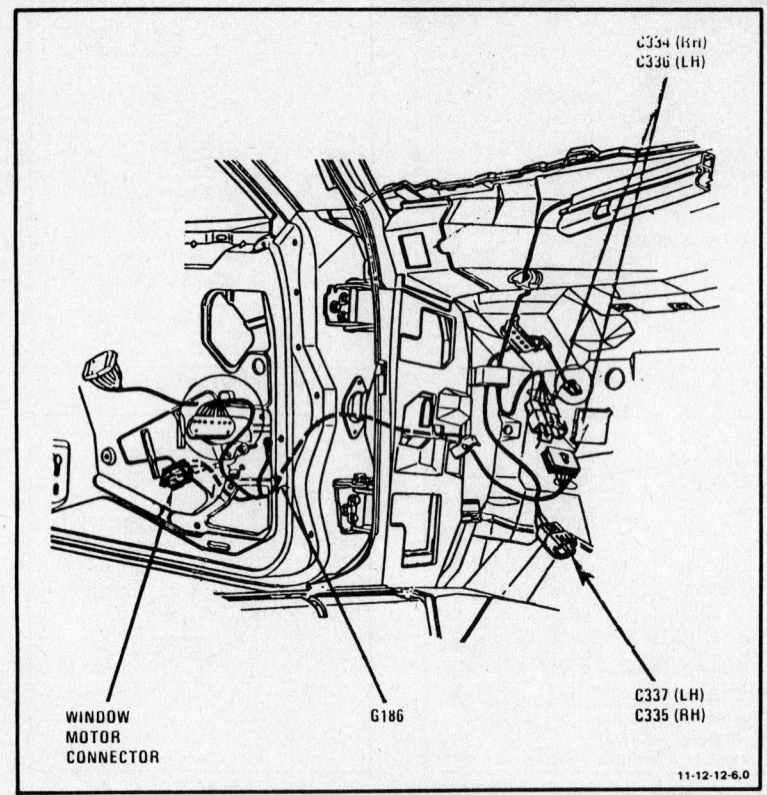

Figure A - LH Door And Shroud

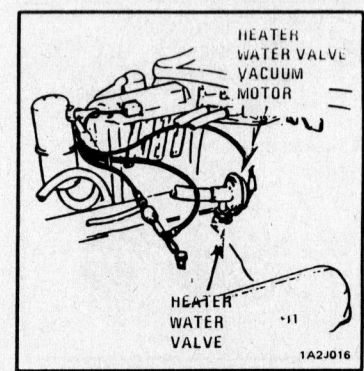

Figure B - RH Rear Corner Of Engine Compartment

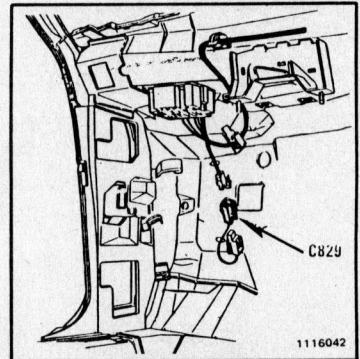

Figure C - RH Rear Of Engine Block

1985-86 Oldsmobile Custom Cruiser

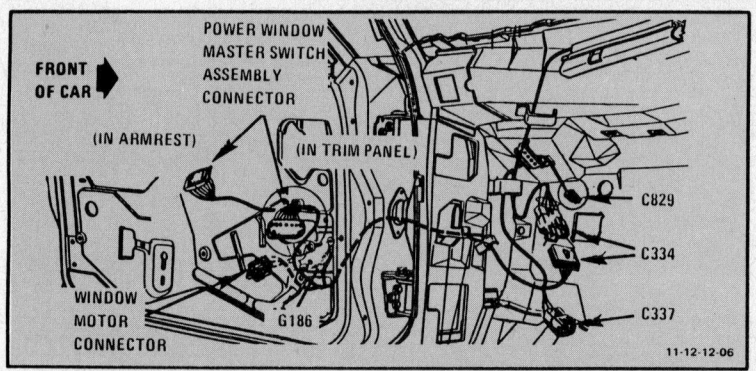

Figure A - LH Front Door And Shroud (Custom Cruiser And Sedan)

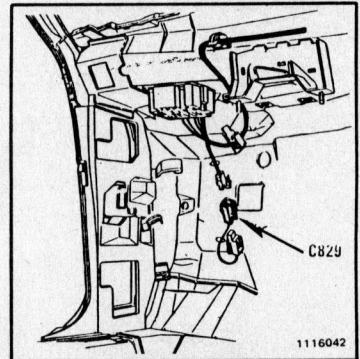

Figure D - LH Shroud

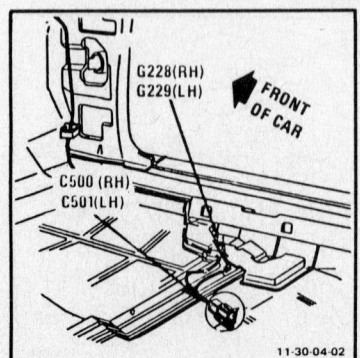

Figure B - RH Front Of Passenger Compartment

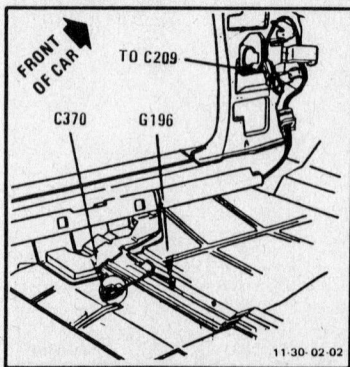

Figure C - LH Front Of Passenger Compartment

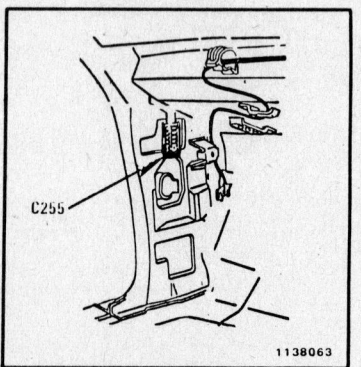

Figure E - Upper LH Shroud

1985-86 Oldsmobile Custom Cruiser

COMPONENT LOCATIONS

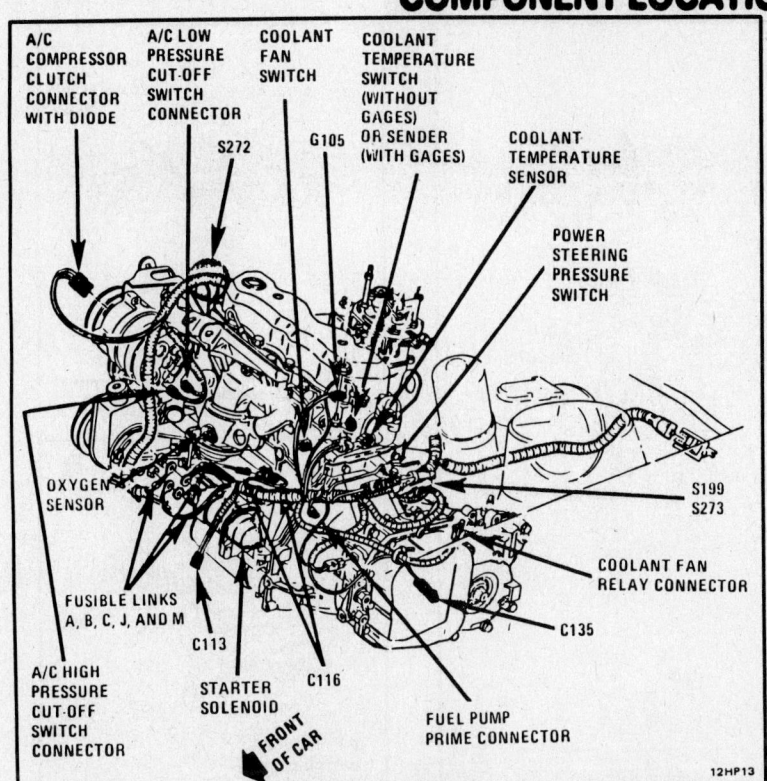

Figure A - Front Of VIN R Engine

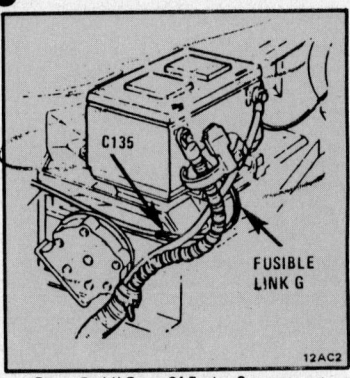

Figure B - LH Front Of Engine Compartment

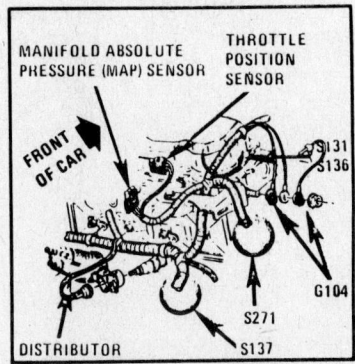

Figure C - RH Rear Of VIN R Engine

1985-86 Oldsmobile Cutlass Clera and Cutlass Cruiser

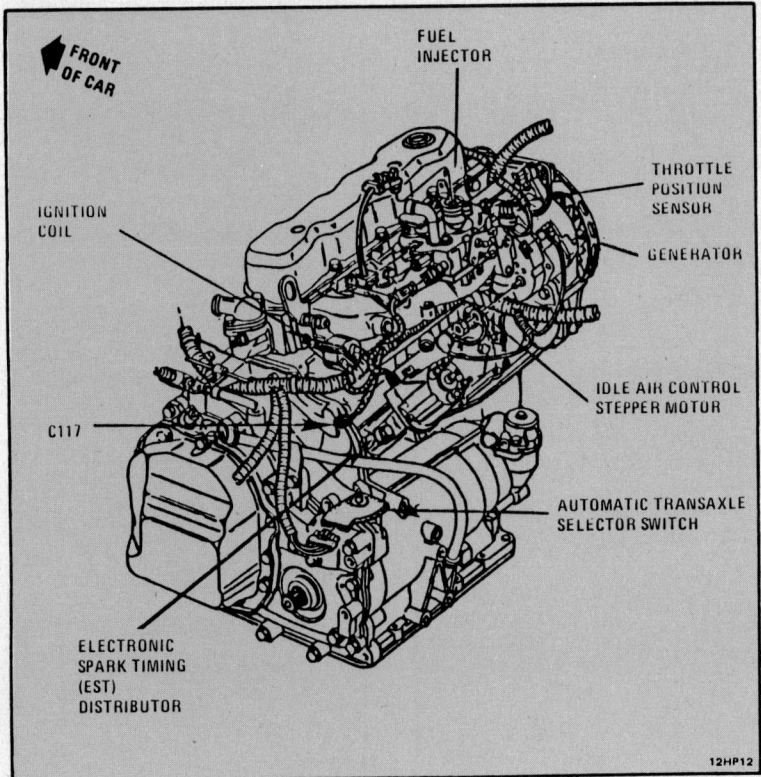

Figure A - LH Rear Of VIN R Engine

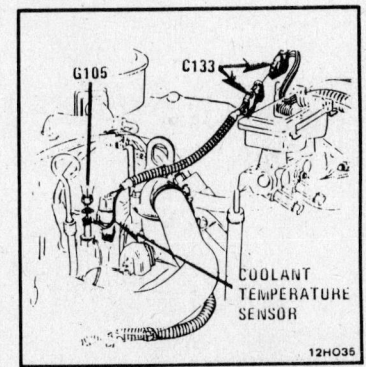

Figure B - LH Side Of VIN R Engine

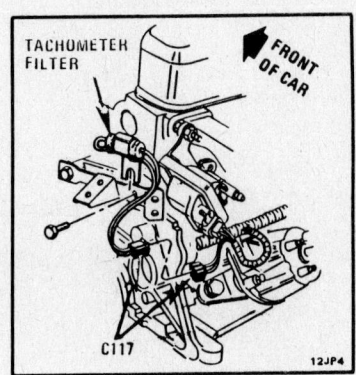

Figure C - Top LH End Of VIN R Engine

1985-86 Oldsmobile Cutlass Clera and Cutlass Cruiser

COMPONENT LOCATIONS

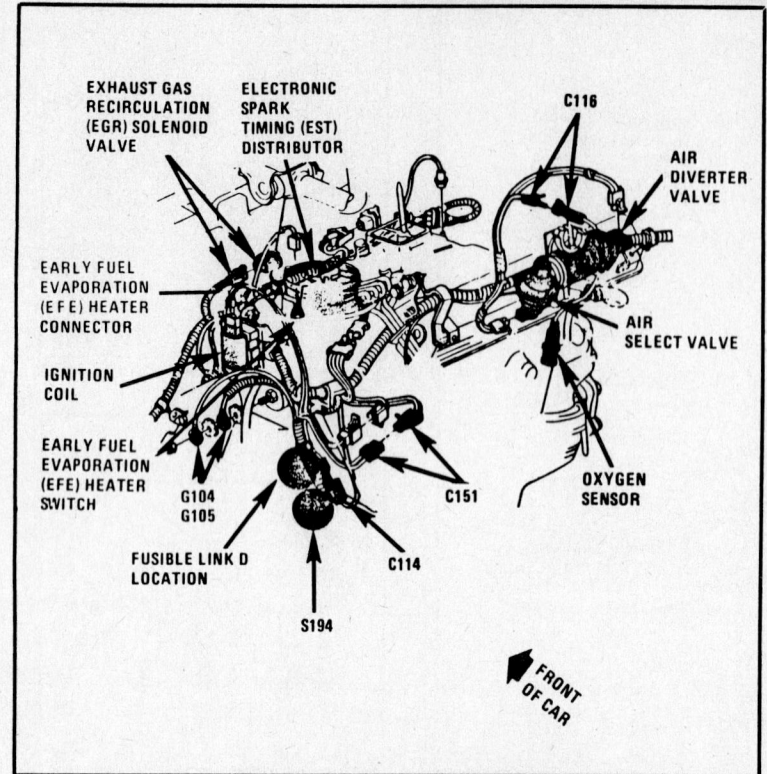

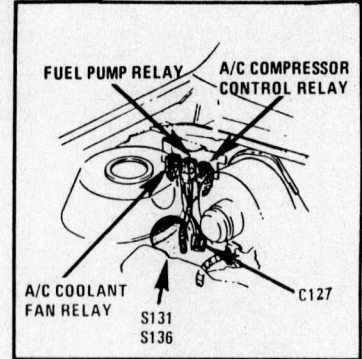

RH Side Of VIN R Engine Dash

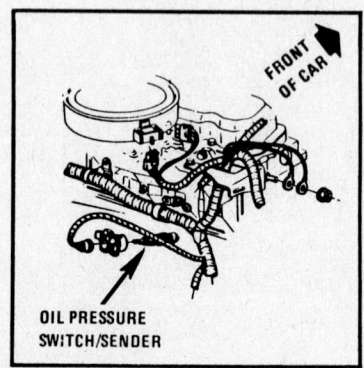

Top RH Rear Of VIN R Engine

Top Of VIN X Engine

1985-86 Oldsmobile Cutlass Ciera and Cutlass Cruiser

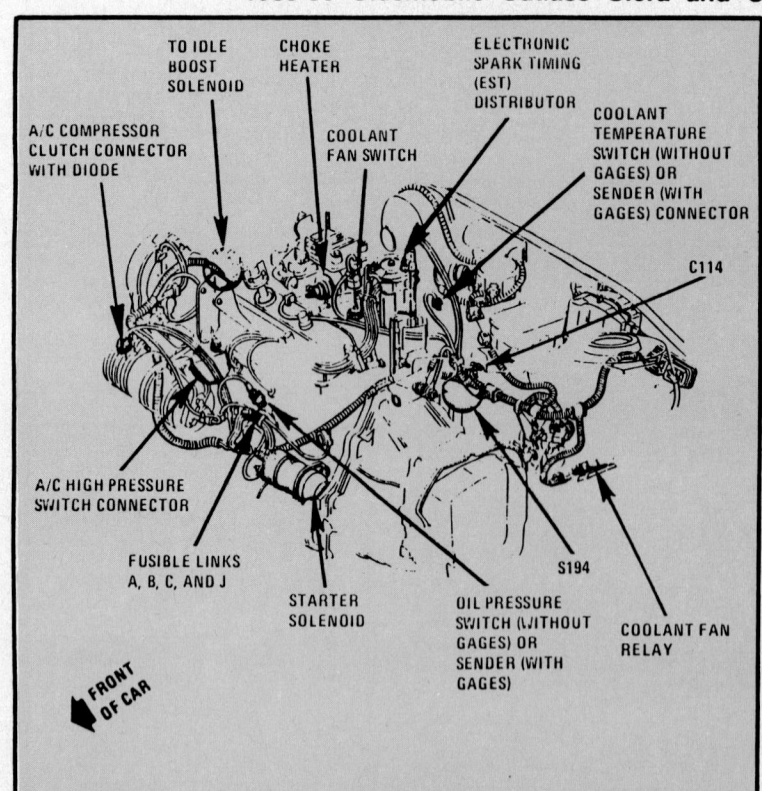

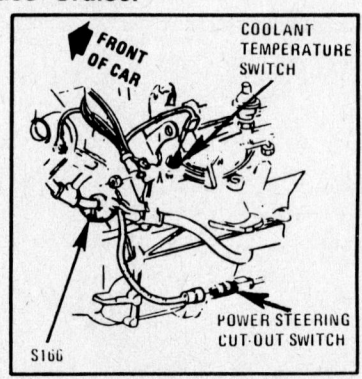

LH Rear Of VIN X Engine

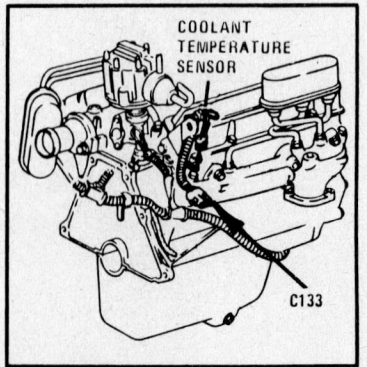

LH Rear Of VIN X Engine (VIN W Similar)

Top Of VIN X Engine

1985-86 Oldsmobile Cutlass Ciera and Cutlass Cruiser

COMPONENT LOCATIONS

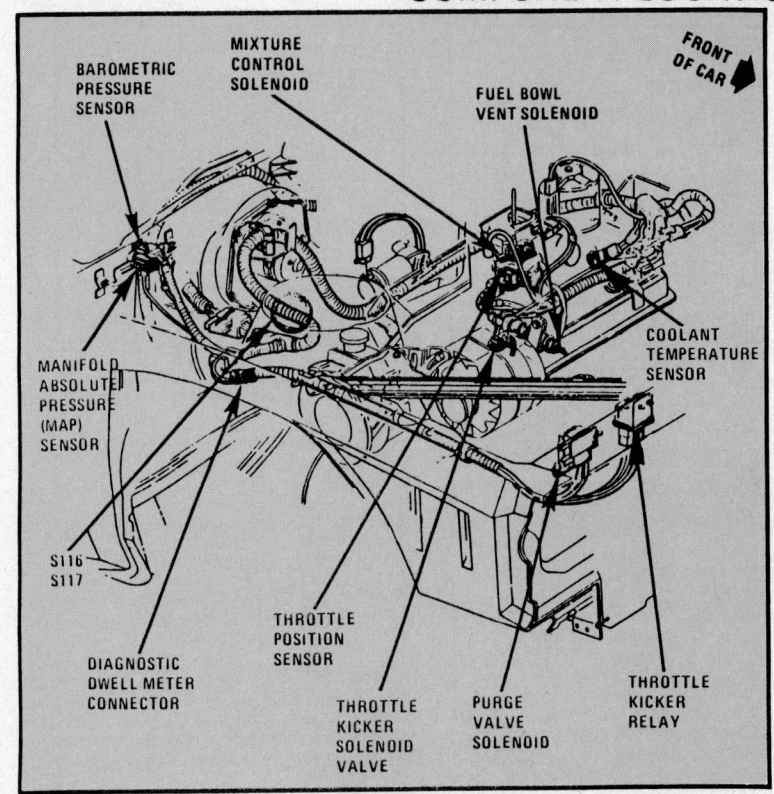

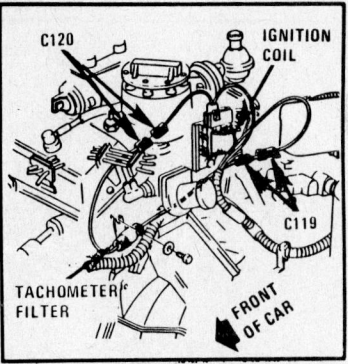

Top LH End Of VIN X Engine

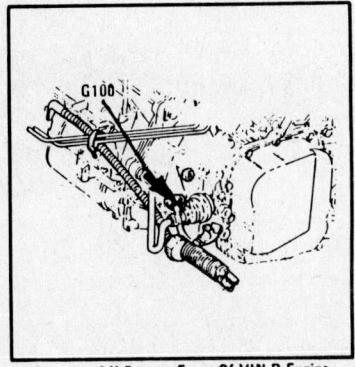

LH Bottom Front Of VIN R Engine

1985-86 Oldsmobile Cutlass Ciera and Cutlass Cruiser

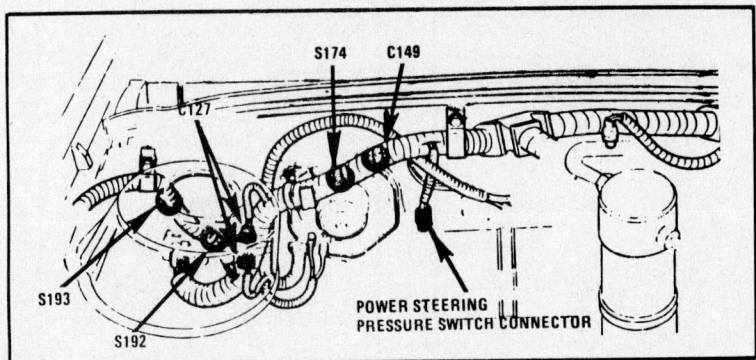

RH Front Of Dash (VIN W)

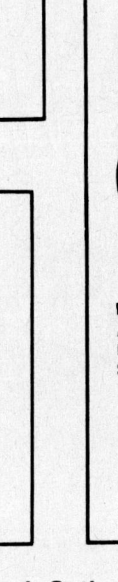

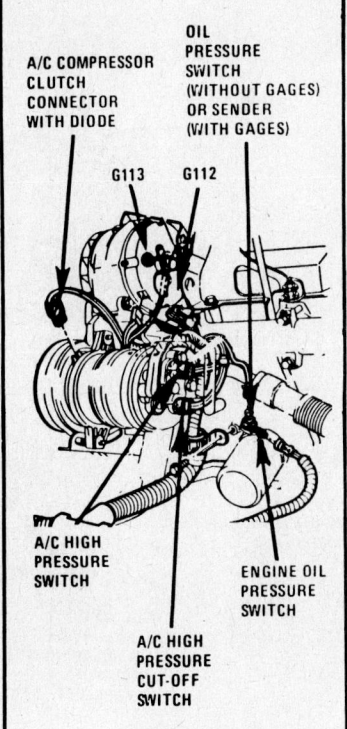

RH Front Of VIN W Engine

LH Front Of Dash (VIN X Shown, Other Similar)

1985-86 Oldsmobile Cutlass Ciera and Cutlass Cruiser

COMPONENT LOCATIONS

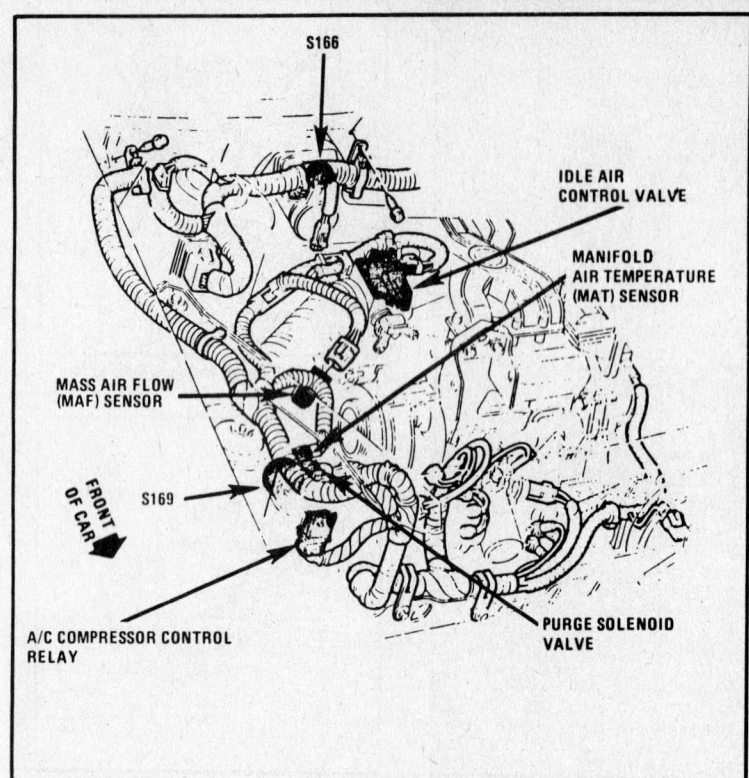

S166

IDLE AIR CONTROL VALVE

MANIFOLD AIR TEMPERATURE (MAT) SENSOR

MASS AIR FLOW (MAF) SENSOR

S169

FRONT OF CAR

A/C COMPRESSOR CONTROL RELAY

PURGE SOLENOID VALVE

Top RH Of VIN W Engine

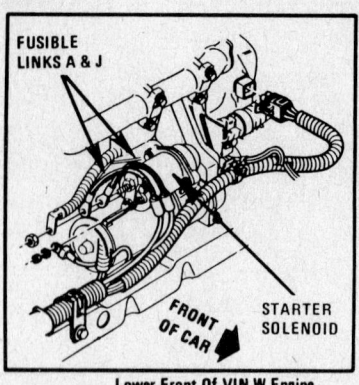

FUSIBLE LINKS A & J

FRONT OF CAR

STARTER SOLENOID

Lower Front Of VIN W Engine

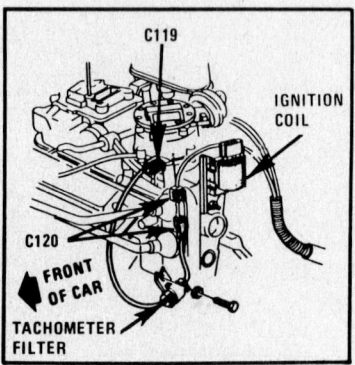

C119

IGNITION COIL

C120

FRONT OF CAR

TACHOMETER FILTER

Top LH End Of VIN W Engine

1985-86 Oldsmobile Cutlass Ciera and Cutlass Cruiser

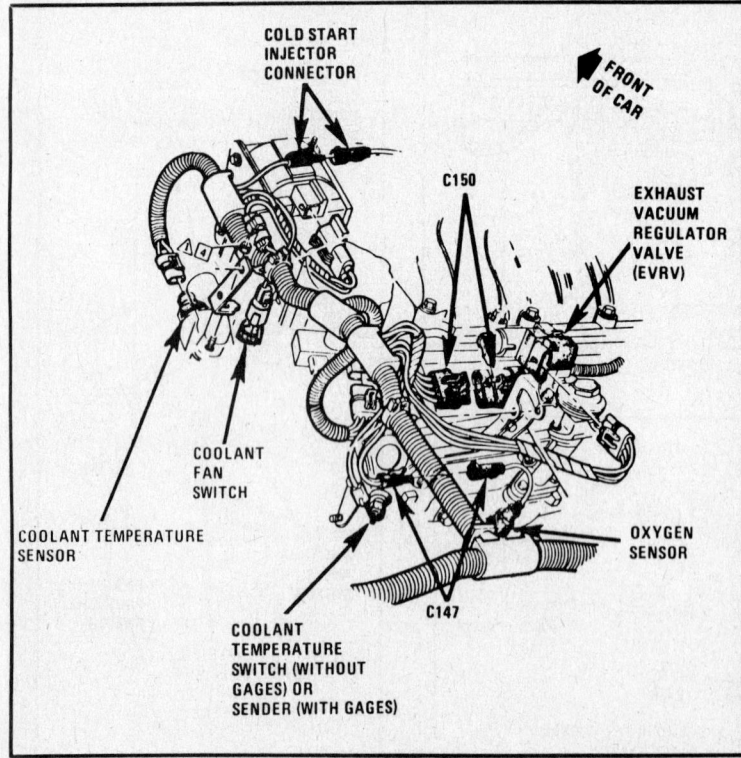

COLD START INJECTOR CONNECTOR

FRONT OF CAR

C150

EXHAUST VACUUM REGULATOR VALVE (EVRV)

COOLANT FAN SWITCH

COOLANT TEMPERATURE SENSOR

OXYGEN SENSOR

C147

COOLANT TEMPERATURE SWITCH (WITHOUT GAGES) OR SENDER (WITH GAGES)

LH Rear Of VIN W Engine

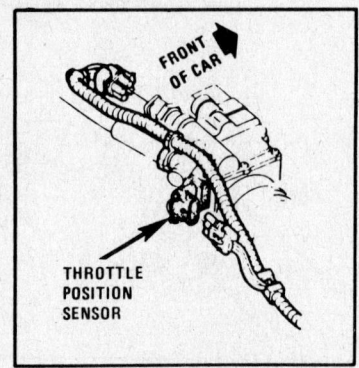

FRONT OF CAR

THROTTLE POSITION SENSOR

Right Side Of Throttle Body On Vin W Engine

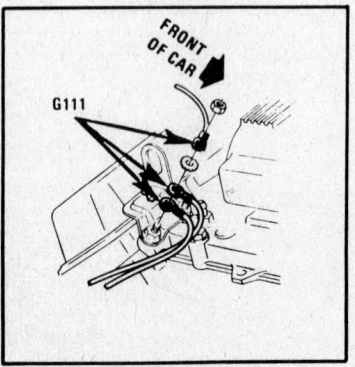

FRONT OF CAR

G111

RH Rear Corner Of VIN B Engine

1985-86 Oldsmobile Cutlass Ciera and Cutlass Cruiser

COMPONENT LOCATIONS

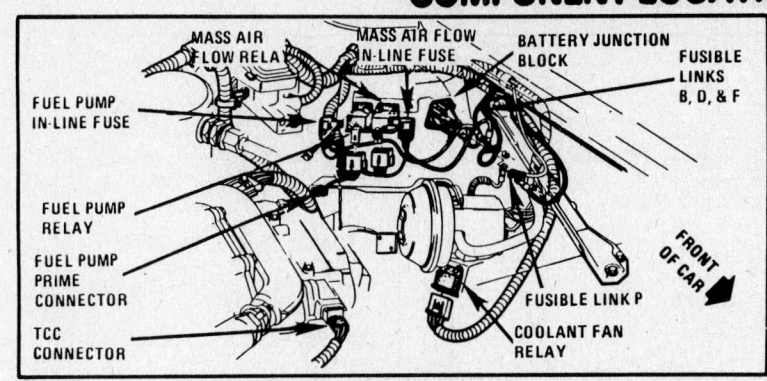

LH Shock Tower (VIN W)

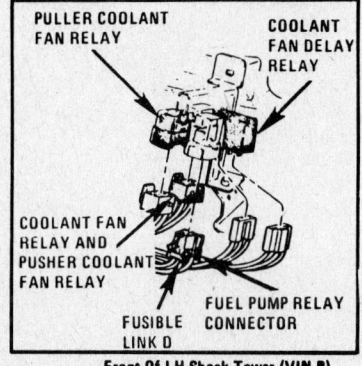

RH Corner Of VIN B Engine Compartment

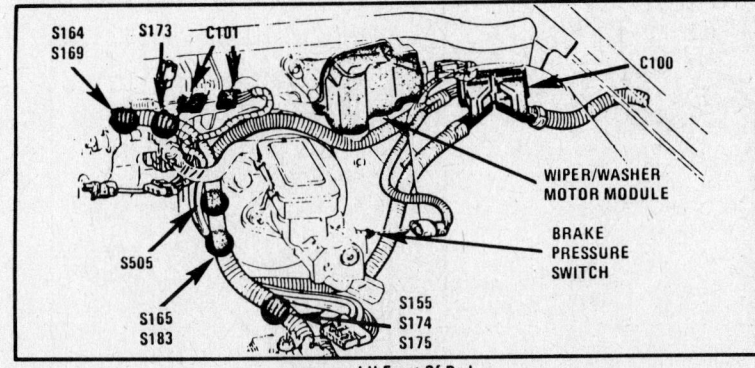

LH Front Of Dash

Front Of LH Shock Tower (VIN B)

1985-86 Oldsmobile Cutlass Clera and Cutlass Cruiser

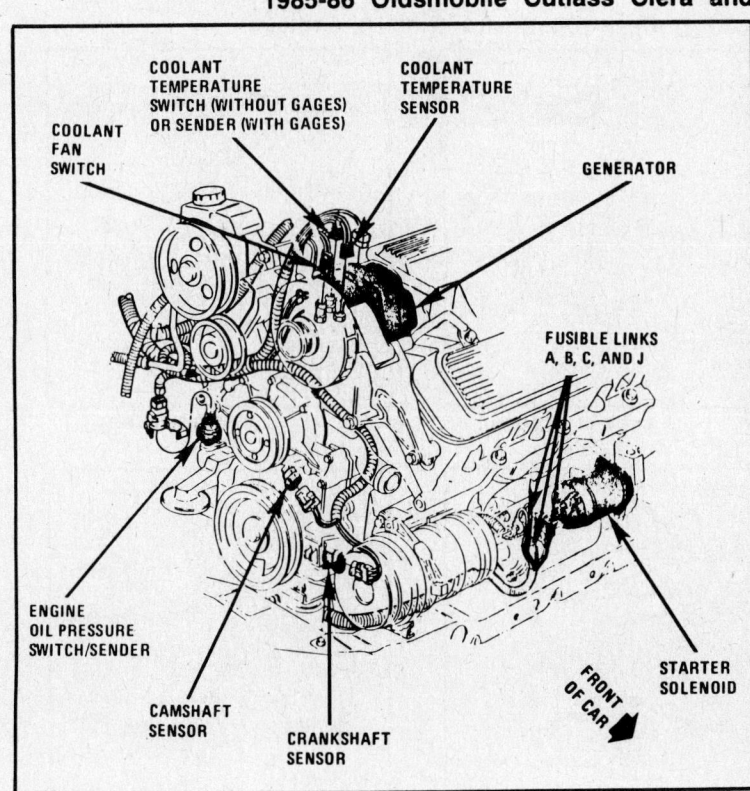

LH Side Of VIN B Engine

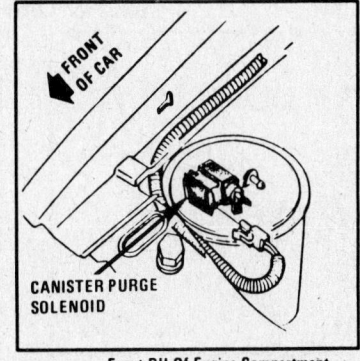

Front RH Of Engine Compartment

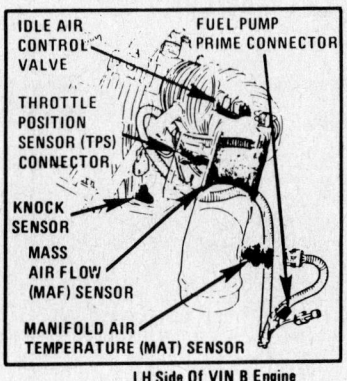

LH Side Of VIN B Engine

1985-86 Oldsmobile Cutlass Clera and Cutlass Cruiser

COMPONENT LOCATIONS

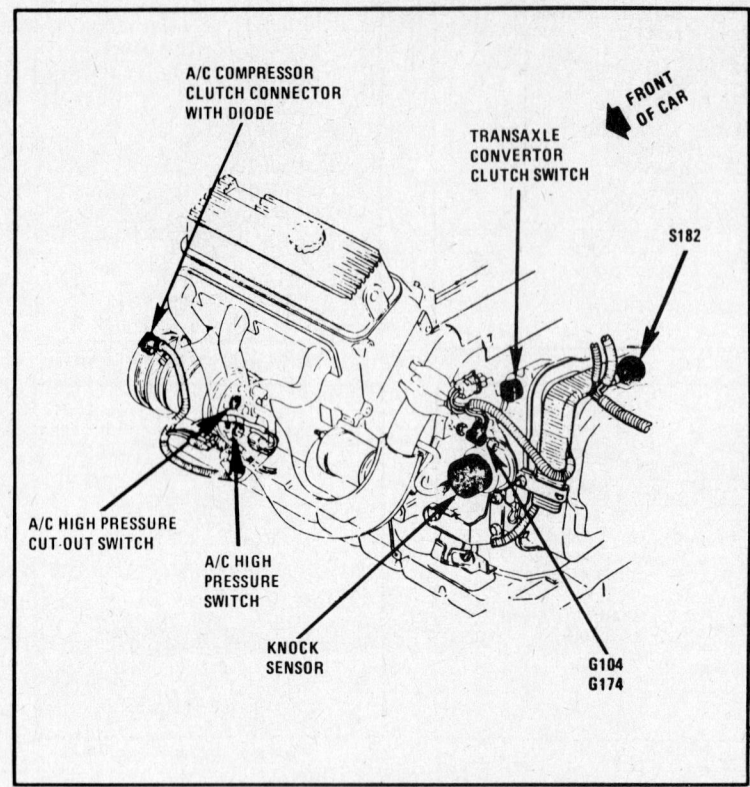

A/C COMPRESSOR CLUTCH CONNECTOR WITH DIODE

TRANSAXLE CONVERTOR CLUTCH SWITCH

S182

FRONT OF CAR

A/C HIGH PRESSURE CUT-OUT SWITCH

A/C HIGH PRESSURE SWITCH

KNOCK SENSOR

G104 G174

Front Of VIN B Engine

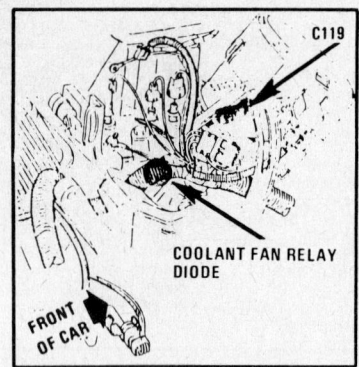

C119

COOLANT FAN RELAY DIODE

FRONT OF CAR

RH Side Of VIN B Engine

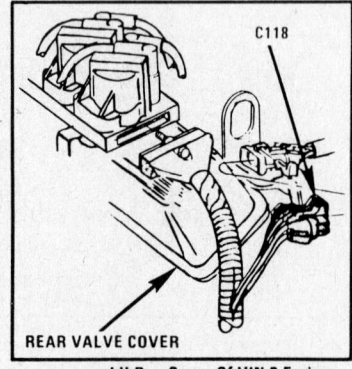

C118

REAR VALVE COVER

LH Rear Corner Of VIN B Engine

1985-86 Oldsmobile Cutlass Ciera and Cutlass Cruiser

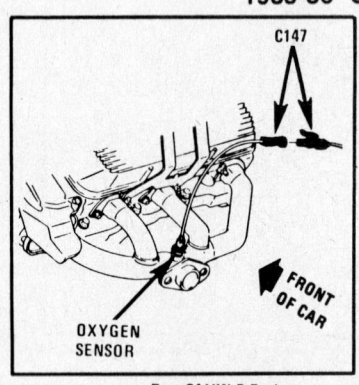

C147

OXYGEN SENSOR

FRONT OF CAR

Rear Of VIN B Engine

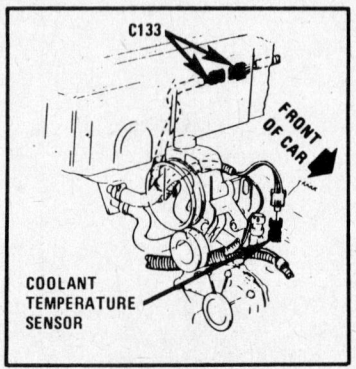

C133

FRONT OF CAR

COOLANT TEMPERATURE SENSOR

Top RH Rear Of VIN B Engine

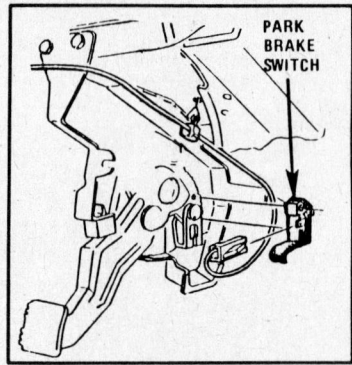

PARK BRAKE SWITCH

Under I/P Driver's Side

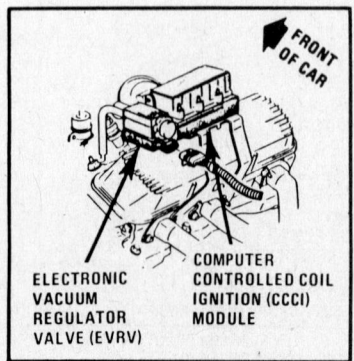

FRONT OF CAR

ELECTRONIC VACUUM REGULATOR VALVE (EVRV)

COMPUTER CONTROLLED COIL IGNITION (CCCI) MODULE

Top Rear Of VIN B Engine

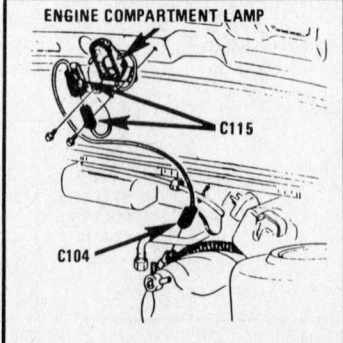

ENGINE COMPARTMENT LAMP

C115

C104

LH Rear Of Engine Compartment

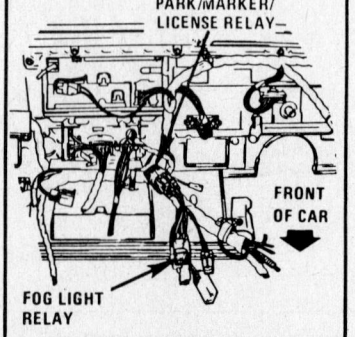

PARK/MARKER/ LICENSE RELAY

FRONT OF CAR

FOG LIGHT RELAY

Behind LH Side Of I/P

1985-86 Oldsmobile Cutlass Ciera and Cutlass Cruiser

COMPONENT LOCATIONS

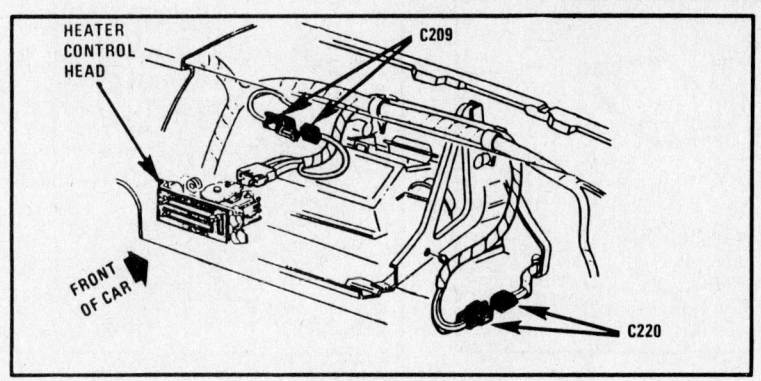

Behind Center Of I/P (Heater)

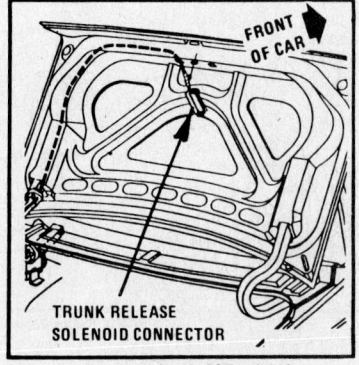

Underside Of Trunk Lid

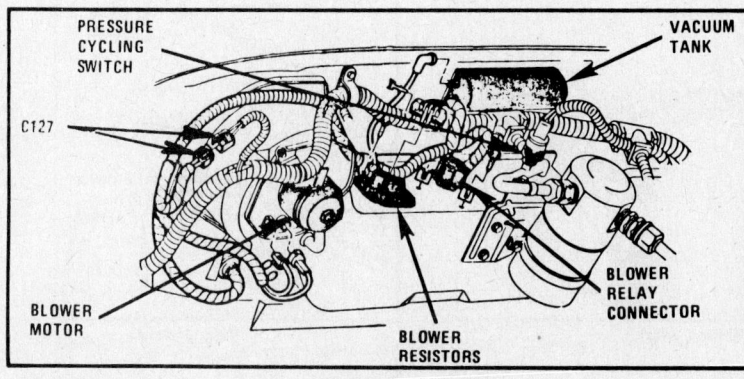

RH Front Of Dash (VIN W)

Underside Of Trunk Lid

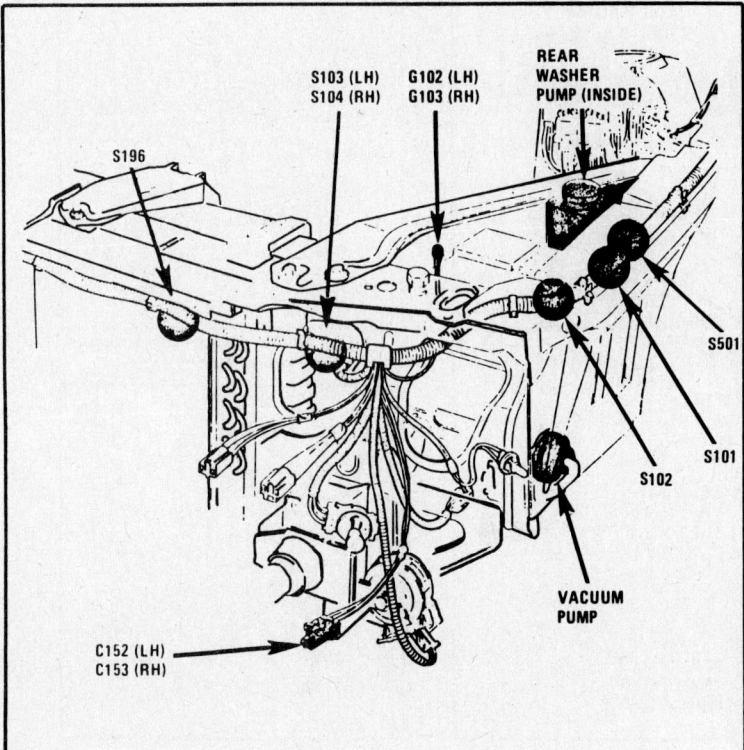

LH Front Of Car

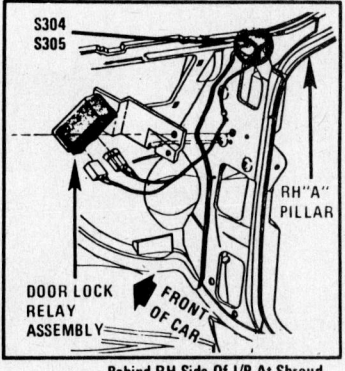

Behind RH Side Of I/P At Shroud

LH Rear Of Trunk

1985-86 Oldsmobile Cutlass Ciera and Cutlass Cruiser

COMPONENT LOCATIONS

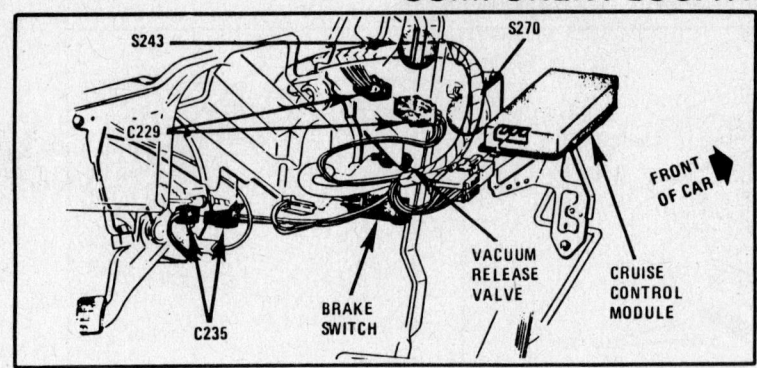

Below LH Side Of I/P

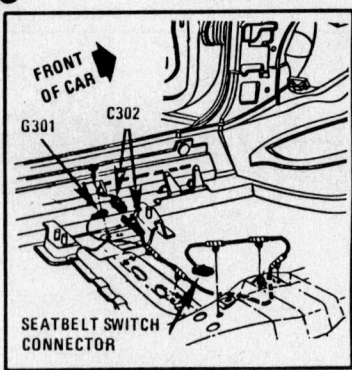

Figure C - Below LH Front Seat

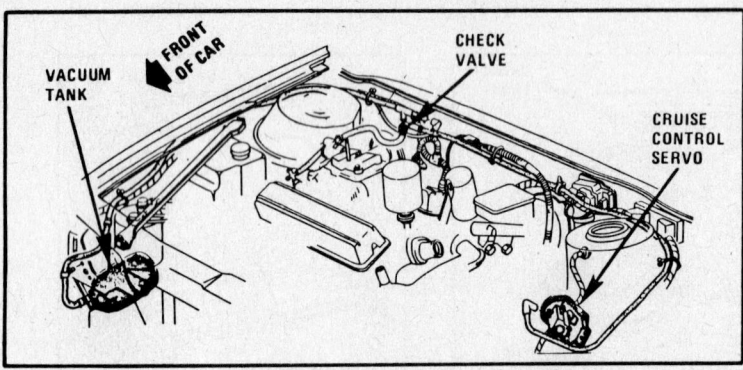

VIN X Engine Compartment (Others Similar)

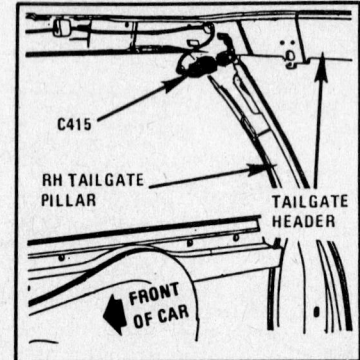

Tailgate Header

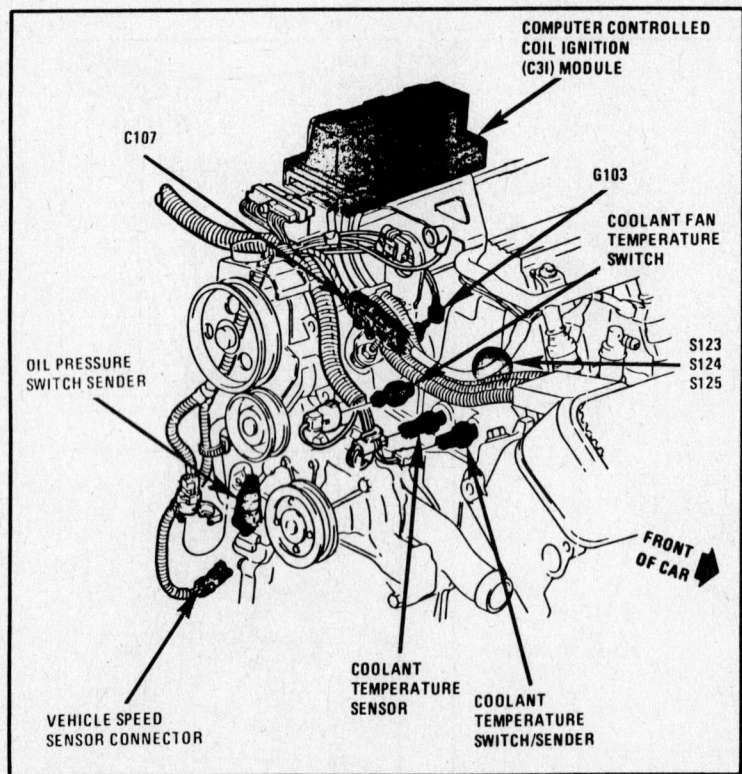

RH End Of VIN L Engine

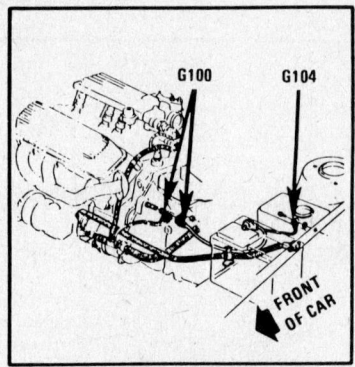

**LH Front Of Engine Compartment
(VIN L Shown, VIN U Similar)**

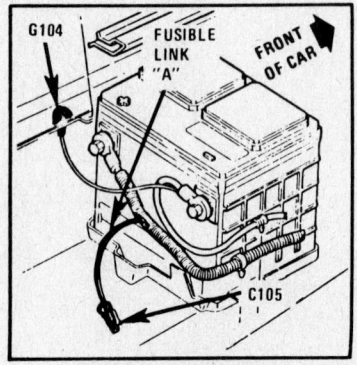

**LH Front Corner Of Engine Compartment
(VIN L Shown VIN U Similar)**

1985-86 Oldsmobile Calais

COMPONENT LOCATIONS

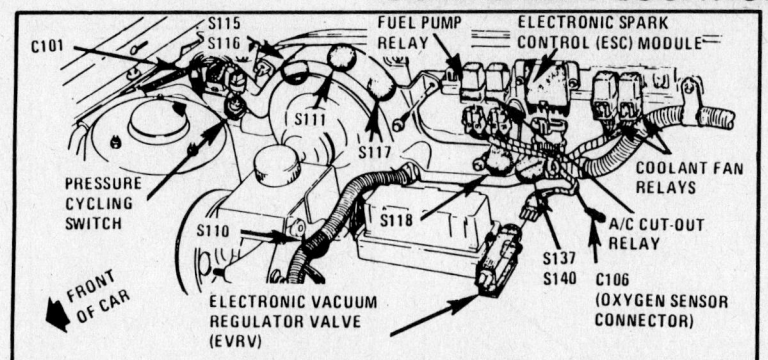

Center To RH Front Of Dash (VIN L)

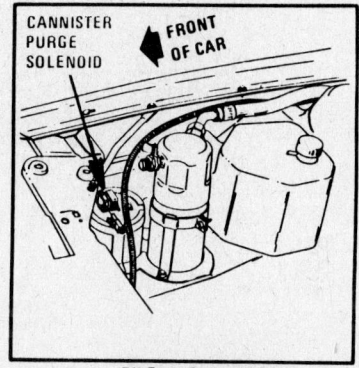

LH Top Of VIN L Engine Compartment

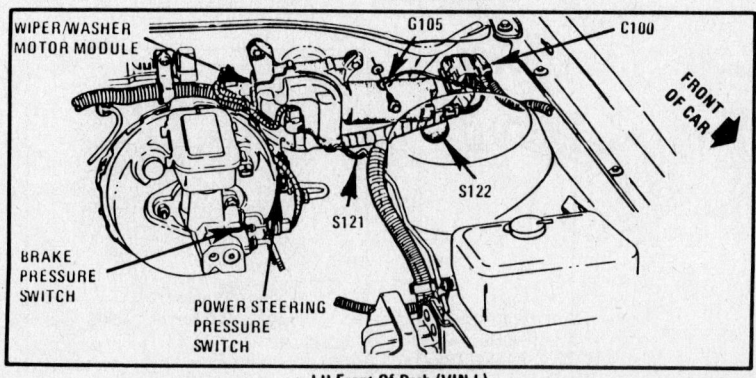

LH Front Of Dash (VIN L)

RH Front Corner Of Engine Compartment (VIN L)

1985-86 Oldsmobile Calais

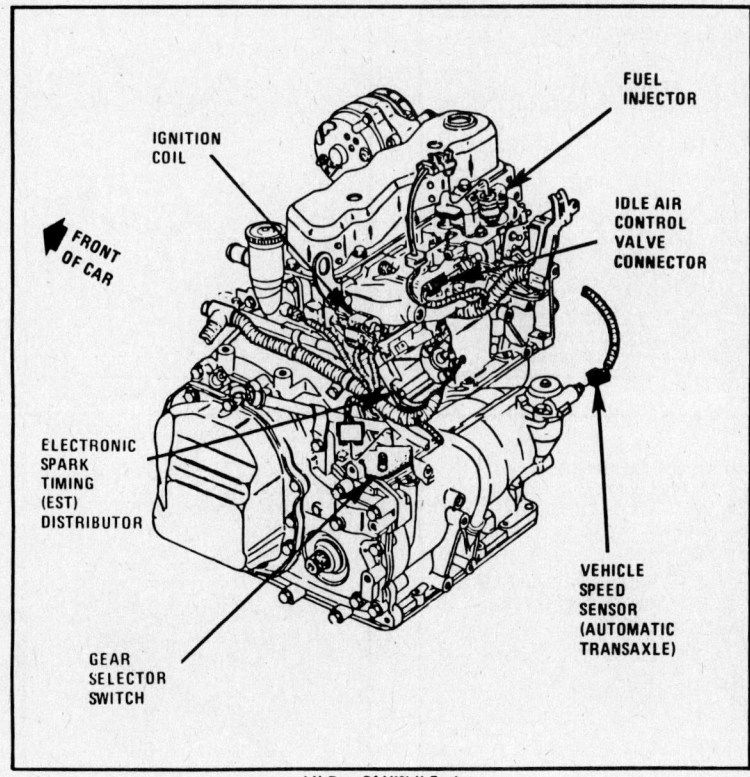

LH Rear Of VIN U Engine

LH Side Of Automatic Transaxle

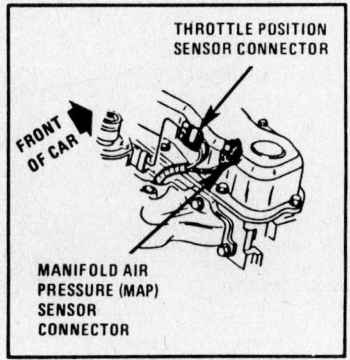

Top RH Rear Of VIN U Engine

1985-86 Oldsmobile Calais

COMPONENT LOCATIONS

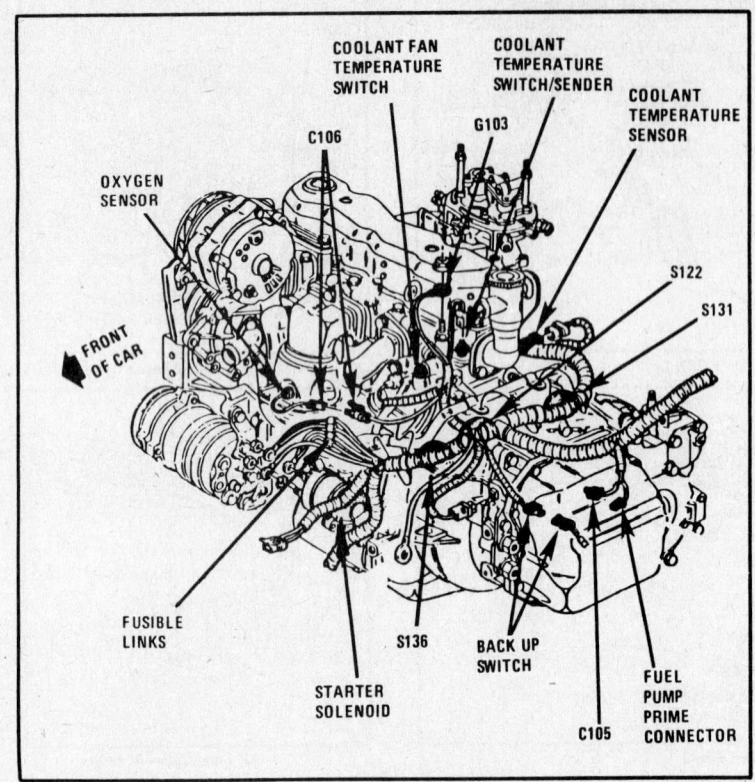

OXYGEN SENSOR

COOLANT FAN TEMPERATURE SWITCH

COOLANT TEMPERATURE SWITCH/SENDER

COOLANT TEMPERATURE SENSOR

C106

G103

S122

S131

FRONT OF CAR

FUSIBLE LINKS

STARTER SOLENOID

S136

BACK UP SWITCH

C105

FUEL PUMP PRIME CONNECTOR

LH Front Of VIN U Engine

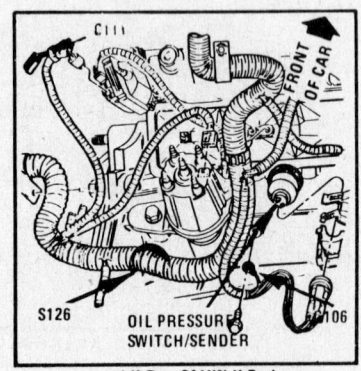

VEHICLE SPEED SENSOR CONNECTOR (MANUAL TRANSAXLE)

FRONT OF CAR

Top Of Transaxle, Rear Of VIN U Engine

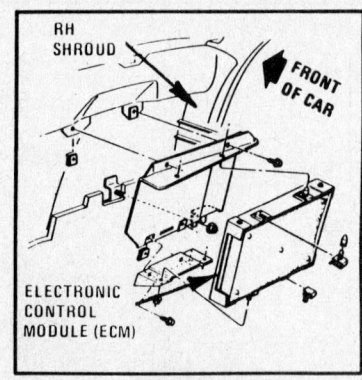

C111

FRONT OF CAR

S126

OIL PRESSURE SWITCH/SENDER

C106

LH Rear Of VIN U Engine

1985-86 Oldsmobile Calais

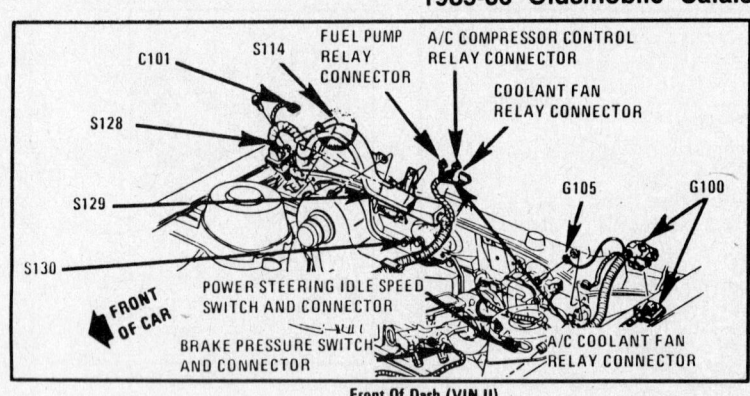

C101

S114

FUEL PUMP RELAY CONNECTOR

A/C COMPRESSOR CONTROL RELAY CONNECTOR

COOLANT FAN RELAY CONNECTOR

S128

S129

S130

G105

G100

FRONT OF CAR

POWER STEERING IDLE SPEED SWITCH AND CONNECTOR

BRAKE PRESSURE SWITCH AND CONNECTOR

A/C COOLANT FAN RELAY CONNECTOR

Front Of Dash (VIN U)

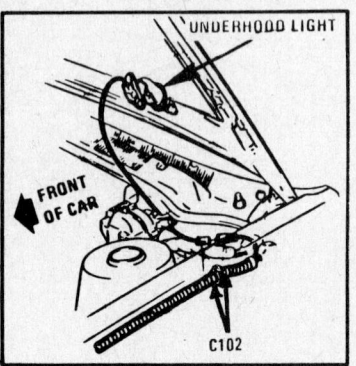

RH SHROUD

FRONT OF CAR

ELECTRONIC CONTROL MODULE (ECM)

Behind RH Side Of I/P

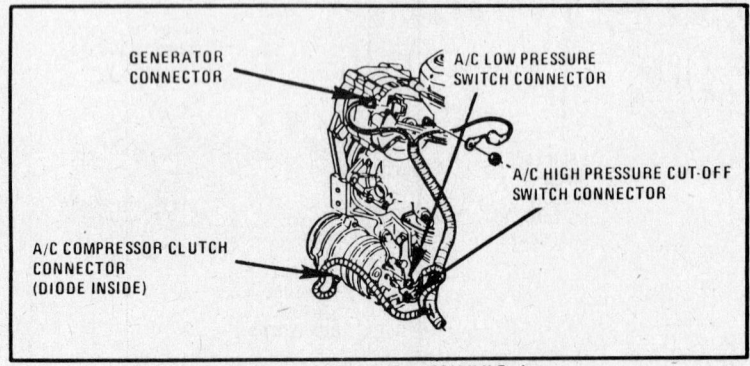

GENERATOR CONNECTOR

A/C LOW PRESSURE SWITCH CONNECTOR

A/C HIGH PRESSURE CUT-OFF SWITCH CONNECTOR

A/C COMPRESSOR CLUTCH CONNECTOR (DIODE INSIDE)

Lower RH Front Of VIN U Engine

UNDERHOOD LIGHT

FRONT OF CAR

C102

LH Rear Corner Of Engine Compartment

1985-86 Oldsmobile Calais

COMPONENT LOCATIONS

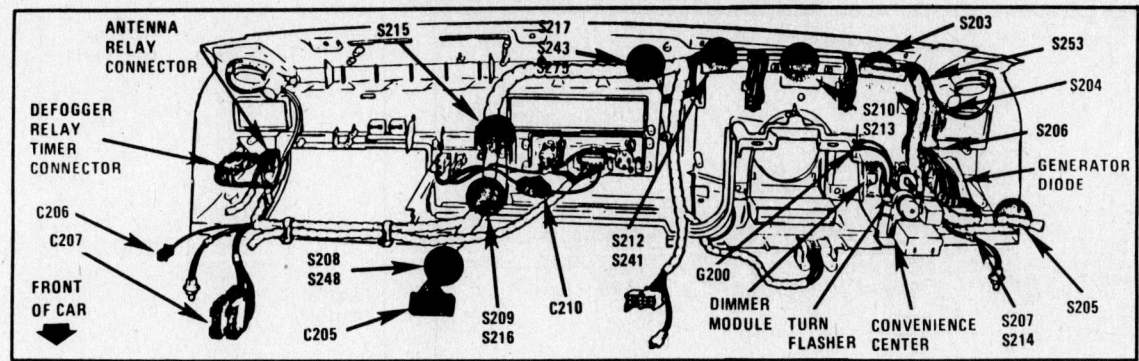

Behind I/P

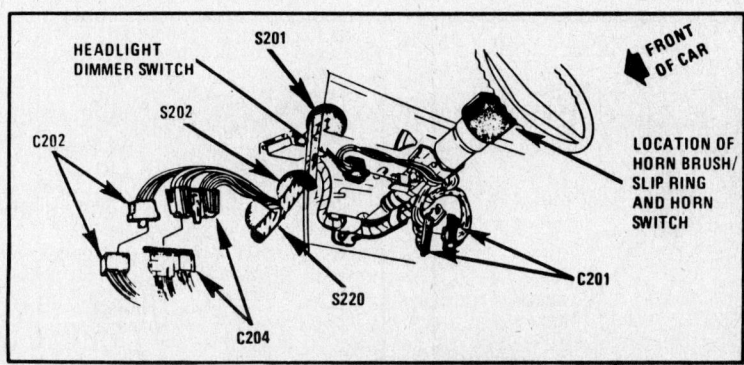

Steering Column And Behind LH Side Of I/P

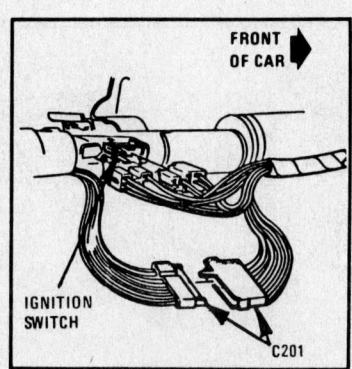

RH Side Of Steering Column

1985-86 Oldsmobile Calais

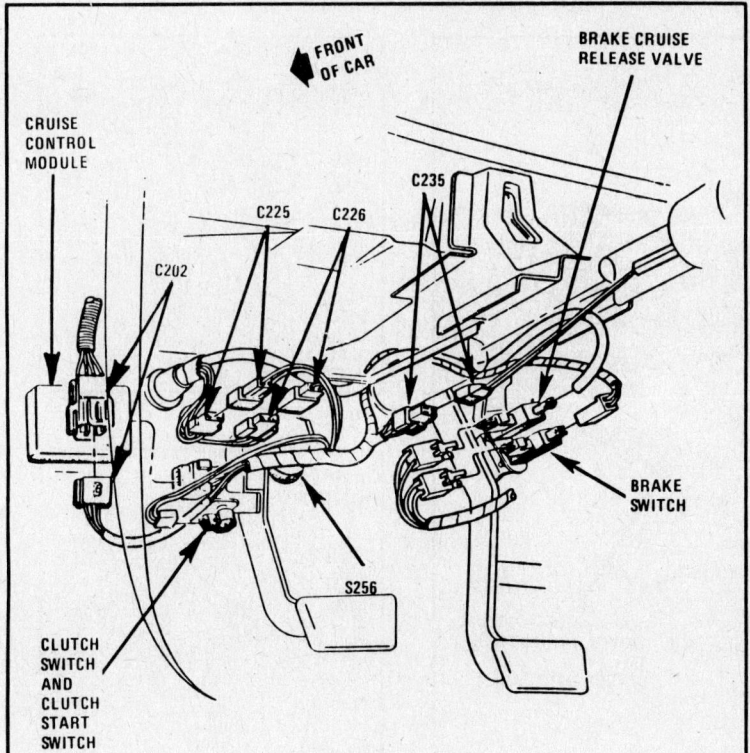

Below LH Side Of I/P

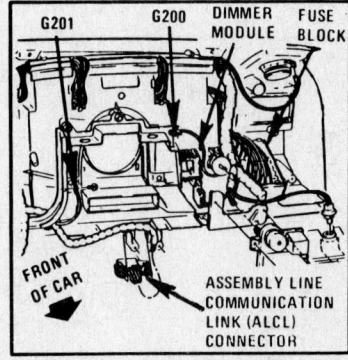

Behind LH Side Of I/P

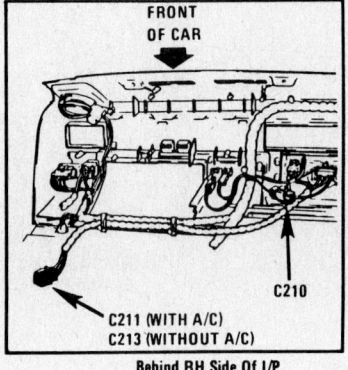

Behind RH Side Of I/P

1985-86 Oldsmobile Calais

COMPONENT LOCATIONS

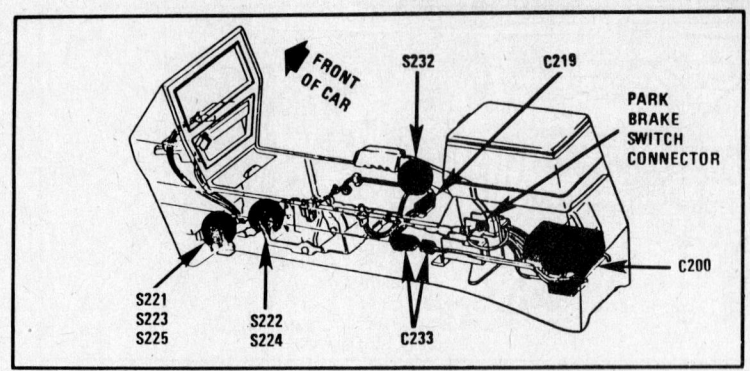

Console

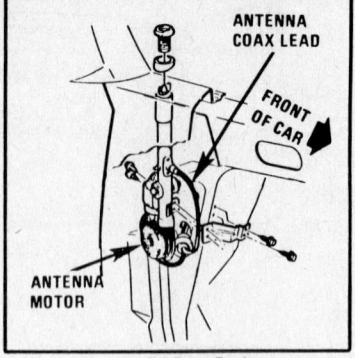

RH Front Fender

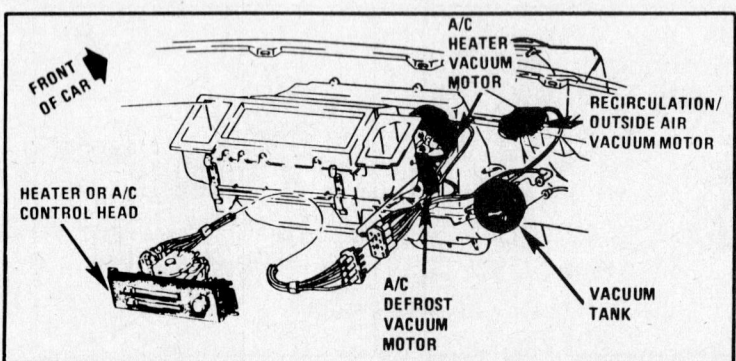

Behind Center And RH Side Of I/P

1985-86 Oldsmobile Calais

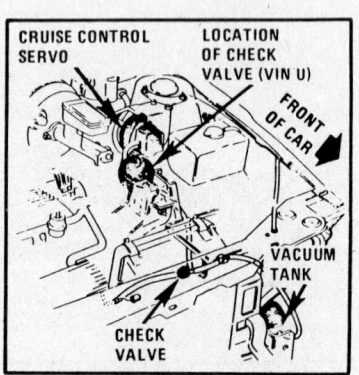

LH Side Of Engine Compartment
(VIN L Shown, VIN U Similar)

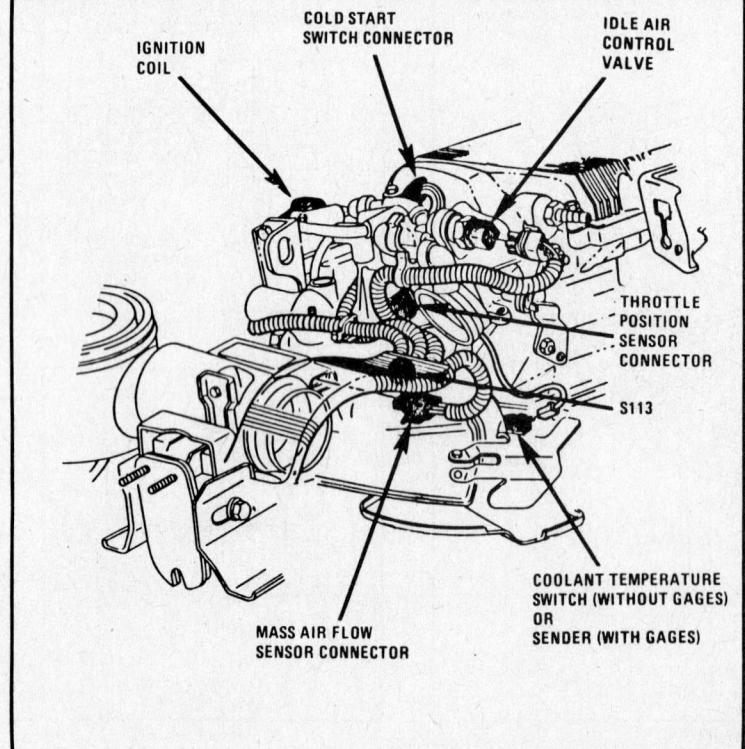

Top LH Rear Of VIN W Engine

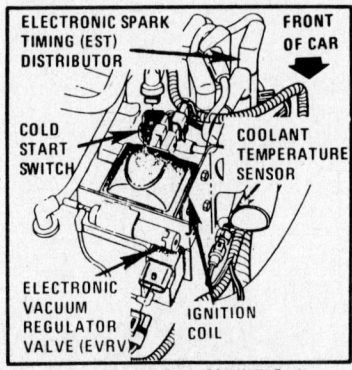

Top LH Front Of VIN W Engine

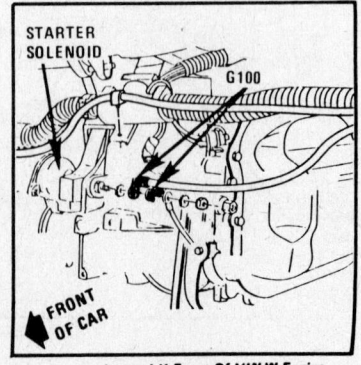

Lower LH Front Of VIN W Engine

1985-86 Oldsmobile Firenza

COMPONENT LOCATIONS

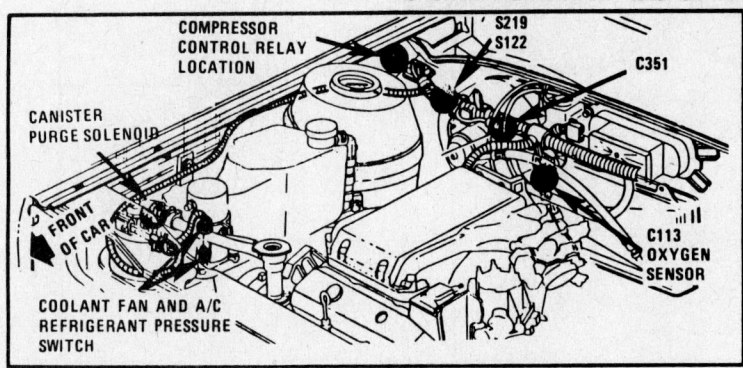

RH Side Of VIN W Engine Compartment

Top RH Rear Of VIN W Engine

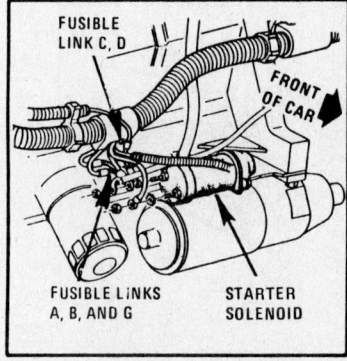

Lower LH Front Of VIN W Engine

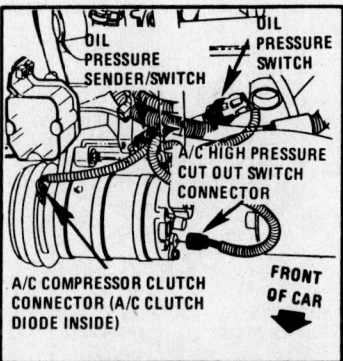

Lower RH Front Of VIN W Engine
VIN P And VIN O Similar

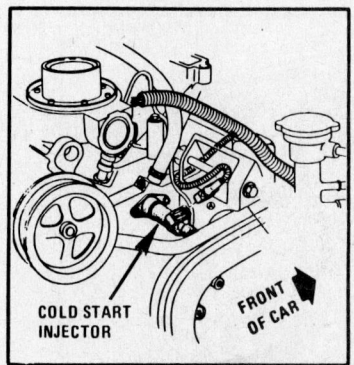

Top RH Of VIN W Engine

1985-86 Oldsmobile Firenza

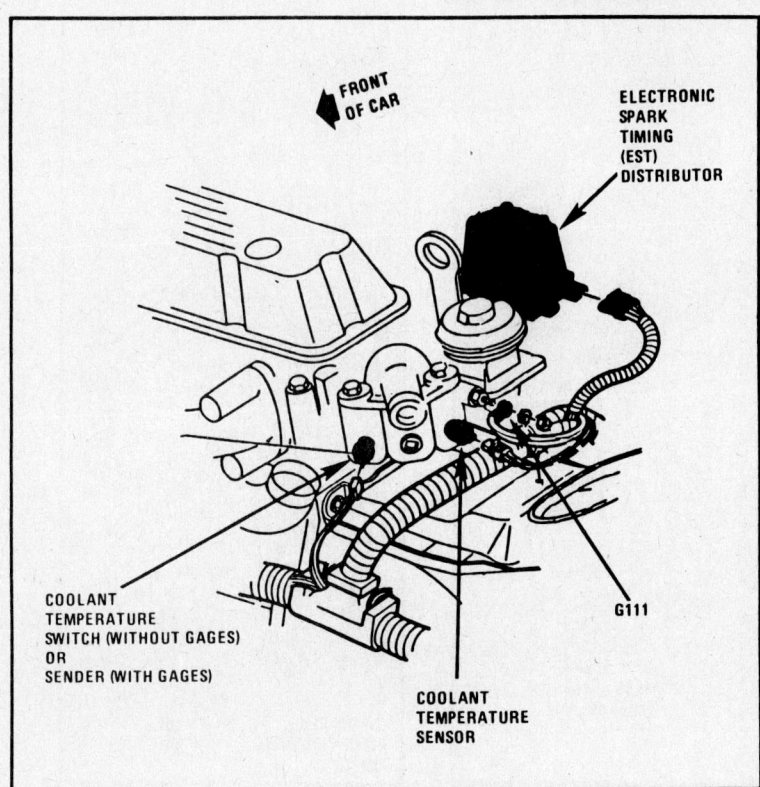

Top LH Front Of VIN P Engine

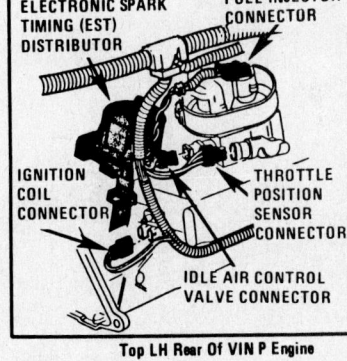

Top LH Rear Of VIN P Engine

Lower LH Front Of VIN P Engine

1985-86 Oldsmobile Firenza

201

COMPONENT LOCATIONS

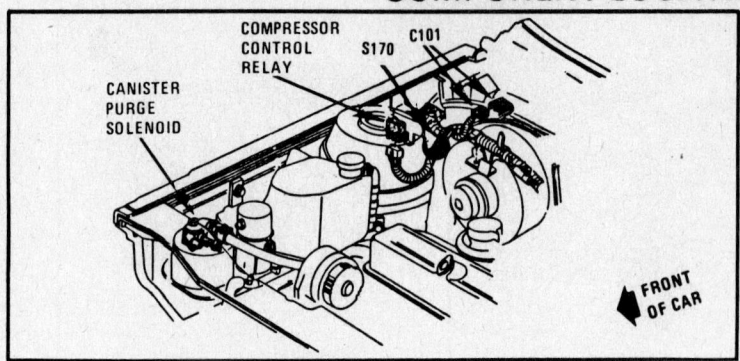

CANISTER PURGE SOLENOID

COMPRESSOR CONTROL RELAY

S170 C101

FRONT OF CAR

RH Side Of VIN P Engine Compartment

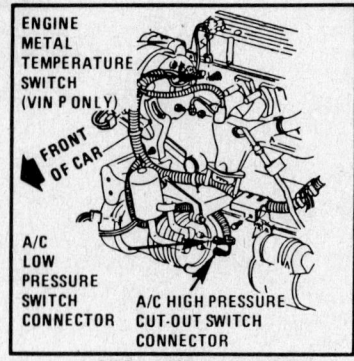

ENGINE METAL TEMPERATURE SWITCH (VIN P ONLY)

FRONT OF CAR

A/C LOW PRESSURE SWITCH CONNECTOR

A/C HIGH PRESSURE CUT-OUT SWITCH CONNECTOR

RH Front Of Engine (VIN P Shown, VIN O Similar)

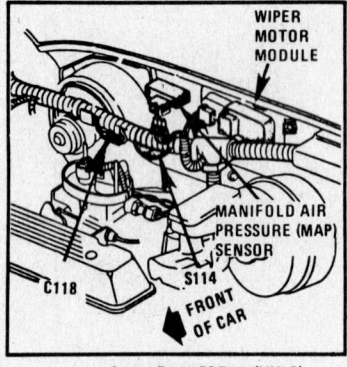

WIPER MOTOR MODULE

MANIFOLD AIR PRESSURE (MAP) SENSOR

C118

S114

FRONT OF CAR

Center Front Of Dash (VIN P)

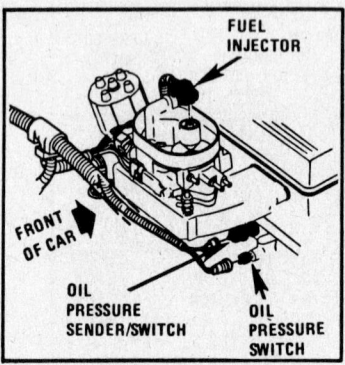

FUEL INJECTOR

FRONT OF CAR

OIL PRESSURE SENDER/SWITCH

OIL PRESSURE SWITCH

Top RH Rear Of VIN P Engine

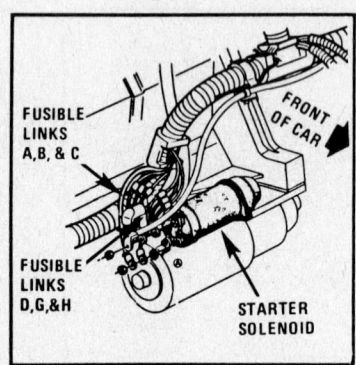

FUSIBLE LINKS A, B, & C

FRONT OF CAR

FUSIBLE LINKS D, G, & H

STARTER SOLENOID

Lower LH Front Of VIN P Engine

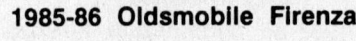

1985-86 Oldsmobile Firenza

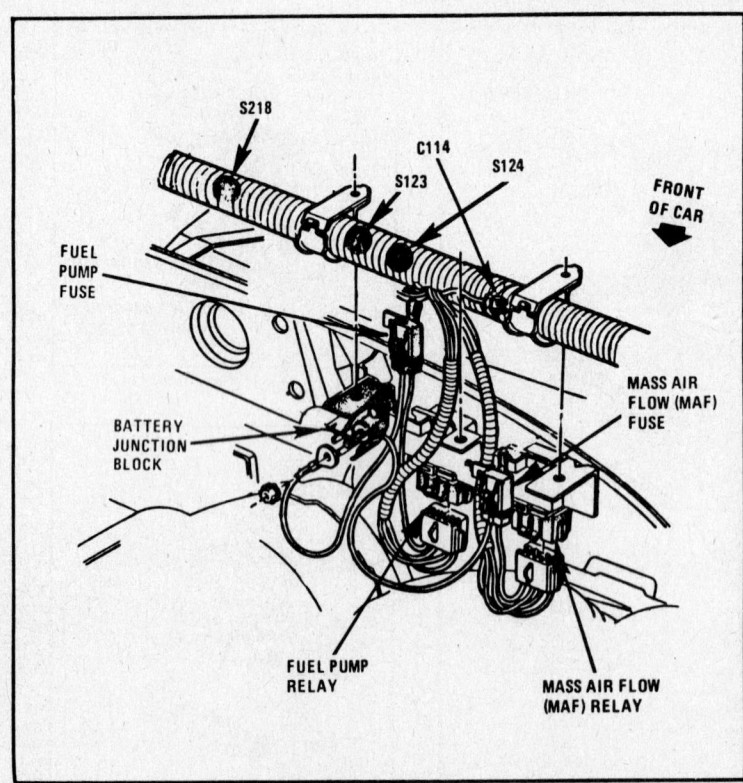

S218

C114 S124

S123

FRONT OF CAR

FUEL PUMP FUSE

MASS AIR FLOW (MAF) FUSE

BATTERY JUNCTION BLOCK

FUEL PUMP RELAY

MASS AIR FLOW (MAF) RELAY

LH Front Of Dash (VIN P Shown, VIN W Similar)

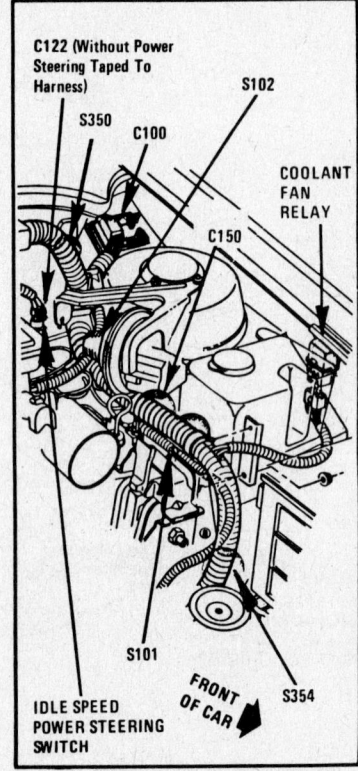

C122 (Without Power Steering Taped To Harness)

S350 C100

S102

C150

COOLANT FAN RELAY

S101

IDLE SPEED POWER STEERING SWITCH

S354

FRONT OF CAR

LH Side Of VIN P Engine Compartment (VIN W Similar)

1985-86 Oldsmobile Firenza

COMPONENT LOCATIONS

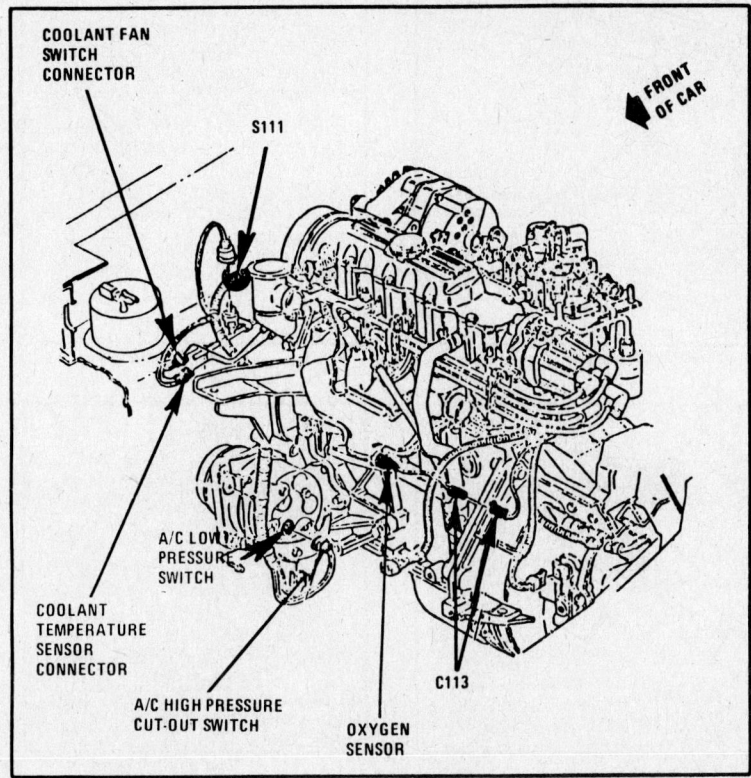

COOLANT FAN
SWITCH
CONNECTOR

S111

FRONT
OF CAR

A/C LOW
PRESSURE
SWITCH

COOLANT
TEMPERATURE
SENSOR
CONNECTOR

A/C HIGH PRESSURE
CUT-OUT SWITCH

C113

OXYGEN
SENSOR

Front Of VIN O Engine

1985-86 Oldsmobile Firenza

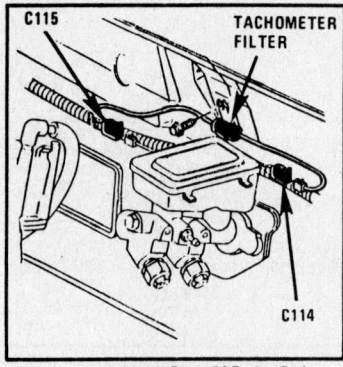

C115

TACHOMETER
FILTER

C114

Upper LH Front Of Engine Dash
(VIN P Shown, VIN W Similar)

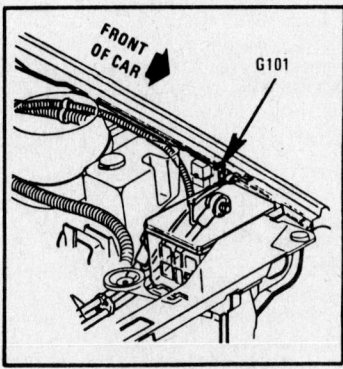

FRONT
OF CAR

G101

LH Front Corner Of VIN P Engine
Compartment (VIN W Similar)

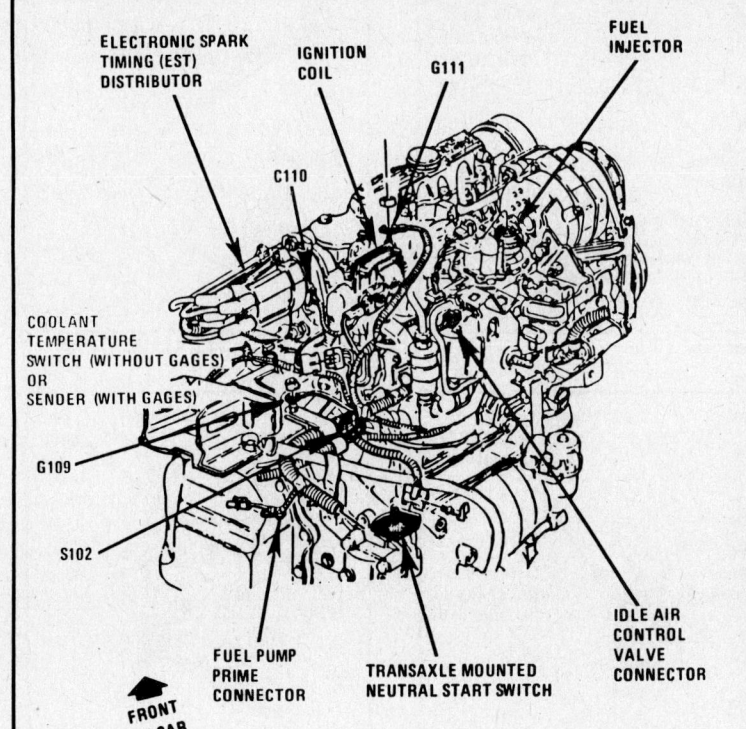

ELECTRONIC SPARK
TIMING (EST)
DISTRIBUTOR

IGNITION
COIL

G111

FUEL
INJECTOR

C110

COOLANT
TEMPERATURE
SWITCH (WITHOUT GAGES)
OR
SENDER (WITH GAGES)

G109

S102

FRONT
OF CAR

FUEL PUMP
PRIME
CONNECTOR

TRANSAXLE MOUNTED
NEUTRAL START SWITCH

IDLE AIR
CONTROL
VALVE
CONNECTOR

LH Rear Of VIN O Engine

1985-86 Oldsmobile Firenza

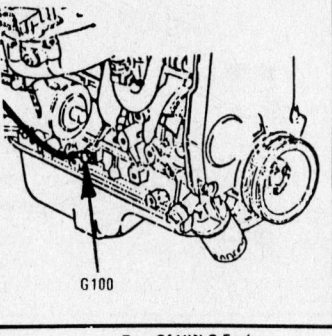

G100

Rear Of VIN O Engine

STARTER
SOLENOID

FUSIBLE LINK
A, B, C & G

Lower LH Of VIN O Engine

COMPONENT LOCATIONS

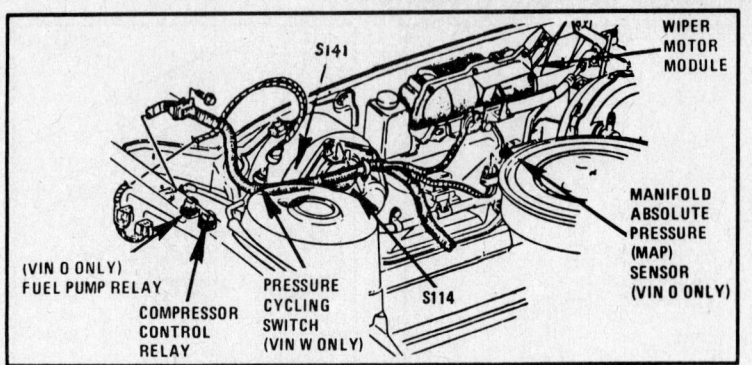

RH Front Of Dash - (VIN O Shown VIN W Similiar)

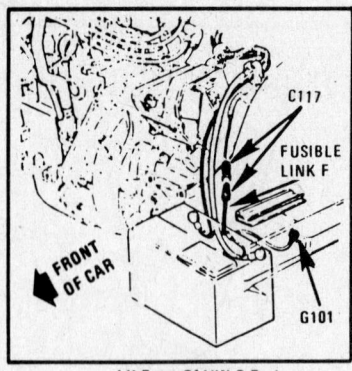

LH Front Of VIN O Engine Compartment

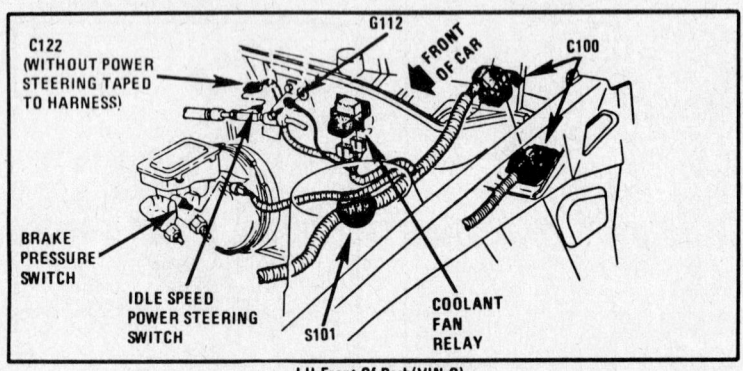

LH Front Of Dash (VIN O)

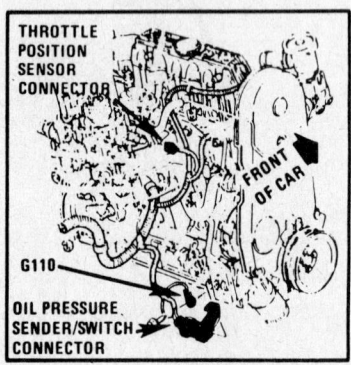

Rear Of VIN O Engine

1985-86 Oldsmobile Firenza

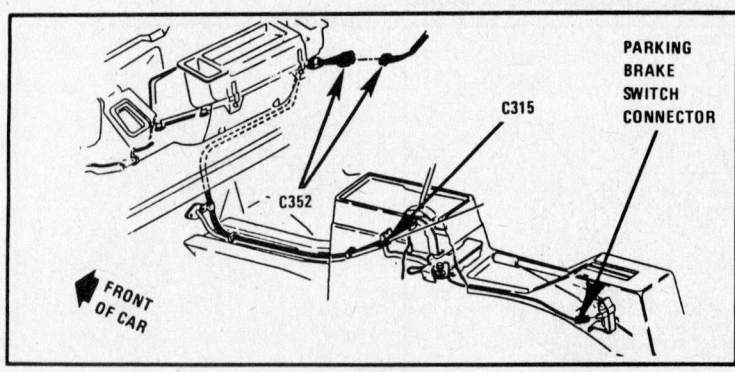

Console With Automatic

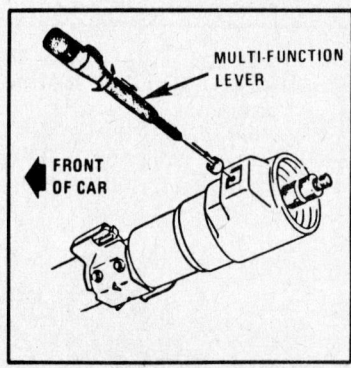

Top LH Side Of Steering Column

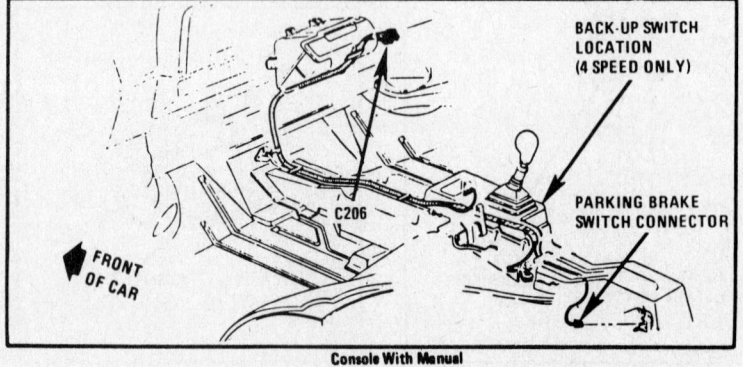

Console With Manual

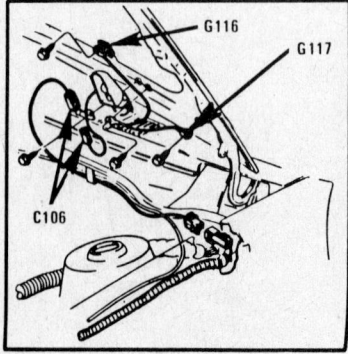

Under Front Hood

1985-86 Oldsmobile Firenza

COMPONENT LOCATIONS

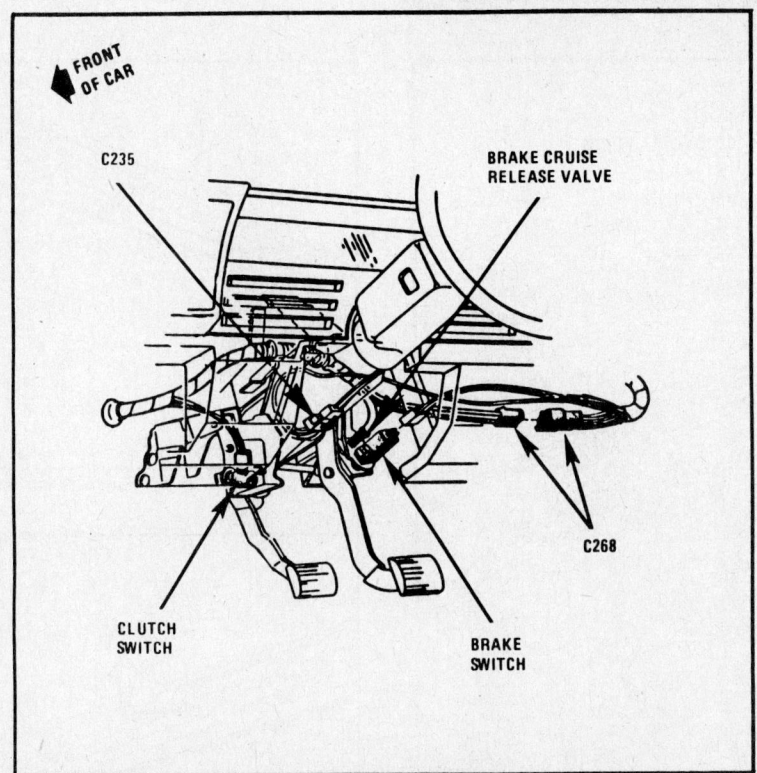

FRONT OF CAR

C235

BRAKE CRUISE RELEASE VALVE

C268

CLUTCH SWITCH

BRAKE SWITCH

Below LH Side Of I/P (Manual)

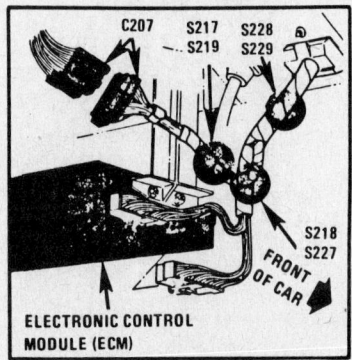

C207   S352 S355 S227   S351 S219

ELECTRONIC CONTROL MODULE (ECM)

S217

Behind RH Side Of I/P
(VIN P Shown, VIN W Similar)

C207   S217 S219   S228 S229

S218 S227

FRONT OF CAR

ELECTRONIC CONTROL MODULE (ECM)

Behind RH Side Of I/P (VIN O)

1985-86 Oldsmobile Firenza

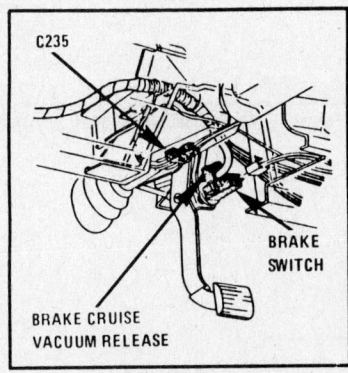

C235

BRAKE SWITCH

BRAKE CRUISE VACUUM RELEASE

Below LH Side Of I/P (Automatic)

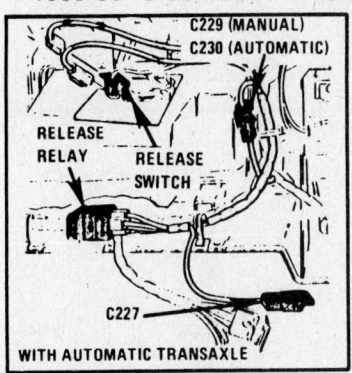

C229 (MANUAL)
C230 (AUTOMATIC)

RELEASE RELAY   RELEASE SWITCH

C227

WITH AUTOMATIC TRANSAXLE

Behind RH Side Of I/P

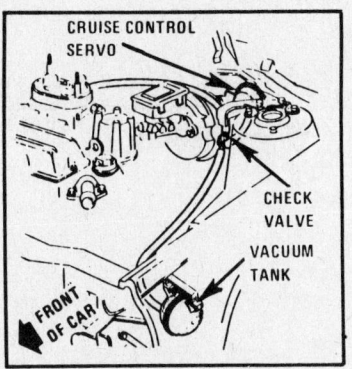

CRUISE CONTROL SERVO

CHECK VALVE

VACUUM TANK

FRONT OF CAR

LH Side Of VIN P Engine Compartment,
VIN O Similiar

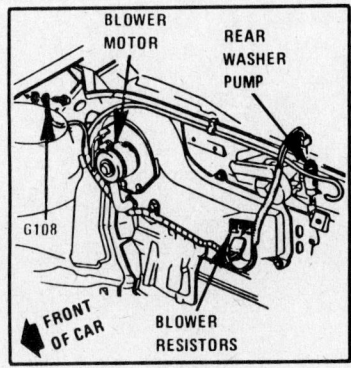

BLOWER MOTOR   REAR WASHER PUMP

G108

FRONT OF CAR

BLOWER RESISTORS

RH Front Of Dash (Without A/C)

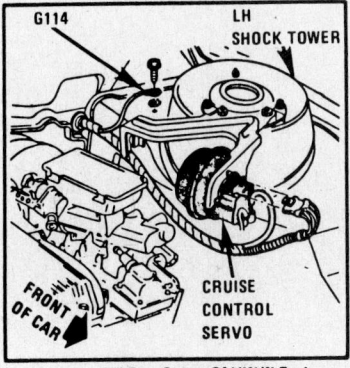

G114   LH SHOCK TOWER

FRONT OF CAR

CRUISE CONTROL SERVO

LH Rear Corner Of VIN W Engine
Compartment

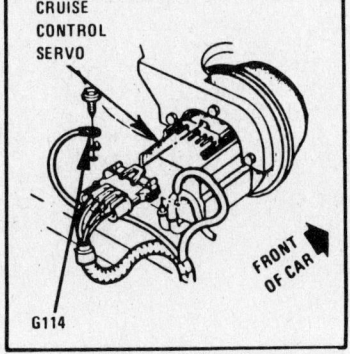

CRUISE CONTROL SERVO

FRONT OF CAR

G114

RH Side Of LH Front Shock Tower,
VIN P And VIN O

1985-86 Oldsmobile Firenza

COMPONENT LOCATIONS

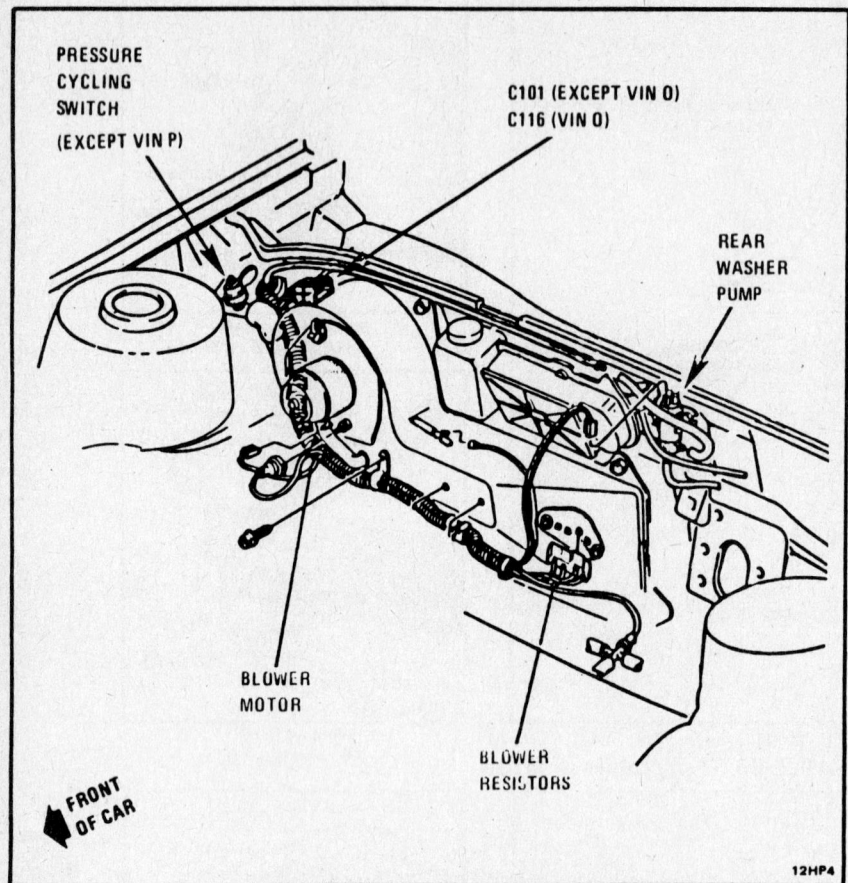

PRESSURE
CYCLING
SWITCH
(EXCEPT VIN P)

C101 (EXCEPT VIN O)
C116 (VIN O)

REAR
WASHER
PUMP

BLOWER
MOTOR

BLOWER
RESISTORS

FRONT
OF CAR

12HP4

Figure A - RH Front Of Dash (With A/C)

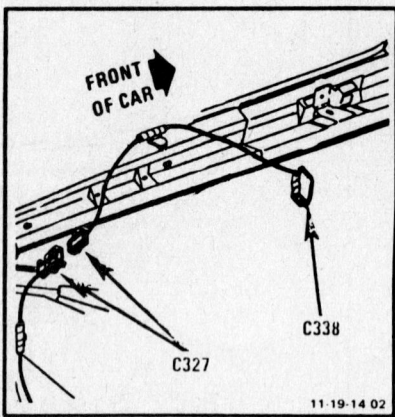

FRONT
OF CAR

C327

C338

11-19-14 02

Figure B - Above LH Rear Window (Hatchback)

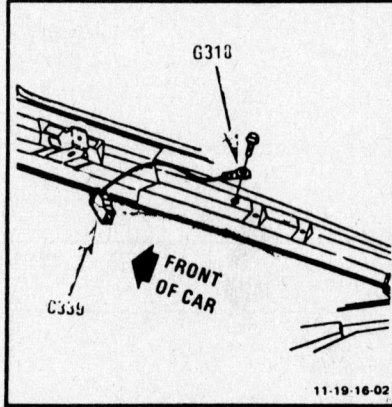

G318

FRONT
OF CAR

C339

11-19-16-02

Figure C - Above RH Rear Window (Hatchback)

1985-86 Oldsmobile Firenza

PONTIAC

Circuit Breaker

1982-84—ALL MODELS

POWER WINDOWS

The circuit breaker that protects the power window circuit, is incorporated with the power window motor, except for the T1000, Grand Prix and Bonneville.

HEADLIGHTS

This circuit breaker is incorporated in the headlight switch.

WINDSHIELD WIPERS

This circuit breaker is incorporated in the winshield wiper motor on all models except the T1000 and the Fiero.

HEADLIGHT DOORS

This circuit breaker is located on the headlight door actuator on all Firebird and Trans Am models.

POWER REMOTE MIRRORS

This circuit breaker is incorporated into the power mirror motors on Bonneville, Grand Prix, Fiero, Parisienne, Firebird and Trans Am.

1985-87—ALL MODELS

HEADLIGHTS

This circuit breaker is incorporated in the headlight switch.

WINDSHIELD WIPERS

This circuit breaker is incorporated in the winshield wiper motor on all models except the T1000 and the Fiero.

POWER REMOTE MIRRORS

This circuit breaker is incorporated into the power mirror motors on Bonneville, Grand Prix, Fiero, Parisienne, Firebird and Trans Am.
This circuit breaker is incorporated in the winshield wiper motor.

POWER WINDOWS

This circuit breaker is incorporated with the power window motors on all models.

Fusible Links

1982-84—ALL MODELS

There are fusible links used on all models and are usally located as follows; On all models there are two fusible links located at the starter solenoid, which are used to protect the charging and lighting circuits. There are two fusible links located at the alternator, used to protect the charging and lighting circuits on the Parisienne, Bonneville, Grand Prix and Firebird four cylinder models.

There is one fusible link used at each headlight door to protect the headlight system on the Firebird and Fiero. There are fusible links used at each glow plug wire on all the diesel models.

There is one fusible link located near the battery positive terminal, which is used for the protection of the electronic control module on the Firebird. There is also a fusible link located at the dash panel bulkhead connector for the cooling fans on the 2000 models.

On the 2000 models, there is one fusible link located at the front fender, which is used for the vacuum pump and a fusible link located in the left rear corner of the engine compartment, which protects the engine compartment light.

There is a fusible link located at the electronic spark timing distributor for the early fuel evaporation heater relay on the Phoenix, 6000 and 6000 STE. There is one fusible link at the starter for the cooling fan on Phoenix, 6000 and 6000 STE.

1985-87—ALL MODELS

On all models there are two fusible links located at the starter solenoid, which are used to protect the charging and lighting circuits. There is one fusible link used at each headlight door to protect the headlight system on the Firebird and Fiero. There are fusible links used at each glow plug wire on all the diesel models.

There is one fusible link located near the battery positive terminal, which is used for the protection of the electronic control module on the Firebird.

There is a fusible link located at the electronic spark timing distributor for the early fuel evaporation heater relay on the Phoenix, 6000 and 6000 STE. There is one fusible link at the starter for the cooling fan on Phoenix, 6000 and 6000 STE.

Relay, Sensors And Computer Locations

1982 AND LATER T1000

- **A/C Compressor Cut-Out Switch**—is located on the accelerator pedal support.
- **A/C-Heater Blower Resistors**—are located in the engine compartment on the lower right side of the A/C-heater assembly.
- **A/C High Speed Blower Relay**—is located in the engine compartment at the center of the A/C heater assembly.
- **A/C Pressure Cycling Switch**—is located on the accumulator /drier.
- **A/C Vacuum Advance Relay**—is located on the left side of the firewall in front of the electronic speed sensor.
- **Assembly Line Diagnostic Line Connector**—is located under the right side of the dash panel.
- **Audio Alarm Module**—is located on the fuse block.
- **"Check Engine" Light Driver**—is located under the right side of the dash panel.
- **Coolant Temperature Sender (Gas)**—is located in the left center of the engine.
- **Coolant Temperature Switch (Diesel)**—is located in the left center of the engine.
- **Diagnostic Dwell Meter Connector**—is taped to the wiring harness, at the rear of the intake manifold.
- **Dropping Resistor**—is located under the glow plug relay assembly cover.
- **Early Fuel Evaporation Temperature Switch**—is located on the left side of the engine.
- **Electronic Control Module (ECM)**—is located under the center of the instrument panel.
- **Electronic Speed Sensor**—is located on the firewall near the bulkhead connector.
- **Fast Idle switch**—is located on the left front side of the engine.

• **Glow Plug Controller (Diesel)** – is located on the right side cowl panel under the instrument panel.
• **Glow Plug Controller Thermal Switch (Diesel)** – is located on the left front side of the engine.
• **Glow Plug Dropping Resistors (Diesel)** – is located on the right front fender apron.
• **Glow Plug Relays (Diesel)** – are located on the right front fender apron.
• **Horn Relay** – is located below the bulkhead connector on the firewall.
• **Key Reminder Buzzer** – is located on the instrument panel near the bulkhead connector.
• **Lamp Reminder Buzzer** – is located on the audio alarm module.
• **Low Vacuum Warning Switch (Diesel)** – is located on the left side of the engine.
• **Oil Pressure Sender (Gas)** – is located on the left front side of the engine.
• **Oil Pressure Switch (Diesel)** – is located on the lower right rear side of the engine below the starter.
• **Oxygen Sensor** – is located in the exhaust manifold.
• **Power Steering Cut-Off Relay** – is located on the left side of the firewall in front of the electronic speed sensor.
• **Rear Defogger Control Timer** – is located on the right side of the instrument panel.
• **Seat Belt Buzzer** – is located below the left side of the dash panel ,on the right side of the fuse block.
• **Speed Sensor** – is located on the left side of the firewall on the gas engines and on the right rear side of the engine on the diesel engines.
• **Throttle Position Sensor** – is located on the throttle body.
• **Torque Converter Vacuum Switch** – is located on the right front of the engine on the diesel engines and on the left side engine cowl on the gas engines.
• **Vacuum Advance Relay** – is located on the left side of the firewall near the electronic speed sensor.

1982-84 BONNEVILLE AND GRAND PRIX

• **A/C Blower Relay** – is located in the blower motor assembly.
• **A/C Cut-Out Switch** – is located on the accelerator pedal.
• **A/C-Heater Blower Resistors** – is located in the heater module in front of the blower motor.
• **A/C Presuure Cycling Switch** – is located on the top of the vacuum tank.
• **A/C Temperature Cut-Out Relay** – is located behind the right front fender apron or at the center of the firewall.
• **A/C Temperature Cut-Out Switch** – is located on the left front side of the engine near the alternator.
• **Altitude Advance Relay (1984 Diesel)** – is located on the upper center of the firewall.
• **Barometric Pressure Sensor** – is located behind the right side of the instrument panel.
• **Brake Pressure Switch** – is located on the rear base of the left front wheel well.
• **"Check Engine" Light Driver Module** – is taped to the instrument panel harness to the left of the glove box.
• **Choke Heater Relay** – is located on the left engine cowl to the right of the steering column.
• **Cold Advance Diode (1984 Diesel)** – is located in the engine harness, to the right of the master cylinder.
• **Cold Inhibit Switch (Diesel)** – is located below the right valve cover.
• **Coolant Temperature Sensor** – is located on the front of ther engine behind the alternator on the V6 engines and on the top left front of the engine ong the V8. Behind the water on the diesel engine.
• **Coolant Temperature Switch** – is located on the top of

the engine behind the alternator or water pump on the V6 and diesel engine and on the left side of the engine near the exhaust manifold on the V8 engines.
• **Cruise Control Unit** – is located under the left side of the dash panel, above the accelerator pedal.
• **Defogger Timer (1982-83)** – is located under the left side of the instrument panel attached to the top of the fuse block.
• **Diesel Electronics Module** – is located behind the instrument panel to the right of the glove box behind the right kick panel.
• **Door Lock Relay** – is located on the lower right kick panel at the bottom access hole.
• **Early Fuel Evaporation (EFE) Relay** – is located on the front of the engine. On the 1984 models this relay is located at the right side of the engine compartment, above the wheel well.
• **Early Fuel Evaporation Solenoid** – is located at the top center of the right valve cover.
• **EGR Cut-Out Relay (1982-83)** – is located on the right front fender well.
• **EGR Solenoid** – is located at the top center of the right valve cover on the V6 engine and on the bracket rear of the right valve cover or top front left side on the V8 engines.
• **Electronic Control Module (ECM)** – is located on the right shroud near the lower access hole.
• **Electronic Spark Control Module (1984)** – is located above the right wheel well on the V6 engine and at the top left side of the engine on the V8 engine.
• **Engine Temperature Switch (Diesel)** – is located below the left valve cover. On the 84 models this switch is located behind the water pump.
• **Fast Idle Relay** – is located on the left side of the engine cowl.
• **Fast Idle Solenoid** – is located on the top of the engine near the front.
• **Fuel Metering Solenoid** – is located on the right side of the carburetor on the V6 engine and/or the top right side of the engine on the V8.
• **Gear Selector Switch** – is attached to the base of the steering column.
• **Glow Plug Controller** – is located at the top left rear of the engine, above the glow plug relay.
• **Glow Plug Relay (Diesel)** – is located on the top of the right front fender well.
• **High Altitude Advance Solenoid (1984 Diesel)** – is located in the fuel line, near the right valve cover.
• **Horn Relay** – is located behind the left side of the instrument panel above the fuse block.
• **Ignition Key Warning Buzzer** – is located behind the left side of the dash panel.
• **Lights-On Buzzer** – is attached to the fuse block.
• **Low Altitude Advance Solenoid (1984 Diesel)** – is located above the right valve cover.
• **Low Altitude Diode (1984 Diesel)** – is located in the engine harness, to the right of the master cylinder.
• **Low Brake Vacuum Delay Module** – is taped to the instrument panel harness above the fuse block.
• **Manifold Absolute Pressure Sensor** – is located on the top right front fender well.
• **Multi-Function Chime Module** – is located behind the instrument panel to the left of the steering column at the convenience center.
• **Oil Pressure Sender/Switch** – is located on the right rear of the engine on the V6 diesel and/or the front of the engine on the other engines.
• **Oxygen Sensor** – is located in the right rear exhaust manifold on the V6 and/or below the the right valve cover on the V8.
• **Power Antenna Relay** – is located behind the right side of the glove box on 1982-83 models on the 84 models the relay is behind the center of the instrument panel to the right of the

radio.

- **Power Door Lock and Power Seat Circuit Breaker**—is located in the fuse block.
- **Seat Belt Timer Buzzer**—is located behind left side of the instrument panel at the convenience center.
- **Theft Deterrent Control Unit**—is located behind the instrument panel to the left of the steering column.
- **Theft Deterrent Diode**—is taped to the instrument panel harness to the left of the steering column.
- **Theft Deterrent Relay**—is located behind the instrument panel to the left of the steering column.
- **Throttle Kicker Relay (1984)**—is located on the firewall near the brake booster.
- **Throttle Position Sensor**—is located at the front of the carburetor.
- **Tone Generator (1984)**—is located at the convenience center.
- **Torque Converter Clutch Switch**—is located on the brake pedal support.
- **Trunk Release Solenoid**—is located at the rear center of the trunk lid, just above the license plate.
- **Turbo Boost Indicator Switch**—is located above the front part of the left front fender well.
- **Vacuum Regulator Vacuum Switch (1984 Diesel)**—is located just forward of the intake manifold crossover.
- **Vacuum Sensor (on the V8)**—is connect to the right front fender well.
- **Vehicle Speed Sensor**—is located behind the speedometer.
- **Wastegate Solenoid**—is located at the rear of the left valve cover.
- **Wide Open Throttle Relay (1984)**—is located at the rear of the engine compartment.
- **Window and Sunroof Circuit Breaker**—is located under the left side of the dash panel, at the fuse block.

1985-87 BONNEVILLE AND GRAND PRIX

- **A/C Blower Relay**—is located on the evaporator case behind the acumulator
- **A/C Compressor Clutch Diode**—is taped to the inside compressor connector on the front of the compressor.
- **A/C Cut-Out Switch**—is located on the accelerator pedal bracket.
- **A/C Fast Idle Solenoid**—is located to the left of the carburetor on the gas engines and on the top center of the engine on the diesel models.
- **A/C-Heater Blower Resistors**—are located on the evaporator case in the engine compartment.
- **A/C Pressure Cycling Switch**—is located on the right side of the firewall on the accumulator.
- **A/C Temperature Cut-Out Relay**—is located behind the right front fender apron or at the center of the firewall.
- **Altitude Advance Relay (Diesel)**—is located on the upper center of the firewall.
- **Ambient Temperature Sensor**—is located under the right side of the dash panel, above rthe blower motor.
- **Anti-Diesel Solenoid**—is located on the left front valve cover.
- **Assembly Line Diagnostic Connector**—is located on the bootom left center of the dash panel.
- **Barometric Pressor Sensor (V6)**—is located behind the right side of the dash panel above the glove box.
- **Barometric Pressor Sensor (V8)**—is located on a braket with the ESC module.
- **Brake Accumulator Pressure Switch**—is located on the left side of the firewall, near the brake booster.
- **Brake Torque Converter Clutch Switch**—is located at the top of the brake pedal support.

- **Camshaft Sensor**—is located at the front center of the engine.
- **"Check Engine" Light Driver**—is taped to the instrumnet panel harness at the left of the glove box.
- **Choke Heater Relay**—is located on the left engine cowl to the right of the steering column.
- **Coolant Temperature Sending Unit**—is located at the top of the engine.
- **Coolant Temperature Sensor**—is located at the top of the engine.
- **Coolant Temperature Switch (3.8L)**—is located behind the water pump at the top of the engine.
- **Coolant Temperature Switch (4.3L)**—is located behind the A/C compressor.
- **Coolant Temperature Switch (V8)**—is located on the left side of the engine, below the exhaust manifold.
- **Crankshaft Sensor**—is located at the front center f the engine.
- **Cruise Control Module**—is located under the left isde of the dash panel, above the accelerator pedal.
- **Defogger Timer Relay**—is located under the left side of the instrument panel attached to the top of the fuse block.
- **Detonation (Knock) Sensor (3.8L)**—is located on the top rear side of the engine.
- **Detonation (Knock) Sensor (4.3L)**—is located on the lower left side of the engine block.
- **Detonation (Knock) Sensor (V8-Gas)**—is located on the lower right side of the engine block in fron tof the starter motor.
- **Diagnonstic Dwell Meter Connector**—is strapped to the wiring harness at the top right side of the engine.
- **Diesel Electronic Control Module (DEC)**—is located behind the right side kick panel.
- **Differential Pressure Sensor**—is located at the right front corner of the engine compartment behind the reservoir compartment.
- **Door Lock Relay**—is located on the lower right kick panel at the bottom access hole.
- **Early Fuel Evaporation (EFE)**—is located at the top of the engine, above the water pump.
- **Early Fuel Evaporation (EFE) Relay (with gauges)**—this relay is located at the left side of the engine compartment, above the wheel well.
- **Early Fuel Evaporation (EFE) Relay (without gauges)**—this relay is located at the right side of the engine compartment, above the wheel well.
- **EGR Temperature Switch (4.3L)**—is located on the intake manifold, in front of the distributor.
- **Electronic Control Module (ECM)**—is located behind the right kick panel.
- **Electronic Level Control Relay**—is located on the electronic level control compressor.
- **Electronic Level Control Sensor**—is located on the rear portion of the crossmember.
- **Electronic Spark Control Module (ESC)**—is located on the bracket at the top of the right front fender well.
- **Electronic Vacuum Regulator Valve Module**—is located at the top center of the right valve cover.
- **EPR Solenoid (Diesel)**—is located on the right valve cover.
- **Fast Idle Relay**—is located on the same bracket as the electronic sapark control module, which is located at the top of the right front fender well.
- **Fuel Control In-Line Fuse**—is located on the bracket next to the ESC module, on the 4.3L V6 engine.
- **Fuel Metering Solenoid (3.8L)**—is located on the carburetor.
- **Fuel Pump Prime Connector**—is located in the wiring harness near the fuel control in-line fuse.
- **Fuel Pump Relay**—is located on a bracket in the right side of the engine compartment.

- **Fuel Shut-Off Solenoid (Diesel)**—is located under the fuel injection pump cover.
- **Gear Selector Switch**—is attached to the base of the steering column.
- **Generator Diode**—is located taped in the harness behind the fuse block.
- **Glow Plug Controller/Relay (Diesel)**—is located on the top right (left on the Cutlass models) valve cover.
- **Glow Plug Relay (Diesel)**—is located on the top of the right front fender well.
- **Headlight Relay**—is located at the front side of the engine compartment, near the headlight.
- **Horn Relay**—is located behind the left side of the instrument panel above the fuse block.
- **Idle Stop Solenoid**—is located on the top of the engine and to the left of the carburetor.
- **Ignition Key Warning Buzzer**—is located behind the left side of the dash panel.
- **In-Car Sensor**—is located at the right side of the dash panel as part of the speaker grille assembly.
- **Low Brake Vacuum Delay Module**—is taped to the instrument panel harness, above the fuse block.
- **Manifold Absolute Pressure Sensor**—is located on the air cleaner on the 4.3L engine and at the right side of the engine compartment above the wheel well on all other engines.
- **Mass Airflow Sensor (EFI)**—is located on the air intake hose at the top left side of the engine compartment.
- **Metering Valve Sensor (Diesel)**—is located on the diesel injection pump.
- **Mixture Control Solenoid**—is located on the front or right side of the carburetor or throttle body.
- **Multi-Function Chime Module**—is located behind the instrument panel to the left of the steering column at the convenience center.
- **Oxygen Sensor**—is located in the exhaust manifold.
- **Power Accessory Circuit Breaker**—is located above the flasher relay in the fuse block.
- **Power Antenna Relay**—is located behind the center of the instrument panel to the right of the radio.
- **Power Master Brake Relay**—is located on top of the electro-hydraulic pump motor below the master cylinder.
- **Seat Belt Timer Buzzer**—is located behind left side of the instrument panel at the convenience center.
- **Theft Deterrent Controller**—is located under the left side of the dash panel, near the kick panel.
- **Theft Deterrent Diode**—is located behind the left side of the dash panel in connector " C-857".
- **Theft Deterrent Relay**—is located behind the instrument panel to the left of the steering column.
- **Third and Fourth Gear Switches**—are located in the middle of the left side of the transmission.
- **Throttle Position Sensor**—is located at the front of the carburetor or on the side of the throttle body.
- **Tone Generator**—is located behind the left side of the dash panel, in the convenience center.
- **Torque Converter Clutch solenoid**—is located in the middle of the left side of the transmission.
- **Trunk Release Solenoid**—is located at the rear of the trunk lid above the license plate.
- **Turbo Boost Gauge Sensor**—is located on the right front inner fender above the wheelwell.
- **Turbo Boost Indicator Switch**—is located on the right front fender , above the wheel well.
- **Twilight Sentinel Amplifier**—is located under the dash panel , near the radio.
- **Twilight Sentinel Photocell**—is located at the top center of the dash panel.
- **Vacuum Sensor**—is located at the rear of the engine above the valve cover.
- **Vehicle Speed Buffer**—is located under the left side of the dash panel, to the right of the steering column.
- **Vehicle Speed Sensor**—is located behind the dash panel and to the right of the steering column.
- **Water-In-Fuel Module (Diesel)**—is located at the top rear side of the engine.
- **Window and Sun Roof Circuit Breaker**—is located in the fuse block.
- **Wiper/Washer Motor Module**—is located on the upper left corner of the firewall in the engine compartment.

1984 PARISIENNE

- **A/C Blower Relay**—on the right side of the engine cowl, in front of the blower motor.
- **A/C Compressor Clutch Diode**—is taped to the inside compressor clutch connector.
- **A/C Compressor Cut-Out Switch**—is located below the left side of the instrument panel on the accelerator plate.
- **A/C-Heater Resistors**—is located on the right side of the engine cowl, infront of the blower motor.
- **A/C Pressure Cycling Switch**—is located on the right side of the ngine cowl, above the front relay.
- **A/C Programmer Unit**—is located behind the right side of the instrument panel.
- **A/C Temperature Cut-Out Relay**—is located on the top center of the engine cowl.
- **A/C Temperature Cut-Out Switch**—is located on the top front of the engine near the left valve cover.
- **Barometric Pressure Sensor (V6)**—is located behind the glove box.
- **Booster Low Vacuum Switch**—is located on the power boost unit.
- **Brake Pressure Switch**—is located under the left side engine cowl, attached to the frame.
- **Cold Inhibit Switch (Diesel)**—is located below the rear portion of the right valve cover.
- **Converter Clutch Switch (Diesel)**—is located on the brake pedal support.
- **Coolant Temperature Sender**—is located on the top left rear of the engine on the diesel models and on the front of the engine on the gas models.
- **Coolant Temperature Sensor (V6)**—is located is located on the front of the engine near the carburetor.
- **Cruise Control Throttle Servo**—is located on the top front portion of the engine.
- **Defogger Timer Relay**—is attached to the top of the fuse block.
- **Detonation (Knock) Sensor**—is located on the top left rear of the engine.
- **Diode Module (Diesel)**—is located on the top center of the engine cowl.
- **Door Lock Control Unit**—is located is attached to the upper right cowl.
- **Door Lock Relay**—is located on the upper right cowl.
- **Door Unlock Relay**—is located on the upper right cowl.
- **Early Fuel Evaporation Relay (V6)**—is located on the front top portion of the engine.
- **Early Fuel Evaporation Solenoid (V6)**—is located on the top center of the right valve cover.
- **EGR Solenoid**—is located on the top center of the right valve cover.
- **Electronic Control Module (ECM)**—is located on the right side kick panel.
- **Engine Temperature Switch (Diesel)**—is located below the rear portion of the left valve cover.
- **Fast Idle Solenoid (Diesel)**—is located on the top center of the engine in front of the injection pump.
- **Gear Selector Switch**—is located on the lower top portion of the steering column.
- **Glow Plug Relay (Diesel)**—is located on the front of the right front wheel well.

- **Glow Plug Thermal Control Unit (Diesel)** – is located on the top of the engine, in front of the fast idle solenoid.
- **Horn Relay** – is attached to the left side of the fuse block.
- **Idle Speed Control Unit (V6)** – is located on the left side of the carburetor.
- **Ignition Key Warning Buzzer** – is attached to the left side of the fuse block.
- **Illuminated Entry Timer** – is located on the upper left shroud, near the junction block.
- **Level Control Height Sensor** – is located on the rear center part of the crossmember.
- **Level Control Relay** – is located on the left front fender well, in front of the level control compressor.
- **Light Switch/Sentinel Control** – is located under the left side of the instrument panel, near the parking brake.
- **Lower Brake Vacuum Relay** – is located behind the instrument panel, to the left of the sterring column.
- **Manifold Absolute Pressure Sensor** – is located on the top of the front wheel well.
- **Mixture Control Solenoid** – is located in the carburetor.
- **Multi-Function Chime Module** – is located is located on the left side of the fuse block.
- **Oil Pressure Switch** – is located on the lower right side of the engine on the (V6) and on the top front left side of the engine on the V8 engines.
- **Oxygen Sensor** – is located on the rear right exhaust manifold on the V6 engine and on the rear left exhaust manifold on the V8 engine.
- **Power Seat Relay** – is located under the left or right seat.
- **Seat Belt Warning Buzzer** – is attached to the left side of the fuse block.
- **Seat Belt Warning Module** – is taped to the harnes located above the fuse block.
- **Temperature Indicator Switch** – is located on the front of the engine near the carburetor on the V6 engine and on the top left side of the engine on the V8 engines.
- **Throttle Position Sensor** – is located on the careburetor.
- **Tailgate Ajar Switch** – is located inside the lower right corner of the tailgate assembly.
- **Tone Generator** – is located under the left side of the instrument panel, near the parking brake.
- **Trunk Release Solenoid** – is located on the rear center of the trunk lid.
- **Twilight Sentinel Amplifier** – is located under the left side of the instrument panel, near the parking brake.
- **Twilight Sentinel Photocell** – is located on the left side of the engine cowl.
- **Vacuum Regulator Switch (Diesel)** – is located on the top center of the engine on the fuel injection pump.
- **Vacuum Sensor** – is located on the right front wheel well.
- **Vehicle Speed Sensor (V6)** – is located behind the instrument panel above the left side of the steering column.
- **Wait Lamp Control Relay (Diesel)** – is located on the top center of the engine cowl.
- **Wiper Motor Relay Diode** – is located in the wipwer motor connector.

1985-87 PARISIENNE

- **A/C Blower Relay** – is located in the engine compartment at the center of the firewall, near the blower motor.
- **A/C Compressor Clutch Diode** – is taped to the inside compressor connector on the front of the compressor.
- **A/C-Heater Blower Resistors** – is located in the engine compartment on the right side of the firewall near the blower motor.
- **A/C Programmer (Tempmatic)** – is located behind the right side of the dash panel.

- **A/C Temperature Cut-Out Relay** – is located on the top right front engine cowl.
- **Ambient Temperature Sensor** – is located in the right air inlet, below screen.
- **Assembly Line Data Link Connector** – is located under the left side of the dash panel, to the right of the steering panel.
- **Audio Alarm Module** – is located on the left side of the fuse block.
- **Automatic Door Lock Controller** – is attached to the upper portion of the right kick panel.
- **Automatic Door Lock Diode** – is located behind the left kick panel, near the lower access hole.
- **Barometeric Pressure Sensor** – is located behind the glove box.
- **Blower and Clutch Control Module** – is located on the top of the blower housing.
- **"Check Engine" Light Driver** – is taped to the instrument panel harness, above the glove box.
- **Coolant Temperature Sensor (3.8L)** – is located on the left front side of the engine.
- **Coolant Temperature Sensor (4.3L)** – is located on the front of the engine below the coolant outlet.
- **Coolant Temperature Sensor (5.0L & 5.7L)** – is located on the front side of the engine, on the coolant outlet.
- **Coolant Temperature Sensor (5.7L Diesel)** – is located on the left front side of the engine.
- **Cruise Control Module** – is located under the left side of the dash, to the left of the steering column.
- **Cruise Control Servo** – is located at the left front side of the engine on the gas models and above the left side valve cover on the diesel models.
- **Defogger Time Relay** – is located on the top of the fuse block.
- **Detonation (Knock) Sensor (6 cyl.)** – is located at the lower left rear side of the engine.
- **Detonation (Knock) Sensor (8 cyl.)** – is located at the right front side of the engine.
- **Diagnostic Dwell Meter Connector (Green)** – is taped the the wiring harness near the carburetor.
- **Diesel Electronic Control Module (DEC)** – is located behind the kick panel.
- **Early Fuel Evaporation Relay (3.8L)** – is located on the top right front engine cowl.
- **Electronic Control Module (ECM)** – is located behind the right kick panel.
- **Electronic Level Control Height Sensor** – is located on the rear center of the rear crossmember.
- **Electronic Level Control Relay** – is located on the left front fender, behind the horn.
- **Electronic Spark Control (ESC) Module** – is located on the right front side of the engine compartment.
- **Fast Idle Relay (4.3L)** – is located in the center of the firewall in the engine compartment.
- **Fuel Pump Relay (4.3L) Relay** – is located on the upper right inner fender panel.
- **Glow Plug Controller Relay (Diesel)** – is located on the top left rear of the engine.
- **Horn Relay** – is attached to the left side of the fuse block.
- **Illuminated Entry Timer** – is located behind the upper portion of the left kick panel, near the junction block.
- **In-Car Sensor** – is located in the right upper part of the dash, to the left of the right speaker.
- **Low Coolant Level Sensor** – is located in the radiator.
- **Manifold Absolute Pressure Sensor** – is located on the air cleaner.
- **Metering Valve Sensor (Diesel)** – is located on the diesel fuel injection pump.
- **Multi-Function Chime Module** – is located in the convenience center.
- **Oxygen Sensor** – is located on the exhaust manifold.

• **Power Antenna Relay**—is located on the bracket under the right side of the instrument panel, to the left of the glove box.
• **Power Door Lock Relay**—is located behind the bottom right kick panel.
• **Power Door Unlock Relay**—is located behind the upper portion of the right side kick panel.
• **Power Master Cylinder Brake In-Line Fuse**—is located under the left side of the dash panel, near the fuse block.
• **Power Master Cylinder Relay**—is located in the connector at the brake reservoir pump motor.
• **Power Seat Relay**—is located on under the right or left seat.
• **Seat Memory Module**—is located under the driver's seat.
• **Starter Interrupt Relay**—is located under the left side of the dash panel, above the steering column.
• **Theft Deterrent Controller**—is located under the left side of the dash, to the right of the steering column.
• **Theft Deterrent Diode**—is located under the left side of the dash panel, near the fuse block.
• **Theft Deterrent In-Line Fuses**—are located above the fuse block taped to the instrument panel wiring harness.
• **Theft Deterrent Relay**—is located at the right of the theft deterrent controller.
• **Throttle Position Sensor**—is located on the carburetor or throttle body.
• **Trailer Relays**—are located on the lower right corner of the fuse block.
• **Twilight Sentinel Amplifier**—is located on a bracket behind the right side of the dash panel.
• **Twilight Sentinel Control**—is located under the left side of the dash, to the right of the steering column.
• **Twilight Sentinel Photocell**—is located on the top left side of the dash panel.
• **Vacuum Sensor**—is located on the right front engine cowl.
• **Vehicle Speed Sensor**—is located behind the instrument panel, is a part of the cluster.
• **Vehicle Speed Sensor Buffer**—is taper top the instrument panel wiring under the left side of the daash near the fuse block.
• **Washer Pump Motor Diode**—is located in the washer motor connector.
• **Water-In-Fuel Module (Diesel)**—is located on top of the fuel filter assembly.
• **Wide Open Throttle Relay**—is located in the engine compartment at the center of the firewall.
• **Window and Sunroof Circuit Breaker**—is located at the top right corner of the fuse block.
• **Wiper Motor Relay Diode**—is located in the wiper motor connector.

1982-84 PHOENIX

• **A/C Clutch Diode**—is located inside the A/C compressor connector.
• **A/C Compressor Relay**—is located in the upper right corner of the engine cowl.
• **A/C Diode**—is located in the A/C harness, near the vacuum tank.
• **A/C-Heater Blower Resistors**—are located on the front of the plenum.
• **A/C High Speed Blower Relay**—is located on the top of the plenum, near the vacuum tank.
• **Audio/Buzzer Alarm Module**—is located on the conveience center.
• **Charging System Relay**—is taped to the instrument panel harness, above the accelerator pedal.
• **"Check Engine" Light Driver**—is taped to the right side of the instrument panel harness.

• **Choke Heater Relay**—is located behind the instrument panel.
• **Coolant Fan Relay**—is located on the left front wheel well.
• **Coolant Temperature Sensor**—is located on the left side of the coolant inlet on the 4 cylinder engines and on the top left front side of the engine on the V6 engines.
• **Defogger Timer/Relay**—is located above the glove box.
• **Door Lock Relay**—is located on the upper center of the right shroud.
• **Early Fuel Evaporation Heater Relay**—is located on the upper right side of the engine cowl.
• **Electronic Control Module (ECM)**—is located behind the instrument panel.
• **Fuel Pump Relay**—is located on the upper right side of the engine cowl.
• **Horn Relay**—is located in the convenience center.
• **Lights-On Buzzer**—is located behind the right side of the instrument panel, near the glove box.
• **Manifold Absolute Pressure Sensor**—is located on the right side of the air filter.
• **Oil Pressure Sender**—is located at the rear of the engine above the distributor on the 4 cylinder engines and above the oil filter on the V6 engines.
• **Oxygen Sensor**—is located in the exhaust manifold.
• **Power Accesories Circuit Breaker**—is located in the buse block.
• **Power Antenna Relay**—is located behind the right side of the instrument panel, near the glove box.
• **Power Window Circuit Breaker**—is located in the fuse block.
• **Throttle Position Sensor**—is located on the throttle body.
• **Vacuum Sensor**—is located in the upper right side of the engine cowl.
• **Vehicle Speed Sensor**—is located as part of the speedometer assembly.
• **Wiper Pulse Module**—is located behind the left side of the instrument panel.

1982-84 2000

• **A/C Ambient Air Sensor**—is located on the engine cowl, above the power steering reservoir.
• **A/C Blower Relay**—is located on the front center of the plenum.
• **A/C Compressor Control Relay**—is located behind the right front shock tower.
• **A/C Compressor Run Relay**—is located behind the right front shock tower.
• **A/C-Heater Blower Resistors**—are located on the front left side of the plenum.
• **Blocking Diode**—is located in the instrument panel harness, near the fuse block.
• **Coolant Fan Relay**—on the left front fender in front of the shock tower.
• **Coolant Temperature Sender**—is located on the left side of the engine, near the coolant outlet.
• **Coolant Temperature Sensor**—is located on the front of the engine on the thermostat housing on the 1.8L engine and on the left side of the engine under the water outlet on the other engines.
• **Cruise Control Throttle Servo**—is located on the bracket on the left front shock tower.
• **Defogger Time Relay**—is located behind the left side of the dash panel.
• **Door Lock Relay**—is located on the upper right side of the steering column support.
• **Electronic Control Module (ECM)**—is located behind the glove box.

- **Fuel Injection Ambient Sensor**—is located on the engine cowl above the washer reservoir.
- **Fuel Pump Relay**—is located on the right engine cowl, behind the shock tower.
- **Hatch/Tailgate/Trunk Release Relay**—is taped to the wire harness, located behind the right side of the radio.
- **Horn Relay**—is located on the conveience center.
- **Idle Speed Motor**—is taped in the EFI harness. to the right of the electronic control module.
- **Manifold Absolute Presure Sensor**—is located on the right shock
- **Oxygen Sensor**—is located in the exhaust manifold.
- **Power Accessories Circuit Breaker**—is located in the fuse block.
- **Power Antenna Relay**—is located behind the instrument panel, below the right side of the radio.
- **Power Window Circuit Breaker**—is located in the fuse block.
- **Throttle Position Sensor**—is located on the throttle body.
- **Torque Converter Clutch Relay (TCC)**—is located on the transmission cowling.
- **Vehicle Speed Sensor**—is located behind the instrument panel, the the right of the steering column.
- **Wiper Pulse Module**—is located below the steering column, above the trim cover.

1985-87 SUNBIRD

- **A/C Blower Relay**—is located on the front center of the plenum.
- **A/C Compressor Control Relay**—is located behind the right front shock tower.
- **A/C Compressor Run Relay**—is located behind the right front shock tower.
- **A/C-Heater Blower Resistors**—are located on the front left side of the plenum.
- **A/C In-Car Temperature Sensor**—is located on the right side of the dash, above the glove box.
- **Assembly Line Diagnostic Link**—is located behind the instrument panel, on the right side of the fuse block.
- **Blocking Diode**—is located in the instrument panel harness, near the bulkhead connector.
- **Coolant Fan Relay**—on the left front fender in front of the shock tower or on the firewall to the left of the brake booster.
- **Coolant Temperature Sender**—is located on the left side of the engine, near the coolant outlet.
- **Coolant Temperature Sensor**—is located on the front of the engine on the thermostat housing on the 1.8L engine and on the left side of the engine under the water outlet on the other engines.
- **Cruise Control Module (2-door)**—is located behind the instrument panel, above the left side of the steering column.
- **Cruise Control Module (4-door)**—is located behind the right side of the dash panel, above the glove box.
- **Defogger Time Relay**—is located behind the left side of the dash panel.
- **Electronic Control Module (ECM)**—is located behind the glove box.
- **Electronic Fuel Injection Ambient Sensor**—is located on the engine cowl above the washer reservoir.
- **Electronic Speed Sensor**—is located on the top right side of the transaxle.
- **Fog Lamp Relays**—are taped to the instrument panel harness, near the fog lamp switch.
- **Fuel Pump In-Line Fuse**—is located on the firewall, behind the brake booster.
- **Fuel Pump Relay**—is located on the right engine cowl,

behind the shock tower or on the firewall, above the brake booster.
- **Hatch/Tailgate/Trunk Release Relay**—is taped to the wire harness, located behind the right side of the radio.
- **Horn Relay**—is located on the conveience center.
- **Knock Sensor**—is located on the right side of the starter below the starter.
- **Low Coolant Module**—is located behind the instrument panel, above the left side of the steering column.
- **Low Coolant Temperature Sensor**—is located in the engine compartment, on the right front side of the radiator.
- **Manifold Absolute Presure Sensor**—is located on the right shock tower.
- **Manifold Air Temperature Sensor**—is located on the engine, underneath or on top of the intake manifold.
- **Mass Airflow Relay**—is located on the firewall, behind the brake booster.
- **Mass Airflow Sensor**—is located on the top of the left side of the engine, behind the air cleaner.
- **Mass Airflow Sensor In-Line Fuse**—is located on the firewall, behind the brake booster.
- **Outside Air Temperature Sensor**—is located inthe engine compartment, behind the right side of the grill.
- **Oxygen Sensor**—is located in the exhaust manifold.
- **Power Accessories/Convertible Top Circuit Breaker**—is located in the fuse block.
- **Power Antenna Relay**—is located behind the instrument panel, below the right side of the radio.
- **Power Door Lock Relay**—is located on the upper right side of the steering column support.
- **Power Unit Dimmer**—is located behind the instrument panel, to the left of the steering column.
- **Power Window Circuit Breaker**—is located in the fuse block.
- **Release Relay**—is taped to the instrument panel harness, behind the radio or glove box.
- **Throttle Position Sensor**—is located on the throttle body. On the 2.8L engine it is located, behind the distributor.
- **Torque Converter Clutch Relay (TCC)**—is located on the transmission cowling.
- **Turbo Release Relay**—is located on the transaxle cowling.
- **Twilight Sentinel Amplifier**—is located behind the instrument panel, to the left of the steering column.
- **Twilight Sentinel Photocell**—is located on the dash panel, on the right side of the defrost vent.
- **Vehicle Speed Sensor**—is located behind the instrument panel, the the right of the steering column.
- **Vehicle Speed Sensor Buffer**—is located behind the instrument cluster, below the speed sensor.

1983-84 6000

- **A/C Blower Resistors**—is located on the right side of the engine cowl.
- **A/C Compressor Relay**—is located on the upper right corner of the engine cowl.
- **A/C Delay Relay**—is located in the upper right corner of the engine cowl.
- **A/C High Pressure Cut-Out Switch**—is located on the left side of the compressor.
- **A/C Temperature Cut-Out Switch**—is located on the top of the engine near the fuel filter.
- **Audio Alarm Module**—is located behind the instrument panel, to the left of the steering column.
- **Charging System Relay**—is located behind the instrument panel, near the fuse block.
- **"Check Engine" Light Driver**—is taped to the instrument panel harness behind the glove box.

- **Choke Relay (Non EFI)**—is located on the convenience center.
- **Coolant Fan Relay**—is located on the left front wheel well on the bracket on the 4 cylinder engine and on the fender panel ahead of the left front shock tower on the V6 engine.
- **Coolant Fan Switch**—is located in front of the engine below the left side valve cover on the 4 cylinder engine and on the top of the V6 engine in front of the distributor.
- **Coolant Temperature Sensor**—is located on the left center side of the 4 cylinder engines and on the top of the V6 engine in front of the distributor.
- **Coolant Temperature Switch**—is located on the top of the engine near the fuel filter.
- **Diagnostic Dwell Meter Connector**—is located near the upper right side of the engine cowl.
- **Diesel Diode Module**—is located on the right side of the engine cowl on a bracket.
- **Early Fuel Evaporation Heater Relay**—is located on the upper right side of the engine cowl.
- **Electronic Control Module (ECM)**—is located behind the right side of the instrument panel.
- **Electronic Level Control Height Sensor**—is located on the frame under the trunk.
- **Electronic Level Control Relay**—is located on the frame behind the left rear wheel well.
- **Fuel Pump Relay**—is located on the upper right side of the engine cowl.
- **Glow Plug Relay (Diesel)**—is located behind the left battery on the wheel well.
- **Headlight-Key-Seat Buzzer**—is located on the convenience center.
- **Heater Blower Resistors**—is located on the right plenum.
- **Horn Relay**—is located on the convenience center.
- **Low Brake Vacuum Relay**—is taped to the instrument panel above the fuse block.
- **Low Brake Vacuum Switch**—is located on top of the brake booster unit.
- **Manifold Absolute Pressure Sensor**—is located in the upper right engine cowl on the 4 cylinder engines and on the behind the right front shock tower on the V6 engines.
- **Oxygen Sensor**—is located in the exhaust manifold.
- **Power Antenna Relay**—is located behind the instrument panel on the rear of the glove box.
- **Power Accessories Circuit Breaker**—is located in the fuse block.
- **Power Window Circuit Breaker**—is located in the fuse block.
- **Thermal Controller (Diesel)**—is located on the top of the engine near the fuel filter.
- **Throttle Position Sensor**—is located on the throttle body.
- **Wait Lamp Control Relay (Diesel)**—is located in the upper right corner of the engine cowl on a bracket.
- **Water-In-Fuel Sensor**—is located in the fuel tank.

1985-87 6000

- **A/C Blower Resistors**—is located on the right side of the engine cowl.
- **A/C Compressor Relay**—is located on the upper right corner of the engine cowl.
- **A/C Delay Relay**—is located in the upper right corner of the engine cowl.
- **A/C Heater Blower Relay**—is located on the plenum, on the right side of the firewall.
- **A/C High Pressure Cut-Out Switch**—is located on the left side of the compressor.
- **A/C Temperature Cut-Out Switch**—is located on top of the engine near the fuel filter.

- **Altitude Advance Relay**—is located on the left inner fender, in front of the shock tower.
- **Assembly Line Diagnostic Link**—is located on the bottom of the instrument oanel, near the steering column.
- **Audio Alarm Module**—is located behind the instrument panel, to the left of the steering column.
- **Barometric Pressure Sensor**—is located on the firewall, at the right side of the blower motor.
- **Buffer Amplifier**—is located behind the right side of the instrument panel, in front of the electronic control module.
- **Charging System Relay**—is located behind the instrument panel, near the fuse block.
- **"Check Engine" Light Driver**—is taped to the instrument panel harness behind the glove box.
- **Choke Relay (Non EFI)**—is located on the convenience center.
- **Constant Run Relay**—is located on the left inner fender wheel well.
- **Coolant Fan In-Line Fuse**—is located in the engine compartment in front of the left front shock tower.
- **Coolant Fan Low-Speed Relay**—is located on the left inner fender wheel well, on a bracket on the 4 cylinder engines and on the fender panel in front of the left front shock tower on the V6 models.
- **Coolant Fan Relay**—is located on the left front wheel well on the bracket on the 4 cylinder engine and on the fender panel ahead of the left front shock tower on the V6 engine.
- **Coolant Fan Switch**—is located in front of the engine below the left side valve cover on the 4 cylinder engine and on the top of the V6 engine in front of the distributor.
- **Coolant Temperature Sensor**—is located on the left center side of the 4 cylinder engines and on the top of the V6 engine in front of the distributor.
- **Coolant Temperature Switch**—is located on the top of the engine near the fuel filter.
- **Cruise Control Module**—is located behind the instrument panel, above the accelerator pedal.
- **Defogger Timer Relay**—is located behind the instrument panel, under the instrument cluster.
- **Diagnostic Dwell Meter Connector**—is located near the upper right side of the engine cowl.
- **Diesel Diode Module**—is located on the right side of the engine cowl on a bracket.
- **Diesel Electronic Controller (DEC)**—is located behind the right side of the instrument panel.
- **Diesel Generator Diode**—is located in the engine harness, to the right of the glow plug controller.
- **Early Fuel Evaporation Heater Relay**—is located on the upper right side of the engine cowl.
- **Electronic Control Module (ECM)**—is located behind the right side of the instrument panel.
- **Electronic Level Control Height Sensor**—is located on the frame under the trunk or in front of the fuel tank on the Wagon models.
- **Electronic Level Control Relay**—is located on the frame behind the left rear wheel well.
- **Fuel Pump Relay**—is located on the upper right side of the engine cowl.
- **Glow Plug Controller/Relay (Diesel)**—is located on the rear of the engine, to the left of the cylinder head.
- **Glow Plug Relay (Diesel)**—is located behind the left battery on the wheel well.
- **Headlight-Key-Seat Buzzer**—is located on the convenience center.
- **Heater Blower Resistors**—is located on the right plenum.
- **High Mount Stop Light Relays**—are located on the left rear wheel well , in the trunk.
- **Horn Relay**—is located on the convenience center.
- **Knock Sensor**—is located on the top left side of the engine, below the front of the oxygen sensor.

- **Low Brake Vacuum Relay**—is taped to the instrument panel above the fuse block.
- **Low Brake Vacuum Switch**—is located on top of the brake booster unit.
- **Manifold Absolute Pressure Sensor**—is located in the upper right engine cowl on the 4 cylinder engines and on the behind the right front shock tower on the V6 engines.
- **Manifold Air Temperature Sensor**—is located in the canister, at the front of the engine compartment.
- **Mass Airflow Relay**—is located in the engine compartment, on the front of the left shock tower.
- **Mass Airflow Sensor In-Line Fuse**—is located in the engine compartment, on the front of the left shock tower.
- **Metering Valve Sesnor (MVS)**—is located on top of the engine.
- **Oxygen Sensor**—is located in the exhaust manifold.
- **Power Accessories Circuit Breaker**—is located in the fuse block.
- **Power Antenna Relay**—is located behind the instrument panel on the rear of the glove box.
- **Power Door Lock Relay**—is located on the right shroud, to the right of the glove box.
- **Power Window Circuit Breaker**—is located in the fuse block.
- **Pulse Relay**—is located on the left inner fender, in ftont of the left front shock tower.
- **Rear Wiper Relay**—is located in the top center of the tailgate.
- **Sentinel Amplifier**—is located behind the center of the instrument panel, behind the ashtray.
- **Speed Sensor**—is located on the top right side of the transaxle.
- **Starter Interrupt Relay**—is located above the ashtray, taped to the instrument panel harness.
- **Theft Deterrent Relay**—is located behind the instrument panel, strapped to the theft deterrent controller.
- **Thermal Controller (Diesel)**—is located on the top of the engine near the fuel filter.
- **Throttle Kicker Relay**—is located on the front of the engine compartment, at the right side of the radiator support.
- **Throttle Position Sensor**—is located on the throttle body.
- **Wait Lamp Control Relay (Diesel)**—is located in the upper right corner of the engine cowl on a bracket.
- **Water-In-Fuel Sensor**—is located in the fuel tank.

1985-87 GRAND AM

- **A/C Compressor Clutch Diode**—is located in the connector at the compressor clutch.
- **A/C Compressor Control Relay (2.5L)**—is located on the relay bracket at the center of the firewall in the engine compartment.
- **A/C Cooling Fan Relay (3.0L)**—is located on the relay bracket at the center of the firewall in the engine compartment.
- **A/C Cut-Out Relay (3.0L)**—is located on the relay bracket at the center of the firewall in the engine compartment.
- **A/C-Heater Blower Motor Relay**—is located on the right side of the firewall in the engine compartment, to the left of the blower motor.
- **Audio Alarm Module**—is located on the fuse block or above the glove box.
- **Computer Control Ignition Module (3.0L)**—is located at the top right rear of the engine.
- **Cooling Fan Relay**—is located is located on the relay bracket at the center of the firewall in the engine compartment.

- **Cooling Fan Resistor (3.0L)**—is located on the lower bracket behind the cooling fan.
- **Coolant Temperature Sensor**—is located at the top right end of the engine (top left on the 2.5L engine).
- **Cruise Control Module**—is attached under the rear of the left side of the dash panel.
- **Defogger Timer Relay**—is located behind the left side f the dash panel, near the fuse block.
- **Driver Information Center Display Module**—is located in the center of the dash, below the radio.
- **Driver Information Center Lights Monitor Module**—is located below the center of the dash panel, in front of the console.
- **Dual Crank Sensor (3.0L)**—is located on the lower right front side of the engine.
- **Electronic Control Module (ECM)**—is located behind the right side kick panel.
- **Electronic Spark Control Module (3.0L)**—is located is located on the relay bracket at the center of the firewall in the engine compartment.
- **Fog Light Relay**—is located on the left front inner fender panel, in front of the shock tower.
- **Fuel Pump Relay**—is located on the relay bracket at the center of the firewall in the engine compartment.
- **Generator Diode (2.5L)**—is located in the instrument panel wiring harness, under the left side of the dash panel.
- **High Mount Stop Lamp Relays**—are located on the left rear wheelwell inside the trunk.
- **Horn Relay**—is located in the instrument panel wiring harness near the fuse block.
- **Illumination Control Relay**—is located behind the center of the instrument panel, in front of the console.
- **Knock (Detonation) Sensor (3.0L)**—is located at the top left side of the engine.
- **Manifold Absolute Pressure Sensor (2.5L)**—is located on the air cleaner assembly.
- **Manifold Absolute Pressure Sensor (3.0L)**—is located on the left side of the engine compartment, behind the radiator.
- **Manifold Airflow Sensor (3.0L)**—is located on the left side of the engine compartment, behind the radiator.
- **Oxygen Sensor**—is located in the exhaust manifold.
- **Power Accessories Circuit Breaker**—is located in the fuse block.
- **Power Antenna Relay**—is located at the right side of the trunk.
- **Power Door Lock Relay Assembly**—is located behind the right side kick panel.
- **Power Window Circuit Breaker**—is located in the fuse block.
- **Remote Dimmer Module**—is located in the instrument panel wiring harness, to the right of the radio.
- **Throttle Postion Sensor**—is located on the throttle body.
- **Vehicle Speed Sensor (ATX)**—is located at the rear of the engine, on the right end of the transaxle.
- **Vehicle Speed Sensor (MTX)**—is located at the rear of the engine, on the top of the transaxle.
- **Vehicle Speed Sensor Buffer Amplifier**—is located behind the right side of the dash panel.
- **Wiper/Washer Motor Module**—is located in the left rear corner of the engine compartment, to the right of the shock tower.

1982-83 FIREBIRD AND TRANS AM

- **A/C Blower Resistors**—are located near the blower motor on the A/C module.
- **A/C Blower Speed High Speed Relay**—is located near the blower module on the A/C module.

- **A/C Compressor Relay** – is located on the left side engine cowl near the brake bosster.
- **A/C Pressure Cycling Switch** – is located on the accumulator/drier.
- **"Check Engine" Light Driver Module** – is taped to the instrument panel harness near the console.
- **Choke Relay** – is located in the convenience center.
- **Coolant Temperature Sensor (4 cyl. and V6)** – is located on the top left side of the engine.
- **Coolant Temperature Sensor (V8 Carb.)** – is located on the lower left side of the engine.
- **Coolant Temperature Sensor (V8 E.F.I.)** – is located on the lower right side of the engine.
- **Coolant Temperature Switch (4 cyl. and V6)** – is located on the top left side of the engine.
- **Coolant Temperature Switch (V8 Carb.)** – is located on the lower left side of the engine.
- **Coolant Temperature Switch (V8 E.F.I.)** – is located on the lower right side of the engine.
- **Cruise Control Servo** – is located on the left rear inner fenser panel.
- **Early Fuel Evaporation Relay** – is located on the upper right side of the engine cowl.
- **Electronic Control Module (ECM)** – is located behind the right side of the instrument panel.
- **Electronic Spark Control Unit** – is located on the left side of the engine cowl.
- **Fuel Pump Relay** – is located on the left side of the engine cowl.
- **Hatch Release Relay** – is located under the front part of the console.
- **Headlight Warning Buzzer** – is located in the convenience center.
- **Hood Louver Relay** – is located on the left side of the engine cowl.
- **Horn Relay** – is located in the convenience center.
- **Knock Sensor (V8)** – is located on the lower right side of the engine.
- **Manifold Absolute Pressure Sensor (4 cyl.)** – is located on the right rear of the engine.
- **Manifold Absolute Pressure Sensor (V8 E.F.I.)** – is located on the left side of the engine cowl.
- **Oxygen Sensor** – is located in the exhaust manifold/
- **Power Antenna Relay** – is located behind the right side of the instrument panel lower cover.
- **Seat Belt Warning Buzzer** – is located in the covenience center.
- **Throttle Kicker Relay (V8)** – is located on the left side of the engine cowl.
- **Vacuum Sensor** – is located on the upper left side of the engine cowl.

1984-87 FIREBIRD AND TRANS AM

- **A/C Blower Relay Assembly (Berlinetta)** – is located under the dash in the module on the A/C plenum housing.
- **A/C Blower Resistors** – are located near the blower motor on the A/C module.
- **A/C Blower Speed High Speed Relay** – is located near the blower module on the A/C module.
- **A/C Compressor Diode** – is taped to the inside of the compressor clutch connector.
- **A/C Compressor Relay** – is located on the left side engine cowl near the brake bosster.
- **A/C Control Module (Berlinetta)** – is located in the right side of the dash panel.
- **A/C-Heater Blower Resistors** – are located on the right side of the engine cowl.
- **A/C Pressure Cycling Switch** – is located on the accumulator/drier.

- **Assembly Line Diagnostic Link** – is located at the convenience center.
- **Barometric Pressure Sensor** – is located on the top right side of the engine cowl.
- **Beam Change Relay (Berlinetta)** – is located inside the light module.
- **Burn Off Relay** – is located behind the ECM.
- **"Check Engine" Light Driver Module** – is taped to the instrument panel harness near the console.
- **Choke Heater Relay** – is located int he convenience center.
- **Coolant Temperature Sensor (4 cyl.)** – is located on the coolant outlet on the front of the engine.
- **Coolant Temperature Sensor (V6)** – is located on the top of the engine behind the A/C cpompressor.
- **Coolant Temperature Sensor (V8)** – is located on the top front of the engine behind the alternator.
- **Coolant Temperature Switch (4 cyl.)** – is located in the rear of the engine, near the oil filler tube.
- **Coolant Temperature Switch (V6)** – is located on the top front section of the engine.
- **Coolant Temperature Switch (V8)** – is located on the left cylinder head below the valve cover.
- **Cooling Fan Relay (V6)** – is located on the left side of the firewall.
- **Cooling Fan Relay (V8)** – is located on the right side of the radiator or the left side of the firewall.
- **Courtesy Light Relay (Berlinetta)** – is located in the light module.
- **Cruise Control Module** – is located behind the right side of the dash.
- **Cruise Control Servo** – is located on the left rear inner fenser panel.
- **Diagnostic Dwell Meter Connector (V6)** – is taped next to the ECM harness, next to the right valve cover.
- **Diagnostic Dwell Meter Connector (V8)** – is taped next to the ECM harness, behind the right shock tower.
- **Early Fuel Evaporation Relay** – is located on the upper right side of the engine cowl.
- **EGR Diagnostic Connector** – is on the top rear section of the engine.
- **Electronic Control Module (ECM)** – is located behind the right side of the instrument panel.
- **Electronic Spark Control Unit** – is located on the left side of the engine cowl.
- **Fast Idle Relay (V6)** – is located behind the right headlight on the side of the radiator.
- **Fast Idle Relay (V8)** – is located on the upper right side of the engine cowl.
- **Flasher Select Relay** – is located inside the light module.
- **Fog Light Relay** – is located on the left rear inner fender panel.
- **Fuel Pump In-Line Fuse** – is located on the right front wheel well in the engine compartment.
- **Fuel Pump Relay** – is located on the left side of the engine cowl.
- **Generator Diode** – is located behind the left side of the dash panel.
- **Hatch Release Relay** – is located under the front part of the console.
- **Headlight Relay** – is located inside the light module.
- **Headlight Warning Buzzer** – is located in the convenience center.
- **Heater Blower Resistors** – are located on the blower motor.
- **Hood Louver Relay** – is located on the left side of the engine cowl.
- **Horn Relay** – is located in the convenience center.
- **Isolation Relay** – is located behind the right headlight.
- **Knock Sensor (V8)** – is located on the lower right side of the engine.

- **Left Turn Signal Relay**—is located inside the light module.
- **Light Control Module (Berlinetta)**—is located under the right side od the dash panel next to the ECM.
- **Light Monitor Module**—is located on the upper left side of the dash panel, above the clutch pedal.
- **Low Blower Relay**—is located on the right side of the firewall, near the blower motor.
- **Manifold Absolute Pressure Sensor**—is located on the front of the air cleaner assembly.
- **Mass Airflow Relay**—is located on the right side of the radiator support bracket.
- **Mass Airflow Sensor (4 cyl.)**—is located on top of the air horn, at the front of the engine compartment.
- **Mass Airflow Sensor (8 cyl.)**—is located on top of the engine.
- **Mass Airflow Sensor In-Line Fuse (V6)**—is located in the right front corner of the engine comaprtment.
- **Mass Airflow Sensor In-Line Fuse (V8)**—is located behind the battery, near the positive battery cable.
- **Oxygen Sensor**—is located in the exhaust manifold/
- **Park/Turn Relay**—is located inside the light module.
- **Power Accessories Circuit Breaker**—is located in the fuse block.
- **Power Antenna Relay**—is located behind the right side of the instrument panel lower cover.
- **Power Door Lock Relay**—is located behind the left kick panel in the lower opening.
- **Power Window/Rear Wiper Circuit Breaker**—is located in the fuse block.
- **Rear Defogger Timer/Relay**—is located below the right side of the dash, near the ECM.
- **Rear Hatch Release Relay**—is located under the console.
- **Right Turn Signal Relay**—is located inside the light module.
- **Seat Belt Warning Buzzer**—is located in the covenience center.
- **Speed Buffer (Berlinetta)**—is located on the left kick panel under the dash.
- **Throttle Kicker Relay (V8)**—is located on the left side of the engine cowl or the right frint inner fender panel.
- **Throttle Position Sensor (4 cyl.)**—is located on the top right side of the engine.
- **Throttle Position Sensor (V6)**—is located on the top front section of the engine.
- **Throttle Position Sensor (V8)**—is located on the top right side of the engine.
- **Vacuum Sensor**—is located on the upper left side of the engine cowl.
- **Vehicle Speed Sensor**—is located on the printed circuit at the rear of the speedometer on all models except Berlinetta. On the Berlinetta the speed sensor is located on the left side of the transmission below the shifter.
- **Wide Open Throttle Relay**—is located in the left rear corner of the engine compartment.
- **Wiper/Washer Motor Module**—is located on the upper left side of the engine cowl.

1984-87 FIERO

- **A/C Compressor Clutch Diode**—is taped to the tinside compressor connector.
- **A/C Compressor Control Relay**—is located on the left side of the rear bulkhead.
- **A/C-Heater Blower Resistors**—is located on the lower right side of the A/C-Heater plenum.
- **A/C Power Relay**—is located in the front compartment, on the right side of the A/C-Heater plenum.
- **Assembly Line Diagnostic Link Connector**—is located at the fron tof the console.
- **Convenience Center**—is located under the right side of the dash panel.
- **Coolant Temperature Sending Unit**—is located on the top left section of the engine.
- **Coolant Temperature Sensor**—is located on the top left side of the engine (it is on the right side of the V6 engine).
- **Cooling Fan Relay**—is located on the left front corner of the front compartment.
- **Cruise Control Module**—is located on the left side of the console, between the seats.
- **Defogger Timer/Relay**—is located on the brake pedal support brace.
- **Door Lock Relays**—is located near the right upper shroud.
- **Electronic Control Module (ECM)**—is located between the seats on the rear bulkhead.
- **Fuel Pump Relay**—is located on the left side of the rear bulkhead.
- **Generator Diode**—is located in the main harness, below the bulkhead grommet.
- **Headlight Actuator Relay**—is located in the front compartment, next to each headlight.
- **High Speed Blower Relay**—is located on the right side of the A/C-Heater plenum.
- **Horn Relay**—is located on the convenience center.
- **In-Line Diode**—is located in the wiring harness, behind the left side of the dash panel.
- **Isolation Relay**—is located on the left side of the front compartment.
- **Manifold Absolute Pressure Sensor**—is located on the right side of the air cleaner.
- **Manifold Air Temperature Sensor**—is located on the top of the engine, near the air cleaner.
- **Oxygen Sensor**—is located on the front side of the engine, at the base of the exhaust manifold.
- **Power Accessories Circuit Breaker**—is located in the fuse block.
- **Power Window Circuit Breaker**—is located in the fuse block.
- **Speed Sensor**—is located on the right side of the transaxle.
- **Throttle Position Sensor**—is located on the right side of the throttle body.
- **Trunk Release Relay**—is located behind the dash panel, near the A/C control panel.
- **Wiper Pulse Module**—is located on the outside of the right steering column bracket.

COMPONENT LOCATIONS

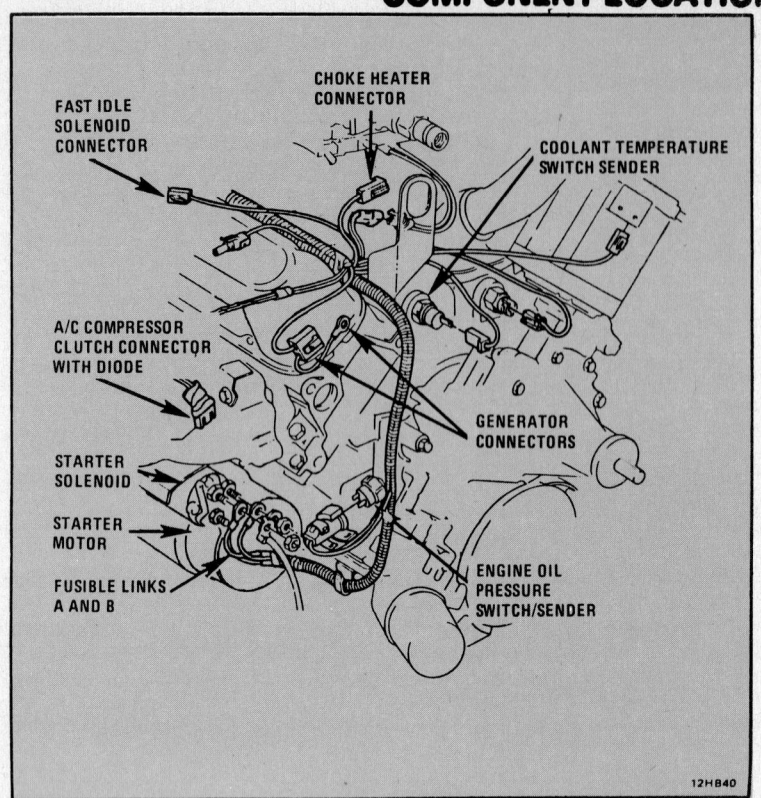

FAST IDLE SOLENOID CONNECTOR

CHOKE HEATER CONNECTOR

COOLANT TEMPERATURE SWITCH SENDER

A/C COMPRESSOR CLUTCH CONNECTOR WITH DIODE

GENERATOR CONNECTORS

STARTER SOLENOID

STARTER MOTOR

FUSIBLE LINKS A AND B

ENGINE OIL PRESSURE SWITCH/SENDER

Figure A - Front Of VIN A Engine (With Gages Shown, Without Gages Similar)

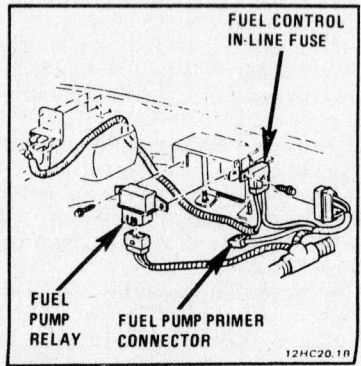

VACUUM SENSOR

RH VALVE COVER

Figure B - RH Rear Of Engine VIN H Shown, VIN A Similar

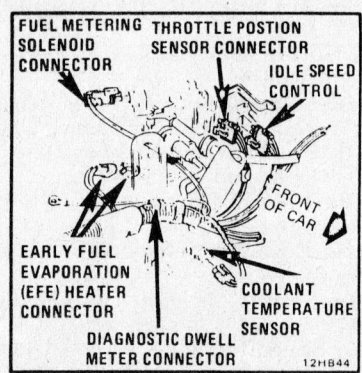

FUEL CONTROL IN-LINE FUSE

FUEL PUMP RELAY

FUEL PUMP PRIMER CONNECTOR

Figure C - RH Side Of VIN Z Engine Compartment

1985-86 Pontiac Grand Prix and Bonneville

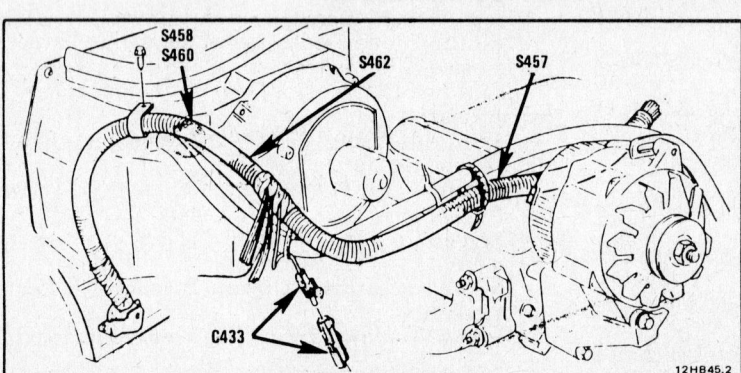

S458 S460

S462

S457

C433

Figure A - RH Side Of Engine Compartment

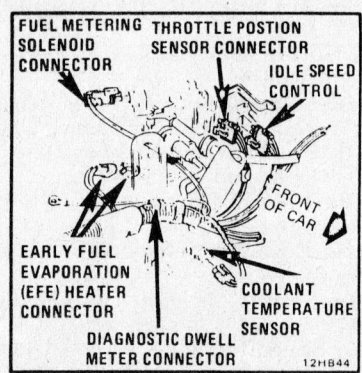

FUEL METERING SOLENOID CONNECTOR

THROTTLE POSTION SENSOR CONNECTOR

IDLE SPEED CONTROL

FRONT OF CAR

EARLY FUEL EVAPORATION (EFE) HEATER CONNECTOR

DIAGNOSTIC DWELL METER CONNECTOR

COOLANT TEMPERATURE SENSOR

Figure D - Top Front Of VIN A Engine

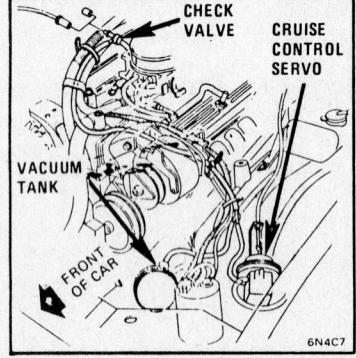

CHECK VALVE

CRUISE CONTROL SERVO

VACUUM TANK

FRONT OF CAR

Figure B - LH Side Of VIN Z Engine Compartment

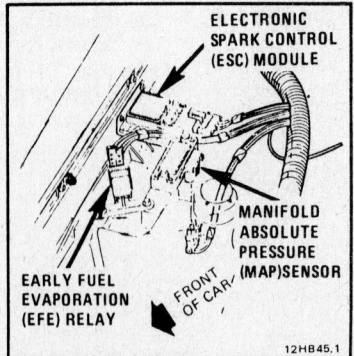

ELECTRONIC SPARK CONTROL (ESC) MODULE

MANIFOLD ABSOLUTE PRESSURE (MAP) SENSOR

EARLY FUEL EVAPORATION (EFE) RELAY

FRONT OF CAR

Figure C - RH Side Of VIN A Engine Compartment

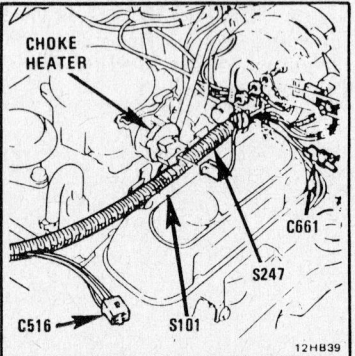

CHOKE HEATER

C661

S247

C516

S101

Figure E - Top Of VIN A Engine

1985-86 Pontiac Grand Prix and Bonneville

COMPONENT LOCATIONS

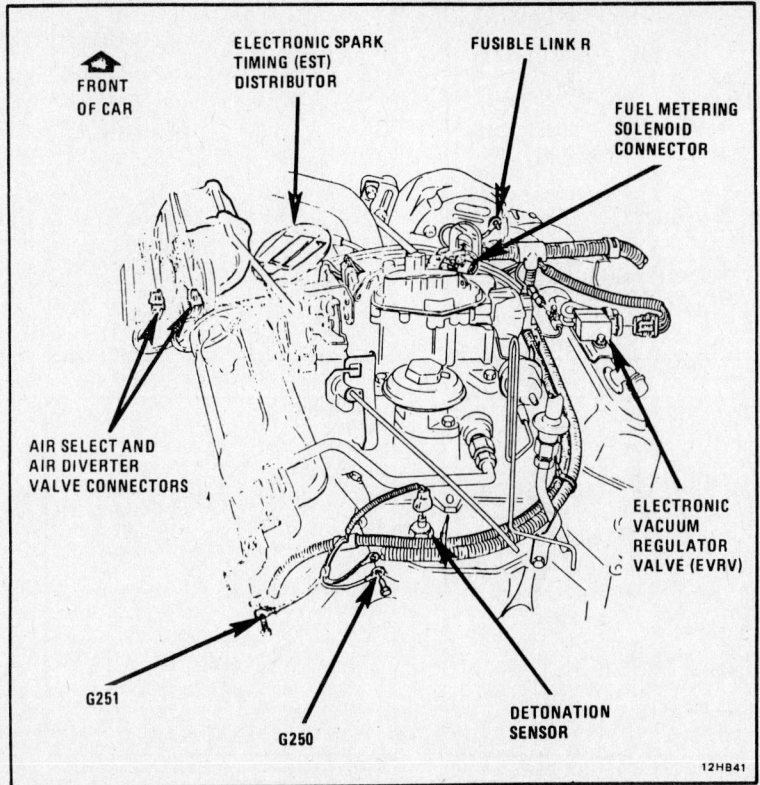

Figure A - Top Of VIN A Engine

1985-86 Pontiac Grand Prix and Bonneville

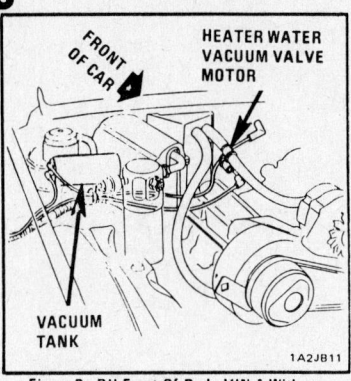

Figure B - RH Front Of Dash, VIN A Without Cruise Control

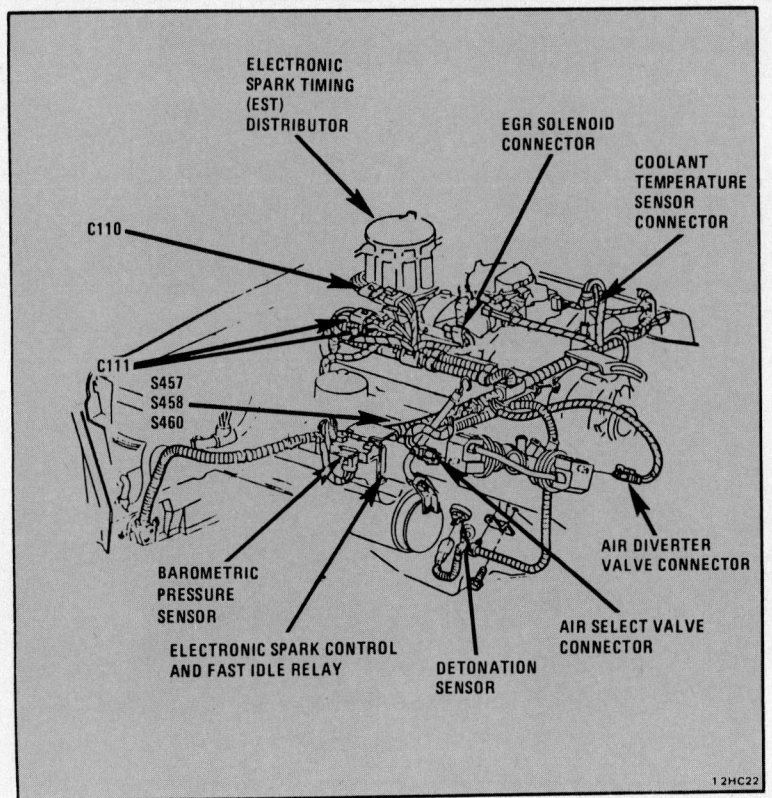

Figure A - RH Side Of VIN H Engine

1985-86 Pontiac Grand Prix and Bonneville

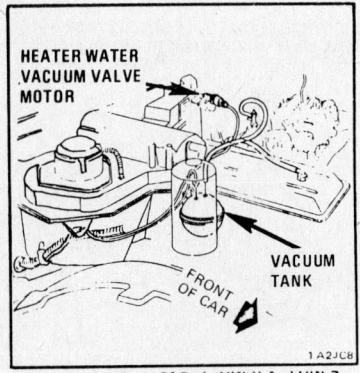

Figure B - RH Front Of Dash, VIN H And VIN Z, Without Cruise Control

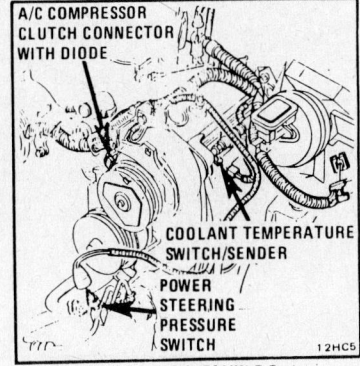

Figure C - LH Side Of VIN Z Engine

COMPONENT LOCATIONS

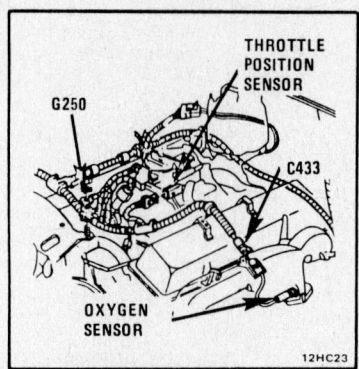

Figure A - LH Side Of VIN H Engine

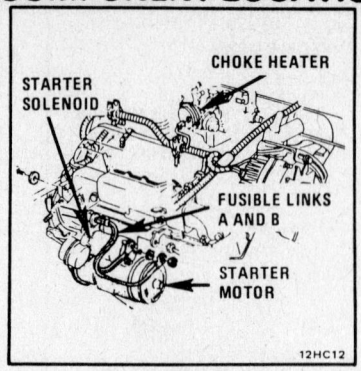

Figure C - RH Side Of VIN H Engine

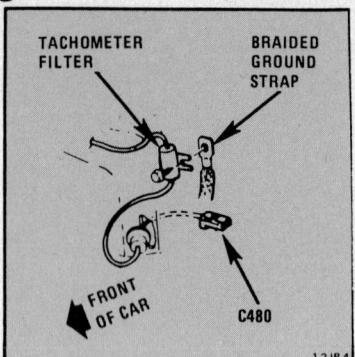

Figure E - Center Of Front Of Dash

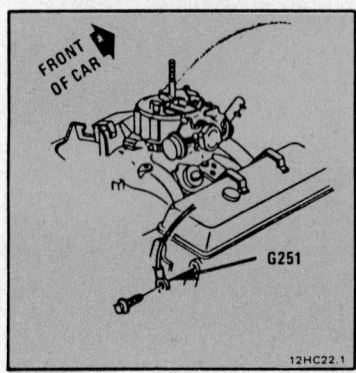

Figure B - Top Of VIN H Engine

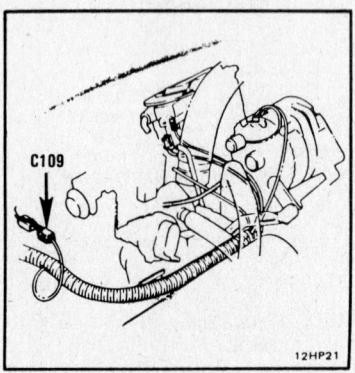

Figure D - Top Of Engine, VIN A Shown, VIN H And VIN Z Similar

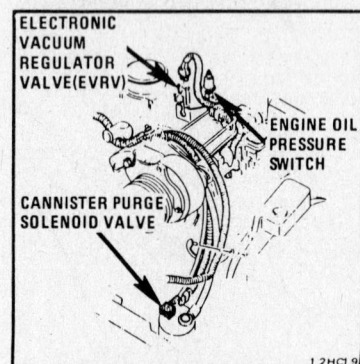

Figure F - LH Side Of VIN Z Engine Compartment

1985-86 Pontiac Grand Prix and Bonneville

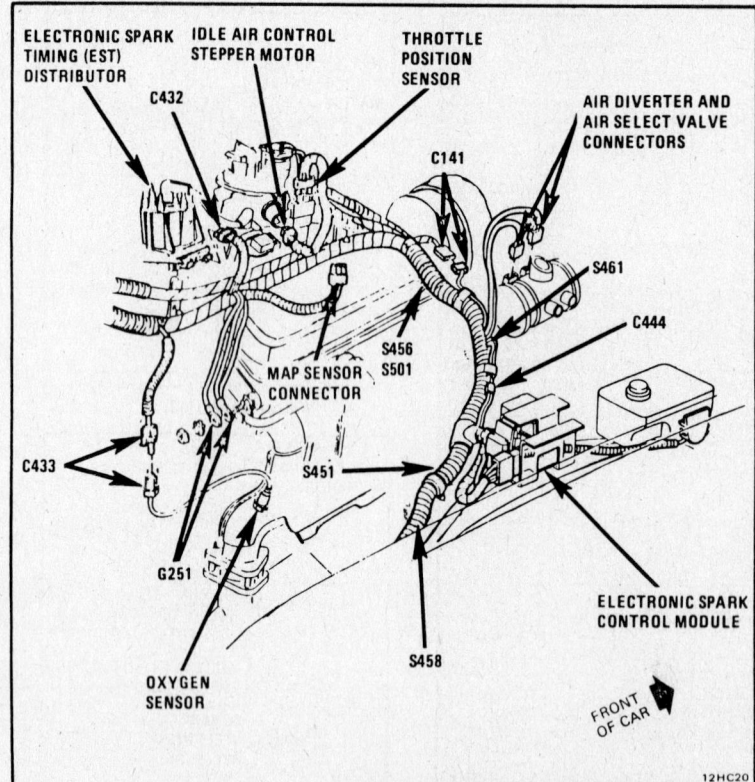

Figure A - RH Side Of VIN Z Engine

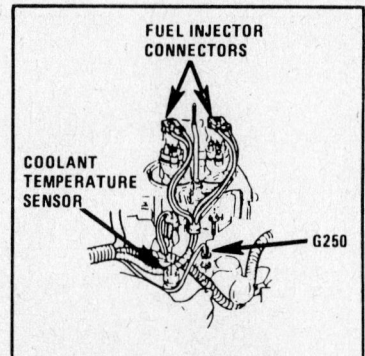

Figure B - Top Of VIN Z Engine

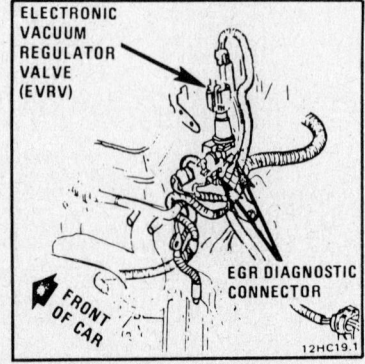

Figure C - Rear Of VIN Z Engine

1985-86 Pontiac Grand Prix and Bonneville

COMPONENT LOCATIONS

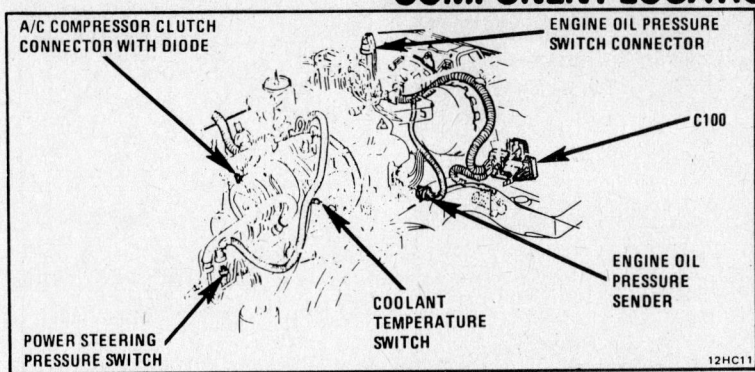

Figure A - LH Side Of VIN H Engine

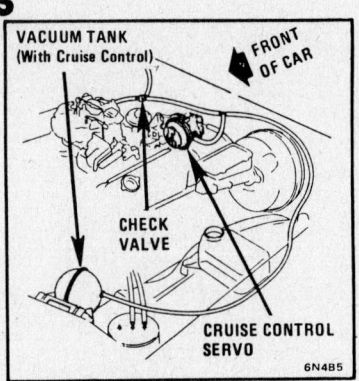

Figure C - Engine Compartment VIN A Shown, VIN H Similar

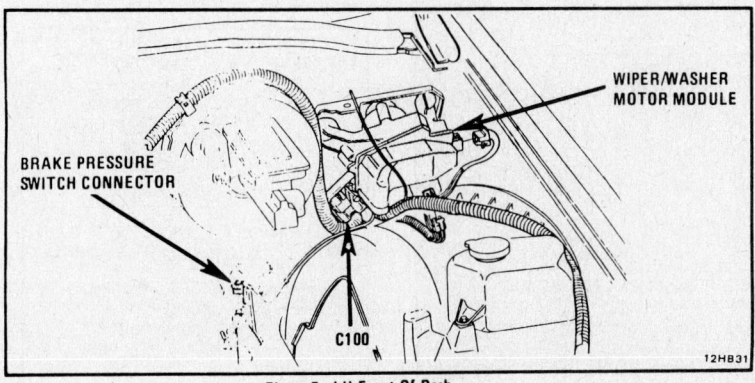

Figure B - LH Front Of Dash

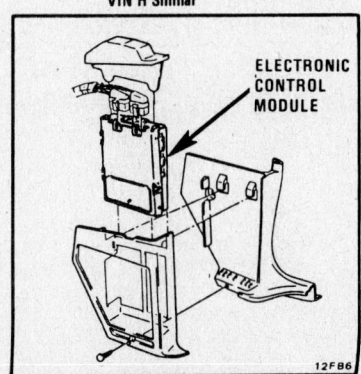

Figure D - RH Shroud

1985-86 Pontiac Grand Prix and Bonneville

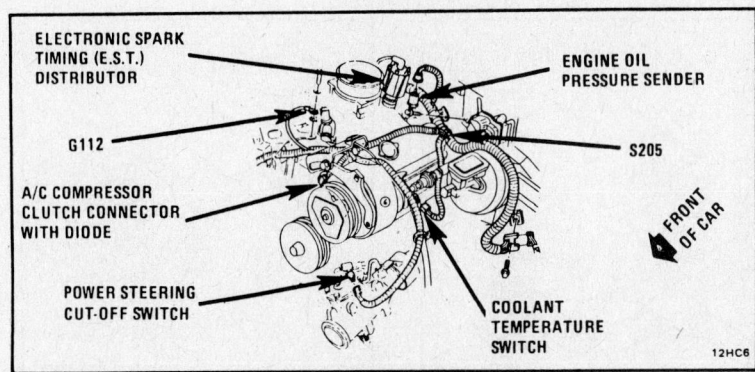

Figure A - LH Side Of Engine (VIN Z)

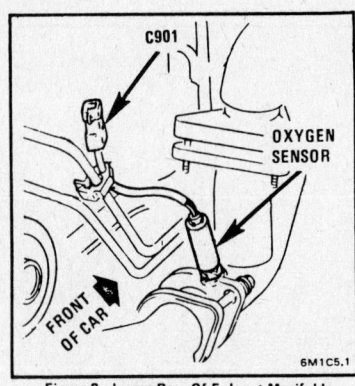

Figure C - Lower Rear Of Exhaust Manifold (VIN Z)

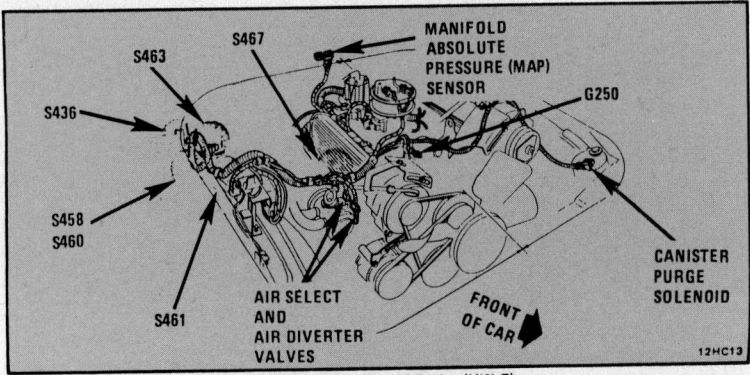

Figure B - RH Side Of Engine (VIN Z)

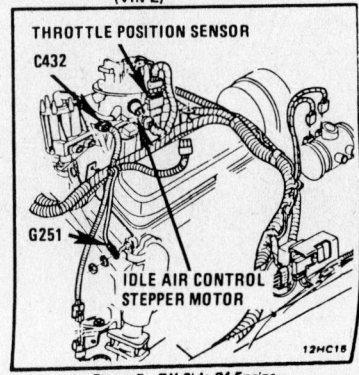

Figure D - RH Side Of Engine

1985-86 Pontiac Parisienne

221

COMPONENT LOCATIONS

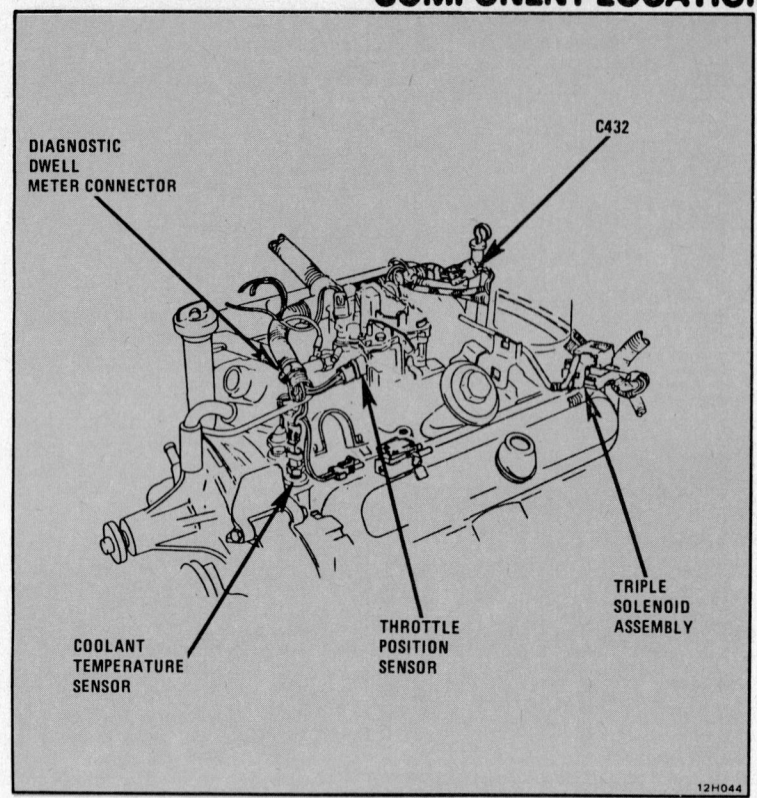

Figure A - Top Of VIN Y Engine

DIAGNOSTIC DWELL METER CONNECTOR

C432

COOLANT TEMPERATURE SENSOR

THROTTLE POSITION SENSOR

TRIPLE SOLENOID ASSEMBLY

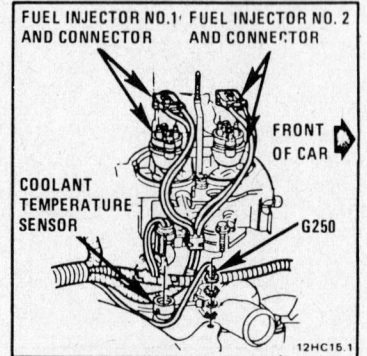

Figure B - RH Side Of Engine Compartment
(VIN Z Shown, VIN H Similar)

BATTERY JUNCTION BLOCK

FUEL CONTROL IN-LINE FUSE

FUEL PUMP RELAY

FUEL PUMP PRIMER CONNECTOR

ELECTRONIC SPARK CONTROL MODULE

FRONT OF CAR

FUEL INJECTOR NO.1 AND CONNECTOR

FUEL INJECTOR NO. 2 AND CONNECTOR

FRONT OF CAR

COOLANT TEMPERATURE SENSOR

G250

Figure C - Top Of Throttle Body (VIN Z)

1985-86 Pontiac Parisienne

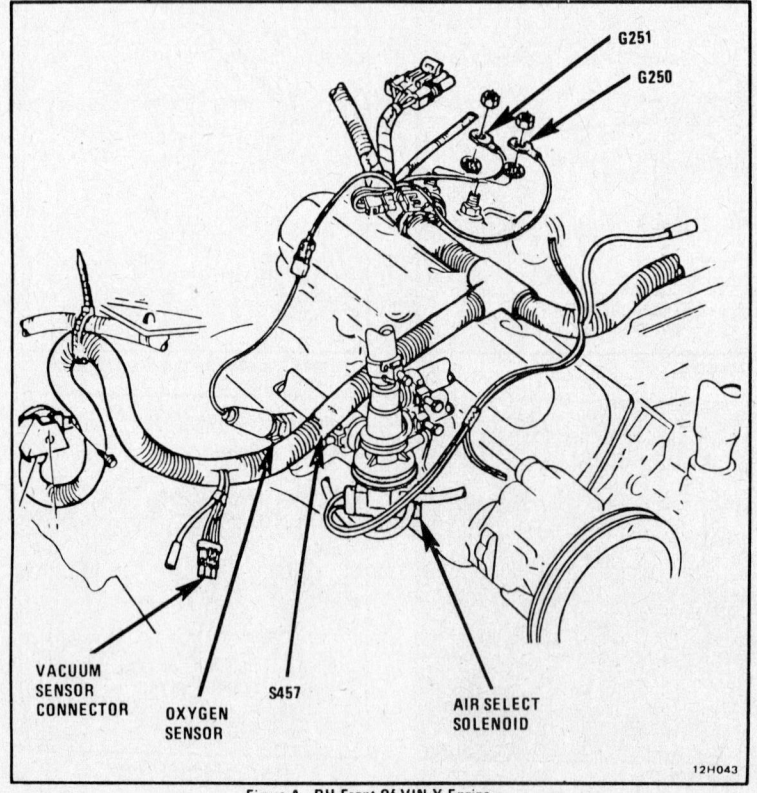

Figure A - RH Front Of VIN Y Engine

G251

G250

VACUUM SENSOR CONNECTOR

OXYGEN SENSOR

S457

AIR SELECT SOLENOID

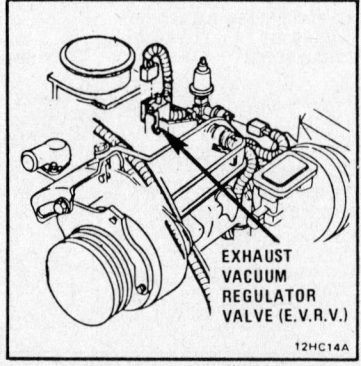

Figure B - LH Side Of VIN Z Engine

EXHAUST VACUUM REGULATOR VALVE (E.V.R.V.)

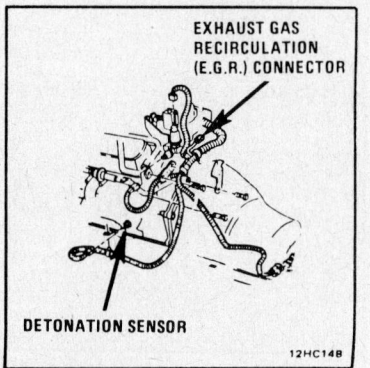

Figure C - LH Rear Of VIN Z Engine

EXHAUST GAS RECIRCULATION (E.G.R.) CONNECTOR

DETONATION SENSOR

1985-86 Pontiac Parisienne

COMPONENT LOCATIONS

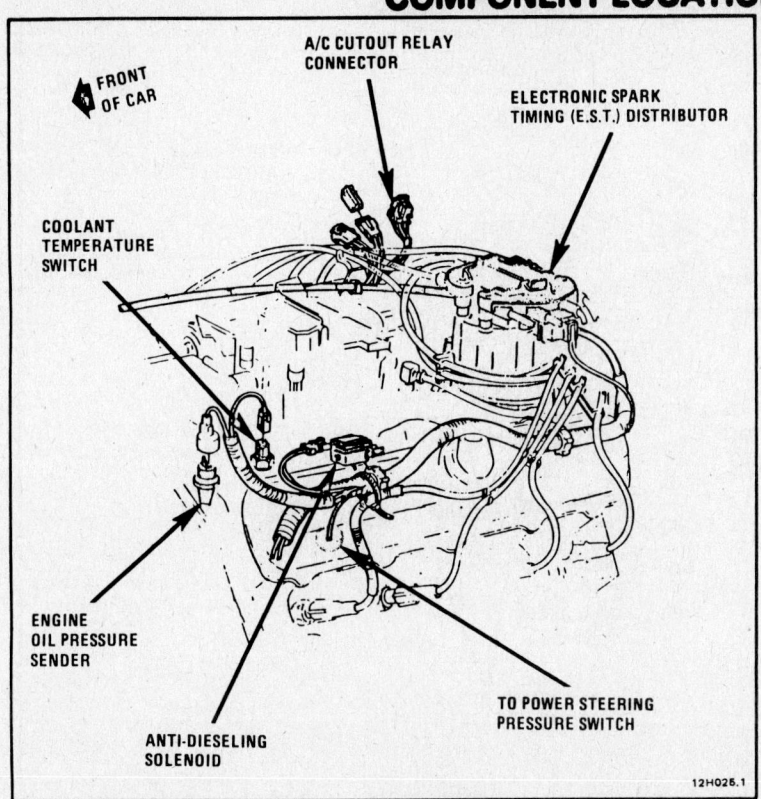

Figure A - Top LH Of VIN Y Motor

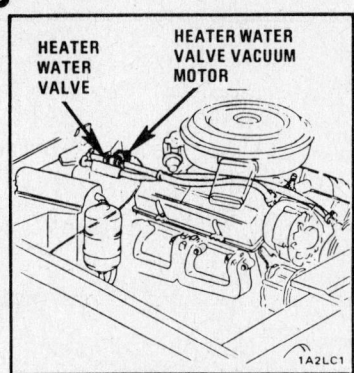

Figure B - RH Side Of Engine (V6 Shown, V8 Similar)

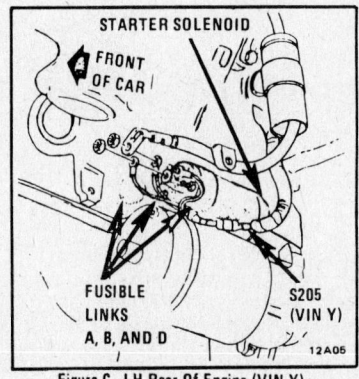

Figure C - LH Rear Of Engine (VIN Y)

1985-86 Pontiac Parisienne

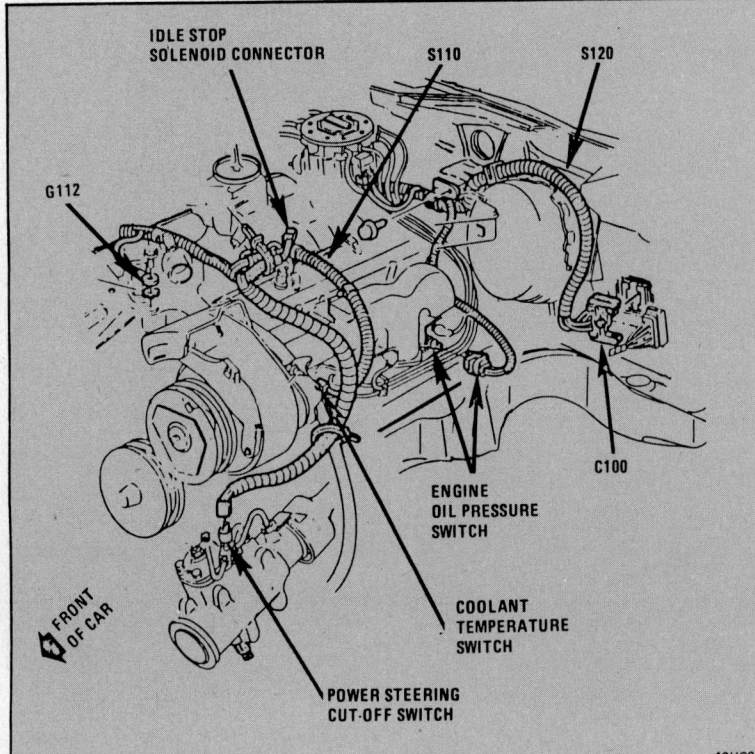

Figure A - LH Side Of Engine Compartment (VIN H)

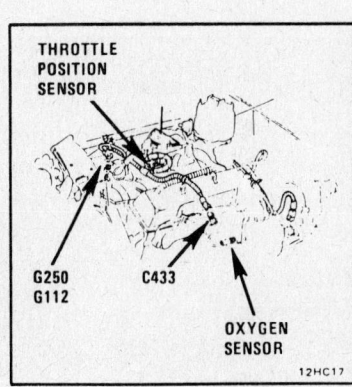

Figure B - Top Of VIN H Engine

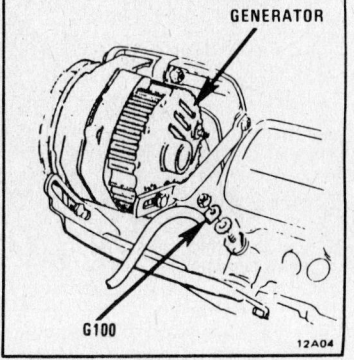

Figure C - LH Front Of Engine (VIN Y)

1985-86 Pontiac Parisienne

COMPONENT LOCATIONS

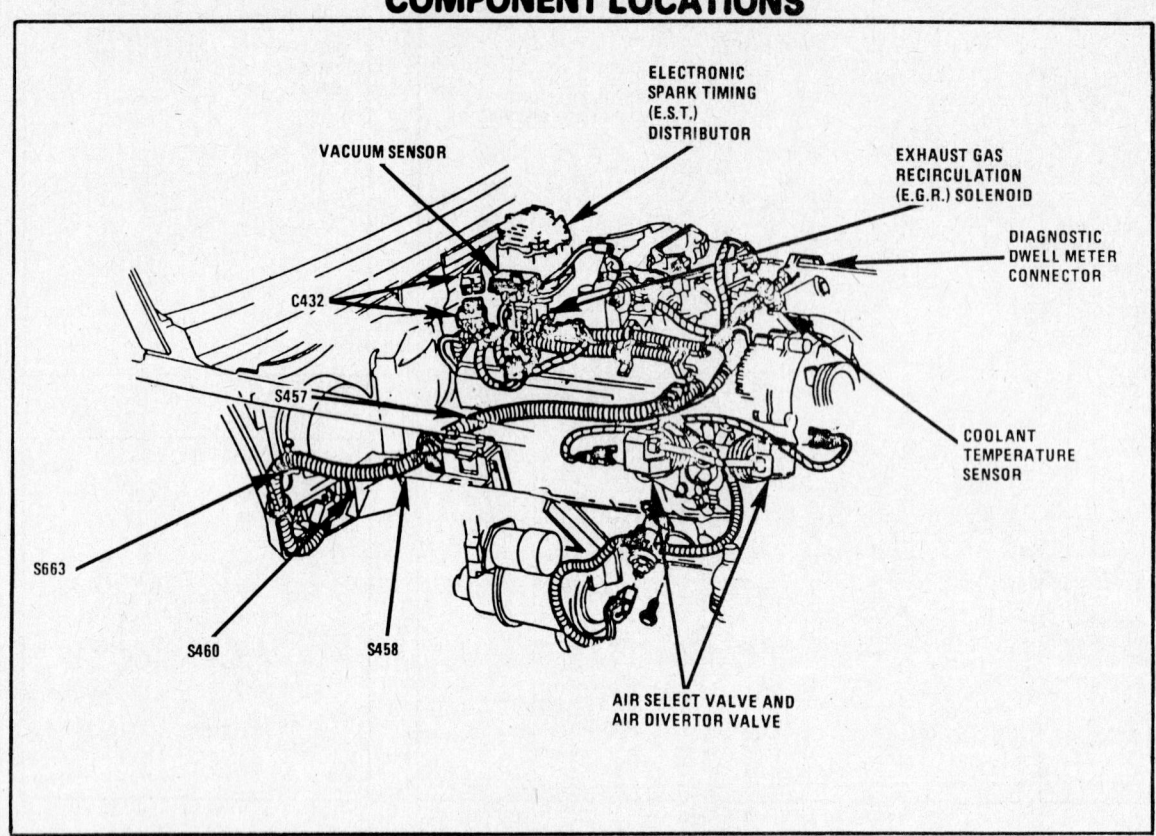

VACUUM SENSOR

ELECTRONIC SPARK TIMING (E.S.T.) DISTRIBUTOR

EXHAUST GAS RECIRCULATION (E.G.R.) SOLENOID

DIAGNOSTIC DWELL METER CONNECTOR

C432

S457

COOLANT TEMPERATURE SENSOR

S663

S460

S458

AIR SELECT VALVE AND AIR DIVERTOR VALVE

1985-86 Pontiac Parisienne

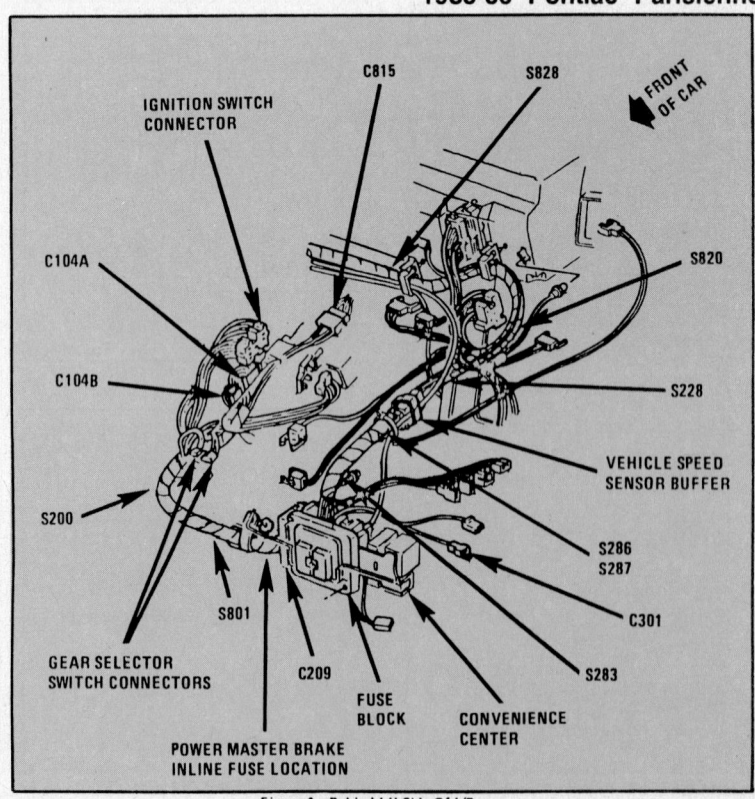

C815

S828

FRONT OF CAR

IGNITION SWITCH CONNECTOR

C104A

S820

C104B

S228

VEHICLE SPEED SENSOR BUFFER

S200

S286
S287

C301

S801

C209

FUSE BLOCK

S283

GEAR SELECTOR SWITCH CONNECTORS

CONVENIENCE CENTER

POWER MASTER BRAKE INLINE FUSE LOCATION

Figure A - Behind LH Side Of I/P

1985-86 Pontiac Parisienne

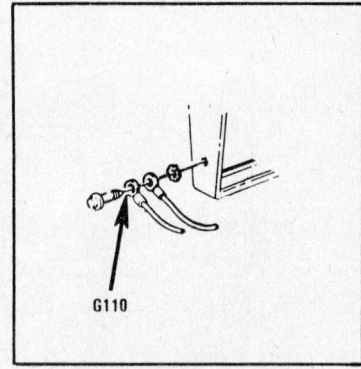

G110

Figure B - LH Steering Column Brace

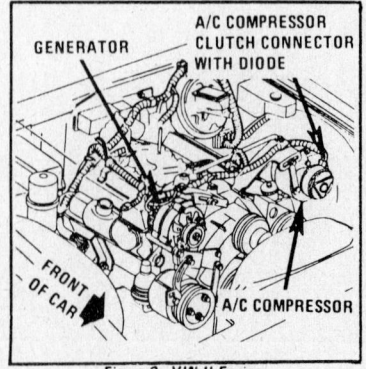

GENERATOR

A/C COMPRESSOR CLUTCH CONNECTOR WITH DIODE

FRONT OF CAR

A/C COMPRESSOR

Figure C - VIN H Engine

COMPONENT LOCATIONS

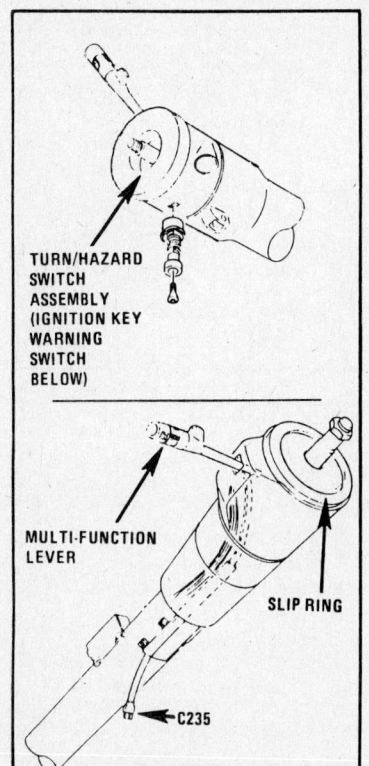

TURN/HAZARD
SWITCH
ASSEMBLY
(IGNITION KEY
WARNING
SWITCH
BELOW)

MULTI-FUNCTION
LEVER

SLIP RING

C235

Figure A - Top Of Steering Column

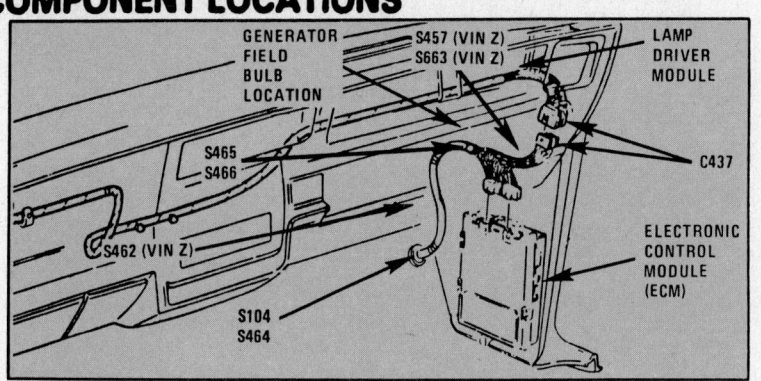

GENERATOR
FIELD
BULB
LOCATION

S457 (VIN Z)
S663 (VIN Z)

LAMP
DRIVER
MODULE

S465
S466

C437

S462 (VIN Z)

ELECTRONIC
CONTROL
MODULE
(ECM)

S104
S464

Figure B - RH Side Of I/P

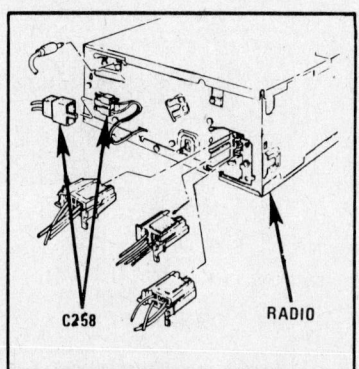

C258

RADIO

Figure C - Center Of I/P Behind Radio

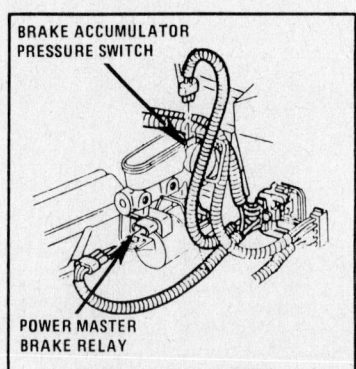

BRAKE ACCUMULATOR
PRESSURE SWITCH

POWER MASTER
BRAKE RELAY

Figure D - LH Front Of Dash
(Station Wagon Only)

1985-86 Pontiac Parisienne

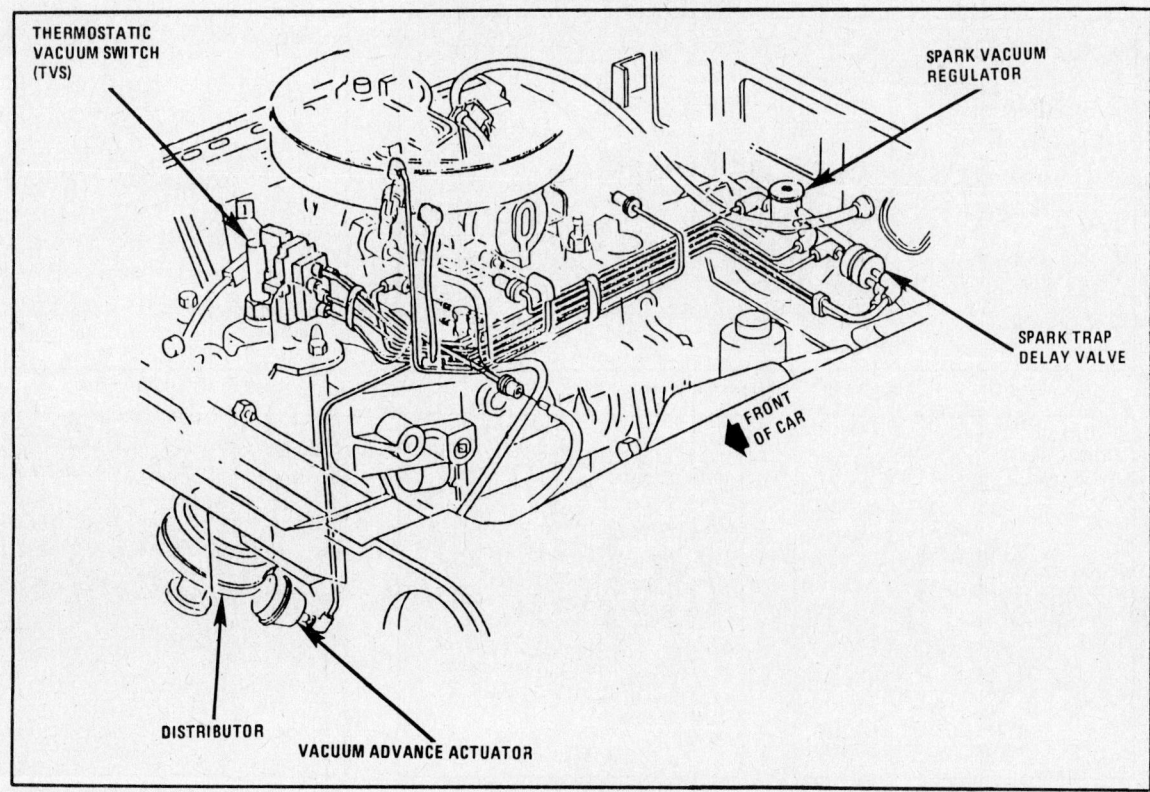

THERMOSTATIC
VACUUM SWITCH
(TVS)

SPARK VACUUM
REGULATOR

SPARK TRAP
DELAY VALVE

FRONT
OF CAR

DISTRIBUTOR

VACUUM ADVANCE ACTUATOR

Figure A - LH Side Of Engine

1985-86 Pontiac 1000

COMPONENT LOCATIONS

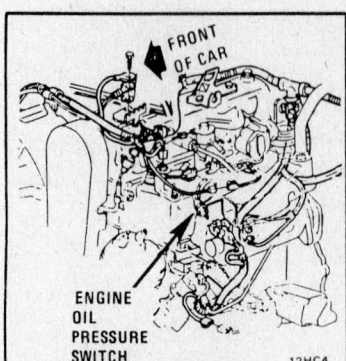

Figure A - LH Side Of Engine

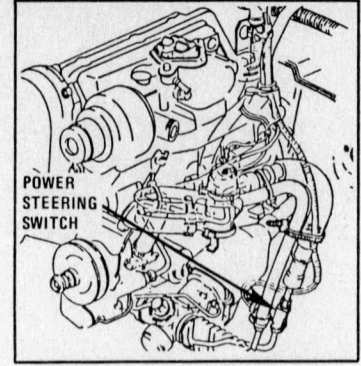

Figure C - LH Side Of Engine Compartment

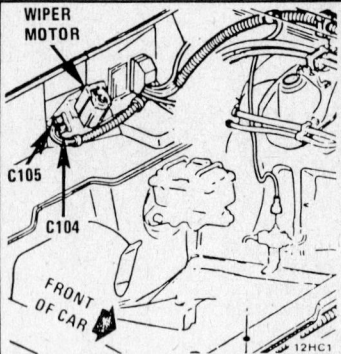

Figure E - Center Front Of Dash

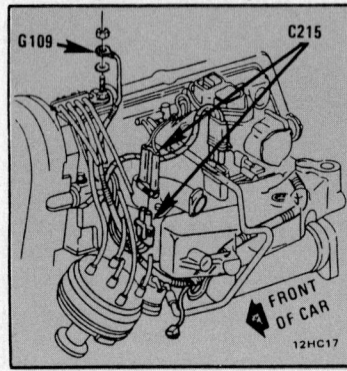

Figure B - LH Side Of Engine

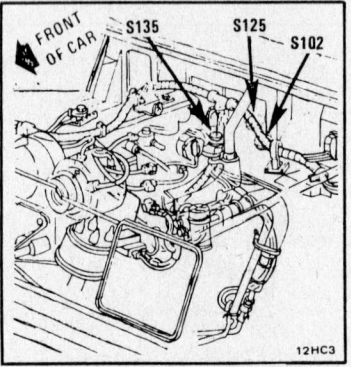

Figure D - Engine Compartment

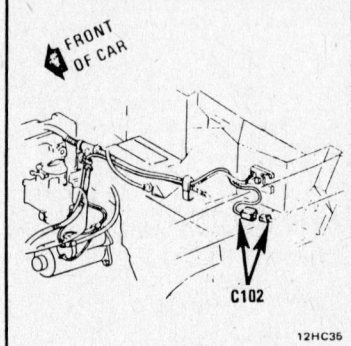

Figure F - LH Front Of Dash

1985-86 Pontiac 1000

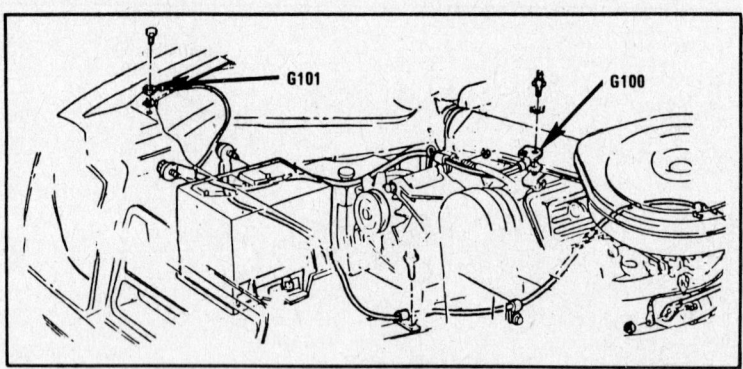

Figure A - RH Side Of Engine Compartment

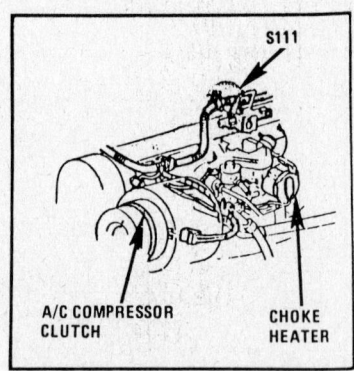

Figure D - Top LH Side Of Engine

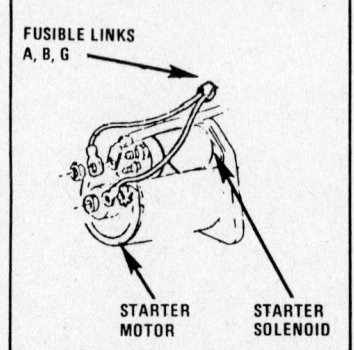

Figure B - Lower LH Side Of Engine

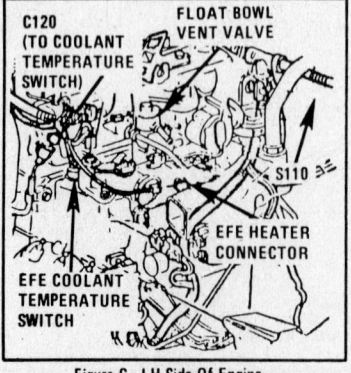

Figure C - LH Side Of Engine

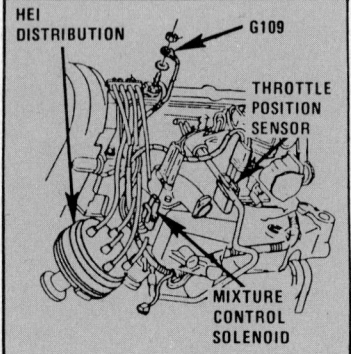

Figure E - LH Side Of Engine

1985-86 Pontiac 1000

COMPONENT LOCATIONS

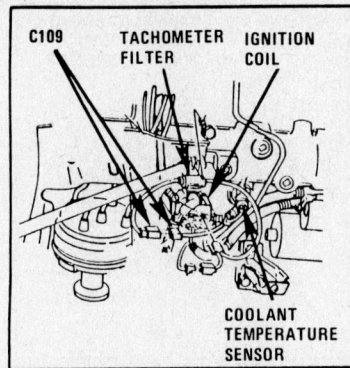

Figure A - LH Side Of Engine

C109 — TACHOMETER FILTER — IGNITION COIL — COOLANT TEMPERATURE SENSOR

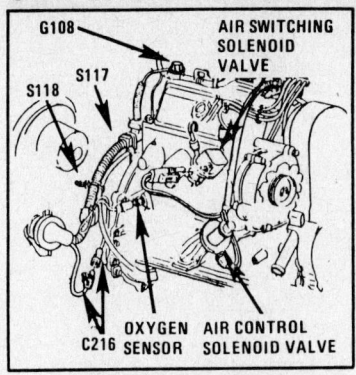

Figure C - RH Side Of Engine

G108 — AIR SWITCHING SOLENOID VALVE — S118 — S117 — OXYGEN SENSOR — C216 — AIR CONTROL SOLENOID VALVE

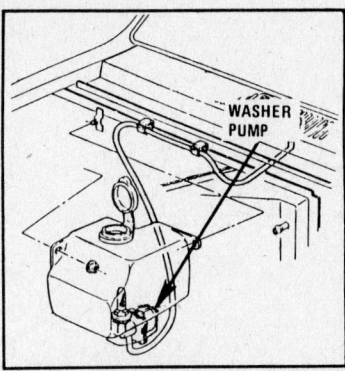

Figure E - RH Fender, Behind Shock Tower

WASHER PUMP

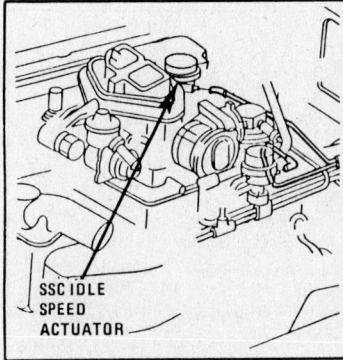

Figure B - Top Of Engine

SSC IDLE SPEED ACTUATOR

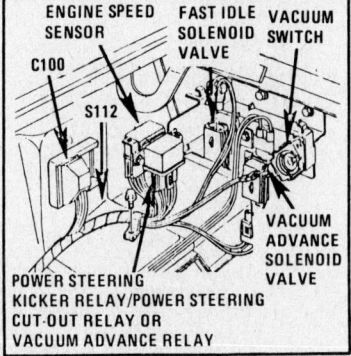

Figure D - LH Dash Area

ENGINE SPEED SENSOR — FAST IDLE SOLENOID VALVE — VACUUM SWITCH — C100 — S112 — VACUUM ADVANCE SOLENOID VALVE — POWER STEERING KICKER RELAY/POWER STEERING CUT-OUT RELAY OR VACUUM ADVANCE RELAY

Figure F - Rear Of Engine

S119

1985-86 Pontiac 1000

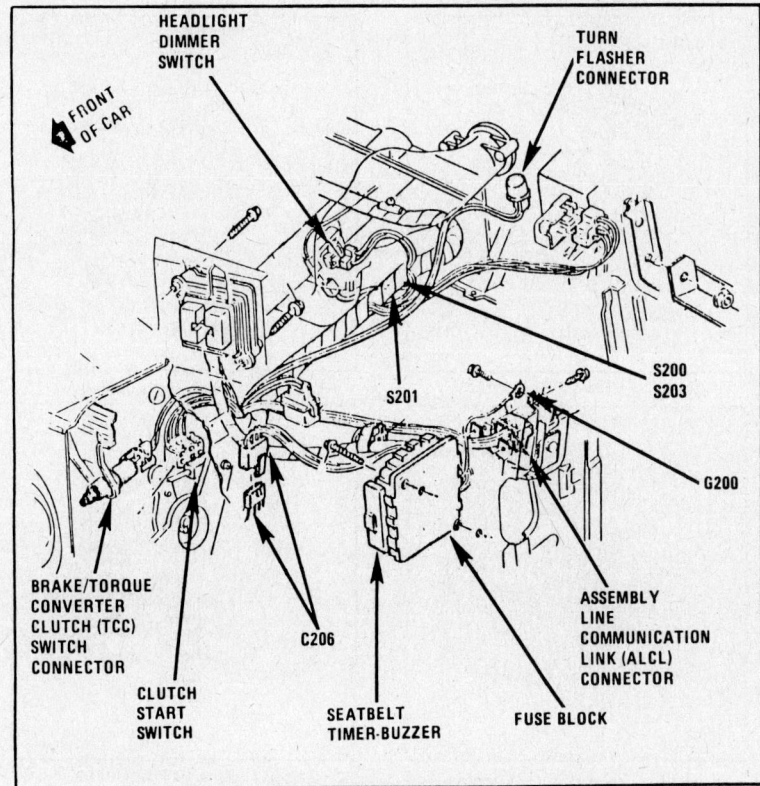

Figure A - Behind LH Side Of I/P

HEADLIGHT DIMMER SWITCH — TURN FLASHER CONNECTOR — FRONT OF CAR — S201 — S200 S203 — G200 — BRAKE/TORQUE CONVERTER CLUTCH (TCC) SWITCH CONNECTOR — C206 — CLUTCH START SWITCH — SEATBELT TIMER-BUZZER — FUSE BLOCK — ASSEMBLY LINE COMMUNICATION LINK (ALCL) CONNECTOR

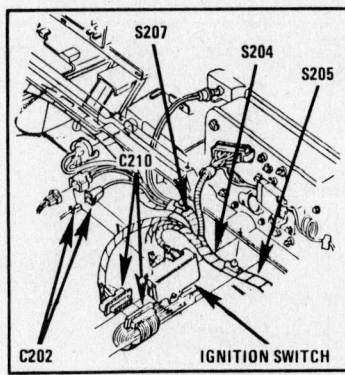

Figure B - LH Side Of I/P

S207 — S204 — S205 — C210 — C202 — IGNITION SWITCH

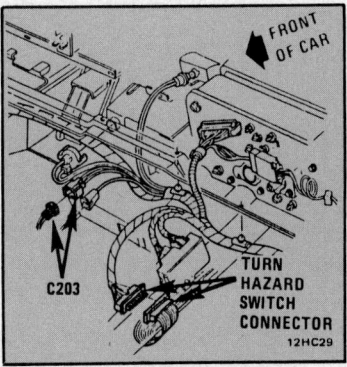

Figure C - Behind LH Side Of I/P

FRONT OF CAR — C203 — TURN HAZARD SWITCH CONNECTOR — 12HC29

1985-86 Pontiac 1000

COMPONENT LOCATIONS

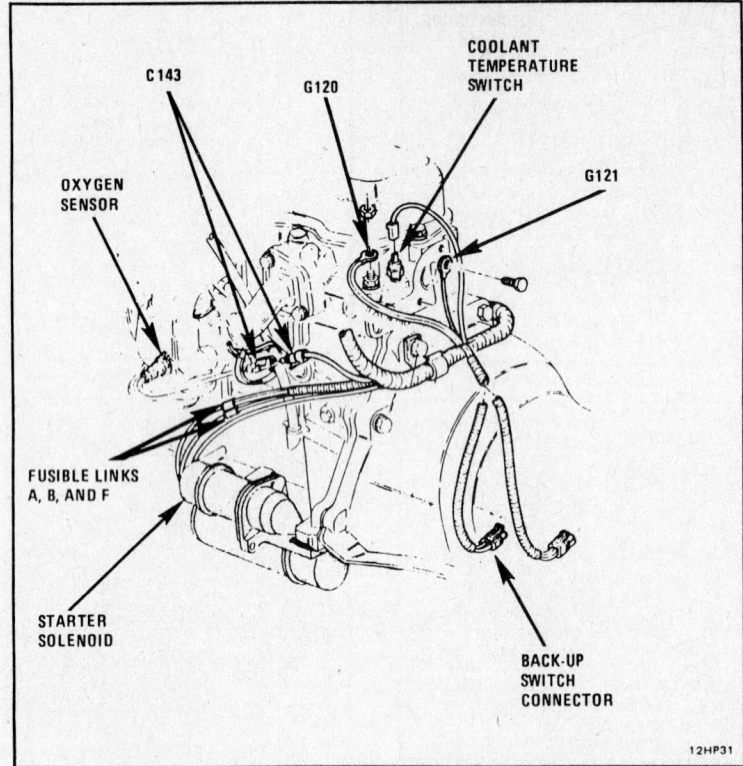

Figure A - LH Rear Of VIN 2 Engine

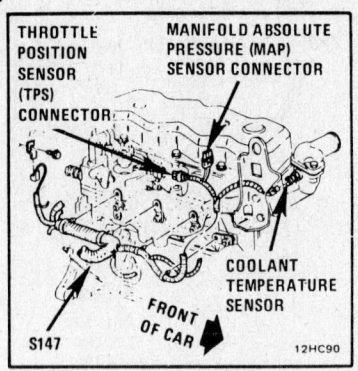

Figure B - RH Side Of VIN 2 Engine

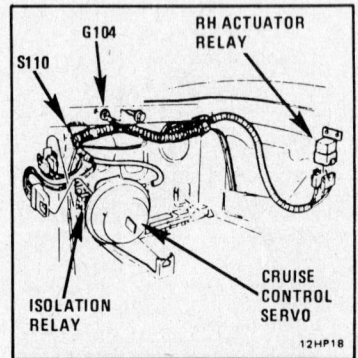

Figure C - RH Front Of Engine Compartment

1985-86 Pontiac Firebird

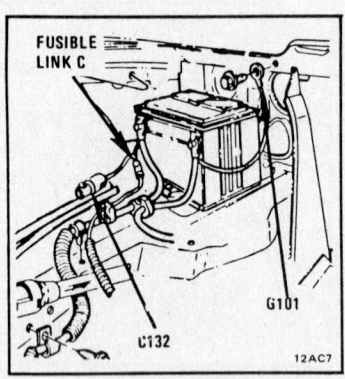

Figure A - LH Front Corner Of VIN 2 Engine

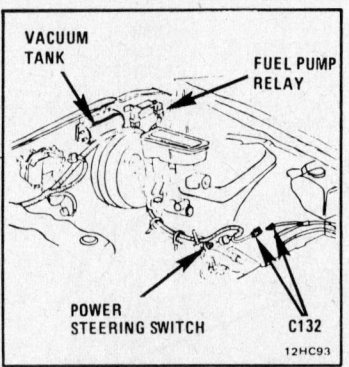

Figure C - LH Rear Corner Of VIN 2

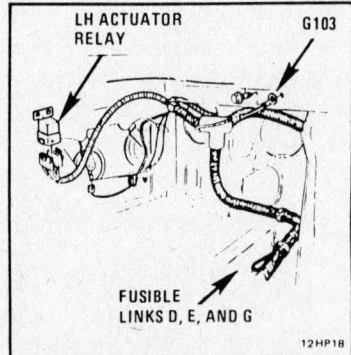

Figure E - LH Front Of Engine Compartment

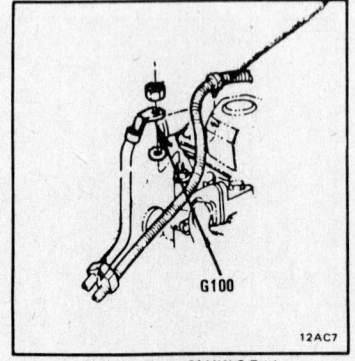

Figure B - Front Of VIN 2 Engine,
LH Side Of Valve Cover

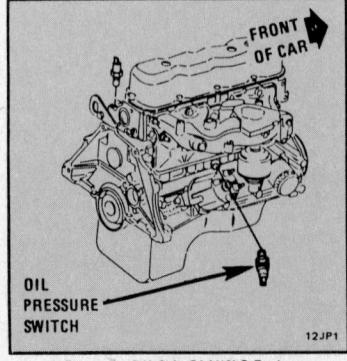

Figure D - RH Side Of VIN 2 Engine

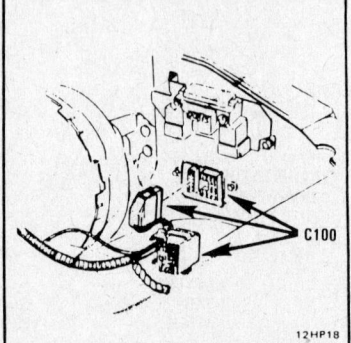

Figure F - Upper LH Front Of Dash

1985-86 Pontiac Firebird

COMPONENT LOCATIONS

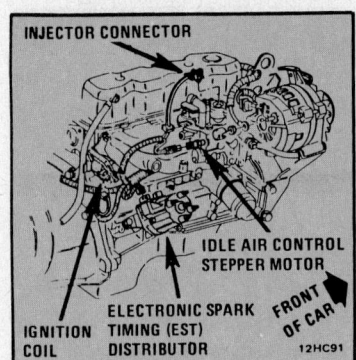

Figure A - RH Side Of VIN 2 Engine

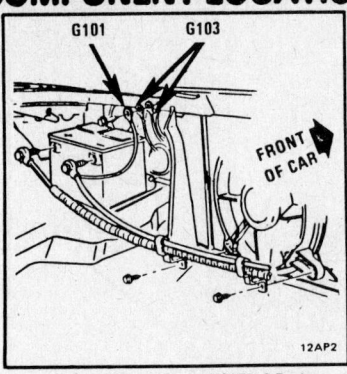

Figure C - LH Front Corner Of VIN S Engine Compartment

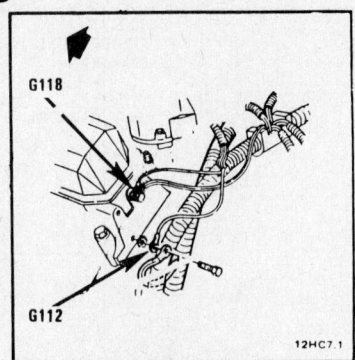

Figure E - LH Rear Of VIN S Engine

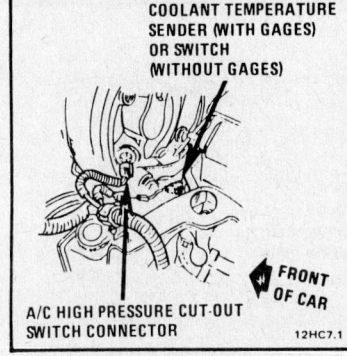

Figure B - LH Side Of VIN S Engine

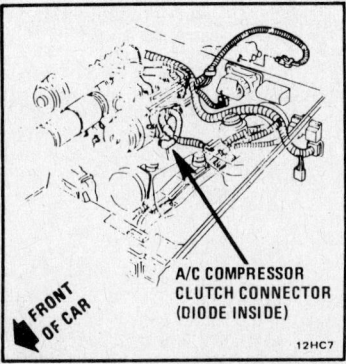

Figure D - LH Side Of VIN S Engine Compartment

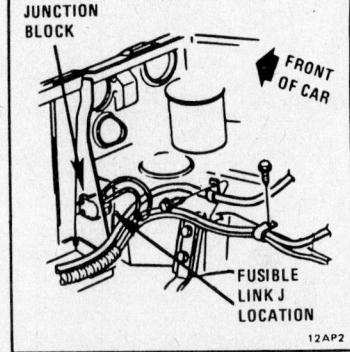

Figure F - RH Side Of VIN S Engine Compartment

1985-86 Pontiac Firebird

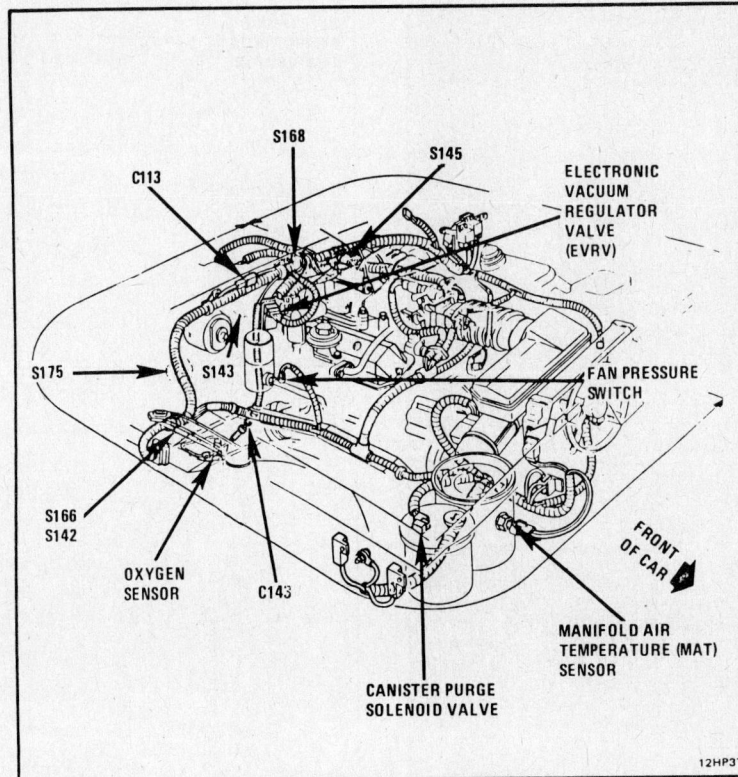

Figure A - VIN S Engine Compartment

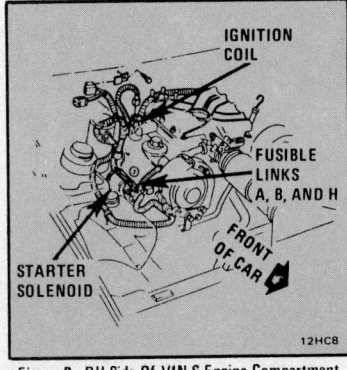

Figure B - RH Side Of VIN S Engine Compartment

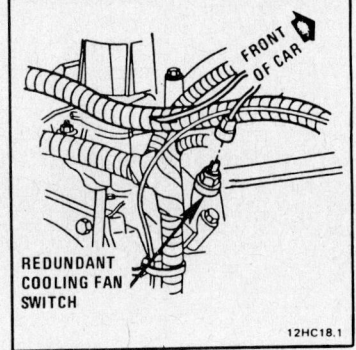

Figure C - Top RH Rear Of VIN S Engine

1985-86 Pontiac Firebird

COMPONENT LOCATIONS

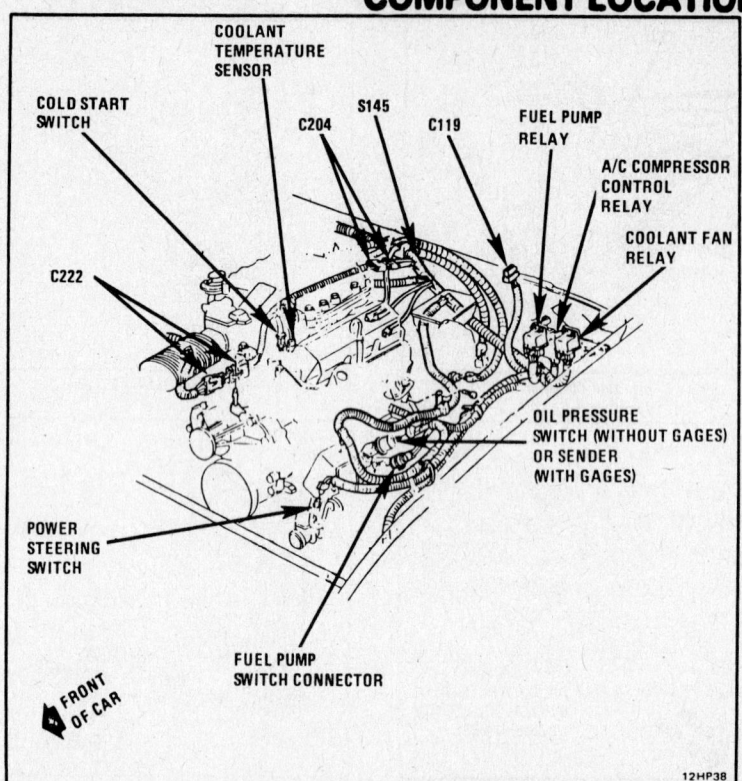

Figure A - LH Side Of VIN S Engine Compartment

1985-86 Pontiac Firebird

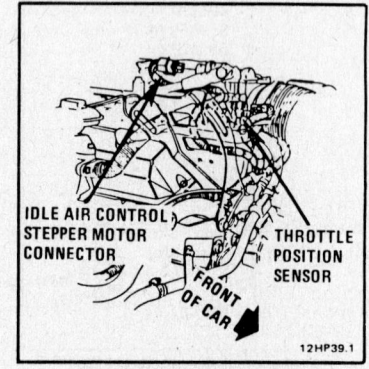

Figure B - Rear Of VIN S LH Cylinder Head

Figure C - RH Side Of VIN S Engine

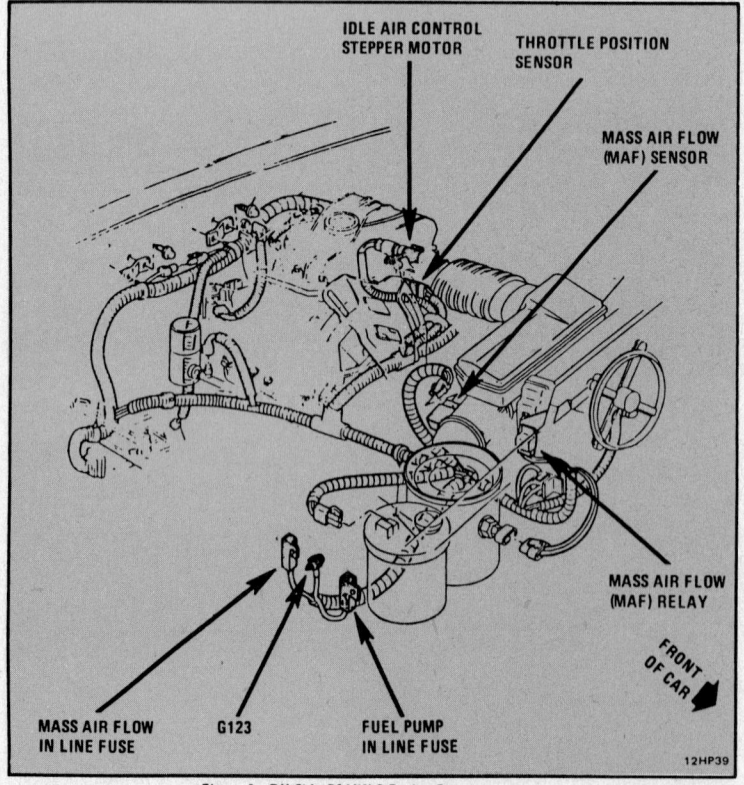

Figure A - RH Side Of VIN S Engine Compartment

1985-86 Pontiac Firebird

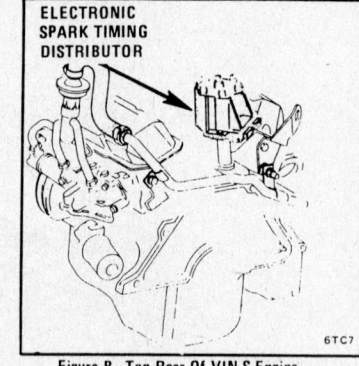

Figure B - Top Rear Of VIN S Engine

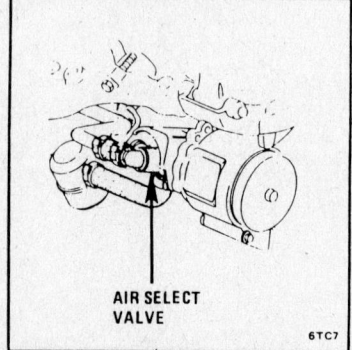

Figure C - Lower RH Side Of VIN S Engine

COMPONENT LOCATIONS

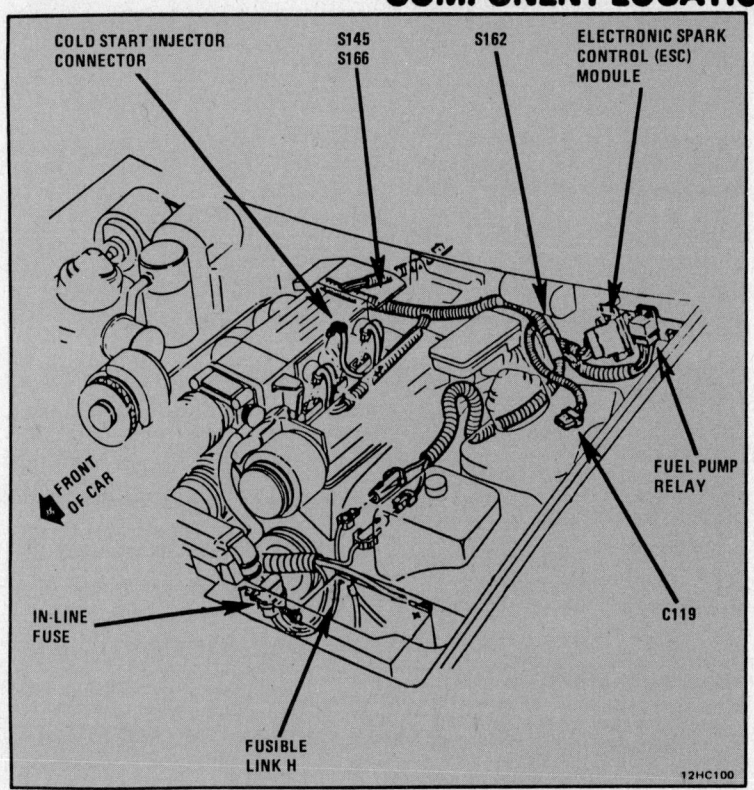

Figure A - LH Side Of VIN F Engine Compartment

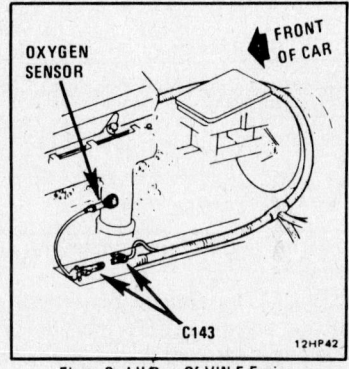

Figure B - Front Of VIN F Engine

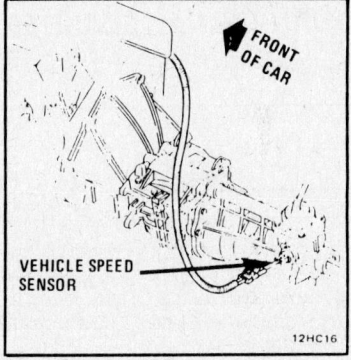

Figure C - LH Rear Of VIN F Engine

1985-86 Pontiac Firebird

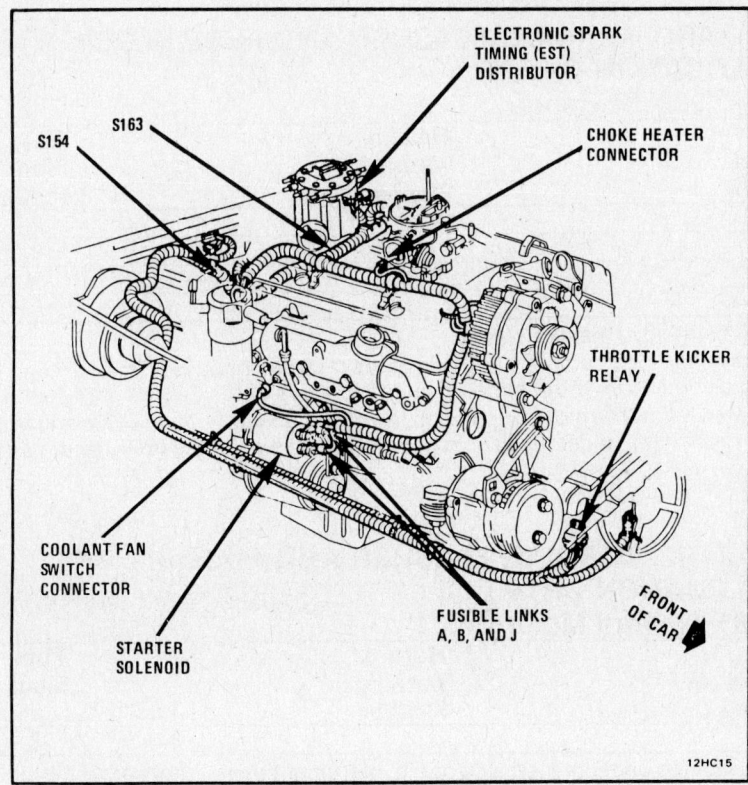

Figure A - RH Side VIN H Engine (VIN G Similar)

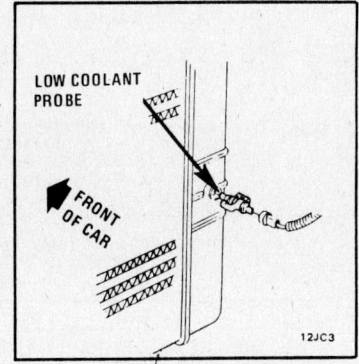

Figure B - LH Side Of Transmission

Figure C - RH Rear Of Radiator (VIN H)

1985-86 Pontiac Firebird

IMPORTS

NOTE: When using this section, some of the components may not be used on a particular vehicle. This is because either the particular component in question was used on an earlier model or a later model. This section is being published from the latest information available at the time of this publication.

TURN SIGNAL FLASHER, HAZARD WARNING FLASHER AND FUSE BLOCK LOCATION CHART
1982-87 Chrysler Corp.—Imports

Model	Turn Signal Flasher	Hazard Warning Flasher	Fuse Block Location
Challenger	1	1	2
Champ	1	1	3
Colt	1	1	3
Colt Vista	1	1	3
Conquest	1	1	3
Sapporo	1	1	2

1 The turn signal and hazard flasher units are installed in the relay box located to the left of the steering column under the instrument panel.
2 The fuse block is located on the left (driver's) kick panel. There are also two 5 amp fuses in-line to the battery and the headlights.
3 The fuse block is located on the cowl under the left side of the instrument panel.

TURN SIGNAL FLASHER, HAZARD WARNING FLASHER AND FUSE BLOCK LOCATION CHART
1982-87 Honda

Model	Turn Signal Flasher	Hazard Warning Flasher	Fuse Block Location
Accord	1	1	2
Civic	1	1	3
Civic CRX/Si	1	1	3
Prelude	1	1	2

1 The turn signal and hazzard flasher units are installed in the fuse block.
2 On 1982 models the fuse block is a flipped down box located on the left side of the instrument panel. On the 83 and later models the fuse block is located behind a door, under the dashboard on the left side of the instrument panel.
3 On the 1982-83 models, the fuse block is located below the glove box and on the right bulkhead. On the 1984 and later models the fuse block is located under a flip down door, under the dashboard on the left side of the instrument panel.

TURN SIGNAL FLASHER, HAZARD WARNING FLASHER AND FUSE BLOCK LOCATION CHART
1985-87 Ford Motor Co.

Model	Turn Signal Flasher	Hazard Warning Flasher	Fuse Block Location
Merkur XR4Ti	1	1	2

1 The turn signal and hazard warning flasher is located under the left side of the instrument panel attached to the steering column support bracket.
2 The fuse block is located in the engine compartment, near the driver's side shock tower.

TURN SIGNAL FLASHER, HAZARD WARNING FLASHER AND FUSE BLOCK LOCATION CHART
1982–87 Mazda

Model	Turn Signal Flasher	Hazard Warning Flasher	Fuse Block Location
626	1	2	2
RX-7	1	1	3
GLC	1	1	2
323	1	1	2

NOTE: There is also a main fuse used on these models to help protect the electrical system and it is located in the engine compartment on either one of the fender aprons.

1 The turn signal and hazard flasher units are located beside the sound warning unit, under the instrument panel.

2 The fuse block is located on the left (driver's) side kick panel.

3 The fuse block is located on the cowl under the left side of the instrument panel.

TURN SIGNAL FLASHER, HAZARD WARNING FLASHER AND FUSE BLOCK LOCATION CHART
1983–87 Mitsubishi

Model	Turn Signal Flasher	Hazard Warning Flasher	Fuse Block Location
Cordia	1	1	2
Galant	1	1	2
Mirage	1	1	2
Starion	1	1	2
Tredia	1	1	2

1 The turn signal and hazard flasher units are installed in the relay box located to the left of the steering column under the instrument panel.

2 The fuse block is located on the cowl under the left side of the instrument panel (behind the trim panel on some of the later models).

TURN SIGNAL FLASHER, HAZARD WARNING FLASHER AND FUSE BLOCK LOCATION CHART
1982–87 Nissan/Datsun

Model	Turn Signal Flasher	Hazard Warning Flasher	Fuse Block Location
200SX	1	1	2
210	3	3	2
280ZX	3	3	4
300ZX	3	3	5
310	6	7	5

TURN SIGNAL FLASHER, HAZARD WARNING FLASHER AND FUSE BLOCK
LOCATION CHART
1982–87 Nissan/Datsun

Model	Turn Signal Flasher	Hazard Warning Flasher	Fuse Block Location
810	3	3	8
Maxima	1	1	2
Pulsar	1	1	5
Pulsar NX	1	1	5
Sentra	1	1	5
Stanza	3	3	9

1 The turn signal and the hazard flasher is located under the left side of the instrument panel on or near the steering column support.
2 The fuse block is located on the cowl under the left side of the instrument panel.
3 The turn signal and the hazard flasher is located under the instrument panel to the right of the steering column.
4 The fuse block is located under the glove box on the right side kick panel.
5 The fuse block is located under the instrument panel on the left (driver's) side kick panel.
6 The turn signal flasher is located under the instrument panel to the right of the steering column.
7 The hazard flasher is located in the fuse block.
8 The fuse block is located in the lower right hand side of the instrument panel, behind a flip down door.
9 The fuse block is located under the glove box on the lower end of the instrument panel.

TURN SIGNAL FLASHER, HAZARD WARNING FLASHER AND FUSE BLOCK
LOCATION CHART
1982–87 Subaru

Model	Turn Signal Flasher	Hazard Warning Flasher	Fuse Block Location
1600	1	1	2
1800	1	1	2
XT Coupe	1	1	3

1 The turn signal and the hazard warning light flasher are a transistor type unit. This unit is installed with a single screw under the left side instrument panel.
2 The fuse block is located on the cowl under the left side of the instrument panel.
3 The fuse block is located in the lower left hand side of the instrument panel, behind a flip down door.

TURN SIGNAL FLASHER, HAZARD WARNING FLASHER AND FUSE BLOCK
LOCATION CHART
1982–87 Toyota

Model	Turn Signal Flasher	Hazard Warning Flasher	Fuse Block Location
Camry	1	1	2
Celica	3	3	2
Corolla FWD	1	1	2
Corolla RWD	4	4	2
Corona	4	4	5
Cressida	3	3	2
MR2	4	4	5
Starlet	4	4	6
Supra	7	7	2
Tercell	4	4	2

TURN SIGNAL FLASHER, HAZARD WARNING FLASHER AND FUSE BLOCK LOCATION CHART
1982–87 Toyota

Model	Turn Signal Flasher	Hazard Warning Flasher	Fuse Block Location
Van	7	7	8

1 The turn signal and hazard warning flashers are located under the left side of the instrument panel.
2 There are three fuse blocks, one is located in the engine compartment on the driver's side wheel well. One on the right side kick panel under the instrument panel and the other on the left side kick panel under the instrument panel. The main fuse block being the one located on the left (driver's) side kick panel. Some of the earlier models only have one fuse block which is usually located on the left kick panel.
3 The turn signal and hazard flasher is located under the instrument panel on or near the left side of the steering column.
4 The turn signal and hazard warning flasher is located on or near the left (driver's) side kick panel.
5 The fuse block is located on the left (driver's) side kick panel.
6 The fuse block is located behind a flip-down door on the cowl of the instrument panel on the left hand side.
7 The turn signal and hazard warning flasher is located under the instrument panel on or near the right side of the steering column.
8 The fuse block is located under the right side of the instrument panel, behind the glove box.

TURN SIGNAL FLASHER, HAZARD WARNING FLASHER AND FUSE BLOCK LOCATION CHART
1982–87 Volkswagon

Model	Turn Signal Flasher	Hazard Warning Flasher	Fuse Block Location
Golf/Cabriolet	1	1	2
GTI	1	1	2
Jetta	1	1	2
Rabbit	1	1	2
Quantum	1	1	2
Scirocco	1	1	2
Volkswagon RWD			
Vanagon	1	1	2

1 The turn signal and hazard warning flasher is located in the fuse/relay block under the left side of the instrument panel.
2 The fuse/relay block is located on the left side of the instrument panel, below the steering column (behind the dashboard bin). To get to the fuses, loosen the bin and fold down the fuse block.

TURN SIGNAL FLASHER, HAZARD WARNING FLASHER AND FUSE BLOCK LOCATION CHART
1982–87 Volvo

Model	Turn Signal Flasher	Hazard Warning Flasher	Fuse Block Location
DL	1	1	2
GL	1	1	2
GLE	1	1	2
GLT	1	1	2
740	3	3	4
760	3	3	4
760 GLE	3	3	4

NOTE: On the electronic fuel injected models, an additional fuse block is located in the engine compartment on the left wheel well. It houses a single fuse protecting the electrical fuel pump.
1 The turn signal and hazard warning flasher is located on the lower left side of the console.
2 The fuse block is located beneath a protective cover, below the instrument panel, on the driver's side kick panel.
3 The turn signal and hazard warning flasher is located in the fuse/relay block, which is located in the center console behind the ashtray.
4 The fuse/relay block is located under a plastic panel in the center console, behind the ashtray.

235

IMPORT VEHICLES

NOTE: When using this section, some of the components may not be used on a particular vehicle. This is because either the particular component in question was used on an earlier model or a later model. This section is being published from the latest information available at the time of this publication.

CIRCUIT BREAKERS, FUSIBLE LINKS, RELAYS, SENSORS AND COMPUTER LOCATIONS

CHRYSLER IMPORTS

Circuit Breakers

ALL MODELS

The Chrysler Import models, protect all the circuits with fuses or relays and do not show any circuit breakers.

Fusible Links

CHAMP, COLT, COLT VISTA AND CONQUEST

AMMETER

There is two fusible links used to protect the ammeter, on is located on the battery wiring harness and the other one is located on the wiring harness along the left side of the engine compartment.

ALTERNATOR

There is a fusible link located on the left side wiring harness, below the ignition coil and it protects the alternator circuit.

STARTER

The starter circuit has a fusible link to protect it and it is located on the battery wire harness.

CHALLENGER AND SAPPORO

AMMETER

The link used to protect the ammeter is located in the fusible link block, on the left front corner of the engine compartment.

HIGH BEAM

Thr fusible link that protects the high beam circuit is located on the light control relay wire harness.

STARTER

This link is located on the wiring harness separating from the positive battery terminal and is used to protect the starter circuit.

IGNITION

The fusible link used to protect the ignition system is located in the fusible link block, on the left front corner of the engine compartment.

NOTE: Depending on the different equipment options on the vehicle, there could be several fusible links used. Before correcting any blown fusible link, try to find out what caused it and replace or repair the problem. Never replace fusible link wire with standard wire, always use wire with hypalon insulation and make sure it is the same gauge as the original wire. The most common wire gauge size and color for the fusible links are as follows; black is 12 gauge, red is 14 gauge, dark blue is 16 gauge, gray is 18 gauge and orange is 20 gauge. On the front wheel drive models most of the fusible links are located in front of the left side shock tower in the engine compartment. On most rear wheel drive models the fusible links are located to the rear of the left front wheel housing.

Relay, Sensors And Computer Locations

CHAMP, CHALLENGER AND SAPPORO

- **A/C High/Low Pressure Cut-Out Switch** – is located on the A/C receiver/drier.
- **Audible Warning Control Unit** – is located behind the glove box.
- **Brake Fluid Level Sensor** – is attached to the brake master cylinder reservoir.
- **Brake/Stop Light Failure Relay** – is located in the relay block, under the left side of the instrument panel.
- **Coolant Temperature Sending Unit** – is located on the left front side of the engine block at the base of the coolant outlet.
- **Cruise Control Unit** – is located under the left side of the instrument panel.
- **Defogger Relay** – is located in the relay block, under the left side of the instrument panel.
- **Dome Light Timer/Relay** – is located in the relay block, under the left side of the instrument panel.
- **Engine Speed Sensor (ESS) Relay** – is located on the left kick panel, above the fuse block.
- **Heater Relay** – is located behind the center console, on the left side of the heater assembly.
- **Intermittent Wiper Relay** – is located on the right front corner of the engine compartment.
- **Light Control Relay** – is located on the left front corner of the engine compartment.
- **Power Window Relay** – is located on the right front corner of the engine compartment, behind the reservoir.
- **Seat Belt Warning Relay** – is located on the right side center console brace.

HONDA

COLT, COLT VISTA AND CONQUEST

- **A/C Cycling Clutch Switch** – is located on the A/C evaporator coil.
- **A/C High/Low Pressure Cut-Out Switch** – is located on the discharge side of the compressor.
- **Air Flow Sensor** – is located in the air cleaner assembly.
- **Blower Relay** – is located on the right side of the firewall near the heater unit.
- **Brake Fluid Level Sensor** – is attached to the brake master cylinder reservoir.
- **Control Relay** – is located on the right side kick panel.
- **Coolant Temperature Sensor** – is located on the bottom of the thermostat housing, in the intake manifold.
- **Cooling Fan Motor Relay** – is located on the relay block, near the driver's side kick panel.
- **Cooling Fan Thermo Sensor** – is located on the bottom left side of the radiator.
- **Detonation (Knock) Sensor** – is located on the left side of the engine.
- **ELC-A/T Control Unit** – is located on or near the left side kick panel.
- **Electronic Control Unit** – is mounted on the passenger's side kick panel.
- **Electronic Controlled Injection (ECI) Unit** – is located in the center of the firewall, near the heater unit.
- **Engine Spark Control Igniter** – is located on the left side of the firewall.
- **Engine Speed Sensor (ESS) Relay** – is located on the left kick panel, above the fuse block.
- **Feedback Carburetor Control (FBC) Unit** – is located in the center of the firewall, near the heater unit.
- **Fuel Cut Solenoid** – is located on the carburetor.
- **Fuel Level Sensor** – is located in the gas tank, but accessible through the spare tire floor.
- **Idle Speed Position Switch** – is installed on the fuel injection mixer assembly.
- **Idle-Up Solenoid Valve** – is located on the left rear corner of the engine compartment.
- **Intake Air Temperature Sensor** – is installed in the air cleaner.
- **Intermittent Wiper Relay** – is located on the left side of the firewall.
- **Oxygen Sensor** – is located in the exhaust manifold.
- **Pressure Sensor** – is located on the firewall.
- **Seat Belt Timer** – in located in the fuse block.
- **Throttle Position Sensor** – is located near the throttle body.
- **Transistor Relay** – is located in the wire harness near the fuse block.

Circuit Breakers

The Honda models protect all the circuits with fuses or relays and do not show any circuit breakers.

Fusible Links

On all Honda models there are one or two fusible links installed near the battery to protect the entire electrical system. All Honda models also use one or two main fuses which are located near the battery and are attached to the fender well.

These fuse are used to protect the electrical system from an overload.

Relay, Sensors And Computer Locations

ACCORD

- **A/C Blower Controller** – is located under the right side of the dash panel.
- **A/C Compressor Clutch Relay** – is in the relay box located on the right side of the engine compartment.
- **A/C Idle Control Solenoid Valves** – is located on the firewall, near the hood release latch.
- **A/C Low Pressure Switch** – Is on the A/C sight glass, near the receiver/drier.
- **Air Intake Temperature Sensor** – is located in the air cleaner housing.
- **Brake Check Relay** – is in the relay box located on the right side of the engine compartment.
- **Brake Fluid Level Sensor** – is located in the brake master cylinder reservoir.
- **Brake Light-Out Sensor** – is located in the left rear lamp assembly.
- **Control Switch Solenoid Valve** – Is located in the emission control box on the right side of the firewall.
- **Cooling Fan Thermo Sensor** – is on the bottom right corner of the radiator.
- **Coolant Temperature Sensor** – is located in the thermostat housing.
- **Cranking Leak Solenoid Valve** – Is located in the emission control box on the right side of the firewall.
- **Cranking Solenoid Valve** – Is located in the emission control box on the right side of the firewall.
- **Cruise Control Solenoid Valve** – is located behind the cruise control actuator.
- **Cruise Control Unit** – is located under the center of the dash panel.
- **EGR Control Solenoid Valve A** – Is located in the emission control box on the right side of the firewall.
- **EGR Control Solenoid Valve B** – Is located in the emission control box on the right side of the firewall.
- **Fuel Flow Solenoid** – is located behind the center console.
- **Fuel Pump Cut-Out Relay** – is located in the fuse/relay block under the left side of the dash panel.
- **Heat/Defrost Solenoid** – is located behind the center console.
- **Lighting Relay** – is located in the fuse/relay block under the left side of the dash panel.
- **Lights-On Control Unit** – is located under the left side of the dash panel.
- **Main Fuel Cut-Off Solenoid** – is located on the carburetor, near the fuel inlet side.
- **Outside Air Solenoid** – is located under the right side of the dash panel, on the right side of the blower motor housing.
- **Power Valve Control Solenoid** – is located in the emission control box on the right side of the firewall.
- **Radiator/Condenser Fan Relay** – is in the relay box located on the right side of the engine compartment.
- **Relay Box** – is located on the right side of the engine compartment, near the battery.

- **Seat Belt/Buzzer Timer** – is located under the center of the dash panel.
- **Slow Fuel Mixture Cut-Off Solenoid** – is located on the carburetor.
- **Speed Sensor** – is located in the transaxle housing near the starter motor.
- **Thermo Sensor** – is located in the cylinder head near the thermostat.
- **Vacuum Holding Solenoid Valve** – is located in the emission box on the right side of the firewall.
- **Vacuum Switch** – is located in the emission box, on the right side of the firewall.
- **Vent/Defrost Solenoid** – is located behind the center console, on the right side of the heater core housing.
- **Windshield Wiper Relay** – is located in the fuse/relay block under the left side of the dash panel.

NOTE: The following components are for the Accord SEi only.

- **A/C Idle Control Solenoid Valve** – is located on the A/C refrigerant lines.
- **Automatic Transmission Idle Control Solenoid Valve** – is located near the left front fender apron.
- **Crank Angle Sensor** – is located near the distributor.
- **Cylinder (CYL) Sensor** – is located in the wiring harness in front of the valve cover on the top of the engine.
- **Electronic Control Unit** – is located under the driver's seat.
- **Fast Idle Control Solenoid Valve** – is located near the left front fender apron.
- **Idle Control Solenoid Valve** – is located near the left front fender apron.
- **Idle Mixture Adjuster Sensor** – This sensor is located in the main control box.
- **Intake Air Temperature Sensor** – is located in the intake manifold.
- **Manifold Air Pressure Sensor** – is located on the air cleaner assembly.
- **Oxygen Sensor** – is located in the exhaust manifold.
- **Throttle Angle sensor** – is located on the throttle body.
- **Top Dead Center (TDC) Sensor** – is located next to the CYL sensor.

CIVIC

- **A/C Blower Controller** – is located under the right side of the dash panel.
- **A/C Compressor Clutch Relay** – is located on the right side of the engine compartment, near the front washer motor.
- **A/C Idle Boost Solenoid Valves** – is located on the firewall, near the hood release latch.
- **A/C Low Pressure Switch** – is located on the high pressure hose near the condenser.
- **Air Intake Temperature Sensor** – is located in the air cleaner housing.
- **Brake Check Relay** – is in the relay box located on the left side of the engine compartment.
- **Brake Fluid Level Sensor** – is located in the brake master cylinder reservoir.
- **Control Switch Solenoid Valve** – is located in the (No.1) emission control box on the right side of the firewall.
- **Coolant Temperature Sensor** – is located in the thermostat housing.
- **Cooling Fan Thermo Sensor** – is on the bottom right corner of the radiator.
- **Cranking Leak Solenoid Valve** – is located in the (No.1) emission control box on the right side of the firewall.
- **Cranking Solenoid Valve** – is located in the (No.1) emission control box on the right side of the firewall.

- **Cruise Control Solenoid Valve** – is located behind the cruise control actuator.
- **Cruise Control Unit** – is located under the center of the dash panel.
- **EGR Control Solenoid Valve A** – is located in the (No.2) emission control box on the left side of the firewall.
- **EGR Control Solenoid Valve B** – is located in the (No.3) emission control box on the left side of the firewall.
- **Fuel Flow Solenoid** – is located behind the center console.
- **Fuel Pump Cut-Out Relay** – is located in the fuse/relay block under the left side of the dash panel.
- **Heat/Defrost Solenoid** – is located behind the center console.
- **Idle Control Solenoid Valve A** – is located in the (NO.1) emission control box on the right side of the firewall.
- **Ignitor Control Unit** – is located in the distributor.
- **Indiactor Amplifier** – is located on the back of the tachometer.
- **Main Fuel Cut-Off Solenoid** – is located on the carburetor, near the fuel inlet side.
- **Outside Air Solenoid** – is located under the right side of the dash panel, on the right side of the blower motor housing.
- **Power Valve Control Solenoid** – is located in the (No.1) emission control box on the right side of the firewall.
- **Radiator/Condenser Fan Relay** – is located on the right side of the engine compartment, near the front washer motor.
- **RPM Sensor** – is installed in the tachometer.
- **Seat Belt/Buzzer Timer** – is located under the left side of the dash panel.
- **Slow Fuel Mixture Cut-Off Solenoid** – is located on the carburetor.
- **Speed Sensor** – is installed in the speedometer.
- **Speed Sensor Amplifier** – is located on the back of the speedometer.
- **Starter Relay** – is located under the left side of the dash panel near the fuse /relay block.
- **Thermo Sensor** – is located in the cylinder head near the thermostat.
- **Throttle Closer Control Unit** – is located above the fuse/relay block.
- **Throttle Closer Solenoid Valve** – is located on a bracket in front of the left front shock tower.
- **Vacuum Holding Solenoid Valve** – is located in the emission box on the right side of the firewall.
- **Vacuum Switch** – is located in the (No.3) emission box, on the left side of the firewall.
- **Vent/Defrost Solenoid** – is located behind the center console, on the right side of the heater core housing.
- **Windshield Wiper Relay** – is located in the fuse/relay block under the left side of the dash panel.

NOTE: The following components are for the Civic CRX-Si only.

- **A/C Idle Control Solenoid Valve** – is located on the A/C refrigerant lines.
- **Automatic Transmission Idle Control Solenoid Valve** – is located near the left front fender apron.
- **Crank Angle Sensor** – is located near the distributor.
- **Cylinder (CYL) Sensor** – is located in the wiring harness in front of the valve cover on the top of the engine.
- **Electronic Control Unit** – is located under the driver's seat.
- **Fast Idle Control Solenoid Valve** – is located near the left front fender apron.
- **Idle Control Solenoid Valve** – is located near the left front fender apron.
- **Idle Mixture Adjuster Sensor** – This sensor is located in the main control box.
- **Intake Air Temperature Sensor** – is located in the in-

take manifold.
- **Manifold Air Pressure Sensor** – is located on the air cleaner assembly.
- **Oxygen Sensor** – is located in the exhaust manifold.
- **Throttle Angle sensor** – is located on the throttle body.
- **Top Dead Center (TDC) Sensor** – is located next to the CYL sensor.

PRELUDE

- **A/C Compressor Clutch Relay** – is located in the left front corner of the engine compartment.
- **A/C Heater Blower Motor Relay** – is located under the right side of the dash panel.
- **A/C Low Pressure Switch** – is located on the high pressure hose near the receiver drier.
- **A/C Thermostatic Switch** – is located on the evaportator housing.
- **Air Suction Control Solenoid Valve** – is located in the (no.1) emission control box on the left side of the engine compartment.
- **Air Suction Vacuum Switch** – is located in the (No.2) emission box, on the right side near the firewall.
- **Air Vent Cut-Off Solenoid Valve** – is located under the air cleaner assembly.
- **Anti-Afterburn Control Solenoid Valve** – is located in the (No.2) emission control box on the right side near the firewall.
- **Auxilliary Slow Fuel Cut-Off Solenoid** – is located on the side of the carburetor.
- **Brake Fluid Level Sensor** – is located in the brake master cylinder.
- **Condensor Fan Relay** – is located in the left front corner of the engine compartment.
- **Control Switch Solenoid Valve** – is located in the (No.1) emission control box on the left side of the engine compartment.
- **Coolant Temperature Sensor** – is located on the front of the intake manifold.
- **Cooling Fan Motor Relay** – is located in the fuse/relay block on the right front fender apron.
- **Cooling Fan Thermo-Sensor** – is located on the bottom right corner of the radiator.
- **Cranking Leak Solenoid Valve** – is located in the (No.1) emission control box on the left side of the engine compartment.
- **Cranking Solenoid Valve** – is located in the (No.1) emission control box on the left side of the engine compartment.
- **Cruise Control Solenoid Valve** – is located behind the cruise control actuator.
- **Cruise Control Unit** – is located under the center of the dash panel.
- **Dimmer Relay** – is located in the fuse/relay block on the right front fender apron.
- **EGR Control Solenoid Valve A** – is located in the (No.1) emission control box on the left side of the engine compartment.
- **EGR Control Solenoid Valve B** – is located in the (No.1) emission control box on the left side of the firewall.
- **Fuel Pump Cut-Off Relay** – is located in the fuse/relay block on the right front fender apron.
- **Headlight Retractor Control Unit** – is located under the center of the dash panel.
- **Headlight Retract Relay** – is located in the left front corner of the engine compartment.
- **Number 1 Idle Control Solenoid Valve** – is located in the (No.1) emission control box on the left side of the engine compartment.
- **Number 2 Idle Control Solenoid Valve** – is located on a bracket near the (No.2) emission control box.
- **Inner Vent Solenoid Valve** – is located under the air cleaner aseembly.
- **Intake Air Temperature Sensor** – is located in the air cleaner.
- **Interior Lighting Timer** – is located under the left side of the dash panel.
- **Intermittent Wiper Relay** – is located in the fuse/relay block under the left side of the dash panel.
- **Lighting Relay** – is located in the fuse/relay block on the right front fender apron.
- **Main Air Jet Solenoid Valve** – is located on the bottom of the air cleaner housing.
- **Main Air Jet Vacuum Switch** – is located in the (No.1) emission box, on the left side of the engine compartment.
- **Oil Pressure Flasher Relay** – is located under the right side of the dash panel.
- **Oxygen Sensor** – is located in the exhaust manifold.
- **Primary Slow Fuel Cut-Off Solenoid** – is located on the fuel inlet side of the carburetor.
- **Rear Defrost Relay** – is located under the left side of the dash panel.
- **Recirculation Solenoids** – are located under the right side of the dash panel.
- **Solenoid Control Unit** – is located under the right side of the dash panel.
- **Speed Sensor** – Is located in the speedometer gear housing.
- **Sunroof Closing Relay** – is located in the fuse/relay block on the right front fender apron.
- **Sunroof Opening Relay** – is located in the fuse/relay block on the right front fender apron.

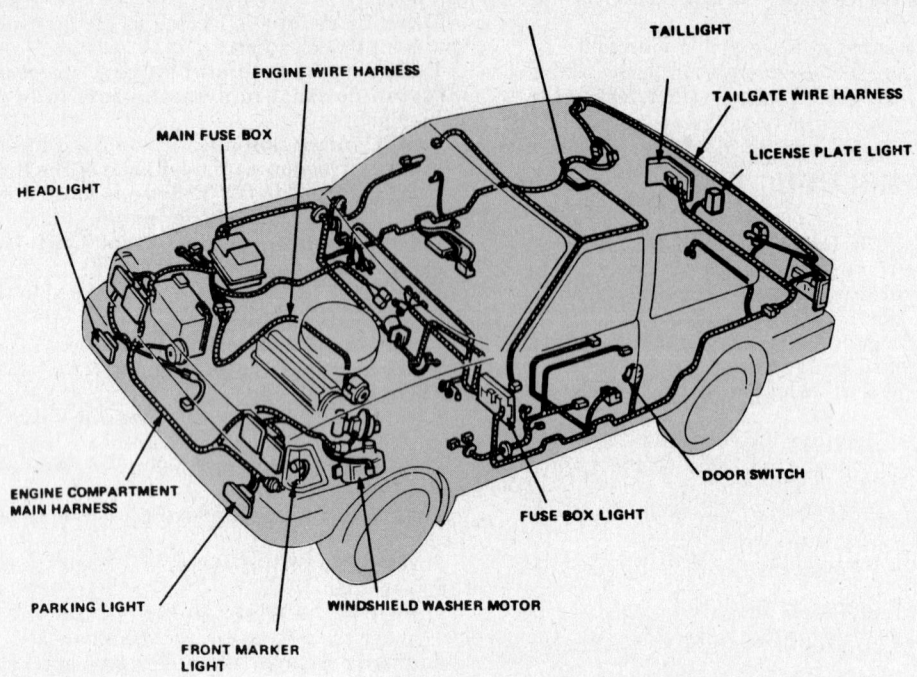

INTERIOR LIGHT/SWITCH

TAILLIGHT

ENGINE WIRE HARNESS

TAILGATE WIRE HARNESS

MAIN FUSE BOX

LICENSE PLATE LIGHT

HEADLIGHT

DOOR SWITCH

ENGINE COMPARTMENT MAIN HARNESS

FUSE BOX LIGHT

PARKING LIGHT

WINDSHIELD WASHER MOTOR

FRONT MARKER LIGHT

Honda Accord Hatchback

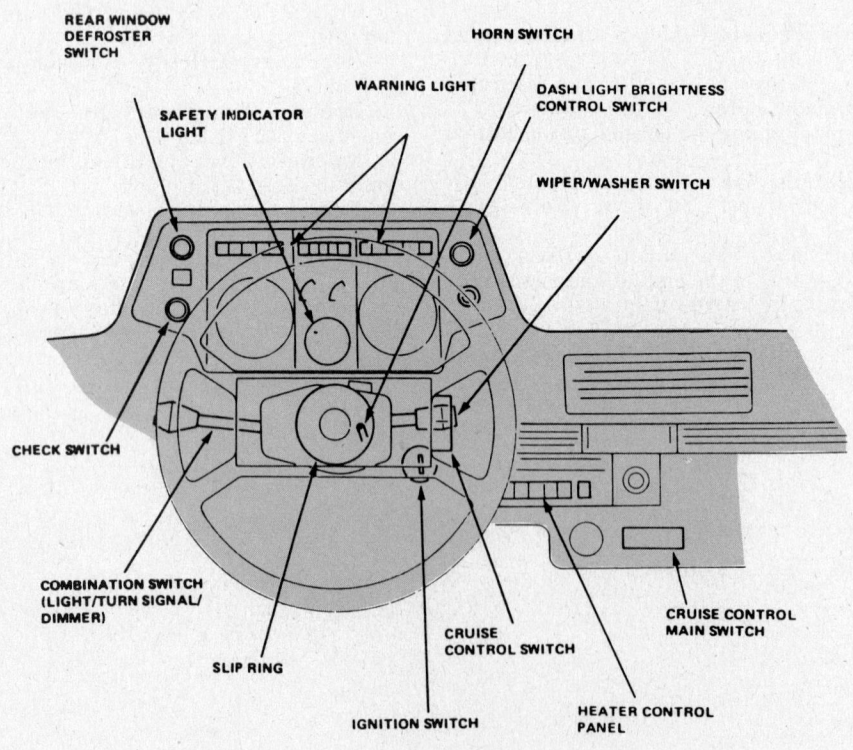

REAR WINDOW DEFROSTER SWITCH

HORN SWITCH

WARNING LIGHT

DASH LIGHT BRIGHTNESS CONTROL SWITCH

SAFETY INDICATOR LIGHT

WIPER/WASHER SWITCH

CHECK SWITCH

COMBINATION SWITCH (LIGHT/TURN SIGNAL/ DIMMER)

CRUISE CONTROL MAIN SWITCH

SLIP RING

CRUISE CONTROL SWITCH

IGNITION SWITCH

HEATER CONTROL PANEL

Honda Accord

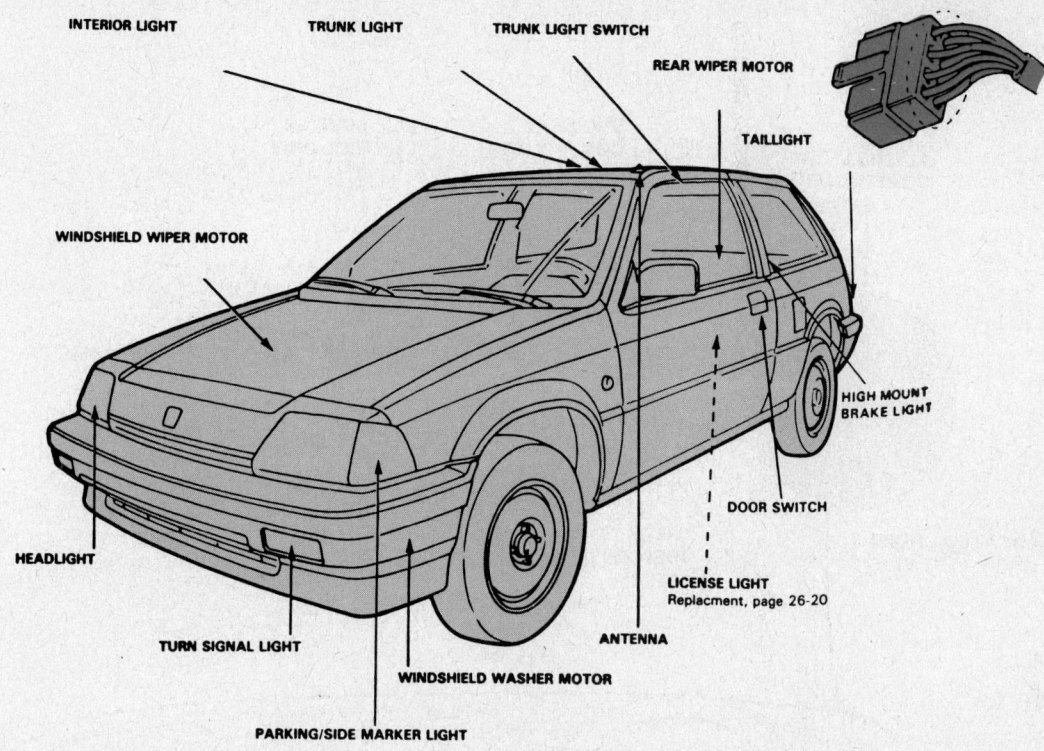

INTERIOR LIGHT

TRUNK LIGHT

TRUNK LIGHT SWITCH

REAR WIPER MOTOR

TAILLIGHT

WINDSHIELD WIPER MOTOR

HIGH MOUNT BRAKE LIGHT

DOOR SWITCH

HEADLIGHT

LICENSE LIGHT
Replacment, page 26-20

TURN SIGNAL LIGHT

WINDSHIELD WASHER MOTOR

ANTENNA

PARKING/SIDE MARKER LIGHT

Honda Civic

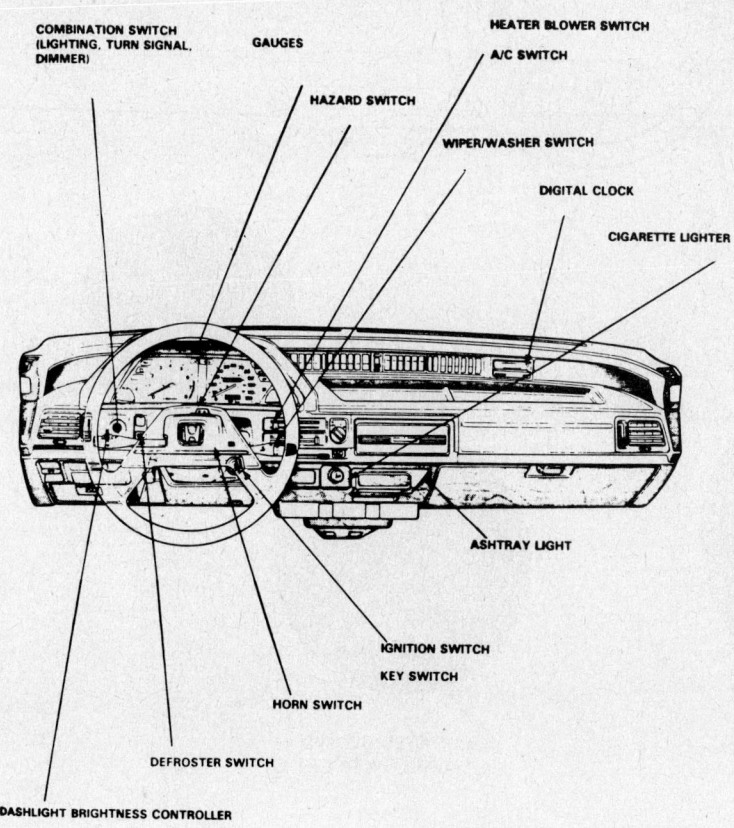

COMBINATION SWITCH
(LIGHTING, TURN SIGNAL, DIMMER)

GAUGES

HEATER BLOWER SWITCH

A/C SWITCH

HAZARD SWITCH

WIPER/WASHER SWITCH

DIGITAL CLOCK

CIGARETTE LIGHTER

ASHTRAY LIGHT

IGNITION SWITCH

KEY SWITCH

HORN SWITCH

DEFROSTER SWITCH

DASHLIGHT BRIGHTNESS CONTROLLER

Honda Civic

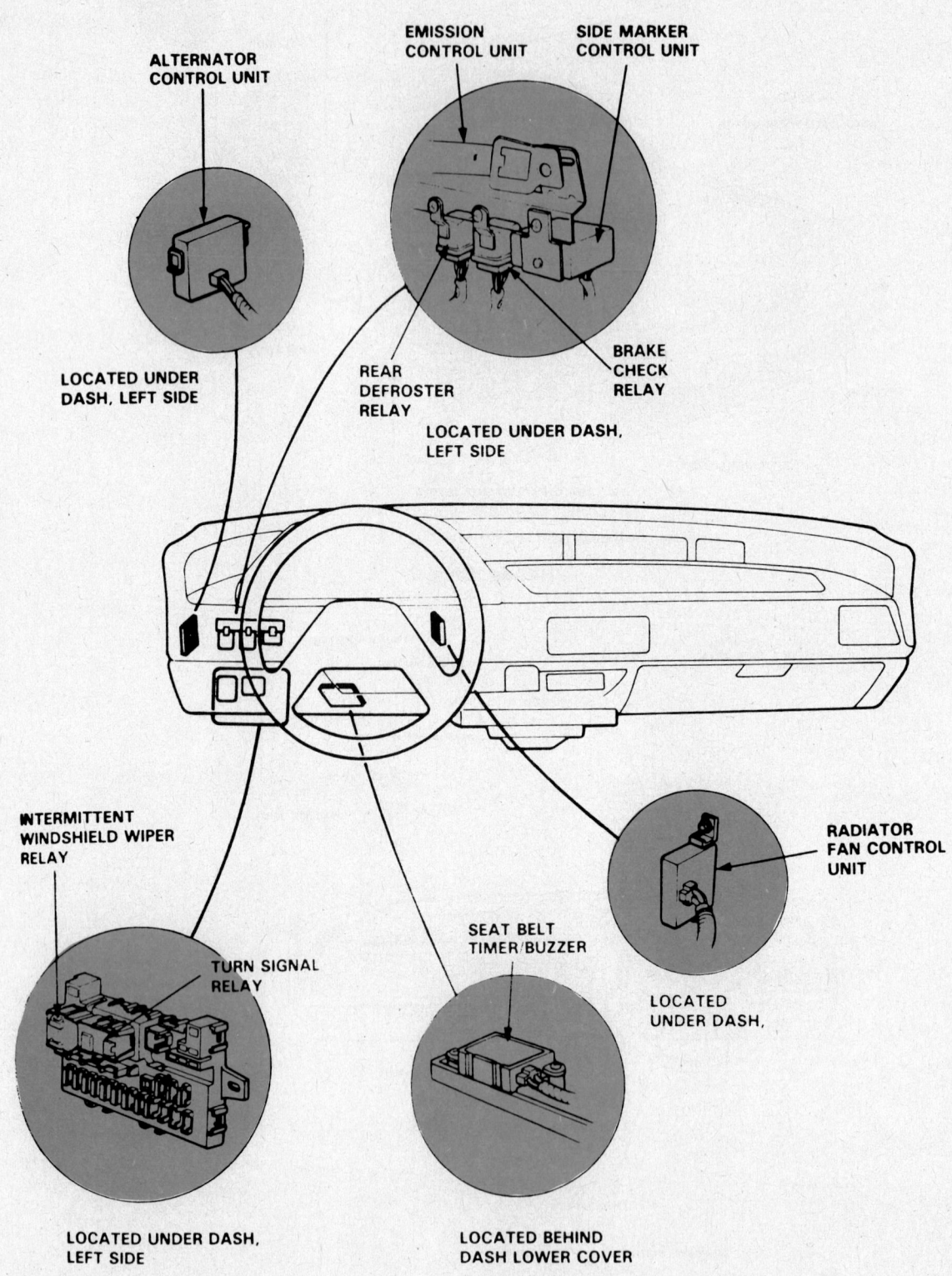

ALTERNATOR
CONTROL UNIT

EMISSION
CONTROL UNIT

SIDE MARKER
CONTROL UNIT

LOCATED UNDER
DASH, LEFT SIDE

REAR
DEFROSTER
RELAY

BRAKE
CHECK
RELAY

LOCATED UNDER DASH,
LEFT SIDE

INTERMITTENT
WINDSHIELD WIPER
RELAY

TURN SIGNAL
RELAY

SEAT BELT
TIMER/BUZZER

RADIATOR
FAN CONTROL
UNIT

LOCATED
UNDER DASH,

LOCATED UNDER DASH,
LEFT SIDE

LOCATED BEHIND
DASH LOWER COVER

Honda Civic

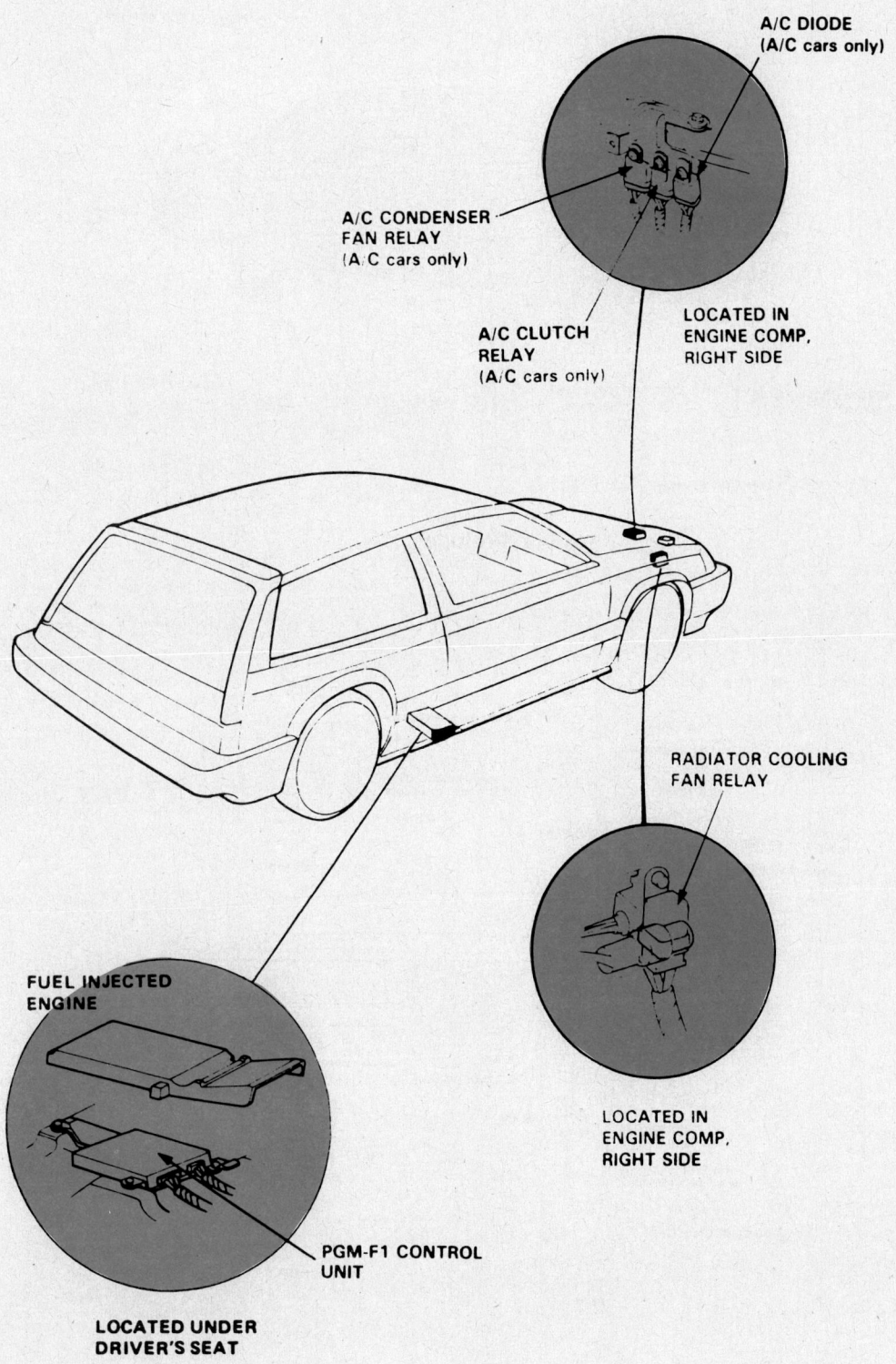

A/C DIODE
(A/C cars only)

A/C CONDENSER
FAN RELAY
(A/C cars only)

A/C CLUTCH
RELAY
(A/C cars only)

LOCATED IN
ENGINE COMP,
RIGHT SIDE

RADIATOR COOLING
FAN RELAY

LOCATED IN
ENGINE COMP,
RIGHT SIDE

FUEL INJECTED
ENGINE

PGM-F1 CONTROL
UNIT

LOCATED UNDER
DRIVER'S SEAT

Honda Civic

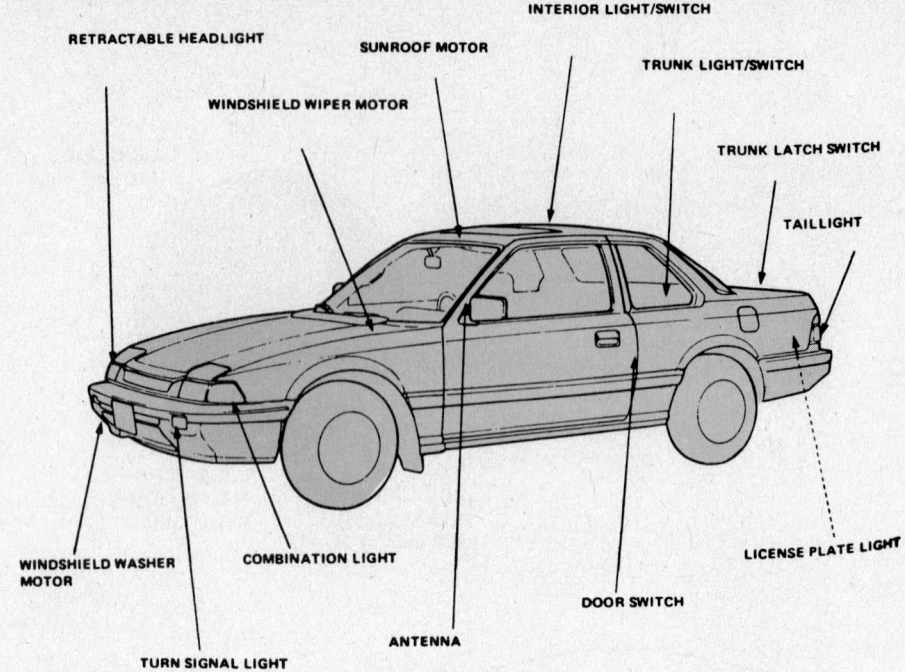

INTERIOR LIGHT/SWITCH

RETRACTABLE HEADLIGHT

SUNROOF MOTOR

TRUNK LIGHT/SWITCH

WINDSHIELD WIPER MOTOR

TRUNK LATCH SWITCH

TAILLIGHT

WINDSHIELD WASHER
MOTOR

COMBINATION LIGHT

LICENSE PLATE LIGHT

DOOR SWITCH

TURN SIGNAL LIGHT

ANTENNA

Honda Prelude

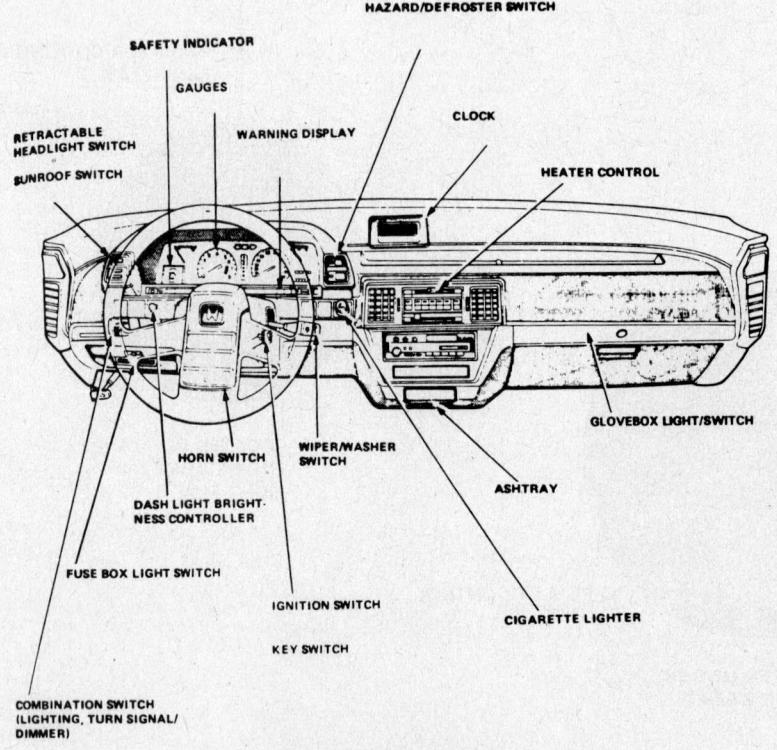

HAZARD/DEFROSTER SWITCH

SAFETY INDICATOR

GAUGES

CLOCK

RETRACTABLE
HEADLIGHT SWITCH

WARNING DISPLAY

HEATER CONTROL

SUNROOF SWITCH

HORN SWITCH

WIPER/WASHER
SWITCH

GLOVEBOX LIGHT/SWITCH

ASHTRAY

DASH LIGHT BRIGHT-
NESS CONTROLLER

FUSE BOX LIGHT SWITCH

IGNITION SWITCH

CIGARETTE LIGHTER

KEY SWITCH

COMBINATION SWITCH
(LIGHTING, TURN SIGNAL/
DIMMER)

Honda Prelude

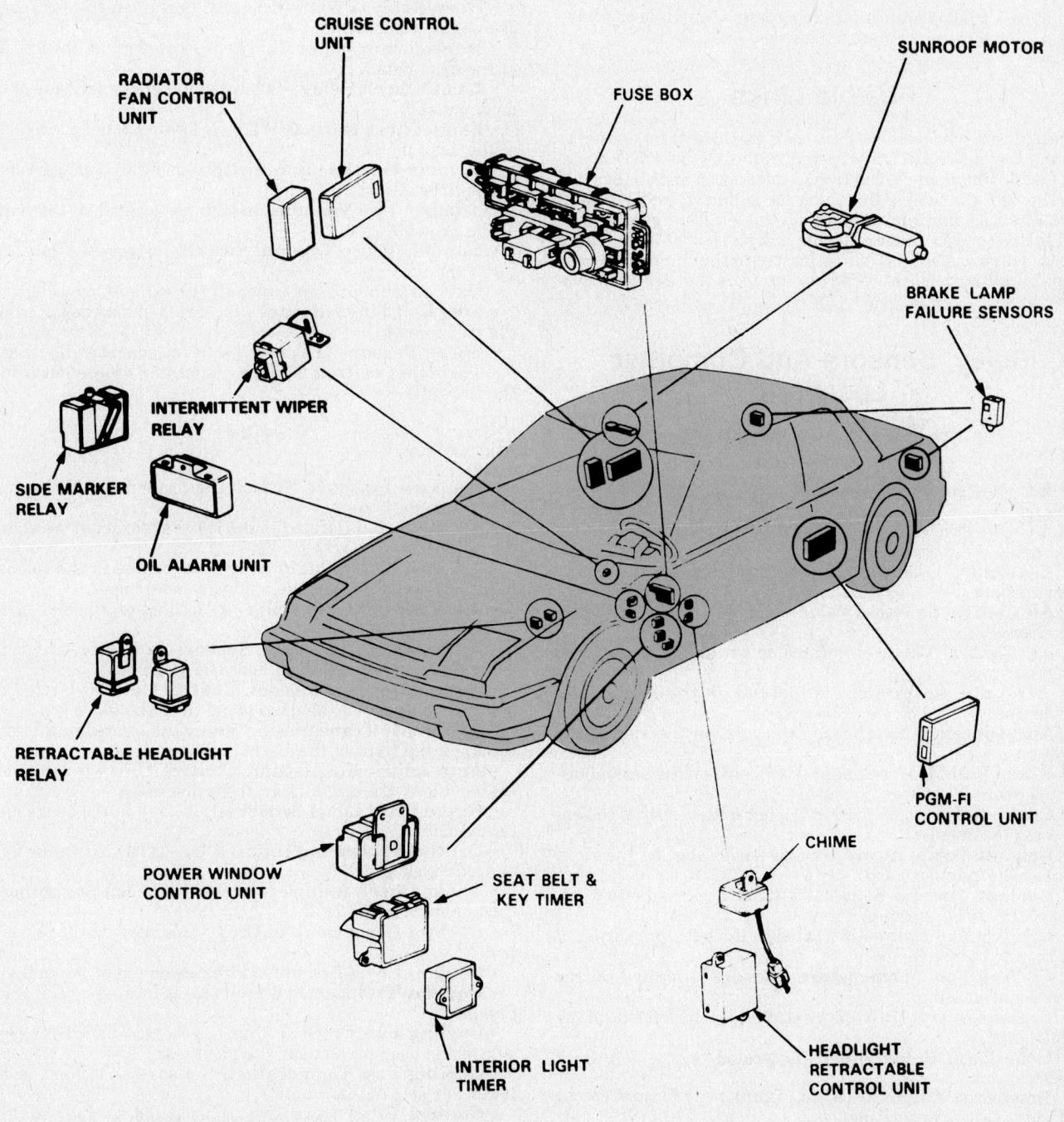

RADIATOR FAN CONTROL UNIT

CRUISE CONTROL UNIT

FUSE BOX

SUNROOF MOTOR

BRAKE LAMP FAILURE SENSORS

INTERMITTENT WIPER RELAY

SIDE MARKER RELAY

OIL ALARM UNIT

RETRACTABLE HEADLIGHT RELAY

POWER WINDOW CONTROL UNIT

SEAT BELT & KEY TIMER

INTERIOR LIGHT TIMER

CHIME

HEADLIGHT RETRACTABLE CONTROL UNIT

PGM-FI CONTROL UNIT

Honda Prelude

MAZDA

Circuit Breakers

The Mazda models protect all the circuits with fuses or relays and do not show any circuit breakers.

Fusible Links

On all Mazda models there are one or two fusible links used to protect the entire electrical system. On the GLC FWD model the fusible link is on the left front fender apron and on the GLC RWD model the fusible link is on the right side radiator support. The RX7 has a fusible link on the left front shock tower and the 626 models have a fusible link on the left front fender apron. There is also a main fuse located in the engine compartment on all models, this fuse also protects the electrical system.

Relay, Sensors And Computer Locations

GLC AND 323 MODELS

- **A/C Control Unit** – is located under the right side of the dash panel.
- **A/C Cut-Out Relay** – is located in the left front corner of the engine compartment.
- **A/C Relay** – is located in the left front corner of the engine compartment.
- **Air Control Solenoid Valve** – is located on the left side of the firewall.
- **Air Control Valve** – is located on the air cleaner next to the reed valve.
- **Air Vent Solenoid** – is located on the side of the carburetor.
- **Anti-Dieseling Solenoid** – is located on the side of the carburetor.
- **Brake Fluid Level Sensor** – is located on the brake master cylinder.
- **Choke Relay** – is located in the left front corner of the engine compartment.
- **Coolant Temperature Sensor** – is located on the right front of the cylinder head.
- **Coolant Thermo Sensor** – is located on the bottom left side of the carburetor.
- **Cooling Fan Relay** – is located in the left front corner of the engine compartment.
- **Cooling Fan Temperature Sensor** – is located on the thermostat housing.
- **Cruise Control Unit** – is located under the left side of the dash panel.
- **Door Lock Relay/Timer** – is located on the left front fender apron.
- **Downshift Solenoid (Auto. Trans.)** – is located on the left side of the transmission case.
- **EGR Solenoid** – is located on the left side of the firewall.
- **Electronic Control Unit (ECU)** – is located under the right side of the dash panel.
- **Engine Speed Control Unit** – is located on the left kick panel.
- **Heat Hazard Sensor** – is located above the catalytic converter.

- **Horn Relay** – is located in the right front corner of the engine compartment.
- **Horn Relay (FWD)** – is located in the left front corner of the engine compartment.
- **Intermittent Wiper Relay** – is located under the left side of the dash panel.
- **Lamp Check Relay** – is located under the left side of the dash panel.
- **Lamp Check Relay (FWD)** – is located under the left side of the dash panel.
- **Number One Vacuum Switch** – is located on the center of the firewall.
- **Number Two Vacuum Switch** – is located on the center of the firewall.
- **Number Three Vacuum Switch** – is located on the center of the firewall.
- **Oxygen Sensor** – is located in the exhaust manifold.
- **Seat Belt Timer/Buzzer** – is located under the left side of the dash panel.
- **Speed Sensor** – is located in the speedometer housing.
- **Throttle Position Sensor** – is located on the left side of the firewall.

RX7

- **A/C Low Pressure Switch** – is located under the right side of the dash panel.
- **A/C Relays** – is located in the left rear corner of the engine compartment.
- **A/C (White) Solenoid Valve** – is located in the solenoid block on the left side of the engine compartment.
- **Air Vent Solenoid Valve** – is located on the side of the carburetor.
- **Atmospheric Pressure Sensor** – is located under the right side of the dash panel near the glove box.
- **Automatic Transmission Control Unit** – is located under the right side of the dash panel near the glove box.
- **Automatic Transmission Relay** – is located in the relay block, on the front of the engine compartment.
- **Auto-Adjust Suspension Control Unit** – is located in the middle of the trunk near, the trunk latch.
- **Brake Fluid Level Sensor** – is located in the brake master cylinder.
- **Central Processing Unit (CPU)** – is located on the driver's side kick panel.
- **Choke/Check Relay** – is located in the left rear corner of the engine compartment.
- **Coolant Level Control Unit** – is located on the left kick panel.
- **Coolant Level Sensor** – is located on top of the radiator.
- **Coolant Temperature Switch** – is located on the water pump.
- **Cooling Fan Control Unit** – is located under the right side of the dash panel near the glove box.
- **Cooling Fan Temperature Sensor** – is located in the lower left side of the radiator.
- **Control Processing Unit** – is located on the left kick panel.
- **Cruise Control Sensor** – is located on the back of the speedometer.
- **Cruise Control Servo** – is located on the right front fender apron.
- **Cruise Control Unit** – is located at the left side of the luggage compartment.

- **Dimmer Relay** – is located in the relay block, on the front of the engine compartment.
- **Downshift Solenoid (Auto.Trans.)** – is located on the left side of the transmission case.
- **Emission Control Unit** – is located under the left side of the dash panel (on the right side kick panel on the later models).
- **Fuel Door Release Solenoid** – is located in the rear quarter panel.
- **Headlight Relay** – is located in the relay block, on the front of the engine compartment.
- **Heat Hazard Sensor** – is located under the right side floor mat.
- **Heater Relay** – is located under the right side of the dash panel near the glove box.
- **Horn Relay** – is located at the left kick panel.
- **Hot Start Relay** – is located in the left rear corner of the engine compartment.
- **Leading Vacuum Control (Brown) Solenoid Valve** – is located in the solenoid block on the left side of the engine compartment.
- **Lock-Up Relay** – is located in the relay block, on the front of the engine compartment.
- **Main Relay (for EGI)** – is located on the left front fender apron.
- **Oil Level Sensor** – is located on the left side of the oil pan.
- **Oil Thermo Sensor** – is located on the left side of the oil pan.
- **Oscillator Control Unit** – is located at the left front corner of the engine compartment.
- **Power Antenna Relay** – is located under the left side of the dash panel (is located in the trunk on the left rear quarter panel, on the later models).
- **Power Steering Control Unit** – is located under the center of the dash panel.
- **Rear Defrost Relay** – is located in the trunk on the left rear quarter panel.
- **Rear Hatch Release Solenoid** – is located in the center of the rear finish panel.
- **Relief (Blue) Solenoid Valve** – is located in the solenoid block on the left side of the engine compartment.
- **Shutter (Yellow) Solenoid Valve** – is located in the solenoid block on the left side of the engine compartment.
- **Starter Cut Relay** – is located on the left front fender
- **Stop Light Checker** – is located on the left kick panel.
- **Switching (Gray) Solenoid Valve** – is located in the solenoid block on the left side of the engine compartment.
- **Theft-Deterrent Control Unit** – is located under the right side of the dash panel near the glove box.
- **Throttle Sensor** – is located on the carburetor throttle linkage.
- **Trailing Vacuum Control (Green) Solenoid Valve** – is located in the solenoid block on the left side of the engine compartment.
- **Turn Cancel And Angle Sensor** – is located in the turn signal assembly.
- **Washer Fluid Level Sensor** – is located in the washer fluid reservoir.

626

- **A/C (3) Relays** – there are two relays located under the right side of the dash panel and one relay located on the left side of the radiator support.
- **Air Control Solenoid Valve** – is located on the left side of the firewall in the engine compartment.
- **Air Solenoid Valve** – is located on the left side of the firewall in the engine compartment.

- **Air-Fuel Solenoid Valve** – is located inside the carburetor.
- **Anti-Dieseling Solenoid** – is located on the side of the carburetor.
- **Auto Adjusting Suspension Control Unit (AAS)** – is located under the passenger's side seat.
- **Brake Fluid Level Sensor** – is located on the brake master cylinder.
- **Coasting Richer Solenoid Valve** – is located on the side of the carburetor.
- **Condenser Fan Relay** – is located in the left front corner of the engine compartment.
- **Coolant Temperature Sensor** – is located on the radiator bottom tank.
- **Coolant Temperature Switch** – is located on the side of the intake manifold.
- **Cooling Fan Motor Relay** – is located in the left front corner of the engine compartment.
- **Cooling Fan Temperature Switch** – is located on the thermostat housing.
- **Cruise Control Actuator** – is located on the left front fender well.
- **Cruise Control Unit** – is located under the left side of the dash panel near the relay block.
- **Door Lock Solenoids** – are located one on each door.
- **Door Lock Timer Unit** – is located under the right side of the dash panel near the kick panel.
- **EGI Control Unit** – is located under the right side of the dash panel.
- **EGR Position Sensor** – is located on top of the EGR valve.
- **EGR Solenoid Valve** – is located on the right side of the
- **Electronic Control Unit (ECU)** – is located under the center of the dash panel.
- **Ignition Relay** – is located on the left front fender apron.
- **Ignition Switch/Door Lock Illumination Timer** – is located under the left side of the dash panel.
- **Intermittent Wiper Relay** – is located under the left side of the dash panel.
- **Headlight (2) Relays** – are located on the left front fender apron.
- **High Mount Stop Light Checker** – is located in the relay block, which is under the left side of the dash panel.
- **Horn Relay** – is located under the left side of the dash panel near the relay block.
- **Key Illumination Timer Unit** – is located in the relay block, which is under the left side of the dash panel.
- **Kickdown Solenoid** – is located on the front of the transaxle.
- **Oxygen Sensor** – is located on the exhaust manifold.
- **Power Steering Solenoid Valve** – is located on the left side of the firewall in the engine compartment.
- **Ride Control (4) Solenoids** – are located on the top of each strut.
- **Ride Control Unit** – is located under the right side of the dash panel.
- **Seat Belt Timer Unit** – is located in the relay block, which is under the left side of the dash panel.
- **Sound Warning Unit** – is located in the relay block, which is under the left side of the dash panel.
- **Starter Cut Relay** – is located in the relay block, which is under the left side of the dash panel.
- **Super Heat Control Unit** – is located under the right side of the dash panel.
- **Theft-Deterent Control Unit** – is located under the driver's side seat.
- **Vacuum Sensor** – is located on the side of the firewall in the engine compartment.
- **Washer Fluid Level Sensor** – is located in the bottom of the washer fluid reservoir.

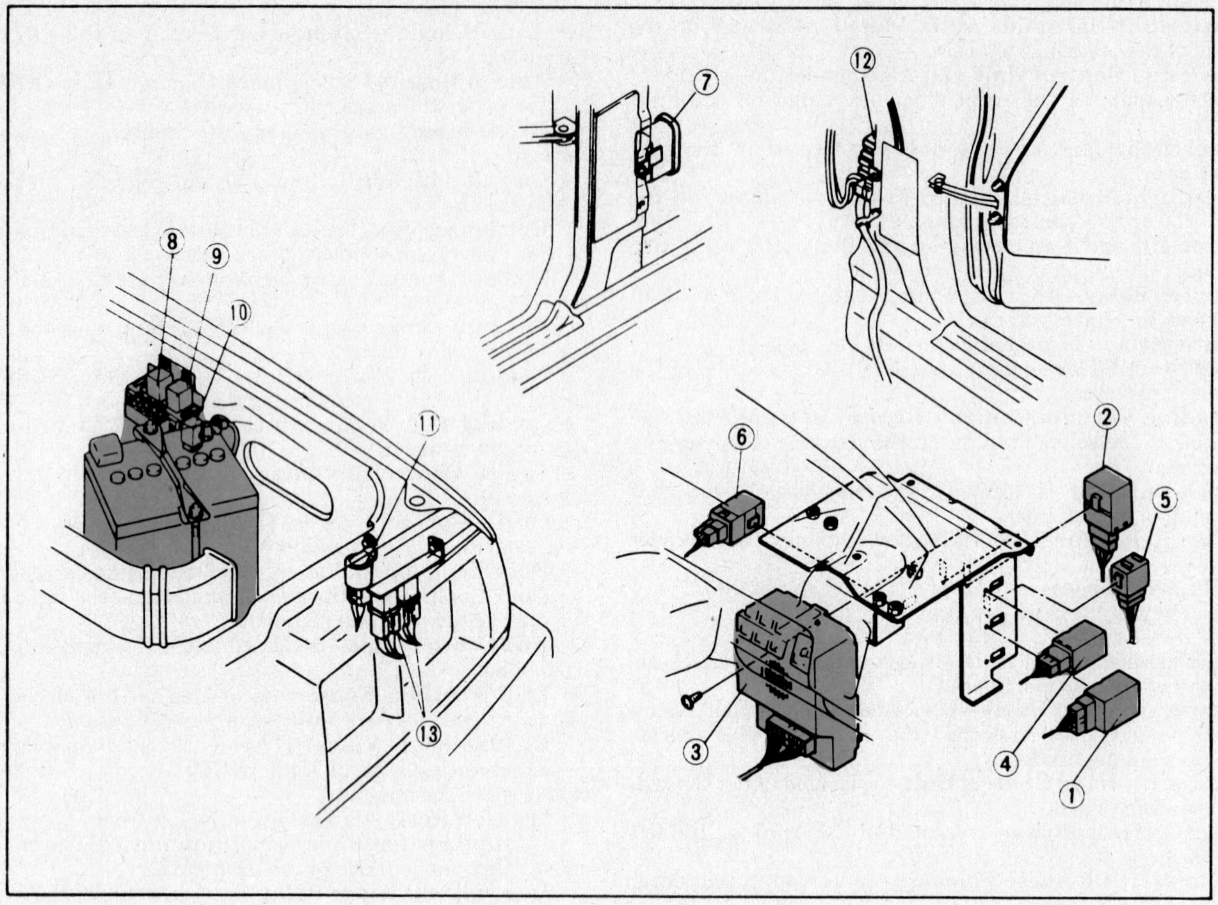

Relays

① Intermittent wipers relay
② Stop and tail light checker
③ Sound warning unit
④ Ignition-switch and door-lock illumination timer
⑤ Seat belt timer
⑥ Flasher unit

⑦ Horn relay
⑧ Headlight relay
⑨ Stop and tail lamp relay
⑩ Ignition relay
⑪ Electric fan relay
⑫ Door lock relay
⑬ Air conditioner relay (optional)

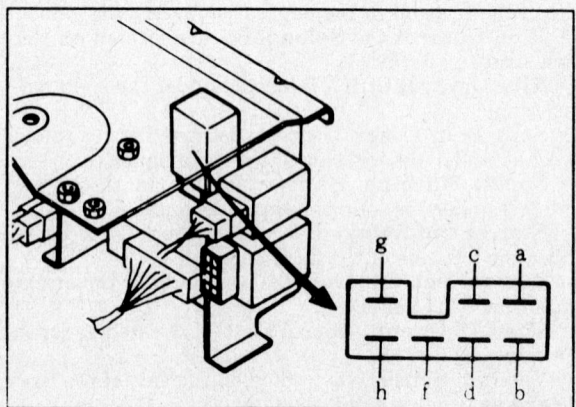

Inspection of Stop Light and Tail Light Checker

1. Use a tester to check for continuity between the various terminals.

Connection terminal	Continuity
a – c	Yes
f – h	Yes
b – d	No
b – g	No

1984-85 Mazda 626

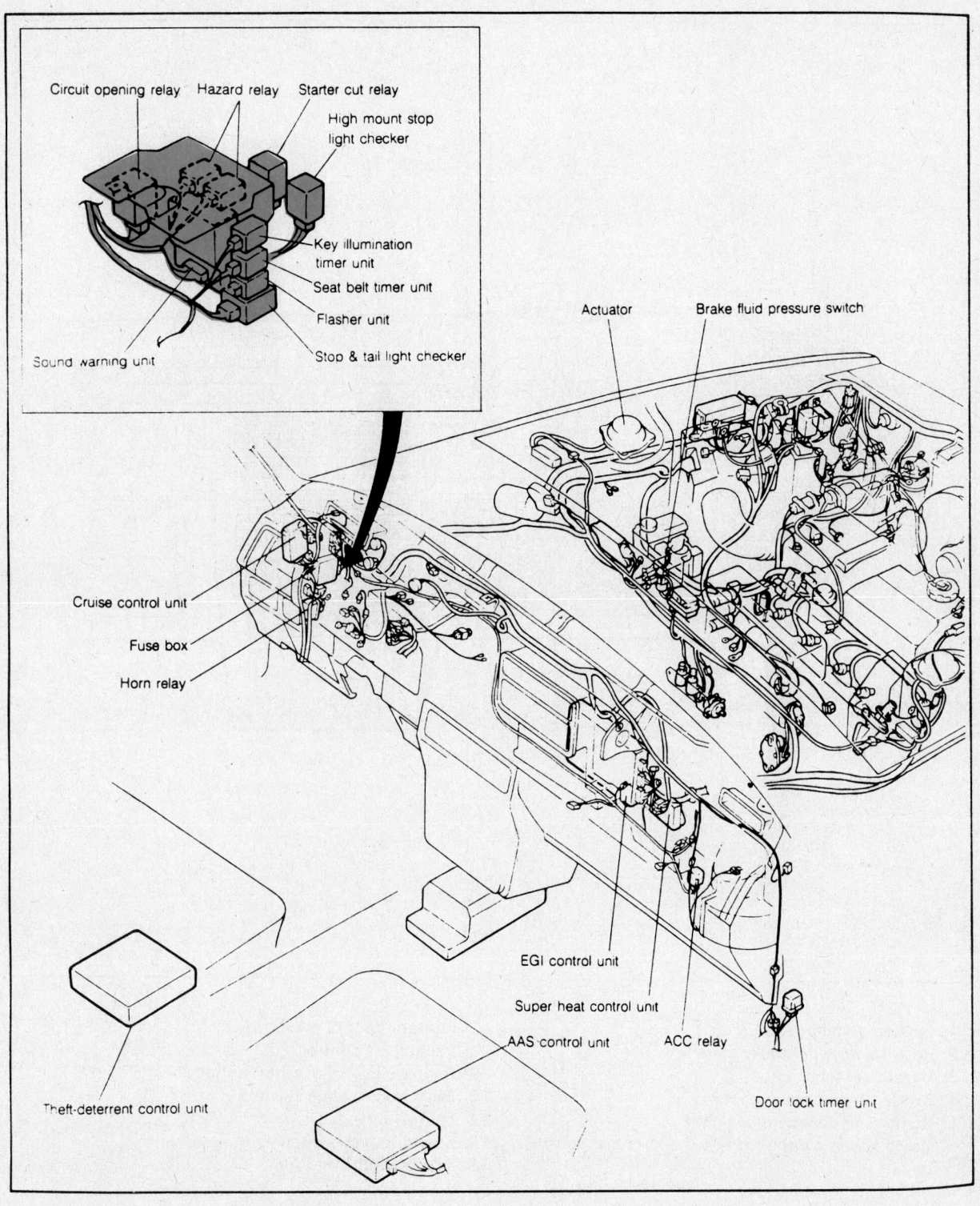

Circuit opening relay · Hazard relay · Starter cut relay
High mount stop light checker
Key illumination timer unit
Seat belt timer unit
Flasher unit
Sound warning unit
Stop & tail light checker

Actuator
Brake fluid pressure switch

Cruise control unit
Fuse box
Horn relay

EGI control unit
Super heat control unit
AAS control unit
ACC relay

Theft-deterrent control unit
Door lock timer unit

1986 Mazda 626

COMPONENT LOCATIONS

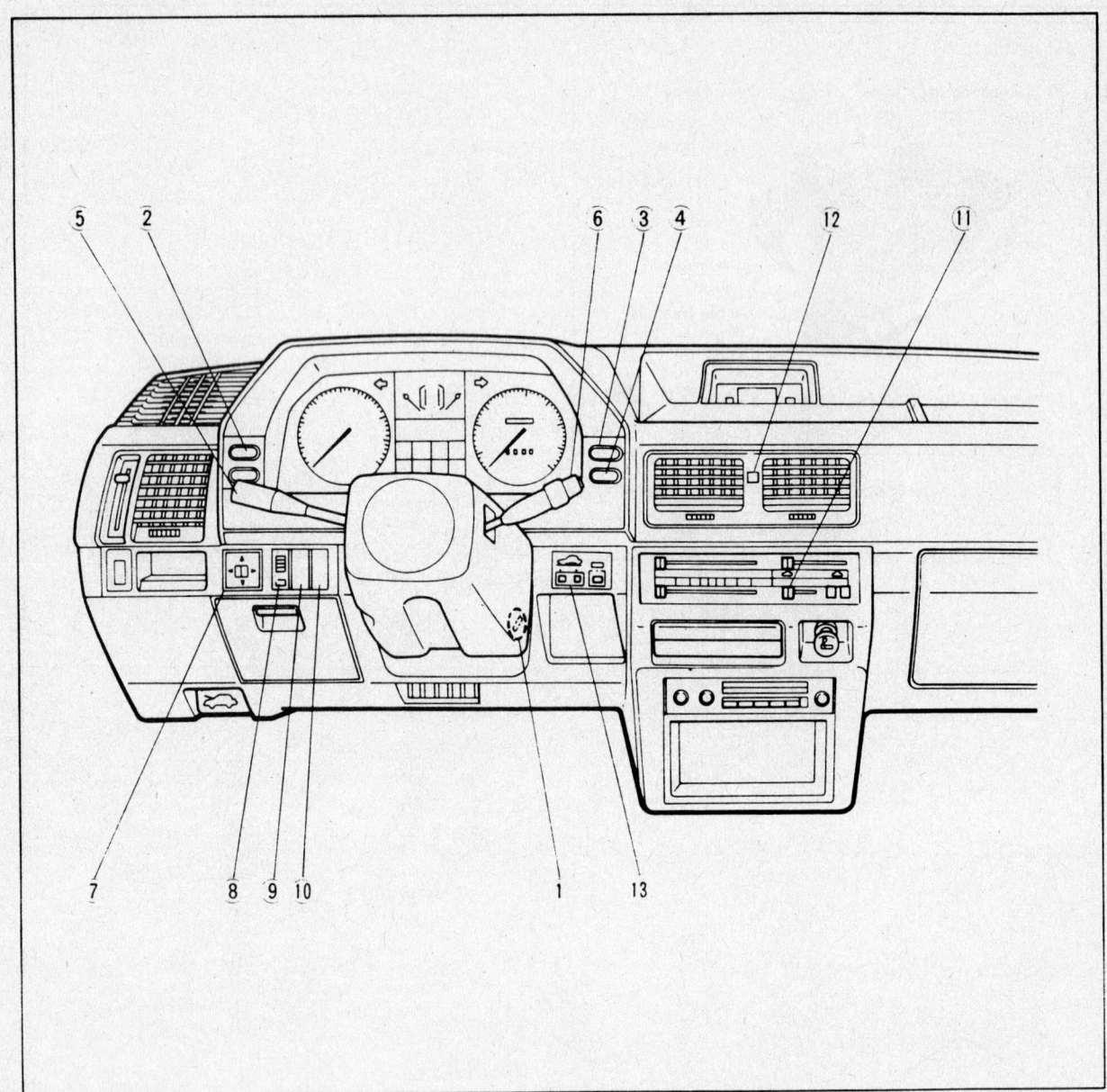

1. Ignition switch
2. Rear window defroster switch
3. Hazard switch
4. Cruise control main switch
5. Combination switch for lights
6. Combination switch for wiper and cruise control

7. Remote control mirror switch
8. Panel light control
9. Rear wiper and washer switch
10. Head light cleaner switch
11. Fan switch
12. Swing louver switch
13. AAS switch

1986 Mazda 626

COMPONENT LOCATIONS

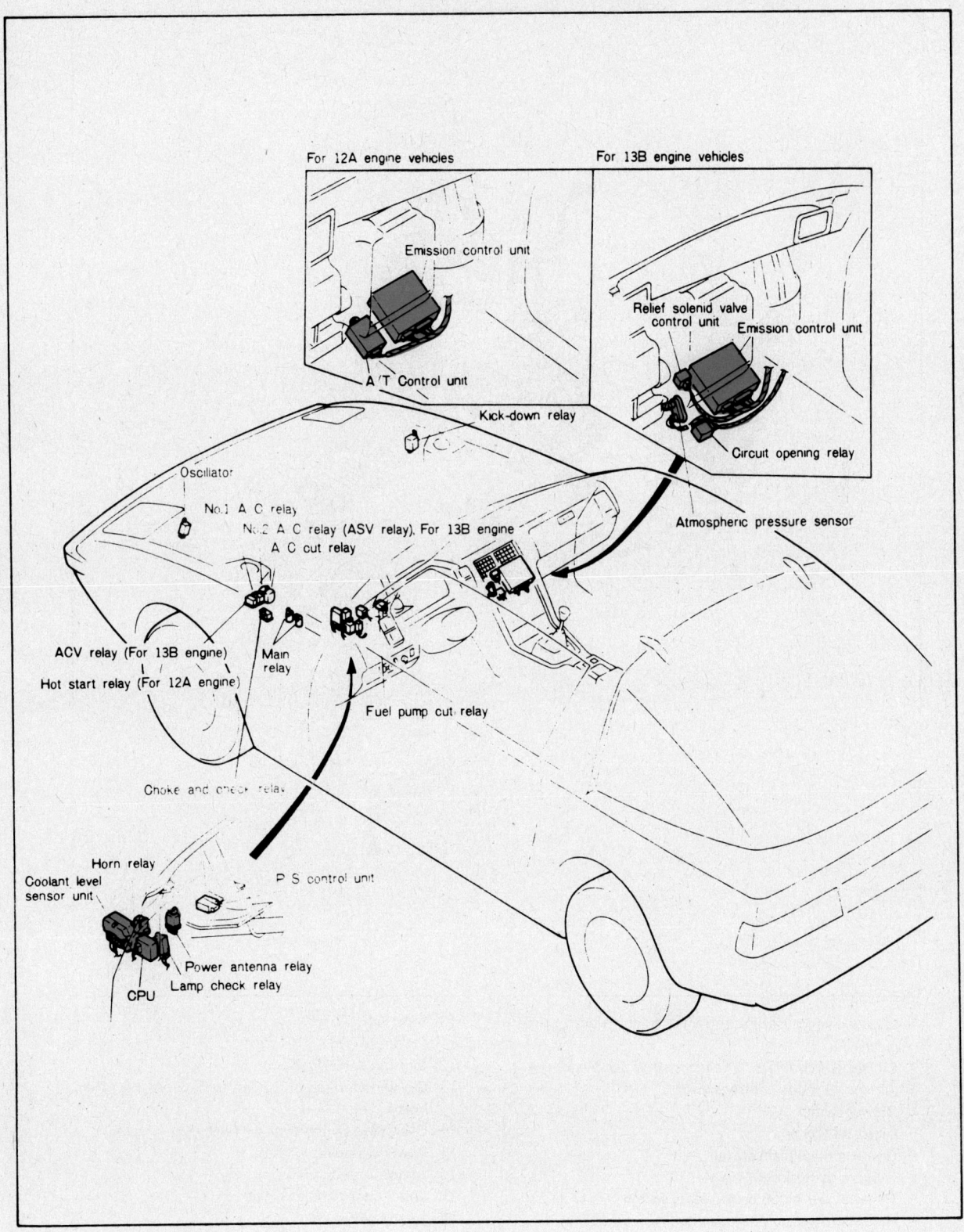

For 12A engine vehicles

Emission control unit

A/T Control unit

For 13B engine vehicles

Relief solenoid valve control unit

Emission control unit

Circuit opening relay

Kick-down relay

Atmospheric pressure sensor

Oscillator

No.1 A/C relay

No.2 A/C relay (ASV relay), For 13B engine

A/C cut relay

ACV relay (For 13B engine)

Hot start relay (For 12A engine)

Main relay

Fuel pump cut relay

Choke and check relay

Horn relay

Coolant level sensor unit

P/S control unit

Power antenna relay

Lamp check relay

CPU

1984-85 Mazda RX-7

COMPONENT LOCATIONS

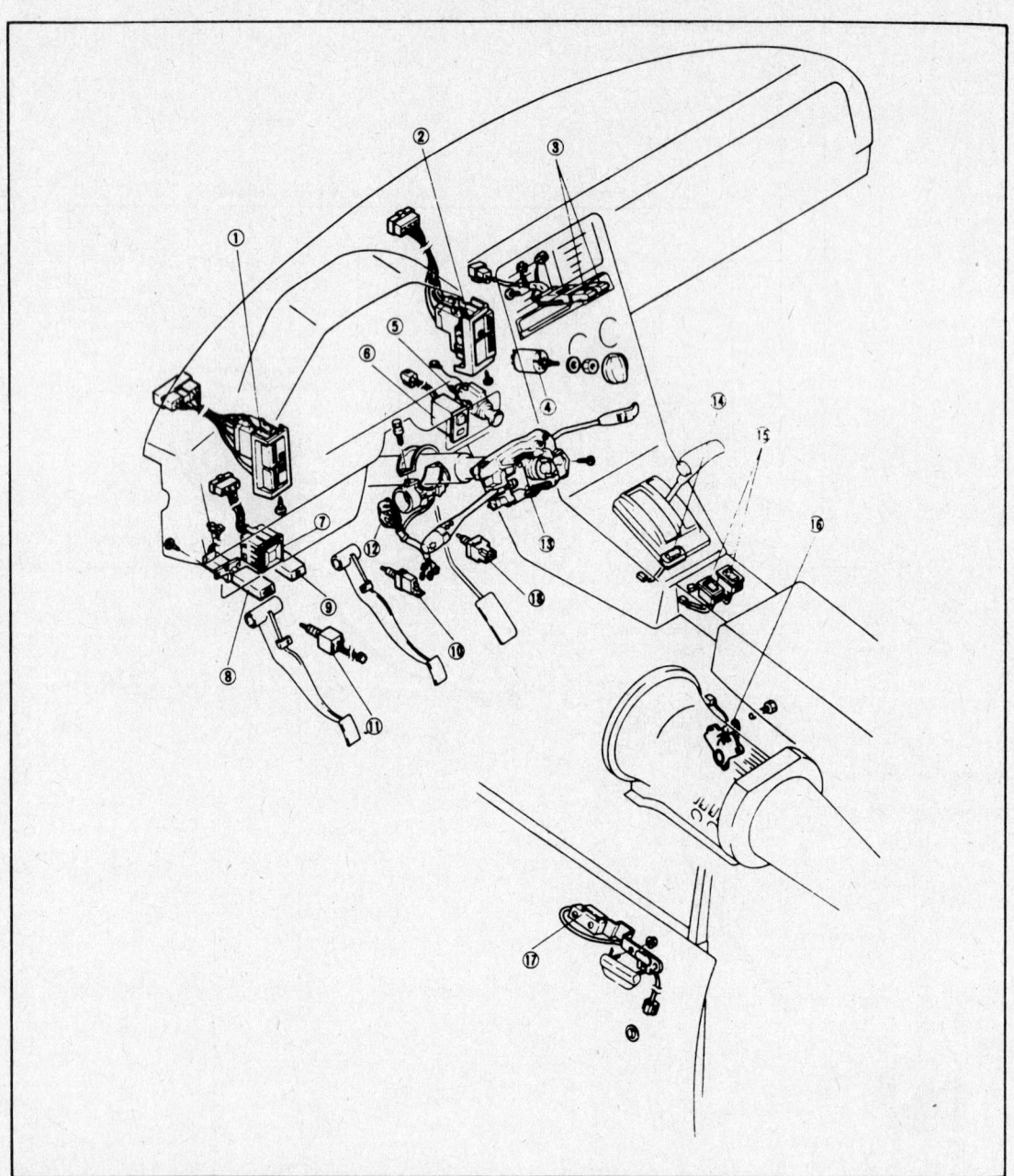

1 Cluster switch (Hazard, retractable light & head light cleaner)
2 Cluster switch (Rear defroster, rear wiper & washer)
3 Air con. & mode control switch
4 Blower switch
5 Cigarette lighter
6 Cruise control main switch
7 Remote control mirror switch
8 Remote glass hatch back release switch
9 Remote fuel door release switch

10 Stop light switch
11 Clutch switch
12 Ignition key switch
13 Combination switch (Light, turn, wiper & washer, horn)
14 Over drive switch (For 4AT vehicle)
15 Power window switches
16 Inhibitor switch
17 Outer door handle switch
18 Kick-down switch

1984-85 Mazda RX-7

COMPONENT LOCATIONS

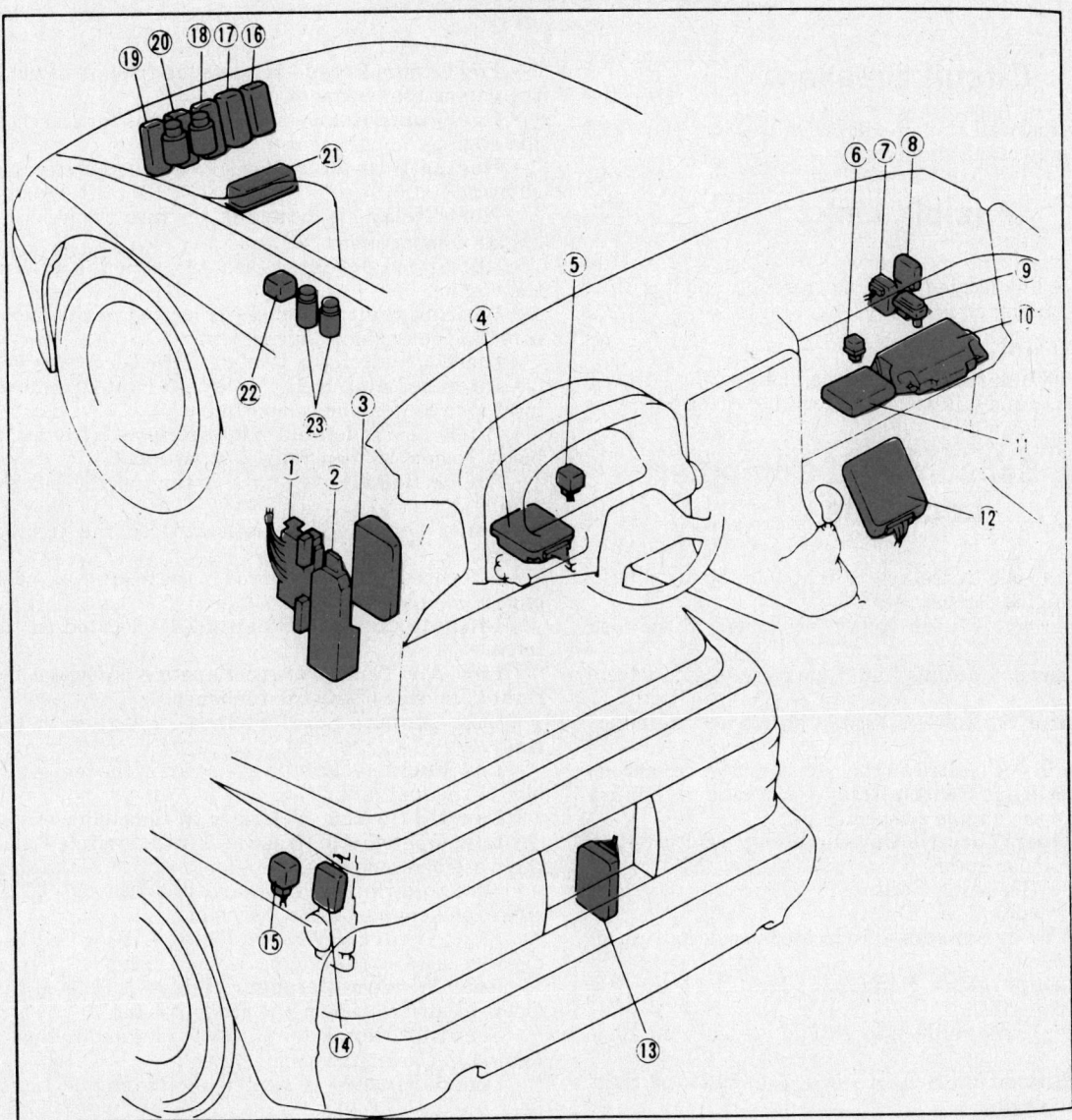

1. Fuse box
2. Central processing unit
   (Turn and hazard, lights off reminder buzzer, key illumination timer, horn relay, seat belt timer, buzzer, ALT. warning light relay, stop light warning relay, key reminder buzzer)
3. Cruise control unit
4. Power steering control unit
5. Circuit opening relay (for EGI)
6. Heater relay
7. Cooling fan control unit
8. 4 A/T control unit
9. Atmospheric pressure sensor
10. Speaker with amplifier
11. Theft-deterrent control unit
12. Emission control unit
13. Auto-adjust suspension control unit
14. Power antenna relay
15. Rear defroster relay
16. Dimmer relay
17. Headlight relay
18. Cooling fan relay
19. Lock-up relay
20. 4 A/T relay
21. Main fuse box
22. Starter cut relay
23. Main relay (for EGI)

1986 Mazda RX-7

MERKUR XR4Ti

Circuit Breakers

This model protects all the circuits with fuses or relays and does not show any circuit breakers.

Fusible Links

STARTER

There is a fusible link located on the starter relay and it is used to protect the starting circuit.

MAIN WIRING HARNESS

There is a fusible link running from the main wiring harness to the starter relay and it is used to protect the wiring harness.

Relay, Sensors And Computer Locations

- **A/C Clutch Cut-Out Relay** — is located in the fuse block, located in the engine compartment.
- **A/C Compressor Clutch Relay** — is located in the fuse block.
- **A/C Condenser Cooling Fan Relay** — is located in the fuse block.
- **A/C Pressure Switch** — is located on the A/C receiver/drier.
- **A/C Solenoid** — is located on the right front fender apron.
- **A/C Temperature Switch Relay** — is located in the fuse block, located in the engine compartment.
- **A/C Wide Open Throttle Cut-Out Relay** — is located on the right front fender apron.
- **Barometric Pressure Sensor** — is located on the right hand side fender apron.
- **Brake Pad Wear Sensors** — are located inside the respective disc pads.
- **Coolant Temperature Sender** — is located on the left hand side of the engine.
- **EGR Control Solenoid** — is located on the left front fender apron.
- **EGR Valve Position Sensor** — is at the top of the right front side of the engine.
- **EGR Vent Solenoid** — is located at the left front fender apron.
- **Electronic Control Assembly (ECA)** — is attached to the lower left side of the cowl.
- **Electronic Engine Control (EEC) Power Relay** — is attached to the lower right side cowl near the electronic control assembly.
- **Engine Coolant Temperature Sensor** — is at the top front of the engine.
- **Engine Cooling Fan Relay** — is located on the left side of the engine on the lower intake manifold.
- **Engine Cooling Fan Temperature Switch** — is located on the left side of the engine on the lower intake manifold.
- **Exhaust Oxygen Sensor** — is located in the left rear side of the engine.

- **Fog Lamps Relay** — is located in the fuse block, located in the engine compartment.
- **Fuel Pump Relay** — is located in the fuse block, located in the engine compartment.
- **Heated Seat Relay** — is located in the steering column support.
- **Horn Relay** — is located in the fuse block, located in the engine compartment.
- **Idle Speed Actuator** — is attached to the left hand side of the engine.
- **Ignition Switch Relay** — is located in the fuse block, located in the engine compartment.
- **Inertia Switch** — is located in the spare tire well.
- **Interior Lamp Delay Relay** — is located in the fuse block, located in the engine compartment.
- **Interval Windshield Wiper Relay** — is located in the fuse block, located in the engine compartment.
- **Knock Sensor** — is at the bottom of the left side of the engine.
- **Lamp Out Module** — is located on the right side cowl panel.
- **Liftgate Relay** — is located in the fuse block, located in the engine compartment.
- **Liftgate Release Solenoid** — is located in the lifgate latch.
- **Low Air Temperature Sensor** — is located behind the right hand side of the front bumper.
- **Low Coolant Level Switch** — is located in the coolant reservoir.
- **Low Fuel Level Switch** — is part of the fuel sender assembly, in the fuel tank.
- **Low Oil Switch** — is located in the engine oil pan.
- **Low Windshield Washer Fluid Switch** — is located in the washer reservoir.
- **Manifold Charge Temperature Sensor** — is on the right side of the engine on the manifold.
- **Rear Interval Wipers Relay** — is located in the fuse block, located in the engine compartment.
- **Rear Window Defogger Relay** — is located in the fuse block, located in the engine compartment.
- **Seat Belt Reminder Relay** — is located in the fuse block, located in the engine compartment.
- **Speed Sensor** — is located in the engine compartment, near the dash panel.
- **Starter Relay** — is located on the right front fender apron.
- **Stop Light Relay** — is located in the fuse block, located in the engine compartment.
- **Thick Film Ignition Module** — is attached to the distributor.
- **Throttle Position Sensor** — is located on the left side of the engine.
- **Tripminder Display Module** — is located behind the center of the instrument panel.
- **Turbo Boost Solenoid** — is located on the right side of the turbocharger.
- **Turbo Overboost Switch** — is located on the left front fender apron.
- **Vane Air Flow Meter** — is located on the front right side of the engine.

MITSUBISHI

Circuit Breakers

These models protect all the circuits with fuses or relays and do not show any circuit breakers.

Fusible Links

CORDIA AND TREDIA

Every circuit except for the starter motor uses fusible links.

STARION

The fusible links consist of a main link and sub links. The main link is connected to the positive terminal of the battery. There are two sub links, and both of them are located in the relay box on the left front fender.

MIRAGE

The fusible links consist of a main link and a sub link. The main link is connected to the positive terminal of the battery. The sub link, is located in the wiring harness across from the alternator on the front radiator mounting support. There is also a fuse connected to the A/C receiver/drier that protects the A/C circuit.

GALANT

The fusible links consist of a main link and sub links. The main link is connected to the positive terminal of the battery. There are two sub links, and both of them are located in the relay box on the left front fender. There is also an in-line fuse used in the sunroof wiring harness to protect the sunroof circuit.

Relay, Sensors And Computer Locations

CORDIA AND TREDIA

- **A/C Condenser Fan Relay** – is located on the A/C evaporator housing.
- **A/C Low Pressure Switch** – is located on the A/C evaporator housing.
- **A/C Relay** – is located on the A/C evaporator housing.
- **A/C Thermo Sensor** – is located in the A/C evaporator housing.
- **A/C Thermo Switch** – is located on the A/C evaporator housing.
- **Bowl Vent Solenoid Valve** – is located on the top of the carburetor.
- **Brake Fluid Sensor** – is located in the master cylinder.
- **Coolant Temperature Sensor** – is located on the side of the intake manifold.
- **Cooling Fan Sensor** – is located in the bottom of the radiator.
- **Dimmer Relay** – is located near the battery on the right inner fender panel.
- **Door Lock Control Relay** – is attached to the bottom of the heater box.

- **Door Lock Power Relay** – is attached to the bottom of the heater box.
- **Door Lock Solenoids** – there is one located behind each door panel.
- **Electronic Control Transmission (ECT) Computer** – is located under the left side of the instrument panel.
- **Engine Speed Sensor** – is located in the left rear corner of the engine compartment.
- **Fuel Cut-Off Solenoid Valve** – is located on the transaxle mounting bracket.
- **Headlight Relay** – is located in the relay box, located in the engine compartment.
- **Heater Relay** – is located under the center of the instrument panel.
- **Ignition Computer** – is located under the left side of the instrument panel.
- **Intermittent Wiper Relay** – is located in the relay box, located in the engine compartment.
- **One-Touch Power Window Relay** – is located in the driver's side door behind the panel.
- **Power Steering Relay** – is located in the relay block attached to the right inner fender panel.
- **Power Window Relay** – is located in the relay box, located in the engine compartment.
- **Radiator Fan Motor Relay** – is located in the relay box, located in the engine compartment.
- **Rear Defrost Relay** – is located under the left side of the instrument panel.
- **Seat Belt Warning Relay** – is located under the left side of the instrument panel.
- **Select Control Relay** – is located under the left side of the instrument panel.
- **Speed Control Switch** – is located under the left side of the instrument panel.
- **Tail Light Relay** – is located in the relay box, located in the engine compartment.
- **Throttle Position Sensor** – is located on the carburetor (or throttle body).
- **Transaxle Select Switch** – is located on the right side of the clutch housing.
- **Transaxle Solenoid Valve** – is located on the transaxle mounting bracket.

STARION

- **A/C Compressor Relay** – is located on the left inner fender panel.
- **A/C Heater Blower Motor Relay** – is located on the blower motor housing.
- **A/C Low Pressure Switch** – is located on the A/C evaporator housing.
- **A/C Power Relay** – is located on the evaporator housing.
- **A/C Thermo Switch** – is located on the A/C evaporator housing.
- **Air Flow Sensor** – is located in the air cleaner housing.
- **Brake Fluid Level Sensor** – is located on the brake master cylinder.
- **Control Relay** – is located above the ECU on the right side cowl.
- **Coolant Temperature Sensor** – is located on the front of the intake manifold.
- **Detonation (Knock) Sensor** – is located on the right front of the engine.

- **Door Lock Relay** – is located in the right side quarter panel.
- **EGR Solenoid** – is located on the left inner fender panel.
- **Electronic Control Unit (ECU)** – is located on the right side of the cowl.
- **Electronic Time/Alarm Control System (ETACS) Unit** – is located on the left front floor crossmember.
- **Engine Spark Control (ESC) Ignitor** – is located on the left inner fender panel.
- **Engine Speed Sensor** – is located on the back of the speedometer housing.
- **'G' Sensor** – is located on the rear floor crossmember.
- **Headlight Lighting Relay** – is located in the left front corner of the engine compartment.
- **Hi/Lo Wiper Relay** – is located in the left front corner of the engine compartment.
- **Idle Speed Control Solenoid** – is located on the injector housing.
- **Idle Speed Switch** – is located on the injector housing.
- **Intake Air Temperature Sensor** – is located in the air cleaner assembly.
- **Left Headlight Pop-Up Relay** – is located in the left front corner of the engine compartment.
- **Manifold Pressure Sensor** – is located in the left rear corner of the engine compartment.
- **Oil Pressure Senor** – is located on the engine block near the oil filter.
- **Overdrive Relay** – is located on the left side cowl, under the instrument panel.
- **Oxygen Sensor** – is located on the exhaust manifold.
- **Passing Control Relay** – is located under the right side of the instrument panel near the radio.
- **Power Antenna Relay** – is located on the left high-floor side panel.
- **Power Window Relay** – is located in the left front corner of the engine compartment.
- **Pressure Sensor** – is located on the left side of the firewall.
- **Radiator Fan Motor Relay** – is located on the left inner fender panel.
- **Rear Brake Lock-Up Control Unit** – is located in the luggage compartment.
- **Rear Brake Lock-Up Modulator** – is located in the right rear corner of the engine compartment.
- **Rear Brake Lock-Up Solenoid Valve** – is located on the rear brake lock-up modulator.
- **Rear Defrost Relay** – is located in the left front corner of the engine compartment.
- **Right Headlight Pop-Up Relay** – is located in the left front corner of the engine compartment.
- **Speed Control Unit** – is located on the left rear inner quarter panel.
- **Speed Control Vacuum Pump Relay** – is located in the right rear corner of the engine compartment.
- **Tail Light Lighting Relay** – is located in the left front corner of the engine compartment.
- **Throttle Position Sensor** – is located on the injector housing.
- **Washer Fluid Level Sensor** – is located on the bottom of the washer reservoir.
- **Wiper Relay** – is located in the left front corner of the engine compartment.

MIRAGE

- **A/C Cycling Clutch Switch** – is located on the A/C evaporator coil.
- **A/C High/Low Pressure Cut-Out Switch** – is located on the discharge side of the compressor.
- **Air Flow Sensor** – is located in the air cleaner assembly.

- **Blower Relay** – is located on the right side of the firewall near the heater unit.
- **Brake Fluid Level Sensor** – is attached to the brake master cylinder reservoir.
- **Control Relay** – is located on the right side kick panel.
- **Coolant Temperature Sensor** – is located on the bottom of the thermostat housing, in the intake manifold.
- **Cooling Fan Motor Relay** – is located on the relay block, behind the driver's side kick panel.
- **Cooling Fan Thermo Sensor** – is located on the bottom left side of the radiator.
- **Detonation (Knock) Sensor** – is located on the left side of the engine.
- **ELC-A/T Control Unit** – is located on or near the left side kick panel.
- **Electronic Control Unit** – is mounted on the passenger's side kick panel.
- **Electronic Controlled Injection (ECI) Unit** – is located in the center of the firewall, near the heater unit.
- **Engine Spark Control Igniter** – is located on the left side of the firewall.
- **Engine Speed Sensor (ESS) Relay** – is located on the left kick panel, above the fuse block.
- **Feedback Carburetor Control (FBC) Unit** – is located in the center of the firewall, near the heater unit.
- **Fuel Cut Solenoid** – is located on the carburetor.
- **Fuel Level Sensor** – is located in the gas tank, but accessible through the spare tire floor.
- **Idle Speed Position Switch** – is installed on the fuel injection mixer assembly.
- **Idle Up Solenoid Valve** – is located on the left rear corner of the engine compartment.
- **Intake Air Temperature Sensor** – is installed in the air cleaner.
- **Intermittent Wiper Relay** – is located on the left side of the firewall.
- **Oxygen Sensor** – is located in the exhaust manifold.
- **Pressure Sensor** – is located on the firewall.
- **Seat Belt Timer** – in located in the fuse block.
- **Throttle Position Sensor** – is located near the throttle body.
- **Transistor Relay** – is located in the wire harness near the fuse block.

GALANT

- **A/C Compressor Relay** – is located in a relay block on the right front fender apron.
- **A/C Fan Relay** – is located in a relay block on the right front fender apron.
- **A/C Low Pressure Switch** – is located on the A/C evaporator housing.
- **A/C Power Relays** – are located on the left side of the engine.
- **A/C Thermo Sensor** – is located in the A/C evaporator housing.
- **A/C Thermo Switch** – is located on the A/C evaporator housing.
- **Air Flow Sensor** – is installed in the air cleaner assembly.
- **Air Suspension Diagnostic Self Check Connector** – is located in the glove box at the top.
- **Auto Temperature Control Unit** – is located under the center of the instrument panel.
- **Bowl Vent Solenoid Valve** – is located of the top of the carburetor.
- **Brake Fluid Sensor** – is located in the master cylinder.
- **Coolant Temperature Sensor** – is located on the side of the intake manifold.

- **Cooling Fan Sensor** – is located in the bottom of the radiator.
- **Defogger Relay** – is located in a relay block under the left side of the instrument panel.
- **Door Lock Solenoids** – there is one located behind each door panel.
- **Duct Sensor** – is located on the right side of the engine.
- **ECS Compressor Relay** – is located on the right front fender apron.
- **Electronic Controlled Suspension (ECS) Unit** – is located in the right rear quarter panel.
- **Electronic Time/Alarm Control System** – is located on or near the left side kick panel.
- **Electronically Controlled Power Steering Sensor** – Is located behind the center console.
- **Engine Speed Sensor** – is located in the left rear corner of the engine compartment.
- **Fuel Cut-Off Solenoid Valve** – is located on the transaxle mounting bracket.
- **'G' Sensor** – is located on the roof headliner.
- **Headlight Lighting Relay** – is located in a relay block on the right front fender apron.
- **Heater Relay** – is located in a relay block under the left side of the instrument panel.
- **Idle Position Switch** – is installed on the fuel injection mixer assembly.
- **Intake Air Temperature Sensor** – is installed in the air cleaner assembly.
- **Multi-Point Fuel Injection Control Relay** – is located on the right side of the firewall.
- **Multi-Point Fuel Injection Control Unit** – is located on the right side of the firewall.

- **Oxygen Sensor** – is located in the exhaust manifold.
- **Photo Sensor** – is located in the engine cowl in front of the windshield.
- **Power Door Lock Relay** – is located in the left side kick panel.
- **Power Window Relay** – is located in a relay block on the right front fender apron.
- **Pressure Sensor** – is located on the firewall.
- **Radiator Fan Motor Relay** – is located in a relay block on the right front fender apron.
- **Room Temperature Sensor** – is located on the roof headliner.
- **Speed Control Switch** – is located under the left side of the instrument panel.
- **Speed Control Unit** – is located near or on the left side kick panel.
- **Tail Light Relay** – is located in a relay block on the right front fender apron.
- **Throttle Position Sensor** – is located on the throttle body.
- **Transaxle Select Switch** – is located on the right side of the clutch housing.
- **Transaxle Solenoid Valve** – is located on the transaxle mounting bracket.
- **Transmission Control Unit** – is located under the center of the instrument panel.
- **Turning Speed Sensor** – is located in the steering column.
- **Wiper Relay** – is located on the right front fender apron.

COMPONENT LOCATIONS

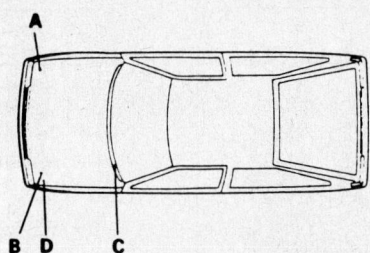

A **Main fusible link**

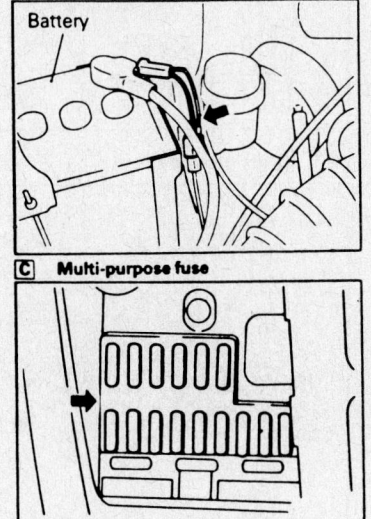

Battery

B **Sub fusible link**

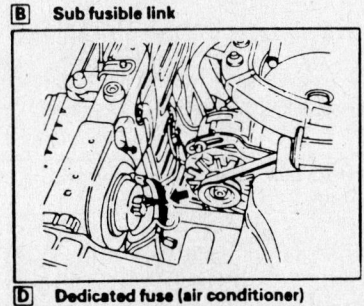

C **Multi-purpose fuse**

D **Dedicated fuse (air conditioner)**

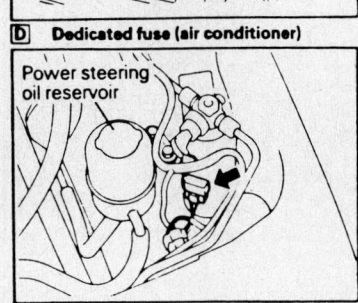

Power steering oil reservoir

Mitsubishi Mirage

257

COMPONENT LOCATIONS

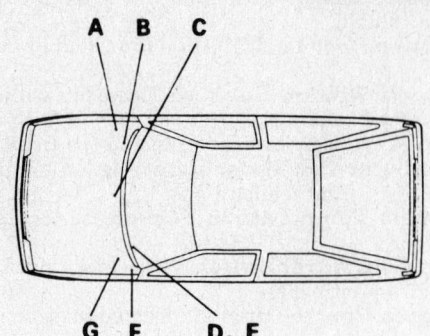

A B C

G F D, E

A Intermittent wiper relay

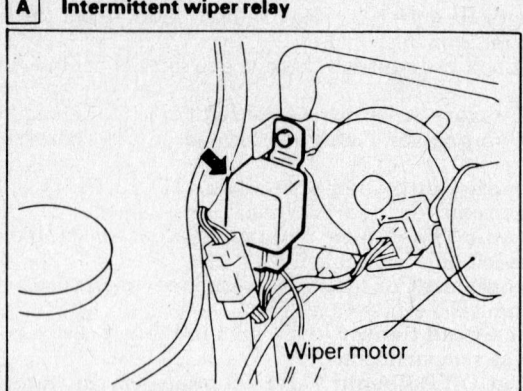

Wiper motor

B Blower relay

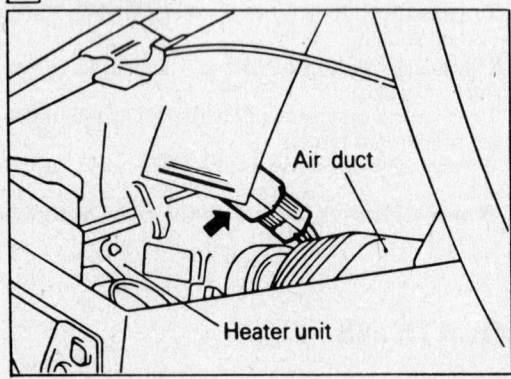

Air duct

Heater unit

C ECI computer and FBC control unit

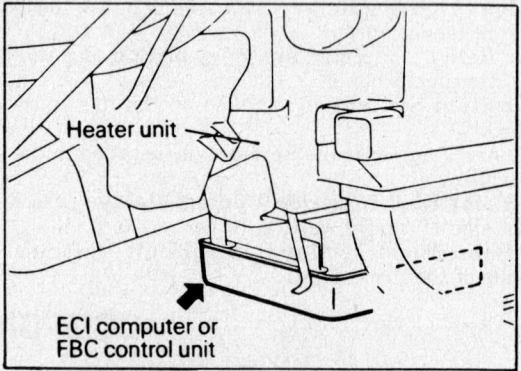

Heater unit

ECI computer or
FBC control unit

D Seat belt timer

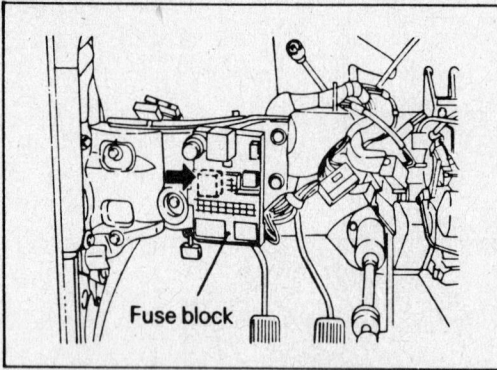

Fuse block

E Radiator fan motor relay and turn-signal and hazard-warning flasher unit

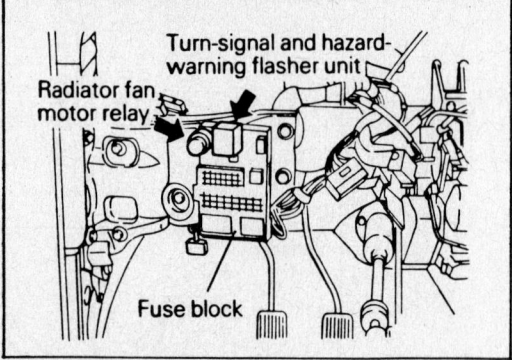

Turn-signal and hazard-warning flasher unit

Radiator fan motor relay

Fuse block

F ELC-A/T control unit, select control unit and ECI control relay

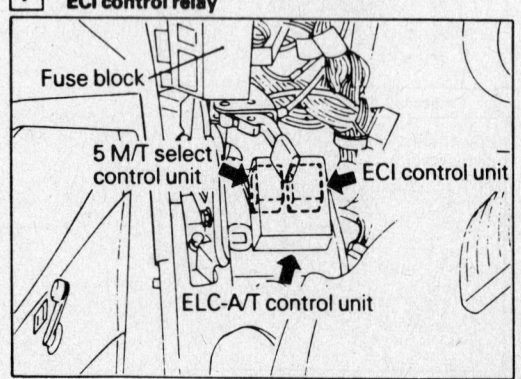

Fuse block

5 M/T select control unit

ECI control unit

ELC-A/T control unit

G Transistor relay

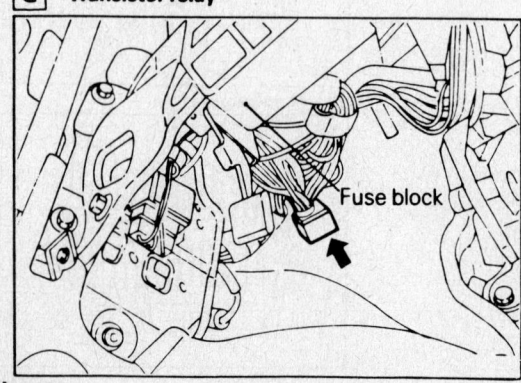

Fuse block

Mitsubishi Mirage

COMPONENT LOCATIONS

Rear

FBC

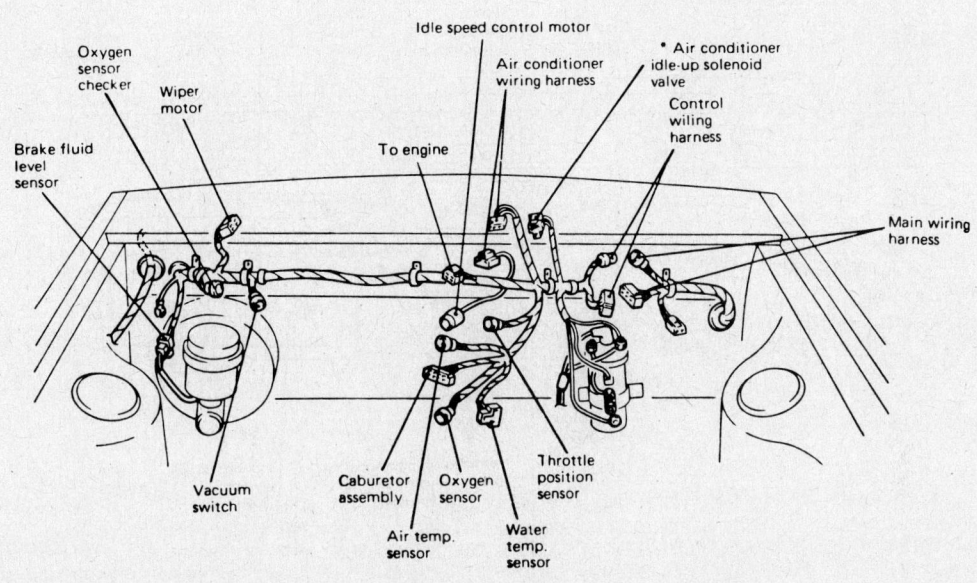

Turbo

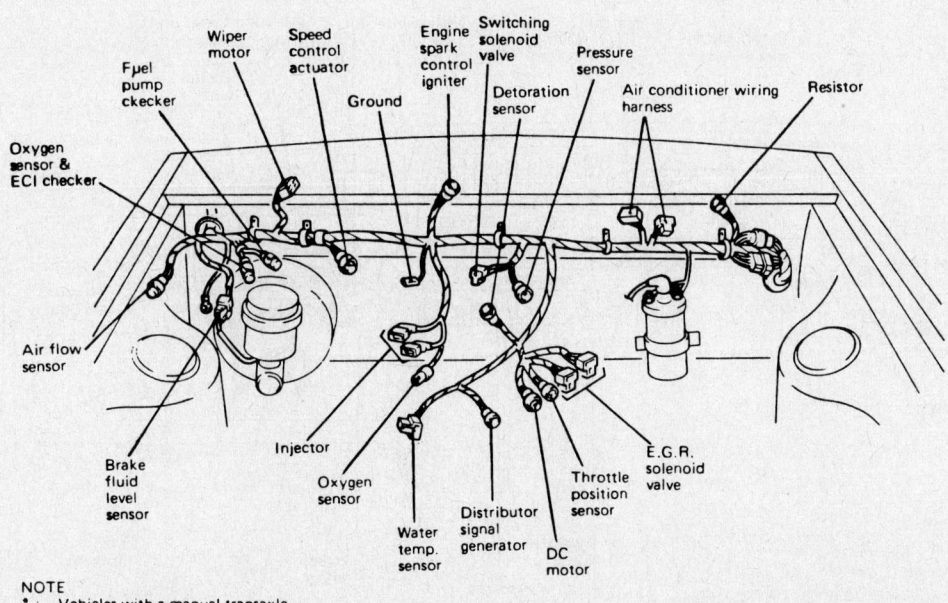

NOTE
* :   Vehicles with a manual transaxle

Mitsubishi Cordia and Tredia

COMPONENT LOCATIONS

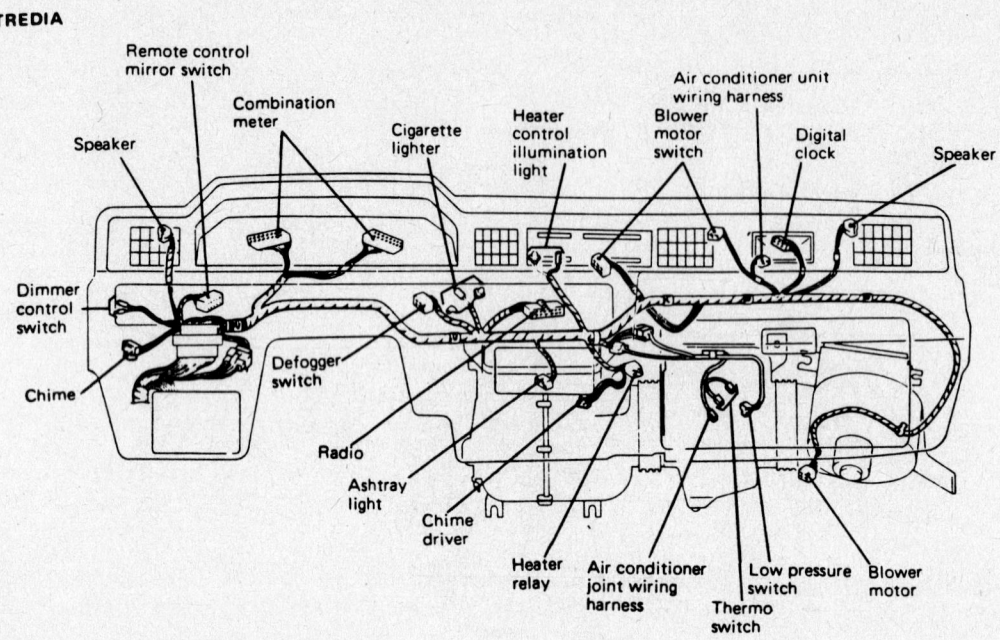

TREDIA

Remote control mirror switch

Combination meter

Speaker

Cigarette lighter

Heater control illumination light

Air conditioner unit wiring harness

Blower motor switch

Digital clock

Speaker

Dimmer control switch

Chime

Defogger switch

Radio

Ashtray light

Chime driver

Heater relay

Air conditioner joint wiring harness

Low pressure switch

Thermo switch

Blower motor

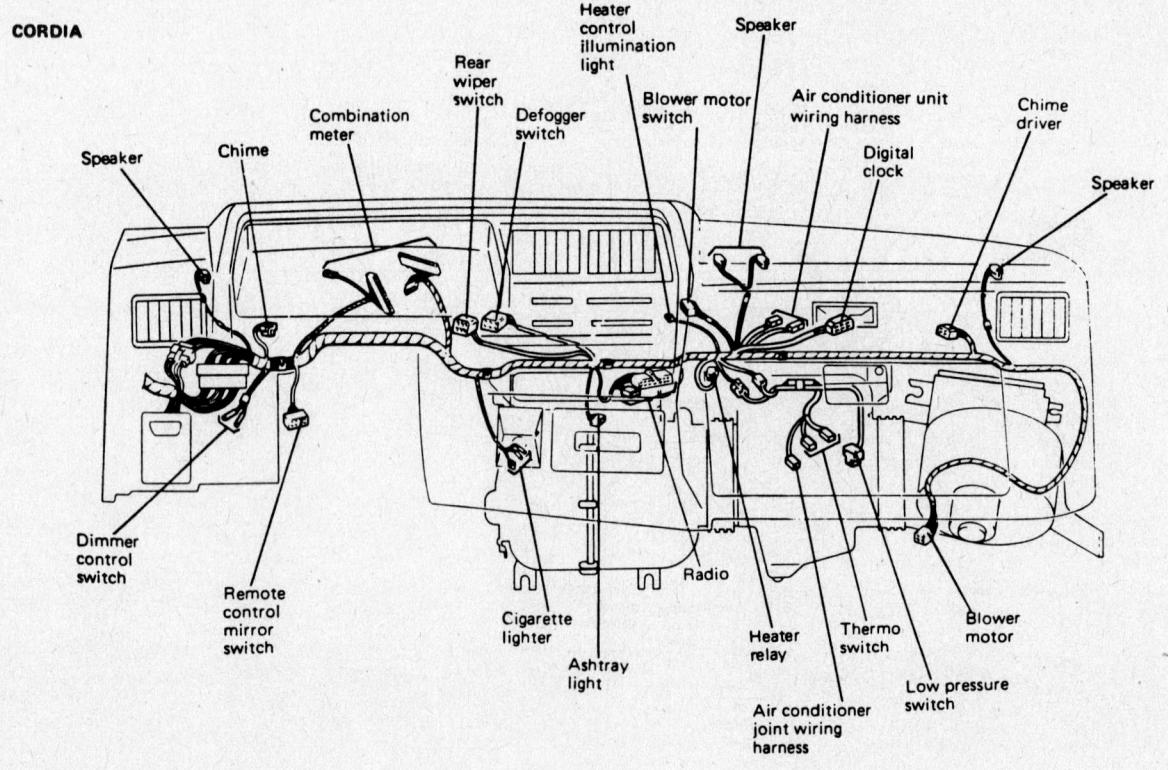

CORDIA

Heater control illumination light

Speaker

Rear wiper switch

Combination meter

Defogger switch

Blower motor switch

Air conditioner unit wiring harness

Digital clock

Chime driver

Speaker

Chime

Speaker

Dimmer control switch

Remote control mirror switch

Cigarette lighter

Ashtray light

Radio

Heater relay

Air conditioner joint wiring harness

Thermo switch

Low pressure switch

Blower motor

Mitsubishi Cordia and Tredia

COMPONENT LOCATIONS

TREDIA

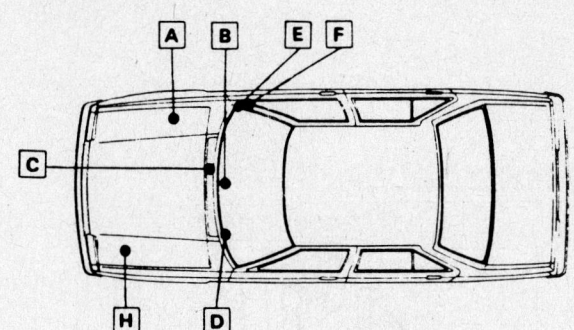

CORDIA

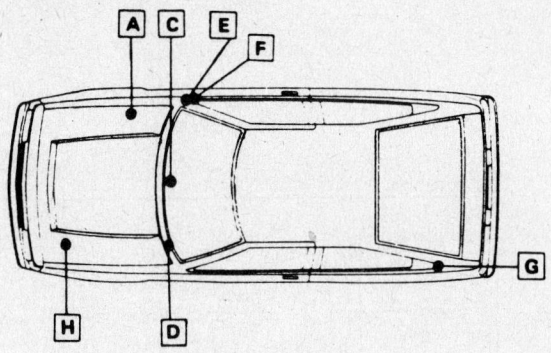

A Relay box inside of engine compartment

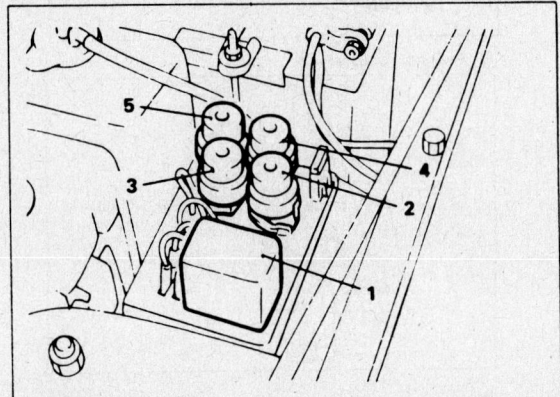

B Bottom of heater unit

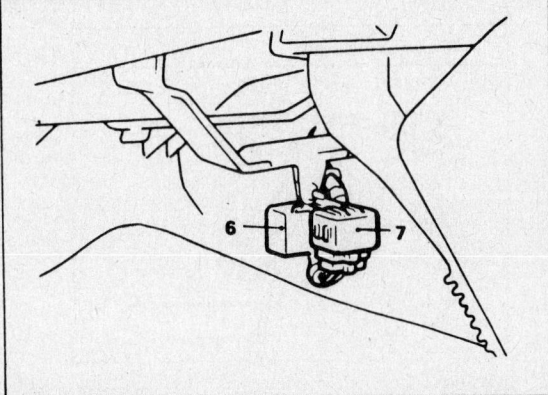

C Left of glove box

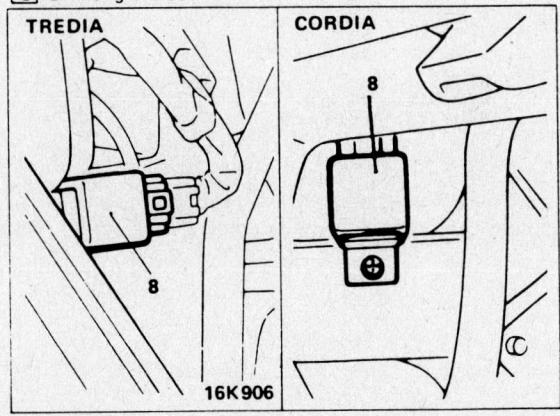

TREDIA   CORDIA

16K 906

D Driver's side firewall (A/T)

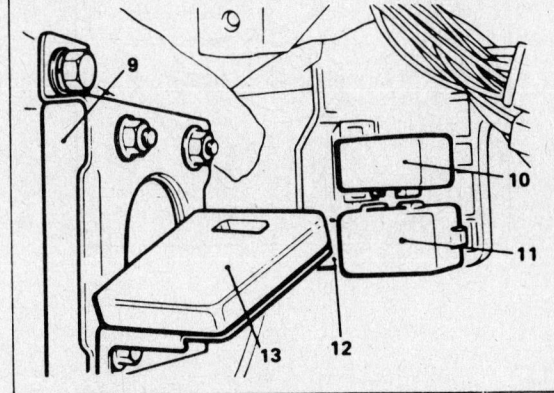

---

1. Intermittent wiper relay	8. Heater realy
2. Headlight relay	9. ELC-A/T control unit
3. Radiator fan motor relay	10. Flasher unit
4. Tail light relay	11. Defogger relay
5. Power window relay	12. Seat belt warning relay
6. Door lock control relay	13. Speed control unit
7. Door lock power realy	

Mitsubishi Cordia and Tredia

COMPONENT LOCATIONS

D Driver's side firewall (M/T)

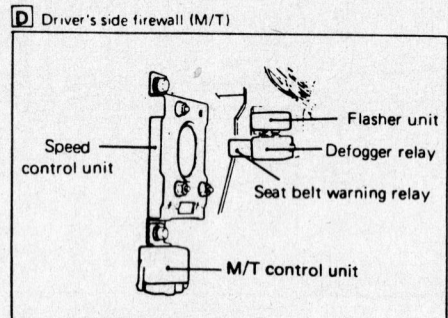

Speed control unit

Flasher unit

Defogger relay

Seat belt warning relay

M/T control unit

E Passenger's side cowl side

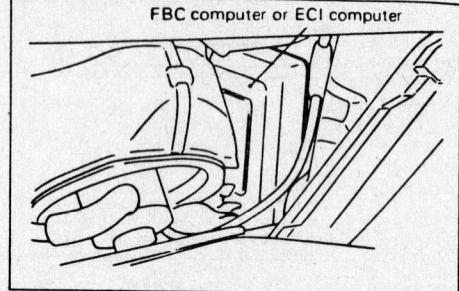

FBC computer or ECI computer

F Passenger's side cowl side

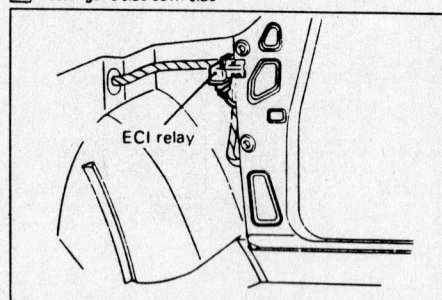

ECI relay

G Rear side panel, left side

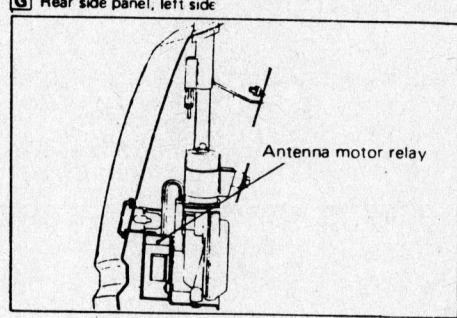

Antenna motor relay

H Front side member, left side

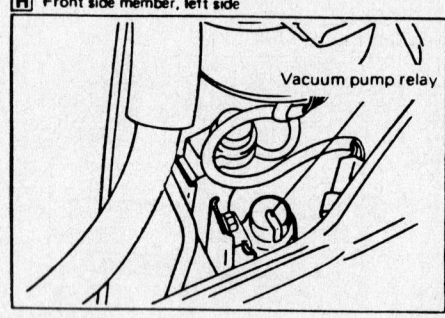

Vacuum pump relay

NOTES
M/T: Manual transaxle
A/T: Automatic transaxle

COMPONENT LOCATIONS

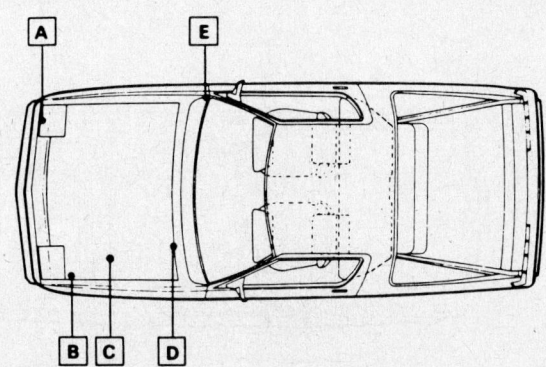

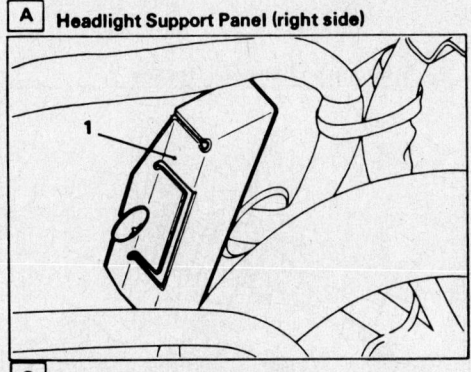

A — Headlight Support Panel (right side)

B — Wheel House Outer (left side)

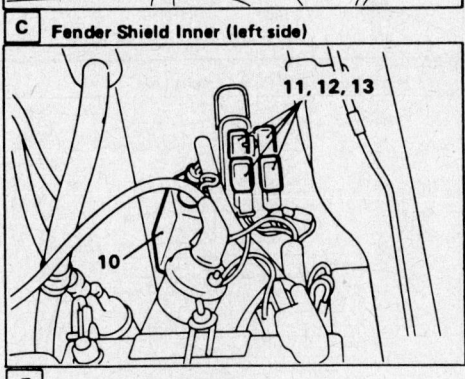

C — Fender Shield Inner (left side)

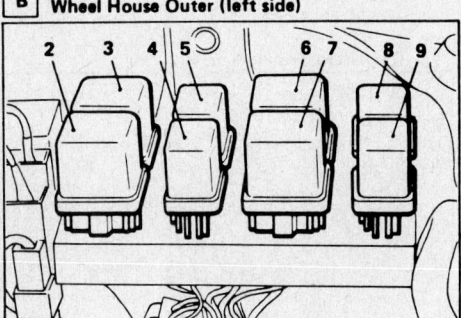

D — Dash Panel (left side)

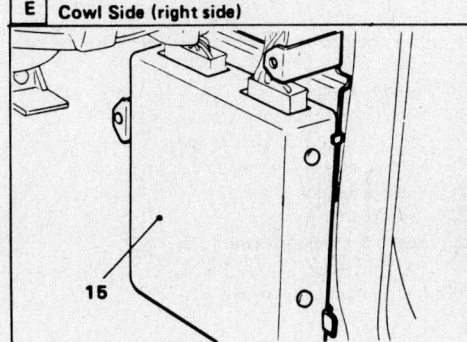

E — Cowl Side (right side)

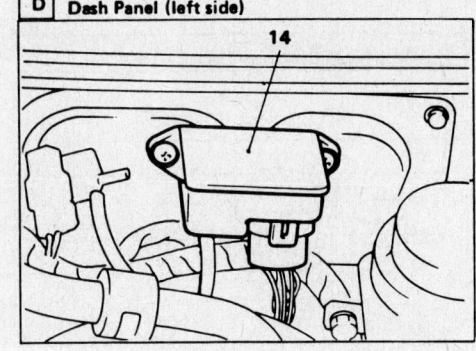

1. Resistor for ECI
2. Pop-up relay (for right headlight)
3. Pop-up relay (for left headlight)
4. Lighting relay (for headlight)
5. Lighting relay (for tail light)
6. Wiper relay (for Low and High)
7. Wiper relay (for ON)
8. Power window relay
9. Rear window defogger relay
10. ESC (Engine Spark Control) igniter
11. Air conditioner relay (for pusher fan)
12. Air conditioner relay (for compressor)
13. Air conditioner relay (for radiator fan control)
14. Pressure sensor
15. ECU (Electronic Control Unit)

Mitsubishi Starion

COMPONENT LOCATIONS

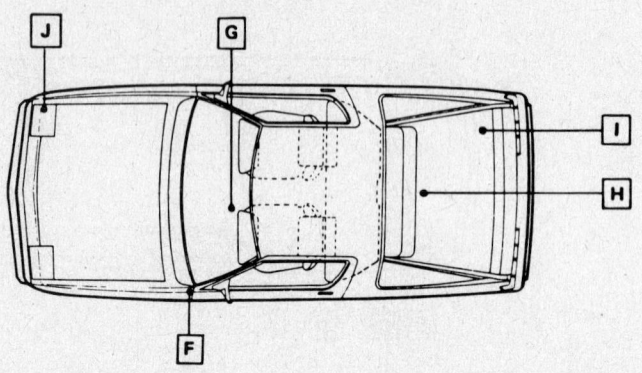

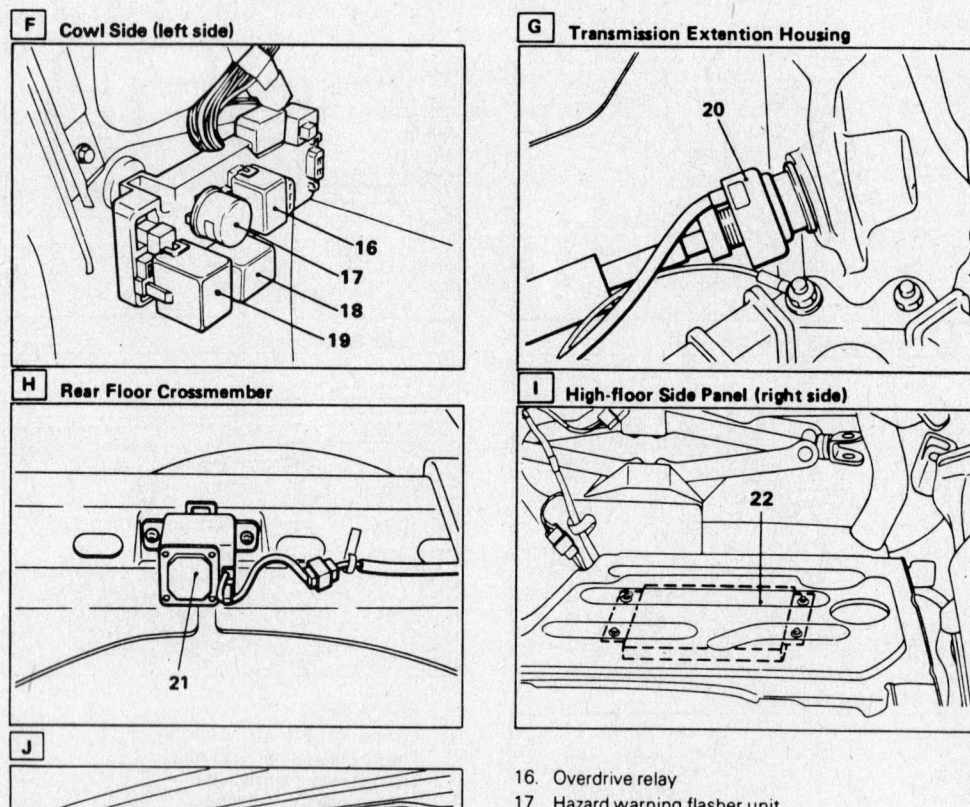

F **Cowl Side (left side)**

16
17
18
19

G **Transmission Extention Housing**

20

H **Rear Floor Crossmember**

21

I **High-floor Side Panel (right side)**

22

J

23
24

16. Overdrive relay
17. Hazard warning flasher unit
18. Rear brake lock-up control relay
19. Turn-signal light flasher unit
20. Pulse generator
21. G-sensor
22. Rear brake lock-up control unit
23. Fog light relay
24. Radiator fan motor relay

Mitsubishi Starion

COMPONENT LOCATIONS

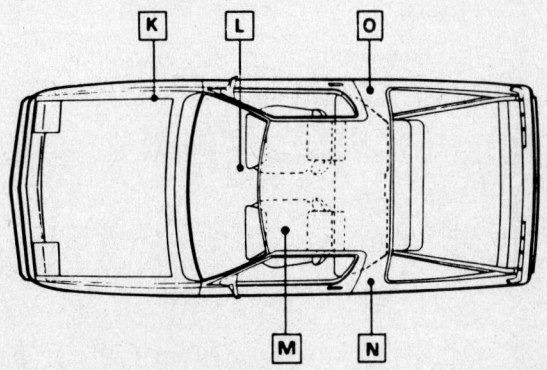

K Wheel House Outer (right side)

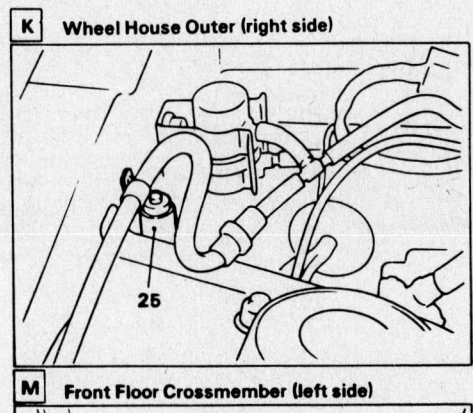

25

L Center Reinforcement (right side)

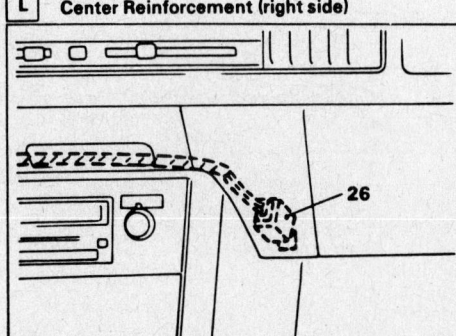

26

M Front Floor Crossmember (left side)

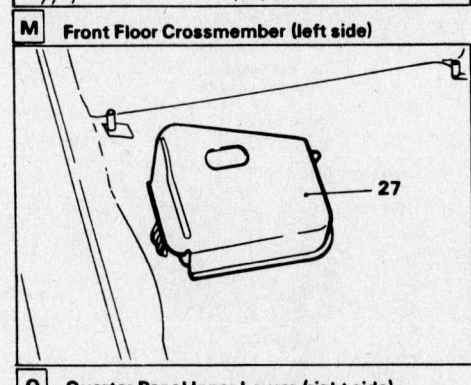

27

N Quarter Panel Inner Lower (left side)

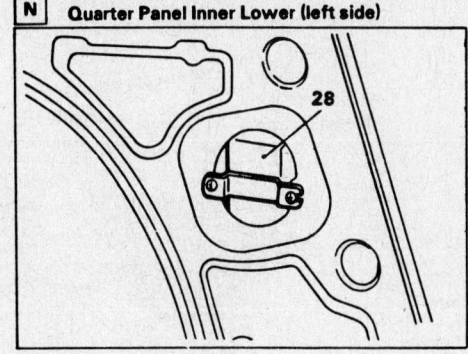

28

O Quarter Panel Inner Lower (right side)

29

25. Speed control vacuum pump relay
26. Passing control relay
27. TAC unit
28. Speed control unit
29. Door lock relay

Mitsubishi Starion

COMPONENT LOCATIONS

Engine compartment — Front (Vehicles with an intercooler)

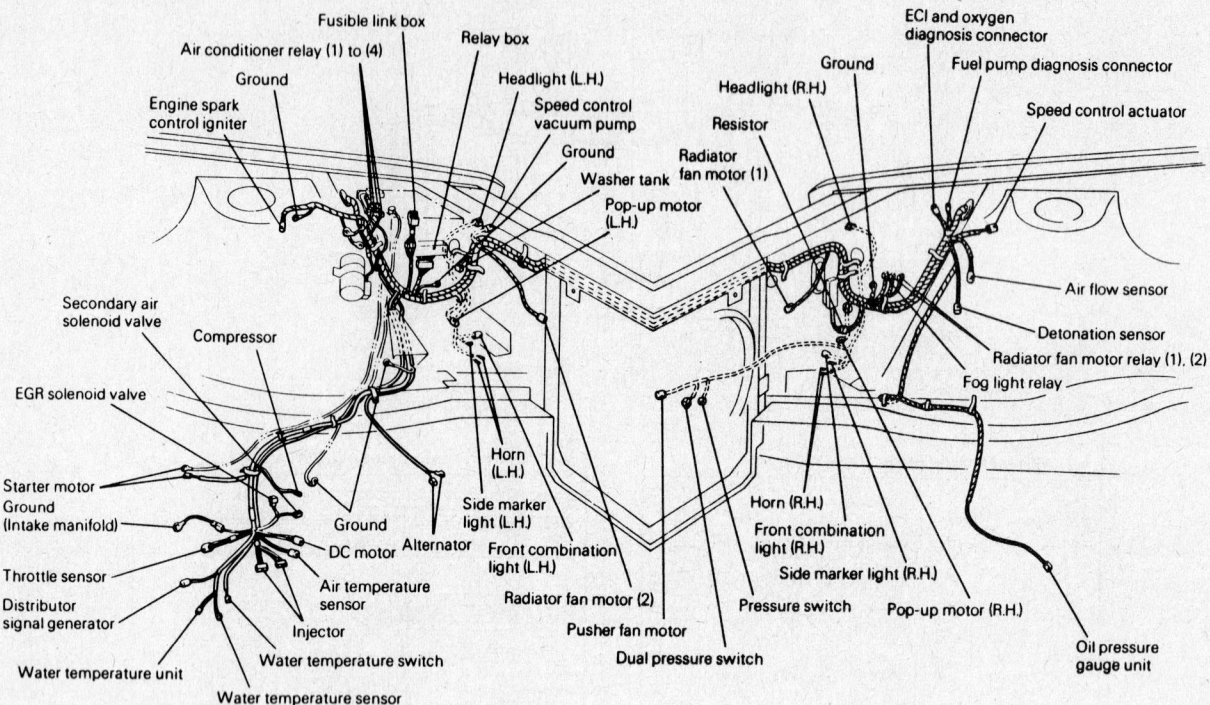

Engine compartment — Front (Vehicles without an intercooler)

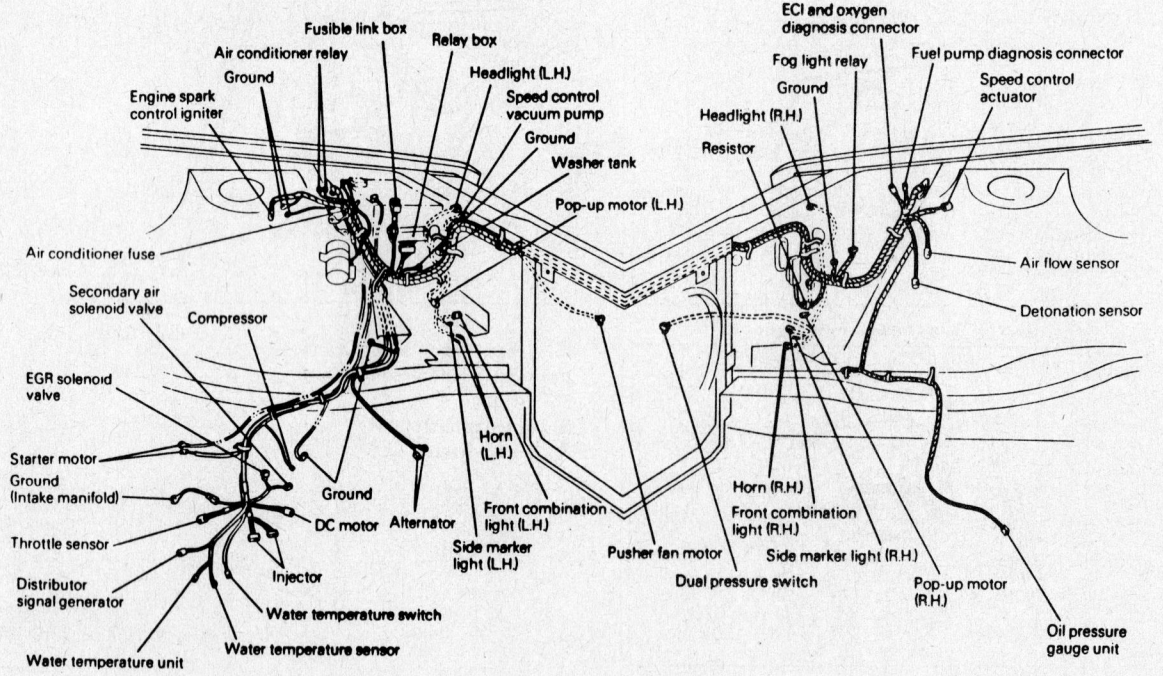

Mitsubishi Starion

COMPONENT LOCATIONS

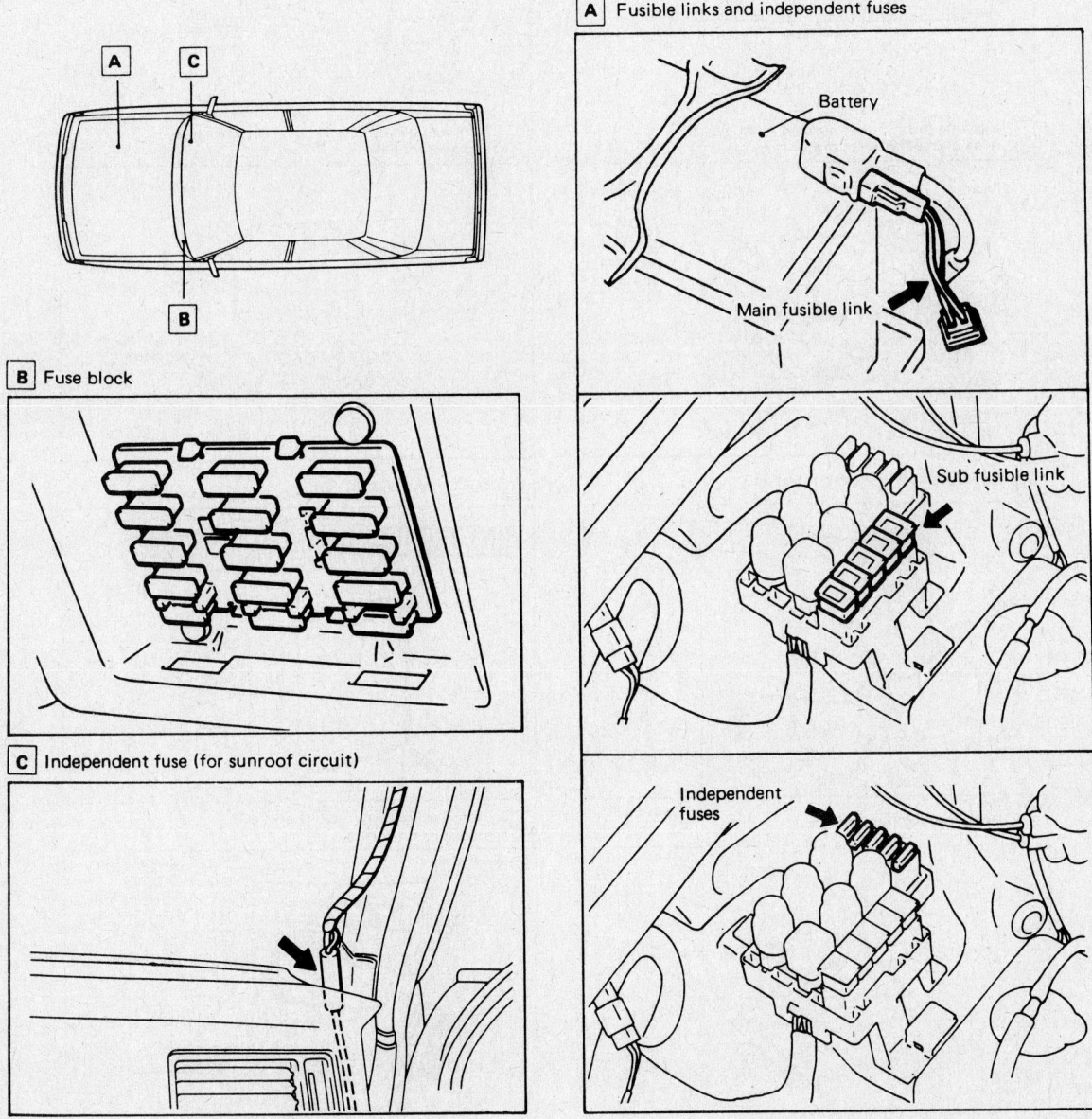

A Fusible links and independent fuses

Battery

Main fusible link

B Fuse block

Sub fusible link

C Independent fuse (for sunroof circuit)

Independent fuses

Mitsubishi Galant

267

COMPONENT LOCATIONS

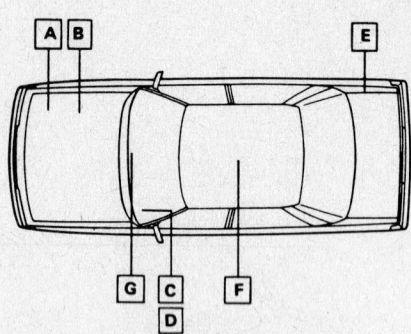

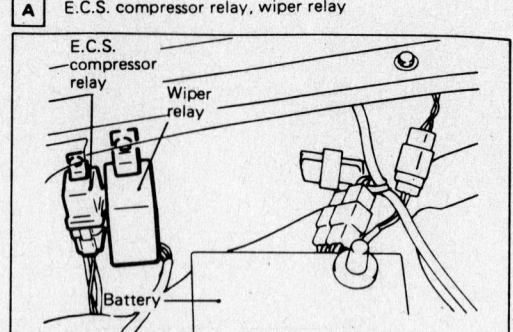

A E.C.S. compressor relay, wiper relay

E.C.S. compressor relay
Wiper relay
Battery

B Lighting relay, Power window relay, Power relay and radiator fan motor relay

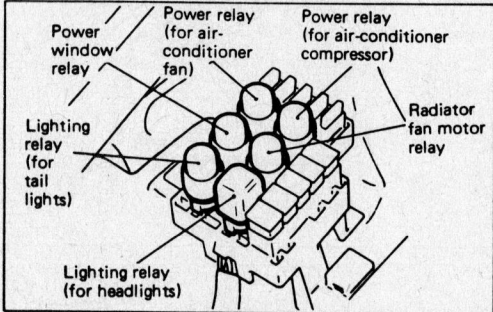

Power window relay
Power relay (for air-conditioner fan)
Power relay (for air-conditioner compressor)
Lighting relay (for tail lights)
Radiator fan motor relay
Lighting relay (for headlights)

C Turn and hazard flasher unit, defogger relay and heater relay

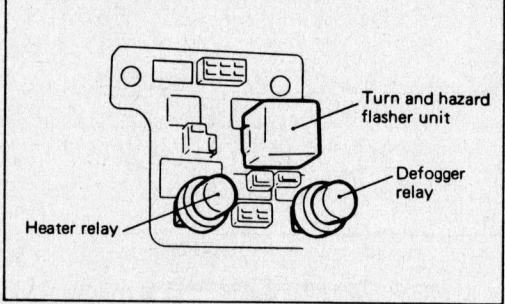

Turn and hazard flasher unit
Defogger relay
Heater relay

D ETACS unit and speed-control unit

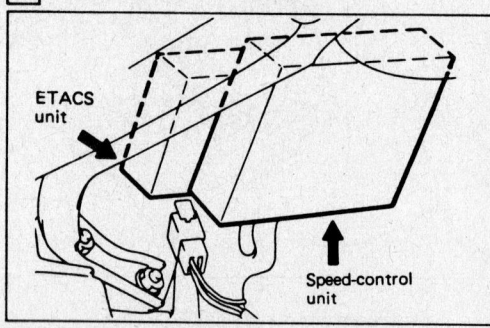

ETACS unit
Speed-control unit

E E.C.S. control unit

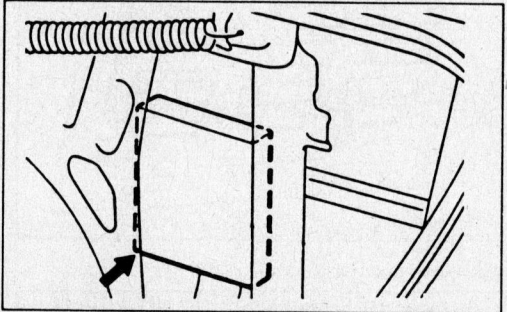

F Room temperature sensor

G Auto temperature control unit and transmission control unit

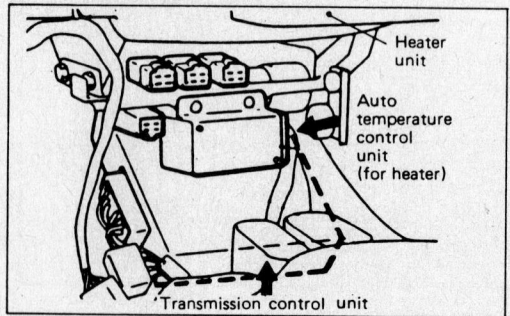

Heater unit
Auto temperature control unit (for heater)
Transmission control unit

NOTE
E.C.S.: Electronic Controlled Suspension
ETACS: Electronic Time and Alarm Control System

Mitsubishi Galant

COMPONENT LOCATIONS

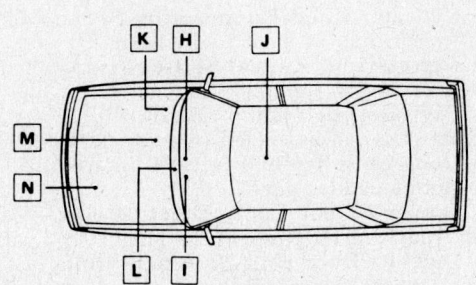

E.P.S. control unit

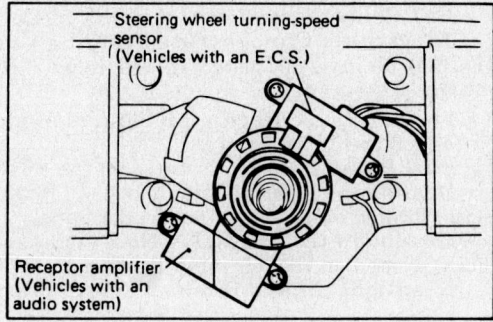

I Steering wheel turning-speed sensor and receptor amplifier

Steering wheel turning-speed sensor (Vehicles with an E.C.S.)

Receptor amplifier (Vehicles with an audio system)

J G sensor

K M.P.I. control unit, M.P.I. control relay

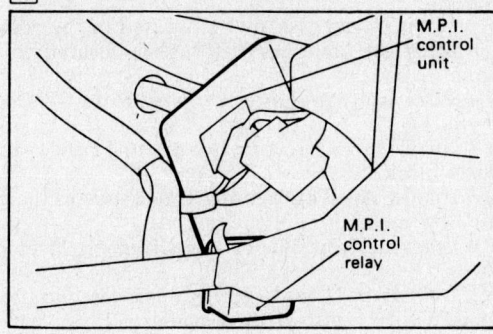

M.P.I. control unit

M.P.I. control relay

L Photo sensor

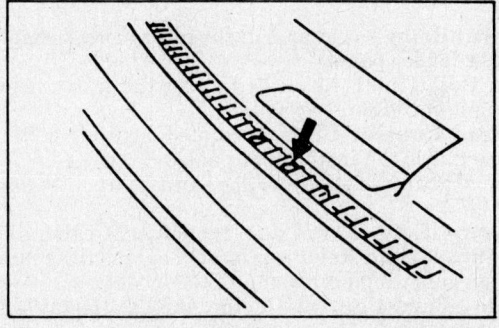

M Duct sensor

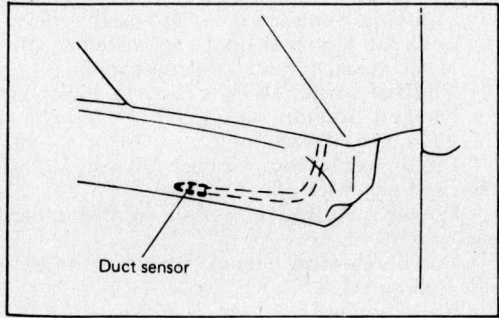

Duct sensor

N Air conditioner power relay

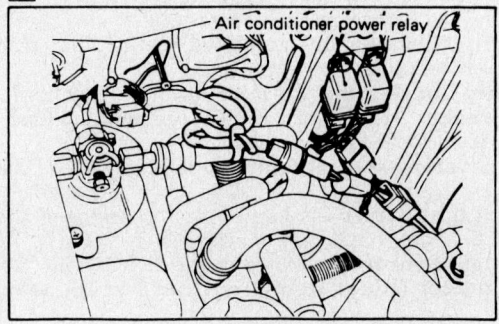

Air conditioner power relay

NOTE
E.P.S.: Electronic controlled Power Steering
M.P.I.: Multi Point Injection

Mitsubishi Galant

269

NISSAN/DATSUN

Circuit Breakers

Most of the models protect all the circuits with fuses or relays. If there are any circuit breakers in use, they will be listed with the relay, sensors and computer locations.

Fusible Links

All models have one fusible link installed in the wire between the battery and alternator (or starter) near the battery (or the relay block) to protect the alternator (or starter) and related circuits.

Relay, Sensors And Computer Locations

200SX

• **A/C Acceleration Cut Switch** – is located near the right hood hinge.
• **A/C Acceleration Cut Timer** – is located under the instrument panel to the right of the center console.
• **A/C Low Pressure Switch** – is located behind the left side of the grille.
• **A/C Magnet Solenoid Valve** – is located on the firewall near the right hood hinge.
• **A/C Relay** – is located on the firewall near the right hood hinge.
• **A/C (Brown) Relay** – is located in the relay block, located on the left inner fender panel.
• **A/C Start Coil Timer** – is located under the instrument panel to the right of the center console.
• **A/C Thermo Control Unit** – is located in front of the evaporator case under the instrument panel.
• **Air Flow Meter** – is incorporated in the air cleaner assembly
• **A.S.C.D Amplifier** – is located on the left kick panel.
• **A.S.C.D. (Blue) Hold Relay** – is located behind the shock tower on the left inner fender panel on SGL models.
• **Automatic Speed Control Device (ASCD) Relay** – is located in the relay block, on SGL models only.
• **Boost Sensor** – is attached to the back side of the right side shock tower, on turbocharged models only.
• **Brake/Tail Light Sensor** – is located on the right rear corner of the vehicle under the trim panel.
• **Bulb (Blue) Check Relay** – is located on the relay block.
• **Circuit Breaker** – is located under the combination flasher unit which is above the brake pedal.
• **Coolant Level Sensor** – is located on the right side of the radiator.
• **Courtesy Light Timer** – is located on the center of the firewall.
• **Crank Angle Sensor** – is located in the distributor.
• **Cruise Control (Blue) Relay** – is located in the relay block.
• **Cruise Control Release Valve** – is located on the right front shock tower below the solenoid valve.
• **Cruise Control Servo Valve** – is located on the right front shock tower above the release valve.
• **Cruise Control Unit** – is located under the right front passenger's seat.

• **Cylinder Head Temperature Sensor** – is located in the left front corner of the cylinder head.
• **Detonation (Knock) Sensor** – is installed in the engine block on the top right side.
• **Digital Touch Entry (Black) Relay** – is located behind the shock tower on the left inner fender panel.
• **Door Lock Timer Digital Control Unit** – is located on the right side kick panel.
• **Driver's Door Lock (Black) Relay** – is located on the right rear quarter panel in the luggage compartment.
• **Driver's Door Unlock (Black) Relay** – is located on the right rear quarter panel in the luggage compartment.
• **E.C.C.S (Green) Relay No.1** – is located in the relay block, located on the left inner fender panel on the SGL models
• **EFI Control Unit** – is located on the left side kick panel.
• **EFI Relay** – is located on the relay block.
• **Electronic Concentrated Engine Control System (ECCS) Relay** – is located in the relay block, on the GL models.
• **Fuel Pressure Regulator Control Module** – is located on the left front shock tower.
• **Fuel Pump Relay** – is located on the relay block.
• **Headlamp (Black) Relay No.1** – is located in the relay block, located on the left inner fender panel.
• **Headlamp (Black) Relay No.2** – is located in the relay block, located on the left inner fender panel.
• **Headlight (Black) Dimmer Relay** – is located on the relay block.
• **Hold Relay** – is located on the right side of the center console.
• **Horn (Gray) Relay** – is located in the relay block.
• **Ignition/Accessory Relay** – is located on the right kick panel.
• **Illumination (Blue) Control Relay** – is located in the relay block.
• **Inhibitor (Gray) Relay Auto. Trans.** – is located in the relay block.
• **Intake Air Temperature Sensor** – is incorporated in the air flow meter.
• **Intermittent Wiper Amplifer** – is located on the relay block
• **Interrupt (Black) Relay** – is located in the relay block on models with theft warning system.
• **Kickdown Solenoid (Auto.Trans.)** – is located in side of the transmission.
• **Lighting Sensor** – is located on the relay block.
• **Lock-Up Control Unit** – is located on the right rear corner of the vehicle under the trim panel.
• **Neutral (Blue) Relay** – is located in the relay block.
• **Oxygen Sensor** – is located in the exhaust manifold on the left side of the engine.
• **Passenger's Door Unlock (Black) Relay** – is located on the right side kick panel.
• **Power Antenna Timer** – is located under the right front passenger seat.
• **Power Window Circuit Breaker** – is located on the right side kick panel.
• **Rain Sensor** – is located in the center of the rear of the hood.
• **Rear Defogger (Brown) Relay** – is located on the right rear quarter panel in the luggage compartment.
• **Relay Block** – is located on the right front inner fender panel on the engine compartment.
• **Retract (Gray) Control Relay** – is located in the relay

block.
- **Retract (Black) Relay Down** – is located in the relay block.
- **Retract (Brown) Relay-Up (w/o theft warning)** – is located in the relay block, on models without theft warning system.
- **Retract (Brown) Relay-Up (w/theft warning)** – is located behind the shock tower on the left inner fender panel on models with theft warning system.
- **Retract (Black) Relay No.1** – is located in the relay block, located on the left inner fender panel.
- **Retract (Black) Relay No.2** – is located in the relay block, located on the left inner fender panel.
- **Selt Belt Chime Timer** – is located on the right side kick panel.
- **Spark Timing Coolant Temperature Switch** – is located on the bottom of the radiator.
- **Speed Sensor** – is attached to the back side of the right side shock tower, on models equipped with a digital type meter.
- **Theft Warning Control Amplifier** – is located on the right side kick panel.
- **Time Control Unit** – is located on the right kick panel.
- **Trunk Release Solenoid (Blue) Relay** – is located on the right rear quarter panel in the luggage compartment.
- **Vacuum Pressure Switch** – is attached to the back side of the right side shock tower, on turbocharged models only.
- **Voice Warning Unit** – is located on the right rear quarter panel in the luggage compartment.
- **Windshield Wiper Relay** – is located on the left inner fender panel.

210

- **Anti-Dieseling Solenoid** – is attached to the carburetor.
- **Auto Choke Relay** – is located in a relay block which is located on the right front fender apron in front of the shock tower.
- **Fuel Cut Relay** – is located in a relay block which is located on the right front fender apron in front of the shock tower.
- **Horn Relay** – is located under the left side of the instrument panel.
- **Inhibitor (A/T) Relay** – is located in a relay block which is located on the right front fender apron in front of the shock tower.
- **Intermittent Wiper Amplifier** – is located on the center of the firewall.
- **Kickdown Switch (A/T)** – is located on the left side of the firewall.
- **Radiator Fan Relay** – is located in a relay block which is located on the right front fender apron in front of the shock tower.
- **Seat Belt Timer Unit** – is located on the left side kick panel.
- **Vacuum Switch** – is located on the front of the intake manifold.
- **Warm-Up Relay No.1** – is located in a relay block which is located on the right front fender apron in front of the shock tower.
- **Warm-Up Relay No.2** – is located in a relay block which is located on the right front fender apron in front of the shock tower.

280ZX AND 280ZX TURBO

- **A/C Coolant Temperature Switch** – is located on the right rear of the engine.
- **A/C In-Car Sensor** – is located behind the glove box.
- **A/C Outside Sensor/Switch** – is located behind the right side of the front license plate.
- **A/C Relay** – is located in a relay block, which is located on the right front inner fender panel.
- **Accessory Relay** – is located on the right side kick panel.
- **Air Flow Meter** – is incorporated in the air cleaner assembly.
- **Air Vent Solenoid Valves** – is located on the upper right side of the firewall.
- **Antenna Timer** – is located on the right side kick panel.
- **A.S.C.D. Relay** – is located on the crossbar under the passenger's seat.
- **Automatic Speed Control Device (ASCD) Controller** – is located on the crossbar under the passenger's seat.
- **Auxiliary Cooling Fan Motor Timer Unit** – is located on the right side kick panel.
- **Boost Gauge Trimmer** – is located under the glove box.
- **Boost Sensor (Turbo models)** – is located on the left front shock tower.
- **Brake Fluid Level Sensor** – is located inside the brake fluid reservoir, at the left rear corner of the engine compartment.
- **Bulb Check Relay** – is located in a relay block, which is located on the right front inner fender panel.
- **Crank Angle Sensor** – is located in the distributor.
- **Cruise Control Servo Valve** – is located on the right front inner fender panel, below the cruise actuator.
- **Cruise Control Solenoid Valve** – is located on the right front inner fender panel, below the cruise actuator.
- **Cruise Control Speed Sensor** – is located inside the back of the speedometer.
- **Cylinder Head Temperature Sensor** – is located in the top of the cylinder head on the left side.
- **Detonation (Knock) Sensor (Turbo models)** – is installed in the engine block on the top left side.
- **Diode Box** – is located on the crossbar under the passenger's seat.
- **Door Lock Timer** – is located on the left side kick panel.
- **E.F.I. Control Unit** – is located on the left side kick panel.
- **Electronic Concentrated Engine Control System (ECCS) Unit** – is located in the left side kick panel.
- **Electronic Fuel Injection (E.F.I) Relay** – is located on the right front inner fender behind the shock tower.
- **Fan Motor Relay (Turbo models)** – is located in a relay block, which is located on the right front inner fender panel.
- **Fuel Pump Relay No.1** – is located on the right side kick panel.
- **Headlight Sensor** – is located in a relay block, which is located on the right front inner fender
- **Horn Relay** – is located on the right front inner fender behind the shock tower.
- **Ignition Relay** – is located on the right side kick panel.
- **Inhibitor Relay (A/T models)** – is located in a relay block, which is located on the right front inner fender panel.
- **Intake Air Temperature Sensor** – is incorporated in the air flow meter.
- **Intermittent Warning Chime** – is located to the left of the steering column.
- **Intermittent Wiper Amplifier** – is located to the left of the steering column.
- **Light Relay** – is located in a relay block, which is located on the right front inner fender panel.
- **Lighting Relay** – is located in a relay block, which is located on the right front inner fender panel.
- **Oxygen Sensor** – is located in the exhaust manifold on the left side of the engine.
- **Power Window Circuit Breaker** – is located on the right side kick panel.
- **Rear Defogger Control** – is located on the crossbar under the driver's seat.
- **Rear Defogger Relay** – is located on the crossbar under the passenger's seat.
- **Room Lamp Timer** – is located on the left side kick panel.

- **Seat Belt Warning Timer Unit** – is located under the glove box.
- **Tail/Stop Lamp Sensor** – is located on the crossbar under the passenger's seat.
- **Thermotime Switch (EFI)** – is located in the front of the engine in the thermostat housing.
- **Throttle Valve Switch** – is located on the throttle chamber.
- **Vacuum Control Modulator (Turbo)** – is located on the lower left front of the engine.
- **Vacuum Pump Relay (Turbo models)** – is located in a relay block, which is located on the right front inner fender panel.
- **Vacuum Switch (Turbo)** – is located under the vacuum tank, at the right front corner under the hood.
- **Warning Display Control Unit** – is located under the glove box.

300ZX AND 300ZX TURBO

- **A/C Low Pressure Switch** – is located on the A/C receiver/drier.
- **A/C Relay** – is located on the evaporator housing, located under the center of the instrument panel.
- **Air Flow Meter** – is attached to the front radiator support cowl.
- **Ambient Temperature Sensor** – is located in the right front corner of the front bumper.
- **Automatic Speed Control Device Control Unit** – is located above the fuse block on the left side kick panel.
- **Automatic Speed Control Device Relay** – is located in the relay block on the right front inner fender panel, in front of the shock tower.
- **Automatic Transmission Relay** – is located in the relay block on the right front inner fender panel, in front of the shock tower (except for turbo models).
- **Auiliary Air Control Relay** – is located above the fuse block on the left side kick panel.
- **Auiliary Air Control Valve** – is located on the left center of the (VG30ET) engine.
- **Auxiliary Driving Lamp Relay** – is located in the relay block on the right front inner fender panel, in front of the shock tower.
- **Blower Relay** – is located above the fuse block on the left side kick panel.
- **Boost Sensor (Turbo models)** – is located near or on the left front shock tower.
- **Bulb Check Relay** – is located in the relay block on the right front inner fender panel, in front of the shock tower.
- **Circuit Breaker (for the power window)** – is located above the fuse block on the left side kick panel.
- **Compressor Relay** – is located in the relay block on the right front inner fender panel, in front of the shock tower.
- **Condenser Fan Motor Relay** – is located in the relay block on the right front inner fender panel, in front of the shock tower.
- **Crank Angle Sensor** – is located in the distributor.
- **Cylinder Head Temperature Sensor** – is located in the top of the cylinder head on the left side.
- **Detonation (Knock) Sensor (Turbo models)** – is installed in the engine block on the right side.
- **EGR Control Solenoid Valve** – is located near the EGR valve on the right rear of the engine.
- **Electronic Concentrated Engine Control System (ECCS) Unit** – is located in the rear of the engine.
- **Electronic Fuel Injection (E.F.I.) Control Unit** – is located on the right side kick panel.

- **Electronic Fuel Injection (Green) Relay** – is located on the right front inner fender panel, after the shock tower.
- **Fan Control Amplifier** – is located on the evaporator housing, located under the center of the instrument panel.
- **Fan Motor Relay (Turbo models)** – is located in the relay block on the right front inner fender panel, in front of the shock tower.
- **Foot Sensor** – is located on the evaporator housing, located under the center of the instrument panel.
- **Fuel Temperature Sensor** – is located in the pressure regulator.
- **Horn Relay** – is located in the relay block on the right front inner fender panel, in front of the shock tower.
- **Idle-Up Solenoid Valve** – is located on the left center of the (VG30ET) engine.
- **Ignition Relay** – is located above the fuse block on the left side kick panel.
- **Inhibitor Relay** – is located in the relay block on the right front inner fender panel, in front of the shock tower.
- **Injection Blower Timer** – is located in the left rear inside quarter panel, just after the driver's side door.
- **Intermittent Wiper Adapter Unit** – is located on the left front inner fender panel, after the shock tower.
- **In-Vehicle Temperature Sensor** – is located in the headliner.
- **Headlight (Black) Relay** – is located on the left front inner fender panel, after the shock tower.
- **Headlight Sensor** – is located on the right front shock tower.
- **Headlight Timer** – is located on the left front inner fender panel, after the shock tower.
- **Headlight Washer Relay** – is located in the relay block on the right front inner fender panel, in front of the shock tower.
- **Intake Air Temperature Sensor** – is incorporated in the air flow meter.
- **Kickdown Switch (A/T models)** – is located above the throttle pedal.
- **Meter Power Unit** – is located under the right side of steering column, on digital type combination meter.
- **Oxygen Sensor** – is located in the exhaust manifold on the left side of the engine.
- **Passing (Brown) Relay** – is located on the left front inner fender panel, after the shock tower.
- **Power Transistor (for the ignition system)** – is located on the left front shock tower.
- **Pressure Regulator Control Solenoid Valve** – is located on the left inner fender panel.
- **Rear Defogger Relay** – is located above the fuse block on the left side kick panel.
- **Resistor (2.2 kilo-ohms) For Tachometer** – is located above the fuse block on the left side kick panel.
- **Speed Sensor** – is located on the right front inner fender panel, after the shock tower.
- **Theft Warning Relay No. 1** – is located in the relay block on the right front inner fender panel, in front of the shock tower.
- **Theft Warning Relay No. 2** – is located in the relay block on the right front inner fender panel, in front of the shock tower.
- **Throttle Valve Switch** – is located on the throttle chamber.
- **Time Control Unit** – is located on the right side kick panel.
- **Uphold (Black) Relay** – is located on the right front inner fender panel, after the shock tower.
- **Vacuum Pump Relay** – is located in the relay block on the right front inner fender panel, in front of the shock tower.
- **Voice Warning Unit** – is located on the right side kick panel.

310

- **40 MPH Amplifier** – is located on the center of the firewall.
- **A/C Low Pressure Switch** – is located on the receiver/drier.
- **A/C Relay** – is located on the left side kick panel, above the hood release handle.
- **Anti-Dieseling Solenoid** – is attached to the carburetor.
- **Automatic Choke Relay** – is located in the relay block on the right front inner fender panel, in front of the shock tower.
- **Cooling Relay** – is located on the cooling unit housing located under the instrument panel in the center of the vehicle.
- **Fan Relay** – is located on the left side kick panel, above the hood release handle.
- **Fast Idle Control Device Actuator** – is located in the middle of the engine on the right side leaning towards the firewall.
- **Fast Idle Control Device Solenoid** – is located on the cooling unit housing located under the instrument panel in the center of the vehicle.
- **Fuel Cut Relay** – is located on the left side kick panel, above the hood release handle.
- **Horn Relay** – is located in the relay block on the right front inner fender panel, in front of the shock tower.
- **Inhibitor Relay (A/T models)** – is located on the left side kick panel, above the hood release handle.
- **Intermittent Warning Chime** – is located on the center of the firewall.
- **Intermittent Wiper Amplifier** – is located in the relay block on the right front inner fender panel, in front of the shock tower.
- **Neutral Relay** – is located in the relay block on the right front inner fender panel, in front of the shock tower.
- **Rear Defogger Relay** – is located on the left side kick panel, above the hood release handle.
- **Seat Belt Warning Timer** – is located on the left side of the steering column under the instrument panel.
- **Sub Cooling Fan Timer** – is located on the left side of the steering column under the instrument panel.
- **Vacuum Switch** – is located on the front of the intake manifold.
- **Warning Relay** – is located in the relay block on the right front inner fender panel, in front of the shock tower.

1980-81 810 MAXIMA

- **A/C Low Pressure Switch** – is located on the receiver/drier.
- **A/C Magnet Valve (Gas Engine)** – is located on the right front shock tower.
- **A/C Relay** – is located on the right front shock tower.
- **A/C Relay (Diesel Engine)** – is located on the right front shock tower.
- **Accessory Relay** – is located in the relay block on the right front inner fender panel, in front of the shock tower.
- **Anti-Dieseling Solenoid** – is attached to the carburetor.
- **Automatic Speed Control Device Controller** – is located on the left side kick panel.
- **Automatic Speed Control Device Relay** – is located in the relay block on the right front inner fender panel, in front of the shock tower.
- **Bulb Check Relay** – is located in the relay block on the right front inner fender panel, in front of the shock tower.
- **Diode** – is located under the right side of the instrument panel, near the kick.
- **Door Lock Circuit Breaker** – is located under the right side of the instrument panel, near the kick.
- **Door Lock Timer** – is located on the left side kick panel.

- **Drop Resistor (Diesel Engine)** – is located on the right front shock tower.
- **EGR Control Unit (Diesel Engine)** – is located on the left side kick panel.
- **Electronic Fuel Injection Control Unit (Sedan)** – is located under the passenger's seat.
- **Electronic Fuel Injection Relay (Gas Engine)** – in the relay block on the right front inner fender panel, in front of the shock tower.
- **Fast Idle Control Device Actuator** – is located in the middle of the engine on the right side leaning towards the firewall.
- **Fast Glow Control Unit (Diesel Engine)** – is located on the left side kick panel.
- **Fuel Filter Amplifier (Diesel Engine)** – is located under the right side of the instrument panel, near the kick.
- **Fuel Pump Relay** – is located in the relay block on the right front inner fender panel, in front of the shock tower.
- **Glow Plug Relay No.1 (Diesel Engine)** – is located on the right front shock tower.
- **Glow Plug Relay No.2 (Diesel Engine)** – is located in the relay block on the right front inner fender panel, in front of the shock tower.
- **Headlight Relay** – is located in the relay block on the right front inner fender panel, in front of the shock tower.
- **Horn Relay** – is located in the relay block on the right front inner fender panel, in front of the shock tower.
- **Inhibitor Relay** – is located in the relay block on the right front inner fender panel, in front of the shock tower.
- **Interior Lamp Timer** – is located in the driver's door.
- **Power Antenna Timer** – is located under the passenger's seat.
- **Power Window Circuit Breaker** – is located under the right side of the instrument panel, near the kick.
- **Power Window/Sun Roof Relay** – is located on the left side kick panel.
- **Safety Relay** – is located in the side of the roof (roof rail).
- **Starter Relay (Diesel Engine)** – is located in the relay block on the right front inner fender panel, in front of the shock tower.
- **Stop/Tail Light Sensor (Wagon)** – is located under the passenger's seat.
- **Stop/Tail Light Sensor (Sedan)** – is located in the right rear quarter panel in the luggage compartment.
- **Sun Roof Slide Relay No.1** – is located in the side of the roof (roof rail).
- **Sun Roof Slide Relay No.2** – is located in the side of the roof (roof rail).
- **Timer Control Unit** – is located under the right side of the instrument panel, near the kick.
- **Vacuum Switch** – is located on the front of the intake manifold.
- **Voice Warning Device** – is under the center of the instrument panel.
- **Wiper Relay** – is located in the relay block on the right front inner fender panel, in front of the shock tower.

1982-83 MAXIMA

- **A/C Low Pressure Switch** – is located on the receiver/drier.
- **A/C Relay** – is located on the right front shock tower.
- **A/C Relay (Diesel Engine)** – is located on the right front shock tower.
- **Accessory Relay** – is located in the relay block on the right front inner fender panel, in front of the shock tower.
- **Auto Glow System Fuse (Diesel)** – is located on the right front shock tower.
- **Brake Fluid Sensor** – is located inside the brake fluid reservoir.

- **Bulb Check Relay** – is located in the relay block on the right front inner fender panel, in front of the shock tower.
- **Coolant Temperature Sensor** – is located in the front of the engine in the thermostat housing.
- **Coolant Thermal Transmitter** – is located in the front of the engine in the thermostat housing.
- **Cruise Control Relay** – is located in the relay block on the right front inner fender panel, in front of the shock tower.
- **Cruise Control Speed Sensor** – is located inside the back of the speedometer.
- **Cruise Control Unit** – is located on the left side kick panel.
- **Cylinder Head Temperature Sensor** – is located on the right rear cylinder head.
- **Diode** – is located under the right side of the instrument panel, near the kick.
- **Door Lock Circuit Breaker** – is located under the right side of the instrument panel, near the kick.
- **Door Lock Timer** – is located on the left side kick panel.
- **Drop Resistor (Diesel Engine)** – is located on the right front shock tower.
- **EGR Control Unit (Diesel Engine)** – is located on the left side kick panel.
- **Electronic Fuel Injection Control Unit (Sedan)** – is located under the passenger's seat.
- **Electronic Fuel Injection Relay (Gas Engine)** – in the relay block on the right front inner fender panel, in front of the shock tower.
- **Fast Glow Control Unit (Diesel Engine)** – is located on the left side kick panel.
- **Fast Idle Control Device Actuator** – is located in the middle of the engine on the right side leaning towards the firewall.
- **Fuel Filter Amplifier (Diesel Engine)** – is located under the right side of the instrument panel, near the kick.
- **Fuel Pump Relay** – is located in the relay block on the right front inner fender panel, in front of the shock tower.
- **Glow Plug Relay No.1 (Diesel Engine)** – is located on the right front shock tower.
- **Glow Plug Relay No.2 (Diesel Engine)** – is located in the relay block on the right front inner fender panel, in front of the shock tower.
- **Headlight Relay** – is located in the relay block on the right front inner fender panel, in front of the shock tower.
- **Horn Relay** – is located in the relay block on the right front inner fender panel, in front of the shock tower.
- **Inhibitor Relay** – is located in the relay block on the right front inner fender panel, in front of the shock tower.
- **Interior Lamp Timer** – is located in the driver's door.
- **Oxygen Sensor** – is located on the lower left side of the engine, in exhaust manifold.
- **Power Antenna Timer** – is located under the passenger's seat.
- **Power Window Circuit Breaker** – is located under the right side of the instrument panel, near the kick.
- **Power Window/Sun Roof Relay** – is located on the left side kick panel.
- **Safety Relay** – is located in the side of the roof (roof rail).
- **Starter Relay (Diesel Engine)** – is located in the relay block on the right front inner fender panel, in front of the shock tower.
- **Stop/Tail Light Sensor (Sedan)** – is located in the right rear quarter panel in the luggage compartment.
- **Stop/Tail Light Sensor (Wagon)** – is located on the right front inner fender.
- **Sun Roof Slide Relay No.1** – is located in the side of the roof (roof rail).
- **Sun Roof Slide Relay No.2** – is located in the side of the roof (roof rail).
- **Thermo Sensor** – is located under the center of the instrument panel. Pressure Sensor – is located on the right side

of the engine next to the oil filter.
- **Timer Control Unit** – is located under the right side of the instrument panel, near the kick.
- **Vacuum Switch** – is located on the front of the intake manifold.
- **Voice Warning Device** – is under the center of the instrument panel.
- **Warning Chime Unit** – is located above the accelerator pedal under the instrument panel.
- **Wiper Relay** – is located in the relay block on the right front inner fender panel, in front of the shock tower.

1984-87 MAXIMA

- **A/C (Brown) Relay** – is located on a relay block, in front of the battery.
- **A/C Clutch (Gray) Relay** – is attached the rear of the left front shock tower, on auto air conditioned models.
- **A/C Hi (Brown) Relay** – is located under the right side of the instrument panel, near the glove box.
- **Accessory (Blue) Relay** – is located in the fuse block.
- **Automatic Speed Control Device Control Unit** – is located under the driver's seat.
- **Automatic Speed Control Device (Blue) Relay** – is located on a relay block, in front of the battery.
- **Automatic Transmission Control Unit** – is located under the driver's seat.
- **Back Door Lock Actuator** – is located in the center panel of the hatchback, on the wagon model.
- **Back Door Unlock (Black) Relay** – is located in the lower luggage compartment on the wagon model.
- **Back Door Unlock (Black) Relay No.1** – is located in the lower luggage compartment on the wagon model.
- **Back Door Unlock (Black) Relay No. 2** – is located in the lower luggage compartment on the wagon model.
- **Bulb Check (Blue) Relay** – is located on the left front inner fender panel.
- **Circuit Breaker** – is located just above the fuse block under the left side of the instrument panel.
- **Cornering Lamp Unit** – is located on the left front inner fender panel.
- **Defogger (Brown) Relay** – is located in the fuse block.
- **Digital Touch Entry Control Unit (Sedan)** – is located on the under side of the rear seat dash panel, on all sedan models except the Euro Sedan Model.
- **Digital Touch Entry Control Unit (Wagon)** – is located in the lower luggage compartment on the wagon model.
- **Diode (for the voice warning system)** – is located on the left inside trunk support on the sedan models.
- **Diode 1, 2, and 3** – are located just above the fuse block under the left side of the instrument panel.
- **Door Lock Relay (Black on GL models)** – is located on the rear tail light panel, inside the luggage compartment.
- **Door Lock (Black) Relay No.1** – is located in the lower luggage compartment on the wagon model.
- **Door Lock Unit** – is located under the driver's seat.
- **Door Unlock Relay No.1 (Black on GL models)** – is located on the rear tail light panel, inside the luggage compartment.
- **Door Unlock (Black) Relay No.2** – is located on a relay block, in front of the battery.
- **Electronic Fuel Injection Control Unit** – is located under the driver's seat.
- **Electronic Fuel Injection (Green) Relay** – is located on a relay block, in front of the battery.
- **Fuel Pump (Green) Relay (Sedan)** – is located on the left inside trunk support on the sedan models.
- **Fuel Pump (Green) Relay (Wagon)** – is located in the lower luggage compartment on the wagon model.

- **Headlight Sensor** – is located behind the right front cornering light.
- **Heater (Blue) Relay** – is attached the rear of the left front shock tower.
- **Hold Relay** – this relay is used for the exhaust gas (oxygen) sensor warning lamp on the needle type meter models and is located behind the time control unit.
- **Horn Relay** – is located on the left front inner fender panel.
- **Ignition (Blue) Relay** – is located in the fuse block.
- **Inhibitor A/T Models (Brown) Relay No.1** – is located on a relay block, in front of the battery.
- **Inhibitor A/T Models (Black) Relay No.2** – is located on the left front inner fender panel.
- **Injector Cooling Fan Motor Timer** – is located on the left front inner fender panel.
- **Power Antenna Motor** – is located in the inside right rear quarter panel, on the sedan models.
- **Power Antenna Timer (Sedan)** – is located in the inside right rear quarter panel, on the sedan models.
- **Power Antenna Timer (Wagon)** – is located on the right kick panel.
- **Power (Black) Relay** – is located in the lower luggage compartment on the wagon model.
- **Power Relay (Black on GL Models)** – is located on the under side of the rear seat dash panel.
- **Power Window (Brown) Relay** – is located in the fuse block.
- **Radiator Fan (Blue) Relay No.1** – is located on a relay block, in front of the battery.
- **Radiator Fan (Blue) Relay No.2** – is located on a relay block, in front of the battery.
- **Radiator Fan (Blue) Relay No.3** – is located on a relay block, in front of the battery.
- **Radiator Fan (Blue) Relay No.4** – is located on the left front inner fender panel.
- **Reset Relay (Blue on GL models)** – is located on the rear tail light panel, inside the luggage compartment.
- **Reset (Blue) Relay** – is located in the lower luggage compartment on the wagon model.
- **Set Relay (Blue on GL models)** – is located on the rear tail light panel, inside the luggage compartment.
- **Set (Blue) Relay** – is located in the lower luggage compartment on the wagon model.
- **Shock Absorber Control Unit (on SE Models)** – is located on the under side of the rear seat dash panel.
- **Speed Sensor** – is located on the center of the firewall, on models equipped with a digital type meter.
- **Stop Lamp (Brown) Relay** – is located on a relay block, in front of the battery.
- **Stop/Tail Light Sensor (Sedan)** – is located in the inside right rear quarter panel, on the sedan models.
- **Stop/Tail Light Sensor (Wagon)** – is located in the inside right rear quarter panel, on the wagon model.
- **Theft Warning Main Control Unit (Sedan)** – is located on the under side of the rear seat dash panel.
- **Theft Warning Main Control Unit (Wagon)** – is located in the lower luggage compartment on the wagon model.
- **Theft Warning (Black) Relay No. 1** – is located on a relay block, in front of the battery.
- **Theft Warning (Black) Relay No. 2** – is located on a relay block, in front of the battery.
- **Theft Warning Sub-Control Unit (Sedan)** – is located on the under side of the rear seat dash panel.
- **Theft Warning Sub-Control Unit (Wagon)** – is located in the lower luggage compartment on the wagon model.
- **Time Control Unit** – is located on the left side kick panel.
- **Trunk Opener Actuator** – is located on the rear tail light panel, inside the luggage compartment.
- **Trunk Opener Relay (Blue on GL Models)** – is located on the under side of the rear seat dash panel.

- **Vacuum Pressure Switch** – is located on the center of the firewall, on auto air conditioned models.
- **Voice Warning Unit** – is located under the passenger's seat.
- **Wiper Relay** – is located on the left front inner fender panel.

PULSAR AND PULSAR NX

- **A/C Condensor Fan (Brown) Relay** – is located in the right front corner of the engine compartment.
- **A/C Fast Idle Solenoid Valve** – is located on the firewall near the right hood hinge.
- **A/C High-Low Pressure Switch** – is located on the top of the reciever-drier.
- **A/C (Blue) Relay** – is located in the right front corner of the engine compartment.
- **A/C Thermo Control Switch** – is located above the evaporator assembly under the instrument panel.
- **Accessory (Black) Relay** – is the top front relay on the left kick panel.
- **Anti-Dieseling Solenoid** – is located on the side of the carburetor.
- **Check Connector** – is located under the right side of the instrument panel.
- **Check (Black) Relay** – is located on the left front inner fender panel, in front of the shock tower.
- **Choke (Gray) Relay** – is located in the left front corner of the engine compartment.
- **Clearance (Blue) Relay** – is located on the right front inner fender panel.
- **Coolant Temperatuire Sensor** – is located on the rear of the engine.
- **Diode (for retract headlight)** – is located on the top of the right side kick panel.
- **Electronic Controlled Carburetor Control Unit** – is located under the driver's side seat.
- **Electronic Controlled Carburetor (Green) Relay** – is located on the right front inner fender panel.
- **Electronic Engine Control (California)** – is located under the driver's side seat.
- **Engine Revolution Control Unit (Federal)** – is located under the left side of the instrument panel.
- **Headlight Control Unit** – is located on the left front corner of the engine compartment.
- **Headlight Dimmer (Black) Relay** – is located in the left front corner of the engine compartment.
- **Hold Relay** – is located on the top of the right side kick panel.
- **Horn Relay** – is located in the left front corner of the engine compartment.
- **Ignition Relay** – is the rear relay on the left side kick panel.
- **Inhibitor (A/T models Black) Relay** – is located in the left front corner of the engine compartment.
- **Intermittent Wiper Amplifier** – is located on the left side of the firewall.
- **Mixture Heater (Black) Relay** – is located in the right front corner of the engine compartment.
- **Mixture Ratio Solenoid Valve (California)** – is located next to the float bowl in the carburetor.
- **Oxygen Sensor** – is located in the exhaust manifold.
- **Rear Window Defogger Relay** – is located under the instrument panel, on the right side of the steering column.
- **Rear Window Defogger Timer** – is located under the instrument panel, on the right side of the steering column.
- **Resistor (for tachometer)** – is located on the right front inner fender panel.
- **Retract (Brown) Relay-Down** – is located on the right front shock tower.

- **Retract (Gray) Relay-H1** – is located on the right front shock tower.
- **Retract (Black) Relay-H2** – is located on the right front shock tower.
- **Retract (Black) Relay-M** – is located on the right front shock tower.
- **Retract (Brown) Relay-Up** – is located on the right front shock tower.
- **Seat Belt Timer** – is located under the center of the instrument panel.
- **Vacuum Sensor** – is located on the left front inner fender panel, in front of the shock tower.
- **Warning Chime** – is located under the center of the instrument panel.

SENTRA

- **A/C Condenser Fan Relay** – is located on the right front corner of the engine compartment.
- **A/C High-Low Pressure Switch** – is located on the receiver drier.
- **A/C Magnet (Solenoid) Valve** – is located on the fire wall near the right hood hinge.
- **A/C Relay** – is located on the right front corner of the engine compartment.
- **A/C Thermo Control Switch** – is located above the evaporator assembly under the instrument panel.
- **Accessory Relay** – is located on the left side kick panel.
- **Anti-Dieseling Solenoid** – is located on the side of the carburetor.
- **Brake/Tail Light Sensor** – is located on the left side of the luggage compartment near the tail lights.
- **Bulb-Check Relay (Diesel)** – is located on the left front corner of the engine compartment.
- **Check Connector** – is located above the left side kick panel.
- **Choke Relay** – is located on the left front corner of the engine compartment.
- **Coolant Temperature Sensor** – is located on the rear of the engine.
- **Coolant Temperature Switches** – are located on the intake manifold in the coolant passage.
- **Crank Angle Sensor** – is located in the base of the distributor.
- **Diode (MPG)** – is located on the left side kick panel.
- **Diode Box (Except MPG)** – is located on the left side kick panel.
- **Dropping Resistor (Diesel)** – is located on the center of the firewall.
- **ECC Control Unit (Calf. & MPG models)** – is located under the driver's seat.
- **EGR Control Unit (Diesel)** – is located under the driver's seat.
- **Electronic Control Carburetor Main Relay** – is located on the right front corner of the engine compartment.
- **Engine Revolution Unit (Calf. & MPG)** – is located on the left side kick panel.
- **Feedback Relay (Calf.& MPG models)** – is located on the right front corner of the engine compartment.
- **Fuel Filter Amplifier (Diesel)** – is located under the left side of the instrument panel.
- **Glow Plug Control Unit (Diesel)** – is located on the right side kick panel.
- **Glow Plug Relay No.1 (Diesel)** – is located on the left front shock tower.
- **Glow Plug Relay No.2 (Diesel)** – is located in the center of the firewall.
- **Headlight Dimmer Relay** – is located on the left front corner of the engine compartment.

- **Horn Relay** – is located on the left front corner of the engine compartment.
- **Ignition Relay** – is located on the left side kick panel.
- **Inhibitor Relay (Auto. Trans.)** – is located on the left front corner of the engine compartment.
- **Intermittent Wiper Amplifier** – is located on the left side of the firewall.
- **Mixture Ratio Solenoid Valve (California)** – is located inside the carburetor next to the float bowl.
- **Mixture Relay (Except MPG models)** – is located on the right front corner of the engine compartment.
- **Oxygen Sensor** – is located in the exhaust manifold.
- **Rear Window Defogger Relay** – is located to the right of the steering column under the instrument panel.
- **Rear Window Defogger Timer** – is located to the right of the steering column under the instrument panel.
- **Seat Belt Timer** – is located behind the radio in the instrument panel.
- **Vacuum Sensor** – is located on the right front inner fender panel.
- **Warm-Up Relay (MPG models)** – is located on the right front corner of the engine compartment.

STANZA

- **A/C Compressor Speed Sensor** – is located on a bracket next to the compressor clutch.
- **A/C Control Relay** – is located under the right side of the instrument panel above the fuse block and under the glove box.
- **A/C High Pressure Cutout Switch** – is located in the high pressure line near the radiator.
- **A/C High Pressure Switch** – is located in the high pressure line near relay bracket in the engine compartment.
- **A/C Low Pressure Switch** – is located on the receiver/drier near the condenser.
- **A/C Magnet Solenoid Valve** – is located on the center of the firewall.
- **A/C (Blue) Relay** – is located on the right rear corner of the engine compartment under the cowl.
- **A/C RPM Sensor** – is located on the compressor.
- **A/C Thermo Control Switch** – is located on the right side of the evaporator assembly under the instrument panel.
- **Accessory Relay** – is located on the right side of the fuse block under the glove box.
- **Anti-Dieseling Solenoid** – are located on the side of the carburetor.
- **Automatic Speed Control Device** – is located in the relay bracket on the right front inner fender panel, in front of the shock tower.
- **Automatic Speed Control Device Control Unit** – is located on the right side kick panel.
- **Brake/Tail Light Sensor** – is located on the right tail housing in trunk.
- **Bulb Check (Blue) Relay** – is located in the relay bracket on the right front inner fender panel, in front of the shock tower.
- **Carburetor Heater (Blue) Relay** – is located on the relay bracket on the right front inner fender panel, in front of the shock tower.
- **Choke (Gray) Relay** – is located on the relay bracket on the right front inner fender panel, in front of the shock tower.
- **Coolant Fan (Blue) Relay** – is located near the radiator filler cap on the fan shroud.
- **Coolant Fan Switch** – is located in the radiator, just below the filler cap.
- **Coolant Temperature Sensor** – is located on the intake manifold below carburetor.
- **Coolant Temperature Switch** – is located on the intake manifold in the coolant passage.

- **Courtesy Light Timer** – is located on the bottom of the left side kick panel.
- **Cruise Control (Black) Relay** – is located on the center section of the fuse block under the glove box.
- **Cruise Control Unit** – is located on the lower left kick panel.
- **Electronic Fuel Injection Control Unit** – is located on the left side kick panel.
- **Electronic Fuel Injection Main (Green) Relay** – is located on the left front inner fender panel.
- **Fast Idle Control Device Actuator** – is located on the side of the carburetor.
- **Fast Idle Control Device Magnet Valve** – is located on the right side of the firewall, on carburetted engines only.
- **Fast Idle Control Device (Blue) Relay** – is located in the relay bracket on the right front inner fender panel, in front of the shock tower.
- **Fast Idle (Blue) Relay** – is located on the upper right side kick panel.
- **Headlight Relay** – is located in the relay block on the right front inner fender panel, in front of the shock tower.
- **Headlight Sensor** – is located on the upper left kick panel.
- **Hold Relay** – is located under the right side of the instrument panel above the fuse block and under the glove box.
- **Horn Relay** – is located in the relay block on the right front inner fender panel, in front of the shock tower.
- **Idle Speed Solenoid Valves** – are located on the side of the carburetor.
- **Idle-Up Relay** – is located in the relay block on the right front inner fender panel, in front of the shock tower.
- **Ignition (Blue) Relay** – is located on the left side of the fuse block under the glove box.
- **Inhibitor Relay** – is located in the relay block on the right front inner fender panel, in front of the shock tower.
- **Intermittent Wiper Amplifier** – is located on the right rear corner of the engine compartment.
- **Power Steering Pressure Switch** – is located in the pressure line below the power steering fluid reservoir.
- **Power Window/Sun Roof Relay** – is located under the right side of the instrument panel above the fuse block and under the glove box.
- **Rear Window Defogger Relay** – is located behind the glove box.
- **Rear Window Defogger Timer** – is located behind the glove box.
- **Seat Belt Chime Timer** – is located in the right side kick panel.
- **Speed Sensor** – is located in the speedometer.
- **Stop/Tail Light Sensor** – is located on the right tail light panel in the luggage compartment.
- **Sun Roof Circuit Breaker** – is located on the right side kick panel.
- **Sun Roof Safety Relay** – is located in the side of the roof (roof rail).
- **Sun Roof Slide Relay No.1** – is located in the side of the roof (roof rail).
- **Sun Roof Slide Relay No.2** – is located in the side of the roof (roof rail).
- **Tachometer Resistor** – is taped to the main wire harness inside the right front wheel well.

STANZA WAGON

- **A/C Condenser Fan Motor (Brown) Relay** – is located in a relay block attached to the right front inner fender panel.
- **A/C (Black) Relay No.1** – is located on the right side kick panel.
- **A/C (Black) Relay No.2** – is located in a relay block attached to the right front inner fender panel.
- **Accessory (Blue) Relay** – is located above the fuse block on the left side kick panel.
- **Automatic Speed Control Device Actuator** – is located on the right side of the firewall.
- **Automatic Speed Control Device Control Unit** – is located under the instrument panel to the right of the steering column.
- **Automatic Speed Control Device (Black) Relay** – is located in a relay block attached to the right front inner fender panel.
- **Bulb Check (Blue) Relay** – is located on the left front inner fender panel.
- **Circuit Breaker (Black)** – is located in the left side kick panel.
- **Electronic Fuel Ignition (Green) Relay** – is located above the fuse block on the left side kick panel.
- **Fuel Pump (Black) Relay** – is located above the fuse block on the left side kick panel.
- **Heater (Black) Relay** – is located on the left front inner fender panel.
- **Horn (Black) Relay** – is located in a relay block attached to the right front inner fender panel.
- **Ignition (Blue) Relay** – is located above the fuse block on the left side kick panel.
- **Inhibitor (Green) Relay** – is located on the left front inner fender panel.
- **Light Warning Chime** – is located under the right side of the instrument panel.
- **Radiator Fan Motor (Brown) Relay** – is located on the left front inner fender panel.
- **Seat Belt Timer/Buzzer** – is located under the right side of the instrument panel.
- **Sun Roof (Black) Relay** – is located on the left side kick panel.
- **Vacuum Pump (Black) Relay** – is located in a relay block attached to the right front inner fender panel.
- **Warning Chime (Brown) Relay** – is located on the left side kick panel.
- **Wiper Amplifier** – is located on the left side of the firewall.

COMPONENT LOCATIONS

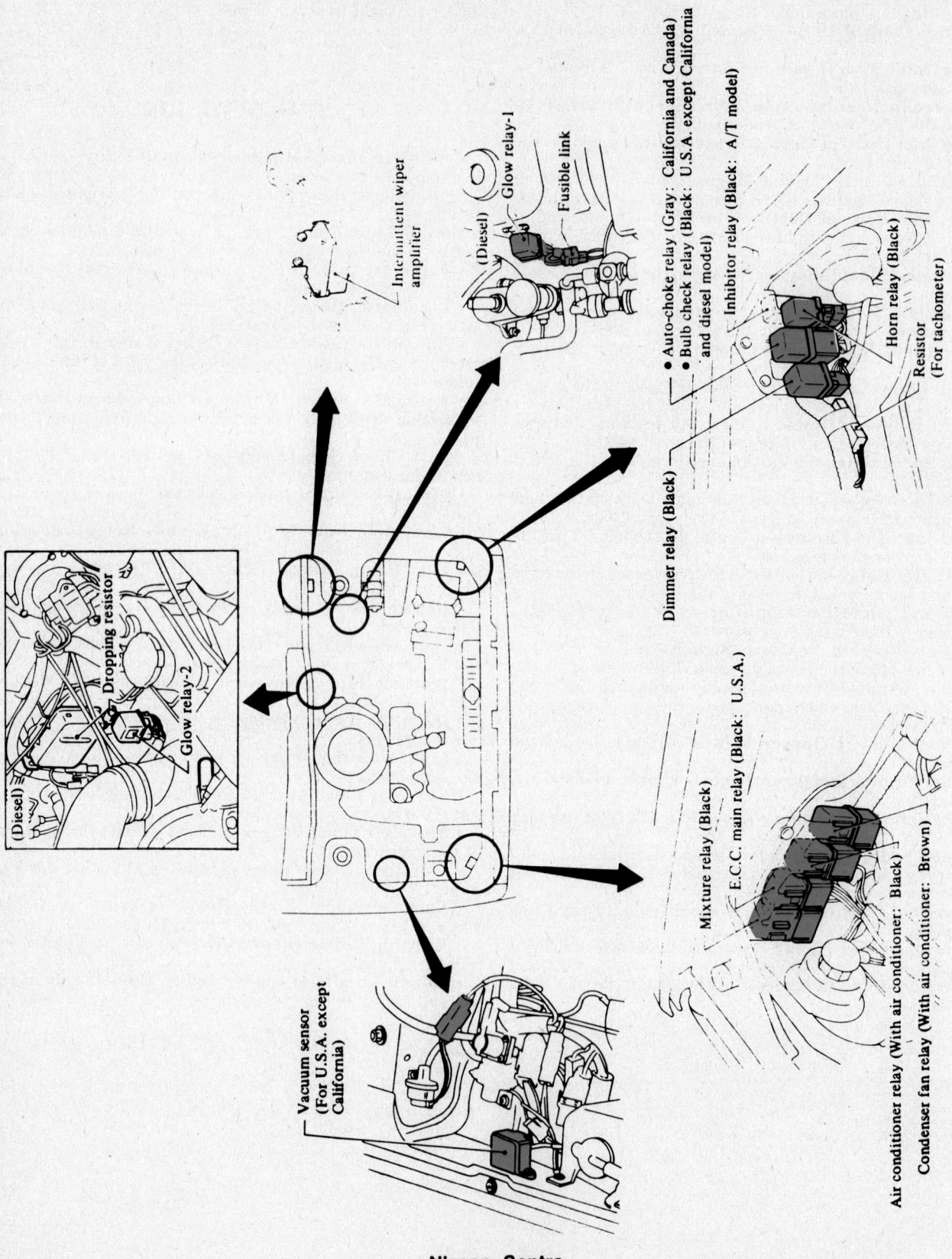

Intermittent wiper amplifier

(Diesel) Glow relay-1

Fusible link

• Auto-choke relay (Gray: California and Canada)
• Bulb check relay (Black: U.S.A. except California and diesel model)

Inhibitor relay (Black: A/T model)

Horn relay (Black)

Resistor (For tachometer)

Dimmer relay (Black)

Dropping resistor

Glow relay-2

(Diesel)

Mixture relay (Black)

E.C.C. main relay (Black: U.S.A.)

Air conditioner relay (With air conditioner: Black)

Condenser fan relay (With air conditioner: Brown)

Vacuum sensor (For U.S.A. except California)

Nissan Sentra

COMPONENT LOCATIONS

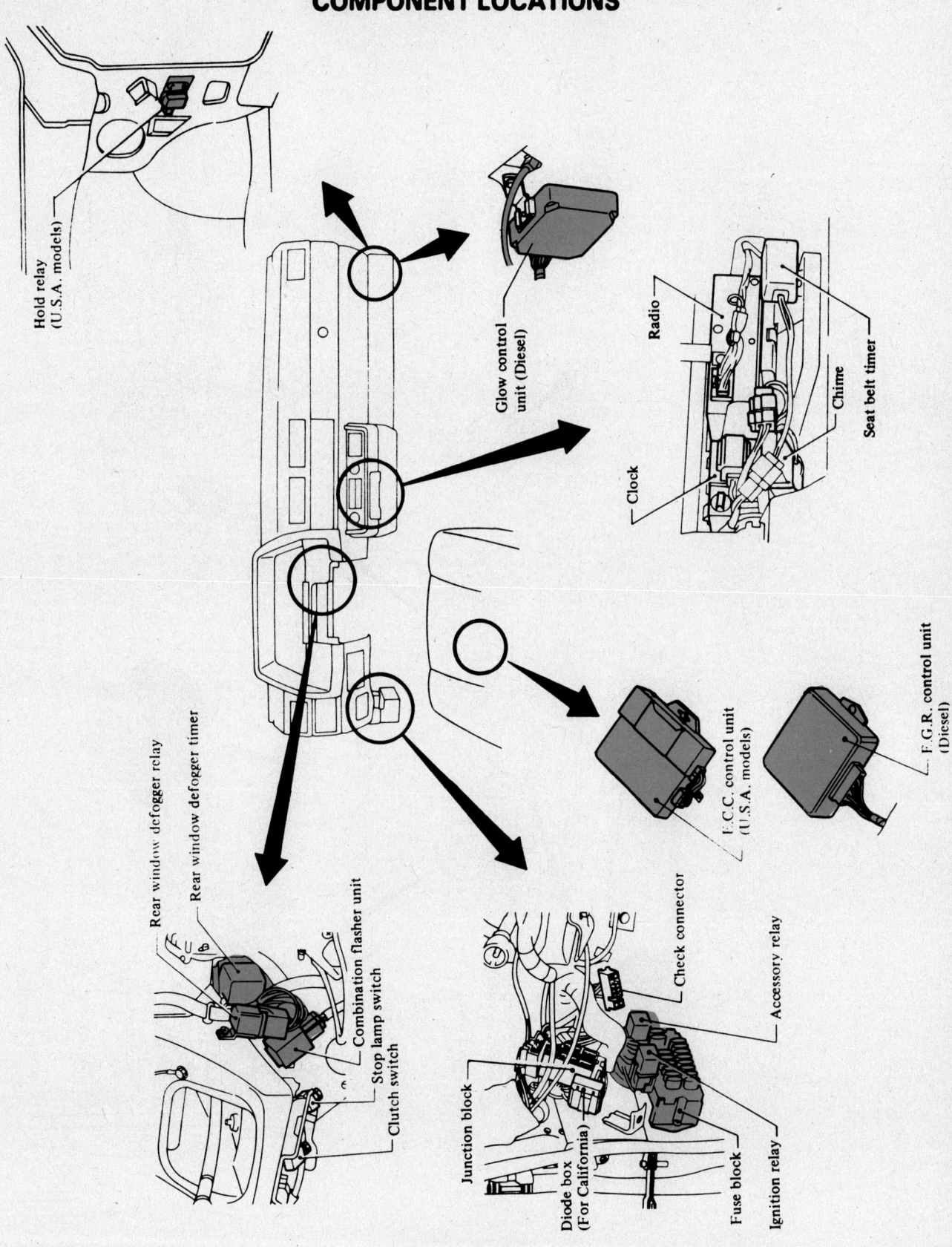

Hold relay (U.S.A. models)

Glow control unit (Diesel)

Radio

Clock

Chime

Seat belt timer

Rear window defogger relay

Rear window defogger timer

Combination flasher unit

Stop lamp switch

Clutch switch

E.C.C. control unit (U.S.A. models)

F.G.R. control unit (Diesel)

Check connector

Accessory relay

Junction block

Diode box (For California)

Fuse block

Ignition relay

Nissan Sentra

COMPONENT LOCATIONS

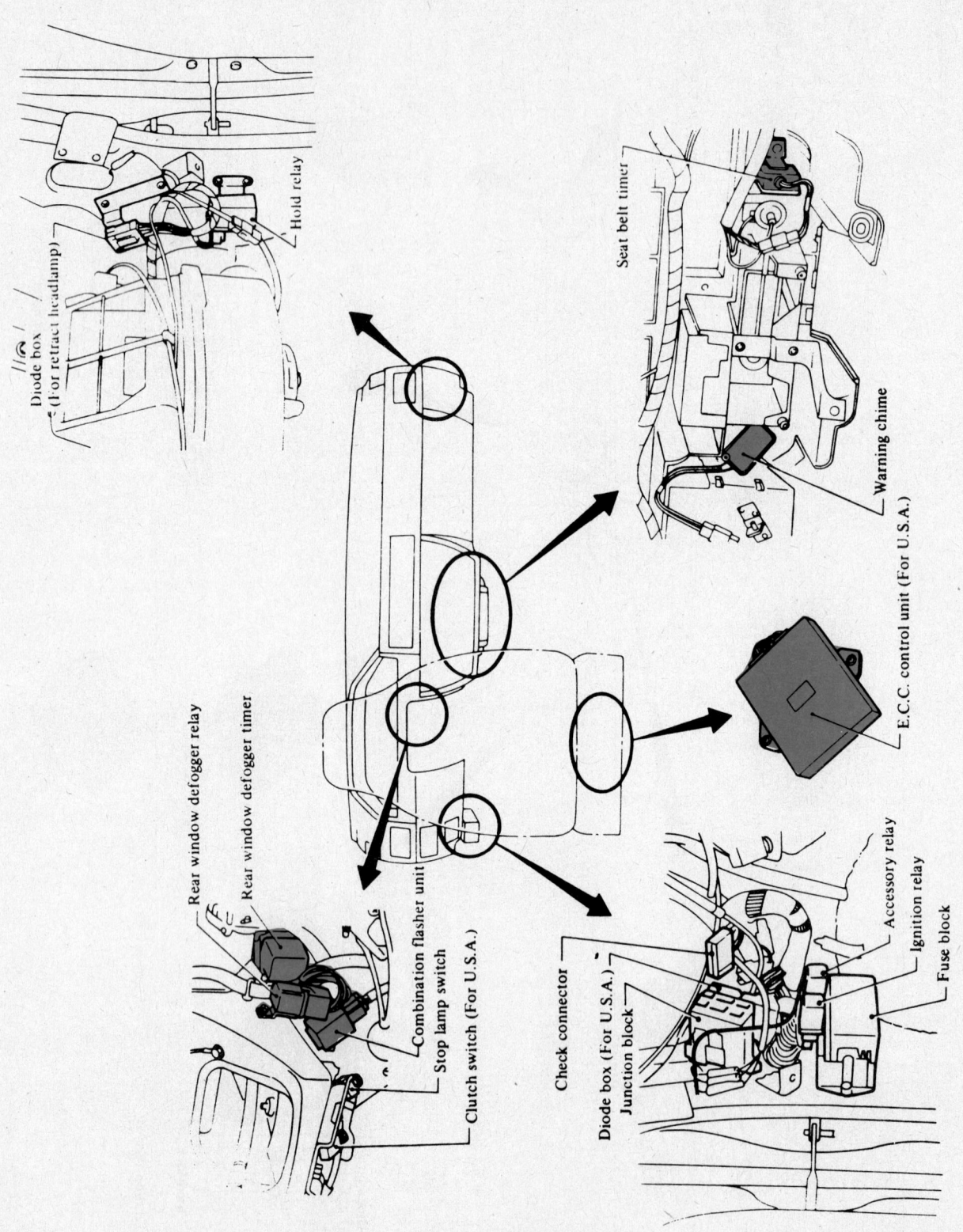

Nissan Pulsar

COMPONENT LOCATIONS

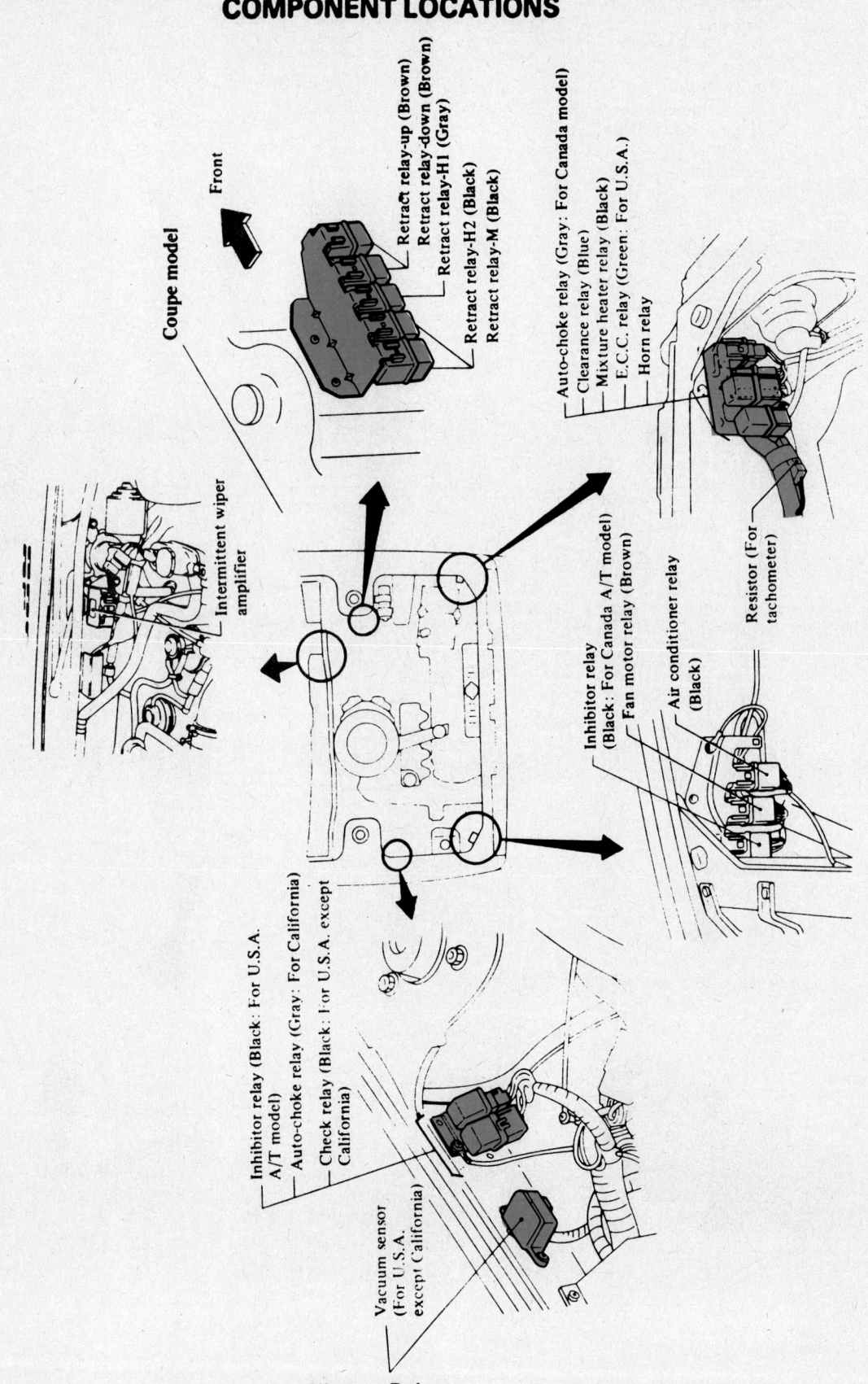

Coupe model

Front

Retract relay-up (Brown)
Retract relay-down (Brown)
Retract relay-H1 (Gray)
Retract relay-H2 (Black)
Retract relay-M (Black)

Auto-choke relay (Gray: For Canada model)
Clearance relay (Blue)
Mixture heater relay (Black)
E.C.C. relay (Green: For U.S.A.)
Horn relay

Intermittent wiper amplifier

Inhibitor relay
(Black: For Canada A/T model)
Fan motor relay (Brown)

Air conditioner relay (Black)

Resistor (For tachometer)

Inhibitor relay (Black: For U.S.A. A/T model)
Auto-choke relay (Gray: For California)
Check relay (Black: For U.S.A. except California)

Vacuum sensor (For U.S.A. except California)

Nissan Pulsar

COMPONENT LOCATIONS

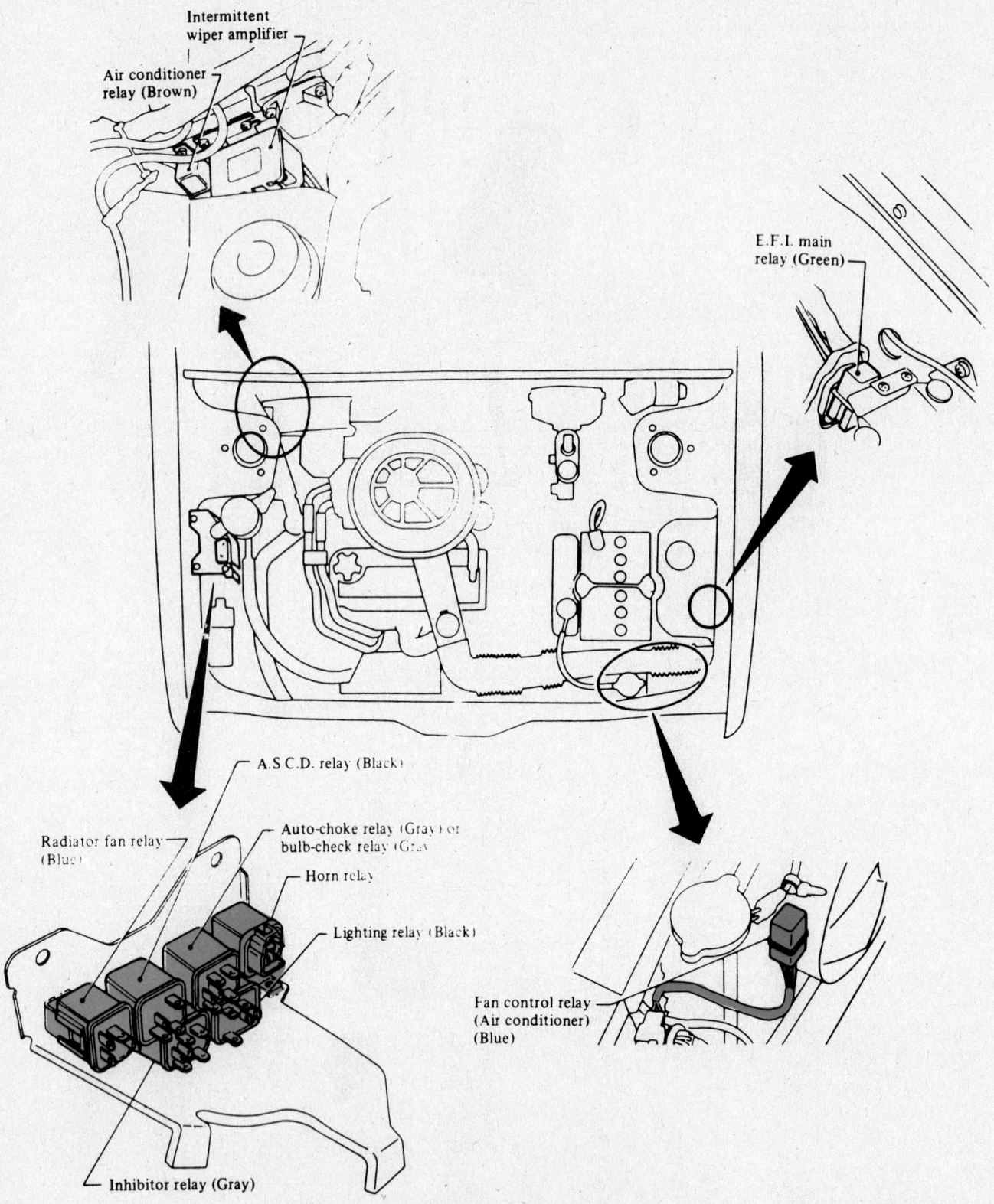

Intermittent wiper amplifier

Air conditioner relay (Brown)

E.F.I. main relay (Green)

A.S.C.D. relay (Black)

Radiator fan relay (Blue)

Auto-choke relay (Gray) or bulb-check relay (Gray)

Horn relay

Lighting relay (Black)

Fan control relay (Air conditioner) (Blue)

Inhibitor relay (Gray)

Nissan Stanza

COMPONENT LOCATIONS

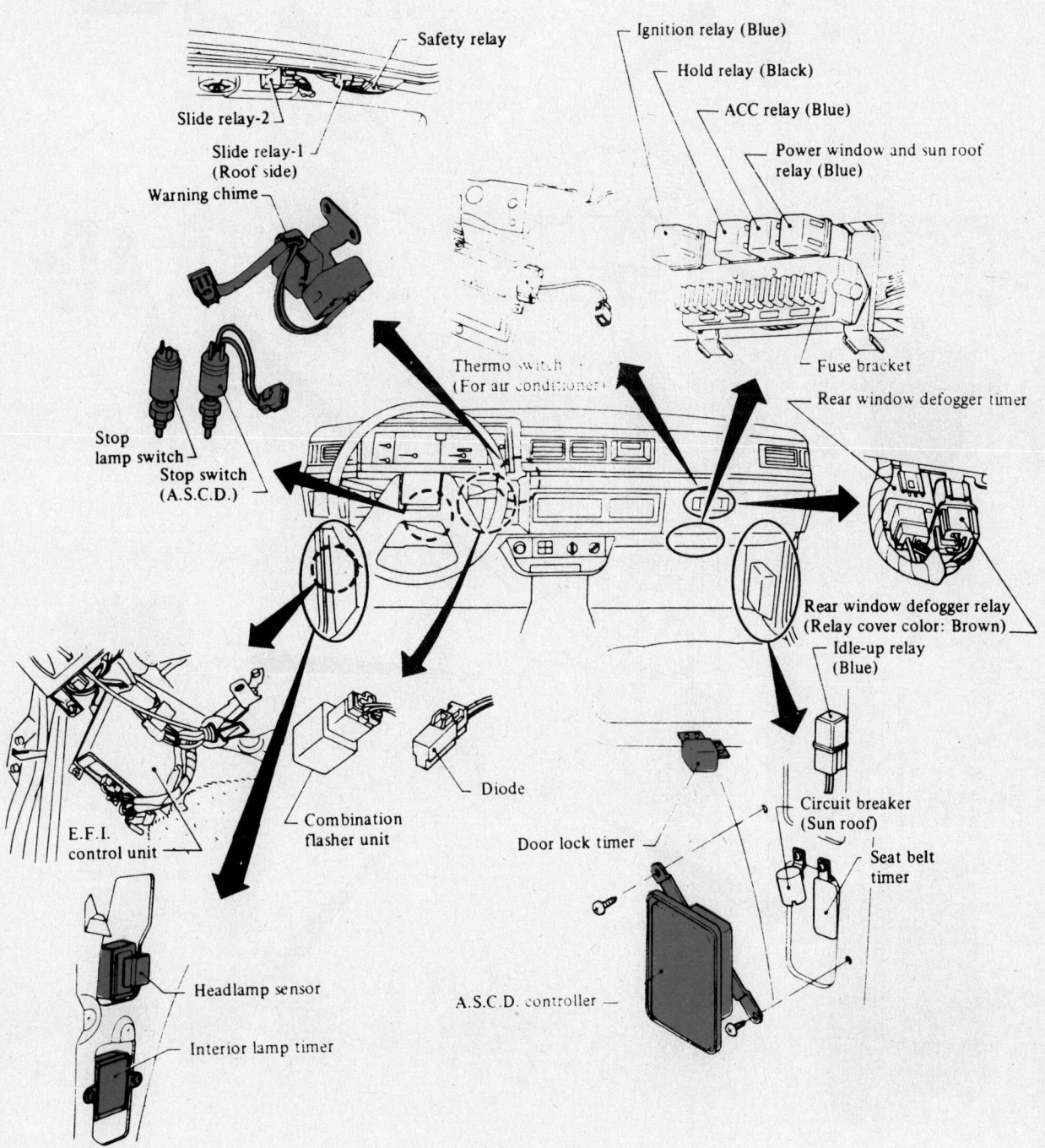

Safety relay

Slide relay-2

Slide relay-1
(Roof side)

Warning chime

Ignition relay (Blue)

Hold relay (Black)

ACC relay (Blue)

Power window and sun roof
relay (Blue)

Thermo switch
(For air conditioner)

Fuse bracket

Rear window defogger timer

Stop
lamp switch

Stop switch
(A.S.C.D.)

E.F.I.
control unit

Combination
flasher unit

Diode

Door lock timer

A.S.C.D. controller

Rear window defogger relay
(Relay cover color: Brown)

Idle-up relay
(Blue)

Circuit breaker
(Sun roof)

Seat belt
timer

Headlamp sensor

Interior lamp timer

Nissan Stanza

COMPONENT LOCATIONS

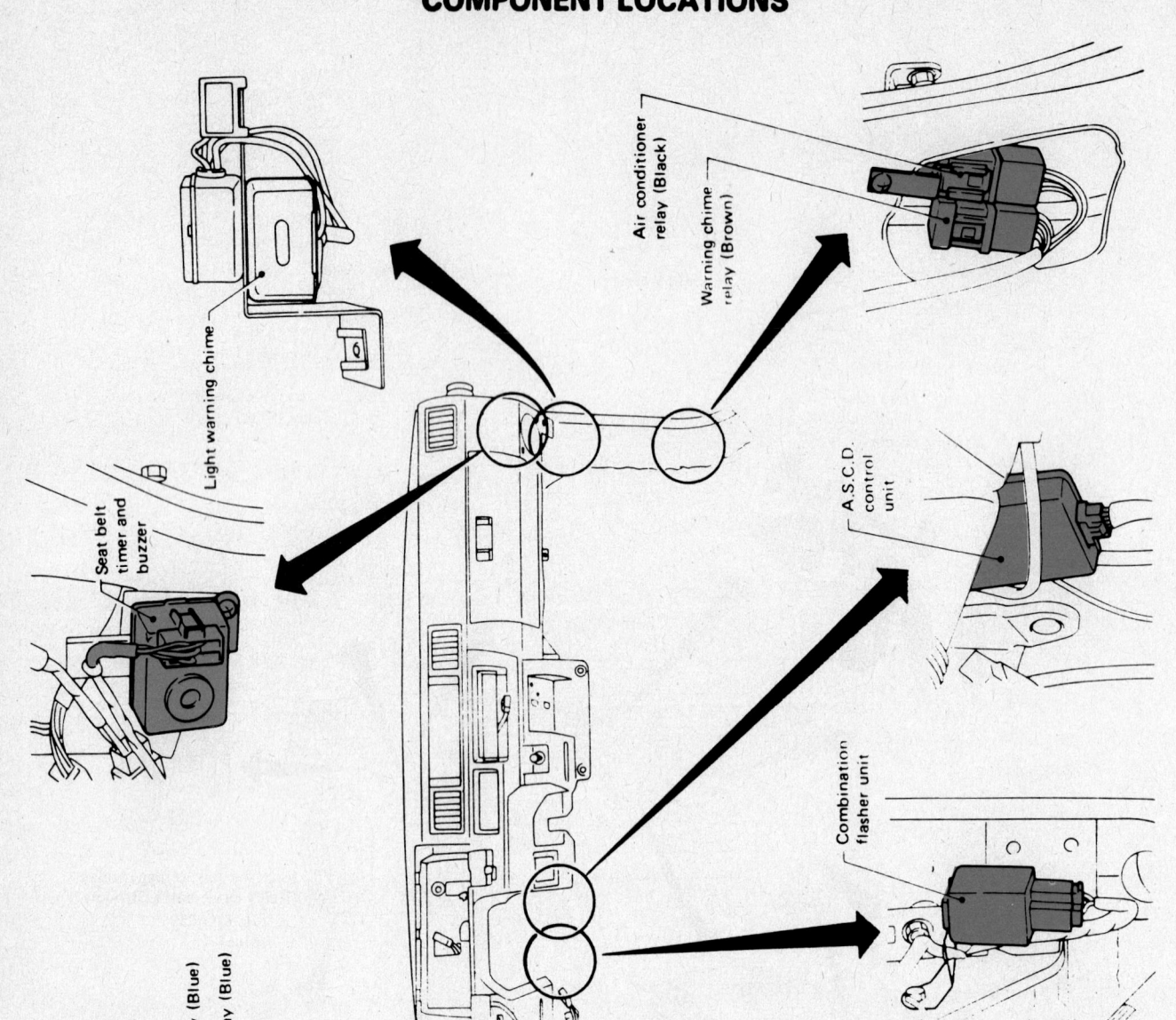

Light warning chime

Air conditioner relay (Black)

Warning chime relay (Brown)

Seat belt timer and buzzer

A.S.C.D. control unit

Combination flasher unit

Fuel pump relay (Black)

E.F.I. relay (Green)

Ignition relay (Blue)

Accessory relay (Blue)

Fuse block

Circuit breaker (Black)

Sun roof relay (Black)

Nissan Stanza Wagon

COMPONENT LOCATIONS

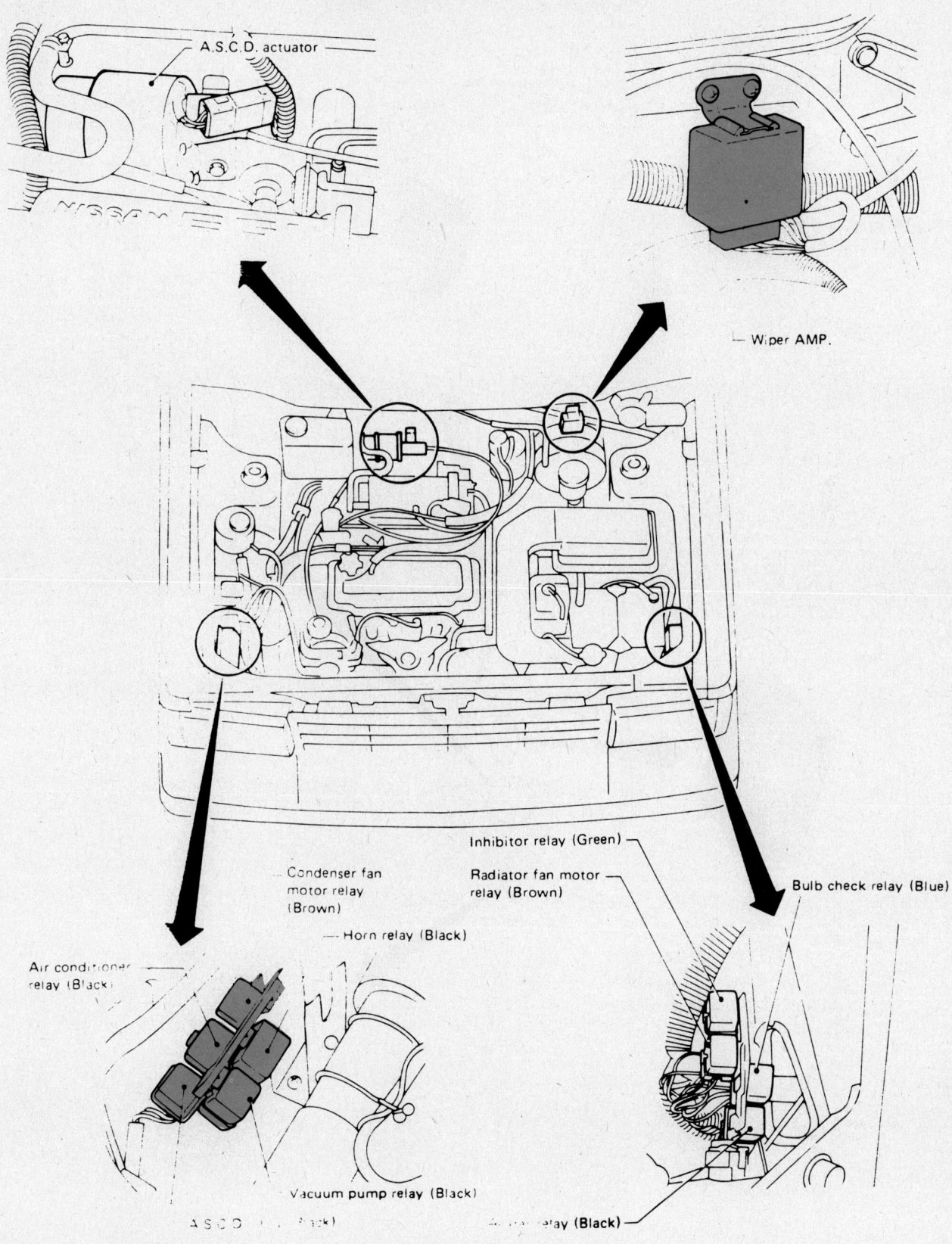

A.S.C.D. actuator

— Wiper AMP.

Inhibitor relay (Green)

Condenser fan
motor relay
(Brown)

Radiator fan motor —
relay (Brown)

Bulb check relay (Blue)

— Horn relay (Black)

Air conditioner
relay (Black)

Vacuum pump relay (Black)

ASCD (Black)

relay (Black)

Nissan Stanza Wagon

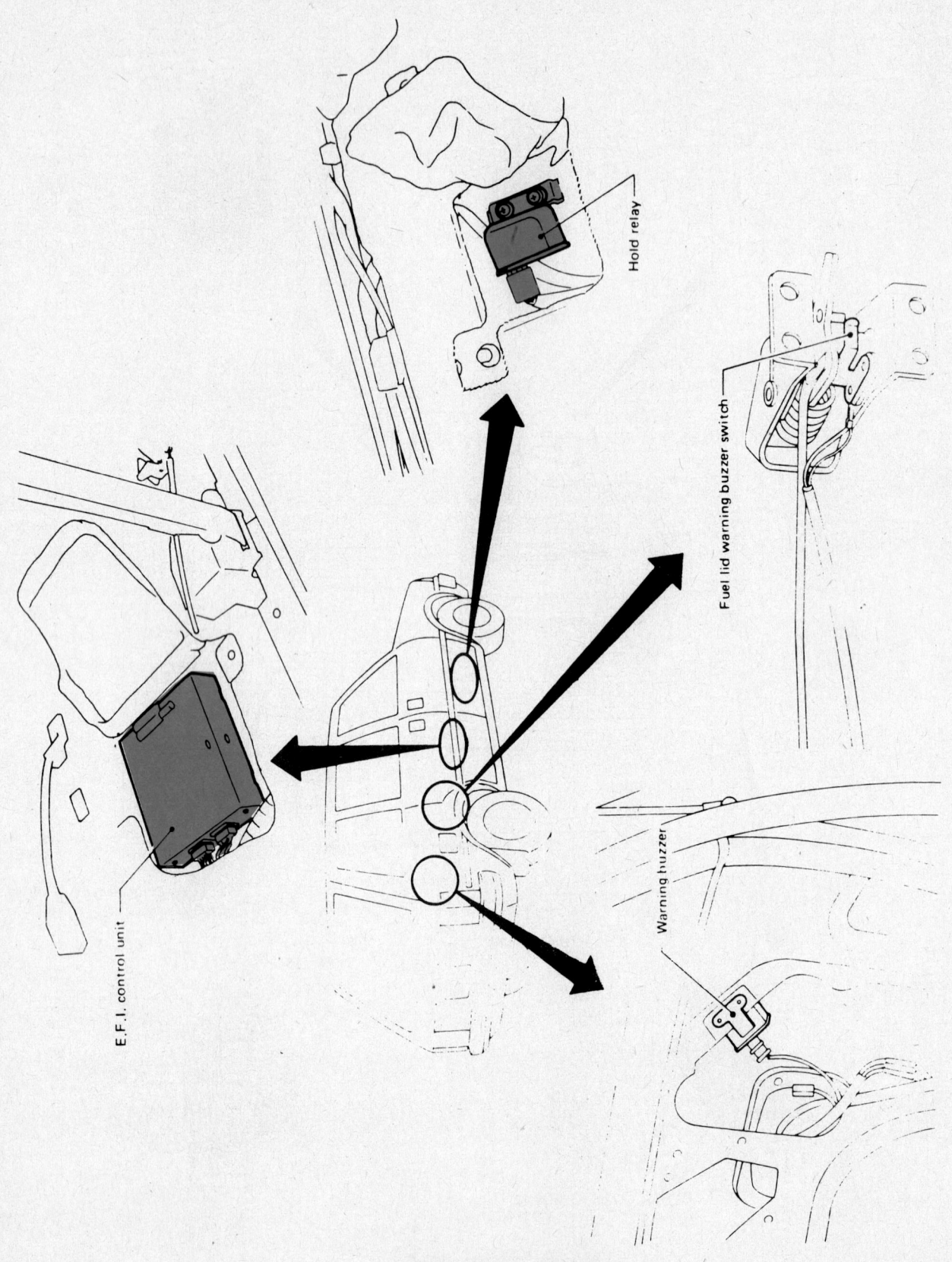

Hold relay

Fuel lid warning buzzer switch

E.F.I. control unit

Warning buzzer

Nissan Stanza Wagon

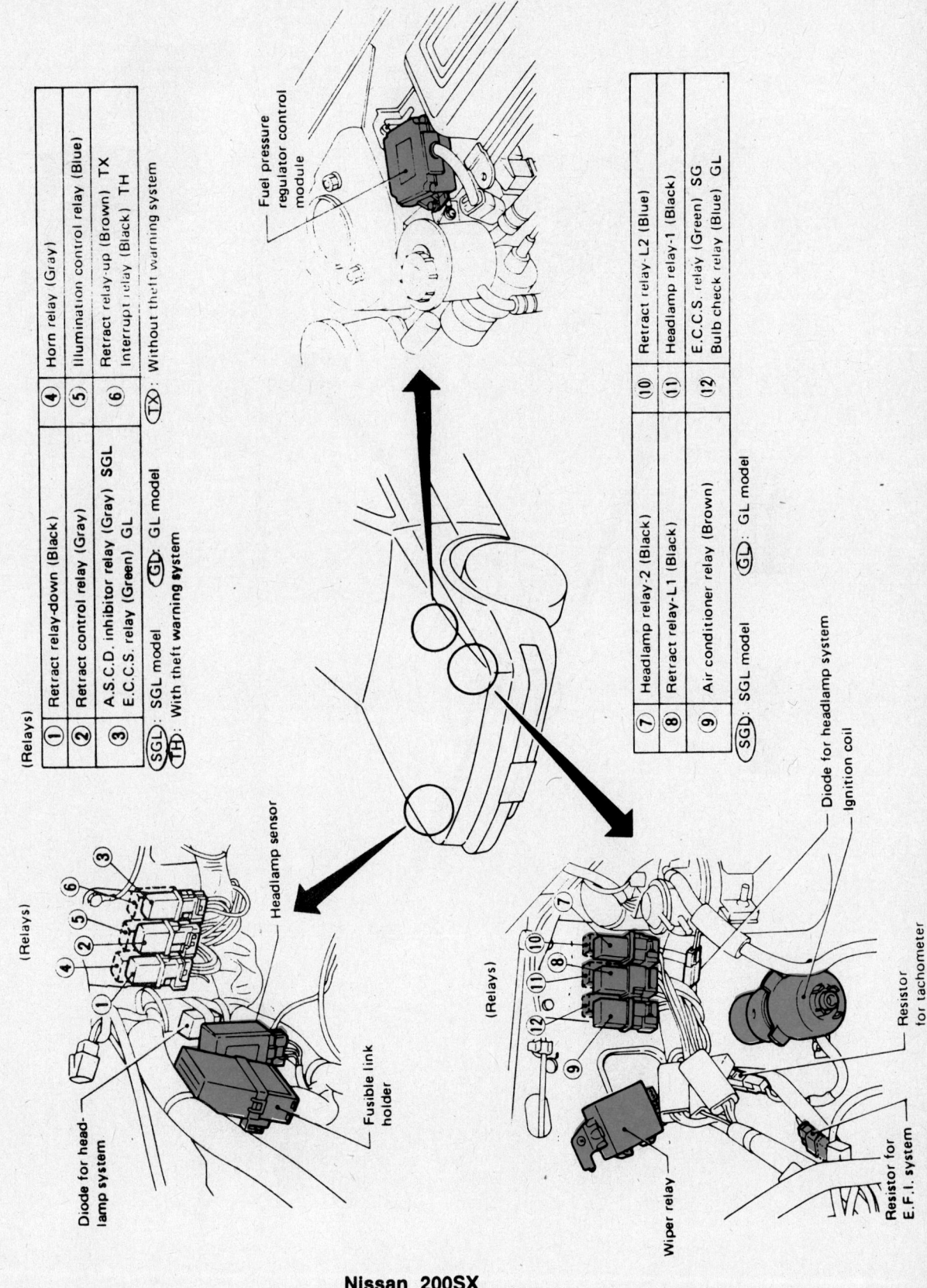

(Relays)

①	Retract relay-down (Black)
②	Retract control relay (Gray)
③	A.S.C.D. inhibitor relay (Gray) SGL E.C.C.S. relay (Green) GL
④	Horn relay (Gray)
⑤	Illumination control relay (Blue)
⑥	Retract relay-up (Brown) TX Interrupt relay (Black) TH

SGL : SGL model   GL : GL model
TX : Without theft warning system
TH : With theft warning system

(Relays)

⑦	Headlamp relay-2 (Black)
⑧	Retract relay-L1 (Black)
⑨	Air conditioner relay (Brown)
⑩	Retract relay-L2 (Blue)
⑪	Headlamp relay-1 (Black)
⑫	E.C.C.S. relay (Green) SG Bulb check relay (Blue) GL

SGL : SGL model   GL : GL model

Fuel pressure regulator control module

Headlamp sensor

Diode for head-lamp system

Fusible link holder

Diode for headlamp system

Ignition coil

Resistor for tachometer

Wiper relay

Resistor for E.F.I. system

Nissan 200SX

287

COMPONENT LOCATIONS

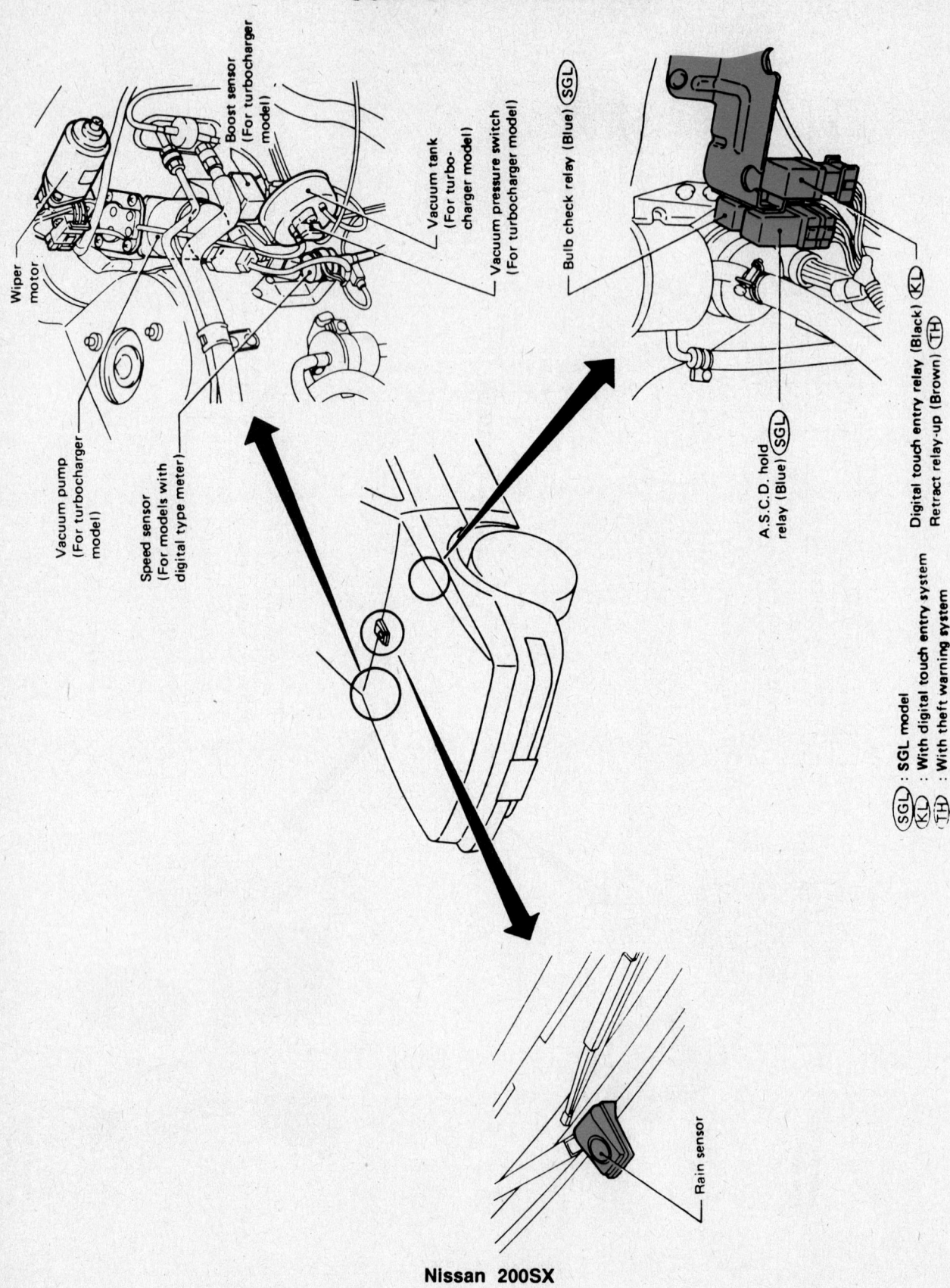

Wiper motor

Vacuum pump (For turbocharger model)

Speed sensor (For models with digital type meter)

Boost sensor (For turbocharger model)

Vacuum tank (For turbo-charger model)

Vacuum pressure switch (For turbocharger model)

Bulb check relay (Blue) SGL

A.S.C.D. hold relay (Blue) SGL

Digital touch entry relay (Black) KL

Retract relay-up (Brown) TH

SGL : SGL model
KL : With digital touch entry system
TH : With theft warning system

Rain sensor

Nissan 200SX

COMPONENT LOCATIONS

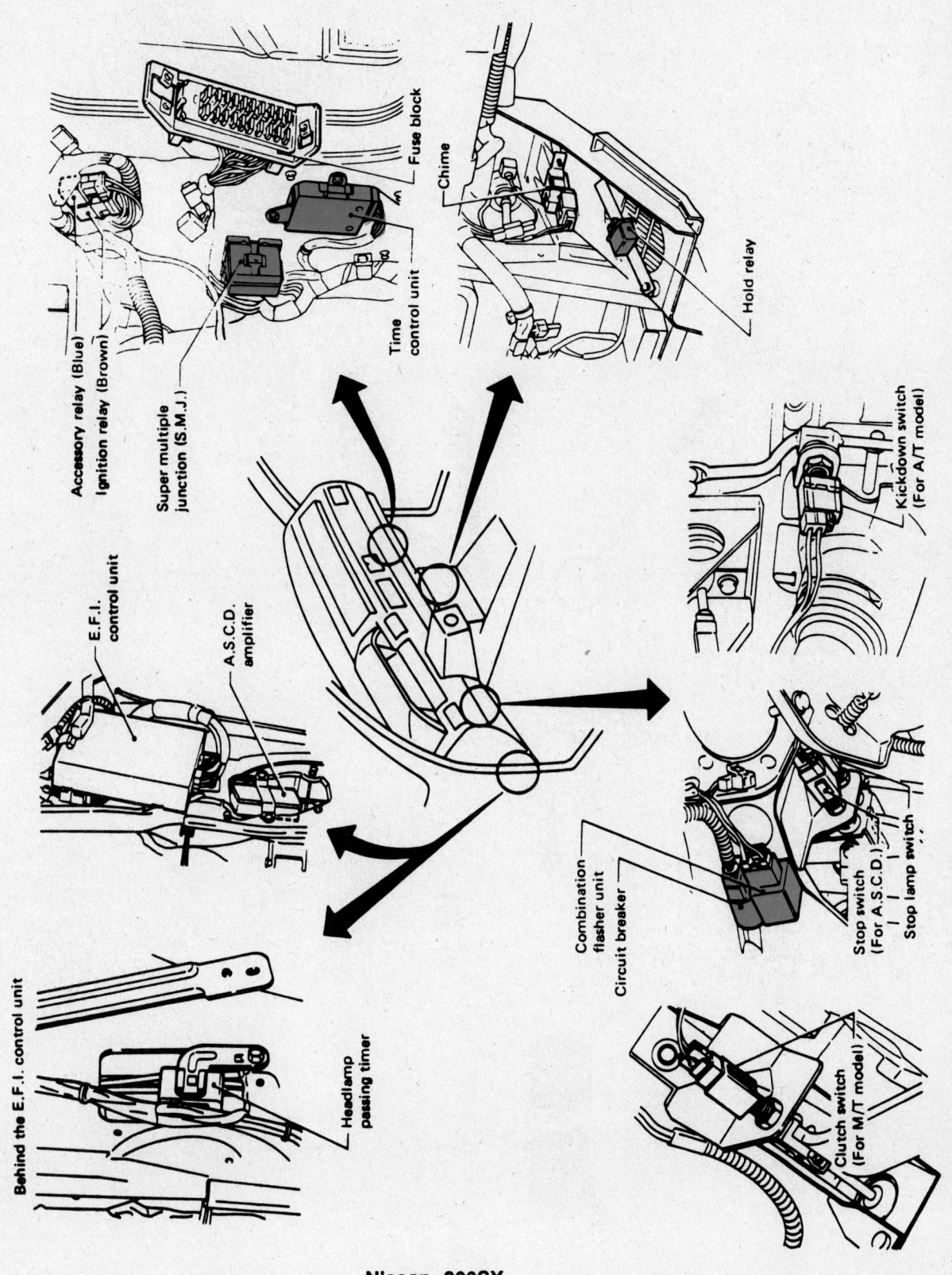

Accesory relay (Blue)
Ignition relay (Brown)
Super multiple junction (S.M.J.)
Time control unit
Fuse block
Chime
Hold relay
Kickdown switch (For A/T model)
E.F.I. control unit
A.S.C.D. amplifier
Combination flasher unit
Circuit breaker
Stop switch (For A.S.C.D.)
Stop lamp switch
Behind the E.F.I. control unit
Headlamp passing timer
Clutch switch (For M/T model)

Nissan 200SX

COMPONENT LOCATIONS

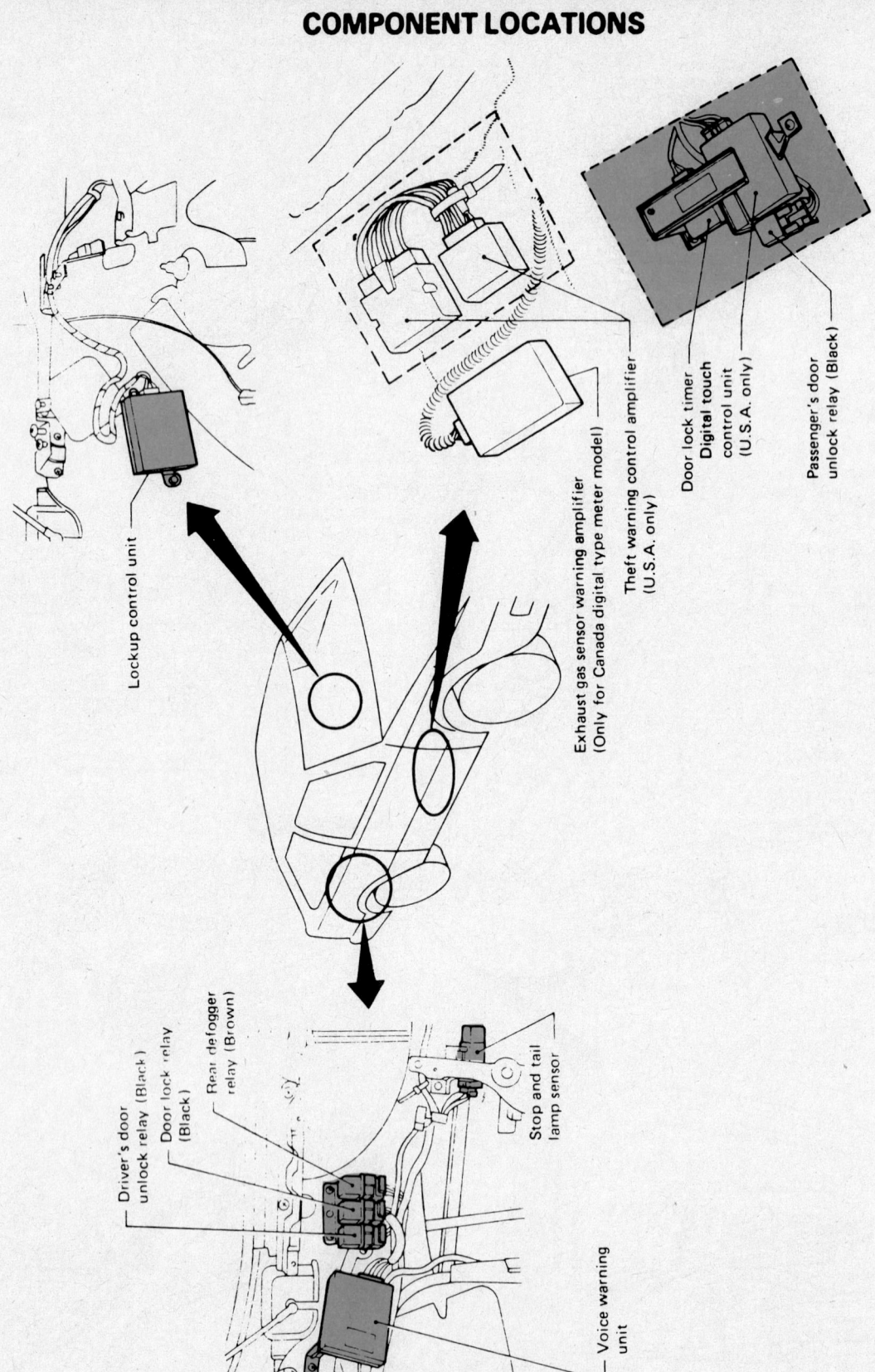

Lockup control unit

Exhaust gas sensor warning amplifier
(Only for Canada digital type meter model)

Theft warning control amplifier
(U.S.A. only)

Door lock timer

Digital touch control unit
(U.S.A. only)

Passenger's door unlock relay (Black)

Driver's door unlock relay (Black)

Door lock relay (Black)

Rear defogger relay (Brown)

Stop and tail lamp sensor

Voice warning unit

Nissan 200SX

COMPONENT LOCATIONS

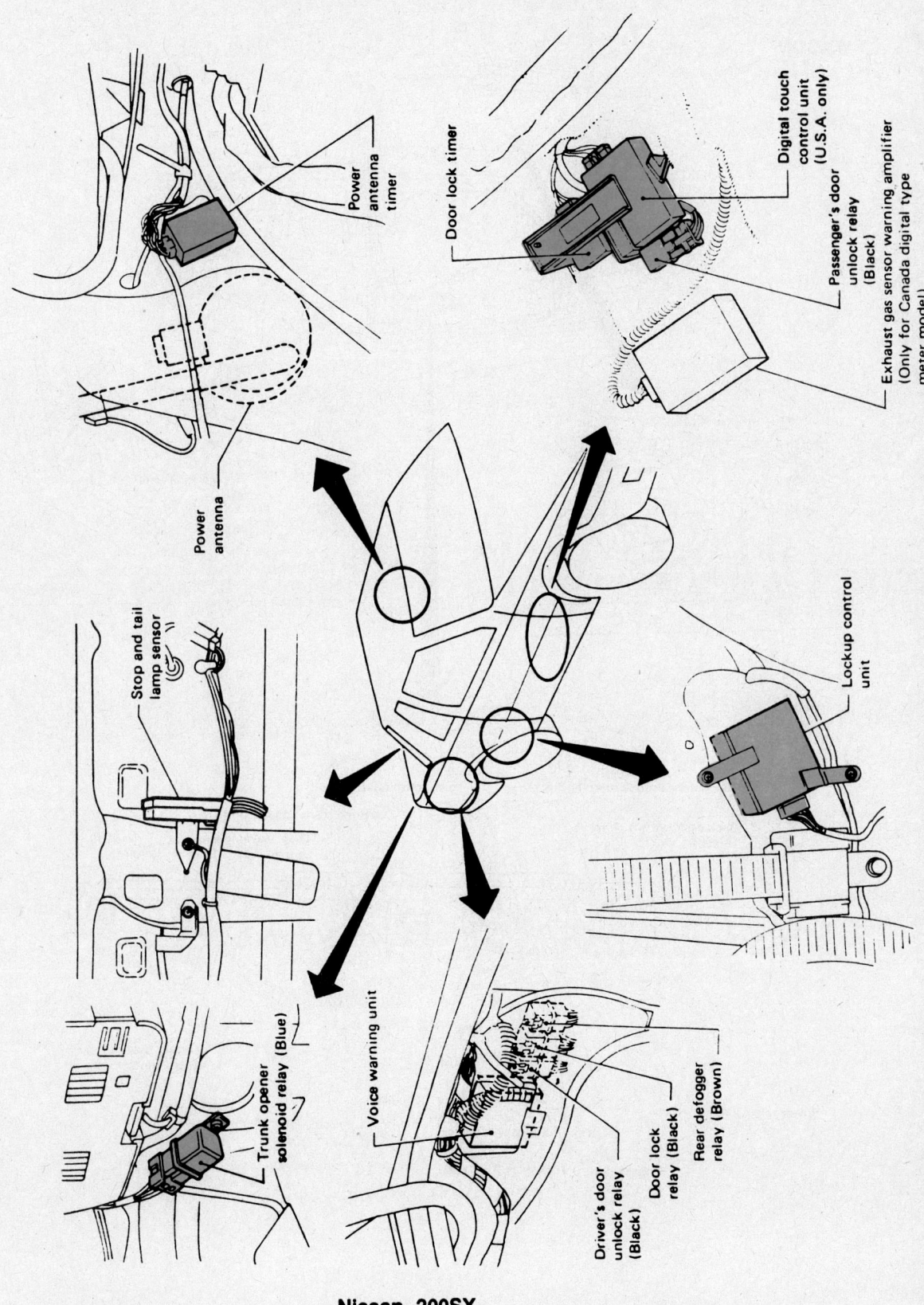

Power antenna timer

Power antenna

Door lock timer

Digital touch control unit (U.S.A. only)

Passenger's door unlock relay (Black)

Exhaust gas sensor warning amplifier (Only for Canada digital type meter model)

Stop and tail lamp sensor

Lockup control unit

Trunk opener solenoid relay (Blue)

Voice warning unit

Driver's door unlock relay (Black)

Door lock relay (Black)

Rear defogger relay (Brown)

Nissan 200SX

WAGON

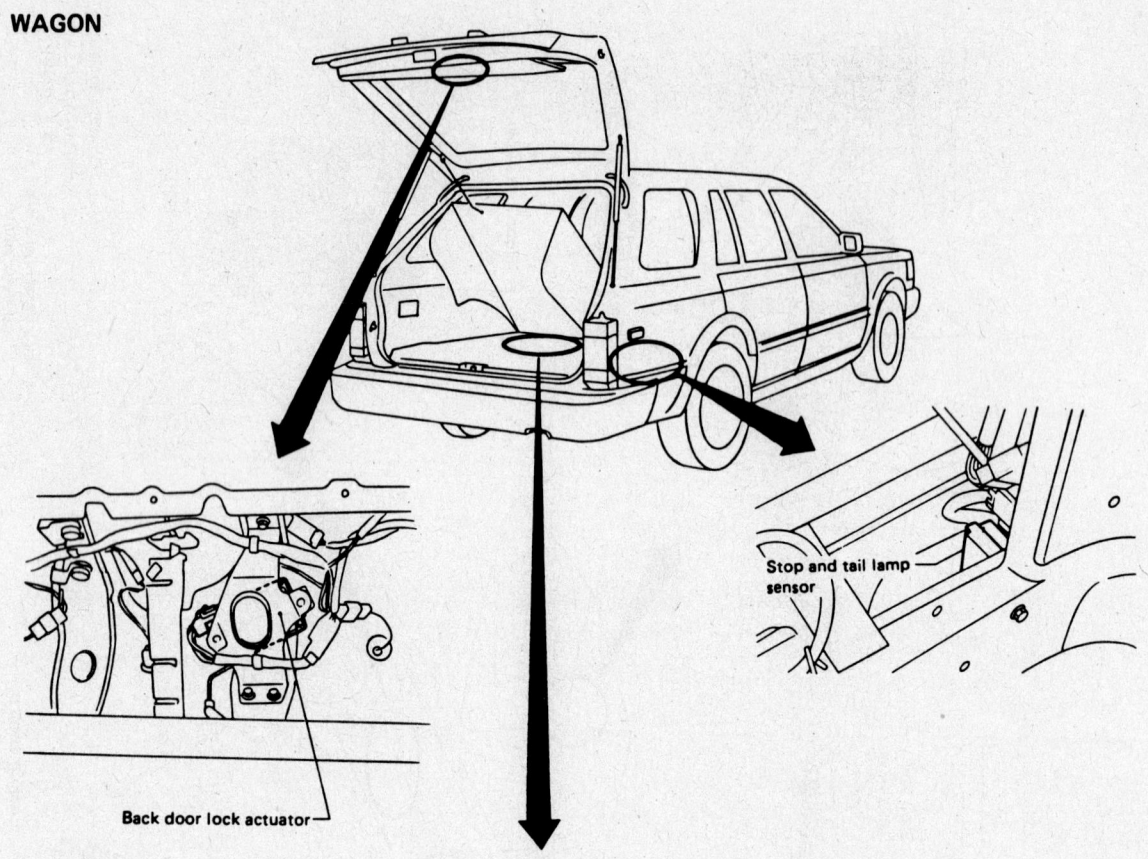

Back door lock actuator

Stop and tail lamp sensor

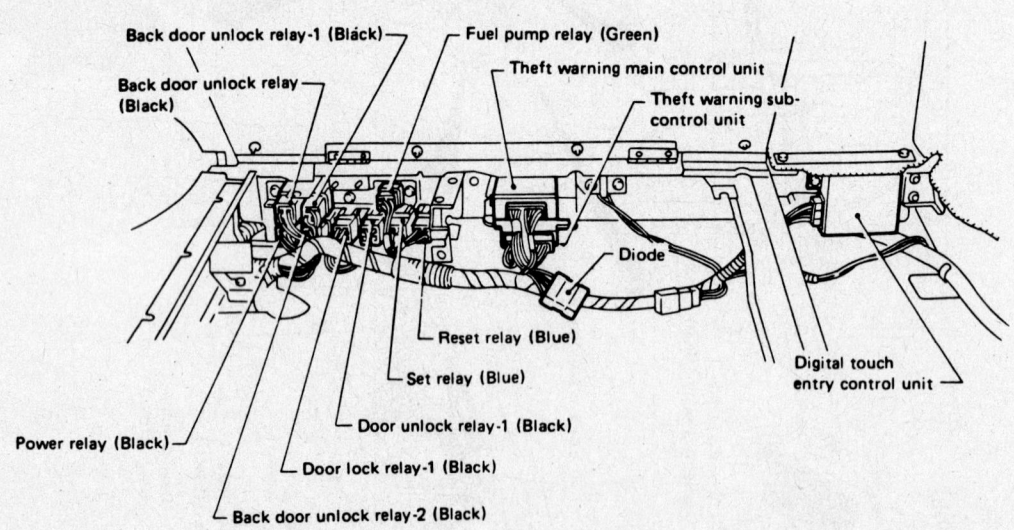

Back door unlock relay-1 (Black)

Back door unlock relay (Black)

Fuel pump relay (Green)

Theft warning main control unit

Theft warning sub-control unit

Diode

Reset relay (Blue)

Set relay (Blue)

Door unlock relay-1 (Black)

Power relay (Black)

Door lock relay-1 (Black)

Back door unlock relay-2 (Black)

Digital touch entry control unit

Nissan Maxima

SEDAN

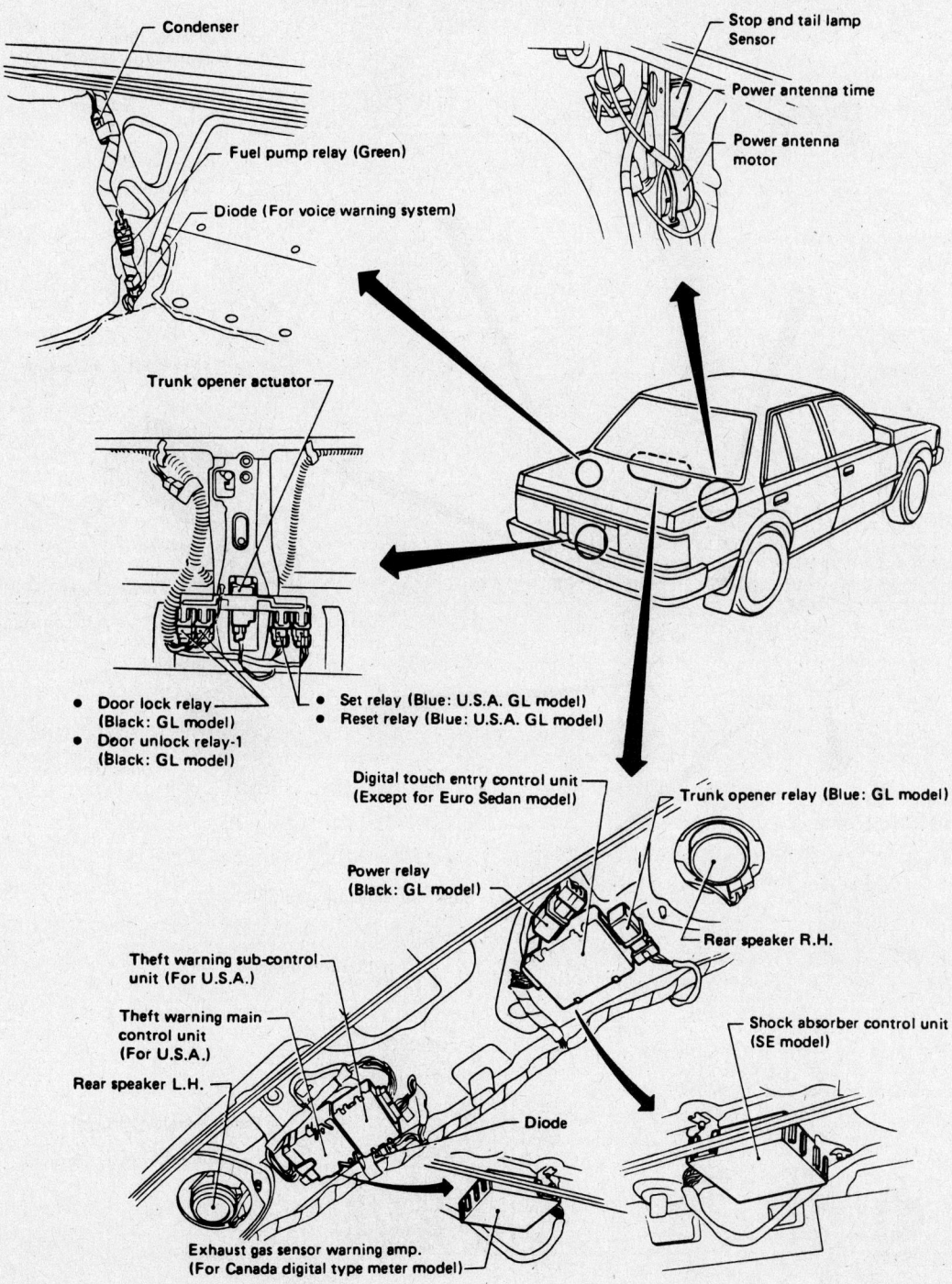

- Condenser
- Fuel pump relay (Green)
- Diode (For voice warning system)

- Stop and tail lamp Sensor
- Power antenna time
- Power antenna motor

Trunk opener actuator

- Door lock relay (Black: GL model)
- Door unlock relay-1 (Black: GL model)

- Set relay (Blue: U.S.A. GL model)
- Reset relay (Blue: U.S.A. GL model)

Digital touch entry control unit (Except for Euro Sedan model)

Trunk opener relay (Blue: GL model)

Power relay (Black: GL model)

Rear speaker R.H.

Theft warning sub-control unit (For U.S.A.)

Theft warning main control unit (For U.S.A.)

Rear speaker L.H.

Shock absorber control unit (SE model)

Diode

Exhaust gas sensor warning amp. (For Canada digital type meter model)

Nissan Maxima

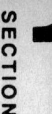
COMPONENT LOCATIONS

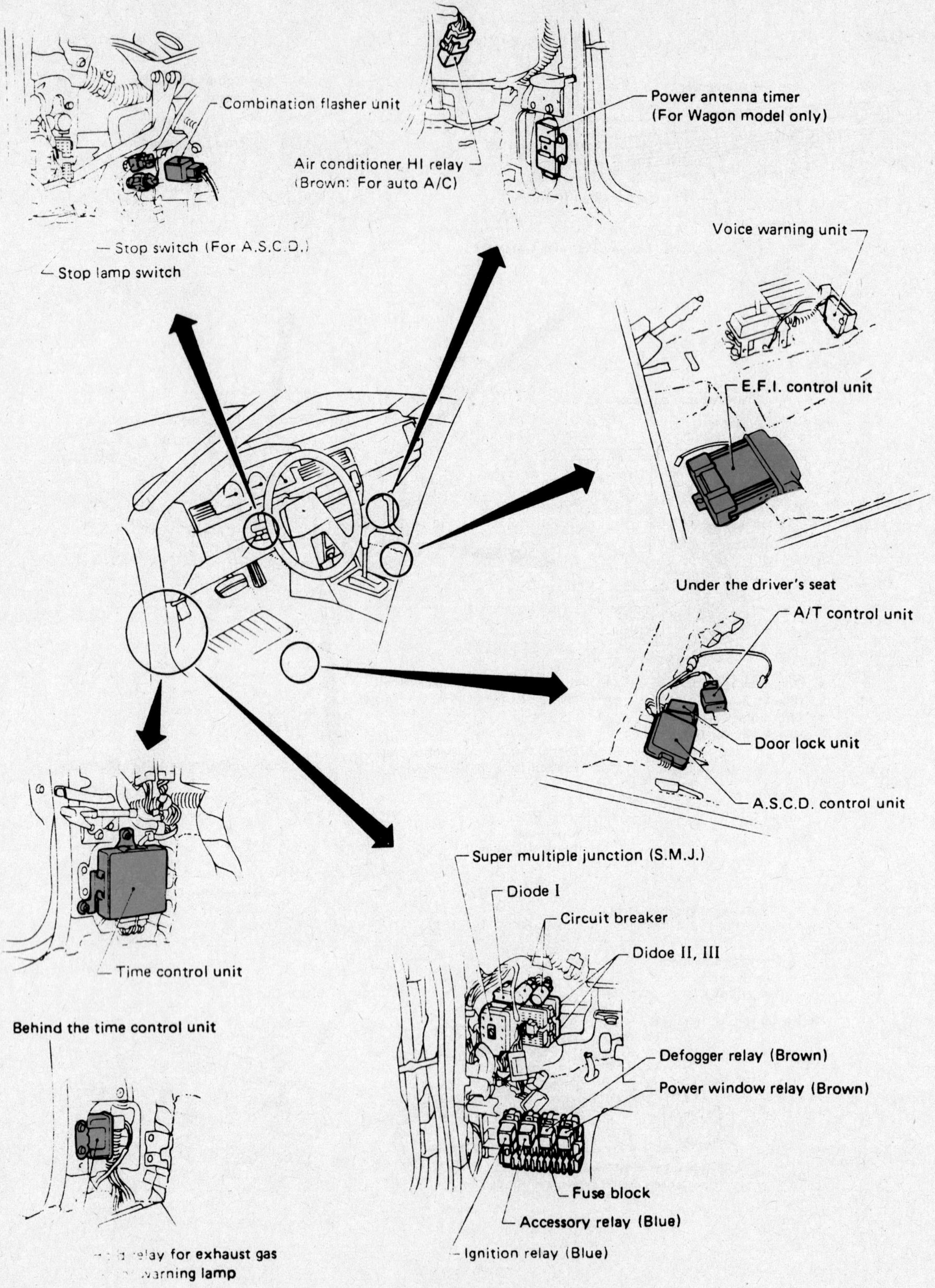

Combination flasher unit

Power antenna timer
(For Wagon model only)

Air conditioner HI relay
(Brown: For auto A/C)

Voice warning unit

— Stop switch (For A.S.C.D.)

Stop lamp switch

E.F.I. control unit

Under the driver's seat

A/T control unit

Door lock unit

A.S.C.D. control unit

— Time control unit

— Super multiple junction (S.M.J.)

— Diode I

— Circuit breaker

— Didoe II, III

Behind the time control unit

Defogger relay (Brown)

Power window relay (Brown)

— Fuse block

— Accessory relay (Blue)

— Ignition relay (Blue)

relay for exhaust gas
warning lamp

Nissan Maxima

COMPONENT LOCATIONS

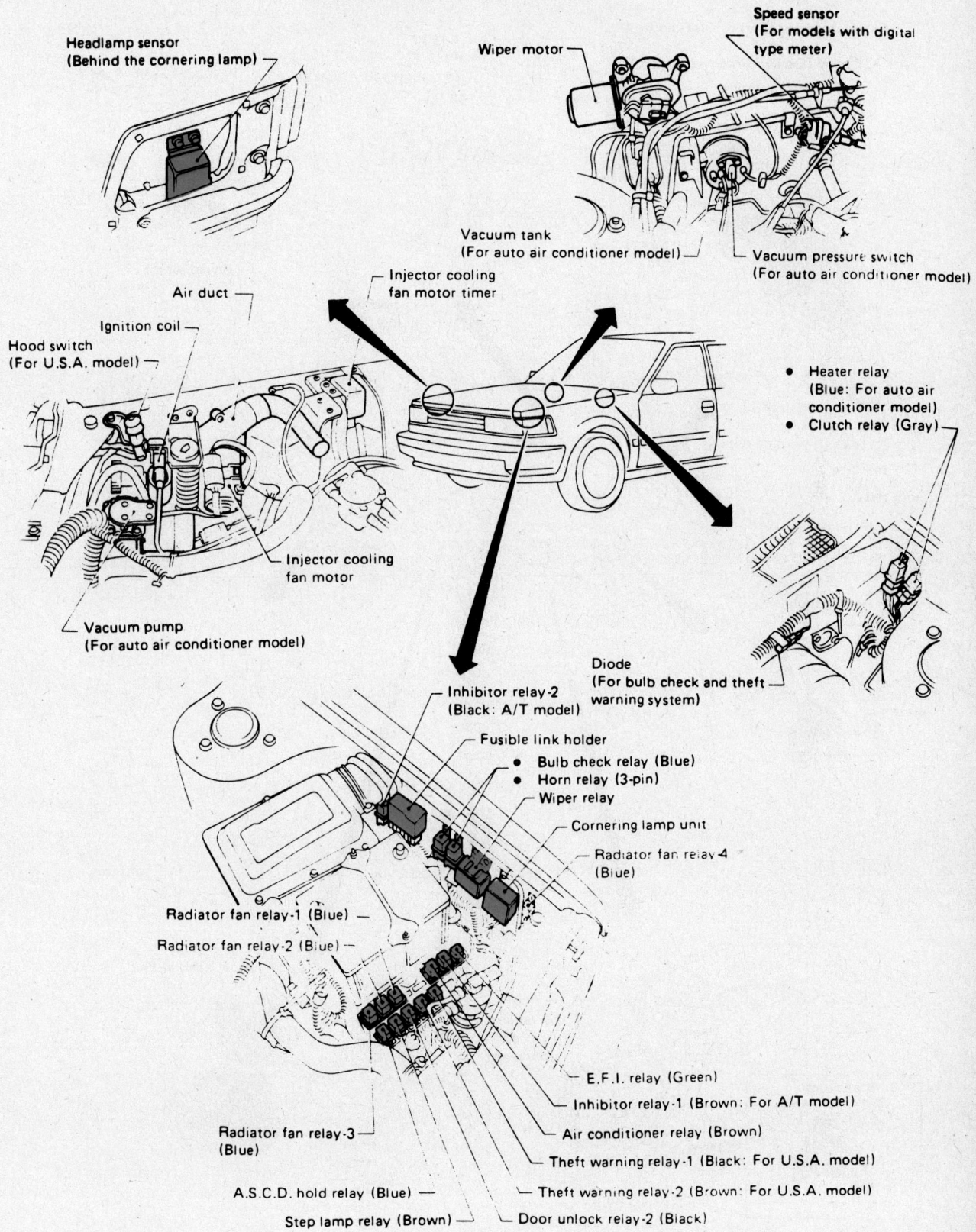

Headlamp sensor
(Behind the cornering lamp)

Wiper motor

Speed sensor
(For models with digital type meter)

Vacuum tank
(For auto air conditioner model)

Vacuum pressure switch
(For auto air conditioner model)

Injector cooling
fan motor timer

Air duct

Ignition coil

Hood switch
(For U.S.A. model)

- Heater relay
  (Blue: For auto air conditioner model)
- Clutch relay (Gray)

Injector cooling
fan motor

Vacuum pump
(For auto air conditioner model)

Diode
(For bulb check and theft warning system)

Inhibitor relay-2
(Black: A/T model)

Fusible link holder
- Bulb check relay (Blue)
- Horn relay (3-pin)
- Wiper relay
- Cornering lamp unit
- Radiator fan relay-4
  (Blue)

Radiator fan relay-1 (Blue)

Radiator fan relay-2 (Blue)

Radiator fan relay-3
(Blue)

A.S.C.D. hold relay (Blue)

Step lamp relay (Brown)

E.F.I. relay (Green)

Inhibitor relay-1 (Brown: For A/T model)

Air conditioner relay (Brown)

Theft warning relay-1 (Black: For U.S.A. model)

Theft warning relay-2 (Brown: For U.S.A. model)

Door unlock relay-2 (Black)

Nissan Maxima

COMPONENT LOCATIONS

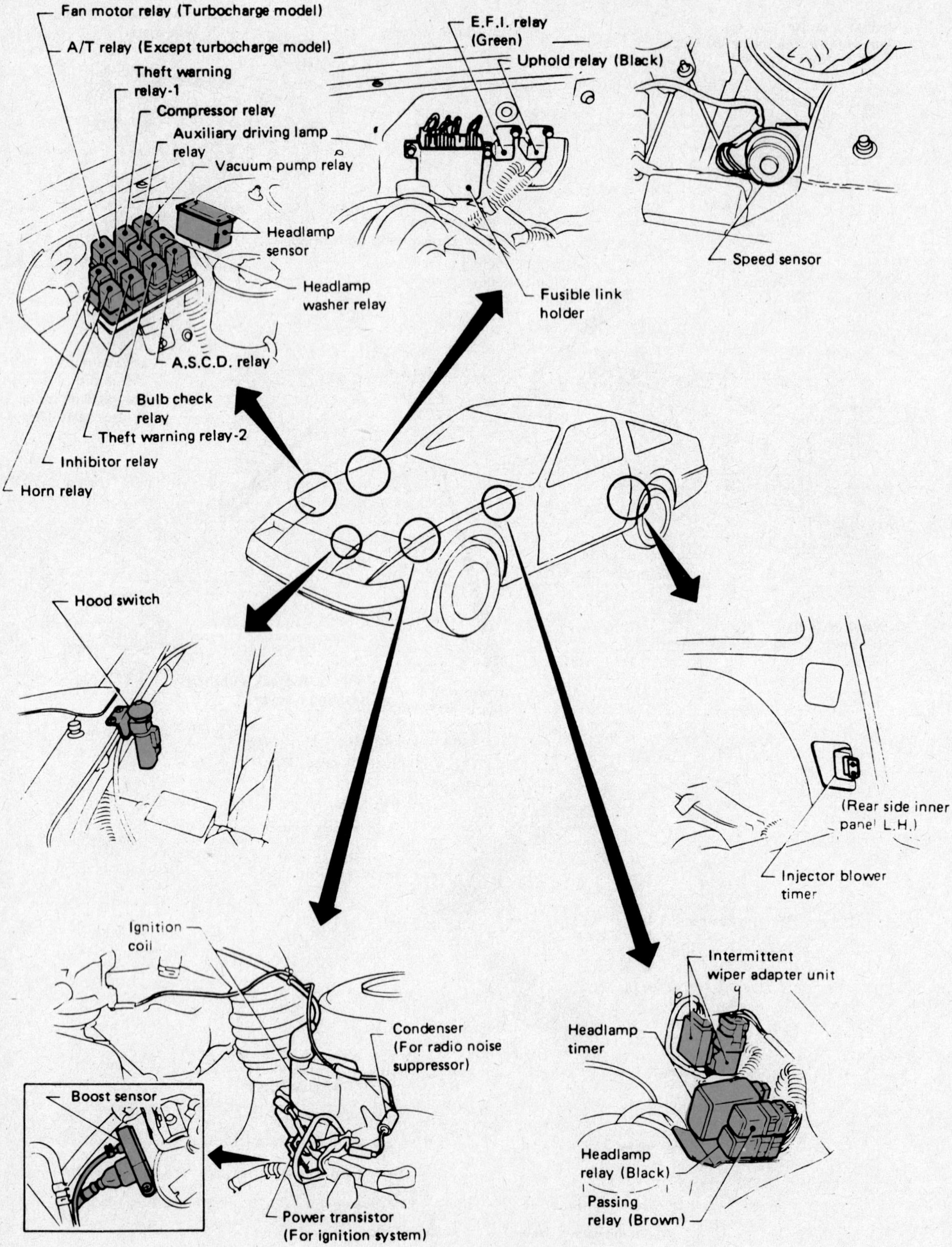

Fan motor relay (Turbocharge model)

A/T relay (Except turbocharge model)

Theft warning relay-1

Compressor relay

Auxiliary driving lamp relay

Vacuum pump relay

Headlamp sensor

Headlamp washer relay

A.S.C.D. relay

Bulb check relay

Theft warning relay-2

Inhibitor relay

Horn relay

E.F.I. relay (Green)

Uphold relay (Black)

Fusible link holder

Speed sensor

Hood switch

(Rear side inner panel L.H.)

Injector blower timer

Ignition coil

Condenser (For radio noise suppressor)

Boost sensor

Power transistor (For ignition system)

Intermittent wiper adapter unit

Headlamp timer

Headlamp relay (Black)

Passing relay (Brown)

Nissan 300ZX

296

COMPONENT LOCATIONS

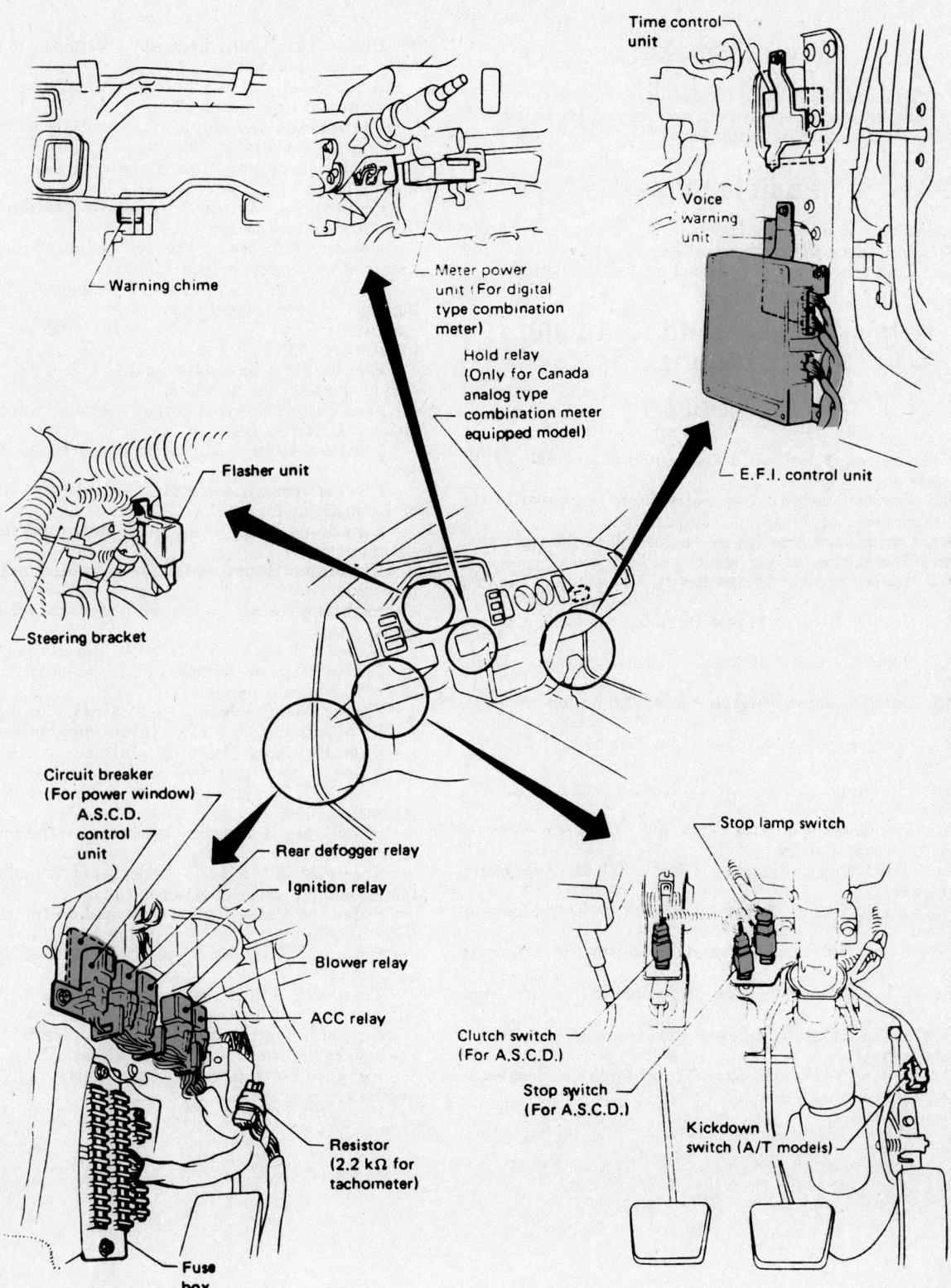

- Warning chime
- Meter power unit (For digital type combination meter)
- Hold relay (Only for Canada analog type combination meter equipped model)
- Time control unit
- Voice warning unit
- E.F.I. control unit
- Flasher unit
- Steering bracket
- Circuit breaker (For power window)
- A.S.C.D. control unit
- Rear defogger relay
- Ignition relay
- Blower relay
- ACC relay
- Resistor (2.2 kΩ for tachometer)
- Fuse box
- Stop lamp switch
- Clutch switch (For A.S.C.D.)
- Stop switch (For A.S.C.D.)
- Kickdown switch (A/T models)

Nissan 300ZX

SUBARU

Circuit Breakers

Most of the models protect all the circuits with fuses or relays. If there are any circuit breakers in use, they will be listed with the relay, sensors and computer locations.

Fusible Links

All models have one or three fusible links and they are usually installed in a relay block which connects into the main wiring harness. This relay block is installed next to the battery.

Relay, Sensors And Computer Locations

ALL MODELS

- **4WD Selector Solenoid** – is located on the side of the transaxle.
- **A/C Condenser Fan Control Relay** – is located in the right rear corner of the engine compartment.
- **A/C Condenser Fan Relay** – is located in the right rear corner of the engine compartment.
- **A/C Heater Blower Motor Relay** – is located on the fuse block bracket.
- **A/C-Heater Blower Motor Resistor** – is located on the outside of the heater case.
- **A/C High Pressure Switch** – is located on top of the receiver/drier.
- **A/C Low Pressure Switch** – is located on top of the receiver/drier.
- **A/C Relay** – is located in the right rear corner of the engine compartment.
- **A/C Thermostatic Sensor** – is located on the evaporator housing.
- **Air Solenoid Valve** – is located in the right rear corner of the engine compartment.
- **Anti-Dieseling Solenoid** – is located on the side of the carburetor.
- **Automatic Choke Relay** – is located under the passenger's seat.
- **Bowl Vent Solenoid Valve** – is located on the carburetor air horn.
- **Brake Fluid Level Sensor** – is located in the brake master cylinder.
- **Brake/Stop Light Checker (Brat)** – is located behind the passenger's seat.
- **Brake/Stop Light Checker (Hatchback)** – is located in the left rear quarter panel.
- **Brake/Stop Light Checker (Wagon)** – is located on the right rear quarter panel.
- **Brake/Stop Light Checker (All others)** – is located on the right tail light assembly.
- **Carburetor Feedback Solenoid** – is located on the air horn on the carburetor.
- **Coolant Temperature Sensor** – is located on the intake manifold.
- **Cooling Fan Control Pressure Switch** – is located on top of the receiver/drier.
- **Cooling Fan Motor Relay** – is located in the right rear corner of the engine compartment.
- **Cooling Fan Temperature Sensor** – is located on the bottom right side of the carburetor.
- **Cruise Control Unit** – is located under the left side of the instrument panel.
- **Electronic Control Module** – is located under the left side of the instrument panel.
- **Fuel Pump Control Unit** – is located under the left side of the instrument panel.
- **Ignition Relay** – is located under the front passenger's seat.
- **Intermittent Wiper Relay** – is located under the left side of the instrument panel.
- **Kickdown Relay** – is located under the left side of the instrument panel.
- **Kickdown Solenoid (A/T)** – is located on the side of the transaxle.
- **Lighting Relay** – is located under the left side of the instrument panel.
- **Oxygen Sensor** – is located on the front exhaust pipe.
- **Power Window Control Unit** – is located in the left side of the instrument panel.
- **Power Window Relay** – is located under the driver's seat.
- **RPM Sensor** – is located in the speedometer.
- **Seat Belt/Key Warning Chime** – is located under the right side of the instrument panel, behind the glove box.
- **Seat Belt Timer** – is located under the left side of the instrument panel.
- **Slow Duty Solenoid** – is located on the intake manifold near the carburetor.
- **Solenoid Valve No.1** – is located on the left side of the intake manifold near the water outlet.
- **Solenoid Valve No.2** – is located on the right of the intake manifold.
- **Solenoid Valve No.3** – is located on the left side of the intake manifold.
- **Transaxle Fluid Temperature Switch (A/T)** – is located on the side of the transaxle extension case.
- **Transfer Clutch Solenoid Valve (A/T)** – is located on the side of the transaxle extension case.
- **Vacuum Switches** – is located in the right rear corner of engine compartment.

TOYOTA

Circuit Breakers

Most of the models protect all the circuits with fuses or relays. If there are any circuit breakers in use, they will be listed with the relay, sensors and computer locations.

Fusible Links

All models have one fusible link and it is usually located in the main battery feed wire near the battery. This link will protect all the circuits except for the starter motor.

Relay, Sensors And Computer Locations

CAMRY

- **A/C Fan Relay** – is located on the number one fuse block, which is located behind the battery in the engine compartment.
- **A/C Micro Switch** – is located on the rear of the A/C control panel.
- **A/C Pressure Switch** – is located in the refrigerant line at the right side of the evaporator housing.
- **Air Flow Meter** – is located in the air intake system, starting at the right front fender panel.
- **Check Engine Connector** – is located at the left rear side of the engine compartment.
- **Coolant Temperature Sensor** – is located in the heater coolant flange at the rear of the engine on the transmission side.
- **Coolant Fan Temperature Switch** – is located in the return flange on the left front side of the engine.
- **Cooling Fan Relay** – is located on the number one fuse block, which is located behind the battery in the engine compartment.
- **Cruise Control Actuator** – is located on the right front shock tower.
- **Cruise Control Computer** – is located behind the right side kick panel.
- **Door Lock Control Relay** – is located under the center of the instrument panel, to the left of the steering column.
- **Electronic Control Transmission Coolant Temperature Switch** – is located in the coolant supply flange in the left front side of the engine.
- **Electronic Control Transmission Speed Sensor** – is located on the right rear side of the transaxle case.
- **Electronic Control Transmission Solenoid Valves** – are located one in each side of the transaxle.
- **Electronic Control Transmission Torque Converter Solenoid Valve** – is located on top of the transaxle.
- **Electronic Control Unit** – is located on the center of the firewall.
- **Electronic Controlled Transmission Computer** – is located under the speaker in the right side of the instrument panel, to the right of the glove box.
- **Electronic Fuel Injection Circuit Opening Relay** – is located on the number one fuse block, which is located behind the battery in the engine compartment.
- **Electronic Fuel Injection Computer** – is located under the center of the instrument panel.
- **Electronic Fuel Injection Main Relay** – is located on the number one fuse block, which is located behind the battery in the engine compartment.
- **Electronic Fuel Injection Resistor** – is located near the air flow meter.
- **Engine Main Relay** – is located on the number one fuse block, which is located behind the battery in the engine compartment.
- **Fade-Out Relay** – is located on the left side kick panel.
- **Front Wiper Relay** – is located under the left side of the instrument panel.
- **Fuel Heater Relay (1C-T Engine)** – is located on the left side kick panel.
- **Glow Plug Current Sensor (Diesel)** – is located on the top of the engine near the top radiator hose.
- **Glow Plug Relays 1 and 2 (Diesel)** – are located on the right hand side fender apron.
- **Glow Plug Resistor (Diesel)** – is located under the glow plug current sensor.
- **Headlight Relay** – is located on the number one fuse block, which is located behind the battery in the engine compartment.
- **Headlight Retainer Relay** – is located under the center of the instrument panel, to the right of the steering column.
- **Heater Circuit Breaker** – is located on fuse block number three, which is located behind the right side kick panel.
- **Heater Relay** – is located on fuse block number three, which is located behind the right side kick panel.
- **Interior Light Relay** – is located above the power circuit breaker next to fuse block number two.
- **Light Failure Sensor** – is located on the right panel in the luggage compartment on the Sedan models.
- **Main/Sun Roof Relay** – is located above the power circuit breaker next to fuse block number two.
- **Oxygen Sensor** – is located in the exhaust manifold.
- **Power Antenna Relay** – is located on the left rear corner of the engine compartment.
- **Power Circuit Breaker** – is located behind the left side kick panel.
- **Power Window Relay** – is located in the power window control unit in the left arm rest.
- **Rear Window Defogger Circuit Breaker** – is located on the fuse block number two, which is located behind the left side kick panel.
- **Rear Window Defogger Relay** – is located on the fuse block number two, which is located behind the left side kick panel.
- **Rear Wiper Relay** – is located in the rear panel.
- **Seat Belt Warning Relay** – is located behind the right kick panel, next to the cruise control computer.
- **Start Injector Time Switch** – is located in the heater coolant flange at the rear of the engine on the transmission side.
- **Tail Light Failure Sensor** – is located on the left panel (right panel on the Sedan) in the luggage compartment.
- **Tail Light Relay** – is located on the fuse block number two, which is located behind the left side kick panel.
- **Throttle Position Sensor** – is located on the throttle body.
- **Vehicle Speed Sensor** – is located behind the speedometer in the instrument panel.

CELICA

- **A/C Circuit Breaker** – is located under the right side of the instrument panel, to the right of the glove box.

• **A/C-Heater Blower Relay** – is located under the right side of the instrument panel, to the right of the glove box.

• **A/C Idle Stabilizer Amplifier** – is attached to the bottom of the evaporator housing.

• **A/C Pressure Switch** – is located on the evaporator housing.

• **A/C Resistor** – is located on the evaporator housing.

• **A/C Thermistor** – is located on the evaporator housing.

• **Air Flow Meter** – is located in the air induction system and is attached to the right front shock tower.

• **Brake Fluid Level Sensor** – is located in the brake fluid reservoir cap.

• **Catalytic Converter Temperature Sensor (Carb.)** – is located in the rear of the catalytic converter.

• **Charge Warning Light Relay** – is located on the number two fuse block, which is located behind the left side kick panel.

• **Circuit Opening Relay** – is located behind the left side kick panel in the bottom corner.

• **Circuit Opening Relay (EFI)** – is located at the right rear corner of the engine compartment.

• **Cold Mixture Heater Relay (Carb.)** – is located on fuse block number one, which is located behind the battery.

• **Cold Start Injector Time Switch (EFI)** – is located in the coolant flange on the right side of the engine, away from the block.

• **Coolant Temperature Sensor** – is located in the coolant flange on the right side of the engine near the block.

• **Cruise Control Actuator** – is located on the right side of the engine.

• **Cruise Control Computer** – is located behind the right side kick panel.

• **Defogger Relay** – is located on the number two fuse block, which is located behind the left side kick panel.

• **Door Lock Control Relay** – is located in the left door.

• **Door Lock Solenoids** – are located one in each door.

• **Electronic Air Control Valve (Carb.)** – is located in the secondary air hose behind the air pump.

• **Electronic Fuel Injection Control Unit** – is located under the right side of the instrument panel, to the right of the glove box.

• **Electronic Fuel Injection Fuel Pump Check Connector** – is located at the rear of the air flow meter.

• **Electronic Fuel Injection Fusible Links** – are located near fuse block number one, which is located behind the battery.

• **Electronic Fuel Injection Main Relay No.1** – is located on fuse block number one, which is located behind the battery.

• **Electronic Fuel Injection Main Relay No.2** – is located in front of the right shock tower in the engine compartment.

• **Electronic Fuel Injection Resistor** – is located on the right front shock tower in the engine compartment.

• **Electronic Fuel Injection Service Connector** – is located near fuse block number one, which is located behind the battery.

• **Emission Control Computer (Carb.)** – is located under the right side of the instrument panel, to the right of the glove box.

• **Emission Control Thermo Switch No.1** – is located in the coolant flange on the right side of the engine, away from the block.

• **Emission Control Thermo Switch No.2** – is located in the coolant flange on the right side of the engine, near the block.

• **Front Wiper Relay** – is located under the right side of the instrument panel, to the right of the glove box.

• **Fuel Cut Solenoid Valve** – is located on the left side of the carburetor.

• **Headlight Dimmer Relay** – is located on fuse block number one, which is located behind the battery.

• **Headlight Relay** – is located on fuse block number one,

which is located behind the battery.

• **Headlight Retractor Control Relay** – is located under the instrument panel, just above the steering column.

• **Headlight Retractor Relay** – is located behind the right headlight assembly.

• **Heater Blower Motor Circuit Breaker** – is located on fuse block number one, which is located behind the battery.

• **Interior Light Control Relay** – is located on the number two fuse block, which is located behind the left side kick panel.

• **Main Power Circuit Breaker** – is located on fuse block number two, which is located behind the left side kick panel.

• **Main Relay (Carb)** – is located on fuse block number one, which is located behind the battery.

• **Outer Vent Control Valve** – is located on the right side of the carburetor.

• **Overdrive Relay (Auto.Trans.)** – is located under the instrument panel to the left of the steering column.

• **Overdrive Solenoid (Auto.Trans.)** – is located on the left side of the transmission.

• **Oxygen Sensor** – is located in the exhaust manifold.

• **Power Window Relay** – is located on the number two fuse block, which is located behind the left side kick panel.

• **Rear Wiper Relay** – is located in the panel behind the left door jam.

• **Seat Belt Warning Relay** – is located under the left side of the instrument panel.

• **Sun Roof/Rear Window Defogger Circuit Breaker** – is located on the number two fuse block, which is located behind the left side kick panel.

• **Sun Roof Relay** – is located on the number two fuse block, which is located behind the left side kick panel.

• **Tail Light Relay** – is located on fuse block number one, which is located behind the battery.

• **Throttle Position Sensor (EFI)** – is located in the throttle body housing.

• **Vacuum Switch (Carb.)** – is located on the right front inner fender panel.

• **Vehicle Speed Sensor** – is located in the rear of the speedometer.

COROLLA FWD

• **A/C Condenser Fan Fusible Link** – is located in the wiring to the condenser fan near the fan shroud.

• **A/C Cut Relay (Diesel)** – is located on the cooling unit under the instrument panel.

• **A/C Fan Relays** – is located in the fuse/relay block attached to the left front inner fender panel, in front of the shock tower.

• **A/C High Pressure Switch** – is located under the battery tray in the engine compartment.

• **A/C Idle Stabilizer Amplifier** – is attached to the bottom of the cooling unit under the instrument panel, behind the glove box.

• **A/C Idle-Up Relay (Diesel)** – is located on the cooling unit under the instrument panel.

• **A/C Low Pressure Switch** – is attached to the bottom of the cooling unit under the instrument panel, behind the glove box.

• **A/C Thermistor** – is attached to the cooling unit under the instrument panel, behind the glove box.

• **Air Shut-Off Valve** – is located in the vacuum line feeding the choke opener on the carburetor.

• **Auxiliary Acceleration Pump** – is located on the carburetor.

• **Charge Light Relay** – is located under the right side of the instrument panel behind the glove box.

• **Coolant Level Warning Switch** – is attached to to the front left shock tower.

- **Coolant Temperature Switch (Diesel)** – is located on the top left side of the engine.
- **Coolant Temperature Switches (Gasoline)** – are located on the rear of the engine near the transaxle.
- **Cooling Fan Relay** – is located in the fuse/relay block attached to the left front inner fender panel, in front of the shock tower.
- **Cruise Control Actuator** – is mounted on the left front inner fender panel.
- **Cruise Control Computer** – is located behind the right side kick panel.
- **Defogger Relay** – is located in the fuse/relay block attached to the right side kick panel.
- **Door Lock Solenoid** – is located inside the driver's side door.
- **Emission Control Computer** – is located under the right side of the instrument panel above the glove box.
- **Heater Relay** – is located in the fuse/relay block attached to the right side kick panel.
- **Glow Plug Current Sensor (Diesel)** – is located on the lower right side of the engine.
- **Glow Plug Relay (Diesel)** – is mounted to the right front inner fender panel.
- **Glow Plug Resistor (Diesel)** – is located on the right top side of the engine.
- **Headlight Relay** – is located in the fuse/relay block attached to the left front inner fender panel, in front of the shock tower.
- **Main Relay** – is located in the fuse/relay block attached to the left front inner fender panel, in front of the shock tower.
- **Neutral Start Switch (Auto. Trans.)** – is located on the transaxle.
- **Power Circuit Breaker** – is located under the right side of the instrument panel behind the glove box.
- **Rear Door Lock Solenoid** – is located inside the left rear door.
- **Seat Belt Relay** – is located under the right side of the instrument panel above the glove box.
- **Starter Relay** – is mounted to the right front inner fender panel.
- **Tail Light Relay** – is located on the fuse/relay block which is located behind the left side kick panel.
- **Throttle Positioner** – is located on the carburetor.
- **Throttle Switch (Diesel)** – is located near the throttle linkage.
- **Vacuum Switch** – is mounted to the right front inner fender panel, behind the shock tower.

COROLLA RWD

- **A/C Heater Blower Relay** – is located under the right side of the instrument panel, above the glove box.
- **A/C Idle Stabilizer Amplifier** – is attached to the bottom of the cooling unit under the instrument panel.
- **A/C Pressure Switch** – is located on the cooling unit under the instrument panel.
- **A/C Relay** – is located in the fuse/relay block attached to the left front inner fender panel, in front of the shock tower.
- **A/C Thermister** – is attached to the cooling unit under the instrument panel.
- **Brake Fluid Level Sensor** – is located in the brake master cylinder reservoir cap.
- **Charge Warning Light Relay** – is located under the right side of the instrument panel.
- **Circuit Opening Relay** – is located under the right side of the instrument panel, to the right of the glove box.
- **Clutch Relay** – is located on the clutch switch, above the clutch pedal.

- **Cold Mixture Heater Relay** – is located on the left front inner fender panel in the engine compartment.
- **Cold Start Injector Time Switch (EFI)** – is located in the coolant flange on the right side of the engine, away from the block.
- **Cruise Control Actuator** – is mounted on the left front inner fender panel.
- **Cruise Control Computer** – is located on the left side kick panel.
- **Electric Air Bleed Control Valve** – is located on the right front inner fender panel.
- **Electronic Fuel Injection Control Unit** – is located on the right side kick panel.
- **Electronic Fuel Injection Main Relay** – is located in the fuse/relay block attached to the left front inner fender panel, in front of the shock tower.
- **Emission Control Computer** – is located under the right side of the instrument panel above the glove box.
- **Emission Control Thermo Switch** – is located in the coolant flange on the right side of the engine.
- **Emission Relay** – is attached to the left front shock tower in the engine compartment.
- **Fuel Solenoid Valves** – are located on the right side of the carburetor.
- **Headlight Relay** – is located in the fuse/relay block attached to the left front inner fender panel, in front of the shock tower.
- **Main Relay** – is located in the fuse/relay block attached to the left front inner fender panel, in front of the shock tower.
- **Neutral Start Switch (Auto. Trans.)** – is located on the transmission.
- **Outer Vent Control Valve** – is located on the right rear side of the cylinder head.
- **Overdrive Relay (Auto. Trans.)** – is located under the instrument panel to the left of the steering column.
- **Overdrive Solenoid (Auto. Trans.)** – is located on the left side of the transmission.
- **Oxygen Sensor** – is located in the exhaust manifold.
- **Power Circuit Breaker** – is located behind the right side kick panel.
- **Retractor Control Relay** – is located under the center of the instrument panel.
- **Retractor Relay** – is located on the left front inner fender panel, in front of the shock tower.
- **Seat Belt Warning Relay** – is located under instrument panel to the right of the steering column.
- **Solenoid Resistor** – is attached to the right front inner fender panel, in front of the shock tower.
- **Tail Light Relay** – is located on the fuse/relay block which is located behind the left side kick panel.
- **Throttle Position Sensor (EFI)** – is located in the throttle body housing.
- **Transmission Control Relay (Auto. Trans.)** – is located under the instrument panel to the right of the steering column.
- **Vacuum Switches** – are located on the right front inner fender panel, in front of the shock tower.
- **Water Temperature Sensor** – is located on the right front side of the engine.

CORONA

- **Brake Fluid Level Warning Switch** – is located in the master cylinder reservoir cap.
- **Charge Light Relay** – is located on the fuse/relay block which is located on the right front inner fender panel in front of the shock tower.
- **Charging Light Relay (with I.C. Regulator)** – is located on the fuse/relay block whick is located on the left front inner fender panel in front of the shock tower.

• **Choke Relay** – is located on the fuse/relay block which is located on the left front inner fender panel in front of the shock tower.

• **Coolant Temperature Sending Unit** – is located near the thermostat housing.

• **Defogger Relay** – is located on the left side kick panel.

• **Emission Control Computer** – is located on the right side kick panel.

• **Fuel Pump Relay** – is located under the right side of the instrument panel.

• **Headlight Dimmer Relay** – is located on the left front shock tower.

• **Headlight Relay** – is located on the fuse/relay block which is located on the right front inner fender panel in front of the shock tower.

• **Heater Relay** – is located on the left side kick panel.

• **Light Reminder Relay** – is located on the right side kick panel.

• **Main Relay** – is located on the fuse/relay block which is located on the right front inner fender panel in front of the shock tower.

• **Outer Vent Control Valve** – is located in the right rear corner of the engine compartment.

• **Oxygen Sensor** – is located in the exhaust manifold.

• **Power Main Relay** – is located on the fuse/relay block which is located on the left front inner fender panel in front of the shock tower.

• **Rear Wiper Relay** – is located on the panel under the hatch back on the liftback models, and on the rear panel in the luggage compartment on the wagon models.

• **Room Light Control Relay** – is located under the right side of the instrument panel, above the glove box.

• **Tail Light Relay** – is located on the left side kick panel.

• **Throttle Positioner** – is located on the carburetor.

• **Vacuum Switch** – is located on the right front shock tower.

• **Wiper Control Relay** – is located on the left side kick panel.

CRESSIDA

• **A/C Ambient Temperature Sensor** – is located on the center of the condenser.

• **A/C Circuit Breaker** – is located behind the right side kick panel.

• **A/C Cut-Out Relay** – is located behind the right side kick panel.

• **A/C-Heater Blower Relay** – is located behind the right side kick panel.

• **A/C Idle Stabilizer Amplifier** – is attached to the side of the evaporator housing.

• **A/C In-Vehicle Temperature Sensor** – is located under the right side of the instrument panel.

• **A/C Pressure Switch** – is located near the expansion valve on the side of the evaporator.

• **Air Flow Meter** – is located in the front of the air induction system.

• **Antenna Control Relay** – is located in the left rear quarter panel near the antenna motor.

• **Automatic Seat Belt Front Limit Switch** – is located on the bottom track in the upper windshield pillar.

• **Automatic Seat Belt Rear Limit Switch** – is located on the bottom track in the door pillar.

• **Automatic Shoulder Belt (ASB) Circuit Breaker** – is located under the right side of the instrument panel, to the right of the ASB computer.

• **Automatic Shoulder Belt Computer** – is located under the right side of the instrument panel.

• **Brake/Stop Light Failure Relay** – is located on fuse/relay block number two, which is located behind the left side kick panel.

• **Charge Warning Light Relay** – is located on fuse/relay block number two, which is located behind the left side kick panel.

• **Cold Start Injection Time Switch** – is located in the coolant flange at the front of the engine, near the block.

• **Coolant Temperature Sensor** – is located in the coolant flange at the front of the engine, away from the block.

• **Cruise Control Actuator** – is located on the front left inner fender panel.

• **Cruise Control Computer** – is located behind the left side kick panel.

• **Defogger Circuit Breaker** – is located on fuse/relay block number two, which is located behind the left side kick panel.

• **Defogger Timer Relay** – is located under the center of the instrument panel.

• **Door Lock Circuit Breaker** – is located on fuse/relay block number two, which is located behind the left side kick panel.

• **Door Lock Control Relay** – is located behind the left side kick panel.

• **Door Lock Relay** – is located under the left side of the instrument panel, behind the air vent.

• **Door Lock Solenoids** – are located in each door, including the lift gate.

• **Electronic Control Transmission Computer** – is located behind the left side kick panel.

• **Electronic Control Transmission Shift Solenoids** – are located on the rear of the transmission.

• **Electronic Control Transmission Speed Sensor** – is located on the left side of the transmission.

• **Electronic Control Transmission Torque Converter Solenoid** – is located on the left side of the transmission.

• **Electronic Fuel Injection Circuit Opening Relay** – is located under the right side of the instrument panel, behind the air vent.

• **Electronic Fuel Injection Control Unit** – is located under the right side of the instrument panel.

• **Electronic Fuel Injection Fuel Pump Check Connector** – is located at the rear of the air flow meter.

• **Electronic Fuel Injection Main Relay No.1** – is located on fuse block number one, which is located behind the battery.

• **Electronic Fuel Injection Resistor** – is located on the front left shock tower in the engine compartment.

• **Electronic Fuel Injection Service Connectors** – are located near fuse block number one, which is located behind the battery.

• **Fade Out Relay** – is located on the right side kick panel.

• **Headlight Cleaner Relay** – is located on the right front inner fender panel.

• **Headlight Relay** – is located on fuse block number one, which is located behind the battery.

• **Heater Circuit Breaker** – is located on the right side kick panel.

• **Ignition Main Relay** – is located on fuse block number one, which is located behind the battery.

• **Interior Light Control Relay** – is located on fuse/relay block number two, which is located behind the left side kick panel.

• **Intermittent Wiper Relay** – is located behind the right side kick panel.

• **Knock Sensor** – is located in the cylinder block.

• **Main Power Circuit Breaker** – is located on fuse block number two, which is located behind the left side kick panel.

• **Music Alarm Relay** – is attached to the left side of the center console.

• **Oxygen Sensor** – is located in the exhaust manifold.

• **Power Window Main Relay** – is located behind the left side kick panel.

- **Power Window Relay** – is located under the center of the instrument panel above the steering column.
- **Rear Window Defogger Relay** – is located on the left side kick panel.
- **Seat Belt Warning Relay** – is located under the center of the instrument panel, above the steering column.
- **Sun Roof Computer** – is located in the under the roof headliner.
- **Super Monitor Computer** – is located in the behind the center console.
- **Tail Light Failure Relay** – is located on fuse/relay block number two, which is located behind the left side kick panel.
- **Tail Light Relay** – is located on fuse block number one, which is located behind the battery.
- **Theft Deterrent Computer** – is located under the center of the instrument panel, above the steering column.
- **Throttle Position Sensor** – is located on the left side of the engine on the throttle body housing.
- **Vacuum Switch** – is located on the right front inner fender panel.
- **Vehicle Speed Sensor** – is located behind the speedometer in the instrument panel.
- **Warm-Up Relay (86°F)** – is located under the instrument panel to the right os the center console.
- **Warm-Up Relay (122°F)** – is located under the instrument panel to the right on the center console.

MR2

- **A/C Ambient Sensor** – is located near the A/C condenser.
- **A/C High Pressure Switch** – is located in the middle of the engine, behind the fuel pump.
- **A/C In-Car Sensor** – is located behind the A/C control panel.
- **A/C Power Servo** – is located behind the center console.
- **Air Flow Meter** – is located in the front of the air induction system.
- **Auxiliary Air Valve** – is located on the throttle body.
- **Brake Fluid Level Warning Switch** – is located in the brake master cylinder reservoir cap.
- **Circuit Opening Relay** – is located on the rear panel of the engine compartment.
- **Coolant Temperature Sensor** – is located on the front of the engine.
- **Cooling Fan Relay** – is located in the relay block located in the luggage compartment.
- **Cooling Fan Temperature Switch** – is located in the right side of the radiator.
- **Cruise Control Actuator** – is located on the firewall in the engine compartment.
- **Cruise Control Computer** – is located on the left rear inner quarter panel of the engine compartment.
- **Cruise Control Vacuum Switch** – is located on the firewall in the engine compartment.
- **Door Lock Circuit Breaker** – is located on the left side kick panel.
- **Door Lock Control Relay** – is located inside the passenger's side.
- **Door Lock Solenoid** – is located inside the passenger's side.
- **EFI Main Relay** – is located on the relay block next to the battery.
- **Electronic Control Unit** – is located on the right side of the firewall in the engine compartment.
- **Headlight Control Relay** – is located under the right side of the instrument panel.
- **Headlight Retainer Relay** – is located under the center of the instrument panel.
- **Heater Relay** – is located on the right side kick panel.
- **Idle-Up Relay** – is located on the cooling unit.

- **Injector Relay** – is located on the relay block next to the battery.
- **Light Retractor Control Relay** – is located on the right front inner fender panel, behind the shock tower.
- **Oxygen Sensor** – is located in the exhaust manifold.
- **Power Window Relay** – is located on the left side kick panel.
- **Seat Belt Warning Relay** – is located behind the left rear (inside) roof rail.
- **Solar Sensor** – is located in the upper left hand corner, under the instrument panel.
- **Solenoid Resistor** – is located on the left side of the firewall.
- **Start Injector Time Switch** – is located on the left rear quarter panel in the engine compartment.
- **Taillight Control Relay** – is located on the left side kick panel.
- **Throttle Position Sensor** – is located on or near the throttle body.
- **Vacuum Pump** – is located on the firewall in the engine compartment.
- **Vacuum Switching Valve** – is attached to the vacuum tank.
- **Water Temperature Sending Unit** – is located on the top right hand side of the engine.

STARLET

- **A/C Fan Relay** – is located on the side of the front washer fluid reservoir.
- **A/C Idle Stabilizer Amplifier** – is located on the right side of the evaporator.
- **A/C In-Car Temperature Sensor** – is located on the top side of the evaporator.
- **A/C Pressure Switch** – is located near the expansion valve on the right side of the evaporator.
- **A/C Relay** – is located behind the right side kick panel.
- **Brake Fluid Level Sensor** – is located in the brake master cylinder reservoir.
- **Charge Warning Light Relay** – is located behind the left side kick panel.
- **Check Engine Connector** – is located in the right rear corner of the engine compartment.
- **Coolant Temperature Sensor** – is located in the coolant flange at the front of the engine block.
- **Coolant Temperature Switch** – is located in the coolant flange at the front of the engine block.
- **Cooling Fan Relay** – is located on the relay block which is located behind the left side kick panel.
- **Electronic Fuel Injection Computer** – is located under the center of the instrument panel, in front of the center console.
- **Electronic Fuel Injection Main Relay** – is located on the relay block which is located behind the left side kick panel.
- **Electronic Fuel Injection Service Connector** – is located in the right rear corner of the engine compartment.
- **Fuel Pump Check Connector** – is located in front of the number one intake runner at the lower end of it.
- **Headlight Control Relay** – is located on the relay block which is located behind the left side kick panel.
- **Ignition Main Relay** – is located on the relay block which is located behind the left side kick panel.
- **Oxygen Sensor** – is located in the exhaust manifold.
- **Oxygen Sensor Check Connector** – is located in the right rear corner of the engine compartment.
- **Rear Wiper Relay** – is located on the rear hatchback.
- **Seat Belt Warning Relay** – is located behind the right side kick panel.
- **Solenoid Resistor** – is located on the left front inner fender panel.

- **Tail Light Control Relay** – is located on the relay block which is located behind the left side kick panel.
- **Throttle Position Sensor** – is located on the throttle body housing.

SUPRA

- **A/C Ambient Temperature Sensor** – is located on the right side of the condensor in the engine compartment.
- **A/C Circuit Breaker** – is located under the right side of the instrument panel, above the glove box.
- **A/C Cut-Out Relay** – is located behind the right side kick panel.
- **A/C Idle Stabilizer Amplifier** – is attached to the bottom of the evaporator housing.
- **A/C In-Car Temperature Sensor** – is located under the center console, at the rear.
- **Air Flow Meter** – is located in the front of the air induction system.
- **Brake Fluid Level Sensor** – is located in the brake master cylinder reservoir cap.
- **Charge Warning Light Relay** – is located on fuse/relay block number two, which is located behind the left side kick panel.
- **Cold Start Injection Time Switch** – is located in the coolant flange in the front of the distributor.
- **Coolant Temperature Sensor** – is located in the coolant flange it the front of the distributor.
- **Cruise Control Actuator** – is located on the front left inner fender panel.
- **Cruise Control Computer** – is located behind the right side kick panel.
- **Defogger Circuit Breaker** – is located on fuse/relay block number two, which is located behind the left side kick panel.
- **Defogger Timer Relay** – is located on fuse/relay block number two, which is located behind the left side kick panel.
- **Door Lock Circuit Breaker** – is located on fuse/relay block number two, which is located behind the left side kick panel.
- **Door Lock Control Relay** – is located in the left door.
- **Door Lock Relay** – is located under the left side of the instrument panel.
- **Door Lock Solenoids** – are located in each door.
- **Electronic Control Transmission Computer** – is located behind the right door jam.
- **Electronic Control Transmission Shift Solenoids** – are located on the rear of the transmission.
- **Electronic Control Transmission Speed Sensor** – is located on the left side of the transmission.
- **Electronic Control Transmission Torque Converter Solenoid** – is located on the left side of the transmission.
- **Electronic Controlled Transmission Diagnostic Terminal** – is located at the rear of the air flow meter, on the right front shock tower.
- **Electronic Fuel Injection Check Connectors** – is located at the rear of the air flow meter.
- **Electronic Fuel Injection Circuit Opening Relay** – is located behind the left side kick panel.
- **Electronic Fuel Injection Control Unit** – is located under the right side of the instrument panel, above the glove box.
- **Electronic Fuel Injection Fuel Pump Check Connector** – is located on the right side of the engine under the air flow meter.
- **Electronic Fuel Injection Fusible Links** – are located on the number one fuse/relay block, located behind the battery.
- **Electronic Fuel Injection Main Relay No.1** – is located on fuse block number one, which is located behind the battery.
- **Electronic Fuel Injection Main Relay No.2** – is located in front of the left front shock tower.

- **Electronic Fuel Injection Resistor** – is located on the left front shock tower in the engine compartment.
- **Fog Light Relay** – is located behind the left side kick panel.
- **Front Wiper Relay** – is located under the right side of the instrument panel, above the glove box.
- **Headlight Cleaner Relay** – is located on the right front shock tower.
- **Headlight Dimmer Relay** – is located on the number one fuse/relay block, which is located behind the battery.
- **Headlight Relay** – is located on fuse block number one, which is located behind the battery.
- **Headlight Retractor Control Relay** – Is located under the instrument panal, above the steering column.
- **Headlight Retractor Relay** – is located on the right front shock tower in the engine compartment.
- **Heater Blower Relay** – is located under the right side of the instrument panel, above the glove box.
- **Heater Double Vacuum Valve** – is located in the heater unit.
- **Heater Power Servo** – is located in the left side of the heater unit.
- **High Speed Fan Relay** – is located behind the right side kick panel.
- **Interior Light Control Relay** – is located on fuse/relay block number two, which is located behind the left side kick panel.
- **Main Power Circuit Breaker** – is located on the left side kick panel.
- **Overdrive Relay (Auto. Trans.)** – is located under the instrument panel. to the right of the steering column.
- **Overdrive Solenoid (Auto.Trans.)** – is located on the left side of the transmission.
- **Oxygen Sensor** – is located in the exhaust manifold.
- **Power Window Main Relay** – is located behind the left side kick panel.
- **Power Window Relay** – is located on fuse/relay block number two, which is located behind the left side kick panel.
- **Rear Wiper Relay** – is located in the panel behind the left door jam.
- **Seat Belt Warning Relay** – is located under the left side of the instrument panel.
- **Solar Sensor** – is located on the cooling unit, under the instrument panel.
- **Sub-Damper Relay No.1** – is located behind the right side kick panel.
- **Sub-Damper Relay No.2** – is located behind the right side kick panel.
- **Sun Roof Relay** – is located on the number two fuse/relay block, which is located behind the left side kick panel.
- **Tail Light Failure Relay** – is located behind the right side kick panel.
- **Tail Light Relay** – is located on fuse block number one, which is located behind the battery.
- **Throttle Position Sensor** – is located on the left side of the engine on the throttle body housing.
- **Vehicle Speed Sensor** – is located behind the speedometer in the instrument panel.
- **Warm-Up Relay (86°F)** – is located under the instrument panel to the right of the center console.
- **Warm-Up Relay (122°F)** – is located under the instrument panel to the right of the center console.

TERCEL

- **4WD Indicator Switch** – is located on the left side of the transmission.
- **4WD Solenoid** – is located on the left side of the transmission attached to the neutral safety switch.

- **A/C Idle Stabilizer Amplifier** – is located on the side of the evaporator housing.
- **A/C Pressure Switch** – is located on the evaporator housing.
- **A/C Relay** – is located on the number one fuse/relay block, which is located on the left front shock tower.
- **A/C Temperature Sensor** – is located on the evaporator housing.
- **A/C Thermister** – is located on the refrigerant line on the cooling unit.
- **Automatic Transmission Fluid Temperature Warning Switch** – is located in the left side of the transmission.
- **Charge Warning Light Relay** – is located on the number three fuse/relay block, which is located behind the right side kick panel.
- **Cold Mixture Heater Relay** – is located on the right front shock tower in the engine compartment.
- **Coolant Temperature Sending Unit** – is located in the upper radiator tank.
- **Coolant Temperature Sensor** – is located in the coolant flange on the right side of the engine block.
- **Cooling Fan Relay** – is located on the number one fuse/relay block, which is located on the left front shock tower.
- **Defogger Circuit Breaker** – is located on the number two fuse/relay block, which is located behind the left side kick panel.
- **Defogger Relay** – is located on the number three fuse/relay block, which is located behind the right side kick panel.
- **Electric Air Bleed Control Valve** – is located on the right front shock tower.
- **Emission Control Computer** – is located under the right side of the instrument panel, above the glove box.
- **Extra Low Gear Indicator Switch** – is located on the left side of the transmission.
- **Fuel Cut-Off Solenoid** – is located on the carburetor.
- **Headlight Control Relay** – is located on the number one fuse/relay block, which is located on the left front shock tower.
- **Headlight Dimmer Relay** – is located on the number one fuse/relay block, which is located on the left front shock tower.
- **Heater Circuit Breaker** – is located on the number three fuse/relay block, which is located behind the right side kick panel.
- **Heater Relay** – is located on the number three fuse/relay block, which is located behind the right side kick panel.
- **Ignition Main Relay** – is located on the number one fuse/relay block, which is located on the left front shock tower.
- **Intermittent Wiper Relay** – is located on the number two fuse/relay block, which is located behind the left side kick panel.
- **Main Power Circuit Breaker** – is located on the number two fuse/relay block, which is located behind the left side kick panel.
- **Main Power Relay** – is located on the number three fuse/relay block, which is located behind the right side kick panel.
- **Outer Vent Control Valve** – is located in the vacuum hose near the charcoal canister.
- **Oxygen Sensor** – is located in the exhaust manifold.
- **Sun Roof Relay** – is located on the number three fuse/relay block, which is located behind the right side kick panel.
- **Tail Light Control Relay** – is located on the number two fuse/relay block, which is located behind the left side kick panel.
- **Vacuum Switches** – is located on the right front inner fender panel.
- **Vacuum Switching Valve** – is attached to the vacuum tank.

VAN

- **A/C Amplifier** – is located on the cooling unit.
- **A/C Cut-Out Relay** – is located on the front of the cooling unit.
- **A/C Magnetic Valve** – is located in the refrigerant line near the expansion valve.
- **A/C Pressure Switch** – is located on the receiver/drier line.
- **A/C Thermister** – is located on the cooling unit.
- **Accelerator Switch** – is located above the accelerator pedal.
- **Air Flow Meter** – is located on the lower left side of the engine.
- **Circuit Opening Relay** – is located in the radiator support panel in the front of the engine compartment.
- **Coolant Thermo Sensor** – is located in or near the thermostat housing.
- **Cruise Control Actuator** – is located under the center of the instrument panel.
- **Dome Light Relay** – is located up under the left side of the instrument panel.
- **Electronic Control Unit** – is located in the driver's side door jam.
- **Electronic Controlled Fuel Injection Main Relay** – is located in the relay block, which is installed under the center of the instrument panel.
- **Engine Service Connectors** – are located behind the air flow meter on the lower left side of the engine.
- **Fusible Link** – is located in the upper left hand corner of the engine compartment (there is also one going to the electronic control unit).
- **Headlight Relay** – is located in the fuse/relay block, which is installed on the right side kick panel.
- **Heater Circuit Breaker** – is located in a relay block under the left side of the instrument panel.
- **Heater Relay** – is located in the relay block, which is installed under the center of the instrument panel.
- **Ignition Relay** – is located in the relay block, which is installed under the center of the instrument panel.
- **Main Power Circuit Breaker** – is located in the fuse/relay block, which is installed on the right side kick panel.
- **Main Power Relay** – is located in the relay block, which is installed under the center of the instrument panel.
- **Oil Level Warning Module** – is located to under the right side of the instrument panel.
- **Oxygen Sensor** – is located in the exhaust manifold.
- **Rear Heater Blower Switch No.1** – is located behind the left center quarter panel of the van.
- **Rear Heater Blower Switch No.2** – is located behind the left center quarter panel of the van.
- **Rear Heater Relay** – is located in the relay block, which is installed under the center of the instrument panel.
- **Rear Windshield Washer Relay** – is located behind the right rear quarter panel.
- **Seat Belt Warning Relay** – is located up under the left side of the instrument panel.
- **Solenoid Resistor** – is located on the lower left side of the engine.
- **Start Injector Time Switch** – is located on the top left side of the engine.
- **Tail Light Relay** – is located in the fuse/relay block, which is installed on the right side kick panel.
- **Throttle Position Sensor** – is located on the throttle body.
- **Unlock Warning Switch** – is located in the center of the rear hatch door.
- **Vacuum Switching Valve** – is located on the vacuum tank.

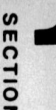

COMPONENT LOCATIONS

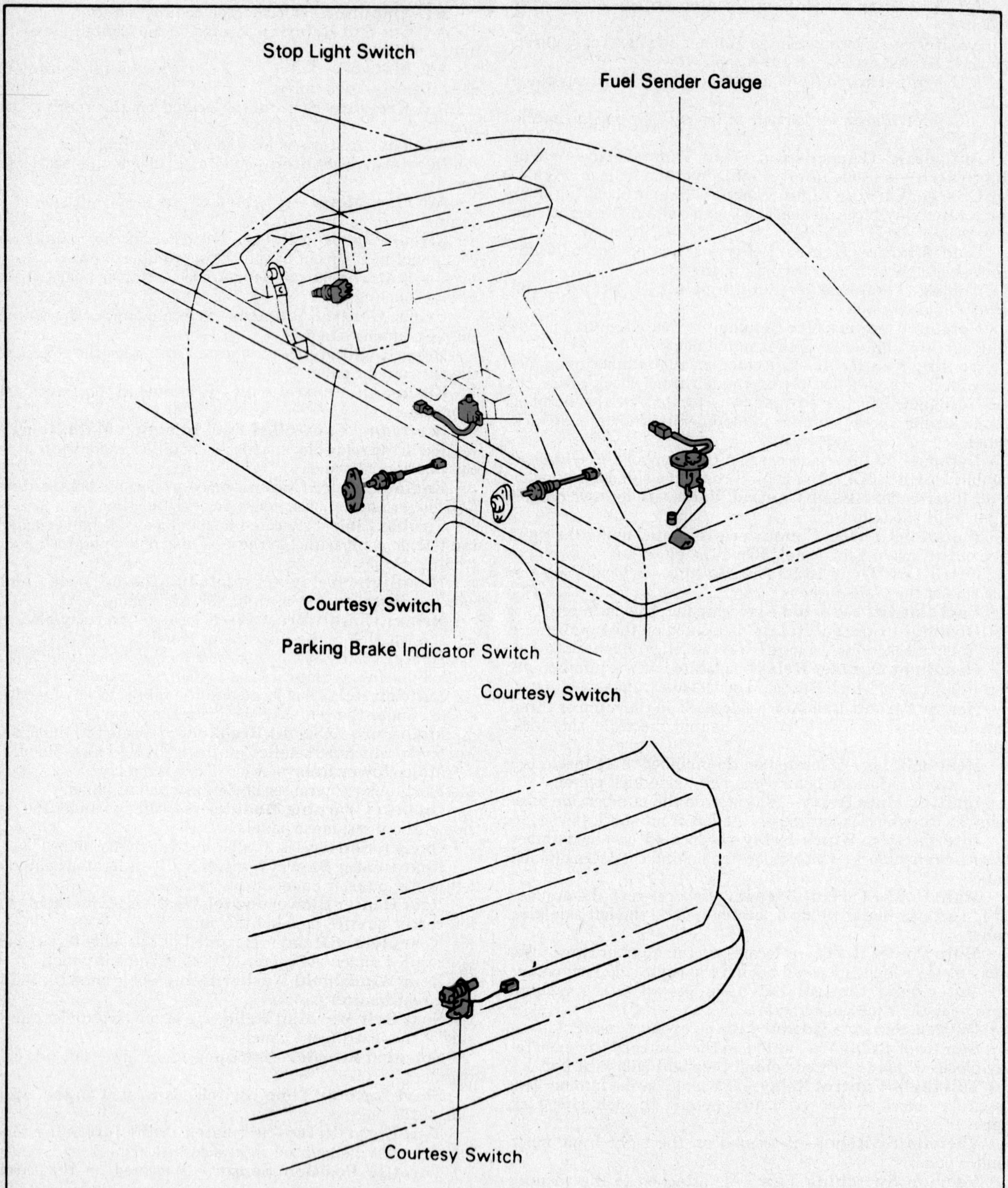

Stop Light Switch

Fuel Sender Gauge

Courtesy Switch

Parking Brake Indicator Switch

Courtesy Switch

Courtesy Switch

Toyota Tercel

COMPONENT LOCATIONS

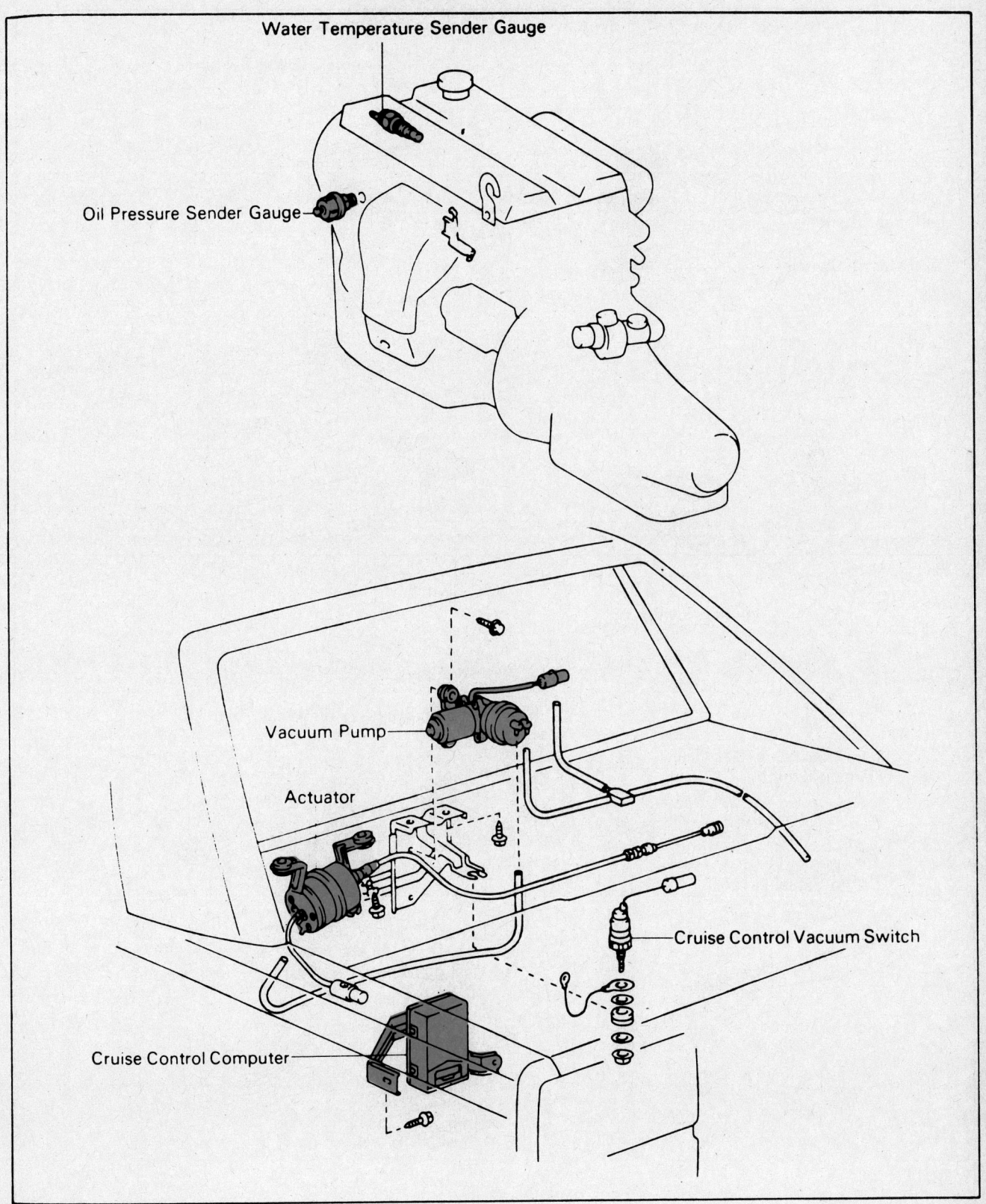

Water Temperature Sender Gauge

Oil Pressure Sender Gauge

Vacuum Pump

Actuator

Cruise Control Vacuum Switch

Cruise Control Computer

Toyota MR2

COMPONENT LOCATIONS

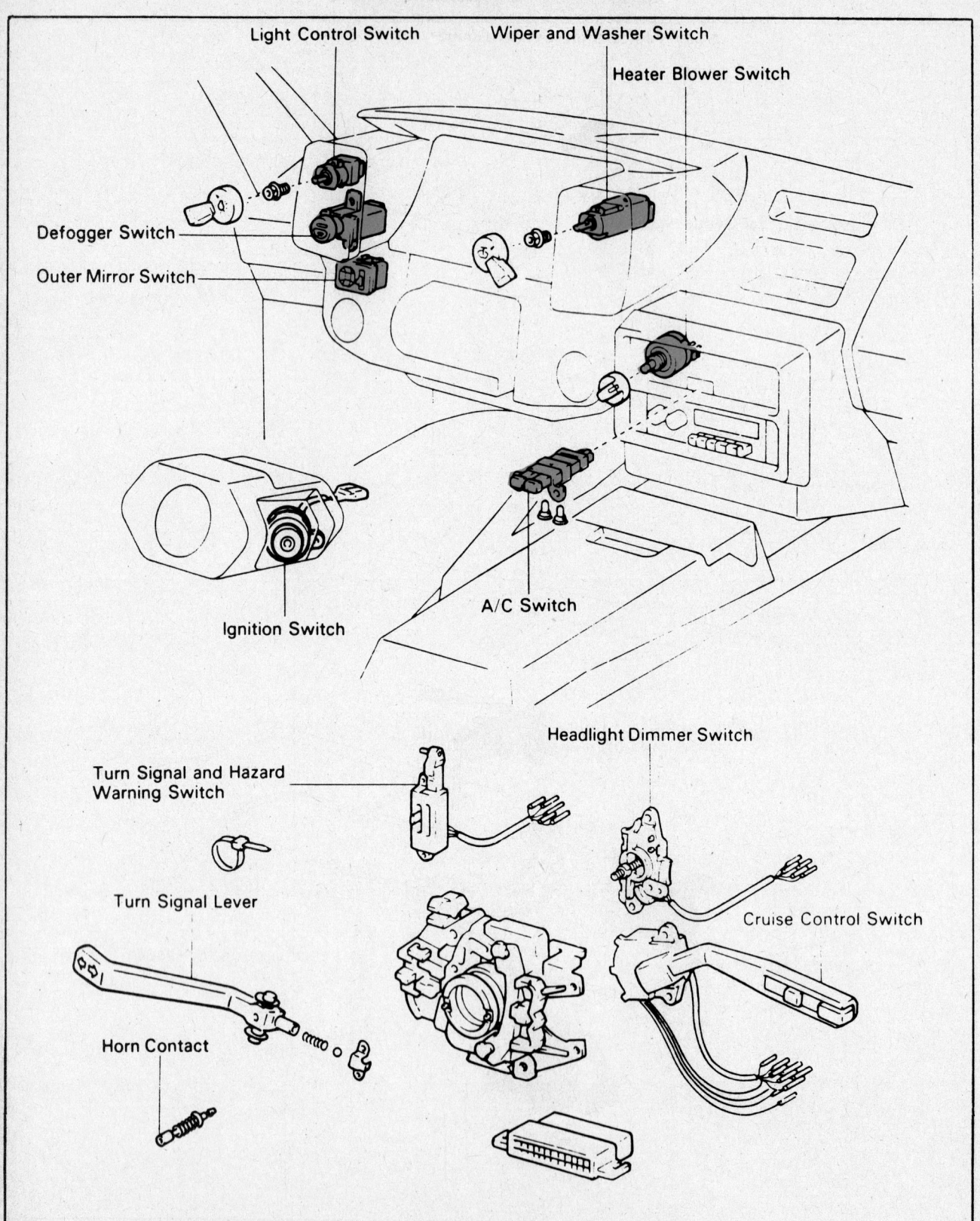

Light Control Switch

Wiper and Washer Switch

Heater Blower Switch

Defogger Switch

Outer Mirror Switch

Ignition Switch

A/C Switch

Headlight Dimmer Switch

Turn Signal and Hazard Warning Switch

Turn Signal Lever

Cruise Control Switch

Horn Contact

Toyota MR2

COMPONENT LOCATIONS

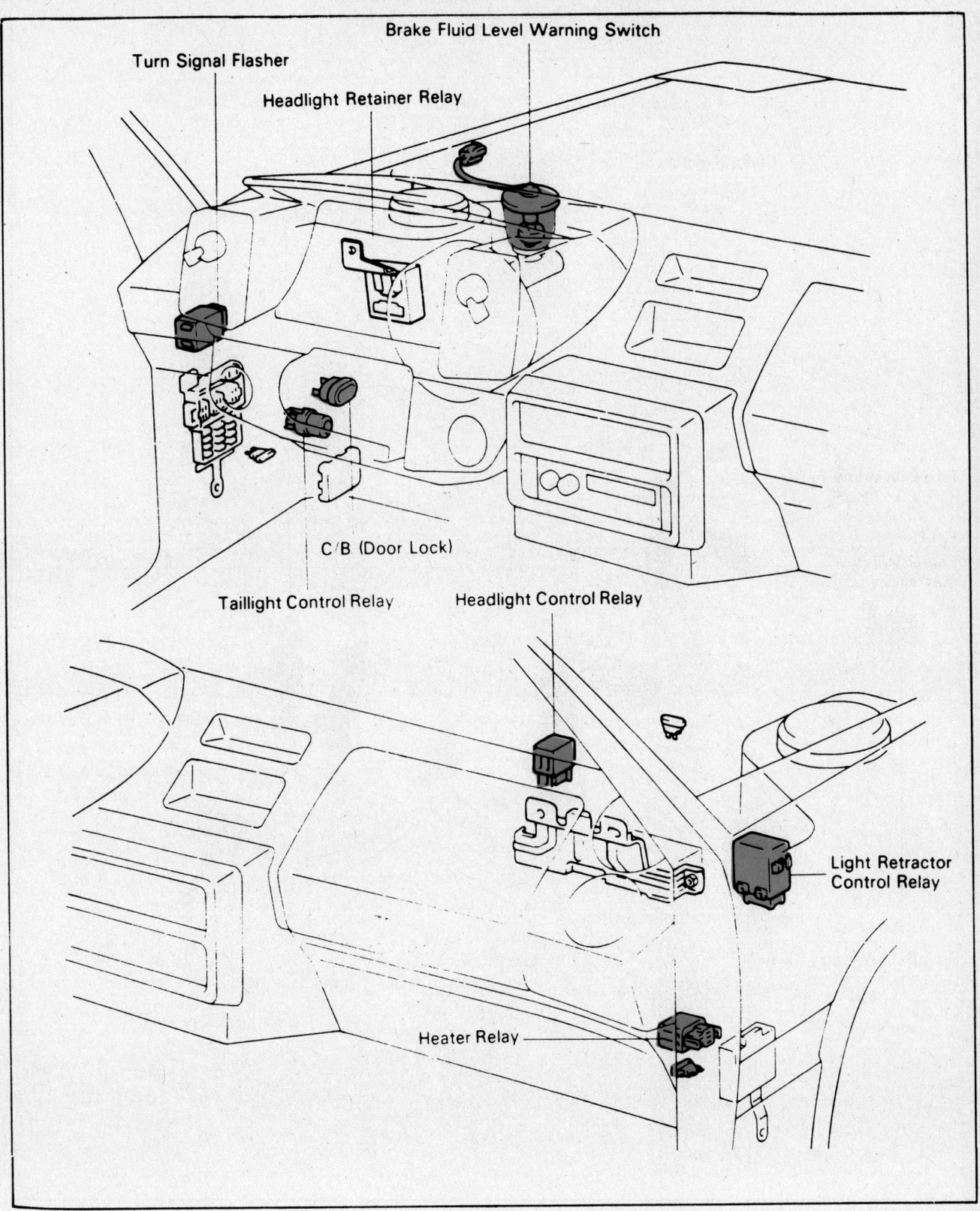

Turn Signal Flasher

Headlight Retainer Relay

Brake Fluid Level Warning Switch

C/B (Door Lock)

Taillight Control Relay

Headlight Control Relay

Light Retractor Control Relay

Heater Relay

Toyota MR2

COMPONENT LOCATIONS

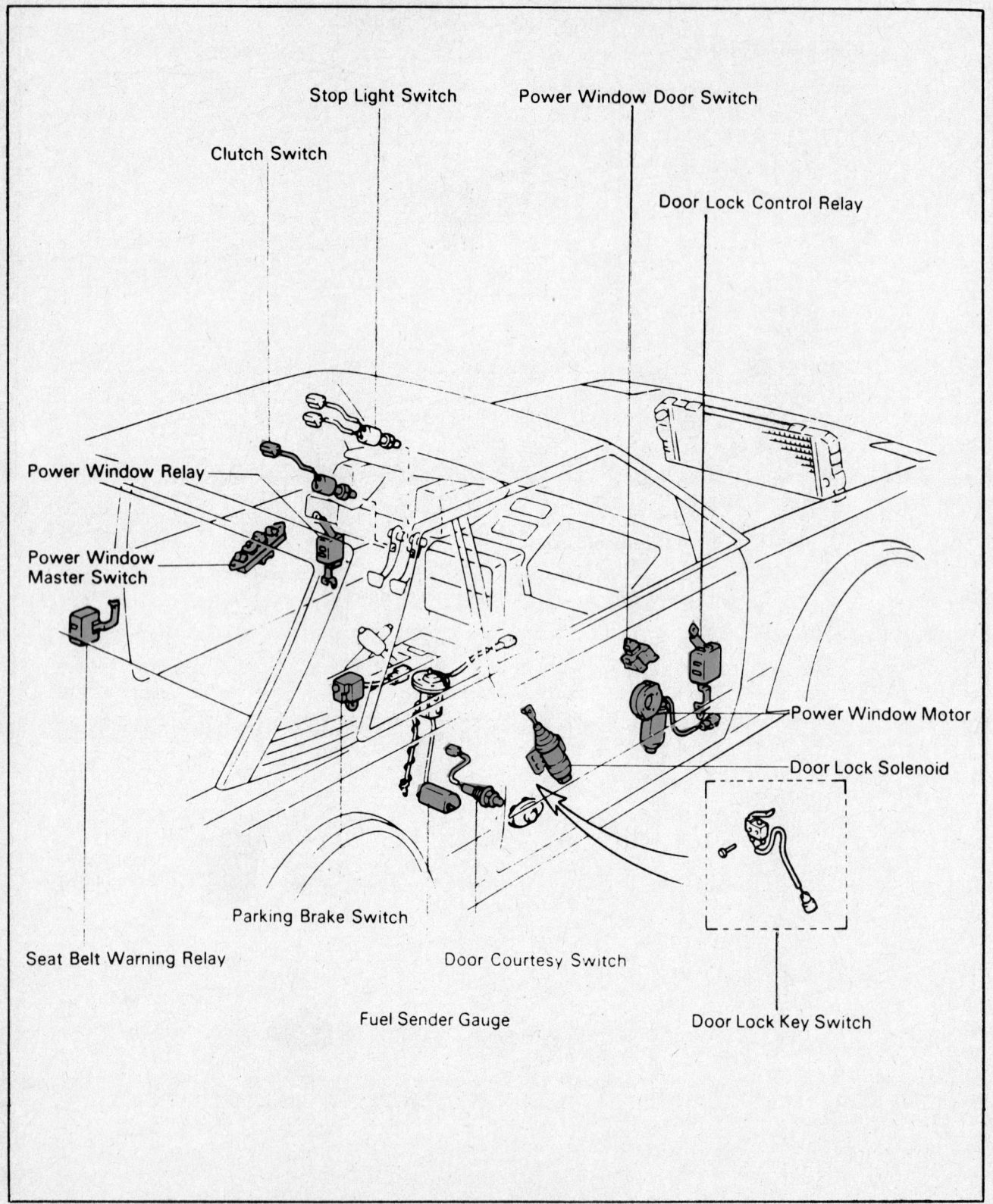

Clutch Switch

Stop Light Switch

Power Window Door Switch

Door Lock Control Relay

Power Window Relay

Power Window Master Switch

Power Window Motor

Door Lock Solenoid

Parking Brake Switch

Seat Belt Warning Relay

Door Courtesy Switch

Fuel Sender Gauge

Door Lock Key Switch

Toyota MR2

COMPONENT LOCATIONS

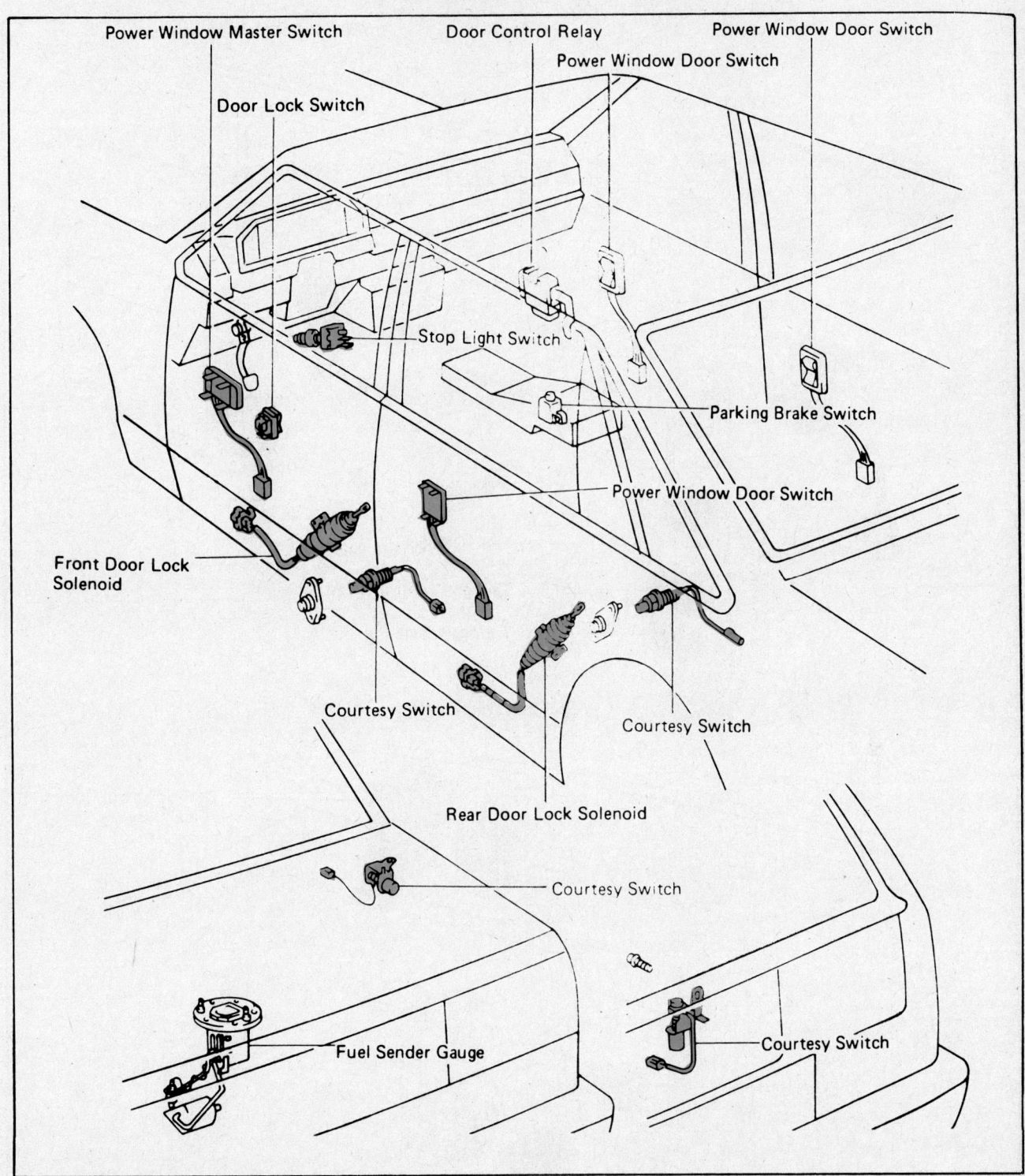

Power Window Master Switch

Door Control Relay

Power Window Door Switch

Door Lock Switch

Power Window Door Switch

Stop Light Switch

Parking Brake Switch

Power Window Door Switch

Front Door Lock Solenoid

Courtesy Switch

Courtesy Switch

Rear Door Lock Solenoid

Courtesy Switch

Fuel Sender Gauge

Courtesy Switch

Toyota Corolla front wheel drive

COMPONENT LOCATIONS

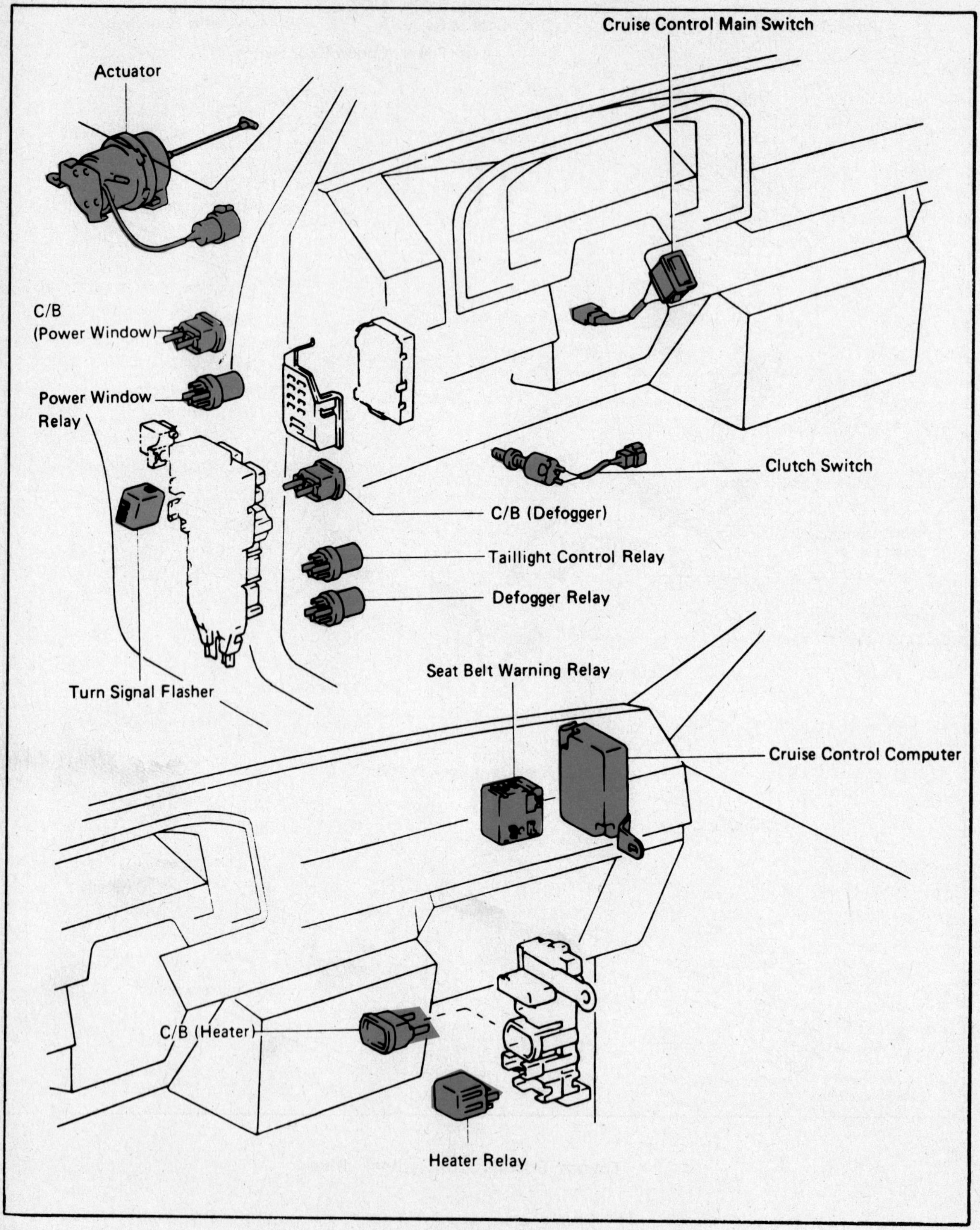

Cruise Control Main Switch

Actuator

C/B (Power Window)

Power Window Relay

Clutch Switch

C/B (Defogger)

Taillight Control Relay

Defogger Relay

Turn Signal Flasher

Seat Belt Warning Relay

Cruise Control Computer

C/B (Heater)

Heater Relay

Toyota Corolla front wheel drive

COMPONENT LOCATIONS

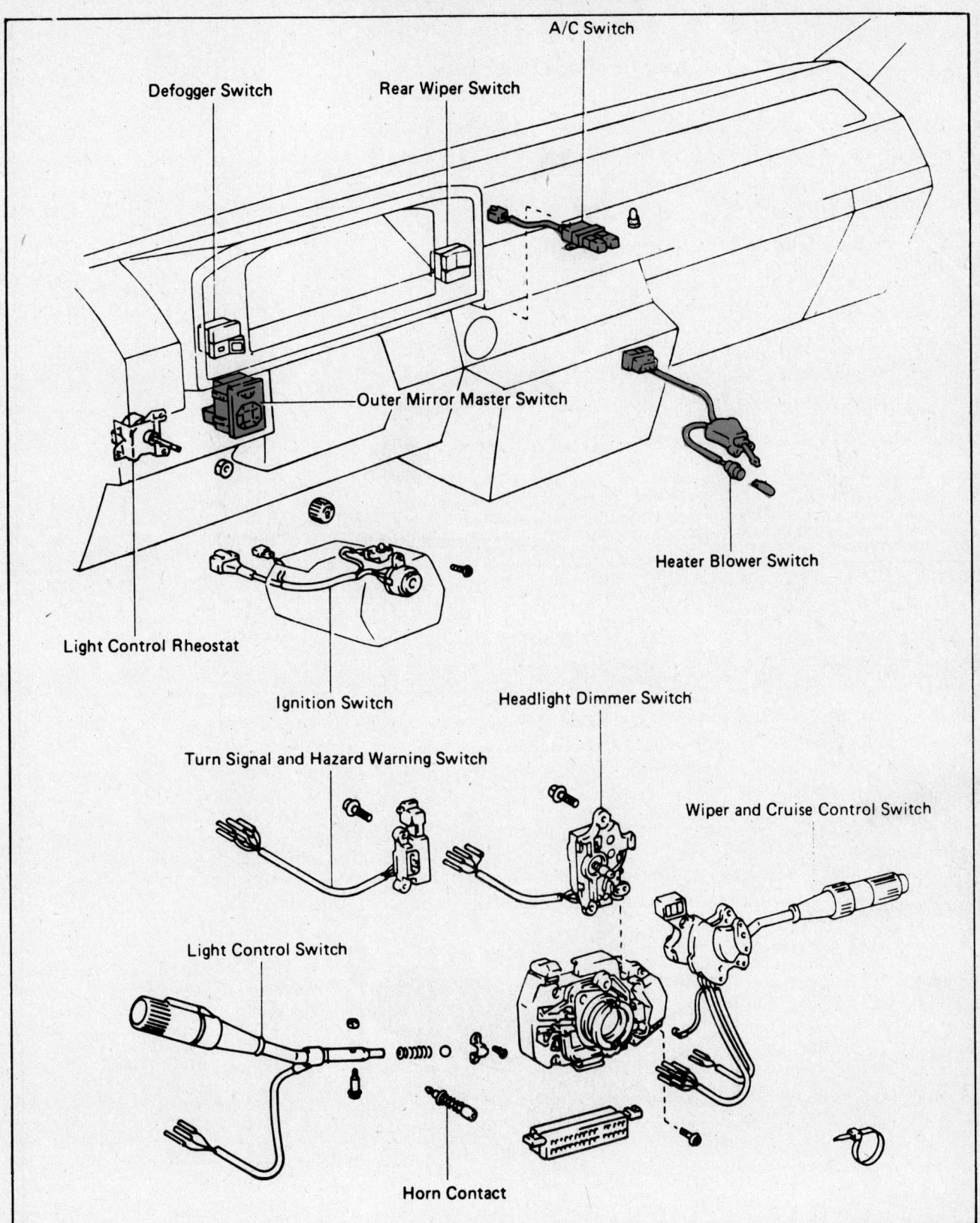

A/C Switch

Defogger Switch

Rear Wiper Switch

Outer Mirror Master Switch

Heater Blower Switch

Light Control Rheostat

Ignition Switch

Headlight Dimmer Switch

Turn Signal and Hazard Warning Switch

Wiper and Cruise Control Switch

Light Control Switch

Horn Contact

Toyota Corolla front wheel drive

COMPONENT LOCATIONS

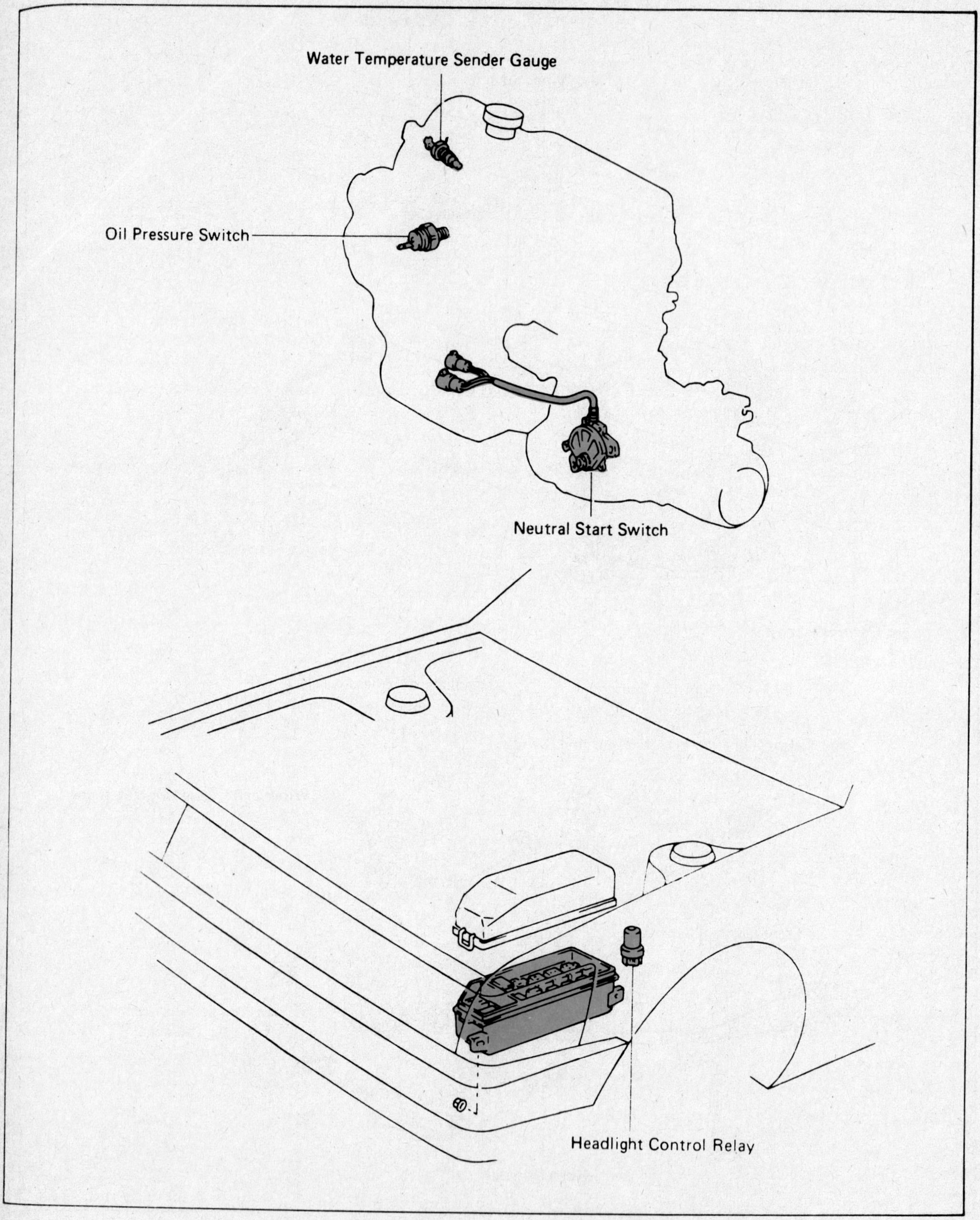

Water Temperature Sender Gauge

Oil Pressure Switch

Neutral Start Switch

Headlight Control Relay

Toyota Corolla front wheel drive

COMPONENT LOCATIONS

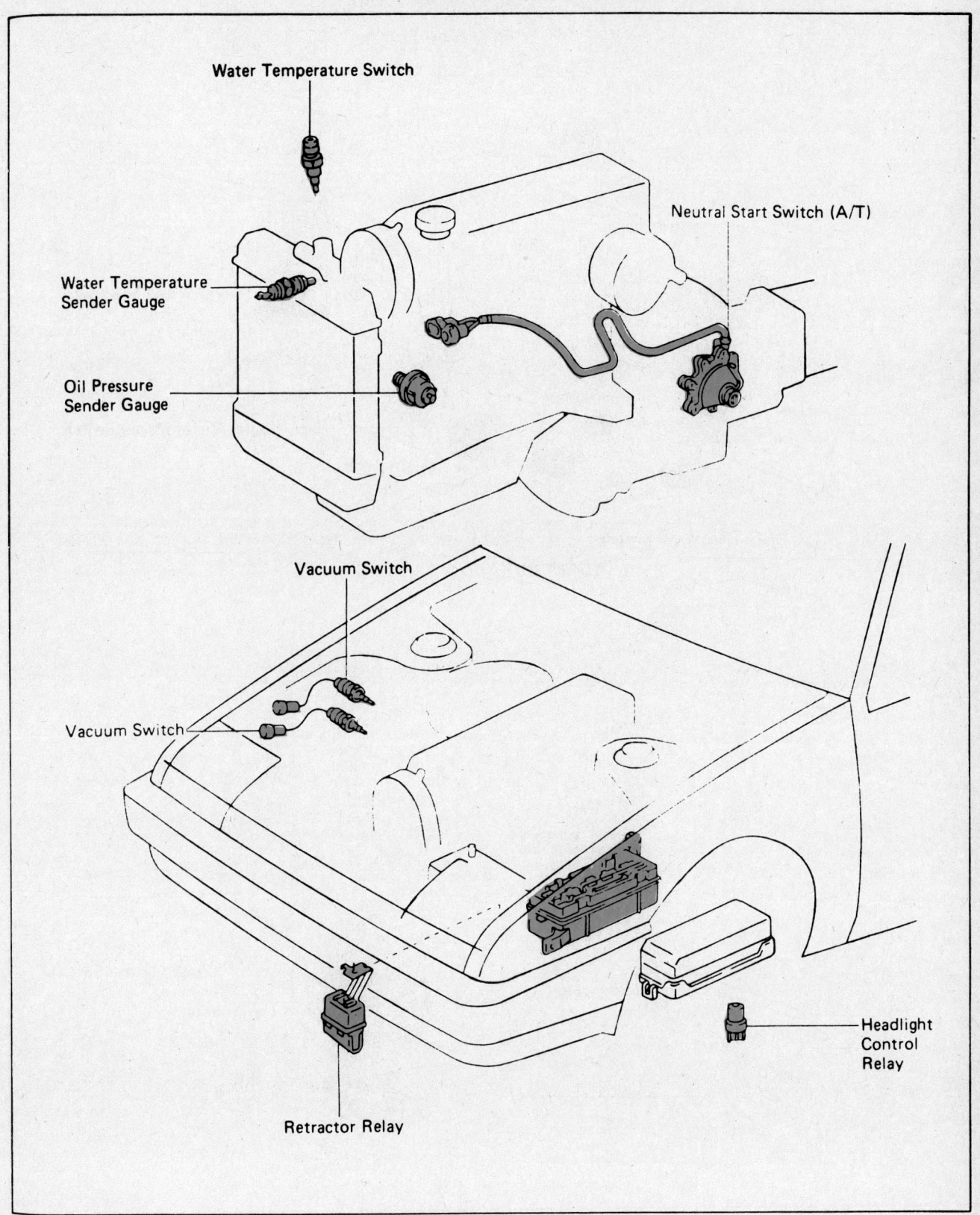

Water Temperature Switch

Neutral Start Switch (A/T)

Water Temperature
Sender Gauge

Oil Pressure
Sender Gauge

Vacuum Switch

Vacuum Switch

Headlight
Control
Relay

Retractor Relay

Toyota Corolla rear wheel drive

COMPONENT LOCATIONS

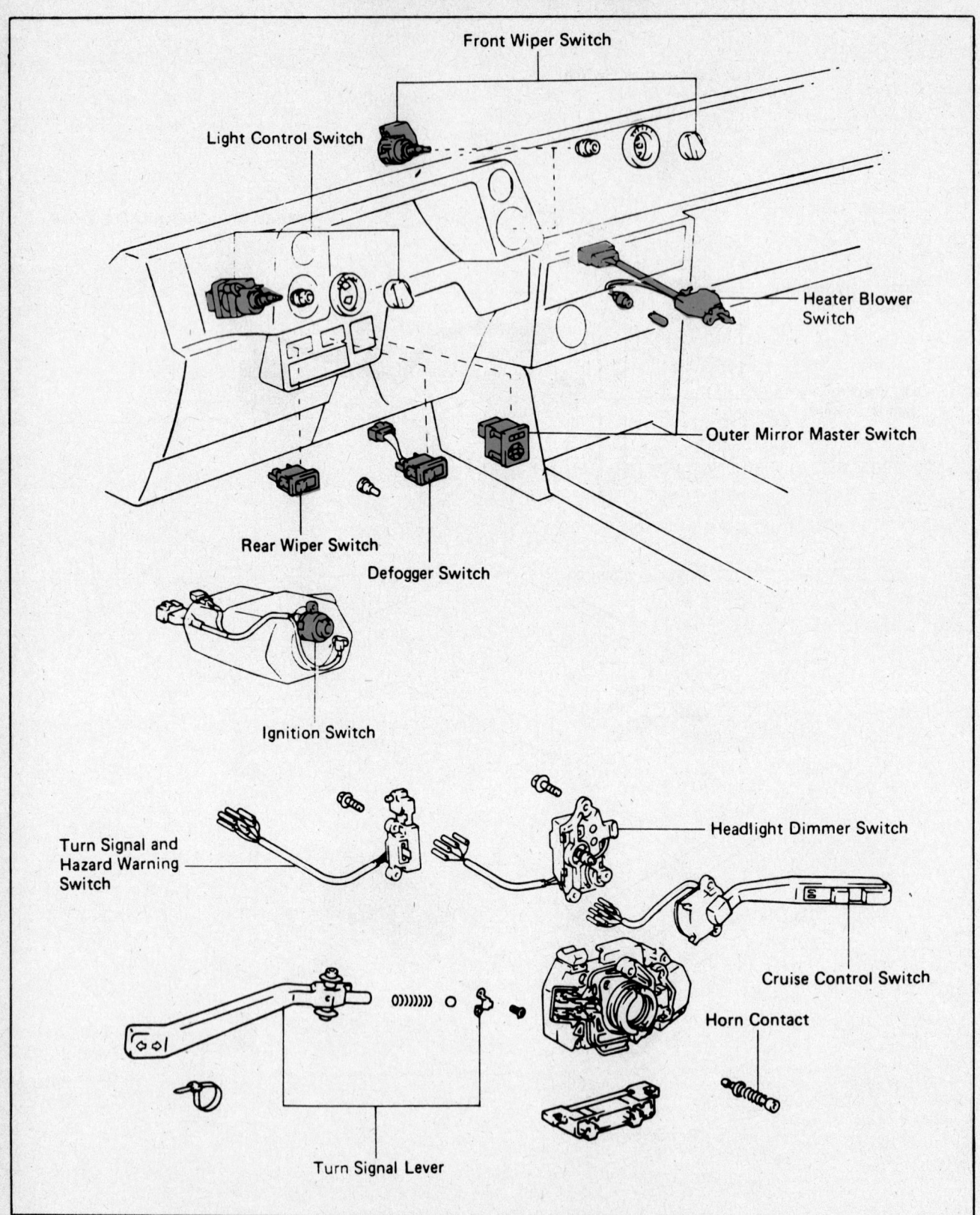

Front Wiper Switch

Light Control Switch

Heater Blower Switch

Outer Mirror Master Switch

Rear Wiper Switch

Defogger Switch

Ignition Switch

Turn Signal and Hazard Warning Switch

Headlight Dimmer Switch

Cruise Control Switch

Horn Contact

Turn Signal Lever

Toyota Corolla rear wheel drive

COMPONENT LOCATIONS

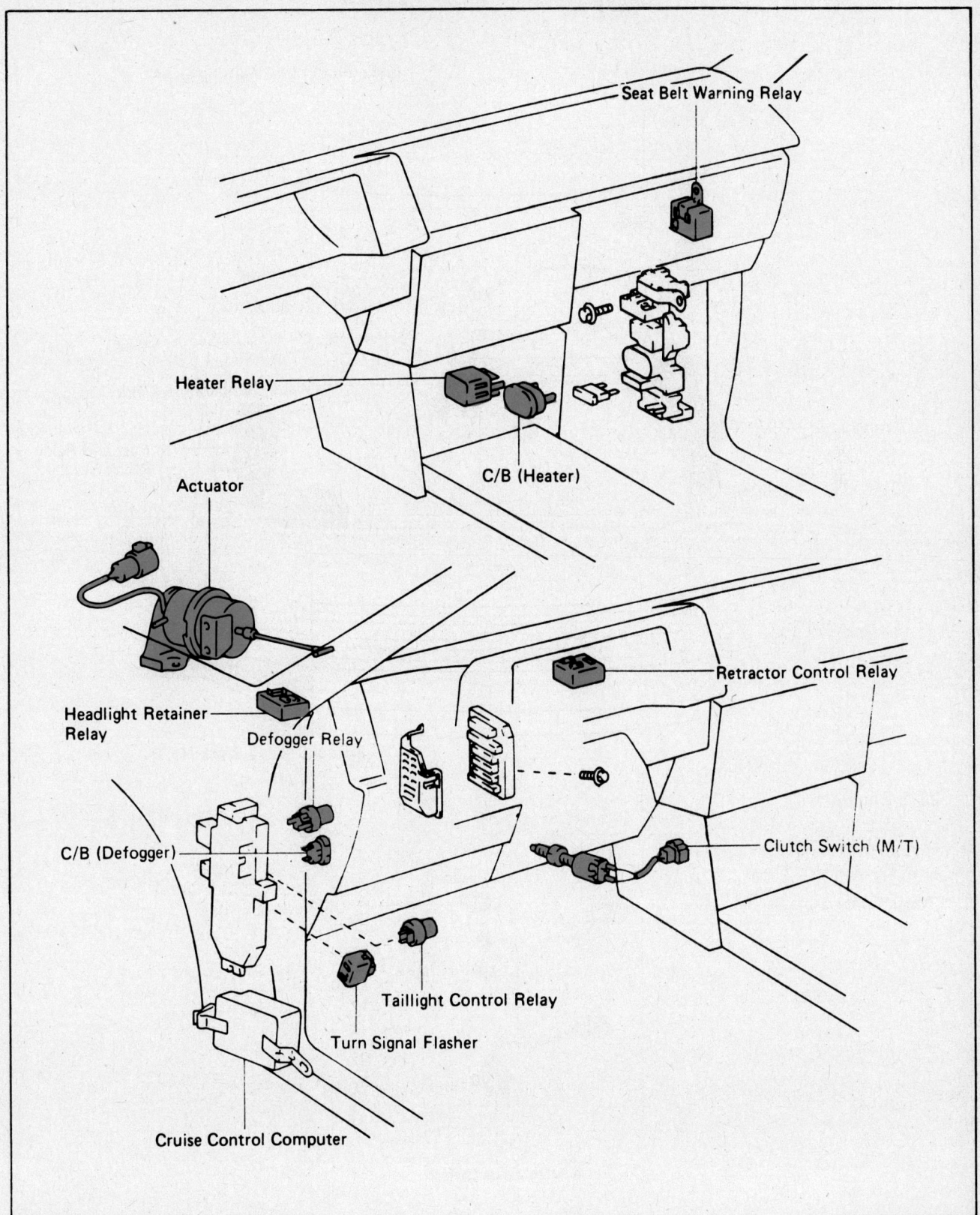

Seat Belt Warning Relay

Heater Relay

C/B (Heater)

Actuator

Headlight Retainer Relay

Defogger Relay

Retractor Control Relay

C/B (Defogger)

Clutch Switch (M/T)

Taillight Control Relay

Turn Signal Flasher

Cruise Control Computer

Toyota Corolla rear wheel drive

COMPONENT LOCATIONS

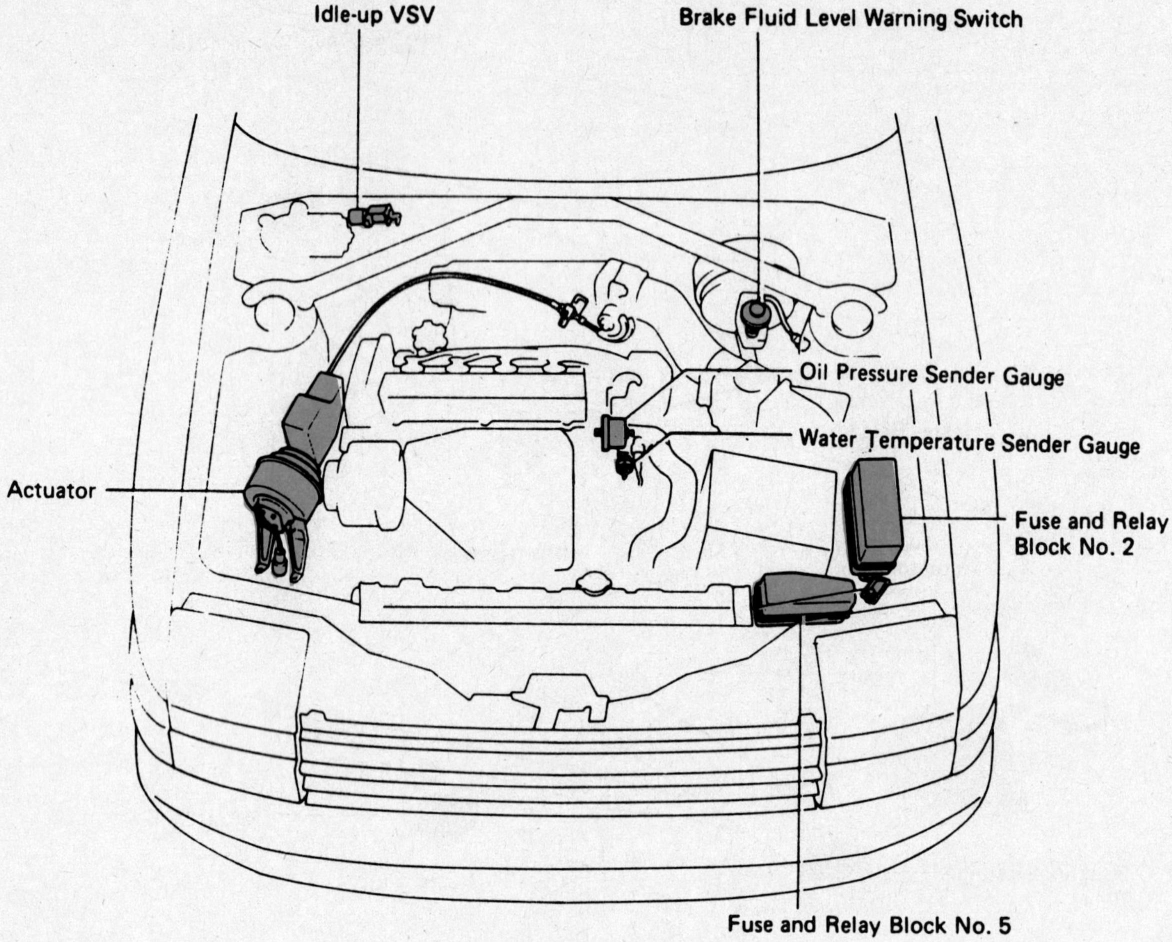

Idle-up VSV

Brake Fluid Level Warning Switch

Oil Pressure Sender Gauge

Water Temperature Sender Gauge

Actuator

Fuse and Relay Block No. 2

Fuse and Relay Block No. 5

2S-E Engine

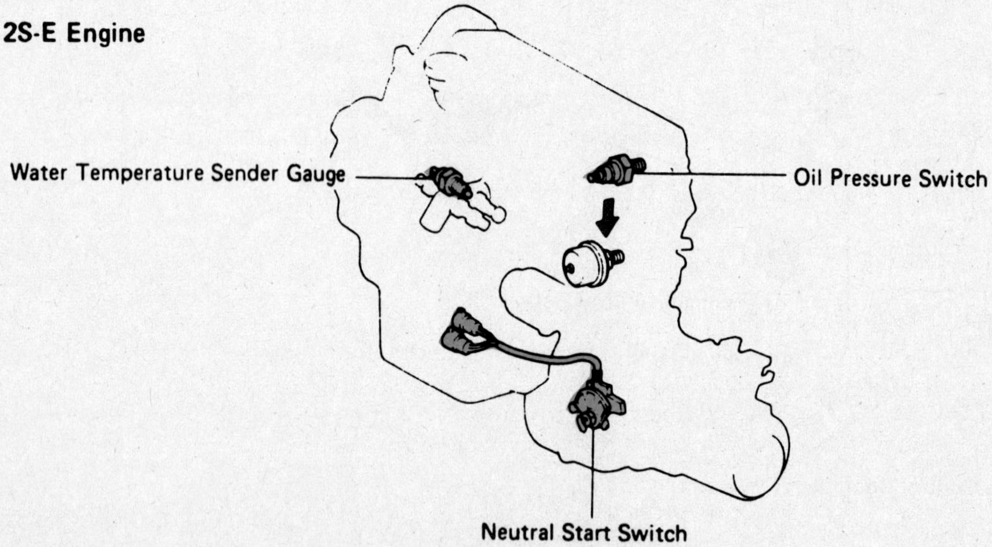

Water Temperature Sender Gauge

Oil Pressure Switch

Neutral Start Switch

Toyota Celica

COMPONENT LOCATIONS

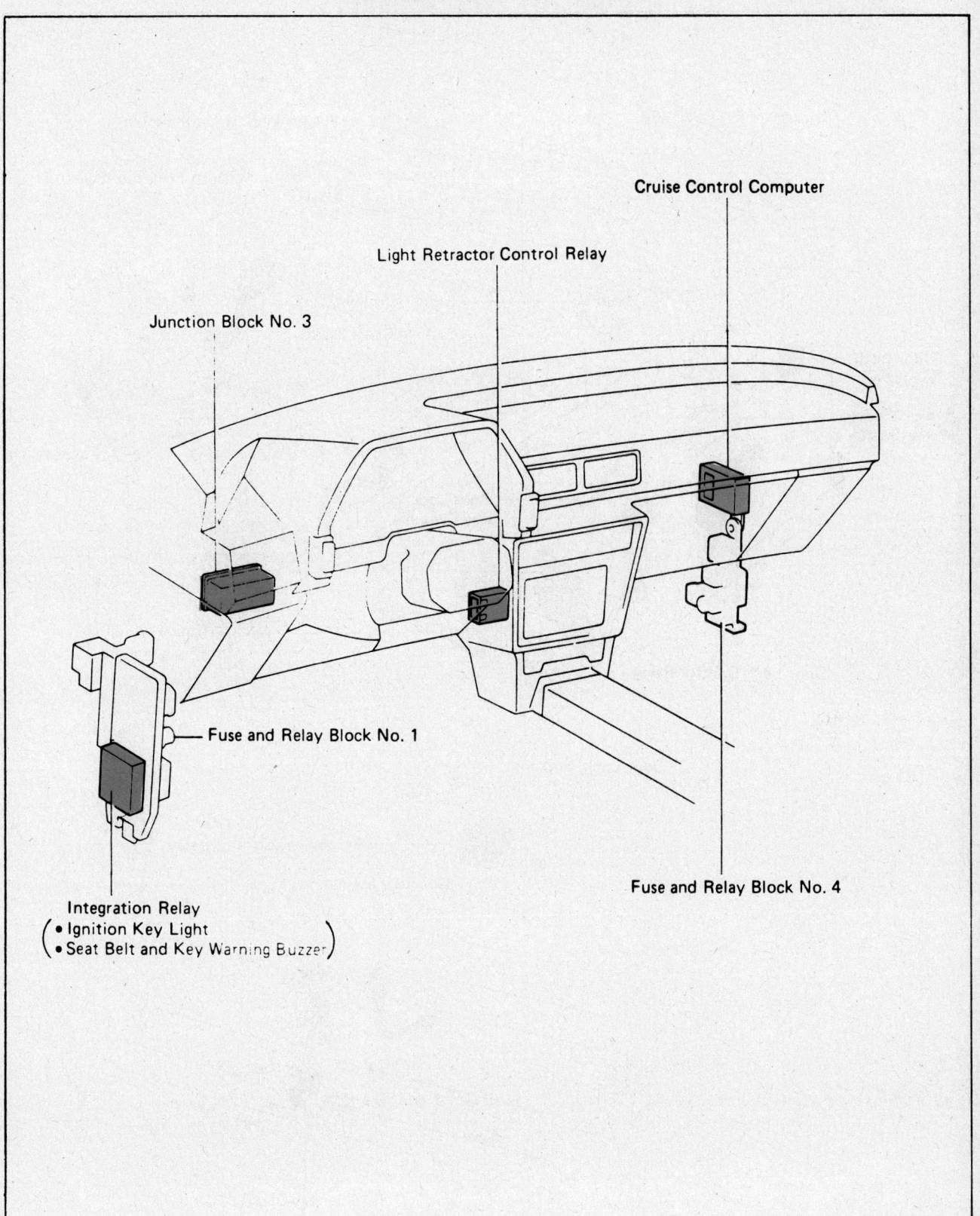

Cruise Control Computer

Light Retractor Control Relay

Junction Block No. 3

Fuse and Relay Block No. 1

Fuse and Relay Block No. 4

Integration Relay
(• Ignition Key Light
• Seat Belt and Key Warning Buzzer)

Toyota Celica

COMPONENT LOCATIONS

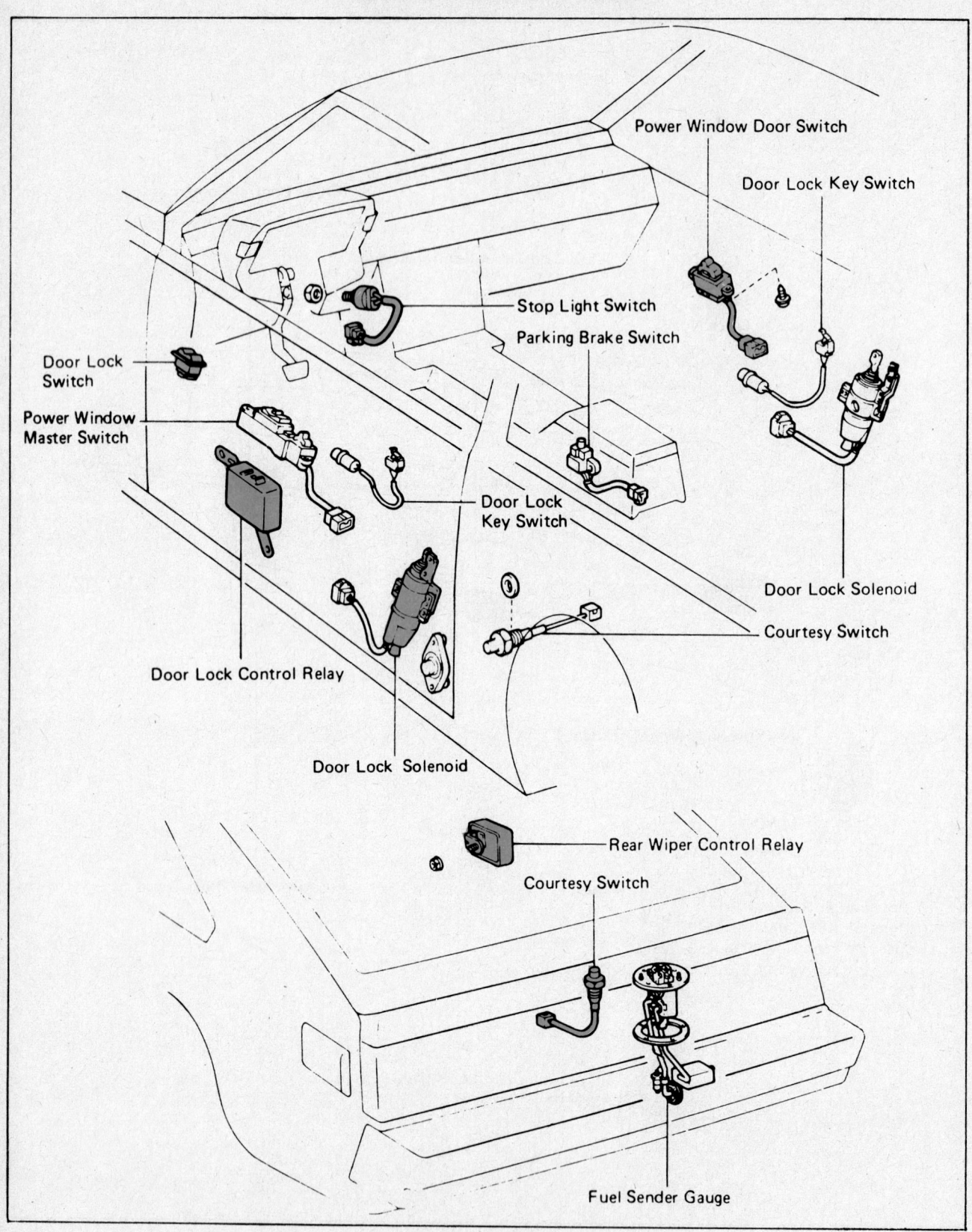

Power Window Door Switch

Door Lock Key Switch

Stop Light Switch

Parking Brake Switch

Door Lock Switch

Power Window Master Switch

Door Lock Key Switch

Door Lock Solenoid

Courtesy Switch

Door Lock Control Relay

Door Lock Solenoid

Rear Wiper Control Relay

Courtesy Switch

Fuel Sender Gauge

Toyota Supra

COMPONENT LOCATIONS

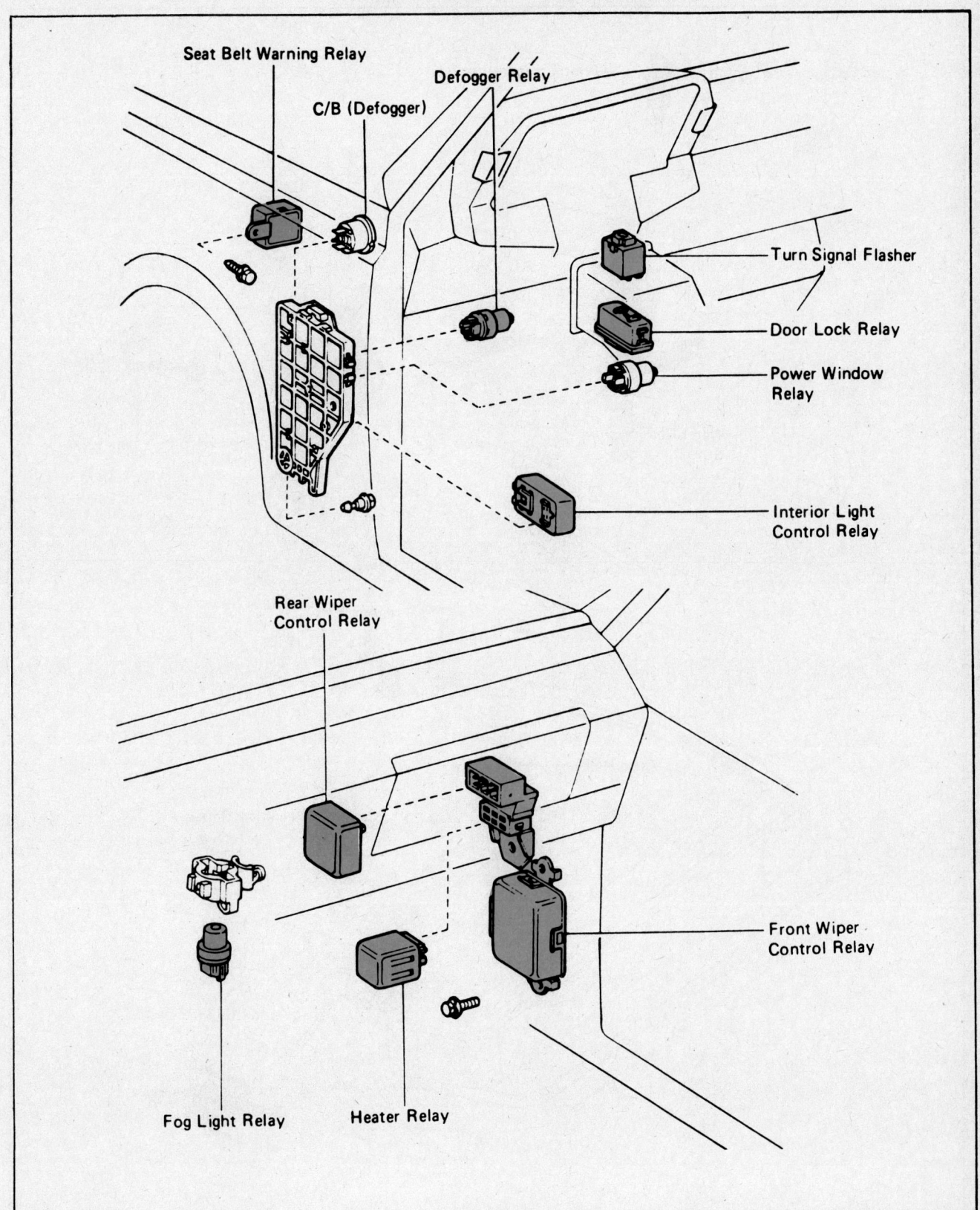

Seat Belt Warning Relay

C/B (Defogger)

Defogger Relay

Turn Signal Flasher

Door Lock Relay

Power Window Relay

Interior Light Control Relay

Rear Wiper Control Relay

Front Wiper Control Relay

Fog Light Relay

Heater Relay

Toyota Supra

COMPONENT LOCATIONS

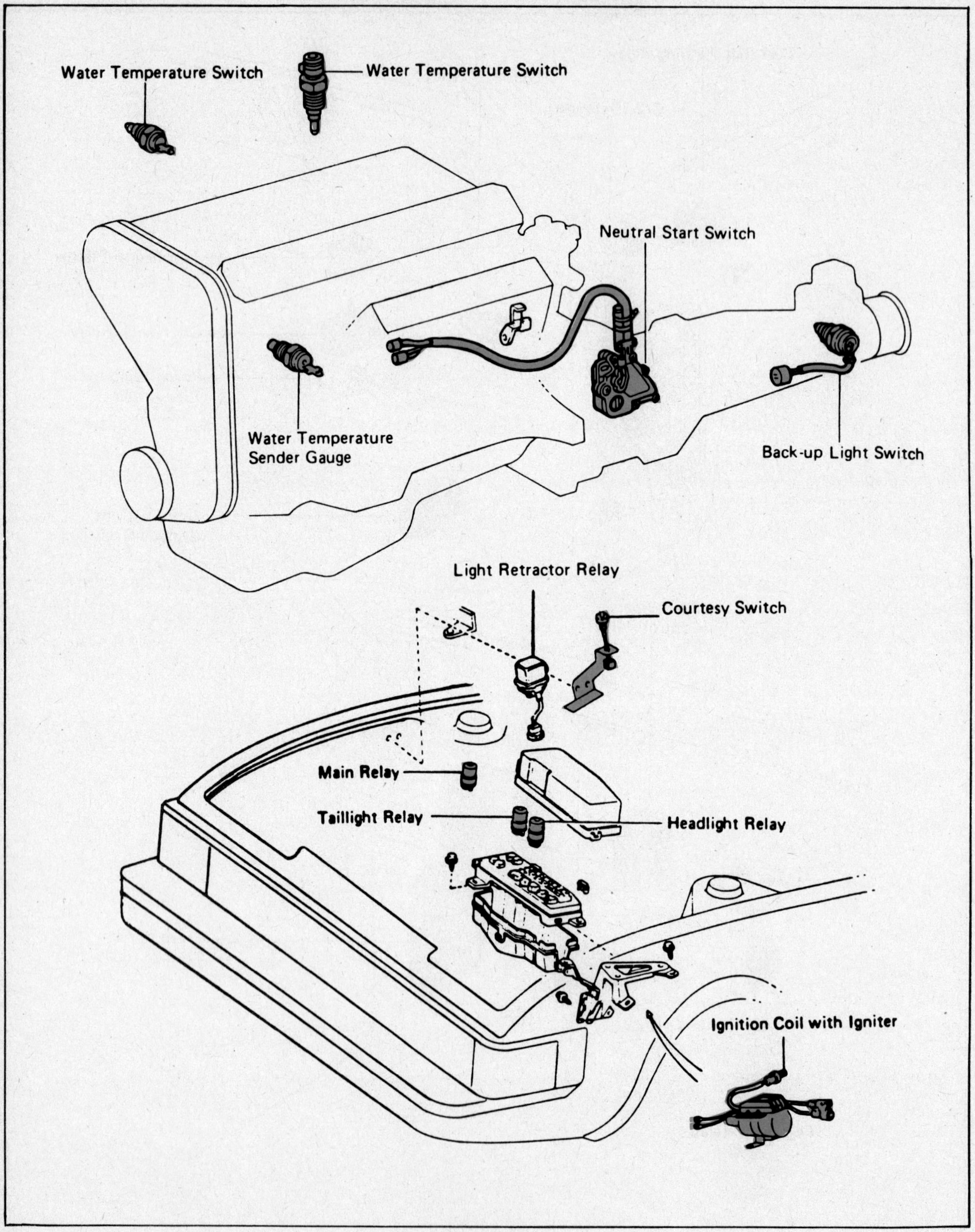

Water Temperature Switch

Water Temperature Switch

Neutral Start Switch

Water Temperature Sender Gauge

Back-up Light Switch

Light Retractor Relay

Courtesy Switch

Main Relay

Taillight Relay

Headlight Relay

Ignition Coil with Igniter

Toyota Supra

COMPONENT LOCATIONS

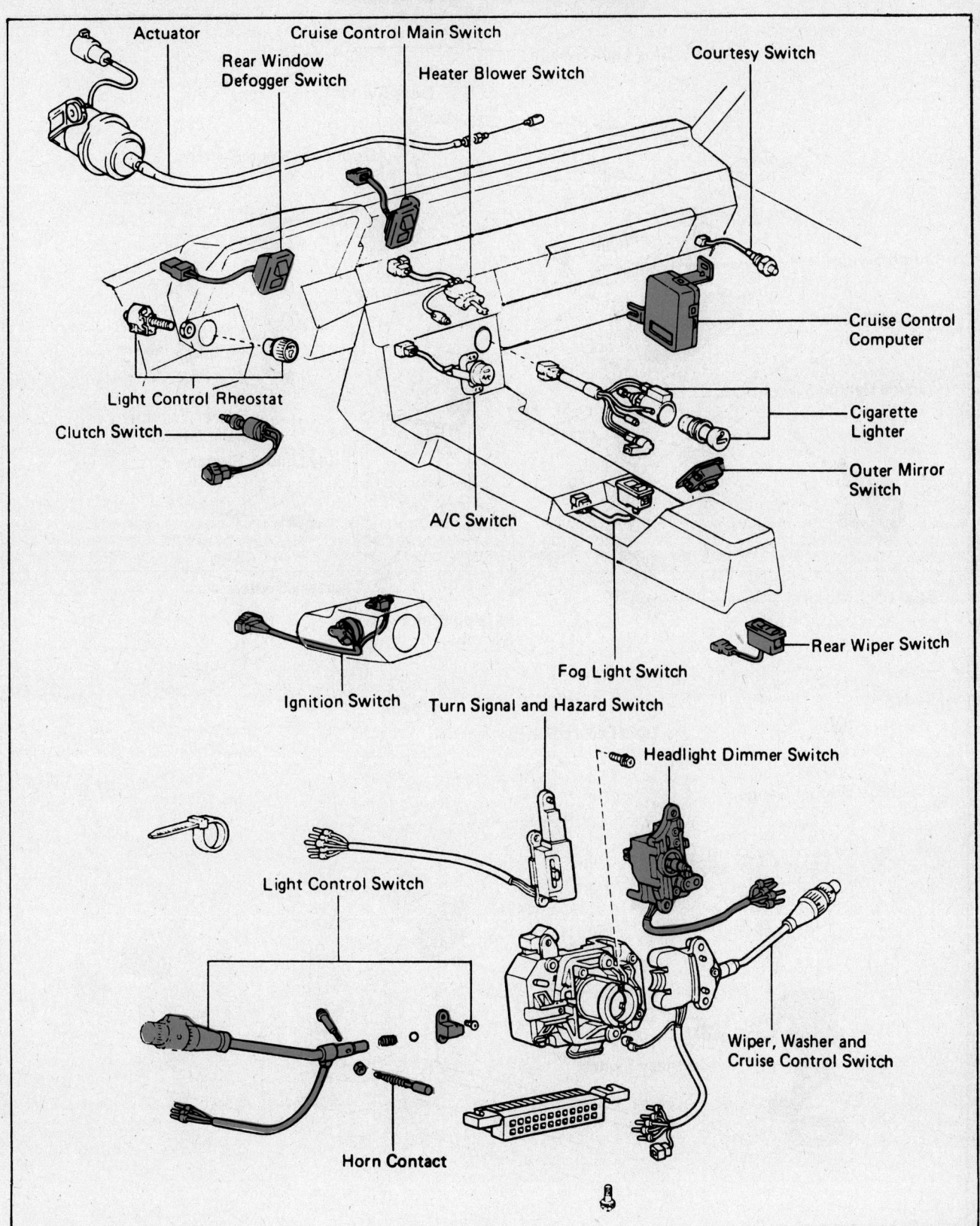

Actuator

Rear Window
Defogger Switch

Cruise Control Main Switch

Heater Blower Switch

Courtesy Switch

Cruise Control
Computer

Cigarette
Lighter

Outer Mirror
Switch

Light Control Rheostat

Clutch Switch

A/C Switch

Rear Wiper Switch

Ignition Switch

Fog Light Switch

Turn Signal and Hazard Switch

Headlight Dimmer Switch

Light Control Switch

Wiper, Washer and
Cruise Control Switch

Horn Contact

Toyota Supra

COMPONENT LOCATIONS

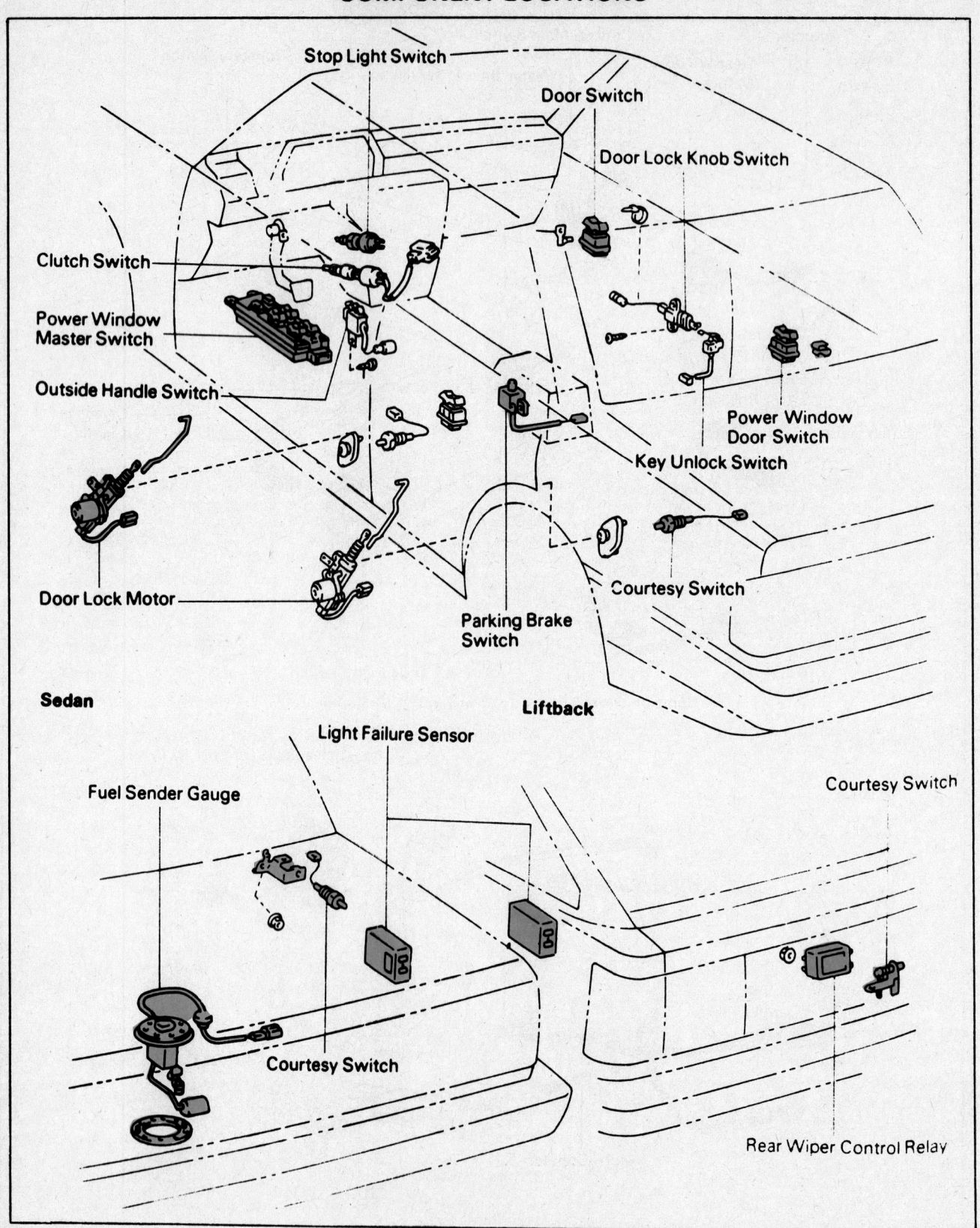

Stop Light Switch

Door Switch

Door Lock Knob Switch

Clutch Switch

Power Window Master Switch

Outside Handle Switch

Power Window Door Switch

Key Unlock Switch

Door Lock Motor

Courtesy Switch

Parking Brake Switch

Sedan

Liftback

Light Failure Sensor

Courtesy Switch

Fuel Sender Gauge

Courtesy Switch

Rear Wiper Control Relay

Toyota Camry

COMPONENT LOCATIONS

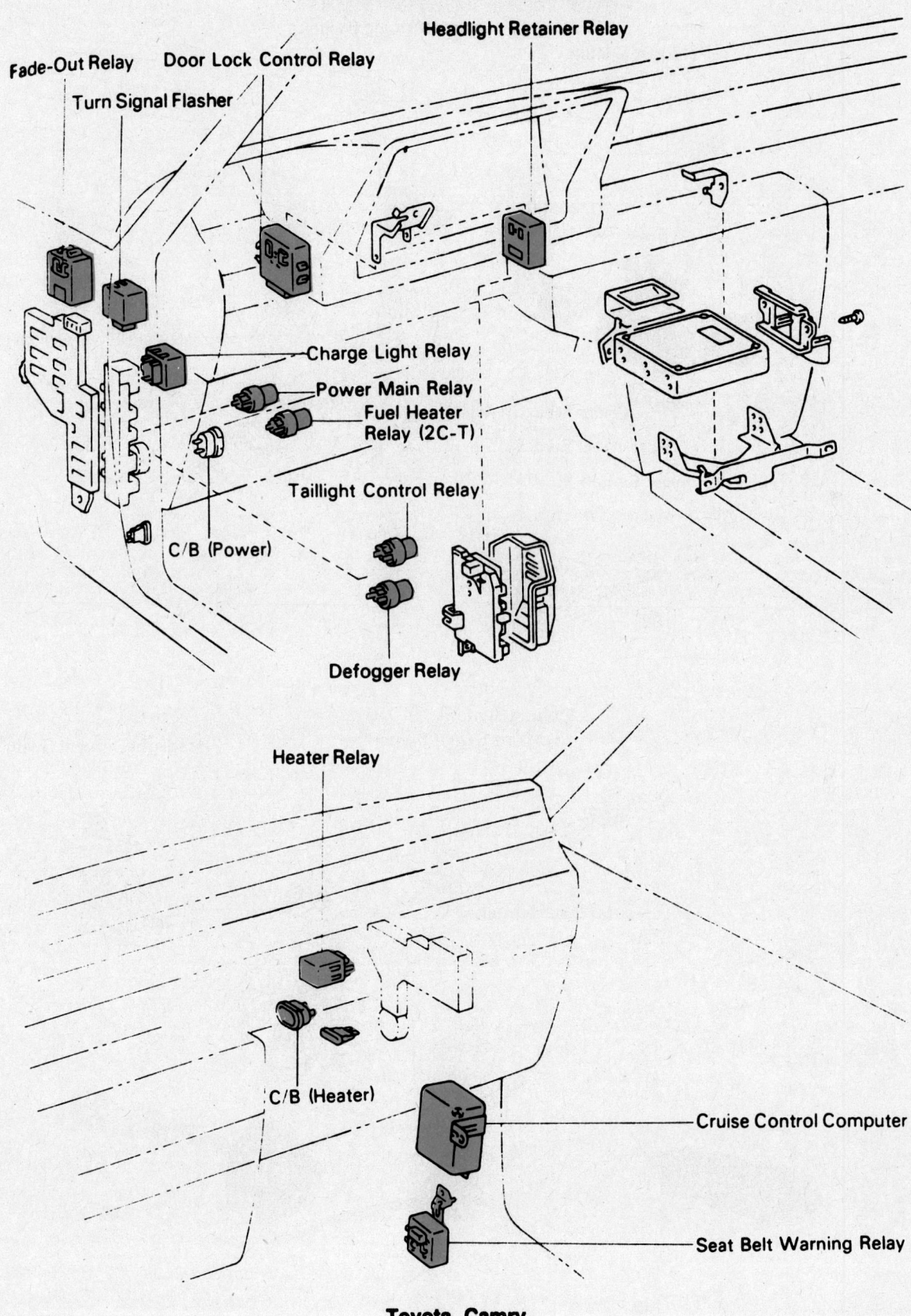

Fade-Out Relay

Turn Signal Flasher

Door Lock Control Relay

Headlight Retainer Relay

Charge Light Relay

Power Main Relay

Fuel Heater Relay (2C-T)

Taillight Control Relay

C/B (Power)

Defogger Relay

Heater Relay

C/B (Heater)

Cruise Control Computer

Seat Belt Warning Relay

Toyota Camry

325

COMPONENT LOCATIONS

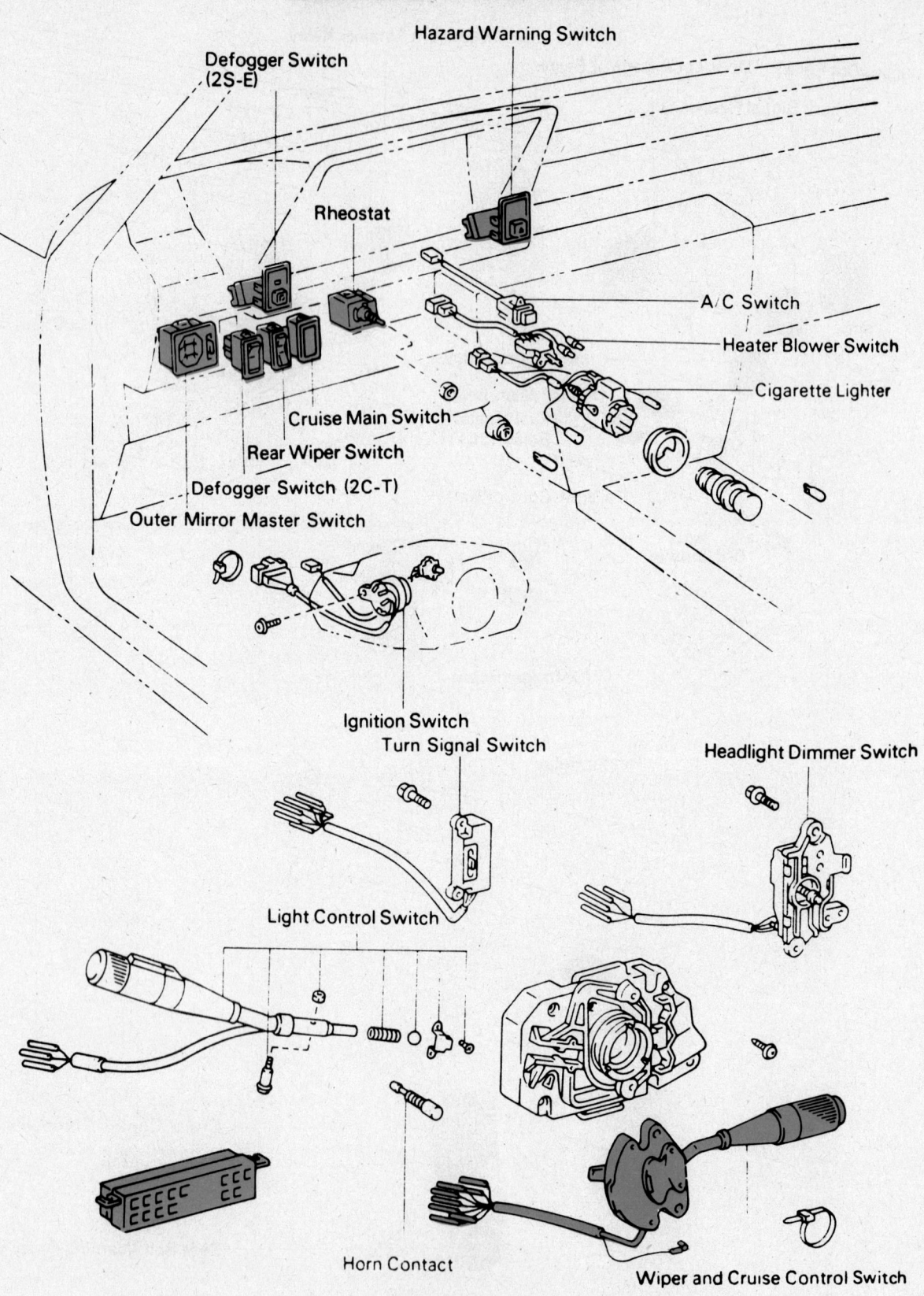

Defogger Switch (2S-E)

Hazard Warning Switch

Rheostat

A/C Switch

Heater Blower Switch

Cigarette Lighter

Cruise Main Switch

Rear Wiper Switch

Defogger Switch (2C-T)

Outer Mirror Master Switch

Ignition Switch
Turn Signal Switch

Headlight Dimmer Switch

Light Control Switch

Horn Contact

Wiper and Cruise Control Switch

Toyota Camry

COMPONENT LOCATIONS

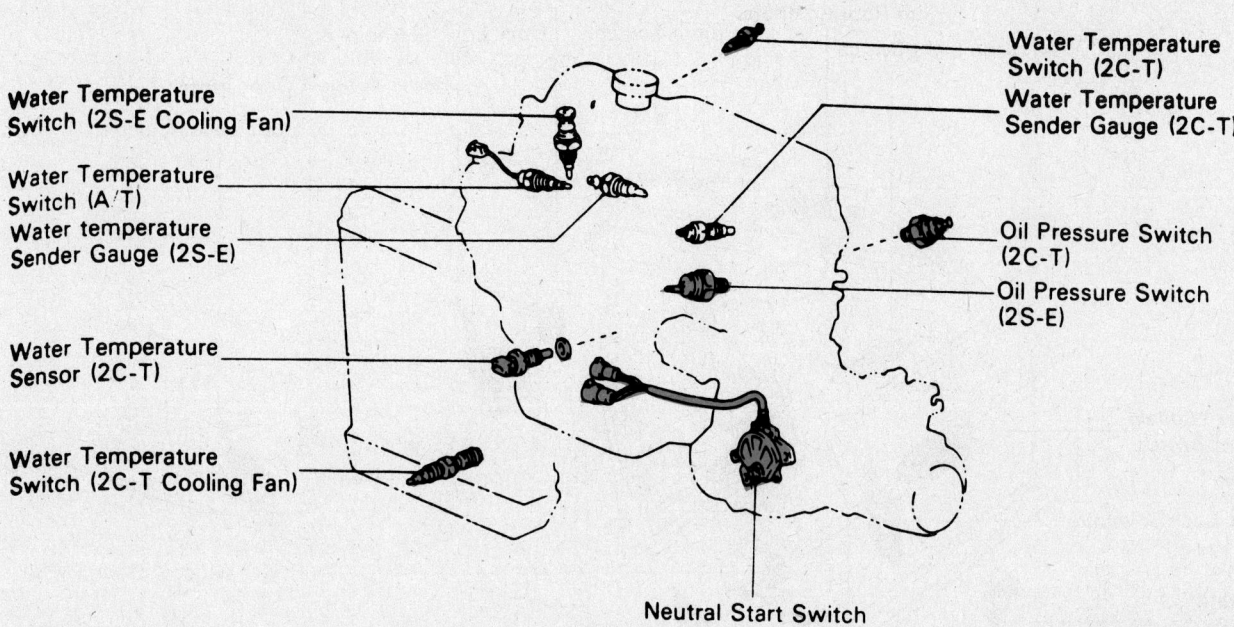

Water Temperature Switch (2S-E Cooling Fan)

Water Temperature Switch (A/T)

Water temperature Sender Gauge (2S-E)

Water Temperature Sensor (2C-T)

Water Temperature Switch (2C-T Cooling Fan)

Water Temperature Switch (2C-T)

Water Temperature Sender Gauge (2C-T)

Oil Pressure Switch (2C-T)

Oil Pressure Switch (2S-E)

Neutral Start Switch

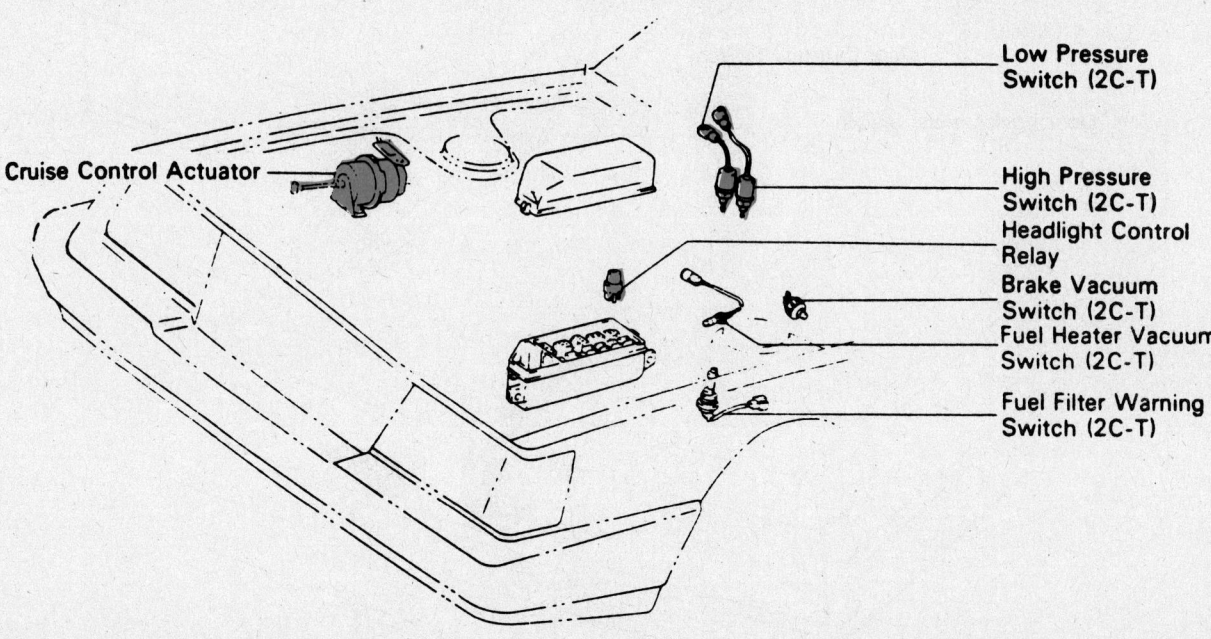

Cruise Control Actuator

Low Pressure Switch (2C-T)

High Pressure Switch (2C-T)

Headlight Control Relay

Brake Vacuum Switch (2C-T)

Fuel Heater Vacuum Switch (2C-T)

Fuel Filter Warning Switch (2C-T)

Toyota Camry

COMPONENT LOCATIONS

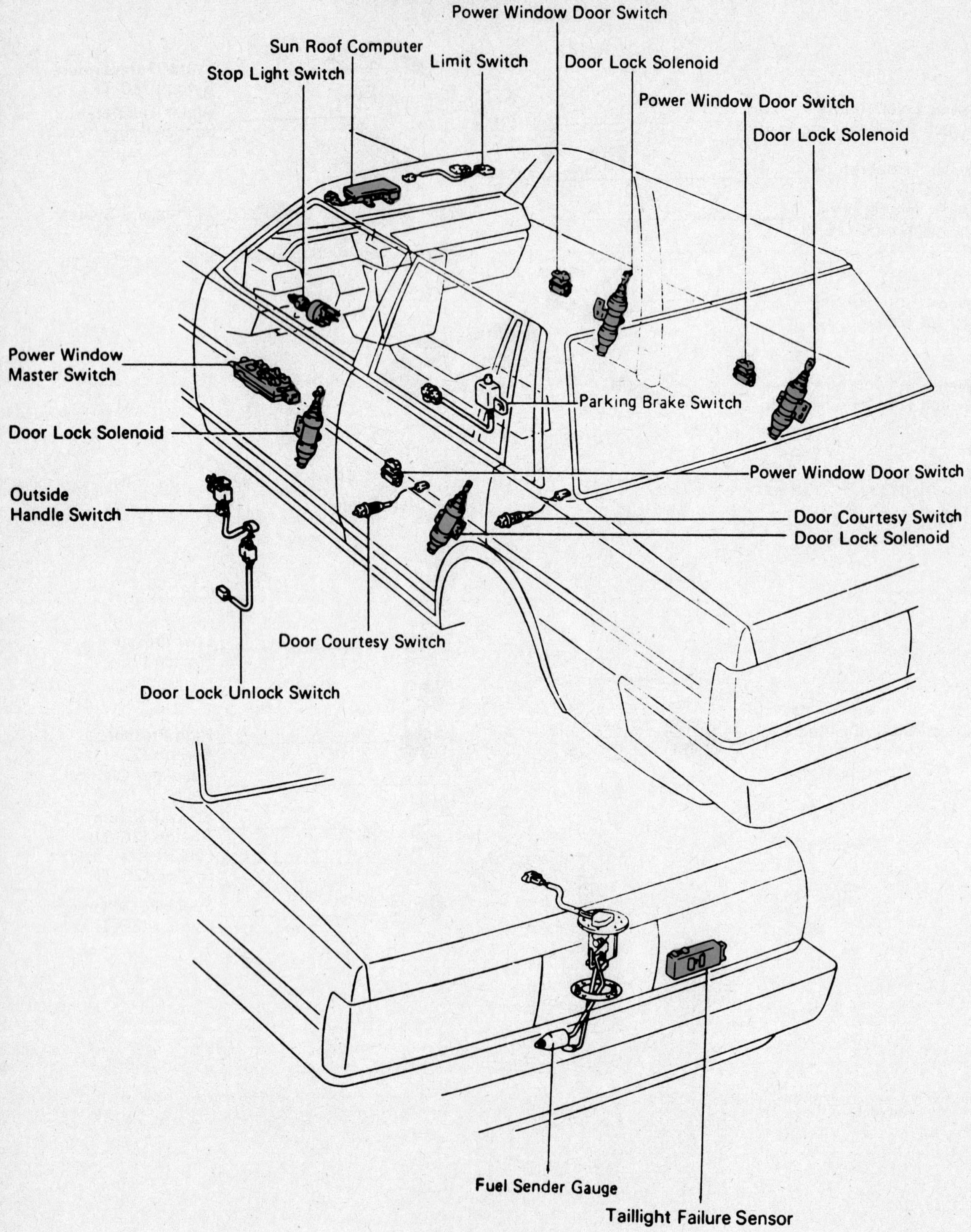

Power Window Door Switch

Sun Roof Computer

Limit Switch

Door Lock Solenoid

Stop Light Switch

Power Window Door Switch

Door Lock Solenoid

Power Window Master Switch

Door Lock Solenoid

Parking Brake Switch

Outside Handle Switch

Power Window Door Switch

Door Courtesy Switch

Door Lock Solenoid

Door Courtesy Switch

Door Lock Unlock Switch

Fuel Sender Gauge

Taillight Failure Sensor

Toyota Cressida

COMPONENT LOCATIONS

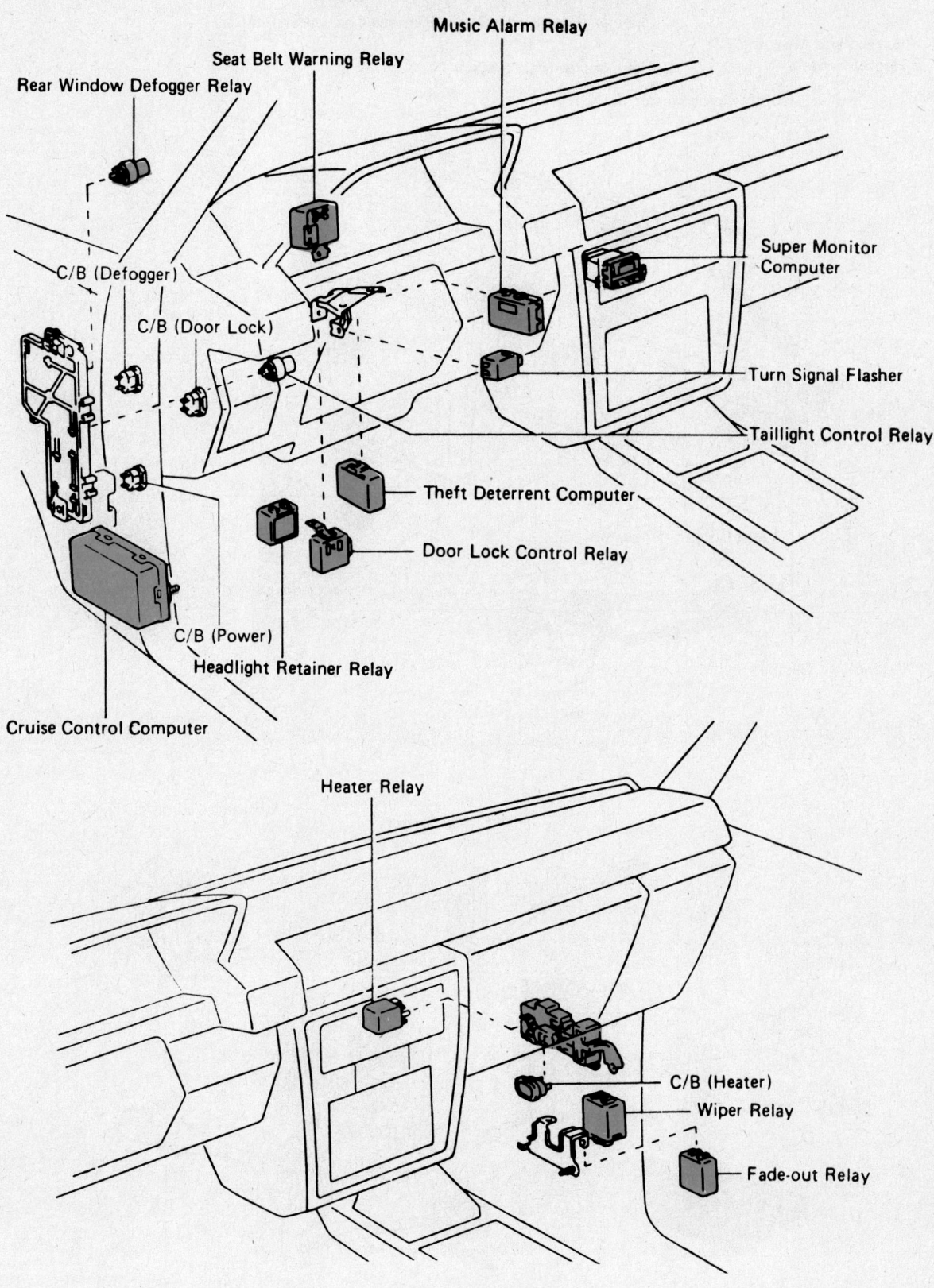

Rear Window Defogger Relay

Seat Belt Warning Relay

Music Alarm Relay

Super Monitor Computer

C/B (Defogger)

C/B (Door Lock)

Turn Signal Flasher

Taillight Control Relay

Theft Deterrent Computer

Door Lock Control Relay

C/B (Power)

Headlight Retainer Relay

Cruise Control Computer

Heater Relay

C/B (Heater)

Wiper Relay

Fade-out Relay

Toyota Cressida

COMPONENT LOCATIONS

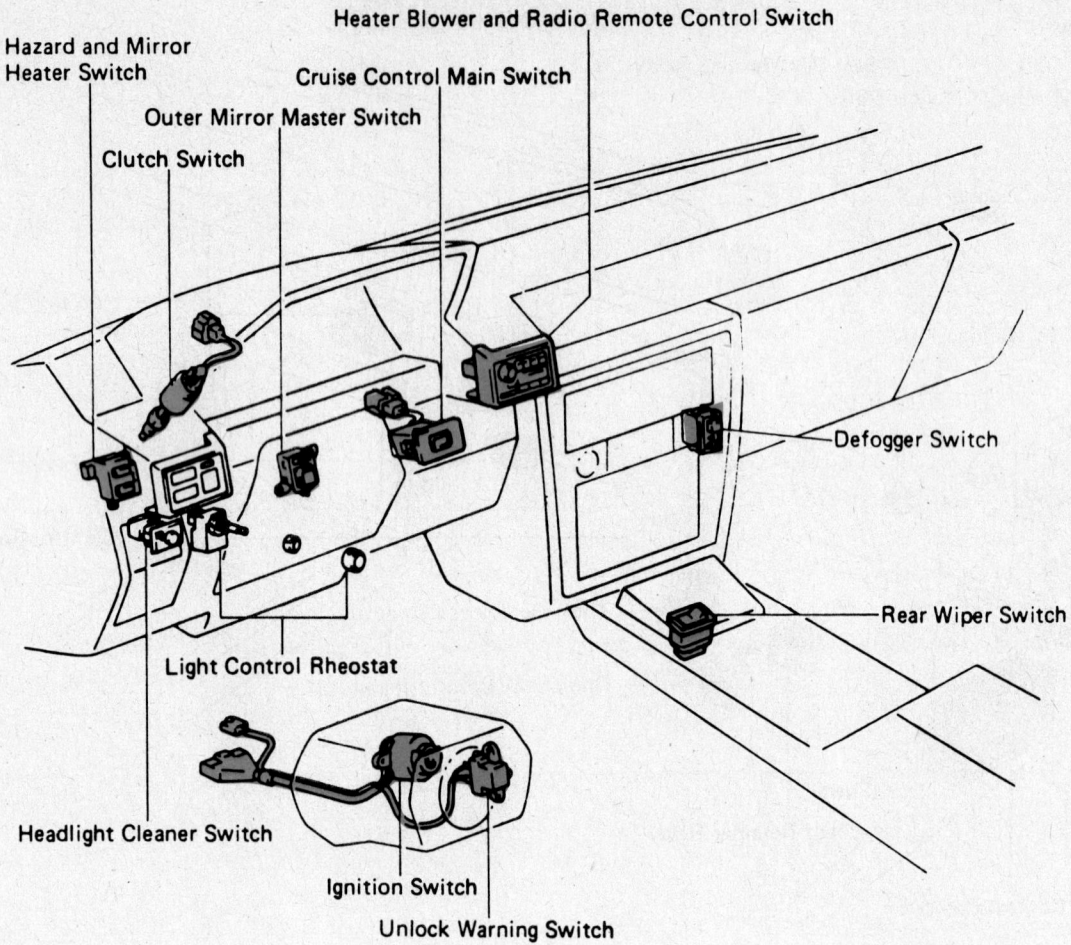

Heater Blower and Radio Remote Control Switch

Hazard and Mirror Heater Switch

Cruise Control Main Switch

Outer Mirror Master Switch

Clutch Switch

Defogger Switch

Rear Wiper Switch

Light Control Rheostat

Headlight Cleaner Switch

Ignition Switch

Unlock Warning Switch

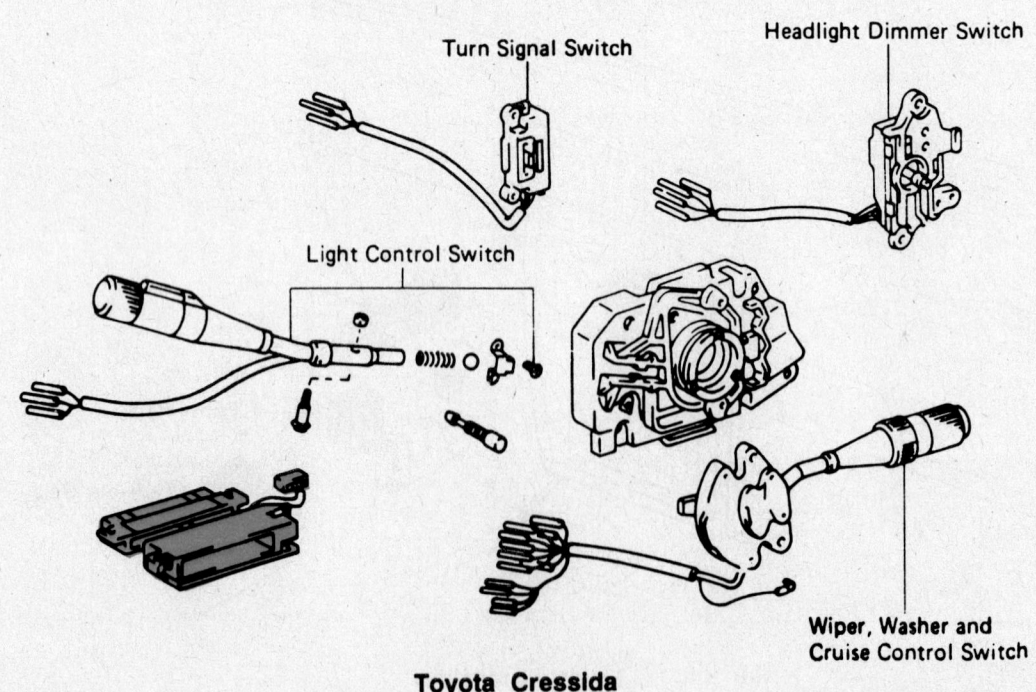

Turn Signal Switch

Headlight Dimmer Switch

Light Control Switch

Wiper, Washer and Cruise Control Switch

Toyota Cressida

COMPONENT LOCATIONS

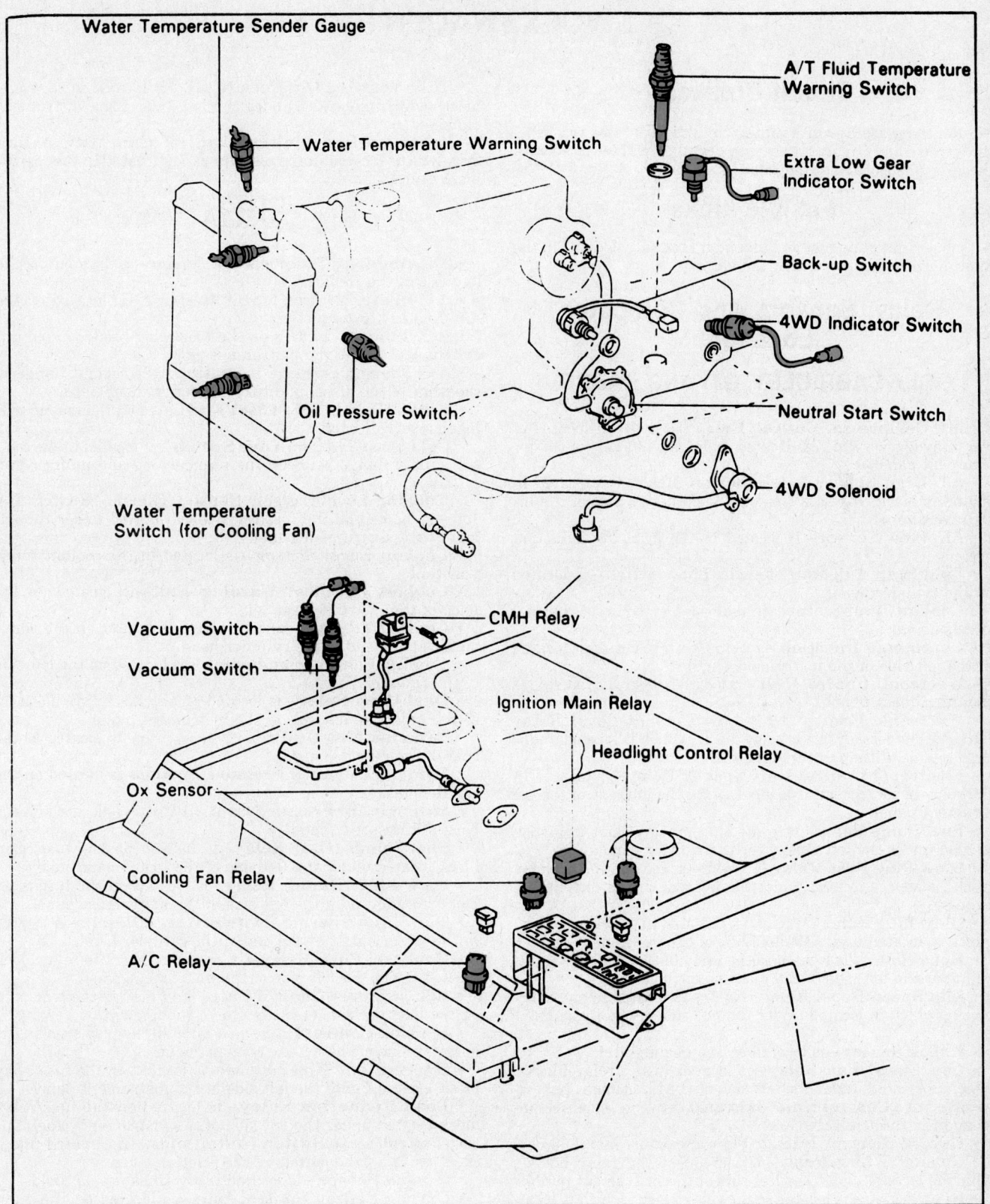

Water Temperature Sender Gauge

Water Temperature Warning Switch

A/T Fluid Temperature Warning Switch

Extra Low Gear Indicator Switch

Back-up Switch

4WD Indicator Switch

Oil Pressure Switch

Neutral Start Switch

4WD Solenoid

Water Temperature Switch (for Cooling Fan)

Vacuum Switch

Vacuum Switch

CMH Relay

Ignition Main Relay

Headlight Control Relay

Ox Sensor

Cooling Fan Relay

A/C Relay

Toyota Tercel

VOLKSWAGEN

Circuit Breakers

Most of the models protect all the circuits with fuses or relays. If there are any circuit breakers in use, they will be listed with the relay, sensors and computer locations.

Fusible Links

All models have one fusible link and it is usually located in the main battery feed wire near the battery.

Relay, Sensors And Computer Locations

GOLF/CABRIOLET, GTI AND RABBIT

- **A/C Compressor Cut-Out Relay (Diesel)** – is located in the relay block , which is located under the left side of the instrument panel.
- **A/C High Blower Relay (not on diesel)** – is located in the relay block, which is located under the left side of the instrument panel.
- **Air Flow Sensor** – is located in the front air induction system.
- **Cold Start Injector Thermo Time switch** – is located on the cylinder head.
- **Coolant Temperature Sensor** – is located in the thermostat housing.
- **Continuous Injection System Control Unit** – is located in the left side of the instrument panel.
- **Electronic Control Unit** – is located under the left side of the instrument panel.
- **Electronic Control Unit Low Coolant Level Relay (Diesel)** – is located in the relay block , which is located under the left side of the instrument panel.
- **Electronic Control Unit Upshift Relay** – is located in the relay block , which is located under the left side of the instrument panel.
- **Fuel Pump Relay** – is located in the relay block , which is located under the left side of the instrument panel.
- **Glow Plug Fuse Relay (Diesel)** – is located in the relay block , which is located under the left side of the instrument panel.
- **Glow Plug Relay (Diesel)** – is located in the relay block , which is located under the left side of the instrument panel.
- **Horn Relay** – is located in the relay block , which is located under the left side of the instrument panel.
- **Idle Speed Boost Relay (Golf)** – is located in the relay block , which is located under the left side of the instrument panel.
- **Knock Sensor** – is located on the engine block.
- **Low Speed Fan Relay** – is located in the relay block , which is located under the left side of the instrument panel.
- **Mixture Control Unit** – is located between the air cleaner and the throttle valve.
- **Oxygen Sensor** – is located in the exhaust manifold.
- **Pulsing Wiper Relay** – is located in the relay block , which is located under the left side of the instrument panel.
- **Rear Wiper** – is located in the relay block , which is located under the left side of the instrument panel.
- **Seat Belt Warning Relay** – is located in the relay block , which is located under the left side of the instrument panel.

- **Time Warning Interlock (Golf)** – is located in the relay block, which is located under the left side of the instrument panel.
- **Transistorized Ignition Control Unit With A Hall Sender** – is located in the plenum panel, located in the instrument panel.

JETTA

- **A/C Ambient Temperature sensor** – is located on the left side of the radiator.
- **A/C-Heater Blower Motor Resistor** – is located on the A/C-Heater blower motor.
- **A/C Relay** – is located on the fuse/relay block located under the left side of the instrument panel.
- **A/C Thermo Switch** – is located in the coolant flange at the front of the diesel and turbo diesel cylinder head.
- **Brake Fluid Level Sensor** – is located on the master cylinder reservoir cap.
- **Cold Start Thermo Time Switch** – is located in the coolant supply flange between the number one and number two cylinders.
- **Coolant Level/Oxygen Sensor Thermo Switch Relay** – is located on the fuse/relay block located under the left side of the instrument panel.
- **Coolant Level Sensor** – is located in the coolant reservoir tank.
- **Coolant Overheat Warning Unit** – is located on the back of the instrument panel.
- **Coolant Temperature Sensor** – is located in the water outlet at the end of the cylinder head.
- **Cooling Fan Thermo Switch** – is located on the left side of the radiator.
- **Dual Horn Relay** – is located on the fuse/relay block located under the left side of the instrument panel.
- **Dynamic Low Oil Presure Switch** – is located at the rear of the cylinder head.
- **Dynamic High Oil Pressure Switch** – is located on the oil filter bracket.
- **Dynamic Oil Pressure Control Unit** – is located on the back of the speedometer.
- **Fuel Pump (Gas) Relay** – is located on the fuse/relay block located under the left side of the instrument panel.
- **Glow Plug (Diesel) Relay** – is located on the fuse/relay block located under the left side of the instrument panel.
- **Glow Plug Thermo Switch Relay (Diesel)** – is located in the water outlet at the end of the cylinder head.
- **Hot Start Pulse Relay** – is located on the fuse/relay block located under the left side of the instrument panel.
- **Idle Stabilzer Control Unit** – is located in the tray area on the left rear side of the engine compartment.
- **Ignition Control Unit** – is located in the tray area on the left rear side of the engine compartment.
- **Intermittent Wiper Relay** – is located on the fuse/relay block located under the left side of the instrument panel.
- **Load Reduction Relay** – is located on the fuse/relay block located under the left side of the instrument panel.
- **Neutral/Start Switch (Auto.Trans.)** – is located under the console, at the bottom of the selector lever.
- **Oxygen Sensor** – is located in the exhaust manifold.
- **Oxygen Sensor Control Unit** – is located on the right side of the glove box.
- **Oxygen Sensor Mileage Counter** – is located in the tray area at the left rear side of the engine compartment.

- **Oxygen Sensor Relay**—is located on the fuse/relay block located under the left side of the instrument panel.
- **Oxygen Sensor Thermo Switch**—is located in the catalytic converter.
- **Rear Wiper Relay**—is located on the fuse/relay block located under the left side of the instrument panel.
- **Seat Belt Interlock Relay**—is located on the fuse/relay block located under the left side of the instrument panel.
- **Seat Belt Warning Relay**—is located on the fuse/relay block located under the left side of the instrument panel.
- **Upshift Indicator Control Unit (Diesel)**—is located on the fuse/relay block under the left side of the instrument panel.
- **Upshift Indicator Top Gear (Diesel) Switch**—is located on the transaxle.

RABBIT

- **A/C Ambient Temperature Sensor**—is located on the left side of the radiator.
- **A/C High Speed Blower Relay**—is located on the cooling unit under the instrument panel.
- **Anti-Diesel Solenoid**—is located on the bracket attached to the side of the carburetor.
- **Bowl Vent Solenoid Valve**—is located on the top of the carburetor.
- **Bulb Check Relay**—is located on the fuse/relay block, which is located under the left side of the instrument panel.
- **Carburetor Feedback Solenoid**—is located on the upper side of the carburetor.
- **Cold Running Vacuum Solenoid**—is located near the carburetor.
- **Cold Start (Carb.) Relay**—is located on the top of the fuse/relay block, which is located under the left side of the instrument panel.
- **Cold Start Thermo Time Switch**—is located in the coolant supply flange between the number one and number two cylinders.
- **Coolant Level Sensor**—is located in the coolant reservoir tank.
- **Coolant Temperature Sensor**—is located in the water outlet at the end of the cylinder head.
- **Cooling Fan Relay**—is located on the fuse/relay block, which is located under the left side of the instrument panel.
- **Cooling Fan Thermo Switch**—is located on the left side of the radiator.
- **Cruise Control Unit**—is located under the left side of the instrument panel.
- **Deceleration Switch**—is located on the bracket attached to the carburetor.
- **Dynamic High Oil Pressure Switch**—is located on the oil filter bracket.
- **Dynamic Low Oil Presuure Switch**—is located at the rear of the cylinder head.
- **Dynamic Oil Pressure Relay**—is located on the fuse/relay block, which is located under the left side of the instrument panel.
- **Electronic Control Unit**—is located under the left side of the instrument panel.
- **Fuel Pump (EFI) Relay**—is located on the fuse/relay block, which is located under the left side of the instrument panel.
- **Glow Plug (Diesel) Relay**—is taped to the right fuse block bracket.
- **Glow Plug (Diesel) Thermo Switch**—is located in the water outlet in the end of the cylinder head.
- **High Speed Blower (Diesel) Relay**—is located on the fuse/relay block, which is located under the left side of the instrument panel.
- **High Speed Cooling Fan Relay**—is located on the fuse/

relay block, which is located under the left side of the instrument panel.
- **Horn Relay**—is located on the fuse/relay block, which is located under the left side of the instrument panel.
- **Hot Start Pulse (EFI) Relay**—is located on the fuse/relay block, which is located under the left side of the instrument panel.
- **Idle Speed Boost Relay**—is attached to the steering column bracket.
- **Idle Stabilizer Control Unit**—is located in the left corner side of the engine compartment.
- **Ignition Control Unit**—is located in the left rear corner of the engine compartment.
- **Intermittent Wiper Relay**—is located on the fuse/relay block, which is located under the left side of the instrument panel.
- **Load Reduction Relay**—is located on the fuse/relay block, which is located under the left side of the instrument panel.
- **Low Coolant Warning (Diesel) Relay**—is located on the fuse/relay block, which is located under the left side of the instrument panel.
- **Manifold Heater (Carb.) Relay**—is located on the fuse/relay block, which is located under the left side of the instrument panel.
- **Neutral/Start Switch (Auto.Trans.)**—is located under the console, at the bottom of the selector lever.
- **Oxygen Sensor**—is located in the exhaust manifold.
- **Oxygen Sensor Control Unit**—is located on the right side of the glove box.
- **Oxygen Sensor Mileage Counter**—is located in the tray area at the rear of the engine compartment.
- **Oxygen Sensor/Power Supply Relay**—is located on the fuse/relay block, which is located under the left side of the instrument panel.
- **Passive Restraint Interlock Relay**—is located on the fuse/relay block, which is located under the left side of the instrument panel.
- **Purge Solenoid Valve**—is located at the center rear of the engine compartment.
- **Rear Wiper Relay**—is located on the fuse/relay block, which is located under the left side of the instrument panel.
- **Seat Belt Warning/Buzzer Relay**—is located on the fuse/relay block, which is located under the left side of the instrument panel.
- **Throttle Valve Switch (1.8L engine)**—is located on the throttle housing.
- **Upshift Indicator Control Unit (Diesel)**—is located on the fuse/relay block, which is located under the left side of the instrument panel.
- **Upshift Indicator Idling (Diesel) Switch**—is located in the sprocket end of the diesel injection pump.
- **Upshift Indicator Load (Diesel) Switch**—is located in the opposite sprocket end of the diesel injection pump.
- **Upshift Indicator Pressure Switch**—is located in the vacuum line running to the distributor vacuum chamber.
- **Upshift Indicator Top Gear (Diesel) Switch**—is located on the transaxle.

QUANTUM

- **4-cyl. A/C Coolant Temperature Switch**—is located in the coolant supply hose near the radiator.
- **4-cyl. Cold Start Thermo Time Switch**—is located in the heater hose flange at the rear of the cylinder head.
- **4-cyl. Coolant Temperature Sending Unit**—is located in the upper left rear side of the cylinder head.
- **4-cyl. Oil Temperature Sensor**—is located on the left front side of the cylinder head.

- **5-cyl. A/C Coolant Temperature Switch** – is located in the coolant supply hose near the expansion tank.
- **5-cyl. Cold Start Thermo Time Switch** – is located in the rear of the cylinder head, below the distributor.
- **5-cyl. Coolant Temperature Sending Unit** – is located in the front of the cylinder head.
- **5-cyl. Idle Stabilzer Control Unit** – is located in the left corner side of the engine compartment.
- **5-cyl. Oil Temperature Sensor** – is located in the oil pump housing.
- **A/C Compressor Cut-Out Switch** – is located below the accelerator pedal.
- **A/C Low-Pressure Cut-Out Switch** – is located in the low pressure refrigerant line on the left side of the radiator.
- **A/C Microswitch** – is located on the side of the heater-A/C control panel.
- **A/C Relay** – is located on the fuse/relay block, which is located under the left side of the instrument panel.
- **A/C Temperature Switch** – is located on the side of the heater-A/C control panel.
- **Cold Start Relay** – is located on the fuse/relay block, which is located under the left side of the instrument panel.
- **Coolant Level (Diesel) Relay** – is located on the fuse/relay block, which is located under the left side of the instrument panel.
- **Coolant Level (Turbo-Diesel) Relay** – is located in the coolant reservoir tank.
- **Coolant Temperature Warning Switch** – is located in the rear of the cylinder head.
- **Cooling Fan Thermo Switch** – is located on the left side of the radiator.
- **Cooling Level Warning Relay/Catalytic Converter Thermo Switch** – is located on the fuse/relay block, which is located under the left side of the instrument panel.
- **Cruise Control Induction Pick-Up** – is located in the back of the speedometer.
- **Cruise Control Unit** – is located under the left side of the instrument panel.
- **Diesel Fuel Cut-Out Solenoid** – is located on the end of the fuel pump, opposite the drive sprocket.
- **Dual Horn Relay** – is located on the fuse/relay block, which is located under the left side of the instrument panel.
- **Dynamic High Oil Pressure Switch** – is located on the oil filter bracket.
- **Dynamic Low Oil pressure Switch** – is located at the rear of the cylinder head.
- **Electronic Control Unit** – is located under the left side of the instrument panel.
- **Fuel Pump (Gas) Relay** – is located on the fuse/relay block, which is located under the left side of the instrument panel.
- **Full Throttle Switch (Turbo-Diesel)** – is located on the top of the injection pump.
- **Glow Plug (Diesel) Relay** – is located on the fuse/relay block, which is located under the left side of the instrument panel.
- **Glow Plug Temperature Sending Unit** – is located in the heater flange at the rear of the cylinder head.
- **Glow Plug (Diesel) Thermo Switch** – is located in the water outlet in the end of the cylinder head.
- **Headlight Washer Relay** – is located on the fuse/relay block, which is located under the left side of the instrument panel.
- **High Speed Blower (Diesel) Relay** – is located on the fuse/relay block, which is located under the left side of the instrument panel.
- **Hot Start Pulse Relay** – is located on the fuse/relay block, which is located under the left side of the instrument panel.
- **Idle Switch (Turbo-Diesel)** – is located on top of the injection pump.

- **Ignition Control Unit** – is located in the left rear corner of the engine compartment.
- **Intermittent Wiper Relay** – is located on the fuse/relay block, which is located under the left side of the instrument panel.
- **Load Reduction Relay** – is located on the fuse/relay block, which is located under the left side of the instrument panel.
- **Neutral/Start Switch (Auto.Trans.)** – is located under the console, at the bottom of the selector lever.
- **Oil Pressure Switch** – is located at the rear of the cylinder head (in front of the dipstick on the 5 cylinder).
- **Oxygen Sensor** – is located in the exhaust manifold.
- **Oxygen Sensor Control Unit** – is located in the tray area on the left rear side of the engine compartment.
- **Oxygen Sensor Mileage Counter** – is located in the tray area on the left rear side of the engine compartment.
- **Oxygen Sensor/Power Supply Relay** – is located on the fuse/relay block, which is located under the left side of the instrument panel.
- **Oxygen Sensor Thermo Switch** – is located in the heater by-pass hose.
- **Power Door Lock Control Solenoid** – is located in the left front door.
- **Power Window Relay** – is located on the fuse/relay block, which is located under the left side of the instrument panel.
- **Rear Wiper Relay** – is located on the fuse/relay block, which is located under the left side of the instrument panel.
- **Seat Belt Warning/Buzzer Relay** – is located on the fuse/relay block, which is located under the left side of the instrument panel.
- **Sun Roof End Stop Switch** – is located in the sun roof motor.
- **Sun Roof Relay** – is located on the sun roof motor.
- **Sun Roof Second Stage Switch** – is located in the sun roof motor.
- **Turbo-Diesel** – in heater flange at the rear of the cylinder head.
- **Upshift Indicator Control Unit** – is located on the fuse/relay block, which is located under the left side of the instrument panel.
- **Upshift Indicator Idling (Turbo-Diesel) Switch** – is located in the sprocket end of the diesel injection pump.
- **Upshift Indicator Load (turb-diesel) Switch** – is located in the opposite sprocket end of the diesel injection pump.
- **Upshift Indicator Pressure Switch** – is located in the vacuum line running to the distributor vacuum chanmber.
- **Upshift Indicator (Diesel) Relay** – is located on the fuse/relay block, which is located under the left side of the instrument panel.
- **Upshift Indicator Top Gear Switch** – is located on the manual transaxle.

SCIROCCO

- **A/C Ambient Temperature Sensor** – is located on the left side of the radiator.
- **A/C-Heater Blower Motor Resistor** – is located on the A/C-Heater blower motor.
- **A/C Relay** – is located on the fuse/relay block, which is located under the left side of the instrument panel.
- **Brake Fluid Level Sensor** – is located on the master cylinder reservoir cap.
- **Cold Start Thermo Time Switch** – is located in the coolant supply flange between the number one and number two cylinders.
- **Coolant Overheat Warning Unit** – is located on the back of the instrument panel.
- **Coolant Temperature Sensor** – is located in the water outlet at the end of the cylinder head.

- **Cooling Fan Thermo Switch** – is located on the left side of the radiator.
- **Catalytic Converter/Coolant Level Control Relay** – is located on the fuse/relay block, which is located under the left side of the instrument panel.
- **Dual Horn Relay** – is located on the fuse/relay block, which is located under the left side of the instrument panel.
- **Dynamic High Oil Pressure Switch** – is located on the oil filter bracket.
- **Dynamic Low Oil Pressure Switch** – ia located at the rear of the cylinder head.
- **Dynamic Oil Pressure Control Unit** – is located on the back of the speedometer.
- **Fuel Pump** – is located on the fuse/relay block, which is located under the left side of the instrument panel.
- **Hot Start Pulse Relay** – is located on the fuse/relay block, which is located under the left side of the instrument panel.
- **Idle Speed Boost Relay** – is located on the fuse/relay block, which is located under the left side of the instrument panel.
- **Idle Stabilizer Control Unit** – is located in the tray area on the left rear side of the engine compartment.
- **Ignition Control Unit** – is located in the tray area on the left rear side of the engine compartment.
- **Intermittent Windshield Wiper Relay** – is located on the fuse/relay block, which is located under the left side of the instrument panel.
- **Load Reduction Relay** – is located on the fuse/relay block, which is located under the left side of the instrument panel.
- **Neutral/Start Switch (Auto.Trans.)** – is located under the console, at the bottom of the selector lever.
- **Oil Temperature Sensor** – is located in the oil filter bracket.
- **Oxygen Sensor** – is located in the exhaust manifold.
- **Oxygen Sensor Control Unit** – is located on the right side of the glove box.
- **Oxygen Sensor Mileage Counter** – is located in the tray area at the left rear side of the engine compartment.
- **Oxygen Sensor/Power Supply Relay** – is located on the fuse/relay block, which is located under the left side of the instrument panel.
- **Oxygen Sensor Thermo Switch** – is located in the catalytic converter.
- **Rear Wiper Relay** – is located on the fuse/relay block, which is located under the left side of the instrument panel.
- **Seat Belt Warning Relay** – is located on the fuse/relay block, which is located under the left side of the instrument panel.
- **Upshift Indicator Control Unit** – is located on the fuse/relay block under the left side of the instrument panel.
- **Upshift Indicator Pressure Switch** – is located in the vacuum line running to the distributor vacuum chamber.
- **Up-Shift Indicator Relay** – is located on the fuse/relay block, which is located under the left side of the instrument panel.

VANAGON

- **Air Circulation Blower Relay (water cooled engines)** – is located under the right side of the instrument panel.
- **Air Intake Sensor** – is located in the air cleaner assembly.
- **Auxiliary Heater Control Unit (water cooled engines)** – is located under the right side of the instrument panel.
- **Auiliary Heater Flame Switch** – is located under the vehicle, on the right side of the heater housing.

- **Auxiliary Heater Glow/Spark Plug (air cooled engines)** – is located under the vehicle, on the top of the heater housing.
- **Auxiliary Heater Glow/Spark Plug (water cooled engines)** – is located under the vehicle, on the the top of the heater housing.
- **Auxiliary Heater Overheat Switch** – is located under the vehicle, on the top of the heater housing.
- **Auxiliary Heater Relay (air cooled engine)** – is located under the right side of the instrument panel.
- **Auxiliary Heater Safety Switch (air cooled engine)** – is located under the instrument panel.
- **Auxiliary Heater Temperature Sensor** – is located under the vehicle, on the right front side of the heater housing.
- **Auxiliary Heater Temperature Switch** – is located in the center of the instrument panel.
- **Auxiliary Ignition Coil (air cooled engines)** – is located under the vehicle, on the left side of the heater housing.
- **Auxiliary Ignition Coil (water cooled engines)** – is located under the vehicle, on the right side of the heater housing.
- **Brake Failure Switch** – is located in the brake master cylinder housing.
- **Compulsory Start Relay (water cooled engines)** – is located under the right side of the instrument panel.
- **Control Unit/Heater Relay (water cooled engines)** – is located under the right side of the instrument panel.
- **Coolant Temperature Sensor (1.9L engine)** – is located in the thermostat housing.
- **Coolant Temperature Sensor (diesel engine)** – is located in the coolant flange at the rear of the cylinder head.
- **Cooling Fan Thermo Switches** – is located on the left side of the radiator.
- **Coolant Level Warning Switch (1.9L engine)** – is located in the coolant reservoir tank.
- **Cylinder Head Temperature Sensor (2.0L engine)** – is located in the rear of the left cylinder head.
- **Double Relay** – is located on the left side of the firewall in the engine comaprtment.
- **EFI Control Unit** – is located on the right side of the engine compartment.
- **EGR/Oxygen Sensor Mileage Counter** – is connected to the speedometer cable under the instrument panel.
- **Flame Switch Relay (water cooled engines)** – is located under the right side of the instrument panel.
- **Fuel Pump Relay (water cooled engines)** – is located under the right side of the instrument panel.
- **Glow Plug Ballast Resistor Relay (water cooled engines)** – is located under the right side of the instrument panel, on the diesel models.
- **Glow Plug Thermo Switch (Diesel)** – is located in the coolant flange on the right side of the cylinder head.
- **Idle Stabilizer Control Unit (Calif.)** – is located on the left side of the engine compartment.
- **Ignition Control Unit** – is located on the left side of the engine compartment.
- **Ignition Key Warning Relay** – is located in the fuse/relay block, which is located under the left side of the instrument panel.
- **Intermittent Wiper Relay** – is located in the fuse/relay block, which is located under the left side of the instrument panel.
- **Load Reduction Relay** – is located in the fuse/relay block, which is located under the left side of the instrument panel.
- **Oil Pressure Switch (1.9L engine)** – is located on top of the oil cooler flange.
- **Oil Pressure Switch (2.0L engine)** – is located at the front of the left cylinder head.
- **Oil Pressure Switch (Diesel)** – is located at the rear of the cylinder head.
- **Oxygen Sensor** – is located in the exhaust system, just

ahead of the catalytic converter.
- **Resistors (2.0L)** – is located on the left side of the firewall in the engine compartment.
- **Speed Limit Switch (Calif.)** – is located in the engine compartment, between the full throttle enrichment switch and the control unit.

- **Thermo Time Switch (1.9L engine)** – is located on the rear of the right cylinder head
- **Throttle Valve Switch (1.9L engine)** – is located on the throttle plate housing.

VOLVO

Circuit Breakers

Most of the models protect all the circuits with fuses or relays. If there are any circuit breakers in use, they will be listed with the relay, sensors and computer locations.

Fusible Links

All models have one fusible link and it is usually located in the main battery feed wire near the battery.

Relay, Sensors And Computer Locations

DL, GL, GLE AND GLT MODELS

• **A/C Relay** – is located at the lower right side of the console.
• **Brake Failure Warning Switch** – is located on the left rear inner fender panel.
• **Bulb Failure Sensor** – is located under the left side of the instrument panel.
• **Central Lock Relay** – is located under the center of the instrument panel.
• **Central Unlock Relay** – is located under the center of the instrument panel.
• **Constant Idle Speed Control Unit (Turbo)** – is located behind the right side kick panel, below the EFI control unit.
• **Constant Idle System Test Point (Blue-White Wire)** – is located in front of the left front shock tower.
• **Coolant Temperature Sensor** – is located on the left rear side of the engine block.
• **Cooling Fan Relay** – is located on the left front inner fender panel in the engine compartment.
• **Cooling Fan Temperature Switch** – is located in the upper radiator hose.
• **Cruise Control Actuator** – is located in the right side of the air cleaner.
• **Cruise Control Governor** – is located in or behind the glove box.
• **Cruise Control Unit** – is located under the right side of the instrument panel.
• **Diesel Control Unit** – is located at the top of the left side kick panel.
• **Electronic Control Unit (for the Constant Idle Speed System)** – is located on the right side of the console.
• **Electronic Control Unit (for the Lambda-Sond System)** – is located on the right side of the console.
• **Electronic Fuel Injection Control Unit** – is located behind the right side kick panel.
• **Electronic Fuel Injection Relay (Non-Turbo)** – is located under the right side of the instrument panel.
• **Electronic Ignition Control Unit** – is located is located at the right front corner of the engine compartment.
• **Front Intermittent Wiper Relay** – is located at the lower left side kick panel.
• **Fuel Pump Relay (Diesel)** – is located behind the left side kick panel.
• **Fuel Pump Relay (Non-Turbo)** – is located under the right side of the instrument panel.
• **Fuel Pump Relay (Turbo)** – is located at the left rear corner of the engine compartment.

• **Glow Plug Control Unit (Diesel)** – is located on the rear of the left front inner fender panel.
• **Glow Plug Relay (Diesel)** – is located at the left center side of the engine comaprtment.
• **Glow Plug Remote Starter Pickup (Diesel)** – is located on the rear of the left front inner fender panel.
• **Glow Plug Stop Valve (Diesel)** – is located at the upper left rear side of the engine block.
• **Glow Plug Temperature Sensor (Diesel)** – is located at the upper left rear side of the engine.
• **Headlight Dimmer Relay** – is located at the left front corner of the engine compartment, near the battery.
• **Interior Light Delay Relay** – is located under the left side of the instrument panel.
• **Knock Sensor (Non-Turbo)** – is located on the left center of the engine block.
• **Lambda System Test Pickup Point (Red Wire)** – is located on the left front inner fender panel.
• **Overdrive Relay** – is located under the center of the instrument panel.
• **Overdrive Solenoid** – is located on the side of the transmission.
• **Overdrive Switch** – is located on the upper left front side of the transmission.
• **Oxygen Sensor** – is located in the exhaust manifold.
• **Oxygen Sensor Relay (Turbo)** – is located on the left front inner fender panel in the engine compartment.
• **Power Window Relay** – is located at the upper right side of the console.
• **Rear Intermittent Wiper Relay** – is located at the lower left front kick panel.
• **Seat Belt Warning Buzzer Relay** – is located under the left side of the steering column bracket.
• **Test Instrument Pickup Point (Non-Turbo)** – is located on the left front shock tower, near the ignition coil.
• **Test Instrument Pickup Point (Turbo)** – is located at the left rear corner of the engine compartment.
• **Throttle Valve Switch** – is located on the throttle body housing.
• **Upper/Lower Beam Switch Relay** – is located on the left front inner fender panel.
• **Voltage Stabilizer** – is located on the back of the instrument cluster circuit board.

740, 760 AND 760 GLE

• **A/C Ambient Temperature Sensor** – is located under the right side of the instrument panel, on the firewall.
• **A/C Compressor Delay Relay** – is located under the right side of the instrument.
• **A/C Coolant Temperature Sensor** – is located in the heater hose at the rear of the engine comaprtment.
• **A/C-Heater Blower Relay** – is located under the right side of the instrument.
• **A/C Idle-Up Solenoid Valve** – is located in the right rear corner of the engine compartment.
• **A/C In-Car Temperature Sensor** – is located under the right side of the instrument panel.
• **A/C Pressure Sensor** – is located at the right rear corner of the engine comaprtment.
• **A/C Programmer Unit** – is located behind the center of the instrument panel.
• **Auxiliary Light Relay** – is located on the fuse/relay

337

block, which is located under a plastic panel in the center console.
- **Brake Failure Warning Switch** — is located in the pressure differential valve, below the master cylinder.
- **Bulb Failure Warning Relay** — is located on the fuse/relay block, which is located under a plastic panel in the center console.
- **Central Locking Door Solenoids** — are located one in each door.
- **Central Locking System Lock Relay** — is located on the fuse/relay block, which is located under a plastic panel in the center console.
- **Central Locking System Unlock Relay** — is located on the fuse/relay block, which is located under a plastic panel in the center console.
- **Constant Idle Speed Control Unit** — is located behind the left side kick panel.
- **Constant Idle Speed Micro Switch** — is located on the inner side of the left air runner.
- **Constant Idle Speed Temperature Sensor** — is located on the left side of the mixture control unit.
- **Constant Idle Speed Test Connector (White/Black Wire)** — is located in the right rear section of the engine compartment.
- **Continuous Injection System Impulse Relay (B-28F engine)** — is located near the coolant expansion tank in the engine compartment.
- **Coolant Temperature Sensor (Gas)** — is located on the right rear inside corner of the left cylinder block.
- **Coolant Temperature Sensor (Turbo-Diesel)** — is located on the left front side of the cylinder block.
- **Cooling Fan/Power Window Relay** — is located on the fuse/relay block, which is located under a plastic panel in the center console.
- **Cooling Fan Temperature Switch** — is located in the left side of the radiator tank.
- **Cruise Control Speed Sensor** — is located on the back of the speedometer.
- **Cruise Control Unit** — is located behind the left side kick panel.
- **Diesel Fuel Shut-Off Solenoid** — is located on the top of the fuel injection pump.
- **Electronic Fuel Injection Impulse Relay** — is located on the left front shock tower.
- **Electronic Fuel Injection Thermal Time Switch** — is located on the right side of the mixture control unit.
- **Electronic Ignition Control Unit** — is located on the right front shock tower.
- **Fog Light Relay** — is located on the fuse/relay block, which is located under a plastic panel in the center console.
- **Fuel Pump (Gas) Relay** — is located on the fuse/relay block, which is located under a plastic panel in the center console.
- **Glow Plug Relay (Diesel)** — is located on the left front shock tower.
- **Glow Plug Temperature Sensor (Diesel)** — is located at the right rear side of the engine.

- **Glow Plug Test Connector** — is located in the left rear section of the engine compartment.
- **Headlight Relay** — is located on the fuse/relay block, which is located under a plastic panel in the center console.
- **Ignition Advance Micro Switch** — is located below the front outer corner of the left air runner.
- **Ignition Advance Relay** — is located on the fuse/relay block, which is located under a plastic panel in the center console.
- **Ignition Ballast Resistor** — is located on the front shock tower.
- **Intermittent Wiper Relay** — is located on the fuse/relay block, which is located under a plastic panel in the center console.
- **Lambda-Sond Relay** — is located on the fuse/relay block, which is located under a plastic panel in the center console.
- **Neutral/Start Switch** — is located on the left side of the transmission.
- **Oil Level Sensor** — is located at the bottom of the engine block, above the oil pan.
- **Oil Level Sensor Relay** — is located on the fuse/relay block, which is located under a plastic panel in the center console.
- **Oil Pressure Control Unit** — is located is located under the rear section of the gearshift console.
- **Oil Pressure Sensor** — is located at the right front side of the engine block.
- **Overdrive Relay** — is located on the fuse/relay block, which is located under a plastic panel in the center console.
- **Oxygen Sensor** — is located in the right exhaust manifold.
- **Oxygen Sensor Control Unit** — is located behind the right side kick panel.
- **Oxygen Sensor Micro Switch** — is located below the front outer corner of the right air runner.
- **Oxygen Sensor Relay** — is located on the fuse/relay block, which is located under a plastic panel in the center console.
- **Oxygen Sensor Test Connector (Red Wire)** — is located in the right rear section of the engine compartment.
- **Oxygen Sensor Thermal Switch** — is located in the coolant passage under the intake manifold.
- **Pressure Differential Switch** — is located on the electronic ignition control unit.
- **Pressure Sensor (Diesel)** — is located at the right center side of the engine.
- **Pressure Warning Relay (Diesel)** — is located on the left front shock tower.
- **Seat Belt Warning Relay/Buzzer** — is located on the fuse/relay block, which is located under a plastic panel in the center console.
- **Starter Motor Service Connector (Pink Wire)** — is located at the left rear corner of the engine comaprtment.
- **Vehicle Speed Sensor** — is located in the differential housing.
- **Washer Reservoir Level Sensor** — is located in the washer reservoir.

FUNDAMENTALS OF ELECTRICITY

In order to be able to successfully troubleshoot and repair any electrical problem, one must first understand the theory behind how electricity works. A clear understanding of how electrical current behaves in a circuit and how components such as solenoids and relays work is essential for correct interpretation of test results. The following section covers basic knowledge necessary to perform all service and testing procedures outlined in this manual. This section should be read before attempting any repair or diagnosis procedures.

All matter is made up of tiny particles called molecules. Each molecule is made up of two or more atoms. Atoms may be divided into even smaller particles called protons, neutrons and electrons. These particles are the same in all matter and differences in materials (hard or soft, conductive or non-conductive) occur only because of the number and arrangement of these particles. In other words, the protons, neutrons and electrons in a drop of water are the same as those in an ounce of lead, there are just more of them (arranged differently) in a lead molecule than in a water molecule. Protons and neutrons packed together form the nucleus of the atom, while electrons orbit around the nucleus much the same way as the planets of the solar system orbit around the sun.

The proton is a small positive natural charge of electricity, while the neutron has no electrical charge. The electron carries a negative charge equal to the positive charge of the proton. Every electrically neutral atom contains the same number of protons and electrons, the exact number of which determines the element. The only difference between a conductor and an insulator is that a conductor possesses free electrons in large quantities, while an insulator has only a few. An element must have very few free electrons to be a good insulator, and vice-versa. When we speak of electricity, we're talking about these free electrons.

In a conductor, the movement of the free electrons is hindered by collisions with the adjoining atoms of the element (matter). This hindrance to movement is called RESISTANCE and it varies with different materials and temperatures. As temperature increases, the movement of the free electrons increases, causing more frequent collisions and therefore increasing resistance to the movement of the electrons. The number of collisions (resistance) also increases with the number of electrons flowing (current). Current is defined as the movement of electrons through a conductor such as a wire. In a conductor (such as copper) electrons can be caused to leave their atoms and move to other atoms. This flow is continuous in that every time an atom gives up an electron, it collects another one to take its place. This movement of electrons is called electric current and is measured in amperes. When 6.28 billion, billion electrons pass a certain point in the circuit in one second, the amount of current flow is called one ampere.

The force or pressure which causes electrons to flow in any conductor (such as a wire) is called VOLTAGE. It is measured in volts and is similar to the pressure that causes water to flow in a pipe. Voltage is the difference in electrical pressure measured between two different points in a circuit. In a 12 volt system, for example, the force measured between the two battery posts is 12 volts. Two important concepts are voltage potential and polarity. Voltage potential is the amount of voltage or electrical pressure at a certain point in the circuit with respect to another point. For example, if the voltage potential at one post of the 12 volt battery is zero, the voltage potential at the other post is 12 volts with respect to the first post. One post of the battery is said to be positive (+); the other post is negative (-) and the conventional direction of current flow is from positive to negative in an electrical circuit. It should be noted that the electron flow in the wire is opposite the current flow. In other words, when the circuit is energized, the current flows from positive to negative, but the electrons actually move from neg-

ative to positive. The voltage or pressure needed to produce a current flow in a circuit must be greater than the resistance present in the circuit. In other words, if the voltage drop across the resistance is greater than or equal to the voltage input, the voltage potential will be zero—no voltage will flow through the circuit. Resistance to the flow of electrons is measured in ohms. One volt will cause one ampere to flow through a resistance of one ohm.

Units Of Electrical Measurement

There are three fundamental characteristics of a direct-current electrical circuit: volts, amperes and ohms.

VOLTAGE in a circuit controls the intensity with which the loads in the circuit operate. The brightness of a lamp, the heat of an electrical defroster, the speed of a motor are all directly proportional to the voltage, if the resistance in the circuit and/or mechanical load on electric motors remains constant. Volt-

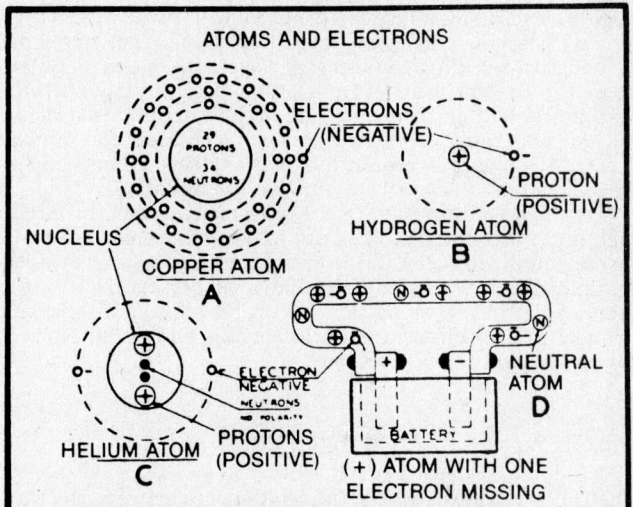

Typical atoms of copper (A), hydrogen (B) and helium (C), showing electron flow through through battery (D)

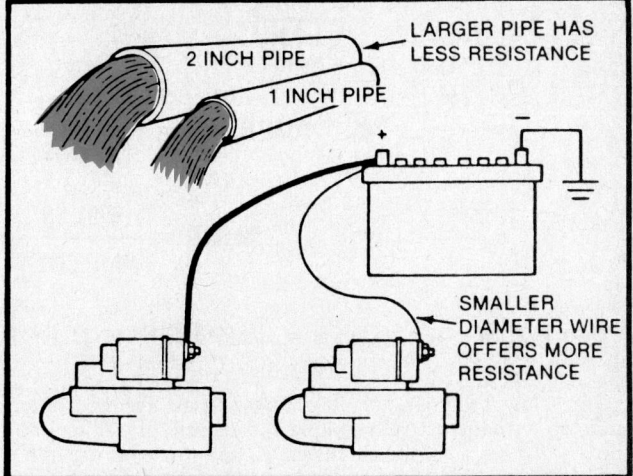

Electrical resistance can be compared to water flow through a pipe. The smaller the wire (pipe), the more resistance to the flow of electrons (water)

age available from the battery is constant (normally 12 volts), but as it operates the various loads in the circuit, voltage decreases (drops).

AMPERE is the unit of measurement of current in an electrical circuit. One ampere is the quantity of current that will flow through a resistance of one ohm at a pressure of one volt. The amount of current that flows in a circuit is controlled by the voltage and the resistance in the circuit. Current flow is directly proportional to resistance. Thus, as voltage is increased or decreased, current is increased or decreased accordingly. Current is decreased as resistance is increased, however, and is increased as resistance is decreased. With little or no resistance in a circuit, current is high.

OHM is the unit of measurement of resistance, represented by the Greek letter Omega (Ω). One ohm is the resistance of a conductor through which a current of one ampere will flow at a pressure of one volt. Electrical resistance can be measured on an instrument called an ohmmeter. The loads (electrical devices) are the primary resistances in a circuit. Loads such as lamps, solenoids, and electric heaters have a resistance that is essentially fixed; at a normal fixed voltage, they will draw a fixed current. Motors, on the other hand, do not have a fixed resistance. Increasing the mechanical load on a motor (such as might be caused by a misadjusted track in a power window system) will decrease the motor speed. The drop in motor rpm has the effect of reducing the internal resistance of the motor because the current draw of the motor varies directly with the mechanical load on the motor, although its actual resistance is unchanged. Thus, as the motor load increases, the current draw of the motor increases, and may increase up to the point where the motor stalls (cannot move the mechanical load).

Circuits are designed with the total resistance of the circuit taken into account. Troubles can arise when unwanted resistances enter into a circuit. If corrosion, dirt, grease, or any other contaminant occurs in places like switches, connectors, and grounds, or if loose connections occur, resistances will develop in these areas. These resistances act like additional loads in the circuit and cause problems.

OHMS LAW

Ohms law is a statement of the relationship between the three fundamental characteristics of an electrical circuit. These rules apply to direct current (DC) only.

$$I = \frac{E}{R} \quad \text{or} \quad \text{AMPERES} = \frac{\text{VOLTS}}{\text{OHMS}}$$

$$R = \frac{E}{I} \quad \text{or} \quad \text{OHMS} = \frac{\text{VOLTS}}{\text{AMPERES}}$$

$$E = I \times R \quad \text{or} \quad \text{VOLTS} = \text{AMPERES} \times \text{OHMS}$$

Ohms law provides a means to make an accurate circuit analysis without actually seeing the circuit. If, for example, one wanted to check the condition of the rotor winding in a alternator whose specifications indicate that the field (rotor) current draw is normally 2.5 amperes at 12 volts, simply connect the rotor to a 12 volt battery and measure the current with an ammeter. If it measures about 2.5 amperes, the rotor winding can be assumed good.

An ohmmeter can be used to test components that have been removed from the vehicle in much the same manner as an ammeter. Since the voltage and the current of the rotor windings used as an earlier example are known, the resistance can be calculated using Ohms law. The formula would be:

$$R = \frac{E}{I} \qquad \text{Where: } E = 12 \text{ volts}, \quad I = 2.5 \text{ amperes}$$

$$R = \frac{12 \text{ volts}}{2.5 \text{ amps}} = 4.8 \text{ ohms}$$

If the rotor resistance measures about 4.8 ohms when checked with an ohmmeter, the winding can be assumed good. By plugging in different specifications, additional circuit information can be determined such as current draw, etc.

Electrical Circuits

An electrical circuit must start from a source of electrical supply and return to that source through a continuous path. Circuits are designed to handle a certain maximum current flow. The maximum allowable current flow is designed higher than the normal current requirements of all the loads in the circuit. Wire size, connections, insulation, etc., are designed to prevent undesirable voltage drop, overheating of conductors, arcing of contacts, and other adverse effects. If the safe maximum current flow level is exceeded, damage to the circuit components will result; it is this condition that circuit protection devices are designed to prevent.

Protection devices are fuses, fusible links or circuit breakers designed to open or break the circuit quickly whenever an overload, such as a short circuit, occurs. By opening the circuit quickly, the circuit protection device prevents damage to the wiring, battery, and other circuit components. Fuses and fusible links are designed to carry a preset maximum amount of current and to melt when that maximum is exceeded, while circuit breakers merely break the connection and may be manually reset. The maximum amperage rating of each fuse is marked on the fuse body and all contain a see-through portion that shows the break in the fuse element when blown. Fusible link maximum amperage rating is indicated by gauge or thickness of the wire. Never replace a blown fuse or fusible link with one of a higher amperage rating.

CAUTION

Resistance wires, like fusible links, are also spliced into conductors in some areas. Do not make the mistake of replacing a fusible link with a resistance wire. Resistance wires are longer than fusible links and are stamped "RESISTOR-DO NOT CUT OR SPLICE."

Circuit breakers consist of two strips of metal which have different coefficients of expansion. As an overload or current flows through the bimetallic strip, the high-expansion metal will elongate due to heat and break the contact. With the circuit open, the bimetal strip cools and shrinks, drawing the strip down until contact is re-established and current flows once again. In actual operation, the contact is broken very quickly if the overload is continuous and the circuit will be repeatedly broken and remade until the source of the overload is corrected.

The self-resetting type of circuit breaker is the one most generally used in automotive electrical systems. On manually reset circuit breakers, a button will pop up on the circuit breaker case. This button must be pushed in to reset the circuit breaker

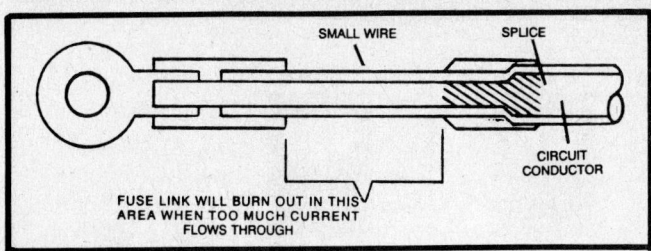

Typical fusible link wire

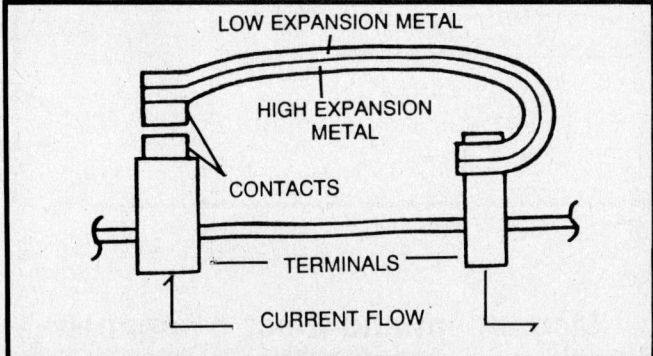

Typical circuit breaker construction

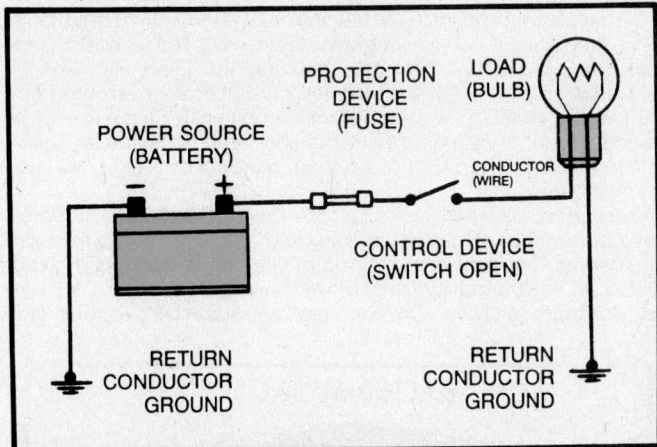

Typical electrical circuit with all essential components

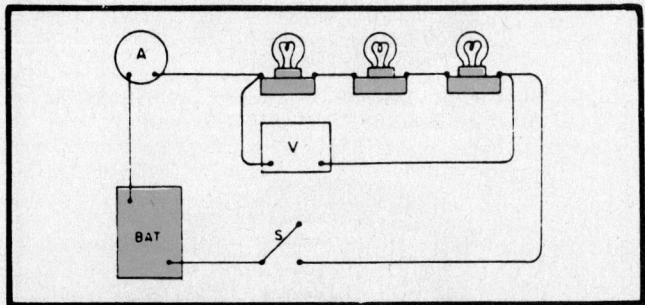

Example of a series circuit

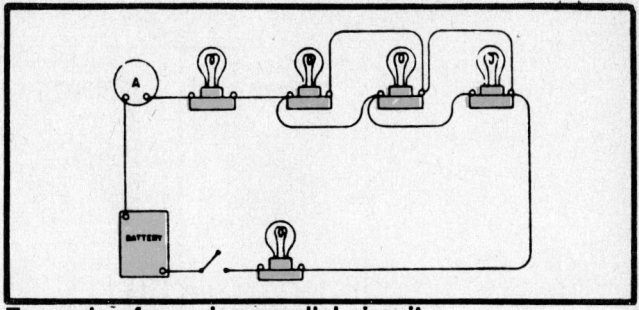

Example of a series-parallel circuit

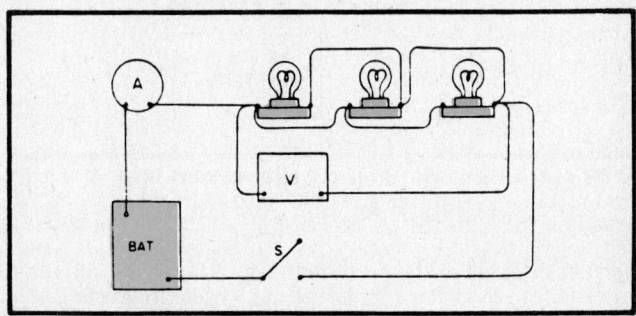

Example of a parallel circuit

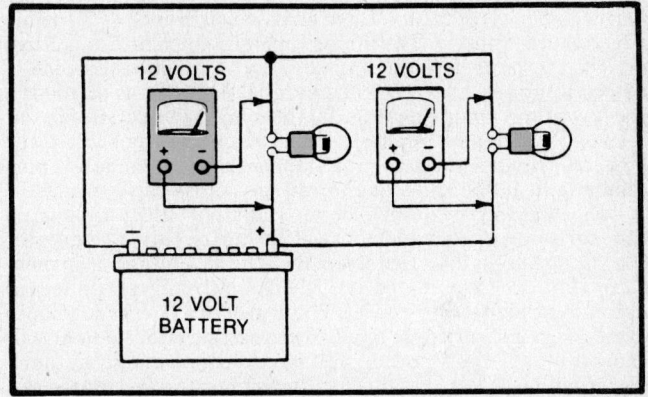

Voltage drop in a parallel circuit. Voltage drop across each lamp is 12 volts

and restore power to the circuit. Always repair the source of the overload before resetting a circuit breaker or replacing a fuse or fusible link. When searching for overloads, keep in mind that the circuit protection devices protect only against overloads between the protection device and ground.

There are two basic types of circuit; Series and Parallel. In a series circuit, all of the elements are connected in chain fashion with the same amount of current passing through each element or load. No matter where an ammeter is connected in a series circuit, it will always read the same. The most important fact to remember about a series circuit is that the sum of the voltages across each element equals the source voltage. The total resistance of a series circuit is equal to the sum of the individual resistances within each element of the circuit. Using ohms law, one can determine the voltage drop across each element in the circuit. If the total resistance and source voltage is known, the amount of current can be calculated. Once the amount of current (amperes) is known, values can be substituted in the Ohms law formula to calculate the voltage drop across each individual element in the series circuit. The individual voltage drops must add up to the same value as the source voltage.

A parallel circuit, unlike a series circuit, contains two or more branches, each branch a separate path independent of the others. The total current draw from the voltage source is the sum of all the currents drawn by each branch. Each branch of a

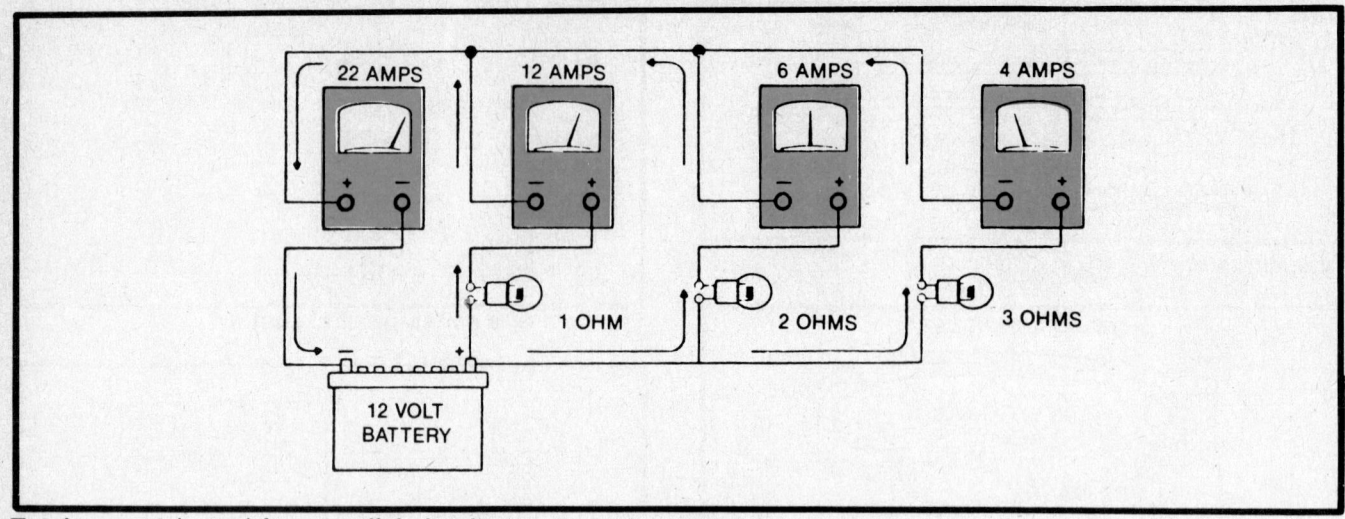

Total current (amps) in a parallel circuit. 4 + 6 + 12 = 22 amps

parallel circuit can be analyzed separately. The individual branches can be either simple circuits, series circuits or combinations of series-parallel circuits. Ohms law applies to parallel circuits just as it applies to series circuits, by considering each branch independently of the others. The most important thing to remember is that the voltage across each branch is the same as the source voltage. The current in any branch is that voltage divided by the resistance of the branch. A practical method of determining the resistance of a parallel circuit is to divide the product of the two resistances by the sum of two resistances at a time. Amperes through a parallel circuit is the sum of the amperes through the separate branches. Voltage across a parallel circuit is the same as the voltage across each branch.

By measuring the voltage drops, you are in effect measuring the resistance of each element within the circuit. The greater the voltage drop, the greater the resistance. Voltage drop measurements are a common way of checking circuit resistances in automotive electrical systems. When part of a circuit develops excessive resistance (due to a bad connection) the element will show a higher than normal voltage drop. Normally, automotive wiring is selected to limit voltage drops to a few tenths of a volt. In parallel circuits, the total resistance is less than the sum of the individual resistances; because the current has two paths to take, the total resistance is lower.

Magnetism and Electromagnets

Electricity and magnetism are very closely associated because when electric current passes through a wire, a magnetic field is created around the wire. When a wire carrying electric current is wound into a coil, a magnetic field with North and South poles is created just like in a bar magnet. If an iron core is placed within the coil, the magnetic field becomes stronger because iron conducts magnetic lines much easier than air. This arrangement is called an electromagnet and is the basic principle behind the operation of such components as relays, buzzers and solenoids.

A relay is basically just a remote-controlled switch that uses a small amount of current to control the flow of a large amount of current. The simplest relay contains an electromagetic coil in series with a voltage source (battery) and a switch. A movable armature made of some magnetic material pivots at one

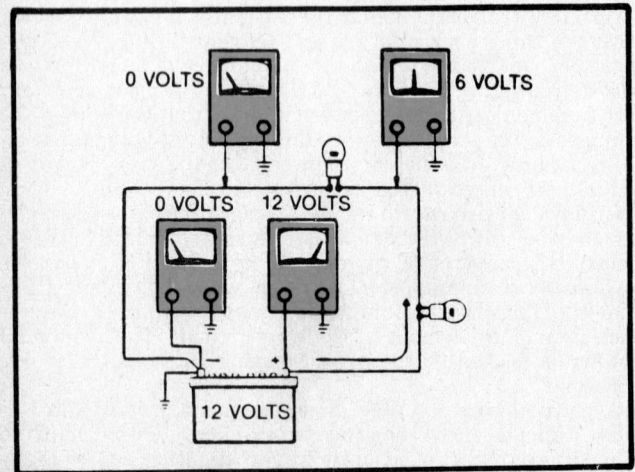

Voltage drop in a series circuit

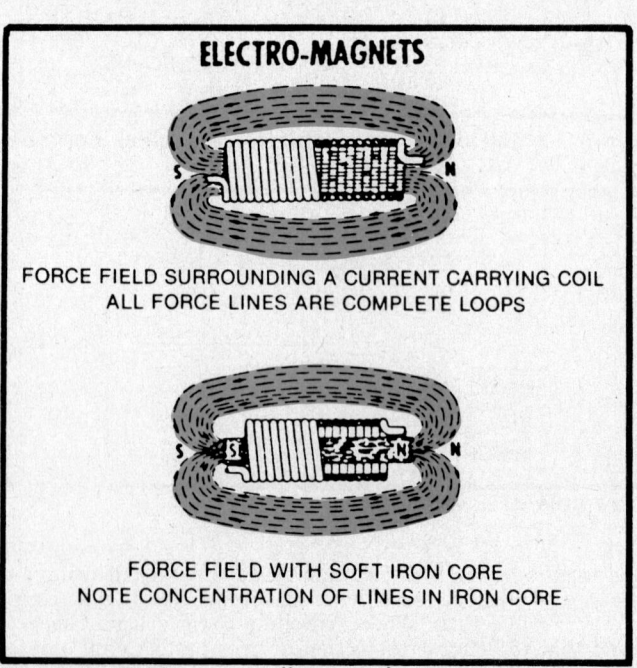

ELECTRO-MAGNETS

FORCE FIELD SURROUNDING A CURRENT CARRYING COIL
ALL FORCE LINES ARE COMPLETE LOOPS

FORCE FIELD WITH SOFT IRON CORE
NOTE CONCENTRATION OF LINES IN IRON CORE

Magnetic field surrounding an electromagnet

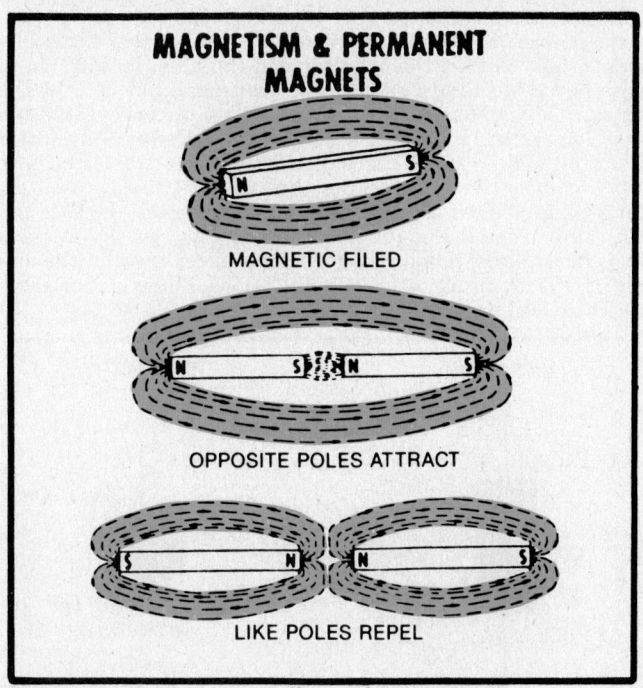

MAGNETISM & PERMANENT MAGNETS

MAGNETIC FILED

OPPOSITE POLES ATTRACT

LIKE POLES REPEL

Magnetic field surrounding a bar magnet

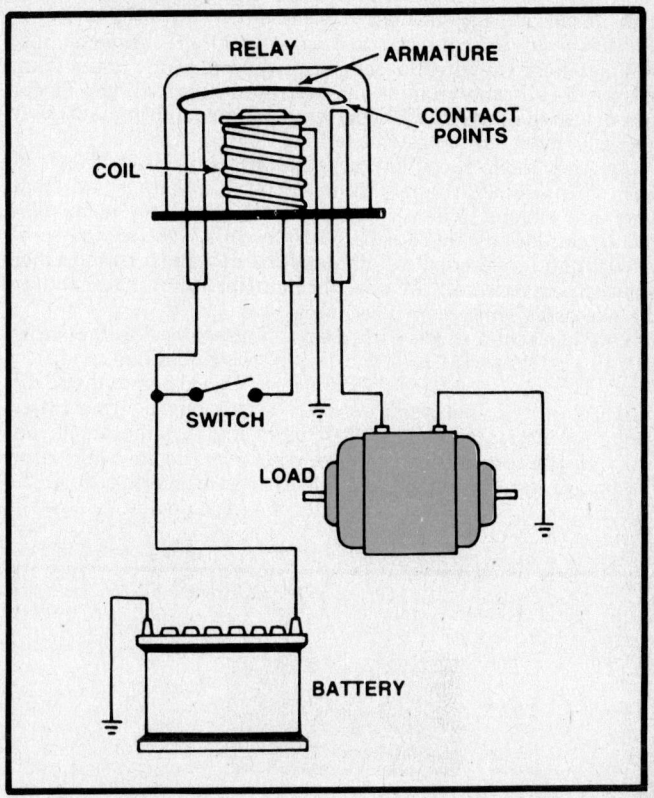

end and is held a small distance away from the electromagnet by a spring or the spring steel of the armature itself. A contact point, made of a good conductor, is attached to the free end of the armature with another contact point a small distance away. When the relay is switched on (energized), the magnetic field created by the current flow attracts the armature, bending it until the contact points meet, closing a circuit and allowing current to flow in the second circuit through the relay to the load the circuit operates. When the relay is switched off (de-energized), the armature springs back and opens the contact points, cutting off the current flow in the secondary, or controlled, circuit. Relays can be designed to be either open or closed when energized, depending on the type of circuit control a manufacturer requires.

A buzzer is similar to a relay, but its internal connections are different. When the switch is closed, the current flows through the normally closed contacts and energizes the coil. When the coil core becomes magnetized, it bends the armature down and breaks the circuit. As soon as the circuit is broken, the spring-loaded armature remakes the circuit and again energizes the coil. This cycle repeats rapidly to cause the buzzing sound.

A solenoid is constructed like a relay, except that its core is allowed to move, providing mechanical motion that can be used to actuate mechanical linkage to operate a door or trunk lock or control any other mechanical function. When the switch is closed, the coil is energized and the movable core is drawn into the coil. When the switch is opened, the coil is de-energized and spring pressure returns the core to its original position.

Basic Solid State

The term "solid state" refers to devices utilizing transistors, diodes and other components which are made from materials known as semiconductors. A semiconductor is a material that is neither a good insulator or a good conductor; principally silicon and germanium. The semiconductor material is specially treated to give it certain qualities that enhance its function, therefore becoming either P-type (positive) or N-type (nega-

tive) material. Most modern semiconductors are constructed of silicon and can be made to change their characteristics depending on whether its function calls for an insulator or conductor.

DIODES

The simplest semiconductor function is that of the diode or rectifier (the two terms mean the same thing). A diode will pass current in one direction only, like a one-way valve, because it has low resistance in one direction and high resistance on the other. Whether the diode conducts or not depends on the polarity of the voltage applied to it. A diode has two electrodes, an anode and a cathode. When the anode receives positive (+) voltage and the cathode receives negative (-) voltage, current can flow easily through the diode. When the voltage is reversed, the diode becomes non-conducting and only allows a very slight amount of current to flow in the circuit. Because the semiconductor is not a perfect insulator, a small amount of reverse current leakage will occur, but the amount is usually too small to consider. The application of voltage to maintain the current flow described is called "forward bias."

A light-emitting diode (LED) is made of a particular type of crystal that glows when current is passed through it. LED's are used in display faces of many digital or electronic instrument clusters. LED's are usually arranged to display numbers (digital readout), but can be used to illuminate a variety of electronic graphic displays.

Like any other electrical device, diodes have certain ratings that must be observed and should not be exceeded. The forward current rating (or bias) indicates how much current can safely pass through the diode without causing damage or destroying it. Forward current rating is usually given in either amperes or milliamperes. The voltage drop across a diode remains constant regardless of the current flowing through it. Small diodes designed to carry low amounts of current need no special provi-

343

sion for dissipating the heat generated in any electrical device, but large current carrying diodes are usually mounted on heat sinks to keep the internal temperature from rising to the point where the silicon will melt and destroy the diode. When diodes are operated in a high ambient temperature environment, they must be de-rated to prevent failure.

Another diode specification is its peak inverse voltage rating. This value is the maximum amount of voltage the diode can safely handle when operating in the blocking mode. This value can be anywhere from 50-1000 volts, depending on the diode, and if exceeded can damage the diode just as too much forward current will. Most semiconductor failures are caused by excessive voltage or internal heat.

One can test a diode with a small battery and a lamp with the same voltage rating. With this arrangement one can find a bad diode and determine the polarity of a good one. A diode can fail and cause either a short or open circuit, but in either case it fails to function as a diode. Testing is simply a matter of connecting the test bulb first in one direction and then the other and making sure that current flows in one direction only. If the diode is shorted, the test bulb will remain on no matter how the light is connected.

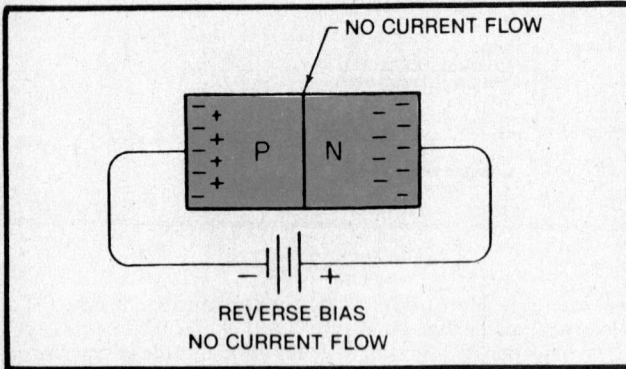

Diode with reverse bias

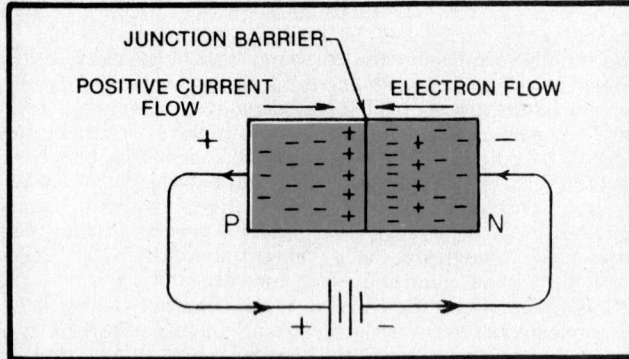

Diode with forward bias

TRANSISTORS

The transistor is an electrical device used to control voltage within a circuit. A transistor can be considered a "controllable diode" in that, in addition to passing or blocking current, the transistor can control the amount of current passing through it. Simple transistors are composed of three pieces of semiconductor material, P and N type, joined together and enclosed in a container. If two sections of P material and one section of N material are used, it is known as a PNP transistor; if the reverse is true, then it is known as an NPN transistor. The two types cannot be interchanged.

Most modern transistors are made from silicon (earlier transistors were made from germanium) and contain three elements; the emitter, the collector and the base. In addition to passing or blocking current, the transistor can control the amount of current passing through it and because of this can function as an amplifier or a switch. The collector and emitter form the main current-carrying circuit of the transistor. The amount of current that flows through the collector-emitter junction is controlled by the amount of current in the base circuit. Only a small amount of base-emitter current is necessary to control a large amount of collector-emitter current (the amplifier effect). In automotive applications, however, the transistor is used primarily as a switch.

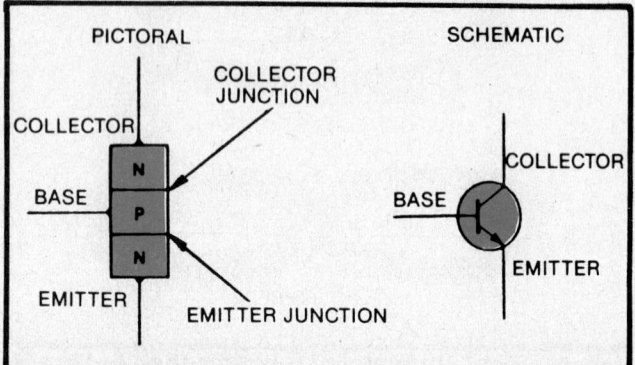

NPN transistor showing both pictorial and schematic illustrations

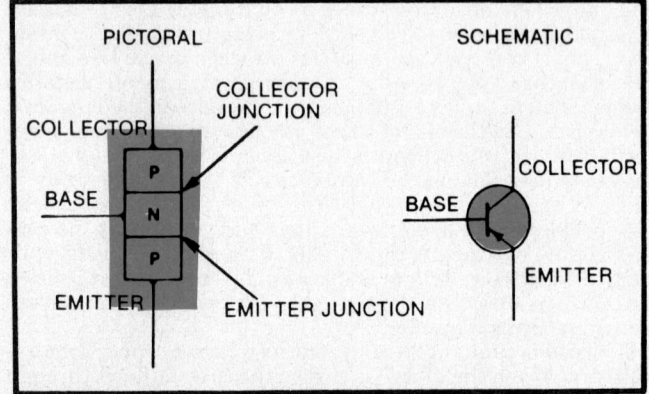

PNP transistor showing both pictorial and schematic illustrations

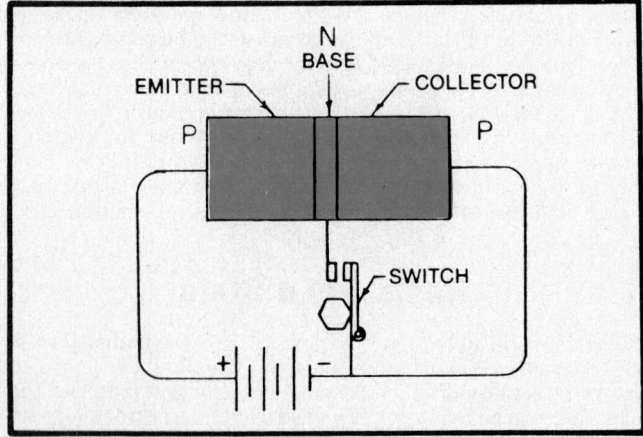

PNP transistor with base switch open (no current flow)

When no current flows in the base-emitter junction, the collector-emitter circuit has a high resistance, like to open contacts of a relay. Almost no current flows through the circuit and transistor is considered OFF. By bypassing a small amount of current into the base circuit, the resistance is low, allowing current to flow through the circuit and turning the transistor ON. This condition is known as "saturation" and is reached when the base current reaches the maximum value designed into the transistor that allows current to flow. Depend-

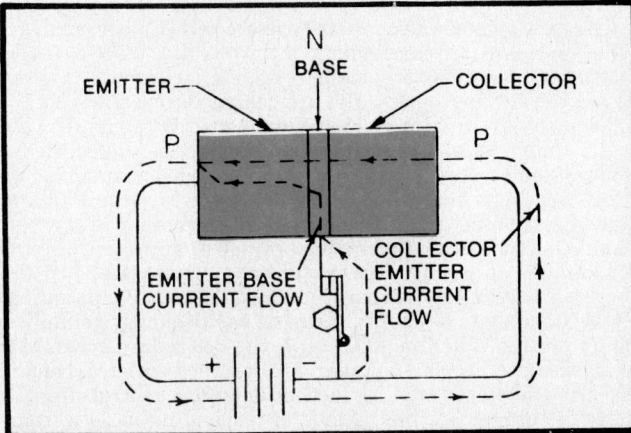

PNP transistor with base switch closed (base emitter and collector emitter current flow)

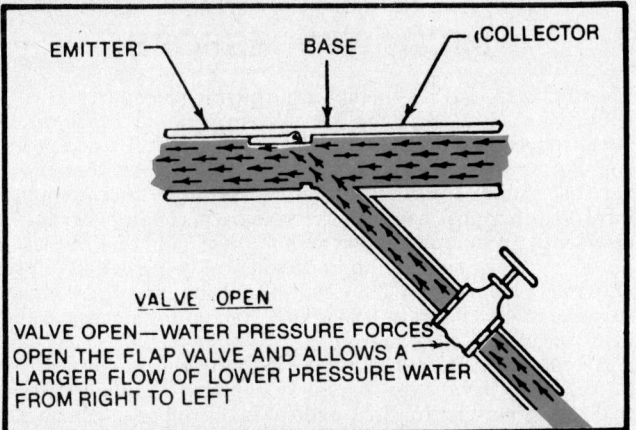

VALVE OPEN

VALVE OPEN—WATER PRESSURE FORCES OPEN THE FLAP VALVE AND ALLOWS A LARGER FLOW OF LOWER PRESSURE WATER FROM RIGHT TO LEFT

Hydraulic analogy to transistor function with base circuit energized

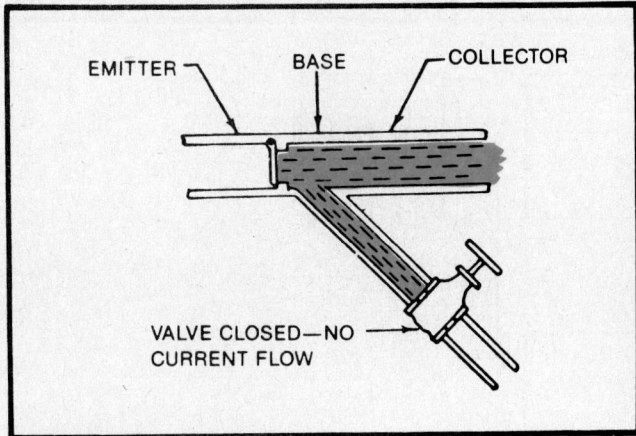

VALVE CLOSED—NO CURRENT FLOW

Hydraulic analogy to transistor function with the base circuit shut off

ing on various factors, the transistor can turn on and off (go from cutoff to saturation) in less than one millionth of a second.

Much of what was said about ratings for diodes applies to transistors, since they are constructed of the same materials. When transistors are required to handle relatively high currents, such as in voltage regulators or ignition systems, they are generally mounted on heat sinks in the same manner as diodes. They can be damaged or destroyed in the same manner if their voltage ratings are exceeded. A transistor can be checked for proper operation by measuring the resistance with an ohmmeter between the base-emitter terminals and then between the base-collector terminals. The forward resistance should be small, while the reverse resistance should be large. Compare the readings with those from a known good transistor. As a final check, measure the forward and reverse resistance between the collector and emitter terminals.

INTEGRATED CIRCUITS

The integrated circuit (IC) is an extremely sophisticated solid state device that consists of a silicone wafer (or chip) which has been doped, insulated and etched many times so that it contains an entire electrical circuit with transistors, diodes, conductors and capacitors miniaturized within each tiny chip. Integrated circuits are often referred to as "computers on a chip" and are largely responsible for the current boom in electronic control technology.

Microprocessors, Computers and Logic Systems

Mechanical or electromechanical control devices lack the precision necessary to meet the requirements of modern control standards, and the ability to respond to a variety of input conditions common to antilock brakes, climate control and electronic suspension operation. To meet these requirements, manufacturers have gone to solid state logic systems and microprocessors to control the basic functions of suspension, brake and temperature control, as well as other systems and accessories.

One of the more vital roles of microprocessor-based systems is their ability to perform logic functions and make decisions. Logic designers use a shorthand notation to indicate whether a voltage is present in a circuit (the number 1) or not present (the number 0), and their systems are designed to respond in different ways depending on the output signal (or the lack of it) from various control devices.

There are three basic logic functions or "gates" used to construct a microprocessor control system: the AND gate, the OR gate or the NOT gate. Stated simply, the AND gate works when voltage is present in two or more circuits which then energize a third (A and B energize C). The OR gate works when voltage is present at either circuit A or circuit B which then energizes circuit C. The NOT function is performed by a solid state device called an "inverter" which reverses the input from a circuit so that, if voltage is going in, no voltage comes out and vice versa. With these three basic building blocks, a logic designer can create complex systems easily. In actual use, a logic or decision making system may employ many logic gates and receive inputs from a number of sources (sensors), but for the most part, all utilize the basic logic gates discussed above.

Stripped to its bare essentials, a computerized decision-making system is made up of three subsystems:
a. Input devices (sensors or switches)
b. Logic circuits (computer control unit)
c. Output devices (actuators or controls)

The input devices are usually nothing more than switches or sensors that provide a voltage signal to the control unit logic circuits that is read as a 1 or 0 (on or off) by the logic circuits.

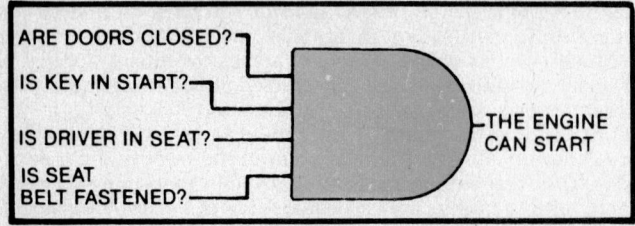

Multiple input AND operation in a typical automotive starting circuit

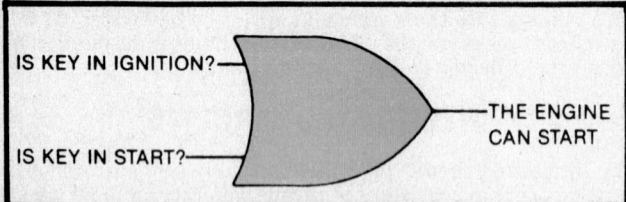

Typical two-input OR circuit operation

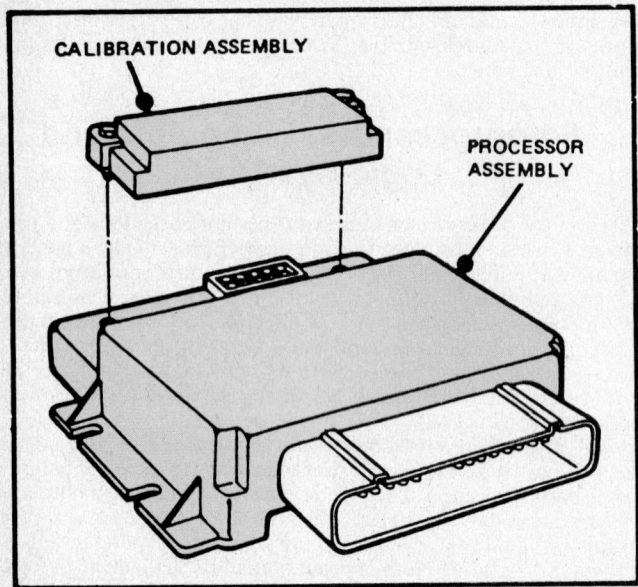

Electronic control assembly

The output devices are anything from a warning light to solenoid-operated valves, motors, linkage, etc. In most cases, the logic circuits themselves lack sufficient output power to operate these devices directly. Instead, they operate some intermediate device such as a relay or power transistor which in turn operates the appropriate device or control. Many problems diagnosed as computer failures are really the result of a malfunctioning intermediate device like a relay and this must be kept in mind whenever troubleshooting any microprocessor-based control system.

The logic systems discussed above are called "hardware" systems, because they consist only of the physical electronic components (gates, resistors, transistors, etc.). Hardware systems do not contain a program and are designed to perform specific or "dedicated" functions which cannot readily be changed. For many simple automotive control requirements, such dedicated logic systems are perfectly adequate. When more complex logic functions are required, or where it may be desirable to alter these functions (e.g. from one model car to another) a true computer system is used. A computer can be programmed through its software to perform many different functions and, if that program is stored on a separate integrated circuit chip called a ROM (Read Only Memory), it can be easily changed simply by plugging in a different ROM with the desired program. Most on-board automotive computers are designed with this capability. The on-board computer method of engine control offers the manufacturer a flexible method of responding to data from a variety of input devices and of controlling an equally large variety of output controls. The computer response can be changed quickly and easily by simply modifying its software program.

MICROPROCESSORS

The microprocessor is the heart of the microcomputer. It is the thinking part of the computer system through which all the data from the various sensors passes. Within the microprocessor, data is acted upon, compared, manipulated or stored for future use. A microprocessor is not necessarily a microcomputer, but the differences between the two are becoming very minor. Originally, a microprocessor was a major part of a microcomputer, but nowadays microprocessors are being called "single-chip microcomputers". They contain all the essential elements to make them behave as a computer, including the most important ingredient—the program.

All computers require a program. In a general purpose computer, the program can be easily changed to allow different tasks to be performed. In a "dedicated" computer, such as most on-board automotive computers, the program isn't quite so easily altered. These automotive computers are designed to per-

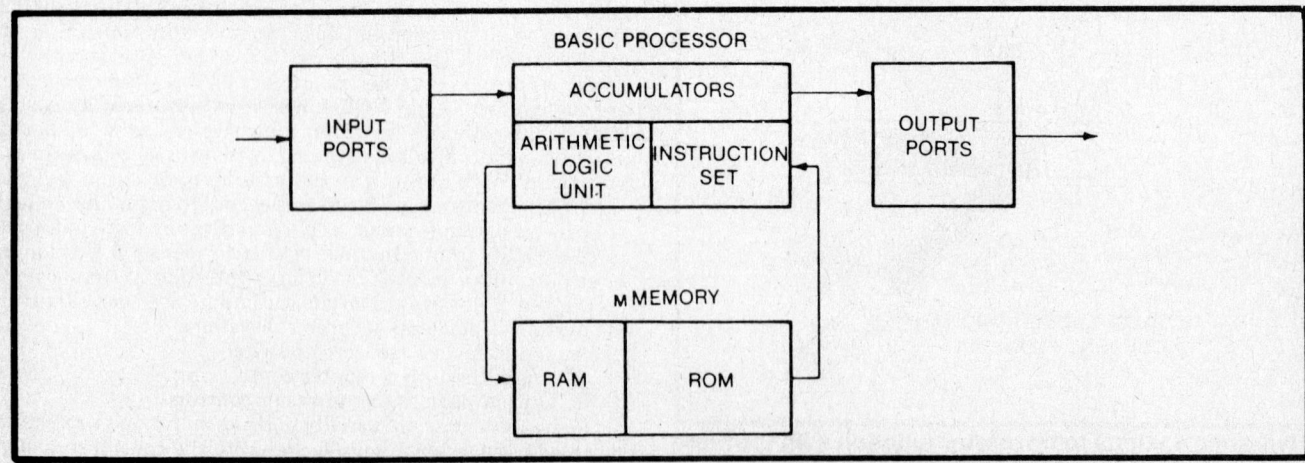

Schematic of typical microprocessor based on-board computer showing essential components

form one or several specific tasks, such as maintaining the passenger compartment temperature at a specific, predetermined level. A program is what makes a computer smart; without a program a computer can do absolutely nothing. The term "software" refers to the program that makes the hardware do what you want it to do.

The software program is simply a listing in sequential order of the steps or commands necessary to make a computer perform the desired task. Before the computer can do anything at all, the program must be fed into it by one of several possible methods. A computer can never be "smarter" than the person programming it, but it is a lot faster. Although it cannot perform any calculation or operation that the programmer himself cannot perform, its processing time is measured in millionths of a second.

Because a computer is limited to performing only those operations (instructions) programmed into its memory, the program must be broken down into a large number of very simple steps. Two different programmers can come up with two different programs, since there is usually more than one way to perform any task or solve a problem. In any computer, however, there is only so much memory space available, so an overly long or inefficient program may not fit into the memory. In addition to performing arithmetic functions (such as with a trip computer), a computer can also store data, look up data in a table and perform the logic functions previously discussed. A Random Access Memory (RAM) allows the computer to store bits of data temporarily while waiting to be acted upon by the program. It may also be used to store output data that is to be sent to an output device. Whatever data is stored in a RAM is lost when power is removed from the system by turning off the ignition key, for example.

Computers have another type of memory called a Read Only Memory (ROM) which is permanent. This memory is not lost when the power is removed from the system. Most programs for automotive computers are stored on a ROM memory chip. Data is usually in the form of a look-up table that saves computing time and program steps. For example, a computer designed to control the amount of distributor advance can have this information stored in a table. The information that determines distributor advance (engine rpm, manifold vacuum and temperature) is coded to produce the correct amount of distributor advance over a wide range of engine operating conditions. Instead of the computer computing the required advance, it simply looks it up in a pre-programmed table. However, not all electronic control functions can be handled in this manner; some must be computed. On an antilock brake system, for example, the computer must measure the rotation of each separate wheel and then calculate how much brake pressure to apply in order to prevent one wheel from locking up and causing a loss of control.

There are several ways of programming a ROM, but once programmed the ROM cannot be changed. If the ROM is made on the same chip that contains the microprocessor, the whole computer must be altered if a program change is needed. For

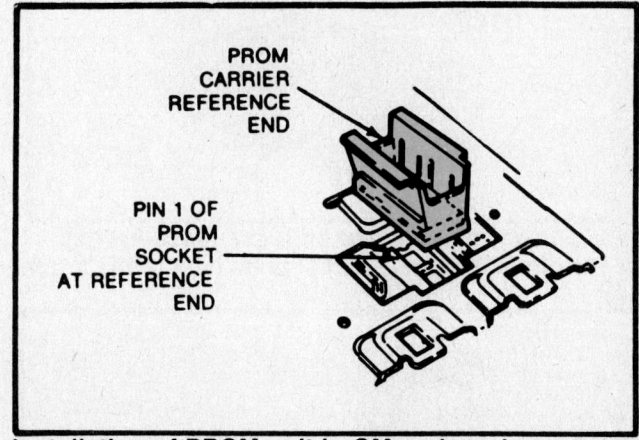

Installation of PROM unit in GM on-board computer

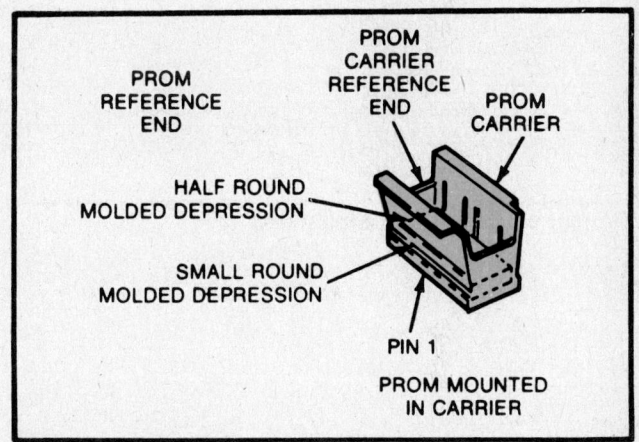

Typical PROM showing carrier and refernce markings for installation

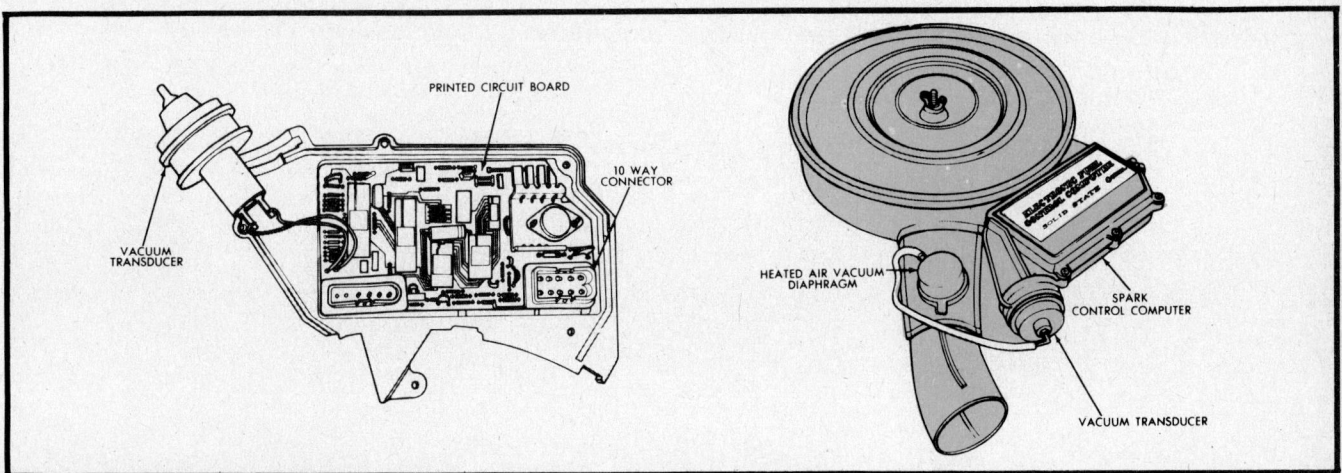

Typical Chrysler combustion assembly showing air cleaner mounting

this reason, a ROM is usually placed on a separate chip. Another type of memory is the Programmable Read Only Memory (PROM) that has the program "burned in" with the appropriate programming machine. Like the ROM, once a PROM has been programmed, it cannot be changed. The advantage of the PROM is that it can be produced in small quantities economi-

cally, since it is manufactured with a blank memory. Program changes for various vehicles can be made readily. There is still another type of memory called an EPROM (Erasable PROM) which can be erased and programmed many times, but they are used only in research and development work, not on production vehicles.

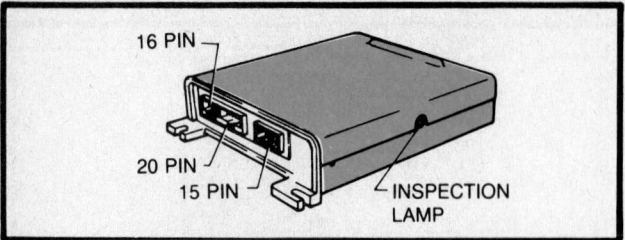

E.C.C.S. control unit used on Nissan models. Except for the pin collectors, all ECU units look pretty much alike

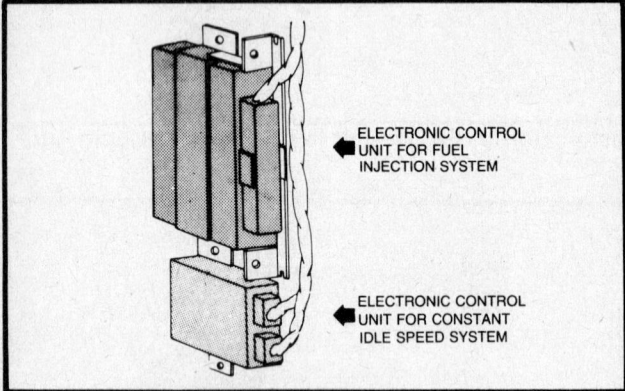

Typical control unit installations

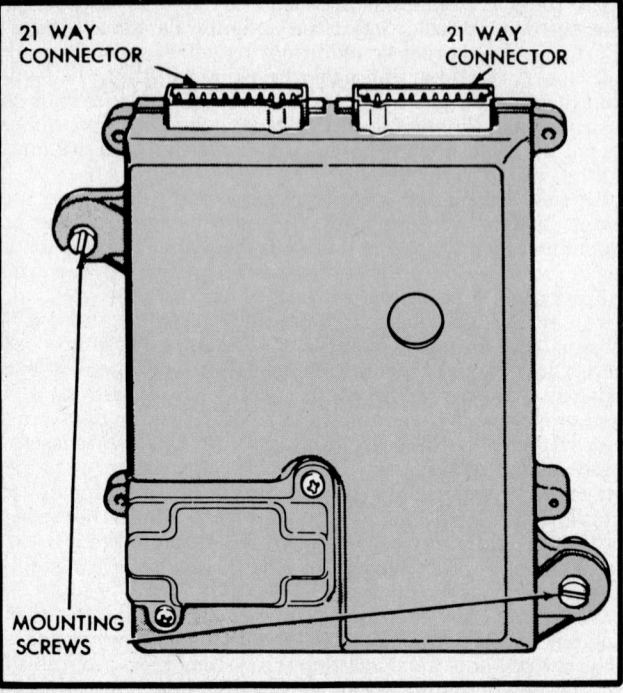

Logic module on Chrysler MFI system showing pin connector locations

DIAGNOSTIC EQUIPMENT AND SPECIAL TOOLS

At the rate which both import and domestic manufacturers are incorporating electronic control systems into their production lines, it won't be long before every new vehicle is equipped with one or more on-board computer. These electronic components (with no moving parts) should theoretically last the life of the car, provided nothing external happens to damage the circuits or memory chips.

While it is true that electronic components should never wear out, in the real world malfunctions do occur. It is also true that any computer-based system is extremely sensitive to electrical voltages and cannot tolerate careless or haphazard testing or service procedures. An inexperienced individual can literally do major damage looking for a minor problem by using the wrong kind of test equipment or connecting test leads or connectors with the ignition switch ON. When selecting test equipment, make sure the manufacturers instructions state that the tester is compatible with whatever type of electronic control system is being serviced. Read all instructions carefully and double check all test points before installing probes or making any connections.

The following section outlines basic diagnosis techniques for dealing with computerized control systems. Along with a general explanation of the various types of test equipment available to aid in servicing modern electronic automotive systems, basic repair techniques for wiring harnesses and connectors is given. Read the basic information before attempting any repairs or testing on any computerized system, to provide the background of information necessary to avoid the most common and obvious mistakes that can cost both time and money. Likewise, the individual system sections for engine controls, fuel injection and feedback carburetors should be read from the beginning to the end before any repairs or diagnosis is attempted. Although the replacement and testing procedures are simple in themselves, the systems are not, and unless one has a thorough understanding of all components and their function within a particular fuel injection system (for example), the logical test sequence these systems demand cannot be followed. Minor malfunctions can make a big difference, so it is important to know how each component affects the operation of the overall electronic system to find the ultimate cause of a problem without replacing good components unnecessarily. It is not enough to use the correct test equipment; the test equipment must be used correctly.

Safety Precautions

CAUTION

Whenever working on or around any computer-based microprocessor control system, always observe these general precautions to prevent the possibility of personal injury or damage to electronic components

• Never install or remove battery cables with the key ON or the engine running. Jumper cables should be connected with the key OFF to avoid power surges that can damage electronic control units. Engines equipped with computer controlled systems should avoid both giving and getting jump starts due to the possibility of serious damage to components from arcing in the engine compartment when connections are made with the ignition ON.
• Always remove the battery cables before charging the battery. Never use a high-output charger on an installed battery or attempt to use any type of "hot shot" (24 volt) starting aid.
• Exercise care when inserting test probes into connectors to insure good connections without damaging the connector or spreading the pins. Always probe connectors from the rear (wire) side, NOT the pin side, to avoid accidental shorting of terminals during test procedures.

• Never remove or attach wiring harness connectors with the ignition switch ON, especially to an electronic control unit.
• Do not drop any components during service procedures and never apply 12 volts directly to any component (like a solenoid or relay) unless instructed specifically to do so. Some component electrical windings are designed to safely handle only 4 or 5 volts and can be destroyed in seconds if 12 volts are applied directly to the connector.
• Remove the electronic control unit if the vehicle is to be placed in an environment where temperatures exceed approximately 176°F (80°C), such as a paint spray booth or when arc or gas welding near the control unit location in the car.

ORGANIZED TROUBLESHOOTING

When diagnosing a specific problem, organized troubleshooting is a must. The complexity of a modern automobile demands that you approach any problem in a logical, organized manner. There are certain troubleshooting techniques that are standard:

1. Establish when the problem occurs. Does the problem appear only under certain conditions? Were there any noises, odors, or other unusual symptoms? Make notes on any symptoms found, including warning lights and trouble codes, if applicable.

2. Isolate the problem area. To do this, make some simple tests and observations; then eliminate the systems that are working properly. Check for obvious problems such as broken wires or split or disconnected vacuum hoses. Always check the obvious before assuming something complicated is the cause.

3. Test for problems systematically to determine the cause once the problem area is isolated. Are all the components functioning properly? Is there power going to electrical switches and motors? Is there vacuum at vacuum switches and/or actuators? Is there a mechanical problem such as bent linkage or loose mounting screws? Doing careful, systematic checks will often turn up most causes on the first inspection without wasting time checking components that have little or no relationship to the problem.

4. Test all repairs after the work is done to make sure that the problem is fixed. Some causes can be traced to more than one component, so a careful verification of repair work is important to pick up additional malfunctions that may cause a problem to reappear or a different problem to arise. A blown fuse, for example, is a simple problem that may require more than another fuse to repair. If you don't look for a problem that caused a fuse to blow, for example, a shorted wire may go undetected.

The diagnostic tree charts are designed to help solve problems by leading the user through closely defined conditions and tests so that only the most likely components, vacuum and electrical circuits are checked for proper operation when troubleshooting a particular malfunction. By using the trouble trees to eliminate those systems and components which normally will not cause the condition described, a problem can be isolated within one or more systems or circuits without wasting time on unnecessary testing. Experience has shown that most problems tend to be the result of a fairly simple and obvious cause, such as loose or corroded connectors or air leaks in the intake system; making careful inspection of components during testing essential to quick and accurate troubleshooting. Frequent references to special test equipment will be found in the text and in the diagnosis charts. These devices or a compatible equivalent are necessary to perform some of the more complicated test procedures listed, but many components can be functionally tested with the quick checks outlined in the "On-Car Service" procedures. Aftermarket testers are available from a variety of sources, as well as from the vehicle manufacturer, but care should be taken that any test equipment being used is designed to diagnose that particular system accurately without damaging the control unit (ECU) or components being tested.

NOTE: Pinpointing the exact cause of trouble in an electrical system can sometimes only be accomplished by the use of special test equipment. The following describes commonly used test equipment and explains how to put it to best use in diagnosis. In addition to the information covered below, the manufacturer's instructions booklet provided with the tester should be read and clearly understood before attempting any test procedures.

TEST EQUIPMENT

Jumper Wires

Jumper wires are simple, yet extremely valuable, pieces of test equipment. Jumper wires are merely wires that are used to bypass sections of a circuit. The simplest type of jumper wire is merely a length of multistrand wire with an alligator clip at each end. Jumper wires are usually fabricated from lengths of standard automotive wire and whatever type of connector (alligator clip, spade connector or pin connector) that is required for

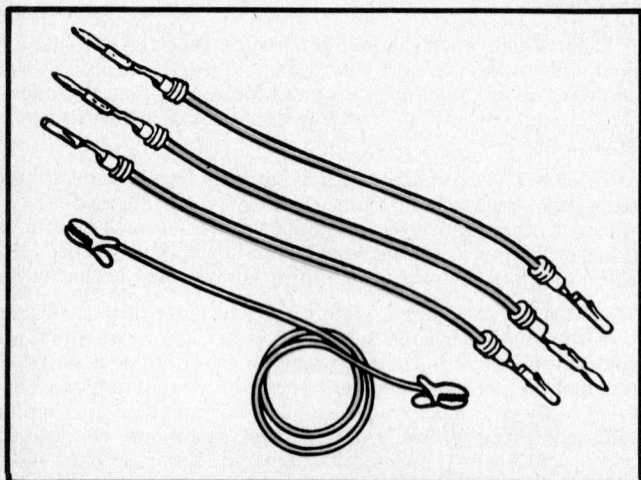

Typical jumper wires with various terminal ends

the particular vehicle being tested. The well-equipped tool box will have several different styles of jumper wires in several different lengths. Some jumper wires are made with three or more terminals coming from a common splice for special-purpose testing. In cramped, hard-to-reach areas it is advisable to have insulated boots over the jumper wire terminals in order to prevent accidental grounding, sparks, and possible fire, especially when testing fuel system components.

Jumper wires are used primarily to locate open electrical circuits, on either the ground (–) side of the circuit or on the hot (+) side. If an electrical component fails to operate, connect the jumper wire between the component and a good ground. If the component operates only with the jumper installed, the ground circuit is open. If the ground circuit is good, but the component does not operate, the circuit between the power feed and component is open. You can sometimes connect the jumper wire directly from the battery to the hot terminal of the component, but first make sure the component uses 12 volts in operation. Some electrical components, such as fuel injectors, are designed to operate on about 4 volts and running 12 volts directly to the injector terminals can burn out the wiring. By inserting an in-line fuseholder between a set of test leads, a fused jumper wire can be used for bypassing open circuits. Use a 5 amp fuse to provide protection against voltage spikes. When in doubt, use a voltmeter to check the voltage input to the component and measure how much voltage is being applied normally. By

moving the jumper wire successively back from the lamp toward the power source, you can isolate the area of the circuit where the open is located. When the component stops functioning, or the power is cut off, the open is in the segment of wire between the jumper and the point previously tested.

--- CAUTION ---
Never use jumpers made from wire that is of lighter gauge than used in the circuit under test. If the jumper wire is of too small gauge, it may overheat and possibly melt. Never use jumpers to bypass high-resistance loads (such as motors) in a circuit. Bypassing resistances, in effect, creates a short circuit which may, in turn, cause damage and fire. Never use a jumper for anything other than temporary bypassing of components in a circuit.

12 Volt Test Light

The 12 volt test light is used to check circuits and components while electrical current is flowing through them. It is used for voltage and ground tests. Twelve volt test lights come in different styles but all have three main parts; a ground clip, a probe, and a light. The most commonly used 12-volt test lights have pick-type probes. To use a 12-volt test light, connect the ground clip to a good ground and probe wherever necessary with the pick. The pick should be sharp so that it can penetrate wire insulation to make contact with the wire, without making a large hole in the insulation. The wrap-around light is handy in hard to reach areas or where it is difficult to support a wire to push a probe pick into it. To use the wrap around light, hook the wire to probed with the hook and pull the trigger. A small pick will be forced through the wire insulation into the wire core.

--- CAUTION ---
Do not use a test light to probe electronic ignition spark plug or coil wires. Never use a pick-type test light to probe wiring on computer controlled systems unless specifically instructed to do so. Any wire insulation that is pierced by the test light probe should be taped and sealed with silicone after testing.

Like the jumper wire, the 12-volt test light is used to isolate opens in circuits. But, whereas the jumper wire is used to bypass the open to operate the load, the 12-volt test light is used to locate the presence of voltage in a circuit. If the test light glows, you know that there is power up to that point; if the 12-volt test light does not glow when its probe is inserted into the wire or connector, you know that there is an open circuit (no power). Move the test light in successive steps back toward the power source until the light in the handle does glow. When it does glow, the open is between the probe and point previously probed.

NOTE: The test light does not detect that 12 volts (or any particular amount of voltage) is present; it only detects that some voltage is present. It is advisable before using the test light to touch its terminals across the battery posts to make sure the light is operating properly.

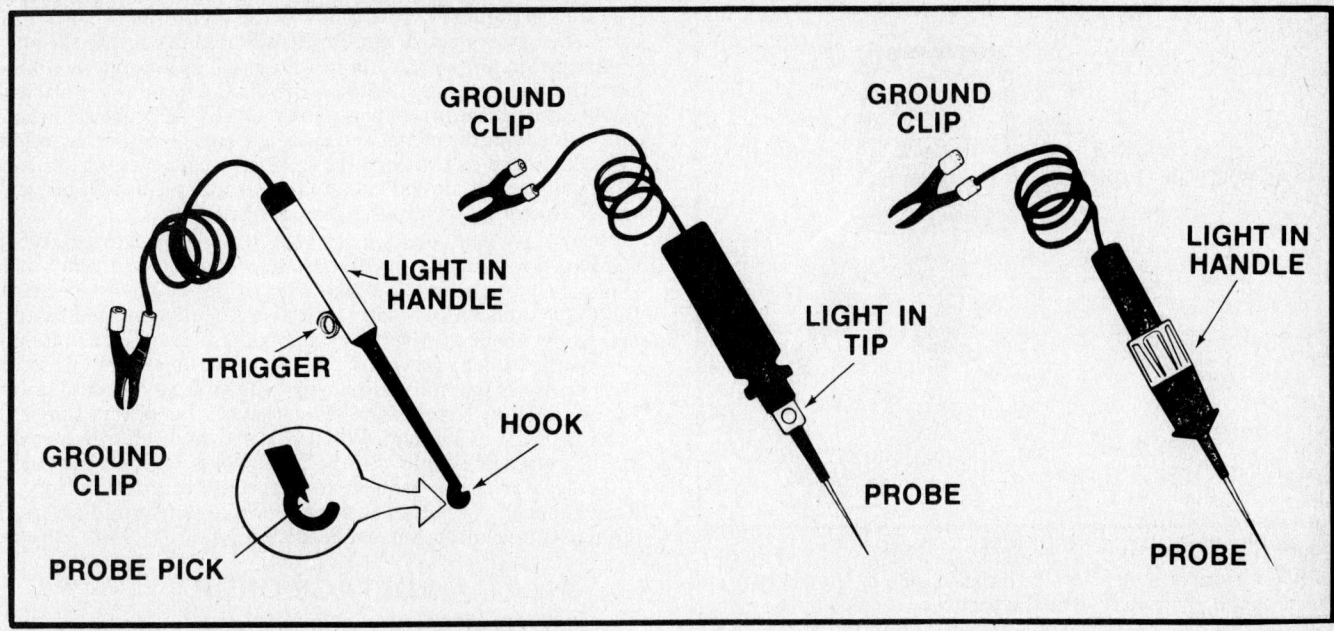

Examples of various types of 12 volt test lights

Self-Powered Test Light

The self-powered test light usually contains a 1.5 volt penlight battery. One type of self-powered test light is similar in design to the 12 volt test light. This type has both the battery and the light in the handle and pick-type probe tip. The second type has the light toward the open tip, so that the light illuminates the contact point. The self-powered test light is dual-purpose piece of test equipment. It can be used to test for either open or short circuits when power is isolated from the circuit (continuity test). A powered test light should not be used on any computer controlled system or component unless specifically instructed to do so. Many engine sensors can be destroyed by even this small amount of voltage applied directly to the terminals.

Open Circuit Testing

To use the self-powered test light to check for open circuits, first isolate the circuit from the vehicle's 12 volt power source by disconnecting the battery or wiring harness connector. Connect the test light ground clip to a good ground and probe sections of the circuit sequentially with the test light. (start from either end of the circuit). If the light is out, the open is between

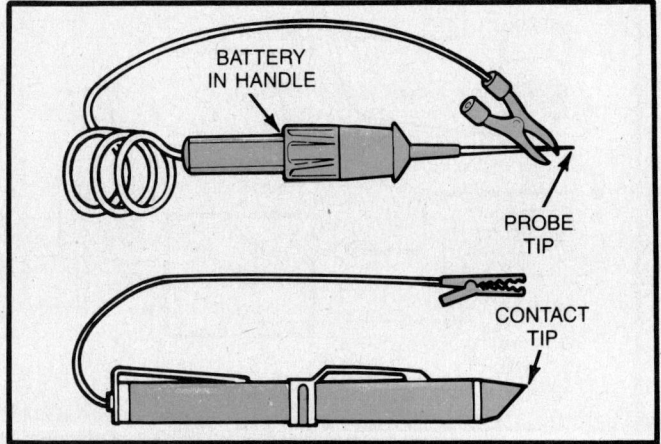

Two types of self-powered test lights

the probe and the circuit ground. If the light is on, the open is between the probe and end of the circuit toward the power source.

Short Circuit Testing

By isolating the circuit both from power and from ground, and using a self-powered test light, you can check for shorts to ground in the circuit. Isolate the circuit from power and ground. Connect the test light ground clip to a good ground and probe any easy-to-reach test point in the circuit. If the light comes on, there is a short somewhere in the circuit. To isolate the short, probe a test point at either end of the isolated circuit (the light should be on). Leave the test light probe connected and open connectors, switches, remove parts, etc., sequentially, until the light goes out. When the light goes out, the short is between the last circuit component opened and the previous circuit opened.

NOTE: The 1.5 volt battery in the test light does not provide much current. A weak battery may not provide enough power to illuminate the test light even when a complete circuit is made (especially if there are high resistances in the circuit). Always make sure that the test battery is strong. To check the battery, briefly touch the ground clip to the probe; if the light glows brightly the battery is strong enough for testing. Never use a self-powered test light to perform checks for opens or shorts when power is applied to the electrical system under test. The 12-volt vehicle power will quickly burn out the 1.5 volt light bulb in the test light.

Voltmeter

A voltmeter is used to measure voltage at any point in a circuit, or to measure the voltage drop across any part of a circuit. It can also be used to check continuity in a wire or circuit by indicating current flow from one end to the other. Voltmeters usually have various scales on the meter dial and a selector switch to allow the selection of different voltages. The voltmeter has a positive and a negative lead. To avoid damage to the meter, always connect the negative lead to the negative (–) side of cir-

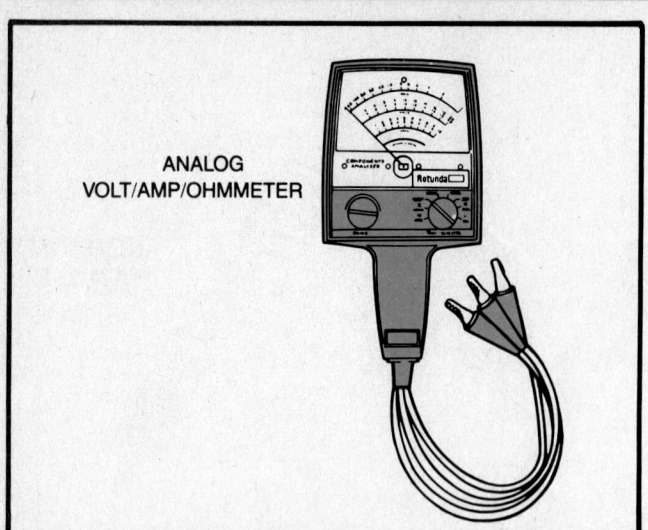

ANALOG
VOLT/AMP/OHMMETER

Typical analog-type voltmeter

cuit (to ground or nearest the ground side of the circuit) and connect the positive lead to the positive (+) side of the circuit (to the power source or the nearest power source). Note that the negative voltmeter lead will always be black and that the positive voltmeter will always be some color other than black (usually red). Depending on how the voltmeter is connected into the circuit, it has several uses.

A voltmeter can be connected either in parallel or in series with a circuit and it has a very high resistance to current flow. When connected in parallel, only a small amount of current will flow through the voltmeter current path; the rest will flow through the normal circuit current path and the circuit will work normally. When the voltmeter is connected in series with a circuit, only a small amount of current can flow through the circuit. The circuit will not work properly, but the voltmeter reading will show if the circuit is complete or not.

Available Voltage Measurement

Set the voltmeter selector switch to the 20V position and connect the meter negative lead to the negative post of the battery. Connect the positive meter lead to the positive post of the battery and turn the ignition switch ON to provide a load. Read the voltage on the meter or digital display. A well-charged bat-

tery should register over 12 volts. If the meter reads below 11.5 volts, the battery power may be insufficient to operate the electrical system properly. This test determines voltage available from the battery and should be the first step in any electrical trouble diagnosis procedure. Many electrical problems, especially on computer controlled systems, can be caused by a low state of charge in the battery. Excessive corrosion at the battery cable terminals can cause a poor contact that will prevent proper charging and full battery current flow.

Normal battery voltage is 12 volts when fully charged. When the battery is supplying current to one or more circuits it is said to be "under load". When everything is off the electrical system is under a "no-load" condition. A fully charged battery may show about 12.5 volts at no load; will drop to 12 volts under medium load; and will drop even lower under heavy load. If the battery is partially discharged the voltage decrease under heavy load may be excessive, even though the battery shows 12 volts or more at no load. When allowed to discharge further, the battery's available voltage under load will decrease more severely. For this reason, it is important that the battery be fully charged during all testing procedures to avoid errors in diagnosis and incorrect test results.

VOLTAGE DROP

When current flows through a resistance, the voltage beyond the resistance is reduced (the larger the current, the greater the reduction in voltage). When no current is flowing, there is no voltage drop because there is no current flow. All points in the circuit which are connected to the power source are at the same voltage as the power source. The total voltage drop always equals the total source voltage. In a long circuit with

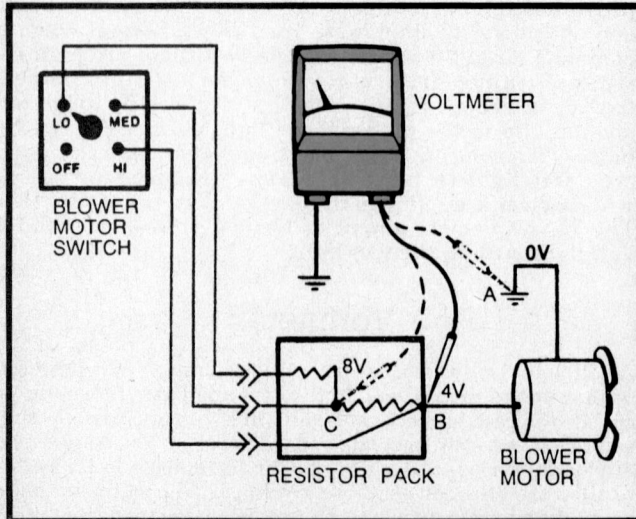

Measuring available voltage in a blower circuit

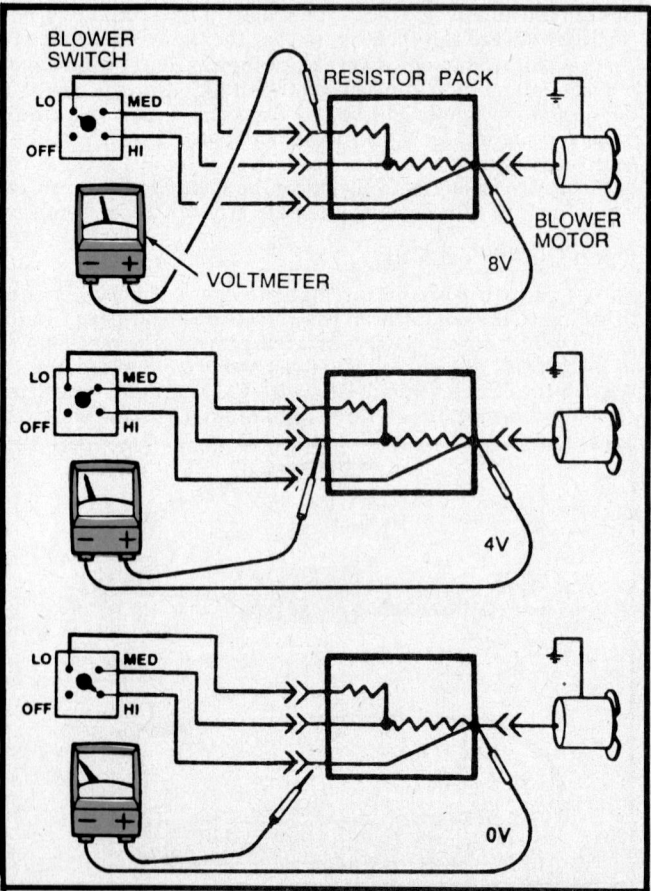

Direct measurement of voltage drops in a circuit

many connectors, a series of small, unwanted voltage drops due to corrosion at the connectors can add up to a total loss of voltage which impairs the operation of the normal loads in the circuit.

Indirect Computation of Voltage Drops

1. Set the voltmeter selector switch to the 20 volt position.
2. Connect the meter negative lead to a good ground.
3. Probe all resistances in the circuit with the positive meter lead.
4. Operate the circuit in all modes and observe the voltage readings.

Direct Measurement of Voltage Drops

1. Set the voltmeter switch to the 20 volt position.
2. Connect the voltmeter negative lead to the ground side of the resistance load to be measured.
3. Connect the positive lead to the positive side of the resistance or load to be measured.
4. Read the voltage drop directly on the 20 volt scale.

Too high a voltage indicates too high a resistance. If, for example, a blower motor runs too slowly, you can determine if there is too high a resistance in the resistor pack. By taking voltage drop readings in all parts of the circuit, you can isolate the problem. Too low a voltage drop indicates too low a resistance. If, for example, a blower motor runs too fast in the MED and/or LOW position, the problem can be isolated in the resistor pack by taking voltage drop readings in all parts of the circuit to locate a possibly shorted resistor. The maximum allowable voltage drop under load is critical, especially if there is more than one high resistance problem in a circuit because all voltage drops are cumulative. A small drop is normal due to the resistance of the conductors.

High Resistance Testing

1. Set the voltmeter selector switch to the 4 volt position.
2. Connect the voltmeter positive lead to the positive post of the battery.
3. Turn on the headlights and heater blower to provide a load.
4. Probe various points in the circuit with the negative voltmeter lead.
5. Read the voltage drop on the 4 volt scale. Some average maximum allowable voltage drops are:
FUSE PANEL—7 volts
IGNITION SWITCH—5volts
HEADLIGHT SWITCH—7 volts
IGNITION COIL (+)—5 volts
ANY OTHER LOAD—1.3 volts

NOTE: Voltage drops are all measured while a load is operating; without current flow, there will be no voltage drop.

Ohmmeter

The ohmmeter is designed to read resistance (ohms) in a circuit or component. Although there are several different styles of ohmmeters, all will usually have a selector switch which permits the measurement of different ranges of resistance (usually the selector switch allows the multiplication of the meter reading by 10, 100, 1000, and 10,000). A calibration knob allows the meter to be set at zero for accurate measurement. Since all ohmmeters are powered by an internal battery (usually 9 volts), the ohmmeter can be used as a self-powered test light. When the ohmmeter is connected, current from the ohmmeter flows through the circuit or component being tested. Since the ohmmeter's internal resistance and voltage are known values, the amount of current flow through the meter depends on the resistance of the circuit or component being tested.

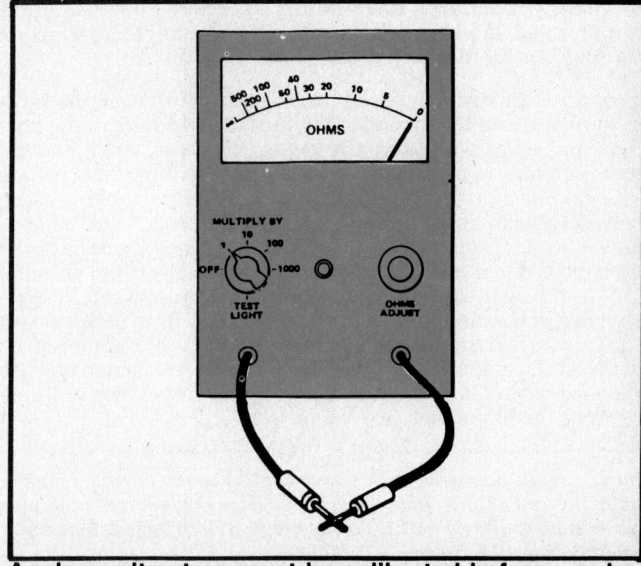

Analog voltmeters must be calibrated before use by touching the probes together and turning the adjustment knob

The ohmmeter can be used to perform continuity test for opens or shorts (either by observation of the meter needle or as a self-powered test light), and to read actual resistance in a circuit. It should be noted that the ohmmeter is used to check the resistance of a component or wire while there is no voltage applied to the circuit. Current flow from an outside voltage source (such as the vehicle battery) can damage the ohmmeter, so the circuit or component should be isolated from the vehicle electrical system before any testing is done. Since the ohmmeter uses its own voltage source, either lead can be connected to any test point.

NOTE: When checking diodes or other solid state components, the ohmmeter leads can only be connected one way in order to measure current flow in a single direction. Make sure the positive (+) and negative (-) terminal connections are as described in the test procedures to verify the one-way diode operation.

In using the meter for making continuity checks, do not be concerned with the actual resistance readings. Zero resistance, or any resistance readings, indicate continuity in the circuit. Infinite resistance indicates an open in the circuit. A high resistance reading where there should be none indicates a problem in the circuit. Checks for short circuits are made in the same manner as checks for open circuits except that the circuit must be isolated from both power and normal ground. Infinite resistance indicates no continuity to ground, while zero resistance indicates a dead short to ground.

Resistance Measurement

The batteries in an ohmmeter will weaken with age and temperature, so the ohmmeter must be calibrated or "zeroed" before taking measurements. To zero the meter, place the selector switch in its lowest range and touch the two ohmmeter leads together. Turn the calibration knob until the meter needle is exactly on zero.

NOTE: All analog (needle) type ohmmeters must be zeroed before use, but some digital ohmmeter models are automatically calibrated when the switch is turned on. Self-calibrating digital ohmmeters do not have an adjusting knob, but its a good idea to check for a zero readout before use by touching the leads together. All computer controlled systems require the use of a digital ohmmeter with at least 10 meagohms impedance for testing. Before

any test procedures are attempted, make sure the ohmmeter used is compatible with the electrical system or damage to the on-board computer could result.

To measure resistance, first isolate the circuit from the vehicle power source by disconnecting the battery cables or the harness connector. Make sure the key is OFF when disconnecting any components or the battery. Where necessary, also isolate at least one side of the circuit to be checked to avoid reading parallel resistances. Parallel circuit resistances will always give a lower reading than the actual resistance of either of the branches. When measuring the resistance of parallel circuits, the total resistance will always be lower than the smallest resistance in the circuit. Connect the meter leads to both sides of the circuit (wire or component) and read the actual measured ohms on the meter scale. Make sure the selector switch is set to the proper ohm scale for the circuit being tested to avoid misreading the ohmmeter test value.

CAUTION

Never use an ohmmeter with power applied to the circuit. Like the self-powered test light, the ohmmeter is designed to operate on its own power supply. The normal 12 volt automotive electrical system current could damage the meter.

Ammeters

An ammeter measures the amount of current flowing through a circuit in units called amperes or amps. Amperes are units of electron flow which indicate how fast the electrons are flowing through the circuit. Since Ohms Law dictates that current flow in a circuit is equal to the circuit voltage divided by the total circuit resistance, increasing voltage also increases the current level (amps). Likewise, any decrease in resistance will increase the amount of amps in a circuit. At normal operating voltage, most circuits have a characteristic amount of amperes, called "current draw" which can be measured using an ammeter. By referring to a specified current draw rating, measuring the amperes, and comparing the two values, one can determine what is happening within the circuit to aid in diagnosis. An open circuit, for example, will not allow any current to flow so the ammeter reading will be zero. More current flows through a

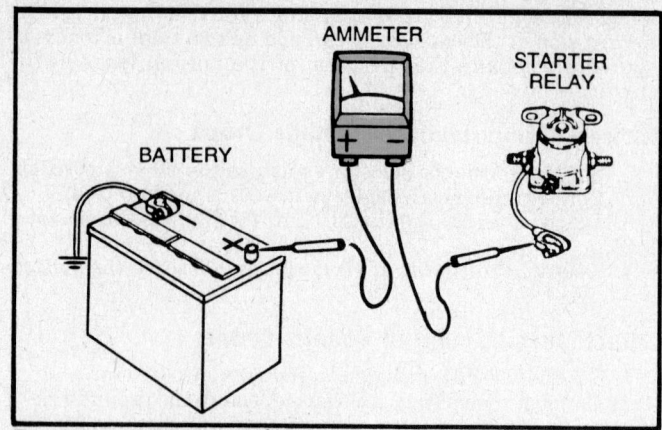

Battery current drain test

heavily loaded circuit or when the charging system is operating.

An ammeter is always connected in series with the circuit being tested. All of the current that normally flows through the circuit must also flow through the ammeter; if there is any other path for the current to follow, the ammeter reading will not be accurate. The ammeter itself has very little resistance to current flow and therefore will not affect the circuit, but it will measure current draw only when the circuit is closed and electricity is flowing. Excessive current draw can blow fuses and drain the battery, while a reduced current draw can cause motors to run slowly, lights to dim and other components to not operate properly. The ammeter can help diagnose these conditions by locating the cause of the high or low reading.

Multimeters

Different combinations of test meters can be built into a single unit designed for specific tests. Some of the more common combination test devices are known as Volt-Amp testers, Tach-Dwell meters, or Digital Multimeters. The Volt-Amp tester is used for charging system, starting system or battery tests and consists of a voltmeter, an ammeter and a variable resistance carbon pile. The voltmeter will usually have at least two ranges for use with 6, 12 and 24 volt systems. The ammeter also has more than one range for testing various levels of battery loads and starter current draw and the carbon pile can be adjusted to offer different amounts of resistance. The Volt-Amp tester has heavy leads to carry large amounts of current and

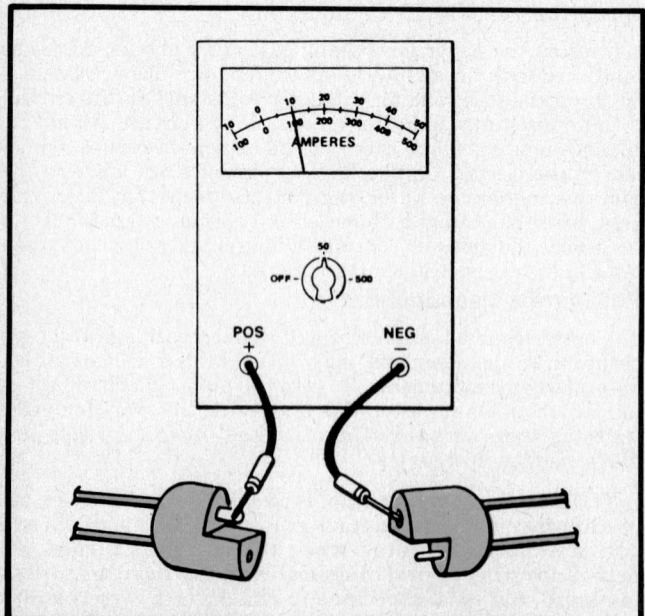

An ammeter must be connected in series with the circuit being tested

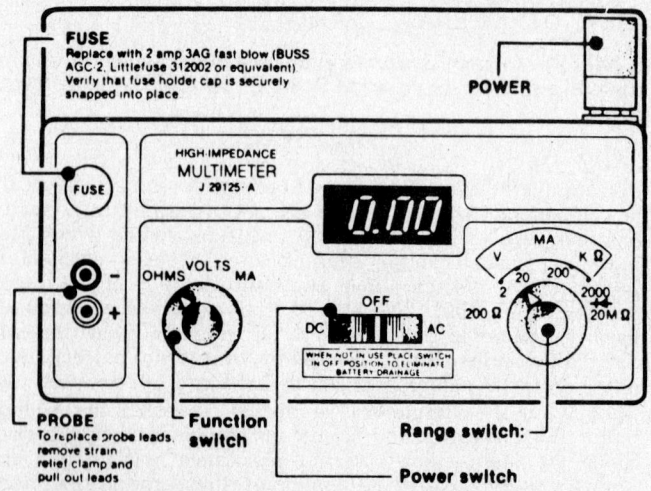

Typical multimeter used to test GM systems

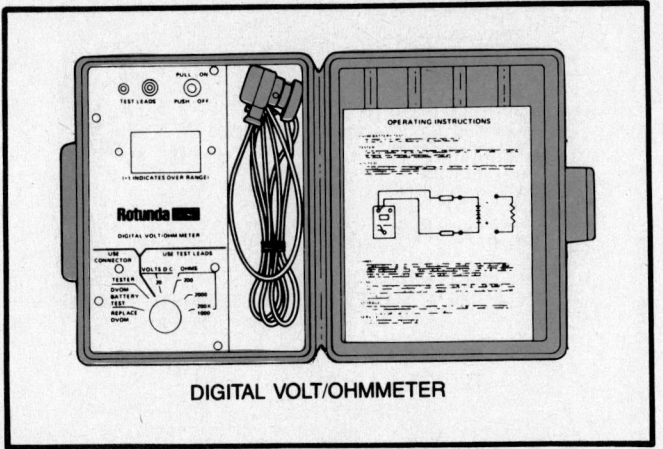

DIGITAL VOLT/OHMMETER

Digital volt-ohmmeter used to test Ford systems

many later models have an inductive ammeter pickup that clamps around the wire to simplify test connections. On some models, the ammeter also has a zero-center scale to allow testing of charging and starting systems without switching leads or polarity. A digital multimeter is a voltmeter, ammeter and ohmmeter combined in an instrument which gives a digital readout. These are often used when testing solid state circuits because of their high input impedence (usually 10 megohms or more).

The tach-dwell meter combines a tachometer and a dwell (cam angle) meter and is a specialized kind of voltmeter. The tachometer scale is marked to show engine speed in rpm and the dwell scale is marked to show degrees of distributor shaft rotation. In most electronic ignition systems, dwell is determined by the control unit, but the dwell meter can also be used to check the duty cycle (operation) of some electronic engine control systems. Some tach-dwell meters are powered by an internal battery, while others take their power from the car bat-

tery in use. The battery powered testers usually require calibration much like an ohmmeter before testing.

Special Test Equipment

A variety of diagnostic tools are available to help troubleshoot and repair computerized engine control systems. The most sophisticated of these devices are the console-type engine analyzers that usually occupy a garage service bay, but there are several types of aftermarket electronic testers available that will allow quick circuit tests of the engine control system by plugging directly into a special connector located in the engine compartment or under the dashboard. Several tool and equipment manufacturers offer simple, hand-held testers that measure various circuit voltage levels on command to check all system components for proper operation. Although these testers usually cost about $300–500, consider that the average computer control unit (or ECM) can cost just as much and the money saved by not replacing perfectly good sensors or components in an attempt to correct a problem could justify the purchase price of a special diagnostic tester the first time it's used.

These computerized testers can allow quick and easy test measurements while the engine is operating or while the car is being driven. In addition, the on-board computer memory can be read to access any stored trouble codes; in effect allowing the computer to tell you where it hurts and aid trouble diagnosis by pinpointing exactly which circuit or component is malfunctioning. In the same manner, repairs can be tested to make sure the problem has been corrected. The biggest advantage these special testers have is their relatively easy hookups that minimize or eliminate the chances of making the wrong connections and getting false voltage readings or damaging the computer accidentally.

NOTE: It should be remembered that these testers check voltage levels in circuits; they don't detect mechanical problems or failed components if the circuit voltage falls within the preprogrammed limits stored in the tester

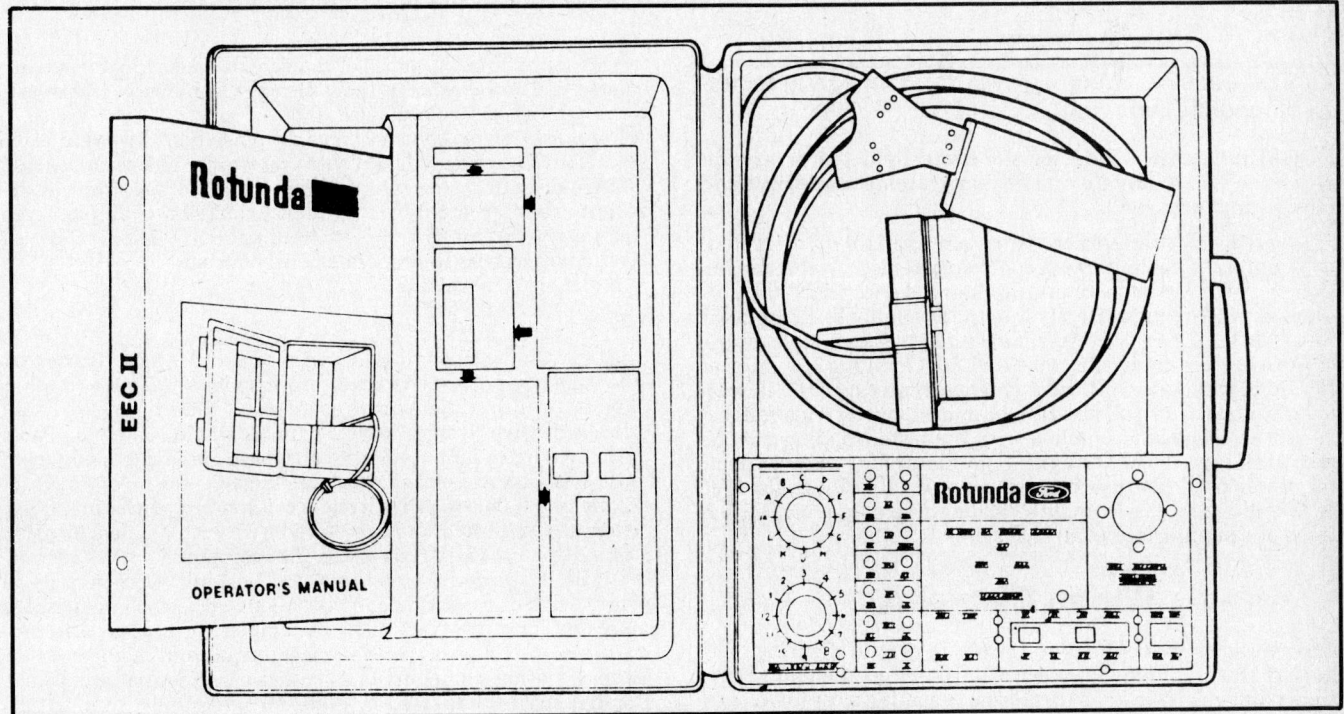

Typical electronic engine control tester used on Ford EEC systems

DIAGNOSTIC EQUIPMENT & SPECIAL TOOLS

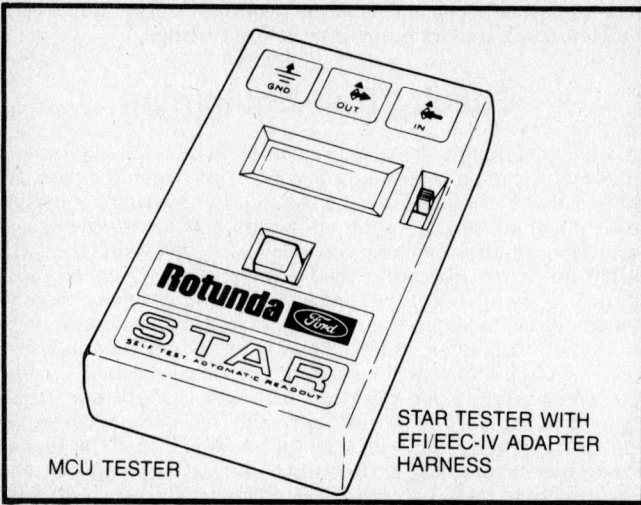

Self-Test and Automatic Readout (STAR) tester used for obtaining trouble codes from Ford MCU and EEC IV systems

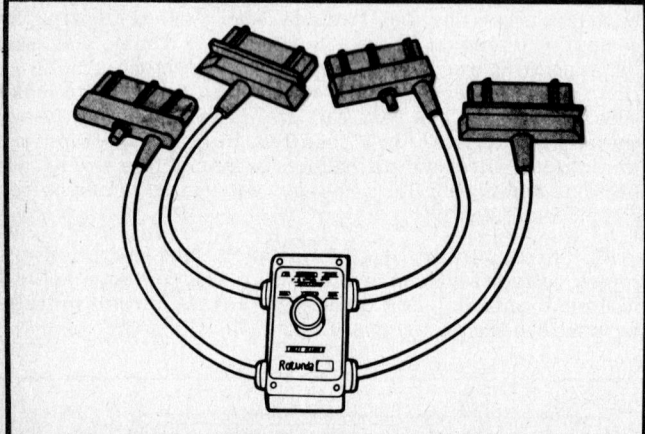

Typical adapter wiring harness for connecting tester to diagnostic terminal

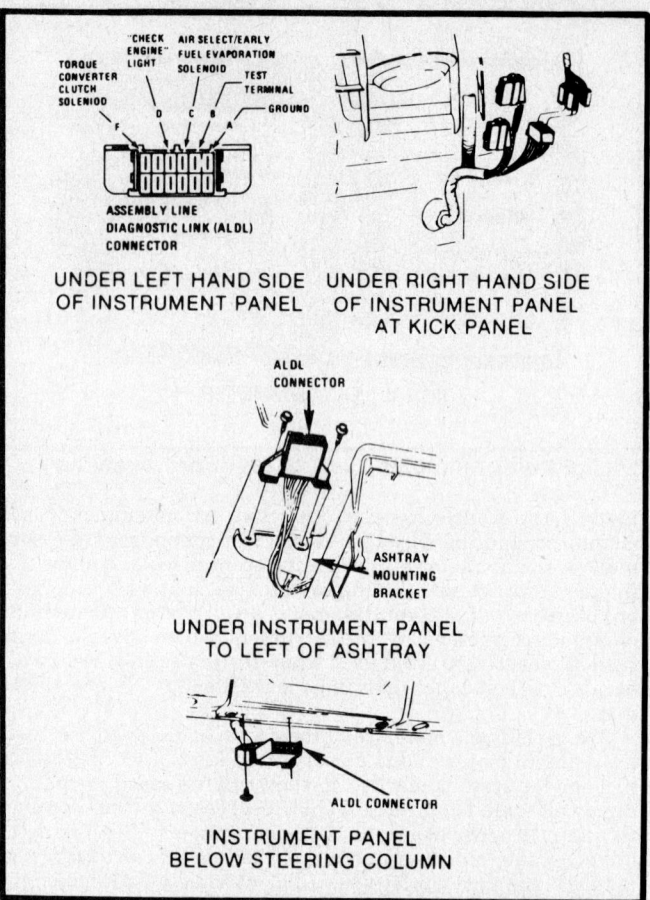

Typical diagnostic terminal locations on GM models. The diagnosis terminals are usually mounted under the dash or in the engine compartment

PROM unit. Also, most of the hand-held testes are designed to work only on one or two systems made by a specific manufacturer.

A variety of aftermarket testers are available to help diagnose different computerized control systems. Owatonna Tool Company (OTC), for example, markets a device called the OTC Monitor which plugs directly into the assembly line diagnostic link (ALDL). The OTC tester makes diagnosis a simple matter of pressing the correct buttons and, by changing the internal PROM or inserting a different diagnosis cartridge, it will work on any model from full size to subcompact, over a wide range of years. An adapter is supplied with the tester to allow connection to all types of ALDL links, regardless of the number of pin terminals used. By inserting an updated PROM into the OTC tester, it can be easily updated to diagnose any new modifications of computerized control systems.

Wiring Diagrams

The average automobile contains about ½ mile of wiring, with hundreds of individual connections. To protect the many wires from damage and to keep them from becoming a confusing tangle, they are organized into bundles, enclosed in plastic or taped together and called wire harnesses. Different wiring harnesses serve different parts of the vehicle. Individual wires are color-coded to help trace them through a harness where sections are hidden from view.

A loose or corroded connection or a replacement wire that is too small for the circuit will add extra resistance and an additional voltage drop to the circuit. A ten percent voltage drop can result in slow or erratic motor operation, for example, even though the circuit is complete. Automotive wiring or circuit conductors can be in any one of three forms:

1. Single strand wire
2. Multistrand wire
3. Printed circuitry

Single strand wire has a solid metal core and is usually used inside such components as alternators, motors, relays and other devices. Multistrand wire has a core made of many small strands of wire twisted together into a single conductor. Most of the wiring in an automotive electrical system is made up of multistrand wire, either as a single conductor or grouped together in a harness. All wiring is color-coded on the insulator, either as a solid color or as a colored wire with an identification stripe. A printed circuit is a thin film of copper or other conductor that is printed on an insulator backing. Occasionally, a printed circuit is sandwiched between two sheets of plastic for more protection and flexibility. A complete printed circuit, consisting of conductors, insulating material and connectors for lamps or other components is called a printed circuit board. Printed circuitry is used in place of individual wires or harnesses in places where space is limited, such as behind instrument panels.

Wire Gauge

Since computer-controlled automotive electrical systems are very sensitive to changes in resistance, the selection of properly sized wires is critical when systems are repaired. The wire gauge number is an expression of the cross section area of the conductor. The most common system for expressing wire size is the American Wire Gauge (AWG) system.

Wire cross section area is measured in circular mils. A mil is one-thousandth of an inch (0.001); a circular mil is the area of a circle one mil in diameter. For example, a conductor $\frac{1}{4}$ inch in diameter is 0.250 in. or 250 mils. The circular mil cross section area of the wire is 250 squared or 62,500 circular mils. Imported car models usually use metric wire gauge designations, which is simply the cross section area of the conductor in square millimeters (mm^2).

Gauge numbers are assigned to conductors of various cross section areas. As gauge number increases, area decreases and the conductor becomes smaller. A 5 gauge conductor is smaller than a 1 gauge conductor and a 10 gauge is smaller than a 5 gauge. As the cross section area of a conductor decreases, resistance increases and so does the gauge number. A conductor with a higher gauge number will carry less current than a conductor with a lower gauge number.

NOTE: Gauge wire size refers to the size of the conductor, not the size of the complete wire. It is possible to have two wires of the same gauge with different diameters because one may have thicker insulation than the other.

12 volt automotive electrical systems generally use 10, 12, 14, 16 and 18 gauge wire. Main power distribution circuits and larger accessories usually use 10 and 12 gauge wire. Battery cables are usually 4 or 6 gauge, although 1 and 2 gauge wires are occasionally used. Wire length must also be considered when making repairs to a circuit. As conductor length increases, so does resistance. An 18 gauge wire, for example, can carry a 10 amp load for 10 feet without excessive voltage drop; however if a 15 foot wire is required for the same 10 amp load, it must be a 16 gauge wire.

An electrical schematic shows the electrical current paths when a circuit is operating properly. It is essential to understand how a circuit works before trying to figure out why it doesn't. Schematics break the entire electrical system down into individual circuits and show only one particular circuit. In a schematic, no attempt is made to represent wiring and components as they physically appear on the vehicle; switches and other components are shown as simply as possible. Face views of harness connectors show the cavity or terminal locations in all multi-pin connectors to help locate test points. The component locator in Chapter One will help in determining the exact location of various components in a particular model of vehicle. If you need to backprobe a connector while it is on the component, the order of the terminals must be mentally reversed. The wire color code can help in this situation, as well as a keyway, lock tab or other reference mark.

Wiring Repairs

Soldering is a quick, efficient method of joining metals permananently. Everyone who has the occasion to make wiring repairs should know how to solder. Electrical connections that are soldered are far less likely to come apart and will conduct electricity much better than connections that are only "pig-tailed" together. The most popular (and preferred) method of soldering is with an electrical soldering gun. Soldering irons are available in many sizes and wattage ratings. Irons with higher wattage ratings deliver higher temperatures and recover lost heat faster. A small soldering iron rated for no more than 50 watts is recommended, especially on electrical systems where excess heat can damage the components being soldered. There are three ingredients necessary for successful soldering; proper flux, good solder and sufficient heat. A soldering flux is necessary to clean the metal of tarnish, prepare it for soldering and to enable the solder to spread into tiny crevices. When soldering, always use a resin flux or resin core solder which is non-corrosive and will not attract moisture once the job is finished. Other types of flux (acid core) will leave a residue tht will attract moisture and cause the wires to corrode. Tin is a unique metal with a low melting point. In a molten state, it dissolves and alloys easily with many metals. Solder is made by mixing tin with lead. The most common proportions are 40/60, 50/50 and 60/40, with the percentage of tin listed first. Low priced solders usually contain less tin, making them very difficult for a beginner to use because more heat is required to melt the solder. A common solder is 40/60 which is well suited for

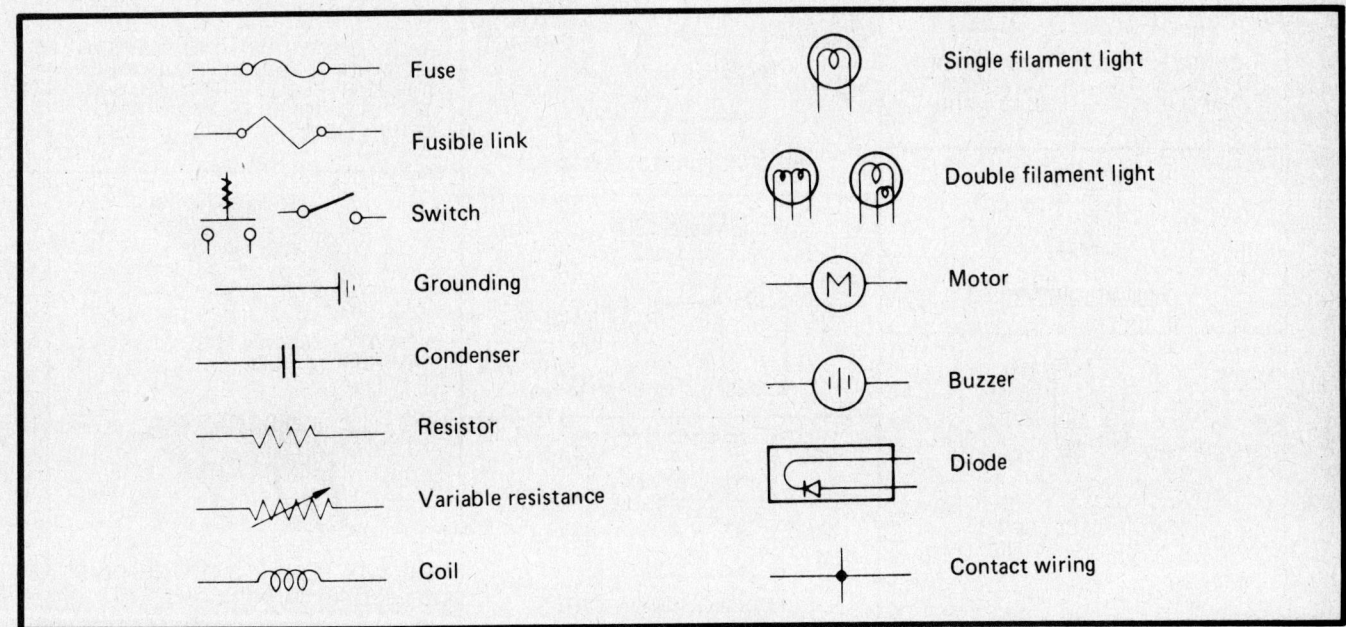

Examples of various electrical symbols found on wiring diagrams

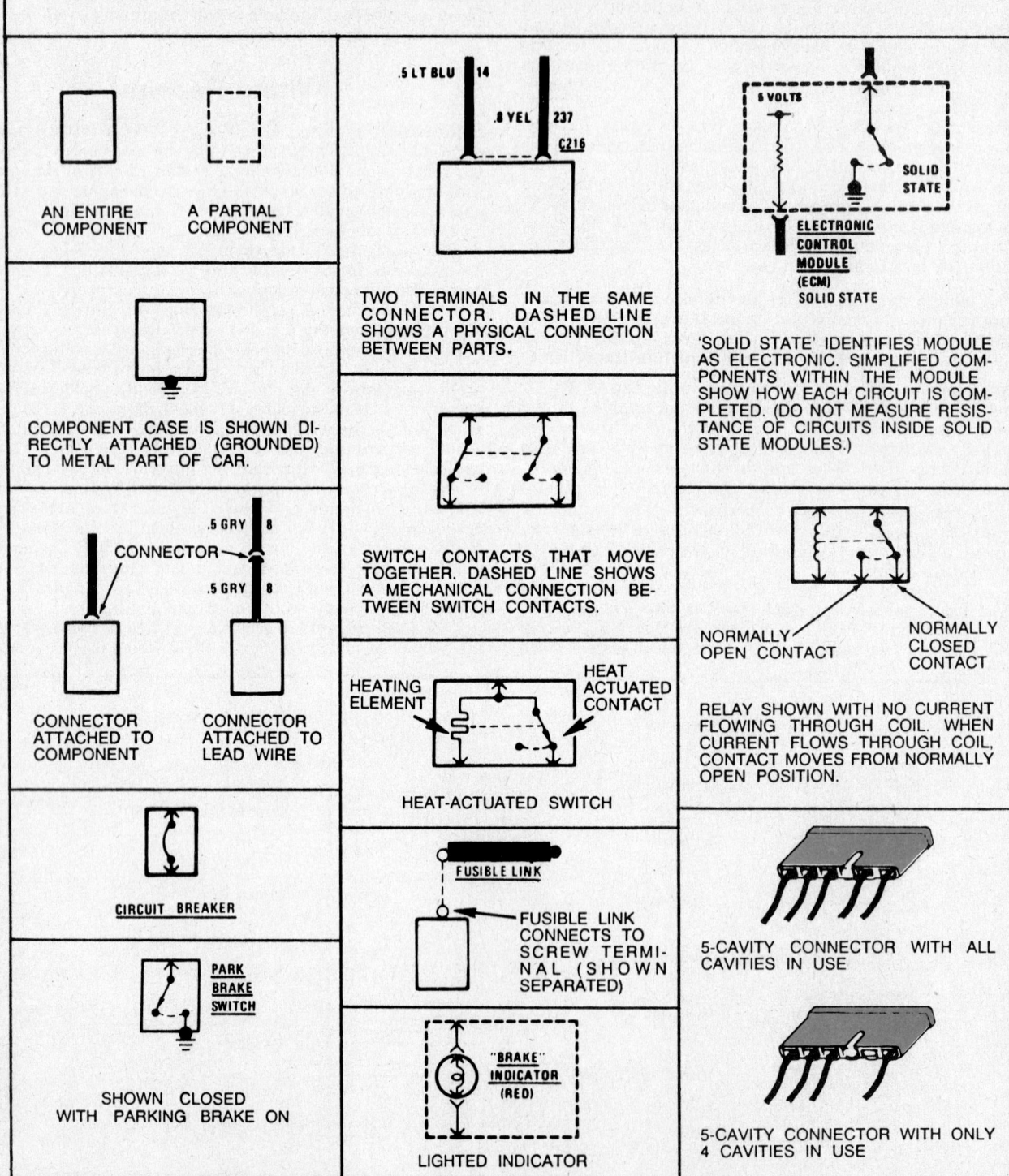

COMMON SYMBOLS FOR AUTOMOTIVE COMPONENTS USED IN SCHEMATIC DIAGRAMS

Automotive service manuals use schematic diagrams to show how electrical and other types of components work, and how such components are connected to make circuits. Components that are shown whole are represented in full lines in a rectangular shape, and are identified by name; where only a part of a component is shown in a schematic diagram, the rectangular shape is outlined with a dashed line.

WIRE IS GROUNDED, AND GROUND IS NUMBERED FOR REFERENCE ON COMPONENT LOCATION TABLE.

WIRE IS INDIRECTLY CONNECTED TO GROUND. (WIRE MAY HAVE ONE OR MORE SPLICES BEFORE IT IS GROUNDED.)

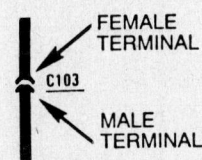

CONNECTOR REFERENCE NO. IS LISTED IN COMPONENT LOCATION TABLE, WHICH ALSO SHOWS TOTAL NO. OF TERMINALS POSSIBLE: C103 (6 CAVITIES).

CIRCUITRY IDENTIFICATION

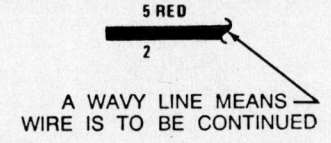

A WAVY LINE MEANS WIRE IS TO BE CONTINUED

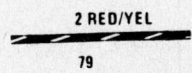

WIRE INSULATION IS ONE COLOR, WITH ANOTHER COLOR STRIPE (EXAMPLE: RED COLOR, WITH YELLOW STRIPE).

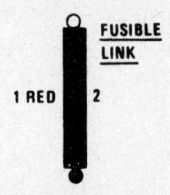

FUSIBLE LINK SHOWS WIRE SIZE AND INSULATION COLOR.

CURRENT PATH IS CONTINUED AS LABLED. THE ARROW SHOWS THE DIRECTION OF CURRENT FLOW, AND IS REPEATED WHERE CURRENT PATH CONTINUES.

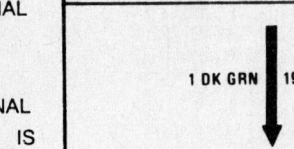

A WIRE IS SHOWN WHICH CONNECTS TO ANOTHER CIRCUIT. THE WIRE IS SHOWN AGAIN ON THAT CIRCUIT.

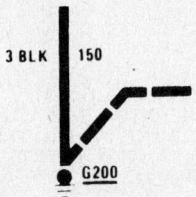

THE DASHED LINE INDICATES THAT THE CIRCUITRY IS NOT SHOWN IN COMPLETE DETAIL BUT IS COMPLETE ON THE INDICATED PAGE.

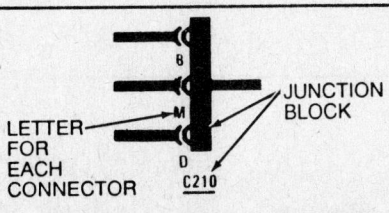

3 CONNECTORS ARE SHOWN CONNECTED TOGETHER AT A JUNCTION BLOCK. FOURTH WIRE IS SOLDERED TO COMMON CONNECTION ON BLOCK.

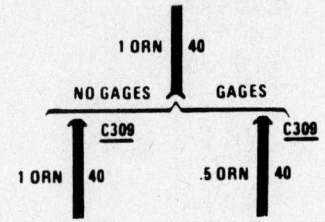

WIRE CHOICES FOR OPTIONS OR DIFFERENT MODELS ARE SHOWN AND LABLED.

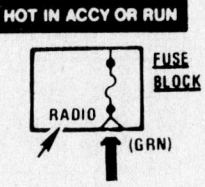

CURRENT CAN FLOW ONLY IN THE DIRECTION OF THE ARROW

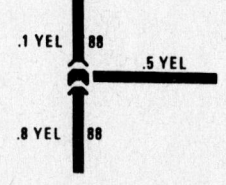

3 WIRES ARE SHOWN CONNECTED TOGETHER WITH A PIGGYBACK CONNECTOR

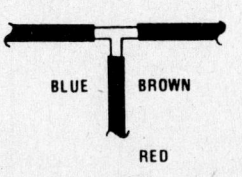

HOSE COLORS ARE SHOWN AT A VACUUM JUNCTION.

359

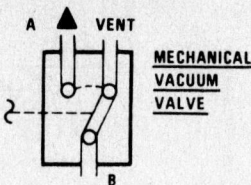

VACUUM SOURCE

MECHANICAL VACUUM VALVE

VACUUM SOURCE

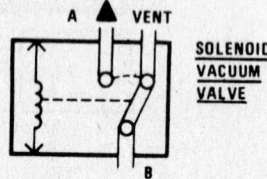

SOLENOID VACUUM VALVE

2-POSITION VACUUM MOTORS

IN THE 'AT REST' POSITION SHOWN, THE VALVE SEALS PORT 'A' AND VENTS PORT 'B' TO THE ATMOSPHERE. WHEN THE VALVE IS MOVED TO THE 'OPERATED' POSITION, VACUUM FROM PORT 'A' IS CONNECTED TO PORT 'B'. THE SOLENOID VACUUM VALVE USES THE SOLENOID TO MOVE THE VALVE.

VACUUM MOTORS OPERATE LIKE ELECTRICAL SOLENOIDS, MECHANICALLY PUSHING OR PULLING A SHAFT BETWEEN TWO FIXED POSITIONS. WHEN VACUUM IS APPLIED, THE SHAFT IS PULLED IN. WHEN NO VACUUM IS APPLIED, THE SHAFT IS PUSHED ALL THE WAY OUT BY A SPRING.

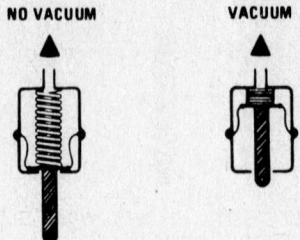

NO VACUUM   VACUUM

SINGLE-DIAPHRAGM MOTOR

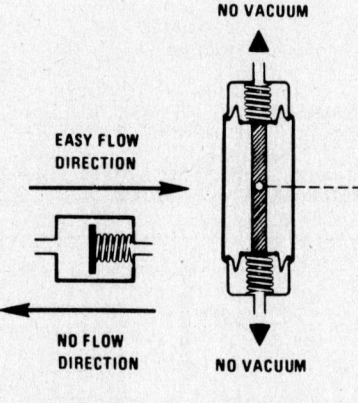

NO VACUUM

EASY FLOW DIRECTION

NO FLOW DIRECTION

NO VACUUM

VACUUM CHECK VALVE

DOUBLE DIAPHRAGM MOTOR

DOUBLE-DIAPHRAGM MOTORS CAN BE OPERATED BY VACUUM IN TWO DIRECTIONS. WHEN THERE IS NO VACUUM, THE MOTOR IS IN THE CENTER 'AT REST' POSITION.

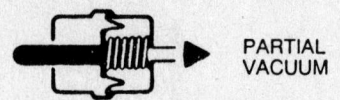

PARTIAL VACUUM

SERVO MOTOR

SOME VACUUM MOTORS, SUCH AS THE SERVO MOTOR IN THE CRUISE CONTROL, CAN POSITION THE ACTUATING ARM AT ANY POSITION BETWEEN FULLY EXTENDED AND FULLY RETRACTED. THE SERVO IS OPERATED BY A CONTROL VALVE THAT APPLIES VARYING AMOUNTS OF VACUUM TO THE MOTOR. THE HIGHER THE VACUUM LEVEL, THE GREATER THE RETRACTION OF THE MOTOR ARM. SERVO MOTORS WORK LIKE THE TWO-POSITION MOTORS; THE ONLY DIFFERENCE IS IN THE WAY THE VACUUM IS APPLIED. SERVO MOTORS ARE GENERALLY LARGER AND PROVIDE A CALIBRATED CONTROL.

METRIC SIZE	AWG SIZES
.22	24
.35	22
.5	20
.8	18
1.0	16
2.0	14
3.0	12
5.0	10
8.0	8
13.0	6
19.0	4
32.0	2

Wire Size Conversion Table

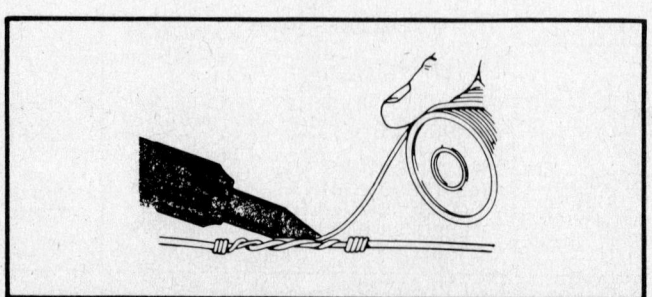

Proper soldering method. Allow the soldering iron to heat the wire first, then apply the solder as shown

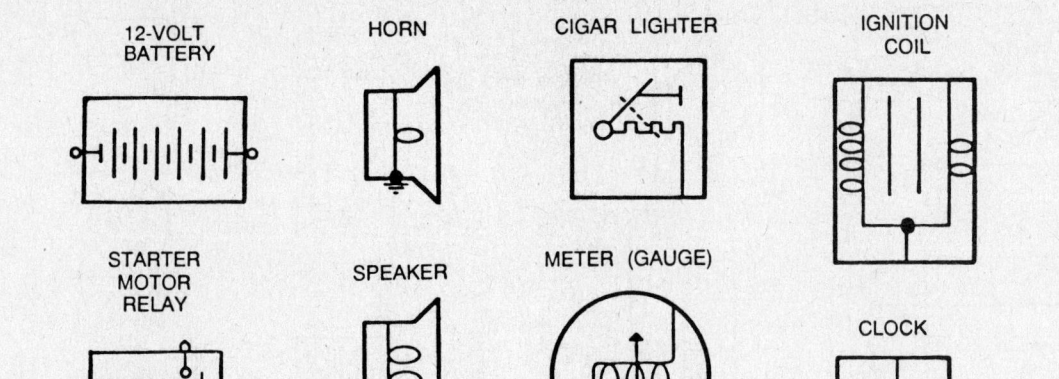

12-VOLT BATTERY

HORN

CIGAR LIGHTER

IGNITION COIL

BUZZER

STARTER MOTOR RELAY

SPEAKER

METER (GAUGE)

CLOCK

WIRE SHIELD

BULBS

SMALL SINGLE FILAMENT

 INDICATORS
 SIDE MARKERS
 LICENSE
 COURTESY
 ILLUMINATION

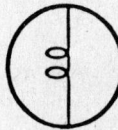

LARGE SINGLE FILAMENT

o CORNERING
o HIGH BEAM
o BACKUP

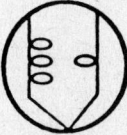

DUAL FILAMENT

o STOP, PARK,
o TURN SIGNAL
o LOW BEAM
o RUNNING

MOTORS

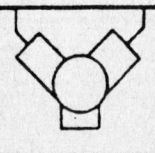

SINGLE-SPEED BIDIRECTIONAL

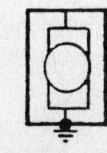

SINGLE-SPEED UNIDIRECTIONAL

TWO-SPEED UNIDIRECTIONAL

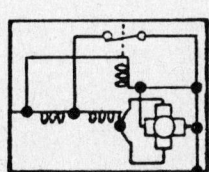

STARTER MOTOR (TYPICAL) FOUR-POLE UNIDIRECTIONAL

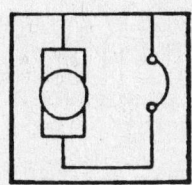

SINGLE-SPEED UNIDIRECTIONAL OR BIDIRECTIONAL DEPENDING ON EXTERNAL CIRCUITRY WITH CIRCUIT BREAKER

Tinning the soldering iron before use

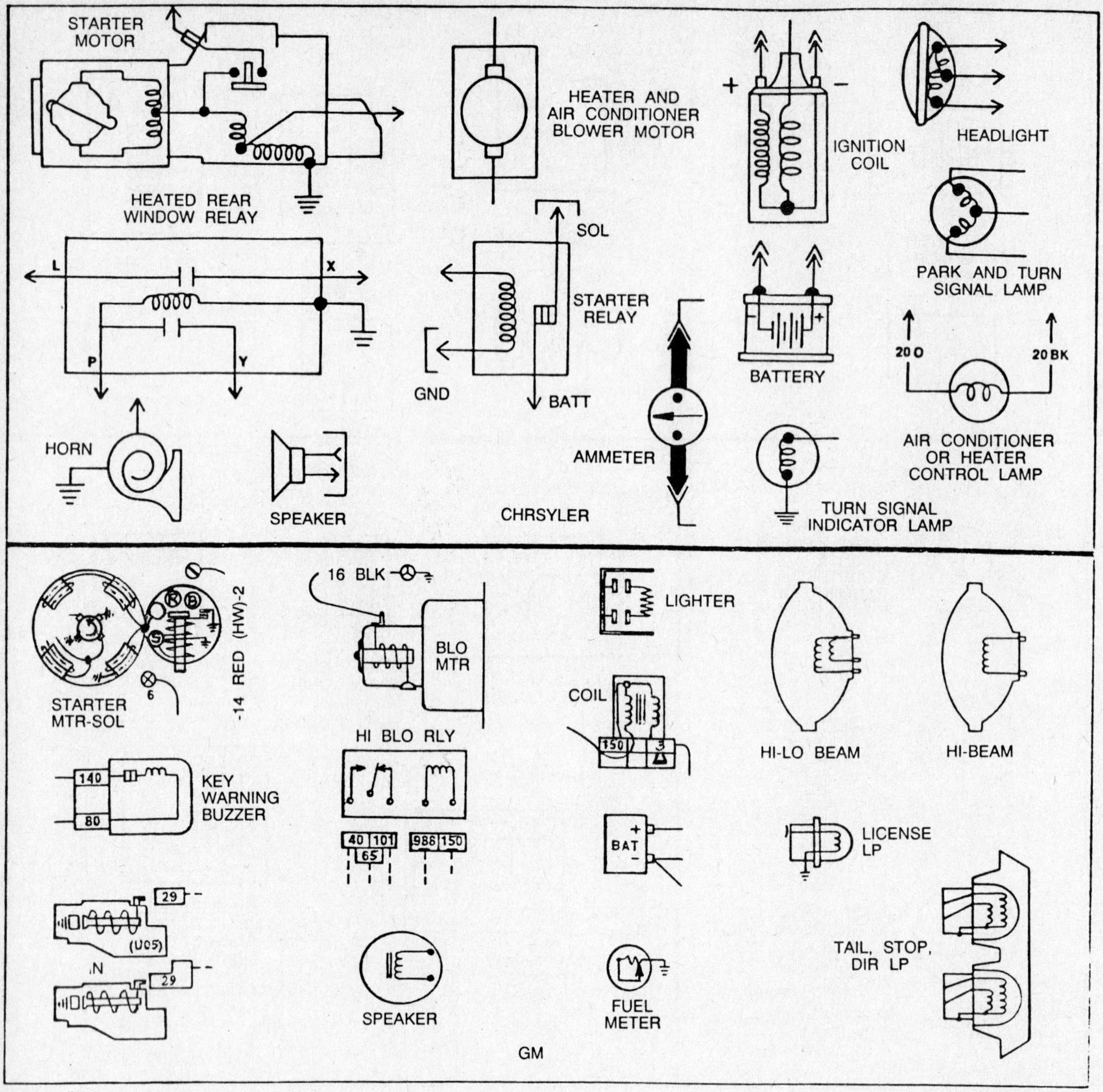

STARTER MOTOR

HEATED REAR WINDOW RELAY

L

X

P

Y

HORN

SPEAKER

HEATER AND AIR CONDITIONER BLOWER MOTOR

SOL

STARTER RELAY

GND

BATT

AMMETER

CHRSYLER

+   IGNITION COIL   −

BATTERY

TURN SIGNAL INDICATOR LAMP

HEADLIGHT

PARK AND TURN SIGNAL LAMP

20 O   20 BK

AIR CONDITIONER OR HEATER CONTROL LAMP

STARTER MTR-SOL

6

−14 RED (HW)-2

KEY WARNING BUZZER

140

80

(U05)

N

29

29

16 BLK

BLO MTR

HI BLO RLY

40 101 65   986 150

SPEAKER

LIGHTER

COIL

150   5

BAT + −

FUEL METER

HI-LO BEAM

HI-BEAM

LICENSE LP

TAIL, STOP, DIR LP

GM

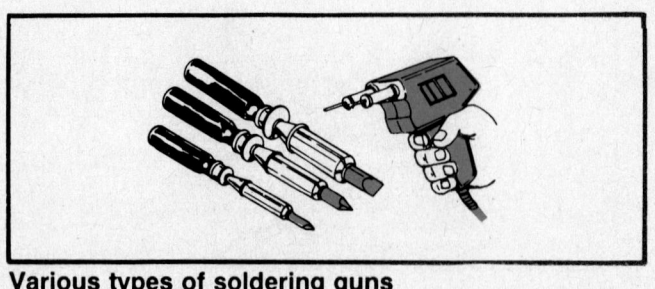

Various types of soldering guns

all-around general use, but 60/40 melts easier, has more tin for a better joint and is preferred for electrical work.

Soldering Techniques

Successful soldering requires that the metals to be joined be heated to a temperature that will melt the solder (usually 360–460°F). Contrary to popular belief, the purpose of the soldering iron is not to melt the solder itself, but to heat the parts being soldered to a temperature high enough to melt the solder when it is touched to the work. Melting flux-cored solder on the soldering iron will usually destroy the effectiveness of the flux.

NOTE: Soldering tips are made of copper for good heat conductivity, but must be "tinned" regularly for quick transference of heat to the project and to prevent the solder from sticking to the iron. To "tin" the iron, simply heat it and touch the flux-cored solder to the tip; the solder will flow over the hot tip. Wipe the excess off with a clean rag, but be careful as the iron will be hot.

After some use, the tip may become pitted. If so, simply dress the tip smooth with a smooth file and "tin" the tip again. An old saying holds that "metals well cleaned are half soldered." Flux-cored solder will remove oxides but rust, bits of insulation and oil or grease must be removed with a wire brush or emery cloth. For maximum strength in soldered parts, the joint must start off clean and tight. Weak joints will result in gaps too wide for the solder to bridge.

If a separate soldering flux is used, it should be brushed or swabben on only those areas that are to be soldered. Most solders contain a core of flux and separate fluxing is unnecessary. Hold the work to be soldered firmly. It is best to solder on a wooden board, because a metal vise will only rob the piece to be soldered of heat and make it difficult to melt the solder. Hold the soldering tip with the broadest face against the work to be soldered. Apply solder under the tip close to the work, using enough solder to give a heavy film between the iron and the piece being soldered, while moving slowly and making sure the solder melts properly. Keep the work level or the solder will run to the lowest part and favor the thicker parts, because these require more heat to melt the solder. If the soldering tip overheats (the solder coating on the face of the tip burns up), it should be retinned. Once the soldering is completed, let the soldered joint stand until cool. Tape and seal all soldered wire splices after the repair has cooled.

Wire Harness and Connectors

The on-board computer (ECM) wire harness electrically connects the control unit to the various solenoids, switches and sensors used by the control system. Most connectors in the engine compartment or otherwise exposed to the elements are protected against moisture and dirt which could create oxidation and deposits on the terminals. This protection is important because of the very low voltage and current levels used by the computer and sensors. All connectors have a lock which se-

WIRE HARNESS REPAIR PROCEDURES

Condition	Location	Correction
Non-continuity	Using the electric wiring diagram and the wiring harness diagram as a guideline, check the continuity of the circuit in question by using a tester, and check for breaks, loose connector couplings, or loose terminal crimp contacts.	**Breaks**—Reconnect the point of the break by using solder. If the wire is too short and the connection is impossible, extend it by using a wire of the same or larger size. Solder. Be careful concerning the size of wire used for the extension. **Loose couplings**—Hold the connector securely, and insert it until there is a definite joining of the coupling. If the connector is equipped with a locking mechanism, insert the connector until it is locked securely. **Loose terminal crimp contacts**—Remove approximately 2 in. (5mm) of the insulation covering from the end of the wire, crimp the terminal contact by using a pair of pliers, and then, in addition, complete the repair by soldering.
	Crimp by using pliers. Solder.	
Short-circuit	Using the electric wiring diagram and the wiring harness diagram as a guideline, check the entire circuit for pinched wires.	Remove the pinched portion, and then repair any breaks in the insulation covering with tape. Repair breaks of the wire by soldering.
Loose terminal	Pull the wiring lightly from the connector. A special terminal removal tool may be necessary for complete removal.	Raise the terminal catch pin, and then insert it until a definite clicking sound is heard. Catch pin

Note: There is the chance of short circuits being caused by insulation damage at soldered points. To avoid this possibility, wrap all splices with electrical tape and use a layer of silicone to seal the connection against moisture. Incorrect repairs can cause malfunctions by creating excessive resistance in a circuit.

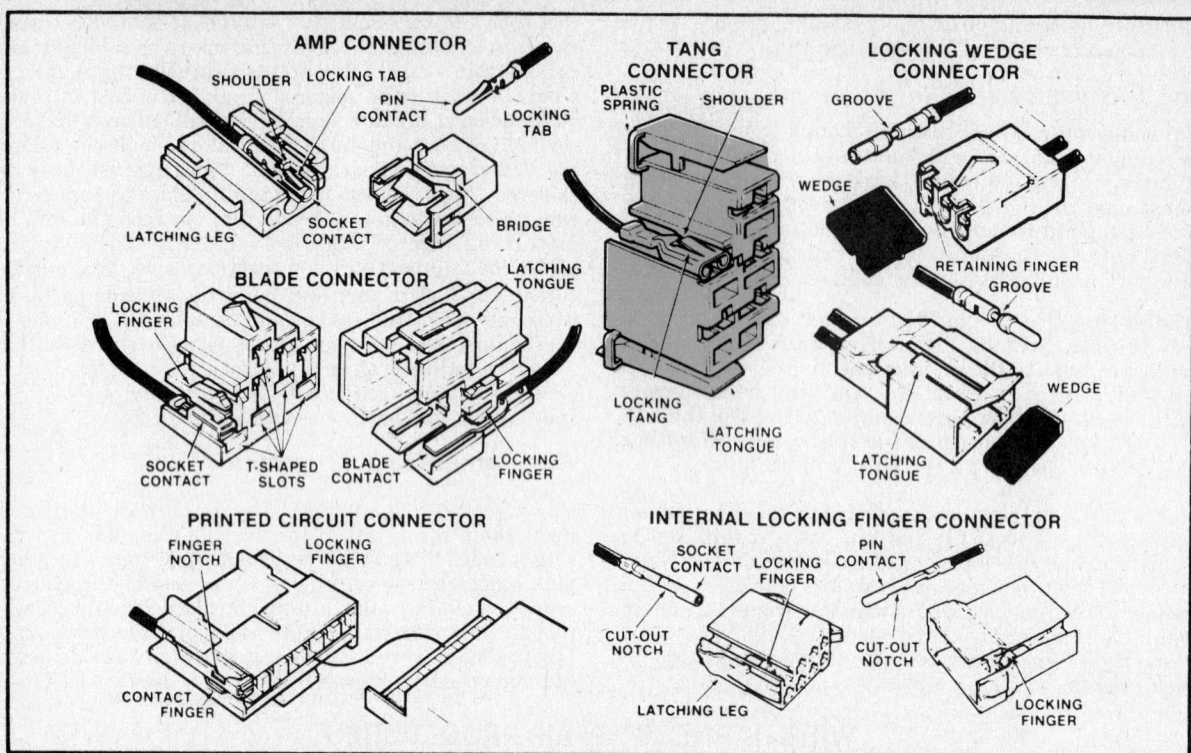

Various types of wiring harness connectors

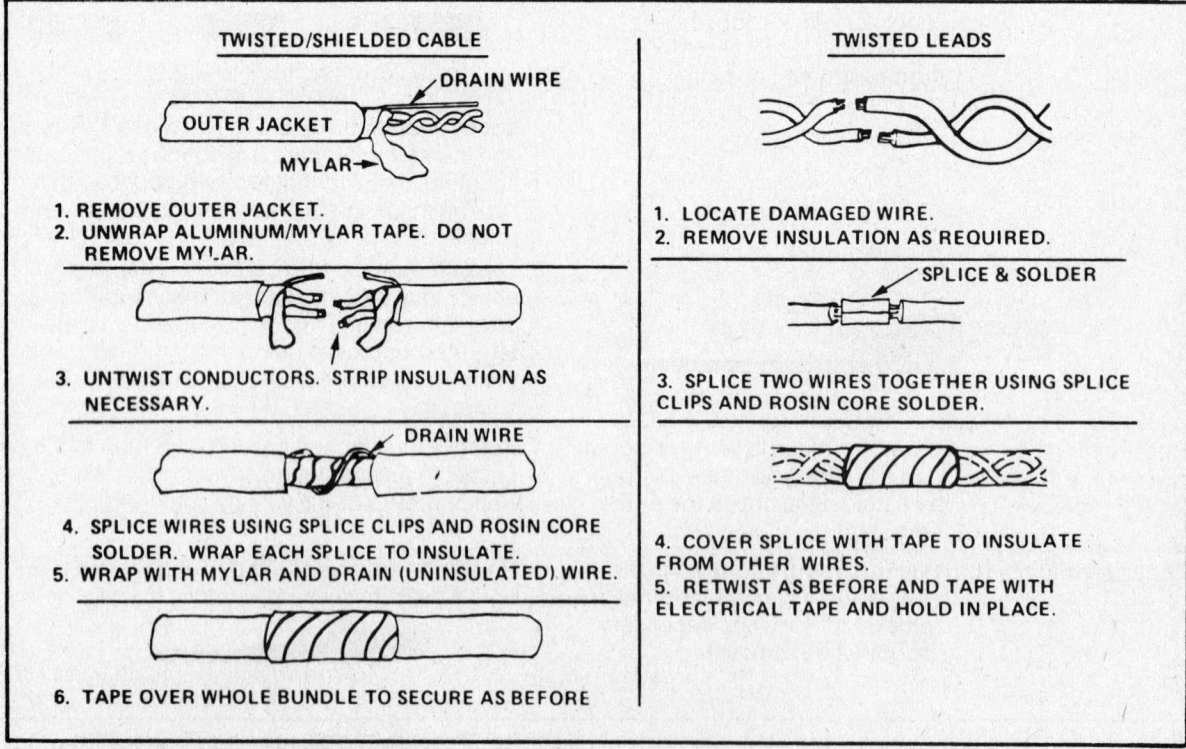

Typical wire harness repair methods

properly seated and all of the sealing rings in place when connecting leads. On some models, a hinge-type flap provides a backup or secondary locking feature for the terminals. Most secondary locks are used to improve the connector reliability by retaining the terminals if the small terminal lock tangs are not positioned properly.

Molded-on connectors require complete replacement of the connection. This means splicing a new connector assembly into the harness. All splices in on-board computer systems should be soldered to insure proper contact. Use care when probing the connections or replacing terminals in them as it is possible to short between opposite terminals. If this happens to the wrong terminal pair, it is possible to damage certain components. Always use jumper wires between connectors for circuit checking and never probe through weatherproof seals.

Open circuits are often difficult to locate by sight because corrosion or terminal misalignment are hidden by the connectors. Merely wiggling a connector on a sensor or in the wiring harness may correct the open circuit condition. This should always be considered when an open circuit or a failed sensor is indicated. Intermittent problems may also be caused by oxidized or loose connections. When using a circuit tester for diagnosis, always probe connections from the wire side. Be careful not to damage sealed connectors with test probes.

All wiring harnesses should be replaced with identical parts, using the same gauge wire and connectors. When signal wires are spliced into a harness, use wire with high temperature insures the male and female terminals together, with a secondary lock holding the seal and terminal into the connector. Both terminal locks must be released when disconnecting ECM connectors.

These special connectors are weather-proof and all repairs require the use of a special terminal and the tool required to service it. This tool is used to remove the pin and sleeve terminals. If removal is attempted with an ordinary pick, there is a good chance that the terminal will be bent or deformed. Unlike standard blade type terminals, these terminals cannot be straightened once they are bent. Make certain that the connectors are sulation only. With the low voltage and current levels found in the system, it is important that the best possible connection at all wire splices be made by soldering the splices together. It is seldom necessary to replace a complete harness. If replacement is necessary, pay close attention to insure proper harness routing. Secure the harness with suitable plastic wire clamps to prevent vibrations from causing the harness to wear in spots or contact any hot components.

NOTE: Weatherproof connectors cannot be replaced with standard connectors. Instructions are provided

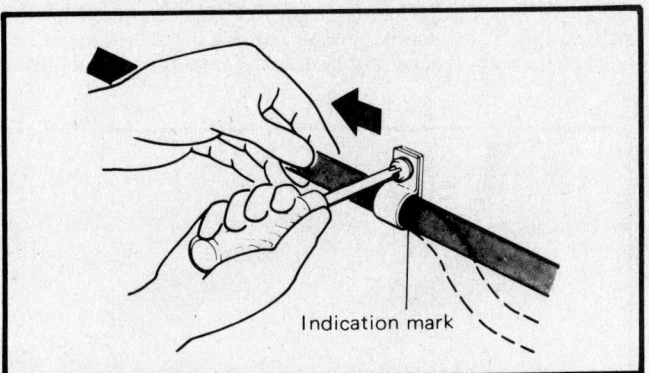

Secure the wiring harness at the indication marks, if used, to prevent vibrations from causing wear and a possible short

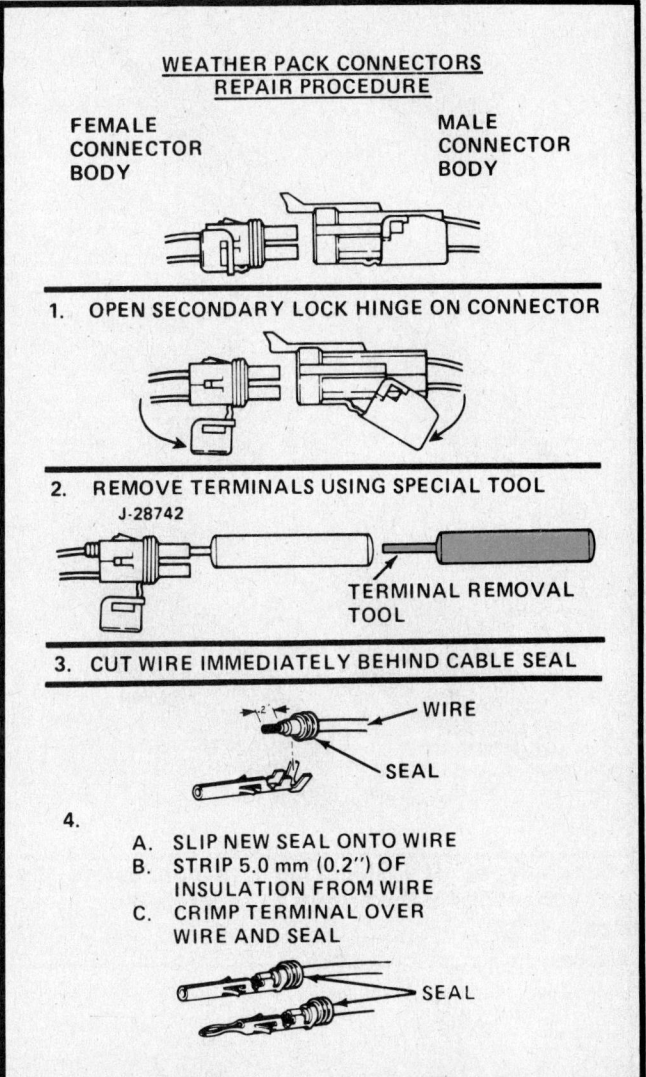

Repairing GM Weatherpak connectors. Note special terminal removal tools

with replacement connector and terminal packages. Some wire harnesses have mounting indicators (usually pieces of colored tape) to mark where the harness is to be secured.

In making wiring repairs, it's important that you always replace damaged wires with wires that are the same gauge as the wire being replaced. The heavier the wire, the smaller the gauge number. Wires are color-coded to aid in identification and whenever possible the same color coded wire should be used for replacement. A wire stripping and crimping tool is necessary to install solderless terminal connectors. Test all crimps by pulling on the wires; it should not be possible to pull the wires out of a good crimp.

Wires which are open, exposed or otherwise damaged are repaired by simple splicing. Where possible, if the wiring harness is accessible and the damaged place in the wire can be located, it is best to open the harness and check for all possible damage. In an inaccessible harness, the wire must be bypassed with a new insert, usually taped to the outside of the old harness.

When replacing fusible links, be sure to use fusible link wire, NOT ordinary automotive wire. Make sure the fusible segment is of the same gauge and construction as the one being replaced and double the stripped end when crimping the terminal con-

DIAGNOSTIC EQUIPMENT & SPECIAL TOOLS

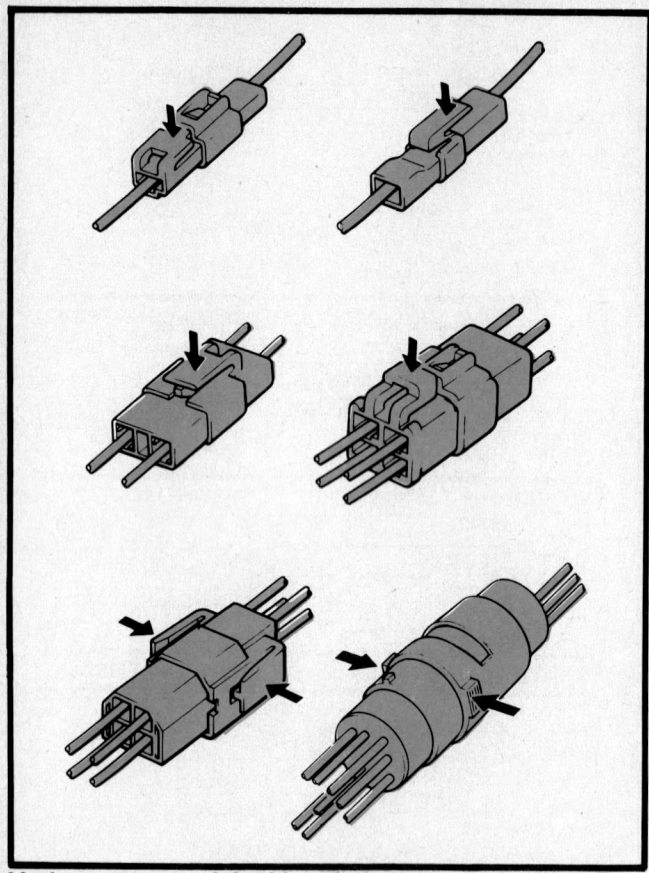

Various types of locking harness connectors. Depress the locks at the arrows to separate the connectors

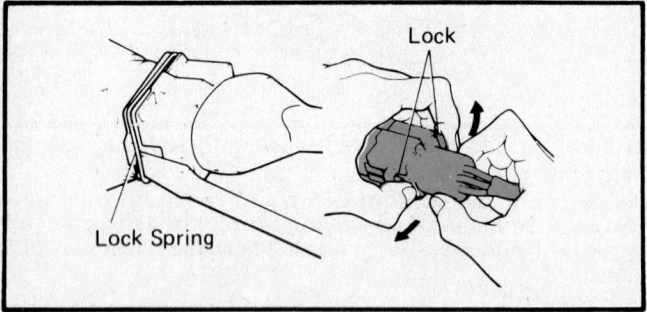

Some electrical connectors use a lock spring instead of the molded locking tabs

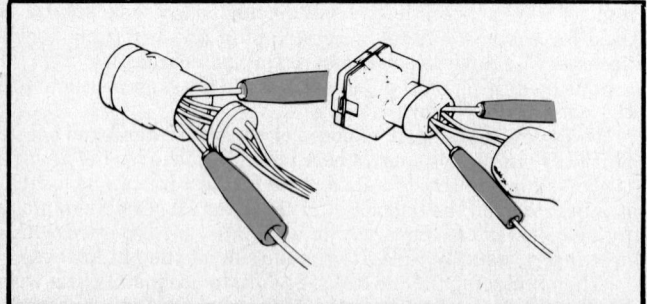

Correct method of testing weatherproof connectors. Do not pierce connector seals with test probes

nector for a good contact. The melted (open) fusible link segment of the wiring harness should be cut off as close to the harness as possible, then a new segment spliced in as described. In the case of a damaged fusible link that feeds two harness wires, the harness connections should be replaced with two fusible link wires so that each circuit will have its own separate protection.

NOTE: Most of the problems caused in the wiring harness are due to bad ground connections. Always check all vehicle ground connections for corrosion or looseness before performing any power feed checks to eliminate the chance of a bad ground affecting the circuit.

Repairing Hard Shell Connectors

Unlike molded connectors, the terminal contacts in hard shell connectors can be replaced. Weatherproof hard-shell connectors with the leads molded into the shell have non-replaceable terminal ends. Replacement usually involves the use of a special terminal removal tool that depress the locking tangs (barbs) on the connector terminal and allow the connector to be removed from the rear of the shell. The connector shell should be replaced if it shows any evidence of burning, melting, cracks, or breaks. Replace individual terminals that are burnt, corroded, distorted or loose.

NOTE: The insulation crimp must be tight to prevent the insulation from sliding back on the wire when the wire is pulled. The insulation must be visibly compressed under the crimp tabs, and the ends of the crimp should be turned in for a firm grip on the insulation.

The wire crimp must be made with all wire strands inside the crimp. The terminal must be fully compressed on the wire strands with the ends of the crimp tabs turned in to make a firm grip on the wire. Check all connections with an ohmmeter to insure a good contact. There should be no measurable resistance between the wire and the terminal when connected.

Mechanical Test Equipment

VACUUM GAUGE

Most gauges are graduated in inches of mercury (in. Hg), although a device called a manometer reads vacuum in inches of water (in. H_2O). The normal vacuum reading usually varies between 18 and 22 in. Hg at sea level. To test engine vacuum, the vacuum gauge must be connected to a source of manifold vacuum. Many engines have a plug in the intake manifold which can be removed and replaced with an adapter fitting. Connect the vacuum gauge to the fitting with a suitable rubber hose or, if no manifold plug is available, connect the vacuum gauge to any device using manifold vacuum, such as EGR valves, etc. The vacuum gauge can be used to determine if enough vacuum is reaching a component to allow its actuation.

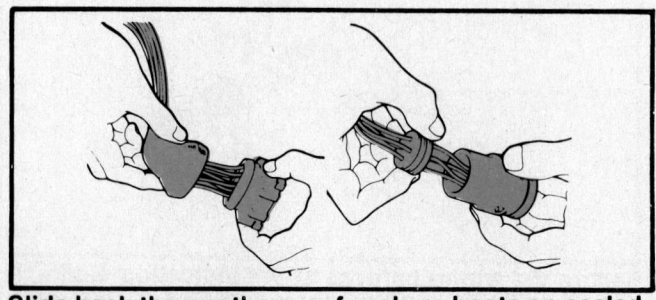

Slide back the weatherproof seals or boots on sealed terminals for testing

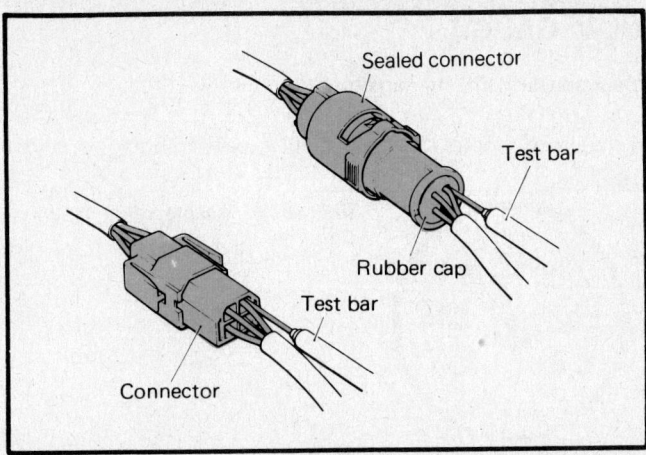

Probe all connectors from the wire side when testing

Sealed connector
Test bar
Rubber cap
Test bar
Connector

HAND VACUUM PUMP

Small, hand-held vacuum pumps come in a variety of designs. Most have a built-in vacuum gauge and allow the component to be tested without removing it from the vehicle. Operate the pump lever or plunger to apply the correct amount of vacuum required for the test specified in the diagnosis routines. The level of vacuum in inches of Mercury (in. Hg) is indicated on the pump gauge. For some testing, an additional vacuum gauge may be necessary.

Intake manifold vacuum is used to operate various systems and devices on late model cars. To correctly diagnose and solve problems in vacuum control systems, a vacuum source is necessary for testing. In some cases, vacuum can be taken from the intake manifold when the engine is running, but vacuum is normally provided by a hand vacuum pump. These hand vacuum pumps have a built-in vacuum gauge that allow testing while the device is still attached to the car. For some tests, an additional vacuum gauge may be necessary.

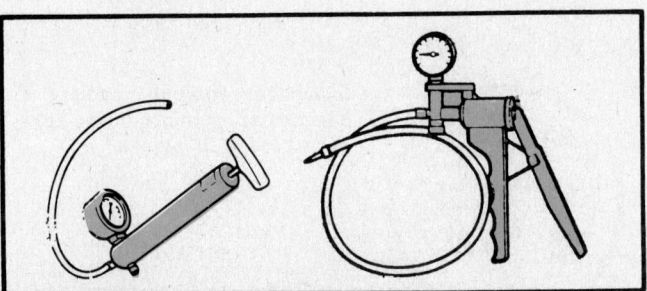

Typical hand vacuum pumps

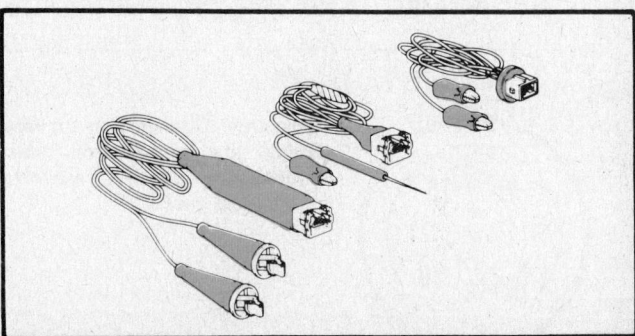

Special purpose test connections for use on some systems made up from factory connectors and jumper wires

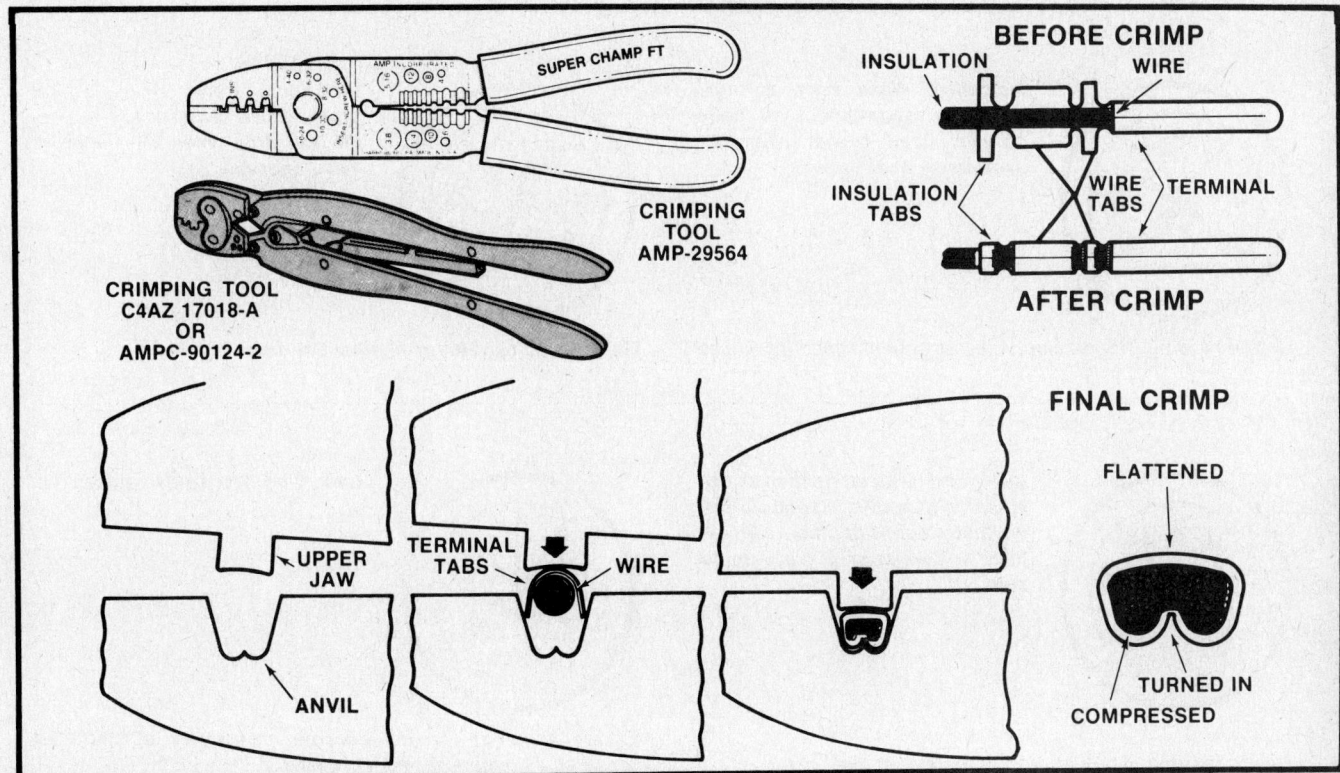

Correct method of crimping terminals with special tool

CRIMPING TOOL AMP-29564
SUPER CHAMP FT
CRIMPING TOOL C4AZ 17018-A OR AMPC-90124-2

BEFORE CRIMP
INSULATION
WIRE
INSULATION TABS
WIRE TABS
TERMINAL
AFTER CRIMP

UPPER JAW
TERMINAL TABS
WIRE
ANVIL

FINAL CRIMP
FLATTENED
TURNED IN
COMPRESSED

USING A VACUUM GAUGE

White needle = steady needle   *Dark needle = drifting needle*

The vacuum gauge is one of the most useful and easy-to-use diagnostic tools. It is inexpensive, easy to hook up, and provides valuable information about the condition of your engine.

Indication: Normal engine in good condition

Gauge reading: Steady, from 17–22 in./Hg.

Indication: Sticking valve or ignition miss

Gauge reading: Needle fluctuates from 15–20 in./Hg. at idle

Indication: Late ignition or valve timing, low compression, stuck throttle valve, leaking carburetor or manifold gasket.

Gauge reading: Low (15–20 in./Hg.) but steady

Indication: Improper carburetor adjustment, or minor intake leak at carburetor or manifold

Gauge reading: Drifting needle

Indication: Weak valve springs, worn valve stem guides, or leaky cylinder head gasket (vibrating excessively at all speeds).

Gauge reading: Needle fluctuates as engine speed increases

Indication: Burnt valve or improper valve clearance. The needle will drop when the defective valve operates.

Gauge reading: Steady needle, but drops regularly

Indication: Choked muffler or obstruction in system. Speed up the engine. Choked muffler will exhibit a slow drop of vacuum to zero.

Gauge reading: Gradual drop in reading at idle

Indication: Worn valve guides

Gauge reading: Needle vibrates excessively at idle, but steadies as engine speed increases

ELECTRONIC DISPLAYS AND INSTRUMENTATION

Application

AMERICAN MOTORS CORPORATION INSTRUMENT CLUSTER APPLICATION

NOTE: Certain forms of electronic controls are used, but digital instrument clusters are not.

1982-86 Eagle
1982-83 Concord
1982-83 Spirit

CHRYSLER CORPORATION ELECTRONIC INSTRUMENT CLUSTER APPLICATION

1982-83 Chrysler Imperial
1984 Chrysler LeBaron
1984 Chrysler E Class
1984-86 Chrysler New Yorker
1984-86 Chrysler Laser
1985-86 Chrysler LeBaron GTS
1984-86 Dodge 600
1984-86 Dodge Daytona
1985-86 Dodge Lancer
1984-86 Plymouth Carvelle (CANADA)
1985-86 Plymouth Carvelle (USA)

FORD MOTOR COMPANY ELECTRONIC INSTRUMENTATION APPLICATION

1982-83 Thunderbird/XR-7
1984 Thunderbird/Cougar
1985-86 Thunderbird/Cougar
(Except Turbo Coupe and XR-7)
1982-83 Continental
1984-86 Mark VII/Continental
1983-84 LTD/Marquis
1986 ½ And Later Aerostar
1986 And Later Taurus/Sable

GENERAL MOTORS CORPORATION ELECTRONIC INSTRUMENTATION APPLICATION

BUICK MOTOR DIVISION

1983-86 Buick Century
1985-86 LeSabre, Electra/Park Avenue
1985-86 Somerset/Skylark
1985-86 Regal
1983-85 Riviera
1986 Riviera

CADILLAC MOTOR CAR DIVISION

1984-86 Cimarron
1985-86 DeVille, Fleetwood Models (RWD)
1985-86 DeVille, Fleetwood Models (FWD)
1982-85 Eldorado/Seville
1986 Eldorado/Seville

CHEVROLET MOTOR DIVISION

1985-86 Cavalier (Type-10)
1985-86 Camaro Berlinetta
1984-86 Corvette

OLDSMOBILE DIVISION

1985-86 Ninety-Eight, Ninety Eight Regency, Delta 88 RoyaleModels
1985-86 Calais
1984-86 Cutlass Ciera
1984-85 Toronado
1986 Toronado

PONTIAC MOTOR DIVISION

1985-86 Pontiac 6000 STE
1985-86 Firebird

INSTRUMENT DISPLAY METHODS

GENERAL INFORMATION

Three basic methods are used by the electronic instruments to display information. The three types are as follows:
1. Light-emitting diode (LED).
2. Vacuum fluorescent display (VF).
3. Liquid crystal display (LCD)

LIGHT-EMITTING DIODE

A diode is a semiconductor device that conducts electricity in only one direction. A light-emitting diode (LED) is made of special semiconductor material that is partially translucent. When current flows through the diode, light is emitted. The diode its self is only part of the LED package. It also requires leads and a plastic lens to defuse the light. For the automotive applications, there is one drawback to the LED system, it can be difficult to see in the bright daylight. Therefore, it is used mainly only on graphic warning displays.

VACUUM FLUORESCENT DISPLAY

A vacuum fluorescent display is made up of digital and/or alpha-numeric characters formed from separate anode segments. These anode segments are coated with phosphor material. There is also a filament in the vacuum fluorescent display. The filament is coated with a material that generates "free"electrons when hot. The electrons are accelerated towards the anode at a high speed and when they strike the phosphor material on the anode, the phosphor material emits a light.

The grid between the filament and the anode is the accelerator. The grid is made of fine wire mesh that allows the electrons to pass through to the anode. Both the grid and the anode operate on a digital logic where, for example, + 5 volts DC is high and - 40 volts DC is low (exact voltages vary from one instrument to another). By putting a high voltage on the appropriate anodes, any number (or letter on fourteen-segment tube) can be illuminated. For example, by putting a high voltage on seg-

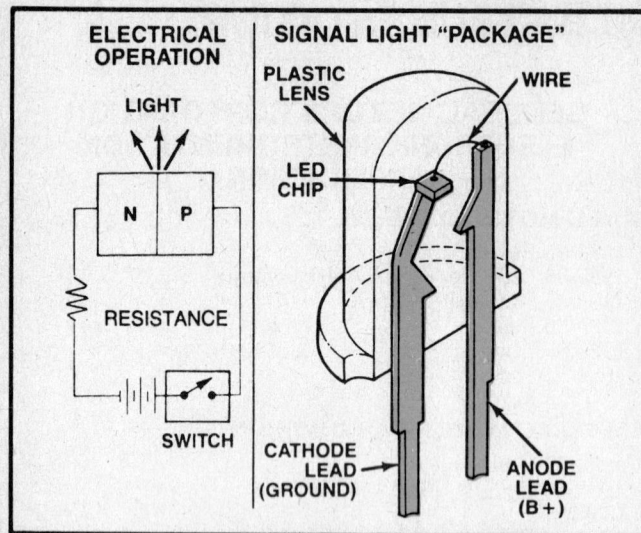

Cross section of Light Emitting Diode (LED)

ments 1, 3, 4, and 7, the number 4 can be illuminated. This occurs because the anodes with high voltage attracts the electrons, while the anodes with low voltage repel the electrons. Remember the basic law of magnetism, "like poles repel, unlike poles attract". This law applies to electrons also. They will be attracted to positively charged components, such as the anodes with high voltage and repelled by the others. The vacuum fluorescent displays are the most common type of display on the electronic instruments.

LIQUID CRYSTAL DISPLAY (LCD)

The heart of the LCD is a special liquid crystal that is contained in a cell. Where the LED emitted its own light, the key to the LCD operation is its ability to reflect ambient light.

The LCD is made up of a vertical polarizer, a liquid crystal cell, a horizontal polarizer and a reflector. Light waves from the sun and most artificial light sources vibrate randomly in many directions. When these light waves are applied to an LCD that has no voltage applied, only vertical light waves pass through the vertical polarizer. But as these waves pass through the liquid crystal, they are gradually rotated 90 degrees to the horizontal position. This rotation occurs because of the way the crystals are laid out in the cell.

Being in a horizontal position, the light waves can pass through the horizontal polarizer to the reflector. The waves reflect off the reflector, back through the horizontal polarizer, the cell and the vertical polarizer to the viewer. Thus, the viewer sees reflected ambient light.

Applying voltage to the LCD causes the crystals to be aligned in a straight line. Therefore, light waves passing through the vertical polarizer cannot pass through the horizontal polarizer. This segment will appear dark to the viewer. Applying voltage to various segments can produce various numbers, letters or other desired figures.

While the LCD is readable in the daytime, which is just the opposite of the LED, it requires use of small lamps in the display to be seen at night.

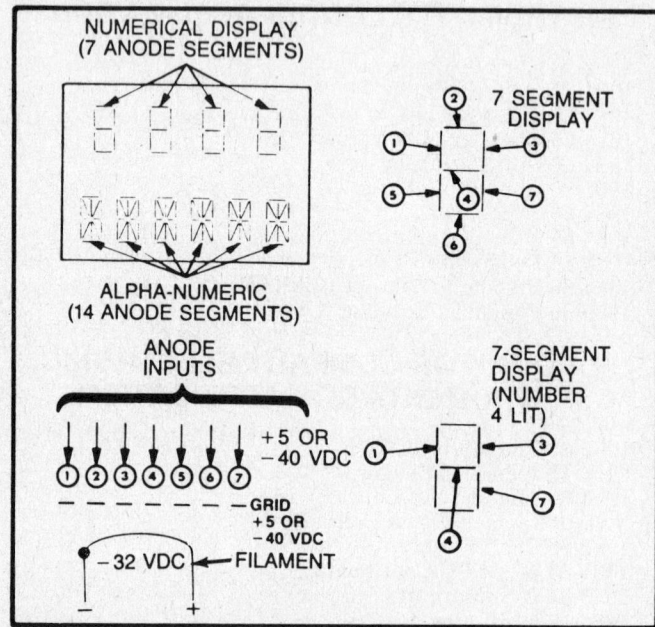

Vacuum Fluorescent Display (VFD)

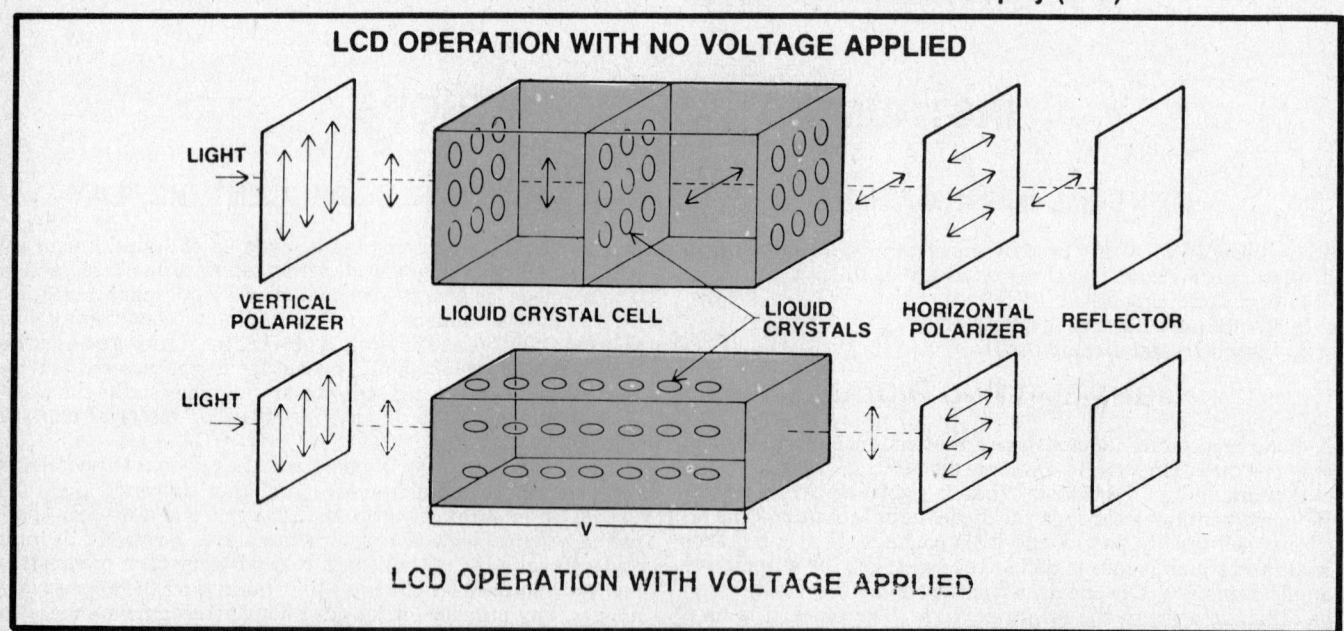

Liquid Crystal Display (LCD), with and without voltage applied

AMERICAN MOTORS CORPORATION INSTRUMENTATION

Application

1982–87 Eagle
1982–83 Concord
1982–83 Spirit

GENERAL INFORMATION

American Motors Corporation continues to use conventional electrically controlled, magnetic type indicating gauges and a cable operated speedometer assembly on its vehicle coverage from 1982 to present.

An electronically operated emission maintenance lamp is located on the instrument cluster of certain emission equipped vehicles and will illuminate after 1000 hours of engine operation, depending upon the vehicle model year and its emission equipment. After performing the required emission service, the E-Cell timer must be replaced. The timer is located in the passenger compartment within the wire harness leading to the ECM.

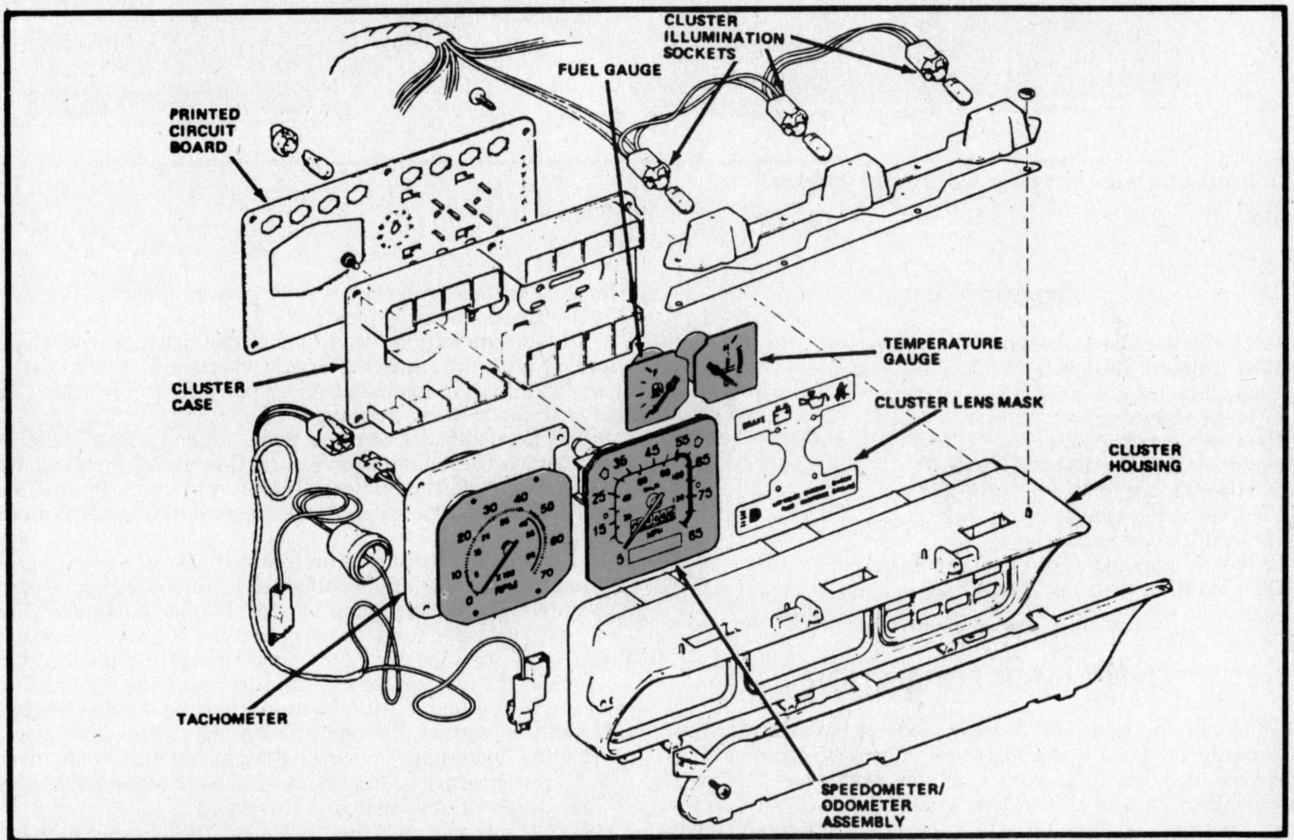

Exploded view of instrument cluster with standard speedometer

CHRYSLER CORPORATION ELECTRONIC INSTRUMENT CLUSTER

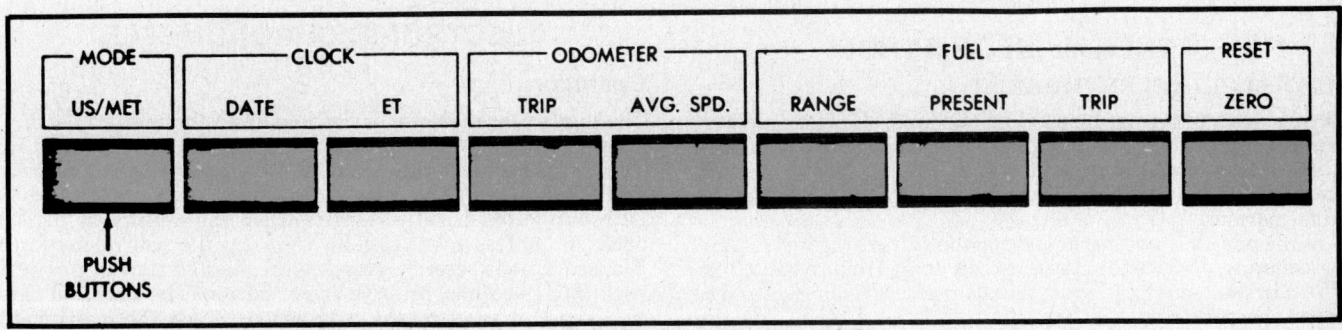

Electronic control button arrangement—1982–83 Chrysler Imperial

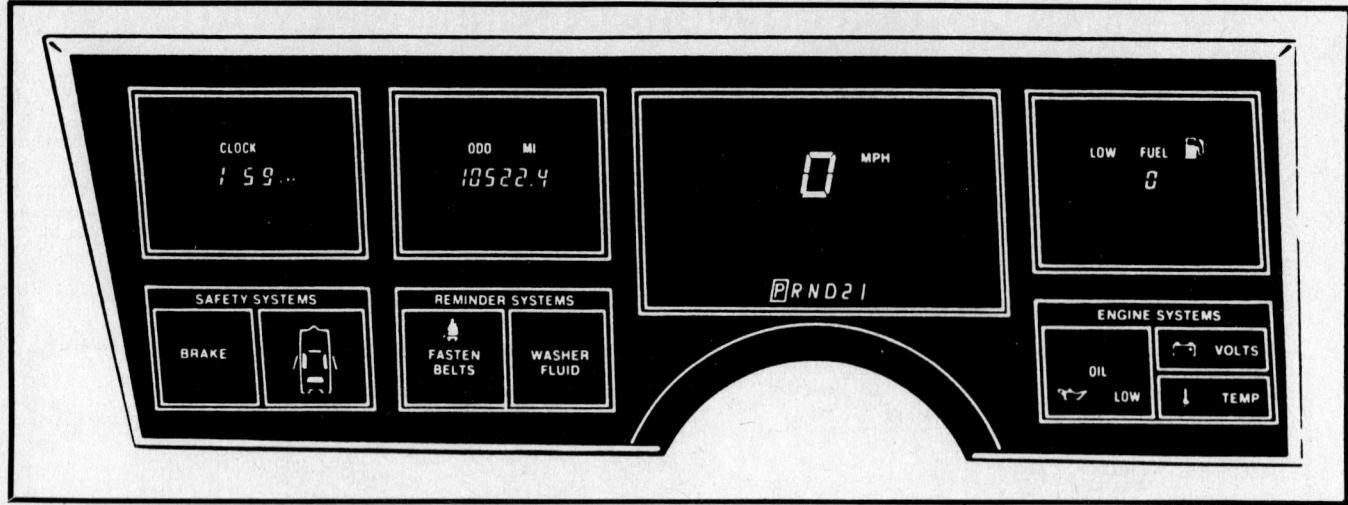

Electronic Cluster — 1982–83 Chrysler Imperial

Application

1982–83 Chrysler Imperial
1984 Chrysler LeBaron
1984 Chrysler E Class
1984–86 Chrysler New Yorker
1984–86 Chrysler Laser
1985–86 Chrysler LeBaron GTS
1984–86 Dodge 600
1984–86 Dodge Daytona
1985–86 Dodge Lancer
1984–86 Plymouth Carvelle (CANADA)
1985–86 Plymouth Carvelle (USA)

GENERAL INFORMATION

The Chrysler Imperial was the first model to have the electronic instrument cluster and information center installed. This was expanded to include other Chrysler, Dodge and Plymouth models, beginning with the 1984 models year. Generally, the basic operation of the electronic cluster and information systems remain the same, with added features, different testing procedures and changes in the configuration of the cluster assemblies from year to year and from model to model.

Cluster Assembly And Information Center

GENERAL INFORMATION

1982–83 CHRYSLER IMPERIAL

A fully electronic instrument cluster is used, allowing the operator to monitor important vehicle functions and to obtain useful travel information at the touch of a button. The entire system is designed to operate without operator supplied information.

Nine push buttons, arranged horizontally on the instrument panel brow, operate the cluster to call up trip information from the microcomputer and to set the odometer, fuel displays and to reset the clock. Two additional buttons are mounted below the instrument panel brow to set the clock time and date. The auto-

matic transmission selector lever position quadrant is located in the speedometer display pod.

All displays may be converted to metric units from the customary U.S. units and back again, when the U.S./METRIC conversion button is depressed. An in-pod indicator is used to identify the mode being displayed.

The four upper electronic pods, (Chronometer, odometer, speedometer and fuel) use vacuum fluorescent displays, while the system condition indicators, (safety systems, reminder system and the engine system) are conventional instrument cluster lamps.

Two levels of display illumination intensity are controlled automatically when the headlamps are on by a photo-detector, mounted in the instrument cluster. Bright blue-green illumination is provided for daytime operation, while reduced illumination is provided for night time driving. A photo-detector overrides the dimmer for day time driving when the headlamps are on. Instrument cluster illumination and display readout illumination can be dimmed by rotating the headlamp switch when the headlamps or parking lamps are on. During normal nighttime operation, the display takes three seconds to dim when the headlamp switch is turned on.

With the exception of the "door ajar" and "washer fluid level" lamps, all safety, reminder and engine system indicators are bulb-checked when the ignition switch is placed in the ON/RUN or START position.

An integral cluster diagnostic system permits rapid item-by-item testing, when placed into the self-diagnostic test mode.

Components

ELECTRONIC CHRONOMETER

Operation

The digital chronometer is capable of displaying time of day, month, day of month and has an elapsed time recorder built-in. The elapsed time feature allows recording of up to 100 hours of ignition ON time. The timer stops when the ignition is turned OFF and automatically restarts when the ignition is turned back on, unless instructed to reset by the control buttons. Elapsed time is reset by pressing the elapsed time button and within five seconds, press the reset button. The time and date can be set or reset by the two buttons below the instrument panel brow.

ELECTRONIC ODOMETER

Operation

Trip distance, or kilometers and average speed are available at the touch of a button from the odometer display. All information is derived from the distance sensor and the internal time base.

Accumulated mileage is up to 99,999.9 miles is permanently and continuously displayed whenever the ignition is in the ON/RUN position. The accumulated mileage is stored in the memory, even if the battery is disconnected. The ODO logo is continuously displayed, along with either MI or H, depending on which mode the electronic cluster is in.

The trip function display will record up to at least 2500 miles (4000 H) of continuous driving. Depressing the TRIP button causes the accumulated mileage, since the last RESET, to be displayed. To clear and reset the trip odometer, the operator must press the TRIP button and within five seconds, press the RESET button. The trip mileage will continue to be displayed until the TRIP button is pressed again , or until the AVG SPD button is pressed.

The AVG SPD button must be depressed to cause the odometer to function as an average speed instrument. The average speed will be displayed in whole numbers for five seconds with the letters AVG SPD displayed below the number. After five seconds, the instrument reverts to its original odometer function. This function may be reset to present speed by pressing the RESET button during the five seconds that the AVG SPD is displayed.

ELECTRONIC DIGITAL SPEEDOMETER

Operation

Large numbers are used on the electronic speedometer assembly to clearly illuminate the vehicle speed for the operator. The numbers are either in miles or kilometers, depending upon the selected mode. Mode selection is made by depressing the U.S./METRIC button on the control panel. The vehicle speed display is updated every one-half second, based on information supplied by the speed sensor located in line in the speed control cable. The sensor detects every eight inches (203mm) of vehicle travel and will transmit this message to the cluster computer. The computer processes this signal, along with the information from the internal time base, to calculate vehicle speed to a ± four percent accuracy over the entire vehicle's speed range.

ELECTRONIC GEAR SELECTOR POSITION DISPLAY (PRND21)

Operation

When the ignition is on, when the driver's seat is occupied, or when either front door is open, this display will indicate which gear is engaged by the transmission selector lever. This is an all-electronic function with no mechanical devices except the steering column mounted switch and back-up lamp switch. This also ties into the door switch, seat switch and ignition key lamp time delay relay so the PRND21 mode will operate anytime the operator is in the vehicle.

CLUSTER ASSEMBLY

Application

1984 Chrysler LeBaron
1984 Chrysler E Class
1984–86 Chrysler New Yorker
1984–86 Chrysler Laser
1984–86 Dodge 600
1984–86 Dodge Daytona
1984–86 Plymouth Caravelle (CANADA)
1985–86 Plymouth Caravelle (USA)

GENERAL INFORMATION

—— CAUTION ——

Disconnect the negative battery cable from the battery before servicing the electronic instrument panel. Reconnect the negative battery cable only when power is needed for test purposes (disconnect after test) or when the repairs are complete.

The electronic instrument cluster uses vacuum fluorescent digital and linear displays to inform the vehicle operator of oil pressure, system voltage, engine temperature, fuel level, speed and odometer readings.

ELECTRONIC CLUSTER DIMMING

The electronic cluster display is dimmed from daytime to nighttime intensity when the headlamp switch control knob is rotated with the switch in the ON position. An addition detent on the headlamp switch will allow daytime intensity while driving in the day time, but the headlamps must be in the ON position

ELAPSED TIMER

The elapsed timer is a vacuum fluorescent display clock with a built-in twenty four hour elapsed timer, which rolls over from minutes-seconds display to hours-minutes display, after accumulated time reaches one hour. In operation, the display can be varied in brightness from an intensity easily readable in sunlight to a soft glow suitable for nighttime viewing. The display is turned off for low power standby operation whenever

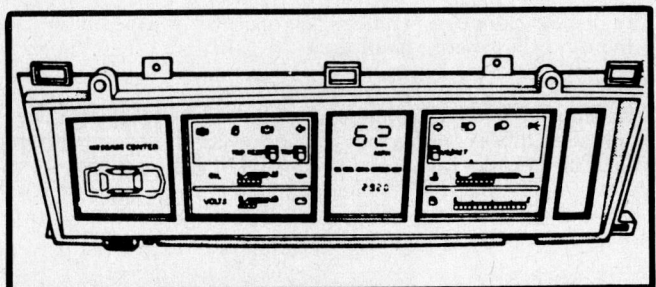

Electronic cluster with message center—typical

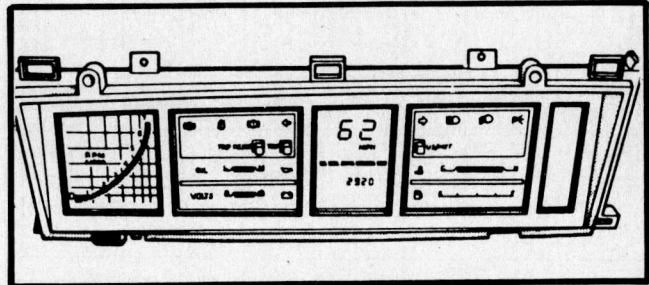

Electronic cluster with tachometer—typical

the ignition key is in the OFF position. The time may be set or the elapsed time may be started, stopped or reset only with the ignition in the ON position.

ELECTRONIC VOICE ALERT WITH ELEVEN FUNCTIONS

The eleven function voice alert system gives the operator up to eleven different audible warnings and messages. All messages are preceded by a group of "BEEPS", followed by a tone. Warning messages are repeated with each "KEY ON" until the unsatisfactory condition is corrected.

Some messages are not heard until the vehicle is in a forward motion. These are controlled by a distance sensor and the backup lamp switch. An OFF/ON switch is located on the module, which is accessible through the glove box, to cancel the voice signal, if desired. All warning lamps and tones will continue to function normally even if the voice alert has been turned off.

ELECTRONIC MONITOR WITH TWENTY FOUR FUNCTIONS

The electronic monitor system gives the operator up to twenty four different audible and visual warnings and messages, depending upon the vehicle equipment. This monitor system includes the electronic monitor module, an electronic voice alert module (above glove box), and the various sensors that supply signals to the monitor module.

The electronic monitor scans the different sensor inputs for warning conditions. When a warning condition is detected, the electronic monitor will display the warning message and send the voice alert module a tone and talk signal.

This signal causes the voice alert module to generate a short tone and speak the appropriate audible message. When more than one warning condition exists, a sequence will be followed for each message, with the monitor alternately displaying each message at a four second rate. When the warning condition can be corrected by the operator, the voice signal will respond with a "THANK YOU".

The systems check button is located on the front of the message center and will put the system into a demonstration mode.

Separate Navigator module—typical

By pressing this button, the system will sound a tone and visually and audibly cycle through some messages. If this button is pressed twice within a half second, the system will shut off until the unit is powered down. The system will automatically return to normal operation after the complete demonstration sequence or when the check button is pressed during the demonstration sequence.

Navigator

GENERAL INFORMATION

1984 AND LATER

The electronic navigator provides the operator with information including time, day of week, date, distance to empty, current fuel efficiency, trip distance, trip average speed, trip fuel efficiency, distance to destination, trip elapsed time, trip fuel consumed, estimated time until arrival and estimated time and date of arrival.

The navigator system includes digital sensors for distance traveled and fuel consumed as well as requiring an analog input from the fuel gauge.

An alpha-numeric vacuum fluorescent display with two rows of ten characters each is used. This display permits information to be displayed so that the function being displayed as well as its value and units of measure are easily recognized.

When the marker lamps are on the display intensity can be controlled by adjusting the panel dimmer control on the headlamp switch. The operator uses a set of momentary contact pushbutton switches to select the information to be displayed, to enter, trip distance, to set time and date and to reset the trip functions. The display is operational when the ignition switch is in its ON position or the time button is pressed. Battery power must be supplied continuously to maintain trip information and timekeeping.

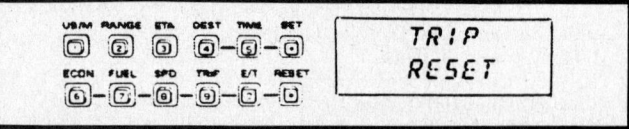

Navigator unit used with Dodge Daytona and Chrysler Laser

NOTE: The time and date functions will be displayed whenever the TIME pushbutton is pressed, even with the ignition in the OFF position.,

Operation

DISPLAY READOUTS

Display readouts may be converted to either U.S. or metric units, or the clock may be changed from a standard twelve hour (AM/PM) format to a twenty-four hour military format by pressing the US/M (number one) pushbutton. When the ignition switch is in the ON position, the electronic navigator will emit a short "BEEP" when any of the buttons are pressed and the display panel responds as the operator selects one of the nine conditions being monitored.

RANGE

Pressing the RANGE (number two) button will display the estimated number of miles that can be driven with the remaining fuel. The range is calculated by multiplying the amount of fuel remaining by the projected fuel efficiency. The range predicted will change every few seconds to a higher or lower number as these factors change.

ETA

The ETA (estimated time of arrival) will display for five seconds, when the button (number three) is pressed, the estimated driving time to arrival. The display will then switch to a continuous display of the estimated time and date that the vehicle will arrive at a previously entered destination. At low speeds, the ETA is calculated using the trip average speed. At normal or higher speeds, the current vehicle speed is used. If the ETA is greater than 100 hours from the present time, "TRIP OVER 100 HOURS" will appear in the display. If the vehicle passes the prearranged destination, "TRIP COMPLETED" will be displayed.

DEST

Pressing the DEST (distance to destination) button (number four) will display the remaining miles to the predetermined destination. To enter the distance to destination, press the DEST button and then within five seconds, press the SET button. The display will then indicate 0 miles. Using thew numbered buttons, enter the distance to the destination in a left to right sequence. Press the SET button again to begin the countdown of distance. The maximum allowable distance setting is 9999 miles. When the destination is reached, the display will show "TRIP COMPLETED" and a short burst of tones will sound.

TIME

Pressing the TIME (number five) button or starting the vehicle will continuously display the time of day, day of the week, month of the year and day of the month. To reset the display, press the TIME button and within five seconds, press the SET button. An arrow will appear on the display indicating hours are to be set. Press and hold the RESET button to advance the setting, or the US/M button to backup the setting. After the hours have been set, press the SET button again and the arrow will point to the minutes. Set the minutes and repeat the procedure for the day, month and date.

Any portion of the display can be bypassed by continuing to press the SET button until the arrow indicates the desired function. When all entry information has been entered, press the SET button a final time and the setting is established.

ECON

Pressing the ECON (number six) button will display the average miles per gallon since the last reset, for a period of five seconds. The display will then switch to a continuously updated reading of present mpg. To reset the average fuel efficiency, press the RESET button while the average mpg is being displayed. The average fuel efficiency reading will be updated about every sixteen seconds. The present fuel efficiency will be updated and displayed every two seconds.

FUEL

The number of gallons of fuel consumed since the last reset, will be displayed by pressing the FUEL (number seven) button. The maximum displayed value will be 999.9 gallons. The display will be updated every several seconds. To reset the display to zero, press the RESET button within five seconds after pressing the FUEL button.

SPD

Pressing the SPD (number eight) button will display the average miles per hour since the last reset. The reading will be updated at least once every eight seconds. The maximum value displayed is eighty-five mph. To reset, press the SPD button and within five seconds, press the RESET button. Since the ETA is based on this average speed, it should be reset after entering distance to destination with DEST button.

TRIP

Pressing the TRIP (number nine) button will continuously display the accumulated trip miles since the last reset. The maximum mileage displayed would be 999.9 miles. When this mileage is reached, the trip display will automatically reset to zero. This display is updated every half second. To reset, press the TRIP button and within five seconds, press the RESET button.

E/T

Pressing the E/T (number 0) button will display the amount of driving time (ignition on) since the last reset. Time is displayed in minutes and seconds for the first half hour after reset, then in hours and minutes. To reset, press the E/T button and within five seconds, press the reset button. The elapsed time will reset automatically after 99 hours and 59 minutes have been displayed.

RESET

The RESET button is used to clear the various functions after they have been displayed. To simultaneously clear all trip information, press the RESET button twice within five seconds after pressing any of the following; ECON, FUEL, SPD, TRIP, or E/T. The display will show TRIP RESET for five seconds.

INTEGRAL TRIP COMPUTER

1986 CHRYSLER NEW YORKER

The instrument cluster includes full instrumentation as well as a new five feature trip computer. The instrument cluster includes the following;
1. Digital speedometer.
2. Digital odometer.
3. Vertical bar gauges with red warning segment to indicate;
   a. Oil pressure.
   b. Electrical system voltage.
   c. Engine coolant temperature.
   d. Fuel level.
4. Warning lamps for the following;
   a. Seat belts.
   b. brake system.
   c. High beam headlamp.
   d. Power loss.
5. Built-in diagnostic routines.
6. Trip computer to include;
   a. Trip miles (trip odometer).
   b. Trip fuel efficiency (average).

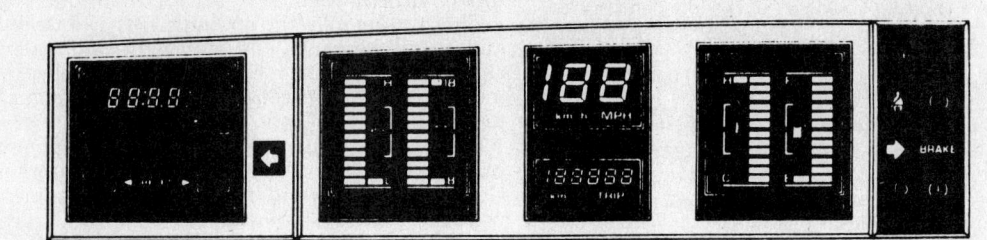

Electronic Voice Alert Diagnostic procedure for Entry and Exit functions—1985-86 models so equipped

c. Instantaneous fuel efficiency.

d. Distance to empty.

e. Trip elapsed time.

To provide this information, digital sensors for distance traveled and fuel consumed are used, as well as the signal output from the fuel gauge module. These inputs are supplied to a single chip microcomputer , which then calculates and displays the results on the front panel of the trip computer. The front panel display is on when the ignition is on. Switching the ignition to the OFF position turns the computer display off but a battery back-up system maintains the computer memory until the ignition is turned back on again. The two momentary contact switches on the trip computer front panel are used by the operator to interface with the computer.

Operation

The operator selects the desired trip computer display by pressing the "STEP" switch on the face of the trip computer. Repeated pressing of the "STEP" switch causes the computer to cycle through all five functions in the following order, "TRIP ODOMETER", "AVERAGE TRIP FUEL EFFICIENCY", "PRESENT FUEL EFFICIENCY","DISTANCE TO EMPTY", and "ELASPED TIME". The "US/M" switch allows the operator to select either U.S. or Metric units for the computer display. Pressing both switches (STEP AND US/M) simultaneously will reset the "TRIP ODOMETER", "AVERAGE TRIP FUEL EFFICIENCY" and "ELASPED TIME" when any of these three are displayed on the trip computer.

TRIP COMPUTER FUNCTIONS

All functions will automatically reset when the battery is disconnected and reconnected. When the battery is reconnected, the computer will display all resettable functions as zero and all reading will be in the US units. When the ignition is in the OFF position, the trip function values are not updated , but are maintained in the computer memory by a battery back-up system. When the ignition switch is turned to the ON position, all functions resume up-dating. The brightness of the computer display is controlled by the same rheostat that controls brightness of the instrument cluster display. The computer has an internal diagnostic program to help locate faults in the system.

TRIP ODOMETER

This function (ODO) displays the distance traveled, in either kilometers or miles, since the computer was last set. The display will show distance traveled to 999.9, in either miles or kilometers, before setting automatically. When the trip odometer automatically resets, the average trip fuel efficiency and elapsed time also resets. This function can also be manually rest by pressing the "STEP" and "US/M" switches simultaneously.

AVERAGE TRIP FUEL EFFICIENCY

This function (ECO AVG) displays the average trip fuel efficiency in either miles/gallon or liter/100 kilometers, obtained since the last reset. The readout for this display is updated approximately every sixteen seconds. This display will automatically reset when either the trip odometer of the elasped time is reset or the "STEP" or "US/M" switches are pressed simultaneously.

PRESENT FUEL EFFICIENCY

This function (ECO) displays the present fuel efficiency of the vehicle in either miles/gallon or liter/100 kilometers. This display is updated and calculated at approximately two second intervals. This function is only reset by disconnection of the battery and is not affected by the reset function.

ESTIMATED DISTANCE TO EMPTY

This function (DTE) displays the estimated distance the vehi-

cle will travel before the fuel tank is empty. This estimate is based on the fuel efficiency history and the remaining fuel in the tank. The fuel efficiency history is an estimate of the future range derived from low and high speed mileages figures in the computer. This display shows the distance to empty in miles or kilometers and is updated every sixteen seconds. This function is non-resetable with the other functions and will continually calculate the distance to empty.

TRIP ELASPED TIME

This function (ET) displays the time the ignition has been in the ON position since the last computer reset. The elapsed time will be displayed in minutes and seconds for the first 59 minutes and 59 seconds and then will be displayed in hours and minutes. The maximum time the computer can store and display is 99 hours and 59 minutes. The elasped time function will then reset, but the other functions will continue. This function can be manually reset by pressing the "STEP" and "US/M" switches simultaneously.

Electronic Voice Alert With 11 Functions

GENERAL INFORMATION

1984 AND LATER – ALL MODELS

Eleven different audible warnings and messages are given to the operator as part of the Electronic Voice Alert system. All messages are proceeded by a group of audible "BEEPS" and followed by a tone. warning messages are repeated with each ignition key ON position, until the malfunctioning condition is corrected.

Some messages are not heard unless the vehicle is in a forward motion. This function is controlled by a distance sensor and the backup lamp switch. To accomplish this, the distance sensor delays selected messages until the vehicle is in motion while the backup lamp switch locks out selected messages when the transmission selector is in the REVERSE position.

A volume control is located in the underside of the module to adjust the desired level of volume. An off/on switch is located on the module and is accessible through the glove box. When moved towards the rear of the vehicle, this switch will cancel only the voice signal, if desired. With the switch turned off, all warning lamps and tones will continue to function normally.

Electronic Monitor + Twenty Four Functions

GENERAL INFORMATION

1984 AND LATER DAYTONA AND LASER

The twenty four function Electronic Monitor system operates basically as does the eleven function Electronic Monitor system, with the exception that thirteen more functions are monitored by the system.

This system give the operator twenty four different audible and visual warnings and messages. This monitor system includes the electronic monitor module, an electronic voice alert module and various sensors which supply signals to the monitor module.

The electronic monitor scans the different sensor inputs for warning conditions. When a warning condition is detected, the electronic monitor will display the warning message, send the voice alert module a tone and talk signal. This causes the voice alert module to speak the appropriate audible message. When more than one warning condition exists, the above sequence will be followed for each message. The monitor will then alternately display each message at a four second rate, When warning conditions, that are operator correctable, are corrected, the monitor will send the voice alert a tone signal. This tone is called a "THANK YOU" tone, which indicates the warning condition has been corrected.

The system check button, located on the front of the message center will put the system into a demonstration mode. By pressing this button, the system will sound a tone and visually and audibly cycle through some messages. If this button is pressed twice within one half second, the system will shut off until the unit is powered down. The system will automatically return to normal operation after the complete demonstration sequence or when the check button is pressed during the demonstration sequence.

A mute switch is located on the electronic voice alert module, which selects the voice alert of the audible tone system desired.

FORD MOTOR COMPANY ELECTRONIC INSTRUMENTATION

Application

1982–83 Thunderbird/XR-7
1984 Thunderbird/Cougar
1985–87 Thunderbird/Cougar
(Except Turbo Coupe and XR-7)
1982–83 Continental
1984–87 Mark VII/Continental
1983–84 LTD/Marquis
1986 ½ And Later Aerostar
1986 And Later Taurus/Sable

GENERAL INFORMATION

The Electronic Instrumentation used in Ford Motor Company vehicles vary with individual components and displays for different models and year applications.

1. Electronic Speedometer
2. Electronic Fuel Indicators
3. Lamp-out Warning, Warning Indicators
4. Graphic Display Warning System
5. Message Center
6. Trip Minder
7. Tone Generator
8. Voice Alert
9. Tachometer
10. Shift Indicator

The major difference between the electronic cluster componens and the conventional cluster components are the method of information display. The electronic cluster components will usually use the same type sensors as the convention-

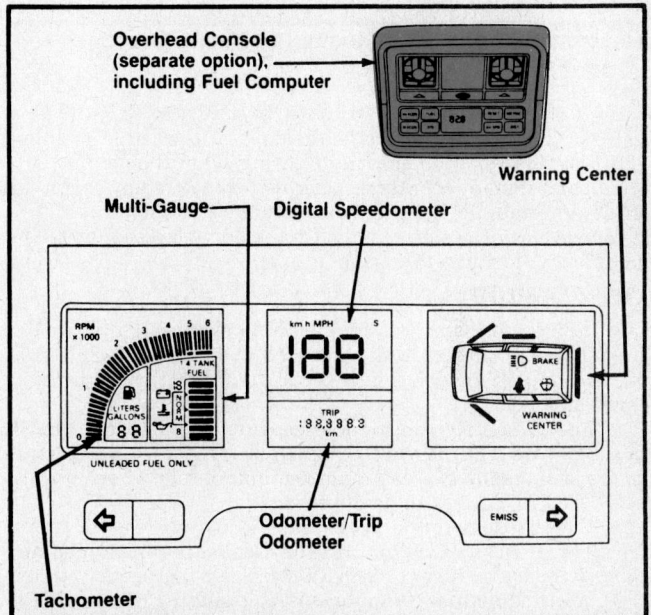

Typical Electronic Instrument Cluster with warning center, typical of Aerostar models

al cluster components. All inputs are essentially the same as used in the standard cluster. The speedometer cable for the electronic speedometer is basically the same as used on the conventional speedometer, but with certain modifications to it or its driven components

ELECTRONIC INSTRUMENT CLUSTER

GENERAL INFORMATION

1982–83 THUNDERBIRD/XR-7
1983 LTD/MARQUIS

The electronic instrument cluster used on these vehicles consists of an electronic speedometer, an electronic fuel gauge and an upper tier of warning lamps. The major difference between the Electronic Instrument Cluster and the standard cluster is the way the information is displayed. The electronic cluster uses the same senders as the standard cluster. All inputs are essentially the same as used in the standard cluster.

Procedures for operation and testing will be included in the general component sections.

1984 THUNDERBIRD/COUGAR, LTD/MARQUIS

The electronic instrument cluster operation is basically the same as in the 1983 models, but differences do exist in physical appearance, displays and diagnosis. Procedure changes will be noted where there are differences in operation of each component.

1985–86 THUNDERBIRD/COUGAR (EXCEPT TURBO COUPE AND XR-7)

The all electronic instrument cluster consists of three electronic modules, a speedometer/odometer, tach/multigauge and fuel computer modules. Warning lamps are also included within the cluster housing assembly. The electronic cluster is only operational when the ignition key is in the RUN position.

The electronic LCD displays get their illumination from bulbs. When the headlamp switch is turned on, the LCD lamp bulbs are switched over to the control of the dimming rheostat via a relay. Tones are sounded via a connection to a remote tone generator.

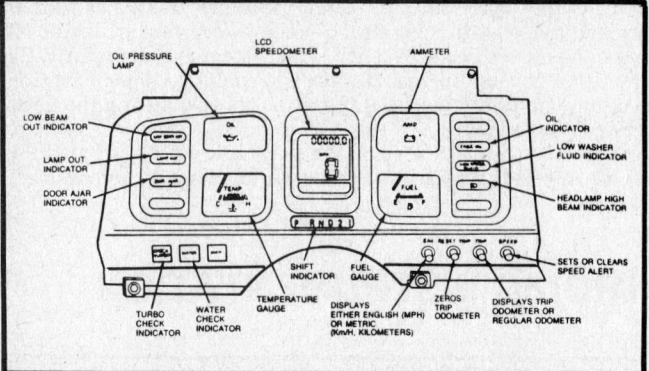

Electronic Instrument Cluster, 1985–86 Thunderbird/Cougar

Each time the ignition switch is first turned from OFF to RUN positions, the electronic displays of the three modules will prove-out by momentarily lighting all of the display segments and then momentarily turning all the display segments off. It is normal for the three displays to be slightly out of synchronization with each other. After the prove-out sequence, the modules will return to normal operation.

1986 ½ AEROSTAR

The 1986 ½ Aerostar has an available electronic instrument cluster that is similar to the one used with the 1985–86 Thunderbird/Cougar models, with certain similarities and differences as follows;

1. The tachometer/multigauge module is almost identical to the one on the Thunderbird/Cougar, except that the analog fuel gauge will display the last quarter tank of fuel when the EXPANDED FUEL button is depressed.

2. The speedometer/odometer module operation is very similar to Thunderbird/Cougar, but the display is rearranged and there is no speed alert or service reminder feature.

3. There is no fuel computer in the cluster.

4. In place of the fuel computer is a warning center that is very similar to the graphic display warning system used in other models.

5. The cluster buttons are located elsewhere on the instrument panel, instead of on the instrument cluster itself. The buttons associated with the fuel computer and speed alert have been eliminated and the EXPANDED FUEL button has been added.

1986 TAURUS/SABLE

In many respects, the 1986 Taurus/Sable electronic instrument cluster is similar to the 1985–86 Thunderbird/Cougar and the 1986 ½ Aerostar electronic clusters. However, there are some significant differences in the type of information displayed and in the way it is displayed.

The all-electronic instrument cluster consists of two electronic modules, a speedometer/odometer/tachometer module and a fuel computer/scanner module. It also contains several warning lamps, as well as the following buttons:

1. MPH/Km/h button which switches the display from english to metric (mph to Km/h) or metric to english (Km/h to mph).

2. ODO SEL button displays trip odometer or the regular odometer.

3. TRIP RESET button, zeros out the trip odometer when the trip odometer is being displayed.

4. SPEED ALARM button sets or clears the speed alert system.

5. FUEL ECON button displays instantaneous fuel economy or average fuel economy.

6. DTE BUTTON displays distance to empty.

7. ECON RESET button resets the average fuel economy when it has been selected.

NOTE: The control buttons are located on a separate switch module.

CLUSTER BUTTONS

1985–86 THUNDERBIRD/COUGAR (EXCEPT TURBO COUPE AND XR-7)

Numerous buttons are positioned along the bottom of the instrument panel and are used in the following capacities;

1. The E/M button switches the display from english to metric (mph to Km/h) or metric to english.

2. The SPEED button sets or clears the speed alert system.

3. The GAUGE button displays four different gauges on it. The temperature gauge will show itself when the power first cones on. When pressing the button for the first time, the oil pressure gauge will show. Pressing the button the second time will bring up the voltage gauge. Pressing it the third time will cause the analog fuel level to be brought to the screen. Pressing it the fourth and fifth times will return the temperature gauge to the screen.

4. The TRIP button displays either the trip odometer or the regular odometer.

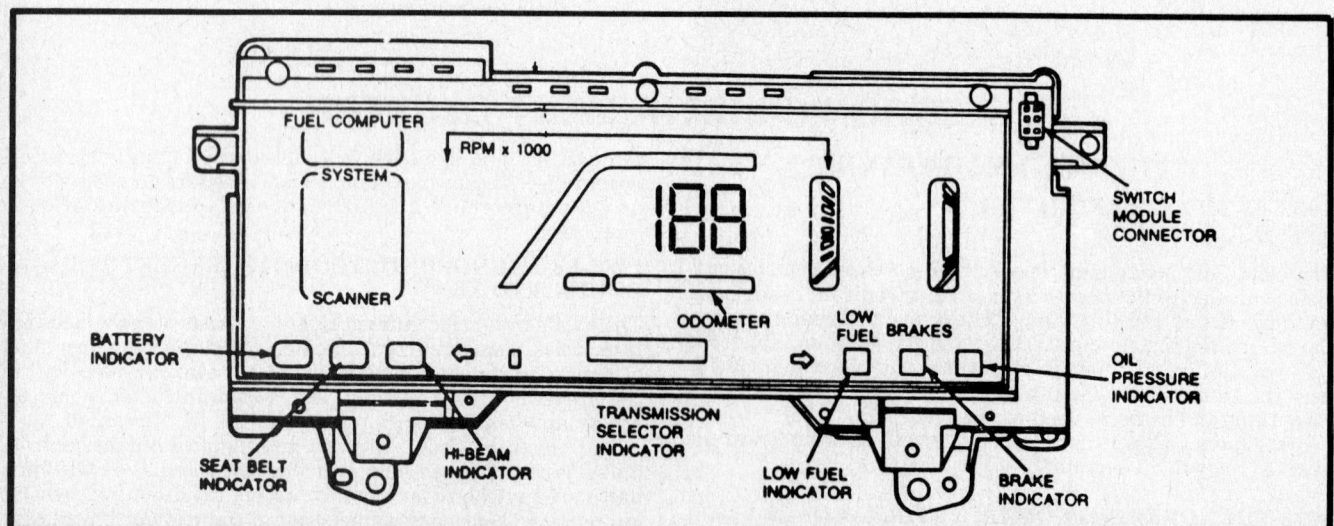

Electronic Instrument Cluster, Taurus/Sable

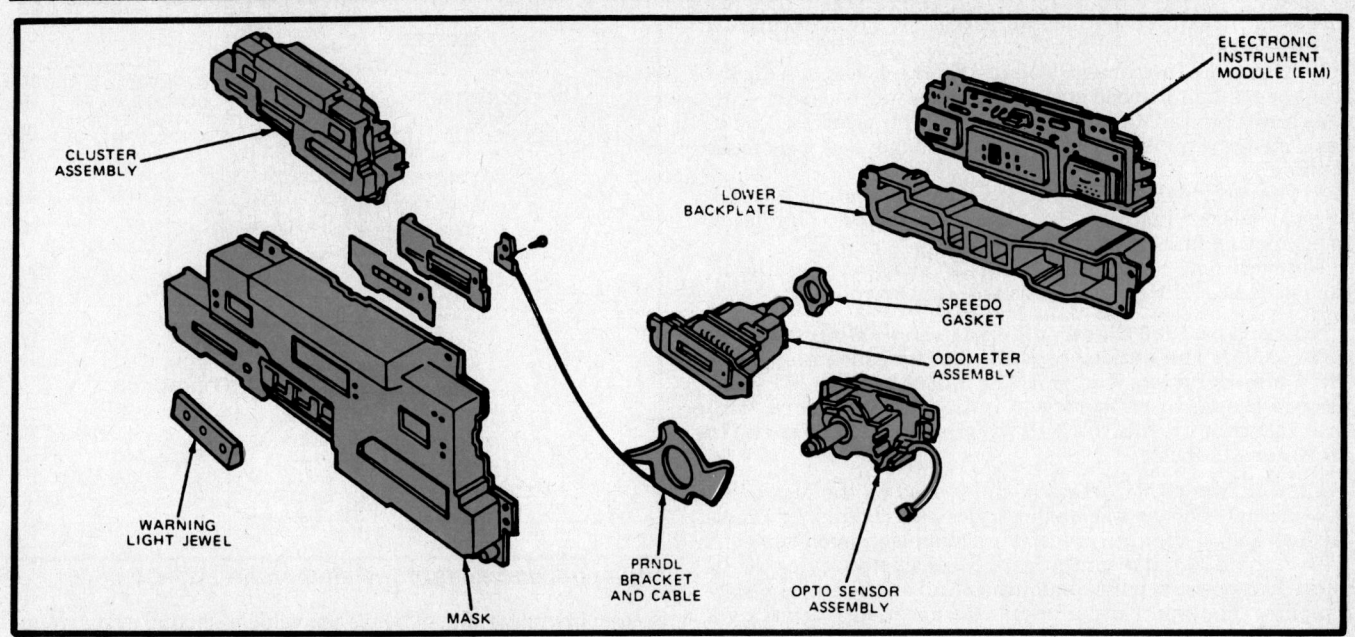

Exploded view of Electronic Instrument Cluster, typical of certain models

5. The RESET (TRIP) button zeros out the trip odometer.

6. The SELECT button displays instantaneous fuel economy, distance to empty, distance or average speed.

7. The RESET (FUEL FUNCTION) button resets the called up fuel computer function.

1982–83 CONTINENTAL

The Electronic Instrument Cluster (EIC) is divided into two sections, the first of which is the electronic feature section and secondly, a conventional feature section.

The electronic feature section consists of the digital speedometer, the electronic fuel gauge and an electronic coolant temperature gauge.

The conventional section consists of a mechanical odometer, transmission select indicator, turn signal indicators and a high beam indicator.

Within the EIC, the speedometer and both gauges share common electronic circuitry, such as power supply, dimming control and a central microcomputer. The input/output interface connections are made via a ribbon connector located at the rear of the assembly.

Operation and testing procedures of the major components will be included in the general component sections.

1984–86 MARK VII/CONTINENTAL

The Continental Electronic Instrument Cluster (EIC) is divided into three sections;

1. Electronic Instrument Module (EIM) consists of a digital fuel gauge, digital speedometer and electronic odometer.

2. Non-Volatile Memory Module (NVMM) provides permanent memory for the odometer, fuel gauge and diagnostic counts.

3. Conventional Feature Section (CFS) consists of a transmission selector indicator, turn signal indicators, high beam indicator and fasten seat belt indicator.

The electronic numerals will appear blue/green and logos, such as GAL, MPH, MILES, etc. will appear yellow

MARK VII – The MARK VII Electronic Instrument Cluster (EIC) is divided into three sections. They have the same fea-

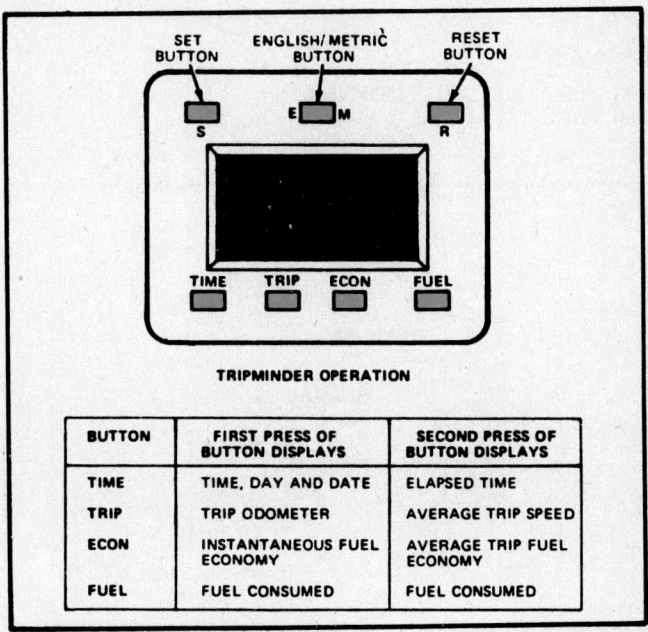

TRIPMINDER OPERATION

BUTTON	FIRST PRESS OF BUTTON DISPLAYS	SECOND PRESS OF BUTTON DISPLAYS
TIME	TIME, DAY AND DATE	ELAPSED TIME
TRIP	TRIP ODOMETER	AVERAGE TRIP SPEED
ECON	INSTANTANEOUS FUEL ECONOMY	AVERAGE TRIP FUEL ECONOMY
FUEL	FUEL CONSUMED	FUEL CONSUMED

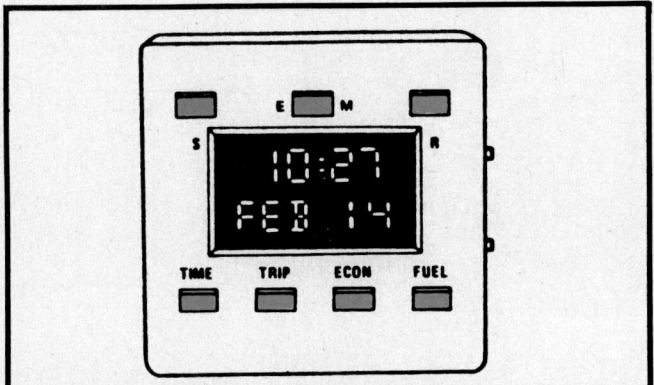

Typical Trip Minder module assembly

Typical Trip Minder operation

ture content as the Continental, except for the conventional feature section;

1. Electronic Instrument Module (EIM) consists of a digital fuel gauge, digital speedometer and electronic odometer.

2. Non-Volatile Memory Module (NVMM) provides permanent memory for the odometer, fuel gauge and diagnostic counts.

3. Conventional Feature Section (CFS) consists of a transmission selector indicator, turn signal indicators, high beam indicator and fasten seat belt indicator.

The electronic numerals will appear blue/green and logos, such as GAL, MPH, MILES, etc. will appear yellow

NOTE: The 1986 Electronic Instrument Module display differs from the earlier modules in the placement of the MPH abbreviation. The earlier models had the MPH display to the right of the speed indication numbers, while the later module has the MPH display under the speed indication numbers.

The Electronic Instrument Modules used on the Mark VII/Continental vehicles is a single service part containing a digital fuel gauge, digital speedometer and electronic odometer. Within the EIM, all displays share common electronic circuitry, such as power supply, dimming control and a central microcomputer. The input/output interface connections are made via a flexible printed circuit connector located at the rear of the cluster assembly. The EIM feature content, function and input/output interface is the same for both the Continental and Mark VII, except for the location and the shape of the flexible printed circuit. As a result, the Mark VII EIM is not interchangable with the Continental EIM. The EIM is powered and at maximum brightness whenever the ignition switch is in the RUN or ACC positions or the door handle is pulled.

ELECTRONIC SPEEDOMETERS AND ODOMETERS

—————— CAUTION ——————

Federal law requires the odometer in any replacement speedometer must register the same mileage as that registered in the removed speedometer. Refer to specific vehicle sections for information on replacement of electronic odometer modules and correct procedures on recording mileages.

Operation

1982–83 THUNDERBIRD/XR7
1983 LTD/MARQUIS

The digital speedometer is located in the center pod of the in-

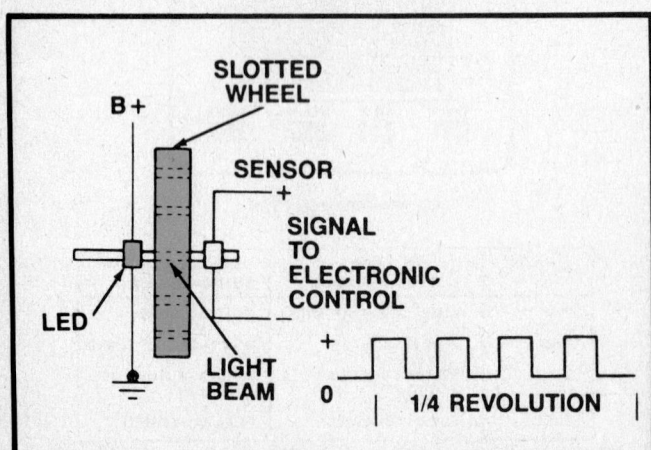

Operation of speed sensor

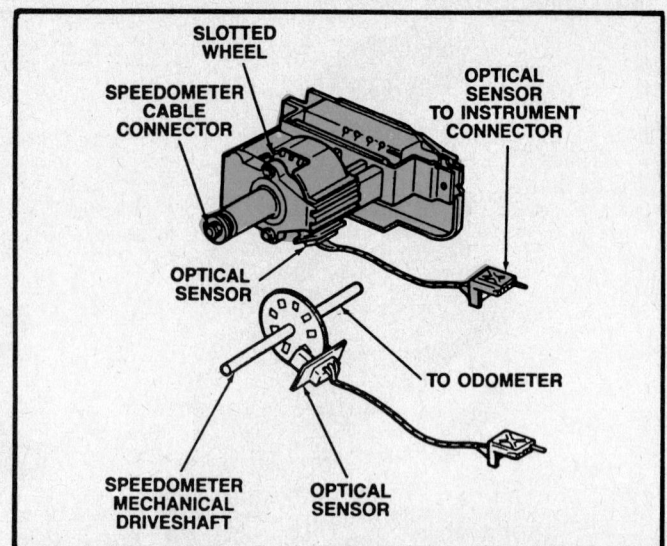

Optical speed sensor installation on speedometer

strument cluster and displays the vehicle's actual speed in numerals.

The difference in the conventional and electronic speedometer heads, is that in the electronic speedometer head, the speedometer cable turns a slotted (16) encoder wheel. As the slotted encoder wheel turns, an optical sensor counts each slot passing by and creates an electrical pulse for each slot. The electrical pulse is sent to the speedometer electronics where the pulses are re-added every 0.45 seconds. The number of pulses generated in this time period is proportional to the speed of the vehicle. The speed is updated and displayed every 0.45 seconds.

NOTE: It is normal for the speedometer to sequence through each number during slow acceleration or deceleration, or to skip several consecutive numbers during more severe stops or starts. It will, however, display the numbers long enough to be read with ease. The speed is displayed regardless if the vehicle is moving forward or backward.

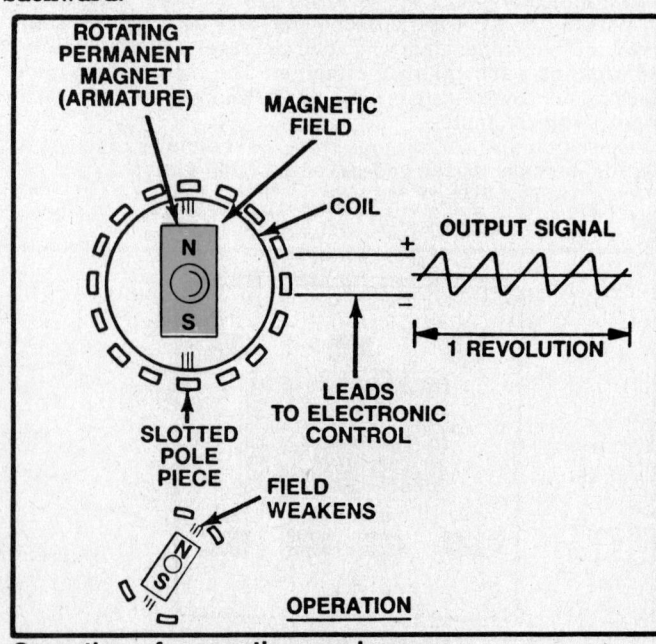

Operation of magnetic speed sensor

The speedometer can be changed to read in either MPH or Km/h. The particular unit of speed is selected by depressing the MPH/Km/h switch button, located on the lower corner of the instrument cluster. Each time the button is depressed, it will change from one unit of speed to the other. The odometer, however, is not responsive to the switch and will always read in miles on U.S. vehicles and kilometers on Canadian vehicles. The highest reading that can be attained on the speedometer is 85 mph and/or 137 Km/h, regardless of a higher vehicle speed.

Each time the ignition switch is first turned from OFF to either RUN or ACC. positions, the speedometer will momentarily display "188 MPH" for prove-out and to insure that all light segments are functional. The speedometer will then will display "0 MPH", providing the vehicle is stopped. There is no speed control sensor used in the speedometer cable on vehicles equipped with the electronic cluster, as the speed signal goes directly from the electronic speedometer to the speed control unit.

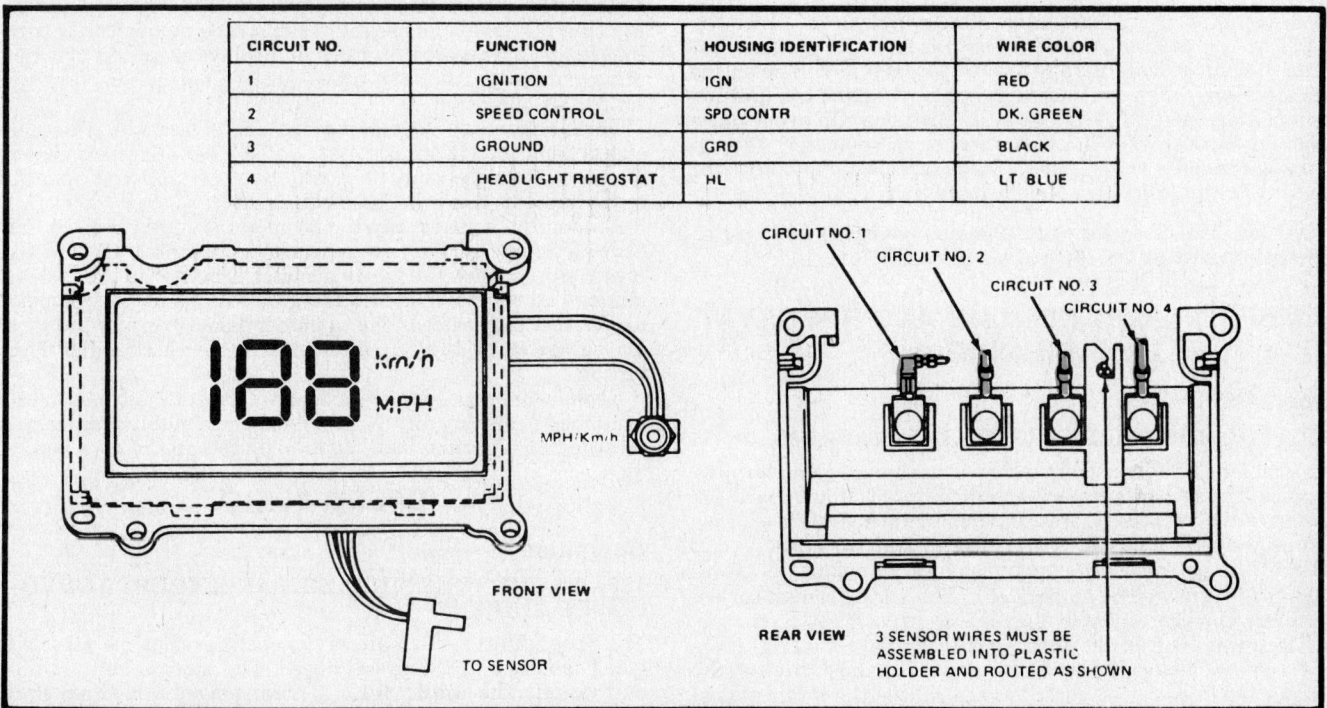

CIRCUIT NO.	FUNCTION	HOUSING IDENTIFICATION	WIRE COLOR
1	IGNITION	IGN	RED
2	SPEED CONTROL	SPD CONTR	DK. GREEN
3	GROUND	GRD	BLACK
4	HEADLIGHT RHEOSTAT	HL	LT BLUE

Electronic speedometer components and circuits, first type

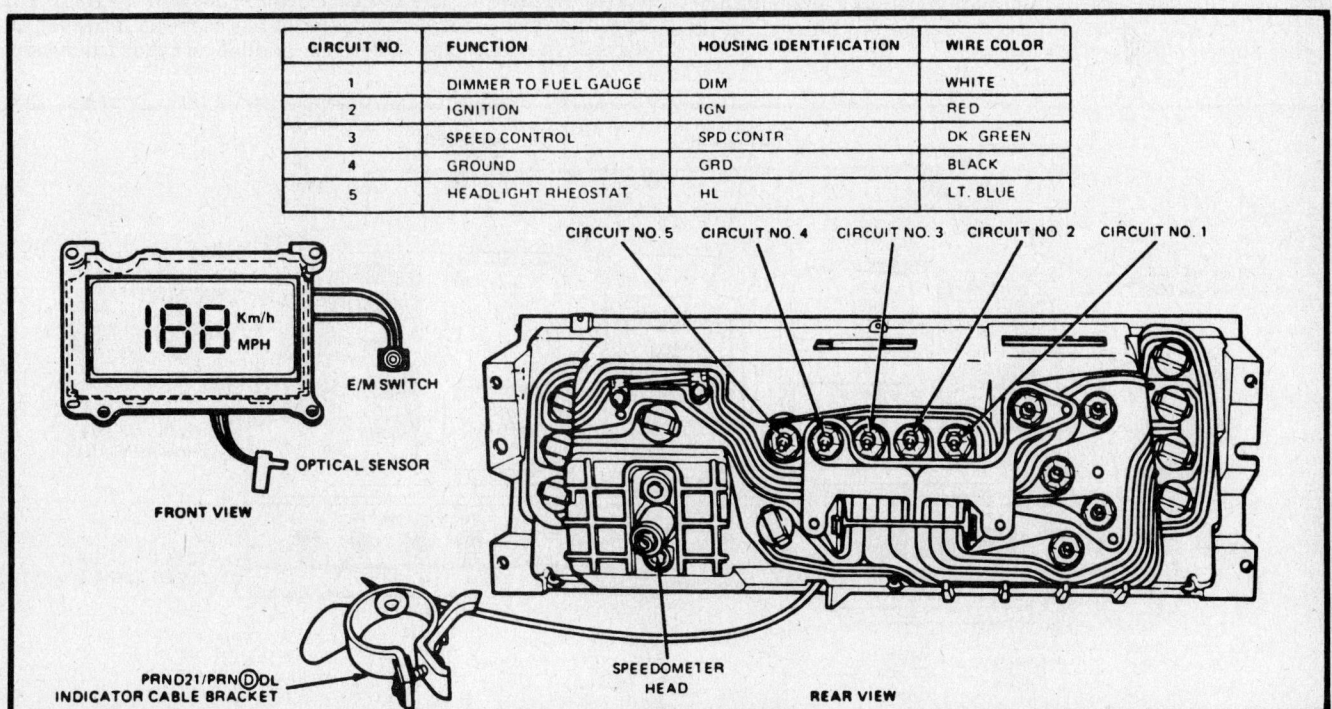

CIRCUIT NO.	FUNCTION	HOUSING IDENTIFICATION	WIRE COLOR
1	DIMMER TO FUEL GAUGE	DIM	WHITE
2	IGNITION	IGN	RED
3	SPEED CONTROL	SPD CONTR	DK. GREEN
4	GROUND	GRD	BLACK
5	HEADLIGHT RHEOSTAT	HL	LT. BLUE

Electronic speedometer components and circuits, second type

1984 LTD/MARQUIS

Display updates are made approximately every one-half second when in the MPH mode and approximately every one-third second when in the Km/h mode. For Canadian and export models, the speedometer has a maximum reading of 180 Km/h (122 mph) and the odometer will have a "K" near the odometer to indicate the odometer is in kilometers.

The speedometer sends speed information to the inputs of the speed control amplifier and tripminder. The signal is DC coupled and bipolar. When the ignition switch is in either the RUN or ACC position, the signal on this line will be either less than -3 volts or more than +3 volts. The signal will be on the negative side when the vehicle is not moving and the ignition switch is in the OFF, RUN or ACC positions. On every pulse from the encoder wheel (slotted wheel on speedometer), the signal will change to the opposite voltage level, which would occur every 100 mm (4 inches) of vehicle motion.

NOTE: The encoder/optical sensor outputs 9942 pulses per kilometer or 16,000 pulses per mile.

AMBIENT LIGHT DIMMING AND RHEOSTAT DIMMING

Operation

1984 THUNDERBIRD/COUGAR, LTD/MARQUIS

An ambient light sensor is included in the speedometer electronics. The sensor is mounted on the printed circuit board, adjacent to the vacuum fluorescent display tube. A clear opening is in the cluster lens and is tunneled through the mask an dial so that the passenger compartment light (ambient light) will fall on the sensor. The amount of light striking the sensor determines the brightness of the display.

Electronics within the speedometer regulate the brightness of the speedometer display and a signal is passed through the cluster flexible printed circuit to control the the brightness of the speedometer display. The same electronics in the speedometer also senses the voltage of the instrument panel dimming rheostat and combines this information with the ambient dimming information. Both of these conditions are linear with no step changes in display brightness.

The ambient sensor will control the display brightness over a 35 to 1 range and the rheostat will control over a 30 to 1 range. When the headlamps and parking lamps are off, the rheostat has no effect and the display brightness will be controlled only by the ambient sensor.

1984–86 THUNDERBIRD/COUGAR(EXCEPT TURBO–COUPE AND XR7)

When the ignition switch is turned to the RUN position, the electronic display will enter a prove-out mode by momentarily lighting all the display segments and then momentarily turning them off. This ensures that all displays segments are operating normally. After the prove-out, the normal displays will return for operation.

The electronic speedometer module receives a speed/distance signal from the transmission mounted magnetic speed sensor. The maximum speedometer readings are 85 mph in the english mode and 199 Km/h in the metric mode.

Accumulated mileage in the odometer is stored in a non-volatile electronic memory every 16 Km/h (10 miles). The mileage is also stored when the ignition switch is turned to the OFF position. The odometer is and integral part of the speedometer and cannot be serviced. The odometer displays either the regular odometer or the trip odometer by depressing the TRIP button.

Replacement speedometer/odometer modules have been programmed to display an "S". Previously accumulated mileage is recorded on a decal which must be placed on the door jam.

SPEED ALERT

Operation

1984–86 THUNDERBIRD/COUGAR (EXCEPT TURBO–COUPE AND XR7)

The Speed Alert system alerts the operator that the vehicle is going faster than the preset speed. The alert is both audible and visual. The word "SPEED" is displayed and three short beeps are sounded.

The preset speed is actuated by accelerating to the desired speed and pressing the SPEED button. The word "SPEED" will appear on the display to show that it has been set. If the vehicle exceeds the preset speed, both the audible and the visual warn-

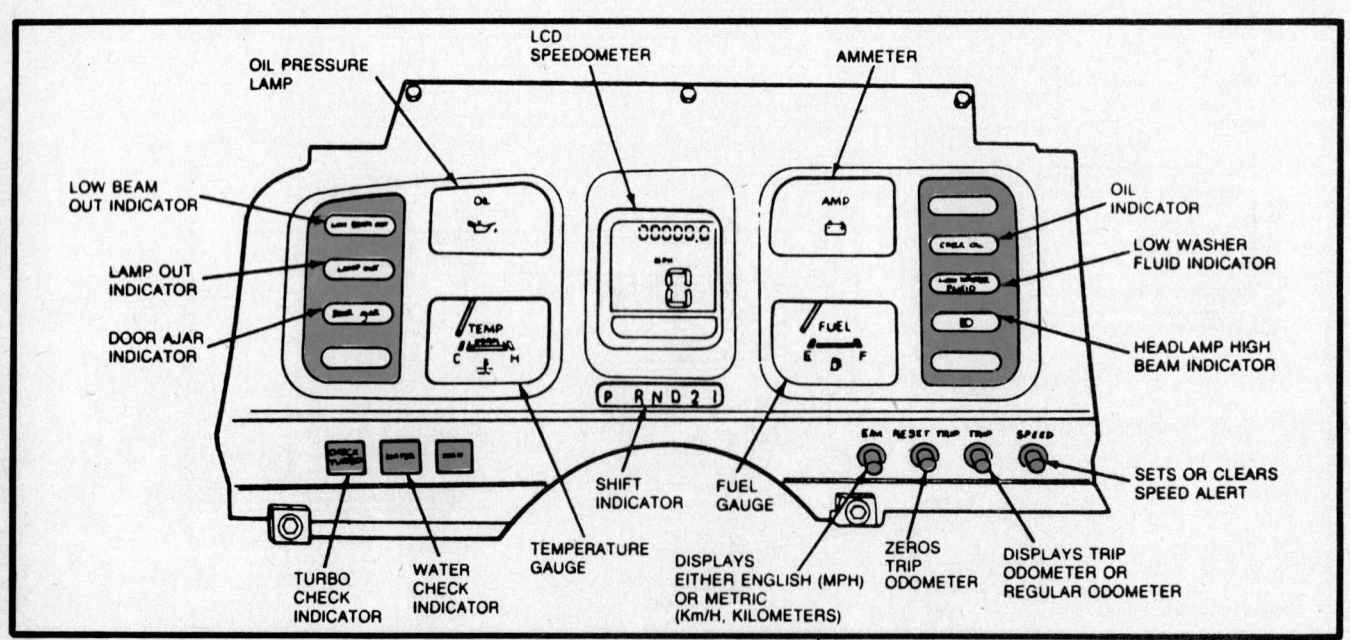

Electronic Instrument Cluster, 1984–86 Thunderbird/Cougar models

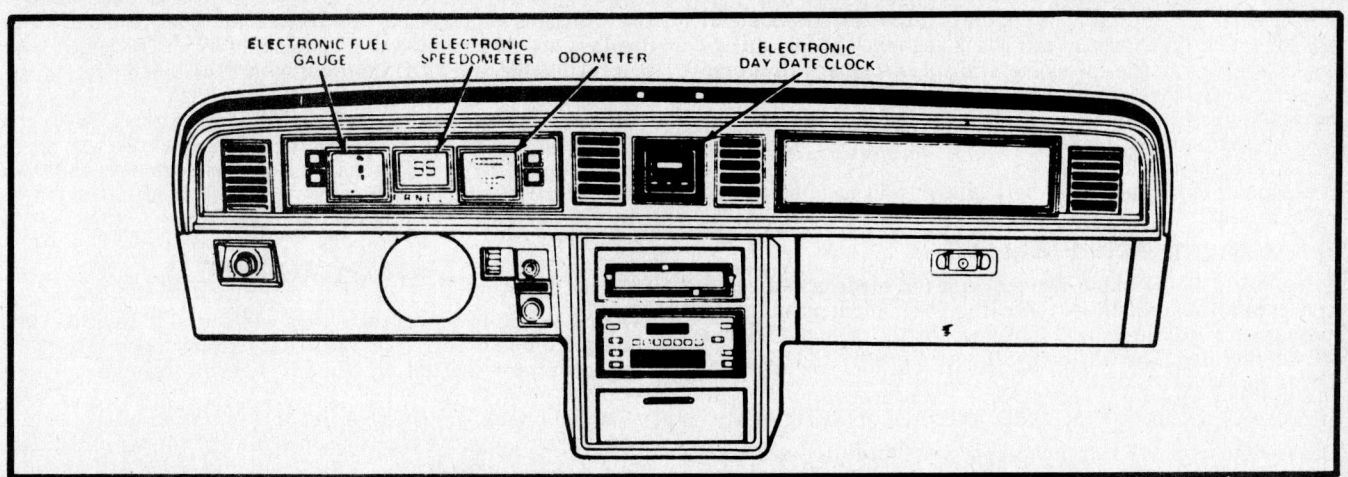

Electronic Instrument Cluster assembly, typical of 1982–84 LTD/Marquis, 1982–84 Thunderbird/Cougar models

ings will alert the operator to slow the vehicle to below the preset speed. The same procedure is used if the speedometer is in the metric mode.

SERVICE INTERVAL REMINDER

Operation

1984–86 THUNDERBIRD/COUGAR (EXCEPT TURBO–COUPE AND XR7)

At approximately 5,000 or 7,500 miles (8,047 or 12,070 km), depending upon engine application, the word "SERVICE" will appear on the electronic display for the first 1.5 miles (2.4 km) to remind the operator that it is time for regular service to be performed on the vehicle.

The reminder is reset for another service interval by pressing the TRIP and TRIP RESET buttons at the same time. The word "SERVICE" will go out and three beeps will be heard to verify that the service reminder has been reset.

DIGITAL SPEEDOMETER

The digital electronic speedometer is located in the center display section of the EIM. It can display vehicle speeds from zero to a maximum of 85 mph or 137 Km/h.

NOTE: Canadian vehicles have a speedometer with a maximum reading of 180 Km/h (112 mph).

For vehicle speed exceeding these limits, the reading is maintained at maximum indication. Under driving conditions, it is normal for the speedometer to display consecutive numbers during slow accelerations and slow decelerations. During fast acceleration and deceleration modes, the speedometer may skip several consecutive numbers. The speed is registered regardless of the forward or backward direction of the vehicle.

SPEED MODE SELECTION

The speedometer can display speeds in either mph or Km/h, depending upon the mode selected. This mode is indicated on the speedometer face to the right of the numerals. The mode is selected by pressing the "Miles/Km" mode selector button, located on the tripminder keyboard. Each time the selector button is pressed, the speedometer will change from one speed mode to the other. When the ignition switch is turned to the RUN or ACC position, the mode last selected when the vehicle was turned off will be provided by the tripminder and displayed on the speedometer display. After disconnecting the battery, the mph mode is automatically selected.

SELF DIAGNOSIS

When the ignition switch is turned to the RUN or ACC posi-

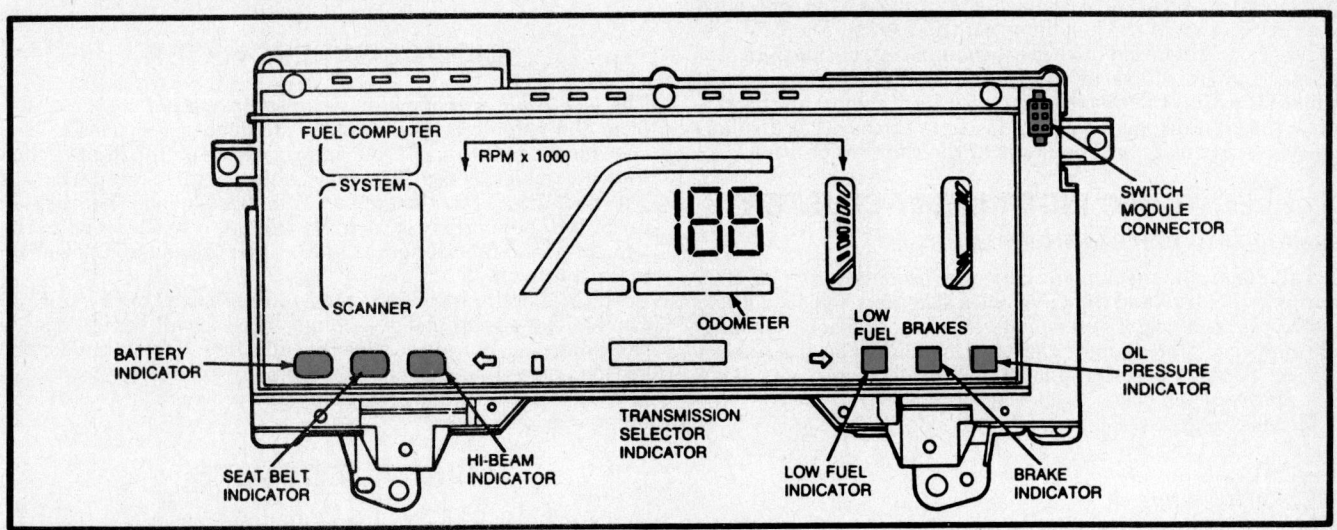

Electronic Instrument Cluster assembly, Taurus/Sable models

tion, or when the outside door handle is lifted, the speedometer will initiate a three second self check sequence which will allow verification of the speedometer display segment illumination. If the speedometer system is in good condition, the following sequence will be observed on the display;
1. All segments will be on.
2. All segment will go off.
3. Mph or Km/h mode will be displayed and the display will indicate zero.

OPEN CIRCUIT SERVICE ALERT

If the optical sensor cable connection is not made or if an open circuit condition exists in the opto sensor diode circuit, the speedometer will turn the "Mph" and "Km/h" on and off at one per second rated. The warning will continue until the malfunction is corrected.

SPEEDOMETER/ODOMETER SYSTEM INTERFACE

The speedometer drives a slotted encoder wheel in the odometer, As the slots on the rotating encoder wheel pass by the optical sensor, the optical sensor generates an electrical pulse for each slot. The electrical pulse is sent to the speedometer electronics, via the optical sensor cable where the number of pulses generated is proportional to the vehicle speed (16,000 pulses per mile). The conventional speedometer cable also drives the mechanical odometer. The odometer shows miles on U.S. vehicles and kilometers from Canadian models. The Canadian models have the letters KM just below the odometer to indicate that the odometer readings are in kilometers.

ELECTRONIC INSTRUMENT MODULE

The Electronic Instrument Module (EIM) is a single service part containing a digital speedometer, an electronic fuel gauge and an electronic engine coolant temperature gauge. Within the EIM, the speedometer and both gauges share common electronic circuitry, such as power supply, dimming control and a central microcomputer. Input/output interface connections are made via a ribbon connector located at the rear of the assembly.

ILLUMINATION

The EIM is illuminated and operational when the ignition switch is in the ON or ACC position. The EIC will illuminate whenever an outside door handle is lifted. The illumination of the displays are at maximum intensity when the head lamp switch is in the OFF position. Pulling the control switch to the parking or headlamp position turns on the EIM's dimming control circuitry and allows the display brightness to be controlled via the rotation of the headlamp control switch. The EIM displays are brighter and have greater dimming control than other electronic displays in the instrument panel. As a result, when adjusting the display intensity from maximum brightness, the EIM displays will dim faster than the other displays and their intensity will be lower in the full dim position.

ELECTRONIC INSTRUMENT CLUSTER

1986 AND LATER TAURUS/SABLE

An all electronic instrument cluster is an option for the 1986 and later Taurus and Sable vehicles. The unit consists of two electronic modules, a speedometer/odometer/tachometer module and and fuel computer/scanner module. The instrument cluster also includes the following warning lamps;
1. Battery.
2. Seat belt.
3. Brake.
4. High beam.
5. Oil pressure.
6. Turnsignals.
The electronic instrument cluster is operational only when the ignition switch is in the RUN position. The electronic LCD displays are illuminated from bulbs and when the headlamps are turned on, the LCD lamp bulbs are switched over to the dimming rheostat through a relay.

Each time the ignition is first turned from the OFF to the RUN position, the electronic displays of the modules will prove out by momentarily lighting all the display segments and then momentarily turning all display segments off. After the proveout, the modules return to normal operation.

SWITCH MODULE

When a switch is depressed, a tone will sound to indicate that the switch has been recognized. Tones are sounded through a tone generator located on the RH steering column opening support.

The following switches control the operation of the switch module, to change the electronic instrument cluster into different operating modes;
1. The MPH/Km/h button switches the display from english to metric (MPH to Km/h or metric to english.
2. The SPEED ALARM button sets or clears the speed alert system.
3. The DTE button displays distance to empty (fuel in tank).
4. The ODO SEL button displays trip odometer, or the regular odometer.
5. The TRIP RESET button zeros out the trip odometer.
6. The FUEL ECON button displays instantaneous fuel economy or average fuel economy.
7. The ECON RESET button resets the average fuel economy.

SPEEDOMETER/ODOMETER/TACHMETER

Operation

The speedometer/odometer/tachometer module goes through a prove-out when powered up and then goes into normal operation, displaying speed and the regular odometer. Four of the seven buttons on the switch module are used to operate speedometer functions. They are as follows:
1. MPH/Km/h–Displays in either English mode of MPH, MILES, MPG or in the metric code, Km/h, Km, L/100Km. This switch controls both the speedo module and the fuel computer module.
2. ODO SEL–Displays trip odometer or regular odometer.
3. TRIP RESET–Resets the trip odometer to zero.
4. SPEED ALARM–Sets or clears the speed alarm.

DIGITAL SPEEDOMETER

The electronic speedometer receives its speed/distance signal from the cableless transmission mounted speed sensor. The speedometer portion of the display consists of 2 ½ digits which indicate vehicle speed. The mode, either english or metric, will also be indicated by the english or metric legends. The display units, either english or metric, will be consistent with the odometer and fuel computer and will be the same at power up or power down.

The maximum speed indicated will be limited to 85 mph (136 Km/h). These readings will be displayed for all vehicle speeds exceeding the maximum speed as indicated. It is normal for the speedometer to display consecutive numbers during slow acceleration or deceleration and to skip consecutive numbers during quick starts or stops.

DIGITAL ODOMETER

The digital odometer displays either miles or kilometers, depending upon the selection made with the MPH/Km/h button.

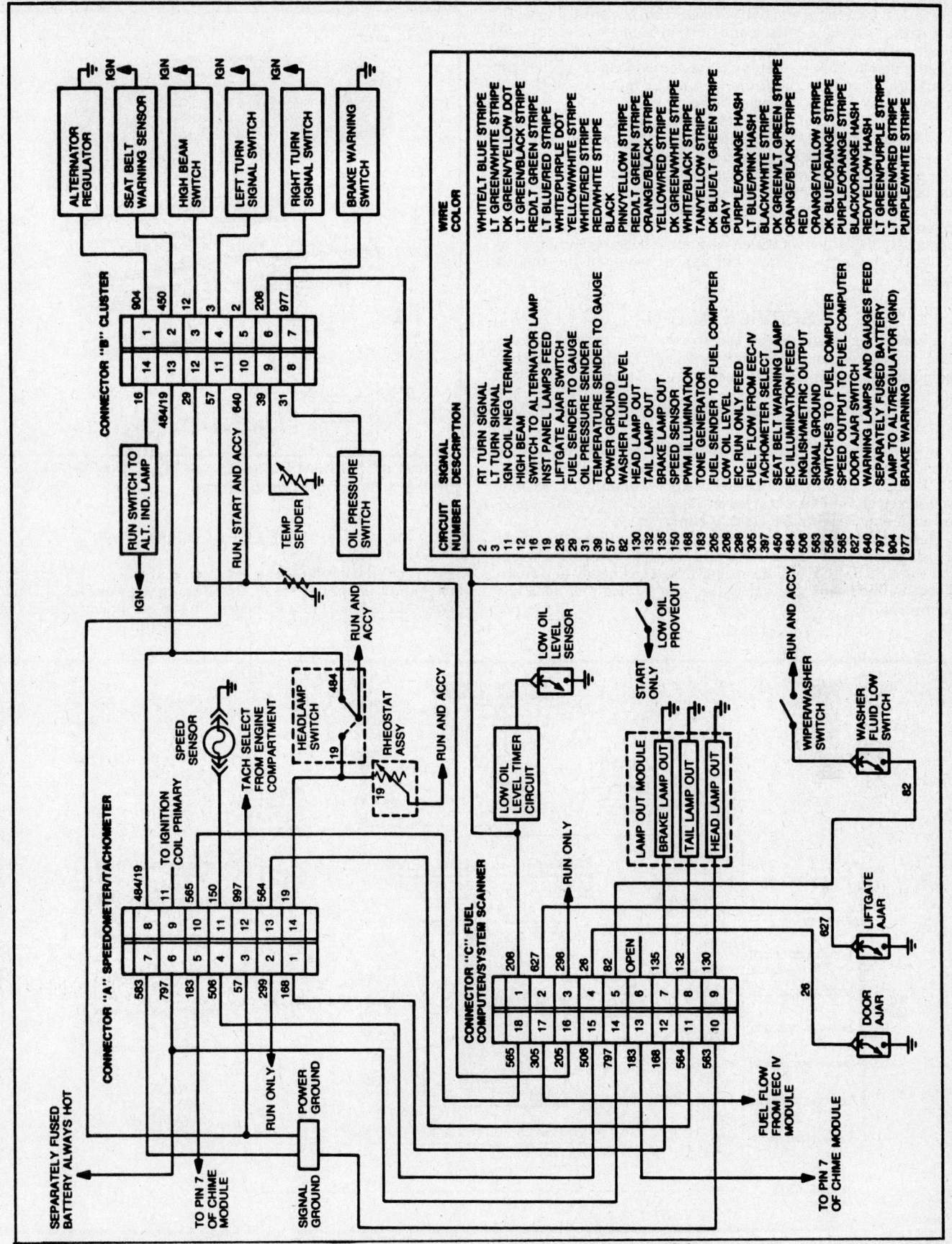

Electronic Instrument Cluster wiring schematic, typical of Taurus/Sable models

The total odometer or the trip odometer can be selected by activating the ODO-SEL button and the trip odometer can be reset by activating the TRIP RESET button while the trip odometer is being displayed. The display of the total odometer of the trip odometer, as well as the units (english or metric) will be the same at power up as at power down.

The accumulated mileage is stored in a non-volatile memory (NVM) every 10 miles (16 Km) and when the ignition switch is turned off. The NVM saves both the total odometer mileage as well as the trip odometer mileage. When the total odometer is displayed, it consists of the legend TRIP, five digits and a decimal point with the leading zeros blanked. When the trip odometer has been reset using the TRIP RESET button, 0.0 will be displayed. Regardless of which odometer is displayed, (TRIP or TOTAL), the legend "Km" will appear when in the metric mode.

SERVICE ALERT

If a condition exists where the speedometer module cannot read a valid odometer memory value from the non-volatile memory, the words ERROR and SERVICE will be displayed.

SERVICE INTERVAL REMINDER

The service interval reminder alerts the operator of regular service time. The service reminder will light the word SERVICE on the display or a period of approximately 30 seconds each time the vehicle is started or the module is powered up after achieving 7200 miles (11,520 Km).

The reminder is reset for another interval by simultaneously pressing the ODO SEL button and the TRIP RESET button. The word SERVICE will disappear from the display and three short audible beeps will verify that the service reminder has been reset.

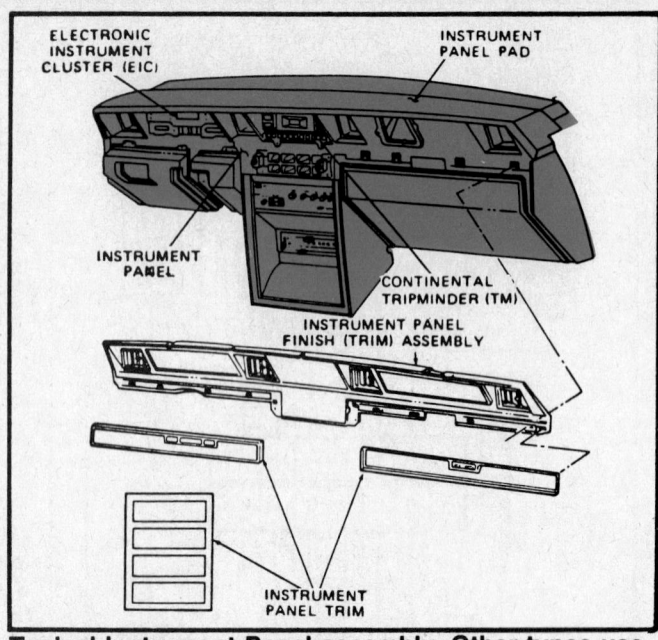

Typical Instrument Panel assembly. Other types use different panel trim mouldings

SPEED ALARM

The speed alarm alerts the operator that the vehicle is going faster than the preset speed, by blinking the word SPEED and giving three short audible beeps. The speed alarm can only be

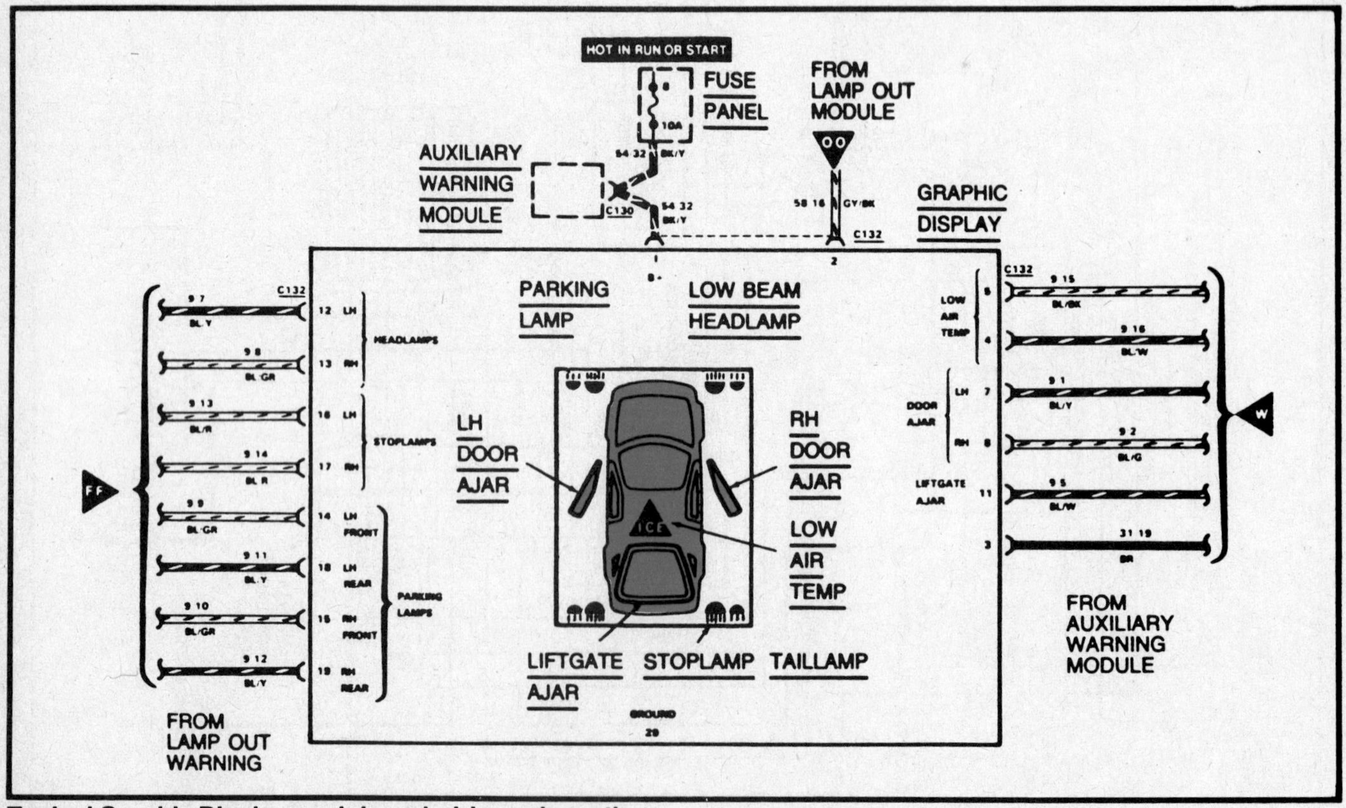

Typical Graphic Display module and wiring schematic

set when the vehicle speed is greater than 20 mph in the english mode or 32 Km/h in the metric mode.

The speed alarm is set at the desired speed by driving 5 mph BELOW the desired speed (5 Km/h in metric mode) and depressing the SPEED ALARM button. The word SPEED will appear to indicate that the alarm has been set. For example, to set the speed alarm at 55 mph, drive 50 mph and depress the SPEED ALARM button. When the vehicle reaches the speed of 55 mph or faster, the alarm will be given until the speed drops below the 55 mph setting.

The speed alarm can be cleared or turned off by again depressing the SPEED ALARM button. The word SPEED will disappear to show that the alarm is no longer set.

If a speed alarm is desired in metric (Km/h), follow the same procedure as outlined, only with the system in the metric mode. Should the mode be changed with the speed alarm in operation, the alarm will be given at an equivalent speed in the newly selected mode.

GENERAL MOTORS CORPORTATION

Electronic Instrument Clusters

GENERAL INFORMATION

The Electronic Instrument Clusters used with the General Motors Corporation vehicle models, use a microprocessor to develop data for fuel supply, coolant temperature, oil pressure, voltage, engine rpm and vehicle speed. The instrument cluster also contains an odometer, warning lamp indicators and, in some vehicle models, an audible alarm. The audible alarm is used to signal low oil pressure, high temperature, low or high voltage and low fuel. With the ignition switch in the RUN position, voltage is applied through the gauges fuse to the battery power input of the electronic instrument cluster. With the light switch in the PARK or HEAD positions, voltage is applied at all times to the lights on dim input. The vehicle's speed is displayed in miles per hour (MPH) or kilometers per hour (Km/h) by selecting either the English or Metric selector switch.

The Electronic Instrument Clusters are vacuum fluorescent operated, with the vehicle information displayed by a variety of indicators, including digital and indicator lights.

No service work can be accomplished on the electronic cluster, since it is serviced as a complete unit. Should repairs be required, it must be returned to an authorized service center for a replacement unit.

--- CAUTION ---

Electrostatic discharge can damage the electronic cluster. Do not touch any electrical component or terminal directly, as static discharge from your body can cause damage to the electronic components of the cluster.

NOTE: When replacing a speedometer or odometer assembly, Federal law requires that the replacement odometer unit be set to show the same mileage as the odometer being replaced. If the same mileage cannot be set, the law requires that the replacement odometer be set to zero and that a label be installed on the driver's door frame to show the date of speedometer/odometer replacement and the accumulated mileage of the replaced odometer. It is a good policy to enter all data on a shop repair order, with the correct date and mileage shown. Have the vehicle owner sign the order, along with an authorized person repair shop signature

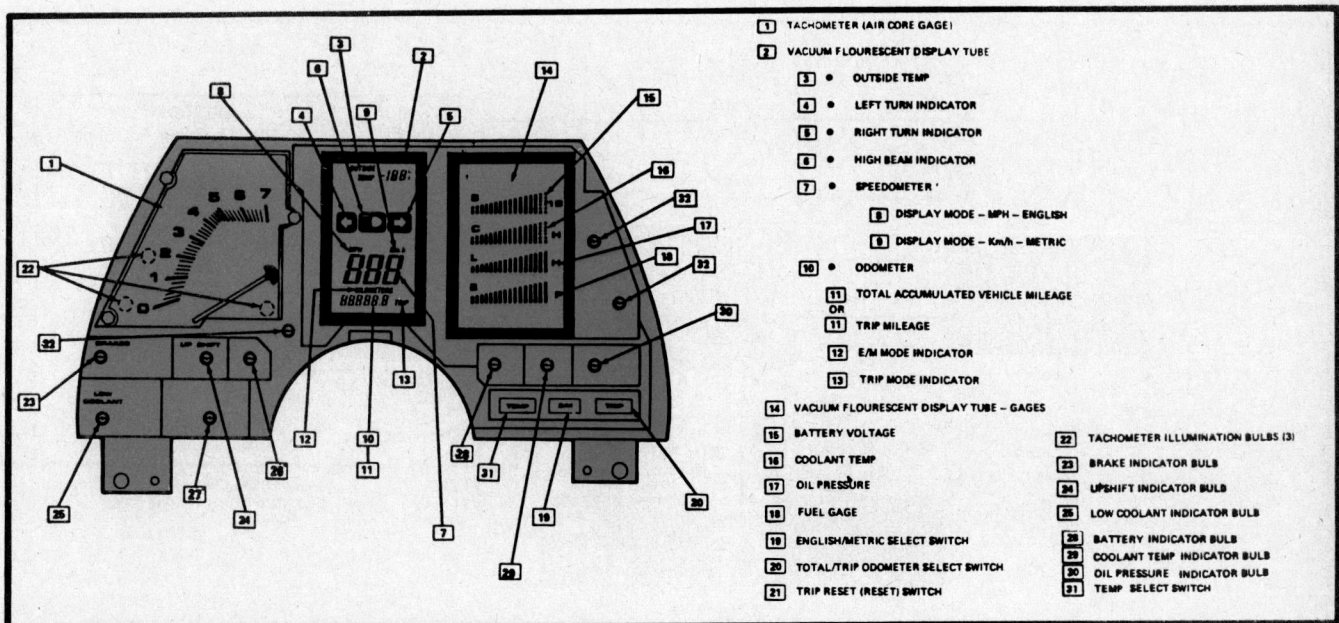

Typical General Motors Electronic Instrument Cluster

QUARTZ ELECTRONIC SPEEDOMETER

GENERAL DESCRIPTION

Quartz electronic speedometers and odometers show vehicle speed, total mileage and trip mileage like their earlier mechanical, cable driven versions did. But these new instrument clusters are driven electronically, instead of by cable.

Quartz electronic speedometer and odometer assemblies include the following components:

1. An odometer driven by electric stepper motor.
2. A speedometer dial and pointer controlled by the magnetic field of two air coils.

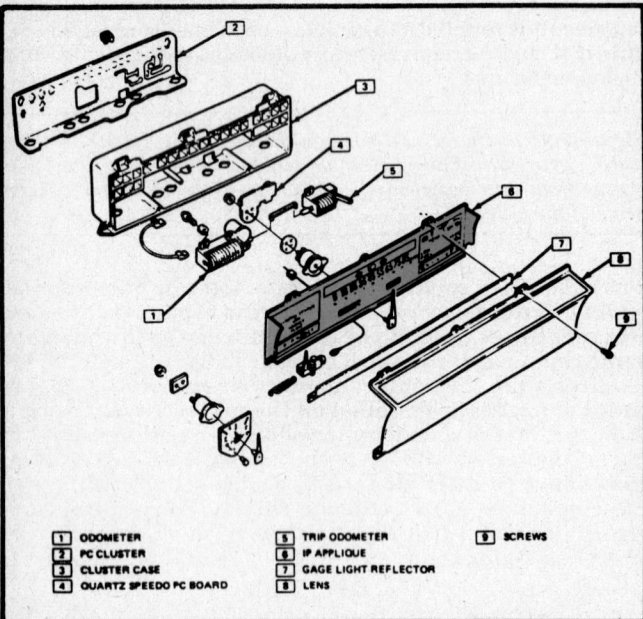

Exploded view of Quartz (Analog) Speedometer Cluster

1	ODOMETER	5	TRIP ODOMETER	9	SCREWS	
2	PC CLUSTER	6	IP APPLIQUE			
3	CLUSTER CASE	7	GAGE LIGHT REFLECTOR			
4	QUARTZ SPEEDO PC BOARD	8	LENS			

3. An electronic printed circuit board with a quartz crystal oscillator, integrated circuits and other electrical components.

The vehicle speed sensor (permanent-magnet generator) is attached to the transmission. The sensor generates vehicle speed information in the form of a sine wave. This signal is fed to the Vehicle Speed Sensor (VSS) buffer amplifier which conditions the signal into a square wave at a frequency proportional to the vehicle speed. The speed signal is used as an input by the Electronic Computer Module (ECM), the Cruise III Control System, and the quartz electronic speedometer circuits.

A quartz crystal oscillator on the speedometer printed circuit board gives an accurate timing signal which with logic and current driver Integrated Circuits (IC) further improve the accuracy of the speed signal.

System Components

QUARTZ SPEEDOMETER CIRCUIT BOARD

The circuit board assembly receives an analog speed signal from the VSS buffer amplifier, shapes it, then generates a modulated square wave output signal at 0.556 Hz/MPH. The signal drives the speedometer/pointer assembly by way of two air-core coils and the odometer stepper motor.

The circuit board is made up of the following:

1. The integrated circuits of a current driver chip and a logic chip mounted on the board.
2. A quartz crystal oscillator.
3. Diodes, resistors and capacitors that serve as buffers and surge suppressors, or provide electromagnetic interference protection.

ODOMETER CIRCUIT

The odometer consists of conventional odometer wheels driven by an electric stepper motor. A frequency-modulated square wave signal from the speedometer circuit controls the rate at which the stepper motor turns the gears on the odometer.

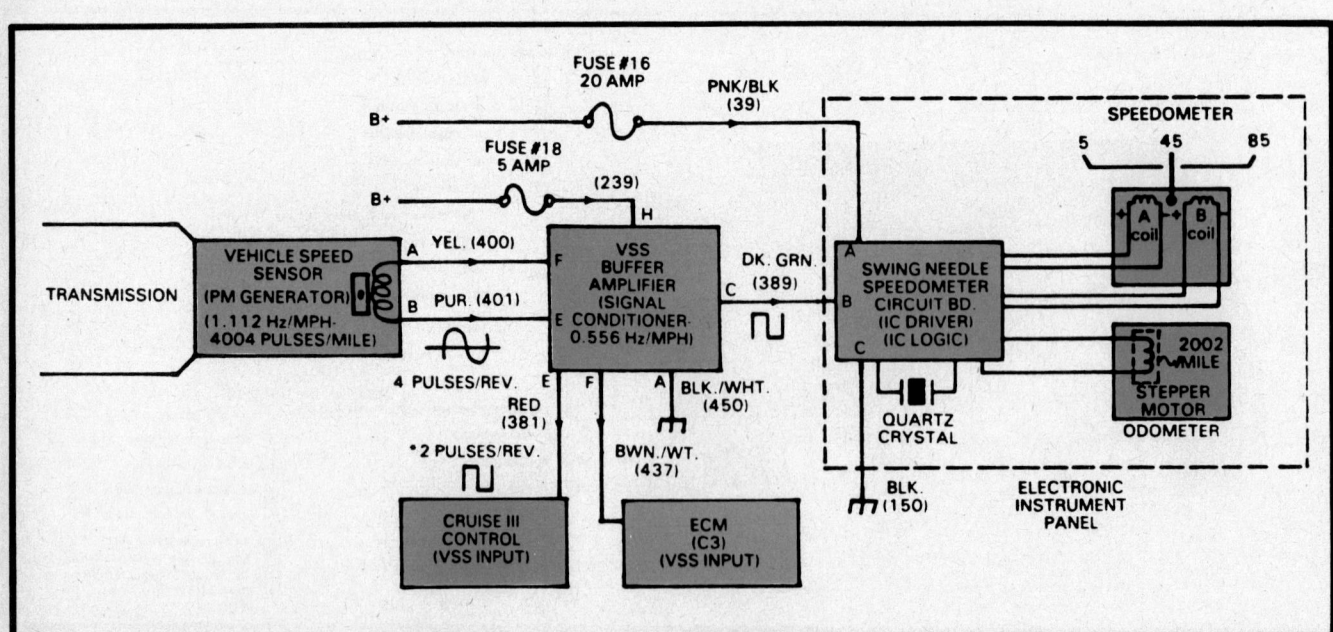

Quartz Speedometer electrical schematic

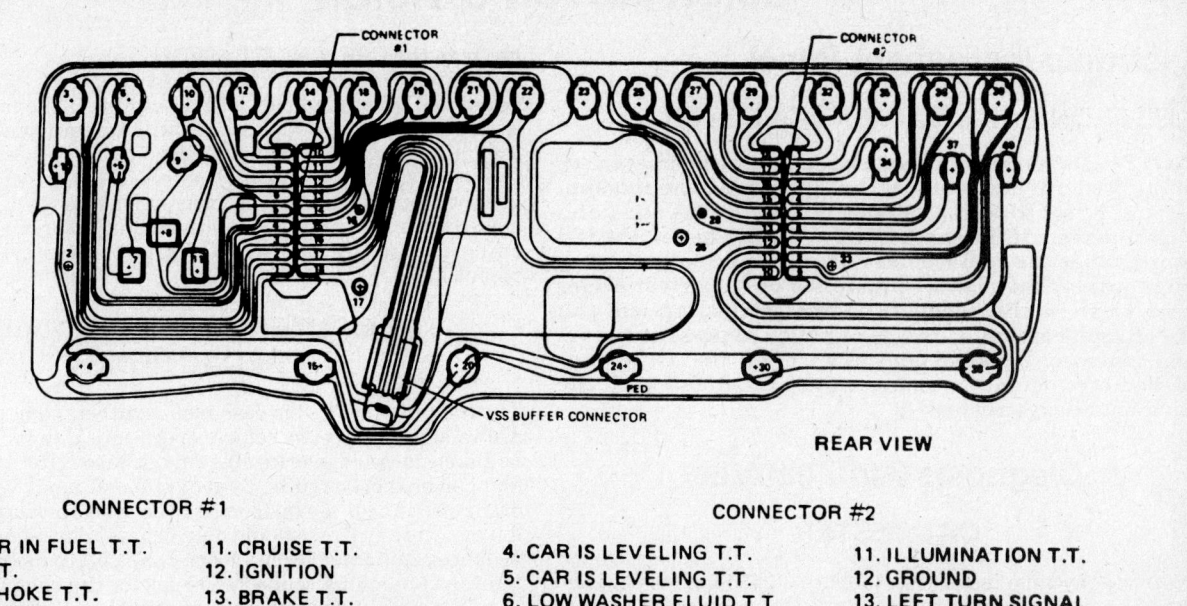

CONNECTOR #1

1. WATER IN FUEL T.T.	11. CRUISE T.T.
2. OIL T.T.	12. IGNITION
3. OIL/CHOKE T.T.	13. BRAKE T.T.
4. WAIT T.T.	14. RIGHT TURN SIGNAL
5. GROUND	15. HIGH BEAM T.T.
6. FUEL SENDER	16. IGNITION—ELECT. SP.
7. TEMPERATURE T.T.	17. SPEED SENSOR
8. VOLTAGE T.T.	18. GROUND—ELECT. SP.
9. & 10. SPARES	T.T. = TELLTALE

CONNECTOR #2

4. CAR IS LEVELING T.T.	11. ILLUMINATION T.T.
5. CAR IS LEVELING T.T.	12. GROUND
6. LOW WASHER FLUID T.T.	13. LEFT TURN SIGNAL
7. LOW WASHER FLUID	14. SEAT BELTS T.T.
8. SECURITY T.T.	15. SEAT BELTS T.T.
9. SECURITY—BATTERY FEED	16. SERVICE ENGINE SOON T.T.
1, 2, 3, 10 & 17 SPARES	18. IGNITION

Use of Mylar for speedometer assembly printed circuit baseboard

AIR CORE GAUGE ASSEMBLY

This assembly consists of two coils (A and B), an armature magnet and a case assembly. It uses the speed signals to display vehicle speed.

Current flowing through the coils generates a magnetic field based on the speed signals. As the field varies, the armature magnet inside the coils rotates and aligns a spindle and pointer (attached to the magnet) with the induced magnetic field. The pointer, thereby indicates the speed on the speedometer dial.

When the current potential across the coils is removed, the pointer should return to zero (MPH). However, some residual flux may remain within the air-core gage case to cause additional rotation, preventing the pointer from resting on zero when the ignition is 'OFF'. When the ignition is turned 'ON,' the pointer should return to zero.

VEHICLE SPEED SENSOR AND VSS BUFFER AMPLIFIER

The VSS develops vehicle speed information in the form of a 1.112 Hz/MPH sine wave. This speed signal is fed into the Buffer Amplifier, where it is shaped and converted into a 0.556 Hz/MPH speed signal. The square wave output signal from the VSS is used by the ECM, the Cruise III Control Module and the quartz Electronic Speedometer.

DIAGNOSIS

No output signal from the vehicle speed sensor would cause the Cruise Control to be inoperative, as well as the speedometer and odometer. Check wiring and connections to begin with. No speed signal input to the Electronic Module could cause vehicle drivability problems, among others. Therefore make certain the problem is not the result of a component failure that is preventing signal input to the instrument cluster. Do not suspect cluster electronics problems, without checking the most accessible parts in the system first.

––––––––––––––––– CAUTION –––––––––––––––––

When checking electronic components sensitive to electrostatic discharge, certain recommended practices must be used. Preventive measures are needed because unprotected electronic parts can be damaged by electrostatic voltages as low as 30 volts generated by an ungrounded person just sliding across the car seat. Under certain low humidity conditions, it is even possible to generate electrostatic voltages as high as 30,000 volts by just walking on a carpet across the room. Practices recommended to prevent electrostatic damage to sensitive components are as follows:

1. Transport static-sensitive parts in protective packaging.
2. Instruct service personnel to wear a wrist strap connected to ground through a one megohm resistor.
3. Use a static-protected work station free of static-producing material (such as styrofoam) when servicing electronic components.
4. Use a floor mat to stand on that is grounded to earth ground through a one megohm resistor.
5. Work in a dust-free work area where Relative Humidity is kept at no less than 30%.

BUICK MOTOR DIVISION

Electronic Instrument Panel

ELECTRONIC INSTRUMENT CLUSTER

NOTE: When replacing a speedometer or odometer assembly, Federal law requires that the replacement odometer unit be set to show the same mileage as the odometer being replaced. If the same mileage cannot be set, the law requires that the replacement odometer be set at zero. It also requires that a label be installed on the driver's door frame to show the previous odometer reading and the date of replacement. It is a good policy to present the vehicle owner with signed copy of a work order, reflecting speedometer/odometer repair work, dated and with the previous mileage recorded.

Diagnosis Aid Features

CRT TESTER

A cathode ray tube tester (Kent Moore J-34914 or its equivalent) is available to help isolate faults that may occur during the CRT operation. Substituting the tool in place of the CRTC will verify the integrity of the picture tube and switching the circuitry that make up the CRT. By connecting the tester directly to the CRT, the CRT can be checked as a unit. Connecting the tester to the vehicle harness, after the CRT has been independently checked out, will determine if the fault is in the wiring or the CRTC. The tester will run automatic tests and then allow individual switch tests.

Should the service facility obtain this type of tester to be used with the CRT system, instructions on its use will be included with the tester. Follow the manufacturer's recommended operating procedures to obtain the tester's maximum potential.

COMPUTER SYSTEM SERVICE PRECAUTIONS

The computer system is designed to withstand normal current draws associated with vehicle operation. However, care must be taken to avoid overloading any of these circuits. In testing for open or short circuits, do not ground or apply voltage to any of the circuits unless instructed to do so by the diagnosis procedures. These circuits should only be tested by using a High Impedance Mulimeter (Kent Moore J-29125A or its equivalent), if the tester remains connected to one of the computers. Power should never be applied or removed to one of the computers with the key in the ON position. Before removing or connecting battery cables, fuses or connectors, always turn the ignition switch to the OFF position.

ELECTRONIC INSTRUMENT CLUSTER

GENERAL INFORMATION

1983-86 BUICK CENTURY

The Electronic Instrument Cluster uses a digital microprocessor to develop data for fuel supply, trip distance and vehicle speed. The electronic instrument panel also contains conventional indicators and a mechanical total miles odometer.

The power to the cluster is through the Courtesy fuse on the

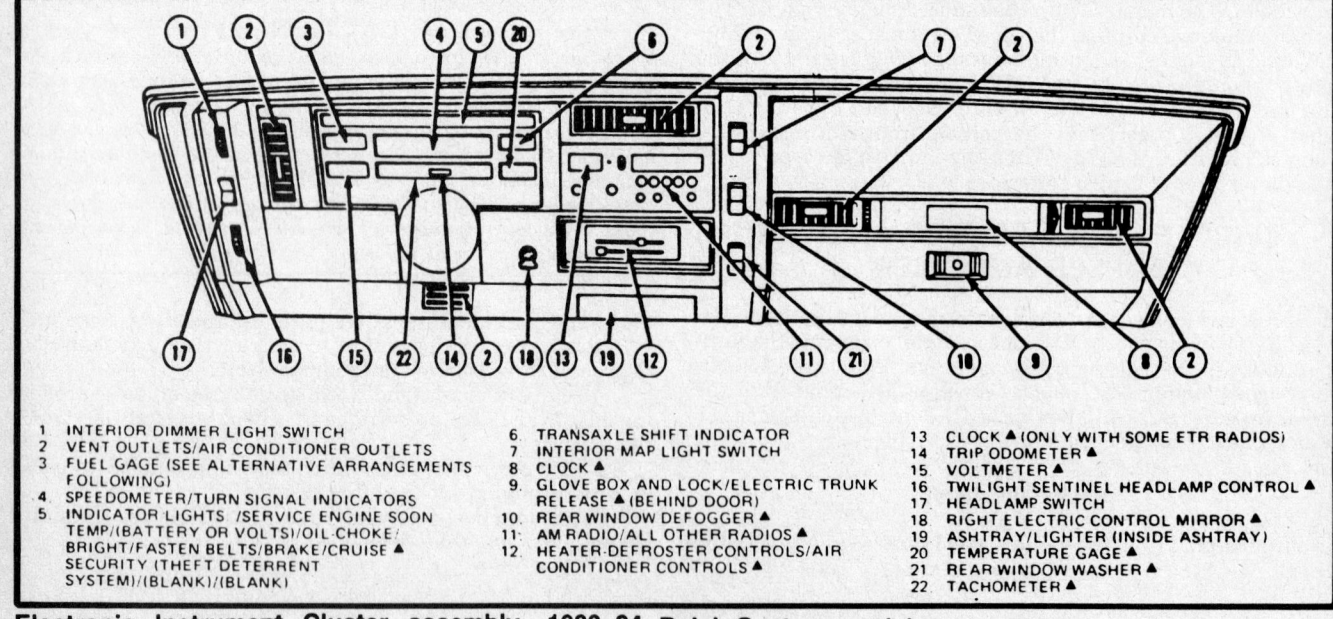

1. INTERIOR DIMMER LIGHT SWITCH
2. VENT OUTLETS/AIR CONDITIONER OUTLETS
3. FUEL GAGE (SEE ALTERNATIVE ARRANGEMENTS FOLLOWING)
4. SPEEDOMETER/TURN SIGNAL INDICATORS
5. INDICATOR LIGHTS /SERVICE ENGINE SOON TEMP/(BATTERY OR VOLTS)/OIL-CHOKE/ BRIGHT/FASTEN BELTS/BRAKE/CRUISE ▲ SECURITY (THEFT DETERRENT SYSTEM)/(BLANK)/(BLANK)
6. TRANSAXLE SHIFT INDICATOR
7. INTERIOR MAP LIGHT SWITCH
8. CLOCK ▲
9. GLOVE BOX AND LOCK/ELECTRIC TRUNK RELEASE ▲ (BEHIND DOOR)
10. REAR WINDOW DEFOGGER ▲
11. AM RADIO/ALL OTHER RADIOS ▲
12. HEATER-DEFROSTER CONTROLS/AIR CONDITIONER CONTROLS ▲
13. CLOCK ▲ (ONLY WITH SOME ETR RADIOS)
14. TRIP ODOMETER ▲
15. VOLTMETER ▲
16. TWILIGHT SENTINEL HEADLAMP CONTROL ▲
17. HEADLAMP SWITCH
18. RIGHT ELECTRIC CONTROL MIRROR ▲
19. ASHTRAY/LIGHTER (INSIDE ASHTRAY)
20. TEMPERATURE GAGE ▲
21. REAR WINDOW WASHER ▲
22. TACHOMETER ▲

Electronic Instrument Cluster assembly, 1983–84 Buick Century models

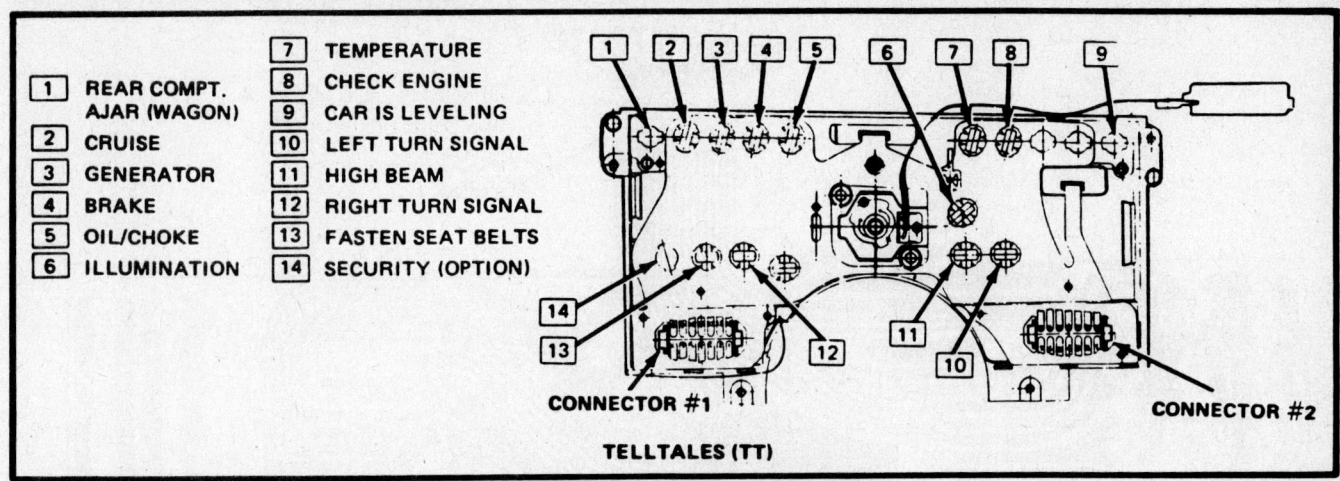

1 REAR COMPT. AJAR (WAGON)	7 TEMPERATURE
2 CRUISE	8 CHECK ENGINE
3 GENERATOR	9 CAR IS LEVELING
4 BRAKE	10 LEFT TURN SIGNAL
5 OIL/CHOKE	11 HIGH BEAM
6 ILLUMINATION	12 RIGHT TURN SIGNAL
	13 FASTEN SEAT BELTS
	14 SECURITY (OPTION)

CONNECTOR #1   CONNECTOR #2

TELLTALES (TT)

Rear of Electronic Instrument cluster, 1983–84 Buick Century models

fuse panel and this power retains the trip odometer memory when the trip odometer is in the OFF position.

When the ignition switch is in the "RUN", "BULB TEST" or "START" positions, voltage is applied through the Gauge fuse to the instrument panel. One second later, all digital display segments come on together as a display test. The display test lasts up to 3 seconds. The display then shows its current data.

When the "E/M" button is depressed, the digital display changes between English units (miles, mph and gallons) and Metric units (km, km/h and liters).

With the light switch in the OFF position, no current is applied to the instrument display dimmer and the digital display shows maximum brightness. With the light switch in the parking lamp-on or headlamp-on position, voltage is applied to the display dimmer enable input at the instrument panel. Current is also applied through the instrument panel dimmer switch, the instrument lamp fuse and the GRY wire to the instrument panel. The voltage on the GRY wire varies as the dimmer control is moved. The digital display illumination varies along with the voltage of the GRY wire, causing the display to dim or become brighter as the GRY wire voltage is reduced or increased.

SPEEDOMETER DISPLAY

With the ignition switch in the "RUN", "BULB TEST" or "START" position, current flows through the gauge fuse to the buffer amplifier and then to ground. As the vehicle moves, the speedometer cable turns the shaft to the mechanical total miles odometer. An infra-red light shines from the vehicle speed sensor onto a rotating field plate in the speedometer. The field plate sends back to the vehicle speed sensor, pulses of light, which are converted by an optical photocell to electrical pulses. The buffer amplifier sends those pulses through wiring (BRN) to the instrument panel display. The pulse rate (speed) is displayed as mph or km/h.

TRIP ODOMETER DISPLAY

The instrument panel display adds up the number of reflected light pulses and advances the trip odometer mileage display. When the trip set button is depressed, the trip odometer returns to "0.0" display. The trip odometer displays tenths of miles until "999.9" and miles from "1000" to "3999". After "3999", the trip odometer returns to a "0.0" display.

DIGITAL INSTRUMENT CLUSTER

GENERAL INFORMATION

1985-86 LESABRE, ELECTRA/PARK AVENUE

The instrument panel has a vacuum fluorescent (VF) digital display for the speedometer and the odometer. The gauge display functions are VF bar graphs. all other displays and indicators within the digital cluster are VF displays as well. All the functions in the cluster are controlled by a solid state microprocessor.

With the light switch in the OFF position, no voltage is applied to the BRN wire and the digital display shows maximum brightness. With the light switch in the PARK or HEAD-LAMP – ON positions, battery voltage is applied to the dimmer input at the instrument panel. Voltage is also applied through the instrument panel illumination input. Voltage applied to the dimmer input varies as the dimmer is moved. The digital display dims as the voltage is reduced to this input.

An English/Metric switch will change the readout modes

from English to Metric or from Metric to English. The following displays are affected:
1. Speedometer.
2. Trip odometer.
3. Seasonal odometer.

Upon powering up, the cluster display will assume the last mode selected. When the ignition switch is turned on, all segments will light up at full intensity, except for the bar graphs, turn signals and the high beam indicator. The bar graphs will run from empty to full, cold to hot, minimum to maximum speed and then reverse. All displays will then revert to their normal readings.

SPEEDOMETER DISPLAY

Speed indication is provided by a speed sensor (PM generator), located in the transaxle. This signal is then sent to the buffer amplifier. The buffer amplifier then outputs a signal of 1.112

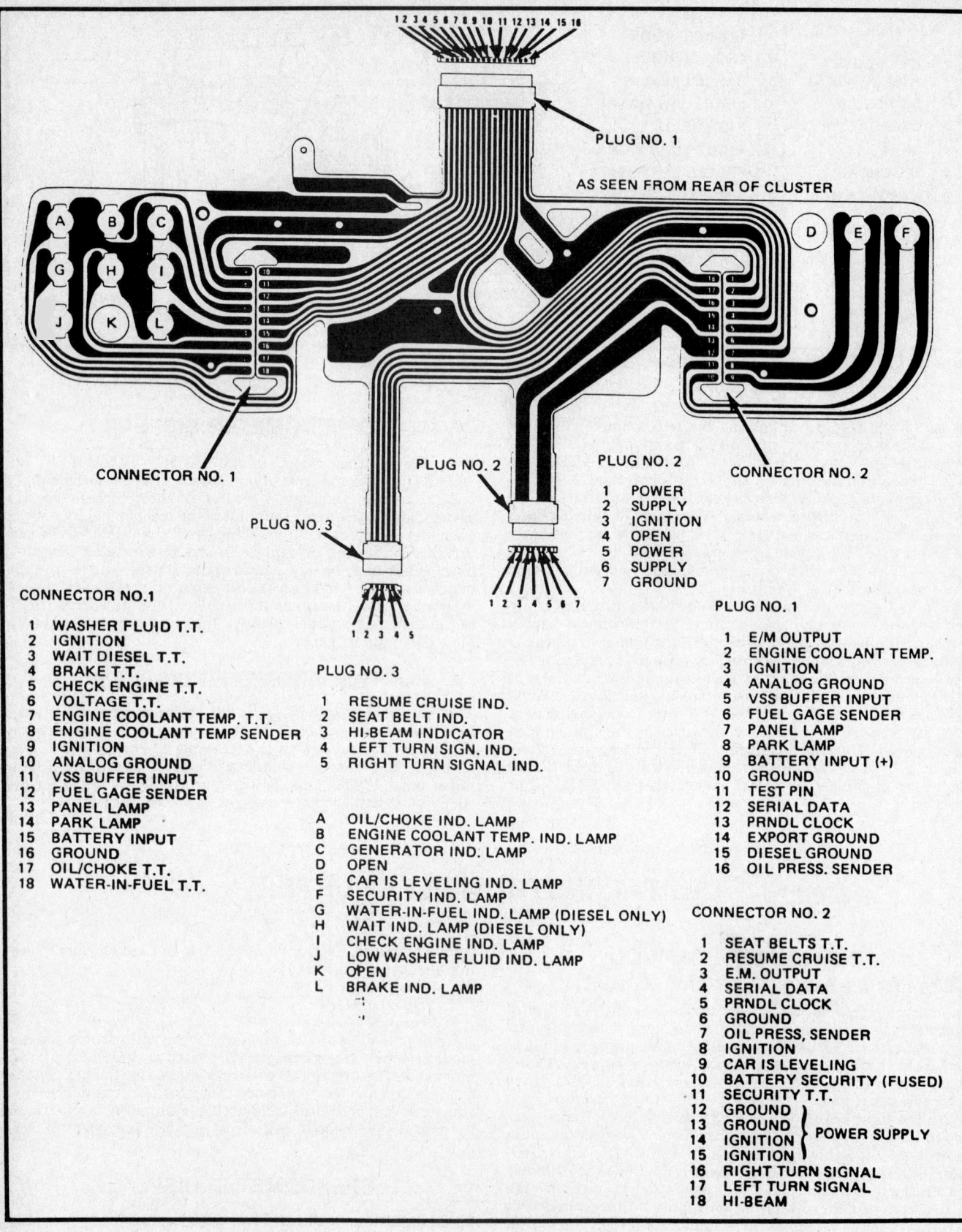

PLUG NO. 1

AS SEEN FROM REAR OF CLUSTER

CONNECTOR NO. 1

PLUG NO. 2

PLUG NO. 2

1 POWER
2 SUPPLY
3 IGNITION
4 OPEN
5 POWER
6 SUPPLY
7 GROUND

CONNECTOR NO. 2

PLUG NO. 3

CONNECTOR NO.1

1 WASHER FLUID T.T.
2 IGNITION
3 WAIT DIESEL T.T.
4 BRAKE T.T.
5 CHECK ENGINE T.T.
6 VOLTAGE T.T.
7 ENGINE COOLANT TEMP. T.T.
8 ENGINE COOLANT TEMP SENDER
9 IGNITION
10 ANALOG GROUND
11 VSS BUFFER INPUT
12 FUEL GAGE SENDER
13 PANEL LAMP
14 PARK LAMP
15 BATTERY INPUT
16 GROUND
17 OIL/CHOKE T.T.
18 WATER-IN-FUEL T.T.

PLUG NO. 3

1 RESUME CRUISE IND.
2 SEAT BELT IND.
3 HI-BEAM INDICATOR
4 LEFT TURN SIGN. IND.
5 RIGHT TURN SIGNAL IND.

A OIL/CHOKE IND. LAMP
B ENGINE COOLANT TEMP. IND. LAMP
C GENERATOR IND. LAMP
D OPEN
E CAR IS LEVELING IND. LAMP
F SECURITY IND. LAMP
G WATER-IN-FUEL IND. LAMP (DIESEL ONLY)
H WAIT IND. LAMP (DIESEL ONLY)
I CHECK ENGINE IND. LAMP
J LOW WASHER FLUID IND. LAMP
K OPEN
L BRAKE IND. LAMP

PLUG NO. 1

1 E/M OUTPUT
2 ENGINE COOLANT TEMP.
3 IGNITION
4 ANALOG GROUND
5 VSS BUFFER INPUT
6 FUEL GAGE SENDER
7 PANEL LAMP
8 PARK LAMP
9 BATTERY INPUT (+)
10 GROUND
11 TEST PIN
12 SERIAL DATA
13 PRNDL CLOCK
14 EXPORT GROUND
15 DIESEL GROUND
16 OIL PRESS. SENDER

CONNECTOR NO. 2

1 SEAT BELTS T.T.
2 RESUME CRUISE T.T.
3 E.M. OUTPUT
4 SERIAL DATA
5 PRNDL CLOCK
6 GROUND
7 OIL PRESS, SENDER
8 IGNITION
9 CAR IS LEVELING
10 BATTERY SECURITY (FUSED)
11 SECURITY T.T.
12 GROUND
13 GROUND   } POWER SUPPLY
14 IGNITION
15 IGNITION
16 RIGHT TURN SIGNAL
17 LEFT TURN SIGNAL
18 HI-BEAM

Rear of Electronic Instrument Cluster, 1985–86 LeSabre, Electra/Park Avenue models

Hertz per mph to the cluster. This signal is then processed by the cluster to display speed in either miles per hour (MPH) or kilometers per hour (KM/H). The maximum speed displayed is 85 MPH or 140 KM/H.

The speed display consists of an 81 segment bar graph. This indicated speed segment will be lit at full intensity. All segments below the indicated speed will be at 30% of full intensity and all segments above the indicated speed will be at 10 % of full intensity. The digits above the bar graph show either English or Metric intervals, depending upon the position of the E/M switch.

ELECTRONIC INSTRUMENT CLUSTER

1985-86 Somerset/Skylark

The electronic instrument cluster has a Vacuum Fluorescent digital display for the speedometer and the odometer. The gauge functions are VF bar graphs and all the functions in the cluster are controlled by a solid state microprocessor.

This cluster may be programmed for different engine/transaxle applications, some of which are not carried over from year to year. The various connections to the Programmed Ground (PG) terminals can be found on the POWER wiring schematic overview.

The tachometer readings and the red lines, the maximum speedometer reading, the shift indicator and the "UNLEADED FUEL ONLY" display are affected by the PG grounds.

DISPLAY DIMMING

With the light switch in the OFF position, no voltage is applied to the Display Dim Enable Input and the digital display will show maximum brightness.

With the light switch in the PARK or HEADLAMP position, battery voltage is applied to the Display Dim Enable Input at the digital cluster. Voltage is also applied through the instrument panel dimmer and the INST LPS fuse (GRY wire) to the Display Dim Input. Voltage is varied as the dimmer is moved and the digital display is dimmed as the voltage is reduced to the input.

SPEEDOMETER DISPLAY

Vehicle speed indication is provided by a speed sensor (PM generator), located in the transaxle. The buffer amplifier is contained within the cluster and supplies the speedometer display module with converted Hertz signal to create a display.

NOTE: If the speed buffer is defective, the instrument cluster must be replaced.

The maximum speed that can be displayed is 85 mph (140 km/h). Above these speeds, the display will flash at a rate of once per second (1 Hertz).

NOTE: Certain instrument digital cluster will have indicator lamps instead of the bar graphs to indicate malfunctions within the systems.

TACHOMETER

The tachometer receives a signal from the ignition coil through the Electronic Fuel Injection Ignition. The tachometer is in the form of a bar graph to 6,000 rpm, with an underlining red line from 4,000 to 6,000 rpm.

ELECTRONIC INSTRUMENT CLUSTER ASSEMBLY

GENERAL INFORMATION

1985-86 REGAL

The electronic instrument cluster has a Vacuum Fluorescent digital display for the speedometer and the odometer. The temperature and fuel gauge functions are VF bar graphs and all the functions in the cluster are controlled by a solid state microprocessor.

DISPLAY DIMMING

With the light switch in the OFF position, no voltage is applied

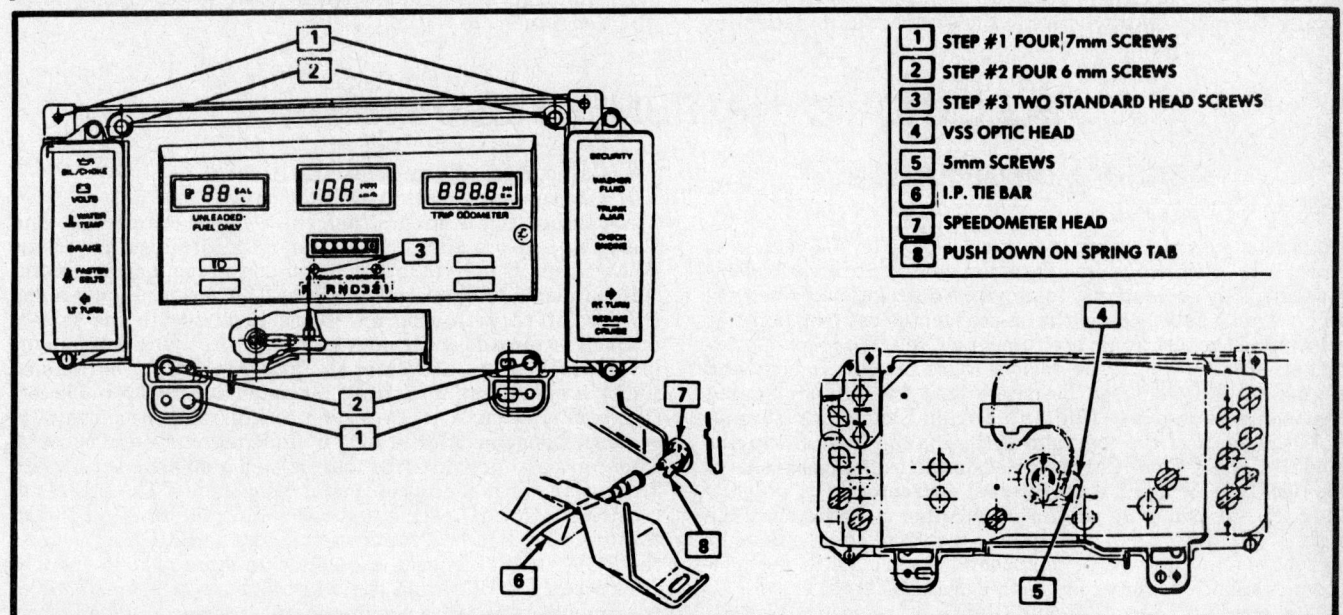

1. STEP #1 FOUR 7mm SCREWS
2. STEP #2 FOUR 6 mm SCREWS
3. STEP #3 TWO STANDARD HEAD SCREWS
4. VSS OPTIC HEAD
5. 5mm SCREWS
6. I.P. TIE BAR
7. SPEEDOMETER HEAD
8. PUSH DOWN ON SPRING TAB

Electronic Instrument Cluster assembly, 1983–85 Riviera, 1985–86 Buick Regal models

to the Display Dim Enable Input and the digital display will show maximum brightness.

With the light switch in the PARK or HEADLAMP position, battery voltage is applied to the Display Dim Enable Input at the digital cluster. Voltage is also applied through the instrument panel dimmer and the INST LPS fuse (GRY wire) to the Display Dim Input. Voltage is varied as the dimmer is moved and the digital display is dimmed as the voltage is reduced to the input.

SPEEDOMETER DISPLAY

Vehicle speed indication is provided by a speed sensor (PM generator), located in the transaxle. The buffer amplifier is contained within the cluster and supplies the speedometer display module with converted Hertz signal to create a display.

NOTE: If the speed buffer is defective, the instrument cluster must be replaced.

The maximum speed that can be displayed is 85 mph (140 km/h). Above these speeds, the display will flash at a rate of once per second (1 Hertz).

NOTE: Certain instrument digital cluster will have indicator lamps instead of the bar graphs to indicate malfunctions within the systems.

ELECTRONIC INSTRUMENT CLUSTER

Digital Cluster
GENERAL INFORMATION

1983-85 RIVIERA

The Digital Cluster uses a microprocessor to interpret data from various sensors and convert it to readings on fuel supply, trip distance and vehicle speed. The cluster also contains some conventional indicators and a mechanical odometer recording total miles.

Current is supplied constantly to the CLK-CIG fuse, and ORN wire to the digital cluster. Current is not interrupted by the ignition switch so that the trip odometer memory will be maintained when the ignition switch is turned off.

Power is supplied through the GAGES fuse to the digital cluster whenever the ignition switch is in "RUN", "BULB TEST", or "START". One second after power is supplied, all the digital display segments come on together as a visual test. After, up to three seconds, the displays show current data. Turning the reset buttons will change the displays for MI (miles), MPH (miles per hour), and GAL (gallons) to metric units km (kilometers), km/h (kilometers per hour), and L (liters).

The cluster is designed so that illumination intensity will always match the light conditions in the car. With the headlight switch off, no voltage is applied to the BRN wire. The digital display will then show maximum brightness. When the light switch is turned to either "Park" or "Head", battery voltage is applied through the BRN wire to the Cluster Illumination in-

put at the digital cluster. Voltage is also applied through the INSTRUMENT PANEL DIMMER, the INST LPS fuse, and the GRY wire to the cluster. The voltage on the GRY wire varies as the dimmer is moved. The digital display illumination dims as the voltage on the GRY wire is reduced.

SPEEDOMETER DISPLAY

With the ignition switch in "Run", "Bulb Test", or "Start", current flows through the GAGES fuse and Vehicle Speed Sensor (VSS) to ground. As the car moves, the speedometer cable is gear driven and turns the shaft which drives the mechanical total miles odometer. An infra-red light is sent by the Vehicle Speed Sensor through a rotating field plate inside the speedometer. This, in turn, reflects the pulses of light onto the Vehicle Speed Sender. These are converted by a photocell to electrical pulses. The vehicle speed sensor sends these pulses to the Digital Cluster through the connector cavity K. The cluster is programmed to convert the number of pulses, measured against actual time elapsed, into MPH or km/h.

TRIP ODOMETER DISPLAY

The digital cluster counts the light pulses and advances the Trip Odometer mileage appropriately. The Trip Odometer displays mileage accumulated since reset up to "3999", after which it returns to "0.0".

ELECTRONIC INSTRUMENT CLUSTER

GENERAL INFORMATION

1986 BUICK RIVIERA

Numerous electronic components are located on the vehicle as a part of an electrical network, designed to control various engine and body subsystems. To provide a description of the overall electronic network and the on-board diagnostic capabilities relating to the electronic instrument cluster, the following explanation is provided. The various codes relating to body and engine malfunctions can be determined from accompanying charts and reference to Chilton's Engine Electronics Manual.

At the heart of the computer system is the Body Computer Module (BCM). The BCM is located on the front drivers side of the floor console and has an internal microprocessor, which is the center for communication with all other components in the system. All sensors and switches are monitored by the BCM or one of the four other major components that complete the computer system. The four components are as follows:
1. Electronic Control Module (ECM)
2. Instrument Panel Cluster (IPC)

3. Cathode Ray Tube Controller (CRTC)
4. Programmer/Heating/Ventilation/AC

A combination of inputs from these major components and the other sensors and switches communicate together to the BCM, either as individual inputs, or on the common communication link called the serial data line. The various inputs to the BMC combine with program instructions within the system memory to provide accurate control over the many subsystems involved. When a subsystem circuit exceeds pre-programmed limits, a system malfunction is indicated and may provide certain back-up functions. Providing control over the many subsystems from the BCM is done by controlling system outputs. This can be either direct of transmitted along the serial data line to one of the four other major components. The process of receiving, storing, testing and controlling information is continuous. The data communication gives the BMC control over the ECM's self-diagnostic capacities in addition to its own.

Between the BCM and the other four major components of the computer system, a communication process has been incorporated which allows the devices to share information and

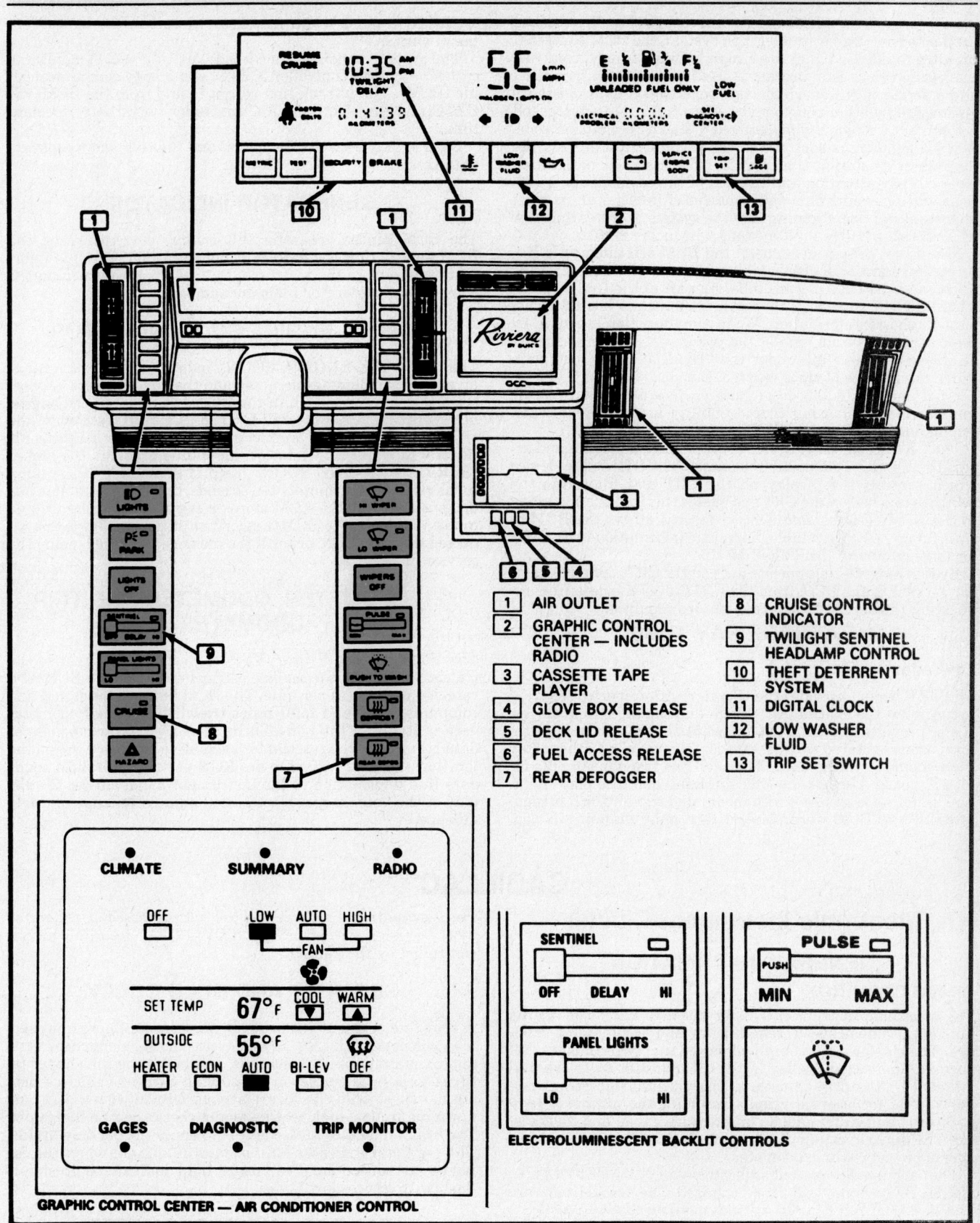

1	AIR OUTLET	**8**	CRUISE CONTROL INDICATOR
2	GRAPHIC CONTROL CENTER — INCLUDES RADIO	**9**	TWILIGHT SENTINEL HEADLAMP CONTROL
3	CASSETTE TAPE PLAYER	**10**	THEFT DETERRENT SYSTEM
4	GLOVE BOX RELEASE	**11**	DIGITAL CLOCK
5	DECK LID RELEASE	**12**	LOW WASHER FLUID
6	FUEL ACCESS RELEASE	**13**	TRIP SET SWITCH
7	REAR DEFOGGER		

GRAPHIC CONTROL CENTER — AIR CONDITIONER CONTROL

CLIMATE   SUMMARY   RADIO

OFF   LOW   AUTO   HIGH
FAN

SET TEMP   67°F   COOL   WARM
OUTSIDE   55°F
HEATER   ECON   AUTO   BI-LEV   DEF

GAGES   DIAGNOSTIC   TRIP MONITOR

ELECTROLUMINESCENT BACKLIT CONTROLS

SENTINEL
OFF   DELAY   HI

PULSE
PUSH
MIN   MAX

PANEL LIGHTS
LO   HI

Electronic Instrument Cluster assembly, 1986 Riviera models

thereby provide for additional control capabilities. In a method similar to that used by a telegraph system, the BCM's internal circuitry rapidly switches to a circuit between 0 and 5 volts like a telegraph key. This process is used to convert information into a series of pulses which represents coded data messages understood by other components. Also, much like a telegraph system, each major component has its own recognition code. When a message is sent out on the serial data line, only the component or station that matches the assigned recognition code will pay attention and the rest of the components or stations will ignore it. This data transfer of information is most important in understanding how the system operates and how to diagnosis possible malfunctions within the system.

In order to access and control the BCM self-diagnostic features, two additional electronic components are necessary, the CRTC and the CRT picture tube. As part of the CRT's "SERVICE MODE" page, a 22 character display area is used to display diagnostic information. When a malfunction is sensed by the computer system, one of the driver warning messages is displayed on the CRT under the "DIAGNOSTIC" category. When the Service Mode is entered, the various BCM, ECM, or IPC parameters, fault codes, inputs, outputs as well as override commands and clearing code capability are displayed when commanded through the CRT.

The CRT becomes the device to enter the diagnostics and access the Service Diagnostic routines. The CRTC is the device which controls the display on the CRT and interprets the switches touched on the CRT and passes this information along to the BCM. This communication process allows the BCM to transfer any of its available diagnostic information to the CRT for display during "SERVICE MODE".

By touching the appropriate pads on the CRT, data messages can be sent to the BCM from the CRTC over the data line, requesting the specific diagnostic feature required.

CATHODE RAY TUBE

Operation

The CRT system provides the operator with fingertip electronic control of the heating/AC system and the radio/tape player. It also provides clock and trip information. This control and information is entered and displayed by the use of a Cathode Ray Tube mounted in the dash. The CRT has two adjustments for viewing ease. The are the CRT dimming and face plate light. The dimming is a pulse width modulated signal which is regulated by the BCM. Incandescent face plate dimming is controlled by a pulse width modulator circuit in the instrument panel cluster.

The systems consists of a cathode ray tube (CRT) monitor, a cathode ray tube controller (CRTC) and a body computer module (BCM). The information is sent to and from the BCM, the CRTC and the electronic A/C controller with the serial data link.

Data is sent between the CRTC and the radio on a separate data link.

GENERATOR INDICATOR

The BCM senses generator (alternator) current. When the BCM detects that the battery is not charging, data line information is sent to the instrument panel cluster to turn on the warning red generator indicator lamp.

SERVICE ENGINE SOON INDICATOR

The "SERVICE ENGINE SOON" indicator lamp warns that an engine problem has occurred and the vehicle needs service. With the ignition switch in the RUN position, but the engine not operating, the lamp will turn on as a bulb test. When the engine is started, the lamp should turn off. If the Electronic Control Module (ECM) detects an engine problem. the amber "SERVICE ENGINE SOON" lamp is turned on. If the lamp turns off in approximately ten seconds, the engine problem has disappeared, but the ECM stores a trouble code. The trouble code will stay in the ECM memory until the battery is disconnected from the ECM or until the memory is cleared, using the service mode.

SPEEDOMETER, ODOMETER AND TRIP ODOMETER

The Vehicle Speed Sensor (VSS) is located at the rear of the transaxle. The sensor sends electrical pulses to the BCM at a rate of 4,000 pulses per mile. The BCM buffers this signal and computes speed and total miles traveled. Seasonal odometer data is stored in the non-volatile memory. The trip odometer data is stored in the resettable "keep-alive" memory. When the ignition switch is turned to the RUN position, the BCM sends data line information to the instrument panel cluster for display of the vehicle speed, total accumulated mileage and trip mileage.

CADILLAC

Electronic Instrument Cluster

GENERAL INFORMATION

1984-86 CIMARRON

The electronic instrument cluster displays all major engine functions, vehicle speed, trip mileage and accumulated mileage. The cluster's self contained power supply illuminates all vacuum fluorescent display, while the indicator bulbs are illuminated by the printed circuit. The vacuum fluorescent displays in the forms of bar graphs, including the voltmeter, temperature gauge, fuel gauge , oil pressure gauge and tachometer. The digital vacuum fluorescent displays are speedometer, odometer and the trip odometer.

The vacuum fluorescent indicators are "TURNSIGNALS", "HIGH BEAM" and "CRUISE" engaged. The bulb telltales are "LOW COOLANT", (V6 cylinder only), "FOG LAMPS", "BRAKES", "CHECK ENGINE", "LOW FUEL", "HAZARD", "FASTEN BELTS" and "SHIFT INDICATOR" (4 cylinder only with manual transmission). These telltale signals originate from conventional sources and are not processed or generated by the cluster, except for the "LOW FUEL" telltale which is controlled by the cluster.

SEGMENT AND BULB CHECK

A complete segment check of all the vacuum fluorescent segments is done with each key-on cycle. The segment check lasts approximately three (3) seconds, at which time the cluster returns to normal operation, displaying current vehicle sensor status. These bulb checks are also performed with the key on, low coolant , low fuel, seat belts and checks engine indicators. The brake indicator bulb check is to apply the parking brake . The fog lamp indicator bulb should illuminate when the fog lamps are turned on. The hazard light indicator bulb should flash with the hazard lamps.

GAUGES AND TACHOMETER

The gauge signal source for the oil pressure gauge is taken

from the engine oil pressure gallery by an ON-OFF gauge. The fuel gauge signal source uses a higher resistance (160 ohm), three wire sending unit, instead of the 90 ohm, two wire sending unit used with the standard cluster.

The input signal for the temperature gauge, voltmeter and the tachometer is from the ECM and is transmitted over the serial data line connected to the cluster.

SPEEDOMETER DISPLAY
Circuit Operation

The vehicle speed sensor generates a signal that indicates the speed of the vehicle. The signal is processed by the solid state vehicle speed sensor buffer to supply inputs to the electronic control module (ECM), the cruise control module and speedometer.

The vehicle speed sensor is mounted in the transaxle. It contains a magnet which rotates near a coil, producing a voltage pulse in the coil. The magnet that is attached to the transaxle turns four times faster than a standard speedometer cable. The coil near the magnet has 4000 pulses per mile generated in it.

The frequency of the AC voltage coming from this coil depends upon the vehicle speed. As the speed increases, so does the number of voltage pulses per second. The vehicle speed sensor buffer takes the voltage pulses from the sensor and uses them to close four solid state output switches. Each output terminal is switched to ground at a rate that is proportional to the speed of the vehicle. The speedometer is switched at the same frequency that the sensor generates. The electronic control module (ECM) and the cruise control use a lower frequency. Their input switches are operated by a circuit that divides the sensor frequency by two.

The maximum speed displayed is 85 mph or 137 kph. Speeds in excess of the maximum speeds are displayed by flashing 85 mph or 137 kmh.

TOTAL ODOMETER DISPLAY

The vehicle distance traveled is computed, based on the input provided by the vehicle speed sensor (VSS). The odometer will display on six digits, indicating with leading zeros up to a 200,000 miles or 321,799 kilometers, depending upon the English/Metric switch mode. The record of distance traveled is retained in a non-volatile memory chip to the nearest ten miles. This means that if all power is removed from the cluster or the car battery is disconnected, up to 9.9 miles can be lost from the current odometer reading. The life of the chip is ten years from the last update. If the non-volatile memory chip is tampered with, or the cluster's microprocessor cannot read from the NVM chip, the odometer display will indicate "ERROR". If the mileage accumulation exceeds 200,000 miles or 321,799 kilometers, the odometer display will indicate "FULL". The NVM chip is removable to allow it to be changed from a defective cluster into a replacement unit.

TRIP ODOMETER

The trip odometer will indicate the number of miles or kilometers the vehicle has traveled since the last time of reset.

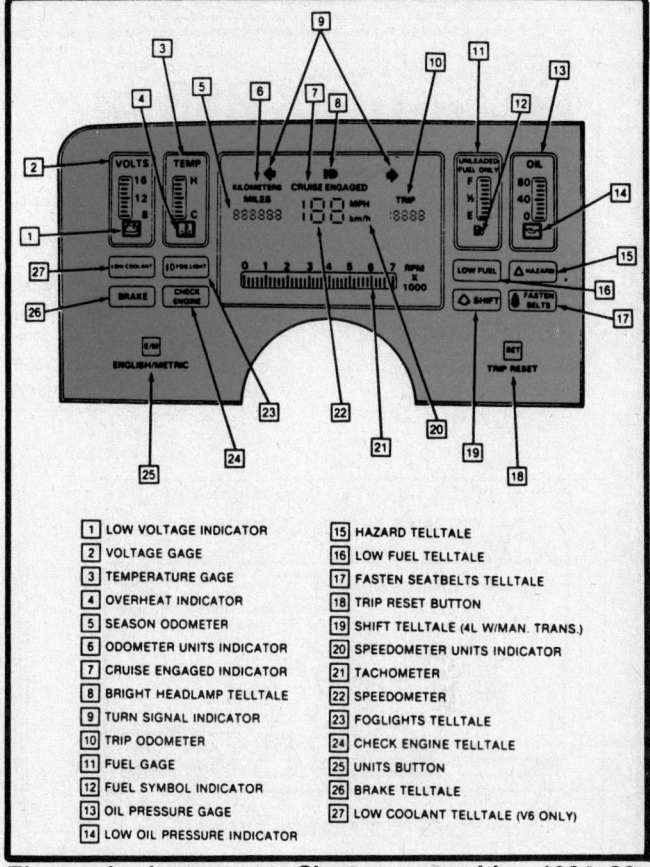

1 LOW VOLTAGE INDICATOR	15 HAZARD TELLTALE
2 VOLTAGE GAGE	16 LOW FUEL TELLTALE
3 TEMPERATURE GAGE	17 FASTEN SEATBELTS TELLTALE
4 OVERHEAT INDICATOR	18 TRIP RESET BUTTON
5 SEASON ODOMETER	19 SHIFT TELLTALE (4L W/MAN. TRANS.)
6 ODOMETER UNITS INDICATOR	20 SPEEDOMETER UNITS INDICATOR
7 CRUISE ENGAGED INDICATOR	21 TACHOMETER
8 BRIGHT HEADLAMP TELLTALE	22 SPEEDOMETER
9 TURN SIGNAL INDICATOR	23 FOGLIGHTS TELLTALE
10 TRIP ODOMETER	24 CHECK ENGINE TELLTALE
11 FUEL GAGE	25 UNITS BUTTON
12 FUEL SYMBOL INDICATOR	26 BRAKE TELLTALE
13 OIL PRESSURE GAGE	27 LOW COOLANT TELLTALE (V6 ONLY)
14 LOW OIL PRESSURE INDICATOR	

Electronic Instrument Cluster assembly, 1984–86 Cimarron models

The trip odometer has four digits and will display the accumulated distance traveled up to 1000 miles or 1608 kilometers depending upon being in the English or Metric mode. The trip odometer will rollover at 1609 kilometers if the last reset was done in the English mode. Also, the trip odometer will; rollover at 621 miles if the last reset was made in the Metric mode.

The trip odometer will retain the accumulated mileage as long as the battery voltage is applied. Should the battery voltage be disconnected, the trip odometer will be erased and be reset to zero when the voltage is re-applied. The trip odometer may be reset anytime by depressing the set button, located to the right of the steering column. The English/Metric switch changes the display mode from English to Metric or Metric to English. The following is a list of the display graphics that are changed when the mode selector switch is operated.
1. Speed to read in mph or kmh.
2. "MPH" and "MILES" or "km/h" and "KILOMETERS" graphics to be lit.
3. Season and trip odometer to convert to either miles or kilometers.

ELECTRONIC INSTRUMENT CLUSTER

DIGITAL SPEEDOMETER
1985 AND LATER DEVILLE, FLEETWOOD MODELS (RWD)
1985 AND LATER DEVILLE, FLEETWOOD MODELS (FWD)

The digital speedometer cluster is considered an optional ac-

cessory for these models. The speedometer cluster is controlled by the same electrical pulses that feed the conventional type speedometer. The speed and odometer displays are of blue-green vacuum fluorescent and includes indications of miles per hour or kilometers per hour for speed and miles or kilometers for mileage accumulation on both a seasonal odometer and a trip odometer. The high beam indicator is also a vacuum fluo-

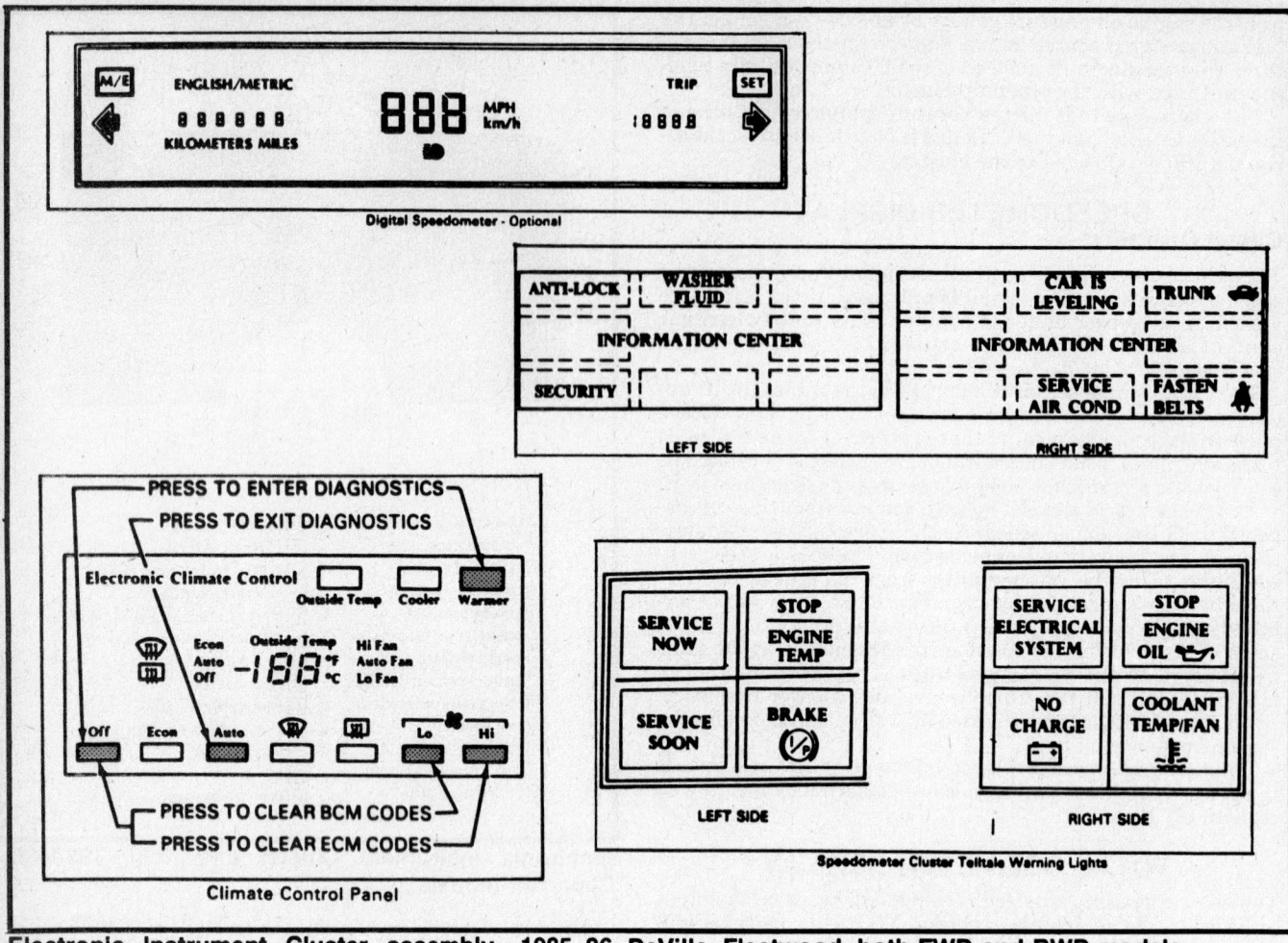

Electronic Instrument Cluster assembly, 1985–86 DeVille, Fleetwood, both FWD and RWD models

rescent display while the turnsignal displays are conventional incandescent bulb indicators.

The mileage information for the season odometer is contained in non-volatile memory circuits within the electronic cluster.

NOTE: Non-volatile means the information is retained in these circuits if the battery is disconnected or power is lost to the digital cluster.

The trip odometer information is stored in volatile memory and will be lost whenever the battery power to the cluster is interrupted. The digital cluster contains a reset button for the trip odometer.

An English/Metric conversion switch is on the digital speedometer cluster. This switch converts speed (mph or km/h), mileage (miles or kilometers), temperature control or outside temperature (F. or C. Degrees) and fuel data (gallons or liters; miles per gallon or liters per 100 kilometers, miles or kilometers).

SPEEDOMETER CLUSTER TELLTALE WARNING LAMPS

The speedometer cluster telltale warning lamps, located on either side of the cluster, are designed to provide high visibility to alert the operator of various vehicle conditions.

The left side includes amber "SERVICE SOON" and "SERVICE NOW" indicators and red "STOP ENGINE TEMP" and "BRAKE" indicators. The right side includes an amber "SERVICE ELECTRICAL SYSTEM" indicator and red "NO CHARGE", "STOP ENGINE OIL" and "COOLANT TEMP/FAN" indicators.

ELECTRONIC INSTRUMENT CLUSTER

GENERAL INFORMATION

1982-85 ELDORADO AND SEVILLE

The digital Instrument cluster is available when the vehicles are equipped with either the gasoline DFI or the Diesel engines. It consists of microprocessor circuitry, three vacuum fluorescent digital displays for fuel remaining, speed and fuel re-

maining (DFI only). Also included on the cluster us an english/metric conversion switch.

Input signals for the cluster microprocessor are from the conventional resistive type fuel tank sending unit (with special calibration), cruise control speed sensor signal from a buffer amplifier and a data from the DFI engine control computer data (if so equipped). Other inputs are the instrument illumination control and parking lamps.

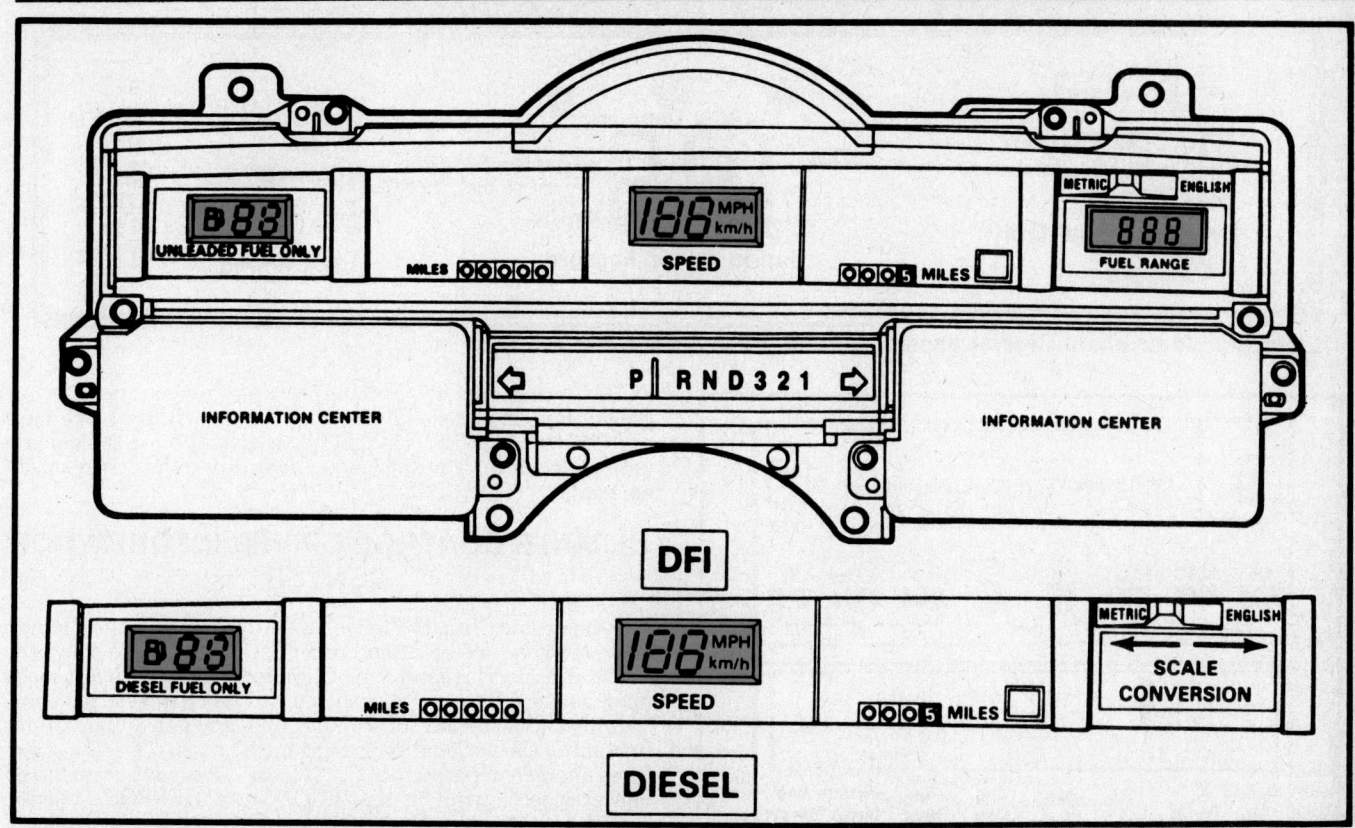

Electronic Instrument Cluster assembly, 1983–85 Eldorado/Seville models

ENGLISH/METRIC CONVERSION SWITCH

The fuel level is displayed in gallons or liters, speed in miles per hour or kilometers per hour and the fuel range (DFI only) in miles or kilometers. The units of measure depend upon the position of the cluster mounted English/Metric conversion switch.

On vehicles equipped with Electronic Climate Control and the fuel data panel, the English/Metric conversion switch converts these displays to degrees celsius and liters per 100 kilometers.

There is no English/Metric conversion for the odometer. The vehicles manufactured for domestic sales are set for miles and vehicles manufactured for Canada and Export are set for kilometers.

ELECTRONIC INSTRUMENT CLUSTER

GENERAL INFORMATION

1986 ELDORADO/SEVILLE

────── CAUTION ──────

Electrostatic discharge can damage the electronic cluster. Do not touch any electrical component or terminal as the static discharge from a person's body can cause damage to the electronic components within the cluster.

GENERAL INFORMATION

The l986 and later Eldorado/Seville models are equipped with a vacuum fluorescent electronic instrument cluster and a Climate Control Driver Information Center. The vehicle information is displayed by a variety of indicators including digital and indicator lights.

There is no service work done on the electronic instrument cluster or the Climate Control Driver Information Center. They are serviced as a complete unit only and if service is required, they must be removed and be obtained or returned through General Motors Parts system or repaired at authorized AC-Delco Repair Centers.

DIGITAL SPEEDOMETER

A digital speedometer cluster, a digital fuel gauge and a digital odometer make up the basic parts of the instrument cluster. The speedometer, odometer and fuel gauge are blue-green vacuum fluorescent displays and include annunciators for speed (mph, km/h), for mileage (miles, kilometers), and for fuel (gallons, liters). The cluster has additional; vacuum fluorescent indicators for high beam, turn signals, low fuel, cruise control engaged and auto dimmer.

A speed sensor, located at the transaxle, sends an electrical pulse to a speed buffer amplifier within the body control module (BCM). The BCM converts the pulses into speed information which is then transferred to the speedometer for display via the data line. The odometer information is also stored in the BCM and transferred to the display via the data line. The mileage information for the season odometer is contained in non-volatile memory circuits within the BCM.

NOTE: Non-volatile means the information is retained within the circuits if the battery is disconnected or power is lost to the BCM.

Electronic Instrument Cluster assembly, 1986 Eldorado/Seville models

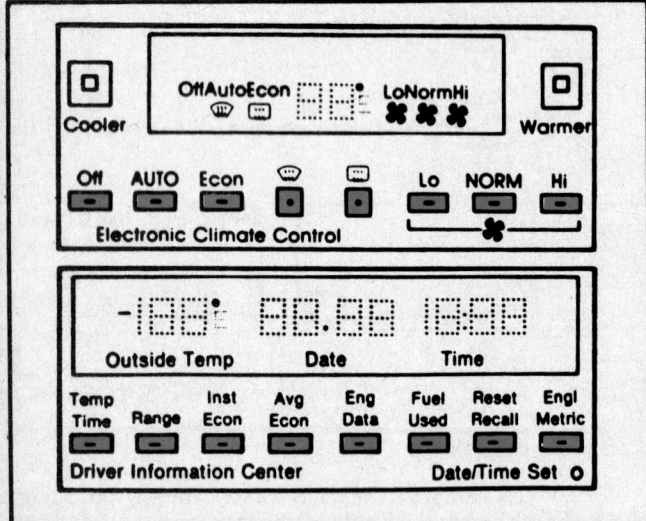

Climate Control Driver Information Center (CCDIC), 1986 Eldorado/Seville models

The trip odometer information is stored in a volatile memory and will be lost when ever the battery power to the BCM is removed. The digital cluster contains the reset switch for the trip odometer.

An English/Metric conversion switch is on the climate control driver information center. This switch converts speed (mph or km/h), mileage (miles or kilometers), temperature control (f. or c. degrees), outside temperature (f. or c. degrees) and fuel data (gallons or liters; miles per gallon or liters per 100 kilometers; miles or kilometers) on the speedometer and the climate control driver information center.

The fuel gauge displays fuel remaining in the fuel tank, in units of gallons or liters, rounded to a whole number. "F" is displayed for fuel levels greater than 16 gallons (61 liters) and an "E" is displayed for a fuel level less than 2 gallons (7.6 liters). A flashing "E" indicates less than one (1) gallon. Also the "LOW

FUEL" indicator is lit when the fuel remaining is less than one gallon. For an additional warning of low fuel level, the message "FUEL LEVEL VERY LOW" is displayed on the climate control driver information center, overriding the driver selected display.

CLIMATE CONTROL DRIVER INFORMATION CENTER

The Electronic Climate Control is the upper half of the Climate Control Driver Information Center (CCDIC), located above the center console. The Electronic Climate Control section is made up of vacuum fluorescent displays and function selector pushbuttons for the heater, air conditioning and defrost operations (including the optional rear defog pushbutton). Operating features include separate "LO", "NORM" (automatic) and "HI" blower speed control for the "ECON" and "DEFROST" modes. The blower speed in the defrost mode is automatically reduced for the first few minutes of a cold start-up when in the "AUTO" mode. It can be overridden by selecting a "HI" blower speed control. To protect the A/C compressor in the event of low refrigerant condition, the BCM automatically switches the climate control system from the "AUTO" to the "ECON" mode, which turns off the compressor.

Below the Electronic Climate Control is the Driver Information Center. This center includes a 20 character dot matrix vacuum fluorescent display and display control buttons. The display control buttons include "TEMP/TIME", "RANGE", "INST ECON", "AVG ECON", "ENG DATA", "FUEL USED", "RESET/RECALL", and "ENGL/METRIC". On vehicle start-up, the information center will display one of the following messages, depending upon the time of the day, "GOOD MORNING", "GOOD AFTERNOON", or "GOOD EVENING", followed by the "ALL MONITORED SYSTEMS OK" display or other vehicle status messages. The operator must acknowledge any vehicle status message by pressing any of the display control buttons or by correcting the condition. After the initial start-up sequence, the operator selected display is shown. At key off, the twilight sentinel delay time is displayed, if the sentinel is turned on.

The "TEMP/TIME" button displays the outside temperature,

Instrument Panel warning lamps, 1986 Eldorado/Seville models

the date and time with the ignition switch in the "ON" position. For convenience with the ignition in the "OFF" position, the date and time can also be displayed by pressing the "TEMP/TIME" button. The "ENG/DATA" button allows one of three engine parameters to be displayed.

1. The first time the "ENG/DATA" button is depressed, engine speed is displayed.

2. With the engine speed displayed, pressing the "ENG/DATA" button again changes the display to show the coolant temperature.

3. The temperature is displayed in F. or C. degrees, depending upon the "ENGL/METRIC" switch position.

4. With the coolant temperature display showing, pressing the "ENG/DATA" button again will change the display to show battery voltage.

5. If the "ENG/DATA" button is depressed again, the display will start over again with the engine speed display.

Fuel data displays consist of "RANGE", "INST ECON" (instantaneous fuel economy), "AVG ECON" (average fuel economy) and "FUEL USED". A feature is selected by depressing the appropriate pushbutton and that feature remains displayed until another is selected."RANGE" is an expected driving range based on fuel remaining in the tank and average fuel economy (calculated on the body computer as a running average, weighted on the most recent driving conditions). The val-

ue is displayed in mph or kilometers, to the nearest whole number. "INST" is a short term (every half second) update of fuel economy, based on a body computer calculation of driving conditions. The value is displayed in miles per gallon or liters per 100 kilometers, rounded off to the nearest whole number.

"AVG ECON" is a display of average fuel economy, calculated by the body computer, as a function of total fuel and miles accumulated since the last operator reset. As long as no reset occurs, the average is continuous and accurate over the accumulated driving mileage.The units displayed are "MPG AVG" or "L/100 km AVG" and displayed to a tenth of a unit. "FUEL USED" is a display of fuel consumption since the last driver reset. The units are displayed in "GAL USED" or "LITERS USED" and displayed to a tenth of a unit. The highest value attainable is 99.9 gallons or 379 liters before the display returns to zero.

The fuel data functions "AVG ECON" and "FUEL USED" can be reset at the operators discretion. The "RESET/RECALL" button is depressed while the individual function is being displayed to start a new series of calculations. The operator can also recall any current vehicle status messages by pressing the "RESET/RECALL" button in any of the other display modes. When any of the fuel data displays are being shown, the Driver information Center also displays the time of day. Time of day is not displayed when the engine data is being shown.

CHEVROLET

Electronic Instrument Cluster

GENERAL OPERATION

1985-86 Chevrolet Cavalier (Type-10)

The digital instrument cluster used on these models is a microprocessor based multi-function information system, which displays vehicle speed, outside temperature, engine speed, fuel level, oil pressure, coolant temperature, battery voltage, odometer information and general information. The displays uses two vacuum florescent tubes and an air core gauge. The tachometer uses the air core gauge with pointer movement for engine RPM display. The speedometer tube displays vehicle speed, outside temperature, total and trip odometer in a digital, English or metric readout. High beam, left and right turn signals are also displayed on the speedometer tube.

The gauge tube displays battery voltage, coolant temperature, oil pressure and fuel level in an analog (16 segment bar graph) form.

Several telltales are also featured including brake, fasten seat belts, low coolant, check engine, and up shift. Battery voltage, engine coolant and oil pressure telltales are also included and work directly with their respective gauges.

OUTSIDE AMBIENT TEMPERATURE DISPLAY

The outside ambient temperature display is a digital readout. The readout will display current outside temperature in the English or Metric mode depending on the last input of the English/Metric switch. The sensor uses a variable resistance to indicate temperature -40°F = 100K ohms, and 167°F = 390 ohms.

SPEEDOMETER DISPLAY

The speedometer readout incorporates a digital display. The speedometer signal is produced from a transmission mounted PM (Permanant magnet) generator which provides a signal, at a rate of 1.11 hz per mile per hour. Vehicle speed data can be displayed in either English or metric mode depending on the last input of the English/Metric switch.

TACHOMETER DISPLAY

The tachometer incorporates an air core gauge and pointer to display engine RPMs. The tachometer signal is produced from the HEI distributor and is filtered before entering the cluster.

ELECTRONIC INSTRUMENT PANEL

Electronic Instrument Cluster

GENERAL INFORMATION

1985-86 CHEVROLET CAMARO BERLINETTA

The Camaro Berlinetta model utilizes a microprocessor based electronic cluster. Vehicle information is displayed with a variety of indicators, which include vacuum fluorescent displays, "OK" to "GO" telltale monitors and conventional air core gauges. The cluster contains electronic components which are sensitive to electrostatic discharge.

NOTE: Care should be taken to avoid touching the printed circuit boards in the cluster as damage to the electronics may result.

SPEEDOMETER

The speedometer uses a buffered square wave signal provided by a permanent magnet generator located in the transmission, to display vehicle speed. Speed data can be displayed in either English or Metric mode depending on the position of the English/Metric switch.

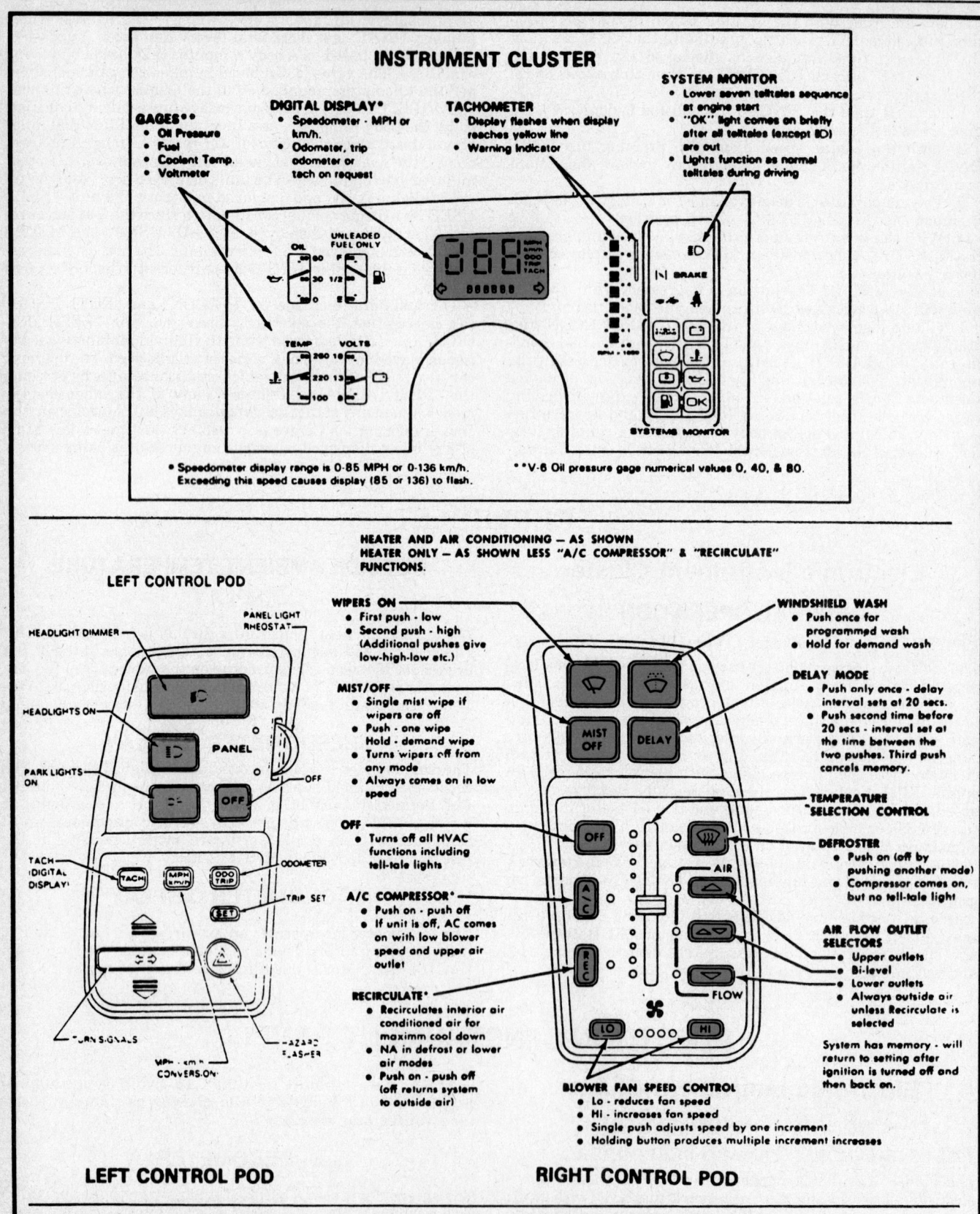

INSTRUMENT CLUSTER

GAGES**
- Oil Pressure
- Fuel
- Coolant Temp.
- Voltmeter

DIGITAL DISPLAY*
- Speedometer - MPH or km/h.
- Odometer, trip odometer or tach on request

TACHOMETER
- Display flashes when display reaches yellow line
- Warning Indicator

SYSTEM MONITOR
- Lower seven telltales sequence at engine start
- "OK" light comes on briefly after all telltales (except ID) are out
- Lights function as normal telltales during driving

- Speedometer display range is 0-85 MPH or 0-136 km/h. Exceeding this speed causes display (85 or 136) to flash.

**V-6 Oil pressure gage numerical values 0, 40, & 80.

HEATER AND AIR CONDITIONING — AS SHOWN
HEATER ONLY — AS SHOWN LESS "A/C COMPRESSOR" & "RECIRCULATE" FUNCTIONS.

LEFT CONTROL POD

- HEADLIGHT DIMMER
- PANEL LIGHT RHEOSTAT
- HEADLIGHTS ON
- PANEL
- PARK LIGHTS ON
- OFF
- TACH (DIGITAL DISPLAY)
- ODOMETER
- TRIP SET
- TURN SIGNALS
- HAZARD FLASHER
- MPH - km/h CONVERSION

WIPERS ON
- First push - low
- Second push - high (Additional pushes give low-high-low etc.)

MIST/OFF
- Single mist wipe if wipers are off
- Push - one wipe Hold - demand wipe
- Turns wipers off from any mode
- Always comes on in low speed

OFF
- Turns off all HVAC functions including tell-tale lights

A/C COMPRESSOR*
- Push on - push off
- If unit is off, AC comes on with low blower speed and upper air outlet

RECIRCULATE*
- Recirculates interior air conditioned air for maximm cool down
- NA in defrost or lower air modes
- Push on - push off (off returns system to outside air)

WINDSHIELD WASH
- Push once for programmed wash
- Hold for demand wash

DELAY MODE
- Push only once - delay interval sets at 20 secs.
- Push second time before 20 secs - interval set at the time between the two pushes. Third push cancels memory.

TEMPERATURE SELECTION CONTROL

DEFROSTER
- Push on (off by pushing another mode)
- Compressor comes on, but no tell-tale light

AIR FLOW OUTLET SELECTORS
- Upper outlets
- Bi-level
- Lower outlets
- Always outside air unless Recirculate is selected

System has memory - will return to setting after ignition is turned off and then back on.

BLOWER FAN SPEED CONTROL
- Lo - reduces fan speed
- Hi - increases fan speed
- Single push adjusts speed by one increment
- Holding button produces multiple increment increases

LEFT CONTROL POD

RIGHT CONTROL POD

Electronic Instrument Cluster and side control pods, 1985–86 Camaro Berlinetta models

ENGLISH AND METRIC MODES

English mode: 0–84 MPH (above 84 MPH, "85" will flash on and off at a rate of two hertz).

Metric mode: 0–136 KPH (above 136 KPH, "137" will flash on and off at a rate of two hertz).

ODOMETER, TRIP ODOMETER, TACHOMETER

The odometer displays, in digital form, the total number of miles or kilometers the vehicle has traveled. The information is retained in a non-volatile memory, and can display an accumulated milage up to 999,999 mile or kilometers. Once one million miles have been accumulated, miles will be replaced by error. The odometer display is a multi-function display, which displays seasonal odo, trip odometer to a tenth of a mile accuracy, and tachometer RPM's all in a digital display. Changing of the displays can be achieved by depressing external momentary switches. Once depressed the digital display of either "Odo", "Trip", or "Tach" will display the information required.

TACHOMETER

The tachometer is also displayed in a analog, (bar graph) form. The tachometer signal is produced from the HEI distributor. There are 64 segments that illuminate from 0 to 7000 RPM. All activated segments flash continuously at 3–4 cycles per second above a specified RPM as follows:
1. LC1 2.8L V6 greater than 5000 rpm.
2. LL1 2.8L V6 (H.O.) greater than 5500 rpm.
3. LG4/LU5 V8 greater than 4400 rpm

AIR CORE GAUGES

The Berlinetta also incorporates four conventional air core gauges with edge lit dials and pointers. These gauges monitor the following:
1. Oil pressure
2. Volts
3. Temp
4. Fuel

"OK TO GO" MONITOR

The purpose of this monitor is, after initial application of ignition, to sequence a test of the following seven telltales, and check for non-sequenced telltales, and finally light the green "OK to GO" telltale.

The "OK to GO" monitor checks the vehicle sensors in the following manner:
1. All lamps illuminate during inital ignition application, to check the bulbs. At the end of crank the "OK to GO" telltale goes off while the non-sequenced lights stay on for one second.
2. Then the sequenced lights go out in a clockwise direction at .5 second intervals. When the sequencing of the telltales is complete and all sequenced and non-sequenced telltales have deactivated, the "OK to GO" telltale is activated for two to three seconds.

DIMMING AND INTENSITY OF DISPLAYS

The electronic displays run at full intensity when the parking lamps are "OFF" and the ignition is "ON". When the parking lamps and the ignition are both "ON", the electronic displays are continuously variable from bright to dim by the panel lamps rheostat. The turn signal indicators are held at full bright at all times.

ELECTRONIC INSTRUMENT CLUSTER

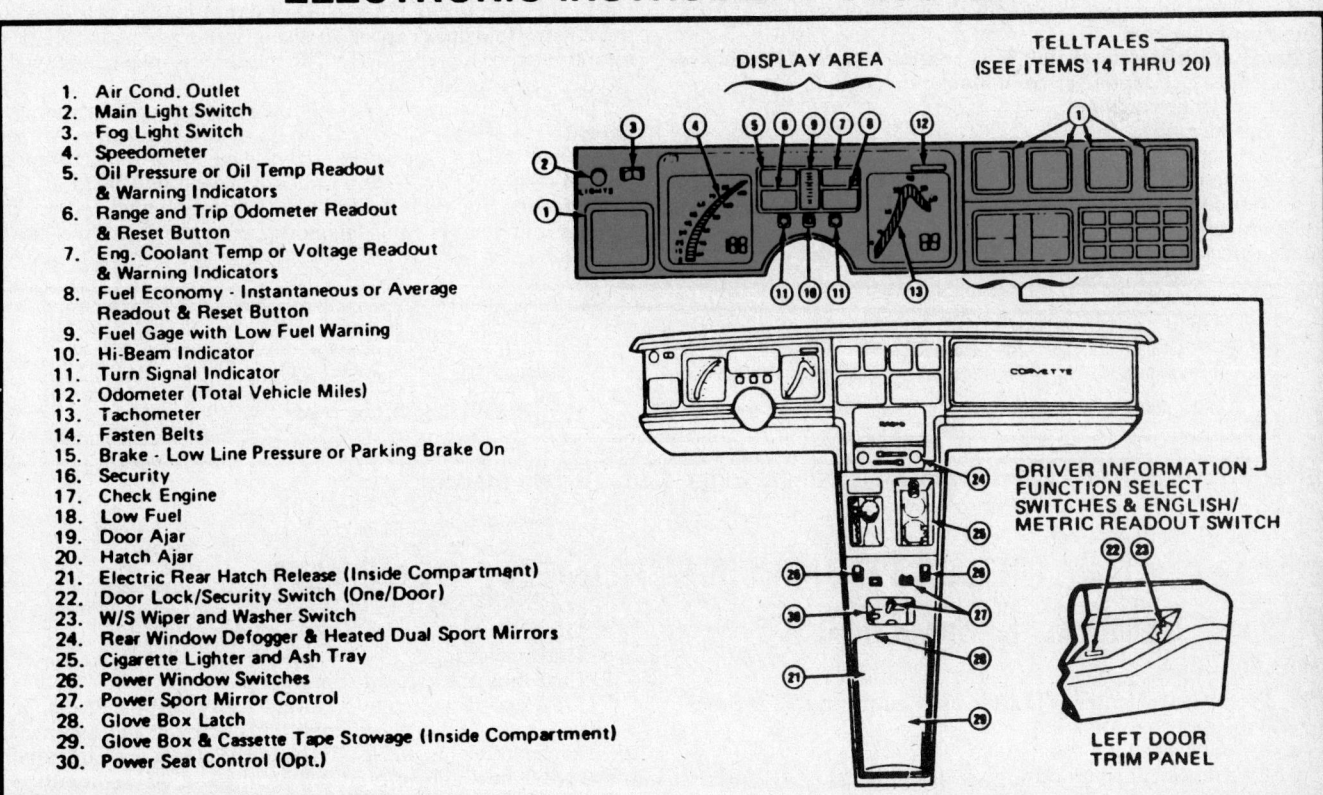

1. Air Cond. Outlet
2. Main Light Switch
3. Fog Light Switch
4. Speedometer
5. Oil Pressure or Oil Temp Readout & Warning Indicators
6. Range and Trip Odometer Readout & Reset Button
7. Eng. Coolant Temp or Voltage Readout & Warning Indicators
8. Fuel Economy - Instantaneous or Average Readout & Reset Button
9. Fuel Gage with Low Fuel Warning
10. Hi-Beam Indicator
11. Turn Signal Indicator
12. Odometer (Total Vehicle Miles)
13. Tachometer
14. Fasten Belts
15. Brake - Low Line Pressure or Parking Brake On
16. Security
17. Check Engine
18. Low Fuel
19. Door Ajar
20. Hatch Ajar
21. Electric Rear Hatch Release (Inside Compartment)
22. Door Lock/Security Switch (One/Door)
23. W/S Wiper and Washer Switch
24. Rear Window Defogger & Heated Dual Sport Mirrors
25. Cigarette Lighter and Ash Tray
26. Power Window Switches
27. Power Sport Mirror Control
28. Glove Box Latch
29. Glove Box & Cassette Tape Stowage (Inside Compartment)
30. Power Seat Control (Opt.)

DRIVER INFORMATION FUNCTION SELECT SWITCHES & ENGLISH/METRIC READOUT SWITCH

LEFT DOOR TRIM PANEL

Electronic Instrument Cluster and Console controls, 1984–86 Corvette models

GENERAL INFORMATION

1984-86 CORVETTE

The instrument cluster that is used on this vehicle is an electronic, microprocessor controlled liquid crystal display type. The speedometer and tachometer readings are displayed digitally and in bar graph formation. A driver information center which is located between the speedometer and the tachometer has an analog fuel gauge display and four multi-function digital displays. The four displays are as follows. Oil pressure or oil temperature display, Coolant temperature or voltage system display, instant or average fuel economy display and trip odometer, range or distance traveled display.

A telltale panel which is located to the right of the cluster above the console incorporates the telltale indicators for low fuel, oil temperature, low oil pressure, coolant temperature and low system voltage which are activated under out of normal range conditions.

A photocell which is located on the face of the cluster provides ambient lighting information to the cluster circuitry which in turn adjusts instrument panel illumination as required.

DIGITAL CLUSTER

The instrument panel digital cluster is a liquid crystal display (LCD) that is a microprocessor based multi-function information system. It displays vehicle speed, rpm and driver information on three LCD displays. It use multi-colored analog (bar graph) displays, digital readouts and warning indicators to inform the driver of the vehicles performance.

The instrument panel digital cluster illumination is controlled by two factors. These factors are, whether the parking lights or headlights are on and the ambient light.

The speedometer and tachometer are displayed in both analog (bar graph) and digital form. The speedometer readout can be displayed in both english and metric by the English/Metric switch. The tachometer readout displays the speed of the engine in revolutions per minute X100. For example (a reading of 32 would mean that the vehicles engine is turning 3200 revolutions per minute).

OLDSMOBILE DIVISION

Electronic Instrument Cluster

DIGITAL CLUSTER

1985-86 NINETY EIGHT, NINETY EIGHT REGENCY, DELTA 88 ROYALE MODELS

The digital cluster is a microprocessor-based multifunction information system which displays vehicle speed, engine temperature, inside and outside ambient temperatures, trip odometer, seasonal odometer, fuel supply, turn signal indication, hi-beam indication and drive modes on three blue-green vacuum fluoresent displays.

An English/Metric switch will change the readout modes from English to Metric or from Metric to English. The following displays are affected:
1. Speedometer.
2. Trip odometer.
3. Seasonal odometer.
4. Ambient temperature.

Upon powering up, the cluster display will assume the last mode selected. When the ignition switch is turned on, all segments will light up at full intensity, except for the bar graphs, turn signals and the high beam indicator. The bar graphs will run from empty to full, cold to hot, minimum to maximum speed and then reverse. All displays will then revert to their normal readings.

SPEEDOMETER DISPLAY

Speed indication is provided by a speed sensor (PM generator), located in the transaxle. This signal is then sent to the buffer amplifier. The buffer amplifier then outputs a signal of 1.112 Hertz per mph to the cluster. This signal is then processed by the cluster to display speed in either miles per hour (MPH) or kilometers per hour (KM/H). The maximum speed displayed is 85 MPH or 140 KM/H.

The speed display consists of an 81 segment bar graph. This indicated speed segment will be lit at full intensity. All segments below the indicated speed will be at 30% of full intensity and all segments above the indicated speed will be at 10 % of full intensity. The digits above the bar graph show either English or Metric intervals, depending upon the position of the E/M switch.

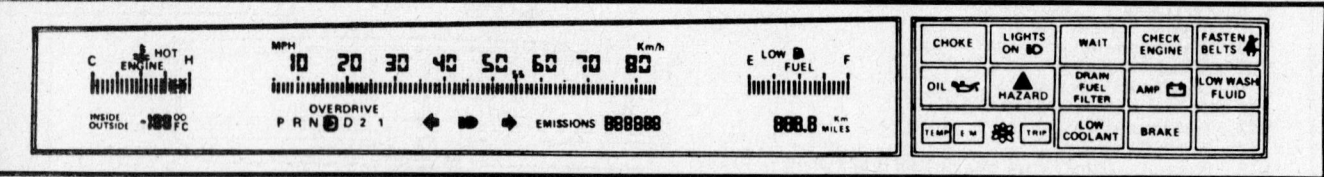

Electronic Instrument Cluster assembly, Ninety Eight, Delta Royale models

ELECTRONIC INSTRUMENT CLUSTER

GENERAL INFORMATION

1985-86 Calais

The electronic instrument cluster uses liquid crystal technology to display the following:
1. Vehicle speed.
2. Engine revolutions through a tachometer.
3. Fuel level.
4. Engine coolant temperature.
5. Oil pressure.
6. Battery voltage.
7. Seasonal and trip odometers.

Vehicle speed is displayed numerically. All other displays, with the exception of the odometer, uses bars or segments to indicate respective levels. When the ignition is turned on, all displays will come on briefly at full brightness. All segments will remain lit momentarily and then return to their proper indications.

NOTE: If any part of the display does not light, the cluster must be replaced.

The cluster also uses conventional warning indicators in conjunction with the gauges. These include the following:
1. Volts.
2. Oil pressure.
3. Up-shift indicator.
4. Check engine.
5. Brake.
6. Hi-beam/turnsignal indicators

On the lower side of the cluster are animated warning indicators. These include the following:
1. Engine coolant temperature.
2. Buckle seat belts.3. Low Fuel.
4. Turn headlamps on.

The cluster display brightness is controlled by a photocell when the headlamps are off. The headlamp switch rheostat and the photocell control brightness when the headlamps are on.

Operation

VEHICLE SPEED INDICATOR

Vehicle speed indication is provided by a speed sensor (PM generator), located in the transaxle. The buffer amplifier is contained within the cluster and supplies the speedometer display module with converted Hertz signal to create a display.

NOTE: If the speed buffer is defective, the instrument cluster must be replaced.

The maximum speed that can be displayed is 85 mph (140 km/h). Above these speeds, the display will flash at a rate of once per second (1 Hertz).

TACHOMETER

The tachometer readings, up to 6,000 rpm, are displayed on a 22 segment bar graph. This is divided into four segments for each 1,000 rpm, up to 4,000 rpm and three segments per 1,000 rpm above 4,000 rpm. The last four segments are red to indicate a warning zone, above 5,000 rpm.

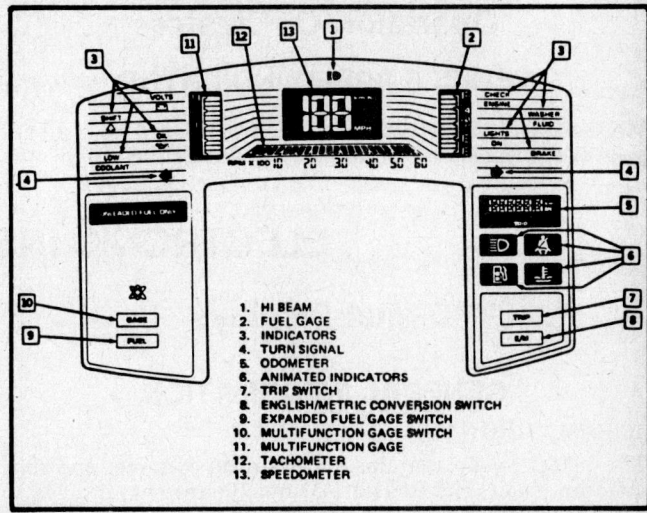

1. HI BEAM
2. FUEL GAGE
3. INDICATORS
4. TURN SIGNAL
5. ODOMETER
6. ANIMATED INDICATORS
7. TRIP SWITCH
8. ENGLISH/METRIC CONVERSION SWITCH
9. EXPANDED FUEL GAGE SWITCH
10. MULTIFUNCTION GAGE SWITCH
11. MULTIFUNCTION GAGE
12. TACHOMETER
13. SPEEDOMETER

Electronic Instrument Cluster assembly, 1985–86 Calais models

MULTIFUNCTION GAUGE

The multifunction gauge displays engine temperature, oil pressure, or battery voltage and is controlled by the "gauge" key.

1. The engine temperature is displayed on a twelve segment scale from hot to cold. The engine temperature is updated every second and the hot temperature indicator is animated when the hot light warning switch is on. Normal temperature readings should be within one bar of the middle of the gauge.

2. The oil pressure gauge is a twelve segment display from low to high pressure. The oil pressure indicator is turned on when the oil pressure is under one segment (14 psi).

3. The voltage display shows battery voltage on a twelve segment display. The display reads from low to high with the sixth segment equal to 12 volts. Only one segment is lit at a time on this gauge, whereas all other gauges display bar graphs of varying heights.

ELECTRONIC INSTRUMENT CLUSTER

OPERATION

1984-86 Cutlass Ciera

The Electronic Instrument Cluster uses bluish-green vacuum fluorescent display tubes to indicate vehicle speed, fuel level and engine coolant temperature.

The vehicle speed is displayed numerically. The fuel and temperature displays use bar graphs to indicate the fuel level and the coolant temperature. When the ignition is turned to the ON position, all displays will come on briefly at full brightness, The bar graph light up slowly from left to right, then return to indicate the current fuel level and coolant temperature.

If any part of the instrument cluster display does not light, the cluster must be removed. It must also be removed if the Vehicle Speed Sensor (VSS) is inoperative. A flashing halo ring around the fuel or temperature display means these is a malfunction in the cluster and must be removed.

The cluster also uses conventional indicator lamps, turn signal indicators, transaxle shift indicator and a cable driven odometer and trip odometer.

The cluster display brightness is controlled by a photocell when the headlamps are off. The headlamp switch rheostat and the photocell control the brightness when the headlamps are on.

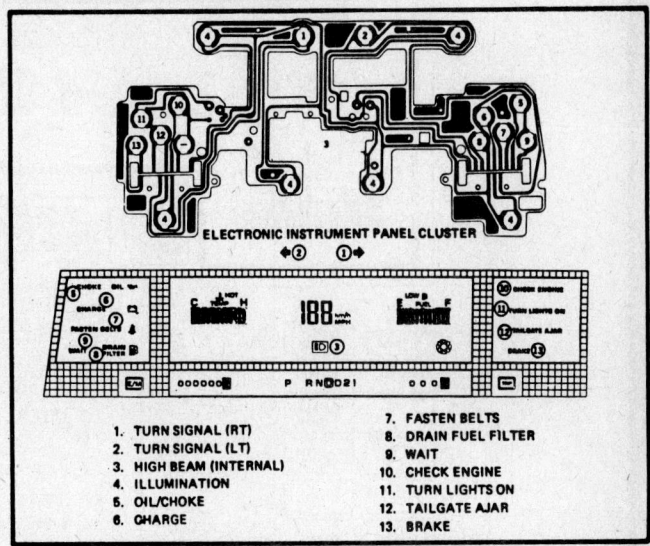

ELECTRONIC INSTRUMENT PANEL CLUSTER

1. TURN SIGNAL (RT)
2. TURN SIGNAL (LT)
3. HIGH BEAM (INTERNAL)
4. ILLUMINATION
5. OIL/CHOKE
6. CHARGE
7. FASTEN BELTS
8. DRAIN FUEL FILTER
9. WAIT
10. CHECK ENGINE
11. TURN LIGHTS ON
12. TAILGATE AJAR
13. BRAKE

Electronic Instrument Cluster assembly, front and rear views, 1984–86 Cutlass Ciera models

ELECTRONIC DISPLAYS & INSTRUMENTATION

Operation Of Cluster

VEHICLE SPEED INDICATOR

When the ignition is turned to the ON position, "188" will appear in the display at full brightness, as will the "km/h" and "mph" symbols. The speed indicator may be changed at any time from English to Metric or vice-versa, by pushing the "E/M" switch. The indicator shows car speed from 3 to 139 km/h or 2 to 84 mph. If the vehicle speed exceeds 139 km/h (or 84 mph), the indicator will show 140 km/h (or 85 mph) and will flash at one cycle per second. Speeds less than 3 km/h (3 mph) will not be displayed.

ELECTRONIC INSTRUMENT CLUSTER

Digital Displays

GENERAL INFORMATION

1984-85 TORONADO

The digital cluster contains a mechanical odometer and shift quadrant indicator. It uses vacuum fluorescent displays to show the following:

1. Vehicle speed.
2. Fuel level.
3. Inside and outside air temperature.
4. Engine temperature.
5. Trip milage.

The vehicle speed indicator uses a signal provided by the vehicle speed sensor, located near the speedometer assembly. An infrared light shines from the vehicle speed buffer, onto a rotating reflector mounted on the shaft. The reflector sends back to the vehicle speed buffer, pulses of light which are converted to electrical impulses. These impulses are counted and displayed at the speedometer.

Vehicle speed is indicated in either English (MPH) or Metric (Km/h) units, depending upon the position of the E/M switch. If the vehicle speed exceeds 85 mph or 137 Km/h, the vehicle speed display will flash about one time per second.

The trip odometer registers the number of miles (or Km/h) traveled since the last time it was reset. After the odometer reaches 999.9 miles (or Km/h), the decimal point is dropped. The odometer will then display completed miles and no tenths. After 4,194 miles (6,710 kilometers) the odometer will reset to zero. The trip odometer display can be changed to read either in English or Metric units by pressing the E/M button. To reset the odometer, press the TRIP button.

The ambient temperature readout will display the inside or outside temperature. Pressing the TEMP button will change the display from inside to outside or vice-versa. It will display the temperature in either Fahrenheit or celsius degrees, depending upon the position of the E/M switch. A memory is built in to the outside ambient temperature circuit. The instrument cluster must receive a speed signal before the outside ambient temperature display will update its self.

The sensor resistance changes with temperature. For example, at 80°F., the resistance is 10,000 ohms and at 38°F., the resistance is 20,000 ohms. This information is calculated by the information processor in the digital cluster as the temperature of the sensors change and is reflected in the cluster readout for inside and outside temperatures .

ANALOG DISPLAYS

The engine coolant temperature indicator uses a 21 segment bar graph display. When the engine temperature causes the 17th segment to light, the X and HOT will flash about one time per second and the Hot tone or voice phrase will be activated. The 17th segment corresponds to a temperature of 259°F. (126°C.)

The coolant temperature sensor resistance changes with temperature. The resistance drops from 2400 ohms with a cold engine, to less than 40 ohms with a very hot engine.

The fuel level indicator also uses a 21 segment bar graph display. When the fuel level is indicated by two segments, the LOW graphics will light up at full cluster intensity and the

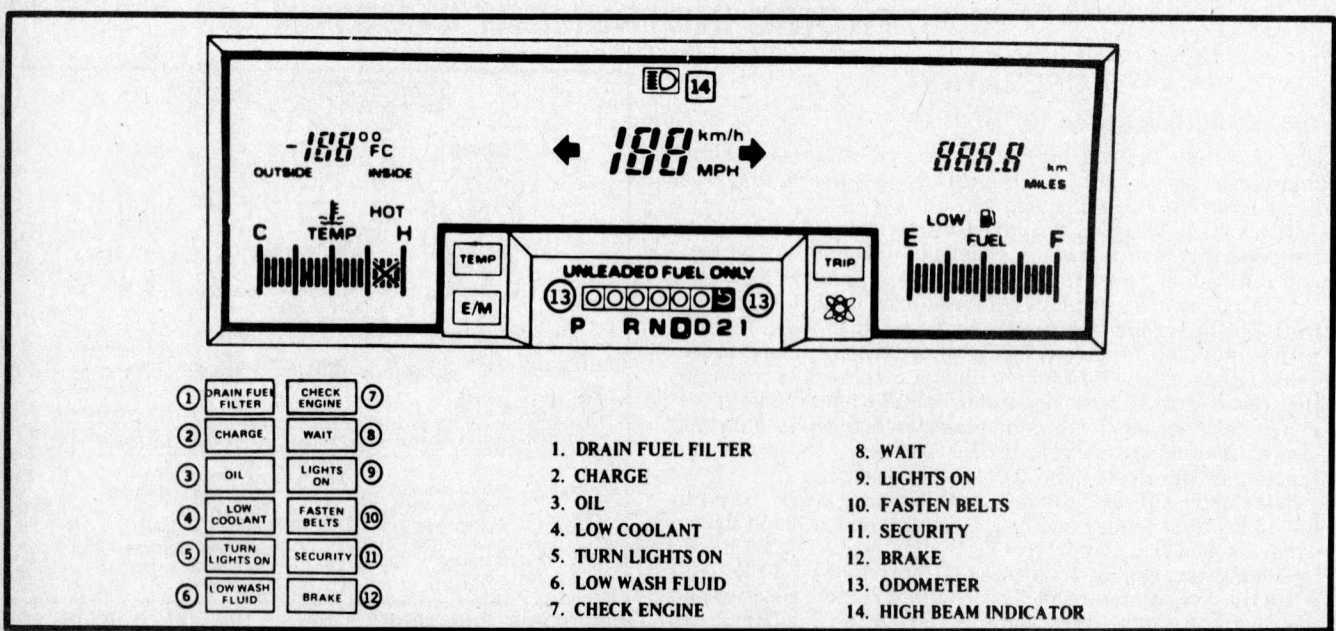

1. DRAIN FUEL FILTER
2. CHARGE
3. OIL
4. LOW COOLANT
5. TURN LIGHTS ON
6. LOW WASH FLUID
7. CHECK ENGINE
8. WAIT
9. LIGHTS ON
10. FASTEN BELTS
11. SECURITY
12. BRAKE
13. ODOMETER
14. HIGH BEAM INDICATOR

Electronic Instrument Cluster assembly, 1984—85 Toronado models

LOW FUEL tone will be activated. When the 2nd segment goes out, the word LOW will flash about one time per second. A delay is built into the fuel sender circuit to prevent fuel sloshing from making the fuel gauge read eradicate.

The resistance of the fuel sender gauge changes with the amount of fuel in the tank. With a full tank, the resistance is 86 ohms and with an empty tank, the resistance is 4 ohms. The information processer is programmed to account for battery voltage changes. Therefore, changes in battery voltage will not affect the fuel gauge reading.

TELLTALE LIGHTS

The Toronado electronic instrument cluster also uses conventional telltale lights, such as the following;
1. Choke (4.1L V6 gasoline engine).
2. Charge indicator.
3. Oil pressure indicator.
4. Low coolant indicator.
5. Low fuel indicator.6. Low washer fluid.
7. Check Engine light (Gasoline engine) or Wait light (Diesel engine).
8.Fasten belts.
9.Lights on.
10. Security system.
11. Brake system.
12. High Beam.

The turnsignal indicators are vacuum fluorescent lights that light up at full intensity whenever the turn signals or hazard warning lamps are used.

POWER-UP SEQUENCE

When the ignition is turned on and after a delay of approximately one second, all the vacuum fluorescent segments will light up at full intensity, except the turn signal indicator lamps. The engine temperature and the fuel level bar graphs will light up from left to right at a uniform rate. The instrument cluster will then hold at full intensity for about $\frac{1}{2}$ second. Each display will then revert to their respective actual values.

DISPLAY INTENSITY

With the parking lights on a cover over the photo cell, the rheostat will control from 40% of full brilliance, down to 1% of full brilliance. When the cover is removed from the photo cell, the photo cell will override the dimming feature of the headlamp switch. With the parking lamps off, the photo cell will have 100% control of the cluster brilliance.

ELECTRONIC INSTRUMENT CLUSTER

GENERAL INFORMATION

1986 OLDSMOBILE TORONADO

Numerous electronic components are located on the vehicle as a part of an electrical network, designed to control various engine and body subsystems. To provide a description of the overall electronic network and the on-board diagnostic capabilities relating to the electronic instrument cluster, the following explanation is provided. The various codes relating to body and engine malfunctions can be determined from accompanying charts and reference to Chilton's Engine Electronics Manual.

At the heart of the computer system is the Body Computer Module (BCM), located behind the glove box. This BCM has an internal microprocessor, which is the center for communication with all other components in the system. All sensors and switches are monitored by the BCM or one of the five other major components that complete the computer system. The five components are as follows:
1. Electronic Control Module (ECM)
2. Instrument Panel Cluster (IPC)
3. Electronic Climate Control Panel (ECC)
4. Programmer/Heating/Ventilation/AC
5. Chime/Voice module

A combination of inputs from these major components and the other sensors and switches communicate together to the BCM, either as individual inputs, or on the common communication link called the serial data line. The various inputs to the BMC combine with program instructions within the system memory to provide accurate control over the many subsystems involved. When a subsystem circuit exceeds pre-programmed limits, a system malfunction is indicated and may provide certain back-up functions. Providing control over the many subsystems from the BCM is done by controlling system outputs. This can be either direct of transmitted along the serial data line to one of the four other major components. The process of receiving, storing, testing and controlling information is continuous. The data communication gives the BMC control over the ECM's self-diagnostic capacities in addition to its own.

Between the BCM and the other five major components of the computer system, a communication process has been incorporated which allows the devices to share information and thereby provide for additional control capabilities. In a method similar to that used by a telegraph system, the BCM's internal circuitry rapidly switches to a circuit between 0 and 5 volts like a telegraph key. This process is used to convert information into a series of pulses which represents coded data messages understood by other components. Also, much like a telegraph system, each major component has its own recognition code. When a message is sent out on the serial data line, only the component or station that matches the assigned recognition code will pay attention and the rest of the components or stations will ignore it. This data transfer of information is most important in understanding how the system operates and how to diagnosis possible malfunctions within the system.

In order to access and control the BCM self diagnostic features, two additional electronic components are necessary, the Instrument Panel Cluster (IPC) and the Electronic Climate Control panel (ECC). As part of the IPC, a 20 character display area called the Information Center is used. During normal engine operation, this area displays "Toronado" or is a Tachmeter, displaying the engine rpm. When a malfunction is sensed by the BCM, one of the driver warning messages is displayed in this area. When the diagnostic mode is entered, the various BCM or ECM diagnostic codes are displayed. In addition to the codes of the ECM/BCM data parameters, discrete inputs and outputs, as well as output override messages are also displayed when commanded for, through the ECC.

The Electronic Comfort Control Panel (ECC) provides the controls for the heating and air conditioning systems. It also becomes the controller to enter the diagnostics and access the BCM self-diagnostics. This communication process allows the BCM to transfer any of its available diagnostic information top the instrument panel for display during service. By pressing the appropriate buttons on the ECC, data messages can be sent to the BCM over the serial data line requesting the specific diagnostic features desired. When in the Override mode of the BCM diagnostics, the amount of Override is displayed at the ECC where the outside and set temperatures are normally displayed.

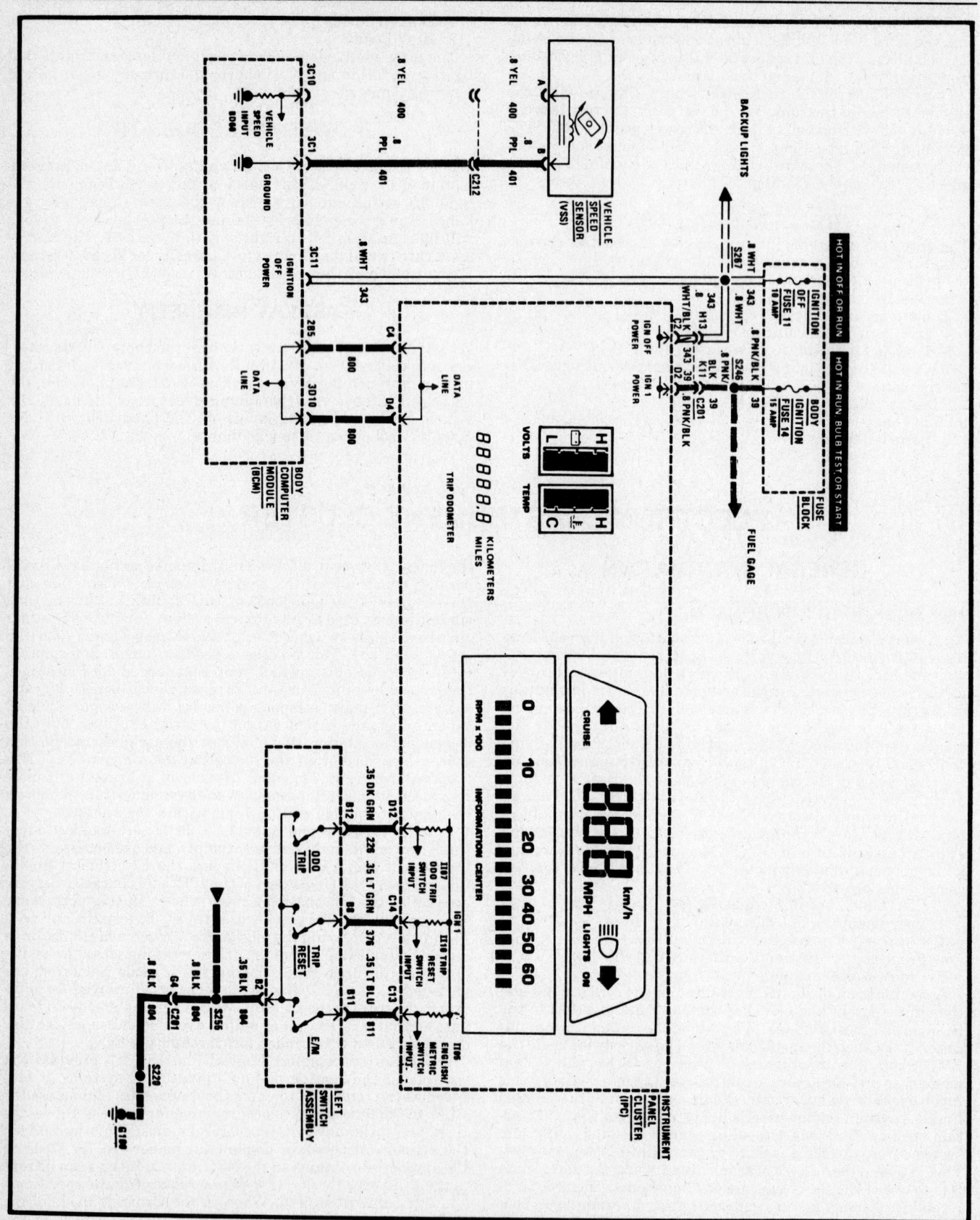

Electrical schematic of Electronic Instrument Cluster assembly, 1986 Toronado models

Electronic Instrument Cluster

— CAUTION —

Electrostatic discharge can damage the electronic cluster. Do not touch any electrical component or terminal as the static discharge from a person's body can cause damage to the electronic components within the cluster.

GENERAL INFORMATION

The l986 and later Toronado models are equipped with a vacuum fluorescent electronic instrument cluster. The vehicle information is displayed by a variety of indicators including digital and indicator lights.

There is no service work done on the electronic instrument cluster. It is serviced as a complete unit only and if service is required, it must be removed and obtained/returned through General Motors Parts system or repaired at authorized AC-Delco Repair Centers.

DIGITAL DISPLAYS

The vehicle speed indicator uses a signal provided by the BMC which is generated by the vehicle speed sensor that is located at the rear of the transaxle. Vehicle speed is indicated in either English (MPH) or Metric (km/h) units, depending upon the position of the E/M buttom, located in the left switch assembly. If the vehicle speed exceeds 85 mph or 140 km/h, the vehicle speed display will flash about one time per second.

The seasonal odometer registers the total miles or kilometers traveled and the milage is stored in the BCM, on a non-volatile EEPROM. If the BCM has to be replaced, the EEPROM must be transferred to the new BCM. If the EEPROM must be replaced, it has to be sent to an authorized Delco Electronic service center, along with the Vehicle Identification Number (VIN), current milage, information on whether or not the vehicle is equipped with voice command, twilight sentinel or if it was built for the U.S. market or a foreign country. The trip odometer registers the number of miles or kilometers traveled since the last time it was reset. The milage is stored in the BCM in a resettable ,keep-alive memory. The trip odometer has a maximum value of 9999.0. To reset the trip odometer, press the "TRIP RESET" button. The seasonal/trip odometer display can be changed to read either English or Metric units by pressing the "E/M" button.

The engine coolant temperature indicator uses a 16 segment bar graph display. When the engine temperature causes the 14th bar to light, the "HOT" tone or voice phrase will be activated and the battery symbol will flash.

The fuel indicator also uses a 16 bar segment bar graph display. When the fuel level is below ¼ tank, the "GAUGE SCALE" button can be pushed to give an expanded quarter tank scale of 10 seconds. If the fuel level gets between two and five gallons, the "LOW FUEL" tone or voice phrase will be activated and the fuel symbol will flash. A delay is built into the fuel sender circuit to prevent fuel sloshing from making the fuel gauge read eradicate.

The voltage indicator is a 16 segment bar graph display. When the battery voltage drops below 11 volts (7th bar), the "CHARGING SYSTEM" tone or voice phrase will be activated and the battery symbol will flash.

The oil pressure indicator is also a 16 bar graph display. When the oil pressure is low (below 1st segment), the "LOW OIL PRESSURE" tone or voice phrase will activate and the oil symbol will flash.

The "PRND21" range indicator is a vacuum fluorescent gauge, located in the lower right hand corner of the instrument cluster. A green box around the letter indicates which gear the transaxle is in. All green boxes will flash at the same time if there is an electrical problem in the quadrant circuit.

INDICATOR LIGHTS

Conventional instrument cluster indicator lights are used, such as the "BRAKE", "SERVICE ENGINE SOON", "LIGHTS ON", "SECURITY" and "SEAT BELTS".

The turnsignal indicator lights are vacuum fluorescent and light up at full intensity whenever the turnsignals or hazard warning lamps are used.

POWER UP SEQUENCE

When the ignition is turned on and after a delay of one second, the graphics will light up at normal operating intensity and the gauges will indicate the condition of the engine at that time.

DISPLAY INTENSITY

With the parking lamps on and a cover over the photocell. the rheostat will control from 40% of full brilliance down to 1% of full brilliance. When the cover is removed from the photocell and a bright light is placed in front of the photocell, the photocell will override the dimming feature of the headlamp switch. With the headlamp/parking lamps off, the photocell will have 100% control of the cluster brilliance.

"ODO/TRIP" BUTTON

When the "ODO/TRIP" button is depressed, it changes the seasonal odometer to the trip odometer. Pushing the button again will return it to the seasonal odometer.

"TRIP RESET" BUTTON

The "TRIP RESET" button resets the trip odometer back to zero.

"E/M" BUTTON

The "ENGLISH/METRIC" (E/M) button changes the speedometer, odometers, A/C temperature, the driver's information and service diagnostics from English to Metric and visa versa.

"SYSTEM MONITOR"BUTTON

Whmen the "SYSTEM MONITOR" button is depressed, if displays any malfunctioning system in the computer system, based on the information center display. The monitor button must be pushed again to display another malfunction or the "WOW" mode. The "WOW" mode will display after all malfunctions are listed or if no malfunctions exist. In the "WOW" mode, all indicators will light up at full intensity, the bar graphs, speedometer and the odometers will light up from low scale to high and back to low and then hold a full scale for about one second. The "MONITOR" button must be held in to continue the "WOW" mode sequence.

"FUEL ECON" BUTTON

Pushing the "FUEL ECONOMY" button once will display "instantaneous miles (kilometers) per gallon" on the information center display. Pushing the button twice will display "average miles (kilometers) per gallon". Fuel economy is calculated on the last 25 miles of driving.

"RANGE" BUTTON

Displays the mileage range the vehicle can go with the present fuel available at the present speed on the information center display.

"FUEL USED" BUTTON

Displays in the information center display how much fuel was used since the "RESET" button was pushed.

"GAUGE SCALE" BUTTON

The "GAUGE SCALE" button expands the fuel gauge to show "E" to ¼ portion for 10 seconds.

"TACHOMETER" BUTTON

When the "TACHOMETER" button is depressed, the tachometer information is displayed in the information center display. The tachometer will remain on display until there is a malfunction message displayed or when one of the other "DRIVER INFORMATION" buttons is selected.

CANCELLING TRIP MONITOR FUNCTIONS

To cancel the trip monitor functions as listed, press the "TACH" button.

PONTIAC MOTOR DIVISION

Electronic Instrument Cluster

DIGITAL CLUSTER

1985-86 PONTIAC 6000 STE, FIREBIRD

The electronic instrument cluster is a microprocessor-based multifunction information system which displays vehicle speed, engine rpm, volt meter, coolant temperature, trip odometer, fuel supply, oil pressure, turn signal indication, hi-beam indication, service engine soon light, anti-lock brake warning light, brake system warning light, seat belt reminder light, and driver information center.

NOTE:The driver information center comes on the 1985-86 6000 STE and Grand Am.

An English/Metric switch will change the readout modes from English to Metric or from Metric to English. The following displays are affected:
1. Speedometer.
2. Odometer.
3. Trip Odometer.

Upon powering up, the cluster display will assume the last mode selected. When the ignition switch is turned on, all segments will light up at full intensity, except for the bar graphs, turn signals and the high beam indicator. The bar graphs will run from empty to full, cold to hot, minimum to maximum speed and then reverse. All displays will then revert to their normal readings.

SPEEDOMETER DISPLAY

Speed indication is provided by a speed sensor (PM generator), located in the transaxle. This signal is then sent to the buffer amplifier. The buffer amplifier then outputs a signal of 1.112 Hertz per mph to the cluster. This signal is then processed by the cluster to display speed in either miles per hour (MPH) or kilometers per hour (KM/H).

The speedometer display is a digital read-out. This indicated speed segment will be lit at full intensity. All segments below the indicated speed will be at 30% of full intensity and all segments above the indicated speed will be at 10% of full intensity. The letters above the digital read-out show either English or Metric intervals, depending upon the position of the E/M switch.

FUEL INDICATION DISPLAY

The fuel supply is displayed on a bar graph consisting of 16 segments that light sequentially from empty to full. The bar graph will light at full intensity to the level of the fuel in the tank and the remaining bars beyond that point will be lit at 10% of full intensity. When the fourth segment goes out, the remaining segments will be amber and the amber word "LOW" will come on. When the second bar goes out, the amber word "LOW" will flash on and off.

When the amber word "LOW" comes on, the chime module will be activated. An anti-slosh delay is programmed into the computer to minimize the effect of tilt and slosh in the fuel tank.

In the case of an open fuel sender circuit, the fuel display will be completely blank. In cases of shorted fuel display sender, the fuel supply display will show empty with the amber word "LOW" flashing on and off.

ENGINE COOLANT TEMPERATURE DISPLAY

The engine temperature is displayed on a bar graph of 14 segments, which light sequentially from 120° to 260° F. The segments will be lit at full intensity up to engine temperature indication, while the remaining segments will be lit at 10% of full intensity. When the engine temperature reaches 200° F., causing the 10th segment to light (counting from 120 to 260), the engine temperature warning light will come on and a warning chime will sound.

The engine temperature warning light is controlled by a thermal switch which senses engine coolant temperatures.

When the ignition switch is turned to "START" position, a test circuit is closed and the light will come on to indicate whether it is functioning properly.

ODOMETER

A six digit odometer will indicate up to 99,999.9 miles or kilometers, depending upon the position of the English/Metric switch mode. Total car mileage will be maintained in a non-volatile memory chip to the nearest mile. The life of the non-volatile memory chip is ten years minimum from the last update.

P, R, N, D, 2, 1 SHIFT QUADRANT DISPLAY

The shift quadrant indicates the position of the transaxle gear. The gear selected will be indicated by a solid amber box surrounding the respective blue-green character.

On a power up, the amber box will be lit around the selected gear. In the case of a problem in the quadrant circuit, the display will flash ('86 and later models, display will flash for two minutes), then all of the amber boxes will be lit.

TRIP ODOMETER

The trip odometer will indicate the number of miles or kilometers (depending upon the position of the "E/M" switch) that the vehicle has traveled since the last time the trip odometer was reset.

Accumulated trip mileage will be retained during vehicle shut-off. When cranking the engine to start and the voltage falls below 7 volts, a memory will be retained for a maximum of 50 milliseconds.

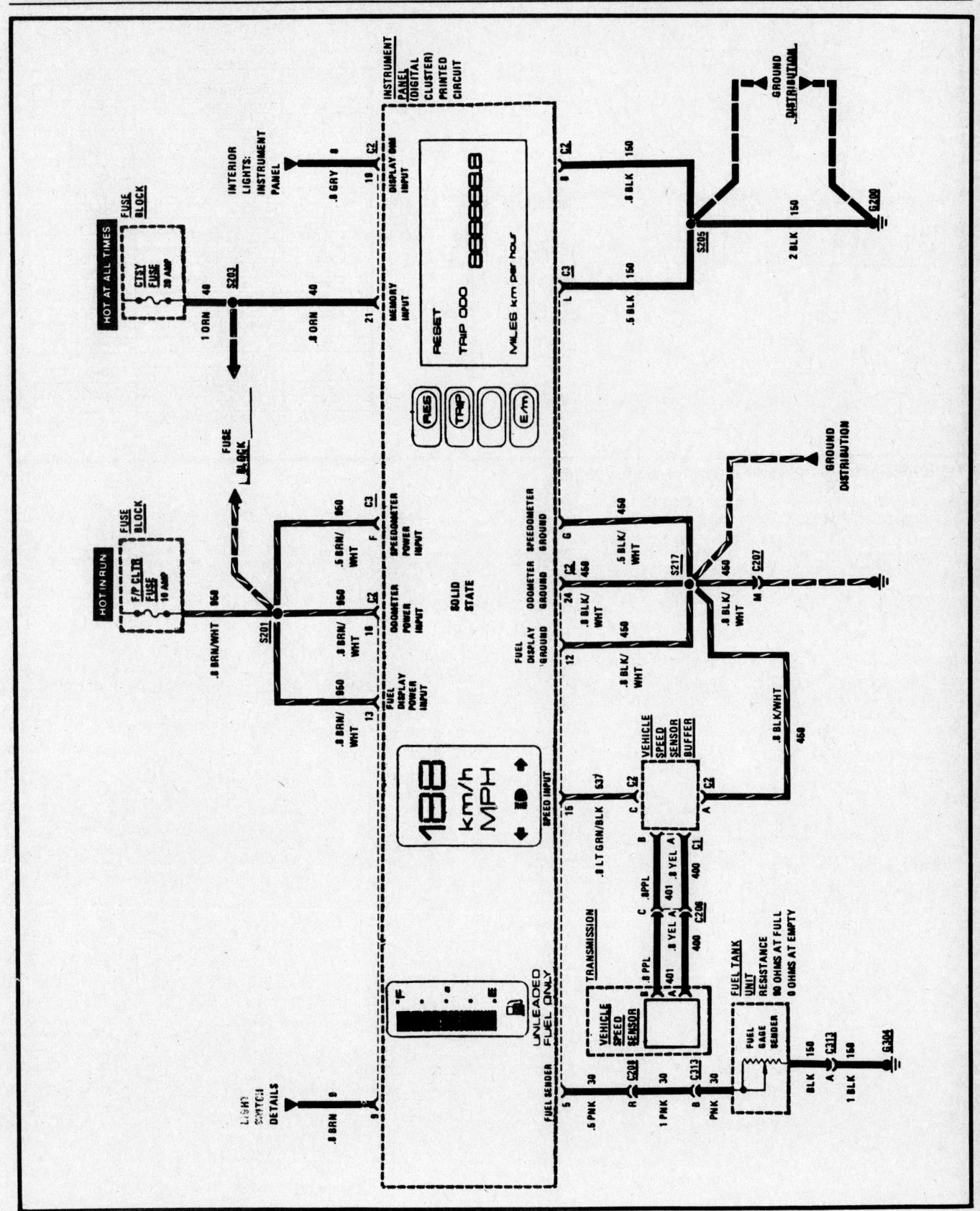

Electrical schematic of Electronic Instrument Cluster assembly, typical of Pontiac Motor Division usage

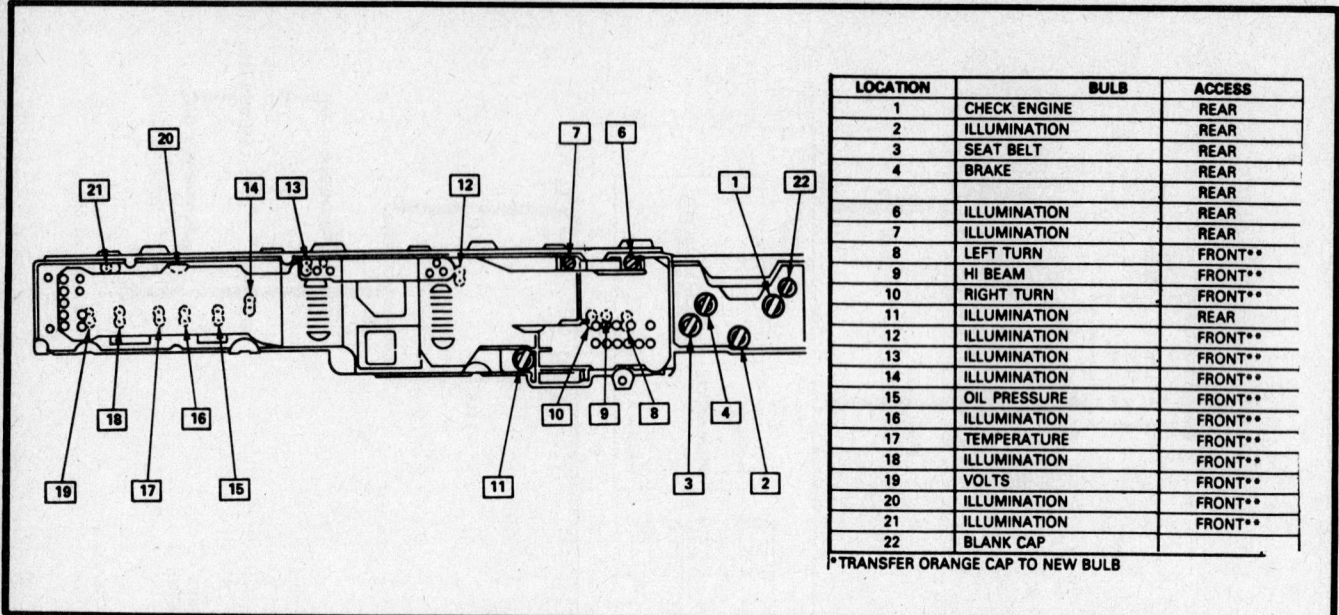

LOCATION	BULB	ACCESS
1	CHECK ENGINE	REAR
2	ILLUMINATION	REAR
3	SEAT BELT	REAR
4	BRAKE	REAR
		REAR
6	ILLUMINATION	REAR
7	ILLUMINATION	REAR
8	LEFT TURN	FRONT**
9	HI BEAM	FRONT**
10	RIGHT TURN	FRONT**
11	ILLUMINATION	REAR
12	ILLUMINATION	FRONT**
13	ILLUMINATION	FRONT**
14	ILLUMINATION	FRONT**
15	OIL PRESSURE	FRONT**
16	ILLUMINATION	FRONT**
17	TEMPERATURE	FRONT**
18	ILLUMINATION	FRONT**
19	VOLTS	FRONT**
20	ILLUMINATION	FRONT**
21	ILLUMINATION	FRONT**
22	BLANK CAP	

**TRANSFER ORANGE CAP TO NEW BULB

Typical Electronic cluster indicator bulb usage.

INDEX

GM BODY COMPUTER MODULE (BCM)

1985 and Later Cadillac Models

On 1985 and later Cadillac models are several electronic components which can be used to provide valuable self-diagnostic information. These components are part of an electronic network designed to control various engine and body subsystems.

At the heart of the self-diagnostic system is the Body Computer Module or BCM. The BCM is located behind the glove compartment opening and has an internal microprocessor which is used to control various vehicle functions based upon monitored sensor and switch inputs. Vehicles have an Electronic Control Module or ECM which provides microprocessor control for various engine and emission related functions. The ECM, located to the right side of the instrument panel, plays the major role in providing self-diagnostic capabilities for those subsystems which it controls.

On vehicles equipped with both an ECM and a BCM, a communication process has been incorporated which allows the two modules to share information and thereby provide for additional control capability. In a method similar to that used by a telegraph key operator, each module's internal circuitry rapidly switches a circuit between 0 and 5 volts. This process is used to convert information into a series of pulses which represent coded data messages understood by the other component. In other words, they can talk to one another.

One of the data messages transferred from the BCM is a request for specific ECM diagnositc action. This action may affect an ECM controlled output or require the ECM to transfer some information back to the BCM. This communication gives the BCM control over the ECM's self-diagnostic capabilities in addition to its own.

In order to access and control the self-diagnostic features available to the BCM, two additional electronic components are utilized. Located to the right of the steering column is the Climate Control Panel (CCP). Located to the left of the steering column is either the Fuel Data Center (FDC) used with gasoline engines, or the Diesel Data Center (DDC) used with diesel engines. These devices provide displays and keyboard switches used with several BCM controlled subsystems, such as the electronic climate control, fuel level display, etc. This display and keyboard information is transferred over single wire data circuits which carry coded data messages back and forth between the BCM and display panels. This communication process (known as "multiplexing") allows the BCM to transfer any of its available diagnostic information to the instrument panel for display during service. By depressing the appropriate buttons on the CCP, data messages can be sent to the BCM requesting the specific diagnostic features required.

BCM Controlled Subsystems

- Electronic Climate Control (ECC)
- Rear Defogger
- Outside Temp Display
- SERVICE AIR COND Indicator
- Diesel Fast Idle Solenoid
- Cooling Fans Control
- Diesel COOLANT TEMP/FAN Indicator
- Data Center Display Information
- Vacuum Fluorescent Display Dimming
- Computer Self-Diagnostics
- Retained Accessory Power

ECM Controlled Subsystems

- COOLANT TEMP/FAN Indicator
- CHECK ELECTRICAL SYSTEM Indicator
- Fuel Injection System
- Electronic Spark Timing (EST)
- Idle Speed Control
- Exhaust Gas Recirculation (EGR)
- Air Injection Reactor (AIR)
- Early Fuel Evaporation (EFE)
- Charcoal Canister Purge
- SERVICE SOON Indicator
- SERVICE NOW Indicator
- Viscous Converter Clutch
- Computer Self-Diagnostics
- Cruise Control

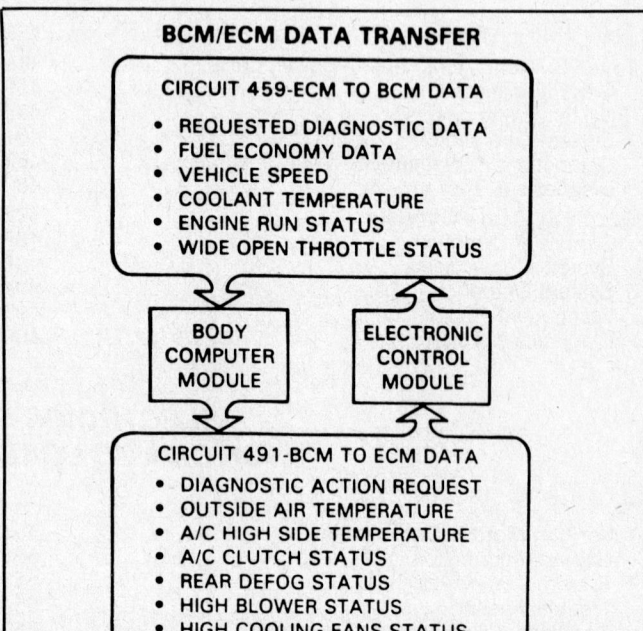

Schematic of information shared by the on-board computers

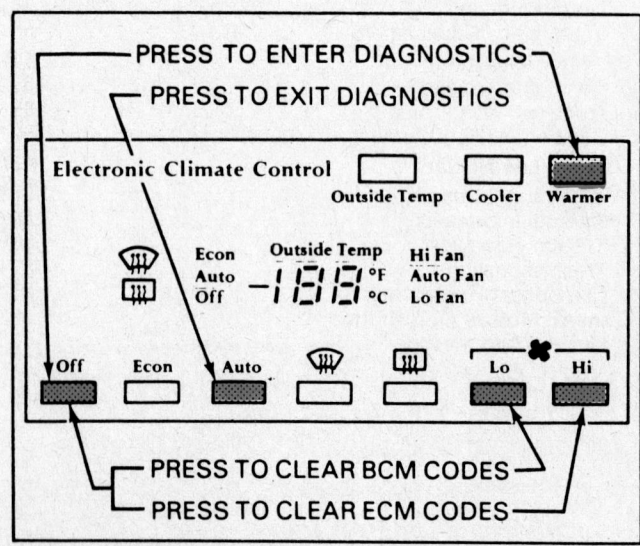

Climate Control Panel (CCP) used to access diagnostic system

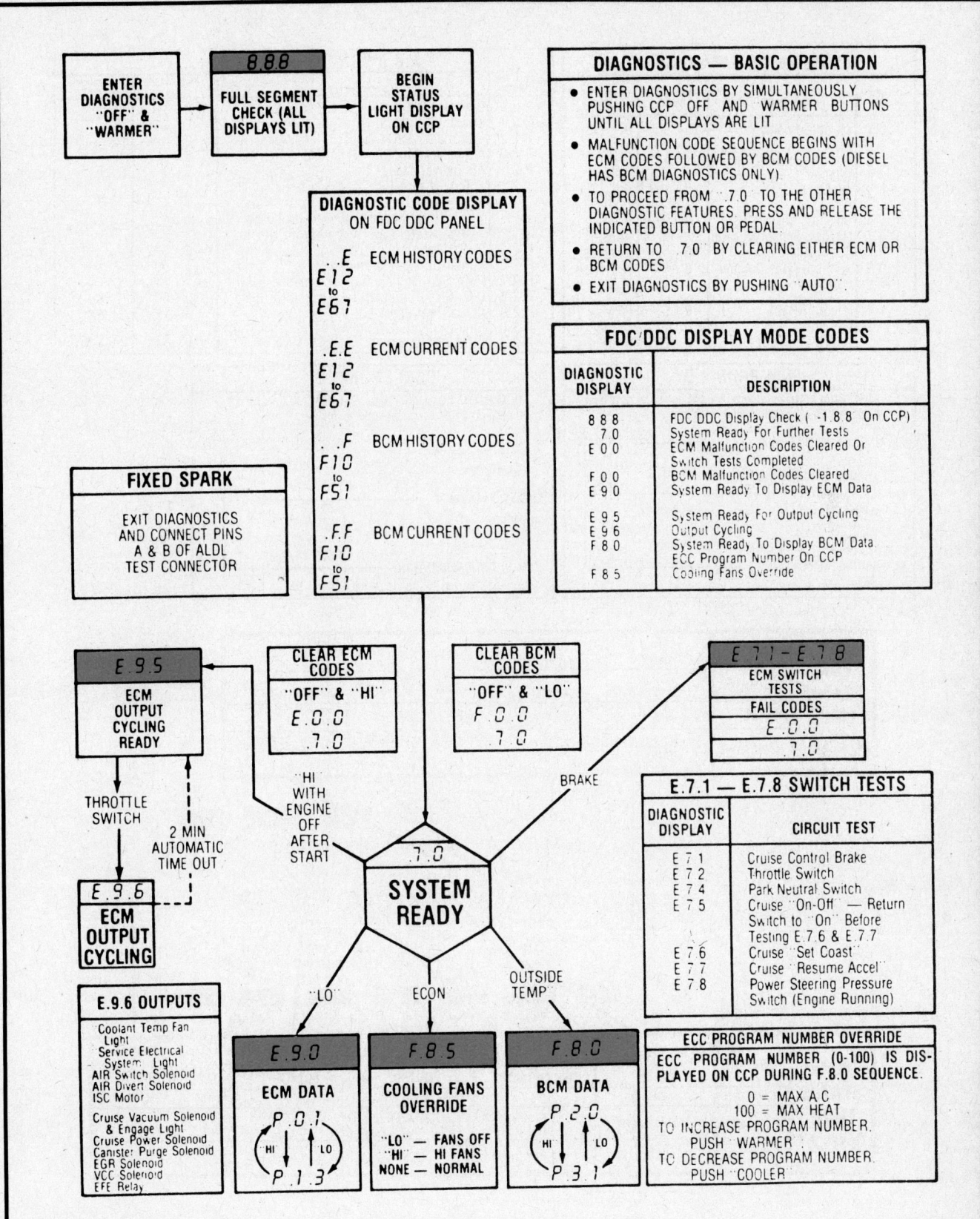

Cadillac FWD Deville and Fleetwood computer diagnostic system

E.9.0 ENGINE DATA DISPLAY

PARAMETER NUMBER	PARAMETER	PARAMETER RANGE	DISPLAY UNITS
P.0.1	Throttle Position	-10 - 90	Degrees
P.0.2	MAP	14 - 109	kPa
P.0.3	Computed BARO	61 - 103	kPa
P.0.4	Coolant Temperature	-40 - 151	°C
P.0.5	MAT	-40 - 151	°C
P.0.6	Injector Pulse Width	0 - 99.9	ms
P.0.7	Oxygen Sensor Voltage	0 - 1.14	Volts
P.0.8	Spark Advance	0 - 52	Degrees
P.0.9	Ignition Cycle Counter	0 - 50	Key Cycles
P.1.0	Battery Voltage	0 - 25.5	Volts
P.1.1	Engine RPM	0 - 6370	RPM ÷ 10
P.1.2	Car Speed	0 - 255	MPH
P.1.3	ECM PROM I.D.	0 - 255	Code

F.8.0 BCM DATA DISPLAY

PARAMETER NUMBER	PARAMETER		PARAMETER RANGE	DISPLAY UNITS
P.2.0	Commanded Blower Voltage		-3.3 - 18.0	Volts
P.2.1	Coolant Temperature		-40 - 215	°C
P.2.2	Commanded Air Mix Door Position		0 - 100	%
P.2.3	Actual Air Mix Door Position		0 - 100	%
P.2.4	Air Delivery Mode		0 - 7	Code
	0 = Max A C	4 = Off		
	1 = A C	5 = Normal Purge		
	2 = Intermediate	6 = Cold Purge		
	3 = Heater	7 = Front Defog		
P.2.5	In-Car Temperature		-40 - 102	°C
P.2.6	Actual Outside Temperature		-40 - 93	°C
P.2.7	High Side Temperature (Condenser Out)		-40 - 215	°C
P.2.8	Low Side Temperature (Evaporator In)		-40 - 93	°C
P.2.9	Actual Fuel Level		0 - 19.0	Gallons
P.3.0	Ignition Cycle Counter		0 - 99	Key Cycles
P.3.1	BCM PROM I.D.		0 - 255	Code

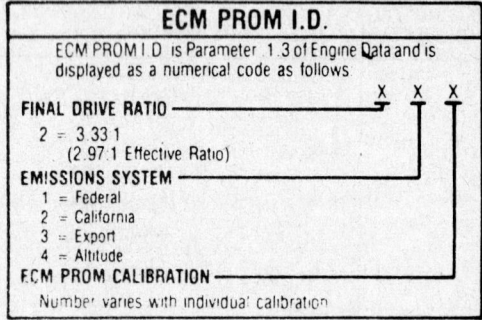

ECM PROM I.D.

ECM PROM I.D. is Parameter .1.3 of Engine Data and is displayed as a numerical code as follows

X X X

FINAL DRIVE RATIO
2 = 3.33:1
(2.97:1 Effective Ratio)

EMISSIONS SYSTEM
1 = Federal
2 = California
3 = Export
4 = Altitude

ECM PROM CALIBRATION
Number varies with individual calibration

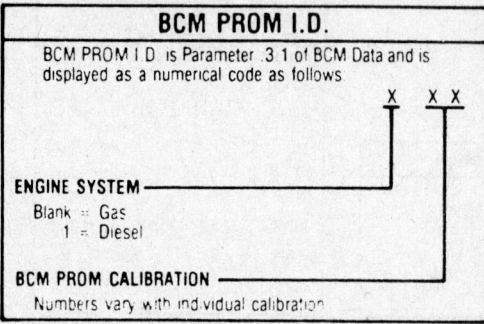

BCM PROM I.D.

BCM PROM I.D. is Parameter .3.1 of BCM Data and is displayed as a numerical code as follows

X X X

ENGINE SYSTEM
Blank = Gas
1 = Diesel

BCM PROM CALIBRATION
Numbers vary with individual calibration

ECM STATUS LIGHT DISPLAY						
	LIGHT ON	IN 4th GEAR	VCC ENABLED	CLOSED THROTTLE	RICH	CLOSED LOOP
	LIGHT OFF	NOT IN 4TH GEAR	VCC DISABLED	OPEN THROTTLE	LEAN	OPEN LOOP
	INDICATOR	(4th gear symbol)	(VCC symbol)	Off	Econ	Auto
	FUNCTION	4TH GEAR INPUT	VCC OUTPUT	THROTTLE SWITCH INPUT	OXYGEN SENSOR INPUT	ECM OPERATING MODE

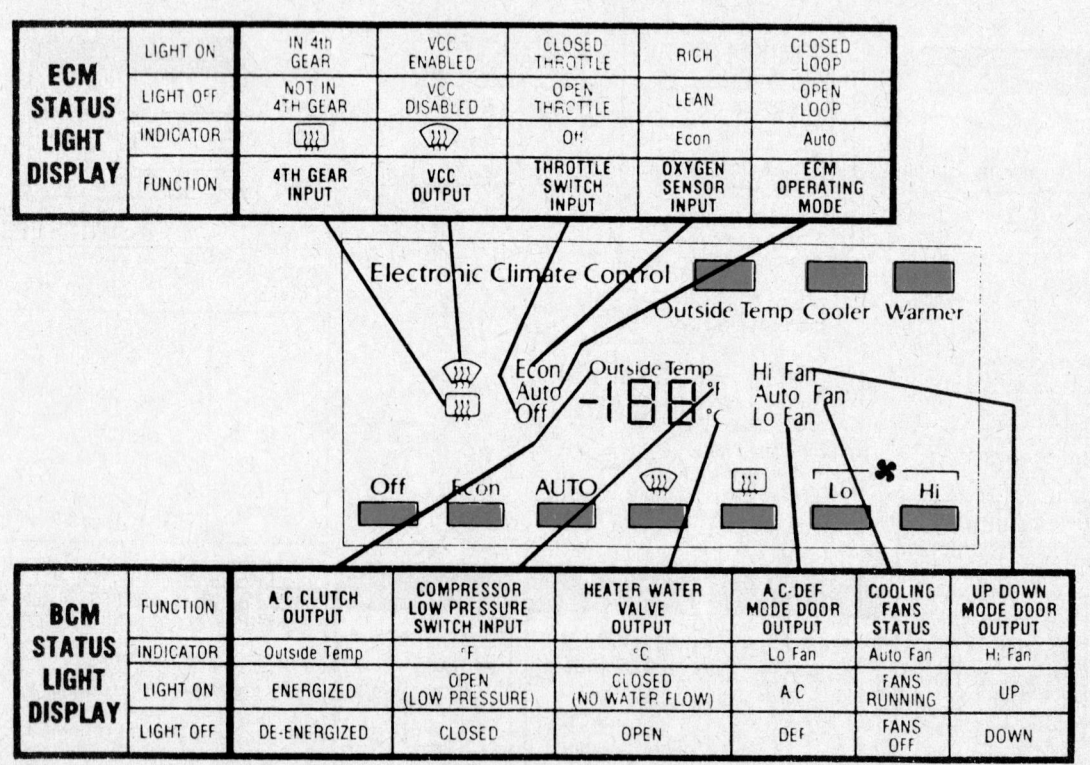

BCM STATUS LIGHT DISPLAY						
	FUNCTION	A C CLUTCH OUTPUT	COMPRESSOR LOW PRESSURE SWITCH INPUT	HEATER WATER VALVE OUTPUT	A C-DEF MODE DOOR OUTPUT	COOLING FANS STATUS	UP DOWN MODE DOOR OUTPUT
	INDICATOR	Outside Temp	°F	°C	Lo Fan	Auto Fan	Hi Fan
	LIGHT ON	ENERGIZED	OPEN (LOW PRESSURE)	CLOSED (NO WATER FLOW)	A C	FANS RUNNING	UP
	LIGHT OFF	DE-ENERGIZED	CLOSED	OPEN	DEF	FANS OFF	DOWN

Cadillac FWD Deville and Fleetwood computer diagnostic system

Self-Diagnostic System

TROUBLE CODES

In the process of controlling its various subsystems, the ECM and BCM continually monitor operating conditions for possible system malfunctions. By comparing system conditions against standard operating limits programmed into the computer memory, certain circuit and component malfunctions can be detected. A two digit numerical Trouble Code is stored in the computer memory when a problem is detected by this self-diagnostic system. These trouble codes can later be displayed to aid in repair of the system.

Certain system malfunctions require that the vehicle operator be alerted to the problem so as to avoid prolonged operation, which may cause more extensive damage. In this case, warning lights on the dash panel illuminate to indicate the need for service. If a particular malfunction would result in unacceptable system operation, the computer will attempt to minimize the effects of the malfunction by taking "Failsoft" action. Failsoft action is any attempt by the computer to compensate for the detected problem by, for example, substituting a fixed input value for a sensor circuit that is found to be open or shorted. The PROM contains preprogrammed, emergency values to be used in just such a situation. This process is sometimes referred to as a "Limp Home Mode" of operation.

ACTIVATING DIAGNOSTIC MODE

To enter the diagnostic mode, turn the ignition switch ON and press the OFF and WARMER buttons on the climate control panel simultaneously and hold them down until all display panel segments illuminate to indicate the beginning of the diagnostic readout. Diagnosis should not be attempted unless all segments of the display are working properly, or false code numbers could be read.

Once the display segment check is completed, any trouble codes stored in the computer memory will be displayed on the Data Center panel as follows:

1. Display of trouble codes will begin with "8.8.8" display on the panel for one second, followed by an "..E" which indicates the beginning of the stored trouble codes. The first pass of trouble codes includes all detected malfunctions whether they are currently present or not. If no trouble codes are stored, the "..E" display will be bypassed.

2. The lowest numbered ECM trouble code will be displayed for approximately two seconds, with all ECM codes prefixed with an "E" (E12, E13, etc.). Progressively higher numbered ECM codes will be displayed consecutively for two seconds until the highest code present has been displayed.

3. Once the first pass of trouble codes is complete, the panel will display ".E.E" to indicate the beginning of the second pass. On the second pass, only the "hard" trouble codes will be displayed, indicating a currently present malfunction. Codes displayed on the first pass are "intermittent" problems and if no hard failures are stored, the ".E.E" display will be bypassed.

4. Once all the stored ECM codes have been displayed, the BCM trouble codes will appear in the same manner. All BCM trouble codes are prefixed by an "F" (F12, F13, etc.), the display "..F" precedes the first pass and the display ".F.F" precedes the second pass.

5. After all ECM and BCM trouble codes have been displayed, or if no codes were stored, the Data Center will display ".7.0" to indicate that the system is ready for the next diagnostic feature to be selected.

NOTE: If a Code E51 is currently being detected, it will be displayed continuously until the technician exits the diagnostic mode. During the display of Code E51, none of the other diagnostic features (switch tests, output cycling, etc.) will be possible.

6. To exit the diagnostic mode, depress the AUTO button on the climate control panel, or turn the ignition OFF for 10 seconds. Trouble codes are not erased when this is done and the temperature setting will reappear in the Display Center.

7. To clear (erase) the trouble codes from the ECM memory, enter the diagnostic mode and depress the OFF and HI buttons on the climate control panel simultaneously and hold them down until "E.O.O" is displayed. To clear trouble codes from the BCM memory, depress the OFF and LO buttons simultaneously until "F.O.O" is displayed. After "E.O.O" or "F.O.O" is displayed, ".7.O" will appear. With ".7.O" displayed, turn the ignition OFF for at least 10 seconds before re-entering the diagnostic mode.

System Status Display

While in the diagnostic mode, the mode indicators on the climate control panel are used to indicate the status of certain system operating modes. The different modes of operation are indicated by the status light either being turned ON or OFF as follows:

ECM/BCM SYSTEM STATUS

Indicator	System Operating Mode
AUTO	Closed Loop Fuel Control—illuminates when coolant and oxygen sensors reach operating temperature.
ECON	Rich exhaust signal from oxygen sensor. Should flash on and off as ECM constantly adjusts mixture.
OFF	Closed throttle switch signal to ECM. Should go out when throttle is applied.
FRONT DEFOG	VCC engagement signal from ECM. Actual operation depends on VCC system integrity.
REAR DEFOG	Open 4th gear pressure switch. Should only come on while 4th gear is engaged.
OUTSIDE TEMP	ECC compressor clutch engagement signal from BCM. Actual operation depends on compressor clutch integrity.
AUTO FAN	Cooling fan operation signal to BCM from cooling fan control module. Indicator light Should be off when fans are off.
HI FAN	BCM signal to Up-Down mode door to divert air flow up away from heater outlet. Should be off whenever ECC system is in Heater or Normal Purge modes.
LO FAN	BCM signal to A/C-DEF mode door to divert air flow to the A/C outlets. Should be off whenever ECC system is in Heater, Intermediate, Defrost or Cold Purge modes.

ECM/BCM SYSTEM STATUS

Indicator	System Operating Mode
°F	Open refrigerant low pressure switch signal to BCM. Will illuminate when ambient temperature falls below −5°F due to pressure temperature relationship of refrigerant 12. Should be off under all other conditions.
°C	BCM signal to heater water valve to block coolant flow through the heater core. Should be off except when air mix door is commanded to MAX A/C position.

Indicator lights on climate control panel will illuminate if the electrical signal described is present in the ECM/BCM circuit. Actual operation of controlled components depends on component subsystem integrity.
ECM Electronic Control Module
BCM Body Control Module
VCC Viscous Converter Clutch
ECC Electronic Climate Control

ECM Switch Test Series

The engine must be running and Code .7.0 must be displayed on the Data Center panel before the switch tests can begin. To start the switch test sequence, depress and release the brake pedal. The switch tests will begin as the display switches from Code .7.0 to Code E.7.1. If the display fails to switch to code E.7.1, the ECM is not processing the brake signal.

As each code is displayed, the associated switch must be cycled within 10 seconds or the code will be recorded in the ECM memory as a failure. After the ECM recognizes a test as passing, or after 10 seconds elapses without the proper cycling being recognized, the display automatically advances to the next switch test code. The switch test sequence is as follows:

1. With Code E.7.1 displayed, depress and release the brake pedal to test the cruise control brake circuit.
2. With Code E.7.2 displayed, depress the throttle from the idle position to an open throttle position and then slowly release the throttle. The ECM will check the throttle switch for proper operation.
3. With Code E.7.4 displayed and the brakes applied, shift the transmission lever into Reverse and then Neutral to check the operation of the Park/Neutral switch.

NOTE: On cars without cruise control, Codes E.7.5, E.7.6 and E.7.7 will be displayed but cannot be performed during the switch tests. When these codes are displayed during the switch tests, allow each code to reach its 10 second limit. After 10 seconds, the display will advance to the next code. Allow Codes E.7.5, E.7.6 and E.7.7 to display for 30 seconds. Since these codes will be recorded as failures in the switch test sequence, a display of E.0.0 will never come up at the completion of the tests. To confirm proper operation of the remaining switch, Code E.7.8 must be observed as having advanced within 10 seconds. If the code cannot be advanced within 10 seconds, it should be considered a failed test.

4. With Code E.7.5 displayed, switch the cruise control switch from OFF to ON to OFF to check the operation of this switch.

5. With Code E.7.6 displayed and with the cruise switch ON, depress and release the SET/COAST button to check switch operation.
6. With Code E.7.7 displayed and with the cruise control switch ON, depress and release the RESUME/ACCELERATE switch to check its operation.
7. With Code E.7.8 displayed and the engine running, turn the wheels from straight ahead to full right or left, then return to straight ahead. This checks the power steering pressure switch operation.
8. When the switch tests are complete, the ECM will display the switch codes that did not test properly. Each failed code will be displayed beginning with the lowest number. The codes will not disappear until the affected switch circuit has been repaired and retested.
9. After the switch tests are completed and all circuits pass, the Data Center displays E.0.0 and then returns to Code .7.0 to indicate that all of the switch circuits are functioning properly.

ECM Data Display

Code .7.0 must be displayed on the Data Center panel before the diagnostics can begin to display the ECM data series. To display the ECM data information, proceed as follows:

1. Depress and release the LO button on the climate control panel. The ECM data series begins as the display switches from Code .7.0 to Code E.9.0. It is possible to leave the ECM data series at any time and return to Code .7.0 by clearing the ECM or BCM codes.
2. To advance the display, depress the HI button on the climate control panel. To return to a lower number parameter or jump directly from E.9.0 to the end of the parameter list (P.1.3), depress the LO button.
3. When troubleshooting a malfunction, the ECM data display can be used to compare the vehicle with problems to a vehicle which is functioning normally. See the ECM Parameter Chart for an explanation of each display.

When the ECM data display is initiated, the Data Center will display a parameter check (P.0.1, P.0.2, etc.) for one second and then a number will be displayed for nine seconds to indicate the parameter value. The display will continue to repeat this sequence of events until moved to another parameter.

BCM DATA PARAMETERS

Display	Parameter
P.2.0	Blower voltage ①
P.2.1	Coolant temperature (°C)
P.2.2	Air mix door position (%) ②
P.2.3	Actual air mix door position (%)
P.2.4	Air delivery mode (0–7) ③
P.2.5	In-car temperature (°C)
P.2.6	Outside temperature (°C)
P.2.7	High side temperature (°C) ④
P.2.8	Low side temperature (°C) ⑤
P.2.9	Fuel level (gals) ①
P.3.0	Ignition cycle counter ⑥
P.3.1	BCM PROM ID number

① A decimal point will appear before the last digit
② A valve close to 0% represents a cold air mix while a valve
 close to 100% indicates a warm air mix
③ 0 = MAX A/C
 1 = A/C
 2 = Intermediate
 3 = Heater
 4 = Off
 5 = Normal purge
 6 = Cold purge
 7 = Defrost
④ Condenser output
⑤ Evaporator input
⑥ The number of times the ignition has been cycled to OFF
 since a BCM trouble code was last detected. After 100 ignition cycles without any malfunction, all BCM codes are
 cleared and the counter reset to zero.

ECM Output Cycling

This mode can be initiated after E.9.5 is displayed on the Data Center panel. The E.9.5 display can be reached by depressing the HI button on the climate control panel while Code .7.0 is displayed. The ECM output cycling mode (Code E.9.6) turns the ECM outputs on and off. To enter the output cycling mode, proceed as follows:

1. Start the engine and allow it to idle.
2. Turn the cruise control switch ON so the outputs will cycle.
3. Turn the engine OFF, then within two seconds turn the ignition ON.
4. Enter diagnostics and display Code E.9.5.
5. Depress the accelerator pedal (throttle switch open) and release it (throttle switch closed). The ECM output cycling mode begins as the display switches from Code E.9.5 to Code E.9.6. It is possible to leave the ECM output cycling mode at any time and return to .7.0 by clearing the ECM or BCM codes.

NOTE: If the display doesn't advance to Code E.9.6, refer to Code E.7.2 of the switch tests.

6. The output cycling mode will end automatically after two minutes of cycling and the display will switch from Code E.9.6 to Code E.9.5. The outputs will cycle on and off every three seconds until the two minute automatic shutoff occurs. The only exception to this three second cycle is the cruise control power valve which cycles continuously. If additional output cycling is desired, recycle the throttle switch.

BCM Data Display

Code .7.0 must be displayed on the Data Center panel before diagnostics can begin to display the BCM data series. To display the BCM data information, proceed as follows:

1. Depress and release the OUTSIDE TEMP button on the climate control panel. The BCM data series begins as the display switches from Code .7.0 to Code F.8.0. It is possible to leave the BCM data series at any time and return to Code .7.0 by clearing the ECM or BCM codes.
2. To advance the display, depress the HI button on the climate control panel. To return to a lower number parameter or jump directly from F.8.0 to the end of the parameter list (P.3.1), depress the LO button on the climate control panel.
3. When troubleshooting a malfunction, the BCM data display can be used to compare the vehicle with a problem to a vehicle which is functioning properly. See the BCM Parameter Chart for an explanation of each display.

ECM DATA PARAMETERS

Display	Parameter
P.0.1	Throttle angle in degrees
P.0.2	MAP valve in kilopascals (kPa)
P.0.3	BARO valve in kilopascals (kPa)
P.0.4	Coolant temperature (°C)
P.0.5	Manifold air temperature (°C)
P.0.6	Injector pulse width in milliseconds ①
P.0.7	Oxygen sensor voltage
P.0.8	Spark advance in degrees ②
P.0.9	Ignition cycle counter ③
P.1.0	Battery voltage ①
P.1.1	Engine speed in rpm/10 ④
P.1.2	Road speed in mph
P.1.3	ECM PROM ID number

MAP Manifold Air Pressure
BARO Ambient barometric pressure
① A decimal point will appear before the last digit
② Valve should agree with timing light ± 2°
③ After 50 ignition cycles without any malfunction being detected, all ECM codes are cleared and the counter is reset to zero.
④ For example; 120 = 1200 rpm

When the BCM data display is first initiated, the Data Center will display a parameter check (P.2.0, P.3.1, etc.) for one second and then a number will be displayed for nine seconds to indicate the parameter value. This display will continue to repeat this sequence of events until the display is moved to another parameter.

ECC Program Override

During the display of BCM data on the Data Center, the climate control panel will display a two-digit number which represents the Electronic Climate Control (ECC) program number. This number represents various levels of heating and cooling effort. As F.8.0 first appears on the Data Center, the climate control panel will begin displaying the program number which is currently being used by the ECC system. As operating conditions change, this number will automatically change in response.

The automatic calculation of program number can be bypassed by a manual override feature using the WARMER and COOLER buttons. While in the F.8.0 mode, pressing the WARMER button will increase the program number at a controlled rate until the value of 100 is reached. 100 represents the MAX HEAT mode of ECC operation. Pressing the COOLER button will decrease the program number until the value of 0 is reached, which represents the MAX A/C mode of operation.

This manual override will continue until the F.8.0 mode is exited. This allows control of the program number (from 0 to 100) while simultaneously observing the reaction of any BCM data parameters.

Cooling Fans Override

Code .7.0 must be displayed on the Data Center panel before the cooling fans override feature can be selected. This feature allows manual override of the BCM automatic control of cooling fan speed. To manually command either HIGH FAN or FAN OFF, proceed as follows:

1. Depress and release the ECON button on the climate control panel. The cooling fans override mode begins as the display switches from Code .7.0 to Code F.8.5. It is possible to leave the cooling fans override mode at any time and return to .7.0 by clearing the ECM or BCM codes.

2. To command HIGH FAN operation, hold in the HI button on the climate control panel. Fan speed should increase until the maximum speed is achieved. Releasing the HI button will return the calculation of fan speed to automatic BCM control.

3. To command FAN OFF, hold in the LO button on the climate control panel. Fan speed should decrease until the fans are completely stopped. Releasing the LO button will return the calculation of fan speed to automatic BCM control.

Self-Diagnostic System Check

The self-diagnostic system check is an organized approach for identifying a problem caused by the on-board computer controlled electronics. Understanding the chart and using it correctly will reduce diagnosis time and prevent the unnecessary replacement of parts.

A two second bulb check of the SERVICE AIR COND telltale when the ignition is switched ON confirms battery, ignition and ground integrity to the BCM. SERVICE NOW and SERVICE SOON telltales illuminate during cranking to confirm battery, ignition and ground integrity to the ECM.

The Climate Control Panel (CCP) and Fuel/Diesel Data Center (FDC/DDC) must be functional in order to use the self-diagnostic system. Check that the panels illuminate and respond when the buttons are depressed. After entering diagnostics, record all displayed trouble codes and note those displayed during both the first and second pass. Codes displayed during the first pass only are "intermittents" and may require a visual inspection of circuitry to isolate. Codes displayed during the second pass are "hard" malfunctions which can be diagnosed using the trouble charts. Malfunctions which are not detected by a trouble code or switch test could be mechanical (rather than electrical) in nature and a visual check for binding linkage, disconnected vacuum hoses, etc. should be undertaken before attempting any electrical diagnosis procedures.

SELF-DIAGNOSTIC SYSTEM CHECK

- IF YOU HAVE NOT REVIEWED THE BASIC INFORMATION ON HOW TO USE THE COMPUTOR SELF-DIAGNOSTICS, GO TO THE INTRODUCTION OF THIS SECTION.

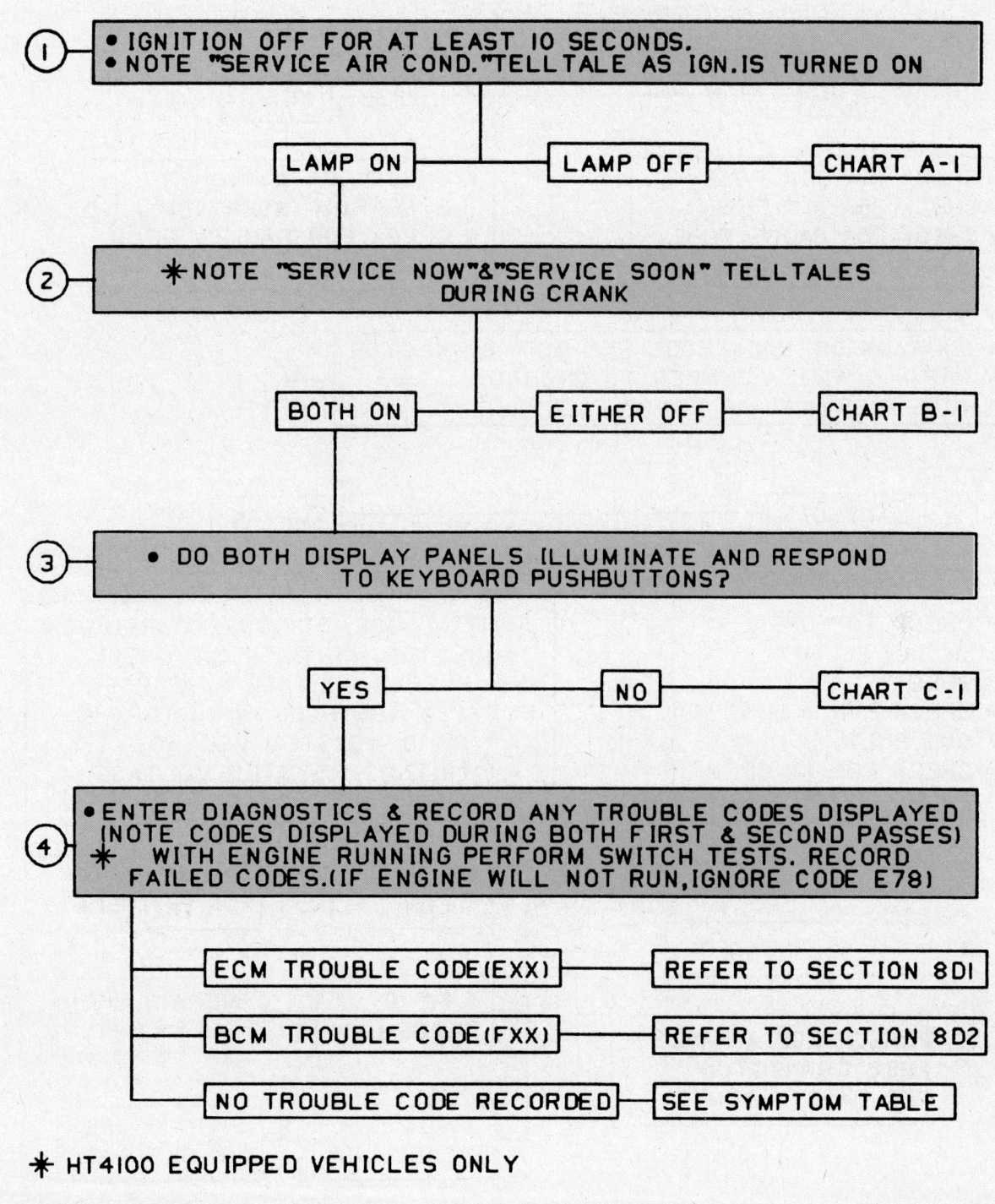

① • IGNITION OFF FOR AT LEAST 10 SECONDS.
  • NOTE "SERVICE AIR COND."TELLTALE AS IGN.IS TURNED ON

LAMP ON — LAMP OFF — CHART A-1

② ✳NOTE "SERVICE NOW"&"SERVICE SOON" TELLTALES DURING CRANK

BOTH ON — EITHER OFF — CHART B-1

③ • DO BOTH DISPLAY PANELS ILLUMINATE AND RESPOND TO KEYBOARD PUSHBUTTONS?

YES — NO — CHART C-1

④ • ENTER DIAGNOSTICS & RECORD ANY TROUBLE CODES DISPLAYED (NOTE CODES DISPLAYED DURING BOTH FIRST & SECOND PASSES)
  ✳ WITH ENGINE RUNNING PERFORM SWITCH TESTS. RECORD FAILED CODES.(IF ENGINE WILL NOT RUN,IGNORE CODE E78)

ECM TROUBLE CODE(EXX) — REFER TO SECTION 8DI

BCM TROUBLE CODE(FXX) — REFER TO SECTION 8D2

NO TROUBLE CODE RECORDED — SEE SYMPTOM TABLE

✳ HT4100 EQUIPPED VEHICLES ONLY

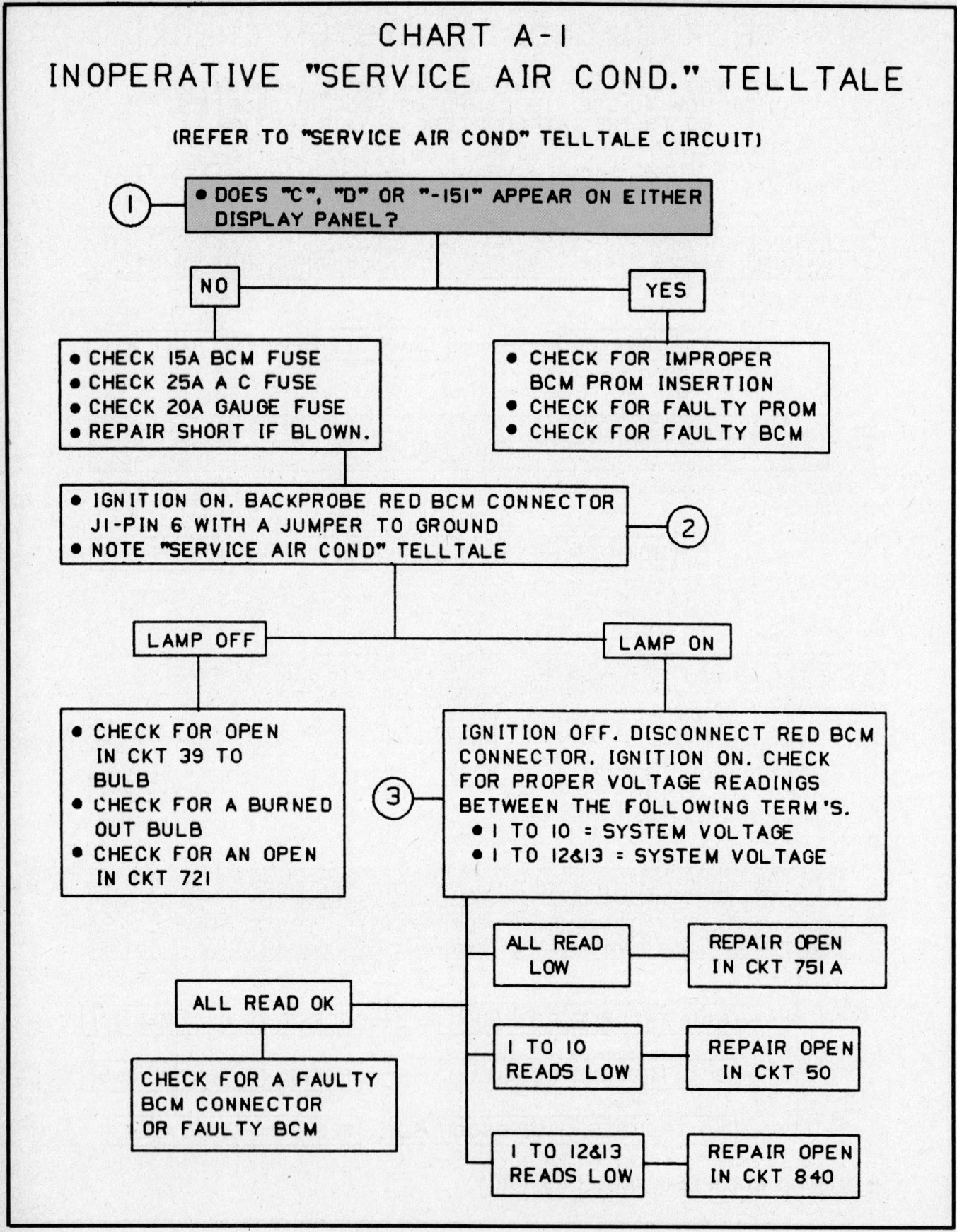

CHART A-1
INOPERATIVE "SERVICE AIR COND." TELLTALE

(REFER TO "SERVICE AIR COND" TELLTALE CIRCUIT)

① • DOES "C", "D" OR "-151" APPEAR ON EITHER DISPLAY PANEL?

NO

- CHECK 15A BCM FUSE
- CHECK 25A A C FUSE
- CHECK 20A GAUGE FUSE
- REPAIR SHORT IF BLOWN.

YES

- CHECK FOR IMPROPER BCM PROM INSERTION
- CHECK FOR FAULTY PROM
- CHECK FOR FAULTY BCM

② • IGNITION ON. BACKPROBE RED BCM CONNECTOR J1-PIN 6 WITH A JUMPER TO GROUND
- NOTE "SERVICE AIR COND" TELLTALE

LAMP OFF

- CHECK FOR OPEN IN CKT 39 TO BULB
- CHECK FOR A BURNED OUT BULB
- CHECK FOR AN OPEN IN CKT 721

LAMP ON

③ IGNITION OFF. DISCONNECT RED BCM CONNECTOR. IGNITION ON. CHECK FOR PROPER VOLTAGE READINGS BETWEEN THE FOLLOWING TERM'S.
- 1 TO 10 = SYSTEM VOLTAGE
- 1 TO 12&13 = SYSTEM VOLTAGE

ALL READ LOW → **REPAIR OPEN IN CKT 751A**

ALL READ OK

CHECK FOR A FAULTY BCM CONNECTOR OR FAULTY BCM

1 TO 10 READS LOW → **REPAIR OPEN IN CKT 50**

1 TO 12&13 READS LOW → **REPAIR OPEN IN CKT 840**

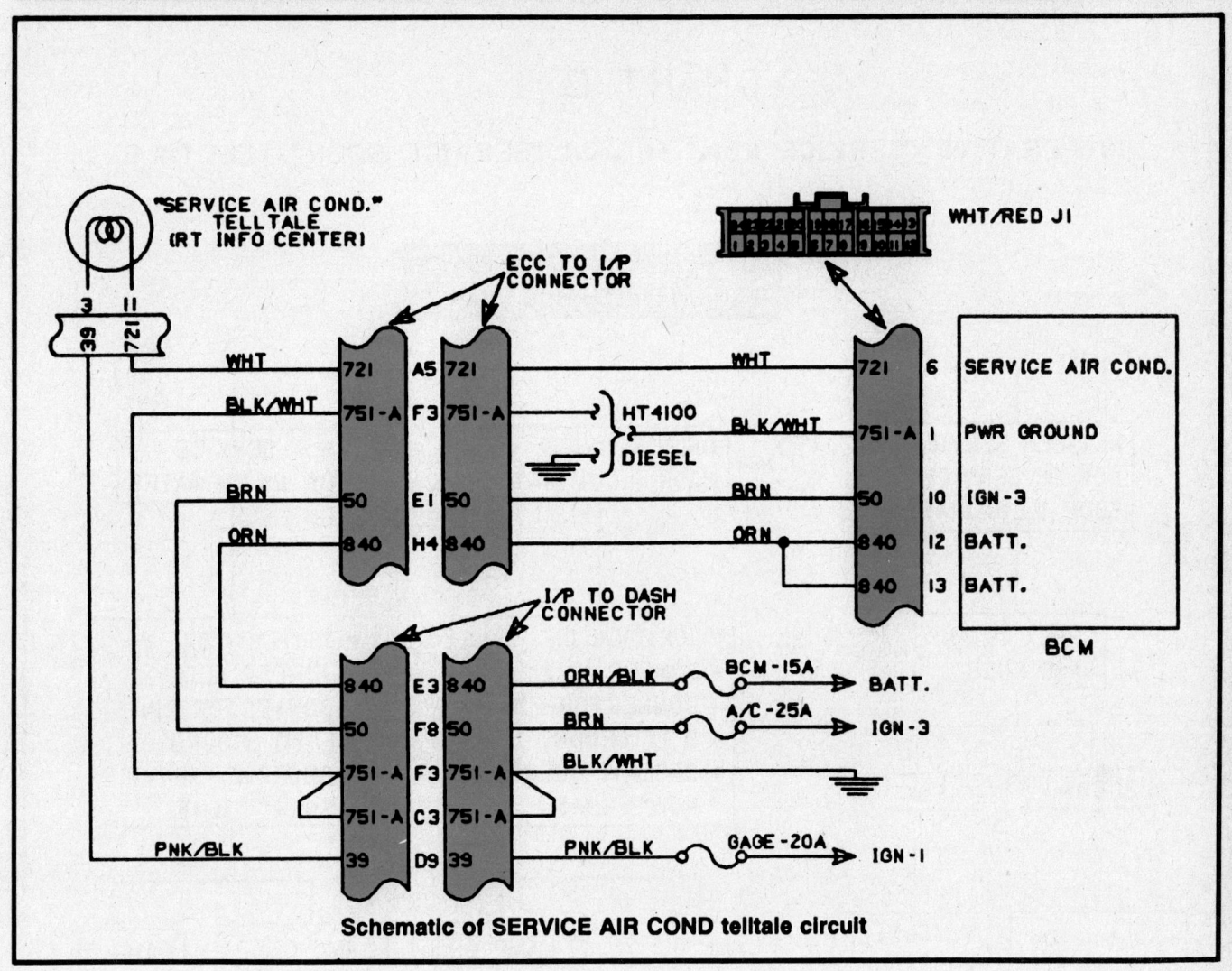

Schematic of SERVICE AIR COND telltale circuit

CHART A-1 — SERVICE AIR COND TELLTALE INOPERATIVE

1. If the SERVICE AIR COND telltale does not illuminate when the ignition is switched ON and a "c", "d" or "-151" appears on one of the displays, the BCM microprocessor is not functioning properly. This could be due to improper PROM insertion or failed components in the BCM.

2. If the SERVICE AIR COND telltale cannot be illuminated by providing a ground to circuit 721, the problem is in the bulb circuitry.

3. If the bulb can be illuminated, then battery, ignition and ground integrity must be checked to the BCM. If the circuits check OK, the BCM connector or BCM is faulty.

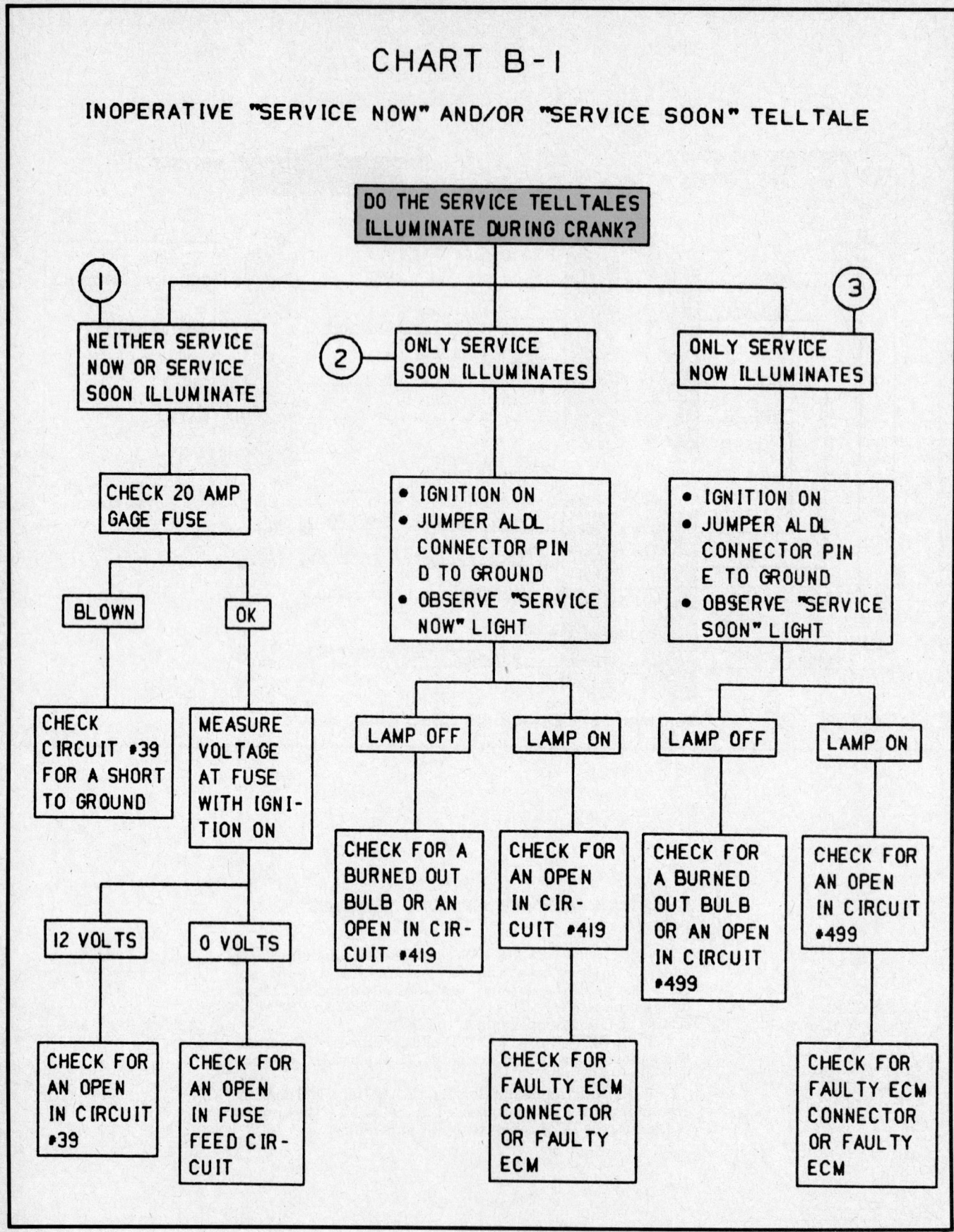

CHART B-1

INOPERATIVE "SERVICE NOW" AND/OR "SERVICE SOON" TELLTALE

DO THE SERVICE TELLTALES ILLUMINATE DURING CRANK?

① NEITHER SERVICE NOW OR SERVICE SOON ILLUMINATE

② ONLY SERVICE SOON ILLUMINATES

③ ONLY SERVICE NOW ILLUMINATES

CHECK 20 AMP GAGE FUSE

BLOWN

OK

- IGNITION ON
- JUMPER ALDL CONNECTOR PIN D TO GROUND
- OBSERVE "SERVICE NOW" LIGHT

- IGNITION ON
- JUMPER ALDL CONNECTOR PIN E TO GROUND
- OBSERVE "SERVICE SOON" LIGHT

CHECK CIRCUIT #39 FOR A SHORT TO GROUND

MEASURE VOLTAGE AT FUSE WITH IGNITION ON

LAMP OFF

LAMP ON

LAMP OFF

LAMP ON

12 VOLTS

0 VOLTS

CHECK FOR A BURNED OUT BULB OR AN OPEN IN CIRCUIT #419

CHECK FOR AN OPEN IN CIRCUIT #419

CHECK FOR A BURNED OUT BULB OR AN OPEN IN CIRCUIT #499

CHECK FOR AN OPEN IN CIRCUIT #499

CHECK FOR AN OPEN IN CIRCUIT #39

CHECK FOR AN OPEN IN FUSE FEED CIRCUIT

CHECK FOR FAULTY ECM CONNECTOR OR FAULTY ECM

CHECK FOR FAULTY ECM CONNECTOR OR FAULTY ECM

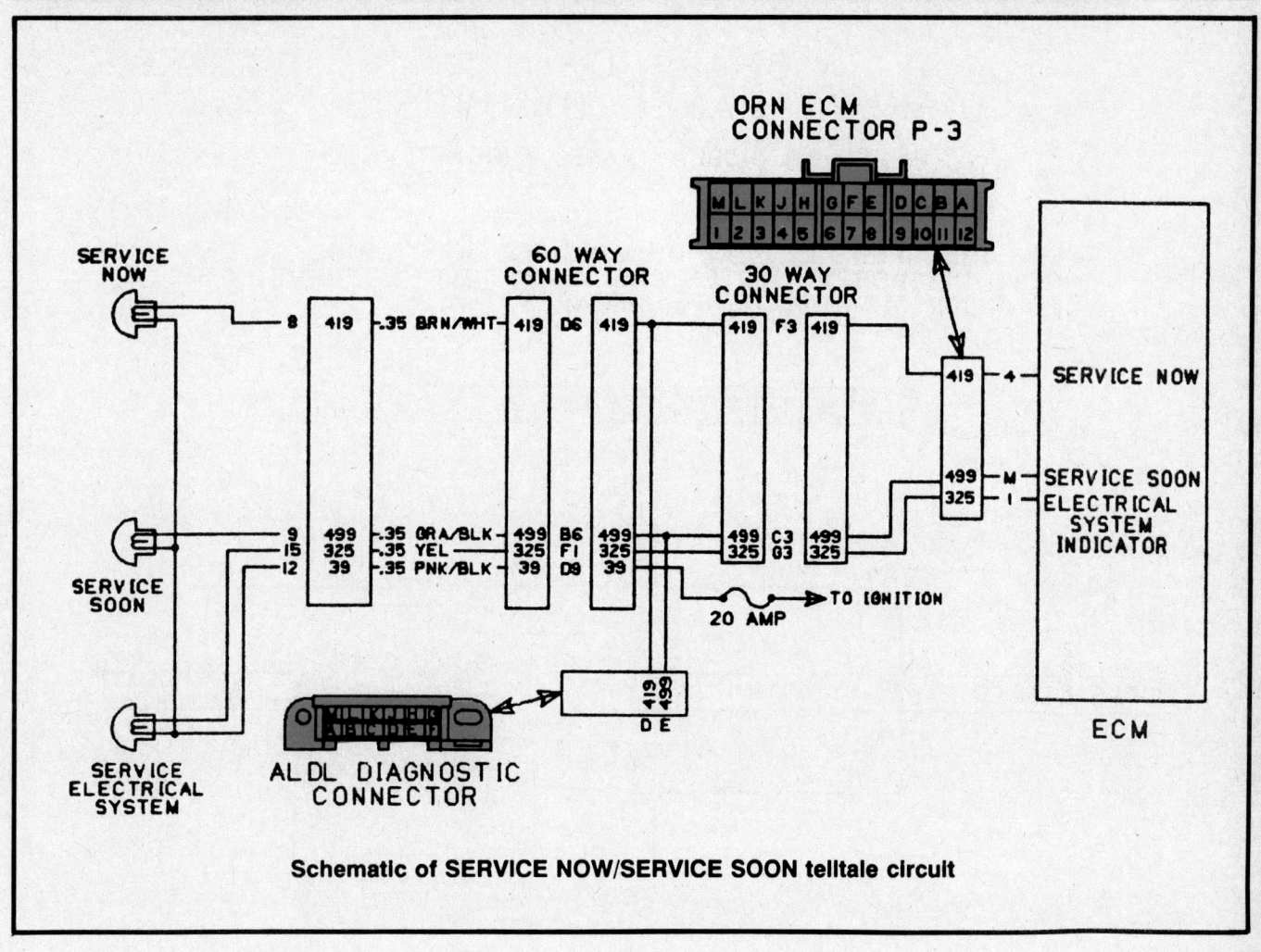

Schematic of SERVICE NOW/SERVICE SOON telltale circuit

CHART B-1 — SERVICE NOW/SERVICE SOON TELLTALE INOPERATIVE

1. If the SERVICE SOON or SERVICE NOW telltales do not illuminate during cranking, check the 20 amp fuse. If the fuse is blown, check for a short to ground in circuit 39. If the fuse is OK, measure the voltage at the fuse with the ignition ON. Make all test connections with the ignition switched OFF, then turn ON the ignition and read the voltmeter. If the voltmeter indicates 12 volts to the fuse, check circuit 39 for an open wire. If the voltage reading is zero, the open circuit is between the ignition switch and the fuse.

2. If the SERVICE SOON telltale operates normally, the power circuit 39 is OK and the cause of the problem is the bulb or the ground side of the bulb. The ECM is responsible for turning on the SERVICE NOW telltale by grounding circuit 419.

The ECM activity can be simulated by jumpering the ALDL connector pin D to ground. If the light comes on, check circuit 419 for an open wire to the ECM. If circuit 419 is OK, check for a faulty ECM connector or a faulty ECM. If the bulb does not illuminate, the cause is a burned out bulb or an open wire in circuit 419.

3. If the SERVICE NOW telltale operates normally, the power circuit 39 is OK and the cause of the problem is the bulb or the ground side of the bulb. The ECM is responsible for turning on the SERVICE SOON light by grounding circuit 499. The ECM activity can be simulated by jumpering the ALDL connector pin E to ground. If the light comes on, check circuit 499 for an open wire to the ECM. If circuit 499 is OK, check for a faulty ECM connector or faulty ECM. If the bulb does not light, the cause is a burned out bulb or an open in circuit 499.

CHART C-1
DISPLAY PANEL DIAGNOSIS
(REFER TO DISPLAY PANEL CIRCUIT)

- FOR IMPROPER- DISPLAY DIMMING SEE SECTION 8C
- SELF-DIAGNOSTIC SYSTEM CHECK MUST BE PERFORMED FIRST
- TURN IGNITION ON. TURN HEADLAMPS OFF.

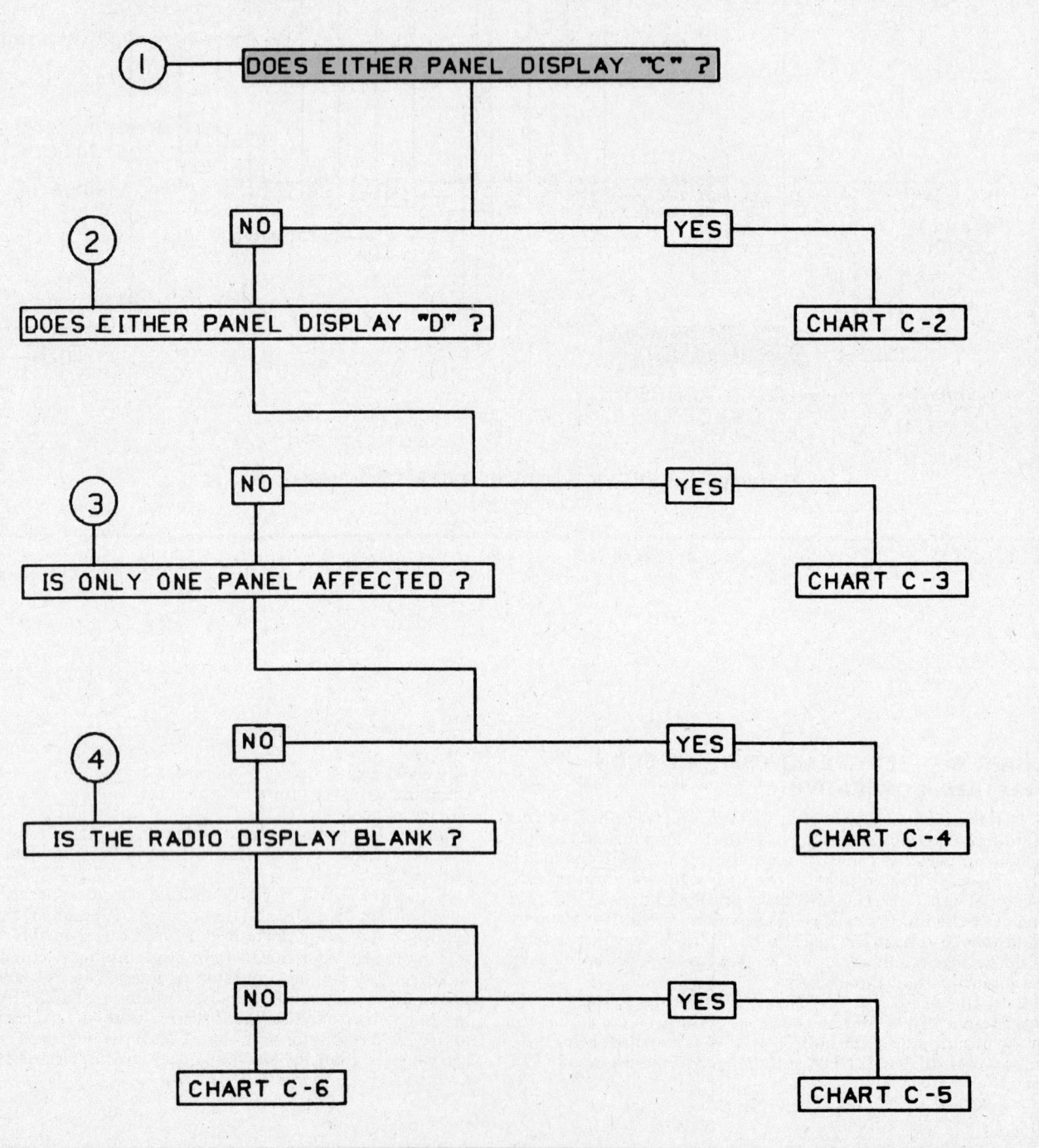

(1) DOES EITHER PANEL DISPLAY "C" ?

(2) NO — YES — CHART C-2

DOES EITHER PANEL DISPLAY "D" ?

(3) NO — YES — CHART C-3

IS ONLY ONE PANEL AFFECTED ?

(4) NO — YES — CHART C-4

IS THE RADIO DISPLAY BLANK ?

NO — YES

CHART C-6 — CHART C-5

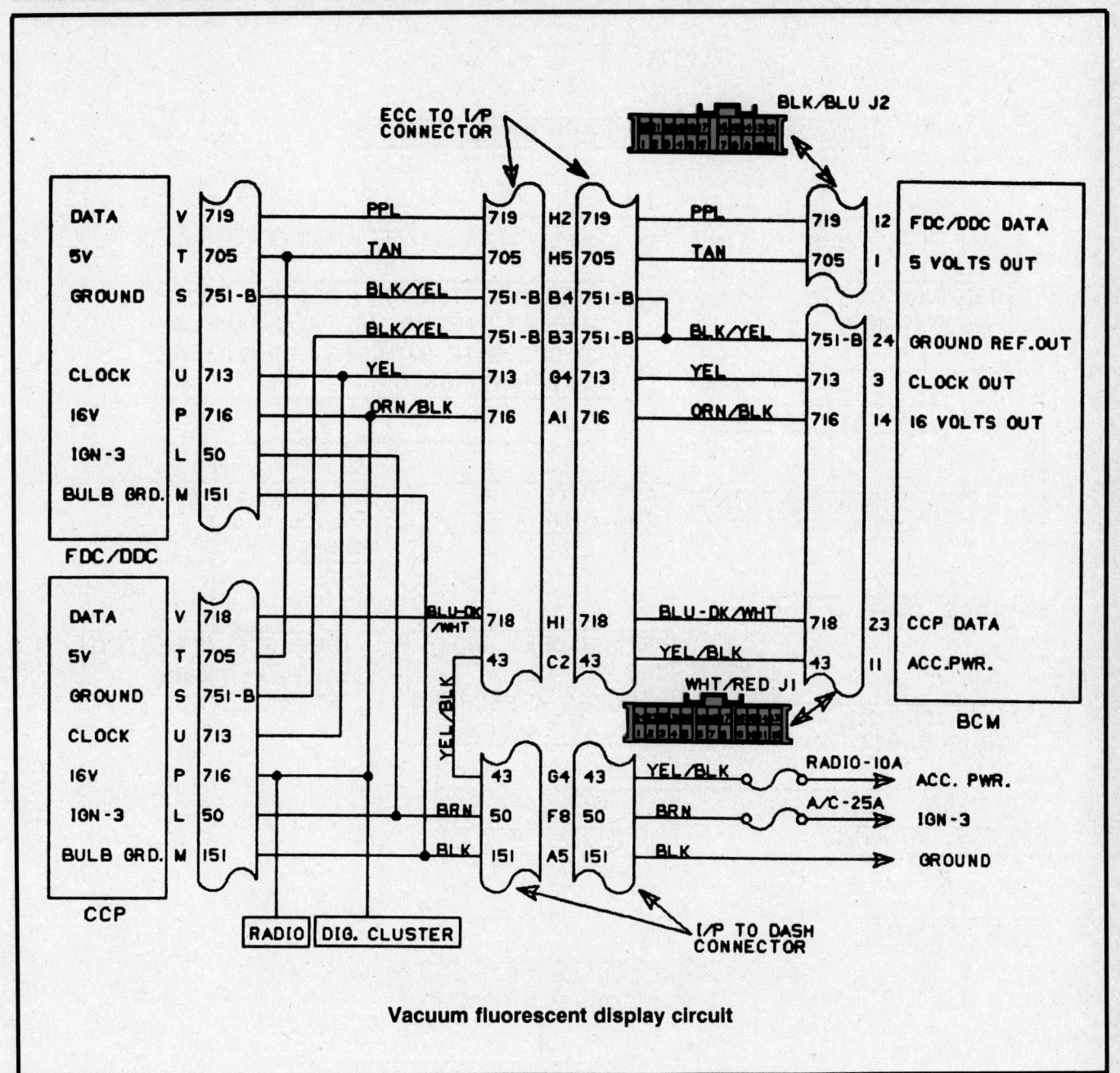

Vacuum fluorescent display circuit

CHART C-1 – DISPLAY PANEL DIAGNOSIS

1. A "c" displayed on one or both panels indicates a loss of the "clock" signal to the affected panel.

2. A "d" displayed on either panel indicates a loss of the "data" signal to the affected panel.

3. If one panel is affected, only branches of the critical circuits to that panel require investigation.

4. If both panels and the radio are blank, a loss of 16 volts is indicated. This signal is produced by the BCM when the accessory power circuit receives voltage. If the radio displays properly, all remaining critical circuits will require investigation

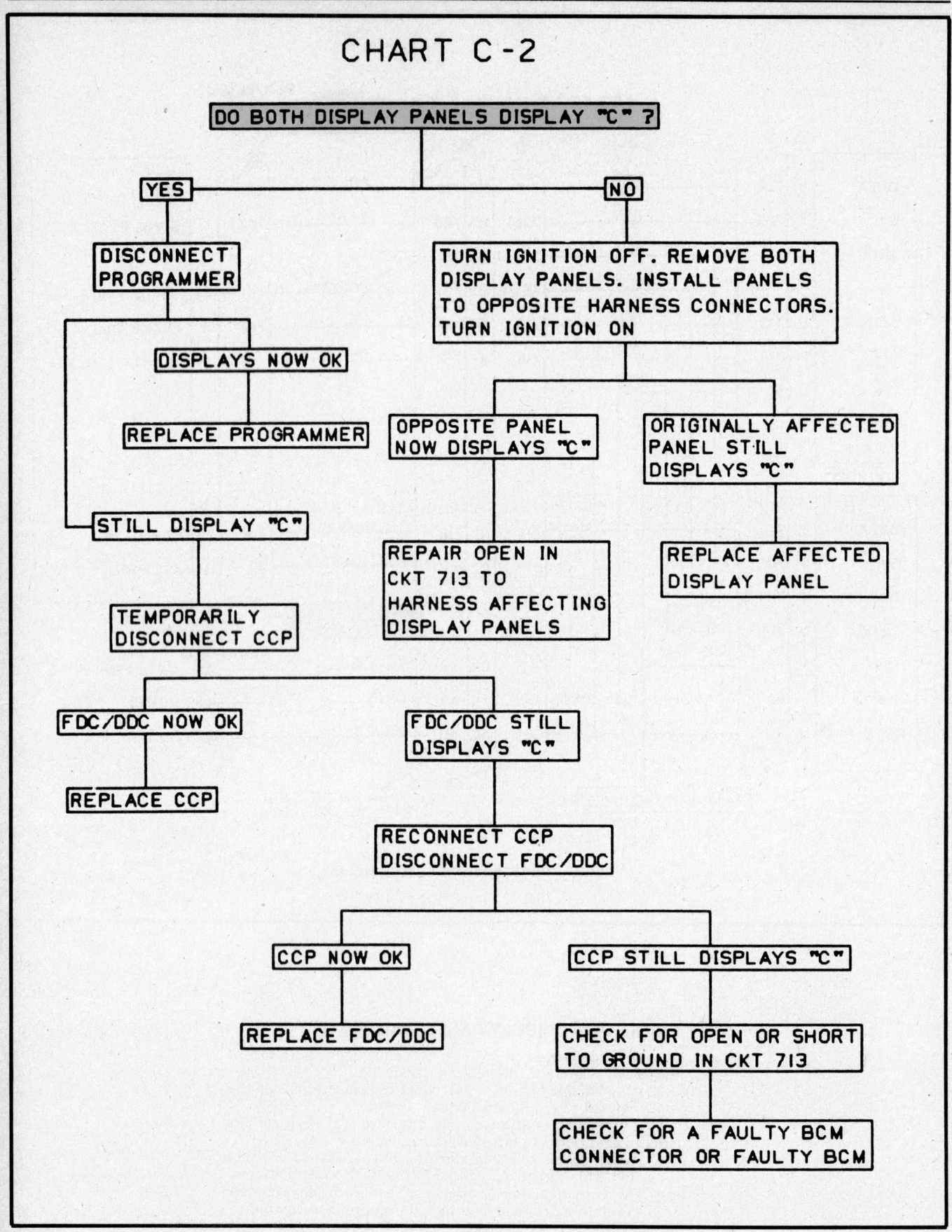

CHART C-2

DO BOTH DISPLAY PANELS DISPLAY "C" ?

YES — NO

DISCONNECT PROGRAMMER

TURN IGNITION OFF. REMOVE BOTH DISPLAY PANELS. INSTALL PANELS TO OPPOSITE HARNESS CONNECTORS. TURN IGNITION ON

DISPLAYS NOW OK

OPPOSITE PANEL NOW DISPLAYS "C"

ORIGINALLY AFFECTED PANEL STILL DISPLAYS "C"

REPLACE PROGRAMMER

STILL DISPLAY "C"

REPAIR OPEN IN CKT 713 TO HARNESS AFFECTING DISPLAY PANELS

REPLACE AFFECTED DISPLAY PANEL

TEMPORARILY DISCONNECT CCP

FDC/DDC NOW OK

FDC/DDC STILL DISPLAYS "C"

REPLACE CCP

RECONNECT CCP DISCONNECT FDC/DDC

CCP NOW OK

CCP STILL DISPLAYS "C"

REPLACE FDC/DDC

CHECK FOR OPEN OR SHORT TO GROUND IN CKT 713

CHECK FOR A FAULTY BCM CONNECTOR OR FAULTY BCM

CHART C-3

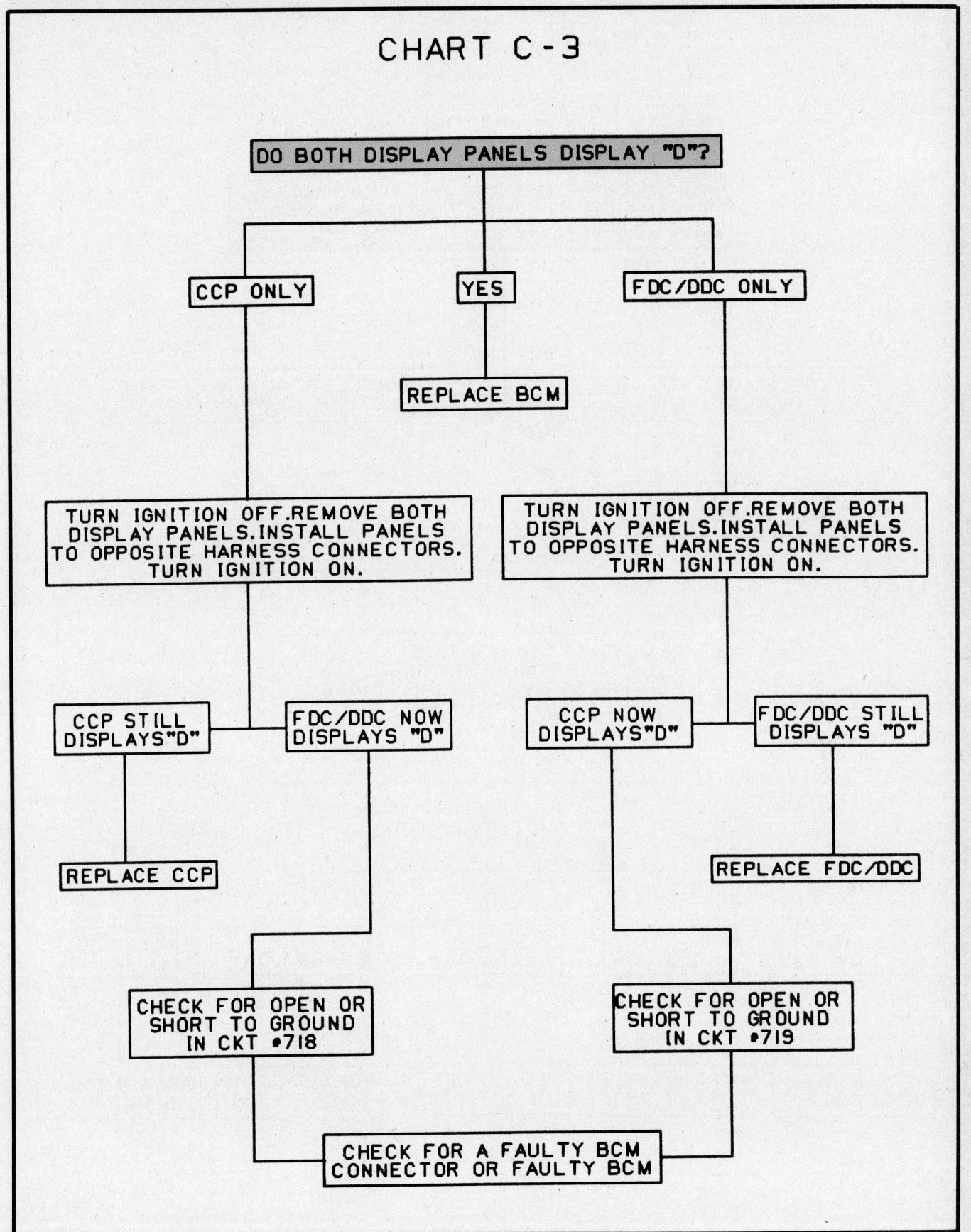

DO BOTH DISPLAY PANELS DISPLAY "D"?

CCP ONLY | YES | FDC/DDC ONLY

REPLACE BCM

TURN IGNITION OFF. REMOVE BOTH DISPLAY PANELS. INSTALL PANELS TO OPPOSITE HARNESS CONNECTORS. TURN IGNITION ON.

TURN IGNITION OFF. REMOVE BOTH DISPLAY PANELS. INSTALL PANELS TO OPPOSITE HARNESS CONNECTORS. TURN IGNITION ON.

CCP STILL DISPLAYS "D" | FDC/DDC NOW DISPLAYS "D"

CCP NOW DISPLAYS "D" | FDC/DDC STILL DISPLAYS "D"

REPLACE CCP

REPLACE FDC/DDC

CHECK FOR OPEN OR SHORT TO GROUND IN CKT ●718

CHECK FOR OPEN OR SHORT TO GROUND IN CKT ●719

CHECK FOR A FAULTY BCM CONNECTOR OR FAULTY BCM

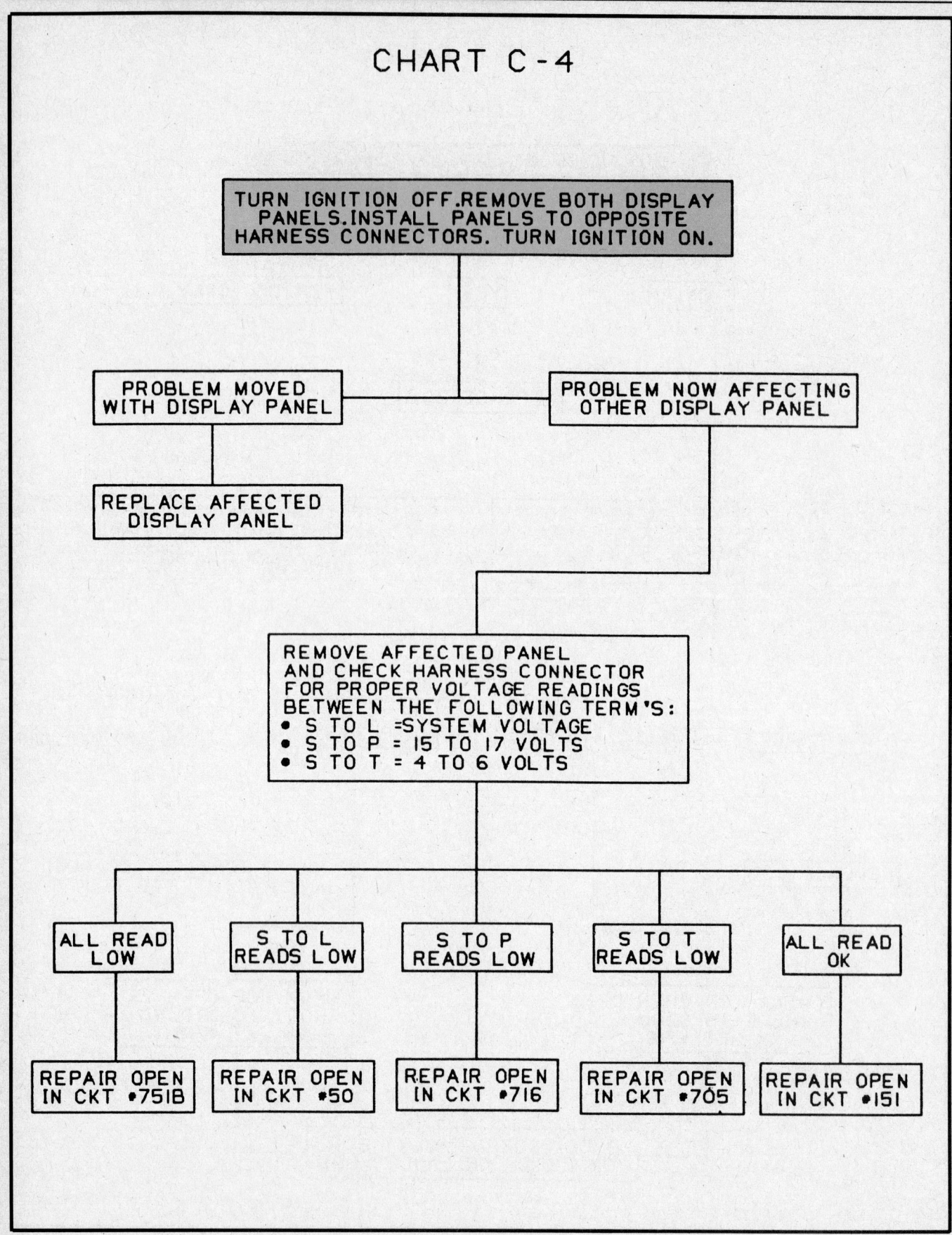

CHART C-4

TURN IGNITION OFF. REMOVE BOTH DISPLAY PANELS. INSTALL PANELS TO OPPOSITE HARNESS CONNECTORS. TURN IGNITION ON.

PROBLEM MOVED WITH DISPLAY PANEL

PROBLEM NOW AFFECTING OTHER DISPLAY PANEL

REPLACE AFFECTED DISPLAY PANEL

REMOVE AFFECTED PANEL AND CHECK HARNESS CONNECTOR FOR PROPER VOLTAGE READINGS BETWEEN THE FOLLOWING TERM'S:
- S TO L = SYSTEM VOLTAGE
- S TO P = 15 TO 17 VOLTS
- S TO T = 4 TO 6 VOLTS

ALL READ LOW

S TO L READS LOW

S TO P READS LOW

S TO T READS LOW

ALL READ OK

REPAIR OPEN IN CKT #751B

REPAIR OPEN IN CKT #50

REPAIR OPEN IN CKT #716

REPAIR OPEN IN CKT #705

REPAIR OPEN IN CKT #151

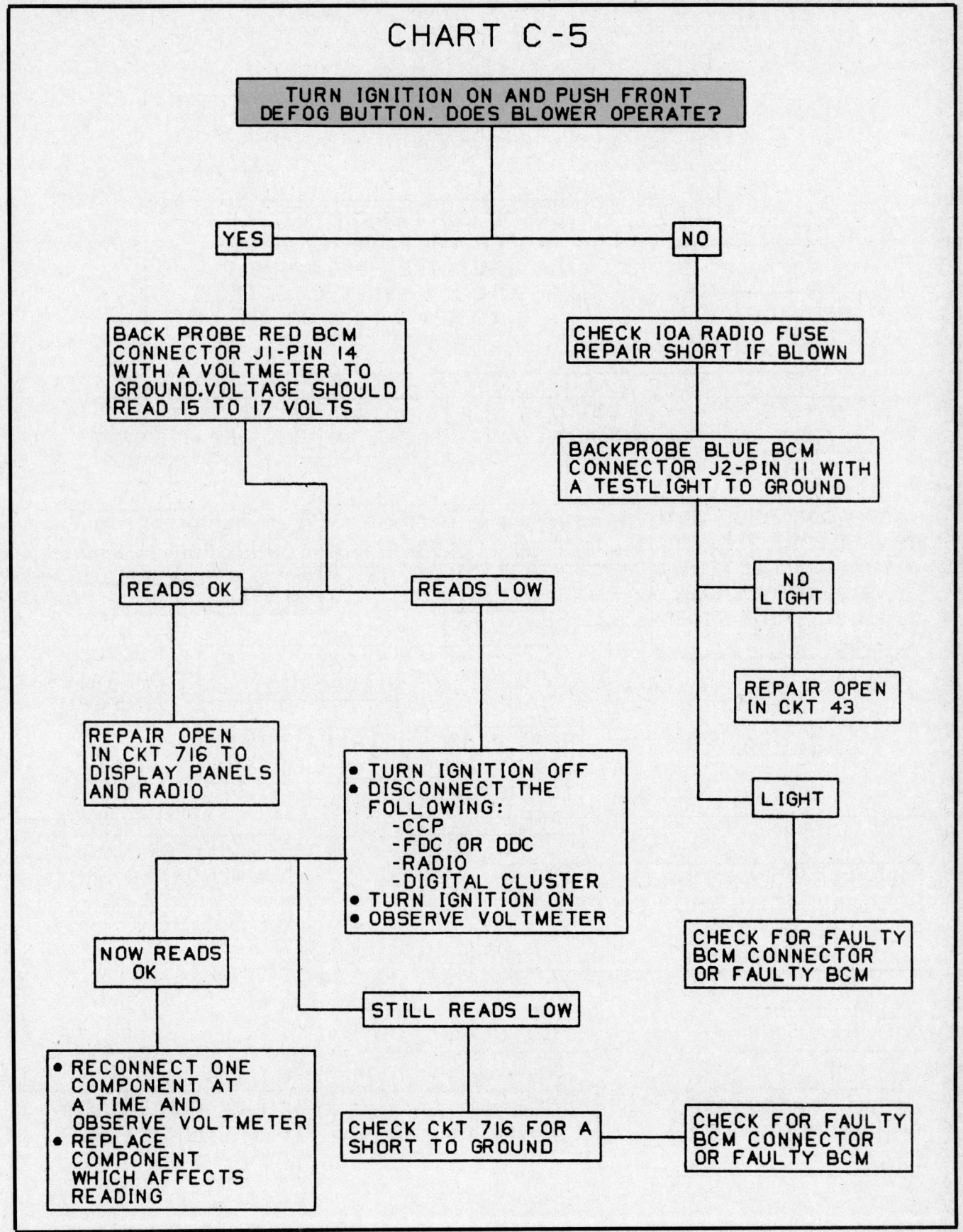

CHART C-5

TURN IGNITION ON AND PUSH FRONT DEFOG BUTTON. DOES BLOWER OPERATE?

YES

NO

BACK PROBE RED BCM CONNECTOR J1-PIN 14 WITH A VOLTMETER TO GROUND. VOLTAGE SHOULD READ 15 TO 17 VOLTS

CHECK 10A RADIO FUSE REPAIR SHORT IF BLOWN

BACKPROBE BLUE BCM CONNECTOR J2-PIN 11 WITH A TESTLIGHT TO GROUND

READS OK

READS LOW

NO LIGHT

REPAIR OPEN IN CKT 43

REPAIR OPEN IN CKT 716 TO DISPLAY PANELS AND RADIO

- TURN IGNITION OFF
- DISCONNECT THE FOLLOWING:
  - CCP
  - FDC OR DDC
  - RADIO
  - DIGITAL CLUSTER
- TURN IGNITION ON
- OBSERVE VOLTMETER

LIGHT

CHECK FOR FAULTY BCM CONNECTOR OR FAULTY BCM

NOW READS OK

STILL READS LOW

- RECONNECT ONE COMPONENT AT A TIME AND OBSERVE VOLTMETER
- REPLACE COMPONENT WHICH AFFECTS READING

CHECK CKT 716 FOR A SHORT TO GROUND

CHECK FOR FAULTY BCM CONNECTOR OR FAULTY BCM

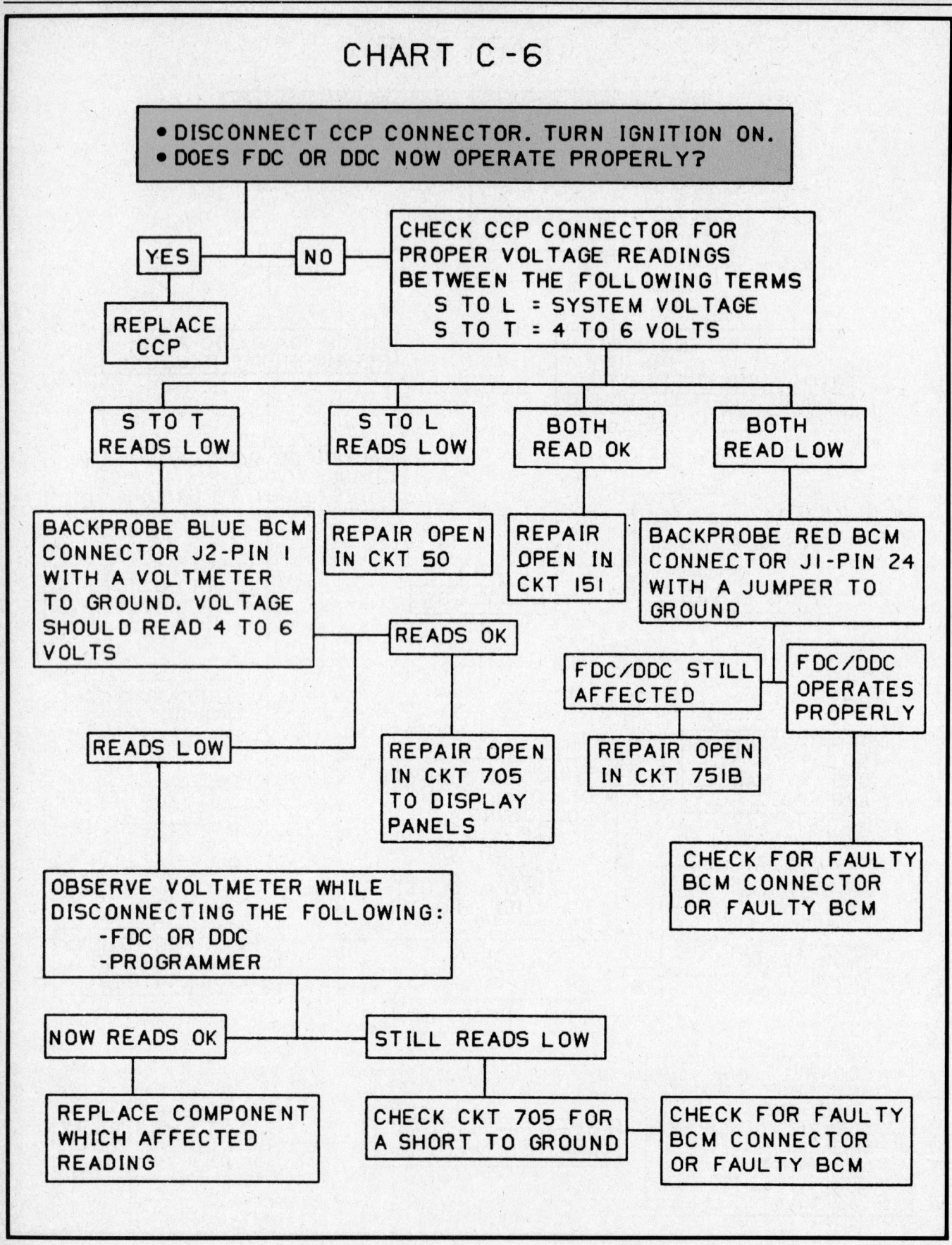

CHART C-6

- DISCONNECT CCP CONNECTOR. TURN IGNITION ON.
- DOES FDC OR DDC NOW OPERATE PROPERLY?

YES → REPLACE CCP

NO → CHECK CCP CONNECTOR FOR PROPER VOLTAGE READINGS BETWEEN THE FOLLOWING TERMS
S TO L = SYSTEM VOLTAGE
S TO T = 4 TO 6 VOLTS

S TO T READS LOW → BACKPROBE BLUE BCM CONNECTOR J2-PIN 1 WITH A VOLTMETER TO GROUND. VOLTAGE SHOULD READ 4 TO 6 VOLTS

S TO L READS LOW → REPAIR OPEN IN CKT 50

BOTH READ OK → REPAIR OPEN IN CKT 151

BOTH READ LOW → BACKPROBE RED BCM CONNECTOR J1-PIN 24 WITH A JUMPER TO GROUND

READS OK → REPAIR OPEN IN CKT 705 TO DISPLAY PANELS

READS LOW → OBSERVE VOLTMETER WHILE DISCONNECTING THE FOLLOWING:
-FDC OR DDC
-PROGRAMMER

FDC/DDC STILL AFFECTED → REPAIR OPEN IN CKT 751B

FDC/DDC OPERATES PROPERLY → CHECK FOR FAULTY BCM CONNECTOR OR FAULTY BCM

NOW READS OK → REPLACE COMPONENT WHICH AFFECTED READING

STILL READS LOW → CHECK CKT 705 FOR A SHORT TO GROUND → CHECK FOR FAULTY BCM CONNECTOR OR FAULTY BCM

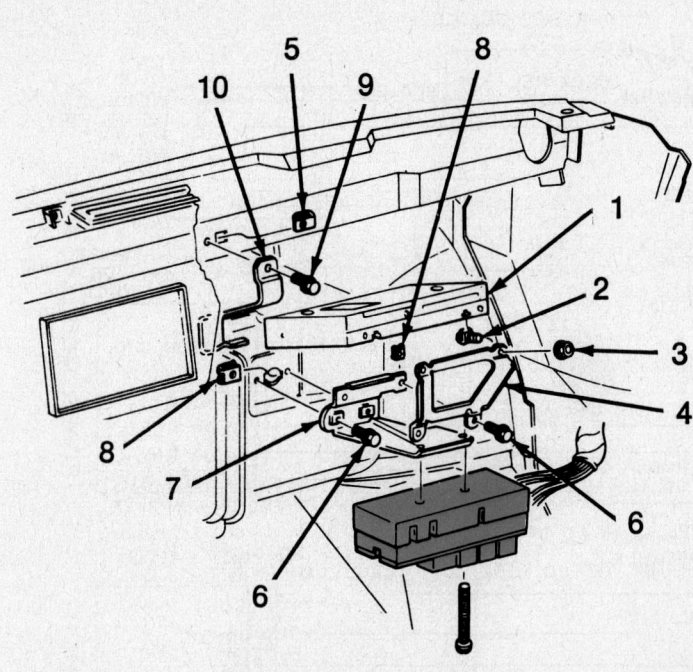

1. Module assembly
2. Bolt assembly
3. Nut assembly
4. Bracket
5. Nut
6. Screw
7. Bracket
8. Nut
9. Screw
10. Bracket

Location of Body Computer and accessory relay center

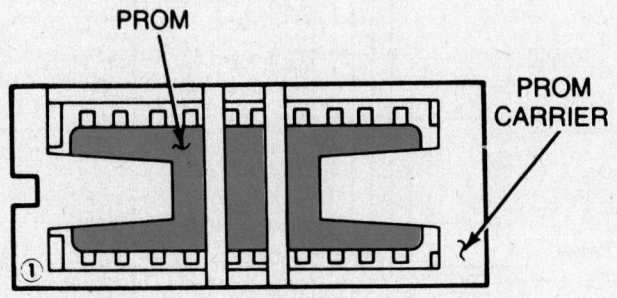

NOTCH IN PROM REFERENCED
TO SMALLER NOTCH IN
CARRIER AND THE ①

PROM to carrier orientation

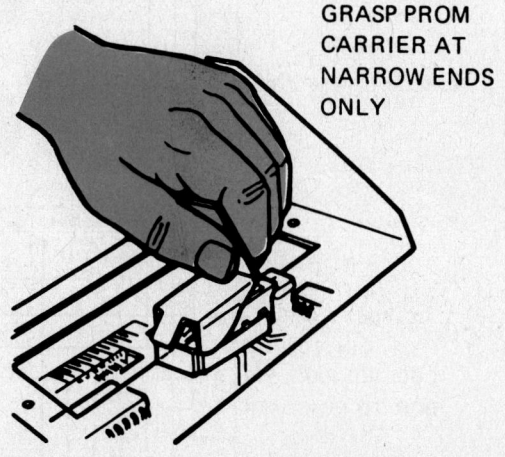

GRASP PROM
CARRIER AT
NARROW ENDS
ONLY

PROM replacement with removal tool

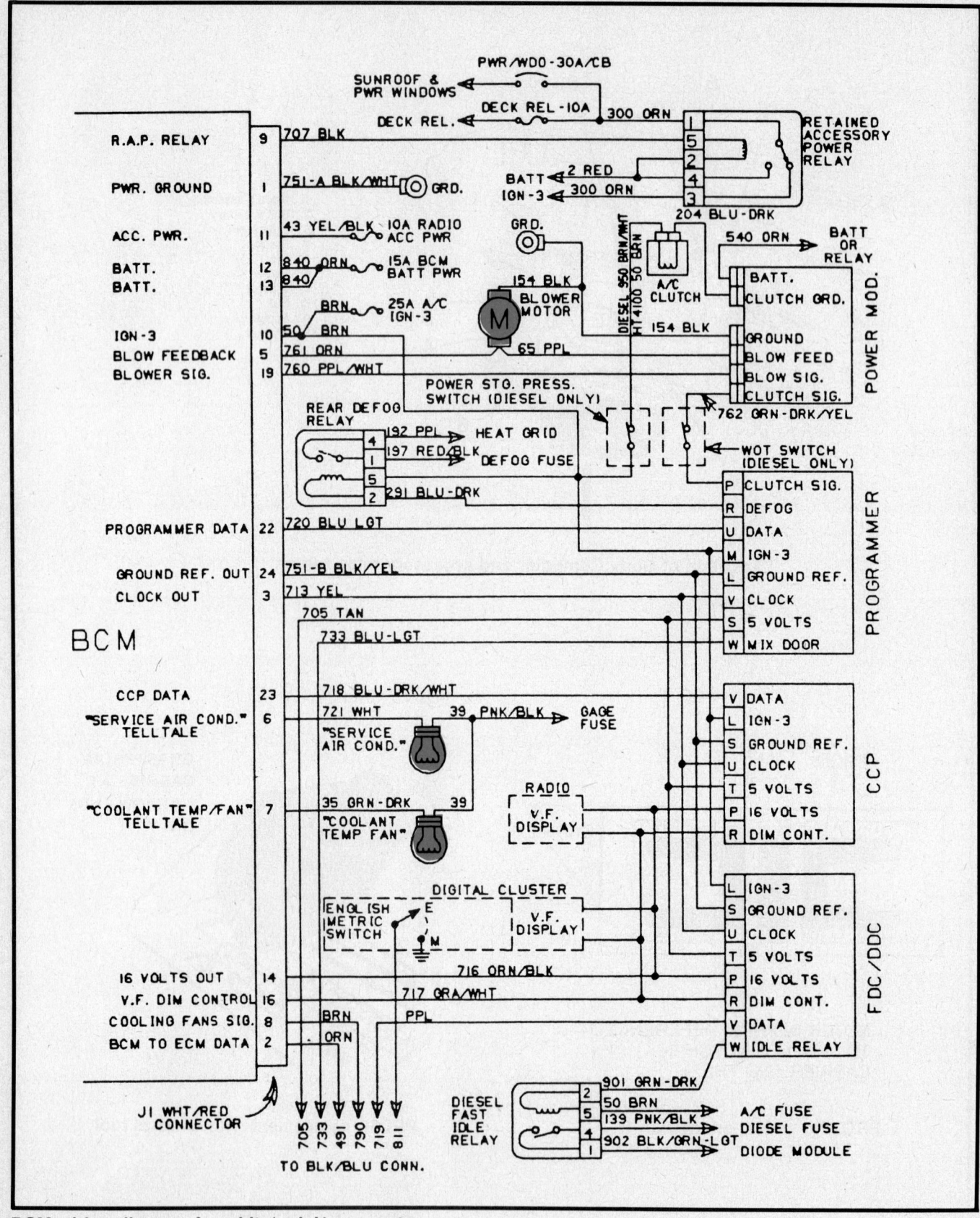

BCM wiring diagram for white/red J1 connector

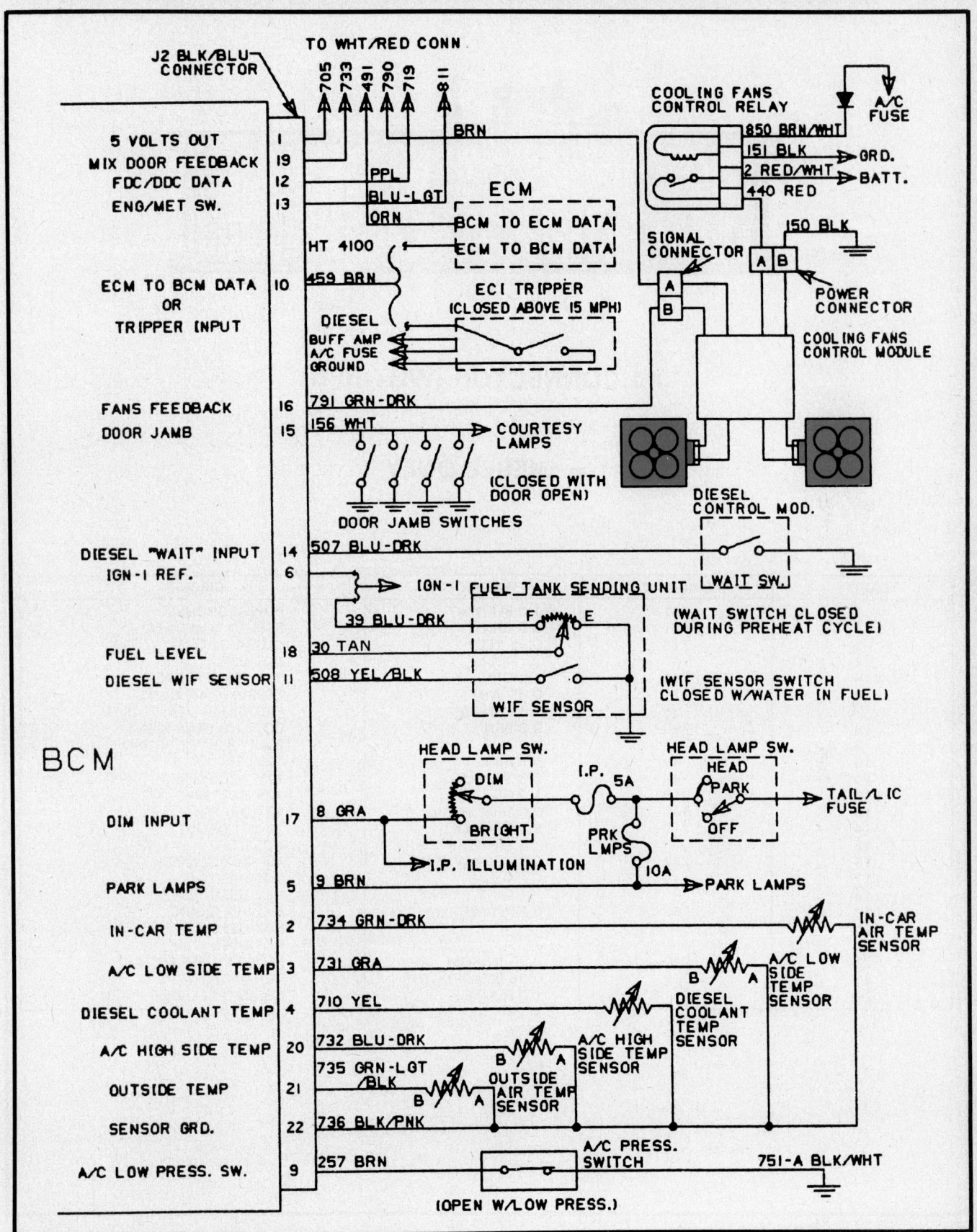

BCM wiring diagram for black/blue J2 connector

J-1 CONNECTOR (WHT/RED)

( ) = DIESEL ONLY

CAVITY	CIRCUIT #	WIRE COLOR	CIRCUIT
1	751-A	1.0 BLK/WHT	POWER GROUND
2	491	0.5 ORN	BCM TO ECM DATA
3	713	0.35 YEL	CLOCK OUT
4	—	—	NOT USED
5	761	1.0 ORN	BLOWER FEEDBACK
6	721	0.35 WHT	"SERVICE AIR COND"
7	35	0.8 GRN-DRK	("COOLANT TEMP/FAN")
8	790	0.8 BRN	COOLING FANS SIGNAL
9	707	0.8 BLK	R.A.P. RELAY GROUND
10	50	0.8 BRN	12V IGNITION-3
11	43	0.8 YEL/BLK	12V ACC POWER
12	840	1.0 ORN	12V BATTERY
13	840	1.0 ORN	12V BATTERY
14	716	0.8 ORN/BLK	16 VOLTS OUT
15	—	—	NOT USED
16	717	0.35 GRA/WHT	V.F. DIM CONTROL
17	—	—	NOT USED
18	—	—	NOT USED
19	760	0.5 PPL/WHT	BLOWER SIGNAL
20	—	—	NOT USED
21	—	—	NOT USED
22	720	0.35 BLU-LGT	PROGRAMMER DATA
23	718	0.35 BLU-DRK/WHT	CCP DATA
24	751-B	1.0 BLK/YEL	GROUND REF. OUT

Pin locations on BCM J1 connector

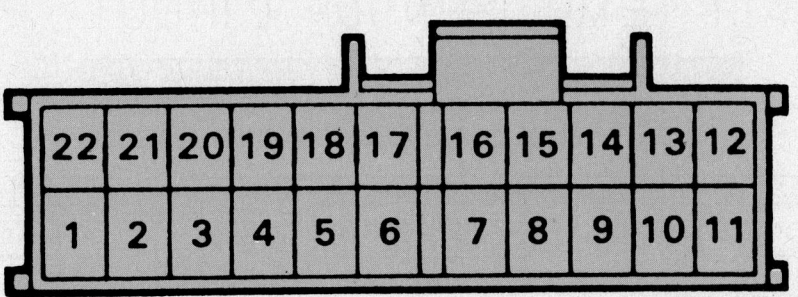

J-2 CONNECTOR (BLK/BLU)

(   ) = DIESEL ONLY

CAVITY	CIRCUIT #	WIRE COLOR	CIRCUIT
1	705	0.8 TAN	5 VOLTS OUT
2	734	0.35 GRN-DRK	IN-CAR TEMP
3	731	0.5 GRA	A/C LOW SIDE TEMP
4	710	0.8 YEL	(DIESEL COOLANT TEMP)
5	9	0.5 BRN	PARK LAMPS
6	39(239)	0.8 PNK/BLK	12V IGNITION-1 REF.
7	—	—	NOT USED
8	—	—	NOT USED
9	257	0.8 BRN	A/C LOW PRESSURE
10	459	0.35 BRN	ECM TO BCM DATA (ECI TRIPPER)
11	508	0.8 YEL/BLK	(WIF SENSOR)
12	719	0.35 PPL	FDC DATA (DDC DATA)
13	811	0.5 BLU-LGT	ENG/MET SWITCH
14	507	0.5 BLU-DRK	(WAIT SWITCH)
15	156	0.5 WHT	DOOR JAMB
16	791	0.8 GRN-DRK	FANS FEEDBACK
17	8	0.5 GRA	DIM INPUT
18	30	0.5 TAN	FUEL LEVEL
19	733	0.5 BLU-LGT	MIX DOOR FEEDBACK
20	732	0.5 BLU-DRK	A/C HIGH SIDE TEMP
21	735	0.35 GRN-LGT/BLK	OUTSIDE TEMP
22	736	0.35 BLK/PNK	SENSOR GROUND

Pin locations on BCM J2 connector

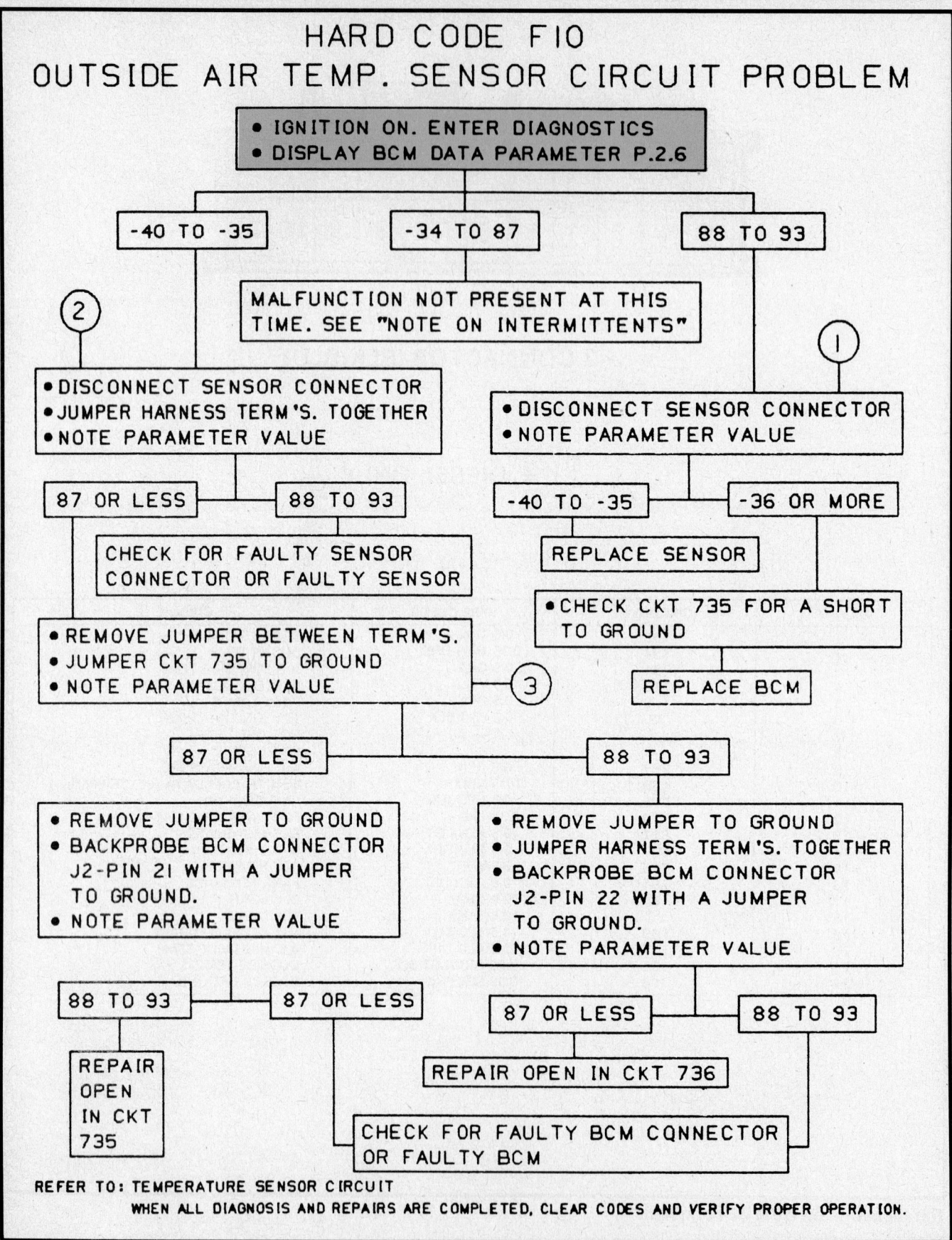

HARD CODE F1O
OUTSIDE AIR TEMP. SENSOR CIRCUIT PROBLEM

- IGNITION ON. ENTER DIAGNOSTICS
- DISPLAY BCM DATA PARAMETER P.2.6

| -40 TO -35 | -34 TO 87 | 88 TO 93 |

MALFUNCTION NOT PRESENT AT THIS TIME. SEE "NOTE ON INTERMITTENTS"

(2)

(1)

- DISCONNECT SENSOR CONNECTOR
- JUMPER HARNESS TERM'S. TOGETHER
- NOTE PARAMETER VALUE

- DISCONNECT SENSOR CONNECTOR
- NOTE PARAMETER VALUE

| 87 OR LESS | 88 TO 93 |

| -40 TO -35 | -36 OR MORE |

CHECK FOR FAULTY SENSOR CONNECTOR OR FAULTY SENSOR

REPLACE SENSOR

- REMOVE JUMPER BETWEEN TERM'S.
- JUMPER CKT 735 TO GROUND
- NOTE PARAMETER VALUE

(3)

- CHECK CKT 735 FOR A SHORT TO GROUND

REPLACE BCM

| 87 OR LESS | 88 TO 93 |

- REMOVE JUMPER TO GROUND
- BACKPROBE BCM CONNECTOR J2-PIN 21 WITH A JUMPER TO GROUND.
- NOTE PARAMETER VALUE

- REMOVE JUMPER TO GROUND
- JUMPER HARNESS TERM'S. TOGETHER
- BACKPROBE BCM CONNECTOR J2-PIN 22 WITH A JUMPER TO GROUND.
- NOTE PARAMETER VALUE

| 88 TO 93 | 87 OR LESS |

| 87 OR LESS | 88 TO 93 |

REPAIR OPEN IN CKT 735

REPAIR OPEN IN CKT 736

CHECK FOR FAULTY BCM CONNECTOR OR FAULTY BCM

REFER TO: TEMPERATURE SENSOR CIRCUIT
WHEN ALL DIAGNOSIS AND REPAIRS ARE COMPLETED, CLEAR CODES AND VERIFY PROPER OPERATION.

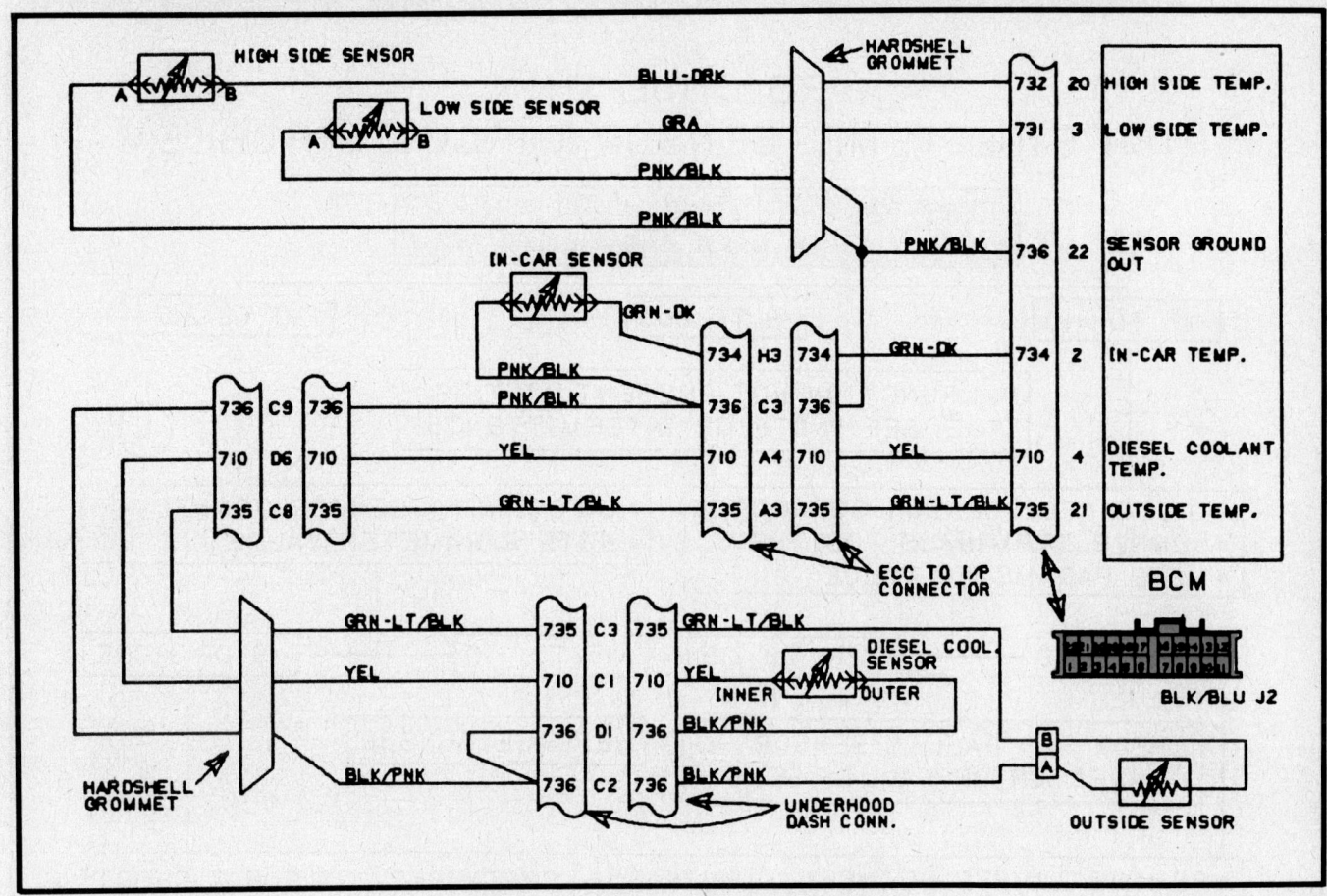

Schematic of temperature sensors circuit

CODE F10 – OUTSIDE AIR TEMPERATURE SENSOR CIRCUIT PROBLEM

NOTE: If this code is NOT displayed during the second pass of diagnostic codes, it is an intermittent failure and cannot be diagnosed using this procedure. For an intermittent code, refer to "Note On Intermittents" at the end of this text.

The Outside Air Temperature Sensor uses a thermistor to control the signal voltage to the BCM. The BCM applies a voltage on circuit 735 to the sensor. When the sensor is cold its resistance is high, therefore the BCM will see a high signal voltage. As the sensor warms, its resistance becomes less and the signal voltage is pulled low through the sensor ground, circuit 736. This signal voltage will vary between 5V (open ckt) and 0V (shorted ckt). Code F10 will set if the signal voltage indicates less than -34°C (open ckt) or over 87°C (shorted ckt). These conditions can be observed in BCM data display as an "Outside Temp" reading (parameter P.2.6) outside the range of -34° to 87°C.

1. If the shorted circuit reading changes to an open circuit reading after disconnecting the sensor, the BCM and wiring are OK.

2. If the open circuit reading changes to a shorted circuit reading after jumpering the sensor terminals, the BCM and wiring are OK.

3. By applying a ground to various points in the circuits, an open can be isolated by observing whether the parameter display can be changed from the open reading to the shorted reading.

Note On Intermittents

A Code F10 will be stored in memory whenever the ambient temperature drops below approximately -34°C (-29°F). This code should be ignored if this cause is suspected. If an intermittent Code F10 is being set, manipulate the related wiring while observing BCM data parameter P.2.6. If the failure is induced, the reading will jump from its normal value to a reading outside the range of -34° to 87°C.

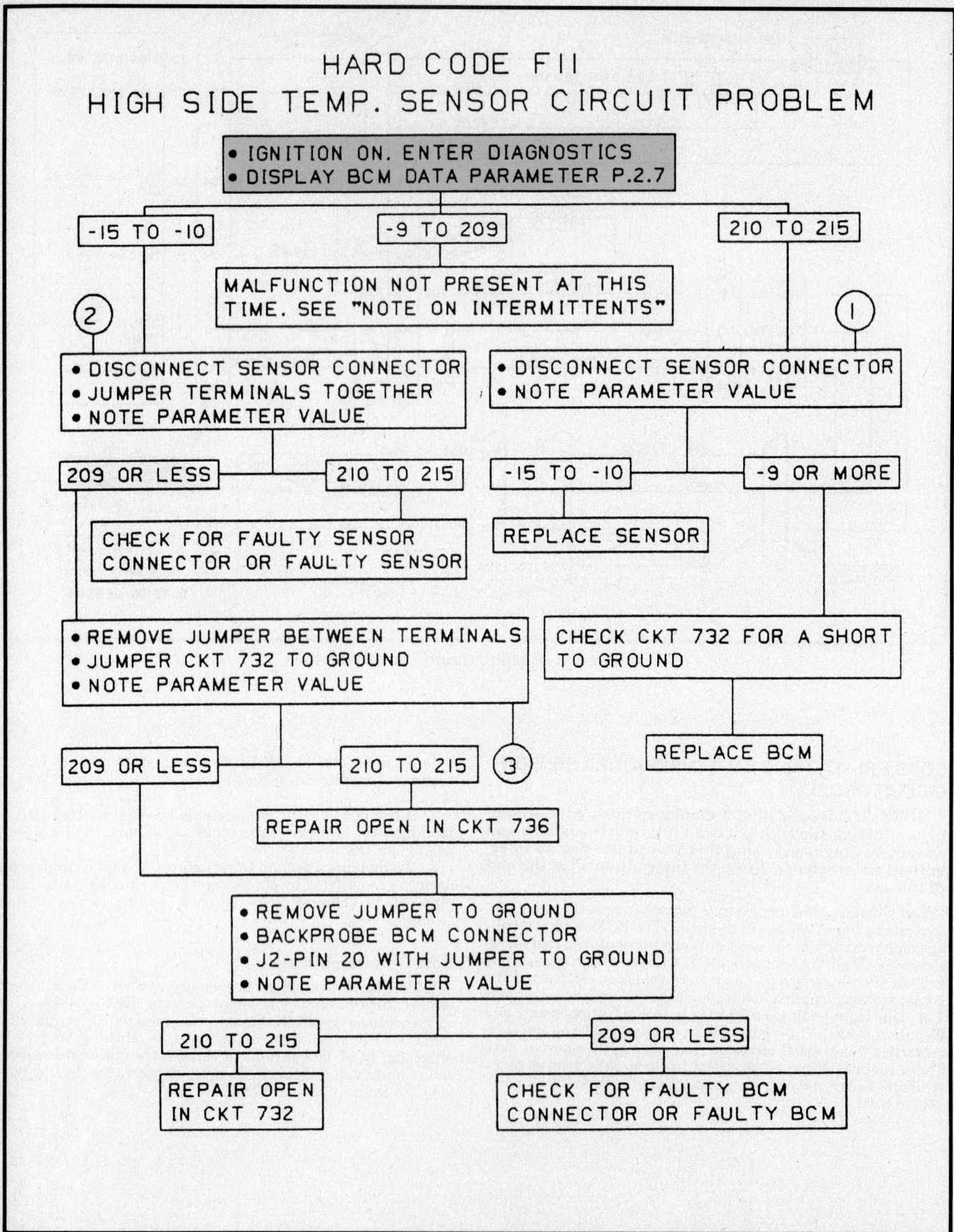

HARD CODE FII
HIGH SIDE TEMP. SENSOR CIRCUIT PROBLEM

- IGNITION ON. ENTER DIAGNOSTICS
- DISPLAY BCM DATA PARAMETER P.2.7

-15 TO -10 | -9 TO 209 | 210 TO 215

MALFUNCTION NOT PRESENT AT THIS TIME. SEE "NOTE ON INTERMITTENTS"

(2)

- DISCONNECT SENSOR CONNECTOR
- JUMPER TERMINALS TOGETHER
- NOTE PARAMETER VALUE

(1)

- DISCONNECT SENSOR CONNECTOR
- NOTE PARAMETER VALUE

209 OR LESS | 210 TO 215

-15 TO -10 | -9 OR MORE

CHECK FOR FAULTY SENSOR CONNECTOR OR FAULTY SENSOR

REPLACE SENSOR

- REMOVE JUMPER BETWEEN TERMINALS
- JUMPER CKT 732 TO GROUND
- NOTE PARAMETER VALUE

CHECK CKT 732 FOR A SHORT TO GROUND

209 OR LESS | 210 TO 215 (3)

REPLACE BCM

REPAIR OPEN IN CKT 736

- REMOVE JUMPER TO GROUND
- BACKPROBE BCM CONNECTOR
- J2-PIN 20 WITH JUMPER TO GROUND
- NOTE PARAMETER VALUE

210 TO 215 | 209 OR LESS

REPAIR OPEN IN CKT 732

CHECK FOR FAULTY BCM CONNECTOR OR FAULTY BCM

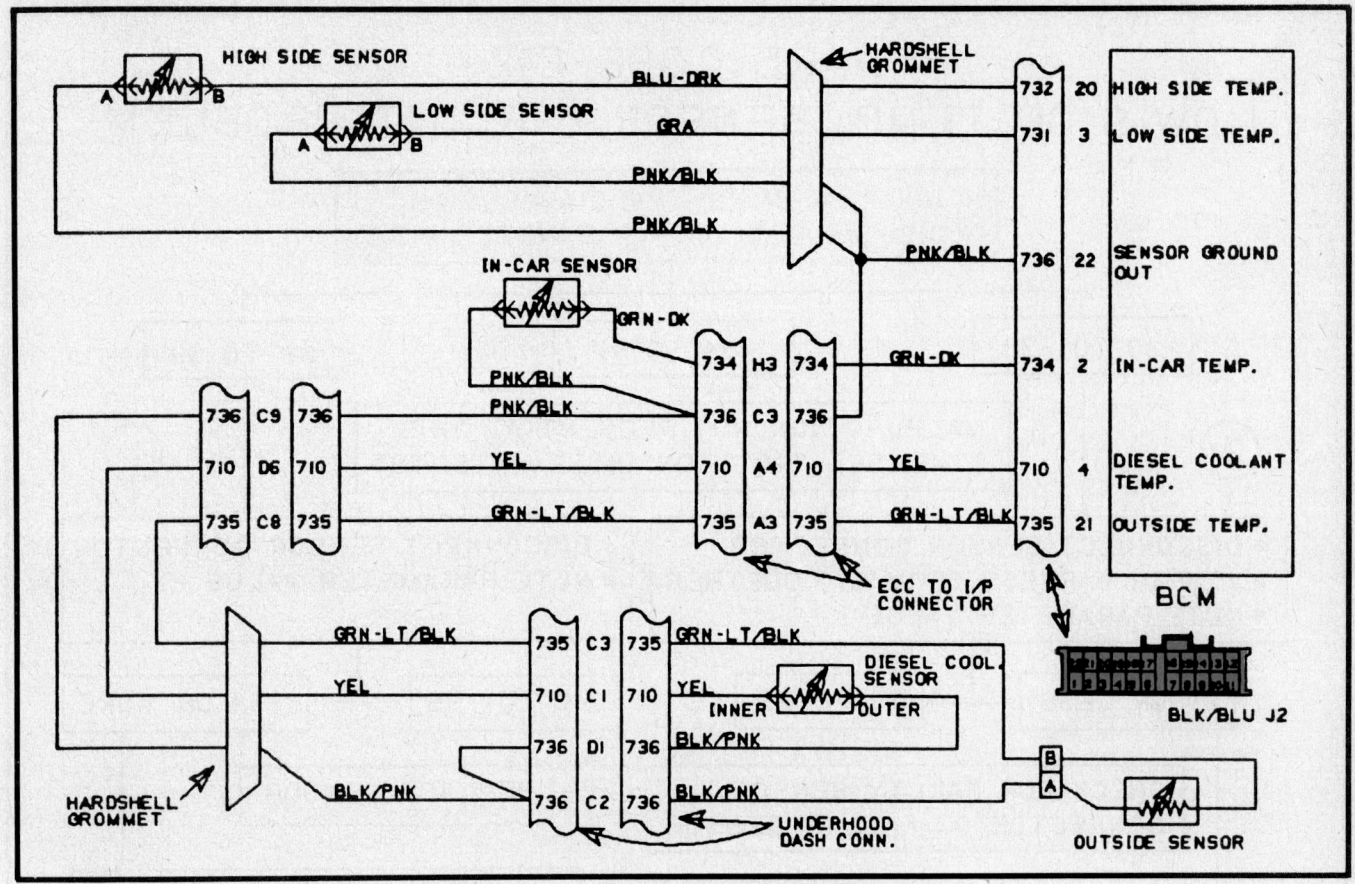

Schematic of temperature sensors circuit

CODE F11—A/C HIGH SIDE TEMPERATURE SENSOR CIRCUIT PROBLEM

NOTE: If this code is NOT displayed during the second pass of diagnostic codes, it is an intermittent failure and cannot be diagnosed using this procedure. For an intermittent code, refer to "Note On Intermittents" at the end of this text.

The A/C High Side Temperature Sensor uses a thermistor to control the signal voltage to the BCM. The BCM applies a voltage on circuit 732 to the sensor. When the sensor is cold its resistance is high, therefore the BCM will see a high signal voltage. As the sensor warms, its resistance becomes less and the signal voltage is pulled low through the sensor ground circuit 736. This signal voltage will vary between 5V (open ckt) and 0V (shorted ckt). Code F11 will set if the signal voltage indicates less than -9°C (open ckt) or over 209°C (shorted ckt). These conditions can be observed in BCM data display as an

"A/C High Side Temp" reading (parameter P.2.7) outside the range of -9°C to 209°C.

1. If the shorted circuit reading changes to an open circuit reading after disconnecting the sensor, the BCM and wiring are OK.

2. If the open circuit reading changes to a shorted circuit reading after jumpering the sensor terminals, the BCM and wiring are OK.

3. By applying a ground to various points in the circuits, an open can be isolated by observing whether the parameter display can be changed from the open reading to the shorted reading.

Note On Intermittents

If an intermittent Code F11 is being set, manipulate the related wiring while observing BCM data parameter P.2.7. If the failure is induced, the reading will jump from its normal value to a reading outside the range of -9°C to 209°C.

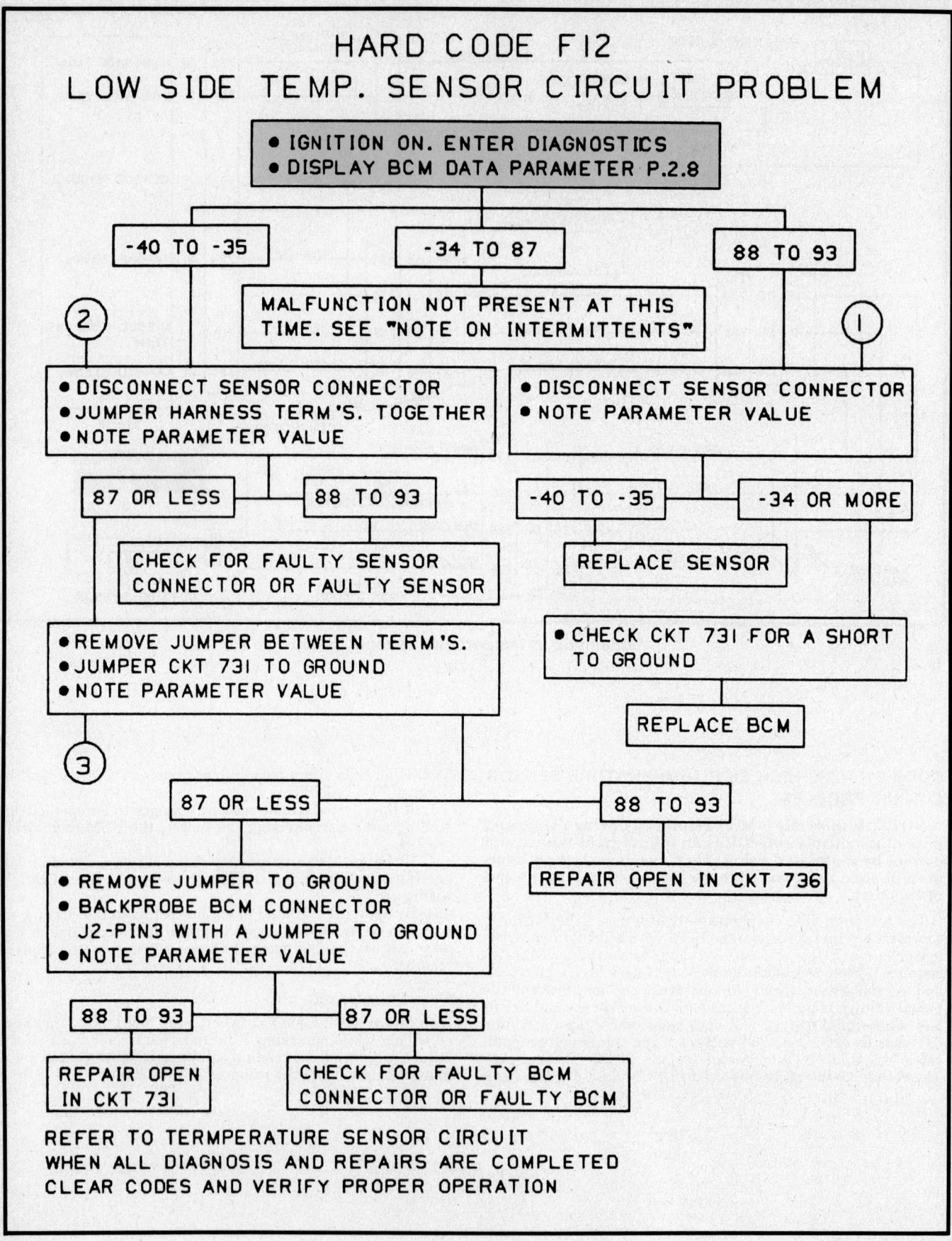

HARD CODE F12
LOW SIDE TEMP. SENSOR CIRCUIT PROBLEM

- IGNITION ON. ENTER DIAGNOSTICS
- DISPLAY BCM DATA PARAMETER P.2.8

| -40 TO -35 | -34 TO 87 | 88 TO 93 |

MALFUNCTION NOT PRESENT AT THIS TIME. SEE "NOTE ON INTERMITTENTS"

2

1

- DISCONNECT SENSOR CONNECTOR
- JUMPER HARNESS TERM'S. TOGETHER
- NOTE PARAMETER VALUE

- DISCONNECT SENSOR CONNECTOR
- NOTE PARAMETER VALUE

| 87 OR LESS | 88 TO 93 |

| -40 TO -35 | -34 OR MORE |

CHECK FOR FAULTY SENSOR CONNECTOR OR FAULTY SENSOR

REPLACE SENSOR

- REMOVE JUMPER BETWEEN TERM'S.
- JUMPER CKT 731 TO GROUND
- NOTE PARAMETER VALUE

- CHECK CKT 731 FOR A SHORT TO GROUND

REPLACE BCM

3

| 87 OR LESS | 88 TO 93 |

- REMOVE JUMPER TO GROUND
- BACKPROBE BCM CONNECTOR J2-PIN3 WITH A JUMPER TO GROUND
- NOTE PARAMETER VALUE

REPAIR OPEN IN CKT 736

| 88 TO 93 | 87 OR LESS |

REPAIR OPEN IN CKT 731

CHECK FOR FAULTY BCM CONNECTOR OR FAULTY BCM

REFER TO TERMPERATURE SENSOR CIRCUIT
WHEN ALL DIAGNOSIS AND REPAIRS ARE COMPLETED
CLEAR CODES AND VERIFY PROPER OPERATION

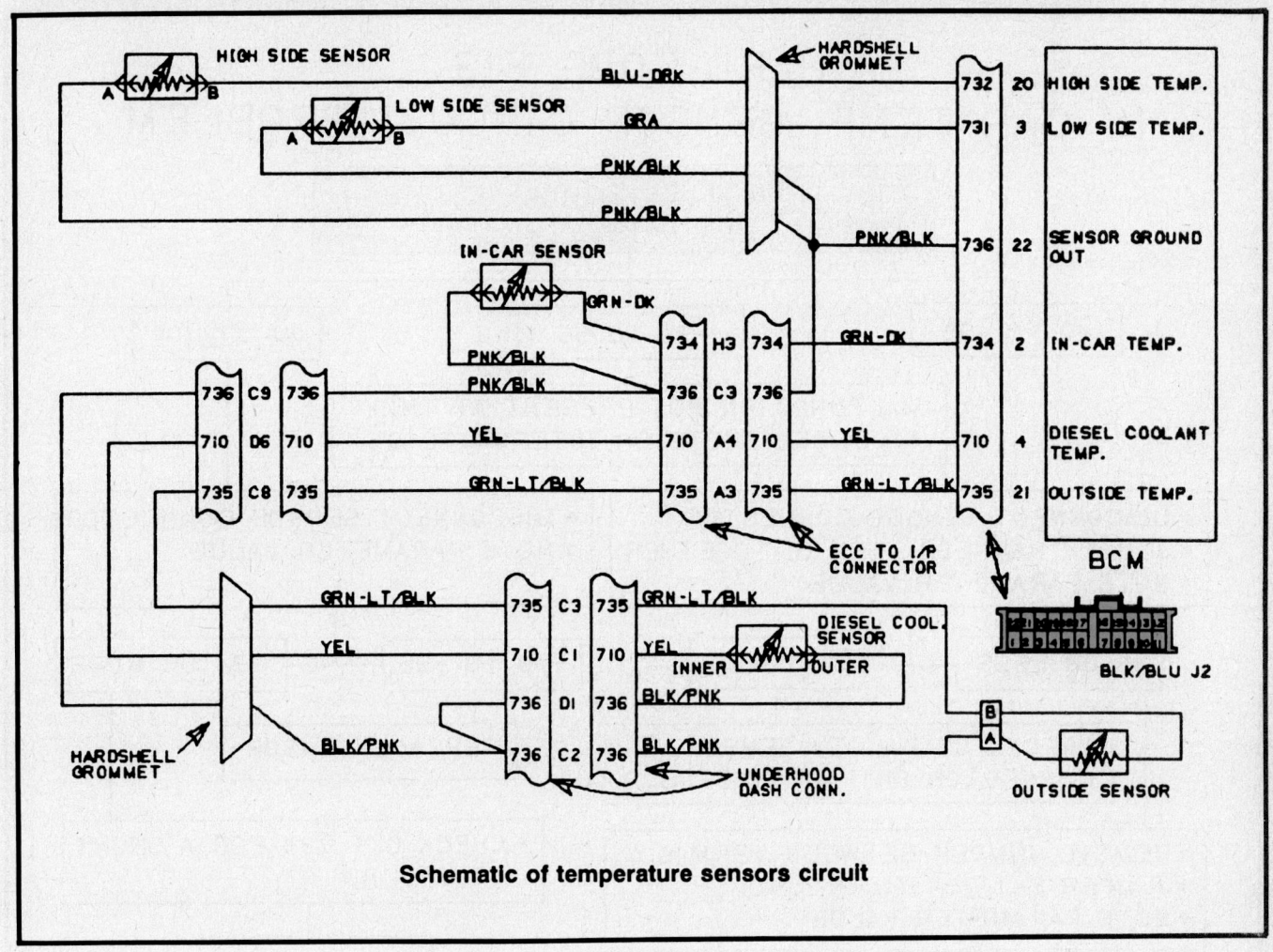

Schematic of temperature sensors circuit

CODE F12—A/C LOW SIDE TEMPERATURE SENSOR CIRCUIT PROBLEM

NOTE: If this code is NOT displayed during the second pass of diagnostic codes, it is an intermittent failure and cannot be diagnosed using this procedure. For an intermittent code, refer to "Note On Intermittents" at the end of this text.

The A/C Low Side Temperature Sensor uses a termistor to control the signal voltage to the BCM. The BCM applies a voltage on circuit 731 to the sensor. When the sensor is cold its resistance is high, therefore the BCM will see a high signal voltage. As the sensor warms, its resistance becomes less and the signal voltage is pulled low through the sensor ground, circuit 736. This signal voltage will vary between 5V (open ckt) and 0V (shorted ckt). Code F12 will set if the signal voltage indicates less than -34°C (open ckt) or over 87°C (shorted ckt). These conditions can be observed in BCM data display as an

"A/C Low Side Temp" reading (parameter P.2.8) outside the range of -34° to 87°C.

1. If the shorted circuit reading changes to an open circuit reading after disconnecting the sensor, the BCM and wiring are OK.

2. If the open circuit reading changes to a shorted circuit reading after jumpering the sensor terminals, the BCM an wiring are OK.

3. By applying a ground to various points in the circuits, an open can be isolated by observing whether the parameter display can be changed from the open reading to the shorted reading.

Note On Intermittents

If an intermittent Code F12 is being set, manipulate the related wiring while observing BCM data parameter P.2.8. If the failure is induced, the reading will jump from its normal value to a reading outside the range of -34° to 87°C.

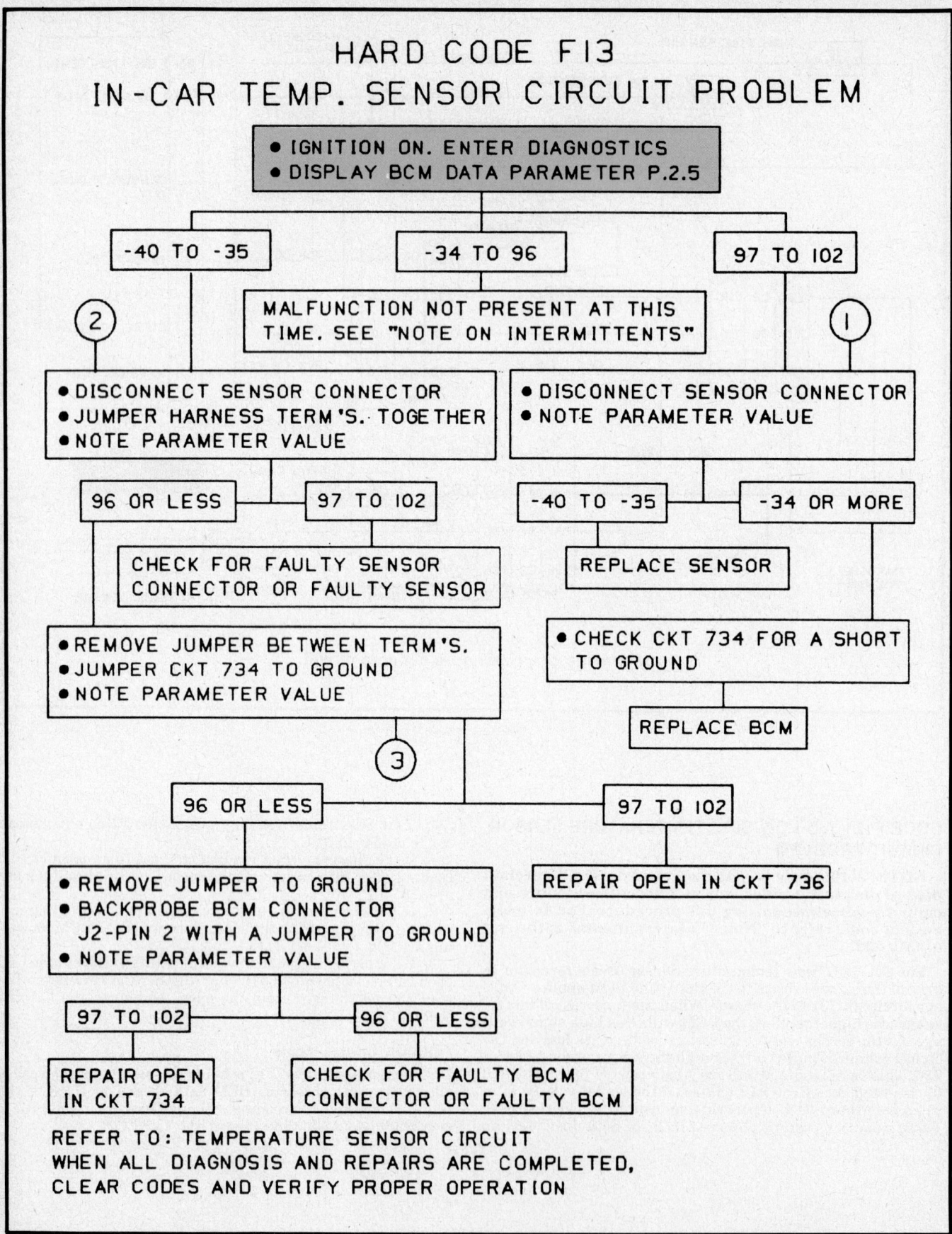

HARD CODE F13
IN-CAR TEMP. SENSOR CIRCUIT PROBLEM

- IGNITION ON. ENTER DIAGNOSTICS
- DISPLAY BCM DATA PARAMETER P.2.5

-40 TO -35 | -34 TO 96 | 97 TO 102

MALFUNCTION NOT PRESENT AT THIS TIME. SEE "NOTE ON INTERMITTENTS"

(2)

- DISCONNECT SENSOR CONNECTOR
- JUMPER HARNESS TERM'S. TOGETHER
- NOTE PARAMETER VALUE

(1)

- DISCONNECT SENSOR CONNECTOR
- NOTE PARAMETER VALUE

96 OR LESS | 97 TO 102

CHECK FOR FAULTY SENSOR CONNECTOR OR FAULTY SENSOR

-40 TO -35 | -34 OR MORE

REPLACE SENSOR

- REMOVE JUMPER BETWEEN TERM'S.
- JUMPER CKT 734 TO GROUND
- NOTE PARAMETER VALUE

- CHECK CKT 734 FOR A SHORT TO GROUND

REPLACE BCM

(3)

96 OR LESS | 97 TO 102

REPAIR OPEN IN CKT 736

- REMOVE JUMPER TO GROUND
- BACKPROBE BCM CONNECTOR J2-PIN 2 WITH A JUMPER TO GROUND
- NOTE PARAMETER VALUE

97 TO 102 | 96 OR LESS

REPAIR OPEN IN CKT 734

CHECK FOR FAULTY BCM CONNECTOR OR FAULTY BCM

REFER TO: TEMPERATURE SENSOR CIRCUIT
WHEN ALL DIAGNOSIS AND REPAIRS ARE COMPLETED,
CLEAR CODES AND VERIFY PROPER OPERATION

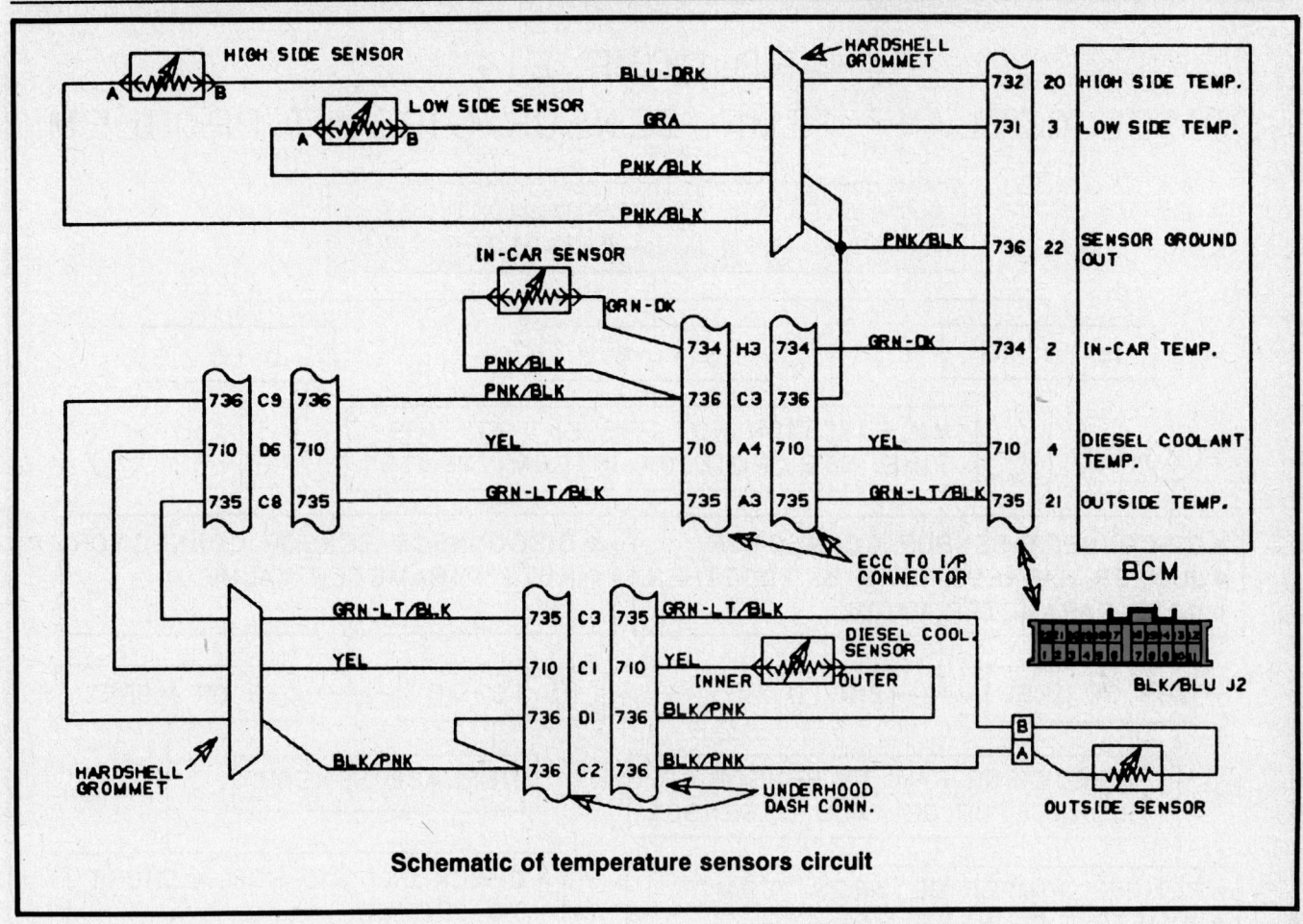

Schematic of temperature sensors circuit

CODE F13—IN-CAR TEMPERATURE SENSOR CIRCUIT PROBLEM

NOTE: If this code is NOT displayed during the second pass of diagnostic codes, it is an intermittent failure and cannot be diagnosed using this procedure. For an intermittent code, refer to "Note on Intermittents" at the end of this text.

The In-Car Temperature Sensor uses a thermistor to control the signal voltage to the BCM. The BCM applies a voltage on circuit 734 to the sensor. When the sensor is cold its resistance is high, therefore the BCM will see a high signal voltage. As the sensor warms, its resistance becomes less and the signal voltage is pulled low through the sensor ground, circuit 736. This signal voltage will vary between 5V (open ckt) and 0V (shorted ckt). Code F13 will set if the signal voltage indicates less than -34°C (open ckt) or over 96°C (shorted ckt). These conditions can be observed in BCM data display as an "In-Car

Temp" reading (parameter P.2.5) outside the range of -34°C to 96°C.

1. If the shorted circuit reading changes to an open circuit reading after disconnecting the sensor, the BCM and wiring are OK.

2. If the open circuit reading changes to a shorted circuit reading after jumpering the sensor terminals, the BCM and wiring are OK.

3. By applying a ground to various points in the circuits, an open can be isolated by observing whether the parameter display can be changed from the open reading to the shorted reading.

Note On Intermittents

If an intermittent Code F13 is being set, manipulate the related wiring while observing BCM data parameter P.2.5. If the failure is induced, the reading will jump its normal value to a reading outside the range of -34° to 96°C.

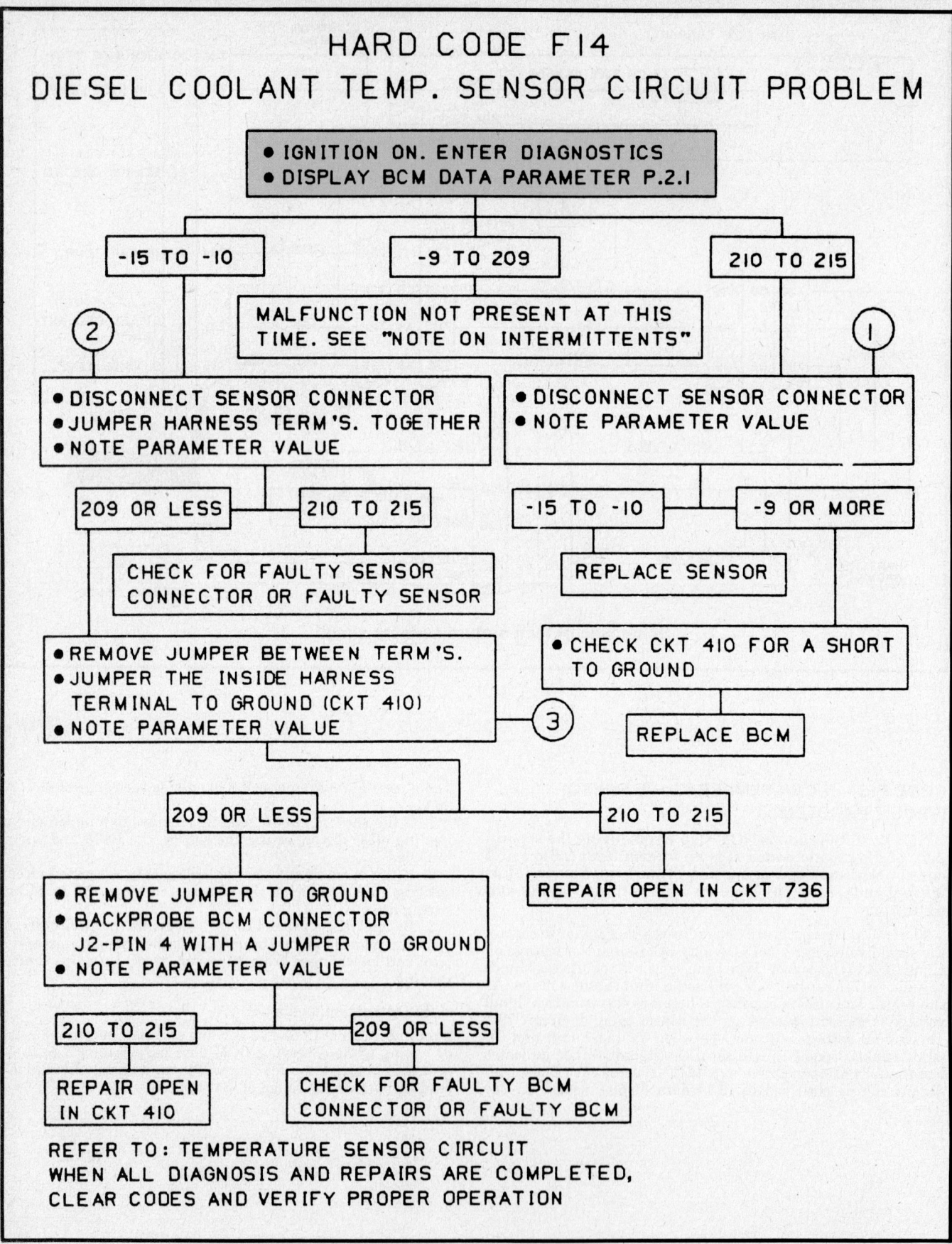

HARD CODE FI4
DIESEL COOLANT TEMP. SENSOR CIRCUIT PROBLEM

- IGNITION ON. ENTER DIAGNOSTICS
- DISPLAY BCM DATA PARAMETER P.2.I

-15 TO -10 | -9 TO 209 | 210 TO 215

MALFUNCTION NOT PRESENT AT THIS TIME. SEE "NOTE ON INTERMITTENTS"

(2)

(1)

- DISCONNECT SENSOR CONNECTOR
- JUMPER HARNESS TERM'S. TOGETHER
- NOTE PARAMETER VALUE

- DISCONNECT SENSOR CONNECTOR
- NOTE PARAMETER VALUE

209 OR LESS | 210 TO 215

-15 TO -10 | -9 OR MORE

CHECK FOR FAULTY SENSOR CONNECTOR OR FAULTY SENSOR

REPLACE SENSOR

- REMOVE JUMPER BETWEEN TERM'S.
- JUMPER THE INSIDE HARNESS TERMINAL TO GROUND (CKT 410)
- NOTE PARAMETER VALUE

(3)

- CHECK CKT 410 FOR A SHORT TO GROUND

REPLACE BCM

209 OR LESS | 210 TO 215

- REMOVE JUMPER TO GROUND
- BACKPROBE BCM CONNECTOR J2-PIN 4 WITH A JUMPER TO GROUND
- NOTE PARAMETER VALUE

REPAIR OPEN IN CKT 736

210 TO 215 | 209 OR LESS

REPAIR OPEN IN CKT 410

CHECK FOR FAULTY BCM CONNECTOR OR FAULTY BCM

REFER TO: TEMPERATURE SENSOR CIRCUIT
WHEN ALL DIAGNOSIS AND REPAIRS ARE COMPLETED,
CLEAR CODES AND VERIFY PROPER OPERATION

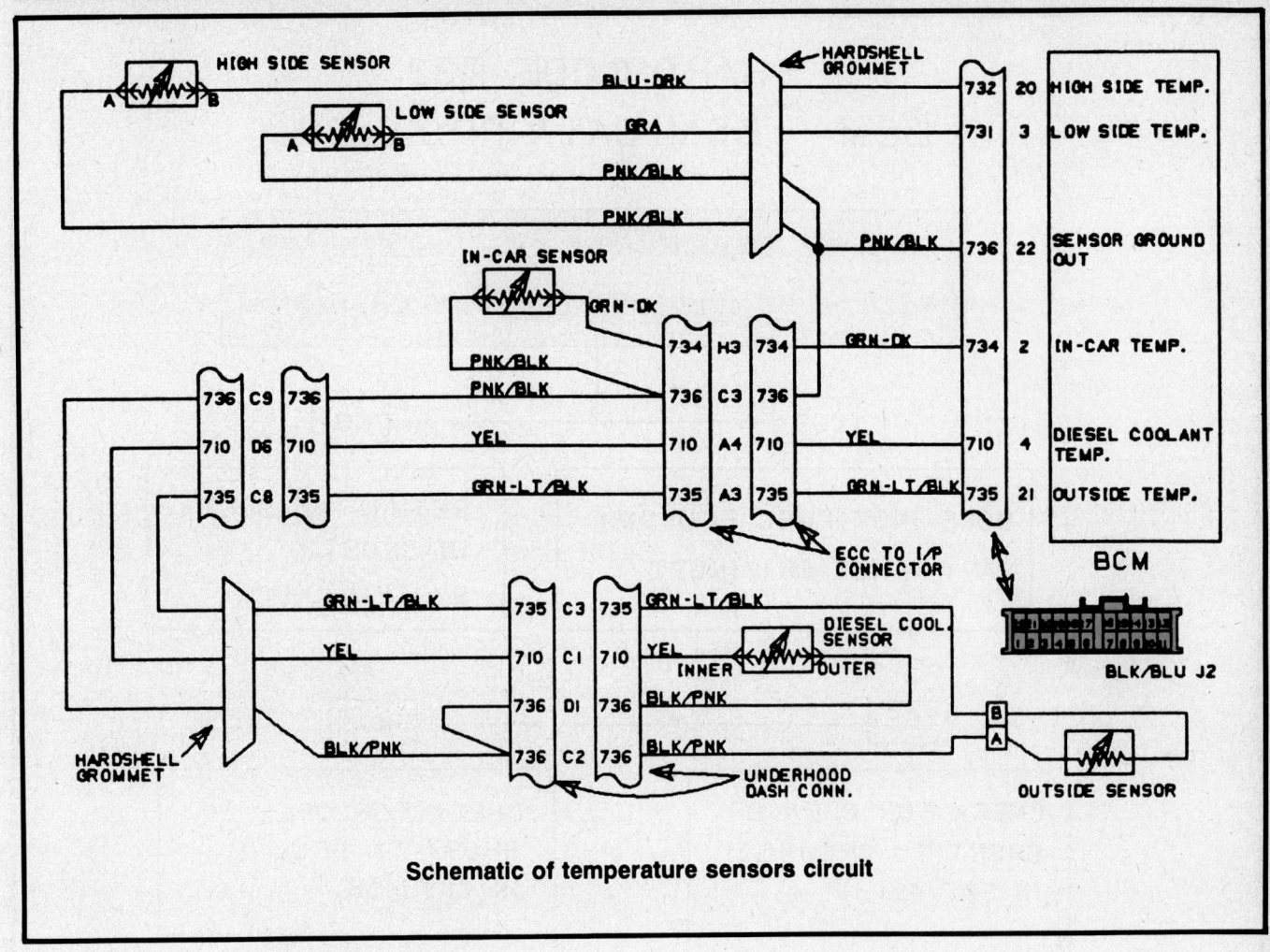

Schematic of temperature sensors circuit

CODE F14 – DIESEL COOLANT TEMPERATURE SENSOR CIRCUIT PROBLEM

NOTE: If this code is NOT displayed during the second pass of diagnostic codes, it is an intermittent failure and cannot be diagnosed using this procedure. For an intermittent code, refer to "Note on Intermittents" at the end of this text.

The Diesel Coolant Temperature Sensor uses a thermistor to control the signal voltage to the BCM. The BCM applies a voltage on circuit 410 to the sensor. When the sensor is cold its resistance is high, therefore the BCM will see a high signal voltage. As the sensor warms, its resistance becomes less and the signal voltage is pulled low through the sensor ground, circuit 736. This signal voltage will vary between 5V (open ckt) and 0V (shorted ckt). Code F14 will set if the signal voltage indicates less than -9°C (open ckt) or over 209°C (shorted ckt). These conditions can be observed in BCM data display as a

"Coolant Temp" reading (parameter P.2.1) outside the range of -9° to 209°C.

1. If the shorted circuit reading changes to an open circuit reading after disconnecting the sensor, the BCM and wiring are OK.

2. If the open circuit reading changes to a shorted circuit reading after jumpering the sensor terminals, the BCM and wiring are OK.

3. By applying a ground to various points in the circuits, an open can be isolated by observing whether the parameter display can be changed from the open reading to the shorted reading.

Note On Intermittents

If an intermittent Code F14 is being set, manipulate the related wiring while observing BCM data parameter P.2.1. If the failure is induced, the reading will jump from its normal value to a reading outside the range of -9° to 209°C.

447

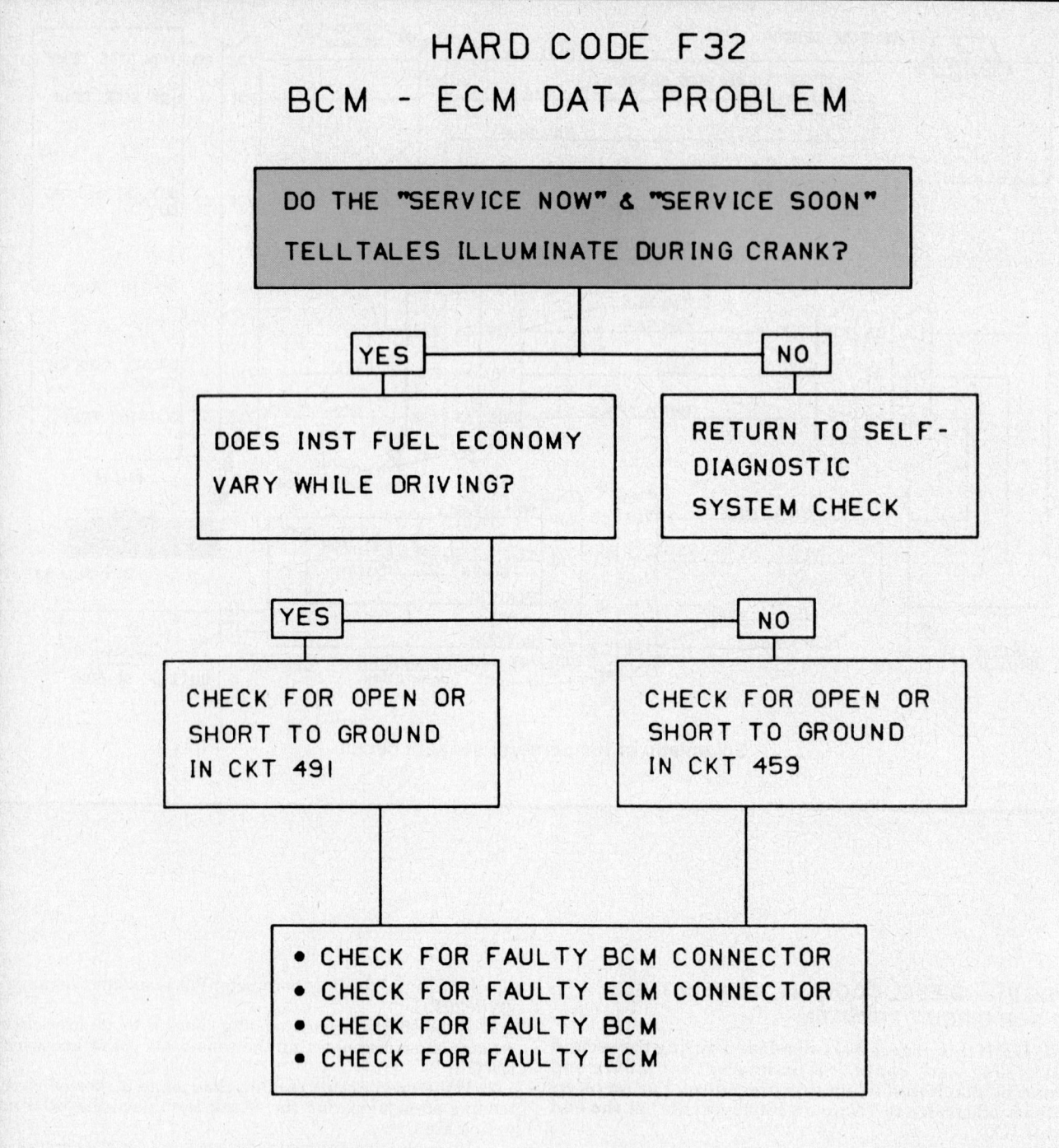

HARD CODE F32
BCM - ECM DATA PROBLEM

DO THE "SERVICE NOW" & "SERVICE SOON" TELLTALES ILLUMINATE DURING CRANK?

YES → DOES INST FUEL ECONOMY VARY WHILE DRIVING?

NO → RETURN TO SELF-DIAGNOSTIC SYSTEM CHECK

YES → CHECK FOR OPEN OR SHORT TO GROUND IN CKT 491

NO → CHECK FOR OPEN OR SHORT TO GROUND IN CKT 459

- CHECK FOR FAULTY BCM CONNECTOR
- CHECK FOR FAULTY ECM CONNECTOR
- CHECK FOR FAULTY BCM
- CHECK FOR FAULTY ECM

REFER TO: DATA CIRCUITS

WHEN ALL DIAGNOSIS AND REPAIRS ARE COMPLETED, CLEAR CODES AND VERIFY PROPER OPERATION.

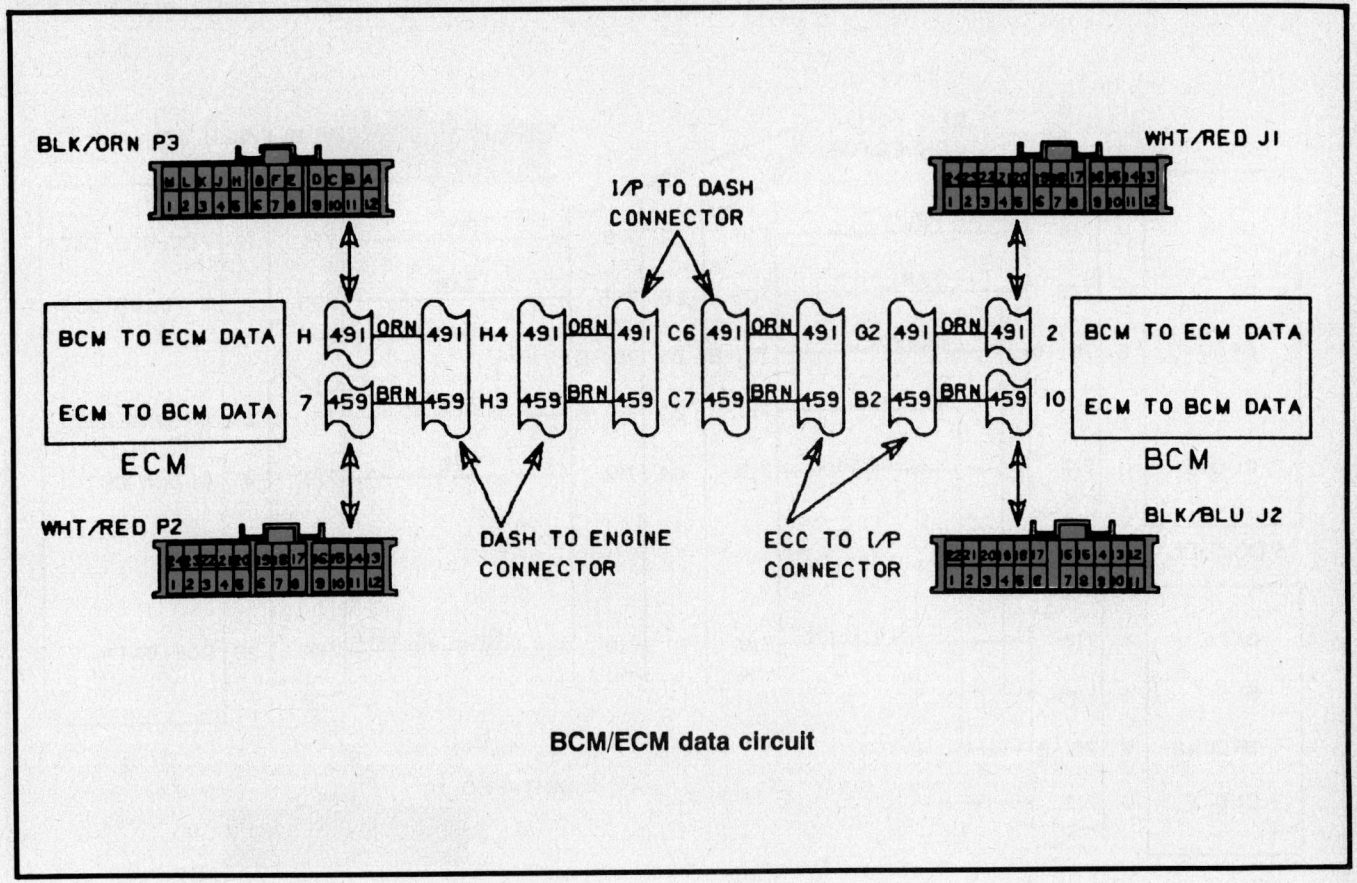

BCM/ECM data circuit

CODE F32 — BCM-ECM DATA PROBLEM

NOTE: If this code is NOT displayed during the second pass of diagnostic codes, it is an intermittent failure and cannot be diagnosed using this procedure. For an intermittent code, refer to "Note On Intermittents" at the end of this text.

Code F32 is set by the BCM if a problem is detected transferring data back and forth the the ECM. If a hard Code F32 is displayed upon entering diagnostics. One of the following conditions exist:

1. ECM to BCM data malfunction (ckt 459). If the BCM fails to receive data from the ECM over circuit 459, Code F32 will be set immediately and the BCM will stop sending data to the ECM over circuit 491. When the ECM stops receiving data over circuit 491 it will set a Code E47 in its memory, however, this code cannot be displayed since it would have to be sent over circuit 459 to the BCM. The loss of data to the BCM will result in a faulty instantaneous fuel economy reading of "0 MPG" at all times.

2. BCM to ECM data malfunction (ckt 491). If the ECM fails to receive data from the BCM over circuit 491, Code E47 will be set immediately by the ECM, however, data will continue to be sent to the BCM over circuit 459. Since the BCM continues to receive data, Code F32 is not set immediately and the instantaneous fuel economy reading will remain accurate. Upon entering diagnostics the BCM will attempt to request diagnostic data from the ECM but cannot due to the malfunction in circuit 491. If diagnostic data is not received shortly after diagnostics

is entered, the BCM will set F32 and will be unable to display the E47 stored in ECM memory.

If a hard code F32 is displayed, first check to see if the ECM can illuminate its service telltales during crank. If not, the ECM is not operating properly and should be diagnosed using the Self-Diagnostic System Check. If the telltales work properly, observe the instantaneous fuel economy while the vehicle is moving. A malfunction in circuit 459 will result in a constant reading of 0 MPG. If the reading varies normally, the cause of the Code F32 is a malfunction in circuit 491. If no circuit problem can be found, one of the two modules is unable to process the data and should be replaced.

Note On Intermittents

The following conditions will result in intermittent BCM-ECM data codes F32 and/or E47:

1. Momentary open or short in circuit 459. Results in both F32 and E47.

2. Momentary open or short in circuit 491. Results in E47 only.

3. Momentary loss of ignition (ckt 50), battery (ckt 840) or ground (ckt 751-A) to BCM. Results in E47 and intermittent display panel operation.

4. Momentarily loss of ignition (ckt 639) to ECM. Results in F32 and intermittent engine operation.

5. Momentary loss of battery (ckt 480) or ground (ckt 450) to ECM. Result sin F32, E52 and intermittent engine operation.

6. Momentary BCM PROM problem. Results in E47, F51 and intermittent display of "-151" on CCP.

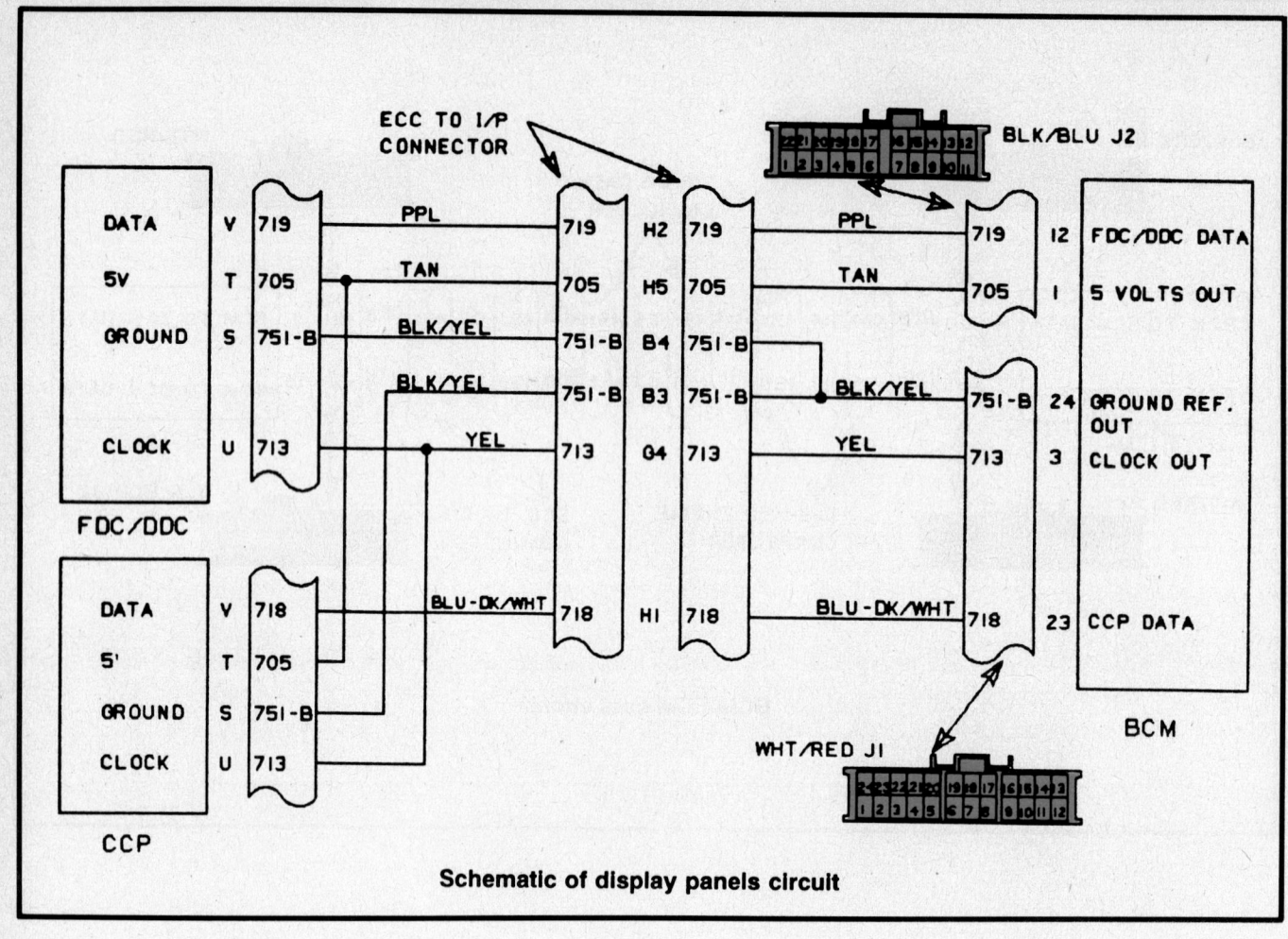

Schematic of display panels circuit

INTERMITTENT CODES F30 AND/OR F31 — DISPLAY PANELS TO BCM DATA PROBLEM

Code F30 is set if the BCM is unable to receive data from the Climate Control Panel. Code F31 indicates that the same condition exists between the BCM and Fuel Data Panel or Diesel Data Panel. If a malfunction should occur in a circuit common to both display panels, both codes will be stored in BCM memory.

Due to the failure mode of codes F30 and F31 they will only be displayed if the problem is intermittent. When these codes are currently failing the displays do not function properly which prohibits the use of diagnostics. Listed below are the symptoms and malfunctions which would result in one or both codes being displayed after the problem corrects itself. One or more of the following symptoms is associated with each circuit malfunction and is referenced in parenthesis:
1. Panel displays "d"
2. Panel displays "c"
3. Panel frozen, dim or blank
4. Displays flash on and off

Code F30 Only — CCP-BCM Data Problem
- Ckt 718 open or short to ground (1)
- CCP branch of ckt 713 open (2)
- CCP branch of ckt 751-B open (3)
- CCP branch of ckt 705 open (3)

- Faulty CCP (1, 2, 3 or 4)
- Faulty BCM (1)

Code F31 Only — FDC/DDC-BCM Data Problem
- Ckt 719 open or short to ground (1)
- FDC/DDC branch of ckt 713 open (2)
- FDC/DDC branch of ckt 751-B open (3)
- FDC/DDC branch of ckt 705 open (3)
- Faulty FDC/DDC (1, 2, 3 or 4)
- Faulty BCM (1)

Both Codes F30 and F31 — Symptoms Affect Both Displays
- Common branch of ckt 713 open (2)
- Ckt 713 short to ground (2)
- Common branch of ckt 751-B open (3)
- Common branch of ckt 705 open (3)
- Ckt 705 short to ground (3, 4)
- Faulty BCM (1, 2, 3, 4)

If an intermittent Code F30 and/or F31 is being set, manipulate the related wiring while observing the display panels. If the failure is induced, the associated symptom will appear. This will help to isolate the location of the malfunction. If the failure is induced but cannot be isolated to a given circuit, follow the "Self-Diagnostic System Check" which is designed to locate display malfunctions which are currently failing.

HARD OR INTERMITTENT CODE F40
AIR MIX DOOR PROBLEM

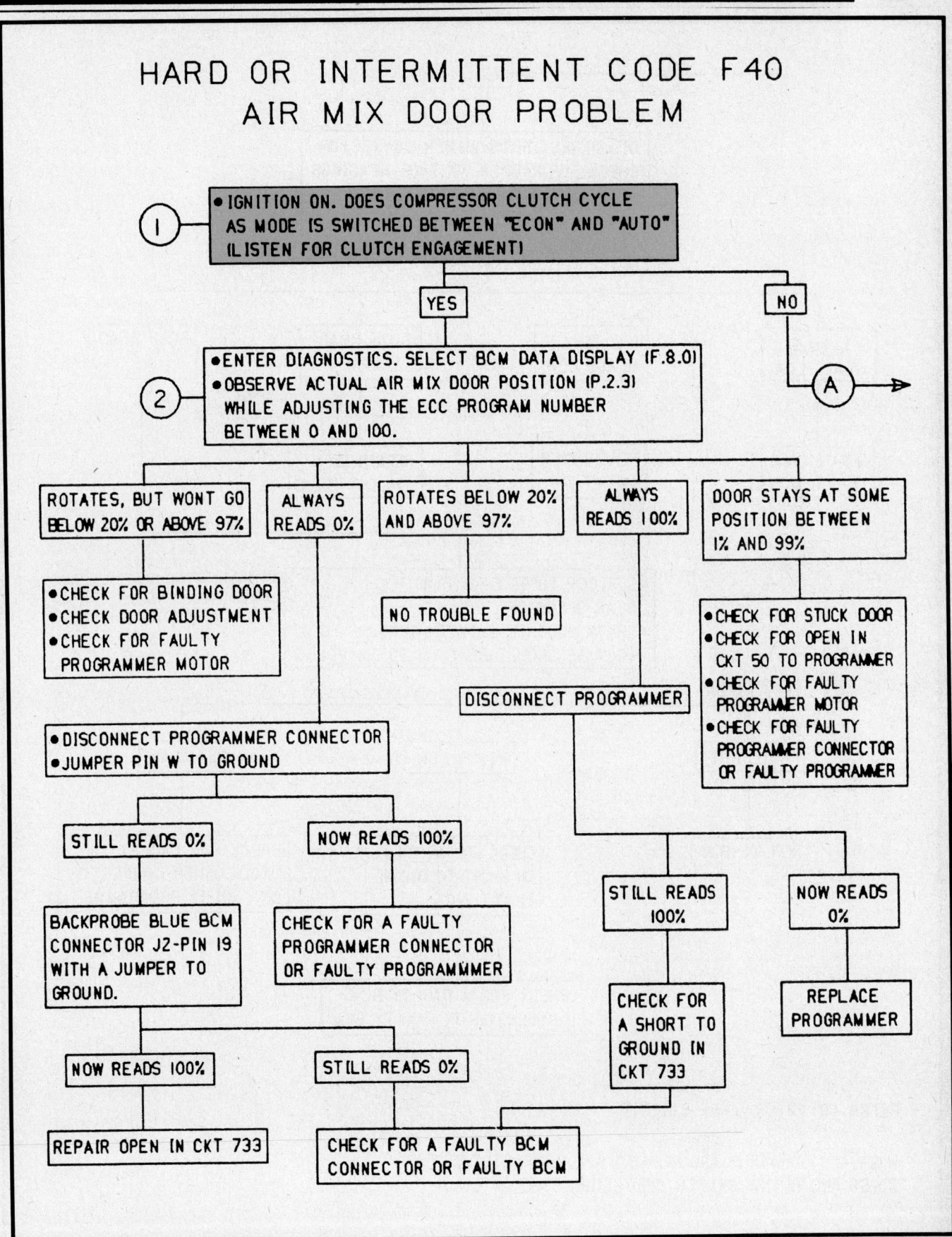

1 • IGNITION ON. DOES COMPRESSOR CLUTCH CYCLE AS MODE IS SWITCHED BETWEEN "ECON" AND "AUTO" (LISTEN FOR CLUTCH ENGAGEMENT)

YES   NO

2 • ENTER DIAGNOSTICS. SELECT BCM DATA DISPLAY (F.8.0)
• OBSERVE ACTUAL AIR MIX DOOR POSITION (P.2.3) WHILE ADJUSTING THE ECC PROGRAM NUMBER BETWEEN 0 AND 100.

A →

ROTATES, BUT WONT GO BELOW 20% OR ABOVE 97%

ALWAYS READS 0%

ROTATES BELOW 20% AND ABOVE 97%

ALWAYS READS 100%

DOOR STAYS AT SOME POSITION BETWEEN 1% AND 99%

• CHECK FOR BINDING DOOR
• CHECK DOOR ADJUSTMENT
• CHECK FOR FAULTY PROGRAMMER MOTOR

NO TROUBLE FOUND

• CHECK FOR STUCK DOOR
• CHECK FOR OPEN IN CKT 50 TO PROGRAMMER
• CHECK FOR FAULTY PROGRAMMER MOTOR
• CHECK FOR FAULTY PROGRAMMER CONNECTOR OR FAULTY PROGRAMMER

• DISCONNECT PROGRAMMER CONNECTOR
• JUMPER PIN W TO GROUND

DISCONNECT PROGRAMMER

STILL READS 0%

NOW READS 100%

BACKPROBE BLUE BCM CONNECTOR J2-PIN 19 WITH A JUMPER TO GROUND.

CHECK FOR A FAULTY PROGRAMMER CONNECTOR OR FAULTY PROGRAMMMER

STILL READS 100%

NOW READS 0%

NOW READS 100%

STILL READS 0%

CHECK FOR A SHORT TO GROUND IN CKT 733

REPLACE PROGRAMMER

REPAIR OPEN IN CKT 733

CHECK FOR A FAULTY BCM CONNECTOR OR FAULTY BCM

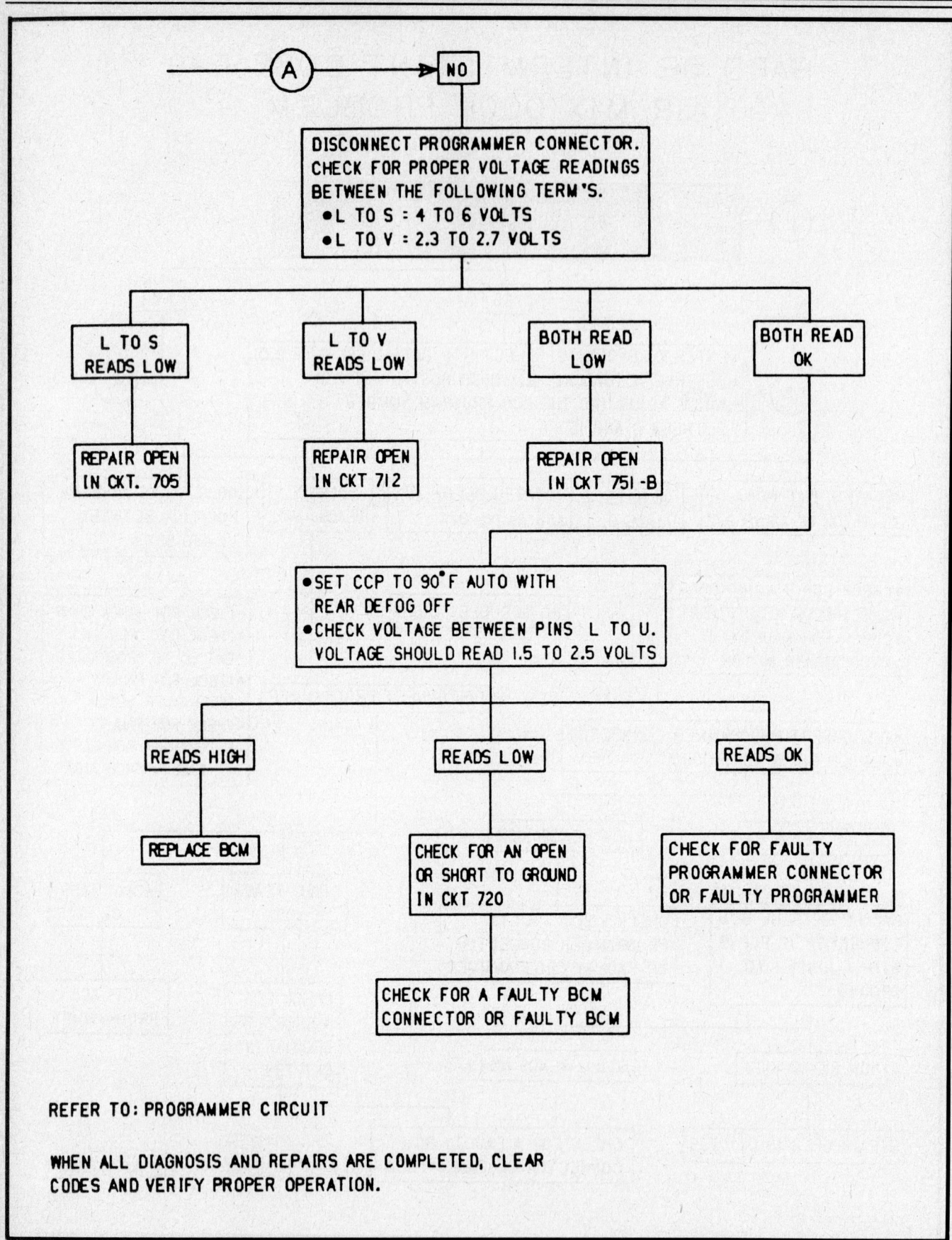

A → NO

DISCONNECT PROGRAMMER CONNECTOR.
CHECK FOR PROPER VOLTAGE READINGS
BETWEEN THE FOLLOWING TERM'S.
- L TO S = 4 TO 6 VOLTS
- L TO V = 2.3 TO 2.7 VOLTS

L TO S
READS LOW

L TO V
READS LOW

BOTH READ
LOW

BOTH READ
OK

REPAIR OPEN
IN CKT. 705

REPAIR OPEN
IN CKT 712

REPAIR OPEN
IN CKT 751-B

- SET CCP TO 90°F AUTO WITH
  REAR DEFOG OFF
- CHECK VOLTAGE BETWEEN PINS L TO U.
  VOLTAGE SHOULD READ 1.5 TO 2.5 VOLTS

READS HIGH

READS LOW

READS OK

REPLACE BCM

CHECK FOR AN OPEN
OR SHORT TO GROUND
IN CKT 720

CHECK FOR FAULTY
PROGRAMMER CONNECTOR
OR FAULTY PROGRAMMER

CHECK FOR A FAULTY BCM
CONNECTOR OR FAULTY BCM

REFER TO: PROGRAMMER CIRCUIT

WHEN ALL DIAGNOSIS AND REPAIRS ARE COMPLETED, CLEAR
CODES AND VERIFY PROPER OPERATION.

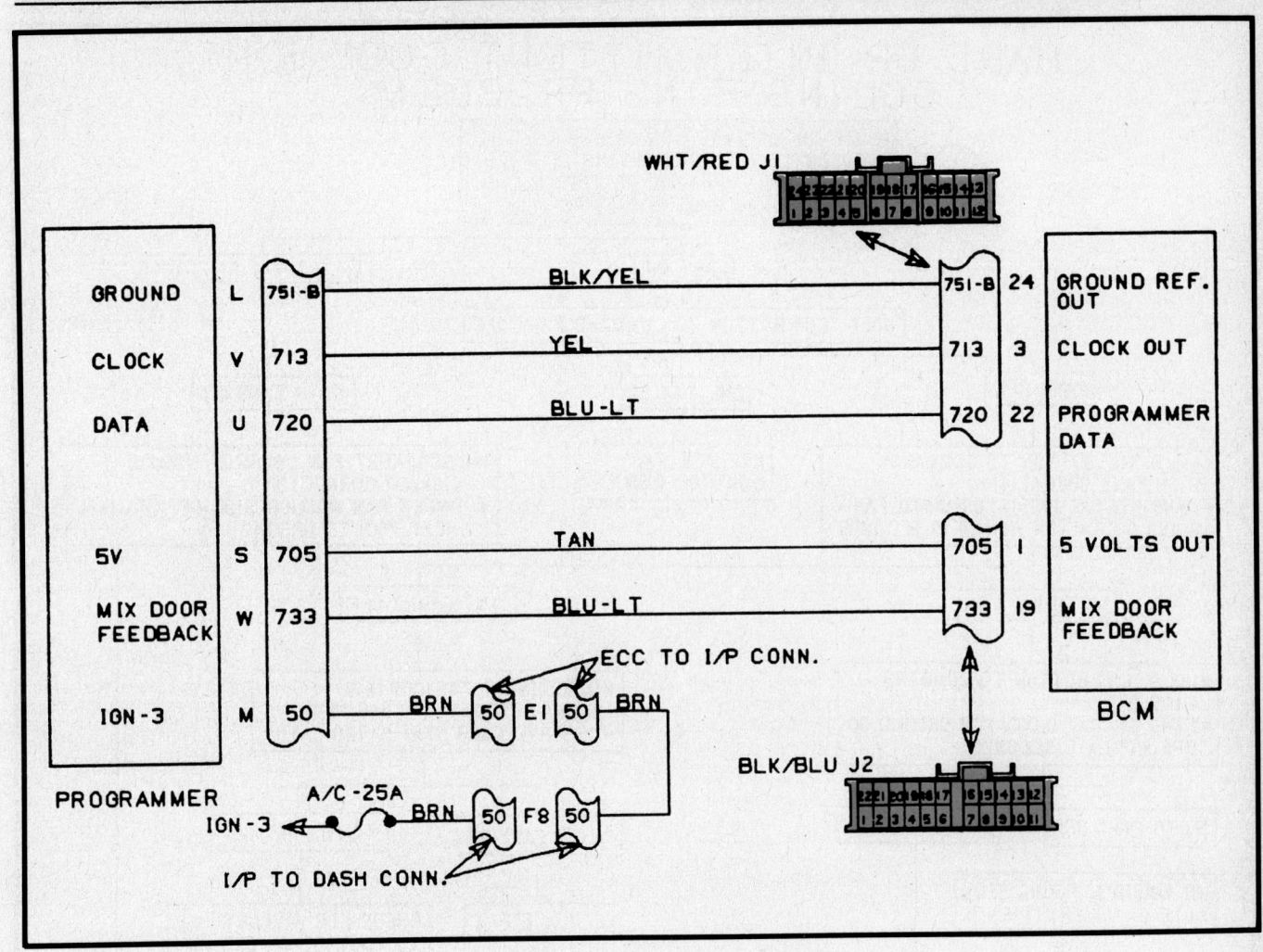

Schematic of programmer circuit

CODE F40—AIR MIX DOOR PROBLEM

NOTE: The following procedure is designed to account for intermittent codes. If no malfunction is uncovered using this procedure, it will indicate that the system is OK at this time. Refer to "Note On Intermittents" at the end of this text if further investigation is necessary.

Code F40 is set by the BCM if it is unable to move the Air Mix Door. The BCM requests the door to move over the data circuit (ckt 720) to the programmer. The programmer then supplies voltage to a D.C. motor which drives the Air Mix Door. The BCM monitors a feedback pot in the D.C motor which varies between 0 and 5 volts depending on its position. If the door is requested to move but the feedback voltage does not change, the BCM checks to see if the door has reached its mechanical limit of travel. If the door is not at its mechanical limit the BCM stores Code F40 to indicate that the door is not responding to it's command.

1. If Code F40 is stored and the compressed clutch does not operate, then the BCM's output requests are not being received

by the programmer over circuit 720 or the programmer is unable to process the data. If the clutch does operate then data is being received since both commands are sent by the BCM over circuit 720.

2. Operation of the Air Mix Door can be evaluated in BCM data display by observing "actual" Air Mix Door position (parameter P.2.3) while changing the ECC program number. As the program number is changed from 0 (max A/C) to 100 (max heat), the door position should vary between its mechanical limits of travel (below 20% and above 97%). Readings of 0% or 100% indicate a malfunction in the feedback circuit (ckt 733) back to the BCM while fixed or restricted readings within the range of travel indicate improper door movement.

Note On Intermittents

If an intermittend Code F40 is being set, manipulate the related wiring while observing "actual" Air Mix Door position (parameter P.2.3) movement. If the failure is induced, the door position will either stop or jump to an extreme value (0 or 100%). This will help in isolating the location of the malfunction.

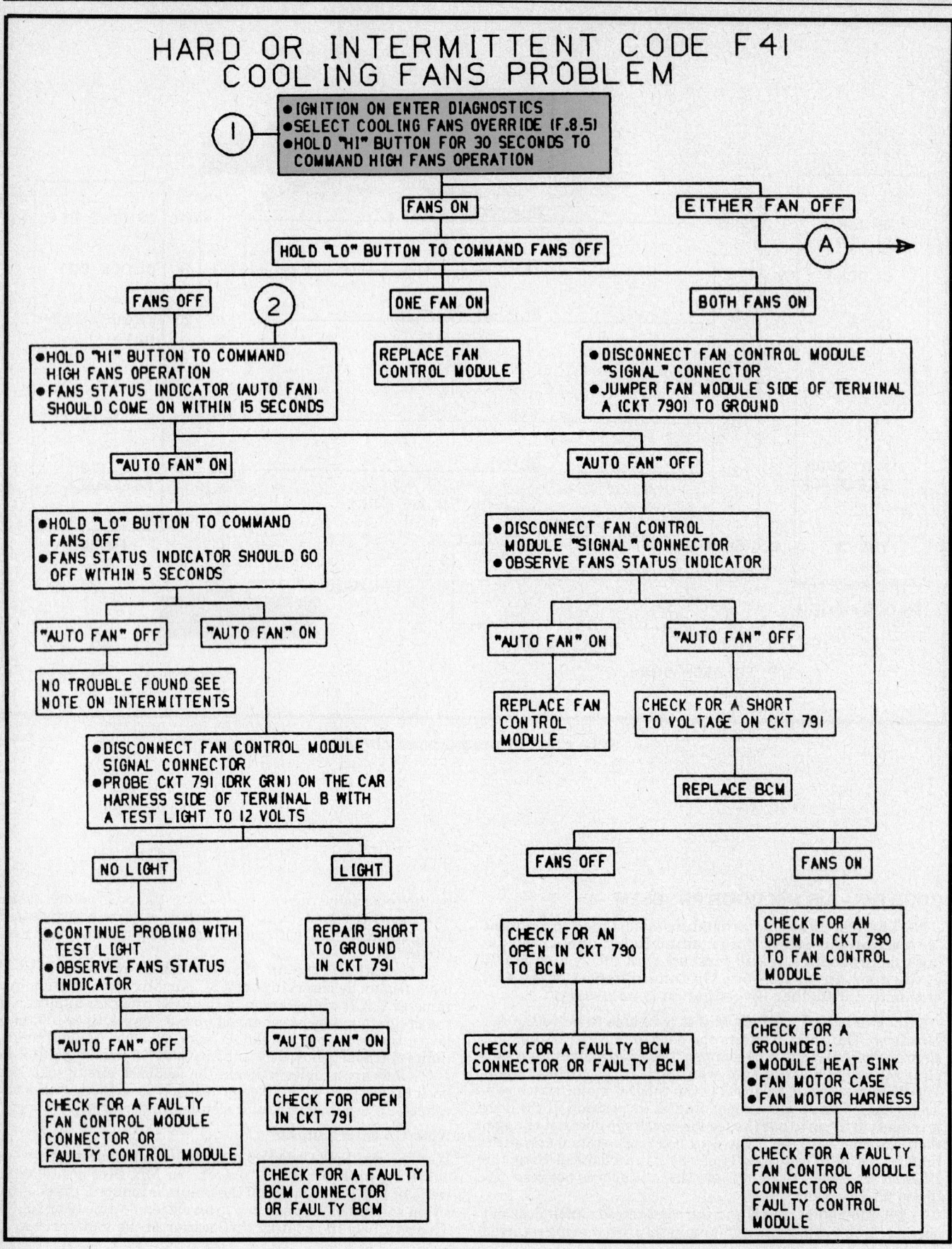

HARD OR INTERMITTENT CODE F41
COOLING FANS PROBLEM

1
- IGNITION ON ENTER DIAGNOSTICS
- SELECT COOLING FANS OVERRIDE (F.8.5)
- HOLD "HI" BUTTON FOR 30 SECONDS TO COMMAND HIGH FANS OPERATION

FANS ON

EITHER FAN OFF → A

HOLD "LO" BUTTON TO COMMAND FANS OFF

FANS OFF   2

ONE FAN ON

BOTH FANS ON

- HOLD "HI" BUTTON TO COMMAND HIGH FANS OPERATION
- FANS STATUS INDICATOR (AUTO FAN) SHOULD COME ON WITHIN 15 SECONDS

REPLACE FAN CONTROL MODULE

- DISCONNECT FAN CONTROL MODULE "SIGNAL" CONNECTOR
- JUMPER FAN MODULE SIDE OF TERMINAL A (CKT 790) TO GROUND

"AUTO FAN" ON

"AUTO FAN" OFF

- HOLD "LO" BUTTON TO COMMAND FANS OFF
- FANS STATUS INDICATOR SHOULD GO OFF WITHIN 5 SECONDS

- DISCONNECT FAN CONTROL MODULE "SIGNAL" CONNECTOR
- OBSERVE FANS STATUS INDICATOR

"AUTO FAN" OFF

"AUTO FAN" ON

"AUTO FAN" ON

"AUTO FAN" OFF

NO TROUBLE FOUND SEE NOTE ON INTERMITTENTS

REPLACE FAN CONTROL MODULE

CHECK FOR A SHORT TO VOLTAGE ON CKT 791

- DISCONNECT FAN CONTROL MODULE SIGNAL CONNECTOR
- PROBE CKT 791 (DRK GRN) ON THE CAR HARNESS SIDE OF TERMINAL B WITH A TEST LIGHT TO 12 VOLTS

REPLACE BCM

NO LIGHT

LIGHT

FANS OFF

FANS ON

- CONTINUE PROBING WITH TEST LIGHT
- OBSERVE FANS STATUS INDICATOR

REPAIR SHORT TO GROUND IN CKT 791

CHECK FOR AN OPEN IN CKT 790 TO BCM

CHECK FOR AN OPEN IN CKT 790 TO FAN CONTROL MODULE

"AUTO FAN" OFF

"AUTO FAN" ON

CHECK FOR A FAULTY BCM CONNECTOR OR FAULTY BCM

CHECK FOR A GROUNDED:
- MODULE HEAT SINK
- FAN MOTOR CASE
- FAN MOTOR HARNESS

CHECK FOR A FAULTY FAN CONTROL MODULE CONNECTOR OR FAULTY CONTROL MODULE

CHECK FOR OPEN IN CKT 791

CHECK FOR A FAULTY BCM CONNECTOR OR FAULTY BCM

CHECK FOR A FAULTY FAN CONTROL MODULE CONNECTOR OR FAULTY CONTROL MODULE

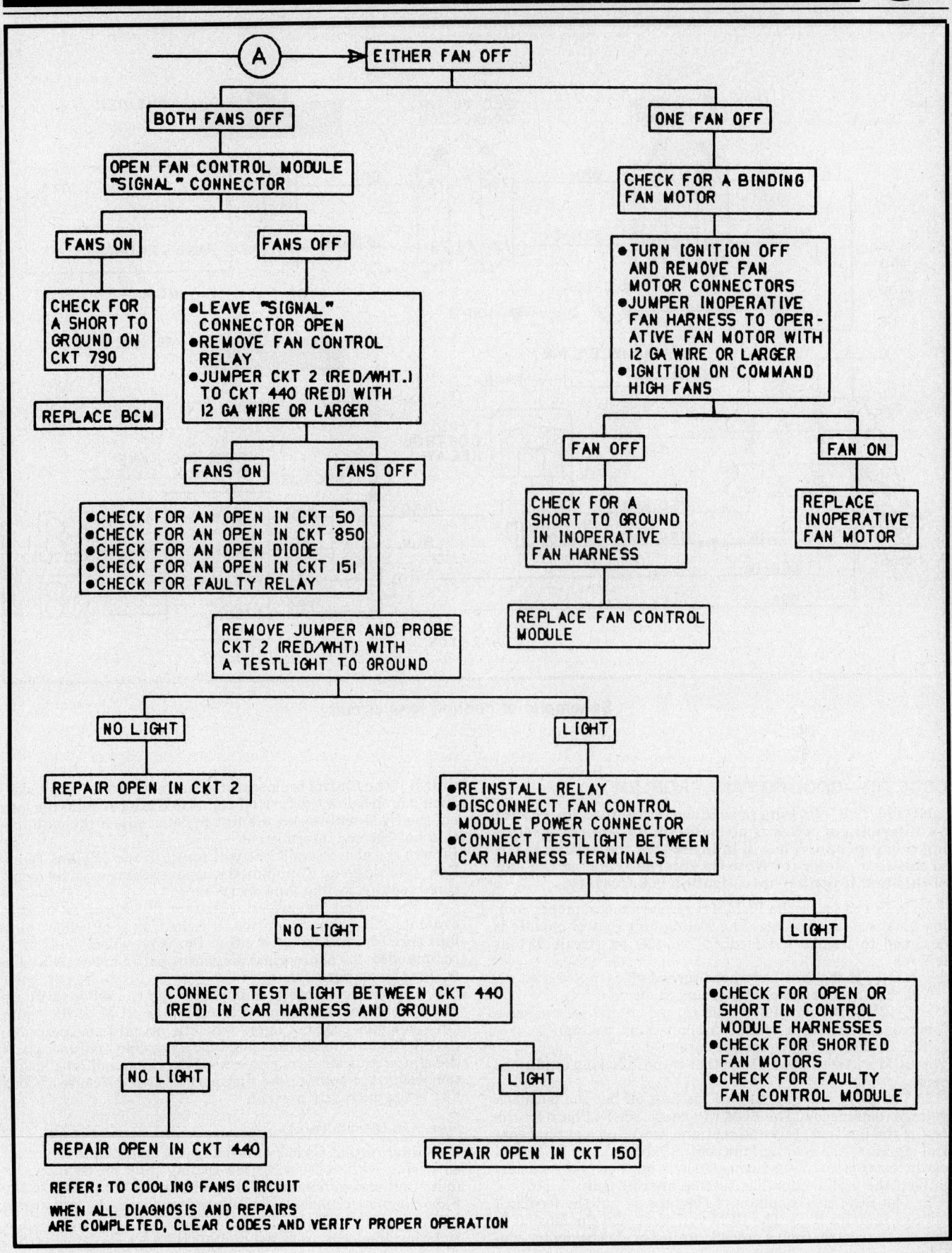

Ⓐ → EITHER FAN OFF

BOTH FANS OFF

OPEN FAN CONTROL MODULE "SIGNAL" CONNECTOR

FANS ON

CHECK FOR A SHORT TO GROUND ON CKT 790

REPLACE BCM

FANS OFF
- LEAVE "SIGNAL" CONNECTOR OPEN
- REMOVE FAN CONTROL RELAY
- JUMPER CKT 2 (RED/WHT.) TO CKT 440 (RED) WITH 12 GA WIRE OR LARGER

FANS ON
- CHECK FOR AN OPEN IN CKT 50
- CHECK FOR AN OPEN IN CKT 850
- CHECK FOR AN OPEN DIODE
- CHECK FOR AN OPEN IN CKT 151
- CHECK FOR FAULTY RELAY

FANS OFF

REMOVE JUMPER AND PROBE CKT 2 (RED/WHT) WITH A TESTLIGHT TO GROUND

NO LIGHT

REPAIR OPEN IN CKT 2

LIGHT
- REINSTALL RELAY
- DISCONNECT FAN CONTROL MODULE POWER CONNECTOR
- CONNECT TESTLIGHT BETWEEN CAR HARNESS TERMINALS

NO LIGHT

CONNECT TEST LIGHT BETWEEN CKT 440 (RED) IN CAR HARNESS AND GROUND

NO LIGHT

REPAIR OPEN IN CKT 440

LIGHT

REPAIR OPEN IN CKT 150

LIGHT
- CHECK FOR OPEN OR SHORT IN CONTROL MODULE HARNESSES
- CHECK FOR SHORTED FAN MOTORS
- CHECK FOR FAULTY FAN CONTROL MODULE

ONE FAN OFF

CHECK FOR A BINDING FAN MOTOR

- TURN IGNITION OFF AND REMOVE FAN MOTOR CONNECTORS
- JUMPER INOPERATIVE FAN HARNESS TO OPERATIVE FAN MOTOR WITH 12 GA WIRE OR LARGER
- IGNITION ON COMMAND HIGH FANS

FAN OFF

CHECK FOR A SHORT TO GROUND IN INOPERATIVE FAN HARNESS

REPLACE FAN CONTROL MODULE

FAN ON

REPLACE INOPERATIVE FAN MOTOR

REFER: TO COOLING FANS CIRCUIT

WHEN ALL DIAGNOSIS AND REPAIRS ARE COMPLETED, CLEAR CODES AND VERIFY PROPER OPERATION

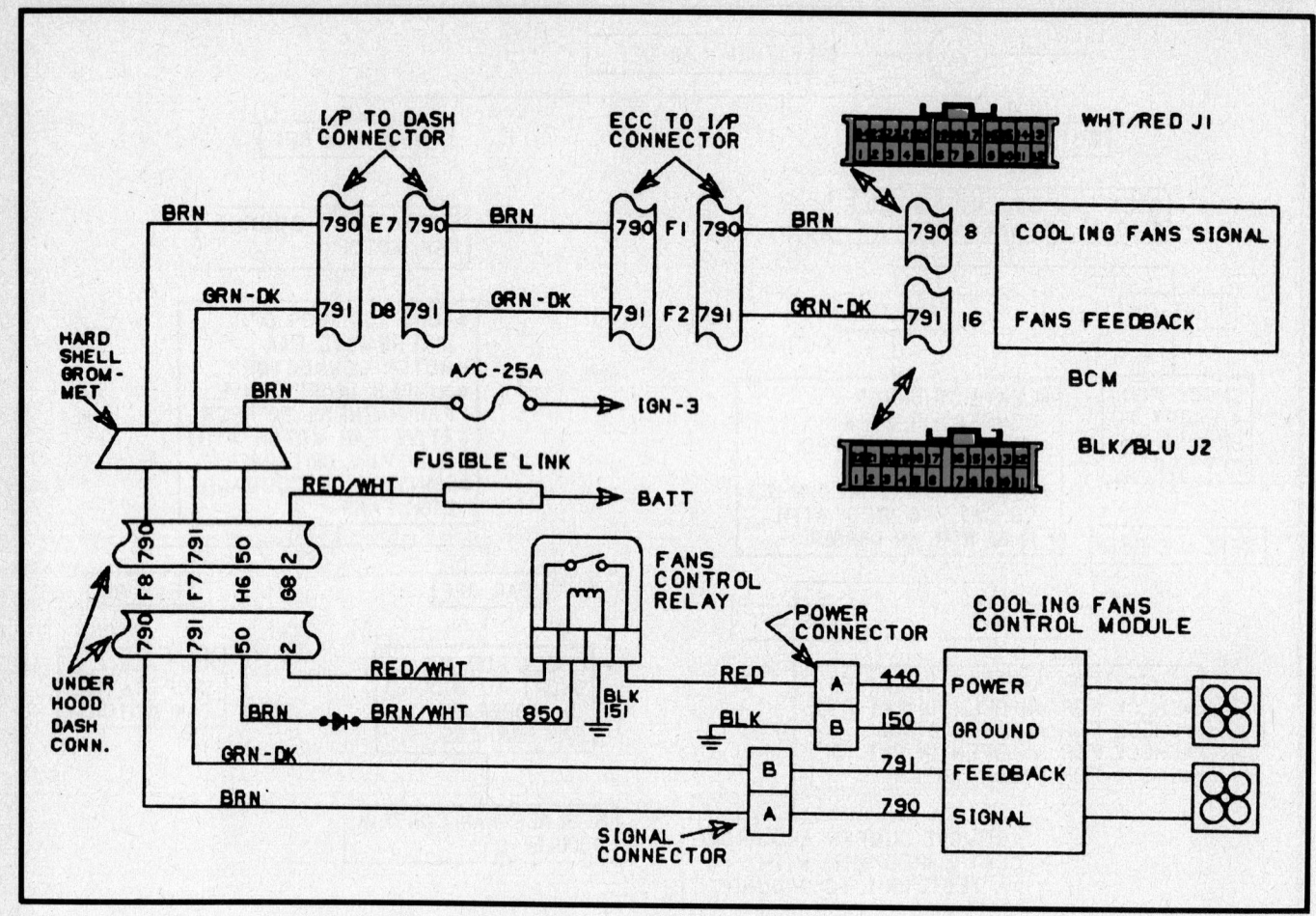

Schematic of cooling fans circuit

CODE F41—COOLING FANS PROBLEM

NOTE: The following procedure is designed to account for intermittent codes. If no malfunction is uncovered using this procedure, it will indicate that the system is OK at this time. Refer to "Note On Intermittents" at the end of this text if further investigation is necessary.

Code F41 is set by the BCM if it receives the improper cooling fans feedback voltage. The cooling fans control module is designed to change the feedback voltage on circuit 791 as follows:

    a. 12V if the fans have been turned off

    b. 0V if the fans have been turned on

    c. 12V if the fans have been turned on and an excessive current draw exists (stalled or shorted fan motors)

    d. 0V if both fan connectors are open.

The BCM will set Code F41 if either of the following conditions exist:

1. The BCM has commanded the fans off but the feedback voltage remains low. The BCM will keep Code F41 hard for the rest of the ignition cycle and continue providing a normal control signal to the cooling fans control module. The BCM will again test this condition during the next ignition cycle to determine if the malfunction has become intermittent.

2. The BCM has commanded the fans on but the feedback voltage remains high. The BCM will command the fans off to protect the system from a possible stalled or shorted motor con-

dition. If the control temperatures (coolant and A/C high side) should drop below the turn off points and later require the fans on, the BCM will repeat the test to determine if the malfunction has become intermittent.

Both of the above conditions will result in the "Coolant Temp/ Fan" telltale being illuminated whenever the control temperatures require cooling fans operation.

1. The cooling fans override feature (F.8.5) can be used to evaluate the system operation. If either fan is off when "high fans" are commanded or if either fan is on when "fans off" is commanded, the appropriate diagnostic path can be followed to isolate the malfunction.

2. The cooling fans status indicator can be used to evaluate the feedback signal being received by the BCM. If the "auto fan" indicator does not agree with the actual fans operation, circuit 791 must be investigated for a possible malfunction. If the status indictor does agree with the command fans operation within the appropriate time period, then the cause of Code F41 is not currently present.

Note On Intermittents

If an intermittent Code F41 is being set, manipulate the related wiring while observing the cooling fans status indicator (auto fan) and commanding "High Fans" or "Fans Off" in the F.8.5 diagnostic mode. If the failure is induced, the fans status will not agree with the command operation. This will help in isolating the location of the malfunction.

HARD OR INTERMITTENT
CODES F46, F47 AND/OR F48

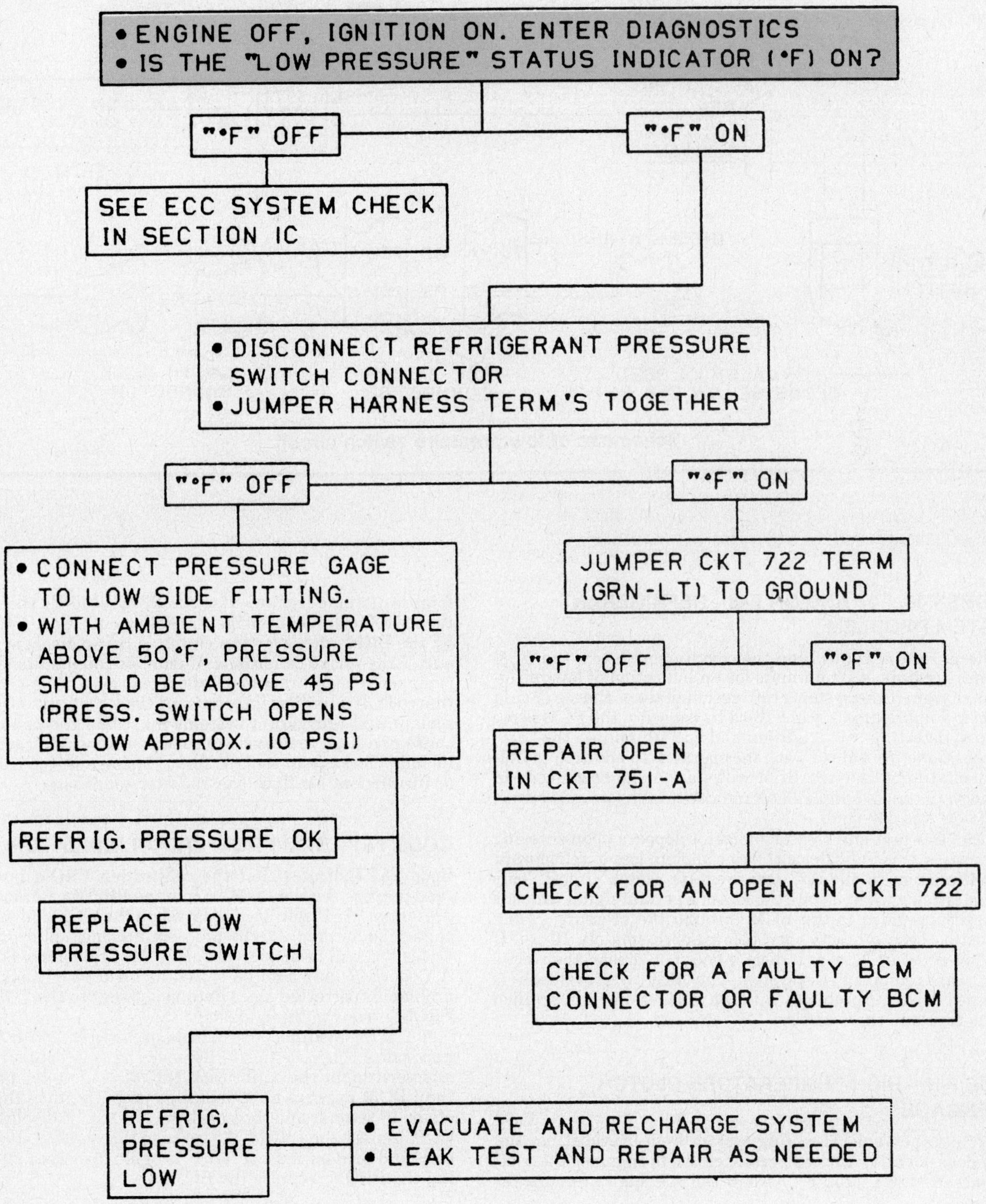

- ENGINE OFF, IGNITION ON. ENTER DIAGNOSTICS
- IS THE "LOW PRESSURE" STATUS INDICATOR (°F) ON?

"°F" OFF

"°F" ON

SEE ECC SYSTEM CHECK IN SECTION IC

- DISCONNECT REFRIGERANT PRESSURE SWITCH CONNECTOR
- JUMPER HARNESS TERM'S TOGETHER

"°F" OFF

"°F" ON

- CONNECT PRESSURE GAGE TO LOW SIDE FITTING.
- WITH AMBIENT TEMPERATURE ABOVE 50°F, PRESSURE SHOULD BE ABOVE 45 PSI (PRESS. SWITCH OPENS BELOW APPROX. IO PSI)

JUMPER CKT 722 TERM (GRN-LT) TO GROUND

"°F" OFF

"°F" ON

REPAIR OPEN IN CKT 751-A

REFRIG. PRESSURE OK

REPLACE LOW PRESSURE SWITCH

CHECK FOR AN OPEN IN CKT 722

CHECK FOR A FAULTY BCM CONNECTOR OR FAULTY BCM

REFRIG. PRESSURE LOW

- EVACUATE AND RECHARGE SYSTEM
- LEAK TEST AND REPAIR AS NEEDED

REFER TO: LOW PRESSURE SWITCH CIRCUIT

WHEN ALL DIAGNOSIS AND REPAIRS ARE COMPLETED, CLEAR CODES AND VERIFY PROPER OPERATION.

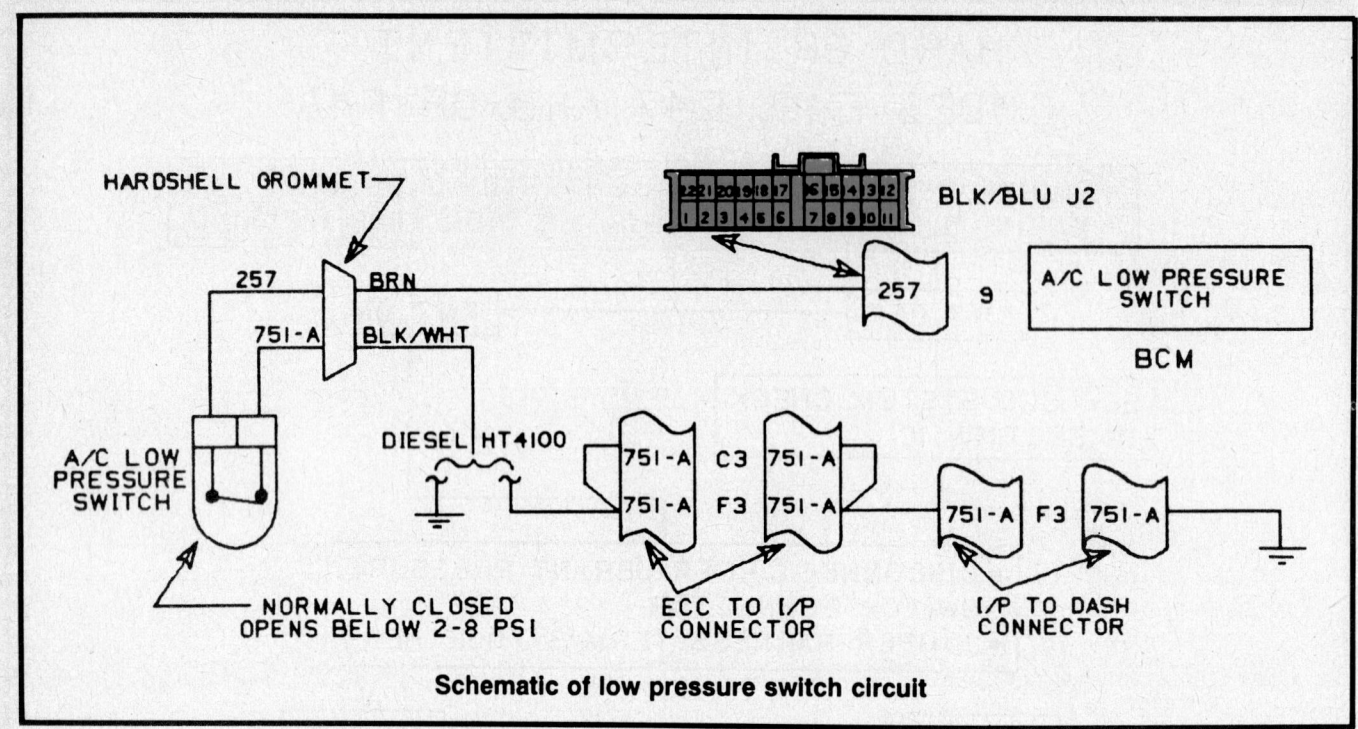

Schematic of low pressure switch circuit

CODES F46, F47 AND/OR F48 — REFRIGERANT SYSTEM PROBLEM

In the process of controlling the compressor clutch, the BCM monitors certain system inputs for an indication of low refrigerant charge. If the systems refrigerant state of charge should fall below approximately one third its capacity, the BCM is capable of detecting this condition and will illuminate the "Service Air Cond" telltale to warn the operator. In addition to illuminating the telltale the BCM will store a diagnostic code in memory. Codes F47 and F48 all indicate that a low refrigerant condition was detected.

If the "low pressure" status indicator appears upon entering diagnostics, this indicates either a complete loss of refrigerant or malfunction in the A/C low pressure switch circuit. This charge is designed to isolate the loss of a ground signal which is normally provided to the BCM through the pressure switch contacts. These contacts open below approximately 10 psi. If the "low pressure" status indicator does not appear, then some refrigerant remains in the system. The "ECC System Check" is designed to isolate problems with the refrigerant system which might result in these codes.

CODE F49 — HIGH TEMPERATURE CLUTCH DISENGAGE

To protect the vehicles cooling system from overheating, the BCM does not allow the compressor clutch to engage if the coolant exceeds 126°C (259°F). Also, if the A/C high pressure re-

frigerant temperature exceeds 93°C (200°F) the clutch is turned off to prevent refrigerant "blow-out". Code F49 is stored by the BCM whenever the clutch is being disengaged due to one of the above conditions. Customer complaints of "insufficient cooling" or "engine overheating" may be associated with this code. If a hard or intermittent Code F has been sorted, the coolant and refrigerant systems must be investigated for the cause of a high temperature condition. Possible causes would include blockage in coolant flow, blockage in refrigerant flow or insufficient air flow over radiator/condenser.

CODE F51 — BCM PROM ERROR INDICATOR

Code F51 indicates that the calibration PROM is not being read properly by the BCM. While the PROM error condition is present a "-151" will be displayed on the CCP and diagnostics cannot be entered. IF the problem becomes intermittent, the Codes F51 will be displayed during the first pass of BCM codes. A Code E47 may also be stored as an intermittent after the problem is corrected since data is not sent to the ECM while a PROM error condition exists.

A PROM installed backwards or installed with bent pins may cause this code to set. Remove the trap door on the BCM and verify that the calibration PROM is installed properly. If the PROM appears to be installed properly, turn the ignition off for 10 seconds and then back on. If "-151" is displayed on the CCP, replace the PROM. Again turn the ignition off for 10 seconds and then back on. If "-151" is again displayed after replacing the PROM, replace the BCM.

ANTILOCK BRAKE APPLICATION CHART
Domestic Models

Make	Year	Vehicle Model	System Manufacturer	Ref. Type
Buick	1986	Electra (C-Body)	Teves	1
	1986	Park Ave (C-Body)	Teves	1
Cadillac	1986	Deville (C-Body)	Teves	1
	1986	Fleetwood Limo (C-Body)	Teves	1
Chevrolet	1986	Corvette	Bosch	2
Lincoln	1985–86	Continental, Mark VII	Teves	3
	1986	Town Car	Teves	3
Oldsmobile	1986	Ninety-Eight (C-Body)	Teves	1
	1986	Regency (C-Body)	Teves	1
Pontiac	1986	6000 (A-Body)	Teves	1

ANTILOCK BRAKE APPLICATION CHART
Import Models

Make	Year	Vehicle Model	System Manufacturer	Ref. Type
Chrys. Corp.	1984–86	Conquest	Mitsubishi	4
Mitsubishi	1983–86	Starion	Mitsubishi	4

TYPE 1
TEVES SYSTEM
GENERAL MOTORS "A & C-BODY" Cars

General Information

The Antilock brake system used on the General Motors "A & C" body cars works on all four wheels. A combination of wheel speed sensors and a microprocessor can determine when a wheel is about to lock-up and adjust the brake pressure to maintain the best braking. This system helps the driver maintain the control of the vehicle under heavy braking conditions.

-------- CAUTION --------

Some procedures in this section require that hydraulic lines, hoses and fitting be disconnected for inspection or testing purposes. Before disconnecting any hydraulic lines, hoses or fittings, BE SURE THAT THE ACCUMULATOR IS FULLY DEPRESSURIZED as described in this section. Failure to depressurize the hydraulic accumulator may result in personal injury.

System Components

The Antilock brake system consists of a pump motor assembly, fluid accumulator, pressure switch, fluid reservoir with an integral filter, hydraulic booster/master cylinder, four wheel speed sensors, Electronic Brake Control Module (known as the EBCM), and a valve block assembly. A wiring harness with specific fuses and relays connects the major system components to the EBCM which controls the Antilock brake system.

ELECTRONIC BRAKE CONTROL MODULE

The EBCM microcomputer monitors the speed of each wheel to determine if any of the wheels are beginning to lock-up. If lock-up of a wheel is detected, the brake pressures are automatically adjusted to provide for maximum braking without wheel lock.

The EBCM is a separate computer used exclusively for control of the Antilock brake system and is located in the passenger's side dash close-out panel on "A-Body" cars or driver's side dash close-out panel on "C-Body" cars. The EBCM provides outputs to the hydraulic unit and the "Antilock" warning light based on the controller logic and the EBCM inputs described below.

EBCM Inputs

IGNITION ENABLE

This input receives voltage from the battery whenever the ignition switch is in the "RUN" position. Upon receiving an ignition enable input, the EBCM performs a self-check and "wakes up".

WHEEL SPEED SENSORS

A wheel speed sensor is located at each wheel and transmits wheel speed information to the EBCM by means of a small AC voltage that is dependent on the wheel speed. This voltage is

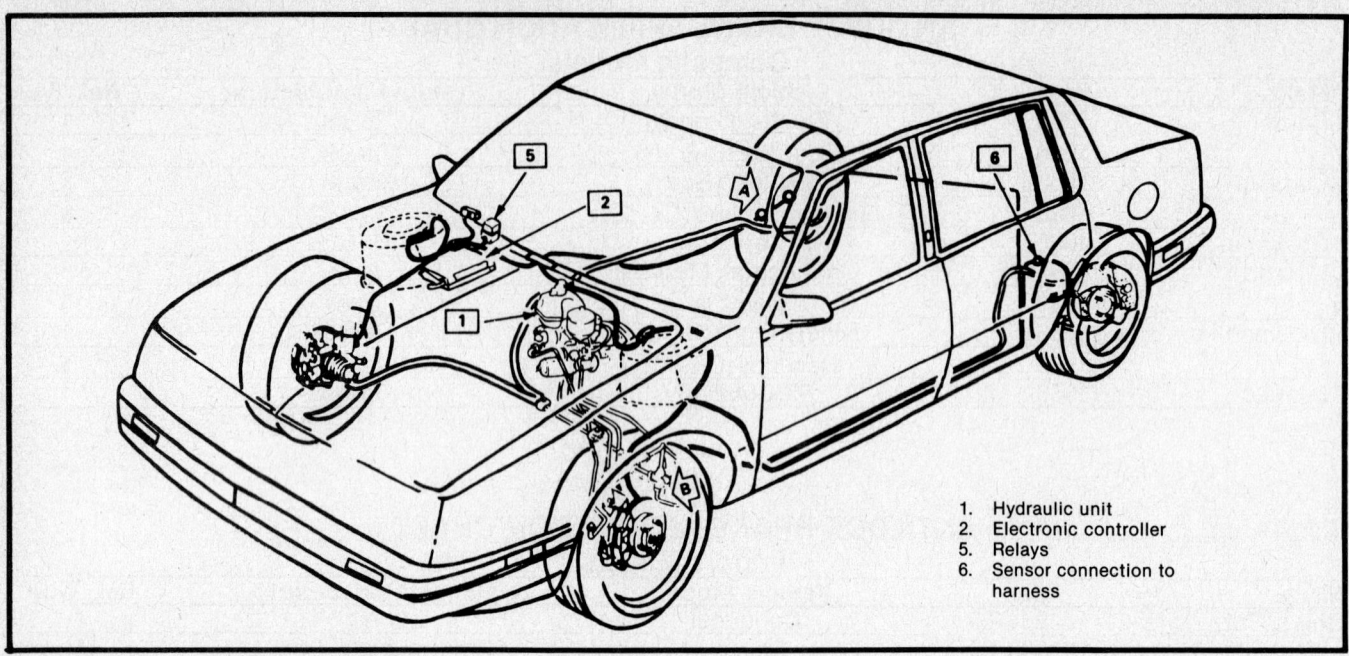

1. Hydraulic unit
2. Electronic controller
5. Relays
6. Sensor connection to harness

A-Body antilock brake system

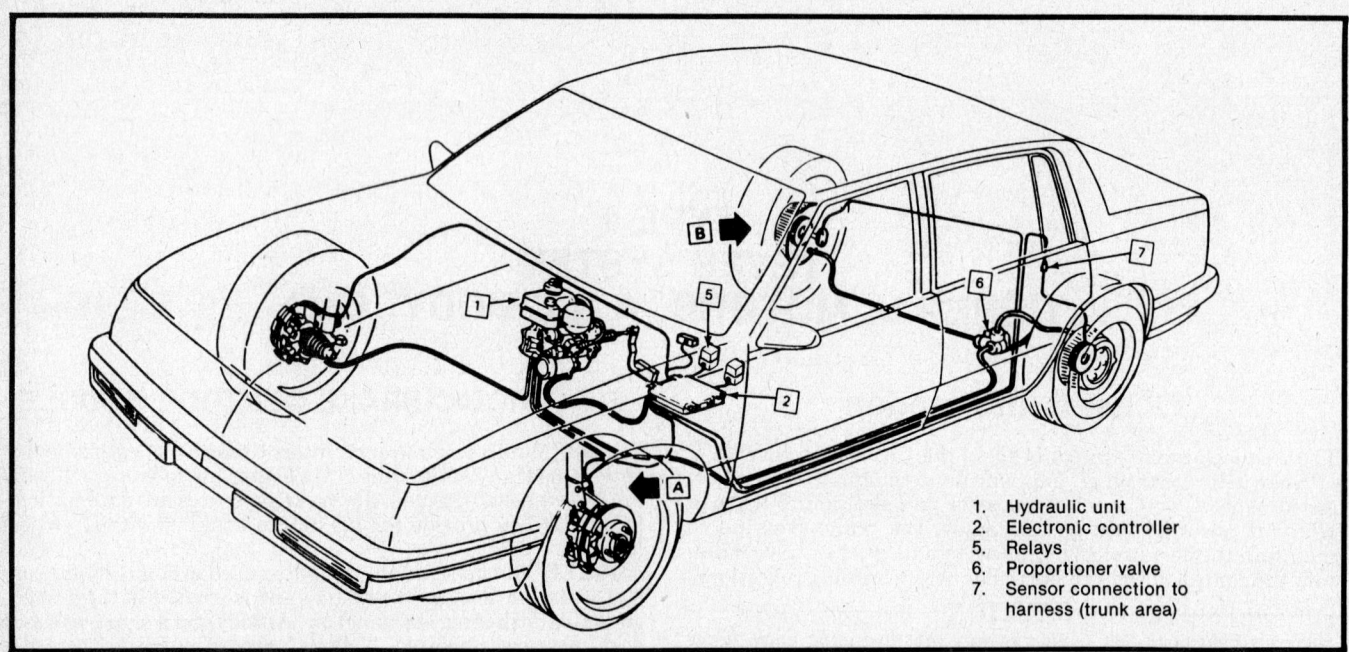

1. Hydraulic unit
2. Electronic controller
5. Relays
6. Proportioner valve
7. Sensor connection to harness (trunk area)

C-Body antilock brake system

generated by magnetic induction caused by passing a toothed sensor ring past a stationery sensor. The EBCM calculates wheel speed for each wheel based on the frequency of the AC voltage received from the sensor.

LOW FLUID AND LOW PRESSURE

The low brake fluid and low brake pressure inputs consist of a continuous loop circuit which runs through the fluid level sensor and pressure switch on the hydraulic unit. If a low fluid condition is detected, the fluid sensor will open the circuit. Likewise if low pressure is detected at the accumulator, the pressure switch will open the circuit. Any time an open circuit is detected on the low fluid/pressure input circuit, the antilock function is inhibited.

EBCM Outputs
SOLENOID VALVES (VALVE BLOCK)

Each hydraulic brake circuit: left front, right front, and rear, is equipped with two non-serviceable solenoid valves for fluid intake and output. These valve are actuated by a 12 volt signal from the EBCM when the antilock mode is activated and act singly or in combination to provide pressure increase, holding

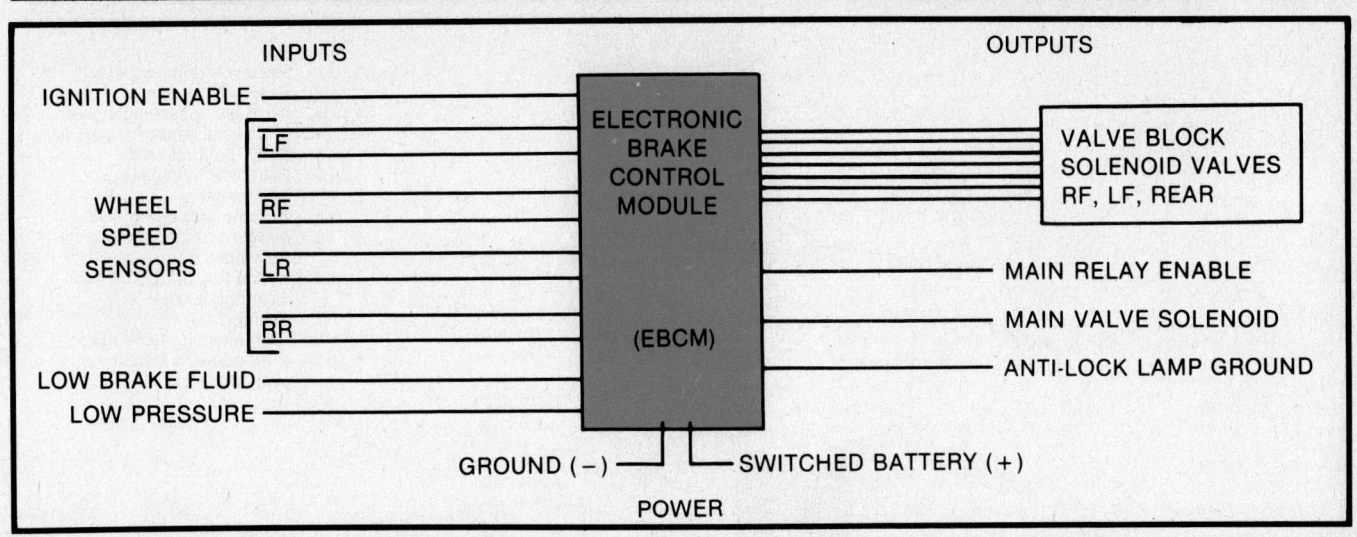

INPUTS
OUTPUTS

IGNITION ENABLE

ELECTRONIC BRAKE CONTROL MODULE

LF
RF
LR
RR

WHEEL SPEED SENSORS

(EBCM)

LOW BRAKE FLUID
LOW PRESSURE

VALVE BLOCK SOLENOID VALVES RF, LF, REAR

MAIN RELAY ENABLE

MAIN VALVE SOLENOID

ANTI-LOCK LAMP GROUND

GROUND (−)
SWITCHED BATTERY (+)

POWER

Electronic brake control module

pressure, or decrease depending on the wheel speed sensor signal.

During normal braking (not in the antilock mode), no voltage is sent to these valves. The inlet valve is normally open and the outlet valve is normally closed.

MAIN RELAY ENABLE

The main relay provides the switched battery power to the EBCM. The relay provides battery voltage only after the EBCM receives an ignition enable input. If the main relay in not active, the antilock system is disabled. The EBCM energizes the main relay by providing 12 volts to the main relay enable output at all times except after a fault has been detected in the antilock brake system.

MAIN VALVE SOLENOID

The main valve solenoid is located in the hydraulic unit and is activated by the EBCM main valve solenoid circuit only when antilock braking is required. During antilock braking, The EBCM provides 12 volts to the main valve solenoid output.

ANTILOCK LAMP GROUND

When a fault in the antilock brake system is detected by the EBCM, the "Antilock" light output is grounded, turning on the "Antilock" light.

HYDRAULIC UNIT

The main components of the hydraulic unit are the hydraulic booster/master cylinder, valve block assembly, pump motor assembly, pressure switch, accumulator and the fluid level sensor.

When the brake pedal is depressed, the booster/master cylinder operates the front brakes in the normal manner and also provides modulated accumulator pressure to the rear brakes.

The valve block assembly is a series of solenoid controlled valves which can cycle very quickly to increase and reduce hydraulic pressure to each wheel. The pump and the motor assembly supplies high pressure brake fluid to the accumulator. This high pressure fluid is used for the power assist and also to apply the rear brakes.

The pressure switch monitors the pressure that is maintained in the accumulator. When the pressure drops below the pressure limit, the pressure switch activates the pump motor relay which turns on the pump. Once the pressure reaches the upper pressure limit the pressure switch deactivates the relay and shuts down the pump. In the event of a pressure leak or a

pump failure, the pressure switch will signal the EBCM to shut-down the Antilock function. The pressure switch will also light the "BRAKE" lamp located in the instrument panel.

The accumulator is a pressure storage device which can hold brake fluid under very high pressures. The accumulator has an internal diaphragm with nitrogen trapped on one side. As the pump fills the accumulator, the diaphragm moves and compresses the trapped nitrogen.

The fluid level sensor is located in the fluid reservoir cap. It has two functions. It can signal the EBCM that there is a low fluid condition. The EBCM with then shut-down the Antilock function. The fluid level sensor will also light the red "BRAKE" lamp located in the instrument panel.

System Operation

NORMAL & ANTILOCK BRAKING

Under normal driving conditions the Antilock brake system functions the same as a standard brake system. However, during the detection of wheel lock-up a slight bump or a kick-back will be felt in the brake pedal. This "bump" felt in the pedal will be followed by a series of short pulsations which occur in rapid succession. The brake pedal pulsations will continue until there is no longer a need for the antilock function or until the car is stopped. A slight ticking or popping noise may be heard during brake applications with antilock. This noise is normal and indicates that the antilock system is being used. When the antilock system is being used, the brake pedal may rise even as the brakes are being applied. This is normal. Maintaining a constant force on the pedal will provide the shortest stopping distance.

BRAKE PEDAL TRAVEL

Vehicles equipped with the Antilock Brake System may be stopped by applying normal force to the brake pedal. Although there is no need to push the brake pedal beyond the point where it stops or holds the vehicle, by applying more force the pedal will continue to travel toward the floor. This extra brake travel is normal.

ANTILOCK WARNING LIGHT

Vehicles equipped with the Antilock Brake System will have

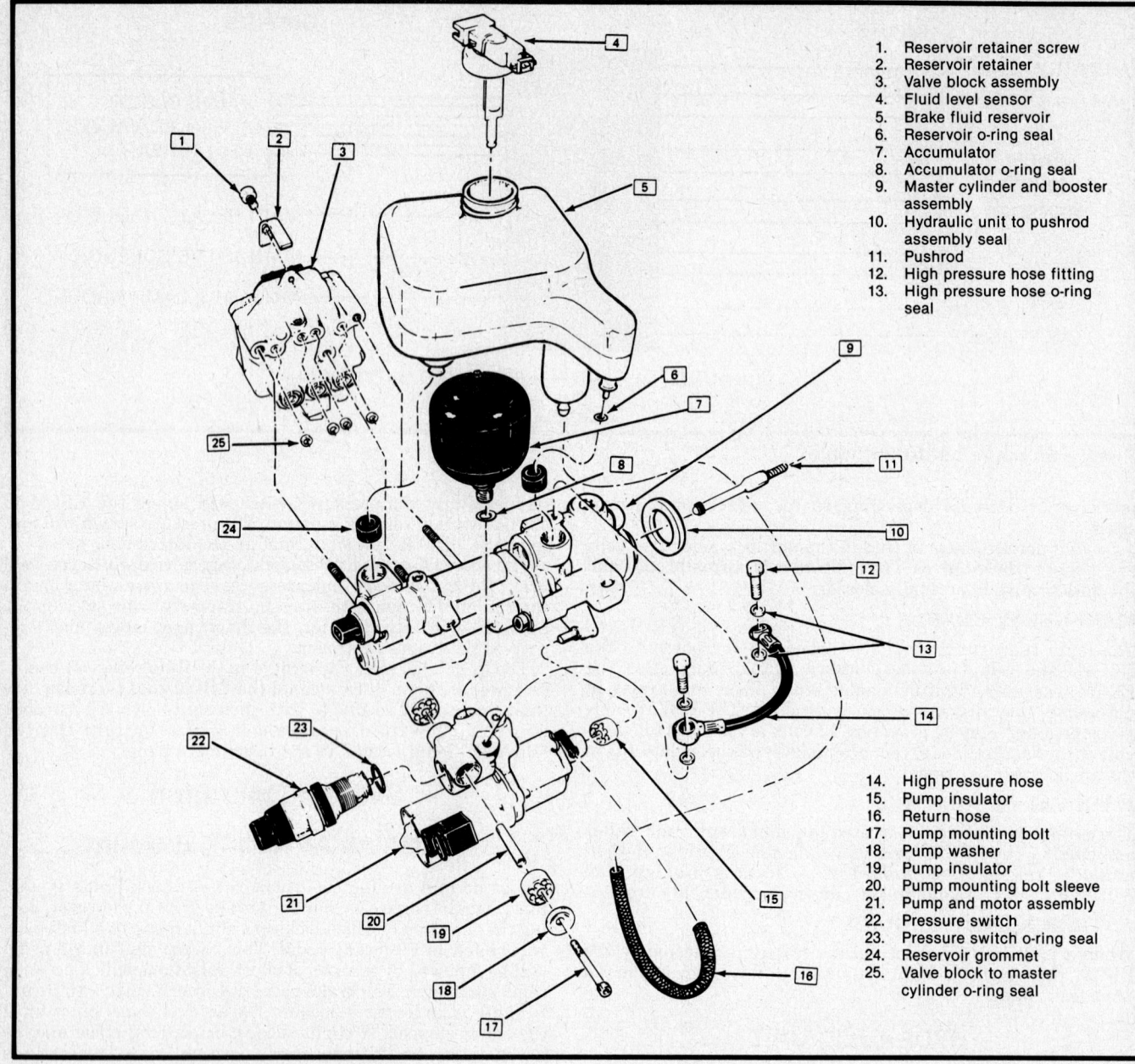

1. Reservoir retainer screw
2. Reservoir retainer
3. Valve block assembly
4. Fluid level sensor
5. Brake fluid reservoir
6. Reservoir o-ring seal
7. Accumulator
8. Accumulator o-ring seal
9. Master cylinder and booster assembly
10. Hydraulic unit to pushrod assembly seal
11. Pushrod
12. High pressure hose fitting
13. High pressure hose o-ring seal

14. High pressure hose
15. Pump insulator
16. Return hose
17. Pump mounting bolt
18. Pump washer
19. Pump insulator
20. Pump mounting bolt sleeve
21. Pump and motor assembly
22. Pressure switch
23. Pressure switch o-ring seal
24. Reservoir grommet
25. Valve block to master cylinder o-ring seal

Hydraulic unit—antilock brake system

an amber warning light in the instrument panel marked "ANTILOCK". This warning light will illuminate if a malfunction in the antilock brake system is detected by the electronic controller. In case of an electronic malfunction, the controller will turn on the "ANTILOCK" warning light and shut-down the antilock brakeing function. If the "ANTILOCK" warning light and the red "BRAKE" warning light come on at the same time, there may be something wrong with the hydraulic brake system. If ONLY the "ANTILOCK" light is on, normal braking with full assit is operational.

The "ANTILOCK" light will turn on during the starting of the engine and will usually stay on for approximately 3 seconds after the ignition switch is returned to the "RUN" position. In some cases the "ANTILOCK" light may stay on as long as 30 seconds. This may be normal operation. If the light stays on longer than 30 seconds after starting the engine, or comes

on and stays on while driving, the brake system should be inspected for a malfunction.

BRAKE SYSTEM WARNING LIGHT

The Antilock Brake System uses a two circuit design so that some braking capacity is still available if hydraulic pressure is lost in one circuit. A "BRAKE" warning light is located at the left hand side of the instrument cluster and is designed to alert the driver of conditions that could result in reduced braking ability.

The "BRAKE" warning light should turn on briefly during engine starting and should remain on whenever the parking brake is not fully released. If the "BRAKE" warning light stays on longer than 30 seconds after starting the engine, or comes on and stays on while driving, there may be a malfunction in the brake hydraulic system.

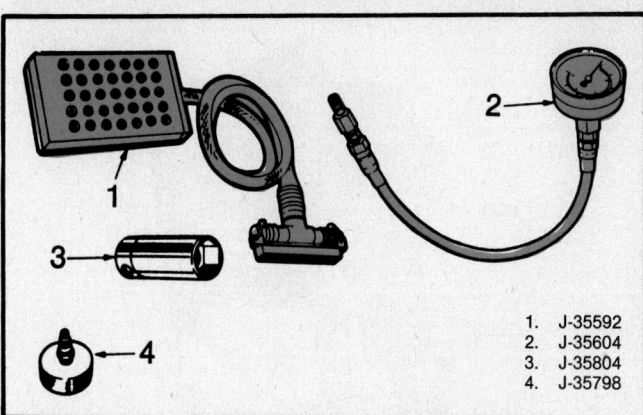

1.	J-35592
2.	J-35604
3.	J-35804
4.	J-35798

Special tools—antilock brake service

Component Replacement

── CAUTION ──

Some procedures in this section require that hydraulic lines, hoses and fitting be disconnected for inspection or testing purposes. Before disconnecting any hydraulic lines, hoses or fittings, BE SURE THAT THE ACCUMULATOR IS FULLY DEPRESSURIZED as described in this section. Failure to depressurize the hydraulic accumulator may result in personal injury.

DEPRESSURIZING THE HYDRAULIC ACCUMULATOR

• Depressurize the Hydraulic Accumulator before performing any service.
• With the ignition turned OFF and the negative battery cable disconnected, apply and release the brake pedal a minimum of 20 times using approximately 50 lbs. force on the pedal. A noticeable change in pedal feel will occur when the accumulator is completely discharged.

SPECIAL TOOLS

The following special tools are required for service of the Antilock Brake System:
• Tool No. J–35798 Bleeder Adapter
• Tool No. J–35592 Break Out Box
• Tool No. J–35804 Pressure Switch Socket
• Tool No. J–35604 Pressure Gauge

FILLING AND BLEEDING PROCEDURE

NOTE: DO NOT allow the pump to run more than 60 seconds at one time. If the pump must rum longer, allow the pump to cool several minutes between 60 second runs.

Checking & Filling

• With the ignition turned OFF and the negative battery cable disconnected, apply and release the brake pedal a minimum of 20 times using approximately 50 lbs. force on the pedal. A noticeable change in pedal feel will occur when the accumulator is completely discharged. Fill the reservoir to the full mark with Dot 3 brake fluid.

NOTE: Use only Dot 3 brake fluid from a clean, sealed container. Use of Dot 5 silicone fluid is not recommended. Internal damage to the pump components may result.

PRESSURE BLEEDING

Only the front brakes should be pressure bled. The rear brakes will bleed without the use of pressure equipment. Only diaphragm type pressure bleeding equipment should be used to prevent air, moisture and other contaminants from entering the system.

NOTE: The front brakes may be manually bled by conventional bleeding methods. The rear brakes should be bled according to the procedures given below.

Front Brake Circuit

1. Disconnect the wiring sensor from the fluid level sensor and remove the sensor.
2. Install the special tool No. J–35798 in place of the sensor.
3. Attach the brake bleeder to the adapter tool No. J–35798 and charge to 20 psi (138 kPa).
4. Attach a bleeder hose to one front bleeder valve and submerge the other end in a container of clean brake fluid.
5. Open the bleeder valve.
6. Allow the fluid to flow from the bleeder until no air bubbles are seen in the brake fluid.
7. Close the bleeder valve.
8. Repeat Steps 4–7 on the other front bleeder valve.
9. Check the fluid level and adjust as necessary.
10. Remove the brake bleeding equipment and adapters, install and connect the fluid level sensor.

Rear Brake Circuit

1. Turn the ignition on and allow the system to charge. (Listen for the pump motor, it will stop when the system is charged.)
2. Attach a bleeder hose to one of the rear bleeder valves and submerge the other end in a container of clean brake fluid.
3. Open the bleeder valve.
4. With the ignition on, slightly depress the brake pedal for at least 10 seconds.
5. Allow the fluid to flow from the bleeder until no air bubbles are seen in the brake fluid. Repeat the Step above if necessary.
6. Close the bleeder valve.
7. Repeat Steps 2–6 on the other rear bleeder valve.
8. Fill the fluid reservoir to the maximum level mark, following the "checking & filling" procedure above.

HYDRAULIC UNIT REPLACEMENT

1. Disconnect the negative battery cable.
2. Depressurize the accumulator by applying and releasing the brake pedal a minimum of 20 times using approximately 50 lbs. force on the pedal. A noticeable change in pedal feel will occur when the accumulator is completely discharged.
3. Label and disconnect all electrical connections to the unit.
4. Remove the pump bolt and move the energy unit to the side to gain access to the brake lines.
5. Disconnect the three lines connected to the valve block. Use a second wrench to prevent the line from twisting.
6. Disconnect the line attaching the hydraulic unit to the combination valve.
7. From the inside of the car, disconnect the pushrod from the brake pedal.
8. Push the dust boot foreward, past the hex on the pushrod.
9. Separate the pushrod halves by unthreading the two pieces.
10. Remove the two unit-to-pushrod bracket bolts and remove the Hydraulic unit.

NOTE: The front half of the pushrod will remain locked into the hydraulic unit.

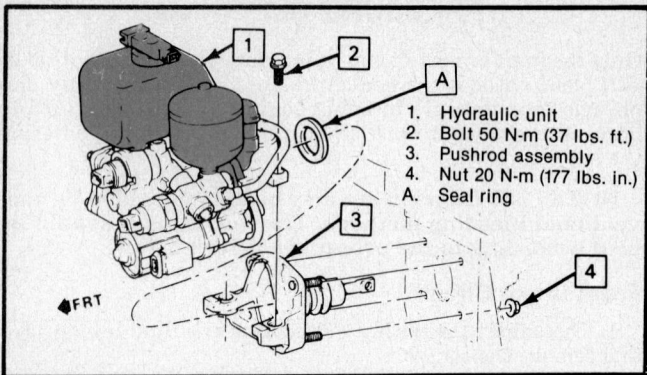

1. Hydraulic unit
2. Bolt 50 N·m (37 lbs. ft.)
3. Pushrod assembly
4. Nut 20 N·m (177 lbs. in.)
A. Seal ring

Hydraulic unit replacement

To install:
11. Install the Hydraulic unit to the support bracket.
12. Install the support bracket bolts and torque them to 37 ft. lbs.
13. Thread the two halves of the pushrod together and tighten.
14. Reposition the dust boot.
15. Connect the line from the combination valve to the hydraulic unit.
16. Connect the three lines to the valve block, reposition the energy unit as necessary.
17. Install all the electrical connections to the unit.
18. Connect the negative battery cable.
19. Bleed the brake system. Refer to the "Filling and Bleeding" procedure above.

PUMP AND MOTOR ASSEMBLY REPLACEMENT

1. Disconnect the negative battery cable.
2. Depressurize the accumulator by applying and releasing the brake pedal a minimum of 20 times using approximately 50 lbs. force on the pedal. A noticeable change in pedal feel will occur when the accumulator is completely discharged.
3. Disconnect the electrical connector from the pressure switch and the electric motor. Remove the fluid from the reservoir.
4. Remove the hydraulic accumulator and O-ring.
5. Disconnect the high pressure hose fitting connected to the pump.
6. Remove the pressure hose assembly and O-rings.
7. Disconnect the wire clip then, pull the return hose fitting out of the pump body.
8. Remove the bolt attaching the pump and motor assembly to the main body.
9. Remove the pump and motor assembly by sliding it off of the locating pin.

NOTE: Replace the insulators if damaged or deteriorated.

To install:
10. Install the pump amd motor assembly to the main body.
11. Install the bolt attaching the pump and motor assembly to the main body.
12. Connect the pressure hose assembly.
13. Connect the return hose and fitting into the pump body. Install the wire clip.
14. Install the bolt, O-rings and fitting of the high pressure hose to the pump assembly.
15. Connect the electrical connector to the pump motor.
16. Connect the negative battery cable.

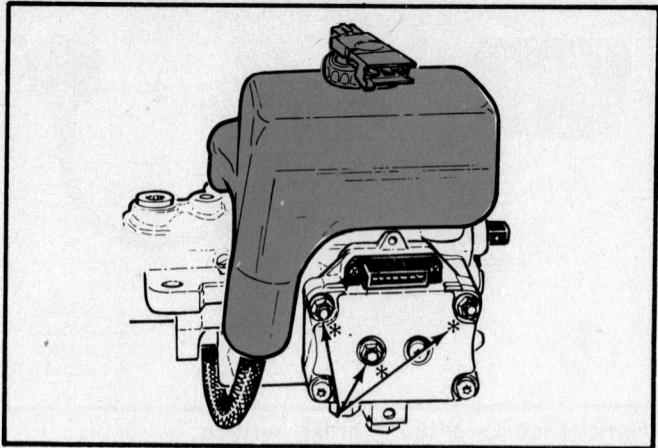

Valve block removal—remove the 3 nuts marked by the arrows

VALVE BLOCK ASSEMBLY REPLACEMENT

1. Disconnect the negative battery cable.
2. Depressurize the accumulator by applying and releasing the brake pedal a minimum of 20 times using approximately 50 lbs. force on the pedal. A noticeable change in pedal feel will occur when the accumulator is completely discharged.
3. Remove the hydraulic unit as described above.
4. Remove the three nuts and washers show in the illustration.
5. Remove the valve block assembly and O-rings by sliding the valve block off of the studs.
To install:
6. Lubricate the O-rings with brake fluid.
7. Install the valve block and O-rings onto the master cylinder body.
8. Install the three nuts and washers removed in Step 4.
9. Install the hydraulic unit.
10. Install the negative battery cable.
11. Following the procedures given in this section under "Filling and Bleeding", refill and bleed the system.

PRESSURE WARNING SWITCH REPLACEMENT

1. Disconnect the negative battery cable.
2. Depressurize the accumulator by applying and releasing the brake pedal a minimum of 20 times using approximately 50 lbs. force on the pedal. A noticeable change in pedal feel will occur when the accumulator is completely discharged.
3. Disconnect the electrical connector from the pressure/warning switch.
4. Remove the pressure/warning switch using special tool No. J–35804.
5. Remove the O-ring from the switch.
To install:
6. Lubricate the O-ring with clean brake fluid.
7. Install the O-ring on the pressure/warning switch.
8. Install the switch and tighten to 17 ft. lbs. using special tool No. J–35804.
9. Connect the electrical connector to the pressure/warning switch.
10. Connect the negative battery cable.
11. Turn the ignition to the "ON" position. The "Brake" light should go out within 60 seconds.
12. Check for leakage around the switch.

HYDRAULIC ACCUMULATOR REPLACEMENT

1. Disconnect the negative battery cable.
2. Depressurize the accumulator by applying and releasing the brake pedal a minimum of 20 times using approximately 50 lbs. force on the pedal. A noticeable change in pedal feel will occur when the accumulator is completely discharged.
3. Unscrew the hydraulic accumulator from the hydraulic unit.
4. Remove the O-ring from the accumulator.
To install:
5. Lubricate a new O-ring with clean brake fluid and install it on the accumulator.
6. Install the accumulator and tighten to 17 ft. lbs.
7. Connect the negative battery cable.
8. Turn the ignition to the "ON" position. The "Brake" light should go out within 60 seconds.
9. Check for leakage around the accumulator.

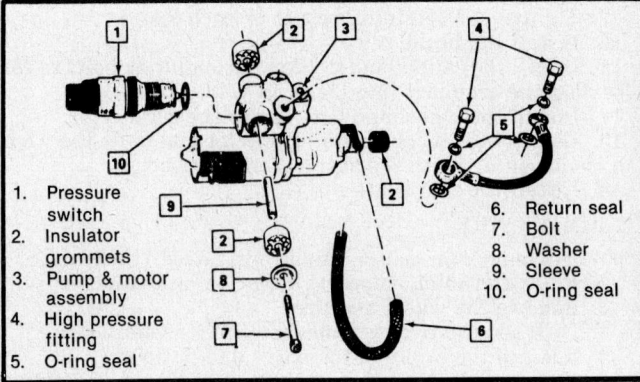

1. Pressure switch
2. Insulator grommets
3. Pump & motor assembly
4. High pressure fitting
5. O-ring seal
6. Return seal
7. Bolt
8. Washer
9. Sleeve
10. O-ring seal

Energy unit assembly

BRAKE FLUID RESERVOIR AND SEAL REPLACEMENT

1. Disconnect the negative battery cable.
2. Depressurize the accumulator by applying and releasing the brake pedal a minimum of 20 times using approximately 50 lbs. force on the pedal. A noticeable change in pedal feel will occur when the accumulator is completely discharged.
3. Remove the return hose and drain the brake fluid into a container and discard the fluid.
4. Disconnect the two wire connectors from the fluid level sensor assembly.
5. Remove the reservoir to block mounting bolt.
6. Remove the reservoir by carefully prying between the reservoir and the master cylinder.
To install:
7. Lubricate the seals with clean brake fluid.
8. Install the seals and O-ring into the master cylinder body.
9. Push the reservoir into the master cylinder until it is fully seated.
10. Install the reservoir to valve block mounting bracket bolt.
11. Connect the two wire connectors to the reservoir cap.
12. Connect the sump hose to the reservoir.
13. Refill the reservoir with clean brake fluid. Refer to the procedure on "Filling and Bleeding".
14. Connect the negative battery cable.

SENSOR AIR GAP ADJUSTMENT

Front Wheel

1. Raise and safely support the car on jackstands.

2. Remove the wheel and tire.
3. Remove the sensor retaining bolt.
4. Loosen the sensor lock bolt.
5. Inspect the face of the sensor for abnormal wear or damage. If necessary replace the sensor.
6. If the sensor is to be reused, clean the face of the sensor of all traces of the paper spacer, dirt, dust, etc.
To install:
7. Reposition the sensor and install the retaining bolt.
8. Tighten the sensor retaining bolt to 84 inch lbs.
9. Adjust the air gap to 0.028 in. (0.7mm) using a nonferous feeler gauge.
10. Tighten the sensor lock bolt to 22 inch lbs.
11. Install the wheel and tire. Lower the car.

Rear Wheel
A-BODY CARS

1. Raise and safely support the car on jackstands.
2. Remove the wheel and tire.
3. Remove the caliper mounting bolts and suspend the caliper with a piece of wire. DO NOT allow the caliper to hang from the brake hose.
4. Remove the brake rotor. Remove the sensor retaining bolt and remove the sensor.
5. Inspect the face of the sensor for abnormal wear or damage. If necessary replace the sensor.
6. If the sensor is to be reused, clean the face of the sensor of all traces of the paper spacer, dirt, dust, etc.
To install:
7. Reposition the sensor and install the retaining bolt.
8. Adjust the air gap to 0.028 in. (0.7mm) using a nonferous feeler gauge.
9. Tighten the retaining bolt to 85 inch lbs.
10. Install the brake rotor.
11. Install the caliper and tighten the mounting bolts to 28 ft. lbs.
12. Install the wheel and tire. Lower the car.

C-BODY CARS

1. Raise and safely support the car on jackstands.
2. Remove the wheel and tire.
3. Remove the brake drum.
4. Remove the brake shoe closest to the sensor.
5. Remove the sensor retaining bolt and remove the sensor.
6. Inspect the face of the sensor for abnormal wear or damage. If necessary replace the sensor.
7. If the sensor is to be reused, clean the face of the sensor of all traces of the paper spacer, dirt, dust, etc.
To install:
8. Reposition the sensor and install the retaining bolt.
9. Adjust the air gap to 0.028 in. (0.7mm) using a non-ferous feeler gauge.
10. Tighten the retaining bolt to 85 inch lbs.
11. Install the brake shoe and brake drum.
12. Install the wheel and tire. Lower the car.

WHEEL SENSOR REPLACEMENT

Front Wheel

1. Raise and safely support the car on jackstands.
2. Disconnect the wheel sensor connector from the wiring harness.
3. Remove the sensor retaining screw.
4. Remove the wheel sensor.
To install:

NOTE: New wheel sensors are equipped with a paper spacer that will properly gap the sensor when placed against the sensor ring. The air gap adjustment is not necessary.

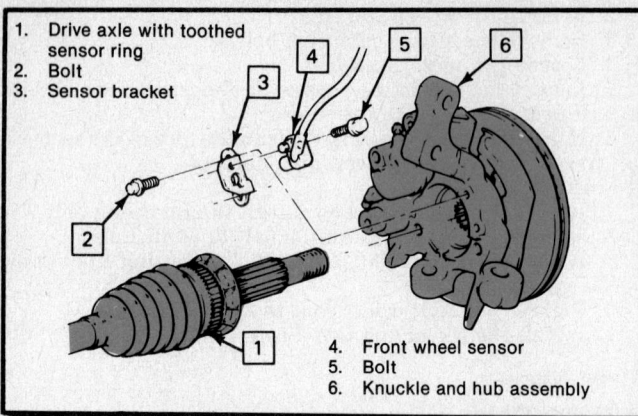

1. Drive axle with toothed sensor ring
2. Bolt
3. Sensor bracket
4. Front wheel sensor
5. Bolt
6. Knuckle and hub assembly

Front wheel speed sensor mounting—A & C Body

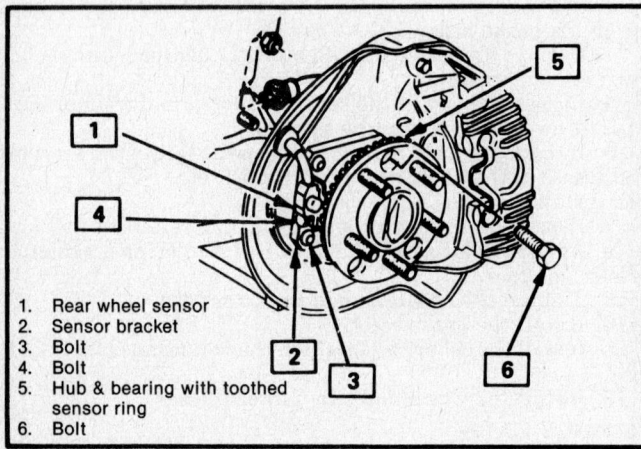

1. Rear wheel sensor
2. Sensor bracket
3. Bolt
4. Bolt
5. Hub & bearing with toothed sensor ring
6. Bolt

Rear wheel sensor—A-Body

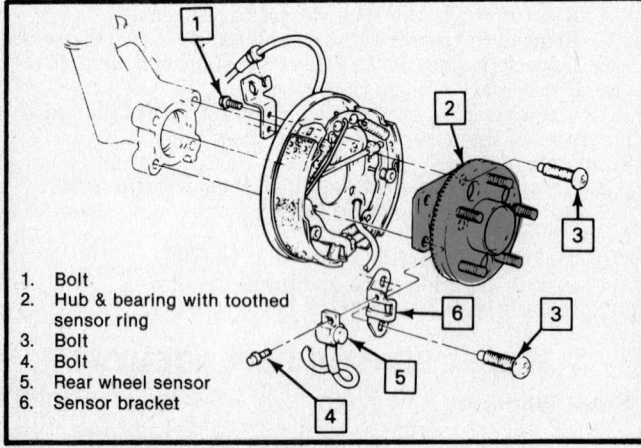

1. Bolt
2. Hub & bearing with toothed sensor ring
3. Bolt
4. Bolt
5. Rear wheel sensor
6. Sensor bracket

Rear wheel sensor—C-Body

5. Reposition the sensor and install the retaining bolt.
6. Tighten the sensor retaining bolt to 84 inch lbs.
7. Adjust the air gap to 0.028 in. (0.7mm) using a nonferous feeler gauge.
8. Tighten the sensor lock bolt to 22 inch lbs.
9. Connect the wheel sensor connector and route the wiring to avoid contact with the suspension components.
10. Lower the car.

Rear Wheel
A-BODY CARS

1. Remove the lower section of the rear seat and disconnect the sensor connector located beneath it.
2. Raise and safely support the car on jackstands.
3. Remove the wheel and tire.
4. Remove the caliper mounting bolts and suspend the caliper with a piece of wire. DO NOT allow the caliper to hang from the brake hose.
5. Remove the brake rotor.
6. Remove the sensor retaining bolt and remove the sensor.
To install:

NOTE: New wheel sensors are equipped with a paper spacer that will properly gap the sensor when placed against the sensor ring. The air gap adjustment is not necessary.

7. Install the wheel sensor.
8. Adjust the air gap to 0.028 in. (0.7mm) using a nonferous feeler gauge.
9. Tighten the retaining bolt to 85 inch lbs.
10. Install the brake rotor.
11. Install the caliper and tighten the mounting bolts to 28 ft. lbs. Pop the grommet into place.
12. Install the wheel and tire. Lower the car.
13. Connect the wheel sensor connector and route the wiring to avoid contact with the suspension components.
14. Install the rear seat.

C-BODY CARS

1. Disconnect the sensor connector located in the trunk area.
2. Raise and safely support the car on jackstands.
3. Remove the wheel and tire.
4. Drill out the two grommet retaining rivets.
5. Remove the brake drum, shoes and hardware.
6. Remove the sensor retaining screw and remove the sensor.
To install:

NOTE: New wheel sensors are equipped with a paper spacer that will properly gap the sensor when placed against the sensor ring. The air gap adjustment is not necessary.

7. Install the wheel sensor.
8. Adjust the air gap to 0.028 in. (0.7mm) using a nonferous feeler gauge.
9. Tighten the retaining bolt to 85 inch lbs.
10. Install the brake shoes, hardware, and drum.
11. Pop rivet the grommet into place.
12. Install the wheel and tire. Lower the car.
13. Connect the wheel sensor connector and route the wiring to avoid contact with the suspension components.

Diagnosis & Testing

Diagnosis of a malfunction on this antilock brake system involves three basic steps which must be followed in order to isolate the fault, correctly determine its cause and repair the problem in the least amount of time. The proper diagnostic procedure consists of the following:
- Pre-Diagnosis Inspection
- Light Sequence Determination
- Component Test Charts

INSTALLING THE BREAK-OUT BOX

Certain diagnostic procedures in this section require that a Break-Out box, special tool No. J–35592, be connected to the

35-pin Electronic Brake Control Module (EBCM) connector using the following procedure:

1. Remove the two retainers holding the EBCM to the dash close-out panel (driver's side on the "C-Body" cars, and passenger's side on the "A-Body") and lower the EBCM into the passenger compartment.

2. Depress the looking plate and remove the 35-pin connector from the EBCM using a rocking motion, rotating the connector toward the forward end of the module.

3. Inspect the 35-pin connector for damage. Plug the J–35592 Beak-Out box connector into the 35-pin harness connector.

INSTALLING THE PRESSURE GAUGE

Certain diagnostic procedures in this section require that a Pressure Gauge, special tool No. J–35604, be connected to the energy unit to read accumulator pressure. The following procedure should be used to connect the gauge:

1. Depressurize the accumulator as described under "Depressurizing the Hydraulic Accumulator".

2. Remove the "Banjo Bolt" pressure hose fitting from the pump body. Be careful not to drop the two O-ring seals when removing the fitting.

3. Install one of the O-ring seals on the pressure gauge fitting and insert the gauge fitting into the pressure hose coupling.

4. Install the second O-ring seal on the gauge fitting on the underside of the pressure hose and thread the gauge fitting into the pump body. Tighten the fitting to 15 ft. lbs.

5. When removing the gauge and installing the pressure fitting, inspect the O-ring seals for cuts or damage. Replace any damaged seals.

PRE-DIAGNOSIS INSPECTION

The Pre-Diagnosis Inspection consists of a quick visual check of specific components that could cause an apparent Antilock system malfunction. Performing this quick test may uncover a simple failure which may be the cause of an inoperative system. This check should be the first step in analyzing a problem in this Antilock system. When performing this check refer to the illustrations for connector and ground locations.

LIGHT SEQUENCE DETERMINATION

The second step in analyzing a problem of this Antilock Brake System is determination of the warning light behavior. As described under "System Operation" above, this Antilock brake system uses two warning lamps, including a red "BRAKE" warning light on the left side of the instrument panel and an amber "ANTILOCK" light in the left hand Driver Information Center. By observing when these lights are lit, specific components and sub-systems of the brake system may be isolated as a likely cause of a system malfunction. The normal indicator lamp sequence is shown in the illustration. In this illustration and in the "LAMP SEQUENCE CHART", indicator lamp sequences are shown graphically as described below.

Vehicle Status

Each light sequence is divided into seven areas which represent vehicle status, with the behavior of the "BRAKE" and "ANTILOCK" lights represented in the horizontal rows below the vehicle status headers. The vehicle status headers may be interpreted as shown in the "Normal Indicator Light Sequence" chart.

Light Status

The "BRAKE" and "ANTILOCK" light status is indicated by

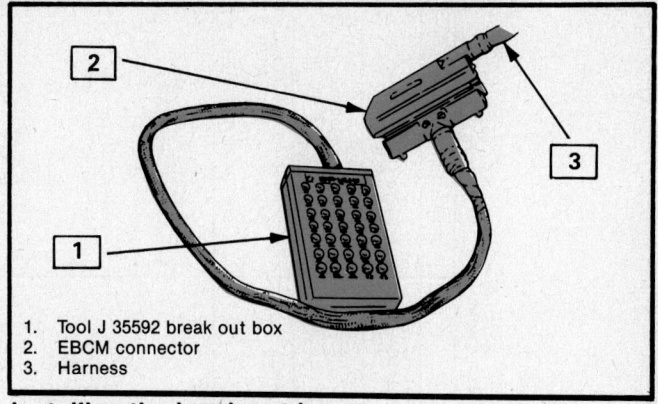

1. Tool J 35592 break out box
2. EBCM connector
3. Harness

Installing the break out box

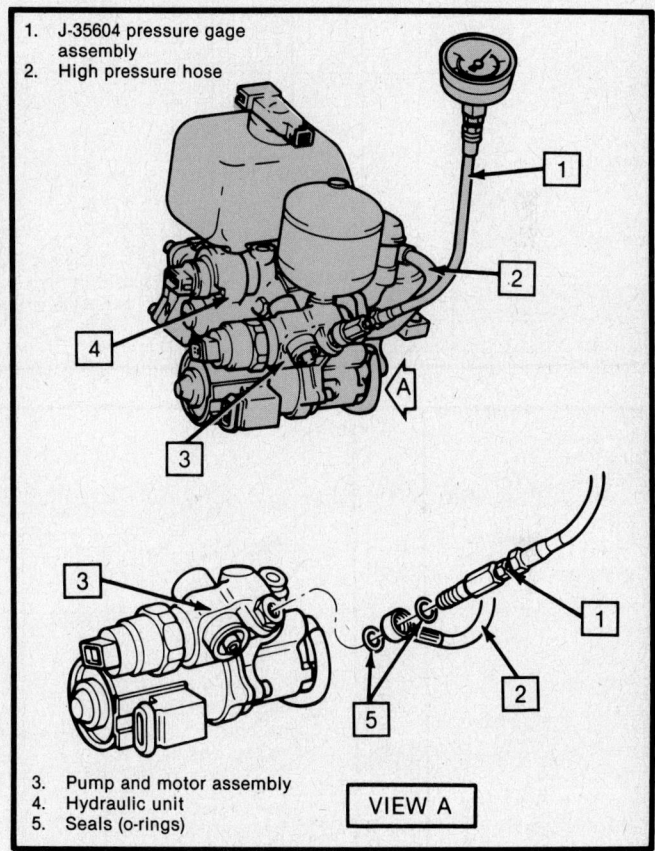

1. J-35604 pressure gage assembly
2. High pressure hose

3. Pump and motor assembly
4. Hydraulic unit
5. Seals (o-rings)

VIEW A

Installing the pressure gauge

the shaded areas in the horizontal rows below each vehicle status header. The right hand diagonal shading indicates illumination of the "ANTILOCK" light, while left hand diagonal shading indicates illumination of the "BRAKE" light. A vehicle status block which is not entirely shaded means that the light is on for only part of the test period.

LAMP SEQUENCE TEST PROCEDURE

The Lamp Sequence Test Procedure should be used to determine the correct light sequence to be used for futher diagnosis.

1. Determine the vehicle operators complaint as accurately as possible. If reduced braking ability is described, use caution in evaluating the vehicle.

ITEM	PRE-DIAGNOSIS INSPECTION — INSPECT FOR:	CORRECTIVE ACTION
BRAKE FLUID RESERVOIR, HYDRAULIC UNIT	— LOW FLUID LEVEL — EXTERNAL LEAKS	— FILL RESERVOIR — REPAIR LEAKS AS REQUIRED
PARKING BRAKE	FULL RELEASE	— RELEASE PARKING BRAKE — ADJUST CABLE OR VACUUM RELEASE VALVE IF REQUIRED
BATTERY	ADEQUATE CHARGE ("GREEN EYE")	— CHARGE OR REPLACE BATTERY AS REQUIRED — SERVICE CHARGING SYSTEM AS REQUIRED
FUSES • ELECTRONIC BRAKE FUSE — 5 AMP — LOCATED IN FUSE PANEL (FUSE #5)	BLOWN FUSE	— REPLACE FUSE AND VERIFY OPERATION
• MAIN RELAY FUSE — 30 AMP WITH RED WIRE — LOCATED IN FUSE HOLDER ON RELAY BRACKET	BLOWN FUSE	— REPLACE FUSE AND VERIFY OPERATION
• PUMP MOTOR FUSE — 30 AMP WITH YELLOW WIRE — LOCATED IN FUSE HOLDER ON RELAY BRACKET	BLOWN FUSE	— REPLACE FUSE AND VERIFY OPERATION
CONNECTORS • MAIN RELAY — CONNECTOR WITH 5 WIRES ATTACHED • PUMP MOTOR RELAY — CONNECTOR WITH 4 WIRES ATTACHED • PRESSURE SWITCH • PUMP MOTOR • MAIN VALVE • VALVE BLOCK • FLUID LEVEL SENSOR — 3-WIRE CONNECTOR • ELECTRONIC BRAKE — 2-WIRE CONNECTOR • ELECTRONIC BRAKE CONTROL MODULE (EBCM)	— PROPER ENGAGEMENT OF CONNECTOR — LOOSE WIRES IN CONNECTOR	— PROPERLY ENGAGE CONNECTORS — REPAIR LOOSE WIRES
GROUNDS • BODY GROUNDS — LOCATED ON STUD AT LEFT FENDER RAIL • HYDRAULIC UNIT GROUND — ON HYDRAULIC UNIT • ELECTRONIC BRAKE GROUND — ON GENERATOR BRACKET	— LOOSE CONNECTIONS — BROKEN EYELETS — CORROSION	— TIGHTEN — REPAIR WIRE OR EYELET — CLEAN CONTACT SURFACES

Pre-Diagnosis inspection chart

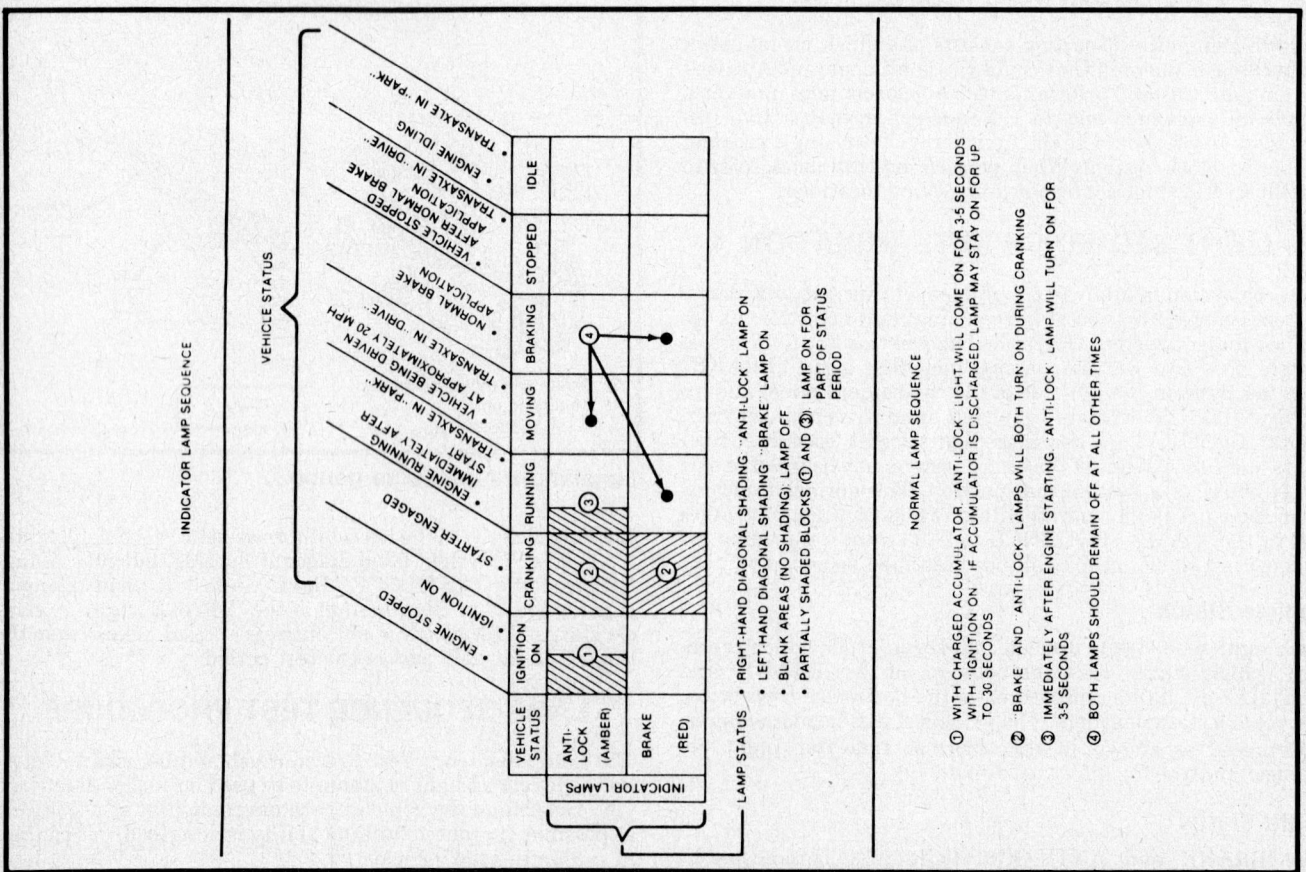

Normal indicator light sequence chart

INDICATOR LAMP SEQUENCE

LAMP STATUS •
- RIGHT-HAND DIAGONAL SHADING "ANTI-LOCK" LAMP ON
- LEFT-HAND DIAGONAL SHADING "BRAKE" LAMP ON
- BLANK AREAS (NO SHADING) LAMP OFF
- PARTIALLY SHADED BLOCKS ① AND ② LAMP ON FOR PART OF STATUS PERIOD

NORMAL LAMP SEQUENCE

① WITH CHARGED ACCUMULATOR, "ANTI-LOCK" LIGHT WILL COME ON FOR 3-5 SECONDS WITH IGNITION ON. IF ACCUMULATOR IS DISCHARGED, LAMP MAY STAY ON FOR UP TO 30 SECONDS

② "BRAKE" AND "ANTI-LOCK" LAMPS WILL BOTH TURN ON DURING CRANKING

③ IMMEDIATELY AFTER ENGINE STARTING, "ANTI-LOCK" LAMP WILL TURN ON FOR 3-5 SECONDS

④ BOTH LAMPS SHOULD REMAIN OFF AT ALL OTHER TIMES

LAMP SEQUENCE CHART

SEE LAMP SEQUENCE DETERMINATION PROCEDURE
IN THIS SECTION BEFORE USING THIS CHART

SEQUENCE NUMBER	LAMP SEQUENCE	SYMPTOM DESCRIPTION	PERFORM TEST
1	LAMPS / IGNITION ON / CRANKING / RUNNING / MOVING / BRAKING / STOPPED / IDLE — "ANTI-LOCK" / BRAKE	NORMAL LAMP SEQUENCE WITH — EXCESSIVE PEDAL TRAVEL OR SPONGY PEDAL — ANTI-LOCK BRAKING OPERATION OR VALVE CYCLING DURING NORMAL STOPS ON DRY PAVEMENT — POOR VEHICLE TRACKING DURING ANTI-LOCK BRAKING	H C D
2	LAMPS / IGNITION ON / ... "ANTI-LOCK" / BRAKE	CONTINUOUS "ANTI-LOCK" LAMP NORMAL "BRAKE" LAMP	A
3	LAMPS / IGNITION ON / ... "ANTI-LOCK" / BRAKE	"ANTI-LOCK" LAMP COMES ON AFTER VEHICLE STARTS MOVING NORMAL BRAKE LAMP	C
4	LAMPS / IGNITION ON / ... "ANTI-LOCK" / BRAKE	NO "ANTI-LOCK" LAMP WHILE CRANKING NORMAL "BRAKE" LAMP	E
5	LAMPS / IGNITION ON / ... "ANTI-LOCK" / BRAKE	NO "ANTI-LOCK" LAMP NORMAL "BRAKE" LAMP	F
6	LAMPS / IGNITION ON / ... "ANTI-LOCK" / BRAKE	INTERMITTANT "ANTI-LOCK" LAMP WHILE DRIVING NORMAL "BRAKE" LAMP	G
7	LAMPS / IGNITION ON / ... "ANTI-LOCK" / BRAKE	CONTINUOUS "ANTI-LOCK" LAMP CONTINUOUS "BRAKE" LAMP	B
8	LAMPS / IGNITION ON / ... "ANTI-LOCK" / BRAKE	"ANTI-LOCK" AND "BRAKE" LAMPS COME ON WHILE BRAKING	B
9	LAMPS / IGNITION ON / ... "ANTI-LOCK" / BRAKE	NORMAL "ANTI-LOCK" LAMP CONTINUOUS "BRAKE" LAMP	B
10	LAMPS / IGNITION ON / ... "ANTI-LOCK" / BRAKE	NORMAL OR CONTINUOUS "ANTI-LOCK" LAMP FLASHING "BRAKE" LAMP	B

Indicator Light Sequence Chart

2. Turn the ignition "OFF" for at least 15 seconds.

3. Turn the ignition "ON" and observe the "BRAKE" and "ANTILOCK" lights.

    a. If the accumulator has been discharged, both of the indicator lights may remain on for approximately 30 seconds. If this occurs, allow the lights to turn off and turn the ignition "OFF" for another 15 seconds.

    b. If the lights go out within 30 seconds, go to Step 5.

4. Turn the ignition "ON" and observe the warning lights. Now, the "BRAKE" light should remain off, and the "ANTILOCK" light should come on for 3–6 seconds and then go out.

5. Turn the ignition to the "START" position and observe the warning lights. While the ignition is in this position both of the warning lights should illuminate.

6. When the engine starts, release the key to the "RUN" position and observe the warning lights. The "BRAKE" light should turn off immediately and the "ANTILOCK" light should remain on for 3–6 seconds and then go off.

7. Drive the car at a maximum speed of 20 mph for a short

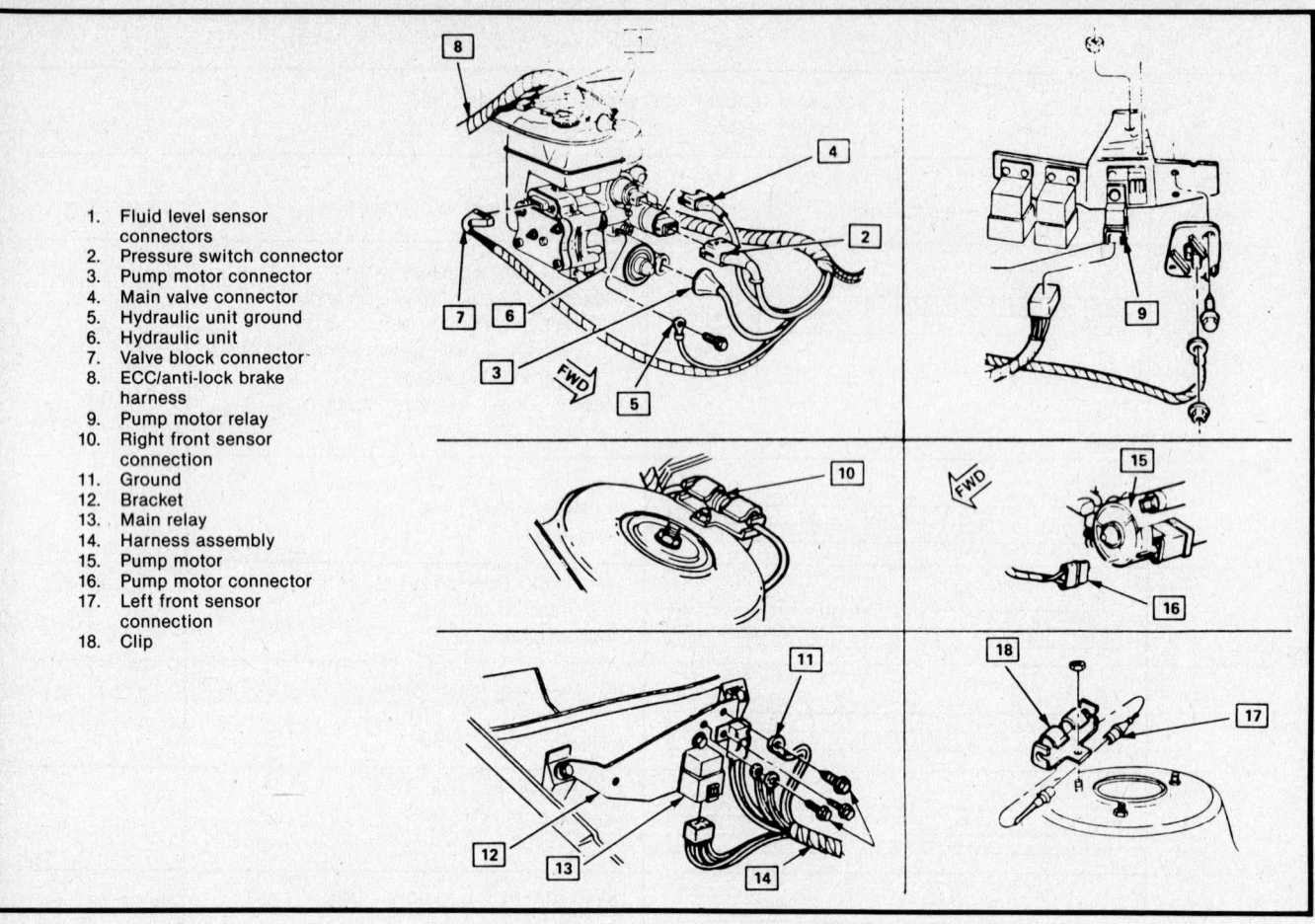

1. Fluid level sensor connectors
2. Pressure switch connector
3. Pump motor connector
4. Main valve connector
5. Hydraulic unit ground
6. Hydraulic unit
7. Valve block connector
8. ECC/anti-lock brake harness
9. Pump motor relay
10. Right front sensor connection
11. Ground
12. Bracket
13. Main relay
14. Harness assembly
15. Pump motor
16. Pump motor connector
17. Left front sensor connection
18. Clip

Connector locations—A-Body

period of time and observe the warning lights. Both of the lights should remain off for this step and for the remainder of the test. Note as accurately as possible the condition under which either light comes on.

8. Stop the car using normal brake pressure. Both lights should remain off.

9. Place the transaxle in "PARK" and allow the car to idle for a few seconds. Observe the warning lights. Both should remain off.

10. From the information obtained in this test above, determine the light sequence and/or symptom shown in the "Indicator Light Sequence Chart" which most closely matches the behavior of the complaint and perform the tests indicated.

INTERMITTENT PROBLEMS

The diagnostic procedures in this section may or may not be helpful in determining the cause of an intermittent problem in the Antilock Brake System electrical components. Most of the time, the fault must be present to locate the problem effectively using the Pin-Out checks and Trouble Shooting Charts.

A light sequence description from the driver of the vehicle may be helpful in locating the "probable" component or circuit in the case of an intermittent failure. Use the Lamp Sequence Chart, if a good description of the light behavior can be obtained.

Most intermittent problems are caused by faulty electrical connections or wiring. When an intermittent failure is encountered, check the suspected circuits for:

• Poor mating of the connector halves or terminals not fully seated in the connector body.

• Improperly formed or damaged terminals. All connector terminals in a problem circuit should be carefully reformed to increase the contact tension.

• Poor terminal to wire connection. This requires removing the terminal from the connector body to inspect it.

If a visual inspection does not find the cause of the problem, operate the car with the EBCM connected in an attempt to duplicate the condition and use the Lamp Sequence Chart to isolate the potential cause.

Circuits that could possibly cause intermittent operation of the "ANTILOCK" light include:

• EBCM switch loop circuit (low fluid/pressure sensors)—intermittent open.

• Main relay circuit—interuption in coil or switched battery power.

• Wheel speed sensor circuit—low or intermittent output.

• Ignition enable circuit—interuption of the 12 volt input.

WIRING SCHEMATIC AND CONNECTOR FACES

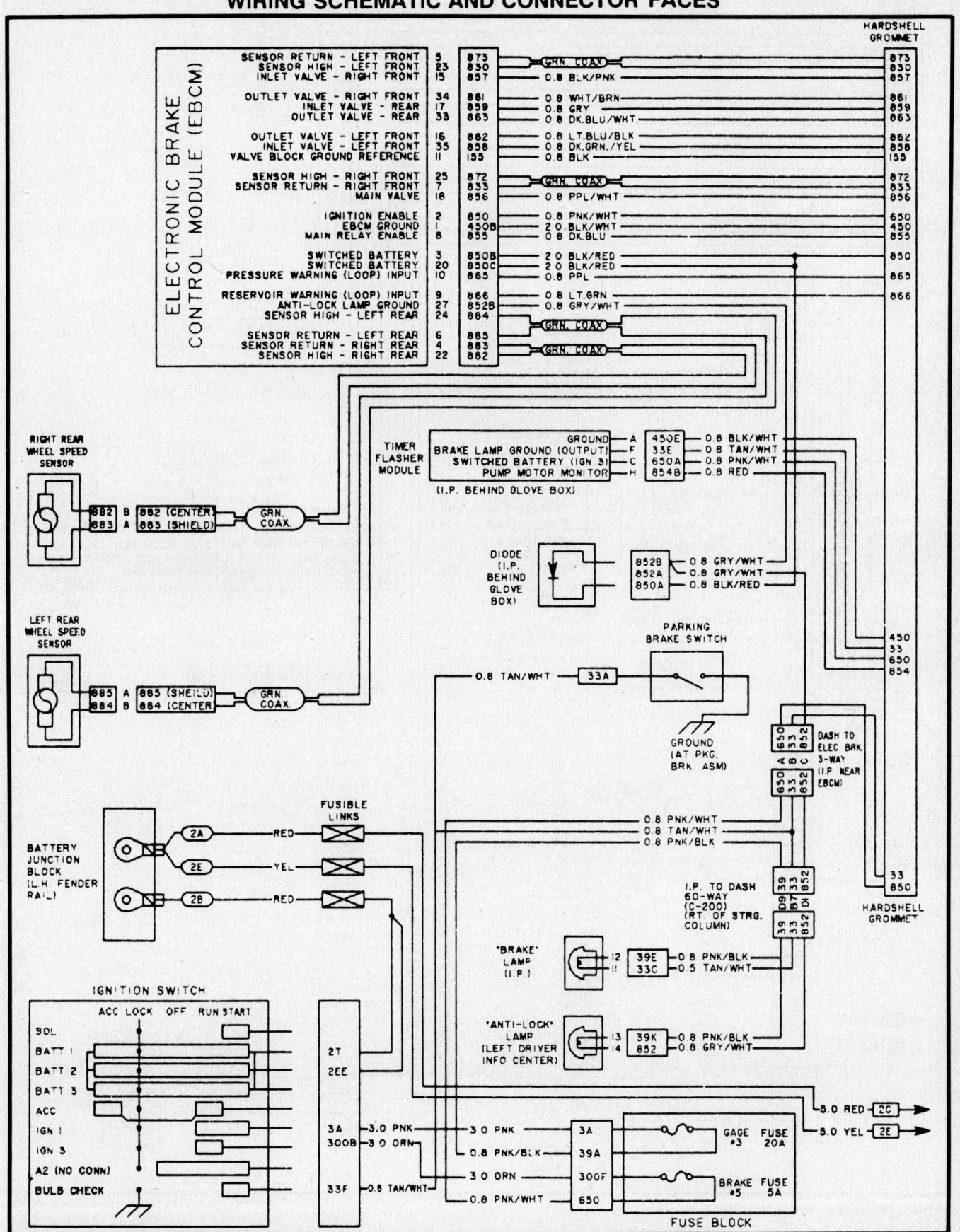

Antilock brake system wiring schematic

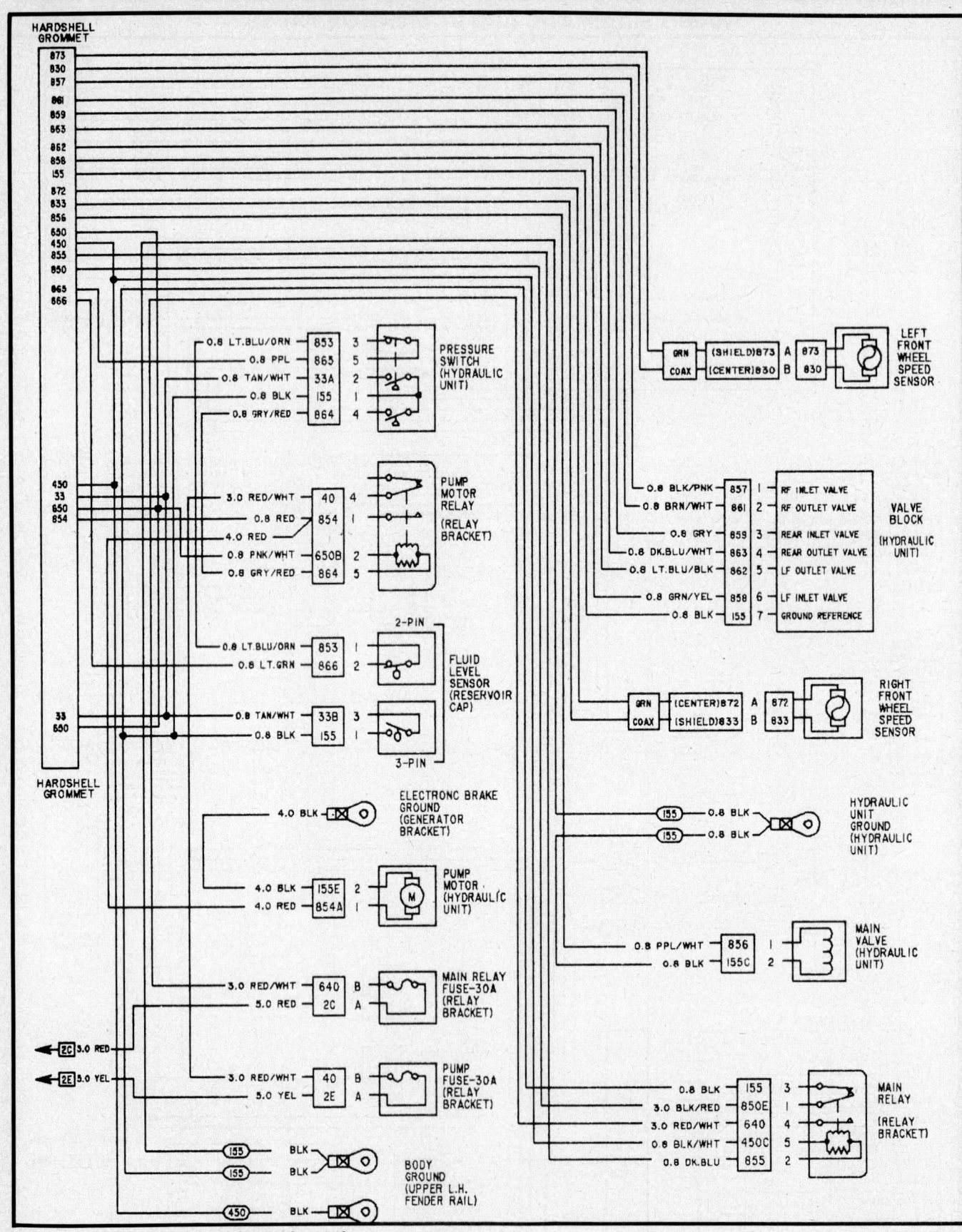

Antilock brake system wiring schematic

DIODE CONNECTOR

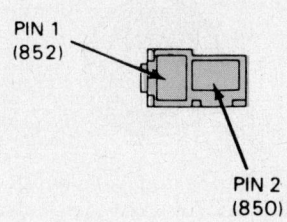

PIN 1
(852)

PIN 2
(850)

MAIN VALVE CONNECTOR

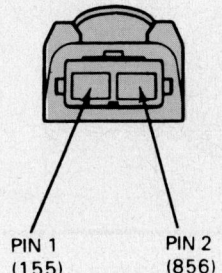

PIN 1
(155)

PIN 2
(856)

PUMP MOTOR CONNECTOR

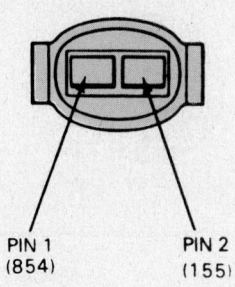

PIN 1
(854)

PIN 2
(155)

FLUID LEVEL SENSOR CONNECTOR (3 PIN)

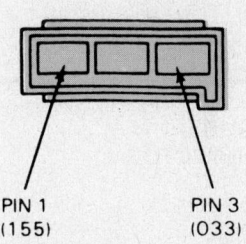

PIN 1
(155)

PIN 3
(033)

FLUID LEVEL SENSOR CONNECTOR (2 PIN)

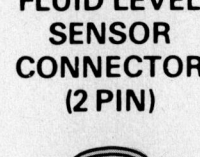
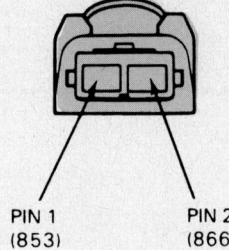

PIN 1
(853)

PIN 2
(866)

FLUID LEVEL SENSOR (2 PIN)

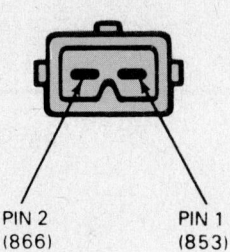

PIN 2
(866)

PIN 1
(853)

WHEEL SPEED SENSOR CONNECTORS

LEFT FRONT

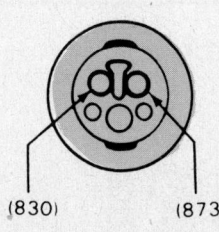

(830)   (873)

RIGHT FRONT

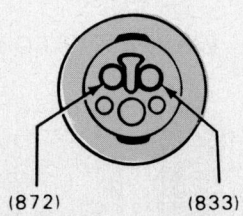

(872)   (833)

LEFT REAR

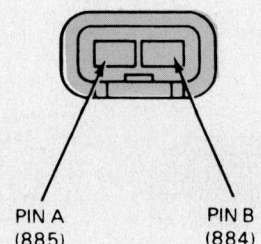

PIN A
(885)

PIN B
(884)

RIGHT REAR

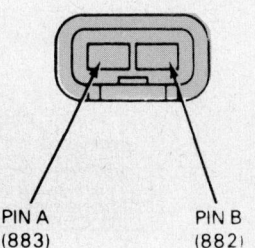

PIN A
(883)

PIN B
(882)

WHEEL SPEED SENSOR CONNECTORS

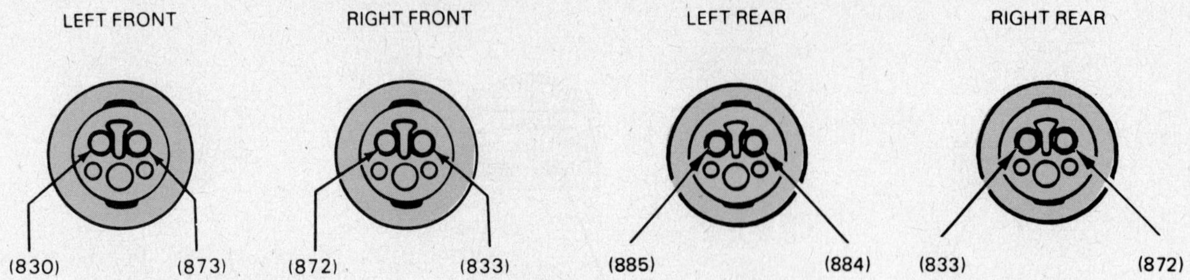

LEFT FRONT	RIGHT FRONT	LEFT REAR	RIGHT REAR
(830) (873)	(872) (833)	(885) (884)	(833) (872)

MAIN RELAY CONNECTOR

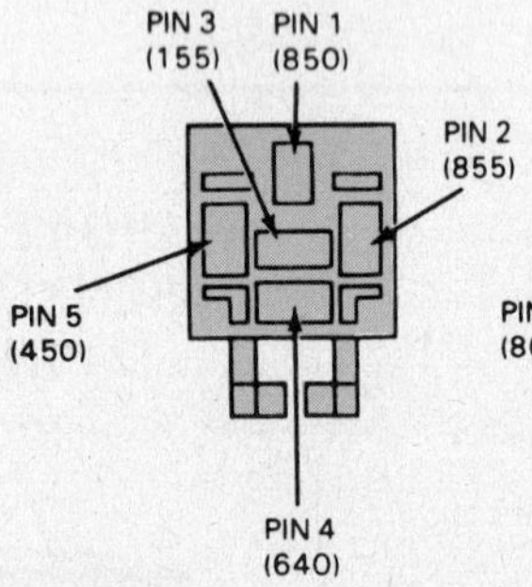

PIN 3 (155) PIN 1 (850)
PIN 2 (855)
PIN 5 (450)
PIN 4 (640)

PUMP RELAY CONNECTOR

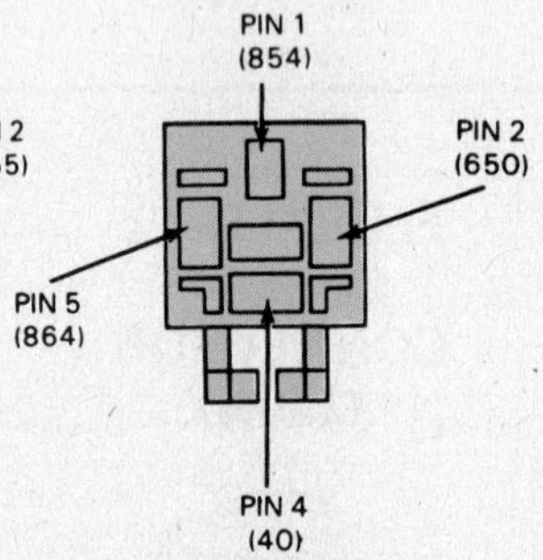

PIN 1 (854)
PIN 2 (650)
PIN 5 (864)
PIN 4 (40)

MAIN FUSE

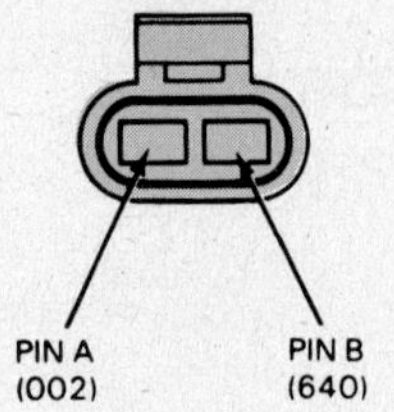

PIN A (002) PIN B (640)

PUMP FUSE

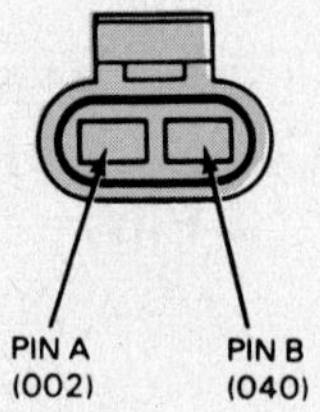

PIN A (002) PIN B (040)

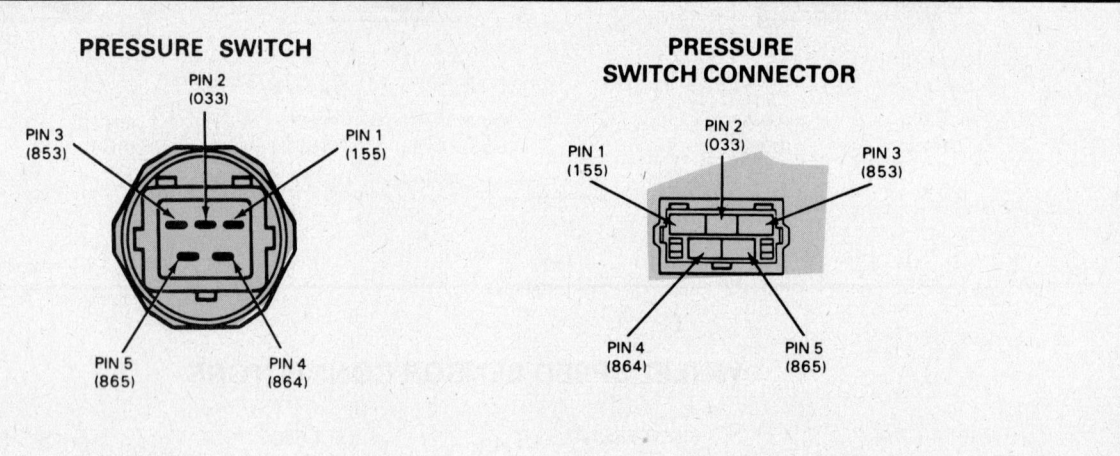

PRESSURE SWITCH

PIN 2 (033)
PIN 3 (853) PIN 1 (155)
PIN 5 (865) PIN 4 (864)

PRESSURE SWITCH CONNECTOR

PIN 1 (155) PIN 2 (033) PIN 3 (853)
PIN 4 (864) PIN 5 (865)

VALVE BLOCK

PIN 1 (857)
PIN 2 (861)
PIN 3 (859)
PIN 4 (863)
PIN 5 (862)
PIN 6 (858)
PIN 7 (155)

VALVE BLOCK CONNECTOR

PIN 1 (857)
PIN 2 (861)
PIN 3 (859)
PIN 4 (863)
PIN 5 (862)
PIN 6 (858)
PIN 7 (155)

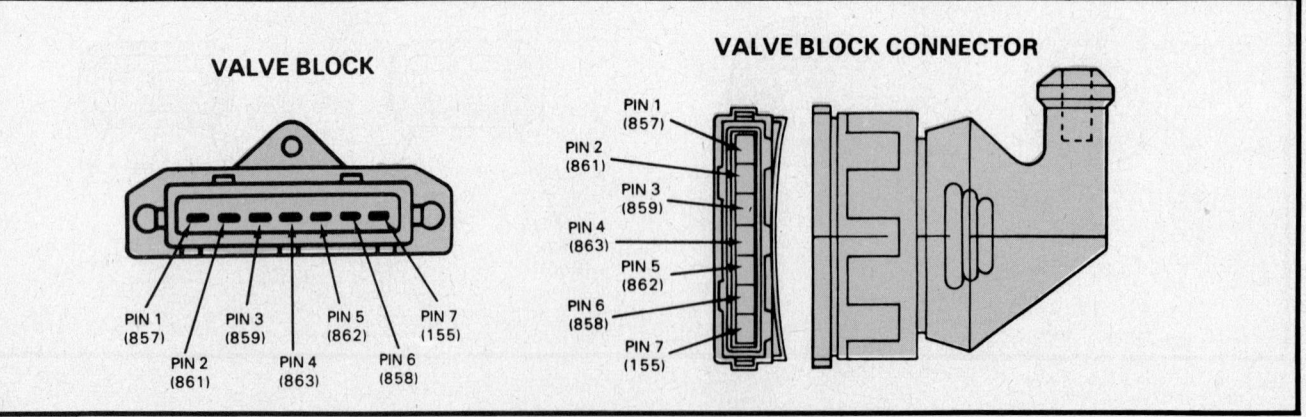

TIMER LOGIC MODULE CONNECTOR

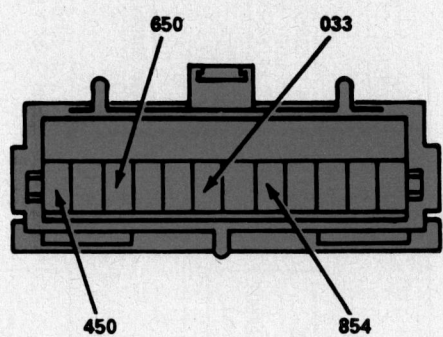

CIRCUIT NUMBER	WIRE COLOR	CIRCUIT DESCRIPTION
002	RED OR YELLOW	(+) SUPPLY, PUMP (YELLOW) MAIN (RED)
033	TAN-WHITE STRIPE	"BRAKE" INDICATOR GROUND CIRCUIT
040	RED-WHITE STRIPE	PUMP MOTOR RELAY SECONDARY SUPPLY CIRCUIT
155	BLACK	SYSTEM GROUND CIRCUIT
450	BLACK-WHITE STRIPE	SYSTEM GROUND CIRCUIT
640	RED-WHITE STRIPE	MAIN RELAY SECONDARY SUPPLY CIRCUIT
650	BROWN-WHITE STRIPE	IGNITION ENABLE TO EBCM & PUMP RELAY
850	BROWN SPLICED TO BLACK-RED STRIPE	EBCM SUPPLY CIRCUIT
852	GRAY-DOUBLE WHITE STRIPE	ANTILOCK INDICATOR TO EBCM GROUND WIRE
853	BLUE-LIGHT ORANGE STRIPE	FLUID LEVEL SENSOR TO PRESSURE SWITCH (CHECK LOOP)
854	RED SPLICED TO PINK-BLACK STRIPE	SUPPLY CIRCUIT TO PUMP MOTOR FROM PUMP RELAY
855	DARK BLUE	MAIN RELAY PRIMARY SUPPLY CIRCUIT
856	PURPLE-WHITE STRIPE	MAIN VALVE SUPPLY CIRCUIT
857	BLACK-PINK STRIPE	RIGHT FRONT INLET VALVE SUPPLY CIRCUIT
858	GREEN-YELLOW STRIPE	LEFT FRONT INLET VALVE SUPPLY CIRCUIT
859	GRAY	REAR INLET VALVE SUPPLY CIRCUIT
861	BROWN-WHITE STRIPE	RIGHT FRONT OUTLET VALVE SUPPLY CIRCUIT
862	LIGHT BLUE-BLACK STRIPE	LEFT FRONT OUTLET VALVE SUPPLY CIRCUIT
863	DARK BLUE-WHITE STRIPE	REAR OUTLET VALVE SUPPLY CIRCUIT
864	GRAY-RED STRIPE	PUMP MOTOR RELAY "PULL-IN" GROUND CIRCUIT
865	PURPLE	EBCM TO PRESSURE SWITCH (CHECK LOOP)
866	LIGHT GREEN	EBCM TO FLUID LEVEL SENSOR (CHECK LOOP)
901	RED-DOUBLE YELLOW STRIPE	EBCM TO EBCM CONNECT CIRCUIT
830	GREEN COAXIAL CABLE	LEFT FRONT SENSOR (+)
873	GREEN COAXIAL CABLE	LEFT FRONT SENSOR (–)
884	GREEN COAXIAL CABLE	LEFT REAR SENSOR (+)
885	GREEN COAXIAL CABLE	LEFT REAR SENSOR (–)
833	GREEN COAXIAL CABLE	RIGHT FRONT SENSOR (+)
872	GREEN COAXIAL CABLE	RIGHT FRONT SENSOR(–)
882	GREEN COAXIAL CABLE	RIGHT REAR SENSOR (+)
883	GREEN COAXIAL CABLE	RIGHT REAR SENSOR (–)

Connector face circuit number and description

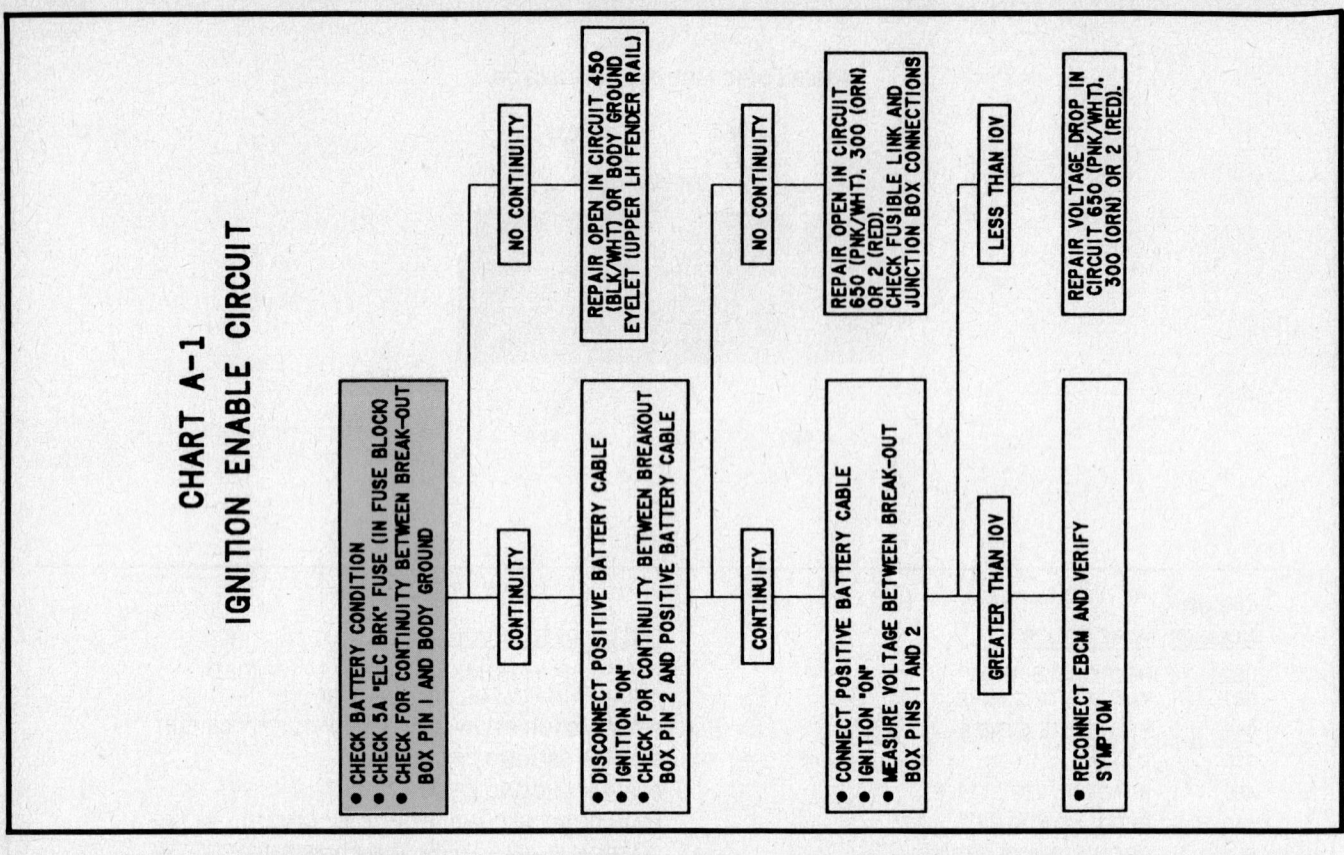

CHART A-1
IGNITION ENABLE CIRCUIT

TEST A
PIN-OUT CHECKS

- CONNECT BREAK-OUT BOX J-35592 to 35-PIN EBCM HARNESS CONNECTOR AS DESCRIBED IN THIS SECTION
- PERFORM CHECKS WITH HIGH IMPEDANCE DIGITAL MULTIMETER J-34029-A OR EQUIVALENT
- ALL CHECKS ARE MADE WITH ENGINE STOPPED

CIRCUIT TO BE TESTED	IGNITION SWITCH POSITION	MULTIMETER SCALE/RANGE	MEASURE BETWEEN PIN NUMBERS	SPECIFICATION	IF RESULT NOT WITHIN SPECIFICATION, SEE CHART
IGNITION ENABLE	RUN	20 DCV	2(+),1(−)	10 V MINIMUM	A-1
MAIN RELAY GROUND	OFF	200 Ω	1,3	CONTINUITY	A-2
MAIN RELAY COIL	OFF	200 Ω	1,20	CONTINUITY	A-3
	OFF	200 Ω	1,8	45-105 Ω	
BEFORE PERFORMING THIS TEST: REMOVE GAGE FUSE (FUSE #3) FROM FUSE PANEL. PLACE FUSED JUMPER BETWEEN BREAK-OUT BOX PINS 2 & 8					
MAIN RELAY POWER	ON	20 DCV	3(+),1(−)	10 V MINIMUM	A-4
	ON	20 DCV	20(+),1(−)	10 V MINIMUM	
BEFORE PROCEEDING: REMOVE JUMPER FROM PINS 2 & 8. INSTALL GAGE FUSE					
EBCM SWITCH LOOP	OFF	200 Ω	9,10	LESS THAN 5 Ω	A-5
	OFF	200 Ω	1,9	NO CONTINUITY	A-6
RR SENSOR RESISTANCE	OFF	2k Ω	4,22	800-1400 Ω	A-7
LF SENSOR RESISTANCE	OFF	2k Ω	5,23	800-1400 Ω	A-8
LR SENSOR RESISTANCE	OFF	2k Ω	6,24	800-1400 Ω	A-9
RF SENSOR RESISTANCE	OFF	2k Ω	7,25	800-1400 Ω	A-10
MAIN VALVE SOLENOID	OFF	200 Ω	11,18	2-5 Ω	A-11
VALVE BLOCK GROUND	OFF	200 Ω	1,11	LESS THAN 2 Ω	A-12
RF INLET VALVE	OFF	200 Ω	11,15	5-7 Ω	A-13
LF INLET VALVE	OFF	200 Ω	11,35	5-7 Ω	A-14
REAR INLET VALVE	OFF	200 Ω	11,17	5-7 Ω	A-15
RF OUTLET VALVE	OFF	200 Ω	11,34	3-5 Ω	A-16
LF OUTLET VALVE	OFF	200 Ω	11,16	3-5 Ω	A-17
REAR OUTLET VALVE	OFF	200 Ω	11,33	3-5 Ω	A-18
DIODE	OFF	DIODE ⊿	27(+),3(−)	CONTINUITY	A-19
	OFF	DIODE ⊿	3(+),27(−)	NO CONTINUITY	

* (+) OR (−) INDICATES MULTI-METER POLARITY

IF ALL TEST RESULTS ARE WITHIN SPECIFICATION, RECONNECT EBCM AND VERIFY CONTINUOUS "ANTI-LOCK" LAMP OPERATION

- IF NORMAL OPERATION RESUMES, SEE NOTE ON INTERMITTANTS
- IF LAMP REMAINS ON, SEE CHART A-20

Test "A" — Pin-out checks

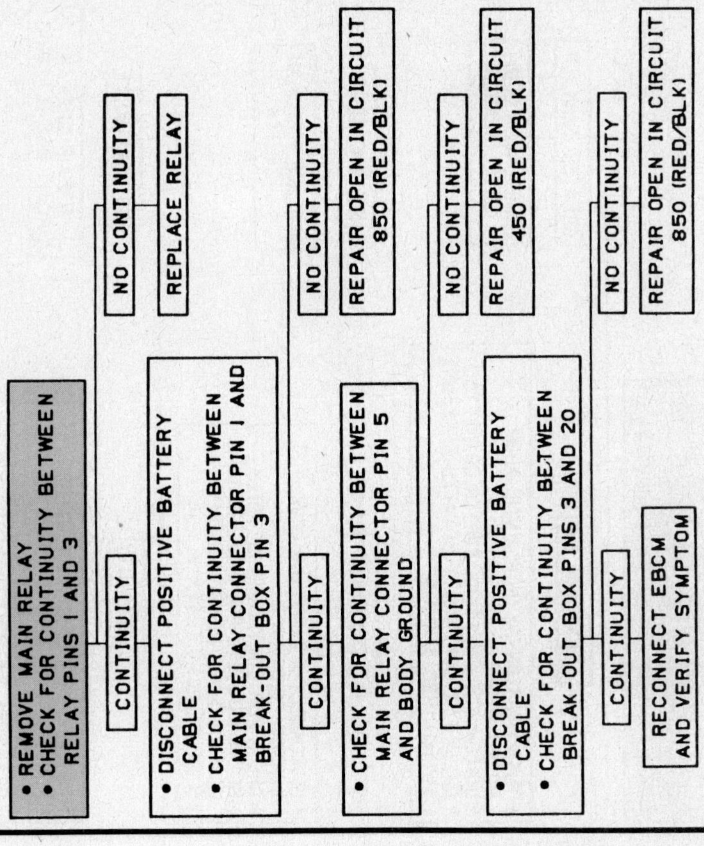

CHART A-3
MAIN RELAY COIL CIRCUIT

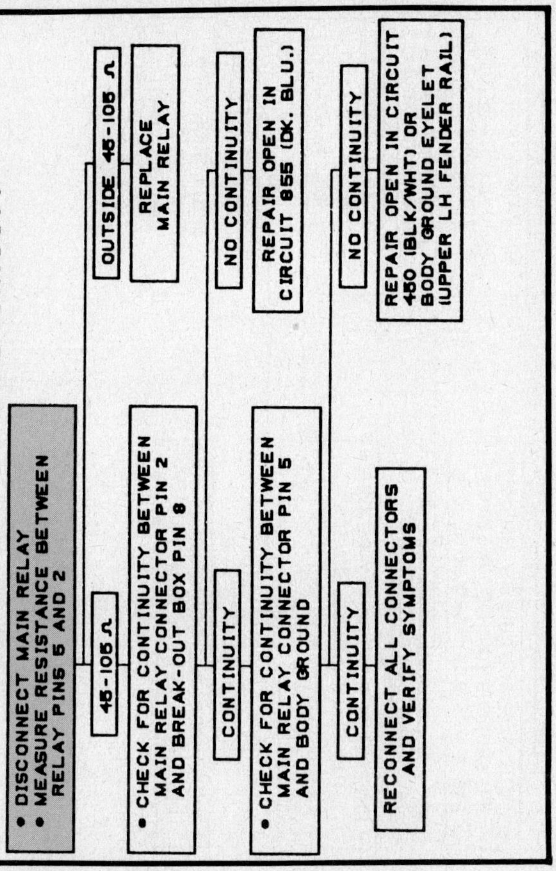

- DISCONNECT MAIN RELAY
- MEASURE RESISTANCE BETWEEN RELAY PINS 5 AND 2

45-105 Ω
- CHECK FOR CONTINUITY BETWEEN MAIN RELAY CONNECTOR PIN 2 AND BREAK-OUT BOX PIN 8

OUTSIDE 45-105 Ω
→ REPLACE MAIN RELAY

CONTINUITY
- CHECK FOR CONTINUITY BETWEEN MAIN RELAY CONNECTOR PIN 5 AND BODY GROUND

NO CONTINUITY
→ REPAIR OPEN IN CIRCUIT 855 (DK. BLU.)

CONTINUITY
- RECONNECT ALL CONNECTORS AND VERIFY SYMPTOMS

NO CONTINUITY
→ REPAIR OPEN IN CIRCUIT 450 (BLK/WHT) OR BODY GROUND EYELET (UPPER LH FENDER RAIL)

CHART A-4
MAIN RELAY POWER CIRCUIT

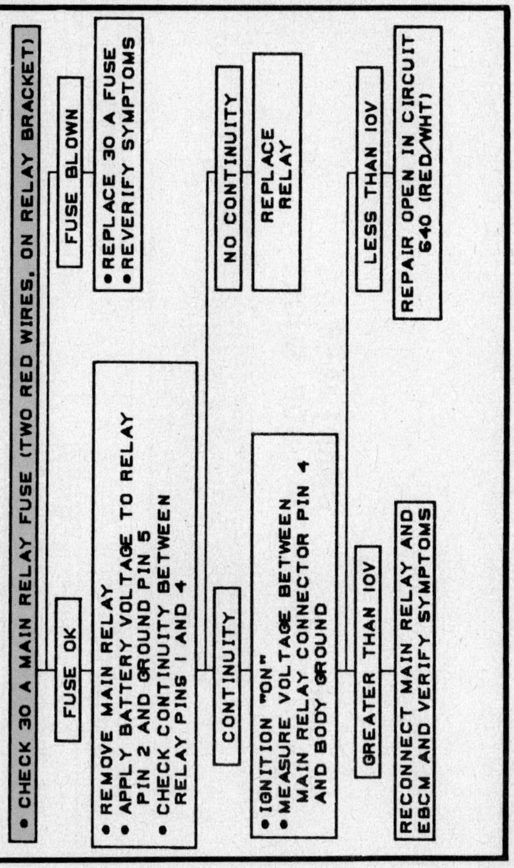

- CHECK 30 A MAIN RELAY FUSE (TWO RED WIRES, ON RELAY BRACKET)

FUSE OK
- REMOVE MAIN RELAY
- APPLY BATTERY VOLTAGE TO RELAY PIN 2 AND GROUND PIN 5
- CHECK CONTINUITY BETWEEN RELAY PINS 1 AND 4

FUSE BLOWN
- REPLACE 30 A FUSE
- REVERIFY SYMPTOMS

CONTINUITY
- IGNITION "ON"
- MEASURE VOLTAGE BETWEEN MAIN RELAY CONNECTOR PIN 4 AND BODY GROUND

NO CONTINUITY
→ REPLACE RELAY

GREATER THAN 10V
→ RECONNECT MAIN RELAY AND EBCM AND VERIFY SYMPTOMS

LESS THAN 10V
→ REPAIR OPEN IN CIRCUIT 640 (RED/WHT)

CHART A-2
MAIN RELAY GROUND CIRCUIT

- REMOVE MAIN RELAY
- CHECK FOR CONTINUITY BETWEEN RELAY PINS 1 AND 3

CONTINUITY
- DISCONNECT POSITIVE BATTERY CABLE
- CHECK FOR CONTINUITY BETWEEN MAIN RELAY CONNECTOR PIN 1 AND BREAK-OUT BOX PIN 3

NO CONTINUITY
→ REPLACE RELAY

CONTINUITY
- CHECK FOR CONTINUITY BETWEEN MAIN RELAY CONNECTOR PIN 5 AND BODY GROUND

NO CONTINUITY
→ REPAIR OPEN IN CIRCUIT 850 (RED/BLK)

CONTINUITY
- DISCONNECT POSITIVE BATTERY CABLE
- CHECK FOR CONTINUITY BETWEEN BREAK-OUT BOX PINS 3 AND 20

NO CONTINUITY
→ REPAIR OPEN IN CIRCUIT 450 (RED/BLK)

CONTINUITY
- RECONNECT EBCM AND VERIFY SYMPTOM

NO CONTINUITY
→ REPAIR OPEN IN CIRCUIT 850 (RED/BLK)

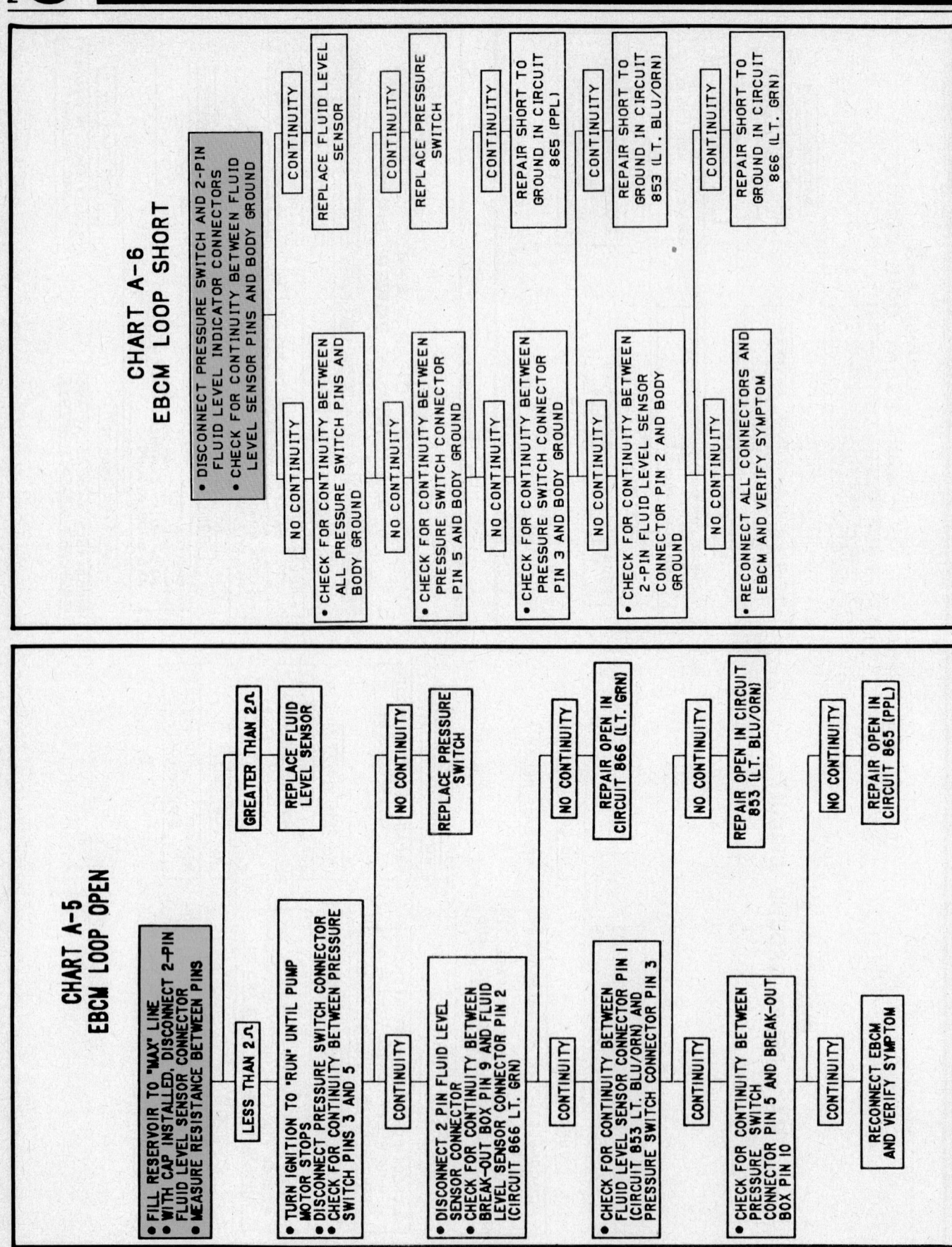

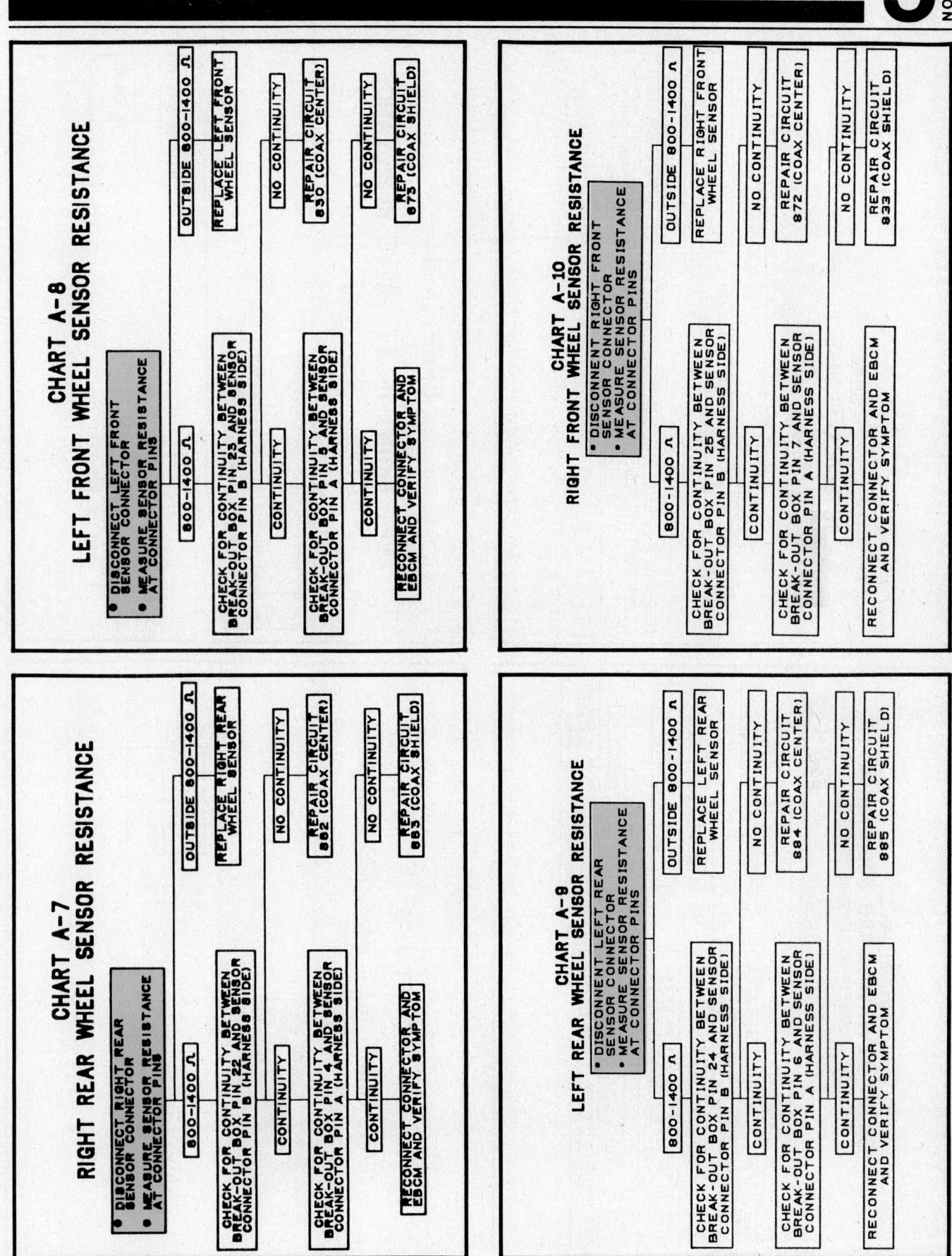

CHART A-8
LEFT FRONT WHEEL SENSOR RESISTANCE

- DISCONNECT LEFT FRONT SENSOR CONNECTOR
- MEASURE SENSOR RESISTANCE AT CONNECTOR PINS

OUTSIDE 800-1400 Ω → REPLACE LEFT FRONT WHEEL SENSOR

800-1400 Ω

CHECK FOR CONTINUITY BETWEEN BREAK-OUT BOX PIN 23 AND SENSOR CONNECTOR PIN B (HARNESS SIDE)
- NO CONTINUITY → REPAIR CIRCUIT 830 (COAX CENTER)
- CONTINUITY

CHECK FOR CONTINUITY BETWEEN BREAK-OUT BOX PIN 5 AND SENSOR CONNECTOR PIN A (HARNESS SIDE)
- NO CONTINUITY → REPAIR CIRCUIT 673 (COAX SHIELD)
- CONTINUITY

RECONNECT CONNECTOR AND EBCM AND VERIFY SYMPTOM

CHART A-10
RIGHT FRONT WHEEL SENSOR RESISTANCE

- DISCONNECT RIGHT FRONT SENSOR CONNECTOR
- MEASURE SENSOR RESISTANCE AT CONNECTOR PINS

OUTSIDE 800-1400 Ω → REPLACE RIGHT FRONT WHEEL SENSOR

800-1400 Ω

CHECK FOR CONTINUITY BETWEEN BREAK-OUT BOX PIN 25 AND SENSOR CONNECTOR PIN B (HARNESS SIDE)
- NO CONTINUITY → REPAIR CIRCUIT 872 (COAX CENTER)
- CONTINUITY

CHECK FOR CONTINUITY BETWEEN BREAK-OUT BOX PIN 7 AND SENSOR CONNECTOR PIN A (HARNESS SIDE)
- NO CONTINUITY → REPAIR CIRCUIT 833 (COAX SHIELD)
- CONTINUITY

RECONNECT CONNECTOR AND EBCM AND VERIFY SYMPTOM

CHART A-7
RIGHT REAR WHEEL SENSOR RESISTANCE

- DISCONNECT RIGHT REAR SENSOR CONNECTOR
- MEASURE SENSOR RESISTANCE AT CONNECTOR PINS

OUTSIDE 800-1400 Ω → REPLACE RIGHT REAR WHEEL SENSOR

800-1400 Ω

CHECK FOR CONTINUITY BETWEEN BREAK-OUT BOX PIN 22 AND SENSOR CONNECTOR PIN B (HARNESS SIDE)
- NO CONTINUITY → REPAIR CIRCUIT 882 (COAX CENTER)
- CONTINUITY

CHECK FOR CONTINUITY BETWEEN BREAK-OUT BOX PIN 4 AND SENSOR CONNECTOR PIN A (HARNESS SIDE)
- NO CONTINUITY → REPAIR CIRCUIT 883 (COAX SHIELD)
- CONTINUITY

RECONNECT CONNECTOR AND EBCM AND VERIFY SYMPTOM

CHART A-8
LEFT REAR WHEEL SENSOR RESISTANCE

- DISCONNECT LEFT REAR SENSOR CONNECTOR
- MEASURE SENSOR RESISTANCE AT CONNECTOR PINS

OUTSIDE 800-1400 Ω → REPLACE LEFT REAR WHEEL SENSOR

800-1400 Ω

CHECK FOR CONTINUITY BETWEEN BREAK-OUT BOX PIN 24 AND SENSOR CONNECTOR PIN B (HARNESS SIDE)
- NO CONTINUITY → REPAIR CIRCUIT 884 (COAX CENTER)
- CONTINUITY

CHECK FOR CONTINUITY BETWEEN BREAK-OUT BOX PIN 6 AND SENSOR CONNECTOR PIN A (HARNESS SIDE)
- NO CONTINUITY → REPAIR CIRCUIT 885 (COAX SHIELD)
- CONTINUITY

RECONNECT CONNECTOR AND EBCM AND VERIFY SYMPTOM

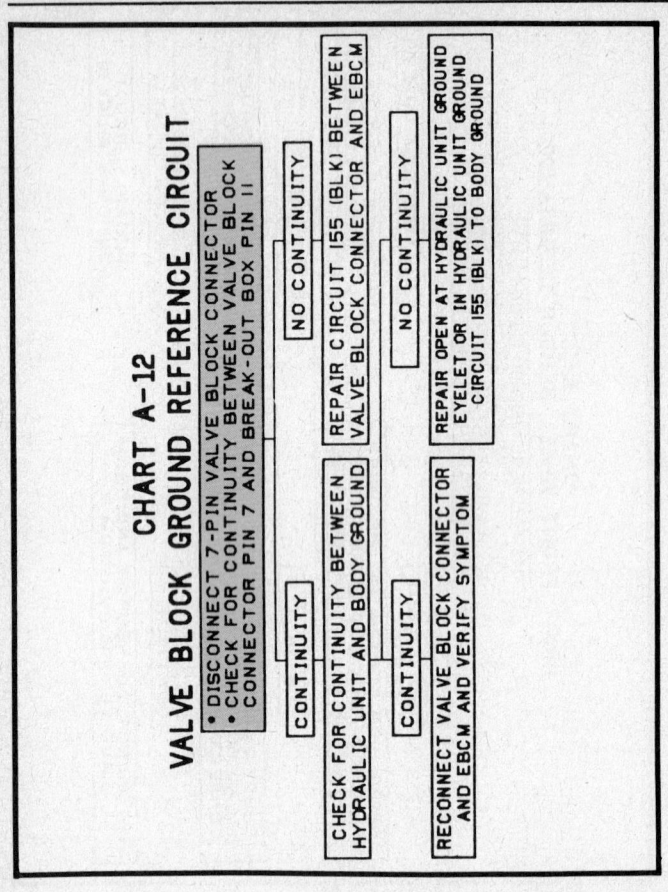

CHART A-12
VALVE BLOCK GROUND REFERENCE CIRCUIT

- DISCONNECT 7-PIN VALVE BLOCK CONNECTOR
- CHECK FOR CONTINUITY BETWEEN VALVE BLOCK CONNECTOR PIN 7 AND BREAK-OUT BOX PIN 11

CHECK FOR CONTINUITY BETWEEN HYDRAULIC UNIT AND BODY GROUND

- CONTINUITY / NO CONTINUITY

NO CONTINUITY → REPAIR CIRCUIT 155 (BLK) BETWEEN VALVE BLOCK CONNECTOR AND EBCM

CONTINUITY → RECONNECT VALVE BLOCK CONNECTOR AND EBCM AND VERIFY SYMPTOM

NO CONTINUITY → REPAIR OPEN AT HYDRAULIC UNIT GROUND EYELET OR IN HYDRAULIC UNIT GROUND CIRCUIT 155 (BLK) TO BODY GROUND

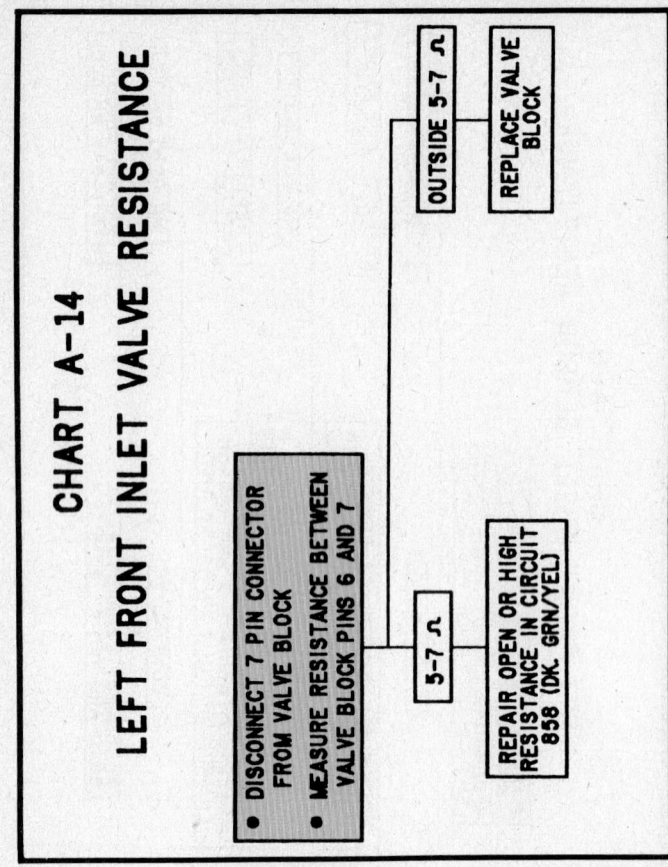

CHART A-14
LEFT FRONT INLET VALVE RESISTANCE

- DISCONNECT 7 PIN CONNECTOR FROM VALVE BLOCK
- MEASURE RESISTANCE BETWEEN VALVE BLOCK PINS 6 AND 7

5-7 Ω

OUTSIDE 5-7 Ω → REPLACE VALVE BLOCK

REPAIR OPEN OR HIGH RESISTANCE IN CIRCUIT 858 (DK. GRN/YEL)

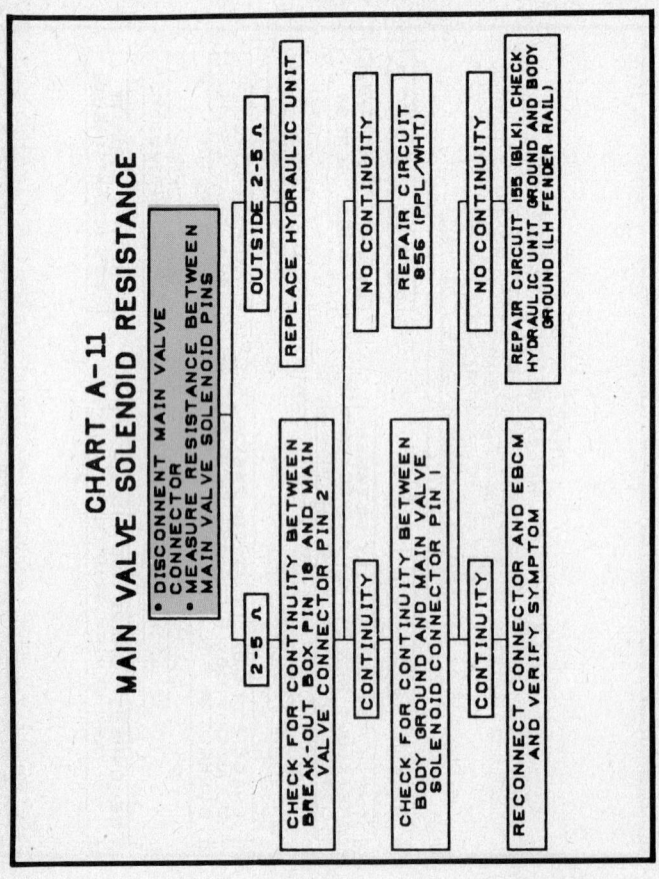

CHART A-11
MAIN VALVE SOLENOID RESISTANCE

- DISCONNECT MAIN VALVE CONNECTOR
- MEASURE RESISTANCE BETWEEN MAIN VALVE SOLENOID PINS

2-5 Ω

OUTSIDE 2-5 Ω → REPLACE HYDRAULIC UNIT

CHECK FOR CONTINUITY BETWEEN BREAK-OUT BOX PIN 18 AND MAIN VALVE CONNECTOR PIN 2

CONTINUITY / NO CONTINUITY

NO CONTINUITY → REPAIR CIRCUIT 856 (PPL/WHT)

CHECK FOR CONTINUITY BETWEEN BODY GROUND AND MAIN VALVE SOLENOID CONNECTOR PIN 1

CONTINUITY / NO CONTINUITY

NO CONTINUITY → REPAIR CIRCUIT 155 (BLK). CHECK HYDRAULIC UNIT GROUND AND BODY GROUND (LH FENDER RAIL)

CONTINUITY → RECONNECT CONNECTOR AND EBCM AND VERIFY SYMPTOM

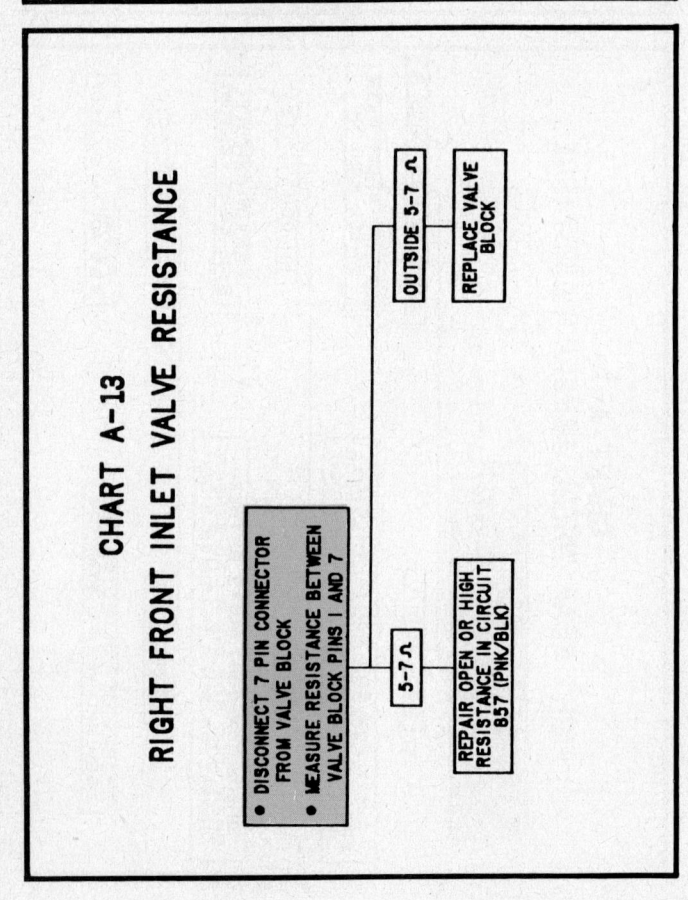

CHART A-13
RIGHT FRONT INLET VALVE RESISTANCE

- DISCONNECT 7 PIN CONNECTOR FROM VALVE BLOCK
- MEASURE RESISTANCE BETWEEN VALVE BLOCK PINS 1 AND 7

5-7 Ω

OUTSIDE 5-7 Ω → REPLACE VALVE BLOCK

REPAIR OPEN OR HIGH RESISTANCE IN CIRCUIT 857 (PNK/BLK)

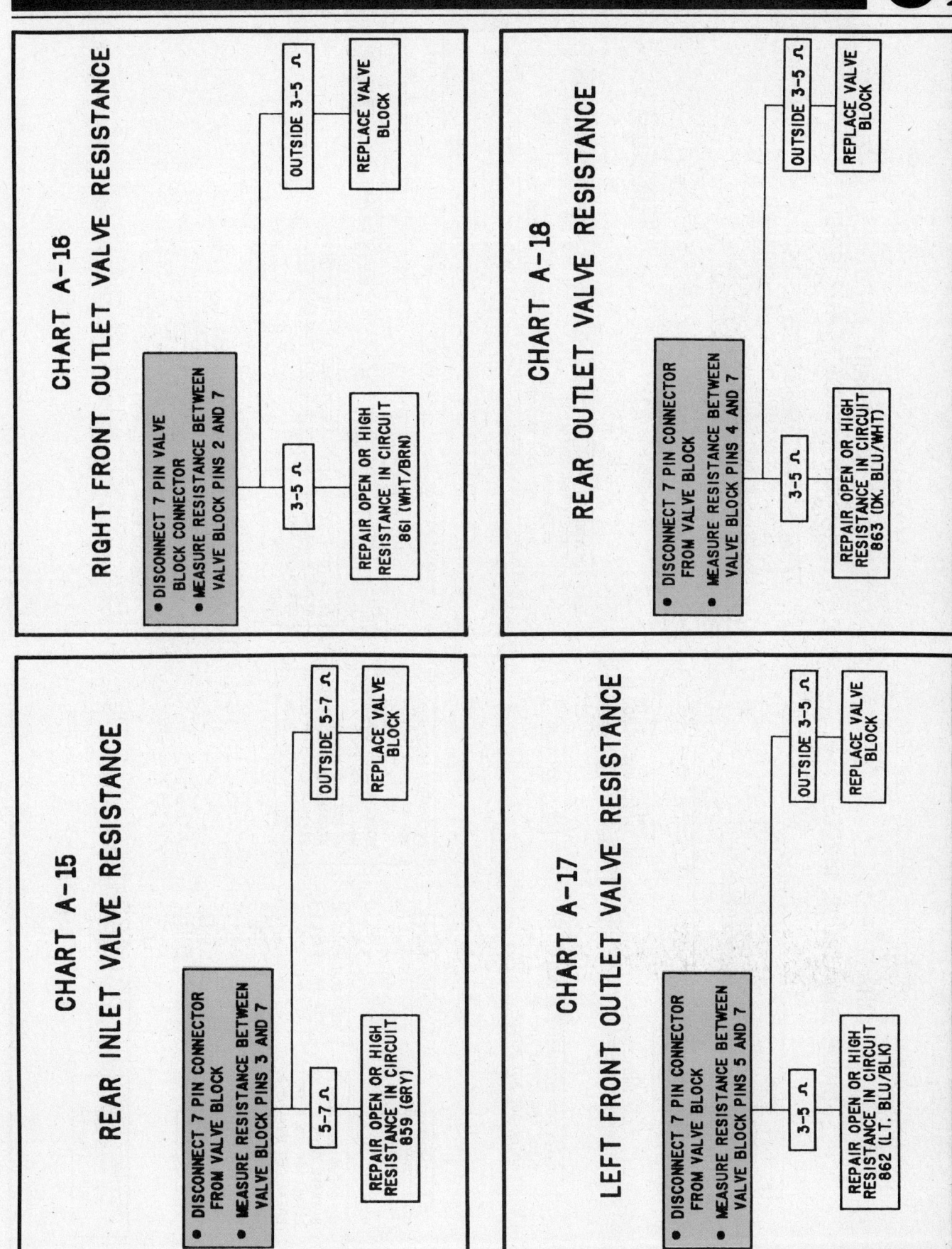

CHART A-16
RIGHT FRONT OUTLET VALVE RESISTANCE

- DISCONNECT 7 PIN VALVE BLOCK CONNECTOR
- MEASURE RESISTANCE BETWEEN VALVE BLOCK PINS 2 AND 7

3-5 Ω → REPAIR OPEN OR HIGH RESISTANCE IN CIRCUIT 861 (WHT/BRN)

OUTSIDE 3-5 Ω → REPLACE VALVE BLOCK

CHART A-18
REAR OUTLET VALVE RESISTANCE

- DISCONNECT 7 PIN CONNECTOR FROM VALVE BLOCK
- MEASURE RESISTANCE BETWEEN VALVE BLOCK PINS 4 AND 7

3-5 Ω → REPAIR OPEN OR HIGH RESISTANCE IN CIRCUIT 863 (DK. BLU/WHT)

OUTSIDE 3-5 Ω → REPLACE VALVE BLOCK

CHART A-15
REAR INLET VALVE RESISTANCE

- DISCONNECT 7 PIN CONNECTOR FROM VALVE BLOCK
- MEASURE RESISTANCE BETWEEN VALVE BLOCK PINS 3 AND 7

5-7 Ω → REPAIR OPEN OR HIGH RESISTANCE IN CIRCUIT 859 (GRY)

OUTSIDE 5-7 Ω → REPLACE VALVE BLOCK

CHART A-17
LEFT FRONT OUTLET VALVE RESISTANCE

- DISCONNECT 7 PIN CONNECTOR FROM VALVE BLOCK
- MEASURE RESISTANCE BETWEEN VALVE BLOCK PINS 5 AND 7

3-5 Ω → REPAIR OPEN OR HIGH RESISTANCE IN CIRCUIT 862 (LT. BLU/BLK)

OUTSIDE 3-5 Ω → REPLACE VALVE BLOCK

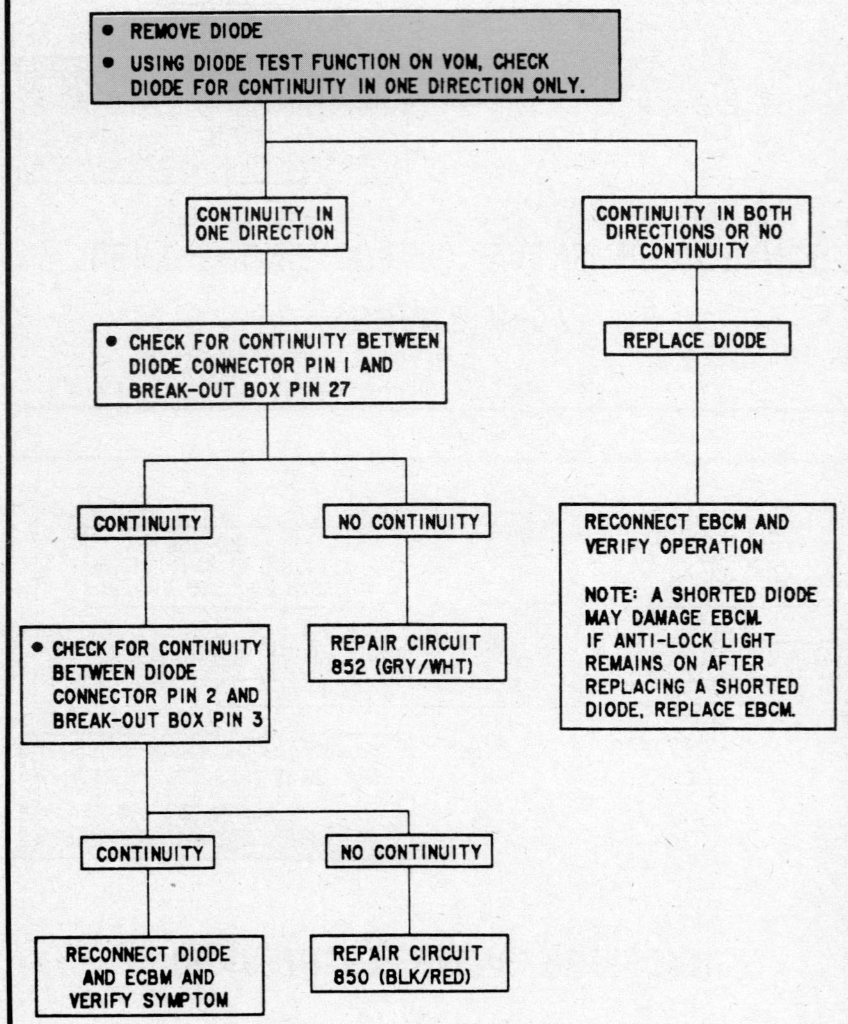

CHART A-20 "ANTI-LOCK" LAMP CIRCUIT

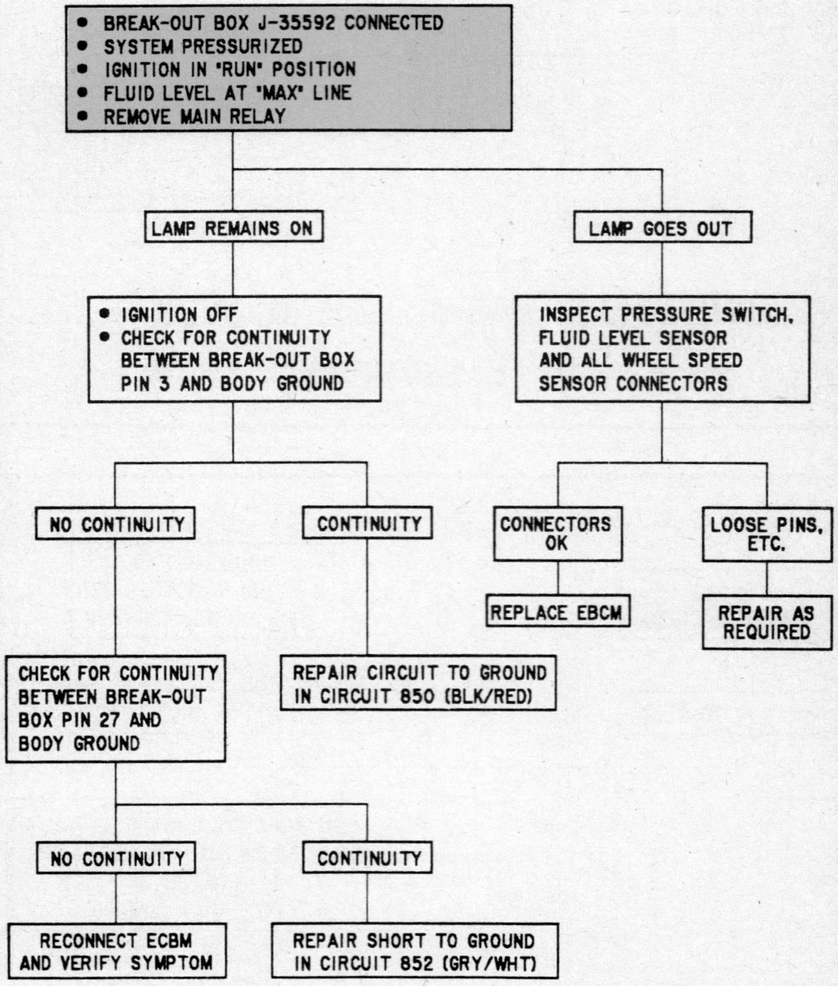

- BREAK-OUT BOX J-35592 CONNECTED
- SYSTEM PRESSURIZED
- IGNITION IN "RUN" POSITION
- FLUID LEVEL AT "MAX" LINE
- REMOVE MAIN RELAY

LAMP GOES OUT → INSPECT PRESSURE SWITCH, FLUID LEVEL SENSOR AND ALL WHEEL SPEED SENSOR CONNECTORS
- LOOSE PINS, ETC. → REPAIR AS REQUIRED
- CONNECTORS OK → REPLACE EBCM

LAMP REMAINS ON → IGNITION OFF; CHECK FOR CONTINUITY BETWEEN BREAK-OUT BOX PIN 3 AND BODY GROUND
- CONTINUITY → REPAIR CIRCUIT TO GROUND IN CIRCUIT 850 (BLK/RED)
- NO CONTINUITY → CHECK FOR CONTINUITY BETWEEN BREAK-OUT BOX PIN 27 AND BODY GROUND
  - CONTINUITY → REPAIR SHORT TO GROUND IN CIRCUIT 852 (GRY/WHT)
  - NO CONTINUITY → RECONNECT ECBM AND VERIFY SYMPTOM

CHART A-19 DIODE AND DIODE CIRCUIT

- REMOVE DIODE
- USING DIODE TEST FUNCTION ON VOM, CHECK DIODE FOR CONTINUITY IN ONE DIRECTION ONLY.

CONTINUITY IN BOTH DIRECTIONS OR NO CONTINUITY → REPLACE DIODE → RECONNECT EBCM AND VERIFY OPERATION

NOTE: A SHORTED DIODE MAY DAMAGE EBCM. IF ANTI-LOCK LIGHT REMAINS ON AFTER REPLACING A SHORTED DIODE, REPLACE EBCM.

CONTINUITY IN ONE DIRECTION → CHECK FOR CONTINUITY BETWEEN DIODE CONNECTOR PIN I AND BREAK-OUT BOX PIN 27
- NO CONTINUITY → REPAIR CIRCUIT 852 (GRY/WHT)
- CONTINUITY → CHECK FOR CONTINUITY BETWEEN DIODE CONNECTOR PIN 2 AND BREAK-OUT BOX PIN 3
  - NO CONTINUITY → REPAIR CIRCUIT 850 (BLK/RED)
  - CONTINUITY → RECONNECT DIODE AND ECBM AND VERIFY SYMPTOM

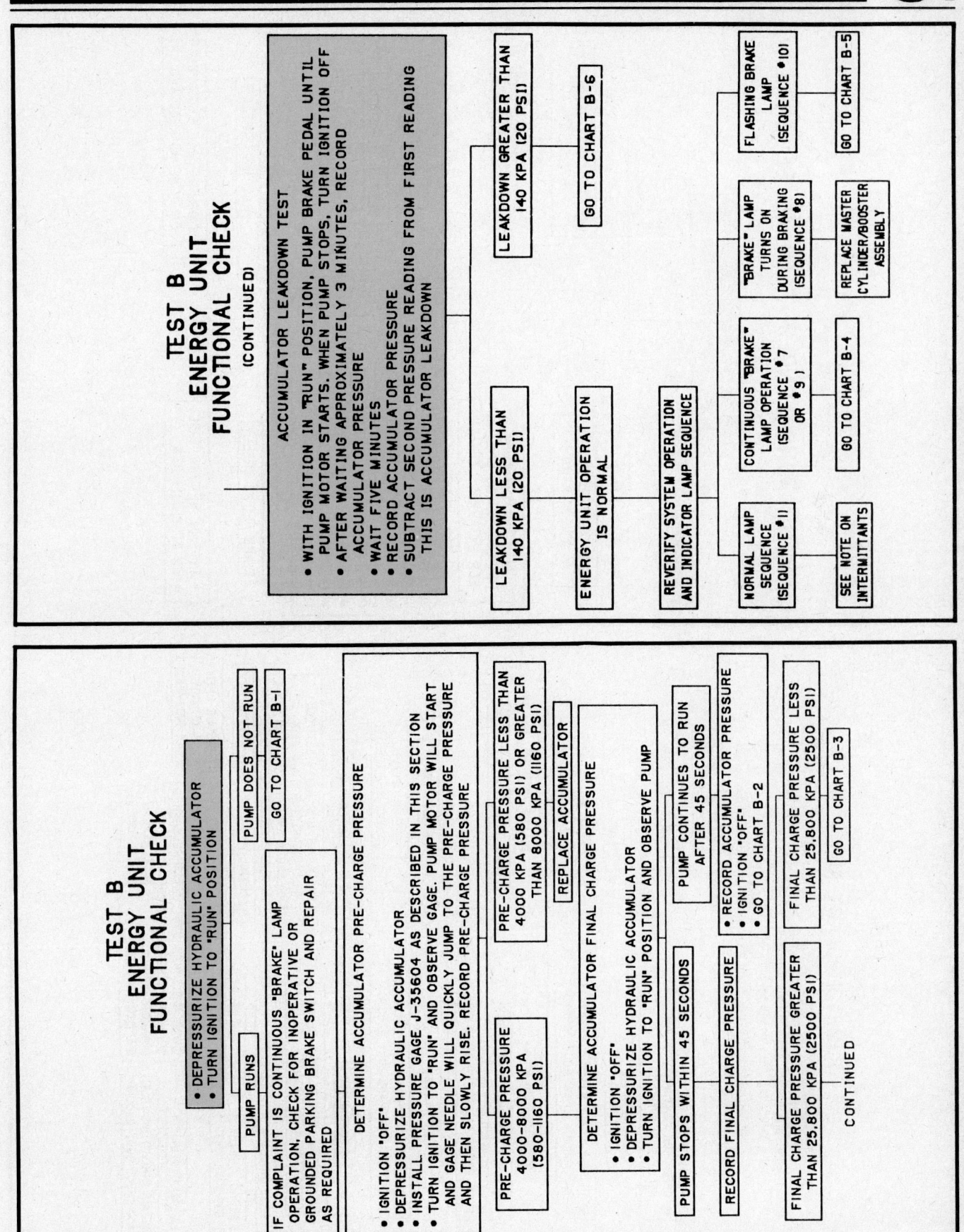

TEST B
ENERGY UNIT
FUNCTIONAL CHECK
(CONTINUED)

ACCUMULATOR LEAKDOWN TEST

- WITH IGNITION IN "RUN" POSITION, PUMP BRAKE PEDAL UNTIL PUMP MOTOR STARTS. WHEN PUMP STOPS, TURN IGNITION OFF
- AFTER WAITING APPROXIMATELY 3 MINUTES, RECORD ACCUMULATOR PRESSURE
- WAIT FIVE MINUTES
- RECORD ACCUMULATOR PRESSURE
- SUBTRACT SECOND PRESSURE READING FROM FIRST READING THIS IS ACCUMULATOR LEAKDOWN

LEAKDOWN GREATER THAN 140 KPA (20 PSI)

GO TO CHART B-6

LEAKDOWN LESS THAN 140 KPA (20 PSI)

ENERGY UNIT OPERATION IS NORMAL

REVERIFY SYSTEM OPERATION AND INDICATOR LAMP SEQUENCE

NORMAL LAMP SEQUENCE (SEQUENCE #11)

SEE NOTE ON INTERMITTANTS

CONTINUOUS "BRAKE" LAMP OPERATION (SEQUENCE #7 OR #9)

GO TO CHART B-4

"BRAKE" LAMP TURNS ON DURING BRAKING (SEQUENCE #8)

REPLACE MASTER CYLINDER/BOOSTER ASSEMBLY

FLASHING BRAKE LAMP (SEQUENCE #10)

GO TO CHART B-5

TEST B
ENERGY UNIT
FUNCTIONAL CHECK

- DEPRESSURIZE HYDRAULIC ACCUMULATOR
- TURN IGNITION TO "RUN" POSITION

PUMP RUNS

PUMP DOES NOT RUN

GO TO CHART B-1

IF COMPLAINT IS CONTINUOUS "BRAKE" LAMP OPERATION, CHECK FOR INOPERATIVE OR GROUNDED PARKING BRAKE SWITCH AND REPAIR AS REQUIRED

DETERMINE ACCUMULATOR PRE-CHARGE PRESSURE

- IGNITION "OFF"
- DEPRESSURIZE HYDRAULIC ACCUMULATOR
- INSTALL PRESSURE GAGE J-35604 AS DESCRIBED IN THIS SECTION
- TURN IGNITION TO "RUN" AND OBSERVE GAGE. PUMP MOTOR WILL START AND GAGE NEEDLE WILL QUICKLY JUMP TO THE PRE-CHARGE PRESSURE AND THEN SLOWLY RISE. RECORD PRE-CHARGE PRESSURE

PRE-CHARGE PRESSURE 4000-8000 KPA (580-1160 PSI)

PRE-CHARGE PRESSURE LESS THAN 4000 KPA (580 PSI) OR GREATER THAN 8000 KPA (1160 PSI)

REPLACE ACCUMULATOR

DETERMINE ACCUMULATOR FINAL CHARGE PRESSURE

- IGNITION "OFF"
- DEPRESSURIZE HYDRAULIC ACCUMULATOR
- TURN IGNITION TO "RUN" POSITION AND OBSERVE PUMP

PUMP STOPS WITHIN 45 SECONDS

PUMP CONTINUES TO RUN AFTER 45 SECONDS

- RECORD ACCUMULATOR PRESSURE
- IGNITION "OFF"
- GO TO CHART B-2

RECORD FINAL CHARGE PRESSURE

FINAL CHARGE PRESSURE GREATER THAN 25,800 KPA (2500 PSI)

FINAL CHARGE PRESSURE LESS THAN 25,800 KPA (2500 PSI)

GO TO CHART B-3

CONTINUED

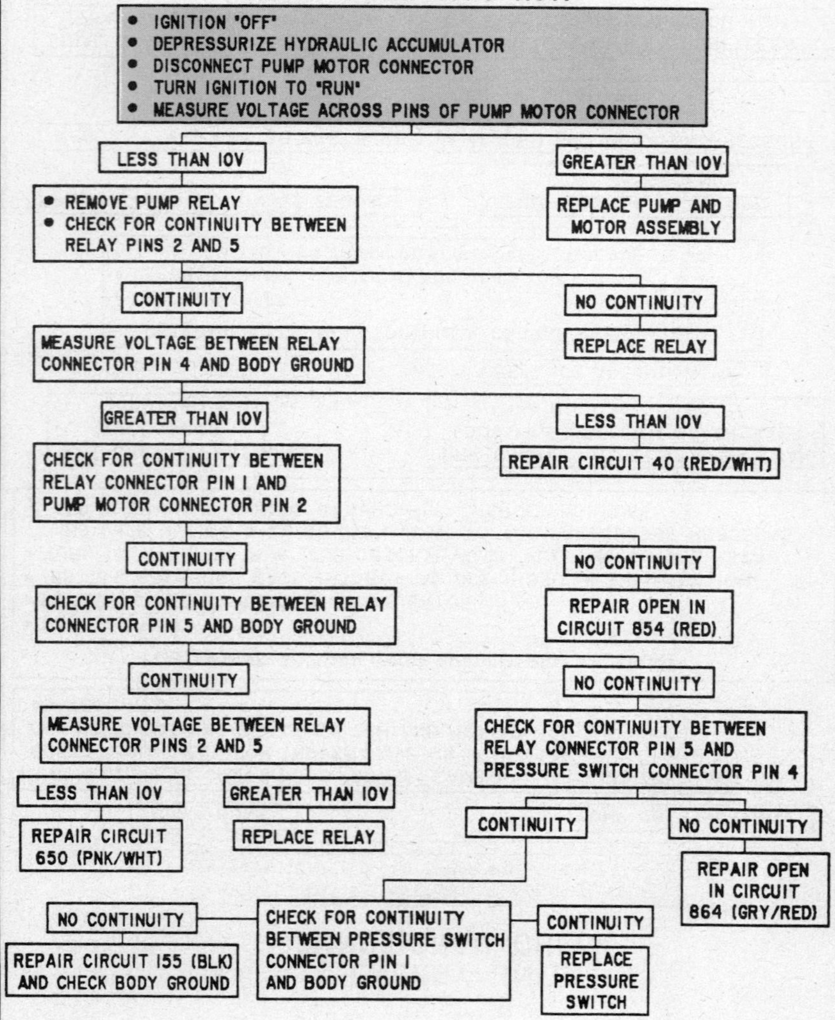

CHART B-2
PUMP RUNS LONGER THAN 45 SECONDS

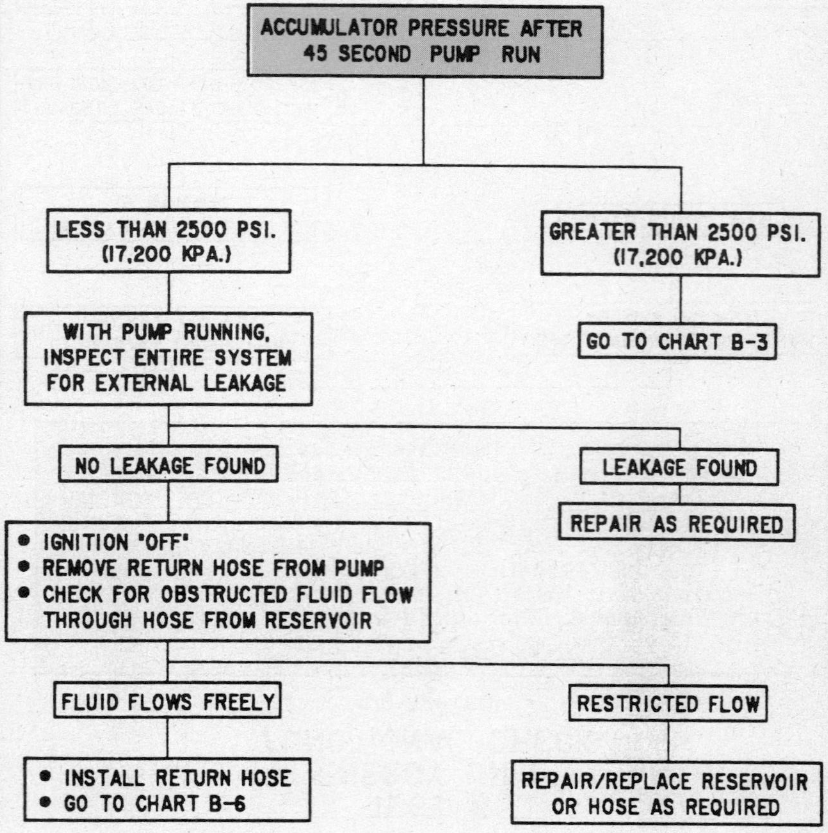

- ACCUMULATOR PRESSURE AFTER 45 SECOND PUMP RUN
  - GREATER THAN 2500 PSI. (17,200 KPA.)
    - GO TO CHART B-3
  - LESS THAN 2500 PSI. (17,200 KPA.)
    - WITH PUMP RUNNING, INSPECT ENTIRE SYSTEM FOR EXTERNAL LEAKAGE
      - LEAKAGE FOUND
        - REPAIR AS REQUIRED
      - NO LEAKAGE FOUND
        - IGNITION "OFF"
        - REMOVE RETURN HOSE FROM PUMP
        - CHECK FOR OBSTRUCTED FLUID FLOW THROUGH HOSE FROM RESERVOIR
          - RESTRICTED FLOW
            - REPAIR/REPLACE RESERVOIR OR HOSE AS REQUIRED
          - FLUID FLOWS FREELY
            - INSTALL RETURN HOSE
            - GO TO CHART B-6

CHART B-1
PUMP DOES NOT RUN

- IGNITION "OFF"
- DEPRESSURIZE HYDRAULIC ACCUMULATOR
- DISCONNECT PUMP MOTOR CONNECTOR
- TURN IGNITION TO "RUN"
- MEASURE VOLTAGE ACROSS PINS OF PUMP MOTOR CONNECTOR
  - GREATER THAN 10V
    - REPLACE PUMP AND MOTOR ASSEMBLY
  - LESS THAN 10V
    - REMOVE PUMP RELAY
    - CHECK FOR CONTINUITY BETWEEN RELAY PINS 2 AND 5
      - CONTINUITY
        - MEASURE VOLTAGE BETWEEN RELAY CONNECTOR PIN 4 AND BODY GROUND
          - NO CONTINUITY
            - REPLACE RELAY
          - GREATER THAN 10V
            - CHECK FOR CONTINUITY BETWEEN RELAY CONNECTOR PIN 1 AND PUMP MOTOR CONNECTOR PIN 2
              - LESS THAN 10V
                - REPAIR CIRCUIT 40 (RED/WHT)
              - CONTINUITY
                - CHECK FOR CONTINUITY BETWEEN RELAY CONNECTOR PIN 5 AND BODY GROUND
                  - NO CONTINUITY
                    - REPAIR OPEN IN CIRCUIT 854 (RED)
                  - CONTINUITY
                    - MEASURE VOLTAGE BETWEEN RELAY CONNECTOR PINS 2 AND 5
                      - NO CONTINUITY
                        - CHECK FOR CONTINUITY BETWEEN RELAY CONNECTOR PIN 5 AND PRESSURE SWITCH CONNECTOR PIN 4
                          - NO CONTINUITY
                            - REPAIR OPEN IN CIRCUIT 864 (GRY/RED)
                          - CONTINUITY
                            - CHECK FOR CONTINUITY BETWEEN PRESSURE SWITCH CONNECTOR PIN 1 AND BODY GROUND
                              - CONTINUITY
                                - REPLACE PRESSURE SWITCH
                              - NO CONTINUITY
                                - REPAIR CIRCUIT 155 (BLK) AND CHECK BODY GROUND
                      - GREATER THAN 10V
                        - REPLACE RELAY
                      - LESS THAN 10V
                        - REPAIR CIRCUIT 650 (PNK/WHT)

484

CHART B-3
PRESSURE SWITCH PERFORMANCE

I. SWITCH STATUS - PRESSURIZED
- TURN IGNITION TO "RUN" UNTIL PUMP STOPS
- IGNITION "OFF"
  - NOTE: IF PUMP CONTINUES TO RUN AFTER 45 SECONDS, TURN IGNITION OFF AND PROCEDE
- CHECK PRESSURE SWITCH PINS FOR THE FOLLOWING CONDITIONS USING VOM

MEASURE BETWEEN PINS	SCALE	SPECIFICATION
1,2	200 Ω	NO CONTINUITY
1,4	200 Ω	NO CONTINUITY
3,5	200 Ω	CONTINUITY
ALL PINS,BODY GROUND	200 Ω	NO CONTINUITY

IF ANY CONDITION IS NOT MET, REPLACE PRESSURE SWITCH

II. SWITCH STATUS - DEPRESSURIZED
- DEPRESSURIZE HYDRAULIC ACCUMULATOR
- CHECK PRESSURE SWITCH PINS FOR THE FOLLOWING CONDITIONS USING VOM

MEASURE BETWEEN PINS	SCALE	SPECIFICATION
1,2	200 Ω	CONTINUITY
1,4	200 Ω	CONTINUITY
3,5	200 Ω	NO CONTINUITY
ALL PINS,BODY GROUND	200 Ω	NO CONTINUITY

IF ANY CONDITION IS NOT MET, REPLACE PRESSURE SWITCH

CONTINUED →

CHART B-3
(CONTINUED)

III. SWITCH THRESHOLDS
- DEPRESSURIZE HYDRAULIC ACCUMULATOR
- INSTALL PRESSURE GAGE J-35604 AS DESCRIBED IN THIS SECTION
- CONNECT PRESSURE SWITCH CONNECTOR AND TURN IGNITION TO "RUN" UNTIL PUMP STOPS
- USING VOM, MONITOR FOR CONTINUITY BETWEEN PRESSURE SWITCH PINS AS SHOWN BELOW WHILE SLOWLY BLEEDING OFF ACCUMULATOR PRESSURE BY PUMPING THE BRAKE PEDAL. CONTINUITY SHOULD BE GAINED OR LOST AS INDICATED.
- PRESSURIZE SYSTEM BETWEEN EACH TEST BY RECONNECTING PRESSURE SWITCH AND TURNING IGNITION TO "RUN" UNTIL PUMP STOPS

MEASURE BETWEEN PINS	SWITCH STATUS	PRESSURE RANGE
1,4	CONTINUITY SHOULD BE GAINED AT:	1980-2080 PSI (13,650-14,350 KPA)
1,2	CONTINUITY SHOULD BE GAINED AT:	1500-1550 PSI (10,350-10,700 KPA)
3,5	CONTINUITY SHOULD BE LOST AT:	1500-1550 PSI (10,350-10,700 KPA)

IF ANY CONDITION IS NOT MET, REPLACE PRESSURE SWITCH

- DEPRESSURIZE HYDRAULIC ACCUMULATOR
- WITH IGNITION OFF, CONNECT PRESSURE SWITCH CONNECTOR
- TURN IGNITION TO "RUN" AND OBSERVE GAGE, "ANTI-LOCK" LAMP, "BRAKE" LAMP AND PUMP MOTOR. EVENTS SHOULD OCCUR AT PRESSURES INDICATED IN CHART BELOW

EVENT	PRESSURE
"ANTI-LOCK" LAMP TURNS OFF	1900-1975 PSI (13,100-13,600 KPA)
"BRAKE" LAMP TURNS OFF	1900-1975 PSI (13,100-13,600 KPA)
PUMP MOTOR STOPS	2550-2670 PSI (17,580-18,400 KPA)

IF ANY CONDITION IS NOT MET, REPLACE PRESSURE SWITCH

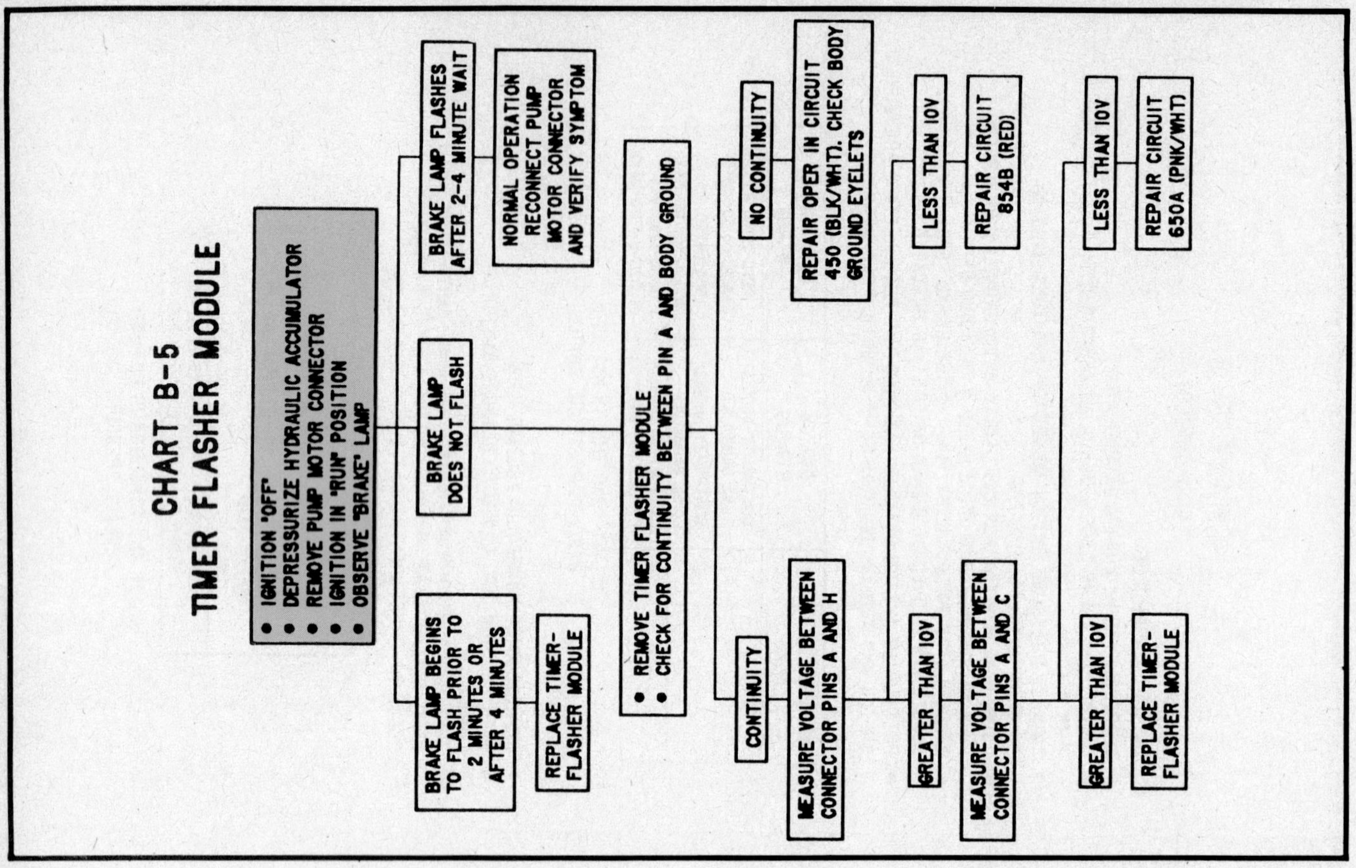

CHART B-5
TIMER FLASHER MODULE

- IGNITION "OFF"
- DEPRESSURIZE HYDRAULIC ACCUMULATOR
- REMOVE PUMP MOTOR CONNECTOR
- IGNITION IN "RUN" POSITION
- OBSERVE "BRAKE" LAMP

BRAKE LAMP BEGINS TO FLASH PRIOR TO 2 MINUTES OR AFTER 4 MINUTES
→ REPLACE TIMER-FLASHER MODULE

BRAKE LAMP FLASHES AFTER 2-4 MINUTE WAIT
→ NORMAL OPERATION RECONNECT PUMP MOTOR CONNECTOR AND VERIFY SYMPTOM

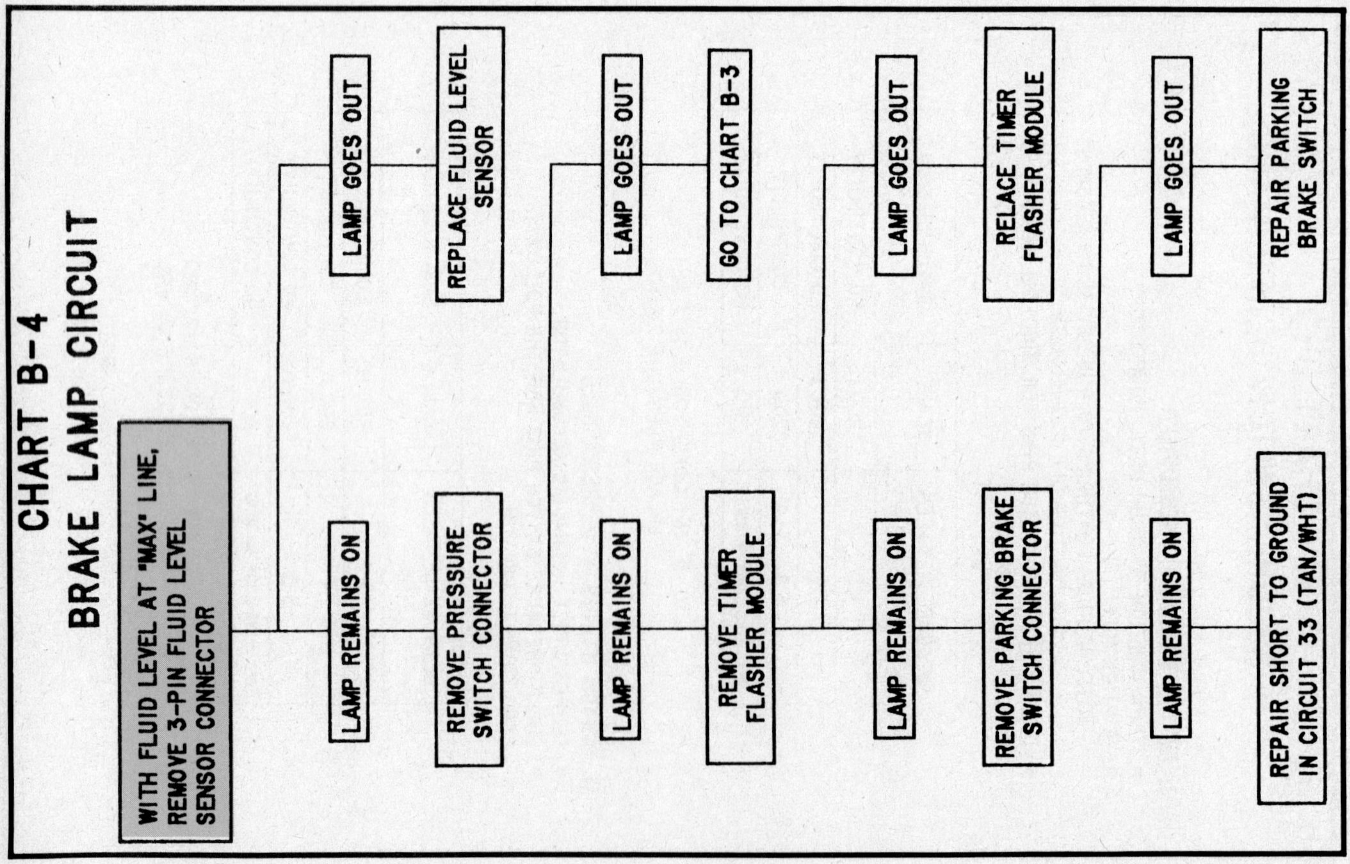

BRAKE LAMP DOES NOT FLASH
→ - REMOVE TIMER FLASHER MODULE
  - CHECK FOR CONTINUITY BETWEEN PIN A AND BODY GROUND

CONTINUITY
→ MEASURE VOLTAGE BETWEEN CONNECTOR PINS A AND H

NO CONTINUITY
→ REPAIR OPEN IN CIRCUIT 450 (BLK/WHT). CHECK BODY GROUND EYELETS

GREATER THAN 10V
→ MEASURE VOLTAGE BETWEEN CONNECTOR PINS A AND C

LESS THAN 10V
→ REPAIR CIRCUIT 854B (RED)

GREATER THAN 10V
→ REPLACE TIMER-FLASHER MODULE

LESS THAN 10V
→ REPAIR CIRCUIT 650A (PNK/WHT)

CHART B-4
BRAKE LAMP CIRCUIT

WITH FLUID LEVEL AT "MAX" LINE, REMOVE 3-PIN FLUID LEVEL SENSOR CONNECTOR

LAMP GOES OUT
→ REPLACE FLUID LEVEL SENSOR

LAMP REMAINS ON
→ REMOVE PRESSURE SWITCH CONNECTOR

LAMP GOES OUT
→ GO TO CHART B-3

LAMP REMAINS ON
→ REMOVE TIMER FLASHER MODULE

LAMP GOES OUT
→ RELACE TIMER FLASHER MODULE

LAMP REMAINS ON
→ REMOVE PARKING BRAKE SWITCH CONNECTOR

LAMP GOES OUT
→ REPAIR PARKING BRAKE SWITCH

LAMP REMAINS ON
→ REPAIR SHORT TO GROUND IN CIRCUIT 33 (TAN/WHT)

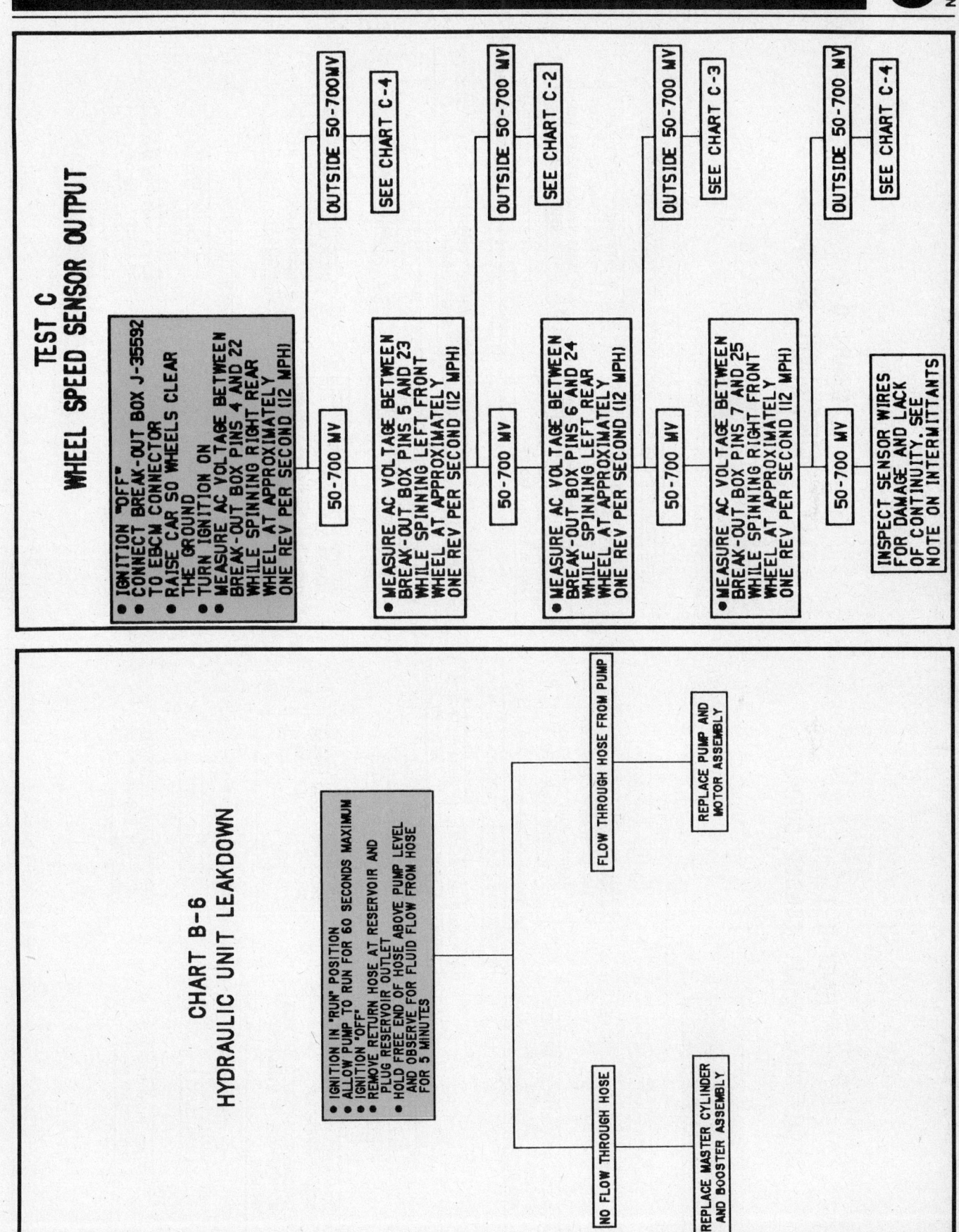

TEST C
WHEEL SPEED SENSOR OUTPUT

- IGNITION "OFF"
- CONNECT BREAK-OUT BOX J-35592 TO EBCM CONNECTOR
- RAISE CAR SO WHEELS CLEAR THE GROUND
- TURN IGNITION ON
- MEASURE AC VOLTAGE BETWEEN BREAK-OUT BOX PINS 4 AND 22 WHILE SPINNING RIGHT REAR WHEEL AT APPROXIMATELY ONE REV PER SECOND (12 MPH)

50-700 MV

- MEASURE AC VOLTAGE BETWEEN BREAK-OUT BOX PINS 5 AND 23 WHILE SPINNING LEFT FRONT WHEEL AT APPROXIMATELY ONE REV PER SECOND (12 MPH)

50-700 MV

- MEASURE AC VOLTAGE BETWEEN BREAK-OUT BOX PINS 6 AND 24 WHILE SPINNING LEFT REAR WHEEL AT APPROXIMATELY ONE REV PER SECOND (12 MPH)

50-700 MV

- MEASURE AC VOLTAGE BETWEEN BREAK-OUT BOX PINS 7 AND 25 WHILE SPINNING RIGHT FRONT WHEEL AT APPROXIMATELY ONE REV PER SECOND (12 MPH)

50-700 MV

OUTSIDE 50-700MV

SEE CHART C-4

OUTSIDE 50-700 MV

SEE CHART C-2

OUTSIDE 50-700 MV

SEE CHART C-3

OUTSIDE 50-700 MV

SEE CHART C-4

INSPECT SENSOR WIRES FOR DAMAGE AND LACK OF CONTINUITY. SEE NOTE ON INTERMITTANTS

CHART B-6
HYDRAULIC UNIT LEAKDOWN

- IGNITION IN "RUN" POSITION
- ALLOW PUMP TO RUN FOR 60 SECONDS MAXIMUM
- IGNITION "OFF"
- REMOVE RETURN HOSE AT RESERVOIR AND PLUG RESERVOIR OUTLET
- HOLD FREE END OF HOSE ABOVE PUMP LEVEL AND OBSERVE FOR FLUID FLOW FROM HOSE FOR 5 MINUTES

NO FLOW THROUGH HOSE

REPLACE MASTER CYLINDER AND BOOSTER ASSEMBLY

FLOW THROUGH HOSE FROM PUMP

REPLACE PUMP AND MOTOR ASSEMBLY

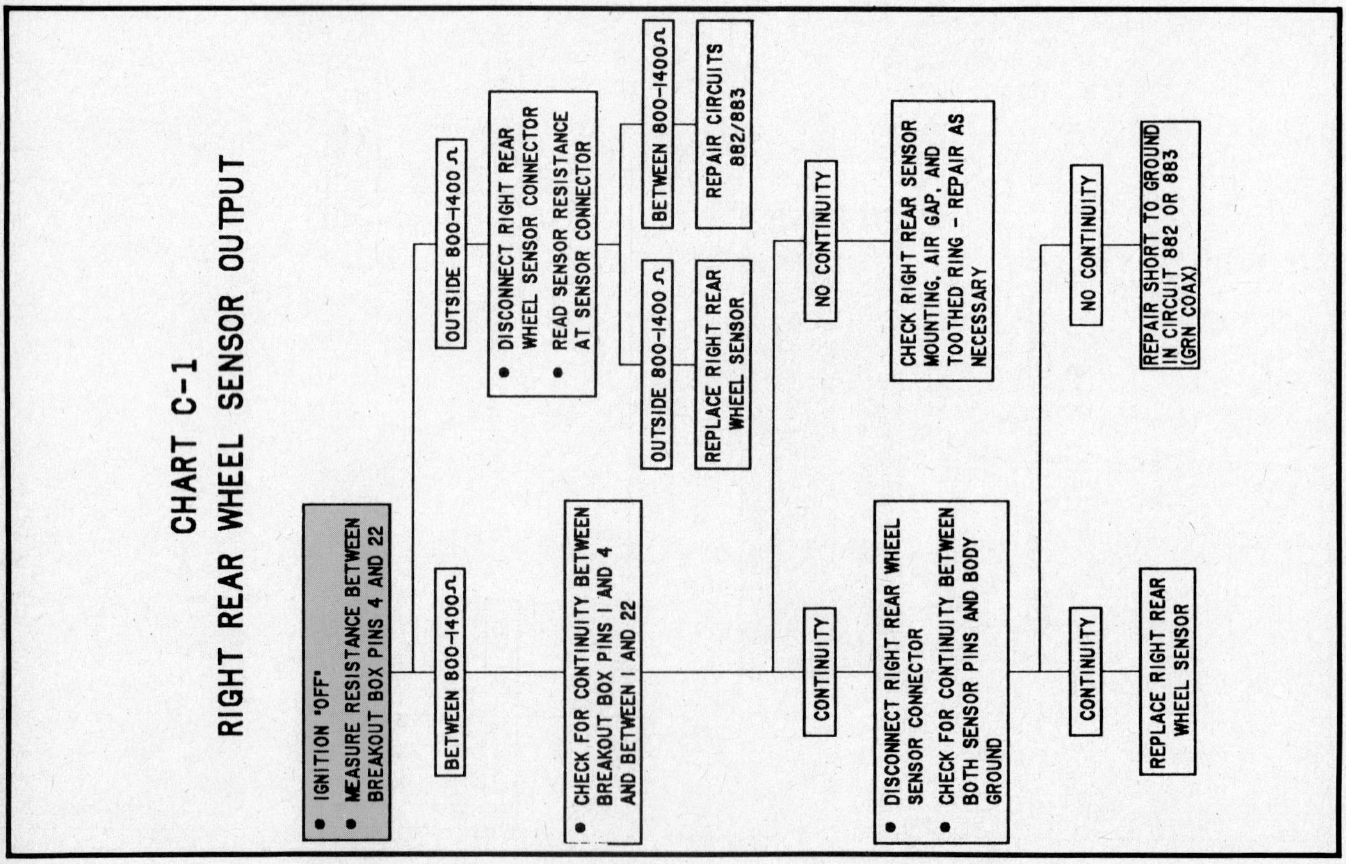

CHART C-2
LEFT FRONT WHEEL SENSOR OUTPUT

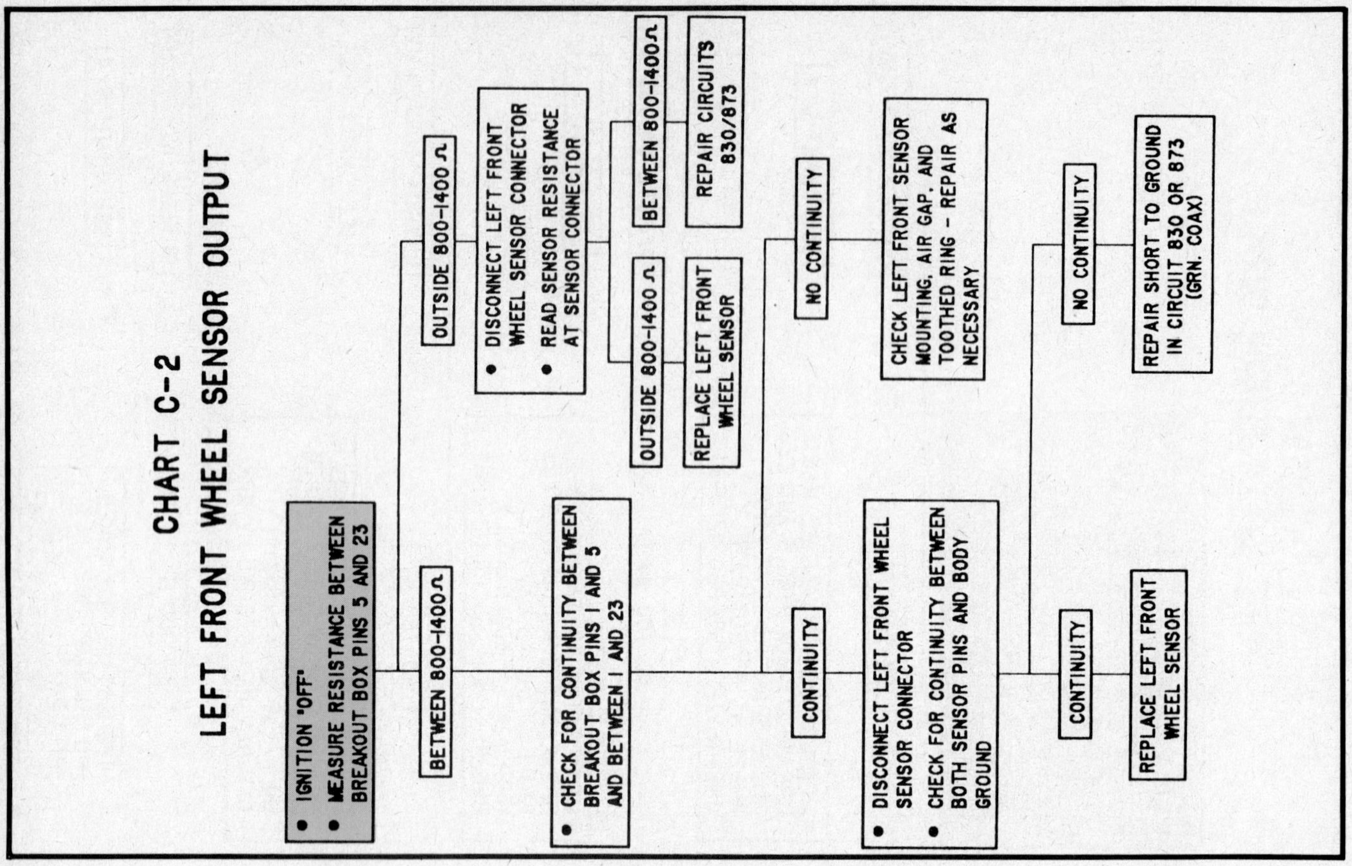

- IGNITION "OFF"
- MEASURE RESISTANCE BETWEEN BREAKOUT BOX PINS 5 AND 23

BETWEEN 800-1400 Ω

- CHECK FOR CONTINUITY BETWEEN BREAKOUT BOX PINS 1 AND 5 AND BETWEEN 1 AND 23

CONTINUITY

- DISCONNECT LEFT FRONT WHEEL SENSOR CONNECTOR
- CHECK FOR CONTINUITY BETWEEN BOTH SENSOR PINS AND BODY GROUND

CONTINUITY

REPLACE LEFT FRONT WHEEL SENSOR

OUTSIDE 800-1400 Ω

- DISCONNECT LEFT FRONT WHEEL SENSOR CONNECTOR
- READ SENSOR RESISTANCE AT SENSOR CONNECTOR

BETWEEN 800-1400 Ω

REPAIR CIRCUITS 830/873

OUTSIDE 800-1400 Ω

REPLACE LEFT FRONT WHEEL SENSOR

NO CONTINUITY

CHECK LEFT FRONT SENSOR MOUNTING, AIR GAP, AND TOOTHED RING — REPAIR AS NECESSARY

NO CONTINUITY

REPAIR SHORT TO GROUND IN CIRCUIT 830 OR 873 (GRN. COAX)

CHART C-1
RIGHT REAR WHEEL SENSOR OUTPUT

- IGNITION "OFF"
- MEASURE RESISTANCE BETWEEN BREAKOUT BOX PINS 4 AND 22

BETWEEN 800-1400 Ω

- CHECK FOR CONTINUITY BETWEEN BREAKOUT BOX PINS 1 AND 4 AND BETWEEN 1 AND 22

CONTINUITY

- DISCONNECT RIGHT REAR WHEEL SENSOR CONNECTOR
- CHECK FOR CONTINUITY BETWEEN BOTH SENSOR PINS AND BODY GROUND

CONTINUITY

REPLACE RIGHT REAR WHEEL SENSOR

OUTSIDE 800-1400 Ω

- DISCONNECT RIGHT REAR WHEEL SENSOR CONNECTOR
- READ SENSOR RESISTANCE AT SENSOR CONNECTOR

BETWEEN 800-1400 Ω

REPAIR CIRCUITS 882/883

OUTSIDE 800-1400 Ω

REPLACE RIGHT REAR WHEEL SENSOR

NO CONTINUITY

CHECK RIGHT REAR SENSOR MOUNTING, AIR GAP, AND TOOTHED RING — REPAIR AS NECESSARY

NO CONTINUITY

REPAIR SHORT TO GROUND IN CIRCUIT 882 OR 883 (GRN COAX)

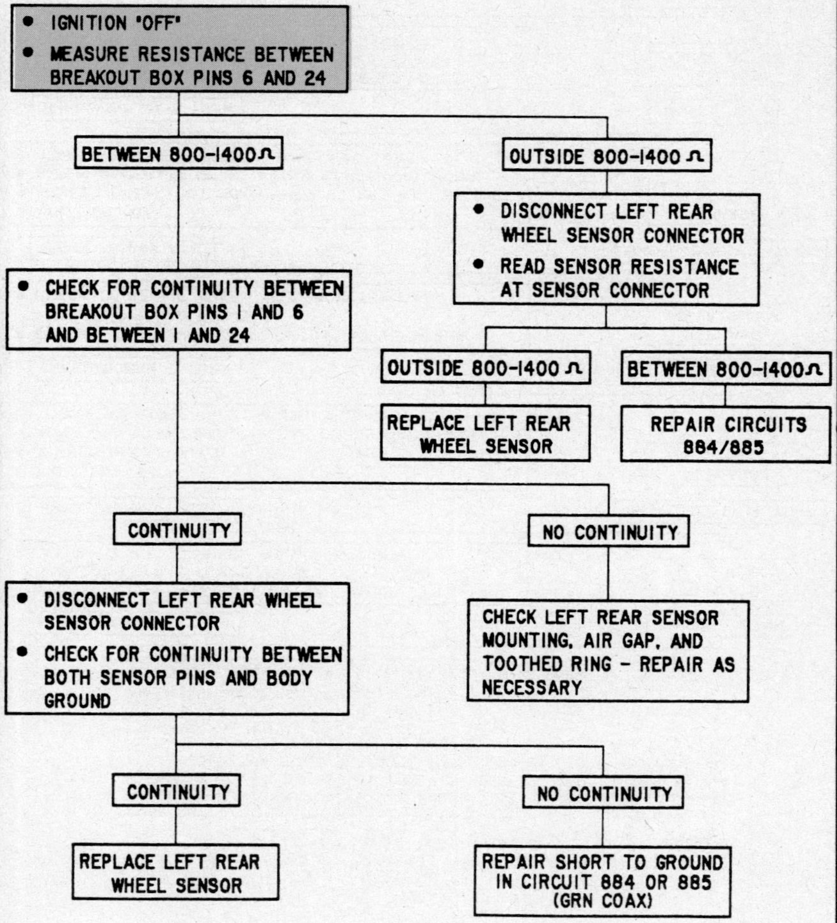

CHART C-4
RIGHT FRONT WHEEL SENSOR OUTPUT

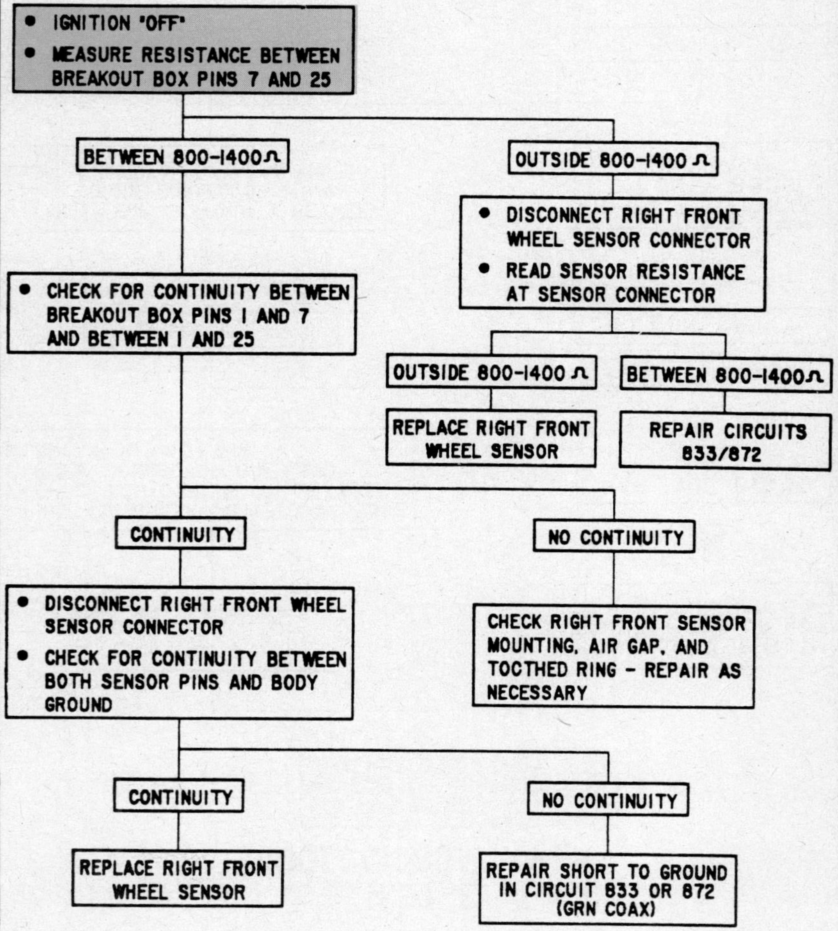

- IGNITION "OFF"
- MEASURE RESISTANCE BETWEEN BREAKOUT BOX PINS 7 AND 25

BETWEEN 800-1400 Ω

- CHECK FOR CONTINUITY BETWEEN BREAKOUT BOX PINS I AND 7 AND BETWEEN I AND 25

  - CONTINUITY
    - DISCONNECT RIGHT FRONT WHEEL SENSOR CONNECTOR
    - CHECK FOR CONTINUITY BETWEEN BOTH SENSOR PINS AND BODY GROUND
      - CONTINUITY → REPLACE RIGHT FRONT WHEEL SENSOR
      - NO CONTINUITY → REPAIR SHORT TO GROUND IN CIRCUIT 833 OR 872 (GRN COAX)

  - NO CONTINUITY → CHECK RIGHT FRONT SENSOR MOUNTING, AIR GAP, AND TOOTHED RING – REPAIR AS NECESSARY

OUTSIDE 800-1400 Ω

- DISCONNECT RIGHT FRONT WHEEL SENSOR CONNECTOR
- READ SENSOR RESISTANCE AT SENSOR CONNECTOR

  - BETWEEN 800-1400 Ω → REPAIR CIRCUITS 833/872
  - OUTSIDE 800-1400 Ω → REPLACE RIGHT FRONT WHEEL SENSOR

CHART C-3
LEFT REAR WHEEL SENSOR OUTPUT

- IGNITION "OFF"
- MEASURE RESISTANCE BETWEEN BREAKOUT BOX PINS 6 AND 24

BETWEEN 800-1400 Ω

- CHECK FOR CONTINUITY BETWEEN BREAKOUT BOX PINS I AND 6 AND BETWEEN I AND 24

  - CONTINUITY
    - DISCONNECT LEFT REAR WHEEL SENSOR CONNECTOR
    - CHECK FOR CONTINUITY BETWEEN BOTH SENSOR PINS AND BODY GROUND
      - CONTINUITY → REPLACE LEFT REAR WHEEL SENSOR
      - NO CONTINUITY → REPAIR SHORT TO GROUND IN CIRCUIT 884 OR 885 (GRN COAX)

  - NO CONTINUITY → CHECK LEFT REAR SENSOR MOUNTING, AIR GAP, AND TOOTHED RING – REPAIR AS NECESSARY

OUTSIDE 800-1400 Ω

- DISCONNECT LEFT REAR WHEEL SENSOR CONNECTOR
- READ SENSOR RESISTANCE AT SENSOR CONNECTOR

  - BETWEEN 800-1400 Ω → REPAIR CIRCUITS 884/885
  - OUTSIDE 800-1400 Ω → REPLACE LEFT REAR WHEEL SENSOR

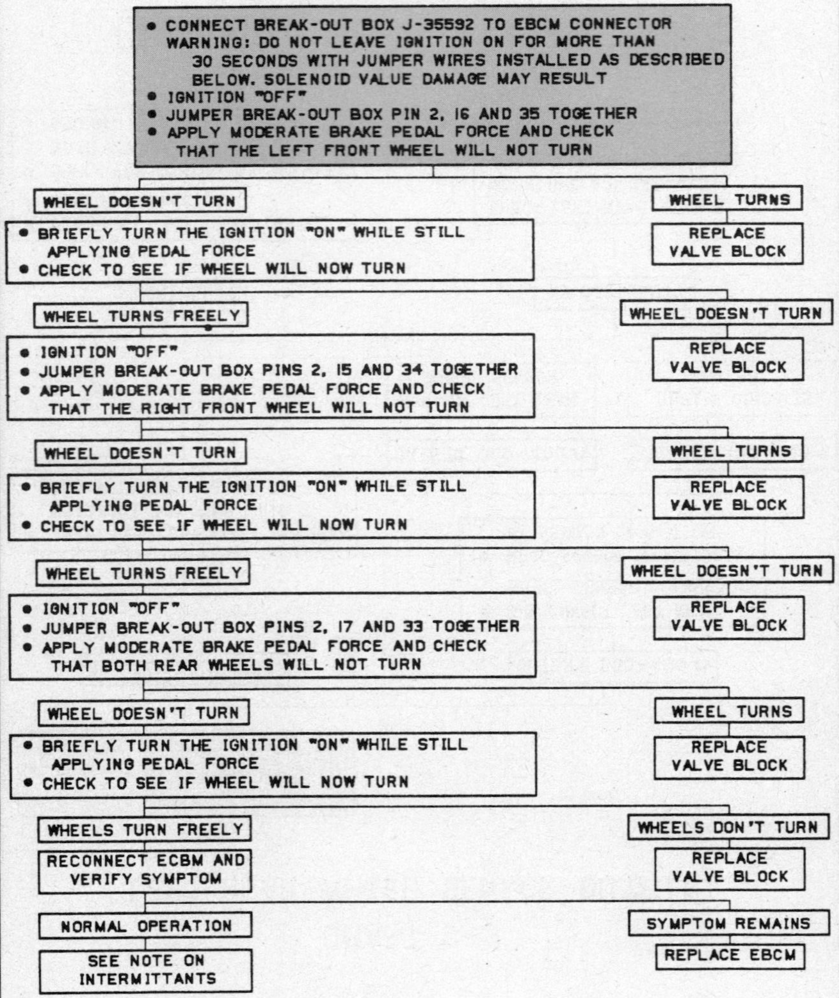

TEST E
DIODE CIRCUIT OPEN

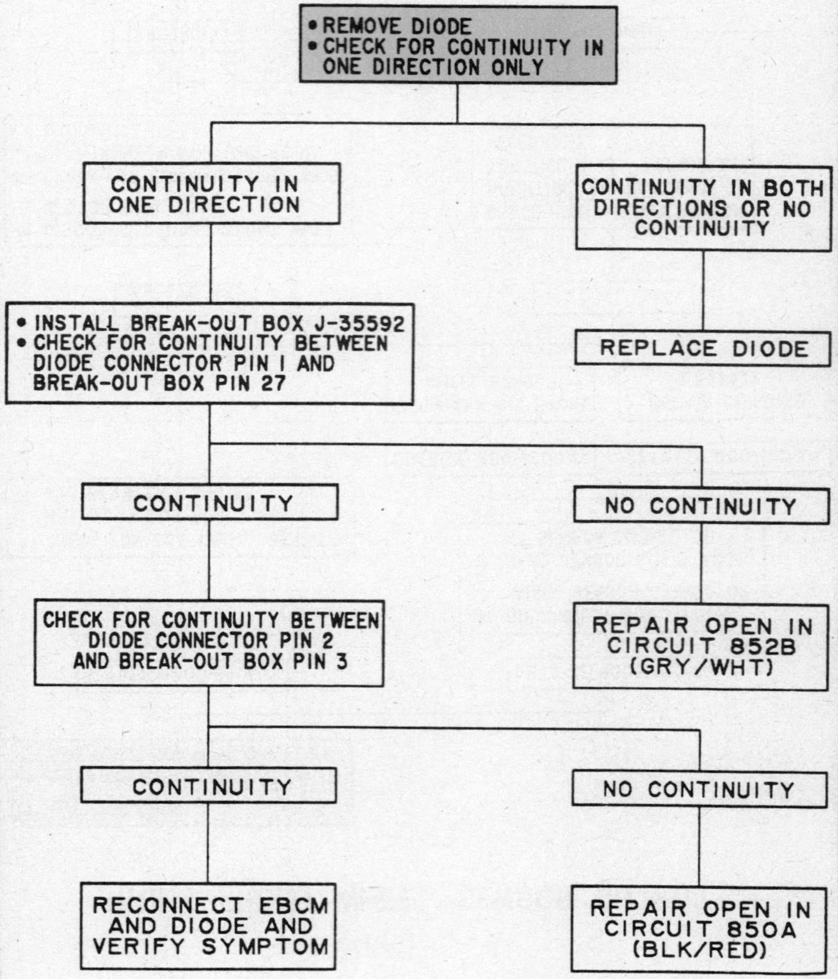

- REMOVE DIODE
- CHECK FOR CONTINUITY IN ONE DIRECTION ONLY

CONTINUITY IN BOTH DIRECTIONS OR NO CONTINUITY → REPLACE DIODE

CONTINUITY IN ONE DIRECTION →
- INSTALL BREAK-OUT BOX J-35592
- CHECK FOR CONTINUITY BETWEEN DIODE CONNECTOR PIN 1 AND BREAK-OUT BOX PIN 27

NO CONTINUITY → REPAIR OPEN IN CIRCUIT 852B (GRY/WHT)

CONTINUITY → CHECK FOR CONTINUITY BETWEEN DIODE CONNECTOR PIN 2 AND BREAK-OUT BOX PIN 3

NO CONTINUITY → REPAIR OPEN IN CIRCUIT 850A (BLK/RED)

CONTINUITY → RECONNECT EBCM AND DIODE AND VERIFY SYMPTOM

TEST D
SOLENOID VALVE OPERATION

- CONNECT BREAK-OUT BOX J-35592 TO EBCM CONNECTOR
  WARNING: DO NOT LEAVE IGNITION ON FOR MORE THAN 30 SECONDS WITH JUMPER WIRES INSTALLED AS DESCRIBED BELOW. SOLENOID VALUE DAMAGE MAY RESULT
- IGNITION "OFF"
- JUMPER BREAK-OUT BOX PIN 2, 16 AND 35 TOGETHER
- APPLY MODERATE BRAKE PEDAL FORCE AND CHECK THAT THE LEFT FRONT WHEEL WILL NOT TURN

WHEEL DOESN'T TURN →
- BRIEFLY TURN THE IGNITION "ON" WHILE STILL APPLYING PEDAL FORCE
- CHECK TO SEE IF WHEEL WILL NOW TURN
  - WHEEL TURNS → REPLACE VALVE BLOCK

WHEEL TURNS FREELY →
- IGNITION "OFF"
- JUMPER BREAK-OUT BOX PINS 2, 15 AND 34 TOGETHER
- APPLY MODERATE BRAKE PEDAL FORCE AND CHECK THAT THE RIGHT FRONT WHEEL WILL NOT TURN
  - WHEEL DOESN'T TURN → REPLACE VALVE BLOCK

WHEEL DOESN'T TURN →
- BRIEFLY TURN THE IGNITION "ON" WHILE STILL APPLYING PEDAL FORCE
- CHECK TO SEE IF WHEEL WILL NOW TURN
  - WHEEL TURNS → REPLACE VALVE BLOCK

WHEEL TURNS FREELY →
- IGNITION "OFF"
- JUMPER BREAK-OUT BOX PINS 2, 17 AND 33 TOGETHER
- APPLY MODERATE BRAKE PEDAL FORCE AND CHECK THAT BOTH REAR WHEELS WILL NOT TURN
  - WHEEL DOESN'T TURN → REPLACE VALVE BLOCK

WHEEL DOESN'T TURN →
- BRIEFLY TURN THE IGNITION "ON" WHILE STILL APPLYING PEDAL FORCE
- CHECK TO SEE IF WHEEL WILL NOW TURN
  - WHEEL TURNS → REPLACE VALVE BLOCK

WHEELS TURN FREELY → RECONNECT ECBM AND VERIFY SYMPTOM
- WHEELS DON'T TURN → REPLACE VALVE BLOCK
- SYMPTOM REMAINS → REPLACE EBCM

NORMAL OPERATION → SEE NOTE ON INTERMITTANTS

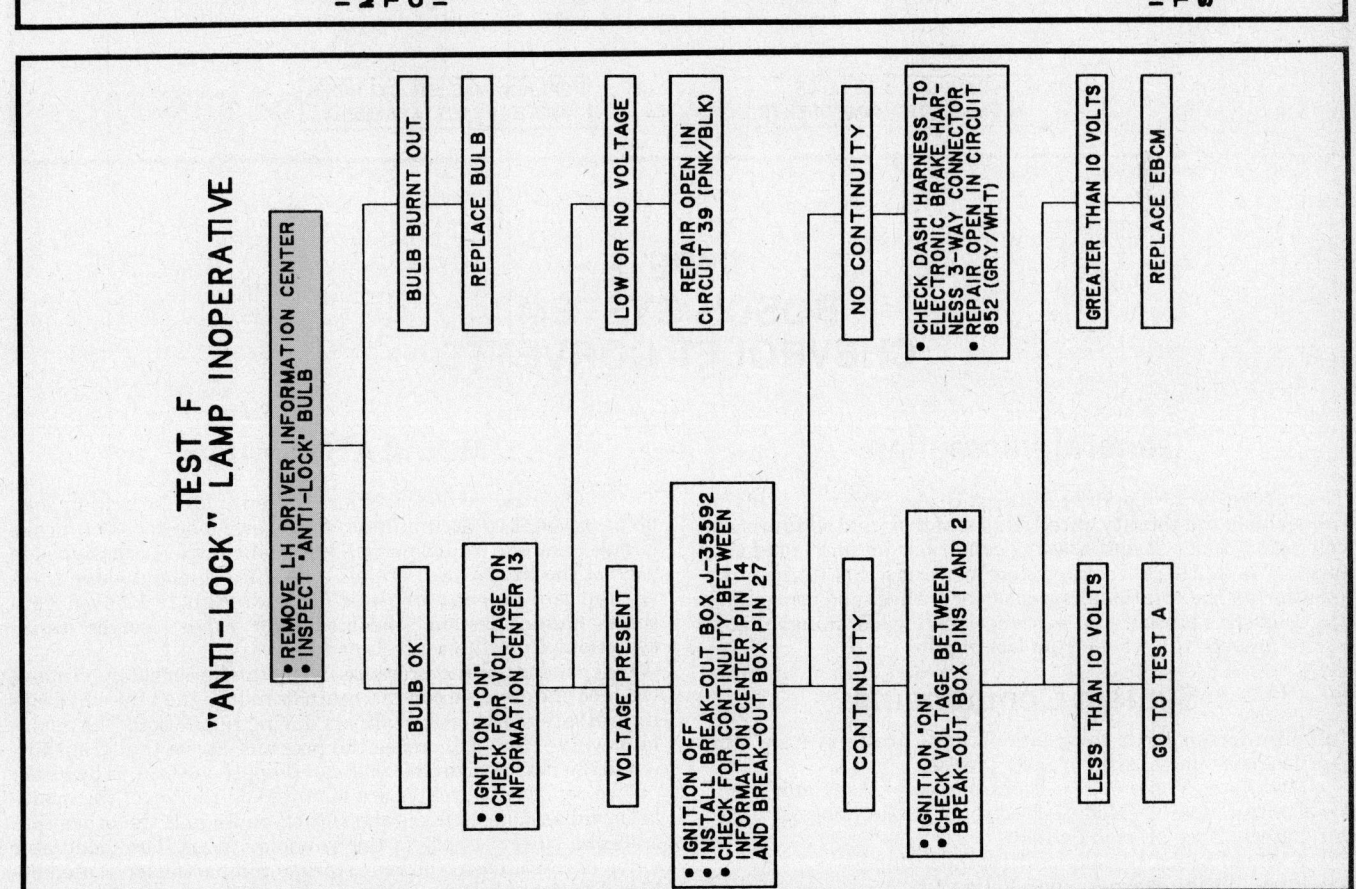

TEST G
INTERMITTANT "ANTI-LOCK" LAMP WHILE DRIVING

INTERUPTIONS IN THE FOLLOWING CIRCUITS AND OTHERS MAY CAUSE THE "ANTI-LOCK" LAMP TO LIGHT INTERMITTANTLY. THIS LIST DOES NOT INCLUDE ALL POSSIBILITIES, BUT IN-CLUDES THOSE CIRCUITS MOST LIKELY TO CAUSE AN INTERMITTANT "ANTI-LOCK" LAMP.

- EBCM SWITCH LOOP, INCLUDING
  - CIRCUIT 866 (LT. GRN) FROM EBCM TO FLUID LEVEL SENSOR
  - 2-PIN FLUID LEVEL SENSOR SWITCH
  - CIRCUIT 853 (LT. BLU/ORN) FROM FLUID LEVEL SENSOR TO PRESSURE SWITCH
  - CIRCUIT 865 (PPL) FROM PRESSURE SWITCH TO EBCM

- IGNITION ENABLE CIRCUIT, INCLUDING
  - BRAKE FUSE (#5 IN FUSE BLOCK, 5A)
  - CIRCUIT 650 (PNK/WHT) FROM FUSE TO EBCM

- MAIN RELAY CIRCUITS, INCLUDING
  - CIRCUIT 855 (DK. BLU) FROM EBCM TO RELAY COIL
  - CIRCUIT 450 (BLK/WHT) FROM RELAY COIL TO GROUND

- ALL WHEEL SPEED SENSOR CIRCUITS

INSPECT CONNECTORS AND WIRES IN THESE CIRCUITS. IF NO TROUBLE IS FOUND, SEE NOTE ON INTERMITTANTS IN THIS SECTION AND PERFORM TEST A

TEST F
"ANTI-LOCK" LAMP INOPERATIVE

- REMOVE LH DRIVER INFORMATION CENTER
- INSPECT "ANTI-LOCK" BULB

BULB BURNT OUT → REPLACE BULB

BULB OK
- IGNITION "ON"
- CHECK FOR VOLTAGE ON INFORMATION CENTER 13

VOLTAGE PRESENT

LOW OR NO VOLTAGE → REPAIR OPEN IN CIRCUIT 39 (PNK/BLK)

- IGNITION OFF
- INSTALL BREAK-OUT BOX J-35592
- CHECK FOR CONTINUITY BETWEEN INFORMATION CENTER PIN 14 AND BREAK-OUT BOX PIN 27

CONTINUITY

NO CONTINUITY →
- CHECK DASH HARNESS TO ELECTRONIC BRAKE HAR-NESS 3-WAY CONNECTOR
- REPAIR OPEN IN CIRCUIT 852 (GRY/WHT)

- IGNITION "ON"
- CHECK VOLTAGE BETWEEN BREAK-OUT BOX PINS 1 AND 2

GREATER THAN 10 VOLTS → REPLACE EBCM

LESS THAN 10 VOLTS → GO TO TEST A

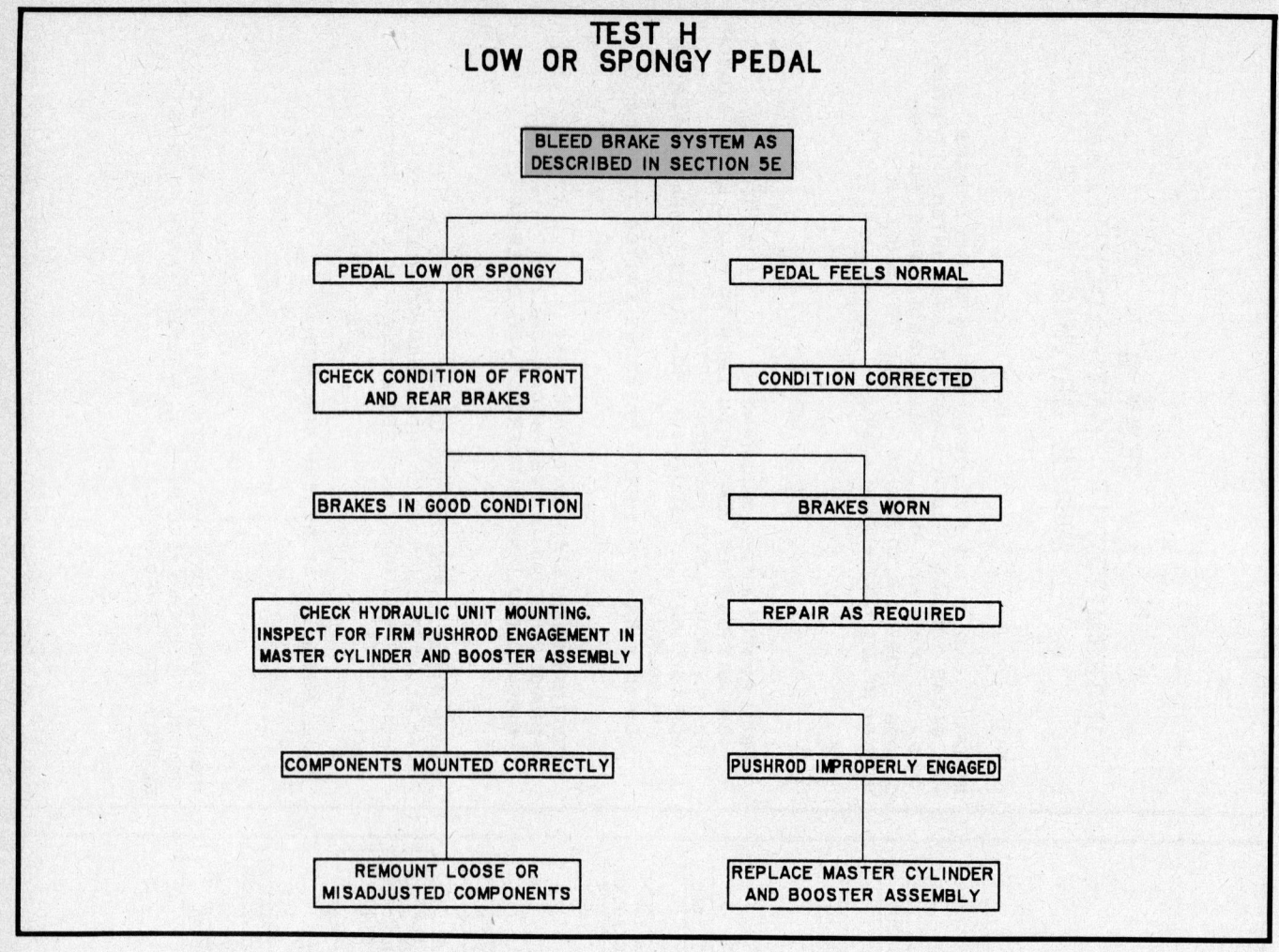

TEST H
LOW OR SPONGY PEDAL

BLEED BRAKE SYSTEM AS DESCRIBED IN SECTION 5E

PEDAL LOW OR SPONGY | PEDAL FEELS NORMAL

CHECK CONDITION OF FRONT AND REAR BRAKES | CONDITION CORRECTED

BRAKES IN GOOD CONDITION | BRAKES WORN

CHECK HYDRAULIC UNIT MOUNTING. INSPECT FOR FIRM PUSHROD ENGAGEMENT IN MASTER CYLINDER AND BOOSTER ASSEMBLY | REPAIR AS REQUIRED

COMPONENTS MOUNTED CORRECTLY | PUSHROD IMPROPERLY ENGAGED

REMOUNT LOOSE OR MISADJUSTED COMPONENTS | REPLACE MASTER CYLINDER AND BOOSTER ASSEMBLY

TYPE 2
BOSCH SYSTEM
CHEVROLET CORVETTE

General Infomation

The purpose of the Corvette Antilock Brake System is to maintain vehicle steerability, directional stability, and optimum deceleration under severe braking conditions on most road surfaces. The Antilock brake system performs this function by monitoring the rotational speed of each wheel and controlling the brake line pressure to each wheel during a braking maneuver to prevent the wheel from locking-up.

System Components

In conjunction with the conventional brake system, the Antilock system consists of the following:
- Modulator Valve (Valve-Brake Pressure Modulator)
- Control Module (Module-Electronic Brake Control)
- Lateral Acceleration Switch
- 4-Wheel Speed Sensors and Toothed Rings
- Fuse, Wiring Harness, and Relay

MODULATOR VALVE

The modulator valve consists of three rapidly switching solenoid valves, two accumulator chambers, (one for each brake circuit), and the return pump. One solenoid valve is assigned to each of the front wheel brakes. The third solenoid valve is assigned to the rear brakes. This design is known as a three-channel system. The modulator valve receives its instructions from the control module.

Independent of the pressure in the tandem master cylinder, the modulator valve can maintain or reduce the brake hydraulic pressure to the brake calipers during regulation. The modulator valve cannot increase the pressure above that transmitted to the master cylinder, nor can it apply the brakes by itself.

Two replaceable relays are mounted on the top of the modulator valve. One controls the return pump and the other controls the power supply to the solenoid valves. The modulator valve is mounted in the rear storage compartment located behind the driver's seat.

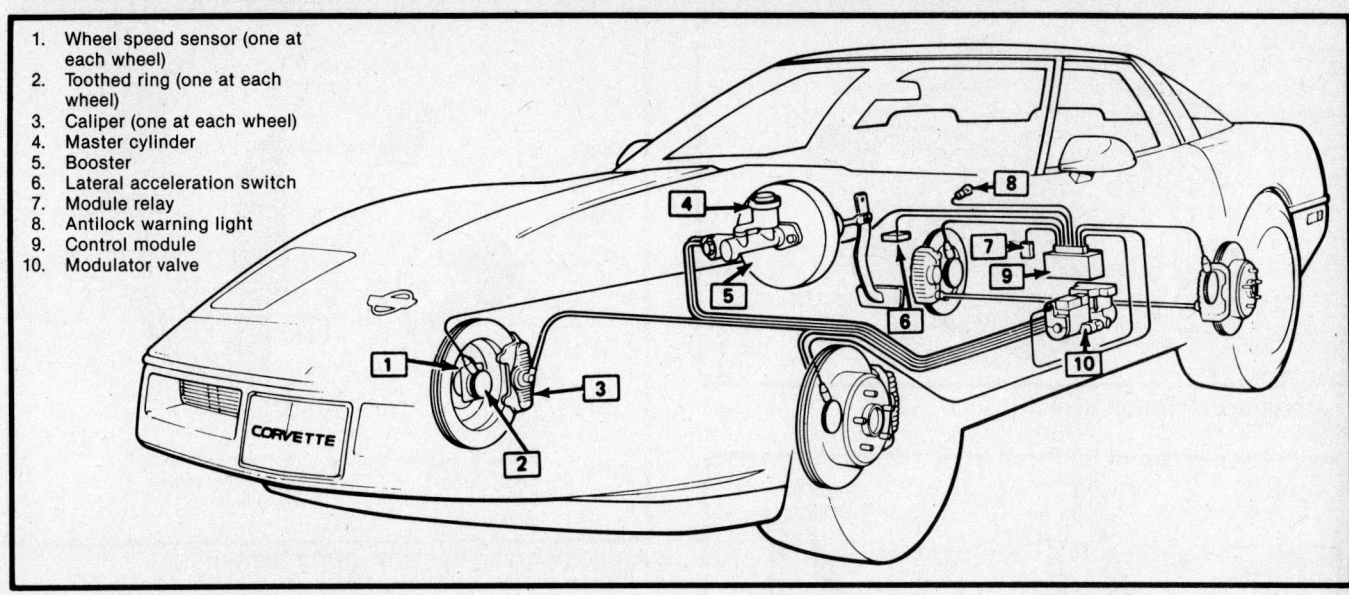

1. Wheel speed sensor (one at each wheel)
2. Toothed ring (one at each wheel)
3. Caliper (one at each wheel)
4. Master cylinder
5. Booster
6. Lateral acceleration switch
7. Module relay
8. Antilock warning light
9. Control module
10. Modulator valve

Corvette antilock brake system

NOTE: The modulator valve cannot be repaired. Only the relays may be replaced. If a problem occurs in the modulator valve, it must be replaced as an assembly.

ELECTRONIC BRAKE CONTROL MODULE

The EBCM is constructed of two circuit boards. Components such as resistors, diodes, transistors and large integrated circuits are mounted on the boards. These intergrated circuits contain thousands of transistors, resistors and diodes mounted on a single silicon (IC) chip. The circuit boards are housed in the control module and are surrounded by a light alloy case.

Wheel acceleration, deceleration, and slip values are calculated from the electronic signals generated by the wheel speed sensors, which are proportional to the speed of the tire/wheel. The control module calculates these values and produces control commands for the electro-mechanically controlled hydraulic modulator valves.

The control module is located in the rear storage compartment behind the driver's seat.

NOTE: The control module cannot be repaired. If a problem occurs in the control module, it must be replaced as an assembly.

LATERAL ACCELERATION SWITCH

The Lateral Acceleration Switch is basically two mercury switches connected in series. It is used to detect if the vehicle is traveling faster than a given cornering speed. When this speed is exceeded, one of the two mercury switches opens up and sends a signal to the control module.

The Lateral Acceleration Switch is located underneath the A/C control head on the floorpan.

NOTE: The Lateral Acceleration Switch cannot be repaired and can only be tested using the "ABS TESTER". If a problem occurs in the switch it must be replaced.

WHEEL SPEED SENSORS

The rotational speed of the wheels is detected by the inductive

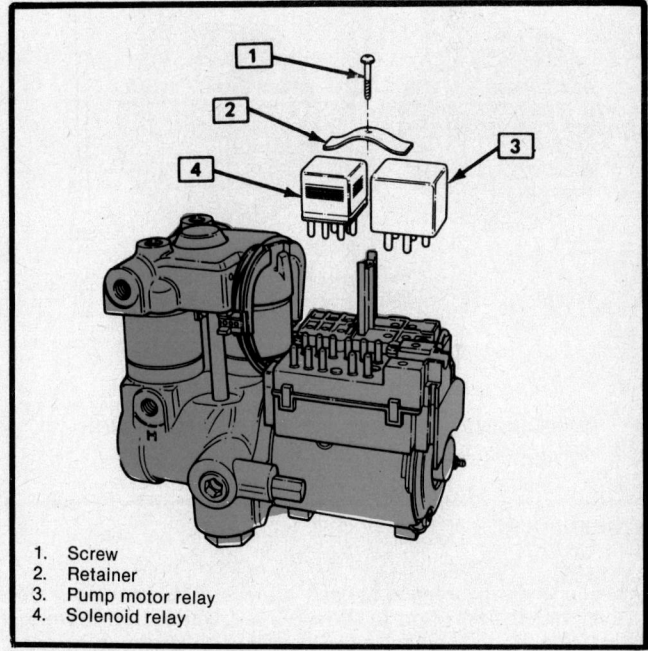

1. Screw
2. Retainer
3. Pump motor relay
4. Solenoid relay

Modulator valve assembly

Electronic brake control module

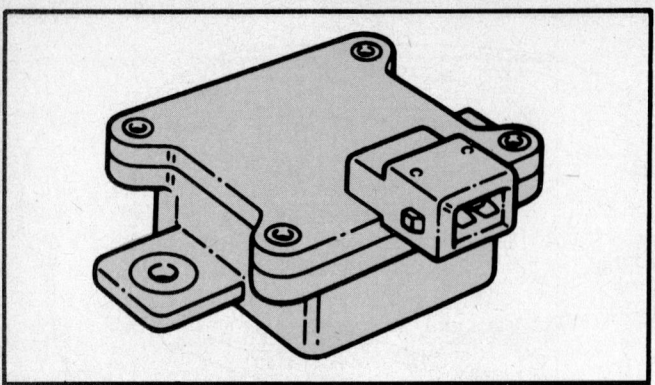

Lateral acceleration switch

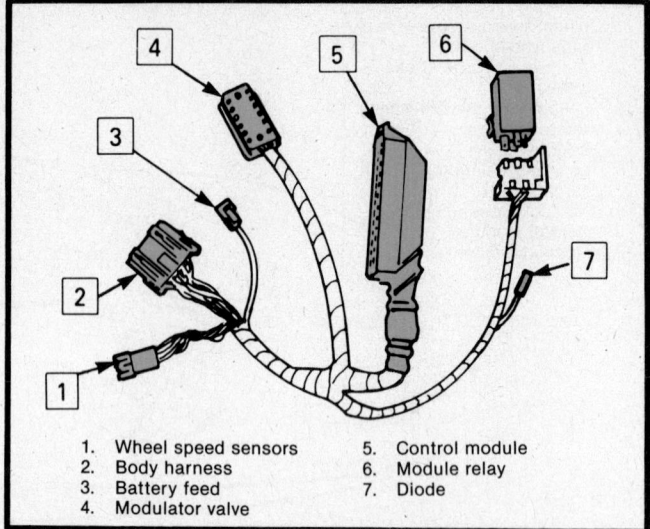

1. Wheel speed sensors
2. Body harness
3. Battery feed
4. Modulator valve
5. Control module
6. Module relay
7. Diode

Antilock brake system wiring harness

the wheel speed sensors, lateral acceleration switch, power and stop light switch information to the electronic control module and also outputs the current signal to the modulator valves and the "ANTILOCK" warning light.

The ABS system has its own wiring harness, located in the rear storage compartment behind the driver's seat, which is connected to the standard wiring harness.

The module relay is installed in the circuit between the battery, fuse and the electronic control module to protect the electronic control module from damage due to a possible voltage spike caused by a defective alternator regulator.

CIRCUIT PROTECTION

A fuse located in the main fuse block, labeled "BRAKE", provides protection for the main power feed circuit of the ABS electrical system. The "GAUGE" fuse is also tied into the main power feed to the Antilock Brake System.

System Operation

When the ignition is switched to the on position, the amber "ANTILOCK" warning light in the instrument panel lights. When the engine is started it goes out similar to the battery charge warning light. If the antilock brake system warning light does not go out or illuminates permanently while driving, it indicates a problem with the Antilock Brake System.

Upon starting the vehicle, the control module performs a functional check of the electrical circuitry (Self-Test). The test cycle itself checks the components of the monitoring circuit as well as the logic section. For this reason the control module is fed with given test sample signals to check if the correct output signals are available.

Since the Antilock Brake System may not be used everyday, there is an additional test which actually runs the modulator valve. This check is done to insure that the system is functioning correctly. Each time the ignition is first turned on and the vehicle reaches 4 mph, the test begins. This can be heard and, if the driver's foot is on the brake pedal it can be felt.

The ABS system continuously monitors the following components:
- Modulator Valve
- Electronic Control Module
- Lateral Acceleration Switch
- Wheel Speed Sensors
- Wiring Harness and Relays

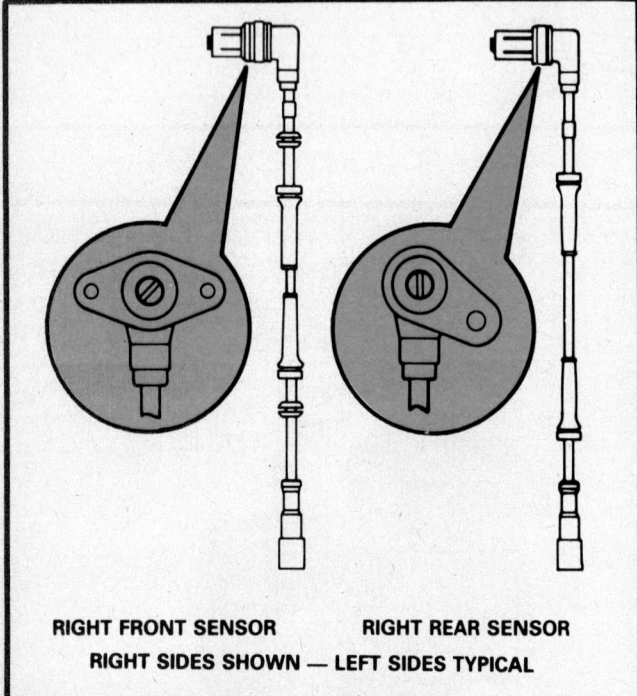

RIGHT FRONT SENSOR　　**RIGHT REAR SENSOR**
RIGHT SIDES SHOWN — LEFT SIDES TYPICAL

Wheel speed sensors

wheel speed sensors, one at each wheel and the resulting electric signal is passed on to the control module. In a system of this type with four wheel speed sensors, the rotational speed of each wheel is measure individually.

On the three-channel system, the front wheels are controlled individually, and the rear wheels together. The control of the rear wheels works on the "Select Low" principle. "Select Low" means that the tire with the lower tire to road co-efficient, (i.e., the greater tendency to lock) determines the level of control.

The wheel speed sensors are mounted in the knuckles. The toothed rings are pressed into the front hub and bearing assemblies and the rear halfshaft spindles.

NOTE: The Wheel Speed Sensors cannot be repaired or adjusted. If a problem occurs in the sensor it must be replaced.

WIRING HARNESS AND RELAY

The Antilock Brake System wiring harness provides a path for

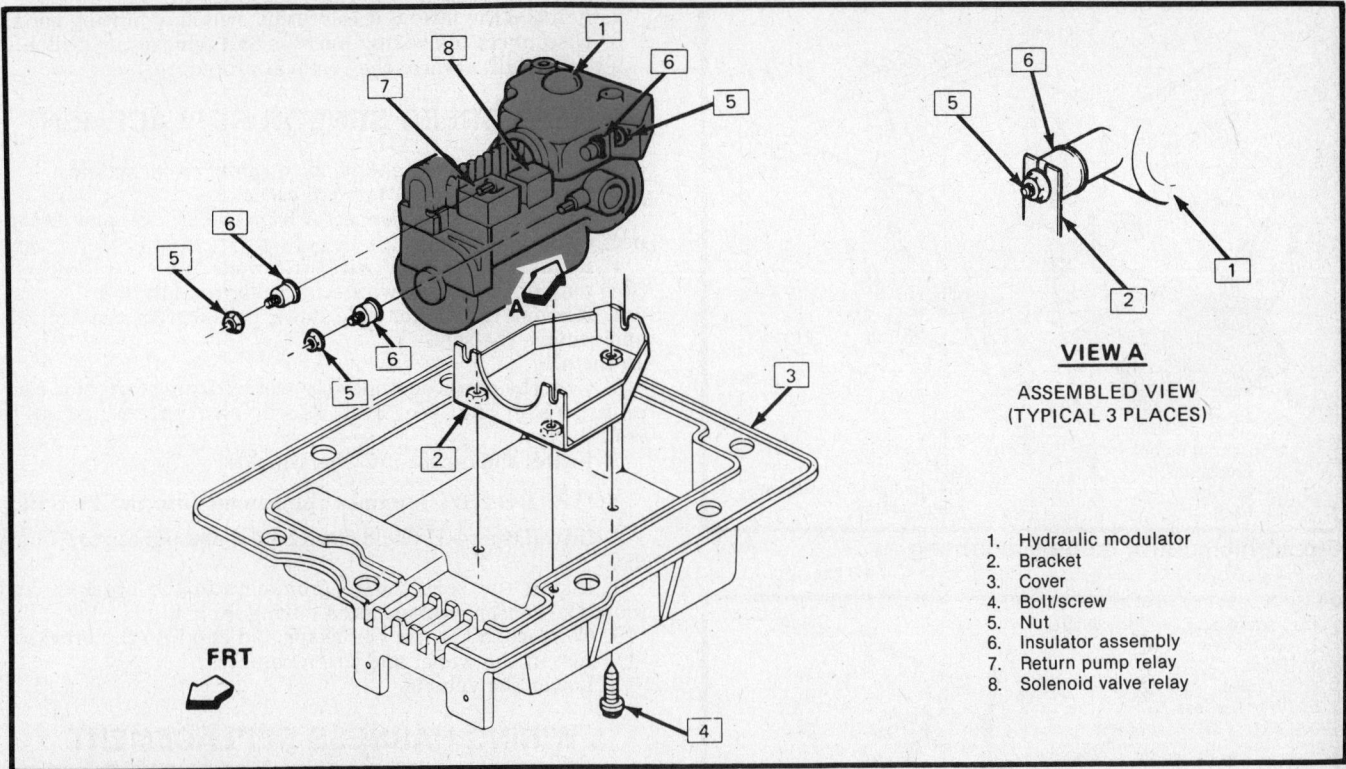

Bosch modulator valve assembly

1. Hydraulic modulator
2. Bracket
3. Cover
4. Bolt/screw
5. Nut
6. Insulator assembly
7. Return pump relay
8. Solenoid valve relay

VIEW A

ASSEMBLED VIEW
(TYPICAL 3 PLACES)

The electronic control module also monitors its own supply voltage. If the supply voltage drops below a specified value, the antilock brake system will be shut off and the amber "ANTILOCK" warning light comes on. When the supply voltage returns to or exceeds the specified minimum value, the light will go off. If a problem occurs with the antilock brake system, the "antilock" light will come on and the system will be shut off. The system will remain off until the car is restarted at which time the functional (self-test) check is repeated.

NOTE: During a problem with the antilock brake system, the conventional system remains fully operational providing it is not faulty.

Component Replacement

MODULATOR VALVE REPLACEMENT

1. Disconnect the negative battery cable.
2. Remove the storage tray and insulation.
3. Disconnect and remove the entire ABS wiring harness from the storage compartment. Refer to "Wiring Harness Replacement" for this procedure.
4. Disconnect the modulator valve ground from the body harness.
5. Label, then disconnect the five brake lines from the modulator valve.
6. Loosen the three nuts holding the modulator valve to the bracket.

NOTE: When removing the modulator valve from the storage compartment, protect the interior from possible damage caused by the spillage of brake fluid.

7. Remove the modulator valve from the storage compartment.

8. Wipe any brake fluid from the bottom of the storage compartment.
To install:
9. Transfer the ground wire and the insulators to the new modulator valve.
10. Install the modulator valve to the bracket and tighten the nuts to 7 ft. lbs.
11. Remove the shipping caps from the modulator valve and connect the brake lines to their correct positions. Tighten the brake lines to 13 ft. lbs.
12. Connect the modulator valve ground wire.
13. Install the ABS wiring harness.

NOTE: When installing the wiring harness, be certain that all the connectors are securely connected.

14. Connect the negative battery cable.
15. Bleed the brake system.
16. Install the insulation and the storage tray.

ELECTRONIC CONTROL MODULE REPLACEMENT

1. Disconnect the negative battery cable.
2. Remove the storage tray and insulation.
3. Disconnect the electronic control module connector by depressing the spring clip located under the neck of the connector.
4. Remove the module relay from the electronic control module.
5. Remove the two electronic control module mounting bolts.
6. Remove the control module.
7. To install, reverse the removal procedure.

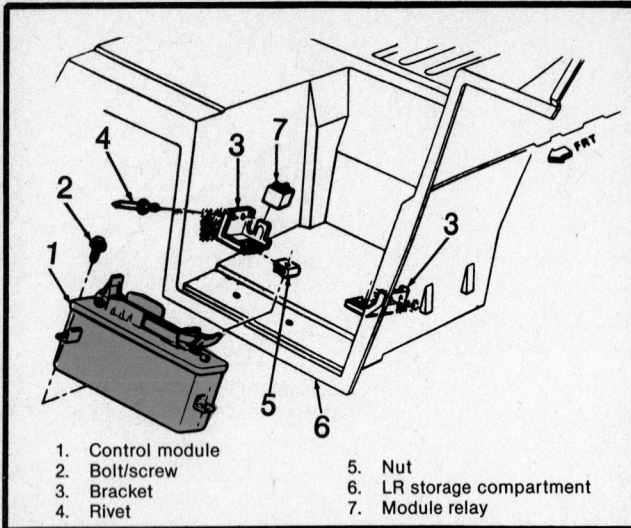

1. Control module
2. Bolt/screw
3. Bracket
4. Rivet

5. Nut
6. LR storage compartment
7. Module relay

Electronic control module mounting

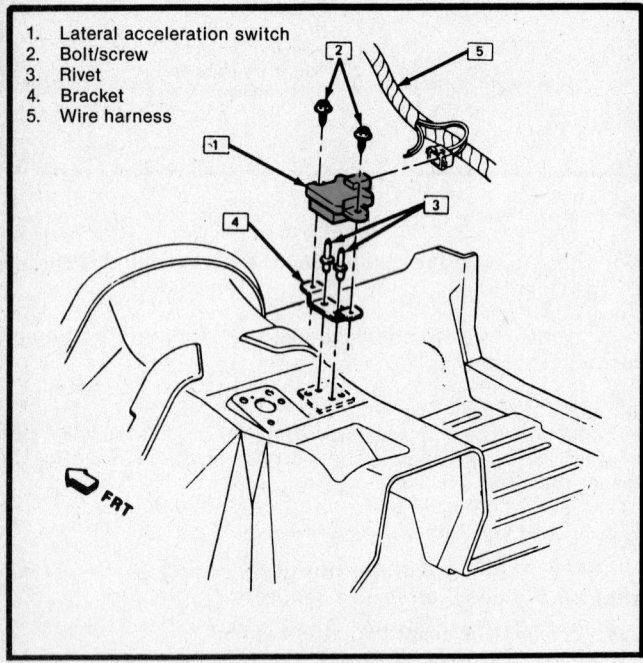

1. Lateral acceleration switch
2. Bolt/screw
3. Rivet
4. Bracket
5. Wire harness

Lateral acceleration switch mounting

NOTE: The electronic control module must be installed correctly to insure the wiring harness connector comes in from the correct side. The electronic control module connector must be securely connected.

LATERAL ACCELERATION SWITCH REPLACEMENT

1. Disconnect the negative battery cable.
2. Remove the screws retaining the instrument cluster trim plate.
3. Remove the screw retaining the "I.P" accessory trim plate and then remove the trim plate.
4. Remove the screws retaining the console trim plate.
5. Rotate the trim plate and disconnect the lighter.
6. Remove the "A/C" control head.

7. Remove the lateral acceleration switch mounting bolts.
8. Disconnect the wiring harness and remove the switch.
9. To install, reverse the removal procedure.

WHEEL SPEED SENSOR REPLACEMENT

1. Raise the vehicle and support safely on jackstands.
2. Remove the wheel and tire assembly.
3. Unclip the sensor connector from the bracket and disconnect it.
4. Remove the sensor wire grommets from the brackets, take note of the sensor wire routing for installation.
5. Remove the sensor hold down bolt(s) from the knuckle and remove the sensor.
To install:
6. Coat the new wheel speed sensor with anti-corrosion compound (GM Part No. 9981128 or equivalent) prior to installation.
7. Install the sensor into the knuckle.

NOTE: DO NOT hammer the sensor into the knuckle.

8. Install the sensor hold down bolt(s) and tighten to 27 inch lbs.
9. Install the sensor wire grommets to the brackets and route the sensor wire as noted during Step 4.
10. Connect the sensor connector and clip into the bracket.
11. Install the wheel and tire assembly.
12. Lower the vehicle.

WIRING HARNESS REPLACEMENT

1. Disconnect the negative battery cable.
2. Remove the storage tray and installation.
3. Disconnect the following wiring harness connectors:
   a. Electronic Control Module—depress the spring clip located under the neck of the connector and remove it.
   b. Modulator Valve—remove the two screws from the harness retainer and remove the connector.
   c. Battery Feed—disconnect the 12 gauge red wire.
   d. Wheel Speed Sensor—disconnect.
   e. Body Harness—disconnect.
   f. Module Relay—remove the module relay from the electronic control module bracket and disconnect it.
4. To install, reverse the removal procedure.

NOTE: When installing the harness, make sure all the connectors of the wiring harness are securely connected.

Diagnosis & Testing

PRELIMINARY CHECKS

While encountering an Antilock Brake System problem, such as the "ANTILOCK" warning light on, perform the following preliminary checks before performing the diagnostig procedure.
• Check that the car is equipped with an updated electronic control module relay which can be identified by a "green dot" on the side.
• Check that the electronic control module connector is securely connected.
• Check that all the other antilock brake system connectors are securely connected.
• Check the "BRAKE" and "GAUGE" fuses.

PRECAUTIONS

• If welding is to be performed with an electric arc welder, the control module must be unplugged.
• During painting work, the electronic control module may

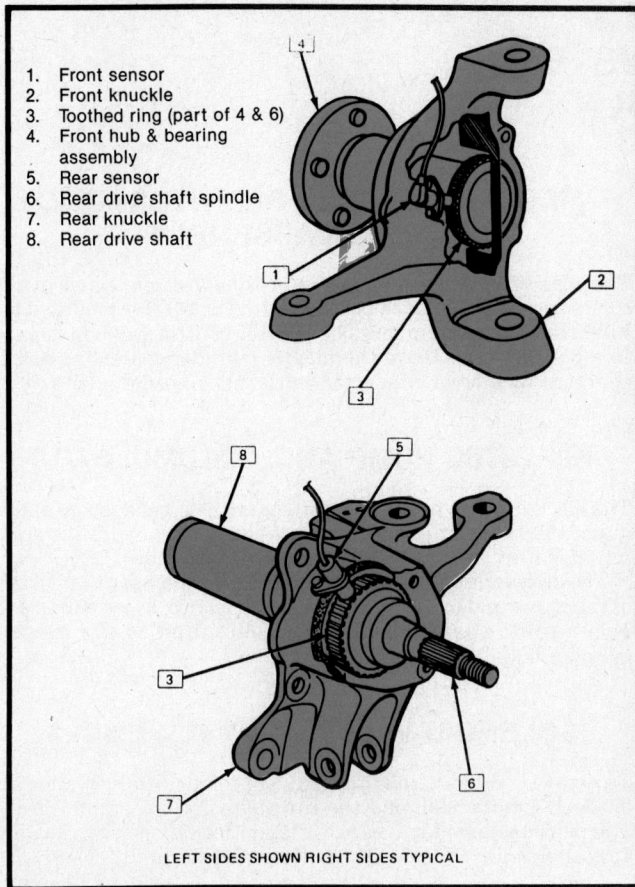

1. Front sensor
2. Front knuckle
3. Toothed ring (part of 4 & 6)
4. Front hub & bearing assembly
5. Rear sensor
6. Rear drive shaft spindle
7. Rear knuckle
8. Rear drive shaft

LEFT SIDES SHOWN RIGHT SIDES TYPICAL

Wheel speed sensor mounting

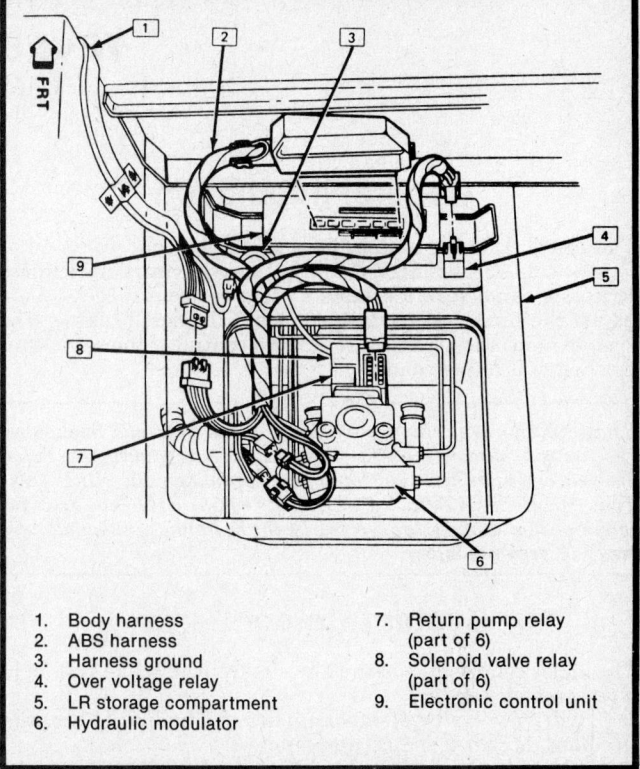

1. Body harness
2. ABS harness
3. Harness ground
4. Over voltage relay
5. LR storage compartment
6. Hydraulic modulator
7. Return pump relay (part of 6)
8. Solenoid valve relay (part of 6)
9. Electronic control unit

Wiring harness and relay mounting

be subjected to a maximum temperature of 95°C for short periods and a maximum temperature of 85°C for longer periods up to 2 hours.

• After replacing the modulator valve, electronic control module, wheel speed sensors and/or wiring harness, as well as work performed after accidents, the entire ABS system must be checked using the ABS diagnostic tester.

NOTE: Make sure that the hydraulic brake lines are routed properly during component replacement. If the brake lines happen to get swapped (i.e., inlet vs. outlet), it can be detected in one of the two following ways: one being the ABS diagnostic tester or by actually doing an antilock stop, at which time the wheels will do the opposite of what they're supposed to, namely lock-up.

• DO NOT use a fast charger for starting the engine.
• Disconnect the battery from the vehicle while fast charging.
• DO NOT disconnect the battery from the vehicle while the engine is running.
• Check that all the wiring connectors are securely connected.
• DO NOT connect or disconnect the wiring harness plug of the electronic control module with the ignition switched "ON".
• DO NOT attemp to repair the modulator valve. The entire assembly must be replaced. Exceptions to this are the two relays, both of which may be replaced. No screws on the modulator valve may be loosened apart from the brake-line connec-

tions. After loosening it is no longer possible to get the brake circuits leak-tight.

• When replacing the modulator valve, it must be replaced through the access in the rear storage compartment. Be sure to protect the interior from damage which may be caused from the spillage of brake fluid. DO NOT attempt to remove the bottom of the rear storage compartment to replace the modulator valve.

• Wipe out the bottom of the rear storage compartment when replacing the modulator valve.

• DO NOT allow suspension components to be supported by the wheel sensor wires.

• The wheel speed sensors are a tight fit into the knuckle and are to be pushed in by hand. DO NOT hammer the sensors into position.

• There are four "individual" wheel speed sensors and must be installed in their respective locations. Each replacement wheel speed sensor is identified with a white tag, (located 20mm from the neck of the sensor) labeled "L" (left) and "R" (right).

• Wheel and tire assemblies are to be removed when replacing wheel speed sensors.

• Wheel speed sensors must be given an anti-corrosion coating before installation to prevent galvanic corrosion. DO NOT use grease.

• DO NOT use silicone brake fluid.

• Always note the routing, position, mounting, and locations of all of the components, wiring connectors, clips, brackets, brake lines, etc., when performing service on the ABS system. Proper operation of the antilock brake system can only be achieved if the system is restored to its original equipment condition.

TYPE 3
TEVES SYSTEM
LINCOLN

General Infomation

The Antilock brake system used on the Lincoln works on all four wheels. A combination of wheel speed sensors and a microprocessor can determine when a wheel is about to lock-up and adjust the brake pressure to maintain the best braking. This system helps the driver maintain the control of the vehicle under heavy braking conditions.

--- CAUTION ---

Some procedures in this section require that hydraulic lines, hoses and fitting be disconnected for inspection or testing purposes. Before disconnecting any hydraulic lines, hoses or fittings, BE SURE THAT THE ACCUMULATOR IS FULLY DEPRESSURIZED as described in this section. Failure to depressurize the hydraulic accumulator may result in personal injury.

System Components

The major components of the Lincoln antilock brake system include the following:
- Hydraulic Unit—Master cylinder and hydraulic booster
- Electric pump and accumulator
- Solenoid valve body assembly
- Electronic Brake Control Module—Electronic controller
- Reservoir
- Four wheel speed sensors

MASTER CYLINDER AND HYDRAULIC BOOSTER ASSEMBLY

The master cylinder and brake booster are connected in the convention front-to-back position with the booster mounted behind the master cylinder. The booster control valve is located in a parallel bore above the master cylinder centerline and is operated by a lever connected to the brake pedal push rod.

ELECTRIC PUMP AND ACCUMULATOR

The electric pump is high pressure pump designed to run at frequent intervals for short periods to charge the hydraulic accumulator that supplies the service brake system.

The accumulator is a gas-filled pressure chamber that is part of the pump and motor assembly. The electric motor, pump and accumulator assembly is shock mounted to the master cylinder/booster assembly.

SOLENOID VALVE BODY ASSEMBLY

The valve body contains three pairs of solenoid valves, one pair for each front wheel, and the third pair for both rear wheels. The paired solenoid valves are inlet/outlet valves with the inlet valve normally open and the outlet valve normally closed. The

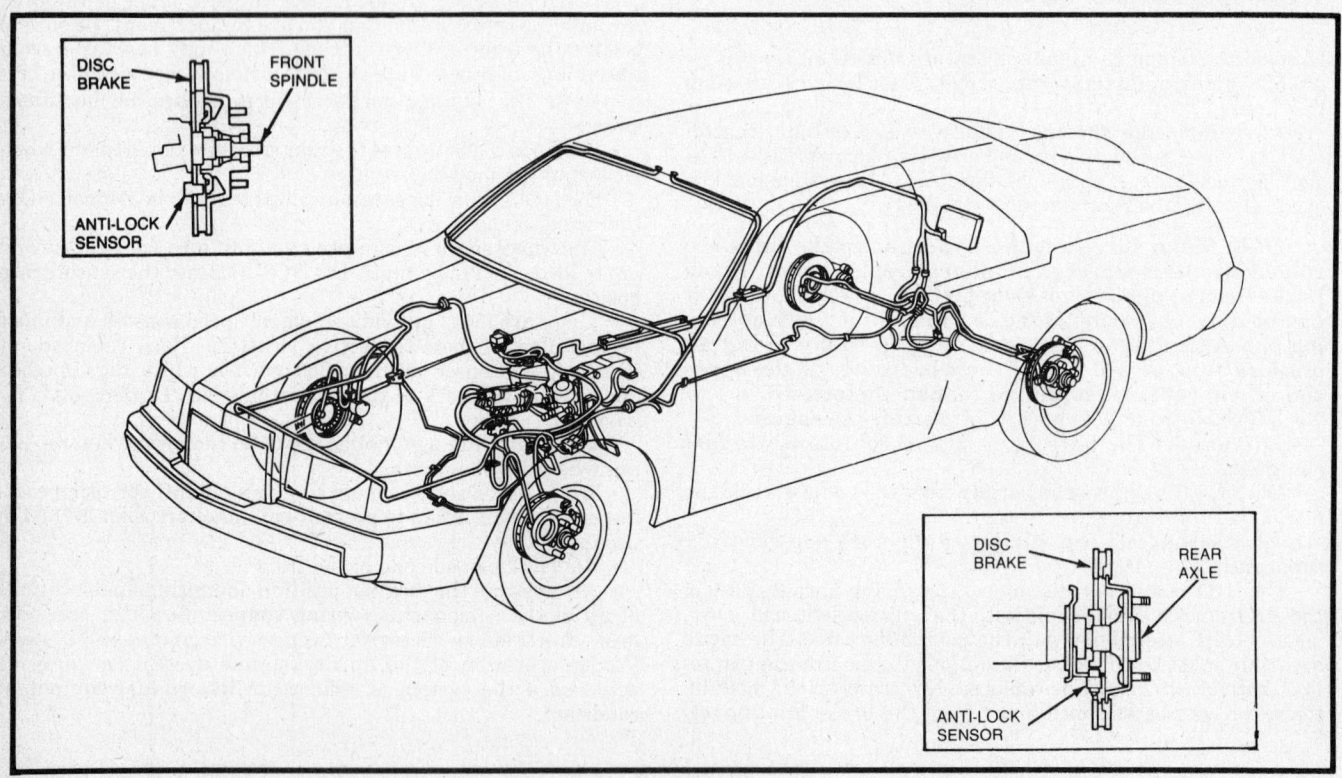

Lincoln antilock brake system

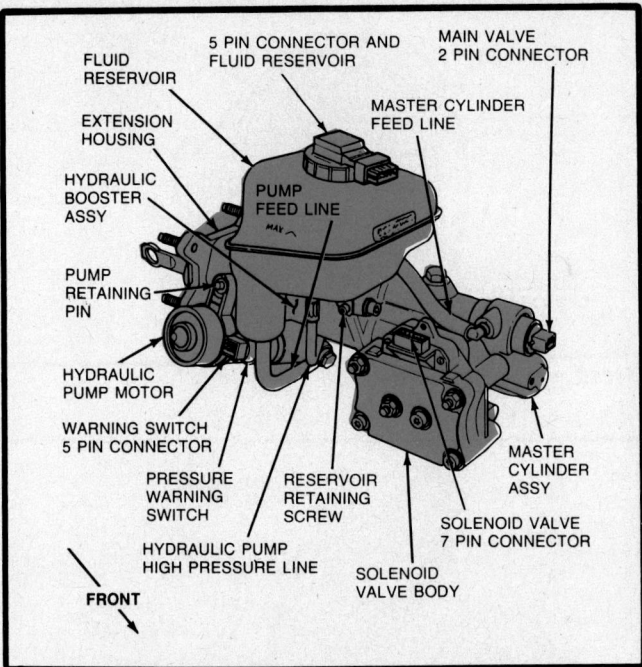

Master cylinder and hydraulic booster assembly

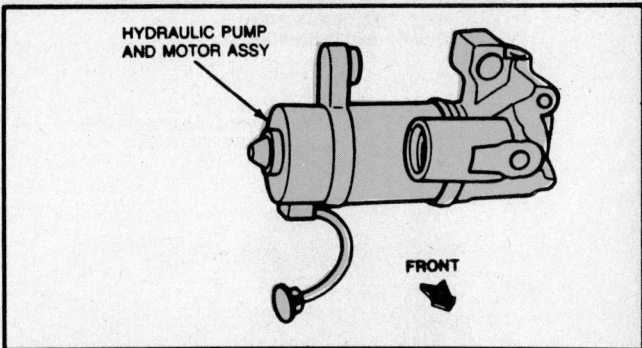

Electric motor and pump assembly

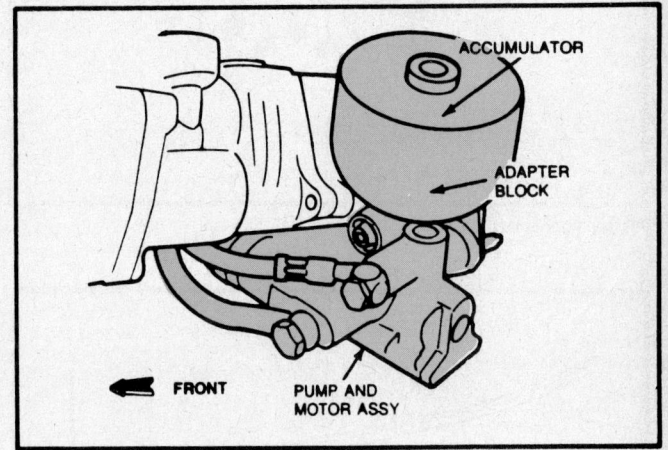

Accumulator assembly

valve body is bolted to the inboard side of the master cylinder/booster assembly.

FLUID RESERVOIR AND WARNING SWITCHES

The reservoir assembly is a translucent plastic container having two main chambers. Integral fluid level switches are part of the reservoir cap assembly with one electrical connector pointing foreward for the wire harness connections. Two low pressure hoses lead from the reservoir, one is attached to the hydraulic pump assembly and the other to the master cylinder housing.

The reservoir is mounted to the hydraulic unit with a screw and bracket and a push-in tube outlet that seats in a grommet located in the brake booster housing.

WHEEL SPEED SENSORS

There are four electronic sensor assemblies, each with a 104 tooth ring in the antilock brake system. Each sensor is connected to the electronic brake control module through a wiring harness. The front sensors are bolted to brackets which are mounted to the front spindles. The front toothed sensor rings are pressed onto the inside of the front rotors. Each sensor has an adjustable air gap between the sensor head and the toothed sensor ring. The front sensor air gap is 0.043 in. (1.1mm) and is set using a non-magnetic feeler gauge.

The rear sensors are bolted to brackets which are mounted to the rear disc brake axle adapters. The toothed rings are pressed on the axle shafts, inboard of the axle shaft flange. The rear sensor air gap is 0.026 in. (0.65mm) and is set using a non--magnetic feeler gauge.

ELECTRONIC BRAKE CONTROL MODULE

The EBCM microcomputer monitors the speed of each wheel to determine if any of the wheels are beginning to lock-up. If lock--up of a wheel is detected, the brake pressures are automatical-

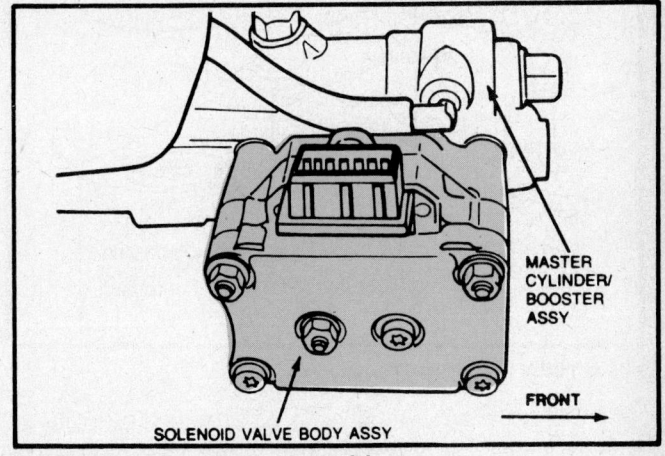

Solenoid valve block assembly

ly adjusted to provide for maximum braking without wheel lock.

The EBCM monitors system operation during normal driving as well as during antilock braking. Under normal driving conditions the antilock brake system functions the same as a standard brake system. However, during the detection of wheel lock-up a slight bump or a kick-back will be felt in the brake pedal. This "bump" felt in the pedal will be followed by a series of short pulsations which occur in rapid succession. The brake pedal pulsations will continue until there is no longer a need for the antilock function or until the car is stopped. A

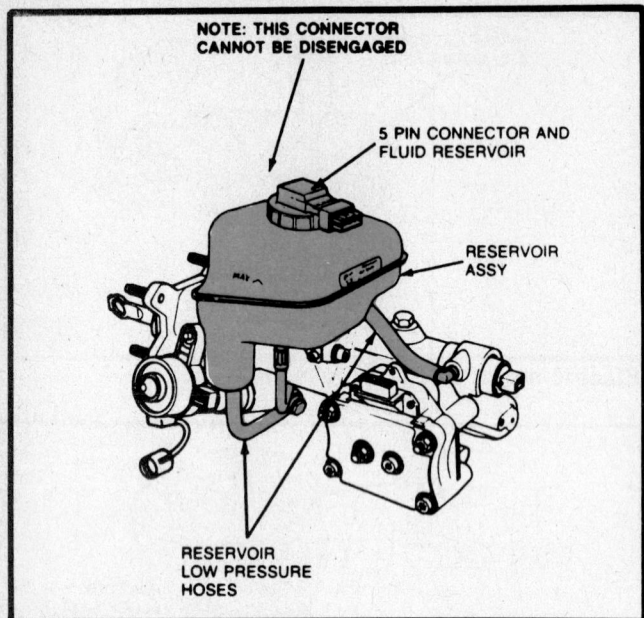

Fluid reservoir assembly

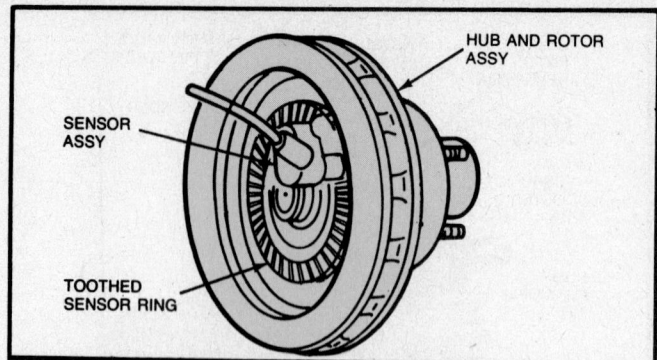

Front wheel speed sensor

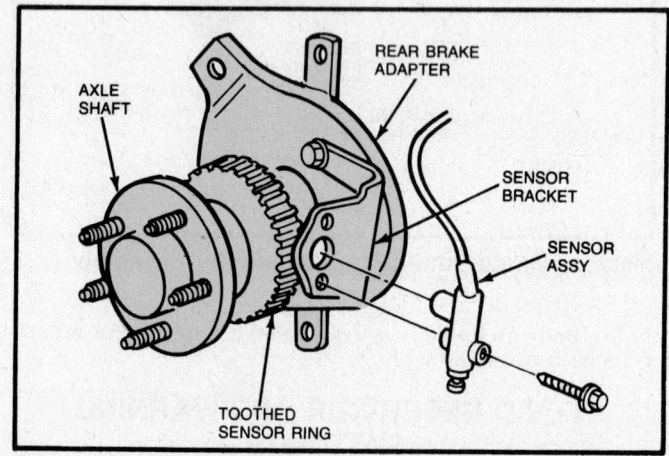

Rear wheel speed sensor

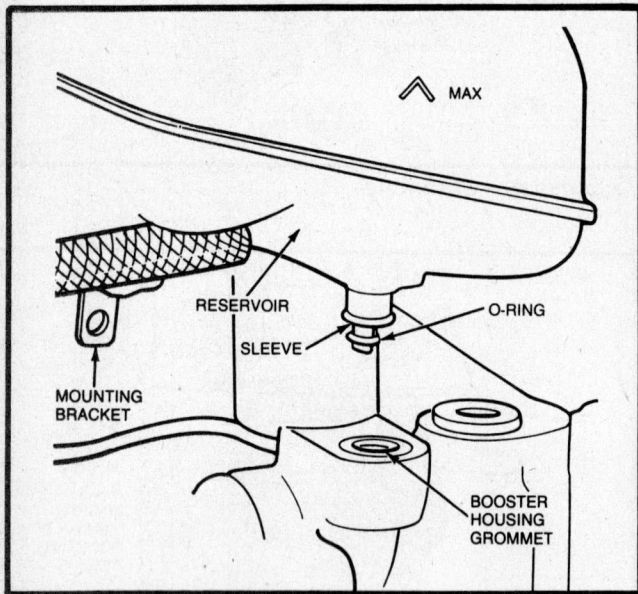

Fluid reservoir mounting

slight ticking or popping noise may be heard during brake applications with antilock. This noise is normal and indicates that the antilock system is being used.

When the antilock system is being used, the brake pedal may rise even as the brakes are being applied. This is normal. Maintaining a constant force on the pedal will provide the shortest stopping distance.

System Operation

The hydraulic pump maintains a pressure between 2030–2610 psi in the accumulator and is connected by a high pressure hose to the booster chamber and a control valve. When the brakes are applied, a scissor-lever mechanism activates the control valve and a pressure, proportional to the pedal travel, enters the booster chamber. This pressure is transmitted through the normally open solenoid valve through the proportioning valve to the rear brakes. The same pressure moves the booster piston against the master cylinder piston, shutting off the central valves in the master cylinder. This applies pressure to the front wheels through the two front normally open solenoid valves.

The Electronic Brake Control Module monitors the electromechanical components of the system. A malfunction in the antilock brake system will cause the module to shut off or inhibit the antilock system. However, normal power assisted braking remains operational. Malfunctions are indicated by one of the two warning lights inside the vehicle.

The four wheel antilock brake system is self monitoring. When the ignition switch is turned to the "RUN" position, the electronic brake control module will perform a preliminary self check on the antilock electrical system indicated by a 3–4 second illumination of the "CHECK ANTILOCK BRAKES" light in the over head console. During operation of the vehicle, including both normal and antilock braking, the electronic brake control module continually monitors all electrical antilock functions as well as many hydraulic performance characteristics.

During most malfunctions in the antilock brake system, the amber "CHECK ANTILOCK BRAKES" and/or "BRAKE" light will be illuminated. The sequence of these warning lights combined with other problem symptoms determine the appropriate tests to perform. The diagnostic test will then pin point the exact components causing the malfunction.

Component Replacement

CAUTION

Some procedures in this section require that hydraulic lines, hoses and fitting be disconnected for inspection or testing purposes. Before disconnecting any hydraulic lines, hoses or fittings, BE SURE THAT THE ACCUMULATOR IS FULLY DEPRESSURIZED as described in this section. Failure to depressurize the hydraulic accumulator may result in personal injury.

DEPRESSURIZING THE HYDRAULIC ACCUMULATOR

• Depressurize the Hydraulic Accumulator before performing any service.
• With the ignition turned OFF and the negative battery cable disconnected, apply and release the brake pedal a minimum of 20 times using approximately 50 lbs. force on the pedal. A noticeable change in pedal feel will occur when the accumulator is completely discharged.

SPECIAL TOOLS

The following special tools are required for service of the Antilock Brake System:
• Tool No. T71P–4621–A Pinion Bearing Cone Remover
• Tool No. T85P–20202–A Antilock Ring Gear Remover
• Tool No. T85P–20202–B Antilock Ring Gear Replacer

FILLING AND BLEEDING PROCEDURE

NOTE: DO NOT allow the pump to run more than 60 seconds at one time. If the pump must run longer, allow the pump to cool several minutes between 60 second runs.

Checking & Filling
• With the ignition turned ON, pump the brake pedal until the hydraulic pump motor starts.
• Wait until the motor shuts off.
• Check the brake fluid level. If the level is below the "MAX" line on the reservoir, add fluid to bring the level to this point.

NOTE: DO NOT fill over the "MAX" fill line. Overfilling of the reservoir may cause the fluid to overflow when the accumulator discharges during normal operation. Use only Dot 3 brake fluid from a clean, sealed container. Use of Dot 5 silicone fluid is not recommended. Internal damage to the pump components may result.

PRESSURE BLEEDING

Only the front brakes should be pressure bled. The rear brakes will bleed without the use of pressure equipment. Only diaphragm type pressure bleeding equipment should be used to prevent air, moisture and other contaminants from entering the system.

NOTE: The front brakes may be manually bled by conventional bleeding methods. The rear brakes should be bled according to the procedures given below.

Rear Brake Circuit
1. Turn the ignition on and allow the system to charge. (Listen for the pump motor, it will stop when the system is charged.)
2. Attach a bleeder hose to one of the rear bleeder valves and submerge the other end in a container of clean brake fluid.
3. Open the bleeder valve.

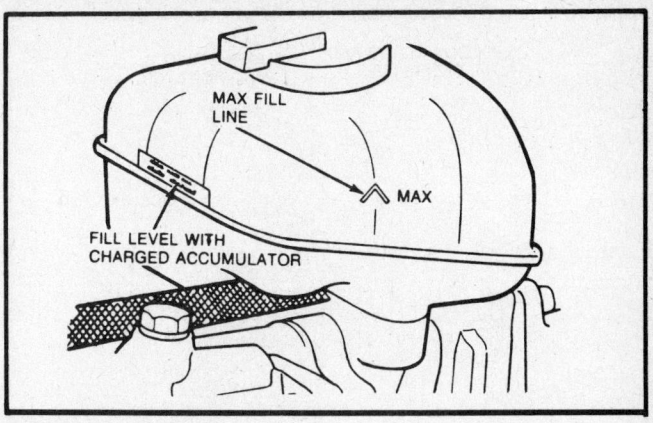

Reservoir fill level

4. With the ignition on, slightly depress the brake pedal for at least 10 seconds.
5. Allow the fluid to flow from the bleeder until no air bubbles are seen in the brake fluid. Repeat the step above if necessary.
6. Close the bleeder valve.
7. Repeat Steps 2–6 on the other rear bleeder valve.
8. Fill the fluid reservoir to the maximum level mark, following the "checking & filling" procedure above.

HYDRAULIC UNIT REPLACEMENT

1. Disconnect the negative battery cable.
2. Depressurize the accumulator by applying and releasing the brake pedal a minimum of 20 times using approximately 50 lbs. force on the pedal. A noticeable change in pedal feel will occur when the accumulator is completely discharged.
3. Label and disconnect all electrical connections to the unit.
4. Disconnect the brake lines connected to the solenoid valve body. Plug the threaded tube openings in the valve body to prevent the loss of brake fluid.
5. From the inside of the car, disconnect the pushrod from the brake pedal as follows:
   a. Disconnect the stoplight switch wires at the connector on the brake pedal.
   b. Remove the hairpin connector at the stoplight switch on the brake pedal and slide the pin far enough for the switch outer hole to clear the pin. Remove the switch using a twisting motion, being careful not to damage the switch.
6. Inside the engine compartment, remove the booster from the dash panel.
To install:
7. Install the Hydraulic unit with the rubber boot to the engine side of the dash panel with the four mounting studs and the push rod inserted in the proper holes.
8. Inside the passenger compartment, loosely start the four retaining lock nuts on the hydraulic unit studs.
9. Connect the push rod to the brake pedal pin as follows:
   a. Install the inner nylon washer, push rod and bushing on the brake pedal pin.
   b. Position the stoplight switch so the switch slot straddles the push rod on the brake pedal pin with the switch outer hole just clearing the pin. Slide the switch onto the pedal pin until the switch outer hole is completely on the pin. Install the outer nylon washer and secure the assembly with the hairpin retainer.
   c. Install the stoplight switch wire connector to the switch. Tighten the four hydraulic unit locknuts to 13–25 ft. lbs.
10. Connect the brake lines to the valve body one at a time

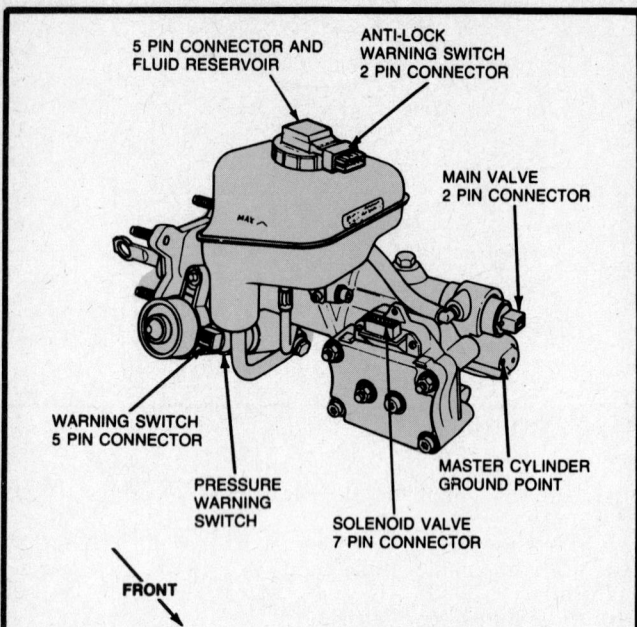

Hydraulic unit

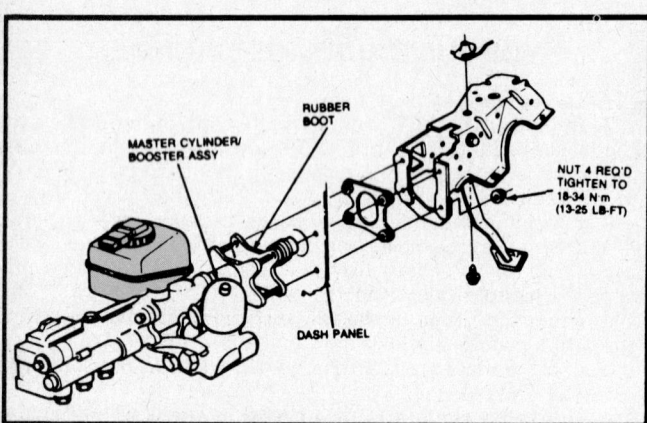

Hydraulic unit mounting

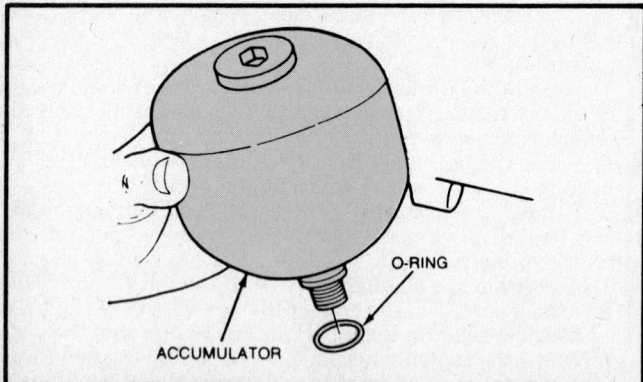

Hydraulic accumulator assembly

starting with the rear brake line (line to the right front wheel), while removing the plugs.

11. Install all electrical connections to the unit.

12. Connect the negative battery cable.
13. Bleed the brake system. Refer to the "Filling and Bleeding" procedure above.

HYDRAULIC ACCUMULATOR REPLACEMENT

1. Disconnect the negative battery cable.
2. Depressurize the accumulator by applying and releasing the brake pedal a minimum of 20 times using approximately 50 lbs. force on the pedal. A noticeable change in pedal feel will occur when the accumulator is completely discharged.
3. Using an 8mm hex wrench unscrew the hydraulic accumulator from the hydraulic unit.
4. Remove the O-ring from the accumulator.
To install:
5. Lubricate a new O-ring with clean brake fluid and install it on the accumulator.
6. Install the accumulator and tighten to 30–34 ft. lbs.
7. Connect the negative battery cable.
8. Turn the ignition to the "ON" position. The "Check Antilock Brakes" light should go out within 60 seconds.
9. Check for leakage around the accumulator.

PUMP AND MOTOR ASSEMBLY REPLACEMENT

1. Disconnect the negative battery cable.
2. Depressurize the accumulator by applying and releasing the brake pedal a minimum of 20 times using approximately 50 lbs. force on the pedal. A noticeable change in pedal feel will occur when the accumulator is completely discharged.
3. Disconnect the electrical connector from the pressure switch and the electric motor. Remove the fluid from the reservoir.
4. Remove the hydraulic accumulator and O-ring.
5. Remove the suction line between the reservoir and the pump at the reservoir by twisting the hose and pulling.
6. Disconnect the high pressure hose fitting connected to the pump. Remove the pressure hose assembly and O-rings.
8. Using a 6mm hex wrench remove the bolt attaching the pump and motor assembly to the extension housing located directly under the accumulator.

NOTE: Use a long extension and a U-joint from the front of the hydraulic unit to remove this bolt. Check and save the thick spacer between the extension housing and the shock mount.

9. Move the pump and motor assembly inboard (toward the engine) to remove the assembly from the retaining pin located on the inboard side of the extension housing.
To install:
10. Install the pump and motor assembly onto the retaining pin and swing the pump outboard into position. Install the allen head bolt and thick spacer and tighten to 5–7 ft. lbs.
11. Install the sealing bolt on the pressure hose to the booster housing under the reservoir. Inspect and replace the O-rings, if necessary. Be sure that the O-rings are on each side of the banjo fitting. Tighten the bolt to 12
15 ft. lbs.
12. Connect the suction hose to the fluid reservoir being careful to minimize fluid loss when removing the vacuum nipple and installing the hose.
13. Lubricate a new O-ring with clean brake fluid and install it on the accumulator.
14. Install the accumulator and tighten to 30–34 ft. lbs.
15. Connect the electrical connectors to the pump motor and pressure warning switch.
16. Connect the negative battery cable.

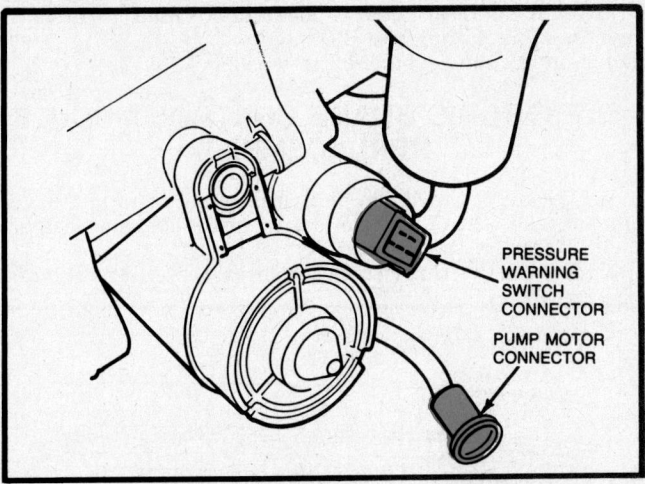

Pressure switch and pump motor connections

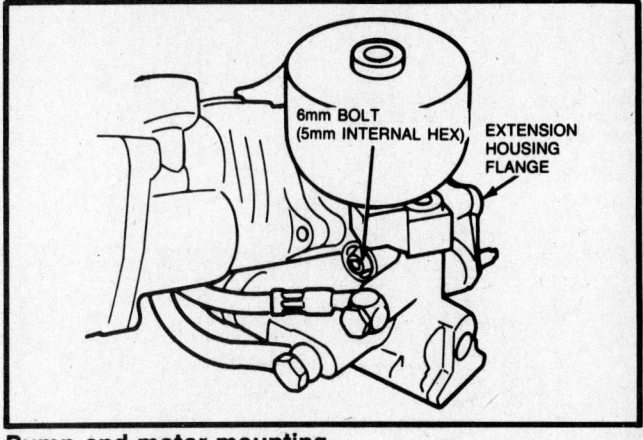

Pump and motor mounting

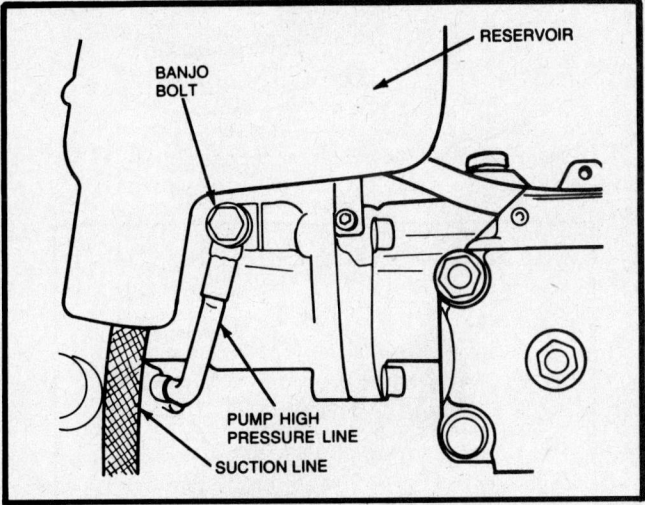

Suction and high pressure line locations

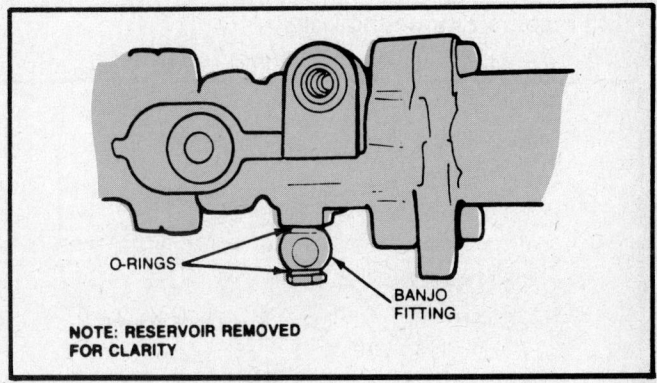

NOTE: RESERVOIR REMOVED FOR CLARITY

Pressure line mounting

17. Turn the ignition to the "ON" position. The "Check Antilock Brakes" light should go out within 60 seconds.

VALVE BLOCK ASSEMBLY REPLACEMENT

1. Disconnect the negative battery cable.
2. Depressurize the accumulator by applying and releasing the brake pedal a minimum of 20 times using approimately 50 lbs. force on the pedal. A noticeable change in pedal feel will occur when the accumulator is completely discharged.
3. Remove the hydraulic unit as described above.
4. Using a 13mm hex socket remove the 3 nuts and washers show in the illustration which are holding the valve block to the master cylinder.
5. Remove the valve block assembly and O-rings by sliding the valve block off of the studs.
To install:
6. Fit four new square-cut O-rings lubricated with brake fluid, in the four ports of the valve block mounting face.
7. Install the valve block and O-rings onto the master cylinder body.
8. Install the three nuts and new washers, tighten to 15–21 ft. lbs.
9. Install the hydraulic unit.

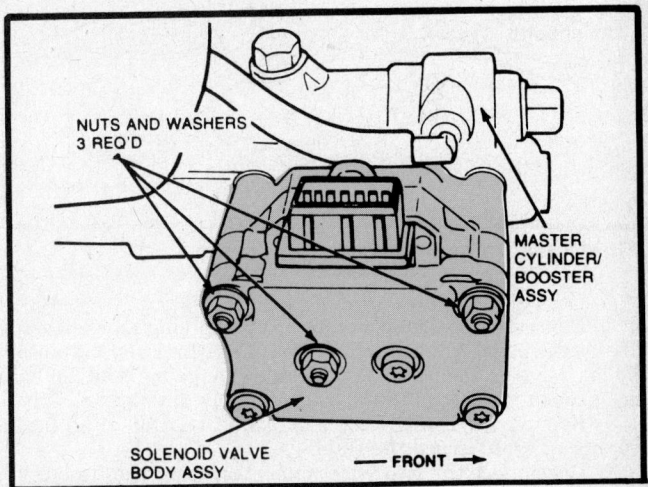

Valve block removal—remove the 3 nuts marked by the arrows

10. Install the negative battery cable.
11. Following the procedures given in this section under "Filling and Bleeding", refill and bleed the system.
12. Check for leaks at the valve block matting surfaces and tube seats.

BRAKE FLUID RESERVOIR REPLACEMENT

1. Disconnect the negative battery cable.

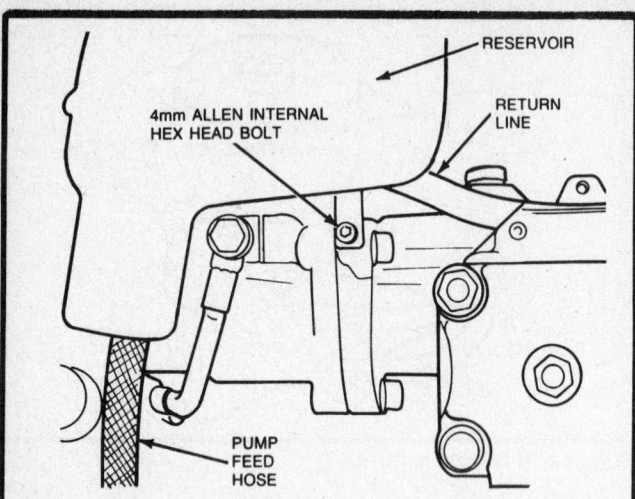

Fluid reservoir mounting bolt

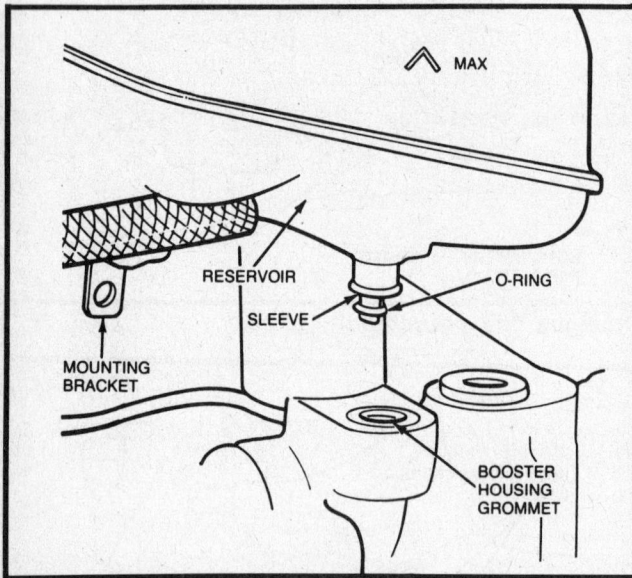

Fluid reservoir removal

2. Depressurize the accumulator by applying and releasing the brake pedal a minimum of 20 times using approximately 50 lbs. force on the pedal. A noticable change in pedal feel will occur when the accumulator is completely discharged.

3. Remove the return hose and drain the brake fluid into a container and discard the fluid.

4. Disconnect the two wire connectors from the fluid level sensor assembly.

5. Remove the 4mm reservoir to block mounting bolt.

6. Remove the reservoir by carefully prying between the reservoir and the master cylinder.

To install:

7. Lubricate the seals with clean brake fluid.

8. Install the seals and O-ring into the master cylinder body.

9. Push the reservoir into the master cylinder until it is fully seated.

10. Install the reservoir to valve block mounting bracket bolt and tighten to 35–53 inch lbs.

11. Connect the two wire connectors to the reservoir cap.

12. Connect the sump hose to the reservoir.

13. Refill the reservoir with clean brake fluid. Refer to the procedure on "Filling and Bleeding".

14. Connect the negative battery cable.

ELECTRONIC BRAKE CONTROL MODULE REPLACEMENT

1. Disconnect the 35-pin electrical connector from the electronic brake control module located in the luggage compartment in front of the forward trim panel.

2. Remove the three screws holding the electronic brake

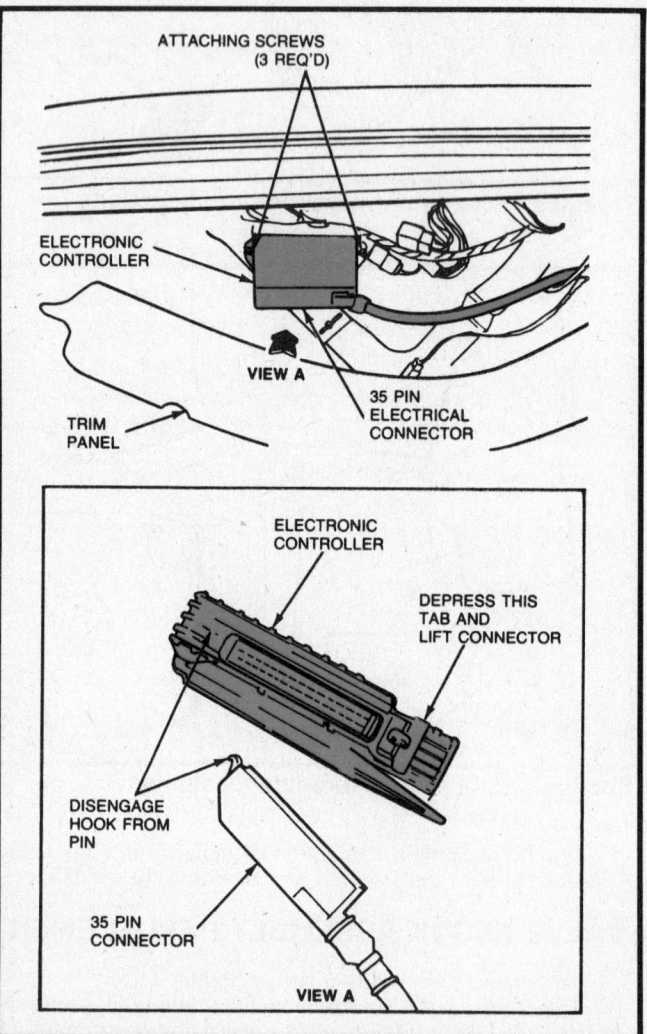

Electronic brake control module mounting

control module to the seat back brace and remove the control module.

3. Installation is the reverse of removal. Be sure that the connector is properly snapped into position.

PRESSURE WARNING SWITCH REPLACEMENT

NOTE: If the pressure warning switch is being replaced with a new one, the pump motor relay should also be replaced.

1. Disconnect the negative battery cable.

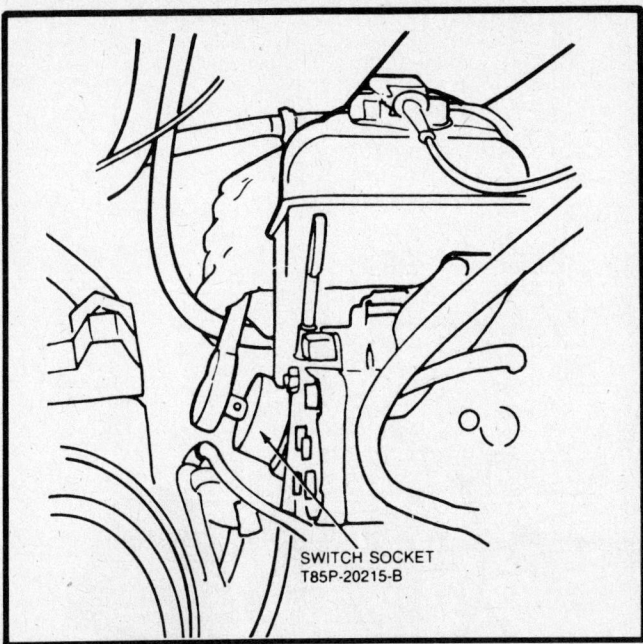

Removing pressure warning switch

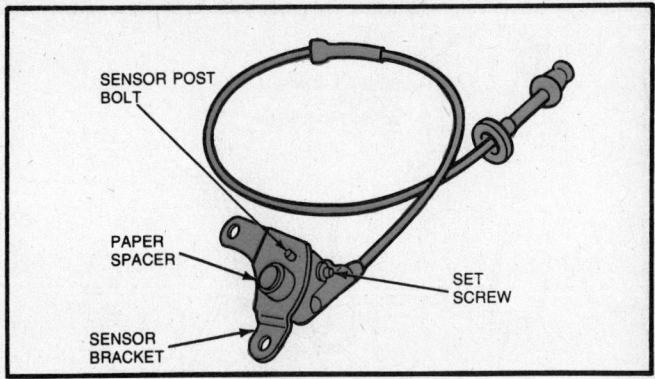

Front wheel speed sensor assembly

2. Depressurize the accumulator by applying and releasing the brake pedal a minimum of 20 times using approximately 50 lbs. force on the pedal. A noticeable change in pedal feel will occur when the accumulator is completely discharged.

3. Disconnect the electrical connectors from the valve body (7-pin) and the pressure/warning switch (5-pin).

4. Remove the pressure/warning switch using special tool No. T85P–20215–B, or equivalent, a 1/2 inch to 3/8 inch adapter, and a 3/8 inch ratchet.

5. Remove the O-ring from the switch.

To install:

6. Lubricate the O-ring with clean brake fluid.

7. Install the O-ring on the pressure/warning switch.

8. Install the switch and tighten to 15–25 ft. lbs. using special tool No. T85P–20215–B, or equivalent.

9. Connect the electrical connectors to the valve body and pressure/warning switch.

10. Connect the negative battery cable.

11. Turn the ignition to the "ON" position. The "Brake" light should go out within 60 seconds.

12. Check for leakage around the switch.

WHEEL SENSOR REPLACEMENT

Front

1. From the inside of the engine compartment, disconnect the electrical connector from the right and left sensor.

2. Raise the vehicle and support on jackstands. Disengage the wire grommet at the right and left hand shock tower and pull the sensor cable connector through the hole. Be careful no to damage the connector.

3. Remove the sensor wire from the bracket on the shock strut and the side rail.

4. Loosen the 5mm set screw holding the sensor to the sensor bracket post. Remove the sensor through the hole in the disc brake splash shield.

5. To remove the sensor bracket or the sensor bracket post, in case of damage, the caliper and the hub and rotor assembly must be removed. After removing the hub and rotor assembly, remove the two brake splash shield attaching bolts which attach the sensor bracket.

NOTE: If the toothed sensor ring is damaged, follow the procedure under "Toothed sensor ring replacement".

To install:

6. Install the sensor bracket to the sensor bracket post, if it was removed. Tighten the post retaining bolt to 40–60 inch lbs. and the splash shield attaching bolts to 10–15 ft. lbs. Install the hub and rotor assembly and the caliper.

7. If a sensor is to be re-used or adjusted, the pole face must be clean of all foreign material. Carefully scrape the pole face with a dull knife, or similar tool to ensure that the sensor slides freely on the post. Glue a new front paper spacer on the pole face (front paper spacer is marked with an "F" and is 0.043 in. (1.1mm) thick). Also the steel sleeve around the post bolt must be rotated to provide a new surface for the set screw to indent and lock onto.

8. Install the sensor through the brake shield onto the sensor bracket post. Be sure the paper spacer on the sensor is intact and does not come off during installation.

9. Push the sensor bracket toward the sensor ring until the new paper spacer contacts the ring. Hold the sensor against the sensor ring and tighten the 5mm set screw to 21–26 inch lbs.

10. Insert the sensor cable into the bracket on the shock strut, rail bracket; then through the inner fender apron to the engine compartment and seat the grommet.

11. Lower the vehicle and from inside the engine compartment, connect the sensor electrical connection.

12. Check the function of the sensor by driving the vehicle and observing the "CHECK ANTILOCK BRAKES" light in the overhead console as described under "System Operation".

Rear

1. From inside the luggage compartment, disconnect the wheel sensor electrical connector located behind the foreward luggage compartment trim panel.

2. Lift the luggage compartment carpet and push the sensor wire grommet through the hole in the luggage compartment floor.

3. Raise the vehicle and support safely on jackstands. Remove the wheel and tire assembly.

4. Carefully remove the wheel sensor wiring from the axle shaft housing. The wiring harness has three different types of retainers. The inboard retainer is a clip located on top of the differential housing. The second retainer is a C-clip located in the center of the axle shaft housing. Pull rearward on the clip to disengage the clip from the axle housing.

NOTE: DO NOT bend the clip open beyond the amount necessary to remove the clip from the axle housing.

The third clip is at the connection between the rear wheel brake tube and the flexible hose. Remove the hold-down bolt and open the clip to remove the harness.

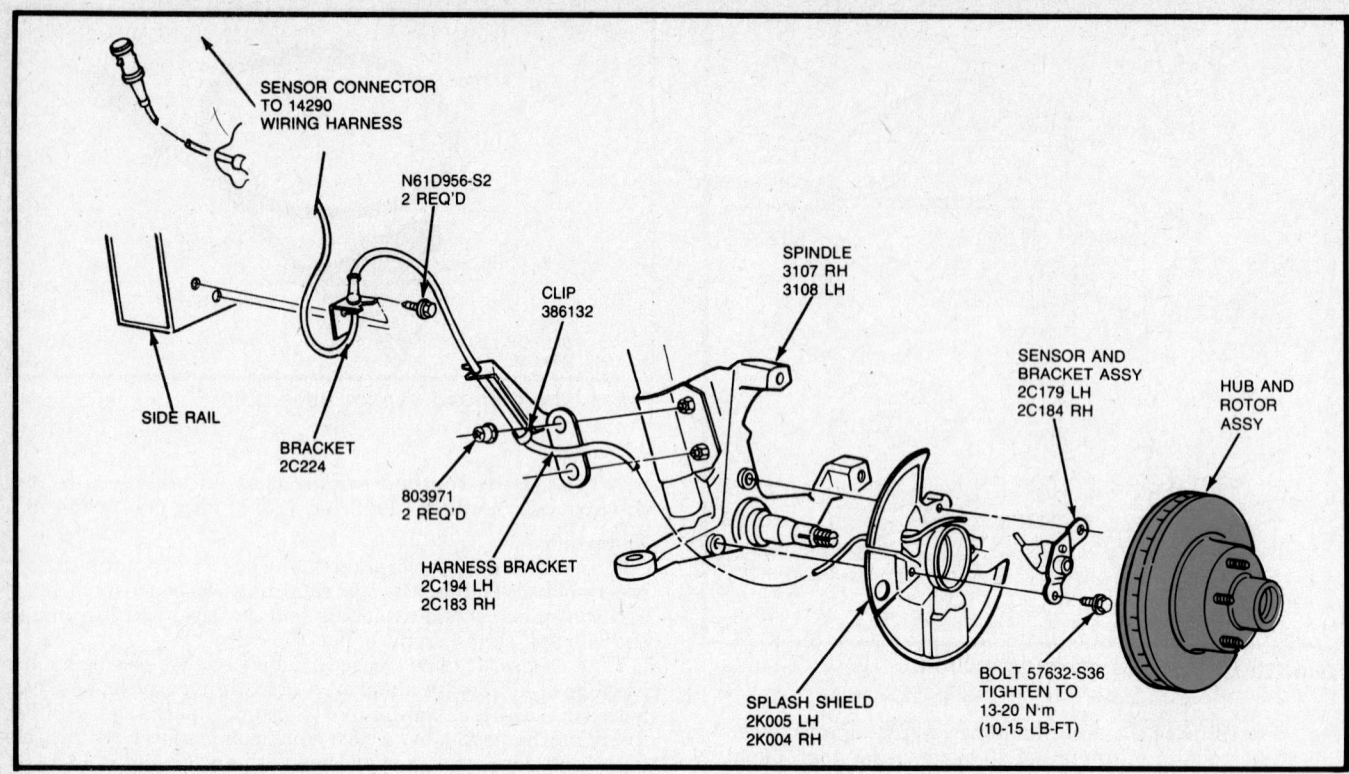

Front wheel sensor mounting

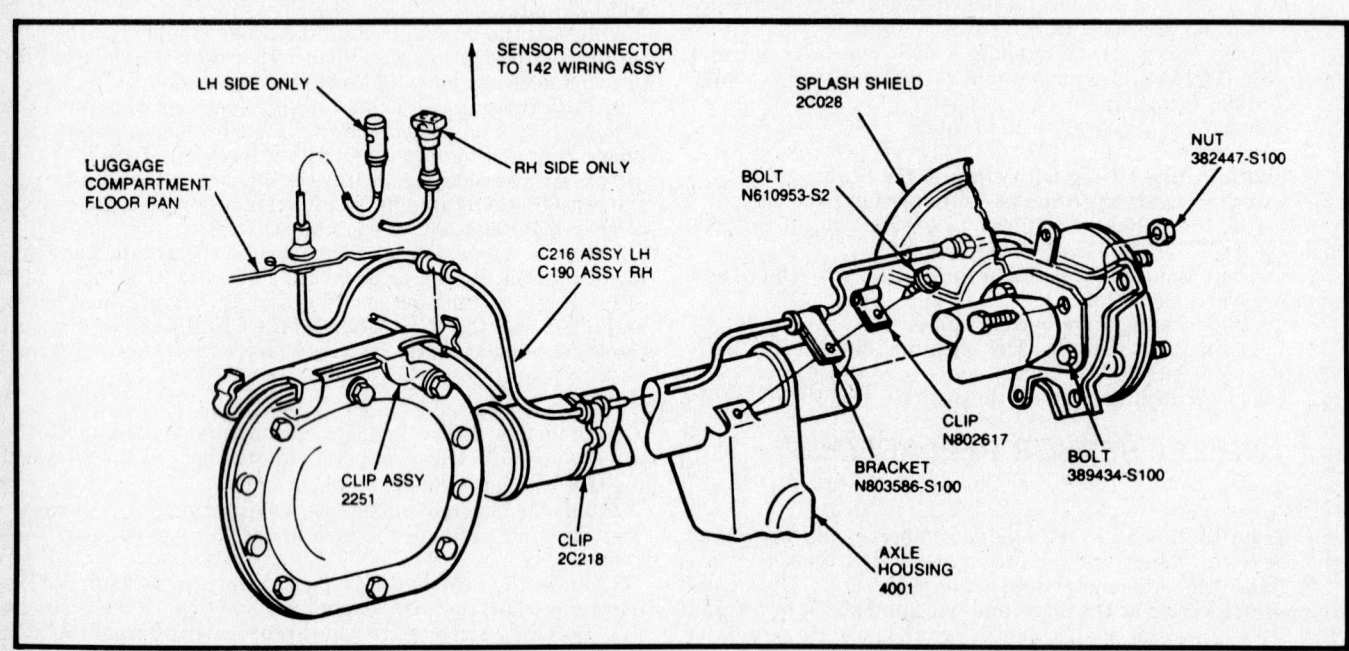

Rear wheel sensor mounting

5. Remove the rear wheel caliper and rotor assemblies.

6. Remove the wheel speed sensor 10mm hex head retaining bolt. Slip the grommet out of the rear brake splash shield and pull the sensor wire outward through the hole.

7. Inspect the sensor bracket for possible damage. If damaged, remove the two 6mm self tapping screws attaching the bracket to the axle adapter and remove the bracket.

NOTE: If the toothed sensor ring is damaged, follow the procedure under "Toothed sensor ring replacement".

To install:

8. If removed, install the sensor bracket. Tighten the screws to 11–15 ft. lbs.

9. Loosen the 5mm set screw on the sensor and ensure that the sensor slides freely on the sensor bracket post.

10. If a sensor is to be re-used or adjusted, the pole face must be clean of all foreign material. Carefully scrape the pole face with a dull knife, or similar tool to ensure that the sensor slides freely on the post. Glue a new rear paper spacer on the pole face (rear paper spacer is marked with an "R" and is 0.026 in. (0.65mm) thick).

If desired, a feeler gauge may be used instead of a paper spacer (if used, remove the paper spacer prior to adjusting). Also the steel sleeve around the post bolt must be rotated to provide a new surface for the set screw to indent and lock onto.

11. Insert the sensor into the large hole in the sensor bracket and install the 10mm hex head retaining bolt into the sensor bracket post. Tighten the bolt to 40–60 inch lbs.

12. Push the sensor toward the toothed ring until the new paper sensor makes contact with the sensor ring. Hold the sensor against the toothed ring and tighten the 5mm set screw to 21–26 inch lbs.

13. Install the caliper and rotor.

14. Push the wire and connector through the splash shield hole and engage the grommet into the shield eyelet. Install the sensor wire in the retainers along the axle housing.

15. Push the connector through the hole in the luggage compartment and seat the grommet in the luggage compartment floorpan.

16. From inside the luggage compartment, connect the cable electrical connector. Install the carpet as necessary.

17. Check the function of the sensor by driving the vehicle and observing the "CHECK ANTILOCK BRAKES" light in the overhead console as described under "System Operation".

TOOTHED SENSOR RING REPLACEMENT

Front

1. Raise and support the vehicle on jackstands.
2. Remove the wheel and tire assembly.
3. Remove the caliper and rotor assemblies.
4. Position the rotor assembly on an arbor press with the wheel studs facing up.

NOTE: Press each stud individually and carefully only until they contact the surface of the sensor ring.

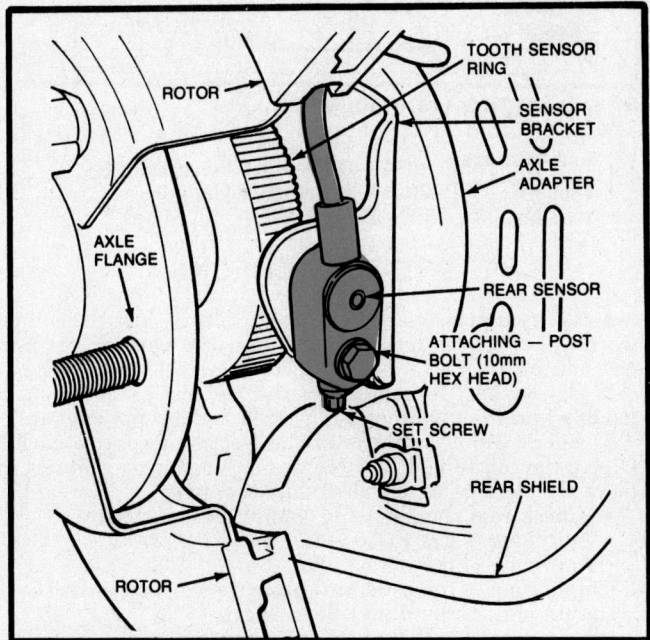

Rear wheel sensor assembly

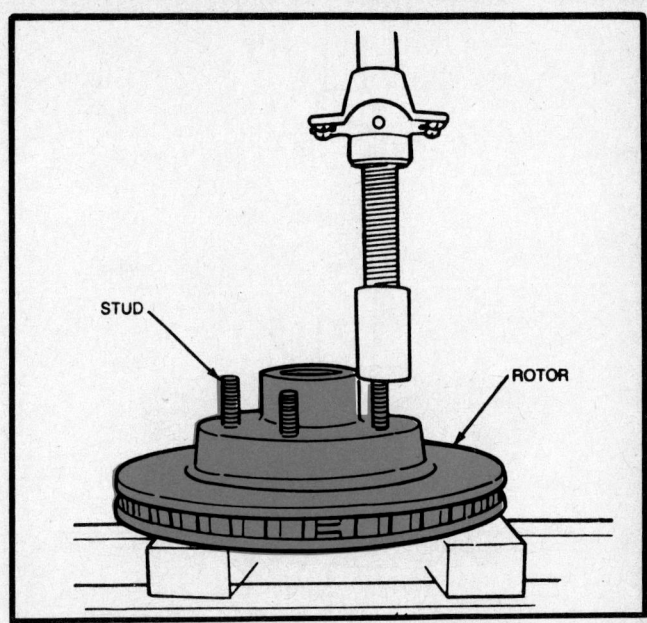

Pressing the front wheel studs individually

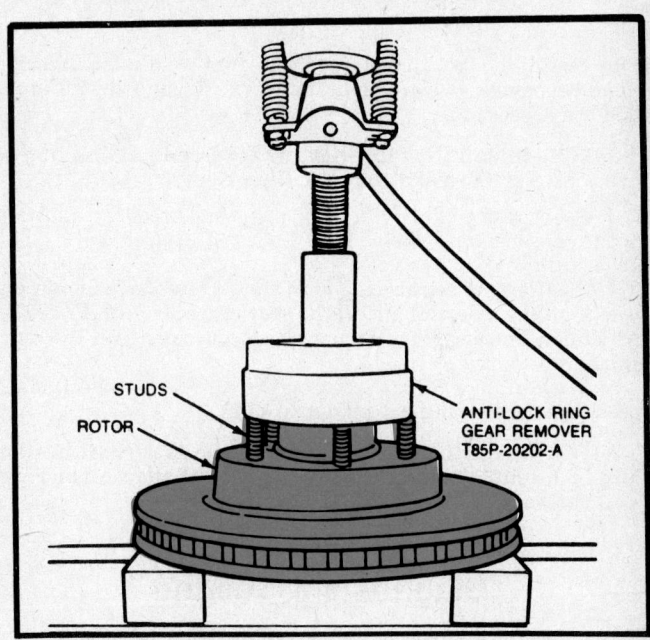

Pressing the wheel studs and the sensor ring

5. Position the special tool No. T85P–20202–A "Antilock Ring Gear Remover", or equivalent, on top of the studs and press the five studs and sensor ring out of the rotor assembly together.

To install:

6. Install the wheel studs into the rotor, one stud at a time.

7. Position the sensor ring on the rotor. Press the sensor ring onto the rotor using the special tool No. T85P–20202–B "Antilock Ring Gear Replacer", or equivalent, until the sensor ring is seated.

8. Install the rotor and caliper assemblies.

9. Install the wheel and tire assembly. Lower the vehicle.

Rear

1. Remove the rear axle shaft.

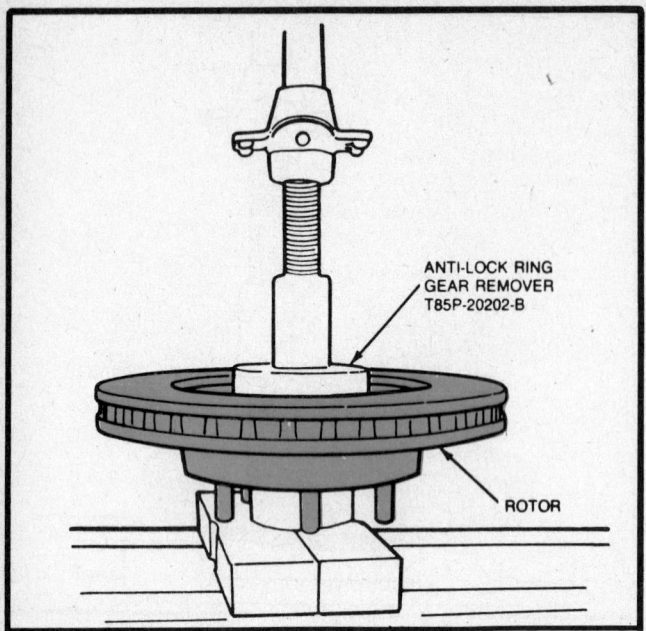

Pressing on the front wheel studs and sensor ring

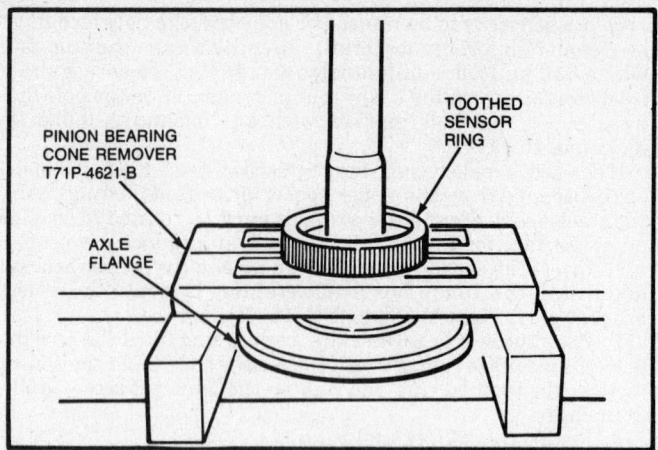

Removing the rear sensor ring from the rear axle

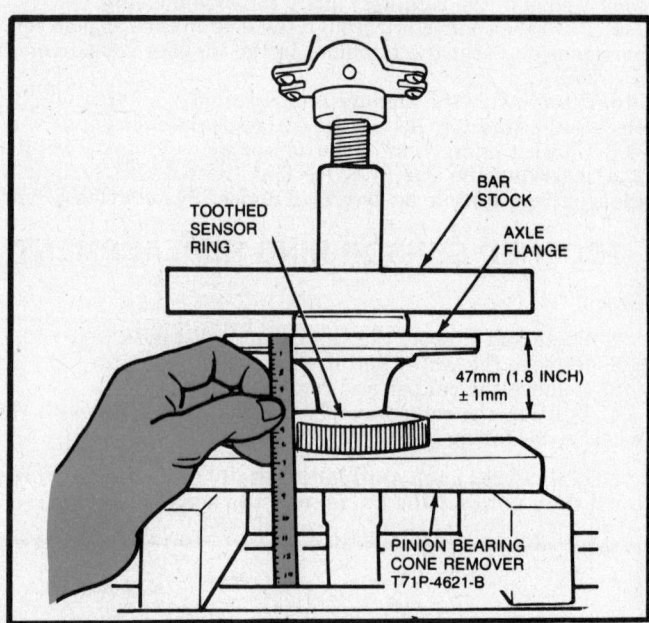

Rear wheel sensor installation

2. Install the special tool No. T71P–4621–A "Pinion Bearing Cone Remover" or equivalent, between the axle shaft flange and the sensor ring.

NOTE: Install the tool with the recessed portion of the inner surface toward the axle flange.

3. Position the axle in an arbor press and press the axle out of the sensor ring.
To install:
4. Position the sensor ring with the recessed side facing inboard, on the axle and install the special tool No. T71P–4621–A "Pinion Bearing Cone Remover" or equivalent, on the axle shaft.
5. With a piece of bar stock on the top of the axle flange, press the sensor ring onto the axle shaft.

NOTE: Press the sensor ring onto the axle shaft until a gap of 1.8 in. (47mm) between the face of the sensor ring and the face of the flange is obtained.

6. Install the axle shaft and related parts.

Diagnosis & Testing

Make sure the diagnostic procedures are used in the sequence and step-by-step order as indicated.

NOTE: Following the wrong sequence or bypassing steps will lead to unnecessary replacement of parts, and/or incorrect resolution of the symptom.

The diagnostic procedure consists of four section:
1. Pre-Test Checks.
2. Quick Tests.
3. Lamp Light Symptom Chart.
4. Diagnostic Tests (including the electrical schematic).

SPECIAL TOOLS

The following special tools are required for service of the Antilock Brake System:
• Tool No. T85P–50–ASA Antilock Harness Adapter
• Tool No. T83L–50–EEC IV Breakout Box
• Tool No. T85P–20215–B Pressure Switch Socket
• Tool No. T85P–20215–A Pressure Gauge
• Tool No. 007–00001 Digital Volt-Ohm Meter

PRE-TEST CHECKS

1. Verify that the parking brake is fully released, the brake warning switch is not grounded, and the battery has been checked.
2. Check that the contacts of the 35-pin electronic control module harness are properly inserted and are not damaged.
3. Check the 35 contacts of the electronic control module (electronic controller). If there are any damaged contacts replace the electronic control module assembly.
4. Check that the following connections are secure:
• 7-pin plug of the valve unit.
• 2-pin plug of the main valve.
• 5-pin plug of the combined pressure warning switch.
• 5-pin plug of the fluid reservoir cap.
• 2-pin plugs of all 4 wheel speed sensors.
• 2- and 4-pin plugs on each end of the motor jumper wire, if it is used.

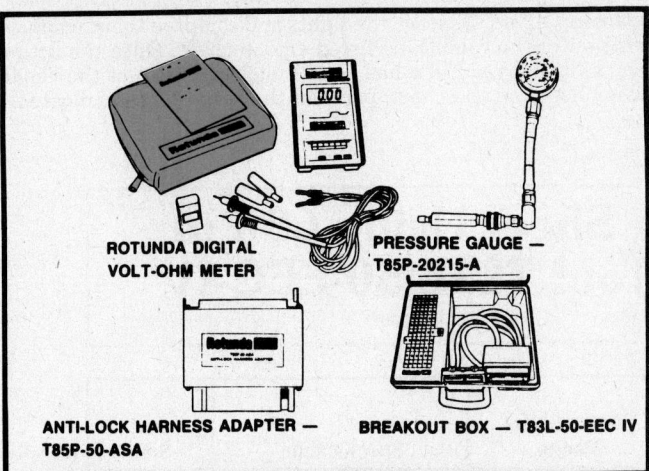

Antilock brake diagnosis—Special tools

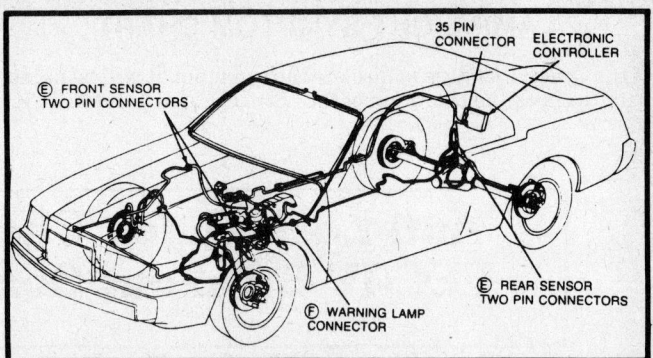

Pre-Test electrical locations

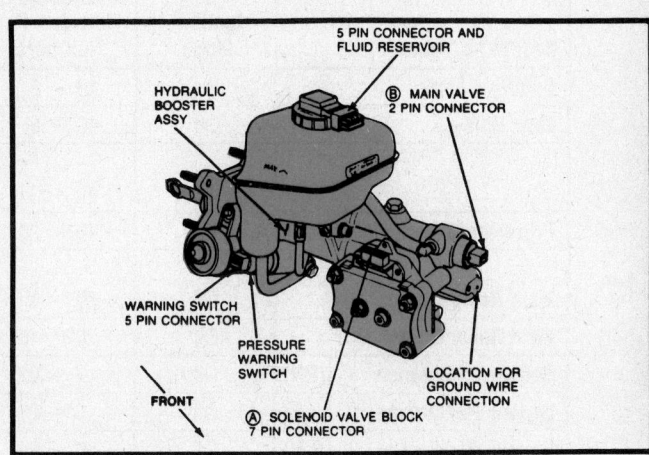

Hydraulic unit electrical locations

Anti-Lock Concerns

TEST STEP	RESULT ▶	ACTION TO TAKE
1.0 PRE-TEST CHECKS		
• Perform Pre-Test Checks.	(OK) ▶	GO to Step **2.0**.
	(⊘) ▶	CORRECT problem indicated.
2.0 QUICK TESTS		
• Perform Quick Tests.	(OK) ▶	CHECK warning lamp operation for conditions indicated in Light Symptom Chart. PERFORM the specific Diagnostic Test indicated, (A through K).
	(⊘) ▶	PERFORM the specific Diagnostic Test indicated, (A through K).

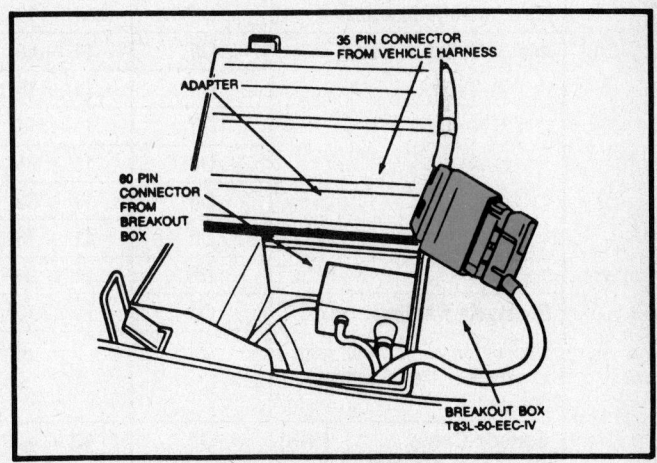

Breakout box hookup for Quick test

• 2 relay plugs located near the brake fluid reservoir inside the plastic box attached to the dash.
• Ground wire attached on the front of the hydraulic booster assembly.
• Ground wire in the luggage compartment near the 35-pin control module plug.
• Ground wire from the negative battery terminal to the fender sheet metal, to the wiring harness through the 2-pin connector.
5. Check that all relays, diodes and fuse links are intact and/or properly inserted.
6. Check that all battery cable connections are clean and tight.
7. Check the ground terminals of the electronic control module and the hydraulic unit.

QUICK CHECK TESTS

The Quick Check Tests require the use of the following special tools:

• Tool No. T85P–50–ASA Antilock Harness Adapter
• Tool No. T83L–50–EEC IV Breakout Box
• Tool No. 007–00001 Digital Volt-Ohm Meter

All Quick Tests are performed in the vehicle luggage compartment using the EEC IV Breakout Box and Harness Adapter. These tests lead to a specific Diagnostic Test that will in most cases, identify the fault. If the fault is not found by the Quick Test, use the "Light Symptom Chart" to identify the proper diagnostic procedure.

LAMP LIGHT SYMPTOM CHART

If the Quick Test does not isolate the symptom, it will be necessary to check the operation of the "BRAKE" and "ANTILOCK" warning lights. Observe the lights and compare their on/off operation to the conditions listed on the chart. Once the actual warning light pattern has been matched to one of the conditions listed on the chart, perform the specific test indicated.

Anti-Lock Quick Check Sheet Using 60-Pin EEC-IV Breakout Box, Tool T83L-50-EEC-IV

Item to be Tested		Ignition Mode	Measure Between Pin Numbers	Tester Scale/ Range	Specification	Test Step
Battery Check		On	40 + 2	Volts	10 minimum	A-1
Main Relay		Off	40 + 8	Ohms	45 Ohms — 105 Ohms	A-6
			Place a jumper between pins 2 & 8			
		On	40 + 3	Volts	10 minimum	A-7
Power from Main Relay		On	40 + 20	Volts	10 minimum	A-3
			Remove jumper from pins 2 & 8			
Main Relay Circuit		Off	40 + 3	Continuity	Continuity	A-2
Main Relay Circuit		Off	20 + 40	Continuity	Continuity	A-3a
Sensor Resistance	(RR)	Off	4 + 22	K Ohms	800 to 1400 Ohms	A-8
Sensor Resistance	(LF)	Off	5 + 23	K Ohms	800 to 1400 Ohms	A-9
Sensor Resistance	(LR)	Off	6 + 24	K Ohms	800 to 1400 Ohms	A-10
Sensor Resistance	(RF)	Off	7 + 25	K Ohms	800 to 1400 Ohms	A-11
Main Valve Resistance		Off	11 + 18	Ohms	2 Ohms to 5.5 Ohms	A-12
Inlet & Outlet Valves		Off	11 + 40	Continuity	Continuity	A-19
		Off	11 + 15	Ohms	5 Ohms to 8 Ohms	A-13
		Off	11 + 17	Ohms	5 Ohms to 8 Ohms	A-14
		Off	11 + 35	Ohms	5 Ohms to 8 Ohms	A-15
		Off	11 + 33	Ohms	3 Ohms to 6 Ohms	A-16
		Off	11 + 16	Ohms	3 Ohms to 6 Ohms	A-17
		Off	11 + 34	Ohms	3 Ohms to 6 Ohms	A-18
Reservoir Warning		On	9 + 10	Ohms	Less than 5 Ohms	A-4a
Lift Fluid Level Indicator from Reservoir (Float at bottom position)		Off	9 + 10	Ohms	Infinite (Open Circuit)	A-5a
Sensor Cable Continuity Shielding to Ground	(RR)	Off	40 + 4	Continuity	No Continuity	B-1a
	(LF)	Off	40 + 5	Continuity	No Continuity	B-2a
	(LR)	Off	40 + 6	Continuity	No Continuity	B-3a
	(RF)	Off	40 + 7	Continuity	No Continuity	B-4a
Sensor Voltage (Rotate wheels at 1 revolution per second minimum) (Shut off air suspension switch in luggage compartment with vehicle on hoist).	(RR)	Off	4 + 22	AC Millivolts	50-700 Millivolts	C-5
	(LF)	Off	5 + 23	AC Millivolts	50-700 Millivolts	C-6
	(LR)	Off	6 + 24	AC Millivolts	50-700 Millivolts	C-7
	(RF)	Off	7 + 25	AC Millivolts	50-700 Millivolts	C-8

Diagnostic light symptom chart

Legend:
- ▨ (hatched) = "Check Anti-Lock Brakes" Warning Lamp On.
- ▬ (black) = "Brake" Warning Lamp On.

Symptom (With Parking Brake Released)	Warning Lamps	Diagnostic Test to be Performed
Normal Light Sequence		
Normal Warning Lamps Sequences. (System OK)	Check Anti-lock (Amber) / Brake (Red)	
Abnormal Warning Lamps Sequences.		
• "Check Anti-Lock Brakes" Warning Lamp On. Normal "Brake" Warning Lamp Sequence.	Check Anti-lock (Amber) / Brake (Red)	A
• "Check Anti-Lock Brakes" Warning Lamp On After Starting Engine. Normal "Brake" Warning Lamp Sequence.	Check Anti-lock (Amber) / Brake (Red)	B
• "Check Anti-Lock Brakes" Warning Lamp Comes On Again After Vehicle Starts Moving. Normal "Brake" Warning Lamp Sequence.	Check Anti-lock (Amber) / Brake (Red)	C
• False Cycling of Anti-Lock System Normal Warning Lamp Sequence.	Check Anti-lock (Amber) / Brake (Red)	C
• "Check Anti-Lock Brakes" Warning Lamp and "Brake" Warning Lamp On.	Check Anti-lock (Amber) / Brake (Red)	D
• Pump Motor Runs More Than 60 Seconds. Normal Warning Lamp Sequence.	Check Anti-lock (Amber) / Brake (Red)	D
• "Check Anti-Lock Brakes" Warning Lamp Intermittently On. Normal "Brake" Warning Lamp Sequence.	Check Anti-lock (Amber) / Brake (Red)	E
• Normal "Check Anti-Lock Brakes" Warning Lamp Sequence. "Brake" Warning Lamp On.	Check Anti-lock (Amber) / Brake (Red)	F
• No "Check Anti-Lock Brakes" Warning Lamp During Test Cycle. Normal "Brake" Warning Lamp Sequence.	Check Anti-lock (Amber) / Brake (Red)	G
• Spongy Brake Pedal. Normal Warning Lamp Sequence.	Check Anti-lock (Amber) / Brake (Red)	H
• Poor Vehicle Tracking During Anti-Lock Braking. Normal Warning Lamp Sequence.	Check Anti-lock (Amber) / Brake (Red)	J
• No Boost (High Brake Pedal Effort) Anti-Lock Lamp On Only. No "Brake" Warning Lamp.	Check Anti-lock (Amber) / Brake (Red)	K

Warning Lights Sequence columns: Ignition On, Cranking Engine, Engine Running, Vehicle Moving, Braking with/without Anti-Lock, Vehicle Stopped, Engine Idle, Ignition Off.

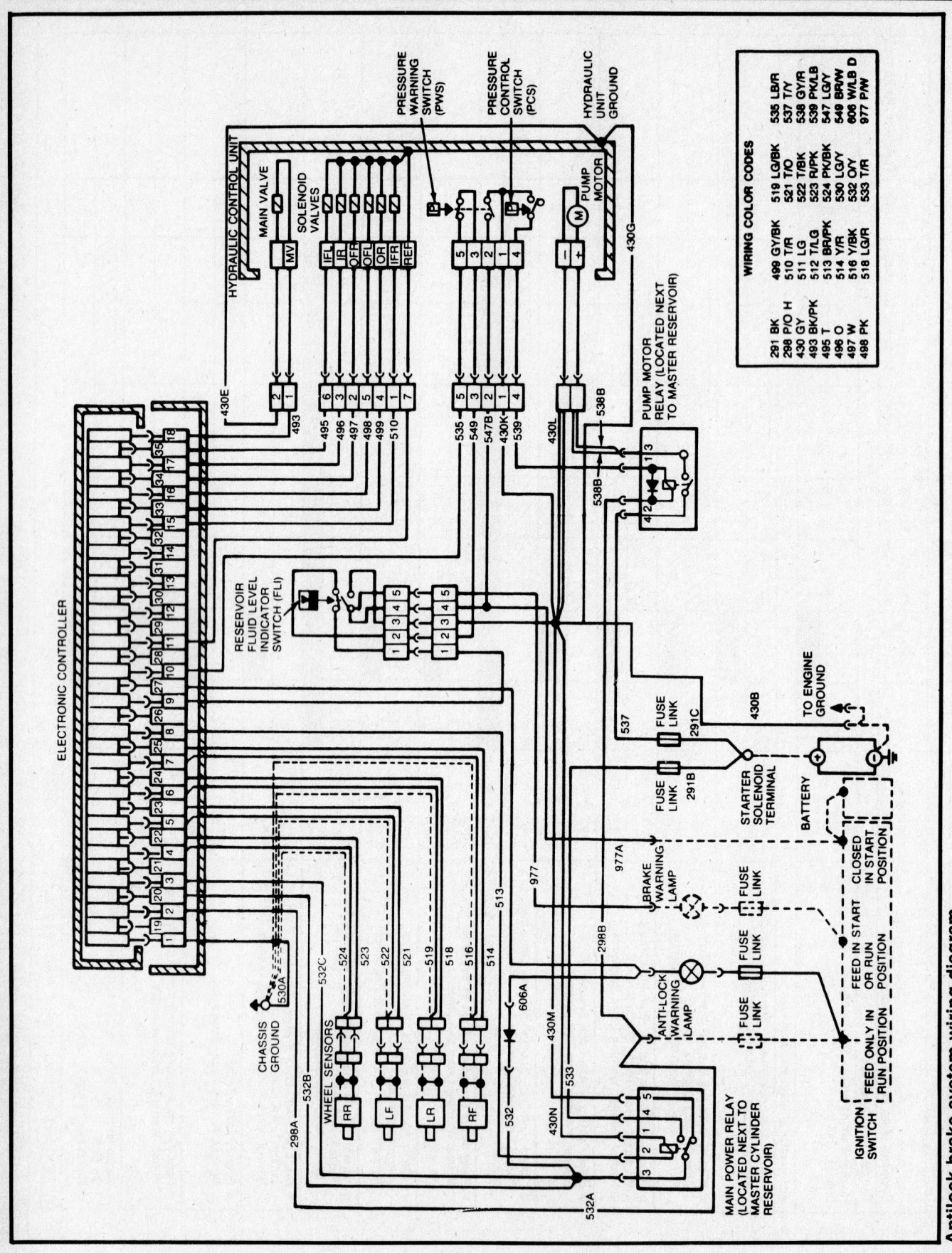

Antilock brake system wiring diagram

Anti-Lock Warning Lamp On (With Brake Warning Lamp Off) — Test A

TEST STEP	RESULT		ACTION TO TAKE
A1a CHECK ELECTRONIC CONTROLLER TO GROUND WIRE			
• Check: — fuse link to anti-lock warning lamp. — battery.			
• Remove positive battery cable.			
• Check continuity between Breakout box pin 40 and body ground.	Continuity	(OK)	GO to Step A1b.
	No continuity	(not OK)	SERVICE or REPLACE cable harness (Circuit 530 or 530A).
A1B CHECK IGNITION TO ELECTRONIC CONTROLLER WIRE			
• Check continuity between Breakout box Pin 2 and ignition switch wire 298.	Continuity	(OK)	RECONNECT positive battery cable. CHECK for power at ignition switch pin with switch ON. If okay, connect electronic controller and reverify symptom.
	No continuity	(not OK)	SERVICE or REPLACE cable harness (Circuit 298A).
A2 CHECK MAIN RELAY SECONDARY CIRCUIT (NORMAL)			
• Turn ignition switch OFF.			
• Check for continuity between Breakout box Pins 40 and 3.	Continuity	(OK)	GO to A3.
	No continuity	(not OK)	GO to A2a.

Anti-Lock Warning Lamp On (With Brake Warning Lamp Off) — Test A

WARNING LIGHTS SEQUENCE

Warning Lamps	Ignition On	Cranking Engine	Engine Running	Vehicle Moving	Braking with/without Anti-Lock	Vehicle Stopped	Engine Idle	Ignition Off
Check Anti-Lock (Amber)								
Brake (Red)								

TEST STEP	RESULT		ACTION TO TAKE
A1 35-PIN PLUG TESTING			
• Turn ignition switch OFF.			
• Disconnect 35-Pin plug from electronic controller.			
• Connect EEC-IV Breakout box with Tool T83L-50-EEC-IV or equivalent, anti-lock test adapter Tool T85P-50-ASA or equivalent, to the anti-lock 35-Pin plug wiring harness.			
• Set multi-meter to read volts DC.			
• Turn ignition switch ON.			
• Measure voltage between Breakout box Pins 40 and 2.	Over 10V	(OK)	GO to Step A2.
	Under 10V	(not OK)	GO to Step A1a.

RETAINING PIN — ELECTRONIC CONTROLLER — RETAINING CLIP — 35 PIN CONNECTOR — RETAINING HOOK — 35 PIN CONNECTOR — BREAKOUT BOX T83L-50-EEC-IV — ADAPTER

With Anti-Lock Warning Lamp On (With Brake Warning Lamp Off) — Test A

TEST STEP	RESULT	ACTION TO TAKE
A3 CHECK MAIN RELAY SECONDARY CIRCUIT (NORMAL) • Check for continuity between Breakout box Pins 40 and 20.	Continuity (OK) No continuity (NOT OK)	GO to Step A4. GO to Step A3a.
A3a CHECK MAIN RELAY SECONDARY CIRCUIT WIRING HARNESS • Remove main relay. • Check for continuity between main relay socket Pin 3 and Breakout box Pin 20. MAIN RELAY CONNECTOR — PIN NO.3	Continuity (OK) No continuity (NOT OK)	CONNECT main relay and electronic controller and reverify symptom. SERVICE or REPLACE cable harness (Circuit 532B).
A4 CHECK FLI AND PWS CIRCUIT • Turn ignition switch ON. • Set multi-meter to read resistance. • Measure the resistance between Breakout box Pins 9 and 10.	Less than 5 ohms (OK) Greater than 5 ohms (NOT OK)	GO to Step A5. GO to Step A4a.
A4a CHECK FLI ANTI-LOCK WARNING CIRCUIT • Disconnect 5-Pin plug on reservoir Fluid Level Indicator (FLI). • Measure resistance between fluid level indicator electrical socket Pins 1 and 2 (with brake fluid level at maximum mark on reservoir). PIN NO.5 / PIN NO.4 / PIN NO.3 / PIN NO.2 / PIN NO.1 — 5-PIN FLUID LEVEL INDICATOR	Less than 2 ohms (OK) Greater than 2 ohms (NOT OK)	GO to Step A4b. REPLACE fluid level indicator.

Anti-Lock Warning Lamp On (With Brake Warning Lamp Off) — Test A

TEST STEP	RESULT	ACTION TO TAKE
A2a CHECK MAIN RELAY SECONDARY CIRCUIT (NORMAL) • Disconnect main relay from socket. • Check for continuity between main relay socket Pins 3 and 5. MAIN POWER RELAY — PIN NO.5 / PIN NO.3	Continuity (OK) No continuity (NOT OK)	GO to Step A2b. REPLACE main power relay.
A2b CHECK MAIN RELAY SECONDARY CIRCUIT WIRING HARNESS • Disconnect positive battery cable. • Check for continuity between main relay socket Pin 3 and Breakout box Pin 3. MAIN RELAY CONNECTOR — PIN NO.3	Continuity (OK) No Continuity (NOT OK)	GO to Step A2c. SERVICE or REPLACE cable harness (Circuit 532C or 532A).
A2c CHECK MAIN RELAY SECONDARY CIRCUIT WIRING HARNESS • Check for continuity between main relay socket Pin 5 and body ground. MAIN RELAY CONNECTOR — PIN NO.5	Continuity (OK) No continuity (NOT OK)	RECONNECT main relay, electronic controller and battery cable and reverify symptom. SERVICE or REPLACE cable harness (Circuit 522).

Anti-Lock Warning Lamp On (With Brake Warning Lamp Off) — Test A

TEST STEP	RESULT	ACTION TO TAKE
A4b CHECK PWS ANTI-LOCK WARNING CIRCUIT • Disconnect 5-Pin plug at pressure warning switch (PWS). • Check for continuity between pressure warning switch socket Pins 3 and 5. PRESSURE WARNING SWITCH	Continuity (OK) No continuity	GO to Step A4c. REPLACE pressure warning switch and pump motor relay.
A4c CHECK ELECTRONIC MODULE TO FLI WIRE • Check for continuity between Breakout box Pin 9 and FLI 5-Pin plug Pin 1. FLUID LEVEL INDICATOR CONNECTOR	Continuity (OK) No continuity	GO to Step A4d. SERVICE or REPLACE cable harness (Circuit 512).
A4d CHECK FLI TO PWS WIRE • Check for continuity between Pin 2 of 5-Pin fluid level plug (harness side) and 5-Pin pressure warning switch plug (harness side) Pin 3. FLUID LEVEL INDICATOR CONNECTOR / PRESSURE WARNING SWITCH CONNECTOR	Continuity (OK) No continuity	GO to Step A4e. SERVICE or REPLACE cable harness (Circuit 549).
A4e PWS TO ELECTRONIC CONTROLLER WIRE • Check for continuity between 5-Pin pressure warning switch plug (harness side) Pin 5 and Breakout box Pin 10. PRESSURE WARNING SWITCH CONNECTOR	Continuity (OK) No continuity	TURN Ignition OFF. CONNECT all electrical connections. Reverify symptom. SERVICE or REPLACE cable harness (Circuit 535).
A5 ISOLATION TEST FLI AND PWS • Check for continuity between Breakout box Pin 9 and body ground.	Continuity (OK) No continuity	GO to Step A5a. GO to Step A6.

515

Anti-Lock Warning Lamp On (With Brake Warning Lamp Off) — Test A

TEST STEP	RESULT	ACTION TO TAKE
A5d CHECK CONTINUITY BETWEEN PWS PINS 3 AND 5 AND BODY GROUND • Check for continuity from PWS 5-Pin socket Pins (pressure warning switch side) 3 and body ground and 5 and body ground. PIN NO.3 PIN NO.5 — PRESSURE WARNING SWITCH	Continuity No continuity	REPLACE Pressure Warning Switch and Pump Motor Relay. GO to Step A5e.
A5e CHECK PWS CONNECTOR PIN 5 AND GROUND • Check for continuity between 5-Pin PWS plug, Pin 5 (harness side) and body ground. PIN NO.5 — PRESSURE WARNING SWITCH CONNECTOR	Continuity No continuity	SERVICE or REPLACE Circuit 535. CONNECT all plugs and reverify symptom.
A6 CHECK MAIN RELAY PRIMARY CIRCUIT RESISTANCE • Turn ignition switch OFF. • Set multi-meter to read resistance. • Measure resistance between Breakout box Pins 40 and 8.	Resistance between 45 and 105 ohms Any other reading	GO to Step A7. GO to Step A6a.

Anti-Lock Warning Lamp On (With Brake Warning Lamp Off) — Test A

TEST STEP	RESULT	ACTION TO TAKE
A5a CHECK FLUID LEVEL INDICATOR PIN NO. 2 • Disconnect FLI 5-Pin plug and check for continuity between FLI socket Pin 2 and body ground and Pin 1 and body ground. PIN NO.1 PIN NO.2 PIN NO.3 PIN NO.4 PIN NO.5 — FLUID LEVEL INDICATOR	Continuity No continuity	REPLACE FLI. GO to Step A5b.
A5b CHECK FLUID LEVEL INDICATOR PIN NO. 1 • Check for continuity between FLI plug Pin 1 (harness side) and body ground. PIN NO.1 PIN NO.2 PIN NO.3 PIN NO.4 PIN NO.5 — FLUID LEVEL INDICATOR	Continuity No continuity	SERVICE or REPLACE Circuit 512. GO to Step A5c.
A5c CHECK FLUID LEVEL INDICATOR PIN NO. 2 • Disconnect 5-Pin plug from PWS. Check for continuity between FLI plug Pin 2 (harness side) and body ground. PIN NO.1 PIN NO.2 PIN NO.3 PIN NO.4 PIN NO.5 — FLUID LEVEL INDICATOR	Continuity No continuity	SERVICE or REPLACE Circuit 549. GO to Step A5d.

Anti-Lock Warning Lamp On (With Brake Warning Lamp Off) — Test A

TEST STEP	RESULT	ACTION TO TAKE
A6c CHECK MAIN RELAY PRIMARY TO GROUND WIRE • Check continuity between main relay socket Pin 1 and ground.	Continuity (OK)	RECONNECT all electrical connections and reverify symptom.
	No continuity	SERVICE or REPLACE cable harness (Circuit 430N).
A7 CHECK MAIN RELAY SECONDARY (ACTIVATED) • Place a jumper wire between Breakout box Pins 2 and 8. • Set multi-meter to read volts DC. • Turn ignition switch ON. • Measure voltage between Breakout box Pins 40 and 3.	Over 10 V DC (OK)	GO to Step A8.
	Under 10 V DC	CHECK fuse F5. REMOVE jumper wire and GO to Step A7a.
A7a CHECK MAIN RELAY SECONDARY CIRCUIT (ACTIVE) • Disconnect main relay from socket. • Apply power (battery positive and ground) to main relay Pins 1 and 2. • Check for continuity between main relay Pins 3 and 4.	Continuity (OK)	GO to Step A7b.
	No continuity	REPLACE main power relay.

Anti-Lock Warning Lamp On (With Brake Warning Lamp Off) — Test A

TEST STEP	RESULT	ACTION TO TAKE
A6a CHECK MAIN RELAY PRIMARY COIL RESISTANCE • Disconnect main relay from socket. • Set multi-meter on resistance. • Measure resistance between main relay Pins 1 and 2.	Resistance between 45 and 105 ohms (OK)	GO to Step A6b.
	Any other reading	REPLACE main power relay.
A6b CHECK MAIN RELAY PRIMARY TO ELECTRONIC CONTROLLER WIRE • Check continuity between main relay socket Pin 2. ... and Breakout box Pin 8.	Continuity (OK)	GO to Step A6c.
	No continuity	SERVICE or REPLACE cable harness (Circuit 513).

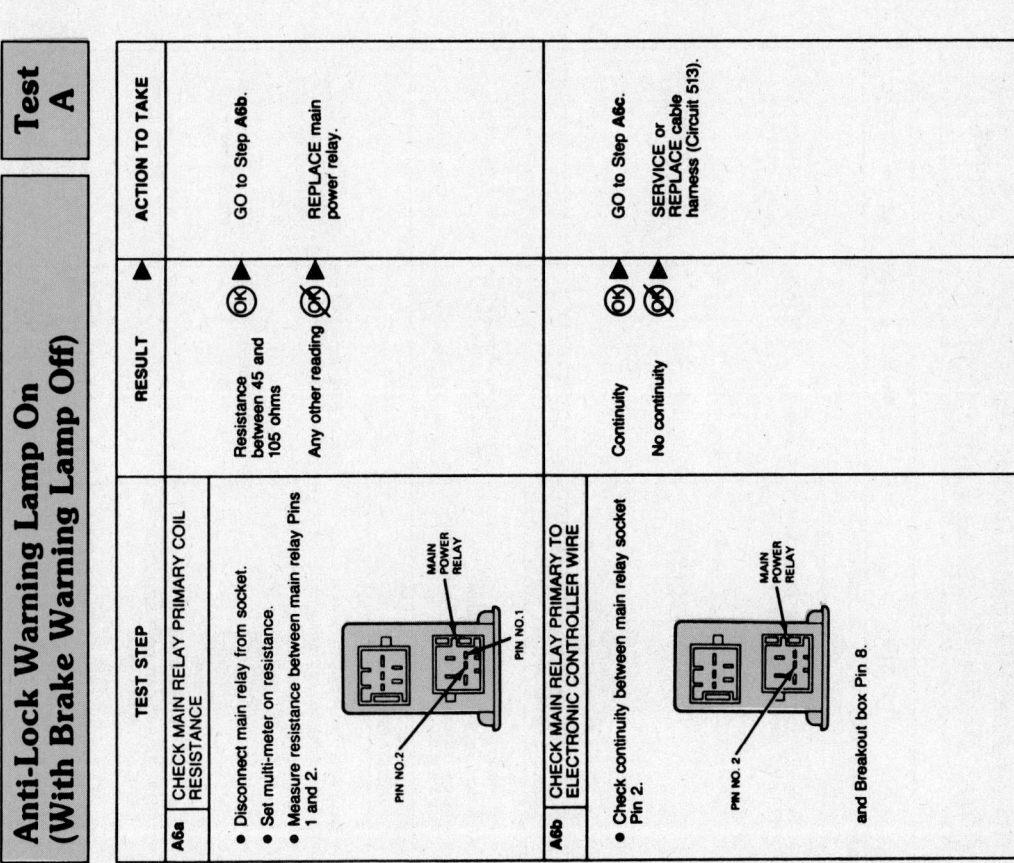

Anti-Lock Warning Lamp On (With Brake Warning Lamp Off) — Test A

TEST STEP	RESULT	ACTION TO TAKE
A9a MEASURE FRONT LEFT SENSOR RESISTANCE • Disconnect sensor plug (left front). • Measure resistance of sensor at sensor plug. *LH FRONT SENSOR*	800 to 1400 ohms (0.8 to 1.4K ohms) ⊘OK	REPAIR or REPLACE cable harness (Circuit 521 or 522).
	Any other reading ⊘	REPLACE left front wheel sensor.
A10 MEASURE LEFT REAR SENSOR CIRCUIT RESISTANCE • Measure resistance between Breakout box Pins 6 and 24.	800 to 1400 ohms (0.8 to 1.4K ohms) ⊘OK	GO to Step A11.
	Any other reading ⊘	GO to Step A10a.
A10a MEASURE LEFT REAR SENSOR RESISTANCE • Disconnect sensor plug (left rear). • Measure resistance of sensor at left rear sensor plug. *LH REAR SENSOR*	800 to 1400 ohms (0.8 to 1.4K ohms) ⊘OK	REPAIR or REPLACE cable harness (Circuit 518 or 519).
	Any other reading ⊘	REPLACE left rear wheel sensor.
A11 MEASURE RIGHT FRONT SENSOR CIRCUIT RESISTANCE • Measure resistance between Breakout box Pins 7 and 25.	800 to 1400 ohms (0.8 to 1.4K ohms) ⊘OK	GO to Step A12.
	Any other reading ⊘	GO to Step A11a.

Anti-Lock Warning Lamp On (With Brake Warning Lamp Off) — Test A

TEST STEP	RESULT	ACTION TO TAKE
A7b CHECK MAIN RELAY SECONDARY CIRCUIT POWER WIRE • Check continuity between main relay socket Pin 4 and positive battery terminal. *MAIN POWER RELAY — PIN NO.4*	Continuity ⊘OK	RECONNECT main relay and reverify symptom.
	No continuity ⊘	SERVICE or REPLACE cable harness (Circuit 533) or fuse link (Circuit 291B).
A8 MEASURE RIGHT REAR SENSOR CIRCUIT RESISTANCE • Turn ignition switch OFF. • Set multi-meter to read resistance. • Measure resistance between Breakout box Pins 4 and 22.	800 to 1400 ohms (0.8 to 1.4K ohms) ⊘OK	GO to Step A9.
	Any other reading ⊘	Go to Step A8a.
A8a MEASURE RIGHT REAR SENSOR RESISTANCE • Disconnect sensor plug (right rear). • Set multi-meter to read resistance. • Measure resistance of sensor at sensor plug. *RH REAR SENSOR*	800 to 1400 ohms (0.8 to 1.4K ohms) ⊘OK	SERVICE or REPLACE cable harness (Circuit 523 or 524).
	Any other reading ⊘	REPLACE right rear wheel sensor.
A9 MEASURE FRONT LEFT SENSOR CIRCUIT RESISTANCE • Measure resistance between Breakout box Pins 5 and 23.	800 to 1400 ohms (0.8 to 1.4K ohms) ⊘OK	GO to Step A10.
	Any other reading ⊘	GO to Step A9a.

Anti-Lock Warning Lamp On (With Brake Warning Lamp Off)

Test A

TEST STEP	RESULT	▲	ACTION TO TAKE
A11a MEASURE RIGHT FRONT SENSOR RESISTANCE			
• Disconnect sensor plug (right front). • Measure resistance of sensor at sensor plug. RH FRONT SENSOR	800 to 1400 ohms (0.8 to 1.4K ohms)	OK ▶	SERVICE or REPLACE cable harness (Circuit 514 or 516).
	Any other reading	⊗ ▶	REPLACE right front wheel sensor.
A12 MEASURE MAIN VALVE CIRCUIT RESISTANCE			
• Turn ignition switch OFF. • Set multi-meter to read resistance. • Measure the resistance between Breakout box Pins 11 and 18.	2 to 5 ohms	OK ▶	GO to Step **A13**.
	Any other reading	⊗ ▶	GO to Step **A12a**.
A12a MEASURE MAIN VALVE RESISTANCE			
• Disconnect main valve 2-Pin plug. • Measure resistance between the main valve electrical Pins 1 and 2. PIN NO.1 PIN NO.2	2 to 5.5 ohms	OK ▶	REPLACE or SERVICE cable harness (Circuit 430E or 493).
	Any other reading	⊗ ▶	REPLACE hydraulic unit.
A13 MEASURE RIGHT FRONT INLET VALVE CIRCUIT RESISTANCE			
• Measure resistance between Breakout box Pins 11 and 15.	5 to 8 ohms	OK ▶	GO to Step **A14**.
	Any other reading	⊗ ▶	GO to Step **A13a**.

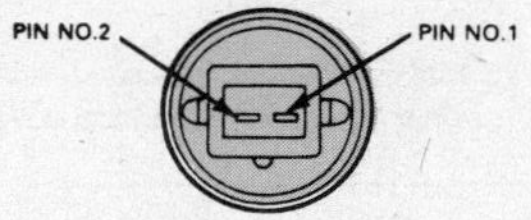

Anti-Lock Warning Lamp On (With Brake Warning Lamp Off)

Test A

TEST STEP	RESULT	▲	ACTION TO TAKE
A13a MEASURE RIGHT FRONT INLET VALVE RESISTANCE			
• Disconnect valve block 7-Pin plug. • Measure resistance between valve block socket electrical Pins 7 and 1. PIN NO.1 PIN NO.7 VALVE BLOCK 7-PIN CONNECTOR	5 to 8 ohms	OK ▶	REPLACE or REPAIR cable harness (Circuit 510).
	Any other reading	⊗ ▶	REPLACE solenoid valve block unit. RECONNECT 7-Pin plug.
A14 MEASURE REAR INLET VALVE CIRCUIT RESISTANCE			
• Measure resistance between Breakout box Pins 11 and 17.	5 to 8 ohms	OK ▶	GO to Step **A15**.
	Any other reading	⊗ ▶	GO to Step **A14a**.

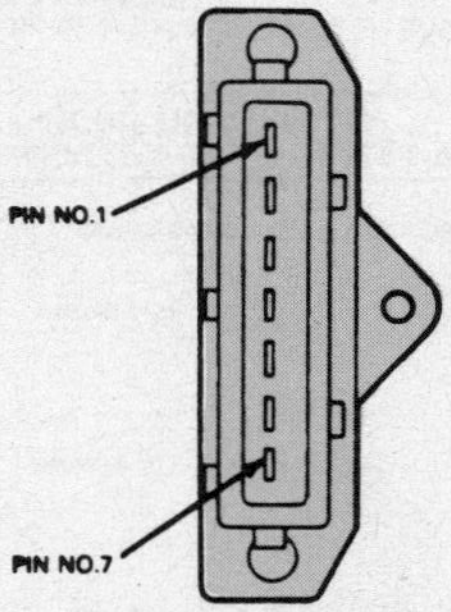

Anti-Lock Warning Lamp On (With Brake Warning Lamp Off) — Test A

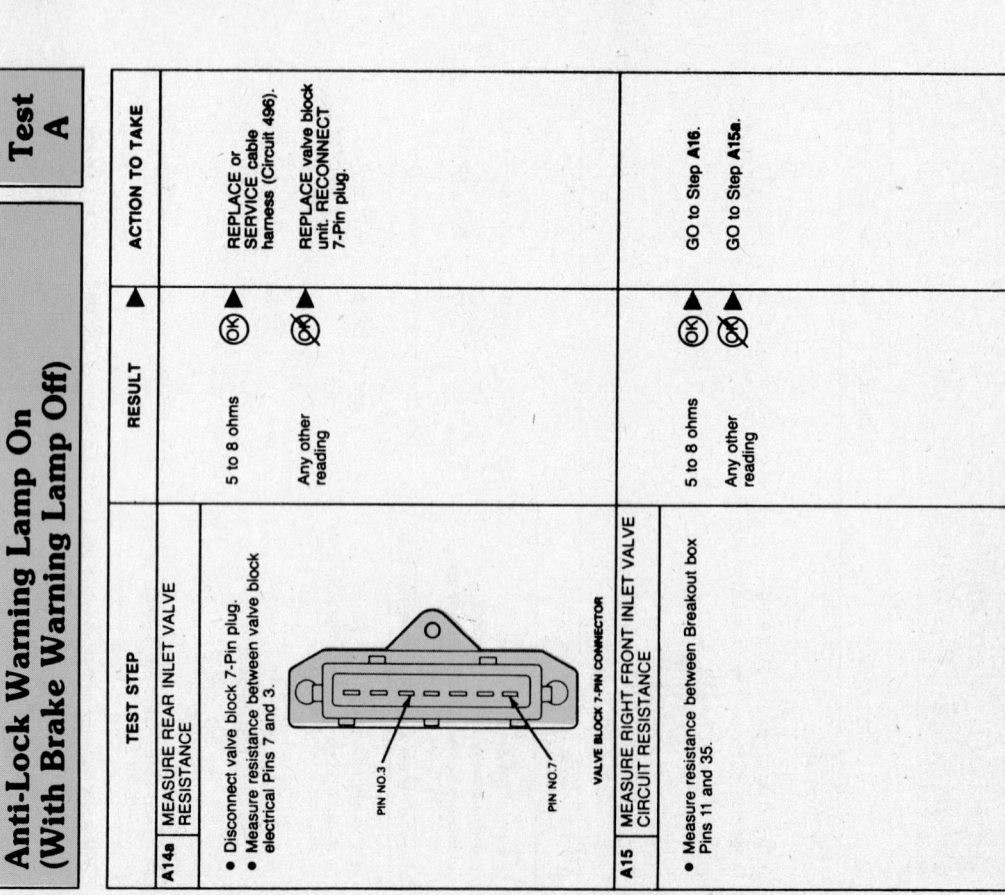

TEST STEP	RESULT		ACTION TO TAKE
A15a MEASURE RIGHT FRONT INLET VALVE RESISTANCE • Disconnect valve block 7-Pin plug. • Measure resistance between valve block electrical Pins 7 and 6.	5 to 8 ohms	OK ▲	REPLACE or SERVICE cable harness (Circuit 495).
	Any other reading	NOT OK ▲	REPLACE valve block unit. RECONNECT 7-Pin plug.
A16 MEASURE REAR OUTLET VALVE CIRCUIT RESISTANCE • Measure resistance between Breakout box Pins 11 and 33.	3 to 6 ohms	OK ▲	GO to Step A17.
	Any other reading	NOT OK ▲	GO to Step A16a.

VALVE BLOCK 7-PIN CONNECTOR — PIN NO.6, PIN NO.7

Anti-Lock Warning Lamp On (With Brake Warning Lamp Off) — Test A

TEST STEP	RESULT		ACTION TO TAKE
A14a MEASURE REAR INLET VALVE RESISTANCE • Disconnect valve block 7-Pin plug. • Measure resistance between valve block electrical Pins 7 and 3.	5 to 8 ohms	OK ▲	REPLACE or SERVICE cable harness (Circuit 496).
	Any other reading	NOT OK ▲	REPLACE valve block unit. RECONNECT 7-Pin plug.
A15 MEASURE RIGHT FRONT INLET VALVE CIRCUIT RESISTANCE • Measure resistance between Breakout box Pins 11 and 35.	5 to 8 ohms	OK ▲	GO to Step A16.
	Any other reading	NOT OK ▲	GO to Step A15a.

VALVE BLOCK 7-PIN CONNECTOR — PIN NO.3, PIN NO.7

Anti-Lock Warning Lamp On (With Brake Warning Lamp Off) — Test A

TEST STEP	RESULT	ACTION TO TAKE
A17a MEASURE LEFT FRONT OUTLET VALVE RESISTANCE • Disconnect valve block 7-Pin plug. • Measure resistance between valve block electrical Pins 7 and 5. PIN NO.5 PIN NO.7 VALVE BLOCK 7-PIN CONNECTOR	3 to 6 ohms (OK) ▶ Any other reading (not OK) ▶	REPLACE or SERVICE cable harness (Circuit 498). REPLACE valve block unit, RECONNECT 7-Pin plug.
A18 MEASURE FRONT RIGHT OUTLET VALVE CIRCUIT RESISTANCE • Measure resistance between Breakout box Pins 11 and 34.	3 to 6 ohms (OK) ▶ Any other reading (not OK) ▶	GO to Step A19. GO TO Step A18a.

Anti-Lock Warning Lamp On (With Brake Warning Lamp Off) — Test A

TEST STEP	RESULT	ACTION TO TAKE
A16a MEASURE REAR OUTLET VALVE RESISTANCE • Disconnect valve block 7-Pin plug. • Measure resistance between valve block electrical Pins 7 and 4. PIN NO.4 PIN NO.7 VALVE BLOCK 7-PIN CONNECTOR	3 to 6 ohms (OK) ▶ Any other reading (not OK) ▶	REPLACE or SERVICE cable harness (Circuit 499). REPLACE valve block unit, RECONNECT 7-Pin plug.
A17 MEASURE LEFT FRONT OUTLET VALVE CIRCUIT RESISTANCE • Measure resistance between Breakout box Pins 11 and 16.	3 to 6 ohms (OK) ▶ Any other reading (not OK) ▶	GO to Step A18. GO to Step A17a.

Anti-Lock Warning Lamp On (With Brake Warning Lamp Off) — Test A

TEST STEP	RESULT	ACTION TO TAKE
A19a TEST VALVE PLUG PIN NO. 7 • Disconnect valve block 7-Pin plug. • Measure resistance between valve block electrical Pin 7 and body ground. PIN NO. 7 VALVE BLOCK 7-PIN CONNECTOR	Less than 2 ohms ▶ ⊘OK⊘	REPLACE or SERVICE cable harness (Circuit 511).
	Greater than 2 ohms ▶ ⊘	GO to Step A19b.
A19b CHECK VALVE BODY GROUND WIRE • Remove negative (−) ground strap from battery. • Check for continuity between valve body and body ground.	Continuity ▶ ⊘	REPLACE valve block unit (internal ground problem).
	No or Poor continuity ▶ ⊘	SERVICE or REPLACE hydraulic unit ground strap (Circuit 430G).

Anti-Lock Warning Lamp On (With Brake Warning Lamp Off) — Test A

TEST STEP	RESULT	ACTION TO TAKE
A18a MEASURE FRONT RIGHT OUTLET VALVE RESISTANCE • Disconnect valve block 7-Pin plug. • Measure resistance between valve block electrical Pins 7 and 2. PIN NO. 2 PIN NO. 7 VALVE BLOCK 7-PIN CONNECTOR	3 to 6 ohms ▶ ⊘OK⊘	REPLACE or SERVICE cable harness (Circuit 497).
	Any other reading ▶ ⊘	REPLACE valve block unit. RECONNECT 7-Pin plug.
A19 CHECK VALVE BODY GROUND CIRCUIT • Measure resistance between Breakout box Pins 11 and 40.	Less than 2 ohms ▶ ⊘	GO to Step A20.
	Greater than 2 ohms ▶ ⊘	GO TO Step A19a.

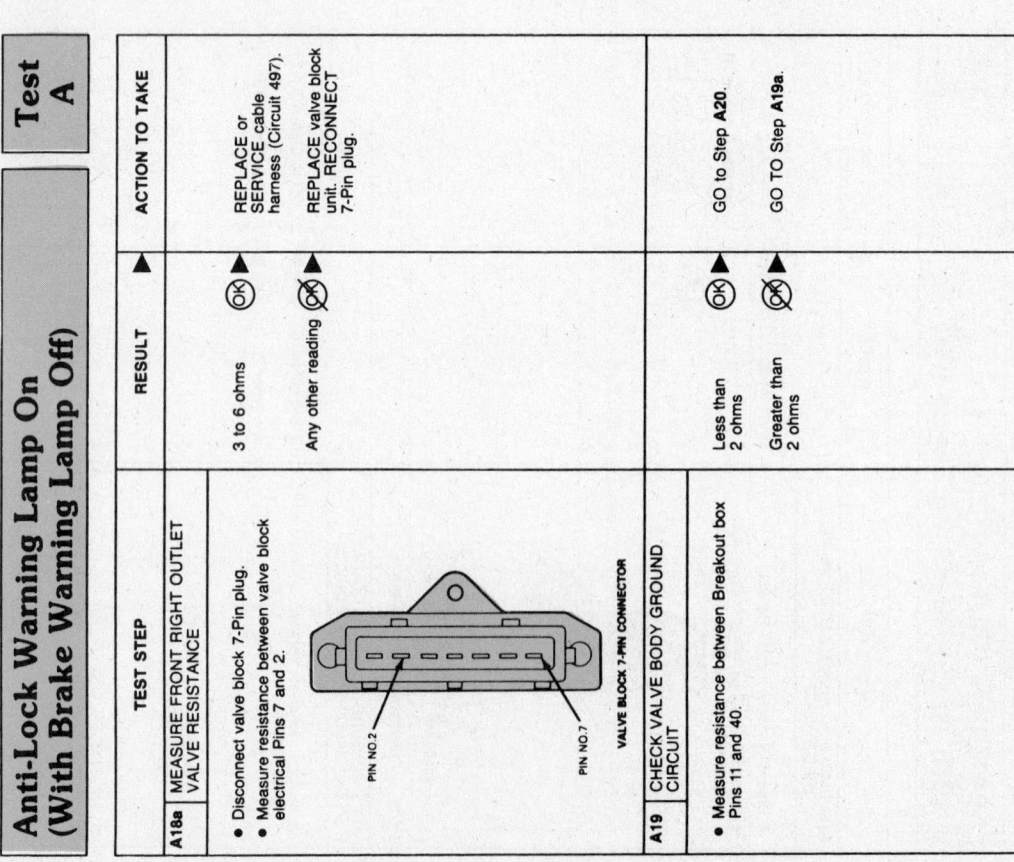

Anti-Lock Warning Lamp On (With Brake Warning Lamp Off)

Test A

TEST STEP	RESULT	ACTION TO TAKE
A21 CHECK PWS BRAKE LAMP CIRCUIT (WITH PRESSURE)		
• Reconnect pressure warning switch 5-Pin plug. • Turn ignition switch ON. • When pump motor stops, turn ignition switch OFF. • Disconnect pressure warning switch 5-Pin plug again. • Check for continuity between pressure warning switch electrical Pins 1 and 2.	Continuity ⊗	REPLACE pressure warning switch.
	No continuity ⊘	GO to Step **A22** and pump motor relay.

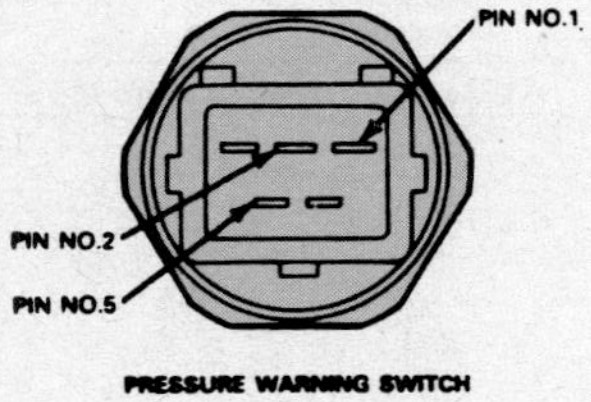

PRESSURE WARNING SWITCH
PIN NO.1 / PIN NO.2 / PIN NO.5

Anti-Lock Warning Lamp On (With Brake Warning Lamp Off)

Test A

TEST STEP	RESULT	ACTION TO TAKE
A20 CHECK PWS BRAKE LAMP CIRCUIT (NO PRESSURE)		
• Vehicle must be cooled to room temperature. • Discharge the brake system as follows: a. Turn ignition switch OFF. b. Pump brake pedal at least 20 times until you feel the pedal become hard. • Disconnect pressure warning switch 5-Pin plug. • Check continuity between pressure warning switch electrical Pins 1 and 2.	Continuity ⊗	GO to Step **A21**.
	No continuity ⊘	REPLACE pressure warning switch and pump motor relay.

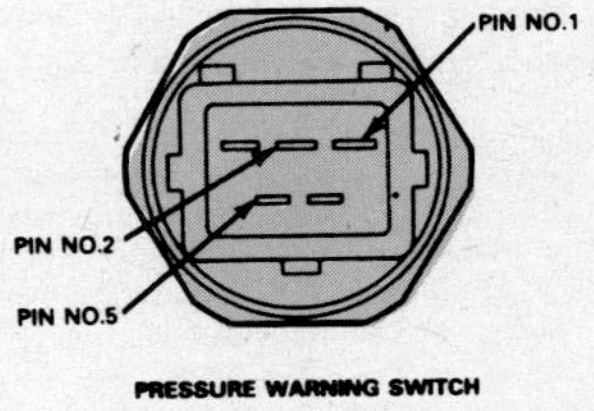

PRESSURE WARNING SWITCH
PIN NO.1 / PIN NO.2 / PIN NO.5

Anti-Lock Warning Lamp On (With Brake Warning Lamp Off) — Test A

TEST STEP	RESULT	ACTION TO TAKE
A23 CHECK PWS HARNESS GROUND • Check for continuity between pressure warning switch 5-Pin plug Pin 1 and body ground. PRESSURE WARNING SWITCH	Continuity (OK) No continuity (not OK)	GO to Step **A24**. REPLACE or SERVICE cable harness (Circuit 430K).

A24 REVERIFY SYSTEM SYMPTOM
• Reconnect all electrical connections.
• Reinstall high pressure banjo bolt.
WARNING: Before disconnecting any hydraulic lines, you must ensure that the brake hydraulic pressure system is discharged.
• Discharge the brake system as follows:
  a. Turn ignition switch OFF.
  b. Pump brake pedal at least 20 times until you feel the pedal become hard.
• Reverify symptom.
	Symptom not present
	
	Symptom still present
		FAULT may have been a loose electrical connection.
		
		REPLACE electronic control module.

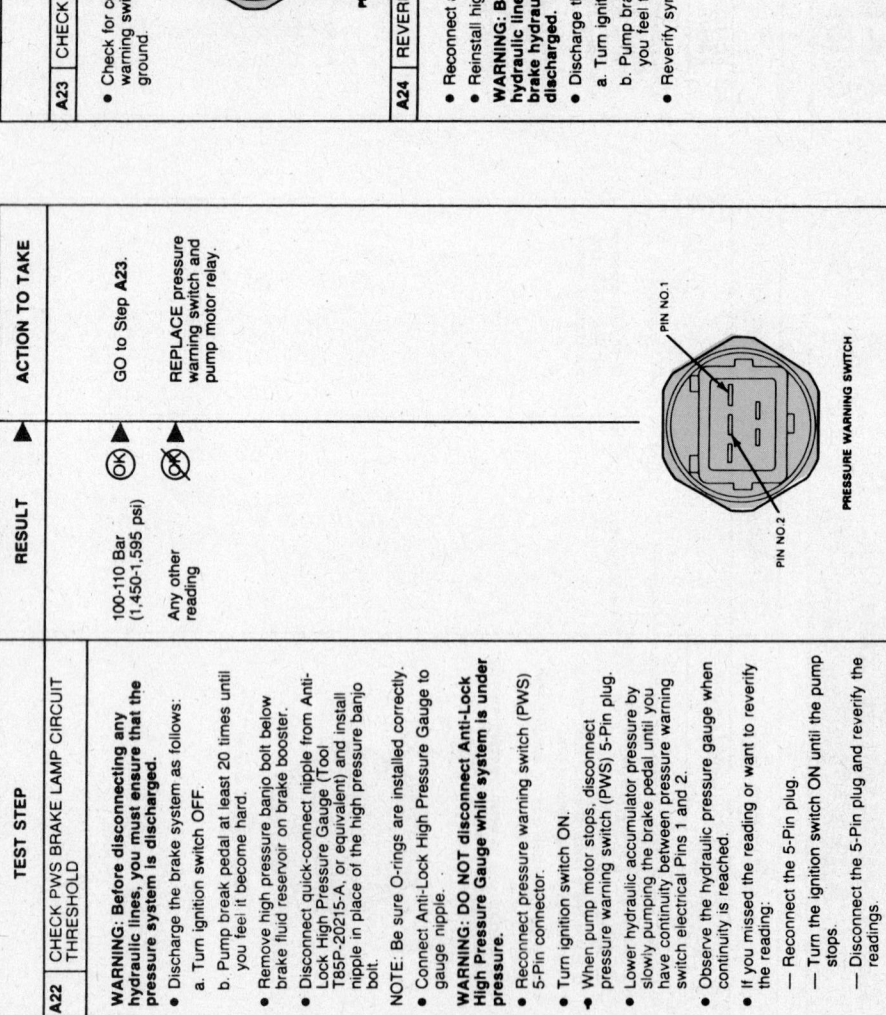

Anti-Lock Warning Lamp On (With Brake Warning Lamp Off) — Test A

TEST STEP	RESULT	ACTION TO TAKE

A22 CHECK PWS BRAKE LAMP CIRCUIT THRESHOLD
 	
WARNING: Before disconnecting any hydraulic lines, you must ensure that the pressure system is discharged.
• Discharge the brake system as follows:
  a. Turn ignition switch OFF.
  b. Pump brake pedal at least 20 times until you feel it become hard.
• Remove high pressure banjo bolt below brake fluid reservoir on brake booster.
• Disconnect quick-connect nipple from Anti-Lock High Pressure Gauge (Tool T85P-20215-A, or equivalent) and install nipple in place of the high pressure banjo bolt.
NOTE: Be sure O-rings are installed correctly.
• Connect Anti-Lock High Pressure Gauge to gauge nipple.
WARNING: DO NOT disconnect Anti-Lock High Pressure Gauge while system is under pressure.
• Reconnect pressure warning switch (PWS) 5-Pin connector.
• Turn ignition switch ON.
• When pump motor stops, disconnect pressure warning switch (PWS) 5-Pin plug.
• Lower hydraulic accumulator pressure by slowly pumping the brake pedal until you have continuity between pressure warning switch electrical Pins 1 and 2.
• Observe the hydraulic pressure gauge when continuity is reached.
• If you missed the reading or want to reverify the reading:
  — Reconnect the 5-Pin plug.
  — Turn the ignition switch ON until the pump stops.
  — Disconnect the 5-Pin plug and reverify the readings.
	100-110 Bar (1,450-1,595 psi) (OK)
	
	Any other reading (not OK)
		GO to Step **A23**.
		
		REPLACE pressure warning switch and pump motor relay.

PRESSURE WARNING SWITCH — PIN NO.1 — PIN NO 2

Anti-Lock Lamp On After Engine Starts (Brake Warning Lamp Off) — Test B

WARNING LIGHTS SEQUENCE

Warning Lamps	Ignition On	Cranking Engine	Engine Running	Vehicle Moving	Braking with/without Anti-Lock	Vehicle Stopped	Engine Idle	Ignition Off
Check Anti-Lock (Amber)								
Brake (Red)								

TEST STEP	RESULT		ACTION TO TAKE
B1 CHECK CONTINUITY OF CIRCUIT 524 • Ignition switch Off. • Disconnect 35-Pin plug from controller. • Connect EEC-IV Breakout box with Anti-Lock Test Adapter to the Anti-Lock 35-Pin plug wiring harness. • Check for continuity between Breakout box Pins 40 and 4.	Continuity	▶	GO to Step **B1a.**
	No continuity	▶	GO to Step **B2.**
B1a CHECK CONTINUITY OF RIGHT REAR SENSOR • Disconnect wheel sensor plug (right rear). • Check for continuity between each sensor plug pin (sensor side) and vehicle ground. RH REAR SENSOR	Continuity	▶	REPLACE sensor (right rear).
	No continuity	▶	REPLACE or REPAIR cable harness. RECONNECT sensor plug.
B2 CHECK CONTINUITY OF CIRCUIT 522 • Check for continuity between Breakout box Pins 40 and 5.	Continuity	▶	GO to Step **B2a.**
	No continuity	▶	GO to Step **B3.**

Anti-Lock Lamp On After Engine Starts (Brake Warning Lamp Off) — Test B

TEST STEP	RESULT		ACTION TO TAKE
B2a CHECK CONTINUITY OF LEFT FRONT SENSOR • Disconnect wheel sensor plug (left front). • Check for continuity between each sensor plug pin (sensor side) and vehicle ground. LH FRONT SENSOR	Continuity	▶	REPLACE sensor (left front).
	No continuity	▶	REPLACE or REPAIR cable harness. RECONNECT sensor plug.
B3 CHECK CONTINUITY OF CIRCUIT 519 • Check for continuity between Breakout box Pins 40 and 6.	Continuity	▶	GO to Step **B3a.**
	No continuity	▶	GO to Step **B4.**
B3a CHECK CONTINUITY OF LEFT REAR SENSOR • Disconnect sensor plug (left rear). • Check for continuity between each sensor plug pin (sensor side) and vehicle ground. LH REAR SENSOR	Continuity	▶	REPLACE sensor (left rear).
	No continuity	▶	REPLACE or REPAIR cable. RECONNECT sensor plug.

Test C

Anti-Lock Warning Lamp On After Vehicle Starts To Move Or False Cycling Of Anti-Lock System

WARNING LIGHTS SEQUENCE

Warning Lamps	Ignition On	Cranking Engine	Engine Running	Vehicle Moving	Braking with/without Anti-Lock	Vehicle Stopped	Engine Idle	Ignition Off
Check Anti-Lock (Amber)	▨		▨	▨				
Brake (Red)		■						

WARNING LIGHTS SEQUENCE

Warning Lamps	Ignition On	Cranking Engine	Engine Running	Vehicle Moving	Braking with/without Anti-Lock	Vehicle Stopped	Engine Idle	Ignition Off
Check Anti-Lock (Amber)	▨		▨					
Brake (Red)		■						

TEST STEP	RESULT ▲	ACTION TO TAKE ▲
C1 MEASURE RIGHT REAR SENSOR CIRCUIT RESISTANCE • Turn ignition switch OFF. • Set multi-meter to read resistance. • Measure resistance between Breakout box Pins 4 and 22.	800 to 1400 ohms (0.8 to 1.4K ohms) ⊘OK	GO to Step **C2**.
	Any other reading ⊗ (not OK)	Go to Step **C1a**.
C1a MEASURE RIGHT REAR SENSOR RESISTANCE • Disconnect sensor plug (right rear). • Set multi-meter to read resistance. • Measure resistance of sensor at sensor plug.	800 to 1400 ohms (0.8 to 1.4K ohms) ⊘OK	SERVICE or REPLACE cable harness (Circuit 523 or 524).
	Any other reading ⊗ (not OK)	REPLACE right rear wheel sensor.

RH REAR SENSOR

Test B

Anti-Lock Lamp On After Engine Starts (Brake Warning Lamp Off)

TEST STEP	RESULT ▲	ACTION TO TAKE ▲
B4 CHECK CONTINUITY OF CIRCUIT 516 • Check for continuity between Breakout box Pins 40 and 7.	Continuity ⊗ (not OK)	GO to Step **B4a**.
	No continuity ⊘OK	Test complete. If Anti-Lock lamp pattern remains, REPEAT Test B.
B4a CHECK CONTINUITY OF RIGHT FRONT SENSOR • Disconnect wheel sensor plug (right front). • Check for continuity between each sensor plug pin (sensor side) and vehicle ground.	Continuity ⊗ (not OK)	REPLACE right front sensor.
	No continuity ⊘OK	REPLACE or REPAIR cable harness. RECONNECT sensor plug.

RH FRONT SENSOR

Anti-Lock Warning Lamp On After Vehicle Starts To Move Or False Cycling Of Anti-Lock System — Test C

TEST STEP	RESULT		ACTION TO TAKE
C3a MEASURE LEFT REAR SENSOR RESISTANCE • Disconnect sensor plug (left rear). • Measure resistance of sensor at left rear sensor plug. LH REAR SENSOR	800 to 1400 ohms (0.8 to 1.4K ohms)	OK ▲	SERVICE or REPLACE cable harness (Circuit 518 or 519).
	Any other reading	⊘ ▲	REPLACE left rear wheel sensor.
C4 MEASURE RIGHT FRONT SENSOR CIRCUIT RESISTANCE • Measure resistance between Breakout box Pins 7 and 25.	800 to 1400 ohms (0.8 to 1.4K ohms)	OK ▲	GO to Step **C5**.
	Any other reading	⊘ ▲	GO to Step **C4a**.
C4a MEASURE RIGHT FRONT SENSOR RESISTANCE • Disconnect sensor plug (right front). • Measure resistance of sensor at sensor plug. RH FRONT SENSOR	800 to 1400 ohms (0.8 to 1.4K ohms)	OK ▲	SERVICE or REPLACE cable harness (Circuit 514 or 516).
	Any other reading	⊘ ▲	REPLACE right front wheel sensor.

Anti-Lock Warning Lamp On After Vehicle Starts To Move Or False Cycling Of Anti-Lock System — Test C

TEST STEP	RESULT		ACTION TO TAKE
C2 MEASURE FRONT LEFT SENSOR CIRCUIT RESISTANCE • Measure resistance between Breakout box Pins 5 and 23.	800 to 1400 ohms (0.8 to 1.4K ohms)	OK ▲	GO to Step **C3**.
	Any other reading	⊘ ▲	GO to Step **C2a**.
C2a MEASURE FRONT LEFT SENSOR RESISTANCE • Disconnect sensor plug (left front). • Measure resistance of sensor at sensor plug. LH FRONT SENSOR	800 to 1400 ohms (0.8 to 1.4K ohms)	OK ▲	REPAIR or REPLACE cable harness (Circuit 521 or 522).
	Any other reading	⊘ ▲	REPLACE left front wheel sensor.
C3 MEASURE LEFT REAR SENSOR CIRCUIT RESISTANCE • Measure resistance between Breakout box Pins 6 and 24.	800 to 1400 ohms (0.8 to 1.4K ohms)	OK ▲	GO to Step **C4**.
	Any other reading	⊘ ▲	GO to Step **C3a**.

Anti-Lock Warning Lamp On After Vehicle Starts To Move Or False Cycling Of Anti-Lock System — Test C

TEST STEP	RESULT	ACTION TO TAKE
C5 CHECK RIGHT REAR SENSOR • Turn ignition switch OFF. • Turn air suspension switch in luggage compartment OFF. • Place vehicle on hoist and raise wheels clear of ground. Refer to Pre-Delivery Manual Section 50-04. • Disconnect 35-Pin plug from electronic controller and connect EEC-IV Breakout box with Anti-Lock Test Adapter to the Anti-Lock 35-Pin wiring harness connector. • Set multi-meter on voltage range (2V-AC). • Measure voltage between Breakout box Pins 4 and 22 while spinning the right rear wheel at approximately 1 revolution per second.	Between 0.05 and 0.70 Vac (OK)	GO to Step **C6**.
	Less than 0.05 or more than 0.70 Vac	CHECK sensor mounting, air gap, or toothed wheel mounting. CORRECT as required.
C6 CHECK LEFT FRONT SENSOR • Measure voltage between Breakout box Pins 5 and 23 while spinning left front wheel at approximately 1 revolution per second.	Between 0.05 and 0.70 Vac	GO to Step **C7**.
	Less than 0.05 or more than 0.70 Vac	CHECK sensor mounting, air gap, or toothed wheel mounting. CORRECT as required.
C7 CHECK LEFT REAR SENSOR • Measure voltage between Breakout box Pins 6 and 24 while spinning the left rear wheel at approximately 1 revolution per second.	Between 0.05 and 0.70 Vac	GO to Step **C8**.
	Less than 0.05 or more than 0.07 Vac	CHECK wheel sensor mounting, air gap, or toothed wheel mounting. CORRECT as required.

Anti-Lock Warning Lamp on After Vehicle Starts to Move or False Cycling of Anti-Lock System — Test C

TEST STEP	RESULT	ACTION TO TAKE
C8 CHECK RIGHT FRONT SENSOR • Measure voltage between Breakout box Pins 7 and 25 while spinning the right front wheel at approximately 1 revolution per second.	Between 0.05 and 0.70 Vac	GO to Step **C9**.
	Less than 0.05 or more than 0.70 Vac	CHECK wheel sensor mounting, air gap, or toothed wheel mounting. CORRECT as required.
C9 CHECK FRONT WHEEL BEARINGS • Check front wheel bearing end play. • Inspect each toothed sensor ring visually for damaged teeth. NOTE: Turn air suspension switch ON when vehicle is off hoist.	Loose or damaged parts	ADJUST bearings or REPLACE faulty parts.
	Not loose or damaged	REVERIFY symptom.

Anti-Lock Warning Lamp And Brake Warning Lamp On And/Or Pump Motor Runs More Than 60 Seconds — Test D

D1a PUMP MOTOR UNIT

TEST STEP	RESULT		ACTION TO TAKE
• Disconnect 4-Pin plug on pump motor unit. • Turn ignition switch On. • Set multi-meter on 20 Volt DC. • Connect meter to the 4-Pin plug on the harness side. (Use one negative and one positive pin). • Observe voltmeter.	More than 10V DC	OK	CHECK brake reservoir filter and/or suction hose. REPLACE if necessary. GO to **D2**.
	Less than 10V DC	(not OK)	GO to **D1b**.

4-PIN MOTOR CONNECTOR — POSITIVE PIN, NEGATIVE PIN, NEGATIVE PIN, POSITIVE PIN

D1b CHECK FUSE LINK

TEST STEP	RESULT		ACTION TO TAKE
• Check for voltage at Circuits 537, 538a and 538b.		OK	GO to **D1c**.
		(not OK)	SERVICE short to ground on Circuits 537, 538a and 538b. REPLACE fuse link as necessary.

Anti-Lock Warning Lamp And Brake Warning Lamp On And/Or Pump Motor Runs More Than 60 Seconds — Test D

WARNING LIGHTS SEQUENCE

Warning Lamps	Ignition On	Cranking Engine	Engine Running	Vehicle Moving	Braking with/without Anti-Lock	Vehicle Stopped	Engine Idle	Ignition Off
Check Anti-Lock (Amber)								
Brake (Red)								

WARNING LIGHTS SEQUENCE

Warning Lamps	Ignition On	Cranking Engine	Engine Running	Vehicle Moving	Braking with/without Anti-Lock	Vehicle Stopped	Engine Idle	Ignition Off
Check Anti-Lock (Amber)								
Brake (Red)								

D1 ACCUMULATOR: PRE-CHARGE

TEST STEP	RESULT		ACTION TO TAKE
• Vehicle must be cooled to room temperature. • **WARNING:** Before disconnecting any hydraulic lines, you must ensure that the pressure system is discharged. • To discharge hydraulic accumulator pressure, turn ignition OFF, pump brake pedal at least 20 times until you feel it become hard. • Remove high pressure banjo bolt below brake fluid reservoir on brake booster. • Install Anti-Lock Pressure Gauge Tool T85P-20215A or equivalent. • Turn ignition switch On and read accumulator precharge pressure. (Gauge needle will spring to this point). Note: Gauge needle reading should spring to 40-90 bar (600-1325 psi) and climb to 16,203-19,306 Kpa bar (2350-2800 psi). • If reading was missed, discharge accumulator as described and repeat ignition ON sequence.	4137-9135 kPa (600-1325 psi)	OK	GO to Step **D2**.
	Under 4137 kPa (600 psi)	(not OK)	REPLACE accumulator.
	Over 9135 kPa (1325 psi)	(not OK)	REPLACE accumulator.
	No pressure increase	(not OK)	GO to Step **D1a**.

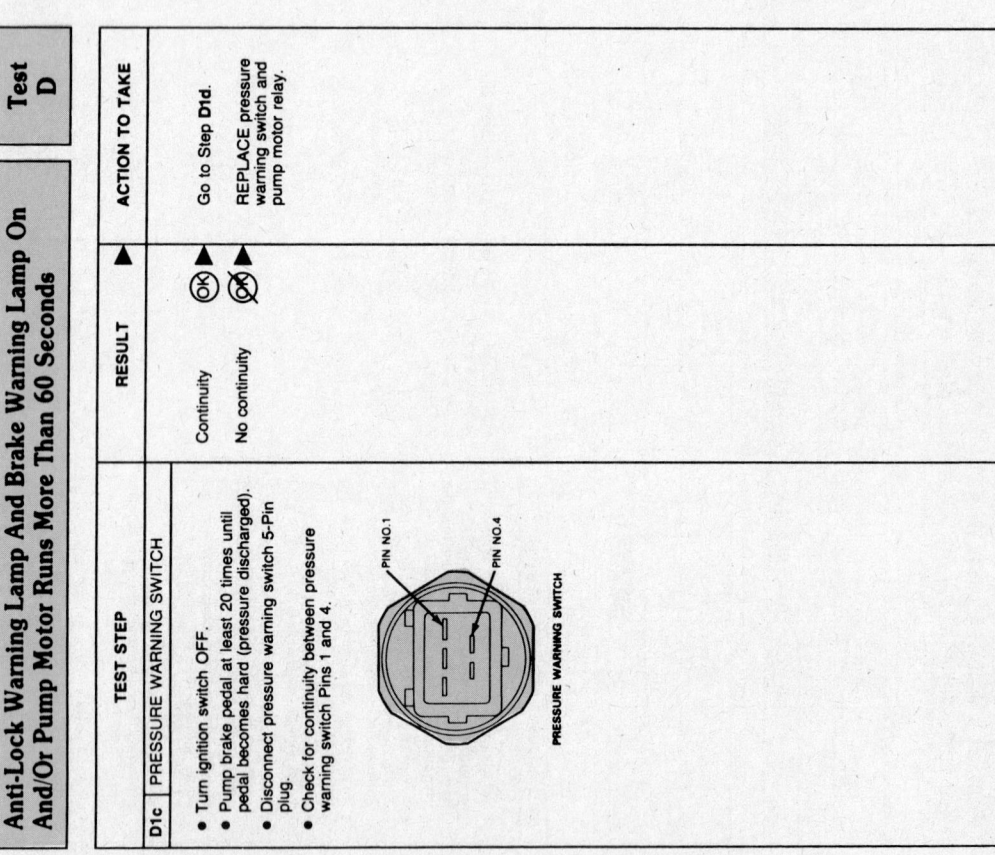

Anti-Lock Warning Lamp And Brake Warning Lamp On And/Or Pump Motor Runs More Than 60 Seconds

Test D

TEST STEP	RESULT	ACTION TO TAKE
D1d CHECK PUMP MOTOR LINE CONTINUITY		
• Turn ignition switch OFF. • Remove positive battery cable from battery. • Disconnect pump motor relay. PUMP MOTOR RELAY • Check continuity between battery positive cable and motor relay socket Pin 4 (harness side). PIN NO. 4 PUMP MOTOR RELAY CONNECTOR	Continuity ✔ No continuity ✘	RECONNECT battery positive cable and GO to Step **D1e**. SERVICE or REPLACE cable harness to pump motor relay.

Anti-Lock Warning Lamp And Brake Warning Lamp On And/Or Pump Motor Runs More Than 60 Seconds

Test D

TEST STEP	RESULT	ACTION TO TAKE
D1c PRESSURE WARNING SWITCH		
• Turn ignition switch OFF. • Pump brake pedal at least 20 times until pedal becomes hard (pressure discharged). • Disconnect pressure warning switch 5-Pin plug. • Check for continuity between pressure warning switch Pins 1 and 4. PIN NO. 1 PIN NO. 4 PRESSURE WARNING SWITCH	Continuity ✔ No continuity ✘	Go to Step **D1d**. REPLACE pressure warning switch and pump motor relay.

Anti-Lock Warning Lamp And Brake Warning Lamp On And/Or Pump Motor Runs More Than 60 Seconds — Test D

TEST STEP	RESULT	ACTION TO TAKE
D1h CHECK PUMP MOTOR RELAY • Set multi-meter on 200 ohm scale. • Connect meter to motor relay Pins 1 and 2.	45 to 105 Ohms (OK) Other (not OK)	GO to Step **D1i**. REPLACE motor relay and pressure warning switch.
D1i CHECK PUMP MOTOR RELAY (CONTINUED) • Connect meter and check continuity between motor relay Pins 3 and 4.	No continuity (OK) Continuity (not OK)	GO to Step **D1j**. REPLACE motor relay and pressure warning switch.

Anti-Lock Warning Lamp And Brake Warning Lamp On And/Or Pump Motor Runs More Than 60 Seconds — Test D

TEST STEP	RESULT	ACTION TO TAKE
D1e CABLE HARNESS PRESSURE WARNING SWITCH • Check for continuity between pressure warning switch 5-Pin plug Pin 1 (harness side) and ground.	Continuity (OK) No continuity (not OK)	GO to Step **D1f**. REPLACE or REPAIR cable harness (Circuit 430K).
D1f CHECK CONTINUITY CIRCUIT 539 • Connect meter to 5-Pin plug Pin 4 (harness side) and motor relay socket Pin 1 (harness side). • Check for continuity.	Continuity (OK) No continuity (not OK)	GO to Step **D1g**. REPLACE or REPAIR cable harness (Circuit 539).
D1g CHECK CONTINUITY CIRCUIT 298 • Connect multi-meter to motor relay socket Pin 2 (harness side) and ignition switch lock pin (On). • Check continuity.	Continuity (OK) No continuity (not OK)	GO to Step **D1h**. REPLACE or REPAIR cable harness (Circuit 298B).

Anti-Lock Warning Lamp And Brake Warning Lamp On And/Or Pump Motor Runs More Than 60 Seconds — Test D

TEST STEP	RESULT	ACTION TO TAKE
D1j CHECK PUMP MOTOR RELAY (CONTINUED) • Connect battery to motor relay terminals 1 and 2. • Check continuity between relay Pins 3 and 4 with multi-meter. PIN NO.2 PIN NO.3 PIN NO.4 PIN NO.1 PIN NO.5	Continuity (OK)	END of Test. RECONNECT all electrical plugs and relay. REVERIFY symptom.
	No continuity (not OK)	REPLACE motor relay and pressure warning switch.
D2 CHECK PUMP MOTOR • Turn ignition switch OFF. • Pump brake pedal at least 20 times, until brake pedal becomes hard. • Connect 4-Pin motor plug. • Turn ignition switch ON. • Measure time pump takes to shut OFF.	Under 60 seconds (OK)	GO to Step D3.
	Over 60 seconds (or motor never turns on) (not OK)	CHECK for corroded connections at: • Motor 4-Pin plug. • Body ground (Circuit 430F). • Motor relay Pin 4 socket (Circuit 537). • Battery to Pin 4. GO to Step D2a.
D2a CHECK PUMP MOTOR UNIT • Turn ignition switch OFF. • Pump brake pedal 20 times to discharge system. • Connect ammeter between battery positive cable and battery positive terminal. • Turn Off any electrical components. • Turn ignition switch ON. • Measure pump motor current.	Current more than 25 amps (not OK)	REPLACE pump motor unit and high pressure hose.
	Current less than 25 amps (OK)	GO to Step D2b.

Anti-Lock Warning Lamp And Brake Warning Lamp On And/Or Pump Motor Runs More Than 60 Seconds — Test D

TEST STEP	RESULT	ACTION TO TAKE
D2b CHECK VOLTAGE TO PUMP MOTOR • Turn ignition switch OFF. • Pump brake pedal to discharge pressure system. • Connect voltmeter in parallel at 2-Pin motor plug. • Set meter to 20 Volts DC range. • Turn ignition switch ON.	With pump running: Voltage over 8 Volts DC (OK)	GO to Step D3.
	Voltage under 8 Volts DC (not OK)	CHECK Circuits 430F, 538A, 538B, Pin 4 to battery and relay Pins 3 and 4 for voltage drop. REPAIR or REPLACE as necessary.
D3 CHECK HYDRAULIC UNIT • Turn ignition switch ON; wait until pump motor stops. Wait 3 more minutes to stabilize gauge pressure. • Read pressure gauge. • Wait 5 minutes and read pressure gauge again to determine the pressure loss over those 5 minutes.	Pressure loss less than 10 bar (140 psi) on gauge (OK)	GO to Step D4.
	More than 10 bar (140 psi) (not OK)	CHECK for external leakage at hydraulic unit and REPAIR. If no external leakage is found, GO to Step D3a.

Anti-Lock Warning Lamp And Brake Warning Lamp On And/Or Pump Motor Runs More Than 60 Seconds — Test D

TEST STEP	RESULT	ACTION TO TAKE
D4 CHECK PUMP PRESSURE		
• With the pressure gauge still attached and ignition switch still On, pump brake pedal to decrease pressure until pump motor restarts.	► 13100-15169 kPa (1900-2200 psi) when pump starts (OK)	GO to Step **D5**.
	Less than or more than 13100-15169 kPa (1900-2200 psi) (not OK)	REPLACE pressure warning switch and pump motor relay.
D5 CHECK PRESSURE WARNING SWITCH		
• With the ignition switch still On and the pressure gauge connected, observe the pressure when the pump motor stops running.	► 16203 kPa (2350-2800 psi) when pump motor stops (OK)	If pump motor takes longer than 60 seconds to reach 16203 kPa (2350-2800 psi), REPLACE pump/ motor assembly and high pressure hose. If pump motor takes less than 60 seconds, REVERIFY symptom.
	Less than 16203 kPa (2350 psi) or over 19306 kPa (2800 psi) (not OK)	REPLACE pressure warning switch and pump motor relay.

Anti-Lock Warning Lamp And Brake Warning Lamp On And/Or Pump Motor Runs More Than 60 Seconds — Test D

TEST STEP	RESULT	ACTION TO TAKE
D3a CHECK FOR LEAKAGE		
• Turn ignition switch OFF. • Pump brake pedal to discharge pressure system. • Turn ignition switch ON. • When pump motor stops, turn ignition switch OFF. • Quickly remove low pressure pump suction line and plug reservoir fitting with large rubber vacuum nipple. • Observe if brake fluid seeps from the low pressure line.	► If line seeps fluid	REPLACE pump/ motor assembly and high pressure hose.
	► If line does not seep fluid	REPLACE hydraulic unit.

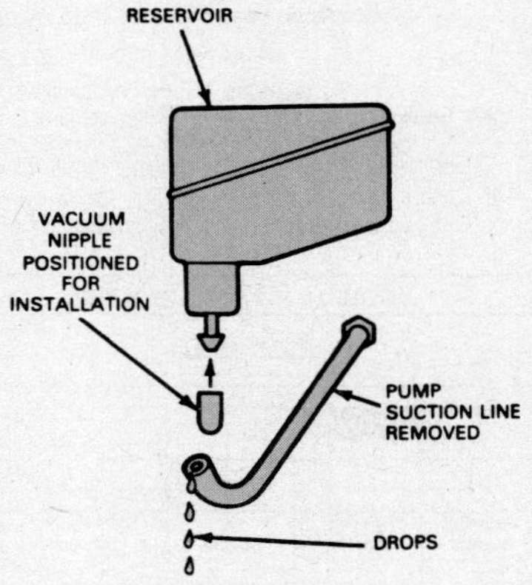

RESERVOIR

VACUUM NIPPLE POSITIONED FOR INSTALLATION

PUMP SUCTION LINE REMOVED

DROPS

Anti-Lock Warning Lamp Intermittently On — Test E

TEST STEP	RESULT	ACTION TO TAKE
E1b CHECK PWS ANTI-LOCK WARNING CIRCUIT (NO PRESSURE) • Turn ignition switch Off. • Pump brake pedal to discharge pressure system. • Disconnect 5-Pin plug at pressure warning switch (PWS). • Check for continuity between pressure warning switch Pins 3 and 5.	No Continuity (OK) Continuity (not OK)	GO to Step E1c. SERVICE pressure warning switch and pump motor relay.
E1c CHECK ELECTRONIC MODULE TO FLI WIRE • Check for continuity between Breakout box Pin 9 and FLI 5-Pin plug Pin 1 (harness side).	Continuity (OK) No continuity (not OK)	GO to Step E1d. REPLACE or SERVICE cable harness (Circuit 512).

Anti-Lock Warning Lamp Intermittently On — Test E

WARNING LIGHTS SEQUENCE

Warning Lamps	Ignition On	Cranking Engine	Engine Running	Vehicle Moving	Braking with/without Anti-Lock	Vehicle Stopped	Engine Idle	Ignition Off
Check Anti-Lock (Amber)								
Brake (Red)								

TEST STEP	RESULT	ACTION TO TAKE
E1 CHECK FLI AND PWS CIRCUIT • Disconnect 35-Pin plug from electronic controller. • Connect EEC-IV Breakout box, T83L-50-EEC-IV with Anti-Lock Test Adapter T85P-50-ASA or equivalent to the Anti-Lock 35-Pin plug wiring harness. • Turn ignition switch ON. • Set multi-meter to read resistance. • Measure the resistance between Breakout box Pins 9 and 10.	Less than 5 ohms (OK) Greater than 5 ohms (not OK)	GO to Step E2. GO to Step E1a.
E1a CHECK FLI ANTI-LOCK WARNING CIRCUIT • Disconnect 5-Pin plug on reservoir fluid level indicator (FLI). • Measure resistance between electrical Pins 1 and 2 (with brake fluid at maximum fluid level).	Less than 2 ohms (OK) Greater than 2 ohms (not OK)	GO to Step E1b. REPLACE fluid level indicator.

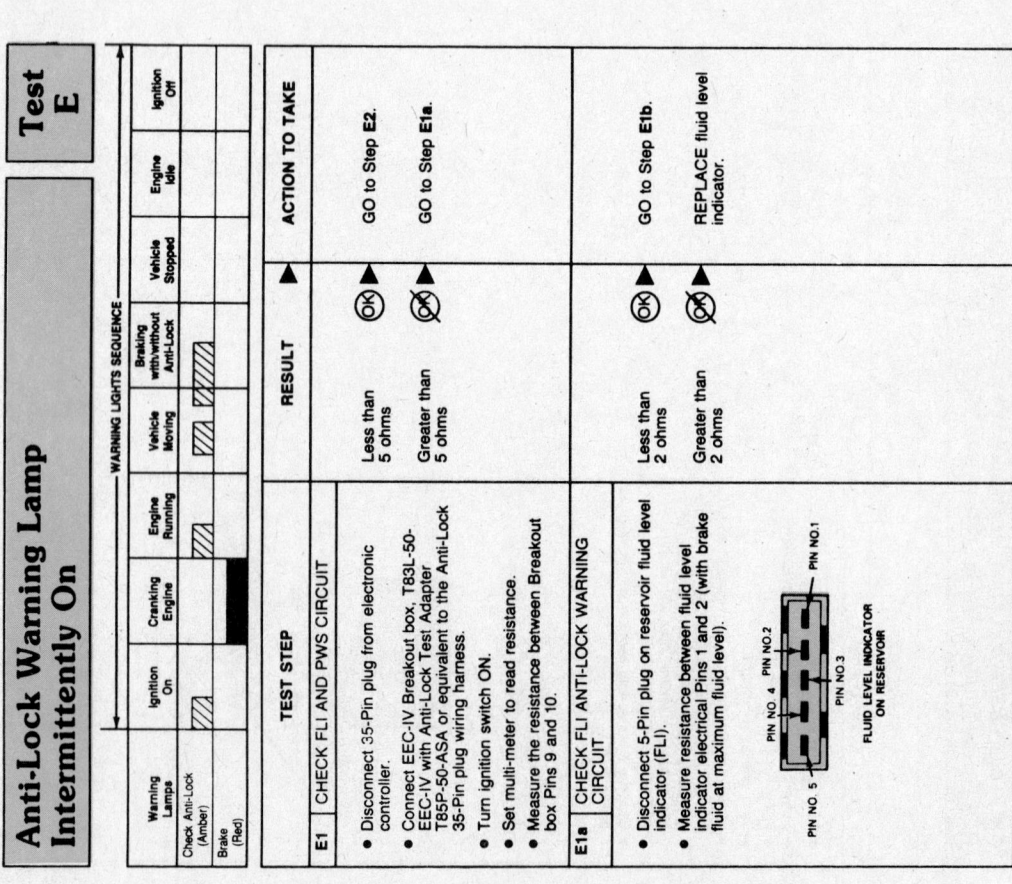

Anti-Lock Warning Lamp Intermittently On — Test E

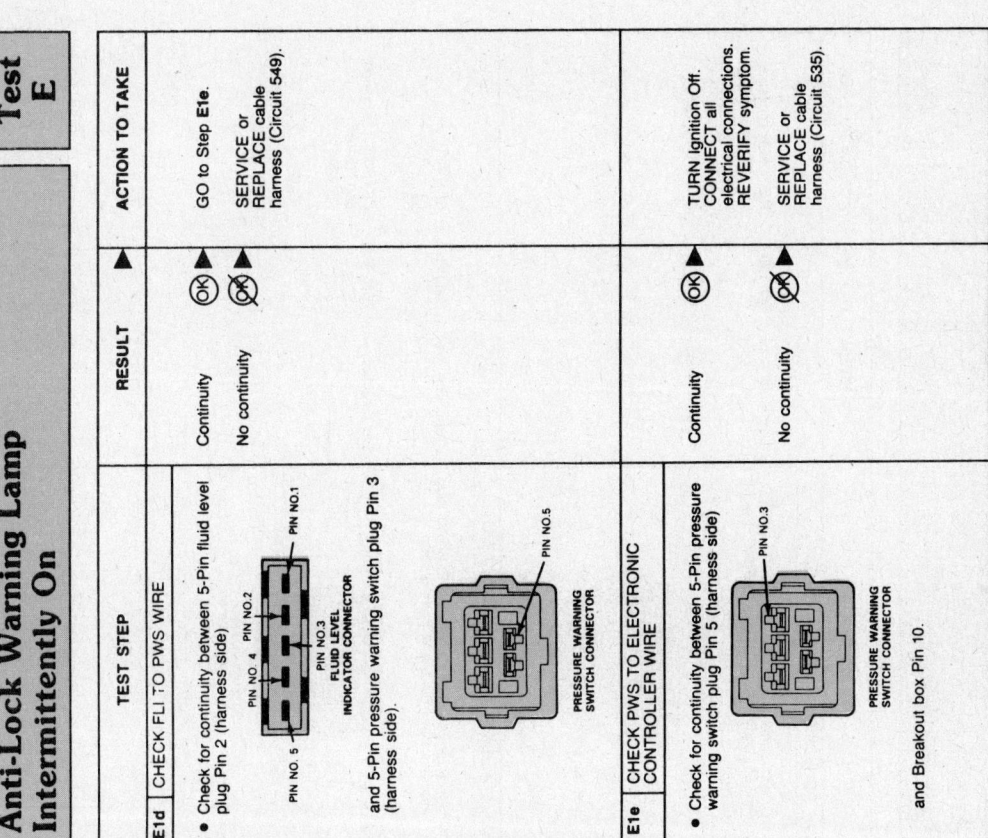

TEST STEP	RESULT	ACTION TO TAKE
E2 CHECK ISOLATION TEST FLI AND PWS		
• Check for continuity between Breakout box Pin 9 and body ground.	Continuity	GO to Step E2a.
	No continuity	REVERIFY symptom.
E2a CHECK CONTINUITY OF FLI SWITCH		
• Disconnect FLI plug and check for continuity between socket Pin 1 and Pins 3, 4, and 5 and Pin 2 and Pins 3, 4, and 5.	Continuity	REPLACE FLI.
	No continuity	GO to Step E2b.
E2b CHECK CONTINUITY CIRCUIT 512		
• Check for continuity between FLI plug Pin 1 (harness side) and body ground.	Continuity	SERVICE or REPLACE (Circuit 512).
	No continuity	GO to Step E2c.
E2c CHECK CONTINUITY CIRCUIT 549		
• Disconnect 5-Pin plug from PWS. Check for continuity between FLI plug Pin 2 (harness side) and body ground.	Continuity	SERVICE or REPLACE (Circuit 549).
	No continuity	GO to Step E2d.

(FLUID LEVEL INDICATOR CONNECTOR — PIN NO.1, PIN NO.2, PIN NO.3, PIN NO.4, PIN NO.5)

Anti-Lock Warning Lamp Intermittently On — Test E

TEST STEP	RESULT	ACTION TO TAKE
E1d CHECK FLI TO PWS WIRE		
• Check for continuity between 5-Pin fluid level plug Pin 2 (harness side) and 5-Pin pressure warning switch plug Pin 3 (harness side).	Continuity	GO to Step E1e.
	No continuity	SERVICE or REPLACE cable harness (Circuit 549).
E1e CHECK PWS TO ELECTRONIC CONTROLLER WIRE		
• Check for continuity between 5-Pin pressure warning switch plug Pin 5 (harness side) and Breakout box Pin 10.	Continuity	TURN Ignition Off. CONNECT all electrical connections. REVERIFY symptom.
	No continuity	SERVICE or REPLACE cable harness (Circuit 535).

(FLUID LEVEL INDICATOR CONNECTOR — PIN NO.1, PIN NO.2, PIN NO.3, PIN NO.4, PIN NO.5)
(PRESSURE WARNING SWITCH CONNECTOR — PIN NO.3, PIN NO.5)

Anti-Lock Warning Lamp Intermittently On — Test E

TEST STEP	RESULT ▶	ACTION TO TAKE
E2d CHECK CONTINUITY OF PWS		
• Check for continuity from PWS 5-Pin socket Pin 3 to body ground, and from Pin 5 to body ground.	Continuity — NOT OK ▶	REPLACE pressure warning switch and pump motor relay.
	No continuity — OK ▶	GO to Step **E2e**.
E2e CHECK CONTINUITY CIRCUIT 535		
• Check for continuity between 5-Pin PWS plug (harness side) Pin 5 and body ground.	Continuity — NOT OK ▶	SERVICE or REPLACE (Circuit 535).
	No continuity — OK ▶	CONNECT all plugs and REVERIFY symptom.

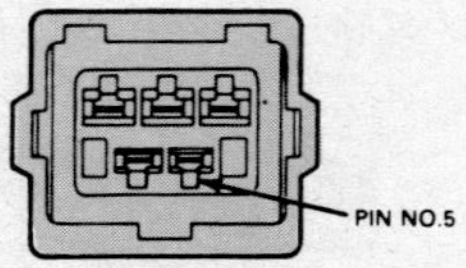

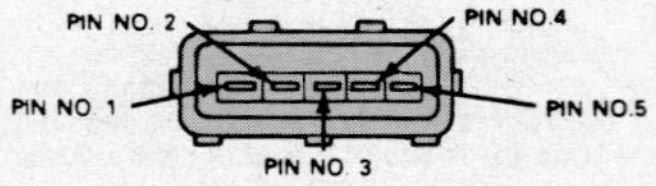

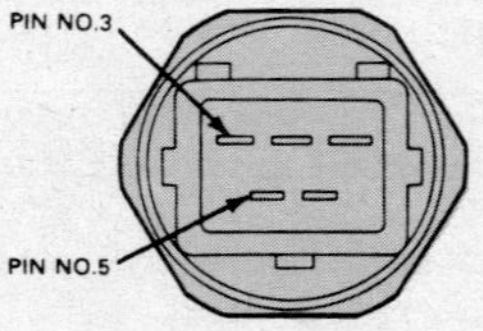

PIN NO.3
PIN NO.5
PRESSURE WARNING SWITCH

PIN NO.5
PRESSURE WARNING SWITCH CONNECTOR

Brake Warning Lamp On (With Anti-Lock Lamp Off, Parking Brake Released And Brake Lining Wear Checked) — Test F

WARNING LIGHTS SEQUENCE

Warning Lamps	Ignition On	Cranking Engine	Engine Running	Vehicle Moving	Braking with/without Anti-Lock	Vehicle Stopped	Engine Idle	Ignition Off
Check Anti-Lock (Amber)	▨		▨					
Brake (Red)	■	■	■	■	■	■	■	

TEST STEP	RESULT ▶	ACTION TO TAKE
F1 CHECK BRAKE FLUID LEVEL		
• Turn ignition switch ON. • Pump brake pedal until pump motor starts. • When pump motor stops check brake fluid level.	Low — NOT OK ▶	CHECK system for external leaks. SERVICE as required.
	Normal — OK ▶	GO to Step **F2**.
F2 CHECK CONTINUITY FLI SWITCH		
• Disconnect 5-Pin plug on fluid reservoir cap. • Set multi-meter on 200 ohm range. Connect to reservoir warning cap Pins 3 and 4.	Above 10 ohms — OK ▶	GO to Step **F3**.
	Below 10 ohms — NOT OK ▶	REPLACE 5-Pin fluid level indicator cap.

PIN NO. 2
PIN NO.4
PIN NO. 1
PIN NO.5
PIN NO. 3
FLUID RESERVOIR CAP

No Anti-Lock Warning Lamp On When Ignition Switch Turned On — Test G

WARNING LIGHTS SEQUENCE

Warning Lamps	Ignition On	Cranking Engine	Engine Running	Vehicle Moving	Braking with/without Anti-Lock	Vehicle Stopped	Engine Idle	Ignition Off
Check Anti-Lock (Amber)								
Brake (Red)		■						

	TEST STEP	RESULT	ACTION TO TAKE
G1	CHECK FUSE AND FUSE LINKS • Check fuse Three in-line fuse links with ignition turned ON.	Fuse Links (OK) ▲ Fuse Links (not OK) ▲	GO to Step G2. SERVICE or REPLACE as required.
G2	CHECK WARNING LAMP BULB • Check warning lamp bulb.	(OK) ▲ (not OK) ▲	GO to Step G3. REPLACE.
G3	CHECK WARNING LAMP OPERATION • Turn ignition switch ON. • Disconnect 35 Pin connector from control module.	If Anti-Lock lamp goes ON ▲ If Anti-Lock lamp is not ON ▲	SERVICE or REPLACE Circuit 606. SERVICE or REPLACE connector to 14401 wire harness.

Brake Warning Lamp On (With Anti-Lock Lamp Off, Parking Brake Released And Brake Lining Wear Checked) — Test F

	TEST STEP	RESULT	ACTION TO TAKE
F3	CHECK CONTINUITY PWS SWITCH (CONTINUED) • Turn ignition switch ON, wait until motor stops running. • Disconnect Pressure Warning Switch 5-Pin plug and connect multi-meter to Pins 1 and 2 (switch side). • Check for continuity. PIN NO. 1 / PIN NO. 2 PRESSURE WARNING SWITCH	Continuity (not OK) ▲ No continuity (OK) ▲	REPLACE pressure warning switch and pump motor relay. GO to Step F4.
F4	CHECK WIRING CONTINUITY • Check cable harness 430H, 512, 547B, 547A, 549, 977 Circuits. (Refer to vehicle Wiring Diagram.)	(OK) ▲ (not OK) ▲	CHECK parking brake electrical circuit workshop manual. REVERIFY symptom. SERVICE or REPLACE as required.

Poor Vehicle Tracking During Anti-Lock Function (Warning Lamp Off) — Test J

Warning Lamps	Ignition On	Cranking Engine	Engine Running	Vehicle Moving	Vehicle Stopped	Braking with/without Anti-Lock	Engine Idle	Ignition Off
Check Anti-Lock (Amber)	▨		▨					
Brake (Red)		■						

TEST STEP	RESULT	ACTION TO TAKE
J1 VERIFY CONDITION		
• Verify condition exists as reported. • Turn air suspension off. • Bleed brake system per shop manual for Anti-Lock brake system. • Turn air suspension on when vehicle is off hoist.	Vehicle tracks properly ▲	Condition corrected.
	Vehicle still tracks poorly ▲	GO to **J2**.
J2 CHECK ANTI-LOCK OPERATION — LEFT FRONT WHEEL		
• Turn air suspension off. • Lift vehicle and rotate wheels to assure they turn freely. • Turn ignition switch OFF. • Disconnect 35-Pin plug from electronic controller. • Connect EEC-IV Breakout box. Tool T83L-50-EEC-IV with Anti-Lock test adapter, Tool T85P-50-ASA to the Anti-Lock 35-Pin plug wiring harness. • Short Pins 2, 16 and 35 to each other at Breakout box. • Apply moderate brake pedal effort and check that left front wheel will not turn. • Check to see that left front wheel turns freely with ignition switch ON. • Turn air suspension on when vehicle is off hoist. **CAUTION: DO NOT LEAVE IGNITION ON FOR MORE THAN 1 MINUTE MAXIMUM, OR SOLENOID VALVE DAMAGE MAY RESULT.**	If wheel turns freely ▲	TURN ignition switch Off. DISCONNECT wire leads. Go to Step **J3**.
	If wheel does not turn freely or pedal drops ▲	REPLACE solenoid valve block.

Spongy Brake Pedal With/Without Anti-Lock Function (No Warning Lamp) — Test H

Warning Lamps	Ignition On	Cranking Engine	Engine Running	Vehicle Moving	Vehicle Stopped	Braking with/without Anti-Lock	Engine Idle	Ignition Off
Check Anti-Lock (Amber)	▨		▨					
Brake (Red)		■						

TEST STEP	RESULT	ACTION TO TAKE
H1 CHECK COMPONENT MOUNTING		
• Check for proper brake pedal and hydraulic unit attachment. • Bleed brakes as outlined.	Pedal still spongy ⊗ ▲	GO to Step **H2**.
	Pedal feels normal OK ▲	Condition corrected.
H2 BLEED BRAKE SYSTEM		
• Turn off air suspension switch in luggage compartment. • Rebleed brake system. • Turn on air suspension switch when vehicle is off hoist.	Pedal still spongy ⊗ ▲	REPLACE hydraulic unit.
	Pedal feels normal OK ▲	Condition corrected.

Test K — No Booster; Anti-Lock Warning Lamp On

WARNING LIGHTS SEQUENCE

Warning Lamps	Ignition ON	Cranking Engine	Engine Running	Vehicle Moving	Braking with/without Anti-Lock	Vehicle Stopped	Engine Idle	Ignition OFF
Check Anti-Lock (Amber)								
Brake (Red)								

	TEST STEP	RESULT	ACTION TO TAKE
K1	CHECK CONTINUITY PWS SWITCH		
	• Turn ignition switch ON, wait until motor stops running. • Disconnect 5-Pin plug from Pressure Warning Switch (PWS). • Check continuity between Pins 1 and 4 (switch side).	▲ Continuity (OK) ▲ No continuity	▲ SERVICE wire from Pin 1 to ground. REPLACE Pressure warning switch and pump motor relay.

PIN NO. 1 PIN NO. 4

PRESSURE WARNING SWITCH

Test J — Poor Vehicle Tracking During Anti-Lock Function (Warning Lamp Off)

	TEST STEP	RESULT	ACTION TO TAKE
J3	CHECK ANTI-LOCK OPERATION — RIGHT FRONT WHEEL		
	• Turn air suspension off. • Short Pins 2, 15 and 34 to each other at Breakout box. • Apply moderate brake effort. Check that right front wheel does not turn. • Check that right front wheel turns freely with ignition switch ON. **CAUTION: DO NOT LEAVE IGNITION ON MORE THAN 1 MINUTE MAXIMUM OR SOLENOID VALVE DAMAGE MAY RESULT.**	▲ Wheel turns freely ▲ Wheel does not turn freely or brake pedal drops	▲ TURN ignition switch OFF. DISCONNECT wire leads. GO to Step J4. REPLACE solenoid valve block.
J4	CHECK ANTI-LOCK OPERATION — REAR WHEELS		
	• Turn air suspension off. • Short Pins 2, 17 and 33 to each other at Breakout box. • Apply moderate brake pedal pressure. Check that rear wheels will not turn. • Check that rear wheels turn freely with ignition switch ON. • Turn air suspension on when vehicle is off hoist. **CAUTION: DO NOT LEAVE IGNITION ON MORE THAN 1 MINUTE MAXIMUM OR SOLENOID VALVE DAMAGE MAY RESULT.**	▲ Wheels turn freely ▲ Wheels do not turn freely or brake pedal drops	▲ TURN ignition switch Off. DISCONNECT wire lead and Breakout box. LOWER vehicle. REVERIFY symptom. REPLACE solenoid valve block.

TYPE 4
MITSUBISHI SYSTEM
CHRYS. CORP./MITSUBISHI

General Infomation

The Mitsubishi antilock brake system is an automatic brake control system designed to achieve maximum braking efficiency for quick stops on wet or icy road surfaces, and to reduce the possibility of vehicle skidding. This system, however, is designed for rear wheel control only. If the front wheels become locked, the brakes will not be automatically controlled.

System Components

The rear brake antilock system is composed of the following five units:
- PULSE GENERATOR—Generates a rotation pulse in accordance with the speed of the rear wheels.
- G-SENSOR—Generates a voltage in accordance with the reduction of the vehicle speed.
- CONTROL UNIT (Electric Control Module)—Controls each of the signals.
- MODULATOR—Controls the pressure of the brake fluid.
- FAIL INDICATION LIGHT—Illuminates in the event of a malfunction of the control unit.

System Operation

PULSE GENERATOR

The pulse generator is composed of a permanent magnet, a coil and a rotor. It is installed at the speedometer exit port of the transmission. The rotor is rotated by the speedometer drive gear. The magnetic flux generated from the permanent magnet varies according to the rotation of the rotor, and an AC voltage is generated in the coil.

The AC voltage is proportionate to the rotational speed of the rotor, and the frequency varies. Accordingly, the speed of the wheels is detected by using the frequency variations of the AC voltage generated by the pulse generator.

The frequency of the generated voltage is the average value of the speed of the left and right wheels.

G-SENSOR

The G-sensor is composed of a differential transformer, a control circuit (printed circuit board), etc. It is located in the floor of the luggage compartment.

The core within the differential transformer is usually stationery at the center of the coil; however, when a reduction in speed is applied, the core moves and a voltage corresponding to the amount of displacement of the core is generated. In other words, the amount of the reduction in vehicle speed is detected.

CONTROL UNIT (ELECTRONIC CONTROL MODULE)

The control unit is located inside the luggage compartment. It receives the signals from the pulse generator, the G-sensor, and the brake switch (which is also used as the stoplight switch), and transmits the brake fluid pressure control signal to the modulator (the solenoid valve section), or in the event of an open circuit, the condition is detected. The brake system is

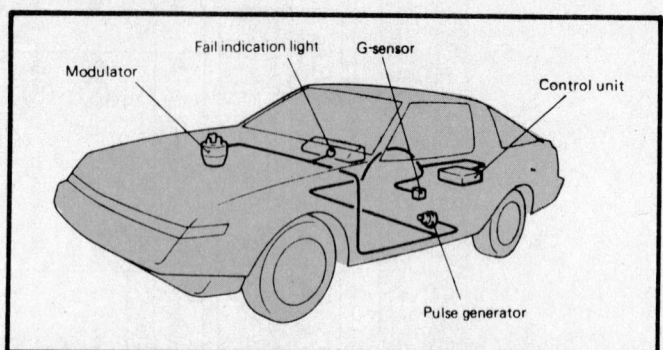

Mitsubishi antilock brake system components

returned to conventional operation, and the fail indicator light illuminates to warn the driver of a malfunction.

In addition, if an open circuit occurs in the wiring of the control unit power supply, the G-sensor, the inside of the pulse generator, or the brake switch (input wiring), or if the stop light bulb burns out, the brake system is returned to conventional operation, and the fail indicator light illuminates in the same way to warn the driver.

The signal to lower the brake fluid pressure of the rear brakes causes the modulator release valve to operate in the event that the amount of slipping of the tires on the road surface becomes greater than the specified value which is determined in accordance with the speed reduction of the wheels and also in the event that the speed reduction of the wheels becomes greater than the specified value in relationship to the reduction of the vehicle speed. Note that there is no antilock control of the rear brakes when the vehicle speed is 5 mph or less.

Operation Outline

The control unit determines the ideal vehicle speed reduction curve in accordance with the input signals from the G-sensor and the pulse generator. As shown in the illustration, the ideal vehicle speed reduction and the actual speed reduction of the wheels are compared. If the actual speed reduction of the wheels is greater (if the rotational speed of of the wheels is slowing down too rapidly), the brake fluid pressure for the rear brakes is decreased, the rate of the speed reduction of the wheels is also decreased, and the ideal vehicle speed reduction rate is restored. On the other hand, if the actual speed reduction of the wheels is smaller (if the rotational speed of the wheels is slowing down too slowly), the brake fluid pressure for the rear wheels is increased, the rate of speed reduction of the wheels is also increased, and the ideal wheel speed reduction rate is restored. In this way, the wheels are controlled to maintain the ideal rate of speed reduction.

Fail-Safe Function

The fail-safe function causes the control unit to cease operation, the brake system to return to conventional operation, and the fail indicator light to illuminate in the event that any of the following malfunctions occur in the rear antilock brake control system:
- The wiring of the solenoid valve used for vacuum control of the modulator becomes disconnected.

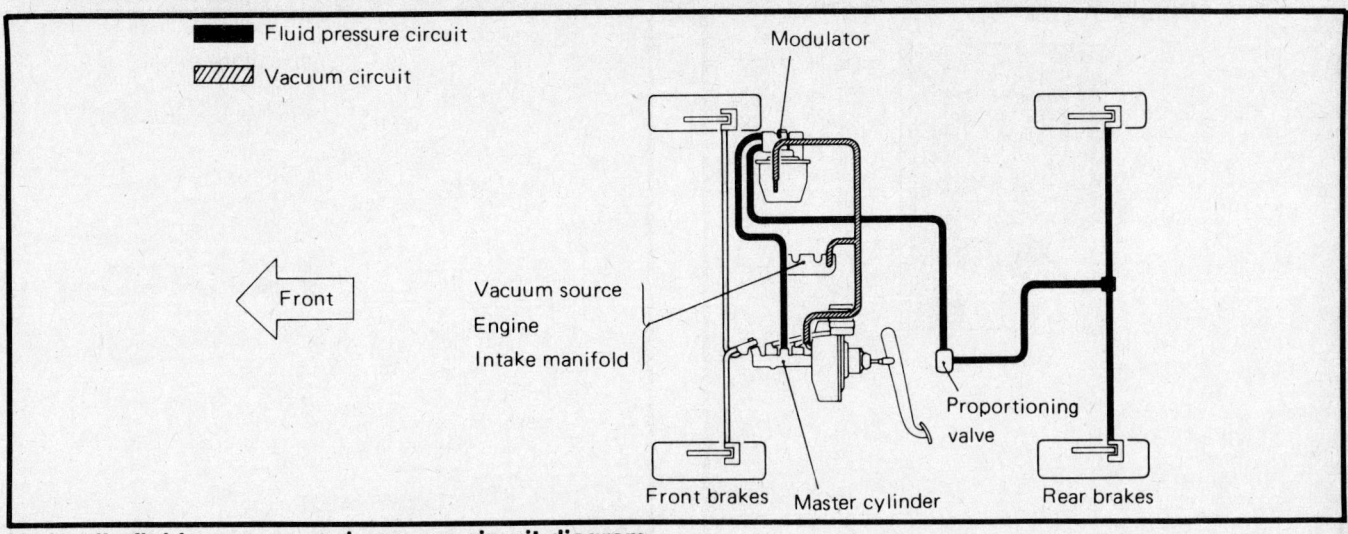

Hydraulic fluid pressure and vacuum circuit diagram

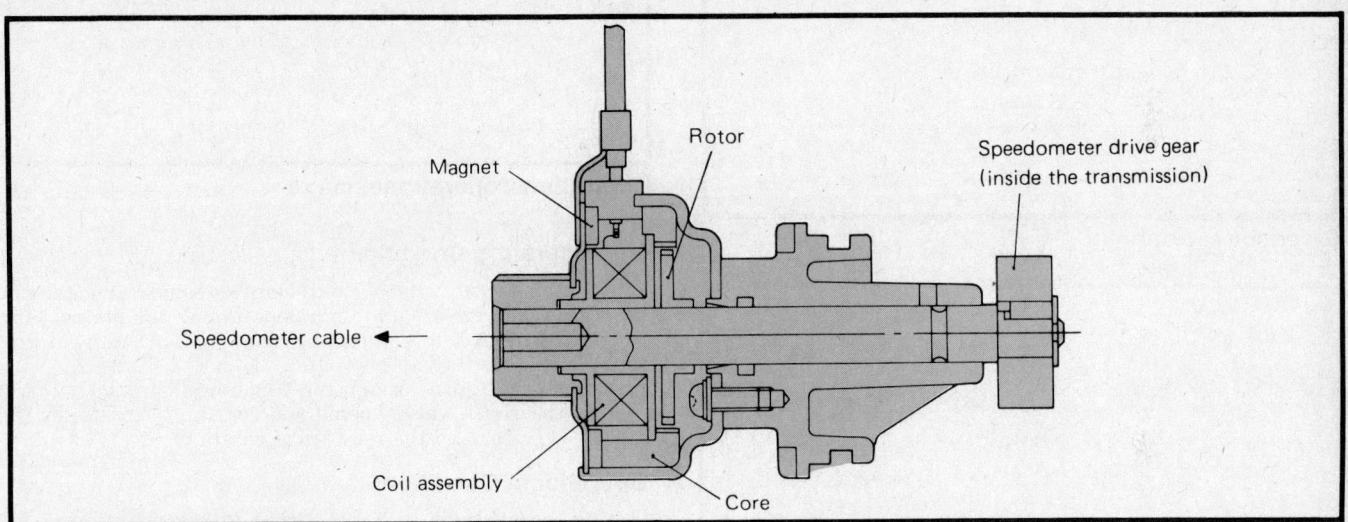

Pulse generator assembly

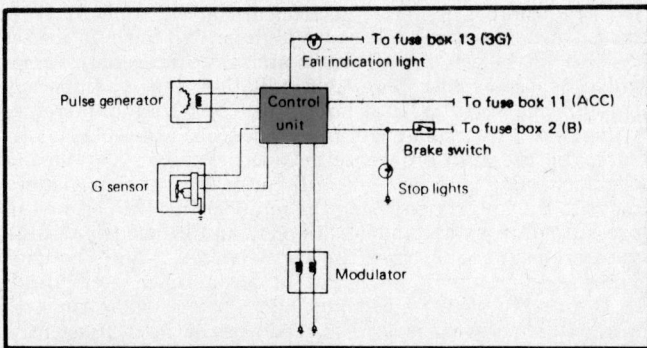

Electrical circuit diagram

- The solenoid valve used for vacuum control of the modulator operates continuously for five seconds or longer.
- The wiring to the brake switch becomes disconnected.
- A problem occurs inside the pulse generator, or the wiring of the pulse generator becomes disconnected.
- A problem occurs in the G-sensor, or the wiring of the G-sensor becomes disconnected.

- The wiring of the stop light becomes disconnected.
If the fail indicator light illuminates, refer to the "Diagnosis & Testing" section.

Control Unit Function Check

Run the engine for five seconds or longer while the vehicle is not in motion. Next, turn the ignition key to the "LOCK" position, depress the brake pedal, and then, while keeping the brake pedal depressed, turn the ignition key back to the "ON" position. At this time, confirm that the operation sound of the modulator solenoid valve can be heard. If this sound can be heard, the control unit is functioning properly.

In other words, self-diagnosis of the control unit is done by causing the solenoid valve to operate.

MODULATOR

The modulator receives the control signal from the control unit, and controls the brake fluid pressure for the rear brakes.

The modulator is composed of a brake fluid pressure control section to control the brake fluid pressure for the rear brakes, a vacuum pressure drive section to drive the brake fluid pressure control section, and a solenoid valve to control the vacuum pressure of the vacuum pressure drive section.

541

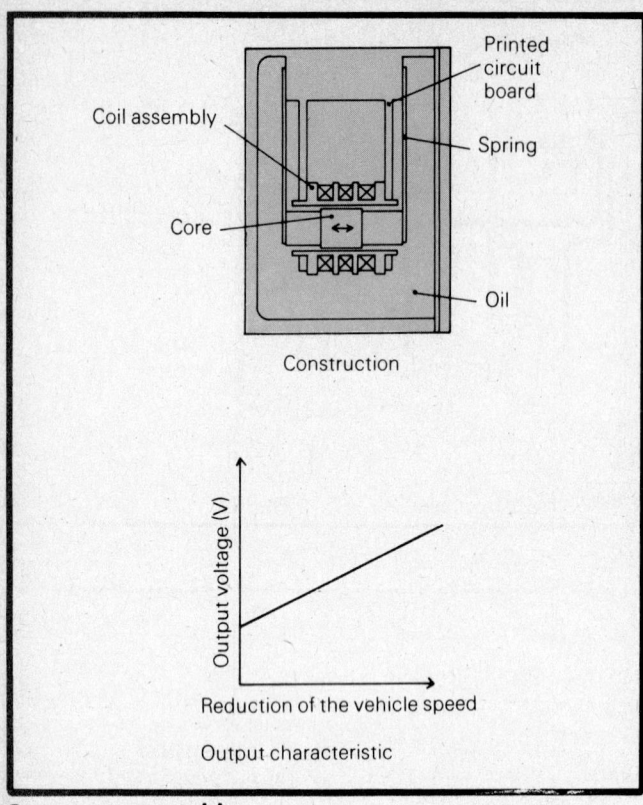

Construction

Output characteristic

G-sensor assembly

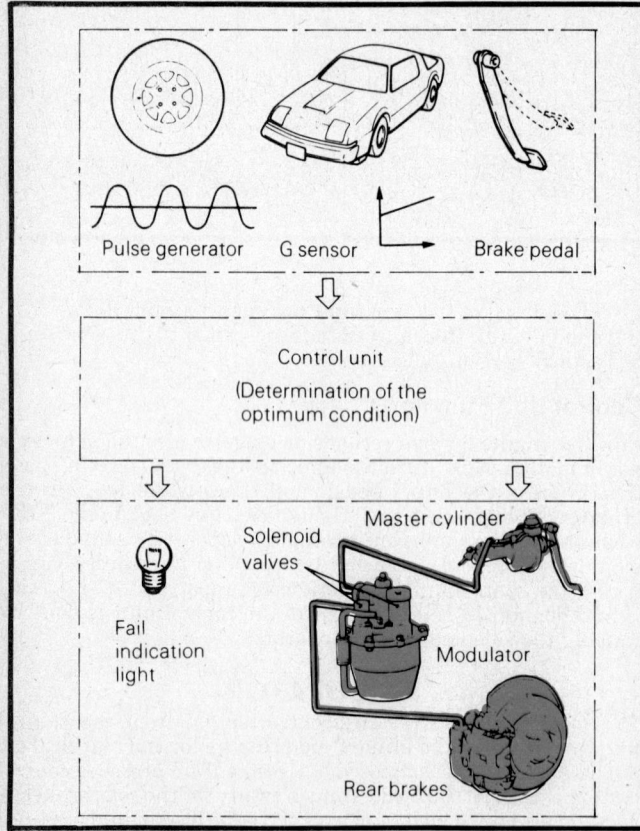

Pulse generator   G sensor   Brake pedal

Control unit
(Determination of the
optimum condition)

Fail
indication
light

Solenoid
valves

Master cylinder

Modulator

Rear brakes

Control unit operation

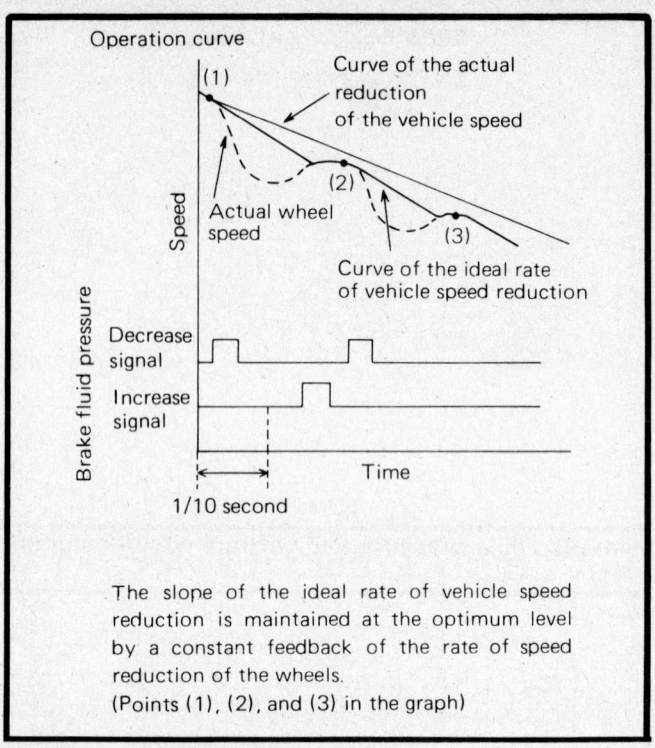

Operation curve

The slope of the ideal rate of vehicle speed reduction is maintained at the optimum level by a constant feedback of the rate of speed reduction of the wheels.
(Points (1), (2), and (3) in the graph)

Control unit operational curve

Non-operating Condition

When the solenoid valves (the release solenoid valve and the build-up solenoid valve) are not operational, the pressures in compartments A and B become equal because of the opening of the release seat B. For this reason, the brake fluid plunger is pressed to the right through the vacuum piston by the main spring, the check valve opens, and continuity exists for the master cylinder and the rear brake circuit.

Operational Condition

During operation:
1. Reduction of the brake fluid pressure for the rear brakes: If the signal for reduction of the brake fluid pressure is output from the control unit, the electric current will flow to the release solenoid valve, the release plunger will move to the left, release valve seat "A" will open, and, simultaneously, release valve seat "B" will close. Air will flow into chamber "B" through the air filter, to the air intake port, and to the release valve seat "A". When chamber "B" reaches atmospheric pressure, the pressure difference between chamber "A" (vacuum condition) and chamber "B" will cause the vacuum piston to move to the left, compressing the main spring. The brake fluid pressure plunger will move to the left simultaneously with the vacuum piston and close the check valve. When the check valve is closed, the flow of brake fluid from the master cylinder to the rear brakes is disrupted, and, at the same time, the brake fluid pressure is decreased because of the increase in the capacity of brake fluid in chamber "C".
2. Slow restoration of the normal brake fluid pressure for the rear brakes to a normal level;
Once the brake fluid pressure to the rear brakes has been reduced, the brake fluid pressure reduction signal will cease to be output, the release solenoid will return to its non-operating condition, and the air intake to chamber "B" will be stopped. Because the atmospheric pressure of chamber "B" passes through the orfice, the pressure in chamber "B" will gradually change from atmospheric pressure to a vacuum; and, as a re-

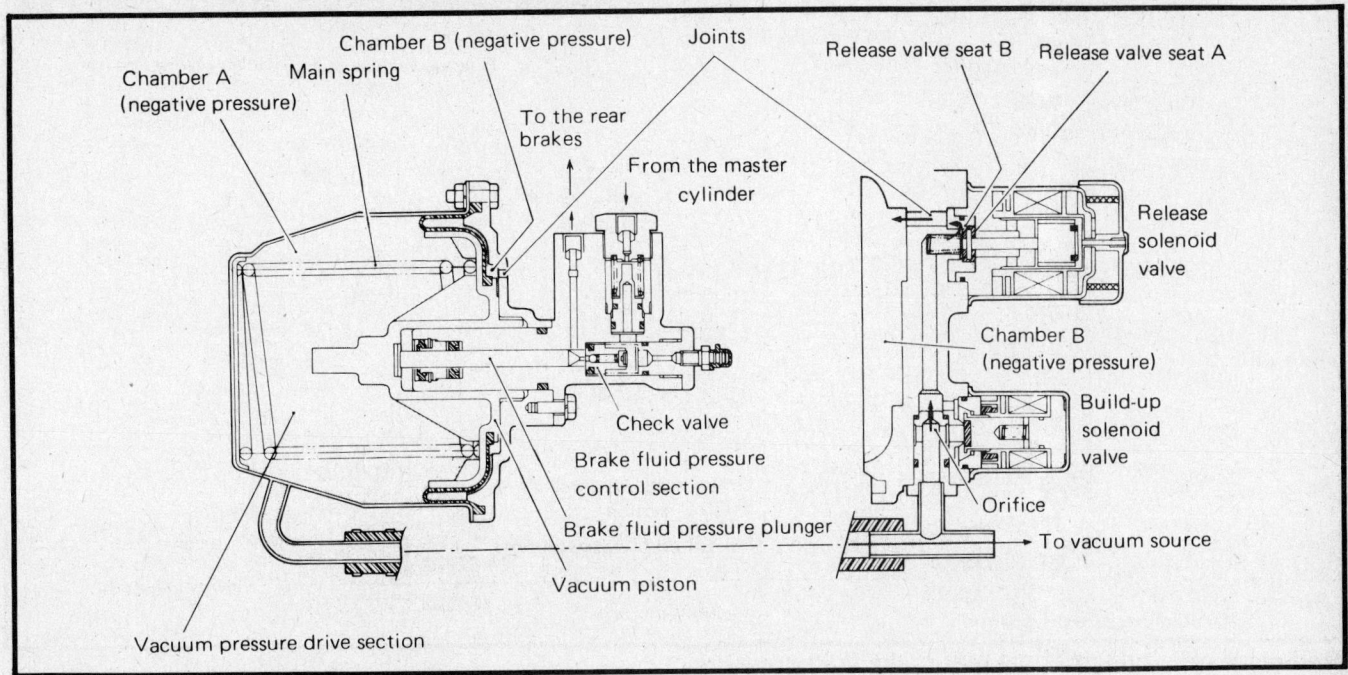

Modulator—non-operating condition

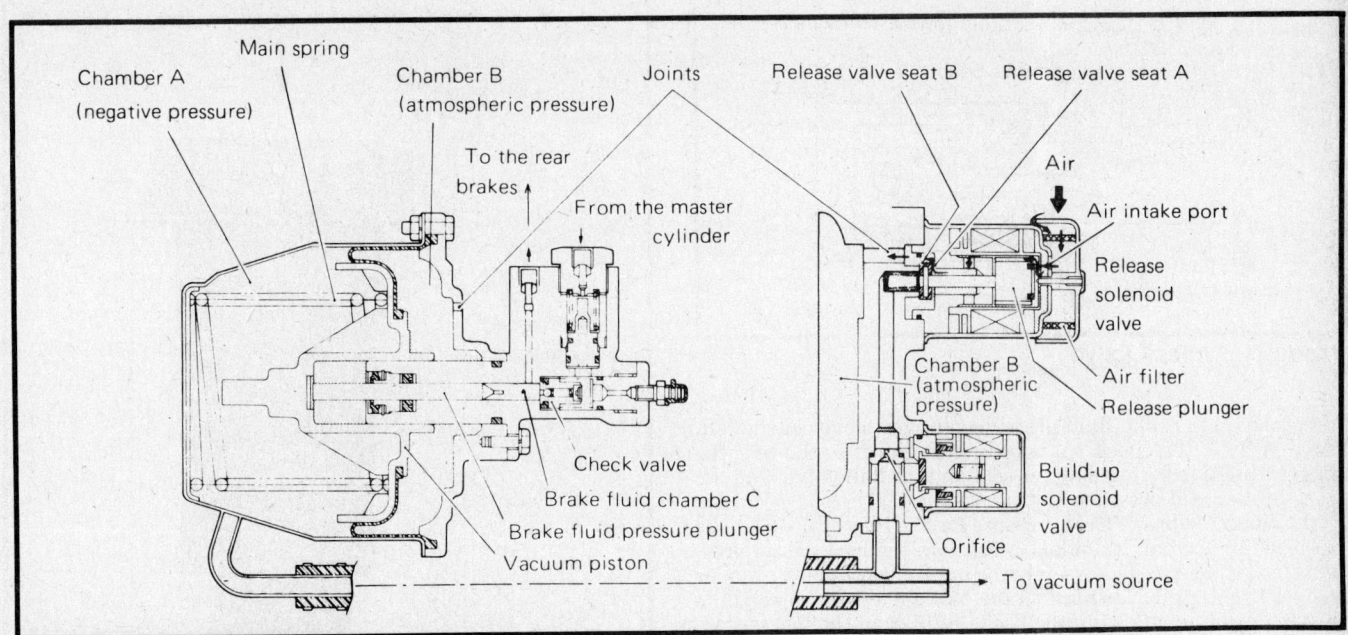

Modulator—reduction in rear brake fluid pressure

sult, the pressure difference between chamber "A" and chamber "B" will gradually disappear. The brake fluid plunger will be pushed back to the right by the force of the main spring, the condition will be the same as when not operating, and the normal level of brake fluid pressure will be supplied to the rear brakes.

3. Quick restoration of the brake fluid pressure for the rear brakes to the normal level;
The electric current will flow to the build-up solenoid valve, the build-up plunger will move to the right, and the build-up valve seat will open. Because the pressure reduction of chamber "B" is done through the orfice and the build-up valve seat,

the pressure of chamber "A" and chamber "B" will quickly equalize.

NOTE: If the brake fluid pressure is reduced too much and the level of wheel speed reduction becomes significantly lower then the desired level, the build-up solenoid valve will operate to rapidly archive the desired level of speed reduction.

Check Valve Functions

1. When the brake fluid pressure for the rear brakes is to be

543

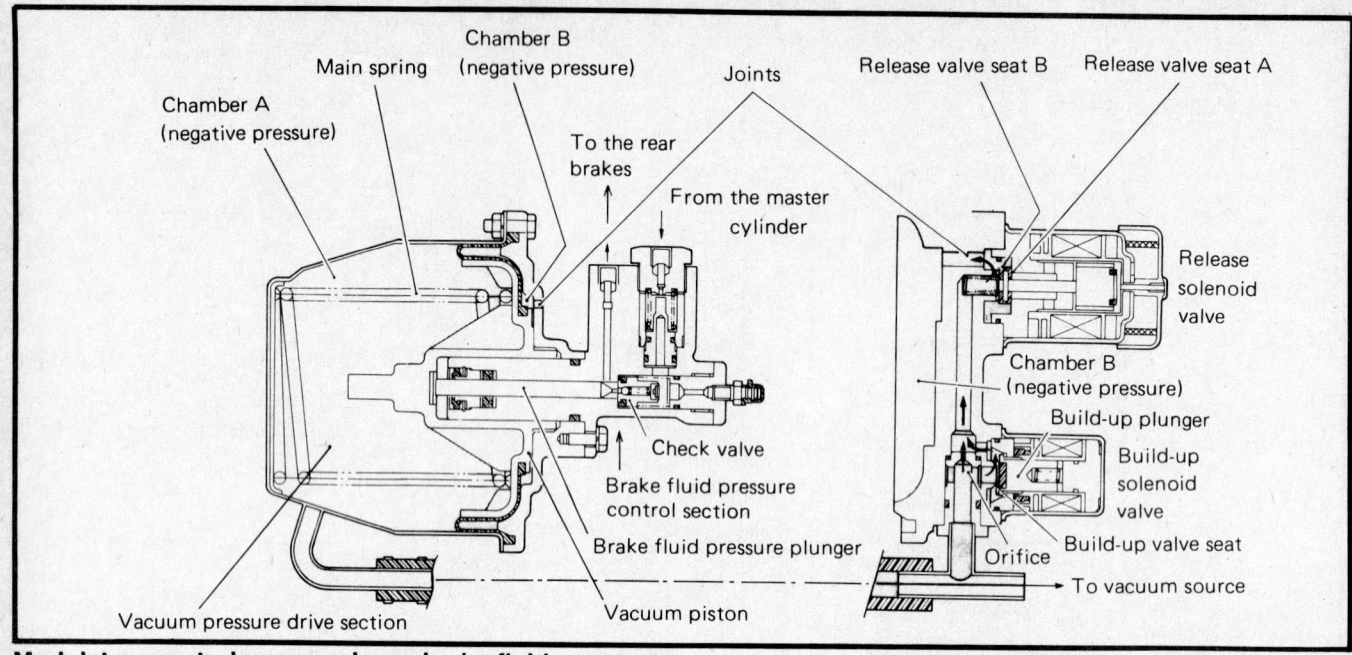

Modulator—restoring normal rear brake fluid pressure

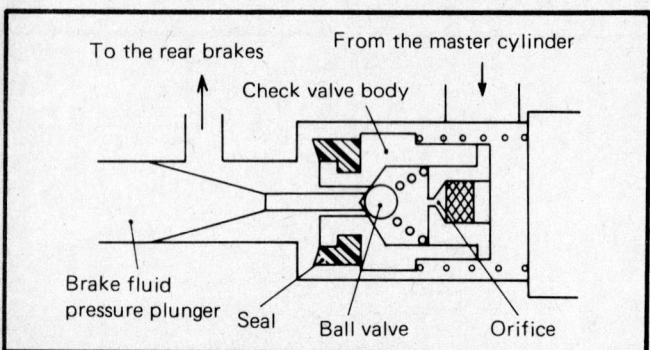

Modulator check valve

decreased, the brake fluid pressure plunger moves to the left. At this time, the check valve body also moves to the left, the brake fluid line is closed by the seal and the ball valve, and the rear brake fluid pressure is decreased.

2. When the brake fluid pressure for the rear brakes is to be restored to normal, a sudden increase in the brake fluid pressure is avoided as follows: The brake fluid pressure plunger moves to the right, pushing on the ball valve which opens the brake fluid line, allowing the brake fluid from the master cylinder to pass through the orifice and gradually flow to the rear brakes.

Choke Valve Function

Extreme increase in the master cylinder brake fluid pressure will occur when the brake pedal is operated suddenly during quick stops etc. The choke valve prevents sudden increase in the rear brake fluid pressure to allow the system to correctly perform the control function even during sudden braking. The brake fluid flows freely to the rear brakes until the brake fluid pressure of the master cylinder reaches 711 psi, as shown in the illustration.

When the brake fluid pressure reaches 711 psi, the stepped diameter piston will press the cut-in spring upward, and contact the plug. The brake fluid will pass only through the

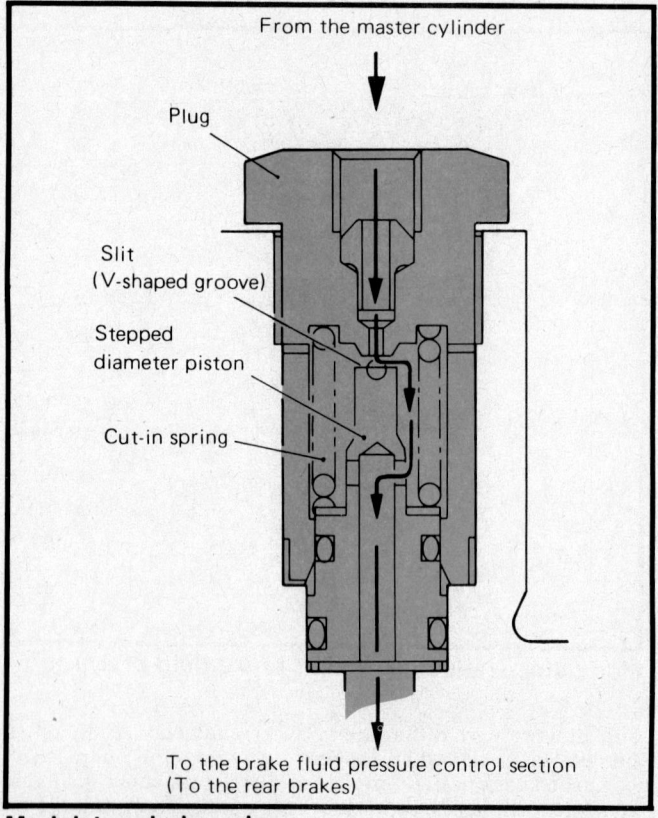

Modulator choke valve

V-shaped groove, thus limiting the rate of increase of the brake fluid pressure to the rear brakes.

FAIL INDICATION LIGHT

If any malfunction occurs in the rear brake antilock control

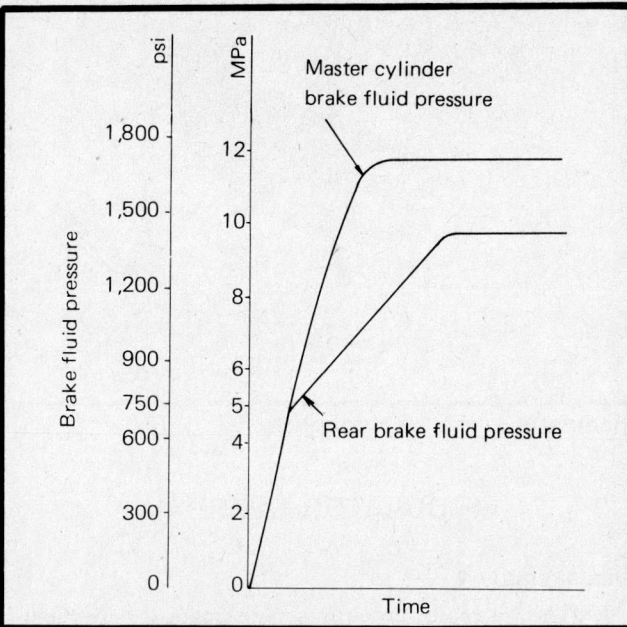

Choke valve pressure curve

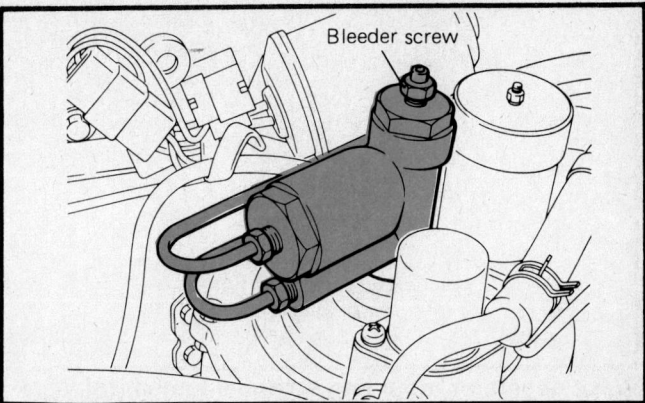

Modulator bleeder screw location

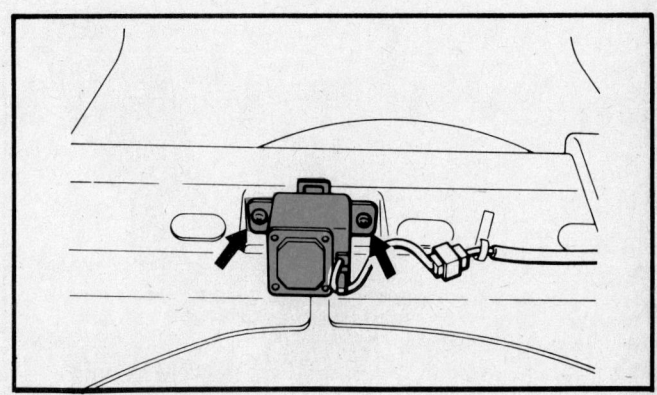

G-sensor mounting

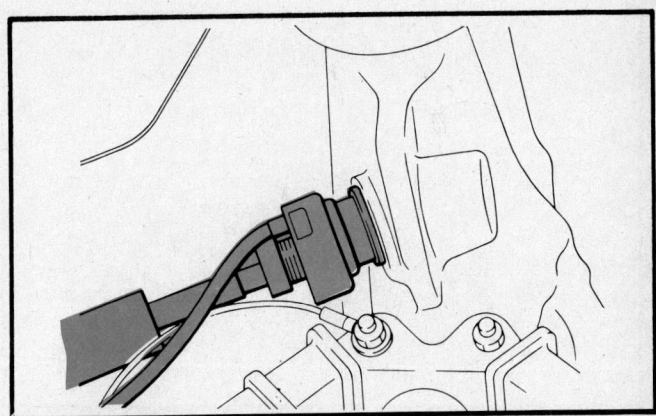

Pulse generator mounting

system, a signal from the control unit will cause the fail indicator light to illuminate and warn the driver of the malfunction. In addition, the light will illuminate for approximately three seconds when the ignition key is set to the "ON" position in order to provide confirmation that the light is connected and performing properly.

If the light does not illuminate, there is a malfunction of the light or the light circuit.

If the light remains on, there is a malfunction of the rear brake antilock control system.

Component Replacement

BLEEDING THE BRAKE SYSTEM

The Mitsubishi rear antilock brake system should be bled in the conventional manner following the component order below:
1. Rear wheel caliper—right side
2. Rear wheel caliper—left side
3. Bleeder screw on the hydraulic modulator
4. Front wheel calipers

G-SENSOR REPLACEMENT

NOTE: When removing the G-sensor, be careful not to subject it to any impact or violent shaking.

1. Disconnect the negative battery cable.
2. From inside the luggage compartment, disconnect the electrical connector.
3. Remove the two screws and remove the G-sensor.
To install:
4. With the vehicle parked on a level surface, mount the G-sensor using a level to be sure it is perfectly horizontal.
5. Connect the electrical connector and the negative battery cable.

PULSE GENERATOR REPLACEMENT

1. Disconnect the speedometer cable at the pulse generator side.

2. Remove the pulse generator.
To install:
3. Reverse the removal procedures above, on models with manual transmission, count the number of speedometer driven gear teeth and select the mark on the sleeve of the pulse generator which indicates that number of teeth. Align the selected mark with the reference mark on the extension housing.

CONTROL UNIT REPLACEMENT

1. Disconnect the negative battery cable.
2. From its position beneath the high floor side of the luggage compartment, remove the four mounting bolts.

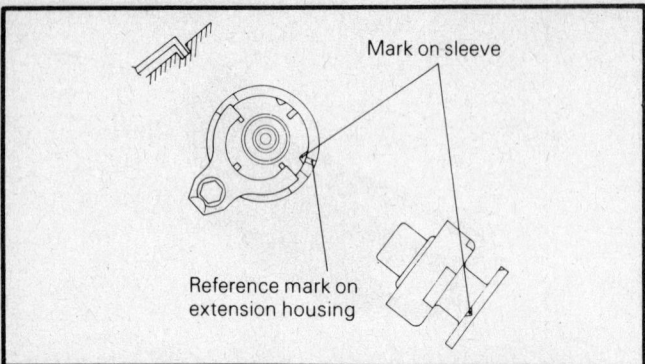

Pulse generator mounting — manual transmission vehicles

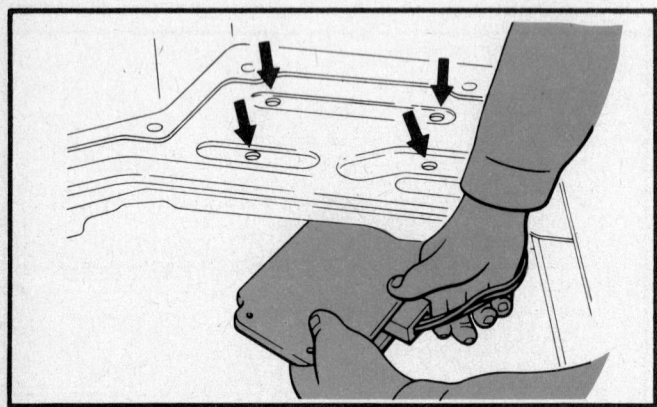

Control unit mounting

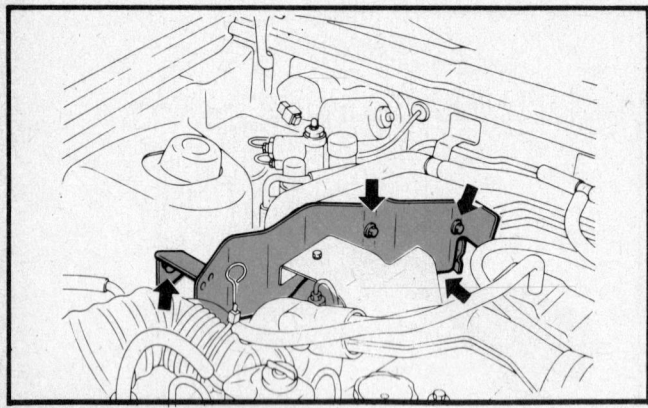

Modulator heat protector

3. Lower the control unit and disconnect the electrical connector.
4. To install, reverse the removal procedure above.

MODULATOR REPLACEMENT

1. Disconnect the negative battery cable.
2. Remove the modulator heat protector.
3. Remove the vacuum hose, the brake tube and the connector for the solenoid valve.
4. Remove the modulator bracket from the bulkhead, and then remove the modulator.
5. To install, reverse the removal procedure above.

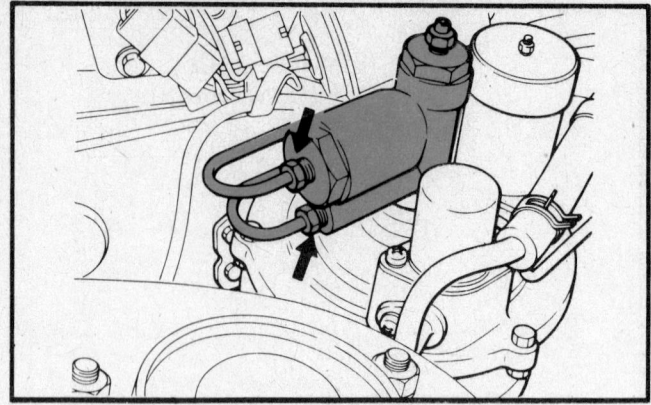

Modulator brake tube connections

MODULATOR OVERHAUL

Disassembly

NOTE: No repair or replacement parts, except those in the service kit, are available for servicing the rear brake antilock control system modulator. If a part is lost or damaged, the entire modulator must be replaced.

1. Disconnect the vacuum hose, brake lines and electrical wiring from the modulator.
2. Remove the two mounting bolts from the hydraulic cylinder and pull the hydraulic cylinder from the vacuum cylinder. Seal the hole in the vacuum cylinder to prevent dirt from entering it.
3. Pull the plunger from the hydraulic cylinder and protect the surfaces of the plunger from damage. With a pointed piece of plastic or similar tool, remove the dust seal from the bottom of the hydraulic cylinder.
4. With the snap ring plier tip as shown in the illustration, remove the snap ring, being careful not to damage the inner surface of the hydraulic cylinder. Then pull out the cup retainer and back-up ring. If necessary use a long nose plier to lightly hold the cup retainer and pull it out.
5. Remove the cup seal with a brass wire with an L-shaped end.
6. Put the black painted portion of the hydraulic cylinder into a soft jaw vise and remove the bleeder cap. Remove the O-ring from the bleeder cap with a pointed piece of plastic or trim tool.
7. Remove the check valve spring, check valve piston, and the check valve seal from the hydraulic cylinder. Using a clean cloth and your thumb, pull the check valve seal off the check valve piston.
8. Re-position the hydraulic cylinder in the vise and remove the valve cap, gasket, choke valve spring, and spring seat.
9. Hold the end of the choke valve piston with long nose pliers and pull the choke valve piston and bushing from the hydraulic cylinder. Push the choke valve piston out of the bushing with your fingers.
10. Remove the O-rings from the choke valve with a pointed piece of plastic or trim tool.
11. Clean all parts and inspect for wear or damage.

Assembly

NOTE: No repair or replacement parts, except those in the service kit, are available for servicing the rear brake antilock control system modulator. If a part is lost or damaged, the entire modulator must be replaced.

1. Coat the O-rings with SAE J1703 or equivalent DOT 3

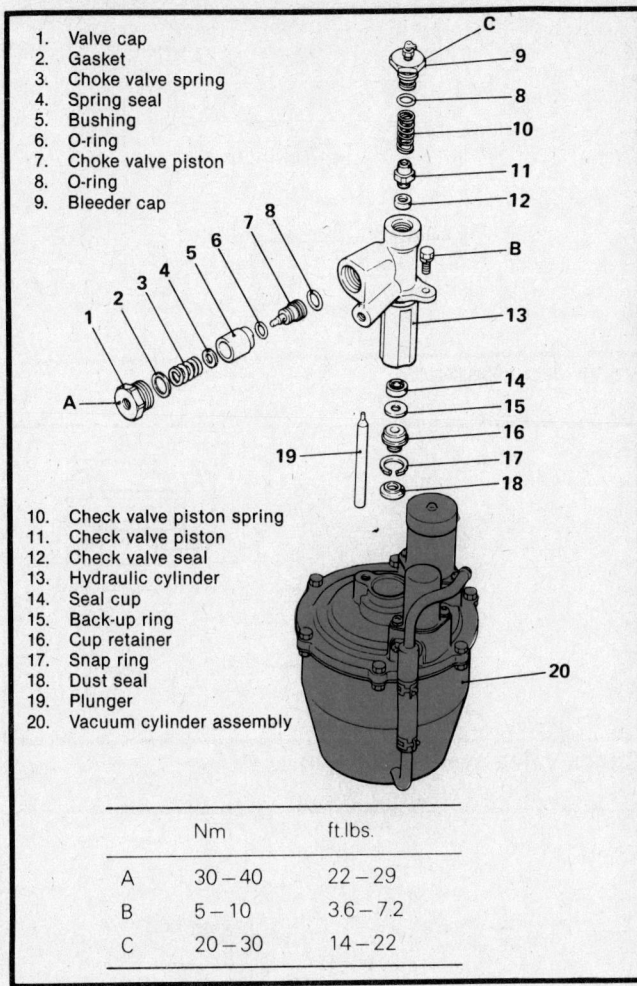

1. Valve cap
2. Gasket
3. Choke valve spring
4. Spring seal
5. Bushing
6. O-ring
7. Choke valve piston
8. O-ring
9. Bleeder cap

10. Check valve piston spring
11. Check valve piston
12. Check valve seal
13. Hydraulic cylinder
14. Seal cup
15. Back-up ring
16. Cup retainer
17. Snap ring
18. Dust seal
19. Plunger
20. Vacuum cylinder assembly

	Nm	ft.lbs.
A	30 – 40	22 – 29
B	5 – 10	3.6 – 7.2
C	20 – 30	14 – 22

Modulator exploded view

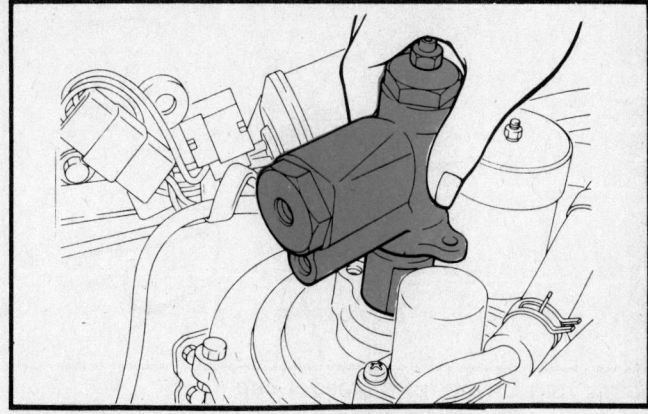

Removing the hydraulic cylinder from the vacuum cylinder

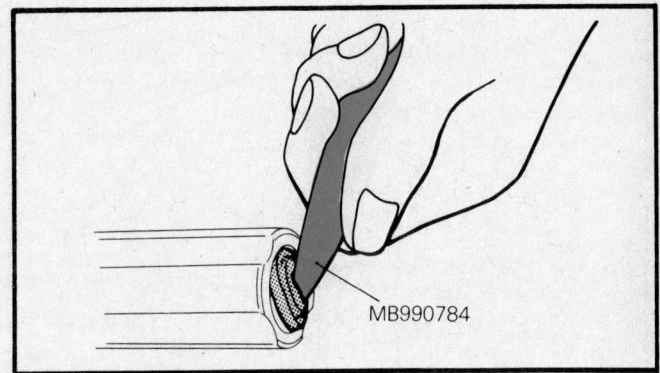

MB990784

Dust seal removal

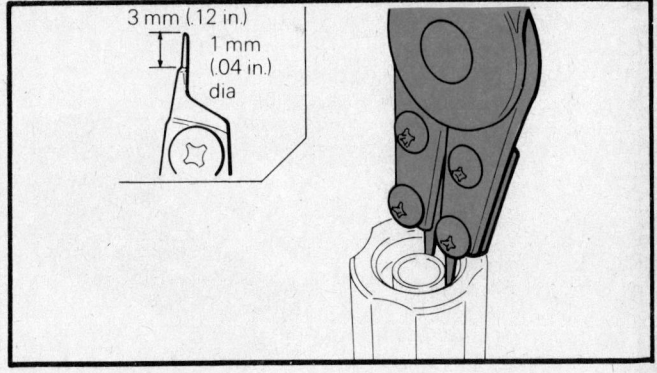

3 mm (.12 in.)

1 mm (.04 in.) dia

Snap-ring removal

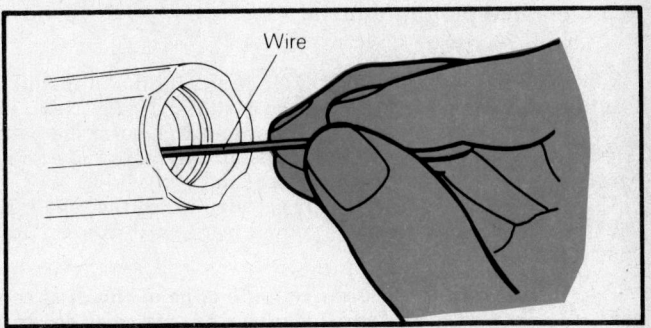

Wire

Cup seal removal

brake fluid and install them on the choke valve piston.

2. Assemble the choke valve piston and bushing first; and then install them together into the hydraulic cylinder. Make sure to replace the gasket with a new one.

3. Install the spring seat, choke valve spring, gasket, and the valve cap in that order into the hydraulic cylinder. Make sure to replace the gasket with a new one.

4. Tighten the valve cap to 22–29 ft. lbs. The clearance between the cap and the cylinder should be 0.004–0.020 in. (0.1–0.5mm).

5. Coat the check valve seal with brake fluid and install it on the check valve piston with the larger inner diameter of the seal facing toward the outside.

NOTE: If the check valve seal is installed upside down, the rear brake antilock control system will become inoperative.

6. Install the check valve seal end first into the hydraulic cylinder. Next, install the check valve spring.

NOTE: If the check valve is installed upside down, the rear brake antilock control system will become inoperative.

7. Coat the O-ring with DOT 3 brake fluid and install it on the bleeder cap. Install the bleeder cap and tighten to 15–22 ft. lbs.

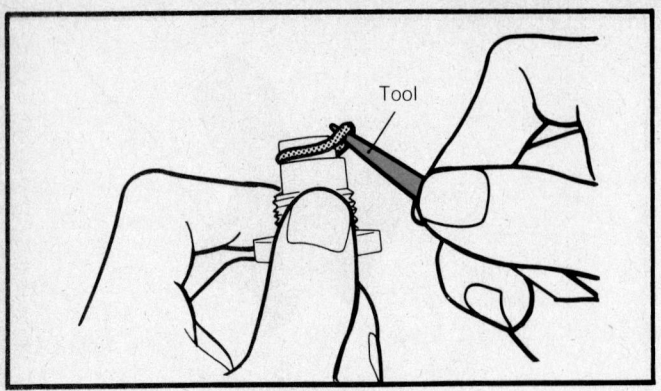

Removing O-ring from bleeder cap

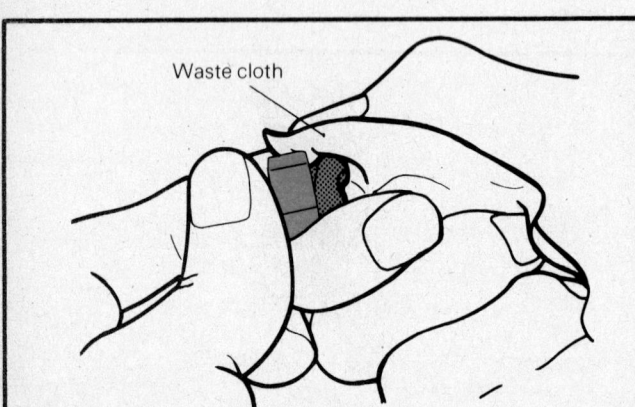

Removing the check valve seal

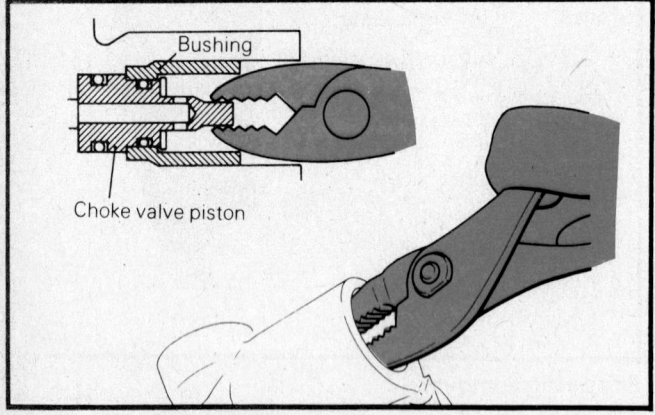

Choke valve piston removal

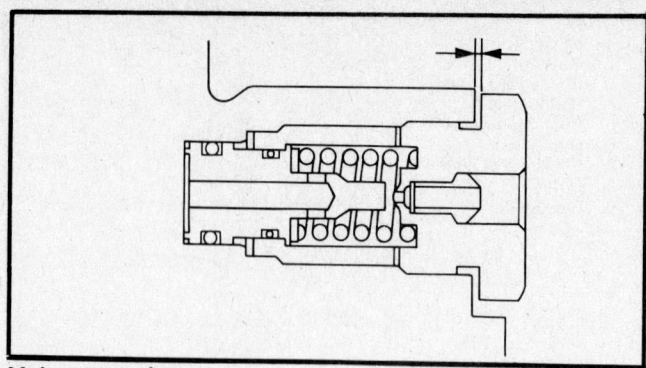

Valve cap clearance

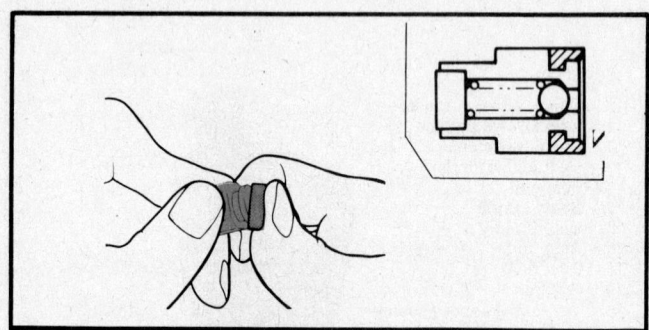

Check valve seal installation

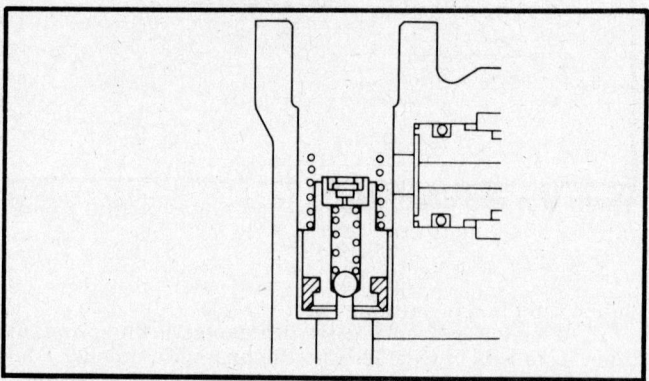

Check valve installation

8. Coat the cup seal with DOT 3 brake fluid and install it with its lipped side first into the hydraulic cylinder. Next, install the back-up ring, the cup retainer (large outer diameter first) into the hydraulic cylinder. Install the snap ring into its groove and make sure it is fully seated.

9. Coat the dust seal with grease supplied in the repair kit and push the dust seal with your fingers until it snaps into place on the cup retainer.

NOTE: DO NOT force the outside edge of the dust seal too far into the hydraulic cylinder, since a certain amount of clearance must be provided between the dust seal and the snap ring.

10. Install the plunger with the smaller diameter end first into the hydraulic cylinder.

11. Install the hydraulic cylinder to the vacuum cylinder assembly.

12. Connect the vacuum hose, brake lines, and electrical connections.

13. Bleed the air from the modulator first, and then the rear brakes.

Diagnosis & Testing

PRECAUTIONS

• Because there is such a large number of transistor circuits, the system could be easily and instantly damaged if a terminal is improperly contacted during a check for a malfunction.

• DO NOT open the cover of the control unit to inspect the internal parts. The unit might easily be damaged if a part is mistakenly touched, or if dust or other foreign particles enter the unit.

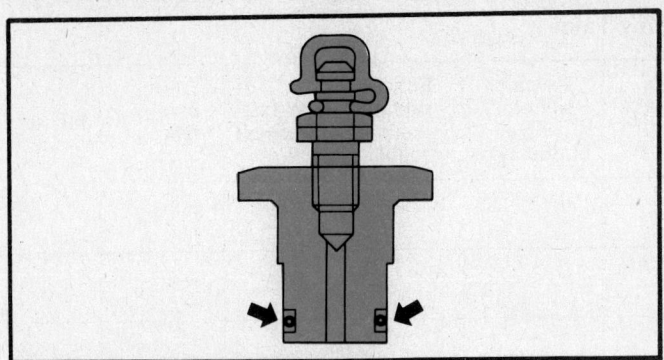

Bleeder cap O-ring installation

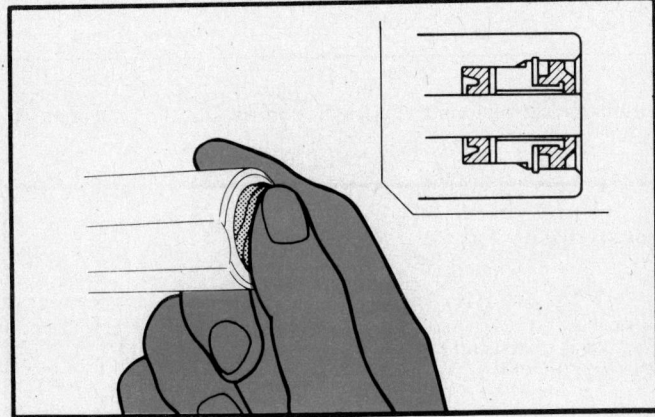

Dust seal installation

• The connections of the battery must never be reversed. During the replacement of the battery, be sure to set the ignition key to the "LOCK" position, and connect the new battery carefully so there are no mistakes.

• During replacement procedures, be careful not to expose any of the components to any violent shaking or impacts. Special care must be observed in the handling of the G-sensor; however, all of the other components of the rear antilock brake system should also be handled with care.

• When checking the system with a circuit tester, be careful not to mistakenly touch an adjacent terminal, or to connect the tester to the wrong terminal. If this occurs, the system could be easily and instantly damaged.

• If the system is being checked during rainy weather, be careful not to allow water to get into any of the components.

• The G-sensor is filled with a special oil. If it is opened, it can no longer be used.

REAR BRAKE ANTILOCK CONTROL SYSTEM TEST

1. Operate the engine for five seconds or longer while the vehicle is not moving, turn the ignition key to the "LOCK" position, and then depress the brake pedal. Turn the ignition key from the "LOCK" position to the "ON" position, and confirm that the sound of the modulator operating can be heard. If the operating sound can be heard, the solenoid valve is functioning properly.

NOTE: The sound of the modulator operating should be a dull clicking sound.

2. Raise the vehicle on a jack (the rear wheels should be completely off the ground), and then support the vehicle on rigid racks. Block the front wheels.

3. Warm up the engine, set the shift lever to second gear position, depress the accelerator pedal, and maintain the speedometer reading at approximately 19 mph.

4. Keep the accelerator pedal depressed in the same position, and then depress the brake pedal suddenly.

5. The brakes will attempt to stop the rotation of the rear wheel; however, because the operation of the rear brake antilock control system will cut off the supply of brake fluid pressure, the rotation of the rear wheels will be restored. This reduction and increase process should keep repeating itself.

TROUBLESHOOTING

If a malfunction occurs in the rear brake antilock control system, follow the troubleshooting procedure to check the system. Check all the components (including the wiring harness) except the control unit. If there are no malfunctions in any of the components, replace the control unit.

Before beginning the troubleshooting procedure, check each of the following items:

1. The conditions of the wiring harness and components of the rear brake antilock control system.

2. Check the master cylinder, the brake booster, the rear brakes, and other brake related components.

PULSE GENERATOR TESTING

1. Measure the resistance between the terminals. If the resistance is not within 600–800 ohms, replace the pulse generator.

2. Measure the resistance between the terminals and the case.

3. The resistance should be infinity. If continuity exists, replace the pulse generator.

G-SENSOR TESTING

1. Check that the G-sensor is mounted correctly to the vehicle body. (The vehicle should be empty, and on a flat, level surface.)

2. Check that the mounting is correct by using a level. If the G-sensor varies 1 or more from the horizontal position, use a suitable shim to adjust it to be perfectly horizontal.

3. Check that there is no oil leakage. If any oil exists, replace the sensor.

4. Measure the voltage of the G-sensor when it is laid down in accordance with the following procedures:

   a. Check the voltage across terminal "R" of the control unit and ground for 7.0–7.5 volts. A voltage reading other than 7.0–7. 5 volts indicates a faulty control unit.

NOTE: Be sure to set the multimeter to the volt range before making the measurement to protect the control unit from possible damage.

   b. Remove the G-sensor and the ground to the car body wire.

   c. Turn the G-sensor with the mark facing upward. Measure the voltage across terminal "G" of the G-sensor and the ground. If the voltage is not 4.8 volts 0.2 volts, replace the G-sensor.

RELEASE SOLENOID VALVE AND BUILD-UP SOLENOID VALVE TESTING

Measure the resistance values values of the solenoid valve terminals for both of the solenoid valves. If the resistance value

Troubleshooting Table

Symptom \ Components to be checked	Fuse No.10	Fuse No. 2	Pulse generator	G-sensor	Brake switch	Release solenoid valve (modulator)	Build-up solenoid valve (modulator)	Wiring harness	Stop lights	Modulator
Fail indication light illuminates	○		○	○	○	○	○	○	○	
No self-diagnosis (Refer to P. 5-35.)	○	○			○	○		○	○	
Weak brakes (Braking power is insufficient)			○	○			○			○
Brakes lock (High tendency to skid)	○	○	○	○	○	○		○	○	○

NOTE
Check the system by following the troubleshooting table. If no malfunction can be found, replace the control unit and then recheck the system to see if the malfunction still exists.

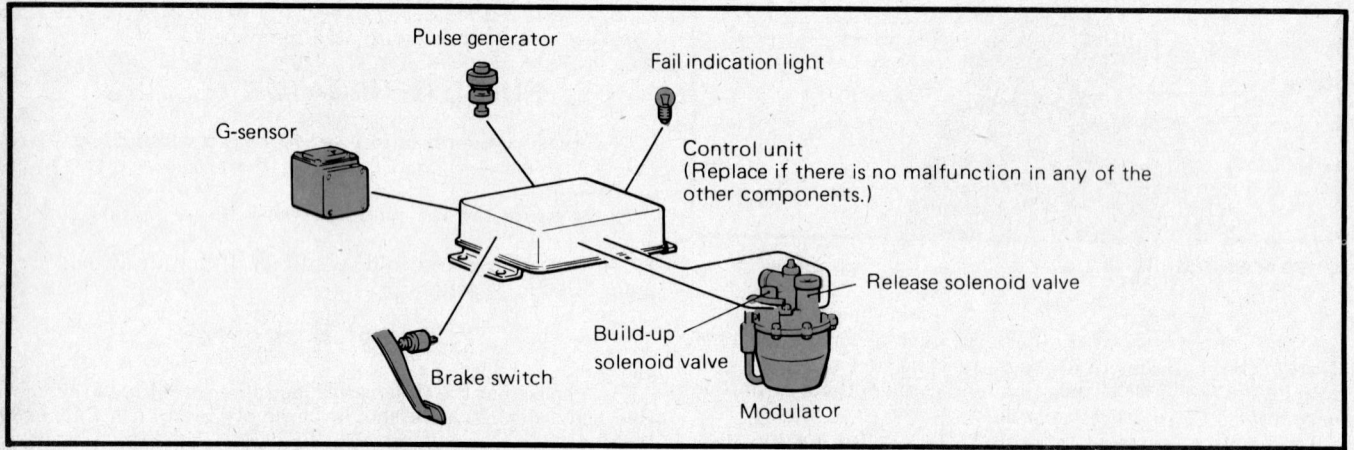

Components of the rear antilock brake control system

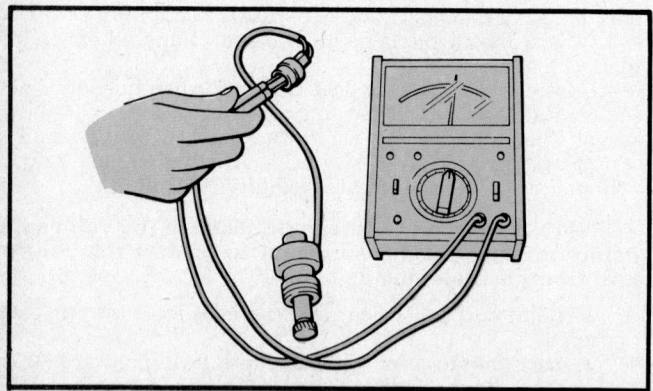

Checking the resistance of the pulse generator

for the release solenoid valve is not with 3.8–4.8 ohms, replace the valve; if the resistance value for the build–up solenoid valve is not within 4.5–5.5 ohms, replace the valve. If a multimeter is not available, check the solenoid valves by listening to the operating sound when voltage is applied to them. If the operating sound cannot be heard, replace the solenoid valves.

NOTE: If a battery is to be connected to test the solenoid valves, do not connect it for more than one minute.

MODULATOR VACUUM LINE TEST

1. Check the vacuum lines (including the brake booster lines) for vacuum leakage caused by loose, disconnected or cracked hoses.
2. Check the vacuum check valves (for the modulator and the brake booster) for any abnormal condition such as clogging, etc.

MODULATOR OPERATIONAL TEST

NOTE: The following test requires the use of two pressure gauges rated 0–2,133 psi or more.

1. Connect two pressure gauges, one to the rear brake exit point of the modulator "B", and the other between the master cylinder and the modulator "A".
2. Let the engine run at idling speed.
3. Hold the brake pedal at the point which will result in a reading of about 711 psi on the pressure gauge connected to the rear brake exit point of the modulator.
4. While watching pressure gauge "B", operate the release

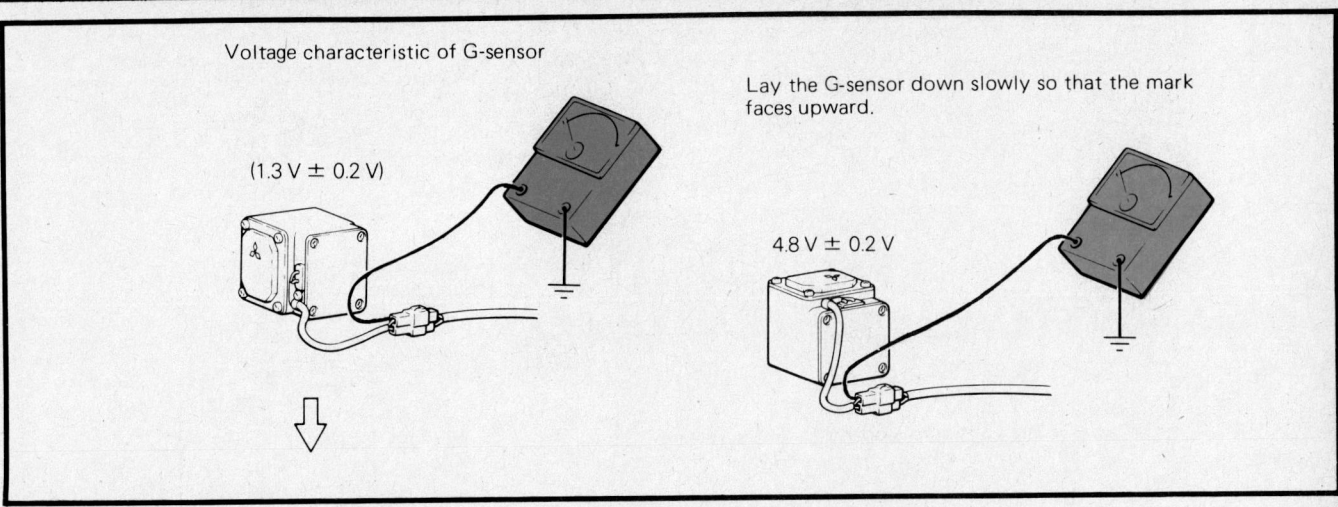

Voltage characteristic of G-sensor

Lay the G-sensor down slowly so that the mark faces upward.

(1.3 V ± 0.2 V)

4.8 V ± 0.2 V

Voltage readings on the G-sensor

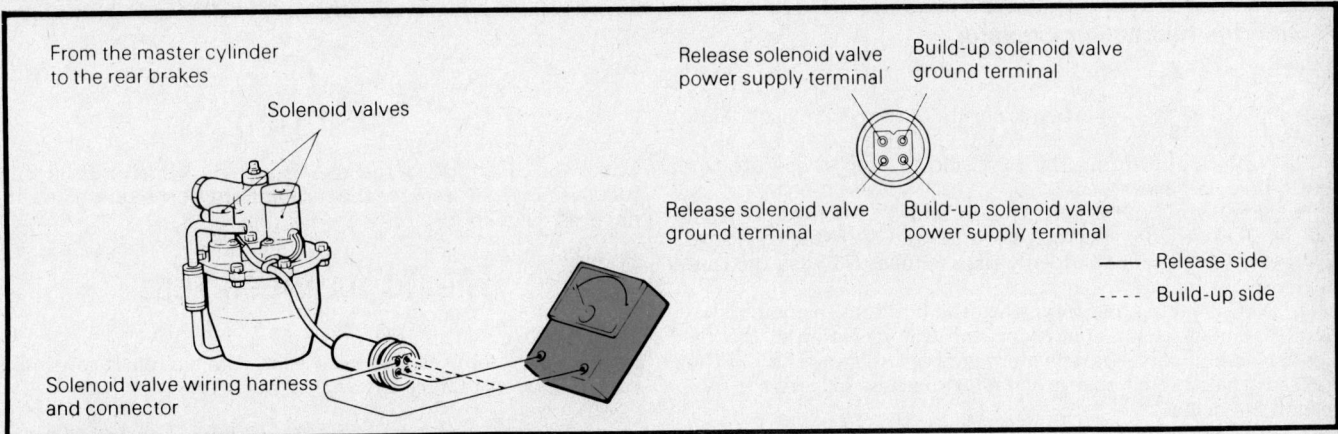

From the master cylinder to the rear brakes

Solenoid valves

Release solenoid valve power supply terminal

Build-up solenoid valve ground terminal

Release solenoid valve ground terminal

Build-up solenoid valve power supply terminal

—— Release side

---- Build-up side

Solenoid valve wiring harness and connector

Checking the solenoid valves with a multimeter

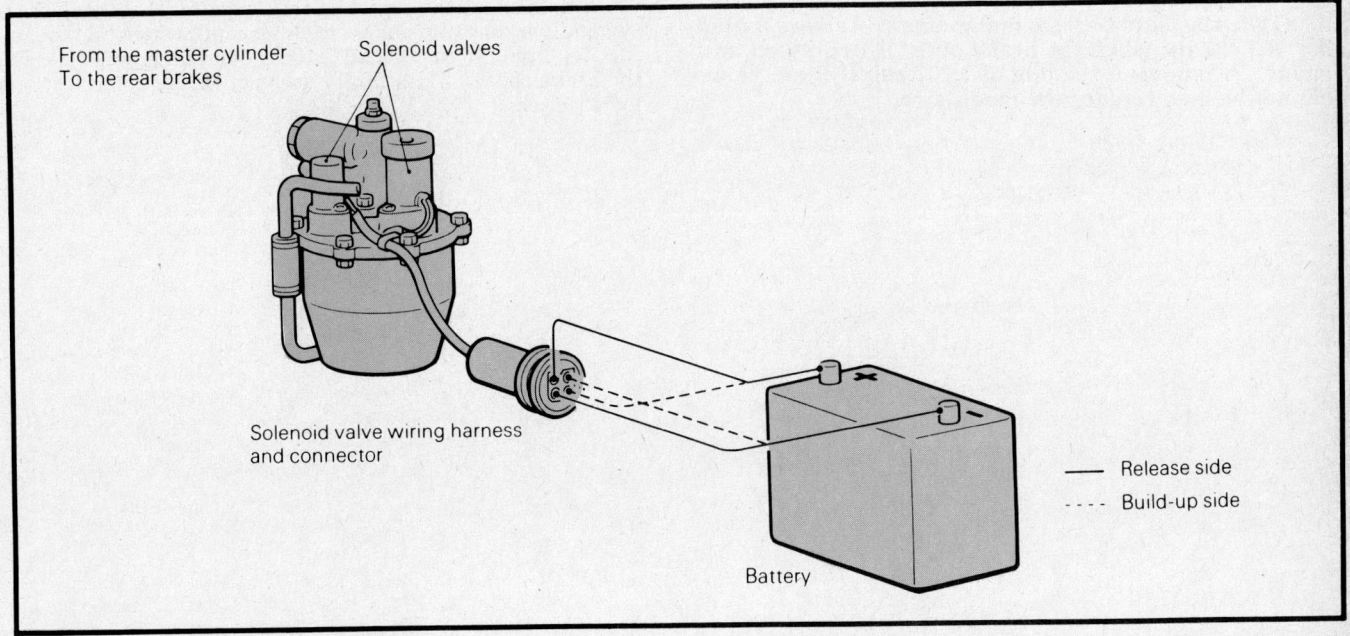

From the master cylinder To the rear brakes

Solenoid valves

Solenoid valve wiring harness and connector

—— Release side

---- Build-up side

Battery

Checking the solenoid valves with

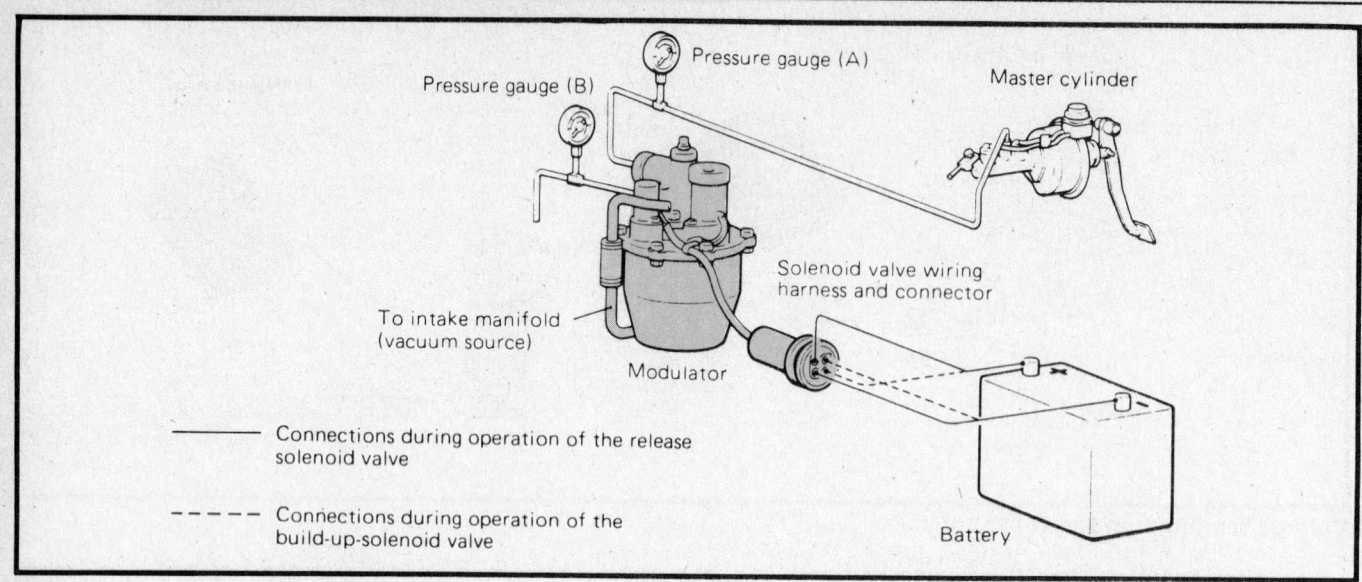

Testing the hydraulic modulator

Testing the hydraulic modulator

solenoid valve. The condition is normal if the reading suddenly drops to almost 0 psi.

5. While maintaining the condition in Step 4, operate the build-up solenoid valve.

6. Then, while in the condition in Step 5, stop the operation of the release solenoid valve while watching the pressure gauge. If the pressure suddenly rises to about 711 psi, the condition is normal.

7. Repeat Step 4 and then, with the build-up solenoid valve in the non-operating condition, stop the operation of the release solenoid valve while watching pressure gauge "B". If the pressure rises about one second later to about 711 psi, the condition is normal.

8. With both the solenoid valves in the non-operating condition, increase the fluid pressure of the master cylinder, and check the relationship with the rear brake fluid pressure.

NOTE: Check to be sure that gauge "B" shows a reading of 1,422 psi when the brake pedal is depressed until gauge "A" shows a reading of 1,707 psi. If these values cannot be met, replace the modulator.

FUSE TEST

Check the continuity of the fuse using a multimeter. If continuity does not exist, replace the fuse and check the related wiring harness for a short-circuit.

WIRING HARNESS TEST

Use a multimeter or continuity tester to check the continuity in the wiring harness between each component. If continuity does not exist, replace the wiring harness.

STOP LIGHT SWITCH TEST

Check to be sure the switch is set correctly. If not, adjust the switch. Use a multimeter to check for continuity while causing the stop lights to turn on and off (by depressing and releasing the brake pedal). If continuity does not exist, replace the stop light switch.

AMERICAN MOTORS

General Information

The load leveling system automatically adjusts the rear height with changes in the vehicle loading. The system consists of a compressor assembly, exhaust solenoid, air dryer, compressor relay, air adjustable shock absorbers, height sensor, air tubing, wiring and a pressure limiter.

Adjustment is accomplished by means of the on board compressor. The electrically operated compressor is mounted in the engine compartment. Although the compressor is controlled automatically, it can be switched to manual by means of a three position switch which is located in the compressor mounting bracket in most applications.

When the three position switch is in the automatic mode, the the compressor is operated by the height sensor and compressor relay.

System Components

COMPRESSOR

The compressor assembly is a positive displacement single piston air pump which is powered by a permanent magnet motor. The compressor head casting contains the piston, intake and exhaust valves plus a solenoid operated exhaust which releases air from the system when energized.

NOTE: The compressor is not a serviceable item. if diagnostic testing indicates that the compressor has malfunctioned, replace the compressor as an assembly only. Do not attempt to repair it.

AIR DRYER

The air dryer, which is attached to the compressor output provides a dual function. It contains a dry chemical which absorbs moisture from the sir before it is delivered to the shocks and returns the moisture to the air when it is exhausted.

The air dryer also contains a valve arrangement which maintains a minimum air pressure in the system between 7–14 psi.

EXHAUST SOLENOID

The exhaust solenoid, which provides a dual function, is located in the compressor assembly. When energized, it exhausts air from the system. This operation is controlled by the height sensor. The solenoid also acts as a relief valve to limit maximum output pressure of the compressor.

COMPRESSOR RELAY

The relay is located on the compressor bracket. It is a single pole/single throw type switch. When energized, it completes the 12 volt circuit to the compressor motor. This operation is controlled by the height sensor.

HEIGHT SENSOR

The height sensor, which is an electronic device, controls the compressor relay and exhaust solenoid ground circuit.

To prevent falsely activating the exhaust solenoid circuit or the compressor relay, during normal driving motions, the height sensor provides a 7–15 second delay before either circuit is completed.

The sensor also will limit the time the compressor or exhaust solenoid is energized to a maximum time of 3 ½ minutes. The time limit is designed to prevent unnecessary running time of the compressor in the event of a system leak or exhaust solenoid malfunction. Turning the ignition "off and on" will reset the electronic timer circuit to the 3 ½ minute maximum run time.

The electronic timer circuit is also reset for each change in exhaust and compressor signals from the height sensor. The height sensor, on most vehicles, is located on the side sill in the rear of the vehicle with the sensor actuator arm attached to the rear axle housing by means of a short link.

ADJUSTABLE AIR SHOCKS

The adjustable air shock is essentially a conventional shock absorber encased in an air chamber. The shocks are constructed with a rubber sleeve attached to the shock reservoir and dust tube. This creates a flexible chamber which will extend the shock absorber when air pressure is increased in the air chamber. When air pressure is released, the weight of the vehicle collapses the shock absorber.

SYSTEM OPERATION

Raising The Vehicle

When weight is added to the rear of the vehicle, the body is forced downward which causes the height sensor actuating arm to rotate upward. This action causes the height sensor to electrically start the internal time delay circuit. When the time delay (7–15 seconds) has occurred, the sensor then completes the compressor relay circuit. With the relay energized, the 12 volt circuit to the compressor is complete and the compressor runs, sending air to the air adjustable shock absorbers through air lines.

As the shocks inflate, the vehicle body moves upward which begins rotating the height sensor actuating arm back towards the position the arm had before the weight addition. When the body reaches the original trim height ($\pm \frac{3}{4}$"), the sensor opens the compressor relay circuit, which in turn shuts off the compressor.

Lowering The Vehicle

A high body condition has the effect of rotating the height sensor actuating arm downward. The height sensor then senses the high condition and starts the time delay circuit. When the time delay (7–15 seconds) has elasped, The sensor completes the exhaust solenoid circuit. With the exhaust solenoid energized, air escapes from the shocks through the air dryer and exhaust solenoid valve.

As the vehicle body lowers, the height sensor actuating arm is rotated toward its original position. When the vehicle body reaches its original height ($\pm \frac{3}{4}$") the sensor opens the exhaust valve solenoid circuit, which prevents the further escape of air.

A minimum air pressure of 7–14 psi is maintained on the vehicle. The minimum pressure provides improved ride characteristics while the vehicle has a minimum load. The compressor relief valve is designed to operate at 120–150 psi.

Troubleshooting

If the system is rendered inoperative and the vehicle remains low when weight is added, refer to the diagnostic procedure charts. Also refer to the charts if the compressor runs for two to three minutes every time the ignition is turned on.

SYSTEM OPERATION

Testing

1. With the vehicle on a level surface, measure the distance between the bumper and the floor.
2. Turn the ignition on.
3. Apply approximately 200 pounds to the trunk of the vehicle. There should be a 7–15 second delay before the compressor is activated and the vehicle starts to raise. The vehicle should raise to within $\frac{3}{4}$ inch of the measurement made in Step 1.
4. Failure of the vehicle to return to $\frac{3}{4}$ inch of the original position could be due to improper adjustment of the height sensor.

COMPRESSOR

Testing

The following test can be performed with the compressor either on the vehicle or on the bench.

1. Disconnect the wiring from the compressor motor and the exhaust solenoid terminals.
2. Disconnect the existing pressure line from the dryer and attach pressure gauge J-22124A or equivalent to the dryer fitting.
3. Connect a 12 volt (+) power supply to the compressor through an ammeter and note the following:
   a. Current draw should not exceed 14 amps.
   b. When the gauge reads approximately 100 psi minimum, shut off the compressor and note if pressure is maintained or it leaks down (allow pressure to stabilize).
   c. If the compressor is permitted to run until it reaches maximum output pressure of 120–150 psi, the solenoid exhaust valve will act as a pressure relief valve. The resulting leak down when the compressor is shut off will indicate a false leak.
4. If the compressor fails to meet specifications, refer to the diagnostic charts.

HEIGHT SENSOR

Testing

1. Turn the ignition off then on. This will reset the height sensor timer circuitry to the 3 $\frac{1}{2}$ minute maximum run time.
2. Raise and support the vehicle safely.

NOTE: Be sure that the rear wheels or the axle housing are supported as close as possible to the trim height dimension. Inspect the wiring for proper connections along with the harness ground.

3. Disconnect the link from the height sensor arm.
4. Move the sensor arm up. There should be a 7–15 second delay before the compressor begins operating and the air shocks inflate. As soon as the air shock begin to fill, stop the compressor by moving the sensor arm downward.
5. Move the sensor arm down below the position where the compressor stopped. There should be a 7–15 second delay before the shocks are able to be deflated.

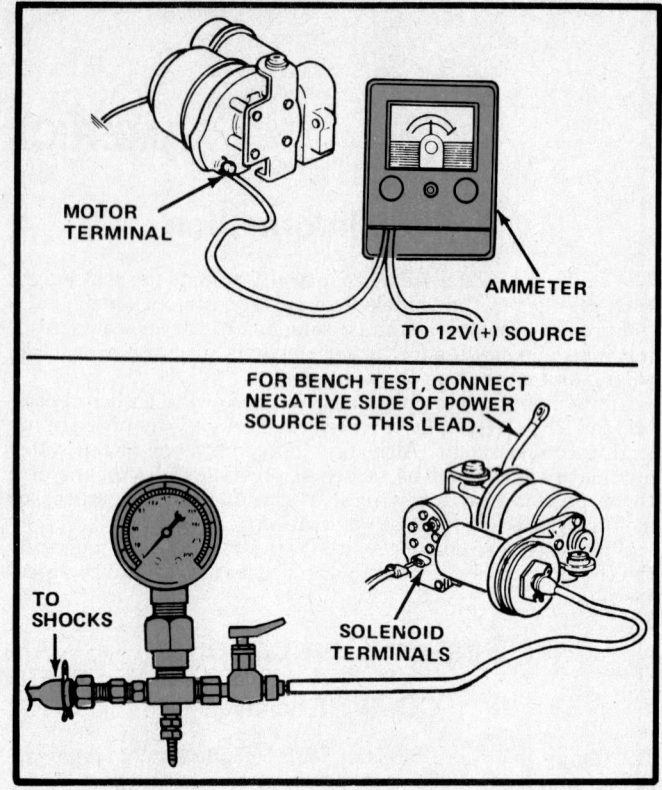

Compressor performance test connections

6. Reconnect the link to the height sensor arm before making any adjustments.

TRIM HEIGHT

Adjustment

NOTE: The link must be attached to the metal arm when making the adjustment.

1. Loosen the locknut securing the metal arm to the height sensor plastic arm.
2. To increase the vehicle trim height, move the black plastic actuator arm upward to the top of slot and tighten the locknut.
3. To lower the vehicle trim height, follow Step 1 and move the plastic arm downward to the bottom of the slot.

NOTE: If all the adjustments are used, inspect the vehicle for proper trim height.

SYSTEM LEAK

Testing

1. Connect pressure gauge J-22124-A or equivalent into the system between the dryer and the system air line. Make sure that the shut off valve is on the compressor side of the gauge.
2. With the shut off valve open, apply air pressure through the service valve on the gauge until a reading of 100–120 is obtained.
3. If a leak is indicated, close the shut off valve and continue to observe for a pressure drop.
4. If the gauge pressure continues to drop, the leak is external to the compressor.

Diagnosis Procedure

IMPORTANT: Always cycle ignition "OFF" and "ON" before starting test to reset height sensor time limit accumulators. If car is allowed to remain in a CAR LOW or CAR HIGH condition for more than 3½ minutes with ignition switch on, BE SURE to cycle ignition "ON" and "OFF" before continuing tests. A test light is necessary for system diagnosis.

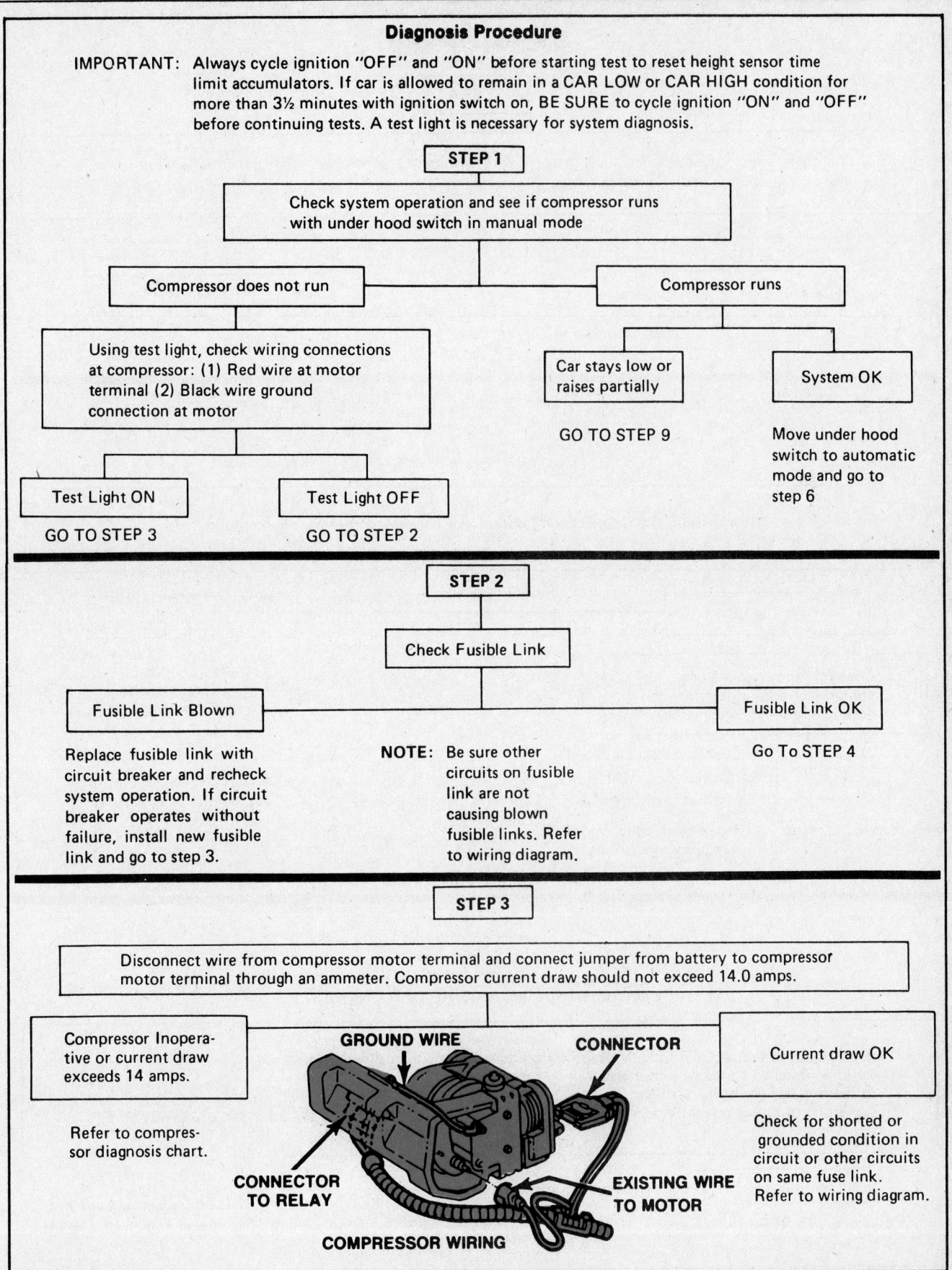

STEP 1

Check system operation and see if compressor runs with under hood switch in manual mode

Compressor does not run

Using test light, check wiring connections at compressor: (1) Red wire at motor terminal (2) Black wire ground connection at motor

Test Light ON

GO TO STEP 3

Test Light OFF

GO TO STEP 2

Compressor runs

Car stays low or raises partially

GO TO STEP 9

System OK

Move under hood switch to automatic mode and go to step 6

STEP 2

Check Fusible Link

Fusible Link Blown

Replace fusible link with circuit breaker and recheck system operation. If circuit breaker operates without failure, install new fusible link and go to step 3.

NOTE: Be sure other circuits on fusible link are not causing blown fusible links. Refer to wiring diagram.

Fusible Link OK

Go To STEP 4

STEP 3

Disconnect wire from compressor motor terminal and connect jumper from battery to compressor motor terminal through an ammeter. Compressor current draw should not exceed 14.0 amps.

Compressor Inoperative or current draw exceeds 14 amps.

Refer to compressor diagnosis chart.

GROUND WIRE

CONNECTOR

CONNECTOR TO RELAY

EXISTING WIRE TO MOTOR

COMPRESSOR WIRING

Current draw OK

Check for shorted or grounded condition in circuit or other circuits on same fuse link. Refer to wiring diagram.

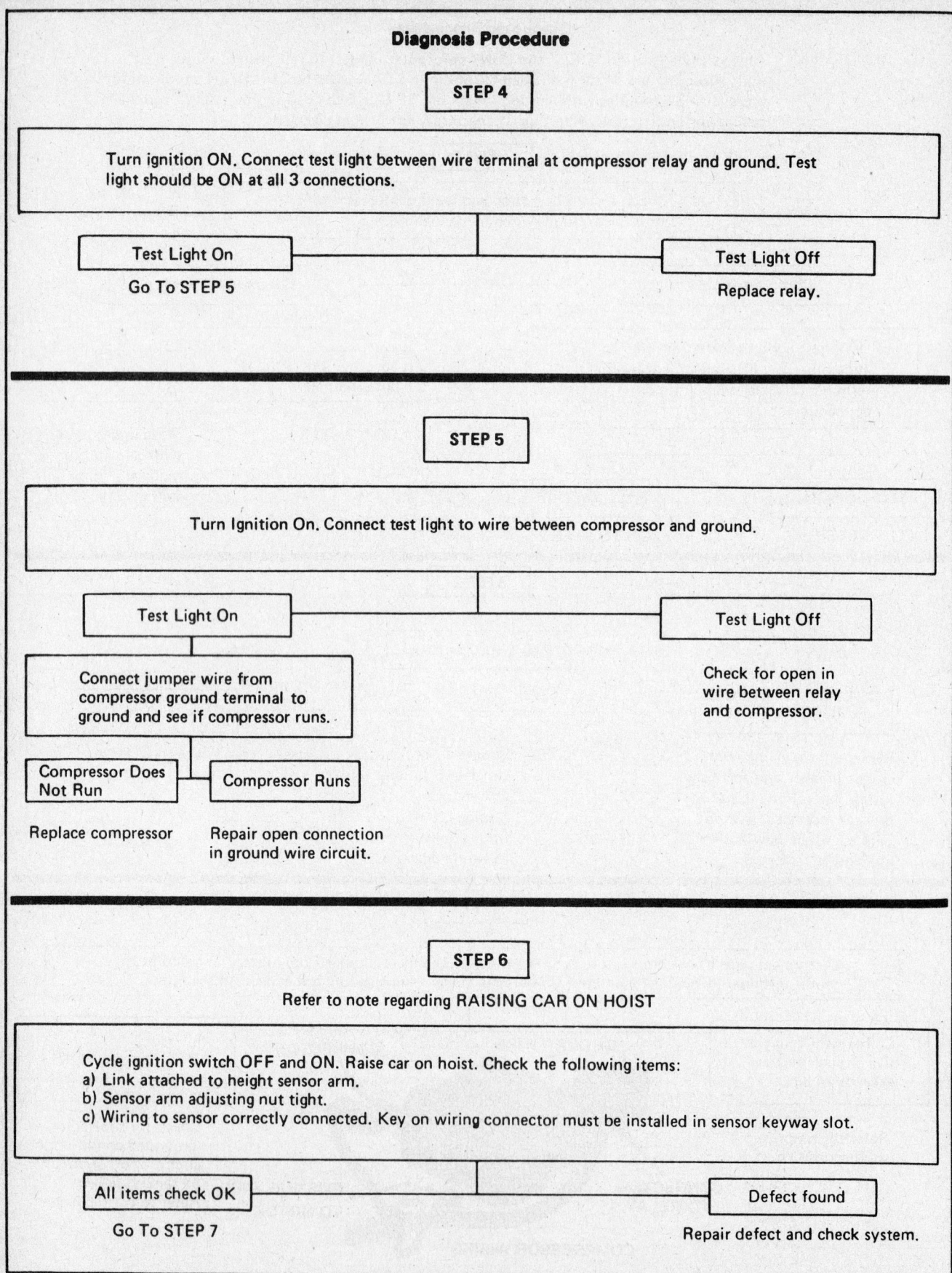

Diagnosis Procedure

STEP 4

Turn ignition ON. Connect test light between wire terminal at compressor relay and ground. Test light should be ON at all 3 connections.

Test Light On

Go To STEP 5

Test Light Off

Replace relay.

STEP 5

Turn Ignition On. Connect test light to wire between compressor and ground.

Test Light On

Connect jumper wire from compressor ground terminal to ground and see if compressor runs.

Compressor Does Not Run

Compressor Runs

Replace compressor

Repair open connection in ground wire circuit.

Test Light Off

Check for open in wire between relay and compressor.

STEP 6

Refer to note regarding RAISING CAR ON HOIST

Cycle ignition switch OFF and ON. Raise car on hoist. Check the following items:
a) Link attached to height sensor arm.
b) Sensor arm adjusting nut tight.
c) Wiring to sensor correctly connected. Key on wiring connector must be installed in sensor keyway slot.

All items check OK

Go To STEP 7

Defect found

Repair defect and check system.

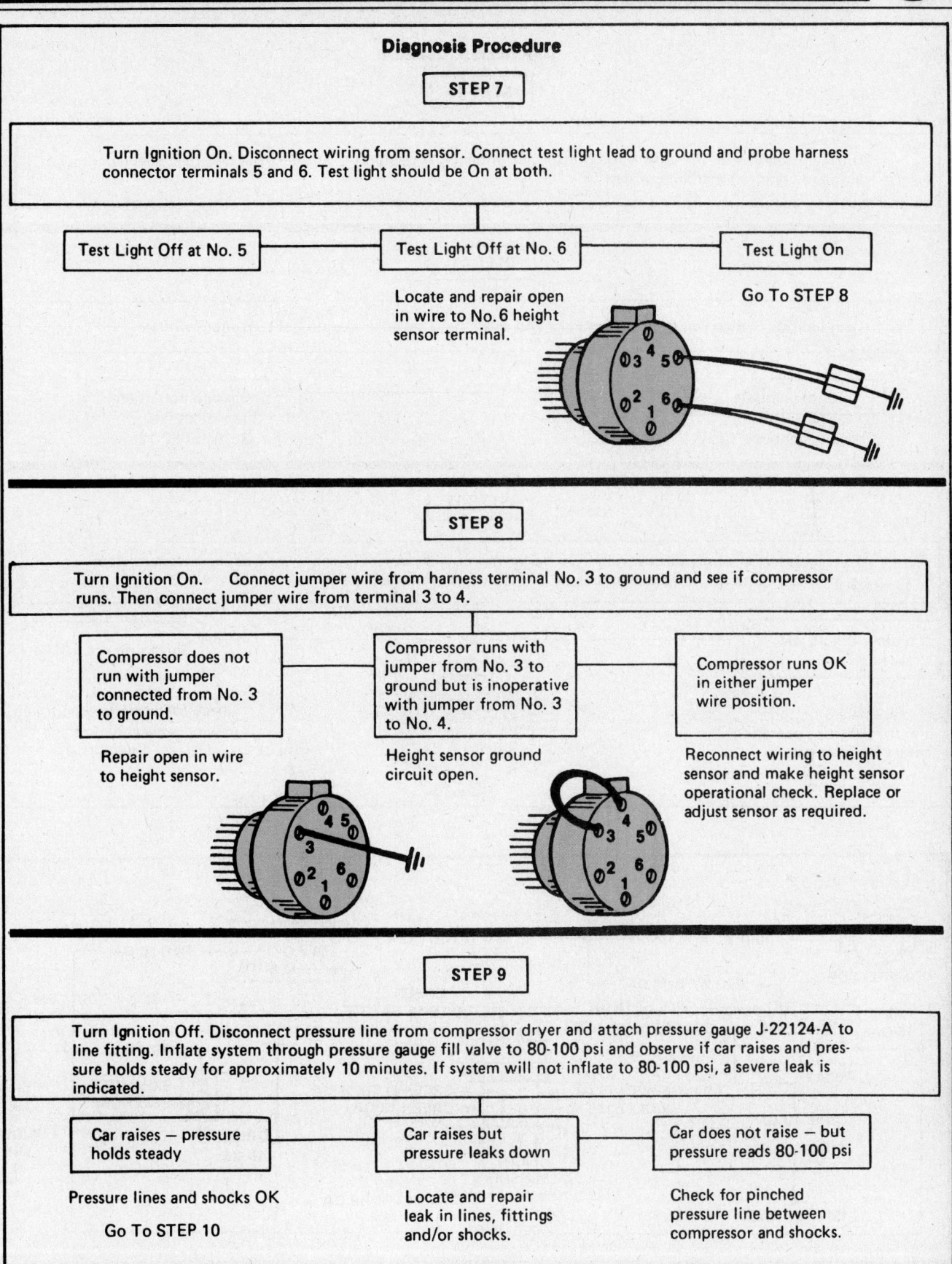

Diagnosis Procedure

STEP 7

Turn Ignition On. Disconnect wiring from sensor. Connect test light lead to ground and probe harness connector terminals 5 and 6. Test light should be On at both.

Test Light Off at No. 5	Test Light Off at No. 6	Test Light On
	Locate and repair open in wire to No. 6 height sensor terminal.	Go To STEP 8

STEP 8

Turn Ignition On.   Connect jumper wire from harness terminal No. 3 to ground and see if compressor runs. Then connect jumper wire from terminal 3 to 4.

Compressor does not run with jumper connected from No. 3 to ground.	Compressor runs with jumper from No. 3 to ground but is inoperative with jumper from No. 3 to No. 4.	Compressor runs OK in either jumper wire position.
Repair open in wire to height sensor.	Height sensor ground circuit open.	Reconnect wiring to height sensor and make height sensor operational check. Replace or adjust sensor as required.

STEP 9

Turn Ignition Off. Disconnect pressure line from compressor dryer and attach pressure gauge J-22124-A to line fitting. Inflate system through pressure gauge fill valve to 80-100 psi and observe if car raises and pressure holds steady for approximately 10 minutes. If system will not inflate to 80-100 psi, a severe leak is indicated.

Car raises – pressure holds steady	Car raises but pressure leaks down	Car does not raise – but pressure reads 80-100 psi
Pressure lines and shocks OK Go To STEP 10	Locate and repair leak in lines, fittings and/or shocks.	Check for pinched pressure line between compressor and shocks.

Electronic Chassis Controls

Diagnosis Procedure

STEP 10

Turn Ignition Switch Off. Check compressor performance. If compressor/dryer check OK, re-connect wiring to compressor and go to step 11.

STEP 11

Turn Ignition Switch On. Raise car on hoist and check height sensor operation. See if shocks inflate.

Shocks inflate	Shocks do not inflate
Check system operation.	Go To STEP 12

STEP 12

Turn Ignition On. Disconnect wiring from height sensor and connect jumper wire from harness connector terminals No. 3 to No. 4 to run compressor. See if shocks inflate and car raises.

Shocks inflate and car raises.	Shocks do not inflate
Replace height sensor and check sensor operation before lowering car.	Check for grounded condition in wire between sensor and compressor solenoid valve.

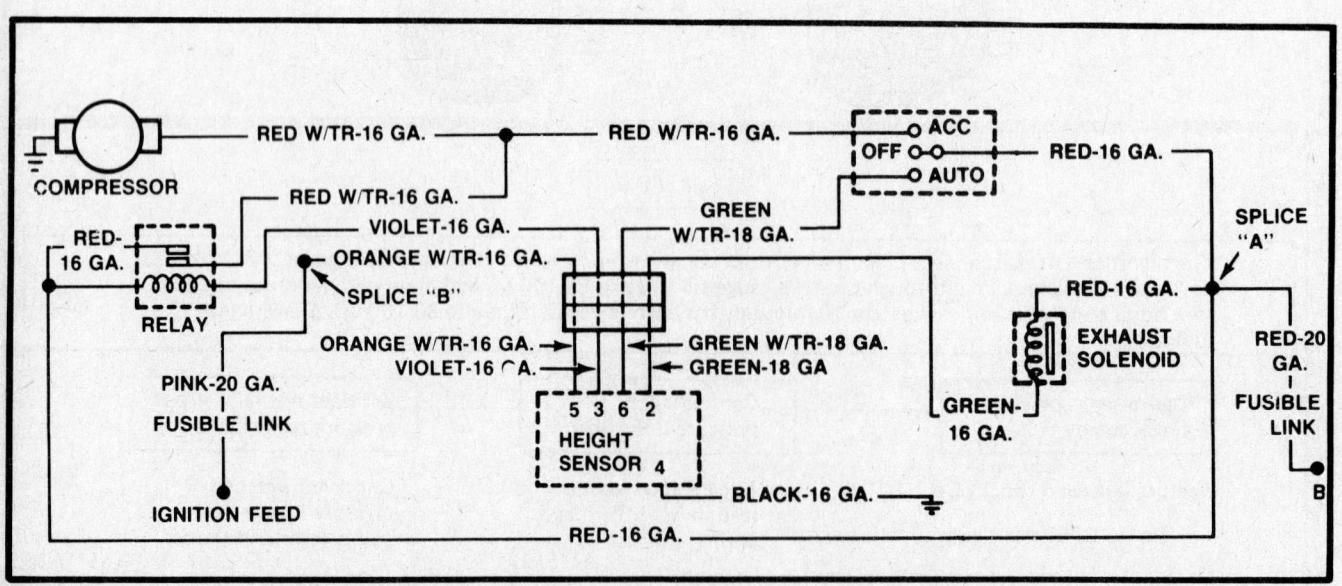

Wiring diagram—automatic load leveling system

558

5. If the gauge does not drop any further, the leak is internal to the compressor.

Component Replacement

COMPRESSOR

Removal and Installation

1. Bleed air from the system.
2. Disconnect the air line at the compressor air dryer.
3. Tag and disconnect electrical connections from the compressor.
4. Remove the compressor mounting bolts. Remove the compressor assembly from the vehicle.
5. Installation is the reverse of the removal procedure. Check compressor for proper operation.

HEIGHT SENSOR

Removal and Installation

1. Raise and support the vehicle safely.
2. Tag and disconnect the connector plug from the height sensor.
3. Disconnect the link from the sensor actuating arm.
4. Loosen and remove the bolts attaching the height sensor to the underbody of the vehicle. Remove the height sensor from the vehicle.
5. Installation is the reverse of the removal procedure.

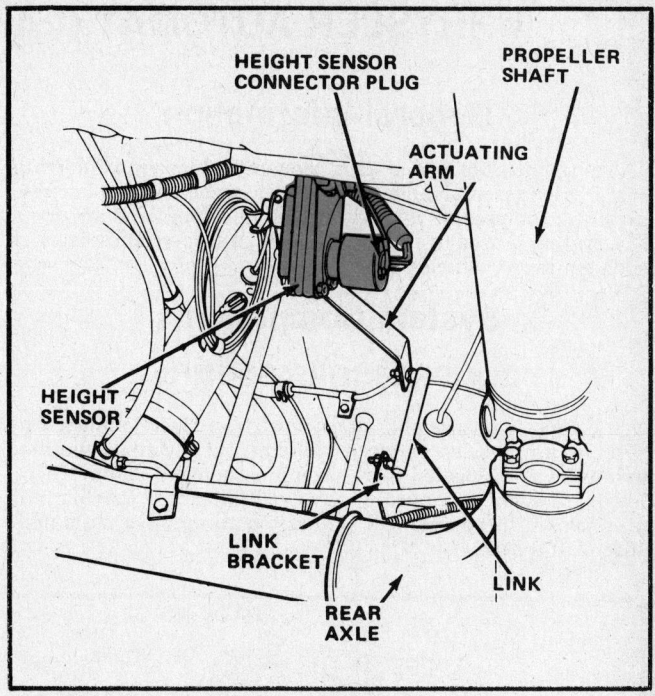

Height sensor

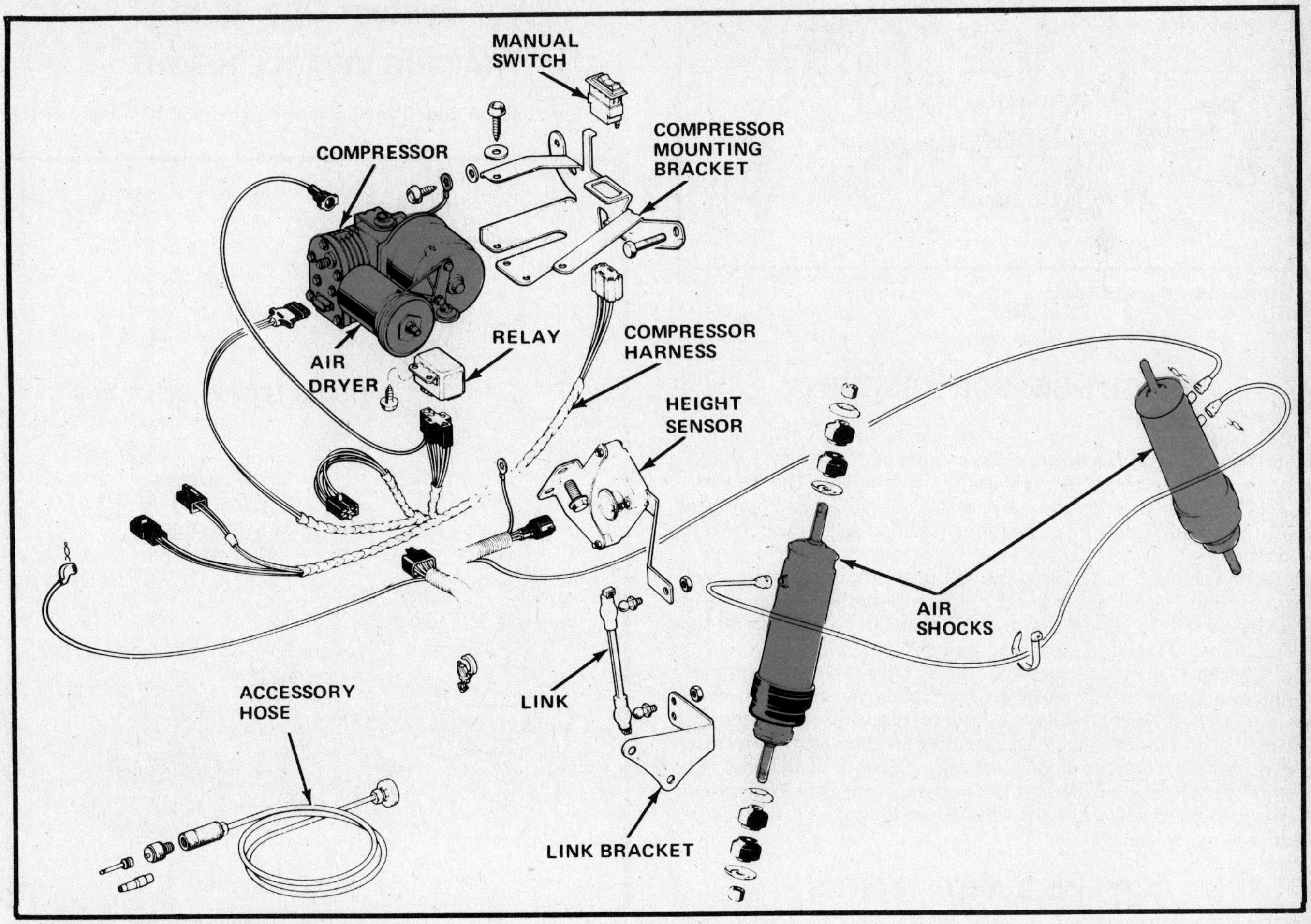

Automatic load leveling system

CHRYSLER AUTOMATIC AIR LOAD LEVELING SYSTEM

General Information

The automatic air load leveling system includes the following: compressor assembly, height sensor assembly, wiring harness, air lines, compressor relay, air shock absorbers and air dryer. The system is used to assist the standard suspension system on such equipped vehicles.

System Components

COMPRESSOR ASSEMBLY

The compressor assembly is driven by an electric motor and supplies air pressure between 120–200 psi. A solenoid operated exhaust valve, located in the compressor head assembly, releases air when energized. This valve limits maximum blow off pressure to 200 psi and will maintain a minimum system pressure of 100 psi.

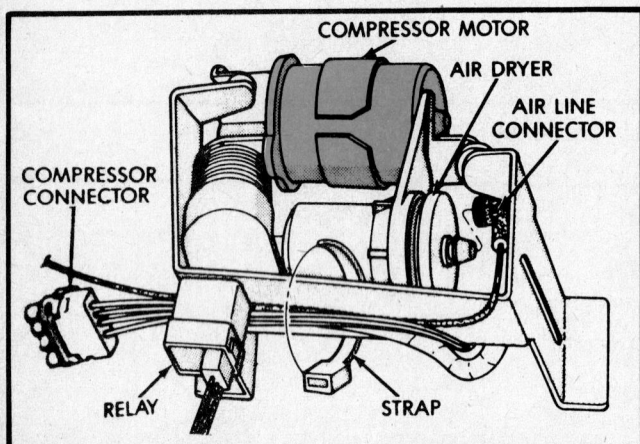

Compressor assembly

HEIGHT SENSOR ASSEMBLY

The height sensor assembly is an electronic device that controls the ground circuits for the compressor relay and the exhaust valve solenoid. An electronic timer within the unit controls the run time from one minute and 45 seconds to three minutes and 30 seconds. This prevents damage to the leveling system.

Also included in the system, is an air replenishment cycle that is controlled by the height sensor assembly. When the ignition switch is turned to the "ON" position, after a 30–60 second delay, the compressor will run 3–5 seconds.

In order to prevent excessive cycling between the compressor and the exhaust solenoid circuits during normal ride conditions a 13–27 second delay is incorporated into the electronic timer. The height sensor is mounted on the right rear frame rail. A link from the sensor actuating arm is attached to the rear of the track bar. When the arm moves up the compressor relay is energized, when the arm moves down the exhaust solenoid is energized.

AIR LINES AND FITTINGS

The air lines are equipped with snap on fittings with two "O"

rings located on the male fittings. A retainer spring locks the male fitting into a groove on the female fitting.

NOTE: When replacing air lines and/or fittings, do not kink air lines or route new components near moving components of the vehicle.

COMPRESSOR RELAY

The relay is mounted to a bracket on the compressor assembly. When the compressor is energized it allows the compressor to operate. The unit is controlled by the height sensor.

AIR ADJUSTABLE SHOCK ABSORBERS

Air shock absorbers are hydraulic shock absorbers with a neoprene bladder sealing the upper and lower sections together, forming an air cylinder.

AIR DRYER

The air dryer is attached to the compressor and is not serviceable. This component serves two purposes; it absorbs moisture from the atmosphere before it enters the system and through internal valving, maintains a residual pressure of 14–21 psi.

System Operation

RAISING VEHICLE HEIGHT

When weight is added to the rear suspension, the body of the

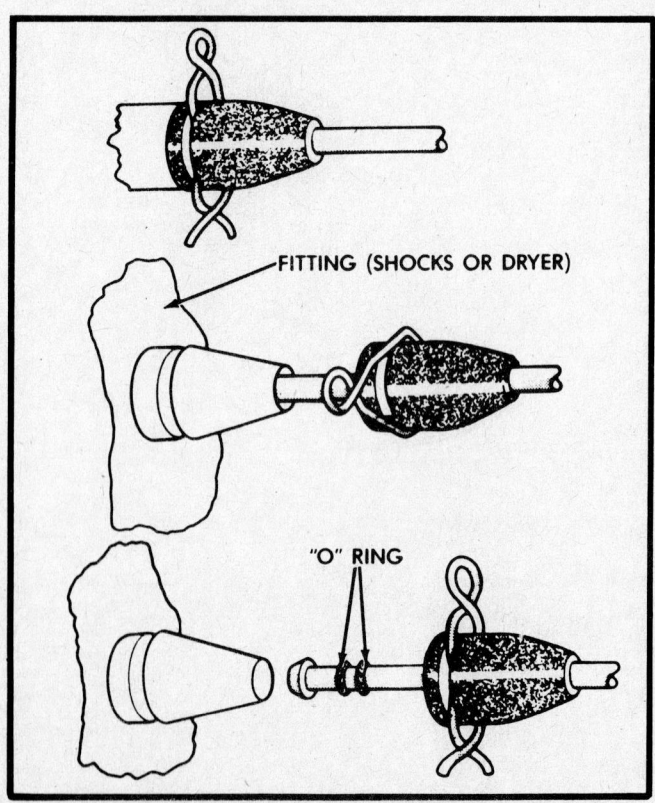

Air hose fittings

vehicle is lowered causing the height sensor actuating arm to rotate upward. This action causes the internal time delay circuit to activate. After a time delay of 13–27 seconds, the sensor grounds pin number 3 and completes the ground circuit to the compressor relay.

When the relay is energized, the compressor motor runs and air is sent through the system. As the shock absorbers inflate, the body moves upward to the corrected position. When the body reaches the corrected level, the sensor stops the compressor operation.

LOWERING VEHICLE HEIGHT

When the weight is removed from the vehicle the body moves upward, causing the height sensor actuating arm to rotate downward and activate the internal time delay circuit.

After a time delay of 13–27 seconds, the sensor activates the exhaust solenoid circuit. Air is exhausted from the shock absorbers through the air dryer and exhaust solenoid to the atmosphere.

As the body lowers, the height sensor actuating arm rotates torwards its original position. When the body reaches the original vehicle height the sensor opens the exhaust solenoid valve circuit.

Troubleshooting

COMPRESSOR

Performance Test

This test can be performed on the vehicle in order to evaluate the compressor current draw, leak down and pressure output.

1. Tag and disconnect the compressor motor wiring harness connector.
2. Disconnect the compressor air line at the air line "T" connector.
3. Connect an air pressure gauge into the air line between the compressor and the air hose tee.
4. Connect an ammeter in series between the orange wire in the wiring harness and the dark green wire to the compressor motor
5. Connect a ground wire from the black wire on the compressor motor to a known ground located on the frame.
6. If the current draw to the compressor motor exceeds 14 amps, replace the compressor assembly.
7. When the air pressure stabilizes at 120 psi, disconnect the positive (+) lead from the connector.

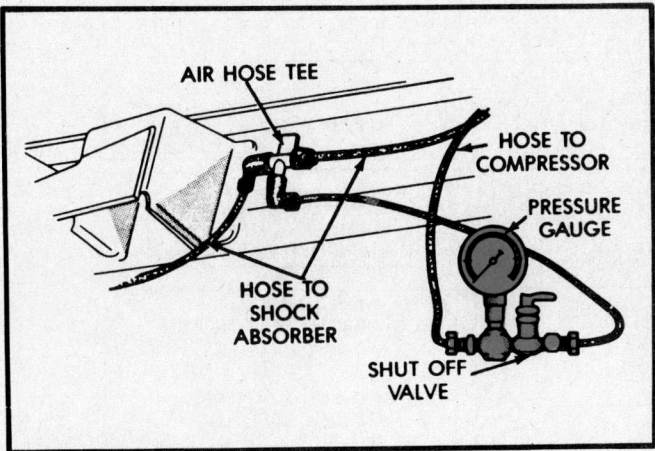

Pressure leak down test

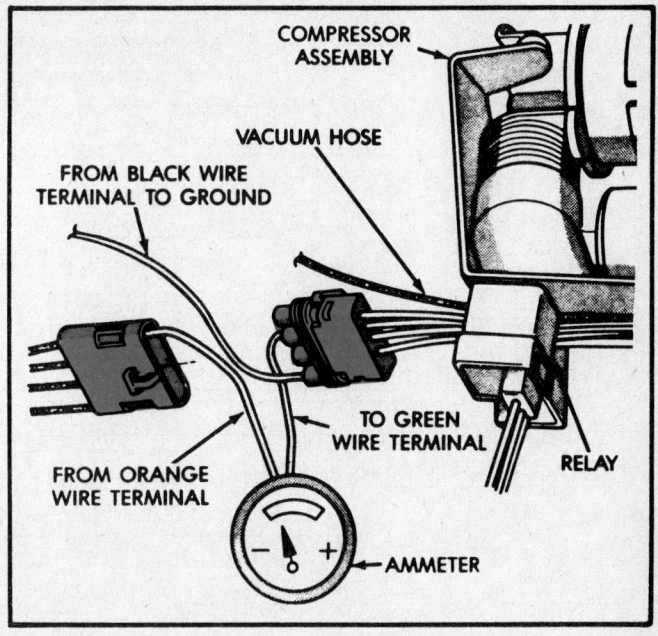

Current draw test

CAUTION

If any of the following conditions exist, replace the compressor assembly.
- Air pressure leaks down below 90 psi before it remains steady.
- Output pressure builds up to less than 110 psi psi when it stabilizes.

If the compressor is allowed to run during this test until it reaches its maximum output pressure (200 psi), the solenoid exhaust valve will act as a pressure relief valve. The resulting leak down after the compressor is shut off will indicate a false leak.

HEIGHT SENSOR

Performance Test

1. Cycle the ignition off then on. This resets the height sensor timer circuit.
2. Raise the vehicle and support safely.
3. Inspect the wiring to see that it is properly secured to the height sensor.
4. Disconnect the link from the height sensor arm and move up. There should be a 13–27 second delay before the compressor turns on and the shocks begin to inflate.

CAUTION

As soon as the shock absorber bladder fills, stop the compressor by moving the sensor arm down as damage to the air bladder can result.

5. There should be a 13–27 second delay after the sensor arm is moved down before the shocks begin to deflate.

Component Replacement

COMPRESSOR

Removal

1. Disconnect the negative battery cable.
2. Raise the vehicle and support safely.

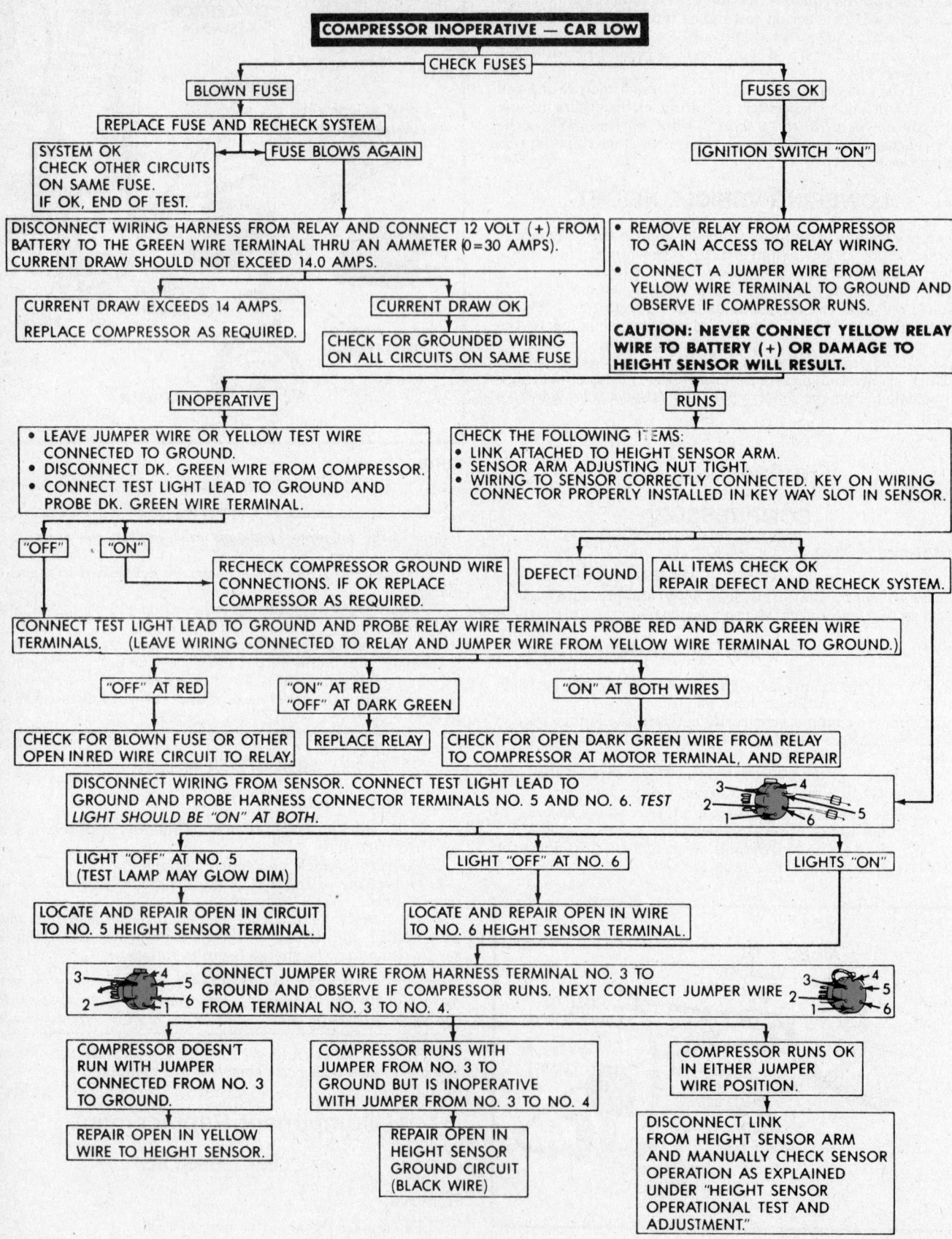

COMPRESSOR INOPERATIVE — CAR LOW

CHECK FUSES

BLOWN FUSE

FUSES OK

REPLACE FUSE AND RECHECK SYSTEM

IGNITION SWITCH "ON"

SYSTEM OK
CHECK OTHER CIRCUITS
ON SAME FUSE.
IF OK, END OF TEST.

FUSE BLOWS AGAIN

DISCONNECT WIRING HARNESS FROM RELAY AND CONNECT 12 VOLT (+) FROM
BATTERY TO THE GREEN WIRE TERMINAL THRU AN AMMETER (0=30 AMPS).
CURRENT DRAW SHOULD NOT EXCEED 14.0 AMPS.

- REMOVE RELAY FROM COMPRESSOR
  TO GAIN ACCESS TO RELAY WIRING.
- CONNECT A JUMPER WIRE FROM RELAY
  YELLOW WIRE TERMINAL TO GROUND AND
  OBSERVE IF COMPRESSOR RUNS.

**CAUTION: NEVER CONNECT YELLOW RELAY
WIRE TO BATTERY (+) OR DAMAGE TO
HEIGHT SENSOR WILL RESULT.**

CURRENT DRAW EXCEEDS 14 AMPS.

REPLACE COMPRESSOR AS REQUIRED.

CURRENT DRAW OK

CHECK FOR GROUNDED WIRING
ON ALL CIRCUITS ON SAME FUSE

INOPERATIVE

RUNS

- LEAVE JUMPER WIRE OR YELLOW TEST WIRE
  CONNECTED TO GROUND.
- DISCONNECT DK. GREEN WIRE FROM COMPRESSOR.
- CONNECT TEST LIGHT LEAD TO GROUND AND
  PROBE DK. GREEN WIRE TERMINAL.

CHECK THE FOLLOWING ITEMS:
- LINK ATTACHED TO HEIGHT SENSOR ARM.
- SENSOR ARM ADJUSTING NUT TIGHT.
- WIRING TO SENSOR CORRECTLY CONNECTED. KEY ON WIRING
  CONNECTOR PROPERLY INSTALLED IN KEY WAY SLOT IN SENSOR.

"OFF"   "ON"

RECHECK COMPRESSOR GROUND WIRE
CONNECTIONS. IF OK REPLACE
COMPRESSOR AS REQUIRED.

DEFECT FOUND

ALL ITEMS CHECK OK
REPAIR DEFECT AND RECHECK SYSTEM.

CONNECT TEST LIGHT LEAD TO GROUND AND PROBE RELAY WIRE TERMINALS PROBE RED AND DARK GREEN WIRE
TERMINALS.   (LEAVE WIRING CONNECTED TO RELAY AND JUMPER WIRE FROM YELLOW WIRE TERMINAL TO GROUND.)

"OFF" AT RED

"ON" AT RED
"OFF" AT DARK GREEN

"ON" AT BOTH WIRES

CHECK FOR BLOWN FUSE OR OTHER
OPEN IN RED WIRE CIRCUIT TO RELAY.

REPLACE RELAY

CHECK FOR OPEN DARK GREEN WIRE FROM RELAY
TO COMPRESSOR AT MOTOR TERMINAL, AND REPAIR

DISCONNECT WIRING FROM SENSOR. CONNECT TEST LIGHT LEAD TO
GROUND AND PROBE HARNESS CONNECTOR TERMINALS NO. 5 AND NO. 6. *TEST
LIGHT SHOULD BE "ON" AT BOTH.*

LIGHT "OFF" AT NO. 5
(TEST LAMP MAY GLOW DIM)

LIGHT "OFF" AT NO. 6

LIGHTS "ON"

LOCATE AND REPAIR OPEN IN CIRCUIT
TO NO. 5 HEIGHT SENSOR TERMINAL.

LOCATE AND REPAIR OPEN IN WIRE
TO NO. 6 HEIGHT SENSOR TERMINAL.

CONNECT JUMPER WIRE FROM HARNESS TERMINAL NO. 3 TO
GROUND AND OBSERVE IF COMPRESSOR RUNS. NEXT CONNECT JUMPER WIRE
FROM TERMINAL NO. 3 TO NO. 4.

COMPRESSOR DOESN'T
RUN WITH JUMPER
CONNECTED FROM NO. 3
TO GROUND.

COMPRESSOR RUNS WITH
JUMPER FROM NO. 3 TO
GROUND BUT IS INOPERATIVE
WITH JUMPER FROM NO. 3 TO NO. 4

COMPRESSOR RUNS OK
IN EITHER JUMPER
WIRE POSITION.

REPAIR OPEN IN YELLOW
WIRE TO HEIGHT SENSOR.

REPAIR OPEN IN
HEIGHT SENSOR
GROUND CIRCUIT
(BLACK WIRE)

DISCONNECT LINK
FROM HEIGHT SENSOR ARM
AND MANUALLY CHECK SENSOR
OPERATION AS EXPLAINED
UNDER "HEIGHT SENSOR
OPERATIONAL TEST AND
ADJUSTMENT."

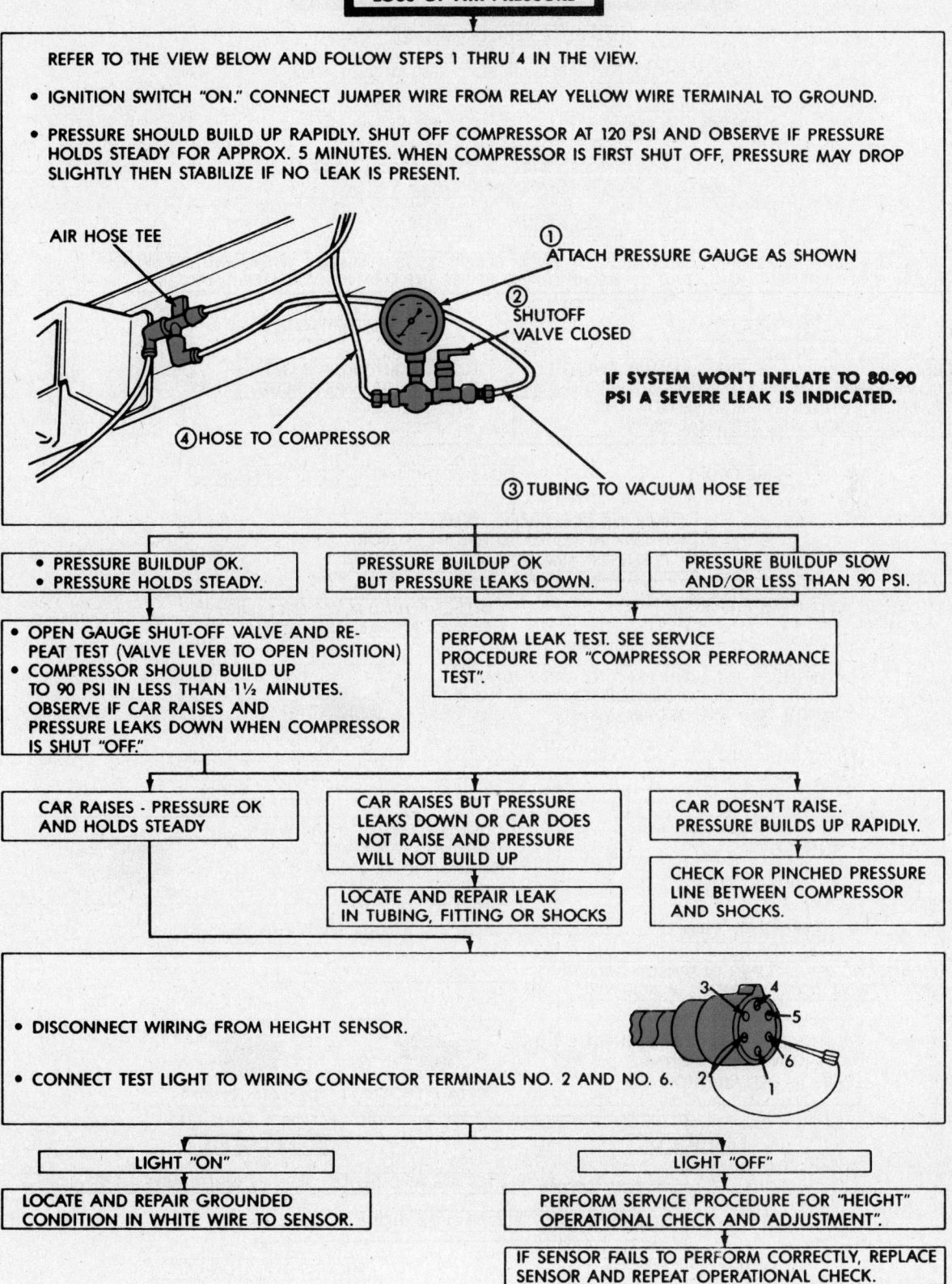

LOSS OF AIR PRESSURE

REFER TO THE VIEW BELOW AND FOLLOW STEPS 1 THRU 4 IN THE VIEW.

- IGNITION SWITCH "ON." CONNECT JUMPER WIRE FROM RELAY YELLOW WIRE TERMINAL TO GROUND.

- PRESSURE SHOULD BUILD UP RAPIDLY. SHUT OFF COMPRESSOR AT 120 PSI AND OBSERVE IF PRESSURE HOLDS STEADY FOR APPROX. 5 MINUTES. WHEN COMPRESSOR IS FIRST SHUT OFF, PRESSURE MAY DROP SLIGHTLY THEN STABILIZE IF NO LEAK IS PRESENT.

AIR HOSE TEE

① ATTACH PRESSURE GAUGE AS SHOWN

② SHUTOFF VALVE CLOSED

IF SYSTEM WON'T INFLATE TO 80-90 PSI A SEVERE LEAK IS INDICATED.

④ HOSE TO COMPRESSOR

③ TUBING TO VACUUM HOSE TEE

- PRESSURE BUILDUP OK.
- PRESSURE HOLDS STEADY.

PRESSURE BUILDUP OK BUT PRESSURE LEAKS DOWN.

PRESSURE BUILDUP SLOW AND/OR LESS THAN 90 PSI.

- OPEN GAUGE SHUT-OFF VALVE AND RE-PEAT TEST (VALVE LEVER TO OPEN POSITION)
- COMPRESSOR SHOULD BUILD UP TO 90 PSI IN LESS THAN 1½ MINUTES. OBSERVE IF CAR RAISES AND PRESSURE LEAKS DOWN WHEN COMPRESSOR IS SHUT "OFF."

PERFORM LEAK TEST. SEE SERVICE PROCEDURE FOR "COMPRESSOR PERFORMANCE TEST".

CAR RAISES - PRESSURE OK AND HOLDS STEADY

CAR RAISES BUT PRESSURE LEAKS DOWN OR CAR DOES NOT RAISE AND PRESSURE WILL NOT BUILD UP

LOCATE AND REPAIR LEAK IN TUBING, FITTING OR SHOCKS

CAR DOESN'T RAISE. PRESSURE BUILDS UP RAPIDLY.

CHECK FOR PINCHED PRESSURE LINE BETWEEN COMPRESSOR AND SHOCKS.

- DISCONNECT WIRING FROM HEIGHT SENSOR.

- CONNECT TEST LIGHT TO WIRING CONNECTOR TERMINALS NO. 2 AND NO. 6.

LIGHT "ON"

LOCATE AND REPAIR GROUNDED CONDITION IN WHITE WIRE TO SENSOR.

LIGHT "OFF"

PERFORM SERVICE PROCEDURE FOR "HEIGHT" OPERATIONAL CHECK AND ADJUSTMENT".

IF SENSOR FAILS TO PERFORM CORRECTLY, REPLACE SENSOR AND REPEAT OPERATIONAL CHECK.

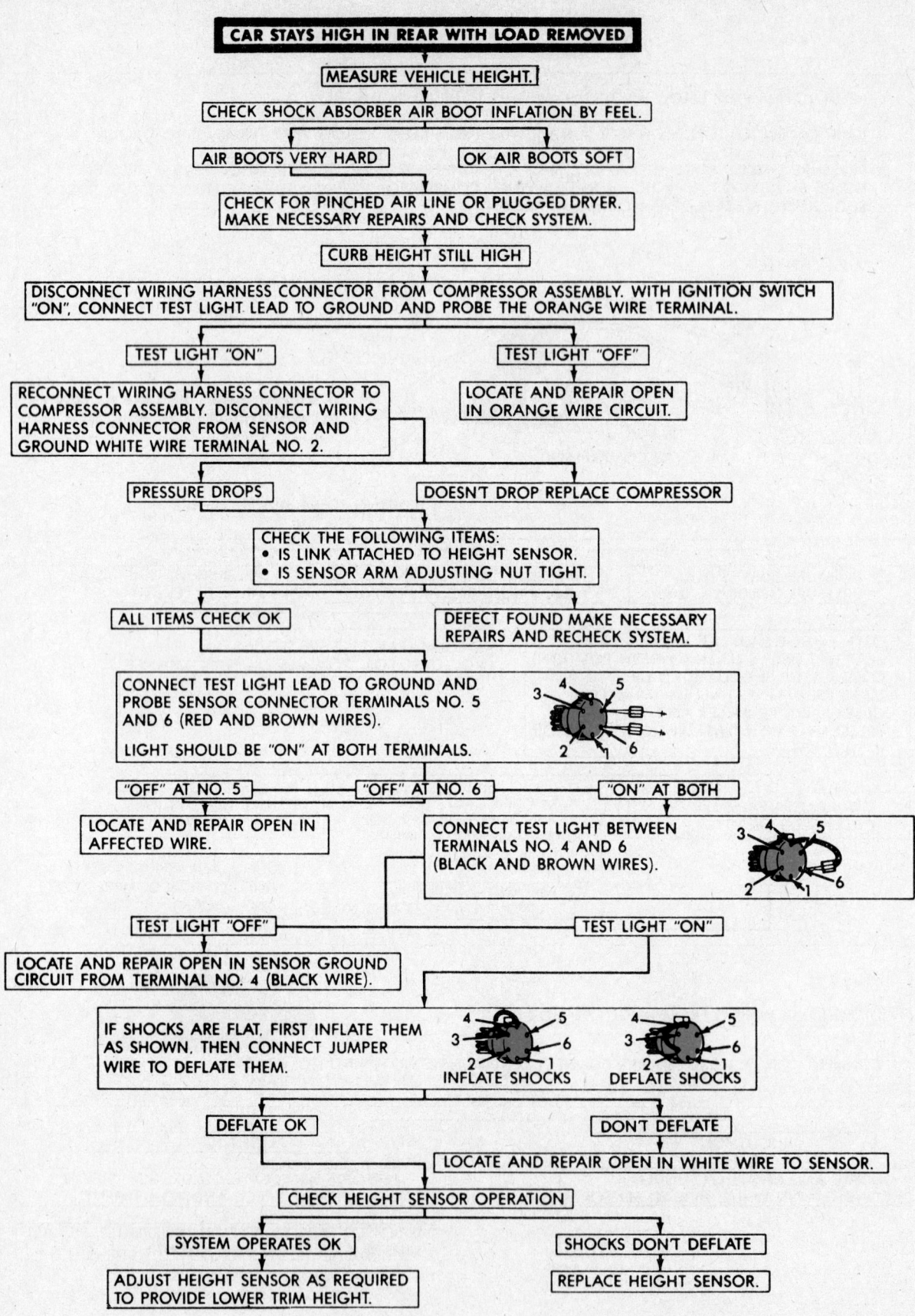

CAR STAYS HIGH IN REAR WITH LOAD REMOVED

MEASURE VEHICLE HEIGHT.

CHECK SHOCK ABSORBER AIR BOOT INFLATION BY FEEL.

AIR BOOTS VERY HARD

OK AIR BOOTS SOFT

CHECK FOR PINCHED AIR LINE OR PLUGGED DRYER. MAKE NECESSARY REPAIRS AND CHECK SYSTEM.

CURB HEIGHT STILL HIGH

DISCONNECT WIRING HARNESS CONNECTOR FROM COMPRESSOR ASSEMBLY. WITH IGNITION SWITCH "ON", CONNECT TEST LIGHT LEAD TO GROUND AND PROBE THE ORANGE WIRE TERMINAL.

TEST LIGHT "ON"

TEST LIGHT "OFF"

RECONNECT WIRING HARNESS CONNECTOR TO COMPRESSOR ASSEMBLY. DISCONNECT WIRING HARNESS CONNECTOR FROM SENSOR AND GROUND WHITE WIRE TERMINAL NO. 2.

LOCATE AND REPAIR OPEN IN ORANGE WIRE CIRCUIT.

PRESSURE DROPS

DOESN'T DROP REPLACE COMPRESSOR

CHECK THE FOLLOWING ITEMS:
• IS LINK ATTACHED TO HEIGHT SENSOR.
• IS SENSOR ARM ADJUSTING NUT TIGHT.

ALL ITEMS CHECK OK

DEFECT FOUND MAKE NECESSARY REPAIRS AND RECHECK SYSTEM.

CONNECT TEST LIGHT LEAD TO GROUND AND PROBE SENSOR CONNECTOR TERMINALS NO. 5 AND 6 (RED AND BROWN WIRES).

LIGHT SHOULD BE "ON" AT BOTH TERMINALS.

"OFF" AT NO. 5

"OFF" AT NO. 6

"ON" AT BOTH

LOCATE AND REPAIR OPEN IN AFFECTED WIRE.

CONNECT TEST LIGHT BETWEEN TERMINALS NO. 4 AND 6 (BLACK AND BROWN WIRES).

TEST LIGHT "OFF"

TEST LIGHT "ON"

LOCATE AND REPAIR OPEN IN SENSOR GROUND CIRCUIT FROM TERMINAL NO. 4 (BLACK WIRE).

IF SHOCKS ARE FLAT, FIRST INFLATE THEM AS SHOWN, THEN CONNECT JUMPER WIRE TO DEFLATE THEM.

INFLATE SHOCKS

DEFLATE SHOCKS

DEFLATE OK

DON'T DEFLATE

LOCATE AND REPAIR OPEN IN WHITE WIRE TO SENSOR.

CHECK HEIGHT SENSOR OPERATION

SYSTEM OPERATES OK

SHOCKS DON'T DEFLATE

ADJUST HEIGHT SENSOR AS REQUIRED TO PROVIDE LOWER TRIM HEIGHT.

REPLACE HEIGHT SENSOR.

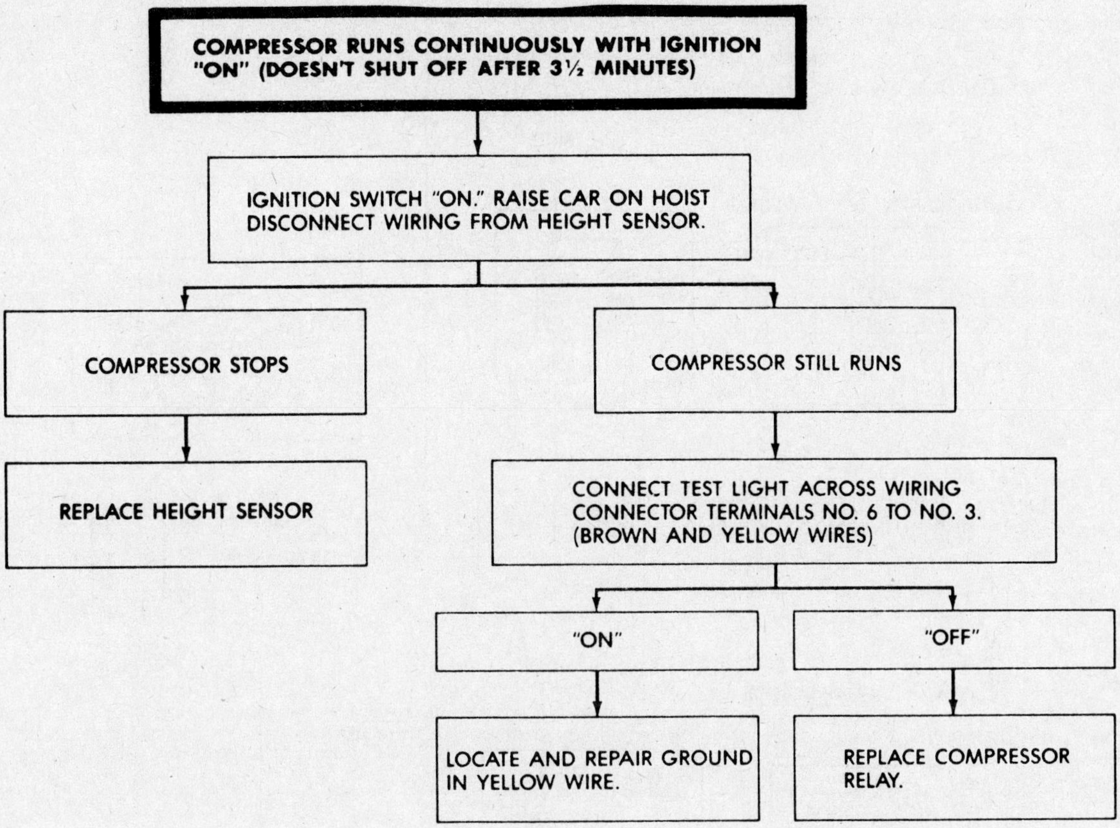

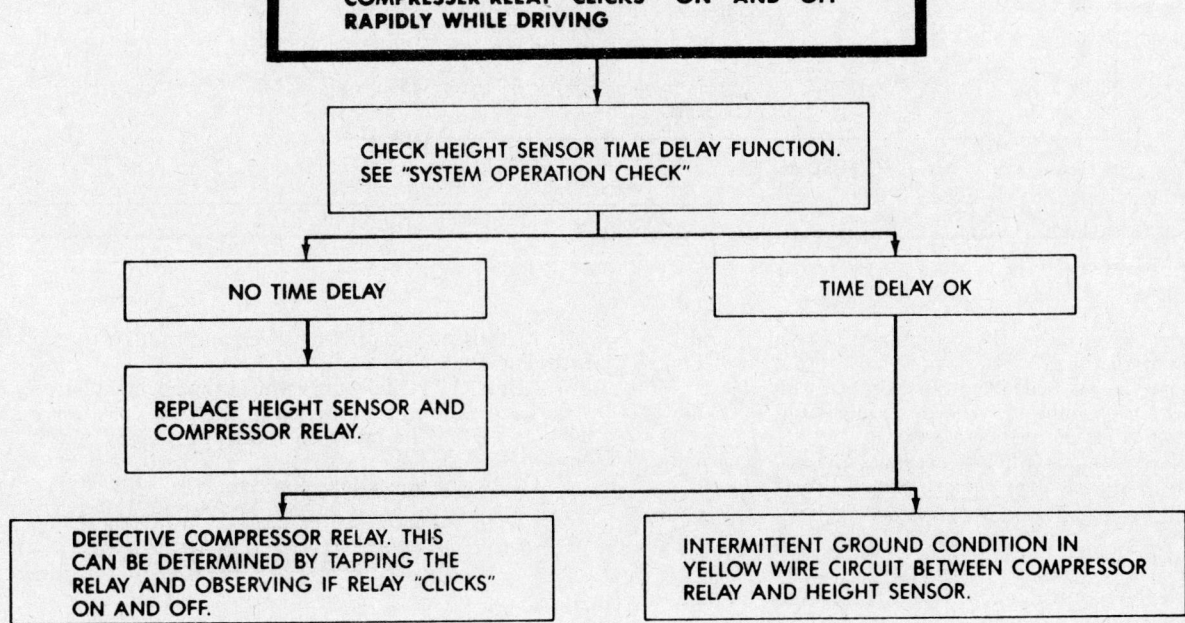

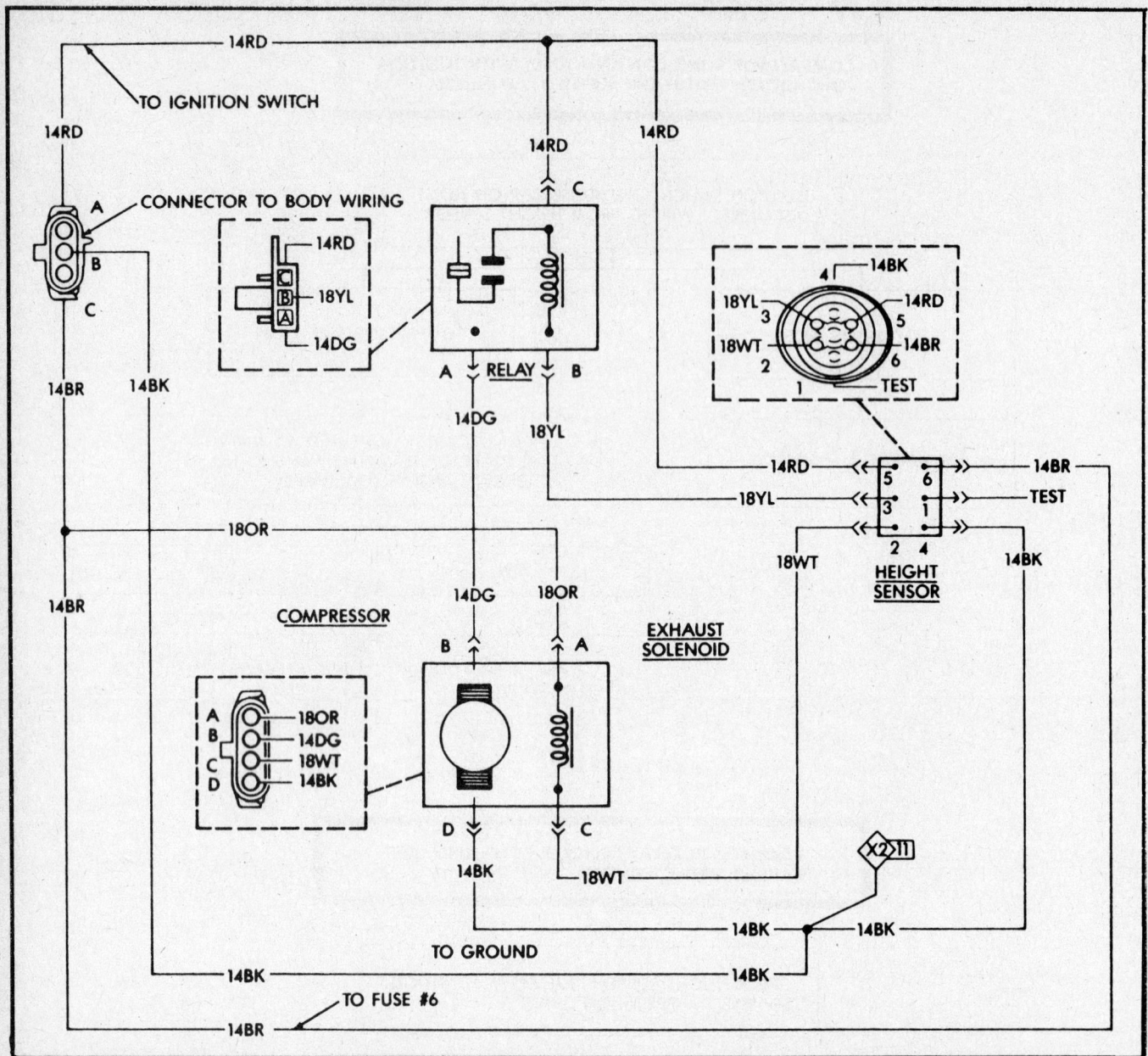

Load leveling schematic

3. Remove cover from the compressor assembly and discharge the air system.
4. Remove the air hose from the electrical connectors.
5. Remove the compressor assembly mounting bolts. Lower the assembly from the vehicle.
6. Remove the mounting bracket bolts and slide the mounting bracket away from the compressor.

Installation

1. Install the mounting bracket on the compressor and install the bolts and tighten to 70 inch pounds (8 Nm).
2. Install the compressor assembly to the frame rail and tighten the bolts to 70 inch pounds (8 Nm).
3. Connect the air hose and electrical connectors to the compressor.

4. Install the compressor cover and tighten the bolts to 70 inch pounds (8 Nm).
5. Lower the vehicle and connect the negative battery cable.
6. Turn the ignition switch to the "ON" position and then back to "OFF" in order to reset the height sensor timing circuits.
7. Check the operation of system.

HEIGHT SENSOR

Removal

1. Disconnect the negative battery cable.
2. Raise the vehicle and support safely.
3. Tag and disconnect the electrical connector and link from the sensor arm.

4. Remove the mounting bolts and remove the height sensor assembly from the frame rail.

Installation

1. Install height sensor assembly and tighten mounting bolts to 70 inch pounds (8 Nm).
2. Connect the link and electrical connector to sensor.
3. Lower the vehicle and connect the negative battery cable.
4. Check system operation.

Adjustment

1. Loosen the lock nut on the sensor arm.
2. To increase vehicle height, move the sensor arm upward and tighten.
3. To decrease vehicle height, move the sensor arm downward and tighten.
4. Check for proper system operation and vehicle height.

COMPRESSOR RELAY

Removal

1. Raise the vehicle and support safely.
2. Remove cover from the compressor assembly.
3. Remove the compressor assembly from the frame rail.
4. Tag and disconnect the electrical connector.
5. Remove the relay mounting screw. Remove the relay.

Installation

1. Position the relay and install the mounting screw.
2. Connect the electrical connection.

3. Install the compressor assembly on the frame rail and tighten to 70 inch pounds (8 Nm).
4. Install the cover on the compressor assembly and tighten to 70 inch pounds (8 Nm).
5. Lower the vehicle. Test system operation.

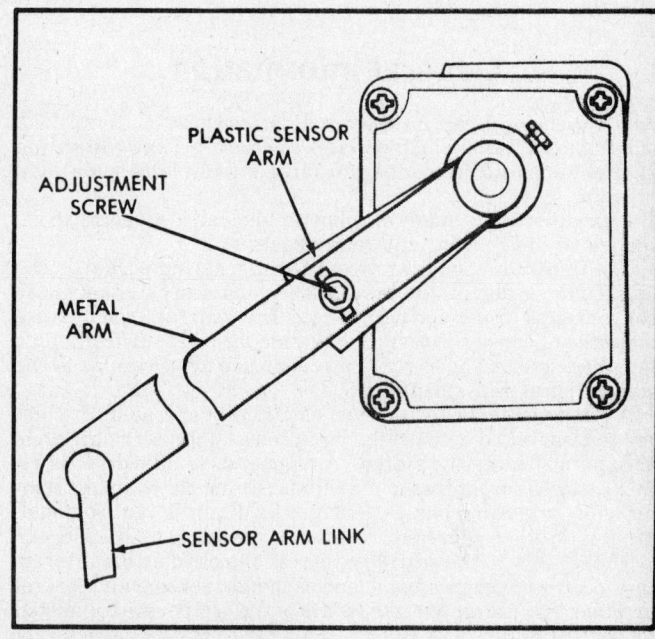

Height sensor adjustment

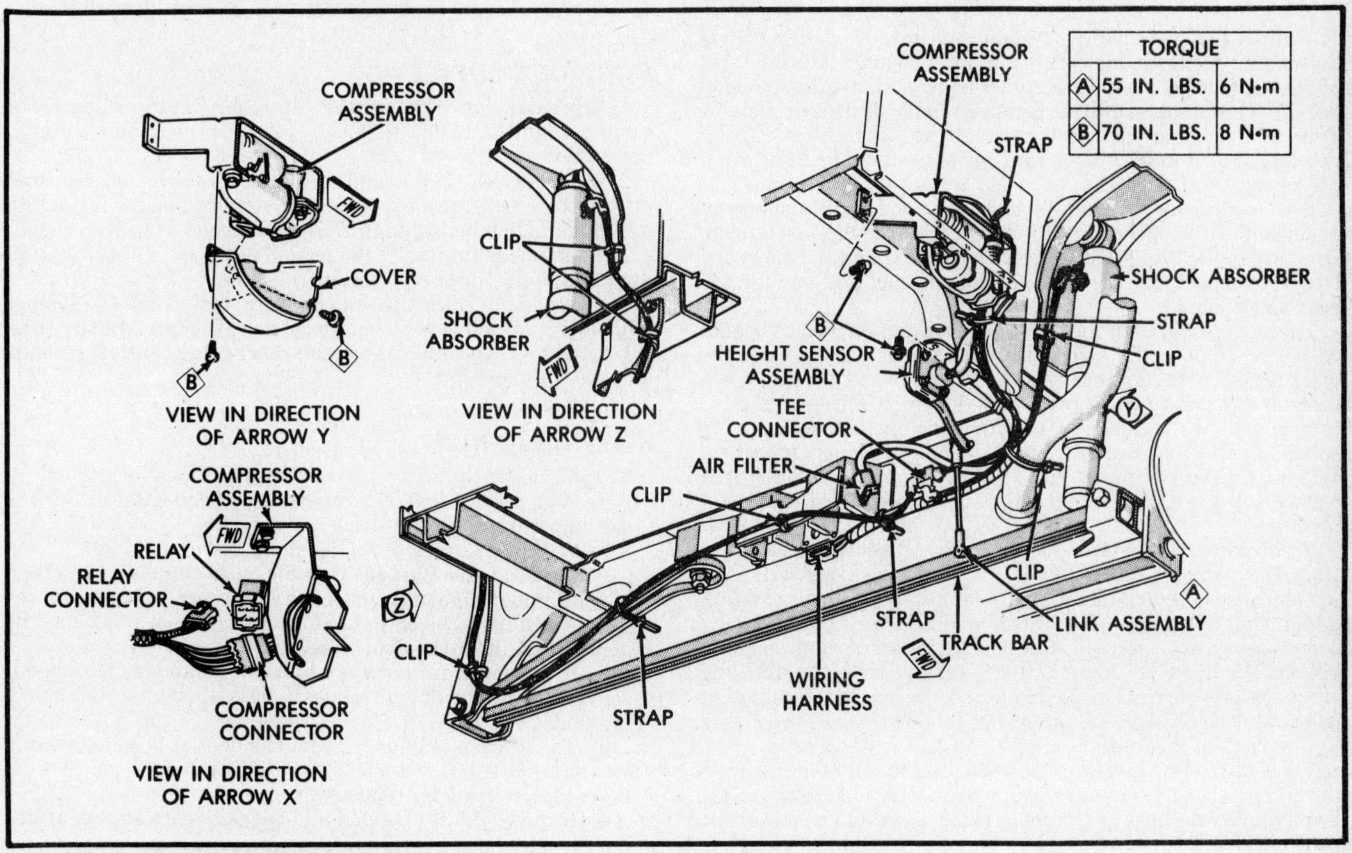

TORQUE		
Ⓐ	55 IN. LBS.	6 N•m
Ⓑ	70 IN. LBS.	8 N•m

Automatic air load levelling system

567

FRONT AND REAR AIR SUSPENSION—1984 AND LATER MARK VII AND LINCOLN CONTINENTAL
1985 AND LATER FORD CROWN VICTORIA AND MERCURY GRAND MARQUIS

General Information

Air suspension is an air operated, microprocessor controlled, suspension system which replaces the conventional coil spring suspension and provides automatic front and rear load leveling.

Four air springs, made of rubber and plastic, support the vehicle load at the front and rear wheels.

The front air springs are mounted to a spring pocket in the crossmember and on the lower suspension arms similar to the conventional front spring system. The rear air springs are mounted ahead of the rear axle outside the body sub frame side members and on the lower rear suspension arms similar to the conventional rear spring system.

A single cylinder piston type electrically operated air compressor, mounted on most fender aprons, supplies the air pressure for operating the system. A regenerative type dryer is attached to the compressor manifold. All air flow during compression or venting passes through the dryer. A vent solenoid, located on the compressor manifold, controls air exhaustion.

The air flow to the entire system is controlled by the interaction of the air compressor, solenoids, height sensors and control modules. All the air operated parts of the system are connected by nylon tubing.

Operation

The air suspension leveling system is operated by adding or removing air from the air springs in order to maintain the level of the vehicle at a predetermined front and rear suspension height. The predetermined distance is known as trim height. Trim height is controlled by the height sensors. Distance from the body to ground will change with tire size and inflation pressure.

The height sensors are attached to the body and suspension arms, and will lengthen or shorten the travel of the suspension. On most applications, three height sensors are used: One at the left front wheel, one at the right front wheel and one for the rear suspension.

The system works in the following manner: As weight is added to the vehicle, the body will settle under the load. As the body lowers, the height sensors shorten (low out of trim), generating a signal to the control module which activates the air compressor (through a relay) and in turn opens the air spring solenoid valves. As the body rises, the height sensors lengthen. When the preset trim height is reached, the air compressor is turned off and the solenoid valves are closed by the control module.

A similar action takes place whenever weight is removed from the vehicle. As weight is removed, the body will rise, which causes the height sensors to lengthen (high out of trim), generating a signal to the control module which opens the air compressor vent solenoid and opens the air spring solenoid valves. As the body lowers, the height sensors shorten and when the preset trim height is reached, the air compressor vent solenoid is closed and the air spring solenoid valves are closed by the control module.

Air required for leveling the vehicle is distributed from the air compressor to each air spring by means of four nylon air lines which originate at the compressor dryer and terminate at the individual air springs. The dryer is a common pressure manifold for all four air lines so orientation of these lines at the compressor is not required. However, the air lines are color coded to identify to which air spring they are attached. The dryer contains a desiccant (silica gel) which drys the compressed air before delivering the air to the springs. During venting of any spring, the previously dried air passes through the dryer to remove moisture from the desiccant. Air required for compression and vent air enter and exit through a common port on the compressor head. Vented air is also controlled by a solenoid valve in the compressor head.

The compressor relay, compressor vent solenoid and all air spring solenoids have internal diodes for electrical noise supression and therefore are polarity sensitive. Care must be taken when servicing these components not to switch the battery feed and ground circuits or component damage will result.

CAUTION

A module controls the air compressor motor (through a relay), vent solenoid and four air spring solenoids to provide the air requirements of the springs. The module also provides power and ground to the height sensors and monitors input from the height sensors and the ignition Run/Brake On/Door Open circuits. These inputs are used by the module to make vehicle levelling decisions which are then carried out by the air system components controlled by the module. For service, the module provides a series of diagnostic tests, a routine for filling the springs and operates a system warning lamp.

The control logic for operating the system is given below:

IGNITION IN OFF

1. Operates for 30 minutes after the ignition switch is turned from Run to Off, then the system is inoperable through the module.
2. Will service down requests (lower vehicle) as required during the 30 minutes except if any height sensor was reading a high vehicle when the ignition was turned from Run to Off. The vent time is limited to ten seconds for the rear springs and approximately three seconds for the front.
3. At one hour after the ignition is turned to Off, the system will correct for a low vehicle if necessary. Compressor run time is limited to 15 seconds for the the rear springs and 30 seconds for the front springs.

IGNITION IN RUN

1. Ignition in the run position for less than 45 seconds.
   a. Will service first rear or front up requests (raise vehicle) immediately if required.
   b. Will not service down requests (lower vehicle).
2. Ignition in the Run position for more than 45 seconds.
   a. If a door(s) is open with the brake not engaged, up requests will be serviced immediately and down requests will be serviced after the door(s) is closed.
   b. If the doors are not open and the brake is not engaged, service all (up or down) requests by a 45 second averaging method.
   c. If the brake is engaged and the door(s) is open, service up requests (raise vehicle) immediately but do not service down (lower vehicle) requests.
   d. If the brake is engaged and the doors are closed, all requests (up or down) will not be serviced except that if a rear up request (raise vehicle) is in progress it will be completed.

GENERAL

1. Down requests (lower vehicle) will not be serviced if any door is open.

2. Requests are serviced in the following order: rear up, front up, rear down, front down.

3. During Ignition In Run, if any up or down requests cannot be serviced within three minutes, the warning lamp will come on and stay on for that ignition cycle. However, only the request which was being serviced is affected. That is, if a time out failure occurred during a left front up correction, the module will continue to service future left front down requests and all right front and rear requests.

4. The rear spring solenoids are always operated in tandem, but the front spring solenoids may operate independently.

5. Front and rear requests (up or down) will never be serviced at the same time.

6. Turning the ignition from Run to Off clears all memory in the module and therefore the warning lamp may not immediately indicate a failure when the ignition is returned to the Run position.

--- **CAUTION** ---

When charging the battery, the ignition switch must be in the OFF position if the air suspension switch is ON or damage to the air compressor relay or motor may occur.

However, use of a battery charger while performing the diagnostic test or air spring fill options is acceptable. Set the charger to a rate to maintain, but not damage the vehicle battery.

ADJUSTMENTS

NOTE: This adjustment procedure must be used prior to alignment, pinion angle or ride height checking. This method causes the system to perform a vent to trim. If the vehicle is significantly colder or warmer than alignment area, time must be allowed for the vehicle to warm or cool to the temperature of the alignment area prior to Steps 1, 2 and 3.

1. Drive onto the alignment rack, position vehicle, turn ignition key off and exit vehicle.

2. Level rack as required, re-enter vehicle and turn ignition to run position (do not start).

3. Allow one minute for vehicle to level, then push trunk release, turn ignition to off position and exit vehicle.

4. Allow 20 seconds for vehicle to vent to trim height (all doors must be closed) then turn air suspension system switch to off position (in trunk on left hand side).

5. Check alignment (pinion angle).

RIDE HEIGHT

The front suspension ride height or "S" dimension is adjusted by moving the front left and/or right lower sensor attaching stud (there are three adjustment positions provided on the bracket). Loosen the attaching screw and adjust up or down as required. A one position change to the sensor attachment point will yield approximately 0.5 inch (12.7 mm) change up or down to the "S" dimension.

The rear suspension ride height "D" dimension is adjusted by moving the rear sensor attaching bracket up or down relative to the right rear upper arm (a slot adjustment is provided on the bracket). Loosen the attaching nut and adjust up or down as required. A one index mark change to the sensor attachment point will yield approximately 0.25 inch (6.35 mm) change up or down to the "D" dimension.

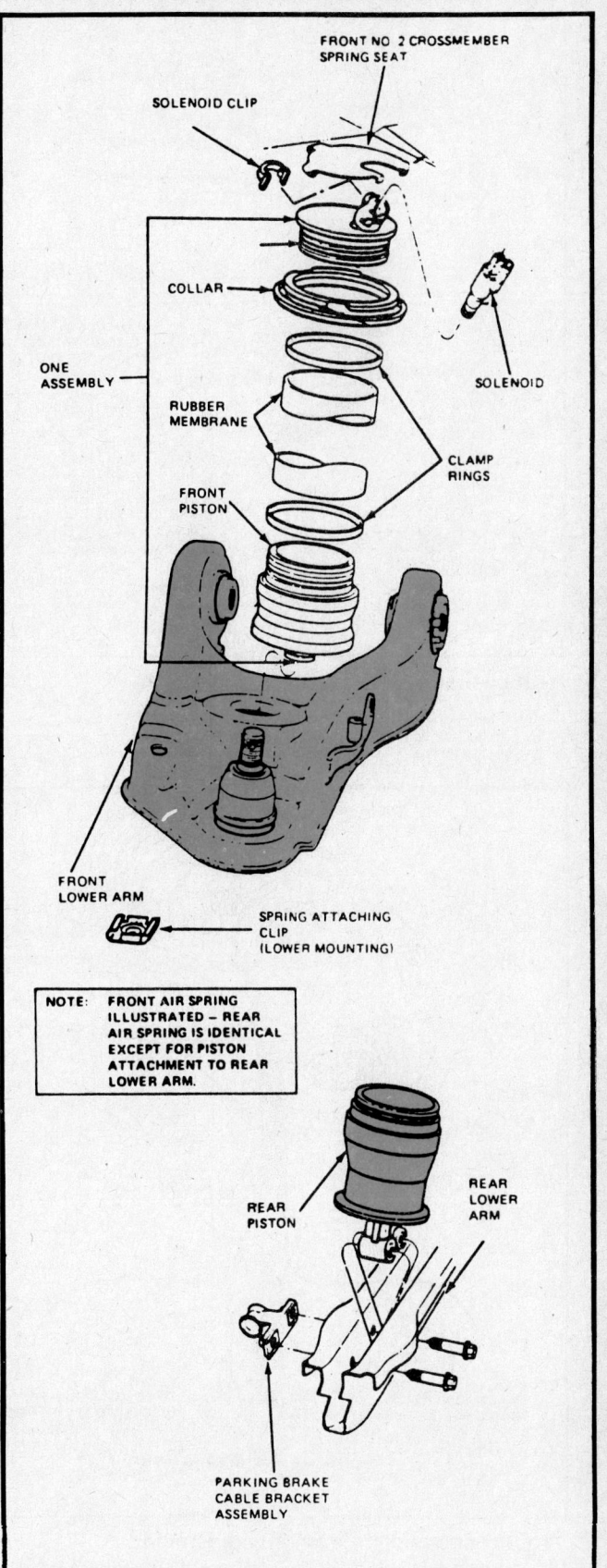

NOTE: FRONT AIR SPRING ILLUSTRATED – REAR AIR SPRING IS IDENTICAL EXCEPT FOR PISTON ATTACHMENT TO REAR LOWER ARM.

Air spring—exploded view

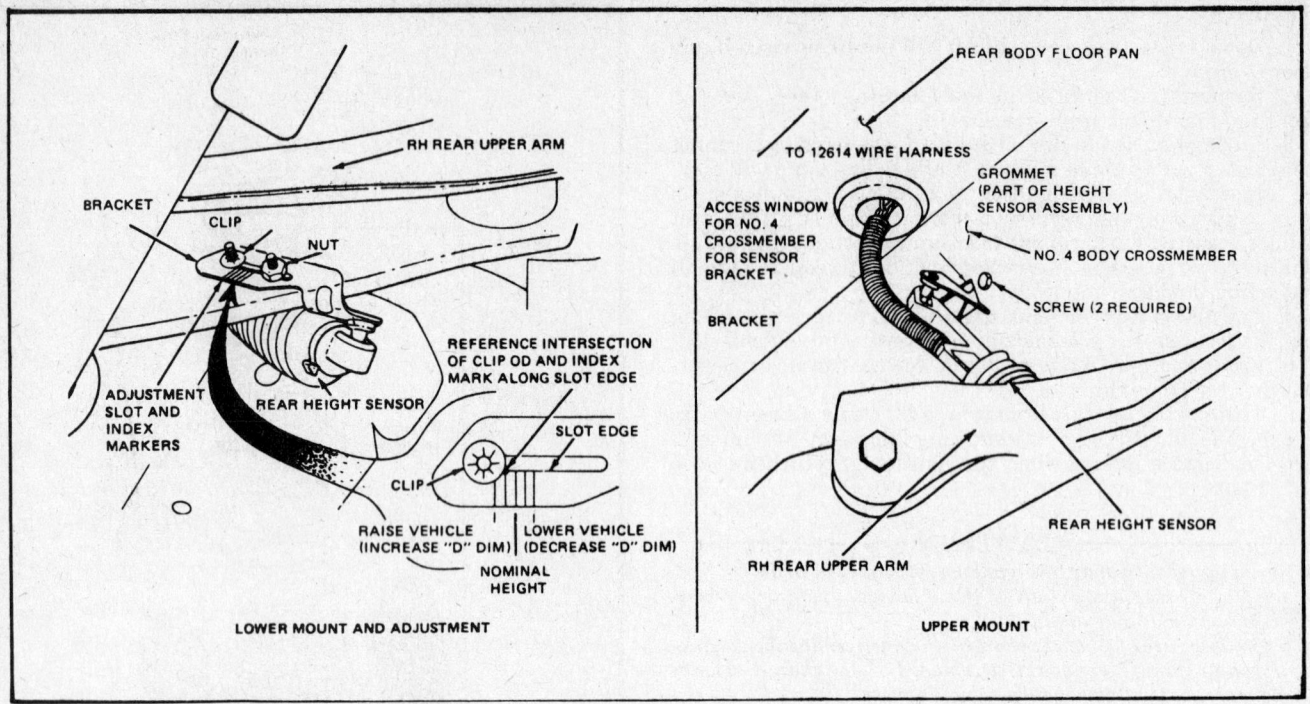

Rear suspension ride height suspension

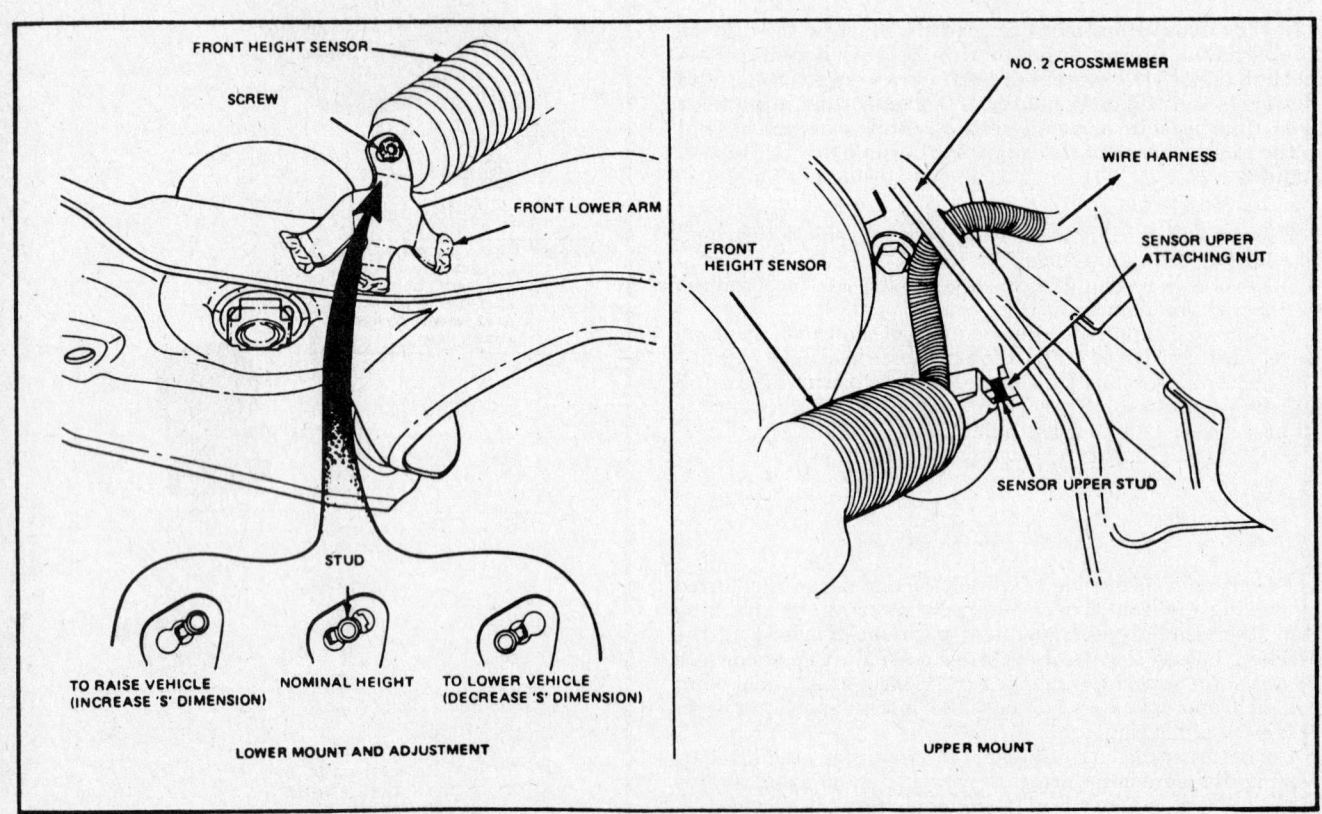

Front suspension ride height adjustment

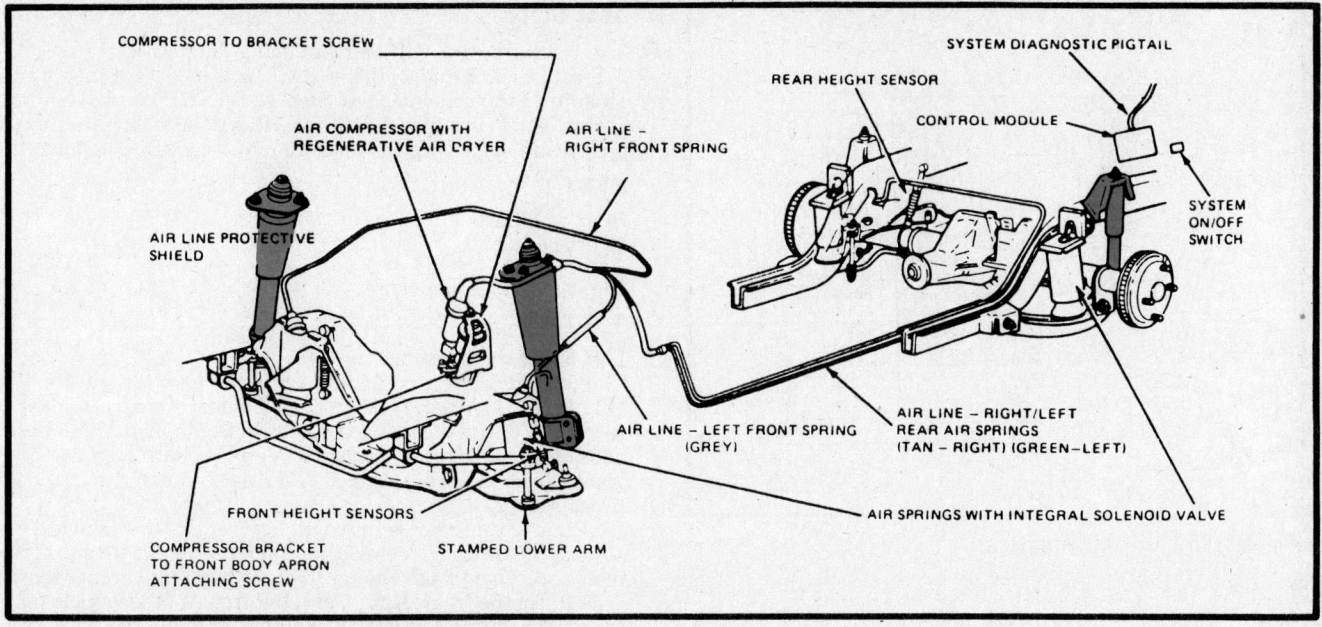

Air spring suspension system—Mark/Continental

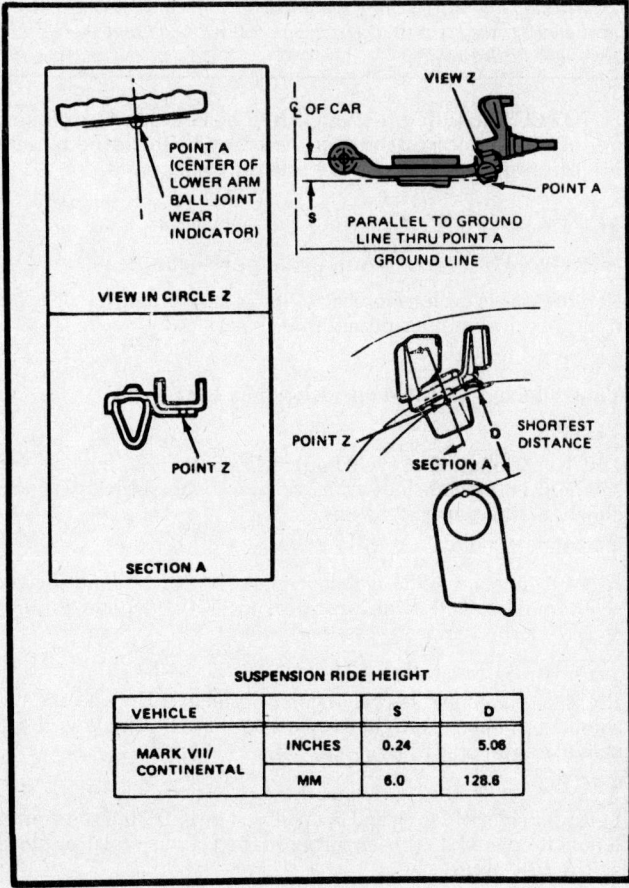

SUSPENSION RIDE HEIGHT			
VEHICLE		S	D
MARK VII/ CONTINENTAL	INCHES	0.24	5.06
	MM	6.0	128.6

Check dimensions "S" and "D"

Troubleshooting

Leak Checks

If the air spring system is suspected of leakage, the standard soap solution check procedure is acceptable.

Warning Lamp (Check Suspension)

The air suspension warning lamp, located in the overhead console, has three main functions.

1. During normal operation with the ignition in the Run position, the lamp glowing continuously indicates a possible air suspension system problem.

2. During diagnostic testing, the lamp blinks at a rate of 1.8 blinks per second to show that diagnostic routine (in the module) has been entered and then blinks the test number that is being run during the test sequence.

3. During the air spring fill routine, the lamp blinks at a rate of one blink every two seconds to show that the air fill routine (in the module) has been entered.

CAUTION

Observation of the warning lamp during normal operation with the ignition switch on, can aid in detecting some system problems.

---

1. On a vehicle operating normally, the warning lamp will glow for approximately one second and then go out when the ignition is turned from the Off to Run position. The lamp does not operate when the ignition is in either the Off or Start position.

2. If the lamp does not go out after turning the ignition from the Off to Run position, it indicates no battery power to the module.

3. If the lamp glows for approximately ½ second, goes out, and then glows continuously after 5–8 seconds, when the ignition is turned from Off to Run position, a height sensor or harness problem is indicated.

4. After the ignition is turned from the Off to Run position, if

571

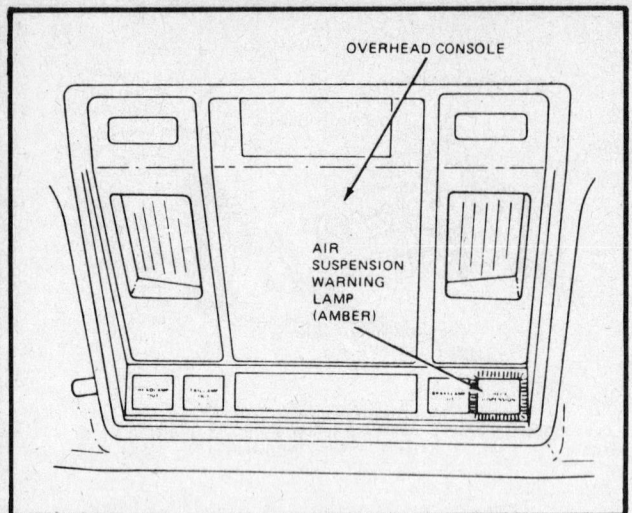

Air suspension warning lamp

the lamp comes on and glows continuously at any time after 8 seconds, a system problem is indicated.

5. Once the warning lamp comes on during an ignition On cycle, it will glow continuously for that ignition On cycle.

6. Erratic operation of the warning lamp (blinking or occasional flashing) during an ignition On cycle indicates a system problem.

DIAGNOSTIC AND AIR FILL INSTRUCTIONS

The control module has the capability of performing either a series of diagnostic tests on the air suspension system or to selectively fill the front and/or rear air springs. Specific instructions for entering diagnostics and test descriptions follow.

Entering Diagnostics

1. Turn On the air suspension switch. The diagnostic pigtail is to be ungrounded.

2. Install battery charger according to manfacturers instruction in order to reduce battery drain.

3. Cycle the ignition from the Off to Run position, hold in the run position for a minimum of five seconds, then return to the Off position. Drivers door is open with all other doors shut.

4. Change the diagnostic pigtail from an ungrounded state to a grounded state by attaching a lead from the diagnostic pigtail to vehicle ground. The pigtail must remain grounded during the spring fill sequence.

5. Turn the ignition switch to the Run position. Do not start the vehicle. The warning lamp will blink continuously at a rate of 1.8 blinks per second to indicate diagnostics has been entered and is ready.

WARNING LAMPS

During diagnostics, the warning lamp continuously blinks either the ready status or the current test number.

DOOR FUNCTION

Each successive transition from door closed to door open will cause the module to advance to the next step in the test sequence.

TERMINATING DIAGNOSTICS

Diagnostics may be terminated and the module returned to normal operational mode at any time by cycling the ignition, actuating the brake or ungrounding the diagnostic pigtail.

Test Steps

The following test will be run during diagnostics.

For tests 1, 2 and 3, PASS/FAIL will be determined by the module at the conclusion of Step A, B or C.

For tests 4 through 10, PASS/FAIL will be determined by the technician observing the operation of a specific component.

TEST 1

Rear Suspension

TEST 2

Right Front Suspension

TEST 3

Left Front Suspension

The following steps occur in each of the first three tests:

1. Raise the (rear, right front, left front) of the vehicle for 15 seconds. Continue raising the vehicle for an additional 15 seconds (30 seconds total) or until a "Vehicle High" signal or an illegal sensor read is received from the (rear, right front, left front) sensor.

2. Lower the (rear, right front, left front) of the vehicle for 30 seconds or until a "Vehicle Low" signal or an illegal sensor read is received from the (rear, right front, left front) sensor.

3. Raise the (rear, right front, left front) of the vehicle for 30 seconds or until a Vehicle Trim signal, or an illegal sensor read is received from the (rear, right front, left front) sensor.

—————————— **CAUTION** ——————————

If the expected signal is not received within the 30 second limit, the test will stop and the warning lamp will turn on continuously. Also, if an illegal sensor read is received, the test will stop and the warning lamp will flash rapidly.

NOTE: The failed test may then be repeated by closing/opening the door or the next test may be initiated by closing/opening the door twice within 15 seconds.

TEST 4

NOTE: Hz (Hertz) = one cycle per second.

Compressor is cycled On/Off at 0.25 Hz. The compressor is limited to cycling a maximum of 50 times.

TEST 5

Vent solenoid is cycled open/closed at 1 Hz.

TEST 6

Left front solenoid is cycled open/closed at 1 Hz. and the vent solenoid is opened. Left front corner of the vehicle will drop slowly as the test progresses.

TEST 7

Right front solenoid is cycled open/closed at 1 Hz. and the vent solenoid is opened. Right front corner of the vehicle will drop slowly as the test progresses.

TEST 8

Right rear solenoid is cycled open/closed at 1 Hz. and the vent solenoid is opened. Right rear corner of the vehicle will drop slowly as the test progresses.

TEST 9

Left rear solenoid is cycled open/closed at 1 Hz. and the vent solenoid is opened. Left rear corner of the vehicle will drop slowly as the test progresses.

TEST 10

Actuating the brake, turning the ignition switch to Off, or disconnecting the diagnostic lead returns the module from diagnostics to the normal operating mode.

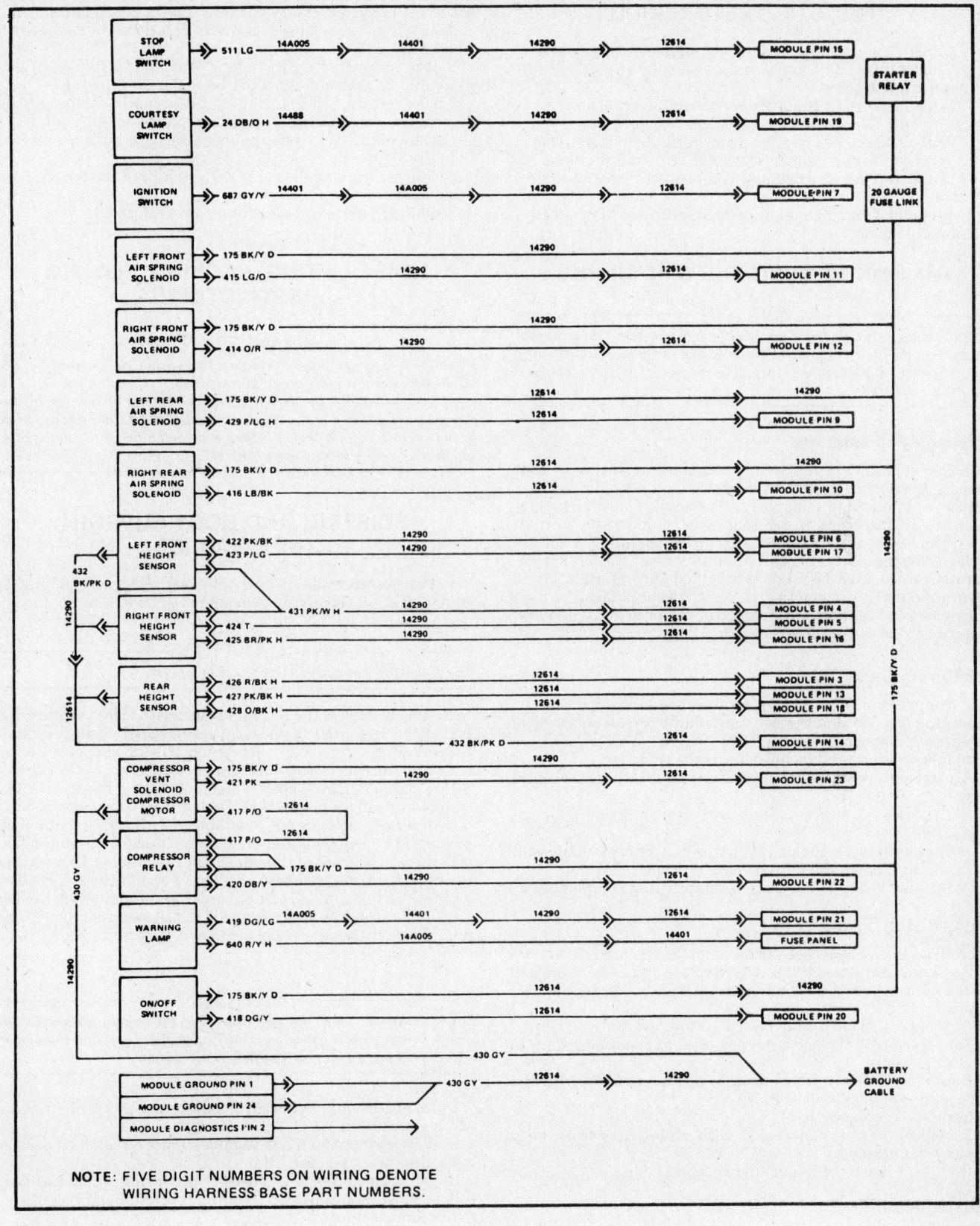

NOTE: FIVE DIGIT NUMBERS ON WIRING DENOTE WIRING HARNESS BASE PART NUMBERS.

Diagnostic tests

DIAGNOSTIC TESTING INDEX

1. Quick Test: Perform system self diagnostic quick test.
2. Pinpoint Test B: Cannot enter/sequence or exit self test diagnostic quick test.
3. Pinpoint Test C: Diagnose sensor related problem.
4. Pinpoint Test D: Diagnose vehicle rear problem.
5. Pinpoint Test E: Diagnose vehicle right front problem.
6. Pinpoint Test F: Diagnose vehicle left front problem.
7. Pinpoint Test G: Diagnose compressor motor electrical problem.
8. Pinpoint Test H: Diagnose compressor vent solenoid electrical problem.

Air Spring System Components

——————————— CAUTION ———————————

Do not remove an air spring under any circumstances when there is pressure in the air spring. Do not remove any components supporting an air spring without either exhausting the air or providing support for the air spring.

———————————————————————————————

Suspension Fasteners

Suspension fasteners are important attaching parts in that they could affect performance of vital components and systems and/or could result in major service expense. They must be replaced with fasteners of the same part number, or with an equivalent part, if replacement becomes necessary. Do not use a replacement part of lesser quality or substitute design. Torque values must be used, as specified, during assembly to assure proper retention of parts. New fasteners must be used whenever old fasteners are loosened or removed and when new component parts are installed.

Air Spring Suspension

Air compressor (less dryer), regenerative dryer, O-rings, mounting bracket and the isolator mounts are all serviced as separate components.

Height sensors and modules are replaceable.

Air springs are replaceable as assemblies (includes solenoid valve).

Air spring solenoid valves and external O-rings are replaceable.

Air lines are replaceable, however, quick connect unions and bulk tubing are available to mend a damaged air line.

Collet and O-ring of the quick connect fitting is replaceable.

Suspension, Front

Gas filled shock absorber struts must be replaced as assemblies. They are not serviceable. Replace only the damaged shock absorber strut. It is not necessary to replace in matched pairs.

Strut upper mounts may be replaced individually.

Air springs are replaced as assemblies. It is not necessary to replace in pairs.

Lower control arm is replaceable as an assembly with the ball joint and bushings included.

Spindle is replaceable.

Stabilizer bar is replaceable with stabilizer bar to body insulators included.

Stabilizer bar to body bushing is replaceable.

Suspension, Rear

The following rear suspension components may be replaced individually:

Gas filled shock absorbers must be replaced as assemblies. They are not servicable. Replace only the damaged shock absorber. It is not necessary to replace in matched pairs.

Air springs are replaced as assemblies. It is not necessary to replace in pairs.

Lower control arms, including both end bushings, are replaceable as assemblies. (Must be replaced in pairs).

Upper control arms, including body end bushings, are replaceable as assemblies. (Must be replaced in pairs).

Upper control arm axle and bushings are replaceable individually. (Must be replaced in pairs).

Stabilizer bar is replaceable with stabilizer bar-to-axle insulator included.

Stabilizer bar-to-body bushings are replaceable.

HOIST LIFTING, JACKING, TOWING RESTRICTIONS

——————————— CAUTION ———————————

The electrical power supply to the air suspension system must be shut off prior to hoisting, jacking or towing an air suspension vehicle. This can be accomplished by disconnecting the battery or turning off the power switch located in the trunk on the left hand side. Failure to do so may result in unexpected inflation or deflation of the air springs which may result in shifting of the vehicle during these operations.

———————————————————————————————

HOISTING AND BODY SUPPORT PROCEDURES

1. Position the vehicle over the hoist and turn the ignition off and shut off the air suspension power switch located in the trunk.

——————————— CAUTION ———————————

The following hoist restriction must be observed.

———————————————————————————————

2. A body hoist is the recommended method for vehicle hoisting. When this hoist is used, raise the vehicle using standard support procedures. The suspension will be supported in rebound by the front struts and rear shock absorbers after the vehicle is lifted. Also support vehicle at four corners with jack stands as a safety precaution. Do not use suspension hoist.

3. If a body hoist is not available, an alternate method approved for vehicle hoisting is to use a standard hydraulic floor jack. Raise the front of the vehicle at the number 2 crossmember until the tires are above the floor. Support the vehicle body with jack stands at each front corner and then lower the floor jack so that the front suspension is in full rebound. Repeat this procedure for the rear suspension except raise the body at the rear jacking location.

——————————— CAUTION ———————————

Power to the air system must be shut off by turning the air suspension switch (in luggage compartment) off or by disconnecting the battery when servicing any air suspension components.

———————————————————————————————

1. Do not attempt to install or inflate any air spring that has become unfolded.
2. Any spring which has unfolded must be refolded prior to installing in a vehicle.
3. Do not attempt to inflate any air spring which has been collasped while uninflated from the rebound hanging position to the jounce stopper.
4. After inflating an air spring in the hanging position, it must be inspected for proper shape.
5. Failure to follow the above procedures may result in a sudden failure of the air spring or suspension system.

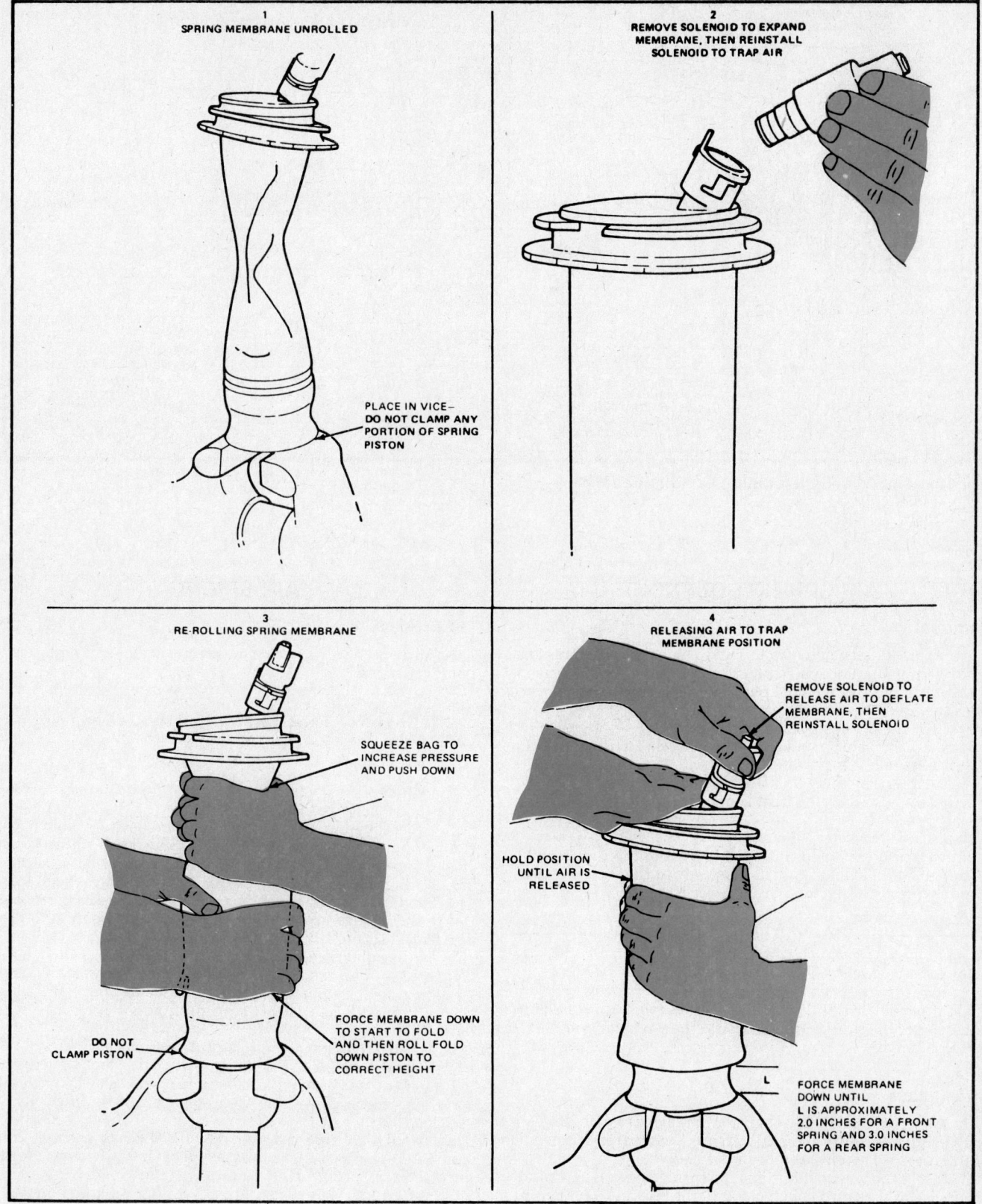

1 SPRING MEMBRANE UNROLLED

PLACE IN VICE—
DO NOT CLAMP ANY
PORTION OF SPRING
PISTON

2 REMOVE SOLENOID TO EXPAND
MEMBRANE, THEN REINSTALL
SOLENOID TO TRAP AIR

3 RE-ROLLING SPRING MEMBRANE

SQUEEZE BAG TO
INCREASE PRESSURE
AND PUSH DOWN

DO NOT
CLAMP PISTON

FORCE MEMBRANE DOWN
TO START TO FOLD
AND THEN ROLL FOLD
DOWN PISTON TO
CORRECT HEIGHT

4 RELEASING AIR TO TRAP
MEMBRANE POSITION

REMOVE SOLENOID TO
RELEASE AIR TO DEFLATE
MEMBRANE, THEN
REINSTALL SOLENOID

HOLD POSITION
UNTIL AIR IS
RELEASED

L

FORCE MEMBRANE
DOWN UNTIL
L IS APPROXIMATELY
2.0 INCHES FOR A FRONT
SPRING AND 3.0 INCHES
FOR A REAR SPRING

Air spring folding procedure

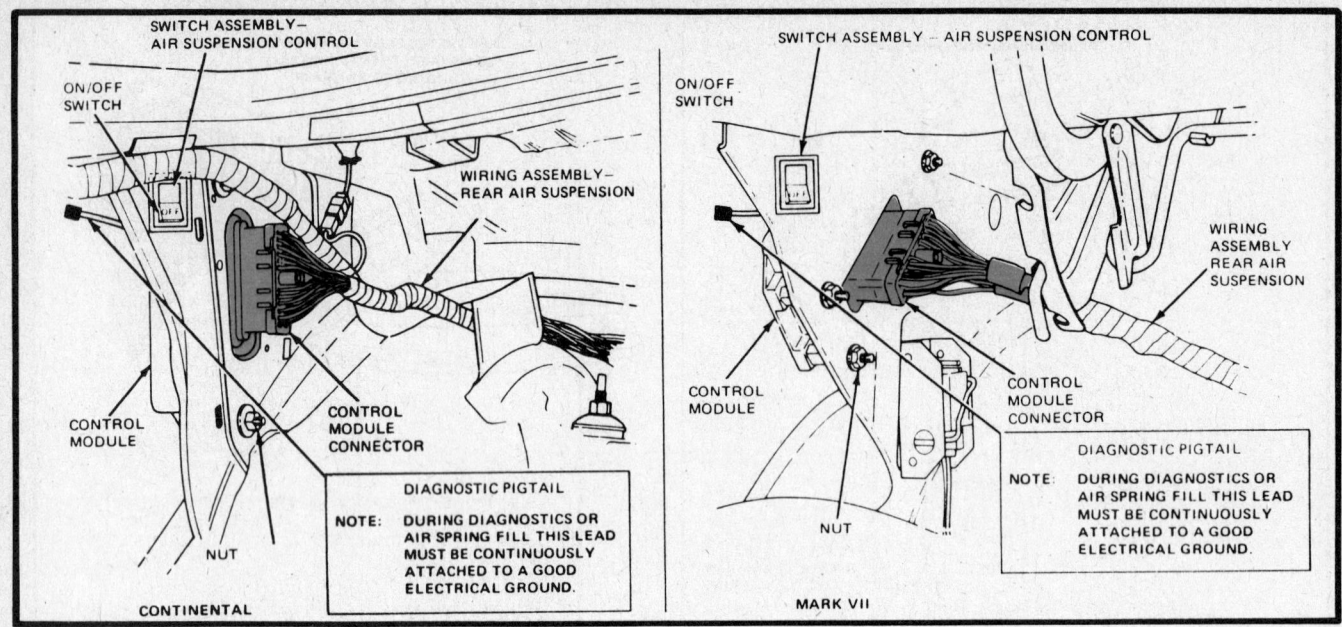

Air suspension switch location Continental/Mark

AIR SPRING SOLENOID

Removal

The air spring solenoid valve has a two stage solenoid pressure relief fitting similar to a radiator cap. A clip is first removed, and rotation of the solenoid out of the spring will release air from the assembly before the solenoid can be removed.

1. Turn the air suspension switch off.
2. Raise the vehicle and support safely. Suspension must be at full rebound.
3. Remove the wheel and tire assembly.
4. Disconnect the electrical connector and then disconnect the air line.
5. Remove the solenoid clip.
6. Rotate the solenoid counterclockwise to the first stop.
7. Pull the solenoid straight outslowly to the second stop to bleed air from the system.

———— CAUTION ————

Do not fully release the solenoid until air is completely bled from the air spring.

8. After the air is fully bled from the system, rotate counterclockwise to the third stop and remove the solenoid from the air spring assembly.

Installation

1. Inspect the solenoid O-ring for abrasions or cuts. Replace the O-ring as required. Lightly grease O-ring area of solenoid with silicone dielectric compound or equivalent.
2. Insert the solenoid into the air spring end cap and rotate clockwise to the third stop, push into the second stop, then rotate clockwise to the first stop.
3. Install the solenoid clip.
4. Connect the air line and the electrical connector.
5. Refile the air spring as outlined below.
6. Install the wheel and tire assembly.

AIR SPRING

Fill Procedure

1. Turn on the air suspension switch. Diagnostic pigtail is to be ungrounded.

NOTE: Lower hoist as required, but do not apply a load to the suspension.

2. Install battery charger according to manufacturers instruction so as to reduce battery drain.
3. Cycle the ignition from the off to run position, hold in the run position for a minimum of five seconds, then return to the off position. Driver's door is open with all other doors shut.
4. Change the diagnostic pigtail from an ungrounded state to a grounded state by attaching a lead from the diagnostic pigtail to the vehicle ground. The pigtail must remain grounded during the spring fill sequence.
5. While applying the brakes, turn the ignition switch to the run position. The door must be open and do not start the vehicle. The warning lamp will blink continuously once every two seconds to indicate the spring pump sequence has been entered.
6. To fill a rear spring(s), close and open the door once. After a six second delay, the rear spring will be filled for 60 seconds.
7. To fill a front spring(s), close and open the door twice. After a six second delay, the front spring will be filled for 60 seconds.
8. To fill front and rear springs, fill the rear springs first. When the rear has finished, close and open the door once to begin the front spring fill.
9. Terminate the air spring fill by turning the ignition switch to off, actuating the brake, or ungrounding the diagnostic pigtail. The diagnostic pigtail must be ungrounded at the end of the spring fill.
10. Lower the hoist completely and start the vehicle. Allow the vehicle to level with the doors closed.

576

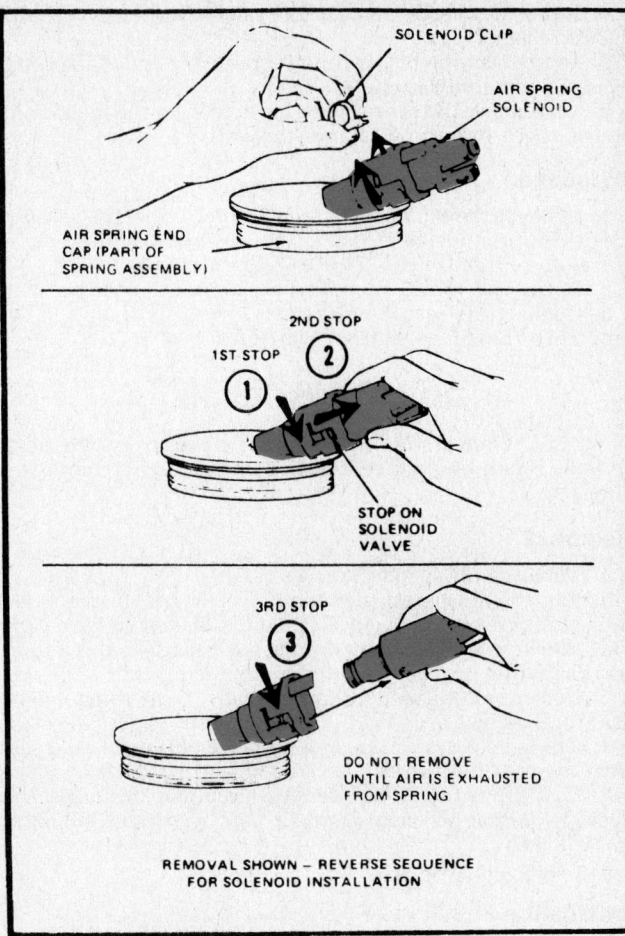

Air spring solenoid removal

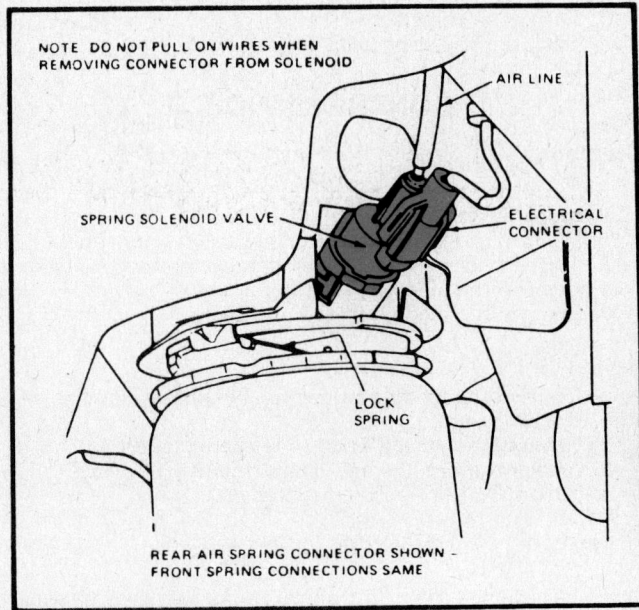

Air spring solenoid connector

AIR SPRING—FRONT OR REAR

Removal

1. Turn the air suspension switch off.
2. Raise the vehicle and support safely. Suspension must be at full rebound.
3. Remove the tire and wheel assembly.
4. Remove the air spring solenoid.
5. Remove the spring to lower arm fasteners. Remove clip for front spring and/or remove bolts for rear spring.
6. Push down on the spring clip on the collar of the air spring and rotate collar counterclockwise to release the spring from the body spring seat.
7. Remove the air spring.

Installation

1. Install air spring solenoid as outlined.
2. Correctly position the solenoid. For LH installation (front or rear spring), the notch on the collar is to be in line with the centerline of the solenoid. For RH installation (front or rear), the flat on the collar is to be in line with the centerline of the solenoid.
3. Install the air spring into the body spring seat, taking care to keep the solenoid air and electrical connections clean and free of damage. Rotate the air spring collar until the spring clip snaps into place. Be sure that the air spring collar is retained by the rolled tabs on the body spring seat.
4. Attach the air line and electrical connector to the solenoid assembly.
5. Align and secure the lower arm to the spring attachment with suspension at full rebound and supported by shock absorbers.

CAUTION

The air springs may be damaged if suspension is allowed to compress before spring is inflated.

6. Replace the tire and wheel assembly.
7. Remove the floor jacks and lower vehicle until the tire and wheel assembly are 1–3 inches above the floor.
8. Refill the air spring(s) as outlined.

AIR COMPRESSOR AND DRYER ASSEMBLY

Removal

1. Turn the air suspension switch off.
2. Tag and disconnect the electrical connector located on the compressor.
3. Remove the air line protector cap from the dryer by releasing the two latching pins located on the bottom of the cap 180 degrees apart.
4. Disconnect the four air lines from the dryer.
5. Remove the screws retaining the air compressor to the mounting bracket.

Installation

1. Position the air compressor and dryer assembly onto the mounting bracket and install the mounting screws.
2. Connect the four air lines into the dryer.
3. Connect the electrical connection.
4. Install the air line protector cap onto the dryer.
5. Turn the air suspension switch on.

DRYER, AIR COMPRESSOR

Removal

1. Turn the air suspension switch off.

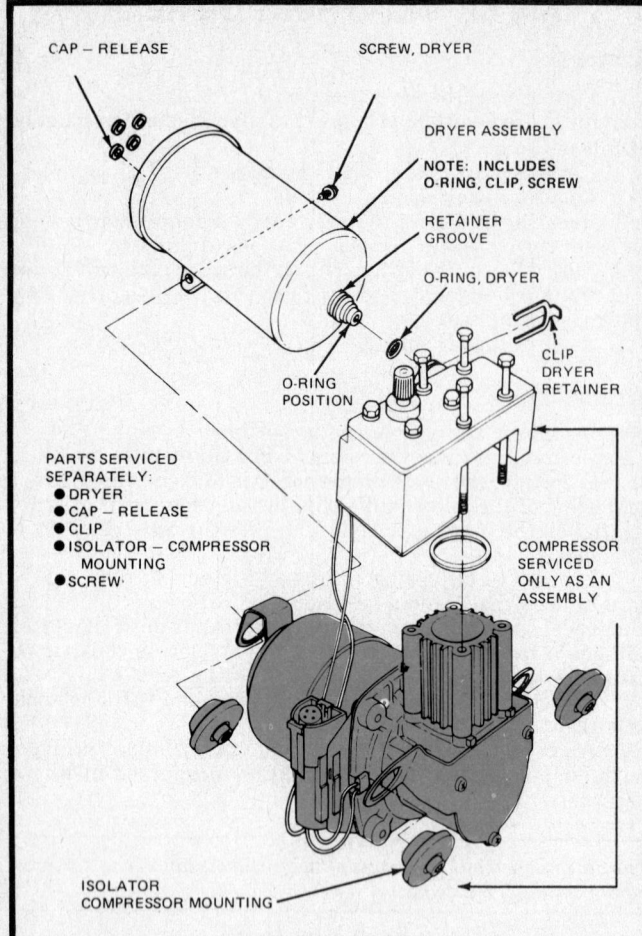

Air compressor and dryer assembly—exploded view

2. Remove the air line protector cap from the dryer by releasing the two latching pins located on the bottom of the cap.
3. Disconnect the four air lines from the dryer.
4. Remove the dryer retaining clip and screw.
5. Remove from the head assembly.

Installation

1. Check to ensure that the old O-ring is not in the head assembly.
2. Check the dryer end to ensure the new O-ring is in its proper position.
3. Insert the dryer into the head assembly and install the retainer clip and screw.
4. Connect the four air lines to the dryer.
5. Install the air line protector cap onto the dryer.
6. Turn the air suspension switch on.

HEIGHT SENSORS—FRONT

Removal

1. Turn the air suspension switch off.
2. Tag and disconnect the sensor electrical connector. The front sensor connectors are located in the engine compartment behind the shock towers.
3. Push the front sensor connector through the access hole in the rear of the shock tower.

4. Raise the vehicle and support safely. Suspension must be at full rebound.
5. Disconnect the bottom and then the top end of the sensor from the attaching stud.
6. Disconnect the sensor wire harness from the plastic clips on the shock tower and remove the sensor.

Installation

1. Connect the top and then the bottom end of the sensor to the attaching studs. Route the sensor electrical connector as required to connect to the vehicle wiring harness.
2. Lower the vehicle.
3. Connect the sensor connector.
4. Turn the air suspension switch on.

HEIGHT SENSOR—REAR

NOTE: When replacing the front air springs, the height sensor must be inspected and replaced if damage is suspected.

Removal

1. Turn the air suspension switch off.
2. Tag and disconnect the sensor electrical connector located in the luggage compartment in front of the forward trim panel. Pull the luggage compartment carpet back for access to the sensor sealing grommet located on the floor pan.
3. Raise the vehicle and support safely. Suspension must be at full rebound.
4. Disconnect the bottom and then the top end of the sensor from the attaching studs.
5. Push upwards on the sealing grommet to unseat then push the sensor through the floor pan hole into the luggage compartment.
6. Lower the vehicle.

Installation

1. Connect the sensor connector and then push the sensor through the floor pan hole being sure to seat the sealing grommet.
2. Replace the luggage compartment carpet.
3. Raise the vehicle and support safely.
4. Connect the top and then the bottom end of the sensor.
5. Lower the vehicle.
6. Turn the air suspension switch on.

CONTROL MODULE

Removal

1. Turn the ignition switch to the off position. Turn the air suspension switch off.
2. Remove the LH luggage compartment trim panel.
3. Tag and disconnect the wiring harness from the module.
4. Remove the module attaching nuts.
5. Remove the module from the vehicle.

Installation

1. Position the module in the vehicle and and secure using the attaching nuts.
2. Connect the wiring harness to the module.
3. Attach the LH luggage compartment trim panel.
4. Turn the air suspension switch on.

NYLON AIR LINE

If a leak is detected in an air line, it can be serviced by carefully cutting the line using a sharp knife to ensure a good, clean, straight cut. Then, install a service fitting.

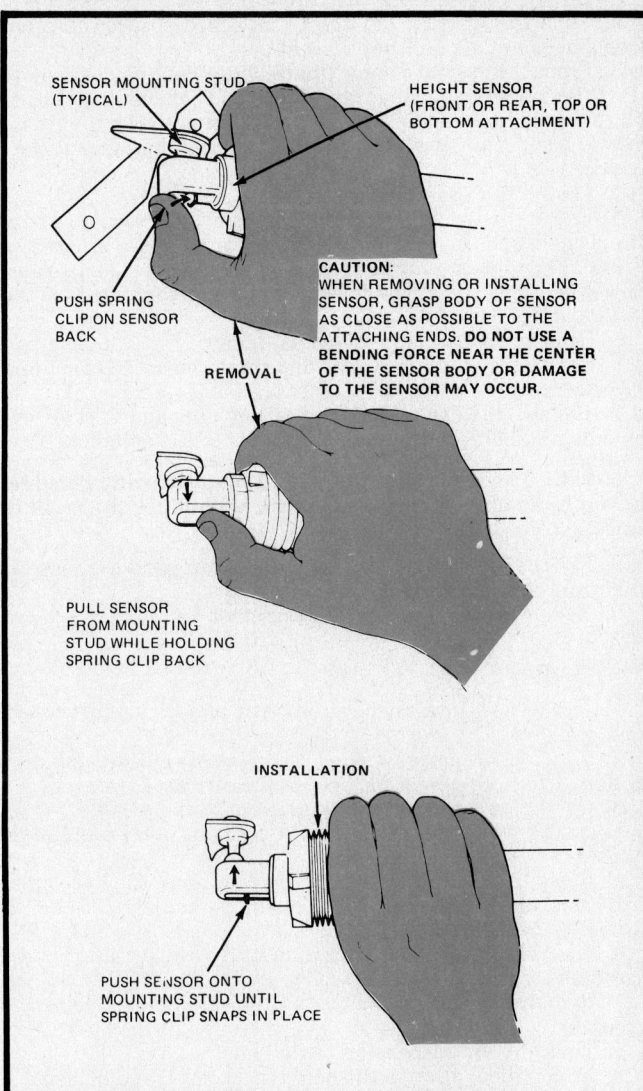

Height sensor—removal and installation

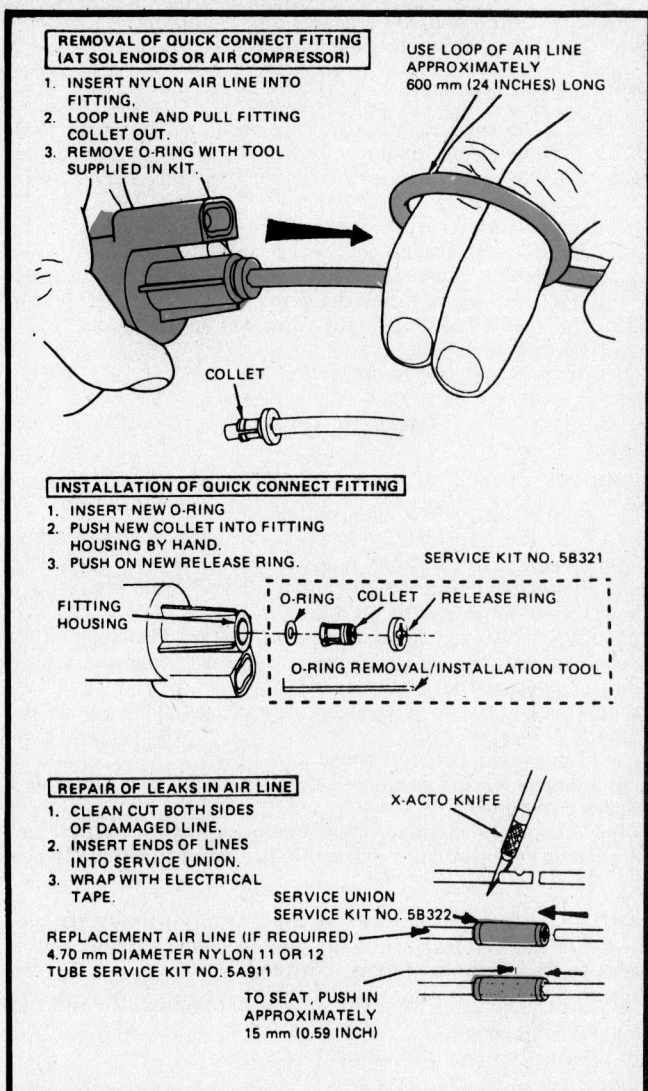

Air line service

QUICK CONNECT FITTINGS

If a leak is detected in any of the quick connect fittings, it can be serviced by using a repair kit containing a new O-ring, collet, release ring and O-ring removal tool. The outer housing of the fitting cannot be serviced.

AIR SUSPENSION SWITCH

Removal and Installation

1. Disconnect the electrical connector.
2. Depress the retaing clips retaining switch to brace, and remove switch.
3. To install; push switch into position in the brace, making sure retaining clips are fully seated.
4. Connect the electrical connector.

COMPRESSOR RELAY

Removal and Installation

1. Disconnect the electrical connector.

2. Remove the screw retaining the relay to the left front shock tower. Remove the relay.
3. Position the relay on the shock tower and install the retaining screw.
4. Connect the electrical connector.

Front Suspension Components

————————— CAUTION —————————
Power to the air system must be shut off by turning the air suspension switch (located in the luggage compartment) off or by disconnecting the battery when servicing any suspension components.
—————————————————————————————

STABILIZER BAR AND/OR BUSHINGS

Removal

1. Turn the air suspension switch off.
2. Raise the vehicle and support safely.
3. Disconnect the stabilazer bar from each link and bushing U-clamps. Remove the stabilizer bar assembly.

4. Remove the adapter brackets and U-clamps.
5. Cut the worn bushings from the stabilizer bars.

Installation

1. Coat the necessary parts of the stabilizer bar with Ford Rubber Suspension Insulator Lubricant, or equivalent, and slide the bushings on the stabilizer bar. Reinstall the U-clamps.
2. Reinstall the adapter brackets on the U-clamps.
3. Using a new nut and bolt, secure each end of the stabilizer bar to the lower suspension arm. Tighten nuts to specification.
4. Using new bolts, clamp the stabilizer bar to the attaching brackets on the side rail. Tighten nuts to specification.
5. Lower the vehicle.
6. Turn the air suspension switch on.

SHOCK STRUT

Removal

1. Turn the air suspension switch off.
2. Turn the ignition key to the unlocked position to allow free movement of the front wheels.
3. From the engine compartment, loosen but do not remove the strut to upper mount attaching nut.
4. Raise the vehicle and support safely. Position safety stands under the lower control arms as far outboard as possible being sure that the lower sensor mounting bracket is clear. Lower hoist until vehicle weight is supported by the lower arms.
5. Remove the tire and wheel assembly.
6. Remove the brake caliper, then rotate out of position and wire securely.
7. Remove the strut to upper mounting attaching nut and then the two lower nuts and bolts attaching the strut to the spindle.

NOTE: The strut should be held firmly during the removal of the last bolt since the gas pressure will cause the strut to fully extend when removed.

8. Lift the strut up from the spindle to compress the rod and then remove the strut.
9. Remove the jounce bumper.

Installation

1. Prime the new strut by extending and compressing the strut rod five times.
2. Install the jounce bumper.
3. Place the strut rod through the upper mount, and hand start and secure a new 16 mm nut.
4. Compress strut, and position onto the spindle.
5. Install two new lower mounting bolts, and hand start nuts.
6. Raise the vehicle to remove vehicle load from the lower control arms, and tighten the lower mounting nuts.
7. Install brake caliper.
8. Install the tire and wheel assembly.
9. Remove the safety stands, and lower the vehicle to the ground.
10. Turn the air suspension switch on.
11. Front wheel alignment should be checked and adjusted if necessary.

UPPER MOUNT ASSEMBLY

Removal

NOTE: Upper mounts are one piece units and cannot be disassembled.

1. Turn the air suspension switch off.

2. Turn the ignition key to the unlocked position to allow free movement of the front wheels.
3. From the engine compartment, loosen but do not remove the three upper mounting retaining nuts. Vehicle should be in place over a hoist and must not be driven with these nuts removed. Do not remove the pop rivet holding the camber plate in position.
4. Loosen the strut rod nut at this time.
5. Raise the vehicle and support safely. Position safety stands under the lower control arms as far outboard as possible being sure that the lower sensor mounting bracket is clear. Lower the hoist until the vehicle weight is supported by the lower control arms.
6. Remove the tire and wheel assembly.
7. Remove the brake caliper and rotate out of position and wire securely.
8. Remove the upper mount retaining nuts and the two lower nuts and bolts that attach the struts to the spindles.

NOTE: The strut should be held firmly during removal of the bolts since the gas pressure will cause the strut to fully extend when removed.

9. Lift the strut up from the spindle to compress the rod, and then remove the strut.
10. Remove the upper mount from strut.

Installation

1. Install new upper mount on strut and hand start a new nut.
2. Position the upper mount studs into the body and start and secure three new nuts. Secure the strut rod nut.
3. Compress the strut and position onto the spindle.
4. Install two new lower mounting bolts, and hand start nuts.
5. Raise the vehicle to remove the load from the lower control arms, and tighten the lower mounting nuts to 126–179 ft. lbs. (170–244 Nm).
6. Install the brake caliper. Install the tire and wheel assembly.
7. Remove the safety stands, and lower the vehicle to the ground.
8. Turn the air suspension switch on.
9. Front wheel alignment should be checked and adjusted if necessary.

SPINDLE ASSEMBLY

Removal

1. Turn the air suspension switch off.
2. Raise the vehicle and support safely.
3. Remove the wheel and tire assembly.
4. Remove the brake caliper, rotor and dust shield.
5. Remove the stabilizer link from the lower control arm assembly.
6. Remove the tie rod end from the spindle.
7. Remove the cotter pin from the ball joint stud nut, and loosen the ball joint nut one or two turns.

——————— CAUTION ———————
DO NOT remove the nut from the ball joint stud at this time.
——————————————————————————

8. Tap the spindle boss to relieve the stud pressure.
9. Place a floor jack under the lower arm, compress the air spring and remove the stud nut.
10. Remove the bolts and nuts attaching the spindle to the shock strut. Compress the shock strut until working clearance is obtained.
11. Remove the spindle assembly.

Installation

1. Place the spindle on the ball joint stud, and install a new stud nut. DO NOT tighten at this time.
2. Lower the shock strut until the attaching holes are in line with the holes in the spindle. Install two new bolts and nuts.
3. Tighten the ball joint stud nut and install cotter pin.
4. Lower the floor jack from under the suspension arm, and remove jack.
5. Tighten the shock strut to spindle attaching nuts.
6. Install the stabilizer bar link and tighten attaching nut.
7. Attach the tie rod end, and tighten the retaining nut.
8. Install the brake dust shield, rotor and caliper.
9. Install the tire and wheel assembly.
10. Remove the safety stands. Lower the vehicle.
11. Turn the air suspension switch on.
12. Front wheel alignment should be checked and adjusted if necessary.

SUSPENSION CONTROL ARM

Removal

1. Turn the air suspension switch off.
2. Raise the vehicle and support safely, so the control arms hang free (full rebound).
3. Remove the wheel and tire assembly.
4. Disconnect the tie rod assembly from the steering spindle.
5. Remove the steering gear bolts, if necessary, and position the gear so that the suspension arm bolt may be removed.
6. Disconnect the stabilizer bar link from the lower arm.
7. Disconnect the lower end of the height sensor from the lower control arm sensor mounting stud. Remove sensor mounting stud and screw from lower arm, noting the position of the stud on the lower arm bracket.
8. Remove the cotter pin from the ball joint stud nut, and loosen the ball joint nut one or two turns. DO NOT remove the nut at this time. Tap the spindle boss to relieve stud pressure.
9. Vent air springs to atmospheric pressure. Refer to air spring solenoid removal. Then reinstall solenoid. Refer to air spring solenoid installation.
10. Remove air spring to lower arm fastening clip.
11. Remove the ball joint nut, and raise the entire strut and spindle assembly (strut, rotor, caliper and spindle). Wire it out of the way in order to gain working room.
12. Remove the suspension arm to crossmember nuts and bolts. Remove the arm from the spindle.

Installation

1. Position the arm into the crossmember and install new arm to crossmember bolts and nuts. DO NOT tighten at this time.
2. Remove the wire from the strut and spindle assembly and attach to the ball joint stud. Install a new ball joint stud nut. DO NOT tighten at this time.
3. Position air springs in the arm and install new fasteners.
4. Attach sensor mounting stud and screw to lower arm in the same position as on the replaced arm. Connect lower end of sensor to lower arm mounting stud.
5. With a suitable jack, raise the suspension arm to curb height.
6. With the jack still in place, tighten the lower arm to crossmember attaching nut to 150–180 ft. lbs. (203–244 Nm).
7. Tighten the ball joint stud nut to 100–120 ft. lbs. (136–163 Nm) and install a new cotter pin. Remove the jack.
8. Install the steering gear to crossmember bolts and nuts (if removed). Hold the bolts and tighten nuts to 90–100 ft. lbs. (122–135 Nm).
9. Position the tie rod assembly into the steering spindle, and install the retaining nut. Tighten the nut to 35 ft. lbs. (47 Nm), and continue tightening the nut to align the next

castellation with cotter pin hole in the stud. Install a new cotter pin.
10. Connect the stabilizer bar link to the lower suspension arm, and tighten the attaching nut to 9–12 ft. lbs. (12–16 Nm).
11. Install the wheel and tire assembly, and lower the vehicle but DO NOT allow tires to touch the ground.
12. Turn the air suspension switch on.
13. Refill the air spring(s) as outlined.
14. Front wheel alignment should be checked and adjusted if necessary.

Rear Suspension Components

─────────────── CAUTION ───────────────
Power to the air system must be shut off by turning the air suspension switch (located in the luggage compartment) off or by disconnecting the battery when servicing any suspension components.
──

SHOCK ABSORBER

Removal

1. Turn the air suspension switch off.
2. Open the luggage compartment and remove the inside trim panels to gain access to the upper shock stud.
3. Loosen but DO NOT remove the shock rod attaching nut.
4. Raise the vehicle and support safely. Position two safety stands under the rear axle. Lower the hoist until the vehicle weight is supported by the rear axle.
5. Remove the upper attaching nut, washer and insulator and then remove the shock protective cover (right shock only) and lower shock absorber cross bolt and nut from the lower shock brackets.
6. From under the vehicle, compress the shock absorber to clear it from the hold in the upper shock tower.

─────────────── CAUTION ───────────────
Shock absorbers will extend unassisted. Do not apply heat or flame to the shock absorber tube during removal.
──

7. Remove the shock absorber from the vehicle.

Installation

1. Prime the new shock absorber by extending and compressing the shock absorber five times.
2. Place the inner washer and insulator on the upper attaching stud. Position stud through the shock tower mounting hole and position an insulator, washer on stud from the luggage compartment. Hand start the attaching nut and secure.
3. Place shock absorbers lower mounting eye between the ears of the lower shock mounting bracket, compressing the shock as required. Insert the bolt, (bolt head must seat on the inboard side of the shock bracket), through the shock bracket and the shock absorber mounting eye. Hand start and then secure the original attaching nut.
4. Install the protective cover, to the RH shock absorber. This is done by inserting the bolt point and nut into the covers open end, sliding the cover over the bolt head. Properly installed, the cover will conceal the bolt point, nut and bolt head. The rounded or closed end of the cover should be pointing inboard.
5. Raise the vehicle and remove the safety stands from under the axle, then lower the vehicle.
6. Reinstall the inside trim panels.
7. Turn the air suspension switch on.

LOWER CONTROL ARM

Removal

NOTE: If one arm arm requires replacement, replace the other arm also.

1. Turn the air suspension switch off.
2. Raise the vehicle and support safely. Suspension will be at full rebound.
3. Remove the wheel and tire assembly.
4. Vent air spring(s) at atmospheric pressure. Refer to air spring solenoid removal. Then reinstall the solenoid. Refer to air spring solenoid installation.
5. Remove the two air spring-to-lower arm bolts and remove the air spring from the lower arm.
6. Remove the frame-to-arm and the axle-to-arm bolts and remove the arm from the vehicle.

Installation

1. Position the lower arm assembly into the front arm brackets, and insert a new arm-to-frame pivot bolt and nut with the nut facing outwards. DO NOT tighten at this time.
2. Position the rear bushing in the axle bracket and install a new arm-to-axle pivot bolt and nut with the nut facing outwards. DO NOT tighten at this time.
3. Install two new air spring-to-arm bolts. DO NOT tighten at this time.
4. Using a suitable jack, raise the axle to curb height. Tighten the lower arm front bolt, the rear pivot bolt and the air spring to arm bolt being sure that the air spring piston is flat on the lower arm. Remove the jack.
5. Replace the wheel and tire assembly.
6. Lower the vehicle.
7. Turn the air suspension switch on.
8. Refill the air springs as outlined.

UPPER CONTROL ARM AND AXLE BUSHING

Removal

NOTE: If one arm requires replacement, replace the other arm also.

1. Turn the air suspension switch off.
2. Raise the vehicle and support safely. Suspension will be at full rebound.
3. On the RH side, detach the rear height sensor from the side arm. Note position of the sensor adjustment bracket on the upper arm.
4. Remove the upper arm-to-axle pivot bolt and nut.
5. Remove upper arm-to-frame pivot bolt and nut. Remove the upper arm from the vehicle.

─────────── **CAUTION** ───────────

If upper arm axle bushing is to be replaced, use the following procedure.

6. Place the upper arm axle bushing remover tool in position, and remove the bushing assembly.
7. Using the installer tool, install the bushing assembly into the bushing ear of the rear axle.

Installation

1. Place the upper arm into the bracket of the body side rail. Insert a new upper arm-to-frame pivot bolt and nut (nut facing outboard) DO NOT tighten at this time.
2. Align the upper arm-to-axle pivot hole with the hole in the axle bushing. If required, raise the axle using a suitable jack to align. Install a new pivot bolt and nut (nut inboard) DO NOT tighten at this time.

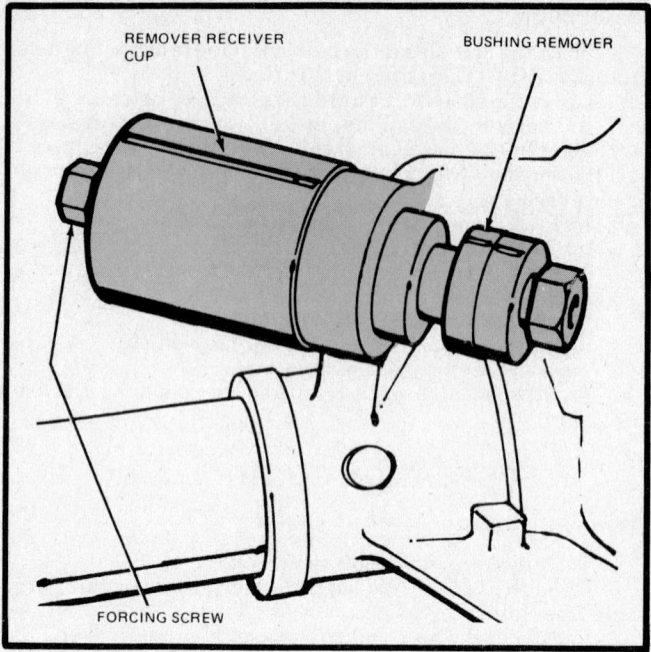

Bushing removal

3. On the RH side, reattach the rear height sensor to the arm. Set the adjustment bracket to the same position as on the replaced arm and tighten nut.
4. Using a suitable jack, raise the axle to curb height, and tighten the front upper arm bolt, and the rear upper arm bolt.
5. Lower the vehicle.
6. Turn the air suspension switch on.

STABILIZER BAR BUSHINGS

Removal

1. Turn the air suspension switch off.

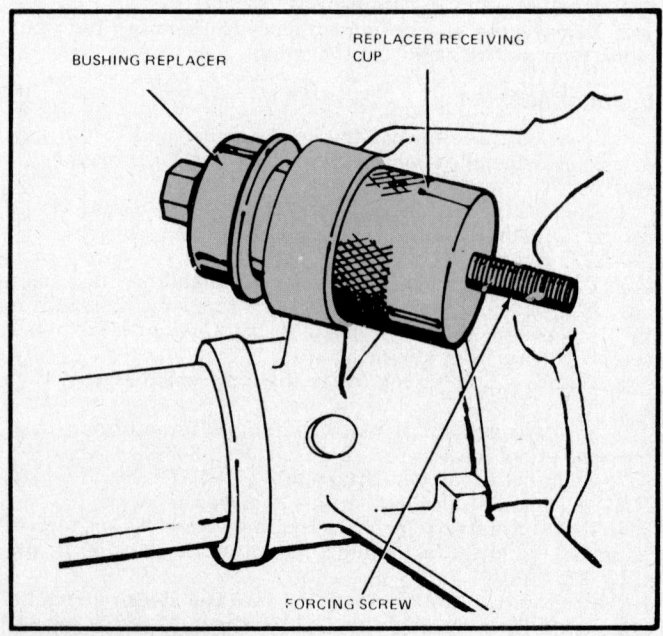

Bushing installation

AIR SUSPENSION BOLT TORQUE SPECIFICATIONS

Front Suspension—Description	Nm	ft. lbs.
Lower arm to No. 2 crossmember—nut	203-244	150-180
Stabilizer bar mounting clamp to bracket—bolt	27-34	20-25
Stabilizer bar to lower arm—nut	12-16	9-12
Spindle to shock strut—nut	203-244	150-180
Shock strut to upper mount—nut	75-125	55-92
Ball joint to spindle—nut	136-163	100-120
Shock upper mount to body—nut	84-102	62-75
Steering gear to No. 2 crossmember—nut	122-136	90-100
Tie rod end to spindle—nut	47-64	35-47
Compressor bracket to frame—bolt	3-5	30-40*
Air compressor to compressor bracket—bolt	3-5	30-40*
Sensor upper attachment to frame—nut	35-46	26-34
Sensor lower attachment to arm—bolt	10-16	8-12

Rear Suspension—Description	Nm	Ft. Lbs.
Shock absorber to frame—nut	26-37	17-27
Upper arm to frame—bolt	135-142	100-105
Upper arm to axle—bolt	122-135	90-100
Lower arm to frame—bolt	135-142	100-105
Lower arm to axle—bolt	122-135	90-100
Shock absorber to clevis bracket bolt	61-81	45-60
Clevis bracket to axle—nut	75-90	55-70
Stabilizer bar to axle—bolt	41-48	30-35
Stabilizer bar to body—nut	17-24	13-18
Air spring to lower arm—bolt	41-48	30-35
Sensor upper bracket to frame—bolt	12-17	110-150*
Sensor lower bracket to arm—nut	8-14	7-10

2. Raise the vehicle and support safely.

3. Disconnect the stabilizer bar from each link and bushing U-clamp. Remove the stabilizer bar assembly.

4. Remove the U-clamps

5. Cut the worn bushings from the stabilizer bar.

Installation

1. Coat the necessary parts of the stabilizer bar with Ford Rubber Suspension Insulator Lubricant or equivalent and slide the new bushings onto the stabilizer bar. Reinstall the U-clamps.

2. Using new bolts and nuts, attach the stabilizer bar to the axle. DO NOT tighten bolts at this time.

3. Using new bolts and nuts, attach the link end of the stabilizer bar to the body. Tighten the link attaching nut and then the axle attaching bolts.

4. Lower vehicle.

5. Turn the air suspension switch on.

GENERAL MOTORS ELECTRONIC LEVEL CONTROL

General Information

The Electronic Level Control (ELC) system automatically adjusts the rear height of the vehicle depending on the vehicle load. The system consists of a compressor assembly, air dryer, exhaust solenoid, compressor relay, height sensor, air adjustable struts, wiring, air tubing and pressure limiter.

System Components

COMPRESSOR

The compressor assembly is a positive displacement rocking piston air pump powered by a 12 volt DC permanent magnet motor. The compressor head casting contains intake and exhaust valves. A solenoid operated exhaust valve, which releases air from the system when energized, is also contained within the compresser assembly. In most applications, the compressor is located on the left side of the engine compartment.

AIR DRYER

The air dryer is attached externally to the compressor output and provides a dual function:

1. It is filled with a dry chemical that absorbs moisture from the atmosphere before it is delivered to the struts and returns the moisture to the atmosphere when it is being exhausted.

2. The air dryer also contains a valving arrangement that maintains 7–14 pounds minimum air pressure in the struts.

EXHAUST SOLENOID

The exhaust solenoid is located in the compressor head assembly and provides a dual function:

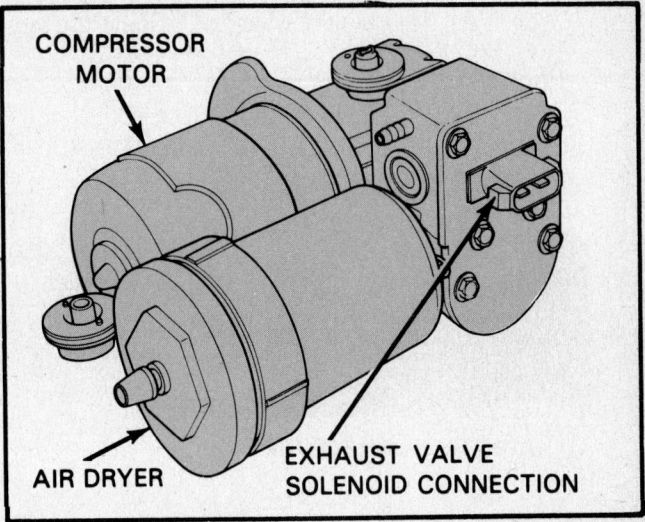

Compressor assembly

1. It exhausts air from the system when energized. The height sensor controls this function.

2. It acts as a blow-off valve to limit maximum pressure output of the compressor.

COMPRESSOR RELAY

The relay, located in the relay panel under the instrument panel, completes the 12 volt circuit to the compressor motor and dash light when energized. The height sensor controls this function. A dual contact relay is used to provide increased system reliability.

HEIGHT SENSOR

The height sensor is an electronic device that controls two basic circuits:

1. Compressor relay coil and indicator light ground circuit.
2. Exhaust solenoid coil ground circuit.

—— CAUTION ——

To prevent falsely actuating the compressor relay or exhaust solenoid circuits during normal ride motions, the sensor circuitry provides a 13–27 second delay before ground is completed to either circuit.

In addition, the sensor electronically limits compressor run time to a maximum of 5 minutes. This time limit function is necessary to prevent continuous compressor operation in the event of a system leak or continuous exhaust solenoid operation.

NOTE: Turning the ignition "on and off" resets the electronic timer circuit to restart the 5 minute maximum run time.

—— CAUTION ——

The ignition must be cycles on to reset the initial timer. The electronic timer circuit is also reset for each change in the exhaust and compressor signal from the height sensor with the ignition on.

The height sensor is mounted to the body sub-frame in the rear with the sensor actuating arm attached to the rear control arm by a short link.

AIR ADJUSTABLE STRUTS

The air adjustable strut is basically an air adjustable strut enclosed in an air chamber. The struts are constructed with a rubber like sleeve attached to the dust tube and strut reservoir. This creates a flexible chamber which will extend the strut

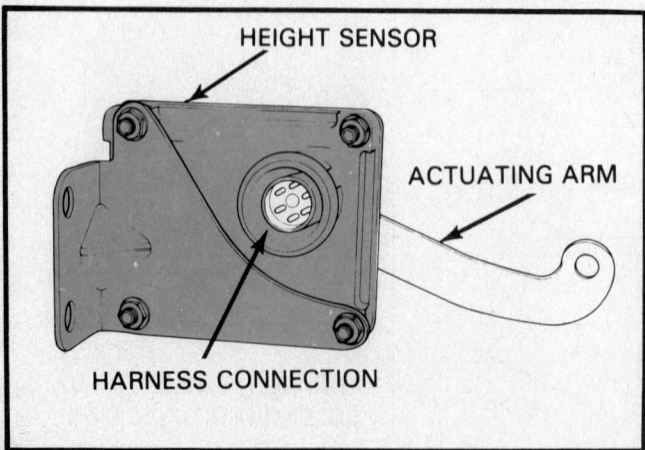

Height sensor—typical

when air pressure in the chamber is increased. When air pressure is reduced, the weight of the vehicle collapses the strut. A minimum air pressure of 7–14 pounds must be maintained at all times.

AIR LINES AND FITTINGS

NOTE: While the lines are flexible for easy routing and handling, care should be taken not to kink them and to keep them from coming in contact with the exhaust system.

Flexible air lines of $\frac{1}{8}$ inch diameter tubing are used throughout the system. A snap on connector is used to attach the air line tubing to the struts, compressor air dryer, and intermediate connector. The connector housing has a retainer spring which snaps into a groove in the fitting, locking the air line into position. All air line fittings are sealed with two "O" rings.

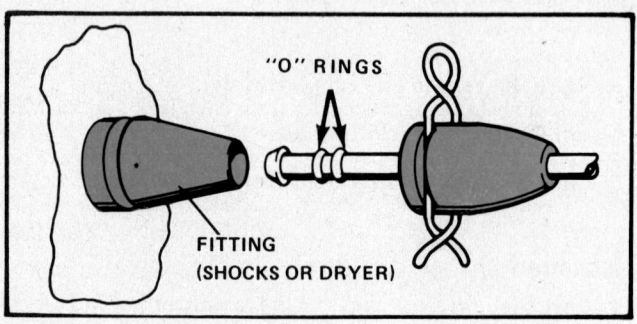

Air line connection

PRESSURE LIMITER VALVE

To insure optimum handling and ride qualities, a pressure limiter valve is used in the system. The valve is located in the engine compartment. In most applications it is in the pressure line which runs from the compressor to the rear of the vehicle and is mounted to the compressor mounting bracket. This limiter valve restricts maximum pressure to the rear struts to 67–74 psi.

SYSTEM OPERATION

Raising the Vehicle

When a load is added to the vehicle, the vehicle body is forced downward causing the height sensor actuating arm to rotate upward. This action causes the internal timing circuit to activate. After an initial time delay of 13–27 seconds, the sensor completes the compressor relay circuit to ground. With the relay energized, the 12 volt circuit to the compressor is complete and the compressor runs sending air to the adjustable struts through the plastic tubing.

As the air struts inflate, the vehicle body moves upward, rotating the height sensor actuating arm back towards its original position before the added carrying weight. Once the body reaches its original height ($\pm$ 1"), the sensor opens the compressor relay circuit and shuts off the compressor.

Lowering the Vehicle

When the load is removed from the rear of the vehicle, the body is forced upward causing the height sensor actuating arm to rotate downward. The downward rotation of the actuating arm causes the internal timing circuit to activate. After an initial delay of 13–27 seconds, the sensor completes the exhaust solenoid circuit to ground. With the exhaust solenoid energized, air begins exhausting out of the shocks back through the air dryer and exhaust solenoid valve into the atmosphere.

As the vehicle body lowers, the height sensor actuating arm is rotated toward its original position. When the vehicle body reaches its original height (± 1″), the sensor opens the exhaust solenoid circuit. This stops air from further escaping.

A minimum air pressure of 14–20 psi is maintained in the struts by the air dryer retention valve. The minimum pressure provides improved ride characteristics when the vehicle is lightly loaded.

Troubleshooting

HEIGHT SENSOR

Performance Test

1. Cycle the ignition off and then on. This will reset the height sensor timing circuit. Move the shift lever from Park to Reverse to Park again with the ignition on in order to reset the internal timer.
2. Raise the vehicle and support safely. Be sure the rear wheels or control arms are supported as close as possible to trim height dimension.
3. Inspect the wiring for secure connection to height sensor and harness ground.
4. Disconnect the link from the height sensor arm.
5. Move the sensor arm up. There should be a 13–27 second delay before the compressor turns on and the shocks begin to inflate. As soon as the shock absorber air boots fill noticeably, stop the compressor by moving the compressor arm down.
6. Move the sensor arm down below position where the compressor stopped. There should be a 13–27 second delay before the struts start to deflate and the vehicle lowers.

HEIGHT SENSOR

Adjustment

NOTE: The attaching link must be securely connected to the sensor actuating arm before any adjustments are made to the vehicle.

1. Loosen the lock nut that secures the metal arm to the plastic sensor arm.
2. To raise the vehicle trim height, move the plastic arm towards the top of the slot and retighten the locknut.
3. To lower the vehicle trim height, move the plastic arm to the bottom of the slot and retighten the lock nut.

COMPRESSOR

Performance Test

1. Tag and disconnect the wiring from the compressor motor and exhaust solenoid terminals.
2. Disconnect the existing pressure line from the dryer and attach pressure gauge J22124–A or equivalent to dryer fitting.
3. Connect a 12 volt (+) power supply to the compressor through an ammeter and note the following:
   a. Current draw should not exceed 14 amps.
   b. When the gauge reads approximately 100 psi minimum, shut off the compressor and observe if pressure is maintained or whether it leaks down.
   c. If the compressor is permitted to run until it reaches its maximum output pressure, the solenoid exhaust valve will act as a pressure relief valve. The resulting leak down when compressor is shut off will indicate a false leak.
4. If the compressor fails to meet these specifications, refer to the Compressor/Dryer Diagnosis Chart.

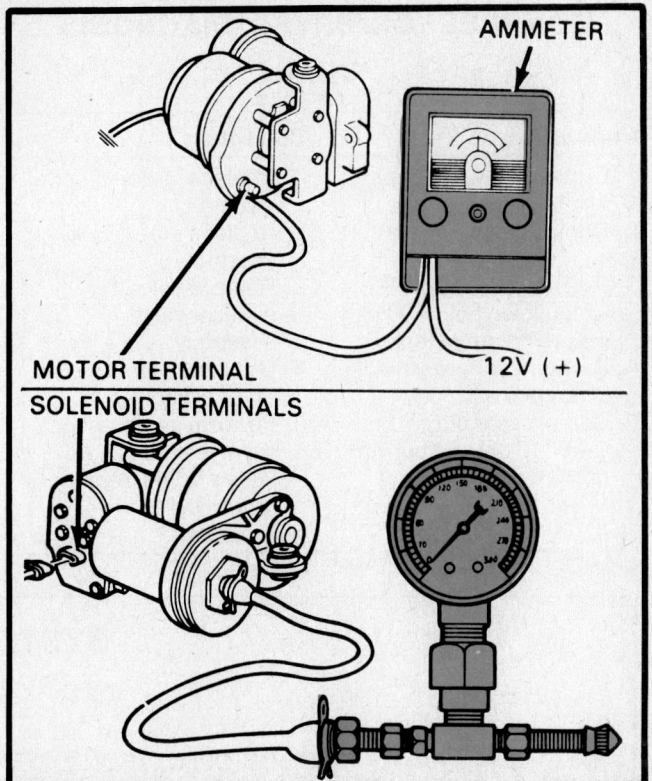

Compressor test connections

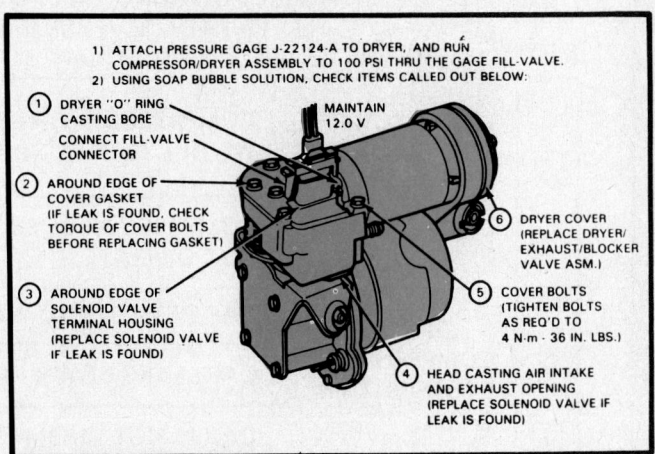

1) ATTACH PRESSURE GAGE J-22124-A TO DRYER, AND RUN COMPRESSOR/DRYER ASSEMBLY TO 100 PSI THRU THE GAGE FILL-VALVE.
2) USING SOAP BUBBLE SOLUTION, CHECK ITEMS CALLED OUT BELOW:

① DRYER "O" RING CASTING BORE
CONNECT FILL-VALVE CONNECTOR

② AROUND EDGE OF COVER GASKET (IF LEAK IS FOUND, CHECK TORQUE OF COVER BOLTS BEFORE REPLACING GASKET)

③ AROUND EDGE OF SOLENOID VALVE TERMINAL HOUSING (REPLACE SOLENOID VALVE IF LEAK IS FOUND)

MAINTAIN 12.0 V

⑥ DRYER COVER (REPLACE DRYER/EXHAUST/BLOCKER VALVE ASM.)

⑤ COVER BOLTS (TIGHTEN BOLTS AS REQ'D TO 4 N·m - 36 IN. LBS.)

④ HEAD CASTING AIR INTAKE AND EXHAUST OPENING (REPLACE SOLENOID VALVE IF LEAK IS FOUND)

Compressor leak test

5. If system checks ok, reconnect all wiring and air line connections.

ELC SYSTEM

Performance Leak Test

1. Attach a pressure gauge between the dryer assembly and the system air line with the shut off valve on the compressor side of the gauge.
2. With the shut off valve open (up), apply air pressure through the service valve on the gauge until the gauge reads 100–120 psi.
3. If a leak is indicated, close the shut off valve (down) and

COMPRESSOR/DRYER DIAGNOSIS CHART

Malfunction	Correction
1. Current draw exceeds 14 amps.	1. Replace motor cylinder assembly.
2. Compressor Inoperative.	2. Replace motor cylinder assembly.
3. Pressure build up OK but leaks down below 90 psi before holding steady.	3. Replace solenoid exhaust valve assembly.
4. Compressor pressure leaks down to 0 psi.	4. Leak test compressor/ dryer assembly.
5. Compressor output less than 110 psi and current draw normal.	5. Perform compressor/ dryer leak test. If no leak is found, replace motor/cylinder assembly.

continue to observe for pressure drop. This action will isolate the compressor from the rest of the system.

4. If the gauge pressure continues to drop, the leak is external to the compressor. Leak test all connections using soap and water.

5. If the gauge pressure does not drop any further, the leak is internal to the compressor.

6. If pressure builds up rapidly, but the vehicle does not raise, inspect the system for pinched pressure lines and/or stuck shocks.

Component Replacement

HEIGHT SENSOR

An oval connector lock is included at the wiring connector to the height control sensor.

If harness disconnection is required, squeeze the oval sides of the connector lock to release the two locking tabs and pull the harness connector from the height sensor plug.

To insure proper circuit connections, the height sensor plug has an indexing slot and a matching boss is molded into the

---

SYSTEM CHECK
INITIAL CONDITIONS

- HOOD OPEN, TRUNK OPEN AND UNLOADED, IGNITION OFF
- CHECK HEIGHT AT REAR WHEELHOUSE OPENING
- IGNITION ON, ENGINE STOPPED
- RESET RUNNING TIME. WITH IGNITION ON, CYCLE SHIFT LEVER PARK-REVERSE-PARK

STEP				NEXT STEP
1	SET INITIAL CONDITIONS. ADD 300 LBS. LOAD TO TRUNK	COMPRESSOR STARTS WITHIN 28 SECONDS	CAR BEGINS TO LEVEL	2
			CAR STANDS LOW	B
		COMPRESSOR DOES NOT OPERATE	CAR STANDS HIGH	D
			STANDING HEIGHT OK	A
2	COMPRESSOR STOPS WITHIN 2 MIN.	CAR RETURNS TO WITHIN 1" OF UNLOADED HEIGHT		3
		CAR LEAKS DOWN -- RAPIDLY OR SLOWLY		B
		CAR IS NOT WITHIN 1" OF UNLOADED HEIGHT	ADJUST SENSOR	1
	COMPRESSOR RUNS CONTINUOUSLY		CHECK HEIGHT SENSOR LINK TO ARM	C
3	REMOVE LOAD FROM TRUNK	EXHAUST STARTS WITHIN 28 SEC.	AFTER 1½-2 MIN. CAR RETURNS TO WITHIN 1" ORIGINAL HEIGHT	STOP
			CONTINUOUS EXHAUST	B
			CAR NOT WITHIN 1" ORIGINAL HEIGHT / REPLACE HEIGHT SENSOR	1
		NO EXHAUST		D

ELC system checks

(A) COMPRESSOR DOES NOT OPERATE

△1	GROUND YELLOW TEST LEAD TO COMPRESSOR	COMPRESSOR RUNS ‡	CHECK CONNECTIONS TO SENSOR	REPAIR	☐1
			TEST HEIGHT SENSOR		A
		COMPRESSOR DOESN'T RUN			△2
△2	APPLY +12V. AND GROUND DIRECTLY TO COMPRESSOR TERMINALS (REMOVE CONNECTORS)	COMPRESSOR RUNS	CHECK RELAY	REPAIR	☐1
			REPLACE FAULTY WIRES AND/OR FUSES†		
		COMPRESSOR DOESN'T RUN	INSPECT COMPRESSOR MOTOR	REPAIR•	☐1

(B) IMPROPER OR CONTINUOUS EXHAUST

▽1	DISCONNECT EXHAUST SOLENOID GROUND YELLOW TEST LEAD	CAR BEGINS TO RAISE	CHECK FOR GROUND IN WHITE WIRE TO EXHAUST SOLENOID	REPAIR•	☐1
			TEST HEIGHT SENSOR		
		CAR DOESN'T MOVE -- OR RAISES AND LEAKS DOWN			▽2
▽2	CHECK FOR LEAKS AND PINCHES IN THE SYSTEM				☐1
	CHECK SOLENOID EXHAUST VALVE		REPAIR•		
	CHECK COMPRESSOR PERFORMANCE		COMPRESSOR LEAK TEST		

(C) COMPRESSOR RUNS CONTINUOUSLY

◇1	RESET RUNNING TIME CYCLE TO REVERSE	DISCONNECT RELAY	COMPRESSOR RUNS	CHECK FOR SHORT IN GREEN WIRE	☐1
			COMPRESSOR STOPS		◇2
◇2	LEAKING OR CONTINUAL EXHAUSTING	YES			(B)
		NO	GROUND AT PIN 3 OF HEIGHT SENSOR	YES — TEST HEIGHT SENSOR — REPAIR	☐1
				NO	◇3
◇3	CHECK FOR GROUND			REPAIR	☐1
	CHECK RELAY				

(D) NO EXHAUST

☐1	RESET RUNNING TIME	POWER AT ORANGE WIRE TO SOLENOID	NO	☐2
			YES	☐3
☐2	TRACE POWER TO SOLENOID THROUGH FUSES	POWER		☐3
		NO POWER	REPLACE FAULTY WIRES AND/OR FUSES	☐1
☐3	WITH CONNECTORS OFF APPLY +12V AND GROUND DIRECTLY TO THE SOLENOID	EXHAUST OPENS	CHECK FOR OPEN IN WHITE WIRE	☐1
			TEST HEIGHT SENSOR — REPAIR•	
		NO EXHAUST	REPLACE EXHAUST SOLENOID VALVE	☐1

• SEE CHART A   • SEE SYSTEM LEAK TEST
‡ IF COMPRESSOR RUNS BUT TELLTALE DOES NOT LIGHT, CHECK BULB.

ELC Diagnostic chart

CHART A — ELECTRICAL CHECKS

NOTICE: THIS CHART SHOULD NOT BE USED UNLESS ALL OTHER PROCEDURES LEADING TO IT HAVE BEEN FOLLOWED IN ORDER TO PREVENT MISDIAGNOSIS.

STEP						NEXT STEP
◁1	IGNITION ON ENGINE STOPPED SELECTOR IN REVERSE	DISCONNECT HARNESS FROM SENSOR	POWER AT TERMINAL 5	YES		◁2
				NO	REPAIR OPEN IN CIRCUIT TO TERMINAL 5 (CHECK FUSE)	1
◁2	POWER AT TERMINAL 6	YES	TEST LIGHT LEAD TO TERMINAL 4; PROBE TERMINAL 6	LIGHT		◁3
				NO LIGHT	REPAIR SYSTEM GROUND	1
		NO	REPAIR OPEN IN CIRCUIT TO TERMINAL 6 (CHECK FUSE)			1
◁3	JUMPER TERMINALS 3 AND 4	COMPRESSOR RUNS; SHOCKS BEGIN TO INFLATE				◁4
		COMPRESSOR DOESN'T RUN	REPAIR OPEN IN CIRCUIT TO TERMINAL 3			1
◁4	JUMPER TERMINALS 2 AND 4	EXHAUST; SHOCK DEFLATE	WIRING OK CHECK SENSOR AND CONNECTOR			1
		NO EXHAUST	REPAIR OPEN IN CIRCUIT TO WIRE 2			1

NOTICE: IGNITION MUST BE OFF WHEN RECONNECTING THE ELC HARNESS TO THE SENSOR.

ELC HARNESS CONNECTOR

1 — NOT USED
2 — EXHAUST SOLENOID
3 — COMPRESSOR RELAY
4 — GROUND
5 — RESET
6 — BATTERY SOURCE, 12V (+)

CHART B — RELAY, FUSE CHECK

NOTICE: THIS CHART SHOULD NOT BE USED UNLESS ALL OTHER PROCEDURES LEADING TO IT HAVE BEEN FOLLOWED IN ORDER TO PREVENT MISDIAGNOSIS.

STEP						NEXT STEP
▷1	IGNITION "ON" ENGINE STOPPED	GROUND YELLOW TEST LEAD	REMOVE RELAY	POWER AT CAVITY 39 E,K = 839	YES		▷2
					NO	REPLACE FUSE	1
	REPLACE RELAY						1
▷2	REPAIR OPEN IN YELLOW WIRE TO COMPRESSOR						1

ELC Diagnostic chart continued

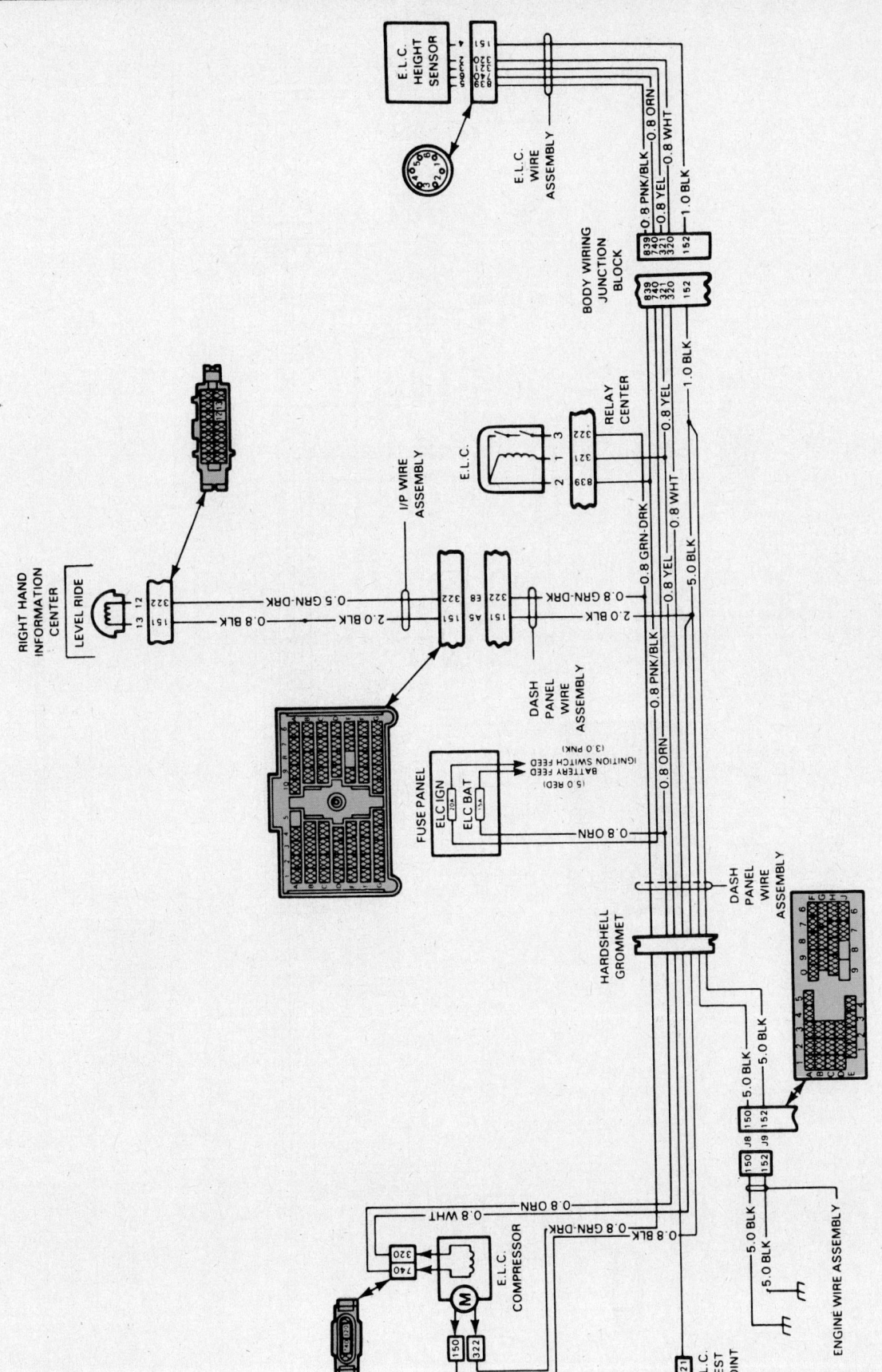

ELC Gas schematic

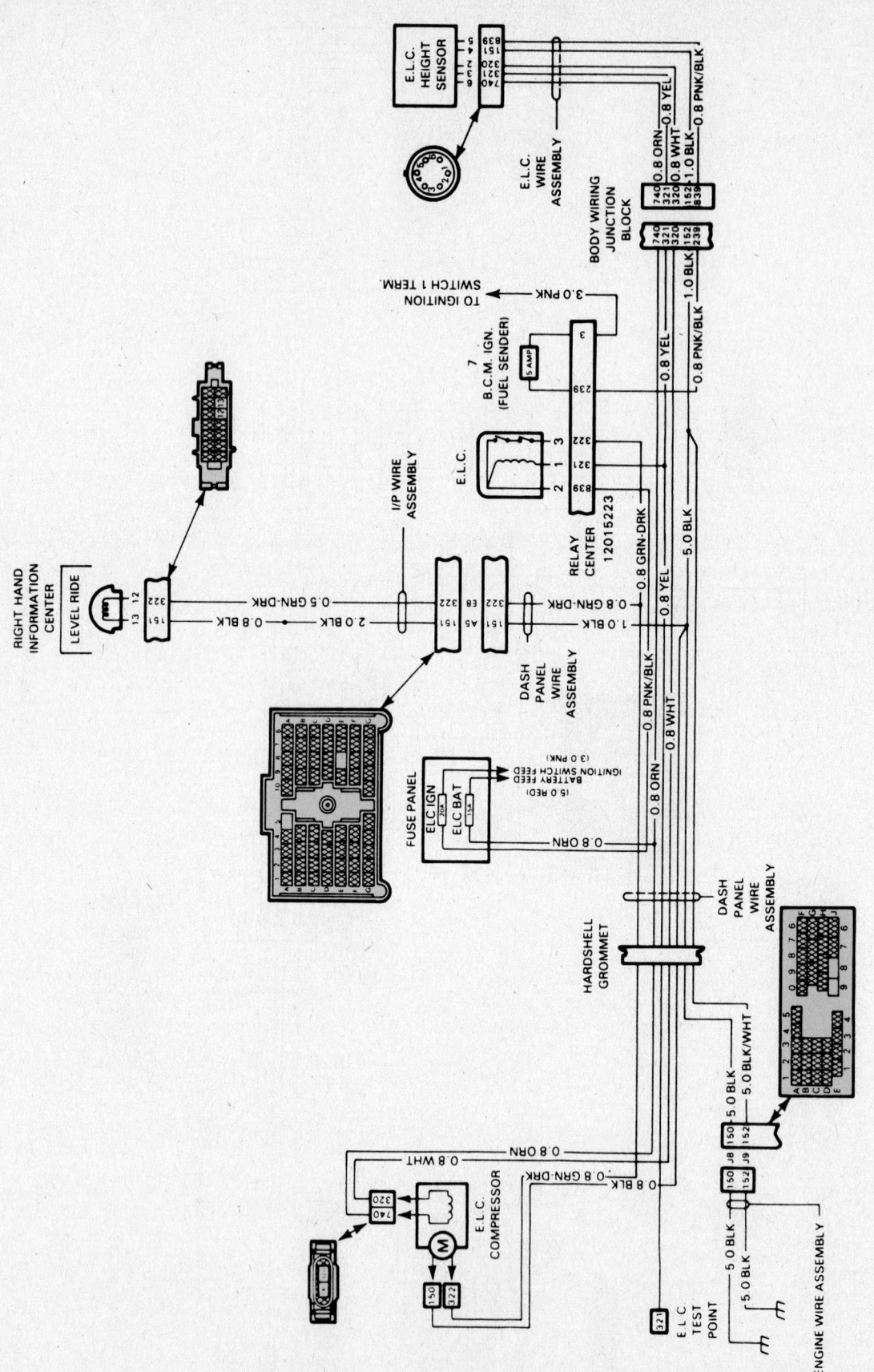

ELC Diesel schematic

outer diameter of the weatherproof connector.

When reconnecting the harness to the sensor, push the sensor into the connector plug until the sloped shoulder on the rear edge of the boss is visible in the plug slot, then push the oval connector lock onto the plug until its two locking tabs snap over the shoulder of the sensor plug.

DISCONNECTING AIR LINES

The air lines include spring clip connections with molded sealing shoulders in the retainer and on the end of the air line with double O-ring seals. Before making any air line disconnection, clean the connector and surrounding area. Squeeze the spring clip to release the connector. To reassemble, moisten the O-rings with vaseline or equivalent lubricant and push the air line and connector fully into the fitting.

COMPRESSOR

Removal

1. Tag and disconnect the electrical connections at the compressor.
2. Remove the limiter retaining clip from the compressor bracket.
3. Remove the rear feed strut lines from the pressure limiter.
4. Remove the compressor mounting bolts.
5. Remove the compressor from the vehicle.

Installation

1. Install the compressor to bracket bolts. Install the compressor assembly.
2. Install the rear strut feed line to the pressure limiter.
3. Install the pressure limiter retaining clip to the compressor bracket. The compressor has a locater dimple for proper positioning.
4. Connect the electrical connection as required. Test system operation.

HEIGHT SENSOR

Removal and Installation

1. Raise the vehicle and support safely.
2. Tag and disconnect the electrical connector from the height sensor.
3. Remove the link from the height sensor arm.
4. Remove the height sensor retaining bolts.
5. Remove the height sensor from the vehicle.
6. Installation is the reverse of the removal procedure. Adjust the vehicle trim height as necessary.

AIR DRYER

Removal

1. Deflate the system through the service valve.
2. Disconnect the high pressure line at the air dryer by revolving the spring clip and removing the tube assembly.
3. Disconnect the air dryer from the compressor mounting.
4. Remove the O-ring from the compressor head.

Installation

Lubricate the dryer O-ring with petroleum jelly or equivalent before installing dryer in head casting.
1. Reverse the removal procedure.
2. Check the system for proper operation and leaks.
3. Adjust the trim height if necessary.

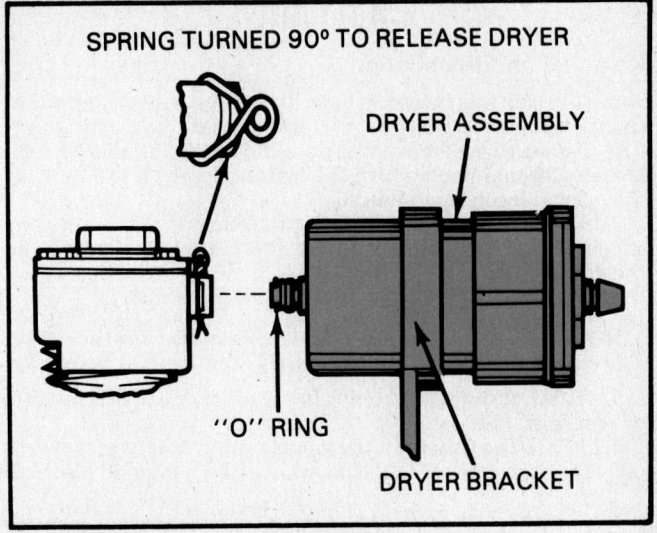

Air dryer—removal and installation

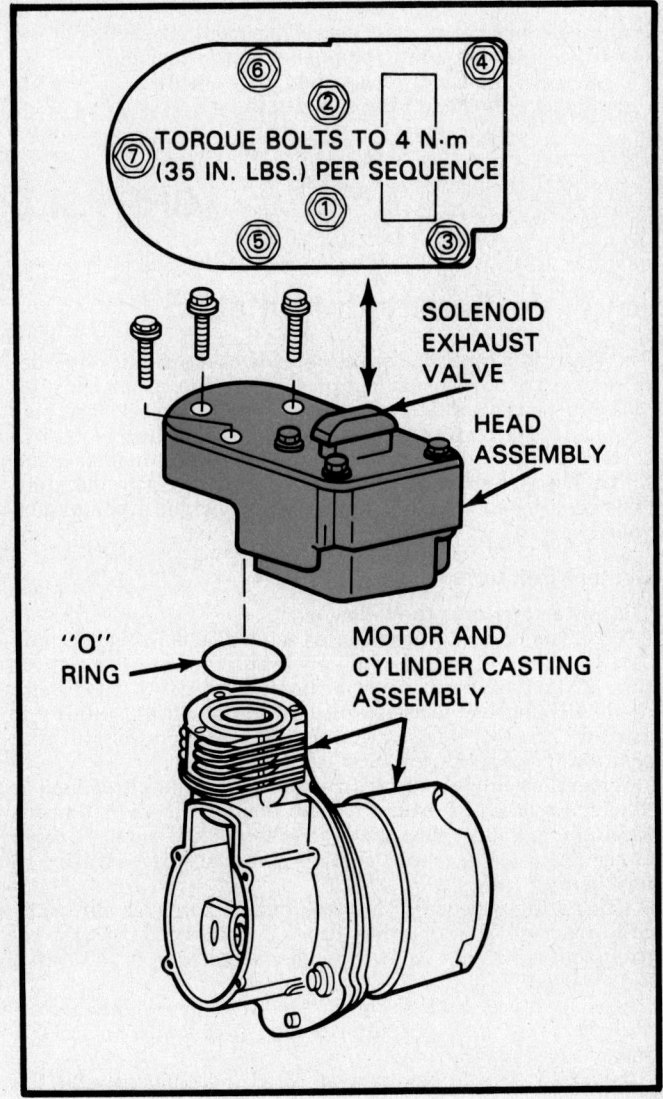

Compressor assembly

AIR LINE

Removal and Installation

Service repair kits include a length of tubing with a snap on fitting plus the necessary parts for splicing into an existing line.
1. Detach the defective line from the shock absorber or compressor depending on which the leak is closer to.
2. Cut the tubing to length.
3. Remove the plastic retainer pin from one of the nuts and slide the replacement tubing into the nut until it bottoms in the rubber seal.
4. Without moving the tubing, tighten the nut.

NOTE: While tightening the nut, a collar on the metal sleeve breaks free. Continue to tighten the nut securely.

5. Attach the original tubing to the other end of the coupling as described above.
6. Secure the tubing to the vehicle in an area where it will not come into contact with the exhaust system or be pinched.

SOLENOID EXHAUST VALVE

Removal and Installation

If the solenoid valve requires replacement, it should be replaced with the complete compressor head assembly.
1. Remove the air dryer as previously outlined.
2. Remove the head assembly retaining bolts.

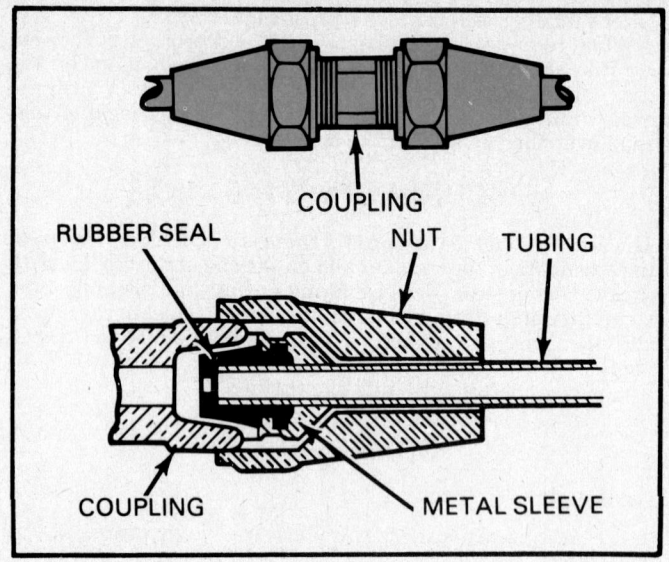

Air line repair

3. Remove the head assembly including the solenoid exhaust valve from the vehicle.
4. When installing, use a new "O" ring with the dryer assembly. Refer to the illustration for torque sequence.

CHRYSLER/MITSUBISHI

General Information

The electronic control suspension utilizes electronics in order to control the suspension characteristics. The spring constant of the suspension and the damping force of the shock absorbers are changed in response to driving conditions. This results in a system that maintains riding comfort and good handling stability. The system also improves driving stability by automatically making adjustments of the vehicle height depending on vehicle speed and load.

System Features

The system features the following;
   Very comfortable riding while the vehicle is being operated under ordinary driving conditions (when the vehicle height is the normal and the suspension characteristic is SOFT). There are few changes of chassis attitude, and handling stability is excellent, on poor roads or during heavy acceleration, turning or braking (AUTO mode, SOFT-HARD).
   When the vehicle is being driven at approximately 25 mph or less on a road which causes a great deal of vibration, the system automatically raises the vehicle height and the suspension characteristics become hard which causes driveability to improve.
   During high speed driving, the vehicle height is automatically reduced. This improves driving stability along with reducing air resistance (vehicle height decreases from NORMAL to LOW).
   Because it is possible to obtain the soft suspension characteristics at speed, this is optimum for long distance driving (SOFT suspension characteristic).
   Since the vehicle height is adjusted independently for the front and rear wheels there is very little change in headlight aiming.

Optical (non-contact) sensors are used which detect the steering angle, acceleration and vehicle height. The reliability of the sensors is high with few malfunctions. In the event of a malfunction, the operation of the system is stopped by a fail-safe function.

System Operation

The suspension system is the McPherson type for the front wheels and the 3 link type for the rear wheels. The wheel alignment, anti-dive geometry and other set values are the same as ordinary suspension systems. The electronic control system makes use of soft coil springs and air springs in both the front struts (3) and the rear shock absorbers (8).
   The driving conditions and road surface conditions are detected by five types of sensors (4, 5, 11, 13 & 14). These conditions are transmitted as data to the electronic control suspension control unit (9). The HARD/SOFT air valves of the front and rear solenoid valves (2 & 6) are activated by the electronic control unit (9), and changeover is made by driving the air actuator (7) for each wheel.
   The front and rear vehicle height sensors (14 & 10) detect the vehicle height. The G sensor (11) and the front vehicle height sensor (14) detect the driving conditions and road surface conditions. This information is transmitted to the suspension control unit (9), this in turn activates either the exhaust solenoid valve or intake solenoid valve. Vehicle height adjustment is made according to the change of the air pressure in the air spring chambers.
   The air pressure system components include the motor driven air compressor (15) and the reserve tank with a built in air dryer. Nylon tubes are used for the routing of the air pressure system.

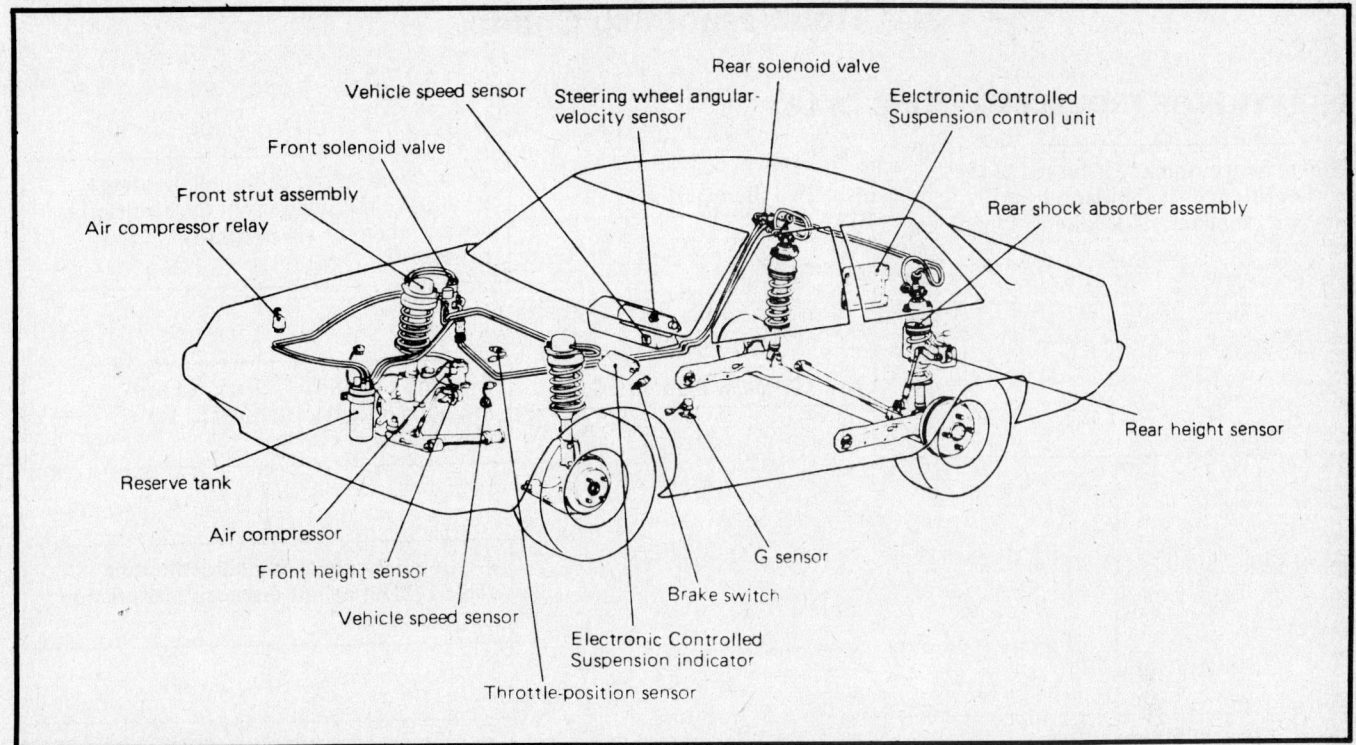

Component location

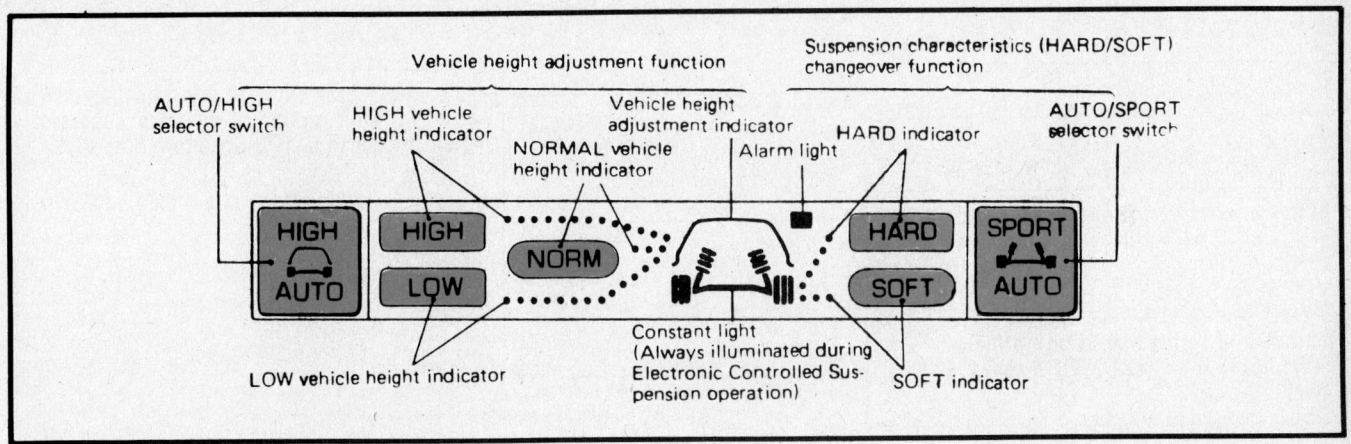

Electronic controlled suspension panel

Troubleshooting

Before beginning any troubleshooting procedures, it is recommended that the following items be inspected.

1. The control unit is connected to a known ground.
2. Unless otherwise indicated, all connectors must be properly connected.
3. The vehicle must be stopped and located on a level surface.
4. All air lines should be inspected for leaks and repaired or replaced as necessary.
5. The battery terminals must be connected properly.
6. Sensors and other electronic circuits must not be disassembled into smaller parts than as supplied as replacement parts.

NOTE: The battery terminals must be disconnected before circuit connectors are disconnected or electrical damage to the system could result.

—————————— **CAUTION** ——————————

The electronically controlled suspension control unit has a fail safe system which maintains driving stability by a self diagnostic system. The system will diagnose abnormal conditions and will terminate automatic suspension control as soon as the abnormal conditions are detected.

The self diagnostic system advises the driver of the condition by turning on an alarm light located on the suspension console panel.

For malfunction diagnosis, it is first necessary to check

Troubleshooting Charts

SELECTION OF TROUBLESHOOTING CHART

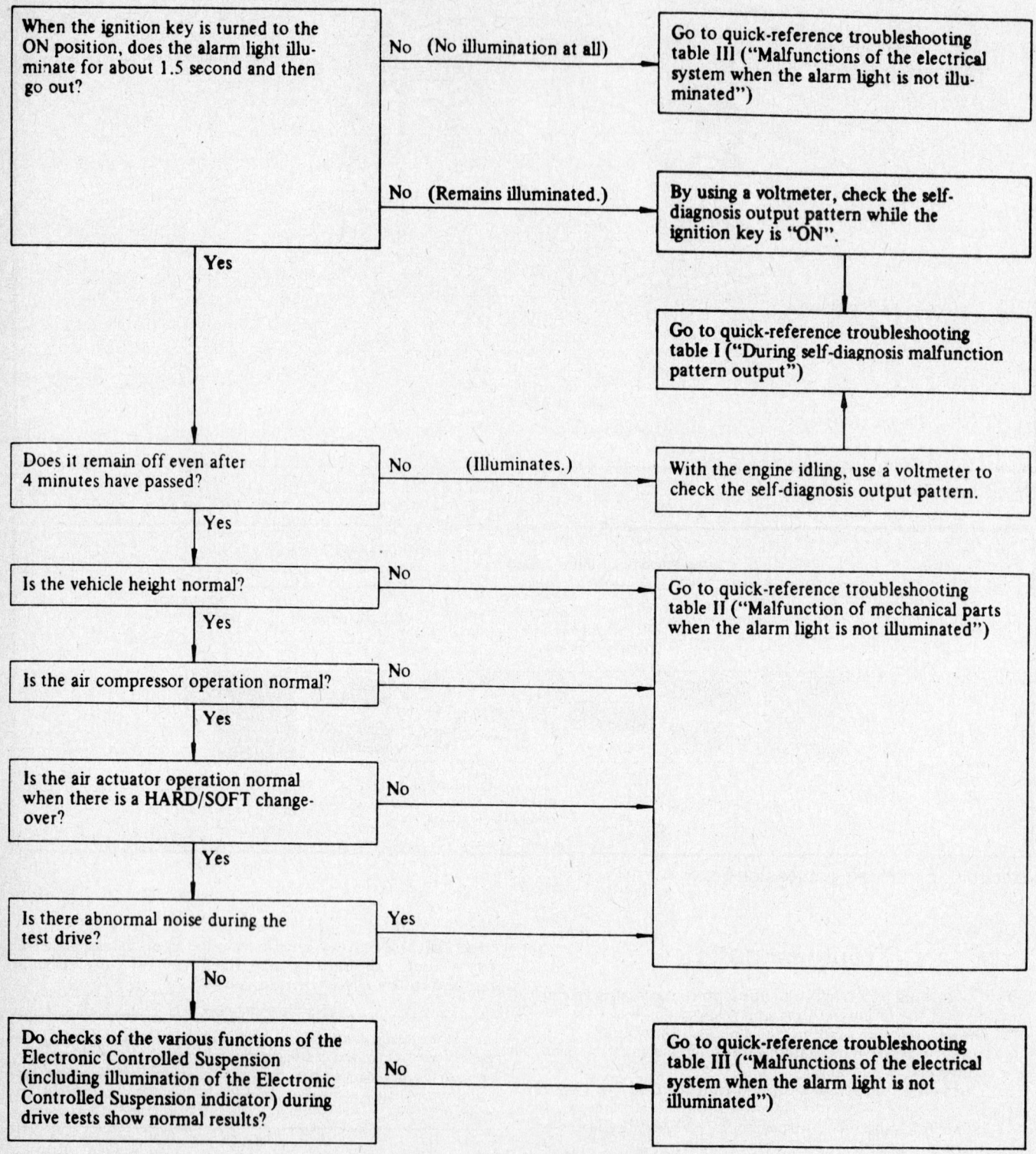

NOTE
1. The "control unit" mentioned during troubleshooting is the Electronic Controlled Suspension control unit.

Troubleshooting table 1

QUICK-REFERENCE TROUBLESHOOTING TABLE I (Self-diagnosis Malfunction Output Patterns and Codes)

Mal-function No.	Self-diagnosis output pattern and output code	Problem (chassis condition)	Probable cause(s)
0	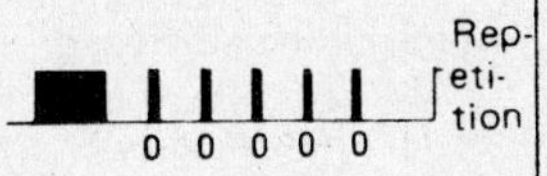 Repetition 0 0 0 0 0	Normal	
1	 0 0 0 0 1	Disconnection or damage of air-valve drive circuit for HARD/SOFT switchover of the front or rear solenoid valve, or a short-circuit of the drive transistor within the control unit. (Alarm light illuminates and SOFT condition remains; no adjustment to HIGH vehicle height.)	• Front or rear solenoid valve connector is disconnected. • Solenoid for HARD/SOFT switchover is damaged or disconnected. • Connector disconnected or harness damaged or disconnected (circuit shown at left). • Malfunction of the control unit (Malfunction of the output transistor)
*2	 0 0 0 1 0	G sensor input circuit is damaged or disconnected. (Alarm light illuminates; condition remains HARD.)	• Disconnection of the G sensor connector • Damage or disconnection within the G sensor • Damage or disconnection of G sensor output circuit harness, or connector is disconnected.
*3	 0 0 0 1 1	Steering angular-velocity sensor input circuit is damaged or disconnected, or there is a malfunction of the steering angular-velocity sensor. (Alarm light illuminates; condition remains HARD.)	• Disconnection of the steering angular-velocity sensor connector • Malfunction of the steering angular-velocity sensor connector • Damage or disconnection of the steering angular-velocity sensor output circuit harness, or disconnection of connector
*4	 1 0 0 0 0	Abnormal condition signal is input from front height sensor, or there is a malfunction of the vehicle-height judgment circuit within the control unit. (The alarm light illuminates, and the vehicle-height adjustment operation stops at that point.) (Note, however, that operation of the air compressor is possible.) **Caution** **Remember that approximately 32 seconds are required for malfunction judgment.**	• Disconnection of front height sensor connector • Malfunction of front height sensor • Damage or disconnection of the front height sensor circuit harness, or disconnection of the connector • Malfunction of the control unit

Troubleshooting table 1 continued

Mal-function No.	Self-diagnosis output pattern and output code	Problem (chassis condition)	Probable cause(s)
*5	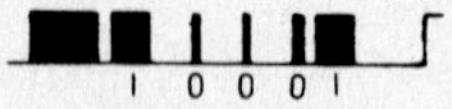 I 0 0 0 1	Abnormal condition signal is input from rear height sensor, or there is a malfunction of the vehicle-height judgment circuit within the control unit. (The alarm light illuminates, and the vehicle-height adjustment operation stops at that point.) (Note, however, that operation of the air compressor is possible.) **Caution** Remember that approximately 32 seconds are required for malfunction judgment.	• Disconnection of rear height sensor connector • Malfunction of rear height sensor • Damage or disconnection of the rear height sensor circuit harness, or disconnection of the connector • Malfunction of the control unit
6	 I 0 0 1 0	Damage or disconnection of the exhaust solenoid valve (in the compressor) or air compressor relay drive circuit, or short-circuit of drive transistor within the control unit. (Note, however, that operation of the air compressor is possible.)	• Disconnection of the exhaust solenoid valve (air compressor) connector • Disconnection of air compressor relay connector • Damaged or disconnected air compressor relay coil • Damaged or disconnected exhaust solenoid valve coil • Damaged or disconnected circuit (shown at left), or disconnection of connector • Malfunction of the control unit (Malfunction of the output transistor)
7	 I 0 0 1 I	Damaged or disconnected front or rear solenoid air valve for vehicle height adjustment, or intake solenoid reserve tank), or short-circuit of drive transistor within control unit (The alarm light illuminates, and the vehicle-height adjustment operation stops at that point.)	• Intake solenoid valve (reserve tank) connector is disconnected. • Intake solenoid coil is damaged or disconnected. • Solenoid coil for vehicle height adjustment is damaged or disconnected. • Circuit shown at left is damaged or disconnected, or connector is disconnected. • Malfunction of the control unit (Malfunction of the output transistor)
8	 I 0 1 0 0	Even though the pressure of the reserve tank is sufficient (pressure switch is OFF), the vehicle height adjustment is not finished even though 3 minutes each or more have passed for the front and rear height adjustments. (The alarm light illuminates, and the vehicle-height adjustment operation stops at that point.)	• Overload • Improper adjustment of the front or rear height sensor • Clogging of the vehicle height adjustment air pressure line • Malfunction of the air spring of the rear shock absorber unit or front strut unit • Malfunction of the control unit (Malfunction of the output transistor)

Troubleshooting table 1 continued

Mal-function No.	Self-diagnosis output pattern and output code	Problem (chassis condition)	Probable cause(s)
9	[output pattern] 1 0 1 0 1	The pressure in the reserve tank is low (pressure switch is ON), and the vehicle height adjustment is not finished even though 3 minutes each or more have passed for the front and rear height adjustments. Or, the air compressor has operated continuously for 4 minutes or more. (The alarm light illuminates, and the vehicle-height adjustment operation stops at that point.)	• Air leakage • Abnormal condition of the air compressor **Caution** **For details, please refer to quick-reference troubleshooting table II ("Malfunction of mechanical parts").**
10	[output pattern] 1 0 1 1 0	The output voltage of the L terminal of the alternator is approximately 5V or less even though the ignition key is at ON and the vehicle speed is approximately 40 km/h (25 mph) or more. [The charge warning light is illuminated. Moreover, the Electronic Controlled Suspension function does not operate when the vehicle is stopped (vehicle speed of approximately 3 km/h (2 mph).] **Caution** **The Electronic Controlled Suspension alarm light does not illuminate. In addition, there is no detection of harness damage or disconnection between the alternator's L terminal and the control unit.**	• Alternator's L terminal output voltage is low (malfunction of the charging system). • The harness is short-circuited between the control unit and the alternator's L terminal.

NOTE
1. If two or more malfunctions occur, only that with the lower number will be indicated.
2. Regarding problems indicated by an asterisk (*), it is possible that the alarm light illumination will stop and the function will return to normal for problems caused by poor connector contact, etc. if the cause remedies itself naturally. It should be noted however that even in this case the diagnosis output pattern is memorized until the ignition key is turned to OFF, and, for that reason, if a malfunction occurs in which the alarm light illuminates from time to time during driving, the self-diagnosis output pattern should be checked, by using a voltmeter, without stopping the engine, and then carefully checking the component (sensor) and harness which are indicated by its malfunction output pattern to be the cause of the malfunction.
Then check whether the problem occurs or not when the connections to the harness and sensor, and the harness for components which move as a result of vibration, are twisted and pulled in order to find the location of the problem.

QUICK-REFERENCE TROUBLESHOOTING TABLE II (Malfunction of Mechanical Parts)

Problem	Probable cause(s)		Remedy
Abnormal vehicle height — When the vehicle is left with the engine stopped, front vehicle height becomes lower than NORM mode position.	Air leakage from joint or pressure line to front strut		Check and repair the air leakage location(s).
	Poor seal of front solenoid valve (for vehicle height)		Replace the front solenoid valve.
	Air leakage at front strut unit		Replace the strut unit.
	Improper adjustment of front height sensor rod		Adjust the front height sensor.
When the vehicle is left with the engine stopped, rear vehicle height becomes lower than NORM mode position.	Air leakage from joint or pressure line to rear shock absorber unit		Check and repair the air leakage location(s).
	Poor seal of rear solenoid valve. (for vehicle height)		Replace the rear solenoid valve.
	Air leakage at rear shock absorber unit		Replace rear shock absorber unit.
	Improper adjustment of rear height sensor rod		Adjust the rear height sensor.
When the vehicle is left with the engine stopped, both the front and rear decrease to a height less than the NORMAL vehicle height.	Improper adjustment of the front and rear height sensor rods.		Adjust the front and rear height sensors.
	Air leakage from the connection part of the pressure line for vehicle height adjustment to the front and/or rear.		Check and repair the air leakage location(s).
Front or rear height is lower than NORMAL vehicle height with the engine running. (Vehicle height adjustment can be made.)	Improper adjustment of the front and rear height sensor rods.		Adjust the front and rear height sensors.
	Air spring rolling diaphragm out of position. (Alarm light illuminates 3 minutes later.)		Check and repair the air springs.
With the vehicle stopped (engine running), the alarm light does not illuminate even though the vehicle height adjustment is not made.	When charge warning light is illuminated	Output drop (approximately 5V or less) of alternator's L terminal	Check and repair the charge system.
	When charge warning light is not illuminated	Short-circuit of harness between control unit and alternator's L terminal	Repair the harness.

Troubleshooting table 2 continued

	Problem	Probable cause (s)		Remedy
Abnormal vehicle height	With the engine running and in the AUTO mode, the vehicle height becomes higher than it should be for NORMAL.	Improper adjustment of the front and rear height sensor rods.		Adjust the front and rear height sensors.
		Incorrect piping connection of the air tube (black) for vehicle height adjustment and the air tube (white) for HARD/SOFT changeover (Alarm light illuminates 3 minutes later.)		Connect the air tubes correctly.
	With the engine idling (vehicle stopped), the front or rear vehicle height automatically repeats up and down functions at approximately 10-second intervals.	Malfunction of the front or rear height sensor (when only element B or element C of height sensor elements A, B, C and D malfunctions)		Replace the front or rear height sensor
Malfunction of the air compressor	Air compressor does not operate even though the engine is running.	Air compressor thermal switch operation (when engine compartment temperature is high)		Open the hood and let the air compressor cool for about 10 minutes or more; then start the engine once again and check.
		Malfunction of electrical system of air compressor motor	Damaged or disconnected compressor motor power-supply circuit	Check (by following the yes/no flow chart) and repair.
			Malfunction of the compressor motor	
			Malfunction of the pressure switch	Replace the pressure switch.
	Air compressor operates with ignition key at ON position (engine stopped).	Damaged or disconnected harness between alternator's L terminal and control unit [pin (17) connector A terminal]		Repair the harness.
	Air compressor starts frequently.	Incorrect activation pressure of pressure switch		Replace the pressure switch.
		Air leakage from connection of air tube of solenoid valve (for HARD/SOFT changeover) and reserve tank (Alarm light illuminates when air compressor operates for 4 minutes or more continuously.)		Check and repair the air leakage location (s).
		Poor seal of the exhaust valve (within the air compressor)		Replace the air compressor assembly.
	Air compressor motor turns slowly.	Weak battery		Charge the battery.
		Improper connector contactor or high harness resistance		Check the connector or repair the harness.
		Malfunction of the air compressor		Replace the air compressor assembly.

ELECTRONIC CHASSIS CONTROLS
ELECTRONIC SUSPENSIONS & AUTOMATIC LOAD LEVELLING SYSTEMS

Troubleshooting table 2 continued

	Problem	Probable cause (s)	Remedy
Poor HARD/SOFT switching	Even though the Electronic Controlled Suspension indicator panel changes to the HARD or SOFT indication, the HARD/SOFT changeover rod of the rear shock absorber or the front strut unit does not turn.	Malfunction of actuator or incorrect installation	Replace the actuator or check the installation and correct if necessary.
		Disconnected or clogged air tube for actuator drive	Repair or replace the air tube.
		Malfunction of HARD/SOFT solenoid valve	Replace the solenoid valve.
		Switching rod at shock absorber side is stuck or moving without load.	Replace the shock absorber assembly.
		Oil leakage at shock absorber	
	When the Electronic Controlled Suspension indicator panel changes to the HARD or SOFT indication, the HARD/SOFT changeover rod of each unit turns, but the suspension characteristics remain HARD or SOFT.	The changeover rod of the rear shock absorber or of the front strut unit is turning without a load.	Replace the front strut unit or the rear shock absorber.
		Oil leakage from front or rear shock absorber (if characteristics remain SOFT)	
		Air spring rolling diaphragm twisted or out of position (if characteristics remain HARD)	Check and repair the air spring.
Abnormal noise	Abnormal noise from front strut or rear shock absorber	Poor contact of spring and spring seat	Repair, or replace the spring pad.
		Contact of spring and diaphragm cover (Buckling due to abnormal spring condition)	Replace the spring.
		Rough noise inside shock absorber or strut unit (Rough noise from cylinder because ring nut is not tight) (Rough noise from piston) (Rough noise from switching valve)	Replace the strut or shock absorber unit.
	Abnormal noise due to loose installation parts	Looseness at installation of front strut or rear shock absorber assembly	Tighten.
		Looseness at installation of actuator or actuator bracket	Tighten.
		Looseness at installation of insulator	Tighten.
		Looseness due to insulator bearing wear	Replace the insulator.
		Looseness at installation of height sensor, or link looseness	Tighten, or replace the height sensor.
		Looseness at installation of solenoid valve, reserve tank or air compressor	Tighten.

Troubleshooting table 3

QUICK-REFERENCE TROUBLESHOOTING TABLE III
(Malfunctions of the Electrical System when the Alarm Light is not illuminated)

No.	Symptom	Check procedures	Judgment — Normal	Judgment — Malfunction	Cause	Remedy
1	The following Electronic Controlled Suspension indicators do not illuminate when the ignition key is turned to the ON position. • AUTO mode indicator (AUTO/SPORT selector) • SOFT indicator • AUTO mode indicator • (AUTO/HIGH selector) • Alarm light • Vehicle height adjustment indicator NOTE It is normal if the alarm light indicates only for a period of apporximately 1.5 second immediately after the ignition key is turned to the ON position.	1. Turn the ignition key to the ON position and then measure the following terminal voltages at the control unit. Terminal No. — Signal P — IG₂ power supply	Battery voltage (approx. 12V)	0V	Fuse No. 12 blown	Replace the fuse.
					Harness damaged or disconnected between fuse No. 12 and control unit (P terminal).	Repair the harness.
		2. Disconnect the 21-pin connector of the control unit, turn the ignition key to the ON position, and then ground the following terminals of the connector at the harness side of the control unit. Terminal No. — Signal 19 — AUTO/SPORT mode indication 2 — SOFT/HARD indication 3 — AUTO/HIGH mode indication 21 — Alarm light 20 — Vehicle height adjustment indication	Indication of grounded circuit illuminates.	No illumination when grounded	Harness damaged or disconnected between fuse No. 12 and the Electronic Controlled Suspension indicator panel (terminal No. 10).	Repair the harness.
					Electronic Controlled Suspension indicator panel bulb is damaged or disconnected.	Replace the bulb.
					Malfunction of Electronic Controlled Suspension indicator panel circuit	Replace the Electronic Controlled Suspension indicator panel.
					Damaged or disconnected harness between Electronic Controlled Suspension indicator panel and control unit terminals	Repair the harness.
		3. The results of checks made in 1 and 2 above are normal, but there is no illumination when the 21-pin connector of the control unit is connected.	–	–	Poor contact of control unit harness connector	Check the connector contacts and repair.
					Malfunction of the control unit	Replace the control unit.
2	The following Electronic Contorolled Suspension indicators do not illuminate when the ignition key is turned to the ON position. • NORMAL vehicle height indicator • Constant light	1. Turn the ignition key to the ON position and then measure the following terminal voltages at the Electronic Controlled Suspension indicators Terminal No. — Signal 10 — IG₂ power supply	Battery voltage (approx. 12V)	0V	Fuse No. 12 blown	Replace the fuse.
					Harness damaged or disconnected between fuse No. 12 and the Electronic Controlled Suspension indicator panel (terminal No. 10).	Repair the harness.
		2. If check in 1 shows no abnormal condition.			NORMAL vehicle height indicator bulb is damaged or disconnected.	Replace the bulb.
			–	–	Circuit malfunction within Electronic Controlled Suspension indicator panel	Replace the Electronic Controlled Suspension indicator panel.

Troubleshooting table 3 continued

No.	Symptom	Check procedures	Judgment Normal	Judgment Malfunction	Cause	Remedy
3	The mode indicator doesn't change from AUTO to SPORT when, with the ignition key at the ON position, the AUTO/SPORT selector is pressed. The AUTO/HIGH switching is normal however.	1. Turn the ignition key to the ON position; then check whether there is a change of the following terminal voltage at the control unit when the AUTO/SPORT selector switch is pressed. Terminal No.: 7 Signal: Mode selector switch	When AUTO/SPORT selector switch is pressed; approx. 4.3V → 0V	Remains approx. 4.3V when switch is pressed.	Damaged or disconnected circuit inside Electronic Controlled Suspension indicator panel, or switch malfunciton	Replace the Electronic Controlled Suspension indicator panel.
		2. Check whether the AUTO mode indicator stops illumination and the SPORT mode indicator illuminates when the 21-pin connector of the control unit is disconnected and the ignition key is turned to the ON position.	The AUTO mode indicator stops illumination and the SPORT mode indicator illuminates.	The AUTO mode indicator remains illuminated. (The SPORT mode indicator does not illuminate.)	Harness short-circuit between Electronic Controlled Suspension indicator panel and control unit (terminal No. 19).	Repair the harness.
				The SPORT mode indicator does not illuminate. (The AUTO mode indicator stops illumination.)	SPORT mode indicator bulb is damaged or disconnected.	Replace the bulb.
					Circuit malfunction within Electronic Controlled Suspension indicator panel	Replace the Electronic Controlled Suspension indicator panel.
		3. The results of checks made in 1 and 2 above are normal, but there is no illumination when the 21-pin connector of the control unit is connected.	–	–	Malfunction of the control unit	Replace the control unit.
4	The mode indicator illumination does not change from AUTO to HIGH when, with the ignition key at the ON position, the AUTO/HIGH selector switch is pressed. The AUTO/SPORT switching is normal however.	1. Turn the ignition key to the ON position; then check whether there is a change of the following terminal voltage at the control unit when the AUTO/HIGH selector swtich is pressed. Terminal No.: 7 Signal: Mode selector switch	When AUTO/HIGH selector switch is pressed: approx. 4.3V → 2V	Remains approx. 4.3V when switch is pressed.	Circuit malfunction within Electronic Controlled Suspension indicator panel	Replace the Electronic Controlled Suspension indicator panel.
		2. Check whether the AUTO mode indicator stops illumination and the HIGH mode indicator illuminates when the 21-pin connector of the control unit is disconnected and the ignition key is turned to the ON position.	The AUTO mode indicator stops illumination and the HIGH mode indicator illuminates.	The AUTO mode indicator remains illuminated.	Harness short-circuit between Electronic Controlled Suspension indicator and control unit (terminal No. 3).	Repair the harness.
				The HIGH mode indicator does not illuminate. (The AUTO mode indicator stops illumination.)	HIGH mode indicator bulb is damaged or disconnected.	Replace the bulb.
					Circuit malfunction within Electronic Controlled Suspension indicator panel	Replace the Electronic Controlled Suspension indicator panel.
		3. The results of checks made in 1 and 2 above are normal, but there is no illumination when the 21-pin connector of the control unit is connected.	–	–	Malfunction of the control unit	Replace the control unit.

Troubleshooting table 3 continued

No.	Symptom	Check procedures	Judgment Normal	Judgment Malfunction	Cause	Remedy
5	Neither the SPORT nor the HIGH mode indicator illuminates when, with the ignition key at the ON position, the AUTO/SPORT and AUTO/HIGH selector switches are pressed.	1. Turn the ignition key to the ON position; then check whether there is a change of the following terminal voltage at the control unit when the AUTO/SPORT selector switch is pressed. Terminal No. 7 — Signal: Mode selector switch	When AUTO/SPORT selector switch is pressed: approx. 4.3V → 0V when AUTO/HIGH selector switch is pressed: approx. 4.3V → 2V	Remains approx. 4.3V when switch is pressed.	Damaged or disconnected circuit inside Electronic Controlled Suspension indicator panel, or switch malfunction	Replace the Electronic Controlled Suspension indicator panel.
					Damaged or disconnected harness between Electronic Controlled Suspension indicator panel and control unit (terminal No. 7).	Repair the harness.
				Remains 0V before and after switch is pressed.	Harness short-circuit between Electronic Controlled Suspension indicator panel and control unit (terminal No. 7)	Repair the harness.
					AUTO/SPORT selector switch always ON	Replace the Electronic Controlled Suspension indicator panel.
					Malfunction of the control unit	Replace the control unit.
				Remains 2V before and after switch is pressed.	AUTO/HIGH selector switch always ON	Replace the Electronic Controlled Suspension indicator panel.
		2. Check whether, after the 21-pin connector of the control unit is disconnected and the ignition key is turned to the ON position, there is any illumination of the SPORT mode indicator and the HIGH mode indicator.	The SPORT mode indicator and HIGH mode indicator illuminate.	Both AUTO mode indicators remain illuminated. (The SPORT mode indicator and the HIGH mode indicator do not illuminate.)	Harness short-circuit between Electronic Controlled Suspension indicator panel and control unit (terminal No. 19 and terminal No. 3)	Repair the harness.
				The SPORT mode indicator and the HIGH mode indicator do not illuminate. (Both AUTO mode indicators stop illumination.)	Indicator bulbs for both the SPORT mode indicator and the HIGH mode indicator and damaged or disconnected.	Replace the bulb.
					Circuit malfunction within Electronic Controlled Suspension indicator panel	Replace the Electronic Controlled Suspension indicator panel.
		3. The results of checks made in 1 and 2 above are normal, but there is no illumination when the 21-pin connector of the control unit is connected.	—	—	Poor contact of the control unit harness connector.	Check the connector contacts and repair.
					Malfunction of the control unit	Replace the control unit.

Troubleshooting table 3 continued

No.	Symptom	Check procedures	Judgment Normal	Judgment Malfunction	Cause	Remedy
6	Operate the AUTO/SPORT selector switch with the engine idling. The illumination of the AUTO mode indicator and the SPORT mode indicator changes each time the switch is pressed, but the HARD mode indicator does not illuminate in the SPORT mode. NOTE The SOFT mode indicator does illuminate, however, in the AUTO mode.	1. Check whether the HARD mode indicator illuminates when the 21-pin connector of the control unit is disconnected and the ignition key is turned to the ON position.	The HARD mode indicator illuminates.	The SOFT mode indicator remains illuminated.	Harness short-circuit between Electronic Controlled Suspension indicator panel and control unit (terminal No. 2).	Repair the harness
				Neither the HARD mode indicator nor the SOFT mode indicator illuminates.	HARD mode indicator bulb is damaged or disconnected.	Replace the bulb.
					Circuit malfunction within Electronic Controlled Suspension indicator panel.	Replace the Electronic Controlled Suspension indicator panel.
		2. The results in 1 are normal, but the HARD mode indicator does not illuminate in the SPORT mode when the 21-pin connector of the control unit is connected.	—	—	Poor contact of the control unit harness connector.	Check the connector contacts and repair.
					Malfunction of the control unit	Replace the control unit.
7	When, with the engine idling, the AUTO/HIGH selector switch is operated, the illumination of the AUTO mode indicator and the HIGH mode indicator changes each time the switch is pressed, but the HIGH mode indicator does not illuminate in the HIGH mode. NOTE The NORMAL vehicle height indicator does illuminate, however, in the AUTO mode.	1. Disconnect the 17-pin connector of the control unit, turn the ignition key to the ON position, and then ground the following connector at the harness side of the control unit. Terminal No. J — Signal: High vehicle height indication	The NORMAL vehicle height indicator stops illumination, and the HIGH vehicle height indicator illuminates.	If the NORMAL vehicle height indicator remains illuminated.	Damaged or disconnected harness between Electronic Controlled Suspension indicator panel and control unit (terminal No. J).	Repair the harness.
					Malfunction of the Electronic Controlled Suspension indicator panel.	Replace the Electronic Controlled Suspension indicator panel.
				If the NORMAL vehicle height indicator stops illumination	HIGH vehicle height indicator bulb is damaged or disconnected.	Replace the bulb.
		2. The results in 1 are normal, but the HIGH vehicle height indicator does not illuminate in the HIGH mode when the 17-pin connector of the control unit is connected.	—	—	Poor contact of the control unit harness connector.	Check the connector contacts and repair.
					Malfunction of the control unit.	Replace the control unit.

Troubleshooting table 3 continued

No.	Symptom	Check procedures	Judgment Normal	Judgment Malfunction	Cause	Remedy
8	When the AUTO/ SPORT selector switch or the AUTO/ HIGH selector switch is operated, the mode indicators for each switch illuminate normally each time the switch is pressed, but the buzzer does not sound.	1. Disconnect the 21-pin connector of the control unit, turn the ignition key to the ACC position, and then ground the following connector at the harness side of the control unit. Terminal No. / Signal 1 / Buzzer	Buzzer sounds continuously during grounding.	Buzzer dosen't sound.	Fuse No. 6 blown	Replace the fuse.
					Buzzer malfunction within column switch	Replace the buzzer.
					Harness is damaged or disconnected between buzzer within column switch and control unit (terminal No. 1).	Repair the harness.
		2. The results in 1 are normal, but the buzzer doesn't sound when the 21-pin connector is connected and a check is made.	–	–	Poor contact of the control unit harness connector.	Check the connector contacts and repair.
					Malfunction of the control unit	Replace the control unit.
9	With the vehicle speed approximately 90 km/h (56 mph) or higher, the LOW vehicle height indicator does not illuminate after approximately 10 seconds have passed. NOTE The AUTO mode indicator and the NORMAL vehicle height, indicator illuminate, however, at this time.	1. Disconnect the 17-pin connector of the control unit, turn the ignition key to the ON position, and then ground the following connector at the harness side of the control unit. Terminal No. / Signal I / LOW vehicle height indication	The NORMAL vehicle height indicator stops illumination, and the LOW vehicle height indicator illuminates.	If the NORMAL vehicle height indicator remains illuminated	Damaged or disconnected harness between Electronic Controlled Suspension indicator panel and control unit (terminal No. I).	Repair the harness.
					Malfunction of the Electronic Controlled Suspension indicator panel	Replace the Electronic Controlled Suspension indicator panel.
				If the NORMAL vehicle height indicator stops illumination	LOW vehicle height indicator bulb is damaged or disconnected.	Replace the bulb.
		2. Connect this connector of the control unit and then, with the vehicle speed sensor activated (by jacking up the front wheels and slowly turning the front wheels), check whether the following control unit terminal voltage change occurs. Terminal No. / Signal 5 / Vehicle speed sensor	Alternates between approximately 4.3V or more and 1.3V or less.	Remains 0V.	Vehicle speed sensor is short-circuited. (Remains ON.)	Replace the vehicle speed sensor.
					Malfunction of the control unit.	Replace the control unit.
				Remains approximately 4.3V or more.	Vehicle speed sensor wiring is damaged or disconnected. (Remains OFF.)	Replace the vehicle speed sensor.
					Harness is damaged or disconnected between the vehicle speed sensor and the control unit (terminal No. 5).	Repair the harness.
		3. When the results in 1 and 2 are normal.	–	–	Malfunction of the control unit	Replace the control unit.

Troubleshooting table 3 continued

No.	Symptom	Check procedures	Judgment		Cause	Remedy
			Normal	Malfunction		
10	When the Electronic Controlled Suspension indicator panel is illuminated, the indicator illumination doesn't dim when the tail lights are switched ON. **NOTE** For models with electronic meters, make the check at the rheostat ON position, because the light does not dim at the rheostat OFF position (when the lever is at the farthest right position).	1. With the ignition key at the ON position and the tail lights switched ON, measure the terminal voltage of the following Electronic Controlled Suspension indicator panel connector. Terminal No. 12 — Signal: Tail lights	Battery voltage (approx. 12V)	0V	Fuse No. 4 (in engine compartment relay box) is blown.	Replace the fuse.
					Harness is damaged or disconnected between fuse no. 4 (in engine compartment relay box) and Electronic Controlled Suspension indicator panel (terminal No. 12).	Repair the harness.
		2. If check in 1 shows no abnormal condition	–	–	Circuit malfunction within Electronic Controlled Suspension indicator panel.	Replace the Electronic Controlled Suspension indicator panel.
11	With the engine idling, the HARD mode indicator remains illuminated even though the AUTO/SPORT mode indicator is AUTO. **NOTE** The AUTO/HIGH mode is AUTO and the NORMAL vehicle height indicator is illuminated.	1. With the engine idling and the G sensor inoperative (horizontal position), measure the following control unit terminal voltage. Terminal No. 16 — Signal: G sensor	Approx. 2.5 – 3.8V	0V	Harness is short-circuited between the G sensor and the control unit (terminal No. 16).	Repair the harness.
					Malfunction of the G sensor output circuit	Replace the G sensor.
		2. Disconnect the 21-pin connector of the control unit, turn the ignition key to the ACC position, and then ground the following connector at the harness side of the control unit. Terminal No. 2 — Signal: SOFT/HARD indication	The HARD mode indicator stops illumination, and the SOFT mode indicator illuminates.	The HARD mode indicator remains illuminated, and the SOFT mode indicator does not illuminate.	Damaged or disconnected harness between Electronic Controlled Suspension indicator and control unit (terminal No. 2).	Repair the harness.
					Circuit malfunction within Electronic Controlled Suspension indicator panel.	Replace the Electronic Controlled Suspension indicator panel.
		3. The results in 1 and 2 are normal, but the HARD mode indicator remains illuminated when the 21-pin connector is connected and a check is made.	–	–	Poor contact of the control unit harness connector.	Check the connector contacts and repair.
					Malfunction of the control unit.	Replace the control unit.

Troubleshooting table 3 continued

No.	Symptom	Check procedures	Judgment Normal	Judgment Malfunction	Cause	Remedy
12	With the engine idling, the SOFT mode indicator remains illuminated even though the AUTO/SPORT mode indicator is SPORT.	1. Check whether the HARD mode indicator illuminates when the 21-pin connector of the control unit is disconnected and the ignition key is turned to the ON position.	The HARD mode indicator illuminates.	The HARD mode indicator doesn't illuminate, and the SOFT mode indicator remains illuminated.	Damaged or disconnected harness between Electronic Controlled Suspension indicator panel and control unit (terminal No. 2).	Repair the harness.
					Circuit malfunction within Electronic Controlled Suspension indicator panel	Replace the Electronic Controlled Suspension indicator panel.
		2. If check in 1 shows no abnormal condition	–	–	Malfunction of the control unit.	Replace the control unit.
13	When the ignition key is turned to the ON position, there is a change to the SPORT mode, but, after the engine is started, the SPORT mode remains even though the AUTO/SPORT selector switch is pressed.	1. Turn the ignition key to the ON position, and, without pressing the AUTO/SPORT selector switch, measure the following control unit terminal voltage. Terminal No.: 7 — Signal: Mode selector switch	Approx. 4.3V	0V	Harness is short-circuited between the Electronic Controlled Suspension indicator panel and the control unit (terminal No. 7).	Repair the harness.
					Malfunction of the AUTO/SPORT selector switch (remains ON)	Replace the Electronic Controlled Suspension indicator panel.
		2. If check in 1 shows no abnormal condition	–	–	Malfunction of the control unit	Replace the control unit.
14	With the engine idling and the AUTO/HIGH mode indicator at AUTO, the HIGH vehicle height indicator or the LOW vehicle height indicator remains illuminated.	1. With the 17-pin connector of the control unit disconnected and the ignition key turned to the ON position, check for illumination of the HIGH vehicle height indicator.	The NORMAL vehicle height indicator illuminates.	The NORMAL vehicle height indicator does not illuminate, and the HIGH vehicle height indicator or the LOW vehicle height indicator remains illuminated.	Harness is short-circuited between the Electronic Controlled Suspension indicator panel and the control unit (terminal No. I or J).	Repair the harness.
					Circuit malfunction within Electronic Controlled Suspension indicator panel.	Replace the Electronic Controlled Suspension indicator panel.
		2. If check in 1 shows no abnormal condition	–	–	Malfunction of the control unit	Replace the control unit.
15	With the engine idling and the AUTO/HIGH mode indicator at HIGH, the NORMAL vehicle height indicator remains illuminated.	1. Disconnect the 17-pin connector of the control unit, turn the ignition key to the ON position, and then ground the following connector at the harness side of the control unit. Terminal No.: J — Signal: HIGH vehicle height indication	The NORMAL vehicle height indicator stops illumination, and the HIGH vehicle height indicator illuminates.	The NORMAL vehicle height indicator remains illuminated, and the HIGH vehicle height indicator does not illuminate.	Damaged or disconnected harness between Electronic Controlled Suspension indicator panel and control unit (terminal No. J).	Repair the harness.
					Circuit malfunction within Electronic Controlled Suspension indicator panel.	Replace the Electronic Controlled Suspension indicator panel.
		2. If check in 1 shows no abnormal condition	–	–	Malfunction of the control unit	Replace the control unit.

Troubleshooting table 3 continued

No.	Symptom	Check procedures	Normal	Malfunction	Cause	Remedy
16	When the ignition key is turned to the ON position, there is a change to the HIGH mode, but, after the engine is started, the HIGH mode remains even though the AUTO/HIGH selector switch is pressed.	1. Turn the ignition key to the ON position, and, without pressing the AUTO/HIGH selector switch, measure the following control unit terminal voltage. Terminal No. 7 — Signal: Mode selector switch	Approx. 4.3V	Approx. 2V	Malfuncton of the AUTO/HIGH selector switch (remains ON)	Replace the Electronic Controlled Suspension indicator panel.
		2. If check in 1 shows no abnormal condition	–	–	Malfucntion of the control unit	Replace the control unit.
17	No functions operate at a vehicle speed of 3 km/h (2 mph) or higher. Example: HARD/SOFT change-over function • No changeover to HARD during the AUTO mode even though the memo-rized vehicle speed [initial setting 150 km/h (94 mph)] is reached or exeeded. • No changeover to HARD when accel-erator is suddenly depressed or steer-ing wheel is suddenly turned. Vehicle height adjust-ment function • No changeover to AUTO mode (NORMAL vehicle height) during the HIGH mode even though the vehicle speed reaches or ex-ceeds approxima-tely 70 km/h (44 mph). • There is a change to the HIGH mode when, at a vehicle speed of approxima-tely 70 km/h (44 mph) or more, the AUTO/HIGH selec-tor switch is pressed.	1. Turn the ignition key to the ON position, and then, with the vehicle speed sensor activated (by jacking up the front wheels and slowly turning the front wheels), check whether the following control unit terminal voltage change occurs. Terminal No. 5 — Signal: Vehicle speed sensor	Alternates between approx-imately 4.3V or more and 1.3V or less.	Remains 0V.	Vehicle speed sensor is short-circuited. (Remains ON.)	Replace the vehicle speed sensor.
					Malfunction of the control unit	Replace the control unit.
				Remains approx-imately 4.3V or more.	Vehicle speed sensor wiring is damaged or disconnected. (Remains OFF.)	Replace the vehicle speed sensor.
					Harness is damaged or disconnected be-tween the vehicle speed sensor and the control unit (terminal No. 5).	Repair the harness.
		2. If check in 1 shows no abnormal condition NOTE At this time, the control condition relative to the vehicle speed by other systems (electronic meter ETACS, etc.) should be normal.	–		Malfunction of the control unit	Replace the control unit.

Troubleshooting table 3 continued

No.	Symptom	Check procedures	Judgment Normal	Judgment Malfunction	Cause	Remedy
18	No changeover to HARD, during the AUTO mode and NORMAL vehicle height, when the accelerator is depressed quickly at a vehicle speed of approximately 3 km/h (2 mph). NOTE At this time, other functions related to the vehicle speed should be normal.	1. Turn the ignition key to the ON position, and then measure the following control unit terminal voltage with the throttle valve fully closed and fully opened. Terminal No. 18 — Signal: Throttle position	Approx. 0.25V when fully closed Approx. 4.8V when fully opened	0V when fully closed and fully opened	Damaged or disconnected wiring of the throttle position sensor	Throttle position sensor
					Harness is damaged or disconnected between the throttle position sensor and the control unit (terminal No. 18).	Remair the harness.
		2. If check in 1 shows no abnormal condition	—	—	Malfunction of the control unit	Replace the control unit.
19	No changeover to HARD, during the AUTO mode and NORMAL vehicle height, when the steering wheel is turned suddenly at a vehicle speed of approximately 40 km/h (25 mph). NOTE At this time, other functions related to the vehicle speed should be normal.	1. Turn the ignition key to the ON position, and then measure the voltage of the steering angular-velocity sensor's power supply terminal (0.3-L line).	Approx. 5V	0V	Harness is damaged or disconnected between the steering angular-velocity sensor and the control unit (sensor power supply, terminal No. Q).	Repair the harness.
					Malfunction of the control unit	Replace the control unit.
		2. Turn the ignition key to the ON position, and then check whether the following control unit voltage changes when the steering wheel is turned. Terminal No. 6 / 17 — Signal: Steering angular-velocity sensor	Repeatedly alternates between approximately 3.8V and 0V.	Remains 0V	Harness is short-circuited between the steering angular-velocity sensor and the control unit (terminal No.6 or No.Q).	Repair the harness.
					Malfunciton (continuity) of the steering angular-velocity sensor output transistor	Replace the steering angular-velocity sensor
				Always remains at approximately 3.8V.	Malfunction (damage) of the steering angular-velocity sensor output transistor	Replace the steering angular-velocity sensor
				(Always remains at approximately 5V.)	(Damaged or disconnected wiring of the steering angular-velocity sensor)	[Self-diagnosis output code 00011 is output, and alarm height illuminates.
		3. When the results of 1 and 2 are normal.	—	—	Malfunciton of the control unit	Replace the control unit.

Troubleshooting table 3 continued

No.	Symptom	Check procedures	Judgment		Cause	Remedy
			Normal	Malfunction		
20	No changeover to HARD when, during AUTO mode and NORMAL vehicle height, the G sensor is switched ON.	1. Turn the ignition key to the ON position, and then measure the voltage of the power supply terminal (0.3-L line) of the G sensor.	Approx. 5V	0V	Harness is damaged or disconnected between the G sensor and the control unit (sensor power supply, terminal No. Q).	Repair the harness.
					Malfunction of the control unit	Replace the control unit.
		2. Check for the following control unit terminal voltage change when, with the ignition key at the ON position, the G sensor is tilted forward and backward (from the horizontal position) approximately 21° or more, or approximately 39° or more to the left and right. Terminal No. 16 — Signal: G sensor	At the horizontal position (G sensor OFF) Approx. 3.8V when tilted (G sensor ON) 0V	Remains 0V no matter whether G sensor is ON or OFF.	Harness is short-circuited between the G sensor and the control unit (terminal No.16).	Repair the harness.
					Malfunction (continuity) of the G sensor output transistor	Replace the G sensor.
				Always remains at approximately 3.8V.	Malfunction (damage) of the G sensor output transistor	Replace the G sensor.
				(Always remains at approximately 5V)	(G sensor wiring is disconnected or damaged.)	[Self-diagnosis output code 00010 is output, and the alarm light illuminates.]
		3. When the results of 1 and 2 are normal.	–	–	Malfunction of the control unit	Replace the control unit.
21	Vehicle height is adjusted when, with the brake pedal depressed, the AUTO/HIGH selector switch is pressed. NOTE The normal condition is for the vehicle height adjustment to be deferred until the stop light switch is OFF or the vehicle speed has reached 3 km/h (2 mph) or higher.	1. With the brake pedal depressed, measure the following control unit terminal voltage. Terminal No. L — Signal: Stop light switch	Approx. 12V	0V	Fuse No. 2 blown.	Replace the fuse.
					Stop light switch is improperly installed.	Correct the installation of the stop light switch.
					Malfunction of the stop light switch.	Replace the stop light switch.
					Harness is damaged or disconnected between the stop light switch and the control unit (terminal No. L).	Repair the harness.
		2. If check in 1 shows no abnormal condition	–	–	Malfunction of the control unit	Replace the control unit.

Compressor troubleshooting

Symptom of Malfunction

Air compressor doesn't operate
while engine is running.

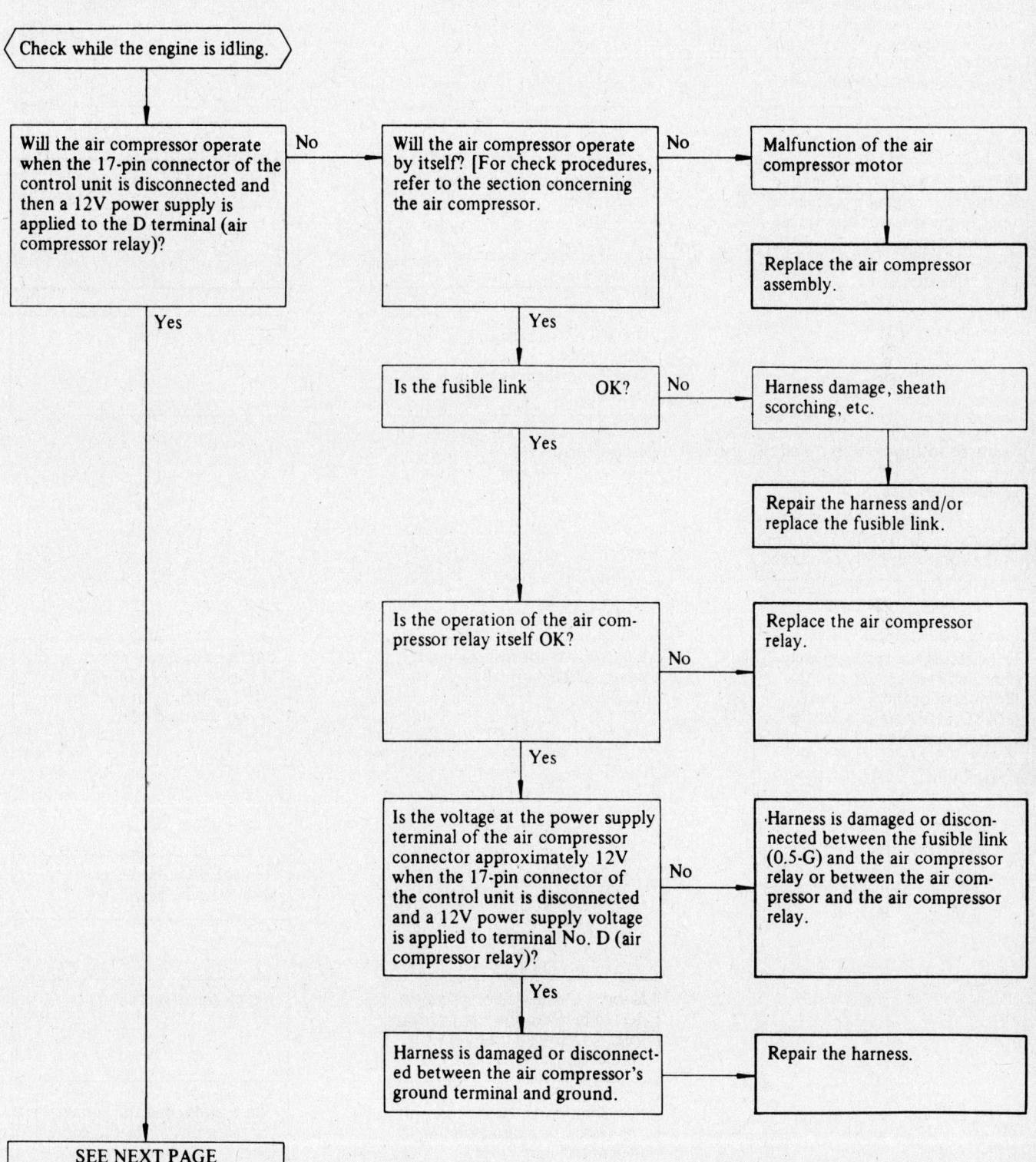

Check while the engine is idling.

Will the air compressor operate when the 17-pin connector of the control unit is disconnected and then a 12V power supply is applied to the D terminal (air compressor relay)?

No → Will the air compressor operate by itself? [For check procedures, refer to the section concerning the air compressor.

No → Malfunction of the air compressor motor → Replace the air compressor assembly.

Yes ↓

Is the fusible link   OK?

No → Harness damage, sheath scorching, etc. → Repair the harness and/or replace the fusible link.

Yes ↓

Is the operation of the air compressor relay itself OK?

No → Replace the air compressor relay.

Yes ↓

Is the voltage at the power supply terminal of the air compressor connector approximately 12V when the 17-pin connector of the control unit is disconnected and a 12V power supply voltage is applied to terminal No. D (air compressor relay)?

No → Harness is damaged or disconnected between the fusible link (0.5-G) and the air compressor relay or between the air compressor and the air compressor relay.

Yes ↓

Harness is damaged or disconnected between the air compressor's ground terminal and ground.

→ Repair the harness.

Yes ↓

SEE NEXT PAGE

Compressor troubleshooting continued

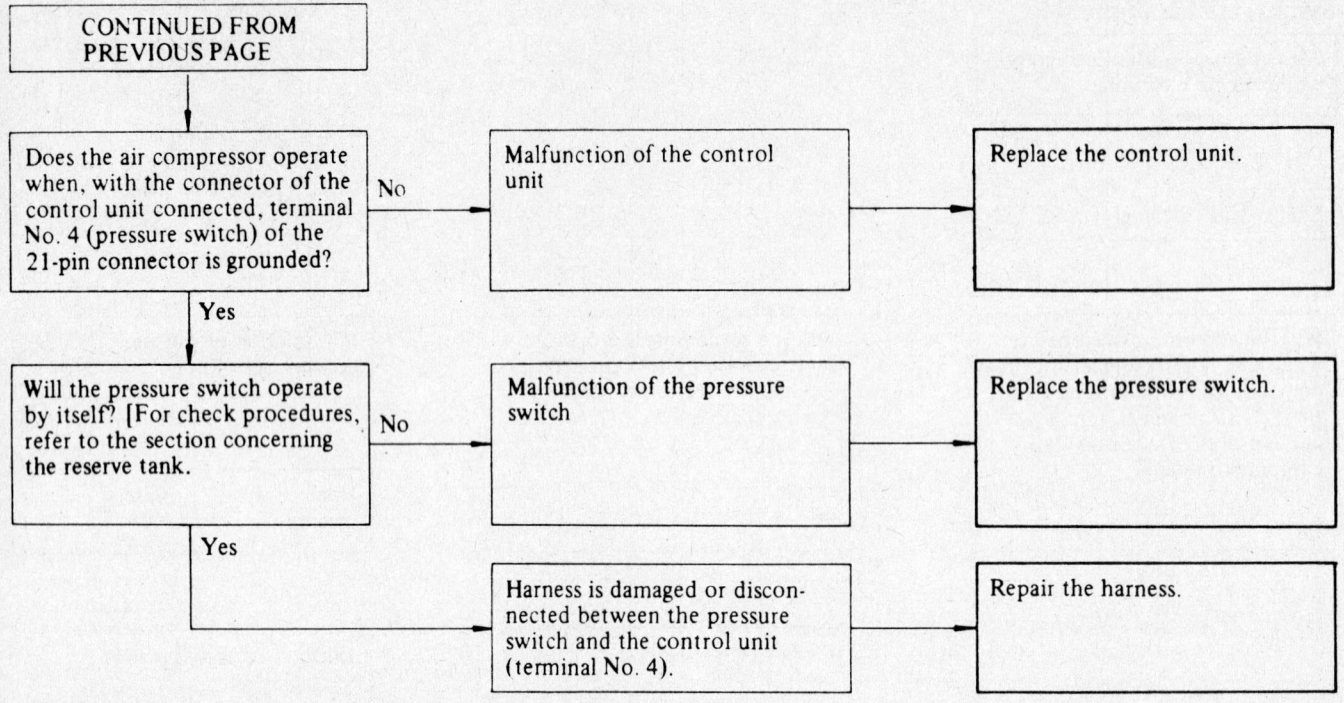

Troubleshooting by using self diagnosis output patterns

Malfunction No. 1

Troubleshooting by using self diagnosis output patterns

Malfunction No. 2

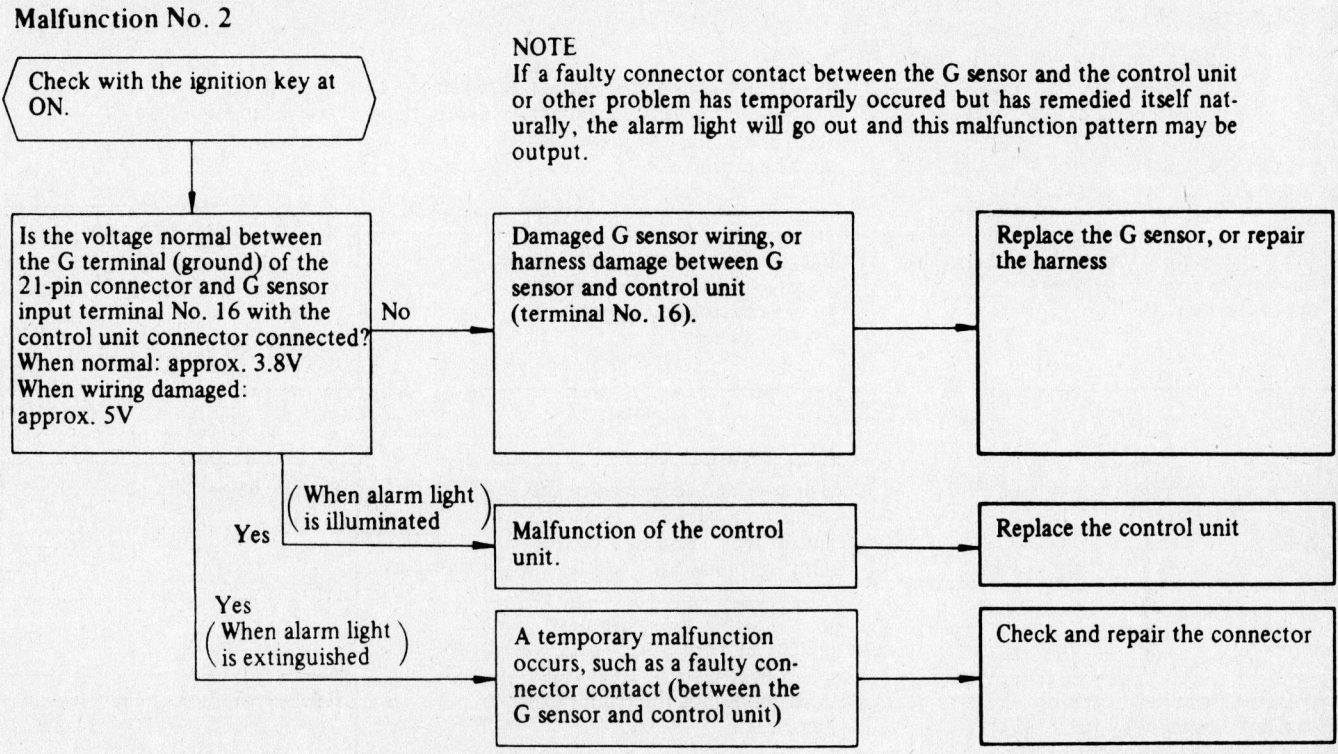

Check with the ignition key at ON.

NOTE
If a faulty connector contact between the G sensor and the control unit or other problem has temporarily occured but has remedied itself naturally, the alarm light will go out and this malfunction pattern may be output.

Is the voltage normal between the G terminal (ground) of the 21-pin connector and G sensor input terminal No. 16 with the control unit connector connected?
When normal: approx. 3.8V
When wiring damaged: approx. 5V

No → Damaged G sensor wiring, or harness damage between G sensor and control unit (terminal No. 16). → Replace the G sensor, or repair the harness

Yes (When alarm light is illuminated) → Malfunction of the control unit. → Replace the control unit

Yes (When alarm light is extinguished) → A temporary malfunction occurs, such as a faulty connector contact (between the G sensor and control unit) → Check and repair the connector

Troubleshooting by using self diagnosis output patterns

Malfunction No. 3

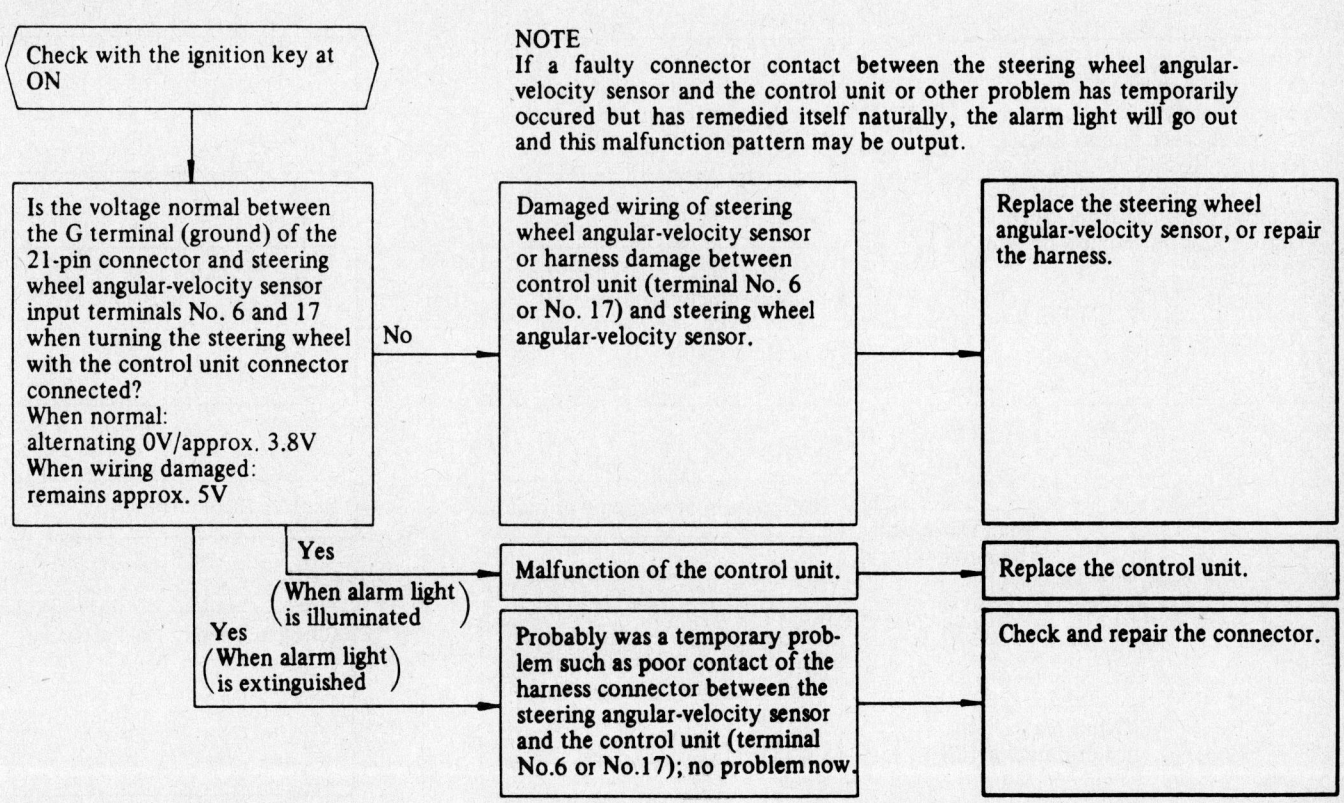

Check with the ignition key at ON

NOTE
If a faulty connector contact between the steering wheel angular-velocity sensor and the control unit or other problem has temporarily occured but has remedied itself naturally, the alarm light will go out and this malfunction pattern may be output.

Is the voltage normal between the G terminal (ground) of the 21-pin connector and steering wheel angular-velocity sensor input terminals No. 6 and 17 when turning the steering wheel with the control unit connector connected?
When normal: alternating 0V/approx. 3.8V
When wiring damaged: remains approx. 5V

No → Damaged wiring of steering wheel angular-velocity sensor or harness damage between control unit (terminal No. 6 or No. 17) and steering wheel angular-velocity sensor. → Replace the steering wheel angular-velocity sensor, or repair the harness.

Yes (When alarm light is illuminated) → Malfunction of the control unit. → Replace the control unit.

Yes (When alarm light is extinguished) → Probably was a temporary problem such as poor contact of the harness connector between the steering angular-velocity sensor and the control unit (terminal No.6 or No.17); no problem now. → Check and repair the connector.

Troubleshooting by using self diagnosis output patterns

Malfunction No. 4

```
Check with the ignition key
at ON
```

NOTE
If a faulty connector contact between the front height sensor and the
control unit or other problem has temporarily occured but has remedied
itself naturally, the alarm light will go out and this malfunction pattern
may be output.

```
Is the voltage between ground and     ──No──▶   Is the voltage between ground    ──No──▶   Malfunction of the control unit
the power supply terminal (0.5-L                and the Q terminal (sensor power
line) of the front height sensor               supply) of the 17-pin connector
approximately 5V?                              of the control unit approxi-
                                               mately 5V?
         │                                              │                                          │
        Yes                                            Yes                                         ▼
         │                                              │                                  Replace the control unit.
         │                                              ▼
         │                                      The harness is damaged or dis-   ──▶   Repair the harness.
         │                                      connected between the front
         │                                      height sensor and the control
         │                                      unit (terminal No. Q).
         ▼
Will the front height sensor          ──No──▶   Malfunction of the front height   ──▶   Replace the front height sensor.
operate normally by itself? [For               sensor
check procedures, refer to the
section concerning the height
sensor. (Refer to page 2-104.)]
         │
        Yes
         ▼
Is there a voltage indication         ──No──▶   The harness is short-circuited    ──▶   Repair the harness.
alternating between 0V and             (Remains  between the front height sensor
approximately 4.3V of the              0V.)      and the control unit (terminal
voltage between ground and                       No. 8, 9, 14 and/or 15).
terminals No.8, 9, 14 and 15 of
the 21-pin connector of the con-      ──No──▶   The harness is damaged or dis-   ──▶   Repair the harness.
trol unit when the front height        (Remains  connected between the front
sensor rod is moved upward and         4.3V.)    height sensor and the control
downward?                                        unit (terminal No. 8, 9, 14 and/
                                                 or 15).
    │         │
   Yes       Yes
    │         │   (When alarm light
    │         │   is illuminated)      ──▶   Malfunction of the control unit   ──▶   Replace the control unit.
    │
    │   (When alarm light
    │   is not illuminated)            ──▶   Probably was a temporary prob-   ──▶   Check and repair the harness
                                             lem such as poor contact of the         connector.
                                             harness connector between the
                                             front height sensor and the con-
                                             trol unit (terminal No. Q8, 9,
                                             14 and/or 15); no problem now.
```

Troubleshooting by using self diagnosis output patterns

Malfunction No. 5

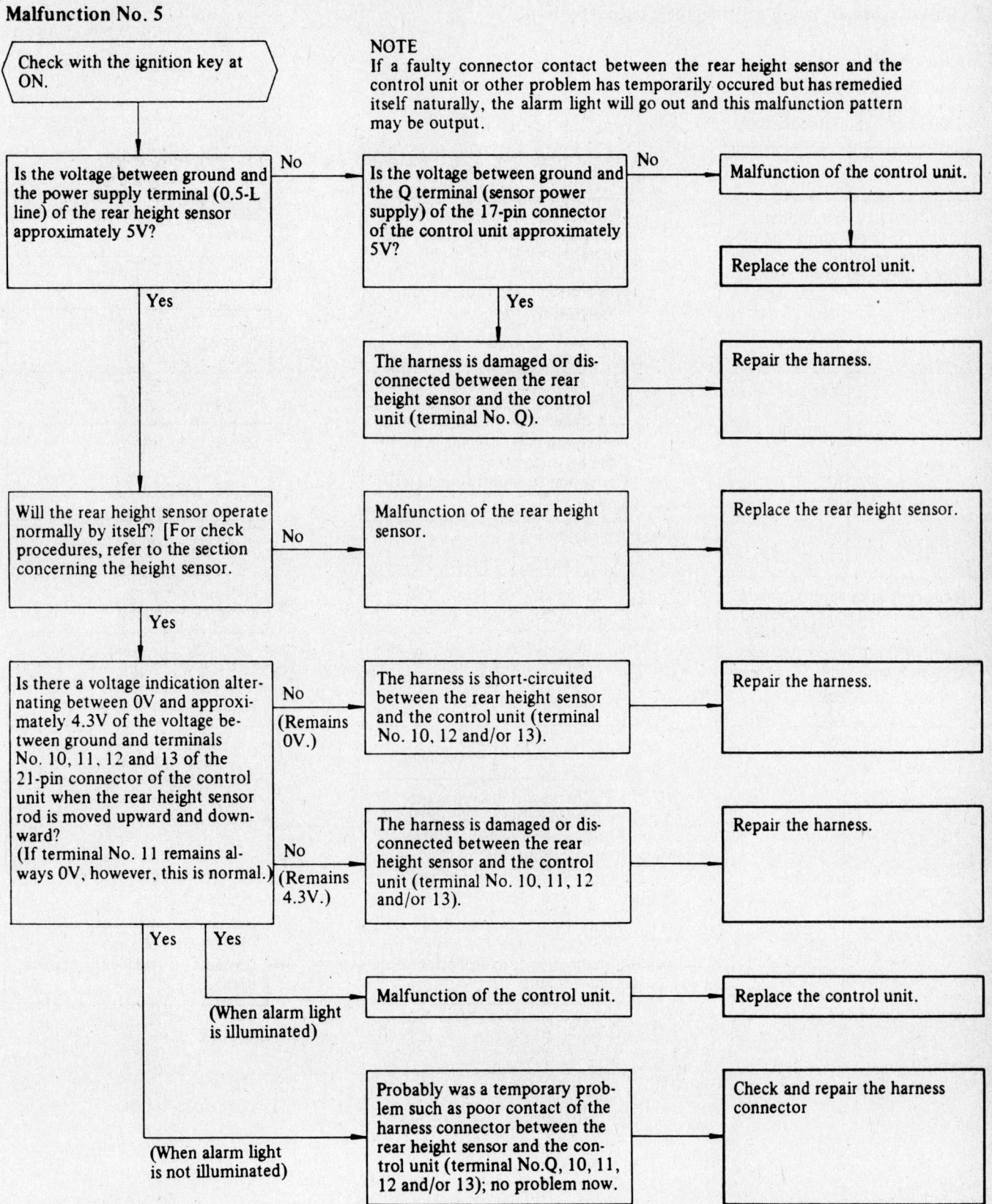

Check with the ignition key at ON.

NOTE
If a faulty connector contact between the rear height sensor and the control unit or other problem has temporarily occured but has remedied itself naturally, the alarm light will go out and this malfunction pattern may be output.

Is the voltage between ground and the power supply terminal (0.5-L line) of the rear height sensor approximately 5V?

— No → Is the voltage between ground and the Q terminal (sensor power supply) of the 17-pin connector of the control unit approximately 5V?

— No → Malfunction of the control unit. → Replace the control unit.

Yes ↓

Yes → The harness is damaged or disconnected between the rear height sensor and the control unit (terminal No. Q). → Repair the harness.

Will the rear height sensor operate normally by itself? [For check procedures, refer to the section concerning the height sensor.

— No → Malfunction of the rear height sensor. → Replace the rear height sensor.

Yes ↓

Is there a voltage indication alternating between 0V and approximately 4.3V of the voltage between ground and terminals No. 10, 11, 12 and 13 of the 21-pin connector of the control unit when the rear height sensor rod is moved upward and downward?
(If terminal No. 11 remains always 0V, however, this is normal.)

— No (Remains 0V.) → The harness is short-circuited between the rear height sensor and the control unit (terminal No. 10, 12 and/or 13). → Repair the harness.

— No (Remains 4.3V.) → The harness is damaged or disconnected between the rear height sensor and the control unit (terminal No. 10, 11, 12 and/or 13). → Repair the harness.

Yes / Yes

(When alarm light is illuminated) → Malfunction of the control unit. → Replace the control unit.

(When alarm light is not illuminated) → Probably was a temporary problem such as poor contact of the harness connector between the rear height sensor and the control unit (terminal No.Q, 10, 11, 12 and/or 13); no problem now. → Check and repair the harness connector

Troubleshooting by using self diagnosis output patterns

Malfunction No. 6

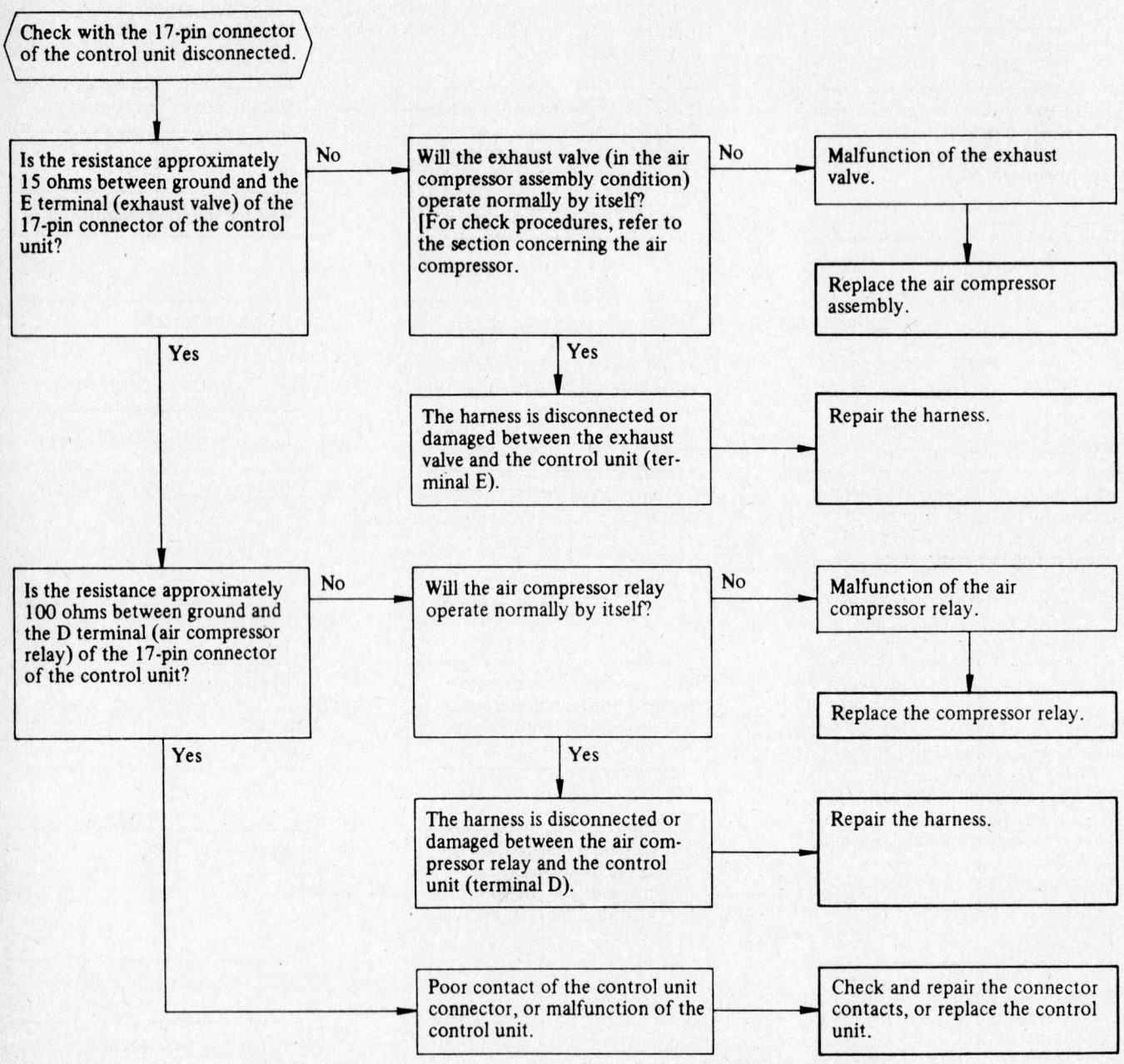

Check with the 17-pin connector of the control unit disconnected.

Is the resistance approximately 15 ohms between ground and the E terminal (exhaust valve) of the 17-pin connector of the control unit? — **No** → Will the exhaust valve (in the air compressor assembly condition) operate normally by itself? [For check procedures, refer to the section concerning the air compressor. — **No** → Malfunction of the exhaust valve. → Replace the air compressor assembly.

Yes ↓ (from exhaust valve question) → The harness is disconnected or damaged between the exhaust valve and the control unit (terminal E). → Repair the harness.

Yes ↓ (from 15 ohms question)

Is the resistance approximately 100 ohms between ground and the D terminal (air compressor relay) of the 17-pin connector of the control unit? — **No** → Will the air compressor relay operate normally by itself? — **No** → Malfunction of the air compressor relay. → Replace the compressor relay.

Yes ↓ (from air compressor relay question) → The harness is disconnected or damaged between the air compressor relay and the control unit (terminal D). → Repair the harness.

Yes ↓ (from 100 ohms question) → Poor contact of the control unit connector, or malfunction of the control unit. → Check and repair the connector contacts, or replace the control unit.

Troubleshooting by using self diagnosis output patterns

Malfunction No. 7

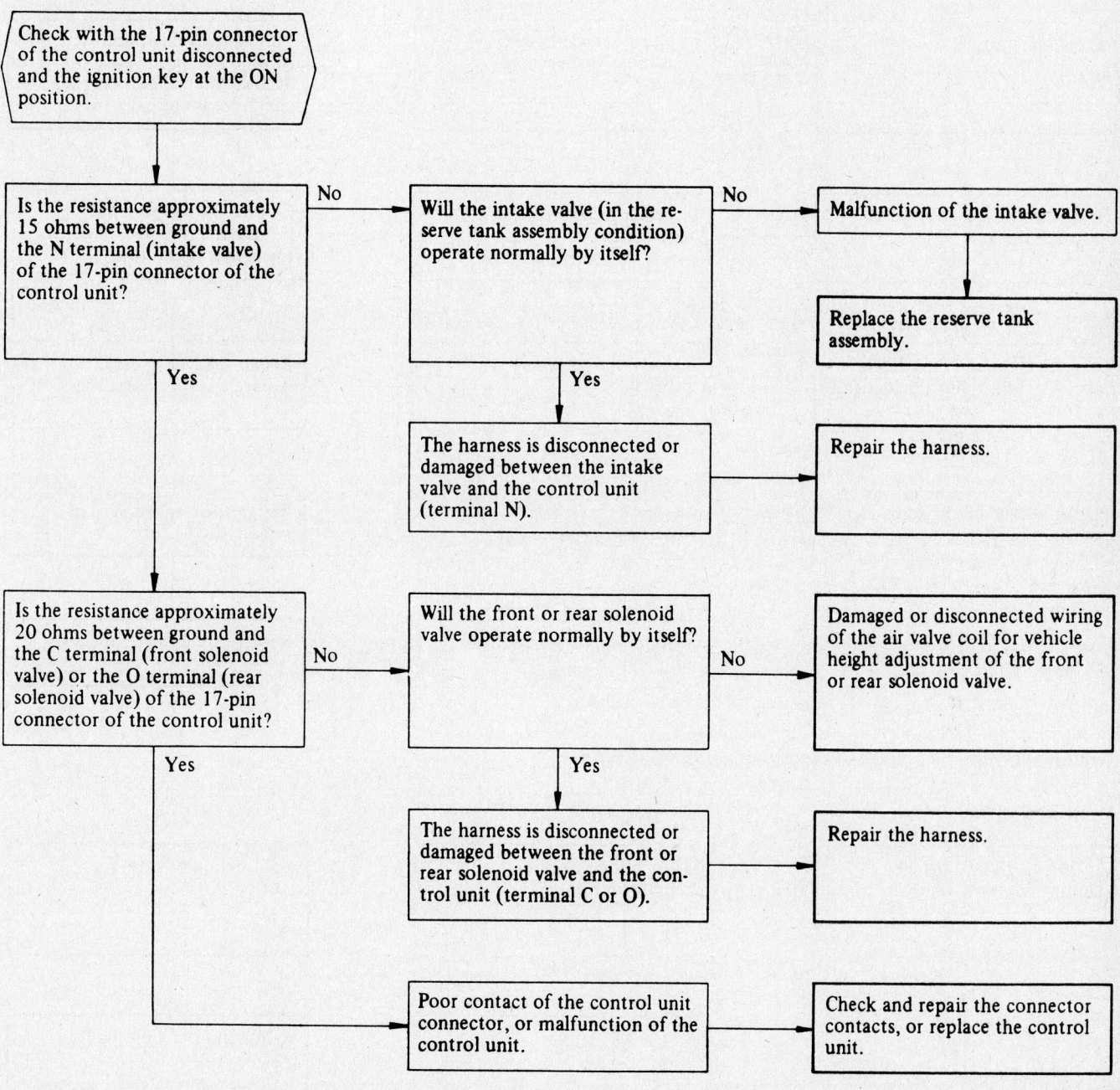

Troubleshooting by using self diagnosis output patterns

Malfunction No. 8

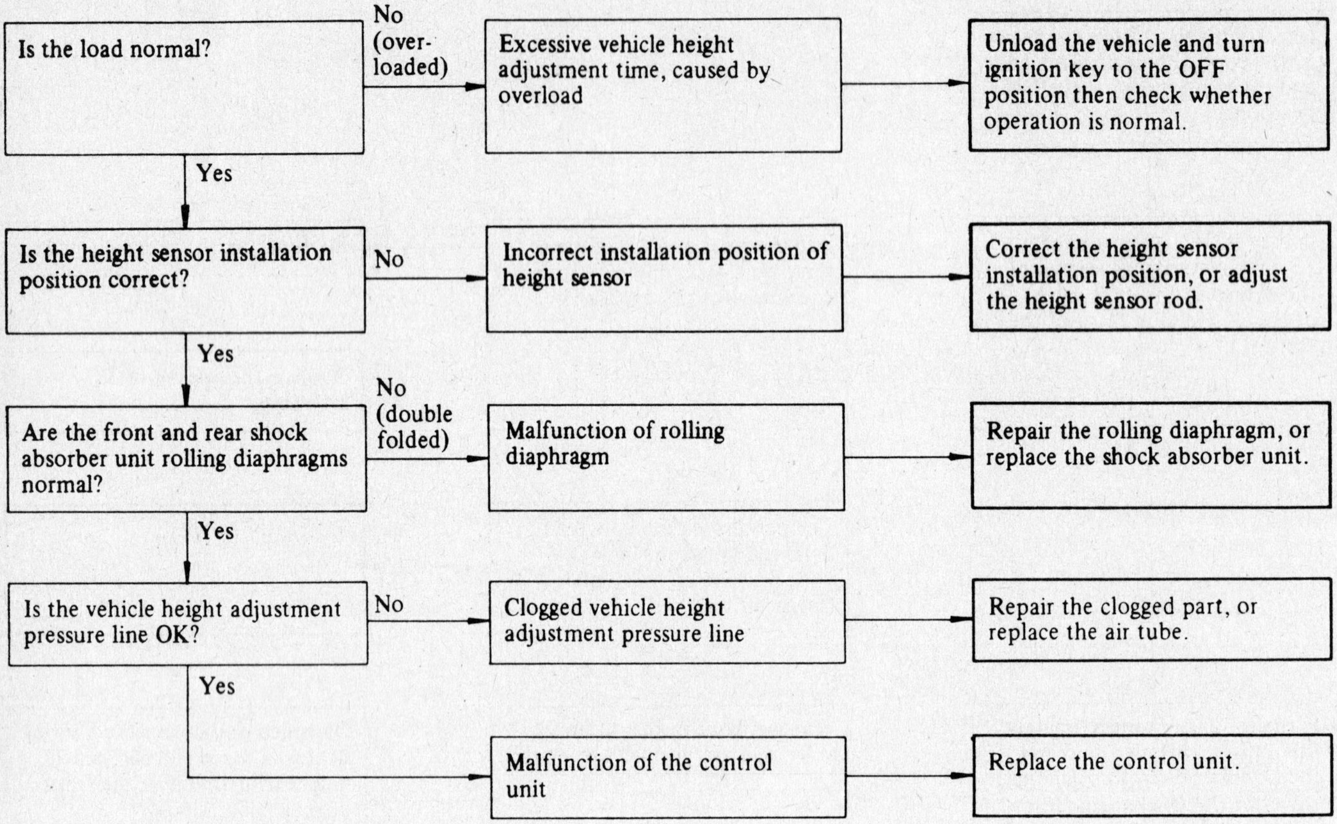

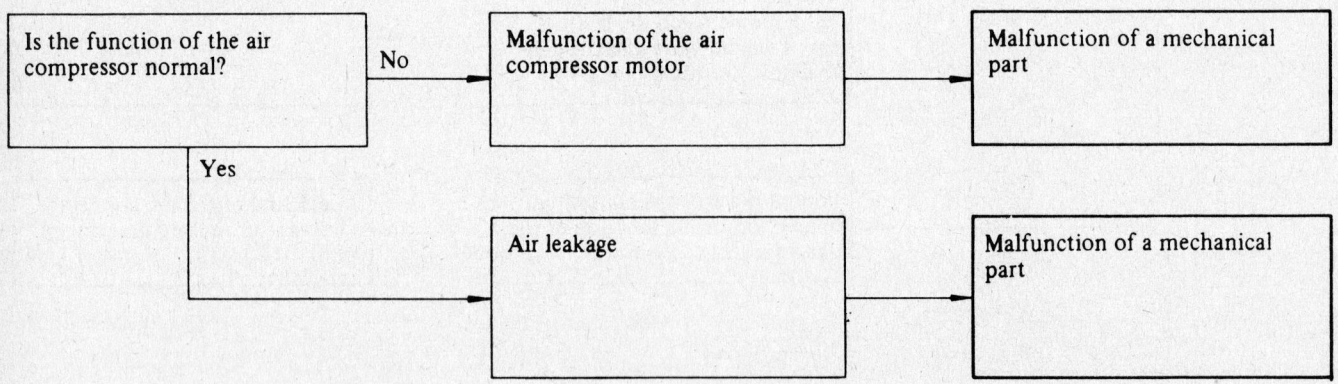

| Is the load normal? | → No (over-loaded) → | Excessive vehicle height adjustment time, caused by overload | → | Unload the vehicle and turn ignition key to the OFF position then check whether operation is normal. |

↓ Yes

| Is the height sensor installation position correct? | → No → | Incorrect installation position of height sensor | → | Correct the height sensor installation position, or adjust the height sensor rod. |

↓ Yes

| Are the front and rear shock absorber unit rolling diaphragms normal? | → No (double folded) → | Malfunction of rolling diaphragm | → | Repair the rolling diaphragm, or replace the shock absorber unit. |

↓ Yes

| Is the vehicle height adjustment pressure line OK? | → No → | Clogged vehicle height adjustment pressure line | → | Repair the clogged part, or replace the air tube. |

↓ Yes

| | | Malfunction of the control unit | → | Replace the control unit. |

Troubleshooting by using self diagnosis output patterns

Malfunction No. 9

| Is the function of the air compressor normal? | → No → | Malfunction of the air compressor motor | → | Malfunction of a mechanical part |

↓ Yes

| | | Air leakage | → | Malfunction of a mechanical part |

618

Troubleshooting by using self diagnosis output patterns

Malfunction No. 10

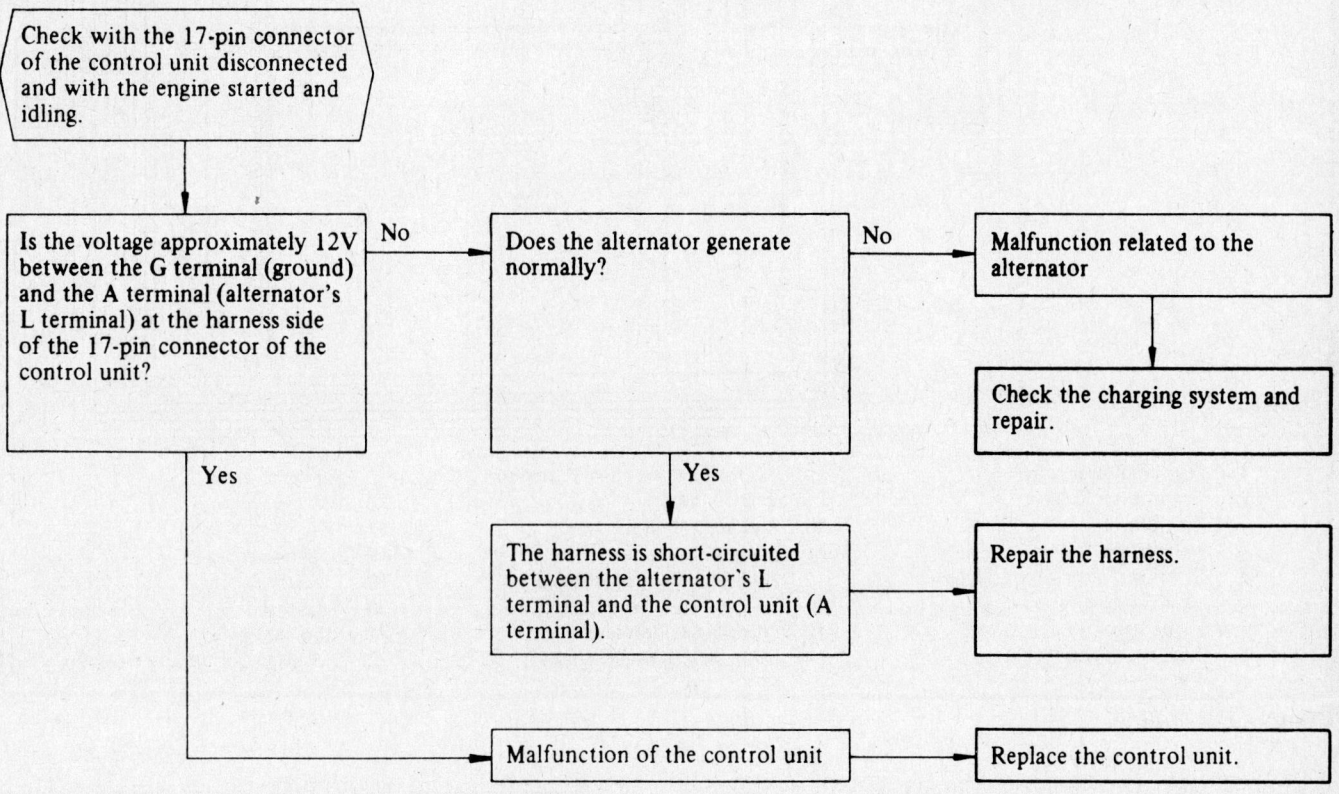

ELECTRONIC CONTROLLED SUSPENSION CONTROL UNIT TERMINALS VOLTAGE CHART
(with connectors connected to control unit)

Terminal No.	Signal	Condition	Terminal voltage E (V)
Ⓐ	Alternator L terminal	Engine stopped (alternator not generating)	More than 0V, less than 5V
		Engine running (alternator generating)	5V or more
Ⓑ	Battery (+B) power supply	Battery connected	10V or more
		Battery not connected	0V
C	Front solenoid valve (for vehicle height adjustment) drive	Height control air valve ON (open)	10V or more
		Height control air valve OFF (closed)	More than 0V, 1V or less

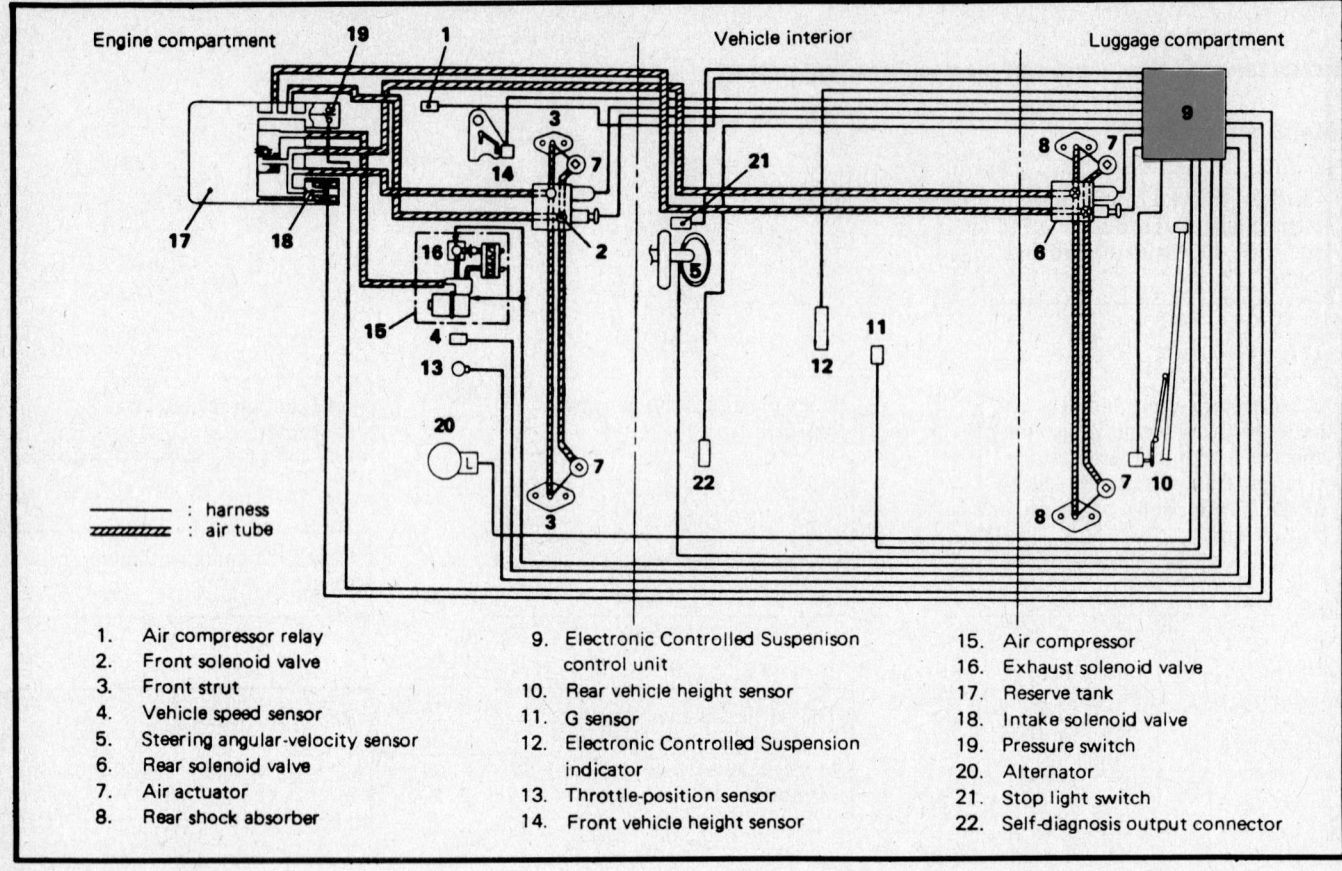

1. Air compressor relay	
2. Front solenoid valve	
3. Front strut	
4. Vehicle speed sensor	
5. Steering angular-velocity sensor	
6. Rear solenoid valve	
7. Air actuator	
8. Rear shock absorber	

9. Electronic Controlled Suspension control unit	
10. Rear vehicle height sensor	
11. G sensor	
12. Electronic Controlled Suspension indicator	
13. Throttle-position sensor	
14. Front vehicle height sensor	

15. Air compressor	
16. Exhaust solenoid valve	
17. Reserve tank	
18. Intake solenoid valve	
19. Pressure switch	
20. Alternator	
21. Stop light switch	
22. Self-diagnosis output connector	

: harness
: air tube

Component outline

whether or not the alarm light is illuminated. After checking to see that the alarm light is not illuminated, check the system's operation and check whether there are malfunctions other than those which cause the alarm light to illuminate.

The alarm light will also illuminate under other conditions such as vehicle overload, insufficient air pressure or vehicle stopped on a steep slope. This does not necessarily mean there is a malfunction in the system.

CAUTION

If vehicle height adjustment is made with the brake pedal held down, a noise may be heard from the suspension. This is not an indication of an abnormal condition.

The sound occurs because all four wheels are locked when the brake pedal is depressed. This action obstructs the movement of the suspension arm which is necessary while vehicle is being adjusted.

TROUBLESHOOTING GUIDE
Chrysler/Mitsubishi

Condition	Cause	Correction
Overload	Height adjustment not finished even though 3 minutes or more have passed.	Stop the engine temporarily, and then re-start after unloading the overload.
Vehicle stopped on steep slope with engine running.	Vehicle height adjustment starts because of load movement while travelling on steep slope, but height adjustment is not completed even though 3 minutes or more have passed.	Move to a flat surface, stop engine, and then re-start.
Vehicle height adjustment occurs frequently when outside temperature is high.	Air pressure is insufficient because the compressor has operated continuously for 4 minutes or more, or the air compressor is not operating because its thermo-switch is OFF, with the result that the vehicle height adjustment is not completed even though 3 minutes or more have passed.	Stop the engine, open the hood and allow the air compressor in the engine compartment to cool; then re-start the engine.

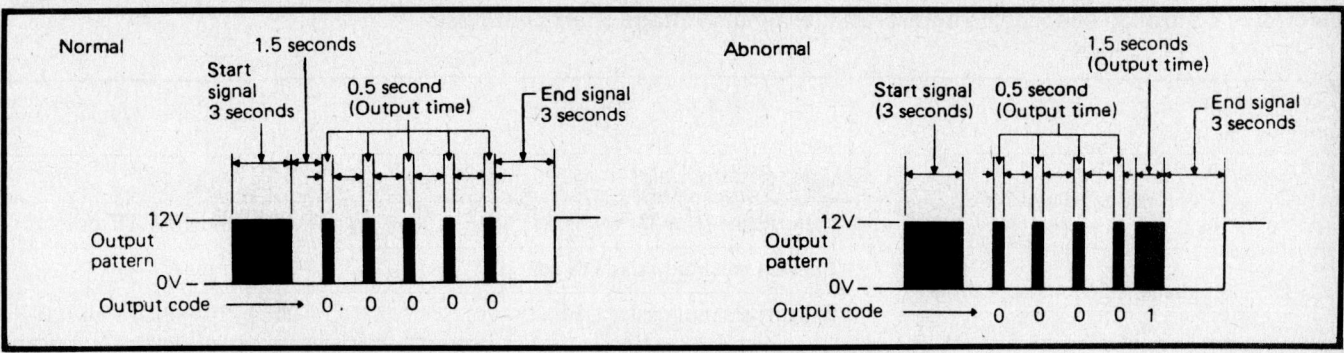

Voltage reading output pattern example

SELF DIAGNOSTIC OUTPUT CODES AND PATTERNS

Self diagnostic output patterns (voltage waveforms generated to the self diagnostic check connector) are patterns shown as waveforms.

By reading the indicator shown on a voltmeter connected to the connector, it is possible to diagnose each malfunction condition. Voltage is indicated by changes in the range of 0 to 12 volts.

The self diagnostic check connector is located inside the glove box at the top. In order to gain access to the connector, the glove compartment must first be removed.

NOTE: Because the voltage generation time is short for some voltmeters, the meter may not read a full 12 volts.

Component Replacement

STRUT ASSEMBLY

Removal and Installation

1. Raise the vehicle and support safely. Remove the wheel and tire assembly.
2. Remove the brake hose bracket from the strut assembly.
3. Remove the strut assembly retaining bolts.
4. Disconnect the air line from the strut assembly. Remove the dust cover.

5. Remove the strut assembly mounting bolts.
6. Remove the strut assembly from the vehicle.
7. Installation is the reverse of the removal procedure. Use new "O" rings on the air lines and attach according to their color.
8. Inspect the system for air leaks and proper operation.

Disassembly

1. Remove the strut assembly from the vehicle as outlined.
2. Secure the strut in a holding fixture. Attach a spring compression tool according to the manufacturers instructions.
3. After spring compression is complete, remove the snap ring. Remove the joint bracket from the strut assembly.
4. Remove the actuator bracket from the strut assembly.
5. Remove the insulator mounting nut. Remove the insulator from the strut assembly.
6. Gradually loosen the spring compression tool, and remove the sub tank, coil spring and lower spring pad from the strut assembly.
7. Remove the "O" ring from the sub tank.

Inspection

1. Inspect the rubber components for deterioration.
2. Check the strut insulator bearing for wear.
3. Inspect the coil spring for damage.
4. Inspect the shock absorber for damage or fluid leakage.

Reassembly

1. Coat a new "O" ring with petroleum jelly or equivalent and install on the sub tank.
2. Attach the strut assembly lower spring pad, coil spring

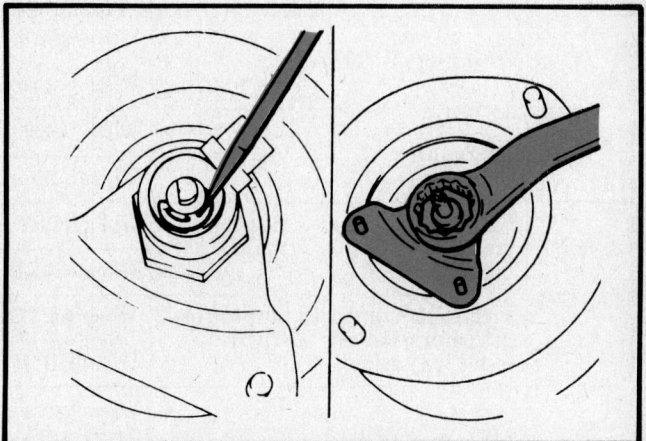

Air line connections

Snap ring and actuator bracket removal

Electronic controlled suspension control unit terminals voltage chart continued

Terminal No.	Signal	Condition	Terminal voltage E (V)
D	Compressor relay drive	Compressor relay ON	10V or more
		Compressor relay OFF	More than 0V, 1V or less
E	Exhaust solenoid valve drive	Exhaust solenoid valve ON (open)	10V or more
		Exhaust solenoid valve OFF (closed)	More than 0V, 1V or less
F	Rear solenoid valve (for HARD/SOFT switching) drive	HARD/SOFT air valve OFF (open)	10V or more
		HARD/SOFT air valve OFF (closed)	More than 0V, 1V or less
Ⓖ	Sensor circuit ground	—	0V
H	Self-diagnosis output	During output	10V or more
		During non-output	More than 0V, 1V or less
I	Electronic Controlled Suspension indicator panel HIGH vehicle height indication	When NORMAL or LOW vehicle height	10V or more
		When HIGH vehicle height	More than 0V, 1V or less
J	Electronic Controlled Suspension indicator panel LOW vehicle height indication	When NORMAL vehicle height	10V or more
		When LOW vehicle height	More than 0V, 1V or less
Ⓚ	Ground	—	0V
Ⓛ	Stop light switch	Stop light switch ON (stop lights illuminated)	10V or more
		Stop light switch OFF (stop lights not illuminated)	More than 0V, 1V or less
M	Front solenoid valve (for HARD/SOFT switching) drive	HARD/SOFT air valve ON (open)	10V or more
		HARD/SOFT air valve OFF (closed)	More than 0V, 1V or less
N	Intake solenoid valve drive	Intake solenoid valve ON (open)	10V or more
		Intake solenoid valve OFF (closed)	More than 0V, 1V or less
O	Rear solenoid valve (for vehicle height adjustment) drive	Height control air valve ON (open)	10V or more
		Height control air valve OFF (closed)	More than 0V, 1V or less
Ⓟ	IG2 power supply	Ignition key at ON position	10V or more
		Ignition key at LOCK, ACC or START position	0V
Q	Power supply for sensor	When control unit is operating	Approx. 5V
		When control unit is not operating	0V
1	Buzzer drive	When buzzer is sounding	More than 0V, 1V or less
		When buzzer is not sounding	10V or more
2	Electronic Controlled Suspension indicator panel SOFT/HARD indication	When SOFT	More than 0V, 1V or less
		When HARD	10V or more
3	Electronic Controlled Suspension indicator panel AUTO/HIGH mode indication	When AUTO mode	More than 0V, 1V or less
		When HIGH mode	10V or more
④	Pressure switch	When pressure switch is ON	More than 0V, 1V or less
		When pressure switch is OFF	4V or more, less than 5V

Electronic controlled suspension control unit terminals voltage chart continued

Terminal No.	Signal			Condition		Terminal voltage E (V)
⑤	Vehicle speed sensor			When vehicle speed sensor is ON		More than 0V, 1.6V or less
				When vehicle speed sensor is OFF		4.5V or more
⑥	Steering angular-velocity sensor		When normal	When photo-interruptor is ON		More than 0V, 1V or less
				When photo-interruptor is OFF		2.5V or more, less than 4V
			When harness is damaged or disconnected			4V or more, less than 5V
⑦	Mode selector switch		AUTO/SPORT selector switch	When switch is ON		More than 0V, 1V or less
				When switch is OFF		4V or more, less than 5V
			AUTO/HIGH selector switch	When switch is ON		Approx. 2V
				When switch is OFF		4V or more, less than 5V
⑧	Height sensor input signal	Front B				When photo-interruptor is ON
⑨		Front D				
⑩		Rear B				More than 0V, 1V or less
⑪		Rear D				
⑫		Rear C				
⑬		Rear A				When photo-interruptor is OFF
⑭		Front C				
⑮		Front A				4V or more, less than 5V
⑯	G sensor		When normal	When G sensor is OFF (photo-interruptor)		More than 0V, 1V or less
				When G sensor is ON (photo-interruptor)		More than 2.5V, less than 4V
			When harness is damaged or disconnected			4V or more, less than 5V
⑰	Steering angular-velocity sensor		When normal	When photo-interruptor is ON		More than 0V, 1V or less
				When photo-interruptor is OFF		2.5V or more, less than 4V
			When harness is damaged or disconnected			4V or more, less than 5V
⑱	Throttle-position sensor			When throttle valve is completely closed		0.4V or more, 1.5V or less
				When throttle valve is completely open		4V or more, less than 5V
19	Electronic Controlled Suspension indicator panel AUTO/SPORT mode indication			When AUTO mode		More than 0V, 1V or less
				When SPORT mode		10V or more
20	Electronic Controlled Suspension indicator panel vehicle height adjustment indication			When vehicle height adjustment indicator is illuminated		More than 0V, 1V or less
				When vehicle height adjustment indicator is not illuminated		10V or more
21	Electronic Controlled Suspension indicator panel alarm light			When alarm light is illuminated		More than 0V, 1V or less
				When alarm light is not illuminated		10V or more

Remarks:
Terminal numbers surrounded by a circle indicate input terminals; those not encircled are output terminals.

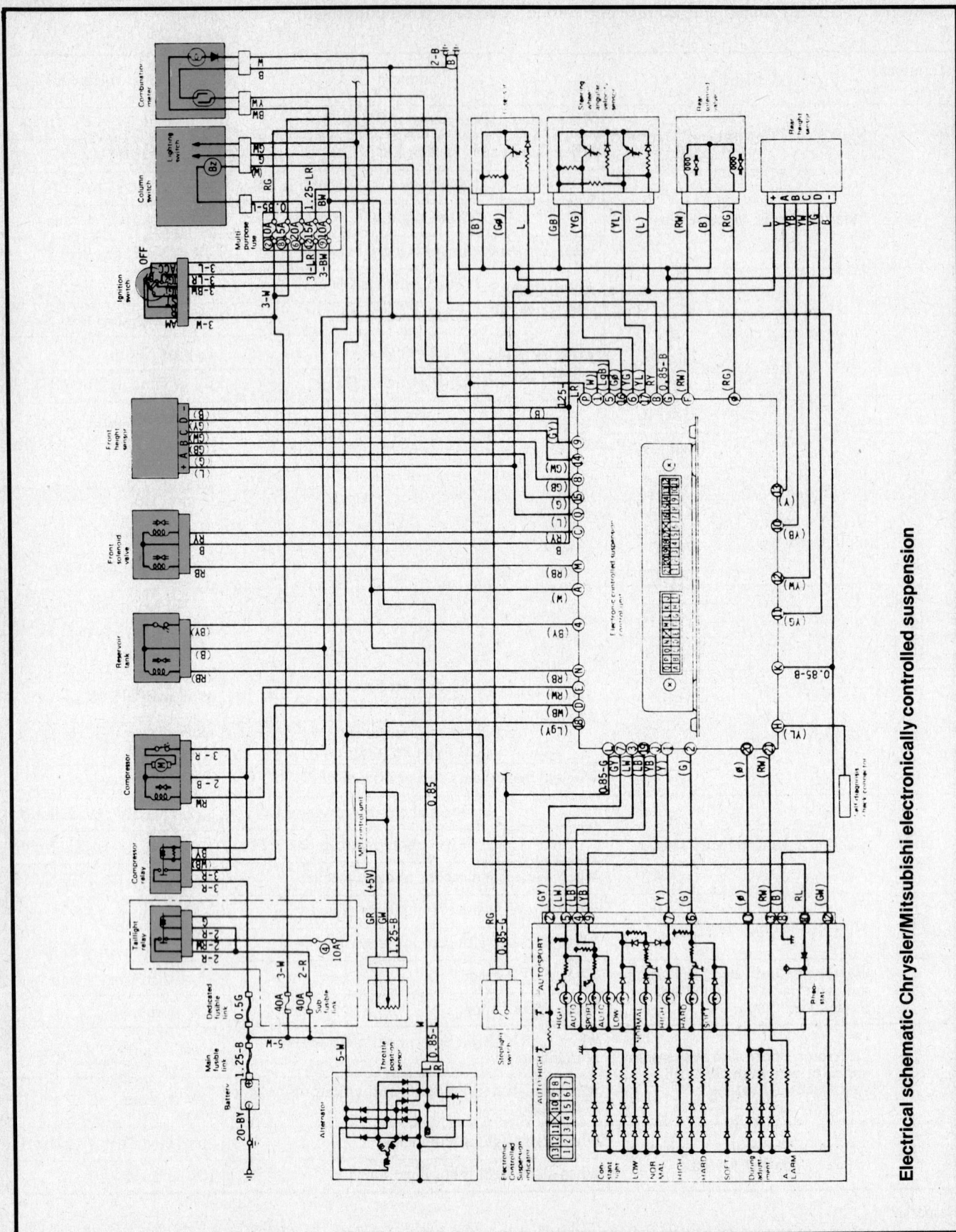

Electrical schematic Chrysler/Mitsubishi electronically controlled suspension

and sub tank. Place the assembly into the spring compression tool and gradually tighten.

CAUTION

When installing the coil spring, install so that the part of the coil spring that has the larger outer diameter is facing downward. While adjusting, make sure the lower edge of the coil spring and of the lower spring pad and sub tank are in correct order. Apply compression while adjusting the notched position of the piston rod by using a wrench to fit the "D" shape of the sub tank and one to fit the notch of the piston rod.

---

3. Install the insulator to the strut assembly and tighten to 58–72 ft. lbs.

4. Remove the compression tool and apply a coating of multipurpose grease (SAE J310a, NLGI grade #2 EP) or equivalent to the insulator bearing channel.

5. Align the notch of the piston rod with the "D" shape of the actuator bracket. Attach the actuator bracket to the strut assembly and tighten the nut to 29–43 ft. lbs.

6. Apply a coating of grease to a new "O" ring and install it to the piston rod.

7. Install the joint to the strut assembly. Attach the snap ring to the piston rod.

8. Inspect the strut to make sure that it turns smoothly. Check the strut assembly for air leakage.

Installation

1. Turn the insulator so that the joint and actuator are at

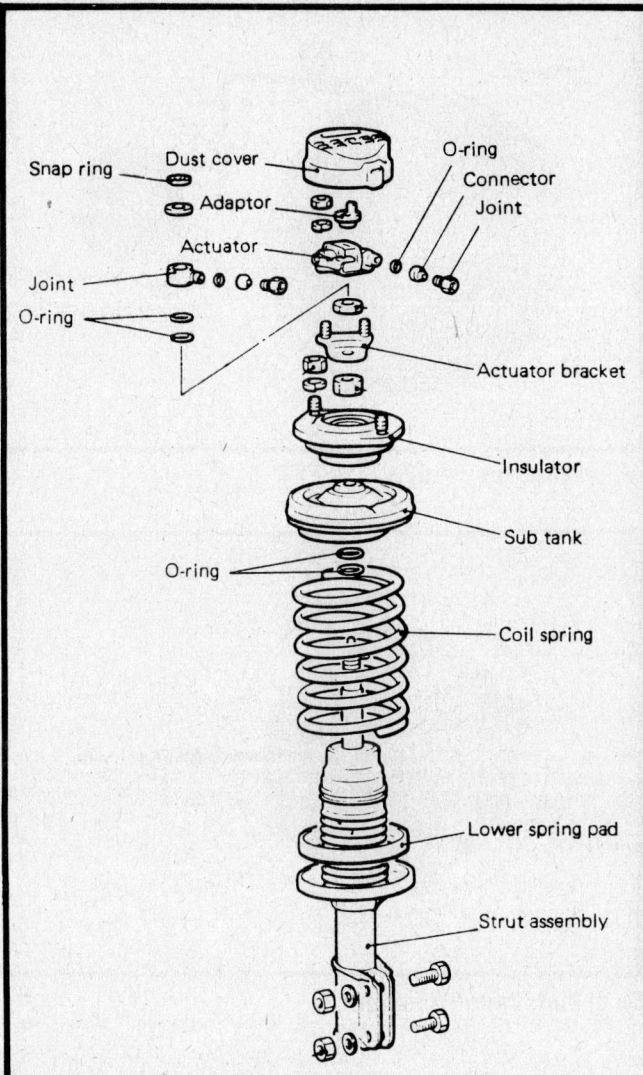

Strut assembly—exploded view

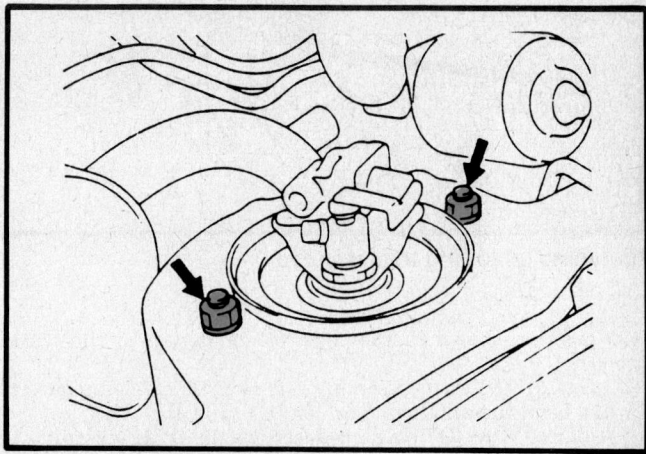

Strut assembly mounting nuts

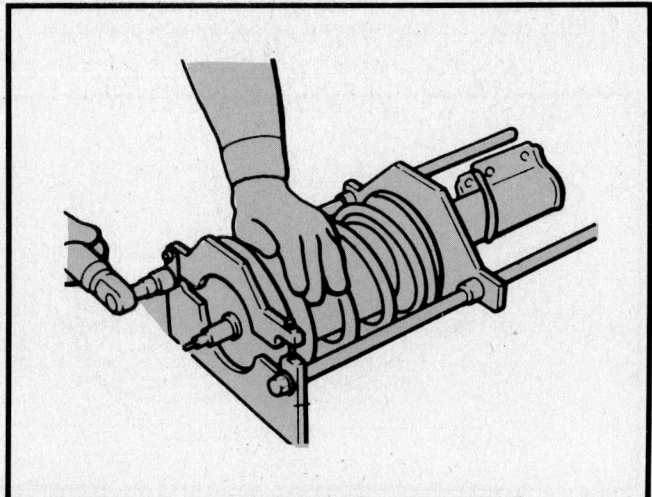

Placement of spring in compression tool

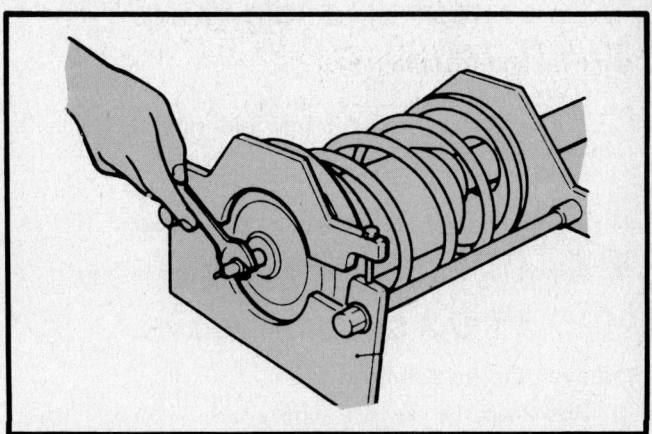

Wrench location to fit the "D" shape of the sub tank

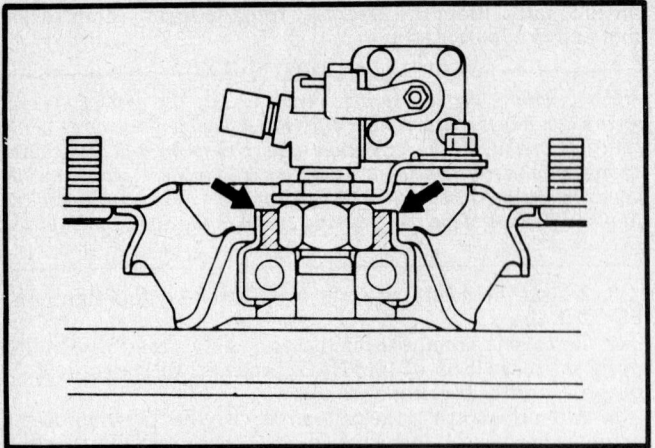

Insulator bearing channel grease location

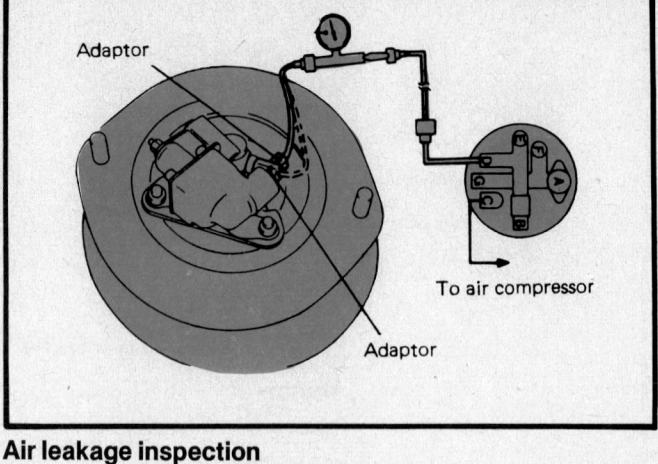

Air leakage inspection

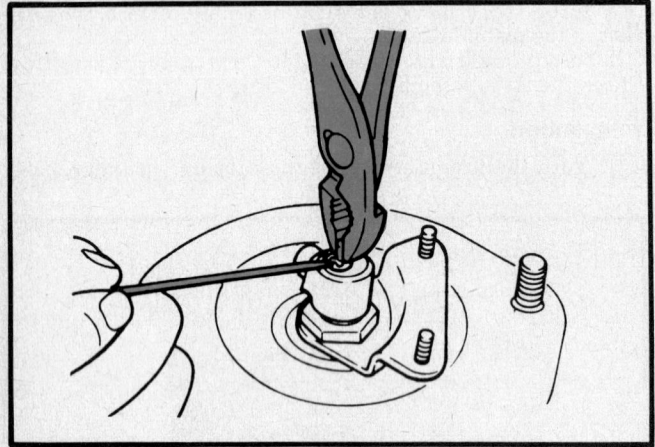

Installing snap ring to piston rod

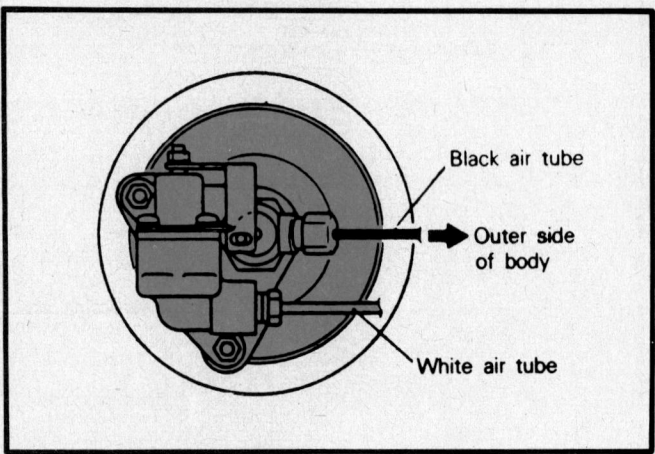

Strut installation position

the position shown in the illustration. Install in the wheel house.

2. Install the strut assembly into the vehicle being careful not to bend the air lines. Tighten to 6–7 ft. lbs.

3. Using new "O" rings, connect the air lines according to color.

4. Inspect the system for proper operation and air leaks.

FRONT SOLENOID VALVE

Removal and Installation

1. Disconnect the negative battery cable.

2. Tag and disconnect the air tube and connections from the solenoid valve.

3. Remove the front solenoid retaining bolts.

4. Remove the solenoid from the vehicle.

5. Installation is the reverse of the removal procedure. Use a new "O" ring upon installation.

6. Inspect for air leakage and proper system operation.

REAR SOLENOID VALVE

Removal and Installation

1. Disconnect the negative battery cable.

2. Remove the rear seat cushion anchor covers. Remove the rear seat cushion retaining bolts.

3. Remove the upper seat back retaining screws. Lifting the seat in an upward motion, remove the rear seat back.

4. Disconnect the air tube and connector attachment from the rear solenoid valve.

5. Remove the rear solenoid valve from the vehicle.

6. Installation is the reverse of the removal procedure.

7. Inspect for air leakage and proper system operation.

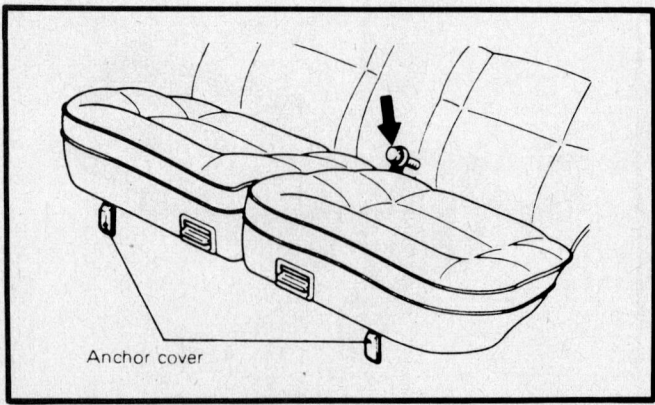

Lower seat retaining bolt location

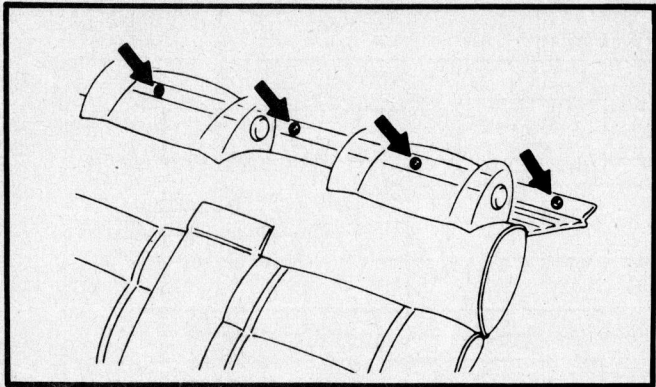

Rear seat back retaining screws

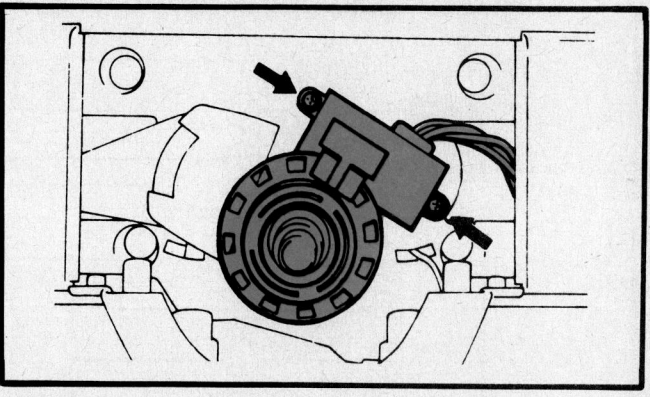

Steering wheel angular velocity sensor location

RESERVE TANK

Removal and Installation

1. Disconnect the battery terminals. Remove the battery from the vehicle.
2. Remove the battery tray from the vehicle in order to gain working clearance.
3. Tag and disconnect the air lines and connectors from the reserve tank.
4. Loosen the reserve tank retaining nuts. Remove the reserve tank from the vehicle.
5. Installation is the reverse of the removal procedure. Inspect for air leakage.

FRONT HEIGHT SENSOR

Removal and Installation

1. Disconnect the negative battery cable.
2. Disconnect the front rod from the lower control arm.
3. Remove the air compressor from the transmission mounting bracket.
4. Tag and disconnect the front wiring harness from the height sensor.
5. Remove the retaining bolts from the front height sensor. Remove the height sensor from the crossmember.
6. Installation is the reverse of the removal procedure.

REAR HEIGHT SENSOR

Removal and Installation

1. Disconnect the nagative battery cable.
2. Disconnect the coupling of the rear height sensor bracket and the rear rod if necessary.
3. Disconnect the wiring connector from the height sensor.
4. Remove the rear height sensor from the rear floor side member. Remove the rear height sensor from the vehicle.
5. Installation is the reverse of the removal procedure.

STEERING WHEEL ANGULAR VELOCITY SENSOR

Removal and Installation

1. Disconnect the negative battery cable.
2. Remove the steering wheel horn pad.
3. Remove the steering wheel retaining bolt.
4. Using a suitable puller, remove the steering wheel.
5. Remove the velocity sensor retaining screws.

6. Disconnect the velocity sensor wiring harness. Remove the sensor from the vehicle.
7. Installation is the reverse of the removal procedure.

ELECTRONIC SUSPENSION CONTROL UNIT

Removal and Installation

1. Disconnect the negative battery cable.
2. Remove the luggage compartment trim from the right side of the trunk compartment.
3. Remove the suspension control unit mounting bolts.
4. Tag and disconnect the electrical connectors.
5. Remove the control unit from the body.
6. Installation is the reverse of the removal procedure.

AIR COMPRESSOR RELAY

Removal and Installation

1. Remove the mounting bolt from the compressor relay.
2. Tag and disconnect the electrical connector from the relay assembly.
3. Remove the relay from the wheel housing.
4. Installation is the reverse of the removal procedure. Inpsect the system for proper operation.

CONSOLE INDICATOR

Removal and Installation

1. Disconnect the negative battery cable.
2. Remove the lower part of the radio panel.

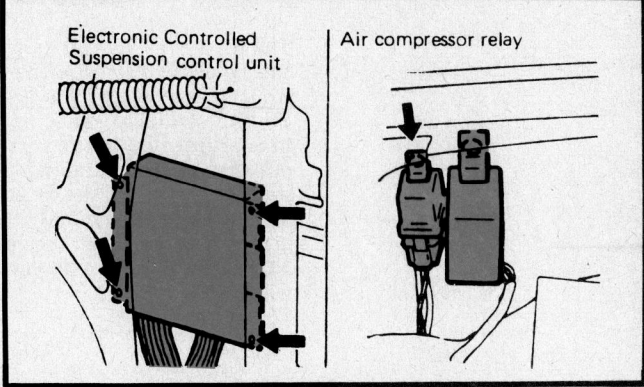

Electronic Controlled Suspension control unit

Air compressor relay

Control unit and relay mounting bolt locations

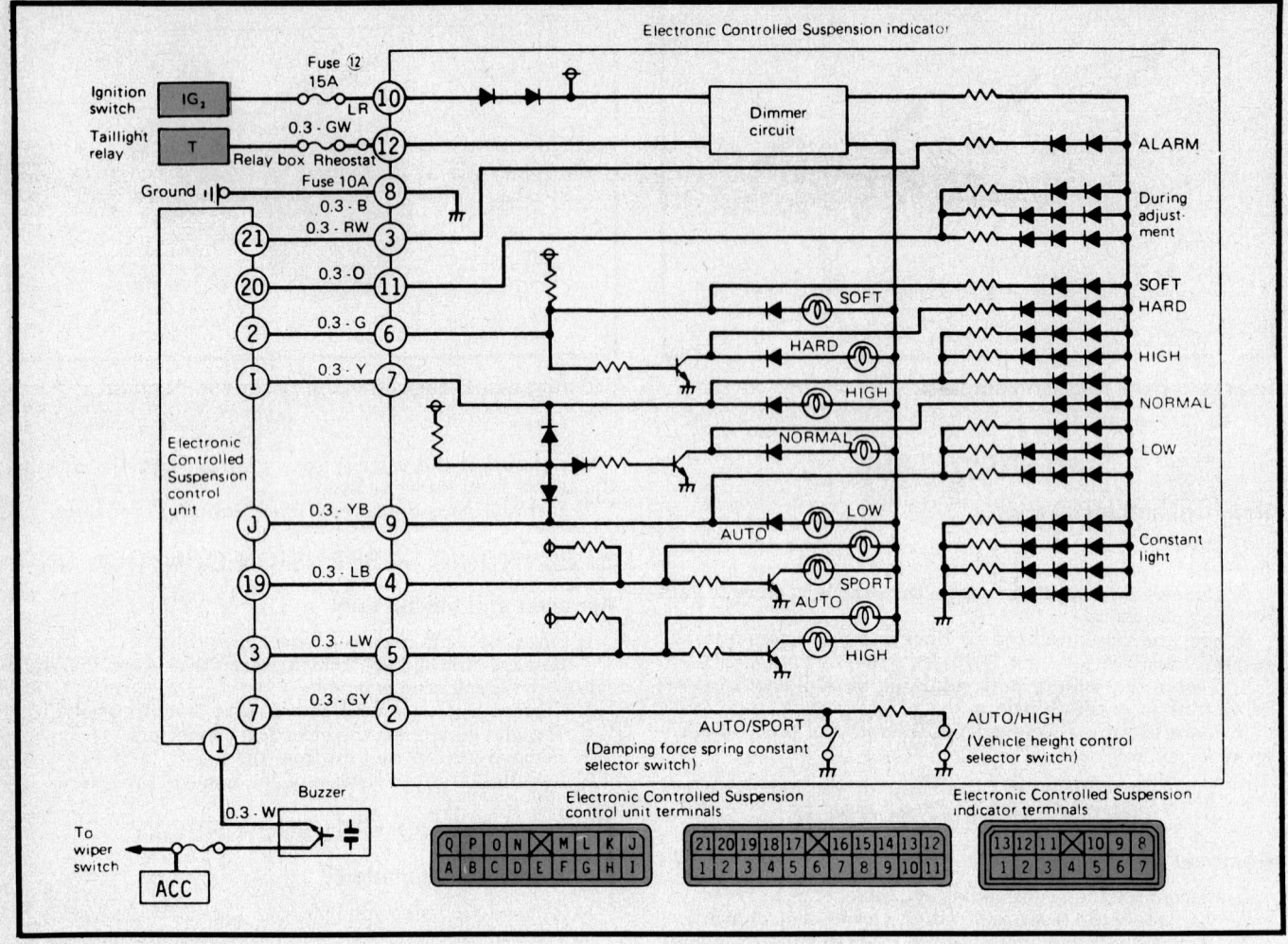

Electronic suspension electrical schematic

3. Remove the radio from the console.
4. Remove the console indicator retaining bolts.
5. Tag and disconnect the electrical connector from the rear

of the indicator.
6. Remove the console indicator from the vehicle.
7. Installation is the reverse of the removal procedure.

MAZDA

General Information

The three-way control damping system switches in the vehicle can be used to select either SPORT or NORMAL mode of the front or rear wheel shock absorber damping force. When the SPORT switch is set to on, the SPORT damping force is applied, regardless of the vehicle speed. When the switch is set to off, the normal damping force is applied. When the AUTO switch is set to on, the control unit allows the SPORT damping force to be applied to only the front wheels if the vehicle speed is over 50 mph. When the vehicle speed is less than 50 mph, the NORMAL damping force is applied to the front and rear wheels.

Troubleshooting

The following troubleshooting guides can be used in diagnosing the automatic adjusting suspension system.

TROUBLESHOOTING GUIDE
Mazda

Condition	Cause	Correction
Body "rolls"	Weak stabilizer	Replace
	Worn or deteriorated stabilizer and suspension arm installation bushing	Replace
	Shock absorber malfunction	Replace
Poor riding comfort	Weak coil spring	Replace
	Malfunction of shock absorber(s)	Replace
Body tilt	Weak coil spring	Replace
	Worn stabilizer and suspension arm installation bushing	Replace
Abnormal noise from suspension system	Poor lubrication or wear of lower arm ball joint	Replace
	Looseness of peripheral connections	Tighten
	Malfunction of shock absorber(s)	Replace
	Worn or deteriorated stabilizer and suspension arm installation bushing	Replace
	Wear or damage of front strut bearing	Replace
"Heavy" steering wheel operation	Lower arm ball joint stuck	Replace
	Ball joints stuck or damaged	Replace
	Ball joints insufficiently lubricated; foreign material; abnormal wear	Lubricate or replace
	Improperly adjusted wheel alignment (toe-in)	Adjust
	Worn or damaged steering gear bushing	Replace
	Improperly adjusted pinion pre-load	Adjust
	Damaged steering gear	Replace
	Insufficient grease on steering gear	Add grease
	Malfunction of steering shaft universal joint	Repair or replace
	Low tire pressure	Adjust
	Abnormal tire wear	Replace
Steering wheel pulls to one side	Weak coil spring	Replace
	Lower arm and stabilizer installation bushing worn or damaged	Replace
	Bent knuckle arm	Replace
	Lower arm deformed or loose	Replace or tighten
	Improperly adjusted wheel alignment (toe-in)	Adjust
	Bent steering linkage	Replace
	Worn wheel bearing	Replace
	Uneven tire pressure	Adjust
	Abnormal tire wear (left and right are worn differently)	Replace
	Brakes dragging	Repair
Steering wheel vibrates	Suspension arm and stabilizer installation bushing worn or deteriorated	Replace
	Worn lower arm ball joint	Replace
	Shock absorber malfunction or looseness	Replace or tighten
	Improperly adjusted wheel alignment (toe-in)	Adjust
	Bent linkage	Replace
	Worn or damaged joints	Replace
	Improperly adjusted pinion pre-load	Adjust
	Worn steering gear bushing	Replace
	Loose steering shaft universal joint	Replace
	Malfunction of wheel bearing	Replace
	Abnormal tire wear	Replace
	Tire tread depth different (left/right)	Replace
	Deformed or unbalanced wheel	Replace or repair
Excessive steering wheel play	Worn or damaged lower arm installation bushing	Replace
	Improperly adjusted pinion pre-load	Adjust
	Worn rack and pinion	Replace
	Worn or damaged joints	Replace
	Loose steering shaft universal joint	Replace

TROUBLESHOOTING GUIDE
Mazda

Condition	Cause	Correction
General instability	Weak coil springs	Replace
	Malfunction of shock absorber(s)	Replace
	Wear or deterioration of lower arm or stabilizer installation bushing	Replace
	Improperly adjusted wheel alignment	Adjust
	Bent linkage	Replace
	Worn or damaged joints	Replace
	Improperly adjusted pinion pre-load	Adjust
	Loose steering shaft universal joint	Replace
	Incorrect tire pressure	Adjust
	Bent or unbalanced wheel	Replace or repair
	Malfunction of wheel bearing	Replace

TROUBLESHOOTING GUIDE
Mazda

Switch Position	Condition		Cause	Correction
Sport	Indicator lights do not illuminate (both front and rear).		Bulb(s) burned out	Replace
			Malfunction of AAS switch	Replace
			Malfunction of control unit	Replace
	Dampers do not become Sport	All 4	Malfunction of control unit	Replace
		Only 1	Malfunction of actuator	Replace
Normal	Dampers do not become Normal	All 4	Malfunction of control unit	Replace
		Only 1	Malfunction of actuator	Replace
Auto	Dampers do not become Sport when vehicle turns corners or curves		Malfunction of angle sensor	Replace
			Malfunction of speed sensor	Replace
			Malfunction of control unit	Replace
	Dampers do not become Sport when vehicle is suddenly accelerated		Malfunction of accelerator switch	Replace
			Malfunction of control unit	Replace
	Dampers do not become Sport when vehicle is suddenly braked		Malfunction of brake pressure switch	Replace
			Malfunction of control unit	Replace
	Dampers do not become Sport when set speed is exceeded		Malfunction of vehicle speed sensor	Replace
			Malfunction of control unit	Replace

INDICATOR LIGHT

Testing

1. Turn the ignition key to the on position.
2. Alternately switch on the SPORT and NORMAL automatic adjusting suspension (AAS) switches. Check that the indicator light illuminates only when the SPORT switch is operated.
3. If it does not illuminate, check for the following:
   a. Disconnect the 21 pin connector from the control unit.
   b. Ground the "O" and "P" terminals of the connector.
   c. Turn the ignition key to the on position.
   d. If the indicator light illuminates, a malfunction of the AAS switch or control unit can be suspected.
   e. If the indicator light does not illuminate, the light bulb has probably burned out.

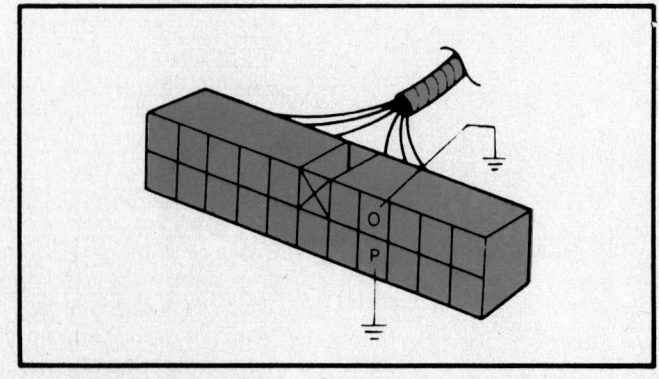

21 pin connector terminals

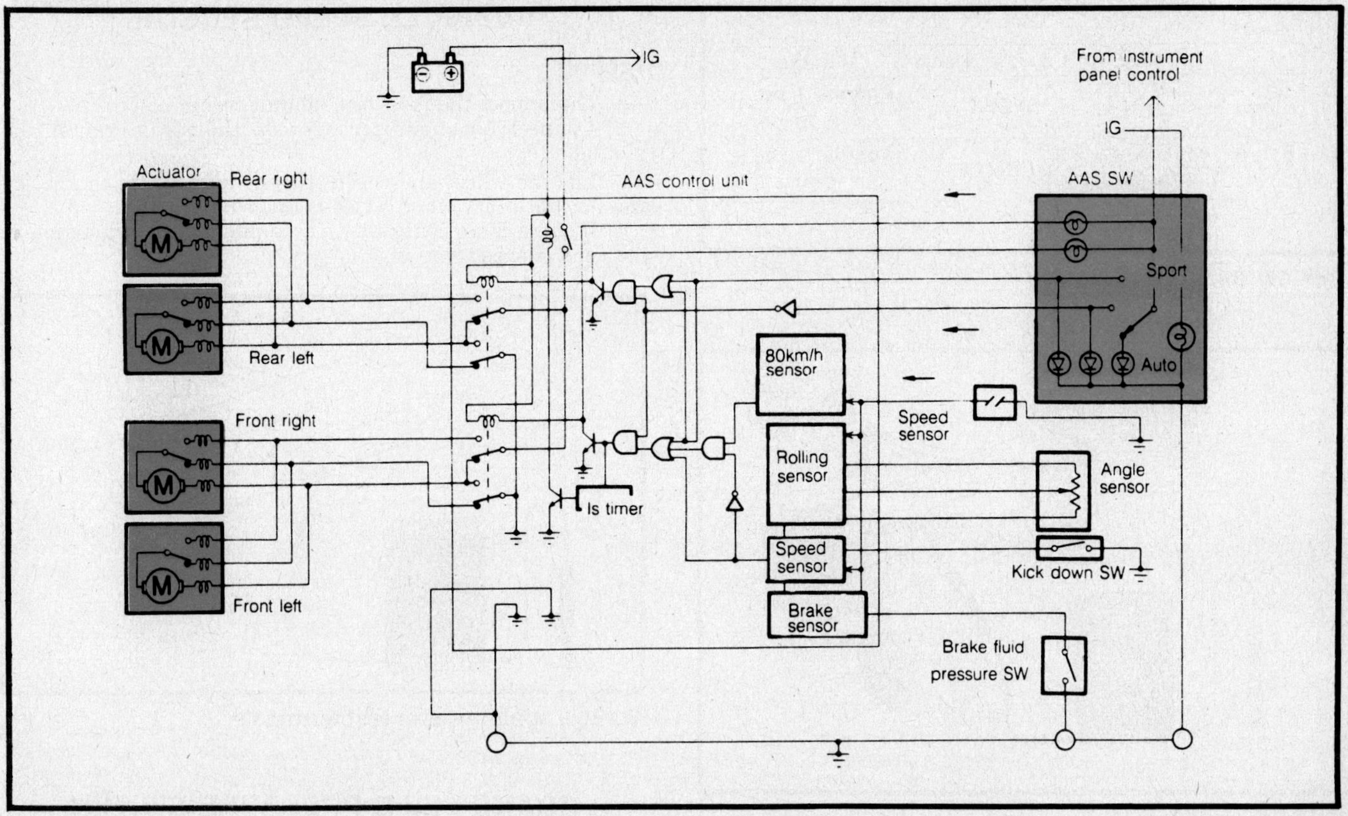

Wiring schematic

ACTUATOR

Testing

1. Turn the ignition key on.
2. Alternator switch on the SPORT and NORMAL switches. The shaft of the actuator, located on the top of the strut assemblies, should rotate.
3. If actuator shaft is not rotating, disconnect the actuator connector from the actuator which is not operating and check the voltage with the ignition key switched on.
4. Voltage should be as indicated.
5. If voltage is not as indicated, replace the defective actuator.

ACTUATOR CIRCUIT

Testing

1. Disconnect the AAS control unit connector.
2. Turn the ignition key on.
3. Voltage and continuity should be as follows;
   a. terminal "M" to body ground-12 volts
   b. terminal "a" to body ground-12 volts
   c. terminal "B" to body ground-continuity
   d. terminal "b" to body ground-continuity
4. If not correct, check or repair the power supply or the ground circuit.

Actuator shaft rotation

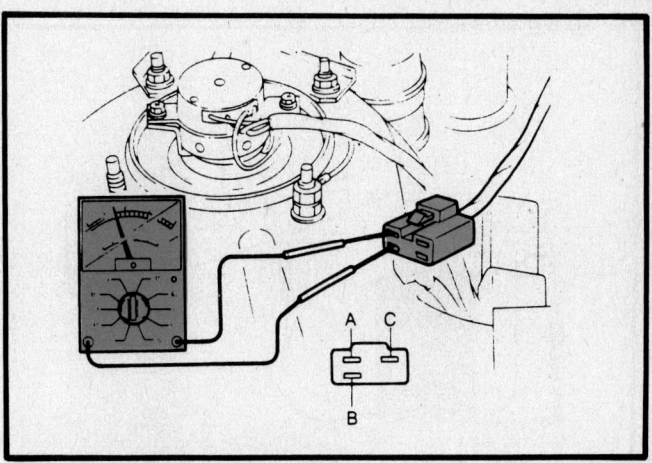

Actuator connector voltage test

	Terminal	AAS switch position	Voltage
Tester probl +	A	SPORT	Approx. 1 sec., 1.2V
−	C		
+	C	NORMAL	Approx. 1 sec., 1.2V
−	B		

Normal voltage test results

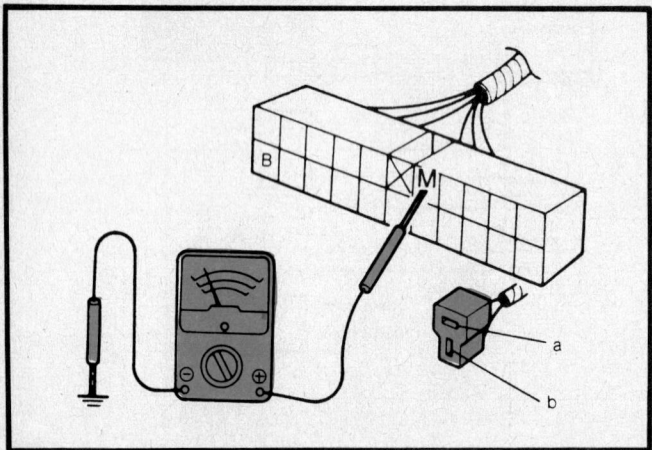

Actuator circuit test connections

AAS SWITCH

Testing

1. Disconnect the AAS control unit connector.
2. Turn the ignition key on.
3. Check the voltage of the "J" terminal. With the switch position in the SPROT mode, a reading of 12 volts should be obtained.
4. Check the voltage of terminal "I". With the switch position in the NORMAL mode, a reading of 12 volts should be obtained.
5. If not correct, there may be a malfunction of the AAS switch or an open circuit in the wiring harness.

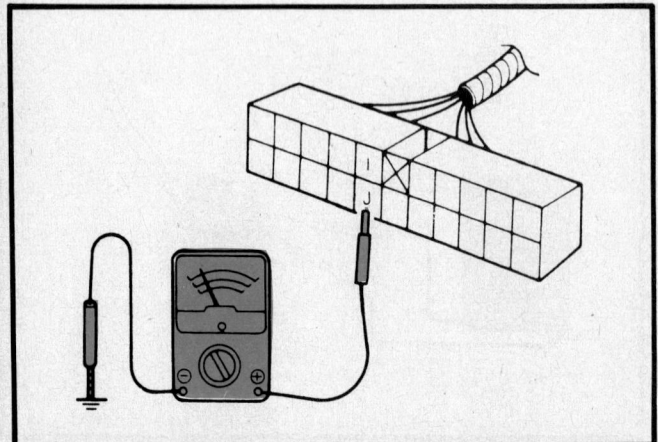

AAS switch terminals

VEHICLE SPEED SENSOR

Testing

1. Disconnect the AAS control unit terminal.
2. Connect an ohmmeter between the "H" terminal and ground.
3. Lift the wheel and check there is alternately continuity and no continuity when a tire is turned manually.
4. If there is no continuity, there may be a malfunction of the vehicle speed sensor.

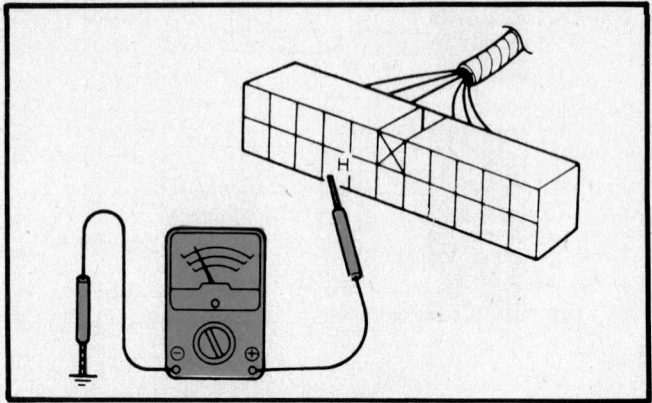

Vehicle speed sensor test terminals

BRAKE FLUID PRESSURE SWITCH

Testing

1. Disconnect the AAS control unit connector.
2. Connect an ohmmeter between the "E" terminal and ground.
3. Continuity should be present when the brake pedal is depressed.
4. No continuity indicates either a defective brake fluid pressure switch or wiring harness short circuit.
5. If continuity is present, replace control unit.

ACCELERATOR/KICKDOWN SWITCH

Testing

1. Disconnect the AAS control unit connector.

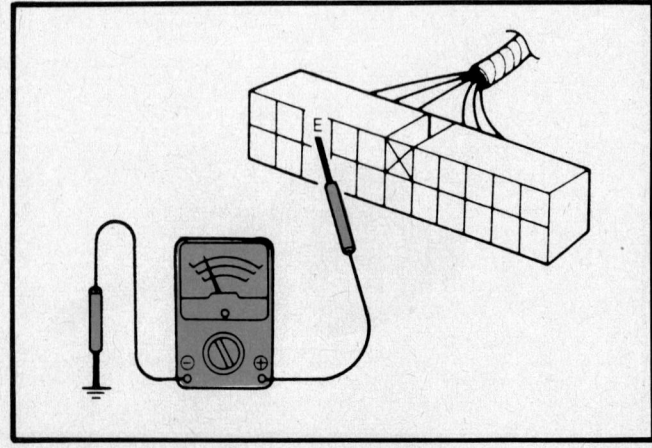

Brake fluid pressure switch terminals

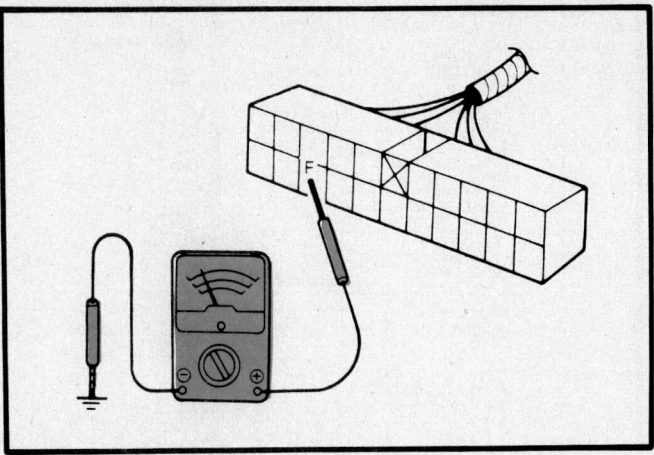

Accelerator kickdown switch terminals

2. Connect an ohmmeter between terminal "F" and ground.
3. There should be no continuity when the accelerator pedal is ¾ depressed.
4. No continuity indicates a malfunction of the kickdown switch.

Component Replacement

STRUT ASSEMBLY

Removal and Installation
FRONT

1. Remove the wheel cover and loosen the lug nuts.
2. Raise the vehicle and support safely. Do not jack it or support it by any of the front suspension members. Remove the wheel and tire assembly.

— CAUTION —

Be sure the vehicle is securely supported. Remember, you will be working underneath it.

3. Remove the brake caliper and disc on all models except the GLC and 626 with front wheel drive.
4. Remove the nuts securing the upper shock mount to the top of the wheel arch.
5. Unfasten the bolts securing the lower end of the shock to the steering knuckle arm.
6. Remove the shock and coil spring as a complete assembly.
7. Installation is the reverse of the removal procedure.

— CAUTION —

The coil springs are retained under considerable pressure. They can exert enough force to cause serious injury. Exercise extreme caution when servicing.

REAR

1. Remove the side trim panels from inside the trunk or the rear seat and trim. Loosen and remove the top mounting nuts from strut mounting block assembly.
2. Loosen the rear wheel lugs. Raise the vehicle and support safely.
3. Remove the rear wheels. Disconnect the flexible brake hose from the strut.
4. Disconnect the trailing arm from the lower side of the strut. Separate the lateral link and strut by removing the bolt assembly.
5. Remove the strut from the lower unit by removing the through nuts and bolts.

6. Remove the strut and brake assembly.

— CAUTION —

The coil springs are retained under considerable pressure. They can exert enough force to cause serious injury. Exercise extreme caution when servicing.

FRONT AND REAR SUSPENSION

Inspection

1. Check the strut cartridge for oil leakage and abnormal noise when compressed.
2. Inspect the mounting block for deterioration or damage.
3. Inspect the dust boot for tears or cracks.
4. Check the bound stopper for wear or damage.
5. Repair or replace all defective parts as required.

COIL SPRING

Removal and Installation From Strut Assembly
FRONT STRUT

1. Secure the strut and spring assembly in a suitable holding fixture.
2. Using tool number 49 G030 640 or equivalent, compress the spring.

— CAUTION —

The coil springs are retained under considerable pressure. They can exert enough force to cause serious injury. Exercise extreme caution when servicing.

3. Remove the piston rod upper nut.
4. Slowly release spring compression tool.

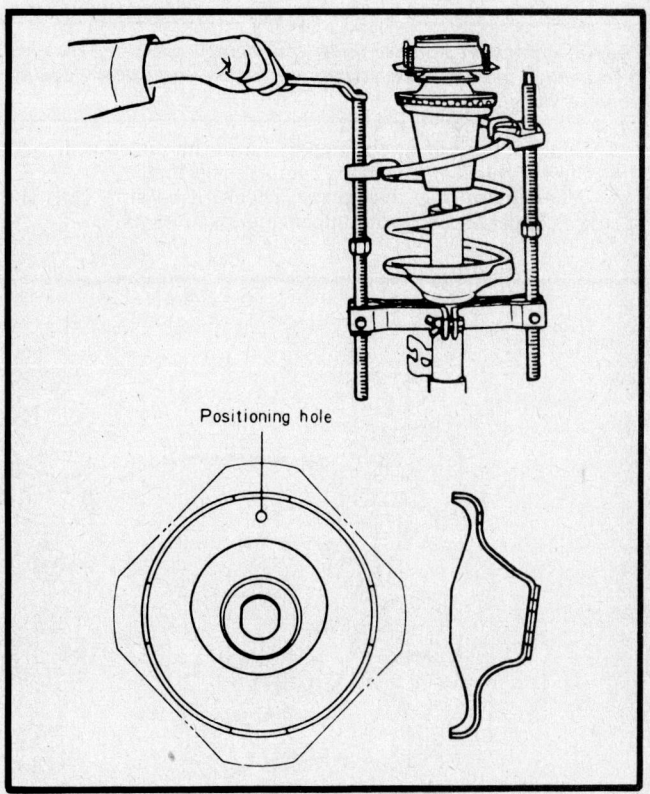

Positioning hole

Spring compressor and positioning hole illustrated

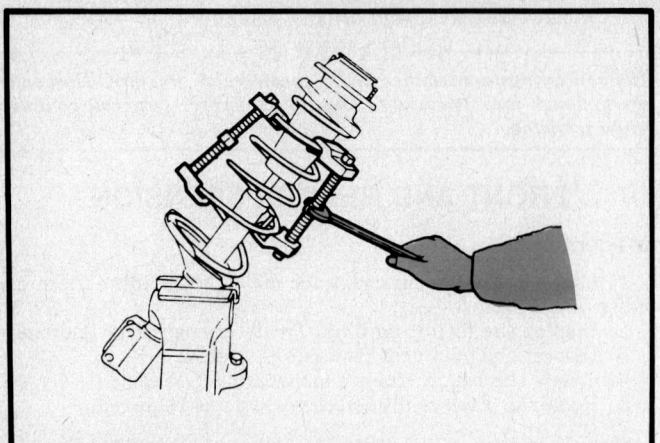

Strut in holding fixture with spring compressor tool

5. When installing the spring, check to be sure that the spring is well seated in the upper and lower seat.

CAUTION

Install the spring so that the spring seat positioning hole faces the inside of the vehicle.

REAR STRUT

1. Secure the strut and spring assembly in a suitable holding fixture.
2. Using tool number 49 G030 700 or equivalent, compress the spring.

CAUTION

The coil springs are retained under considerable pressure. They can exert enough force to cause serious injury. Exercise extreme caution when servicing.

---

3. Remove the nut at the upper end of the piston rod.
4. Slowly release the spring compression tool.
5. When installing the spring, check to be sure that the spring is well seated in the upper and lower seats.

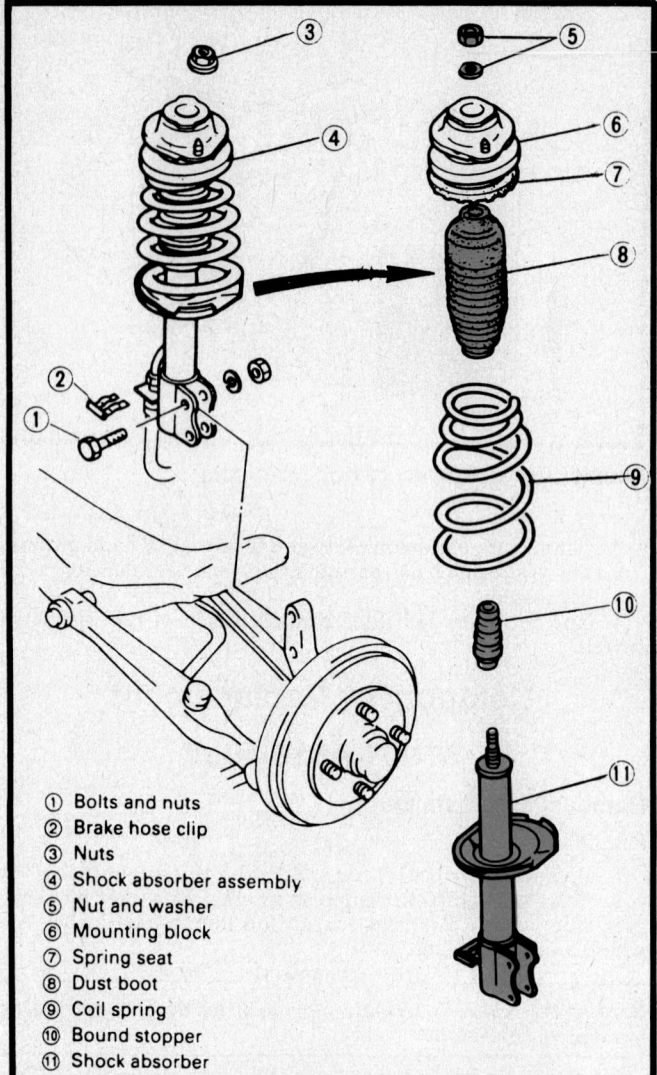

① Bolts and nuts
② Brake hose clip
③ Nuts
④ Shock absorber assembly
⑤ Nut and washer
⑥ Mounting block
⑦ Spring seat
⑧ Dust boot
⑨ Coil spring
⑩ Bound stopper
⑪ Shock absorber

Rear strut and spring assembly—exploded view

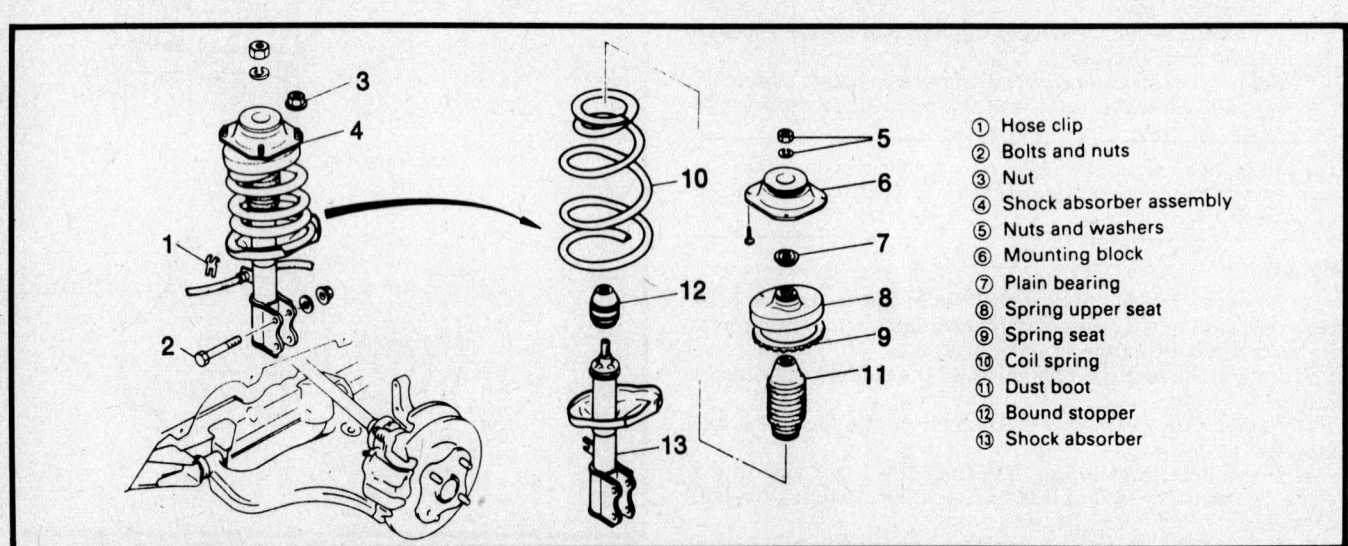

① Hose clip
② Bolts and nuts
③ Nut
④ Shock absorber assembly
⑤ Nuts and washers
⑥ Mounting block
⑦ Plain bearing
⑧ Spring upper seat
⑨ Spring seat
⑩ Coil spring
⑪ Dust boot
⑫ Bound stopper
⑬ Shock absorber

Front strut and spring assembly—exploded view

NISSAN

General Information

The shock absorbers are adjustable for ride from the driver's seat. The shock absorber damping force can be varied by the shock absorber switch located on the front of the center console.

Marks "S", "N" and "F" on the switch stand for "Soft", "Normal" and "Firm" respectively. The switch becomes operable only when the ignition switch is in the "ON" position. After ride level is selected, an indicator light on the console will illuminate.

When the system is normal, only the indicator light for the selected position will come on. If any other condition exists, (example: all three indicator lights come on or go off, or any of the lights flicker), it indicates that there is an abnormalty.

System Operation

Located inside each shock absorber, is a small electric actuator. These actuators operate shutters located within the shock absorbers which reduce or increase the resistance to the fluid as it is forced through the gates by a piston.

Component Replacement

SHOCK ABSORBER SWITCH

Removal and Installation

1. Disconnect the negative battery cable.
2. Remove the plastic trim cover from the selector switch. Do not use excessive force since the trim cover is plastic.
3. Remove the selector switch retaining screws.
4. Tag and disconnect the electrical connector.
5. Remove the selector switch.
6. Installation is the reverse of the removal procedure.

SHOCK ABSORBER STRUT

Removal and Installation

FRONT

1. Disconnect the sub harness connector from the top of the shock tower. Remove the strut mounting bolts.
2. Raise the vehicle and support safely. Remove the wheel and tire assembly.
3. Disconnect and plug the brake hose.
4. Disconnect the tension rod (compression rod on "Z" series) and stabilizer bar from the transverse link if necessary to gain working room.
5. Remove the lower strut mounting bolts.
6. Remove the strut assembly from the vehicle.
7. Installation is the reverse of the removal procedure.

SHOCK ABSORBER STRUT

Removal and Installation

REAR

1. Raise the vehicle and support safely. Remove the wheel and tire assembly.

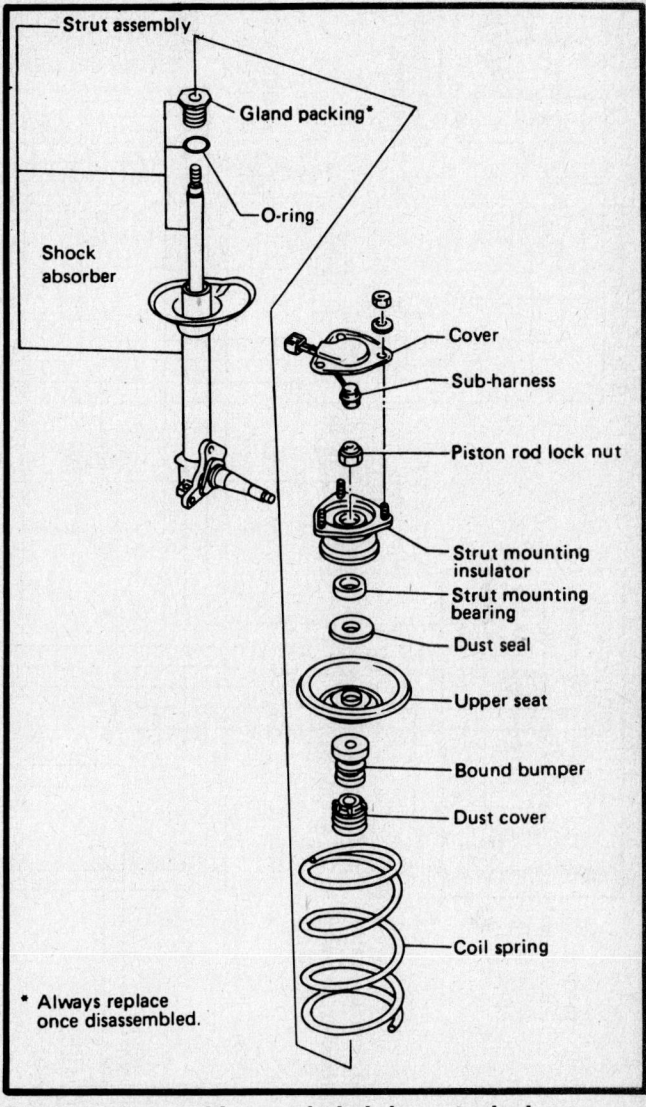

Front strut assembly—exploded view—typical

(Diagram labels: Strut assembly, Gland packing*, O-ring, Shock absorber, Cover, Sub-harness, Piston rod lock nut, Strut mounting insulator, Strut mounting bearing, Dust seal, Upper seat, Bound bumper, Dust cover, Coil spring)

* Always replace once disassembled.

CAUTION

Do not raise the vehicle at the parallel links, radius rod or the stabilizer bar.

---

2. Remove the rear brake assemblies without diconnecting the brake lines. Remove the lock spring.
3. Remove the parallel link retaining bolt, radius rod bolt, stabilizer retaining bolt and the stabilizer connecting rod brackets.
4. Remove the rear seat and parcel shelf if necessary in order to gain access to the strut assembly retaining nuts.
5. Tag and disconnect the electrical connectors from the strut assembly.
6. Remove the strut assembly retaining bolts.
7. Installation is the reverse of the removal procedure.

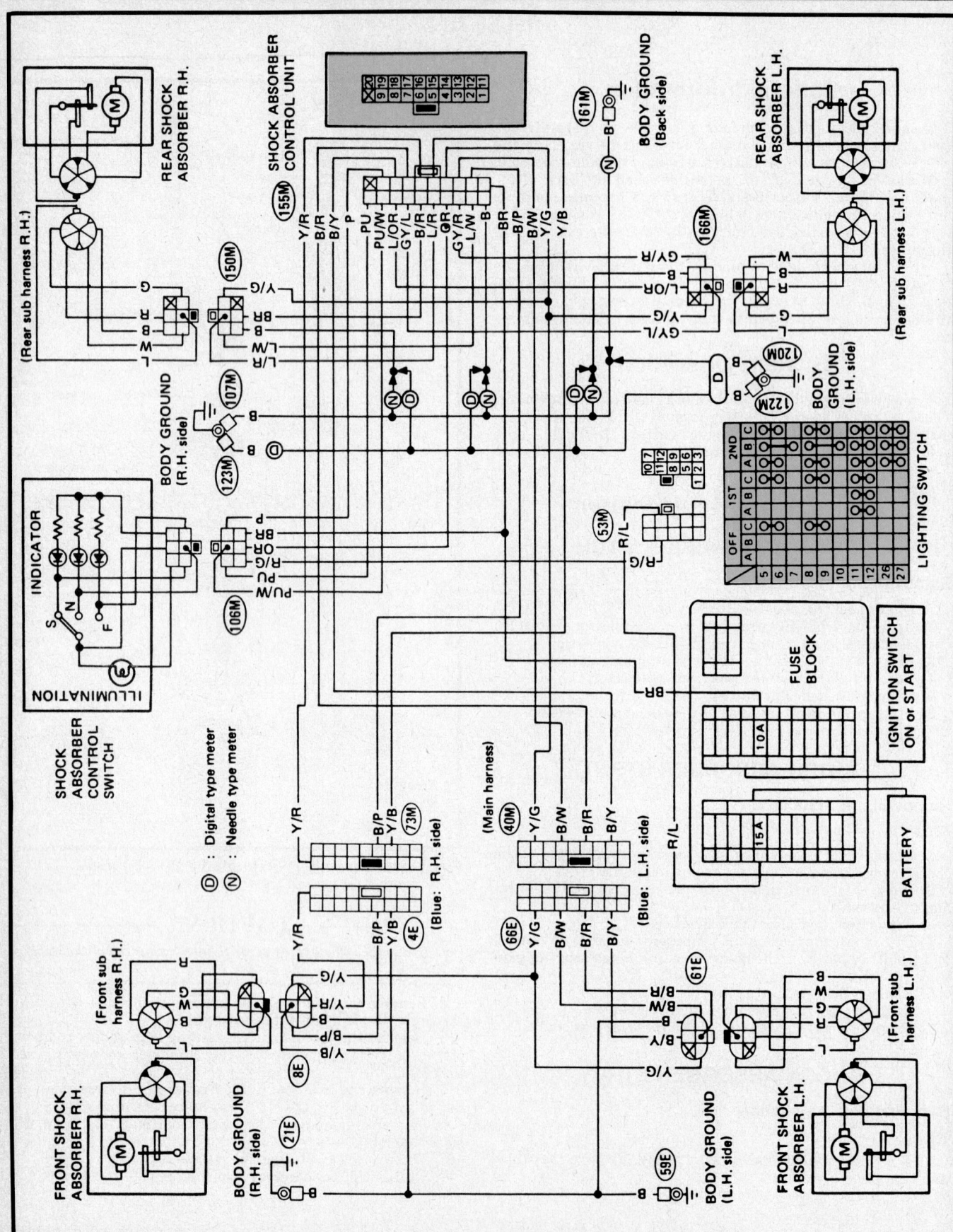

Wiring schematic—adjustable shock absorbers

Troubleshooting

Adjustable shock absorber troubleshooting guide

No.	Phenomenon on switch	Possible cause	Checking method		Corrective action
			Checking procedure	Result	
1	3 lamps all off	• Lamp burnt out • Fuse blown • Harness wire broken	(1) Operate switch and check lamp for lighting condition. (2) Check fuse. (3) Check power and grounding harnesses for broken wires.	One lamp on	Replace burnt out lamp.
				3 lamps all off	(1) Replace fuse. (2) Replace 3 lamps. (3) Repair harness.
2	2 lamps off	• Switch side harness shorted • Switch out of order	Operate switch and check lamp for proper lighting condition.	One lamp on	Repair harness.
				2 lamps always on	(1) Replace switch. (2) Replace harness.
3	3 lamps all on	• Switch side harness shorted • Switch out of order • Controller out of order	Operate switch, check lamp for proper lighting condition.	One lamp off	(1) Replace harness. (2) Replace switch. (3) Replace controller.
				3 lamps on	
4	One lamp on and 2 lamps on and off	• Harness wire broken (Selected signal wire broken)	Operate switch while lamp is going on and off. **Do this with key on.**	Selected ... On Other ... On and off	Repair harness.
		• Motor harness wire broken, or shorted	(1) Connect dummy actuators (motors) in 4 places, and operate switches (for F, N, S), check lamps for proper lighting condition. (2) Check dummy actuators for normal operation in 4 places (Front-Right, Front-Left, Rear-Right, Rear-Left).	Selected ... On 2 others ... On and off	Repair harness.
				Any dummy actuator not operating	
		• Position switch harness wire broken or shorted	Connect dummy actuators in 4 places, and operate switches (for F, N, S), check lamps for proper lighting condition. Further, check 4 places for any actuator operating longer than 4 seconds.	Selected ... On 2 others ... On and off	Repair harness.
				Any place where any actuator is operating more than the specified time after lamp starts to go on and off	

Adjustable shock absorber troubleshooting guide continued

No.	Phenomenon on switch	Possible cause	Checking method		Corrective action
			Checking procedure	Result	
4	One lamp on 2 lamps on and off (continued)	● Wire broken or shorted in motor harness of shock absorber	(1) Changing the connection combinations of the 3 dummy actuators, check 4 shock absorbers one by one using the operation described in (2) below. (2) Turn switch to F, N, S and check lamp for proper lighting condition.	Selected ... On 2 others ... On and off (When connected to shock absorber out of order)	Replace shock absorber.
		● Wire broken or shorted in position switch harness of shock absorber	Same as above.	Same as above.	Same as above.
		● Motor completely locked	Same as above.	Same as above.	Same as above.
		● Motor overloaded (Temporary overload)	(1) Turn key off to stop the lamp from going on and off; then turn key on again and check lamp for proper lighting condition.	Selected ... On 2 others ... Off	Normal. If it is frequent, take action as described in (3) below.
			(2) Check power voltage.	Below 9 V.	Repair power system (Charge battery).
			(3)-1 Changing the connection combinations of the 4 actuators, check each of the 4 shock absorbers in one place described in (3)-2 below. (3)-2 Turn switch to F, N, S, and check lamp for proper lighting condition.	Selected ... On 2 others ... On and off (when connected to overloaded shock absorber)	Replace shock absorber.
		● Controller out of order	Replace with normal controller, and operate switch, check lamp for proper lighting condition.	Selected ... On 2 others ... On and off (Returned to normal state)	Replace controller.

638

Adjustable shock absorber troubleshooting guide continued

No.	Phenomenon on switch	Possible cause	Checking method		Corrective action
			Checking procedure	Result	
5	3 lamps on and off	● Switch malfunction	Turn key off to stop the lamp from going on and off; then turn key on again and check lamp for proper lighting condition.	Selected ... On 2 others ... Off	Replace switch.
		● Switch contact out of order	(1) Operate switch, check lamp for proper lighting condition.	Selected ... On 2 others ... Off	Replace switch.
			(2) Turn switch to original position, and check lamp for occurrence of on and off condition.	3 lamps ... On and off	
		● Harness disconnected	Turn key off to stop the lamp from going on and off; then turn key on again and check lamp for proper lighting condition.	3 lamps ... On and off	Repair harness.

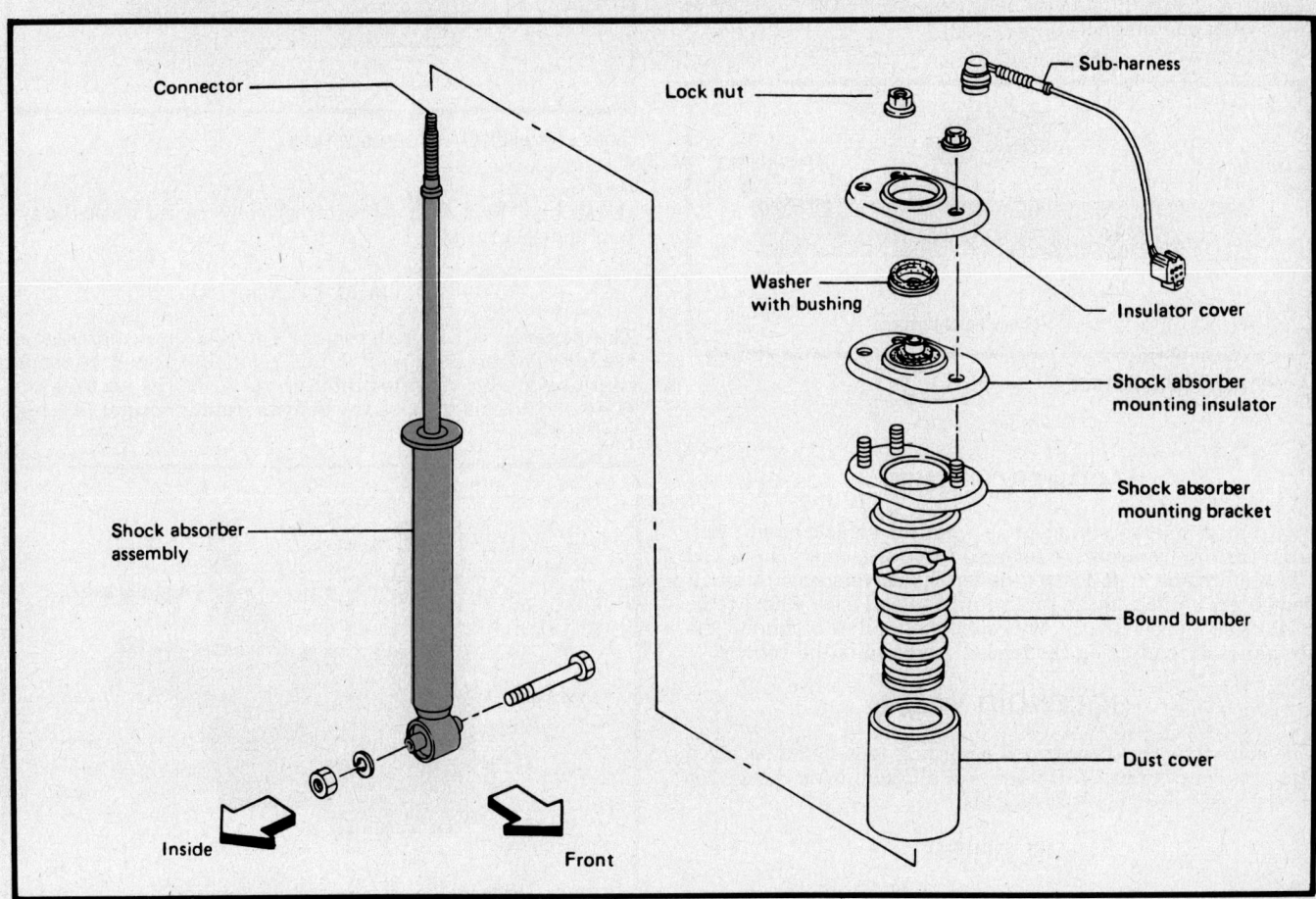

Rear strut assembly—exploded view—typical

SUBARU

General Information

On vehicles equipped with air suspension, vehicle height can be controlled by operation of the height control switch. Two levels of ground clearance can be obtained, either "Normal" or "High".

The system also maintains constant ground clearance regardless of the vehicle load. For this purpose air volume in each air spring is adjusted according to a signal received from the vehicle height sensor. These sensors are installed in each air spring.

The air spring on the four wheel drive vehicle provides riding comfort and stabilized driving when rough roads are encountered. The air spring is adopted in place of the conventional metal spring.

When operating the vehicle in the four wheel drive mode, the height control is automatically set to the high ground clearance position. This will prevent vehicle underbody contact and possible damage with the ground surfaces.

System Components

VEHICLE HEIGHT SENSOR

The vehicle height sensor consists of a switch and magnet. The switch is attached to the body side of the air suspension assembly while the magnet is fixed on the wheel side. Height signal is generated according to the relation between the positions of the switch and magnet.

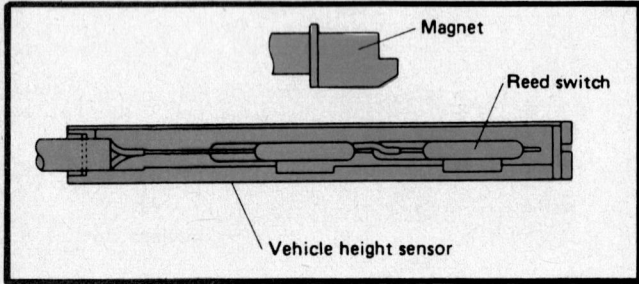

Vehicle height sensor

CONTROL UNIT

The control unit receives signals from the vehicle height sensors. The unit controls the solenoid valve of each air shock and the compressor. It is located under the drivers seat. A small computer, located in the control unit allows each wheel to be controlled independently. This action will allow optimum performance depending on the loaded condition of the vehicle.

SOLENOID VALVE

The solenoid valve is operated according to a signal received from the control unit. This valve will allow air to be charged or discharged from the air suspension.

AIR DRIER

The air drier dries air which flows to the air tank or air spring. The drier is filled with silica gel which will prevent freezing in

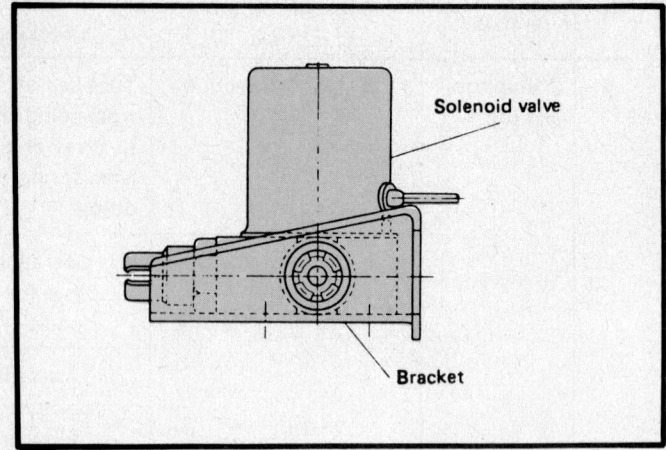

Solenoid valve

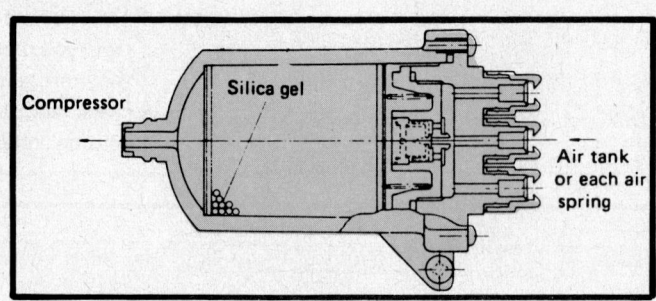

Drier assembly—cross section

the air pipe. The silica gel is refreshed by dry air while the system is discharging.

AIR TANK

The air tank is filled with compressed from the compressor assembly. The pressure switch and solenoid valve used for air charging are incorporated into the air tank. The air tank contains enough air to raise the vehicle from a normal to a high position.

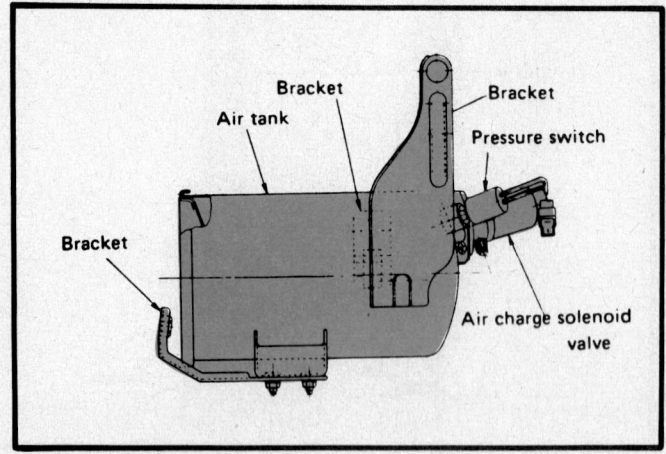

Air tank—cross section

PRESSURE SWITCH

If the pressure in the air tank rises, the pressure sensitive disc pushes the guide pin up to open the moving contact. This in turn opens the switch. When the pressure drops, the switch is closed.

AIR SUSPENSION SHOCK ABSORBERS

Both front and rear air suspension assemblies use air springs in place of the conventional metal springs. A housing, on the outside of the shock absorber, can be stroked through the function of the rolling diaphragm.

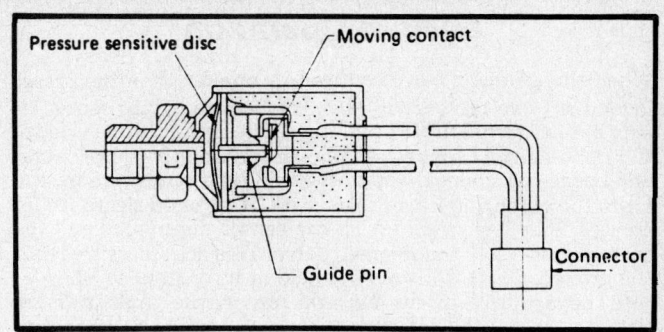

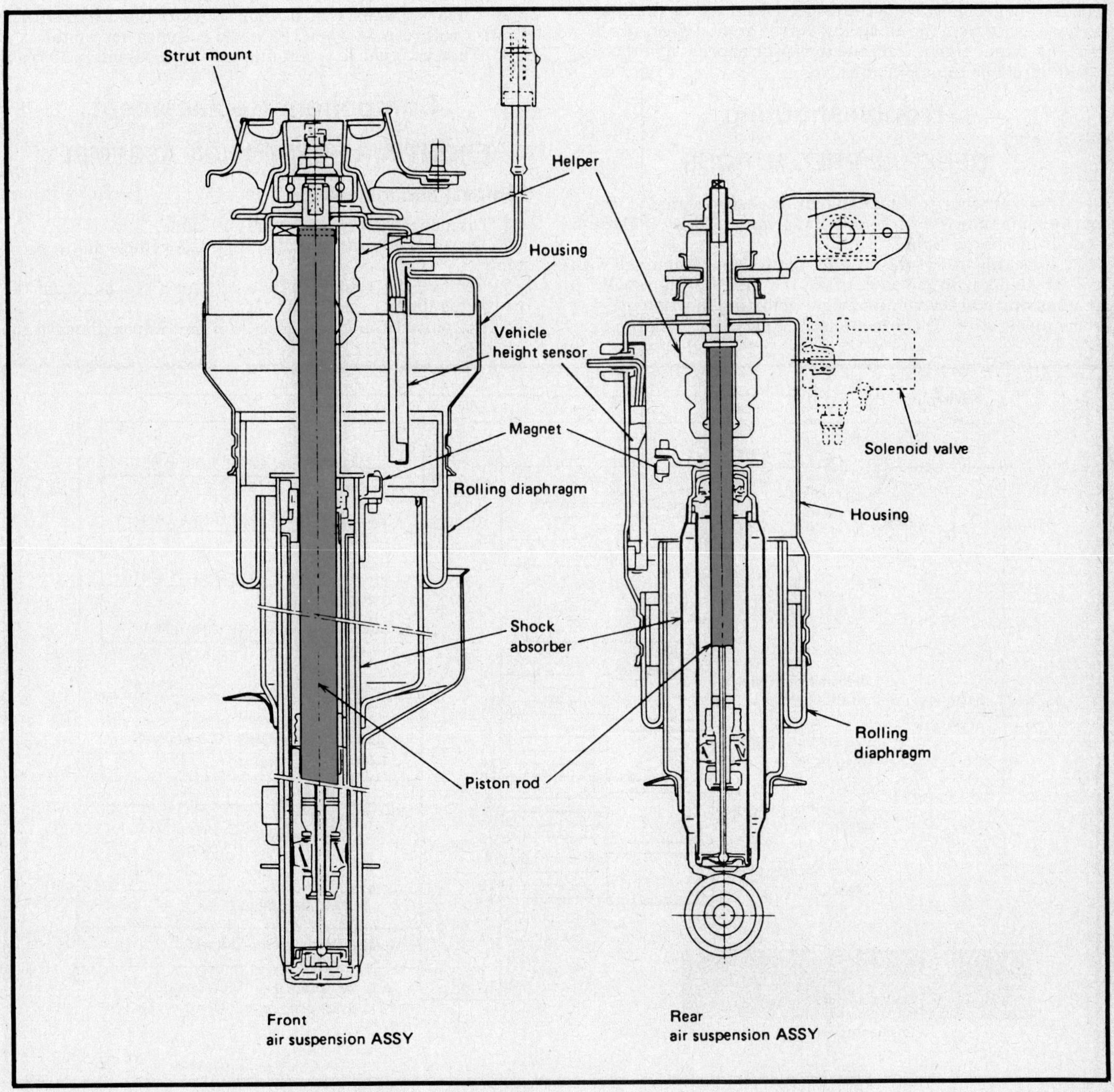

Pressure switch—cross section

Front and rear air suspension assemblies—cross section

System Operation

When the ground clearance becomes smaller than the preset level due to an increase in load, the vehicle height sensor issues a "low" signal. If this condition lasts for a certain period of time, the control unit decides that the ground clearance is low, and opens the solenoid valve which in turn sends compressed air to the air spring from the air tank. As ground clearance increases, the "low" signal from the sensor disappears and the control unit closes the solenoid valve. This action assures that the ground clearance is always held at a constant level.

If the pressure in the air tank drops, the tank pressure switch operates the compressor until the pressure returns to the specified level.

If the ground clearance becomes larger than the preset level due to a load reduction, the sensor issues a "high" signal, and opens the solenoid valve of the respective air spring to allow air to be released from the air spring. As the ground clearance lowers, the "high" signal from the sensor disappears and the control unit closes the solenoid valve.

Troubleshooting

GENERAL PRECAUTIONS

1. If an air charge signal and air discharge signal is issued at the same time from different air springs, priority is given to the air discharge signal.

2. If jacking up is continued for more than 10 minutes with the ignition key in the on position, the indicator light will begin flashing and the vehicle height adjusting function may become inoperative. This is not a fault indication. Turn the ignition key to the off position and proper function will be restored.

3. If one of the wheels is on a bump slightly higher than several centimeters, charging or discharging of air is not performed even when the ignition key is set to on.

4. The air spring of each wheel is controlled independently.

5. When checking the air suspension system, reduce the vehicle load as much as possible.

6. Soapy water may be used to check for an air leak in a suspected area. Do not apply soapy water to a greased portion such as a ball bearing inside of a strut mount.

CAUTION
In addition to the above precautions; the following is to be observed.

The height control remains inoperative in the following cases and is not to be considered abnormal.

1. When the vehicle is making a turn.

2. When one wheel is on a bump or in an extended condition. Control will resume when the wheel becomes horizontal.

3. When the vehicle is running over approximately 55 mph.

Component Replacement

FRONT AIR SUSPENSION ASSEMBLY

Removal and Installation

1. Disconnect the negative battery cable.

2. Loosen the front lug nuts. Raise the vehicle and support safely.

3. Remove the parking brake retaining bracket from the transverse link.

4. Disconnect the brake hose from the caliper. Remove the

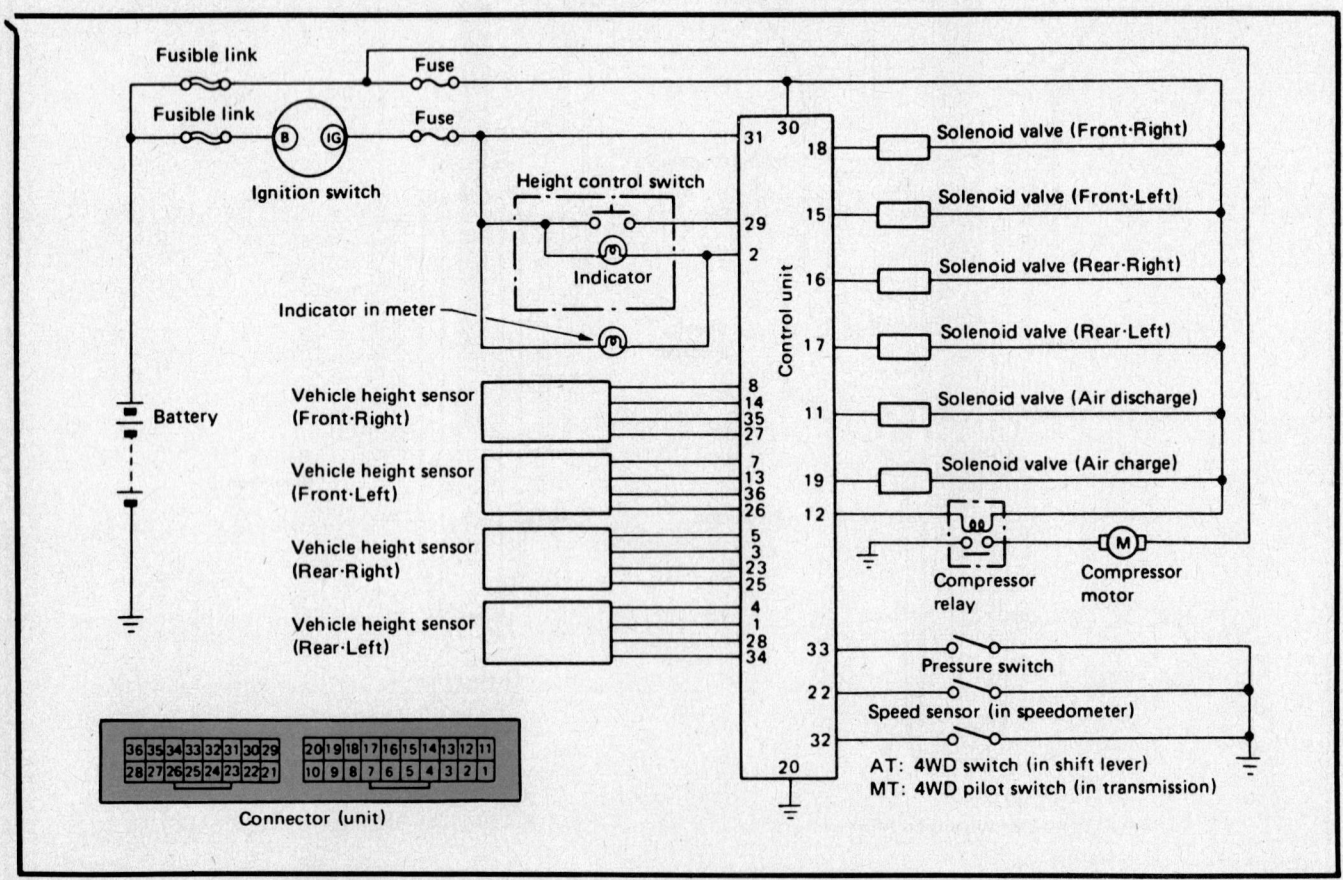

Air suspension wiring schematic

ELECTRONIC CHASSIS CONTROLS

Compressor troubleshooting

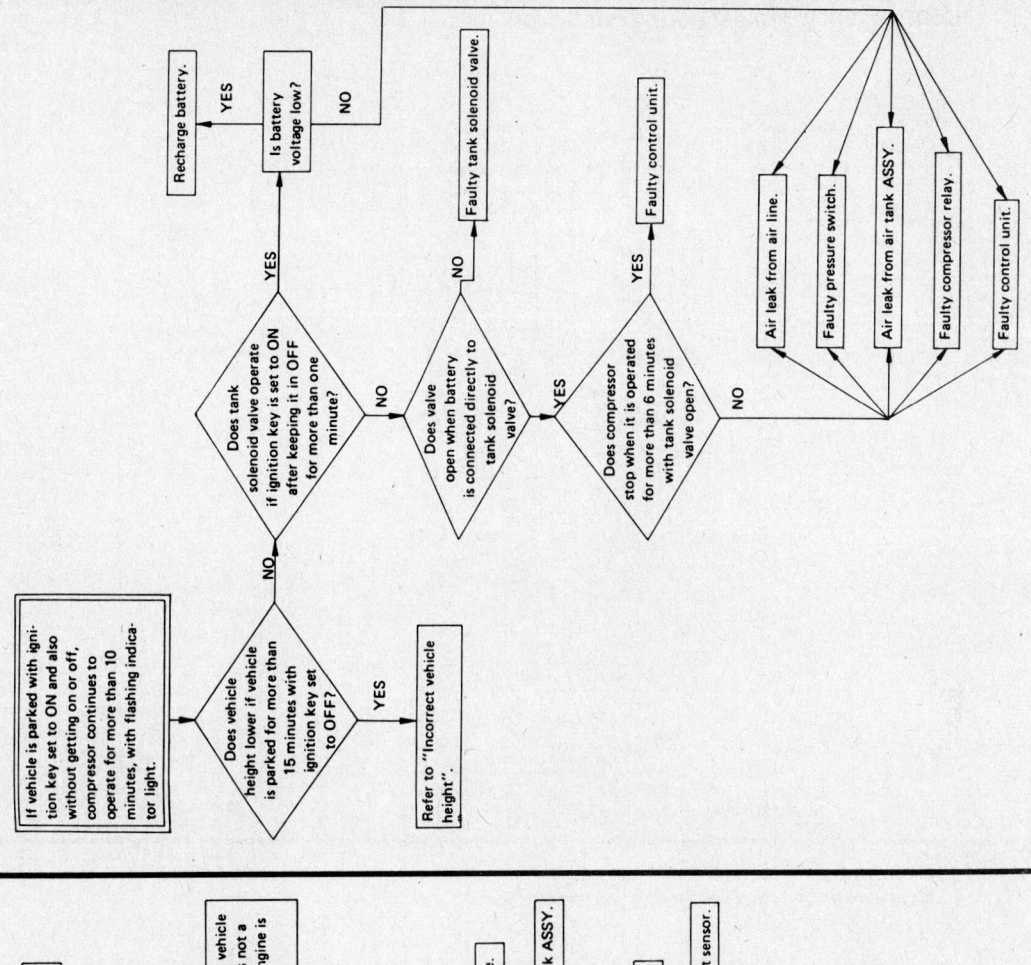

Air suspension troubleshooting

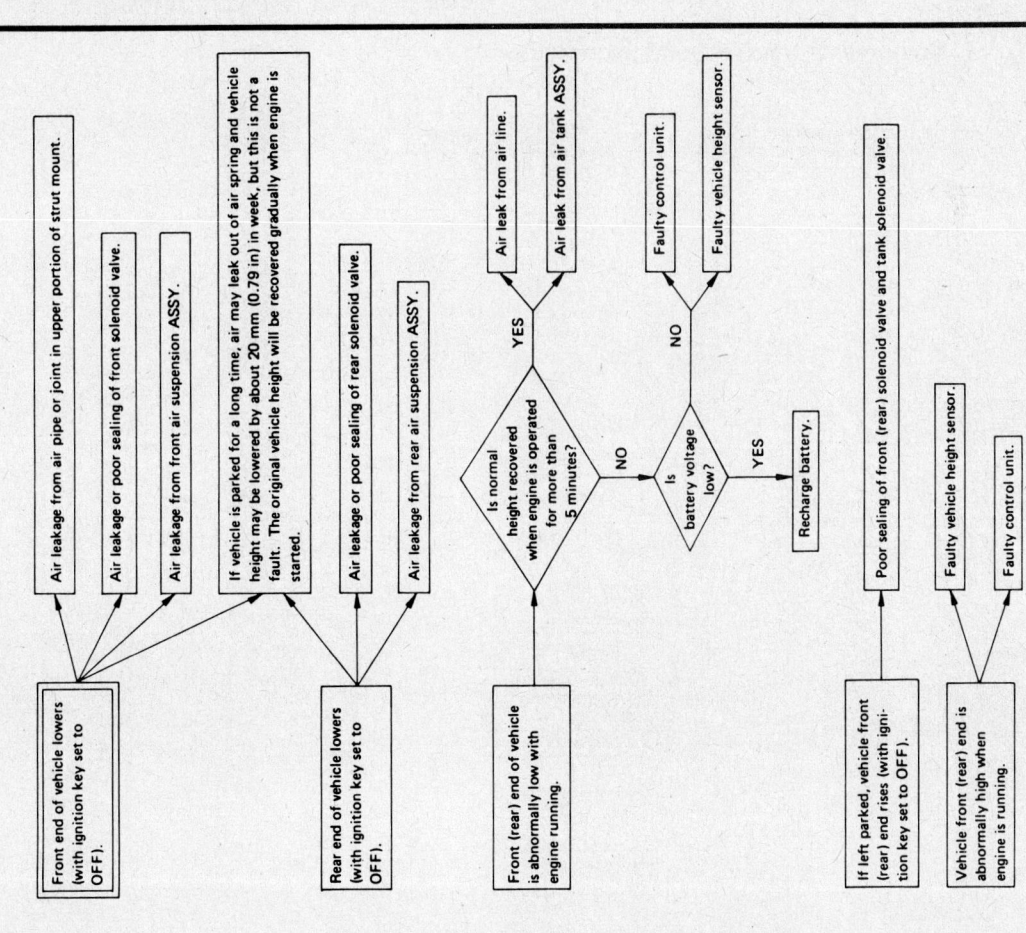

Compressor troubleshooting continued

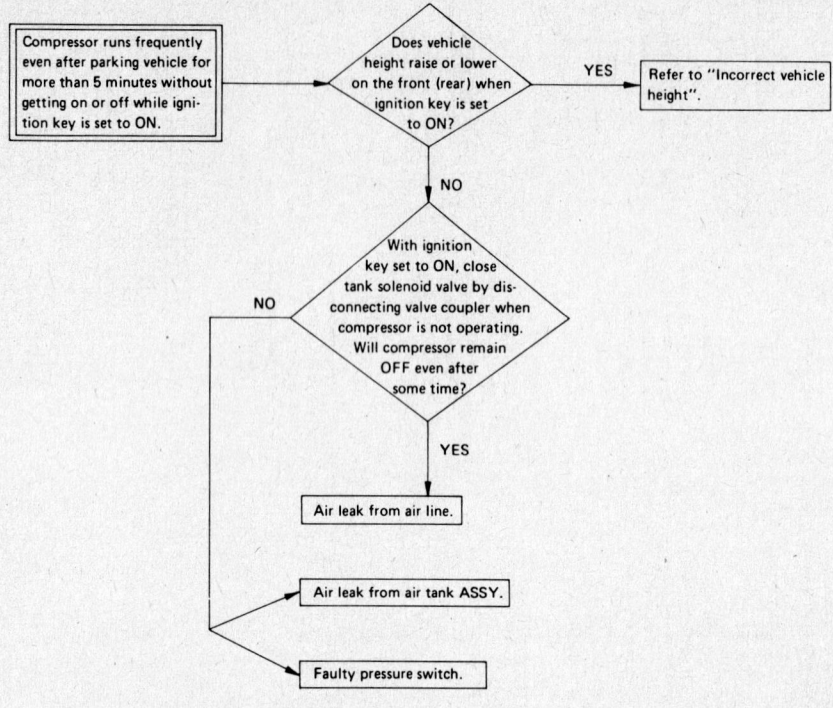

Compressor troubleshooting continued

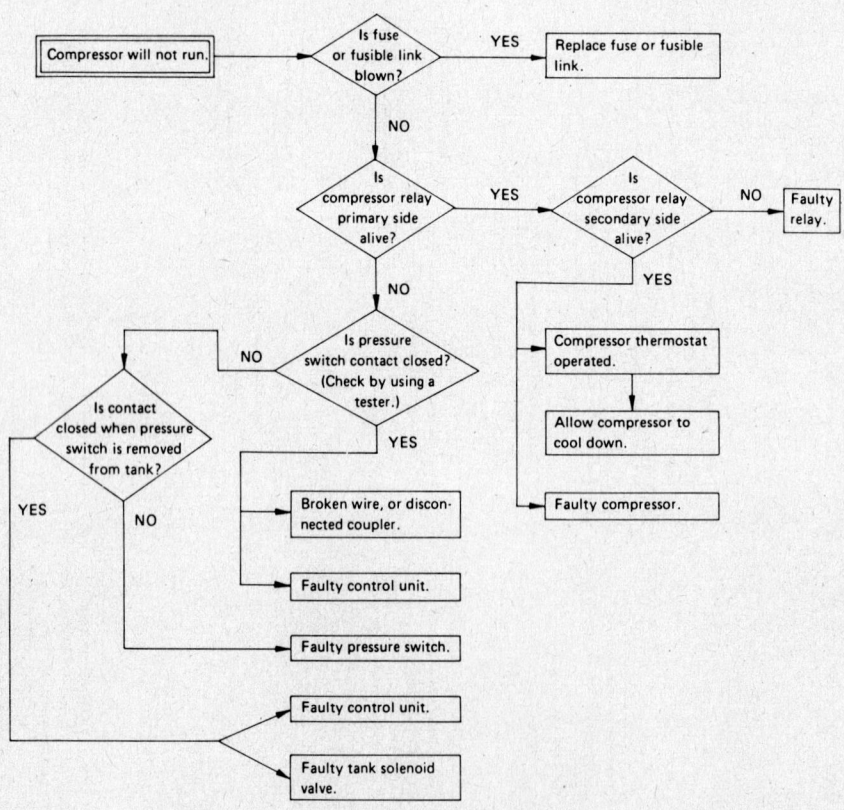

Height control troubleshooting

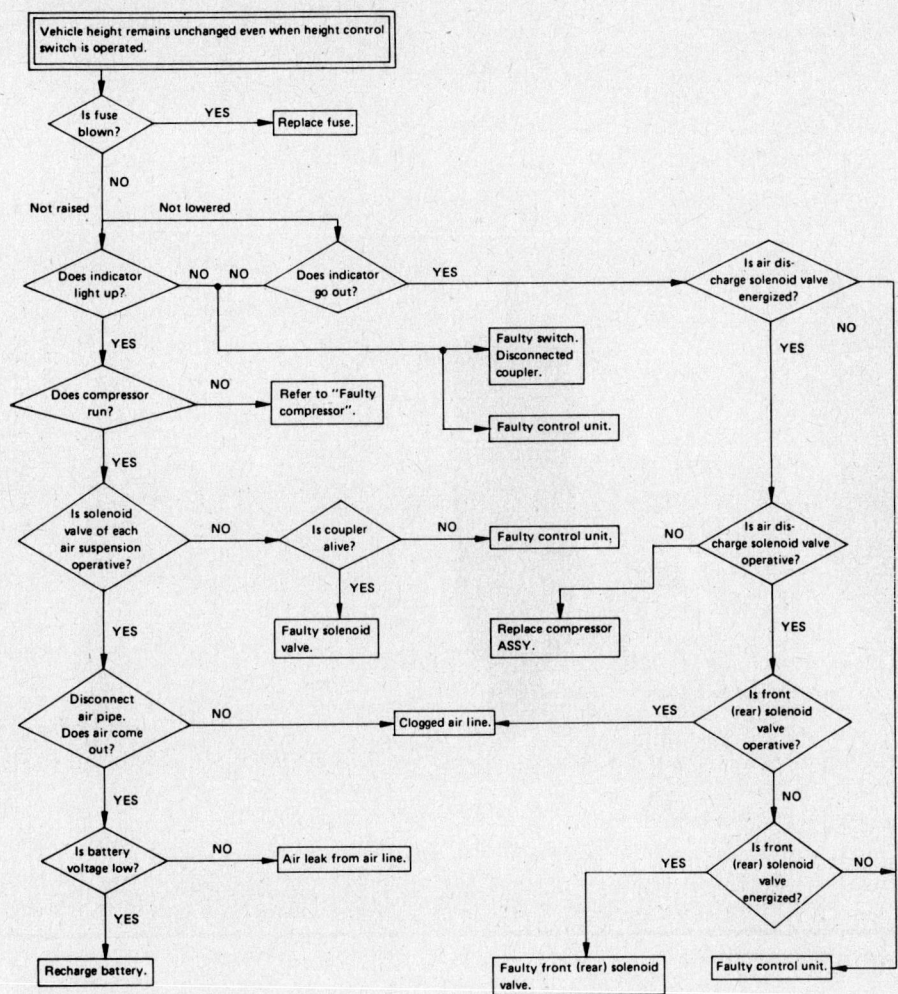

brake hose securing clip and detach the brake hose from the damper strut bracket.

5. Remove the damper strut retaining bolts.

6. Disconnect the air line from the strut assembly.

7. Remove the mud guard to gain working clearance.

8. Remove the vehicle height sensor harness from the clip. Disconnect the harness coupler.

9. Remove the strut assembly retaining bolts. Remove the strut from the vehicle.

10. Installation is the reverse of the removal procedure. Bleed the brakes after installation.

REAR AIR SUSPENSION ASSEMBLY

Removal and Installation

1. Disconnect the negative battery cable.

2. Remove the rear apron protector if necessary in order to gain working clearance.

3. Remove the rear solenoid valve from the air suspension assembly.

4. If replacing the solenoid valve, disconnect the air line from the solenoid valve.

5. Raise the vehicle and support safely. Remove the rear wheel and tire assembly.

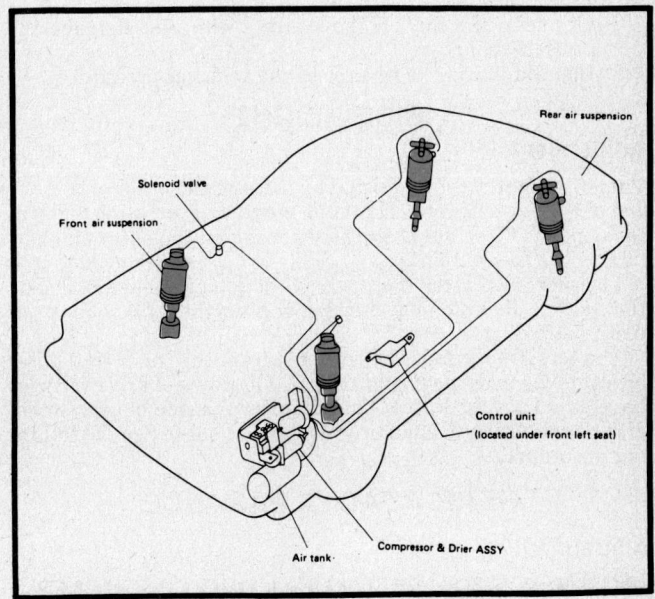

Component layout—typical

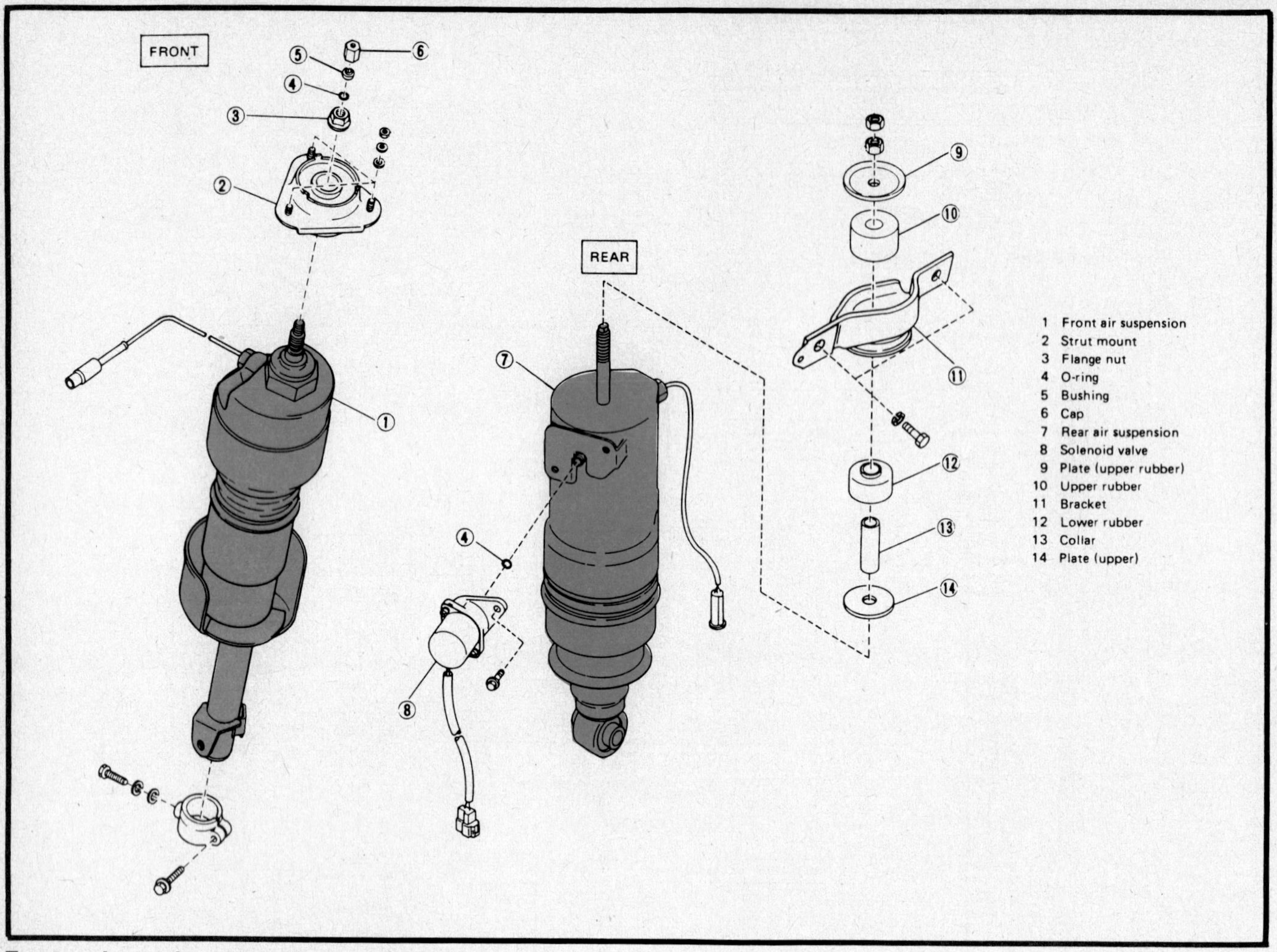

FRONT

REAR

1	Front air suspension
2	Strut mount
3	Flange nut
4	O-ring
5	Bushing
6	Cap
7	Rear air suspension
8	Solenoid valve
9	Plate (upper rubber)
10	Upper rubber
11	Bracket
12	Lower rubber
13	Collar
14	Plate (upper)

Front and rear air suspension assemblies

6. Remove the shock absorber mounting nuts. Remove the washer and bushings.

7. Unfasten the nut on the trailing arm pin. Remove the shock absorber.

8. Installation is the reverse of the removal procedure.

RIDE HEIGHT

Adjustment

Vehicle height can be adjusted by turning the outer and inner end of the torsion bar by the same number of serration teeth in the opposite direction of the arrow mark on the outer end surface of the torsion bar.

Turning the torsion bar in the direction of the arrow lowers the vehicle height, and changes the height 0.20 inches per tooth shifted.

The torsion bar must be removed from the inner and outer brackets to make the adjustment. All four wheel drive vehicles have an adjusting device that will alter the ride height (in addition in addition to adjusting the torsion bars). See the following procedure.

REAR ROAD CLEARANCE

Adjustment

1982 AND LATER FOUR WHEEL DRIVE VEHICLES

1. Measure the height of the vehicle from the lowest point of the rear axle crossmember to the ground.

2. To adjust the rear height, remove the access cover from the service hole in the vehicles floor above the rear axle. Turn the adjusting bolt clockwise to increase the height, counterclockwise to lower it.

COMPRESSOR AND DRIER ASSEMBLY

Removal and Installation

1. Disconnect the negative battery cable.

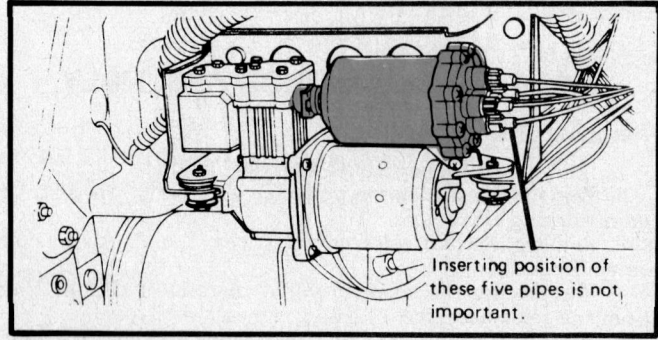

Inserting position of these five pipes is not important.

Compressor and drier assembly

2. Raise the vehicle and support safely. Remove the front left wheel.

3. Remove the mud guard.

4. Using air pipe removal tool number 926520000 or equivalent, disconnect the five air pipes from the drier assembly.

5. Remove the coupler.

6. Remove the compressor and drier assembly retaining bolts. Remove the compressor and drier assembly from the vehicle.

7. Installation is the reverse of the removal procedure.

AIR TANK ASSEMBLY

Removal and Installation

1. Disconnect the negative battery cable.

2. Using air pipe removal tool number 926520000 or equivalent, remove the air pipe from the solenoid valve. Remove the solenoid valve coupler.

3. Remove the left hand turn signal indicator from the front bumper in order to gain working clearance.

4. Remove the air tank assembly retaining bolts and nuts. Remove the air tank and drier assembly.

NOTE: When removing the pressure switch or solenoid valve from the air tank, discharge the air from the tank gradually.

5. Installation is the reverse of the removal procedure. When installing the "O" ring, make sure it is free from dirt and dust and then coat with grease.

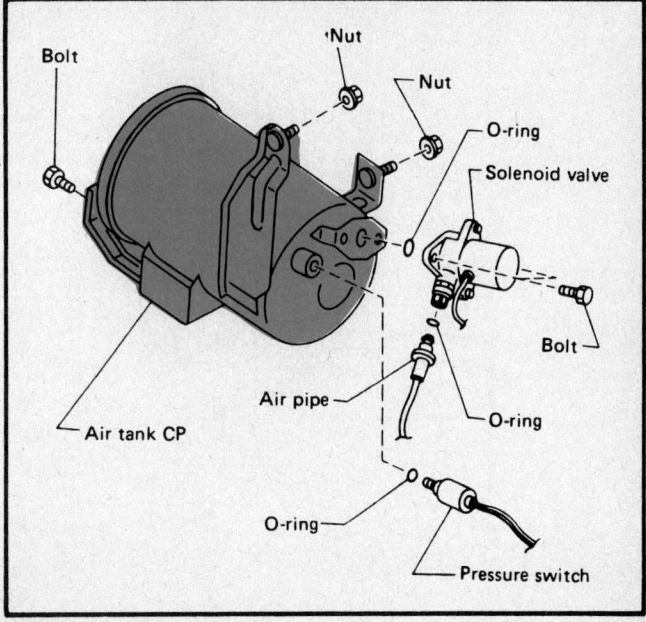

Air tank—exploded view

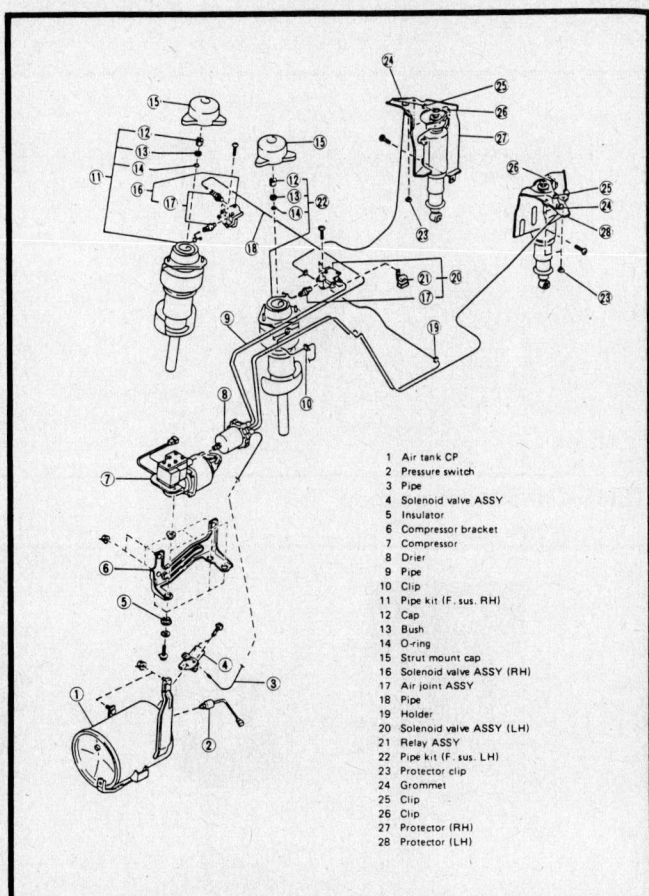

1	Air tank CP
2	Pressure switch
3	Pipe
4	Solenoid valve ASSY
5	Insulator
6	Compressor bracket
7	Compressor
8	Drier
9	Pipe
10	Clip
11	Pipe kit (F. sus. RH)
12	Cap
13	Bush
14	O-ring
15	Strut mount cap
16	Solenoid valve ASSY (RH)
17	Air joint ASSY
18	Pipe
19	Holder
20	Solenoid valve ASSY (LH)
21	Relay ASSY
22	Pipe kit (F. sus. LH)
23	Protector clip
24	Grommet
25	Clip
26	Clip
27	Protector (RH)
28	Protector (LH)

Air line routing for Subaru except XT

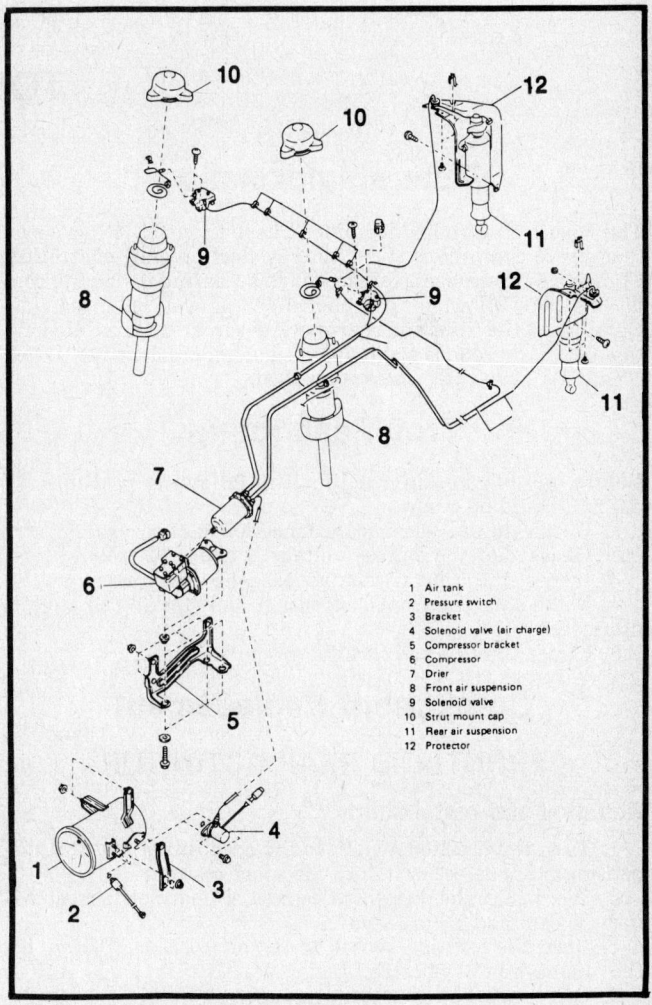

1	Air tank
2	Pressure switch
3	Bracket
4	Solenoid valve (air charge)
5	Compressor bracket
6	Compressor
7	Drier
8	Front air suspension
9	Solenoid valve
10	Strut mount cap
11	Rear air suspension
12	Protector

Air line routing for XT

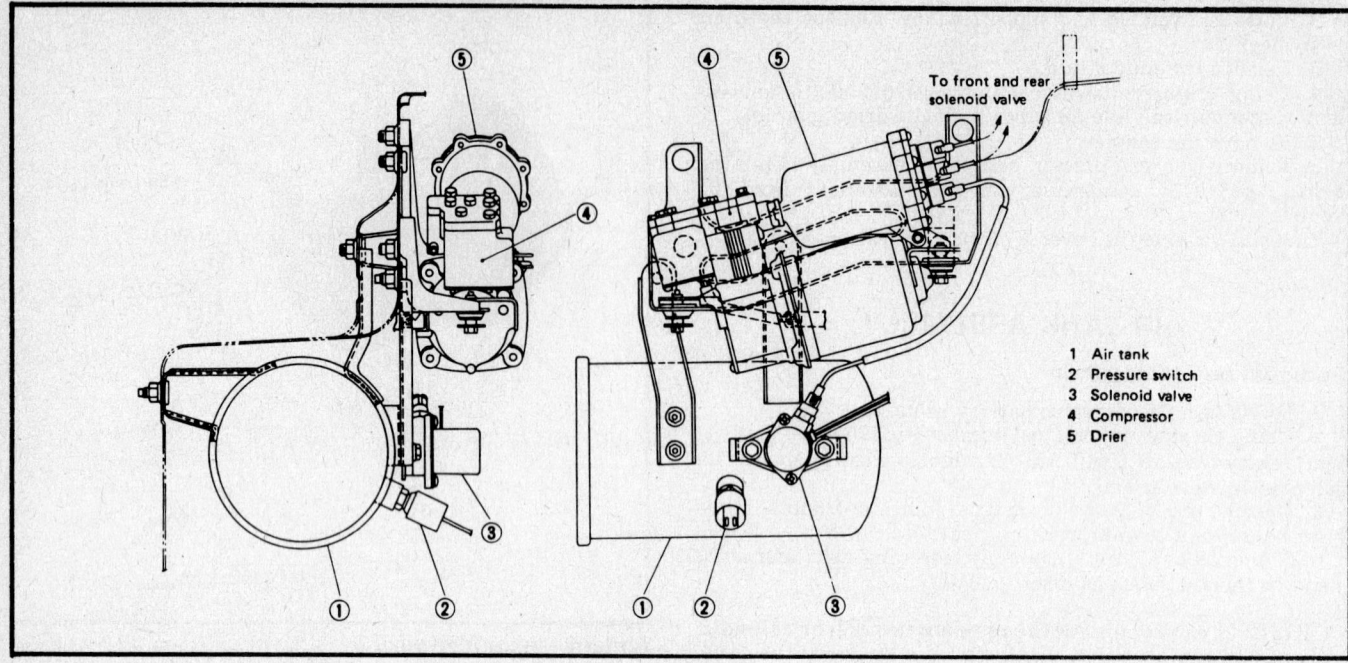

1 Air tank
2 Pressure switch
3 Solenoid valve
4 Compressor
5 Drier

Compressor, air tank and drier assemblies for XT— others similar

TOYOTA

General Information

The Toyota Electronic Modulated Suspension (TEMS) is a system where the vehicle suspension is electronically controlled. Changes in the suspension are made according to driving conditions. This allows for a comfortable and well balanced ride. Damping of the front and rear shock absorbers is controlled automatically to reduce squatting on sudden acceleration. When cornering, body roll is also controlled.

Troubleshooting

Before troubleshooting begins, the following preliminary checks should be made:
1. Check that all electrical connections are secure.
2. Check that the battery voltage is above 12 volts.
3. Inspect the front tire for proper wheel alignment.
4. Make sure the front suspension and steering linkage is lubricated.
5. Check the tire pressure for proper inflation.

Component Replacement

FRONT AND REAR ACTUATOR

Removal and Installation

1. Turn the ignition switch to the on position and the suspension mode select switch to the sport position.
2. Disconnect the diagnostic connector and short circuit terminals Tem and E_2 together.
3. Turn the ignition switch to the off position. Disconnect the negative battery cable.
4. Disconnect the actuator connector.
5. Remove the actuator cover.

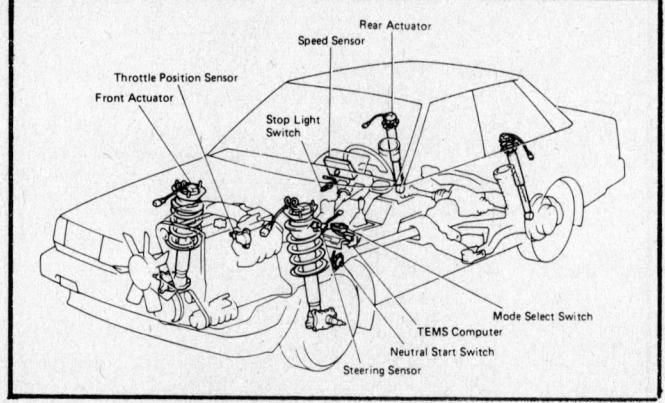

TEMS component location

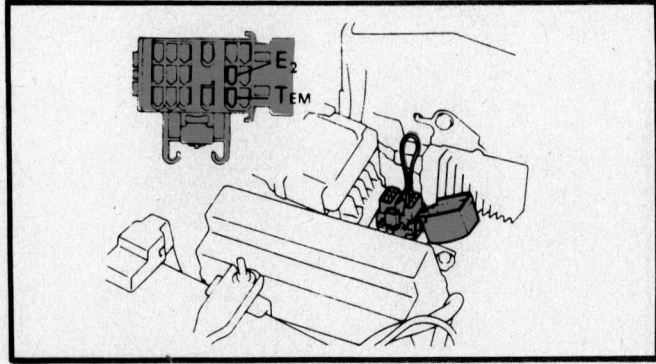

Diagnostic connector shorted

Initial check troubleshooting chart continued

Initial check troubleshooting chart

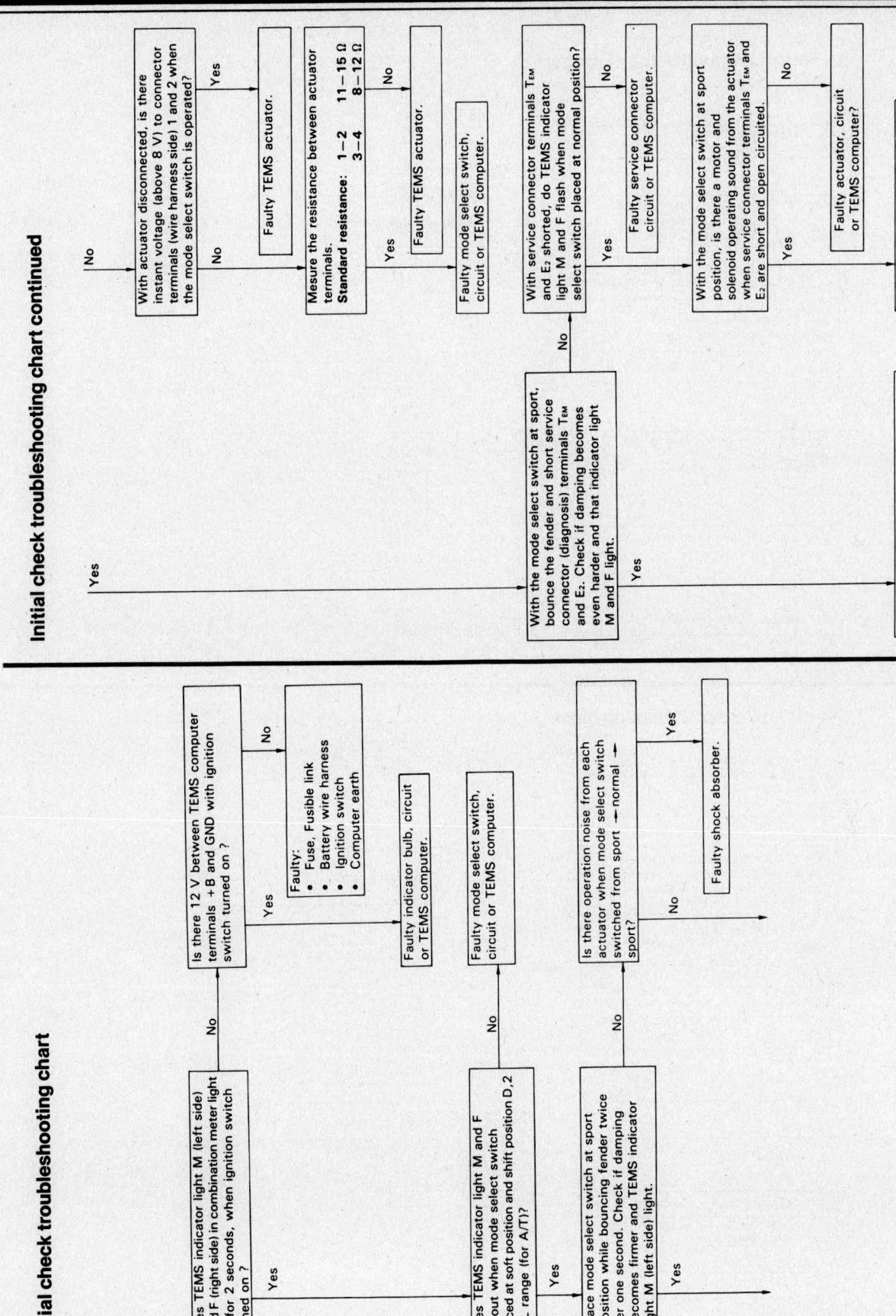

No anti-squat troubleshooting chart

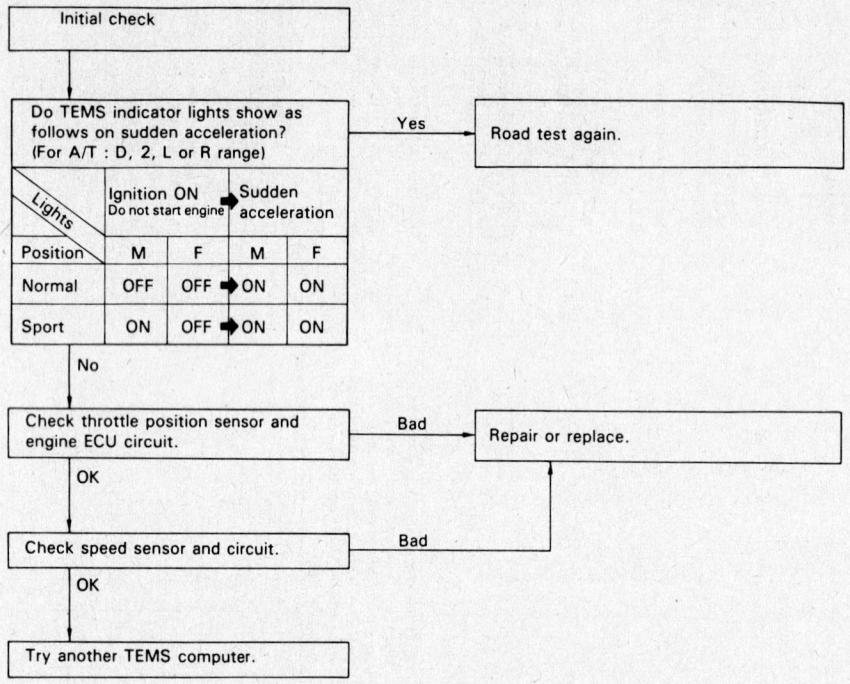

No anti-roll troubleshooting chart

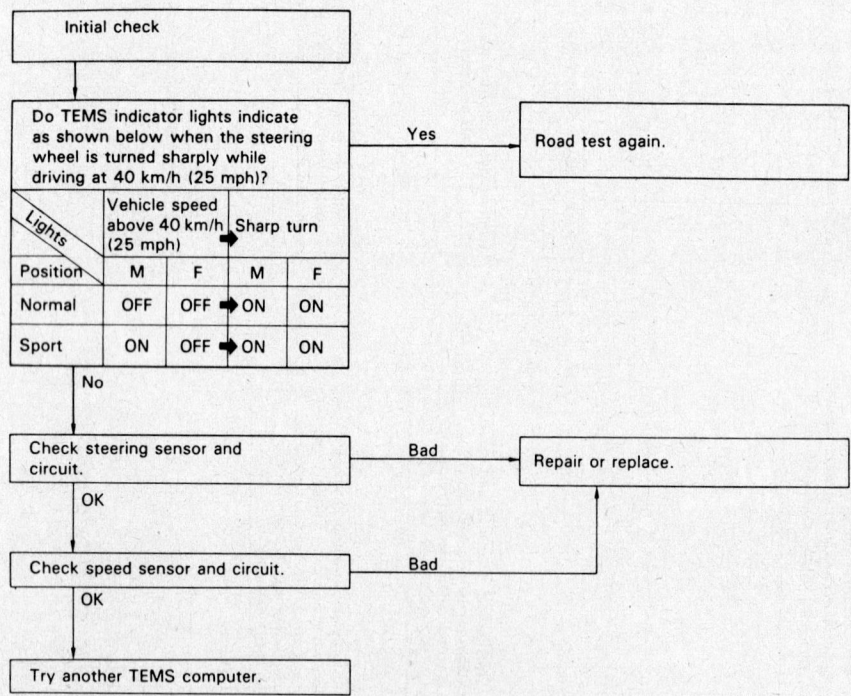

No anti-dive troubleshooting chart

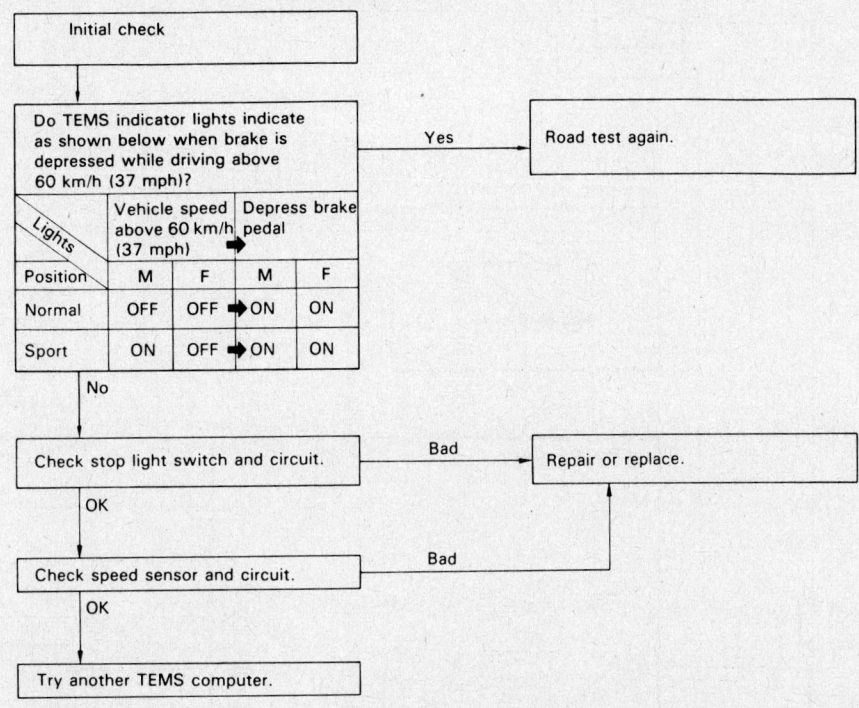

Lights	Vehicle speed above 60 km/h (37 mph)		Depress brake pedal →	
Position	M	F	M	F
Normal	OFF	OFF →	ON	ON
Sport	ON	OFF →	ON	ON

(Initial check → Do TEMS indicator lights indicate as shown below when brake is depressed while driving above 60 km/h (37 mph)? → Yes → Road test again.)

(No → Check stop light switch and circuit. → Bad → Repair or replace.)

(OK → Check speed sensor and circuit. → Bad → Repair or replace.)

(OK → Try another TEMS computer.)

No high speed response troubleshooting chart. The high speed response functions only during normal base auto, and not during sport base auto.

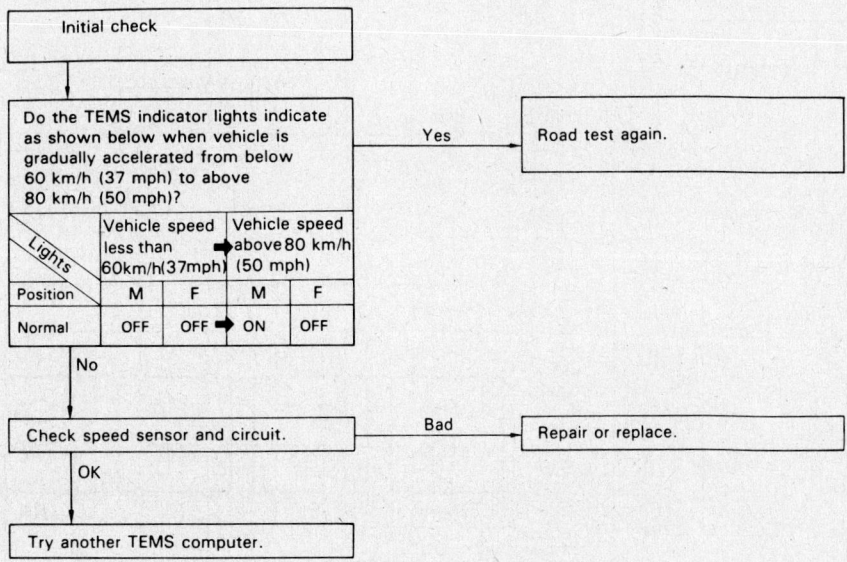

Lights	Vehicle speed less than 60km/h(37mph)		Vehicle speed → above 80 km/h (50 mph)	
Position	M	F	M	F
Normal	OFF	OFF →	ON	OFF

(Initial check → Do the TEMS indicator lights indicate as shown below when vehicle is gradually accelerated from below 60 km/h (37 mph) to above 80 km/h (50 mph)? → Yes → Road test again.)

(No → Check speed sensor and circuit. → Bad → Repair or replace.)

(OK → Try another TEMS computer.)

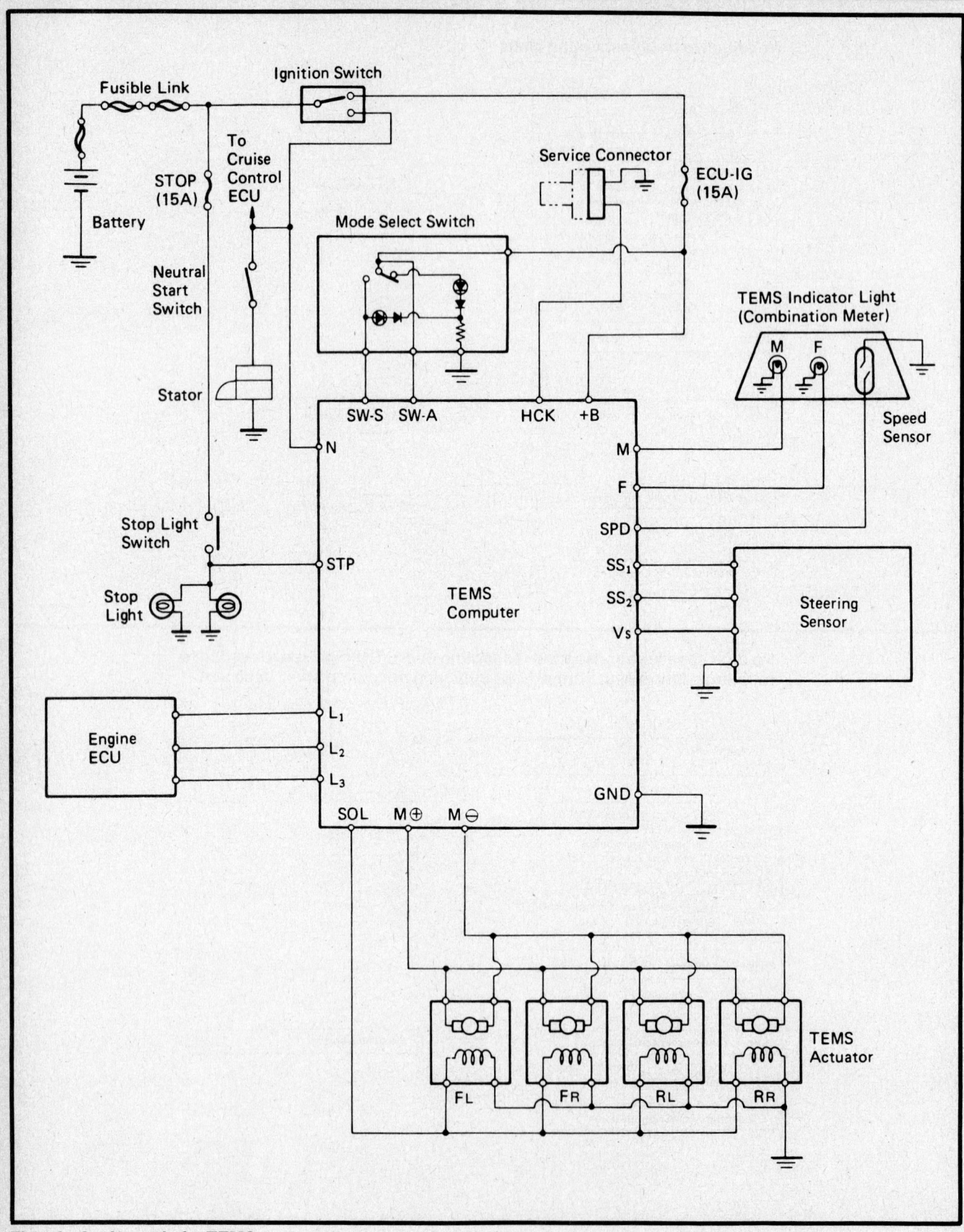

Electrical schematic for TEMS

No anti-shift squat troubleshooting chart (with A/T)

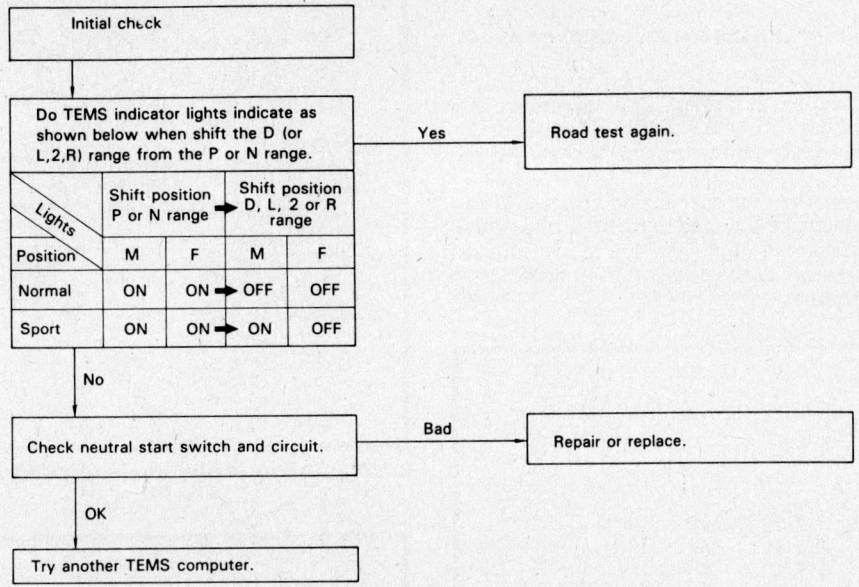

Lights	Shift position P or N range		Shift position D, L, 2 or R range	
Position	M	F	M	F
Normal	ON	ON → OFF	OFF	OFF
Sport	ON	ON → ON	ON	OFF

6. Remove the actuator mounting bolts. Remove the actuator assembly by pulling the actuator out slowly and straight in order to prevent bending of the absorber control rod.

7. Installation is the reverse of the removal procedure. During front actuator installation, fasten the actuator wiring harness so that it faces the front of the vehicle.

STEERING SENSOR DISC

Removal and Installation

1. In order to gain access to the steering sensor and disc, it will first be necessary to remove the steering wheel and column assembly from the vehicle.

Actuator cover removal

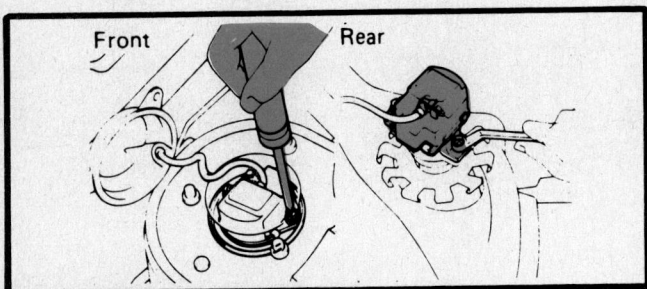

Actuator removal—front and rear

2. Remove the steering wheel from the vehicle in the conventional manner.

3. Remove the necessary trim panels in order to gain access to the steering column retaining bolts.

4. Tag and disconnect all electrical connections from the steering column.

5. Remove the steering column retaining bolts. Remove the steering column from the vehicle.

6. Lightly clamp the center of the intermediate shaft in a soft jawed vise.

7. Remove the snap rings for the steering sensor disc and bearing. Tap out the bearing and remove the bearing.

8. Upon installation, insert a new steering sensor disc with the TOYOTA mark facing the upper side.

9. Press the new steering sensor disc into place using tool number SST 09515 21010 or equivalent. The remaining installation is the reverse of the removal procedure.

FRONT SHOCK ABSORBER

Removal and Installation

1. Raise the vehicle and support safely.

2. Disconnect the brake tube and drain the fluid into a container.

3. Remove the TEMS actuator as outlined elsewhere in this section..

4. Remove the upper shock absorber mounting nuts. Remove the lower mounting nuts.

5. Remove the front shock absorber, front axle hub and brake caliper.

6. Installation is the reverse of the removal procedure. Connect and bleed the brake lines.

REAR SHOCK ABSORBER

Removal and Installation

1. Raise the vehicle and support safely.

2. Remove the brake hose retaining clips.

3. Disconnect the bolt cushion and retainer arm from the suspension. Remove the stabilizer bar end.

4. Place matchmarks on the drive shaft and axle shaft flange. Disconnect the rear axle shaft.

NOTE: Use care when removing the axle shaft so as not to damage the axle boots.

5. Leaving a jack under the rear suspension arm, remove the actuator. Using tool number SST 09278 54011 or equivalent, hold the actuator bracket and remove the shock absorber retaining nuts.

6. Slowly begin to lower the rear suspension arm while being careful not to pull the brake line and parking brake cable.

7. Remove the coil spring and upper and lower insulators.

8. Installation is the reverse of the removal procedure. Connect and bleed the brake lines.

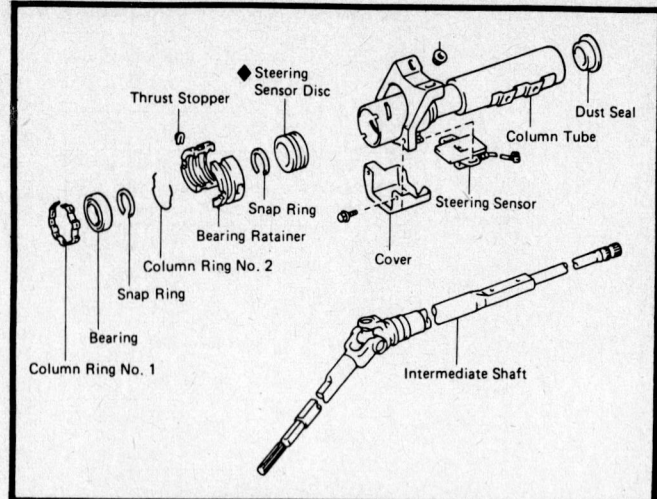

Lower steering column—exploded view

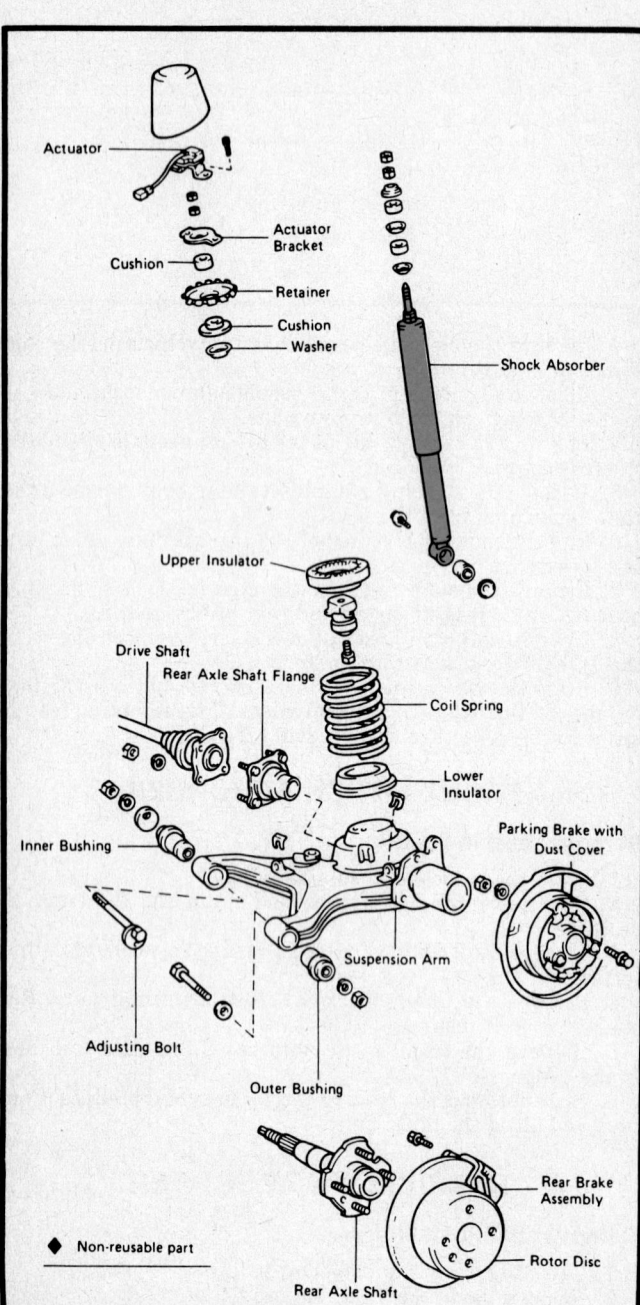

Rear suspension exploded view

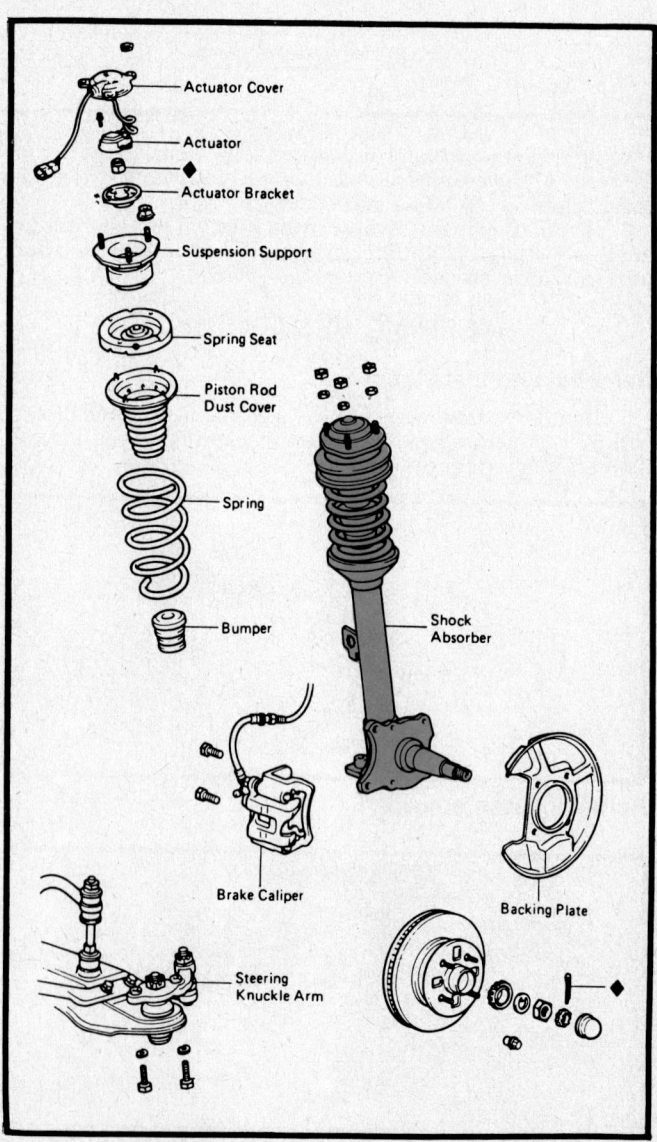

Front axle shock absorber—exploded view

INDEX

INDEX

GENERAL INFORMATION

The cruise control system is an electrically actuated and vacuum controlled system. Most systems consist of a multifunction lever that is located on the steering column. This lever controls the operational functions of the cruise control system. Other systems incorporate the operational functions of the cruise control system on the steering wheel pad. Regardless of the location of the operational controls the systems basically function the same. The control lever or buttons consists of an ON and OFF switch a SET and HOLD button and a RESUME and ACCEL button.

Only factory equipped cruise control units are covered in this manual. If the vehicle is not equipped with factory installed cruise control do not use these procedures to diagnosis and repair a problem.

AMC

DIAGNOSIS AND TESTING PROCEDURES

Whenever a malfunction occurs first verify that the cruise control wiring harness is properly connected to the electronic regulator. A poor connection can cause a complete or intermittent malfunction and is also the only non testable connection in the circuit. For this reason a loose connection may be misdiagnosed as a regulator malfunction. If the wiring harness is properly connected continue with the following tests.

SERVO TEST

NOTE: The servo test can be performed with the servo unit installed in the vehicle.

1. With the ignition switch off, disconnect the servo wire harness connector. Remove the vacuum hose from the brake pedal vent valve nipple, which is located on the servo.
2. Disconnect the servo cable from the throttle linkage at the carburetor.

CRUISE CONTROL DIAGNOSTIC CHART—AMC

Condition	Cause	Correction
System does not engage in "on" position	1. Restricted vacuum hose or no vacuum	1. Locate restriction or air leak and repair
	2. Control switch defective	Replace switch
	3. Regulator defective	Replace regulator
	4. Speed sensor defective	Replace sensor
	5. Brake lamps defective	5. Replace brake lamp bulbs
	6. Brake light switch defective	6. Replace switch
	7. Brake light switch wire	7. Connect wire to switch disconnected
	8. Open circuit between brake light switch and brake lamps	8. Repair open circuit
	9. Mechanical vent valve position improperly adjusted	9. Adjust vent valve position
Resume feature inoperative	1. Defective servo ground connection	1. Check servo ground wire connection and repair as necessary
	2. Control switch defective	2. Replace switch
Accelerate function inoperative	1. Accelerate circuit in regulator inoperative	1. Replace regulator
	2. Control switch defective	2. Replace switch
System re-engages when brake pedal is released	1. Regulator defective	1. Replace regulator
	2. Mechanical vent valve not opening	2. Adjust position or replace valve
	3. Kink in mechanical vent valve hose	3. Reroute hose to remove kink
	4. Brake light switch defective	4. Adjust or replace switch
Carburetor throttle does not return to idle position	1. Improper linkage adjustment	1. Adjust properly (4cyl only)
	2. Improper chain adjustment	2. Adjust chain (4cyl only)
	3. No slack in lost motion link	3. Adjust servo cable (6cyl only)
Road speed changes more than 2 mph when setting speed	1. Centering adjustment set wrong	1. Adjust centering screw
Engine accelerates when started when started	1. No slack in bead chain	1. Adjust chain
	2. Vacuun hose connections reversed at servo	2. Check connection and correct
	3. Servo defective	3. Replace servo

CRUISE CONTROL DIAGNOSTIC CHART—AMC

Condition	Cause	Correction
Automobile continues to accelerate when set button is released	1. Servo defective 2. Regulator defective	1. Replace servo 2. Replace regulator
System engages but slowly loses set speed	1. Air leak at vacuum hose connections or in hoses 2. Air leak at vent valve on brake pedal	1. Check hoses and connection Repair as necessary 2. Replace vent valve
System disengages on level road without applying brake	1. Loose wire connection 2. Loose vacuum hose connection 3. Servo linkage broken 4. Defective brake light switch	1. Repair connection 2. Check vacuum hose connection and repair as necessary 3. Repair linkage 4. Replace switch
Erratic operation	1. Reverse polarity 2. Servo defective 3. Regulator defective	1. Check position of speed sensor wires at connector 2. Replace servo 3. Repalkace regulator

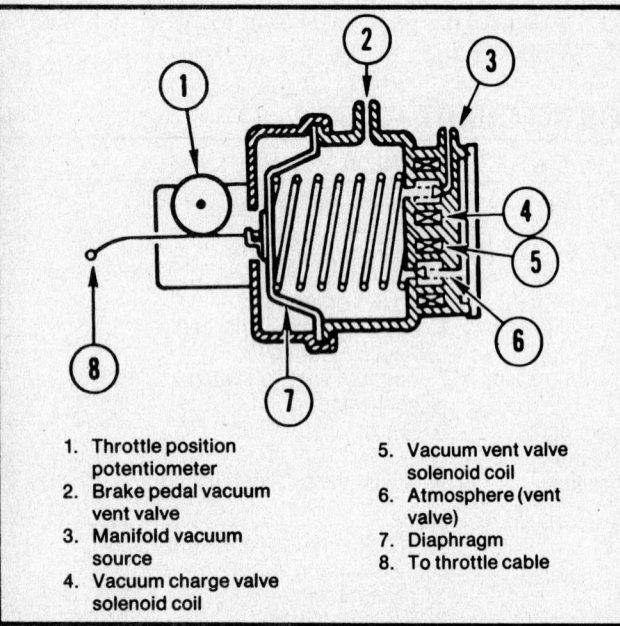

1. Throttle position potentiometer
2. Brake pedal vacuum vent valve
3. Manifold vacuum source
4. Vacuum charge valve solenoid coil
5. Vacuum vent valve solenoid coil
6. Atmosphere (vent valve)
7. Diaphragm
8. To throttle cable

Cross section of cruise control servo (© AMC Corp.)

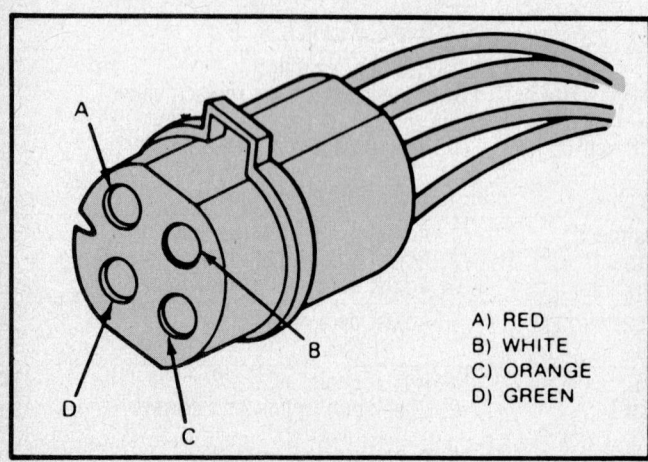

A) RED
B) WHITE
C) ORANGE
D) GREEN

Servo wiring connector (© AMC Corp.)

3. Test the servo unit for shorts to ground.

4. Connect the ohmmeter negative probe to the servo unit mounting stud. Touch the ohmmeter positive probe to the red, the orange and then the white wire terminal of the servo unit wire harness connector.

5. Observe the ohmmeter reading during each test. Infinite resistance should be indicated for each wire terminal.

6. If the ohmmeter reading indicates less than infinite resistance on any wire terminal, the servo unit has a short circuit to ground and must be replaced. The short circuit will also damage the regulator and it too must be replaced. With no load or insufficient load the solid state circuitry in the regulator will be damaged by excessive current flow.

7. If the servo unit does not have a short circuit to ground, continue the test.

8. Connect a vacuum gauge to the brake pedal vent valve nipple. Connect a jumper wire from the chassis ground to the orange wire terminal in the servo unit wire harness connector.

9. Connect one end of a second jumper wire to the battery positive terminal. Do not connect the other end at this time. Start the engine.

10. Momentarily connect the jumper wire attached to the battery positive terminal simultaneously to the red and white wire terminals in the servo unit wire connector.

11. Vacuum should be indicated on the gauge while the jumper wire is in contact with the red and white terminals.

NOTE: With battery voltage applied, the solenoid charge valve is open and the solenoid vent valve is closed. With no voltage applied, the solenoid charge valve is closed and the solenoid vent valve is open.

12. If the servo unit is defective, it must be replaced.

CONTROL SWITCH CONTINUITY TEST

Using a test lamp check the control switch as indicated in the illustration.

SPEED SENSOR TEST

1. Disconnect the speed sensor wire harness connector.

2. Connect a voltmeter, set on the low AC scale, to the speed sensor wire connector terminals.

3. Raise and support the vehicle safely. For Eagle models raise the front and rear of the vehicle if it is not in the two wheel drive mode.

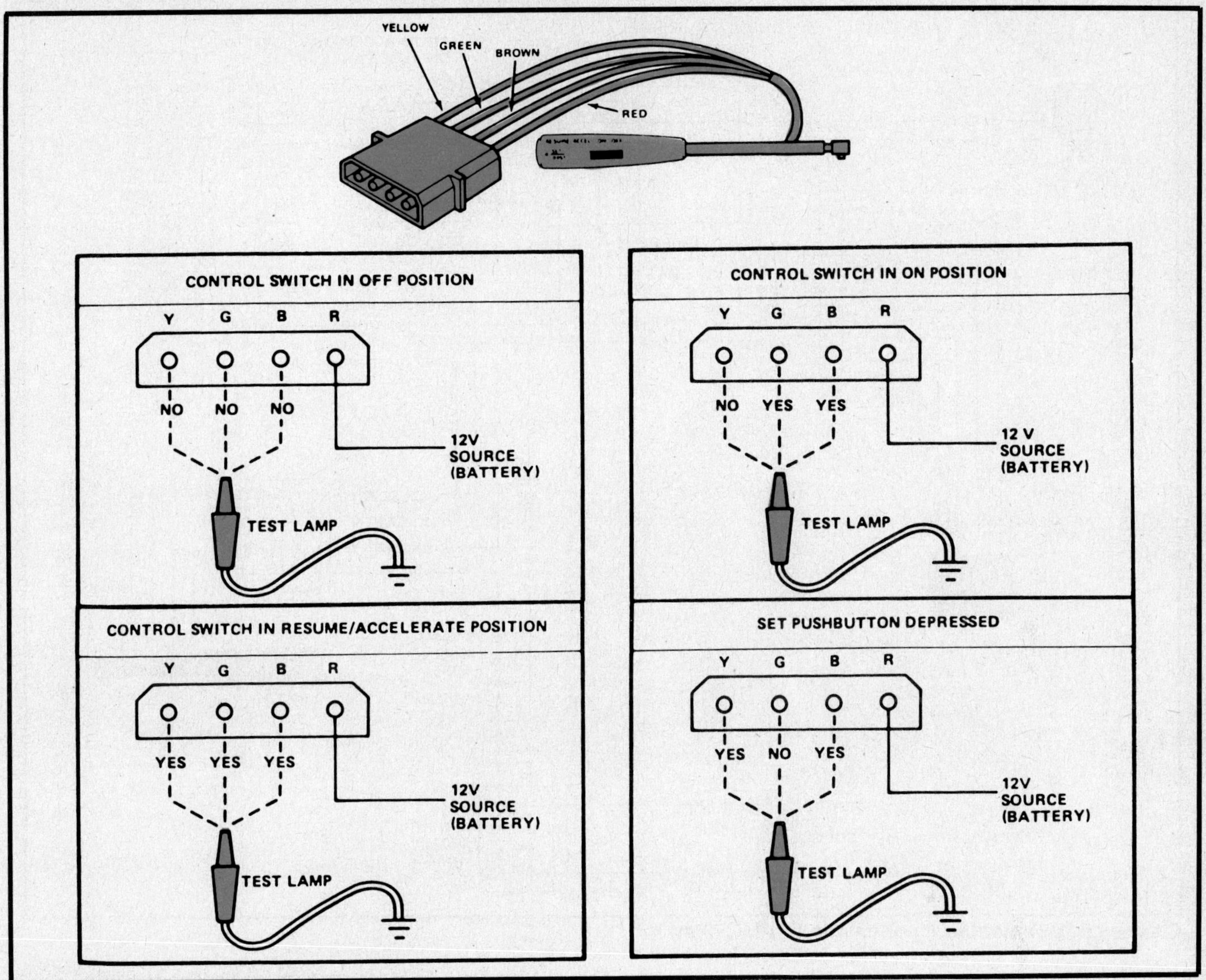

CONTROL SWITCH IN OFF POSITION

Y   G   B   R

NO   NO   NO

12V SOURCE (BATTERY)

TEST LAMP

CONTROL SWITCH IN ON POSITION

Y   G   B   R

NO   YES   YES

12 V SOURCE (BATTERY)

TEST LAMP

CONTROL SWITCH IN RESUME/ACCELERATE POSITION

Y   G   B   R

YES   YES   YES

12V SOURCE (BATTERY)

TEST LAMP

SET PUSHBUTTON DEPRESSED

Y   G   B   R

YES   NO   YES

12V SOURCE (BATTERY)

TEST LAMP

YELLOW   GREEN   BROWN   RED

Cruise control switch continuity test (© AMC Corp.)

4. Operate the engine at about 30 mph and note the voltage. It should be about .9 volt. The voltage should increase about .1 volt for every 10 mph increase in engine speed.

5. Replace the speed sensor assembly if it is found to be defective.

REGULATOR ADJUSTMENT

NOTE: Regulator adjustments are preset by the manufacturer but if all other components in the system appear to be performing properly and the system is still not operating perform the following adjustment.

1. Carefully turn the centering adjustment screw to the ten o'clock position.

2. Carefully turn the low speed adjustment screw to the ten o'clock position.

3. Carefully turn the sensitivity adjustment screw to the full clockwise position.

4. If these adjustments have no effect on the cruise control system, replace the regulator.

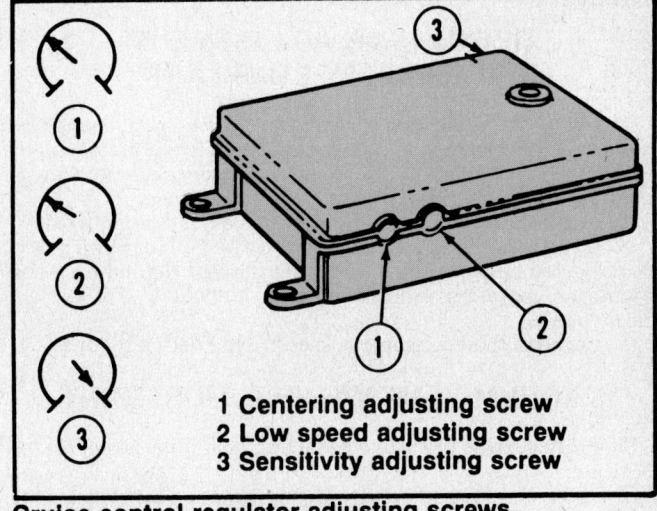

1 **Centering adjusting screw**
2 **Low speed adjusting screw**
3 **Sensitivity adjusting screw**

Cruise control regulator adjusting screws

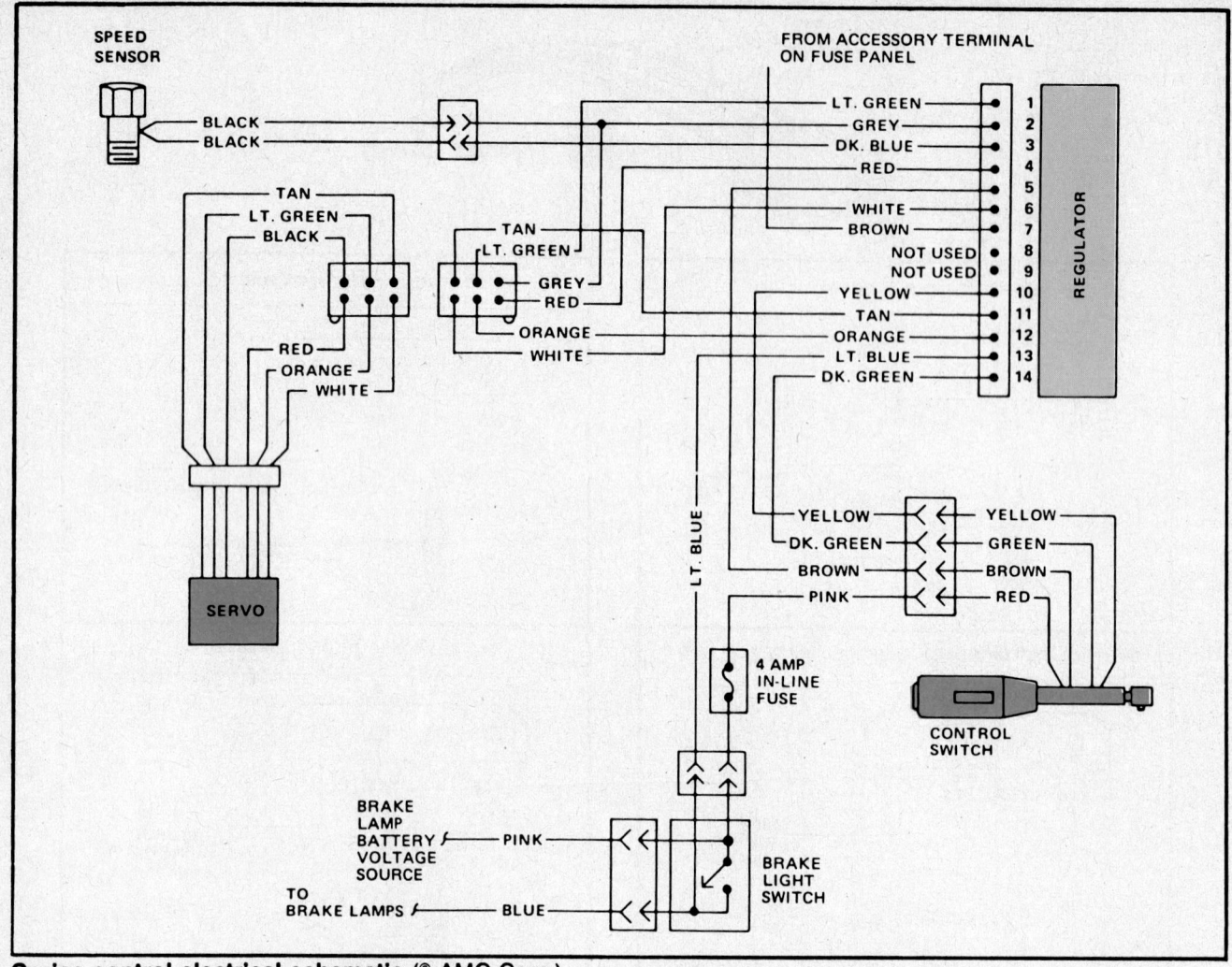

Cruise control electrical schematic (© AMC Corp.)

NOTE: The regulator is the only component in the system that cannot be isolated and tested separately. It must be tested while connected to the rest of the cruise control system.

REGULATOR ADJUSTMENT (DRIVEABILITY COMPLAINT)

1. Drive the vehicle on a level road. If the actual engagement speed is two mph or more above the selected engagement speed, stop the vehicle and turn the regulator centering adjustment screw about $1/16$ of a turn counterclockwise.
2. Recheck the engagement speed. Readjust as required.
3. If the actual engagement speed is two mph or more below the selected engagement speed, stop the vehicle and turn the regulator centering adjustment screw about $1/16$ of a turn clockwise.
4. Recheck the engagement speed. Readjust as required.

VACUUM VENT VALVE ADJUSTMENT

1. Fully depress the brake pedal and hold it in the depressed position.
2. Move the vacuum vent valve toward the bracket on the brake pedal as far as possible.

3. Release the brake pedal. The vacuum vent valve is now adjusted.

Component Replacement

REGULATOR ASSEMBLY

Removal and Installation

NOTE: The regulator is mounted on a bracket and is located under the dash behind the headlight switch.

1. Disconnect the negative battery cable.
2. Remove the regulator mounting screws. Unplug the electrical connector.
3. Using a suitable thin tool, depress the tab inside the hole on the regulator that is marked "terminal release".
4. Remove the regulator assembly from the vehicle.
5. Installation is the reverse of the removal procedure.

SERVO UNIT ASSEMBLY

Removal and Installation

1. Disconnect the negative battery cable.

2. Remove the retaining nuts and cable housing from the servo unit.

3. Spread the clip that connects the cable to the servo unit and remove it.

4. Disconnect the vacuum hoses from the servo unit.

5. Remove the retaining nut and servo unit from the bracket. Note the position of the ground cable.

6. Disconnect the wire harness connector from under the instrument panel. Carefully maneuver the wire harness through the dash panel. Remove the servo unit.

7. Installation is the reverse of the removal procedure.

SERVO CABLE REPLACEMENT

Removal and Installation

1. Disconnect the negative battery cable.

2. Remove the clip and washer from the pin on the bellcrank. Remove the lost motion link.

3. Squeeze the tabs that retain the cable housing in the bracket. Remove the servo cable from the bracket.

4. Remove the retaining nuts and the cable housing from the servo.

5. Spread the clip that connects the cable to the servo and remove the cable.

6. Installation is the reverse of the removal procedure.

CONTROL SWITCH/STALK ASSEMBLY

Removal and Installation

NOTE: The cruise control switch is integral with the turn signal switch and the headlight high beam switch. This switch is not repairable. The complete switch and harness assembly must be replaced if found to be defective.

1. Disconnect the negative battery cable. Remove the lower steering column cover.

2. Disconnect the four wire harness connector located under the dash.

3. If the vehicle is equipped with a tilt column, remove the wires from the connector.

4. Fold back and tape two of the wires to the wire harness. Tie or tape string to the wire harness.

5. If the vehicle is equipped with a standard steering column, tie or tape the string to the wire harness connector.

6. As required remove the steering wheel and related components in order to gain access to the switch/stalk retaining screws.

7. Remove the switch/stalk assembly by pulling the assembly straight out of its housing. Carefully pull the wire harness up through and out of the steering column.

8. Installation is the reverse of the removal procedure.

CHRYSLER CORPORATION

CRUISE CONTROL TROUBLE DIAGNOSIS CHART (1982–83)

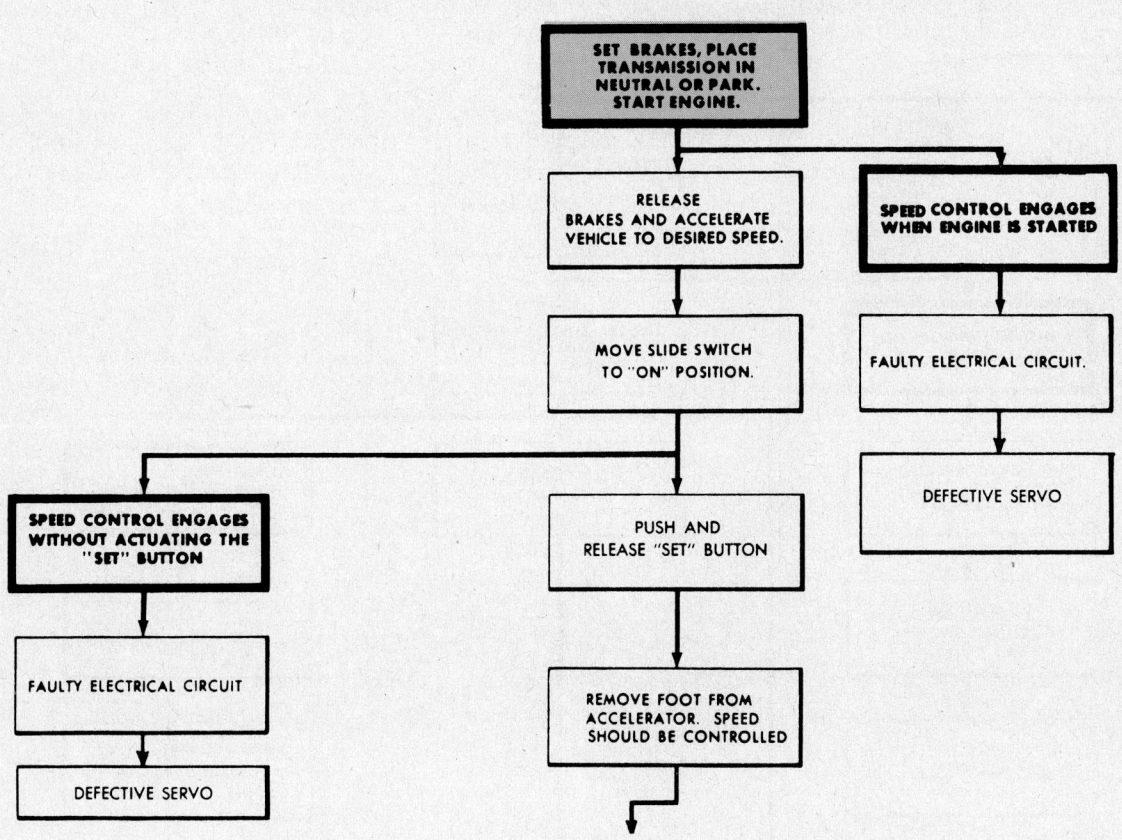

CRUISE CONTROL TROUBLE DIAGNOSIS CHART (1982–83)

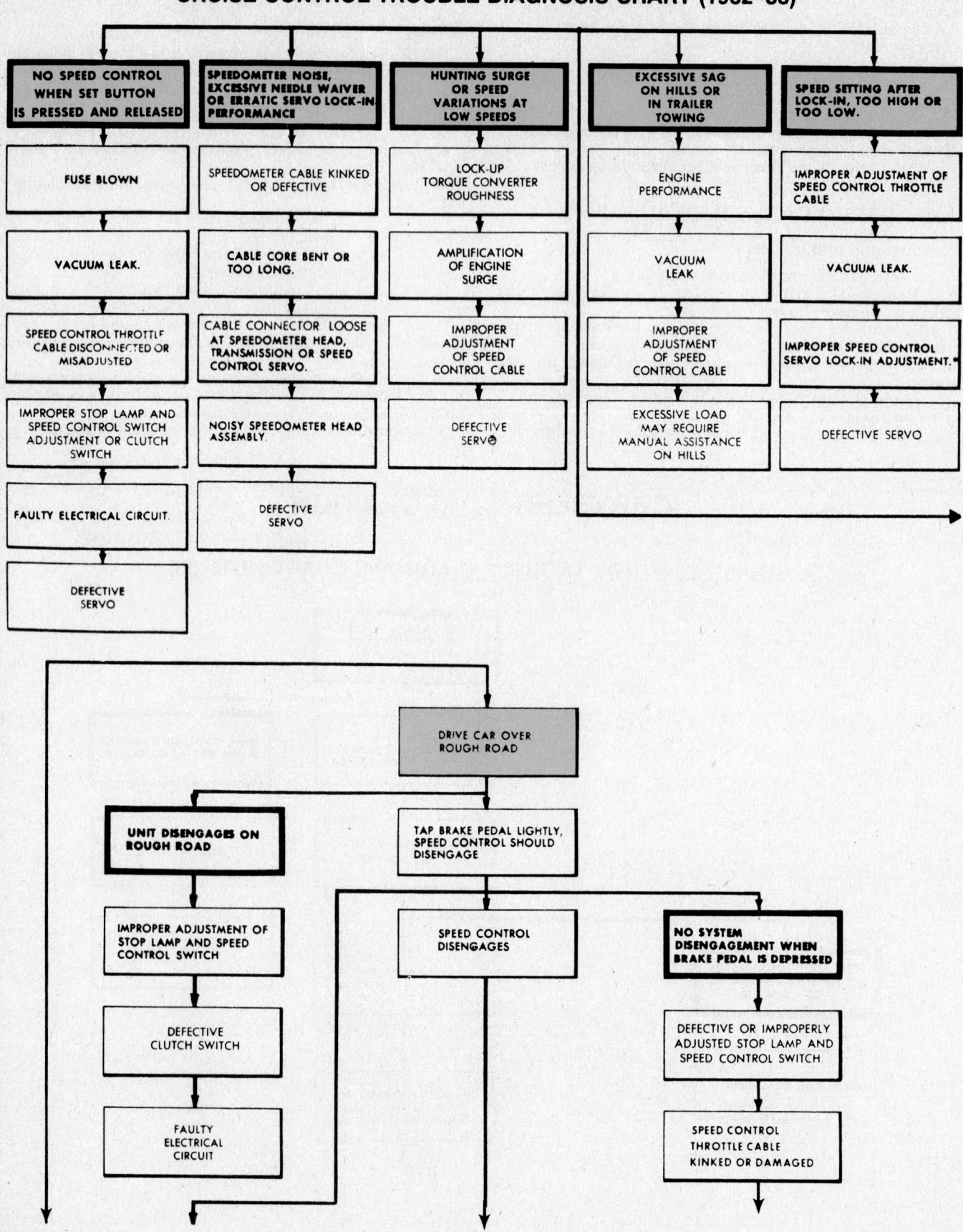

CRUISE CONTROL TROUBLE DIAGNOSIS CHART (1982–83)

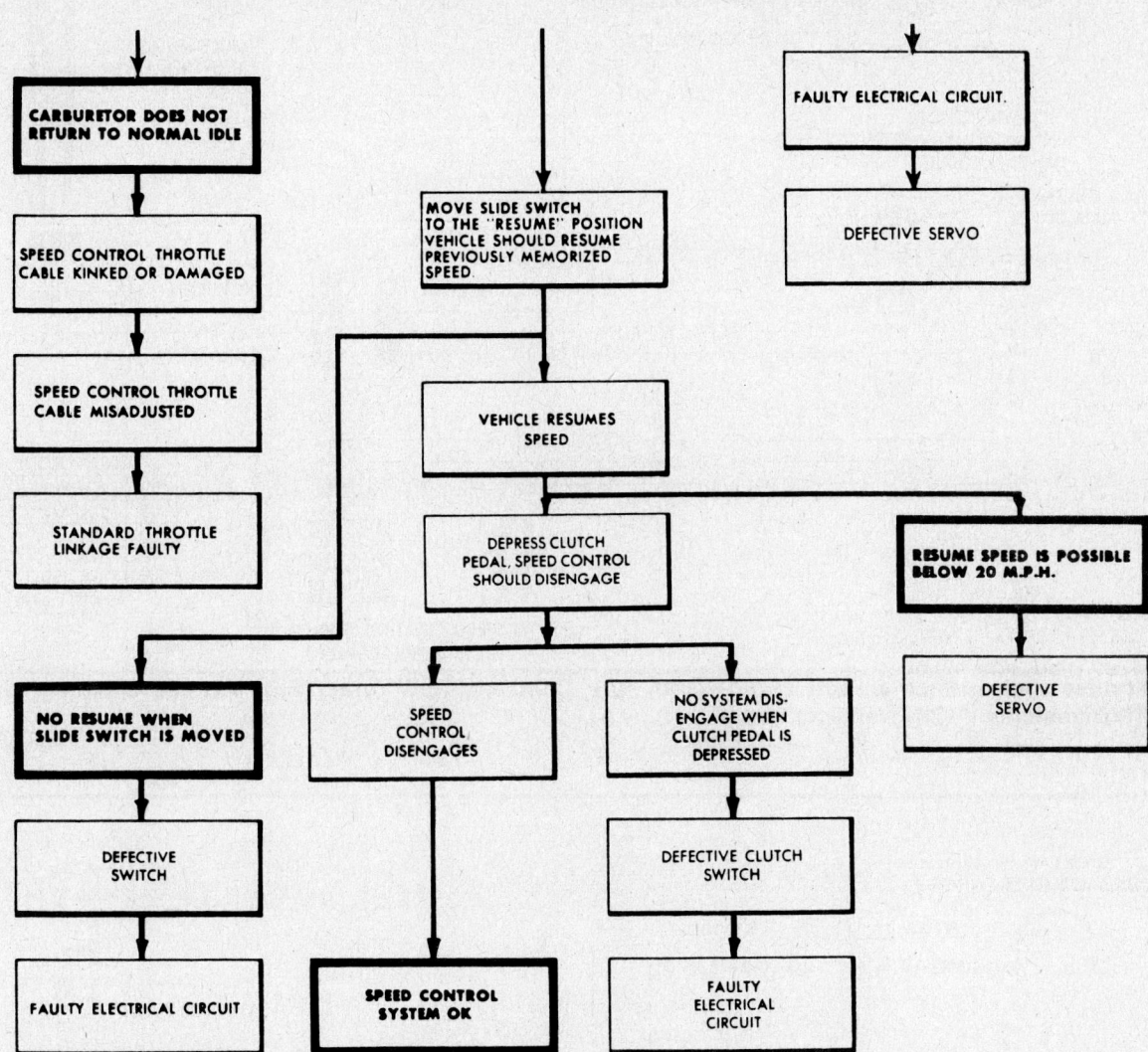

DIAGNOSIS AND TESTING PROCEDURES

Road test the vehicle and verify that the cruise control is malfunctioning. The road test should include attention to the speedometer, as speedometer operation should be smooth and without flutter at all speeds.

A broken or disconnected speedometer cable from the transmission to the cruise control servo will disable both the cruise control system and the vehicle speedometer. Flutter in the speedometer can cause surging in the speed control system. Correct all speedometer problems before proceeding.

If the road test verifies that the speedometer is operating properly and the cruise control system is still not operating and inspection should be made for loose electrical connections at the servo assembly. If the electrical connections are in order continue with the diagnosis procedures.

Conventional Cruise Control System

ELECTRICAL INPUT TO SERVO TEST

The following servo tests are performed at the servo using a test light. Check for a good ground before proceeding. The electrical input to the servo should be checked at the servo terminals.

BROWN WIRE AND RED TRACER

1. Connect the test light between ground and the brown wire with the red tracer.
2. Turn the ignition switch. Turn on the cruise control switch. The test light should be on.
3. Push the set button. The test light should go out and a click should be heard at the servo assembly.

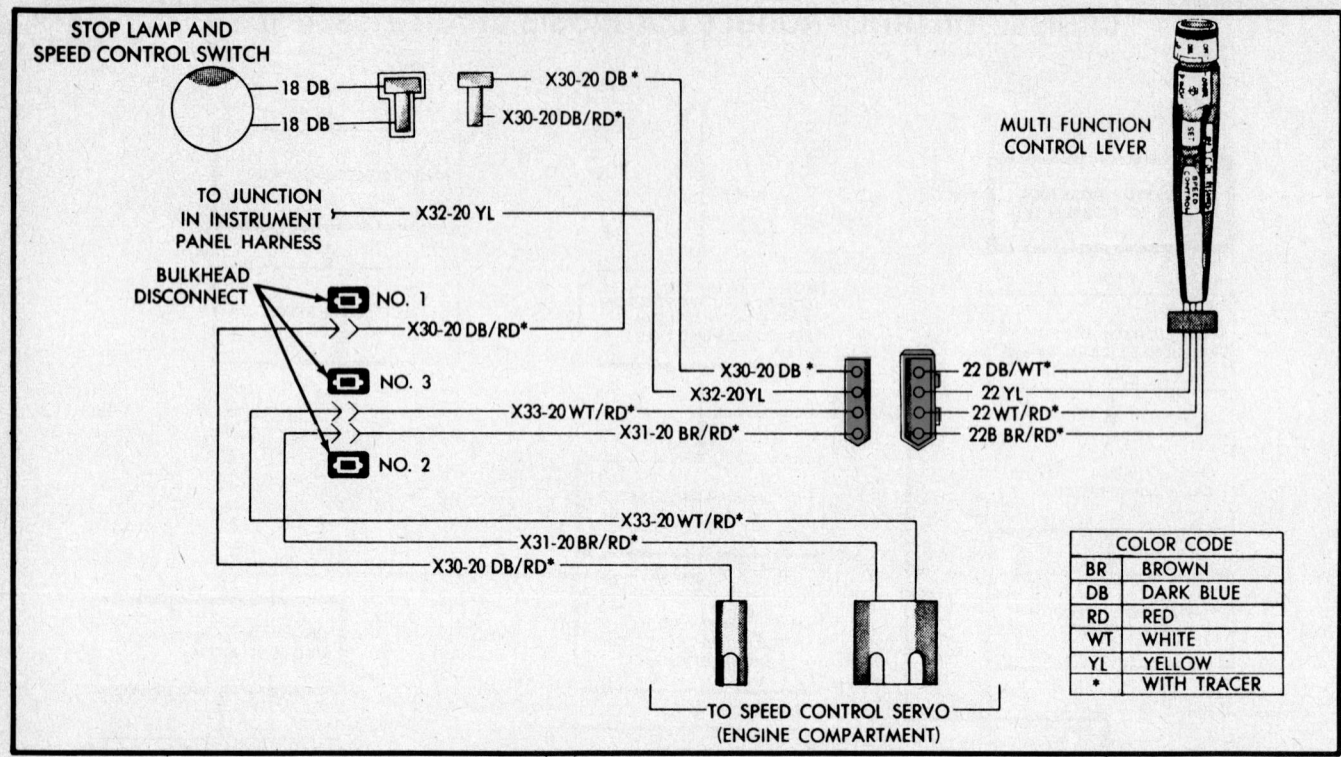

COLOR CODE	
BR	BROWN
DB	DARK BLUE
RD	RED
WT	WHITE
YL	YELLOW
*	WITH TRACER

Typical cruise control electrical schematic – Gran Fury, Caravelle, New Yorker, Fifth Avenue, Diplomat and New-port – RWD vehicles (© Chrysler Corp.)

COLOR CODE	
RD	RED
BR	BROWN
DB	DARK BLUE
YL	YELLOW
WT	WHITE
*	WITH TRACER

Typical cruise control electrical schematic – Cordoba, Mirada and Inperial – RWD vehicles (© Chrysler Corp.)

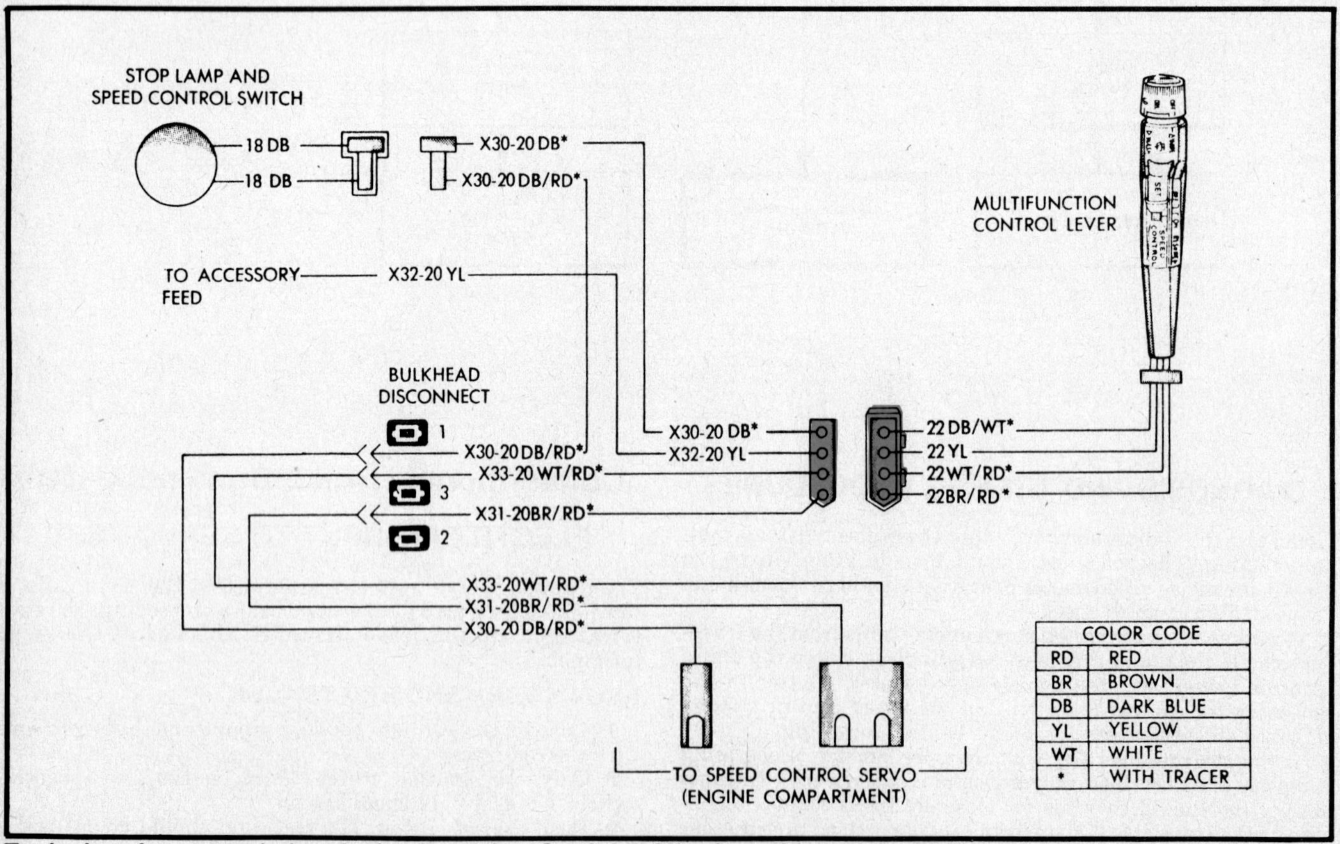

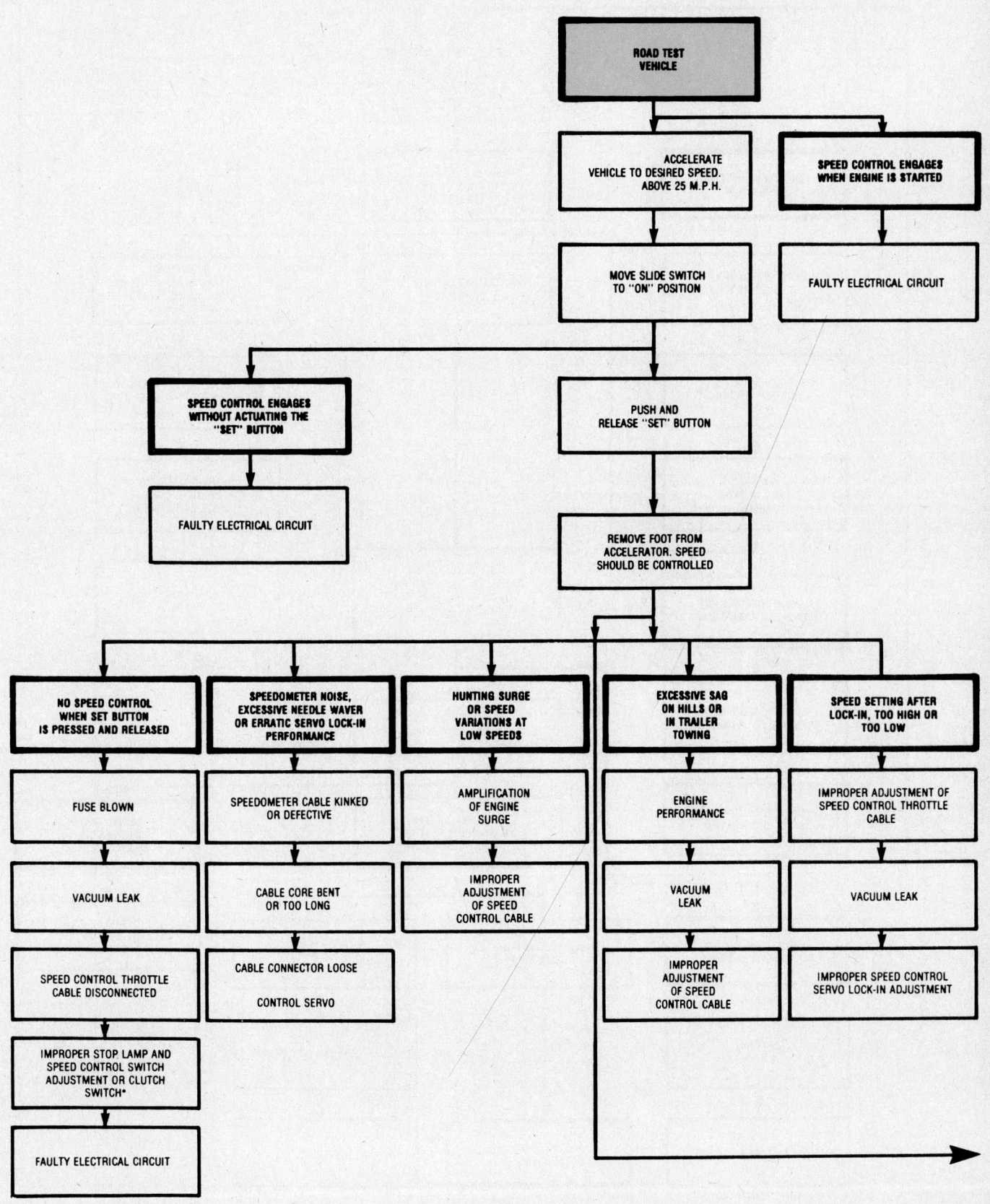

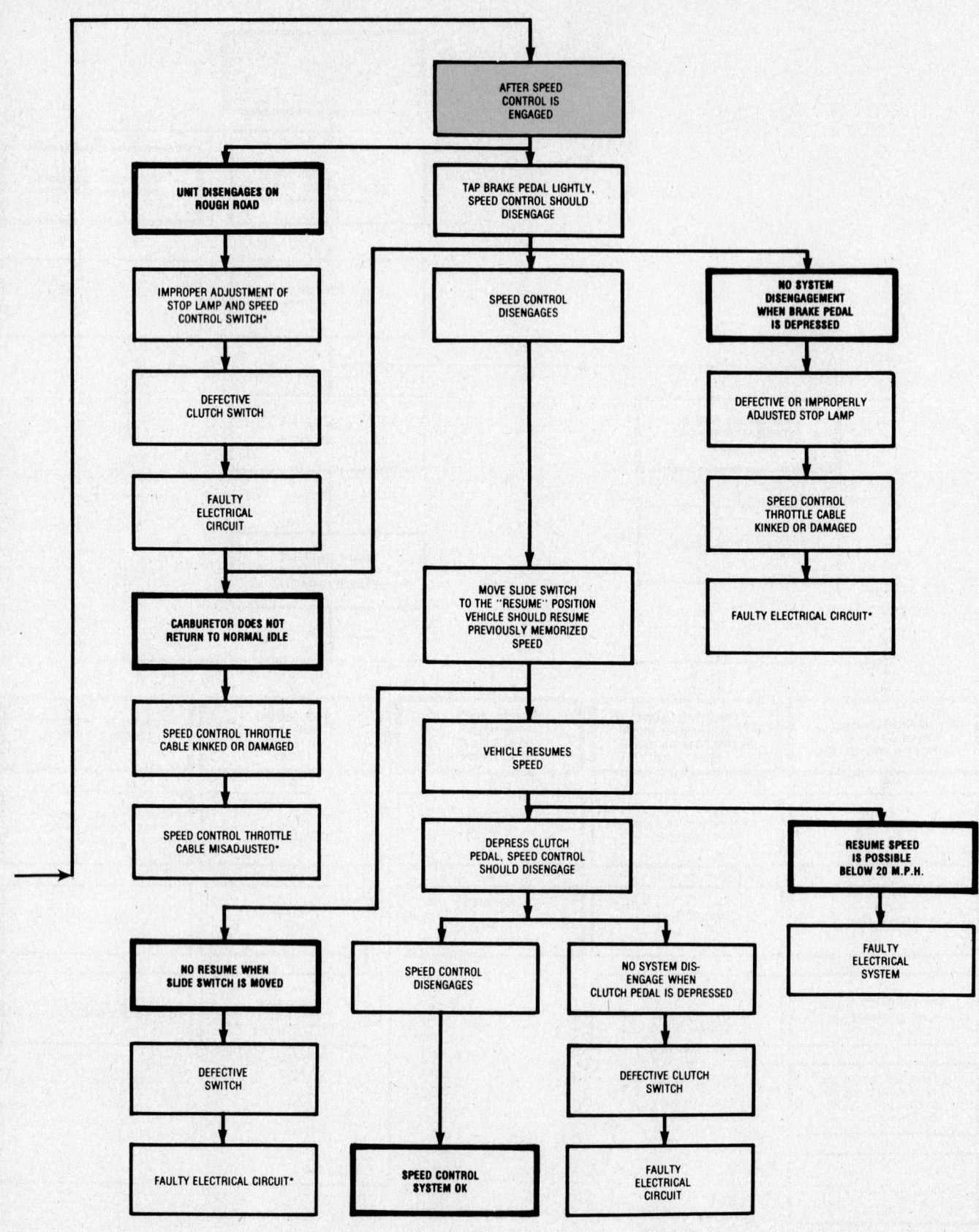

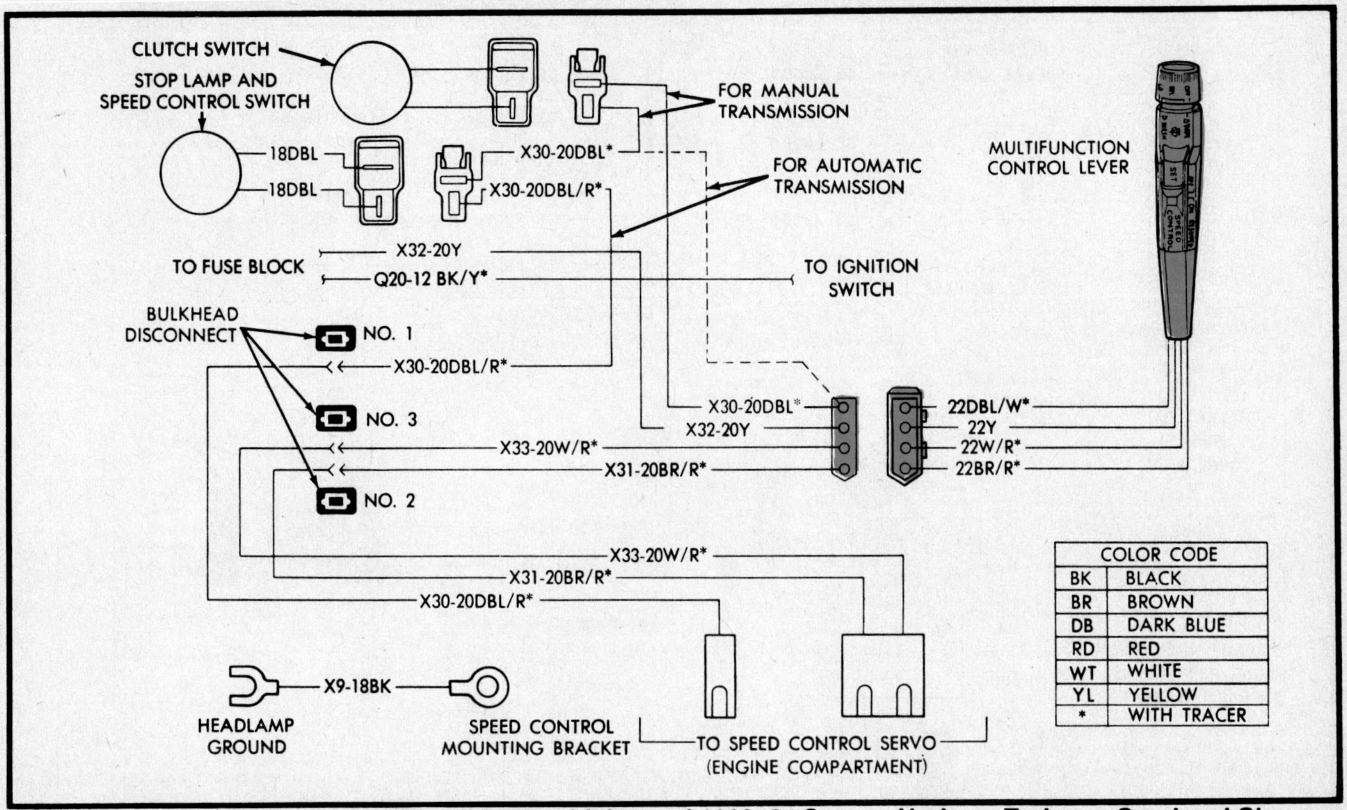

COLOR CODE	
BK	BLACK
BR	BROWN
DB	DARK BLUE
RD	RED
WT	WHITE
YL	YELLOW
*	WITH TRACER

Cruise control electrical schematic – all 1982 vehicles and 1983–84 Scamp, Horizon, Turismo, Omni and Charger (© Chrysler Corp.)

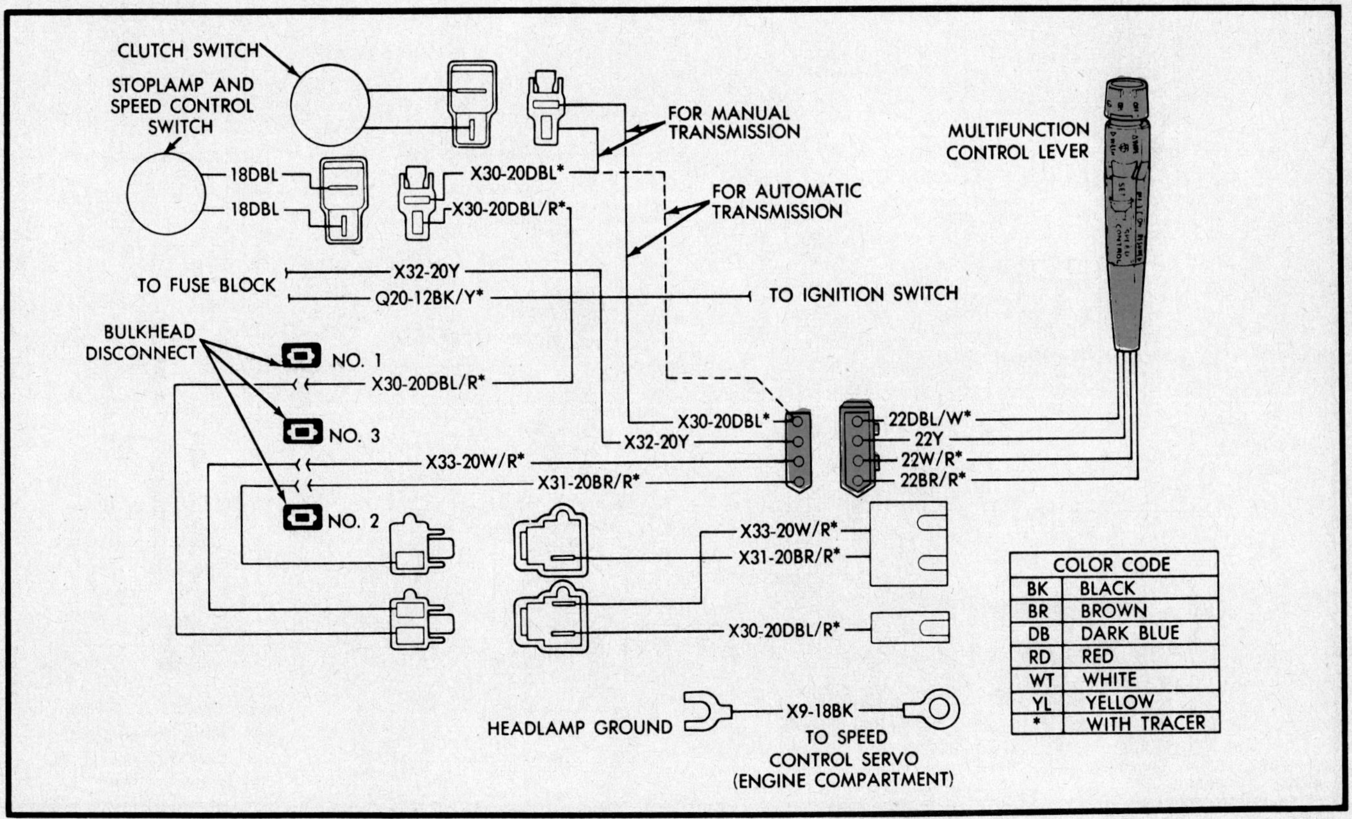

COLOR CODE	
BK	BLACK
BR	BROWN
DB	DARK BLUE
RD	RED
WT	WHITE
YL	YELLOW
*	WITH TRACER

Cruise control electrical schematic – 1983–84 Reliant, Aries, Caravelle, LeBaron, Town and Country, 400, 600, New Yorker, E Class, Daytona and Laser (© Chrysler Corp.)

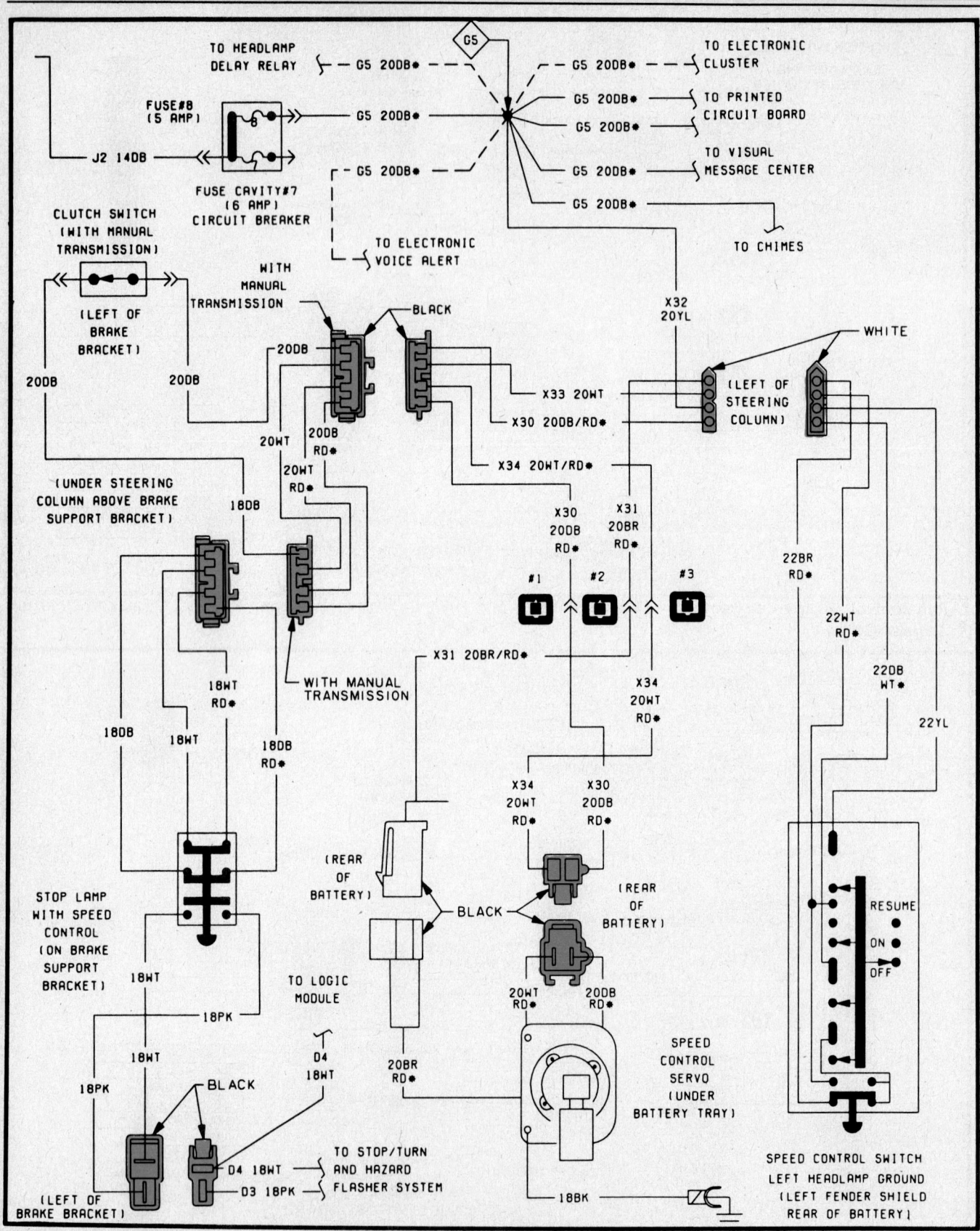

Cruise control electrical schematic—1985 and later Lancer and LeBaron (© Chrysler Corp.)

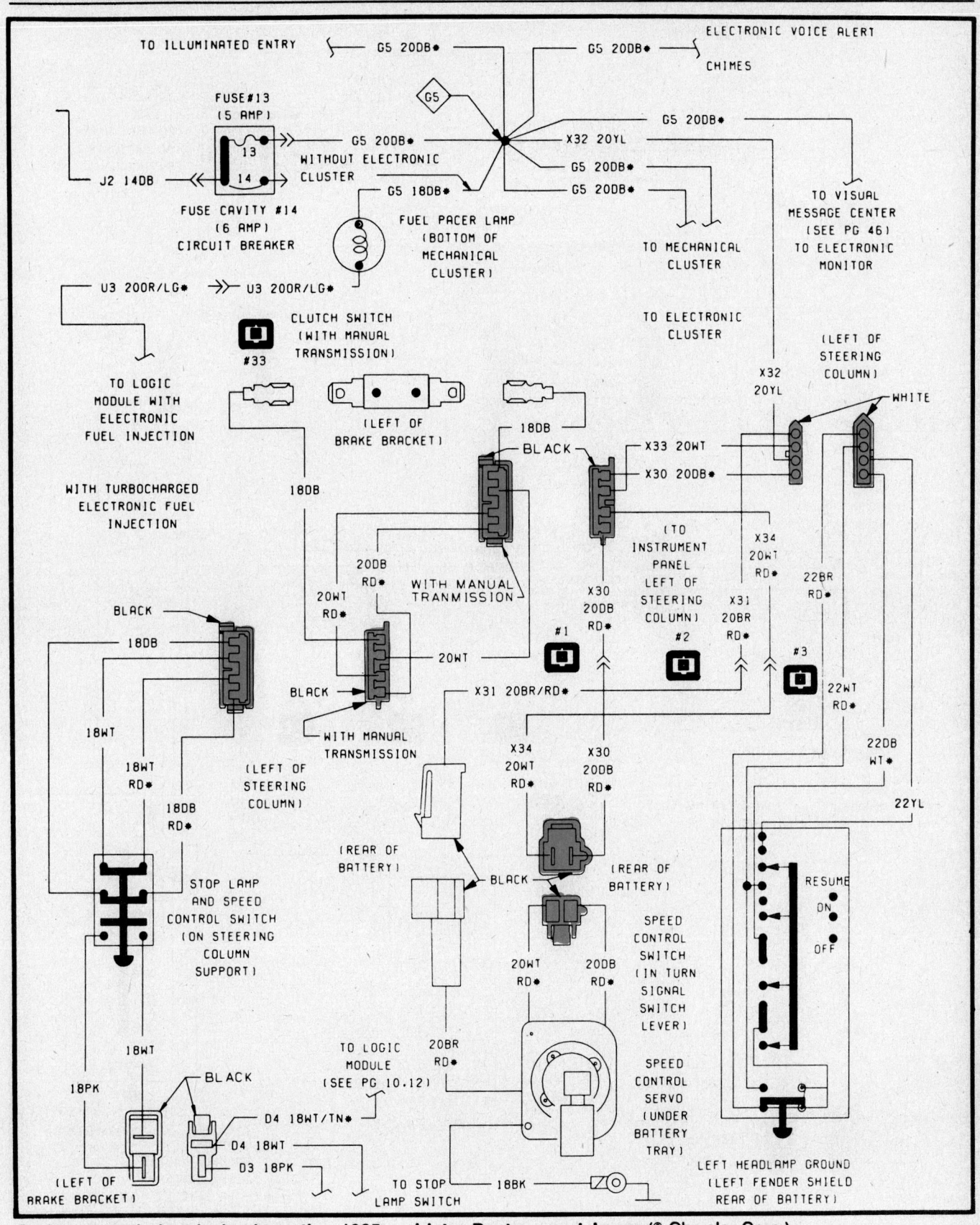

Cruise control electrical schematic—1985 and later Daytona and Laser (© Chrysler Corp.)

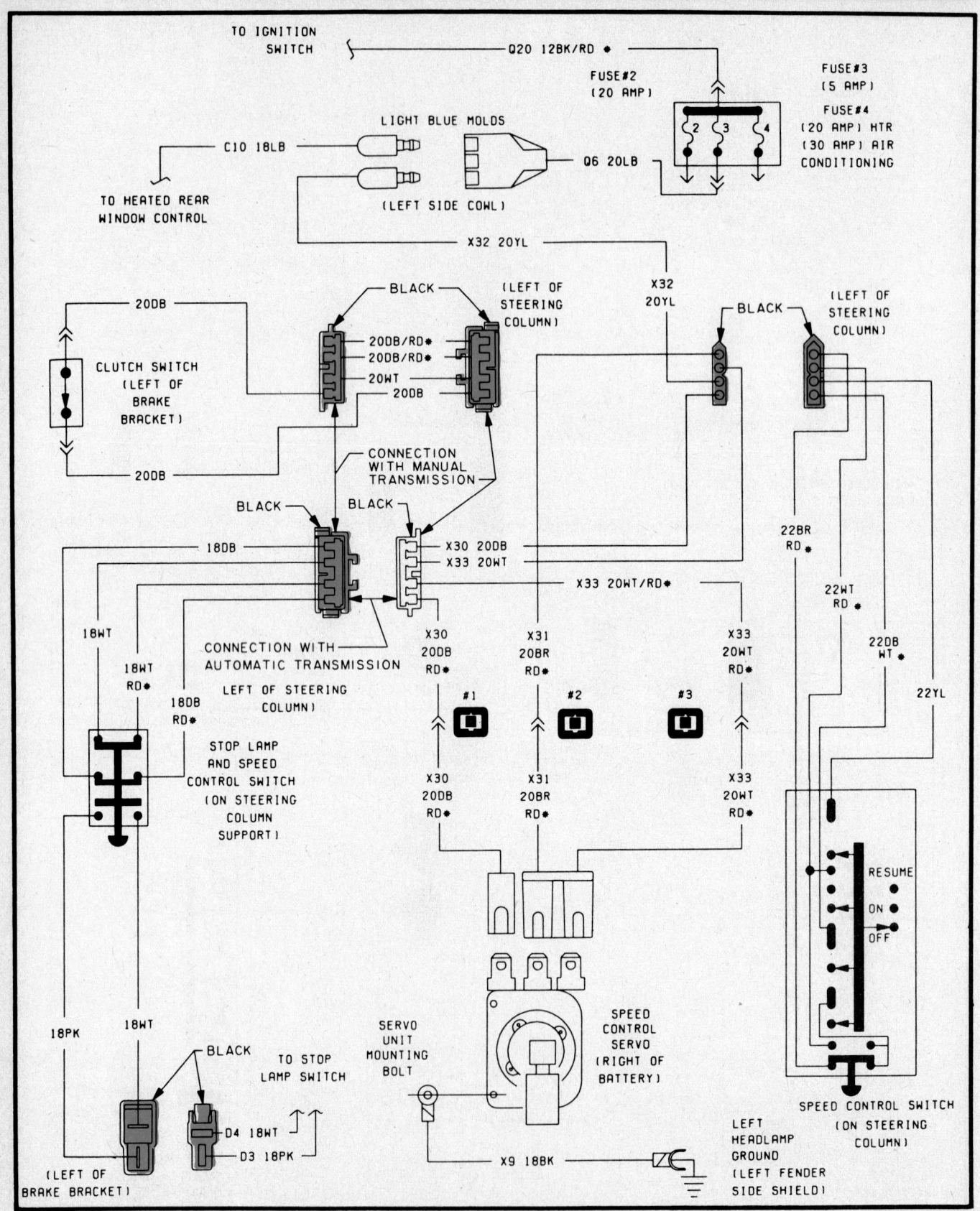

Cruise control electrical schematic—1985 and later Omni, Charger, Turismo and Horizon (© Chrysler Corp.)

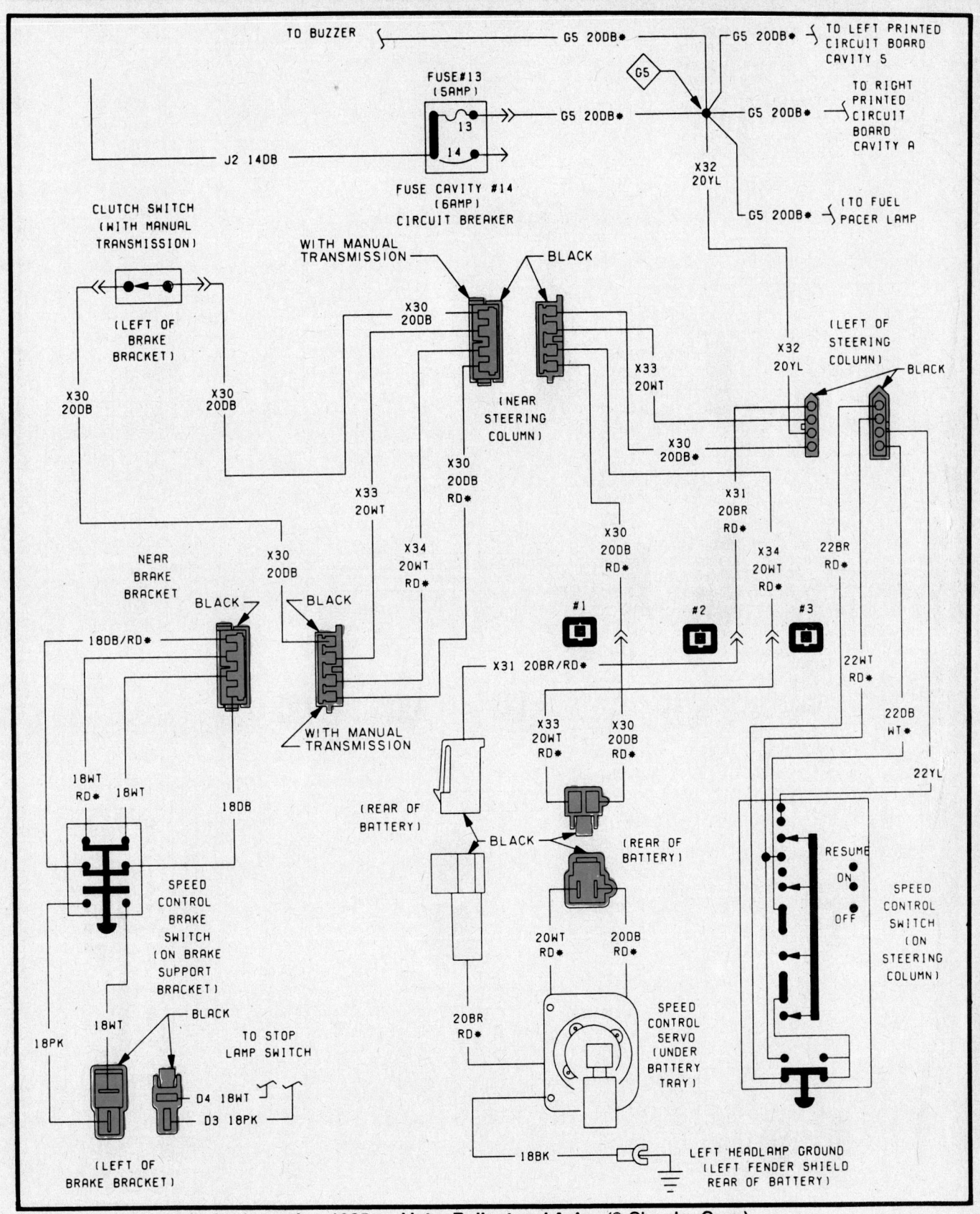

Cruise control electrical schematic — 1985 and later Reliant and Aries (© Chrysler Corp.)

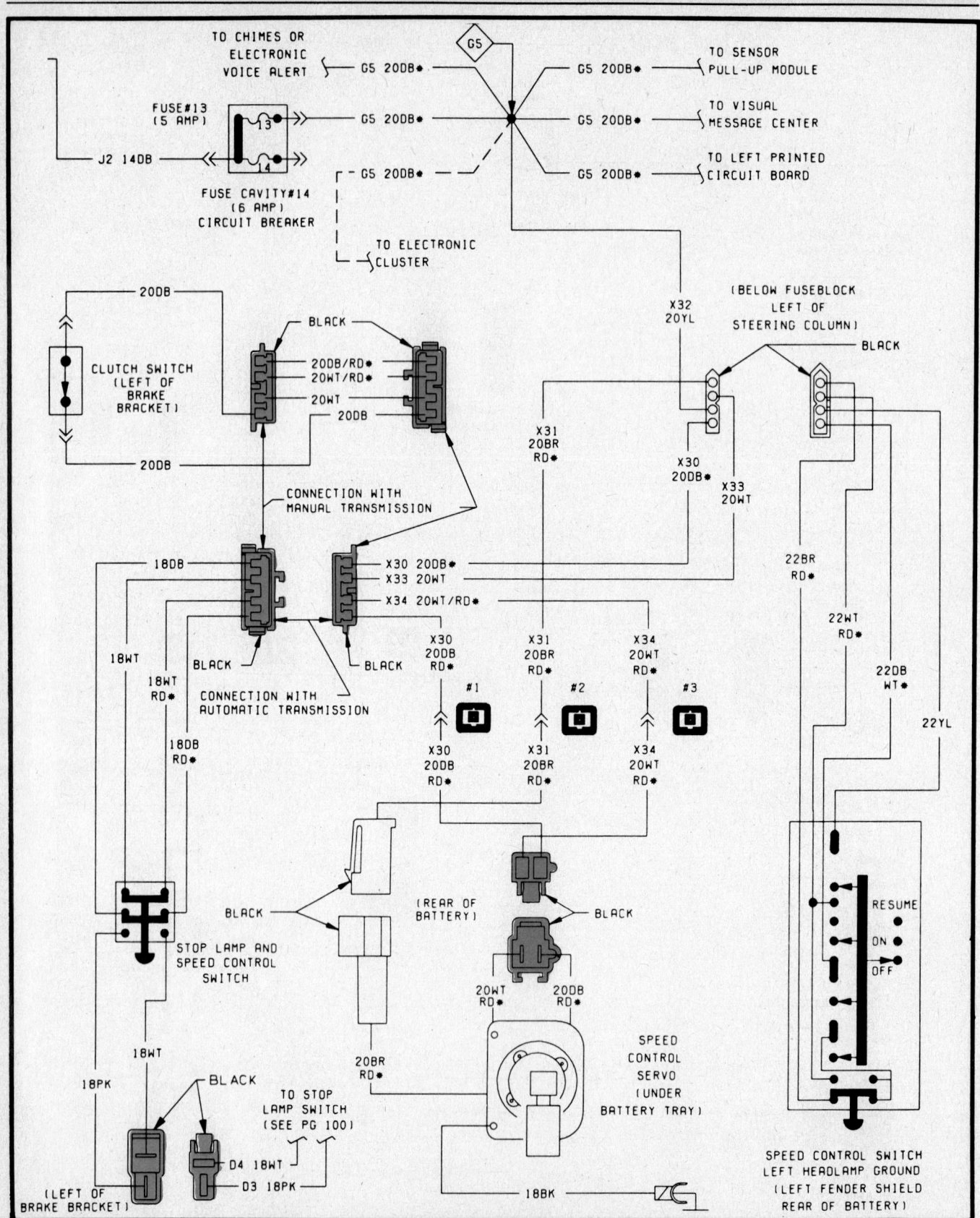

Cruise control electrical schematic—1985 and later Caravelle, 600, LeBaron, Town and Country and New Yorker (© Chrysler Corp.)

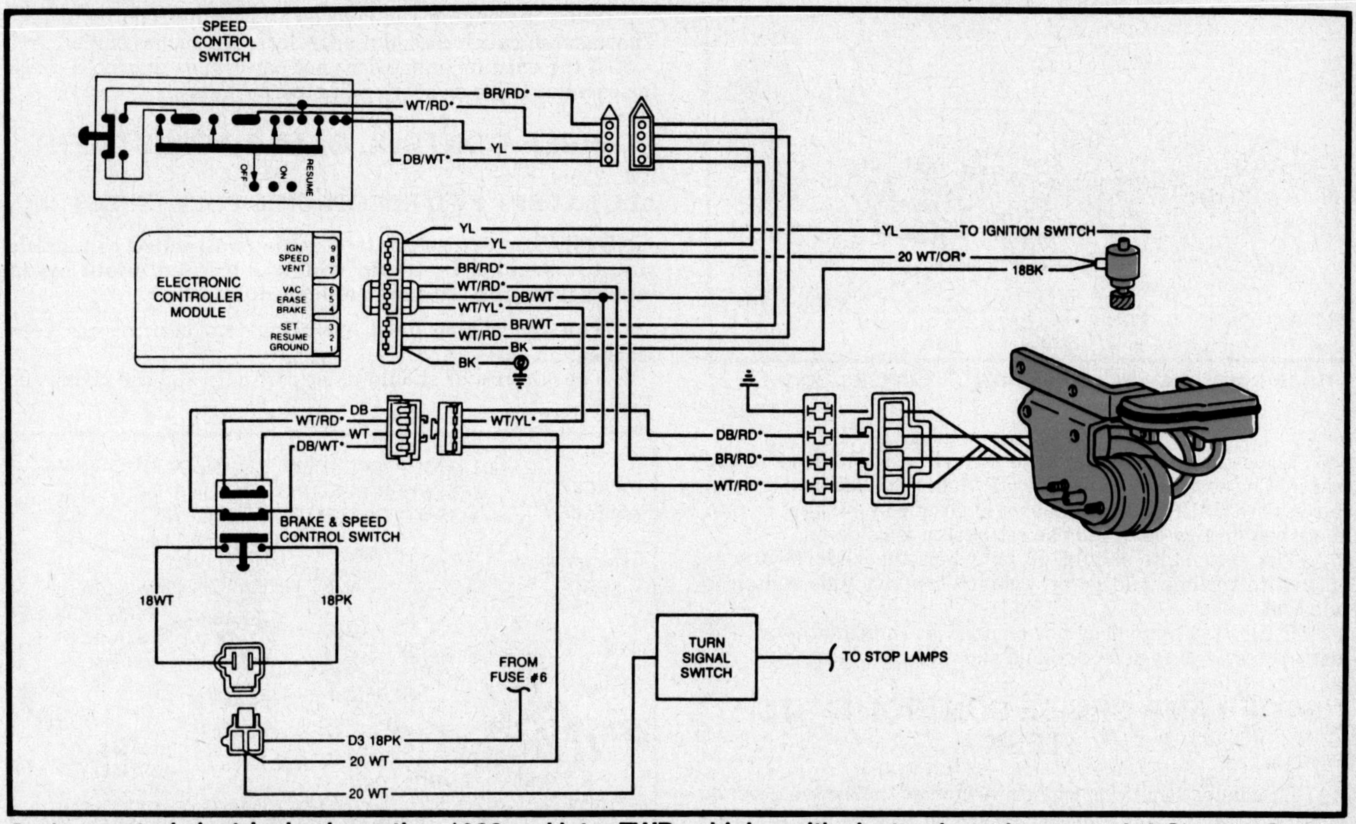

Cruise control electrical schematic – 1986 and later FWD vehicles with electronic cruise control (© Chrysler Corp.)

4. Release the set button. The test light should go on and a click should be heard at the servo assembly.

5. If the test does not respond as indicated, there is a blown fuse, faulty cruise control wiring or a defective cruise control switch.

6. If the clicks are not heard at the servo assembly, the servo assembly is defective.

7. Repair or replace defective components as required.

WHITE WIRE WITH RED TRACER

1. Connect the test light between ground and the white wire with the red tracer.

2. Turn the ignition switch. Turn on the cruise control switch. The test light should be off.

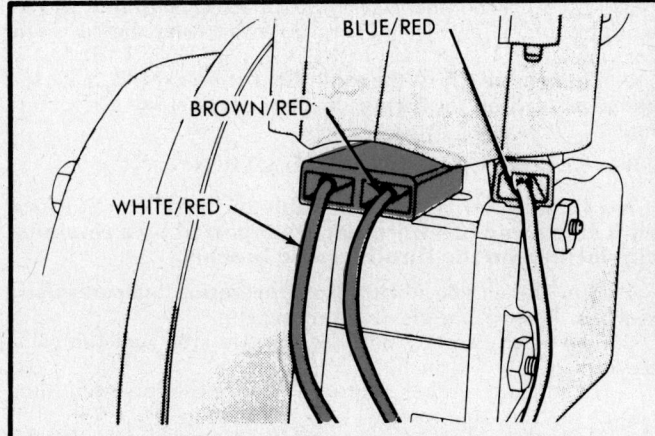

Servo test terminal location (© Chrysler Corp.)

3. Push the set button. The test light should be on while the set button is depressed.

4. If the test does not respond as indicated, there is a defect in the cruise control switch or faulty wiring somewhere in the cruise control system.

5. Repair or replace defective components as required.

BLUE WIRE WITH RED TRACER

1. Connect the test light between ground and the blue wire with the red tracer.

2. Turn the ignition switch. Turn on the cruise control switch. The test light should be on.

3. If the test does not respond as indicated, there is a defect in the cruise control switch, faulty wiring somewhere in the cruise control system, a defective brake switch or a defective clutch switch.

5. Repair or replace defective components as required.

CRUISE CONTROL SWITCH TEST

1. Check the fuse for continuity. Disconnect the four wire electrical connector at the steering column.

2. Connect a twelve volt positive source to the yellow wire terminal in the cruise control (male end) wire harness.

3. Attach one lead of the test light to ground and the other lead to the brown wire with the red tracer terminal.

4. The test light should go on when the cruise control switch is in the on position. The test light should be off when the set button is depressed or when the cruise control switch is in the off position.

5. Move the test light lead to the dark blue wire with the white tracer. The test light should be on when the slide switch is in the one position and off when the slide switch is in off position.

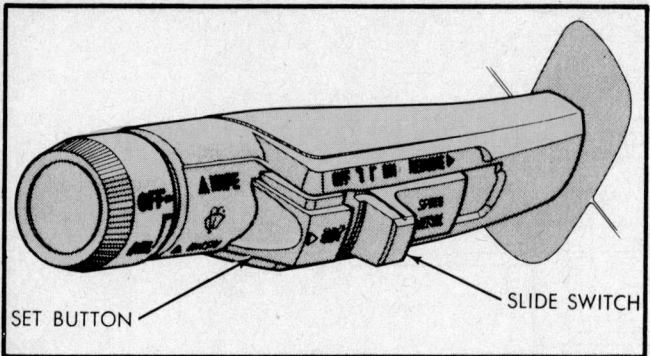

Cruise control switch assembly (© Chrysler Corp.)

6. Move the test light lead to the white wire with the red tracer. The test light should be off when the slide switch is in the on position. The test light should go on when the set button is pushed and go off when the set button is released.

7. The test light should go on when the slide switch is pushed to resume and go off again when the slide switch is released.

8. If the test light does not respond as indicated to all the tests, the switch is defective and should be replaced.

STOP LAMP CRUISE CONTROL SWITCH TEST

1. Disconnect the four way connector at the switch pigtail. Connect a twelve volt source to either terminal of the inner or outer pair.

2. Connect a test light between the other terminal and a good ground. The test light should be on when the brake pedal is in the normal position.

3. The test light should go off when the brake pedal is depressed about three eigths of an inch.

4. Repeat the same test using the other pair of terminals.

5. If the test light does not perform as indicated, the switch is defective or out of adjustment. Correct the problem by adjusting the switch or replacing it.

VACUUM SUPPLY TEST

1. Disconnect the vacuum hose at the servo. Install a vacuum gauge in the hose.

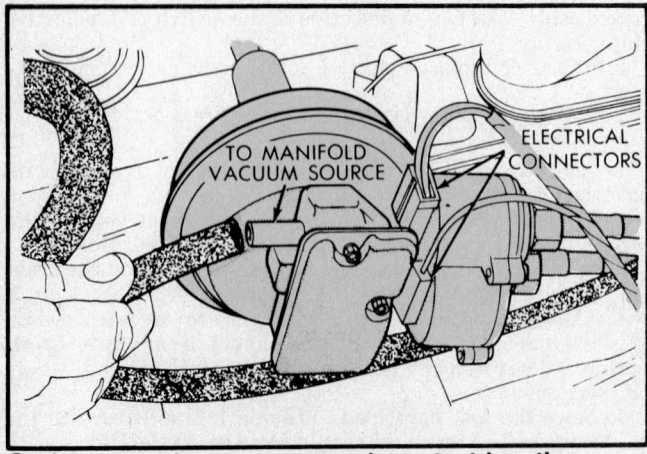

Cruise control servo vacuum hose test location (© Chrysler Corp.)

2. Start the engine and record the vacuum reading at idle. The vacuum gauge should read at least ten inches of mercury.

3. If the vacuum gauge does not perform as indicated check for vacuum leaks or poor engine performance.

CRUISE CONTROL CABLE ADJUSTMENT

ALL EXCEPT FWD ELECTRONIC FUEL INJECTION

NOTE: The cruise control cable is attached to a cable support bracket by a clip which is located about seven inches from the stud on the lost motion link.

1. Run the engine until operating temperature has been reached.

2. The carburetor should be at curb idle and the choke off.

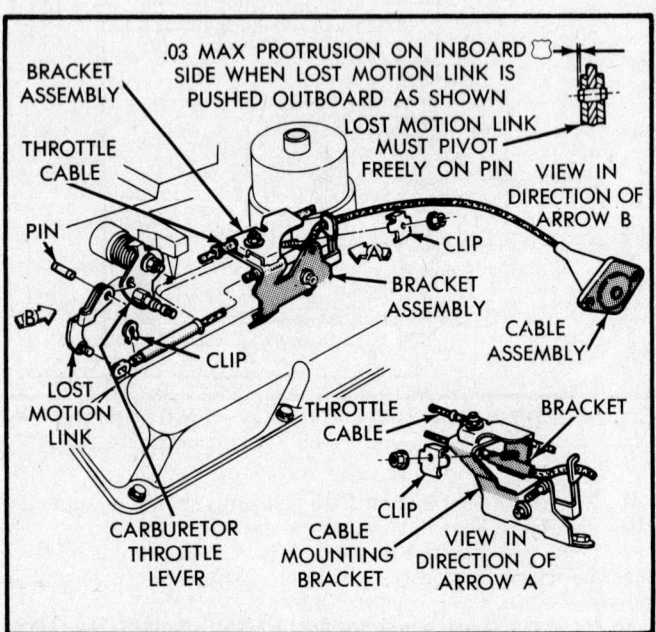

Cruise control cable location and adjustment—Imperial (© Chrysler Corp.)

3. Remove the spring clip from the lost motion link stud. The clearance between the stud and cable clevis should be $\frac{1}{16}$ inch.

4. Insert the gauge pin between the cable clevis and the stud. Loosen the clip at the cable support bracket.

5. Pull all of the slack out of the cable. Do not pull the cable so tight that it moves the throttle away from the curb idle position.

6. Tighten the clip at the cable support bracket. Remove the gauge pin. Install the spring clip on the stud of the lost motion link.

FWD ELECTRONIC FUEL INJECTION

NOTE: The cruise control cable on vehicles equipped with electronic fuel injection is supported by a retaining clip located on the throttle cable bracket.

1. Run the engine until normal operating temperature is reached. Remove the clevis retaining clip.

2. The clearance between the throttle stud and the cable clevis should be $\frac{3}{32}$ inch.

3. To adjust the cable clearance remove the cable retaining clip at the throttle bracket.

4. Pull all the slack out of the cable. Using a $\frac{3}{32}$ inch drill bit or equivalent adjust the clearance. Do not pull the cable so

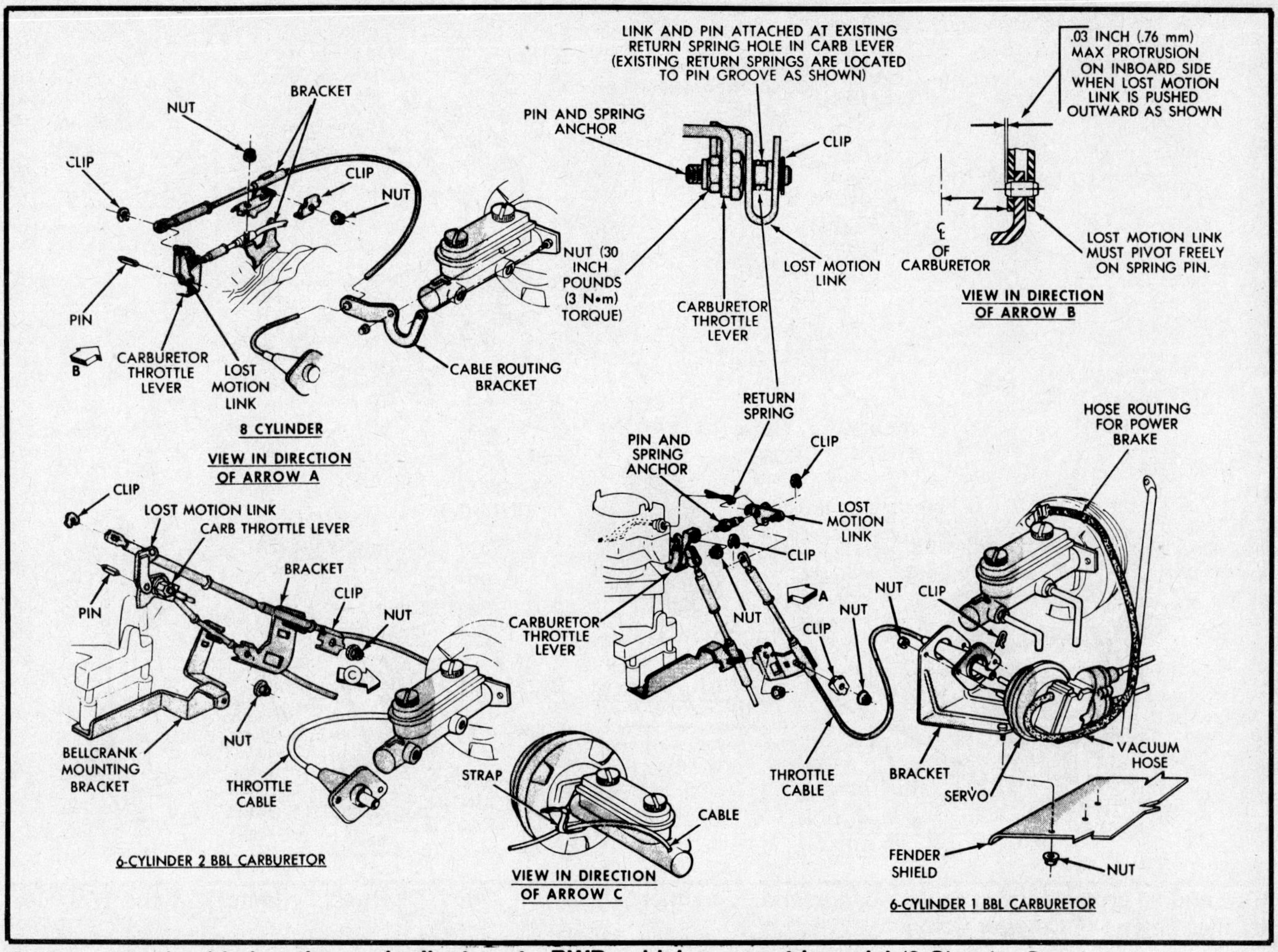

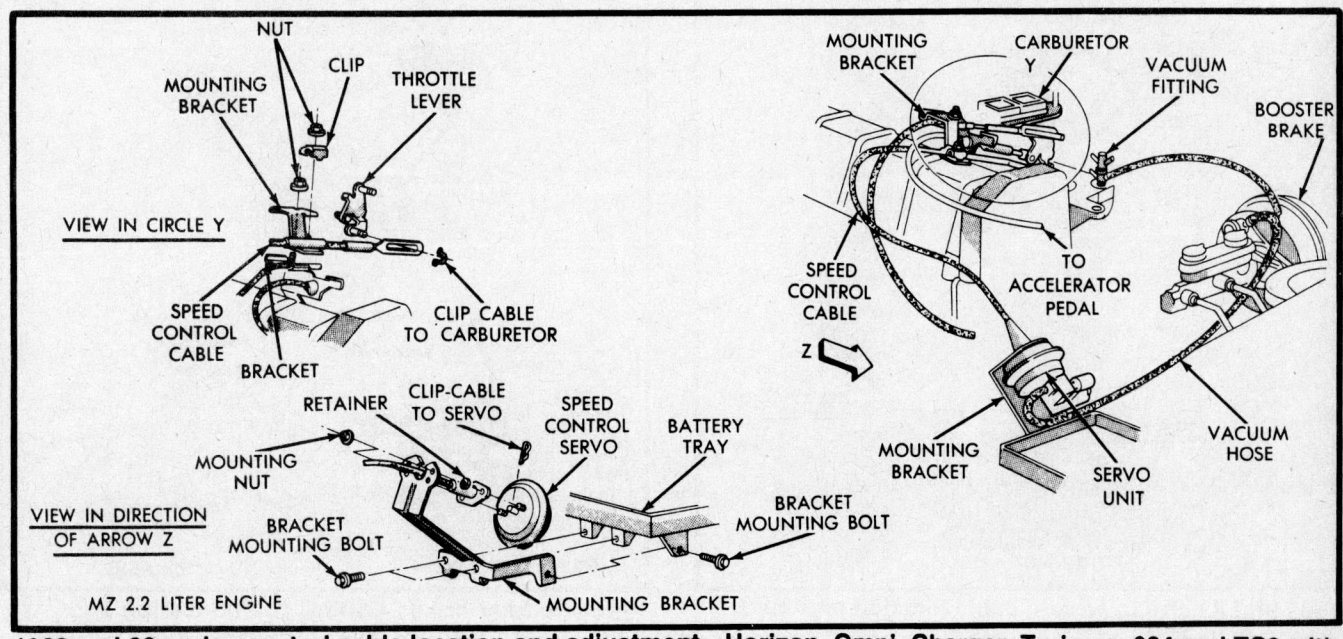

Cruise control cable location and adjustment—RWD vehicles except Imperial (© Chrysler Corp.)

1982 and 83 cruise control cable location and adjustment—Horizon, Omni, Charger, Turismo, 024 and TC3 with 2.2 liter engine (© Chrysler Corp.)

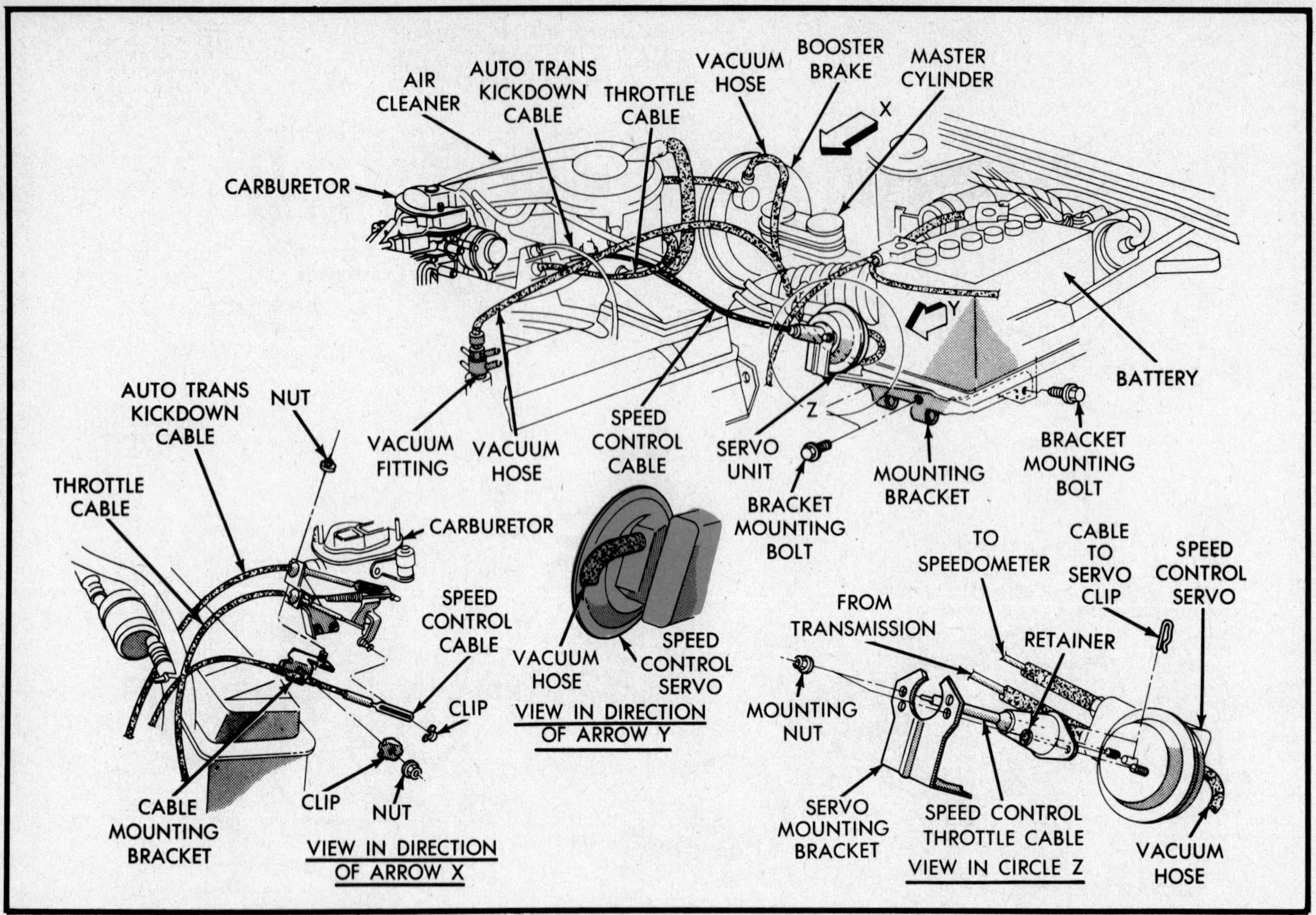

AIR CLEANER

AUTO TRANS KICKDOWN CABLE

THROTTLE CABLE

VACUUM HOSE

BOOSTER BRAKE

MASTER CYLINDER

X

CARBURETOR

BATTERY

AUTO TRANS KICKDOWN CABLE

NUT

VACUUM FITTING

VACUUM HOSE

SPEED CONTROL CABLE

SERVO UNIT

Y

MOUNTING BRACKET

Z

BRACKET MOUNTING BOLT

BRACKET MOUNTING BOLT

THROTTLE CABLE

CARBURETOR

SPEED CONTROL CABLE

CLIP

VACUUM HOSE

SPEED CONTROL SERVO

TO SPEEDOMETER

FROM TRANSMISSION

MOUNTING NUT

RETAINER

CABLE TO SERVO CLIP

SPEED CONTROL SERVO

VIEW IN DIRECTION OF ARROW Y

CABLE MOUNTING BRACKET

CLIP

NUT

VIEW IN DIRECTION OF ARROW X

SERVO MOUNTING BRACKET

SPEED CONTROL THROTTLE CABLE

VIEW IN CIRCLE Z

VACUUM HOSE

1982 and 83 cruise control cable location and adjustment—Horizon, Omni, Charger, Turismo, 024 and TC3 with 1.7 liter engine (© Chrysler Corp.)

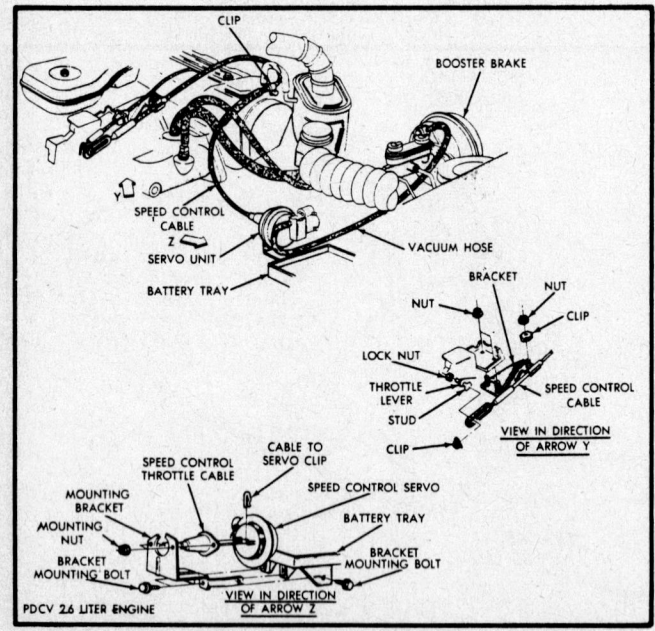

1982 and 83 cruise control cable location and adjustment—Reliant, Aries, LeBaron, Town and Country and 400 with 2.6 liter engine (© Chrysler Corp.)

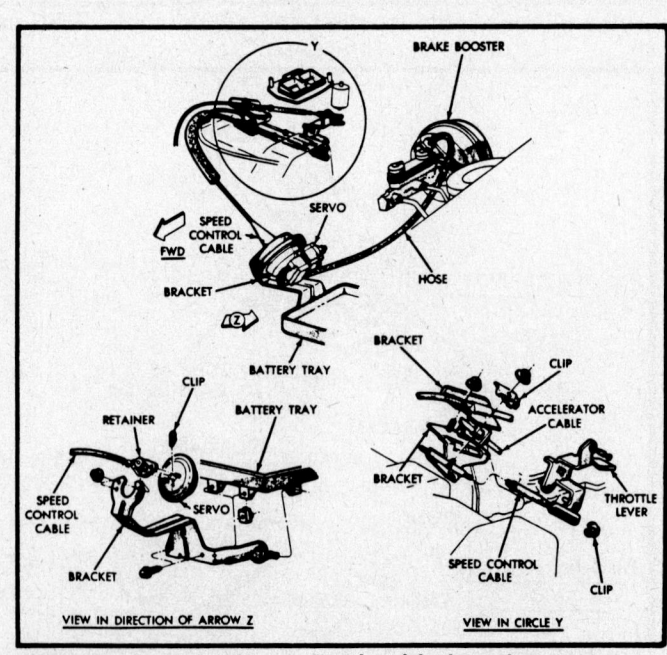

1984 and later cruise control cable location and adjustment—Horizon, Omni, Charger and Turismo (© Chrysler Corp.)

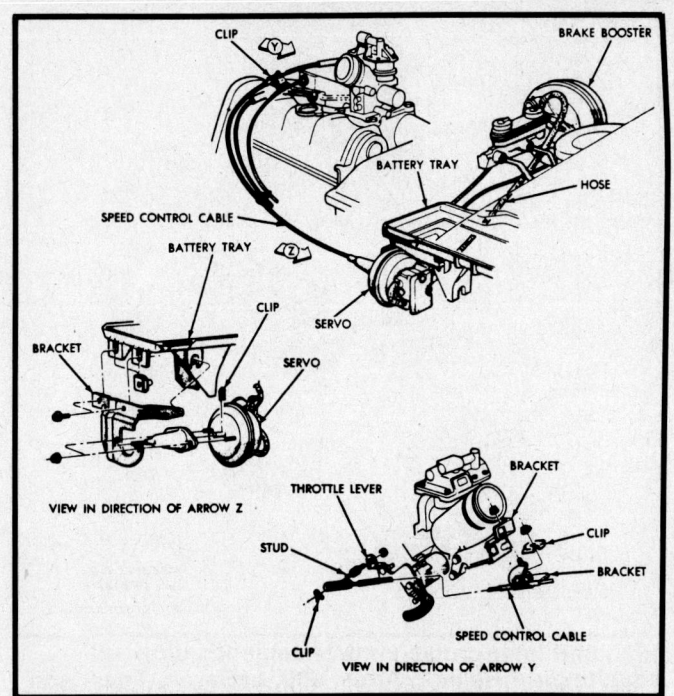

1984 and 85 cruise control cable location and adjustment—Caravelle, 600, New Yorker, Daytona and Laser with 2.2 liter EFI engine (© Chrysler Corp.)

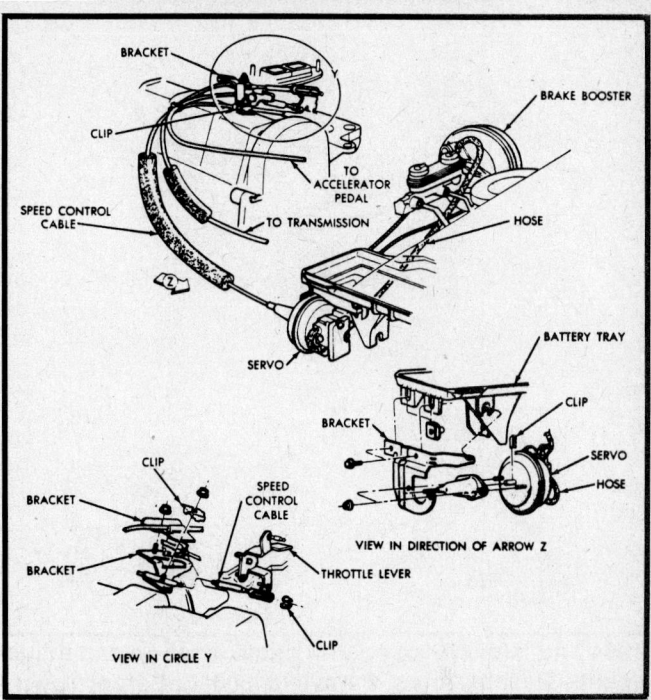

1984 and later cruise control cable location and adjustment—Reliant, Aries, Caravelle, 600, LeBaron, Town and Country, Daytona and Laser (© Chrysler Corp.)

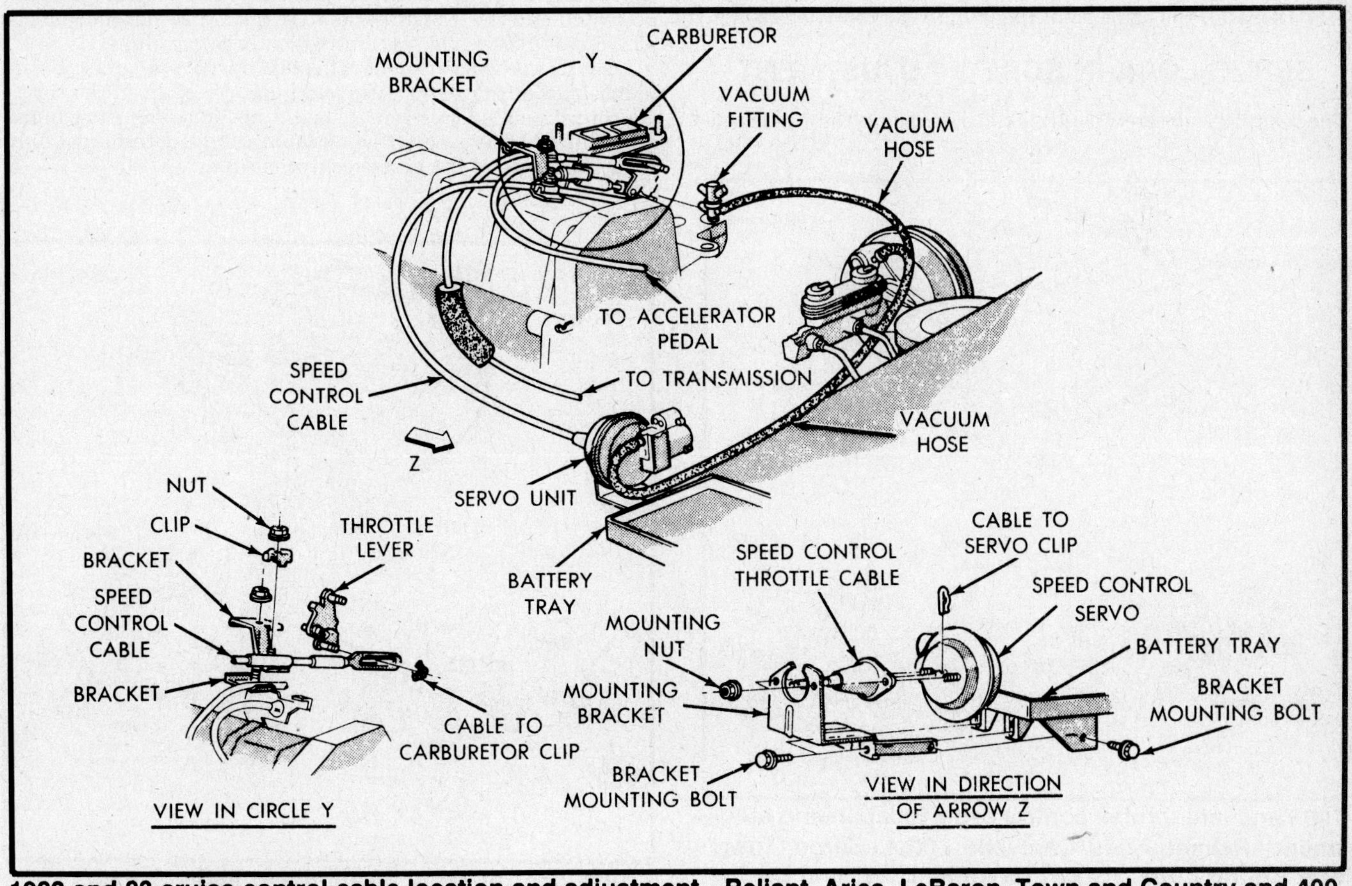

1982 and 83 cruise control cable location and adjustment—Reliant, Aries, LeBaron, Town and Country and 400 with 2.2 liter engine (© Chrysler Corp.)

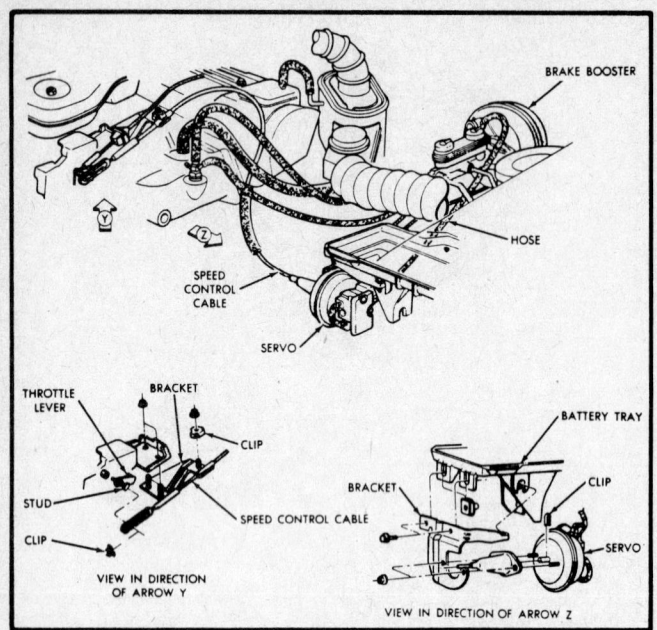

1984 and later cruise control cable location and adjustment—Reliant, Aries, Caravelle, 600, LeBaron, Town and Country, and New Yorker with 2.6 liter engine (© Chrysler Corp.)

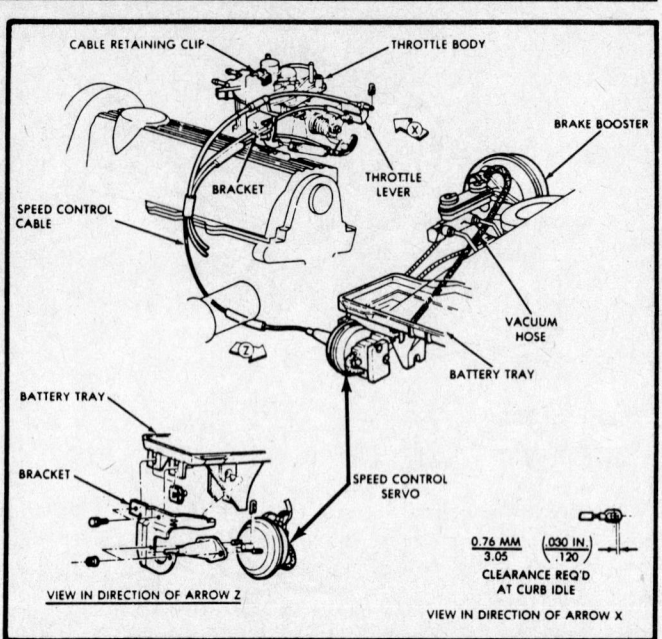

1986 and later cruise control cable location and adjustment—Reliant, Aries, 600, LeBaron, Town and Country, Ner Yorker, Daytona, Laser and Lancer with 2.2 liter EFI engine (© Chrysler Corp.)

tight that it moves the throttle away from the curb idle position.

5. Reinstall the cable retaining clip to the throttle bracket.

SERVO LOCK-IN SCREW ADJUSTMENT

The servo lock-in screw controls the accuracy of the cruise control unit. When the set button is depressed and released at speeds above thirity miles per hour the cruise control system is activated and the system locks-in and should hold the vehicle at virtually the same speed at which it is traveling.

Lock-in accuracy can be affected by poor engine performance, power to weight ratio and improper slack in the throttle control cable. This screw should never be adjusted indiscriminately. The need for adjustment can be determined only after diagnosis of the cruise control system.

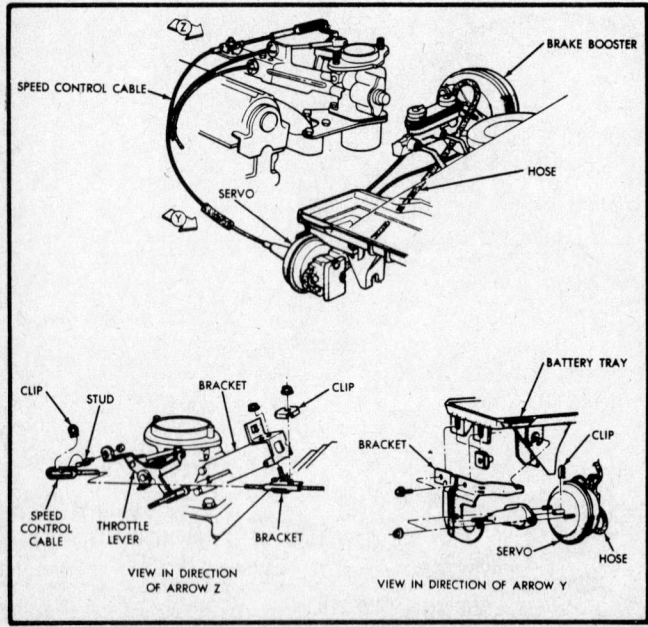

1985 and later cruise control cable location and adjustment—Reliant, Aries, Caravelle, 600, LeBaron, Town and Country, Ner Yorker, Daytona, Laser and Lancer with 2.2 liter EFI Turbo engine (© Chrysler Corp.)

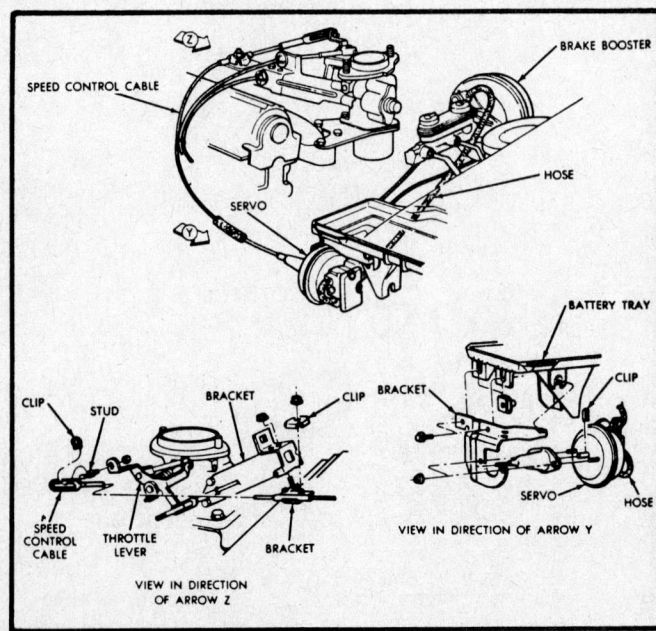

Cruise control cable location and adjustment—Shadow and Sundance with 2.2 liter EFI Turbo engine

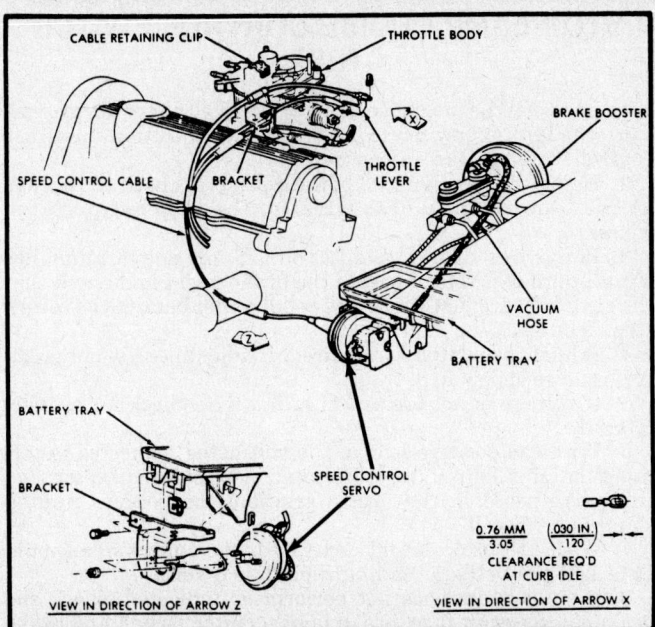

Cruise control cable location and adjustment—Shadow and Sundance with 2.2 liter EFI engine

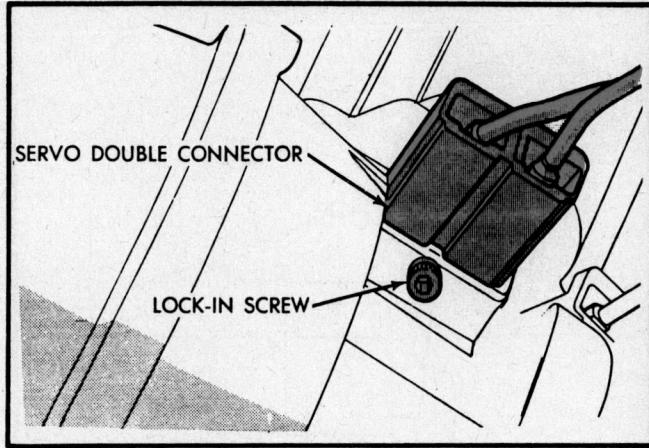

Lock in screw location (© Chrysler Corp.)

NOTE: The lock-in screw adjustment should not exceed two turns of the screw in either direction or damage to the unit may occur.

1. If engine speed drops more than two or three miles per hour when the cruise control is activated the adjusting screw should be turned counterclockwise about $\frac{1}{4}$ turn per mile per hour.

2. If engine speed increases more than two or three miles per hour when the cruise control is activated the adjusting screw should be turned clockwise about $\frac{1}{4}$ turn per mile per hour.

3. If the screw is loose stake the side of the servo housing adjacent to the screw to insure a snug fit.

Electronic Cruise Control System

ELECTRONIC GROUND TEST

Before proceeding with the other tests check for a good valve body and electronic module ground.

To check for valve body ground, connect the test light to the positive battery terminal and touch the probe to the black ground wire terminal at the valve body four way connector. The test light should light. If not check for poor ground connection.

To check for electronic module ground, remove the module from its mounting position in order to make it accessible but still have it connected. Connect the test light to a twelve volt source under the instrument panel and touch the probe to the black ground wire terminal at the module connector. The test light should light. If not check for poor ground connection.

CRUISE CONTROL SWITCH TEST

1. Remove the cruise control module from its mounting, but do not disconnect it from the wiring harness.

2. With the ignition switch in the on position, connect the negative lead of the volt meter to ground. Connect the positive lead of the voltmeter to terminal number two, located on the cruise control module.

3. With the cruise control switch in the off position the voltmeter should read zero.

4. Depress the set button to the set position and the voltmeter should read 12 volts as long as the set position is held.

5. Release the set button button and slide the switch to the resume position the voltmeter should read 12 volts as long as the switch is held in that position.

6. With the positive lead of the voltmeter connected to terminal number three of the cruise control module and the switch in the off position the voltmeter should read zero.

7. Slide the switch to the on position, the voltmeter should read 12 volts. It should also read 12 volts when in the resume position.

8. With the switch in the on position depress the set button. The the voltmeter should read zero.

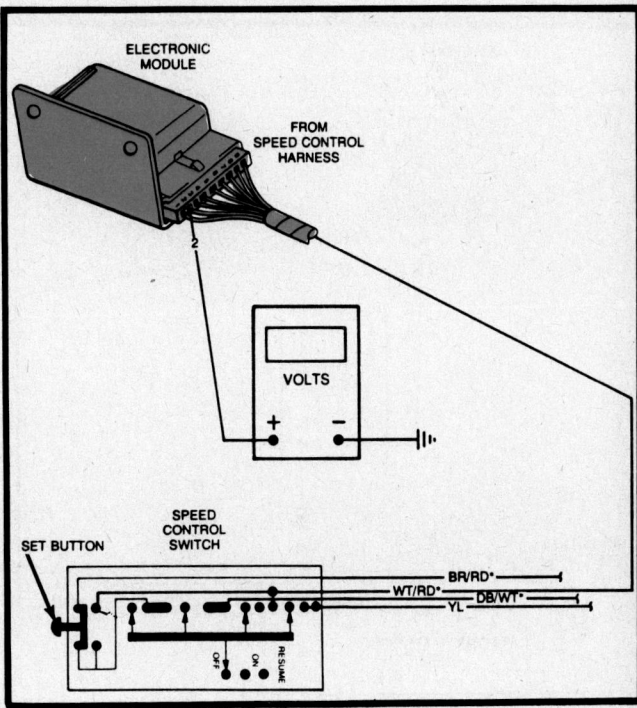

Electronic cruise control switch test connections—test one (© Chrysler Corp.)

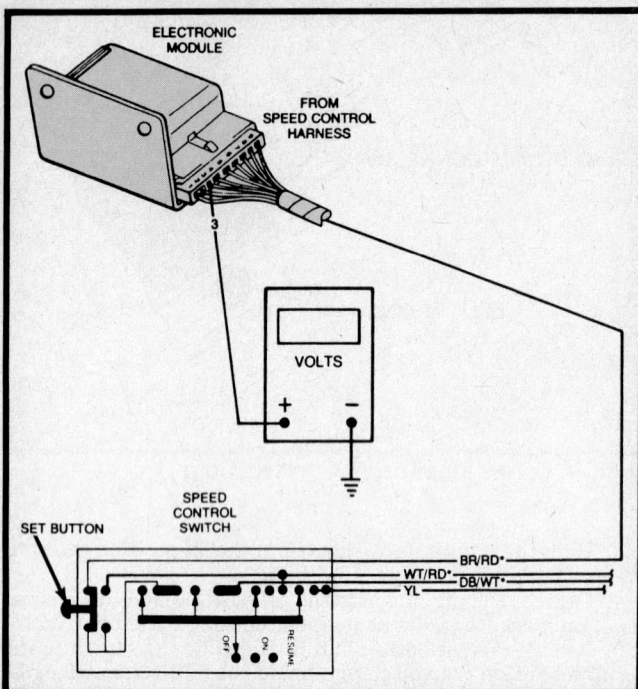

Electronic cruise control switch test connections— test two (© Chrysler Corp.)

9. With the positive lead of the voltmeter connected to terminal number five of the cruise control module and the switch in the off position the voltmeter should read zero.

10. Slide the switch to either the on or the resume position. The voltmeter should read 12 volts.

11. If the voltmeter does not perform as indicated, replace the switch assembly.

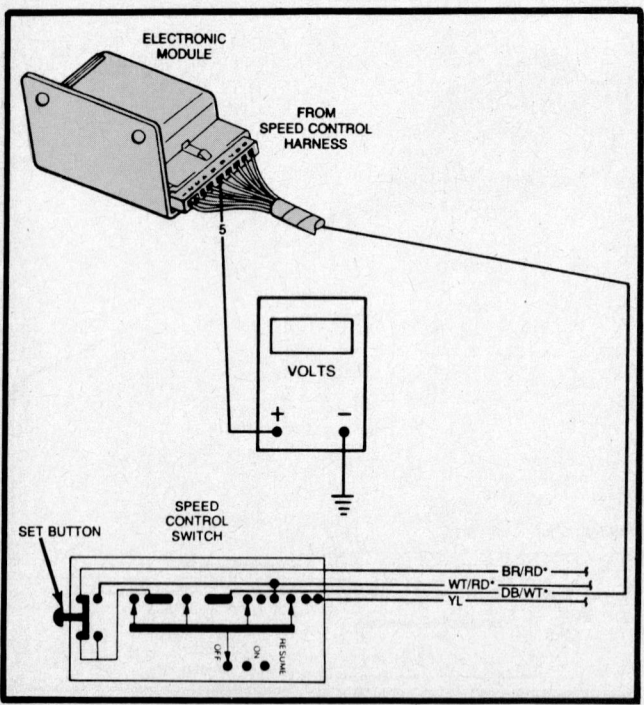

Electronic cruise control switch test connections— test three (© Chrysler Corp.)

STOP LAMP CRUISE CONTROL SWITCH TEST

1. Connect the negative lead of the voltmeter to ground. Turn the ignition switch to the on position. Position the cruise control switch in the on position.

2. Using the positive lead of the voltmeter check for voltage at the blue/red and blue wires of the stop lamp switch connector.

3. Both wires should have 12 volts. If only one terminal has a minimum of 6 volts, operate the brake pedal and check that the click is heard just before the pedal comes back to the return stop.

4. Adjust the switch as required. If adjustment is not possible, replace the switch.

5. If voltage is not present at either wire check for a defective fuse.

6. With the positive lead of the voltmeter connected to terminal number four of the cruise control module connector, and the brake pedal in the return position, the voltage reading should be 0.5 volt.

7. With the brake pedal depressed, the stop lamps should light and the voltage reading should be 6 volts.

8. If the system does not perform as indicated, check the brake lamp circuit fuse, brake lamps, clutch switch and brake switch adjustment.

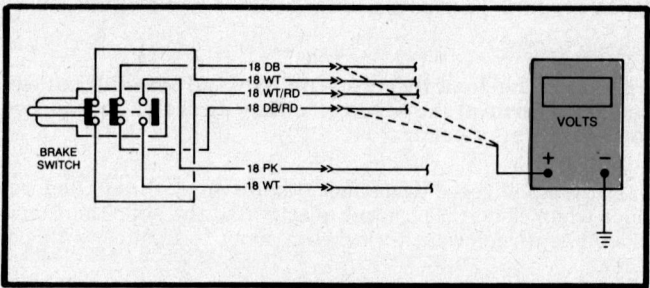

Stop lamp electrical current test points—electronic cruise control (© Chrysler Corp.)

CLUTCH SWITCH TEST (MANUAL TRANSMISSION)

1. Turn the ignition switch to the on position. Position the cruise control switch to the on position.

2. Connect the negative lead of the voltmeter to ground. Connect the positive lead to terminal number four of the cruise control electronic module.

3. Depress the brake pedal and note when the stop lamps light and the voltmeter reads 12 volts.

4. With the brake pedal released depress the clutch pedal. The voltmeter should read 6 volts.

5. If the system does not perform as indicated, readjust the clutch switch or replace it, as required.

SPEED SENSOR TEST

1. Remove the speed sensor from the transaxle.

2. Connect an ohmmeter between the connector terminals of the speed sensor switch.

NOTE: Set the ohmmeter to the lowest setting. A digital ohmmeter should be used. The ohmmeter should have a minimum impedance of 20,000 ohms per volt.

3. Rotate the speed sensor switch one full turn and look for eight pulses on the ohmmeter. If the reading is not correct replace the speed sensor.

4. If the speed sensor is defective fault code 28 will appear in the diagnostic read out code box.

VACUUM SERVO AND RESERVOIR TEST

1. Disconnect the hose connection from the vacuum servo to the valve body. Connect a vacuum pump directly to the vacuum servo.

2. Apply 10 inches HG of vacuum to the servo and note that the throttle is fully applied, and remains so for about one minute.

3. If this cannot be accomplished, either the servo or the mechanical throttle linkage is defective. Readjust or replace defective components as required.

4. Connect the servo directly to the valve body side of the vacuum tank. Connect the vacuum pump into this line using a tee connection.

5. Apply 10 inches HG of vacuum to the servo/tank and note that the throttle is fully applied, and remains so for about one minute.

6. If this cannot be accomplished, check all hose connections, or replace faulty vacuum tank as required.

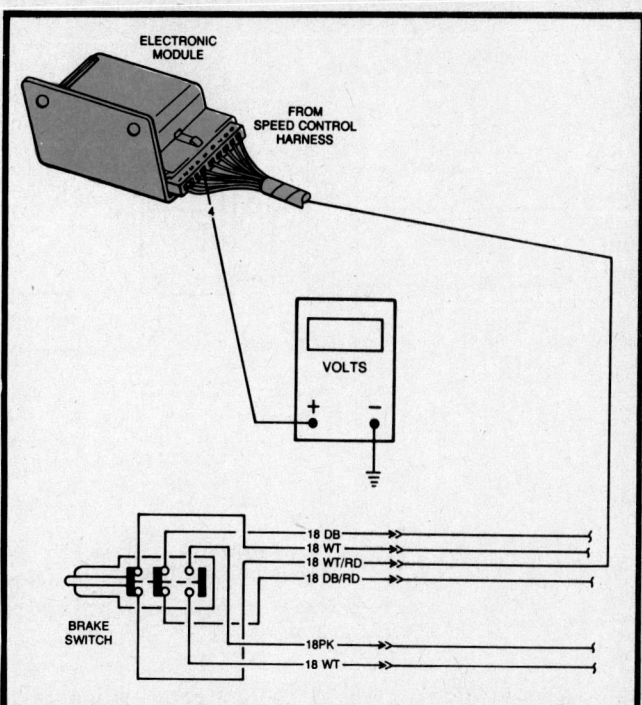

Stop lamp and control module test points—electronic cruise control (© Chrysler Corp.)

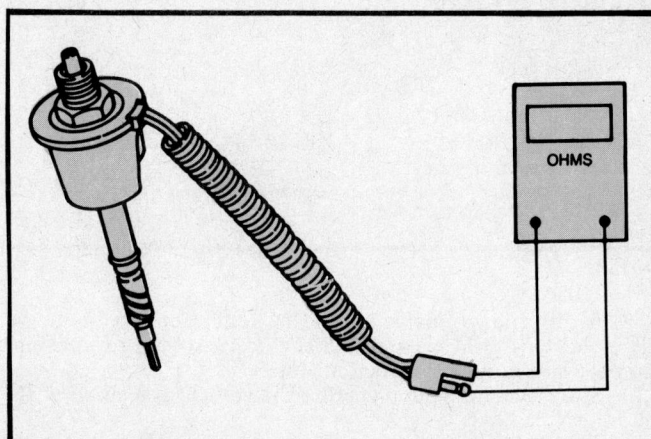

Speed sensor test point location—electronic cruise control (© Chrysler Corp.)

NOTE: The vacuum servo and valve body are both serviced as a single assembly, the vacuum tank can be serviced separately.

VALVE BODY TEST

1. Turn the ignition switch to the on position. With the cruise control switch in the on position, set up the voltmeter to read 12 volts. Connect the negative lead to ground.

2. Disconnect the four way connector going to the valve body. The female valve body main harness terminal with the blue/red wire should measure 12 volts. If not check for loose connections or repair the main harness as required.

3. Connect a jumper wire between the male and female terminals of the blue/red wire. The other three male valve body terminals should now measure 12 volts. If not, replace the cruise control servo assembly.

4. Disconnect the hose connection from the vacuum tank side and connect the vacuum pump to the tank.

5. Apply about 10 inches Hg of vacuum to the tank, using three additional jumper wires.

6. Ground the male valve body terminals with black, brown/red and red/white wires, in that order. Each time a grounding

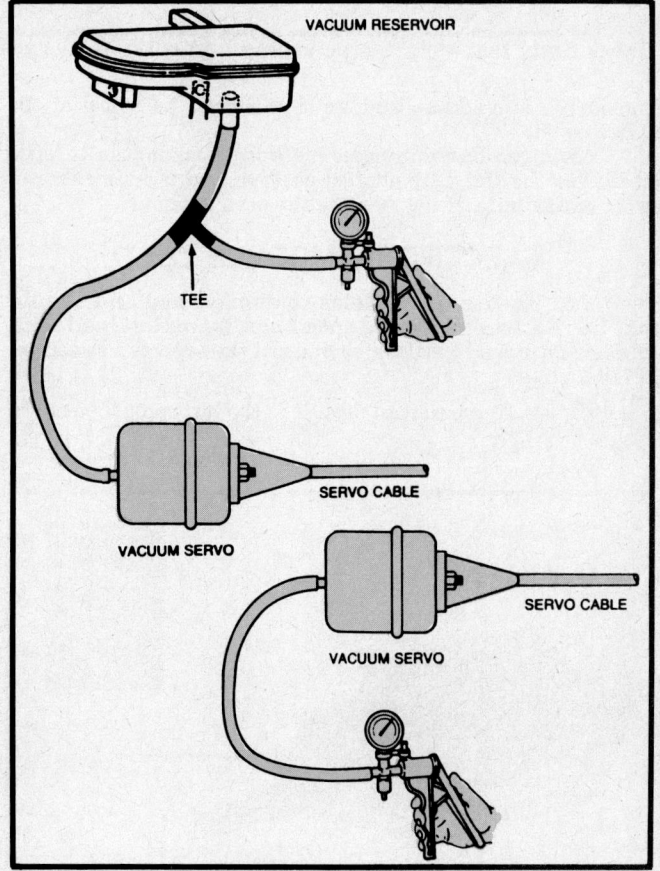

Vacuum sensor and reservoir test—electronic cruise control (© Chrysler Corp.)

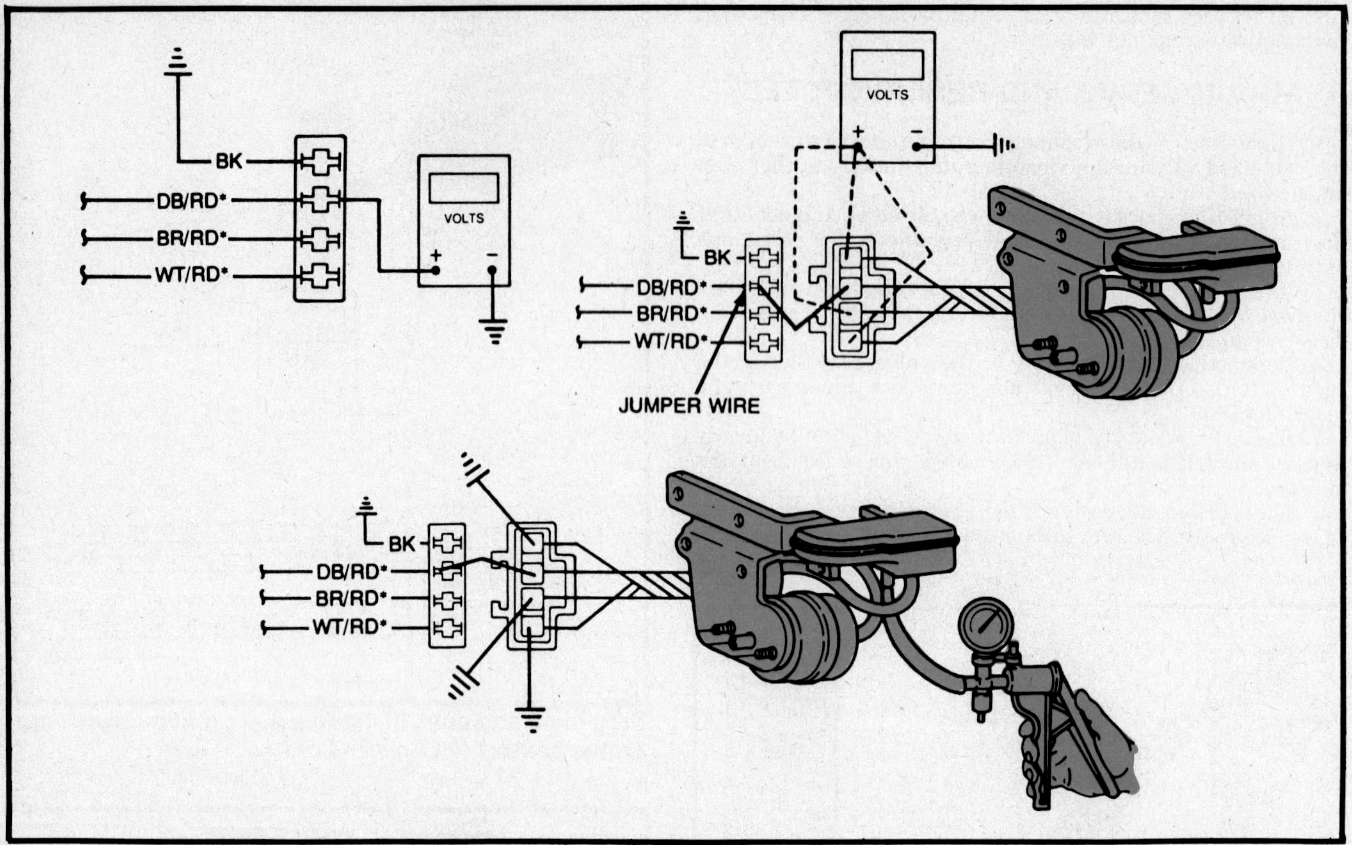

Valve body test—electronic cruise control (© Chrysler Corp.)

connection is made an audible click should be heard at the valve body.

7. When the last ground connection is made, the throttle should so the the fully applied position and remain there at least one minute. If not, replace the sevo assembly.

ELECTRONIC MODULE TEST

NOTE: Electronic modules seldom go bad and should not be replaced if engine speed can be maintained with plus or minus five miles per hour of the selected speed on a level road.

1. The electronic control module is the last component to be tested.

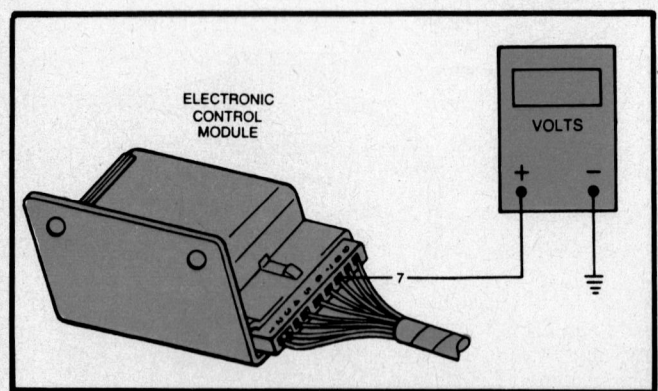

Electronic module test point location—electronic cruise control (© Chrysler Corp.)

2. Set up the voltmeter to read 12 volts. Connect the negative lead to a good ground and the positive lead to terminal number seven on the control module.

3. Start the engine and operate the vehicle at a speed of 40-50 miles per hour.

4. Turn the cruise control switch to the on position, the voltmeter should read 12 volts.

5. Press the cruise control switch set button and than release it. The voltmeter should indicate plus 5 to plus 9 volts and will probably fluctuate 1 or 2 volts at a rapid rate.

6. The cruise control system should be performing throttle control at this time to maintain the set speed satisfactorily, if not replace the control module.

Component Replacement RWD Vehicles

CRUISE CONTROL SERVO

Removal and Installation

1. Disconnect the negative battery cable.
2. Disconnect the speedometer cables from the servo assembly.
3. Disconnect the vacuum hose at the servo. Disconnect the electrical connections at the servo assembly.
4. Remove the two retaining nuts from the servo mounting studs.
5. Pull the servo away from the mounting bracket. Pull the cruise control cable away from the servo in order to expose the cable retaining clip.
6. Remove the clip attaching the servo to the cable. Remove the servo assembly.

7. Installation is the reverse of the removal procedure.

SERVO THROTTLE CABLE ASSEMBLY

Removal and Installation

1. Disconnect the negative battery cable. Remove the air cleaner.
2. Disconnect the cable at the retaining clamp and at the carburetor lost motion link by removing the spring clip.
3. Disconnect the throttle cable at the servo. Remove the cable assembly.
4. Installation is the reverse of the removal procedure. Route the new cable as required. Adjust the cable free play as required.

CRUISE CONTROL SWITCH

Removal and Installation

1. Disconnect the negative battery cable.
2. Remove the lower steering column cover.
3. If equipped with tilt wheel, remove the two steering column mounting nuts and drop the column down from the instrument panel. Remove the screws securing the support bracket to the column jacket and unsnap the four plastic retainer clips. Remove the through wiring.
4. For standard steering columns, remove the through wiring after unsnaping the four plastic retainer clips.
5. Disconnect the cruise control switch electrical connector from the instrument panel harness connector.
6. If equipped with tilt wheel, remove the terminals from the insulator using tool C-4135 or equivalent.
7. Remove the windshield wiper control knob from the end of the lever. Remove the screws retaining the cruise control switch to the column.
8. If equipped with tilt wheel, remove the steering wheel and attach flexible guide wire to the lower end of the cruise control switch harness.
9. For standard steering columns, remove the upper steering column lock housing cover.
10. Carefully remove the switch and harness from the steering column taking care not to damage wires while pulling them up through the column. If equipped with tilt wheel, pull the wires up through the lock housing between the lock plate and the side of the housing, then disconnect the guide wire and remove the switch assembly.
11. Installation is the reverse of the removal procedure.

Component Replacement FWD Vehicles

CRUISE CONTROL SERVO

Removal and Installation

HORIZON, TURISMO, OMNI AND CHARGER

1. Disconnect the negative battery cable.
2. Disconnect the speedometer cables from the servo assembly.
3. Disconnect the vacuum hose at the servo. Disconnect the electrical connections at the servo assembly.
4. Remove the two retaining nuts from the servo mounting studs.
5. Pull the servo away from the mounting bracket. Pull the cruise control cable away from the servo in order to expose the cable retaining clip.
6. Remove the clip attaching the servo to the cable. Remove the servo assembly.
7. Installation is the reverse of the removal procedure.

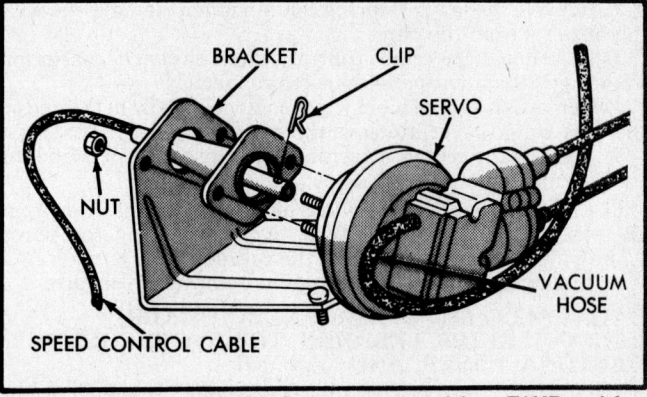

Cruise control cable and servo assembly — RWD vehicles (© Chrysler Corp.)

CARAVELLE, 600, E CLASS, NEW YORKER, RELIANT, ARIES, LEBARON, TOWN AND COUNTRY, DAYTONA, LASER, AND LANCER

1. Disconnect the negative battery cable.
2. Remove the nuts retaining the throttle cable and the mounting bracket to the servo.
3. Remove the screws retaining the servo mounting bracket to the U-nuts on the battery tray.
4. Remove the servo mounting bracket. Disconnect the electrical connectors. Remove the vacuum hose.
5. Disconnect the speedometer cables from the servo.
6. Pull the cable away from the servo to expose the retaining clip. Remove the clip attaching the servo to the cable. Remove the servo assembly.
7. Installation is the reverse of the removal procedure.

CRUISE CONTROL SWITCH

Removal and Installation

HORIZON, TURISMO, OMNI AND CHARGER

1. Disconnect the negative battery cable.

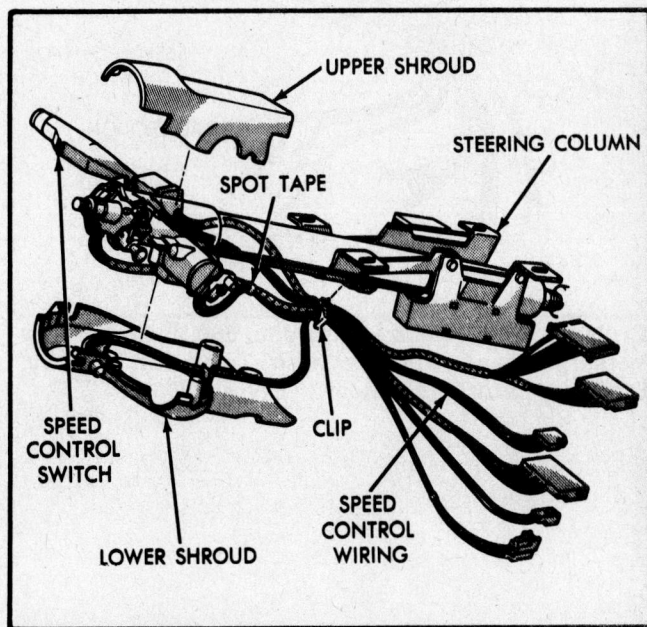

Cruise control switch — Horizon, Turismo, Omni and Charger (© Chrysler Corp.)

2. Remove the lower steering column cover. Remove the wiring harness from the clip.

3. Disconnect the cruise control switch electrical connector from the instrument panel harness connector.

4. Remove the windshield wiper control knob from the end of the turn signal lever. Remove the silencer from the lever.

5. Remove the screws attaching the cruise control switch to the steering column.

6. Carefully remove the switch and the wiring harness from the steering column. Be sure to avoid damaging the wires while pulling them up through the column.

7. Installation is the reverse of the removal procedure.

CARAVELLE, 600, E CLASS, NEW YORKER, RELIANT, ARIES, LEBARON, TOWN AND COUNTRY, DAYTONA, LASER, AND LANCER

1. Disconnect the negative battery cable.

2. Remove the lower steering column cover. Remove the wiring after unsnapping the four plastic retaining clips.

3. Disconnect the cruise control switch electrical connector from the instrument panel harness connector.

4. If equipped with tilt wheel, remove the terminals from the insulator using tool C-4135.

5. Remove the windshield wiper control knob from the end of the turn signal lever. Remove the silencer from the lever.

6. Remove the screws attaching the cruise control switch to the steering column.

7. If equipped with tilt wheel, remove the steering wheel.

Cruise control switch—Caravelle, 600, E Class, New Yorker, Reliant, Aries, LeBaron, Town and Country, Daytona, Laser and Lancer (© Chrysler Corp.)

Attach flexible guide wire to the lower end of the cruise control switch harness.

8. On standard steering columns, remove the upper steering column lock housing cover. Remove the switch and the wiring harness from the steering column. Be sure not to damage the wires while pulling them through the column.

9. If equipped with tilt wheel, pull the wires through the lock housing between the lock plate and the side of the housing. Disconnect the guide wire from the harness.

10. Installation is the reverse of the removal procedure.

Component Replacement—Electronic Cruise Control

CRUISE CONTROL SERVO

Removal and Installation

1. Disconnect the negative battery cable.

2. Remove the nuts retaining the throttle cable to the servo assembly.

3. Pull the cable away from the servo in order to expose the retaining clip. Remove the clip attaching the cable to the servo.

4. Remove the screws retaining the servo mounting bracket to the U-nuts on the battery tray.

5. Remove the servo mounting bracket. Disconnect the electrical connector and the vacuum hose.

6. Remove the servo assembly from the vehicle.

7. Installation is the reverse of the removal procedure.

CRUISE CONTROL SWITCH

Removal and Installation

1. Disconnect the negative battery cable. Remove the lower steering column cover.

2. Remove the through wiring after unsnaping the four plastic retainer clips.

3. Disconnect the cruise control switch electrical connector from the instrument panel harness connector.

4. If equipped with tilt wheel, remove the terminals from the insulator using tool C-4135 or equivalent.

5. Remove the wiper control knob from the end of the turn signal lever. Remove the silencer from the lever.

6. Remove the screws retaining the cruise control switch to the steering column.

7. If the vehicle is equipped with tilt wheel, remove the steering wheel. Attach a flexible guide wire to the lower end of the cruise control switch harness.

8. On regular steering columns, remove the upper steering column lock housing cover. Remove the switch and harness from the column taking care to avoid damaging the wires while pulling them up through the column.

9. If equipped with tilt wheel, pull the wires through the lock housing between the lock plate and the side of the housing. Then disconnect the guide wire from the harness.

10. Installation is the reverse of the removal procedure.

FORD MOTOR COMPANY

CONTINENTAL, THUNDERBIRD, MARK VII, COUGAR, XR7, FAIRMONT, ZEPHYR, GRANADA, LTD, MARQUIS, MUSTANG, CAPRI, LINCOLN TOWN CAR, MARK VI, CROWN VICTORIA AND GRAND MARQUIS

VISUAL INSPECTION

Before performing any tests make a visual inspection of the cruise control system. Check all items in the system for abnormal conditions such as bare broken or disconnected wires and damage to the vacuum hoses. Be sure that the speedometer cables are attached and properly routed. All vacuum hoses must be properly routed and must not have any kinks or bends. Be sure that all electrical connections are complete and tight. The wiring harness must be routed properly.

The servo assembly and actuator cable must operate freely and smoothly. The actuator cable is preadjusted, with 0.094 inch slack. If adjustment is required the cable should be adjusted as tight as possible without opening the throttle plate or increasing the idle speed.

ROAD TEST (SIMULATED)

NOTE: Before performing the simulated road test be sure that the drive wheels are of the ground and supported properly. Failure to do this may result in serious damage.

1. Start the engine. Position the selector lever in drive.
2. Turn on the cruise control.

NOTE: If at any time during the following test, the cruise control system should appear to go out of control and over speed, be prepared to shut the cruise control system down at once using the off switch or the ignition switch.

3. Accelerate and hold the engine speed at about 35 miles per hour.
4. Press the release set/accel button. Hold foot pressure very lightly on the accelerator pedal. Normally speed will continue at 35 miles per hour for a short period of time and then gradually start surging because the engine is not loaded.
5. Press the off button. The engine should drop back to idle. Stop the wheels using the brakes.
6. Press the on button. Accelerate and hold a speed of about 35 miles per hour.
7. Press the hold set/accel button. Slowly remove your foot from the accelerator pedal. The engine speed should gradually increase.
8. When the engine speed reaches about 50 miles per hour, release the set/accel button. The vehicle should maintain that engine speed for a short time before it begins to surge.
9. Press the coast button and hold. The engine should idle. Slow the wheels to about 35 miles per hour. Release the coast button. Engine speed should maintain about 35 miles per hour and surging should soon start.
10. Press and release the brake pedal. The system should shut off and the engine should slow to idle.
11. Accelerate the engine and set the speed to about 50 miles per hour.
12. Brake to about 35 miles per hour and maintain that speed using the accelerator.
13. Depress and release the resume button. The engine speed should return to about 50 miles per hour.

14. If the system does not perform as indicated make a note of the malfunction and repair or replace defective components as required.

CONTROL SWITCH TEST

1. Check to see that the main fuse and the stop lamp fuse are good. If so, disconnect the six way connector at the amplifier assembly.
2. Connect a voltmeter between circuit 151 (light blue/black) and ground. Depress the on button and check for battery voltage.
3. Connect an ohmmeter between circuit 151 (lightblue/black) and ground.
4. Rotate the steering wheel through its full range and make the following checks.
5. Depress the off button and check for a reading between 0–1 ohm. Depress the set/accel button and check for a reading between 714–646 ohms. Depress the coast button and check for a reading between 126–114 ohms. Depress the resume button and check for a reading between 2090–2310 ohms.
6. If the resistance values are not as indicated, remove the steering wheel and check the resistance at the steering wheel switch connector on the hub.
7. If the resistance values are as indicated, check switch assemblies and the ground circuit.
8. Reconnect the six way connector at the amplifier.

SPEED SENSOR TEST WITHOUT ELECTRONIC INSTRUMENT CLUSTER

1. Disconnect the connector at the speed sensor and connect an ohmmeter between the wire connector terminals and the speed sensor end.
2. The ohmmeter should read between 200 and 300 ohms. A reading of zero ohms indicates a shorted coil and the speed sensor should be replaced. A maximum reading indicates an open coil and the speed sensor should be replaced.
3. If the ohmmeter reading is between 200 and 300 ohms, and the speedometer operates properly within needle waver, the speed sensor is probably functioning properly.
4. A speed sensor of known good quality can also be substituted in place of the existing sensor to check for proper operation.

SPEED SENSOR TEST WITH ELECTRONIC INSTRUMENT CLUSTER

NOTE: AC and DC voltage measurements are required in the diagnosis of the cruise control system on vehicles equipped with an electronic instrument cluster. The use of a special diagnostic tool, Beckman 3020- Fluke 8022A or eqvivalent should be used.

The speed signal is provided by the electronic speedometer rather than the speed sensor. To test this system, connect an AC voltmeter across circuit 150 (dark green/white) and the ground leads at the amplifier. With the wheels raised and vehicle speed at about 30 mph the voltmeter should read about 6 to 24 volts. If not refer to the speed signal diagnostic test chart.

DIAGNOSIS AND TESTING PROCEDURES

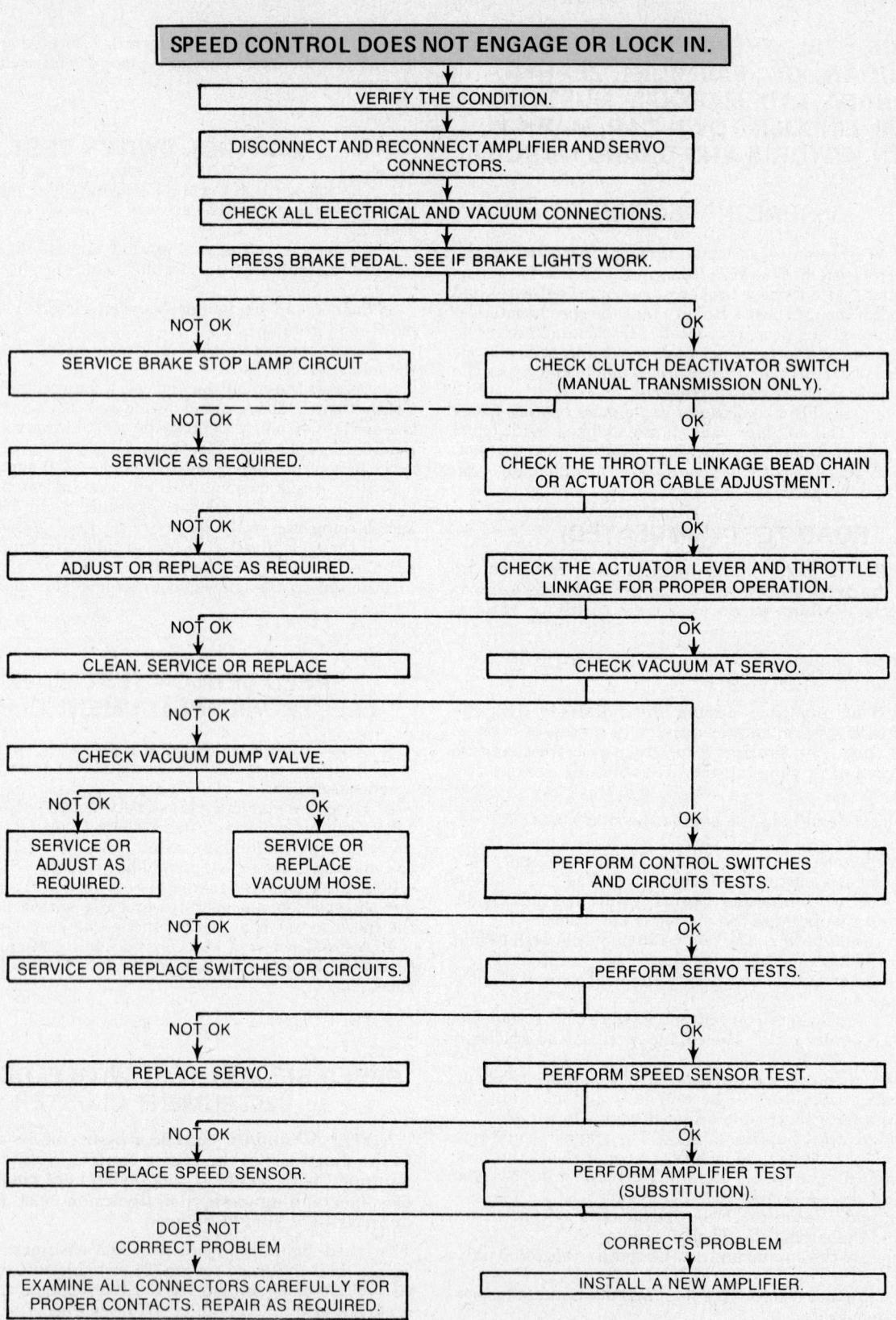

SPEED CONTROL DOES NOT ENGAGE OR LOCK IN.

VERIFY THE CONDITION.

DISCONNECT AND RECONNECT AMPLIFIER AND SERVO CONNECTORS.

CHECK ALL ELECTRICAL AND VACUUM CONNECTIONS.

PRESS BRAKE PEDAL. SEE IF BRAKE LIGHTS WORK.

NOT OK
SERVICE BRAKE STOP LAMP CIRCUIT

OK
CHECK CLUTCH DEACTIVATOR SWITCH (MANUAL TRANSMISSION ONLY).

NOT OK
SERVICE AS REQUIRED.

OK
CHECK THE THROTTLE LINKAGE BEAD CHAIN OR ACTUATOR CABLE ADJUSTMENT.

NOT OK
ADJUST OR REPLACE AS REQUIRED.

OK
CHECK THE ACTUATOR LEVER AND THROTTLE LINKAGE FOR PROPER OPERATION.

NOT OK
CLEAN. SERVICE OR REPLACE

OK
CHECK VACUUM AT SERVO.

NOT OK
CHECK VACUUM DUMP VALVE.

NOT OK
SERVICE OR ADJUST AS REQUIRED.

OK
SERVICE OR REPLACE VACUUM HOSE.

OK
PERFORM CONTROL SWITCHES AND CIRCUITS TESTS.

NOT OK
SERVICE OR REPLACE SWITCHES OR CIRCUITS.

OK
PERFORM SERVO TESTS.

NOT OK
REPLACE SERVO.

OK
PERFORM SPEED SENSOR TEST.

NOT OK
REPLACE SPEED SENSOR.

OK
PERFORM AMPLIFIER TEST (SUBSTITUTION).

DOES NOT CORRECT PROBLEM
EXAMINE ALL CONNECTORS CAREFULLY FOR PROPER CONTACTS. REPAIR AS REQUIRED.

CORRECTS PROBLEM
INSTALL A NEW AMPLIFIER.

* ON LINCOLN CONTINENTAL AND THUNDERBIRD/XR-7 WITH ELECTRONIC INSTRUMENT CLUSTER, PERFORM SPEED SIGNAL TEST

DIAGNOSIS AND TESTING PROCEDURES

NON-ELECTRONIC INSTRUMENT CLUSTER

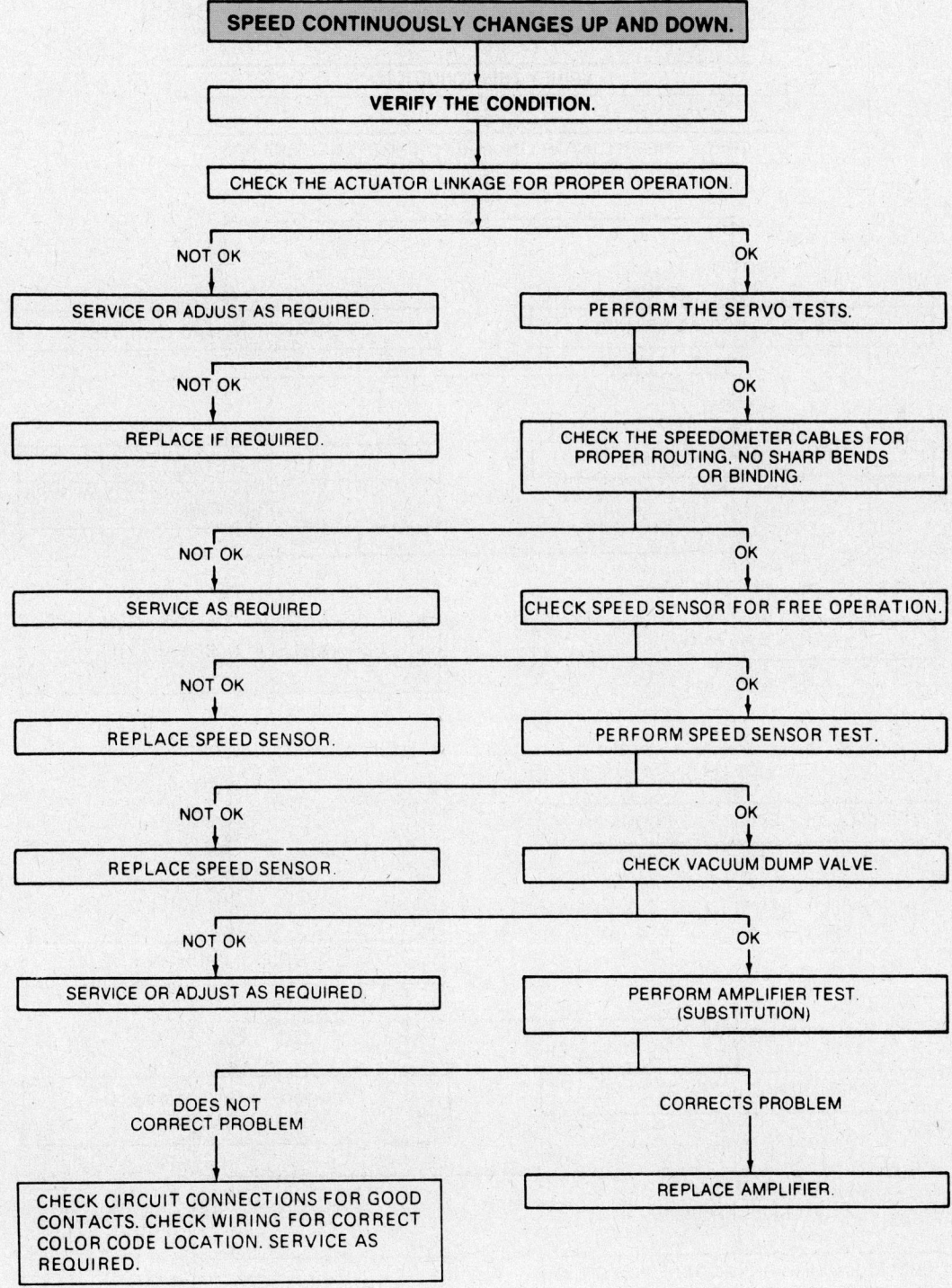

DIAGNOSIS AND TESTING PROCEDURES

ELECTRONIC INSTRUMENT CLUSTER

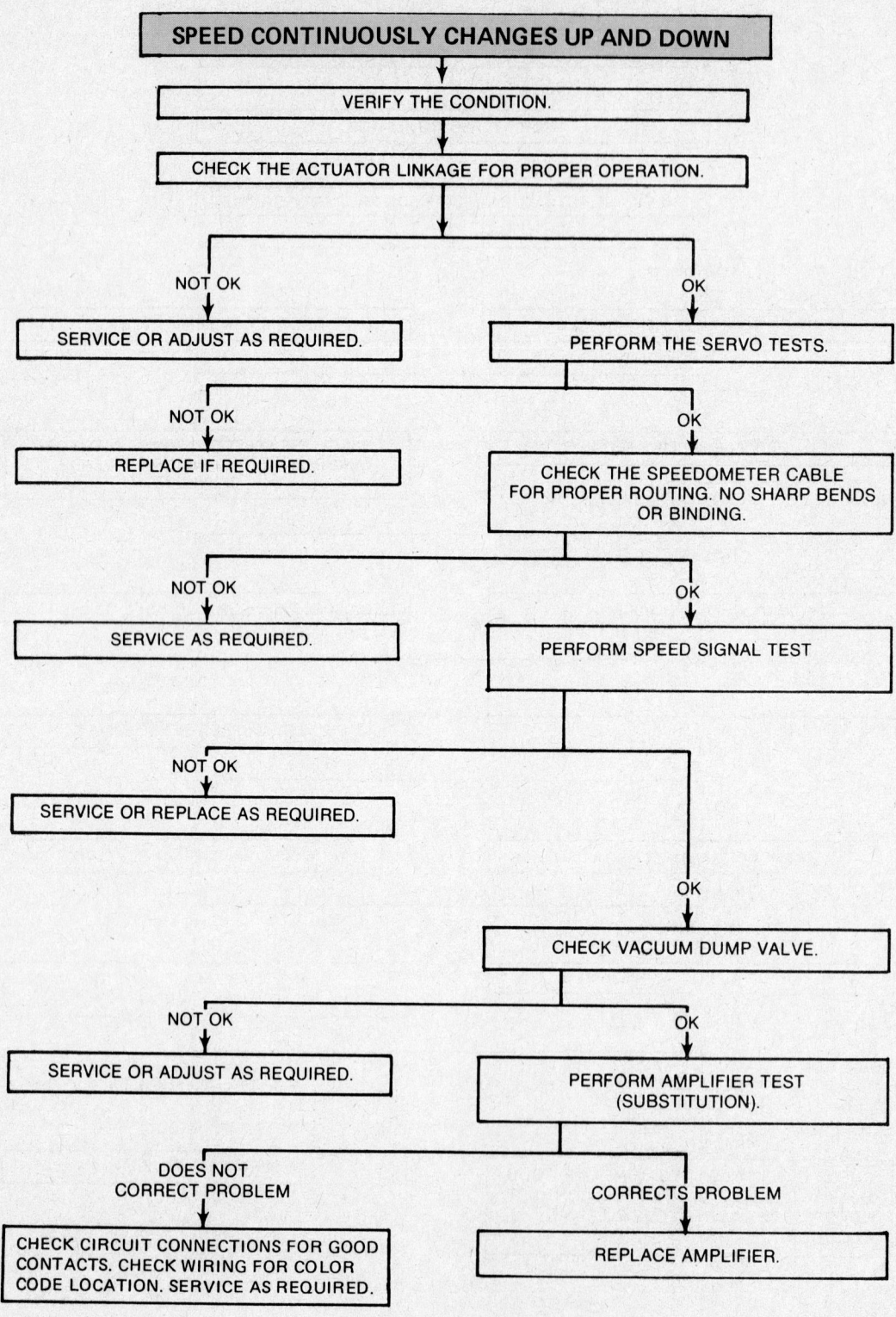

SPEED CONTINUOUSLY CHANGES UP AND DOWN

VERIFY THE CONDITION.

CHECK THE ACTUATOR LINKAGE FOR PROPER OPERATION.

NOT OK → SERVICE OR ADJUST AS REQUIRED.

OK → PERFORM THE SERVO TESTS.

NOT OK → REPLACE IF REQUIRED.

OK → CHECK THE SPEEDOMETER CABLE FOR PROPER ROUTING. NO SHARP BENDS OR BINDING.

NOT OK → SERVICE AS REQUIRED.

OK → PERFORM SPEED SIGNAL TEST

NOT OK → SERVICE OR REPLACE AS REQUIRED.

OK → CHECK VACUUM DUMP VALVE.

NOT OK → SERVICE OR ADJUST AS REQUIRED.

OK → PERFORM AMPLIFIER TEST (SUBSTITUTION).

DOES NOT CORRECT PROBLEM → CHECK CIRCUIT CONNECTIONS FOR GOOD CONTACTS. CHECK WIRING FOR COLOR CODE LOCATION. SERVICE AS REQUIRED.

CORRECTS PROBLEM → REPLACE AMPLIFIER.

DIAGNOSIS AND TESTING PROCEDURES

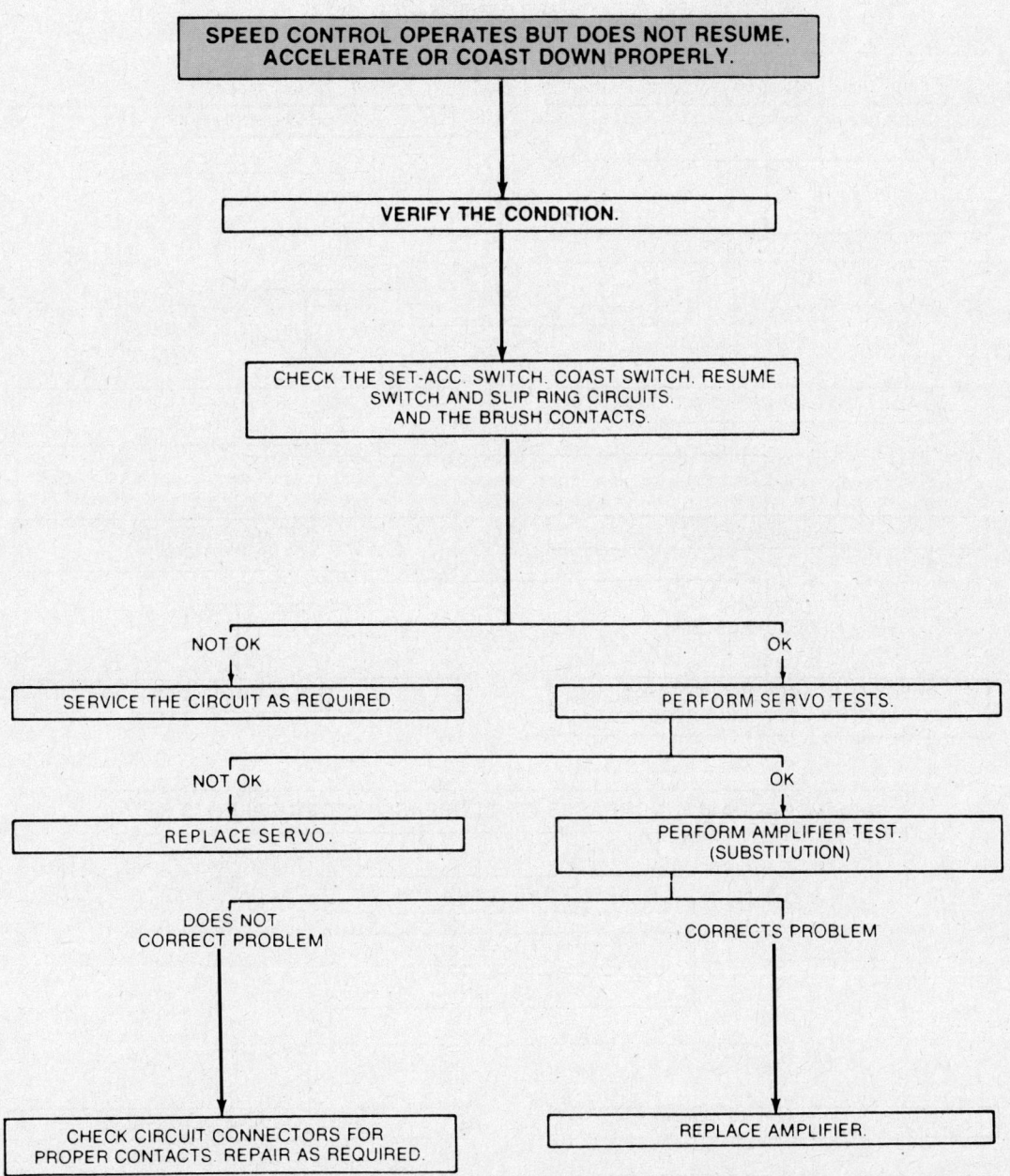

SPEED CONTROL OPERATES BUT DOES NOT RESUME,
ACCELERATE OR COAST DOWN PROPERLY.

VERIFY THE CONDITION.

CHECK THE SET-ACC. SWITCH, COAST SWITCH, RESUME
SWITCH AND SLIP RING CIRCUITS,
AND THE BRUSH CONTACTS.

NOT OK — SERVICE THE CIRCUIT AS REQUIRED.

OK — PERFORM SERVO TESTS.

NOT OK — REPLACE SERVO.

OK — PERFORM AMPLIFIER TEST.
(SUBSTITUTION)

DOES NOT CORRECT PROBLEM — CHECK CIRCUIT CONNECTORS FOR
PROPER CONTACTS. REPAIR AS REQUIRED.

CORRECTS PROBLEM — REPLACE AMPLIFIER.

DIAGNOSIS AND TESTING PROCEDURES

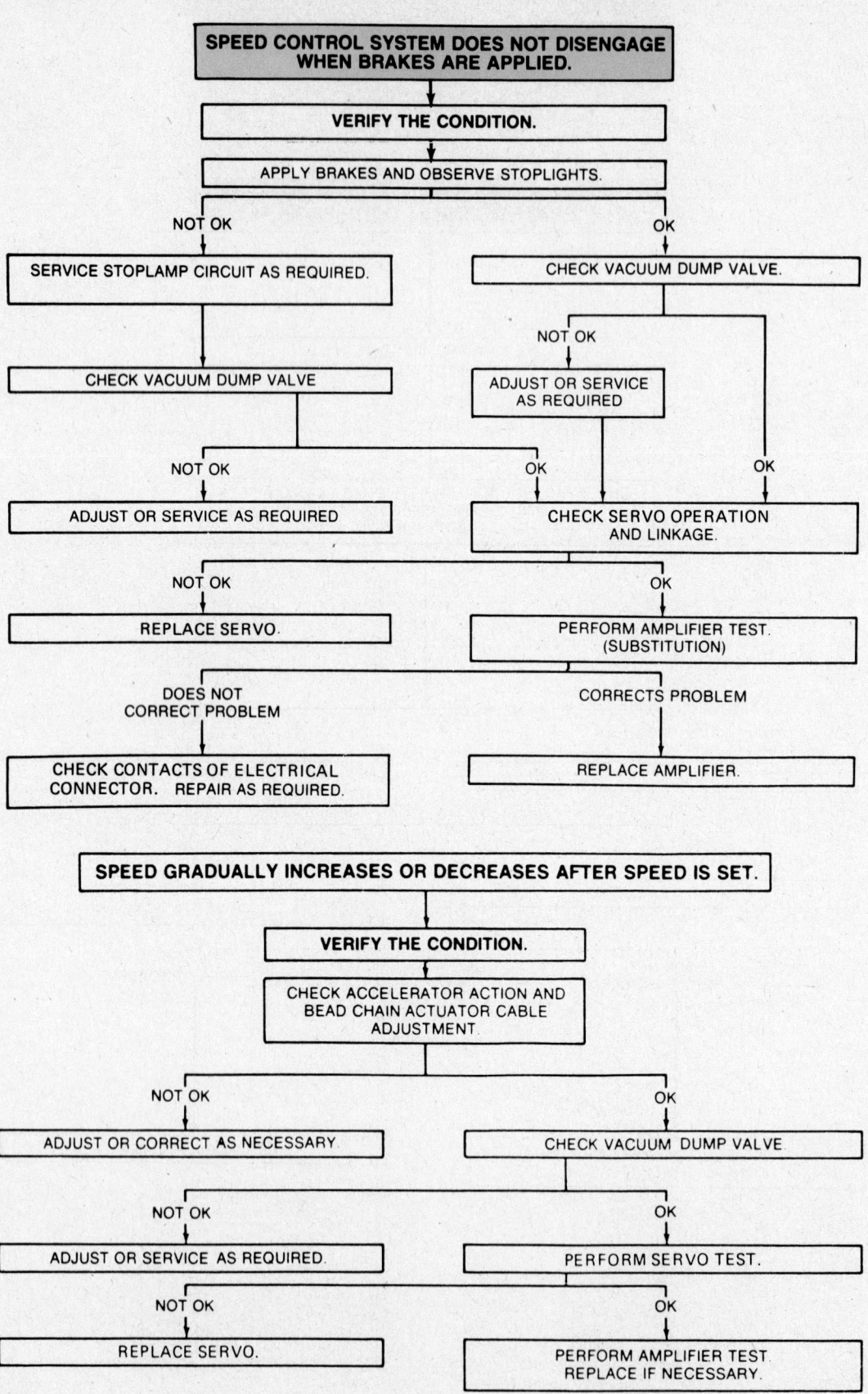

DIAGNOSIS AND TESTING PROCEDURES

NON-ELECTRONIC INSTRUMENT CLUSTER

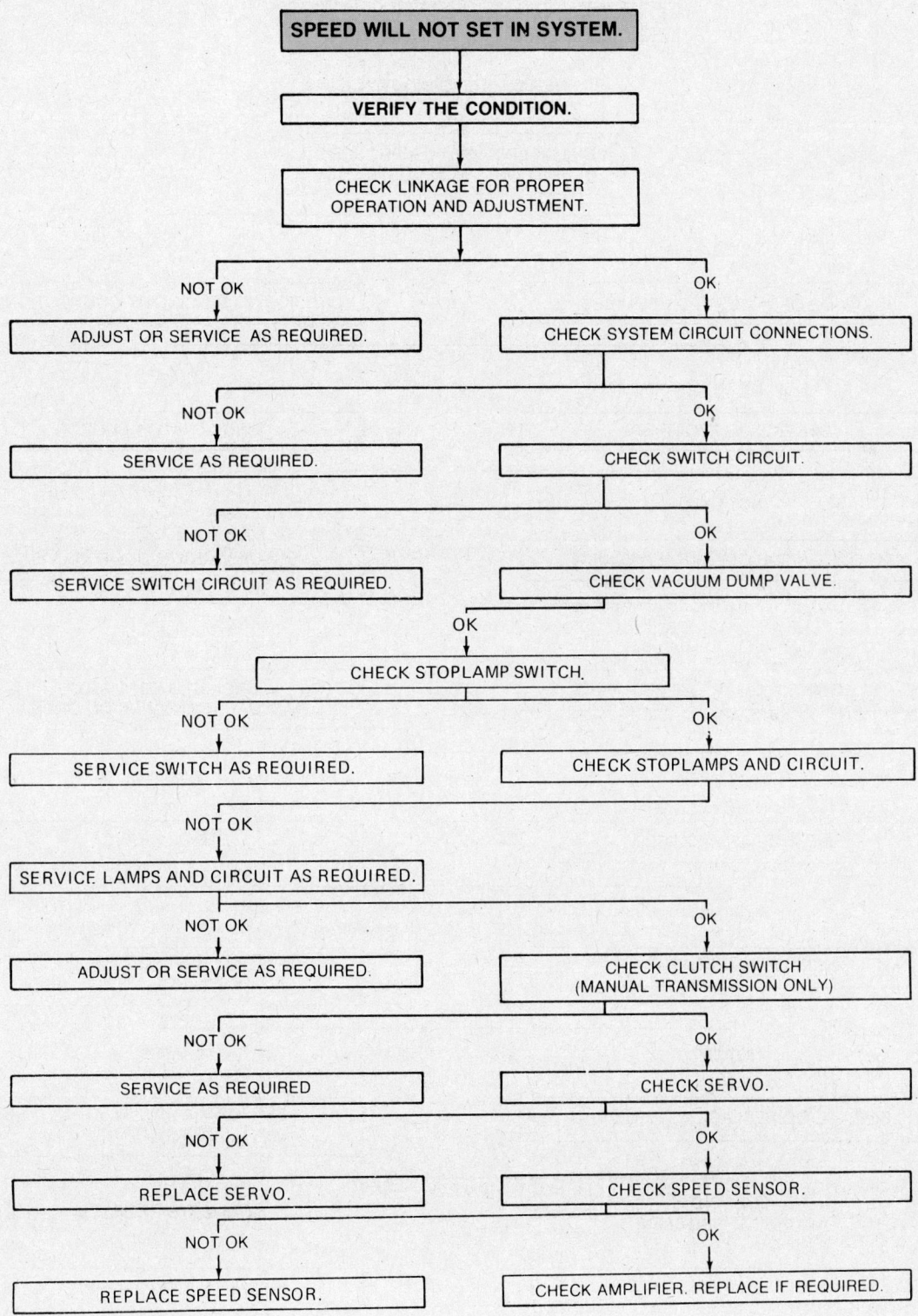

SPEED WILL NOT SET IN SYSTEM.	
VERIFY THE CONDITION.	
CHECK LINKAGE FOR PROPER OPERATION AND ADJUSTMENT.	
NOT OK → ADJUST OR SERVICE AS REQUIRED.	OK → CHECK SYSTEM CIRCUIT CONNECTIONS.
NOT OK → SERVICE AS REQUIRED.	OK → CHECK SWITCH CIRCUIT.
NOT OK → SERVICE SWITCH CIRCUIT AS REQUIRED.	OK → CHECK VACUUM DUMP VALVE.
	OK → CHECK STOPLAMP SWITCH.
NOT OK → SERVICE SWITCH AS REQUIRED.	OK → CHECK STOPLAMPS AND CIRCUIT.
NOT OK → SERVICE LAMPS AND CIRCUIT AS REQUIRED.	
NOT OK → ADJUST OR SERVICE AS REQUIRED.	OK → CHECK CLUTCH SWITCH (MANUAL TRANSMISSION ONLY)
NOT OK → SERVICE AS REQUIRED	OK → CHECK SERVO.
NOT OK → REPLACE SERVO.	OK → CHECK SPEED SENSOR.
NOT OK → REPLACE SPEED SENSOR.	OK → CHECK AMPLIFIER. REPLACE IF REQUIRED.

DIAGNOSIS AND TESTING PROCEDURES

ELECTRONIC INSTRUMENT CLUSTER

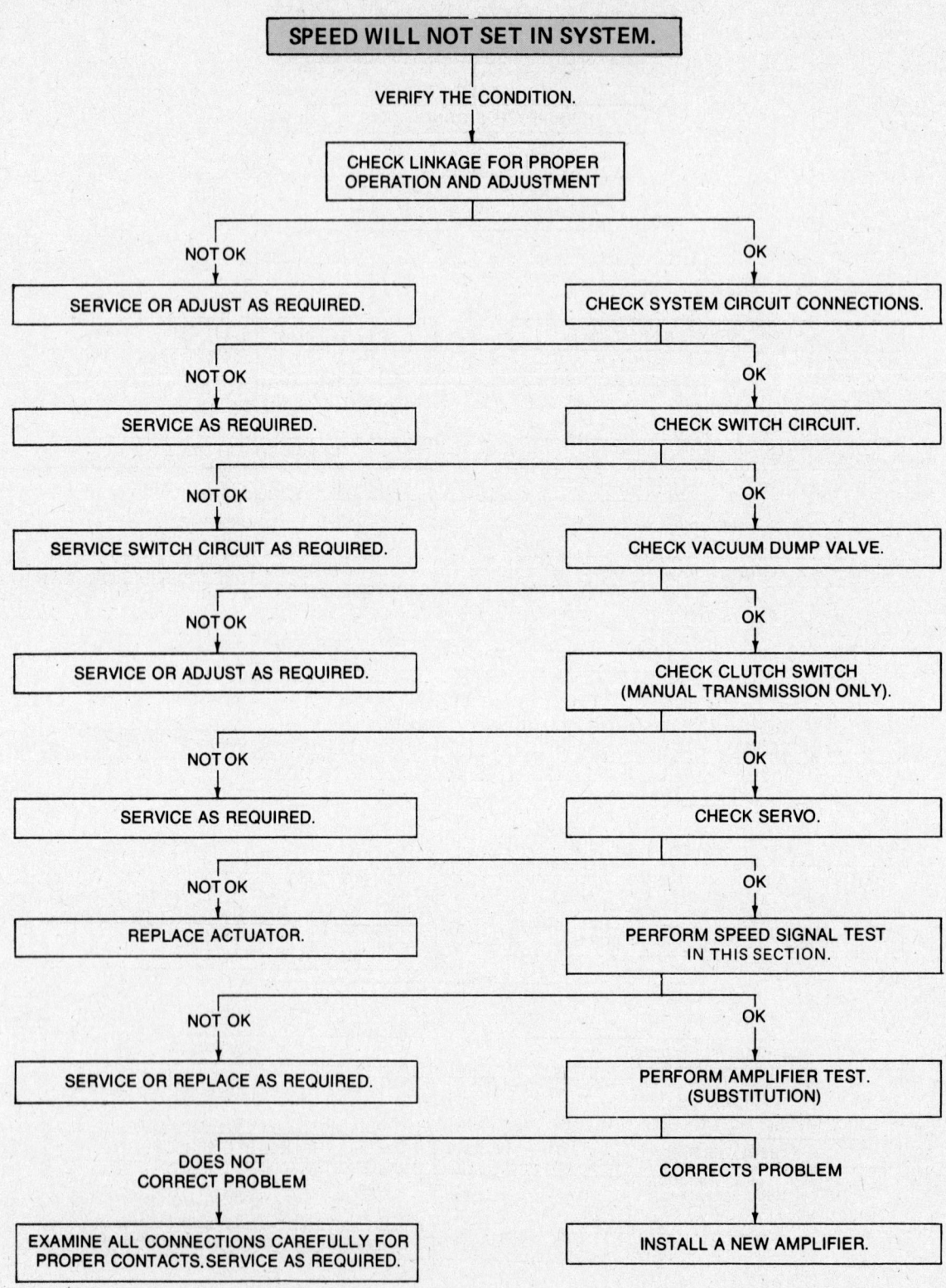

SPEED WILL NOT SET IN SYSTEM.

VERIFY THE CONDITION.

CHECK LINKAGE FOR PROPER OPERATION AND ADJUSTMENT

NOT OK — SERVICE OR ADJUST AS REQUIRED.

OK — CHECK SYSTEM CIRCUIT CONNECTIONS.

NOT OK — SERVICE AS REQUIRED.

OK — CHECK SWITCH CIRCUIT.

NOT OK — SERVICE SWITCH CIRCUIT AS REQUIRED.

OK — CHECK VACUUM DUMP VALVE.

NOT OK — SERVICE OR ADJUST AS REQUIRED.

OK — CHECK CLUTCH SWITCH (MANUAL TRANSMISSION ONLY).

NOT OK — SERVICE AS REQUIRED.

OK — CHECK SERVO.

NOT OK — REPLACE ACTUATOR.

OK — PERFORM SPEED SIGNAL TEST IN THIS SECTION.

NOT OK — SERVICE OR REPLACE AS REQUIRED.

OK — PERFORM AMPLIFIER TEST. (SUBSTITUTION)

DOES NOT CORRECT PROBLEM — EXAMINE ALL CONNECTIONS CAREFULLY FOR PROPER CONTACTS. SERVICE AS REQUIRED.

CORRECTS PROBLEM — INSTALL A NEW AMPLIFIER.

DIAGNOSIS AND TESTING PROCEDURES

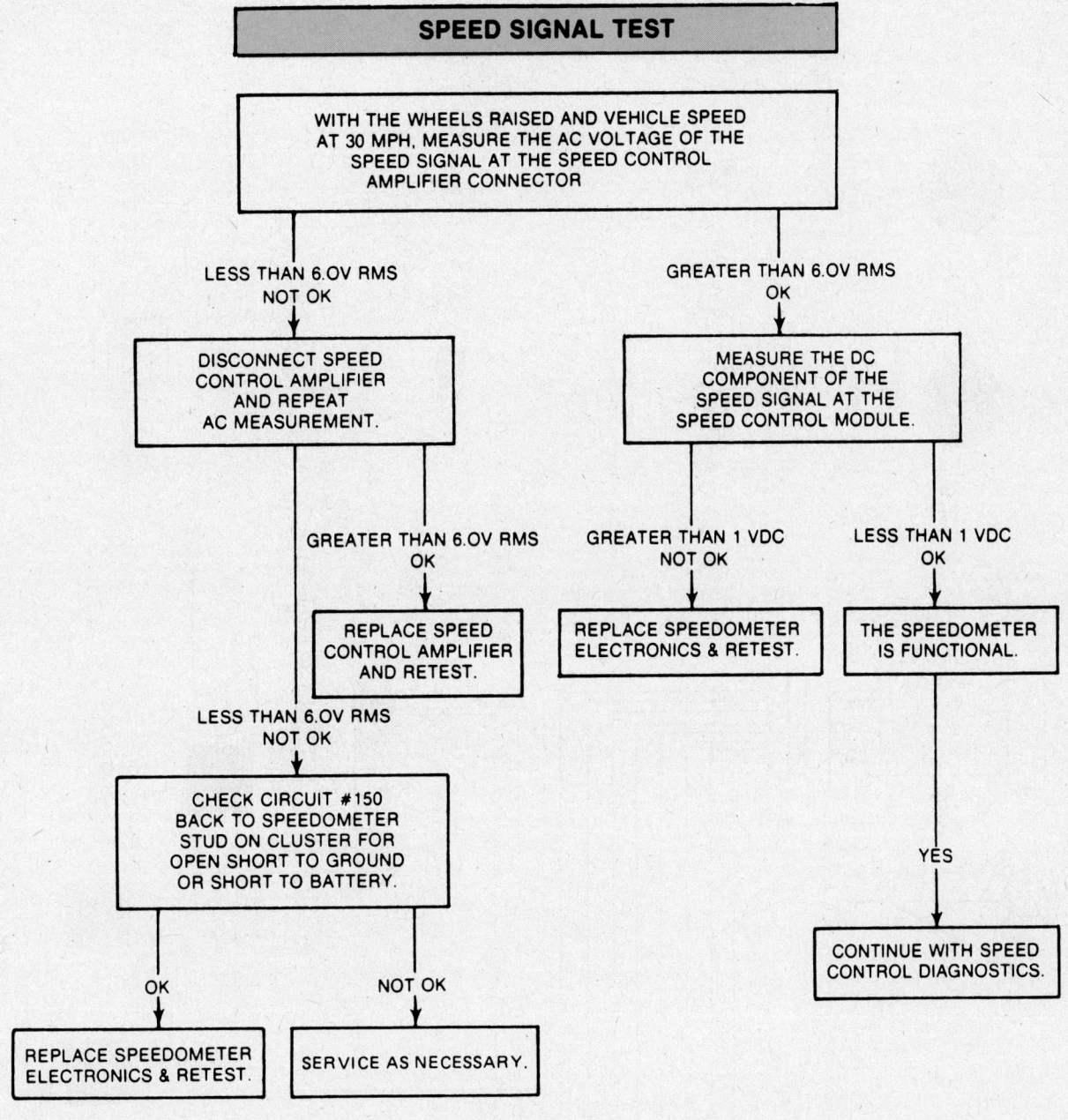

SPEED SIGNAL TEST

WITH THE WHEELS RAISED AND VEHICLE SPEED AT 30 MPH, MEASURE THE AC VOLTAGE OF THE SPEED SIGNAL AT THE SPEED CONTROL AMPLIFIER CONNECTOR

LESS THAN 6.0V RMS
NOT OK

GREATER THAN 6.0V RMS
OK

DISCONNECT SPEED CONTROL AMPLIFIER AND REPEAT AC MEASUREMENT.

MEASURE THE DC COMPONENT OF THE SPEED SIGNAL AT THE SPEED CONTROL MODULE.

GREATER THAN 6.0V RMS
OK

GREATER THAN 1 VDC
NOT OK

LESS THAN 1 VDC
OK

REPLACE SPEED CONTROL AMPLIFIER AND RETEST.

REPLACE SPEEDOMETER ELECTRONICS & RETEST.

THE SPEEDOMETER IS FUNCTIONAL.

LESS THAN 6.0V RMS
NOT OK

CHECK CIRCUIT #150 BACK TO SPEEDOMETER STUD ON CLUSTER FOR OPEN SHORT TO GROUND OR SHORT TO BATTERY.

YES

CONTINUE WITH SPEED CONTROL DIAGNOSTICS.

OK

NOT OK

REPLACE SPEEDOMETER ELECTRONICS & RETEST.

SERVICE AS NECESSARY.

NOTE:

NEVER INSTALL A SPEED CONTROL SENSOR (9E731) AND A TWO-PIECE SPEEDOMETER CABLE ON SUBJECT VEHICLES TO SERVICE AN INOPERATIVE SPEED CONTROL CAUSED BY THE LACK OF A SPEED SIGNAL GENERATED BY THE ELECTRONIC SPEEDOMETER ASSEMBLY.

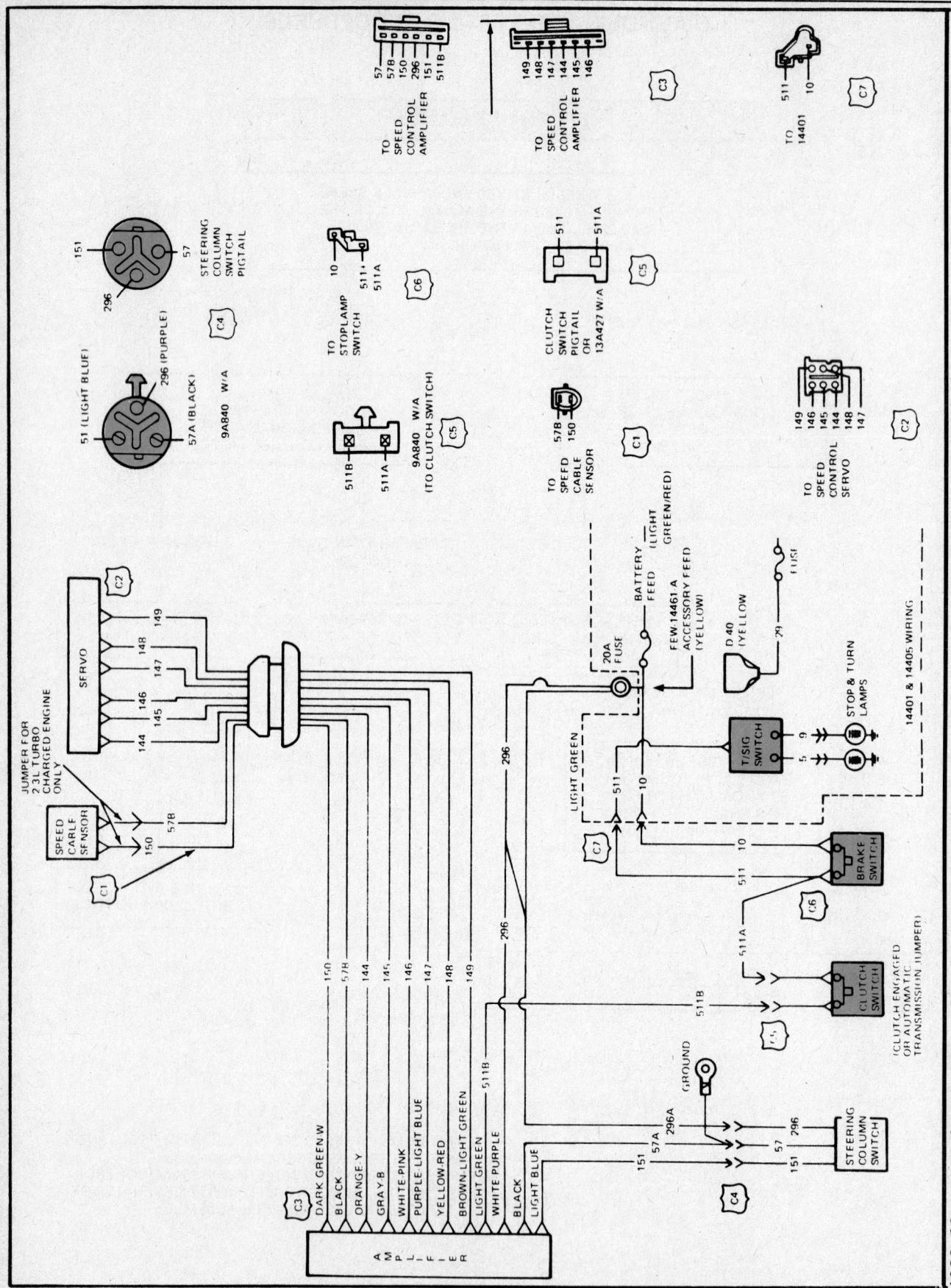

1982–83 except thunderbird, XR7 and Lincoln Continential 1984 and later LTD, Marquis, Mustang and Capri—cruise control wiring and vacuum diaphragm

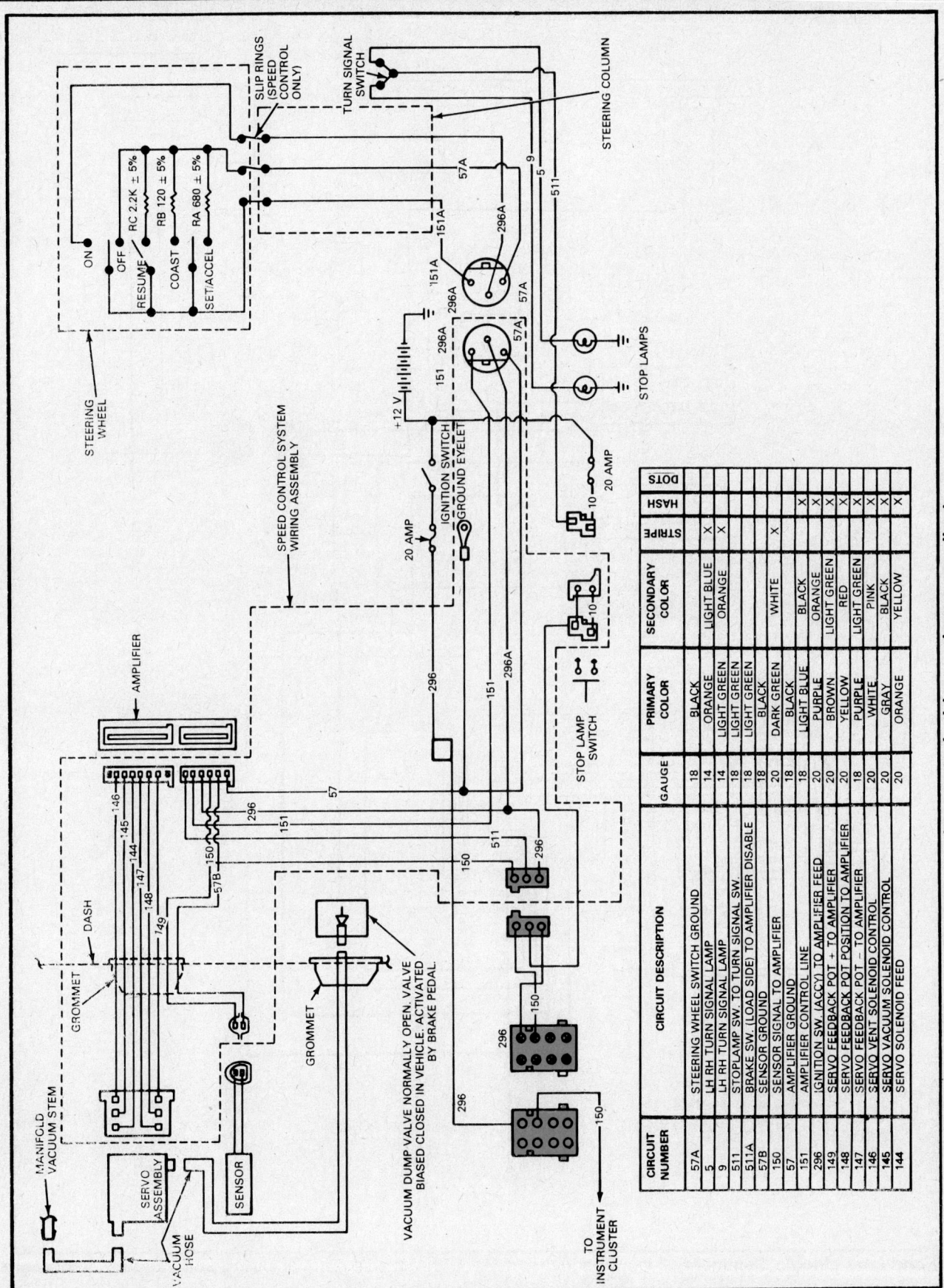

1982 and later thunderbird, XR7 and Cougar — cruise control wiring and vacuum diaphragm

CIRCUIT NUMBER	CIRCUIT DESCRIPTION	GAUGE	PRIMARY COLOR	SECONDARY COLOR	STRIPE	HASH	DOTS
57A	STEERING WHEEL SWITCH GROUND	18	BLACK				
5	LH RH TURN SIGNAL LAMP	14	ORANGE	LIGHT BLUE	X		
9	LH RH TURN SIGNAL LAMP	14	LIGHT GREEN	ORANGE	X		
511	STOPLAMP SW. TO TURN SIGNAL SW.	18	LIGHT GREEN				
511A	BRAKE SW. (LOAD SIDE) TO AMPLIFIER DISABLE	18	LIGHT GREEN				
57B	SENSOR GROUND	18	BLACK				
150	SENSOR SIGNAL TO AMPLIFIER	20	DARK GREEN	WHITE	X		
57	AMPLIFIER GROUND	18	BLACK				
151	AMPLIFIER CONTROL LINE	18	LIGHT BLUE	BLACK		X	X
296	(IGNITION SW. (ACCY.) TO AMPLIFIER FEED	20	PURPLE	ORANGE		X	X
149	SERVO FEEDBACK POT + TO AMPLIFIER	20	BROWN	LIGHT GREEN		X	X
148	SERVO FEEDBACK POT POSITION TO AMPLIFIER	20	YELLOW	RED		X	X
147	SERVO FEEDBACK POT – TO AMPLIFIER	18	PURPLE	LIGHT GREEN		X	X
146	SERVO VENT SOLENOID CONTROL	20	WHITE	PINK		X	X
145	SERVO VACUUM SOLENOID CONTROL	20	GRAY	BLACK		X	X
144	SERVO SOLENOID FEED	20	ORANGE	YELLOW		X	X

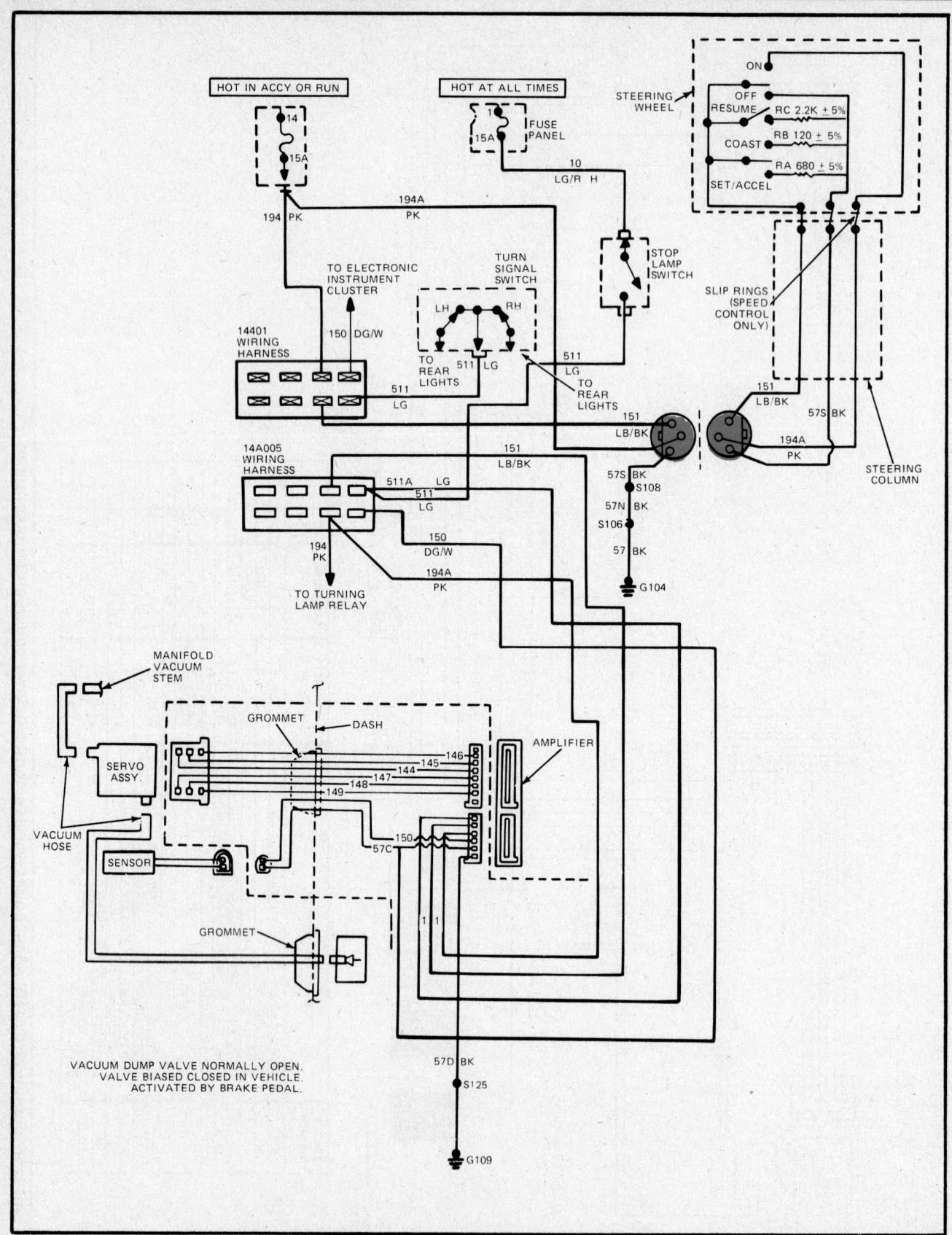

1982 and later Lincoln Continental, Continental and Mark VII—cruise control wiring and vacuum diaphragm

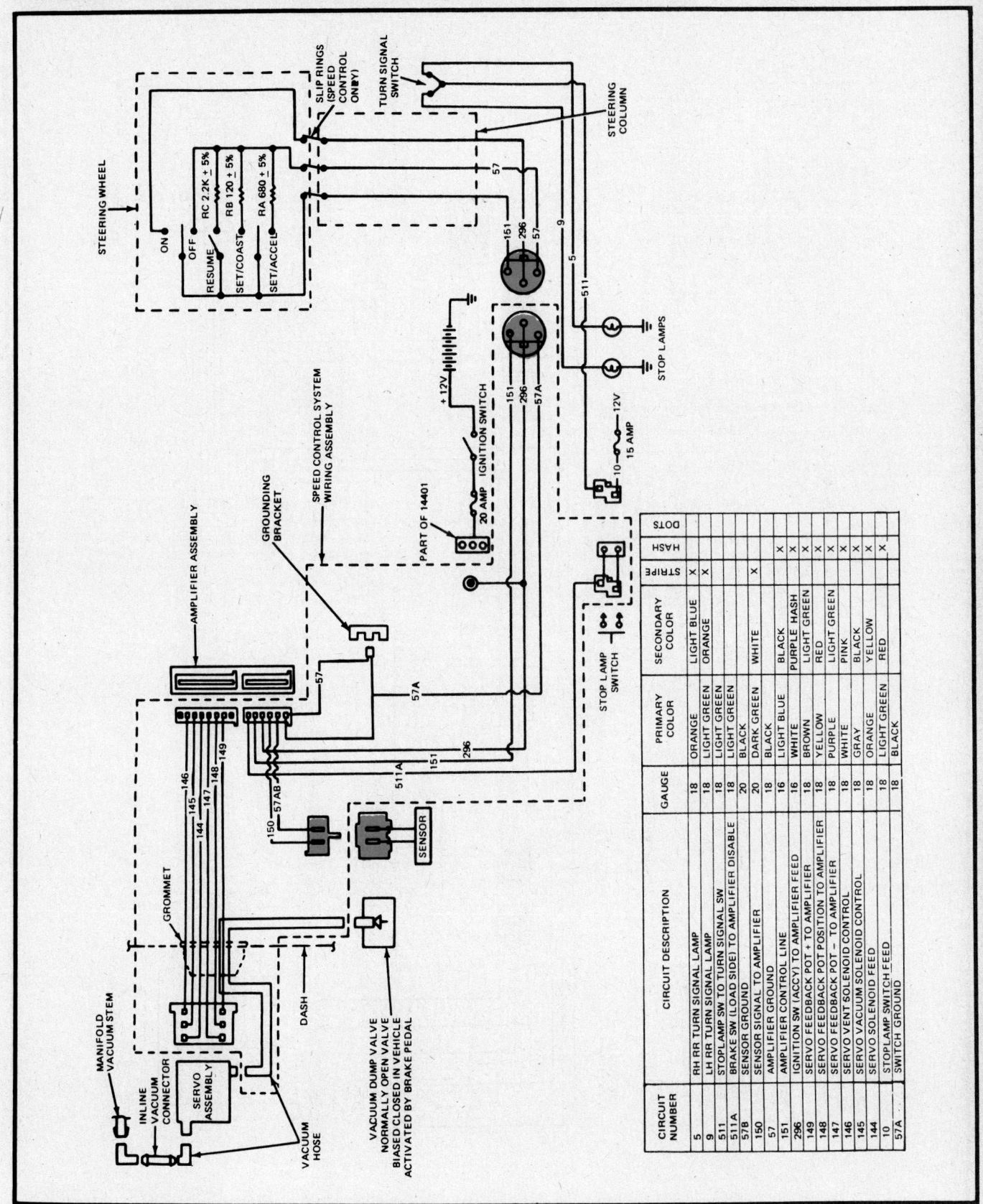

CIRCUIT NUMBER	CIRCUIT DESCRIPTION	GAUGE	PRIMARY COLOR	SECONDARY COLOR	STRIPE	HASH	DOTS
5	RH RR TURN SIGNAL LAMP	18	ORANGE	LIGHT BLUE	X		
9	LH RR TURN SIGNAL LAMP	18	LIGHT GREEN	ORANGE	X		
511	STOPLAMP SW TO TURN SIGNAL SW	18	LIGHT GREEN				
511A	BRAKE SW (LOAD SIDE) TO AMPLIFIER DISABLE	18	LIGHT GREEN				
57B	SENSOR GROUND	20	BLACK				
150	SENSOR SIGNAL TO AMPLIFIER	20	DARK GREEN	WHITE	X		
57	AMPLIFIER GROUND	18	BLACK				
151	AMPLIFIER CONTROL LINE	16	LIGHT BLUE	BLACK		X	X
296	IGNITION SW (ACCY) TO AMPLIFIER FEED	16	WHITE	PURPLE HASH		X	X
149	SERVO FEEDBACK POT + TO AMPLIFIER	18	BROWN	LIGHT GREEN		X	X
148	SERVO FEEDBACK POT POSITION TO AMPLIFIER	18	YELLOW	RED		X	X
147	SERVO FEEDBACK POT − TO AMPLIFIER	18	PURPLE	LIGHT GREEN		X	X
146	SERVO VENT SOLENOID CONTROL	18	WHITE	PINK		X	X
145	SERVO VACUUM SOLENOID CONTROL	18	GRAY	BLACK		X	X
144	SERVO SOLENOID FEED	18	ORANGE	YELLOW		X	X
10	STOPLAMP SWITCH FEED	18	LIGHT GREEN	RED		X	X
57A	SWITCH GROUND	18	BLACK				

1982–83 Ford and Mercury shown, Lincoln Town Car and Mark VI similar — cruise control wiring and vacuum diaphragm

CIRCUIT NUMBER	CIRCUIT DESCRIPTION	GAUGE	PRIMARY COLOR	SECONDARY COLOR	STRIPE
5	RH RR TURN SIGNAL LAMP	18	ORANGE	LIGHT BLUE	
9	LH RR TURN SIGNAL LAMP	18	LIGHT GREEN	ORANGE	
511	STOPLAMP SW TO TURN SIGNAL LAMP	18	LIGHT GREEN		
511A	BRAKE SW (LOAD SIDE) TO AMPLIFIER DISABLE	18	LIGHT GREEN		
57AB	STOPLAMP SW TO AMPLIFIER SW	20	BLACK		
150	SENSOR GROUND	18	DARK GREEN	WHITE	x
151	SENSOR SIGNAL TO AMPLIFIER	18	LIGHT BLUE	BLACK	
296	AMPLIFIER GROUND	16	BLACK		
149	AMPLIFIER CONTROL LINE	16	WHITE	PURPLE HASH	
148	IGNITION SW (ACCY.) TO AMPLIFIER FEED	18	BROWN	LIGHT GREEN	
147	SERVO FEEDBACK POT + TO AMPLIFIER	18	YELLOW	RED	
146	SERVO FEEDBACK POT POSITION TO AMPLIFIER	18	PURPLE	LIGHT GREEN	
145	SERVO FEEDBACK POT − TO AMPLIFIER	18	WHITE	PINK	
144	SERVO VENT SOLENOID CONTROL	18	GRAY	BLACK	
10	SERVO VACUUM SOLENOID CONTROL	18	ORANGE	LIGHT GREEN	
57A	SERVO SOLENOID FEED	18	LIGHT GREEN	YELLOW	
	STOPLAMP SWITCH + FEED		BLACK	RED	
	SWITCH GROUND				

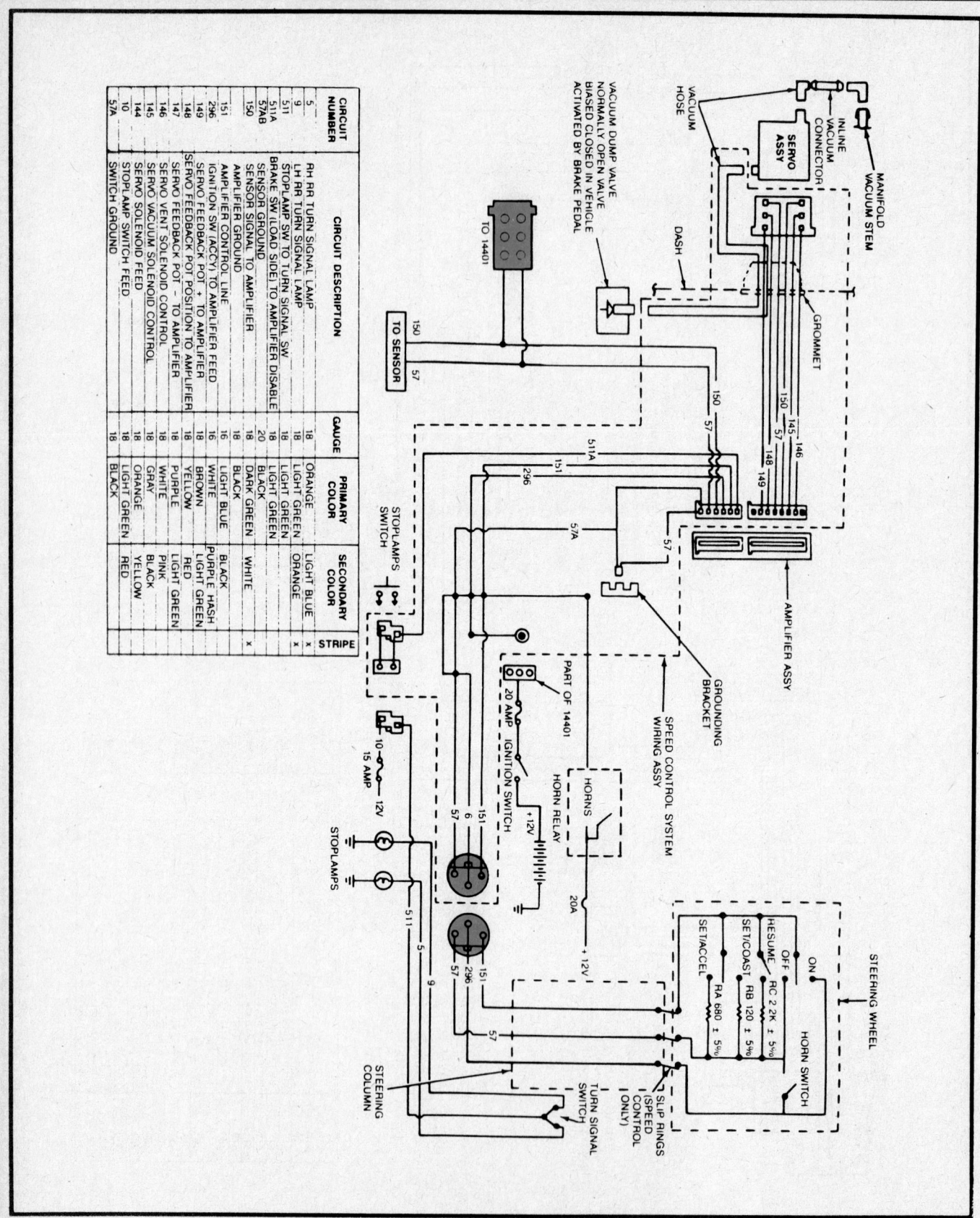

1984 and later Lincoln Town Car, Crown Victoria and Grand Marquis— cruise control wiring and vacuum diaphragm

SERVO ASSEMBLY TEST

1. Separate the eight pin connector at the amplifier. Connect an ohmmeter between circuit 144 (yellow/orange) and circuit 145 (grey/black). A resistance of 40–125 ohms should be recorded.

2. Connect an ohmmeter between circuit 144 (yellow/orange) and circuit 146 (white/pink). A resistance of 60–190 ohms should be recorded.

3. If the proper reading is not obtained, check the wiring and the servo assembly separately for damage. Repair or replace defective components as required.

4. Start the engine and with the servo disconnected from the amplifier connect circuit 144 (orange/yellow) of the servo to the battery positive terminal. Connect circuit 146 (white/pink) of the servo to ground.

5. Momentarily touch circuit 145 (grey/black) of the servo to ground. The servo throttle actuator arm should pull in and the engine speed should increase.

6. The servo throttle actuator arm should hold in that position or slowly release.

7. When circuit 146 (white/pink) is removed from ground the servo throttle actuator arm should release.

8. Replace the servo assembly if it does not perform as indicated.

NOTE: On some vehicles equipped with a diesel engine, check for vacuum supply at the servo. If vacuum is not available check the vacuum pump. If the pump is found to be defective repair or replace it as required.

9. If circuit 144 (orange/yellow) is shorted to either the circuit 146 (white/pink) or circuit 145 (grey/black) it may be necessary to replace the amplifier assembly.

AMPLIFIER TESTS

NOTE: Do not use a test lamp to perform the amplifier tests as excessive current draw will damage electronic components inside the amplifier. Use a voltmeter of 5000 ohm/volt rating or higher.

ON CIRCUIT TEST

1. Turn the ignition switch to the on position. Connect a voltmeter between circuit 296 (white/pink) and ground in the six pin connector at the amplifier.

2. The voltmeter should read battery voltage.

3. Connect the voltmeter between circuit 151 (light blue/black) and ground in the six pin connector at the amplifier.

4. The voltmeter should read battery voltage only when the on switch in the steering wheel is depressed and held.

5. If voltage is not present perform the control switch test.

6. Release the on button the voltmeter should read about 7.8 volts, this indicates that the on circuit is engaged. If the voltmeter reads zero, check for a bad ground at the amplifier.

7. If there is no ground at the amplifier check the system ground connections and wiring. Also check the number 6 and 20 amp fuse.

8. Substitute, but do not install, a known good amplifier and check for proper circuit operation.

BRAKE CIRCUIT TEST (1984 AND LATER)

1. Connect an ohmmeter between circuit 511 (light green) (circuit 10 (red and light green) on Lincoln Town Car, Crown Victoria and Grand Marquis) on the six pin connector and ground. The resistance should be less than 5 ohms.

2. If the resistance is greater than indicated check for improper wiring, burned out stop lamp lights or clutch malfunction, if equipped.

OFF CIRCUIT TEST

1. With the ignition switch in the on position and the voltmeter connected between circuit 151 (light blue/black) of the six pin amplifier connector and ground depress the off switch on the steering wheel.

2. Voltage on the blue wire should drop to zero which indicates that the on circuit is not energized.

3. If voltage does not drop to zero, perform the control switch test. If the control switch checks out good install a good amplifier and recheck the off circuit.

SET ACCEL CIRCUIT TEST

1. With the ignition switch in the on position and the voltmeter connected between circuit 151 (light blue/black) of the six pin amplifier connector and ground depress and hold set/accel button on the steering wheel. The voltmeter should read about 4.5 volts.

2. Rotate the steering wheel back and forth and watch the voltmeter for fluctuations.

3. If voltage varies more than 0.5 volt perform the control switch test.

COAST CIRCUIT TEST

1. With the ignition switch in the on position and the voltmeter connected between circuit 151 (light blue/black) of the six pin amplifier connector and ground depress and hold the coast button on the steering wheel. The voltmeter should read about 1.5 volts.

2. If the circuit checks out good perform the servo assembly test. If the servo test checks out good install a new amplifier and repeat the tests. Do not substitute the amplifier until after performing the servo assembly test.

RESUME CIRCUIT TEST

1. With the ignition switch in the on position and the voltmeter connected between circuit 151 (light blue/black) of the six pin amplifier connector and ground depress and hold the resume button on the steering wheel. The voltmeter should read about 6.5 volts.

2. If the circuit checks out good perform the servo assembly test. If the servo test checks out good install a new amplifier and repeat the tests. Do not substitute the amplifier until after performing the servo assembly test.

BRAKE LIGHT SWITCH AND CIRCUIT TEST

This test is performed when brake pedal application will not disconnect the cruise control system.

1. Check the break light operation with maximum brake pedal effort of about six pounds. If more than about six pounds is required, check the brake actuation of the brake light switch. Repair or replace defective components as required.

2. If the brake light do not work check the fuse, bulbs and the switch. Repair or replace defective components as required.

3. If the brake lights are working properly check for battery voltage at circuit 296 (white/pink) wires at the six pin electrical connector.

4. Depress the brake pedal until the tail lamps light. Check voltage on circuit 810 (brown/light green) at the six pin electrical connector.

5. The difference between the two voltage readings should not exceed 1.5 volts. If the reading is higher, the resistance in the brake light circuit must be found and repaired.

6. There should be no voltage present at circuit 810 (red/light green) with the brake lights off.

Perform the vacuum dump valve test.

VACUUM DUMP VALVE TEST

The vacuum dump valve releases vacuum in the servo assembly whenever the brake pedal is depressed and thus acts as a redundant safety feature. The vacuum dump valve should be checked whenever brake application does not disconnect the cruise control system.

1. Disconnect the vacuum hose (white stripe) from the dump valve servo. Connect a vacuum pump to the hose and pump up the vacuum.

2. If a vacuum cannot be obtained, the hose or the dump valve is leaking. Replace or repair defective components as required.

3. Step on the brake pedal, the vacuum should be released. If not adjust or replace the dump valve.

4. The dump valve black housing must clear the white plastic pad on the brake pedal by 0.050–0.100 inch with the brake pedal pulled to the rearmost position.

CLUTCH SWITCH TEST (MANUAL TRANSMISSION)

The cruise control system is designed to disengage when the clutch pedal is depressed. This is accomplished via a clutch switch. The cruise control system disengage function is operated by opening the circuit between the cruise control module and the brake lamps. This prevents engine over speed when the clutch is depressed and the cruise control system is engaged.

The disengagement switch is a plunger switch that operates when the clutch pedal is depressed and the pedal moves away from the switch plunger. The switch is adjustable and attaches to a mounting bracket on the clutch module assembly.

NOTE: Do not use a test light to perform the clutch switch test, as the light cannot properly indicate the condition of the switch. Do not use a strong magnet near the clutch switch, as it can be affected by magnetic fields

1. Disconnect the clutch pigtail connector from the cruise control harness connector. Connect an ohmmeter to the two switch connector terminals.

2. With the clutch pedal in the full up position, resistance should be less than five ohms.

3. With the clutch pedal depressed, the circuit should be open.

4. If the switch does not perform as indicated, it must be replaced.

SHORTING PLUG TEST (AUTOMATIC TRANSMISSION)

Vehicles equipped with automatic transmission use a shorting plug instead of a clutch switch to regulate the cruise control system operation.

ACTUATOR CABLE ADJUSTMENT

LINKAGE TYPE

1. If equipped with a carburetor, set the choke on the hot idle condition with the throttle positioner solenoid disengaged.

2. Remove the cruise control cable retaining clip. Push the cruise control cable through the adjuster until a slight tension is felt.

3. Insert the cruise control cable retaining clip and snap it into place.

BEAD CHAIN TYPE

Adjust the bead chain in order to obtain a tight chain when the engine is at hot idle. This adjustment should be made in order

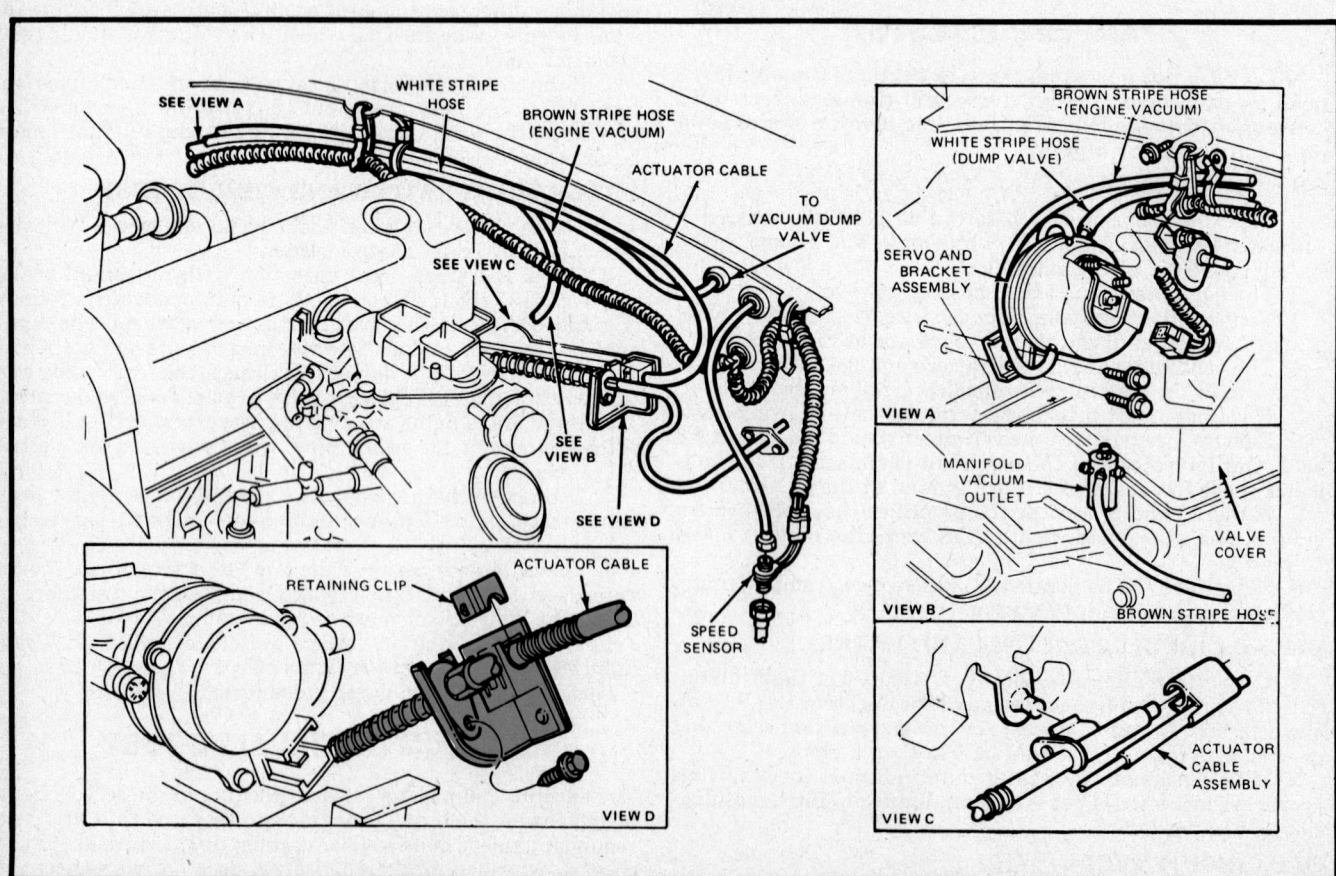

Actuator cable adjustment – 1982–83 Fairmont, Zephyr, Granada, Cougar, Mustang and Capri with 2.3 liter engine

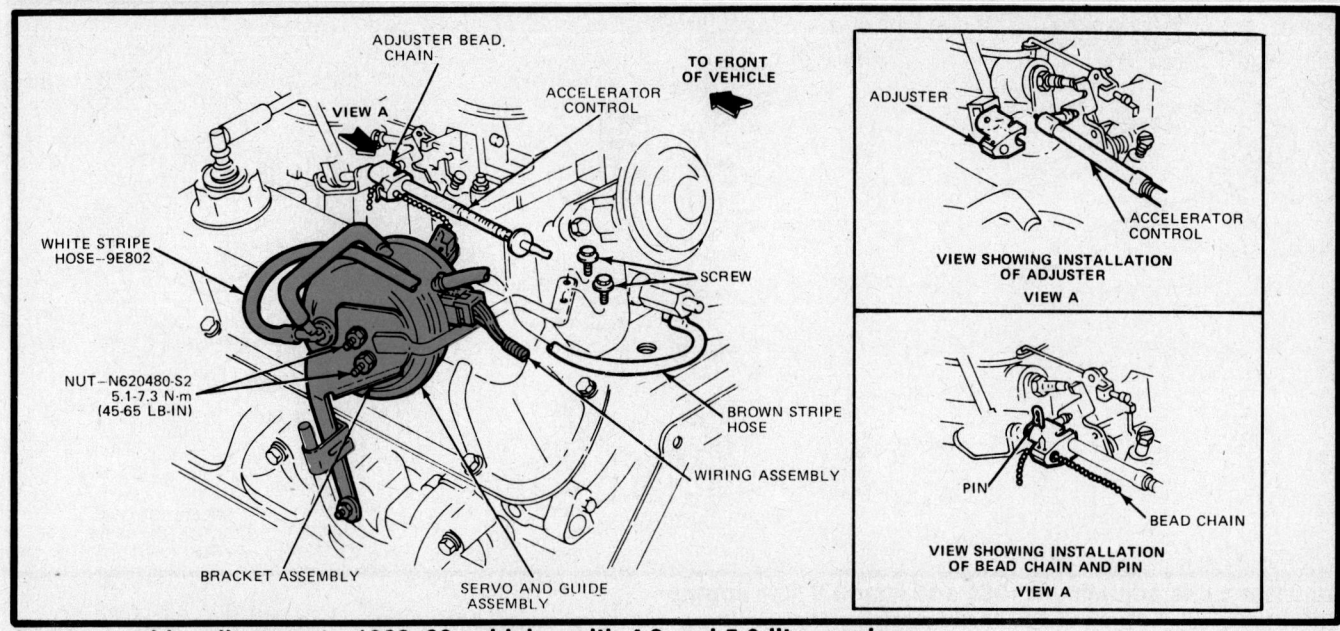

Actuator cable adjustment—1982–83 vehicles with 4.2 and 5.0 liter engines

to take as much slack out of the chain as possible without restricting the carburetor lever from returning to idle. The tighter the chain the better the cruise control system will function. If the vehicle is equipped with a solenoid throttle positioner, perform this adjustment with the throttle positioner disengaged.

VACUUM DUMP VALVE ADJUSTMENT

1. Depress the brake pedal and hold it in that position.
2. Push in the dump valve until the valve collar bottoms against the retaining clip.
3. Position a 0.050–0.10 inch shim between the white button of the valve and the pad on the brake pedal.

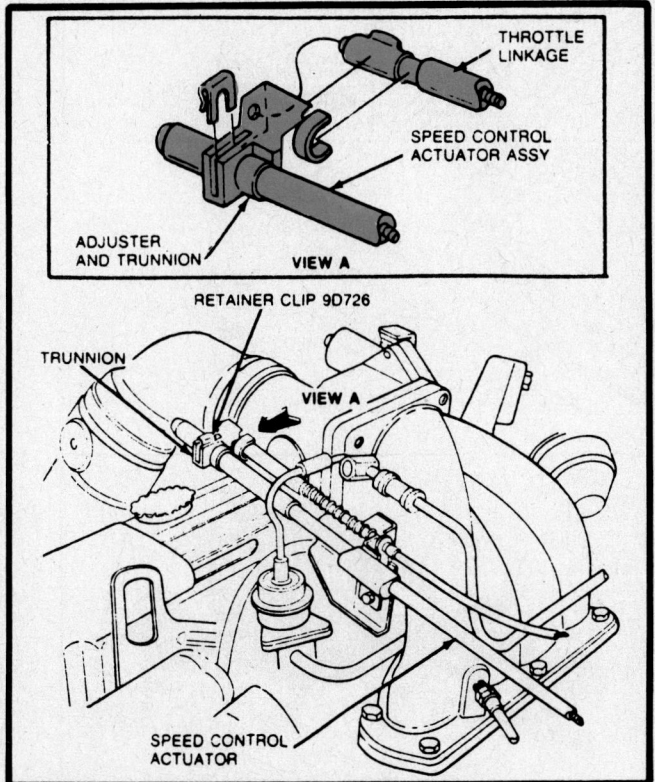

Actuator cable adjustment—1984 and later Thunderbird, Cougar, Mustang and Capri with 2.3 liter electronic fuel injected turbocharged engine

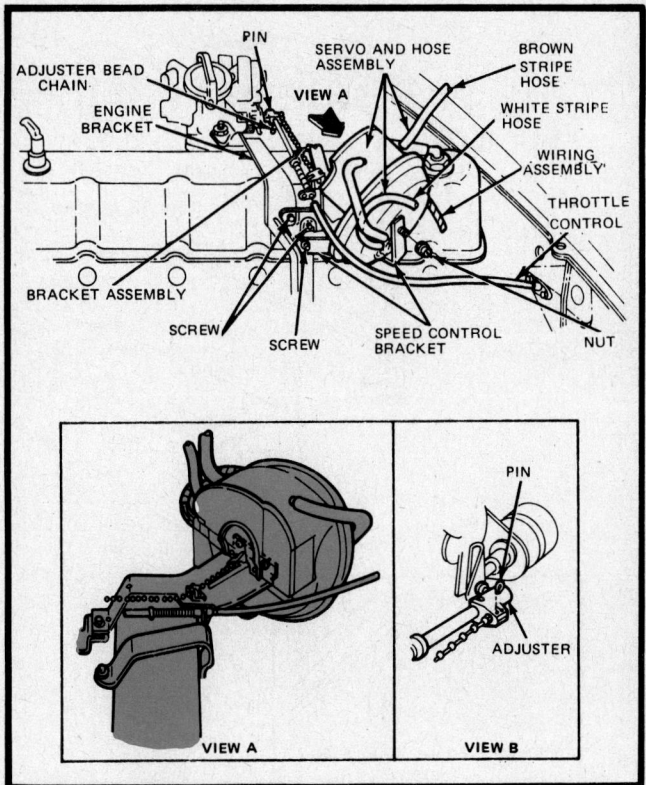

Actuator cable adjustment—1982–83 vehicles with 3.0 liter engine

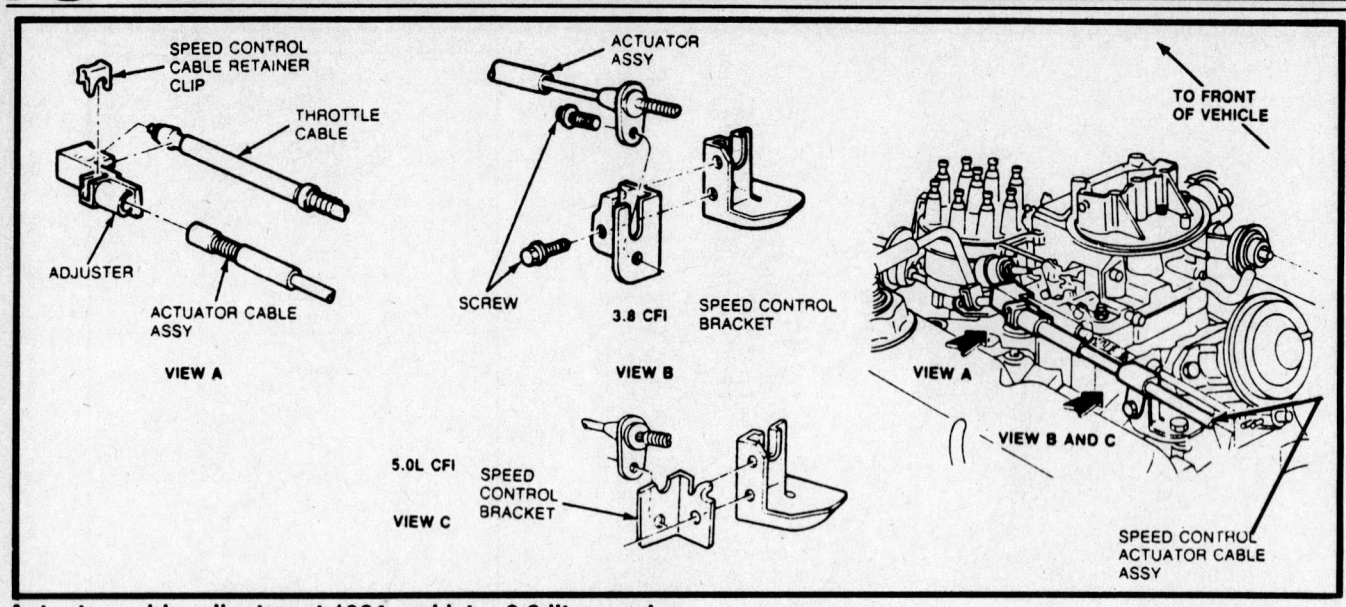

Actuator cable adjustment 1984 and later 3.8 liter engine

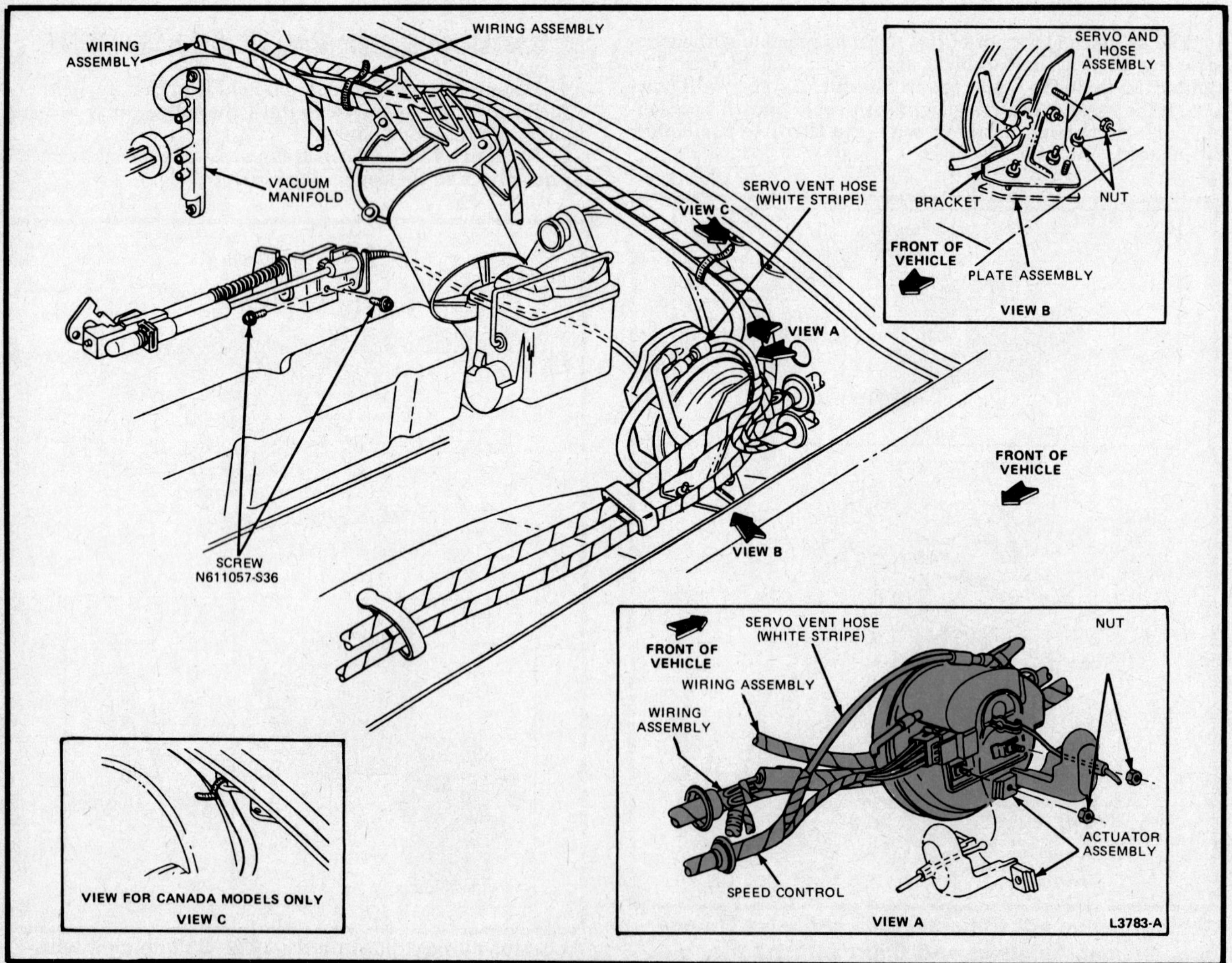

Actuator cable adjustment—Lincoln Town Car, Mark VI, Crown Victoria and Grand Marquis

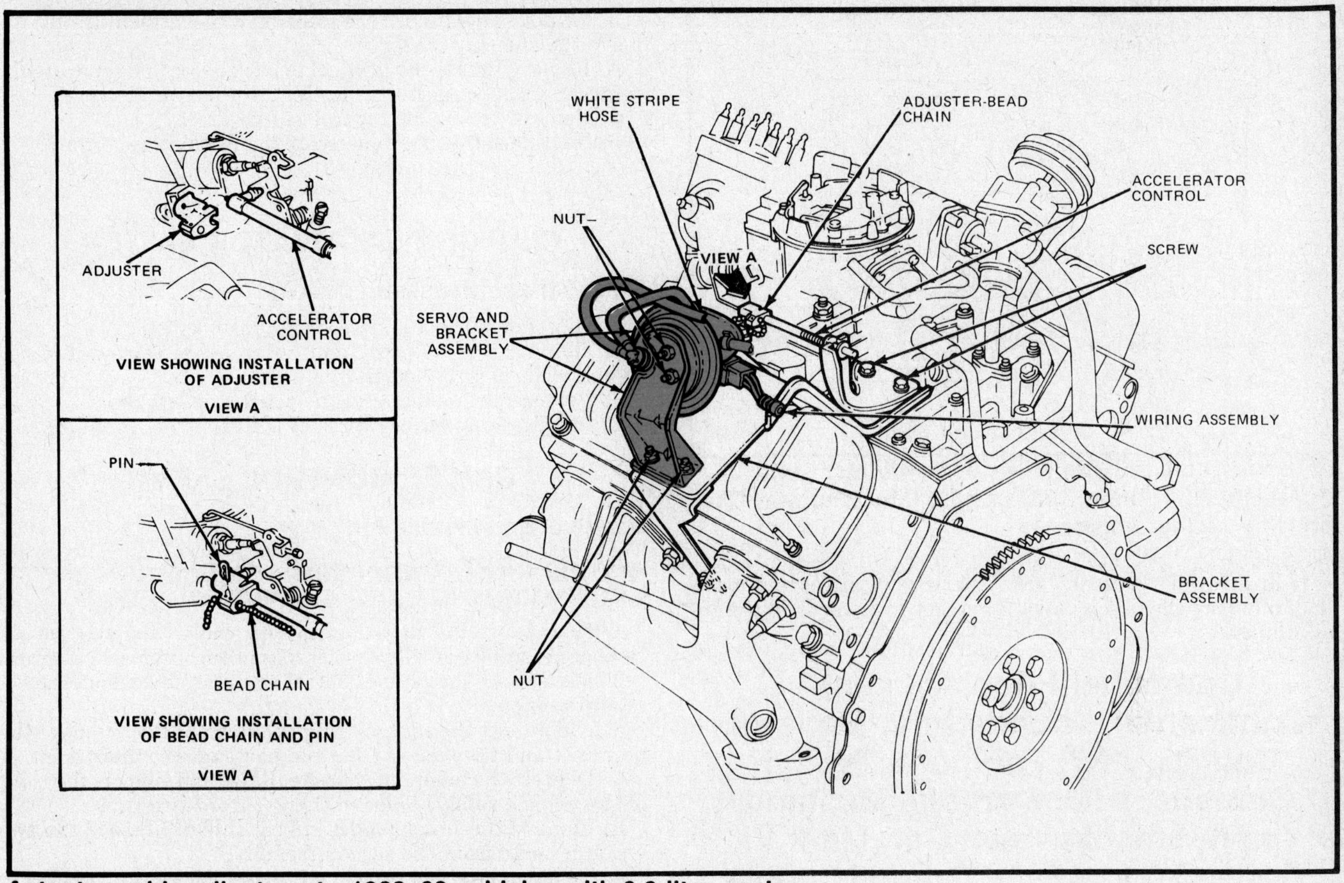

ADJUSTER

ACCELERATOR CONTROL

VIEW SHOWING INSTALLATION OF ADJUSTER

VIEW A

PIN

BEAD CHAIN

VIEW SHOWING INSTALLATION OF BEAD CHAIN AND PIN

VIEW A

WHITE STRIPE HOSE

ADJUSTER-BEAD CHAIN

NUT—

VIEW A

SERVO AND BRACKET ASSEMBLY

NUT

ACCELERATOR CONTROL

SCREW

WIRING ASSEMBLY

BRACKET ASSEMBLY

Actuator cable adjustment—1982–83 vehicles with 3.8 liter engine

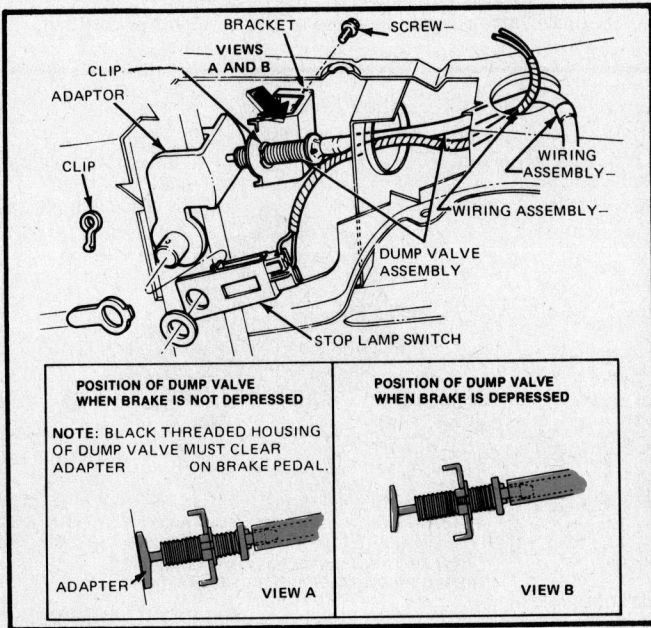

BRACKET

SCREW—

VIEWS A AND B

CLIP

ADAPTOR

CLIP

WIRING ASSEMBLY—

WIRING ASSEMBLY—

DUMP VALVE ASSEMBLY

STOP LAMP SWITCH

POSITION OF DUMP VALVE WHEN BRAKE IS NOT DEPRESSED

POSITION OF DUMP VALVE WHEN BRAKE IS DEPRESSED

NOTE: BLACK THREADED HOUSING OF DUMP VALVE MUST CLEAR ADAPTER ON BRAKE PEDAL.

ADAPTER

VIEW A

VIEW B

Dump valve and brake light switch installation—Lincoln Town Car, Mark VII, Crown Victoria and Grand Marquis

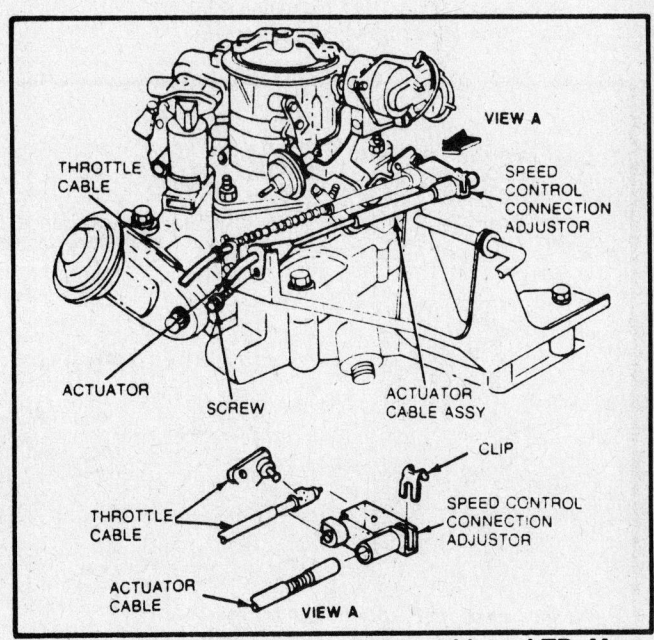

VIEW A

THROTTLE CABLE

SPEED CONTROL CONNECTION ADJUSTOR

ACTUATOR

SCREW

ACTUATOR CABLE ASSY

CLIP

THROTTLE CABLE

SPEED CONTROL CONNECTION ADJUSTOR

ACTUATOR CABLE

VIEW A

Actuator cable adjustment—1984 and later LTD, Marquis, Mustang and Capri with 2.3 liter non turbocharged engine

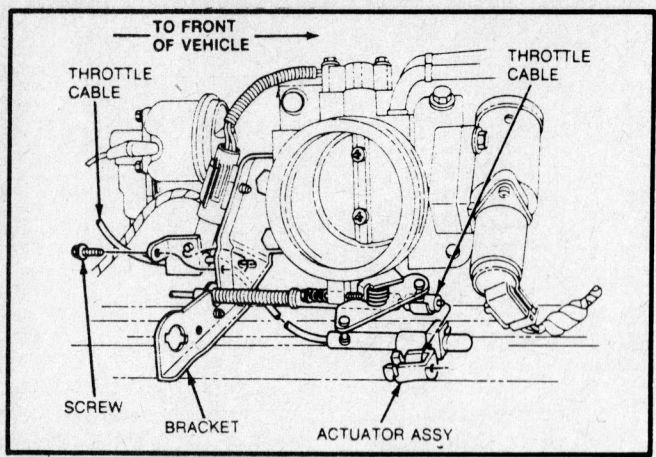

Actuator cable adjustment—1984 and later Mark VII, Continental, Thunderbird, Cougar, Mustang and Capri with 5.0 liter engine

4. Firmly pull the brake pedal rearward to its normal position, allowing the dump valve to ratchet backwards in the retaining clip.

Component Replacement— Continental, Thunderbird, Mark VII, Cougar, XR7, Fairmont, Zephyr, Granada, LTD, Marquis, Mustang, Capri, Lincoln Town Car, Mark VI, Crown Victoria and Grand Marquis

CRUISE CONTROL SWITCH

Removal and Installation

1. Disconnect the negative battery cable.
2. Remove the steering wheel hub cover.
3. Remove and discard the steering wheel attaching nut. Remove the steering wheel.
4. Remove the steering wheel to back cover and separate the control switch connector from the terminal on the cover.
5. Remove the cruise control switch assembly.
6. Installation is the reverse of the removal procedure.

CLUTCH DEACTIVATOR SWITCH

Removal and Installation

1. Disconnect the negative battery cable.
2. Remove the bracket mounting nuts. Disconnect the switch electrical connector.
3. Remove the switch and the bracket assembly.
4. Installation is the reverse of the removal procedure.

CRUISE CONTROL SERVO

Removal and Installation

ALL EXCEPT LINCOLN TOWN CAR, MARK VI, CROWN VICTORIA AND GRAND MARQUIS

1. Disconnect the negative battery cable. Remove the air cleaner assembly, on all vehicles except turbocharged engines.
2. Disconnect the cruise control actuator cable from the accelerator cable.
3. Disconnect the servo wiring at the amplifier. Remove the grommet and the wiring from the passenger compartment.
4. Depress the emergency brake. Raise and support the front of the vehicle safely. Remove the left front tire.
5. Remove the inner fender splash shield. Remove the two vacuum hoses from the servo assembly.
6. Remove the screws holding the servo mounting bracket to the A-pillar.
7. Remove the nuts from the actuator cable cover at the servo assembly. Remove the cable and the cover. Remove the rubber boot.
8. Remove the nuts attaching the servo assembly to the mounting bracket. Remove the servo assembly.
9. Installation is the reverse of the removal procedure.

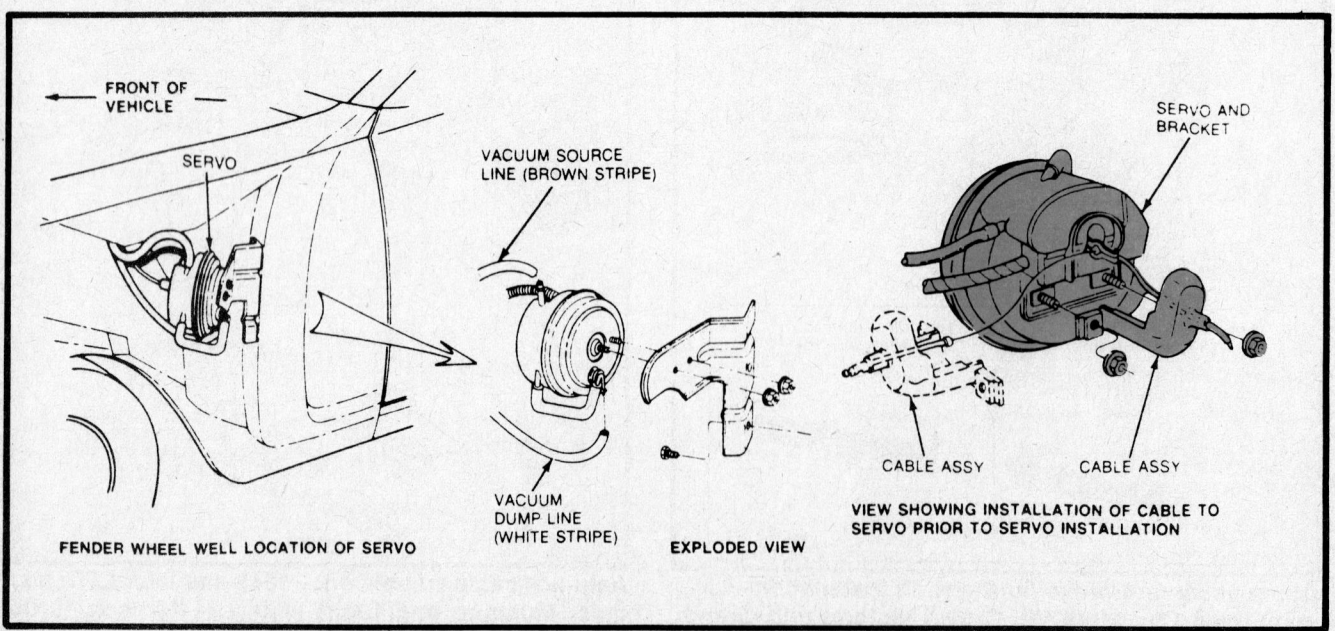

Typical servo assembly mounting except Lincoln Town Car, Mark VI, Crown Victoria and Grand Marquis

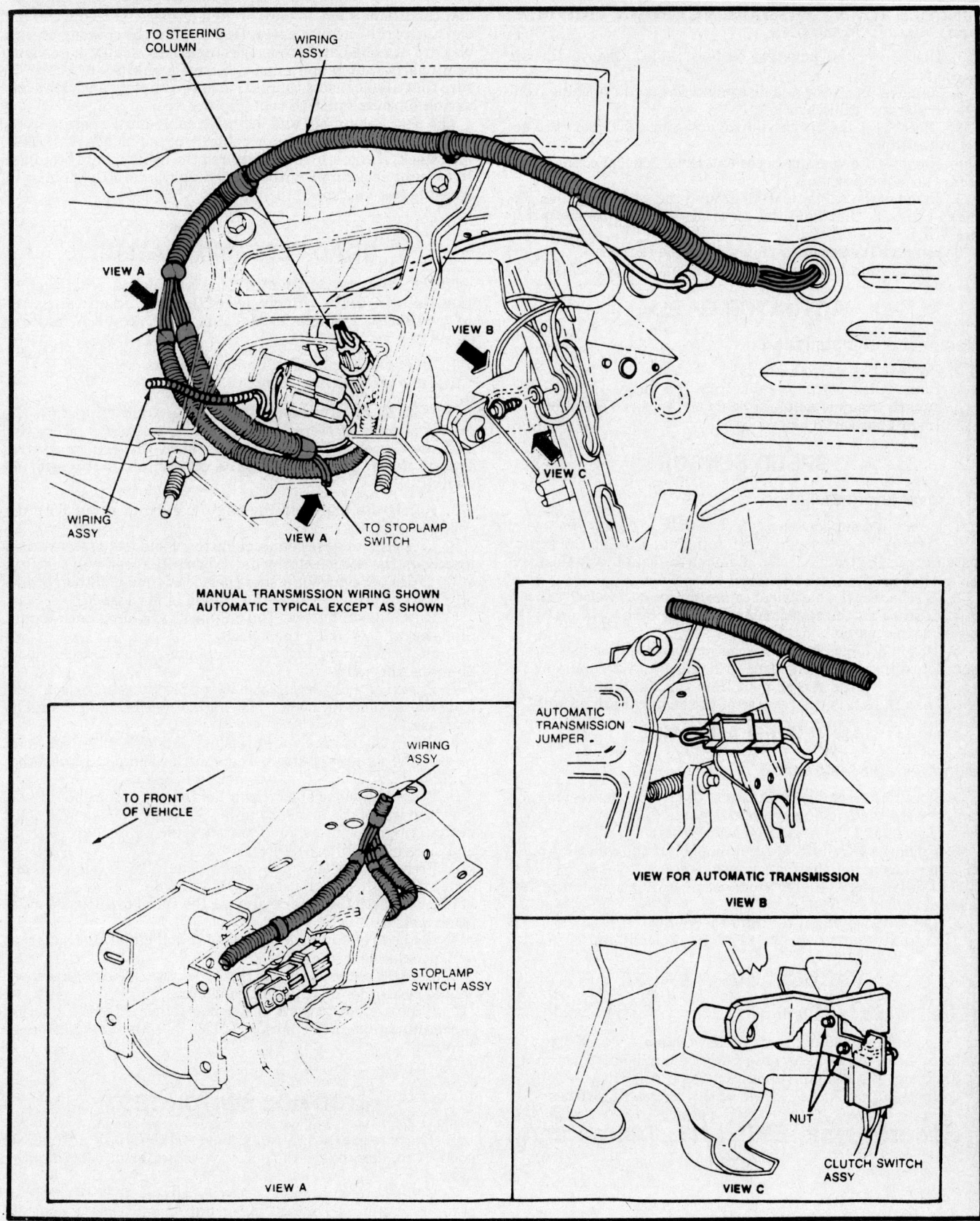

TO STEERING COLUMN

WIRING ASSY

VIEW A

VIEW B

VIEW C

WIRING ASSY

VIEW A

TO STOPLAMP SWITCH

MANUAL TRANSMISSION WIRING SHOWN
AUTOMATIC TYPICAL EXCEPT AS SHOWN

TO FRONT OF VEHICLE

WIRING ASSY

STOPLAMP SWITCH ASSY

VIEW A

AUTOMATIC TRANSMISSION JUMPER

VIEW FOR AUTOMATIC TRANSMISSION
VIEW B

NUT

CLUTCH SWITCH ASSY

VIEW C

Typical cruise control under dash wiring

LINCOLN TOWN CAR, MARK VI, CROWN VICTORIA AND GRAND MARQUIS

1. Disconnect the negative battery cable. Remove the air cleaner.
2. Remove the screw and disconnect the actuator cable from the accelerator cable bracket.
3. Disconnect the cruise control actuator cable from the accelerator cable.
4. Remove the vacuum hoses and the electrical connections from the servo assembly.
5. Remove the cable tie from around the actuator cable. Remove the nuts that hold the servo assembly to its mounting bracket.
6. Remove the servo assembly from the vehicle.
7. Installation is the reverse of the removal procedure.

ACTUATOR CABLE

Removal and Installation

1. Remove the servo assembly.
2. Remove the actuator cable from the servo.
3. Attach the new actuator cable to the servo assembly.
4. Install the servo assembly.

SPEED SENSOR

Removal and Installation

1. Raise and support the vehicle safely.
2. Loosen the speed sensor retaining nut holding the sensor assembly in the transmission. Remove the sensor and the driven gear from the transmission.
3. Disconnect the electrical connector from the speed sensor.
4. Disconnect the speedometer cable by pulling it out of the speed sensor assembly.
5. Do not attempt to remove the spring retainer clip with the speedometer cable in the sensor. Remove the driven gear retainer. Remove the driven gear from the speed sensor.
6. Installation is the reverse of the removal procedure.

AMPLIFIER ASSEMBLY

Removal and Installation

The amplifier assembly is located to the left of the steering column inside the passenger compartment.
1. Disconnect the negative battery cable.
2. Remove the amplifier retaining bolts that hold the amplifier in place under the instrument panel.
3. Disconnect the electrical connectors at the amplifier assembly.
4. Remove the amplifier from the vehicle.
5. Installation is the reverse of the removal procedure.

VACUUM DUMP VALVE

Removal and Installation

1. Disconnect the negative battery cable.
2. Remove the vacuum hose from the dump valve assembly.
3. Remove the dump valve from the bracket.
4. Installation is the reverse of the removal procedure.

Escort, Lynx, EXP, LN7, Tempo and Topaz

VISUAL INSPECTION

Before performing any tests make a visual inspection of the cruise control system. Check all items in the system for abnormal conditions such as bare broken or disconnected wires and damage to the vacuum hoses. Be sure that the speedometer cables are attached and properly routed. All vacuum hoses must be properly routed and must not have any kinks or bends. Be sure that all electrical connections are complete and tight. The wiring harness must be routed properly.

The servo assembly and actuator cable must operate freely and smoothly. The actuator cable is preadjusted, with 0.094 inch slack. If adjustment is required the cable should be adjusted as tight as possible without opening the throttle plate or increasing the idle speed.

ROAD TEST (SIMULATED)

NOTE: Before performing the simulated road test be sure that the drive wheels are of the ground and supported properly. Failure to do this may result in serious damage.

1. Start the engine. Position the selector lever in drive.
2. Turn on the cruise control.

NOTE: If at any time during the following test, the cruise control system should appear to go out of control and over speed, be prepared to shut the cruise control system down at once using the off switch or the ignition switch.

3. Accelerate and hold the engine speed at about 35 miles per hour.
4. Press the release set/accel button. Hold foot pressure very lightly on the accelerator pedal. Normally speed will continue at 35 miles per hour for a short period of time and then gradually start surging because the engine is not loaded.
5. Press the off button. The engine should drop back to idle. Stop the wheels using the brakes.
6. Press the on button. Accelerate and hold a speed of about 35 miles per hour.
7. Press the hold set/accel button. Slowly remove your foot from the accelerator pedal. The engine speed should gradually increase.
8. When the engine speed reaches about 50 miles per hour, release the set/accel button. The vehicle should maintain that engine speed for a short time before it begins to surge.
9. Press the coast button and hold. The engine should idle. Slow the wheels to about 35 miles per hour. Release the coast button. Engine speed should maintain about 35 miles per hour and surging should soon start.
10. Press and release the brake pedal. The system should shut off and the engine should slow to idle.
11. Accelerate the engine and set the speed to about 50 miles per hour.
12. Brake to about 35 miles per hour and maintain that speed using the accelerator.
13. Depress and release the resume button. The engine speed should return to about 50 miles per hour.
14. If the system does not perform as indicated make a note of the malfunction and repair or replace defective components as required.

CONTROL SWITCH TEST

1. Check to see that the main fuse and the stop lamp fuse are good. If so, disconnect the six way connector at the amplifier assembly.
2. Connect a voltmeter between circuit 57B (light blue/black) and ground. Depress the on button and check for battery voltage.
3. Connect an ohmmeter between circuit 57B (lightblue/black) and ground.

DIAGNOSIS AND TESTING PROCEDURES

1982 AND LATER ESCORT, LYNX, TEMPO, TOPAZ, LN7 AND EXP

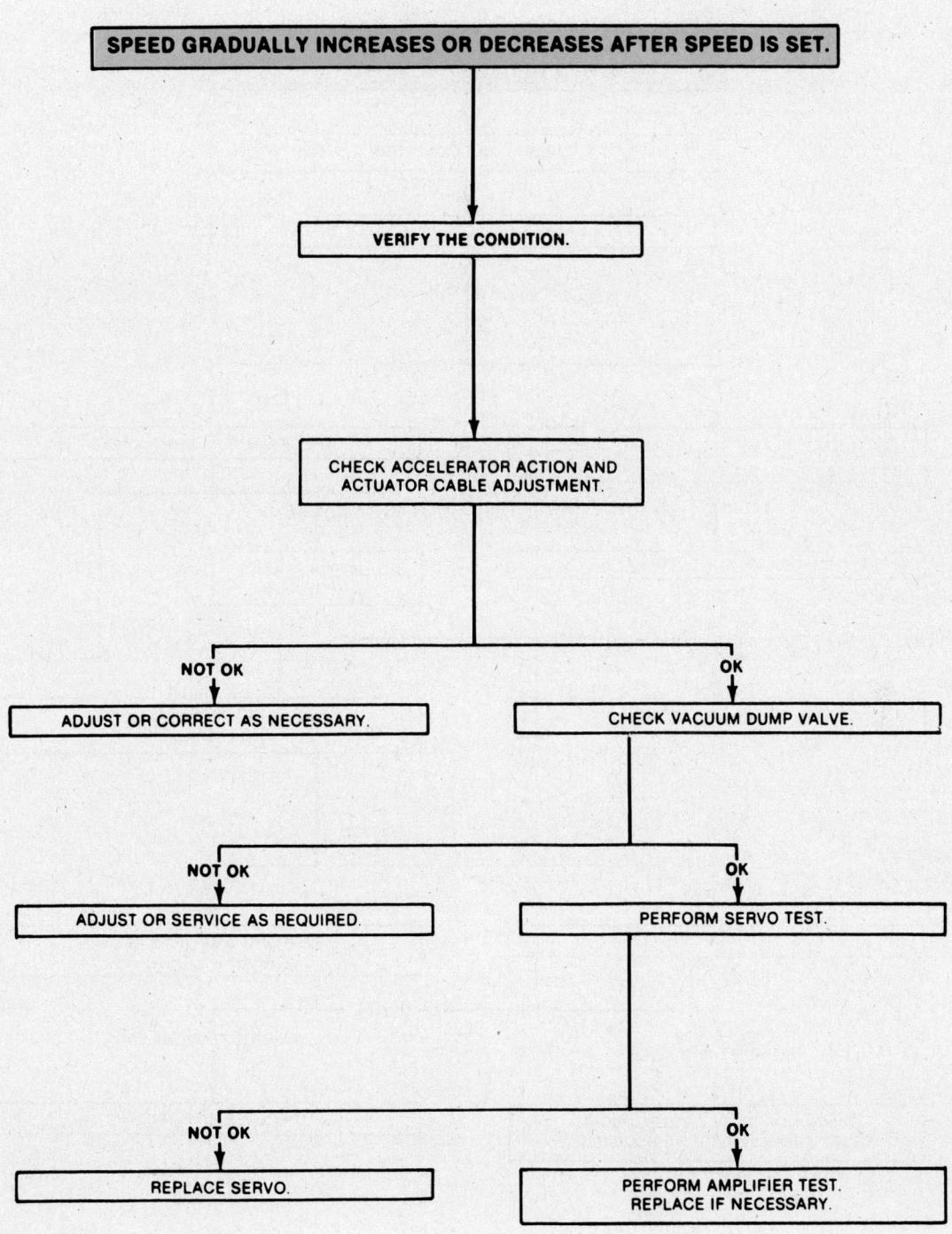

SPEED GRADUALLY INCREASES OR DECREASES AFTER SPEED IS SET.

VERIFY THE CONDITION.

CHECK ACCELERATOR ACTION AND ACTUATOR CABLE ADJUSTMENT.

NOT OK
ADJUST OR CORRECT AS NECESSARY.

OK
CHECK VACUUM DUMP VALVE.

NOT OK
ADJUST OR SERVICE AS REQUIRED.

OK
PERFORM SERVO TEST.

NOT OK
REPLACE SERVO.

OK
PERFORM AMPLIFIER TEST. REPLACE IF NECESSARY.

DIAGNOSIS AND TESTING PROCEDURES

1982 AND LATER ESCORT, LYNX, TEMPO, TOPAZ, LN7 AND EXP

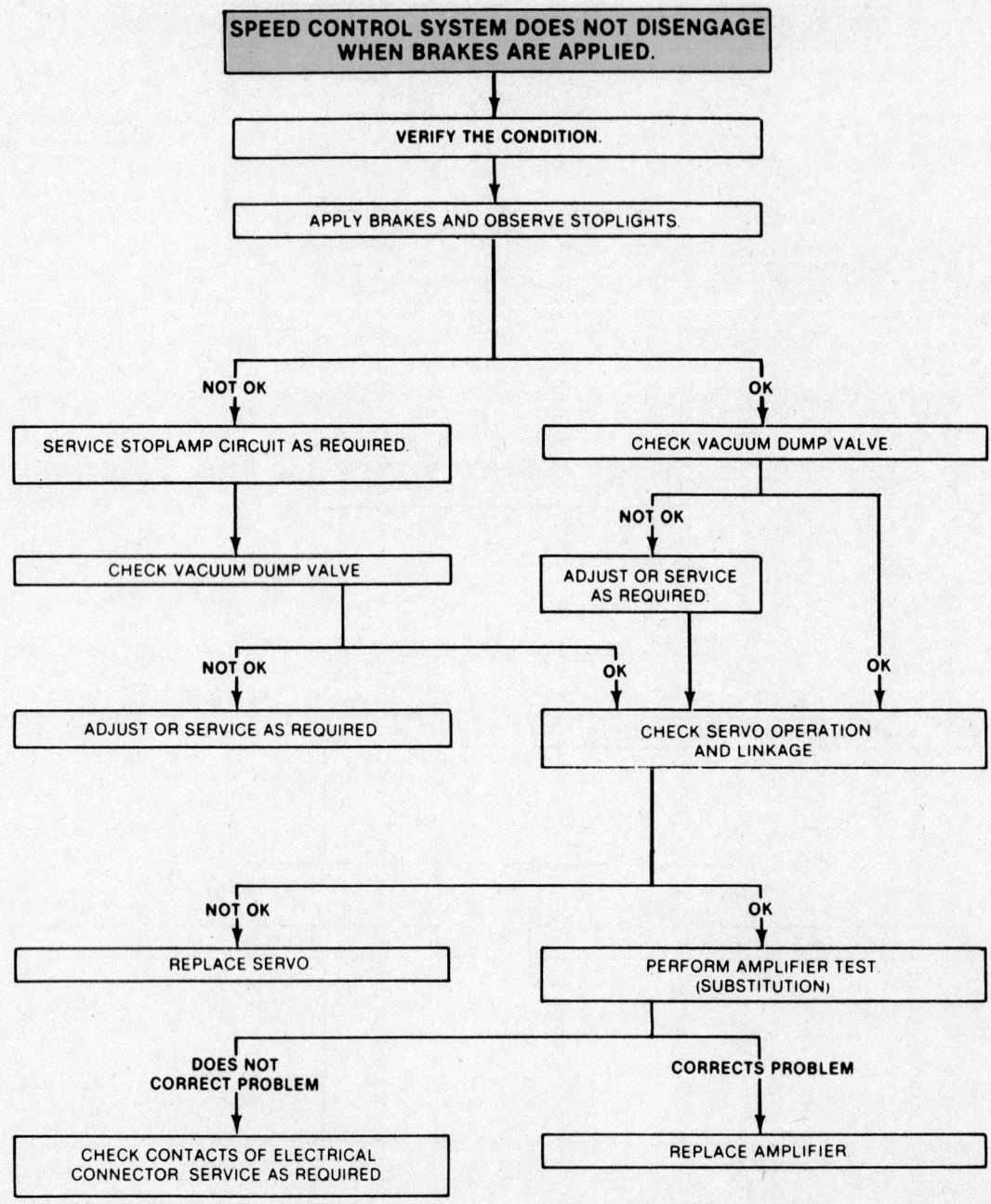

SPEED CONTROL SYSTEM DOES NOT DISENGAGE WHEN BRAKES ARE APPLIED.

VERIFY THE CONDITION.

APPLY BRAKES AND OBSERVE STOPLIGHTS.

NOT OK — SERVICE STOPLAMP CIRCUIT AS REQUIRED.

OK — CHECK VACUUM DUMP VALVE.

CHECK VACUUM DUMP VALVE

NOT OK — ADJUST OR SERVICE AS REQUIRED.

NOT OK — ADJUST OR SERVICE AS REQUIRED

OK

OK — CHECK SERVO OPERATION AND LINKAGE.

NOT OK — REPLACE SERVO

OK — PERFORM AMPLIFIER TEST. (SUBSTITUTION)

DOES NOT CORRECT PROBLEM — CHECK CONTACTS OF ELECTRICAL CONNECTOR. SERVICE AS REQUIRED.

CORRECTS PROBLEM — REPLACE AMPLIFIER.

DIAGNOSIS AND TESTING PROCEDURES

1982 AND LATER ESCORT, LYNX, TEMPO, TOPAZ, LN7 AND EXP

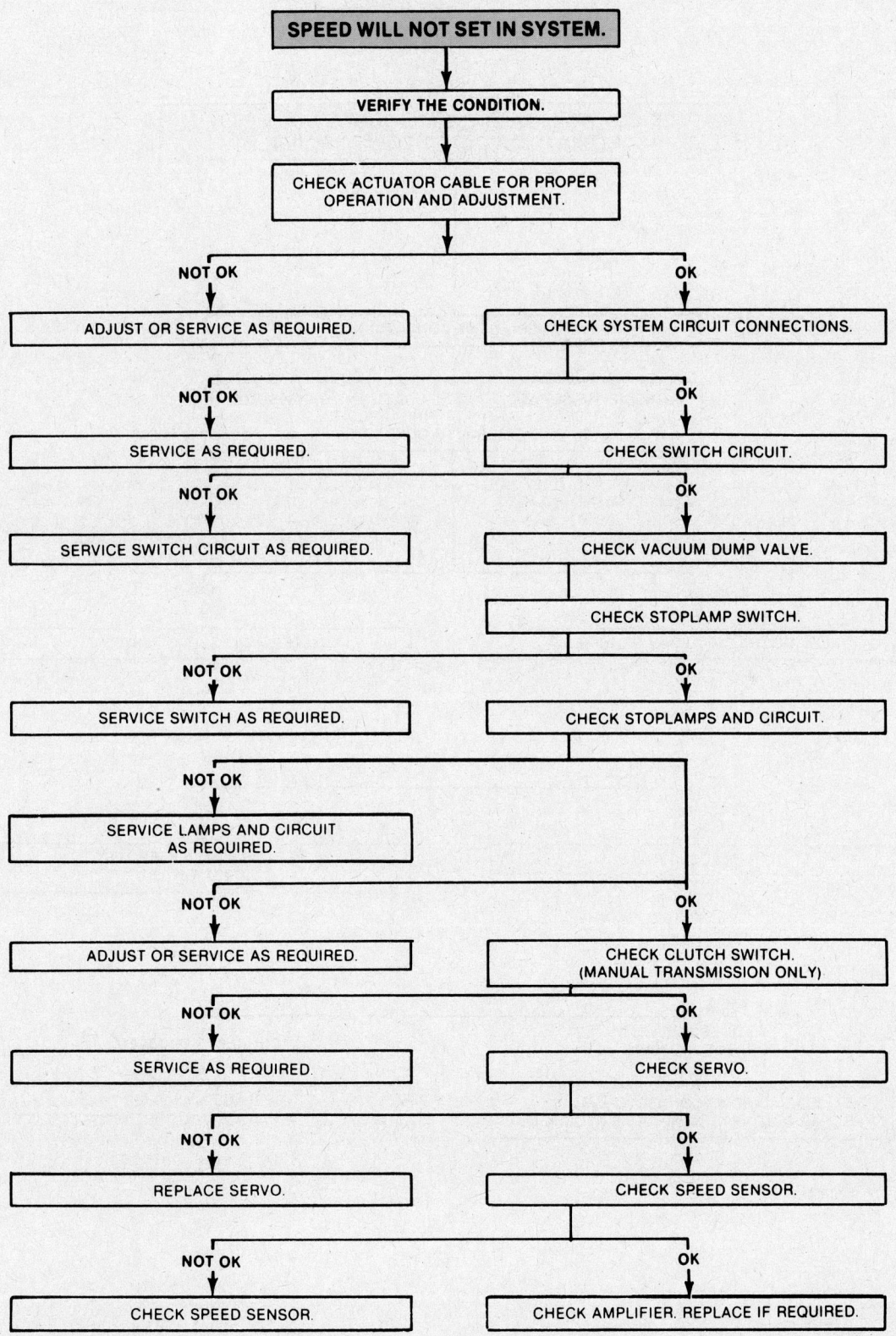

DIAGNOSIS AND TESTING PROCEDURES

1982 AND LATER ESCORT, LYNX, TEMPO, TOPAZ, LN7 AND EXP

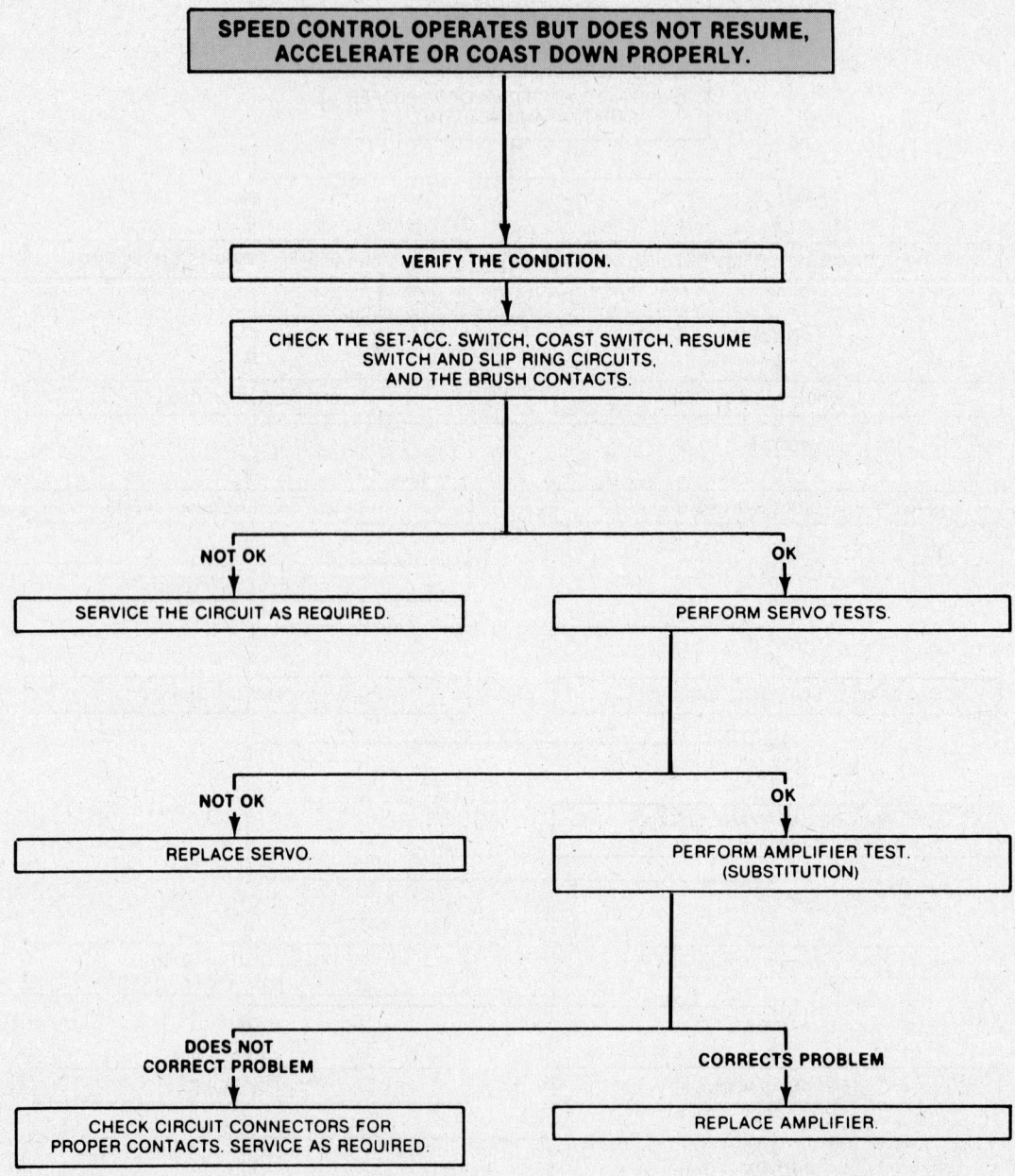

SPEED CONTROL OPERATES BUT DOES NOT RESUME, ACCELERATE OR COAST DOWN PROPERLY.

VERIFY THE CONDITION.

CHECK THE SET-ACC. SWITCH, COAST SWITCH, RESUME SWITCH AND SLIP RING CIRCUITS, AND THE BRUSH CONTACTS.

NOT OK → SERVICE THE CIRCUIT AS REQUIRED.

OK → PERFORM SERVO TESTS.

NOT OK → REPLACE SERVO.

OK → PERFORM AMPLIFIER TEST. (SUBSTITUTION)

DOES NOT CORRECT PROBLEM → CHECK CIRCUIT CONNECTORS FOR PROPER CONTACTS. SERVICE AS REQUIRED.

CORRECTS PROBLEM → REPLACE AMPLIFIER.

DIAGNOSIS AND TESTING PROCEDURES

1982 AND LATER ESCORT, LYNX, TEMPO, TOPAZ, LN7 AND EXP

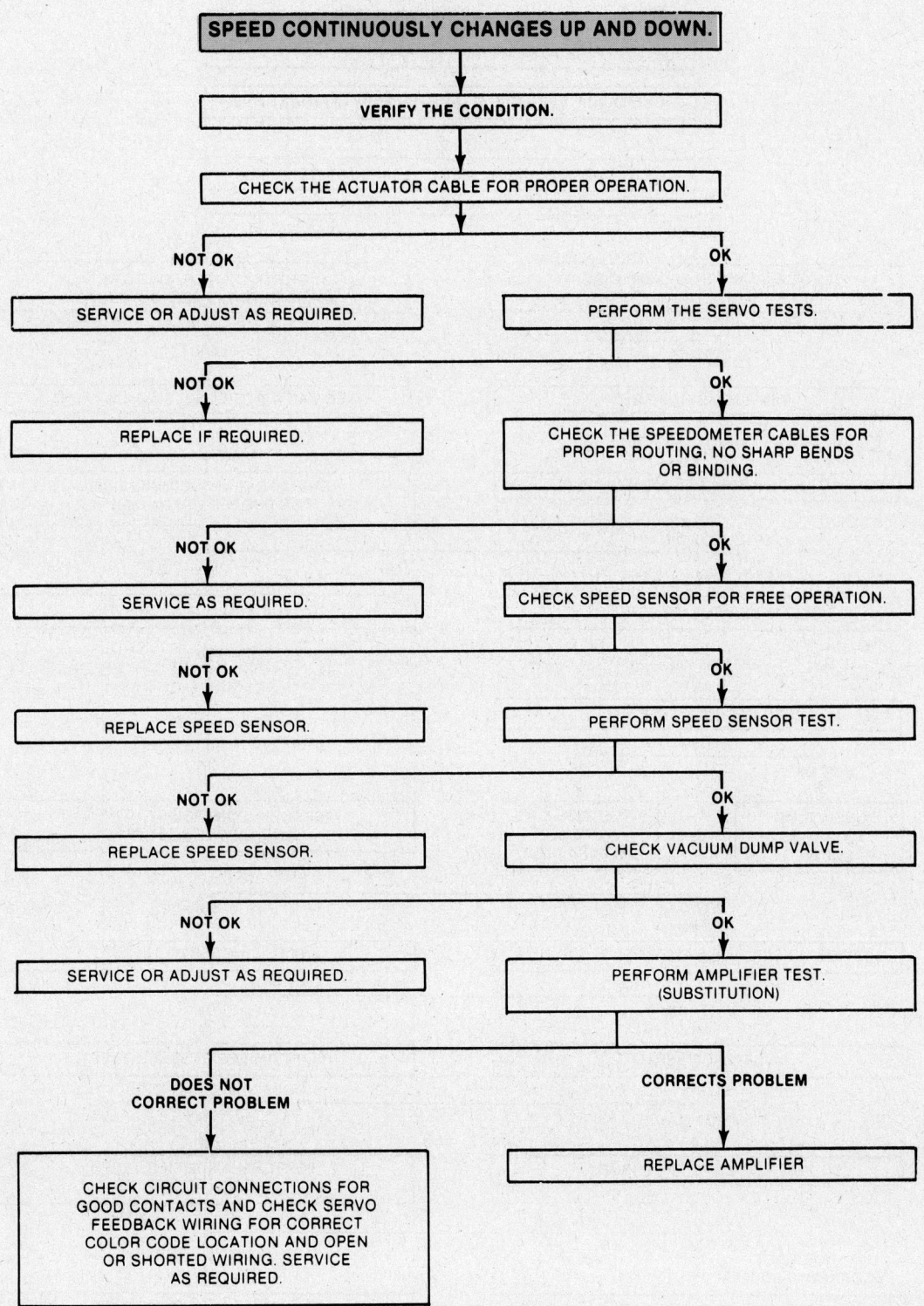

SPEED CONTINUOUSLY CHANGES UP AND DOWN.

VERIFY THE CONDITION.

CHECK THE ACTUATOR CABLE FOR PROPER OPERATION.

NOT OK → SERVICE OR ADJUST AS REQUIRED.

OK → PERFORM THE SERVO TESTS.

NOT OK → REPLACE IF REQUIRED.

OK → CHECK THE SPEEDOMETER CABLES FOR PROPER ROUTING, NO SHARP BENDS OR BINDING.

NOT OK → SERVICE AS REQUIRED.

OK → CHECK SPEED SENSOR FOR FREE OPERATION.

NOT OK → REPLACE SPEED SENSOR.

OK → PERFORM SPEED SENSOR TEST.

NOT OK → REPLACE SPEED SENSOR.

OK → CHECK VACUUM DUMP VALVE.

NOT OK → SERVICE OR ADJUST AS REQUIRED.

OK → PERFORM AMPLIFIER TEST. (SUBSTITUTION)

DOES NOT CORRECT PROBLEM → CHECK CIRCUIT CONNECTIONS FOR GOOD CONTACTS AND CHECK SERVO FEEDBACK WIRING FOR CORRECT COLOR CODE LOCATION AND OPEN OR SHORTED WIRING. SERVICE AS REQUIRED.

CORRECTS PROBLEM → REPLACE AMPLIFIER

711

DIAGNOSIS AND TESTING PROCEDURES

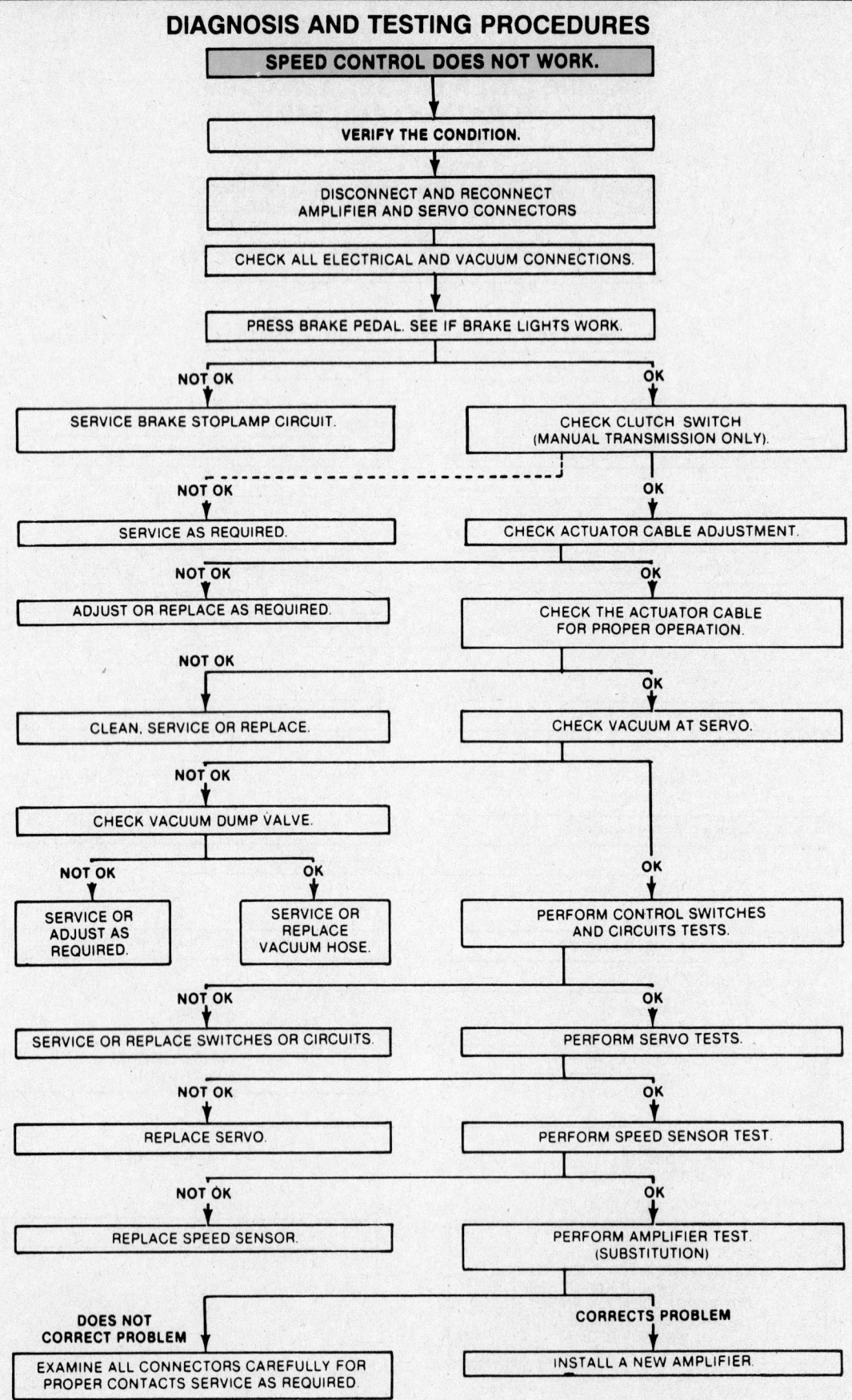

SPEED CONTROL DOES NOT WORK.

VERIFY THE CONDITION.

DISCONNECT AND RECONNECT
AMPLIFIER AND SERVO CONNECTORS

CHECK ALL ELECTRICAL AND VACUUM CONNECTIONS.

PRESS BRAKE PEDAL. SEE IF BRAKE LIGHTS WORK.

NOT OK — SERVICE BRAKE STOPLAMP CIRCUIT.

OK — CHECK CLUTCH SWITCH (MANUAL TRANSMISSION ONLY).

NOT OK — SERVICE AS REQUIRED.

OK — CHECK ACTUATOR CABLE ADJUSTMENT.

NOT OK — ADJUST OR REPLACE AS REQUIRED.

OK — CHECK THE ACTUATOR CABLE FOR PROPER OPERATION.

NOT OK — CLEAN, SERVICE OR REPLACE.

OK — CHECK VACUUM AT SERVO.

NOT OK — CHECK VACUUM DUMP VALVE.

NOT OK — SERVICE OR ADJUST AS REQUIRED.

OK — SERVICE OR REPLACE VACUUM HOSE.

OK — PERFORM CONTROL SWITCHES AND CIRCUITS TESTS.

NOT OK — SERVICE OR REPLACE SWITCHES OR CIRCUITS.

OK — PERFORM SERVO TESTS.

NOT OK — REPLACE SERVO.

OK — PERFORM SPEED SENSOR TEST.

NOT OK — REPLACE SPEED SENSOR.

OK — PERFORM AMPLIFIER TEST. (SUBSTITUTION)

DOES NOT CORRECT PROBLEM — EXAMINE ALL CONNECTORS CAREFULLY FOR PROPER CONTACTS SERVICE AS REQUIRED.

CORRECTS PROBLEM — INSTALL A NEW AMPLIFIER.

4. Rotate the steering wheel through its full range and make the following checks.

5. Depress the off button and check for a reading between 0–1 ohm. Depress the set/accel button and check for a reading between 714–646 ohms. Depress the coast button and check for a reading between 126–114 ohms. Depress the resume button and check for a reading between 2310–2090 ohms.

6. If the resistance values are not as indicated, remove the steering wheel and check the resistance at the steering wheel switch connector on the hub.

7. If the resistance values are as indicated, check switch assemblies and the ground circuit.

8. Reconnect the six way connector at the amplifier.

SPEED SENSOR TEST

1. Disconnect the connector at the speed sensor and connect an ohmmeter between the wire connector terminals and the speed sensor end.

2. The ohmmeter should read about 200 ohms. A reading of zero ohms indicates a shorted coil and the speed sensor should be replaced. A maximum reading indicates an open coil and the speed sensor should be replaced.

3. If the ohmmeter reading is about 200 ohms, and the speedometer operates properly within needle waver, the speed sensor is probably functioning properly.

4. A speed sensor of known good quality can also be substituted in place of the existing sensor to check for proper operation.

SERVO ASSEMBLY TEST

1. Separate the eight pin connector at the amplifier. Connect an ohmmeter between circuit 144 (yellow/orange) and circuit 145 (grey/black). A resistance of 40–125 ohms should be recorded.

2. Connect an ohmmeter between circuit 144 (yellow/orange) and circuit 146 (white/pink). A resistance of 60-190 ohms should be recorded.

3. If the proper reading is not obtained, check the wiring and the servo assembly separately for damage. Repair or replace defective components as required.

4. Start the engine and with the servo disconnected from the amplifier connect circuit 144 (orange/yellow) of the servo to the battery positive terminal. Connect circuit 146 (white/pink) of the servo to ground.

5. Momentarily touch circuit 145 (grey/black) of the servo to ground. The servo throttle actuator arm should pull in and the engine speed should increase.

6. The servo throttle actuator arm should hold in that position or slowly release.

7. When circuit 146 (white/pink) is removed from ground the servo throttle actuator arm should release.

8. Replace the servo assembly if it does not perform as indicated.

NOTE: If the vehicle is equipped with a diesel engine, check for vacuum supply at the servo. If vacuum is not available check the vacuum pump. If the pump is found to be defective repair or replace it as required.

9. If circuit 144 (orange/yellow) is shorted to either the circuit 146 (white/pink) or circuit 145 (grey/black) it may be necessary to replace the amplifier assembly.

AMPLIFIER TESTS

NOTE: Do not use a test lamp to perform the amplifier tests as excessive current draw will damage electronic components inside the amplifier. Use a voltmeter of 5000 ohm/volt rating or higher.

ON CIRCUIT TEST

1. Turn the ignition switch to the on position. Connect a voltmeter between circuit 296 (white/pink) and ground in the six pin connector at the amplifier.

2. The voltmeter should read battery voltage. If battery voltage is not present check the fuse voltage at the horn relay and service as required.

3. Connect the voltmeter between circuit 151 (light blue/black) and ground in the six pin connector at the amplifier.

4. The voltmeter should read battery voltage only when the on switch in the steering wheel is depressed and held.

5. If voltage is not present perform the control switch test.

6. Release the on button the voltmeter should read about 7.8 volts, this indicates that the on circuit is engaged. If the voltmeter reads zero, check for a bad ground at the amplifier.

7. If there is no ground at the amplifier check the system ground connections and wiring. Also check the number 6 and 20 amp fuse.

8. Substitute, but do not install, a known good amplifier and check for proper circuit operation.

BRAKE CIRCUIT TEST (1984 AND LATER)

1. Connect an ohmmeter between circuit 810 (brown/light green) and the six pin amplifier connector and ground. The resistance should be less than 5 ohms.

2. If the resistance is greater than indicated check for improper wiring, burned out stop lamp lights or clutch malfunction, if equipped.

HAND RELAY TEST (1984 AND LATER)

1. Connect the voltmeter between circuit 460 (yellow/light blue) of the relay and ground. The voltmeter should read battery voltage.

2. If battery voltage is not indicated check for voltage on the supply lead, circuit 1 (dark brown) for Tempo and Topaz and circuit 40 (light blue/white) for Escort and Lynx.

3. If voltage is not present replace the relay. If voltage is not available check the fuse and wiring for shorts.

OFF CIRCUIT TEST

1. With the ignition switch in the on position and the voltmeter connected between circuit 151 (light blue/black) of the six pin amplifier connector and ground depress the off switch on the steering wheel.

2. Voltage on the blue wire should drop to zero which indicates that the on circuit is not energized.

3. If voltage does not drop to zero, perform the control switch test. If the control switch checks out good install a good amplifier and recheck the off circuit.

SET ACCEL CIRCUIT TEST

1. With the ignition switch in the on position and the voltmeter connected between circuit 151 (light blue/black) of the six pin amplifier connector and ground depress and hold set/accel button on the steering wheel. The voltmeter should read about 4.5 volts.

2. Rotate the steering wheel back and forth and watch the voltmeter for fluctuations.

3. If voltage varies more than 0.5 volt perform the control switch test.

COAST CIRCUIT TEST

1. With the ignition switch in the on position and the voltmeter connected between circuit 151 (light blue/black) of the six pin amplifier connector and ground depress and hold the coast button on the steering wheel. The voltmeter should read about 1.5 volts.

2. If the circuit checks out good perform the servo assembly test. If the servo test checks out good install a new amplifier and repeat the tests. Do not substitute the amplifier until after performing the servo assembly test.

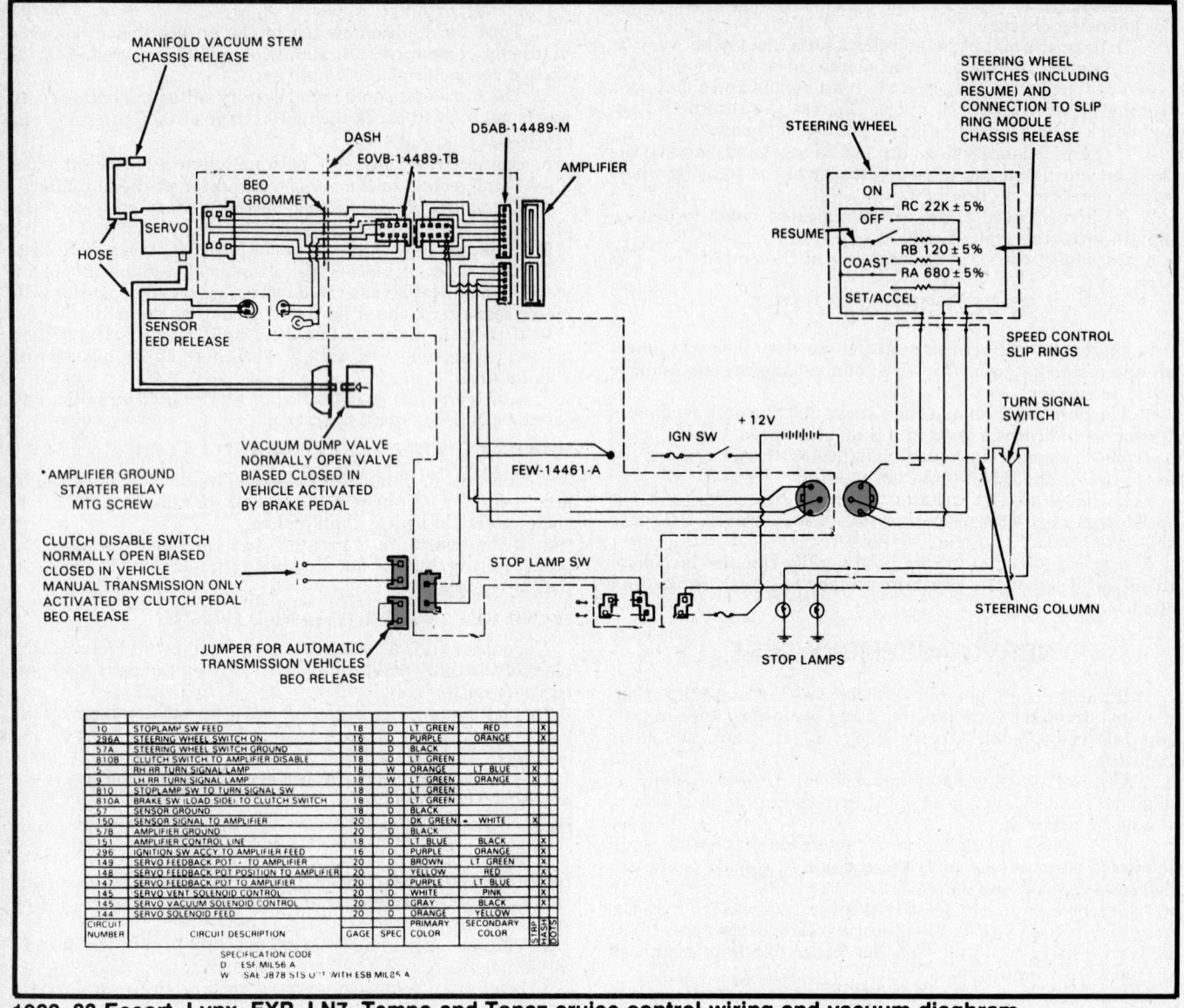

1982–83 Escort, Lynx, EXP, LN7, Tempo and Topaz cruise control wiring and vacuum diaghram

CIRCUIT NUMBER	CIRCUIT DESCRIPTION	GAGE	SPEC	PRIMARY COLOR	SECONDARY COLOR	STRP HASH DOTS
10	STOPLAMP SW FEED	18	D	LT GREEN	RED	X
296A	STEERING WHEEL SWITCH ON	16	D	PURPLE	ORANGE	X
57A	STEERING WHEEL SWITCH GROUND	18	D	BLACK		
810B	CLUTCH SWITCH TO AMPLIFIER DISABLE	18	D	LT GREEN		
5	RH RR TURN SIGNAL LAMP	18	W	ORANGE	LT BLUE	X
9	LH RR TURN SIGNAL LAMP	18	W	LT GREEN	ORANGE	X
810	STOPLAMP SW TO TURN SIGNAL SW	18	D	LT GREEN		
810A	BRAKE SW (LOAD SIDE) TO CLUTCH SWITCH	18	D	LT GREEN		
57	SENSOR GROUND	18	D	BLACK		
150	SENSOR SIGNAL TO AMPLIFIER	20	D	DK GREEN	WHITE	X
57B	AMPLIFIER GROUND	20	D	BLACK		
151	AMPLIFIER CONTROL LINE	18	D	LT BLUE	BLACK	X
296	IGNITION SW ACCY TO AMPLIFIER FEED	16	D	PURPLE	ORANGE	X
149	SERVO FEEDBACK POT + TO AMPLIFIER	20	D	BROWN	LT GREEN	X
148	SERVO FEEDBACK POT POSITION TO AMPLIFIER	20	D	YELLOW	RED	X
147	SERVO FEEDBACK POT TO AMPLIFIER	20	D	PURPLE	LT BLUE	X
145	SERVO VENT SOLENOID CONTROL	20	D	WHITE	PINK	X
145	SERVO VACUUM SOLENOID CONTROL	20	D	GRAY	BLACK	X
144	SERVO SOLENOID FEED	20	D	ORANGE	YELLOW	

SPECIFICATION CODE
D   ESF MIL56 A
W   SAE J878 STS O T WITH ESB MIL85 A

RESUME CIRCUIT TEST

1. With the ignition switch in the on position and the voltmeter connected between circuit 151 (light blue/black) of the six pin amplifier connector and ground depress and hold the resume button on the steering wheel. The voltmeter should read about 6.5 volts.

2. If the circuit checks out good perform the servo assembly test. If the servo test checks out good install a new amplifier and repeat the tests. Do not substitute the amplifier until after performing the servo assembly test.

BRAKE LIGHT SWITCH AND CIRCUIT TEST

This test is performed when brake pedal application will not disconnect the cruise control system.

1. Check the break light operation with maximum brake pedal effort of about six pounds. If more than about six pounds is required, check the brake actuation of the brake light switch. Repair or replace defective components as required.

2. If the brake light do not work check the fuse, bulbs and the switch. Repair or replace defective components as required.

3. If the brake lights are working properly check for battery voltage at circuit 296 (white/pink) wires at the six pin electrical connector.

4. Depress the brake pedal until the tail lamps light. Check voltage on circuit 810 (brown/light green) at the six pin electrical connector.

5. The difference between the two voltage readings should not exceed 1.5 volts. If the reading is higher, the resistance in the brake light circuit must be found and repaired.

6. There should be no voltage present at circuit 810 (red/light green) with the brake lights off.

Perform the vacuum dump valve test.

VACUUM DUMP VALVE TEST

The vacuum dump valve releases vacuum in the servo assembly whenever the brake pedal is depressed and thus acts as a redundant safety feature. The vacuum dump valve should be

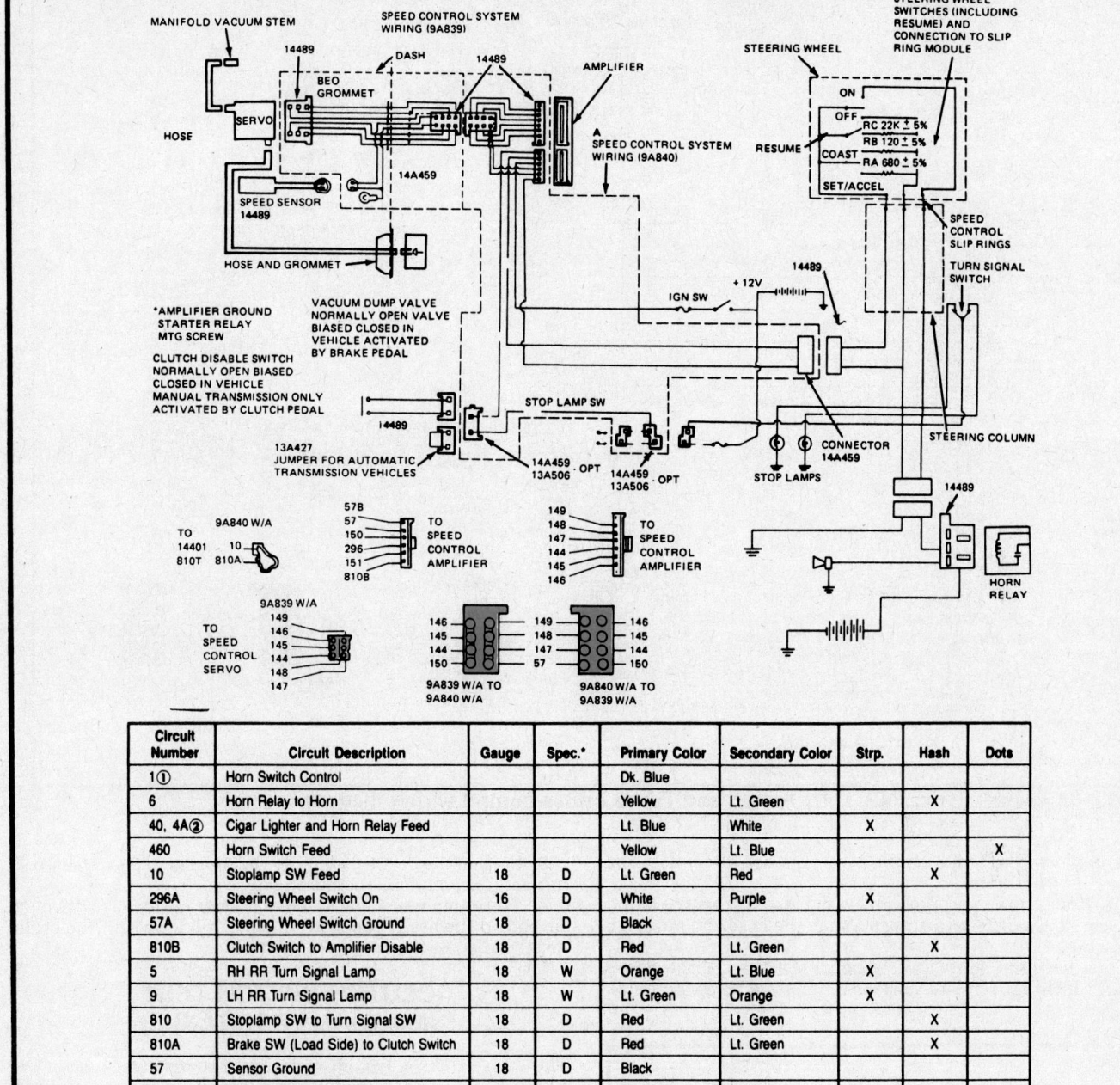

Circuit Number	Circuit Description	Gauge	Spec.*	Primary Color	Secondary Color	Strp.	Hash	Dots
1 ①	Horn Switch Control			Dk. Blue				
6	Horn Relay to Horn			Yellow	Lt. Green		X	
40, 4A ②	Cigar Lighter and Horn Relay Feed			Lt. Blue	White	X		
460	Horn Switch Feed			Yellow	Lt. Blue			X
10	Stoplamp SW Feed	18	D	Lt. Green	Red		X	
296A	Steering Wheel Switch On	16	D	White	Purple	X		
57A	Steering Wheel Switch Ground	18	D	Black				
810B	Clutch Switch to Amplifier Disable	18	D	Red	Lt. Green		X	
5	RH RR Turn Signal Lamp	18	W	Orange	Lt. Blue	X		
9	LH RR Turn Signal Lamp	18	W	Lt. Green	Orange	X		
810	Stoplamp SW to Turn Signal SW	18	D	Red	Lt. Green		X	
810A	Brake SW (Load Side) to Clutch Switch	18	D	Red	Lt. Green		X	
57	Sensor Ground	18	D	Black				
150	Sensor Signal to Amplifier	20	D	Dk. Green	White	X		
57B	Amplifier Ground	20	D	Black				
151	Amplifier Control Line	18	D	Lt. Blue	Black		X	
296	Ignition SW Accy. to Amplifier Feed	16	D	White	Purple	X		
149	Servo Feedback Pot to Amplifier	20	D	Brown	Lt. Green		X	
148	Servo Feedback Pot Position to Amplifier	20	D	Yellow	Red		X	
147	Servo Feedback Pot to Amplifier	20	D	Purple	Lt. Blue		X	
145	Servo Vent Solenoid Control	20	D	White	Pink		X	
145	Servo Vacuum Solenoid Control	20	D	Gray	Black		X	
144	Servo Solenoid Feed	20	D	Orange	Yellow			

*SPECIFICATION CODE
D   ESF-MIL56-A
W   SAE J878 STS Opt with ESB-MIL85-A
① Tempo/Topaz only.
② Escort/Lynx, EXP only.

1984 and later Escort, Lynx, EXP, LN7, Tempo and Topaz cruise control wiring and vacuum diaphragm

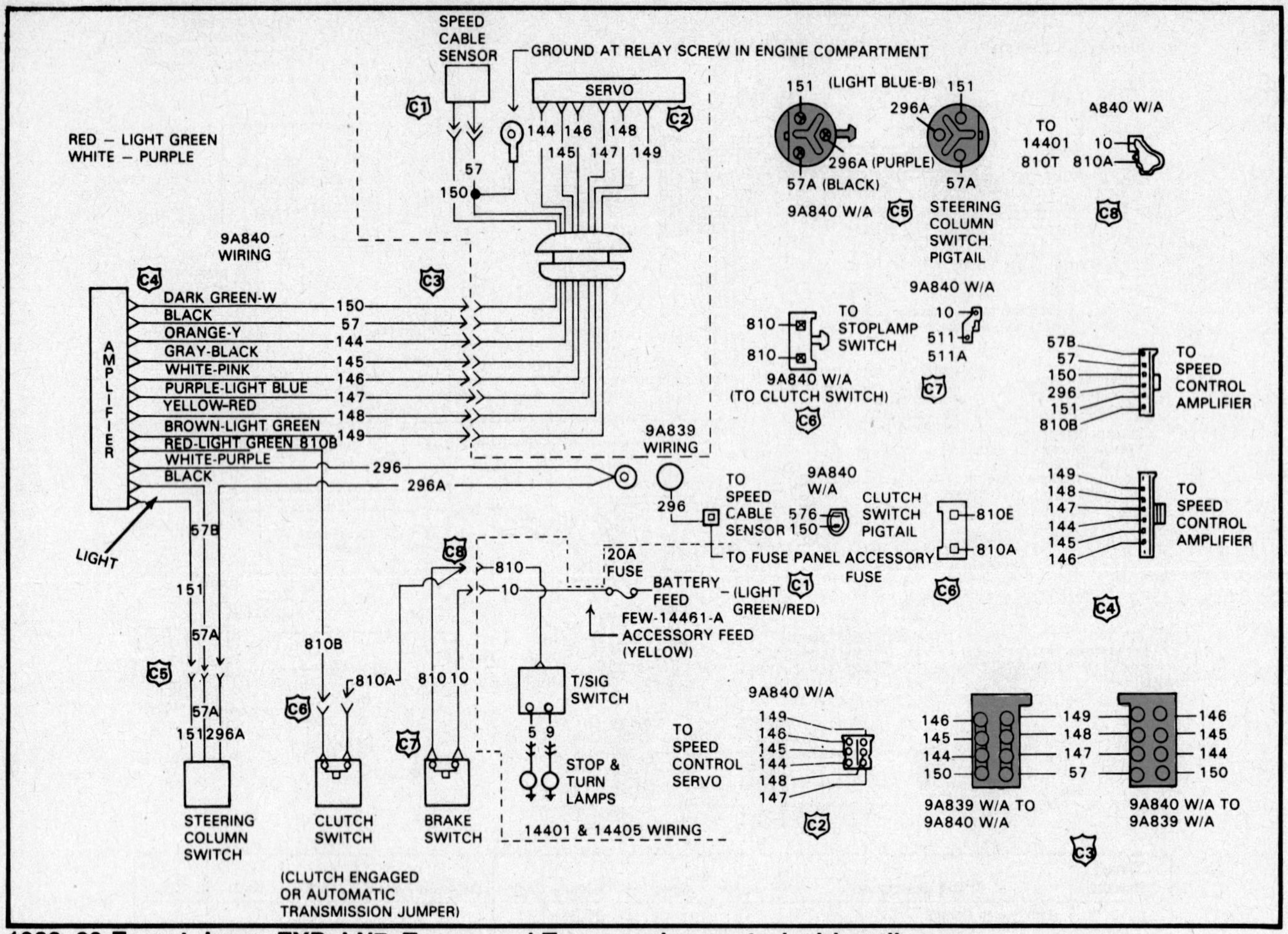

1982–83 Escort, Lynx, EXP, LN7, Tempo and Topaz cruise control wiring diagram

checked whenever brake application does not disconnect the cruise control system.

1. Disconnect the vacuum hose (white stripe) from the dump valve servo. Connect a vacuum pump to the hose and pump up the vacuum.

2. If a vacuum cannot be obtained, the hose or the dump valve is leaking. Replace or repair defective components as required.

3. Step on the brake pedal, the vacuum should be released. If not adjust or replace the dump valve.

4. The dump valve black housing must clear the white plastic pad on the brake pedal by 0.050–0.100 inch with the brake pedal pulled to the rearmost position.

CLUTCH SWITCH TEST (MANUAL TRANSAXLE)

The cruise control system is designed to disengage when the clutch pedal is depressed. This is accomplished via a clutch switch. The cruise control system disengage function is operated by opening the circuit between the cruise control module and the brake lamps. This prevents engine over speed when the clutch is depressed and the cruise control system is engaged.

The disengagement switch is a plunger switch that operates when the clutch pedal is depressed and the pedal moves away from the switch plunger. The switch is adjustable and attaches to a mounting bracket on the clutch module assembly.

NOTE: Do not use a test light to perform the clutch switch test, as the light cannot properly indicate the condition of the switch. Do not use a strong magnet near the clutch switch, as it can be affected by magnetic fields

1. Disconnect the clutch pigtail connector from the cruise control harness connector. Connect an ohmmeter to the two switch connector terminals.

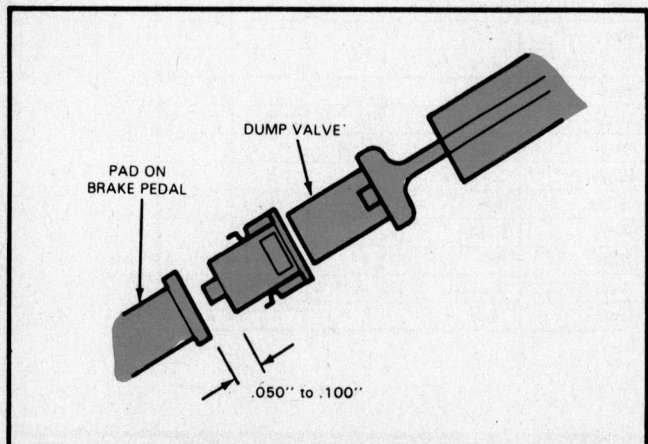

Dump valve location and adjustment–Escort, Lynx, EXP, LN7, Tempo and Topaz

2. With the clutch pedal in the full up position, resistance should be less than five ohms.

3. With the clutch pedal depressed, the circuit should be open.

4. If the switch does not perform as indicated, it must be replaced.

SHORTING PLUG TEST (AUTOMATIC TRANSAXLE)

Vehicles equipped with automatic transaxle use a shorting plug instead of a clutch switch to regulate the cruise control system operation.

ACTUATOR CABLE ADJUSTMENT

ESCORT, LYNX, EXP AND LN7

1. Remove the cable retaining clip.
2. Disengage the throttle positioner. Set the carburetor at hot idle.
3. Pull on the actuator cable end tube in order to take up any slack. Maintain a tight tension on the cable.
4. While holding the cable, insert the cable retaining clip and snap it securely.

TEMPO AND TOPAZ

1. With the engine off, set the throttle linkage so that the throttle plate is closed and the choke linkage is de-cammed.
2. Remove the locking pin. Pull the bead chain through the adjuster.
3. Insert the locking pin in the best hole of the adjuster for tight bead chain without opening the throttle plate.

VACUUM DUMP VALVE ADJUSTMENT

1. Depress the brake pedal and hold it in that position.
2. Push in the dump valve until the valve collar bottoms against the retaining clip.
3. Position a 0.050–0.10 inch shim between the white button of the valve and the pad on the brake pedal.
4. Firmly pull the brake pedal rearward to its normal position, allowing the dump valve to ratchet backwards in the retaining clip.

CLUTCH SWITCH ADJUSTMENT (MANUAL TRANSAXLE)

1. Prop the clutch pedal in the full up position.
2. Loosen the clutch switch mounting screw.
3. Slide the switch forward toward the clutch pedal until the switch plunger cap is 0.030 inch from contacting the switch housing. Tighten the attaching screw.
4. Remove the prop from the clutch pedal. Test drive the vehicle for clutch switch cancellation of the cruise control system.

Component Replacement — Escort, Lynx, EXP, LN7, Tempo and Topaz

CRUISE CONTROL SWITCH

Removal and Installation

1982–85

1. Disconnect the negative battery cable.
2. Remove the stering wheel hub cover by lifting lightly on the outside edges. Do not pry with a sharp instrument.
3. Remove and discard the steering wheel attaching nut. Remove the steering wheel.

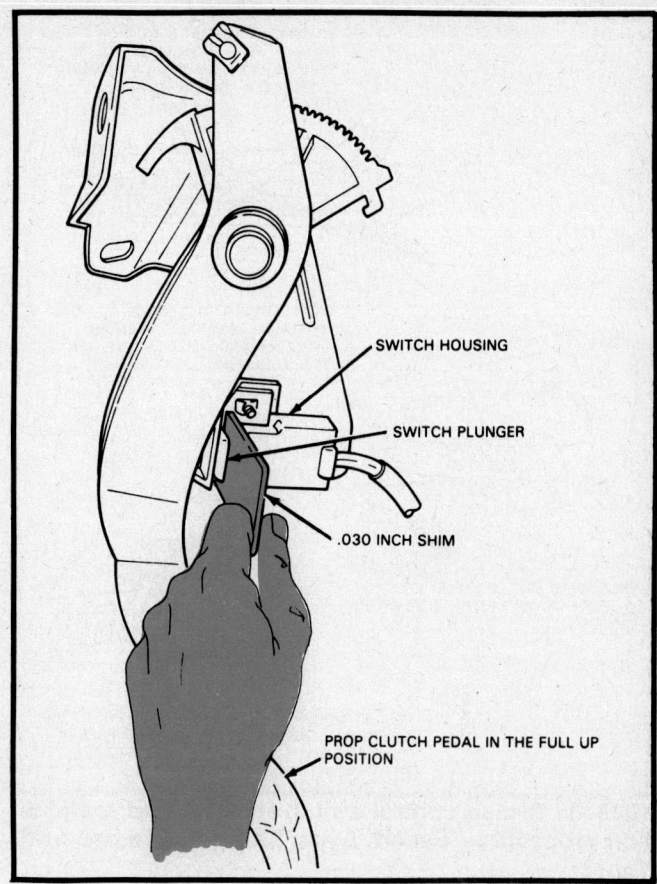

Clutch switch adjustment — Escort, Lynx, EXP, LN7, Tempo and Topaz

4. Remove the steering wheel to back cover and separate the control switch connector from the terminal on the cover.
5. Remove the cruise control switch assembly.
6. Installation is the reverse of the removal procedure.

1986 AND LATER

1. Disconnect the negative battery cable.
2. Remove the steering wheel pad cover. Remove the foam insert.
3. Disconnect the wiring connector from the steering wheel.
4. Disconnect the two horn wire connectors from the steering wheel pad cover.
5. Remove the cruise control switches from the steering wheel pad cover.
6. Installation is the reverse of the removal procedure.

GROUND BRUSH

Removal and Installation

1. Disconnect the negative battery cable. Remove the steering wheel horn pad. Remove and discard the steering wheel attaching nut. Remove the steering wheel.
2. Remove the steering column lower trim shroud.
3. Remove the straps securing the brush assembly wire at the ignition switch and column tube.
4. Separate the cruise control brush wire harness at the connector.
5. Remove the screw securing the brush assembly to the upper bearing retainer plate.
6. Remove the brush assembly wire and connector assembly through the opening in the upper bearing retainer plate.

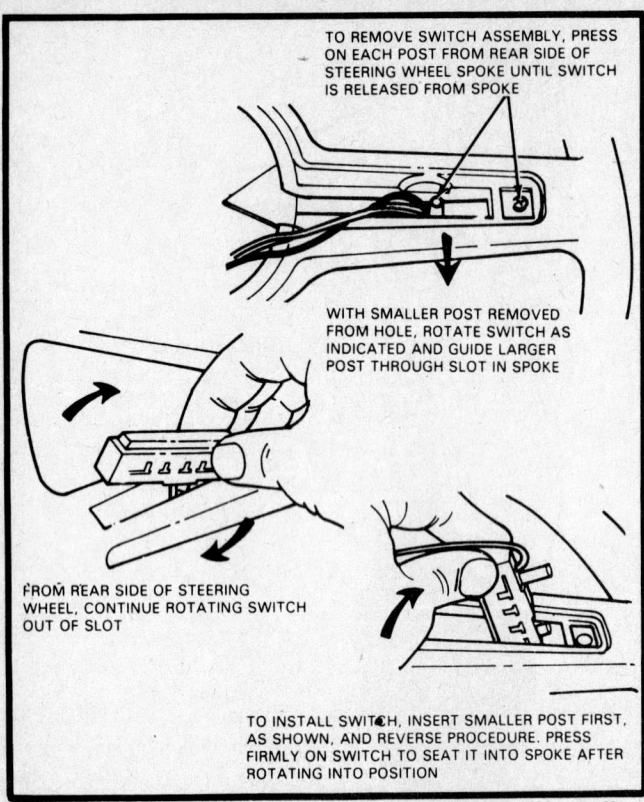

1982–85 Cruise control switch removal and installation procedure—Escort, Lynx, EXP, LN7, Tempo and Topaz

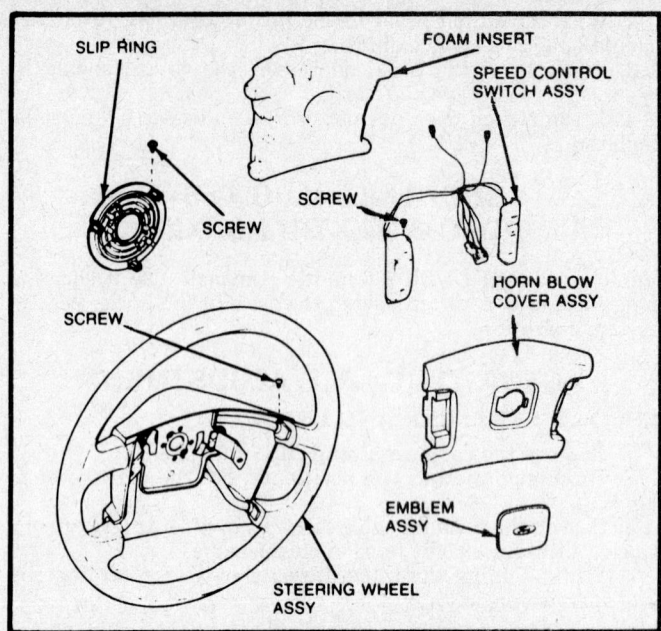

1986 and later cruise control switch assembly—Escort, Lynx, EXP, LN7, Tempo and Topaz

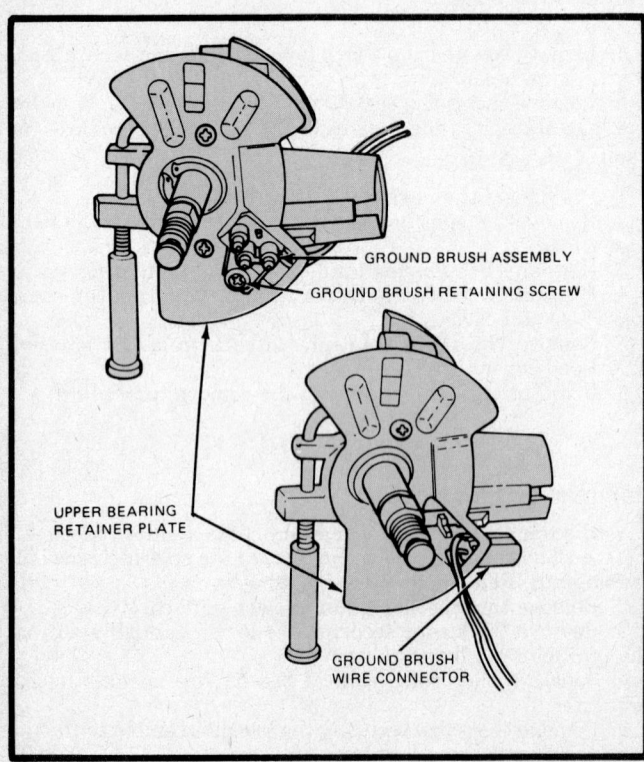

Ground brush assembly—Escort, Lynx, EXP, LN7, Tempo and Topaz

7. Installation is the reverse of the removal procedure. Install a new steering wheel bolt and torque 30 to 35 ft. lbs.

CRUISE CONTROL SERVO

Removal and Installation
ESCORT, LYNX, EXP AND LN7

1. Disconnect the negative battery cable. Remove the air cleaner assembly.
2. Remove the push pin and disconnect the cruise control actuator cable from the accelerator cable bracket.
3. Disconnect the cruise control actuator cable with the adjuster from the accelerator cable.
4. Remove the vacuum hoses from the servo assembly. Remove the electrical connections from the servo assembly.
5. Remove the nuts holding the servo assembly to its mounting bracket.
6. Remove the servo and the cable assembly. Remove the nuts holding the cable cover to the servo assembly. Pull off the cover and remove the cable assembly.
7. Installation is the reverse of the removal procedure.

TEMPO AND TOPAZ

1. Disconnect the negative battery cable.
2. Remove the screw and disconnect the cruise control actuator cable from the accelerator cable bracket.
3. Disconnect the cruise control actuator cable with the adjuster, from the accelerator cable.
4. Remove the vacuum hoses from the servo assembly. Disconnect the electrical connections from the servo assembly.
5. Remove the nuts holding the servo assembly to its mounting bracket.
6. Remove the servo and the cable assembly. Remove the nuts holding the cable cover to the servo assembly. Pull off the cover and remove the cable assembly.
7. Installation is the reverse of the removal procedure.

ACTUATOR CABLE

Removal and Installation

1. Remove the servo assembly.
2. Remove the actuator cable from the servo.
3. Attach the new actuator cable to the servo assembly.
4. Install the servo assembly.

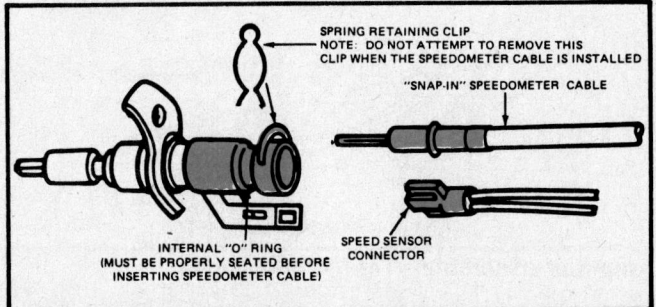

Speed sensor installation—Escort, Lynx, EXP, LN7, Tempo and Topaz

SPEED SENSOR

Removal and Installation

1. Raise and support the vehicle safely.
2. Loosen the speed sensor retaining nut holding the sensor assembly in the transaxle.
3. Disconnect the electrical connector from the speed sensor.
4. Disconnect the speedometer cable by pulling it out of the speed sensor assembly.

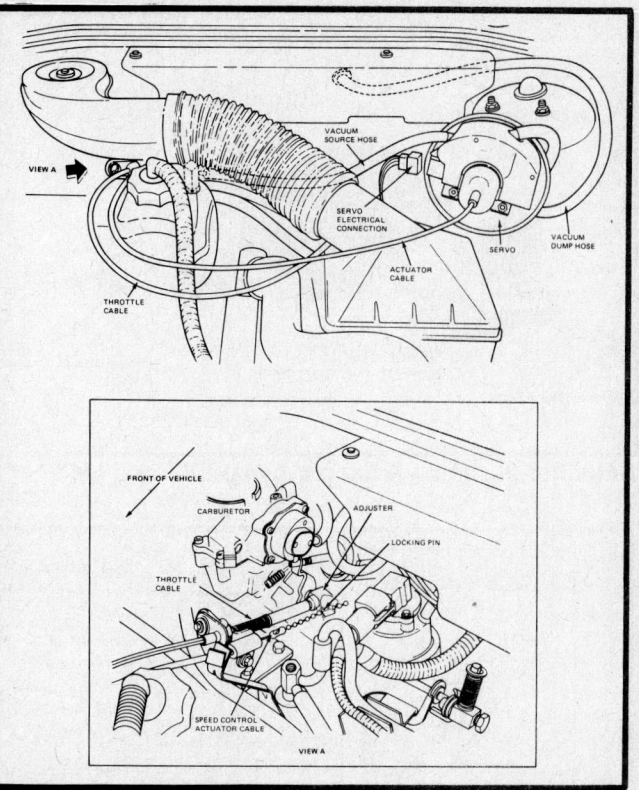

Cruise control assembly—Tempo and Topaz with gas engine

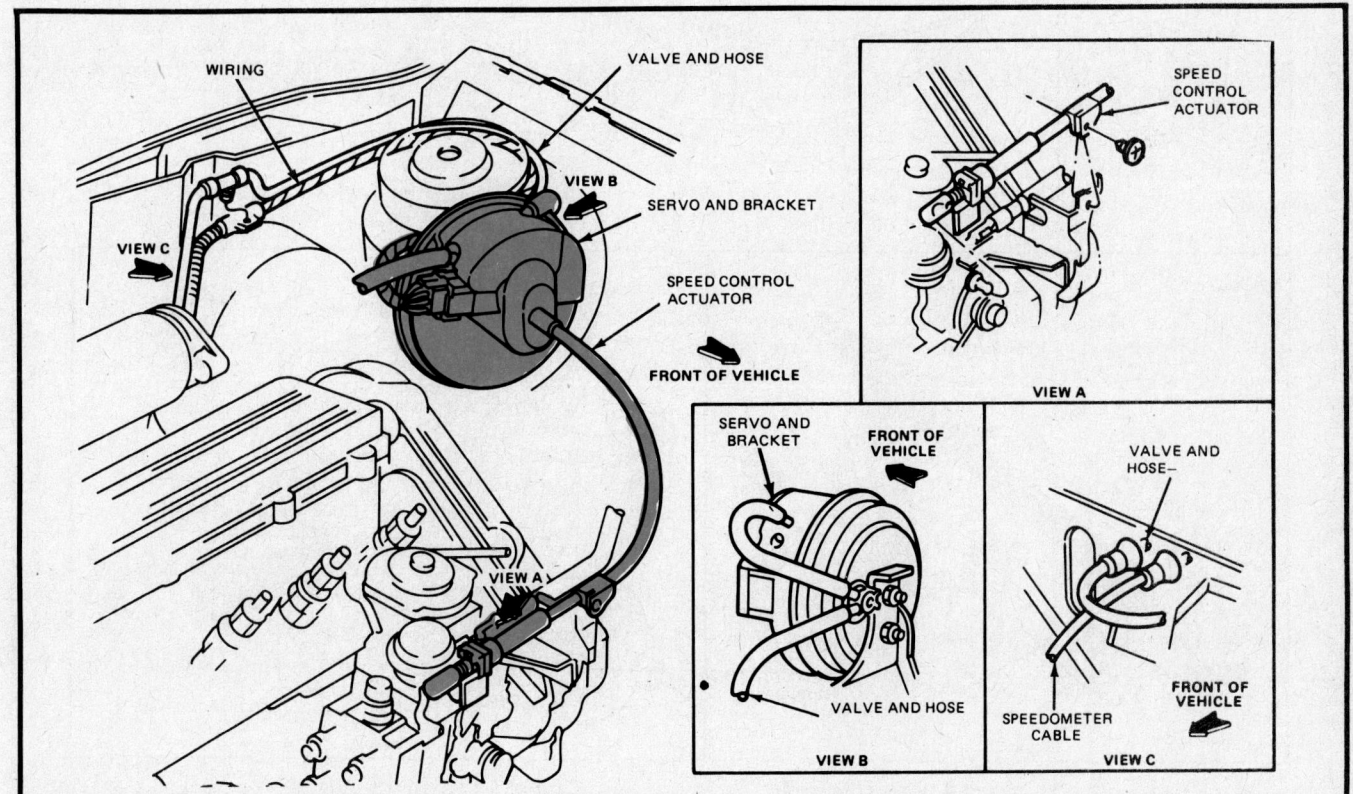

Cruise control assembly—Escort, Lynx, EXP, LN7, Tempo and Topaz with diesel engine

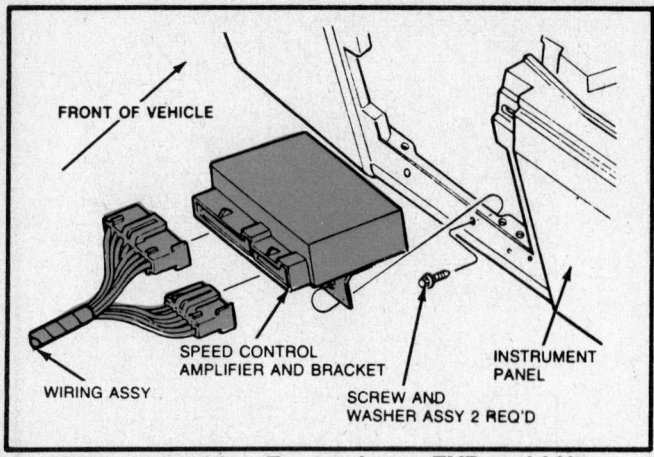

Amplifier assembly—Escort, Lynx, EXP and LN7

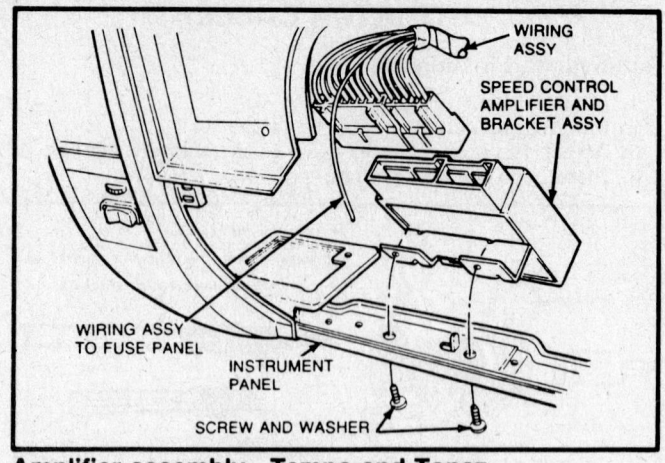

Amplifier assembly—Tempo and Topaz

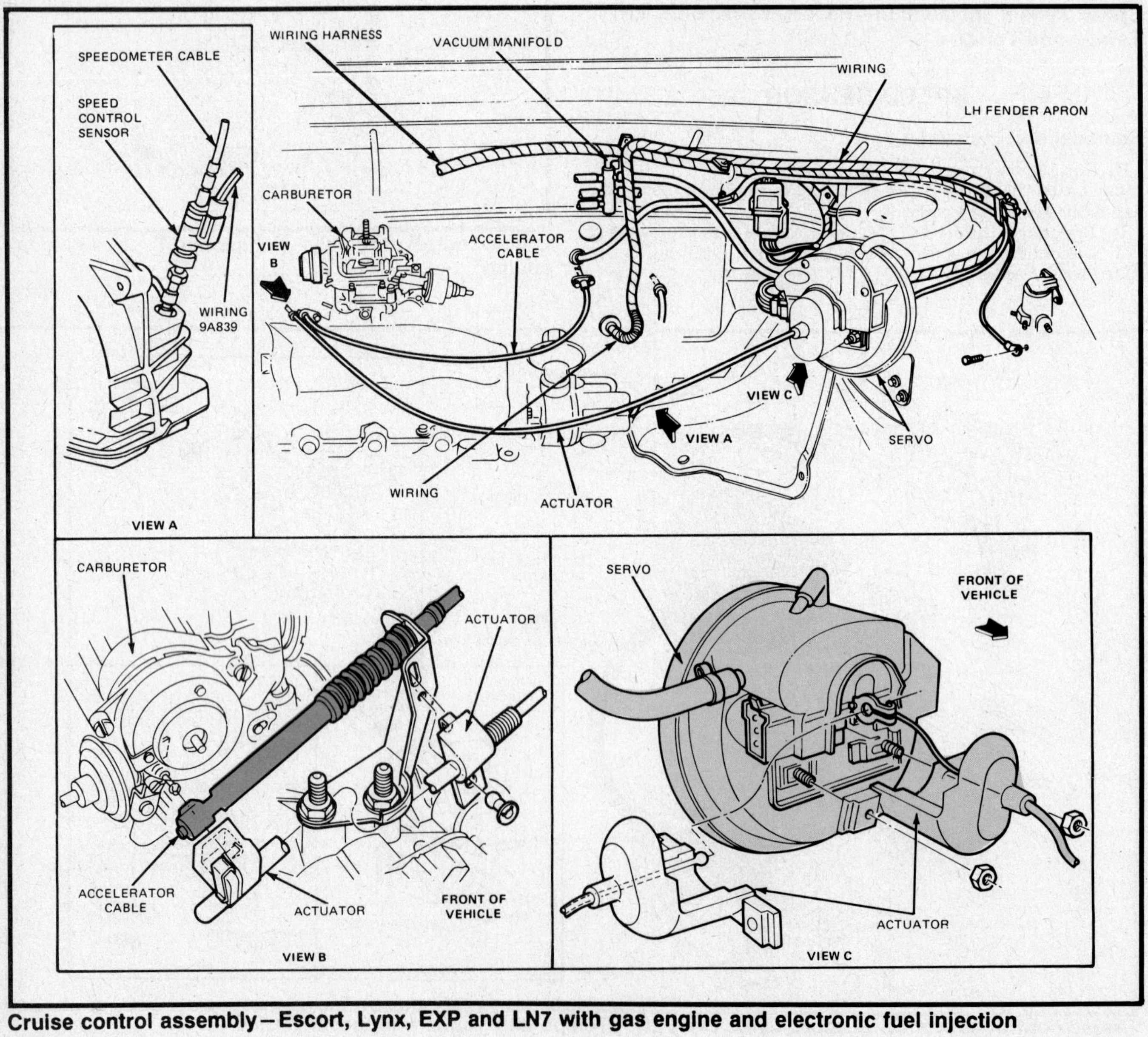

Cruise control assembly—Escort, Lynx, EXP and LN7 with gas engine and electronic fuel injection

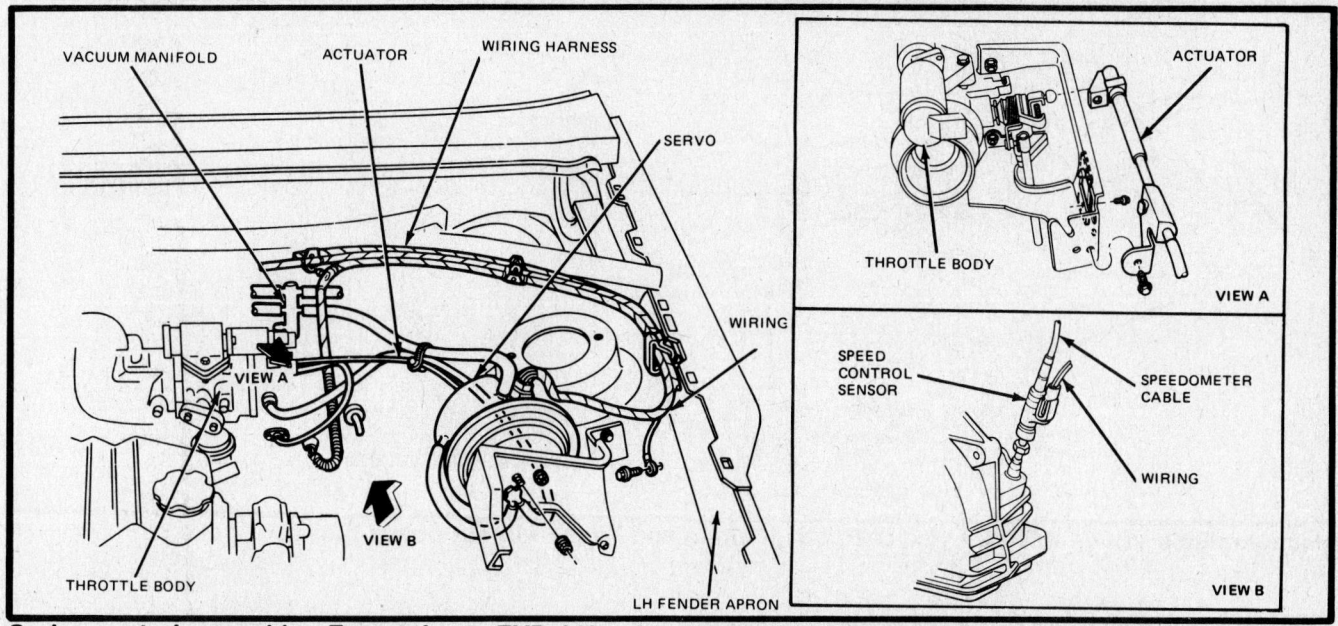

Cruise control assembly—Escort, Lynx, EXP, LN7 with gas engine and electronic fuel injection

5. Do not attempt to remove the spring retainer clip with the speedometer cable in the sensor.
6. Installation is the reverse of the removal procedure.

AMPLIFIER ASSEMBLY

Removal and Installation

1. Disconnect the negative battery cable.
2. Remove the amplifier retaining bolts that hold the amplifier in place under the instrument panel.
3. Disconnect the electrical connectors at the amplifier assembly.
4. Remove the amplifier from the vehicle.
5. Installation is the reverse of the removal procedure.

VACUUM DUMP VALVE

Removal and Installation

1. Disconnect the negative battery cable.
2. Remove the vacuum hose from the dump valve assembly.
3. Remove the dump valve from the bracket.
4. Installation is the reverse of the removal procedure.

CLUTCH SWITCH (MANUAL TRANSAXLE)

Removal and Installation

1. Disconnect the negative battery cable.
2. Remove the clutch switch bracket mounting screw.

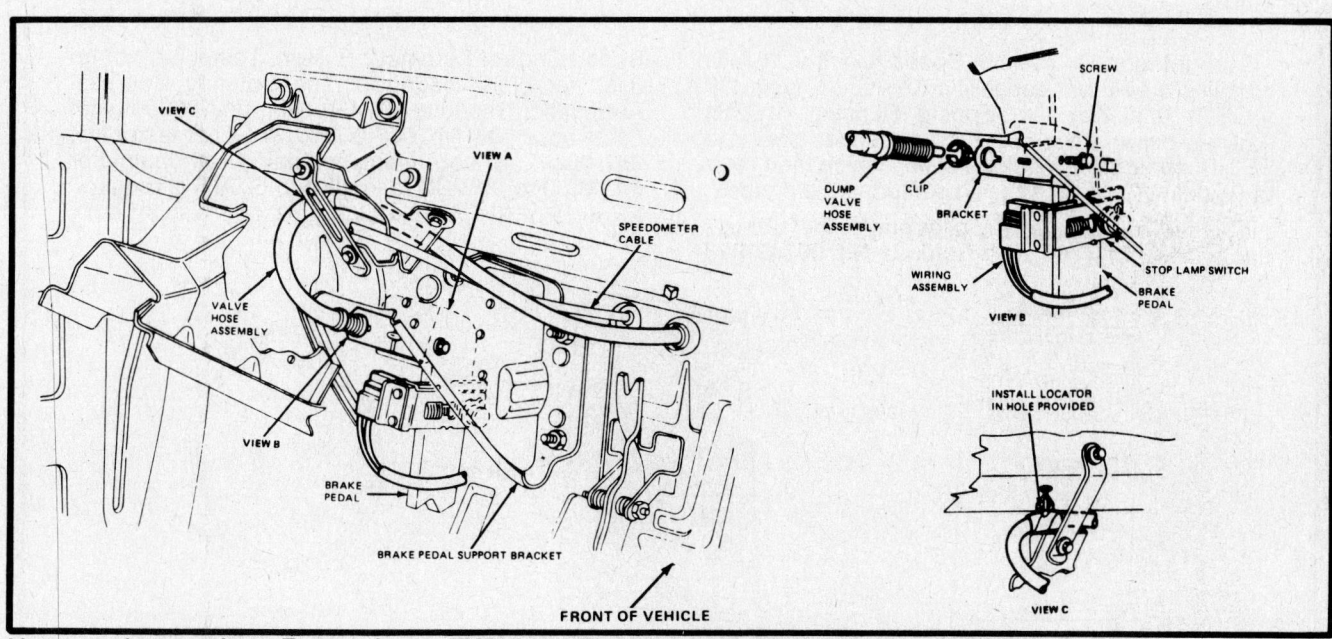

Vacuum dump valve—Escort, Lynx, EXP, LN7, Tempo and Topaz with power brakes

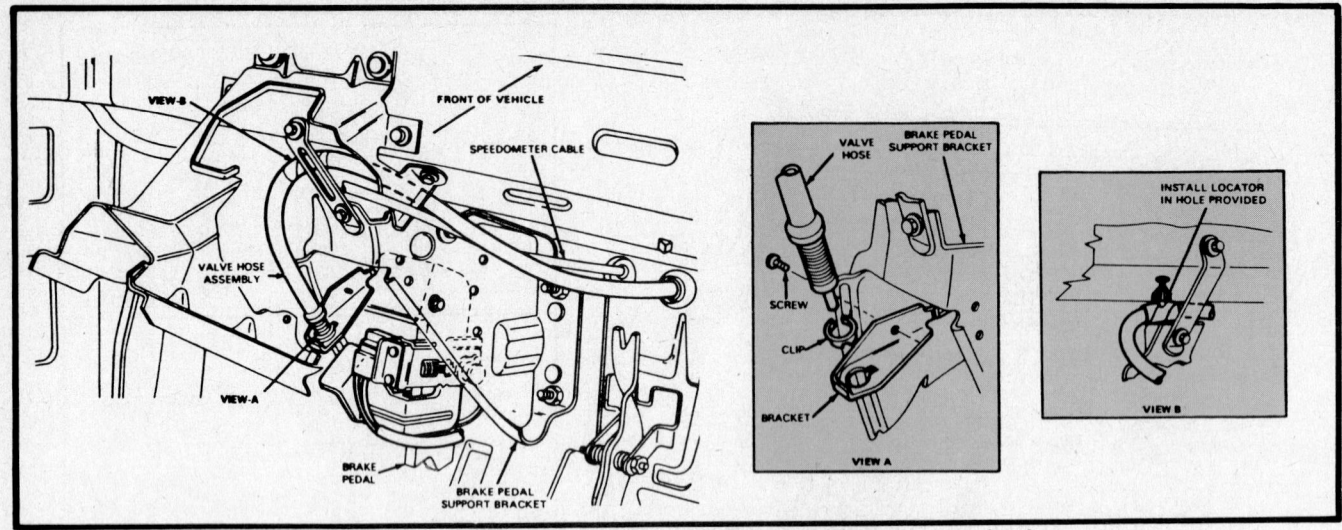

Vacuum dump valve—Escort, Lynx, EXP, LN7, Tempo and Topaz without power brakes

3. Disconnect the electrical connector from the switch assembly.

4. Remove the clutch switch and bracket assembly.

5. Remove the clutch switch from the bracket assembly.

6. Installation is the reverse of the removal procedure.

Taurus and Sable
VISUAL INSPECTION

Before performing any tests make a visual inspection of the cruise control system. Check all items in the system for abnormal conditions such as bare broken or disconnected wires and damage to the vacuum hoses. Be sure that the speedometer ca-

bles are attached and properly routed. All vacuum hoses must be properly routed and must not have any kinks or bends. Be sure that all electrical connections are complete and tight. The wiring harness must be routed properly.

DIAGNOSIS AND TESTING PROCEDURES

NOTE: The following diagnosis procedures are to be performed only with the use of special diagnostic tools that are available through the Ford Motor Company. Anyone who departs from the instructions or special tools that are used here must first establish that he compromises neither his personal safety nor the vehicle integrity by his choice of methods or tools.

TAURUS AND SABLE TESTING PROCEDURES

The Integrated Vehicle Speed Control (IVSC) contains a self-test capability. Key On, Engine Off (KOEO) and Key On, Engine Running (KOER) routines output error codes, in a manner similar to EEC-IV subsystem "Quick Tests", which then refer to Pinpoint Tests for specific component diagnosis.

The self-test capability applies only to the Taurus/ Sable IVSC for 1986. The Rotunda No. 007-00013

Speed Control Automatic System Tester cannot be used for IVSC diagnosis. The Rotunda Self-Test Automatic Readout (STAR) No. 007-00004 with cable assembly No. 007-00010; or STAR tester No. 007-00017; or equivalent, or Analog volt-ohmmeter (VOM), 0 to 20 VDC (alternate to STAR) is required to perform the IVSC Quick Test and display error codes.

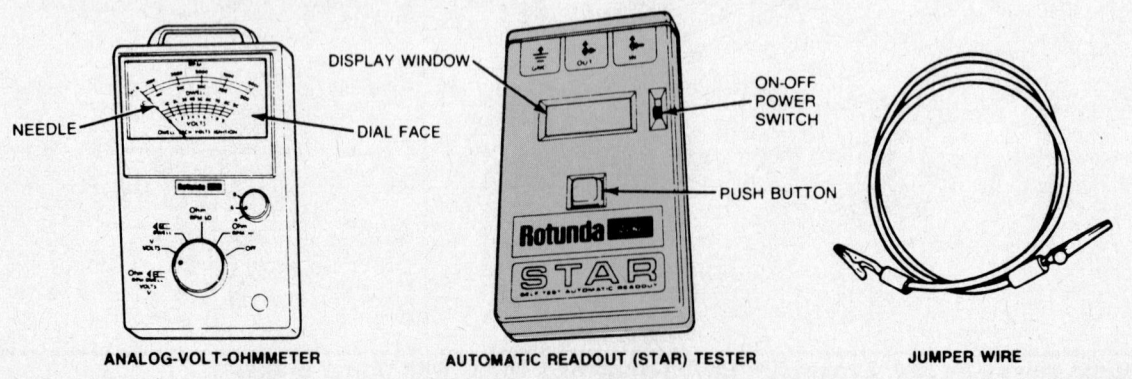

ANALOG-VOLT-OHMMETER   AUTOMATIC READOUT (STAR) TESTER   JUMPER WIRE

TAURUS AND SABLE TESTING PROCEDURES

A Rotunda Breakout Box T83L-5D EEC-IV or equivalent can also be used for convenience during Pinpoint Testing.

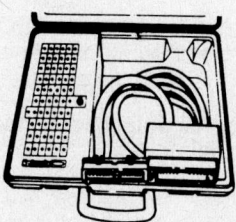

BREAKOUT BOX

Testing for the IVSC is divided into two formats: the Quick Test and Pinpoint Tests. The Quick Test is a functional IVSC system test. The Pinpoint Tests are specific component test.

The Quick Test checks all IVSC components except the speed sensor, which must be tested separately. To test and service the IVSC system, perform the Quick Test first. If the system passes, check the speed sensor. If failure codes are generated, do only the Pinpoint Test specified by that particular failure code.

After all test and services have been completed, repeat the entire Quick Test to verify that the IVSC system operates properly.

Quick Test

Description

The Quick Test is a functional test of the IVSC system consisting of basic Test Steps (described below). These Steps must be carefully followed in sequence. Otherwise, mis-diagnosis or the replacement of non-faulty components may result.

Quick Test Steps

1. Visual check and Vehicle Preparation:
   - Checks for obvious faults.
   - Properly prepares the vehicle for testing.
2. Equipment Hookup:
   - Ensures that the proper equipment for gathering test data is ready, prior to testing.
3. Key On, Engine Off Self-Test:
   - Is a static check of IVSC inputs and outputs.
4. Key On, Engine Running Self-Test:
   - Is a dynamic check of the IVSC with the engine in operation.

WARNING: ANYONE WHO DEPARTS FROM THE INSTRUCTION PROVIDED IN THIS PUBLICATION MUST FIRST ESTABLISH THAT HE COMPROMISES NEITHER HIS PERSONAL SAFETY NOR THE VEHICLE INTEGRITY BY HIS CHOICE OF METHODS, TOOLS OR PARTS.

Visual Check and Vehicle Preparation

Correct test results for the Quick Test are dependent on the proper operation of related non-IVSC components systems. It may be necessary to correct faults in these areas before the IVSC will pass the Quick Test.

Before hooking up any equipment to diagnose the IVSC system, make the following checks:

1. Check all engine vacuum hoses for:
   - Leaks or pinched hoses (servo to dump valve and servo to manifold vacuum).

perform some of the inspections. (Note the location of each pin before disassembly.)

3. Check the EEC-IV ECA and IVSC sensors and actuators for physical damage.
4. Perform all safety steps required to start and run operation vehicle tests.
5. Apply the emergency brake. Place the shift lever in PARK (NEUTRAL for manual transmission).

TAURUS AND SABLE TESTING PROCEDURES

2. Check the IVSC and EEC system wiring harness electrical connections for:
   - Proper connections.
   - Loose or detached connectors, wires and terminals.
   - Corrosion.
   - Proper routing of harness.

   It may be necessary to disconnect or disassemble the connector assembly to

6. Turn off all electrical loads such as the radio, lamps, air conditioner, etc. Be sure doors are closed whenever readings are made.
7. Verify engine coolant is at the specified level.
8. Start the engine and idle until the upper radiator hose is hot and pressurized and the throttle is off fast idle.
9. Turn the ignition key off.
10. Service items as required, and proceed to equipment hookup.

Equipment Hookup

Using the STAR tester:
- Turn the ignition key off.
- Connect the color-coded adapter cable leads to the STAR tester.
- Connect the adapter cable's two service connectors to the vehicle's appropriate Self-Test connectors.

After equipment hookup, go on to Self-Testing.

Using analog voltmeter:

- Turn ignition key off.
- Connect a jumper wire from Self-Test input (STI) to Pin 2, Signal Return on the Self-Test connector (refer to the diagram below).
- Set analog VOM on a DC voltage range to read from 0 to 15 volts DC. Connect VOM from battery (+) to Pin 4 Self-Test Output (STO), in the Self-Test connector.

After equipment hookup go on to Self-Testing.

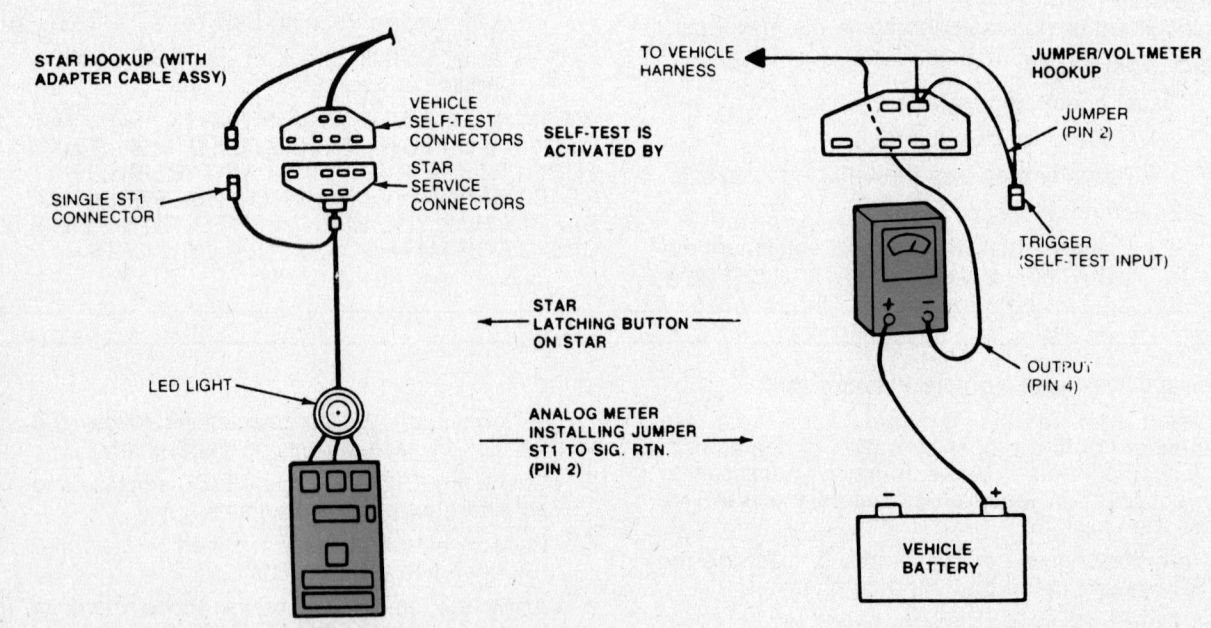

TAURUS AND SABLE TESTING PROCEDURES

Quick Test Self-Test

Quick Test Self-Testing is divided into two specialized test: Key On, Engine Off, and Key On, Engine Running. The Self-Test is not a conclusive test by itself, but is used as a part of the functional Quick Test diagnostic procedure. The processor stores the Self-Test program in its permanent memory. When activated, it checks the IVSC system by testing its functional capability and verifies that various sensors and actuators are connected and operating properly.

The Key On, Engine Off and Engine Running tests are functional tests which only detect faults present at the time of the Self-Test.

Key On, Engine Off Test

At this time, a test of the IVSC system is conducted with power applied and engine at rest.

The fault must be present at the time of testing for errors to be detected in this test.

Key On, Engine Running Test

At this time, a test of the IVSC system is conducted with the engine running. The system is checked under actual operating conditions and at normal operating temperatures. The actuators are exercised and checked for corresponding results.

Service Codes

The EEC-IV system communicates service information to the outside world by way of the Self-Test service codes. These service codes are two-digit numbers representing the results of the Self-Test.

The service codes are transmitted on the Self-Test output (found in the Self-Test connector) in the form of timed pulses, and read by the technician on a voltmeter or on the STAR tester.

Self-Test Output Code Format

DIGIT PULSES ARE 1/2 SECOND "ON" AND 1/2 SECOND "OFF"

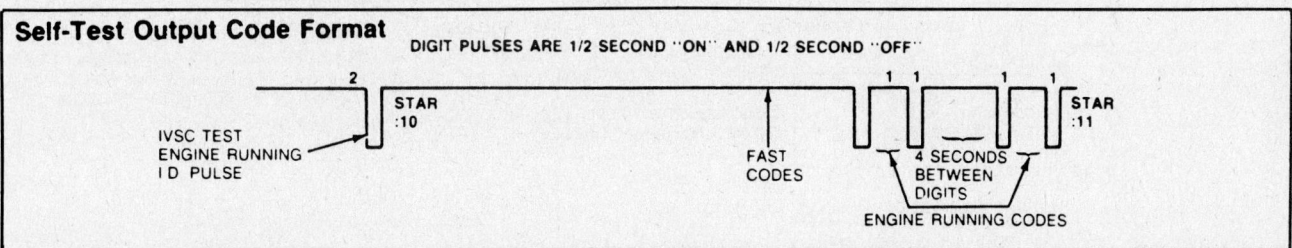

IVSC TEST ENGINE RUNNING I D PULSE · STAR :10 · FAST CODES · 4 SECONDS BETWEEN DIGITS · STAR :11 · ENGINE RUNNING CODES

Reading Codes—Analog Voltmeter

When a service code is reported on the analog voltmeter for a function test, it will represent itself as a pulsing or sweeping movement of the voltmeter's needle across the dial face of the voltmeter. Therefore, a single-digit number of three will be reported by three needle pulses (sweeps). However, as previously stated, a service code is represented by a two-digit number, such as 2-3. As a result, the Self-Tests service code of 2-3 will appear on the voltmeter as two needle pulses (sweeps), then, after a two-second pause, the needle will pulse (sweep) three times.

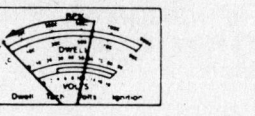

1 NEEDLE PULSE (SWEEP) + 1 NEEDLE PULSE (SWEEP) = 2 NEEDLE PULSES (SWEEPS) FOR 1ST DIGIT

2-SECOND PAUSE BETWEEN DIGITS

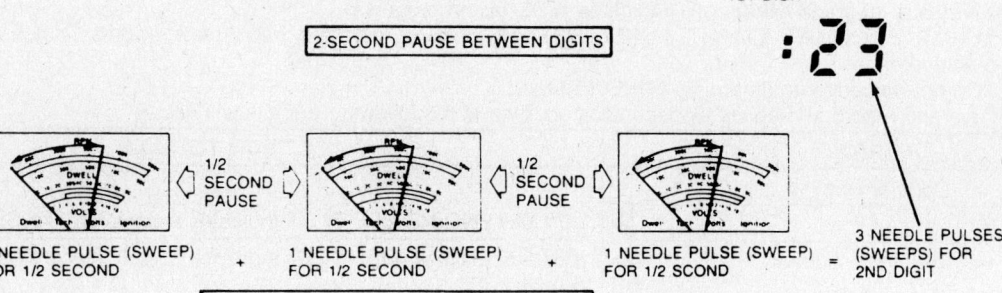

1 NEEDLE PULSE (SWEEP) FOR 1/2 SECOND + 1/2 SECOND PAUSE + 1 NEEDLE PULSE (SWEEP) FOR 1/2 SECOND + 1/2 SECOND PAUSE + 1 NEEDLE PULSE (SWEEP) FOR 1/2 SCOND = 3 NEEDLE PULSES (SWEEPS) FOR 2ND DIGIT

4-SECOND PAUSE BETWEEN SERVICE CODES. WHEN MORE THAN ONE CODE IS INDICATED

TAURUS AND SABLE TESTING PROCEDURES

Reading Codes—Self-Test Automatic Readout (STAR) Rotunda 007-00004, or STAR Rotunda 007-00017, or Equivalent

After hooking up the STAR tester and turning on its power switch, the tester will run a display check and the numerals 88 will begin to flash in the display window. A steady 00 will then appear to signify that the STAR tester is ready to start the Self-Test and receive the test's service codes.

To receive the service codes, press the pushbutton at the front of the STAR tester. The button will latch down, and a colon will appear in the display window in front of the 00 numerals. The colon must be displayed to receive the service codes.

If for any reason the technician wishes to clear the display window during the Self-Test, he must turn off the vehicle's engine, press the tester's pushbuttons once to unlatch it (colon will disappear), then press the button again to latch down the button (colon will appear again). Every time the STAR tester is turned off, the low battery indicator (LO BAT) should show briefly at the upper left corner to the tester's display window. If the LO BAT indicator shows steadily at any other time during the operation of the STAR tester with any service code, turn its power switch to OFF and replace the 9-volt battery in the tester.

The STAR tester will display the last service code received, even after it has been disconnected from the vehicle. It will hold the service code on the display until the power is turned off or the pushbutton is unlatched and relatched.

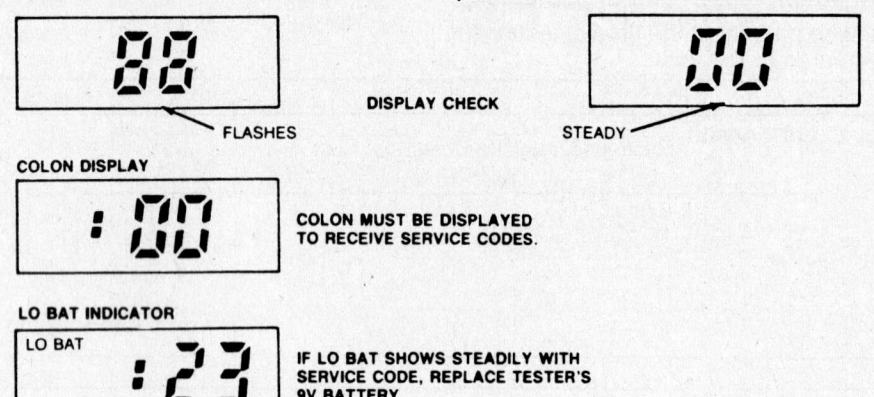

DISPLAY CHECK — FLASHES — STEADY

COLON DISPLAY — COLON MUST BE DISPLAYED TO RECEIVE SERVICE CODES.

LO BAT INDICATOR — IF LO BAT SHOWS STEADILY WITH SERVICE CODE, REPLACE TESTER'S 9V BATTERY.

QUICK TEST: KEY ON, ENGINE OFF (KOEO) SELF-TEST

A	CODE OUTPUT

To activate the KOEO IVSC test, do the following:
- Place transaxle shift lever in PARK (AXOD or ATX) or NEUTRAL (MTX).
- Leave single STI connector unplugged; plug in multipin self-test connector.
- Turn on STAR tester by moving slide switch to ON position.
- Press STAR pushbutton.
- Turn ignition key to RUN position.
- Press speed control ON switch.
- Observe code 10 on STAR display (indicates IVSC test in progress).
- Press speed control OFF, COAST, ACCEL, RESUME buttons; top brake pedal once; depress clutch pedal once (if so equipped).
NOTE: Do not depress throttle during KOEO self-test.
- Observe and record all Service Codes indicated. One of the following outputs will occur.

RESULTS		ACTION TO TAKE
Code Displayed		
11	▶	KEY ON ENGINE OFF TEST indicates a pass. GO To Step B.
Any other code(s)	▶	KEY ON ENGINE OFF TEST indicates a fault. Record codes and GO To Step B.
NO CODES OUTPUTTED	▶	Repeat SELF-TEST and verify that no service codes are present. GO To Pinpoint Test Step Q1.

TAURUS AND SABLE TESTING
PROCEDURES

QUICK TEST: KEY ON, ENGINE OFF (KOEO) SELF-TEST — Continued

B	RESULTS AND ACTION TO TAKE

- Using the KEY ON ENGINE OFF service codes from Step A, follow the instructions in the ACTION TO TAKE column in this step.
- When more than one service code is received always start with the first code received.
- Whenever a service is made, REPEAT QUICK TEST.

NOTE: Before proceeding to the specified Pinpoint Test, read the instructions on how to use the Pinpoint Tests at the beginning of the Pinpoint Test section.

RESULT	ACTION TO TAKE
ON DEMAND SERVICE CODES	
23	► GO to Engine/Emissions Diagnosis Manual . After service, return to this section and REPEAT Quick Test.
47	► GO to Pinpoint Test Step A1 .
48	► Go to Pinpoint Test Step A3 .
49	►
53	► GO to Pinpoint Test Step A5 .
63	► GO to Engine/Emissions Diagnosis Manual . After service, return to this section and REPEAT Quick Test.
74	► GO go Engine/Emissions Diagnosis Manual". After service, return to this section and REPEAT Quick Test.
75	► GO to Pinpoint Test Step B1 .
67	►
	GO to Pinpoint Test Step B4 .
81	►
82	► GO to Engine/Emissions Diagnosis Manual . After service, return to this section and REPEAT Quick Test.
	GO to Pinpoint Test Step C1 .
NOTE: Service codes 23, 53, 63 and 67 are common with EEC-IV Diagnostics.	GO to Pinpoint Test Step C5 .

QUICK TEST: KEY ON, ENGINE RUNNING (KOER) SELF-TEST

A	CODE OUTPUT

Before running KOER Self-Test. start the engine and idle until the upper radiator hose is hot and pressurized, with the throttle off fast idle and the idle stabilized.

To activate the KOER self-test, do the following:

- Connect STAR self-test and STF connectors.
- Turn on STAR tester by moving slide switch to ON position.
- Press speed control ON switch.
- Within 15 seconds, press STAR pushbutton.
- Observe code 10 on STAR display (indicates IVSC test in progress).
- Observe and record all Service Codes indicated. One of the following outputs will occur.

NOTE: Do not depress throttle or brake pedal during the KOER Self-Test. This procedure must be followed exactly to obtain IVSC KOER Self-Test.

NOTE: The engine may stall at test exit. Turn off the ignition to prevent entry into EEC-IV Key On, Engine Off Self-Test.

RESULTS	ACTION TO TAKE
Code Displayed	
11	► ENGINE RUNNING SELF-TEST indicates a pass. If the drive symptom is currently present, GO To DIAGNOSTIC BY SYMPTOM. Otherwise testing is complete, IVSC system is OK.
ANY OTHER CODE(S)	► ENGINE RUNNING SELF-TEST indicates a fault. GO To STEP B.
NO CODES OUTPUTTED	► Repeat SELF-TEST and verify that no service codes are present, then GO To Pinpoint Test Step Q1.

TAURUS AND SABLE TESTING
PROCEDURES

QUICK TEST: KEY ON, ENGINE RUNNING (KOER) SELF-TEST

B	RESULTS AND ACTION TO TAKE

- Using the ENGINE RUNNING service codes from Step A, follow the instructions in the ACTION TO TAKE column in this step.
- When more than one service code is received, always start service with the first code received.
- Whenever a service is made. REPEAT QUICK TEST.

RESULT	ACTION TO TAKE
ENGINE RUNNING SERVICE CODES	
27	▶ Go to Pinpoint Test Step E1.
28	▶ GO to Pinpoint Test Step E3.
36	▶ Go to Pinpoint Test Step D1.
37	▶ GO to Pinpoint Test Step F1.

Pinpoint Tests

Instructions for Using the Pinpoint Tests

- Do not run any of the following Pinpoint Tests unless you are so instructed by the Quick Test. Each Pinpoint Test assumes that a fault has been detected in the system with direction to enter a specific service routine. Doing any Pinpoint Test without direction from the Quick Test may produce incorrect results and cause replacement of non-defective components.

- Do not replace any parts unless the test result indicates that they should be replaced.

- When more than one service code is received, always start service with the first code received.

- Do not measure voltage or resistance at the ECA or connect any test lights to it, unless otherwise specified.

- Isolate both ends of a circuit, and turn the ignition key off whenever checking for shorts or continuity, unless otherwise specified.

- Disconnect solenoids and switches from the harness before measuring for continuity, resistance, or energizing by way of 12-volt source, unless otherwise instructed.

- In using the Pinpoint Tests, follow each Step in order, starting from the first Step in the appropriate test. Follow each Step until the fault is found.

- After completing any service to the IVSC system, verify that all components are properly reconnected and repeat the Quick Test.

- An open is defined as any resistance reading greater than 5 ohms unless otherwise specified.

- A short is defined as any resistance reading less than 10,000 ohms to ground, unless otherwise specified.

TAURUS AND SABLE TESTING PROCEDURES

- Refer to the following wiring diagram as necessary during Pinpoint Testing.

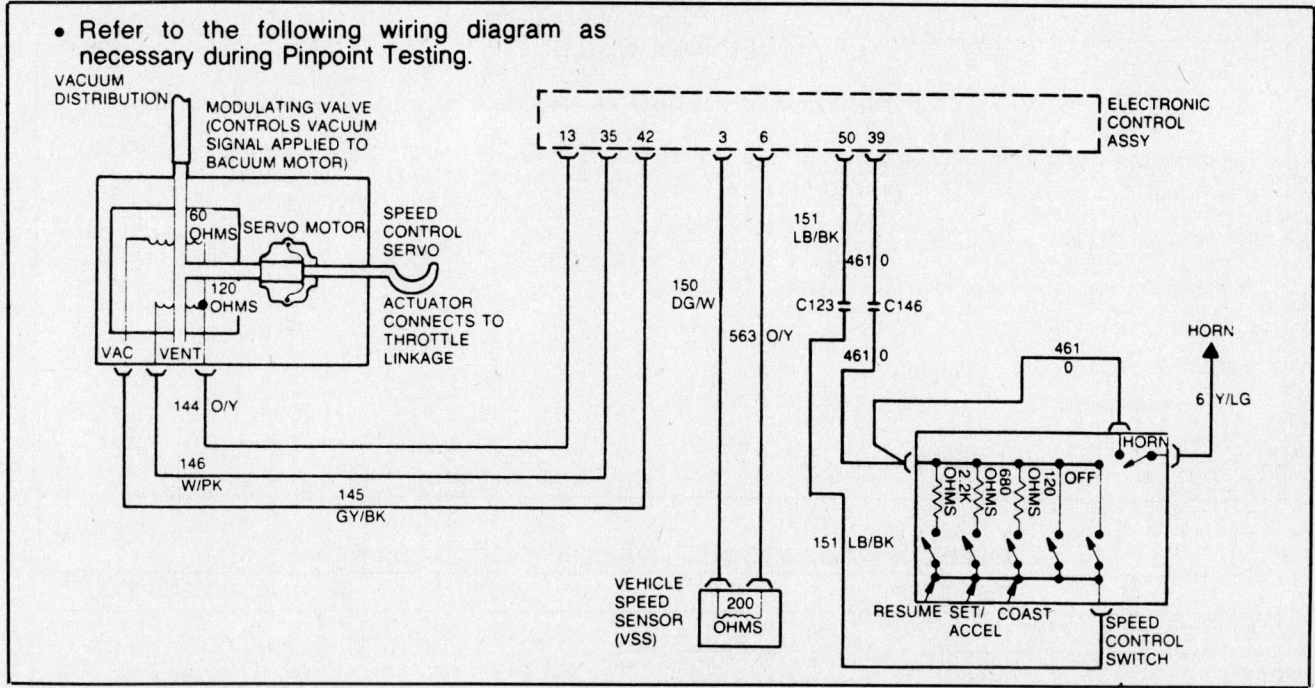

DIAGNOSTIC BY SYMPTOM

SYMPTOM	RESULT ▶	ACTION TO TAKE
• Speed control does not work. • Code "11" displayed on QUICK TESTS.	▶	GO to **G**.

SPEED CONTROL SWITCHES — PINPOINT TEST A

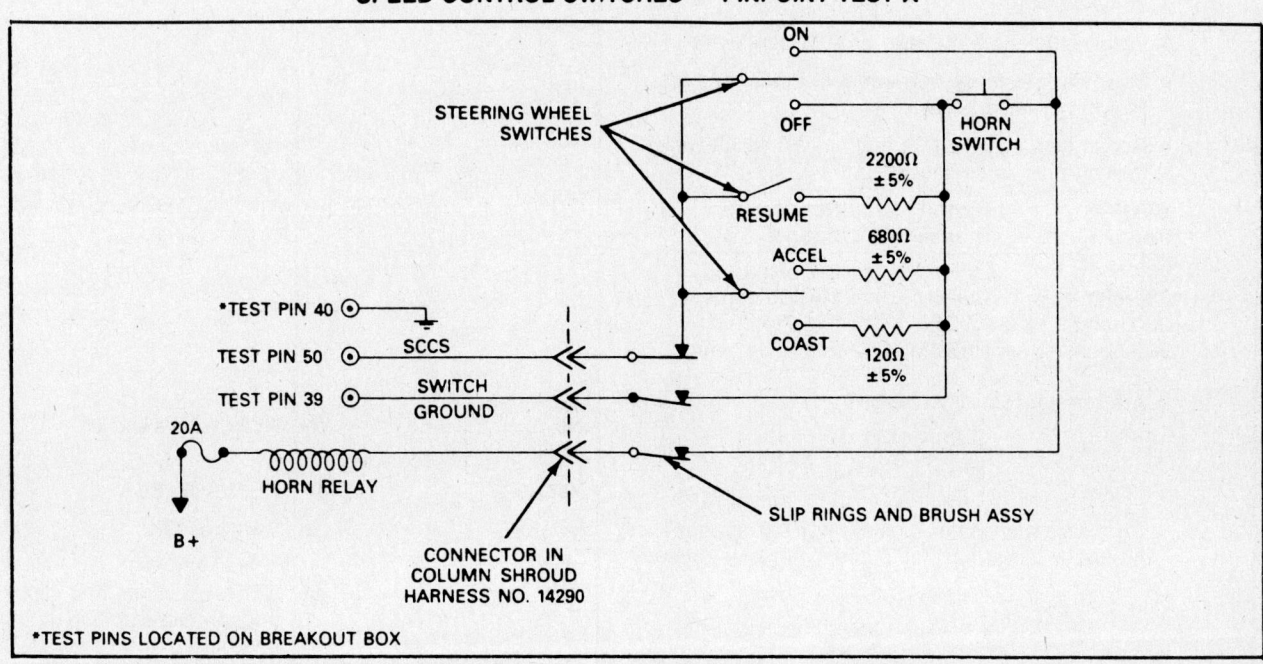

TAURUS AND SABLE TESTING PROCEDURES

STOP-WARNING

You should enter this Pinpoint Test only when a Service Code 47, 48 or 49 is received in the KOEO Self-Test.

To prevent the replacement of good components, be aware that the following non-IVSC areas may be at fault:

- Horn relay
- Fuse

This Pinpoint Test is intended to diagnose only the following:

- Speed control switches
- Brush assembly
- Slip ring assembly
- Wiring harness
- ECA

SPEED CONTROL SWITCHES — PIN POINT TEST A — Continued

	TEST STEP	RESULT	▶	ACTION TO TAKE
A1	SERVICE CODE 47			
	• Did you press the OFF, COAST, ACCEL, and RESUME buttons during the IVSC KOEO Self-Test?	Yes	▶	GO to **A2**.
		No	▶	RERUN IVSC KOEO Self-Test.
A2	SWITCH DOES NOT FUNCTION			
	• Key Off, wait 10 seconds. • Disconnect ECA 60 Pin connector. Inspect for damaged pins, corrosion, loose wires, etc. Service as necessary. • Install Breakout box, leave ECA disconnected. • Measure resistance between test Pin 50 and test Pin 39 per table below. • Rotate steering wheel through its full range while making resistance checks. **DVOM Range / Button Pressed / Resistance Range** 200 ohm — OFF — 0-4 ohms 200 ohm — COAST — 114-126 ohms 2000 ohm — ACCEL — 646-714 ohms 5000 ohm — RESUME — 2090-2310 ohms • Are resistances within range?			
		No	▶	REPLACE switches.
		Yes	▶	REPLACE ECA.
	• Do resistance values fluctuate within the ranges, or go above the ranges, as steering wheel is rotated?	No	▶	Switches OK.
		Yes	▶	CLEAN brushes and slip rings, relubricate slip rings.

TAURUS AND SABLE TESTING
PROCEDURES

SPEED CONTROL SWITCHES — PINPOINT TEST A — Continued

	TEST STEP	RESULT	▶	ACTION TO TAKE
A3	SERVICE CODE 48			
	• Did you press the OFF, COAST, ACCEL, and RESUME buttons during the IVSC KOEO Quick Test?	Yes	▶	GO to **A4**.
		No	▶	RERUN IVSC KOEO QUICK TEST.
A4	SWITCH IS STUCK			
	• Key off, wait 10 seconds.	Yes	▶	REPLACE switches.
	• Disconnect ECA 60 Pin connector. Inspect for damaged pins, corrosion, loose wires, etc. Service as necessary.	No	▶	REPLACE ECA.
	• Install Breakout box, leave ECA disconnected.			
	• DVOM on 5000 ohm scale.			
	• Is resistance reading between 0 ohms and 2310 ohms?			
A5	SERVICE CODE 49			
	• Did you press the OFF, COAST, ACCEL, and RESUME buttons during the IVSC KOEO QUICK TEST?	Yes	▶	GO to **A6**.
		No	▶	RERUN IVSC KOEO QUICK TEST.
A6	GROUND CIRCUIT TO SWITCHES OPEN			
	• Key off, wait 10 seconds.	Yes	▶	SERVICE open circuit between EEC-IV connector Pin 39 and switch plug ground terminal.
	• Disconnect ECA 60 Pin connector. Inspect for damaged pins, corrosion, loose wires, etc. Service as necessary.			
	• Install Breakout box, leave ECA disconnected.			
	• Disconnect speed control switch plug in steering column shroud.	No	▶	REPLACE ECA.
	• DVOM on 200 ohm scale.			
	• Measure resistance between test Pin 39 and ground terminal in 14290 half of disconnected switch plug.			
	• Is resistance reading greater than 5 ohms?			

TAURUS AND SABLE TESTING PROCEDURES
BRAKE ON/OFF (BOO) — PINPOINT TEST B

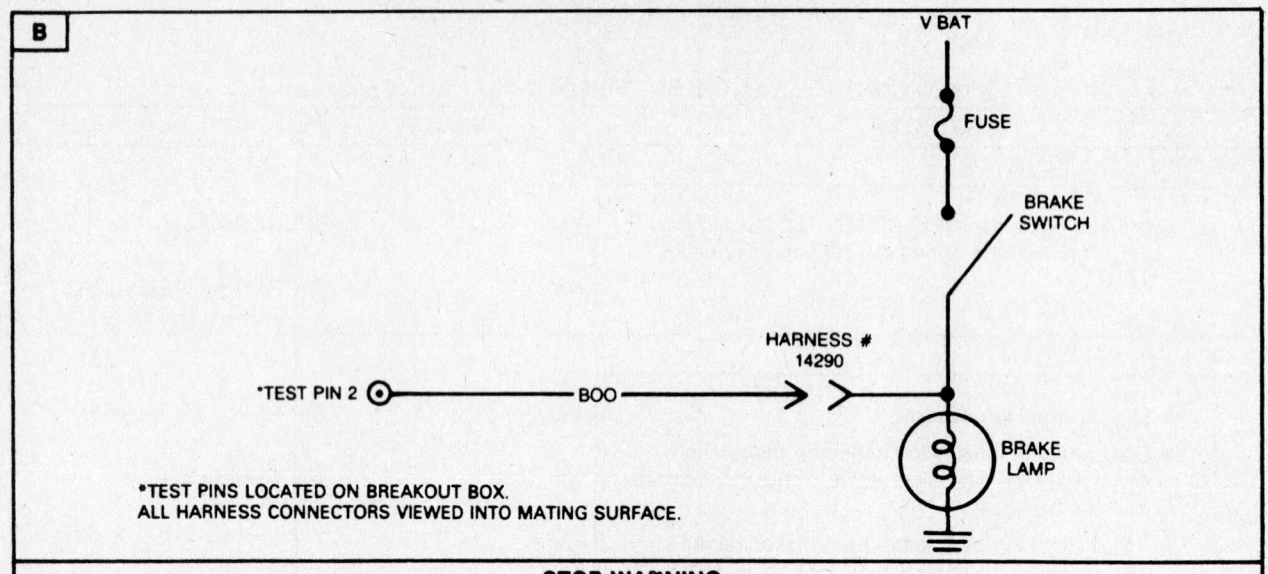

B

V BAT

FUSE

BRAKE SWITCH

HARNESS # 14290

*TEST PIN 2 ——— BOO ———▶ >

BRAKE LAMP

*TEST PINS LOCATED ON BREAKOUT BOX.
ALL HARNESS CONNECTORS VIEWED INTO MATING SURFACE.

STOP-WARNING

You should enter this Pinpoint Test only when a Service Code 74 or 75 is received in the KOEO Self-Test.

To prevent the replacement of good components, be aware that the following non-IVSC areas may be at fault:

● Brake lamp, brake switch, and fuse

This pinpoint test is intended to diagnose only the following:

● BOO circuit

● ECA

BRAKE ON/OFF (BOO) — PINPOINT TEST B — Continued

TEST STEP	RESULT	▶	ACTION TO TAKE
B1 SERVICE CODE 74			
● Did you press brake during the KOEO Self-Test?	Yes	▶	GO to **B2**.
	No	▶	RERUN KOEO Self-Test, PRESS brake once during test.
B2 BOO CIRCUIT CYCLING			
● Key off, wait 10 seconds.	Yes	▶	REPLACE ECA. RETEST.
● Disconnect ECA 60 Pin connector. Inspect for damaged pins, corrosion, loose wires, etc. Service as necessary.	No	▶	GO to **B3**.
● Install Breakout box, leave ECA disconnected.			
● DVOM on 20V scale.			
● Measure voltage between test Pin 2 and test Pin 40 at the Breakout box while depressing and releasing brake.			
● Does the voltage cycle?			

TAURUS AND SABLE TESTING
PROCEDURES

BRAKE ON/OFF (BOO) — PINPOINT TEST B — Continued

TEST STEP	RESULT	▶	ACTION TO TAKE
B3 BOO CIRCUIT SHORT TO GROUND • Key off. • Breakout box installed. • ECA disconnected. • DVOM on 200 Ohm scale. • Disconnect BOO circuit from 14290 harness (12 pin connector). • Measure resistance between test Pin 2 at the Breakout box and ground. • Is resistance reading greater than 5 ohms?	No Yes	▶ ▶	SERVICE BOO circuit short to ground. GO to Shop Manual Section 32-20 to SERVICE stoplamp circuit.
B4 BOO CIRCUIT CYCLING CODE 75 • Key off, wait 10 seconds. • Disconnect ECA 60 Pin connector. Inspect for damaged pins, corrosion, loose wires, etc. Service as necessary. • Install Breakout box, leave ECA disconnected. • DVOM on 20V scale. • Measure voltage between test Pin 2 and test Pin 40 at the Breakout box while depressing and releasing brake. • Does the voltage cycle?	Yes No	▶ ▶	REPLACE ECA. RERUN QUICK TEST. GO to **B5**.
B5 BOO CIRCUIT SHORT TO POWER • Key off. • Breakout box installed. • ECA disconnected. • DVOM on 20V scale. • Disconnect BOO circuit from 14290 harness (12 pin connector). • Measure voltage between test Pin 2 at the Breakout box and Engine Block Ground. • Is voltage reading greater than 10.5V?	Yes No	▶ ▶	SERVICE BOO circuit short to power. BOO circuit OK. GO to Shop Manual Section 32-20 to SERVICE stoplamp circuit.

POWER ACCESSORIES
CRUISE CONTROL SYSTEMS

TAURUS AND SABLE TESTING PROCEDURES

SERVO SOLENOIDS — PINPOINT TEST C

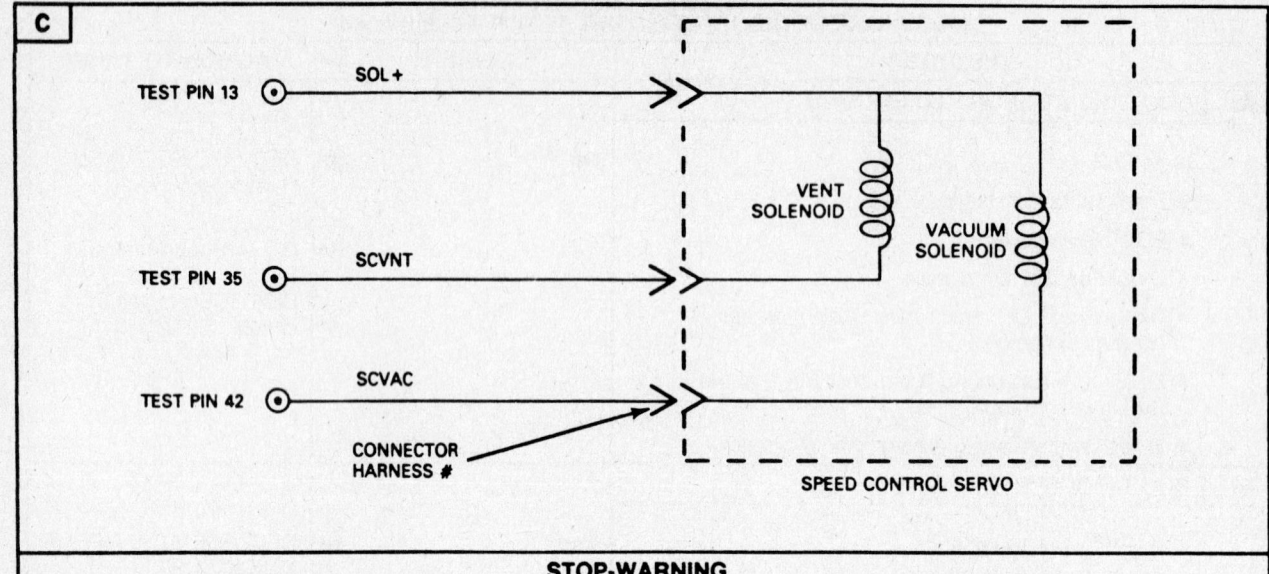

STOP-WARNING

You should enter this Pinpoint Test only when a Service Code 81 or 82 is received in the KOEO Self-Test.

This Pinpoint Test is intended to diagnose only the following:

- Servo vent solenoid
- Servo vacuum solenoid
- Circuits SOL +, SCVNT, and SCVAC
- ECA

SERVO SOLENOIDS — PINPOINT TEST C — Continued

TEST STEP	RESULT	ACTION TO TAKE
C1 VENT SOLENOID TEST		
• Key off. • Disconnect ECA 60 Pin connector. Inspect for damaged pins, corrosion, loose wires, etc. Service as necessary. • Install Breakout box, leave ECA disconnected. • DVOM on 200 ohm scale. • Measure resistance between test Pin 13 and test Pin 35.	Resistance is between 100 and 150 ohms Resistance is less than 100 ohms Resistance is greater than 150 ohms	▶ REPLACE ECA. REPEAT QUICK TEST. ▶ REPLACE servo. REPEAT QUICK TEST. ▶ GO to **C2**.
C2 CHECK CONTINUITY OF SOL + CIRCUIT		
• Disconnect harness connector from the servo. • DVOM on 200 ohm scale. • Measure resistance between test Pin 13 and SOL + circuit at the harness connector.	Resistance is greater than 5 ohms Resistance is less than 5 ohms	▶ SERVICE open circuit. REPEAT QUICK TEST. ▶ GO to **C3**.

TAURUS AND SABLE TESTING
PROCEDURES

SERVO SOLENOIDS — PINPOINT TEST C — Continued

TEST STEP	RESULT ▶	ACTION TO TAKE
C3 CHECK CONTINUITY OF SCVNT CIRCUIT • Disconnect harness connector from the servo. • DVOM on 200 ohm scale. • Measure resistance between test Pin 35 and SCVNT circuit at the harness connector.	Resistance is greater than 5 ohms ▶ Resistance is less than 5 ohms ▶	SERVICE open circuit. REPEAT QUICK TEST. GO to **C4**.
C4 MEASURE SCVNT SOLENOID RESISTANCE • Disconnect harness connector from the servo. • DVOM on 200 ohm scale. • Measure resistance between SOL+ and SCVNT circuit pins on the servo connector.	Resistance is greater than 150 ohms ▶	REPLACE servo. REPEAT QUICK TEST.
SERVICE CODE 82		
C5 VACUUM SOLENOID TEST • Key off. • Disconnect ECA 60 Pin connector. Inspect for damaged pins, corrosion, loose wires, etc. Service as necessary. • Install Breakout box, leave ECA disconnected. • DVOM on 200 ohm scale. • Measure resistance between test Pin 13 and test Pin 42.	Resistance is between 40 and 75 ohms ▶ Resistance is less than 40 ohms ▶ Resistance is greater than 75 ohms ▶	REPLACE ECA. REPEAT QUICK TEST. REPLACE servo. REPEAT QUICK TEST. GO to **C6**.

SERVO SOLENOIDS — PINPOINT TEST C — Continued

TEST STEP	RESULT ▶	ACTION TO TAKE
C6 CHECK CONTINUITY OF SOL+ CIRCUIT • Disconnect harness connector from the servo. • DVOM on 200 ohm scale. • Measure resistance between test Pin 13 and SOL+ circuit at the harness connector.	Resistance is greater than 5 ohms ▶ Resistance is less than 5 ohms ▶	SERVICE open circuit. REPEAT QUICK TEST. GO to **C7**.
C7 CHECK CONTINUITY OF SCVAC CIRCUIT • Disconnect harness connector from the servo. • DVOM on 200 ohm scale. • Measure resistance between test Pin 42 and SCVAC circuit at the harness connector.	Resistance is greater than 5 ohms ▶ Resistance is less than 5 ohms ▶	SERVICE open circuit. REPEAT QUICK TEST. REPLACE servo. REPEAT QUICK TEST.

TAURUS AND SABLE TESTING PROCEDURES

SPEED DOES NOT INCREASE DURING DYNAMIC TEST — PINPOINT TEST D

D	STOP-WARNING

You should enter this Pinpoint Test only when Service Code 36 is received in the KOER Self-Test.

This Pinpoint Test is intended to diagnose only the following:

- Actuator cable
- Vacuum hose connections
- Dump valve adjustment
- ECA

TEST STEP	RESULT	►	ACTION TO TAKE
D1 SERVICE CODE 36 • Repeat KOER Self-Test of QUICK TEST. Be sure that the speed control ON button is pressed before pressing the STAR push button.	Code 36 still present No Code 36	► ►	GO to **D2**. Increase vehicle speed test passed. SERVICE any other service code(s) as necessary.
D2 CHECK ACTUATOR CABLE CONNECTION TO THROTTLE BODY • Is actuator cable attached to throttle body accelerator linkage?	Yes No	► ►	GO to **D3**. CONNECT servo cable to throttle body accelerator linkage. REPEAT QUICK TEST.
D3 CHECK VACUUM HOSES • Is servo vacuum supply hose connected to the servo and the vacuum manifold? • Is dump value hose connected to the servo and to the dump valve?	Yes No	► ►	GO to **D4**. CONNECT hoses. REPEAT QUICK TEST.
D4 CHECK DUMP VALVE ADJUSTMENT • Is the dump valve adjusted properly so that the valve is closed when the brake pedal is not depressed?	Yes No	► ►	REPLACE ECA. REPEAT QUICK TEST. ADJUST dump valve. REPEAT QUICK TEST.

TAURUS AND SABLE TESTING
PROCEDURES

DOES NOT HOLD SPEED DURING DYNAMIC TEST — PINPOINT TEST E

E	STOP-WARNING

You should enter this Pinpoint Test only when Service Codes 27 and/or 28 are received in the KOER Self-Test.

This Pinpoint Test is intended to diagnose only the following:

• Speed control servo

• Vacuum hose connections (servo to manifold and servo to dump valve)

TEST STEP		RESULT	▶	ACTION TO TAKE
E1	SERVICE CODE 27			
	• Repeat Engine Running Self-Test of QUICK TEST. Be sure that the speed control ON button is pressed before pressing the STAR push button.	Code 27 still present?	▶	GO to **E2**.
		No Code 27	▶	Servo leaks down test passed. SERVICE any other service code(s) as necessary.
E2	CHECK VACUUM HOSES			
	• Is servo vacuum supply hose tightly connected to the servo and the vacuum manifold, and free of cuts and cracks?	Yes	▶	REPLACE servo. REPEAT QUICK TEST.
	• Is dump valve hose tightly connected to the servo and dump valve, and free of cuts and cracks?	No	▶	SERVICE vacuum hoses. REPEAT QUICK TEST.
E3	SERVICE CODE 28			
	• REPEAT engine running SELF-TEST of QUICK TEST. Be sure that the speed control ON button is pressed before pressing the STAR push button.	Code 28 still present?	▶	REPLACE servo. REPEAT QUICK TEST.
		No Code 27	▶	Servo leaks up test passed. SERVICE any other service code(s) as necessary.

TAURUS AND SABLE TESTING
PROCEDURES

SPEED DOES NOT DECREASE DURING DYNAMIC TEST — PINPOINT TEST F

F	STOP-WARNING		

You should enter this Pinpoint Test only when a Service Code 37 is received in the KOER Self-Test.

This Pinpoint Test is intended to diagnose only the following:

- Actuator cable
- Throttle shaft and linkage
- Throttle position sensor
- ECA

TEST STEP		RESULT ▶	ACTION TO TAKE
F1	SERVICE CODE 37		
	• Repeat KOER Self-Test of QUICK TEST. Be sure that the speed control ON button is pressed before pressing the STAR push button.	Code 37 still present?	▶ GO to **F2**.
		No Code 37	▶ Decrease vehicle speed test passed. SERVICE any other service code(s) as necessary.
F2	CHECK FOR THROTTLE SHAFT/LINKAGE BINDING		
	• Is the throttle shaft or throttle linkage binding, maintaining a part throttle opening?	Yes	▶ SERVICE to eliminate binding. REPEAT QUICK TEST.
		No	▶ GO to **F3**.
F3	CHECK FOR SPEED CONTROL LINKAGE BINDING		
	• Is the actuator cable binding?	Yes	▶ REPLACE the actuator cable. REPEAT QUICK TEST.
		No	▶ GO to **F4**.
F4	CHECK FOR THROTTLE POSITION SENSOR BINDING		
	• Is throttle position sensor binding at a part throttle opening?	Yes	▶ REPLACE the throttle position sensor. REPEAT QUICK TEST.
		No	▶ REPLACE the ECA. REPEAT QUICK TEST.

TAURUS AND SABLE TESTING PROCEDURES
SPEED SENSOR — PINPOINT TEST G

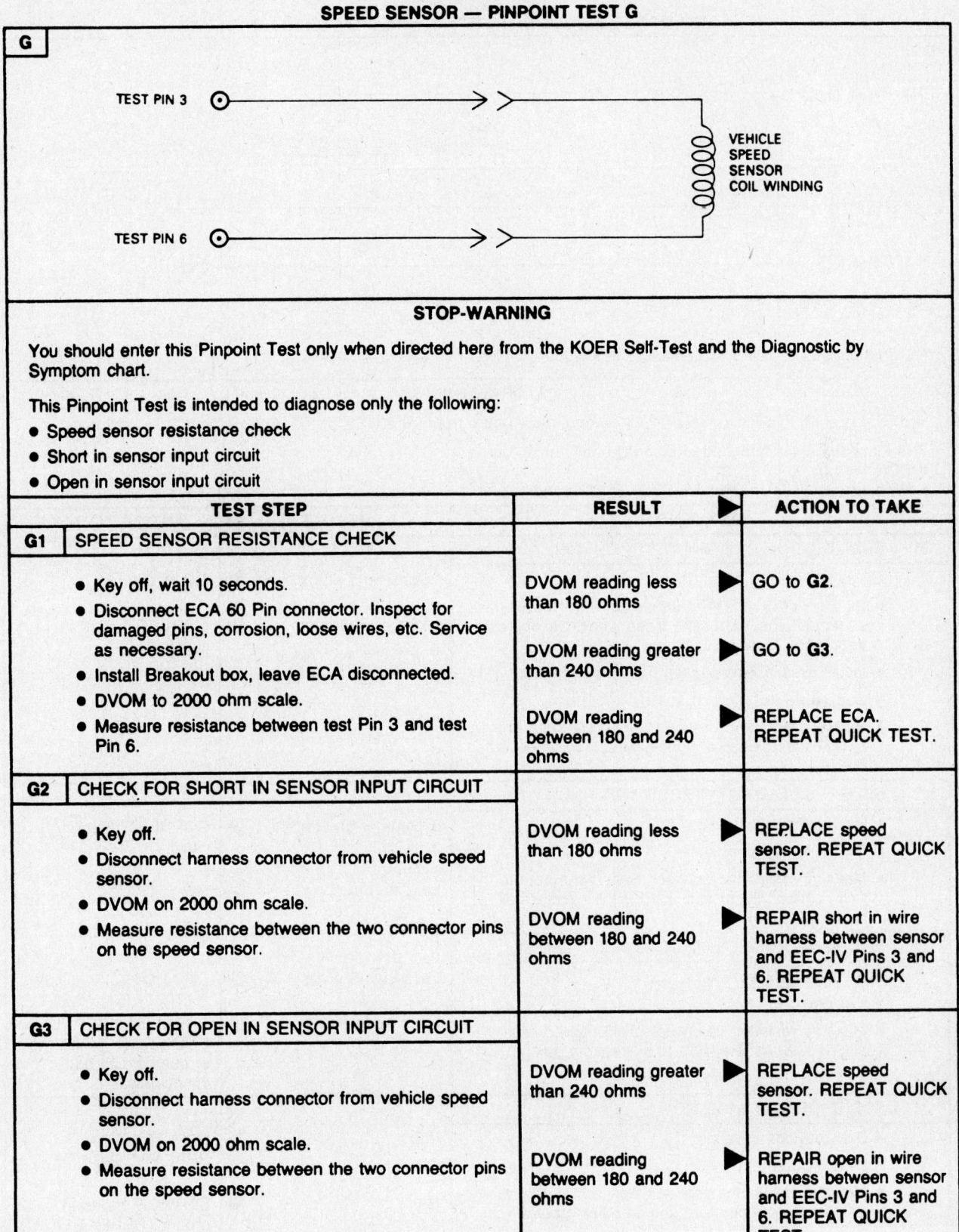

G

TEST PIN 3 ⊙

TEST PIN 6 ⊙

VEHICLE
SPEED
SENSOR
COIL WINDING

STOP-WARNING

You should enter this Pinpoint Test only when directed here from the KOER Self-Test and the Diagnostic by Symptom chart.

This Pinpoint Test is intended to diagnose only the following:

- Speed sensor resistance check
- Short in sensor input circuit
- Open in sensor input circuit

TEST STEP	RESULT ▶	ACTION TO TAKE
G1 SPEED SENSOR RESISTANCE CHECK • Key off, wait 10 seconds. • Disconnect ECA 60 Pin connector. Inspect for damaged pins, corrosion, loose wires, etc. Service as necessary. • Install Breakout box, leave ECA disconnected. • DVOM to 2000 ohm scale. • Measure resistance between test Pin 3 and test Pin 6.	DVOM reading less than 180 ohms ▶ DVOM reading greater than 240 ohms ▶ DVOM reading between 180 and 240 ohms ▶	GO to **G2**. GO to **G3**. REPLACE ECA. REPEAT QUICK TEST.
G2 CHECK FOR SHORT IN SENSOR INPUT CIRCUIT • Key off. • Disconnect harness connector from vehicle speed sensor. • DVOM on 2000 ohm scale. • Measure resistance between the two connector pins on the speed sensor.	DVOM reading less than 180 ohms ▶ DVOM reading between 180 and 240 ohms ▶	REPLACE speed sensor. REPEAT QUICK TEST. REPAIR short in wire harness between sensor and EEC-IV Pins 3 and 6. REPEAT QUICK TEST.
G3 CHECK FOR OPEN IN SENSOR INPUT CIRCUIT • Key off. • Disconnect harness connector from vehicle speed sensor. • DVOM on 2000 ohm scale. • Measure resistance between the two connector pins on the speed sensor.	DVOM reading greater than 240 ohms ▶ DVOM reading between 180 and 240 ohms ▶	REPLACE speed sensor. REPEAT QUICK TEST. REPAIR open in wire harness between sensor and EEC-IV Pins 3 and 6. REPEAT QUICK TEST.

739

TAURUS AND SABLE TESTING PROCEDURES

NO CODES, CODES NOT LISTED — PINPOINT TEST Q

Q

TEST PIN 46 — SIGNAL RETURN

SELF-TEST CONNECTOR

PIGTAIL CONNECTOR

TEST PIN 17 — STO

TEST PIN 48 — STI

TO SELF-TEST INPUT

TEST PIN 40 — GROUND

TEST PIN 60 — GROUND

TO BAT. GRD. PIGTAIL

TEST PINS ON BREAKOUT BOX. ALL HARNESS CONNECTORS VIEWED INTO MATING SURFACE.

STOP-WARNING

You should enter this Pinpoint Test only when directed here from the KOER or KOEO Self-Test.

This Pinpoint Test is intended to diagnose only the following:
- ECA
- Harness circuits: signal return, STO, STI, Ground

TEST STEP	RESULT	▶	ACTION TO TAKE
Q1 SELF-TEST INPUT CONTINUITY CHECK			
• Key off, wait 10 seconds. • Disconnect ECA 60 Pin connector and inspect for damaged pins, corrosion, loose wires. Service as necessary. • Install Breakout box, leave ECA disconnected. • Set DVOM to 200 ohm scale. • Measure resistance between Self-Test input at the Self-Test single pin connector and test Pin 48 at the Breakout box.	Less than 5 ohms 5 ohms or greater	▶ ▶	GO to **Q2**. CORRECT open in circuit.
Q2 SELF-TEST OUTPUT CIRCUIT CONTINUITY CHECK			
• Breakout box installed. • DVOM to 200 ohm scale. • Measure resistance between Self-Test output at the Self-Test connector and test Pin 17 at the Breakout box.	5 ohms or greater Less than 5 ohms	▶ ▶	CORRECT open in circuit. GO to **Q3**.
Q3 EGO SENSOR GROUND CONTINUITY CHECK			
• Breakout box installed. • Key off. • Measure resistance between EGO ground on engine and test Pin 49 at the Breakout box.	Less than 5 ohms 5 ohms or greater	▶ ▶	GO to **Q4**. CHECK and SERVICE EGO sensor ground wire or open circuit bad connection.
Q4 STO SHORT TO GROUND			
• Breakout box installed. • DVOM on 200,000 ohm scale. • Measure resistance between Self-Test output at Self-Test connector and engine block ground. • Is resistance greater than 10,000 ohms?	Yes No	▶ ▶	REPLACE ECA. REPEAT QUICK TEST. SERVICE shorts to ground. REPEAT QUICK TEST.

Model	Description
007-00004 with 007-00010	Self-Test Automatic Readout (STAR) with Cable Assembly
007-00017	Self-Test Automatic Readout (STAR)
T83L-50-EEC-IV Rotunda 014-00322	Breakout Box
014-00407	Digital Volt-Ohmmeter (DVOM)

ACTUATOR CABLE ADJUSTMENT

Taurus and Sable

3.0 LITER ENGINE

1. Remove the cruise control actuator cable retaining clip.
2. Push the actuator cable through the adjuster until slight tension is felt.
3. Insert the cable retaining clip and snap it into place.

2.5 LITER ENGINE

1. Remove then locking pin. Pull the bead chain through the adjuster.
2. Insert the locking pin in the best hole of the adjuster for a tight bead chain without opening the throttle plate.

VACUUM DUMP VALVE ADJUSTMENT

The vacuum dump valve is movable in its mounting on the brake pedal assembly. It should be adjusted so that it is closed when the brake pedal is in its normal position, and open when the brake pedal is depressed. Use a hand vacuum pump to accomplish this.

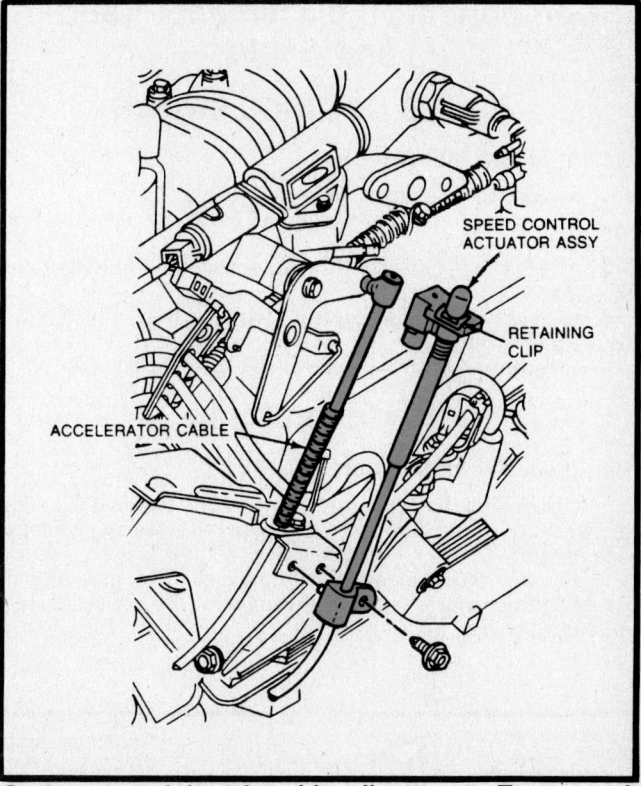

Cruise control throttle cable adjustment – Taurus and Sable with 3.0 liter engine

CLUTCH SWITCH ADJUSTMENT (MANUAL TRANSAXLE)

1. Prop the clutch pedal in the full up position.
2. Loosen the clutch switch mounting screw.
3. Slide the switch forward toward the clutch pedal until the switch plunger cap is 0.030 inch from contacting the switch housing. Tighten the attaching screw.
4. Remove the prop from the clutch pedal. Test drive the vehicle for clutch switch cancellation of the cruise control system.

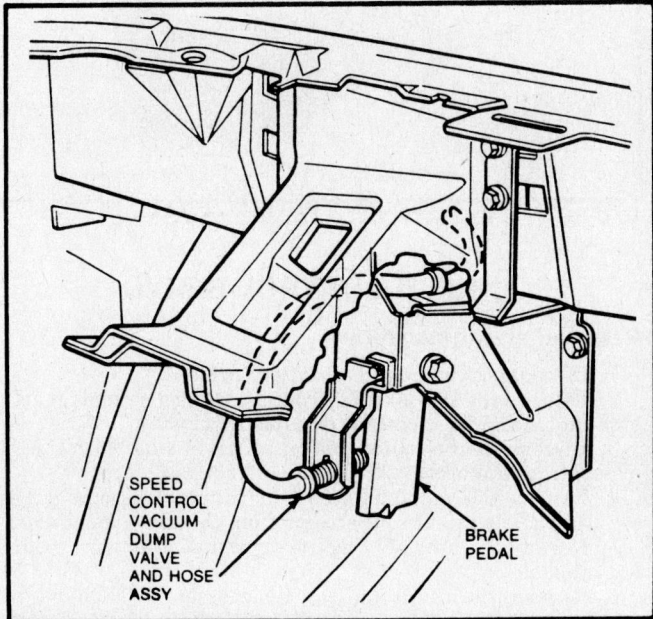

Dump valve location and adjustment – Taurus and Sable

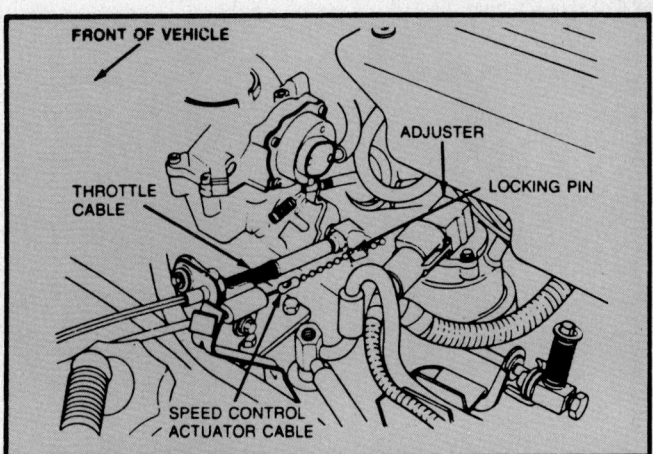

Cruise control throttle cable adjustment – Taurus and Sable with 3.5 liter engine

Component Replacement—Taurus and Sable

CRUISE CONTROL SWITCH

Removal and Installation

1. Disconnect the negative battery cable.
2. Remove the steering wheel pad cover. Remove the foam insert.
3. Disconnect the wiring connector from the slip ring terminal.
4. Remove the cruise control switches from the steering wheel pad cover.
5. Installation is the reverse of the removal procedure.

GROUND BRUSH

Removal and Installation

1. Disconnect the negative battery cable. Remove the steering wheel trim pad. Remove and discard the steering wheel attaching nut.
2. Remove the steering wheel upper shaft by grasping the rim of the steering wheel and pulling on it. Do not use a steering wheel puller.

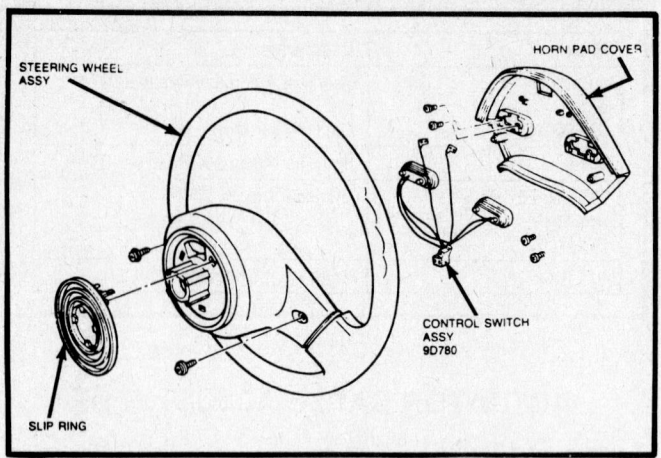

Cruise control switch assembly—Taurus and Sable

3. If equipped with tilt wheel remove the tilt lever.
4. Remove the ignition lock cylinder. Remove the lower trim shroud.
5. Separate the cruise control brush wire harness at the connector. Remove the wire harness connectors from the steering column.
5. Remove the screw securing the brush assembly to the upper bearing retainer plate.
6. Installation is the reverse of the removal procedure. Install a new steering wheel bolt and torque 50 to 62 ft. lbs.

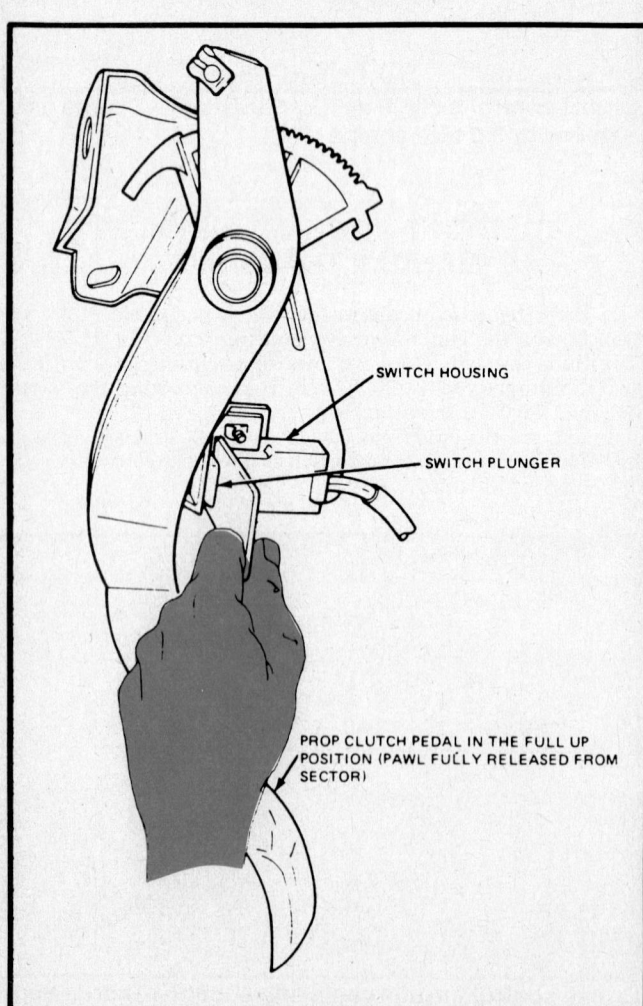

Clutch switch adjustment—Taurus and Sable

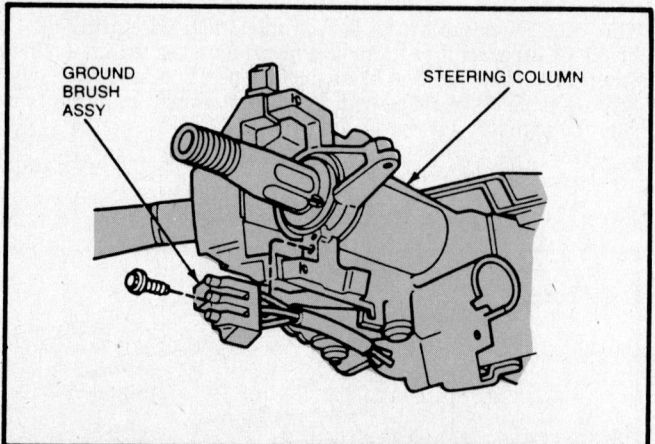

Ground brush assembly—Taurus and Sable

CRUISE CONTROL SERVO

Removal and Installation

1. Disconnect the negative battery cable.
2. Remove the screw and disconnect the cruise control actuator cable from the accelerator cable bracket.
3. Disconnect the cruise control actuator cable with the adjuster, from the accelerator cable.
4. Remove the vacuum hoses from the servo assembly. Disconnect the electrical connections from the servo assembly.
5. Remove the nuts holding the servo assembly to its mounting bracket.
6. Remove the servo and the cable assembly. Remove the nuts holding the cable cover to the servo assembly. Pull off the cover and remove the cable assembly.
7. Installation is the reverse of the removal procedure.

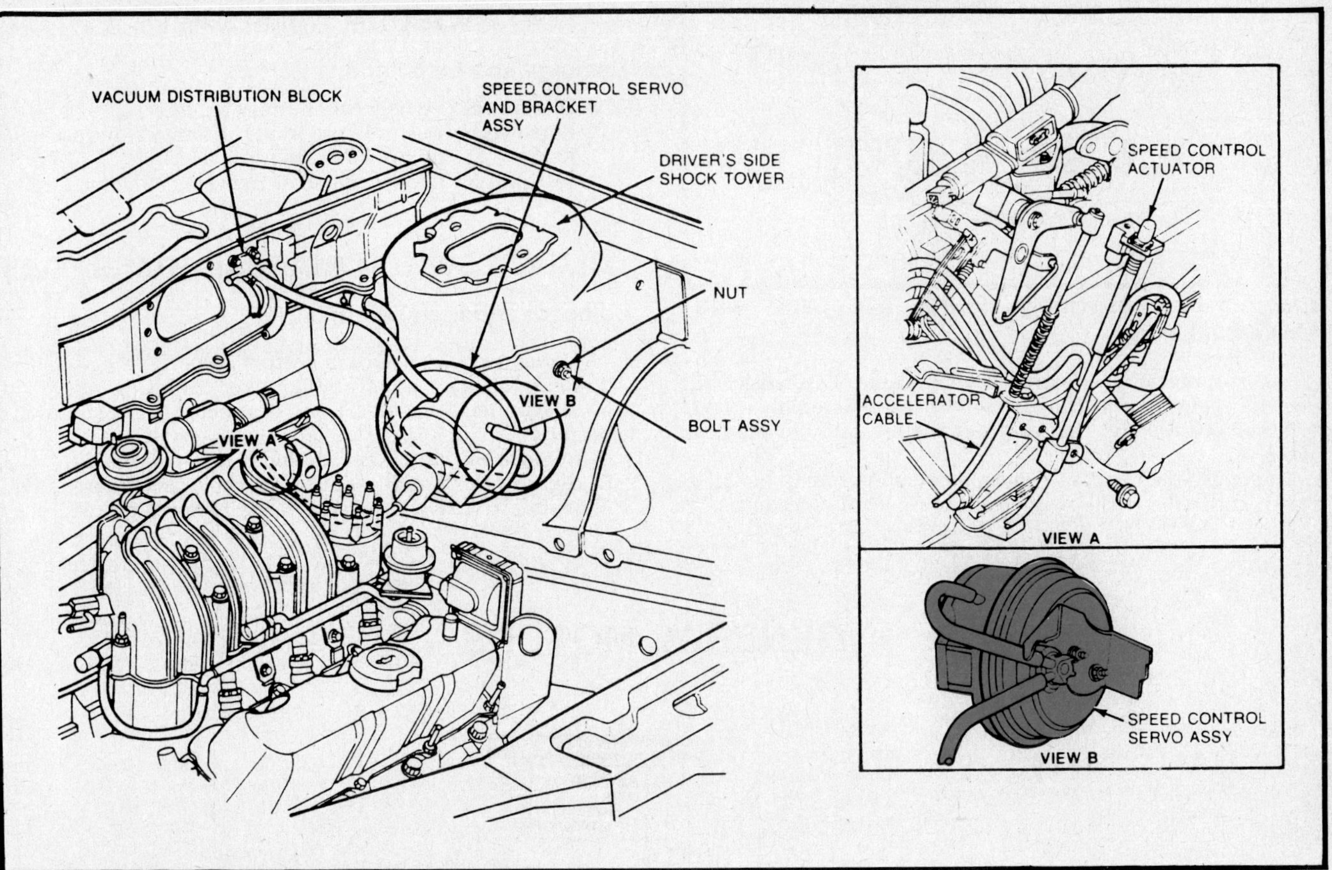

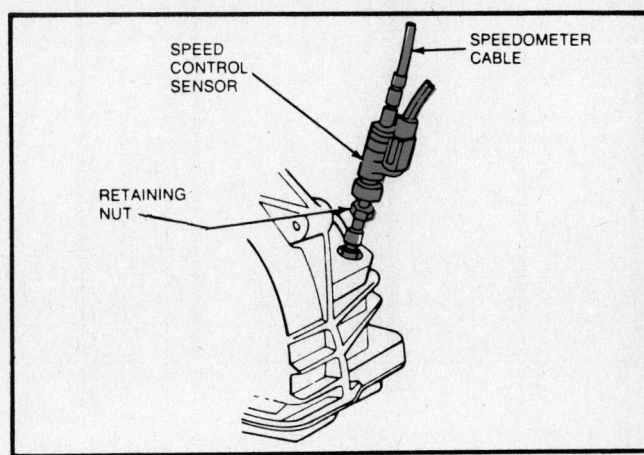

Cruise control assembly—Taurus and Sable

ACTUATOR CABLE

Removal and Installation

1. Remove the servo assembly.
2. Remove the actuator cable from the servo.
3. Attach the new actuator cable to the servo assembly.
4. Install the servo assembly.

SPEED SENSOR

Removal and Installation

ALL EXCEPT AXOD

1. Raise and support the vehicle safely.
2. Loosen the speed sensor retaining nut holding the sensor assembly in the transaxle.
3. Disconnect the electrical connector from the speed sensor.
4. Disconnect the speedometer cable by pulling it out of the speed sensor assembly.
5. Do not attempt to remove the spring retainer clip with the speedometer cable in the sensor.
6. Installation is the reverse of the removal procedure.

AXOD

1. Raise and support the vehicle safely.
2. Remove the bolt retaining the cruise control speed sensor to the transaxle.
3. Disconnect the electrical connector and the speedometer cable from the speed sensor.
4. Disconnect the speedometer cable by pulling it out of the speed sensor.

5. Do not attempt to remove the spring retainer clip with the speedometer cable in the sensor.
6. Remove the driven gear retainer. Remove the driven gear from the sensor.
7. Installation is the reverse of the removal procedure.

EEC–IV ELECTRONIC CONTROL ASSEMBLY (ECA)

The electronic control assembly is located behind the glove compartment, under the instrument panel.

Speed sensor assembly—Taurus and Sable except AXOD transaxle

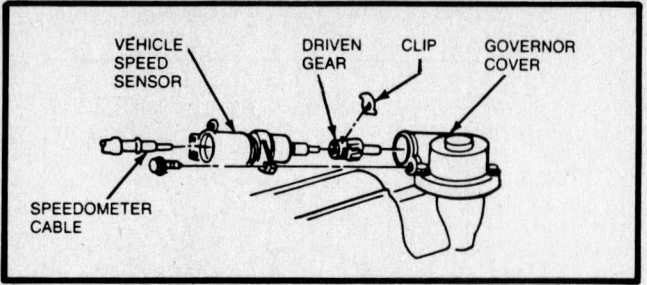

Speed sensor assembly—Taurus and Sable with AXOD transaxle

1. Disconnect the engative battery cable. Disconnect the electrical connector at the electronic control assembly.
2. Remove the clip that attaches the assembly to the dash panel.
3. Remove the electronic control assembly from the vehicle.
4. Installation is the reverse of the removal procedure.

VACUUM DUMP VALVE

Removal and Installation

1. Disconnect the negative battery cable.
2. Remove the vacuum hose from the dump valve assembly.
3. Remove the dump valve from the bracket.
4. Installation is the reverse of the removal procedure.

CLUTCH SWITCH (MANUAL TRANSAXLE)

Removal and Installation

1. Disconnect the negative battery cable.
2. Remove the clutch switch bracket mounting screw.
3. Disconnect the electrical connector from the switch assembly.
4. Remove the clutch switch and bracket assembly.
5. Remove the clutch switch from the bracket assembly.
6. Installation is the reverse of the removal procedure.

GENERAL MOTORS

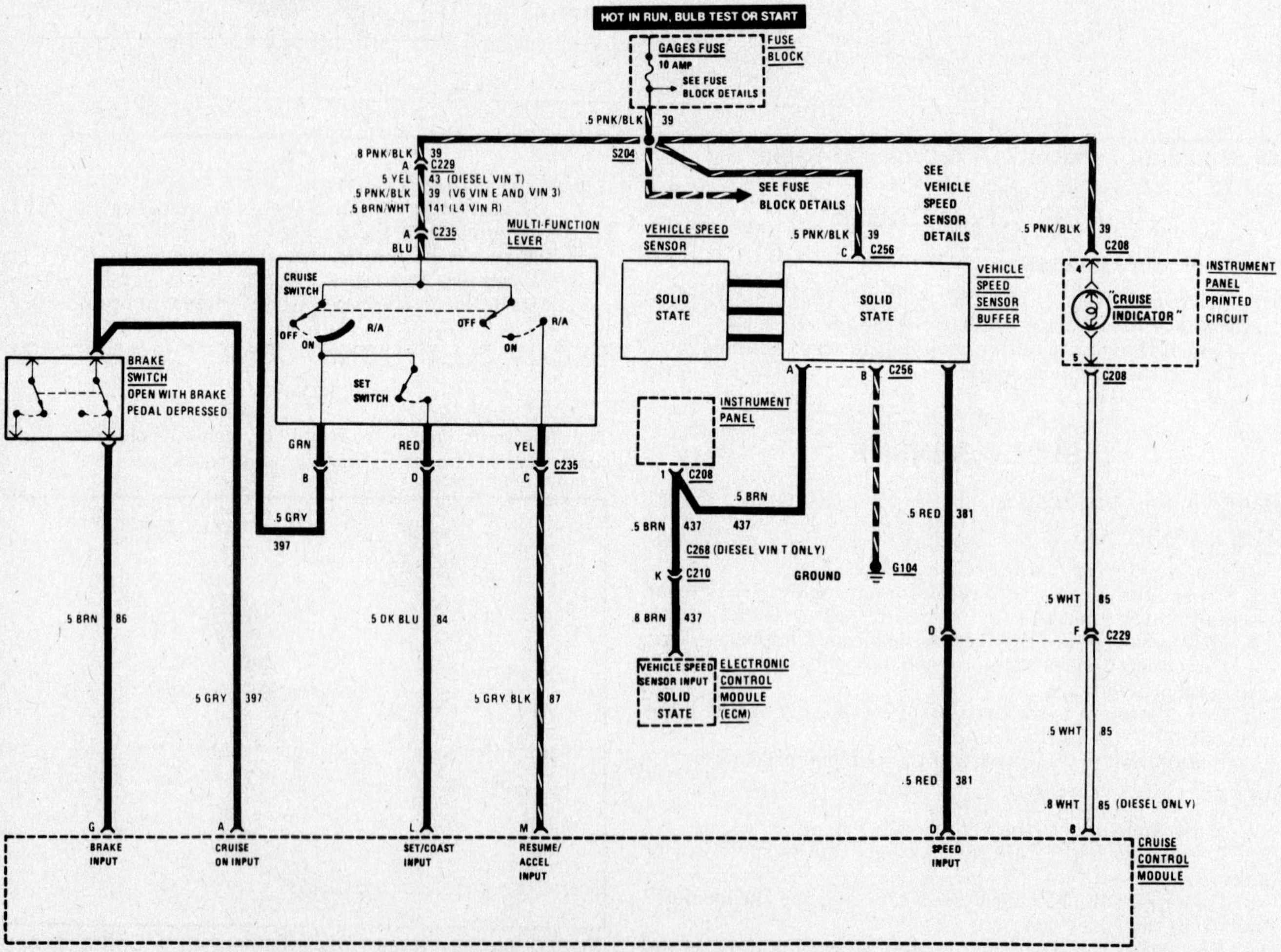

Typical cruise control electrical schematic with digital cluster—1985 "A" body (Century shown)

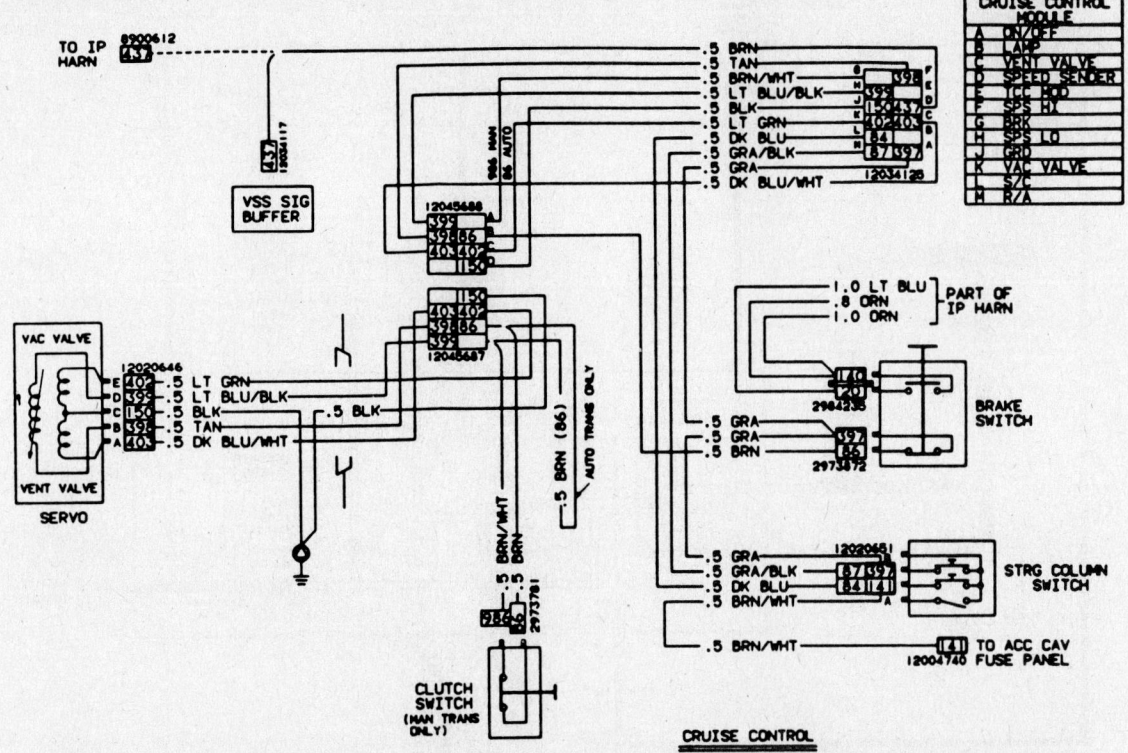

Typical cruise control electrical schematic—1985 and later "J" body (Cavalier shown)

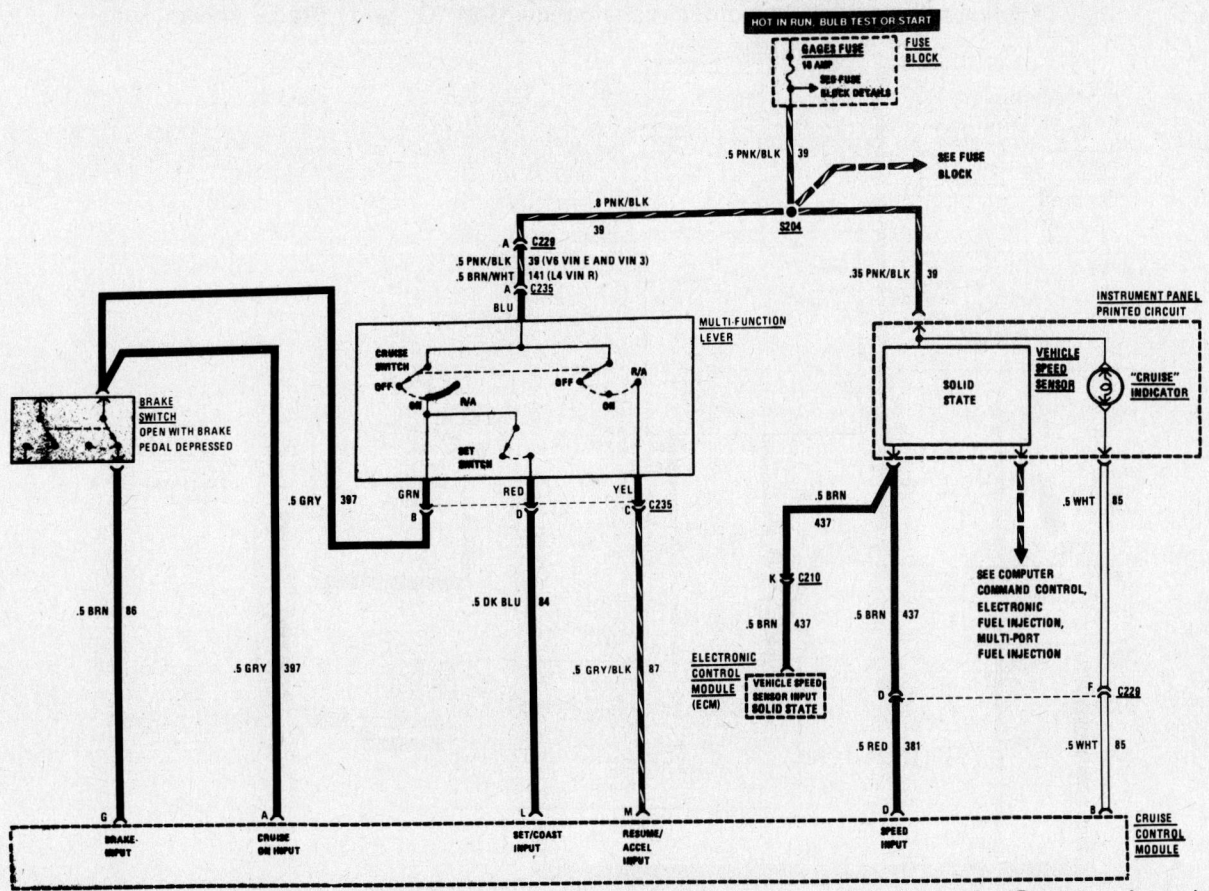

Typical cruise control electrical schematic without digital cluster—1985 "A" body (Century shown)

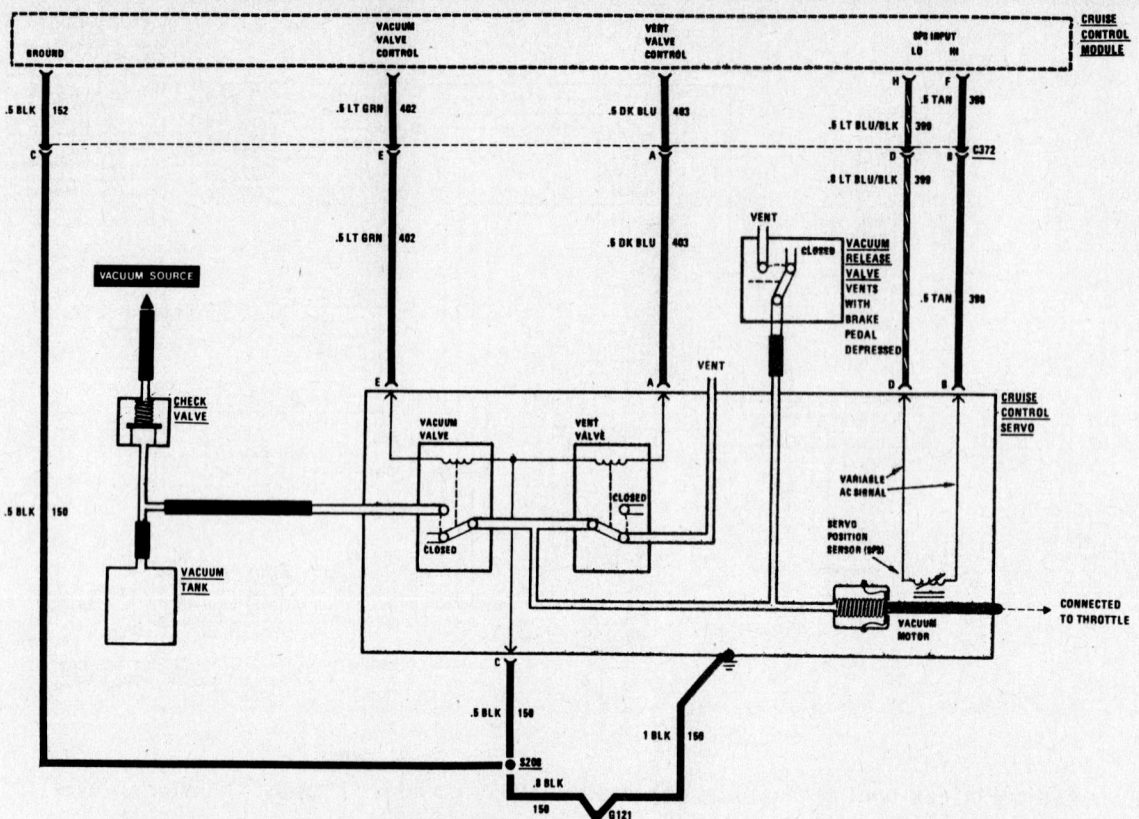

Typical cruise control electrical schematic — 1984 "G" body (Regal shown)

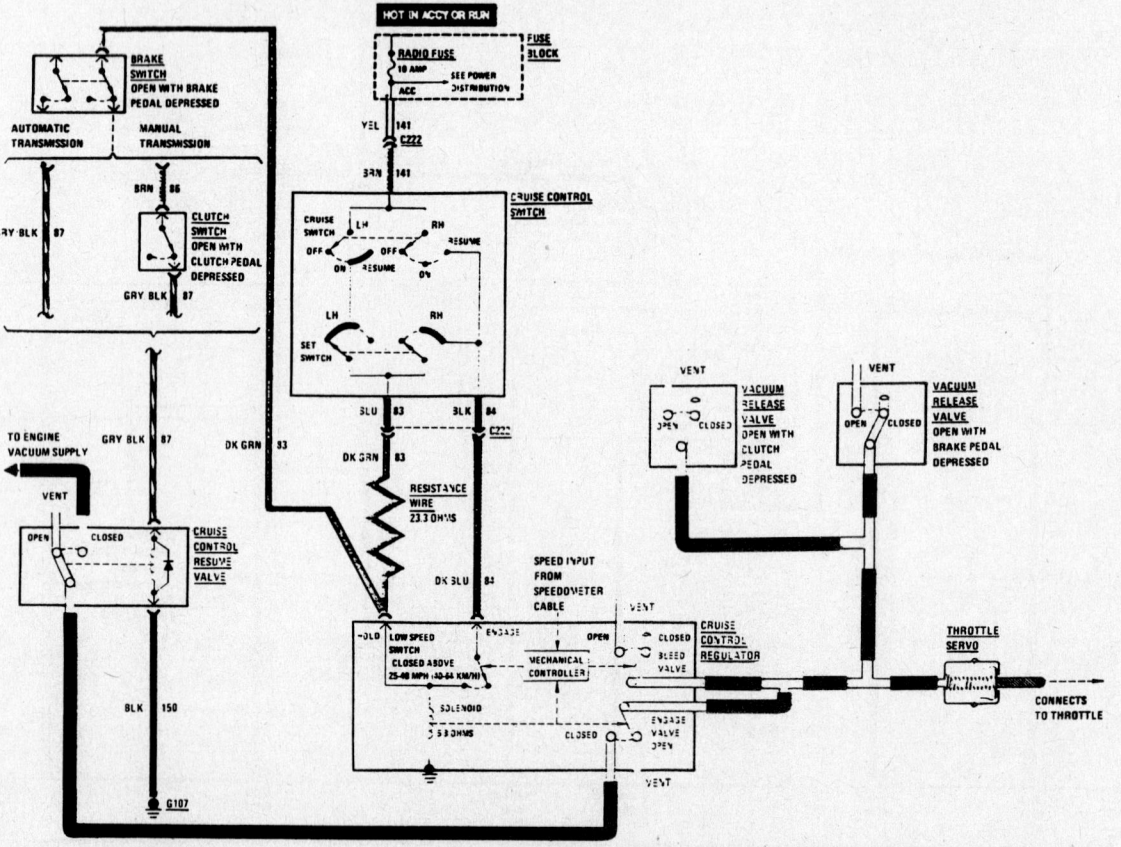

Typical cruise control electrical schematic — 1982–84 "J" body (Cavalier shown)

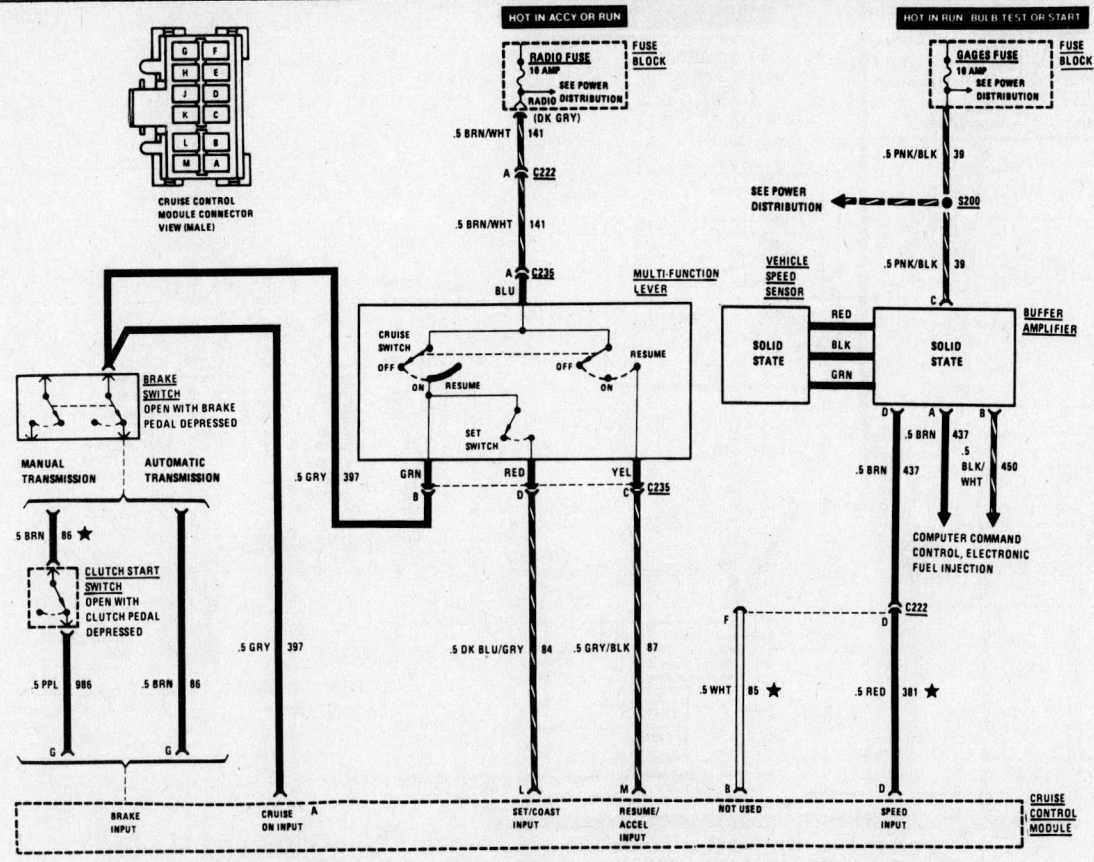

Typical cruise control electrical schematic—1984 "X" body (Phenoix shown)

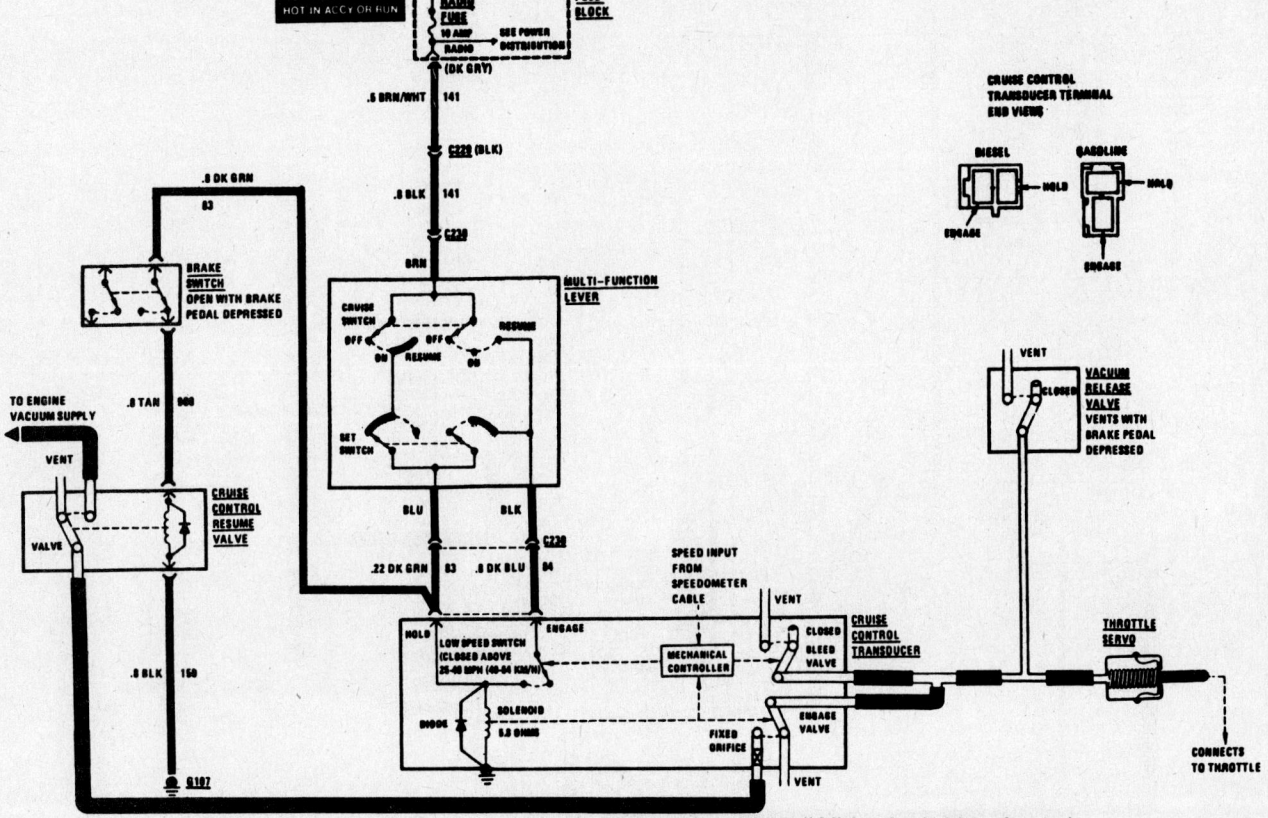

Typical cruise control electrical schematic—1985 "A" body (6000 shown)

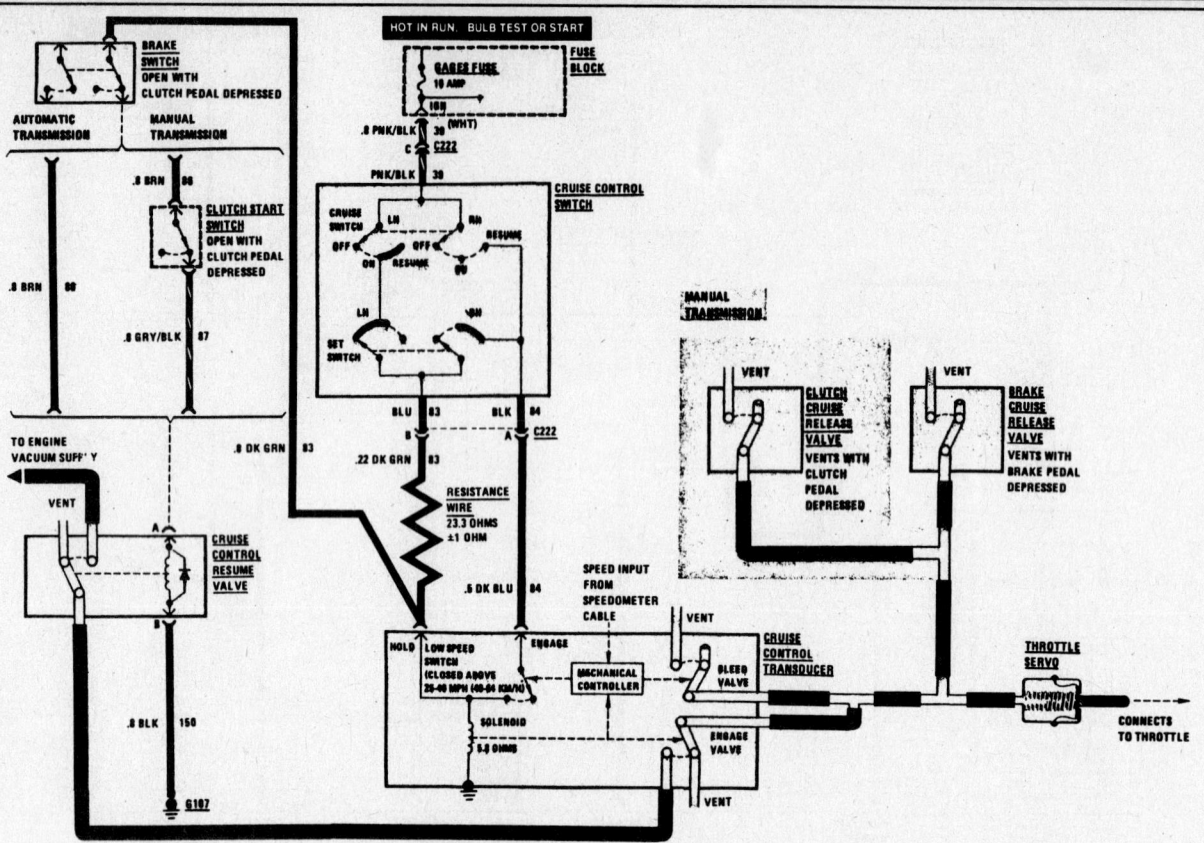

Typical cruise control electrical schematic—1983 "F" body (Firebird shown)

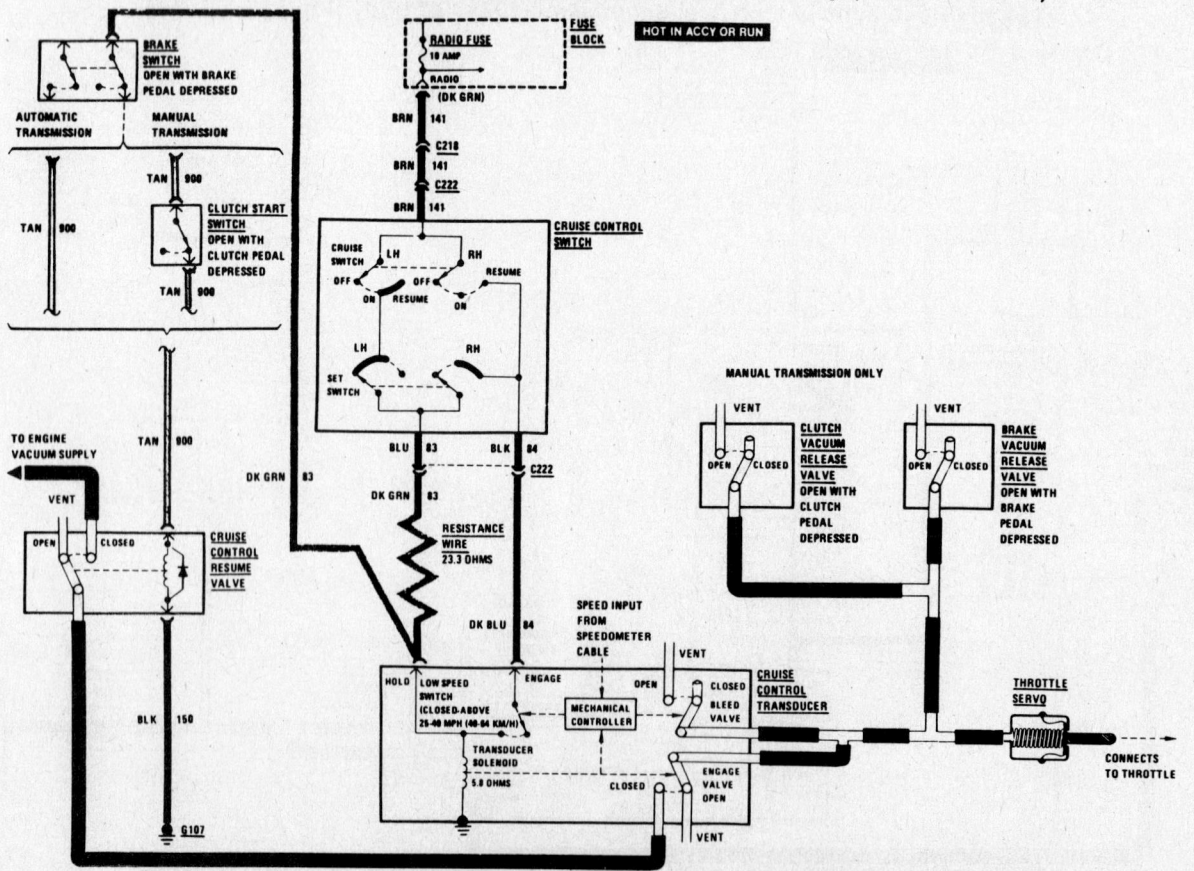

Typical cruise control electrical schematic—1982 "X" body (Phenoix shown)

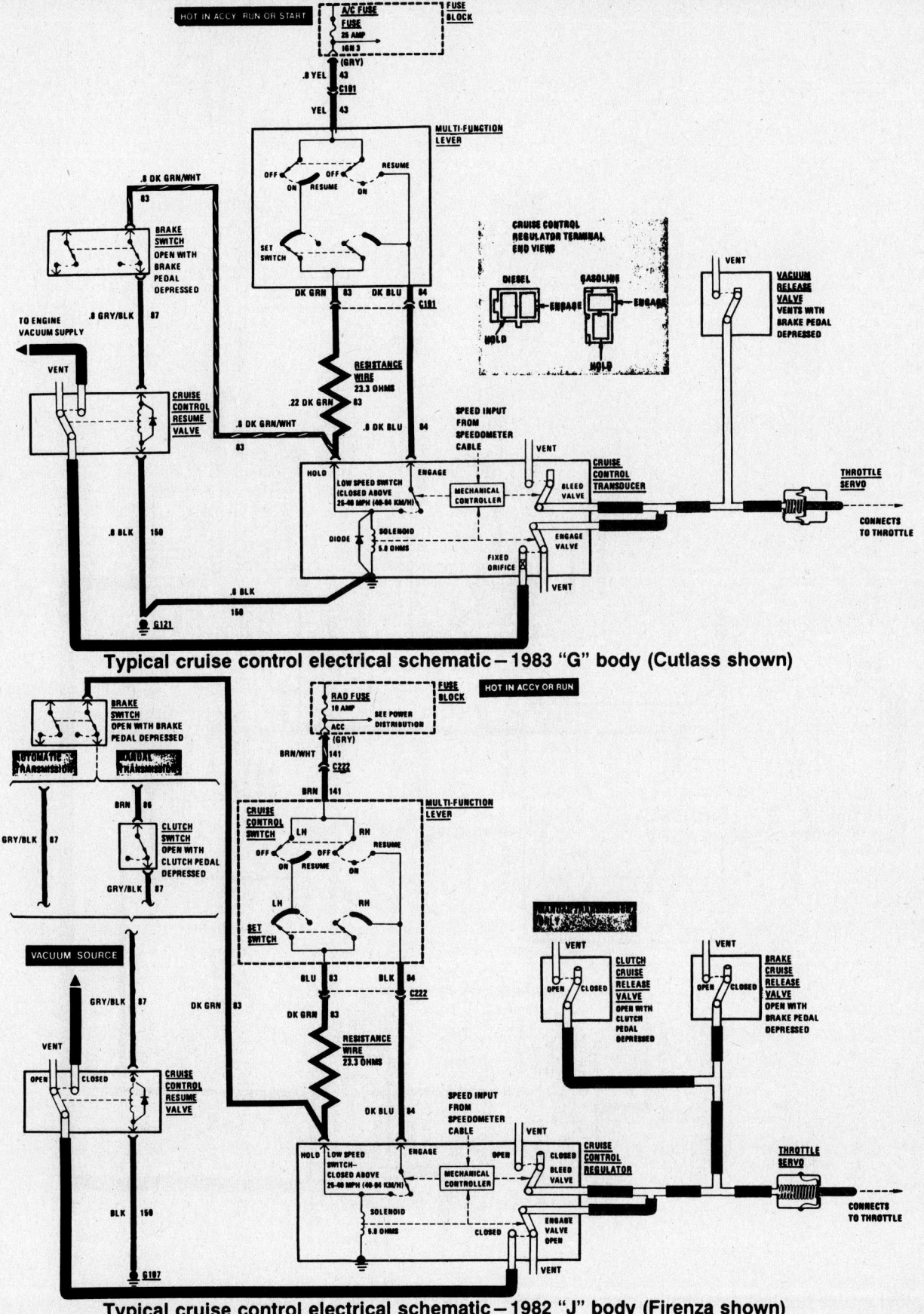

Typical cruise control electrical schematic—1983 "G" body (Cutlass shown)

Typical cruise control electrical schematic—1982 "J" body (Firenza shown)

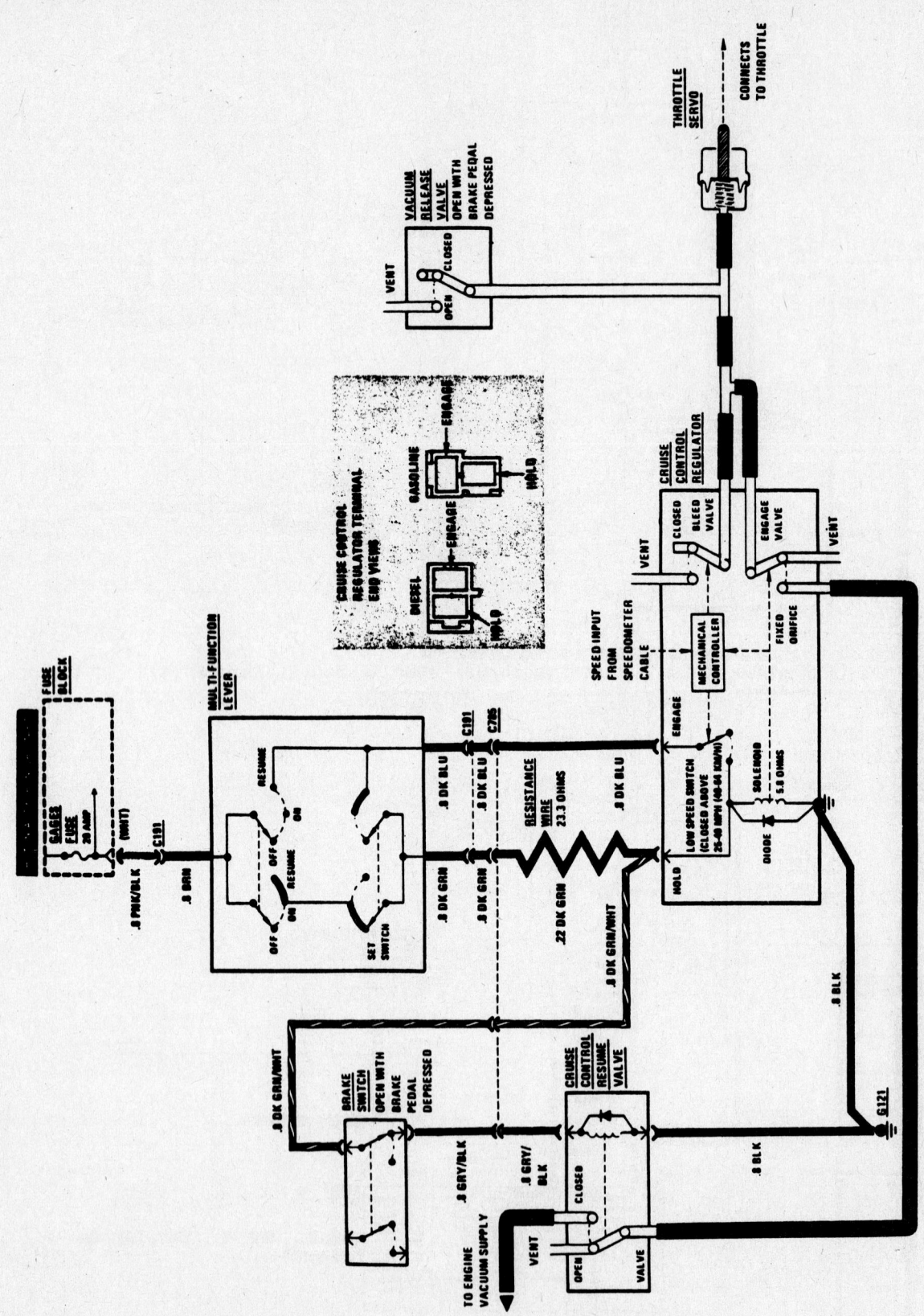

Typical cruise control electrical schematic — 1982 "G" body (Cutlass shown)

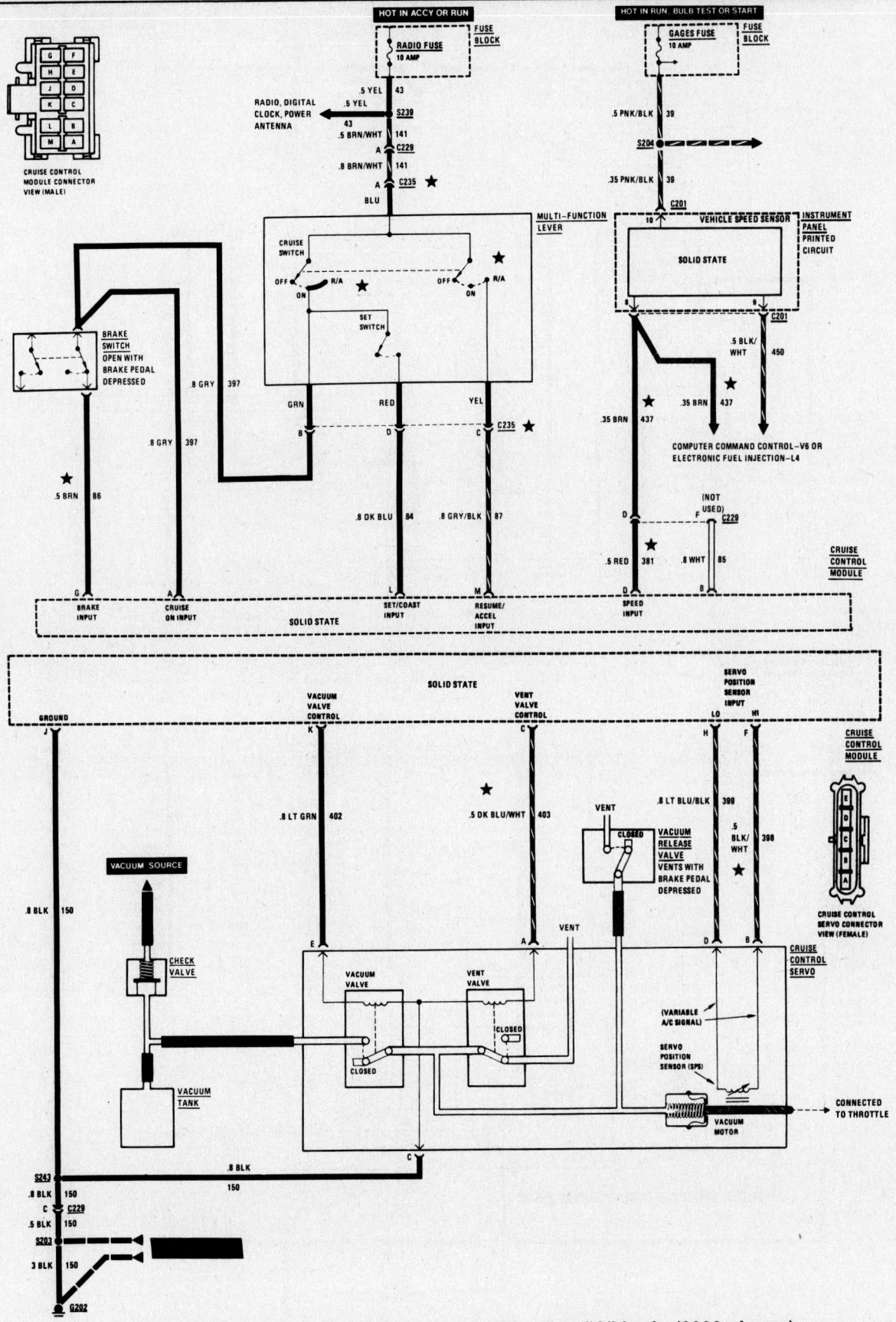

Typical cruise control electrical schematic—1984 "A" body (6000 shown)

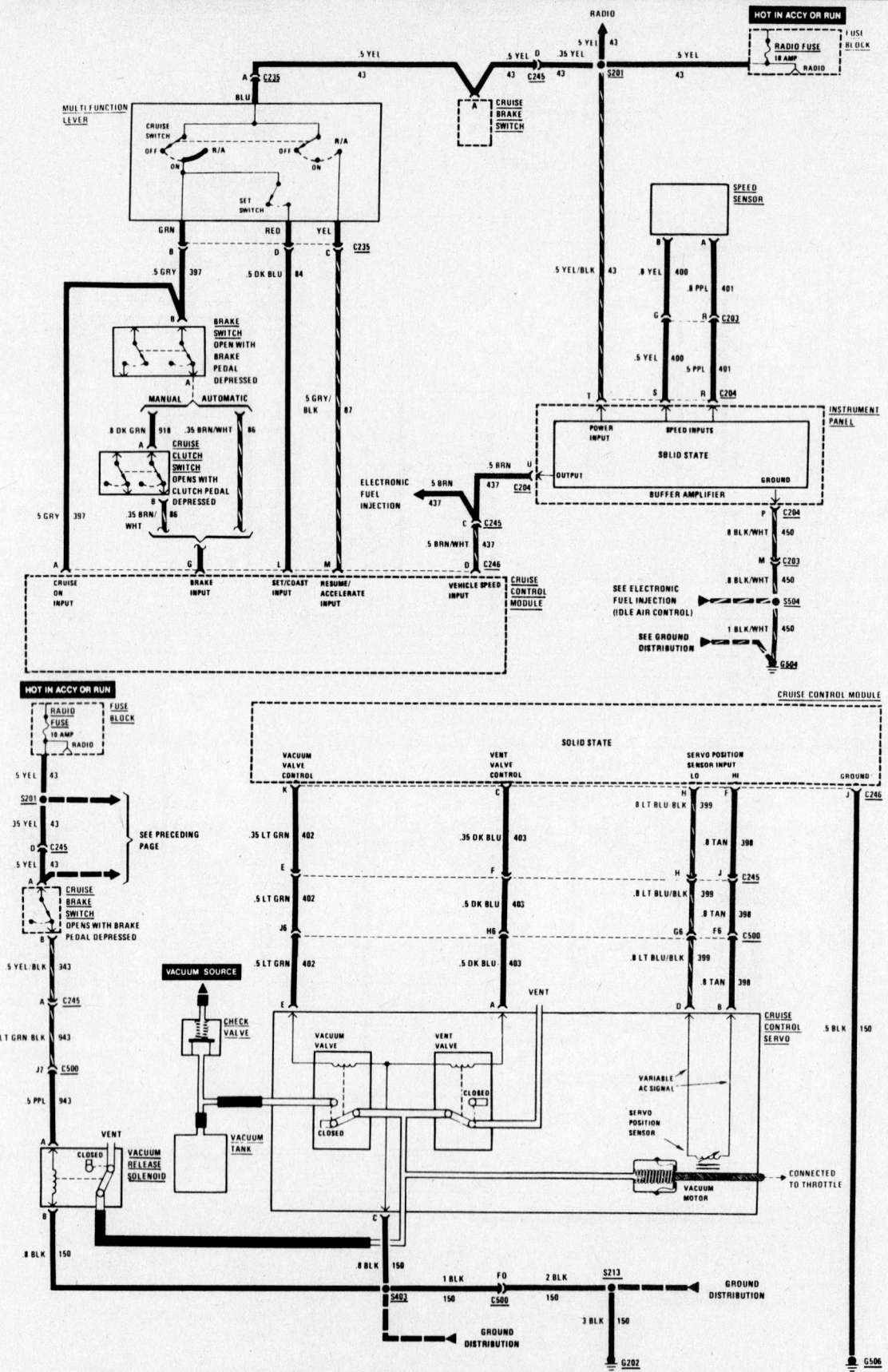

Typical cruise control electrical schematic—1985 and later "P" body (Fiero)

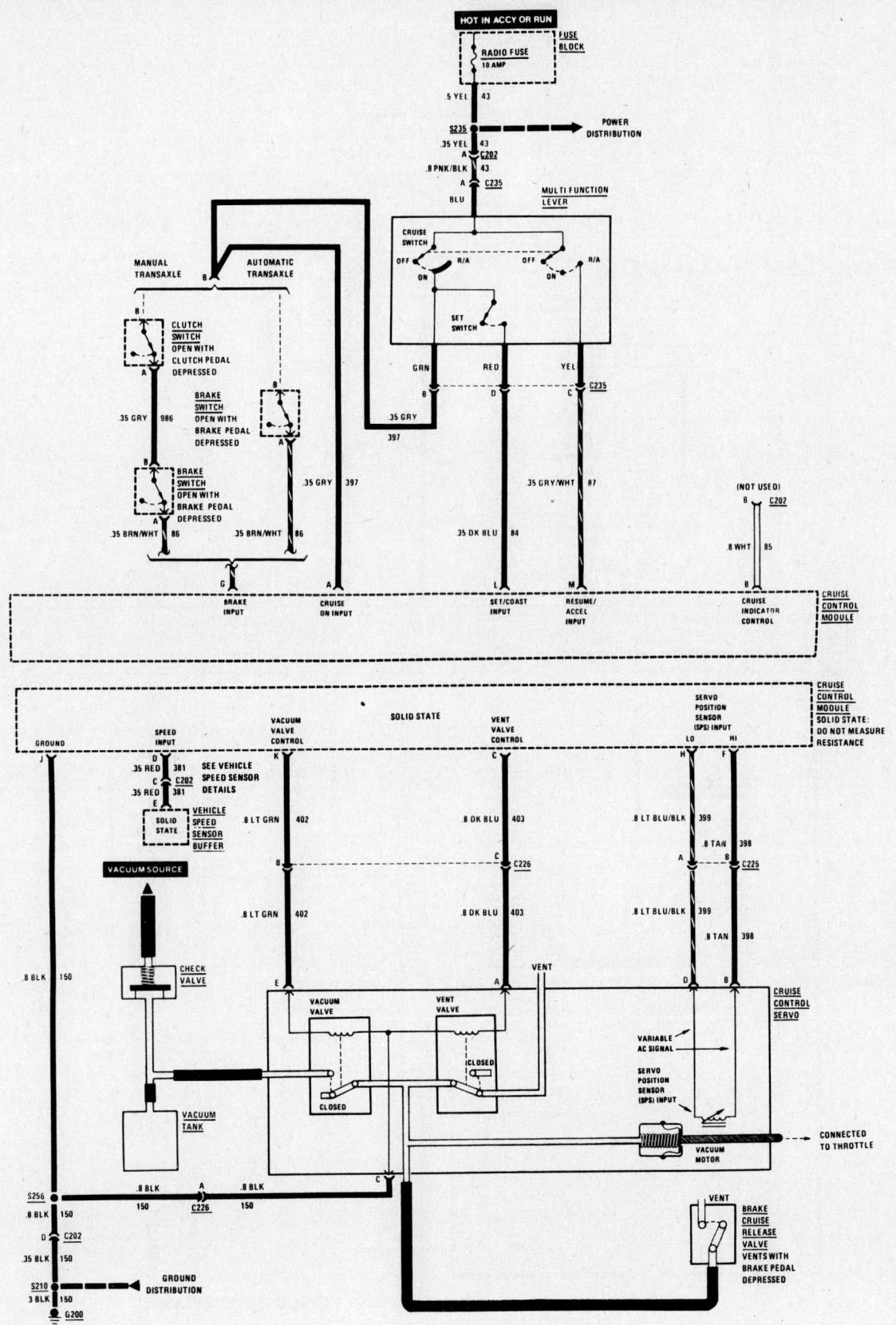

Typical cruise control electrical schematic—1985 and later "N" body (Gran Am shown)

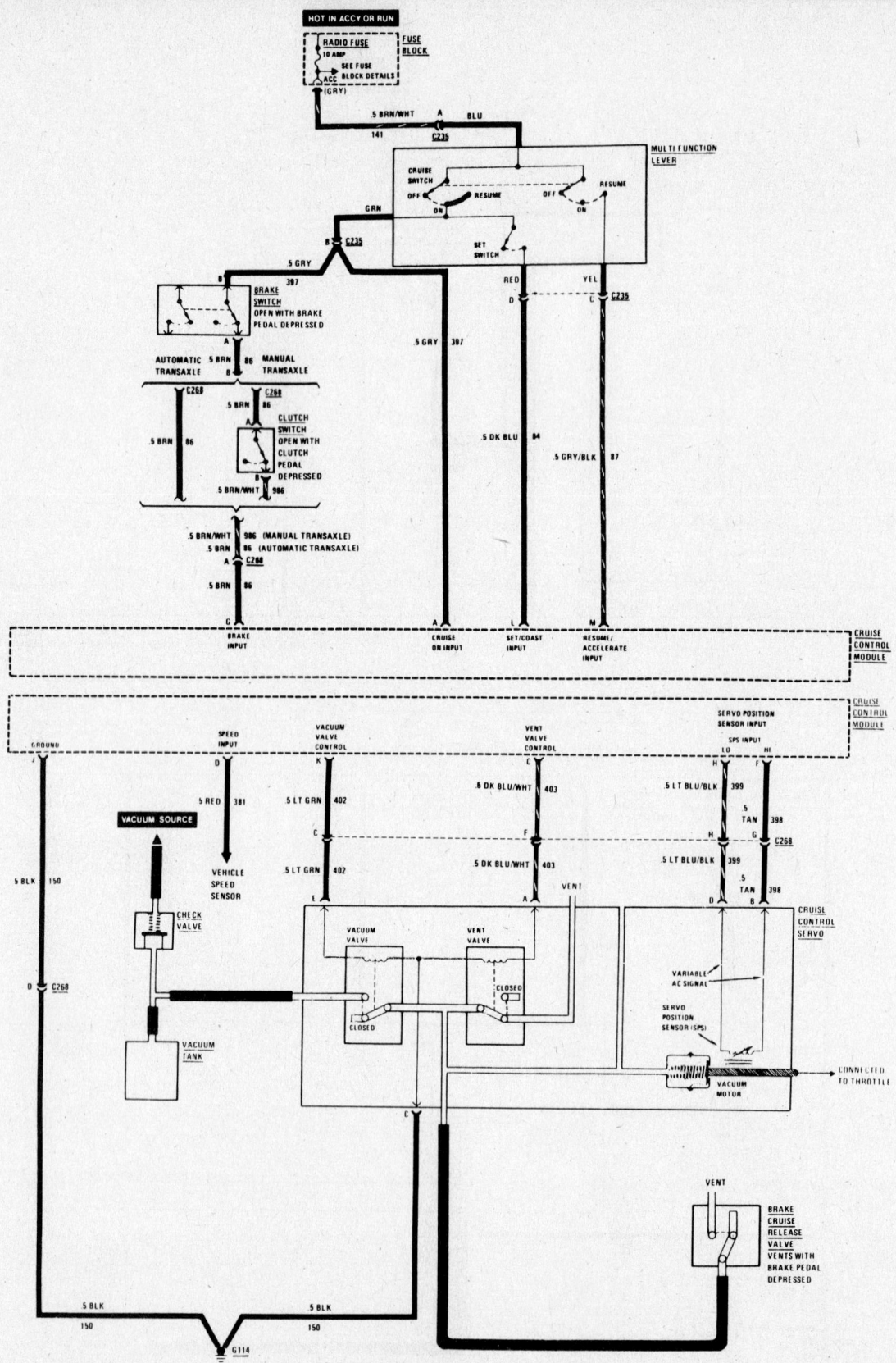

Typical cruise control electrical schematic—1985 and later "J" body (Sunbird shown)

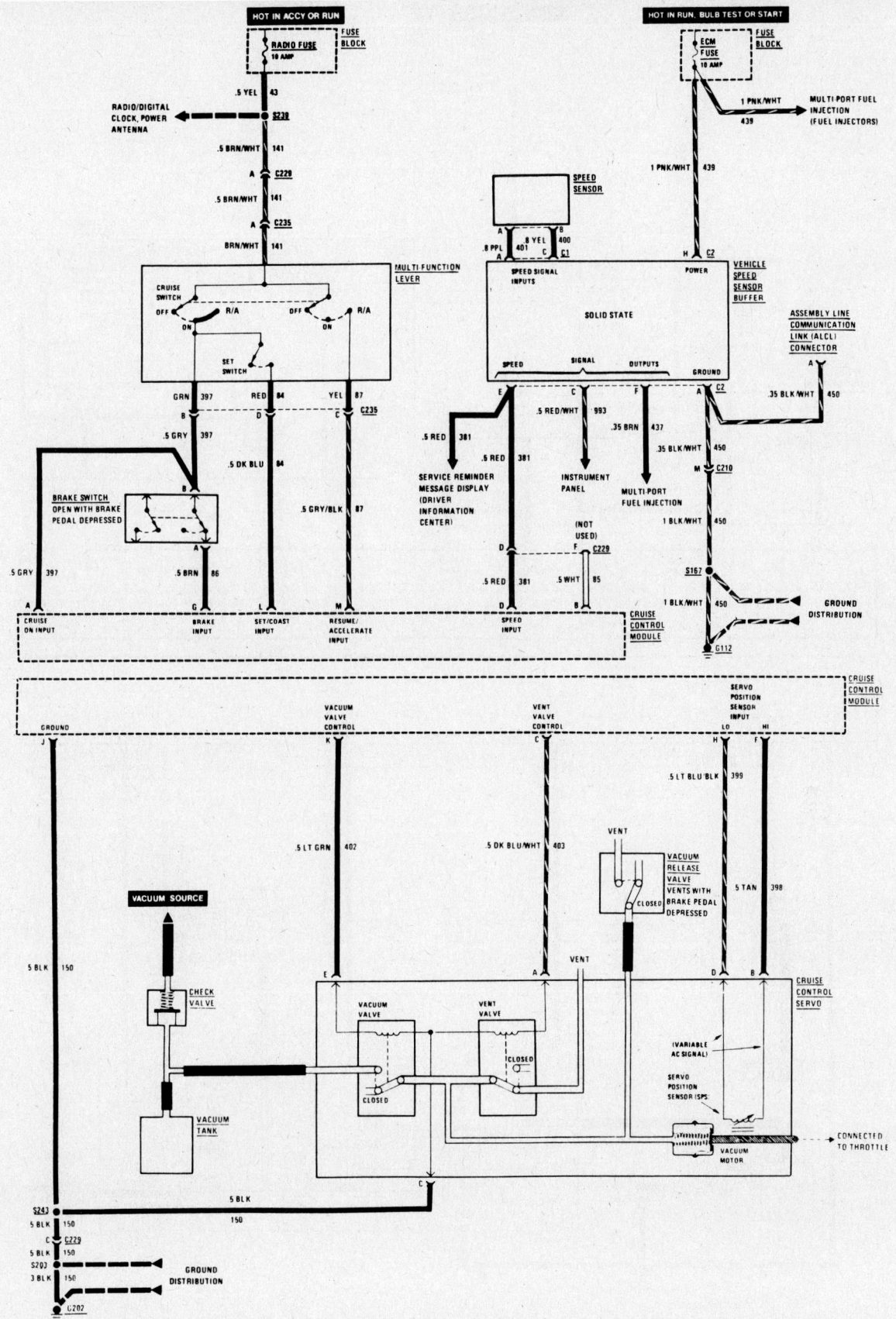

Typical cruise control electrical schematic — 1985 and later "A" body (6000 shown)

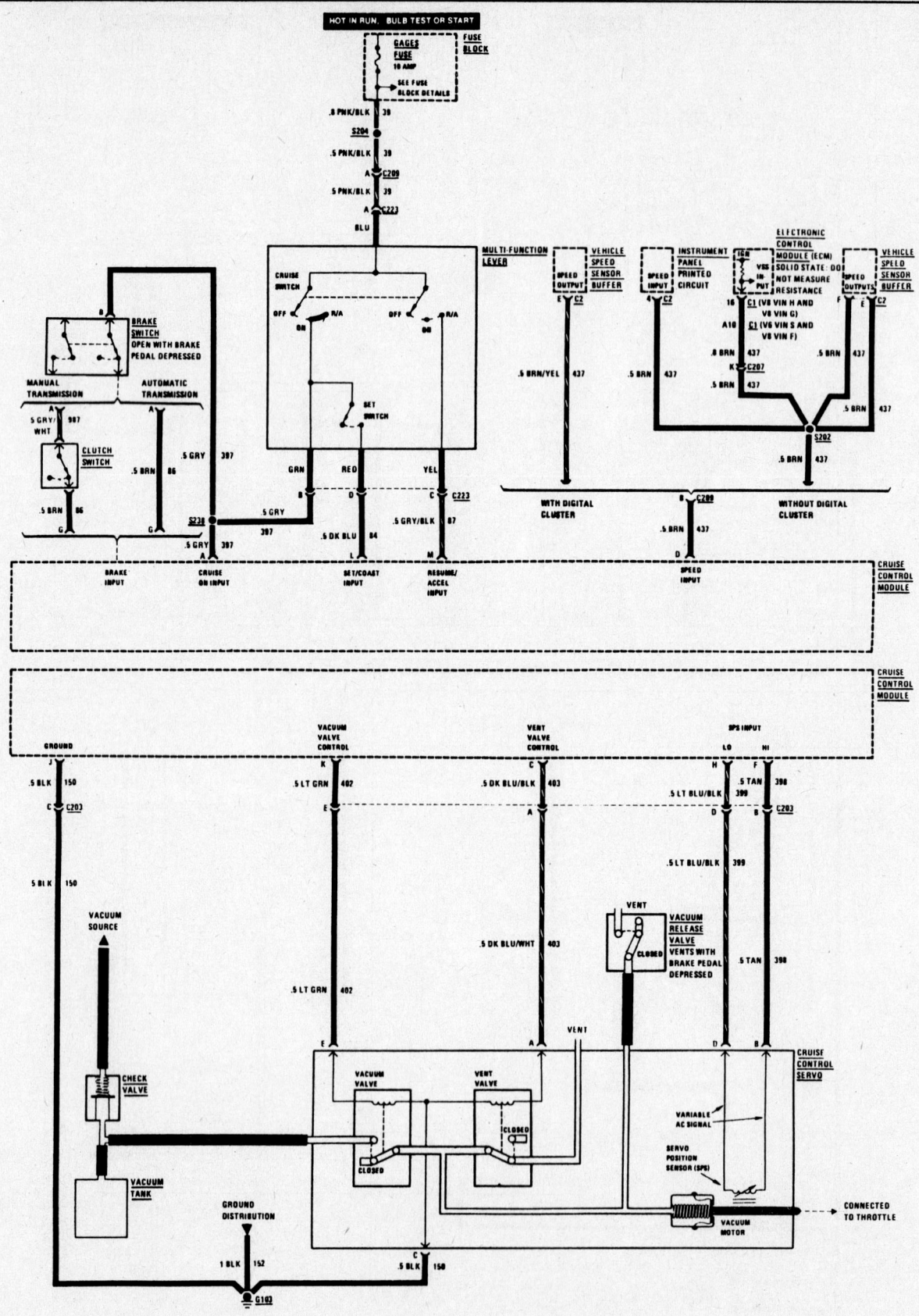

Typical cruise control electrical schematic—1985 and later "F" body (Firebird shown)

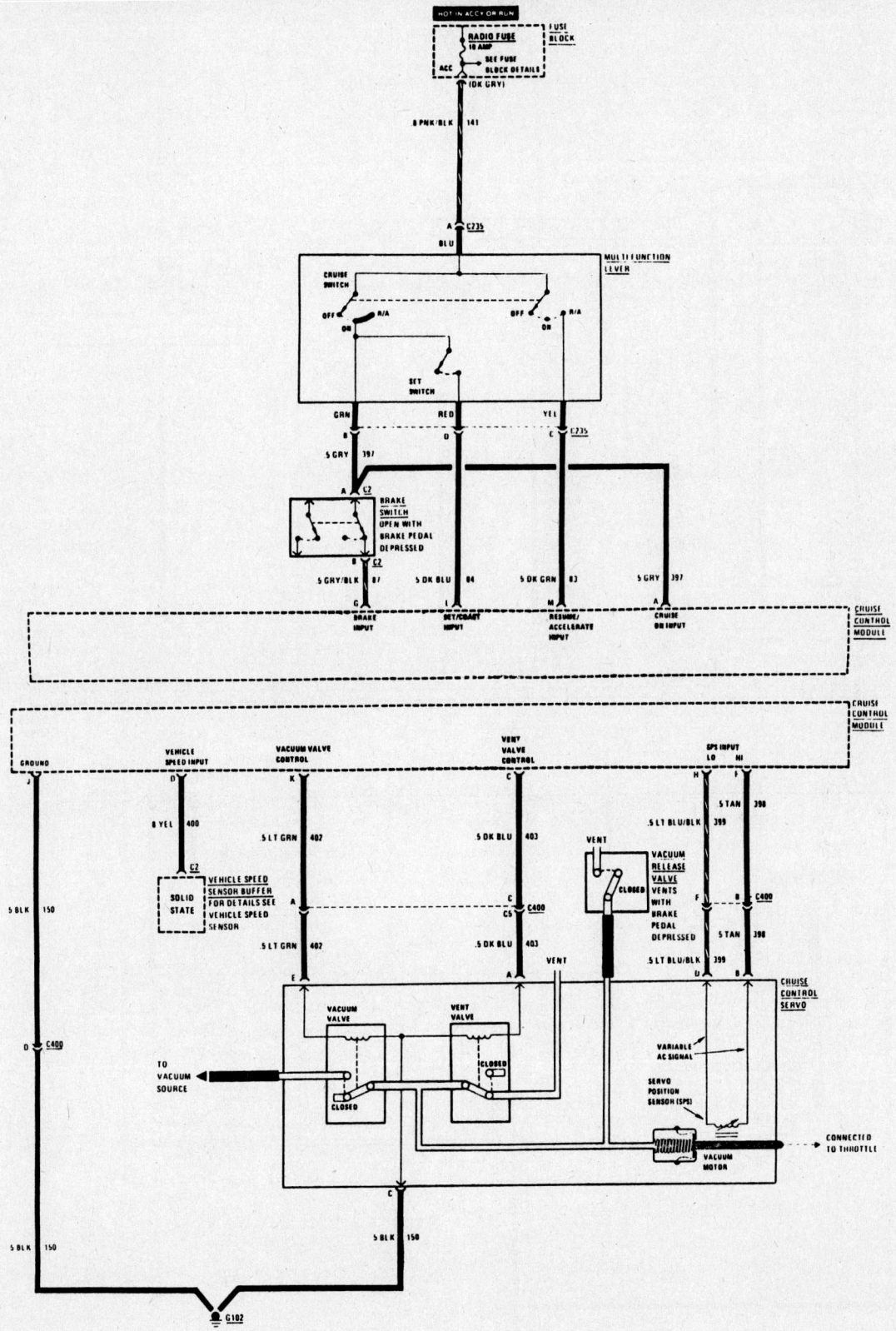

Typical cruise control electrical schematic—1985 and later "B" body (Parisienne shown)

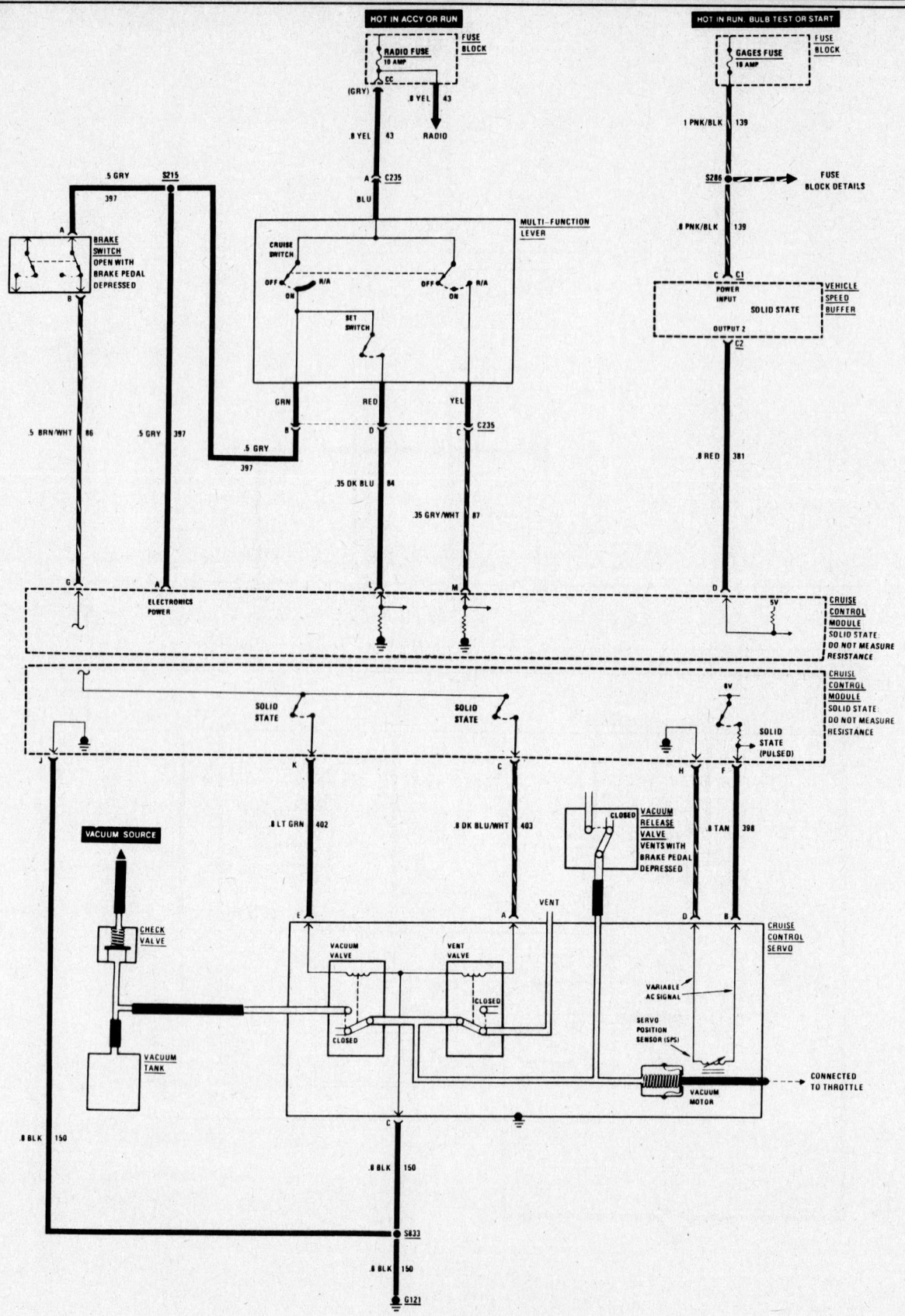

Typical cruise control electrical schematic—1985 and later "G" body (Grand Prix and Bonneville shown)

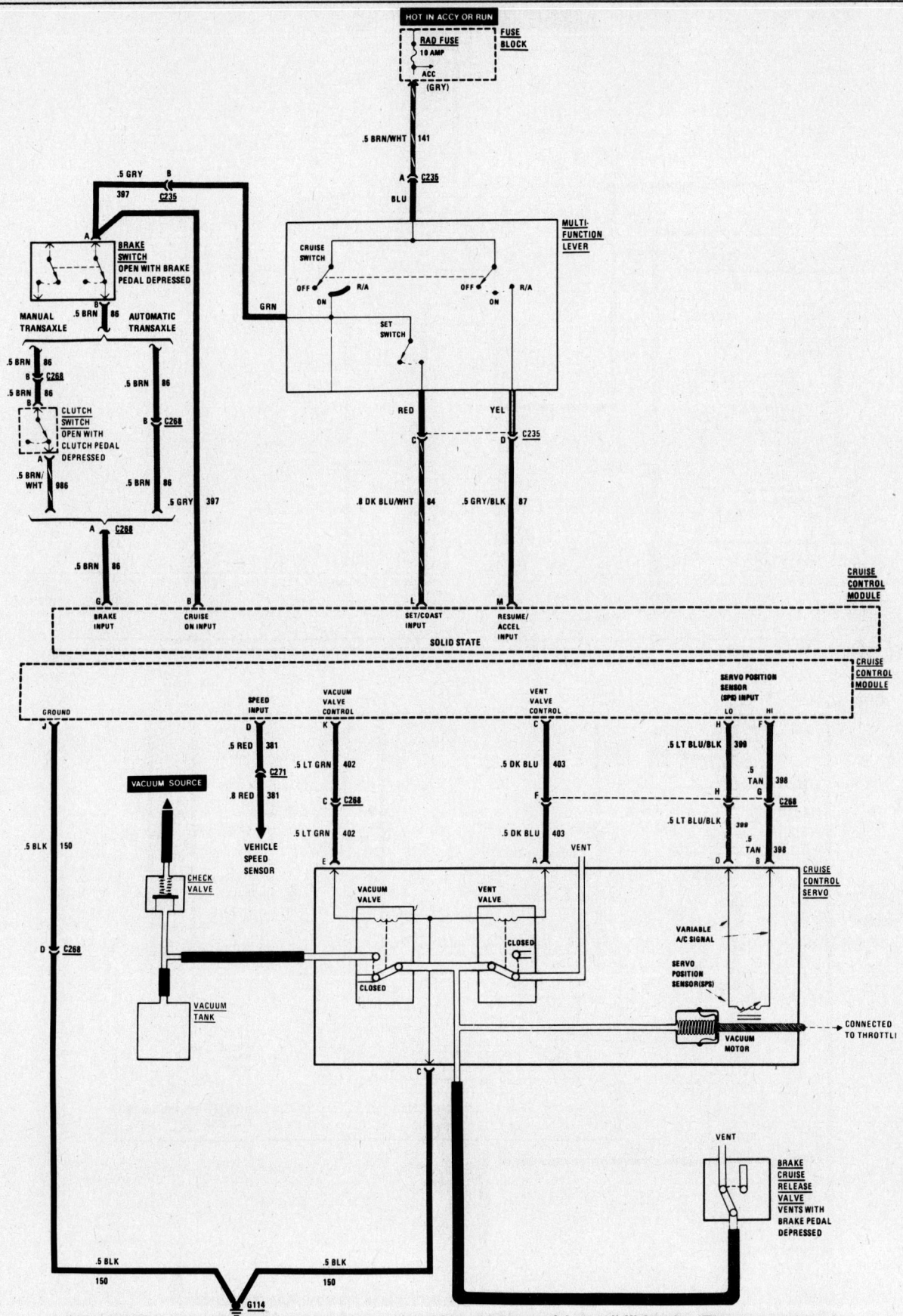

Typical cruise control electrical schematic—1985 and later "J" body (Firenza shown)

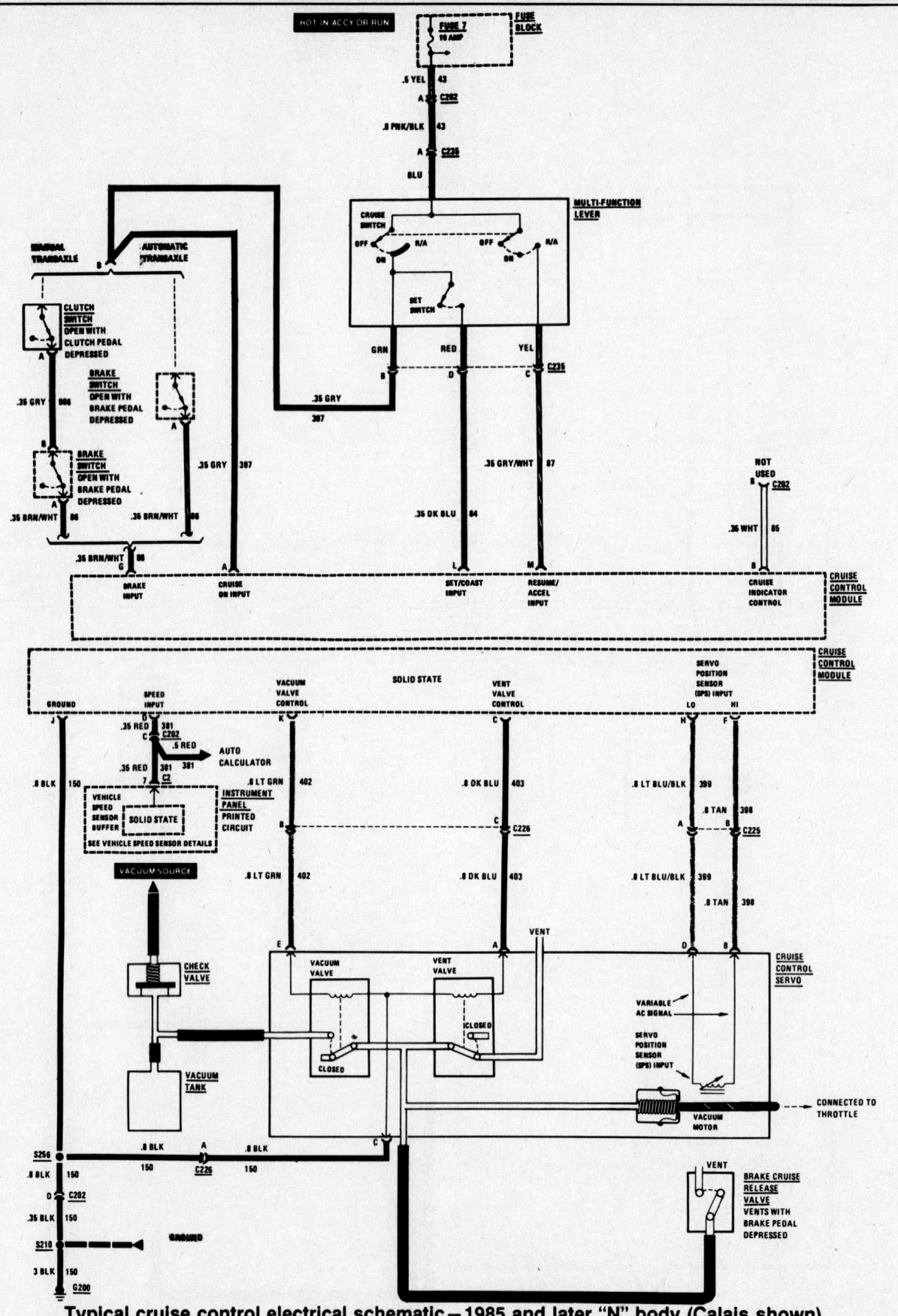

Typical cruise control electrical schematic—1985 and later "N" body (Calais shown)

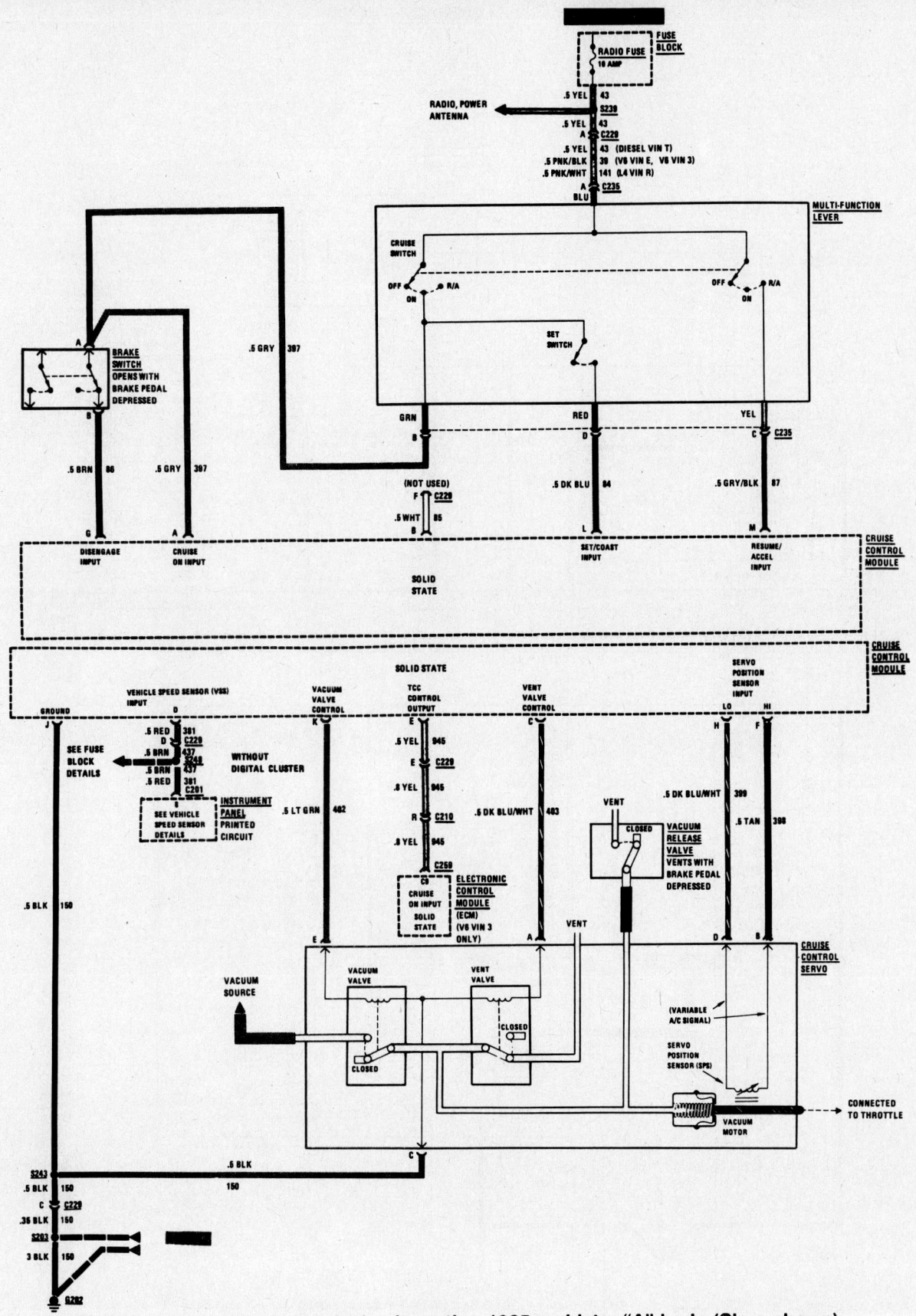

Typical cruise control electrical schematic—1985 and later "A" body (Ciera shown)

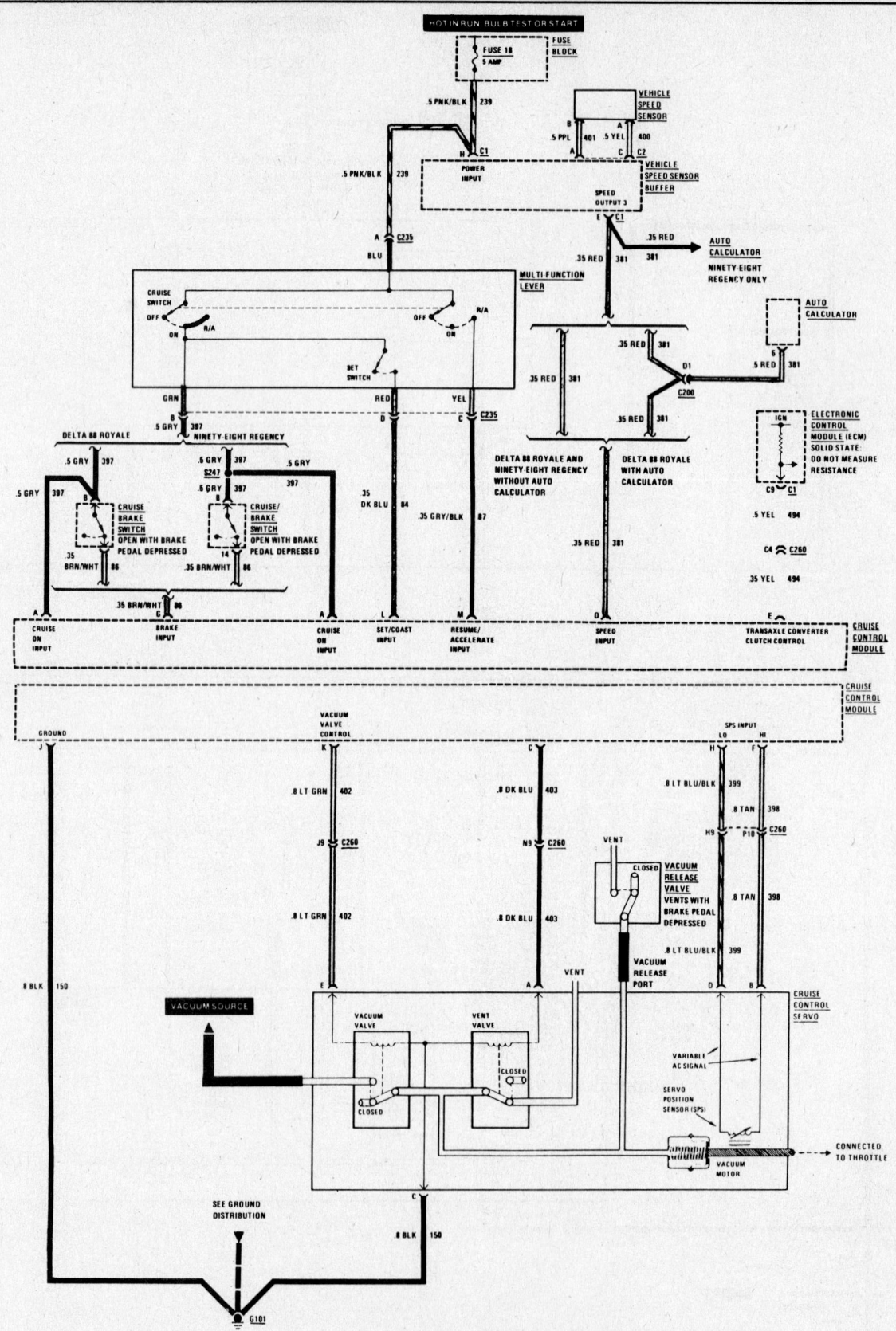

Typical cruise control electrical schematic—1985 and later "C" body

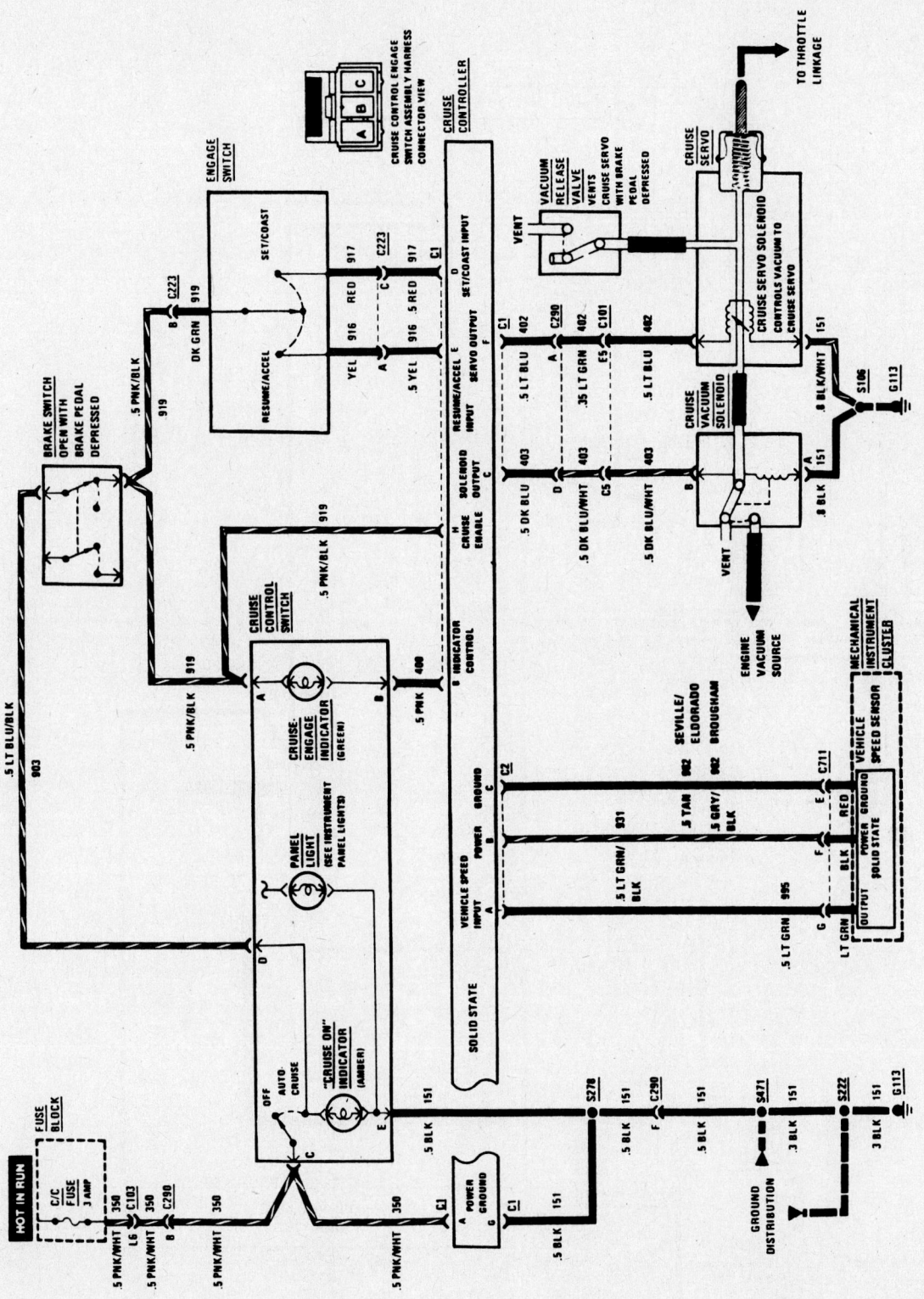

Typical cruise control electrical schematic — 1984 "E", "K" and "C" body with diesel engine, with digital instrument cluster

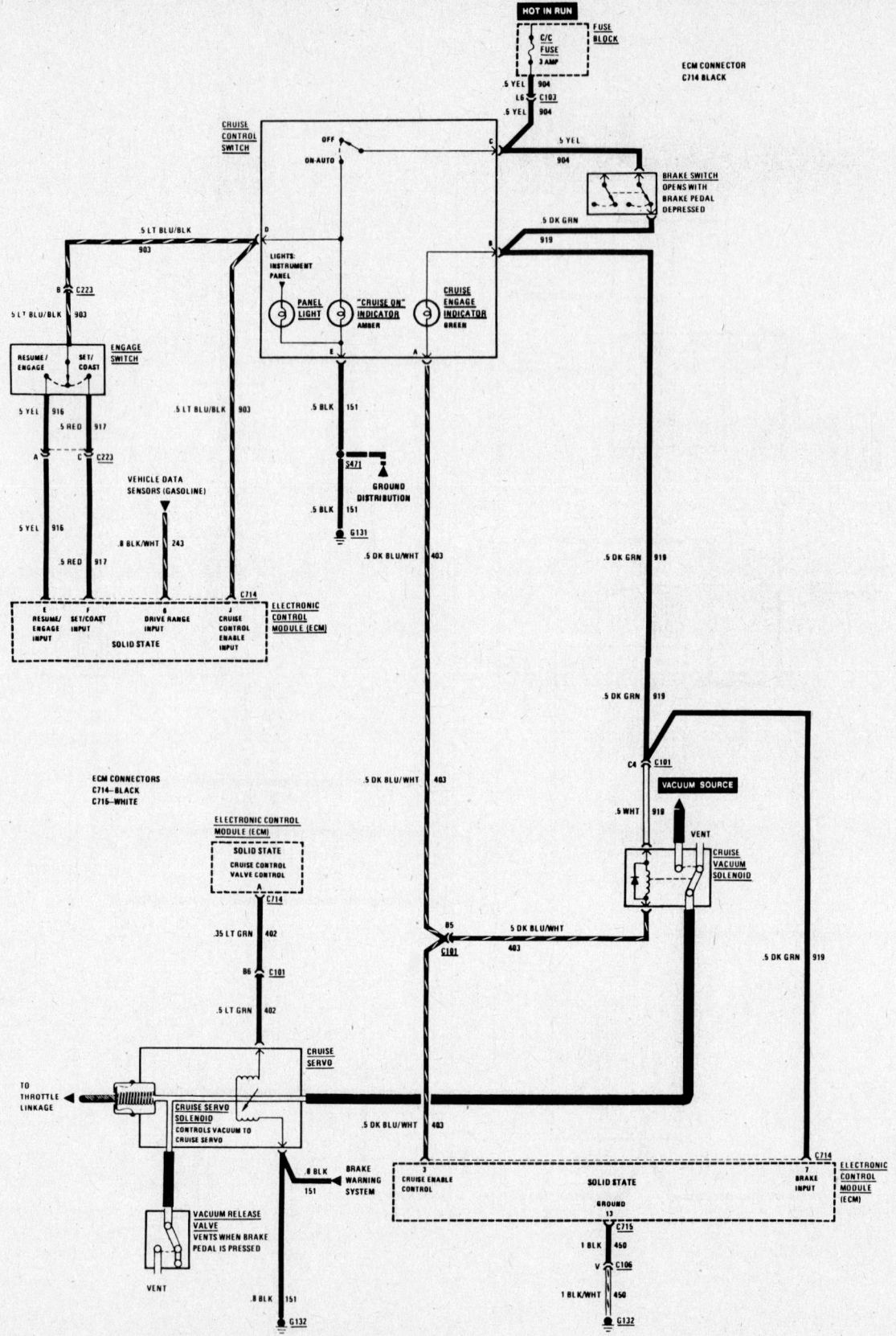

Typical cruise control electrical schematic—1985 "E", "K" and "C" body with gas engine (Eldorado, Seville and RWD DeVille shown)

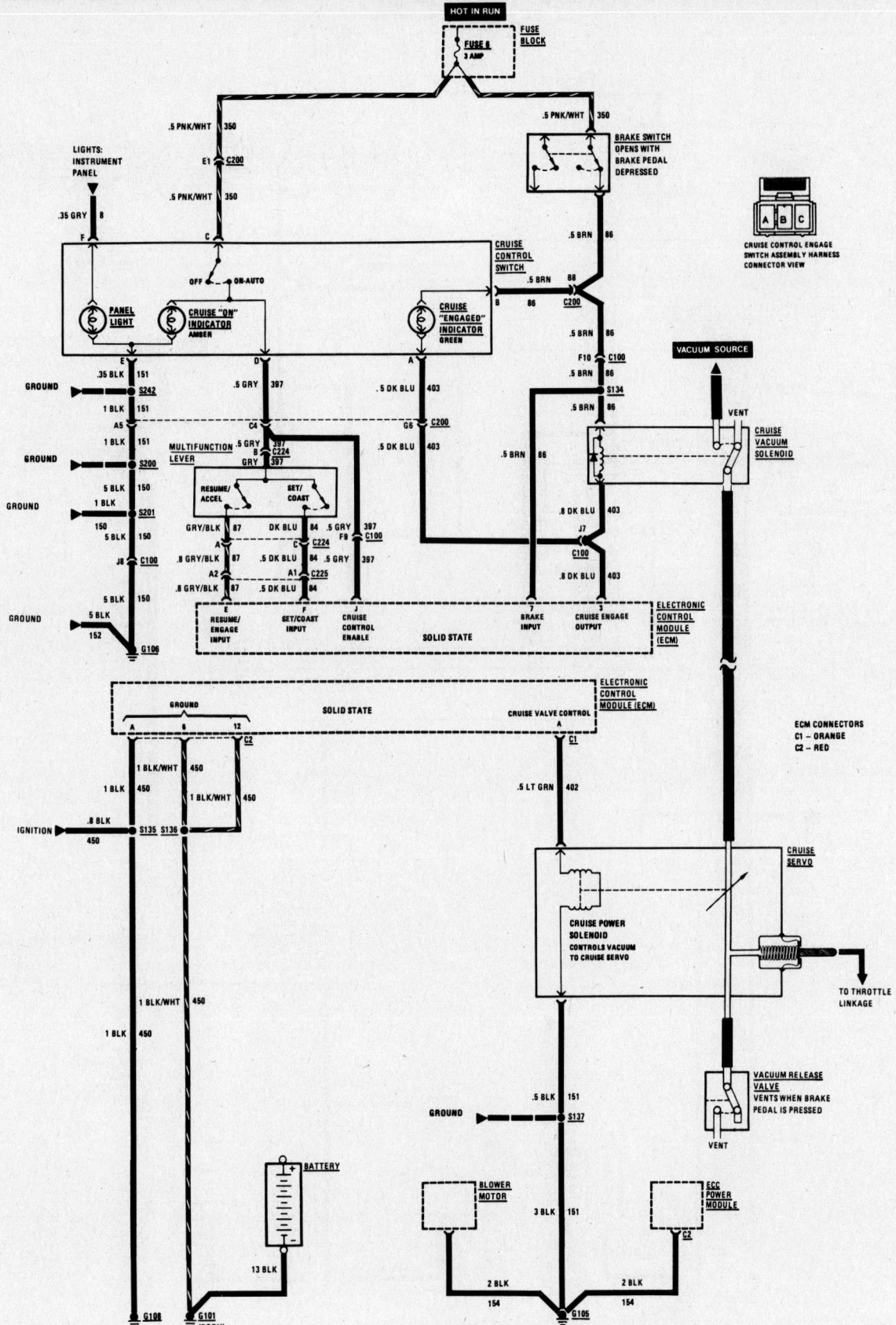

Typical cruise control electrical schematic—1985 and later "C" body with diesel engine (FWD DeVille shown)

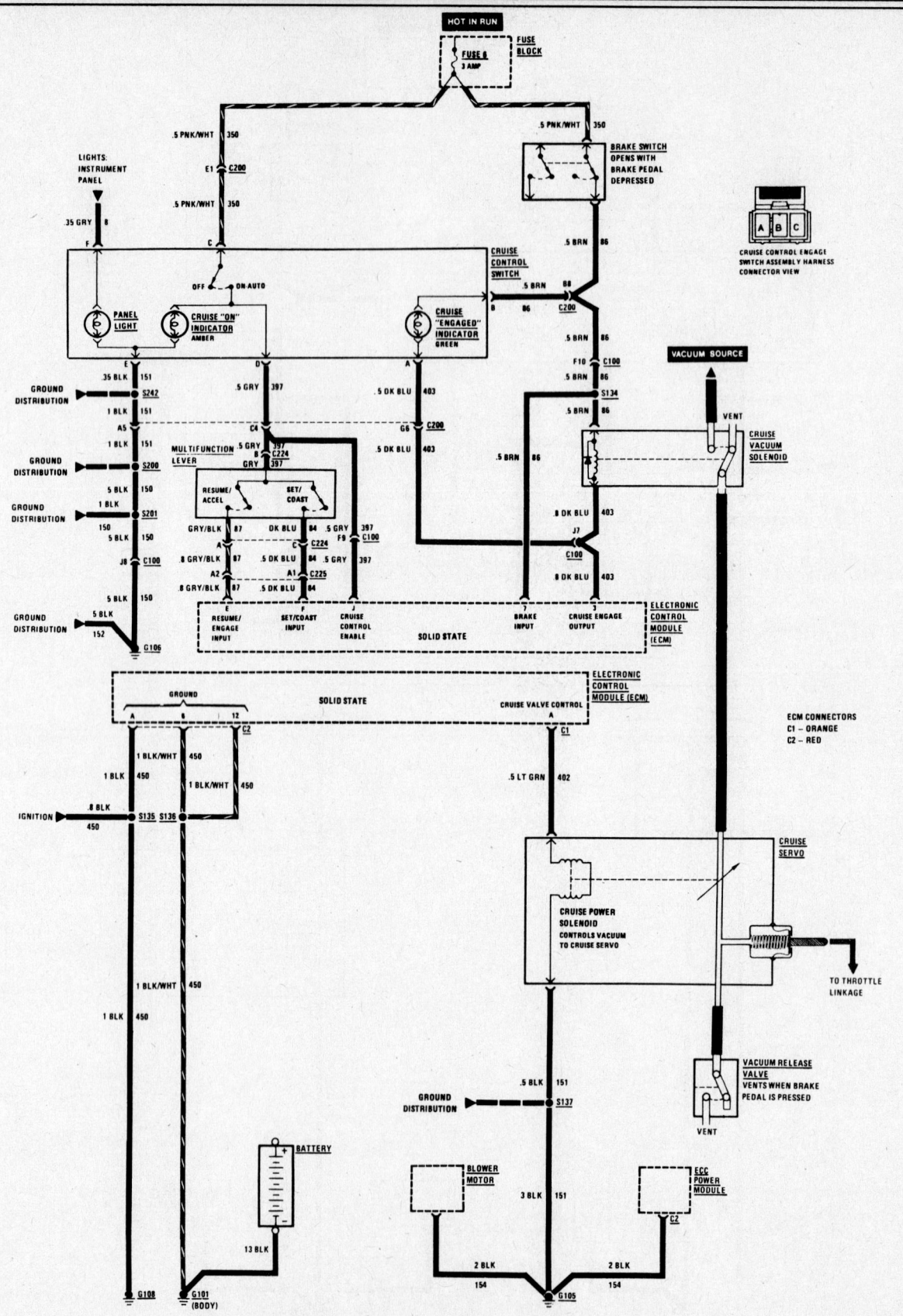

Typical cruise control electrical schematic—1985 and later "C" body with gas engine (FWD DeVille shown)

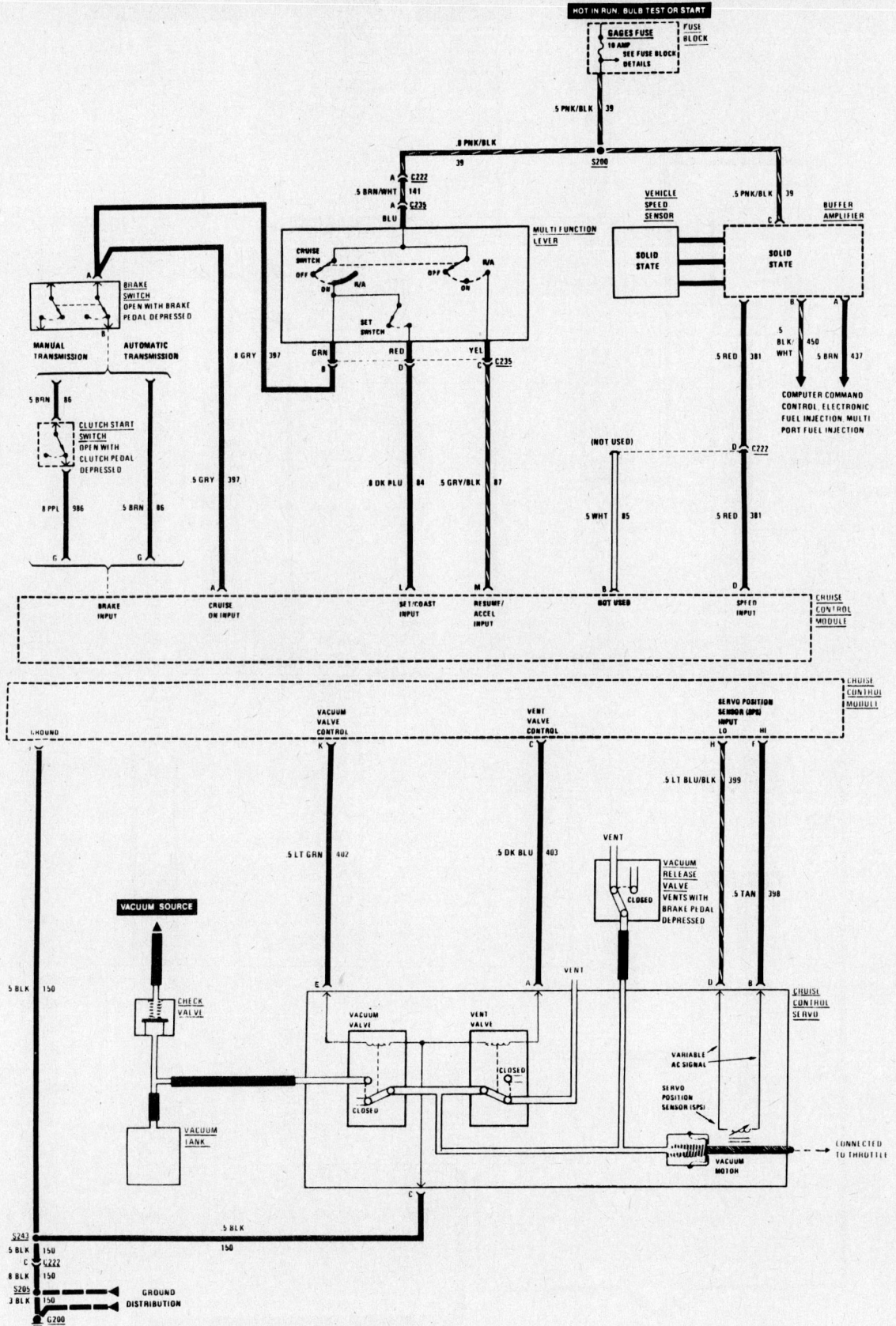

Typical cruise control electrical schematic – 1985 "X" body (Skylark shown)

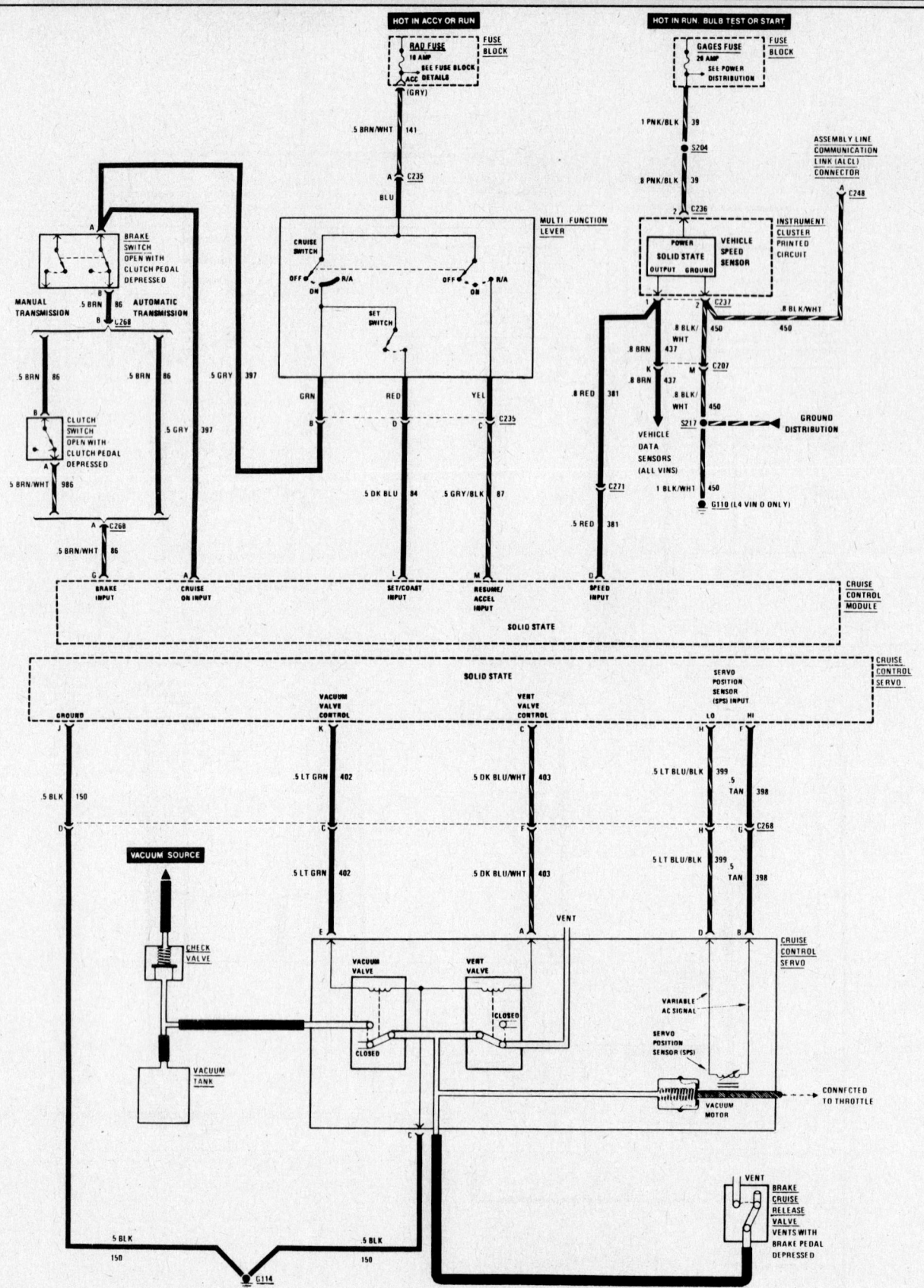

Typical cruise control electrical schematic—1985 and later "J" body (Skyhawk shown)

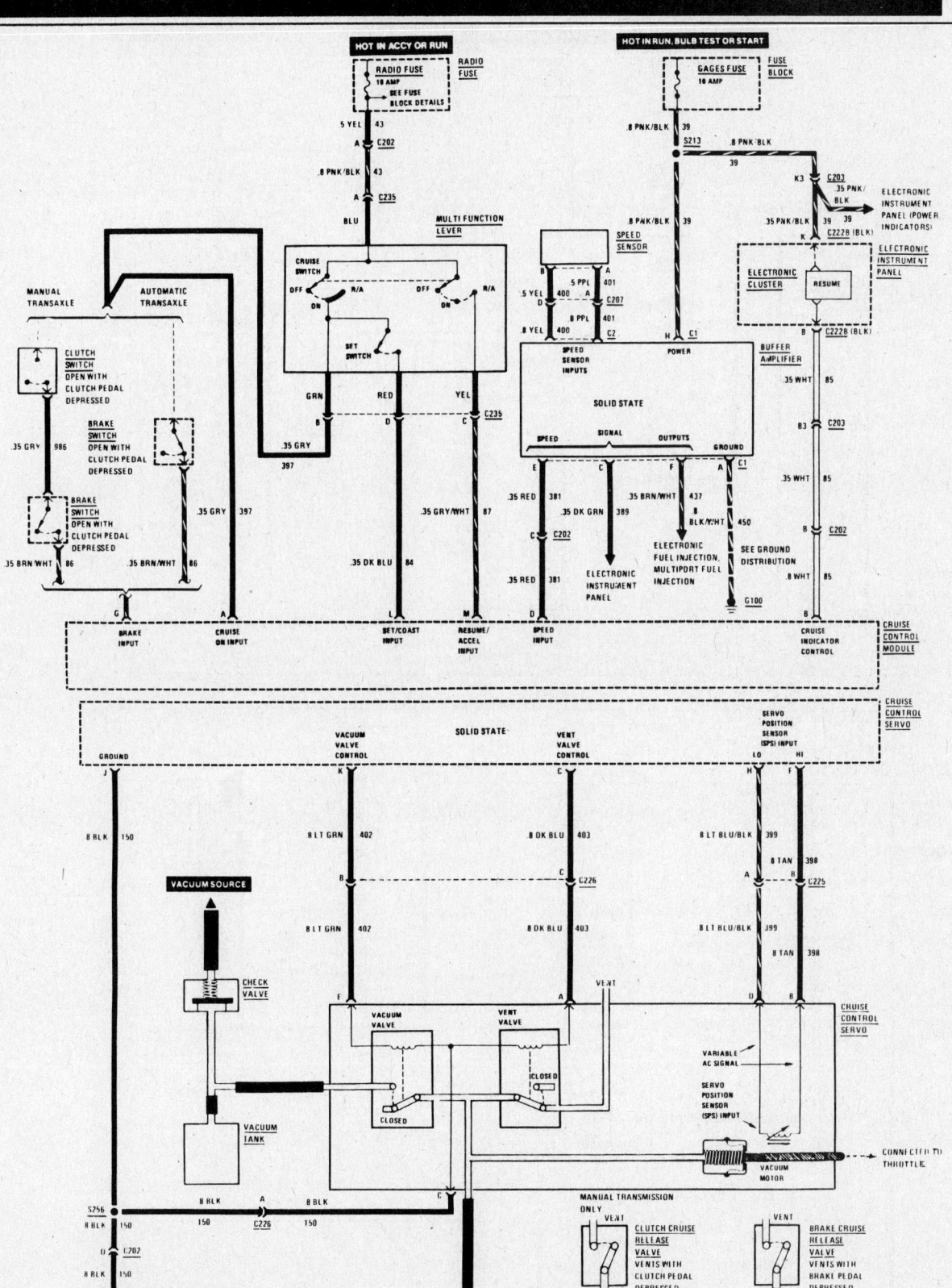

Typical cruise control electrical schematic—1985 and later "N" body (Somerset shown)

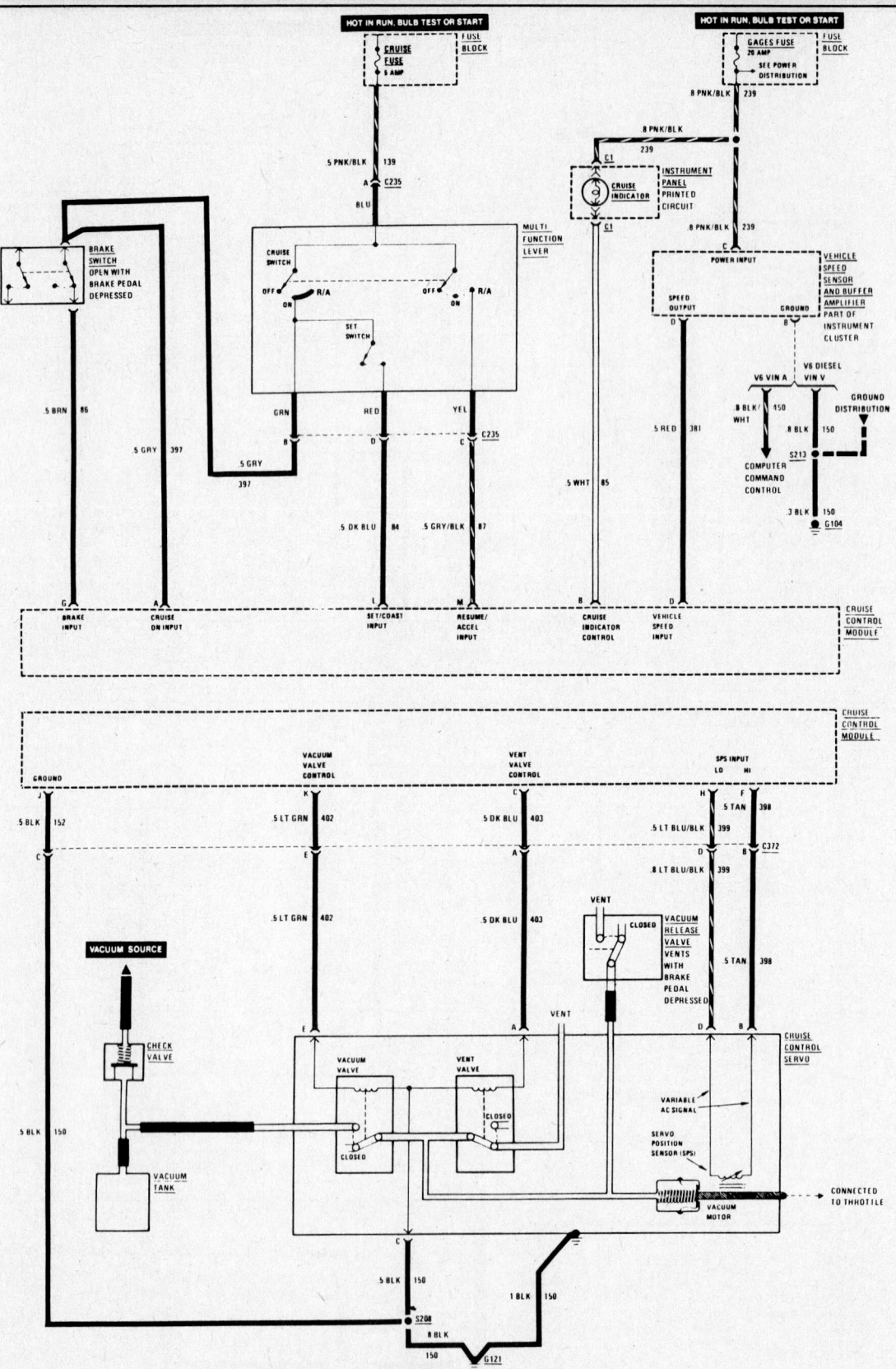

Typical cruise control electrical schematic — 1985 and later "G" body (Regal shown)

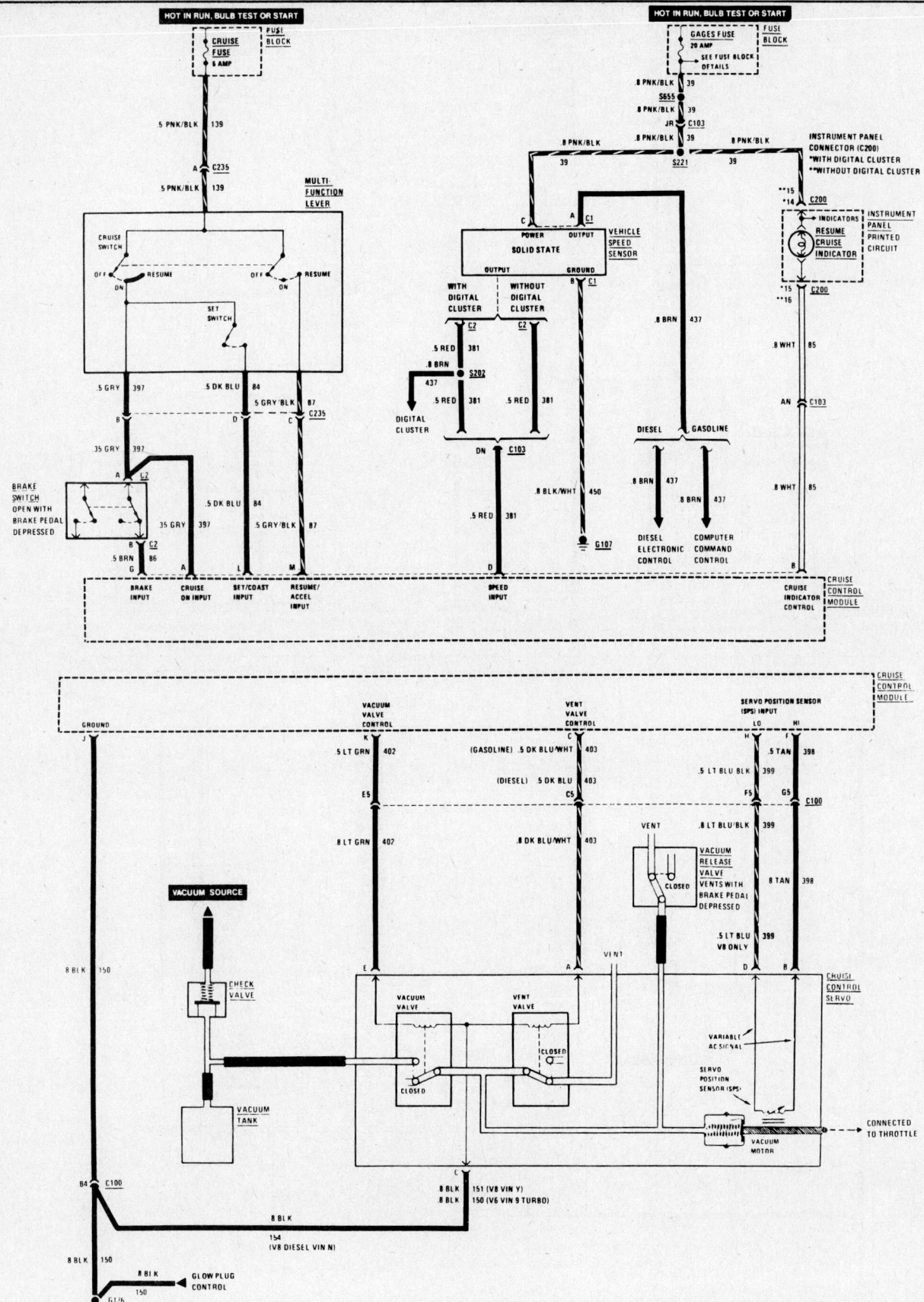

Typical cruise control electrical schematic — 1985 "E" body (Riviera shown)

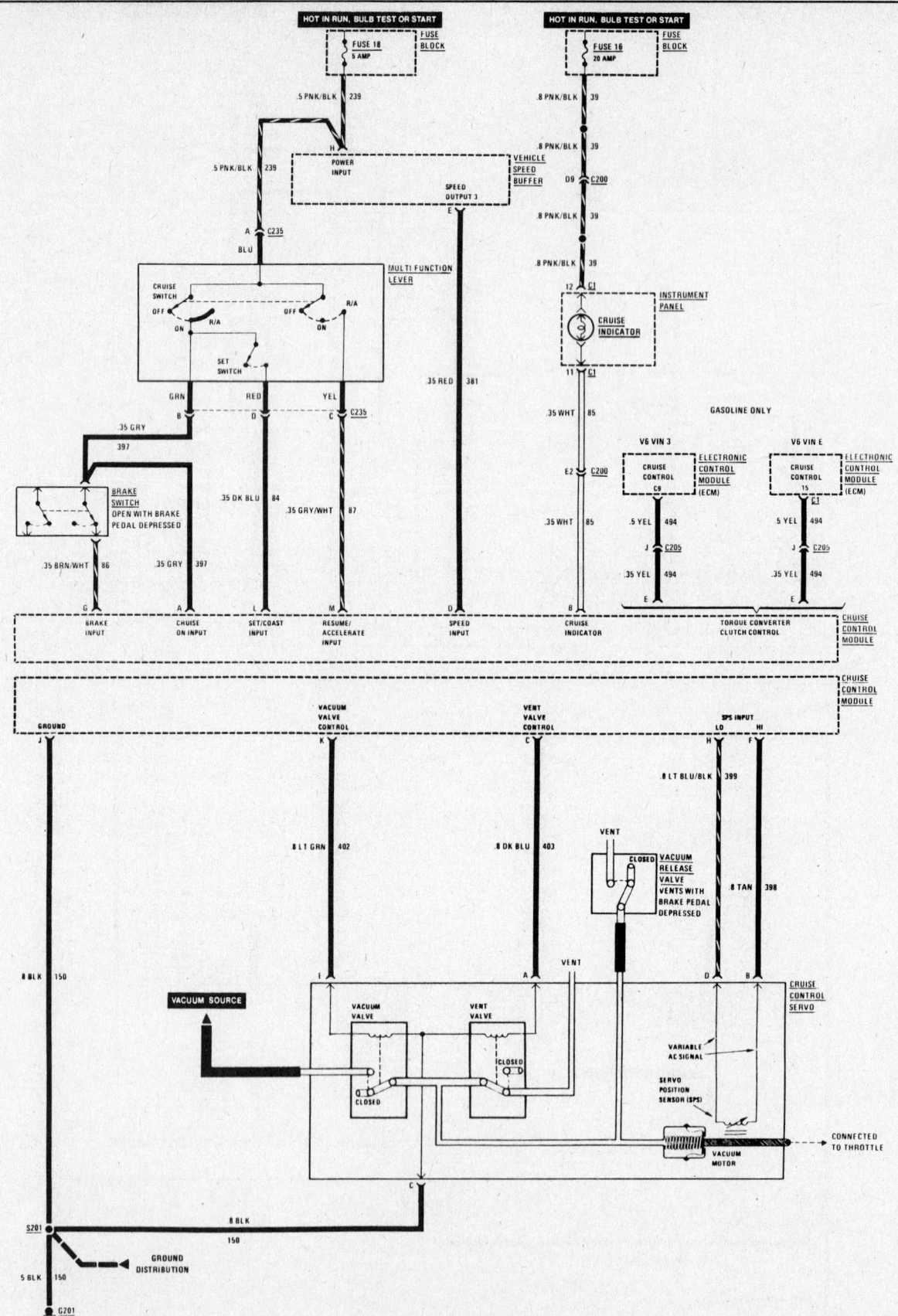

Typical cruise control electrical schematic – 1985 and later "C" body(Park Avenue shown)

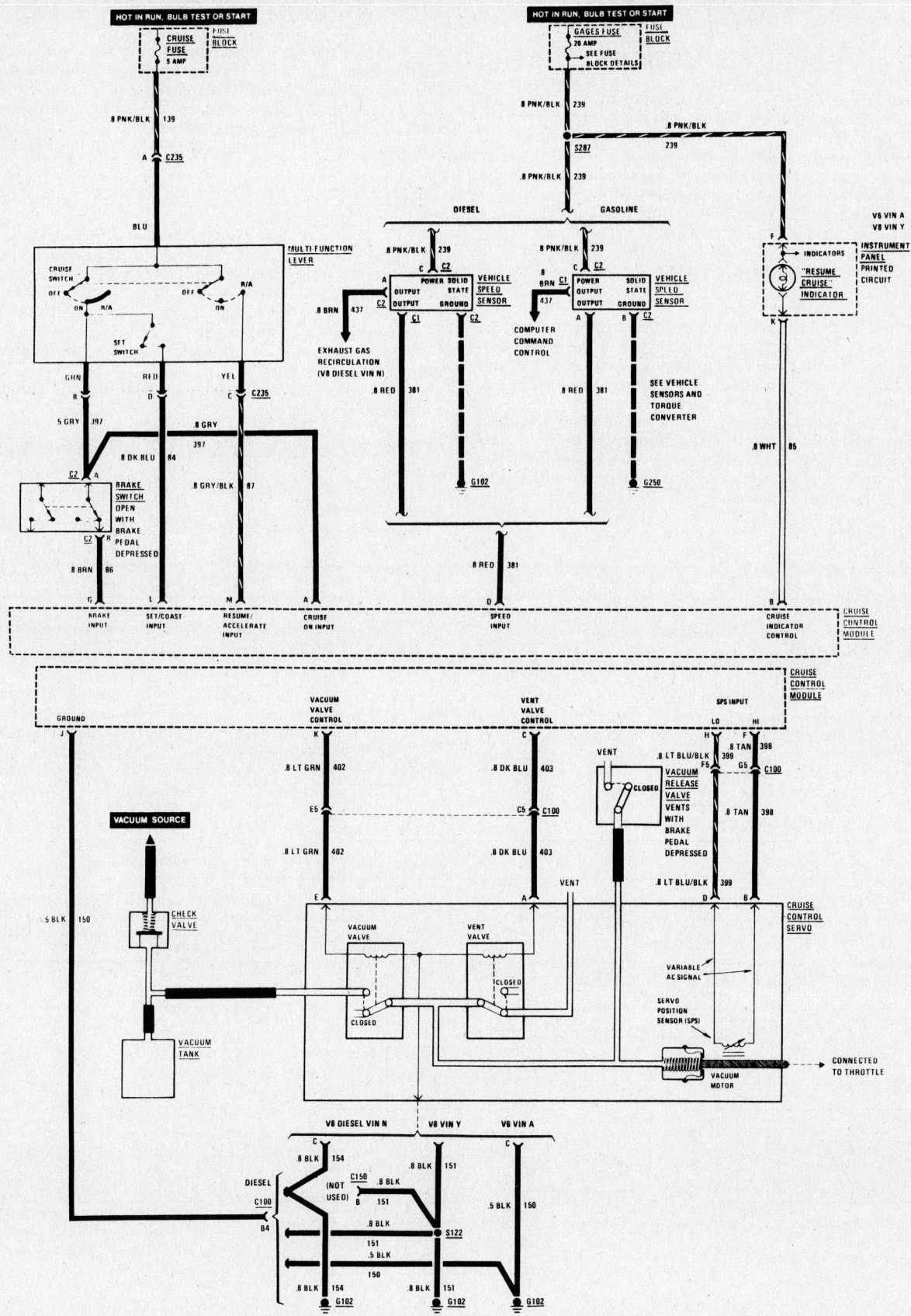

Typical cruise control electrical schematic—1985 "B" body (LeSabre shown)

Buick

VISUAL INSPECTION

Before performing any tests make a visual inspection of the cruise control system. Check all items in the system for abnormal conditions such as bare broken or disconnected wires and damage to the vacuum hoses. Be sure that the speedometer cables are attached and properly routed. All vacuum hoses must be properly routed and must not have any kinks or bends. Be sure that all electrical connections are complete and tight. The wiring harness must be routed properly.

SERVO TEST

1982–83

To determine the condition of the servo diaphragm, remove the vacuum hose from the servo assembly. Apply 14 inches of vacuum to the tube opening and hold in in place for about one minute. The vacuum should not leak down more than 5 inches. If vacuum leaks, replace the servo assembly.

Another test consists of removing the vacuum hose attached to the servo assembly, than push the diaphragm in, hold your finger over the nipple and the diaphragm should remain in the pushed in position. If the servo assembly does not perform as indicated it should be replaced.

1984 and Later

VACUUM LEAK TEST (1982–83)

The vacuum release valves, the resume valve and all the connecting hoses can be checked by applying 15 inches of vacuum to each component and then sealing off the component for about one minute. The vacuum should not leak down more than 5 inches. Repair or replace defective components as required.

ELECTRICAL SYSTEM TEST (1982–83)

1. Check the cruise control fuse and electrical connector.
2. Check all electrical connections. Disconnect and reconnect after checking for bent, broken or dirty mating tabs.
3. Check the electrical release switch as follows. Unplug the connector at the switch. Connect an ohmmeter to the two terminals on the switch assembly.
4. Depress the brake or clutch pedal. The ohmmeter should not indicate continuity.
5. Release the pedal, the ohmmeter should indicate continunity.

CONTROL LEVER SWITCH TEST (1982–83)

1. Disconnect the electrical connector at the cruise control engagement switch.
2. Connect an ohmmeter to the brown and blue wires.

TEST		NORMAL REACTION
1	Apply 12 volts dc to servo pins A and E. Then ground servo pin C. NOTE: Pin A to pin C closes the normally-open vent valve; whereas, pin E to pin C opens the normally-closed vacuum valve.	Servo should full stroke. If not, check vacuum hoses to the vacuum supply.
2	Remove the 12 volts dc source voltage from SERVO pin E.	The servo should hold a full stroke. If not, go to step 3. If servo holds, go to step 4.
3	Disconnect vacuum brake release at servo and plug vacuum release port on the servo. Momentarily apply 12 volts dc to pin E to allow servo to full stroke.	If the servo holds its position, adjust the brake vacuum release valve or replace the valve.
4	Turn ignition "ON".	Vacuum release valve should engage.
5	Turn ignition "OFF" and disconnect vacuum valve harness connector at valve. Then turn ignition "ON".	If the brake switch is properly adjusted, battery voltage should be present across the two connector terminals on the switch. No battery voltage indicates an open circuit. See Figures 9B-6, 9B-8 and 9B-40.

Vacuum servo tests—1984 and later Buick

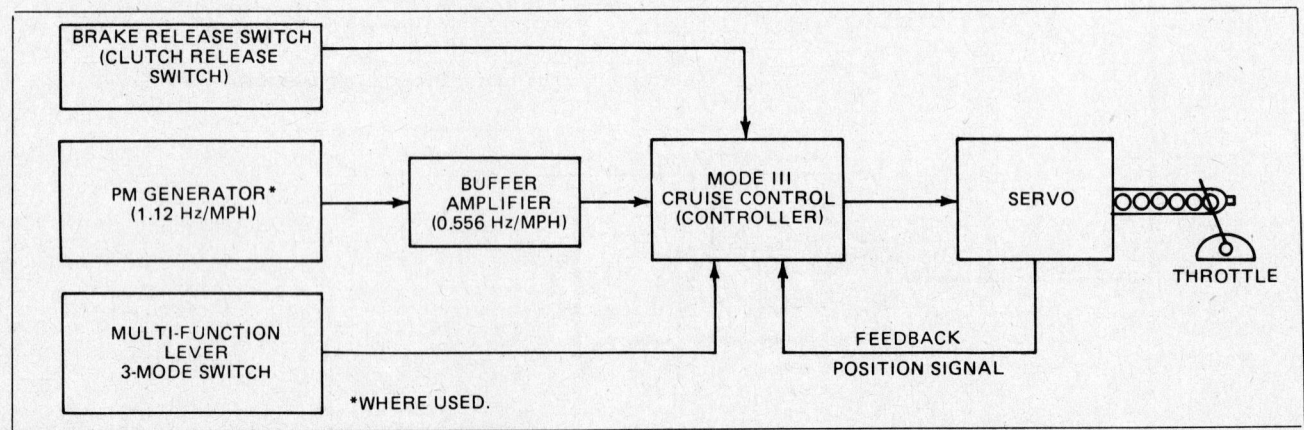

Cruise control system III component diagram

3. Slide the resume switch to the on position. The ohmmeter should indicate continuity. Push the engage button all the way in and and open circuit should be indicated.

4. Connect an ohmmeter to the brown and black wires, with the resume switch still in the on position. An open circuit should be indicated.

5. Depress the engage button and release it half way. Continuity should exist.

6. Connect an ohmmeter to the blue and black wires with the resume switch still in the on position. With the engaged button released, no continuity should be present.

7. With the engaged button depressed and half way released continuity should exist.

HARNESS AND TRANSDUCER ELECTRICAL TEST (1982–83)

1. Using an ohmmeter engage, with the engagement switch connector disconnected, check the resistance of the dark green wire in the wiring harness. If the transducer is grounded properly, the ohmmeter should indicate between 29 and 36 ohms.

2. If resistance is above or below specification, disconnect the connector at the transducer and at the resume solenoid.

3. Measure the resistance of the dark green wire. It should indicate a resistance reading of 23 ohms, plus or minus one ohm. If the reading is not as indicated the wiring harness should be replaced.

4. With the connectors of the transducer disconnected, measure the resistance of the solenoid coil by connecting the ohmmeter to the hold terminal and ground. A reading of 5 to 6 ohms should be indicated.

5. If a reading of 4 ohms or less is obtained there is excessive resistance in the circuit. If a reading of 6 ohms or more is indicated the transducer should be checked.

TRANSDUCER TEST (1982–83)

The only test that is possible to check the transducer assembly is the transducer orifice tube adjustment. Before adjusting the transducer assembly be sure that all vacuum hoses are in good condition. Be sure that all electrical connections are correct. Be sure that the electrical and vacuum release valves are working properly.

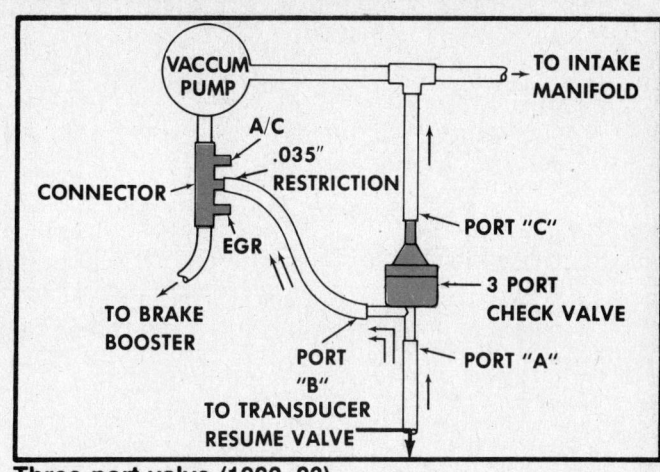

Three port valve (1982–83)

VACUUM REGULATOR TEST (1982–83)

If the vehicle is equipped with a diesel engine a vacuum regulator valve is used. This vacuum regulator valve regulates the vacuum from the engine mounted vacuum pump. To test the regulator use a vacuum pump. The vacuum level should be about 6 in. hg. or slightly higher if cold. If the valve does not perform as indicated it must be replaced.

VACUUM PUMP ASSISTED SYSTEMS TEST (1982–83)

1. Blow low air pressure into port "A" while port "B" is plugged. Then plug port "A" and blow low air pressure into port "B".

2. In both cases air should exit port "C". If not clean or replace the check valve.

3. To check the air flow in the other direction, blow low air pressure into port "C". No air should come out of port "A" or port "B".

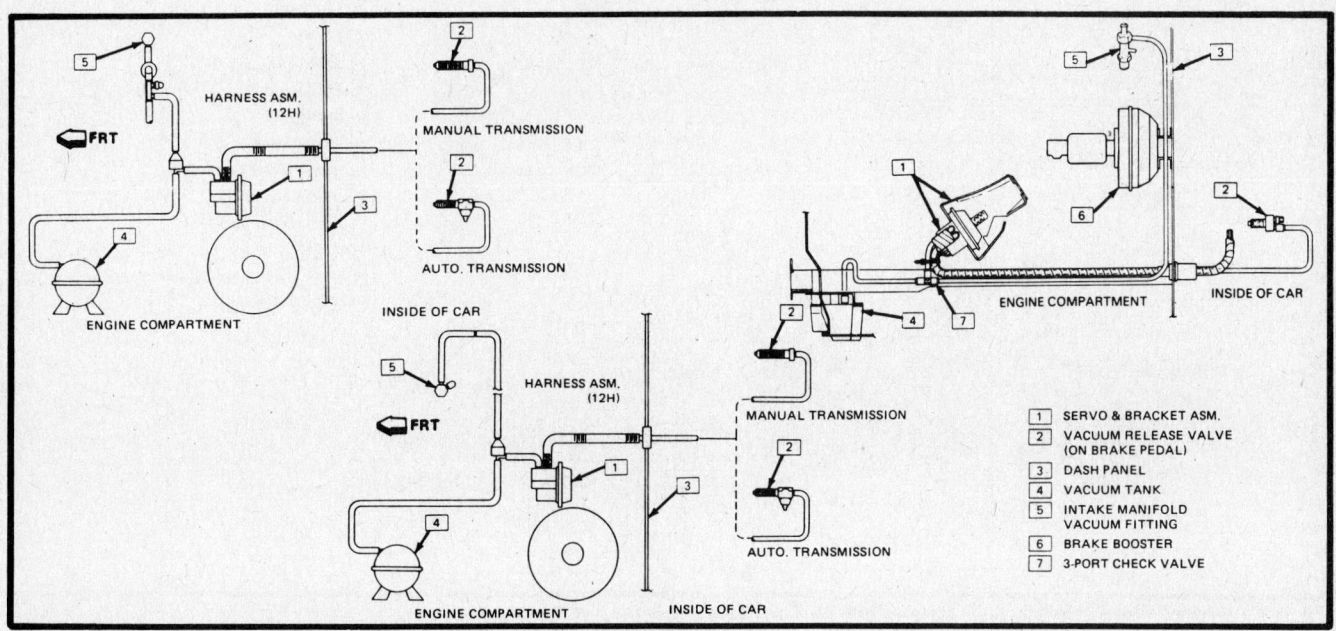

Cruise control vacuum schematic – 1986 and later Skylark

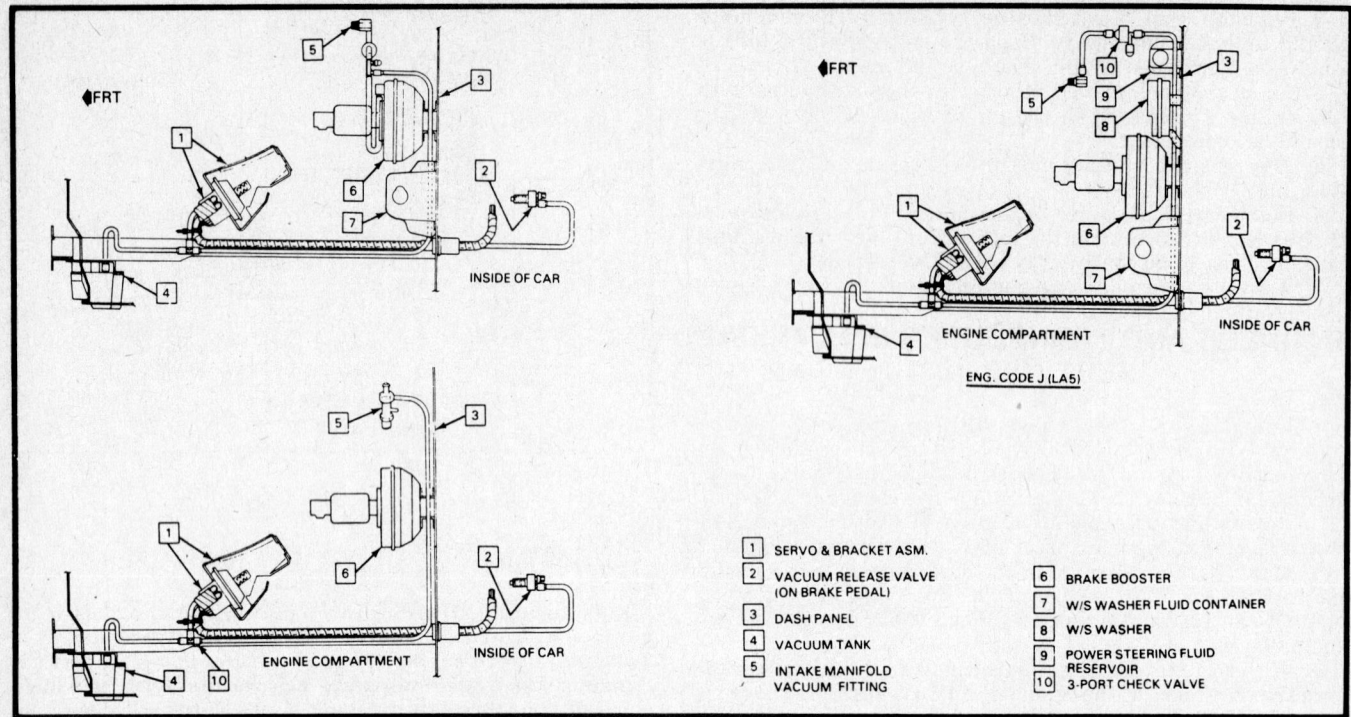

1	SERVO & BRACKET ASM.
2	VACUUM RELEASE VALVE (ON BRAKE PEDAL)
3	DASH PANEL
4	VACUUM TANK
5	INTAKE MANIFOLD VACUUM FITTING

6	BRAKE BOOSTER
7	W/S WASHER FLUID CONTAINER
8	W/S WASHER
9	POWER STEERING FLUID RESERVOIR
10	3-PORT CHECK VALVE

Cruise control vacuum schematic – 1984–85 Skylark

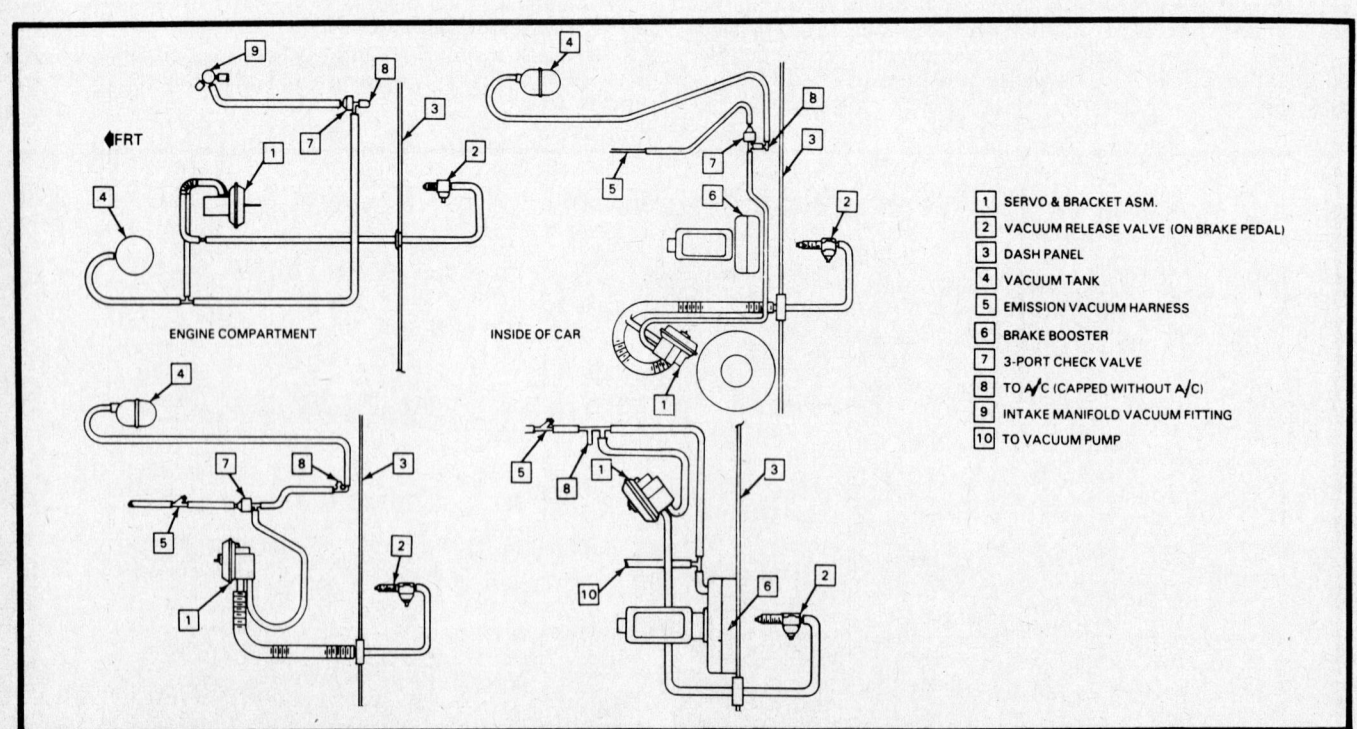

1	SERVO & BRACKET ASM.
2	VACUUM RELEASE VALVE (ON BRAKE PEDAL)
3	DASH PANEL
4	VACUUM TANK
5	EMISSION VACUUM HARNESS
6	BRAKE BOOSTER
7	3-PORT CHECK VALVE
8	TO A/C (CAPPED WITHOUT A/C)
9	INTAKE MANIFOLD VACUUM FITTING
10	TO VACUUM PUMP

Cruise control vacuum schematic – 1984–85 Century

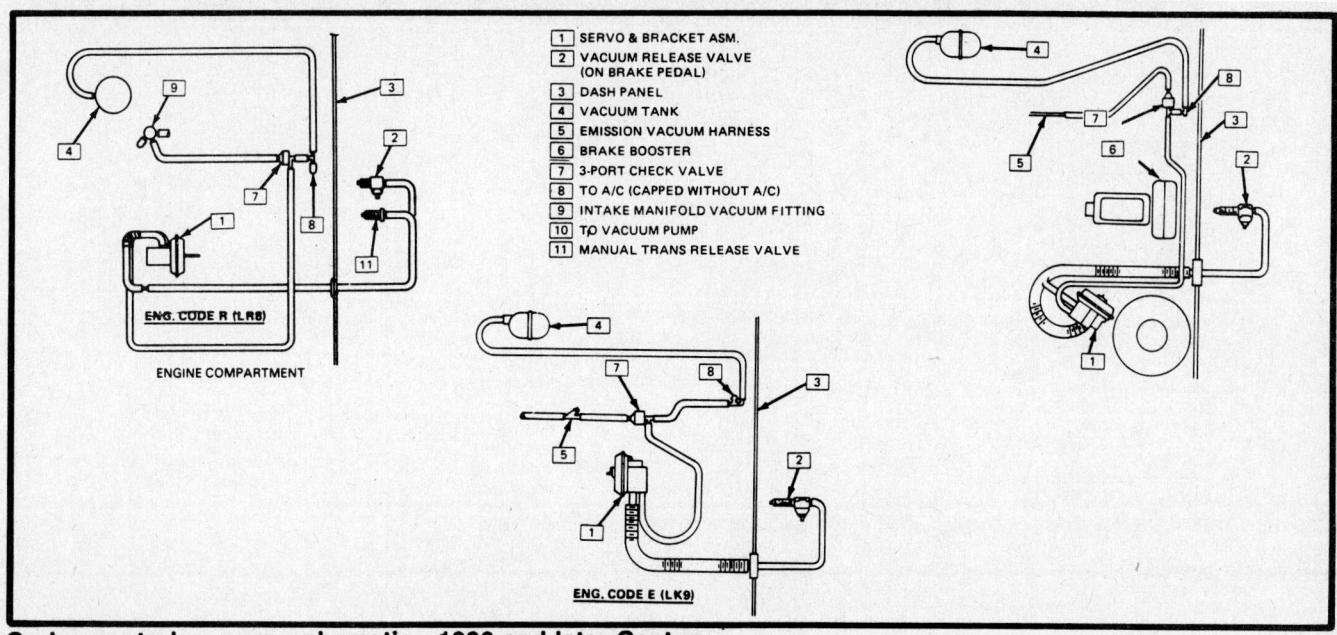

1 SERVO & BRACKET ASM.
2 VACUUM RELEASE VALVE (ON BRAKE PEDAL)
3 DASH PANEL
4 VACUUM TANK
5 EMISSION VACUUM HARNESS
6 BRAKE BOOSTER
7 3-PORT CHECK VALVE
8 TO A/C (CAPPED WITHOUT A/C)
9 INTAKE MANIFOLD VACUUM FITTING
10 TO VACUUM PUMP
11 MANUAL TRANS RELEASE VALVE

Cruise control vacuum schematic—1986 and later Century

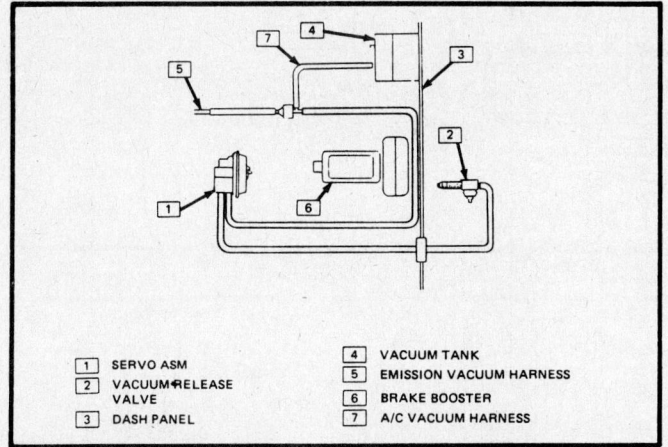

1 SERVO ASM
2 VACUUM RELEASE VALVE
3 DASH PANEL
4 VACUUM TANK
5 EMISSION VACUUM HARNESS
6 BRAKE BOOSTER
7 A/C VACUUM HARNESS

Cruise control vacuum schematic—1986 and later Electra and LeSabre

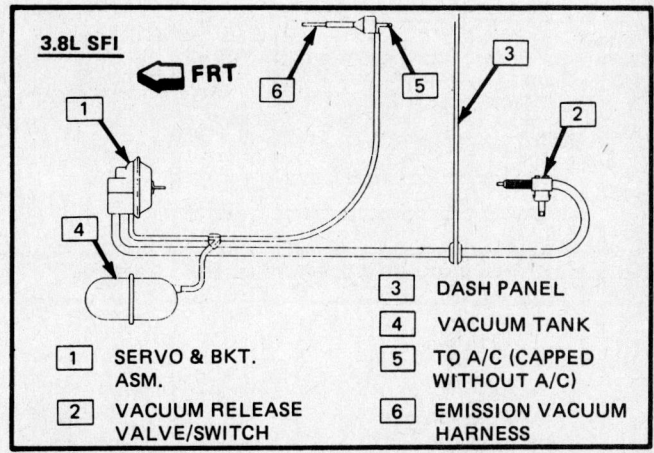

1 SERVO & BKT. ASM.
2 VACUUM RELEASE VALVE/SWITCH
3 DASH PANEL
4 VACUUM TANK
5 TO A/C (CAPPED WITHOUT A/C)
6 EMISSION VACUUM HARNESS

Cruise control vacuum schematic—1986 and later Riviera

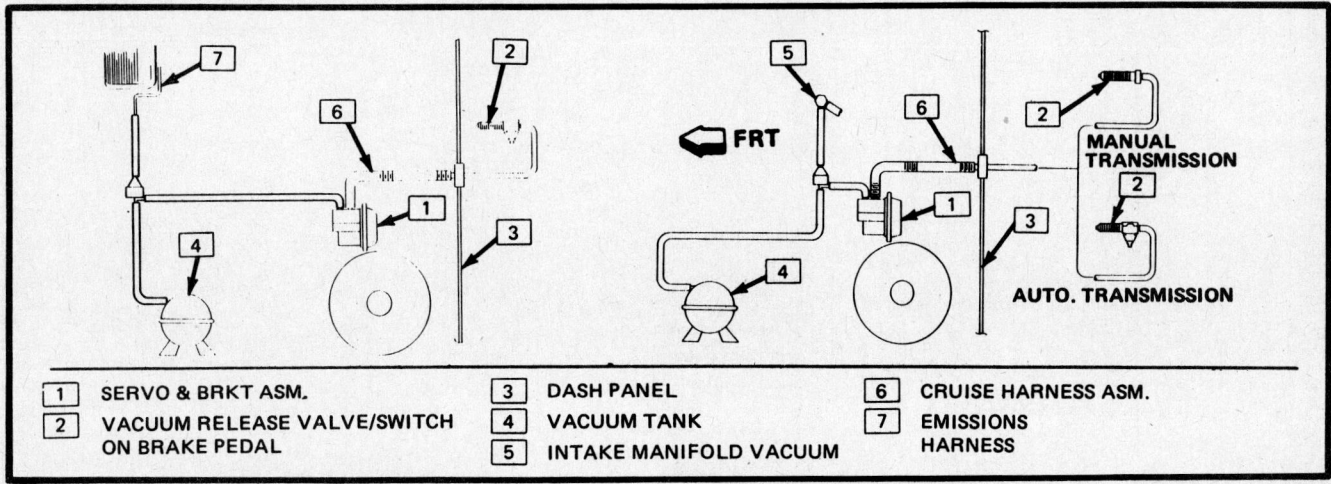

1 SERVO & BRKT ASM.
2 VACUUM RELEASE VALVE/SWITCH ON BRAKE PEDAL
3 DASH PANEL
4 VACUUM TANK
5 INTAKE MANIFOLD VACUUM
6 CRUISE HARNESS ASM.
7 EMISSIONS HARNESS

Cruise control vacuum schematic—1985 and later Somerset

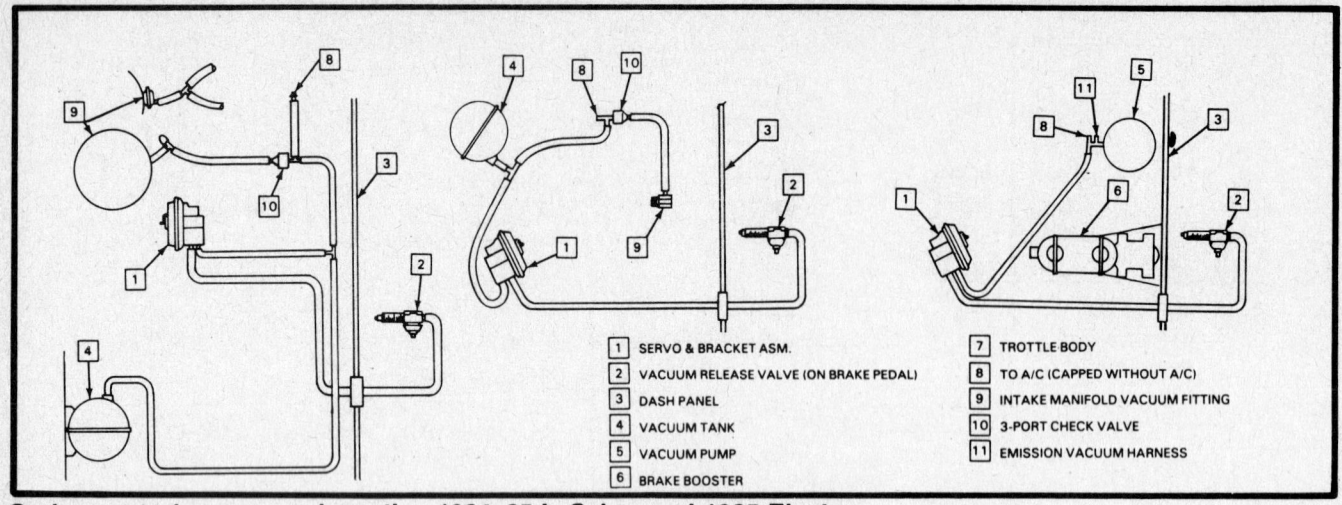

1	SERVO & BRACKET ASM.		7	TROTTLE BODY
2	VACUUM RELEASE VALVE (ON BRAKE PEDAL)		8	TO A/C (CAPPED WITHOUT A/C)
3	DASH PANEL		9	INTAKE MANIFOLD VACUUM FITTING
4	VACUUM TANK		10	3-PORT CHECK VALVE
5	VACUUM PUMP		11	EMISSION VACUUM HARNESS
6	BRAKE BOOSTER			

Cruise control vacuum schematic—1984–85 LeSabre and 1985 Electra

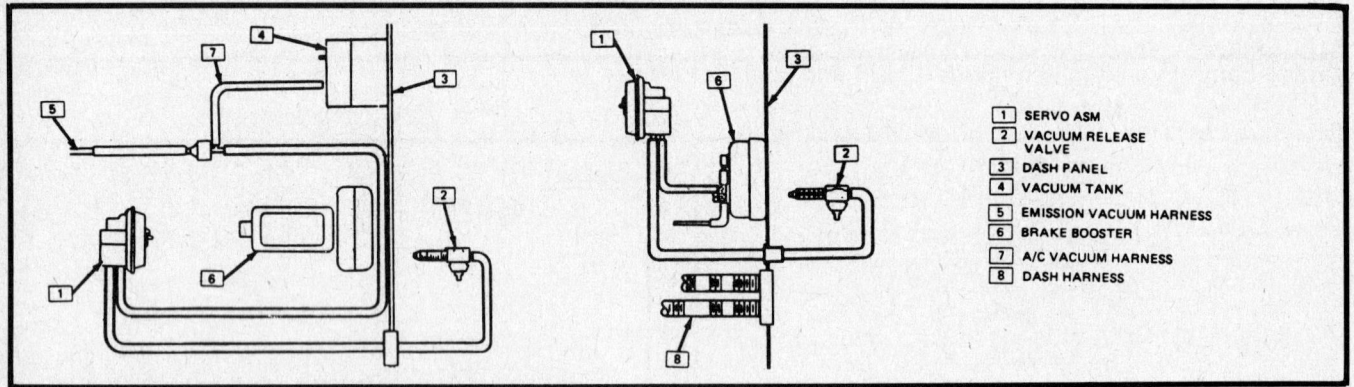

1	SERVO ASM
2	VACUUM RELEASE VALVE
3	DASH PANEL
4	VACUUM TANK
5	EMISSION VACUUM HARNESS
6	BRAKE BOOSTER
7	A/C VACUUM HARNESS
8	DASH HARNESS

Cruise control vacuum schematic—1985 Electra

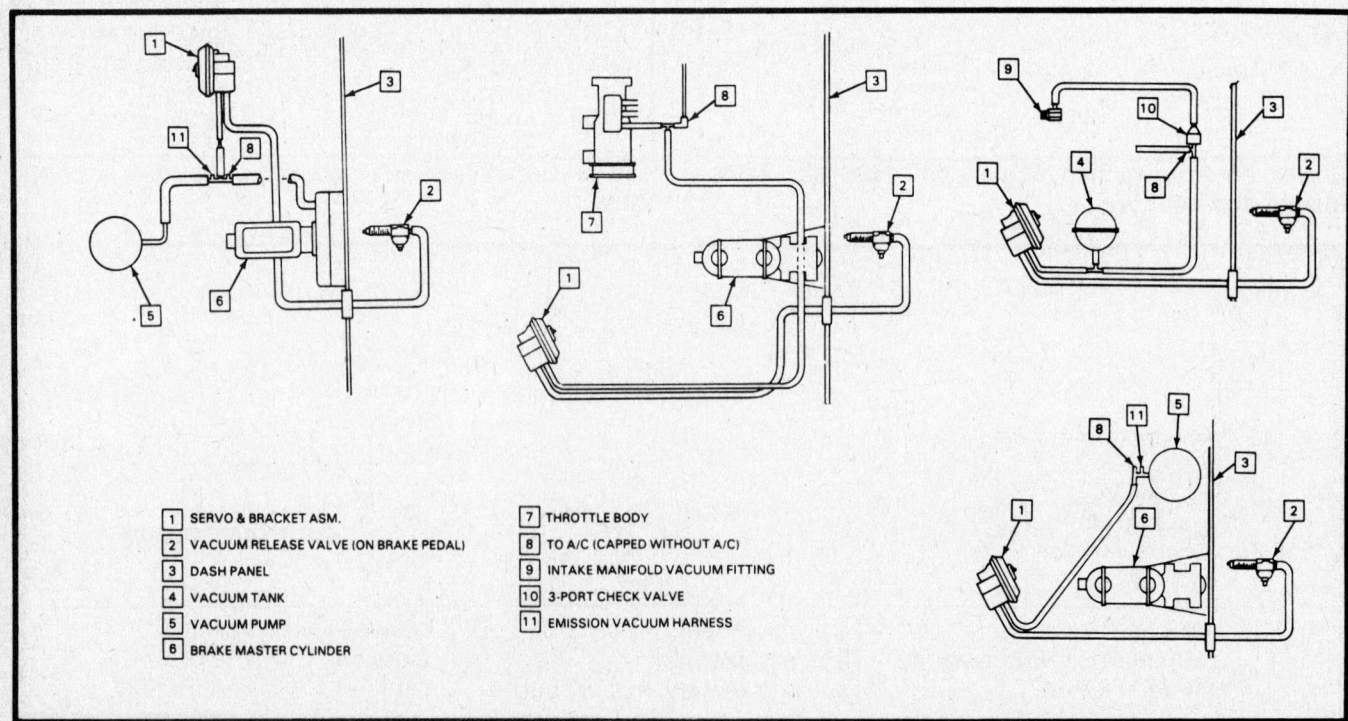

1	SERVO & BRACKET ASM.		7	THROTTLE BODY
2	VACUUM RELEASE VALVE (ON BRAKE PEDAL)		8	TO A/C (CAPPED WITHOUT A/C)
3	DASH PANEL		9	INTAKE MANIFOLD VACUUM FITTING
4	VACUUM TANK		10	3-PORT CHECK VALVE
5	VACUUM PUMP		11	EMISSION VACUUM HARNESS
6	BRAKE MASTER CYLINDER			

Cruise control vacuum schematic—1984–85 Riviera

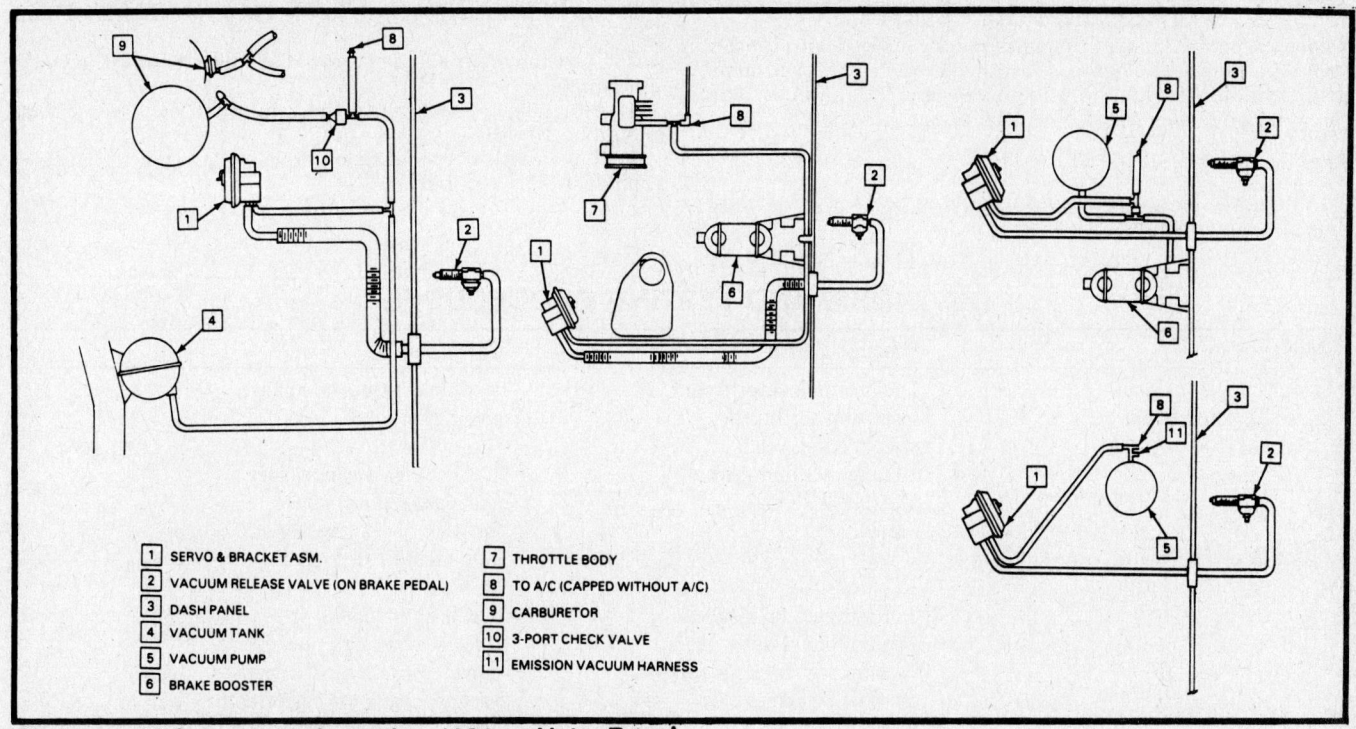

1   SERVO & BRACKET ASM.
2   VACUUM RELEASE VALVE (ON BRAKE PEDAL)
3   DASH PANEL
4   VACUUM TANK
5   VACUUM PUMP
6   BRAKE BOOSTER

7   THROTTLE BODY
8   TO A/C (CAPPED WITHOUT A/C)
9   CARBURETOR
10   3-PORT CHECK VALVE
11   EMISSION VACUUM HARNESS

Cruise control vacuum schematic – 1984 and later Regal

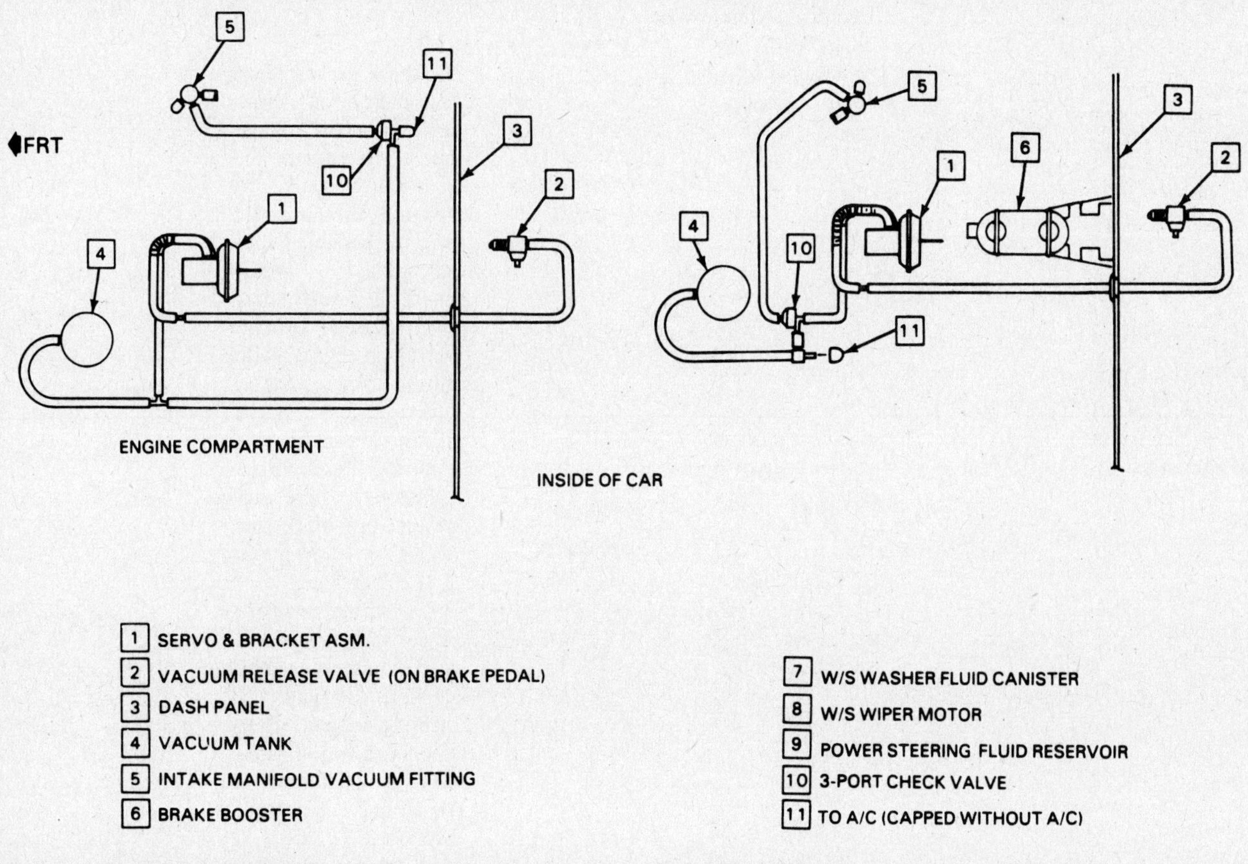

◀FRT

ENGINE COMPARTMENT

INSIDE OF CAR

1   SERVO & BRACKET ASM.
2   VACUUM RELEASE VALVE (ON BRAKE PEDAL)
3   DASH PANEL
4   VACUUM TANK
5   INTAKE MANIFOLD VACUUM FITTING
6   BRAKE BOOSTER

7   W/S WASHER FLUID CANISTER
8   W/S WIPER MOTOR
9   POWER STEERING FLUID RESERVOIR
10   3-PORT CHECK VALVE
11   TO A/C (CAPPED WITHOUT A/C)

Cruise control vacuum schematic – 1984–85 Skylark

VACUUM PUMP TEST

A vacuum pump is used on some vehicles equipped with the 2.5 liter TBI engine. The pump is installed in the same location as the mechanical fuel pump would be for non TBI engines. The vacuum pump is operated by a lobe on the camshaft.

Testing

1. Remove the vacuum lines from both ports at the pump. Plug the hose openings.

2. Install a vacuum gauge to the inlet port of the vacuum pump.

3. Start the engine and operate it at idle. Observe the vacuum gauge.

4. After about one minute the minimum vacuum reading should be 15.0 HG.

5. If not within specification, repair or replace defective components as required.

DIAGNOSIS AND TESTING PROCEDURES

Condition	Possible Cause	Correction
System inoperative but cruise light comes on.	1. Throttle linkage from servo unit to throttle disconnected.	1. Connect throttle linkage and adjust.
	2. Large vacuum leak. Vacuum hose disconnected.	2. Check all vacuum lines and connections. Check for torn or leaking servo unit. Repair or replace as required.
	3. Restricted or plugged vacuum line. Faulty vacuum regulator (diesel only) or incorrect check valve orientation (vacuum pump only).	3. Check for kinks or collapsed vacuum line. Remove restriction. Replace vacuum regulator or correct check valve orientation.
	4. Brake pedal vacuum release valve or brake electrical switch out of adjustment.	4. Adjust or replace as necessary.
	5. Resume solenoid valve inoperative	5. Check for voltage at solenoid (2 volts with ignition on.) If voltage, check ground wire and repair. Investigate "engage" circuit for 12 volts or possible faulty solenoid. If no voltage, check for proper adjustment of brake switch, wiring or engage switch. Repair as necessary.
System inoperative and cruise light stays off.	1. Loose electrical connections or open wiring.	1. Check and secure all electrical connectors, transducer, cruise engage switch, fuse block, and repair cut or open wiring.
	2. Fuse blown.	2. Replace fuse.
	3. Malfunctioned turn signal and engage switch assembly.	3. Substitute new turn signal and engage switch assembly by plugging into connector at bottom of steering column. Check operation and, if satisfactory, install new turn signal and engage switch assembly.
	4. Malfunctioned transducer.	4. Replace.

Condition	Possible Cause	Correction
Speed increases after engagement.	1. Speedometer cable (needle) fluctuates due to speedo cable or housing bent, kinked or misrouted.	1. Correct as necessary.
	2. Transducer orifice tube out of adjustment.	2. Adjust.
	3. Transducer malfunction.	3. Replace.
Speed drops off after engagement.	1. Throttle linkage too loose. Vacuum leak or restriction.	1. Check for damaged, disconnected, pinched, or kinked hoses. Repair or replace as required. Adjust throttle linkage.
	2. Transducer orifice tube out of adjustment.	2. Adjust.
Surging	1. Check for restricted vacuum line from engine to transducer.	1. Repair or replace.
	2. Check to insure that servo unit will full stroke.	2. Replace servo unit.
	3. Transducer malfunction.	3. Replace.
	4. Check valve stuck closed (vacuum pump only) or missing.	4. Install or re-orient check valve as necessary.
Speed Drops Off Excessively on Inclines	1. Throttle linkage too loose.	1. Adjust.
	2. Vacuum source hose restricted.	2. Repair or Replace.
	3. Cruise system not connected to auxiliary vacuum pump.	3. Correct (See vacuum schematics).
	4. Check valve reversed or stuck open (vacuum pump only).	4. Re-orient or replace as necessary.

Cruise control trouble diagnosis chart (1982–83)

PRELIMINARY CHECKS

1. Check Servo Chain or rod adjustment. Must have minimum slack.
2. Check vacuum hoses. Must be in good condition - no restrictions or leaks.
3. Check drive cable routings. No kinks or sharp bends.
4. Check throttle linkage or cable for binding.
5. Check adjustment of electrical release switch and vacuum release valve.
6. Check engagement switch operation.
7. If steps 1 through 6 do not solve the problem, continue with diagnosis.

CRUISE CONTROL INOPERATIVE

1. Check radio fuse. If blown, check wiring for short circuit and repair. A shorted resume solenoid diode could also cause blow fuse.
2. If fuse and preliminary checks ok, resume solenoid must be checked. Start engine and check source vacuum at resume solenoid (refer to picture at right). Disconnect the two wire connector at resume solenoid. Use jumper wire to ground terminal which had black wire connected to it. Apply 12 volts to terminal which had tan wire connected to it. Disconnect outlet vacuum hose (going to B fitting on transducer). Vacuum should be present. If not, replace resume solenoid. Applying voltage incorrectly to resume solenoid could damage diode. If above checks ok, stop engine and reconnect electrical and vacuum connections.
3. To make test below, turn ignition to RUN position and off/on/resume switch to ON. Disconnect the two wire connector at transducer (Engage-Hold Terminals).
4. Connect 12 volt test light to ground and to engage wire in connector. Push engage/coast button in part way to engage position.
5. Repeat test on hold wire in connector.

TEST LIGHT OFF AT ONE WIRE ONLY

Test engagement switch. (See test procedure) Check for open circuit in wire if test light did not light. Repair or replace part that checks bad.

TEST LIGHT ON AT BOTH WIRES (MAY BE DIM ON HOLD WIRE)

Check for poor ground at transducer. If ok, remove transducer for repair.

TEST LIGHT OFF AT BOTH WIRES

Check for open circuit in brown/white wire from fuse panel to off/on/resume switch. If circuit ok, check engagement switch operation and replace if necessary.

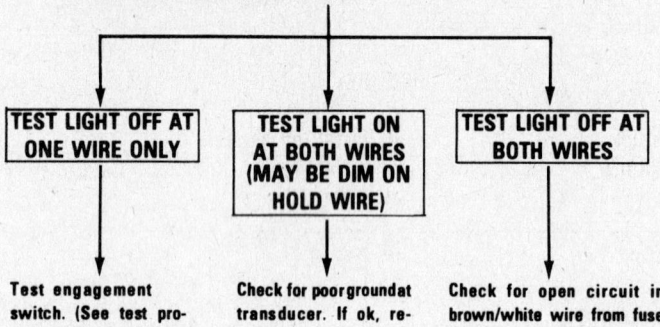

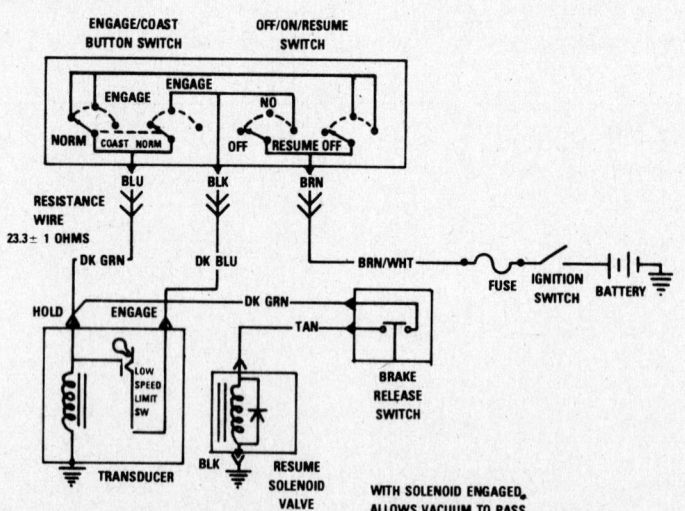

ENGAGEMENT SWITCH TEST PROCEDURE			
USE A SELF POWERED TEST LIGHT. LIGHT WILL BE ON FOR EACH TEST IF SWITCH IS GOOD. CONNECTOR TERMINALS AND COLOR 1 — BROWN, 2 — BLUE, 3 — BLACK			

SWITCH POSITIONS		TERMINALS		
ENGAGE BUTTON	RESUME SWITCH	1 to 2	1 to 3	2 to 3
Released	on	closed	open	open
Fully Depressed	on	open	open	closed
Partially Released	on	closed	closed	closed
Released	resume	closed	closed	closed
Released	off	open	open	open

Cruise control diagnosis (1982–83)

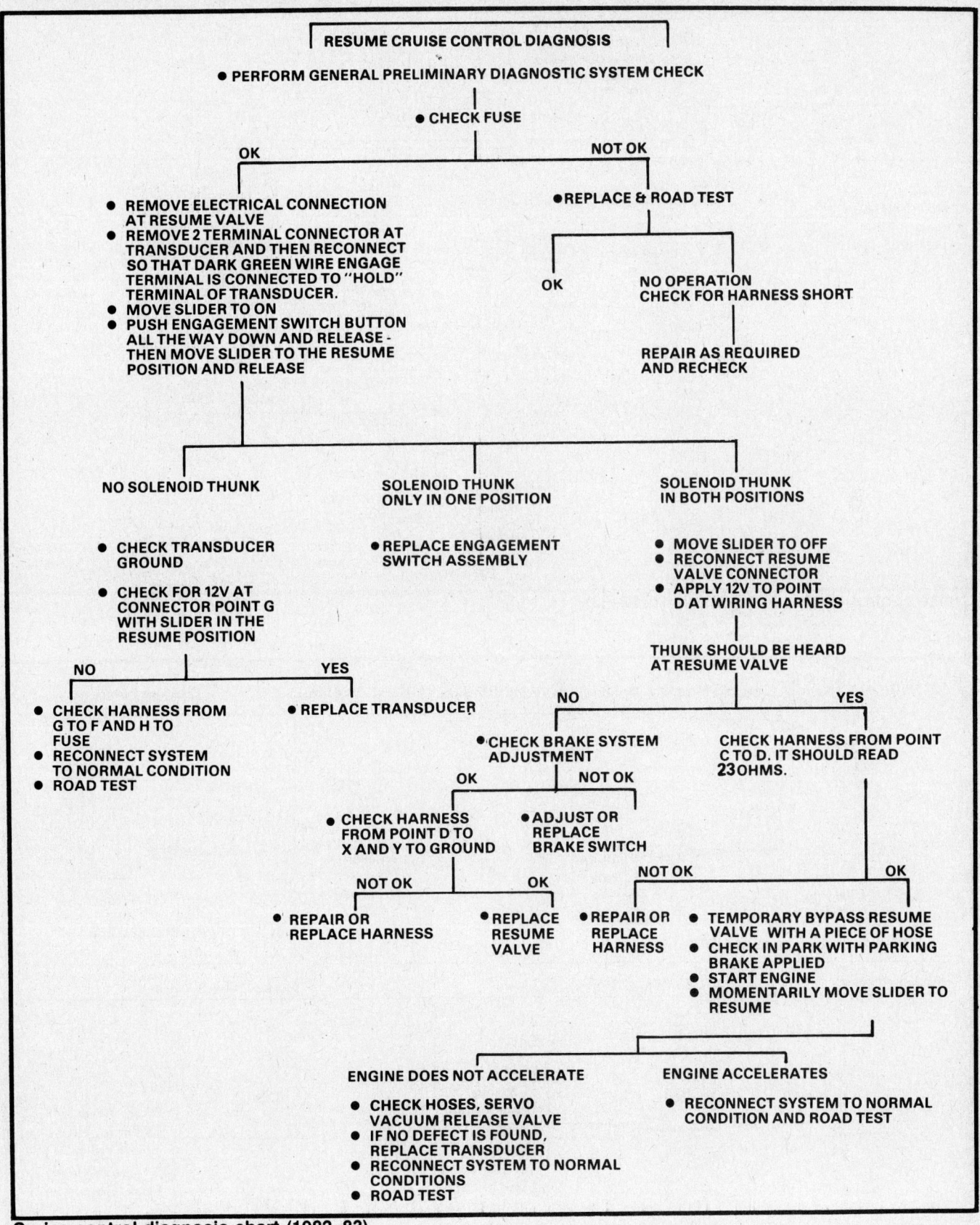

RESUME CRUISE CONTROL DIAGNOSIS

- PERFORM GENERAL PRELIMINARY DIAGNOSTIC SYSTEM CHECK

- CHECK FUSE

OK

- REMOVE ELECTRICAL CONNECTION AT RESUME VALVE
- REMOVE 2 TERMINAL CONNECTOR AT TRANSDUCER AND THEN RECONNECT SO THAT DARK GREEN WIRE ENGAGE TERMINAL IS CONNECTED TO "HOLD" TERMINAL OF TRANSDUCER.
- MOVE SLIDER TO ON
- PUSH ENGAGEMENT SWITCH BUTTON ALL THE WAY DOWN AND RELEASE - THEN MOVE SLIDER TO THE RESUME POSITION AND RELEASE

NOT OK

- REPLACE & ROAD TEST

OK

NO OPERATION CHECK FOR HARNESS SHORT

REPAIR AS REQUIRED AND RECHECK

NO SOLENOID THUNK

- CHECK TRANSDUCER GROUND
- CHECK FOR 12V AT CONNECTOR POINT G WITH SLIDER IN THE RESUME POSITION

SOLENOID THUNK ONLY IN ONE POSITION

- REPLACE ENGAGEMENT SWITCH ASSEMBLY

SOLENOID THUNK IN BOTH POSITIONS

- MOVE SLIDER TO OFF
- RECONNECT RESUME VALVE CONNECTOR
- APPLY 12V TO POINT D AT WIRING HARNESS

THUNK SHOULD BE HEARD AT RESUME VALVE

NO

- CHECK HARNESS FROM G TO F AND H TO FUSE
- RECONNECT SYSTEM TO NORMAL CONDITION
- ROAD TEST

YES

- REPLACE TRANSDUCER

- CHECK BRAKE SYSTEM ADJUSTMENT

OK

- CHECK HARNESS FROM POINT D TO X AND Y TO GROUND

NOT OK

- ADJUST OR REPLACE BRAKE SWITCH

YES

CHECK HARNESS FROM POINT C TO D. IT SHOULD READ 23 OHMS.

NOT OK

- REPAIR OR REPLACE HARNESS

OK

- REPLACE RESUME VALVE

NOT OK

- REPAIR OR REPLACE HARNESS

OK

- TEMPORARY BYPASS RESUME VALVE WITH A PIECE OF HOSE
- CHECK IN PARK WITH PARKING BRAKE APPLIED
- START ENGINE
- MOMENTARILY MOVE SLIDER TO RESUME

ENGINE DOES NOT ACCELERATE

- CHECK HOSES, SERVO VACUUM RELEASE VALVE
- IF NO DEFECT IS FOUND, REPLACE TRANSDUCER
- RECONNECT SYSTEM TO NORMAL CONDITIONS
- ROAD TEST

ENGINE ACCELERATES

- RECONNECT SYSTEM TO NORMAL CONDITION AND ROAD TEST

Cruise control diagnosis chart (1982–83)

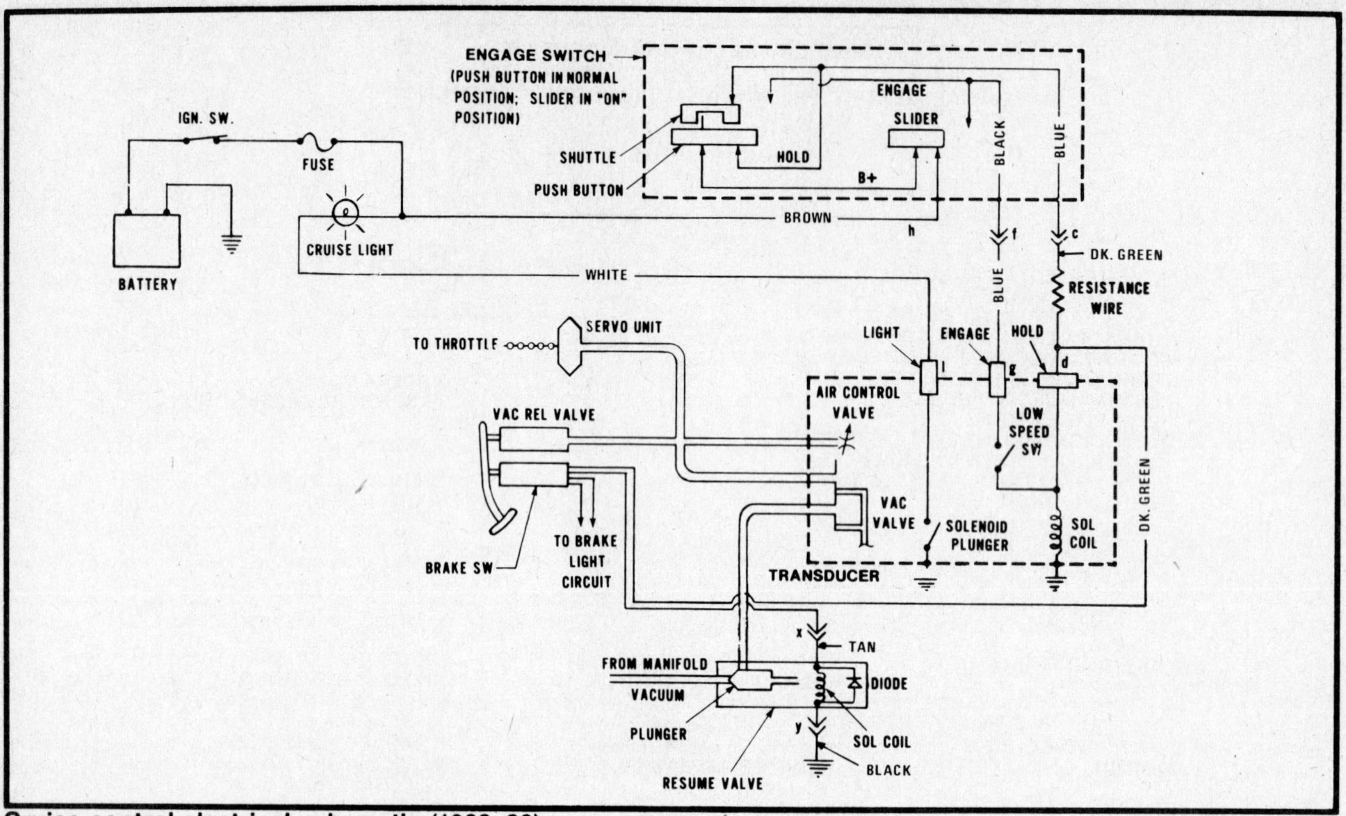

Cruise control electrical schematic (1982–83)

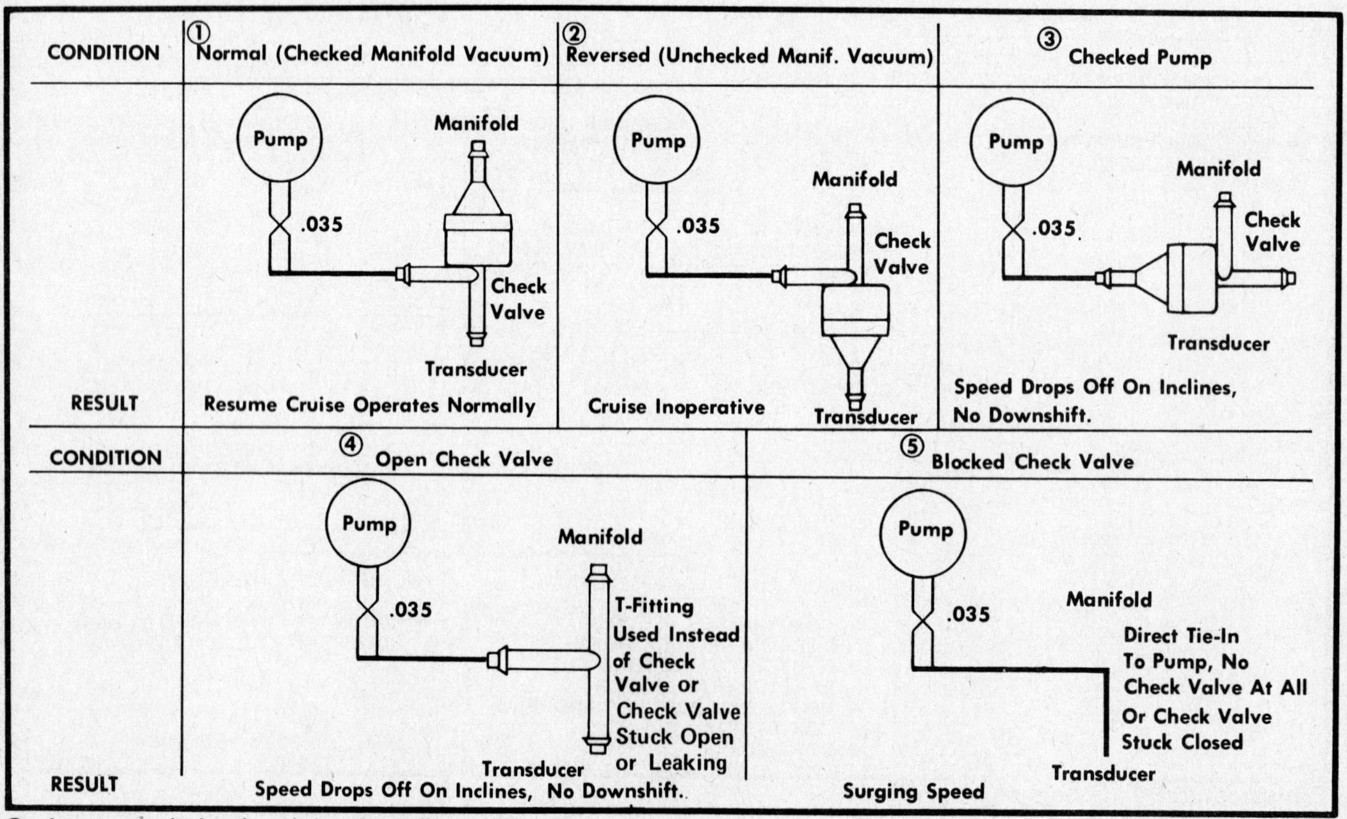

CONDITION	① Normal (Checked Manifold Vacuum)	② Reversed (Unchecked Manif. Vacuum)	③ Checked Pump
RESULT	Resume Cruise Operates Normally	Cruise Inoperative	Speed Drops Off On Inclines, No Downshift.

CONDITION	④ Open Check Valve	⑤ Blocked Check Valve
RESULT	Speed Drops Off On Inclines, No Downshift.	Surging Speed

Cruise control check valve orientation (1982–83)

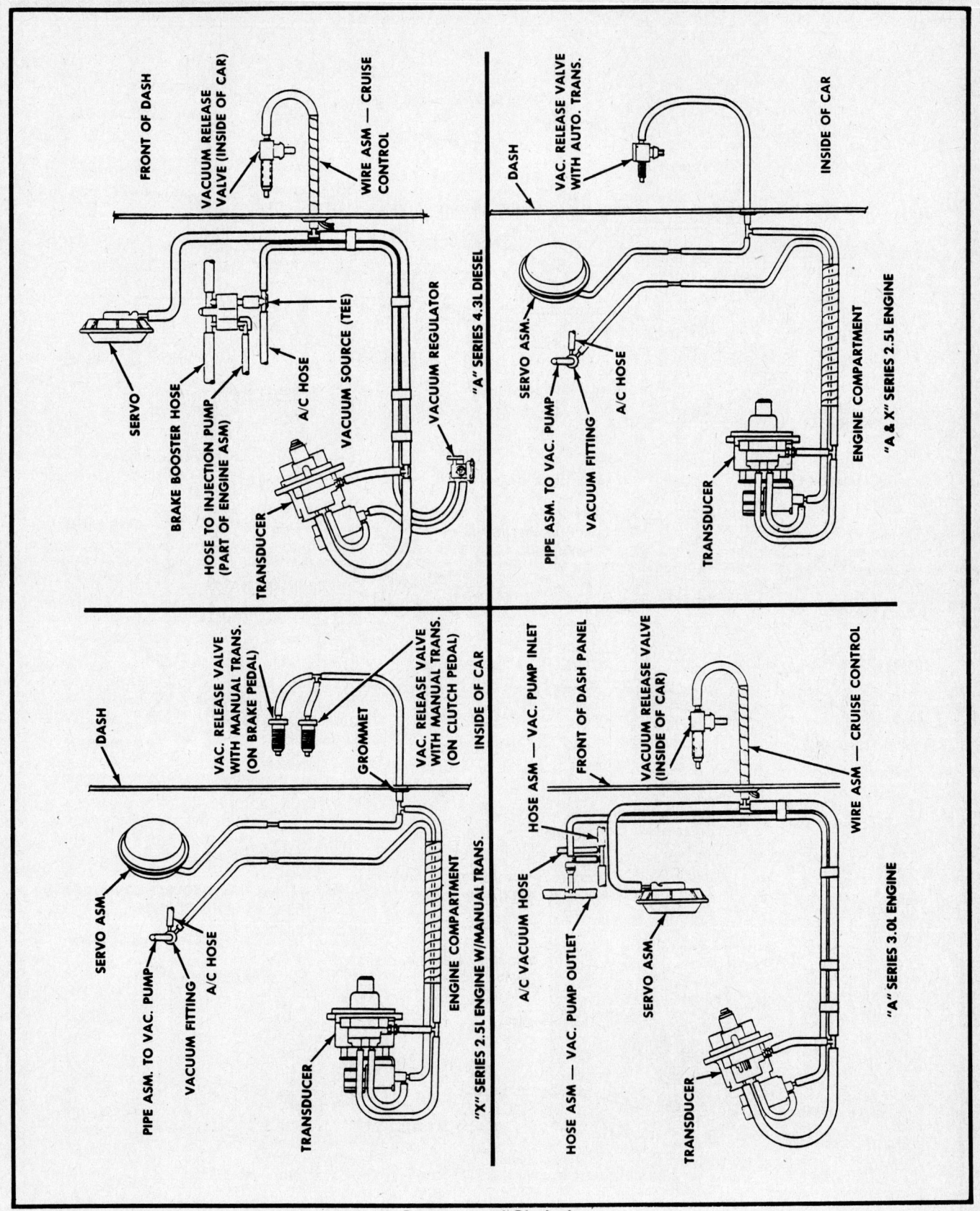

FRONT OF DASH

VACUUM RELEASE VALVE (INSIDE OF CAR)

WIRE ASM — CRUISE CONTROL

SERVO

BRAKE BOOSTER HOSE

HOSE TO INJECTION PUMP (PART OF ENGINE ASM)

A/C HOSE

VACUUM SOURCE (TEE)

VACUUM REGULATOR

TRANSDUCER

"A" SERIES 4.3L DIESEL

VAC. RELEASE VALVE WITH AUTO. TRANS.

DASH

INSIDE OF CAR

SERVO ASM.

PIPE ASM. TO VAC. PUMP

VACUUM FITTING

A/C HOSE

TRANSDUCER

ENGINE COMPARTMENT

"A & X" SERIES 2.5L ENGINE

DASH

VAC. RELEASE VALVE WITH MANUAL TRANS. (ON BRAKE PEDAL)

VAC. RELEASE VALVE WITH MANUAL TRANS. (ON CLUTCH PEDAL)

GROMMET

INSIDE OF CAR

SERVO ASM.

PIPE ASM. TO VAC. PUMP

VACUUM FITTING

A/C HOSE

TRANSDUCER

ENGINE COMPARTMENT

"X" SERIES 2.5L ENGINE W/MANUAL TRANS.

A/C VACUUM HOSE

HOSE ASM — VAC. PUMP INLET

FRONT OF DASH PANEL

VACUUM RELEASE VALVE (INSIDE OF CAR)

WIRE ASM — CRUISE CONTROL

HOSE ASM — VAC. PUMP OUTLET

SERVO ASM

TRANSDUCER

"A" SERIES 3.0L ENGINE

Cruise control vacuum schematic—1982–83 Century and Skylark

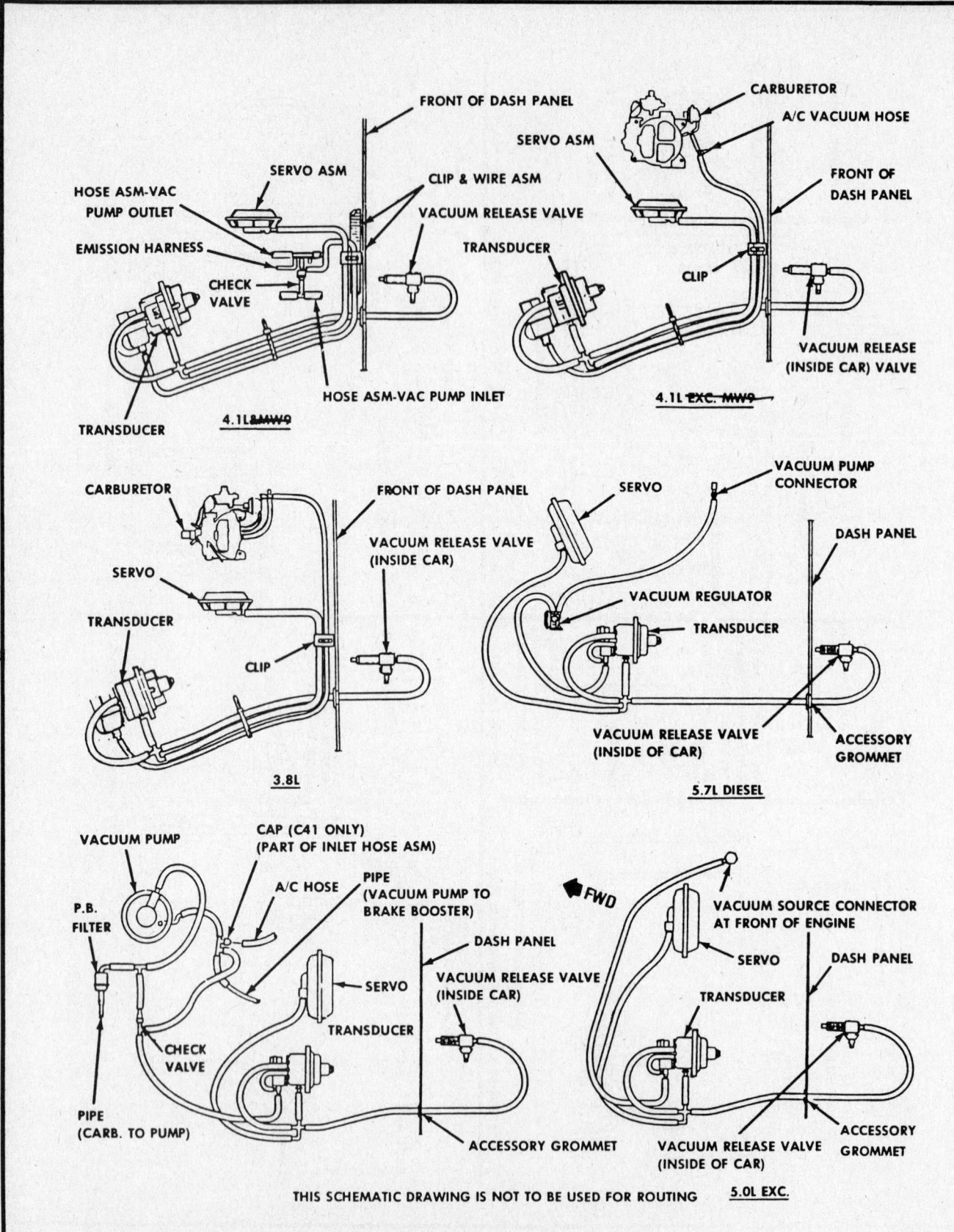

HOSE ASM-VAC PUMP OUTLET

SERVO ASM

EMISSION HARNESS

FRONT OF DASH PANEL

CLIP & WIRE ASM

VACUUM RELEASE VALVE

TRANSDUCER

CHECK VALVE

HOSE ASM-VAC PUMP INLET

TRANSDUCER

4.1L & MW9

CARBURETOR

SERVO ASM

A/C VACUUM HOSE

FRONT OF DASH PANEL

CLIP

VACUUM RELEASE (INSIDE CAR) VALVE

4.1L EXC. MW9

CARBURETOR

SERVO

TRANSDUCER

CLIP

FRONT OF DASH PANEL

VACUUM RELEASE VALVE (INSIDE CAR)

3.8L

VACUUM PUMP CONNECTOR

SERVO

DASH PANEL

VACUUM REGULATOR

TRANSDUCER

VACUUM RELEASE VALVE (INSIDE OF CAR)

ACCESSORY GROMMET

5.7L DIESEL

VACUUM PUMP

CAP (C41 ONLY) (PART OF INLET HOSE ASM)

A/C HOSE

PIPE (VACUUM PUMP TO BRAKE BOOSTER)

P.B. FILTER

DASH PANEL

SERVO

VACUUM RELEASE VALVE (INSIDE CAR)

TRANSDUCER

CHECK VALVE

PIPE (CARB. TO PUMP)

ACCESSORY GROMMET

FWD

VACUUM SOURCE CONNECTOR AT FRONT OF ENGINE

SERVO

DASH PANEL

TRANSDUCER

ACCESSORY GROMMET

VACUUM RELEASE VALVE (INSIDE OF CAR)

5.0L EXC.

THIS SCHEMATIC DRAWING IS NOT TO BE USED FOR ROUTING

Cruise control vacuum schematic—1982–83 LeSabre and Electra

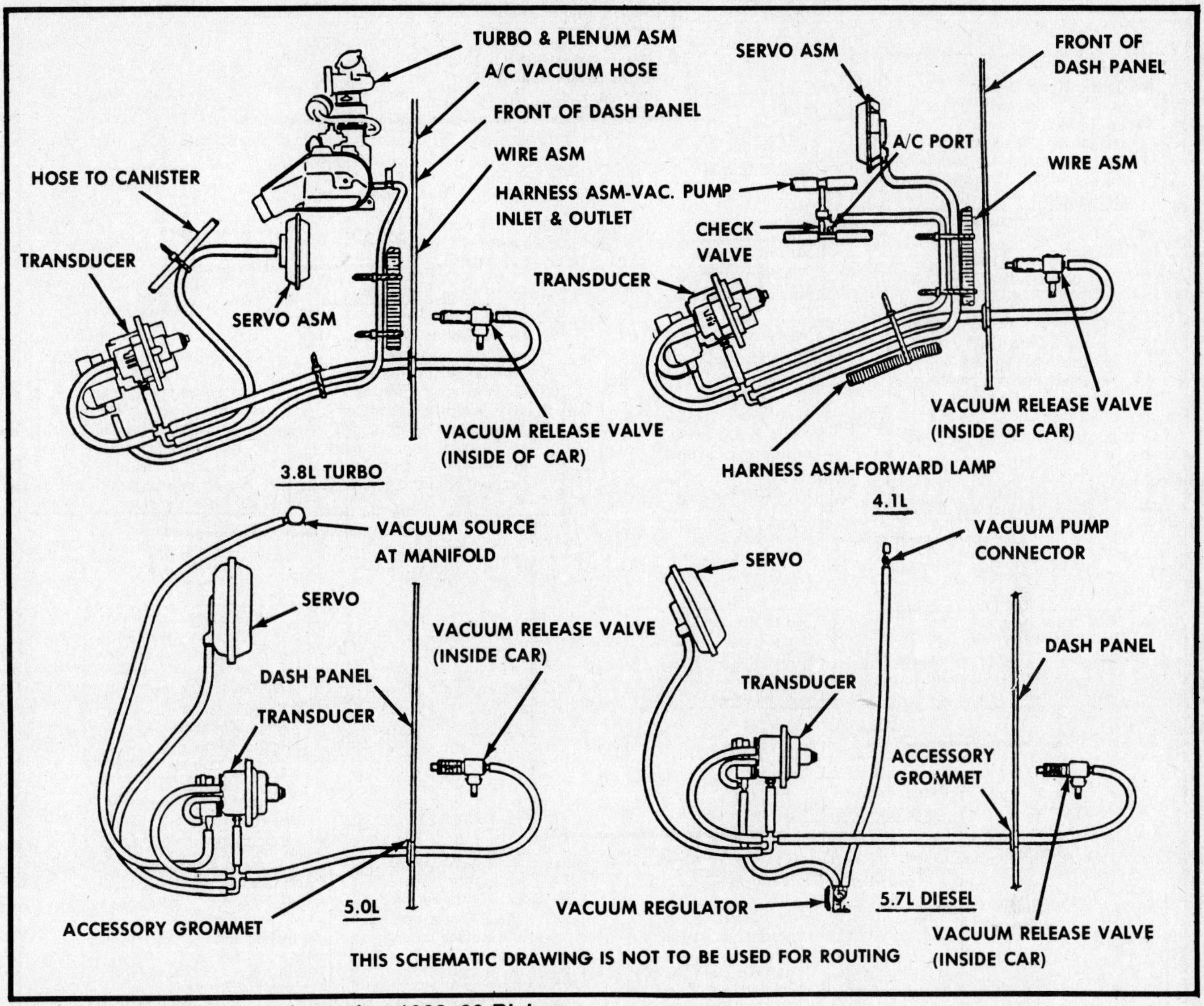

TURBO & PLENUM ASM
A/C VACUUM HOSE
FRONT OF DASH PANEL
WIRE ASM
HOSE TO CANISTER
HARNESS ASM-VAC. PUMP INLET & OUTLET
TRANSDUCER
SERVO ASM
VACUUM RELEASE VALVE (INSIDE OF CAR)
3.8L TURBO
SERVO ASM
FRONT OF DASH PANEL
A/C PORT
WIRE ASM
CHECK VALVE
TRANSDUCER
VACUUM RELEASE VALVE (INSIDE OF CAR)
HARNESS ASM-FORWARD LAMP
4.1L
VACUUM SOURCE AT MANIFOLD
SERVO
VACUUM RELEASE VALVE (INSIDE CAR)
DASH PANEL
TRANSDUCER
ACCESSORY GROMMET
5.0L
SERVO
VACUUM PUMP CONNECTOR
DASH PANEL
TRANSDUCER
ACCESSORY GROMMET
VACUUM REGULATOR
5.7L DIESEL
VACUUM RELEASE VALVE (INSIDE CAR)
THIS SCHEMATIC DRAWING IS NOT TO BE USED FOR ROUTING

Cruise control vacuum schematic – 1982–83 Riviera

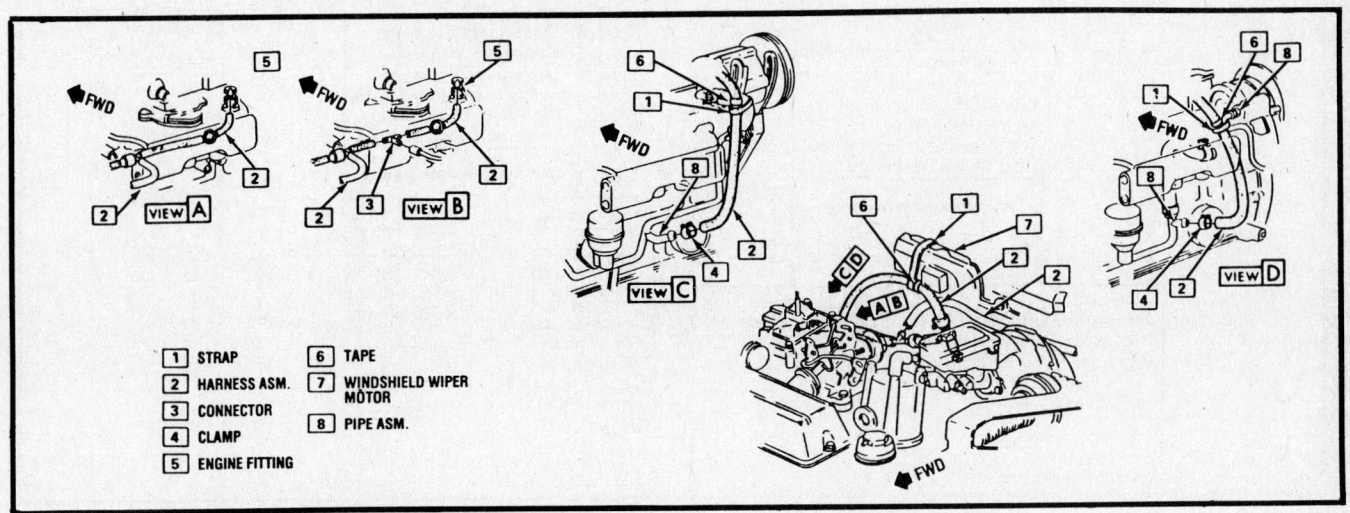

FWD
VIEW A
VIEW B
VIEW C
VIEW D
1 STRAP
2 HARNESS ASM.
3 CONNECTOR
4 CLAMP
5 ENGINE FITTING
6 TAPE
7 WINDSHIELD WIPER MOTOR
8 PIPE ASM.

Cruise control vacuum schematic – 1982–83 Skyhawk

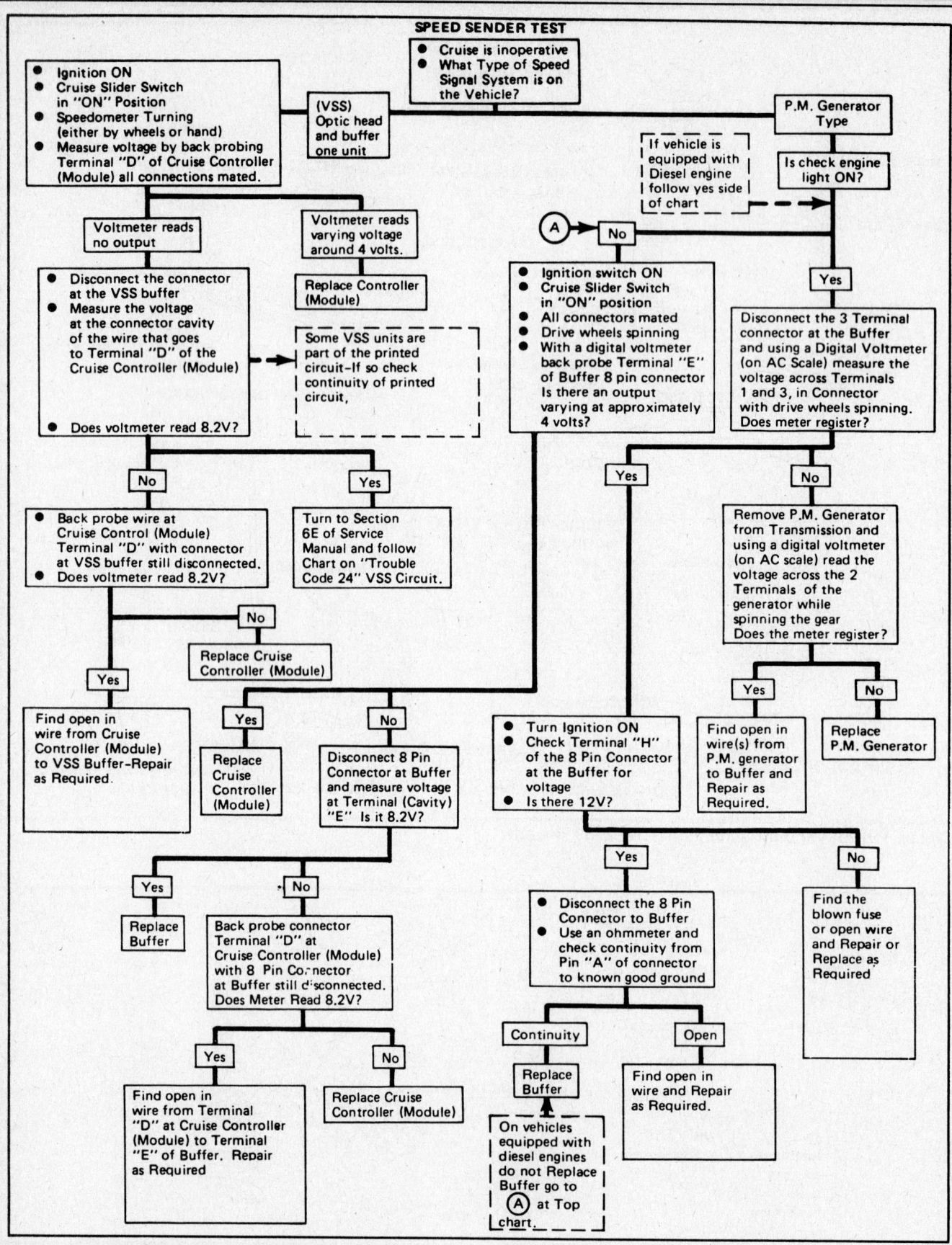

Cruise control diagnosis—1984 and later Buick

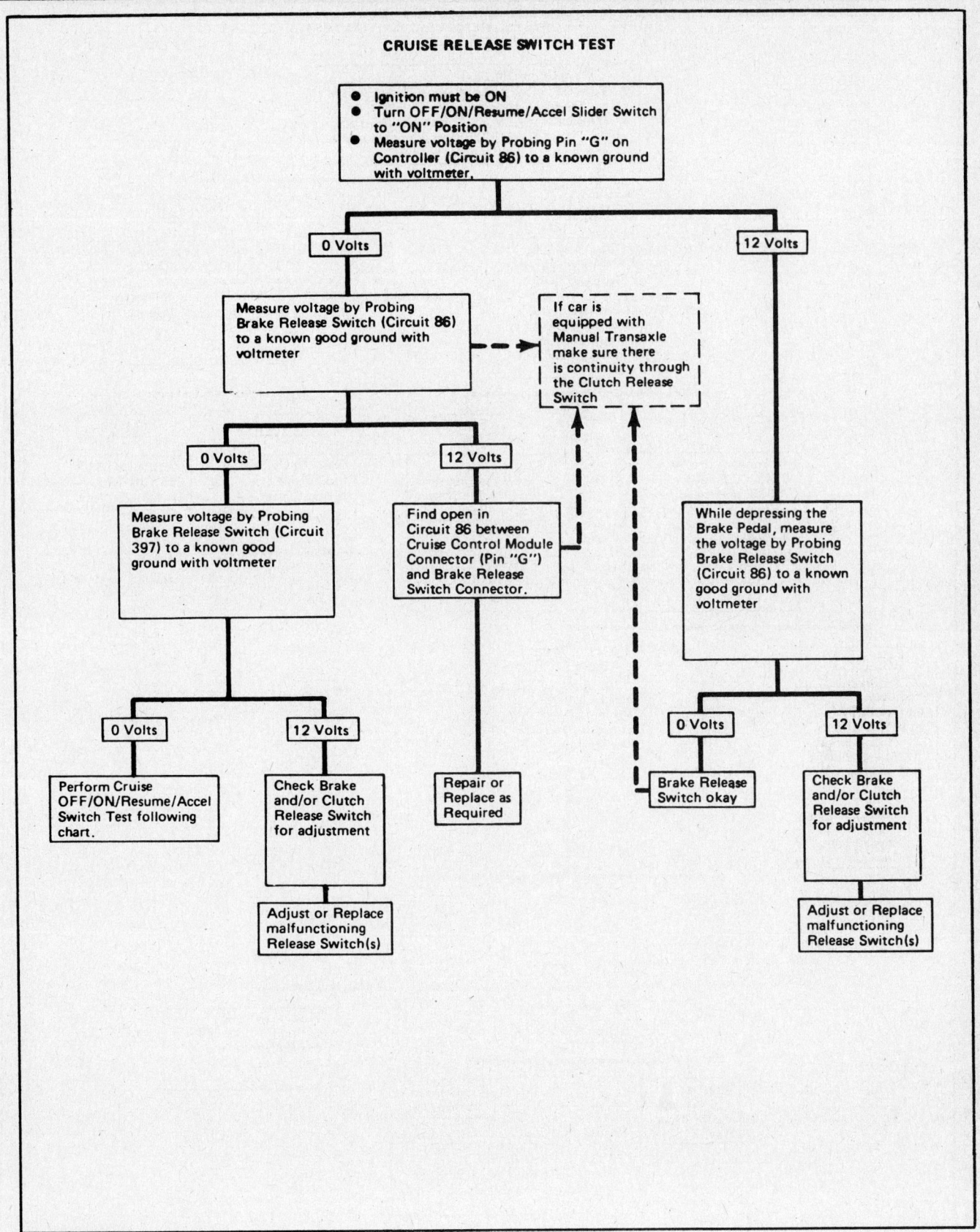

CRUISE RELEASE SWITCH TEST

- Ignition must be ON
- Turn OFF/ON/Resume/Accel Slider Switch to "ON" Position
- Measure voltage by Probing Pin "G" on Controller (Circuit 86) to a known ground with voltmeter.

0 Volts

12 Volts

Measure voltage by Probing Brake Release Switch (Circuit 86) to a known good ground with voltmeter

If car is equipped with Manual Transaxle make sure there is continuity through the Clutch Release Switch

0 Volts

12 Volts

Measure voltage by Probing Brake Release Switch (Circuit 397) to a known good ground with voltmeter

Find open in Circuit 86 between Cruise Control Module Connector (Pin "G") and Brake Release Switch Connector.

While depressing the Brake Pedal, measure the voltage by Probing Brake Release Switch (Circuit 86) to a known good ground with voltmeter

0 Volts

12 Volts

0 Volts

12 Volts

Perform Cruise OFF/ON/Resume/Accel Switch Test following chart.

Check Brake and/or Clutch Release Switch for adjustment

Repair or Replace as Required

Brake Release Switch okay

Check Brake and/or Clutch Release Switch for adjustment

Adjust or Replace malfunctioning Release Switch(s)

Adjust or Replace malfunctioning Release Switch(s)

Cruise control diagnosis—1984 and later Buick

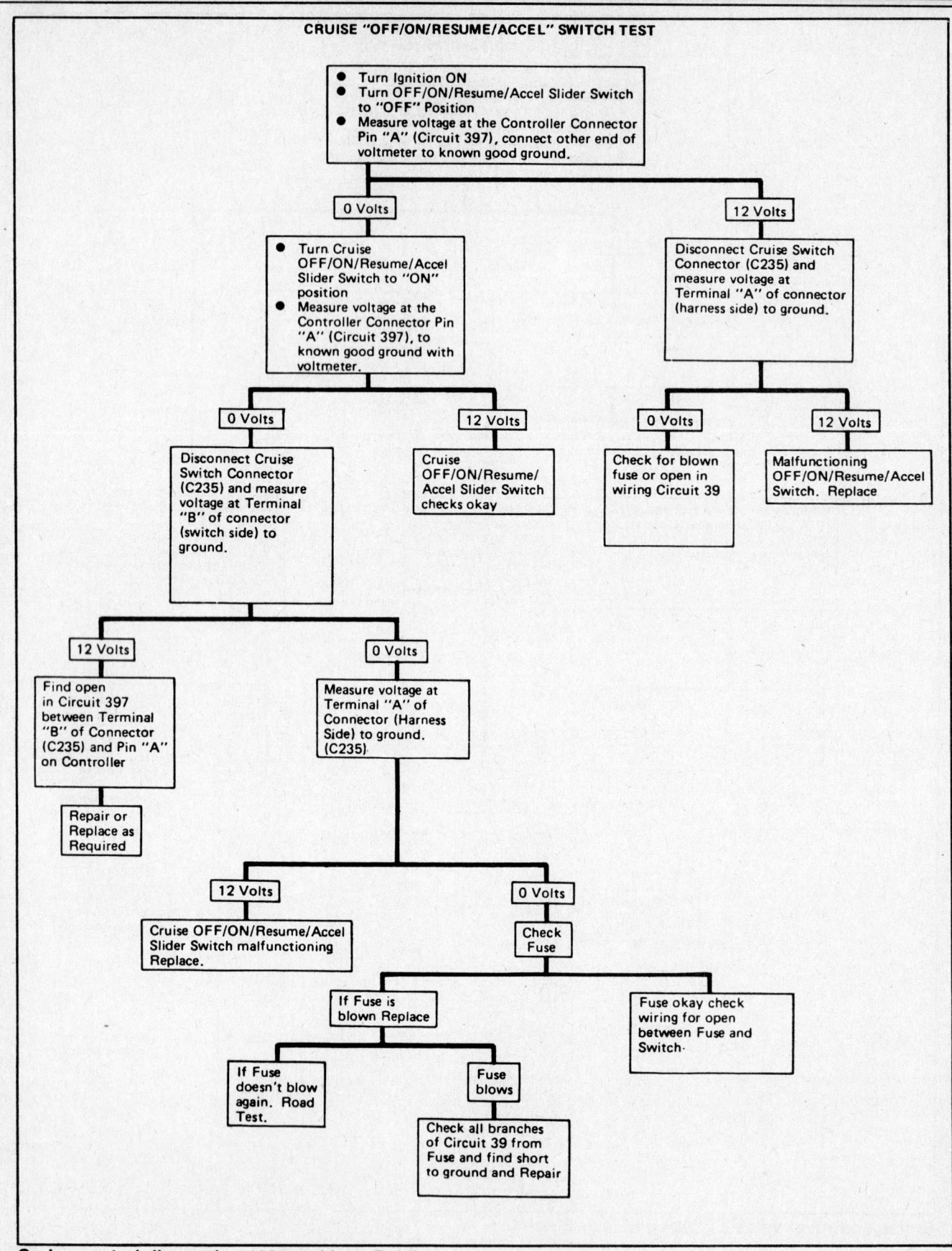

CRUISE "OFF/ON/RESUME/ACCEL" SWITCH TEST

- Turn Ignition ON
- Turn OFF/ON/Resume/Accel Slider Switch to "OFF" Position
- Measure voltage at the Controller Connector Pin "A" (Circuit 397), connect other end of voltmeter to known good ground.

0 Volts

- Turn Cruise OFF/ON/Resume/Accel Slider Switch to "ON" position
- Measure voltage at the Controller Connector Pin "A" (Circuit 397), to known good ground with voltmeter.

0 Volts

Disconnect Cruise Switch Connector (C235) and measure voltage at Terminal "B" of connector (switch side) to ground.

12 Volts

Cruise OFF/ON/Resume/Accel Slider Switch checks okay

12 Volts

Find open in Circuit 397 between Terminal "B" of Connector (C235) and Pin "A" on Controller

Repair or Replace as Required

0 Volts

Measure voltage at Terminal "A" of Connector (Harness Side) to ground. (C235)

12 Volts

Cruise OFF/ON/Resume/Accel Slider Switch malfunctioning Replace.

0 Volts

Check Fuse

If Fuse is blown Replace

If Fuse doesn't blow again. Road Test.

Fuse blows

Check all branches of Circuit 39 from Fuse and find short to ground and Repair

Fuse okay check wiring for open between Fuse and Switch.

12 Volts

Disconnect Cruise Switch Connector (C235) and measure voltage at Terminal "A" of connector (harness side) to ground.

0 Volts

Check for blown fuse or open in wiring Circuit 39

12 Volts

Malfunctioning OFF/ON/Resume/Accel Switch. Replace

Cruise control diagnosis—1984 and later Buick

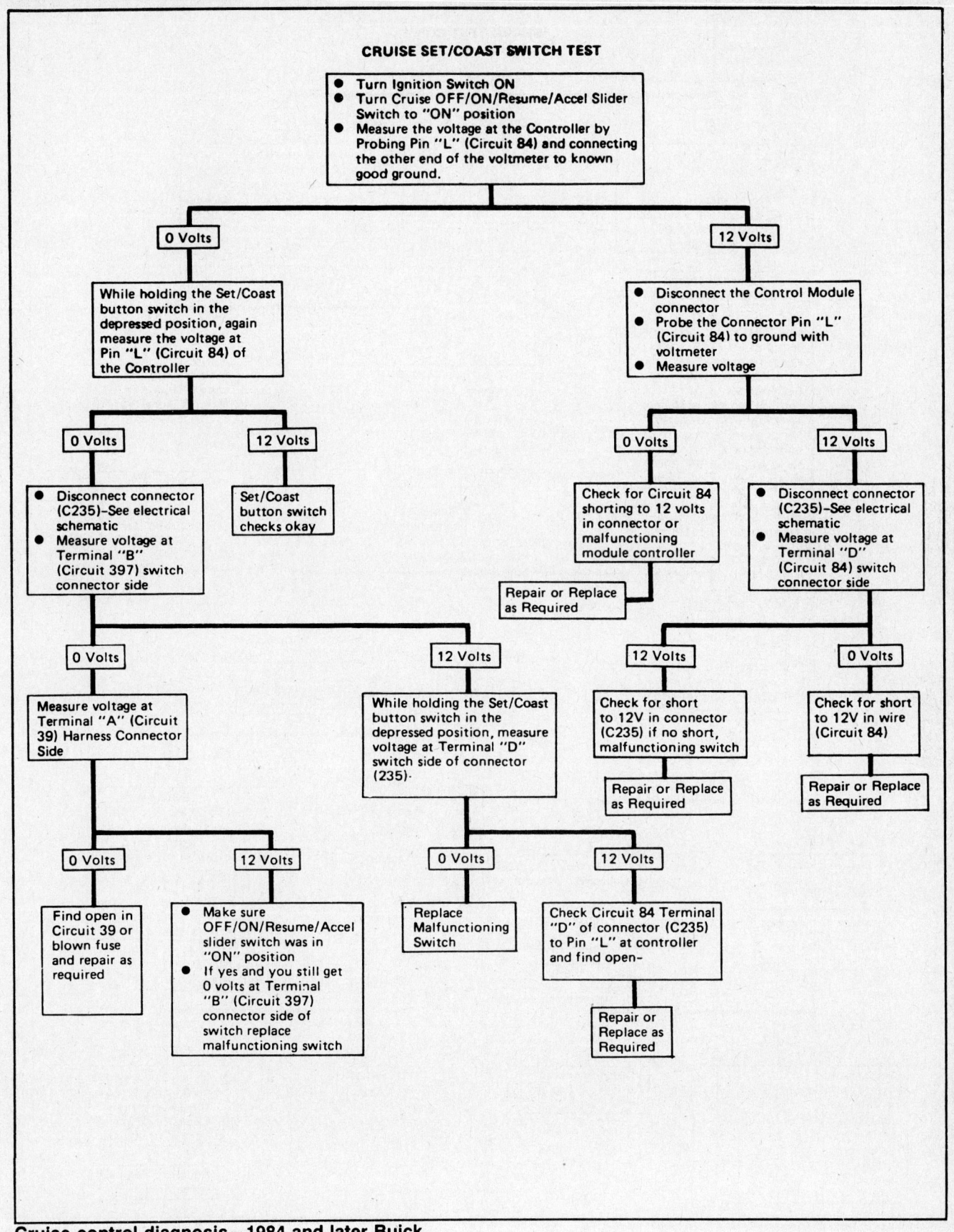

CRUISE SET/COAST SWITCH TEST

- Turn Ignition Switch ON
- Turn Cruise OFF/ON/Resume/Accel Slider Switch to "ON" position
- Measure the voltage at the Controller by Probing Pin "L" (Circuit 84) and connecting the other end of the voltmeter to known good ground.

0 Volts

While holding the Set/Coast button switch in the depressed position, again measure the voltage at Pin "L" (Circuit 84) of the Controller

0 Volts

- Disconnect connector (C235)–See electrical schematic
- Measure voltage at Terminal "B" (Circuit 397) switch connector side

0 Volts

Measure voltage at Terminal "A" (Circuit 39) Harness Connector Side

0 Volts

Find open in Circuit 39 or blown fuse and repair as required

12 Volts

- Make sure OFF/ON/Resume/Accel slider switch was in "ON" position
- If yes and you still get 0 volts at Terminal "B" (Circuit 397) connector side of switch replace malfunctioning switch

12 Volts

Set/Coast button switch checks okay

12 Volts

While holding the Set/Coast button switch in the depressed position, measure voltage at Terminal "D" switch side of connector (235).

0 Volts

Replace Malfunctioning Switch

12 Volts

Check Circuit 84 Terminal "D" of connector (C235) to Pin "L" at controller and find open–

Repair or Replace as Required

12 Volts

- Disconnect the Control Module connector
- Probe the Connector Pin "L" (Circuit 84) to ground with voltmeter
- Measure voltage

0 Volts

Check for Circuit 84 shorting to 12 volts in connector or malfunctioning module controller

Repair or Replace as Required

12 Volts

- Disconnect connector (C235)–See electrical schematic
- Measure voltage at Terminal "D" (Circuit 84) switch connector side

12 Volts

Check for short to 12V in connector (C235) if no short, malfunctioning switch

Repair or Replace as Required

0 Volts

Check for short to 12V in wire (Circuit 84)

Repair or Replace as Required

Cruise control diagnosis – 1984 and later Buick

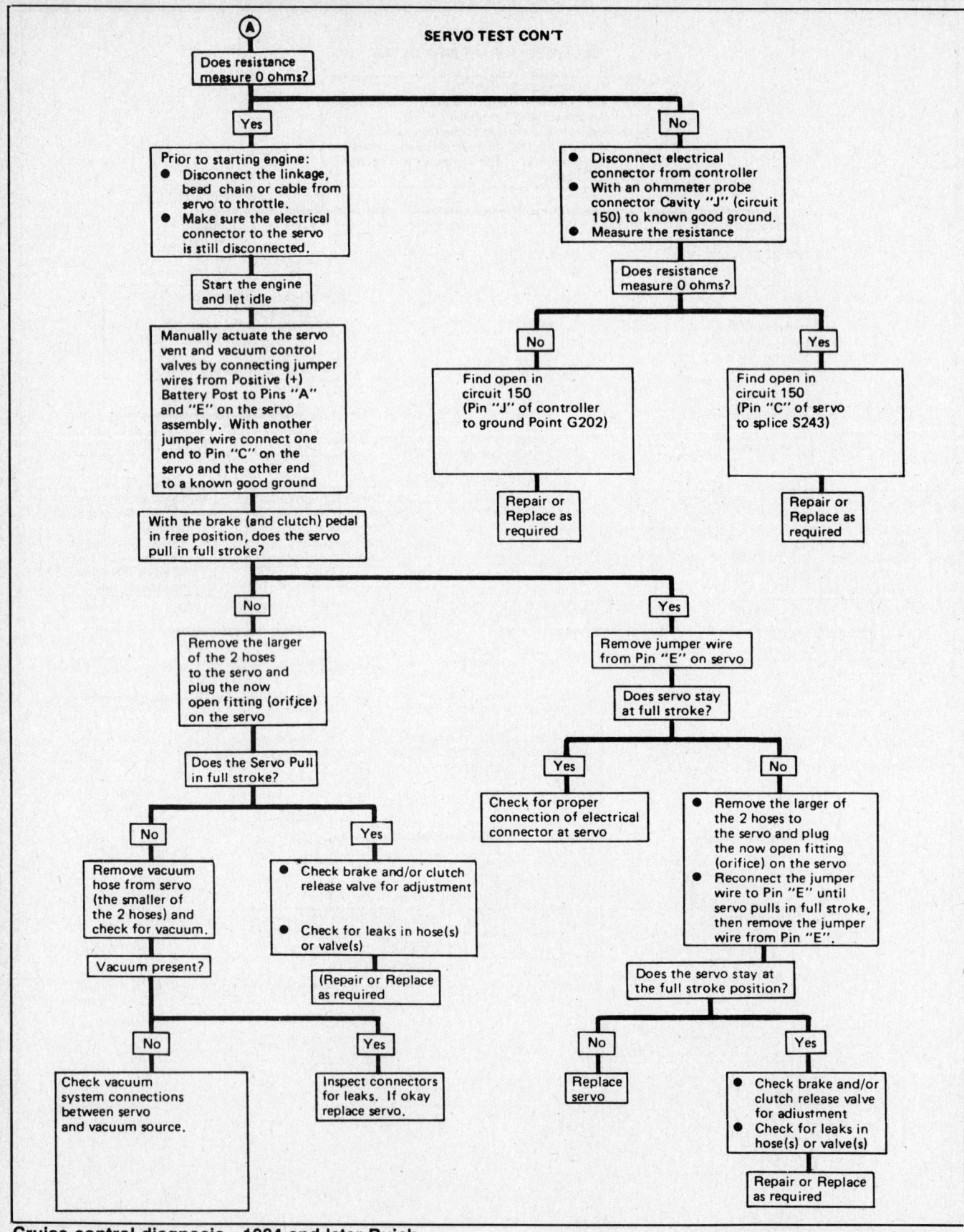

SERVO TEST CON'T

(A) Does resistance measure 0 ohms?

Yes

Prior to starting engine:
• Disconnect the linkage, bead chain or cable from servo to throttle.
• Make sure the electrical connector to the servo is still disconnected.

Start the engine and let idle

Manually actuate the servo vent and vacuum control valves by connecting jumper wires from Positive (+) Battery Post to Pins "A" and "E" on the servo assembly. With another jumper wire connect one end to Pin "C" on the servo and the other end to a known good ground

With the brake (and clutch) pedal in free position, does the servo pull in full stroke?

No

Remove the larger of the 2 hoses to the servo and plug the now open fitting (orifjce) on the servo

Does the Servo Pull in full stroke?

No

Remove vacuum hose from servo (the smaller of the 2 hoses) and check for vacuum.

Vacuum present?

No

Check vacuum system connections between servo and vacuum source.

Yes

Inspect connectors for leaks. If okay replace servo.

Yes

• Check brake and/or clutch release valve for adjustment
• Check for leaks in hose(s) or valve(s)

(Repair or Replace as required)

No

Disconnect electrical connector from controller
• With an ohmmeter probe connector Cavity "J" (circuit 150) to known good ground.
• Measure the resistance

Does resistance measure 0 ohms?

No

Find open in circuit 150 (Pin "J" of controller to ground Point G202)

Repair or Replace as required

Yes

Find open in circuit 150 (Pin "C" of servo to splice S243)

Repair or Replace as required

Yes

Remove jumper wire from Pin "E" on servo

Does servo stay at full stroke?

Yes

Check for proper connection of electrical connector at servo

No

• Remove the larger of the 2 hoses to the servo and plug the now open fitting (orifice) on the servo
• Reconnect the jumper wire to Pin "E" until servo pulls in full stroke, then remove the jumper wire from Pin "E".

Does the servo stay at the full stroke position?

No

Replace servo

Yes

• Check brake and/or clutch release valve for adjustment
• Check for leaks in hose(s) or valve(s)

Repair or Replace as required

Cruise control diagnosis—1984 and later Buick

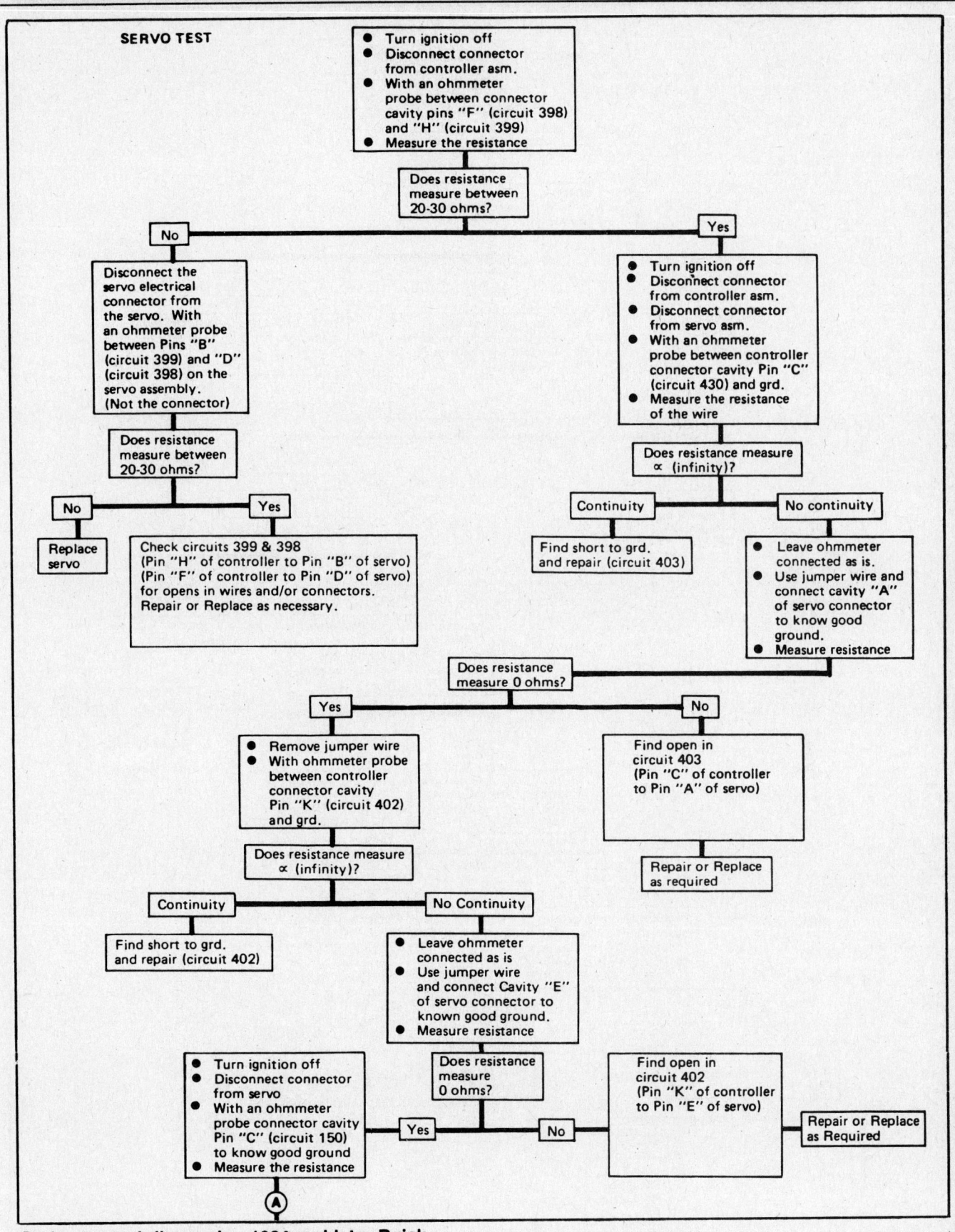

SERVO TEST

- Turn ignition off
- Disconnect connector from controller asm.
- With an ohmmeter probe between connector cavity pins "F" (circuit 398) and "H" (circuit 399)
- Measure the resistance

Does resistance measure between 20-30 ohms?

No → Disconnect the servo electrical connector from the servo. With an ohmmeter probe between Pins "B" (circuit 399) and "D" (circuit 398) on the servo assembly. (Not the connector)

Does resistance measure between 20-30 ohms?

- **No** → Replace servo
- **Yes** → Check circuits 399 & 398 (Pin "H" of controller to Pin "B" of servo) (Pin "F" of controller to Pin "D" of servo) for opens in wires and/or connectors. Repair or Replace as necessary.

Yes →
- Turn ignition off
- Disconnect connector from controller asm.
- Disconnect connector from servo asm.
- With an ohmmeter probe between controller connector cavity Pin "C" (circuit 430) and grd.
- Measure the resistance of the wire

Does resistance measure ∝ (infinity)?

- **Continuity** → Find short to grd. and repair (circuit 403)
- **No continuity** →
  - Leave ohmmeter connected as is.
  - Use jumper wire and connect cavity "A" of servo connector to know good ground.
  - Measure resistance

Does resistance measure 0 ohms?

- **Yes** →
  - Remove jumper wire
  - With ohmmeter probe between controller connector cavity Pin "K" (circuit 402) and grd.

  Does resistance measure ∝ (infinity)?
  - **Continuity** → Find short to grd. and repair (circuit 402)
  - **No Continuity** →
    - Leave ohmmeter connected as is
    - Use jumper wire and connect Cavity "E" of servo connector to known good ground.
    - Measure resistance

- **No** → Find open in circuit 403 (Pin "C" of controller to Pin "A" of servo)

  Repair or Replace as required

Does resistance measure 0 ohms?
- Turn ignition off
- Disconnect connector from servo
- With an ohmmeter probe connector cavity Pin "C" (circuit 150) to know good ground
- Measure the resistance

- **Yes**
- **No** → Find open in circuit 402 (Pin "K" of controller to Pin "E" of servo)

  Repair or Replace as Required

Ⓐ

Cruise control diagnosis—1984 and later Buick

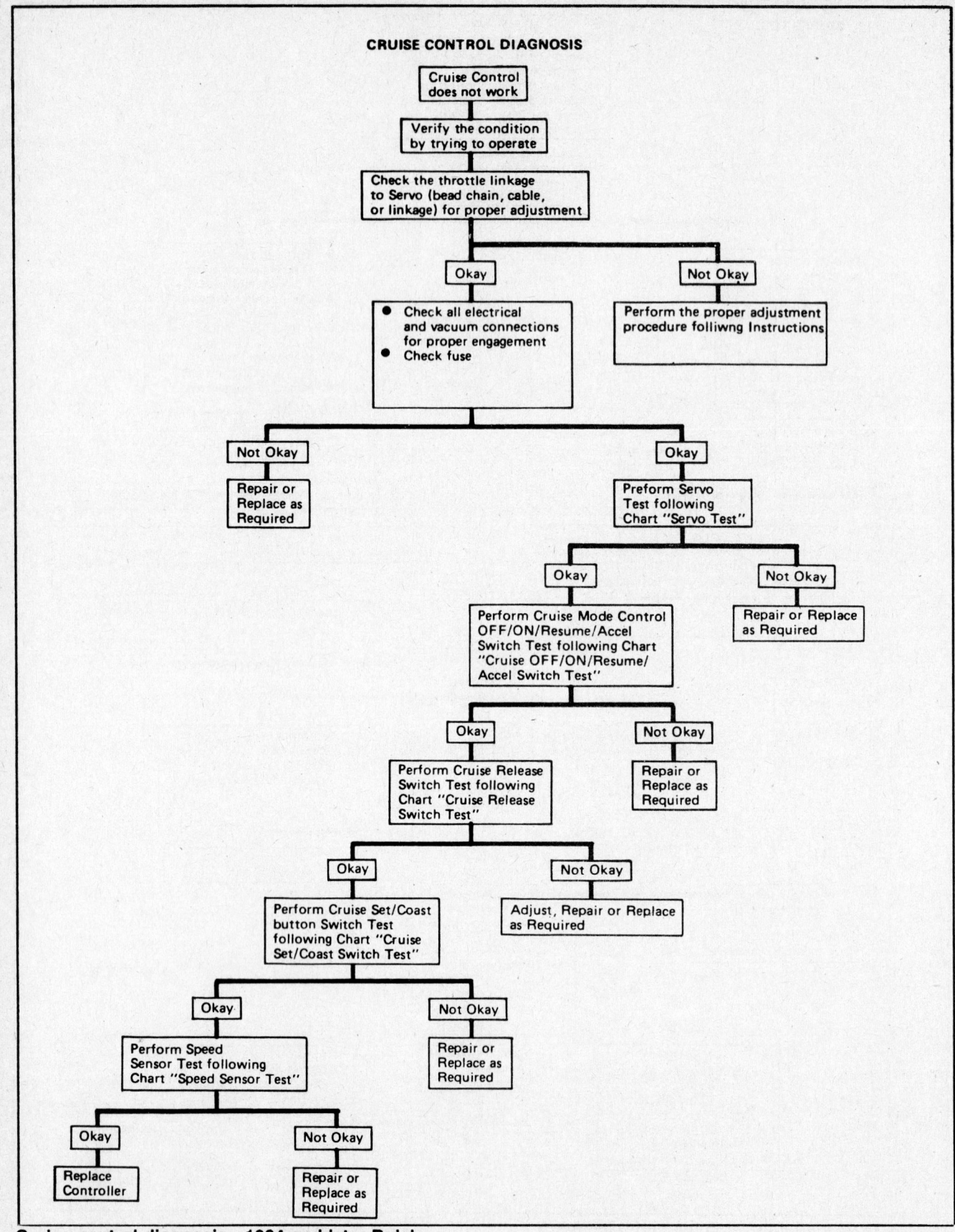

Cruise control diagnosis—1984 and later Buick

**CONTROL SWITCH
CONTINUITY CHECK**

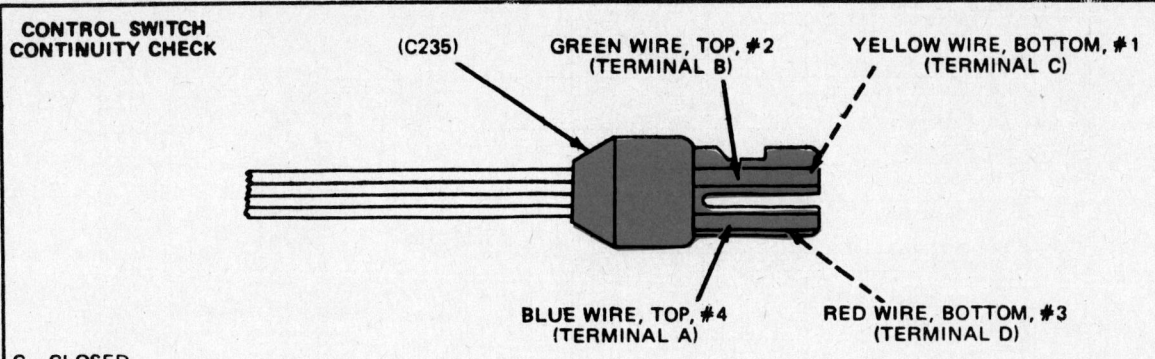

(C235)

GREEN WIRE, TOP, #2
(TERMINAL B)

YELLOW WIRE, BOTTOM, #1
(TERMINAL C)

BLUE WIRE, TOP, #4
(TERMINAL A)

RED WIRE, BOTTOM, #3
(TERMINAL D)

C – CLOSED
O – OPEN

SET/COAST (S/C) SW	POSITION SLIDER	1-2	1-3	1-4	2-3	2-4	3-4
NORMAL	OFF	O	O	O	O	O	O
NORMAL	ON	O	O	O	O	C	O
NORMAL	R/A	C	O	C	O	C	O
DEPRESSED	OFF	O	O	O	C	O	O
DEPRESSED	ON	O	O	O	C	C	C
DEPRESSED	R/A	C	C	C	C	C	C

CRUISE CONTROLLER (MODULE) CHECKS AT CONNECTOR

- IGNITION ON
- CONTROLLER DISCONNECTED

PIN	FUNCTION	VOLTAGE TO GND	RESISTANCE	CONDITIONS
G	BRAKE INPUT	12 V 0 V	— —	BRAKE (AND CLUTCH) NOT DEPRESSED SLIDER SWITCH "ON" BRAKE (AND/OR CLUTCH) DEPRESSED SLIDER SWITCH "ON"
L	SET/COAST INPUT	12 V 0 V 0 V	— — —	SLIDER SWITCH "ON" – SET/COAST DEPRESSED SLIDER SWITCH "ON" – SET/COAST NORMAL SLIDER SWITCH "OFF" – SET/COAST NORMAL
M	RESUME/ ACCEL. INPUT	12 V 0 V 0 V	— — —	SLIDER SWITCH "R/A" POSITION SLIDER SWITCH "ON" – SET/COAST DEPRESSED OR NORMAL SLIDER SWITCH "OFF" – SET/COAST DEPRESSED OR NORMAL
J	GROUND	—	0Ω	MEASURED TO VEHICLE GROUND
A	ON/OFF INPUT	12 V 0 V	— —	SLIDER SWITCH "ON" SLIDER SWITCH "OFF" – SET/COAST DEPRESSED OR NORMAL
B	INDICATOR LAMP	12 V	—	CRUISE ARMED
F H	SPS HIGH SPS LOW	— —	$20 \text{-} 30 \Omega$ 0Ω	MEASURED BETWEEN PINS F & H – SERVO CONNECTED MEASURED BETWEEN PINS F & H – SERVO DISCONNECTED
D	SPEED SIGNAL	→	→	SEE CHART (DIAGNOSTIC) ON SPEED SENDER TEST
K	VACUUM VALVE CONTROL	— —	$30 \text{-} 50 \Omega$ $\infty \Omega$	MEASURED TO GROUND – SERVO CONNECTED MEASURED TO GROUND – SERVO NOT CONNECTED
C	VENT VALVE CONTROL	— —	$30 \text{-} 50 \Omega$ $\infty \Omega$	MEASURED TO GROUND – SERVO CONNECTED MEASURED TO GROUND – SERVO NOT CONNECTED

SERVO CHECKS

- SERVO CONNECTOR DISCONNECTED
- MEASURE AT SERVO PINS

PIN	FUNCTION	RESISTANCE	CONDITIONS
D B	SPS HIGH SPS LOW	$20 \text{-} 30 \Omega$	MEASURED BETWEEN PINS D AND B (IF MEASURED RESISTANCE IS NOT STATED VALVE, REPLACE SERVO)
A	VENT VALVE	$30 \text{-} 50 \Omega$	MEASURED BETWEEN PINS A AND C (IF MEASURED RESISTANCE IS NOT STATED VALVE, REPLACE SERVO)
E	VACUUM VALVE	$30 \text{-} 50 \Omega$	MEASURED BETWEEN PINS E AND C (IF MEASURED RESISTANCE IS NOT STATED VALVE, REPLACE SERVO)

Cruise control servo, controller and switch checking procedure – 1984 and later Buick

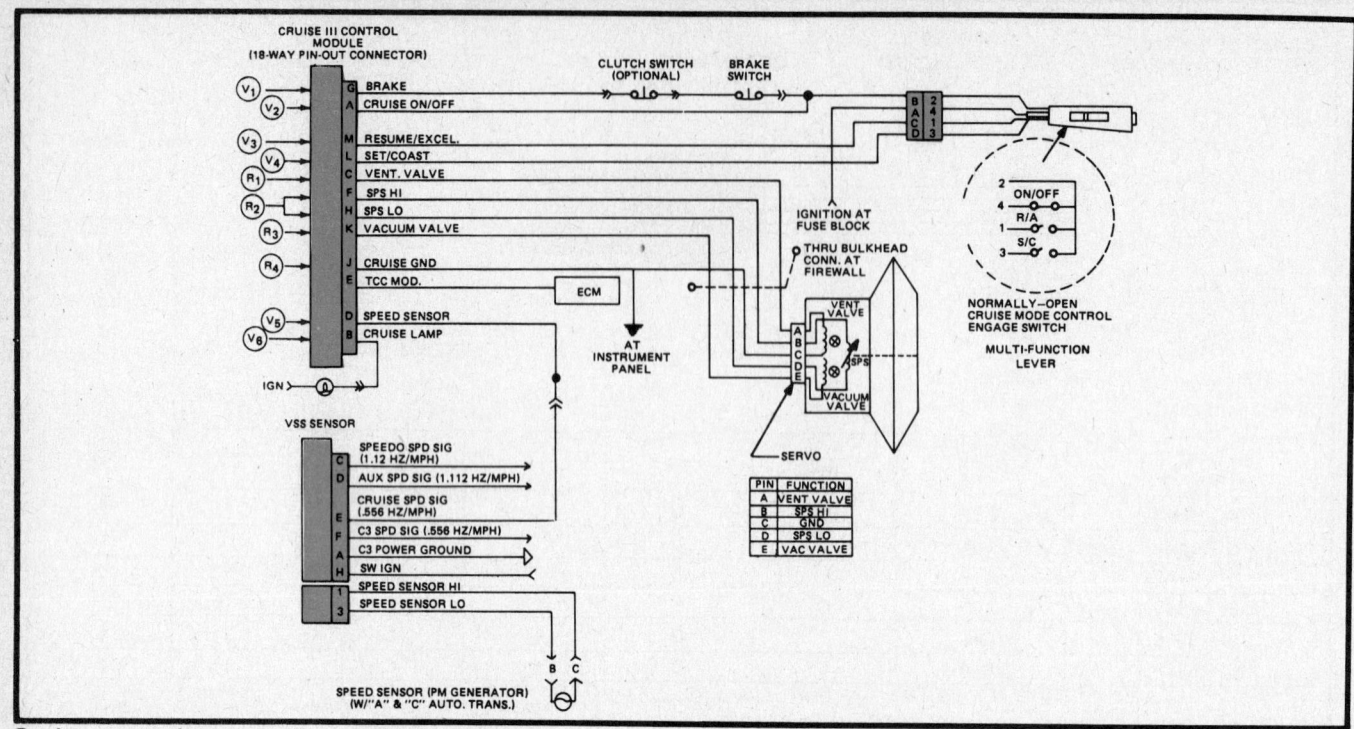

Cruise control system III electrical schematic—1984 and later Buick

SERVO ASSEMBLY LINKAGE ADJUSTMENT

For servo linkage adjustments refer to the proper illustration.

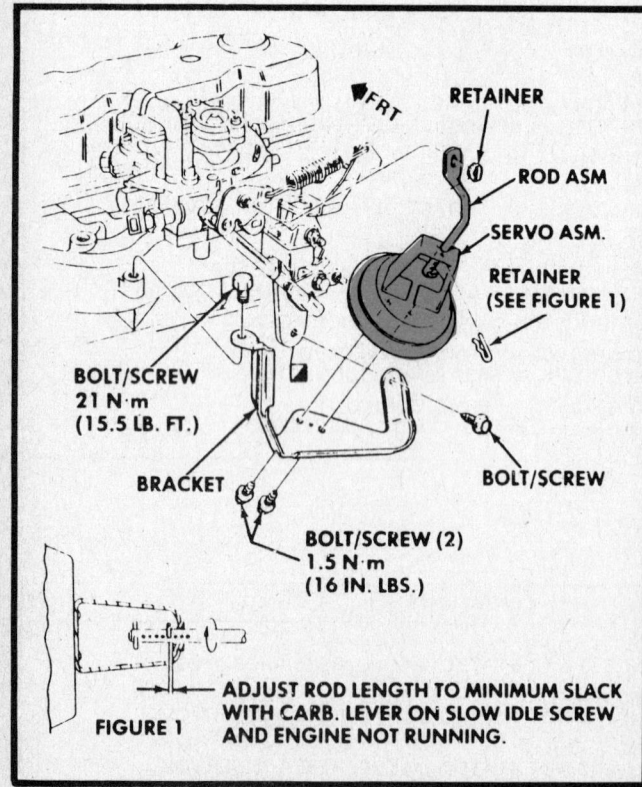

ADJUST ROD LENGTH TO MINIMUM SLACK WITH CARB. LEVER ON SLOW IDLE SCREW AND ENGINE NOT RUNNING.

FIGURE 1

Servo and linkage adjustment—1982–83 Century and Skylark with 2.5 liter TBI engine

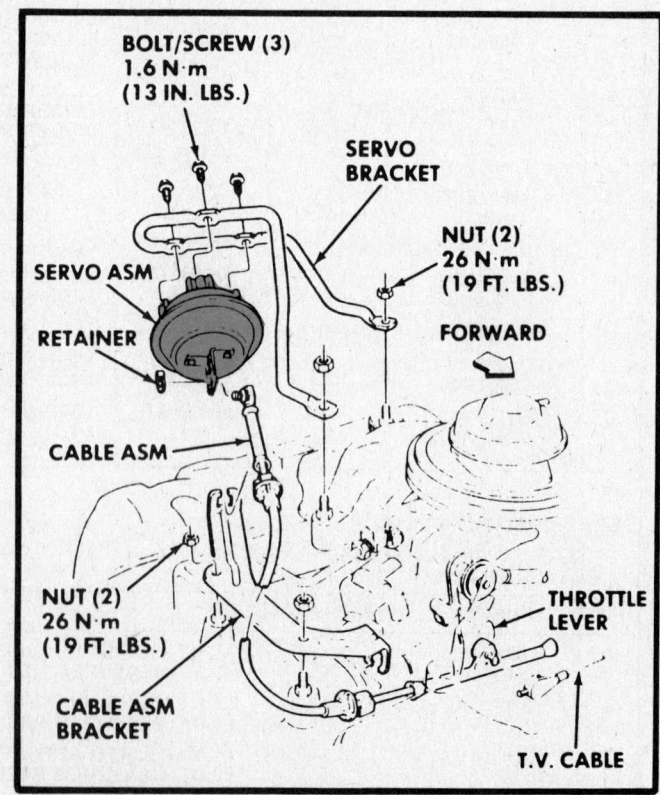

Servo and linkage adjustment—1982–83 Century with V6 diesel engine

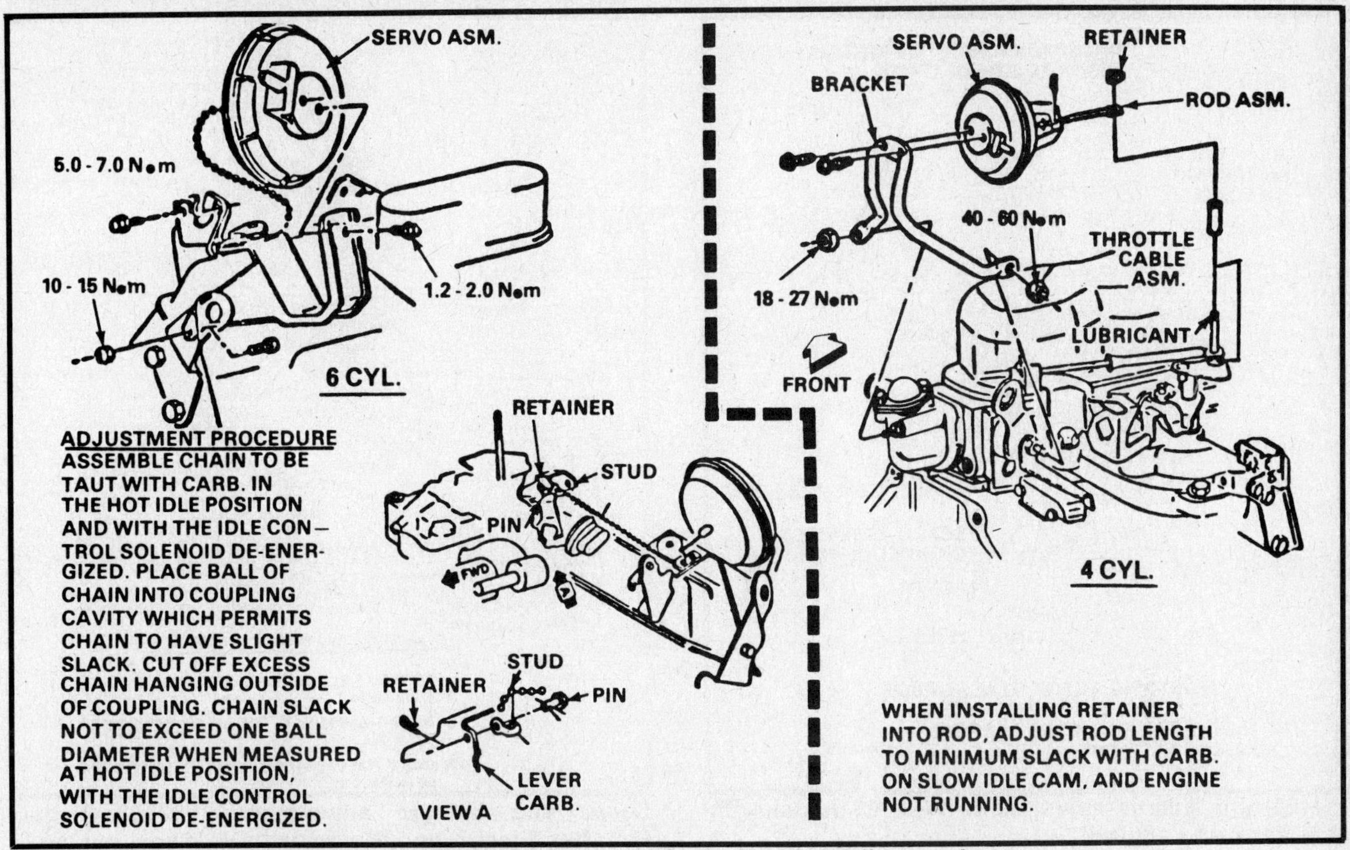

SERVO ASM.

5.0 - 7.0 N•m

10 - 15 N•m

1.2 - 2.0 N•m

6 CYL.

ADJUSTMENT PROCEDURE
ASSEMBLE CHAIN TO BE TAUT WITH CARB. IN THE HOT IDLE POSITION AND WITH THE IDLE CON—TROL SOLENOID DE-ENERGIZED. PLACE BALL OF CHAIN INTO COUPLING CAVITY WHICH PERMITS CHAIN TO HAVE SLIGHT SLACK. CUT OFF EXCESS CHAIN HANGING OUTSIDE OF COUPLING. CHAIN SLACK NOT TO EXCEED ONE BALL DIAMETER WHEN MEASURED AT HOT IDLE POSITION, WITH THE IDLE CONTROL SOLENOID DE-ENERGIZED.

RETAINER

STUD

PIN

FWD

RETAINER

STUD

PIN

LEVER CARB.

VIEW A

SERVO ASM.   RETAINER

BRACKET   ROD ASM.

40 - 60 N•m

18 - 27 N•m

THROTTLE CABLE ASM.

LUBRICANT

FRONT

4 CYL.

WHEN INSTALLING RETAINER INTO ROD, ADJUST ROD LENGTH TO MINIMUM SLACK WITH CARB. ON SLOW IDLE CAM, AND ENGINE NOT RUNNING.

Servo and linkage adjustment—1982–83 Century and Skylark with 2.8 liter engine

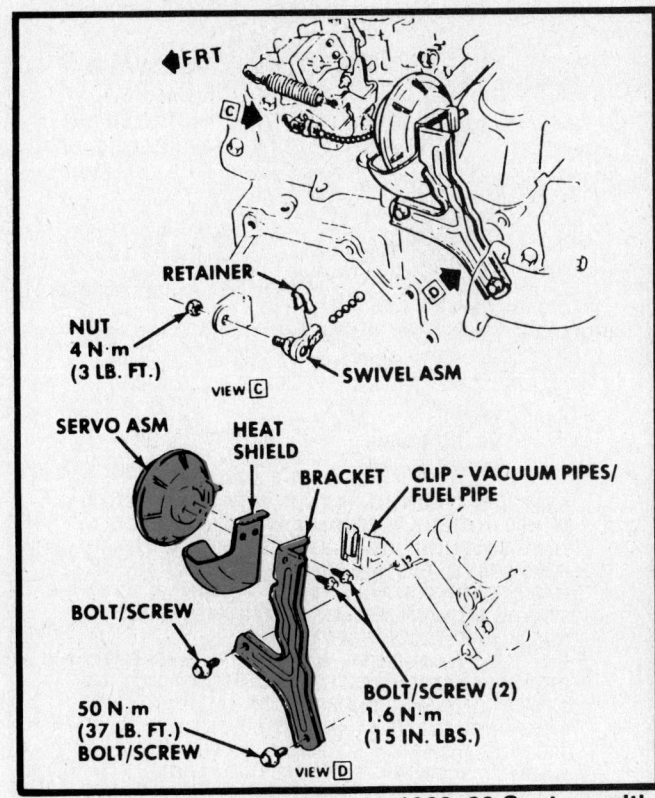

FRT

RETAINER

NUT
4 N·m
(3 LB. FT.)

SWIVEL ASM

VIEW C

SERVO ASM   HEAT SHIELD   BRACKET   CLIP - VACUUM PIPES/ FUEL PIPE

BOLT/SCREW

50 N·m
(37 LB. FT.)
BOLT/SCREW

BOLT/SCREW (2)
1.6 N·m
(15 IN. LBS.)

VIEW D

Servo and linkage adjustment—1982–83 Century with 3.0 liter engine

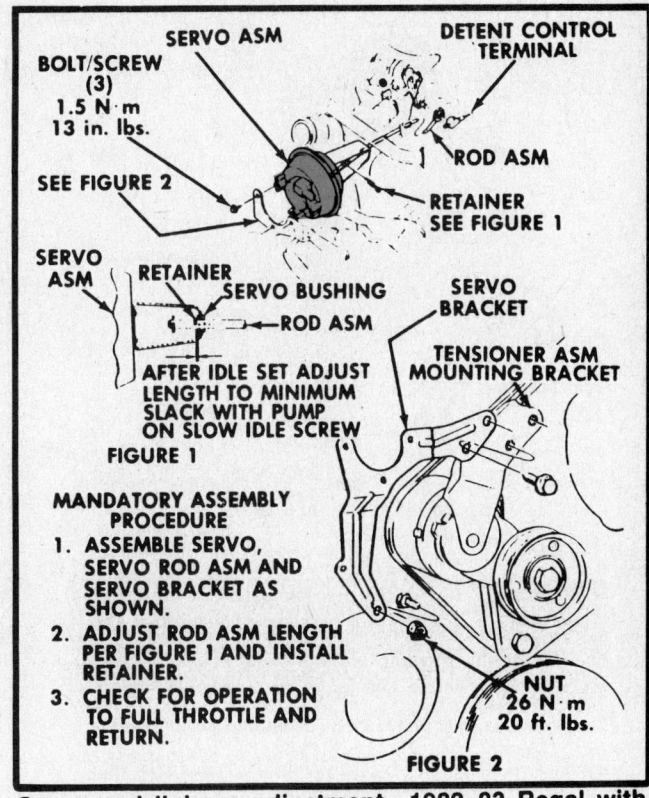

SERVO ASM   DETENT CONTROL TERMINAL

BOLT/SCREW (3)
1.5 N·m
13 in. lbs.

SEE FIGURE 2

ROD ASM

RETAINER SEE FIGURE 1

SERVO ASM   RETAINER   SERVO BUSHING   ROD ASM

SERVO BRACKET

AFTER IDLE SET ADJUST LENGTH TO MINIMUM SLACK WITH PUMP ON SLOW IDLE SCREW

TENSIONER ASM MOUNTING BRACKET

FIGURE 1

MANDATORY ASSEMBLY PROCEDURE
1. ASSEMBLE SERVO, SERVO ROD ASM AND SERVO BRACKET AS SHOWN.
2. ADJUST ROD ASM LENGTH PER FIGURE 1 AND INSTALL RETAINER.
3. CHECK FOR OPERATION TO FULL THROTTLE AND RETURN.

NUT
26 N·m
20 ft. lbs.

FIGURE 2

Servo and linkage adjustment—1982–83 Regal with V6 diesel engine

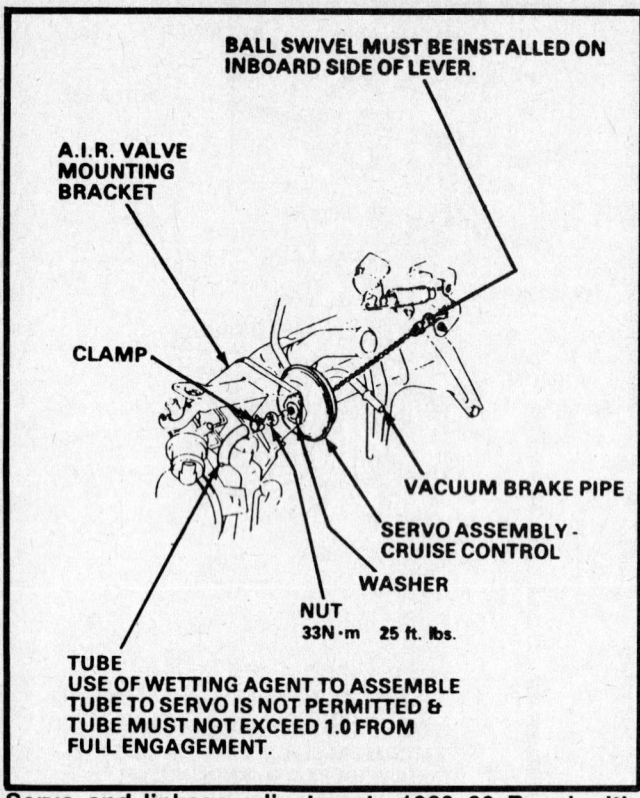

BALL SWIVEL MUST BE INSTALLED ON INBOARD SIDE OF LEVER.

A.I.R. VALVE MOUNTING BRACKET

CLAMP

VACUUM BRAKE PIPE

SERVO ASSEMBLY - CRUISE CONTROL

WASHER

NUT 33N·m 25 ft. lbs.

TUBE USE OF WETTING AGENT TO ASSEMBLE TUBE TO SERVO IS NOT PERMITTED & TUBE MUST NOT EXCEED 1.0 FROM FULL ENGAGEMENT.

Servo and linkage adjustment—1982–83 Regal with 3.8 liter turbo engine

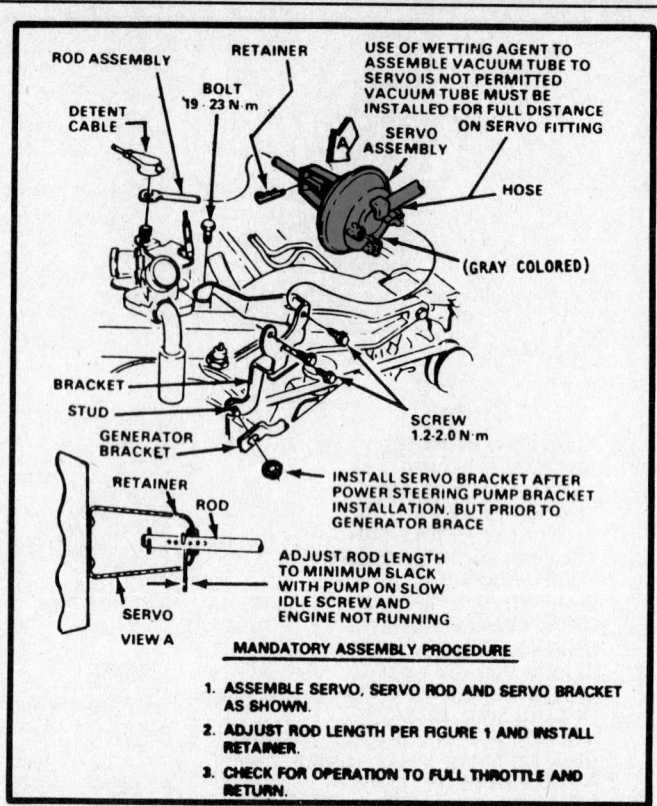

ROD ASSEMBLY

RETAINER

DETENT CABLE

BOLT 19·23 N·m

USE OF WETTING AGENT TO ASSEMBLE VACUUM TUBE TO SERVO IS NOT PERMITTED VACUUM TUBE MUST BE INSTALLED FOR FULL DISTANCE ON SERVO FITTING

SERVO ASSEMBLY

HOSE

(GRAY COLORED)

BRACKET

STUD

GENERATOR BRACKET

SCREW 1.2-2.0 N·m

RETAINER

ROD

SERVO VIEW A

INSTALL SERVO BRACKET AFTER POWER STEERING PUMP BRACKET INSTALLATION, BUT PRIOR TO GENERATOR BRACE

ADJUST ROD LENGTH TO MINIMUM SLACK WITH PUMP ON SLOW IDLE SCREW AND ENGINE NOT RUNNING

MANDATORY ASSEMBLY PROCEDURE

1. ASSEMBLE SERVO, SERVO ROD AND SERVO BRACKET AS SHOWN.
2. ADJUST ROD LENGTH PER FIGURE 1 AND INSTALL RETAINER.
3. CHECK FOR OPERATION TO FULL THROTTLE AND RETURN.

Servo and linkage adjustment—1982–83 Regal, LeSabre, Electra and Riviera with V8 diesel engine

TUBE

NUT 4N·m 2.5 ft. lbs.

RETAINER· CRUISE CHAIN

VIEW B

3.8L BALL STUD & SWIVEL ASSEMBLY

4N·m 2.5 ft. lbs.

RETAINER

SERVO UNIT & CHAIN ASSEMBLY

SCREW 1.2 - 2.0 N·m

BRACKET· SERVO UNIT

BOLT 50N·m 37 ft. lbs.

VIEW A

SWIVEL ASM

VIEW B 4.1L

E.F.E. CLIP

ASSEMBLE CHAIN TO BE TAUT WITH CARBURETOR IN THE HOT IDLE POSITION AND WITH THE IDLE CONTROL SOLENOID DE-ENERGIZED. PLACE CHAIN INTO SWIVEL CAVITIES WHICH PERMIT CHAIN TO HAVE SLIGHT SLACK. PLACE RETAINER OVER SWIVEL AND CHAIN ASSEMBLY. RETAINER MUST BE POSITIONED BETWEEN BALLS. VIEW D. CUT OFF CHAIN FLUSH WITH SIDE OF SWIVEL TO REMOVE EXCESS LENGTH. CHAIN SLACK NOT TO EXCEED ONE HALF DIAMETER OF BALL STUD (3.8) WHEN MEASURED AT HOT IDLE POSITION, WITH THE IDLE CONTROL SOLENOID DE-ENERGIZED AND SWIVEL DISCONNECTED FROM BALL STUD REF. VIEW C.

BALL SWIVEL MUST BE INSTALLED ON OUTBOARD SIDE OF LEVER.

USE OF WETTING AGENT TO ASSEMBLE TUBE TO SERVO IS NOT PERMITTED & TUBE MUST NOT EXCEED 1.0 FROM FULL ENGAGEMENT.

Servo and linkage adjustment—1982–83 Regal with 3.8 liter and 4.1 liter engine

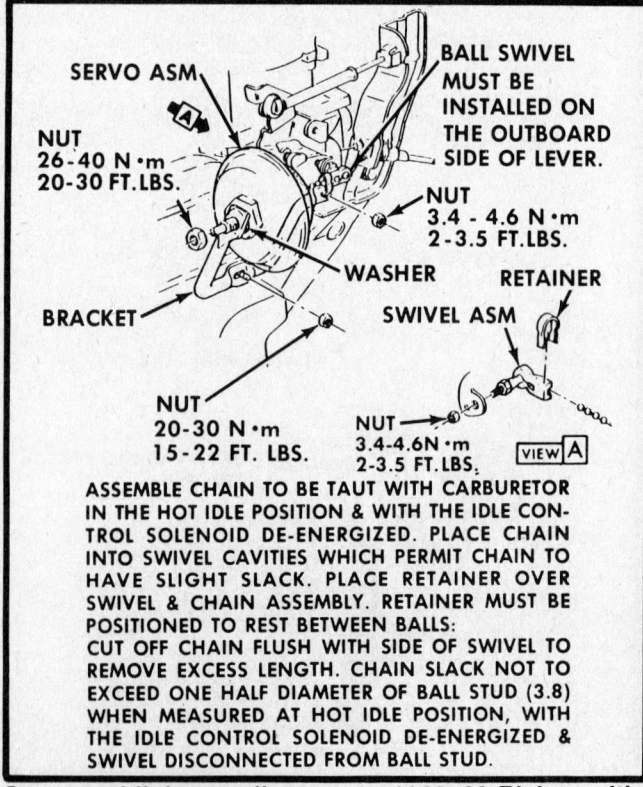

SERVO ASM

NUT 26-40 N·m 20-30 FT.LBS.

BALL SWIVEL MUST BE INSTALLED ON THE OUTBOARD SIDE OF LEVER.

NUT 3.4 - 4.6 N·m 2-3.5 FT.LBS.

WASHER

RETAINER

BRACKET

SWIVEL ASM

NUT 20-30 N·m 15-22 FT. LBS.

NUT 3.4-4.6N·m 2-3.5 FT.LBS.

VIEW A

ASSEMBLE CHAIN TO BE TAUT WITH CARBURETOR IN THE HOT IDLE POSITION & WITH THE IDLE CONTROL SOLENOID DE-ENERGIZED. PLACE CHAIN INTO SWIVEL CAVITIES WHICH PERMIT CHAIN TO HAVE SLIGHT SLACK. PLACE RETAINER OVER SWIVEL & CHAIN ASSEMBLY. RETAINER MUST BE POSITIONED TO REST BETWEEN BALLS:
CUT OFF CHAIN FLUSH WITH SIDE OF SWIVEL TO REMOVE EXCESS LENGTH. CHAIN SLACK NOT TO EXCEED ONE HALF DIAMETER OF BALL STUD (3.8) WHEN MEASURED AT HOT IDLE POSITION, WITH THE IDLE CONTROL SOLENOID DE-ENERGIZED & SWIVEL DISCONNECTED FROM BALL STUD.

Servo and linkage adjustment—1982–83 Riviera with 3.8 liter turbo engine

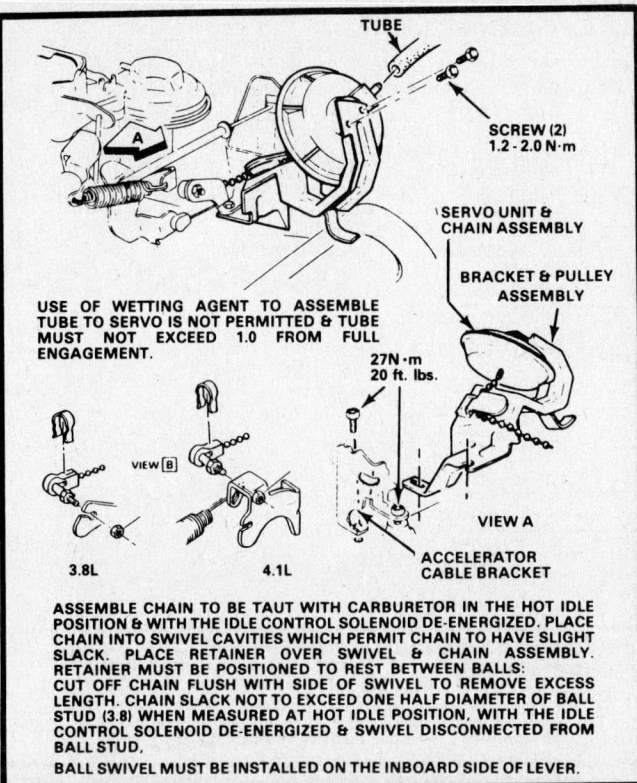

USE OF WETTING AGENT TO ASSEMBLE TUBE TO SERVO IS NOT PERMITTED & TUBE MUST NOT EXCEED 1.0 FROM FULL ENGAGEMENT.

ASSEMBLE CHAIN TO BE TAUT WITH CARBURETOR IN THE HOT IDLE POSITION & WITH THE IDLE CONTROL SOLENOID DE-ENERGIZED. PLACE CHAIN INTO SWIVEL CAVITIES WHICH PERMIT CHAIN TO HAVE SLIGHT SLACK. PLACE RETAINER OVER SWIVEL & CHAIN ASSEMBLY. RETAINER MUST BE POSITIONED TO REST BETWEEN BALLS: CUT OFF CHAIN FLUSH WITH SIDE OF SWIVEL TO REMOVE EXCESS LENGTH. CHAIN SLACK NOT TO EXCEED ONE HALF DIAMETER OF BALL STUD (3.8) WHEN MEASURED AT HOT IDLE POSITION, WITH THE IDLE CONTROL SOLENOID DE-ENERGIZED & SWIVEL DISCONNECTED FROM BALL STUD.

BALL SWIVEL MUST BE INSTALLED ON THE INBOARD SIDE OF LEVER.

Servo and linkage adjustment — 1982–83 LeSabre and Electra with 3.8 liter and 4.1 liter engine

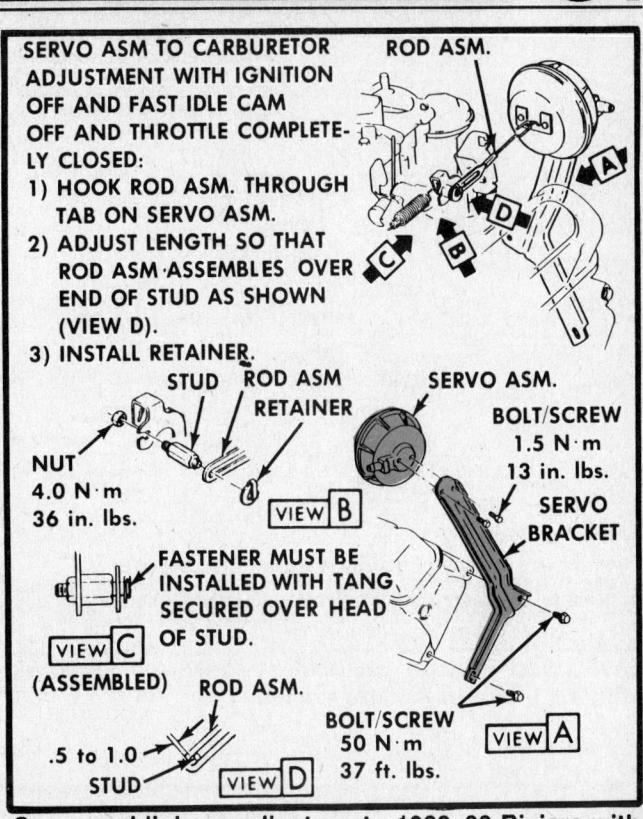

SERVO ASM TO CARBURETOR ADJUSTMENT WITH IGNITION OFF AND FAST IDLE CAM OFF AND THROTTLE COMPLETELY CLOSED:
1) HOOK ROD ASM. THROUGH TAB ON SERVO ASM.
2) ADJUST LENGTH SO THAT ROD ASM ASSEMBLES OVER END OF STUD AS SHOWN (VIEW D).
3) INSTALL RETAINER.

FASTENER MUST BE INSTALLED WITH TANG SECURED OVER HEAD OF STUD.

Servo and linkage adjustment — 1982–83 Riviera with 4.1 liter engine

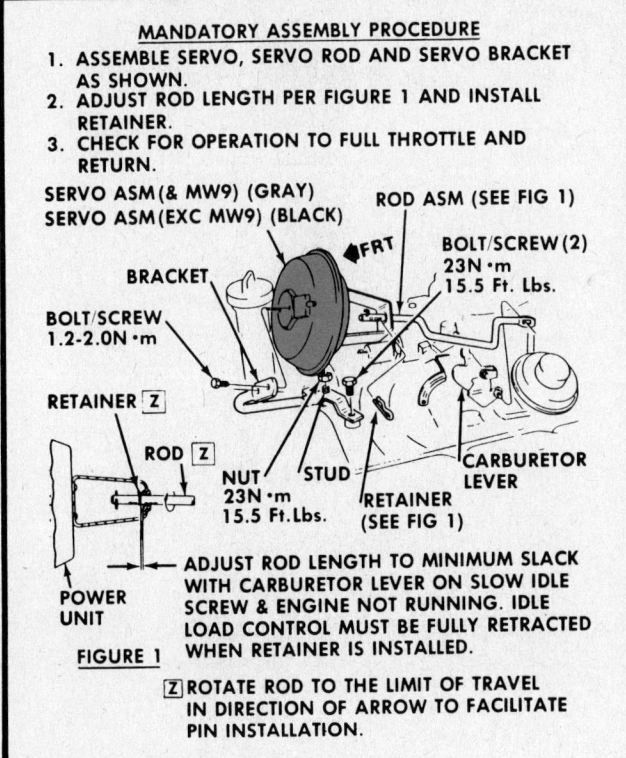

MANDATORY ASSEMBLY PROCEDURE
1. ASSEMBLE SERVO, SERVO ROD AND SERVO BRACKET AS SHOWN.
2. ADJUST ROD LENGTH PER FIGURE 1 AND INSTALL RETAINER.
3. CHECK FOR OPERATION TO FULL THROTTLE AND RETURN.

ADJUST ROD LENGTH TO MINIMUM SLACK WITH CARBURETOR LEVER ON SLOW IDLE SCREW & ENGINE NOT RUNNING. IDLE LOAD CONTROL MUST BE FULLY RETRACTED WHEN RETAINER IS INSTALLED.

FIGURE 1

Z ROTATE ROD TO THE LIMIT OF TRAVEL IN DIRECTION OF ARROW TO FACILITATE PIN INSTALLATION.

Servo and linkage adjustment — 1982–83 LeSabre, Electra and Riviera with 5.0 liter engine

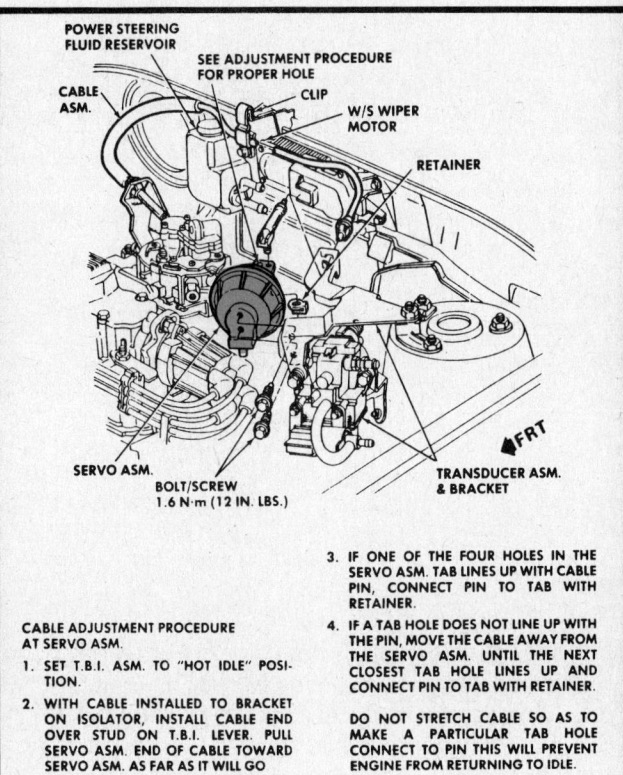

CABLE ADJUSTMENT PROCEDURE AT SERVO ASM.
1. SET T.B.I. ASM. TO "HOT IDLE" POSITION.
2. WITH CABLE INSTALLED TO BRACKET ON ISOLATOR, INSTALL CABLE END OVER STUD ON T.B.I. LEVER. PULL SERVO ASM. END OF CABLE TOWARD SERVO ASM. AS FAR AS IT WILL GO

3. IF ONE OF THE FOUR HOLES IN THE SERVO ASM. TAB LINES UP WITH CABLE PIN, CONNECT PIN TO TAB WITH RETAINER.

4. IF A TAB HOLE DOES NOT LINE UP WITH THE PIN, MOVE THE CABLE AWAY FROM THE SERVO ASM. UNTIL THE NEXT CLOSEST TAB HOLE LINES UP AND CONNECT PIN TO TAB WITH RETAINER.

DO NOT STRETCH CABLE SO AS TO MAKE A PARTICULAR TAB HOLE CONNECT TO PIN THIS WILL PREVENT ENGINE FROM RETURNING TO IDLE.

Servo and linkage adjustment — 1982–83 Skyhawk with 1.8 liter TBI engine

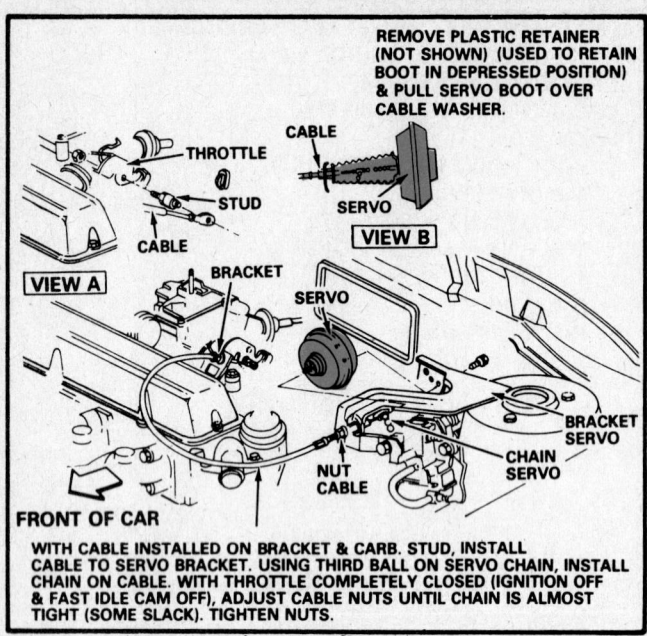

Servo and linkage adjustment—1982–83 Skyhawk with 1.8 liter and 2.0 liter engine

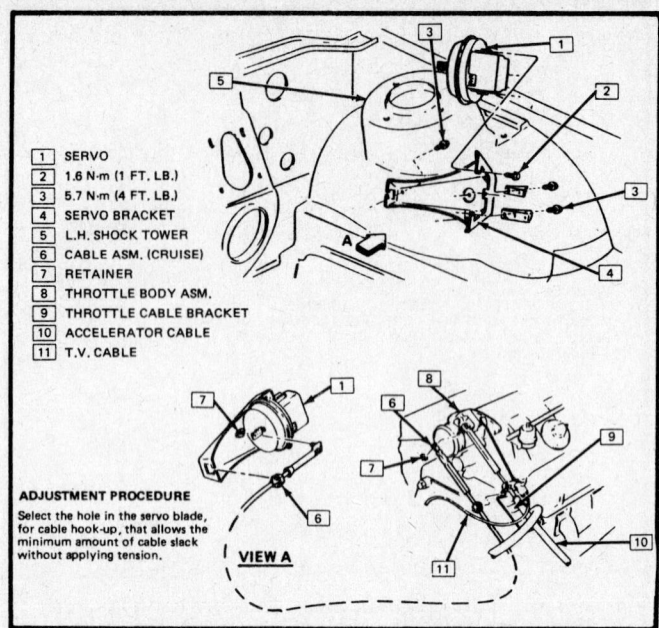

Servo and linkage adjustment—1985 Century with 3.8 liter SFI engine

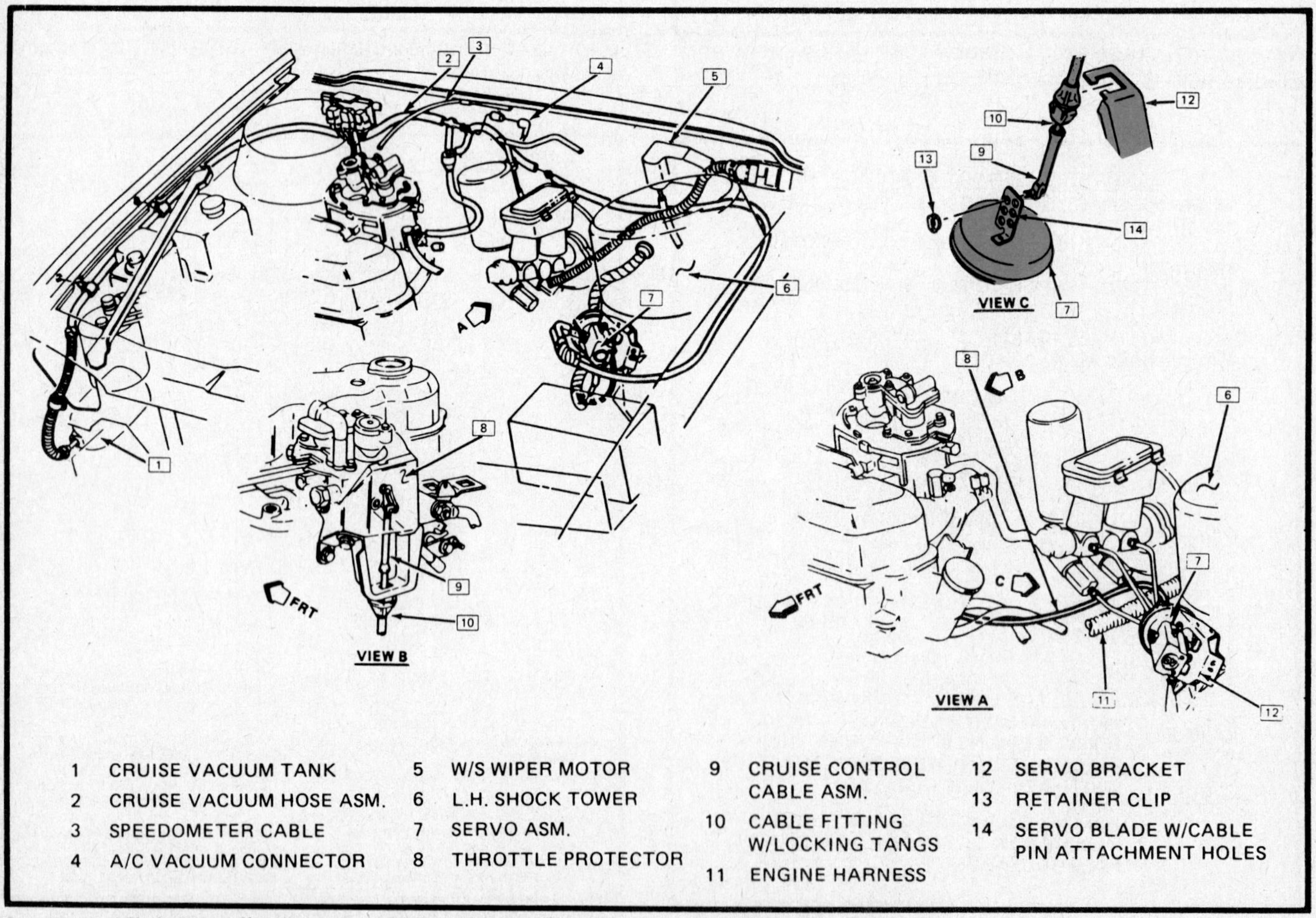

1	CRUISE VACUUM TANK	5	W/S WIPER MOTOR	9	CRUISE CONTROL CABLE ASM.	12	SERVO BRACKET
2	CRUISE VACUUM HOSE ASM.	6	L.H. SHOCK TOWER			13	RETAINER CLIP
3	SPEEDOMETER CABLE	7	SERVO ASM.	10	CABLE FITTING W/LOCKING TANGS	14	SERVO BLADE W/CABLE PIN ATTACHMENT HOLES
4	A/C VACUUM CONNECTOR	8	THROTTLE PROTECTOR	11	ENGINE HARNESS		

Servo and linkage adjustment—1986 and later Century with 2.5 liter TBI engine

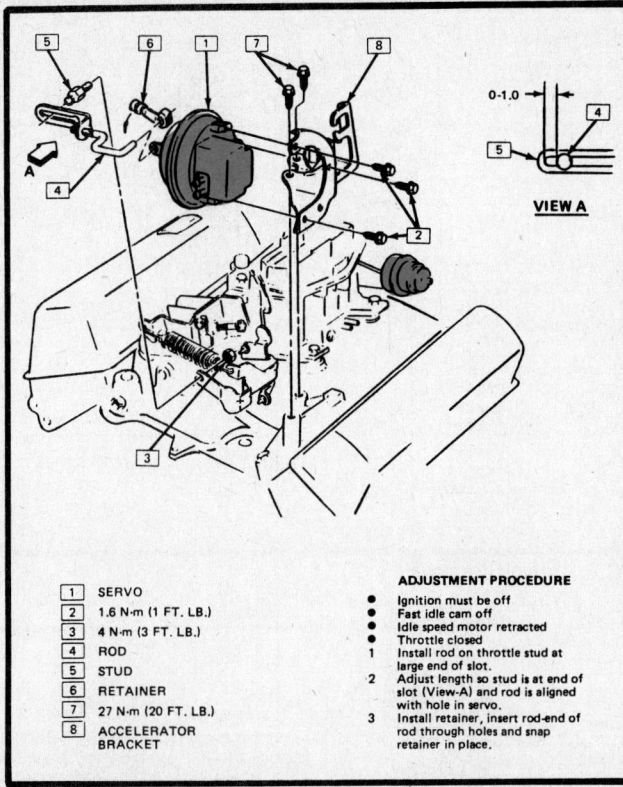

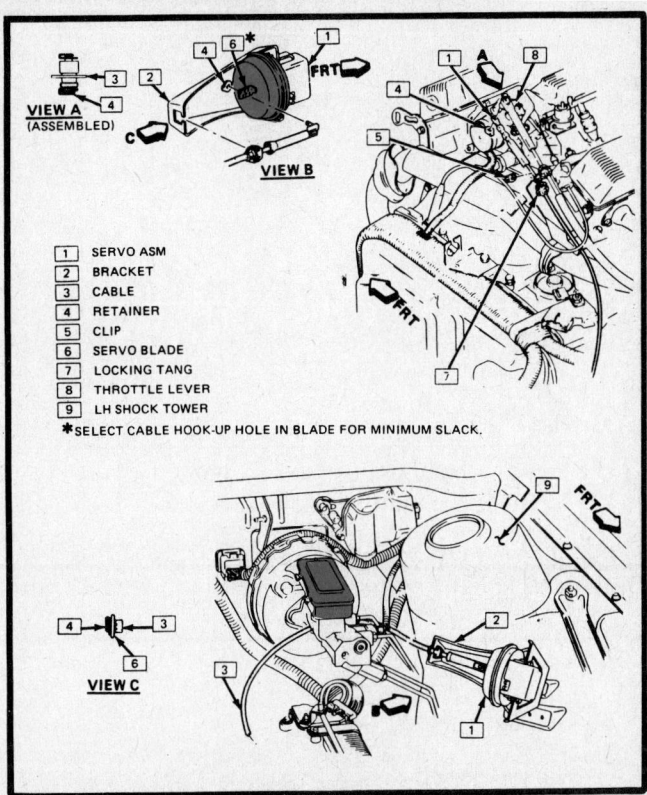

1	SERVO ASM
2	BRACKET
3	CABLE
4	RETAINER
5	CLIP
6	SERVO BLADE
7	LOCKING TANG
8	THROTTLE LEVER
9	LH SHOCK TOWER

✱ SELECT CABLE HOOK-UP HOLE IN BLADE FOR MINIMUM SLACK.

1	SERVO
2	1.6 N·m (1 FT. LB.)
3	4 N·m (3 FT. LB.)
4	ROD
5	STUD
6	RETAINER
7	27 N·m (20 FT. LB.)
8	ACCELERATOR BRACKET

ADJUSTMENT PROCEDURE
- Ignition must be off
- Fast idle cam off
- Idle speed motor retracted
- Throttle closed
1. Install rod on throttle stud at large end of slot.
2. Adjust length so stud is at end of slot (View-A) and rod is aligned with hole in servo.
3. Install retainer, insert rod-end of rod through holes and snap retainer in place.

Servo and linkage adjustment—1985 Century with 3.0 liter engine

Servo and linkage adjustment—1986 and later Century with 3.8 liter SFI engine

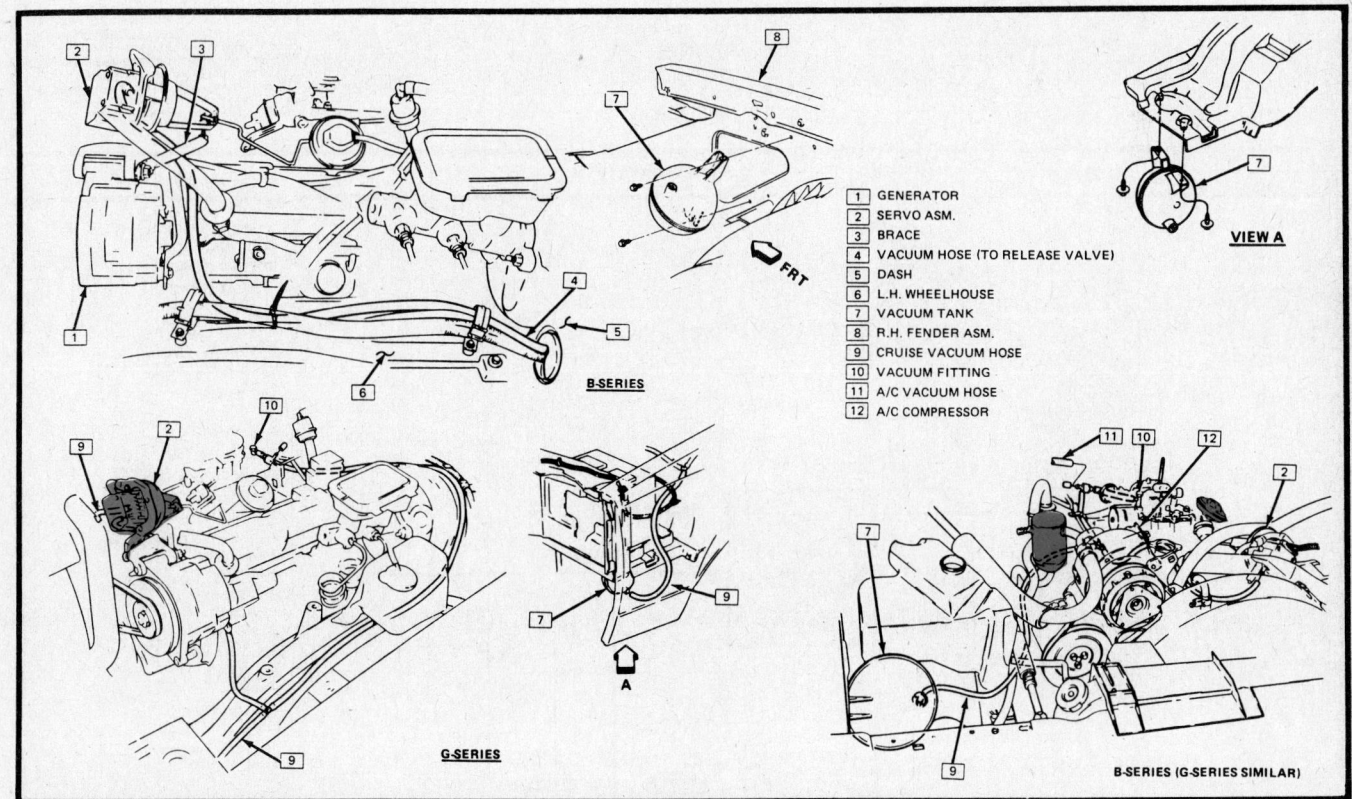

1	GENERATOR
2	SERVO ASM.
3	BRACE
4	VACUUM HOSE (TO RELEASE VALVE)
5	DASH
6	L.H. WHEELHOUSE
7	VACUUM TANK
8	R.H. FENDER ASM.
9	CRUISE VACUUM HOSE
10	VACUUM FITTING
11	A/C VACUUM HOSE
12	A/C COMPRESSOR

Servo and linkage adjustment—1986 and later Regal with 5.0 liter engine

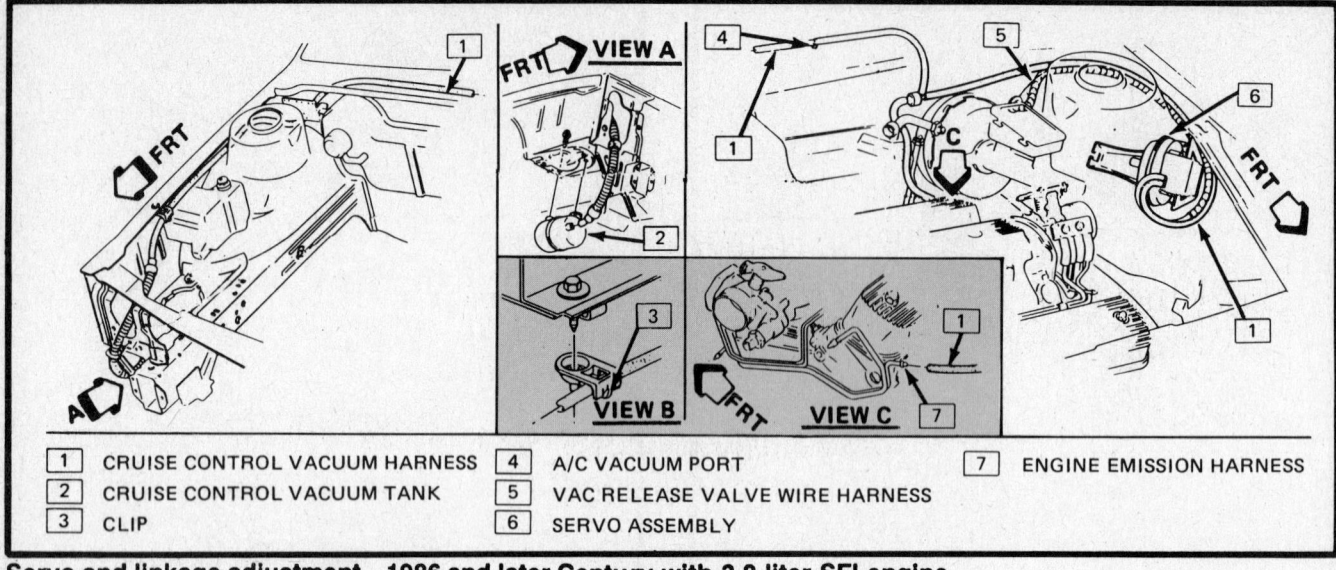

1	CRUISE CONTROL VACUUM HARNESS	4	A/C VACUUM PORT	7	ENGINE EMISSION HARNESS	
2	CRUISE CONTROL VACUUM TANK	5	VAC RELEASE VALVE WIRE HARNESS			
3	CLIP	6	SERVO ASSEMBLY			

Servo and linkage adjustment—1986 and later Century with 3.8 liter SFI engine

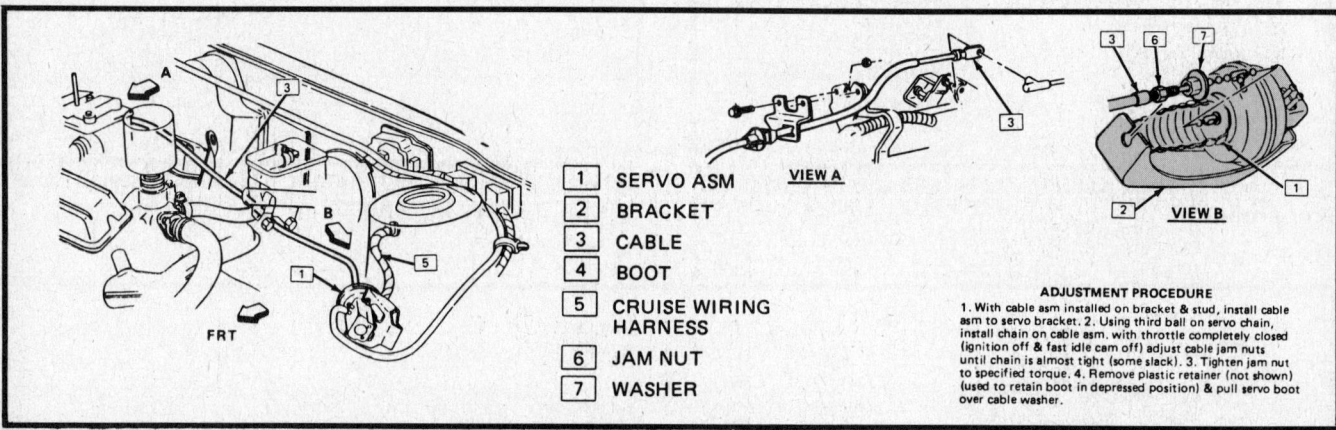

1	SERVO ASM
2	BRACKET
3	CABLE
4	BOOT
5	CRUISE WIRING HARNESS
6	JAM NUT
7	WASHER

ADJUSTMENT PROCEDURE

1. With cable asm installed on bracket & stud, install cable asm to servo bracket. 2. Using third ball on servo chain, install chain on cable asm. with throttle completely closed (ignition off & fast idle cam off) adjust cable jam nuts until chain is almost tight (some slack). 3. Tighten jam nut to specified torque. 4. Remove plastic retainer (not shown) (used to retain boot in depressed position) & pull servo boot over cable washer.

Servo and linkage adjustment—1985 Century with 2.8 liter engine

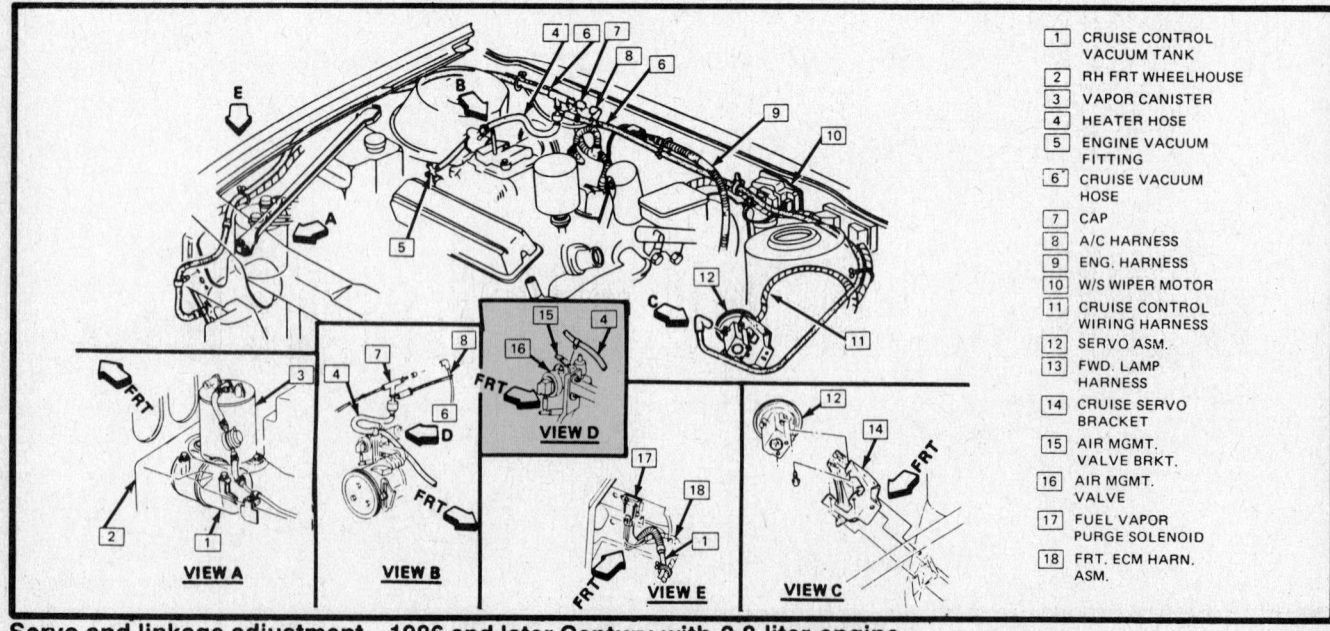

1	CRUISE CONTROL VACUUM TANK
2	RH FRT WHEELHOUSE
3	VAPOR CANISTER
4	HEATER HOSE
5	ENGINE VACUUM FITTING
6	CRUISE VACUUM HOSE
7	CAP
8	A/C HARNESS
9	ENG. HARNESS
10	W/S WIPER MOTOR
11	CRUISE CONTROL WIRING HARNESS
12	SERVO ASM.
13	FWD. LAMP HARNESS
14	CRUISE SERVO BRACKET
15	AIR MGMT. VALVE BRKT.
16	AIR MGMT. VALVE
17	FUEL VAPOR PURGE SOLENOID
18	FRT. ECM HARN. ASM.

Servo and linkage adjustment—1986 and later Century with 2.8 liter engine

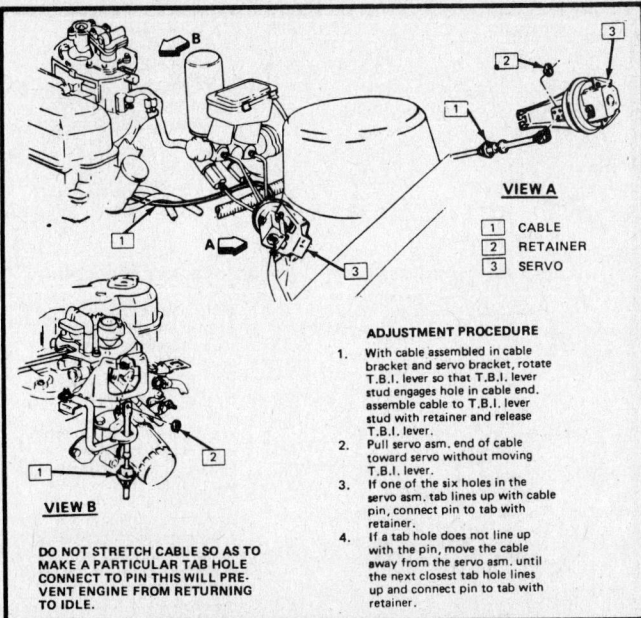

ADJUSTMENT PROCEDURE

1. With cable assembled in cable bracket and servo bracket, rotate T.B.I. lever so that T.B.I. lever stud engages hole in cable end. assemble cable to T.B.I. lever stud with retainer and release T.B.I. lever.
2. Pull servo asm. end of cable toward servo without moving T.B.I. lever.
3. If one of the six holes in the servo asm. tab lines up with cable pin, connect pin to tab with retainer.
4. If a tab hole does not line up with the pin, move the cable away from the servo asm. until the next closest tab hole lines up and connect pin to tab with retainer.

DO NOT STRETCH CABLE SO AS TO MAKE A PARTICULAR TAB HOLE CONNECT TO PIN THIS WILL PREVENT ENGINE FROM RETURNING TO IDLE.

1	CABLE
2	RETAINER
3	SERVO

Servo and linkage adjustment—1984–85 Skylark and Century with 2.5 liter TBI engine

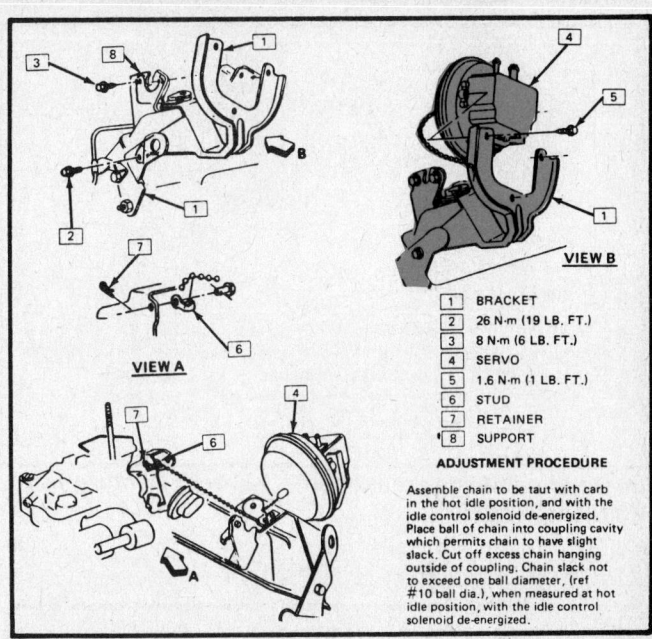

1	BRACKET
2	26 N·m (19 LB. FT.)
3	8 N·m (6 LB. FT.)
4	SERVO
5	1.6 N·m (1 LB. FT.)
6	STUD
7	RETAINER
8	SUPPORT

ADJUSTMENT PROCEDURE

Assemble chain to be taut with carb in the hot idle position, and with the idle control solenoid de-energized. Place ball of chain into coupling cavity which permits chain to have slight slack. Cut off excess chain hanging outside of coupling. Chain slack not to exceed one ball diameter, (ref #10 ball dia.), when measured at hot idle position, with the idle control solenoid de-energized.

Servo and linkage adjustment—1984–85 Skylark with 2.8 liter engine

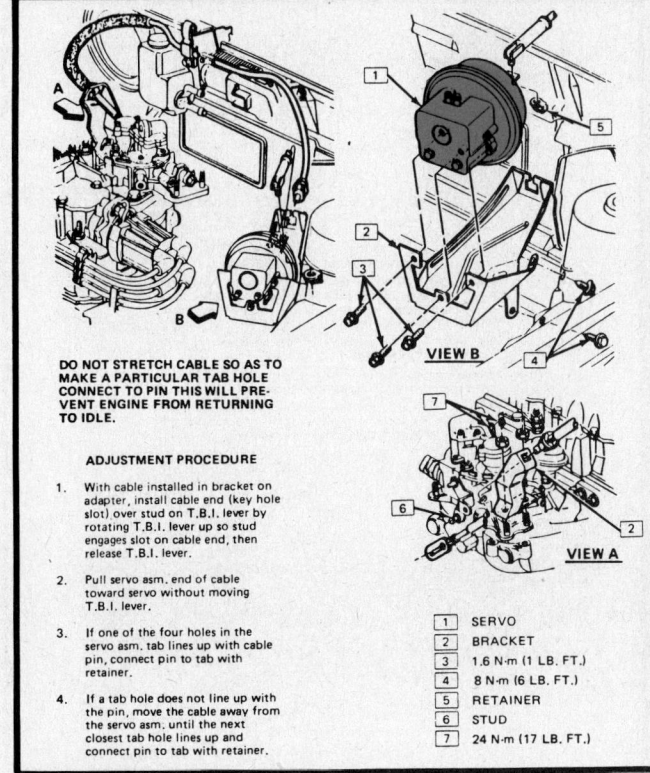

DO NOT STRETCH CABLE SO AS TO MAKE A PARTICULAR TAB HOLE CONNECT TO PIN THIS WILL PREVENT ENGINE FROM RETURNING TO IDLE.

ADJUSTMENT PROCEDURE

1. With cable installed in bracket on adapter, install cable end (key hole slot) over stud on T.B.I. lever by rotating T.B.I. lever up so stud engages slot on cable end, then release T.B.I. lever.
2. Pull servo asm. end of cable toward servo without moving T.B.I. lever.
3. If one of the four holes in the servo asm. tab lines up with cable pin, connect pin to tab with retainer.
4. If a tab hole does not line up with the pin, move the cable away from the servo asm. until the next closest tab hole lines up and connect pin to tab with retainer.

1	SERVO
2	BRACKET
3	1.6 N·m (1 LB. FT.)
4	8 N·m (6 LB. FT.)
5	RETAINER
6	STUD
7	24 N·m (17 LB. FT.)

Servo and linkage adjustment—1984–85 Skylark with 1.8 liter engine

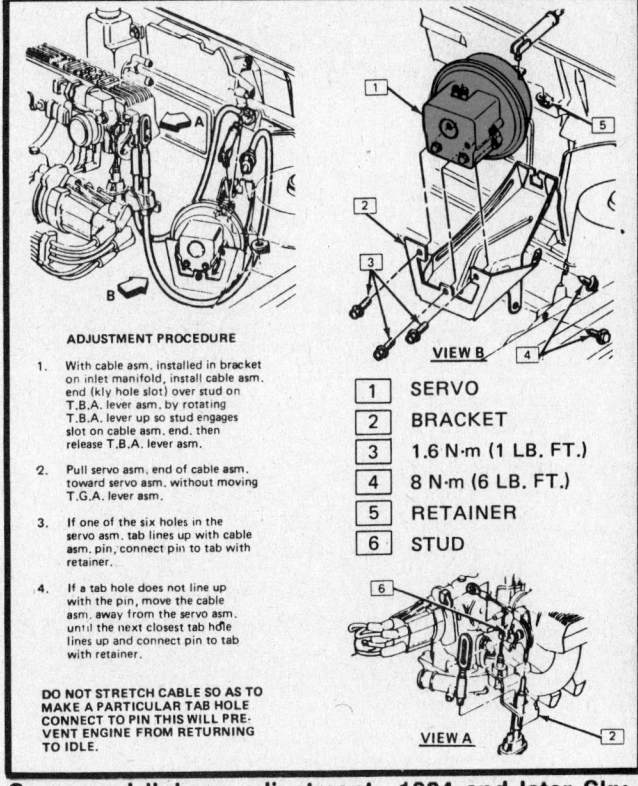

ADJUSTMENT PROCEDURE

1. With cable asm. installed in bracket on inlet manifold, install cable asm. end (kly hole slot) over stud on T.B.A. lever asm., by rotating T.B.A. lever up so stud engages slot on cable asm. end, then release T.B.A. lever asm.
2. Pull servo asm. end of cable asm. toward servo asm. without moving T.G.A. lever asm.
3. If one of the six holes in the servo asm. tab lines up with cable asm. pin, connect pin to tab with retainer.
4. If a tab hole does not line up with the pin, move the cable asm. away from the servo asm. until the next closest tab hole lines up and connect pin to tab with retainer.

DO NOT STRETCH CABLE SO AS TO MAKE A PARTICULAR TAB HOLE CONNECT TO PIN THIS WILL PREVENT ENGINE FROM RETURNING TO IDLE.

1	SERVO
2	BRACKET
3	1.6 N·m (1 LB. FT.)
4	8 N·m (6 LB. FT.)
5	RETAINER
6	STUD

Servo and linkage adjustment—1984 and later Skylark with 1.8 liter Turbo/MFI engine

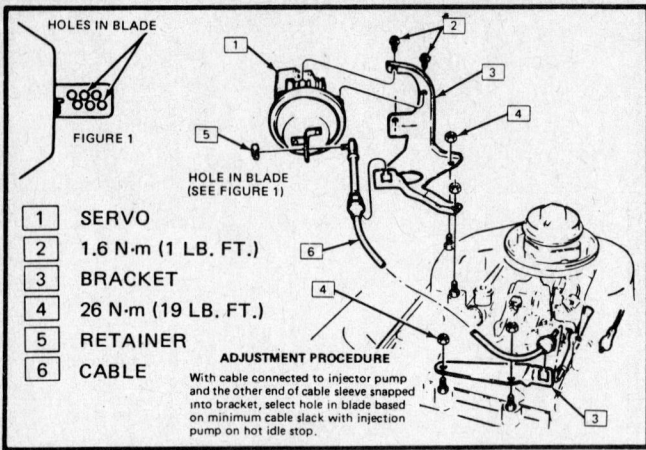

1	SERVO
2	1.6 N·m (1 LB. FT.)
3	BRACKET
4	26 N·m (19 LB. FT.)
5	RETAINER
6	CABLE

ADJUSTMENT PROCEDURE

With cable connected to injector pump and the other end of cable sleeve snapped into bracket, select hole in blade based on minimum cable slack with injection pump on hot idle stop.

Servo and linkage adjustment—1984–85 Century with V6 diesel engine

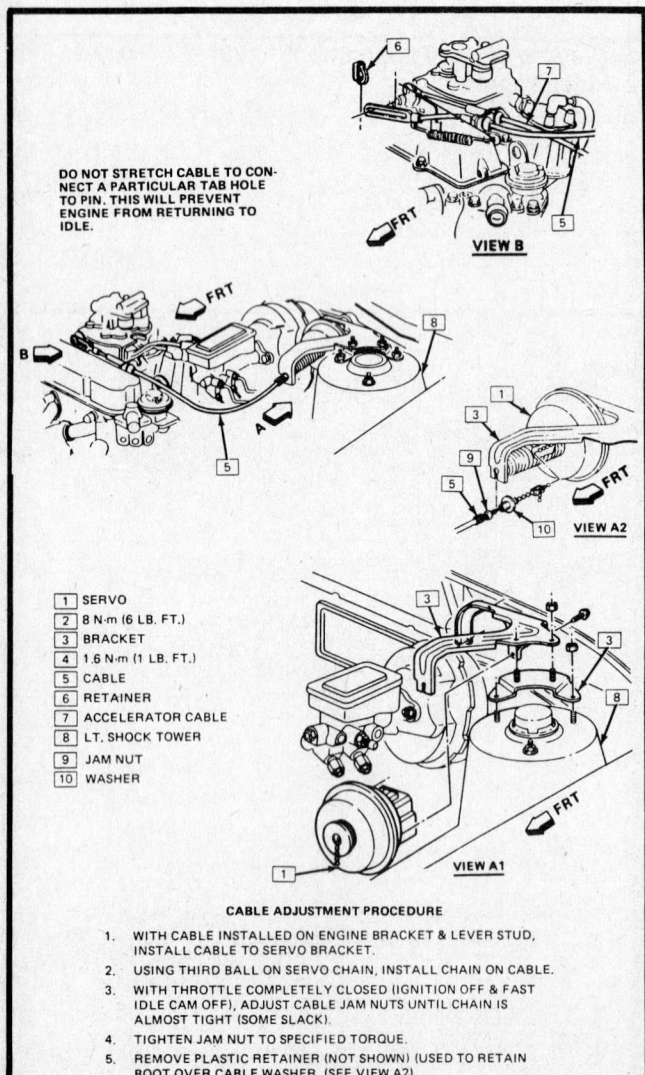

DO NOT STRETCH CABLE TO CONNECT A PARTICULAR TAB HOLE TO PIN. THIS WILL PREVENT ENGINE FROM RETURNING TO IDLE.

1	SERVO
2	8 N·m (6 LB. FT.)
3	BRACKET
4	1.6 N·m (1 LB. FT.)
5	CABLE
6	RETAINER
7	ACCELERATOR CABLE
8	LT. SHOCK TOWER
9	JAM NUT
10	WASHER

CABLE ADJUSTMENT PROCEDURE

1. WITH CABLE INSTALLED ON ENGINE BRACKET & LEVER STUD, INSTALL CABLE TO SERVO BRACKET.
2. USING THIRD BALL ON SERVO CHAIN, INSTALL CHAIN ON CABLE.
3. WITH THROTTLE COMPLETELY CLOSED (IGNITION OFF & FAST IDLE CAM OFF), ADJUST CABLE JAM NUTS UNTIL CHAIN IS ALMOST TIGHT (SOME SLACK).
4. TIGHTEN JAM NUT TO SPECIFIED TORQUE.
5. REMOVE PLASTIC RETAINER (NOT SHOWN) (USED TO RETAIN BOOT OVER CABLE WASHER, (SEE VIEW A2).

Servo and linkage adjustment—1986 and later Skyhawk with 2.0 liter TBI engine

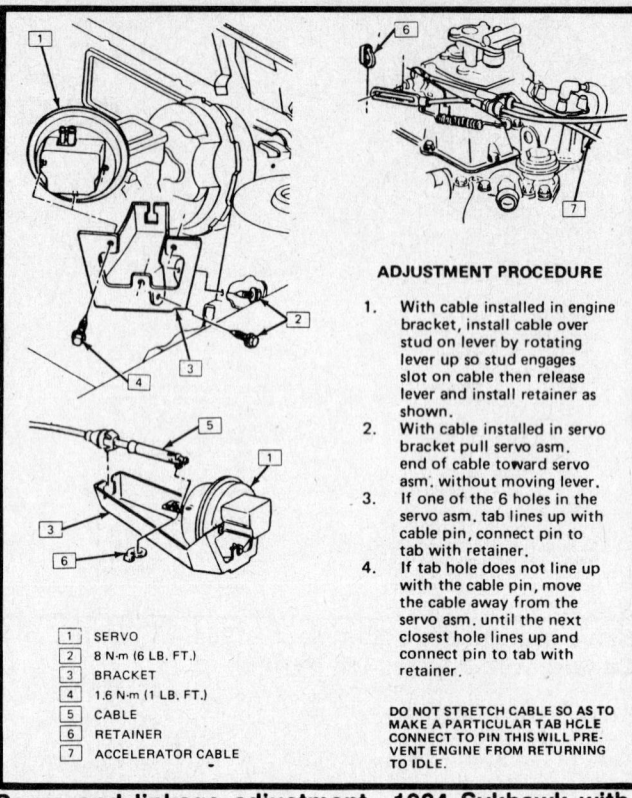

ADJUSTMENT PROCEDURE

1. With cable installed in engine bracket, install cable over stud on lever by rotating lever up so stud engages slot on cable then release lever and install retainer as shown.
2. With cable installed in servo bracket pull servo asm. end of cable toward servo asm. without moving lever.
3. If one of the 6 holes in the servo asm. tab lines up with cable pin, connect pin to tab with retainer.
4. If tab hole does not line up with the cable pin, move the cable away from the servo asm. until the next closest hole lines up and connect pin to tab with retainer.

DO NOT STRETCH CABLE SO AS TO MAKE A PARTICULAR TAB HOLE CONNECT TO PIN THIS WILL PREVENT ENGINE FROM RETURNING TO IDLE.

1	SERVO
2	8 N·m (6 LB. FT.)
3	BRACKET
4	1.6 N·m (1 LB. FT.)
5	CABLE
6	RETAINER
7	ACCELERATOR CABLE

Servo and linkage adjustment—1984 Sykhawk with 2.0 liter TBI engine

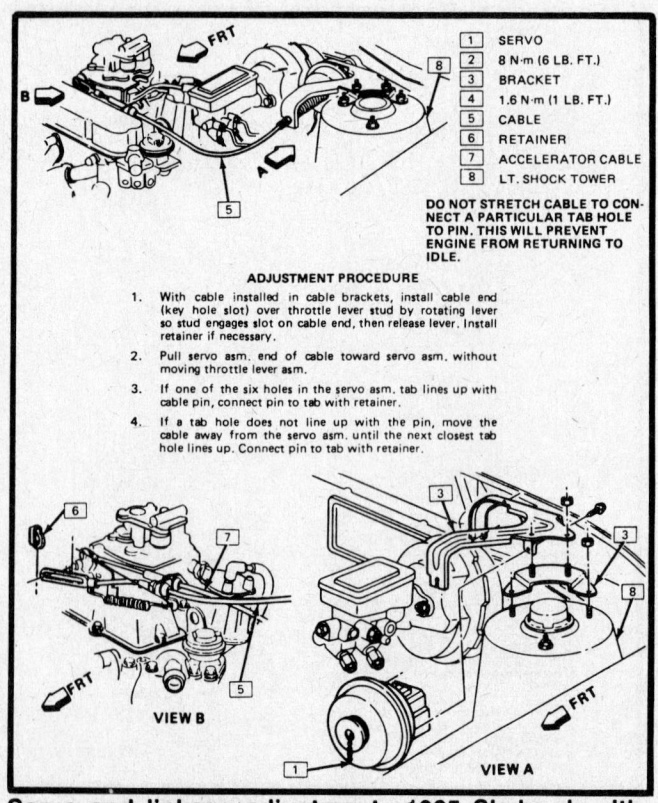

1	SERVO
2	8 N·m (6 LB. FT.)
3	BRACKET
4	1.6 N·m (1 LB. FT.)
5	CABLE
6	RETAINER
7	ACCELERATOR CABLE
8	LT. SHOCK TOWER

DO NOT STRETCH CABLE TO CONNECT A PARTICULAR TAB HOLE TO PIN. THIS WILL PREVENT ENGINE FROM RETURNING TO IDLE.

ADJUSTMENT PROCEDURE

1. With cable installed in cable brackets, install cable end (key hole slot) over throttle lever stud by rotating lever so stud engages slot on cable end, then release lever. Install retainer if necessary.
2. Pull servo asm. end of cable toward servo asm. without moving throttle lever asm.
3. If one of the six holes in the servo asm. tab lines up with cable pin, connect pin to tab with retainer.
4. If a tab hole does not line up with the pin, move the cable away from the servo asm. until the next closest tab hole lines up. Connect pin to tab with retainer.

Servo and linkage adjustment—1985 Skyhawk with 2.0 liter TBI engine

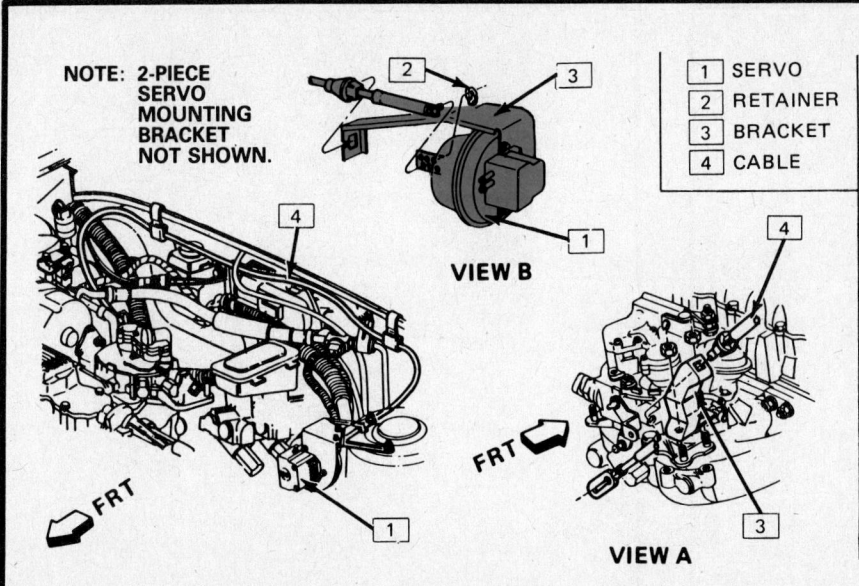

ADJUSTMENT PROCEDURE

1	SERVO
2	RETAINER
3	BRACKET
4	CABLE

NOTE: 2-PIECE SERVO MOUNTING BRACKET NOT SHOWN.

VIEW B

VIEW A

FRT

1. With cable installed in cable brackets, install cable end (key hole slot) over throttle lever stud by rotating lever so stud engages slot on cable end, then release lever. Install retainer if necessary.
2. Pull servo asm. end of cable toward servo asm. without moving throttle lever asm.
3. If one of the six holes in the servo asm. tab lines up with cable pin, connect pin to tab with retainer.
4. If a tab hole does not line up with the pin, move the cable away from the servo asm. until the next closest tab hole lines up. Connect pin to tab with retainer.

CAUTION Do not stretch cable to connect a particular tab hole to pin. This will prevent engine from returning to idle.

Servo and linkage adjustment—1986 and later Skylark with 1.8 liter TBI engine

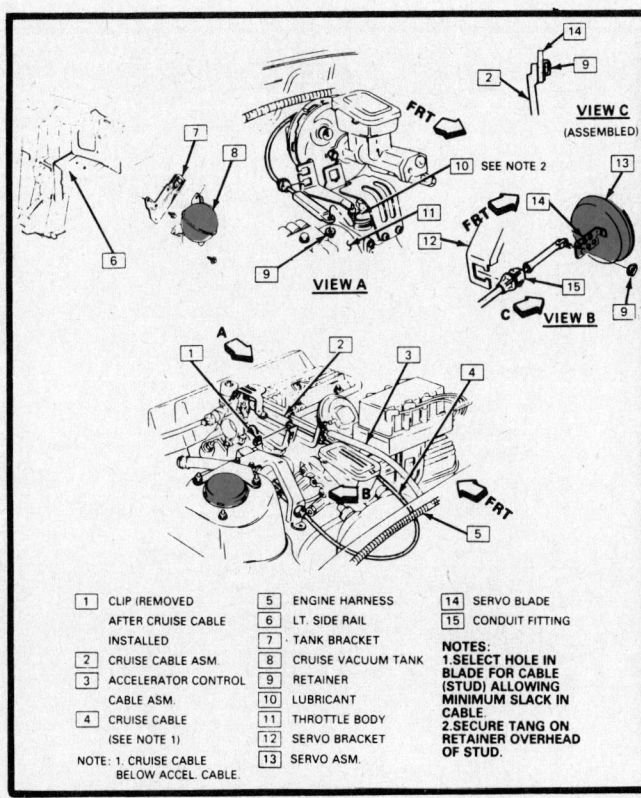

VIEW C (ASSEMBLED)

SEE NOTE 2

VIEW A

VIEW B

FRT

1	CLIP (REMOVED AFTER CRUISE CABLE INSTALLED	5	ENGINE HARNESS	14	SERVO BLADE
2	CRUISE CABLE ASM.	6	LT. SIDE RAIL	15	CONDUIT FITTING
3	ACCELERATOR CONTROL CABLE ASM.	7	TANK BRACKET		
4	CRUISE CABLE (SEE NOTE 1)	8	CRUISE VACUUM TANK		
		9	RETAINER		
		10	LUBRICANT		
		11	THROTTLE BODY		
		12	SERVO BRACKET		
		13	SERVO ASM.		

NOTE: 1. CRUISE CABLE BELOW ACCEL. CABLE.

NOTES: 1.SELECT HOLE IN BLADE FOR CABLE (STUD) ALLOWING MINIMUM SLACK IN CABLE. 2.SECURE TANG ON RETAINER OVERHEAD OF STUD.

Servo and linkage adjustment—1985 and later Somerset and 1986 and later Skylark with 3.0 liter MFI engine

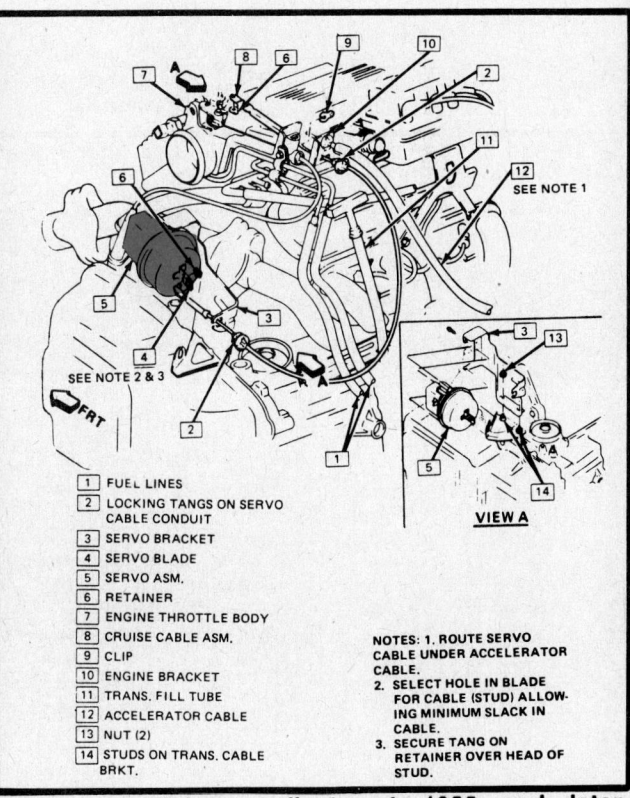

SEE NOTE 1

SEE NOTE 2 & 3

FRT

VIEW A

1	FUEL LINES
2	LOCKING TANGS ON SERVO CABLE CONDUIT
3	SERVO BRACKET
4	SERVO BLADE
5	SERVO ASM.
6	RETAINER
7	ENGINE THROTTLE BODY
8	CRUISE CABLE ASM.
9	CLIP
10	ENGINE BRACKET
11	TRANS. FILL TUBE
12	ACCELERATOR CABLE
13	NUT (2)
14	STUDS ON TRANS. CABLE BRKT.

NOTES: 1. ROUTE SERVO CABLE UNDER ACCELERATOR CABLE.
2. SELECT HOLE IN BLADE FOR CABLE (STUD) ALLOWING MINIMUM SLACK IN CABLE.
3. SECURE TANG ON RETAINER OVER HEAD OF STUD.

Servo and linkage adjustment—1986 and later LeSabre with 3.8 liter SFI and 3.0 liter MFI engine

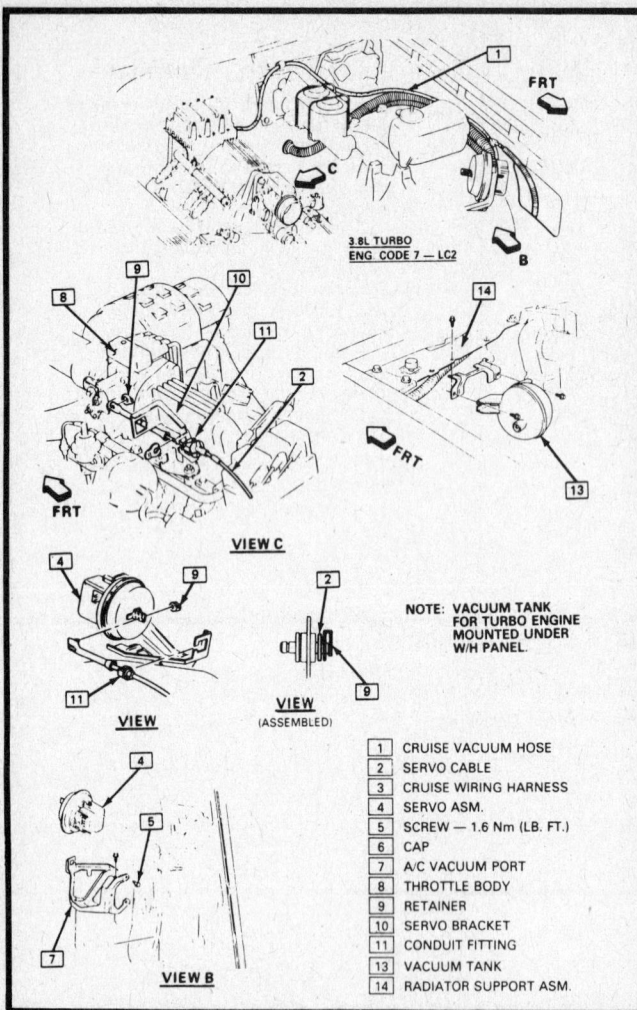

NOTE: VACUUM TANK FOR TURBO ENGINE MOUNTED UNDER W/H PANEL.

1	CRUISE VACUUM HOSE
2	SERVO CABLE
3	CRUISE WIRING HARNESS
4	SERVO ASM.
5	SCREW — 1.6 Nm (LB. FT.)
6	CAP
7	A/C VACUUM PORT
8	THROTTLE BODY
9	RETAINER
10	SERVO BRACKET
11	CONDUIT FITTING
13	VACUUM TANK
14	RADIATOR SUPPORT ASM.

3.8L TURBO
ENG. CODE 7 — LC2

VIEW C

VIEW

VIEW
(ASSEMBLED)

VIEW B

Servo and linkage adjustment—1984 and later Regal with 3.8 liter SFI engine

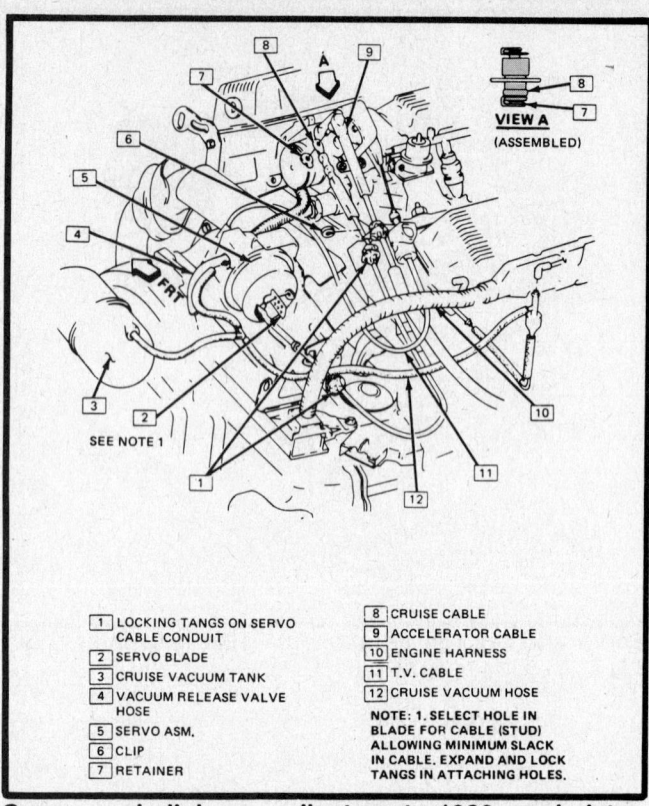

SEE NOTE 1

VIEW A
(ASSEMBLED)

1	LOCKING TANGS ON SERVO CABLE CONDUIT	8	CRUISE CABLE
2	SERVO BLADE	9	ACCELERATOR CABLE
3	CRUISE VACUUM TANK	10	ENGINE HARNESS
4	VACUUM RELEASE VALVE HOSE	11	T.V. CABLE
5	SERVO ASM.	12	CRUISE VACUUM HOSE
6	CLIP		
7	RETAINER		

NOTE: 1. SELECT HOLE IN BLADE FOR CABLE (STUD) ALLOWING MINIMUM SLACK IN CABLE. EXPAND AND LOCK TANGS IN ATTACHING HOLES.

Servo and linkage adjustment—1986 and later LeSabre, Electra and Riviera with 3.8 liter SFI and 3.0 liter MFI engine

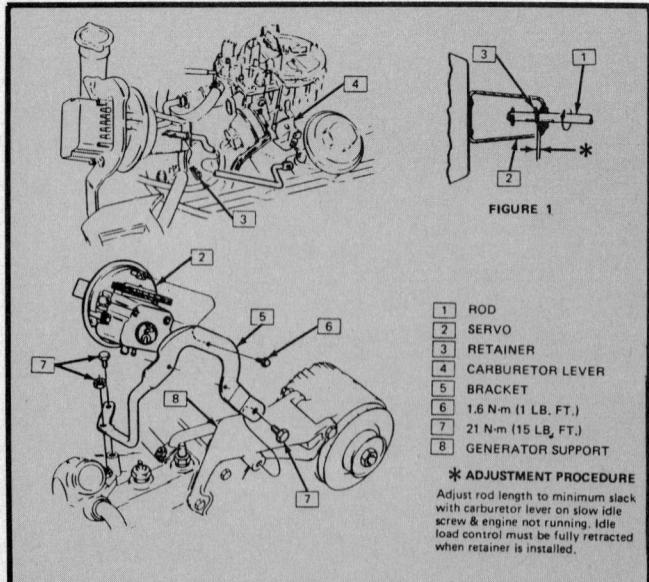

FIGURE 1

1	ROD
2	SERVO
3	RETAINER
4	CARBURETOR LEVER
5	BRACKET
6	1.6 N·m (1 LB. FT.)
7	21 N·m (15 LB. FT.)
8	GENERATOR SUPPORT

✳ ADJUSTMENT PROCEDURE

Adjust rod length to minimum slack with carburetor lever on slow idle screw & engine not running. Idle load control must be fully retracted when retainer is installed.

Servo and linkage adjustment—1984–85 LeSabre and Riviera 1984 Electra with 5.0 liter engine

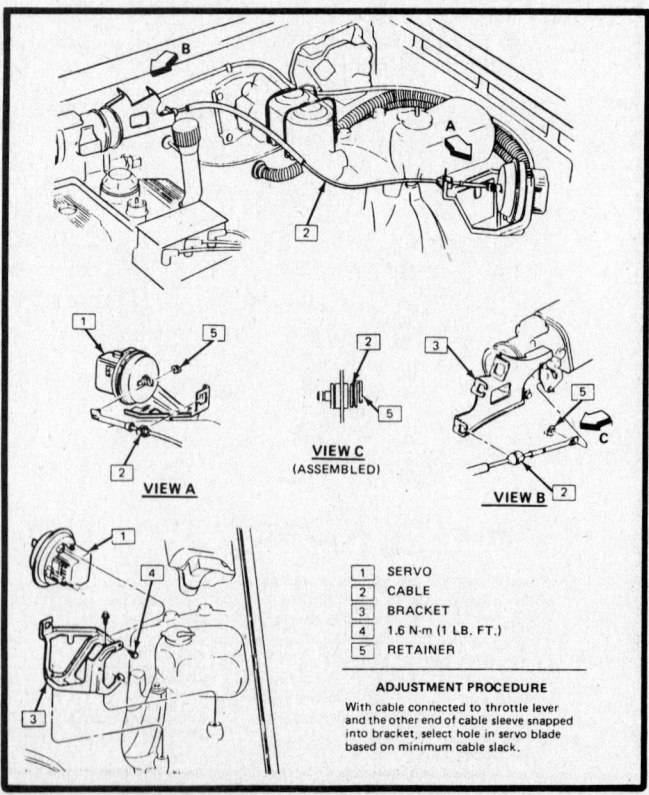

VIEW A

VIEW C
(ASSEMBLED)

VIEW B

1	SERVO
2	CABLE
3	BRACKET
4	1.6 N·m (1 LB. FT.)
5	RETAINER

ADJUSTMENT PROCEDURE

With cable connected to throttle lever and the other end of cable sleeve snapped into bracket, select hole in servo blade based on minimum cable slack.

Servo and linkage adjustment—1984 and later Regal with 3.8 liter Turbo/SFI engine

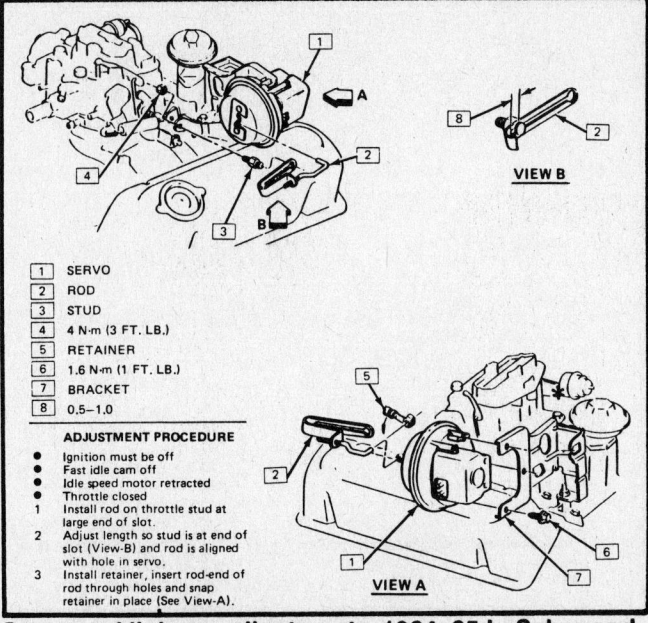

Servo and linkage adjustment—1984–85 LeSabre and 1984 and later Regal with 3.8 liter and 4.1 liter engine

1	SERVO
2	ROD
3	STUD
4	4 N·m (3 FT. LB.)
5	RETAINER
6	1.6 N·m (1 FT. LB.)
7	BRACKET
8	0.5–1.0

ADJUSTMENT PROCEDURE
- Ignition must be off
- Fast idle cam off
- Idle speed motor retracted
- Throttle closed
1 Install rod on throttle stud at large end of slot.
2 Adjust length so stud is at end of slot (View-B) and rod is aligned with hole in servo.
3 Install retainer, insert rod-end of rod through holes and snap retainer in place (See View-A).

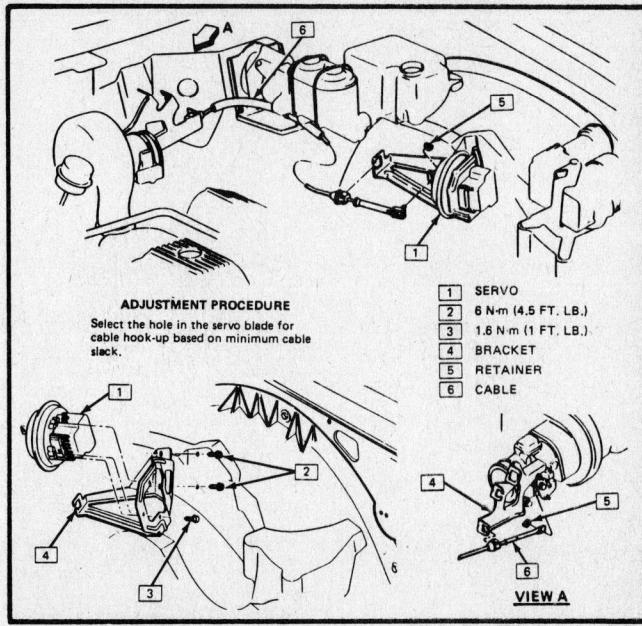

Servo and linkage adjustment—1984–85 Riviera with 3.8 liter Turbo/SFI engine

ADJUSTMENT PROCEDURE
Select the hole in the servo blade for cable hook-up based on minimum cable slack.

1	SERVO
2	6 N·m (4.5 FT. LB.)
3	1.6 N·m (1 FT. LB.)
4	BRACKET
5	RETAINER
6	CABLE

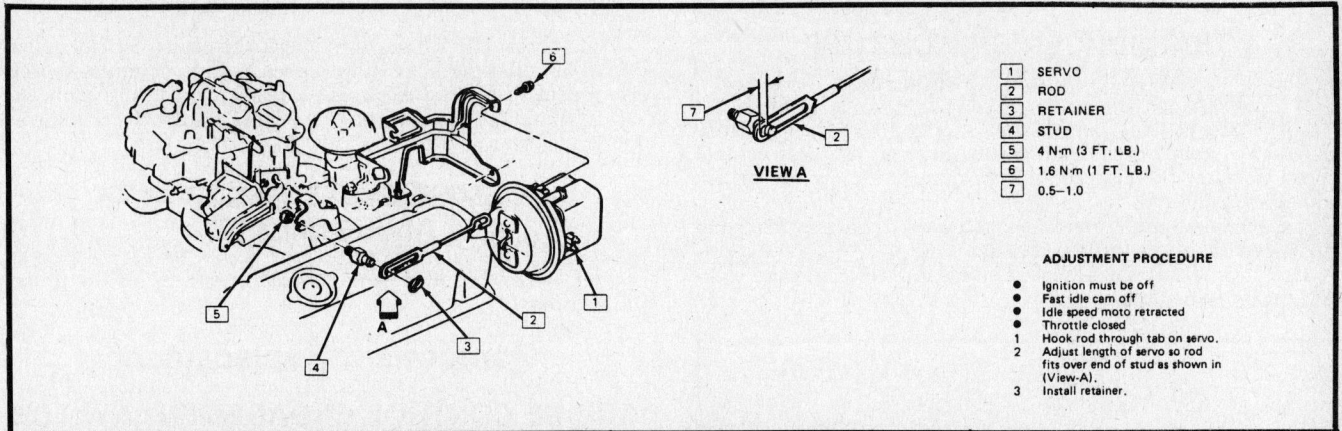

Servo and linkage adjustment—1984–85 Riviera with 4.1 liter engine

1	SERVO
2	ROD
3	RETAINER
4	STUD
5	4 N·m (3 FT. LB.)
6	1.6 N·m (1 FT. LB.)
7	0.5–1.0

ADJUSTMENT PROCEDURE
- Ignition must be off
- Fast idle cam off
- Idle speed moto retracted
- Throttle closed
1 Hook rod through tab on servo.
2 Adjust length of servo so rod fits over end of stud as shown in (View-A).
3 Install retainer.

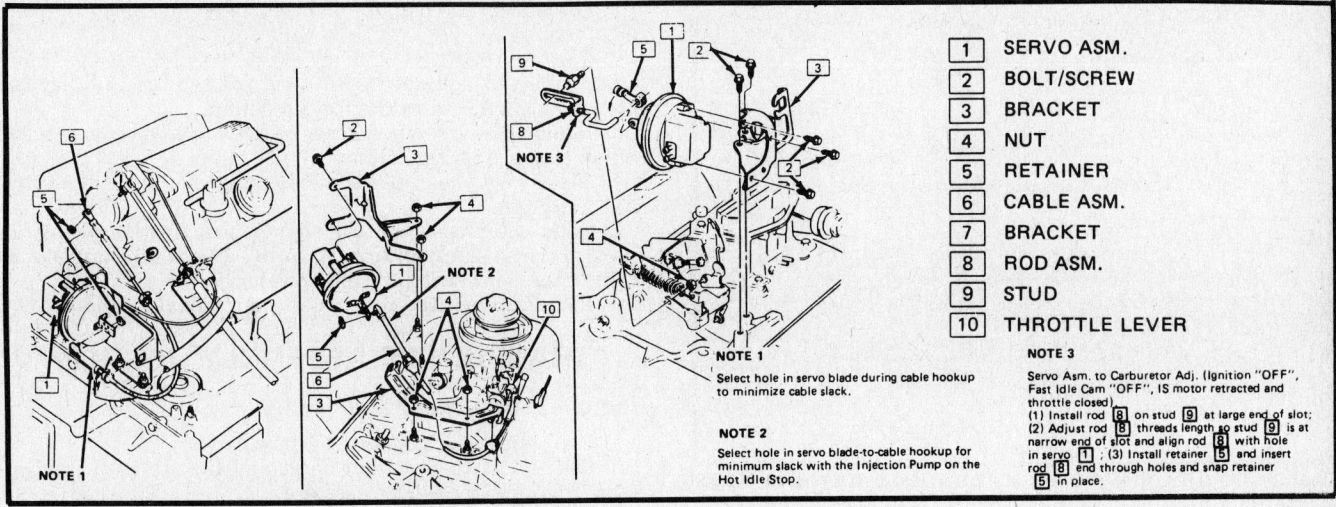

Servo and linkage adjustment—1985 and later Electra

1	SERVO ASM.
2	BOLT/SCREW
3	BRACKET
4	NUT
5	RETAINER
6	CABLE ASM.
7	BRACKET
8	ROD ASM.
9	STUD
10	THROTTLE LEVER

NOTE 1
Select hole in servo blade during cable hookup to minimize cable slack.

NOTE 2
Select hole in servo blade-to-cable hookup for minimum slack with the Injection Pump on the Hot Idle Stop.

NOTE 3
Servo Asm. to Carburetor Adj. (Ignition "OFF", Fast Idle Cam "OFF", IS motor retracted and throttle closed)
(1) Install rod 8 on stud 9 at large end of slot; (2) Adjust rod 8 threads length so stud 9 is at narrow end of slot and align rod 8 with hole in servo 1 ; (3) Install retainer 5 and insert rod 8 end through holes and snap retainer 5 in place.

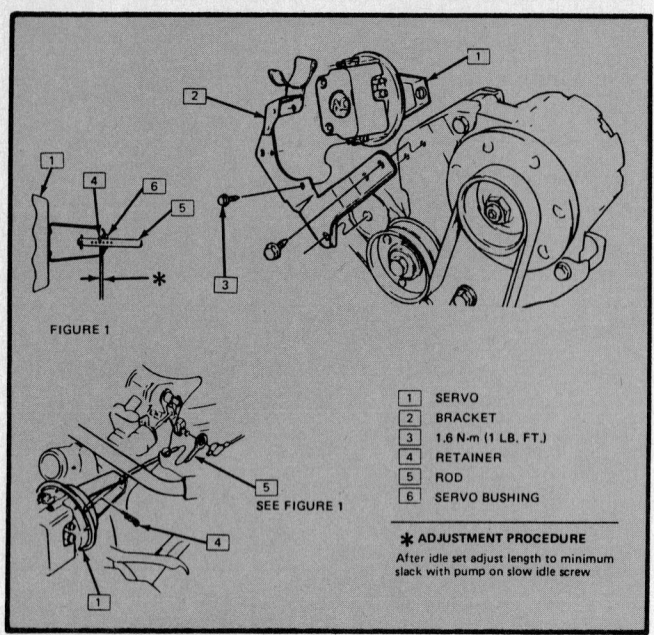

Servo and linkage adjustment—1984–85 Regal with V6 diesel engine

1	SERVO
2	BRACKET
3	1.6 N·m (1 LB. FT.)
4	RETAINER
5	ROD
6	SERVO BUSHING

★ ADJUSTMENT PROCEDURE
After idle set adjust length to minimum slack with pump on slow idle screw

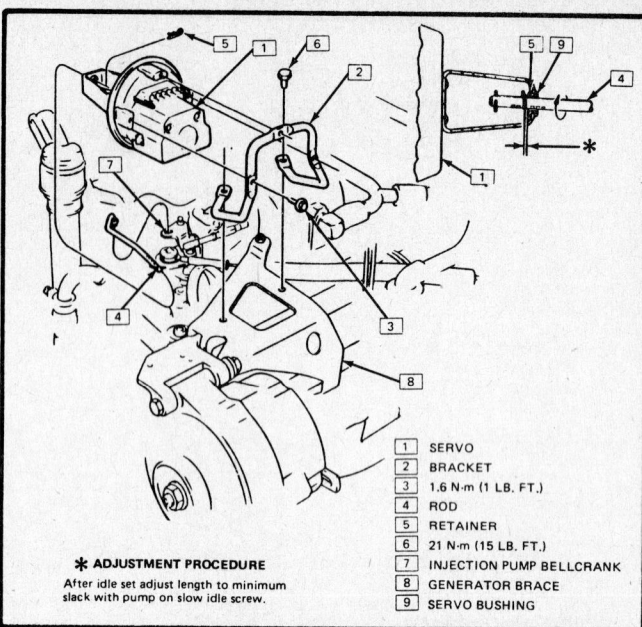

Servo and linkage adjustment—1984–85 Regal, LeSabre, Electra and Riviera with V8 diesel engine

1	SERVO
2	BRACKET
3	1.6 N·m (1 LB. FT.)
4	ROD
5	RETAINER
6	21 N·m (15 LB. FT.)
7	INJECTION PUMP BELLCRANK
8	GENERATOR BRACE
9	SERVO BUSHING

★ ADJUSTMENT PROCEDURE
After idle set adjust length to minimum slack with pump on slow idle screw.

TRANSDUCER ORIFICE TUBE ADJUSTMENT (1982–83)

1. If cruise control speed is consistently above the set cruise control speed screw the orifice tube inward. If cruise control speed is below the set cruise control speed, screw the orifice tube outward.
2. Each one-fourth turn of the orifice tube changes the cruising speed about one mile per hour.
3. After making the adjustment, be sure to secure the locknut to the orifice tube.

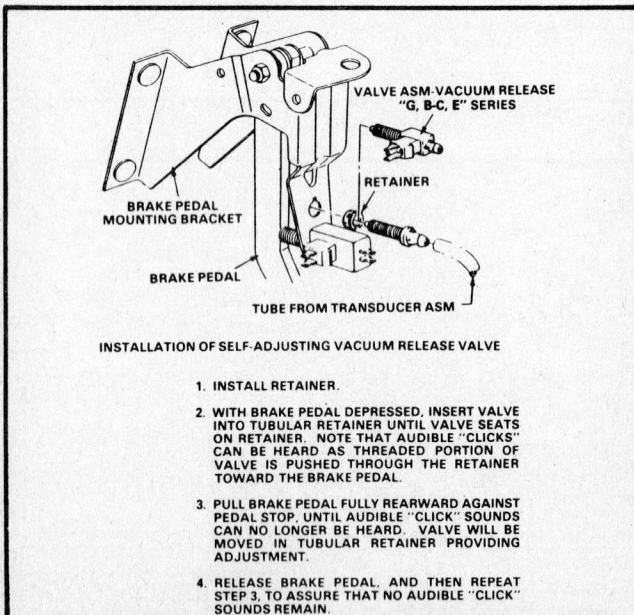

Cruise control release switches—1982 and later Regal, 1982–85 LeSabre and Riviera and 1982–84 Electra

4. Road test the vehicle and check the cruise control operation at 50 miles per hour. If the speed is still not adjusted properly repeat the procedure until the proper results are achieved.
5. If unable to achieve the proper test results the cruise control transducer should be serviced.

RELEASE SWITCH AND VALVE ADJUSTMENTS

For release switch and valve adjustments refer to the proper illustration.

Component Replacement

CRUISE CONTROL ENGAGEMENT SWITCH

Removal and Installation

1. Disconnect the negative battery cable. Remove the steering wheel.
2. Position the turn signal switch in the right turn position. If the vehicle is equipped with a tilt column be sure that the column is positioned in the full up detent.
3. Remove the screw securing the cruise control engagement switch to the steering column.
4. Disconnect the cruise control engagement switch electrical connection.
5. Slide the cruise control engagement switch wiring up through the steering column carefully. Remove the cruise control engagement switch from the vehicle.
6. Installation is the reverse of the removal procedure.

TRANSDUCER ASSEMBLY (1982–83)

Removal and Installation

1. Disconnect the negative battery cable.
2. Disconnect the vacuum hoses and the electrical connections from the transducer assembly.
3. Remove the speedometer cables from the assembly.

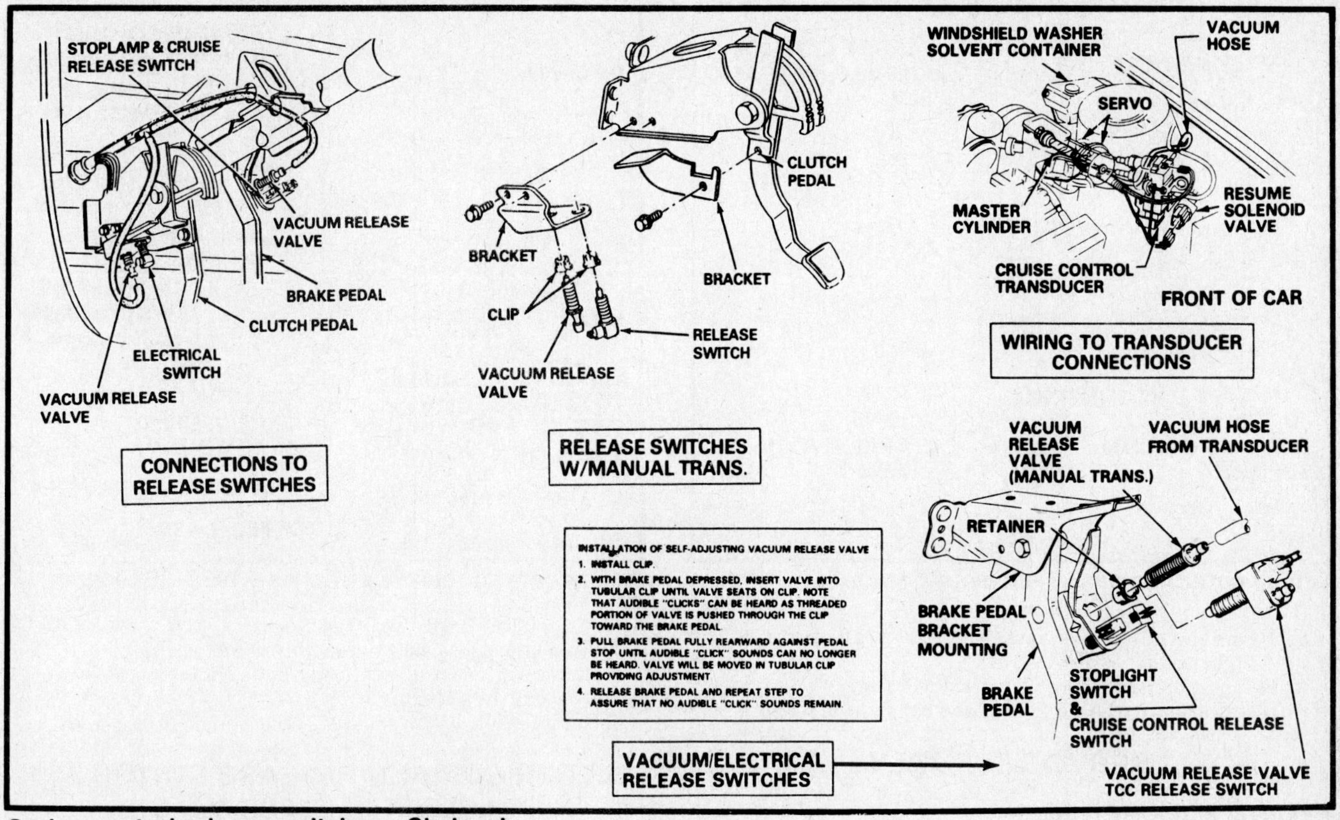

STOPLAMP & CRUISE RELEASE SWITCH

VACUUM RELEASE VALVE

BRAKE PEDAL

CLUTCH PEDAL

ELECTRICAL SWITCH

VACUUM RELEASE VALVE

CONNECTIONS TO RELEASE SWITCHES

CLUTCH PEDAL

BRACKET

CLIP

BRACKET

RELEASE SWITCH

VACUUM RELEASE VALVE

RELEASE SWITCHES W/MANUAL TRANS.

WINDSHIELD WASHER SOLVENT CONTAINER

VACUUM HOSE

SERVO

MASTER CYLINDER

RESUME SOLENOID VALVE

CRUISE CONTROL TRANSDUCER

FRONT OF CAR

WIRING TO TRANSDUCER CONNECTIONS

VACUUM RELEASE VALVE (MANUAL TRANS.)

VACUUM HOSE FROM TRANSDUCER

RETAINER

BRAKE PEDAL BRACKET MOUNTING

BRAKE PEDAL

STOPLIGHT SWITCH & CRUISE CONTROL RELEASE SWITCH

VACUUM RELEASE VALVE TCC RELEASE SWITCH

INSTALLATION OF SELF-ADJUSTING VACUUM RELEASE VALVE
1. INSTALL CLIP.
2. WITH BRAKE PEDAL DEPRESSED, INSERT VALVE INTO TUBULAR CLIP UNTIL VALVE SEATS ON CLIP. NOTE THAT AUDIBLE "CLICKS" CAN BE HEARD AS THREADED PORTION OF VALVE IS PUSHED THROUGH THE CLIP TOWARD THE BRAKE PEDAL.
3. PULL BRAKE PEDAL FULLY REARWARD AGAINST PEDAL STOP UNTIL AUDIBLE "CLICK" SOUNDS CAN NO LONGER BE HEARD. VALVE WILL BE MOVED IN TUBULAR CLIP PROVIDING ADJUSTMENT.
4. RELEASE BRAKE PEDAL AND REPEAT STEP TO ASSURE THAT NO AUDIBLE "CLICK" SOUNDS REMAIN.

VACUUM/ELECTRICAL RELEASE SWITCHES

Cruise control release switches—Skyhawk

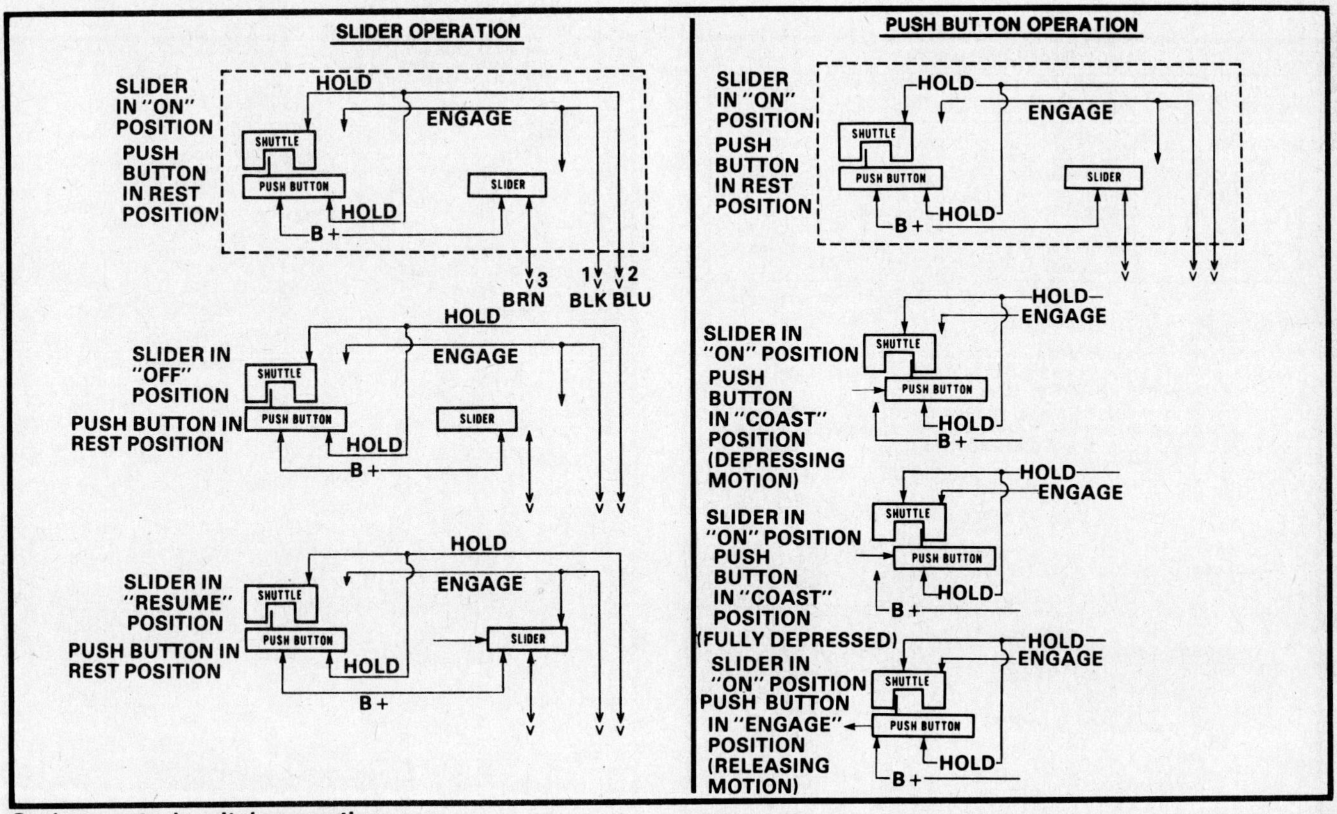

SLIDER OPERATION

SLIDER IN "ON" POSITION PUSH BUTTON IN REST POSITION

HOLD
ENGAGE
SHUTTLE
PUSH BUTTON
SLIDER
HOLD
B +

↓3   ↓1 ↓2
BRN   BLK BLU

SLIDER IN "OFF" POSITION PUSH BUTTON IN REST POSITION

HOLD
ENGAGE
SHUTTLE
PUSH BUTTON
SLIDER
HOLD
B +

SLIDER IN "RESUME" POSITION PUSH BUTTON IN REST POSITION

HOLD
ENGAGE
SHUTTLE
PUSH BUTTON
SLIDER
HOLD
B +

PUSH BUTTON OPERATION

SLIDER IN "ON" POSITION PUSH BUTTON IN REST POSITION

HOLD
ENGAGE
SHUTTLE
PUSH BUTTON
SLIDER
HOLD
B +

SLIDER IN "ON" POSITION PUSH BUTTON IN "COAST" POSITION (DEPRESSING MOTION)

HOLD—ENGAGE
SHUTTLE
PUSH BUTTON
HOLD
B +

SLIDER IN "ON" POSITION PUSH BUTTON IN "COAST" POSITION (FULLY DEPRESSED)

HOLD—ENGAGE
SHUTTLE
PUSH BUTTON
HOLD
B +

SLIDER IN "ON" POSITION PUSH BUTTON IN "ENGAGE" POSITION (RELEASING MOTION)

HOLD—ENGAGE
SHUTTLE
PUSH BUTTON
HOLD
B +

Cruise control switch operation

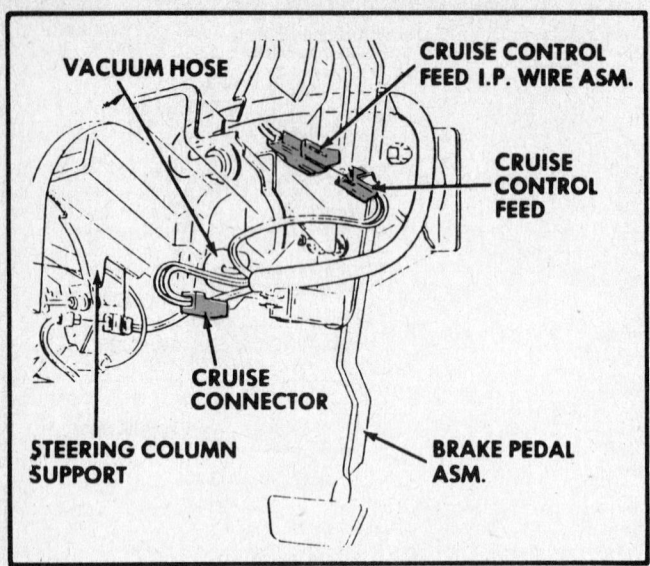

Cruise control release switches—Century

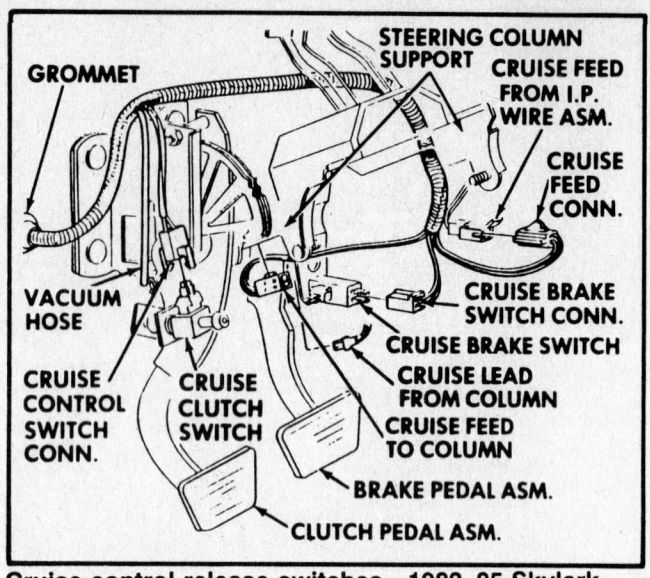

Cruise control release switches—1982–85 Skylark

4. Remove the screws attaching the transducer to the mounting bracket.
5. Remove the transducer from the vehicle.
6. Installation is the reverse of the removal procedure.

SERVO ASSEMBLY

Removal and Installation

1. Disconnect the negative battery cable.
2. Disconnect all electrical and vacuum connections from the servo assembly.

3. Disconnect the servo assembly cable or chain.
4. Remove the servo mounting bolts. Remove the servo assembly from the vehicle.
5. Installation is the reverse of the removal procedure.

ELECTRIC BRAKE RELEASE SWITCH AND VACUUM RELEASE VALVE

Removal and installation

1. Disconnect the negative battery cable.

SWITCH FUNCTION TABLE

TEST ORDER	FUNCTION	SWITCH CONDITION		*TERMINAL CONNECTIONS		
		END BUTTON	**SLIDER	3-2	1-3	2-1
	OFF	RELEASED	OFF	O	O	O
	RESUME	RELEASED	RESUME	C	C	C
	CRUISE	RELEASED	ON	O	O	C
1	COAST	HALF DEPRESSED	ON	O	O	C
2	COAST	FULLY DEPRESSED	ON	C	O	O
3	SET	RELEASING	ON	O	C	C

O = OPEN C = CONTINUITY

* THESE TESTS ARE CONTINUITY TESTS BETWEEN THE TERMINALS SHOWN IN FIGURES IN RESUME CRUISE CONTROL LEVER AND LEVER ELECTRICAL OPERATION.

** THE SLIDER MUST HAVE A DETENT IN THE "ON" AND "OFF" POSITIONS AND MUST RETURN TO THE "ON" DETENT WHEN RELEASED FROM THE RESUME POSITION.

1 – BROWN
2 – BLUE
3 – BLACK

ENGAGE/COAST BUTTON

OFF/ON/RESUME SWITCH

Cruise control lever functional test

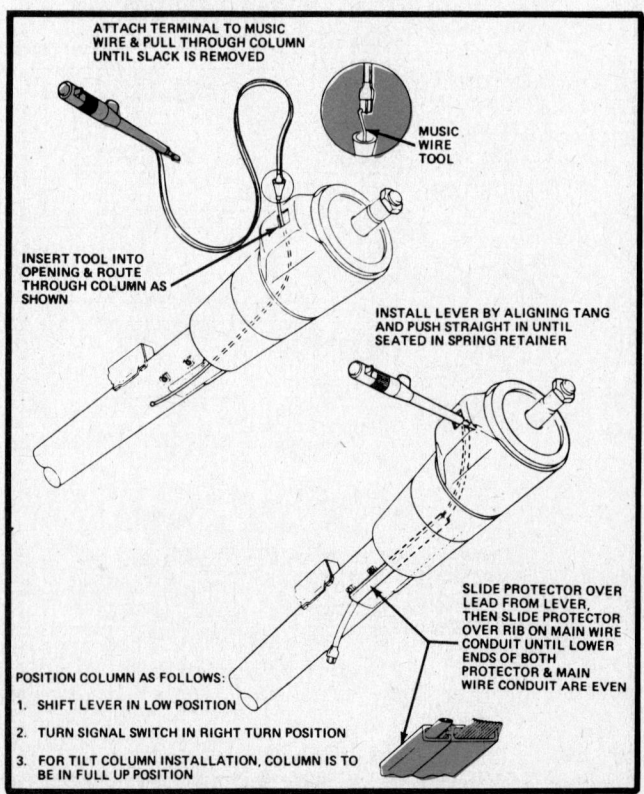

ATTACH TERMINAL TO MUSIC WIRE & PULL THROUGH COLUMN UNTIL SLACK IS REMOVED

MUSIC WIRE TOOL

INSERT TOOL INTO OPENING & ROUTE THROUGH COLUMN AS SHOWN

INSTALL LEVER BY ALIGNING TANG AND PUSH STRAIGHT IN UNTIL SEATED IN SPRING RETAINER

SLIDE PROTECTOR OVER LEAD FROM LEVER, THEN SLIDE PROTECTOR OVER RIB ON MAIN WIRE CONDUIT UNTIL LOWER ENDS OF BOTH PROTECTOR & MAIN WIRE CONDUIT ARE EVEN

POSITION COLUMN AS FOLLOWS:

1. SHIFT LEVER IN LOW POSITION
2. TURN SIGNAL SWITCH IN RIGHT TURN POSITION
3. FOR TILT COLUMN INSTALLATION, COLUMN IS TO BE IN FULL UP POSITION

Cruise control switch installation

2. Remove the switch electrical and vacuum connectors.

3. Remove the switch from its mounting above the brake pedal.

4. Installation is the reverse of the removal procedure.

Adjustment

1. The switch assembly and the valve assembly cannot be adjusted until after the brake booster push rod is assembled to the brake pedal assembly.

2. To adjust the switch depress the brake pedal and insert the switch assembly and valve assembly into their proper retaining clips until fully seated.

3. Pull the pedal back to its fully retracted position. The switch assembly and the valve assembly will move within the retainers of their adjusted position.

4. The switch assembly contacts must open at 3.5mm to 12.5mm of brake pedal travel. Nominal actuation of the brake light switch is 4.5mm.

5. The vacuum release valve assembly must open at 27.0mm to 33.0nn of brake pedal travel.

ELECTRONIC CRUISE CONTROL CONTROL MODULE

Removal and Installation

Note: The electronic cruise control module is normally mounted on or near the accelerator pedal bracket. Location may vary depending upon vehicle model.

1. Disconnect the negative battery cable.

2. Remove the lower steering column filler panel as required. Remove vehicle carpet as required.

3. Disconnect the electrical connectors from the control module.

4. Remove the control module mounting screws. Remove the control module from the vehicle.

6. Installation is the reverse of the removal procedure.

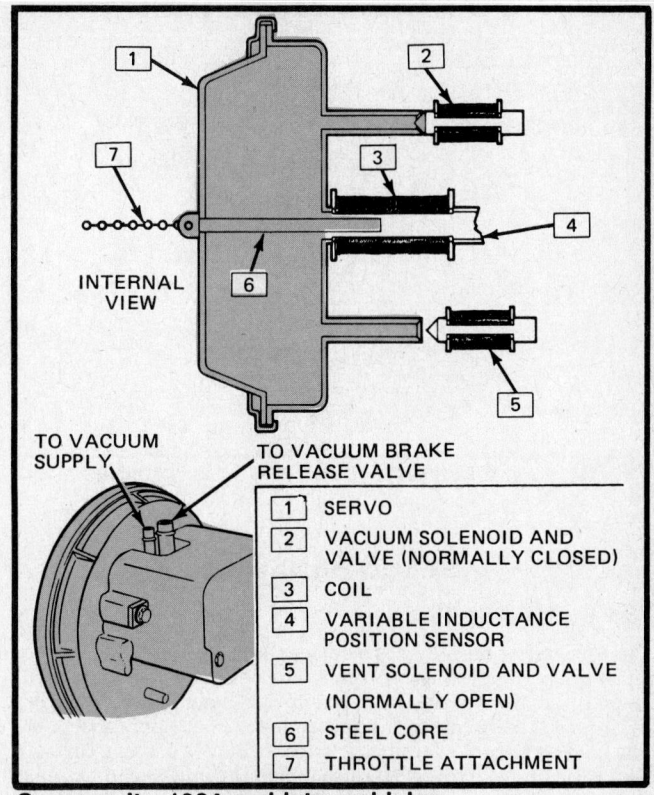

1	SERVO
2	VACUUM SOLENOID AND VALVE (NORMALLY CLOSED)
3	COIL
4	VARIABLE INDUCTANCE POSITION SENSOR
5	VENT SOLENOID AND VALVE (NORMALLY OPEN)
6	STEEL CORE
7	THROTTLE ATTACHMENT

INTERNAL VIEW

TO VACUUM SUPPLY

TO VACUUM BRAKE RELEASE VALVE

Servo unit—1984 and later vehicles

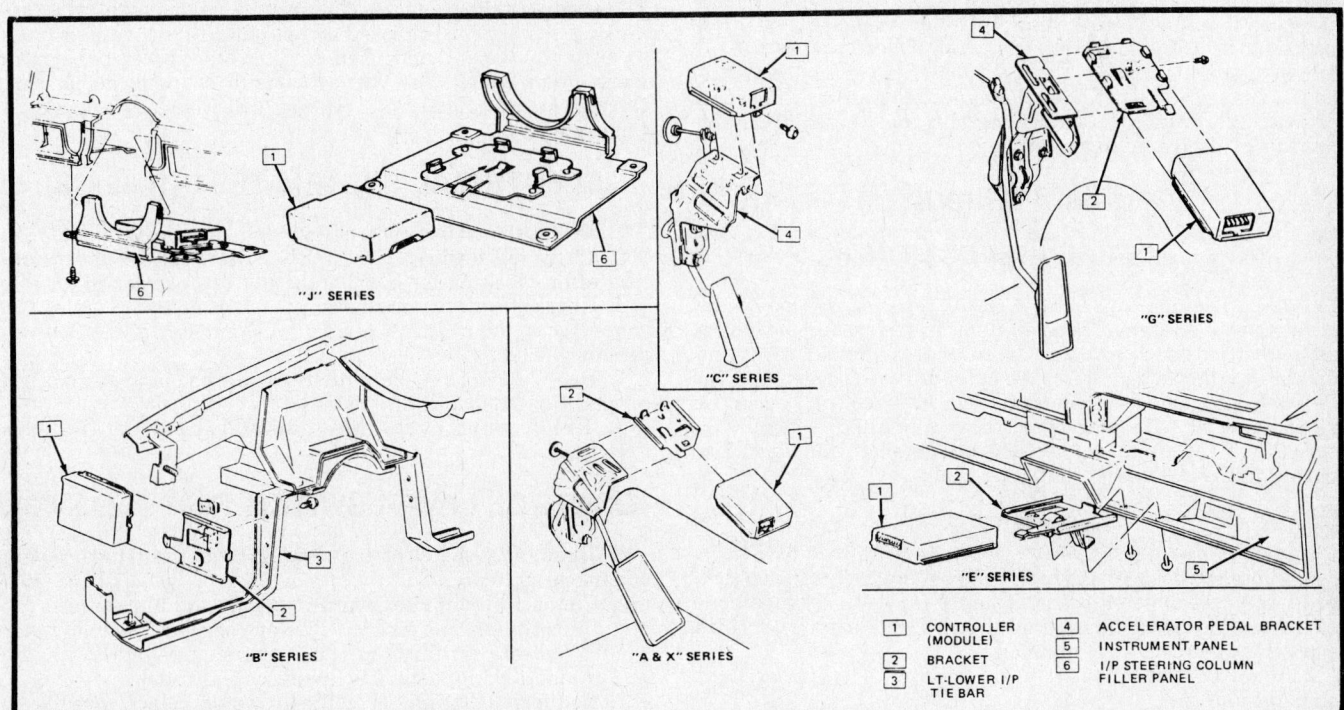

1	CONTROLLER (MODULE)	4	ACCELERATOR PEDAL BRACKET
2	BRACKET	5	INSTRUMENT PANEL
3	LT-LOWER I/P TIE BAR	6	I/P STEERING COLUMN FILLER PANEL

Cruise control electronic control module location—1984 and later

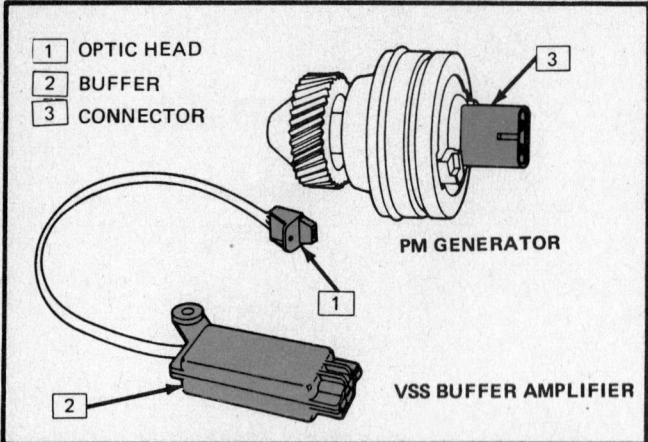

1 OPTIC HEAD
2 BUFFER
3 CONNECTOR

PM GENERATOR

VSS BUFFER AMPLIFIER

Vehicle speed sensors—1984 and later vehicles

SPEED SENSORS

VSS Buffer Amplifier

The VSS buffer amplifier is a device that supplies vehicle speed input to the electronic controller. The optic head portion of the assembly is located in the speedometer head frame. A reflective blade is attached to the speedometer head/cable assembly. The blade spins like a propeller with its blades passing through a light beam from a L.E.D. refractor in the optic head. As each blade enters the light beam, light is reflected back to a photocell that is located in the optic head. This in turn causes a power signal to be sent to a buffer for amplification and signal conditioning. This signal is then sent to the controller for processing and calculation of vehicle speed.

P.M. Generator Speed Signal

The P.M. generator speed signal is a device that supplies vehicle speed input to the electronic controller. Vehicle speed information is provided to the electronic controller by a permanent magnet generator driven by the vehicle transmission. The output frequency of the permanent magnet generator is than routed to a buffer, which in turn will amplify and condition the signal to the electronic controller.

Cadillac – Cimarron

VISUAL INSPECTION

Before performing any tests make a visual inspection of the cruise control system. Check all items in the system for abnormal conditions such as bare broken or disconnected wires and damage to the vacuum hoses. Be sure that the speedometer cables are attached and properly routed. All vacuum hoses must be properly routed and must not have any kinks or bends. Be sure that all electrical connections are complete and tight. The wiring harness must be routed properly.

ROAD TEST

1. Place the dash switch in the off position. Drive the vehicle until the speedometer reads 50 mph. Push the engagement switch button on the turn signal switch and release. The cruise control system should remain off.
2. Place the dash switch in on position. The amber light should come on.
3. Engage the cruise control system by momentarily pushing the turn signal engagement switch button and than releas-

ing it at 50 mph while removing your foot from the accelerator pedal.
4. The green light should come on when the button is released and the system is engaged. The vehicle should maintain the speed of 50 mph.
5. Push the slide switch and hold. The vehicle should accelerate at a controlled rate. Release the slide switch to engage the system to a cruise speed of about 55 mph. The system should now be set to the new speed.
6. Depress the brake pedal about one-half inch. The green light should go out, this confirms the action of the electric brake release switch and the vehicle should now start to slow down.
7. Momentarily depress the slide switch and than release it. The vehicle should accelerate at a controlled rate and resume the previously set speed of 55 mph. The green light should come on when the slide switch is released.
8. Push the engagement switch button all the way in and hold. The green light should go out. Coast to about 50 mph.
9. Release the button in order to engage the system at 50 mph. The green light should come on and the vehicle should maintain that speed.

SERVO TEST (1982–83)

To determine the condition of the servo diaphragm, remove the vacuum hose from the servo assembly. Apply 14 inches of vacuum to the tube opening and hold in in place for about one minute. The vacuum should not leak down more than 5 inches. If vacuum leaks, replace the servo assembly.

Another test consists of removing the vacuum hose attached to the servo assembly, than push the diaphragm in, hold your finger over the nipple and the diaphragm should remain in the pushed in position. If the servo assembly does not perform as indicated it should be replaced.

VACUUM LEAK TEST (1982–83)

The vacuum release valves, the resume valve and all the connecting hoses can be checked by applying 15 inches of vacuum to each component and then sealing off the component for about one minute. The vacuum should not leak down more than 5 inches. Repair or replace defective components as required.

ELECTRICAL SYSTEM TEST (1982–83)

1. Check the cruise control fuse and electrical connector.
2. Check all electrical connections. Disconnect and reconnect after checking for bent, broken or dirty mating tabs.
3. Check the electrical release switch as follows. Unplug the connector at the switch. Connect an ohmmeter to the two terminals on the switch assembly.
4. Depress the brake or clutch pedal. The ohmmeter should not indicate continuity.
5. Release the pedal, the ohmmeter should indicate continunity.

CONTROL LEVER SWITCH TEST (1982–83)

1. Disconnect the electrical connector at the cruise control engagement switch.
2. Connect an ohmmeter to the brown and blue wires.
3. Slide the resume switch to the on position. The ohmmeter should indicate continunity. Push the engage button all the way in and and open circuit should be indicated.
4. Connect an ohmmeter to the brown and black wires, with the resume switch still in the on position. An open circuit should be indicated.

5. Depress the engage button and release it half way. Continunity should exist.

6. Connect an ohmmeter to the blue and black wires with the resume switch still in the on position. With the engaged button released, no continunity should be present.

7. With the engaged button depressed and half way released continunity should exist.

HARNESS AND TRANSDUCER ELECTRICAL TEST (1982–83)

1. Using an ohmmeter engage, with the engagement switch connector disconnected, check the resistance of the dark green wire in the wiring harness. If the transducer is grounded properly, the ohmmeter should indicate between 29 and 36 ohms.

2. If resistance is above or below specification, disconnect the connector at the transducer and at the resume solenoid.

3. Measure the resistance of the dark green wire. It should indicate a resistance reading of 23 ohms, plus or minus one ohm. If the reading is not as indicated the wiring harness should be replaced.

4. With the connectors of the transducer disconnected, measure the resistance of the solenoid coil by connecting the ohmmeter to the hold terminal and ground. A reading of 5 to 6 ohms should be indicated.

5. If a reading of 4 ohms or less is obtained there is excessive resistance in the circuit. If a reading of 6 ohms or more is indicated the transducer should be checked.

RESUME VALVE TEST (1982–83)

1. Disconnect the electrical connector to the transducer hold terminal.

2. Apply 12 volts DC current to the terminal connector cavity. The solenoid should engage.

3. Remove the voltage source and the solenoid should disen-

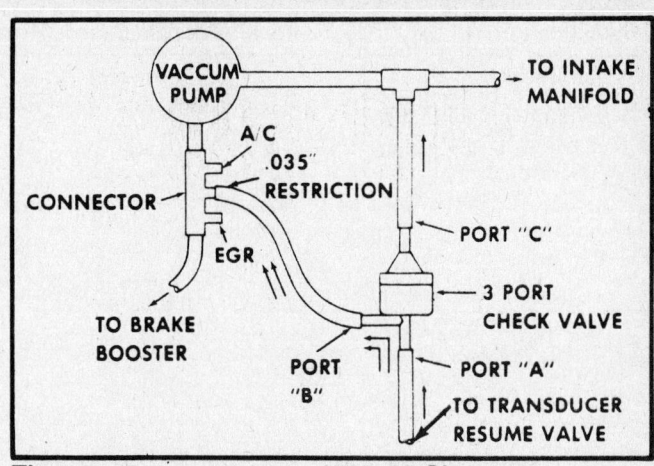

Three port vacuum test—1982–83 Cimarron

gage. A click should be heard each time the solenoid engages and disengages.

4. Do not reverse polarity when applying power. If polarity is reversed the radio noise suppression diode in the solenoid may be damaged.

VACUUM PUMP ASSISTED SYSTEMS TEST (1982–83)

1. Blow low air pressure into port "A" while port "B" is plugged. Then plug port "A" and blow low air pressure into port "B".

2. In both cases air should exit port "C". If not clean or replace the check valve.

3. To check the air flow in the other direction, blow low air pressure into port "C". No air should come out of port "A" or port "B".

DIAGNOSIS AND TESTING PROCEDURES

Condition	Possible Cause	Correction
System inoperative	1. Throttle linkage from servo unit to throttle disconnected.	1. Connect throttle linkage and adjust.
	2. Large vacuum leak. Vacuum hose disconnected.	2. Check all vacuum lines and connections. Check for torn or leaking servo unit. Repair or replace as required.
	3. Restricted or plugged vacuum line. Incorrect check valve valve orientation (vacuum pump).	3. Check for kinks or collapsed vacuum line. Remove restriction. Correct check valve orientation.
	4. Brake pedal vacuum release valve or brake electrical switch out of adjustment.	4. Adjust or replace as necessary.
	5. Resume solenoid valve inoperative	5. Check for voltage at solenoid (2 volts with ignition on.) If voltage, check ground wire and repair. Investigate "engage" circuit for 12

Condition	Possible Cause	Correction
System inoperative 5. volts or possible faulty solenoid. If no voltage, check for proper adjustment of brake switch wiring or engage switch. Repair as necessary.	6. Loose electrical connections or open wiring. 7. Fuse blown. 8. Malfunctioned turn signal and engage switch assembly. 9. Malfunctioned transducer.	1. Check and secure all electrical connectors, transducer, cruise engage switch, fuse block, and repair cut or open wiring. 2. Replace fuse. 3. Substitute new turn signal and engage switch assembly by plugging into connector at bottom of steering column. Check operation and, if satisfactory, install new turn signal and engage switch assembly. 4. Replace
Speed increases after engagement.	1. Speedometer cable (needle) fluctuates due to speedo cable or housing bent, kinked or misrouted. 2. Transducer orifice tube out of adjustment. 3. Transducer malfunction.	1. Correct as necessary. 2. Adjust. 3. Replace.
Speed drops off after engagement.	1. Throttle linkage too loose. Vacuum leak or restriction. 2. Transducer orifice tube out of adjustment.	1. Check for damaged, disconnected, pinched, or kinked hoses. Repair or replace as required. Adjust throttle linkage. 2. Adjust.
Surging	1. Check for restricted vacuum line from engine to transducer. 2. Check to insure that servo unit will full stroke. 3. Transducer malfunction. 4. Check valve stuck closed or missing.	1. Repair or replace. 2. Replace servo unit. 3. Replace. 4. Install or re-orient check valve as necessary.
Speed Drops Off Excessively on Inclines	1. Throttle linkage too loose. 2. Vacuum source hose restricted. 3. Cruise system not connected to auxiliary vacuum pump. 4. Check valve reversed or stuck open.	1. Adjust. 2. Repair or Replace. 3. Correct (See vacuum schematics). 4. Re-orient or replace as necessary.

CRUISE CONTROL DIAGNOSIS

PRELIMINARY CHECKS

1. Check Servo Chain or rod adjustment. Must have minimum slack.
2. Check vacuum hoses. Must be in good condition - no restrictions or leaks.
3. Check drive cable routings. No kinks or sharp bends.
4. Check throttle linkage or cable for binding.
5. Check adjustment of electrical release switch and vacuum release valve.
6. Check engagement switch operation.
7. If steps 1 through 6 do not solve the problem, continue with diagnosis.

CRUISE CONTROL INOPERATIVE

1. Check radio fuse. If blown, check wiring for short circuit and repair. A shorted resume solenoid diode could also cause blow fuse.
2. If fuse and preliminary checks ok, resume solenoid must be checked. Start engine and check source vacuum at resume solenoid (refer to picture at right). Disconnect the two wire connector at resume solenoid. Use jumper wire to ground terminal which had black wire connected to it. Apply 12 volts to terminal which had tan wire connected to it. Disconnect outlet vacuum hose (going to B fitting on transducer). Vacuum should be present. If not, replace resume solenoid. Applying voltage incorrectly to resume solenoid could damage diode. If above checks ok, stop engine and reconnect electrical and vacuum connections.
3. To make test below, turn ignition to RUN position and off/on/resume switch to ON. Disconnect the two wire connector at transducer (Engage-Hold Terminals).
4. Connect 12 volt test light to ground and to engage wire in connector. Push engage/coast button in part way to engage position.
5. Repeat test on hold wire in connector.

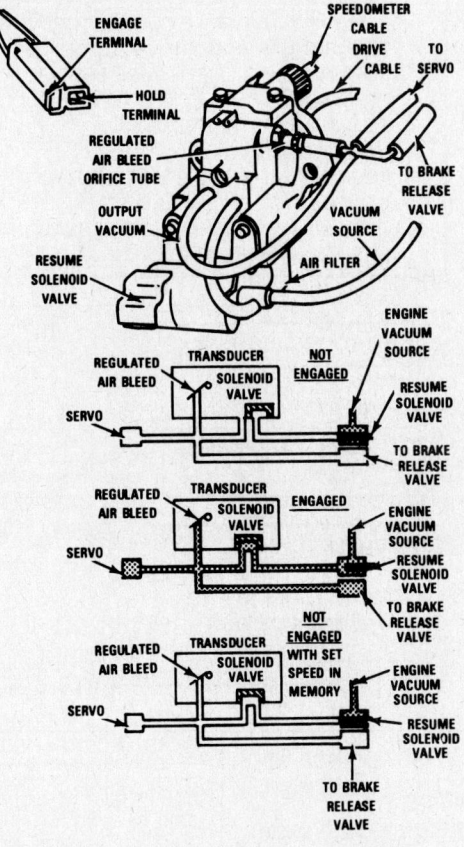

TEST LIGHT OFF AT ONE WIRE ONLY

Test engagement switch. (See test procedure) Check for open circuit in wire if test light did not light. Repair or replace part that checks bad.

TEST LIGHT ON AT BOTH WIRES (MAY BE DIM ON HOLD WIRE)

Check for poor ground at transducer. If ok, remove transducer for repair.

TEST LIGHT OFF AT BOTH WIRES

Check for open circuit in brown/white wire from fuse panel to off/on/resume switch. If circuit ok, check engagement switch operation and replace if necessary.

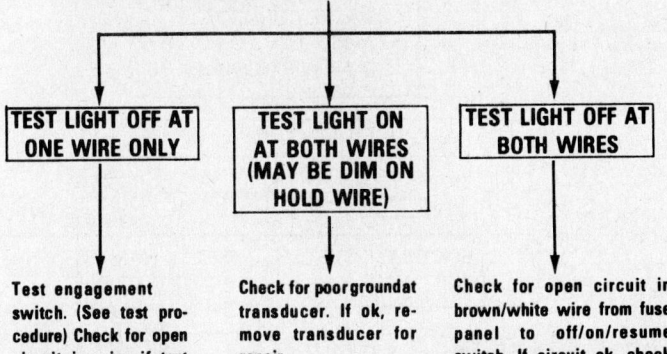

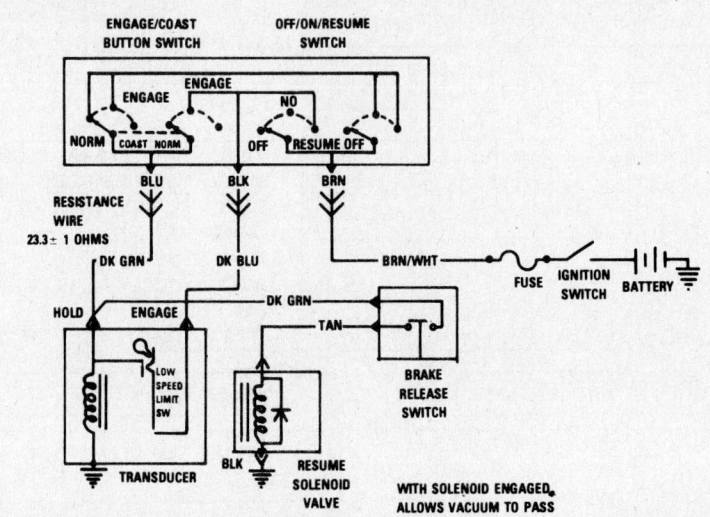

ENGAGEMENT SWITCH TEST PROCEDURE				
USE A SELF POWERED TEST LIGHT. LIGHT WILL BE ON FOR EACH TEST IF SWITCH IS GOOD. CONNECTOR TERMINALS AND COLOR 1 — BROWN, 2 — BLUE, 3 — BLACK				
SWITCH POSITIONS		TERMINALS		
ENGAGE BUTTON	RESUME SWITCH	1 to 2	1 to 3	2 to 3
Released	on	closed	open	open
Fully Depressed	on	open	open	closed
Partially Released	on	closed	closed	closed
Released	resume	closed	closed	closed
Released	off	open	open	open

WITH SOLENOID ENGAGED, ALLOWS VACUUM TO PASS THROUGH IT

SEE SECTION 8 FOR WIRING

Cruise control diagnosis – 1982–83 Cimarron

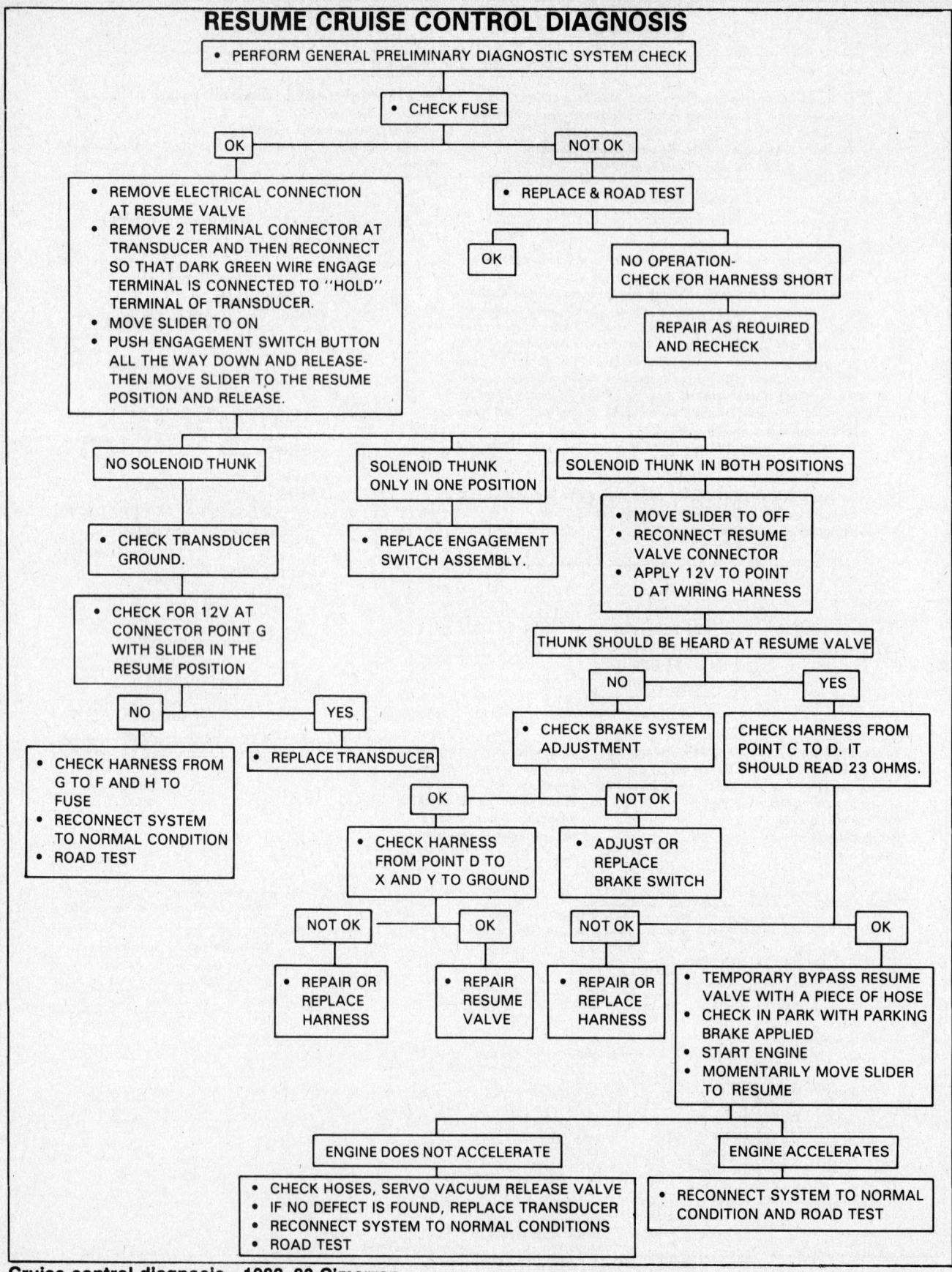

RESUME CRUISE CONTROL DIAGNOSIS

- PERFORM GENERAL PRELIMINARY DIAGNOSTIC SYSTEM CHECK

- CHECK FUSE

OK

- REMOVE ELECTRICAL CONNECTION AT RESUME VALVE
- REMOVE 2 TERMINAL CONNECTOR AT TRANSDUCER AND THEN RECONNECT SO THAT DARK GREEN WIRE ENGAGE TERMINAL IS CONNECTED TO "HOLD" TERMINAL OF TRANSDUCER.
- MOVE SLIDER TO ON
- PUSH ENGAGEMENT SWITCH BUTTON ALL THE WAY DOWN AND RELEASE- THEN MOVE SLIDER TO THE RESUME POSITION AND RELEASE.

NOT OK

- REPLACE & ROAD TEST

OK

NO OPERATION- CHECK FOR HARNESS SHORT

REPAIR AS REQUIRED AND RECHECK

NO SOLENOID THUNK

- CHECK TRANSDUCER GROUND.

- CHECK FOR 12V AT CONNECTOR POINT G WITH SLIDER IN THE RESUME POSITION

NO

- CHECK HARNESS FROM G TO F AND H TO FUSE
- RECONNECT SYSTEM TO NORMAL CONDITION
- ROAD TEST

YES

- REPLACE TRANSDUCER

SOLENOID THUNK ONLY IN ONE POSITION

- REPLACE ENGAGEMENT SWITCH ASSEMBLY.

SOLENOID THUNK IN BOTH POSITIONS

- MOVE SLIDER TO OFF
- RECONNECT RESUME VALVE CONNECTOR
- APPLY 12V TO POINT D AT WIRING HARNESS

THUNK SHOULD BE HEARD AT RESUME VALVE

NO

- CHECK BRAKE SYSTEM ADJUSTMENT

OK

- CHECK HARNESS FROM POINT D TO X AND Y TO GROUND

NOT OK

- REPAIR OR REPLACE HARNESS

OK

- REPAIR RESUME VALVE

NOT OK

- ADJUST OR REPLACE BRAKE SWITCH

NOT OK

- REPAIR OR REPLACE HARNESS

OK

- TEMPORARY BYPASS RESUME VALVE WITH A PIECE OF HOSE
- CHECK IN PARK WITH PARKING BRAKE APPLIED
- START ENGINE
- MOMENTARILY MOVE SLIDER TO RESUME

YES

CHECK HARNESS FROM POINT C TO D. IT SHOULD READ 23 OHMS.

ENGINE DOES NOT ACCELERATE

- CHECK HOSES, SERVO VACUUM RELEASE VALVE
- IF NO DEFECT IS FOUND, REPLACE TRANSDUCER
- RECONNECT SYSTEM TO NORMAL CONDITIONS
- ROAD TEST

ENGINE ACCELERATES

- RECONNECT SYSTEM TO NORMAL CONDITION AND ROAD TEST

Cruise control diagnosis—1982–83 Cimarron

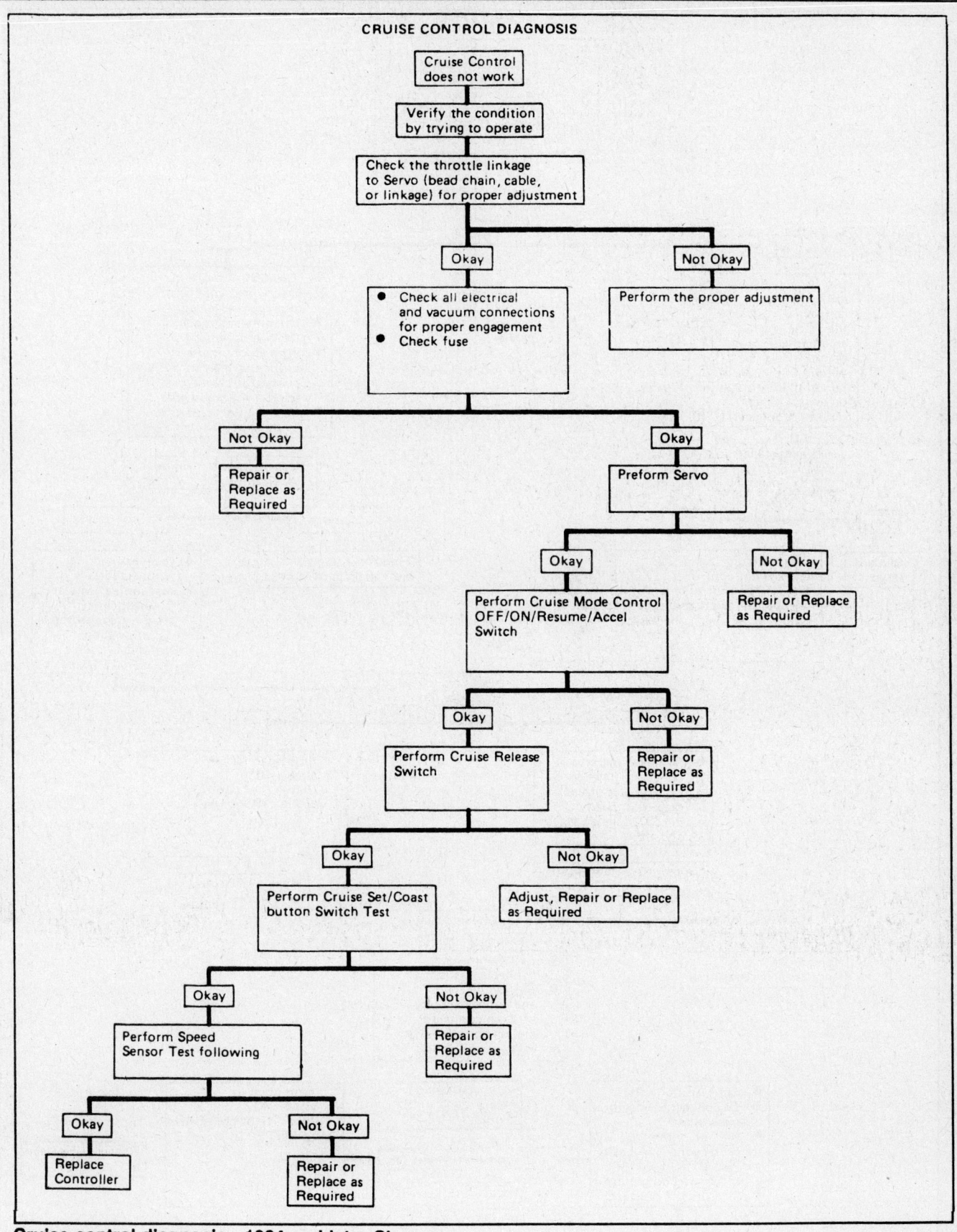

CRUISE CONTROL DIAGNOSIS

Cruise control diagnosis – 1984 and later Cimarron

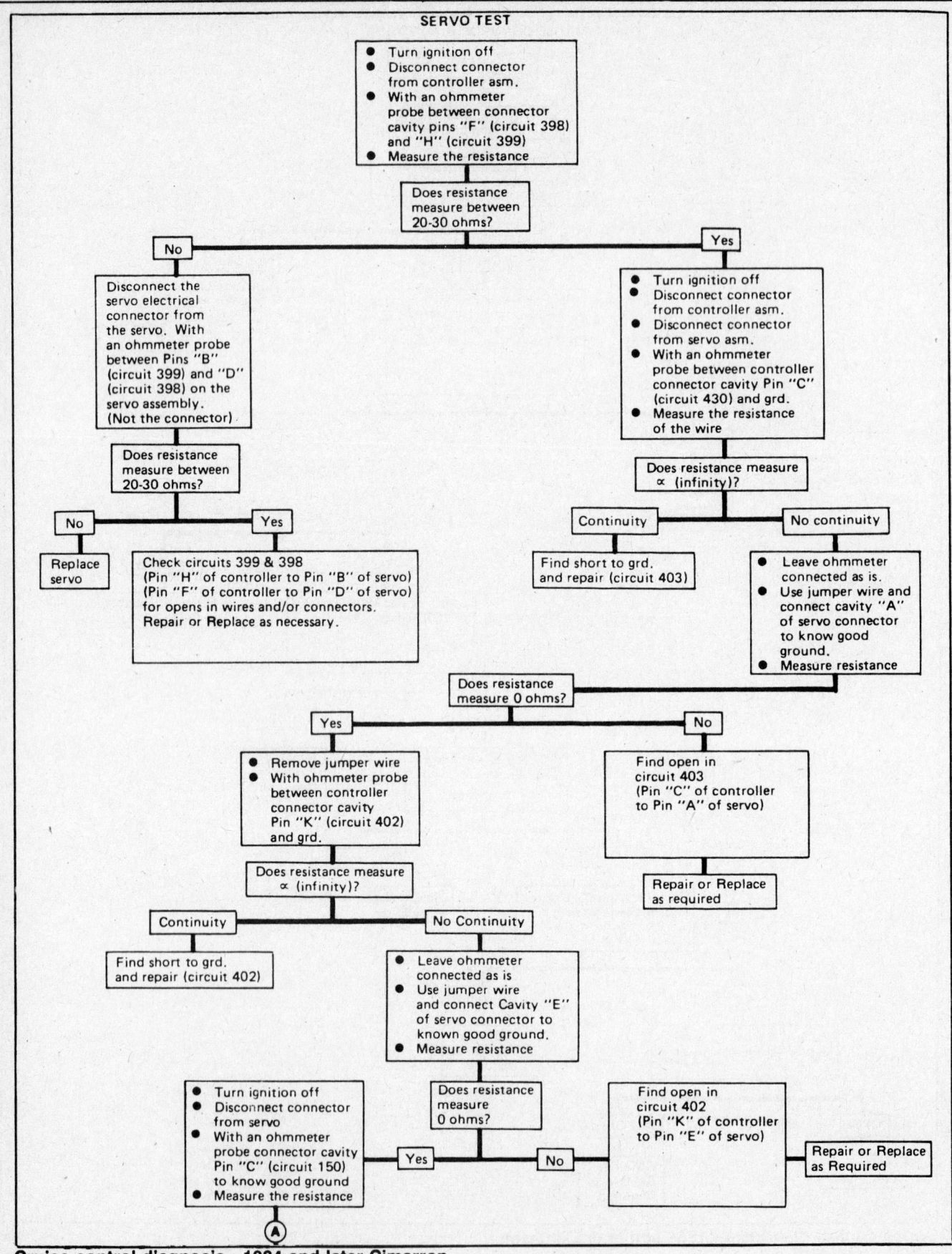

SERVO TEST

- Turn ignition off
- Disconnect connector from controller asm.
- With an ohmmeter probe between connector cavity pins "F" (circuit 398) and "H" (circuit 399)
- Measure the resistance

Does resistance measure between 20-30 ohms?

No

Disconnect the servo electrical connector from the servo. With an ohmmeter probe between Pins "B" (circuit 399) and "D" (circuit 398) on the servo assembly. (Not the connector)

Does resistance measure between 20-30 ohms?

No — Replace servo

Yes — Check circuits 399 & 398 (Pin "H" of controller to Pin "B" of servo) (Pin "F" of controller to Pin "D" of servo) for opens in wires and/or connectors. Repair or Replace as necessary.

Yes

- Turn ignition off
- Disconnect connector from controller asm.
- Disconnect connector from servo asm.
- With an ohmmeter probe between controller connector cavity Pin "C" (circuit 430) and grd.
- Measure the resistance of the wire

Does resistance measure ∝ (infinity)?

Continuity — Find short to grd. and repair (circuit 403)

No continuity
- Leave ohmmeter connected as is.
- Use jumper wire and connect cavity "A" of servo connector to know good ground.
- Measure resistance

Does resistance measure 0 ohms?

Yes
- Remove jumper wire
- With ohmmeter probe between controller connector cavity Pin "K" (circuit 402) and grd.

Does resistance measure ∝ (infinity)?

Continuity — Find short to grd. and repair (circuit 402)

No Continuity
- Leave ohmmeter connected as is
- Use jumper wire and connect Cavity "E" of servo connector to known good ground.
- Measure resistance

No

Find open in circuit 403 (Pin "C" of controller to Pin "A" of servo)

Repair or Replace as required

- Turn ignition off
- Disconnect connector from servo
- With an ohmmeter probe connector cavity Pin "C" (circuit 150) to know good ground
- Measure the resistance

Does resistance measure 0 ohms?

Yes   **No**

Find open in circuit 402 (Pin "K" of controller to Pin "E" of servo)

Repair or Replace as Required

(A)

Cruise control diagnosis—1984 and later Cimarron

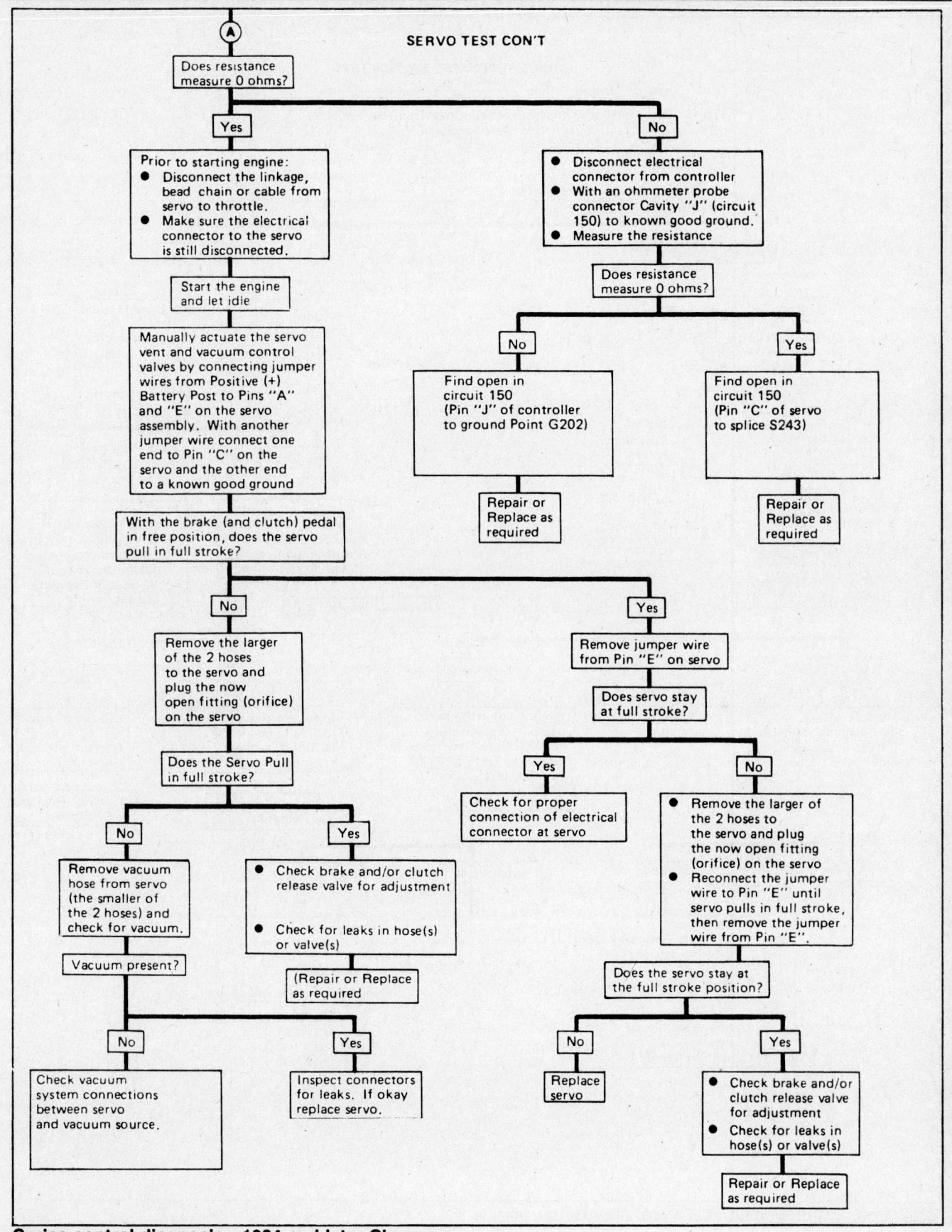

Cruise control diagnosis—1984 and later Cimarron

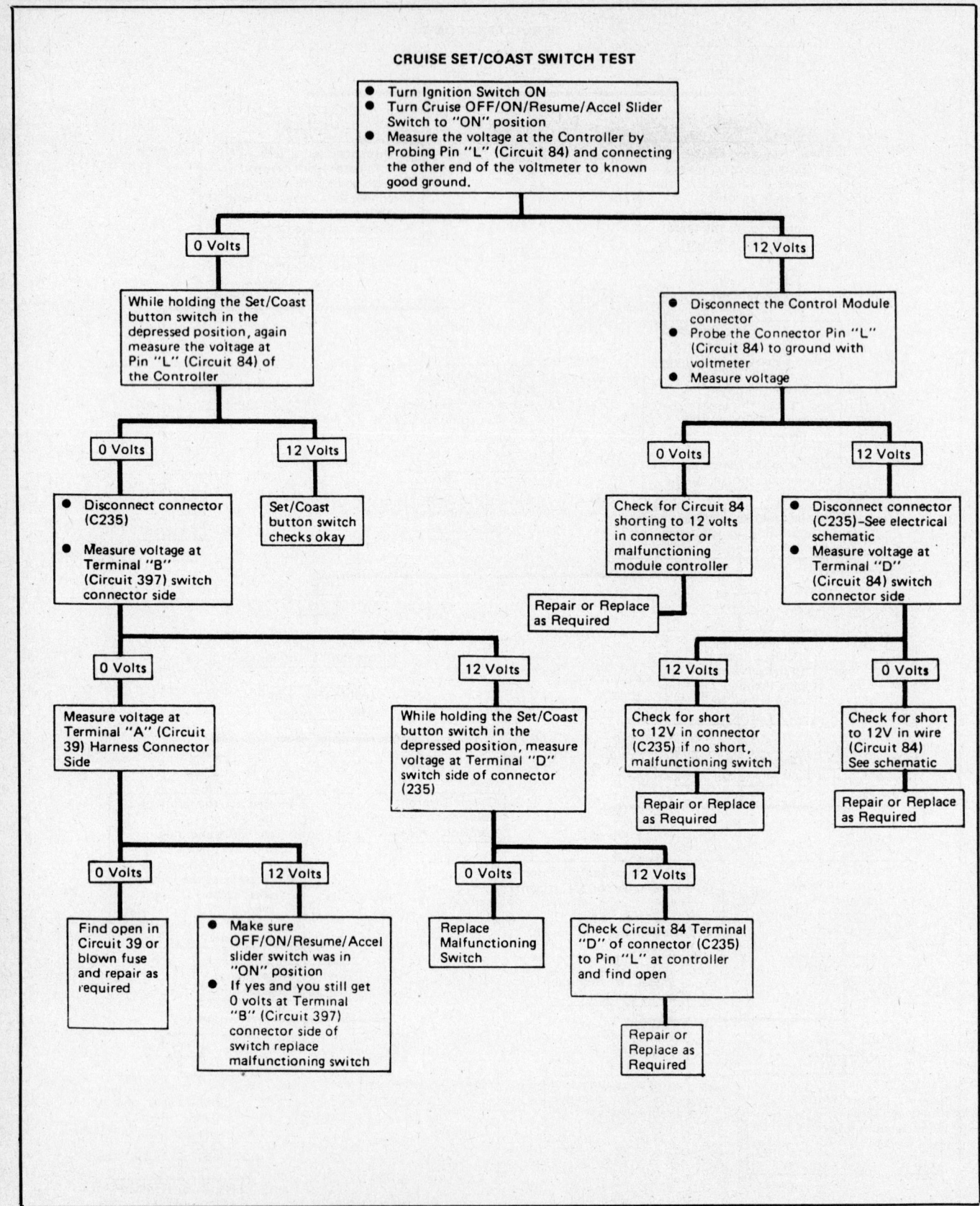

CRUISE SET/COAST SWITCH TEST

- Turn Ignition Switch ON
- Turn Cruise OFF/ON/Resume/Accel Slider Switch to "ON" position
- Measure the voltage at the Controller by Probing Pin "L" (Circuit 84) and connecting the other end of the voltmeter to known good ground.

0 Volts

While holding the Set/Coast button switch in the depressed position, again measure the voltage at Pin "L" (Circuit 84) of the Controller

0 Volts

- Disconnect connector (C235)
- Measure voltage at Terminal "B" (Circuit 397) switch connector side

12 Volts

Set/Coast button switch checks okay

0 Volts

Measure voltage at Terminal "A" (Circuit 39) Harness Connector Side

0 Volts

Find open in Circuit 39 or blown fuse and repair as required

12 Volts

- Make sure OFF/ON/Resume/Accel slider switch was in "ON" position
- If yes and you still get 0 volts at Terminal "B" (Circuit 397) connector side of switch replace malfunctioning switch

12 Volts

While holding the Set/Coast button switch in the depressed position, measure voltage at Terminal "D" switch side of connector (235)

0 Volts

Replace Malfunctioning Switch

12 Volts

Check Circuit 84 Terminal "D" of connector (C235) to Pin "L" at controller and find open

Repair or Replace as Required

12 Volts

- Disconnect the Control Module connector
- Probe the Connector Pin "L" (Circuit 84) to ground with voltmeter
- Measure voltage

0 Volts

Check for Circuit 84 shorting to 12 volts in connector or malfunctioning module controller

Repair or Replace as Required

12 Volts

- Disconnect connector (C235)–See electrical schematic
- Measure voltage at Terminal "D" (Circuit 84) switch connector side

12 Volts

Check for short to 12V in connector (C235) if no short, malfunctioning switch

Repair or Replace as Required

0 Volts

Check for short to 12V in wire (Circuit 84) See schematic

Repair or Replace as Required

Cruise control diagnosis—1984 and later Cimarron

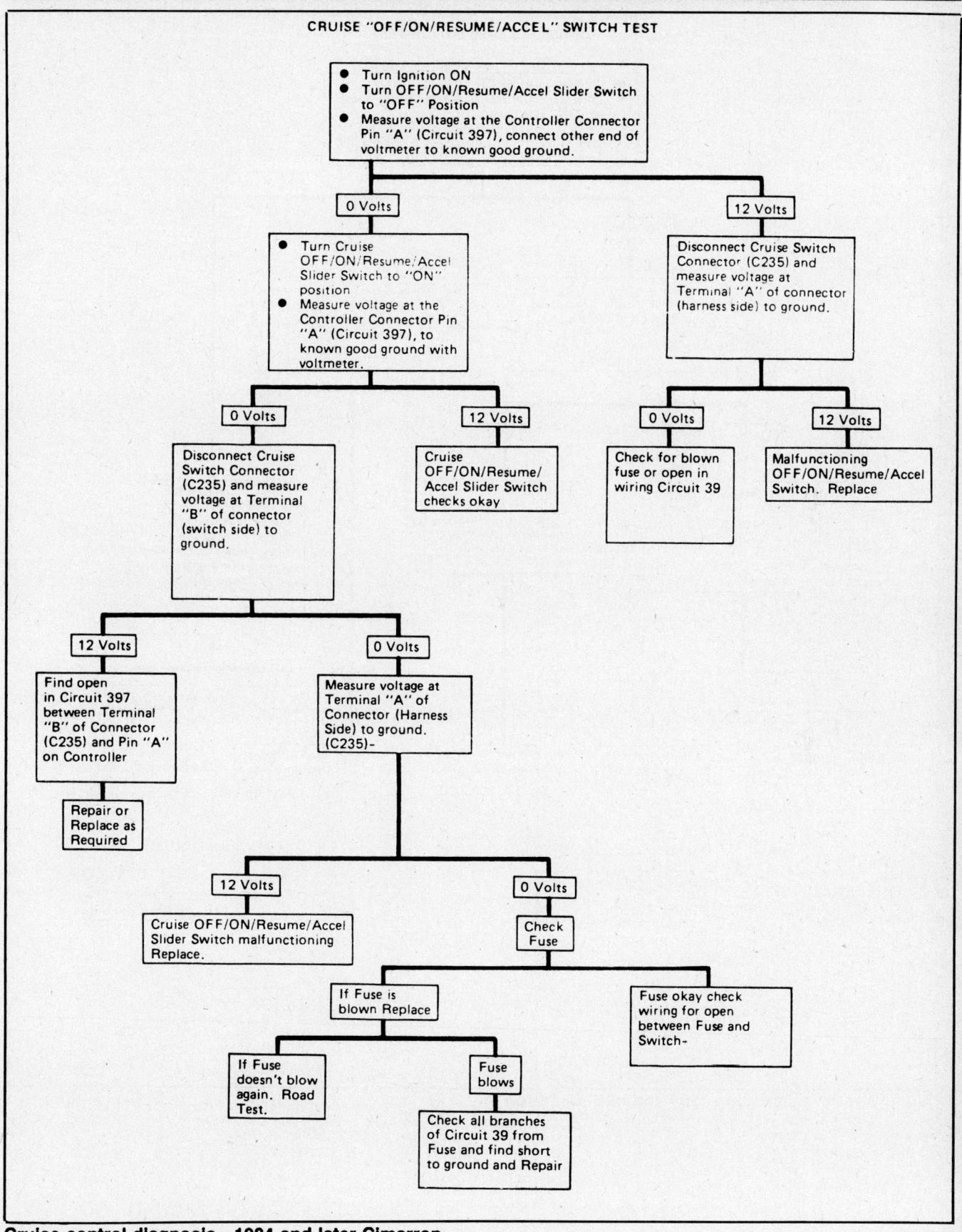

CRUISE "OFF/ON/RESUME/ACCEL" SWITCH TEST

- Turn Ignition ON
- Turn OFF/ON/Resume/Accel Slider Switch to "OFF" Position
- Measure voltage at the Controller Connector Pin "A" (Circuit 397), connect other end of voltmeter to known good ground.

0 Volts

12 Volts

- Turn Cruise OFF/ON/Resume/Accel Slider Switch to "ON" position
- Measure voltage at the Controller Connector Pin "A" (Circuit 397), to known good ground with voltmeter.

Disconnect Cruise Switch Connector (C235) and measure voltage at Terminal "A" of connector (harness side) to ground.

0 Volts

Disconnect Cruise Switch Connector (C235) and measure voltage at Terminal "B" of connector (switch side) to ground.

12 Volts

Cruise OFF/ON/Resume/Accel Slider Switch checks okay

0 Volts

Check for blown fuse or open in wiring Circuit 39

12 Volts

Malfunctioning OFF/ON/Resume/Accel Switch. Replace

12 Volts

Find open in Circuit 397 between Terminal "B" of Connector (C235) and Pin "A" on Controller

Repair or Replace as Required

0 Volts

Measure voltage at Terminal "A" of Connector (Harness Side) to ground. (C235)–

12 Volts

Cruise OFF/ON/Resume/Accel Slider Switch malfunctioning Replace.

0 Volts

Check Fuse

If Fuse is blown Replace

Fuse okay check wiring for open between Fuse and Switch–

If Fuse doesn't blow again. Road Test.

Fuse blows

Check all branches of Circuit 39 from Fuse and find short to ground and Repair

Cruise control diagnosis — 1984 and later Cimarron

821

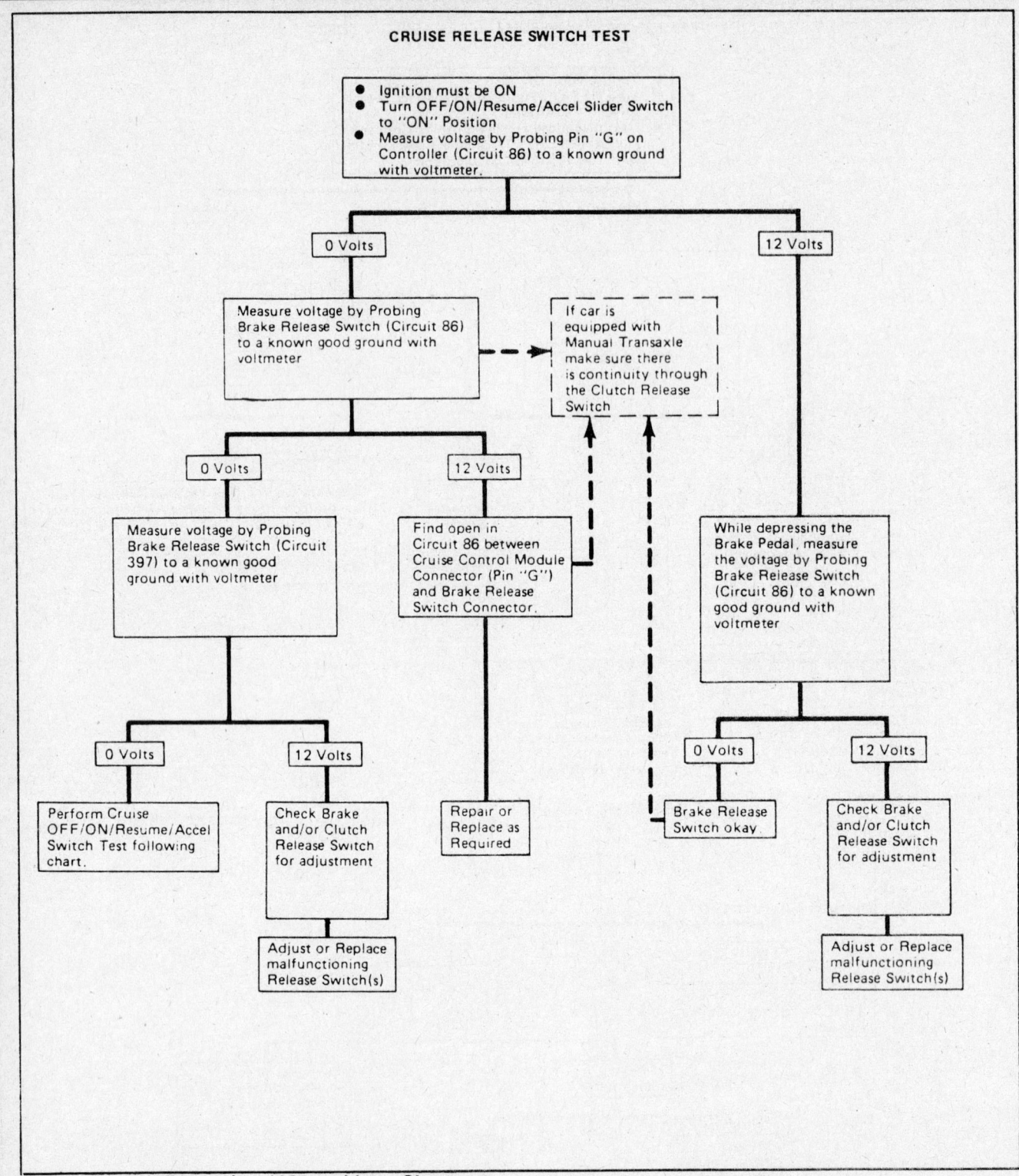

CRUISE RELEASE SWITCH TEST

- Ignition must be ON
- Turn OFF/ON/Resume/Accel Slider Switch to "ON" Position
- Measure voltage by Probing Pin "G" on Controller (Circuit 86) to a known ground with voltmeter.

0 Volts

12 Volts

Measure voltage by Probing Brake Release Switch (Circuit 86) to a known good ground with voltmeter

If car is equipped with Manual Transaxle make sure there is continuity through the Clutch Release Switch

0 Volts

12 Volts

Measure voltage by Probing Brake Release Switch (Circuit 397) to a known good ground with voltmeter

Find open in Circuit 86 between Cruise Control Module Connector (Pin "G") and Brake Release Switch Connector.

While depressing the Brake Pedal, measure the voltage by Probing Brake Release Switch (Circuit 86) to a known good ground with voltmeter

0 Volts

12 Volts

Perform Cruise OFF/ON/Resume/Accel Switch Test following chart.

Check Brake and/or Clutch Release Switch for adjustment

Repair or Replace as Required

0 Volts

12 Volts

Brake Release Switch okay

Check Brake and/or Clutch Release Switch for adjustment

Adjust or Replace malfunctioning Release Switch(s)

Adjust or Replace malfunctioning Release Switch(s)

Cruise control diagnosis—1984 and later Cimarron

822

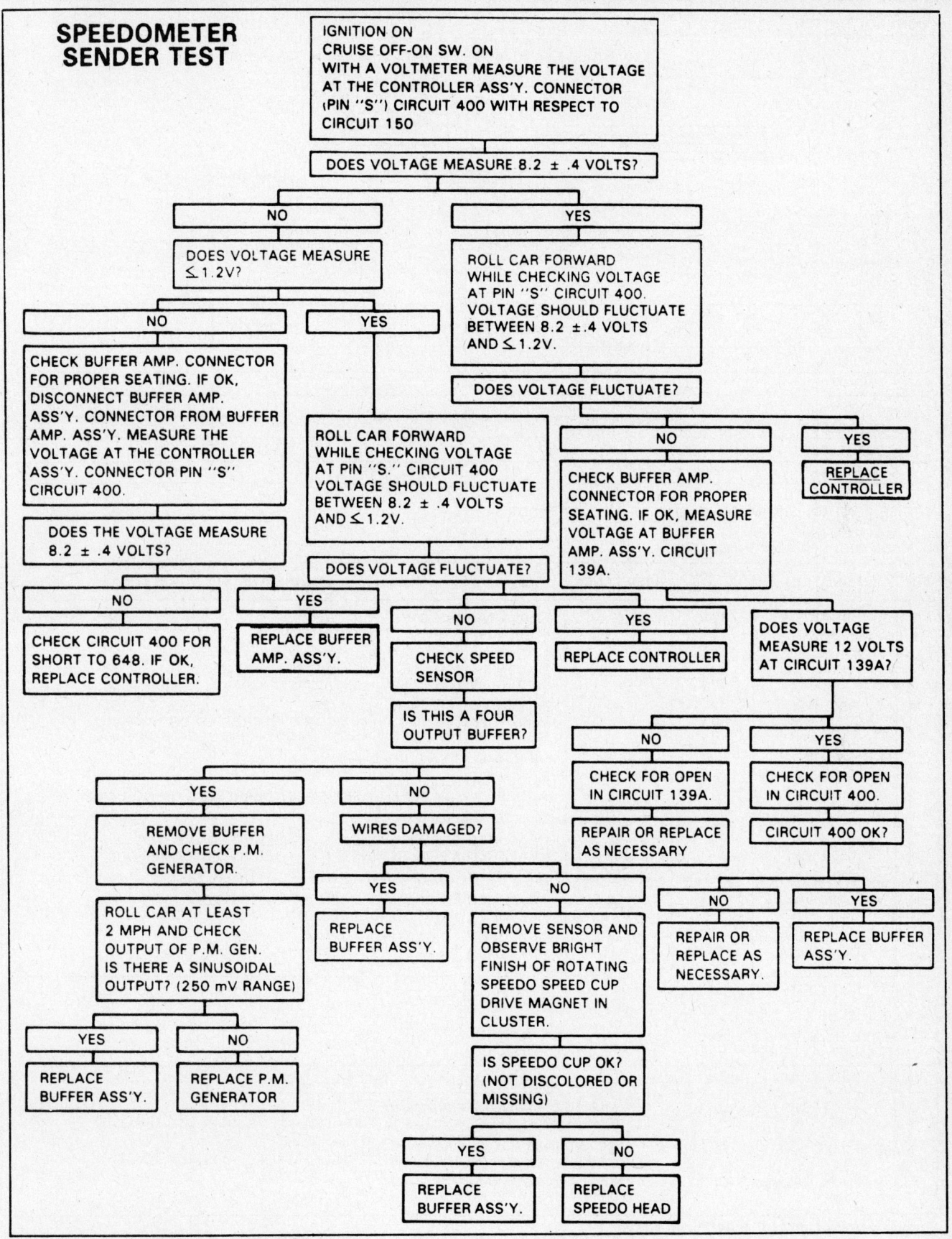

SPEEDOMETER SENDER TEST

IGNITION ON
CRUISE OFF-ON SW. ON
WITH A VOLTMETER MEASURE THE VOLTAGE AT THE CONTROLLER ASS'Y. CONNECTOR (PIN "S") CIRCUIT 400 WITH RESPECT TO CIRCUIT 150

DOES VOLTAGE MEASURE 8.2 ± .4 VOLTS?

- **NO** — DOES VOLTAGE MEASURE ≤ 1.2V?
  - **NO** — CHECK BUFFER AMP. CONNECTOR FOR PROPER SEATING. IF OK, DISCONNECT BUFFER AMP. ASS'Y. CONNECTOR FROM BUFFER AMP. ASS'Y. MEASURE THE VOLTAGE AT THE CONTROLLER ASS'Y. CONNECTOR PIN "S" CIRCUIT 400.
    - DOES THE VOLTAGE MEASURE 8.2 ± .4 VOLTS?
      - **NO** — CHECK CIRCUIT 400 FOR SHORT TO 648. IF OK, REPLACE CONTROLLER.
      - **YES** — REPLACE BUFFER AMP. ASS'Y.
  - **YES** — ROLL CAR FORWARD WHILE CHECKING VOLTAGE AT PIN "S." CIRCUIT 400 VOLTAGE SHOULD FLUCTUATE BETWEEN 8.2 ± .4 VOLTS AND ≤ 1.2 V.
    - DOES VOLTAGE FLUCTUATE?
      - **NO** — CHECK SPEED SENSOR — IS THIS A FOUR OUTPUT BUFFER?
        - **YES** — REMOVE BUFFER AND CHECK P.M. GENERATOR. ROLL CAR AT LEAST 2 MPH AND CHECK OUTPUT OF P.M. GEN. IS THERE A SINUSOIDAL OUTPUT? (250 mV RANGE)
          - **YES** — REPLACE BUFFER ASS'Y.
          - **NO** — REPLACE P.M. GENERATOR
        - **NO** — WIRES DAMAGED?
          - **YES** — REPLACE BUFFER ASS'Y.
          - **NO** — REMOVE SENSOR AND OBSERVE BRIGHT FINISH OF ROTATING SPEEDO SPEED CUP DRIVE MAGNET IN CLUSTER. IS SPEEDO CUP OK? (NOT DISCOLORED OR MISSING)
            - **YES** — REPLACE BUFFER ASS'Y.
            - **NO** — REPLACE SPEEDO HEAD
      - **YES** — REPLACE CONTROLLER
- **YES** — ROLL CAR FORWARD WHILE CHECKING VOLTAGE AT PIN "S" CIRCUIT 400. VOLTAGE SHOULD FLUCTUATE BETWEEN 8.2 ±.4 VOLTS AND ≤ 1.2V.
  - DOES VOLTAGE FLUCTUATE?
    - **NO** — CHECK BUFFER AMP. CONNECTOR FOR PROPER SEATING. IF OK, MEASURE VOLTAGE AT BUFFER AMP. ASS'Y. CIRCUIT 139A.
      - DOES VOLTAGE MEASURE 12 VOLTS AT CIRCUIT 139A?
        - **NO** — CHECK FOR OPEN IN CIRCUIT 139A. REPAIR OR REPLACE AS NECESSARY
        - **YES** — CHECK FOR OPEN IN CIRCUIT 400. CIRCUIT 400 OK?
          - **NO** — REPAIR OR REPLACE AS NECESSARY.
          - **YES** — REPLACE BUFFER ASS'Y.
    - **YES** — REPLACE CONTROLLER

Cruise control diagnosis—1984 Cimarron

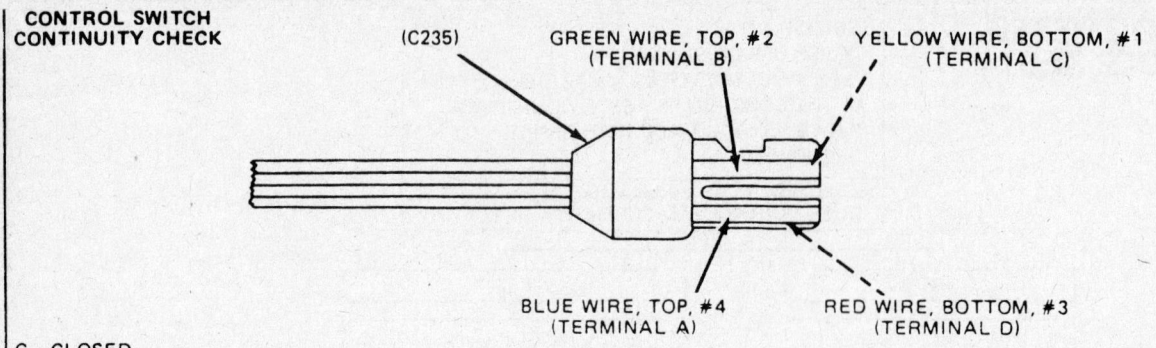

CONTROL SWITCH
CONTINUITY CHECK

(C235)

GREEN WIRE, TOP, #2
(TERMINAL B)

YELLOW WIRE, BOTTOM, #1
(TERMINAL C)

BLUE WIRE, TOP, #4
(TERMINAL A)

RED WIRE, BOTTOM, #3
(TERMINAL D)

C – CLOSED
O – OPEN

SET/COAST (S/C) SW	POSITION SLIDER	1-2	1-3	1-4	2-3	2-4	3-4
NORMAL	OFF	O	O	O	O	O	O
NORMAL	ON	O	O	O	O	C	O
NORMAL	R/A	C	O	C	O	C	O
DEPRESSED	OFF	O	O	O	C	O	O
DEPRESSED	ON	O	O	O	C	C	C
DEPRESSED	R/A	C	C	C	C	C	C

CRUISE CONTROLLER (MODULE) CHECKS AT CONNECTOR

- IGNITION ON
- CONTROLLER DISCONNECTED

PIN	FUNCTION	VOLTAGE TO GND	RESISTANCE	CONDITIONS
G	BRAKE INPUT	12 V 0 V	– –	BRAKE (AND CLUTCH) NOT DEPRESSED BRAKE (AND/OR CLUTCH) DEPRESSED
L	SET/COAST INPUT	12 V 0 V 0 V	– – –	SLIDER SWITCH "ON" – SET/COAST DEPRESSED SLIDER SWITCH "ON" – SET/COAST NORMAL SLIDER SWITCH "OFF" – SET/COAST NORMAL
M	RESUME/ ACCEL. INPUT	12 V 0 V 0 V	– – –	SLIDER SWITCH "R/A" POSITION SLIDER SWITCH "ON" – SET/COAST DEPRESSED OR NORMAL SLIDER SWITCH "OFF" – SET/COAST DEPRESSED OR NORMAL
J	GROUND	–	0 Ω	MEASURED TO VEHICLE GROUND
A	ON/OFF INPUT	12 V 0 V	– –	SLIDER SWITCH "ON" SLIDER SWITCH "OFF" – SET/COAST DEPRESSED OR NORMAL
B	INDICATOR LAMP	12 V	–	CRUISE ARMED
F H	SPS HIGH SPS LOW	– –	20 - 30 Ω 0 Ω	MEASURED BETWEEN PINS F & H – SERVO CONNECTED MEASURED BETWEEN PINS F & H – SERVO DISCONNECTED
D	SPEED SIGNAL	→	→	SEE CHART (DIAGNOSTIC) ON SPEED SENDER TEST
K	VACUUM VALVE CONTROL	– –	30 - 50 Ω ∞ Ω	MEASURED TO GROUND – SERVO CONNECTED MEASURED TO GROUND – SERVO NOT CONNECTED
C	VENT VALVE CONTROL	– –	30 - 50 Ω ∞ Ω	MEASURED TO GROUND – SERVO CONNECTED MEASURED TO GROUND – SERVO NOT CONNECTED

SERVO CHECKS

- SERVO CONNECTOR DISCONNECTED
- MEASURE AT SERVO PINS

PIN	FUNCTION	RESISTANCE	CONDITIONS
D B	SPS HIGH SPS LOW	20 - 30 Ω	MEASURED BETWEEN PINS D AND B (IF MEASURED RESISTANCE IS NOT STATED VALVE, REPLACE SERVO)
A	VENT VALVE	30 - 50 Ω	MEASURED BETWEEN PINS A AND C (IF MEASURED RESISTANCE IS NOT STATED VALVE, REPLACE SERVO)
E	VACUUM VALVE	30 - 50 Ω	MEASURED BETWEEN PINS E AND C (IF MEASURED RESISTANCE IS NOT STATED VALVE, REPLACE SERVO)

Cruise control circuit electronic tests

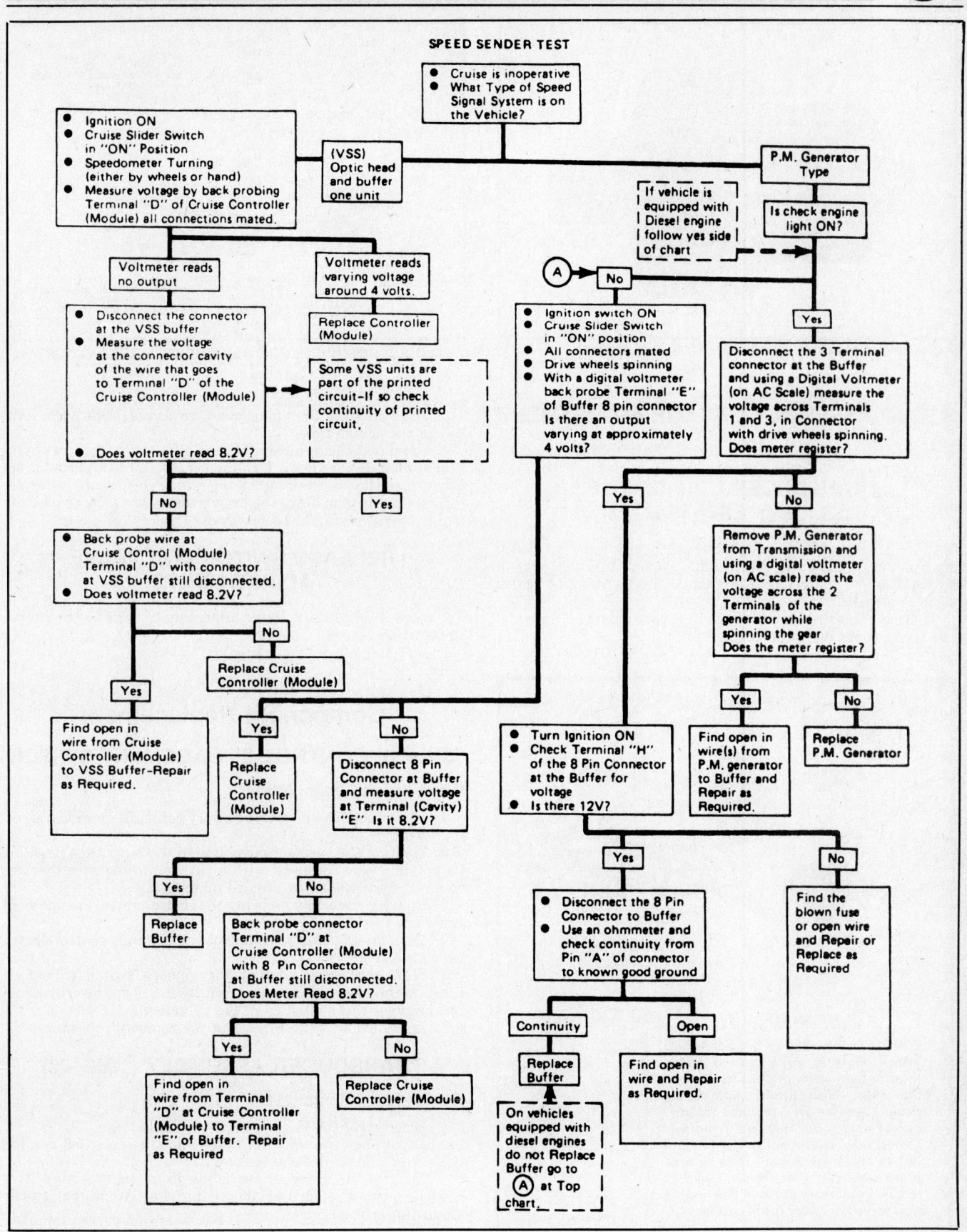

SPEED SENDER TEST

- Cruise is inoperative
- What Type of Speed Signal System is on the Vehicle?

Ignition ON
- Cruise Slider Switch in "ON" Position
- Speedometer Turning (either by wheels or hand)
- Measure voltage by back probing Terminal "D" of Cruise Controller (Module) all connections mated.

(VSS) Optic head and buffer one unit

P.M. Generator Type

If vehicle is equipped with Diesel engine follow yes side of chart

Is check engine light ON?

Voltmeter reads no output

Voltmeter reads varying voltage around 4 volts.

Replace Controller (Module)

A No

- Ignition switch ON
- Cruise Slider Switch in "ON" position
- All connectors mated
- Drive wheels spinning
- With a digital voltmeter back probe Terminal "E" of Buffer 8 pin connector Is there an output varying at approximately 4 volts?

Yes

- Disconnect the connector at the VSS buffer
- Measure the voltage at the connector cavity of the wire that goes to Terminal "D" of the Cruise Controller (Module)
- Does voltmeter read 8.2V?

Some VSS units are part of the printed circuit-If so check continuity of printed circuit.

Disconnect the 3 Terminal connector at the Buffer and using a Digital Voltmeter (on AC Scale) measure the voltage across Terminals 1 and 3, in Connector with drive wheels spinning. Does meter register?

No   Yes

Yes   No

- Back probe wire at Cruise Control (Module) Terminal "D" with connector at VSS buffer still disconnected.
- Does voltmeter read 8.2V?

Remove P.M. Generator from Transmission and using a digital voltmeter (on AC scale) read the voltage across the 2 Terminals of the generator while spinning the gear Does the meter register?

No

Yes

Replace Cruise Controller (Module)

Yes   No

Find open in wire from Cruise Controller (Module) to VSS Buffer-Repair as Required.

Replace Cruise Controller (Module)

Disconnect 8 Pin Connector at Buffer and measure voltage at Terminal (Cavity) "E" Is it 8.2V?

- Turn Ignition ON
- Check Terminal "H" of the 8 Pin Connector at the Buffer for voltage
- Is there 12V?

Yes   No

Find open in wire(s) from P.M. generator to Buffer and Repair as Required.

Replace P.M. Generator

Yes   No

Replace Buffer

Back probe connector Terminal "D" at Cruise Controller (Module) with 8 Pin Connector at Buffer still disconnected. Does Meter Read 8.2V?

Yes

- Disconnect the 8 Pin Connector to Buffer
- Use an ohmmeter and check continuity from Pin "A" of connector to known good ground

No

Find the blown fuse or open wire and Repair or Replace as Required

Yes   No

Find open in wire from Terminal "D" at Cruise Controller (Module) to Terminal "E" of Buffer. Repair as Required

Replace Cruise Controller (Module)

Continuity   Open

Replace Buffer

Find open in wire and Repair as Required.

On vehicles equipped with diesel engines do not Replace Buffer go to **A** at Top chart.

Cruise control diagnosis—1985 and later Cimarron

Permanent magnet generator (PM generator)

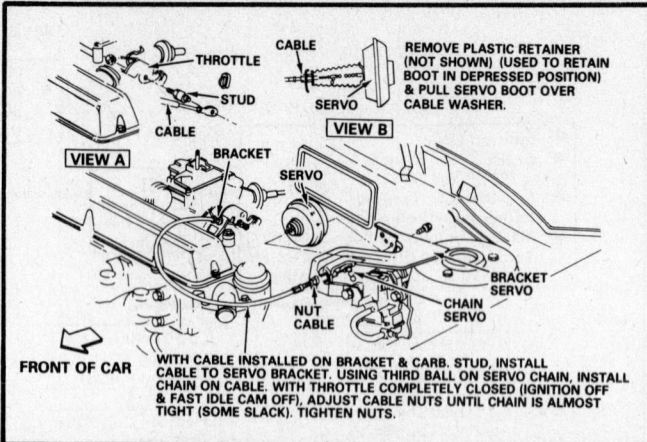

Servo assembly linkage adjustment—1982 Cimarron

SERVO ASSEMBLY LINKAGE ADJUSTMENT

For servo linkage adjustments refer to the proper illustration.

TRANSDUCER ORIFICE TUBE ADJUSTMENT (1982–83)

1. If cruise control speed is consistently above the set cruise control speed screw the orifice tube inward. If cruise control speed is below the set cruise control speed screw the orifice tube owtward.

2. Each one-third turn of the orifice tube changes the cruising speed about one mile per hour.

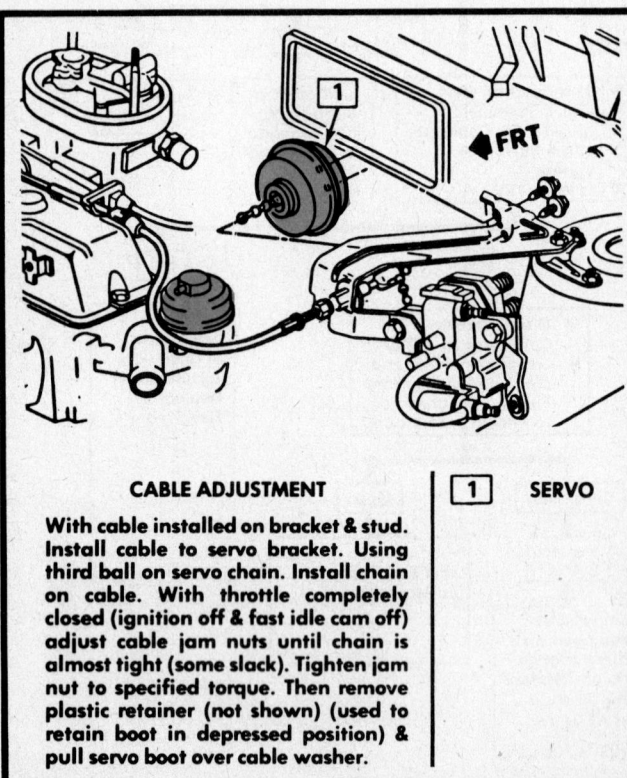

CABLE ADJUSTMENT

With cable installed on bracket & stud. Install cable to servo bracket. Using third ball on servo chain. Install chain on cable. With throttle completely closed (ignition off & fast idle cam off) adjust cable jam nuts until chain is almost tight (some slack). Tighten jam nut to specified torque. Then remove plastic retainer (not shown) (used to retain boot in depressed position) & pull servo boot over cable washer.

☐1 SERVO

Servo assembly linkage adjustment—1983 Cimarron

3. After making the adjustment, be sure to secure the locknut to the orifice tube.

4. Road test the vehicle and check the cruise control operation at 50 miles per hour. If the speed is still not adjusted properly repeat the procedure until the proper results are achieved.

5. If unable to achieve the proper test results the cruise control transducer should be serviced.

RELEASE SWITCH AND VALVE ADJUSTMENTS

For release switch and valve adjustments refer to the proper illustration.

Component Replacement

CRUISE CONTROL ENGAGEMENT SWITCH

Removal and Installation

1. Disconnect the negative battery cable. Remove the steering wheel.

2. Position the turn signal switch in the right turn position. If the vehicle is equipped with a tilt column be sure that the column is positioned in the full up detent.

3. Remove the screw securing the cruise control engagement switch to the steering column.

4. Disconnect the cruise control engagement switch electrical connection.

5. Slide the cruise control engagement switch wiring up through the steering column carefully. Remove the cruise control engagement switch from the vehicle.

6. Installation is the reverse of the removal procedure.

TRANSDUCER ASSEMBLY (1982–83)

Removal and Installation

1. Disconnect the negative battery cable.

2. Disconnect the vacuum hoses and the electrical connections from the transducer assembly.

3. Remove the speedometer cables from the assembly.

4. Remove the screws attaching the transducer to the mounting bracket.

5. Remove the transducer from the vehicle.

6. Installation is the reverse of the removal procedure.

VIEW A
VIEW B
FRONT
FRONT
FRONT
VIEW A
VIEW B

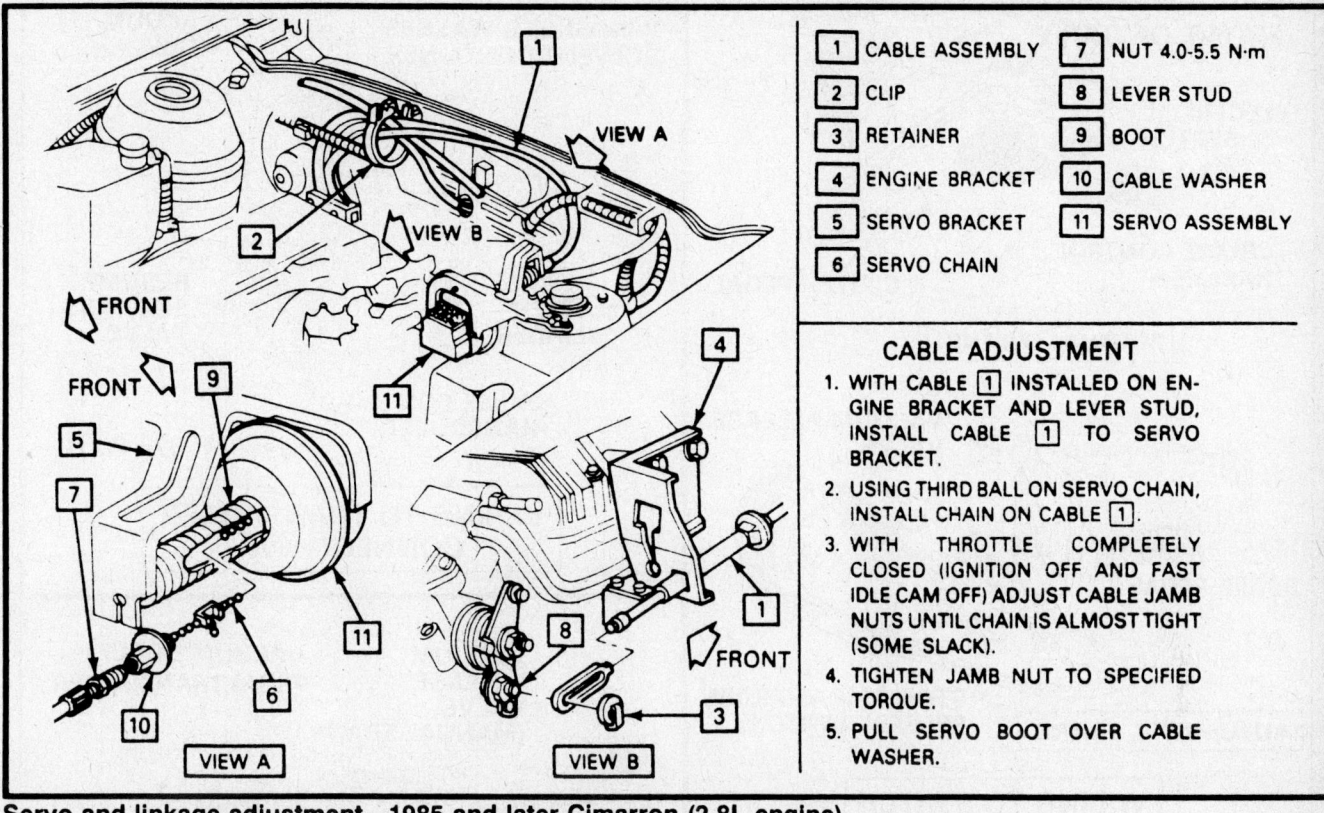

1 CABLE ASSEMBLY	7 NUT 4.0-5.5 N·m
2 CLIP	8 LEVER STUD
3 RETAINER	9 BOOT
4 ENGINE BRACKET	10 CABLE WASHER
5 SERVO BRACKET	11 SERVO ASSEMBLY
6 SERVO CHAIN	

CABLE ADJUSTMENT

1. WITH CABLE 1 INSTALLED ON ENGINE BRACKET AND LEVER STUD, INSTALL CABLE 1 TO SERVO BRACKET.
2. USING THIRD BALL ON SERVO CHAIN, INSTALL CHAIN ON CABLE 1.
3. WITH THROTTLE COMPLETELY CLOSED (IGNITION OFF AND FAST IDLE CAM OFF) ADJUST CABLE JAMB NUTS UNTIL CHAIN IS ALMOST TIGHT (SOME SLACK).
4. TIGHTEN JAMB NUT TO SPECIFIED TORQUE.
5. PULL SERVO BOOT OVER CABLE WASHER.

Servo and linkage adjustment – 1985 and later Cimarron (2.8L engine)

VIEW B
VIEW A
FRONT
NOTE: SNAP OVER STUD END IN DIRECTION OF ARROW.
FRONT
FRONT
VIEW A
VIEW B

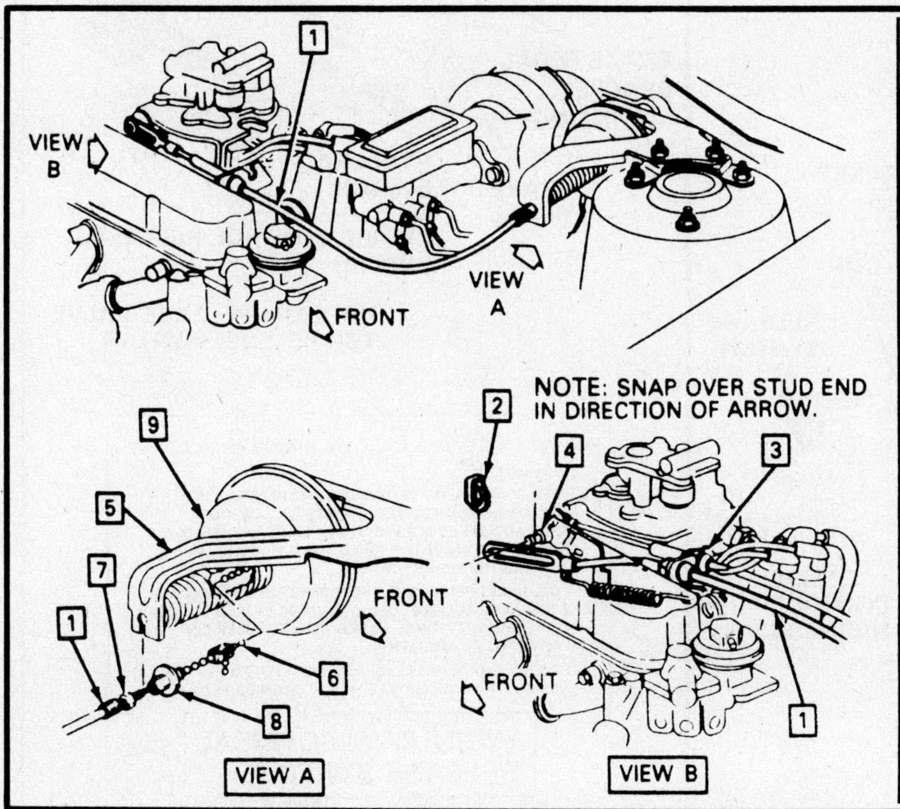

1. CABLE ASSEMBLY
2. RETAINER
3. BRACKET
4. LEVER STUD
5. SERVO BRACKET
6. SERVO CHAIN
7. JAMB NUT 4.0-5.5 N·m
8. CABLE WASHER
9. SERVO ASSEMBLY

CABLE ADJUSTMENT

1. WITH CABLE 1 INSTALLED ON ENGINE BRACKET AND LEVER STUD, INSTALL CABLE 1 TO SERVO BRACKET.
2. USING THIRD BALL ON SERVO CHAIN, INSTALL CHAIN ON CABLE 1.
3. WITH THROTTLE COMPLETELY CLOSED (IGNITION OFF AND FAST IDLE CAM OFF) ADJUST CABLE JAMB NUTS UNTIL CHAIN IS ALMOST TIGHT (SOME SLACK).
4. TIGHTEN JAMB NUT TO SPECIFIED TORQUE.
5. PULL SERVO BOOT OVER CABLE WASHER.

Servo and linkage asjustment – 1985 and later Cimarron (2.0L engine)

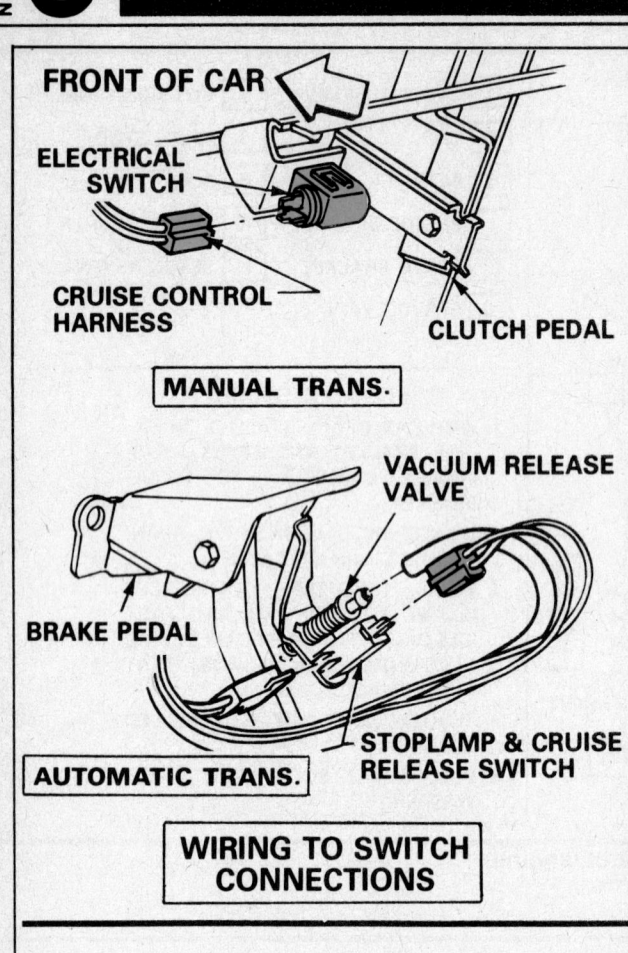

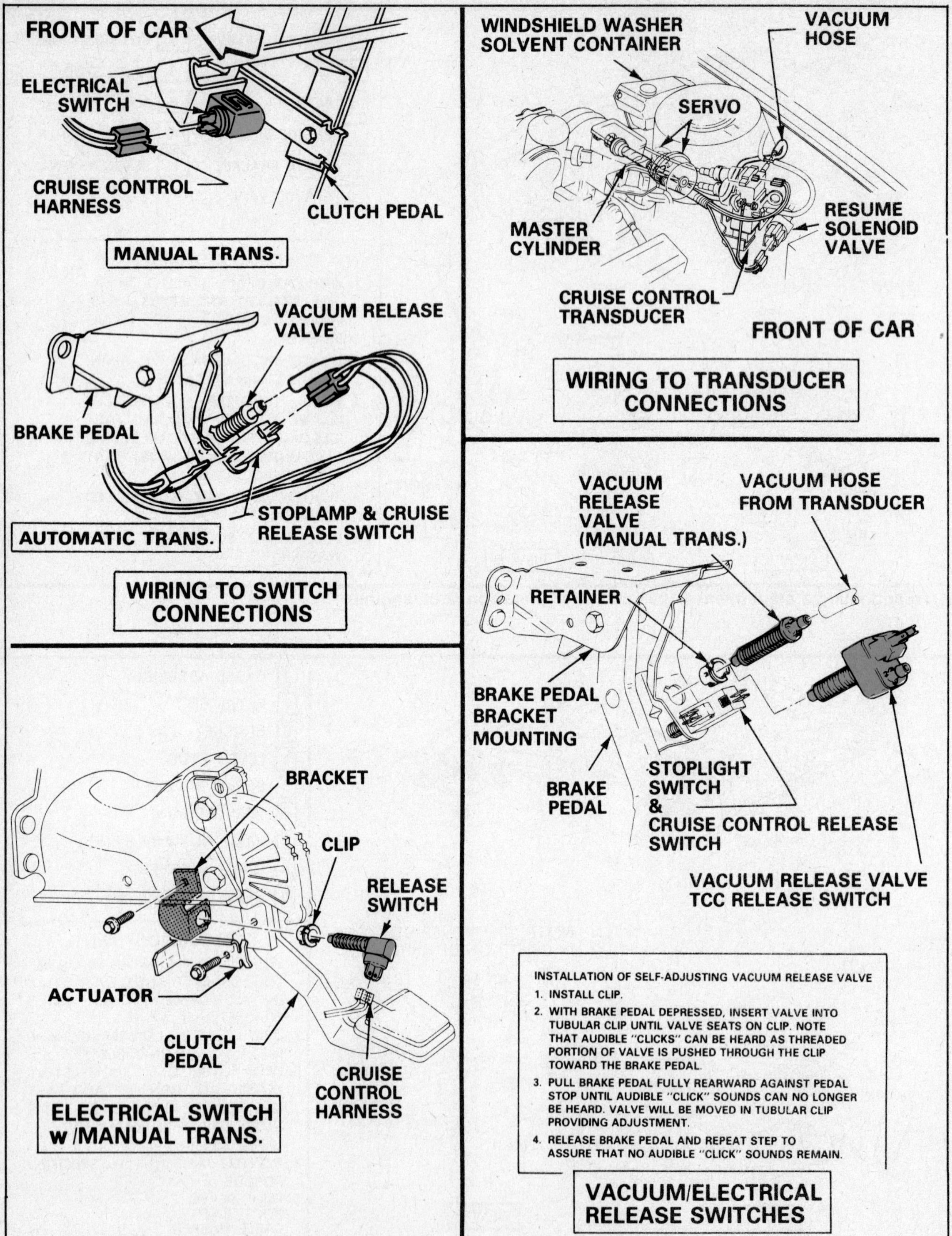

FRONT OF CAR

ELECTRICAL SWITCH

CRUISE CONTROL HARNESS

CLUTCH PEDAL

MANUAL TRANS.

VACUUM RELEASE VALVE

BRAKE PEDAL

STOPLAMP & CRUISE RELEASE SWITCH

AUTOMATIC TRANS.

WIRING TO SWITCH CONNECTIONS

WINDSHIELD WASHER SOLVENT CONTAINER

VACUUM HOSE

SERVO

MASTER CYLINDER

RESUME SOLENOID VALVE

CRUISE CONTROL TRANSDUCER

FRONT OF CAR

WIRING TO TRANSDUCER CONNECTIONS

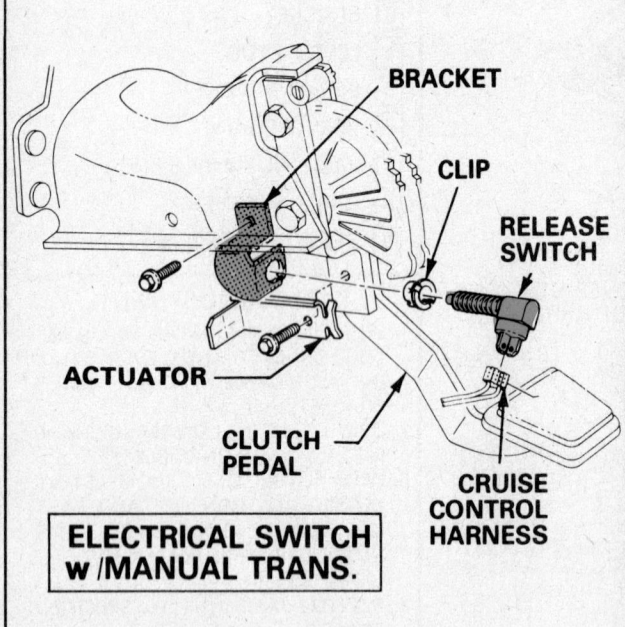

BRACKET

CLIP

RELEASE SWITCH

ACTUATOR

CLUTCH PEDAL

CRUISE CONTROL HARNESS

ELECTRICAL SWITCH w/MANUAL TRANS.

VACUUM RELEASE VALVE (MANUAL TRANS.)

VACUUM HOSE FROM TRANSDUCER

RETAINER

BRAKE PEDAL BRACKET MOUNTING

BRAKE PEDAL

STOPLIGHT SWITCH & CRUISE CONTROL RELEASE SWITCH

VACUUM RELEASE VALVE TCC RELEASE SWITCH

INSTALLATION OF SELF-ADJUSTING VACUUM RELEASE VALVE

1. INSTALL CLIP.
2. WITH BRAKE PEDAL DEPRESSED, INSERT VALVE INTO TUBULAR CLIP UNTIL VALVE SEATS ON CLIP. NOTE THAT AUDIBLE "CLICKS" CAN BE HEARD AS THREADED PORTION OF VALVE IS PUSHED THROUGH THE CLIP TOWARD THE BRAKE PEDAL.
3. PULL BRAKE PEDAL FULLY REARWARD AGAINST PEDAL STOP UNTIL AUDIBLE "CLICK" SOUNDS CAN NO LONGER BE HEARD. VALVE WILL BE MOVED IN TUBULAR CLIP PROVIDING ADJUSTMENT.
4. RELEASE BRAKE PEDAL AND REPEAT STEP TO ASSURE THAT NO AUDIBLE "CLICK" SOUNDS REMAIN.

VACUUM/ELECTRICAL RELEASE SWITCHES

Cruise control release switches—1982–83 Cimarron

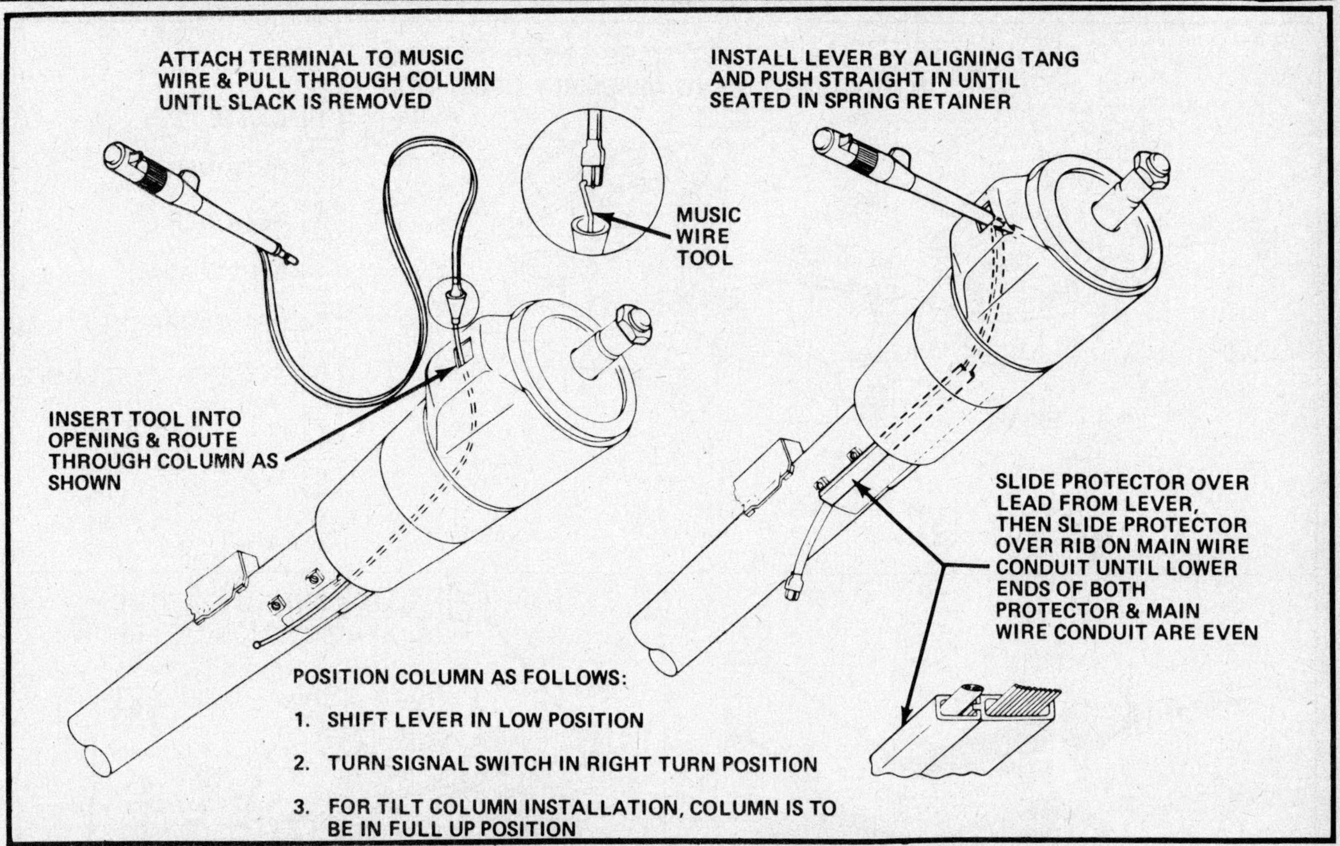

ATTACH TERMINAL TO MUSIC
WIRE & PULL THROUGH COLUMN
UNTIL SLACK IS REMOVED

INSTALL LEVER BY ALIGNING TANG
AND PUSH STRAIGHT IN UNTIL
SEATED IN SPRING RETAINER

MUSIC
WIRE
TOOL

INSERT TOOL INTO
OPENING & ROUTE
THROUGH COLUMN AS
SHOWN

SLIDE PROTECTOR OVER
LEAD FROM LEVER,
THEN SLIDE PROTECTOR
OVER RIB ON MAIN WIRE
CONDUIT UNTIL LOWER
ENDS OF BOTH
PROTECTOR & MAIN
WIRE CONDUIT ARE EVEN

POSITION COLUMN AS FOLLOWS:

1. SHIFT LEVER IN LOW POSITION

2. TURN SIGNAL SWITCH IN RIGHT TURN POSITION

3. FOR TILT COLUMN INSTALLATION, COLUMN IS TO
BE IN FULL UP POSITION

Cruise control engagement switch installation procedure

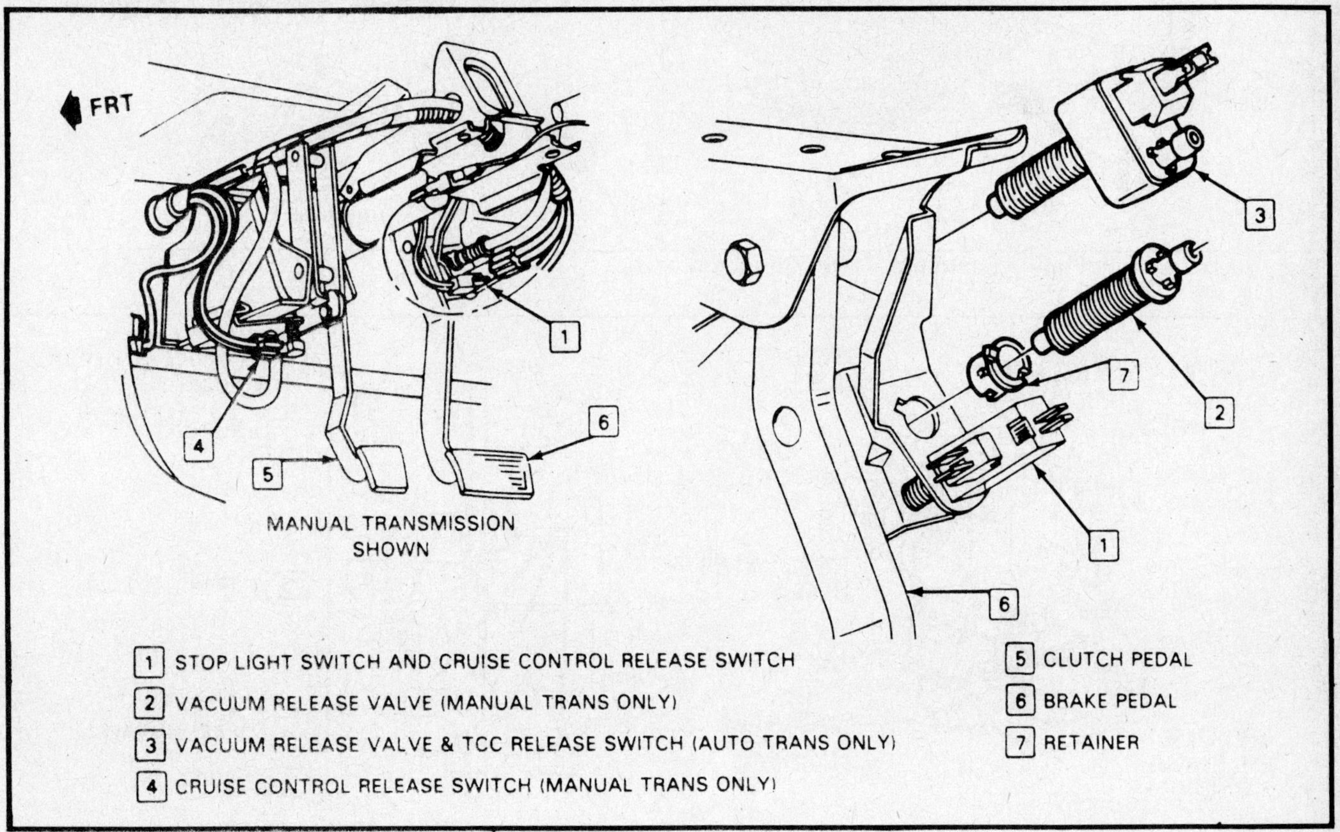

FRT

MANUAL TRANSMISSION
SHOWN

1 STOP LIGHT SWITCH AND CRUISE CONTROL RELEASE SWITCH

2 VACUUM RELEASE VALVE (MANUAL TRANS ONLY)

3 VACUUM RELEASE VALVE & TCC RELEASE SWITCH (AUTO TRANS ONLY)

4 CRUISE CONTROL RELEASE SWITCH (MANUAL TRANS ONLY)

5 CLUTCH PEDAL

6 BRAKE PEDAL

7 RETAINER

Cruise control release switches – 1984 and later Cimarron

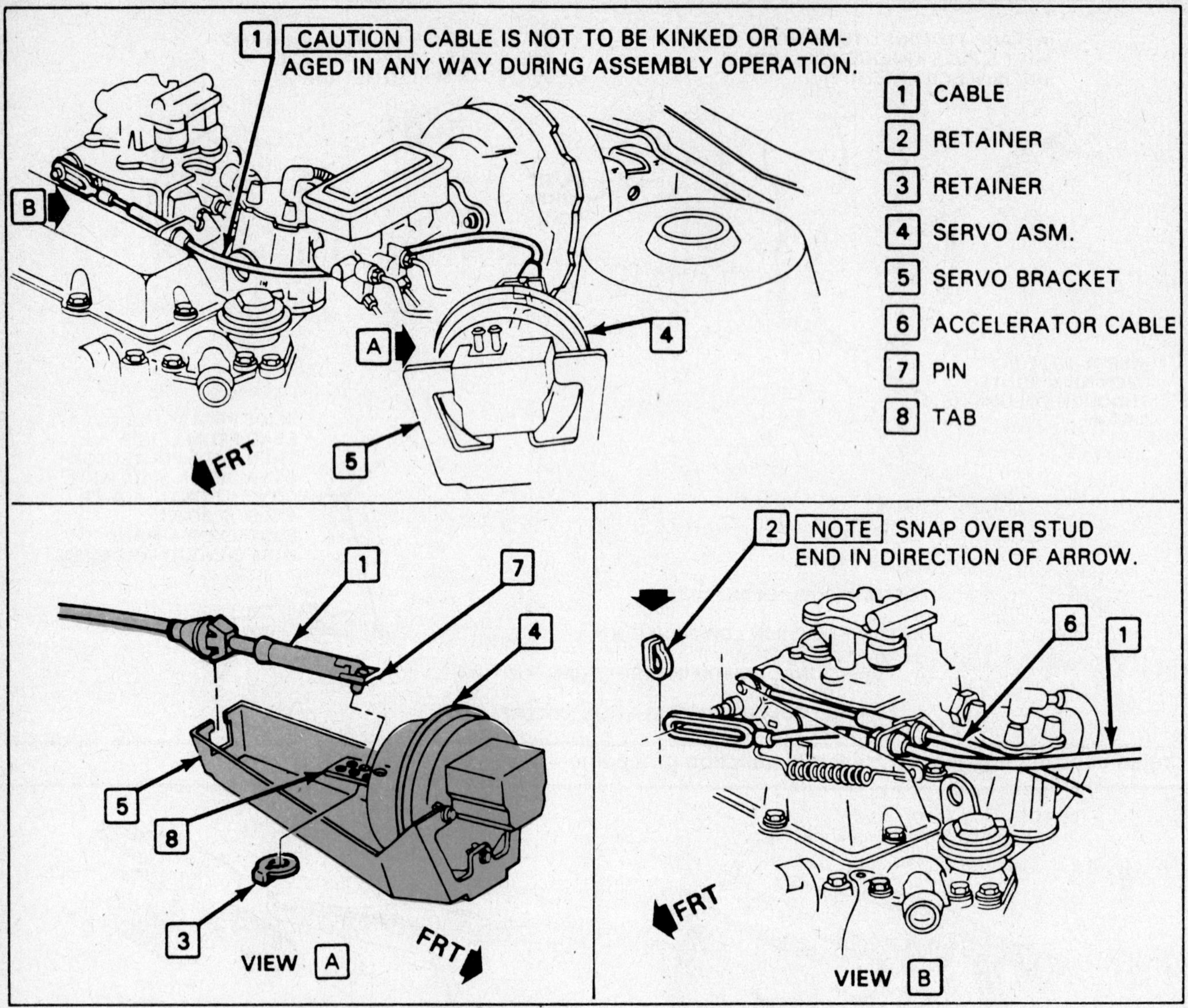

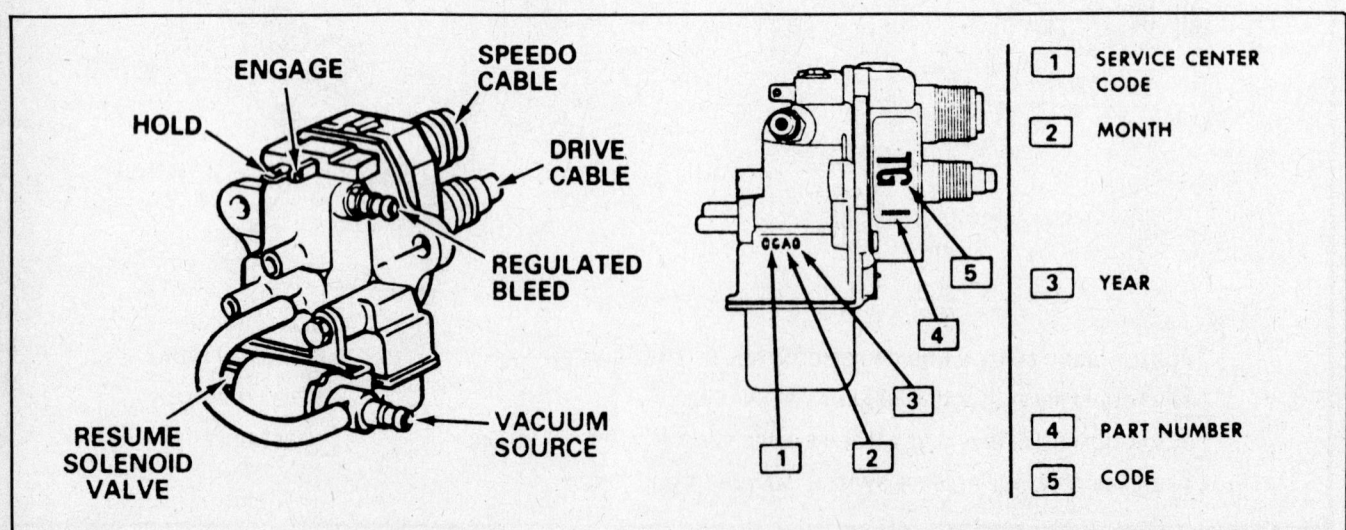

1 CAUTION CABLE IS NOT TO BE KINKED OR DAMAGED IN ANY WAY DURING ASSEMBLY OPERATION.

1	CABLE
2	RETAINER
3	RETAINER
4	SERVO ASM.
5	SERVO BRACKET
6	ACCELERATOR CABLE
7	PIN
8	TAB

FRT

VIEW **A**

FRT

2 NOTE SNAP OVER STUD END IN DIRECTION OF ARROW.

FRT

VIEW **B**

Servo assembly linkage adjustment—1984 Cimarron

ENGAGE

SPEEDO CABLE

HOLD

DRIVE CABLE

REGULATED BLEED

VACUUM SOURCE

RESUME SOLENOID VALVE

1	SERVICE CENTER CODE
2	MONTH
3	YEAR
4	PART NUMBER
5	CODE

Transducer assembly—1982–83 Cimarron

SERVO ASSEMBLY

Removal and Installation

1. Disconnect the negative battery cable.
2. Disconnect all electrical and vacuum connections from the servo assembly.
3. Disconnect the servo assembly cable or chain.
4. Remove the servo mounting bolts. Remove the servo assembly from the vehicle.
5. Installation is the reverse of the removal procedure.

ELECTRONIC CRUISE CONTROL CONTROL MODULE

Removal and Installation

1. Disconnect the negative battery cable.
2. Remove the lower steering column filler panel.
3. Disconnect the electrical connectors from the control module.
4. Remove the control module mounting screws. Remove the control module from the vehicle.
6. Installation is the reverse of the removal procedure.

SPEED SENSORS

VSS Buffer Amplifier

1984 AND LATER

The VSS buffer amplifier is a device that supplies vehicle speed input to the electronic controller. It is used on vehicles that are equipped with the standard instrument panel. The optic head portion of the assembly is located in the speedometer head frame. A reflective blade is attached to the speedometer head/cable assembly. The blade spins like a propeller with its blades passing through a light beam from a L.E.D. refractor in the optic head. As each blade enters the light beam, light is reflected back to a photocell that is located in the optic head. This in turn causes a power signal to be sent to a buffer for amplification and signal conditioning. This signal is then sent to the controller for processing and calculation of vehicle speed.

P.M. Generator Speed Signal

1985 AND LATER

The P.M. generator speed signal is a device that supplies vehicle speed input to the electronic controller. It is used on vehicles equipped with the electronic instrument cluster. Vehicle speed information is provided to the electronic controller by a permanent magnet generator driven by the vehicle transmission. The output frequency of the permanent magnet generator is than routed to a buffer, which in turn will amplify and condition the signal to the electronic controller.

ELECTRIC BRAKE RELEASE SWITCH AND VACUUM RELEASE VALVE

Removal and installation

1. Disconnect the negative battery cable.
2. Remove the switch electrical and vacuum connectors.
3. Remove the switch from its mounting above the brake pedal.
4. Installation is the reverse of the removal procedure.

Adjustment

1. The switch assembly and the valve assembly cannot be adjusted until after the brake booster push rod is assembled to the brake pedal assembly.

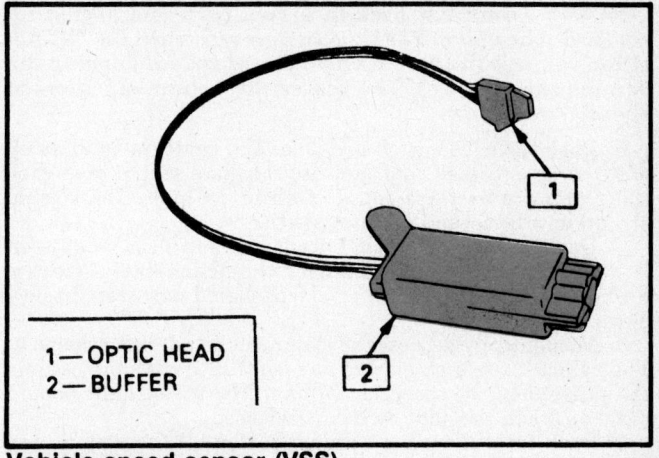

1—OPTIC HEAD
2—BUFFER

Vehicle speed sensor (VSS)

2. To adjust the switch depress the brake pedal and insert the switch assembly and valve assembly into their proper retaining clips until fully seated.
3. Pull the pedal back to its fully retracted position. The switch assembly and the valve assembly will move within the retainers of their adjusted position.
4. The switch assembly contacts must open at 3.5mm to 12.5mm of brake pedal travel. Nominal actuation of the brake light switch is 4.5mm.
5. The vacuum release valve assembly must open at 27.0mm to 33.0nn of brake pedal travel.

Cadillac—1982–85 RWD Deville, 1982 and later RWD Fleetwood, 1982–85 Eldorado and Seville

VISUAL INSPECTION

Before performing any tests make a visual inspection of the cruise control system. Check all items in the system for abnormal conditions such as bare broken or disconnected wires and damage to the vacuum hoses. Be sure that the speedometer cables are attached and properly routed. All vacuum hoses must be properly routed and must not have any kinks or bends. Be sure that all electrical connections are complete and tight. The wiring harness must be routed properly.

ROAD TEST (EXCEPT D.F.I.)

1. Place the dash switch in the off position. Drive the car until the speedometer reads 50 mph. Push the engagement switch button on the turn signal switch and release. The cruise control system should remain off.
2. Place the dash switch in on-auto position. The amber light should come on.
3. Engage the cruise control system by momentarily pushing the turn signal engagement switch button and than releasing it at 50 mph while removing your foot from the accelerator pedal.
4. The green light should come on when the button is released and the system is engaged. The vehicle should maintain the speed of 50 mph.
5. Note the amount, if any, by which the vehicle speed varies from the 50 mph speed when engaged in the cruise mode. This is called lock-in error and can be corrected as required.

NOTE: To adjust lock-in error, turn the adjusting screw on the valve. Turning the screw toward the "S" position reduces the actual engagement speed. Turning the screw toward the "F" increases the actual engagement speed.

6. Push the slide switch and hold. The vehicle should accelerate at a controlled rate. Release the slide switch to engage the system to a cruise speed of about 55 mph. The system should now be set to the new speed.

7. Depress the brake pedal about one-half inch. The green light should go out, this confirms the action of the electric brake release switch and the vehicle should now start to slow down.

8. Momentarily depress the slide switch and than release it. The vehicle should accelerate at a controlled rate and resume the previously set speed of 55 mph. The green light should come on when the slide switch is released.

9. Push the engagement switch button all the way in and hold. The green light should go out. Coast to about 50 mph.

10. Release the button in order to engage the system at 50 mph. The green light should come on and the vehicle should maintain that speed.

ELECTRIC BRAKE RELEASE SWITCH TEST (EXCEPT D.F.I.)

Switch Installed On Vehicle

1. Turn the ignition switch to the on position. Turn the cruise control dash panel switch to the on-auto position.

2. Connect a test light, using the probe of the tool touch the pink/black wire at the brake switch the lamp should light indicating proper feed.

3. Check the switch adjustment with the probe still attached to the pink/black wire. Depress the brake pedal, the light should go out.

4. If the test light did not light at all, position the probe of the tool in the adjacent connector cavity. If the test light works, adjust or replace the switch as required.

5. If the light does not work, the wiring to the switch is defective, repair or replace the wiring as required.

Switch Removed From Vehicle

1. Connect a test light. With the switch plunger extended the test light should be off.

2. With the switch plunger fully depressed the test light should be on.

3. Repair or replace the switch as required.

INSTRUMENT PANEL SWITCH TEST (EXCEPT D.F.I.)

On Vehicle Check

1. Position the ignition switch in the on position. Connect a testlight.

2. Disconnect the three wire connector of the turn signal lever engagement switch harness from the cruise control harness connector.

3. Using the test light, probe the three terminals of the cruise harness connector. First with the instrument panel switch in the off position, then in the on-auto position.

4. In the off position there should be no power to any of the three terminals. In the on-auto position, cavity "B" (pink/black) wire should light the test light. The other two cavities, "A" and "C" (yellow and red) wire should not light.

5. In the on-auto switch position the amber indicator light should come on.

Amber (ON) Light Check

1. Position the ignition switch in the on position. Position the instrument panel switch in the on-auto position.

2. If the amber lamp is not illuminated, check for a burned out bulb, check for open ground, inoperative switch, blown fuse or printed circuit.

3. Position the instrument panel switch in the off position. If the amber lamp is illuminated check for shorted leads or a bad switch.

Green (CRUISE) light Check

1. If the roadtest shows that the green light is not illuminated, Check for a burned out bulb, or a short in the wiring between the switch connector and the controller connector (pink wire in cavity B).

2. With the instrument panel switch in the on-auto position and the ignition switch in the on position, ground cavity "B" in the controller connector. The green lamp should light. If it does light but did not light during the roadtest replace the controller.

3. The amber light should be on to confirm power supply.

ENGAGEMENT SWITCH AND HARNESS

The engagement switch lever can be checked after disconnecting it from the harness and performing the following tests.

With one lead of an ohmmeter connected to the steering column mounting bracket check each terminal of the wiring harness. If any indicate continuity, a short exists and the defective component must be replaced. Move the shift lever through the full range when checking each wire.

ENGAGE SWITCH ON OR OFF CAR TEST			
	INDICATION BETWEEN TERMINALS		
ENGAGE SWITCH	1 TO 2 (YELLOW-GREEN)	1 TO 3 (YELLOW-RED)	2 TO 3 (GREEN-RED)
RELEASED	OPEN	OPEN	OPEN
SLIDE DEPRESSED	CLOSED	OPEN	OPEN
PUSHBUTTON DEPRESSED	OPEN	OPEN	CLOSED

Cruise control engagement switch test

VACUUM CONTROL AND SERVO UNIT SOLENOID VALVES TEST (EXCEPT D.F.I.)

Resistance Test

1. Disconnect the electrical connector at the solenoid valve that is being tested.

2. Connect an ohmmeter to the solenoid valve terminals.

3. Measure the resistance. It should be between 35 and 48 ohms on the servo unit valve and between 23.5 and 27.5 ohms on the vacuum control valve.

4. Repair or replace defective components as required.

Functional Test

1. Disconnect the electrical connector at the solenoid valve that is being tested.

2. Connect a jumper wire from the positive terminal of the battery to one terminal of the valve being tested.

3. Connect another jumper wire to ground.

4. Brush the other end of the grounded jumper wire across the remaining terminal of the valve.

5. Listen for the valve to open and close as you break contact with the terminal. The valves will click twice indicating that each respective valve is functioning properly.

CRUISE CONTROL MODULE (EXCEPT D.F.I.)

No attempt should be made to repair the electronic cruise control module. Check to be sure that the connectors are fully seated. If all other components have been checked and found not to be defective then replace the controller.

Module Current Leakage Test

1. Disconnect the electrical connector at the servo solenoid valve. Position the instrument panel switch to the on-auto position.

2. With the vehicle running at idle, check DC voltage between the connector terminals. It must be less than 1.0 volt.

3. Momentarily increase the idle speed. The voltmeter must indicate less than 1.0 volt DC current.

4. Any indication above 1.0 volt DC current, replace the module.

VACUUM SYSTEM TEST (EXCEPT D.F.I.)

1. Before starting the engine disconnect the bead chain, cable or actuating rod at the servo assembly.

2. Disconnect the electrical connectors at the vacuum control and servo unit solenoid valves.

3. Connect both the vacuum control and the servo unit valves with jumper cables. This is done by connecting jumper wires from the positive terminal of the battery to one terminal on each valve and grounding the remaining terminal on each valve with another set of jumper wires.

4. Start the engine. With the brake pedal in the free position, the diaphragm should pull in to full stroke.

5. Depress the brake pedal down about one inch, the diaphragm should relax to its free position.

6. If the system will not hold vacuum, remove the brake release vent valve hose at the servo unit and plug the servo unit hole.

7. If the servo unit draws down then the problem exists in the brake release vacuum vent system. Inspect the vacuum release hose for leaks, secure connections to the valve and proper adjustment. Correct defects as required.

8. If the servo unit will not draw down, inspect the diaphragm and connectors at the valves for leaks.

SERVO ASSEMBLY LINKAGE ADJUSTMENT

For servo linkage adjustments refer to the proper illustration.

Component Replacement

SERVO ASSEMBLY

Removal and Installation

1. Disconnect the negative battery cable.

2. Disconnect the servo assembly vacuum hoses and electrical connections.

3. Disconnect the throttle actuating chain, cable or rod from the servo assembly.

4. Remove the screws securing the servo assembly and solenoid valve, if equipped, to the mounting bracket. Remove the servo assembly from the vehicle.

DIAGNOSTIC CODES	
CODE	**CIRCUIT AFFECTED**
■■ 12	NO DISTRIBUTOR (TACH) SIGNAL
□ 13	O₂ SENSOR NOT READY
□ 14	SHORTED COOLANT SENSOR CIRCUIT
□ 15	OPEN COOLANT SENSOR CIRCUIT
■■ 16	GENERATOR VOLTAGE OUT OF RANGE
□ 18	OPEN CRANK SIGNAL CIRCUIT
□ 19	SHORTED FUEL PUMP CIRCUIT
■■ 20	OPEN FUEL PUMP CIRCUIT
□ 21	SHORTED THROTTLE POSITION SENSOR CIRCUIT
□ 22	OPEN THROTTLE POSITION SENSOR CIRCUIT
□ 23	EST/BYPASS CIRCUIT PROBLEM
□ 24	SPEED SENSOR CIRCUIT PROBLEM
□ 26	SHORTED THROTTLE SWITCH CIRCUIT
□ 27	OPEN THROTTLE SWITCH CIRCUIT
□ 28	OPEN FOURTH GEAR CIRCUIT
□ 29	SHORTED FOURTH GEAR CIRCUIT
□ 30	ISC CIRCUIT PROBLEM
■■ 31	SHORTED MAP SENSOR CIRCUIT
■■ 32	OPEN MAP SENSOR CIRCUIT
■■ 33	MAP/BARO SENSOR CORRELATION
■■ 34	MAP SIGNAL TOO HIGH
□ 35	SHORTED BARO SENSOR CIRCUIT
□ 36	OPEN BARO SENSOR CIRCUIT
□ 37	SHORTED MAT SENSOR CIRCUIT
□ 38	OPEN MAT SENSOR CIRCUIT
□ 39	TCC ENGAGEMENT PROBLEM
■■ 44	LEAN EXHAUST SIGNAL
■■ 45	RICH EXHAUST SIGNAL
■■ 51	PROM ERROR INDICATOR
▼ 52	ECM MEMORY RESET INDICATOR
▼ 53	DISTRIBUTOR SIGNAL INTERRUPT
▼ 60	TRANSMISSION NOT IN DRIVE
▼ 63	CAR AND SET SPEED TOLERANCE EXCEEDED
▼ 64	CAR ACCELERATION EXCEEDS MAX. LIMIT
▼ 65	COOLANT TEMPERATURE EXCEEDS MAX. LIMIT
▼ 66	ENGINE RPM EXCEEDS MAXIMUM LIMIT
▼ 67	SHORTED SET OR RESUME CIRCUIT
.7.0	SYSTEM READY FOR FURTHER TESTS
.7.1	CRUISE CONTROL BRAKE CIRCUIT TEST
.7.2	THROTTLE SWITCH CIRCUIT TEST
.7.3	DRIVE (ADL) CIRCUIT TEST
.7.4	REVERSE CIRCUIT TEST
.7.5	CRUISE ON/OFF CIRCUIT TEST
.7.6	"SET/COAST" CIRCUIT TEST
.7.7	"RESUME/ACCELERATION" CIRCUIT TEST
.7.8	"INSTANT/AVERAGE" CIRCUIT TEST
.7.9	"RESET" CIRCUIT TEST
.8.0	A/C CLUTCH CIRCUIT TEST
-1.8.8	DISPLAY CHECK
.9.0	SYSTEM READY TO DISPLAY ENGINE DATA
.9.5	SYSTEM READY FOR OUTPUT CYCLING OR IN FIXED SPARK MODE
.9.6	OUTPUT CYCLING
.0.0	ALL DIANOSTICS COMPLETE
■■	TURNS ON "SERVICE NOW" LIGHT
□	TURNS ON "SERVICE SOON" LIGHT
▼	DOES NOT TURN ON ANY TELLTALE LIGHT

NOTE: CRUISE IS DISENGAGED WITH ANY "SERVICE NOW" LIGHT OR WITH CODES 60-67.

Cruise control diagnosis vehicles equipped with DFI — 1982–85 RWD Deville 1982 and later RWD Fleetwood and 1982–85 Eldorado and Seville

DIAGNOSIS AND TESTING PROCEDURES

NO CRUISE CONTROL

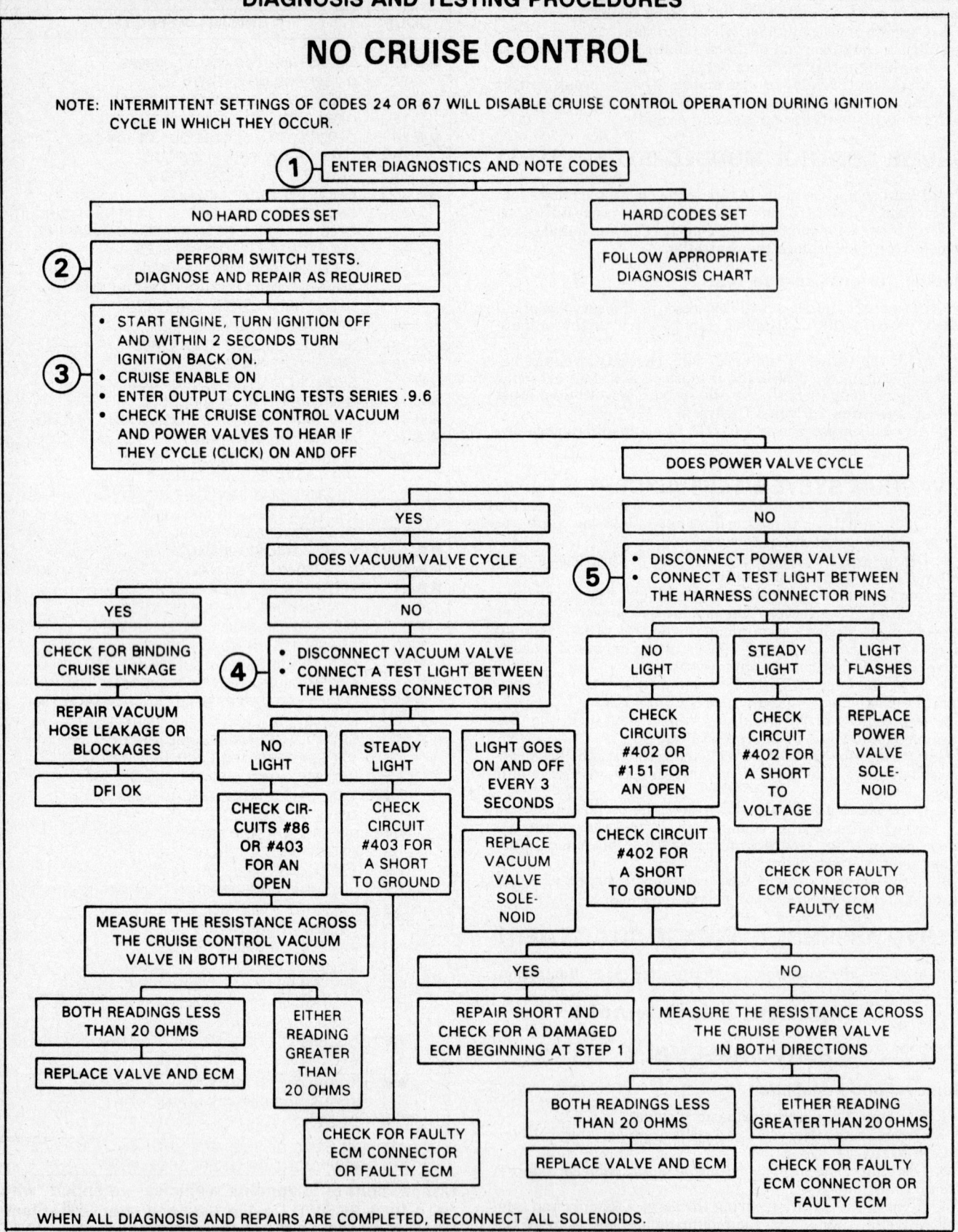

NOTE: INTERMITTENT SETTINGS OF CODES 24 OR 67 WILL DISABLE CRUISE CONTROL OPERATION DURING IGNITION CYCLE IN WHICH THEY OCCUR.

Cruise control diagnosis vehicles equipped with DFI — 1982–85 RWD Deville 1982 and later RWD Fleetwood and 1982–85 Eldorado and Seville

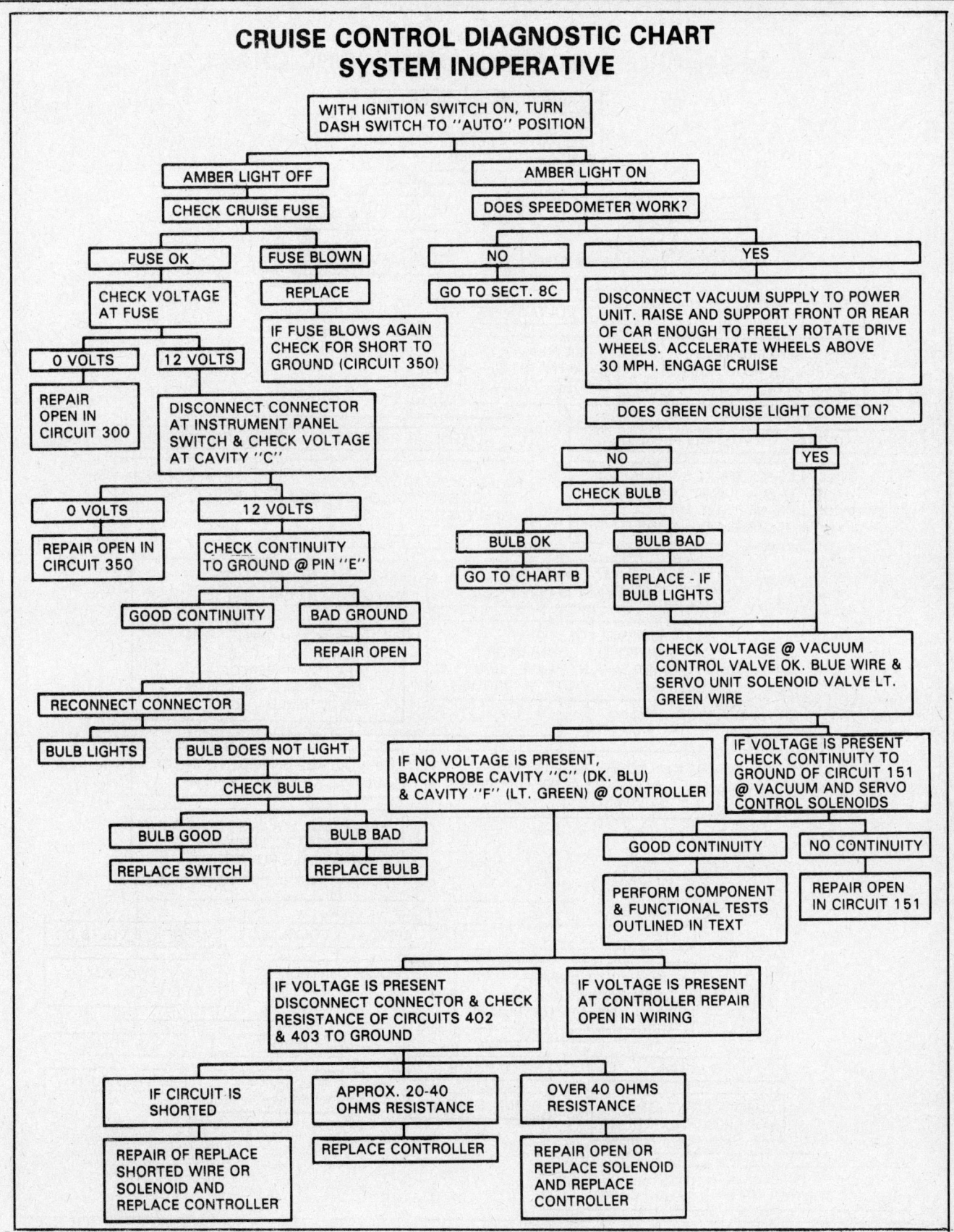

CRUISE CONTROL DIAGNOSTIC CHART
SYSTEM INOPERATIVE

WITH IGNITION SWITCH ON, TURN DASH SWITCH TO "AUTO" POSITION

AMBER LIGHT OFF
CHECK CRUISE FUSE

FUSE OK
CHECK VOLTAGE AT FUSE

FUSE BLOWN
REPLACE
IF FUSE BLOWS AGAIN CHECK FOR SHORT TO GROUND (CIRCUIT 350)

0 VOLTS
REPAIR OPEN IN CIRCUIT 300

12 VOLTS
DISCONNECT CONNECTOR AT INSTRUMENT PANEL SWITCH & CHECK VOLTAGE AT CAVITY "C"

0 VOLTS
REPAIR OPEN IN CIRCUIT 350

12 VOLTS
CHECK CONTINUITY TO GROUND @ PIN "E"

GOOD CONTINUITY

BAD GROUND
REPAIR OPEN

RECONNECT CONNECTOR

BULB LIGHTS

BULB DOES NOT LIGHT
CHECK BULB

BULB GOOD
REPLACE SWITCH

BULB BAD
REPLACE BULB

AMBER LIGHT ON
DOES SPEEDOMETER WORK?

NO
GO TO SECT. 8C

YES
DISCONNECT VACUUM SUPPLY TO POWER UNIT. RAISE AND SUPPORT FRONT OR REAR OF CAR ENOUGH TO FREELY ROTATE DRIVE WHEELS. ACCELERATE WHEELS ABOVE 30 MPH. ENGAGE CRUISE

DOES GREEN CRUISE LIGHT COME ON?

NO
CHECK BULB

YES

BULB OK
GO TO CHART B

BULB BAD
REPLACE - IF BULB LIGHTS

CHECK VOLTAGE @ VACUUM CONTROL VALVE OK. BLUE WIRE & SERVO UNIT SOLENOID VALVE LT. GREEN WIRE

IF NO VOLTAGE IS PRESENT, BACKPROBE CAVITY "C" (DK. BLU) & CAVITY "F" (LT. GREEN) @ CONTROLLER

IF VOLTAGE IS PRESENT CHECK CONTINUITY TO GROUND OF CIRCUIT 151 @ VACUUM AND SERVO CONTROL SOLENOIDS

GOOD CONTINUITY
PERFORM COMPONENT & FUNCTIONAL TESTS OUTLINED IN TEXT

NO CONTINUITY
REPAIR OPEN IN CIRCUIT 151

IF VOLTAGE IS PRESENT DISCONNECT CONNECTOR & CHECK RESISTANCE OF CIRCUITS 402 & 403 TO GROUND

IF VOLTAGE IS PRESENT AT CONTROLLER REPAIR OPEN IN WIRING

IF CIRCUIT IS SHORTED
REPAIR OF REPLACE SHORTED WIRE OR SOLENOID AND REPLACE CONTROLLER

APPROX. 20-40 OHMS RESISTANCE
REPLACE CONTROLLER

OVER 40 OHMS RESISTANCE
REPAIR OPEN OR REPLACE SOLENOID AND REPLACE CONTROLLER

Cruise control diagnosis vehicles equipped with DFI — 1982–85 RWD Deville 1982 and later RWD Fleetwood and 1982–85 Eldorado and Seville

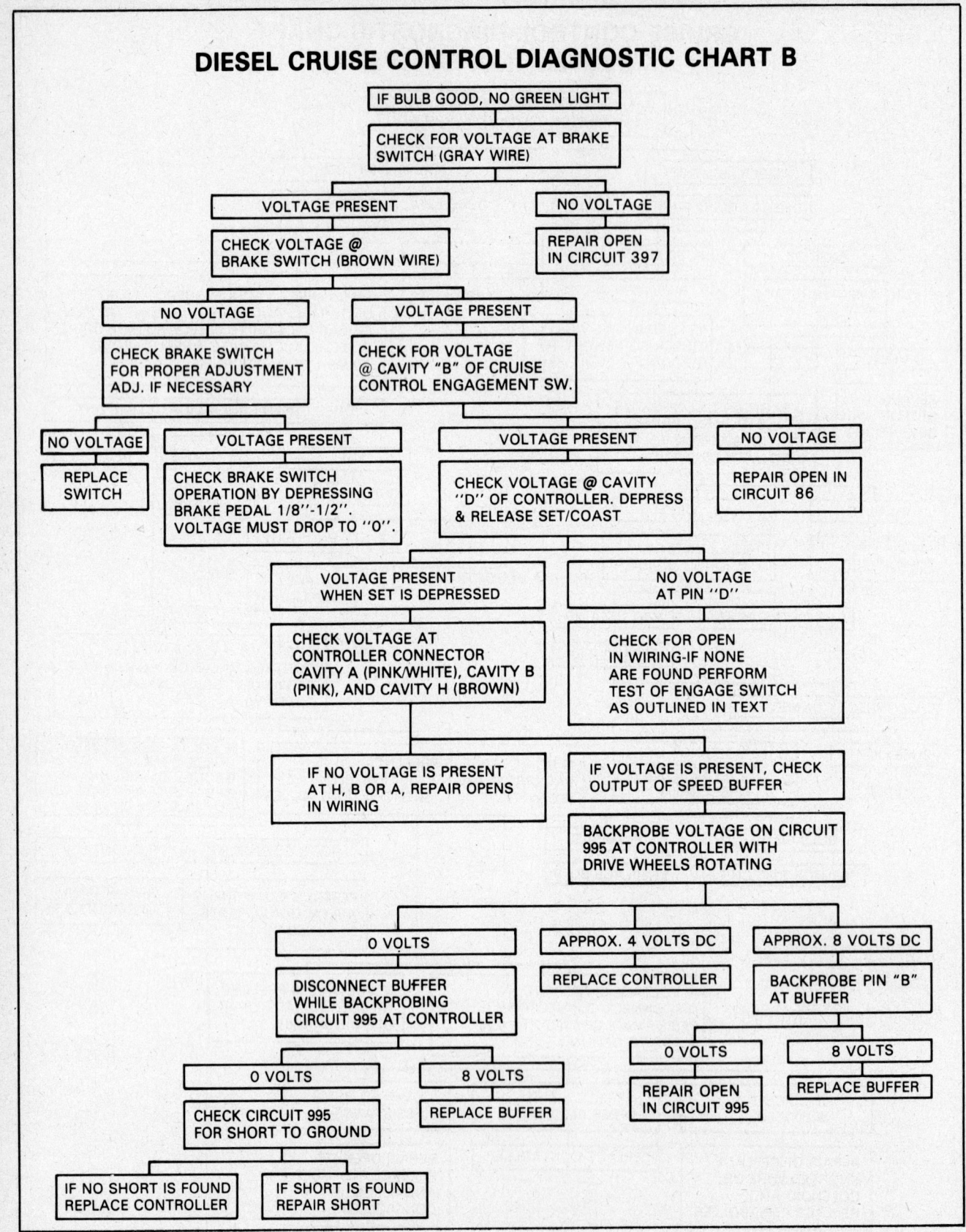

DIESEL CRUISE CONTROL DIAGNOSTIC CHART B

IF BULB GOOD, NO GREEN LIGHT

CHECK FOR VOLTAGE AT BRAKE SWITCH (GRAY WIRE)

VOLTAGE PRESENT

NO VOLTAGE

CHECK VOLTAGE @ BRAKE SWITCH (BROWN WIRE)

REPAIR OPEN IN CIRCUIT 397

NO VOLTAGE

VOLTAGE PRESENT

CHECK BRAKE SWITCH FOR PROPER ADJUSTMENT ADJ. IF NECESSARY

CHECK FOR VOLTAGE @ CAVITY "B" OF CRUISE CONTROL ENGAGEMENT SW.

NO VOLTAGE

VOLTAGE PRESENT

VOLTAGE PRESENT

NO VOLTAGE

REPLACE SWITCH

CHECK BRAKE SWITCH OPERATION BY DEPRESSING BRAKE PEDAL 1/8"-1/2". VOLTAGE MUST DROP TO "0".

CHECK VOLTAGE @ CAVITY "D" OF CONTROLLER. DEPRESS & RELEASE SET/COAST

REPAIR OPEN IN CIRCUIT 86

VOLTAGE PRESENT WHEN SET IS DEPRESSED

NO VOLTAGE AT PIN "D"

CHECK VOLTAGE AT CONTROLLER CONNECTOR CAVITY A (PINK/WHITE), CAVITY B (PINK), AND CAVITY H (BROWN)

CHECK FOR OPEN IN WIRING-IF NONE ARE FOUND PERFORM TEST OF ENGAGE SWITCH AS OUTLINED IN TEXT

IF NO VOLTAGE IS PRESENT AT H, B OR A, REPAIR OPENS IN WIRING

IF VOLTAGE IS PRESENT, CHECK OUTPUT OF SPEED BUFFER

BACKPROBE VOLTAGE ON CIRCUIT 995 AT CONTROLLER WITH DRIVE WHEELS ROTATING

0 VOLTS

APPROX. 4 VOLTS DC

APPROX. 8 VOLTS DC

DISCONNECT BUFFER WHILE BACKPROBING CIRCUIT 995 AT CONTROLLER

REPLACE CONTROLLER

BACKPROBE PIN "B" AT BUFFER

0 VOLTS

8 VOLTS

0 VOLTS

8 VOLTS

CHECK CIRCUIT 995 FOR SHORT TO GROUND

REPLACE BUFFER

REPAIR OPEN IN CIRCUIT 995

REPLACE BUFFER

IF NO SHORT IS FOUND REPLACE CONTROLLER

IF SHORT IS FOUND REPAIR SHORT

Cruise control diagnosis — 1982–85 RWD Deville 1982 and later RWD Fleetwood and 1982–85 Eldorado and Seville

CONDITION	CAUSE	CORRECTION
POWER UNIT DIAPHRAGM RETRACTS MAXIMUM ALLOWABLE OPEN THROTTLE POSITION. A. POSITION OF DASH SWITCH HAS NO EFFECT. VEHICLE RETURNS TO IDLE WITH BRAKE APPLICATION, MAY DUPLICATE WHEN PEDAL IS RELEASED. B. CONDITION OCCURS ONLY WHEN DASH SWITCH IS IN AUTO POSITION. CONDITION WILL CANCEL WHEN PANEL SWITCH IS TURNED OFF.	POWER UNIT SOLENOID VALVE LEAKING VACUUM.	REPLACE VALVE.
	MANIFOLD VACUUM CONNECTED DIRECTLY TO POWER UNIT VACUUM VENT PORT. NO IPSW OR BRAKE APPLY WILL CORRECT THIS.	REROUTE HOSE.
	UNREQUESTED VOLTAGE ON SOLENOID FEED.	DEFECTIVE CONTROLLER — REPLACE.
ERRATIC ENGAGEMENT AND/OR UNWANTED PROGRAM ACCELERATION. NOT TRUE WITH N.O. T/S SWITCH		
WILL NOT CRUISE AT ENGAGED SPEED.	LEAK IN POWER UNIT.	REPLACE. REFER TO VACUUM SYSTEM INSPECTION.
	LEAK IN VACUUM RELEASE VALVE OR HOSE.	REPLACE OR REPAIR. REFER TO VACUUM SYSTEM INSPECTION.
	THROTTLE ACTUATING CABLE OR BEAD CHAIN, OR ROD MISADJUSTED.	READJUST
	KINKED OR DAMAGED SPEEDOMETER CABLE.	REPLACE.
	POWER UNIT SOLENOID VALVE VARIABLE ORIFICE MISADJUSTED.	READJUST.
SYSTEM WILL NOT DISENGAGE WITH BRAKE PEDAL.	BRAKE RELEASE SWITCH INOPERATIVE OR MISADJUSTED.	REPLACE OR ADJUST AS REQUIRED.
CANNOT ENGAGE OR ADJUST CRUISE SPEED DOWNWARD WITH ENGAGE SWITCH.	INOPERATIVE ENGAGE SWITCH.	REPLACE OR REPAIR.
SYSTEM CAN BE ENGAGED BELOW 20 MPH.	DEFECTIVE CONTROLLER.	REPLACE.
HISSING NOISE WHEN BRAKE PEDAL DISENGAGES SYSTEM.	VACUUM RELEASE VALVE OR, RELEASE SWITCH MISADJUSTED.	READJUST VALVE OR REPLACE.
AMBER "ON" LIGHT WILL NOT TURN ON EVEN THOUGH SYSTEM CRUISES SATISFACTORILY.	INOPERATIVE BULB.	REPLACE.
	OPEN PRINTED CIRCUIT ON DASH SWITCH.	REPLACE.
	WIRE HARNESS	REPAIR
"GREEN" OR "AUTO" LIGHT WILL NOT TURN ON EVEN THOUGH SYSTEM CRUISES SATISFACTORILY.	INOPERATIVE BULB.	REPLACE.
	OPEN PRINTED CIRCUIT ON DASH SWITCH OR OPEN IN CRUISE HARNESS.	REPLACE, OR REPAIR.
	DEFECTIVE CONTROLLER.	REPLACE.
	WIRE HARNESS	REPAIR

Cruise control diagnosis – 1982–85 RWD Deville 1982 and later RWD Fleetwood and 1982–85 Eldorado and Seville

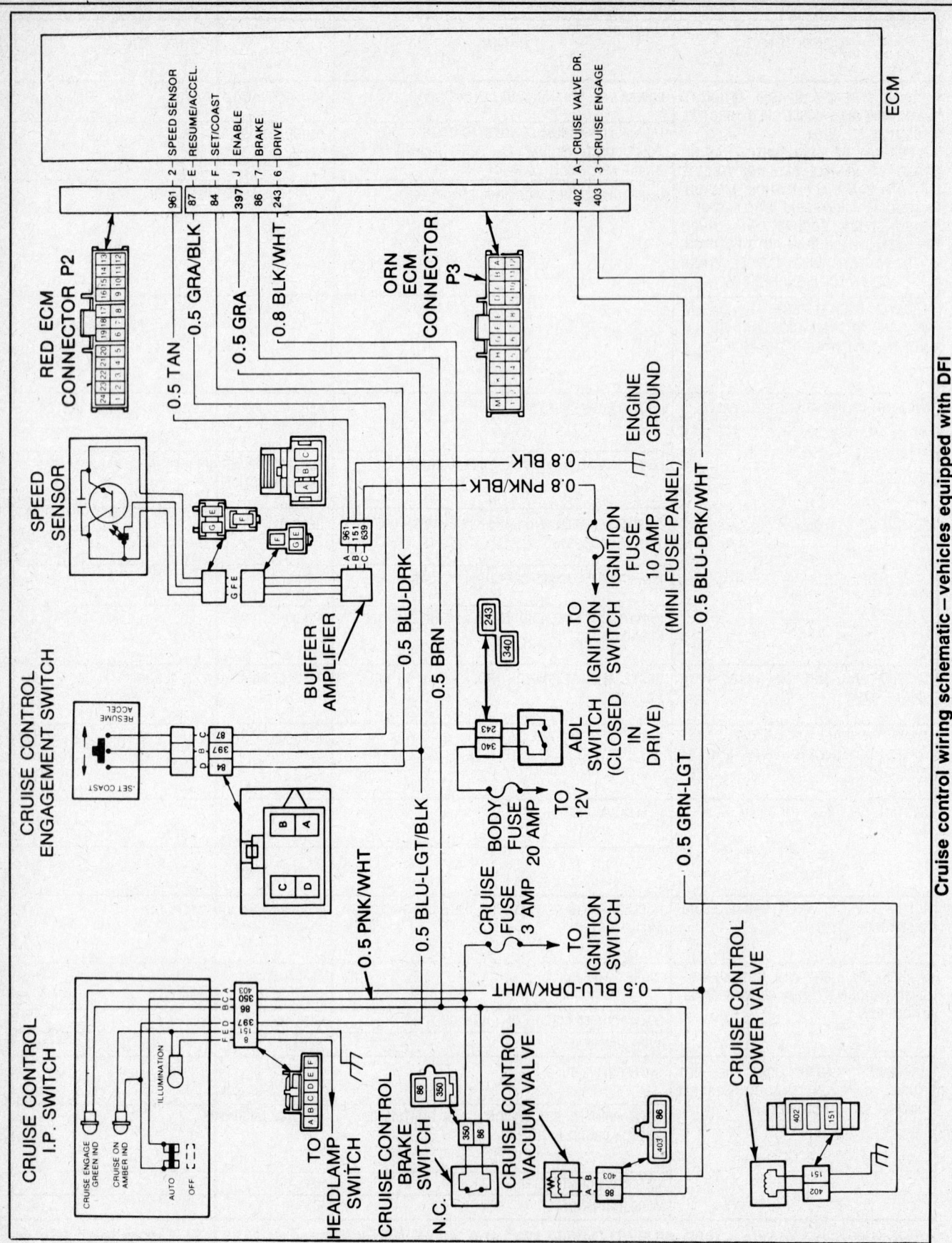

Cruise control wiring schematic—vehicles equipped with DFI

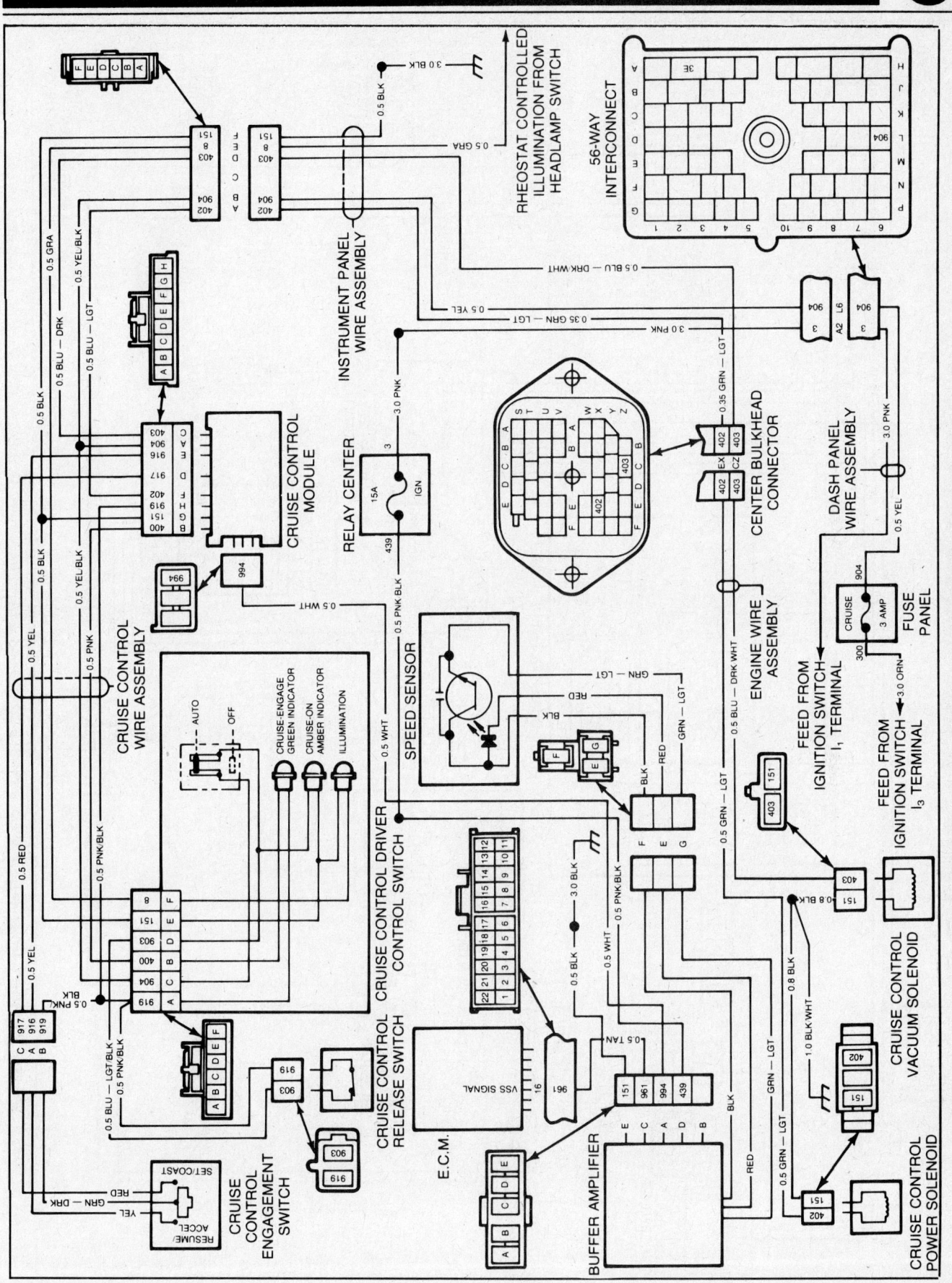

Cruise control wiring schematic—vehicles equipped with 4.1L engine

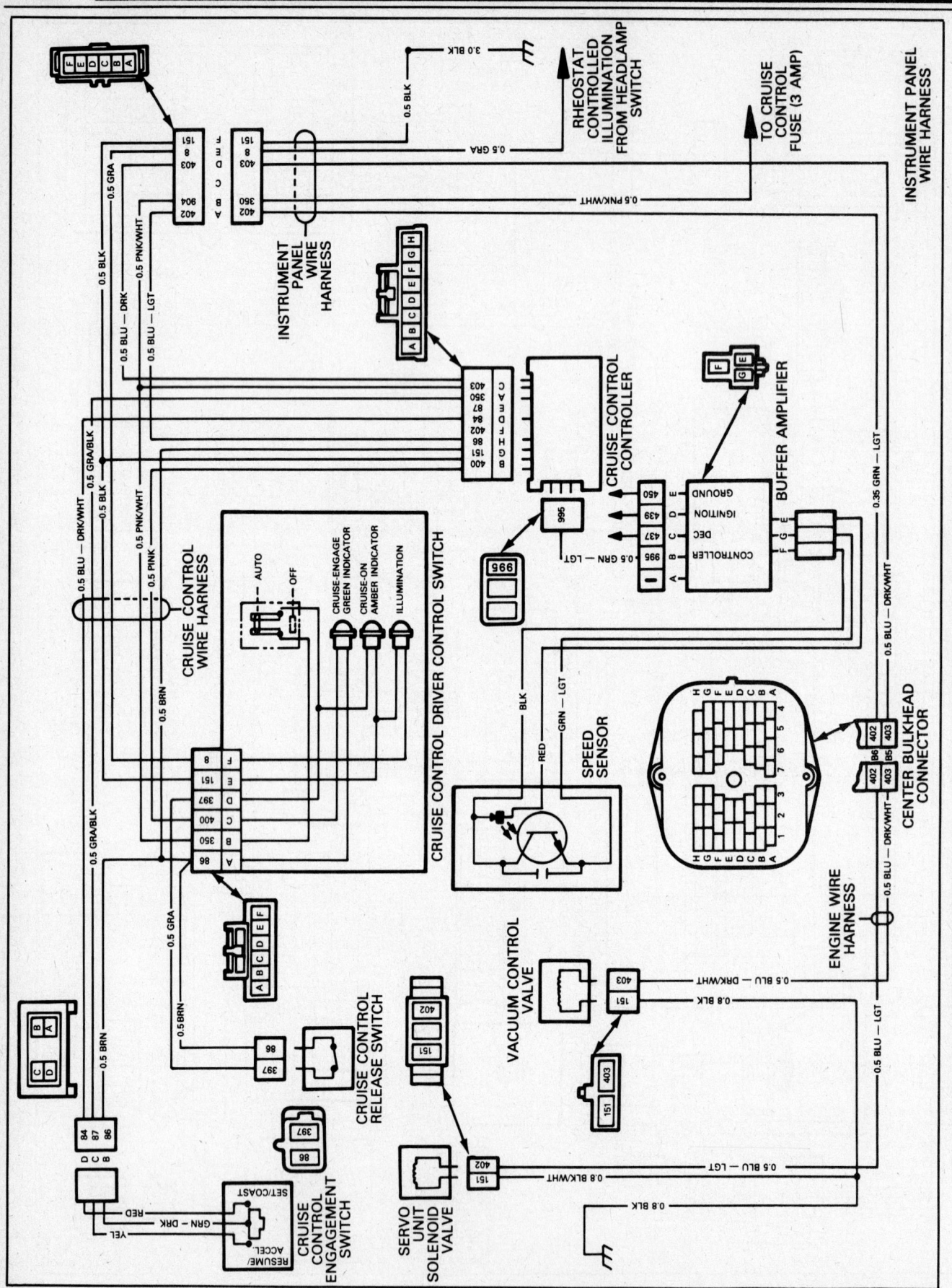

Cruise control wiring schematic—vehicles equipped with diesel engine except Eldorado and Seville

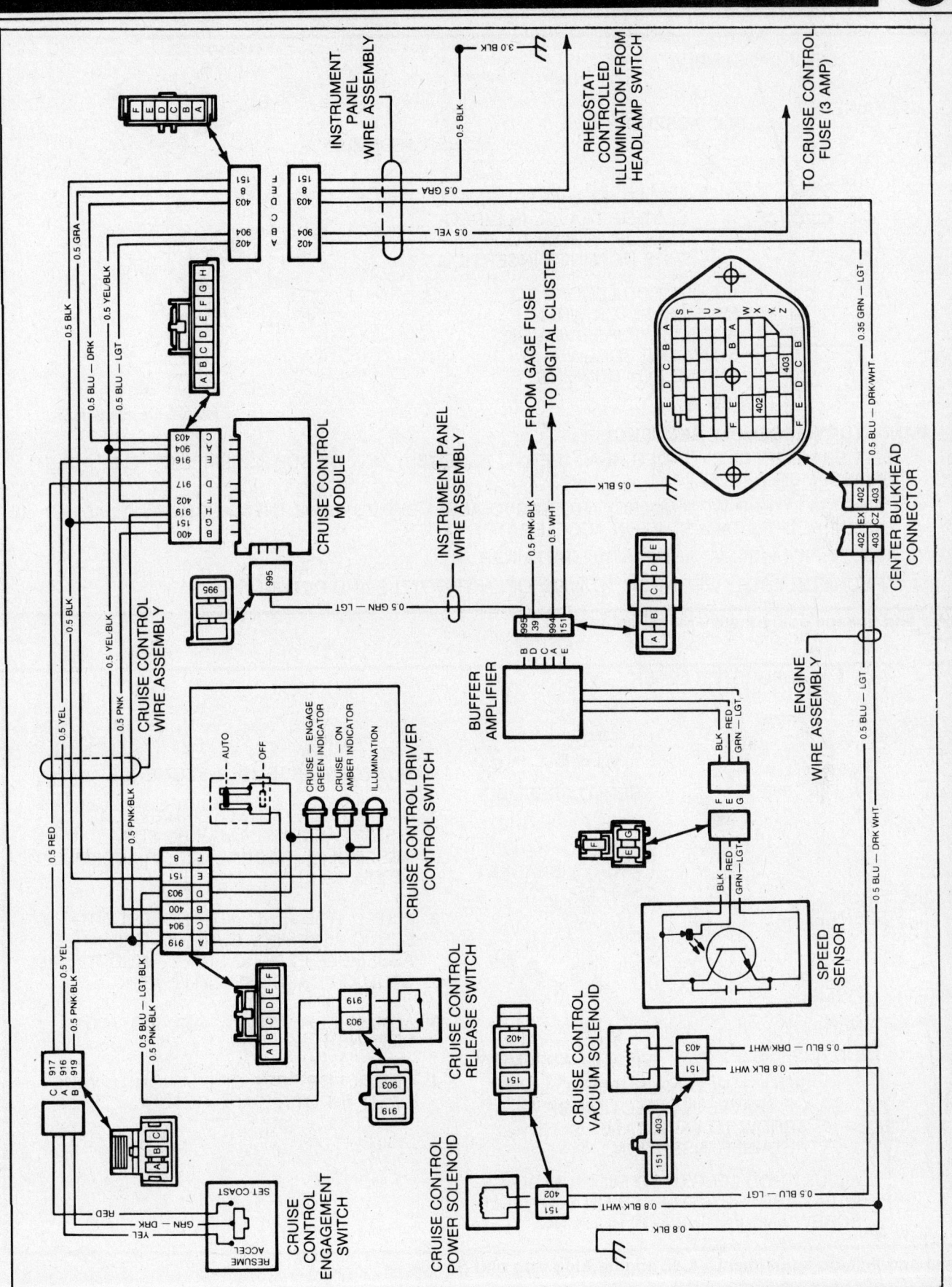

Cruise control wiring schematic—Eldorado and Seville equipped with diesel engine

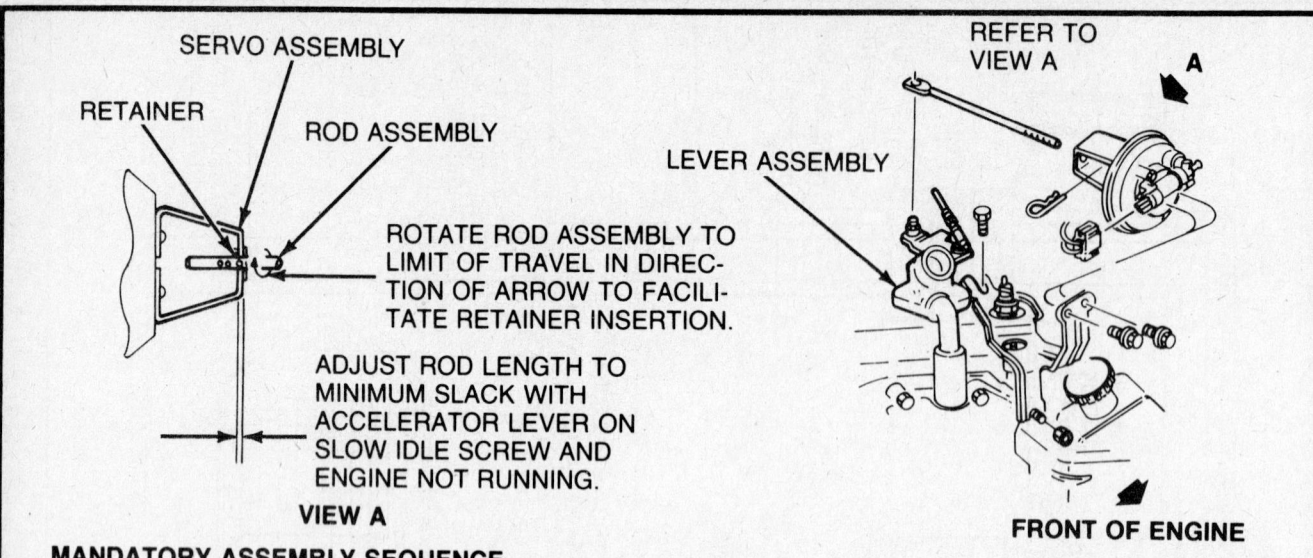

SERVO ASSEMBLY

RETAINER

ROD ASSEMBLY

ROTATE ROD ASSEMBLY TO LIMIT OF TRAVEL IN DIRECTION OF ARROW TO FACILITATE RETAINER INSERTION.

ADJUST ROD LENGTH TO MINIMUM SLACK WITH ACCELERATOR LEVER ON SLOW IDLE SCREW AND ENGINE NOT RUNNING.

VIEW A

REFER TO VIEW A

A

LEVER ASSEMBLY

FRONT OF ENGINE

MANDATORY ASSEMBLY SEQUENCE

1. BOLT BRACKET TO CYLINDER HEAD (SERVO ASSEMBLY MAY BE SUB-ASSEMBLED TO BRACKET OR ASSEMBLED NEXT.)

2. INSERT ROD (END WITH HOLES) INTO SERVO ASSEMBLY BUSHING THEN ASSEMBLE PLASTIC END OF ROD TO BALL-STUD ON ACCELERATOR LEVER.

3. ADJUST PER VIEW "A" AND INSTALL RETAINER.

4. CHECK FOR FREE OPERATION TO WIDE OPEN THROTTLE AND RETURN.

Servo and linkage adjustment – diesel engine

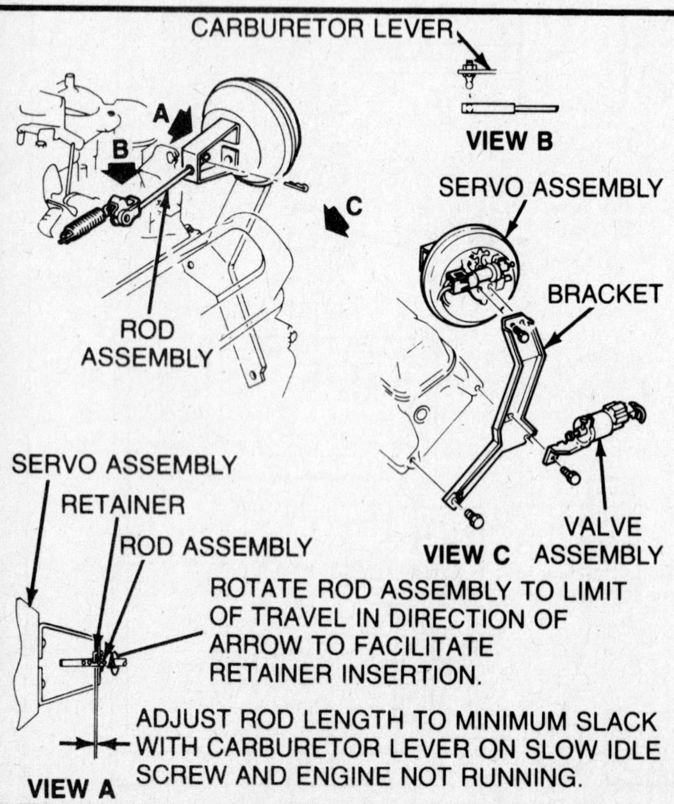

CARBURETOR LEVER

VIEW B

A

B

C

ROD ASSEMBLY

SERVO ASSEMBLY

BRACKET

VALVE ASSEMBLY

VIEW C

SERVO ASSEMBLY

RETAINER

ROD ASSEMBLY

ROTATE ROD ASSEMBLY TO LIMIT OF TRAVEL IN DIRECTION OF ARROW TO FACILITATE RETAINER INSERTION.

ADJUST ROD LENGTH TO MINIMUM SLACK WITH CARBURETOR LEVER ON SLOW IDLE SCREW AND ENGINE NOT RUNNING.

VIEW A

MANDATORY ASSEMBLY SEQUENCE

1. BOLT BRACKET TO CYLINDER HEAD (SERVO ASSEMBLY MAY BE SUB-ASSEMBLED TO BRACKET OR ASSEMBLED NEXT.)

2. INSERT ROD (END WITH HOLES) INTO SERVO ASSEMBLY BUSHING, THEN ASSEMBLE PLASTIC END OF ROD TO BALL STUD ON CARBURETOR LEVER.

3. ADJUST PER VIEW "A" AND INSTALL RETAINER.

4. CHECK FOR FREE OPERATION TO WIDE OPEN THROTTLE AND RETURN.

Servo and linkage adjustment – 4.1L engine Eldorado and Seville

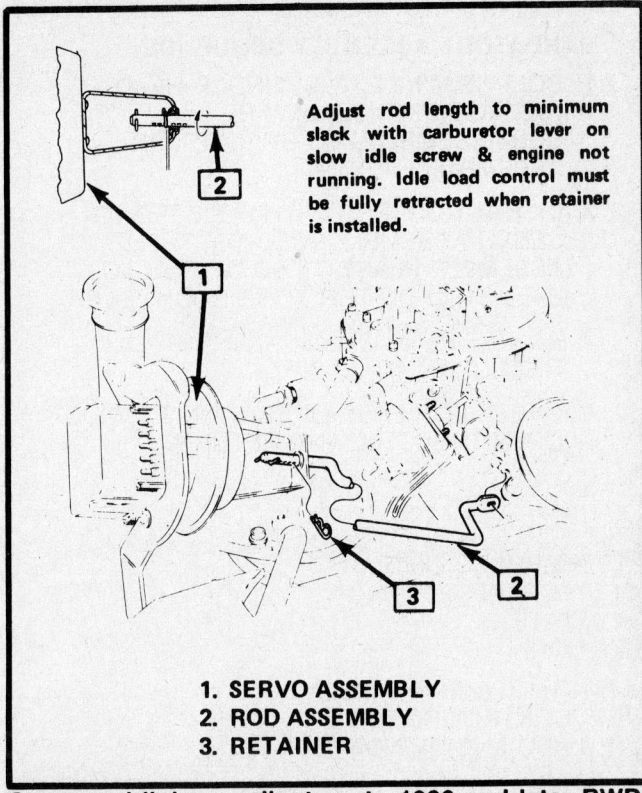

Adjust rod length to minimum slack with carburetor lever on slow idle screw & engine not running. Idle load control must be fully retracted when retainer is installed.

1. SERVO ASSEMBLY
2. ROD ASSEMBLY
3. RETAINER

Servo and linkage adjustment—1986 and later RWD Fleetwood

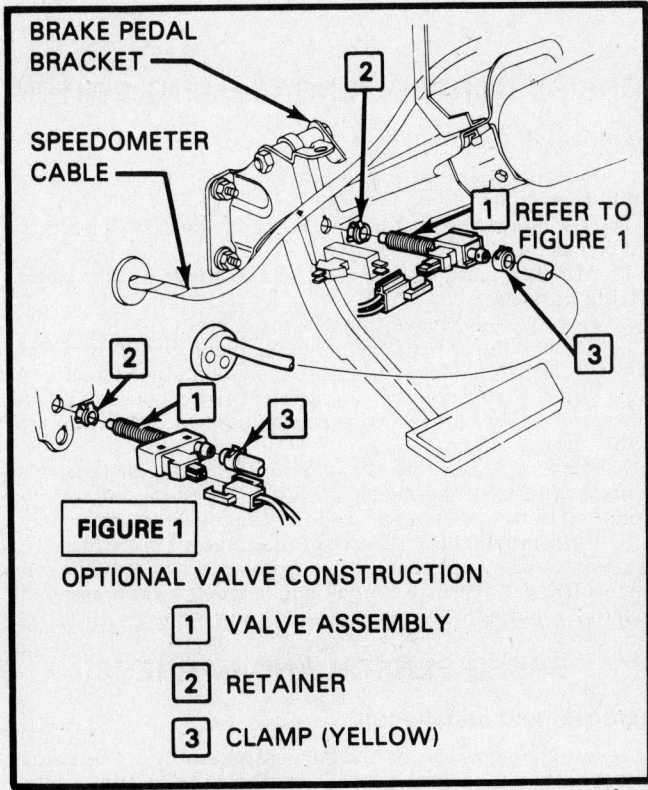

FIGURE 1

OPTIONAL VALVE CONSTRUCTION

1 VALVE ASSEMBLY
2 RETAINER
3 CLAMP (YELLOW)

Cruise control release valve and torque converter clutch release switch

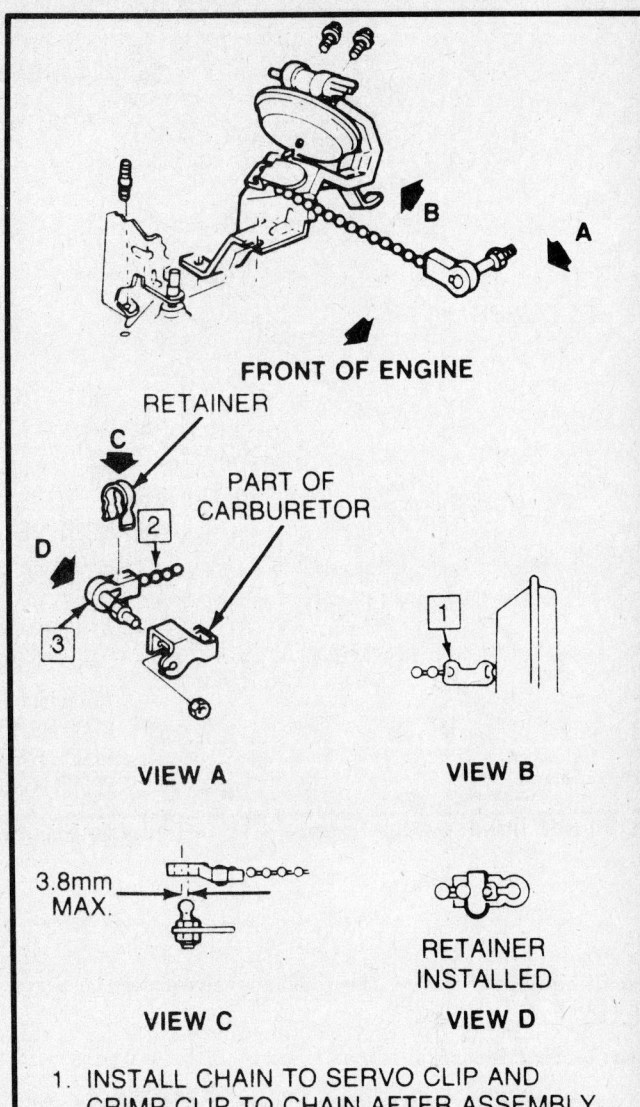

1. INSTALL CHAIN TO SERVO CLIP AND CRIMP CLIP TO CHAIN AFTER ASSEMBLY
2. ASSEMBLE CHAIN TO BE TAUT WITH CARBURETOR IN THE HOT IDLE POSITION WITH THE IDLE CONTROL SOLENOID DE-ENERGIZED. PLACE CHAIN INTO SWIVEL CAVITIES WHICH PERMIT CHAIN TO HAVE SLIGHT SLACK. PLACE RETAINER OVER SWIVEL AND CHAIN ASSEMBLY. RETAINER MUST BE POSITIONED TO REST BETWEEN BALLS, REFER TO VIEW D. CUT OFF CHAIN FLUSH WITH SIDE OF SWIVEL TO REMOVE EXCESS LENGTH. CHAIN SLACK NOT TO EXCEED ONE-HALF DIAMETER OF BALL-STUD WHEN MEASURED AT HOT IDLE POSITION WITH THE IDLE CONTROL SOLE-NOID DE-ENERGIZED AND SWIVEL DISCONNECTED FROM BALL-STUD. REFER TO VIEW C.
3. BALL SWIVEL MUST BE INSTALLED ON THE INBOARD SIDE OF LEVER.

Servo and linkage adjustment—4.1L engine except Eldorado and Seville

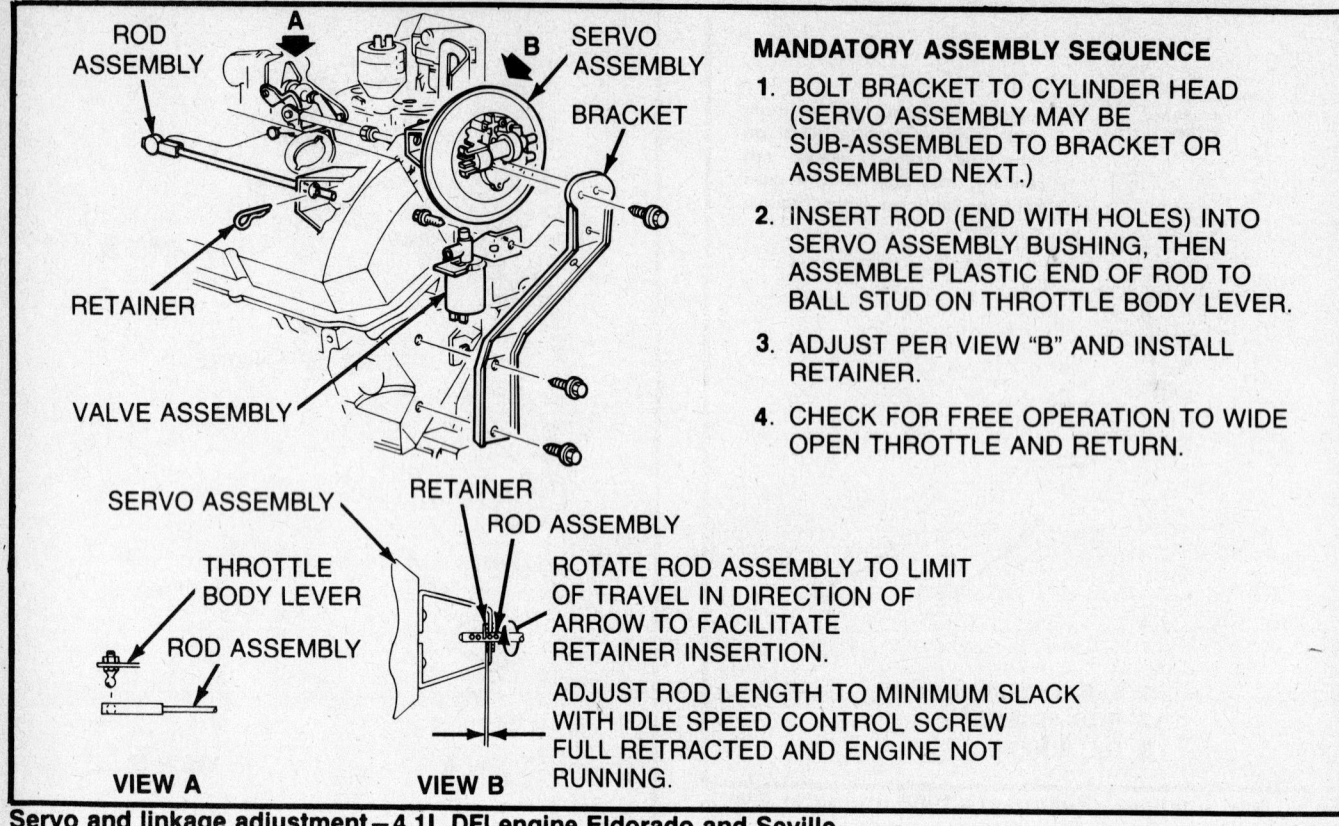

ROD ASSEMBLY

A

B SERVO ASSEMBLY

BRACKET

RETAINER

VALVE ASSEMBLY

SERVO ASSEMBLY

RETAINER

ROD ASSEMBLY

THROTTLE BODY LEVER

ROD ASSEMBLY

ROTATE ROD ASSEMBLY TO LIMIT OF TRAVEL IN DIRECTION OF ARROW TO FACILITATE RETAINER INSERTION.

ADJUST ROD LENGTH TO MINIMUM SLACK WITH IDLE SPEED CONTROL SCREW FULL RETRACTED AND ENGINE NOT RUNNING.

VIEW A

VIEW B

MANDATORY ASSEMBLY SEQUENCE

1. BOLT BRACKET TO CYLINDER HEAD (SERVO ASSEMBLY MAY BE SUB-ASSEMBLED TO BRACKET OR ASSEMBLED NEXT.)

2. INSERT ROD (END WITH HOLES) INTO SERVO ASSEMBLY BUSHING, THEN ASSEMBLE PLASTIC END OF ROD TO BALL STUD ON THROTTLE BODY LEVER.

3. ADJUST PER VIEW "B" AND INSTALL RETAINER.

4. CHECK FOR FREE OPERATION TO WIDE OPEN THROTTLE AND RETURN.

Servo and linkage adjustment—4.1L DFI engine Eldorado and Seville

5. If equipped, remove the solenoid valve from the servo assembly.
6. Installation is the reverse of the removal procedure. Adjust the throttle mechanism as required.

ELECTRIC BRAKE RELEASE SWITCH AND VACUUM RELEASE VALVE

Removal and Installation

1. Disconnect the negative battery cable.
2. Remove the switch electrical and vacuum connectors.
3. Remove the switch from its mounting above the brake pedal.
4. Installation is the reverse of the removal procedure.

Adjustment

1. The switch assembly and the valve assembly cannot be adjusted until after the brake booster push rod is assembled to the brake pedal assembly.
2. To adjust the switch depress the brake pedal and insert the switch assembly and valve assembly into their proper retaining clips until fully seated.
3. Pull the pedal back to its fully retracted position. The switch assembly and the valve assembly will move within the retainers of their adjusted position.
4. The switch assembly contacts must open at 3.5mm to 12.5mm of brake pedal travel. Nominal actuation of the brake light switch is 4.5mm.
5. The vacuum release valve assembly must open at 27.0mm to 33.0mm of brake pedal travel.

CRUISE CONTROL ENGAGEMENT SWITCH

Removal and Installation

1. Disconnect the negative battery cable. Remove the left hand trim panel.
2. Disconnect the cruise control engagement switch electrical connector.
3. Attach a piece of thin wire to the cruise control switch wiring harness.
4. As required remove the steering wheel.
5. Remove the cruise control engagement switch by pulling it out of the detented retaining clip inside the steering column.
6. Pull the cruise control engagement switch harness up and out carefully so that the wire can be used to install the new switch and harness.
7. Removing the protective plastic sheathing for the cruise control wires from the steering column may aid in the removal and installation of the cruise control engagement switch.
8. Installation is the reverse of the removal procedure. The cruise control engagement switch cannot be serviced. The complete turn signal/cruise control engagement switch assembly must be replaced.

SPEED SENSOR AND HARNESS

Removal and Installation

Access to the speed sensor and harness assembly can be gained by partially removing the speedometer cluster and disconnecting the electrical connector at the cluster assembly and electronic controller ends of the harness. Exercise care when re-

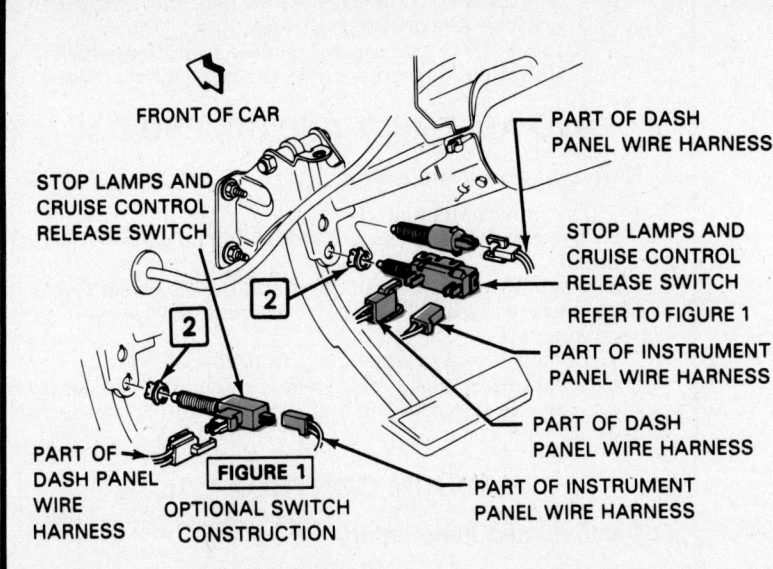

INSTALLATION OF SELF-ADJUSTING VACUUM RELEASE VALVE AND STOP LAMP SWITCH:

1. INSTALL CLIP [2].

2. WITH BRAKE PEDAL DEPRESSED, INSERT SWITCH INTO TUBULAR CLIP UNTIL SWITCH BODY SEATS ON CLIP. NOTE THAT AUDIBLE "CLICKS" CAN BE HEARD AS THE THREADED PORTION OF SWITCH IS PUSHED THROUGH CLIP TOWARD THE BRAKE PEDAL.

3. PULL BRAKE PEDAL FULLY REARWARD AGAINST PEDAL STOP UNTIL AUDIBLE "CLICK" SOUNDS CAN NO LONGER BE HEARD; SWITCH WILL BE MOVED IN TUBULAR CLIP PROVIDING ADJUSTMENT.

4. RELEASE BRAKE PEDAL AND THEN REPEAT STEP 3 TO ASSURE THAT NO AUDIBLE "CLICK" SOUNDS REMAIN.

Cruise control release switches

moving cluster to disconnect speed sensor electrical connector at the back of the cluster. Pulling the cluster too far outward with the speed sensor electrical connector still attached to the cluster could cause damage to the cluster or the connector.

CRUISE CONTROL SPEED SENSOR

Removal and Installation

ELDORADO AND SEVILLE

1. Disconnect the negative battery cable.
2. Remove the lower instrument panel cover.
3. Unclip the relay panel from the twilight sentinel amplifier and the cruise control module mounting bracket, which is located to the left of the steering column.
4. Remove the retaining screws that secure the cruise control module mounting bracket to the instrument panel base assembly.
5. Lower the mounting bracket and disconnect the electrical speed sensor connector from the cruise control module.
6. Remove the instrument panel cluster.
7. With the speed sensor disconnected from the rear of the speedometer cluster, remove it by pulling the harness and the connector through the opening in the instrument panel base assembly.
8. Installation is the reverse of the removal procedure.

BUFFER AMPLIFIER

Removal and Installation

EXCEPT ELDORADO AND SEVILLE

1. Disconnect the negative battery cable.
2. Remove the speedometer cluster.
3. Remove the clip retaining strap holding the buffer amplifier in place.
4. Disconnect the electrical connector from the buffer amplifier assembly.
5. Remove the buffer amplifier assembly from the vehicle.
6. Installation is the reverse of the removal procedure.

ELDORADO AND SEVILLE

1. Disconnect the negative battery cable.

2. Remove the bottom trim panel. Remove the buffer amplifier retaining screws.
3. Disconnect the electrical connections from the buffer amplifier assembly.
4. Remove the buffer amplifier assembly from the vehicle.
5. Installation is the reverse of the removal procedure.

CRUISE CONTROL MODULE

Removal and Installation

EXCEPT ELDORADO AND SEVILLE

1. Disconnect the negative battery cable.
2. Remove the lower steering column cover.
3. Disconnect the electrical connectors from the cruise control module.
4. Remove the screws retaining the cruise control module to the lower steering column cover.
5. Remove the cruise control module from the vehicle.
6. Installation is the reverse of the removal procedure.

ELDORADO AND SEVILLE

1. Disconnect the negative battery cable.

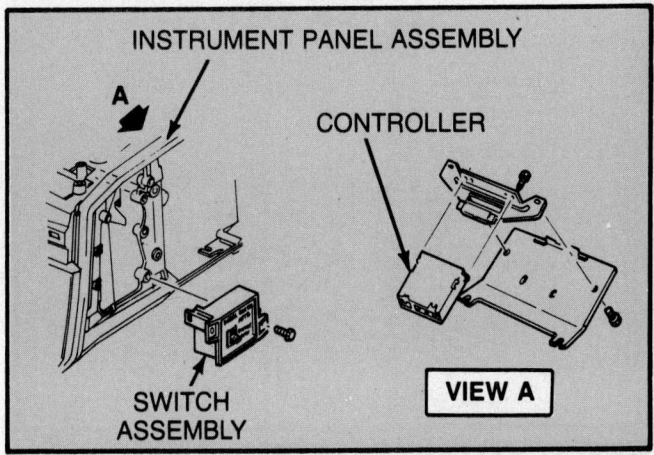

Cruise control electronic module and wiring—typical

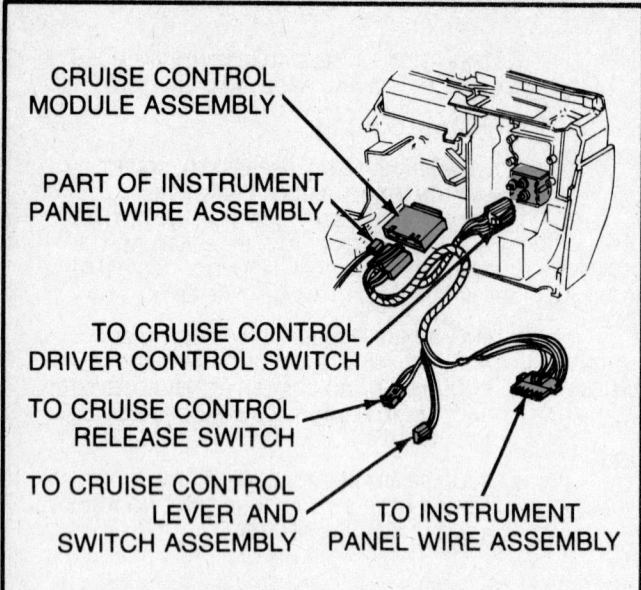

Cruise control electronic module switch assembly location and wiring – typical

2. Remove the lower instrument panel cover.

3. Unclip the relay panel from the twilight sentinel amplifier and the cruise control module mounting bracket, which is located to the left of the steering column.

4. Remove the retaining screws that secure the cruise control module mounting bracket to the instrument panel base assembly.

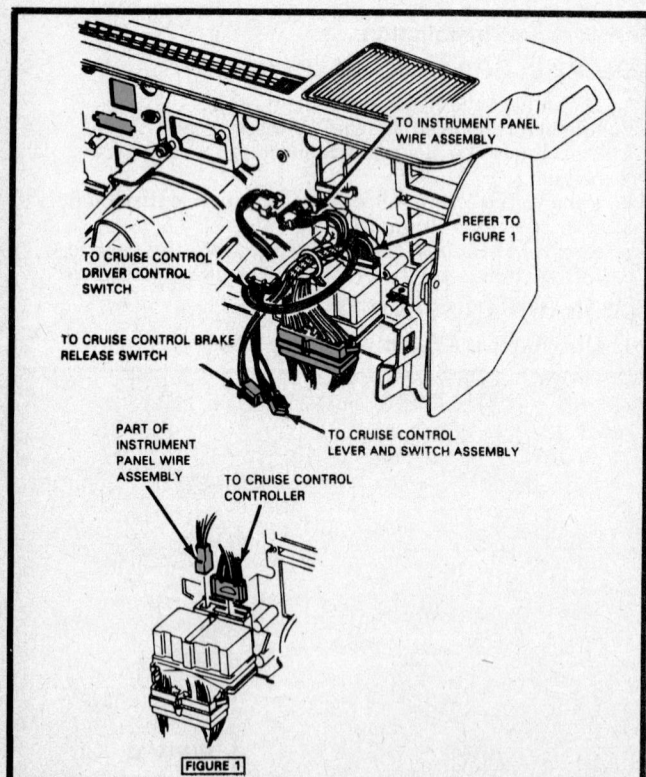

Cruise control electronic controller – Eldorado and Seville

5. Lower the mounting bracket and disconnect the electrical connectors from the cruise control module.

6. Remove the cruise control module from the vehicle.

7. Installation is the reverse of the removal procedure.

SERVO ASSEMBLY AND SOLENOID VALVE

Removal and Installation

1. Disconnect the negative battery cable.

2. Remove the screw securing the solenoid valve to the servo assembly.

3. Disconnect the vacuum hose and the electrical connector from the servo assembly. Pull the solenoid valve away from the servo assembly.

4. Remove the servo assembly from the vehicle.

5. Installation is the reverse of the removal procedure. Be careful not to separate the end cap and filter from the valve body.

VACUUM CONTROL VALVE

Removal and Installation

1. Disconnect the negative battery cable.

2. Disconnect the electrical connector and the vacuum hose from the valve.

3. Remove the screw retaining the valve to the servo assembly mounting bracket or from the front of the dash bracket.

4. Remove the vacuum control valve from the vehicle.

5. Installation is the reverse of the removal procedure.

Cadillac – 1985 and Later FWD Deville and Fleetwood, 1986 and Later Seville and Eldorado

VISUAL INSPECTION

Before performing any tests make a visual inspection of the cruise control system. Check all items in the system for abnormal conditions such as bare broken or disconnected wires and damage to the vacuum hoses. Be sure that the speedometer cables are attached and properly routed. All vacuum hoses must be properly routed and must not have any kinks or bends. Be sure that all electrical connections are complete and tight. The wiring harness must be routed properly.

ROAD TEST
(EXCEPT ELDORADO AND SEVILLE)

1. Place the dash switch in the off position. Drive the car until the speedometer reads 50 mph. Push the engagement switch button on the turn signal switch and release. The cruise control system should remain off.

2. Place the dash switch in on position. The amber light should come on.

3. Engage the cruise control system by momentarily pushing the turn signal engagement switch button and than releasing it at 50 mph while removing your foot from the accelerator pedal.

4. The green light should come on when the button is released and the system is engaged. The vehicle should maintain the speed of 50 mph.

5. Push the slide switch and hold. The vehicle should accelerate at a controlled rate. Release the slide switch to engage the system to a cruise speed of about 55 mph. The system should now be set to the new speed.

6. Depress the brake pedal about one-half inch. The green light should go out, this confirms the action of the electric

brake release switch and the vehicle should now start to slow down.

7. Momentarily depress the slide switch and than release it. The vehicle should accelerate at a controlled rate and resume the previously set speed of 55 mph. The green light should come on when the slide switch is released.

8. Push the engagement switch button all the way in and hold. The green light should go out. Coast to about 50 mph.

9. Release the button in order to engage the system at 50 mph. The green light should come on and the vehicle should maintain that speed.

ENGAGEMENT SWITCH AND HARNESS (EXCEPT ELDORADO AND SEVILLE)

The engagement switch lever can be checked after disconnecting it from the harness and performing the following tests.

With one lead of an ohmmeter connected to the steering column mounting bracket check each terminal of the wiring harness. If any indicate continunity, a short exists and the defective component must be replaced. Move the shift lever through the full range when checking each wire.

ENGAGE SWITCH ON OR OFF CAR TEST			
	INDICATION BETWEEN TERMINALS		
ENGAGE SWITCH	1 TO 2 (YELLOW-GREEN)	1 TO 3 (YELLOW-RED)	2 TO 3 (GREEN-RED)
RELEASED	OPEN	OPEN	OPEN
SLIDE DEPRESSED	CLOSED	OPEN	OPEN
PUSHBUTTON DEPRESSED	OPEN	OPEN	CLOSED

Cruise control engagement switch test—except Eldorado and Seville

VACUUM CONTROL AND SERVO UNIT SOLENOID VALVES TEST (EXCEPT ELDORADO AND SEVILLE)

NOTE: This test can be done automatically on vehicles equipped with D.F.I. by entering the output cycling tests as outlined in diagnosis testing procedures, or by using the following information.

1. Disconnect the electrical connector at the solenoid valve that is being tested.

2. Connect a jumper wire from the positive terminal of the battery to one terminal of the valve being tested.

3. Connect another jumper wire to ground.

4. Brush the other end of the grounded jumper wire across the remaining terminal of the valve.

5. Listen for the valve to open and close as you break contact with the terminal. The valves will click twice indicating that each respective valve is functioning properly.

VACUUM SYSTEM INSPECTION (EXCEPT ELDORADO AND SEVILLE)

1. Disconnect the electrical connectors at the vacuum control valve and the servo unit solenoid valve.

2. Connect both the vacuum control and the servo unit solenoid valves using jumper wires. This is done by connecting jumper wires from the positive terminal of the battery to one terminal on each valve, then ground the remaining terminal on each valve using another set of jumper wires.

3. Turn the ignition switch to the on position, but do not start the engine.

4. With the brake pedal in the free position, the diaphragm should pull in to full stroke.

5. Depress the brake pedal down about one inch, the diaphragm should relax to its free position.

6. If the system will not hold vacuum, remove the brake release vent valve hose at the servo unit and plug the servo unit hole.

7. If the servo unit draws down then the problem exists in the brake release vacuum vent system. Inspect the vacuum release hose for leaks, secure connections to the valve and proper adjustment. Correct defects as required.

8. If the servo unit will not draw down, inspect the diaphragm and connectors at the valves for leaks.

DIAGNOSIS AND TESTING PROCEDURES

NOTE: The following information is to be used in conjunction with the self diagnostic features that are incorporated into the electronic computer of the particular vehicle that you are working on.

Microprocessor controlled subsystems are capable of monitoring operating conditions for possible malfunctions. By comparing the system conditions against the standard operating limits, certain circuit and component malfunctions can be detected. A two digit trouble code is stored in the computer memory when a problem is detected by the self diagnostic system. The trouble codes can later be displayed so that the malfunction can be corrected.

To enter the diagnostic mode, turn the ignition on. Depress the OFF and the WARMER buttons on the climate control panel simultaneously. Hold the buttons in until all the display panel segments illuminate this indicates the beginning of the diagnostic readout. The purpose of illuminating the two display panels is to check that all segments of the displays are functioning properly. If any of the segments are inoperative, the affected display panel will have to be replaced.

After the displays end and the segment check is completed any trouble code that is stored in the computer memory will be displayed on the data center. The trouble codes will appear prefixed with an "E" or "F" to designate which computer detected the malfunction. After all of the codes have been displayed or if no trouble codes are stored ".7.0" will appear on the display.

Trouble codes that are stored in the memory may be cleared by entering the diagnostic mode and then depressing the OFF and HI buttons simultaneously. Hold the buttons in until "E.0.0" appears. Trouble codes that are stored in the memory may be cleared by depressing the OFF and LO buttons simultaneously until "F.0.0" appears. After "E.0.0" or "F.0.0" are displayed ".7.0" will appear. With ".7.0" displayed turn the ignition off for at least ten seconds before re-entering the diagnostic mode.

To get out of the diagnostic mode, depress the AUTO button or tun the ignition switch to the off position for ten seconds. The trouble codes are not erased when this is done. The temperature setting will reappear in the display panel.

Code ".7.0" is a decision point. When code ".7.0" is displayed the diagnostic feature that is needed may be selected. The following selections are available. ECM switch tests, ECM data displays, ECM output cycling, BCM data displays, ECC program override, Cooling fan override and Exit diagnostics or clear codes.

ECM SWITCH TEST

The engine must be running and code ".7.0" must be displayed on the data center panel before the switch testing can be started. To start, depress and release the brake pedal, the switch tests begin as the display switches from code ".7.0" to "E.7.1". As each code is displayed the associated switch must be cycled within ten seconds or the code will be recorded in the memory as a failure. After the ECM recognizes a test as passing the display advances to the next switch test code. The switch tests must be performed in the following order.

1. With code "E.7.1" displayed depress and release the brake pedal to test the cruise control brake circuit.

2. With code "E.7.2" displayed depress the throttle from the idle position to an open throttle position and then slowly release the throttle. This checks the throttle switch for proper operation.

3. With code "E.7.3" displayed and the brakes applied shift the transmission selector lever into reverse and then into neutral. This checks the operation of the park/neutral switch.

4. With code "E.7.5" displayed switch the cruise control instrument panel switch from off to on and then off again. This checks the operation of the switch.

5. With code "E.7.6" displayed and with the cruise control instrument panel switch in the on position depress and release the set/coast button on the engagement lever. This checks the operation of the set/coast function.

6. With code "E.7.7" displayed and with the cruise control instrument panel switch in the on position depress and release the resume/acceleration switch on the engagement lever. This checks the operation of the resume/acceleration function.

7. With code "E.7.8" displayed and the engine running, turn the wheels from the straight ahead position to the full right or left and then back to the straight ahead position again. This checks the power steering pressure switch for proper operation.

8. When the tests are completed the ECM will go back and display the switch coded that did not test properly. Each code that did not pass will be displayed beginning with the lowest number.

9. These codes will not disappear until the affected switch circuit has been repaired and retested.

10. After the switch tests have been completed and all circuits pass the control panel will display "E.0.0" and then return to code ".7.0". Code "E.0.0 indicates that all of the switch circuits are operating properly.

ECM OUTPUT CYCLING TEST

This mode can be initiated after code "E.9.5" is displayed. This code can be reached by depressing the HI button while code ".7.0" is displayed. The ECM output cycling mode, code "E.9.6" turns the ECM's outputs on and off. To enter the output cycling mode proceed as follows.

1. Turn the engine on. Turn the engine off and within two seconds turn the ignition on.

2. Enter diagnostics and display code "E.9.5".

3. Depress the accelerator pedal and release it. The ECM output cycling mode begins as the display switches from code "E.9.5" to code "E.9.6".

4. With the cruise control instrument panel switch in the on position the cruise control power solenoid should begin cycling rapidly and the cruise vacuum valve should cycle on and off every three seconds.

5. The output cycling mode will end automatically after two minutes of cycling and the display will switch from code "E.9.6" to code "E.9.5".

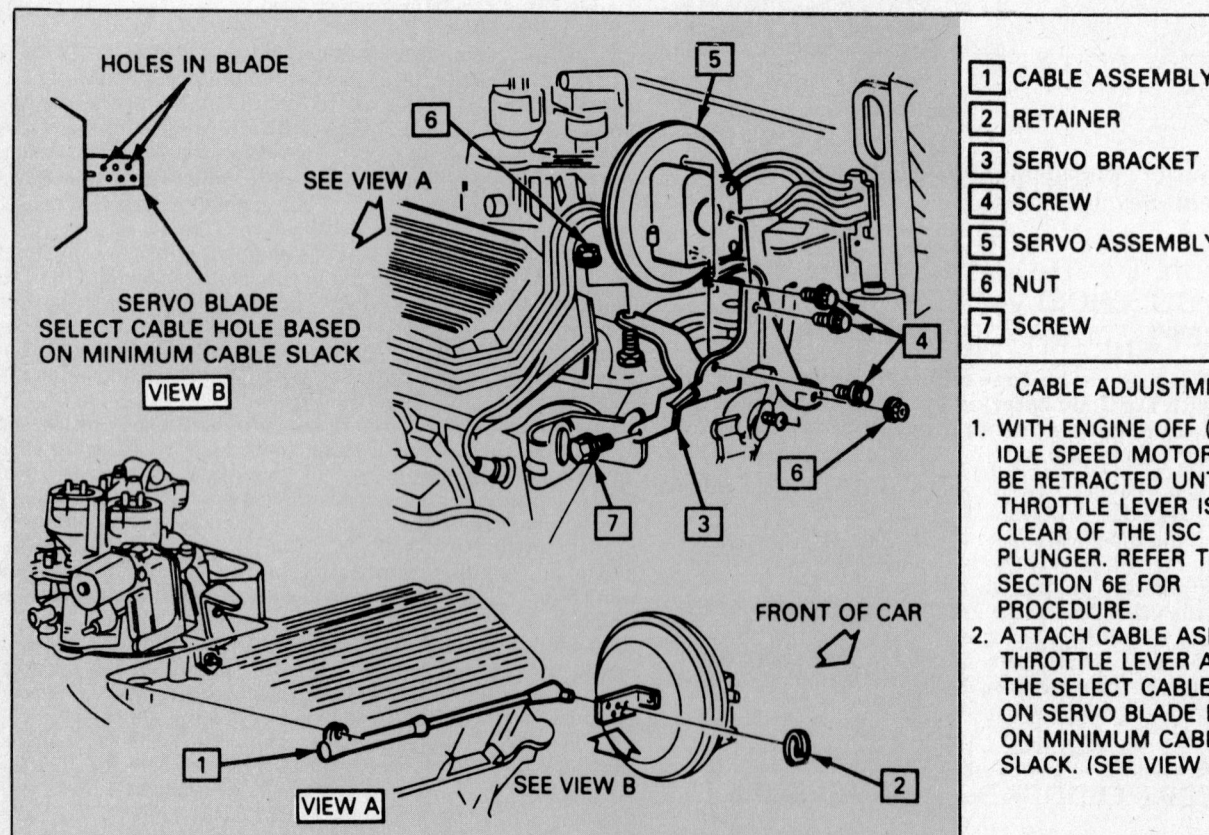

Servo and linkage adjustment—1986 and later Eldorado and Seville

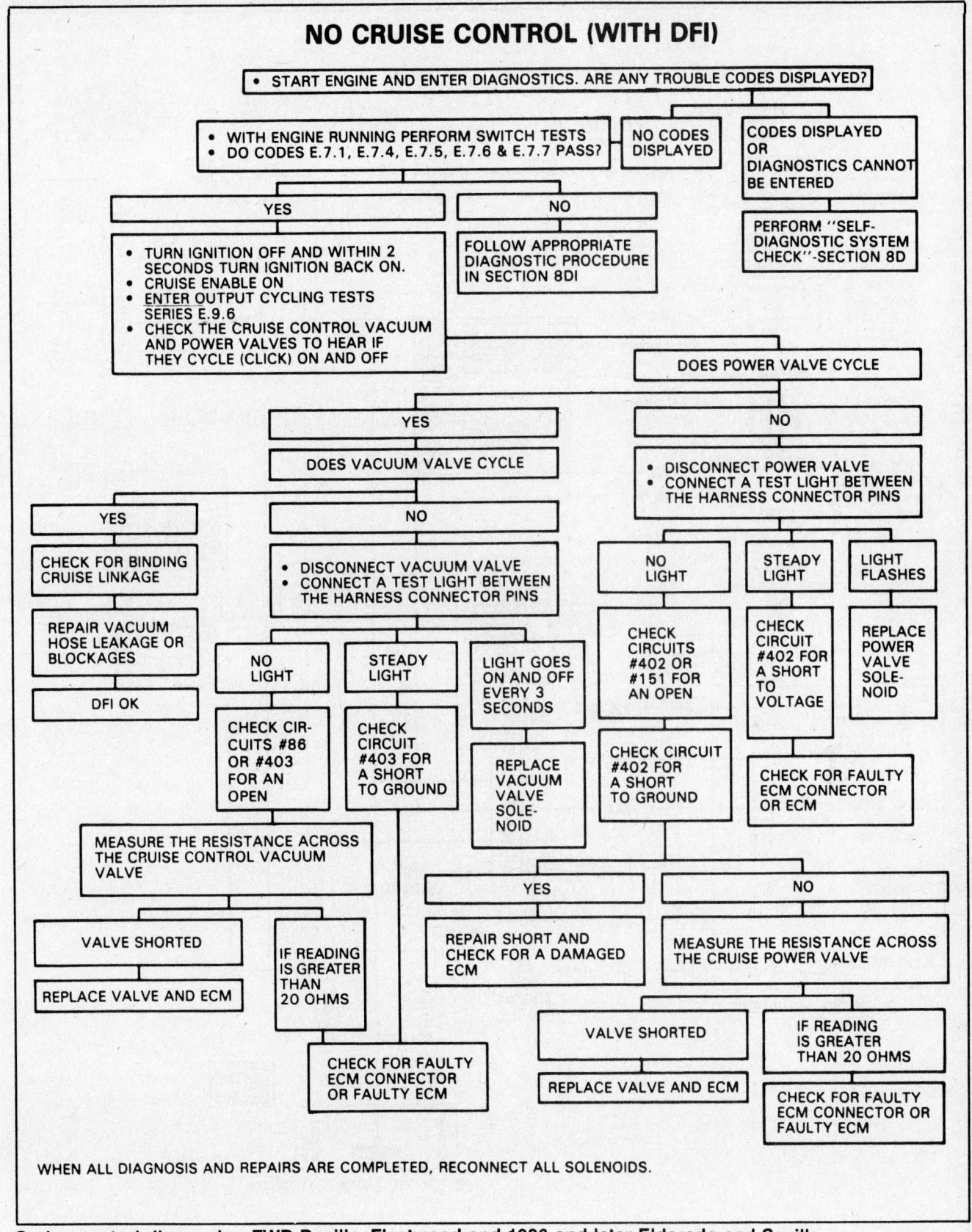

NO CRUISE CONTROL (WITH DFI)

- START ENGINE AND ENTER DIAGNOSTICS. ARE ANY TROUBLE CODES DISPLAYED?

- WITH ENGINE RUNNING PERFORM SWITCH TESTS
- DO CODES E.7.1, E.7.4, E.7.5, E.7.6 & E.7.7 PASS?

NO CODES DISPLAYED

CODES DISPLAYED OR DIAGNOSTICS CANNOT BE ENTERED

PERFORM "SELF-DIAGNOSTIC SYSTEM CHECK"-SECTION 8D

YES
- TURN IGNITION OFF AND WITHIN 2 SECONDS TURN IGNITION BACK ON.
- CRUISE ENABLE ON
- ENTER OUTPUT CYCLING TESTS SERIES E.9.6
- CHECK THE CRUISE CONTROL VACUUM AND POWER VALVES TO HEAR IF THEY CYCLE (CLICK) ON AND OFF

NO
FOLLOW APPROPRIATE DIAGNOSTIC PROCEDURE IN SECTION 8DI

DOES POWER VALVE CYCLE

YES

DOES VACUUM VALVE CYCLE

NO
- DISCONNECT POWER VALVE
- CONNECT A TEST LIGHT BETWEEN THE HARNESS CONNECTOR PINS

YES

CHECK FOR BINDING CRUISE LINKAGE

REPAIR VACUUM HOSE LEAKAGE OR BLOCKAGES

DFI OK

NO
- DISCONNECT VACUUM VALVE
- CONNECT A TEST LIGHT BETWEEN THE HARNESS CONNECTOR PINS

NO LIGHT

STEADY LIGHT

LIGHT FLASHES

CHECK CIRCUITS #402 OR #151 FOR AN OPEN

CHECK CIRCUIT #402 FOR A SHORT TO VOLTAGE

REPLACE POWER VALVE SOLENOID

NO LIGHT

STEADY LIGHT

LIGHT GOES ON AND OFF EVERY 3 SECONDS

CHECK CIRCUITS #86 OR #403 FOR AN OPEN

CHECK CIRCUIT #403 FOR A SHORT TO GROUND

REPLACE VACUUM VALVE SOLENOID

CHECK CIRCUIT #402 FOR A SHORT TO GROUND

CHECK FOR FAULTY ECM CONNECTOR OR ECM

MEASURE THE RESISTANCE ACROSS THE CRUISE CONTROL VACUUM VALVE

YES
REPAIR SHORT AND CHECK FOR A DAMAGED ECM

NO
MEASURE THE RESISTANCE ACROSS THE CRUISE POWER VALVE

VALVE SHORTED

IF READING IS GREATER THAN 20 OHMS

REPLACE VALVE AND ECM

CHECK FOR FAULTY ECM CONNECTOR OR FAULTY ECM

VALVE SHORTED

IF READING IS GREATER THAN 20 OHMS

REPLACE VALVE AND ECM

CHECK FOR FAULTY ECM CONNECTOR OR FAULTY ECM

WHEN ALL DIAGNOSIS AND REPAIRS ARE COMPLETED, RECONNECT ALL SOLENOIDS.

Cruise control diagnosis—FWD Deville, Fleetwood and 1986 and later Eldorado and Seville

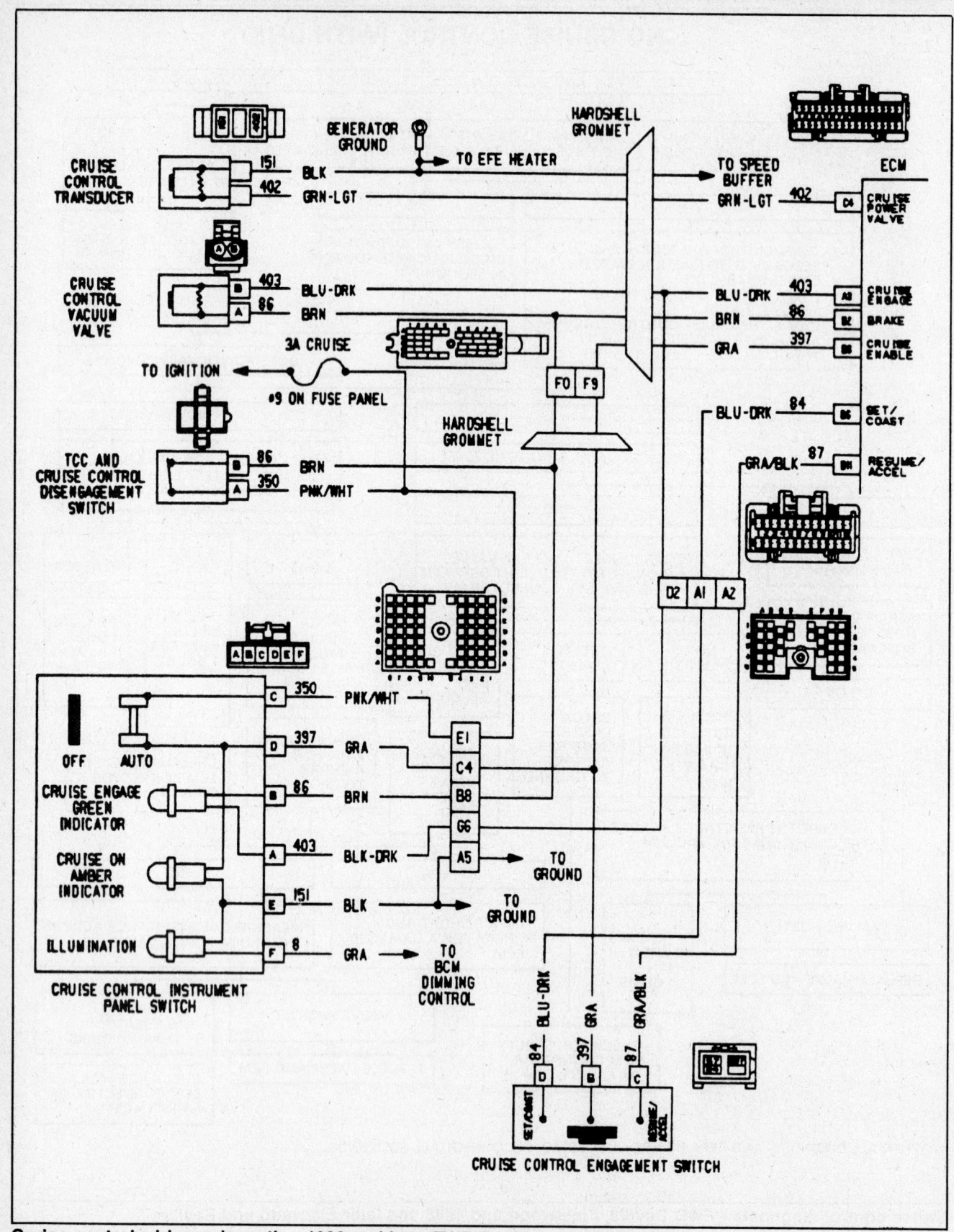

Cruise control wiring schematic—1986 and later FWD Deville and Fleetwood

SERVO ASSEMBLY LINKAGE ADJUSTMENT

For servo linkage adjustments refer to the proper illustration.

Component Replacement

SERVO ASSEMBLY

Removal and Installation

EXCEPT ELDORADO AND SEVILLE

1. Disconnect the negative battery cable.
2. Disconnect the electrical connector from the servo assembly solenoid valve.
3. Disconnect the throttle actuating rod from the servo assembly.
4. Remove the screws securing the servo assembly and the vacuum control valve. Remove the servo assembly from the vehicle.
5. Installation is the reverse of the removal procedure.

ELDORADO AND SEVILLE

1. Disconnect the negative battery cable.
2. Disconnect the electrical connector from the servo assembly. Disconnect the vacuum hoses from the servo assembly.
3. Disconnect the throttle actuating cable from the assembly.
4. Remove the screws securing the servo assembly to its mounting. Remove the servo assembly from the vehicle.
5. Installation is the reverse of the removal procedure. Adjust the servo assembly cable as required.

ELECTRIC BRAKE RELEASE SWITCH AND VACUUM RELEASE VALVE

Removal and installation

1. Disconnect the negative battery cable.
2. Remove the switch electrical and vacuum connectors.
3. Remove the switch from its mounting above the brake pedal.
4. Installation is the reverse of the removal procedure.

Adjustment

1. The switch assembly and the valve assembly cannot be adjusted until after the brake booster push rod is assembled to the brake pedal assembly.
2. To adjust the switch depress the brake pedal and insert the switch assembly and valve assembly into their proper retaining clips until fully seated.
3. Pull the pedal back to its fully retracted position. The switch assembly and the valve assembly will move within the retainers of their adjusted position.
4. The switch assembly contacts must open at 3.5mm to 12.5mm of brake pedal travel. Nominal actuation of the brake light switch is 4.5mm.
5. The vacuum release valve assembly must open at 27.0mm to 33.0mm of brake pedal travel.

CRUISE CONTROL ENGAGEMENT SWITCH

Removal and Installation

EXCEPT ELDORADO AND SEVILLE

1. Disconnect the negative battery cable. Remove the left hand trim panel.
2. Disconnect the cruise control engagement switch electrical connector.
3. Attach a piece of thin wire to the cruise control switch wiring harness.

4. As required remove the steering wheel.
5. Remove the cruise control engagement switch by pulling it out of the detented retaining clip inside the steering column.
6. Pull the cruise control engagement switch harness up and out carefully so that the wire can be used to install the new switch and harness.
7. Removing the protective plastic sheathing for the cruise control wires from the steering column may aid in the removal and installation of the cruise control engagement switch.
8. Installation is the reverse of the removal procedure. The cruise control engagement switch cannot be serviced. The complete turn signal/cruise control engagement switch assembly must be replaced.

ELDORADO AND SEVILLE

1. Disconnect the negative battery cable.
2. Remove the screws retaining the steering wheel pad to the steering wheel.
3. Remove the cruise control switch connector. Remove the horn lead.
4. Remove the screws retaining the horn contact assembly. Remove the nuts attaching the retainer and the cruise control switch assembly.
5. Remove the resume switch button. Remove the trim plate.
6. Installation is the reverse of the removal procedure.

SPEED SENSOR

Removal and Installation

1. Disconnect the negative battery cable.
2. Raise and support the vehicle safely.
3. Disconnect the speed sensor electrical connector. Remove the speed sensor retainer.

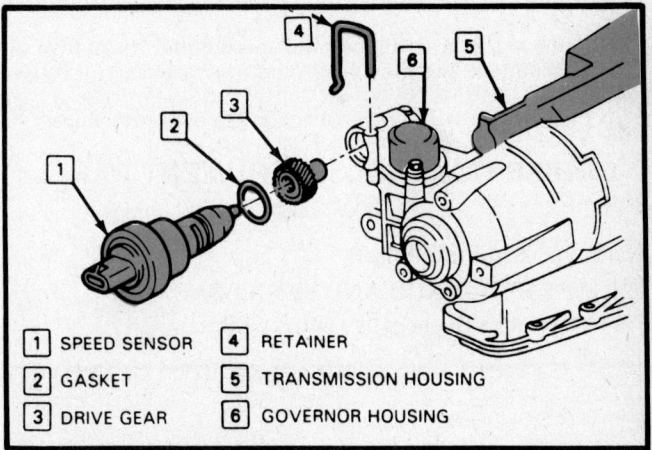

1 SPEED SENSOR		**4** RETAINER	
2 GASKET		**5** TRANSMISSION HOUSING	
3 DRIVE GEAR		**6** GOVERNOR HOUSING	

Speed sensor assembly

4. Remove the speed sensor and the drive gear from the transmission.
5. Installation is the reverse of the removal procedure. The retainer must be seated on the speed sensor assembly motor governor cover.

BUFFER AMPLIFIER

Removal and Installation

EXCEPT ELDORADO AND SEVILLE

1. Disconnect the negative battery cable.
2. Remove the right hand trim panel. Remove the glove box assembly.

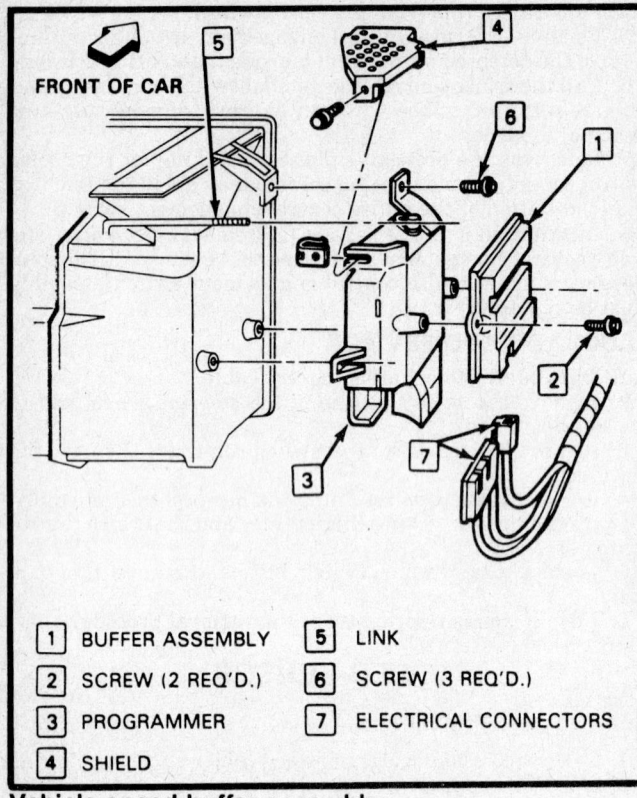

1 BUFFER ASSEMBLY   5 LINK
2 SCREW (2 REQ'D.)   6 SCREW (3 REQ'D.)
3 PROGRAMMER   7 ELECTRICAL CONNECTORS
4 SHIELD

Vehicle speed buffer assembly

3. Remove the buffer assembly shield. Remove the retaining link.
4. Remove the programmer and speed buffer assembly.
5. Disconnect the electrical connectors from the buffer assembly.
6. Installation is the reverse of the removal procedure.

CRUISE CONTROL INSTRUMENT PANEL SWITCH

Removal and Installation
EXCEPT ELDORADO AND SEVILLE

1. Disconnect the negative battery cable.

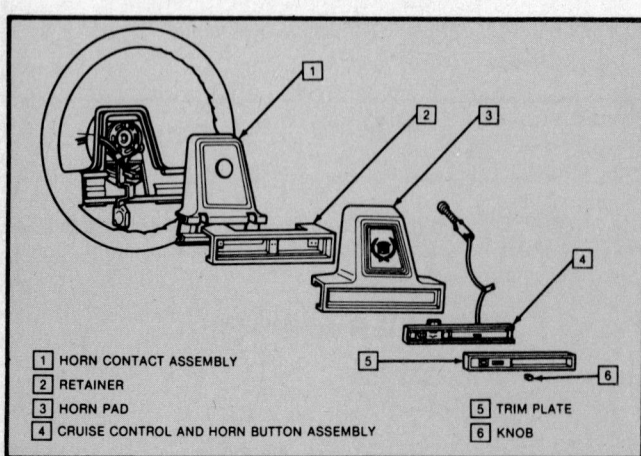

1 HORN CONTACT ASSEMBLY
2 RETAINER
3 HORN PAD
4 CRUISE CONTROL AND HORN BUTTON ASSEMBLY
5 TRIM PLATE
6 KNOB

Cruise control switch assembly—1986 and later Eldorado and Seville

2. Remove the trim plate. Remove the switch retaining screws.
3. Remove the switch assembly from its mounting. Disconnect the electrical connectors from the switch assembly.
4. Installation is the reverse of the removal procedure.

ELDORADO AND SEVILLE

1. Disconnect the negative battery cable.
2. Remove the left hand lower sound insulator.
3. Remove the cruise control switch retainer. Remove the switch assembly from its mounting.
4. Disconnect the switch electrical connectors.
5. Installation is the reverse of the removal procedure.

Chevrolet

VISUAL INSPECTION

Before performing any tests make a visual inspection of the cruise control system. Check all items in the system for abnormal conditions such as bare broken or disconnected wires and damage to the vacuum hoses. Be sure that the speedometer cables are attached and properly routed. All vacuum hoses must be properly routed and must not have any kinks or bends. Be sure that all electrical connections are complete and tight. The wiring harness must be routed properly.

SERVO TEST (1982–83)

To determine the condition of the servo diaphragm, remove the vacuum hose from the servo assembly. Apply 14 inches of vacuum to the tube opening and hold in in place for about one minute. The vacuum should not leak down more than 5 inches. If vacuum leaks, replace the servo assembly.

Another test consists of removing the vacuum hose attached to the servo assembly, than push the diaphragm in, hold your finger over the nipple and the diaphragm should remain in the pushed in position. If the servo assembly does not perform as indicated it should be replaced.

VACUUM LEAK TEST (1982–83)

The vacuum release valves, the resume valve and all the connecting hoses can be checked by applying 15 inches of vacuum to each component and then sealing off the component for about one minute. The vacuum should not leak down more than 5 inches. Repair or replace defective components as required.

ELECTRICAL SYSTEM TEST (1982–83)

1. Check the cruise control fuse and electrical connector.
2. Check all electrical connections. Disconnect and reconnect after checking for bent, broken or dirty mating tabs.
3. Check the electrical release switch as follows. Unplug the connector at the switch. Connect an ohmmeter to the two terminals on the switch assembly.
4. Depress the brake or clutch pedal. The ohmmeter should not indicate continuity.
5. Release the pedal, the ohmmeter should indicate continunity.

CONTROL LEVER SWITCH TEST (1982–83)

1. Disconnect the electrical connector at the cruise control engagement switch.
2. Connect an ohmmeter to the brown and blue wires.
3. Slide the resume switch to the on position. The ohmmeter

should indicate continunity. Push the engage button all the way in and and open circuit should be indicated.

4. Connect an ohmmeter to the brown and black wires, with the resume switch still in the on position. An open circuit should be indicated.

5. Depress the engage button and release it half way. Continunity should exist.

6. Connect an ohmmeter to the blue and black wires with the resume switch still in the on position. With the engaged button released, no continunity should be present.

7. With the engaged button depressed and half way released continunity should exist.

HARNESS AND TRANSDUCER ELECTRICAL TEST (1982–83)

1. Using an ohmmeter engage, with the engagement switch connector disconnected, check the resistance of the dark green wire in the wiring harness. If the transducer is grounded properly, the ohmmeter should indicate between 29 and 36 ohms.

2. If resistance is above or below specification, disconnect the connector at the transducer and at the resume solenoid.

3. Measure the resistance of the dark green wire. It should indicate a resistance reading of 23 ohms, plus or minus one ohm. If the reading is not as indicated the wiring harness should be replaced.

4. With the connectors of the transducer disconnected, measure the resistance of the solenoid coil by connecting the ohmmeter to the hold terminal and ground. A reading of 5 to 6 ohms should be indicated.

5. If a reading of 4 ohms or less is obtained there is excessive resistance in the circuit. If a reading of 6 ohms or more is indicated the transducer should be checked.

TRANSDUCER TEST (1982–83)

The only test that is possible to check the transducer assembly is the transducer orifice tube adjustment. Before adjusting the transducer assembly be sure that all vacuum hoses are in good condition. Be sure that all electrical connections are correct. Be sure that the electrical and vacuum release valves are working properly.

VACUUM REGULATOR TEST (1982–83)

If the vehicle is equipped with a diesel engine a vacuum regulator valve is used. This vacuum regulator valve regulates the vacuum from the engine mounted vacuum pump. To test the regulator use a vacuum pump. The vacuum level should be about 6 in. hg. or slightly higher if cold. If the valve does not perform as indicated it must be replaced.

VACUUM PUMP ASSISTED SYSTEMS TEST (1982–83)

1. Blow low air pressure into port "A" while port "B" is plugged. Then plug port "A" and blow low air pressure into port "B".

2. In both cases air should exit port "C". If not clean or replace the check valve.

3. To check the air flow in the other direction, blow low air pressure into port "C". No air should come out of port "A" or port "B".

VACUUM PUMP TEST

A vacuum pump is used on all 1983 Camaros equipped with the 2.5 liter TBI engine. The pump is installed in the same location as the mechanical fuel pump would be for non TBI engines. The vacuum pump is operated by a lobe on the camshaft.

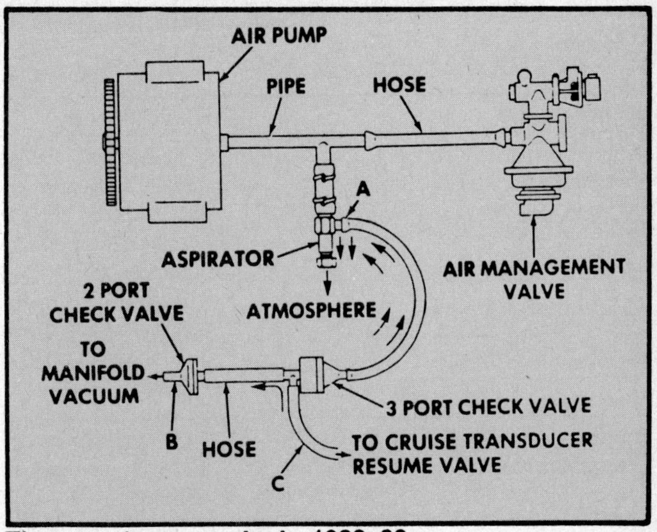

Three port vacuum test—1982–83

Testing

1. Remove the vacuum lines from both ports at the pump. Plug the hose openings.

2. Install a vacuum gauge to the inlet port of the vacuum pump.

3. Start the engine and operate it at idle. Observe the vacuum gauge.

4. After about one minute the minimum vacuum reading should be 15.0 HG.

5. If not within specification, repair or replace defective components as required.

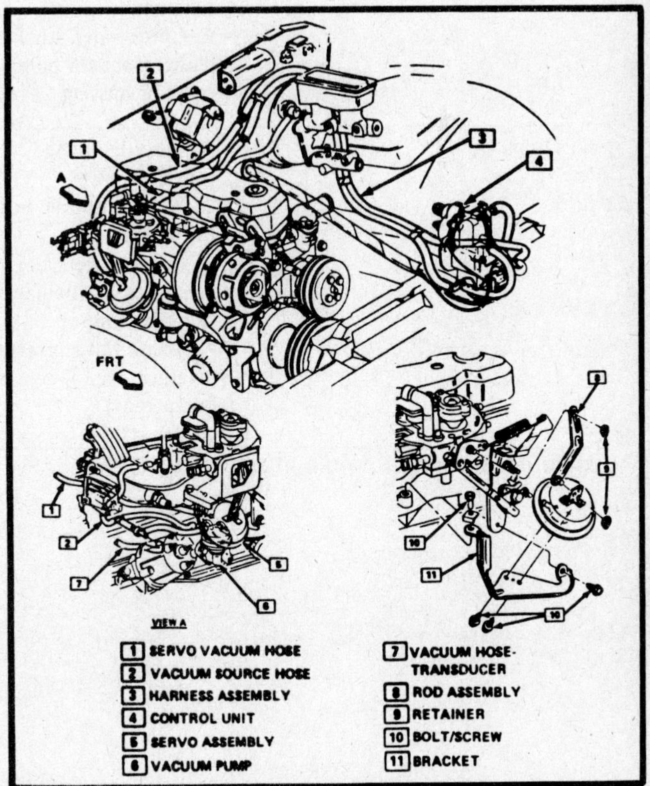

Vacuum pump location and house routing—1983 Camaro

DIAGNOSIS AND TESTING PROCEDURES

Condition	Possible Cause	Correction
Speed increases after engagement.	1. Speedometer cable (needle) fluctuates due to speedo cable or housing bent, kinked or misrouted. 2. Transducer orifice tube out of adjustment. 3. Transducer malfunction.	1. Correct as necessary. 2. Adjust. 3. Replace.
Speed drops off after engagement.	1. Throttle linkage too loose. Vacuum leak or restriction. 2. Transducer orifice tube out of adjustment.	1. Check for damaged, disconnected, pinched, or kinked hoses. Repair or replace as required. Adjust throttle linkage. 2. Adjust.
Surging	1. Check for rstricted vacuum line from engine to transducer. 2. Check to insure that servo unit will full stroke. 3. Transducer malfunction. 4. Check valve stuck closed (vacuum pump only) or missing.	1. Repair or replace. 2. Replace servo unit. 3. Replace. 4. Install or re-orient check valve as necessary.
Speed Drops Off Excessively on Inclines	1. Throttle linkage too loose. 2. Vacuum source hose restricted. 3. Cruise system not connected to auxiliary vacuum pump. 4. Check valve reversed or stuck open (vacuum pump only).	1. Adjust. 2. Repair or Replace. 3. Correct (See vacuum schematics). 4. Re-orient or replace as necessary.

Cruise control Trouble diagnosis chart (1982–83)

CRUISE CONTROL DIAGNOSIS

PRELIMINARY CHECKS

1. Check Servo Chain or rod adjustment. Must have minimum slack.
2. Check vacuum hoses. Must be in good condition - no restrictions or leaks.
3. Check drive cable routings. No kinks or sharp bends.
4. Check throttle linkage or cable for binding.
5. Check adjustment of electrical release switch and vacuum release valve.
6. Check engagement switch operation.
7. If steps 1 through 6 do not solve the problem, continue with diagnosis.

CRUISE CONTROL INOPERATIVE

1. Check radio fuse. If blown, check wiring for short circuit and repair. A shorted resume solenoid diode could also cause blow fuse.
2. If fuse and preliminary checks ok, resume solenoid must be checked. Start engine and check source vacuum at resume solenoid (refer to picture at right). Disconnect the two wire connector at resume solenoid. Use jumper wire to ground terminal which had black wire connected to it. Apply 12 volts to terminal which had tan wire connected to it. Disconnect outlet vacuum hose (going to B fitting on transducer). Vacuum should be present. If not, replace resume solenoid. Applying voltage incorrectly to resume solenoid could damage diode. If above checks ok, stop engine and reconnect electrical and vacuum connections.
3. To make test below, turn ignition to RUN position and off/on/resume switch to ON. Disconnect the two wire connector at transducer (Engage-Hold Terminals).
4. Connect 12 volt test light to ground and to engage wire in connector. Push engage/coast button in part way to engage position.
5. Repeat test on hold wire in connector.

TEST LIGHT OFF AT ONE WIRE ONLY

Test engagement switch. (See test procedure) Check for open circuit in wire if test light did not light. Repair or replace part that checks bad.

TEST LIGHT ON AT BOTH WIRES (MAY BE DIM ON HOLD WIRE)

Check for poor ground at transducer. If ok, remove transducer for repair.

TEST LIGHT OFF AT BOTH WIRES

Check for open circuit in brown/white wire from fuse panel to off/on/resume switch. If circuit ok, check engagement switch operation and replace if necessary.

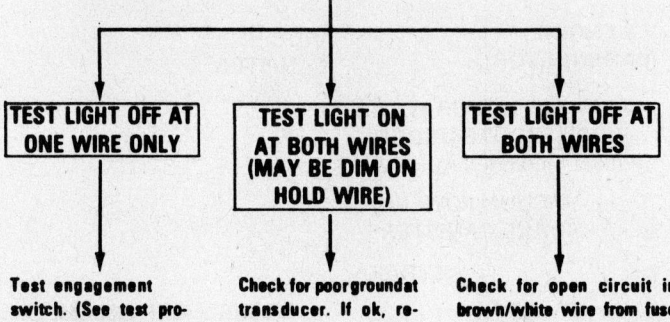

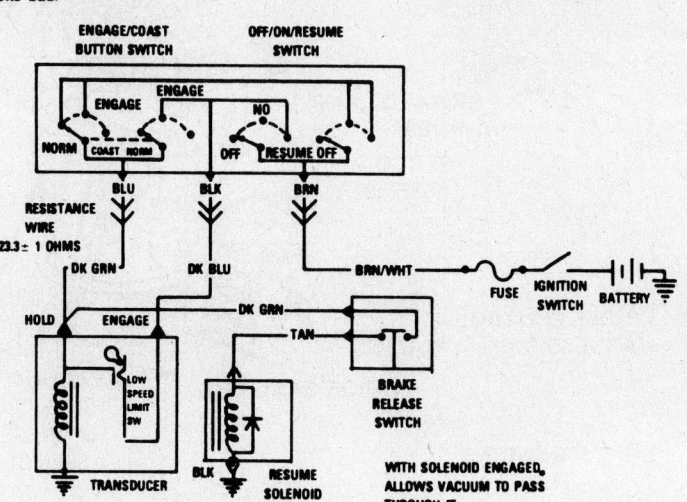

ENGAGE TERMINAL
SPEEDOMETER CABLE DRIVE CABLE TO SERVO
HOLD TERMINAL
REGULATED AIR BLEED ORIFICE TUBE
OUTPUT VACUUM
RESUME SOLENOID VALVE
TO BRAKE RELEASE VALVE
VACUUM SOURCE
AIR FILTER

REGULATED AIR BLEED — TRANSDUCER SOLENOID VALVE — NOT ENGAGED
SERVO — ENGINE VACUUM SOURCE — RESUME SOLENOID VALVE — TO BRAKE RELEASE VALVE

REGULATED AIR BLEED — TRANSDUCER SOLENOID VALVE — ENGAGED
SERVO — ENGINE VACUUM SOURCE — RESUME SOLENOID VALVE — TO BRAKE RELEASE VALVE

REGULATED AIR BLEED — TRANSDUCER SOLENOID VALVE — NOT ENGAGED WITH SET SPEED IN MEMORY
SERVO — ENGINE VACUUM SOURCE — RESUME SOLENOID VALVE — TO BRAKE RELEASE VALVE

ENGAGE/COAST BUTTON SWITCH
OFF/ON/RESUME SWITCH

ENGAGEMENT SWITCH TEST PROCEDURE				
USE A SELF POWERED TEST LIGHT. LIGHT WILL BE ON FOR EACH TEST IF SWITCH IS GOOD. CONNECTOR TERMINALS AND COLOR 1 — BROWN, 2 — BLUE, 3 — BLACK				
SWITCH POSITIONS		TERMINALS		
ENGAGE BUTTON	RESUME SWITCH	1 to 2	1 to 3	2 to 3
Released	on	closed	open	open
Fully Depressed	on	open	open	closed
Partially Released	on	closed	closed	closed
Released	resume	closed	closed	closed
Released	off	open	open	open

ENGAGE
NORM COAST NORM
NO OFF RESUME OFF

BLU BLK BRN
RESISTANCE WIRE 23.3 ± 1 OHMS
DK GRN DK BLU BRN/WHT FUSE IGNITION SWITCH BATTERY
HOLD ENGAGE DK GRN TAN
LOW SPEED LIMIT SW
BRAKE RELEASE SWITCH
TRANSDUCER BLK RESUME SOLENOID VALVE
WITH SOLENOID ENGAGED, ALLOWS VACUUM TO PASS THROUGH IT

Cruise control diagnosis (1982–83)

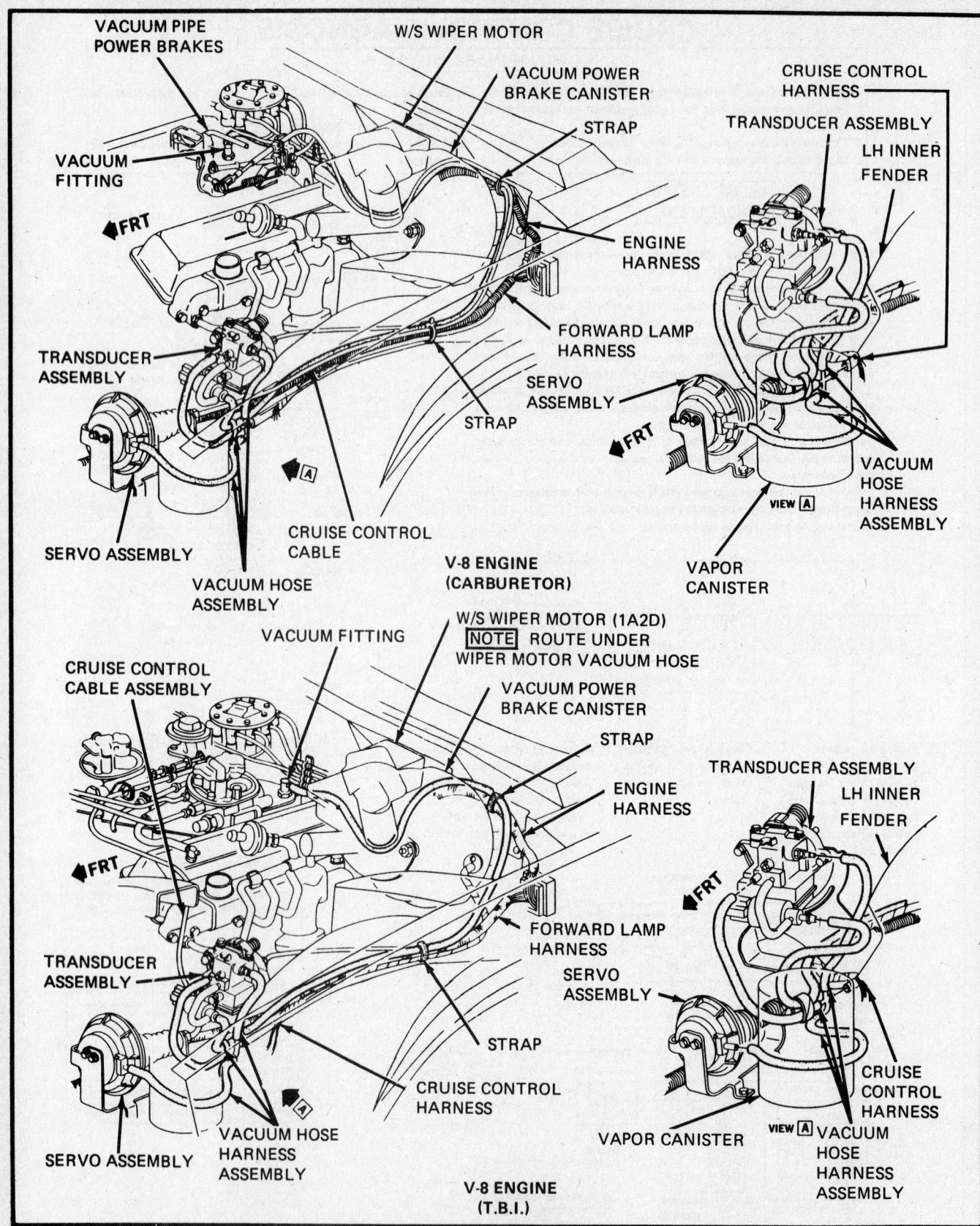

VACUUM PIPE POWER BRAKES

W/S WIPER MOTOR

VACUUM POWER BRAKE CANISTER

STRAP

CRUISE CONTROL HARNESS

VACUUM FITTING

TRANSDUCER ASSEMBLY

LH INNER FENDER

FRT

ENGINE HARNESS

TRANSDUCER ASSEMBLY

FORWARD LAMP HARNESS

SERVO ASSEMBLY

STRAP

SERVO ASSEMBLY

VACUUM HOSE HARNESS ASSEMBLY

CRUISE CONTROL CABLE

V-8 ENGINE (CARBURETOR)

VIEW A

VAPOR CANISTER

VACUUM HOSE HARNESS ASSEMBLY

VACUUM FITTING

W/S WIPER MOTOR (1A2D)
NOTE ROUTE UNDER WIPER MOTOR VACUUM HOSE

CRUISE CONTROL CABLE ASSEMBLY

VACUUM POWER BRAKE CANISTER

STRAP

ENGINE HARNESS

TRANSDUCER ASSEMBLY

LH INNER FENDER

FRT

FRT

FORWARD LAMP HARNESS

TRANSDUCER ASSEMBLY

SERVO ASSEMBLY

STRAP

CRUISE CONTROL HARNESS

CRUISE CONTROL HARNESS

SERVO ASSEMBLY

VACUUM HOSE HARNESS ASSEMBLY

CRUISE CONTROL HARNESS

VAPOR CANISTER

VIEW A

VACUUM HOSE HARNESS ASSEMBLY

V-8 ENGINE (T.B.I.)

Cruise control vacuum schematic—1982–83 Camaro with V8 engine

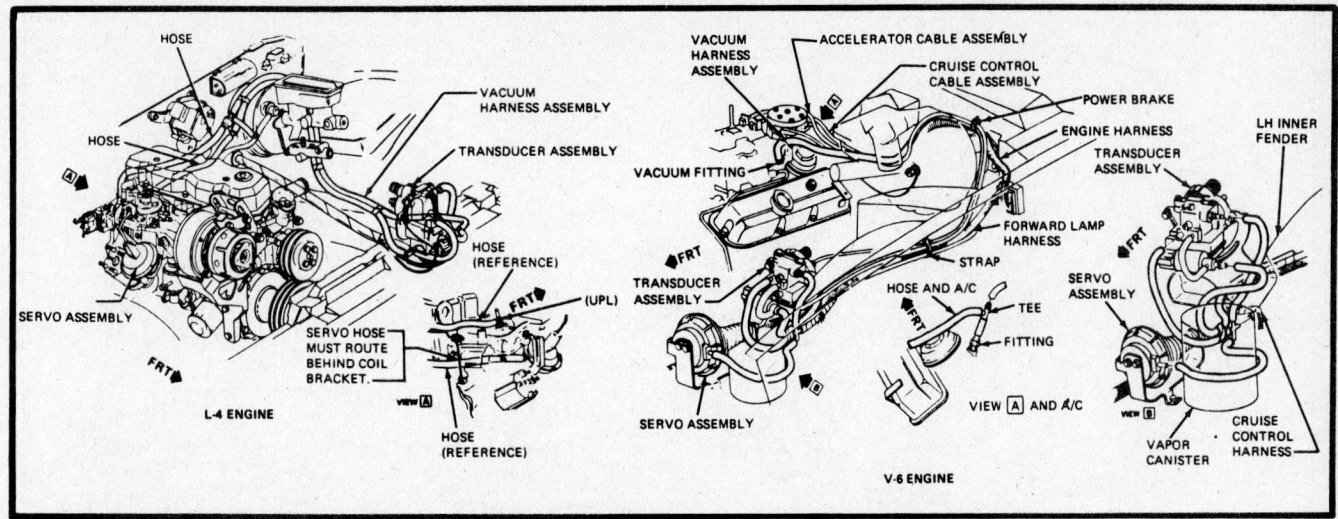

Cruise control vacuum schematic — 1982–83 Camaro with four and six cylinder engines

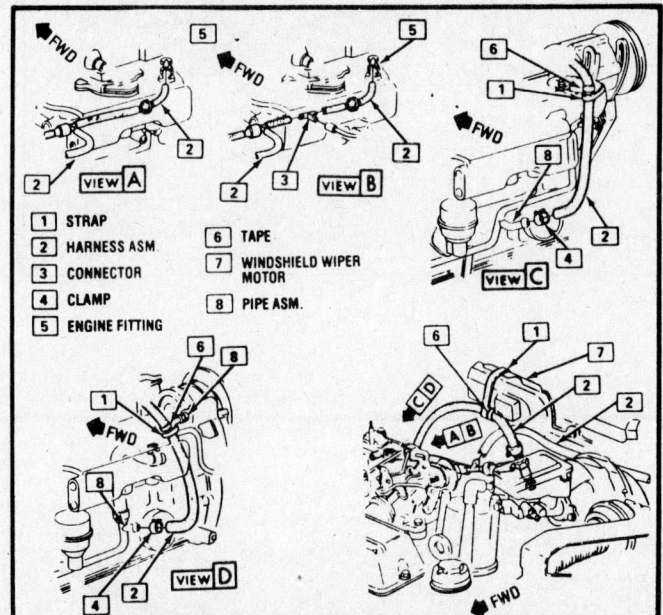

Cruise control vacuum schematic — 1982–83 Cavalier

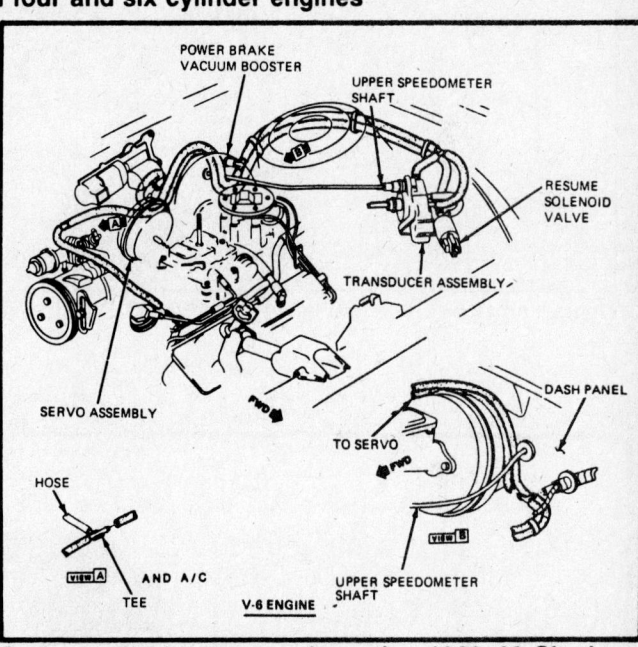

Cruise control vacuum schematic — 1982–83 Citation and Celebrity with V6 engine

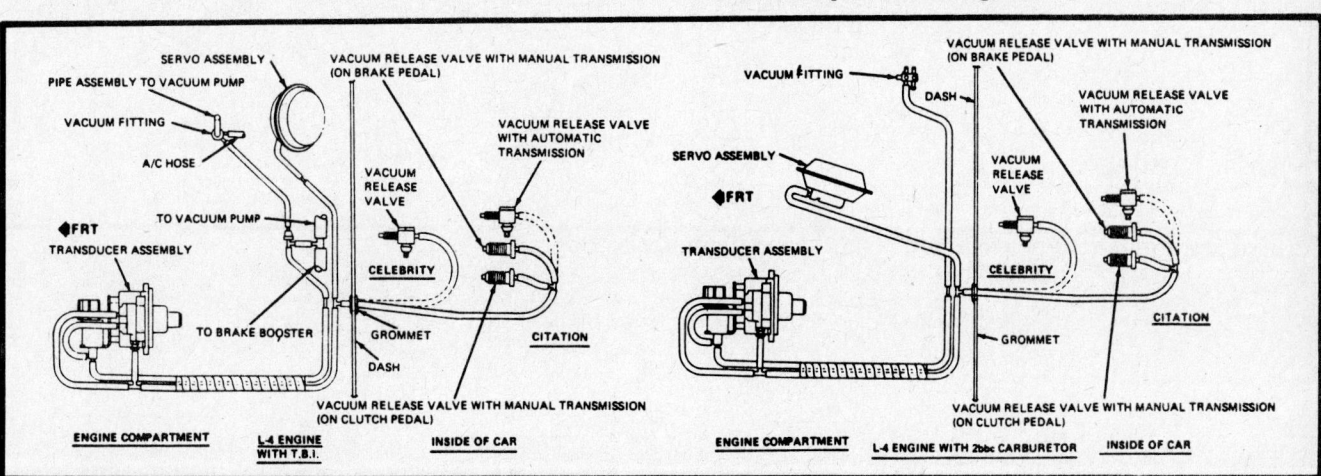

Cruise control vacuum schematic — 1982–83 Citation and Celebrity with four cylinder engine

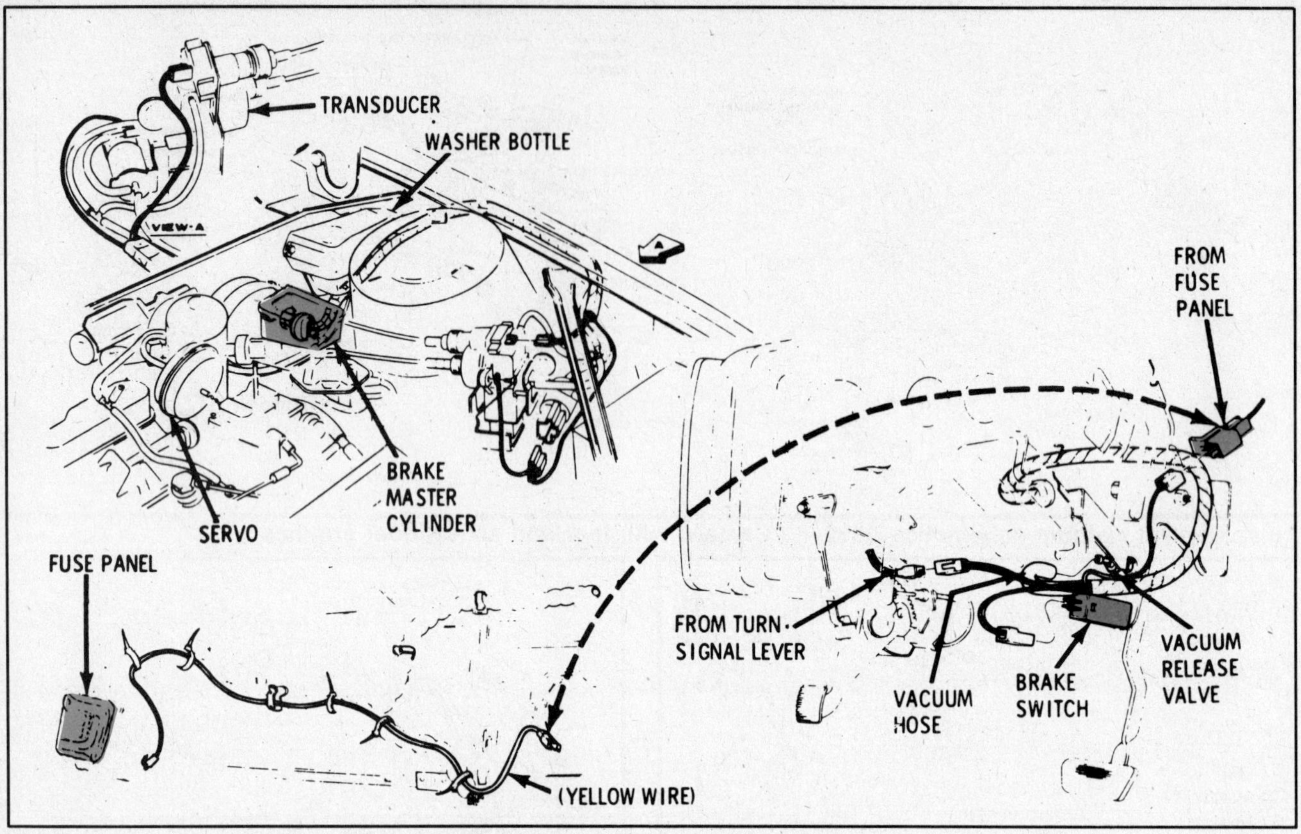

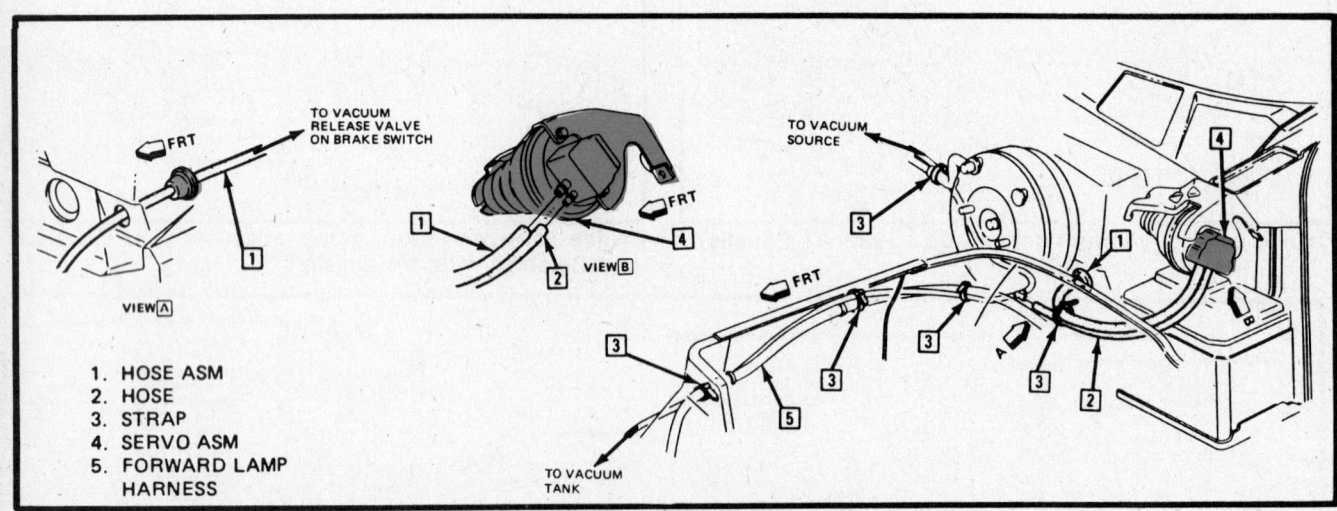

Cruise control electrical wiring—1982–83 Citation and Celebrity

TRANSDUCER

WASHER BOTTLE

FROM FUSE PANEL

BRAKE MASTER CYLINDER

SERVO

FUSE PANEL

FROM TURN SIGNAL LEVER

VACUUM HOSE

BRAKE SWITCH

VACUUM RELEASE VALVE

(YELLOW WIRE)

VIEW A

TO VACUUM RELEASE VALVE ON BRAKE SWITCH

FRT

VIEW B

TO VACUUM SOURCE

FRT

TO VACUUM TANK

VIEW A

1. HOSE ASM
2. HOSE
3. STRAP
4. SERVO ASM
5. FORWARD LAMP HARNESS

Cruise control vacuum schematic—1985 and later Corvette

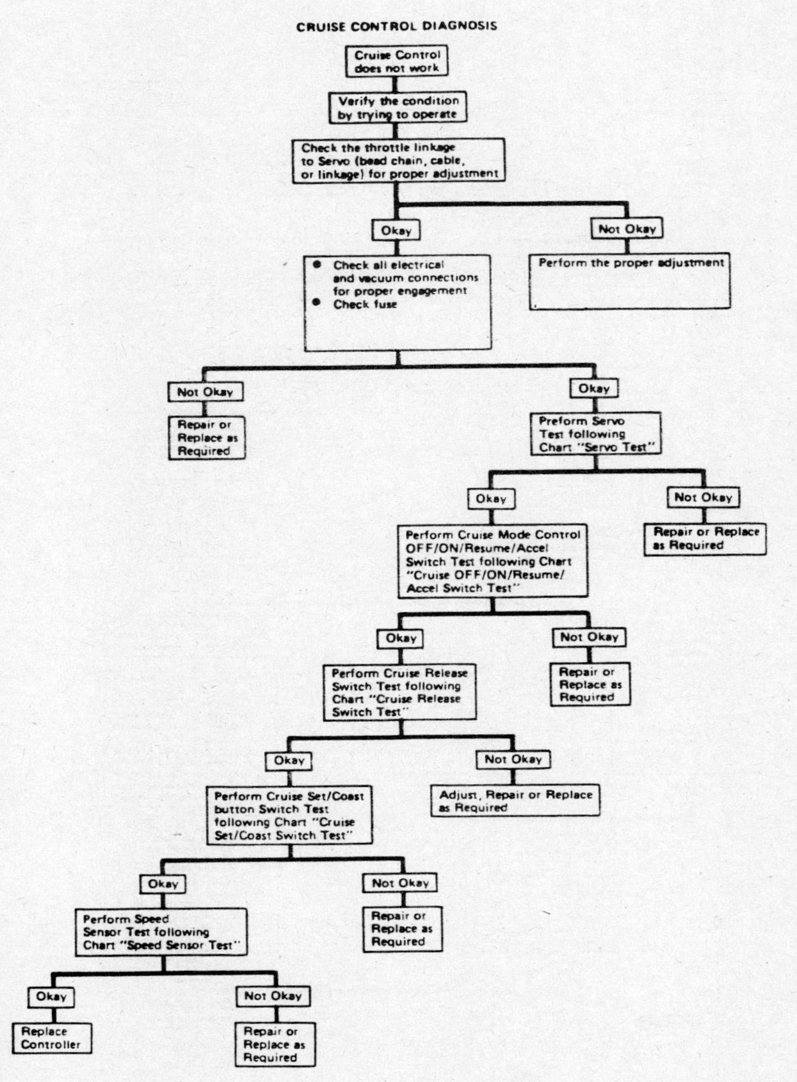

Cruise control diagnosis — 1984 and later Chevrolet

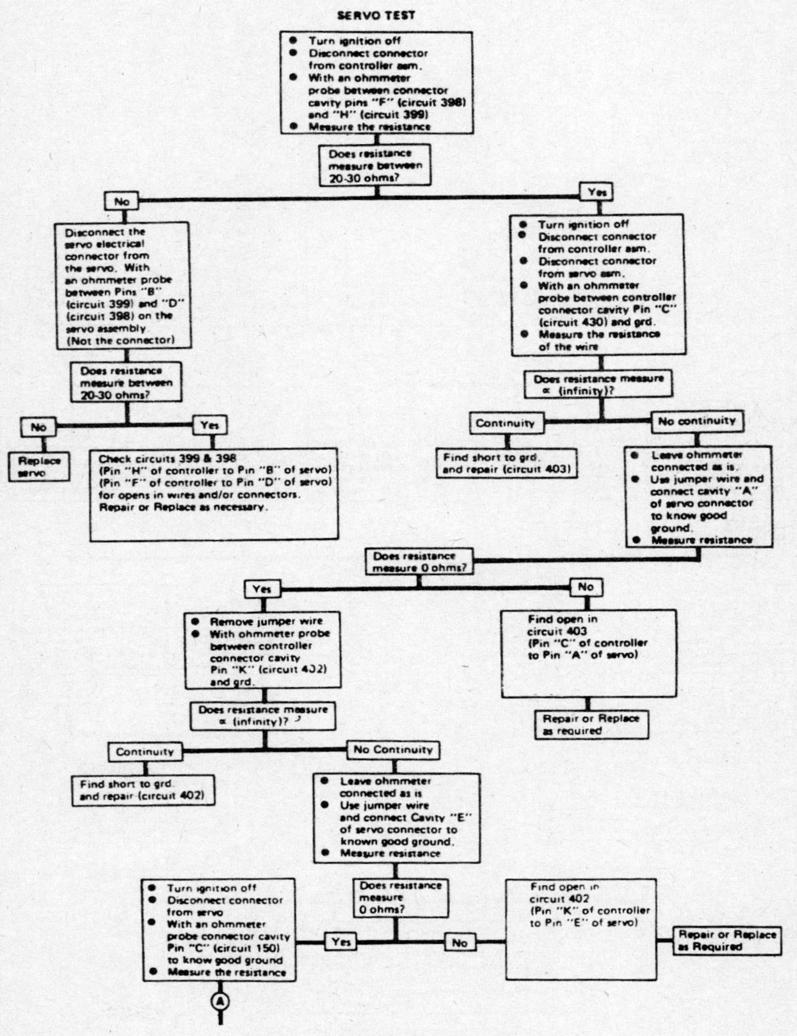

SERVO TEST

- Turn ignition off
- Disconnect connector from controller asm.
- With an ohmmeter probe between connector cavity pins "F" (circuit 398) and "H" (circuit 399)
- Measure the resistance

Does resistance measure between 20-30 ohm?

Yes:
- Turn ignition off
- Disconnect connector from controller asm.
- Disconnect connector from servo
- With an ohmmeter probe between controller connector cavity Pin "C" (circuit 430) and grd. Measure the resistance of the wire

Does resistance measure at (infinity)?

No continuity:
- Leave ohmmeter connected as is.
- Use jumper wire to connect cavity "A" of servo connector to know good ground. Measure resistance

No:
Find open in circuit 403 (Pin "C" of controller to Pin "A" of servo)

Continuity:
Find short to grd. and repair (circuit 403)

Repair or Replace as required

No:
Disconnect the servo electrical connector from the servo. With an ohmmeter probe between Pins "B" (circuit 399) and "D" (circuit 398) on the servo assembly (Not the connector)

Does resistance measure between 20-30 ohm?

Yes:
Check circuits 399 & 398 (Pin "H" of controller to Pin "B" of servo) (Pin "F" of controller to Pin "D" of servo) for opens in wires and/or connections. Repair or Replace as necessary.

No:
Replace servo

Does resistance measure 0 ohms?

Yes:
- Remove jumper wire
- With ohmmeter probe between controller connector cavity Pin "K" (circuit 402) and grd.

Does resistance measure at (infinity)?

No Continuity:
- Leave ohmmeter connected as is.
- Use jumper wire and connect Cavity "E" of servo connector to known good ground. Measure resistance

No:
Find open in circuit 403 (Pin "C" of controller to Pin "A" of servo)

Continuity:
Find short to grd. and repair (circuit 402)

No:
Find open in circuit 402 (Pin "K" of controller to Pin "E" of servo)

Does resistance measure 0 ohm?

Yes:
- Turn ignition off
- Disconnect connector from servo
- With an ohmmeter probe between servo cavity Pin "C" (circuit 150) to known good ground
- Measure the resistance

Ⓐ

Repair or Replace as Required

Cruise control diagnosis — 1984 and later Chevrolet

CRUISE CONTROL DIAGNOSIS

Cruise Control does not work.

Verify the condition by trying to operate

Check the throttle linkage to Servo (bead chain, cable, or linkage) for proper adjustment

Not Okay:
Perform the proper adjustment

Okay:
- Check all electrical and vacuum connections for proper engagement
- Check fuse

Not Okay:
Repair or Replace as Required

Okay:
Preform Servo Test following Chart "Servo Test"

Not Okay:
Repair or Replace as Required

Okay:
Perform Cruise Mode Control OFF/ON/Resume/Accel Switch Test following Chart "Cruise OFF/ON/Resume/Accel Switch Test"

Not Okay:
Repair or Replace as Required

Okay:
Perform Cruise Release Switch Test following Chart "Cruise Release Switch Test"

Not Okay:
Adjust, Repair or Replace as Required

Okay:
Perform Cruise Set/Coast button Switch Test following Chart "Cruise Set/Coast Switch Test"

Not Okay:
Repair or Replace as Required

Okay:
Perform Speed Sensor Test following Chart "Speed Sensor Test"

Not Okay:
Repair or Replace as Required

Okay:
Replace Controller

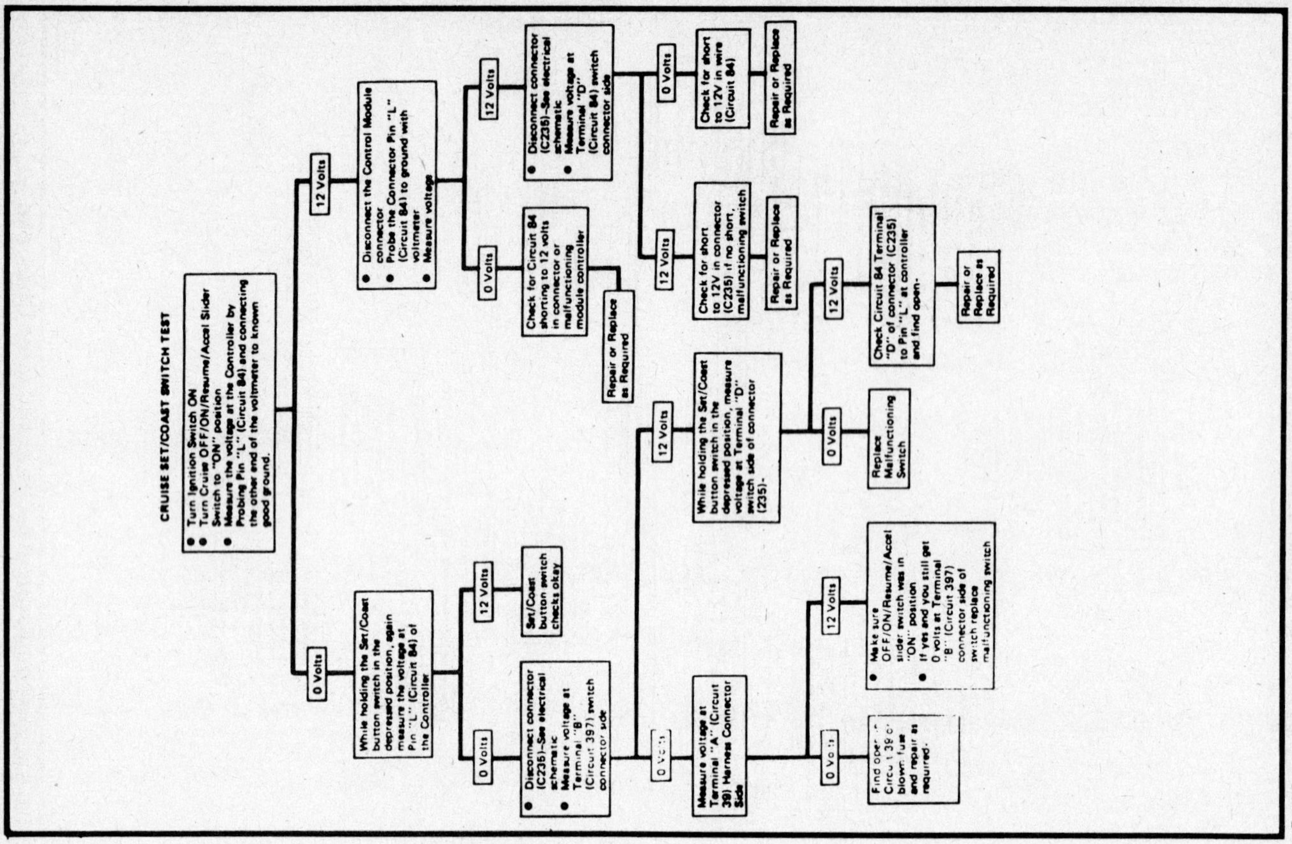

CRUISE SET/COAST SWITCH TEST

- Turn Ignition Switch ON
- Turn Cruise OFF/ON/Resume/Accel Slider Switch to "ON" position
- Measure the voltage at the Controller by Probing Pin "L" (Circuit 84) and connecting the other end of the voltmeter to known good ground.

12 Volts

- Disconnect the Control Module connector
- Probe the Connector Pin "L" (Circuit 84) to ground with voltmeter
- Measure voltage

12 Volts

- Disconnect connector (C235)—See electrical schematic. Measure voltage at Terminal "D" (Circuit 84) switch connector side

0 Volts — Check for short to 12V in wire (Circuit 84) — Repair or Replace as Required

0 Volts — Check for Circuit 84 shorting to 12 volts in connector or malfunctioning module controller — Repair or Replace as Required

12 Volts — Check for short to 12V in connector (C235) if no short, malfunctioning switch — Repair or Replace as Required

12 Volts — Check Circuit 84 Terminal "D" of connector (C235) to Pin "L" at controller and find open— — Repair or Replace as Required

0 Volts

While holding the Set/Coast button switch in the depressed position, measure voltage at Terminal "D" switch side of connector (235)-

12 Volts — Replace Malfunctioning Switch

0 Volts

- Make sure OFF/ON/Resume/Accel slider switch was in "ON" position
- If yes and you still get 0 volts at Terminal "B" (Circuit 397) connector side of switch replace malfunctioning switch

12 Volts

0 Volts

While holding the Set/Coast button switch in the depressed position, again measure the voltage at Pin "L" (Circuit 84) of the Controller

12 Volts — Set/Coast button switch checks okay

0 Volts

- Disconnect connector (C235)-See electrical schematic. Measure voltage at Terminal "B" (Circuit 397) switch connector side

12 Volts

0 Volts — Measure voltage at Terminal "A" (Circuit 39) Harness Connector Side

0 Volts — Find open in Circuit 39 or blown fuse and repair as required.

Cruise control diagnosis — 1984 and later Chevrolet

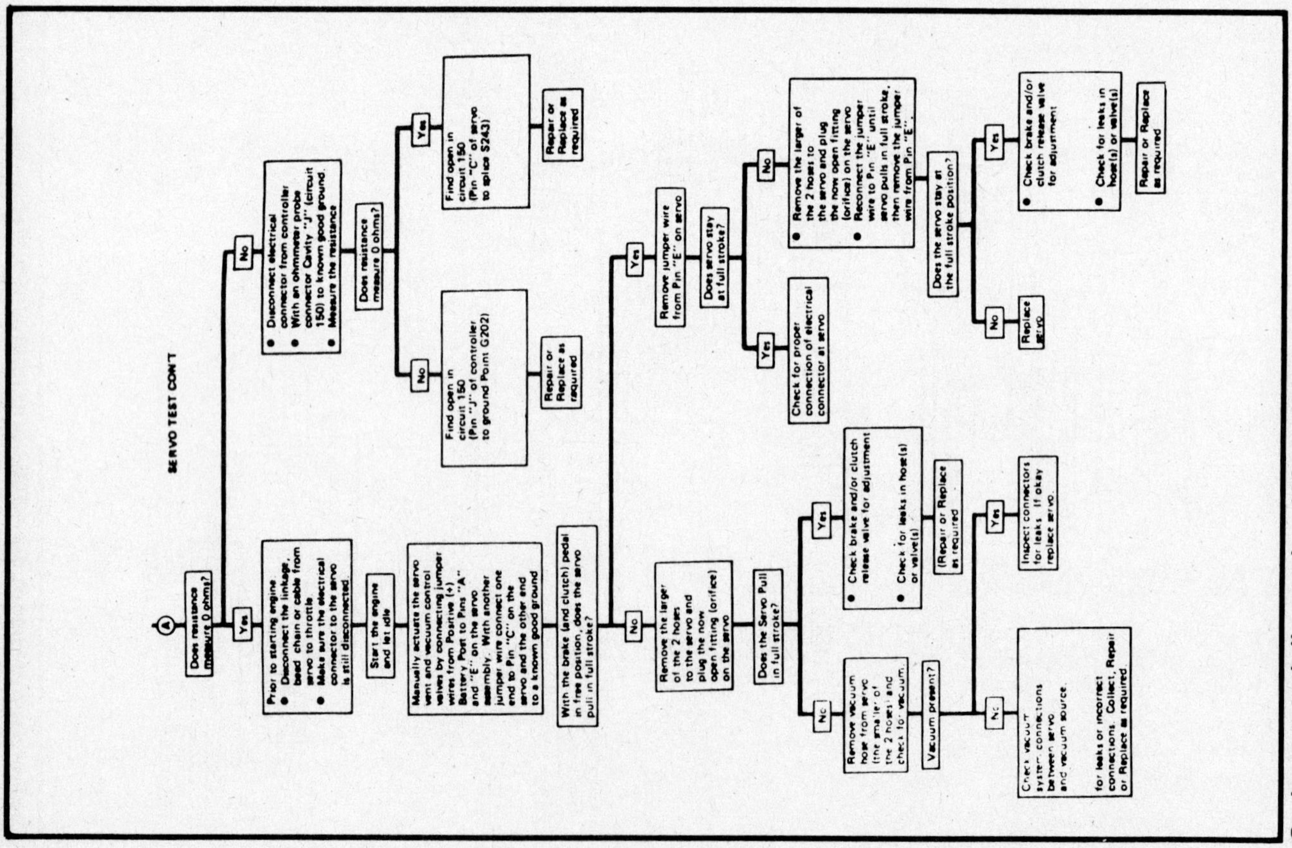

SERVO TEST CON'T

Does resistance measure 0 ohms?

No
- Disconnect electrical connector from controller
- With an ohmmeter probe connector Cavity "J" (circuit 150) to known good ground
- Measure the resistance

Does resistance measure 0 ohms?

Yes — Find open in circuit (Pin "J" of servo to splice S243) — Repair or Replace as required

No — Find open in circuit 150 (Pin "J" of controller to ground Point G202) — Repair or Replace as required

Yes

Prior to starting engine
- Disconnect the linkage bead chain or cable from servo to throttle
- Make sure electrical connector to the servo is still disconnected

Start the engine and let idle

Manually actuate the servo vent and vacuum control valves by connecting jumper wires from Positive (+) Battery "Port to Pins "A" and "E" on the servo assembly. With another jumper wire connect one end to Pin "C" on the servo and the other end to a known good ground

With the brake (and clutch) pedal in free position, does the servo pull in full stroke?

Yes — Remove jumper wire from Pin "E" on servo

Does servo stay at full stroke?

Yes — Check for proper connection of electrical connector at servo

No
- Remove the larger of the 2 hoses to the servo and plug the now open fitting (orifice) on the servo
- Reconnect the jumper wire to Pin "E" until servo pulls in full stroke, then remove the jumper wire from Pin "E"

Does the servo stay at the full stroke position?

Yes
- Check brake and/or clutch release valve for adjustment
- Check for leaks in hose(s) or valve(s)
- Repair or Replace as required

No — Replace servo

No

Remove the larger of the 2 hoses to the servo and plug the now open fitting (orifice) on the servo

Does the Servo Pull in full stroke?

Yes
- Check brake and/or clutch release valve for adjustment
- Check for leaks in hose(s) or valve(s)
- (Repair or Replace) as required

Inspect connectors for leaks, if okay replace servo

No

Remove vacuum hose from servo (the smaller of the 2 hoses) and check for vacuum.

Vacuum present?

Yes

No

Check vacuum system connections between servo and vacuum source for leaks or incorrect connections. Collect, Repair or Replace as required.

Cruise control diagnosis — 1984 and later Chevrolet

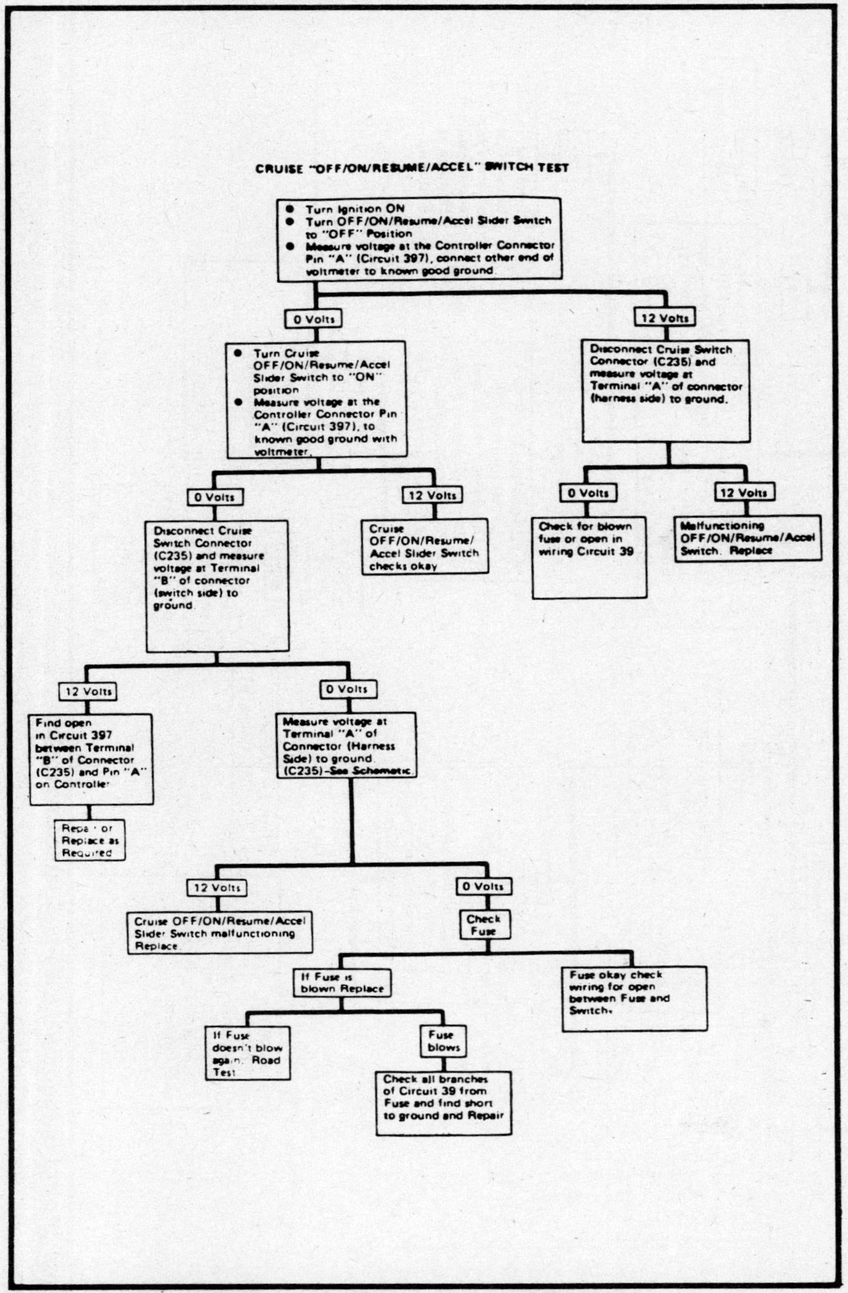

Cruise control diagnosis—1984 and later Chevrolet

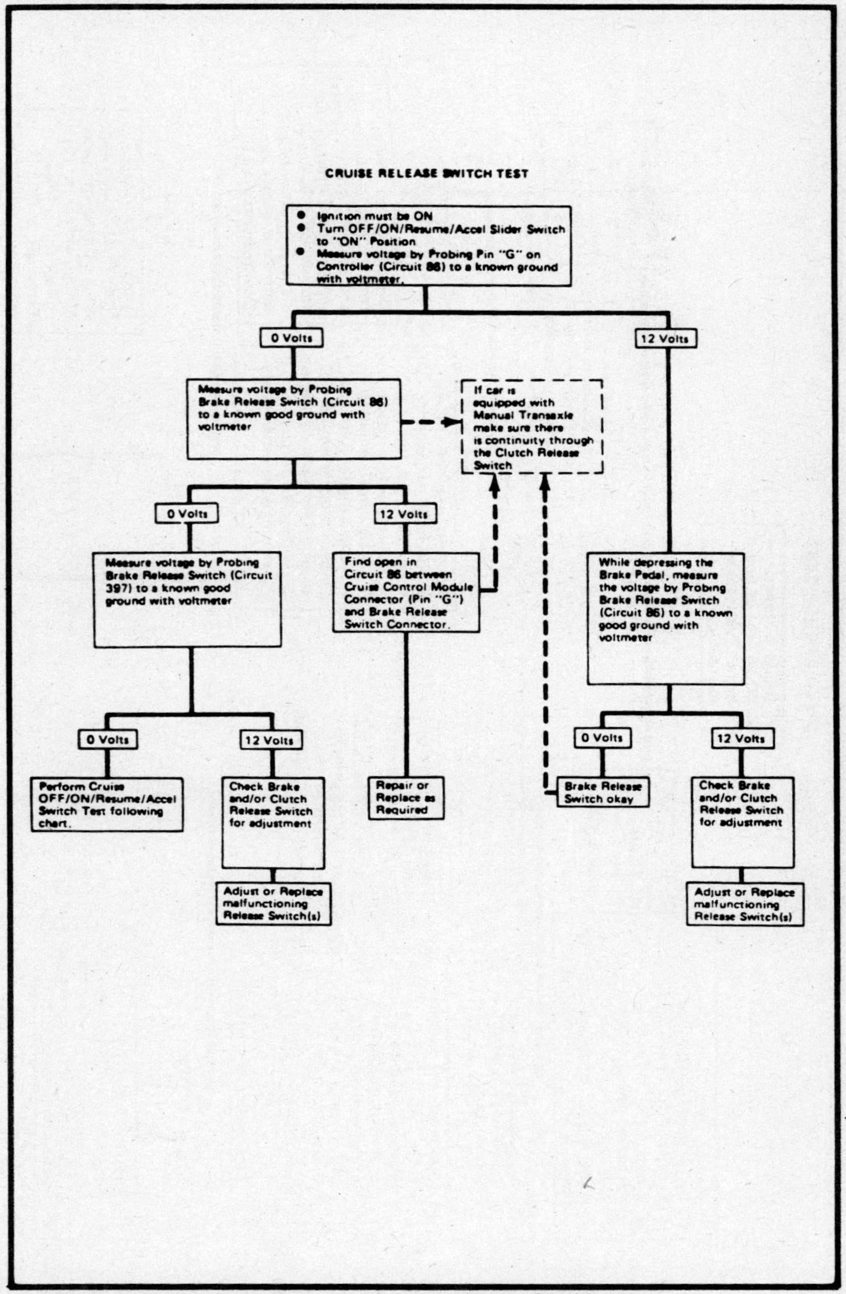

CRUISE RELEASE SWITCH TEST

- Ignition must be ON
- Turn OFF/ON/Resume/Accel Slider Switch to "ON" Position
- Measure voltage by Probing Pin "G" on Controller (Circuit 86) to a known ground with voltmeter.

12 Volts / **0 Volts**

While depressing the Brake Pedal, measure the voltage by Probing Brake Release Switch (Circuit 86) to a known good ground with voltmeter

- **12 Volts** → Check Brake and/or Clutch Release Switch for adjustment → Adjust or Replace malfunctioning Release Switch(s)
- **0 Volts** → Brake Release Switch okay

If car is equipped with Manual Transaxle make sure there is continuity through the Clutch Release Switch

Measure voltage by Probing Brake Release Switch (Circuit 86) to a known good ground with voltmeter

- **12 Volts** → Find open in Circuit 86 between Cruise Control Module Connector (Pin "G") and Brake Release Switch Connector. → Repair or Replace Required
- **0 Volts** → Measure voltage by Probing Brake Release Switch (Circuit 397) to a known good ground with voltmeter
  - **12 Volts** → Check Brake and/or Clutch Release Switch for adjustment → Adjust or Replace malfunctioning Release Switch(s)
  - **0 Volts** → Perform Cruise OFF/ON/Resume/Accel Switch Test following chart.

Cruise control diagnosis—1984 and later Chevrolet

CRUISE "OFF/ON/RESUME/ACCEL" SWITCH TEST

- Turn Ignition ON
- Turn OFF/ON/Resume/Accel Slider Switch to "OFF" Position
- Measure voltage at the Controller Connector Pin "A" (Circuit 397), connect other end of voltmeter to known good ground

- **12 Volts** → Disconnect Cruise Switch Connector (C235) and measure voltage at Terminal "A" of connector (harness side) to ground.
  - **12 Volts** → Malfunctioning OFF/ON/Resume/Accel Switch. Replace
  - **0 Volts** → Check for blown fuse or open in wiring Circuit 39

- **0 Volts**
  - Turn Cruise OFF/ON/Resume/Accel Slider Switch to "ON" position
  - Measure voltage at the Controller Connector Pin "A" (Circuit 397), to known good ground with voltmeter.
    - **12 Volts** → Cruise OFF/ON/Resume/Accel Slider Switch checks okay
    - **0 Volts** → Disconnect Cruise Switch Connector (C235) and measure voltage at Terminal "B" of connector (switch side) to ground
      - **12 Volts** → Find open in Circuit 397 between Terminal "B" of Connector (C235) and Pin "A" on Controller → Repair or Replace as Required
      - **0 Volts** → Measure voltage at Terminal "A" of Connector (Harness Side) to ground (C235) See Schematic
        - **0 Volts** → Check Fuse
          - **0 Volts** → If Fuse is blown Replace
            - Fuse blows → Check all branches of Circuit 39 from Fuse and find short to ground and Repair
            - If Fuse doesn't blow, Road Test
          - Fuse okay check wiring for open between Fuse and Switch.
        - **12 Volts** → Cruise OFF/ON/Resume/Accel Slider Switch malfunctioning Replace

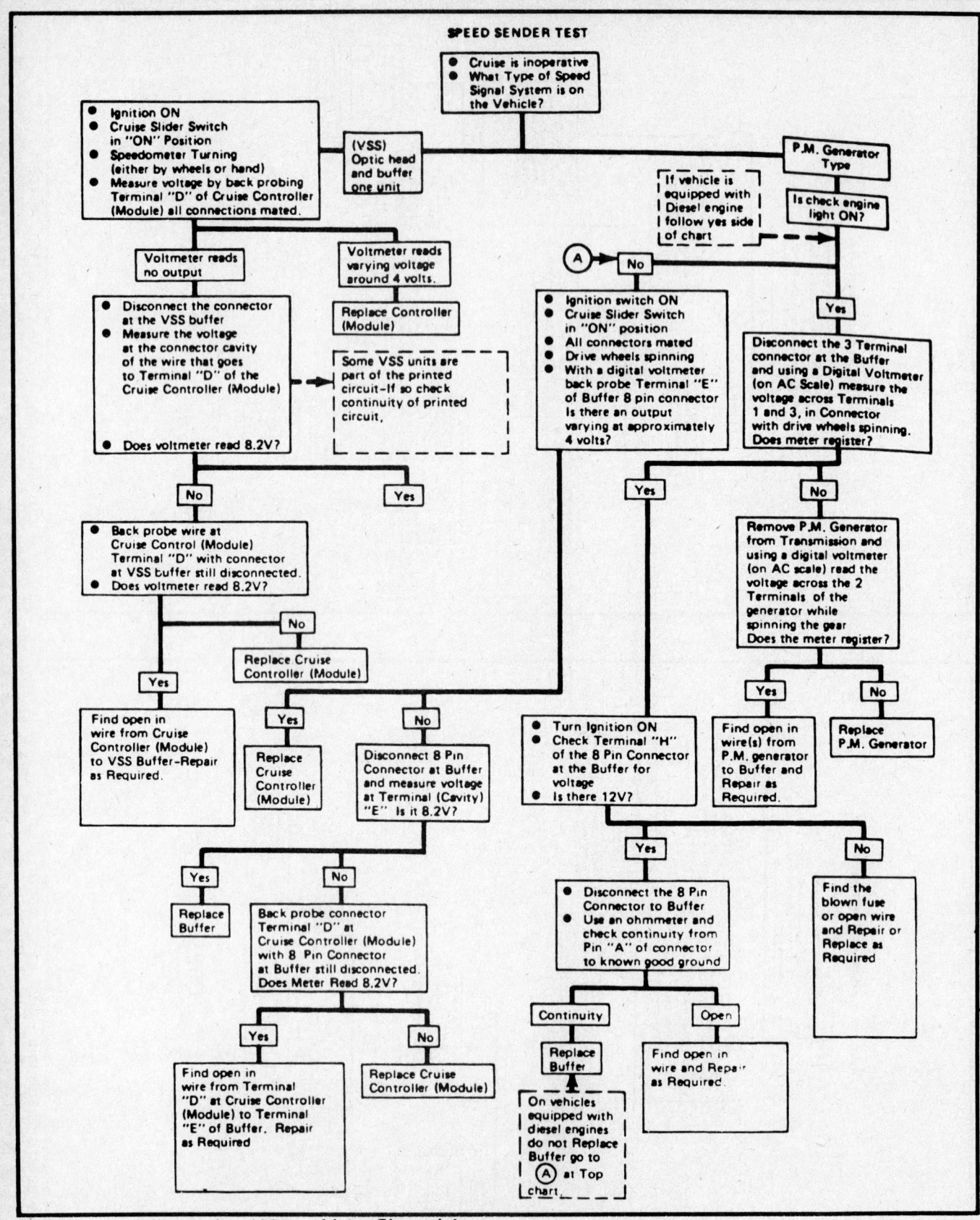

SPEED SENDER TEST

- Cruise is inoperative
- What Type of Speed Signal System is on the Vehicle?

(VSS) Optic head and buffer one unit

P.M. Generator Type

- Ignition ON
- Cruise Slider Switch in "ON" Position
- Speedometer Turning (either by wheels or hand)
- Measure voltage by back probing Terminal "D" of Cruise Controller (Module) all connections mated.

If vehicle is equipped with Diesel engine follow yes side of chart

Is check engine light ON?

Voltmeter reads no output

Voltmeter reads varying voltage around 4 volts.

Replace Controller (Module)

A No

Yes

- Disconnect the connector at the VSS buffer
- Measure the voltage at the connector cavity of the wire that goes to Terminal "D" of the Cruise Controller (Module)

- Does voltmeter read 8.2V?

Some VSS units are part of the printed circuit-If so check continuity of printed circuit.

- Ignition switch ON
- Cruise Slider Switch in "ON" position
- All connectors mated
- Drive wheels spinning
- With a digital voltmeter back probe Terminal "E" of Buffer 8 pin connector Is there an output varying at approximately 4 volts?

Disconnect the 3 Terminal connector at the Buffer and using a Digital Voltmeter (on AC Scale) measure the voltage across Terminals 1 and 3, in Connector with drive wheels spinning. Does meter register?

No

Yes

- Back probe wire at Cruise Control (Module) Terminal "D" with connector at VSS buffer still disconnected.
- Does voltmeter read 8.2V?

Yes

No

Remove P.M. Generator from Transmission and using a digital voltmeter (on AC scale) read the voltage across the 2 Terminals of the generator while spinning the gear Does the meter register?

No

Replace Cruise Controller (Module)

Yes

Find open in wire from Cruise Controller (Module) to VSS Buffer-Repair as Required.

Yes

Replace Cruise Controller (Module)

No

Disconnect 8 Pin Connector at Buffer and measure voltage at Terminal (Cavity) "E" Is it 8.2V?

- Turn Ignition ON
- Check Terminal "H" of the 8 Pin Connector at the Buffer for voltage
- Is there 12V?

Yes

Find open in wire(s) from P.M. generator to Buffer and Repair as Required.

No

Replace P.M. Generator

Yes

No

Replace Buffer

Back probe connector Terminal "D" at Cruise Controller (Module) with 8 Pin Connector at Buffer still disconnected. Does Meter Read 8.2V?

Yes

- Disconnect the 8 Pin Connector to Buffer
- Use an ohmmeter and check continuity from Pin "A" of connector to known good ground

Find the blown fuse or open wire and Repair or Replace as Required

Yes

No

Find open in wire from Terminal "D" at Cruise Controller (Module) to Terminal "E" of Buffer. Repair as Required

Replace Cruise Controller (Module)

Continuity

Open

Replace Buffer

Find open in wire and Repair as Required.

On vehicles equipped with diesel engines do not Replace Buffer go to A at Top chart

Cruise control diagnosis—1984 and later Chevrolet

CONTROL SWITCH CONTINUITY CHECK

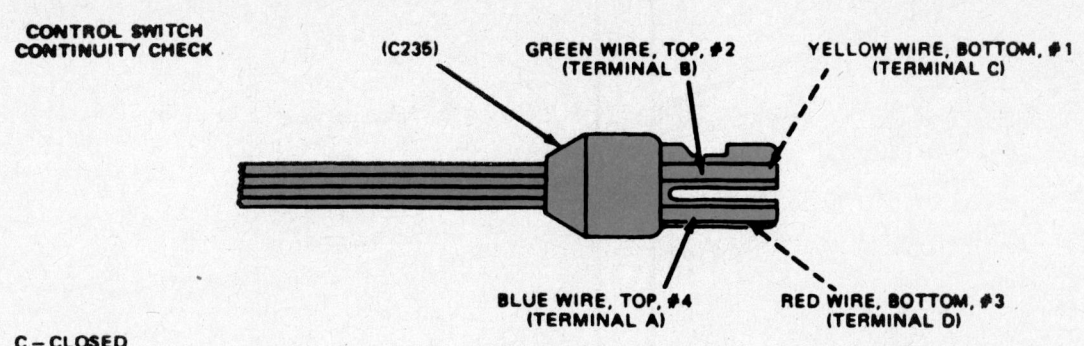

C — CLOSED
O — OPEN

SET/COAST (S/C) SW	POSITION SLIDER	1-2	1-3	1-4	2-3	2-4	3-4
NORMAL	OFF	O	O	O	O	O	O
NORMAL	ON	O	O	O	O	C	O
NORMAL	R/A	C	O	C	O	C	O
DEPRESSED	OFF	O	O	O	C	O	O
DEPRESSED	ON	O	O	O	C	C	C
DEPRESSED	R/A	C	C	C	C	C	C

CRUISE CONTROLLER (MODULE) CHECKS AT CONNECTOR

- IGNITION ON
- CONTROLLER DISCONNECTED

PIN	FUNCTION	VOLTAGE TO GND	RESISTANCE	CONDITIONS
G	BRAKE INPUT	12 V / 0 V	—	BRAKE (AND CLUTCH) NOT DEPRESSED / BRAKE (AND/OR CLUTCH) DEPRESSED
L	SET/COAST INPUT	12 V / 0 V / 0 V	—	SLIDER SWITCH "ON" – SET/COAST DEPRESSED / SLIDER SWITCH "ON" – SET/COAST NORMAL / SLIDER SWITCH "OFF" – SET/COAST NORMAL
M	RESUME/ ACCEL. INPUT	12 V / 0 V / 0 V	—	SLIDER SWITCH "R/A" POSITION / SLIDER SWITCH "ON" – SET/COAST DEPRESSED OR NORMAL / SLIDER SWITCH "OFF" – SET/COAST DEPRESSED OR NORMAL
J	GROUND	—	0 Ω	MEASURED TO VEHICLE GROUND
A	ON/OFF INPUT	12 V / 0 V	—	SLIDER SWITCH "ON" / SLIDER SWITCH "OFF" – SET/COAST DEPRESSED OR NORMAL
B	INDICATOR LAMP	12 V	—	CRUISE ARMED
F / H	SPS HIGH / SPS LOW	—	20-30 Ω / 0 Ω	MEASURED BETWEEN PINS F & H – SERVO CONNECTED / MEASURED BETWEEN PINS F & H – SERVO DISCONNECTED
D	SPEED SIGNAL	→	→	SEE CHART (DIAGNOSTIC) ON SPEED SENDER TEST
K	VACUUM VALVE CONTROL	—	30-50 Ω / ∞ Ω	MEASURED TO GROUND – SERVO CONNECTED / MEASURED TO GROUND – SERVO NOT CONNECTED
C	VENT VALVE CONTROL	—	30-50 Ω / ∞ Ω	MEASURED TO GROUND – SERVO CONNECTED / MEASURED TO GROUND – SERVO NOT CONNECTED

SERVO CHECKS

- SERVO CONNECTOR DISCONNECTED
- MEASURE AT SERVO PINS

PIN	FUNCTION	RESISTANCE	CONDITIONS
D / B	SPS HIGH / SPS LOW	20-30 Ω	MEASURED BETWEEN PINS D AND B (IF MEASURED RESISTANCE IS NOT STATED VALVE, REPLACE SERVO)
A	VENT VALVE	30-50 Ω	MEASURED BETWEEN PINS A AND C (IF MEASURED RESISTANCE IS NOT STATED VALVE, REPLACE SERVO)
E	VACUUM VALVE	30-50 Ω	MEASURED BETWEEN PINS E AND C (IF MEASURED RESISTANCE IS NOT STATED VALVE, REPLACE SERVO)

Cruise control servo, controller and switch checking procedure—1984 and later Chevrolet

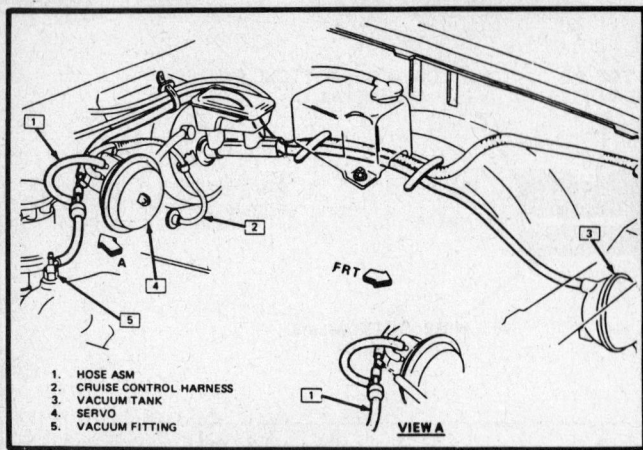

Cruise control vacuum schematic—1985 Monte Carlo and El Camino with V8 engine

1. HOSE ASM
2. CRUISE CONTROL HARNESS
3. VACUUM TANK
4. SERVO
5. VACUUM FITTING

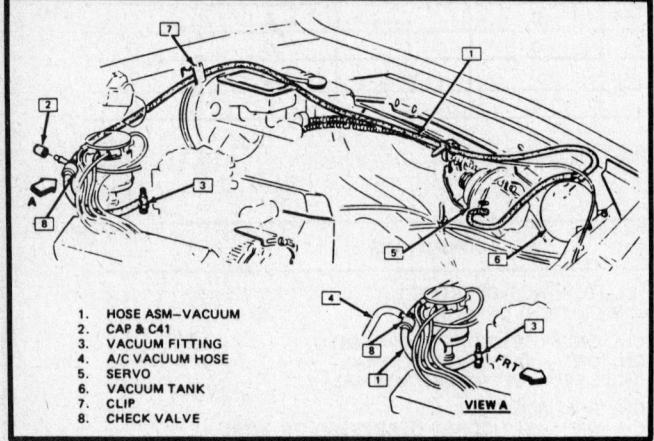

Cruise control vacuum schematic—1985 Impala and 1985 and later Caprice with v8 engine

1. HOSE ASM—VACUUM
2. CAP & C41
3. VACUUM FITTING
4. A/C VACUUM HOSE
5. SERVO
6. VACUUM TANK
7. CLIP
8. CHECK VALVE

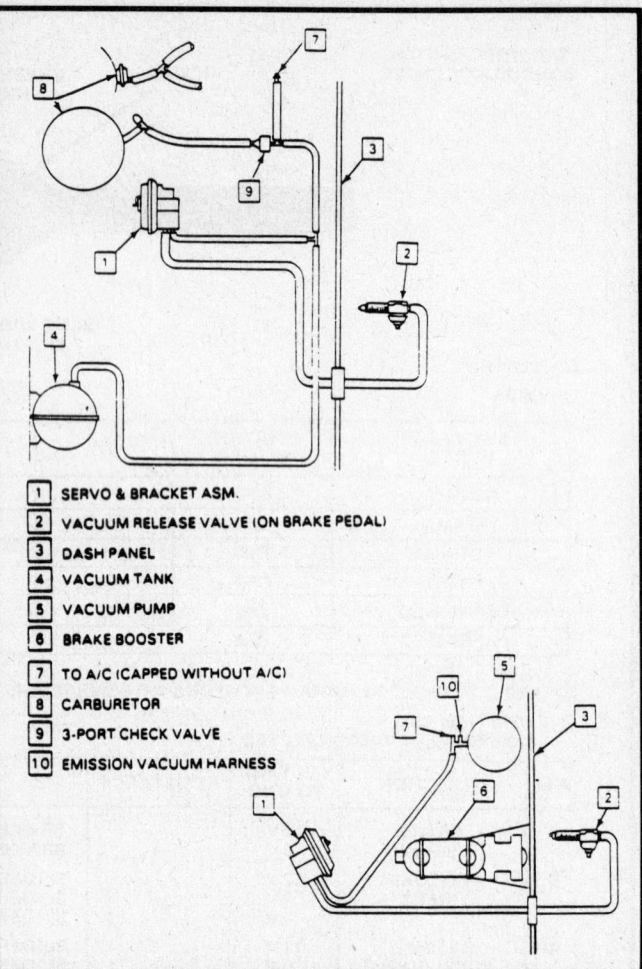

1. SERVO & BRACKET ASM.
2. VACUUM RELEASE VALVE (ON BRAKE PEDAL)
3. DASH PANEL
4. VACUUM TANK
5. VACUUM PUMP
6. BRAKE BOOSTER
7. TO A/C (CAPPED WITHOUT A/C)
8. CARBURETOR
9. 3-PORT CHECK VALVE
10. EMISSION VACUUM HARNESS

Cruise control vacuum schematic—1984 Impala, Caprice, Malibu and Monte Carlo

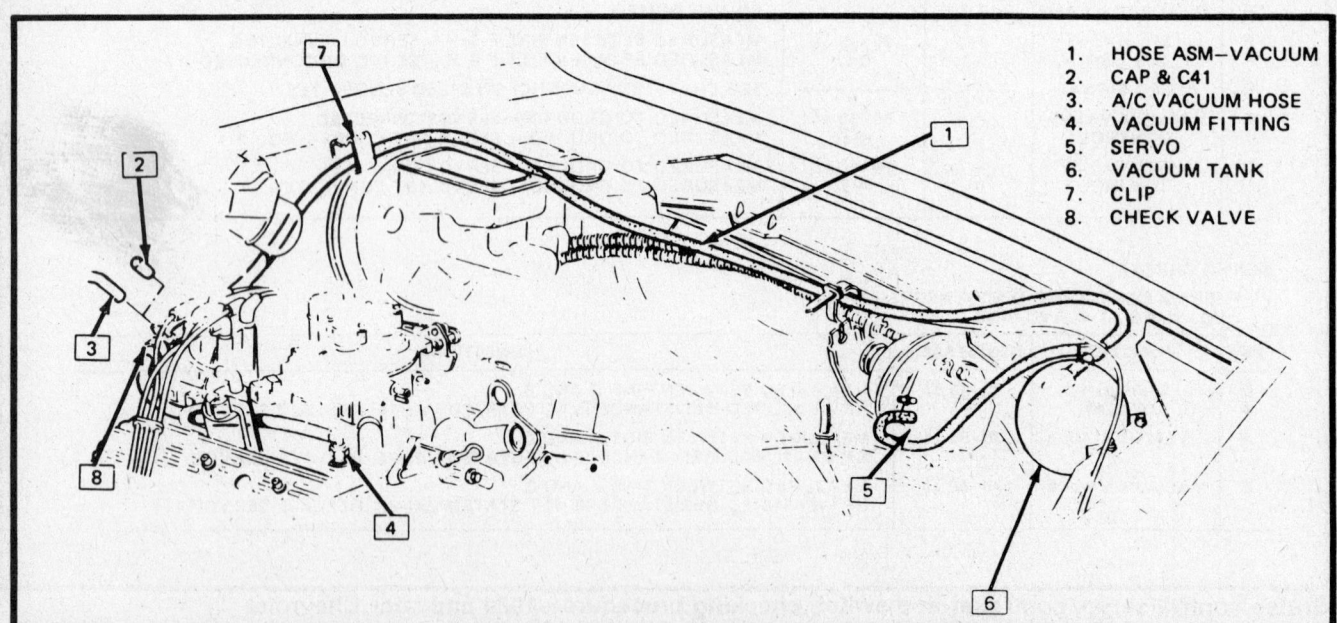

1. HOSE ASM—VACUUM
2. CAP & C41
3. A/C VACUUM HOSE
4. VACUUM FITTING
5. SERVO
6. VACUUM TANK
7. CLIP
8. CHECK VALVE

Cruise control vacuum schematic—1985 Impala and 1985 and later Caprice with 4.3 liter EFI engine

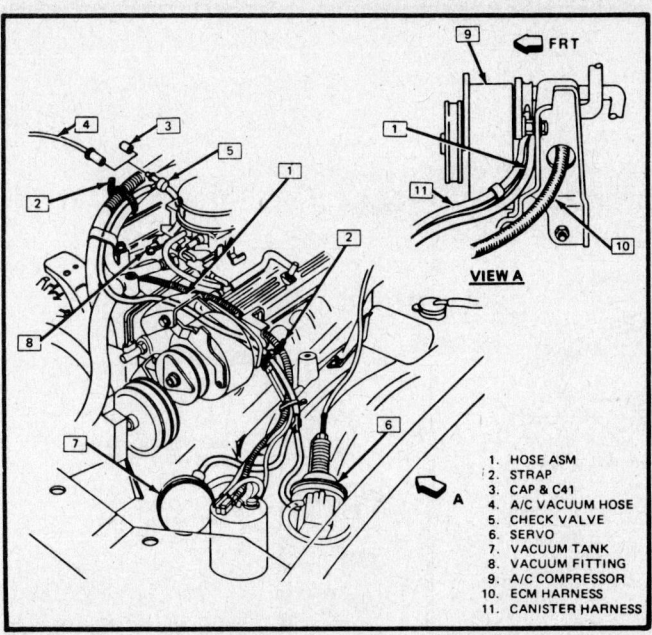

1. HOSE ASM
2. STRAP
3. CAP & C41
4. A/C VACUUM HOSE
5. CHECK VALVE
6. SERVO
7. VACUUM TANK
8. VACUUM FITTING
9. A/C COMPRESSOR
10. ECM HARNESS
11. CANISTER HARNESS

Cruise control vacuum schematic—1985 Monte Carlo with 4.3 liter EFI engine

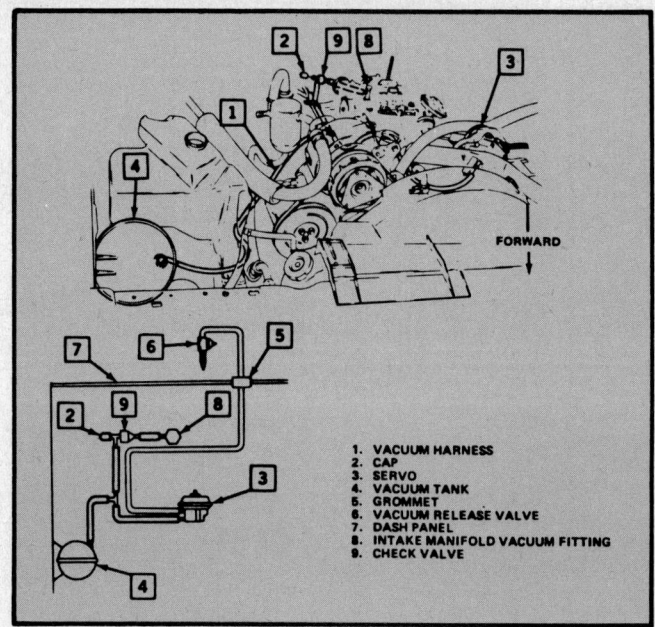

1. VACUUM HARNESS
2. CAP
3. SERVO
4. VACUUM TANK
5. GROMMET
6. VACUUM RELEASE VALVE
7. DASH PANEL
8. INTAKE MANIFOLD VACUUM FITTING
9. CHECK VALVE

Cruise control vacuum schematic—1986 and later Caprice with V8 engine

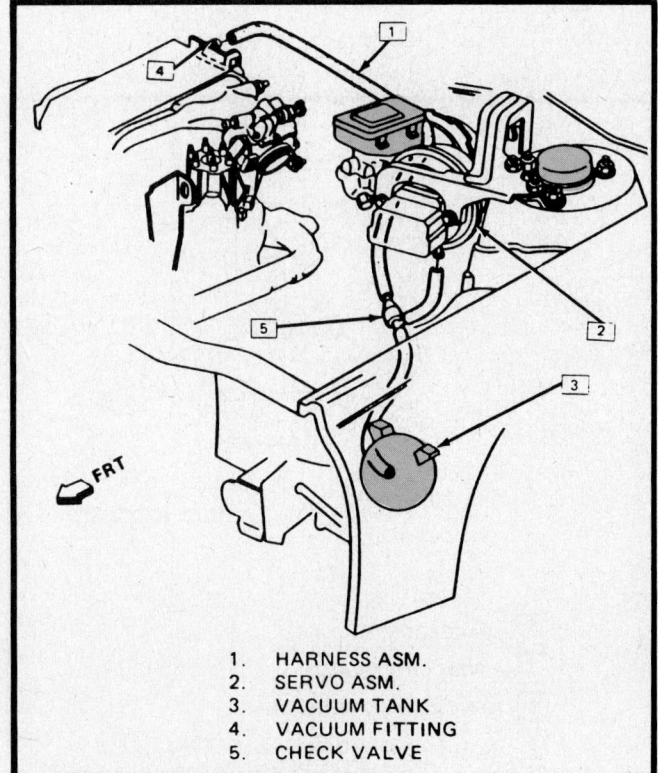

1. HARNESS ASM.
2. SERVO ASM.
3. VACUUM TANK
4. VACUUM FITTING
5. CHECK VALVE

Cruise control vacuum schematic—1985 and later Cavalier with 2.8 liter MFI engine

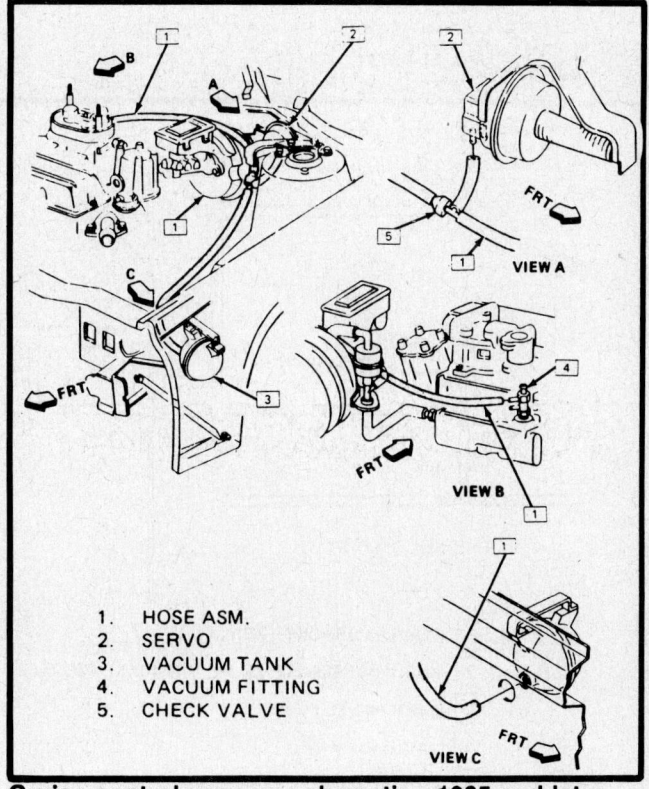

1. HOSE ASM.
2. SERVO
3. VACUUM TANK
4. VACUUM FITTING
5. CHECK VALVE

Cruise control vacuum schematic—1985 and later Cavalier with 2.0 liter EFI engine

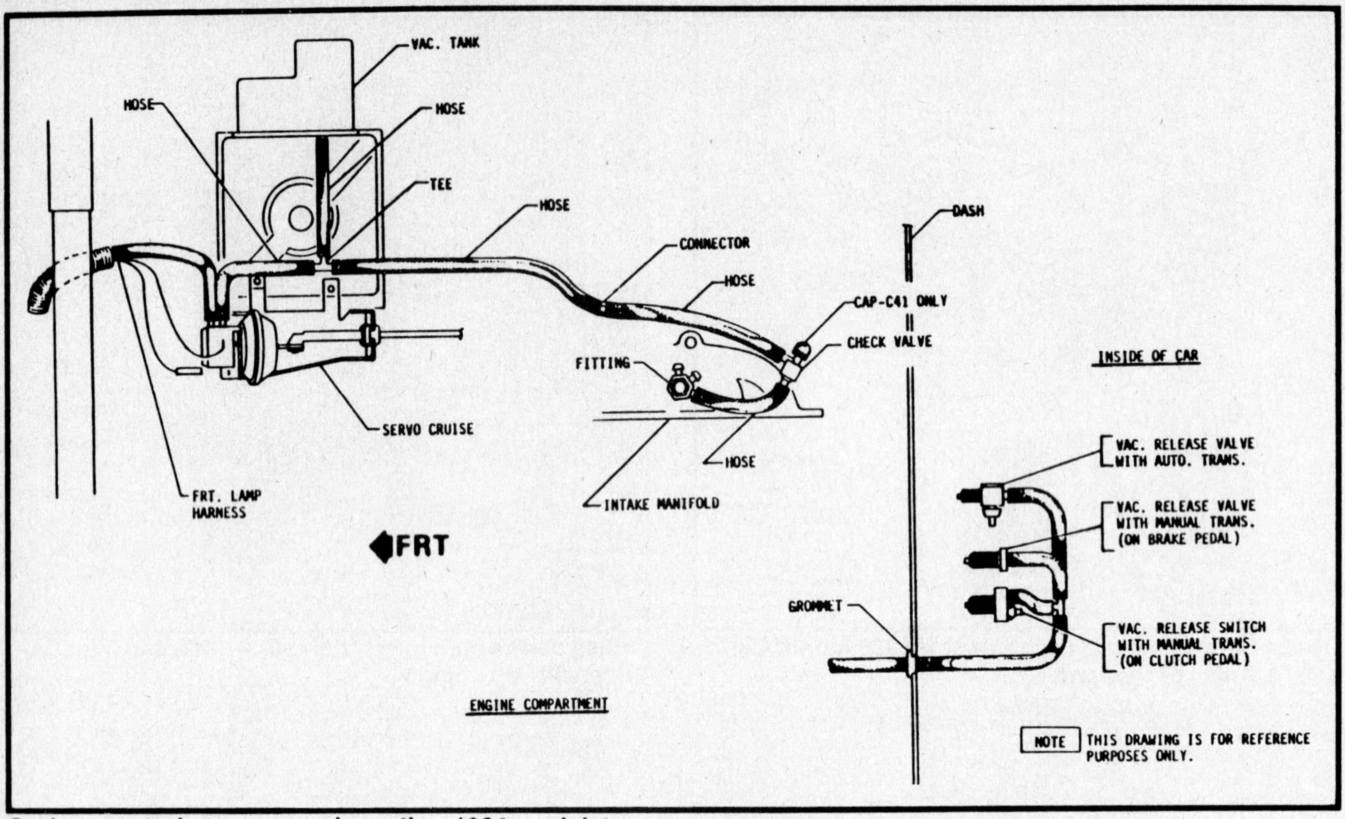

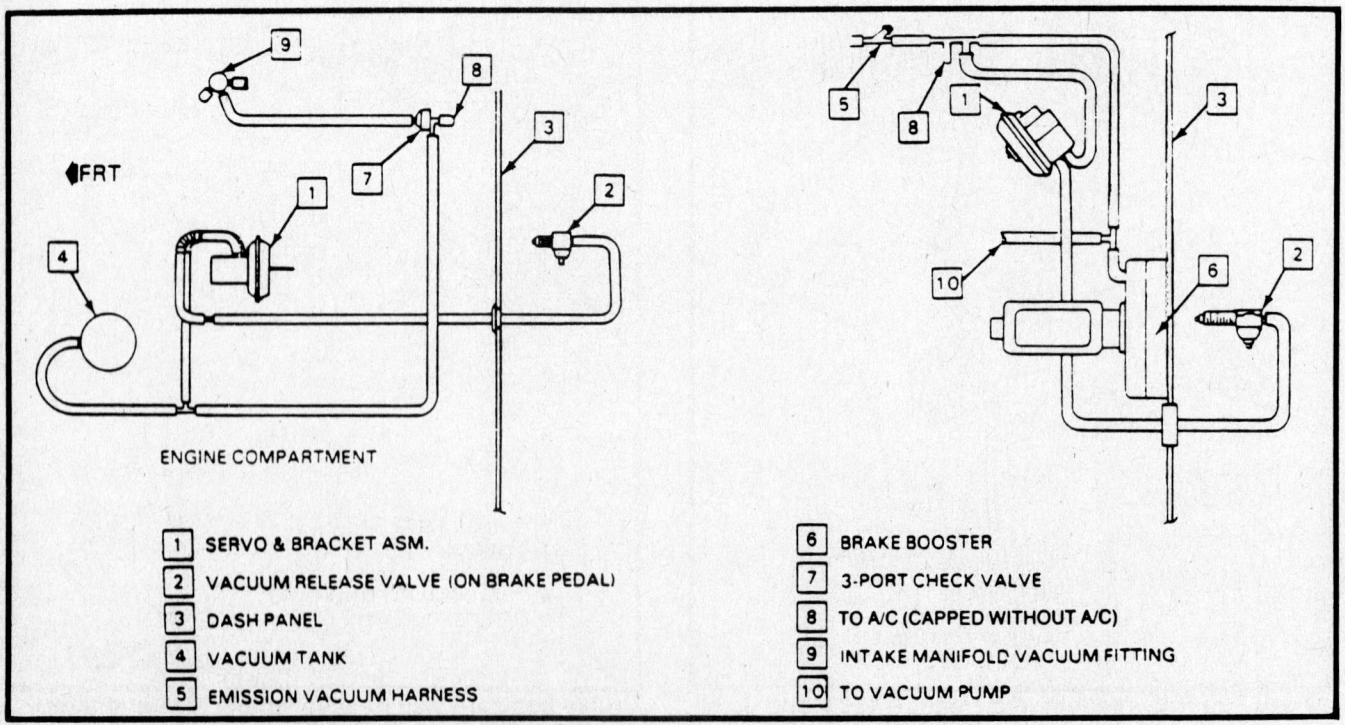

Cruise control vacuum schematic—1984 and later Camaro with 2.5 liter EFI engine

ENGINE COMPARTMENT

1	SERVO & BRACKET ASM.	6	BRAKE BOOSTER
2	VACUUM RELEASE VALVE (ON BRAKE PEDAL)	7	3-PORT CHECK VALVE
3	DASH PANEL	8	TO A/C (CAPPED WITHOUT A/C)
4	VACUUM TANK	9	INTAKE MANIFOLD VACUUM FITTING
5	EMISSION VACUUM HARNESS	10	TO VACUUM PUMP

Cruise control vacuum schematic—1984 Celebrity

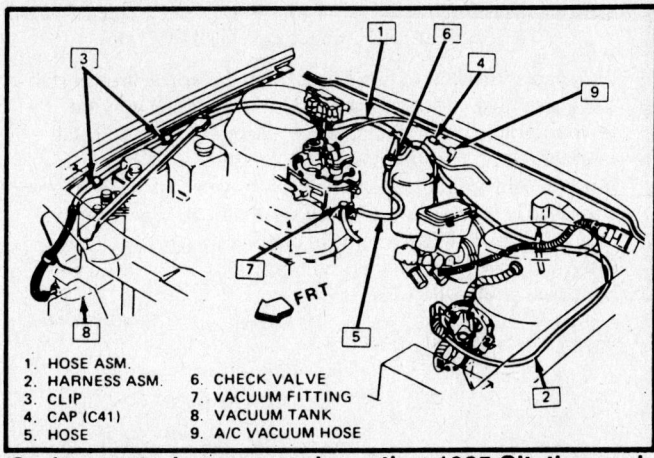

1. HOSE ASM.
2. HARNESS ASM.
3. CLIP
4. CAP (C41)
5. HOSE
6. CHECK VALVE
7. VACUUM FITTING
8. VACUUM TANK
9. A/C VACUUM HOSE

Cruise control vacuum schematic – 1985 Citation and 1985 and later Celebrity with 2.5 liter EFI engine

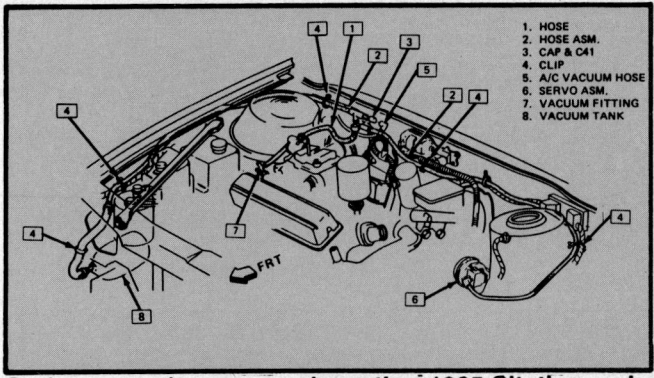

1. HOSE
2. HOSE ASM.
3. CAP & C41
4. CLIP
5. A/C VACUUM HOSE
6. SERVO ASM.
7. VACUUM FITTING
8. VACUUM TANK

Cruise control vacuum schematic – 1985 Citation and 1985 and later Celebrity with V6 engine

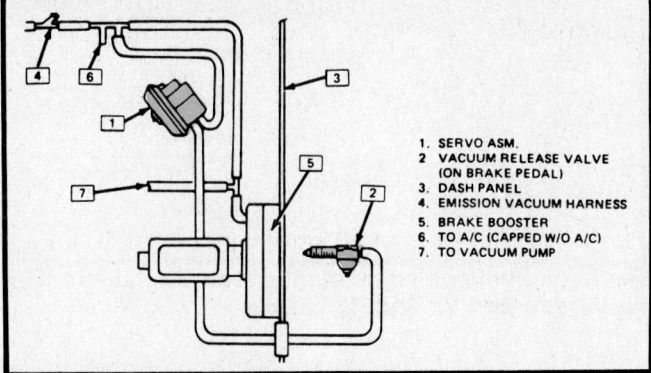

1. SERVO ASM.
2. VACUUM RELEASE VALVE (ON BRAKE PEDAL)
3. DASH PANEL
4. EMISSION VACUUM HARNESS
5. BRAKE BOOSTER
6. TO A/C (CAPPED W/O A/C)
7. TO VACUUM PUMP

Cruise control vacuum schematic – 1985 Celebrity with V6 diesel engine

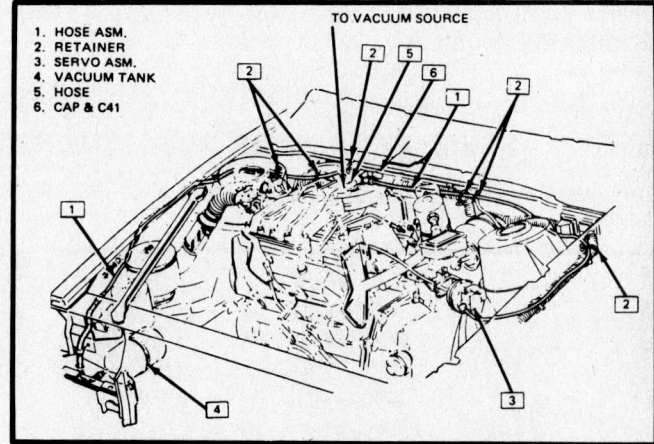

1. HOSE ASM.
2. RETAINER
3. SERVO ASM.
4. VACUUM TANK
5. HOSE
6. CAP & C41

TO VACUUM SOURCE

Cruise control vacuum schematic – 1985 Citation and 1985 and later Celebrity with 2.8 liter MFI engine

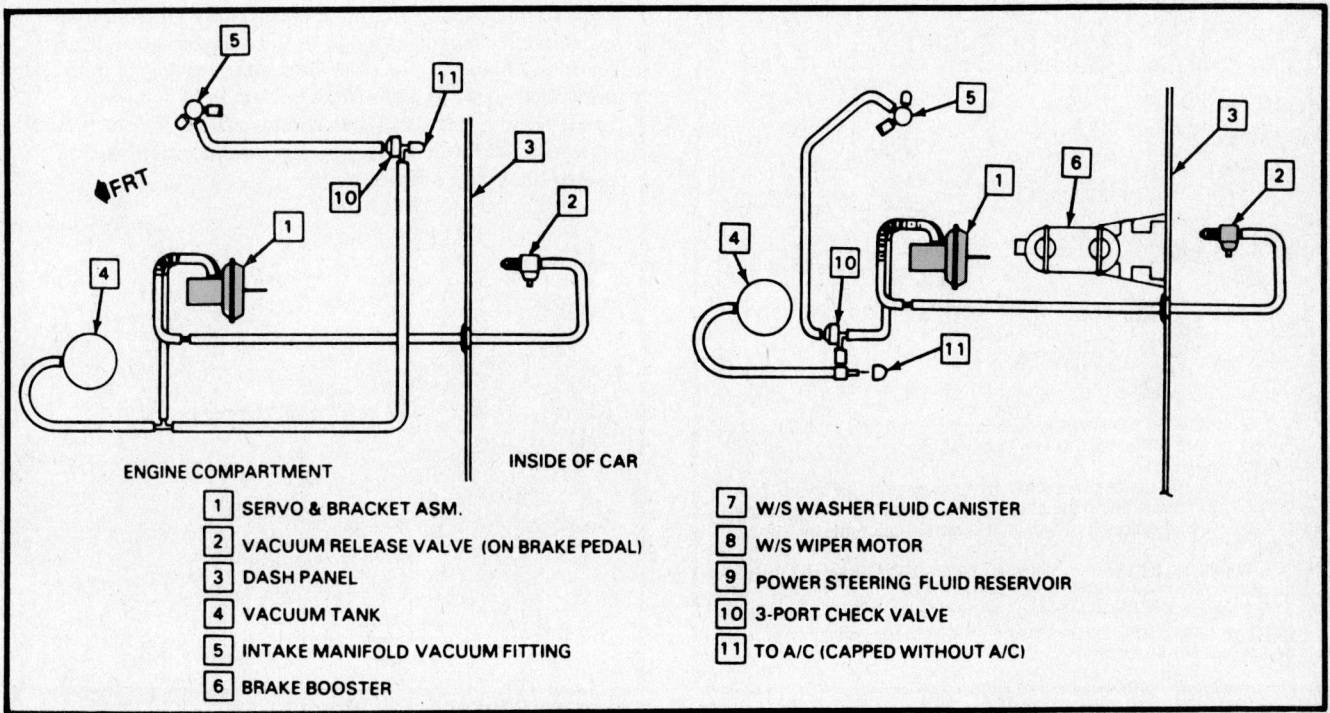

ENGINE COMPARTMENT   INSIDE OF CAR

1	SERVO & BRACKET ASM.
2	VACUUM RELEASE VALVE (ON BRAKE PEDAL)
3	DASH PANEL
4	VACUUM TANK
5	INTAKE MANIFOLD VACUUM FITTING
6	BRAKE BOOSTER
7	W/S WASHER FLUID CANISTER
8	W/S WIPER MOTOR
9	POWER STEERING FLUID RESERVOIR
10	3-PORT CHECK VALVE
11	TO A/C (CAPPED WITHOUT A/C)

Cruise control vacuum schematic – 1984 Citation

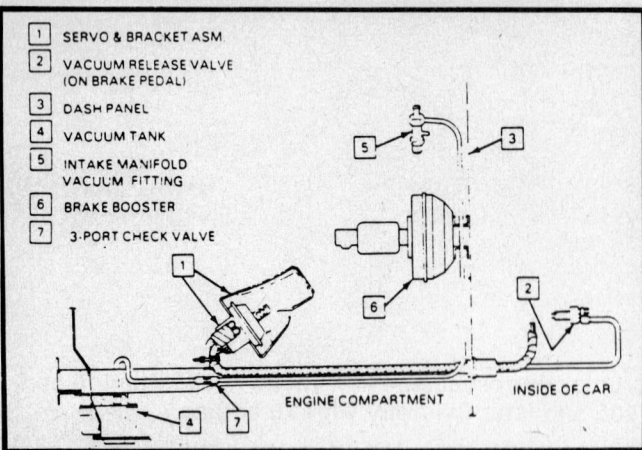

Cruise control vacuum schematic—1984 Cavalier with 2.0 liter EFI engine

1	SERVO & BRACKET ASM
2	VACUUM RELEASE VALVE (ON BRAKE PEDAL)
3	DASH PANEL
4	VACUUM TANK
5	INTAKE MANIFOLD VACUUM FITTING
6	BRAKE BOOSTER
7	3-PORT CHECK VALVE

SERVO ASSEMBLY LINKAGE ADJUSTMENT

For servo linkage adjustments refer to the proper illustration.

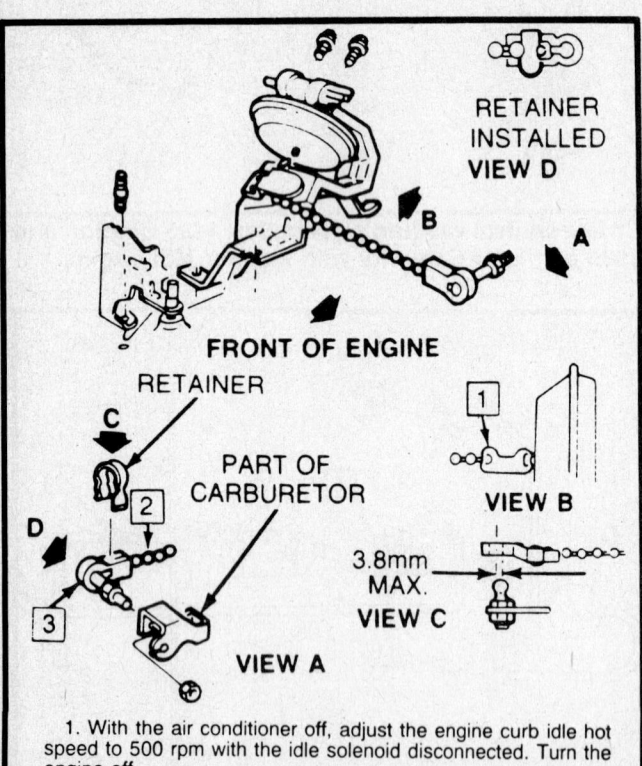

1. With the air conditioner off, adjust the engine curb idle hot speed to 500 rpm with the idle solenoid disconnected. Turn the engine off.
2. Check the bead chain slack by unsnapping the swivel from the ball stud and holding the chain taut at the ball stud. The center of the swivel should extend 1/8 inch beyond the center of the ball stud.
3. Adjust the bead chain slack, as required, by removing the retainer from the swivel and chain assembly.
4. Position the chain into the swivel cavities which permit the chain to have slight slack. Position the retainer over the swivel and the chain assembly.

Servo and linkage adjustment—1982–83 Impala, Caprice, Malibu, Monte Carlo and Corvette (typical)

CRUISE CONTROL CABLE ADJUSTMENT

With cable installed to cable bracket and throttle lever, install cable assembly to servo bracket. Using third ball only on servo assembly chain, install servo assembly chain on cable assembly. With throttle completely closed, (ignition off and fast idle cam off) adjust cable assembly jam nuts until 1.0 mm clearance is between stud pin and end of slot. Tighten cable assembly jam nut. Then remove plastic retainer (not shown) (used to retain boot in depressed position) and pull rubber boot over washer on cable.

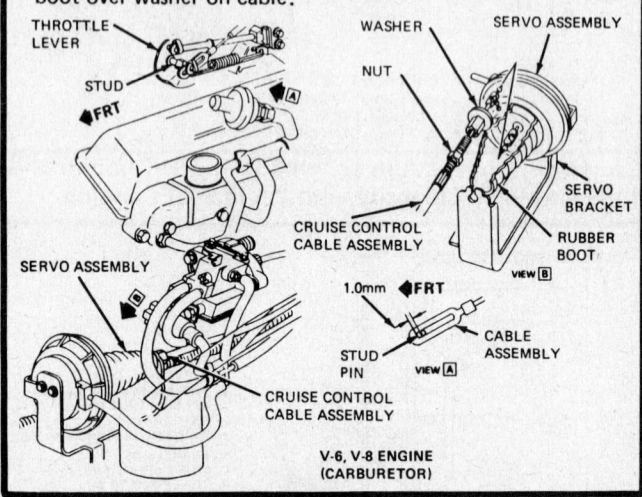

Servo and linkage adjustment—1982–83 Camaro with carburetor and V6 and V8 engine

CRUISE CONTROL CABLE ADJUSTMENT

With cable installed to cable bracket and TBI lever, install cable to servo bracket. Using third ball only on servo chain, install servo chain on cable. With throttle completely closed (ignition off and fast idle cam off), adjust cable jam nuts until cable sleeve at TBI is tight but not holding throttle open. Tighten jam nuts. Then remove plastic retainer (not shown) (used to retain boot in depressed position) and pull rubber boot over washer on cable.

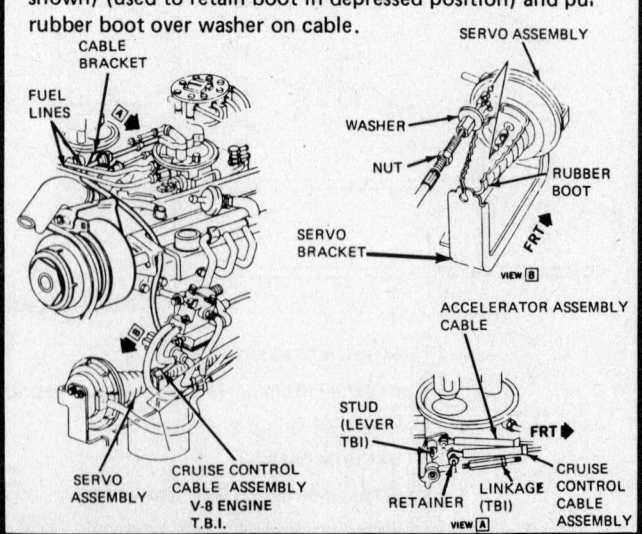

Servo and linkage adjustment—1982–83 Camaro with TBI and V8 engine

Wiring Diagram

Ignition S/W

GAUGE Fuse

STOP Fuse

Parking Brake S/W

Actuator

Stop Light S/W

Control S/W

Speed Sensor

A-8   B-6

OD Solenoid

Cruise Control Computer

Main S/W

Taillight Relay

Clutch S/W

Neutral Start S/W

Starter

Parking Brake Switch   Clutch Switch   Stop Light Switch   Cruise Control Computer   Main Switch

Control Switch   Actuator   Neutral Start Switch   Speed Sensor

B-6   A-8

Cruise control electrical schematic—1985 and later Nova

869

OUTPUT OF DIAGNOSIS CODES

1. INDICATE TYPE A CODE

(a) Turn the ignition switch on.

(b) Turn the main switch and set/coast switch on at the same time.

(c) Meet the conditions listed below.

(d) Read the diagnosis code on the main switch indicator.

No.	Conditions	Indicator Code	Diagnosis
1	Set/coast switch on		Set/coast switch circuit is normal.
2	Accel/resume switch on		Accel/resume switch circuit is normal.
3	Each cancel switch on — Stop light switch, Parking brake switch, Clutch switch, Neutral start switch		Each cancel switch circuit is normal.
4	Drive 40 km/h (25mph) or over		Speed sensor circuit is normal.
5	Drive 40 km/h (25 mph) or below		Speed sensor circuit is normal.

NOTE: Indicator codes appear in order from No. 1.
If there is no indicator code, perform diagnosis and inspection.

2. INDICATE TYPE B CODE

(a) Do not turn ignition switch and main switch off.

(b) Turn the set/coast switch on three times within two seconds.

(c) Read the diagnosis code on the main switch indicator.

No.	Indicator code	Diagnosis
		Normal
11		Actuator circuit is abnormal.
21		Speed sensor signal circuit is abnormal.
23		Speed sensor signal circuit is abnormal.
31		Accel/resume switch circuit is abnormal.
33		Accel/resume switch and set/coast switch is abnormal.

NOTE:
- Indication codes appear with propriety from No. 11.
- Normal code continues 20 seconds and abnormal codes are repeated three times.
- Indication is stopped when vehicle speed is over 16 km/h (10 mph) or main switch is turned off.
- If there is no indication code, perform diagnosis and inspection.

Cruise control system diagnosis — 1985 and later Nova

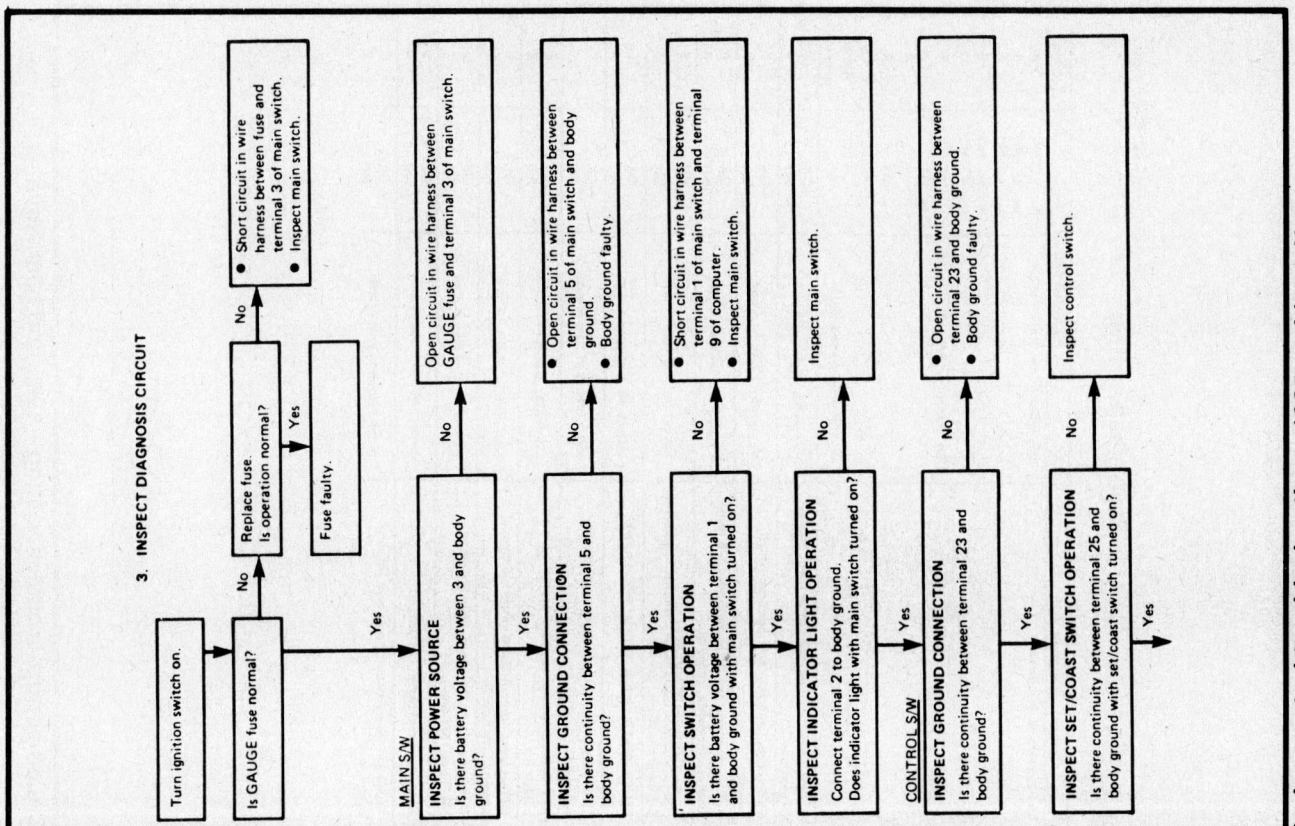

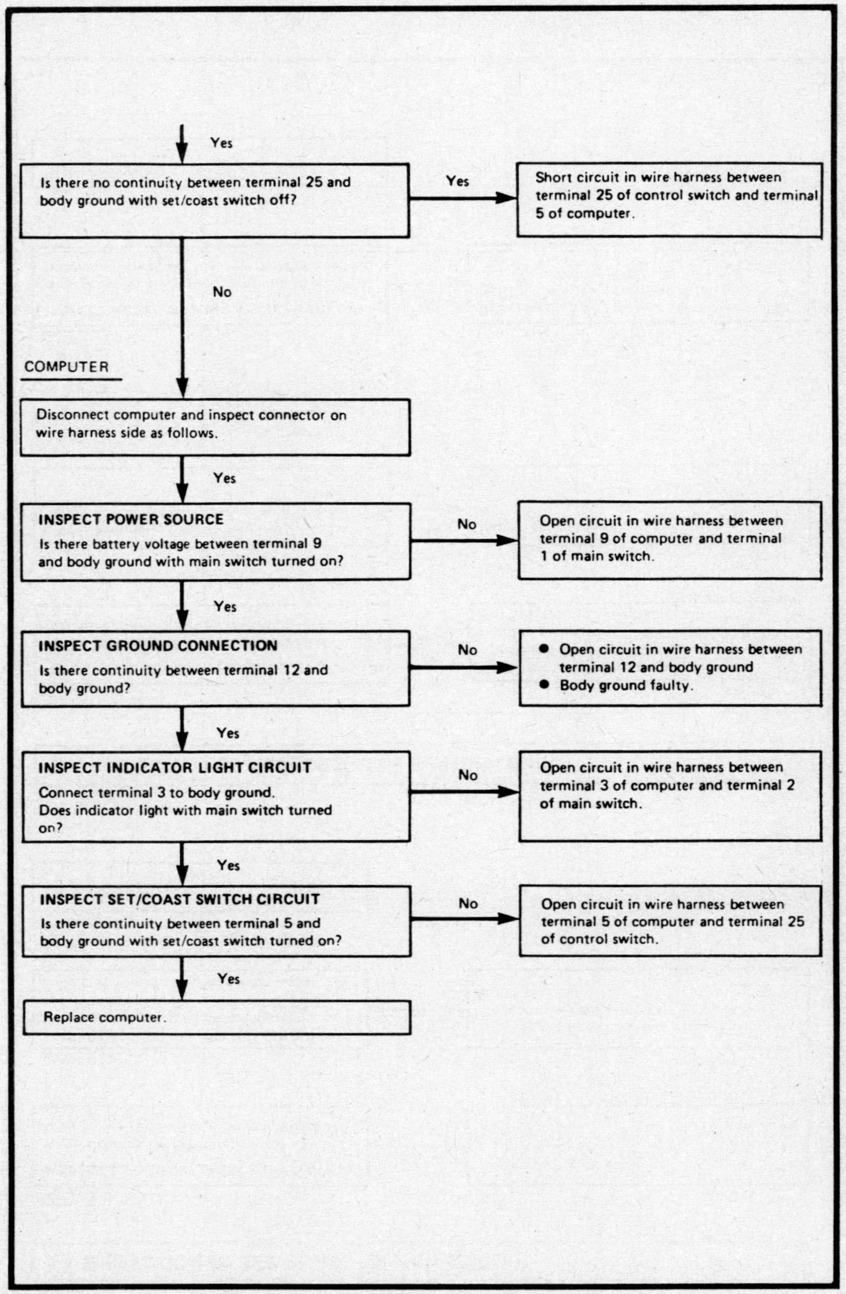

Cruise control troubleshooting – 1985 and later Nova

Top flowchart boxes (upper section):

Short circuit in wire harness between terminal 25 of control switch and terminal 5 of computer.

Is there no continuity between terminal 25 and body ground with set/coast switch off? — **Yes** / **No**

COMPUTER

Disconnect computer and inspect connector on wire harness side as follows.

INSPECT POWER SOURCE
Is there battery voltage between terminal 9 and body ground with main switch turned on? — **Yes** / **No**
Open circuit in wire harness between terminal 9 of computer and terminal 1 of main switch.

INSPECT GROUND CONNECTION
Is there continuity between terminal 12 and body ground? — **Yes** / **No**
- Open circuit in wire harness between terminal 12 and body ground
- Body ground faulty.

INSPECT INDICATOR LIGHT CIRCUIT
Connect terminal 3 to body ground. Does indicator light with main switch turned on? — **Yes** / **No**
Open circuit in wire harness between terminal 3 of computer and terminal 2 of main switch.

INSPECT SET/COAST SWITCH CIRCUIT
Is there continuity between terminal 5 and body ground with set/coast switch turned on? — **Yes** / **No**
Open circuit in wire harness between terminal 5 of computer and terminal 25 of control switch.

Replace computer.

Bottom flowchart boxes (lower section):

3. INSPECT DIAGNOSIS CIRCUIT

Turn ignition switch on.

Is GAUGE fuse normal? — **No** / **Yes**

Replace fuse. Is operation normal? — **No** / **Yes**
- Short circuit in wire harness between fuse and terminal 3 of main switch.
- Inspect main switch.

Fuse faulty.

MAIN S/W

INSPECT POWER SOURCE
Is there battery voltage between 3 and body ground? — **Yes** / **No**
Open circuit in wire harness between GAUGE fuse and terminal 3 of main switch.

INSPECT GROUND CONNECTION
Is there continuity between terminal 5 and body ground? — **Yes** / **No**
- Open circuit in wire harness between terminal 5 of main switch and body ground.
- Body ground faulty.

INSPECT SWITCH OPERATION
Is there battery voltage between terminal 1 and body ground with main switch turned on? — **Yes** / **No**
- Short circuit in wire harness between terminal 1 of main switch and terminal 9 of computer.
- Inspect main switch.

INSPECT INDICATOR LIGHT OPERATION
Connect terminal 2 to body ground. Does indicator light with main switch turned on? — **Yes** / **No**
Inspect main switch.

CONTROL S/W

INSPECT GROUND CONNECTION
Is there continuity between terminal 23 and body ground? — **Yes** / **No**
- Open circuit in wire harness between terminal 23 and body ground.
- Body ground faulty.

INSPECT SET/COAST SWITCH OPERATION
Is there continuity between terminal 25 and body ground with set/coast switch turned on? — **Yes**
Inspect control switch.

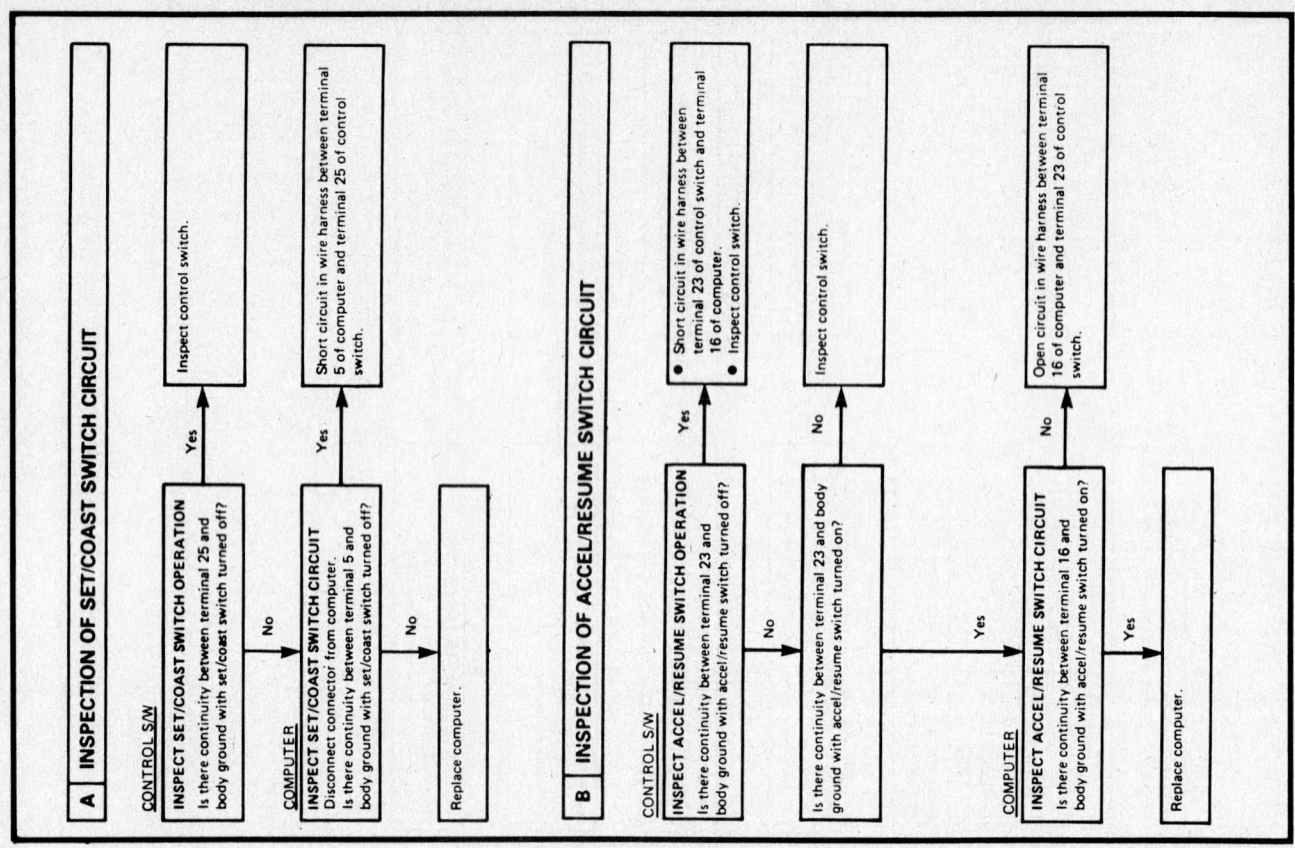

A | INSPECTION OF SET/COAST SWITCH CIRCUIT

CONTROL S/W

INSPECT SET/COAST SWITCH OPERATION
Is there continuity between terminal 25 and body ground with set/coast switch turned off?
- Yes → Inspect control switch.
- No ↓

COMPUTER

INSPECT SET/COAST SWITCH CIRCUIT
Disconnect connector from computer.
Is there continuity between terminal 5 and body ground with set/coast switch turned off?
- Yes → Short circuit in wire harness between terminal 5 of computer and terminal 25 of control switch.
- No → Replace computer.

B | INSPECTION OF ACCEL/RESUME SWITCH CIRCUIT

CONTROL S/W

INSPECT ACCEL/RESUME SWITCH OPERATION
Is there continuity between terminal 23 and body ground with accel/resume switch turned off?
- Yes → • Short circuit in wire harness between terminal 23 of control switch and terminal 16 of computer. • Inspect control switch.
- No ↓

Is there continuity between terminal 23 and body ground with accel/resume switch turned on?
- No → Inspect control switch.
- Yes ↓

COMPUTER

INSPECT ACCEL/RESUME SWITCH CIRCUIT
Is there continuity between terminal 16 and body ground with accel/resume switch turned on?
- No → Open circuit in wire harness between terminal 16 of computer and terminal 23 of control switch.
- Yes → Replace computer.

Troubleshooting

Symptom	Inspection Area			Section
Cruise control cannot be set.	(a) Inspect type A code.	No. 1	NO	A
		No. 2	NO	B
		No. 3	NO	C
		No. 4	NO	D
		No. 5	NO	D
	(b) Inspect type B code.	11		E
		21		D
		23		F
		31		B
		33		A and B
	(c) All codes are normal.			Replace computer
Vehicle speed does not reduce when coast switch turned on.	Inspect No. 1 of type A code.		OK	F
			NO	A
Vehicle does not accelerate when accel switch turned on.	Inspect No. 2 of type A code.		OK	F
			NO	B
Vehicle speed does not return to memorized speed when resume switch turned on.	Inspect No. 2 of type A code.		OK	F
			NO	B
Set speed deviates on high side.	Inspect No. 1 of type A code.		OK	F
Set speed deviates on low side.	Inspect No. 1 of type A code.		NO	A
Vehicle speed fluctuates when set switch turned on.	Inspect No. 1 of type A code.		OK	F
			NO	A
Setting speed does not cancel when brake pedal depressed.	Inspect No. 3 of type A code.		OK	F
			NO	C
Setting speed does not cancel when parking brake pulled.	Inspect No. 3 of type A code.		OK	F
			NO	C
Setting speed does not cancel when clutch pedal depressed (M/T only).	Inspect No. 3 of type A code.		OK	F
			NO	C
Setting speed does not cancel when shifted to "N" range (A/T only).	Inspect No. 3 of type A code.		OK	F
			NO	C
Speed can be set below 20 km/h.	Inspect No. 4 of type A code.		OK	F
			NO	D
Cruise control will not disengage even below 20 km/h.	Inspect No. 5 of type A code.		OK	F
			NO	D

Cruise control troubleshooting—1985 and later Nova

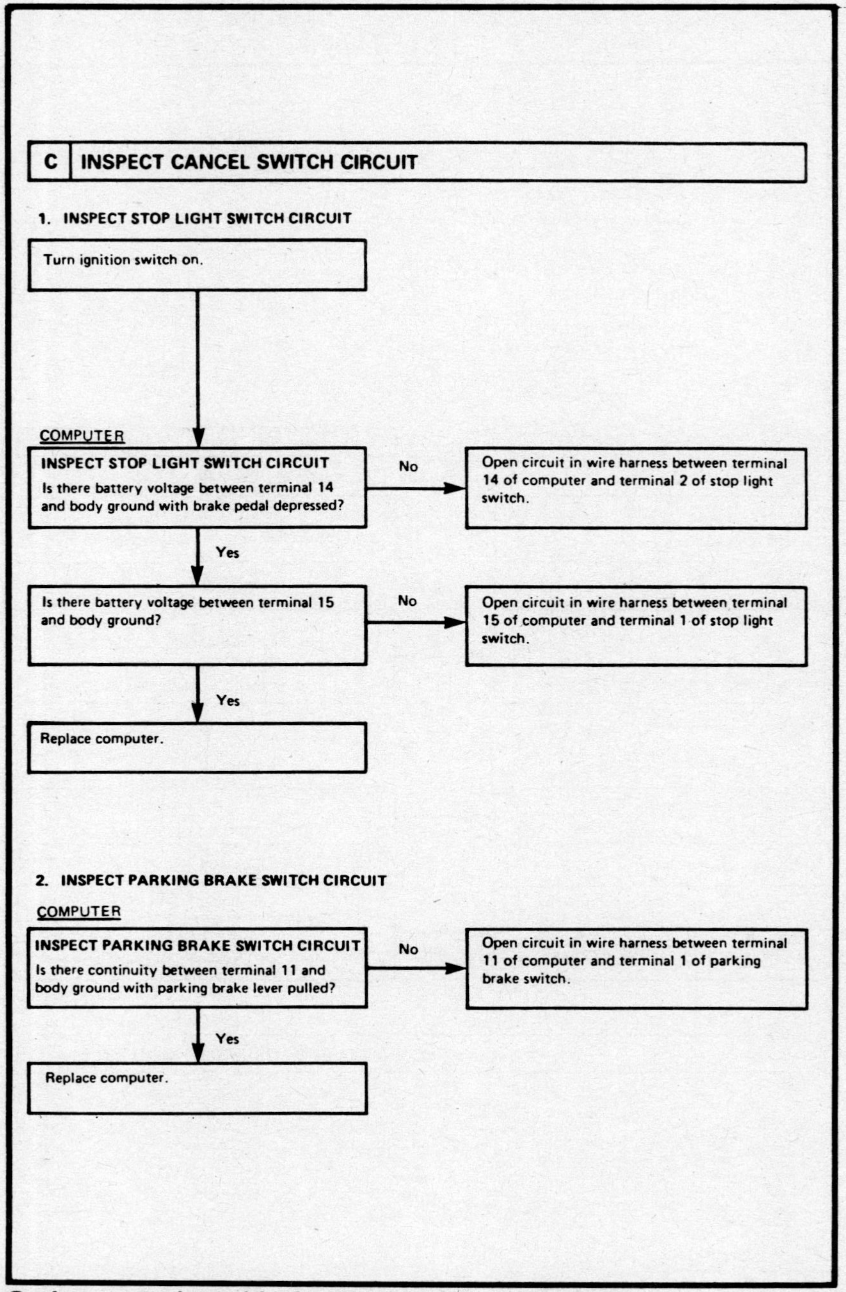

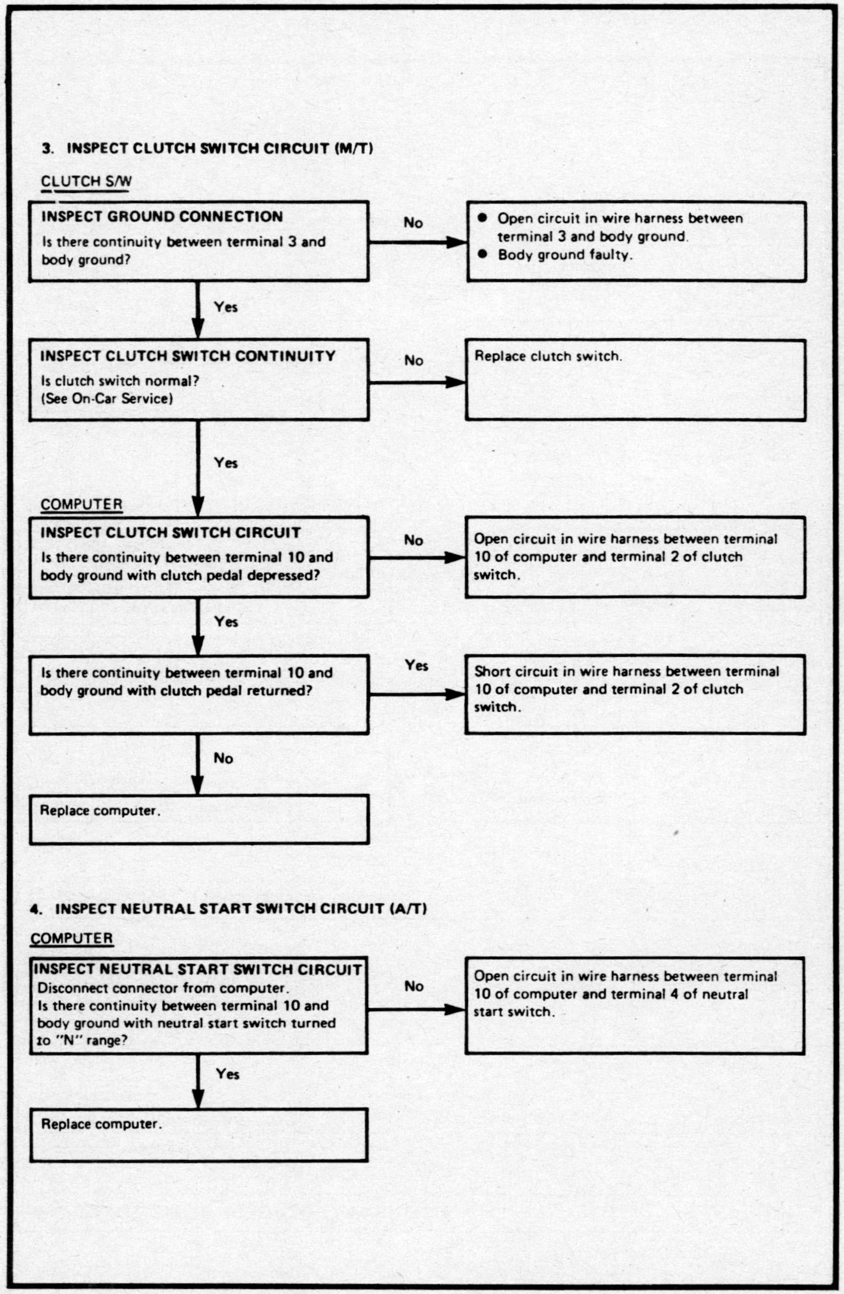

3. INSPECT CLUTCH SWITCH CIRCUIT (M/T)

CLUTCH S/W

INSPECT GROUND CONNECTION
Is there continuity between terminal 3 and body ground?

No →
- Open circuit in wire harness between terminal 3 and body ground
- Body ground faulty.

Yes ↓

INSPECT CLUTCH SWITCH CONTINUITY
Is clutch switch normal?
(See On-Car Service)

No →
Replace clutch switch.

Yes ↓

COMPUTER

INSPECT CLUTCH SWITCH CIRCUIT
Is there continuity between terminal 10 and body ground with clutch pedal depressed?

No →
Open circuit in wire harness between terminal 10 of computer and terminal 2 of clutch switch.

Yes ↓

Is there continuity between terminal 10 and body ground with clutch pedal returned?

Yes →
Short circuit in wire harness between terminal 10 of computer and terminal 2 of clutch switch.

No ↓

Replace computer.

4. INSPECT NEUTRAL START SWITCH CIRCUIT (A/T)

COMPUTER

INSPECT NEUTRAL START SWITCH CIRCUIT
Disconnect connector from computer.
Is there continuity between terminal 10 and body ground with neutral start switch turned to "N" range?

No →
Open circuit in wire harness between terminal 10 of computer and terminal 4 of neutral start switch.

Yes ↓

Replace computer.

C | INSPECT CANCEL SWITCH CIRCUIT

1. INSPECT STOP LIGHT SWITCH CIRCUIT

Turn ignition switch on.

↓

COMPUTER

INSPECT STOP LIGHT SWITCH CIRCUIT
Is there battery voltage between terminal 14 and body ground with brake pedal depressed?

No →
Open circuit in wire harness between terminal 14 of computer and terminal 2 of stop light switch.

Yes ↓

Is there battery voltage between terminal 15 and body ground?

No →
Open circuit in wire harness between terminal 15 of computer and terminal 1 of stop light switch.

Yes ↓

Replace computer.

2. INSPECT PARKING BRAKE SWITCH CIRCUIT

COMPUTER

INSPECT PARKING BRAKE SWITCH CIRCUIT
Is there continuity between terminal 11 and body ground with parking brake lever pulled?

No →
Open circuit in wire harness between terminal 11 of computer and terminal 1 of parking brake switch.

Yes ↓

Replace computer.

Cruise control troubleshooting—1985 and later Nova

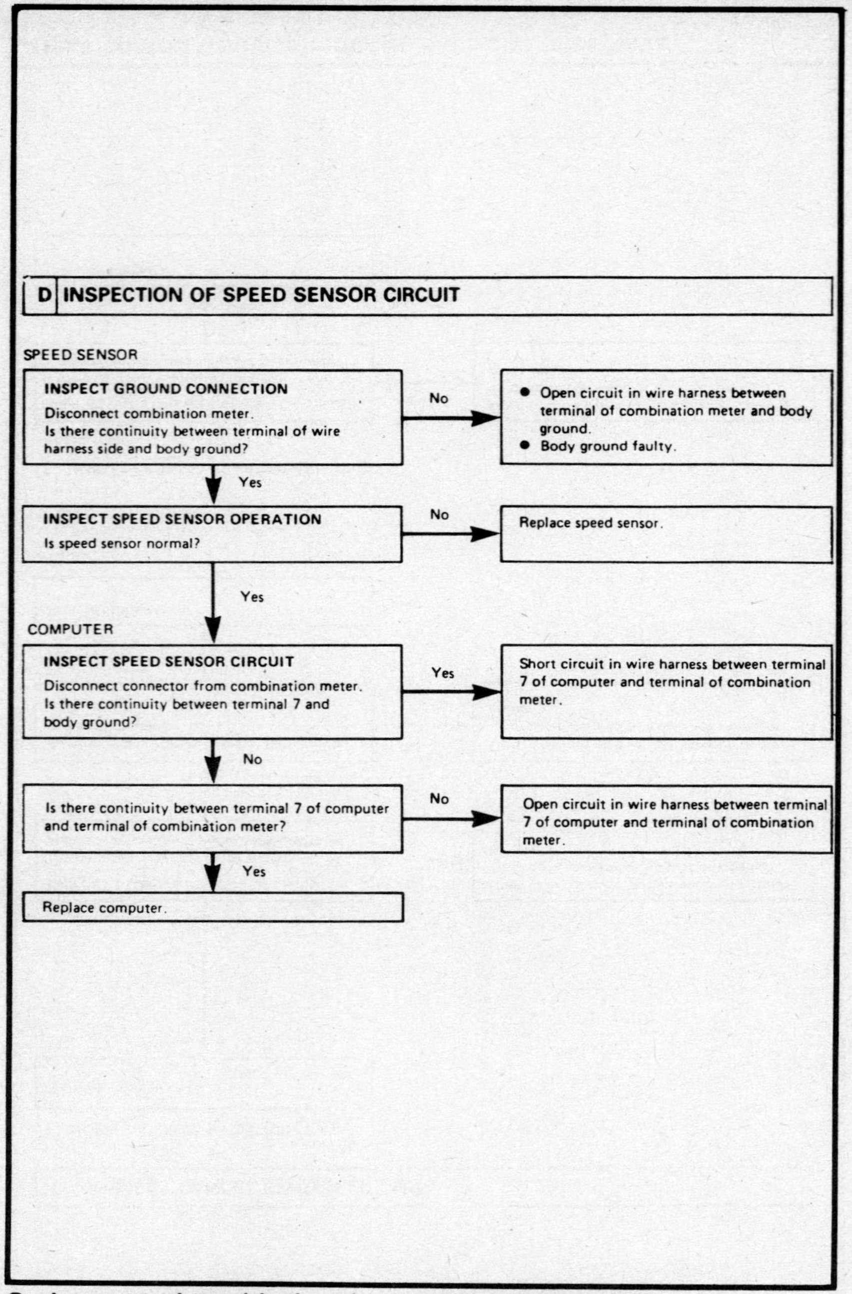

E | INSPECTION OF ACTUATOR OPERATION

ACTUATOR

INSPECT ACTUATOR OPERATION
Remove actuator.
Is actuator normal?
(See On-Car Service)

— No → Replace actuator.

— Yes → Replace computer.

F | INSPECTION OF ACTUATOR CIRCUIT

ACTUATOR

INSPECT ACTUATOR OPERATION
Remove actuator.
Is actuator normal?
(See On-Car Service)

— No → Replace actuator.

— Yes →

STOP LIGHT S/W

INSPECT STOP LIGHT SWITCH OPERATION
Is stop light switch normal?
(See On-Car Service)

— No → Replace stop light switch.

— Yes →

COMPUTER

Disconnect computer and inspect connector on wire harness as follows.

INSPECT RELEASE VALVE CIRCUIT
Is there continuity between terminal 2 and body ground?

— Yes → Short circuit in wire harness between terminal 2 of computer and terminal 3 of actuator.

— No →

D | INSPECTION OF SPEED SENSOR CIRCUIT

SPEED SENSOR

INSPECT GROUND CONNECTION
Disconnect combination meter.
Is there continuity between terminal of wire harness side and body ground?

— No →
- Open circuit in wire harness between terminal of combination meter and body ground.
- Body ground faulty.

— Yes →

INSPECT SPEED SENSOR OPERATION
Is speed sensor normal?

— No → Replace speed sensor.

— Yes →

COMPUTER

INSPECT SPEED SENSOR CIRCUIT
Disconnect connector from combination meter.
Is there continuity between terminal 7 and body ground?

— Yes → Short circuit in wire harness between terminal 7 of computer and terminal of combination meter.

— No →

Is there continuity between terminal 7 of computer and terminal of combination meter?

— No → Open circuit in wire harness between terminal 7 of computer and terminal of combination meter.

— Yes → Replace computer.

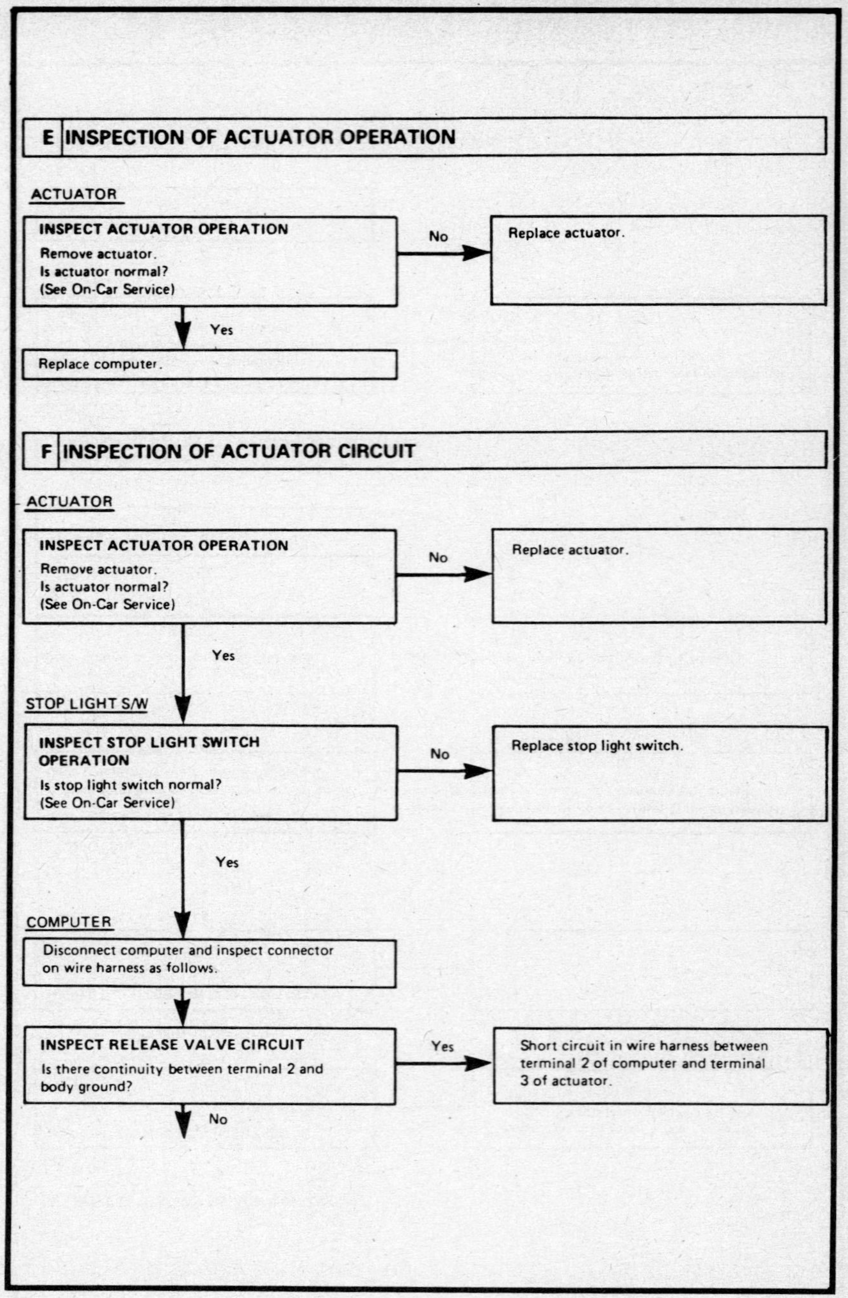

Cruise control troubleshooting — 1985 and later Nova

874

Cruise Control Computer Circuit

INSPECTION OF COMPUTER CIRCUIT

Disconnect the computer and inspect the connector on the wire harness side as shown in the chart below.

Terminal	Connection or Measure item	Check item	tester connection	Condition	Voltage or Resistance value
2	Stop Light Switch and Release Valve	Resistance	2 – 13	Brake pedal returned	About 30
4	Control Valve	Resistance	4 – 13		About 69
5	Control Switch (Set/coast S/W)	Continuity	5 – Body ground	Turn set/coast switch on	Continuity
6	OD Relay			Turn set/coast switch off	Continuity
7	Speed Sensor	Continuity	7 – Body ground	Vehicle moving slowly	1 pulse each 40 cm (15.75 in.)
9	Main Switch	Voltage	9 – Body ground	Turn ignition switch and main switch on	Battery voltage
				Turn ignition switch and/or main switch off	No voltage
10	Clutch Switch or Neutral Start Switch	Continuity	10 – Body ground	Clutch pedal depressed or if shifted into "N" range	Continuity
				Clutch pedal returned or if shifted into any range except "N" range	No continuity
11	Parking Brake Switch	Voltage	11 – Body ground	Parking brake lever pulled	No voltage
				Parking brake lever returned	Battery voltage
12	Body Ground	Continuity	12 – Body ground		Continuity
13	Release Valve and Control Valve				
14	Stop Light Switch	Voltage	14 – Body ground	Brake pedal depressed	Battery voltage
15	STOP Fuse	Voltage	15 – Body ground	Brake pedal returned	No voltage
16	Control Switch (Accel/resume S/W)	Continuity	17 – Body ground	Turn accel/resume switch on	Battery voltage
				Turn accel/resume switch on	Continuity
				Turn accel/resume switch off	No continuity

Cruise control computer circuit diagnosis chart 1985 and later Nova

---

Is resistance value about 68 Ω between terminals 2 and 13 with brake pedal returned?

No →
- Open circuit in wire harness between terminal 13 of computer and terminal 1 of actuator.
- Open circuit in wire harness between terminal 2 of computer and terminal 3 of actuator.

Yes ↓

INSPECT CONTROL VALVE CIRCUIT

Is resistance value about 30 Ω between terminals 4 and 13?

No →
Open or short circuit in wire harness between terminal 4 of computer and terminal 2 of actuator.

Yes ↓

Replace computer.

Is resistance value about 68 Ω between terminals 2 and 13 with brake pedal returned?

No →
- Open circuit in wire harness between terminal 13 of computer and terminal 1 of actuator.
- Open circuit in wire harness between terminal 2 of computer and terminal 3 of actuator.

Yes ↓

INSPECT CONTROL VALVE CIRCUIT

Is resistance value about 30 Ω between terminals 4 and 13?

No →
Open or short circuit in wire harness between terminal 4 of computer and terminal 2 of actuator.

Yes ↓

Replace computer.

Cruise control troubleshooting – 1985 and later Nova

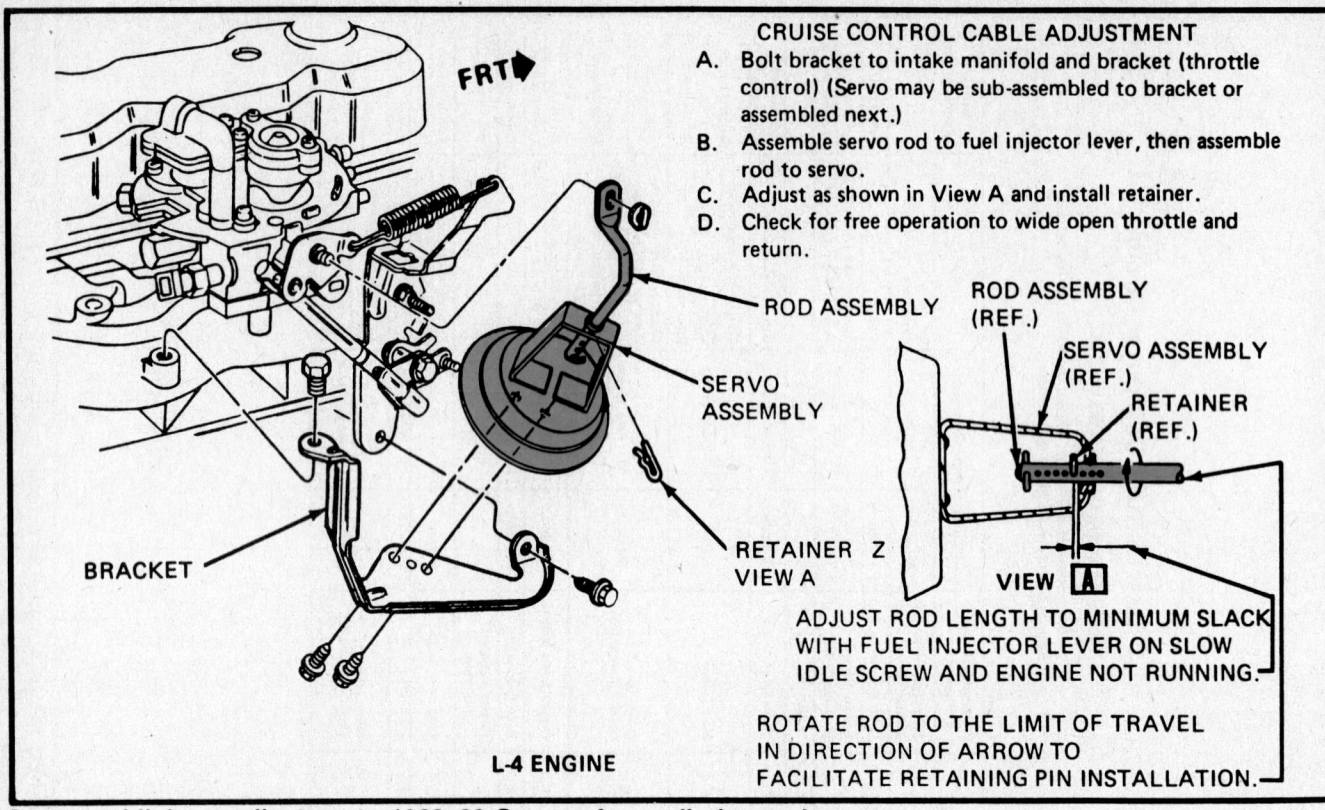

CRUISE CONTROL CABLE ADJUSTMENT

A. Bolt bracket to intake manifold and bracket (throttle control) (Servo may be sub-assembled to bracket or assembled next.)

B. Assemble servo rod to fuel injector lever, then assemble rod to servo.

C. Adjust as shown in View A and install retainer.

D. Check for free operation to wide open throttle and return.

ROD ASSEMBLY

ROD ASSEMBLY (REF.)

SERVO ASSEMBLY (REF.)

RETAINER (REF.)

SERVO ASSEMBLY

RETAINER Z
VIEW A

VIEW A

BRACKET

FRT

L-4 ENGINE

ADJUST ROD LENGTH TO MINIMUM SLACK WITH FUEL INJECTOR LEVER ON SLOW IDLE SCREW AND ENGINE NOT RUNNING.

ROTATE ROD TO THE LIMIT OF TRAVEL IN DIRECTION OF ARROW TO FACILITATE RETAINING PIN INSTALLATION.

Servo and linkage adjustment—1982–83 Camaro four cylinder engine

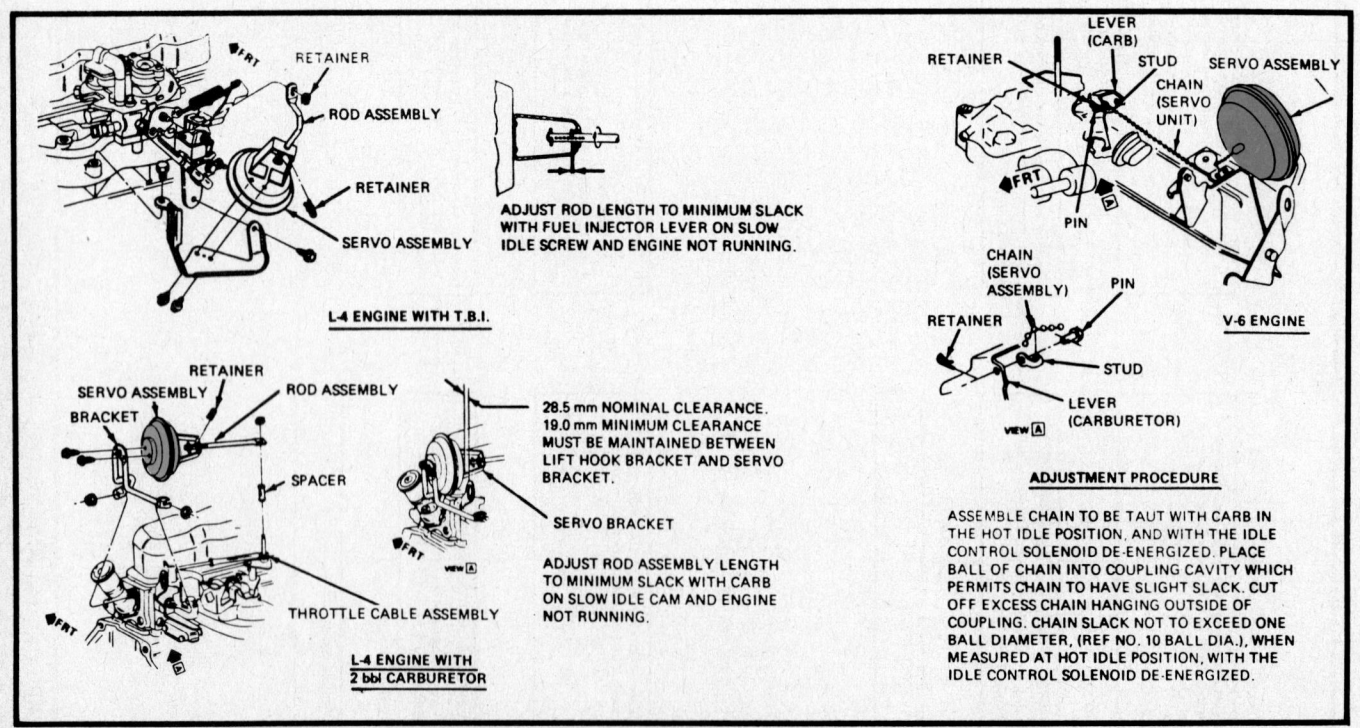

RETAINER

ROD ASSEMBLY

RETAINER

SERVO ASSEMBLY

FRT

L-4 ENGINE WITH T.B.I.

ADJUST ROD LENGTH TO MINIMUM SLACK WITH FUEL INJECTOR LEVER ON SLOW IDLE SCREW AND ENGINE NOT RUNNING.

SERVO ASSEMBLY
BRACKET

RETAINER

ROD ASSEMBLY

SPACER

THROTTLE CABLE ASSEMBLY

FRT

VIEW A

SERVO BRACKET

28.5 mm NOMINAL CLEARANCE. 19.0 mm MINIMUM CLEARANCE MUST BE MAINTAINED BETWEEN LIFT HOOK BRACKET AND SERVO BRACKET.

ADJUST ROD ASSEMBLY LENGTH TO MINIMUM SLACK WITH CARB ON SLOW IDLE CAM AND ENGINE NOT RUNNING.

L-4 ENGINE WITH 2 bbl CARBURETOR

LEVER (CARB)

RETAINER

STUD

SERVO ASSEMBLY

CHAIN (SERVO UNIT)

FRT

PIN

CHAIN (SERVO ASSEMBLY)

PIN

RETAINER

STUD

LEVER (CARBURETOR)

VIEW A

V-6 ENGINE

ADJUSTMENT PROCEDURE

ASSEMBLE CHAIN TO BE TAUT WITH CARB IN THE HOT IDLE POSITION, AND WITH THE IDLE CONTROL SOLENOID DE-ENERGIZED. PLACE BALL OF CHAIN INTO COUPLING CAVITY WHICH PERMITS CHAIN TO HAVE SLIGHT SLACK. CUT OFF EXCESS CHAIN HANGING OUTSIDE OF COUPLING. CHAIN SLACK NOT TO EXCEED ONE BALL DIAMETER, (REF NO. 10 BALL DIA.), WHEN MEASURED AT HOT IDLE POSITION, WITH THE IDLE CONTROL SOLENOID DE-ENERGIZED.

Servo and linkage adjustment—1982–83 Citation and Celebrity

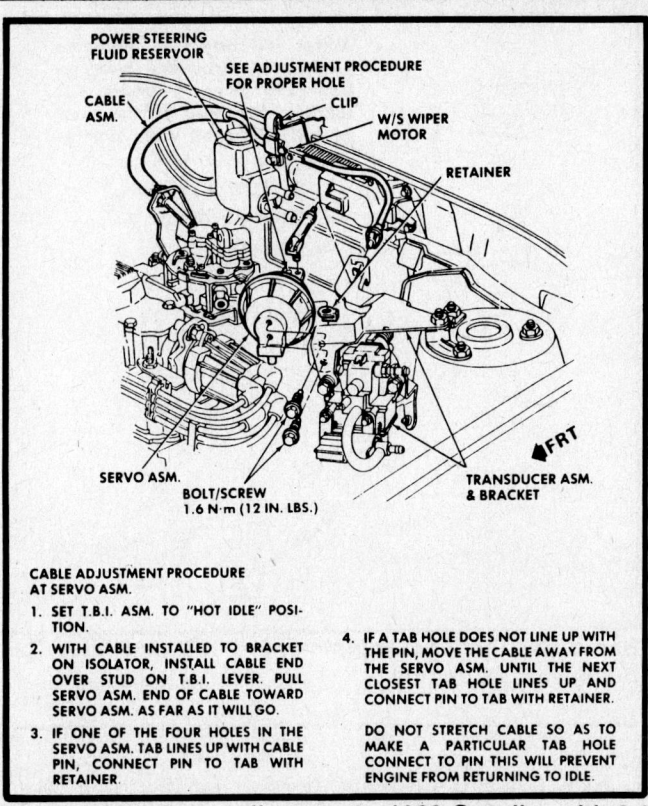

CABLE ADJUSTMENT PROCEDURE AT SERVO ASM.

1. SET T.B.I. ASM. TO "HOT IDLE" POSITION.

2. WITH CABLE INSTALLED TO BRACKET ON ISOLATOR, INSTALL CABLE END OVER STUD ON T.B.I. LEVER. PULL SERVO ASM. END OF CABLE TOWARD SERVO ASM. AS FAR AS IT WILL GO.

3. IF ONE OF THE FOUR HOLES IN THE SERVO ASM. TAB LINES UP WITH CABLE PIN, CONNECT PIN TO TAB WITH RETAINER.

4. IF A TAB HOLE DOES NOT LINE UP WITH THE PIN, MOVE THE CABLE AWAY FROM THE SERVO ASM. UNTIL THE NEXT CLOSEST TAB HOLE LINES UP AND CONNECT PIN TO TAB WITH RETAINER.

DO NOT STRETCH CABLE SO AS TO MAKE A PARTICULAR TAB HOLE CONNECT TO PIN THIS WILL PREVENT ENGINE FROM RETURNING TO IDLE.

Servo and linkage adjustment — 1983 Cavalier with 2.0 liter TBI engine

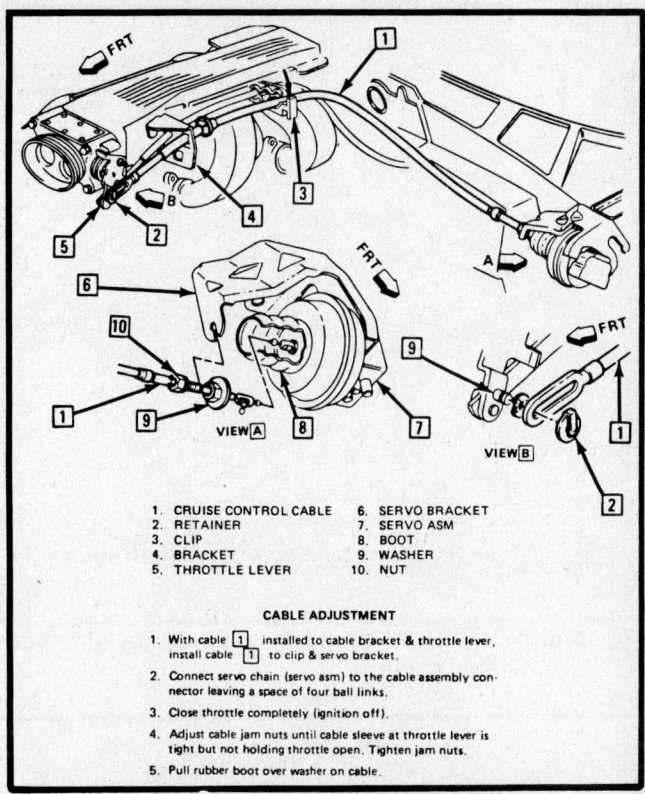

1. CRUISE CONTROL CABLE
2. RETAINER
3. CLIP
4. BRACKET
5. THROTTLE LEVER
6. SERVO BRACKET
7. SERVO ASM
8. BOOT
9. WASHER
10. NUT

CABLE ADJUSTMENT

1. With cable [1] installed to cable bracket & throttle lever, install cable [1] to clip & servo bracket.

2. Connect servo chain (servo asm) to the cable assembly connector leaving a space of four ball links.

3. Close throttle completely (ignition off).

4. Adjust cable jam nuts until cable sleeve at throttle lever is tight but not holding throttle open. Tighten jam nuts.

5. Pull rubber boot over washer on cable.

Servo and linkage adjustment — 1985 and later Corvette

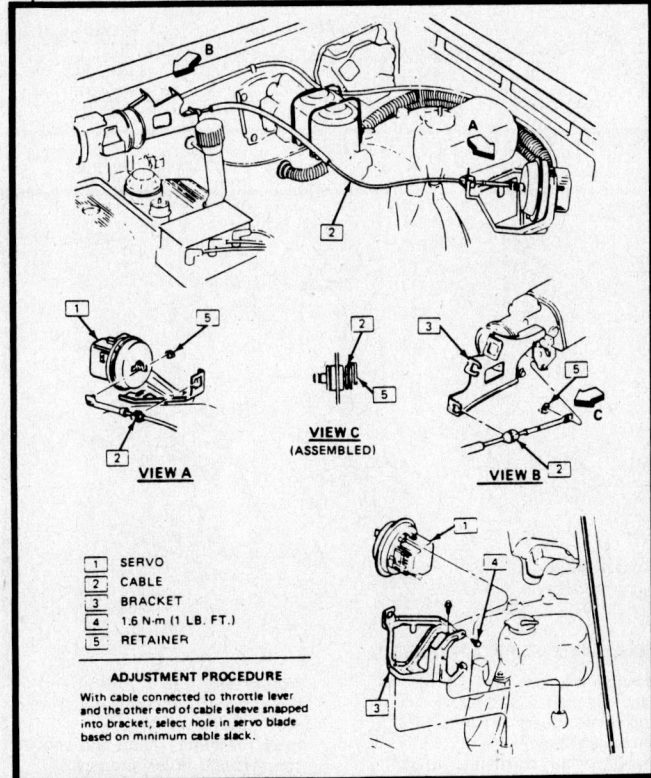

1. SERVO
2. CABLE
3. BRACKET
4. 1.6 N·m (1 LB. FT.)
5. RETAINER

ADJUSTMENT PROCEDURE

With cable connected to throttle lever and the other end of cable sleeve snapped into bracket, select hole in servo blade based on minimum cable slack.

Servo and linkage adjustment — 1984 Impala, Caprice, Malibu, Monte Carlo and El Camino with V8 engine

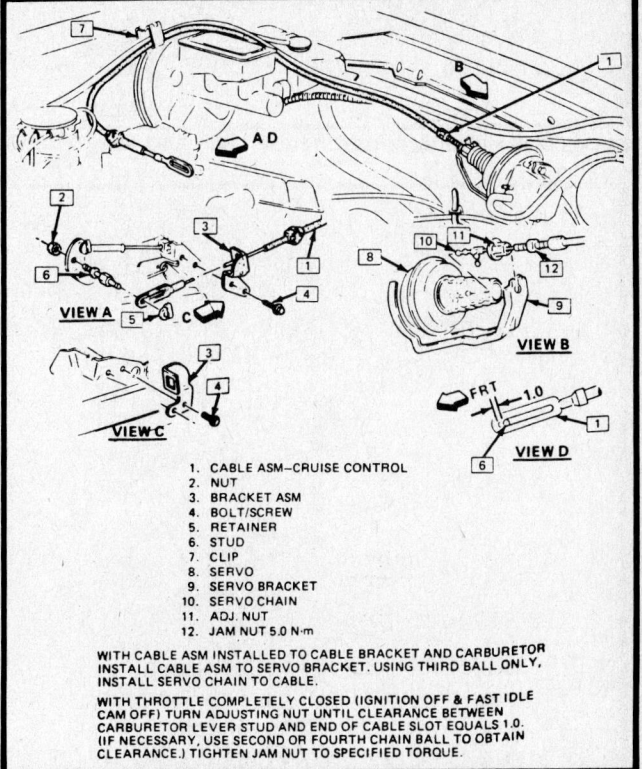

1. CABLE ASM—CRUISE CONTROL
2. NUT
3. BRACKET ASM
4. BOLT/SCREW
5. RETAINER
6. STUD
7. CLIP
8. SERVO
9. SERVO BRACKET
10. SERVO CHAIN
11. ADJ. NUT
12. JAM NUT 5.0 N·m

WITH CABLE ASM INSTALLED TO CABLE BRACKET AND CARBURETOR INSTALL CABLE ASM TO SERVO BRACKET. USING THIRD BALL ONLY, INSTALL SERVO CHAIN TO CABLE.

WITH THROTTLE COMPLETELY CLOSED (IGNITION OFF & FAST IDLE CAM OFF) TURN ADJUSTING NUT UNTIL CLEARANCE BETWEEN CARBURETOR LEVER STUD AND END OF CABLE SLOT EQUALS 1.0. (IF NECESSARY, USE SECOND OR FOURTH CHAIN BALL TO OBTAIN CLEARANCE.) TIGHTEN JAM NUT TO SPECIFIED TORQUE.

Servo and linkage adjustment — 1985 Impala and 1986 and later Caprice

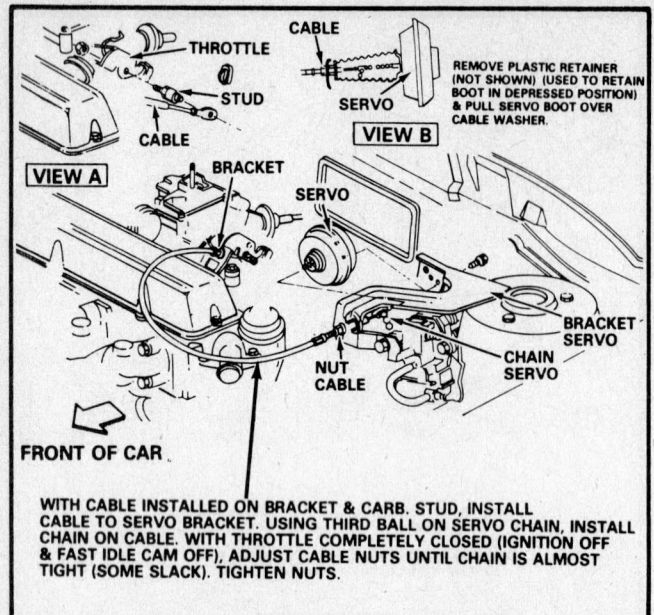

Servo and linkage adjustment—1982–83 Cavalier with 1.8 and 2.0 liter engine

WITH CABLE INSTALLED ON BRACKET & CARB. STUD, INSTALL CABLE TO SERVO BRACKET. USING THIRD BALL ON SERVO CHAIN, INSTALL CHAIN ON CABLE. WITH THROTTLE COMPLETELY CLOSED (IGNITION OFF & FAST IDLE CAM OFF), ADJUST CABLE NUTS UNTIL CHAIN IS ALMOST TIGHT (SOME SLACK). TIGHTEN NUTS.

FRONT OF CAR

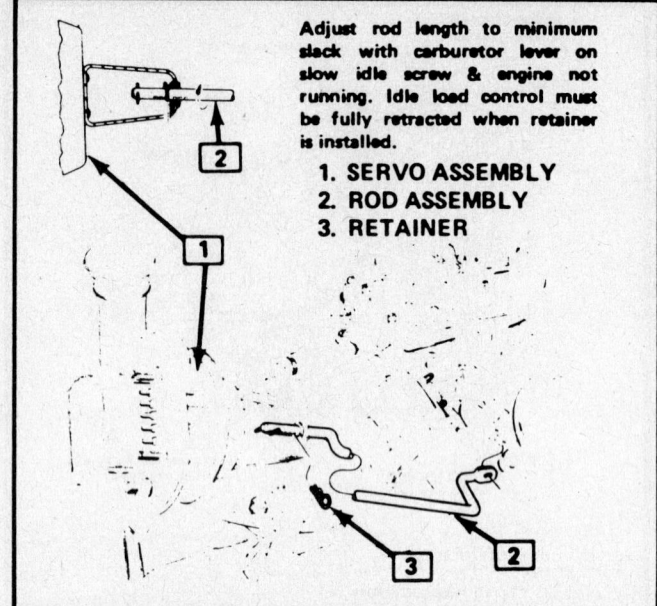

Servo and linkage adjustment—1986 and later Caprice with V8 engine

Adjust rod length to minimum slack with carburetor lever on slow idle screw & engine not running. Idle load control must be fully retracted when retainer is installed.

1. SERVO ASSEMBLY
2. ROD ASSEMBLY
3. RETAINER

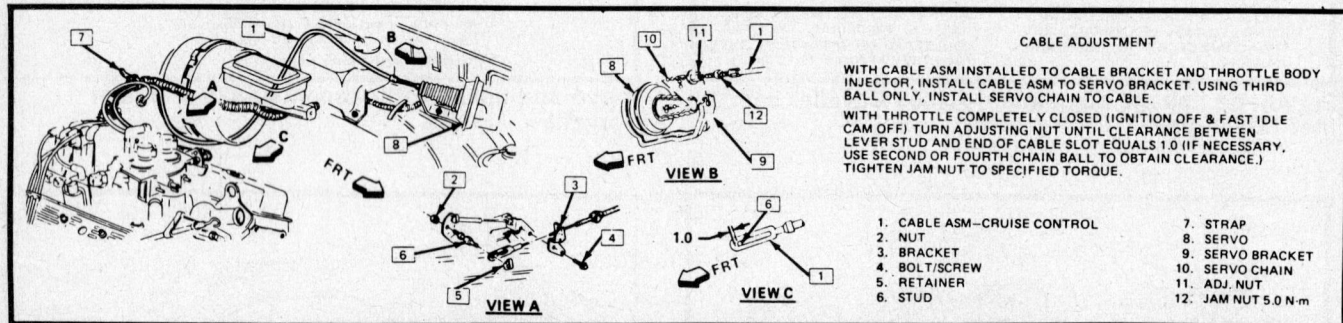

Servo and linkage adjustment—1985 and later Monte Carlo with 4.3 liter EFI V6 engine

CABLE ADJUSTMENT

WITH CABLE ASM INSTALLED TO CABLE BRACKET AND THROTTLE BODY INJECTOR, INSTALL CABLE ASM TO SERVO BRACKET. USING THIRD BALL ONLY, INSTALL SERVO CHAIN TO CABLE.

WITH THROTTLE COMPLETELY CLOSED (IGNITION OFF & FAST IDLE CAM OFF) TURN ADJUSTING NUT UNTIL CLEARANCE BETWEEN LEVER STUD AND END OF CABLE SLOT EQUALS 1.0 (IF NECESSARY, USE SECOND OR FOURTH CHAIN BALL TO OBTAIN CLEARANCE.) TIGHTEN JAM NUT TO SPECIFIED TORQUE.

1. CABLE ASM—CRUISE CONTROL
2. NUT
3. BRACKET
4. BOLT/SCREW
5. RETAINER
6. STUD
7. STRAP
8. SERVO
9. SERVO BRACKET
10. SERVO CHAIN
11. ADJ. NUT
12. JAM NUT 5.0 N·m

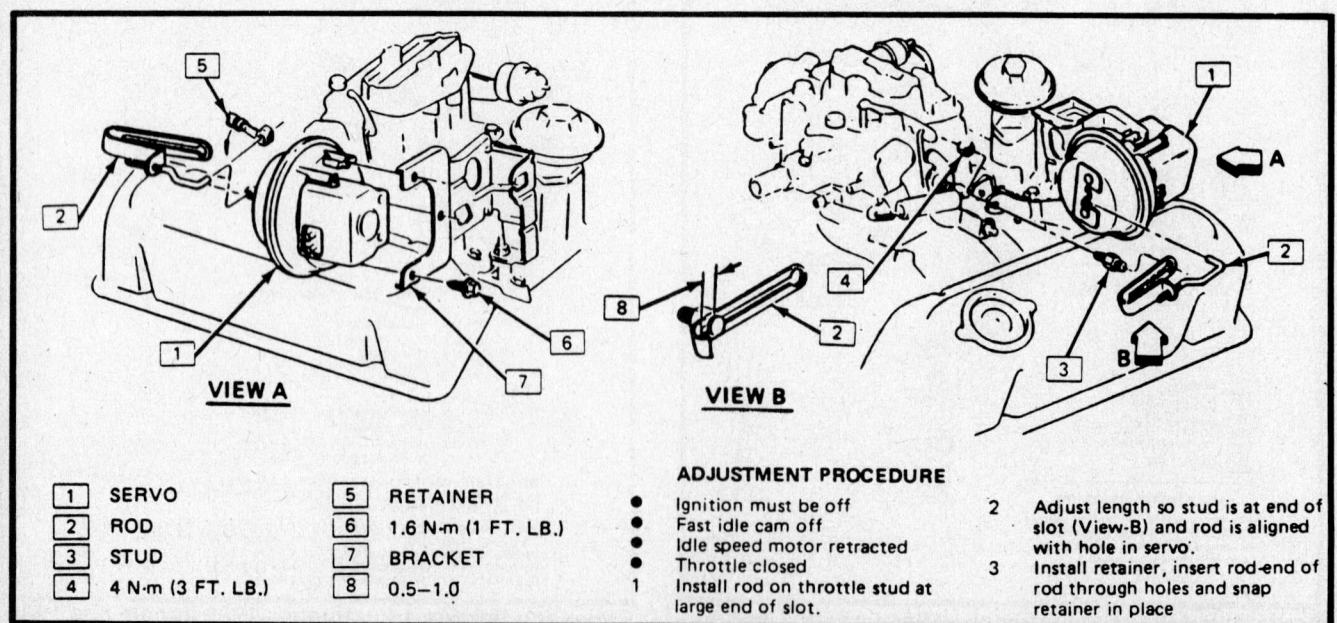

1	SERVO	5	RETAINER
2	ROD	6	1.6 N·m (1 FT. LB.)
3	STUD	7	BRACKET
4	4 N·m (3 FT. LB.)	8	0.5–1.0

ADJUSTMENT PROCEDURE

- Ignition must be off
- Fast idle cam off
- Idle speed motor retracted
- Throttle closed

1. Install rod on throttle stud at large end of slot.

2. Adjust length so stud is at end of slot (View-B) and rod is aligned with hole in servo.

3. Install retainer, insert rod-end of rod through holes and snap retainer in place

Servo and linkage adjustment—1984 Impala, Caprice, Malibu, Monte Carlo and El Camino with V6 engine

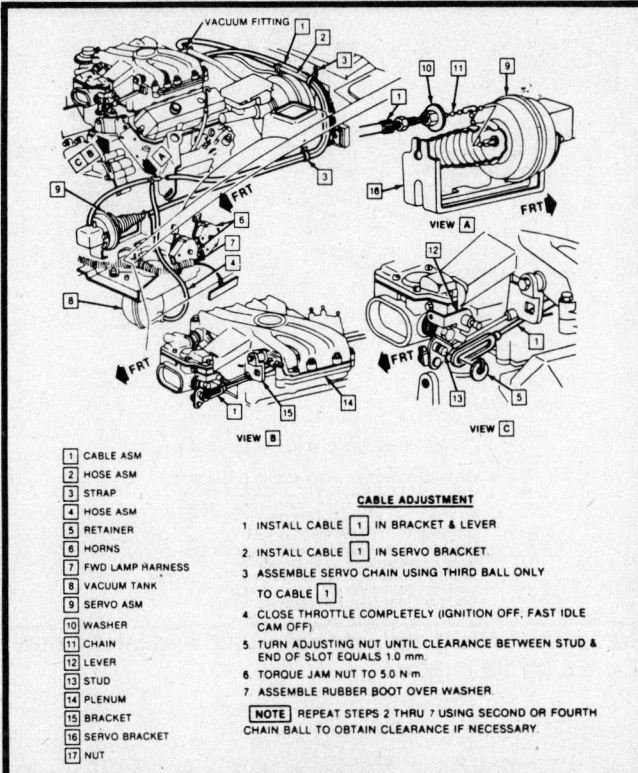

CABLE ADJUSTMENT

1	CABLE ASM
2	HOSE ASM
3	STRAP
4	HOSE ASM
5	RETAINER
6	HORNS
7	FWD LAMP HARNESS
8	VACUUM TANK
9	SERVO ASM
10	WASHER
11	CHAIN
12	LEVER
13	STUD
14	PLENUM
15	BRACKET
16	SERVO BRACKET
17	NUT

1. INSTALL CABLE [1] IN BRACKET & LEVER.
2. INSTALL CABLE [1] IN SERVO BRACKET.
3. ASSEMBLE SERVO CHAIN USING THIRD BALL ONLY TO CABLE [1]
4. CLOSE THROTTLE COMPLETELY (IGNITION OFF, FAST IDLE CAM OFF).
5. TURN ADJUSTING NUT UNTIL CLEARANCE BETWEEN STUD & END OF SLOT EQUALS 1.0 mm.
6. TORQUE JAM NUT TO 5.0 N.m.
7. ASSEMBLE RUBBER BOOT OVER WASHER.

NOTE REPEAT STEPS 2 THRU 7 USING SECOND OR FOURTH CHAIN BALL TO OBTAIN CLEARANCE IF NECESSARY.

Servo and linkage adjustment—1984 and later Camaro with 2.8 liter MFI engine

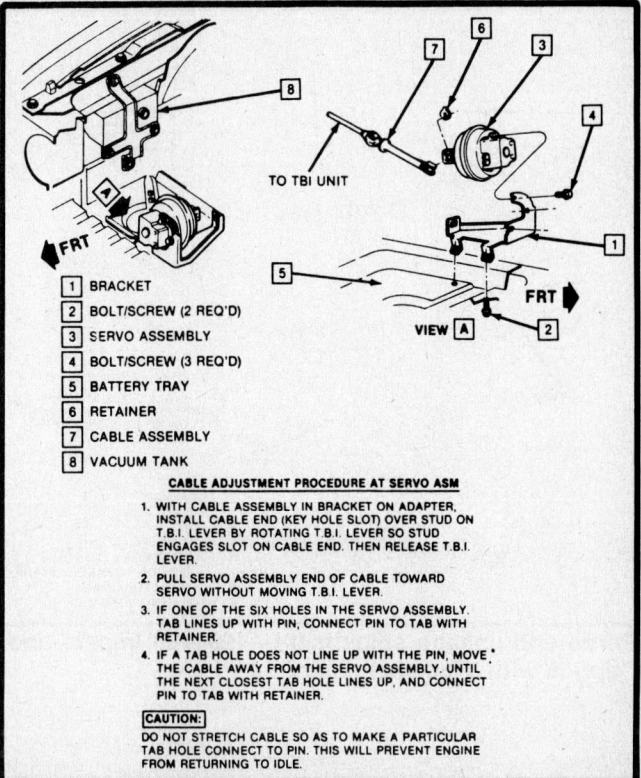

1	BRACKET
2	BOLT/SCREW (2 REQ'D)
3	SERVO ASSEMBLY
4	BOLT/SCREW (3 REQ'D)
5	BATTERY TRAY
6	RETAINER
7	CABLE ASSEMBLY
8	VACUUM TANK

CABLE ADJUSTMENT PROCEDURE AT SERVO ASM

1. WITH CABLE ASSEMBLY IN BRACKET ON ADAPTER, INSTALL CABLE END (KEY HOLE SLOT) OVER STUD ON T.B.I. LEVER BY ROTATING T.B.I. LEVER SO STUD ENGAGES SLOT ON CABLE END. THEN RELEASE T.B.I. LEVER.
2. PULL SERVO ASSEMBLY END OF CABLE TOWARD SERVO WITHOUT MOVING T.B.I. LEVER.
3. IF ONE OF THE SIX HOLES IN THE SERVO ASSEMBLY. TAB LINES UP WITH PIN, CONNECT PIN TO TAB WITH RETAINER.
4. IF A TAB HOLE DOES NOT LINE UP WITH THE PIN, MOVE THE CABLE AWAY FROM THE SERVO ASSEMBLY. UNTIL THE NEXT CLOSEST TAB HOLE LINES UP, AND CONNECT PIN TO TAB WITH RETAINER.

CAUTION:
DO NOT STRETCH CABLE SO AS TO MAKE A PARTICULAR TAB HOLE CONNECT TO PIN. THIS WILL PREVENT ENGINE FROM RETURNING TO IDLE.

Servo and linkage adjustment—1984 and later Camaro with 2.5 liter EFI engine

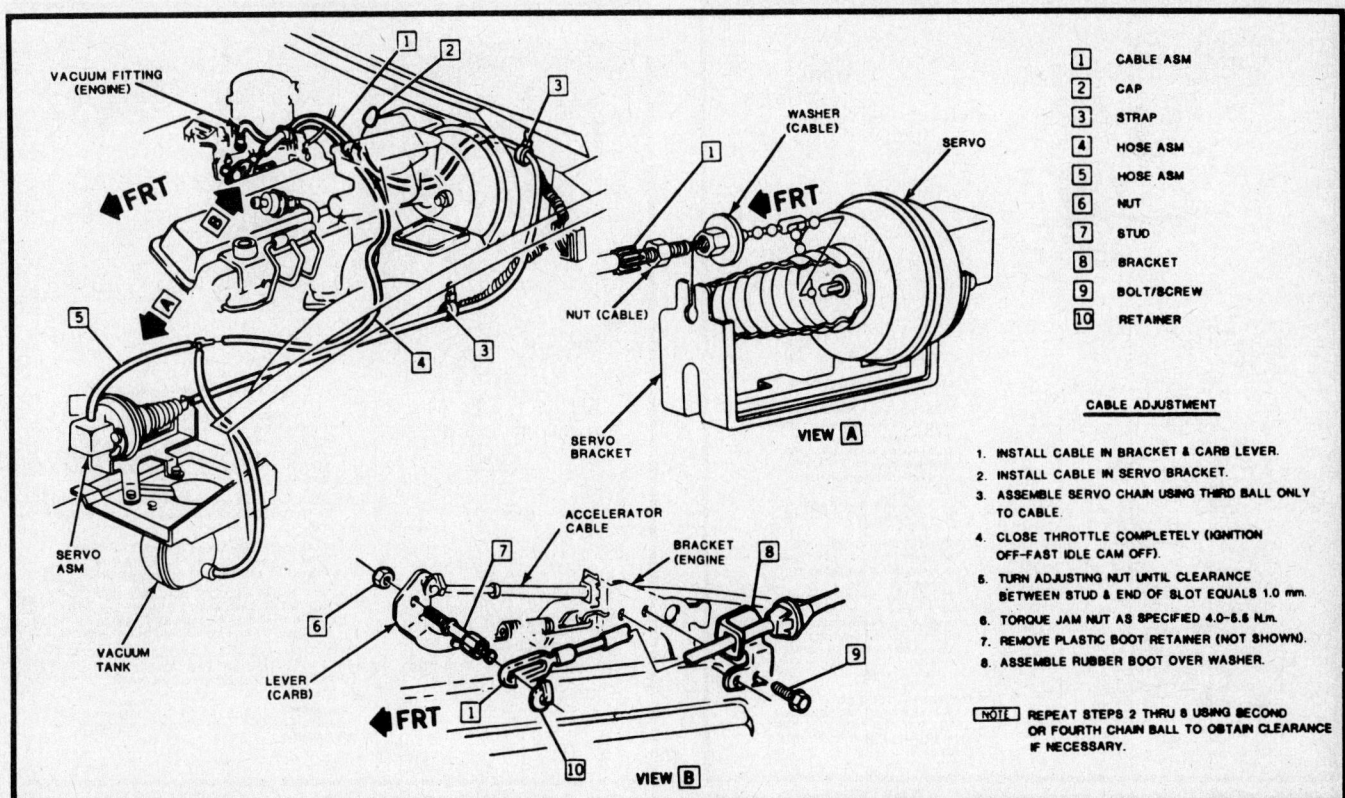

1	CABLE ASM
2	CAP
3	STRAP
4	HOSE ASM
5	HOSE ASM
6	NUT
7	STUD
8	BRACKET
9	BOLT/SCREW
10	RETAINER

CABLE ADJUSTMENT

1. INSTALL CABLE IN BRACKET & CARB LEVER.
2. INSTALL CABLE IN SERVO BRACKET.
3. ASSEMBLE SERVO CHAIN USING THIRD BALL ONLY TO CABLE.
4. CLOSE THROTTLE COMPLETELY (IGNITION OFF—FAST IDLE CAM OFF).
5. TURN ADJUSTING NUT UNTIL CLEARANCE BETWEEN STUD & END OF SLOT EQUALS 1.0 mm.
6. TORQUE JAM NUT AS SPECIFIED 4.0-5.5 N.m.
7. REMOVE PLASTIC BOOT RETAINER (NOT SHOWN).
8. ASSEMBLE RUBBER BOOT OVER WASHER.

NOTE REPEAT STEPS 2 THRU 8 USING SECOND OR FOURTH CHAIN BALL TO OBTAIN CLEARANCE IF NECESSARY.

Servo and linkage adjustment—1984 and later Camaro with 5.0 liter V8 engine

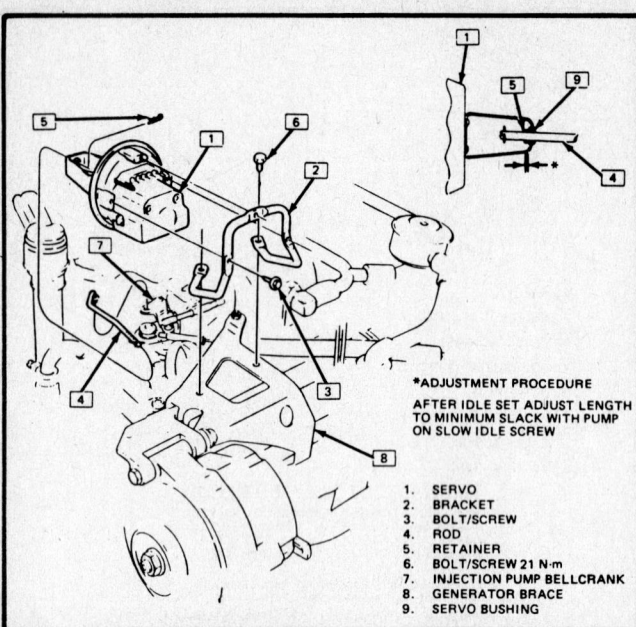

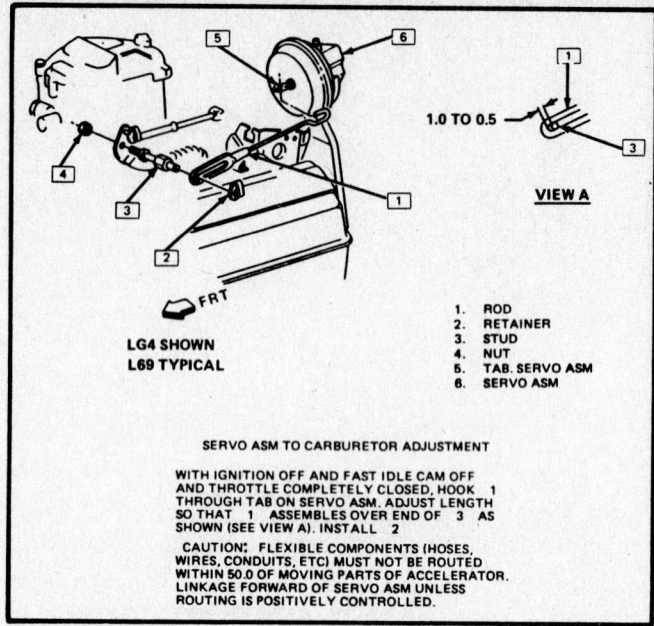

Servo and linkage adjustment—1984–85 Impala and Caprice with V8 diesel engine

Servo and linkage adjustment—1985 and later Monte Carlo with V8 engine

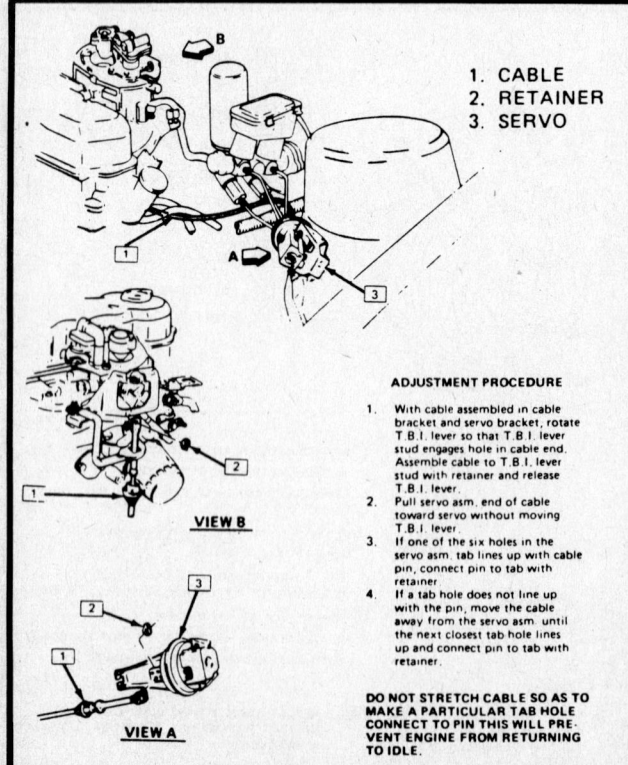

Servo and linkage adjustment—1985 Citation and 1985 and later Celebrity with 2.5 liter EFI engine

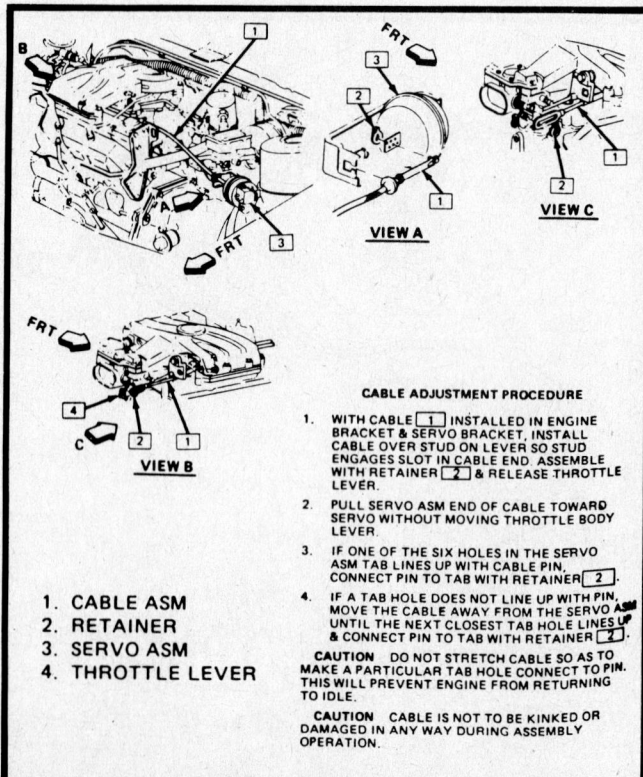

Servo and linkage adjustment—1985 Citation and 1985 and later Celebrity with 2.8 liter MFI engine

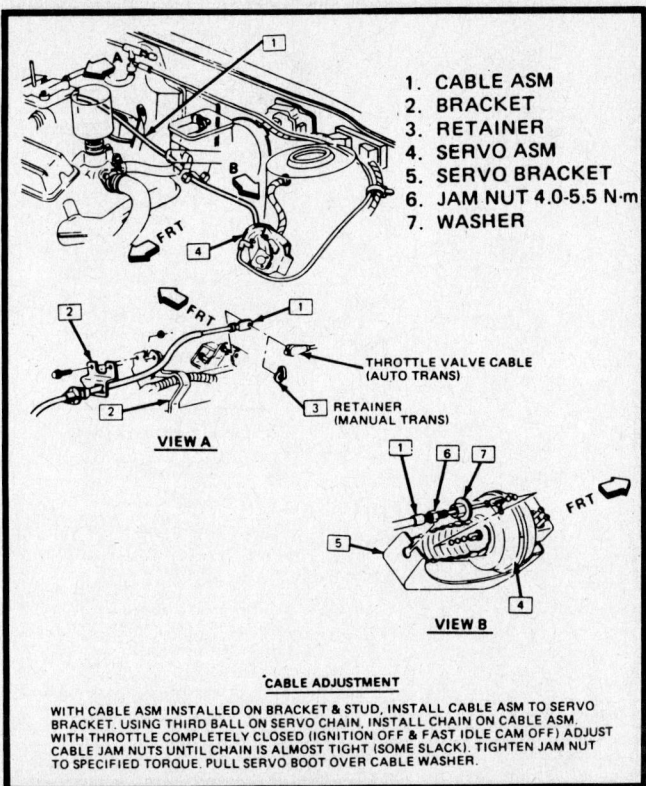

1. CABLE ASM
2. BRACKET
3. RETAINER
4. SERVO ASM
5. SERVO BRACKET
6. JAM NUT 4.0-5.5 N·m
7. WASHER

THROTTLE VALVE CABLE
(AUTO TRANS)

3 RETAINER
(MANUAL TRANS)

VIEW A

FRT

VIEW B

CABLE ADJUSTMENT

WITH CABLE ASM INSTALLED ON BRACKET & STUD, INSTALL CABLE ASM TO SERVO
BRACKET. USING THIRD BALL ON SERVO CHAIN, INSTALL CHAIN ON CABLE ASM.
WITH THROTTLE COMPLETELY CLOSED (IGNITION OFF & FAST IDLE CAM OFF) ADJUST
CABLE JAM NUTS UNTIL CHAIN IS ALMOST TIGHT (SOME SLACK). TIGHTEN JAM NUT
TO SPECIFIED TORQUE. PULL SERVO BOOT OVER CABLE WASHER.

**Servo and linkage adjustment—1985 Citation and
1985 and later Celebrity with 2.8 liter engine**

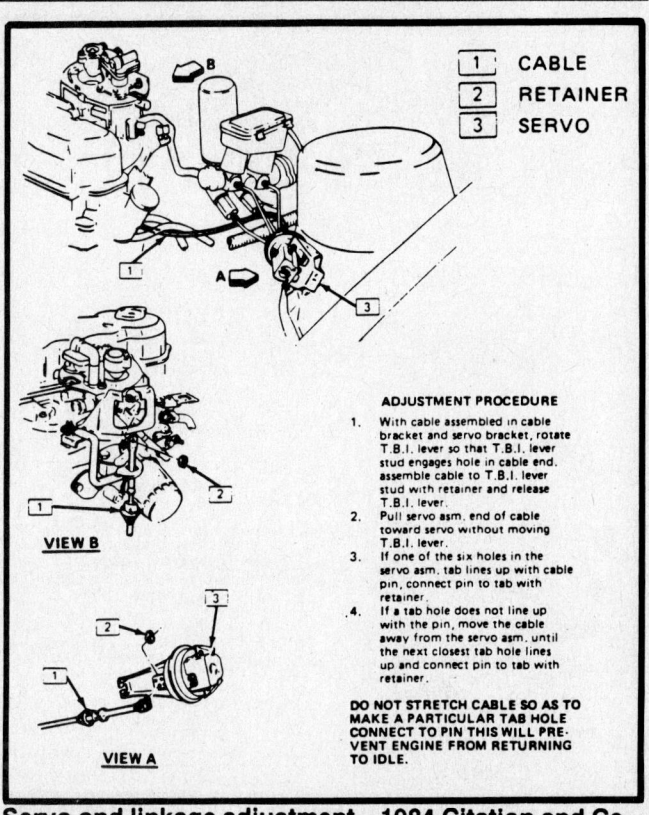

1 CABLE
2 RETAINER
3 SERVO

VIEW B

VIEW A

ADJUSTMENT PROCEDURE

1. With cable assembled in cable
bracket and servo bracket, rotate
T.B.I. lever so that T.B.I. lever
stud engages hole in cable end.
assemble cable to T.B.I. lever
stud with retainer and release
T.B.I. lever.

2. Pull servo asm. end of cable
toward servo without moving
T.B.I. lever.

3. If one of the six holes in the
servo asm. tab lines up with cable
pin, connect pin to tab with
retainer.

4. If a tab hole does not line up
with the pin, move the cable
away from the servo asm. until
the next closest tab hole lines
up and connect pin to tab with
retainer.

**DO NOT STRETCH CABLE SO AS TO
MAKE A PARTICULAR TAB HOLE
CONNECT TO PIN THIS WILL PRE-
VENT ENGINE FROM RETURNING
TO IDLE.**

**Servo and linkage adjustment—1984 Citation and Ce-
lebrity with 2.5 liter EFI engine**

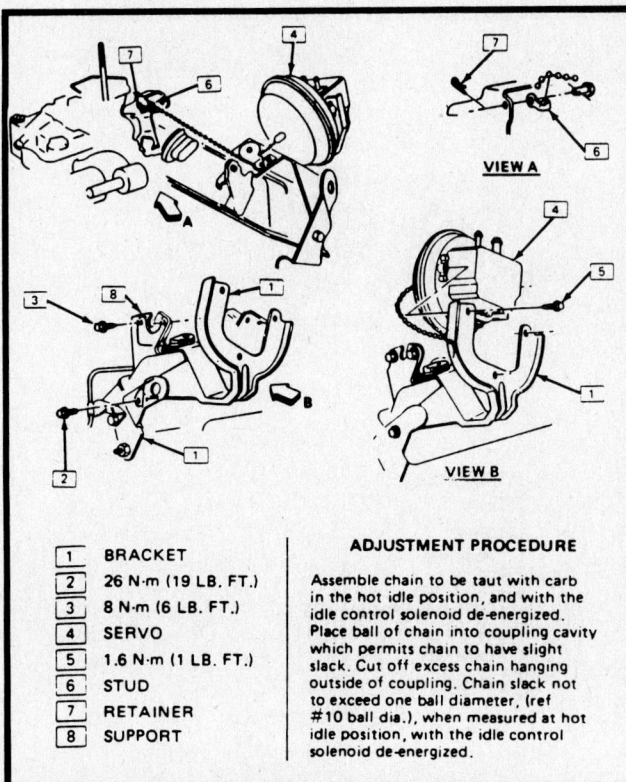

VIEW A

VIEW B

1	BRACKET
2	26 N·m (19 LB. FT.)
3	8 N·m (6 LB. FT.)
4	SERVO
5	1.6 N·m (1 LB. FT.)
6	STUD
7	RETAINER
8	SUPPORT

ADJUSTMENT PROCEDURE

Assemble chain to be taut with carb
in the hot idle position, and with the
idle control solenoid de-energized.
Place ball of chain into coupling cavity
which permits chain to have slight
slack. Cut off excess chain hanging
outside of coupling. Chain slack not
to exceed one ball diameter, (ref
#10 ball dia.), when measured at hot
idle position, with the idle control
solenoid de-energized.

Servo and linkage adjustment—1984 Citation

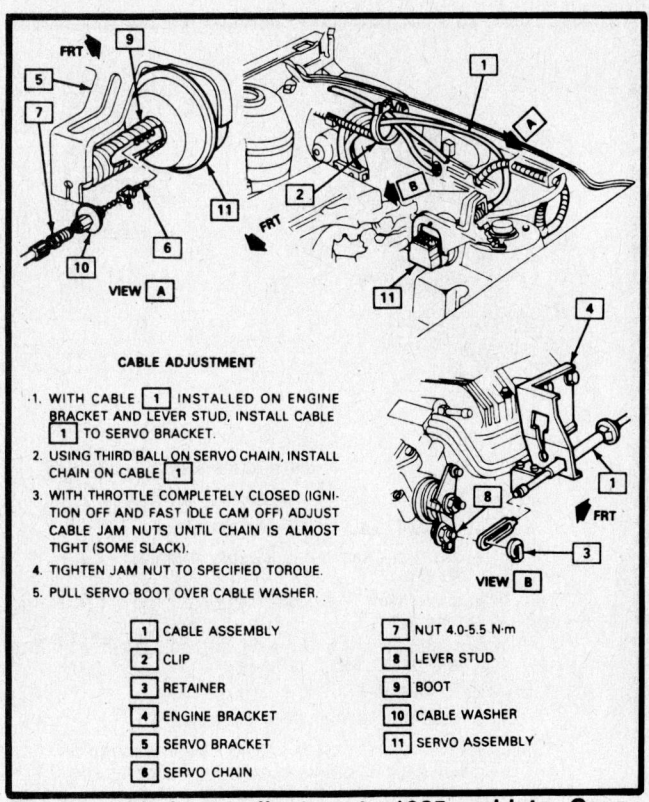

FRT

VIEW A

FRT

VIEW B

FRT

CABLE ADJUSTMENT

1. WITH CABLE 1 INSTALLED ON ENGINE
BRACKET AND LEVER STUD, INSTALL CABLE
1 TO SERVO BRACKET.

2. USING THIRD BALL ON SERVO CHAIN, INSTALL
CHAIN ON CABLE 1.

3. WITH THROTTLE COMPLETELY CLOSED (IGNI-
TION OFF AND FAST IDLE CAM OFF) ADJUST
CABLE JAM NUTS UNTIL CHAIN IS ALMOST
TIGHT (SOME SLACK).

4. TIGHTEN JAM NUT TO SPECIFIED TORQUE.

5. PULL SERVO BOOT OVER CABLE WASHER.

1	CABLE ASSEMBLY	7	NUT 4.0-5.5 N·m
2	CLIP	8	LEVER STUD
3	RETAINER	9	BOOT
4	ENGINE BRACKET	10	CABLE WASHER
5	SERVO BRACKET	11	SERVO ASSEMBLY
6	SERVO CHAIN		

**Servo and linkage adjustment—1985 and later Cava-
lier with 2.8 liter MFI engine**

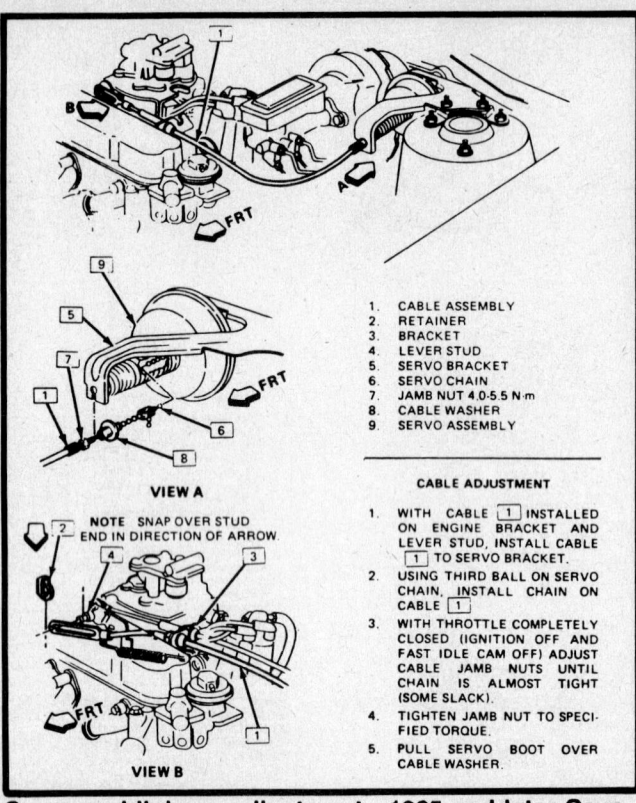

1. CABLE ASSEMBLY
2. RETAINER
3. BRACKET
4. LEVER STUD
5. SERVO BRACKET
6. SERVO CHAIN
7. JAMB NUT 4.0-5.5 N·m
8. CABLE WASHER
9. SERVO ASSEMBLY

VIEW A

NOTE: SNAP OVER STUD END IN DIRECTION OF ARROW.

VIEW B

CABLE ADJUSTMENT

1. WITH CABLE [1] INSTALLED ON ENGINE BRACKET AND LEVER STUD, INSTALL CABLE [1] TO SERVO BRACKET.
2. USING THIRD BALL ON SERVO CHAIN, INSTALL CHAIN ON CABLE [1]
3. WITH THROTTLE COMPLETELY CLOSED (IGNITION OFF AND FAST IDLE CAM OFF) ADJUST CABLE JAMB NUTS UNTIL CHAIN IS ALMOST TIGHT (SOME SLACK).
4. TIGHTEN JAMB NUT TO SPECIFIED TORQUE.
5. PULL SERVO BOOT OVER CABLE WASHER.

Servo and linkage adjustment — 1985 and later Cavalier with 2.0 liter EFI engine

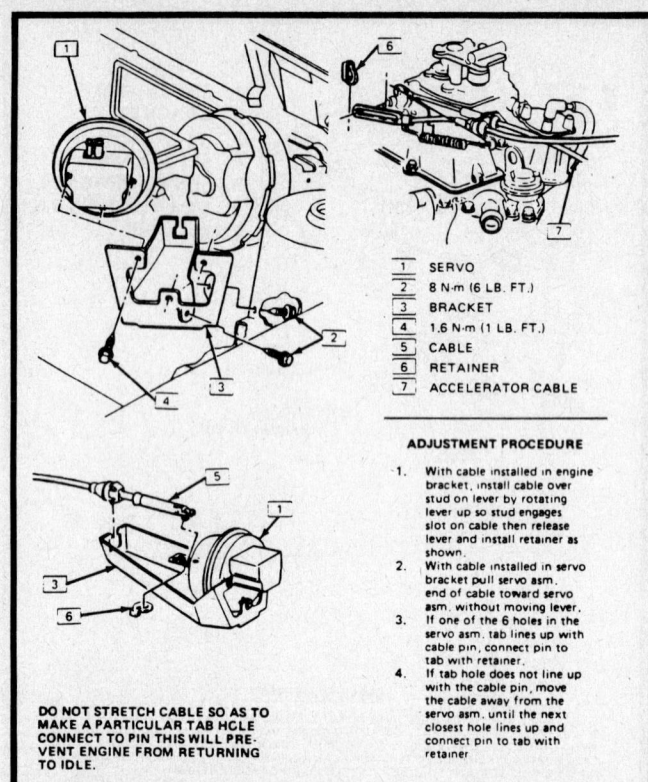

1. SERVO
2. 8 N·m (6 LB. FT.)
3. BRACKET
4. 1.6 N·m (1 LB. FT.)
5. CABLE
6. RETAINER
7. ACCELERATOR CABLE

ADJUSTMENT PROCEDURE

1. With cable installed in engine bracket, install cable over stud on lever by rotating lever up so stud engages slot on cable then release lever and install retainer as shown.
2. With cable installed in servo bracket pull servo asm. end of cable toward servo asm. without moving lever.
3. If one of the 6 holes in the servo asm. tab lines up with cable pin, connect pin to tab with retainer.
4. If tab hole does not line up with the cable pin, move the cable away from the servo asm. until the next closest hole lines up and connect pin to tab with retainer.

DO NOT STRETCH CABLE SO AS TO MAKE A PARTICULAR TAB HOLE CONNECT TO PIN THIS WILL PREVENT ENGINE FROM RETURNING TO IDLE.

Servo and linkage adjustment — 1984 Cavalier with 2.0 liter EFI engine

---

FRT (View A)

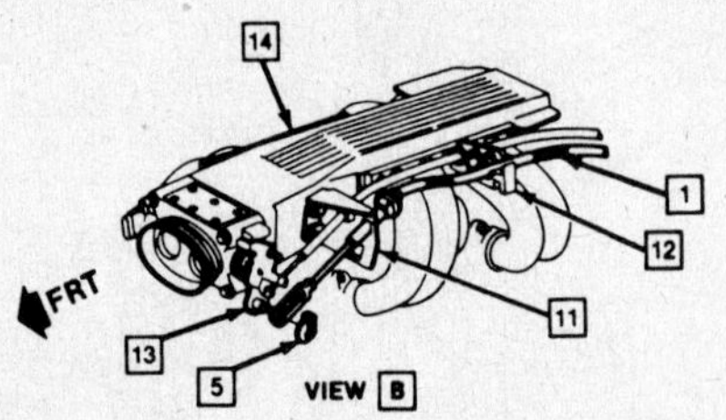

VIEW A

FRT (View B)

VIEW B

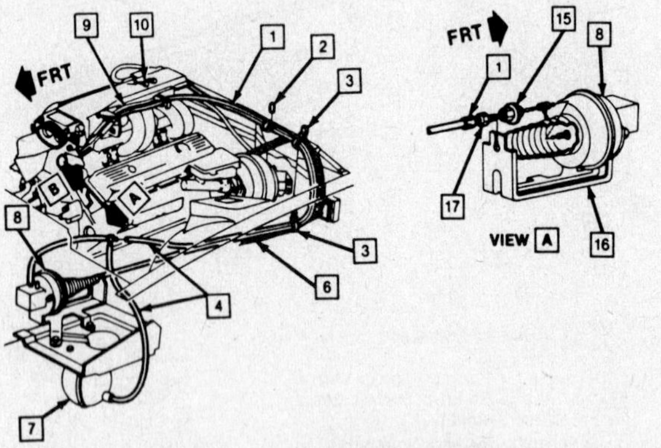

CABLE ADJUSTMENT

1. INSTALL CABLE [1] IN BRACKET & LEVER.
2. INSTALL CABLE [1] IN SERVO BRACKET.
3. ASSEMBLE SERVO CHAIN USING THIRD BALL ONLY TO CABLE.
4. CLOSE THROTTLE COMPLETELY (IGNITION OFF, FAST IDLE CAM OFF).
5. TURN ADJUSTING NUT UNTIL CLEARANCE BETWEEN STUD & END OF SLOT EQUALS 1.0 mm.
6. TORQUE JAM NUT TO 5.0 N·m.
7. ASSEMBLE RUBBER BOOT OVER WASHER.

NOTE REPEAT STEPS 2 THRU 7 USING SECOND OR FOURTH CHAIN BALL TO OBTAIN CLEARANCE IF NECESSARY.

1. CABLE ASM
2. CAP
3. STRAP
4. HOSE ASM
5. RETAINER
6. FWD LAMP HARNESS
7. VACUUM TANK
8. SERVO ASM
9. SPEEDO CABLE
10. VACUUM FITTING
11. BRACKET
12. CLIP
13. LEVER
14. PLENUM
15. WASHER
16. SERVO BRACKET
17. NUT

Servo and linkage adjustment — 1984 and later Camaro with 5.0 liter TPI engine

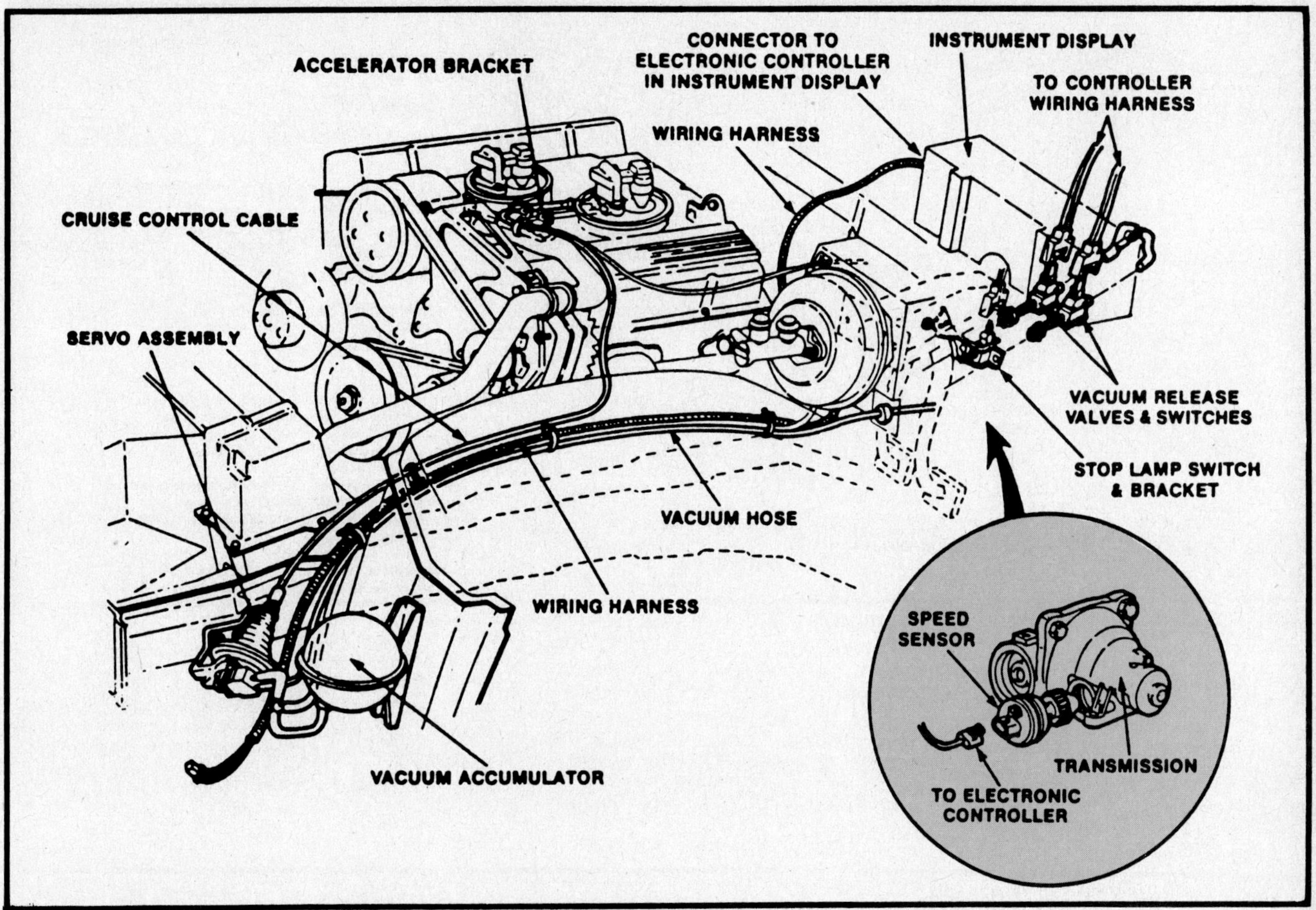

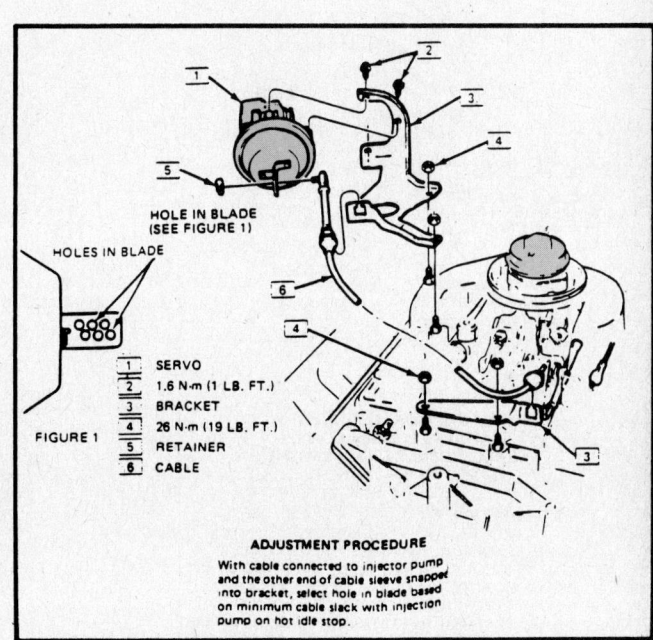

Cruise control electrical schematic—1984 Corvette with Custom Cruise III System

TRANSDUCER ORIFICE TUBE ADJUSTMENT (1982–83)

1. If cruise control speed is consistently above the set cruise control speed screw the orifice tube inward. If cruise control speed is below the set cruise control speed screw the orifice tube outward.

2. Each one-fourth turn of the orifice tube changes the cruising speed about one mile per hour.

3. After making the adjustment, be sure to secure the locknut to the orifice tube.

4. Road test the vehicle and check the cruise control operation at 50 miles per hour. If the speed is still not adjusted properly repeat the procedure until the proper results are achieved.

5. If unable to achieve the proper test results the cruise control transducer should be serviced.

RELEASE SWITCH AND VALVE ADJUSTMENTS

For release switch and valve adjustments refer to the proper illustration.

Servo and linkage adjustment—1984–85 Celebrity with V6 diesel engine

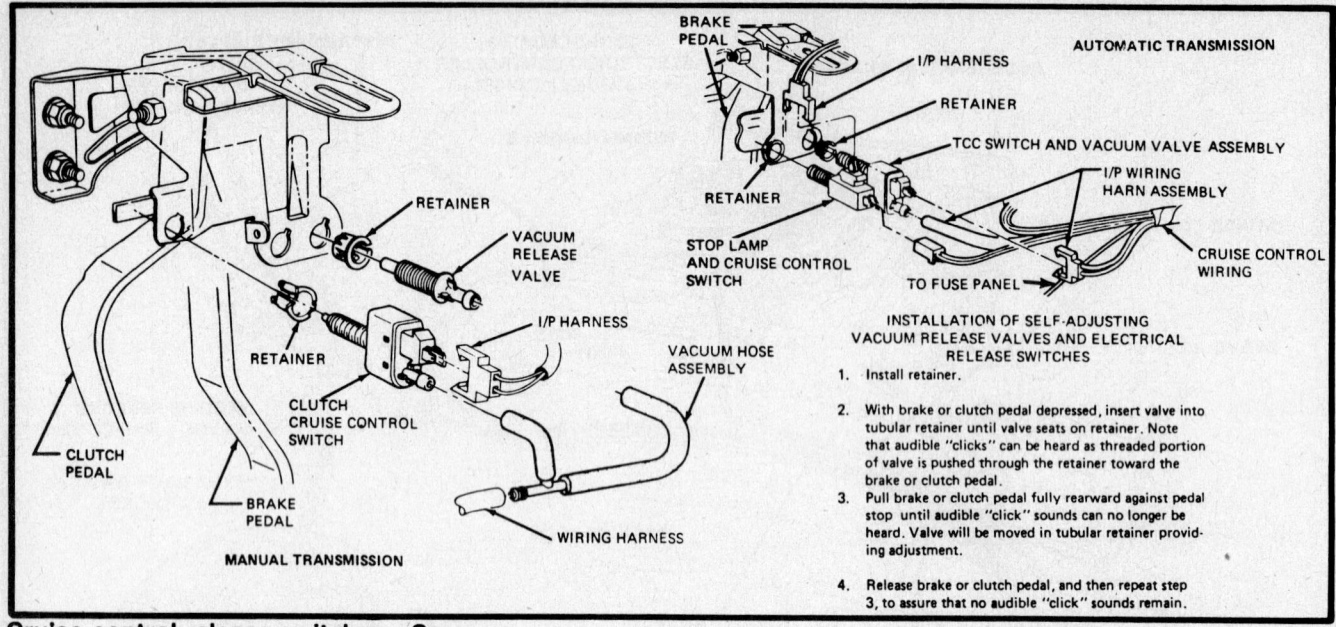

BRAKE PEDAL
I/P HARNESS
AUTOMATIC TRANSMISSION
RETAINER
TCC SWITCH AND VACUUM VALVE ASSEMBLY
I/P WIRING HARN ASSEMBLY
RETAINER
STOP LAMP AND CRUISE CONTROL SWITCH
CRUISE CONTROL WIRING
TO FUSE PANEL

RETAINER
VACUUM RELEASE VALVE
I/P HARNESS
RETAINER
CLUTCH CRUISE CONTROL SWITCH
VACUUM HOSE ASSEMBLY
CLUTCH PEDAL
BRAKE PEDAL
WIRING HARNESS

MANUAL TRANSMISSION

INSTALLATION OF SELF-ADJUSTING VACUUM RELEASE VALVES AND ELECTRICAL RELEASE SWITCHES

1. Install retainer.

2. With brake or clutch pedal depressed, insert valve into tubular retainer until valve seats on retainer. Note that audible "clicks" can be heard as threaded portion of valve is pushed through the retainer toward the brake or clutch pedal.

3. Pull brake or clutch pedal fully rearward against pedal stop until audible "click" sounds can no longer be heard. Valve will be moved in tubular retainer providing adjustment.

4. Release brake or clutch pedal, and then repeat step 3, to assure that no audible "click" sounds remain.

Cruise control release switches—Camaro

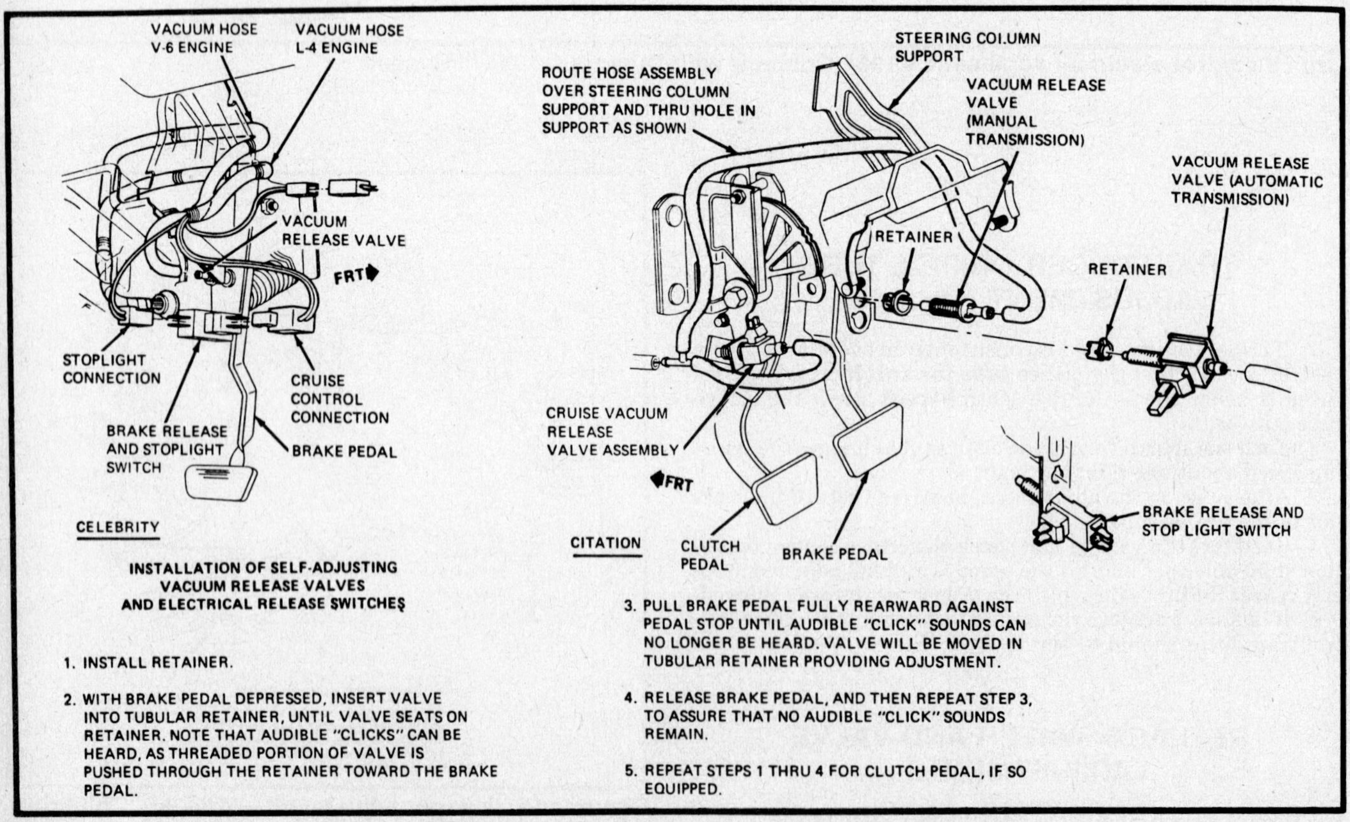

VACUUM HOSE V-6 ENGINE
VACUUM HOSE L-4 ENGINE
ROUTE HOSE ASSEMBLY OVER STEERING COLUMN SUPPORT AND THRU HOLE IN SUPPORT AS SHOWN
STEERING COLUMN SUPPORT
VACUUM RELEASE VALVE (MANUAL TRANSMISSION)
VACUUM RELEASE VALVE (AUTOMATIC TRANSMISSION)
VACUUM RELEASE VALVE
FRT
RETAINER
RETAINER
STOPLIGHT CONNECTION
CRUISE CONTROL CONNECTION
BRAKE RELEASE AND STOPLIGHT SWITCH
BRAKE PEDAL
CRUISE VACUUM RELEASE VALVE ASSEMBLY
FRT
CITATION
CLUTCH PEDAL
BRAKE PEDAL
BRAKE RELEASE AND STOP LIGHT SWITCH

CELEBRITY

INSTALLATION OF SELF-ADJUSTING VACUUM RELEASE VALVES AND ELECTRICAL RELEASE SWITCHES

1. INSTALL RETAINER.

2. WITH BRAKE PEDAL DEPRESSED, INSERT VALVE INTO TUBULAR RETAINER, UNTIL VALVE SEATS ON RETAINER. NOTE THAT AUDIBLE "CLICKS" CAN BE HEARD, AS THREADED PORTION OF VALVE IS PUSHED THROUGH THE RETAINER TOWARD THE BRAKE PEDAL.

3. PULL BRAKE PEDAL FULLY REARWARD AGAINST PEDAL STOP UNTIL AUDIBLE "CLICK" SOUNDS CAN NO LONGER BE HEARD. VALVE WILL BE MOVED IN TUBULAR RETAINER PROVIDING ADJUSTMENT.

4. RELEASE BRAKE PEDAL, AND THEN REPEAT STEP 3, TO ASSURE THAT NO AUDIBLE "CLICK" SOUNDS REMAIN.

5. REPEAT STEPS 1 THRU 4 FOR CLUTCH PEDAL, IF SO EQUIPPED.

Cruise control release switches—Citation and Celebrity

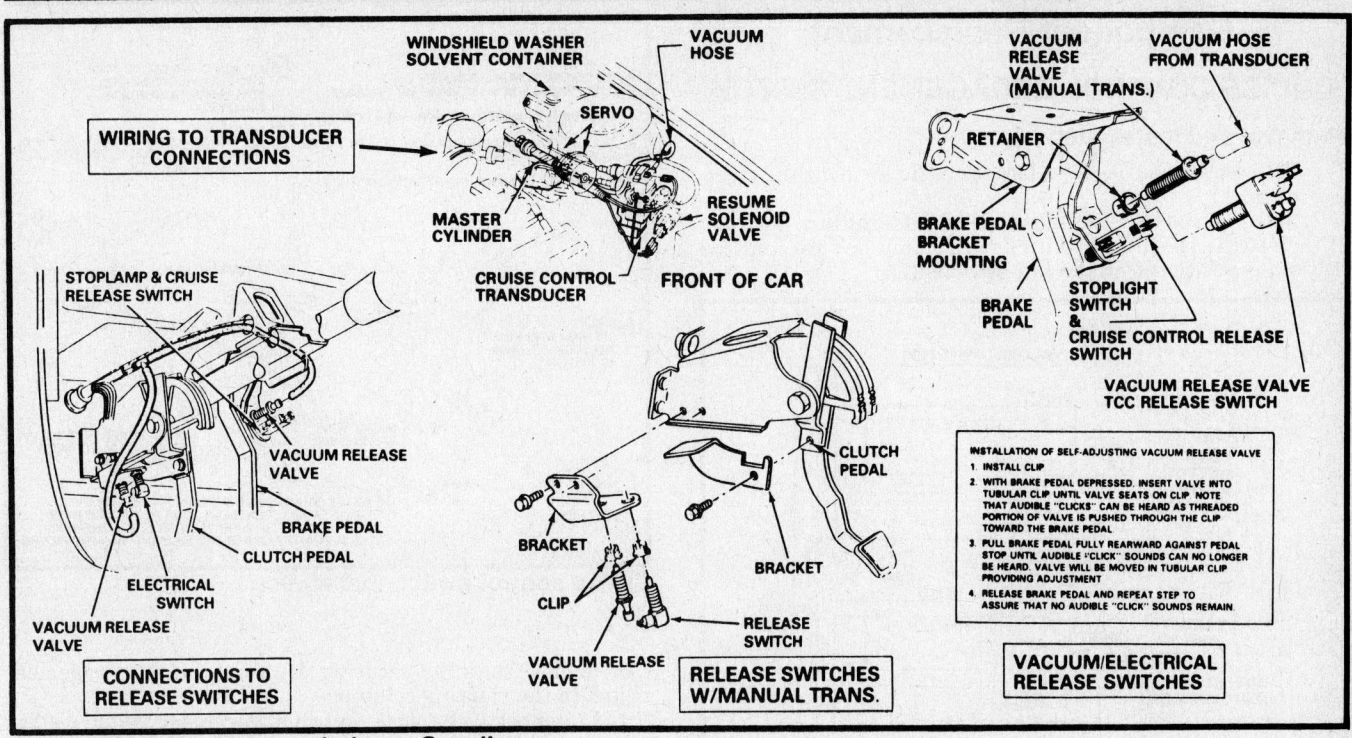

WIRING TO TRANSDUCER CONNECTIONS

WINDSHIELD WASHER SOLVENT CONTAINER

VACUUM HOSE

SERVO

MASTER CYLINDER

RESUME SOLENOID VALVE

CRUISE CONTROL TRANSDUCER

FRONT OF CAR

VACUUM RELEASE VALVE (MANUAL TRANS.)

VACUUM HOSE FROM TRANSDUCER

RETAINER

BRAKE PEDAL BRACKET MOUNTING

BRAKE PEDAL

STOPLIGHT SWITCH & CRUISE CONTROL RELEASE SWITCH

VACUUM RELEASE VALVE TCC RELEASE SWITCH

STOPLAMP & CRUISE RELEASE SWITCH

VACUUM RELEASE VALVE

BRAKE PEDAL

CLUTCH PEDAL

ELECTRICAL SWITCH

VACUUM RELEASE VALVE

CONNECTIONS TO RELEASE SWITCHES

CLUTCH PEDAL

BRACKET

CLIP

BRACKET

RELEASE SWITCH

VACUUM RELEASE VALVE

RELEASE SWITCHES W/MANUAL TRANS.

INSTALLATION OF SELF-ADJUSTING VACUUM RELEASE VALVE
1. INSTALL CLIP
2. WITH BRAKE PEDAL DEPRESSED, INSERT VALVE INTO TUBULAR CLIP UNTIL VALVE SEATS ON CLIP. NOTE THAT AUDIBLE "CLICKS" CAN BE HEARD AS THREADED PORTION OF VALVE IS PUSHED THROUGH THE CLIP TOWARD THE BRAKE PEDAL
3. PULL BRAKE PEDAL FULLY REARWARD AGAINST PEDAL STOP UNTIL AUDIBLE "CLICK" SOUNDS CAN NO LONGER BE HEARD. VALVE WILL BE MOVED IN TUBULAR CLIP PROVIDING ADJUSTMENT
4. RELEASE BRAKE PEDAL AND REPEAT STEP TO ASSURE THAT NO AUDIBLE "CLICK" SOUNDS REMAIN.

VACUUM/ELECTRICAL RELEASE SWITCHES

Cruise control release switches—Cavalier

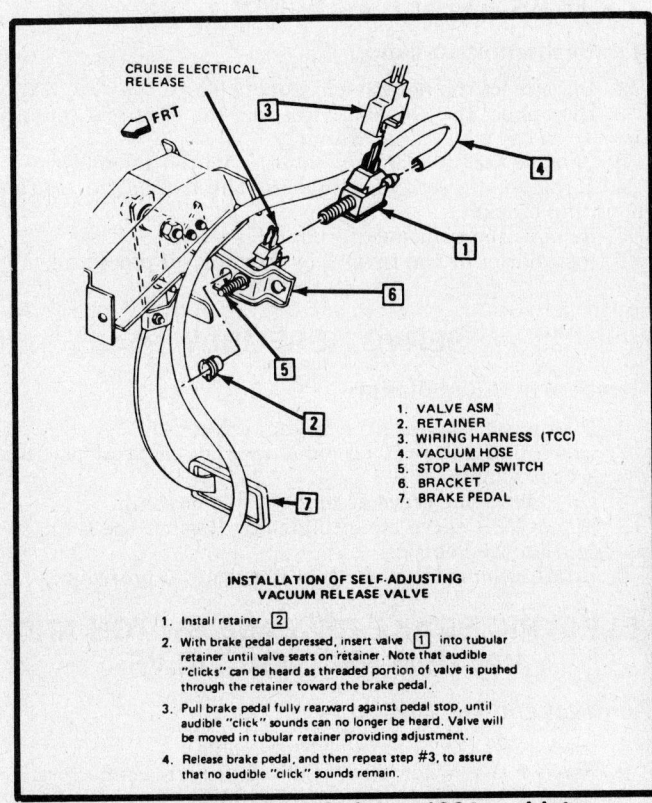

CRUISE ELECTRICAL RELEASE

FRT

1. VALVE ASM
2. RETAINER
3. WIRING HARNESS (TCC)
4. VACUUM HOSE
5. STOP LAMP SWITCH
6. BRACKET
7. BRAKE PEDAL

INSTALLATION OF SELF-ADJUSTING VACUUM RELEASE VALVE
1. Install retainer [2]
2. With brake pedal depressed, insert valve [1] into tubular retainer until valve seats on retainer. Note that audible "clicks" can be heard as threaded portion of valve is pushed through the retainer toward the brake pedal.
3. Pull brake pedal fully rearward against pedal stop, until audible "click" sounds can no longer be heard. Valve will be moved in tubular retainer providing adjustment.
4. Release brake pedal, and then repeat step #3, to assure that no audible "click" sounds remain.

Cruise control release switches—1984 and later Corvette with automatic transmission

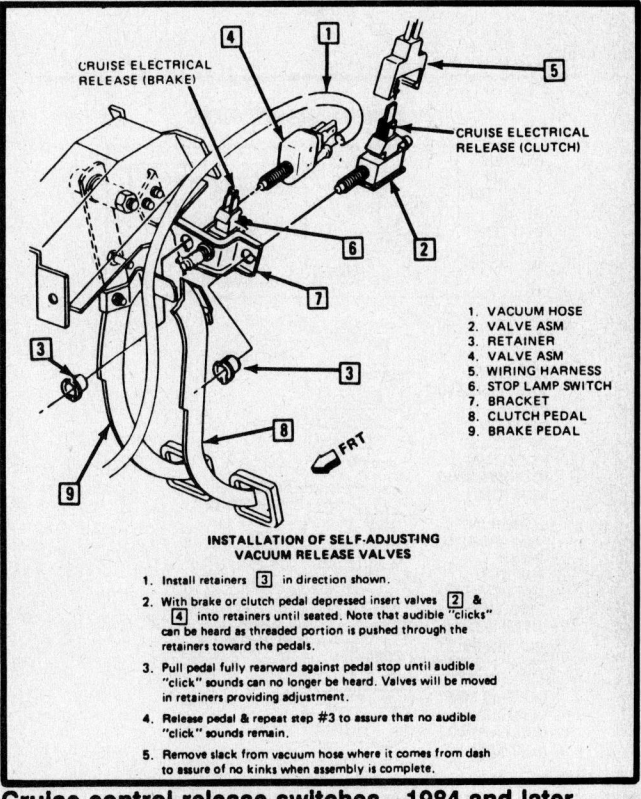

CRUISE ELECTRICAL RELEASE (BRAKE)

CRUISE ELECTRICAL RELEASE (CLUTCH)

FRT

1. VACUUM HOSE
2. VALVE ASM
3. RETAINER
4. VALVE ASM
5. WIRING HARNESS
6. STOP LAMP SWITCH
7. BRACKET
8. CLUTCH PEDAL
9. BRAKE PEDAL

INSTALLATION OF SELF-ADJUSTING VACUUM RELEASE VALVES
1. Install retainers [3] in direction shown.
2. With brake or clutch pedal depressed insert valves [2] & [4] into retainers until seated. Note that audible "clicks" can be heard as threaded portion is pushed through the retainers toward the pedals.
3. Pull pedal fully rearward against pedal stop until audible "click" sounds can no longer be heard. Valves will be moved in retainers providing adjustment.
4. Release pedal & repeat step #3 to assure that no audible "click" sounds remain.
5. Remove slack from vacuum hose where it comes from dash to assure of no kinks when assembly is complete.

Cruise control release switches—1984 and later Corvette with manual transmission

Component Replacement

CRUISE CONTROL ENGAGEMENT SWITCH

Removal and Installation

1. Disconnect the negative battery cable. Remove the steering wheel.
2. Position the turn signal switch in the right turn position. If the vehicle is equipped with a tilt column be sure that the column is positioned in the full up detent.

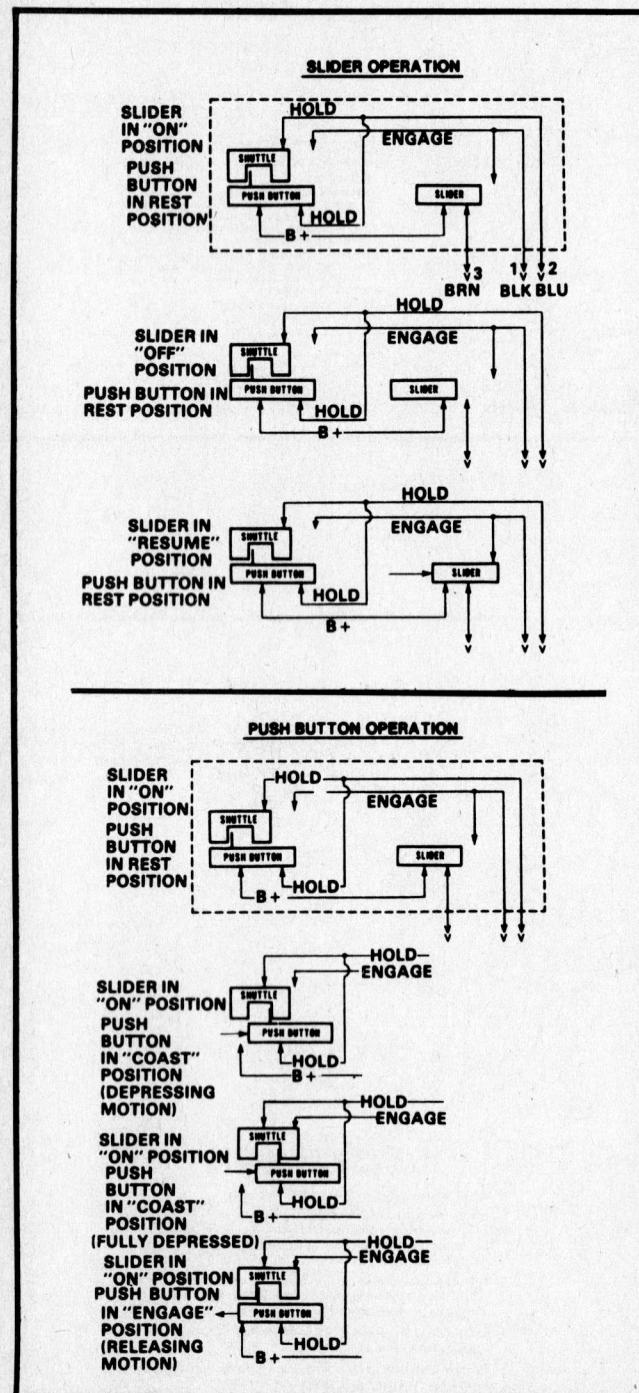

Cruise control electrical schematic—1982–83 switch operation

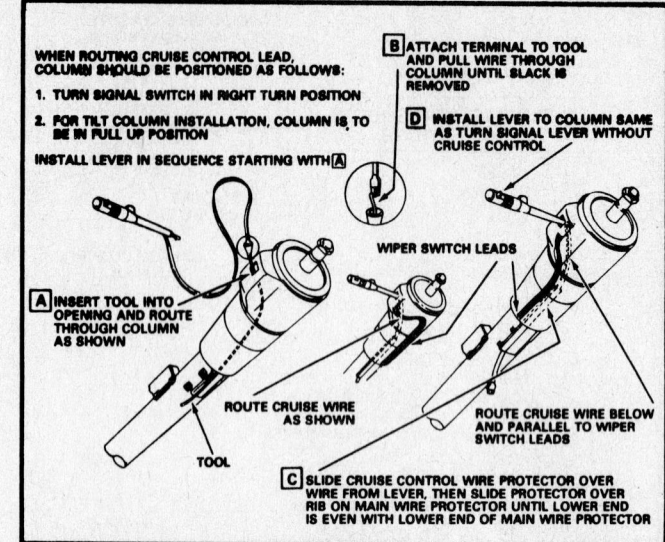

Cruise control switch installation

3. Remove the screw securing the cruise control engagement switch to the steering column.
4. Disconnect the cruise control engagement switch electrical connection.
5. Slide the cruise control engagement switch wiring up through the steering column carefully. Remove the cruise control engagement switch from the vehicle.
6. Installation is the reverse of the removal procedure.

TRANSDUCER ASSEMBLY (1982–83)

Removal and Installation

1. Disconnect the negative battery cable.
2. Disconnect the vacuum hoses and the electrical connections from the transducer assembly.
3. Remove the speedometer cables from the assembly.
4. Remove the screws attaching the transducer to the mounting bracket.
5. Remove the transducer from the vehicle.
6. Installation is the reverse of the removal procedure.

SERVO ASSEMBLY

Removal and Installation

1. Disconnect the negative battery cable.
2. Disconnect all electrical and vacuum connections from the servo assembly.
3. Disconnect the servo assembly cable or chain.
4. Remove the servo mounting bolts. Remove the servo assembly from the vehicle.
5. Installation is the reverse of the removal procedure.

ELECTRIC BRAKE RELEASE SWITCH AND VACUUM RELEASE VALVE

Removal and installation

1. Disconnect the negative battery cable.
2. Remove the switch electrical and vacuum connectors.
3. Remove the switch from its mounting above the brake pedal.
4. Installation is the reverse of the removal procedure.

Adjustment

1. The switch assembly and the valve assembly cannot be adjusted until after the brake booster push rod is assembled to the brake pedal assembly.

2. To adjust the switch depress the brake pedal and insert the switch assembly and valve assembly into their proper retaining clips until fully seated.

3. Pull the pedal back to its fully retracted position. The switch assembly and the valve assembly will move within the retainers of their adjusted position.

4. The switch assembly contacts must open at 3.5mm to 12.5mm of brake pedal travel. Nominal actuation of the brake light switch is 4.5mm.

5. The vacuum release valve assembly must open at 27.0mm to 33.0mm of brake pedal travel.

ELECTRONIC CRUISE CONTROL CONTROL MODULE

Removal and Installation

Note: The electronic cruise control module is normally mounted on or near the accelerator pedal bracket. Location may vary depending upon vehicle model.

1. Disconnect the negative battery cable.

2. Remove the lower steering column filler panel as required. Remove vehicle carpet as required.

3. Disconnect the electrical connectors from the control module.

4. Remove the control module mounting screws. Remove the control module from the vehicle.

6. Installation is the reverse of the removal procedure.

SPEED SENSORS

VSS Buffer Amplifier

The VSS buffer amplifier is a device that supplies vehicle speed input to the electronic controller. The optic head portion of the assembly is located in the speedometer head frame. A reflective blade is attached to the speedometer head/cable assembly. The blade spins like a propeller with its blades passing through a light beam from a L.E.D. refractor in the optic head. As each blade enters the light beam, light is reflected back to a photocell that is located in the optic head. This in turn causes a power signal to be sent to a buffer for amplification and signal conditioning. This signal is then sent to the controller for processing and calculation of vehicle speed.

P.M. Generator Speed Signal

The P.M. generator speed signal is a device that supplies vehicle speed input to the electronic controller. Vehicle speed information is provided to the electronic controller by a permanent

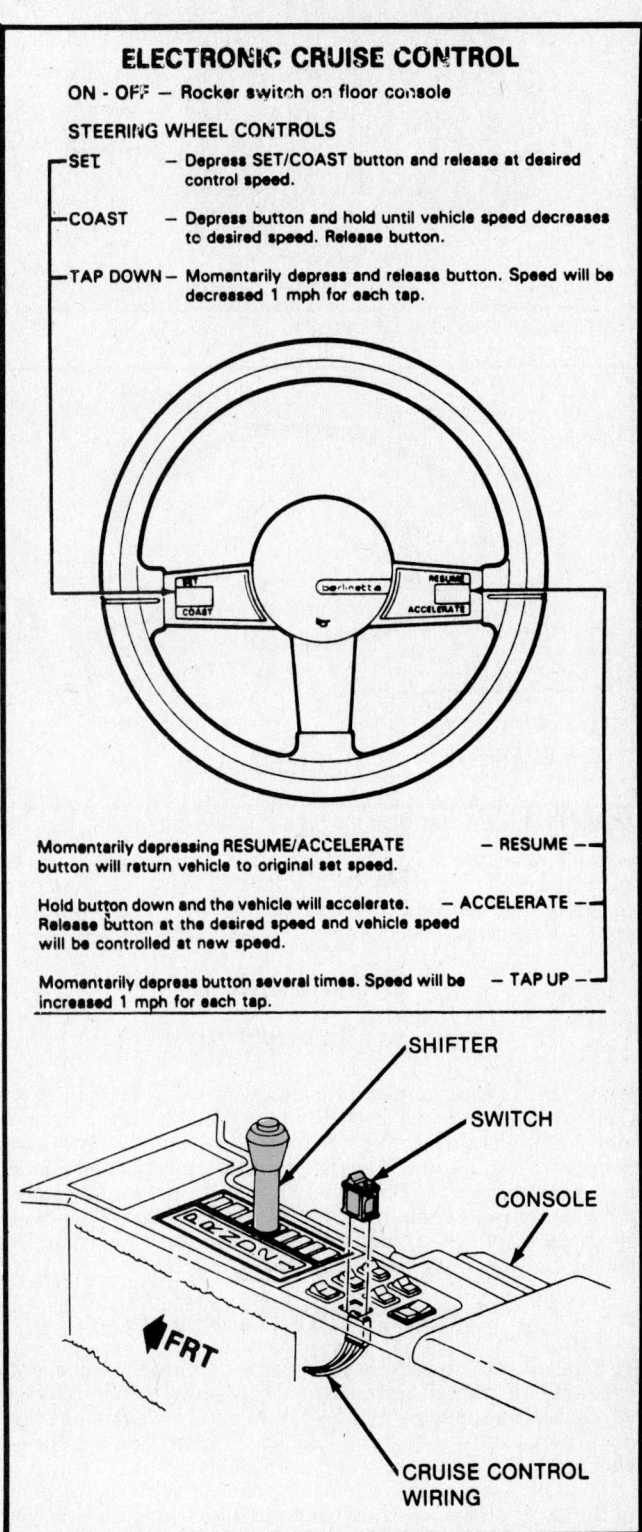

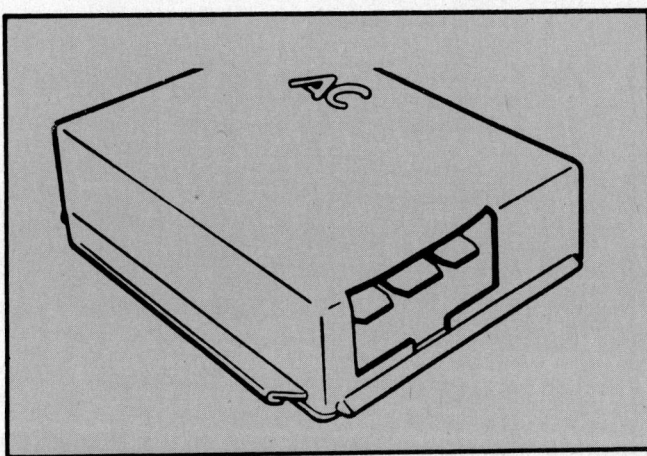

Electronic cruise control module—typical

Cruise control switch location 1984 and later Camaro Berlinetta (1985 and later Shown)

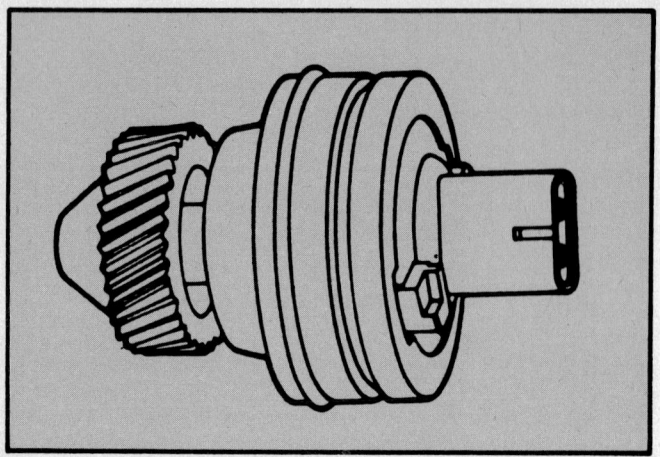

Permanent magnet generator

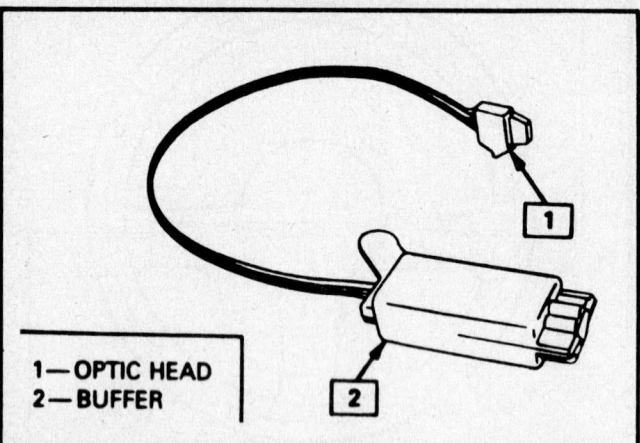

1—OPTIC HEAD
2—BUFFER

Vehicle speed sensor

magnet generator driven by the vehicle transmission. The output frequency of the permanent magnet generator is than routed to a buffer, which in turn will amplify and condition the signal to the electronic controller.

Oldsmobile

VISUAL INSPECTION

Before performing any tests make a visual inspection of the cruise control system. Check all items in the system for abnormal conditions such as bare broken or disconnected wires and damage to the vacuum hoses. Be sure that the speedometer cables are attached and properly routed. All vacuum hoses must be properly routed and must not have any kinks or bends. Be sure that all electrical connections are complete and tight. The wiring harness must be routed properly.

SERVO TEST (1982–83)

To determine the condition of the servo diaphragm, remove the vacuum hose from the servo assembly. Apply 14 inches of vacuum to the tube opening and hold in in place for about one minute. The vacuum should not leak down more than 5 inches. If vacuum leaks, replace the servo assembly.

Another test consists of removing the vacuum hose attached to the servo assembly, than push the diaphragm in, hold your finger over the nipple and the diaphragm should remain in the pushed in position. If the servo assembly does not perform as indicated it should be replaced.

VACUUM LEAK TEST (1982–83)

The vacuum release valves, the resume valve and all the connecting hoses can be checked by applying 15 inches of vacuum to each component and then sealing off the component for about one minute. The vacuum should not leak down more than 5 inches. Repair or replace defective components as required.

ELECTRICAL SYSTEM TEST (1982–83)

1. Check the cruise control fuse and electrical connector.
2. Check all electrical connections. Disconnect and reconnect after checking for bent, broken or dirty mating tabs.
3. Check the electrical release switch as follows. Unplug the connector at the switch. Connect an ohmmeter to the two terminals on the switch assembly.
4. Depress the brake or clutch pedal. The ohmmeter should not indicate continuity.
5. Release the pedal, the ohmmeter should indicate continuity.

CONTROL LEVER SWITCH TEST (1982–83)

1. Disconnect the electrical connector at the cruise control engagement switch.
2. Connect an ohmmeter to the brown and blue wires.
3. Slide the resume switch to the on position. The ohmmeter should indicate continuity. Push the engage button all the way in and and open circuit should be indicated.
4. Connect an ohmmeter to the brown and black wires, with the resume switch still in the on position. An open circuit should be indicated.
5. Depress the engage button and release it half way. Continuity should exist.

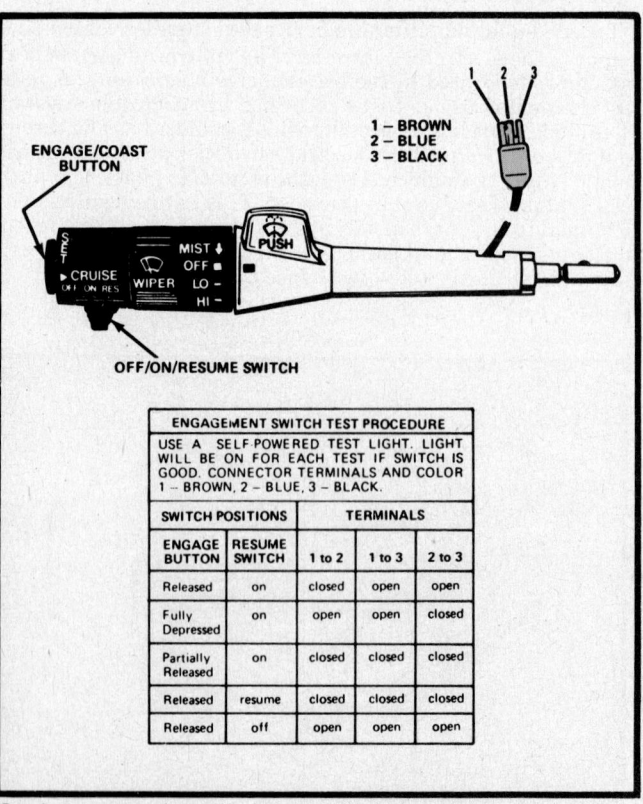

ENGAGE/COAST BUTTON

1 – BROWN
2 – BLUE
3 – BLACK

OFF/ON/RESUME SWITCH

ENGAGEMENT SWITCH TEST PROCEDURE

USE A SELF POWERED TEST LIGHT. LIGHT WILL BE ON FOR EACH TEST IF SWITCH IS GOOD. CONNECTOR TERMINALS AND COLOR 1 – BROWN, 2 – BLUE, 3 – BLACK.

SWITCH POSITIONS		TERMINALS		
ENGAGE BUTTON	RESUME SWITCH	1 to 2	1 to 3	2 to 3
Released	on	closed	open	open
Fully Depressed	on	open	open	closed
Partially Released	on	closed	closed	closed
Released	resume	closed	closed	closed
Released	off	open	open	open

Cruise control engagement switch test

6. Connect an ohmmeter to the blue and black wires with the resume switch still in the on position. With the engaged button released, no continunity should be present.

7. With the engaged button depressed and half way released continunity should exist.

HARNESS AND TRANSDUCER ELECTRICAL TEST (1982–83)

1. Using an ohmmeter engage, with the engagement switch connector disconnected, check the resistance of the dark green wire in the wiring harness. If the transducer is grounded properly, the ohmmeter should indicate between 29 and 36 ohms.

2. If resistance is above or below specification, disconnect the connector at the transducer and at the resume solenoid.

3. Measure the resistance of the dark green wire. It should indicate a resistance reading of 23 ohms, plus or minus one ohm. If the reading is not as indicated the wiring harness should be replaced.

4. With the connectors of the transducer disconnected, measure the resistance of the solenoid coil by connecting the ohmmeter to the hold terminal and ground. A reading of 5 to 6 ohms should be indicated.

5. If a reading of 4 ohms or less is obtained there is excessive resistance in the circuit. If a reading of 6 ohms or more is indicated the transducer should be checked.

TRANSDUCER TEST (1982–83)

The only test that is possible to check the transducer assembly is the transducer orifice tube adjustment. Before adjusting the transducer assembly be sure that all vacuum hoses are in good condition. Be sure that all electrical connections are correct. Be sure that the electrical and vacuum release valves are working properly.

VACUUM REGULATOR TEST (1982–83)

If the vehicle is equipped with a diesel engine a vacuum regulator valve is used. This vacuum regulator valve regulates the vacuum from the engine mounted vacuum pump. To test the regulator use a vacuum pump. The vacuum level should be

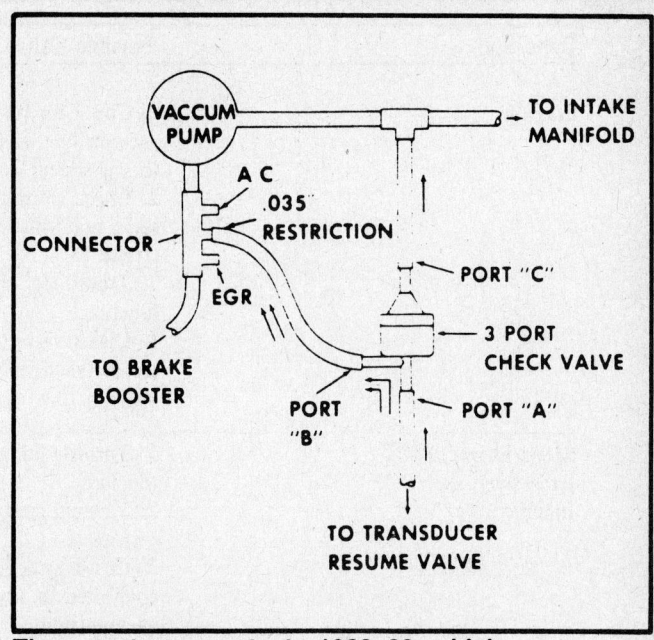

Three port vacuum test – 1982–83 vehicles

about 6 in. hg. or slightly higher if cold. If the valve does not perform as indicated it must be replaced.

VACUUM PUMP ASSISTED SYSTEMS TEST (1982–83)

1. Blow low air pressure into port "A" while port "B" is plugged. Then plug port "A" and blow low air pressure into port "B".

2. In both cases air should exit port "C". If not clean or replace the check valve.

3. To check the air flow in the other direction, blow low air pressure into port "C". No air should come out of port "A" or port "B".

DIAGNOSIS AND TESTING PROCEDURES

Condition	Possible Cause	Correction
Speed increases after engagement.	1. Speedometer cable (needle) fluctuates due to speedo cable or housing bent, kinked or misrouted.	1. Correct as necessary.
	2. Transducer orifice tube out of adjustment.	2. Adjust.
	3. Transducer malfunction.	3. Replace.
Speed drops off after engagement.	1. Throttle linkage too loose. Vacuum leak or restriction.	1. Check for damaged, disconnected, pinched, or kinked hoses. Repair or replace as required. Adjust throttle linkage.
	2. Transducer orifice tube out of adjustment.	2. Adjust.

Condition	Possible Cause	Correction
Surging	1. Check for rstricted vacuum line from engine to transducer.	1. Repair or replace.
	2. Check to insure that servo unit will full stroke.	2. Replace servo unit.
	3. Transducer mal-function.	3. Replace.
	4. Check valve stuck closed (vacuum pump only) or missing.	4. Install or re-orient check valve as necessary.
Speed Drops Off Excessively on Inclines	1. Throttle linkage too loose.	1. Adjust.
	2. Vacuum source hose restricted.	2. Repair or Replace.
	3. Cruise system not connected to auxiliary vacuum pump.	3. Correct
	4. Check valve reversed or stuck open (vacuum pump only).	4. Re-orient or replace as necessary.

Cruise control trouble diagnosis chart (1982–83)

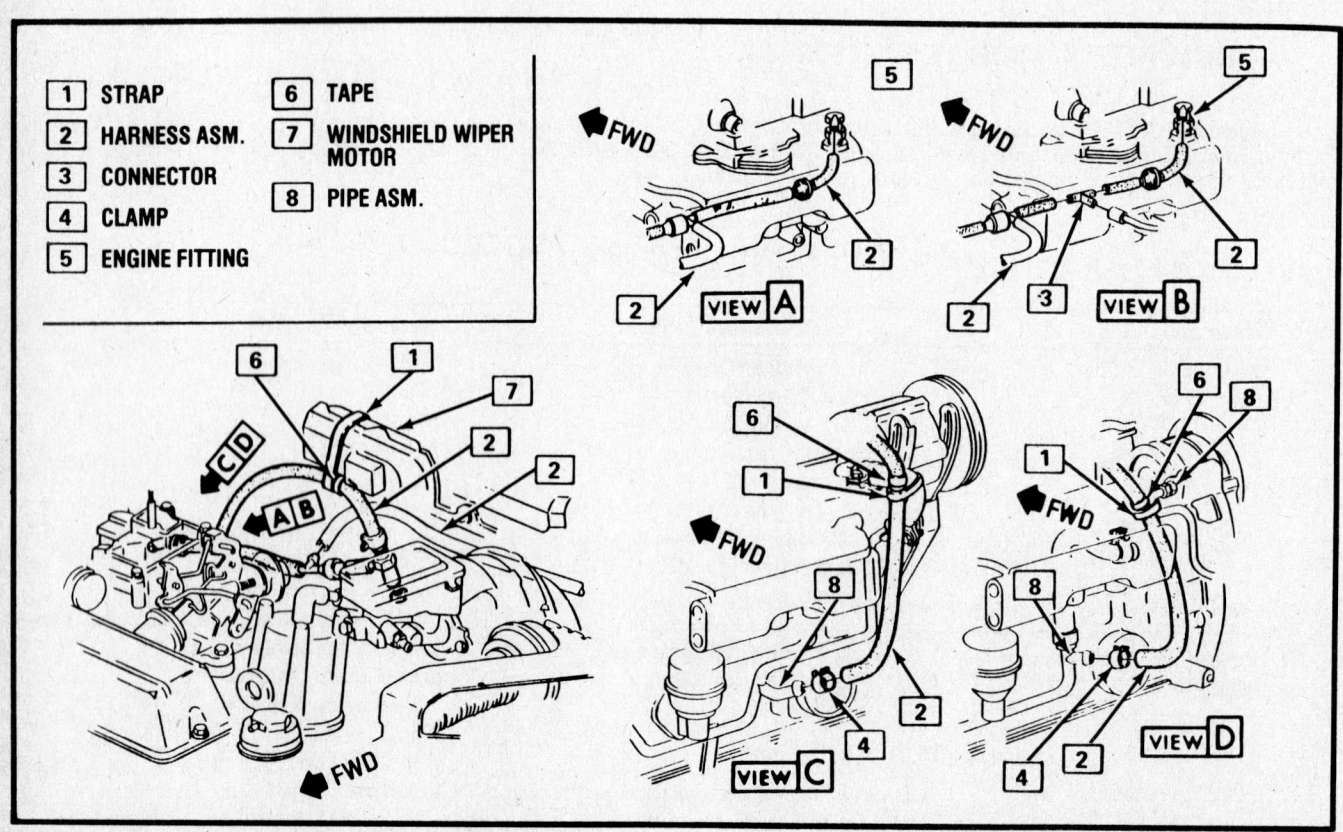

Cruise control vacuum schematic—1982–83 Firenza

CRUISE CONTROL DIAGNOSIS

PRELIMINARY CHECKS

1. Check Servo Chain or rod adjustment. Must have minimum slack.
2. Check vacuum hoses. Must be in good condition - no restrictions or leaks.
3. Check drive cable routings. No kinks or sharp bends.
4. Check throttle linkage or cable for binding.
5. Check adjustment of electrical release switch and vacuum release valve.
6. Check engagement switch operation.
7. If steps 1 through 6 do not solve the problem, continue with diagnosis.

CRUISE CONTROL INOPERATIVE

1. Check radio fuse. If blown, check wiring for short circuit and repair. A shorted resume solenoid diode could also cause blow fuse.
2. If fuse and preliminary checks ok, resume solenoid must be checked. Start engine and check source vacuum at resume solenoid (refer to picture at right). Disconnect the two wire connector at resume solenoid. Use jumper wire to ground terminal which had black wire connected to it. Apply 12 volts to terminal which had tan wire connected to it. Disconnect outlet vacuum hose (going to B fitting on transducer). Vacuum should be present. If not, replace resume solenoid. Applying voltage incorrectly to resume solenoid could damage diode. If above checks ok, stop engine and reconnect electrical and vacuum connections.
3. To make test below, turn ignition to RUN position and off/on/resume switch to ON. Disconnect the two wire connector at transducer (Engage-Hold Terminals).
4. Connect 12 volt test light to ground and to engage wire in connector. Push engage/coast button in part way to engage position.
5. Repeat test on hold wire in connector.

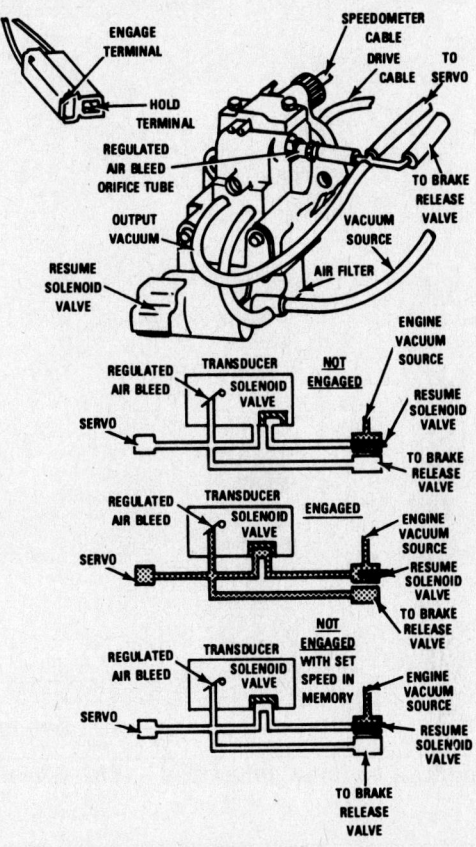

TEST LIGHT OFF AT ONE WIRE ONLY

Test engagement switch. (See test procedure) Check for open circuit in wire if test light did not light. Repair or replace part that checks bad.

TEST LIGHT ON AT BOTH WIRES (MAY BE DIM ON HOLD WIRE)

Check for poor ground at transducer. If ok, remove transducer for repair.

TEST LIGHT OFF AT BOTH WIRES

Check for open circuit in brown/white wire from fuse panel to off/on/resume switch. If circuit ok, check engagement switch operation and replace if necessary.

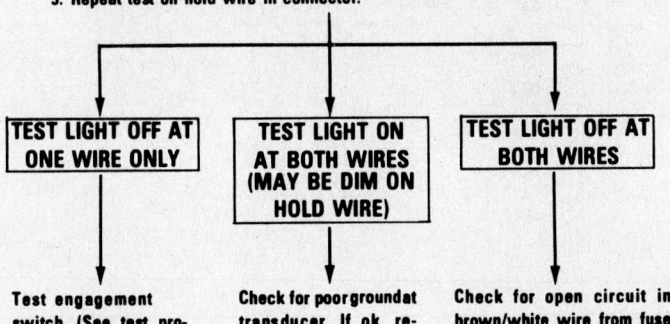

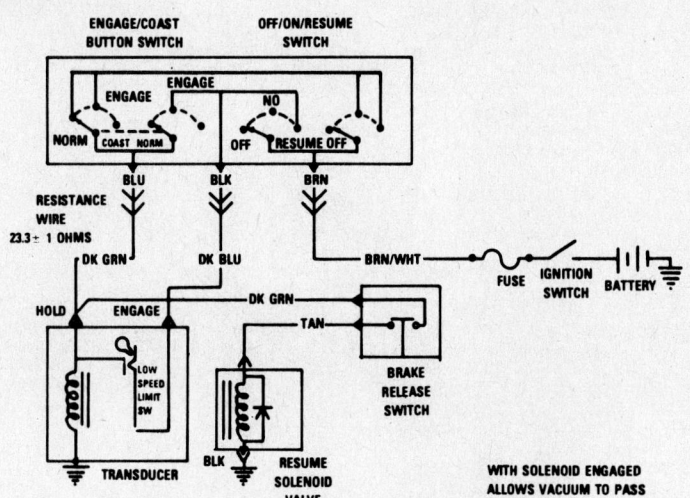

WITH SOLENOID ENGAGED ALLOWS VACUUM TO PASS THROUGH IT

ENGAGEMENT SWITCH TEST PROCEDURE				
USE A SELF POWERED TEST LIGHT. LIGHT WILL BE ON FOR EACH TEST IF SWITCH IS GOOD. CONNECTOR TERMINALS AND COLOR 1 — BROWN, 2 — BLUE, 3 — BLACK				
SWITCH POSITIONS		TERMINALS		
ENGAGE BUTTON	RESUME SWITCH	1 to 2	1 to 3	2 to 3
Released	on	closed	open	open
Fully Depressed	on	open	open	closed
Partially Released	on	closed	closed	closed
Released	resume	closed	closed	closed
Released	off	open	open	open

Cruise control trouble diagnosis chart (1982–83)

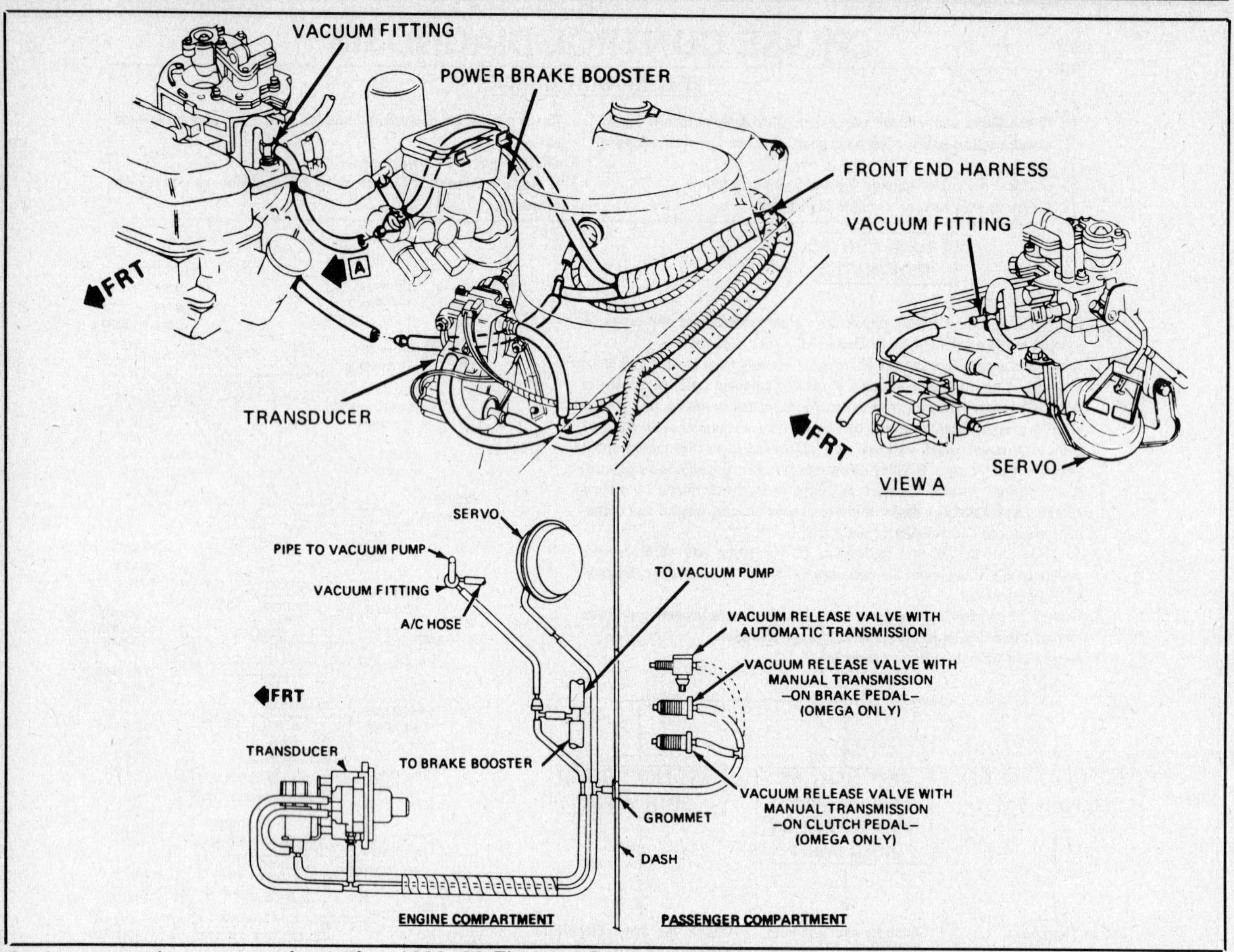

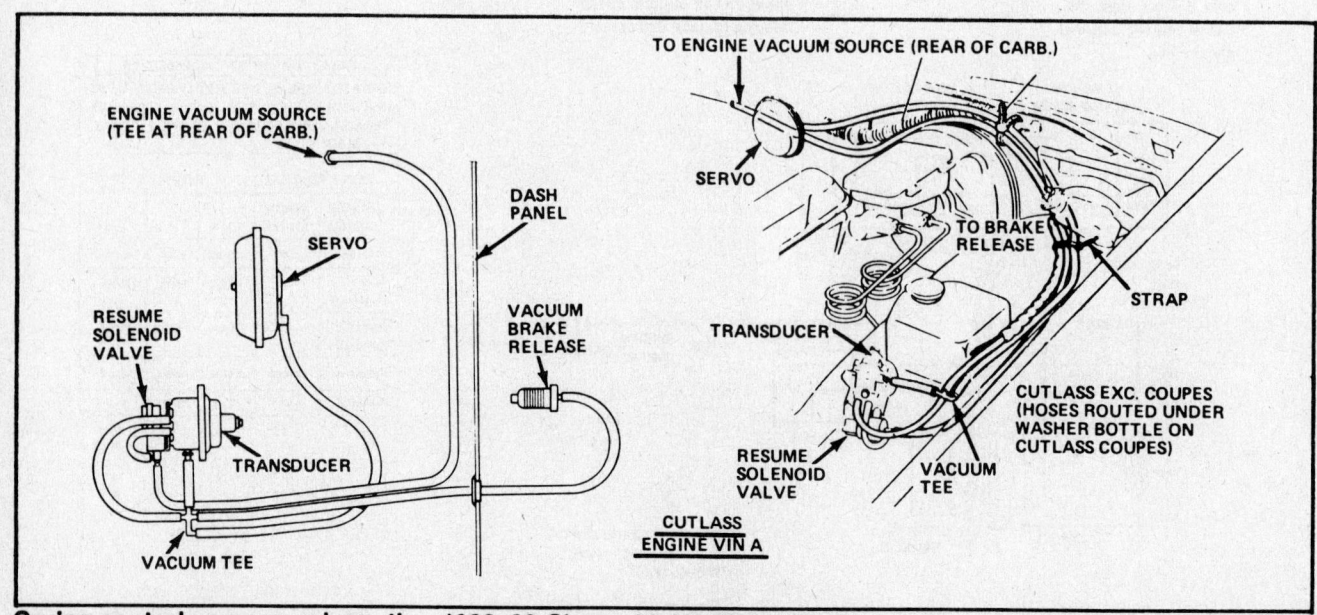

VACUUM FITTING

POWER BRAKE BOOSTER

FRONT END HARNESS

VACUUM FITTING

FRT

A

TRANSDUCER

SERVO

VIEW A

FRT

SERVO

PIPE TO VACUUM PUMP

VACUUM FITTING

A/C HOSE

TO VACUUM PUMP

VACUUM RELEASE VALVE WITH AUTOMATIC TRANSMISSION

VACUUM RELEASE VALVE WITH MANUAL TRANSMISSION
—ON BRAKE PEDAL—
(OMEGA ONLY)

FRT

TRANSDUCER

TO BRAKE BOOSTER

GROMMET

DASH

VACUUM RELEASE VALVE WITH MANUAL TRANSMISSION
—ON CLUTCH PEDAL—
(OMEGA ONLY)

ENGINE COMPARTMENT

PASSENGER COMPARTMENT

Cruise control vacuum schematic—1982–83 Firenza, Omega and Ciera with four cylinder engine

ENGINE VACUUM SOURCE
(TEE AT REAR OF CARB.)

SERVO

DASH PANEL

VACUUM BRAKE RELEASE

RESUME SOLENOID VALVE

TRANSDUCER

VACUUM TEE

TO ENGINE VACUUM SOURCE (REAR OF CARB.)

SERVO

TO BRAKE RELEASE

STRAP

TRANSDUCER

RESUME SOLENOID VALVE

VACUUM TEE

CUTLASS EXC. COUPES
(HOSES ROUTED UNDER WASHER BOTTLE ON CUTLASS COUPES)

**CUTLASS
ENGINE VIN A**

Cruise control vacuum schematic—1982–83 Ciera with V6 diesel engine

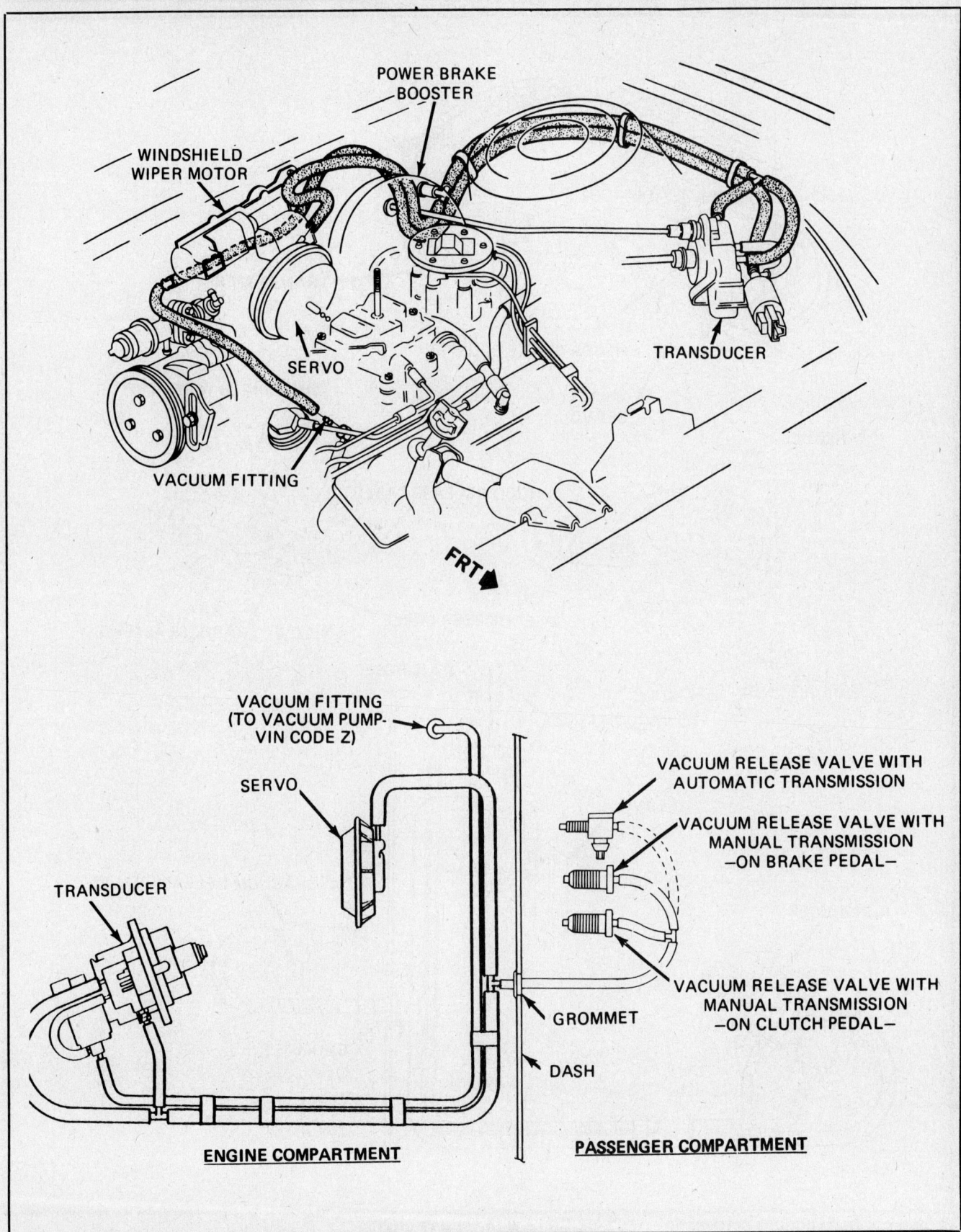

WINDSHIELD WIPER MOTOR

POWER BRAKE BOOSTER

TRANSDUCER

SERVO

VACUUM FITTING

FRT

VACUUM FITTING (TO VACUUM PUMP— VIN CODE Z)

SERVO

TRANSDUCER

VACUUM RELEASE VALVE WITH AUTOMATIC TRANSMISSION

VACUUM RELEASE VALVE WITH MANUAL TRANSMISSION —ON BRAKE PEDAL—

VACUUM RELEASE VALVE WITH MANUAL TRANSMISSION —ON CLUTCH PEDAL—

GROMMET

DASH

ENGINE COMPARTMENT

PASSENGER COMPARTMENT

Cruise control vacuum schematic—1982–83 Omega with V6 gas engine

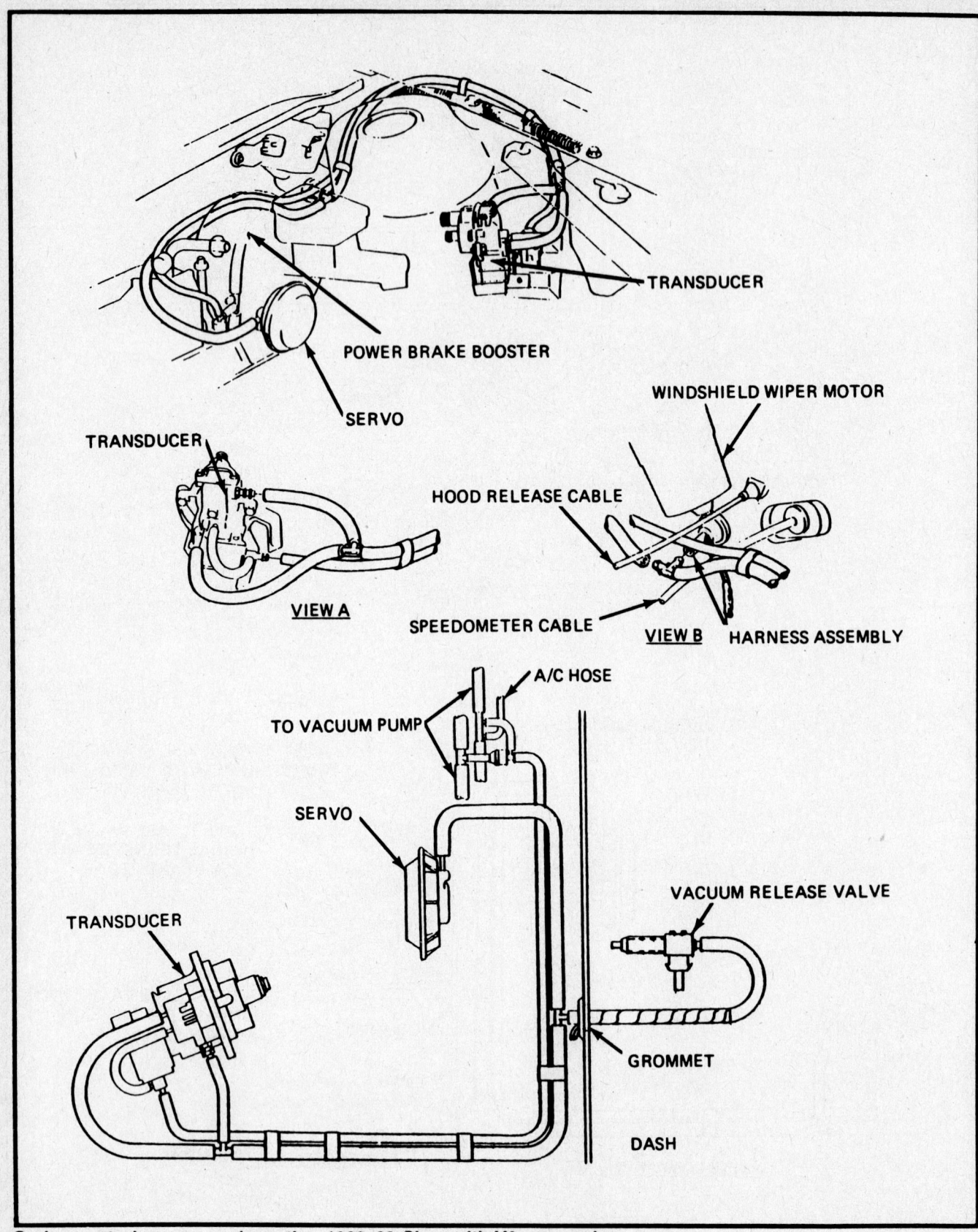

TRANSDUCER

POWER BRAKE BOOSTER

SERVO

TRANSDUCER

VIEW A

WINDSHIELD WIPER MOTOR

HOOD RELEASE CABLE

SPEEDOMETER CABLE

VIEW B

HARNESS ASSEMBLY

A/C HOSE

TO VACUUM PUMP

SERVO

VACUUM RELEASE VALVE

TRANSDUCER

GROMMET

DASH

Cruise control vacuum schematic — 1982–83 Ciera with V6 gas engine

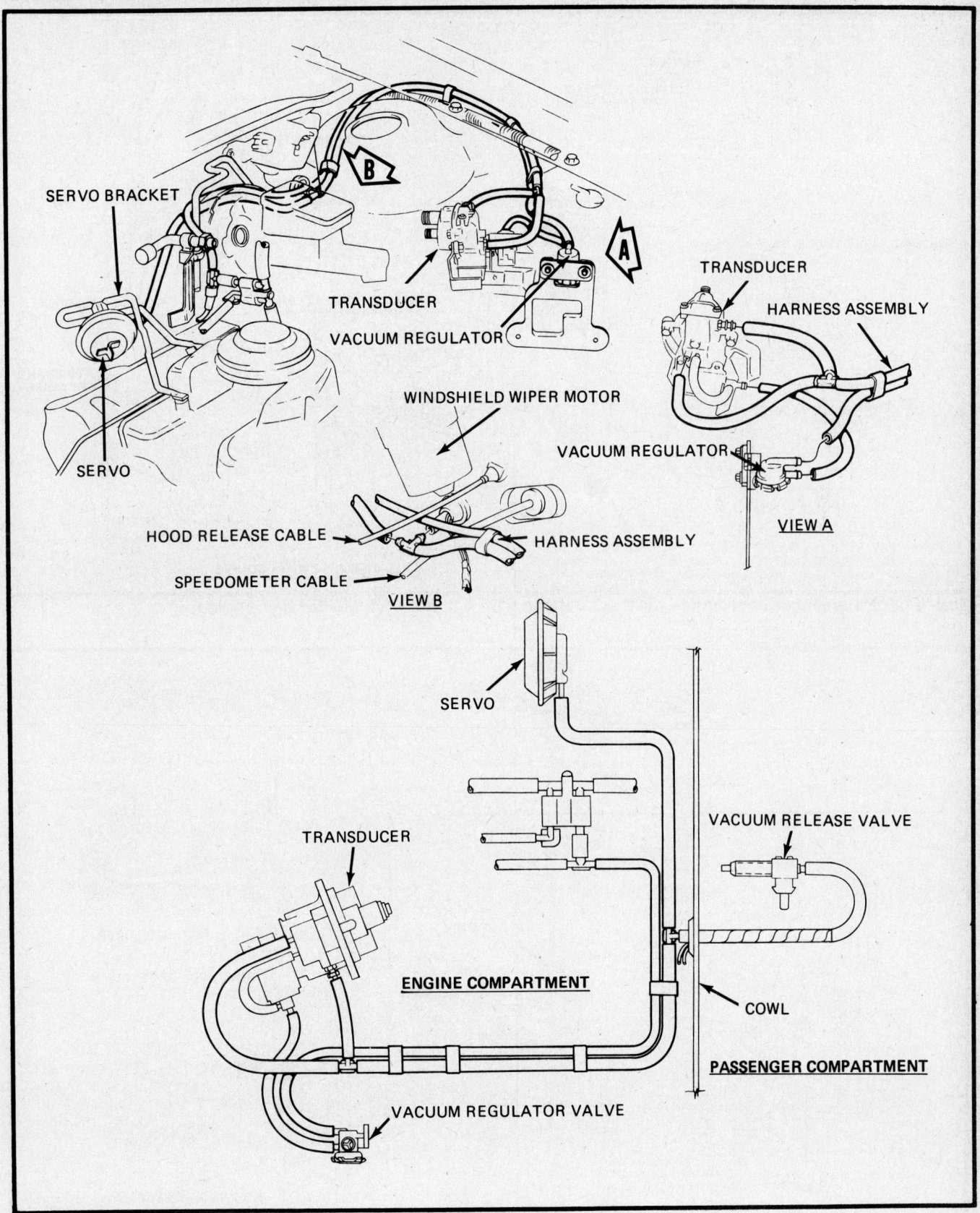

SERVO BRACKET

TRANSDUCER

VACUUM REGULATOR

SERVO

TRANSDUCER

HARNESS ASSEMBLY

VACUUM REGULATOR

VIEW A

WINDSHIELD WIPER MOTOR

HOOD RELEASE CABLE

SPEEDOMETER CABLE

HARNESS ASSEMBLY

VIEW B

SERVO

VACUUM RELEASE VALVE

TRANSDUCER

ENGINE COMPARTMENT

COWL

PASSENGER COMPARTMENT

VACUUM REGULATOR VALVE

Cruise control vacuum schematic – 1982–83 Cutlass with V6 gas engine

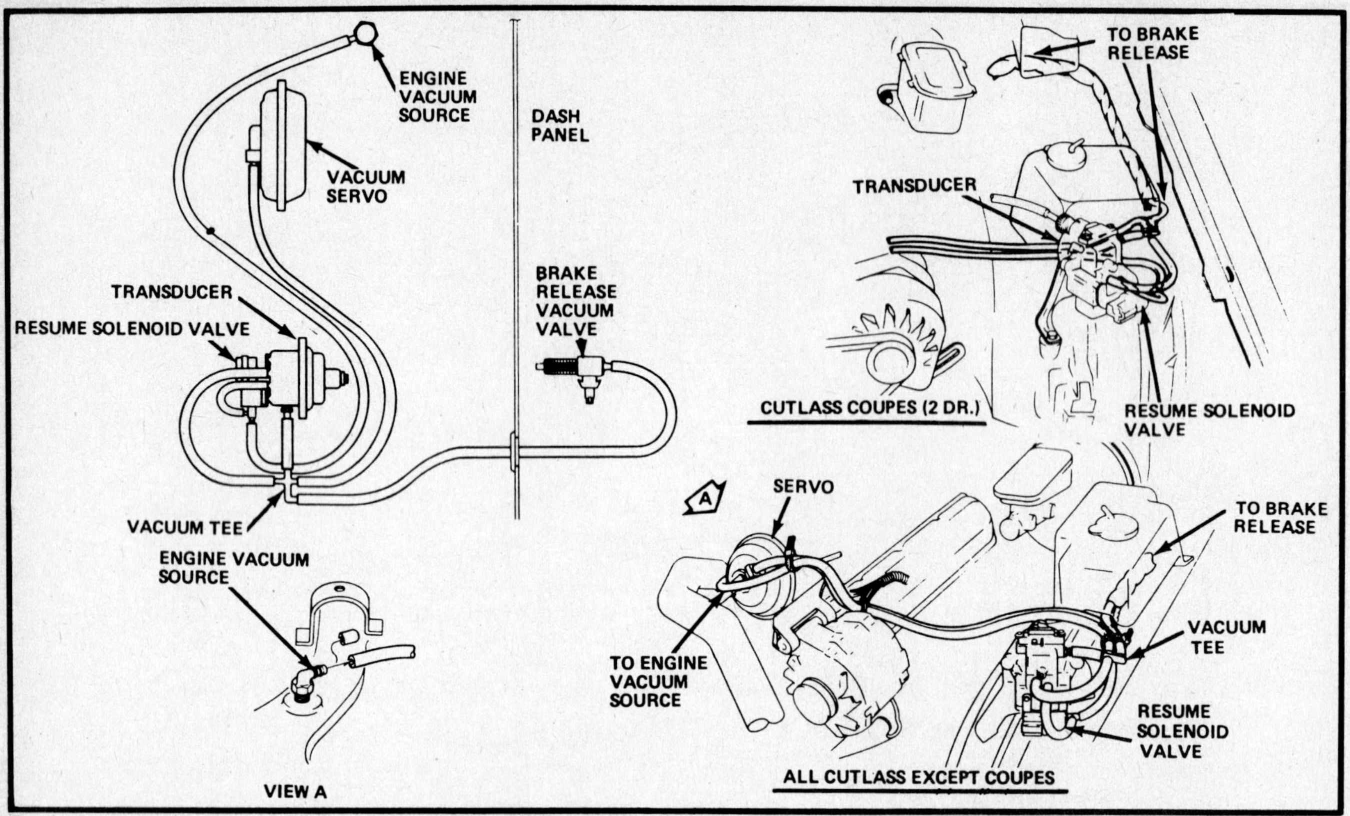

Cruise control vacuum schematic—1982–83 Cutlass with 4.3 liter and 5.0 liter gas engine

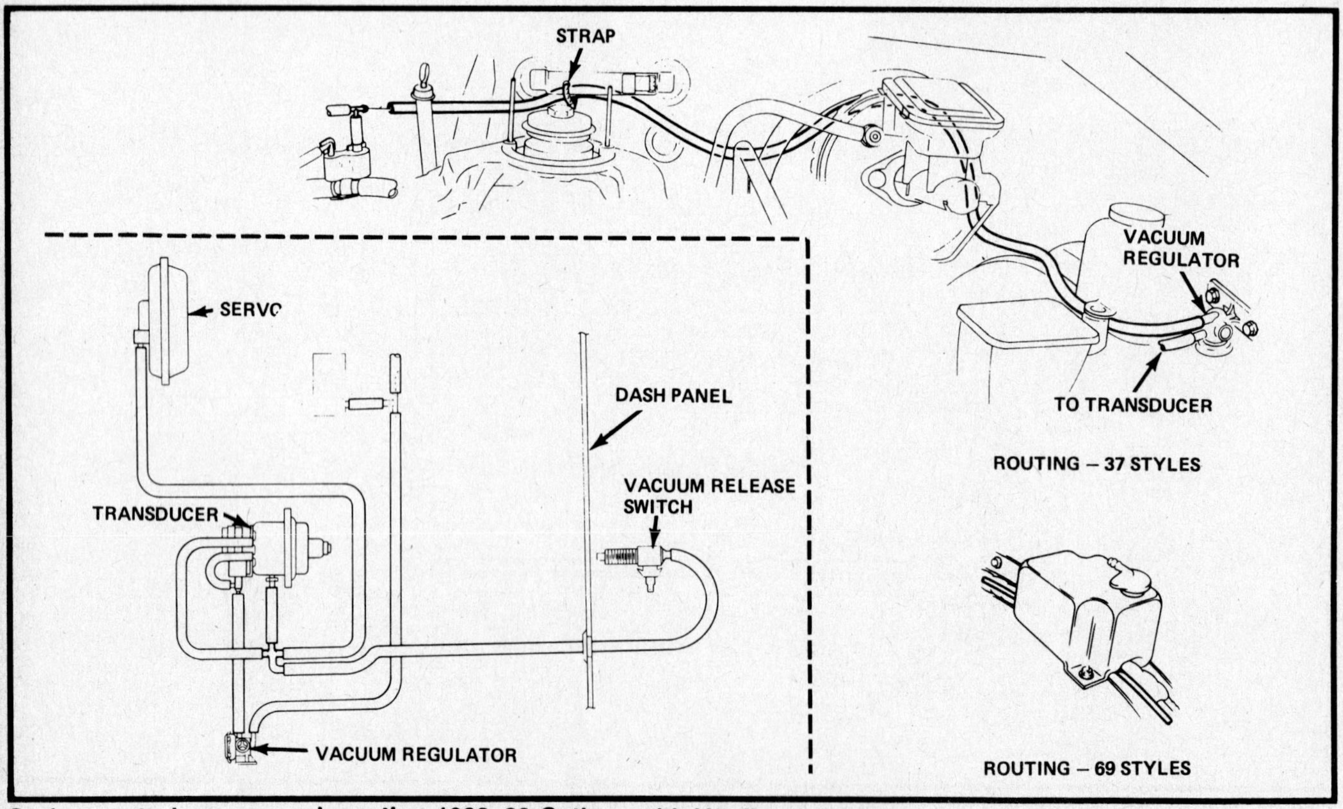

Cruise control vacuum schematic—1982–83 Cutlass with V6 diesel engine

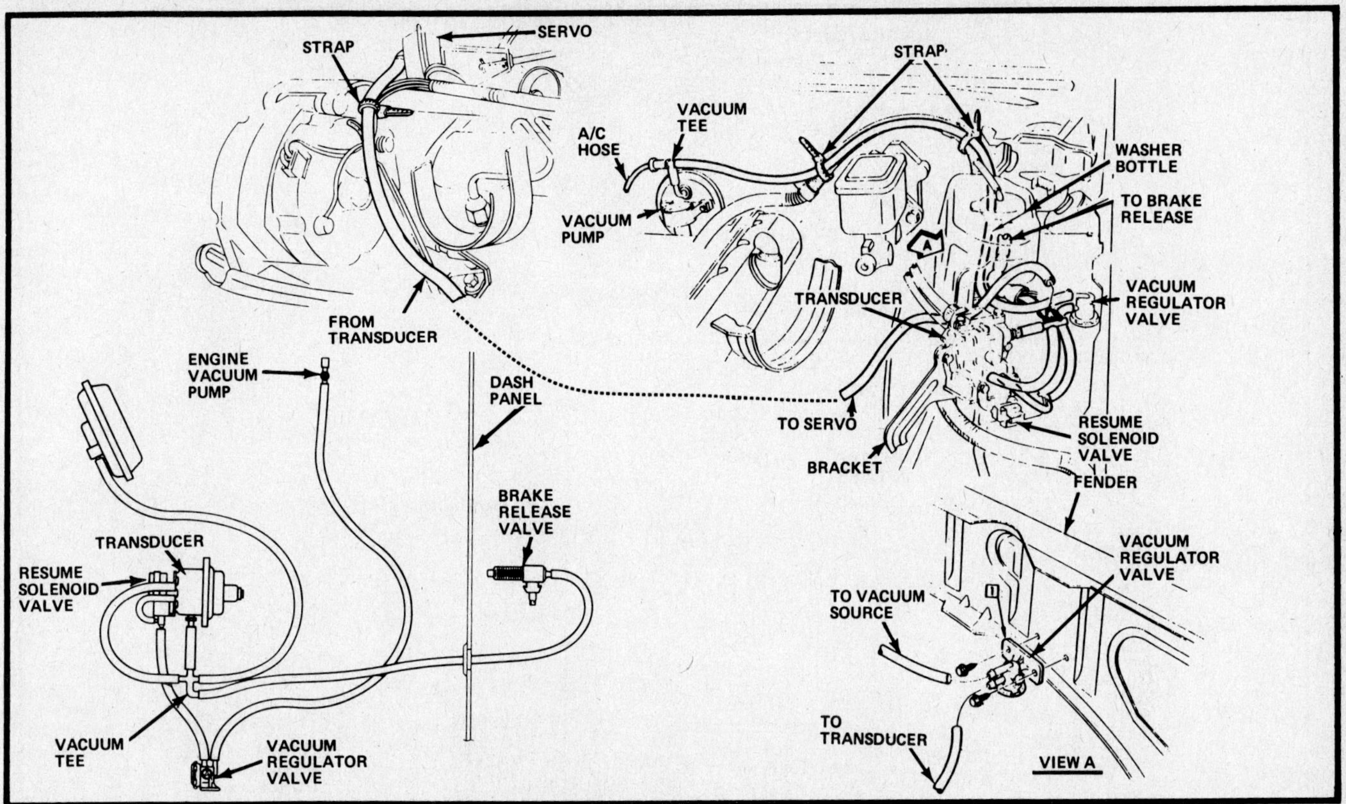

Cruise control vacuum schematic—1982–83 Cutlass with V8 diesel engine

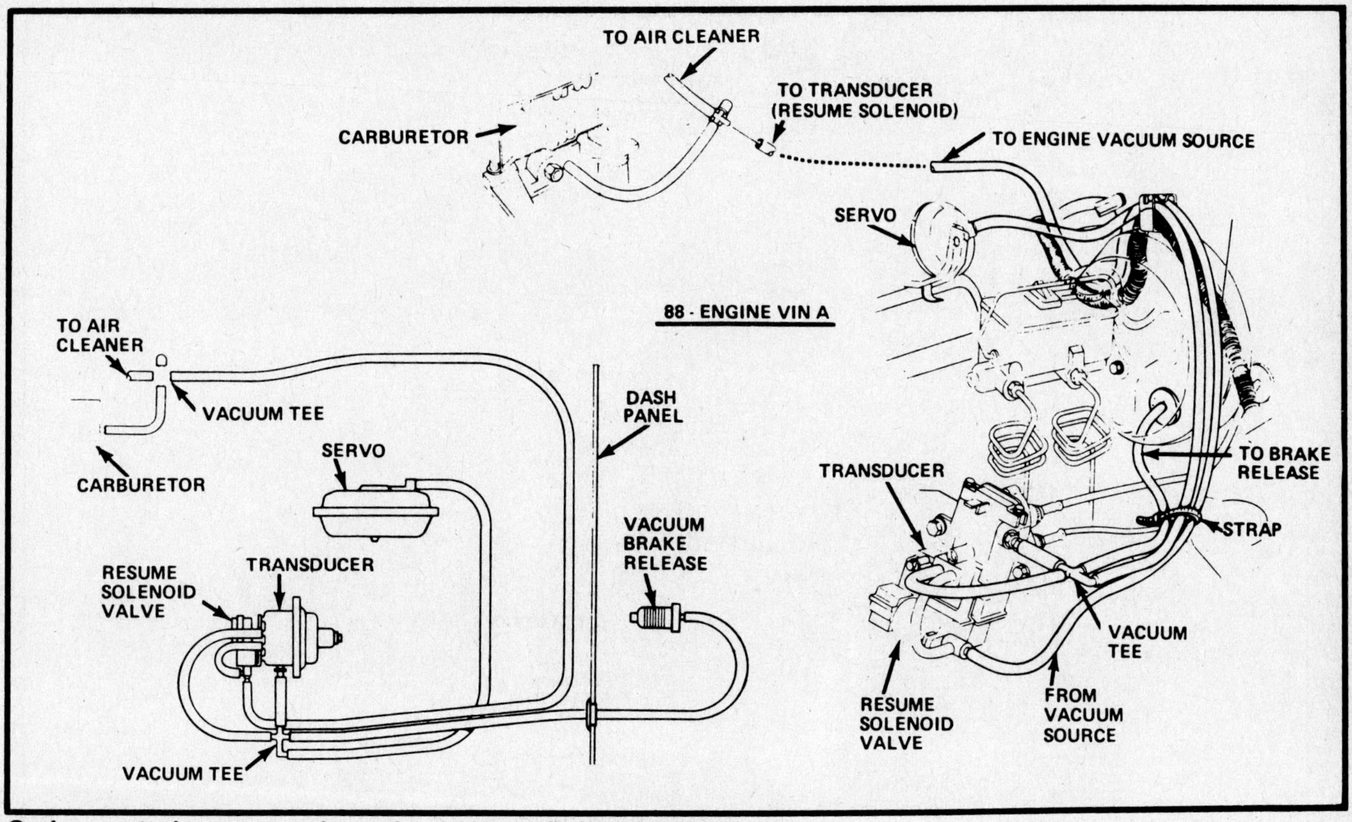

Cruise control vacuum schematic—1982–83 Delta 88 with V6 gas engine

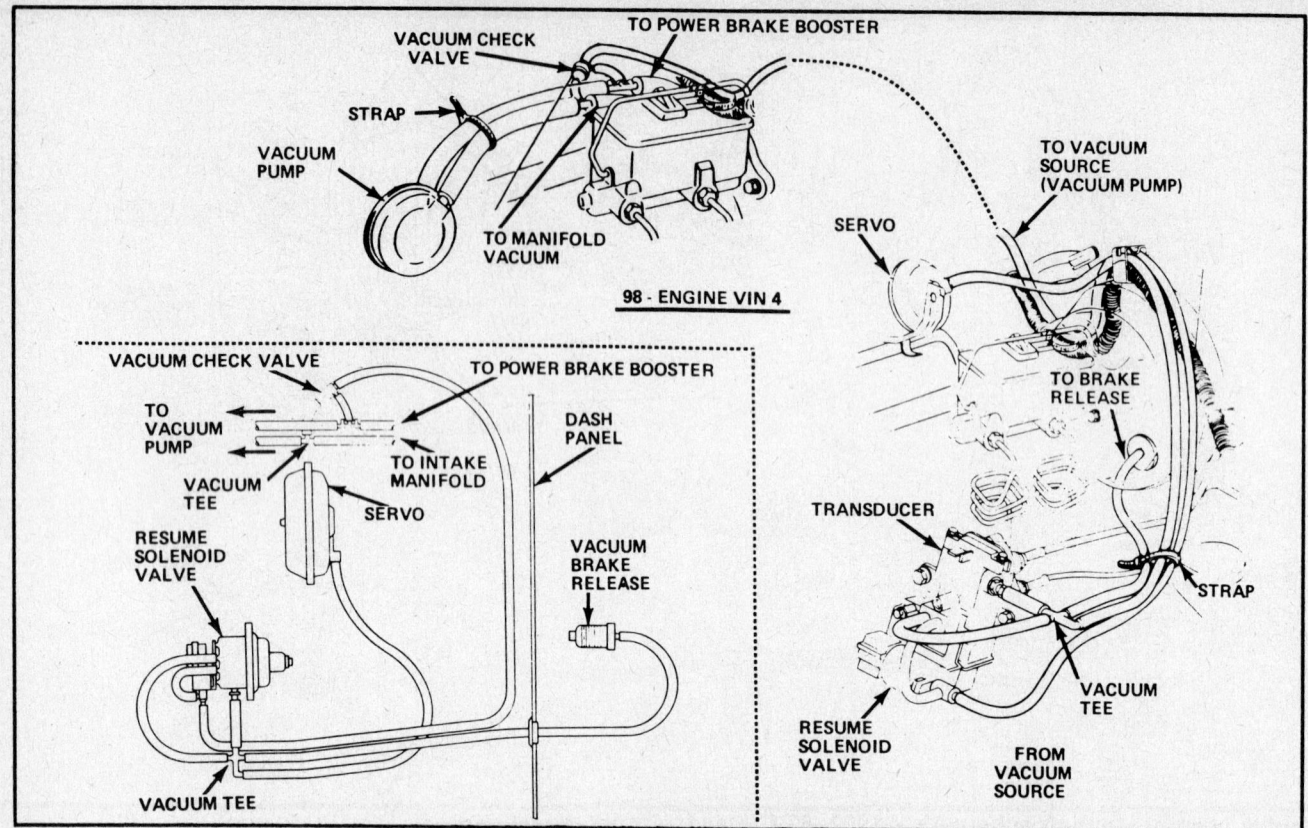

Cruise control vacuum schematic—1982–83 98 with V6 gas engine

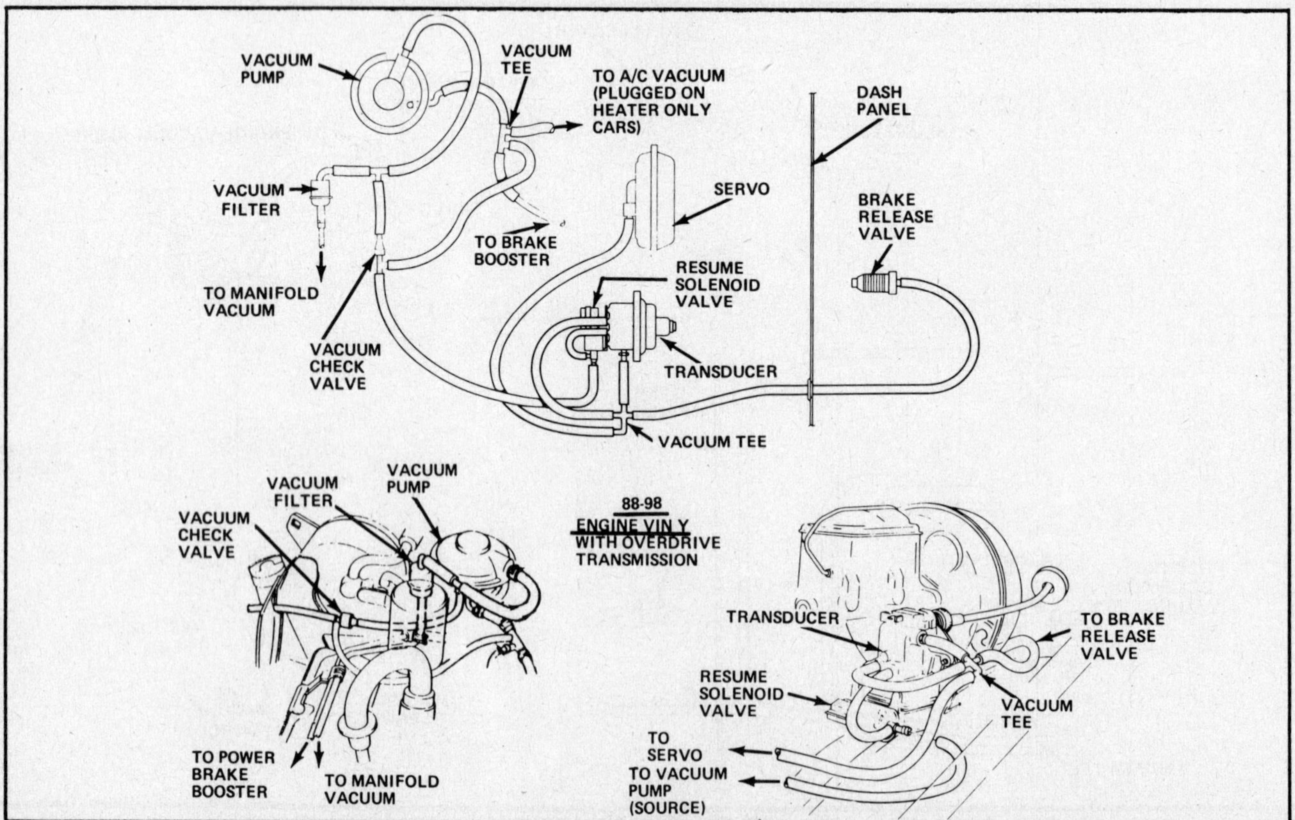

Cruise control vacuum schematic—1982–83 Delta 88 and with V8 gas engine and overdrive transmission

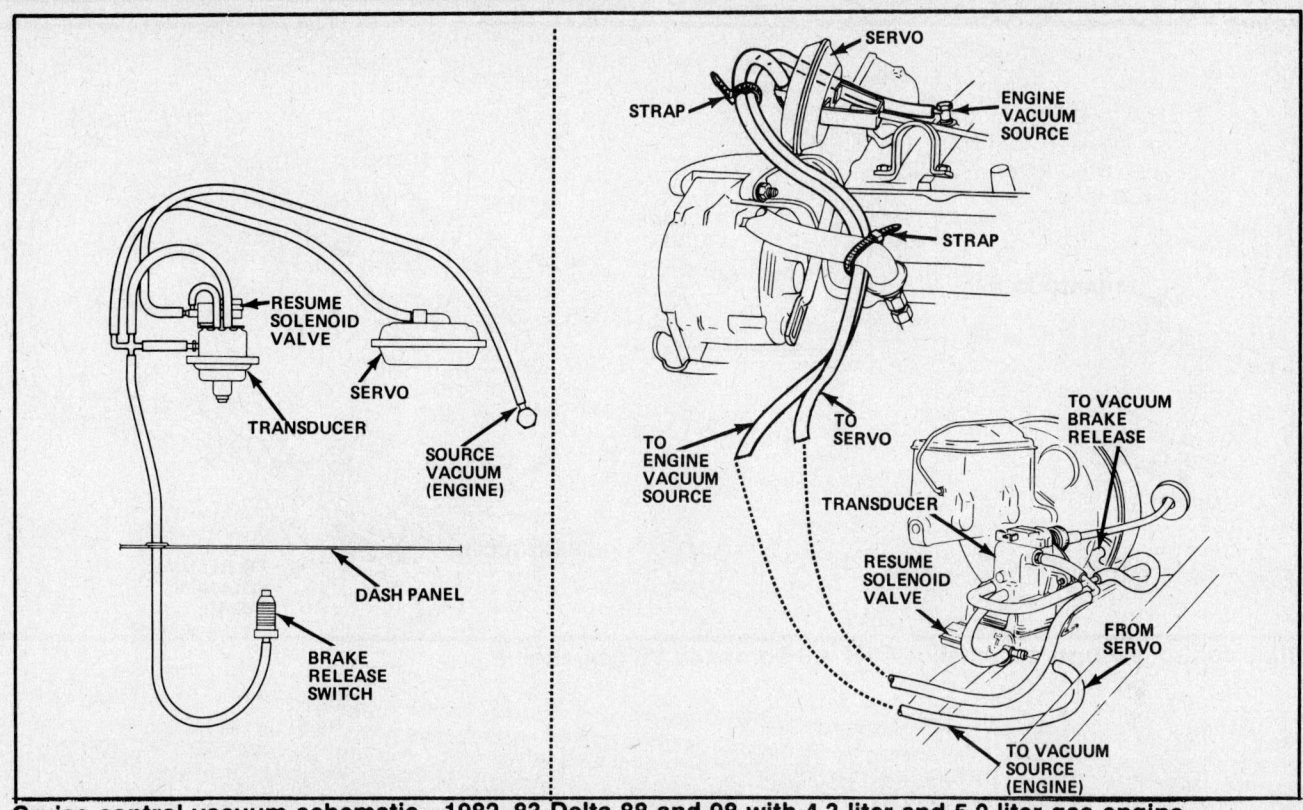

Cruise control vacuum schematic—1982–83 Delta 88 and 98 with 4.3 liter and 5.0 liter gas engine

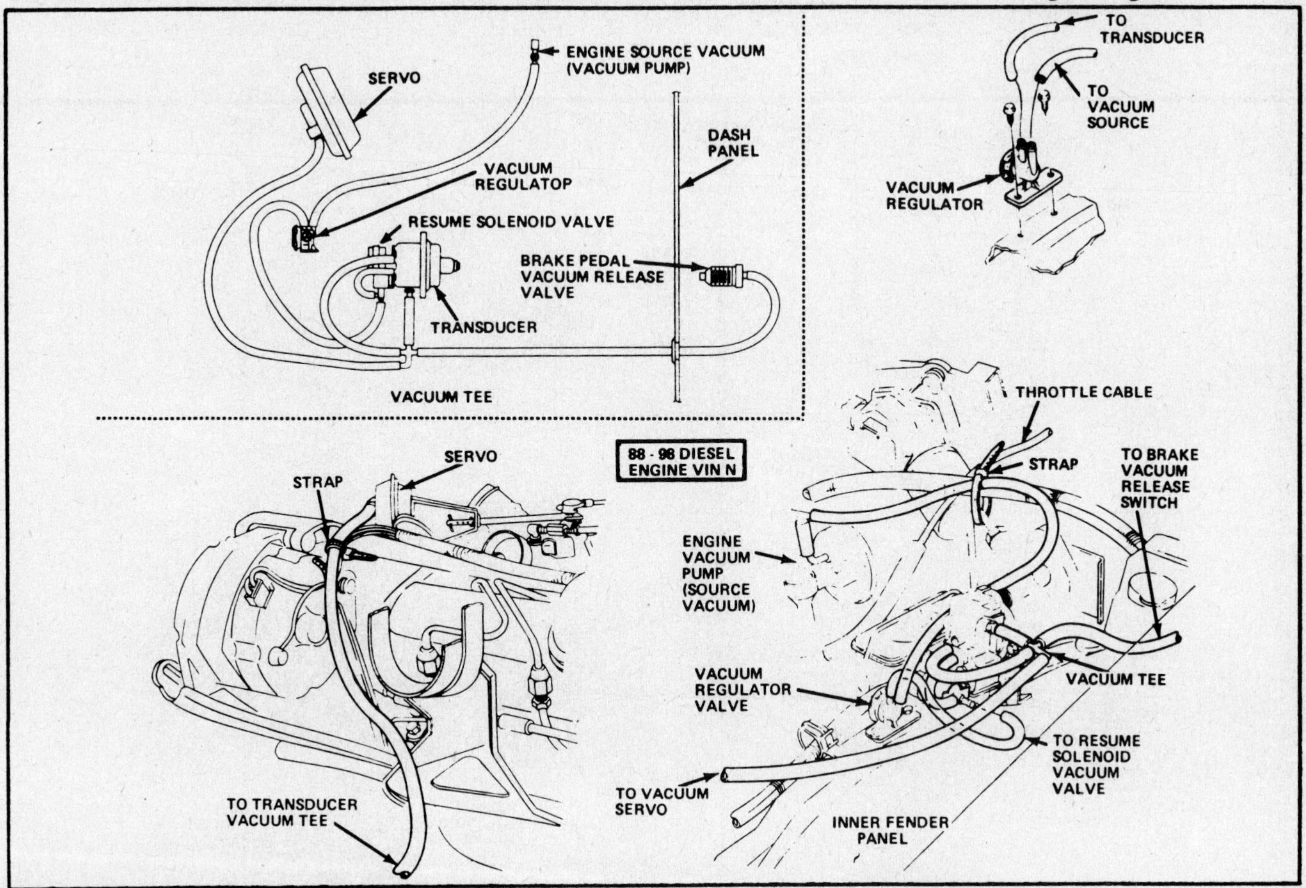

Cruise control vacuum schematic—1982–83 Delta 88 and 98 with V8 diesel engine

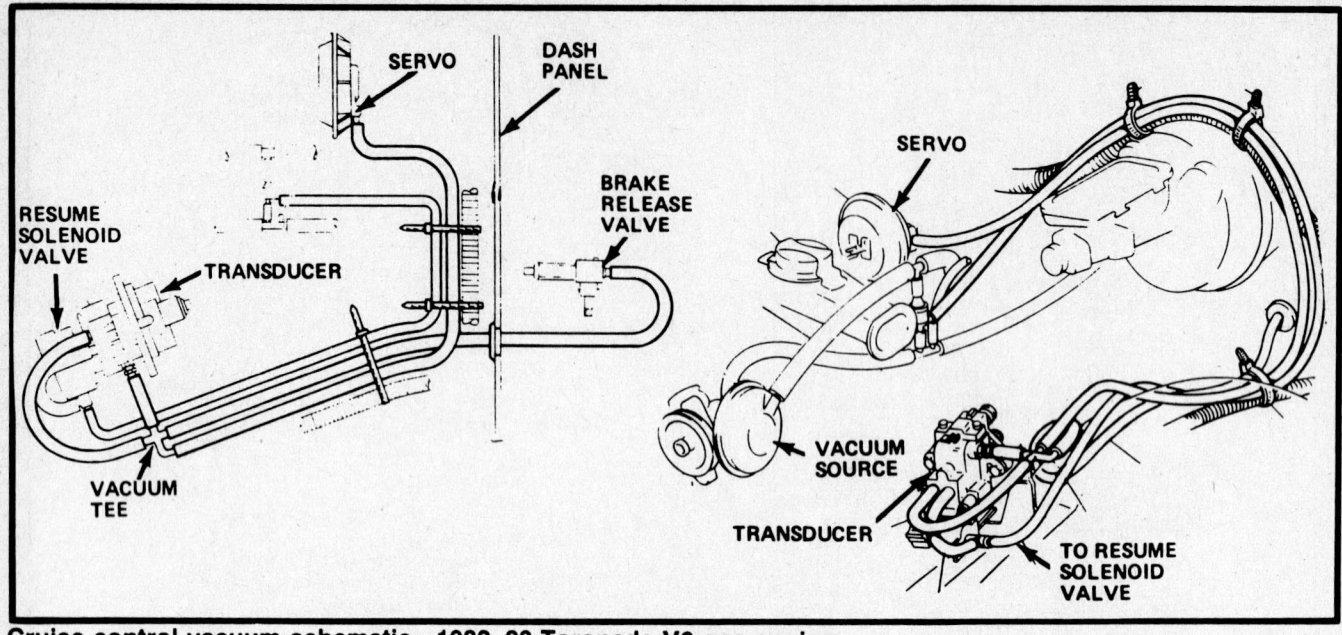

Cruise control vacuum schematic—1982–83 Toronado V6 gas engine

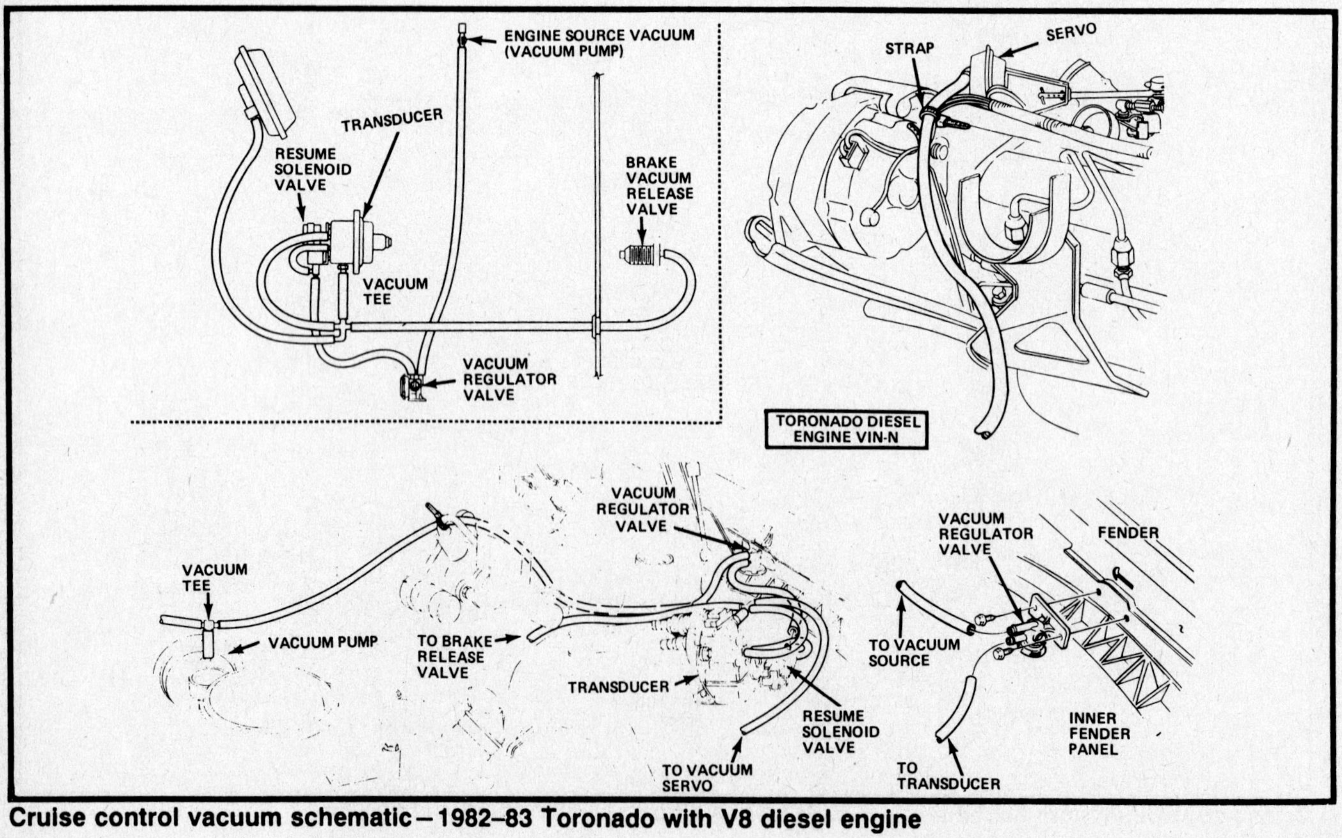

Cruise control vacuum schematic—1982–83 Toronado with V8 diesel engine

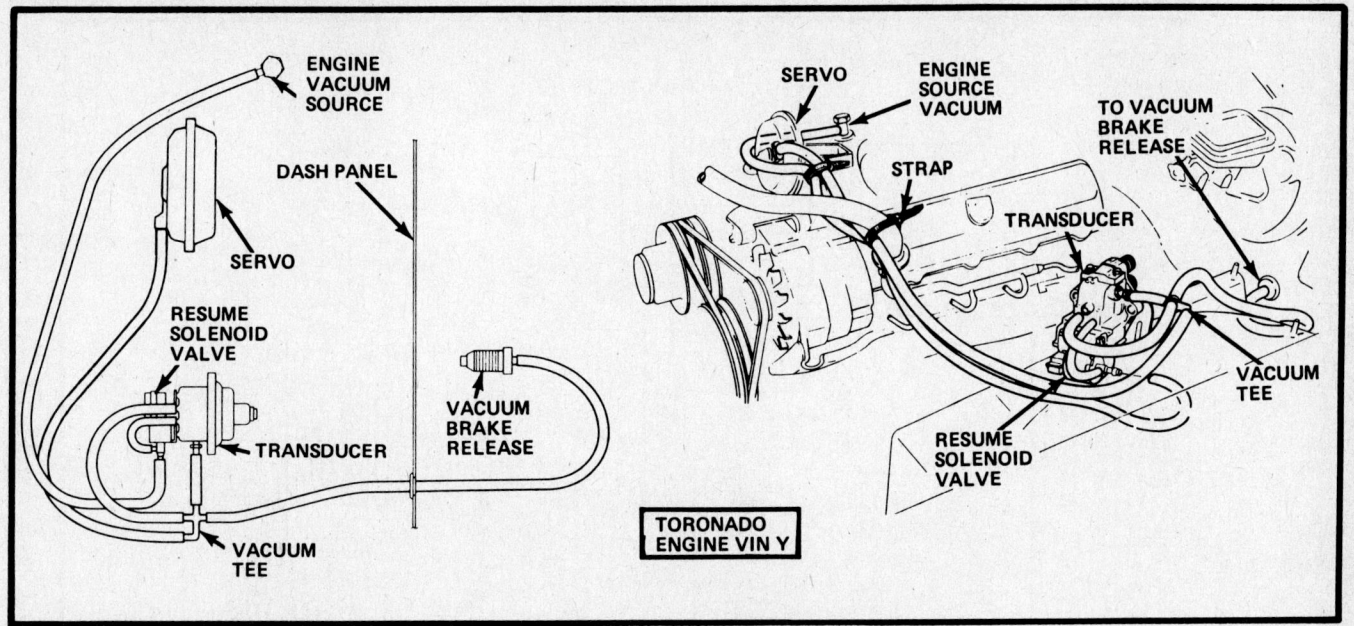

Cruise control vacuum schematic — 1982–83 Toronado with V8 gas engine

SERVO ASSEMBLY LINKAGE ADJUSTMENT

For servo linkage adjustments refer to the proper illustration.

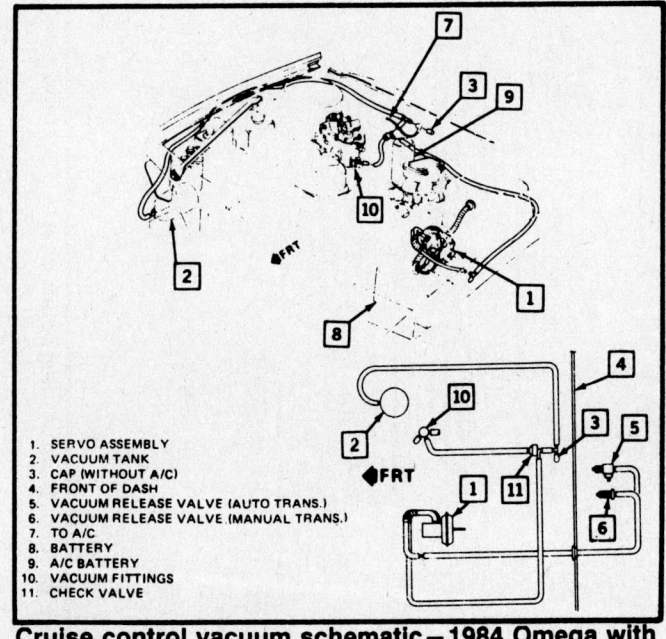

1. SERVO ASSEMBLY
2. VACUUM TANK
3. CAP (WITHOUT A/C)
4. FRONT OF DASH
5. VACUUM RELEASE VALVE (AUTO TRANS.)
6. VACUUM RELEASE VALVE (MANUAL TRANS.)
7. TO A/C
8. BATTERY
9. A/C BATTERY
10. VACUUM FITTINGS
11. CHECK VALVE

Cruise control vacuum schematic — 1984 Omega with 2.5 liter engine

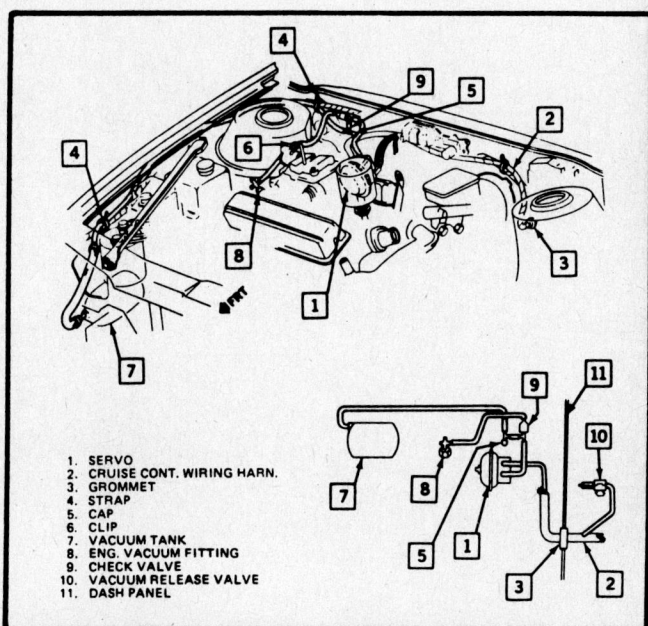

1. SERVO
2. CRUISE CONT. WIRING HARN.
3. GROMMET
4. STRAP
5. CAP
6. CLIP
7. VACUUM TANK
8. ENG. VACUUM FITTING
9. CHECK VALVE
10. VACUUM RELEASE VALVE
11. DASH PANEL

Cruise control vacuum schematic — 1984 Omega with 2.8 liter engine

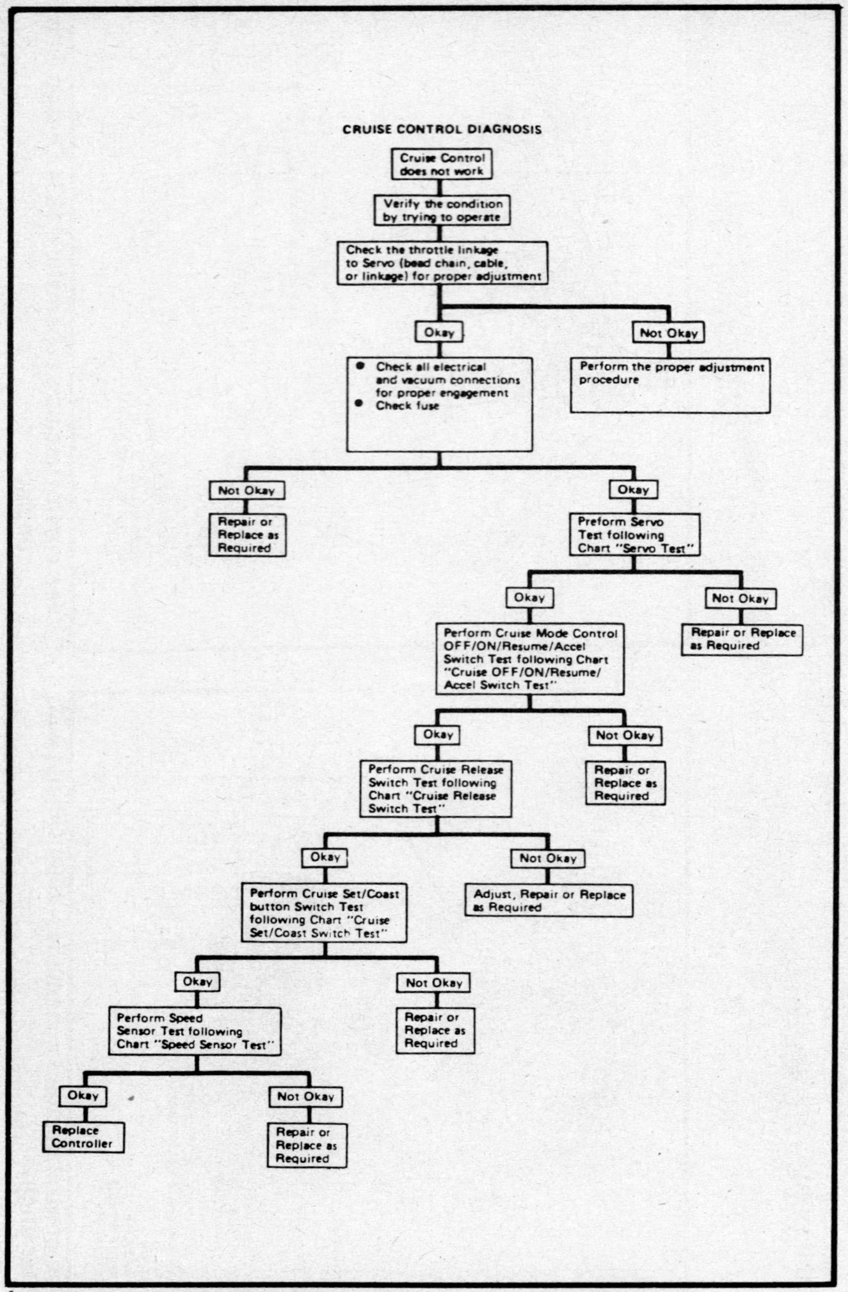

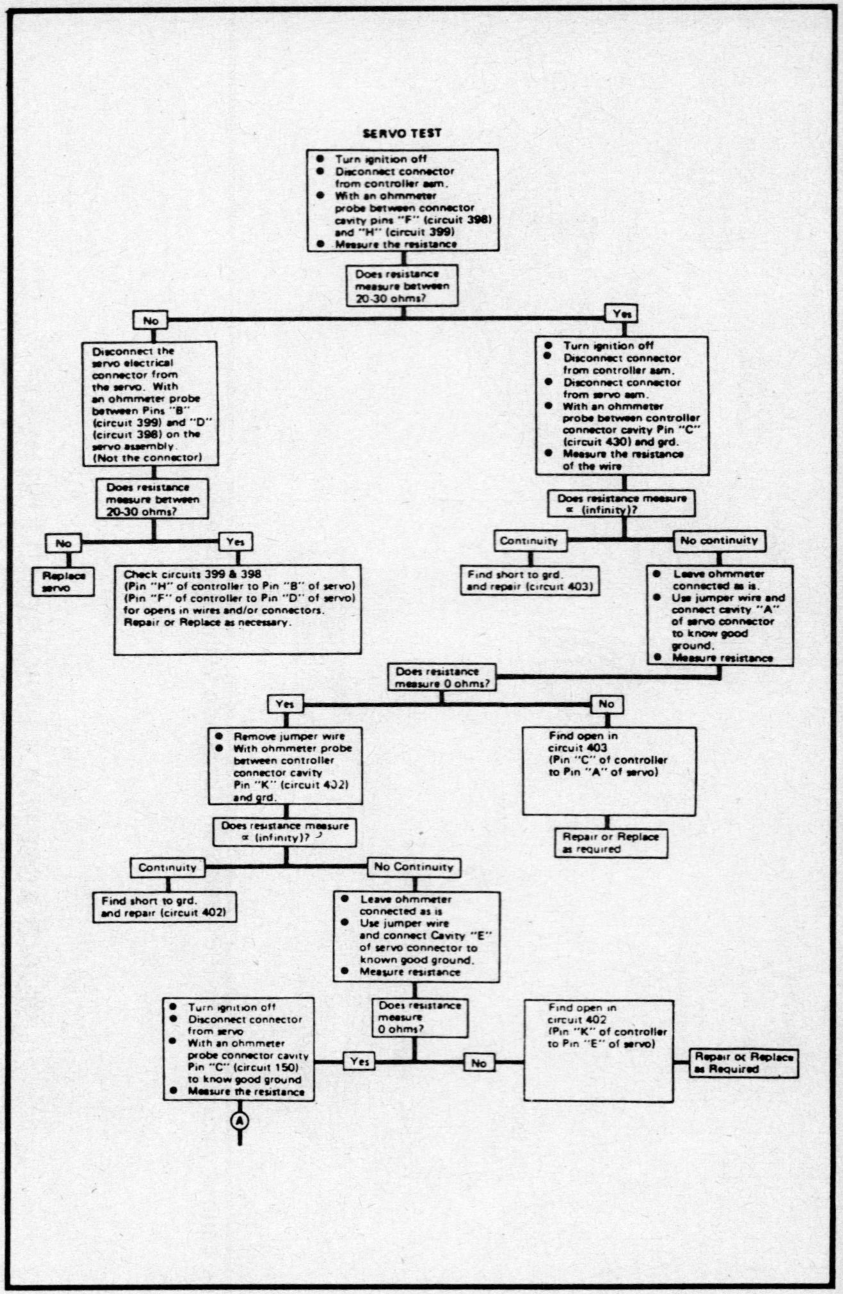

SERVO TEST

- Turn ignition off
- Disconnect connector from controller ass'm.
- With an ohmmeter probe between connector cavity pins "F" (circuit 399) and "H" (circuit 398)
- Measure the resistance

Does resistance measure 20-30 ohms?

Yes:
- Turn ignition off
- Disconnect connector from controller ass'm.
- Disconnect connector from servo ass'm.
- With an ohmmeter probe between controller connector cavity Pin "C" (circuit 430) and grd.
- Measure the resistance of the wire

Does resistance measure ∞ (infinity)?

No continuity:
- Leave ohmmeter connected as is
- Use jumper wire and connect cavity "A" of servo connector to known good ground.
- Measure resistance

Does resistance measure 0 ohms?

No: Find open in circuit 403 (Pin "C" of controller to Pin "A" of servo) — Repair or Replace as required

Yes: Find open in circuit 402 (Pin "K" of controller to Pin "E" of servo) — No

Continuity: Find short to grd. and repair (circuit 403)

No:
- Disconnect the servo electrical connector from the servo. With an ohmmeter probe between Pins "B" (circuit 399) and "D" (circuit 398) on the servo assembly. (Not the connector)

Does resistance measure between 20-30 ohms?

Yes: Check circuit 399 & 398 (Pin "H" of controller to Pin "B" of servo) (Pin "F" of controller to Pin "D" of servo) for opens in wires and/or connectors. Repair or Replace as necessary.

No: Replace servo

- Remove jumper wire
- With ohmmeter probe between controller connector cavity Pin "K" (circuit 432) and grd.

Does resistance measure ∞ (infinity)?

No Continuity:
- Leave ohmmeter connected as is
- Use jumper wire and connect Cavity "E" of servo connector to known good ground.
- Measure resistance

Does resistance measure 0 ohms?

Continuity: Find short to grd. and repair (circuit 402)

Yes:
- Turn ignition off
- Disconnect connector from servo
- With an ohmmeter probe between Pin "C" (circuit 150) to know good ground. Measure the resistance

Repair or Replace as Required

(A)

CRUISE CONTROL DIAGNOSIS

Cruise Control does not work → Verify the condition by trying to operate → Check the throttle linkage to Servo (bead chain, cable, or linkage) for proper adjustment

Not Okay: Perform the proper adjustment procedure

Okay: Check all electrical and vacuum connections for proper engagement — Check fuse

Not Okay: Repair or Replace as Required

Perform Servo Test following Chart "Servo Test"
- Not Okay: Repair or Replace as Required
- Okay: Perform Cruise Mode Control OFF/ON/Resume/Accel Switch Test following Chart "Cruise OFF/ON/Resume/Accel Switch Test"
  - Not Okay: Repair or Replace as Required
  - Okay: Perform Cruise Release Switch Test following Chart "Cruise Release Switch Test"
    - Not Okay: Adjust, Repair or Replace as Required
    - Okay: Perform Cruise Set/Coast button Switch Test following Chart "Cruise Set/Coast Switch Test"
      - Not Okay: Repair or Replace as Required
      - Okay: Perform Speed Sensor Test following Chart "Speed Sensor Test"
        - Not Okay: Repair or Replace as Required
        - Okay: Replace Controller

Cruise control trouble diagnosis chart—1984 and later

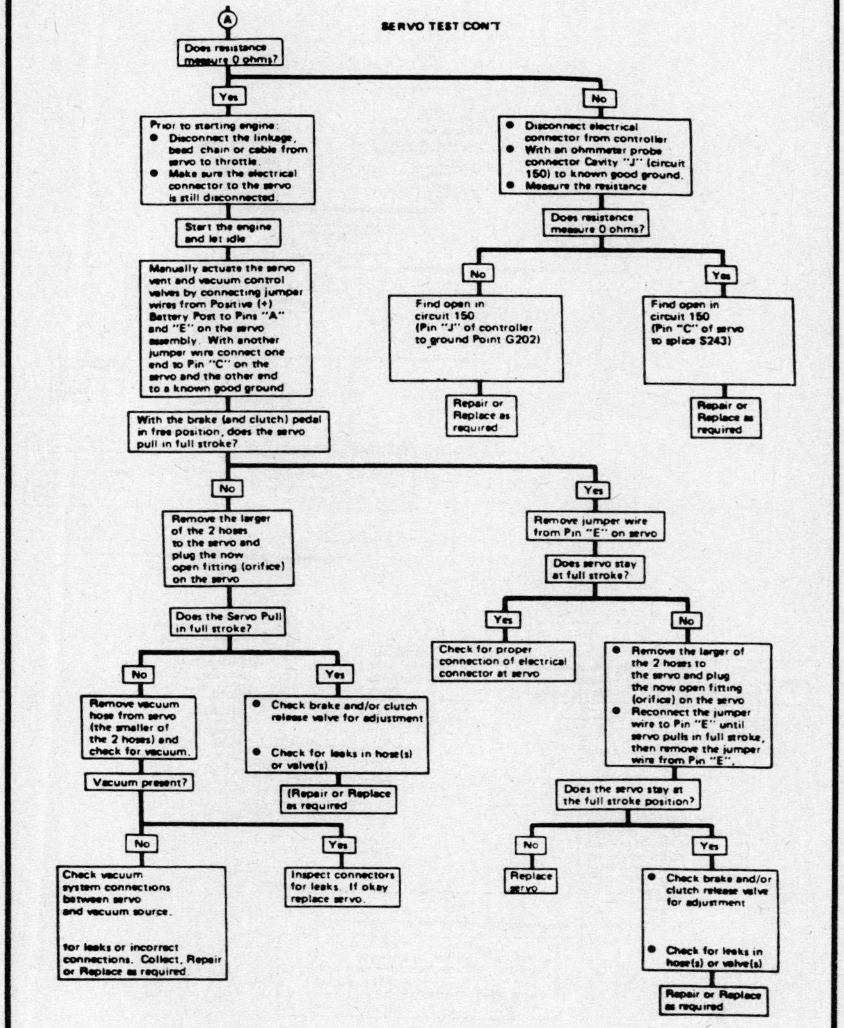

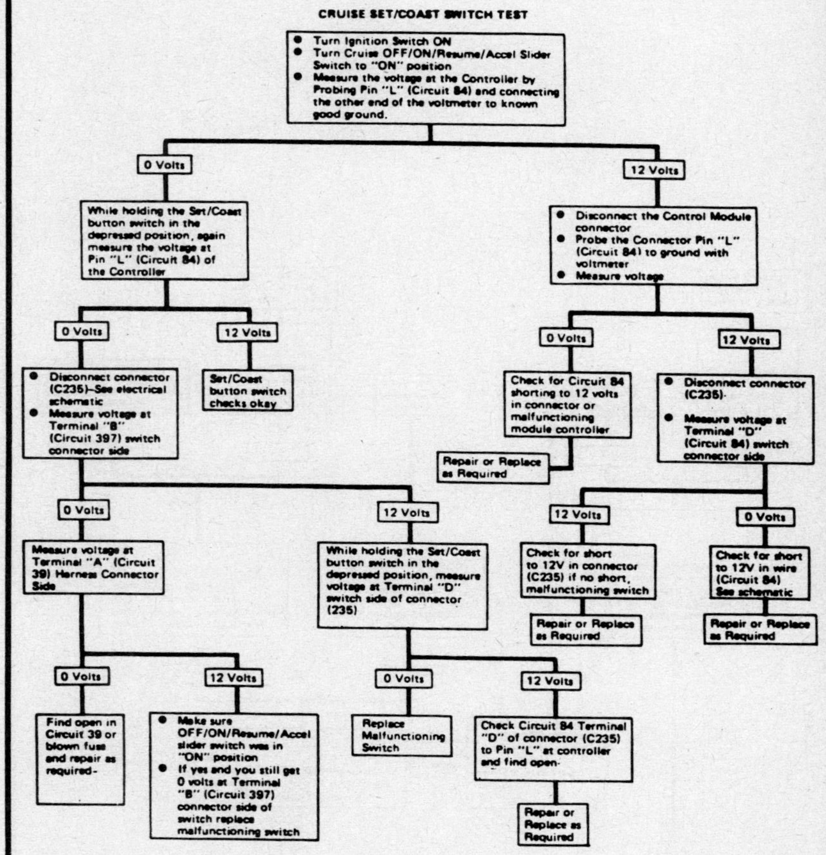

CRUISE SET/COAST SWITCH TEST

- Turn Ignition Switch ON
- Turn Cruise OFF/ON/Resume/Accel Slider Switch to "ON" position
- Measure the voltage at the Controller by Probing Pin "L" (Circuit 84) and connecting the other end of the voltmeter to known good ground.

12 Volts

- Disconnect the Control Module connector
- Probe the Connector Pin "L" (Circuit 84) to ground with voltmeter
- Measure voltage

12 Volts

Disconnect connector (C236).
- Measure voltage at Terminal "D" (Circuit 84) switch connector side

0 Volts → Check for short to 12V in wire (Circuit 84) See schematic → Repair or Replace as Required

0 Volts → Check for Circuit 84 shorting to 12 volts in connector or malfunctioning module controller → Repair or Replace as Required

12 Volts → Check for short to 12V in connector (C235) if no short malfunctioning switch → Repair or Replace as Required

While holding the Set/Coast button switch in the depressed position, measure voltage at Terminal "D" switch connector side of connector (C235)

12 Volts → Check Circuit 84 Terminal "D" of connector (C235) at controller and find open → Repair or Replace as Required

0 Volts → Replace Malfunctioning Switch

0 Volts

While holding the Set/Coast button switch in the depressed position, again measure the voltage at Pin "L" (Circuit 84) of the Controller

12 Volts → Set/Coast button switch checks okay

0 Volts

Disconnect connector (C235)-See electrical schematic Measure voltage at Terminal "B" (Circuit 397) switch connector side

12 Volts → Make sure OFF/ON/Resume/Accel slider switch is in "ON" position. If yes and you still get 0 volts at Terminal "B" (Circuit 397) connector side of switch replace malfunctioning switch

0 Volts

Measure voltage at Terminal "A" (Circuit 39) Harness Connector Side

0 Volts → Find open in Circuit 39 or blown fuse. Detect and repair as required-

---

SERVO TEST CONT

Does resistance measure 0 ohms?

No
- Disconnect electrical connector from controller
- With an ohmmeter probe lead, chain or cable from "J" circuit (Circuit 150) to known good ground.
- Measure the resistance

Does resistance measure 0 ohms?

Yes → Find open in circuit 150 (Pin "J" end of servo to splice S243) → Repair or Replace as required

No → Find open in circuit 150 (Pin "J" of controller to ground Point G202) → Repair or Replace as required

Yes

Prior to starting engine:
- Disconnect the linkage
- Make sure the electrical connector to the servo is still disconnected

Manually actuate the servo vent and vacuum control valves by connecting jumper wire from Positive (+) Battery Post to Pins "A" and "E" on the servo assembly. With another jumper wire connect one end to Pin "C" on the servo and the other end to a known good ground.

Start the engine and let it idle

With the brake (and clutch) pedal in free position, does the servo pull in full stroke?

No

Remove the larger of the 2 hoses to the servo and plug the now open fitting (orifice) on the servo

Does the Servo Pull in full stroke?

Yes
- Check brake and/or clutch release valve for adjustment
- Check for leaks in hose(s) or valve(s)

→ (Repair or Replace as required)

No

Remove vacuum hose from servo (the smaller of the 2 hoses) and check for vacuum.

Vacuum present?

Yes → Inspect connectors for leaks. If okay replace servo.

No → Check vacuum system connections between servo and vacuum source. for leaks or incorrect connections. Correct, Repair or Replace as required.

Yes

Remove jumper wire from Pin "E" on servo

Does servo stay at full stroke?

Yes

Check for proper connection of electrical connector at servo

No
- Remove the larger of the 2 hoses to the servo and plug the now open fitting (orifice) on the servo
- Reconnect the jumper wire to Pin "E" until servo pulls in full stroke, then remove the jumper wire from Pin "E"

Does the servo stay at the full stroke position?

Yes
- Check brake and/or clutch release valve for leaks
- Check for leaks in hose(s) or valve(s)

→ Repair or Replace as required

No → Replace servo

Cruise control trouble diagnosis chart—1984 and later

903

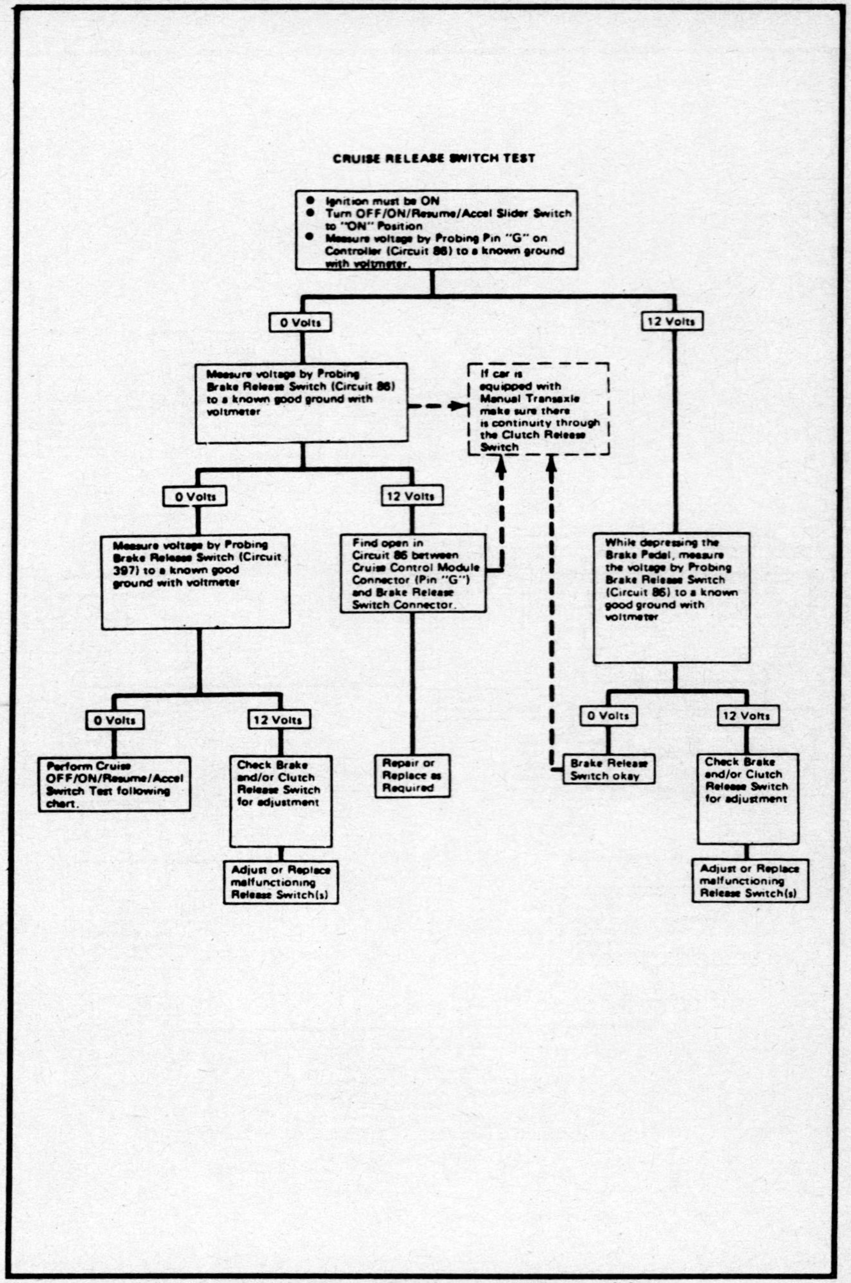

CRUISE RELEASE SWITCH TEST

- Ignition must be ON
- Turn OFF/ON/Resume/Accel Slider Switch to "ON" Position
- Measure voltage by Probing Pin "G" on Controller (Circuit 86) to a known ground with voltmeter.

12 Volts → While depressing the Brake Pedal, measure the voltage by Probing Brake Release Switch (Circuit 86) to a known good ground with voltmeter.
- **12 Volts** → Check Brake and/or Clutch Release Switch for adjustment → Adjust or Replace malfunctioning Release Switch(s)
- **0 Volts** → Brake Release Switch okay

If car is equipped with Manual Transaxle make sure there is continuity through the Clutch Release Switch

0 Volts → Measure voltage by Probing Brake Release Switch (Circuit 86) to a known good ground with voltmeter
- **12 Volts** → Find open in Circuit 86 between Cruise Control Module Connector (Pin "G") and Brake Release Switch Connector. → Repair or Replace as Required
- **0 Volts** → Measure voltage by Probing Brake Release Switch (Circuit 397) to a known good ground with voltmeter
  - **12 Volts** → Check Brake and/or Clutch Release Switch for adjustment → Adjust or Replace malfunctioning Release Switch(s)
  - **0 Volts** → Perform Cruise OFF/ON/Resume/Accel Switch Test following chart.

Cruise control trouble diagnosis chart—1984 and later

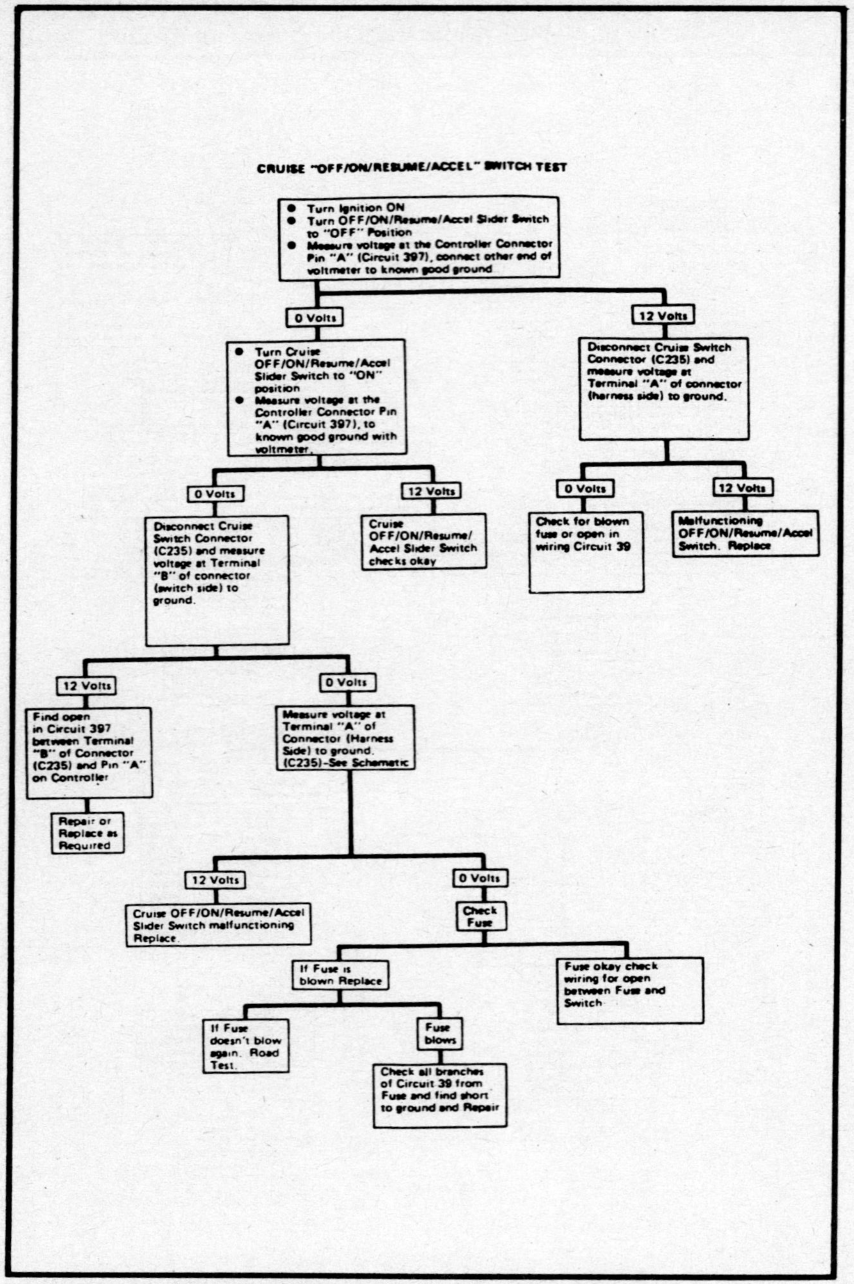

CRUISE "OFF/ON/RESUME/ACCEL" SWITCH TEST

- Turn Ignition ON
- Turn OFF/ON/Resume/Accel Slider Switch to "OFF" Position
- Measure voltage at the Controller Connector Pin "A" (Circuit 397), connect other end of voltmeter to known good ground.

12 Volts → Disconnect Cruise Switch Connector (C235) and measure voltage at Terminal "A" of connector (Harness side) to ground.
- **12 Volts** → Malfunctioning OFF/ON/Resume/Accel Switch. Replace
- **0 Volts** → Check for blown fuse or open in wiring Circuit 39

0 Volts → Turn Cruise OFF/ON/Resume/Accel Slider Switch to "ON" position
- Measure voltage at the Controller Connector Pin "A" (Circuit 397), to known good ground with voltmeter
  - **12 Volts** → Cruise OFF/ON/Resume/Accel Slider Switch checks okay
  - **0 Volts** → Disconnect Cruise Switch Connector (C235) and measure voltage at terminal "B" of connector (switch side) to ground
    - **12 Volts** → Find open in Circuit 397 between Terminal "B" of Connector (C235) and Pin "A" on Controller → Repair or Replace as Required
    - **0 Volts** → Measure voltage at Terminal "A" of Connector (Harness Side) to ground. (C235)—See Schematic
      - **12 Volts** → Cruise OFF/ON/Resume/Accel Slider Switch malfunctioning Replace.
      - **0 Volts** → Check Fuse
        - **If Fuse is blown Replace**
          - If Fuse doesn't blow again. Road Test.
          - Fuse blows → Check all branches of Circuit 39 from Fuse and find short to ground and Repair
        - **Fuse okay check** wiring for open between Fuse and Switch

Cruise control trouble diagnosis chart—1984 and later

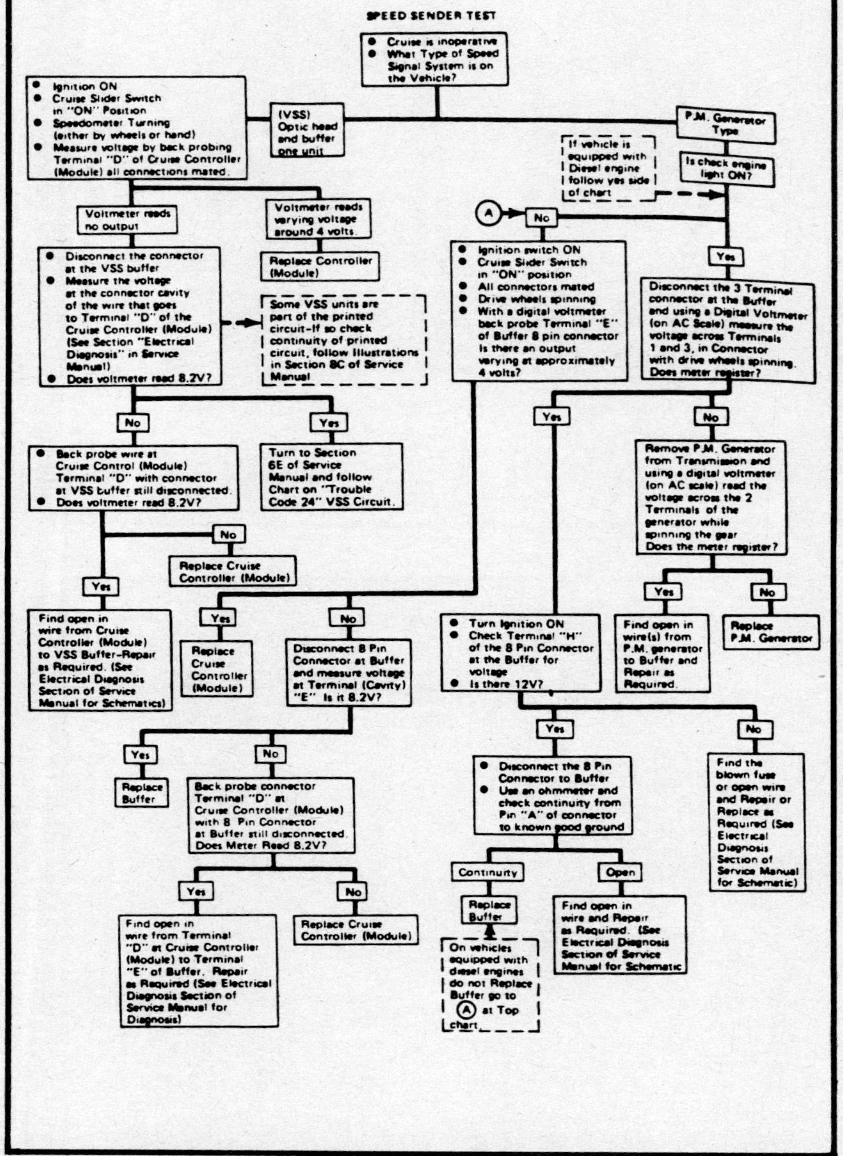

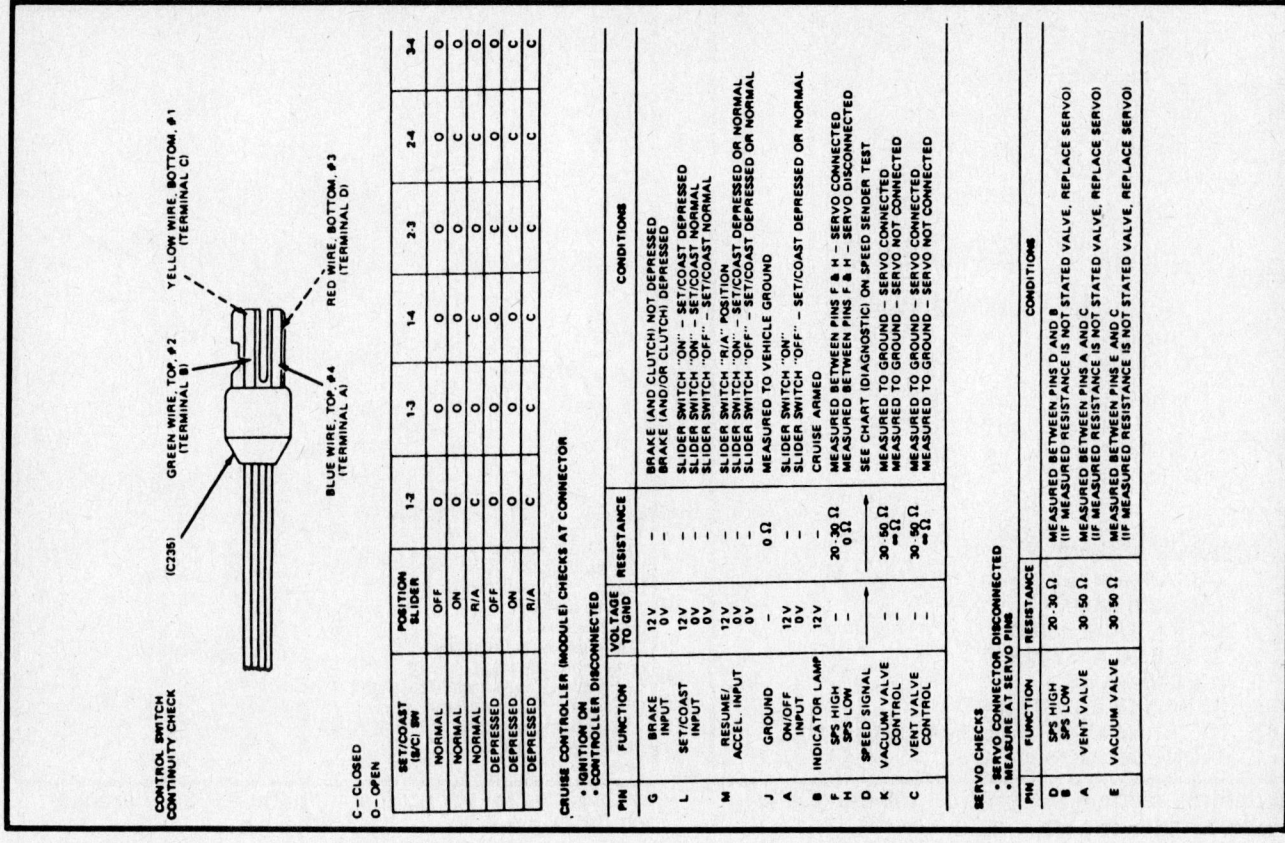

CONTROL SWITCH CONTINUITY CHECK

(C235)

GREEN WIRE, TOP, #2 (TERMINAL B)
YELLOW WIRE, BOTTOM, #1 (TERMINAL C)
BLUE WIRE, TOP, #4 (TERMINAL A)
RED WIRE, BOTTOM, #3 (TERMINAL D)

SET/COAST (S/C) SW	POSITION SLIDER	1-2	1-3	1-4	2-3	2-4
NORMAL	OFF	O	O	O	O	O
NORMAL	ON	O	O	O	C	O
NORMAL	R/A	C	C	C	C	O
DEPRESSED	OFF	O	O	O	O	C
DEPRESSED	ON	O	O	O	C	C
DEPRESSED	R/A	C	C	C	C	C

C – CLOSED
O – OPEN

CRUISE CONTROLLER (MODULE) CHECKS AT CONNECTOR
- IGNITION ON
- CONTROLLER DISCONNECTED

PIN	FUNCTION	POSITION SLIDER	VOLTAGE TO GRD	RESISTANCE	CONDITIONS
G	BRAKE INPUT		12 V	—	BRAKE (AND CLUTCH) NOT DEPRESSED
			0 V	—	BRAKE (AND/OR CLUTCH) DEPRESSED
L	SET/COAST INPUT		12 V	—	SLIDER SWITCH "ON" – SET/COAST DEPRESSED
			0 V	—	SLIDER SWITCH "ON" – SET/COAST NORMAL
			0 V	—	SLIDER SWITCH "OFF" – SET/COAST NORMAL
M	RESUME/ ACCEL. INPUT		12 V	—	SLIDER SWITCH "R/A" POSITION
			0 V	—	SLIDER SWITCH "ON" – SET/COAST DEPRESSED OR NORMAL
			0 V	—	SLIDER SWITCH "OFF" – SET/COAST DEPRESSED OR NORMAL
J	GROUND			0 Ω	MEASURED TO VEHICLE GROUND
A	ON/OFF INPUT		12 V		SLIDER SWITCH "ON"
			0 V		SLIDER SWITCH "OFF" – SET/COAST DEPRESSED OR NORMAL
B	INDICATOR LAMP		12 V		CRUISE ARMED
F H	VACUUM VALVE CONTROL / SPS HIGH SPS LOW			20-30 Ω / 0 Ω	MEASURED BETWEEN PINS F & H – SERVO CONNECTED / MEASURED BETWEEN PINS F & H – SERVO DISCONNECTED
K	SPEED SIGNAL			30-50 Ω	SEE CHART (DIAGNOSTIC) ON SPEED SENDER TEST
C	VENT VALVE CONTROL			30-50 Ω / ∞ Ω	MEASURED TO GROUND – SERVO CONNECTED / MEASURED TO GROUND – SERVO NOT CONNECTED

SERVO CHECKS
- SERVO CONNECTOR DISCONNECTED
- MEASURE AT SERVO PINS

PIN	FUNCTION	RESISTANCE	CONDITIONS
D B	SPS HIGH SPS LOW	20-30 Ω	MEASURED BETWEEN PINS D AND B (IF MEASURED RESISTANCE IS NOT STATED VALUE, REPLACE SERVO)
A	VENT VALVE	30-50 Ω	MEASURED BETWEEN PINS A AND C (IF MEASURED RESISTANCE IS NOT STATED VALUE, REPLACE SERVO)
E	VACUUM VALVE	30-50 Ω	MEASURED BETWEEN PINS E AND C (IF MEASURED RESISTANCE IS NOT STATED VALUE, REPLACE SERVO)

Cruise control servo, controller and switch check—1984 and later

Cruise control trouble diagnosis chart—1984 and later

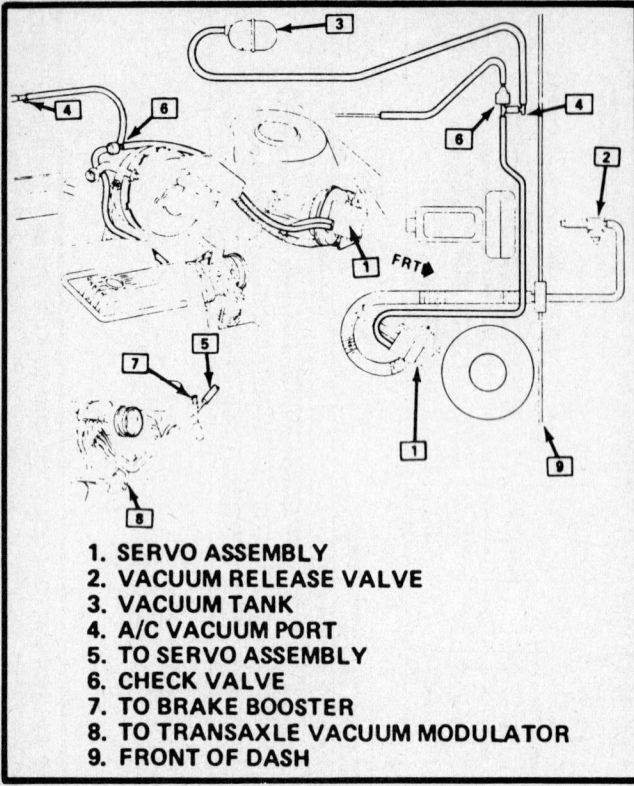

1. SERVO ASSEMBLY
2. VACUUM RELEASE VALVE
3. VACUUM TANK
4. A/C VACUUM PORT
5. TO SERVO ASSEMBLY
6. CHECK VALVE
7. TO BRAKE BOOSTER
8. TO TRANSAXLE VACUUM MODULATOR
9. FRONT OF DASH

Cruise control vacuum schematic—1984 and later Ciera with 3.8 liter engine

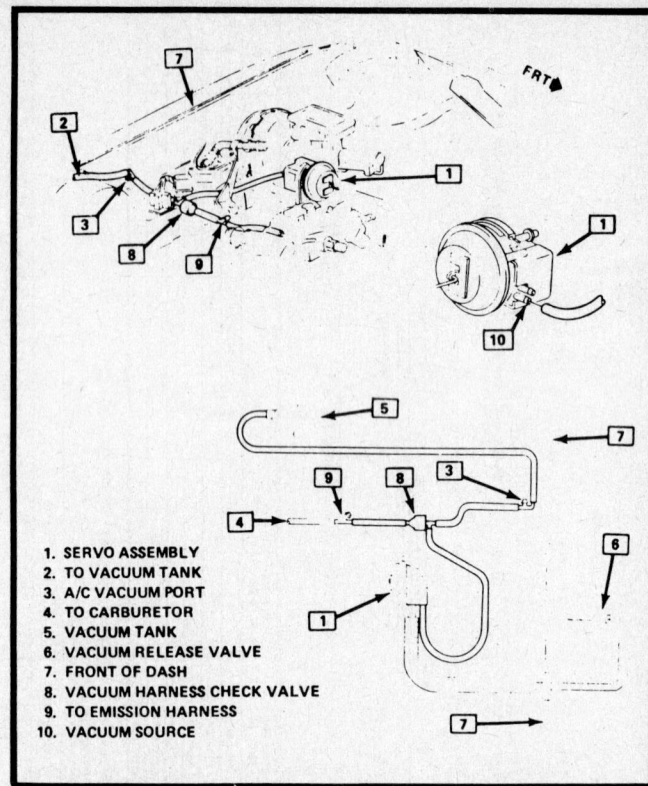

1. SERVO ASSEMBLY
2. TO VACUUM TANK
3. A/C VACUUM PORT
4. TO CARBURETOR
5. VACUUM TANK
6. VACUUM RELEASE VALVE
7. FRONT OF DASH
8. VACUUM HARNESS CHECK VALVE
9. TO EMISSION HARNESS
10. VACUUM SOURCE

Cruise control vacuum schematic—1984 Ciera with 3.0 liter engine

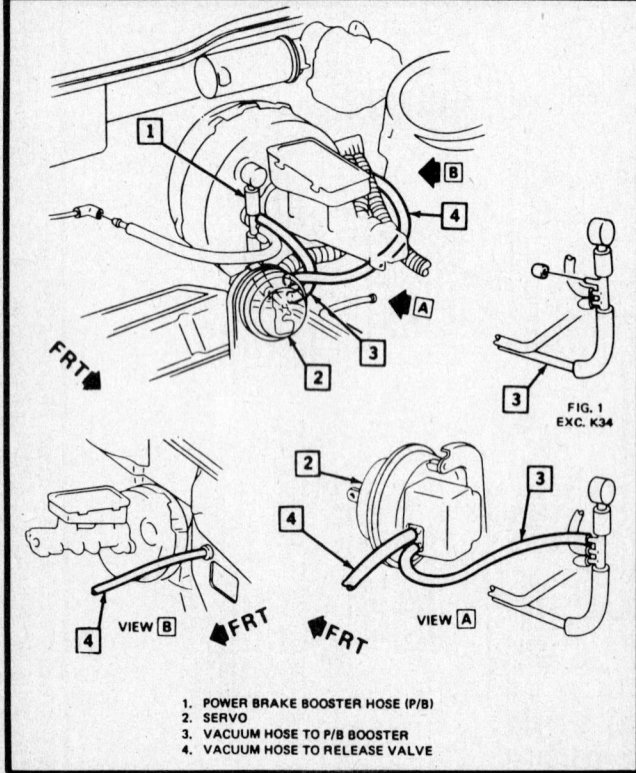

FIG. 1
EXC. K34

1. POWER BRAKE BOOSTER HOSE (P/B)
2. SERVO
3. VACUUM HOSE TO P/B BOOSTER
4. VACUUM HOSE TO RELEASE VALVE

Cruise control vacuum schematic—1985 98 with 3.0 liter engine

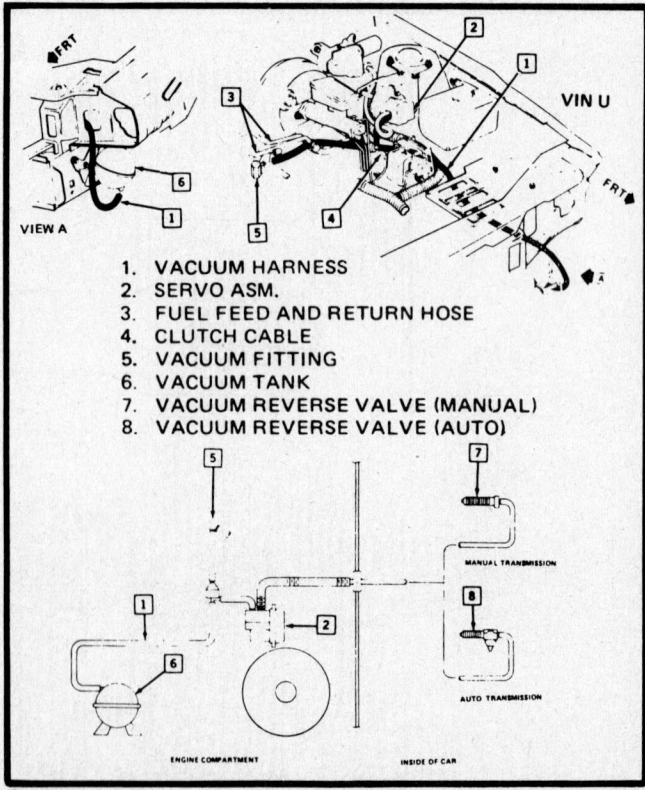

VIEW A

1. VACUUM HARNESS
2. SERVO ASM.
3. FUEL FEED AND RETURN HOSE
4. CLUTCH CABLE
5. VACUUM FITTING
6. VACUUM TANK
7. VACUUM REVERSE VALVE (MANUAL)
8. VACUUM REVERSE VALVE (AUTO)

Cruise control vacuum schematic—1985 Calais with 2.5 liter engine

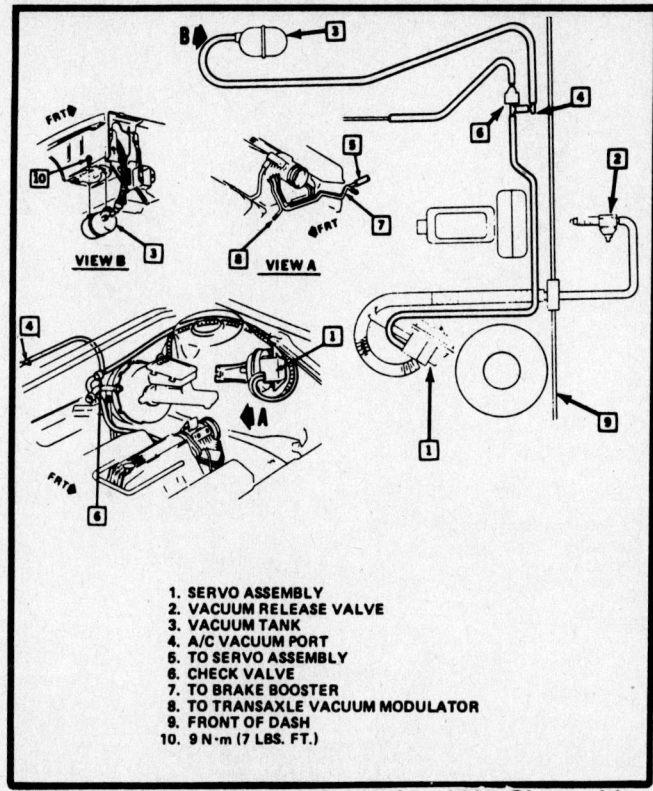

1. SERVO ASSEMBLY
2. VACUUM RELEASE VALVE
3. VACUUM TANK
4. A/C VACUUM PORT
5. TO SERVO ASSEMBLY
6. CHECK VALVE
7. TO BRAKE BOOSTER
8. TO TRANSAXLE VACUUM MODULATOR
9. FRONT OF DASH
10. 9 N·m (7 LBS. FT.)

Cruise control vacuum schematic—1985 Ciera with 3.8 liter engine

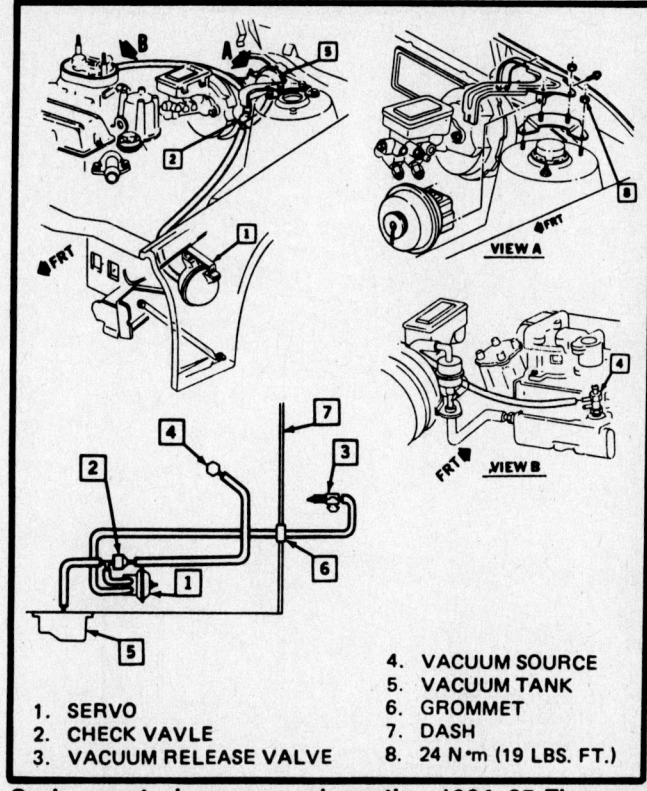

1. SERVO
2. CHECK VAVLE
3. VACUUM RELEASE VALVE
4. VACUUM SOURCE
5. VACUUM TANK
6. GROMMET
7. DASH
8. 24 N·m (19 LBS. FT.)

Cruise control vacuum schematic—1984–85 Firenza with 2.0 liter engine

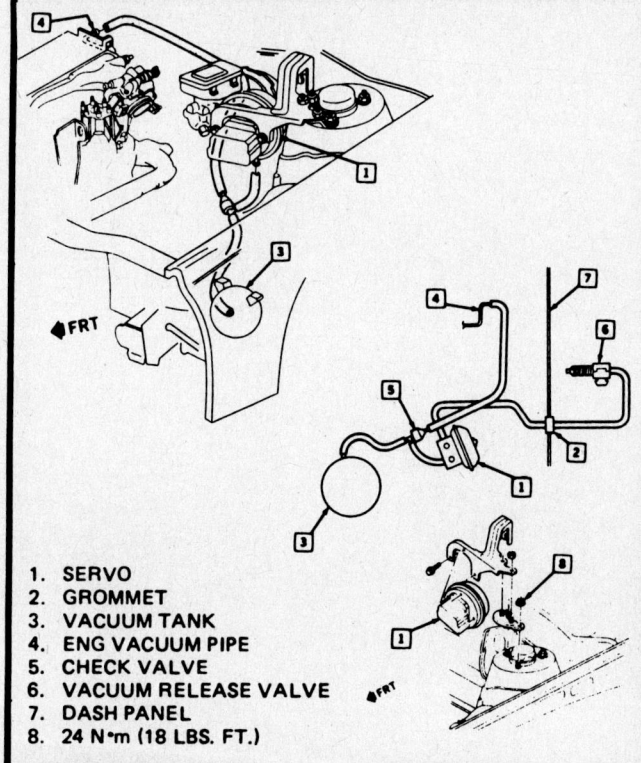

1. SERVO
2. GROMMET
3. VACUUM TANK
4. ENG VACUUM PIPE
5. CHECK VALVE
6. VACUUM RELEASE VALVE
7. DASH PANEL
8. 24 N·m (18 LBS. FT.)

Cruise control vacuum schematic—1985 Firenza with 2.8 liter engine

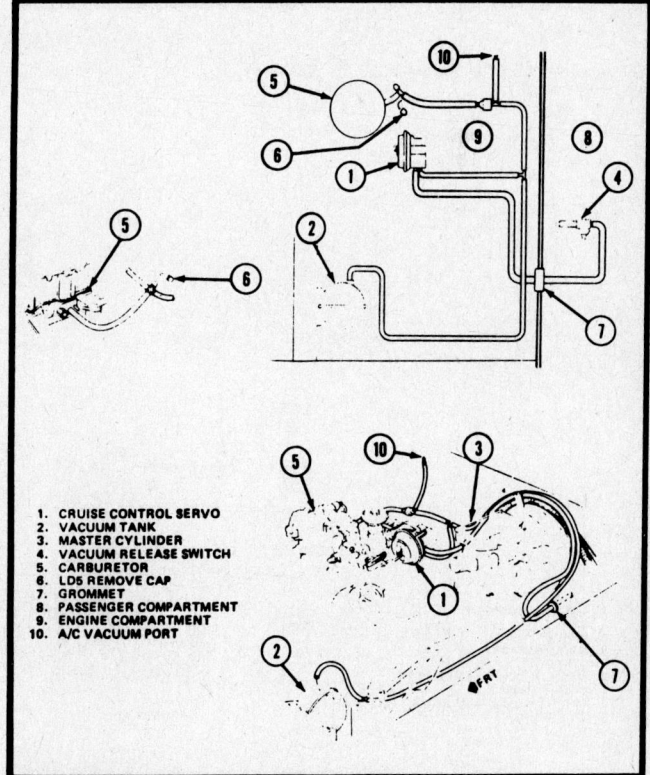

1. CRUISE CONTROL SERVO
2. VACUUM TANK
3. MASTER CYLINDER
4. VACUUM RELEASE SWITCH
5. CARBURETOR
6. LD5 REMOVE CAP
7. GROMMET
8. PASSENGER COMPARTMENT
9. ENGINE COMPARTMENT
10. A/C VACUUM PORT

Cruise control vacuum schematic—1984–85 Cutlass, Delta 88, 98 (1984), Custom cruiser 3.8 liter engine

907

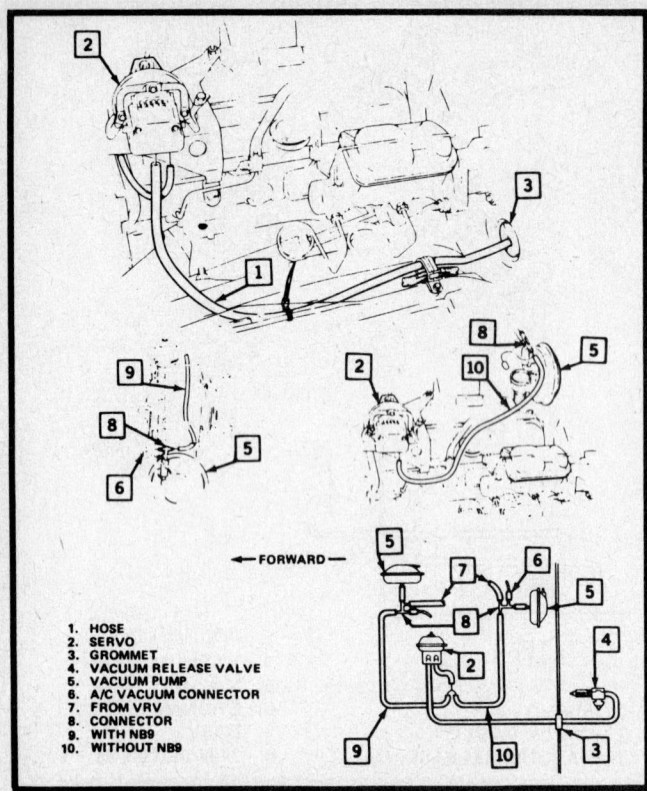

1. HOSE
2. SERVO
3. GROMMET
4. VACUUM RELEASE VALVE
5. VACUUM PUMP
6. A/C VACUUM CONNECTOR
7. FROM VRV
8. CONNECTOR
9. WITH NB9
10. WITHOUT NB9

Cruise control vacuum schematic—1984–85 Cutlass, Delta 88, 98 (1984), Custom Cruiser and Toronado with V8 diesel engine

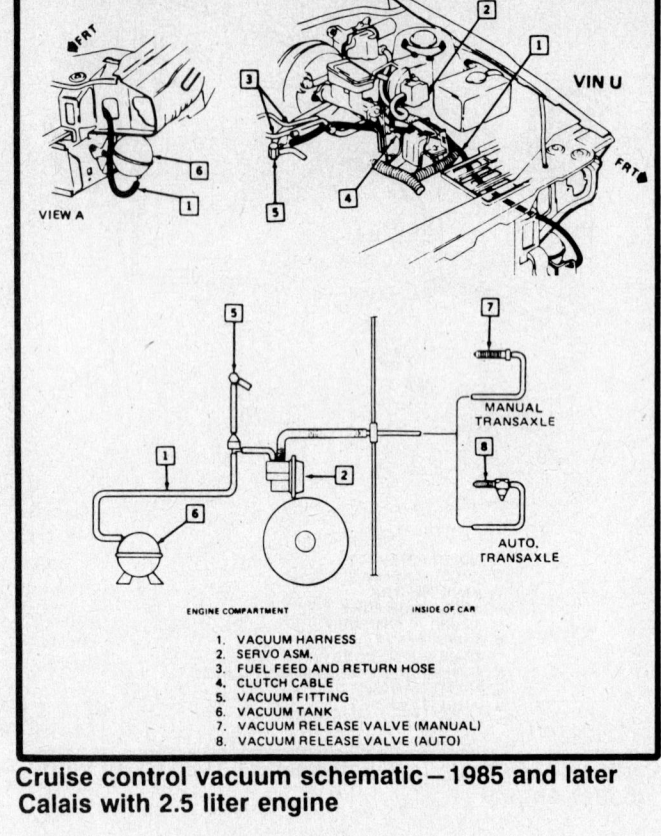

1. VACUUM HARNESS
2. SERVO ASM.
3. FUEL FEED AND RETURN HOSE
4. CLUTCH CABLE
5. VACUUM FITTING
6. VACUUM TANK
7. VACUUM RELEASE VALVE (MANUAL)
8. VACUUM RELEASE VALVE (AUTO)

Cruise control vacuum schematic—1985 and later Calais with 2.5 liter engine

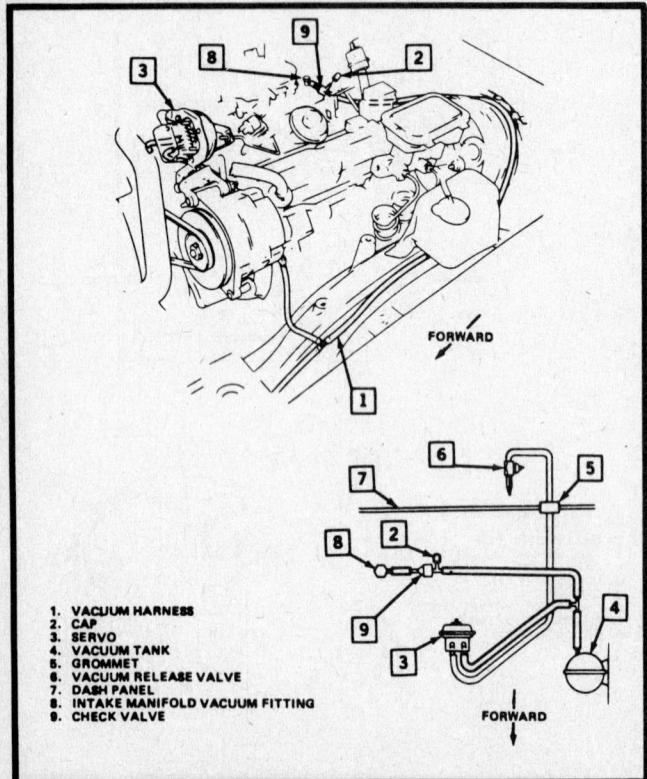

1. VACUUM HARNESS
2. CAP
3. SERVO
4. VACUUM TANK
5. GROMMET
6. VACUUM RELEASE VALVE
7. DASH PANEL
8. INTAKE MANIFOLD VACUUM FITTING
9. CHECK VALVE

Cruise control vacuum schematic—1986 and later Cutlass (four Door) with V8 engine

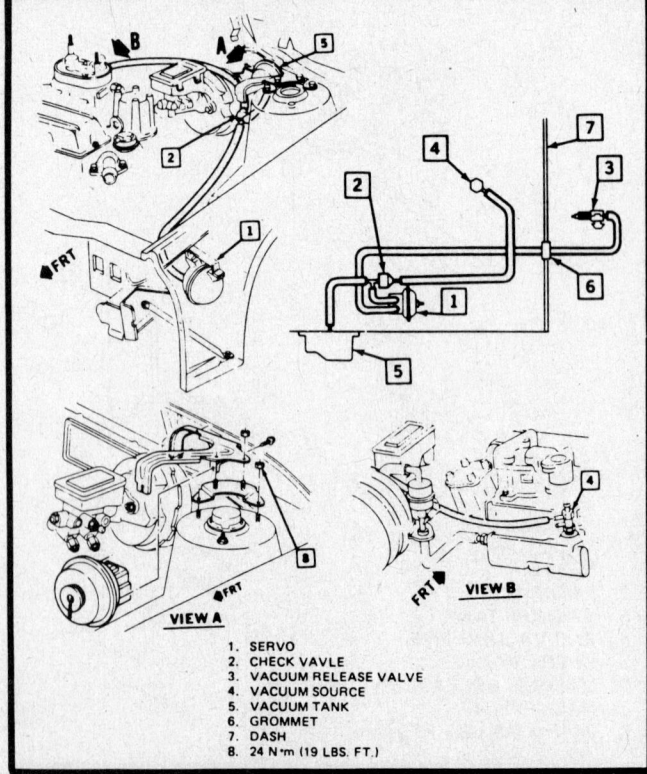

1. SERVO
2. CHECK VAVLE
3. VACUUM RELEASE VALVE
4. VACUUM SOURCE
5. VACUUM TANK
6. GROMMET
7. DASH
8. 24 N·m (19 LBS. FT.)

Cruise control vacuum schematic—1986 and later Firenza with 2.0 liter (EFI) engine

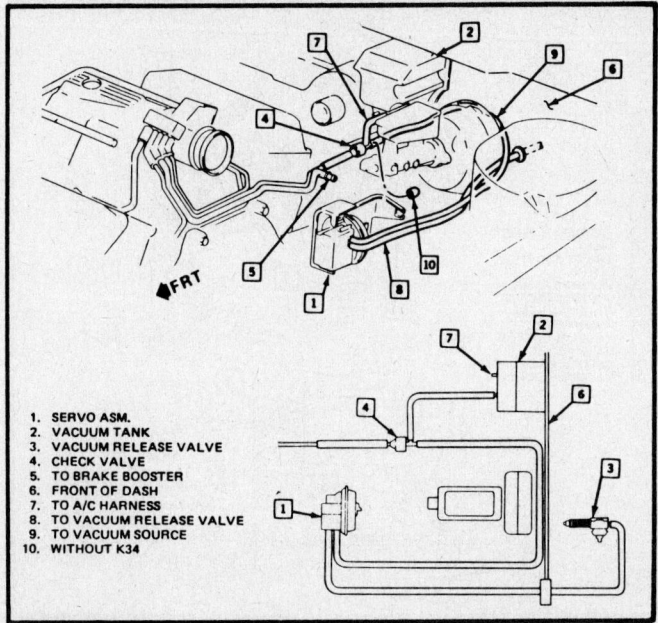

Cruise control vacuum schematic—1985 98 with 3.8 liter engine

1. SERVO ASM.
2. VACUUM TANK
3. VACUUM RELEASE VALVE
4. CHECK VALVE
5. TO BRAKE BOOSTER
6. FRONT OF DASH
7. TO A/C HARNESS
8. TO VACUUM RELEASE VALVE
9. TO VACUUM SOURCE
10. WITHOUT K34

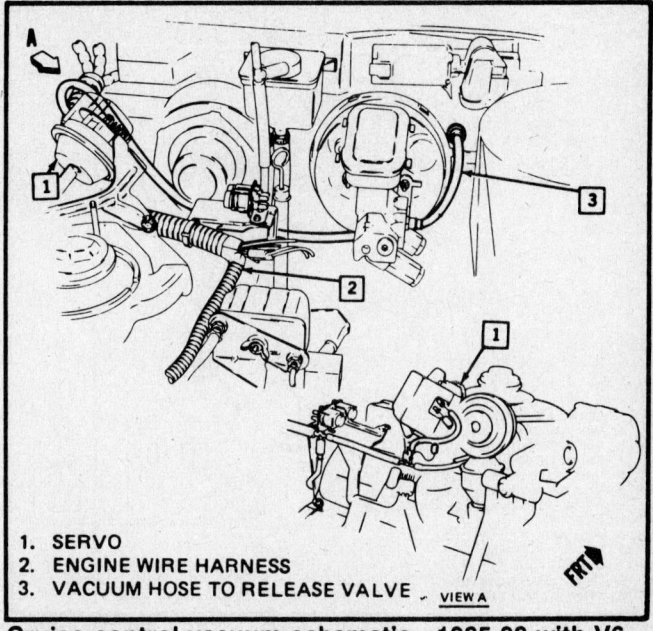

Cruise control vacuum schematic—1985 98 with V6 diesel engine

1. SERVO
2. ENGINE WIRE HARNESS
3. VACUUM HOSE TO RELEASE VALVE

VIEW A

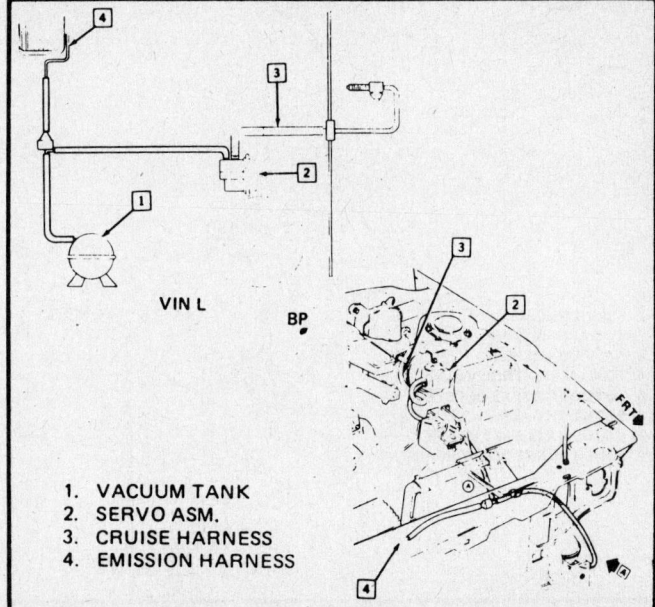

Cruise control vacuum schematic—1985 Calais with 3.0 liter engine

VIN L

1. VACUUM TANK
2. SERVO ASM.
3. CRUISE HARNESS
4. EMISSION HARNESS

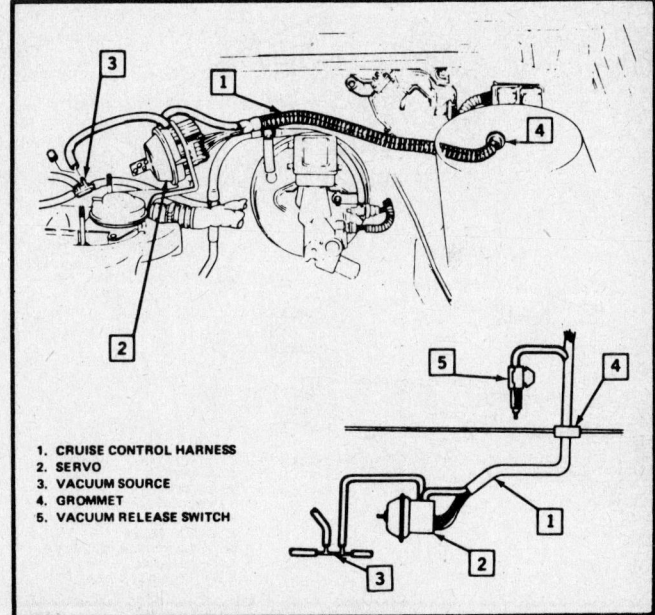

Cruise control vacuum schematic—1984–85 Ciera with V6 diesel engine

1. CRUISE CONTROL HARNESS
2. SERVO
3. VACUUM SOURCE
4. GROMMET
5. VACUUM RELEASE SWITCH

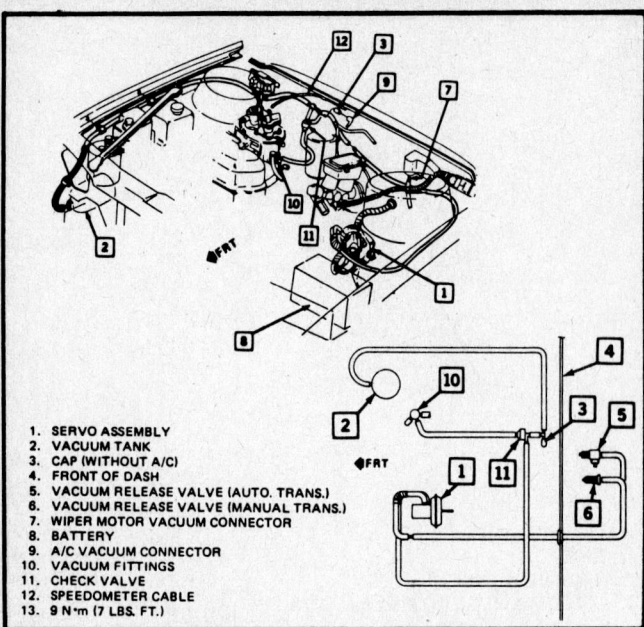

1. SERVO ASSEMBLY
2. VACUUM TANK
3. CAP (WITHOUT A/C)
4. FRONT OF DASH
5. VACUUM RELEASE VALVE (AUTO. TRANS.)
6. VACUUM RELEASE VALVE (MANUAL TRANS.)
7. WIPER MOTOR VACUUM CONNECTOR
8. BATTERY
9. A/C VACUUM CONNECTOR
10. VACUUM FITTINGS
11. CHECK VALVE
12. SPEEDOMETER CABLE
13. 9 N·m (7 LBS. FT.)

Cruise control vacuum schematic—1984–85 Ciera with 2.5 liter engine

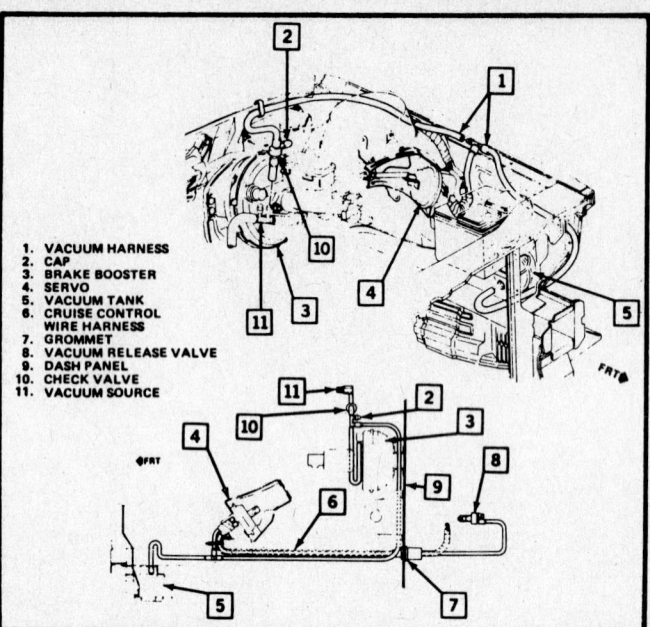

1. VACUUM HARNESS
2. CAP
3. BRAKE BOOSTER
4. SERVO
5. VACUUM TANK
6. CRUISE CONTROL WIRE HARNESS
7. GROMMET
8. VACUUM RELEASE VALVE
9. DASH PANEL
10. CHECK VALVE
11. VACUUM SOURCE

Cruise control vacuum schematic—1984 Firenza with 1.8 liter engine

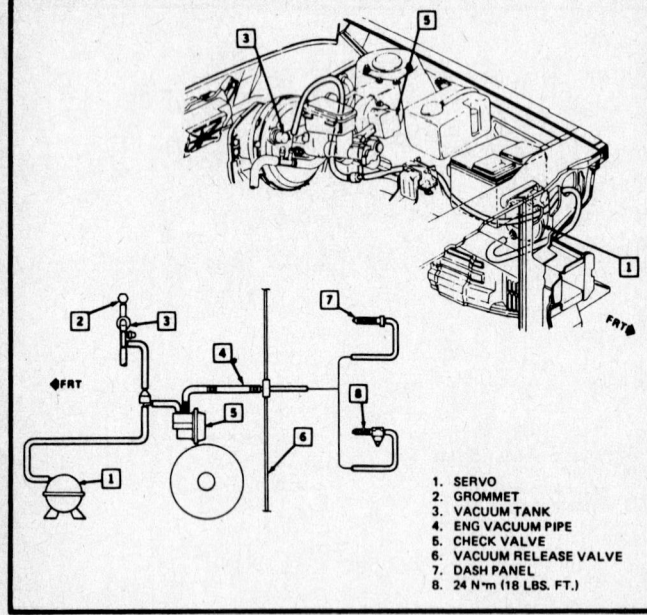

1. SERVO
2. GROMMET
3. VACUUM TANK
4. ENG VACUUM PIPE
5. CHECK VALVE
6. VACUUM RELEASE VALVE
7. DASH PANEL
8. 24 N·m (18 LBS. FT.)

Cruise control vacuum schematic—1985 Firenza with 1.8 liter engine

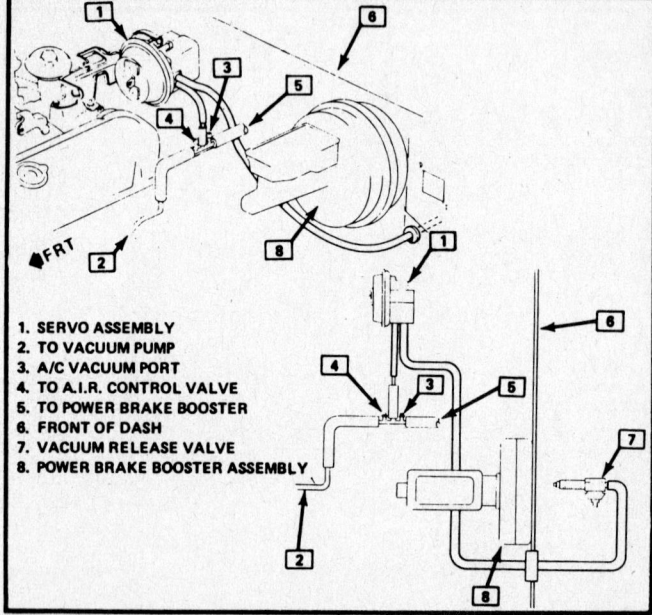

1. SERVO ASSEMBLY
2. TO VACUUM PUMP
3. A/C VACUUM PORT
4. TO A.I.R. CONTROL VALVE
5. TO POWER BRAKE BOOSTER
6. FRONT OF DASH
7. VACUUM RELEASE VALVE
8. POWER BRAKE BOOSTER ASSEMBLY

Cruise control vacuum schematic—1984 Cutlass, Delta 88, 98, Custom Cruiser Toronado with 4.1 liter engine

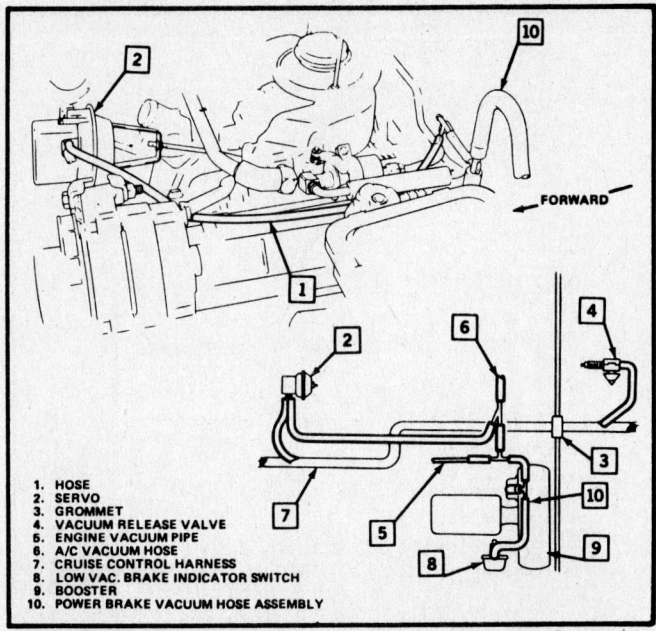

1. HOSE
2. SERVO
3. GROMMET
4. VACUUM RELEASE VALVE
5. ENGINE VACUUM PIPE
6. A/C VACUUM HOSE
7. CRUISE CONTROL HARNESS
8. LOW VAC. BRAKE INDICATOR SWITCH
9. BOOSTER
10. POWER BRAKE VACUUM HOSE ASSEMBLY

Cruise control vacuum schematic—1984–85 Cutlass with V6 diesel engine

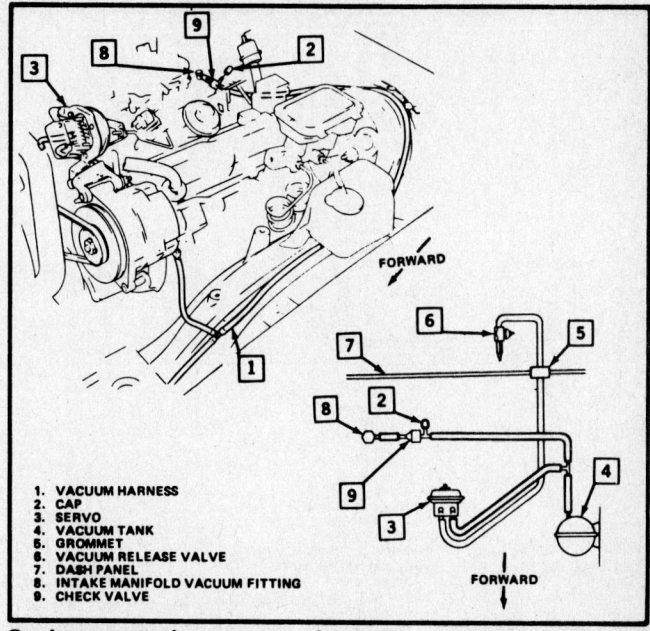

1. VACUUM HARNESS
2. CAP
3. SERVO
4. VACUUM TANK
5. GROMMET
6. VACUUM RELEASE VALVE
7. DASH PANEL
8. INTAKE MANIFOLD VACUUM FITTING
9. CHECK VALVE

Cruise control vacuum schematic—1984–85 Cutlass with V6 gas engine

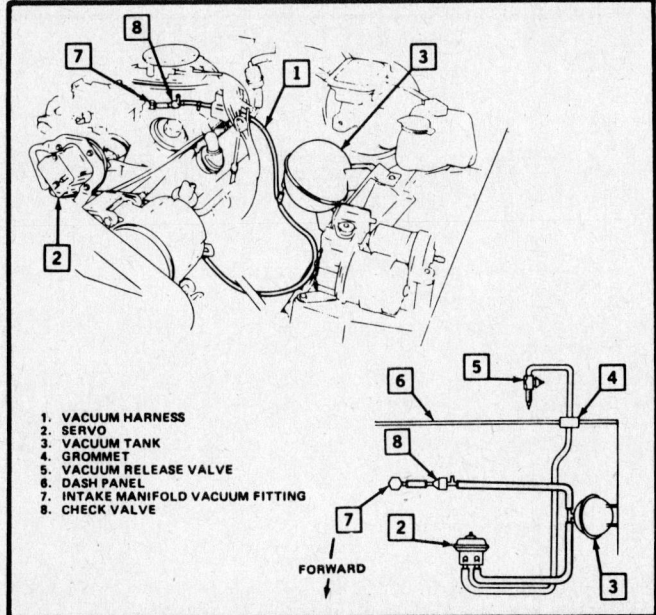

1. VACUUM HARNESS
2. SERVO
3. VACUUM TANK
4. GROMMET
5. VACUUM RELEASE VALVE
6. DASH PANEL
7. INTAKE MANIFOLD VACUUM FITTING
8. CHECK VALVE

Cruise control vacuum schematic—1984–85 Toronado with V8 gas engine

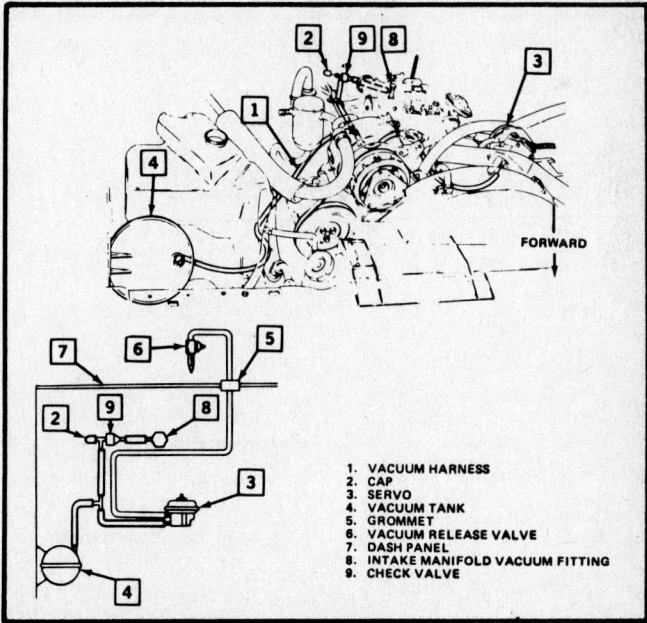

1. VACUUM HARNESS
2. CAP
3. SERVO
4. VACUUM TANK
5. GROMMET
6. VACUUM RELEASE VALVE
7. DASH PANEL
8. INTAKE MANIFOLD VACUUM FITTING
9. CHECK VALVE

Cruise control vacuum schematic—1984–85 Delta 88 and 1984 98 with V8 gas engine

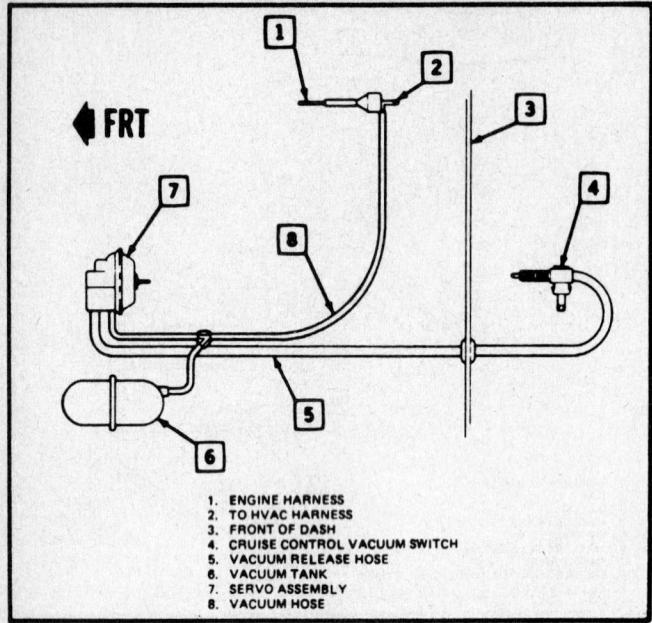

Cruise control vacuum schematic—1986 and later
Toronado

1. ENGINE HARNESS
2. TO HVAC HARNESS
3. FRONT OF DASH
4. CRUISE CONTROL VACUUM SWITCH
5. VACUUM RELEASE HOSE
6. VACUUM TANK
7. SERVO ASSEMBLY
8. VACUUM HOSE

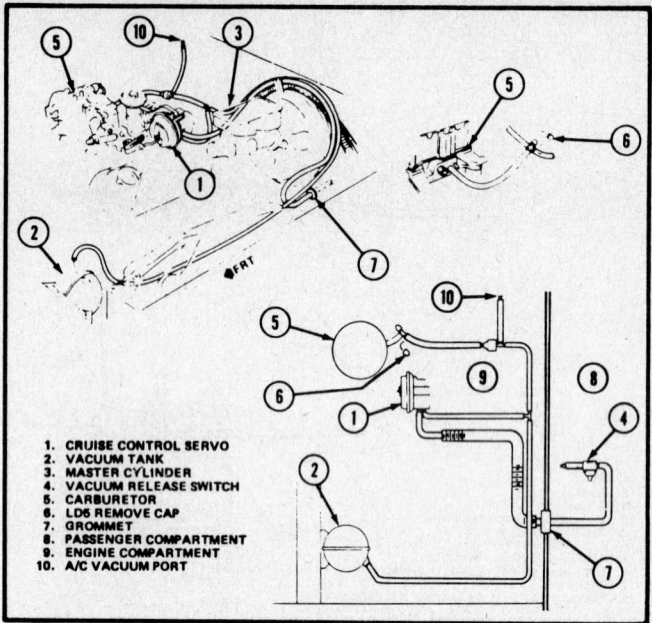

Cruise control vacuum schematic—1986 and later
Cutlass with V6 gas engine

1. CRUISE CONTROL SERVO
2. VACUUM TANK
3. MASTER CYLINDER
4. VACUUM RELEASE SWITCH
5. CARBURETOR
6. LD5 REMOVE CAP
7. GROMMET
8. PASSENGER COMPARTMENT
9. ENGINE COMPARTMENT
10. A/C VACUUM PORT

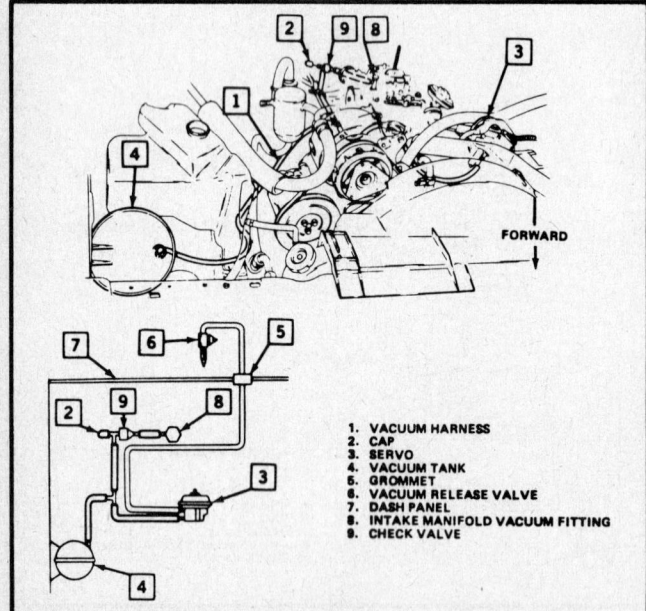

Cruise control vacuum schematic—1986 and later
Custom Cruiser with V8 engine

1. VACUUM HARNESS
2. CAP
3. SERVO
4. VACUUM TANK
5. GROMMET
6. VACUUM RELEASE VALVE
7. DASH PANEL
8. INTAKE MANIFOLD VACUUM FITTING
9. CHECK VALVE

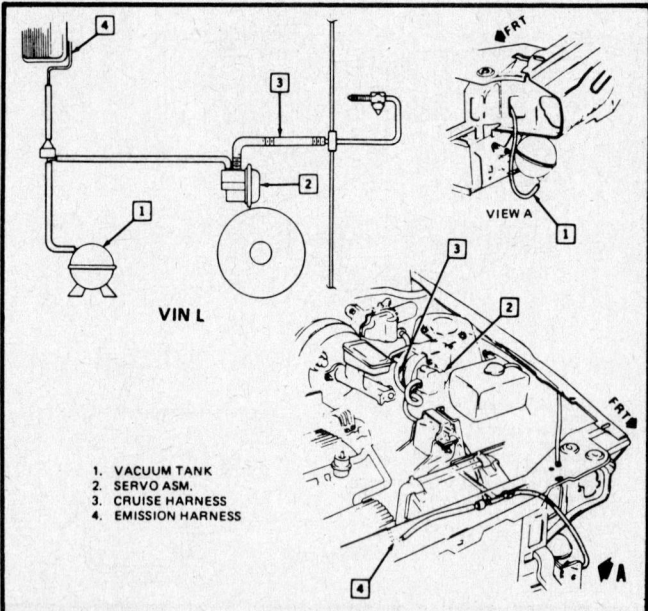

Cruise control vacuum schematic—1985 ands later
Calais with 3.0 liter engine

1. VACUUM TANK
2. SERVO ASM.
3. CRUISE HARNESS
4. EMISSION HARNESS

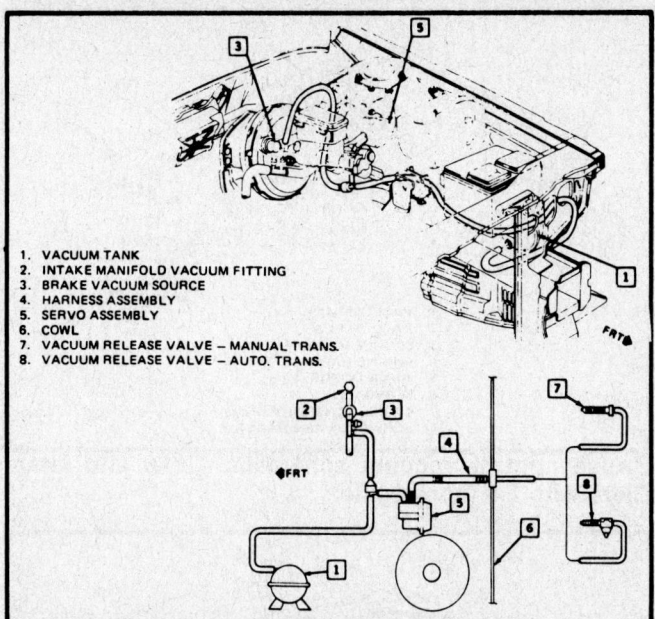

1. VACUUM TANK
2. INTAKE MANIFOLD VACUUM FITTING
3. BRAKE VACUUM SOURCE
4. HARNESS ASSEMBLY
5. SERVO ASSEMBLY
6. COWL
7. VACUUM RELEASE VALVE – MANUAL TRANS.
8. VACUUM RELEASE VALVE – AUTO. TRANS.

Cruise control vacuum schematic – 1986 and later Firenza with 1.8 liter (EFI) engine

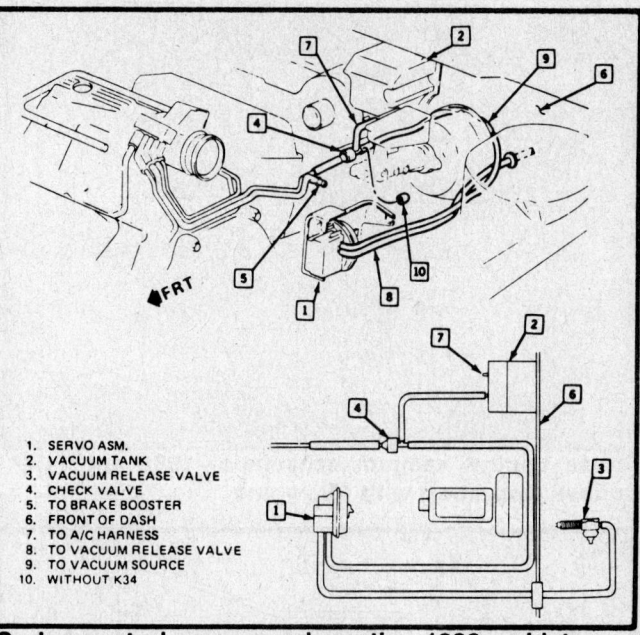

1. SERVO ASM.
2. VACUUM TANK
3. VACUUM RELEASE VALVE
4. CHECK VALVE
5. TO BRAKE BOOSTER
6. FRONT OF DASH
7. TO A/C HARNESS
8. TO VACUUM RELEASE VALVE
9. TO VACUUM SOURCE
10. WITHOUT K34

Cruise control vacuum schematic – 1986 and later Delta 88 and 98 with V6 engine

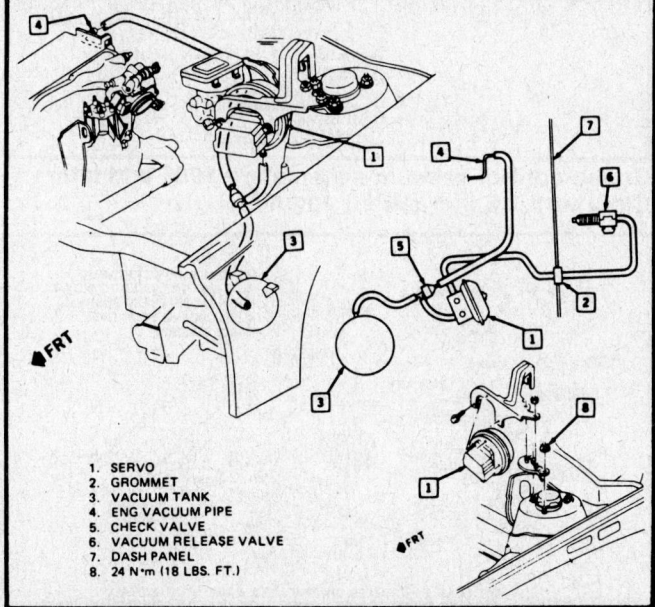

1. SERVO
2. GROMMET
3. VACUUM TANK
4. ENG VACUUM PIPE
5. CHECK VALVE
6. VACUUM RELEASE VALVE
7. DASH PANEL
8. 24 N·m (18 LBS. FT.)

Cruise control vacuum schematic – 1986 and later Firenza with 2.8 liter (MPFI) engine

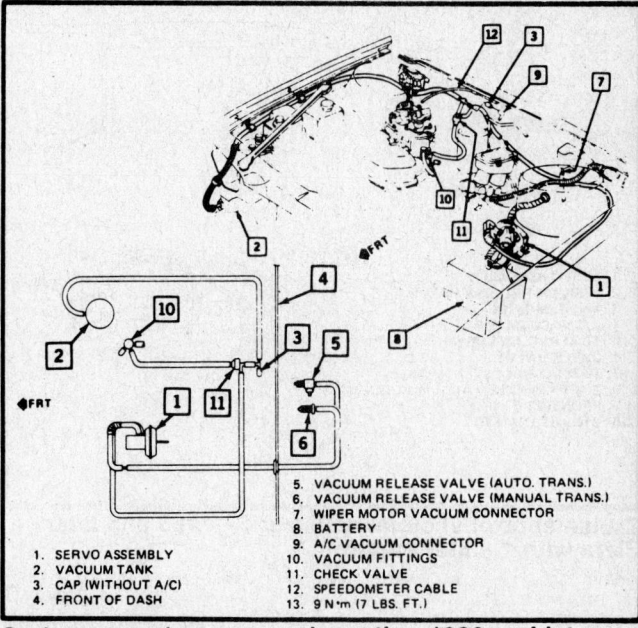

1. SERVO ASSEMBLY
2. VACUUM TANK
3. CAP (WITHOUT A/C)
4. FRONT OF DASH
5. VACUUM RELEASE VALVE (AUTO. TRANS.)
6. VACUUM RELEASE VALVE (MANUAL TRANS.)
7. WIPER MOTOR VACUUM CONNECTOR
8. BATTERY
9. A/C VACUUM CONNECTOR
10. VACUUM FITTINGS
11. CHECK VALVE
12. SPEEDOMETER CABLE
13. 9 N·m (7 LBS. FT.)

Cruise control vacuum schematic – 1986 and later Ciera with 2.5 liter engine

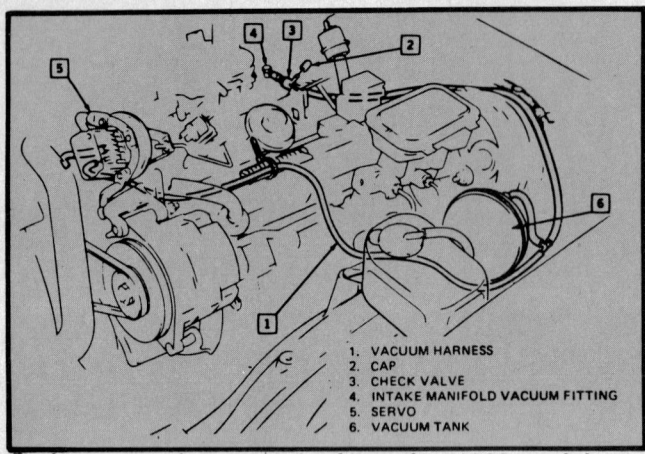

1. VACUUM HARNESS
2. CAP
3. CHECK VALVE
4. INTAKE MANIFOLD VACUUM FITTING
5. SERVO
6. VACUUM TANK

Cruise control vacuum schematic—1986 and later Cutlass (two door) with V8 engine

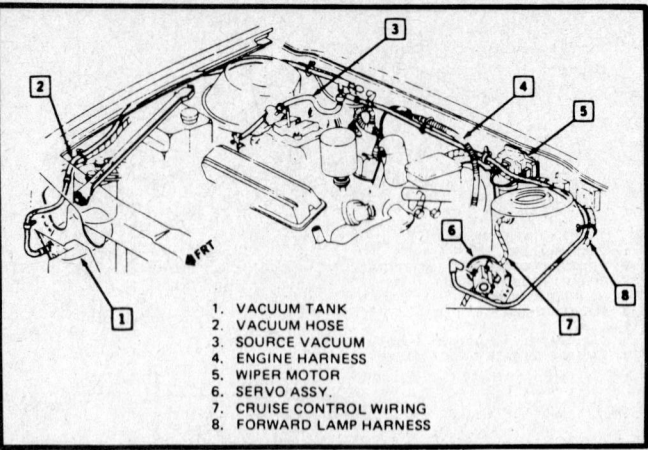

1. VACUUM TANK
2. VACUUM HOSE
3. SOURCE VACUUM
4. ENGINE HARNESS
5. WIPER MOTOR
6. SERVO ASSY.
7. CRUISE CONTROL WIRING
8. FORWARD LAMP HARNESS

Cruise control vacuum schematic—1986 and later Ciera with 2.8 liter engine

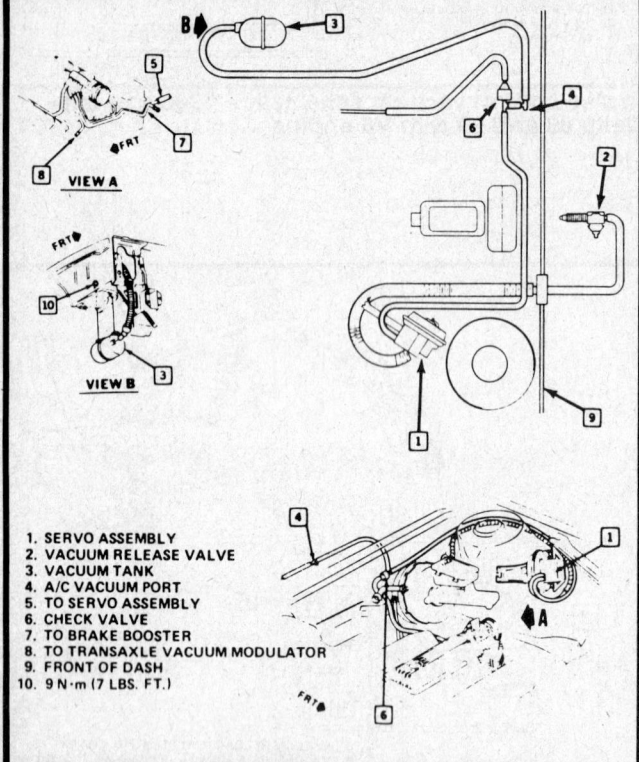

1. SERVO ASSEMBLY
2. VACUUM RELEASE VALVE
3. VACUUM TANK
4. A/C VACUUM PORT
5. TO SERVO ASSEMBLY
6. CHECK VALVE
7. TO BRAKE BOOSTER
8. TO TRANSAXLE VACUUM MODULATOR
9. FRONT OF DASH
10. 9 N·m (7 LBS. FT.)

Cruise control vacuum schematic—1986 and later Ciera with 2.8 liter engine

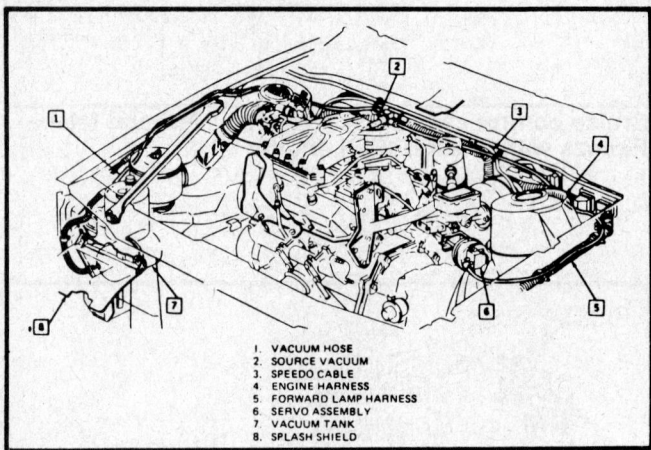

1. VACUUM HOSE
2. SOURCE VACUUM
3. SPEEDO CABLE
4. ENGINE HARNESS
5. FORWARD LAMP HARNESS
6. SERVO ASSEMBLY
7. VACUUM TANK
8. SPLASH SHIELD

Cruise control vacuum schematic—1986 and later Ciera with 2.8 liter (MPFI) engine

TRANSDUCER ORIFICE TUBE ADJUSTMENT (1982–83)

1. If cruise control speed is consistently above the set cruise control speed screw the orifice tube inward. If cruise control speed is below the set cruise control speed screw the orifice tube outward.

2. Each one-fourth turn of the orifice tube changes the cruising speed about one mile per hour.

3. After making the adjustment, be sure to secure the locknut to the orifice tube.

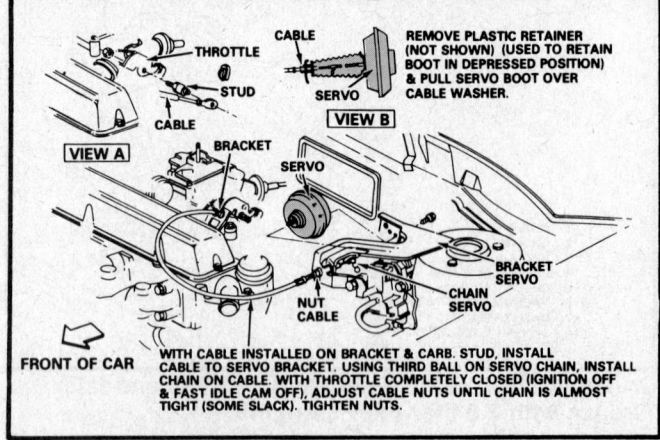

REMOVE PLASTIC RETAINER (NOT SHOWN) (USED TO RETAIN BOOT IN DEPRESSED POSITION) & PULL SERVO BOOT OVER CABLE WASHER.

WITH CABLE INSTALLED ON BRACKET & CARB. STUD, INSTALL CABLE TO SERVO BRACKET. USING THIRD BALL ON SERVO CHAIN, INSTALL CHAIN ON CABLE. WITH THROTTLE COMPLETELY CLOSED (IGNITION OFF & FAST IDLE CAM OFF), ADJUST CABLE NUTS UNTIL CHAIN IS ALMOST TIGHT (SOME SLACK). TIGHTEN NUTS.

Servo and linkage adjustment—1982–83 Firenza with 1.8 liter and 2.0 liter engine

4. Road test the vehicle and check the cruise control operation at 50 miles per hour. If the speed is still not adjusted properly repeat the procedure until the proper results are achieved.

5. If unable to achieve the proper test results the cruise control transducer should be serviced.

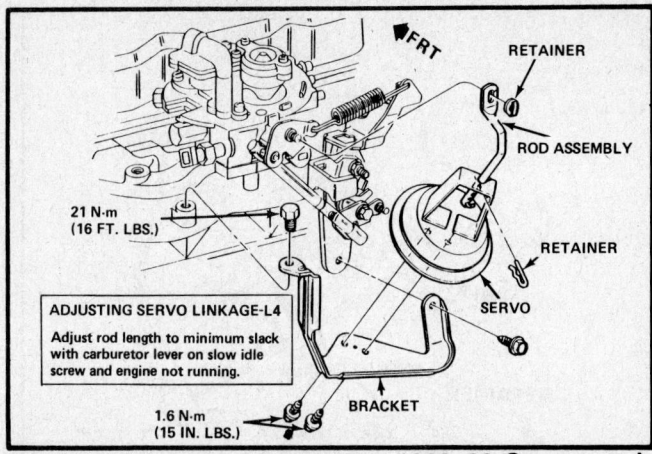

Servo and linkage adjustment — 1982–83 Omega and Ciera with four cylinder engine

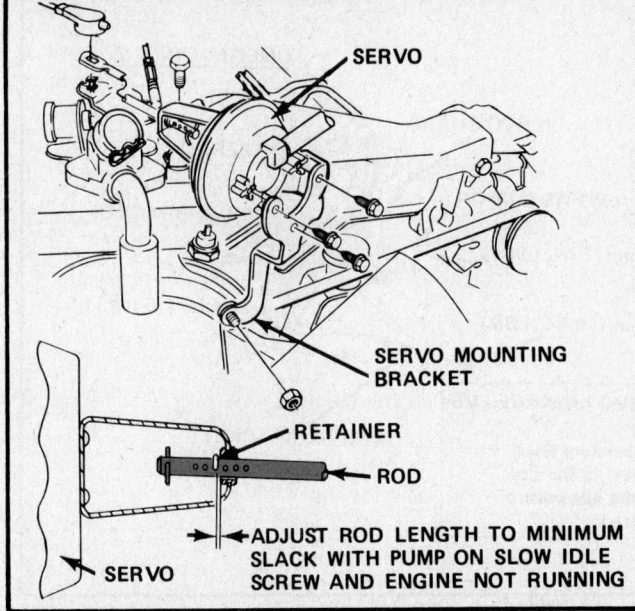

Servo and linkage adjustment — 1982–83 Cutlass, Delta 88, 98 and Toronado with V8 diesel engine

ADJUSTING SERVO LINKAGE-L4

Adjust rod length to minimum slack with carburetor lever on slow idle screw and engine not running.

21 N·m (16 FT. LBS.)

1.6 N·m (15 IN. LBS.)

SERVO

SERVO MOUNTING BRACKET

RETAINER

ROD

ADJUST ROD LENGTH TO MINIMUM SLACK WITH PUMP ON SLOW IDLE SCREW AND ENGINE NOT RUNNING

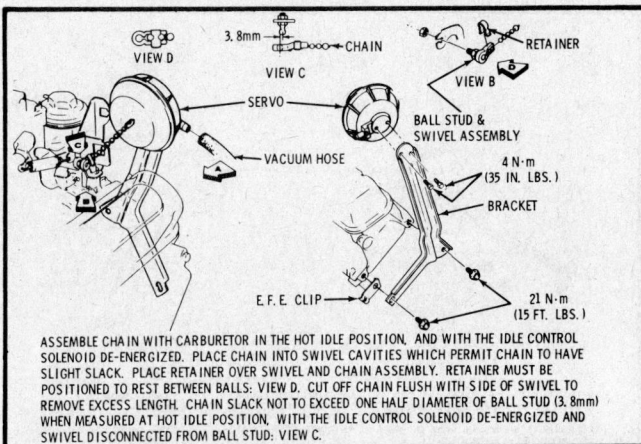

Servo and linkage adjustment — 1982–83 Cutlass with V6 gas engine

ASSEMBLE CHAIN WITH CARBURETOR IN THE HOT IDLE POSITION, AND WITH THE IDLE CONTROL SOLENOID DE-ENERGIZED. PLACE CHAIN INTO SWIVEL CAVITIES WHICH PERMIT CHAIN TO HAVE SLIGHT SLACK. PLACE RETAINER OVER SWIVEL AND CHAIN ASSEMBLY. RETAINER MUST BE POSITIONED TO REST BETWEEN BALLS: VIEW D. CUT OFF CHAIN FLUSH WITH SIDE OF SWIVEL TO REMOVE EXCESS LENGTH. CHAIN SLACK NOT TO EXCEED ONE HALF DIAMETER OF BALL STUD (3.8mm) WHEN MEASURED AT HOT IDLE POSITION, WITH THE IDLE CONTROL SOLENOID DE-ENERGIZED AND SWIVEL DISCONNECTED FROM BALL STUD: VIEW C.

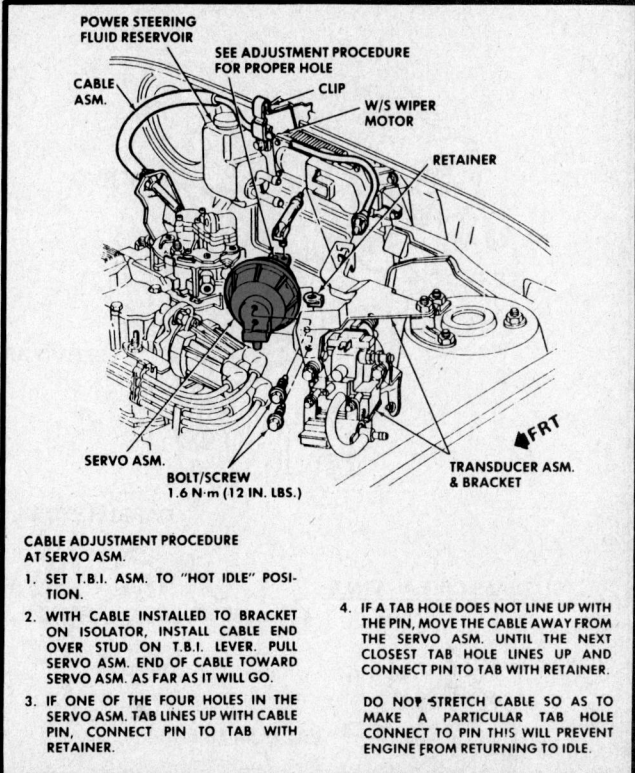

Servo and linkage adjustment — 1982–83 Firenza with TBI

CABLE ADJUSTMENT PROCEDURE AT SERVO ASM.

1. SET T.B.I. ASM. TO "HOT IDLE" POSITION.

2. WITH CABLE INSTALLED TO BRACKET ON ISOLATOR, INSTALL CABLE END OVER STUD ON T.B.I. LEVER. PULL SERVO ASM. END OF CABLE TOWARD SERVO ASM. AS FAR AS IT WILL GO.

3. IF ONE OF THE FOUR HOLES IN THE SERVO ASM. TAB LINES UP WITH CABLE PIN, CONNECT PIN TO TAB WITH RETAINER.

4. IF A TAB HOLE DOES NOT LINE UP WITH THE PIN, MOVE THE CABLE AWAY FROM THE SERVO ASM. UNTIL THE NEXT CLOSEST TAB HOLE LINES UP AND CONNECT PIN TO TAB WITH RETAINER.

DO NOT STRETCH CABLE SO AS TO MAKE A PARTICULAR TAB HOLE CONNECT TO PIN THIS WILL PREVENT ENGINE FROM RETURNING TO IDLE.

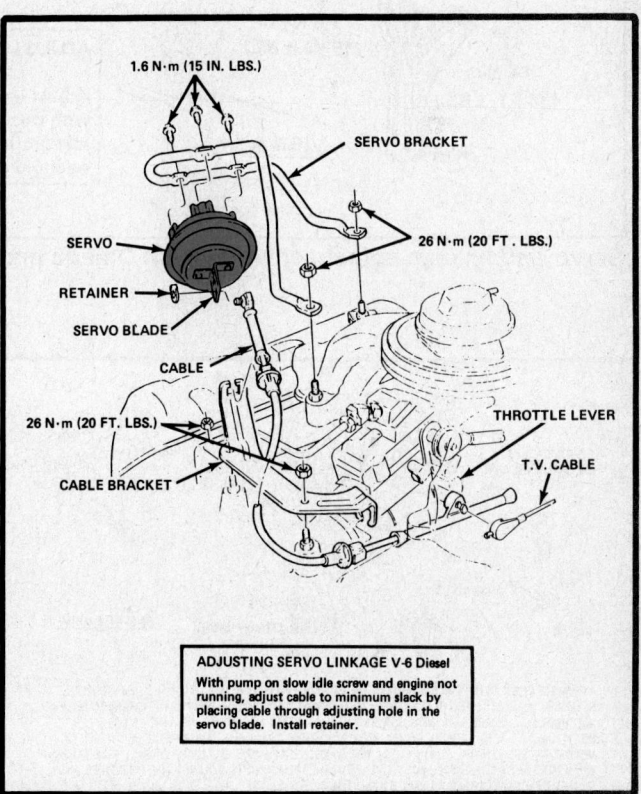

Servo and linkage adjustment — 1982–83 Omega and Ciera with V6 diesel engine

ADJUSTING SERVO LINKAGE V-6 Diesel

With pump on slow idle screw and engine not running, adjust cable to minimum slack by placing cable through adjusting hole in the servo blade. Install retainer.

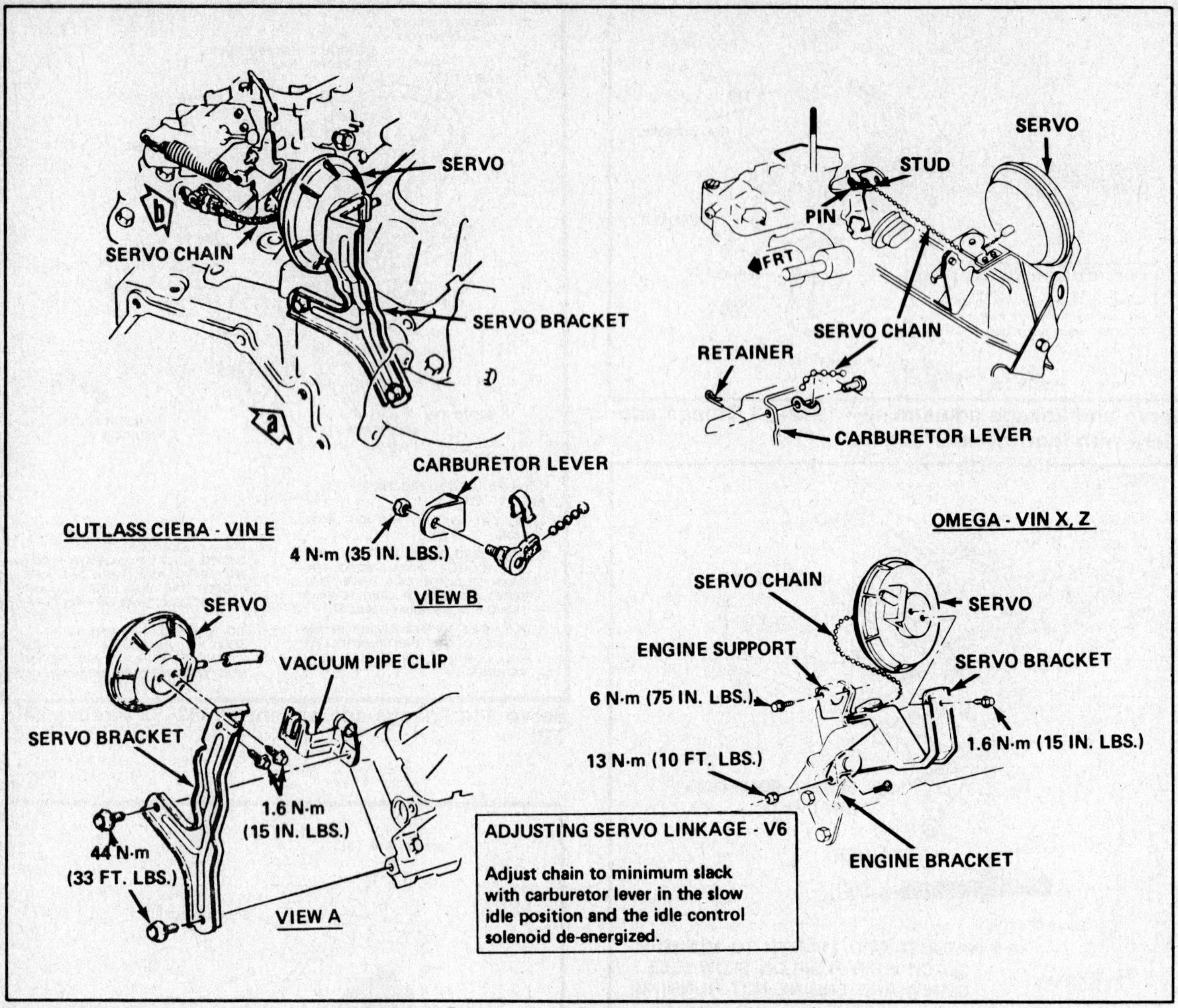

SERVO

SERVO CHAIN

SERVO BRACKET

STUD

PIN

FRT

SERVO

SERVO CHAIN

RETAINER

CARBURETOR LEVER

CARBURETOR LEVER

CUTLASS CIERA - VIN E

4 N·m (35 IN. LBS.)

VIEW B

OMEGA - VIN X, Z

SERVO

VACUUM PIPE CLIP

SERVO BRACKET

1.6 N·m (15 IN. LBS.)

44 N·m (33 FT. LBS.)

VIEW A

SERVO CHAIN

SERVO

ENGINE SUPPORT

SERVO BRACKET

6 N·m (75 IN. LBS.)

1.6 N·m (15 IN. LBS.)

13 N·m (10 FT. LBS.)

ENGINE BRACKET

ADJUSTING SERVO LINKAGE - V6

Adjust chain to minimum slack with carburetor lever in the slow idle position and the idle control solenoid de-energized.

Servo and linkage adjustment—1982–83 Omega and Ciera with V6 gas engine

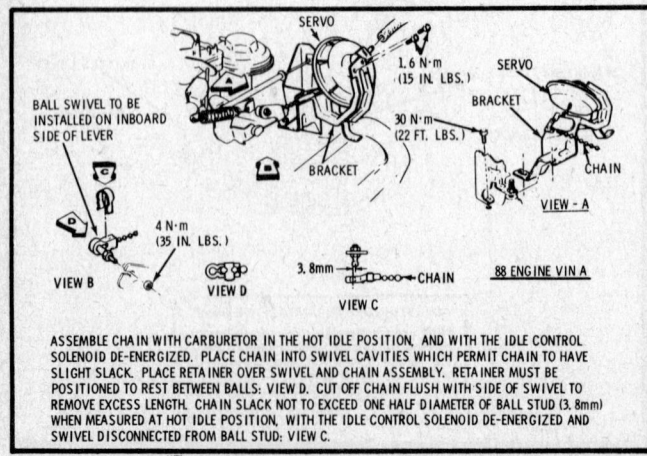

Servo and linkage adjustment—1982–83 Delta 88 and 98 with V6 gas engine

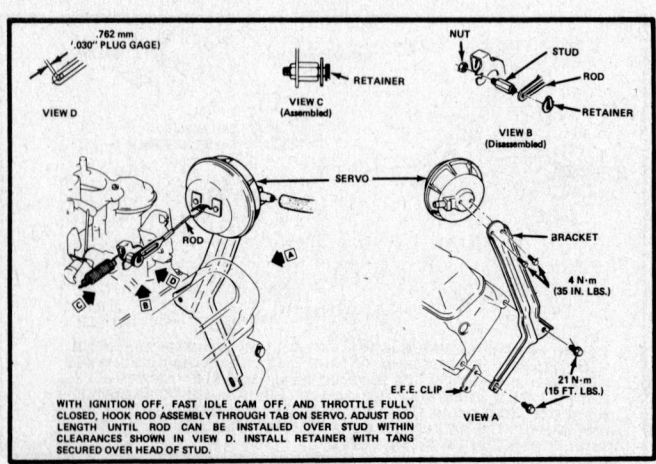

Servo and linkage adjustment—1982–83 Toronado with V6 gas engine

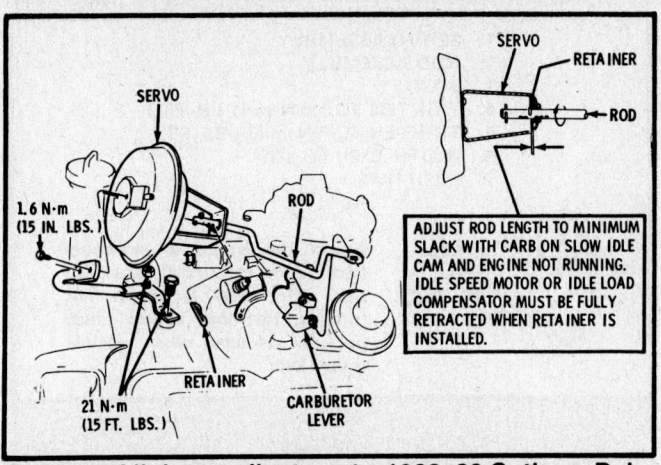

Servo and linkage adjustment—1982–83 Cutlass, Delta 88, 98 and Toronado with 5.0 liter gas engine

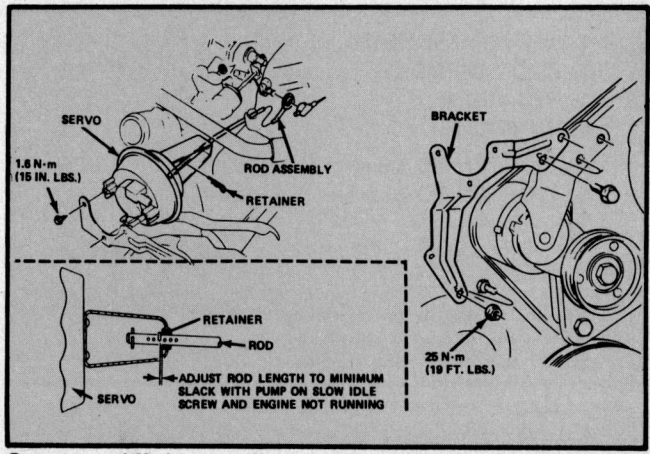

Servo and linkage adjustment—1982–83 Cutlass with V6 diesel engine

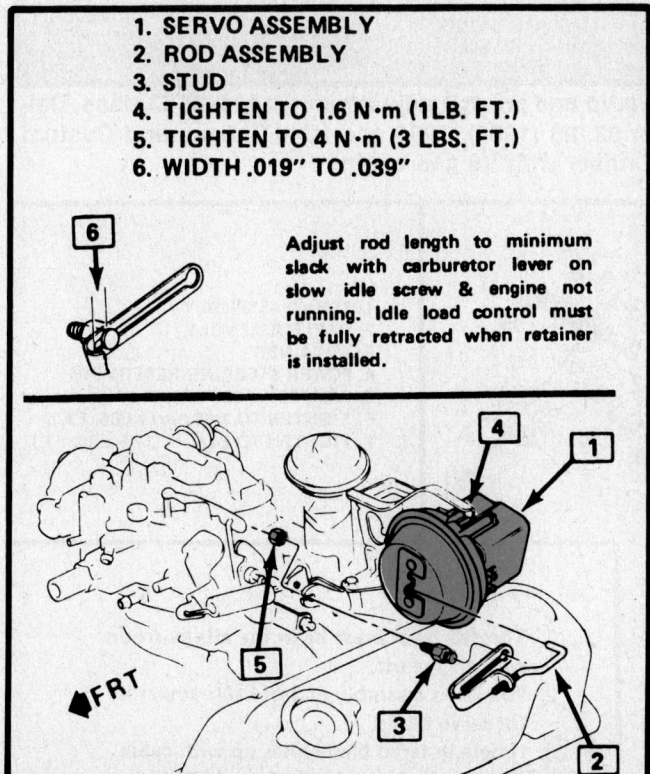

1. SERVO ASSEMBLY
2. ROD ASSEMBLY
3. STUD
4. TIGHTEN TO 1.6 N·m (1LB. FT.)
5. TIGHTEN TO 4 N·m (3 LBS. FT.)
6. WIDTH .019" TO .039"

Adjust rod length to minimum slack with carburetor lever on slow idle screw & engine not running. Idle load control must be fully retracted when retainer is installed.

Servo and linkage adjustment—1984–85 Cutlass, Delta 88, 98 and Custom Cruiser with 3.8 liter engine

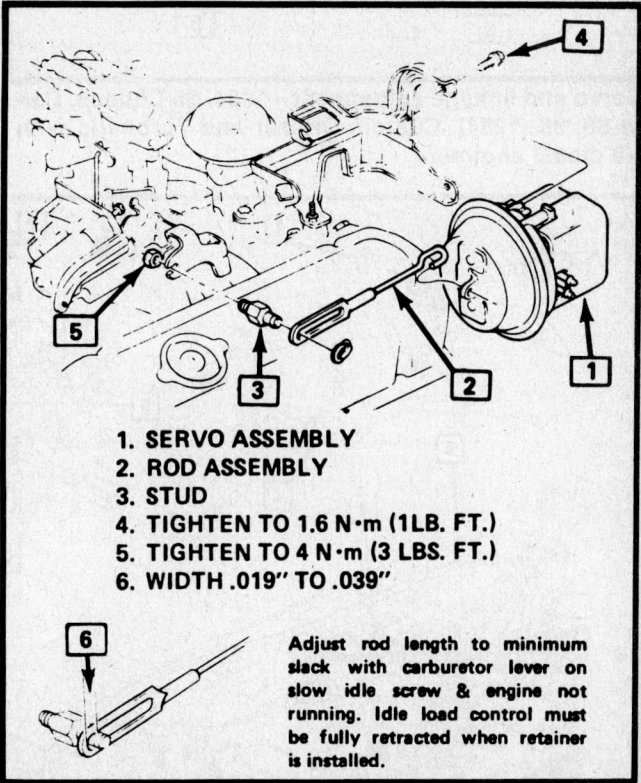

1. SERVO ASSEMBLY
2. ROD ASSEMBLY
3. STUD
4. TIGHTEN TO 1.6 N·m (1LB. FT.)
5. TIGHTEN TO 4 N·m (3 LBS. FT.)
6. WIDTH .019" TO .039"

Adjust rod length to minimum slack with carburetor lever on slow idle screw & engine not running. Idle load control must be fully retracted when retainer is installed.

Servo and linkage adjustment—1984–85 Toronado with 4.1 liter engine

1. SERVO ASSEMBLY
2. ROD ASSEMBLY
3. RETAINER
4. BRACKET
5. TIGHTEN TO 1.6 N·m (1 LB. FT.)
6. TIGHTEN TO 21 N·m (16 LBS. FT.)

Adjust rod length to minimum slack with pump on slow idle screw and engine not running.

Servo and linkage adjustment — 1984–85 Cutlass, Delta 88, 98 (1984), Custom Cruiser and Toronado with V8 diesel engine

1. SERVO ASSEMBLY
2. ROD ASSEMBLY
3. STUD
4. TIGHTEN TO 1.6 N·m (1 LB. FT.)
5. TIGHTEN TO 4 N·m (3 LBS. FT.)
6. WIDTH .019'' TO .039''
7. PUSH NUT

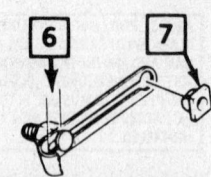

Adjust rod length to minimum slack with carburetor lever on slow idle screw & engine not running. Idle load control must be fully retracted when retainer is installed.

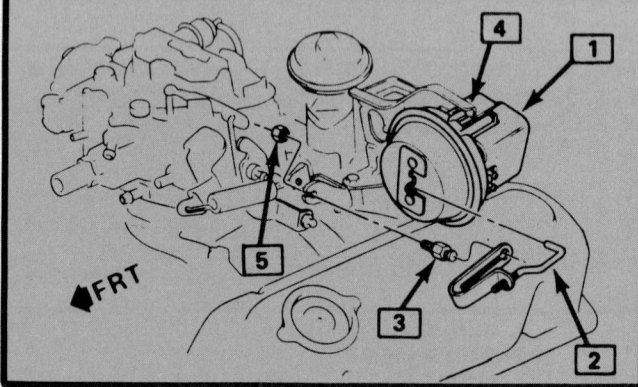

Servo and linkage adjustment — 1984–85 Cutlass, Delta 88, 98 (1984), 1986 and later Cutlass and Custom Cruiser with V6 gas engine

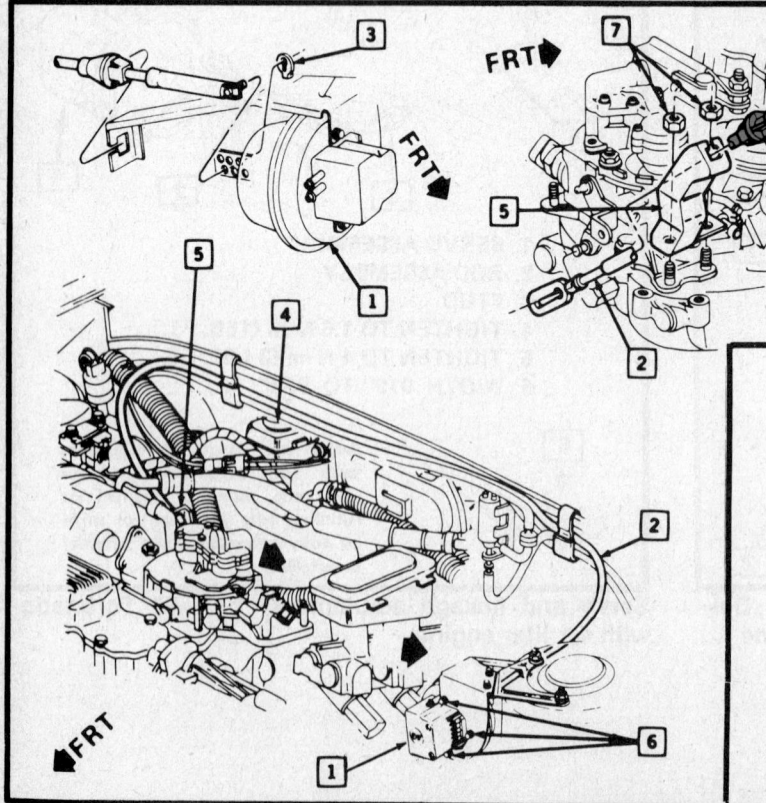

1. SERVO ASSEMBLY
2. CABLE ASSEMBLY
3. RETAINER
4. POWER STEERING RESERVOIR
5. ADAPTER ASSEMBLY
6. TIGHTEN TO 1.6 N·m (1 LBS. FT.)
7. TIGHTEN TO 24 N·m (17.5 LBS. FT.)

1. Throttle lever must be in the idle position with engine off.
2. Pull servo assembly end of cable toward the servo blade.
3. If hole in servo blade lines up with cable pin, install pin in that hole and install retainer.
4. If hole does not align with the pin, install pin in the next hole away from servo assembly.

CAUTION: Do not stretch cable as this will prevent engine from returning to idle.

Servo and linkage adjustment — 1984–85 Firenza with 1.8 liter engine

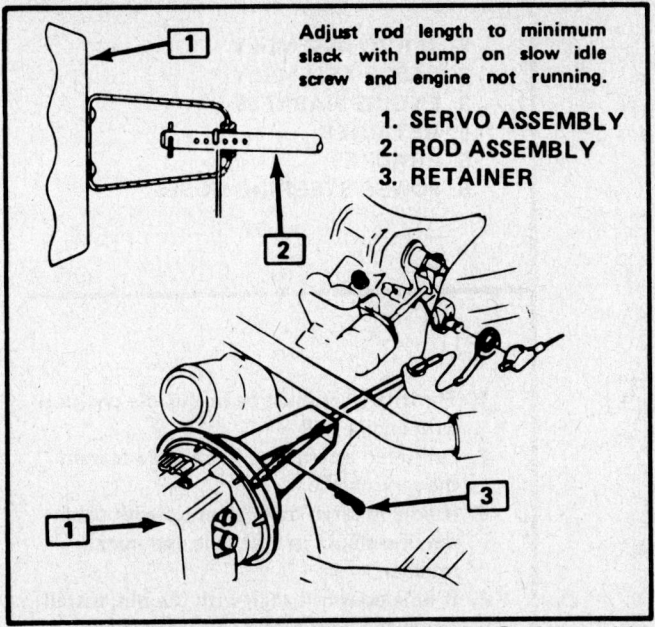

Adjust rod length to minimum slack with pump on slow idle screw and engine not running.

1. SERVO ASSEMBLY
2. ROD ASSEMBLY
3. RETAINER

Servo and linkage adjustment — 1984–85 Cutlass with V6 diesel engine

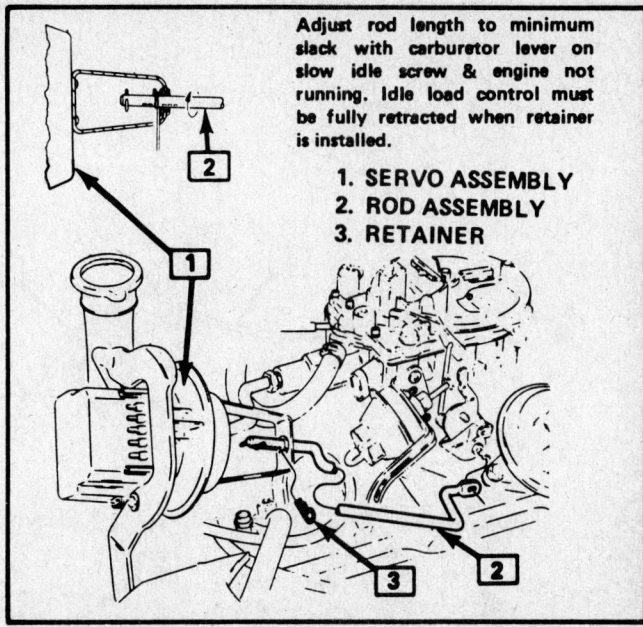

Adjust rod length to minimum slack with carburetor lever on slow idle screw & engine not running. Idle load control must be fully retracted when retainer is installed.

1. SERVO ASSEMBLY
2. ROD ASSEMBLY
3. RETAINER

Servo and linkage adjustment — 1984–85 Cutlass, Delta 88, 98 (1984), Custom Cruiser, Toronado, 1986 and later Cutlass and Custom Cruiser with 5.0 liter engine

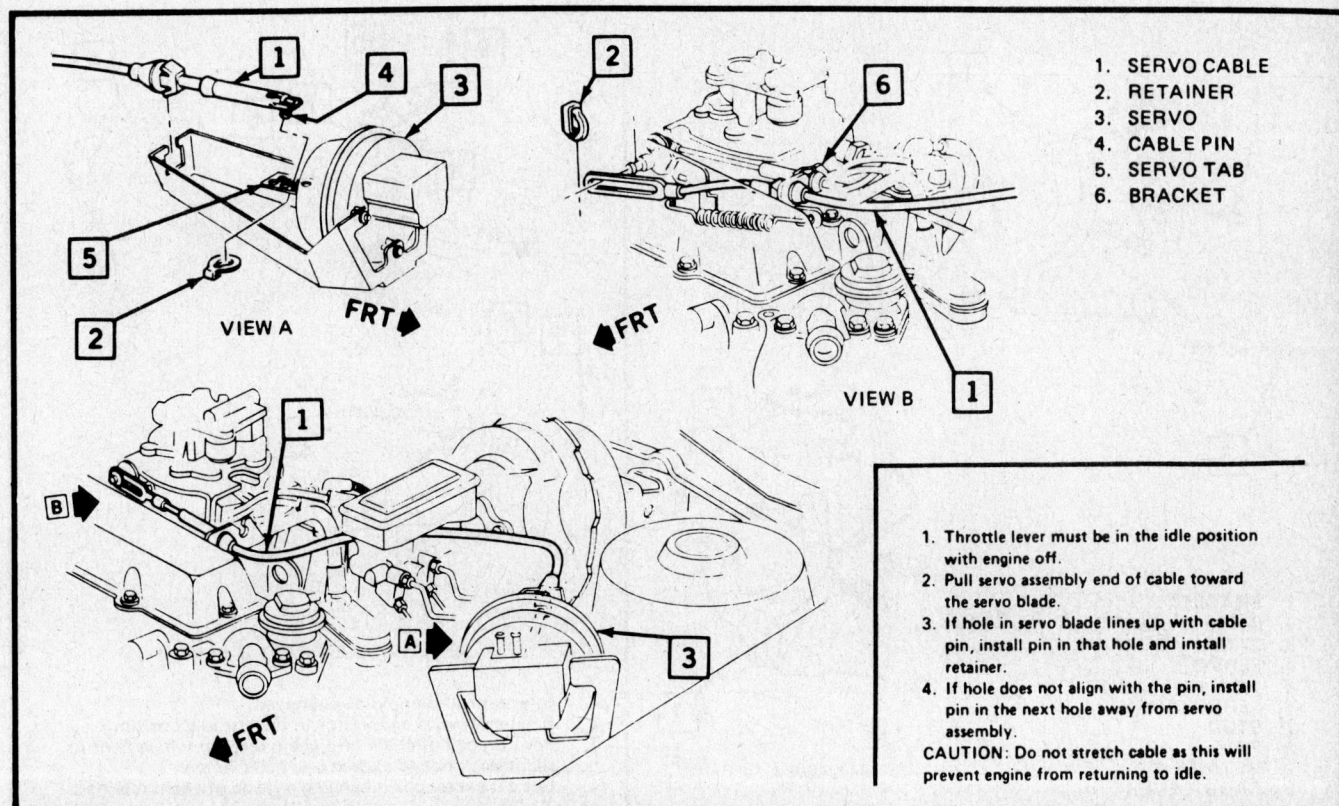

1. SERVO CABLE
2. RETAINER
3. SERVO
4. CABLE PIN
5. SERVO TAB
6. BRACKET

VIEW A

VIEW B

FRT

1. Throttle lever must be in the idle position with engine off.
2. Pull servo assembly end of cable toward the servo blade.
3. If hole in servo blade lines up with cable pin, install pin in that hole and install retainer.
4. If hole does not align with the pin, install pin in the next hole away from servo assembly.

CAUTION: Do not stretch cable as this will prevent engine from returning to idle.

Servo and linkage adjustment — 1984–85 Firenza with 2.0 liter engine

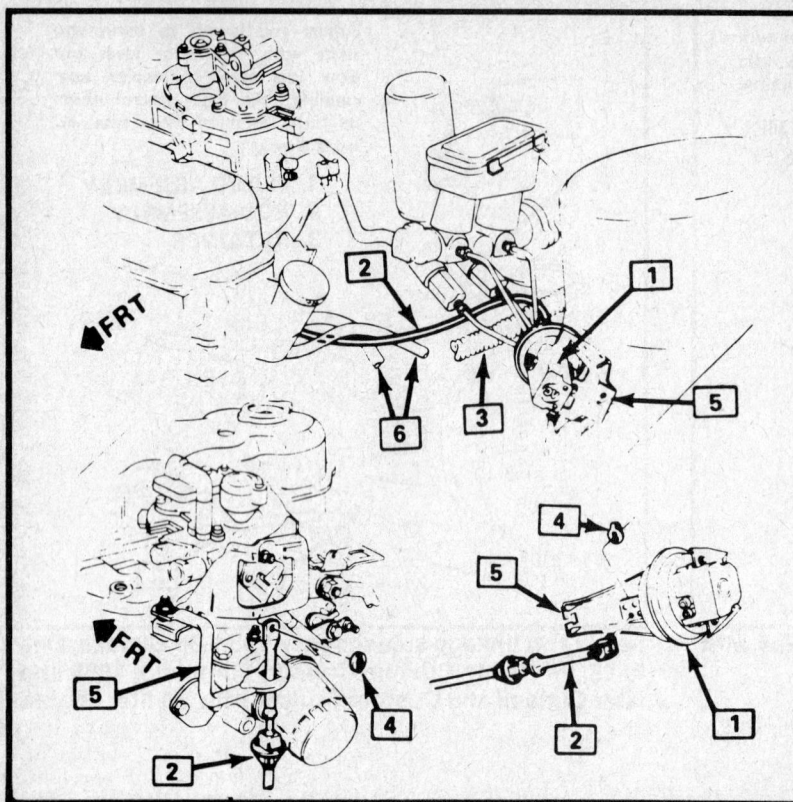

1. SERVO ASSEMBLY
2. CABLE ASSEMBLY
3. ENGINE HARNESS
4. RETAINER
5. BRACKET
6. POWER STEERING HOSES

1. Throttle lever must be in the idle position with engine off.
2. Pull servo assembly end of cable toward the servo blade.
3. If hole in servo blade lines up with cable pin, install pin in that hole and install retainer.
4. If hole does not align with the pin, install pin in the next hole away from servo assembly.

CAUTION: Do not stretch cable as this will prevent engine from returning to idle.

Servo and linkage adjustment—1984 Omega and Ciera with 2.5 liter engine

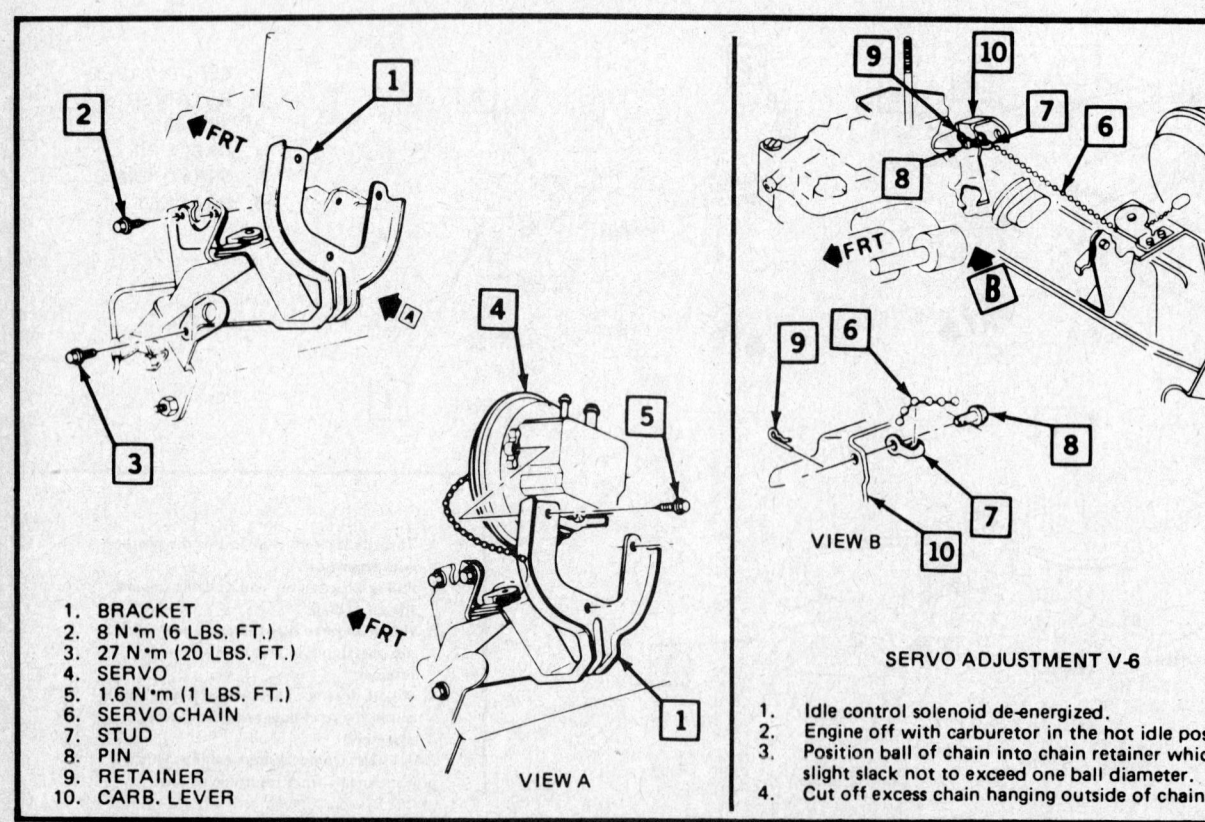

1. BRACKET
2. 8 N·m (6 LBS. FT.)
3. 27 N·m (20 LBS. FT.)
4. SERVO
5. 1.6 N·m (1 LBS. FT.)
6. SERVO CHAIN
7. STUD
8. PIN
9. RETAINER
10. CARB. LEVER

VIEW A

SERVO ADJUSTMENT V-6

1. Idle control solenoid de-energized.
2. Engine off with carburetor in the hot idle position.
3. Position ball of chain into chain retainer which permits slight slack not to exceed one ball diameter.
4. Cut off excess chain hanging outside of chain retainer.

Servo and linkage adjustment—1984 Omega and Ciera with 2.8 liter engine

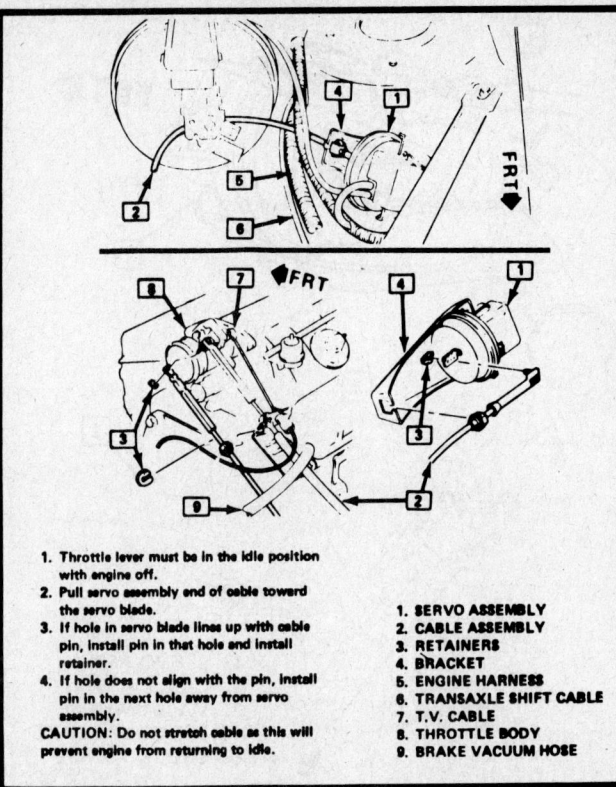

1. Throttle lever must be in the idle position with engine off.
2. Pull servo assembly end of cable toward the servo blade.
3. If hole in servo blade lines up with cable pin, install pin in that hole and install retainer.
4. If hole does not align with the pin, install pin in the next hole away from servo assembly.
CAUTION: Do not stretch cable as this will prevent engine from returning to idle.

1. SERVO ASSEMBLY
2. CABLE ASSEMBLY
3. RETAINERS
4. BRACKET
5. ENGINE HARNESS
6. TRANSAXLE SHIFT CABLE
7. T.V. CABLE
8. THROTTLE BODY
9. BRAKE VACUUM HOSE

Servo and linkage adjustment—1984 Ciera with 3.8 liter engine

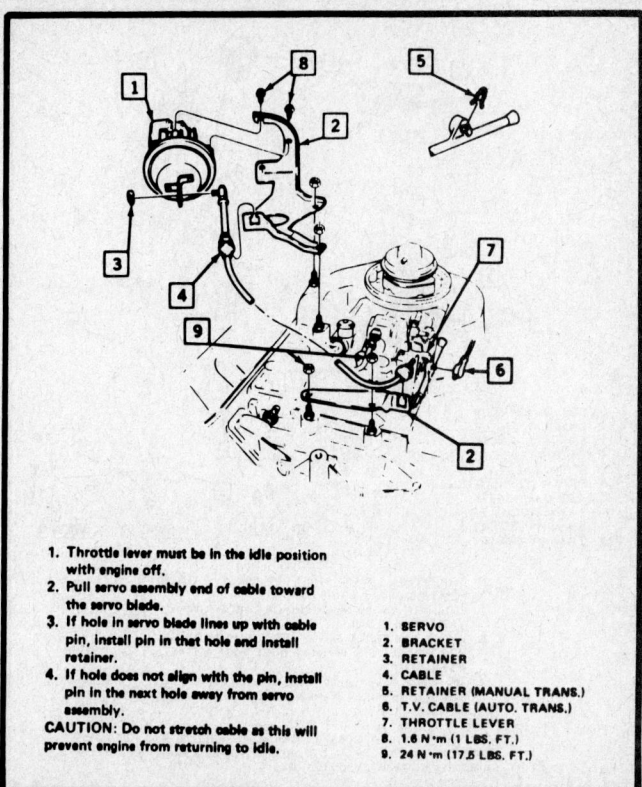

1. Throttle lever must be in the idle position with engine off.
2. Pull servo assembly end of cable toward the servo blade.
3. If hole in servo blade lines up with cable pin, install pin in that hole and install retainer.
4. If hole does not align with the pin, install pin in the next hole away from servo assembly.
CAUTION: Do not stretch cable as this will prevent engine from returning to idle.

1. SERVO
2. BRACKET
3. RETAINER
4. CABLE
5. RETAINER (MANUAL TRANS.)
6. T.V. CABLE (AUTO. TRANS.)
7. THROTTLE LEVER
8. 1.6 N·m (1 LBS. FT.)
9. 24 N·m (17.5 LBS. FT.)

Servo and linkage adjustment—1984–85 Cutlass Cruiser with V6 diesel engine

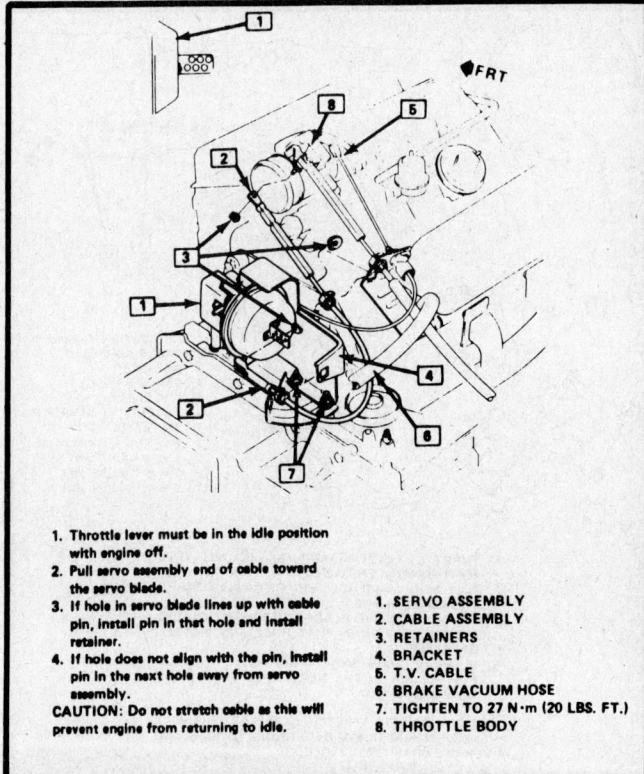

1. Throttle lever must be in the idle position with engine off.
2. Pull servo assembly end of cable toward the servo blade.
3. If hole in servo blade lines up with cable pin, install pin in that hole and install retainer.
4. If hole does not align with the pin, install pin in the next hole away from servo assembly.
CAUTION: Do not stretch cable as this will prevent engine from returning to idle.

1. SERVO ASSEMBLY
2. CABLE ASSEMBLY
3. RETAINERS
4. BRACKET
5. T.V. CABLE
6. BRAKE VACUUM HOSE
7. TIGHTEN TO 27 N·m (20 LBS. FT.)
8. THROTTLE BODY

Servo and linkage adjustment—1985 and later 98 with 3.8 liter engine

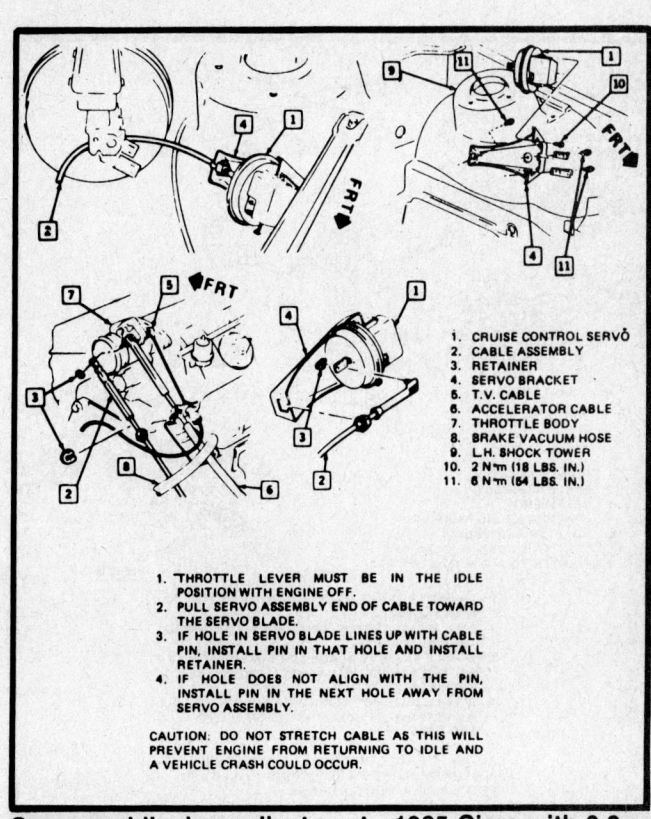

1. THROTTLE LEVER MUST BE IN THE IDLE POSITION WITH ENGINE OFF.
2. PULL SERVO ASSEMBLY END OF CABLE TOWARD THE SERVO BLADE.
3. IF HOLE IN SERVO BLADE LINES UP WITH CABLE PIN, INSTALL PIN IN THAT HOLE AND INSTALL RETAINER.
4. IF HOLE DOES NOT ALIGN WITH THE PIN, INSTALL PIN IN THE NEXT HOLE AWAY FROM SERVO ASSEMBLY.
CAUTION: DO NOT STRETCH CABLE AS THIS WILL PREVENT ENGINE FROM RETURNING TO IDLE AND A VEHICLE CRASH COULD OCCUR.

1. CRUISE CONTROL SERVO
2. CABLE ASSEMBLY
3. RETAINER
4. SERVO BRACKET
5. T.V. CABLE
6. ACCELERATOR CABLE
7. THROTTLE BODY
8. BRAKE VACUUM HOSE
9. L.H. SHOCK TOWER
10. 2 N·m (18 LBS. IN.)
11. 6 N·m (54 LBS. IN.)

Servo and linkage adjustment—1985 Ciera with 3.8 liter engine

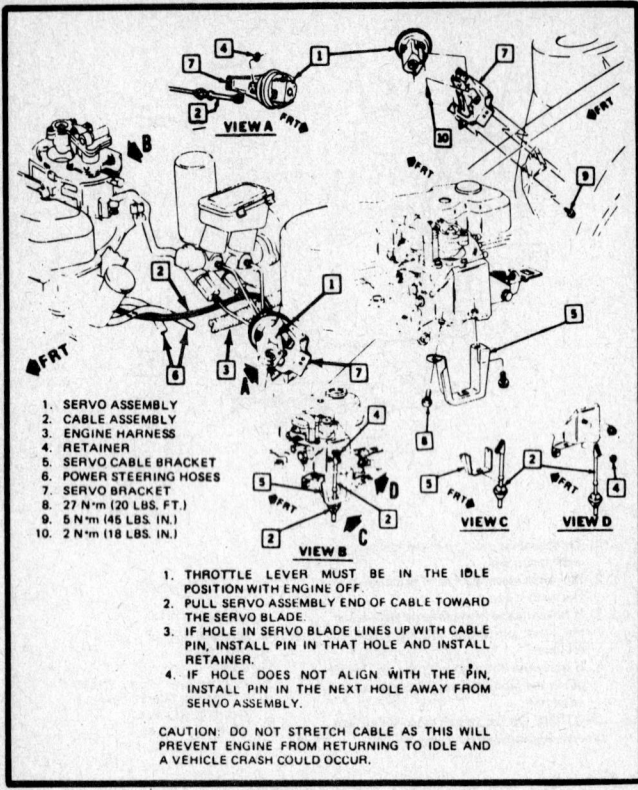

1. SERVO ASSEMBLY
2. CABLE ASSEMBLY
3. ENGINE HARNESS
4. RETAINER
5. SERVO CABLE BRACKET
6. POWER STEERING HOSES
7. SERVO BRACKET
8. 27 N·m (20 LBS. FT.)
9. 5 N·m (45 LBS. IN.)
10. 2 N·m (18 LBS. IN.)

1. THROTTLE LEVER MUST BE IN THE IDLE POSITION WITH ENGINE OFF.
2. PULL SERVO ASSEMBLY END OF CABLE TOWARD THE SERVO BLADE.
3. IF HOLE IN SERVO BLADE LINES UP WITH CABLE PIN, INSTALL PIN IN THAT HOLE AND INSTALL RETAINER.
4. IF HOLE DOES NOT ALIGN WITH THE PIN, INSTALL PIN IN THE NEXT HOLE AWAY FROM SERVO ASSEMBLY.

CAUTION: DO NOT STRETCH CABLE AS THIS WILL PREVENT ENGINE FROM RETURNING TO IDLE AND A VEHICLE CRASH COULD OCCUR.

Servo and linkage adjustment—1985 Ciera with 2.5 liter engine

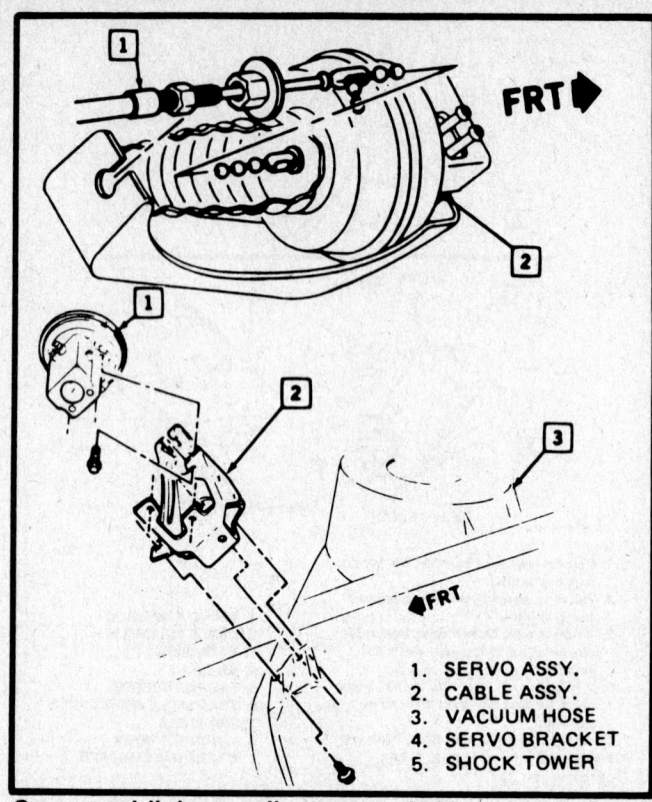

1. SERVO ASSY.
2. CABLE ASSY.
3. VACUUM HOSE
4. SERVO BRACKET
5. SHOCK TOWER

Servo and linkage adjustment—1986 and later Ciera and Cutlass Cruiser with V6 engine

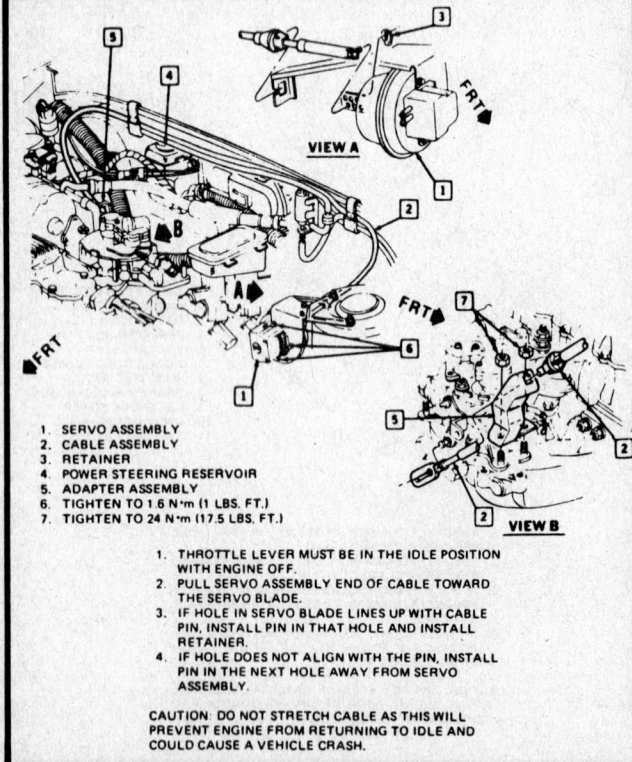

1. SERVO ASSEMBLY
2. CABLE ASSEMBLY
3. RETAINER
4. POWER STEERING RESERVOIR
5. ADAPTER ASSEMBLY
6. TIGHTEN TO 1.6 N·m (1 LBS. FT.)
7. TIGHTEN TO 24 N·m (17.5 LBS. FT.)

1. THROTTLE LEVER MUST BE IN THE IDLE POSITION WITH ENGINE OFF.
2. PULL SERVO ASSEMBLY END OF CABLE TOWARD THE SERVO BLADE.
3. IF HOLE IN SERVO BLADE LINES UP WITH CABLE PIN, INSTALL PIN IN THAT HOLE AND INSTALL RETAINER.
4. IF HOLE DOES NOT ALIGN WITH THE PIN, INSTALL PIN IN THE NEXT HOLE AWAY FROM SERVO ASSEMBLY.

CAUTION: DO NOT STRETCH CABLE AS THIS WILL PREVENT ENGINE FROM RETURNING TO IDLE AND COULD CAUSE A VEHICLE CRASH.

Servo and linkage adjustment—1986 and later Firenza with 1.8 liter (EFI) engine

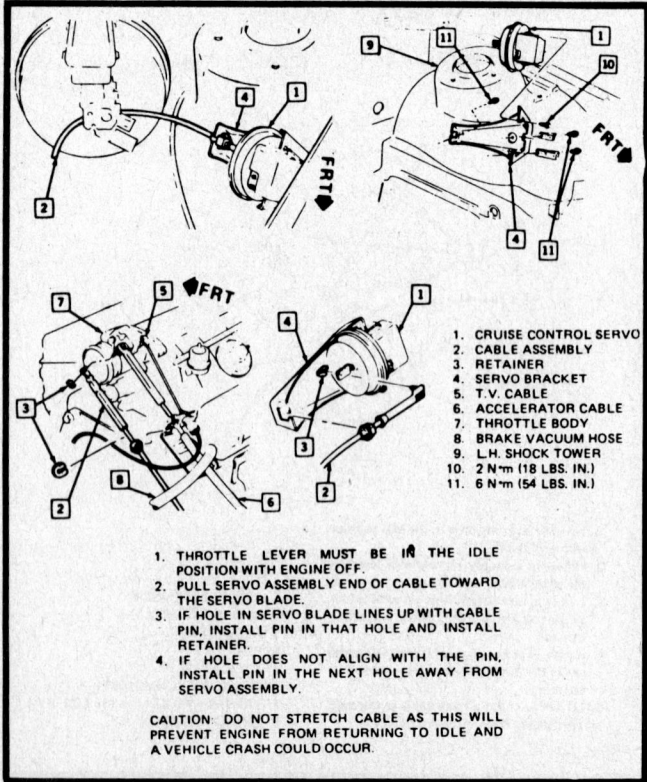

1. CRUISE CONTROL SERVO
2. CABLE ASSEMBLY
3. RETAINER
4. SERVO BRACKET
5. T.V. CABLE
6. ACCELERATOR CABLE
7. THROTTLE BODY
8. BRAKE VACUUM HOSE
9. L.H. SHOCK TOWER
10. 2 N·m (18 LBS. IN.)
11. 6 N·m (54 LBS. IN.)

1. THROTTLE LEVER MUST BE IN THE IDLE POSITION WITH ENGINE OFF.
2. PULL SERVO ASSEMBLY END OF CABLE TOWARD THE SERVO BLADE.
3. IF HOLE IN SERVO BLADE LINES UP WITH CABLE PIN, INSTALL PIN IN THAT HOLE AND INSTALL RETAINER.
4. IF HOLE DOES NOT ALIGN WITH THE PIN, INSTALL PIN IN THE NEXT HOLE AWAY FROM SERVO ASSEMBLY.

CAUTION: DO NOT STRETCH CABLE AS THIS WILL PREVENT ENGINE FROM RETURNING TO IDLE AND A VEHICLE CRASH COULD OCCUR.

Servo and linkage adjustment—1986 and later Ciera and Cutlass Cruiser with 3.8 liter (SFI) engine

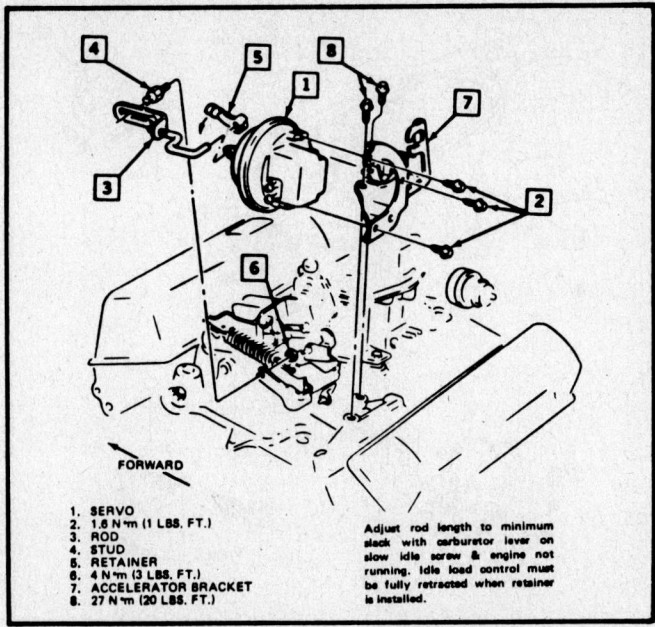

1. SERVO
2. 1.6 N·m (1 LBS. FT.)
3. ROD
4. STUD
5. RETAINER
6. 4 N·m (3 LBS. FT.)
7. ACCELERATOR BRACKET
8. 27 N·m (20 LBS. FT.)

Adjust rod length to minimum slack with carburetor lever on slow idle screw & engine not running. Idle load control must be fully retracted when retainer is installed.

Servo and linkage adjustment—1984–85 Omega and Ciera with 3.0 liter engine

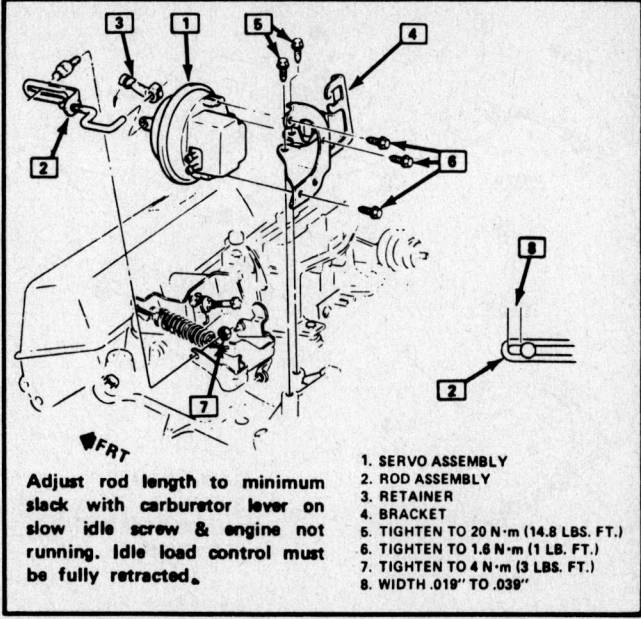

Adjust rod length to minimum slack with carburetor lever on slow idle screw & engine not running. Idle load control must be fully retracted.

1. SERVO ASSEMBLY
2. ROD ASSEMBLY
3. RETAINER
4. BRACKET
5. TIGHTEN TO 20 N·m (14.8 LBS. FT.)
6. TIGHTEN TO 1.6 N·m (1 LB. FT.)
7. TIGHTEN TO 4 N·m (3 LBS. FT.)
8. WIDTH .019″ TO .039″

Servo and linkage adjustment—1985 and later 98 with 3.0 liter engine

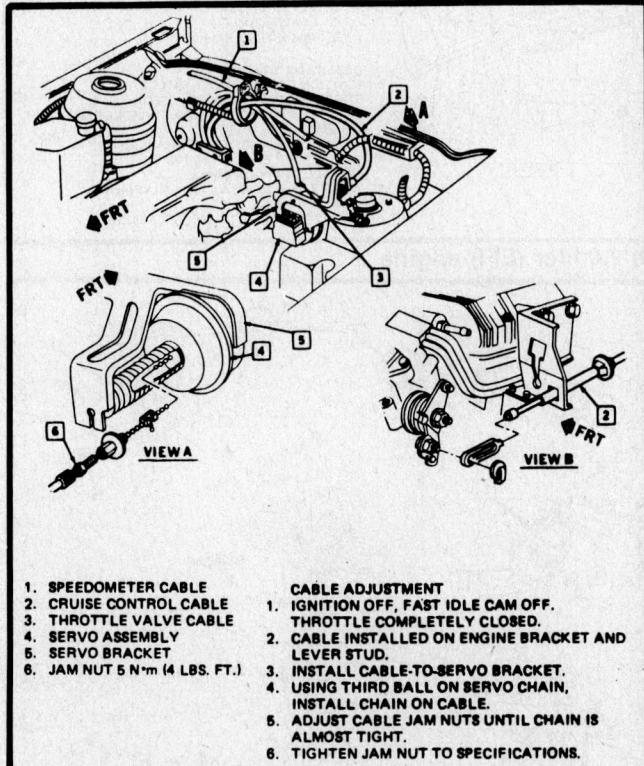

1. SPEEDOMETER CABLE
2. CRUISE CONTROL CABLE
3. THROTTLE VALVE CABLE
4. SERVO ASSEMBLY
5. SERVO BRACKET
6. JAM NUT 5 N·m (4 LBS. FT.)

CABLE ADJUSTMENT
1. IGNITION OFF, FAST IDLE CAM OFF. THROTTLE COMPLETELY CLOSED.
2. CABLE INSTALLED ON ENGINE BRACKET AND LEVER STUD.
3. INSTALL CABLE-TO-SERVO BRACKET.
4. USING THIRD BALL ON SERVO CHAIN, INSTALL CHAIN ON CABLE.
5. ADJUST CABLE JAM NUTS UNTIL CHAIN IS ALMOST TIGHT.
6. TIGHTEN JAM NUT TO SPECIFICATIONS.

Servo and linkage adjustment—1985 Firenza with 2.8 liter engine

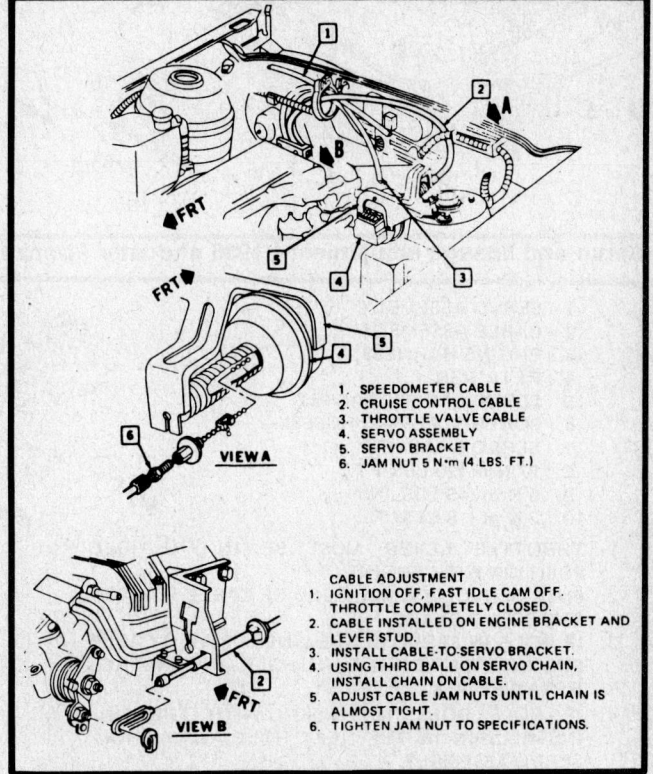

1. SPEEDOMETER CABLE
2. CRUISE CONTROL CABLE
3. THROTTLE VALVE CABLE
4. SERVO ASSEMBLY
5. SERVO BRACKET
6. JAM NUT 5 N·m (4 LBS. FT.)

CABLE ADJUSTMENT
1. IGNITION OFF, FAST IDLE CAM OFF. THROTTLE COMPLETELY CLOSED.
2. CABLE INSTALLED ON ENGINE BRACKET AND LEVER STUD.
3. INSTALL CABLE-TO-SERVO BRACKET.
4. USING THIRD BALL ON SERVO CHAIN, INSTALL CHAIN ON CABLE.
5. ADJUST CABLE JAM NUTS UNTIL CHAIN IS ALMOST TIGHT.
6. TIGHTEN JAM NUT TO SPECIFICATIONS.

Servo and linkage adjustment—1986 and later Firenza with 2.8 liter (MPFI) engine

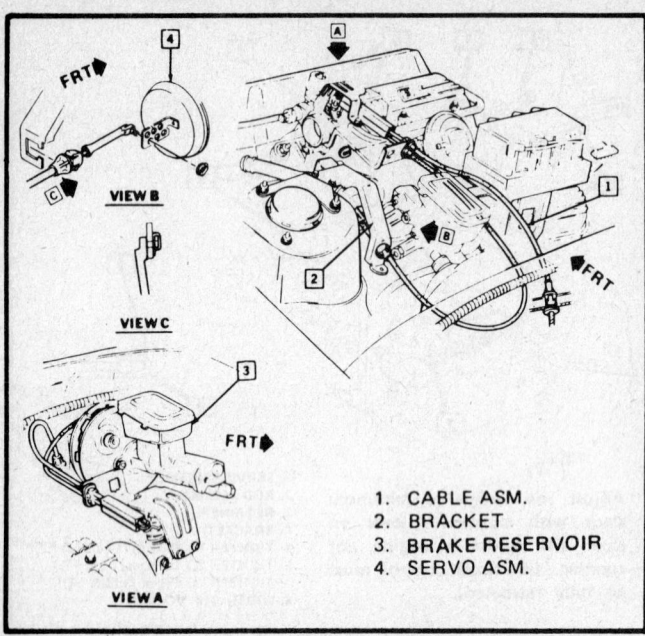

1. CABLE ASM.
2. BRACKET
3. BRAKE RESERVOIR
4. SERVO ASM.

Servo and linkage adjustment—1985 and later Calais with V6 (MPFI) engine

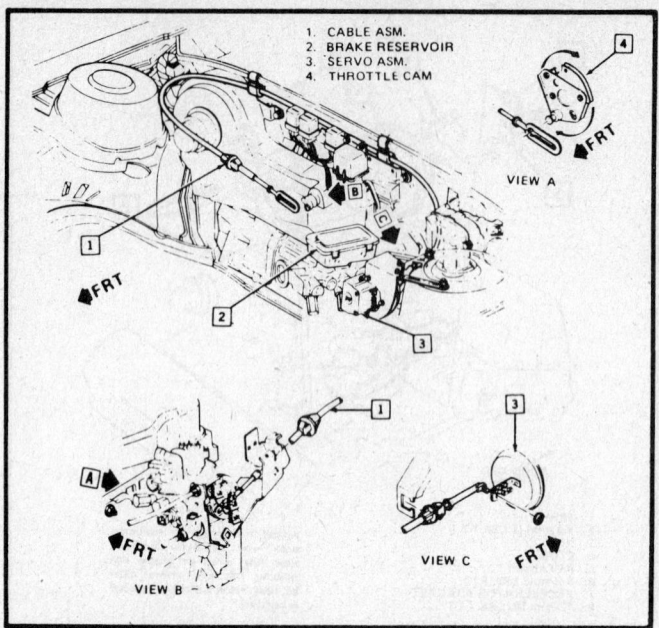

1. CABLE ASM.
2. BRAKE RESERVOIR
3. SERVO ASM.
4. THROTTLE CAM

Servo and linkage adjustment—1985 and later Calais with 2.5 liter (EFI) engine

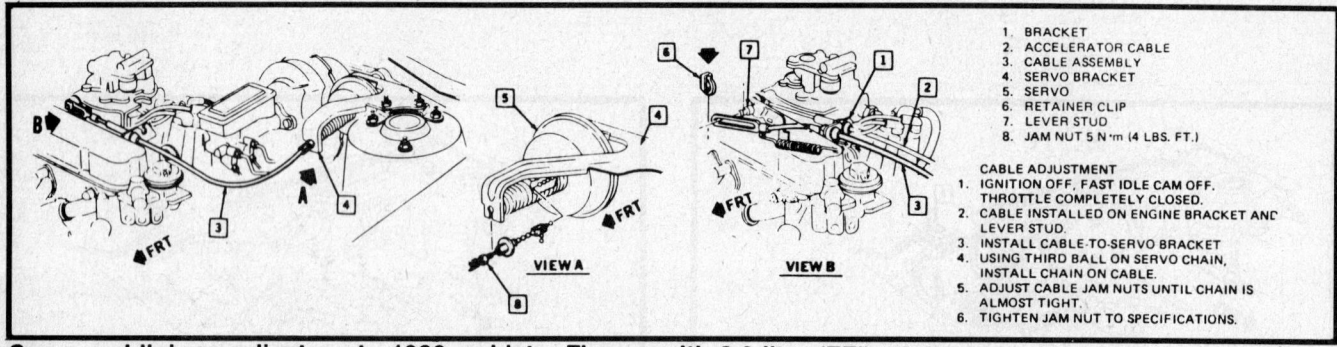

1. BRACKET
2. ACCELERATOR CABLE
3. CABLE ASSEMBLY
4. SERVO BRACKET
5. SERVO
6. RETAINER CLIP
7. LEVER STUD
8. JAM NUT 5 N·m (4 LBS. FT.)

CABLE ADJUSTMENT
1. IGNITION OFF, FAST IDLE CAM OFF. THROTTLE COMPLETELY CLOSED.
2. CABLE INSTALLED ON ENGINE BRACKET AND LEVER STUD.
3. INSTALL CABLE-TO-SERVO BRACKET.
4. USING THIRD BALL ON SERVO CHAIN, INSTALL CHAIN ON CABLE.
5. ADJUST CABLE JAM NUTS UNTIL CHAIN IS ALMOST TIGHT.
6. TIGHTEN JAM NUT TO SPECIFICATIONS.

Servo and linkage adjustment—1986 and later Firenza with 2.0 liter (EFI) engine

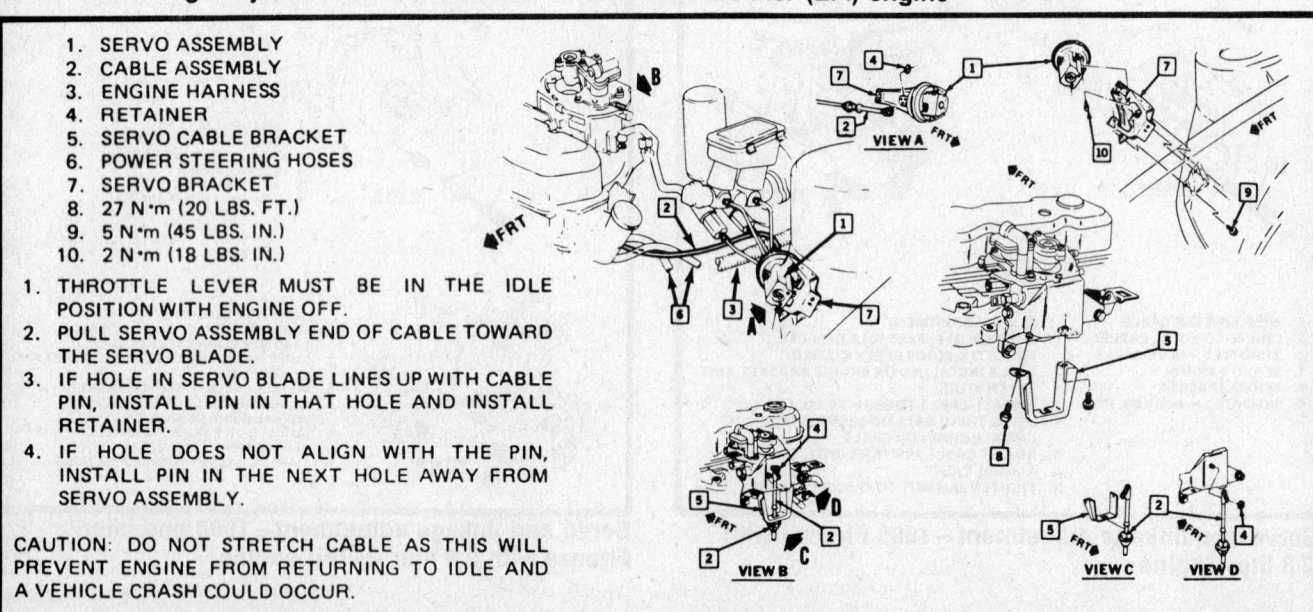

1. SERVO ASSEMBLY
2. CABLE ASSEMBLY
3. ENGINE HARNESS
4. RETAINER
5. SERVO CABLE BRACKET
6. POWER STEERING HOSES
7. SERVO BRACKET
8. 27 N·m (20 LBS. FT.)
9. 5 N·m (45 LBS. IN.)
10. 2 N·m (18 LBS. IN.)

1. THROTTLE LEVER MUST BE IN THE IDLE POSITION WITH ENGINE OFF.
2. PULL SERVO ASSEMBLY END OF CABLE TOWARD THE SERVO BLADE.
3. IF HOLE IN SERVO BLADE LINES UP WITH CABLE PIN, INSTALL PIN IN THAT HOLE AND INSTALL RETAINER.
4. IF HOLE DOES NOT ALIGN WITH THE PIN, INSTALL PIN IN THE NEXT HOLE AWAY FROM SERVO ASSEMBLY.

CAUTION: DO NOT STRETCH CABLE AS THIS WILL PREVENT ENGINE FROM RETURNING TO IDLE AND A VEHICLE CRASH COULD OCCUR.

Servo and linkage adjustment—1986 and later Ciera and Cutlass Cruiser with 2.5 liter (EFI) engine

RELEASE SWITCH AND VALVE ADJUSTMENTS

For release switch and valve adjustments refer to the proper illustration.

Component Replacement

CRUISE CONTROL ENGAGEMENT SWITCH

Removal and Installation

1. Disconnect the negative battery cable. Remove the steering wheel.
2. Position the turn signal switch in the right turn position. If the vehicle is equipped with a tilt column be sure that the column is positioned in the full up detent.
3. Remove the screw securing the cruise control engagement switch to the steering column.
4. Disconnect the cruise control engagement switch electrical connection.
5. Slide the cruise control engagement switch wiring up through the steering column carefully. Remove the cruise control engagement switch from the vehicle.
6. Installation is the reverse of the removal procedure.

TRANSDUCER ASSEMBLY (1982–83)

Removal and Installation

1. Disconnect the negative battery cable.
2. Disconnect the vacuum hoses and the electrical connections from the transducer assembly.
3. Remove the speedometer cables from the assembly.
4. Remove the screws attaching the transducer to the mounting bracket.
5. Remove the transducer from the vehicle.
6. Installation is the reverse of the removal procedure.

SERVO ASSEMBLY

Removal and Installation

1. Disconnect the negative battery cable.
2. Disconnect all electrical and vacuum connections from the servo assembly.
3. Disconnect the servo assembly cable or chain.
4. Remove the servo mounting bolts. Remove the servo assembly from the vehicle.
5. Installation is the reverse of the removal procedure.

ELECTRIC BRAKE RELEASE SWITCH AND VACUUM RELEASE VALVE

Removal and installation

1. Disconnect the negative battery cable.
2. Remove the switch electrical and vacuum connectors.
3. Remove the switch from its mounting above the brake pedal.
4. Installation is the reverse of the removal procedure.

Adjustment

1. The switch assembly and the valve assembly cannot be adjusted until after the brake booster push rod is assembled to the brake pedal assembly.
2. To adjust the switch depress the brake pedal and insert the switch assembly and valve assembly into their proper retaining clips until fully seated.

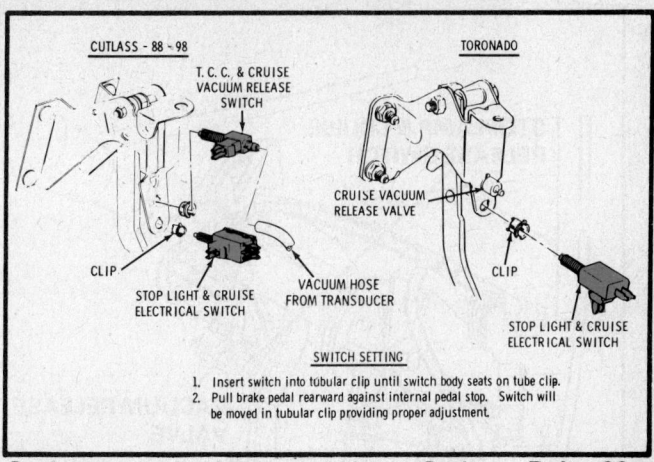
Cruise control release switches—Cutlass, Delta 88, 98 and Toronado

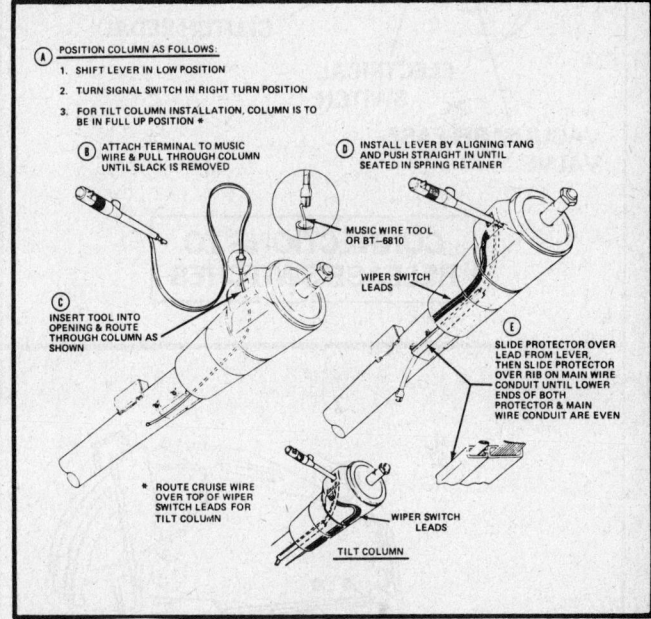
Cruise control engagement switch lever installation procedure

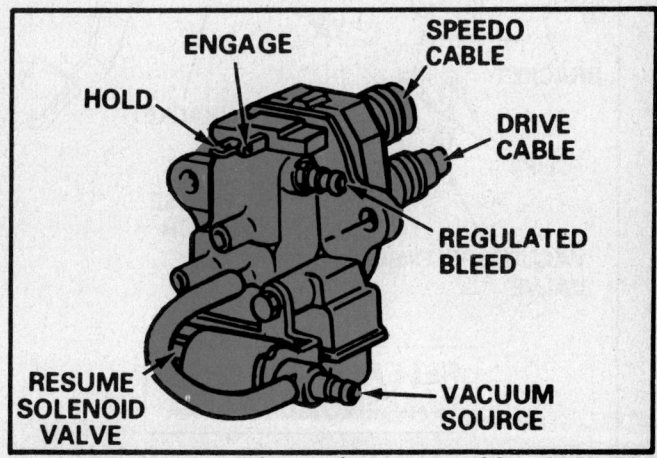
Typical cruise control transducer assembly—1982–83

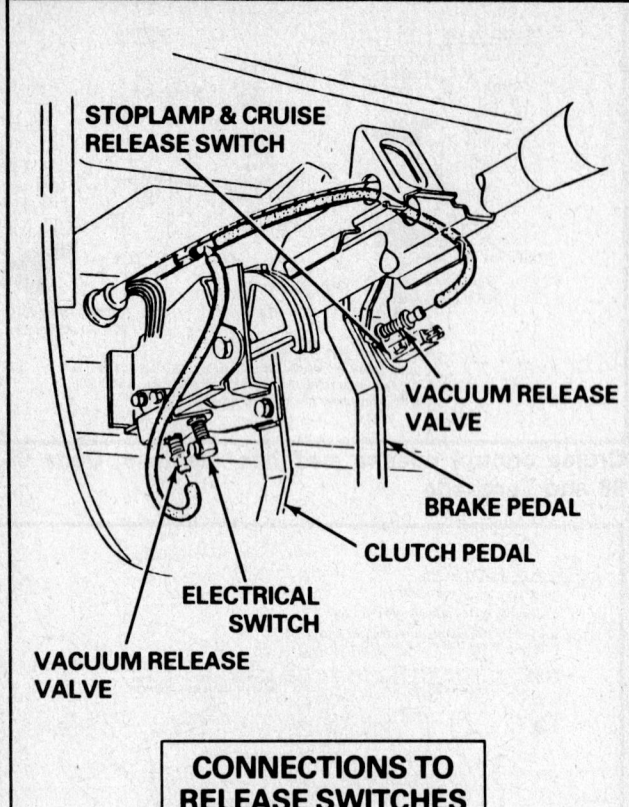

STOPLAMP & CRUISE
RELEASE SWITCH

VACUUM RELEASE
VALVE

BRAKE PEDAL

CLUTCH PEDAL

ELECTRICAL
SWITCH

VACUUM RELEASE
VALVE

**CONNECTIONS TO
RELEASE SWITCHES**

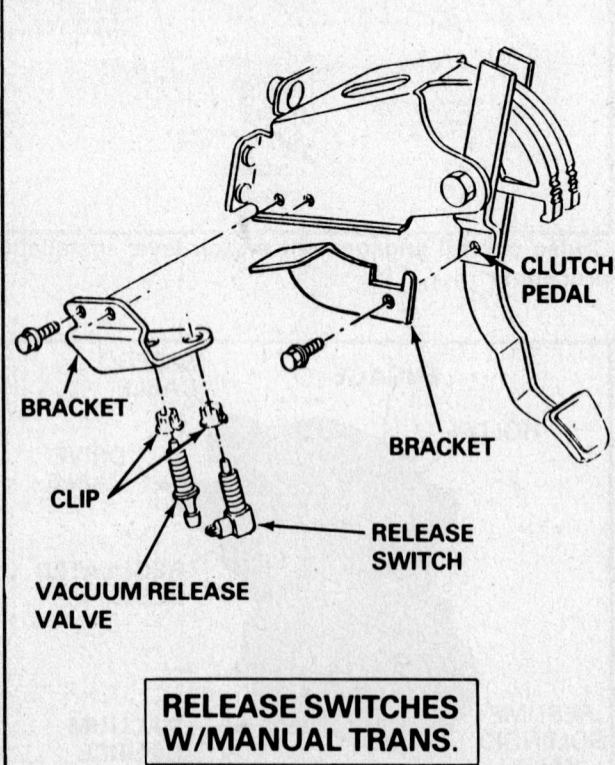

CLUTCH
PEDAL

BRACKET

BRACKET

CLIP

RELEASE
SWITCH

VACUUM RELEASE
VALVE

**RELEASE SWITCHES
W/MANUAL TRANS.**

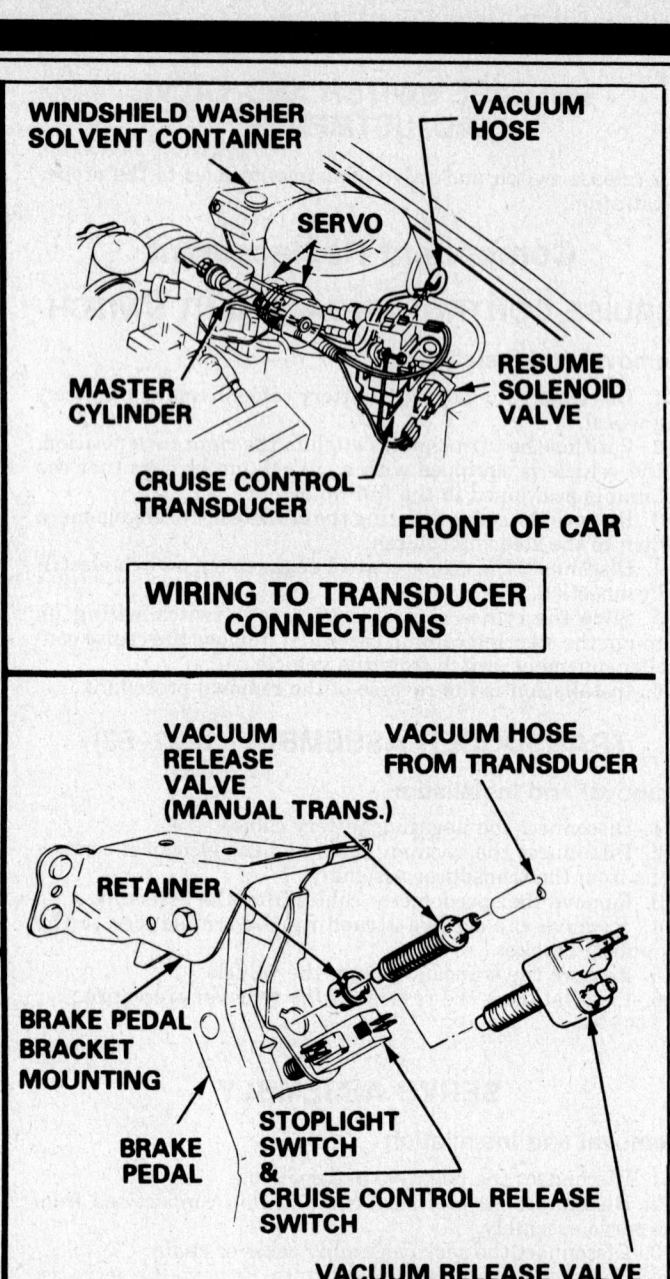

WINDSHIELD WASHER
SOLVENT CONTAINER

VACUUM
HOSE

SERVO

MASTER
CYLINDER

RESUME
SOLENOID
VALVE

CRUISE CONTROL
TRANSDUCER

FRONT OF CAR

**WIRING TO TRANSDUCER
CONNECTIONS**

VACUUM
RELEASE
VALVE
(MANUAL TRANS.)

VACUUM HOSE
FROM TRANSDUCER

RETAINER

BRAKE PEDAL
BRACKET
MOUNTING

BRAKE
PEDAL

STOPLIGHT
SWITCH
&
CRUISE CONTROL RELEASE
SWITCH

VACUUM RELEASE VALVE
TCC RELEASE SWITCH

INSTALLATION OF SELF-ADJUSTING VACUUM RELEASE VALVE

1. INSTALL CLIP.
2. WITH BRAKE PEDAL DEPRESSED, INSERT VALVE INTO TUBULAR CLIP UNTIL VALVE SEATS ON CLIP. NOTE THAT AUDIBLE "CLICKS" CAN BE HEARD AS THREADED PORTION OF VALVE IS PUSHED THROUGH THE CLIP TOWARD THE BRAKE PEDAL.
3. PULL BRAKE PEDAL FULLY REARWARD AGAINST PEDAL STOP UNTIL AUDIBLE "CLICK" SOUNDS CAN NO LONGER BE HEARD. VALVE WILL BE MOVED IN TUBULAR CLIP PROVIDING ADJUSTMENT.
4. RELEASE BRAKE PEDAL AND REPEAT STEP TO ASSURE THAT NO AUDIBLE "CLICK" SOUNDS REMAIN.

**VACUUM/ELECTRICAL
RELEASE SWITCHES**

Cruise control release switches—Firenza, Omega and Ciera

RESUME CRUISE CONTROL TRANSDUCER USAGE						
SERIES	3.8L V6	4.1L V6	4.3L V8	5.0L V8	•5.7L V8 DIESEL	•4.3L V6 DIESEL
CUTLASS	RH		RH	RK	RS	RS
88-98	RH	RH	RH	RK	RS	
TORONADO		RH		RK	RS	

TRANSDUCER CODE	LOW SPEED LIMIT SETTING*	*LOW SPEED LIMIT SETTING PREVENTS CRUISE CONTROL ENGAGEMENT BELOW THE SPECIFIED SPEED AND IS NOT ADJUSTABLE
RH	30 - 35 MPH	
RK	35 - 40 MPH	•SOME EARLY PRODUCTION DIESEL ENGINES WILL USE TRANSDUCER RW WITH A LOW SPEED LIMIT SETTING OF 25 - 30 MPH.
RS	35 - 40 MPH	

Transducer usage and identification chart — 1982–83 Cutlass, Delta 88, 98 and Toronado

3. Pull the pedal back to its fully retracted position. The switch assembly and the valve assembly will move within the retainers of their adjusted position.

4. The switch assembly contacts must open at 3.5mm to 12.5mm of brake pedal travel. Nominal actuation of the brake light switch is 4.5mm.

5. The vacuum release valve assembly must open at 27.0mm to 33.0nn of brake pedal travel.

ELECTRONIC CRUISE CONTROL CONTROL

MODULE

Removal and Installation

Note: The electronic cruise control module is normally mounted on or near the accelerator pedal bracket. Location may vary depending upon vehicle model.

1. Disconnect the negative battery cable.
2. Remove the lower steering column filler panel as required. Remove vehicle carpet as required.
3. Disconnect the electrical connectors from the control module.
4. Remove the control module mounting screws. Remove the control module from the vehicle.
6. Installation is the reverse of the removal procedure.

SPEED SENSORS

VSS Buffer Amplifier

The VSS buffer amplifier is a device that supplies vehicle speed input to the electronic controller. The optic head portion of the assembly is located in the speedometer head frame. A reflective blade is attached to the speedometer head/cable assembly. The blade spins like a propeller with its blades passing through a light beam from a L.E.D. refractor in the optic head. As each blade enters the light beam, light is reflected back to a photocell that is located in the optic head. This in turn causes a power signal to be sent to a buffer for amplification and signal conditioning. This signal is then sent to the controller for processing and calculation of vehicle speed.

RESUME CRUISE CONTROL TRANSDUCER USAGE				
SERIES	2.5L L4	2.8L V-6	3.0L V-6	4.3L V-6 DIESEL
CUTLASS CIERA	RB		RB	RX
OMEGA	RB	RB		

TRANSDUCER CODE	LOW SPEED LIMIT SETTING*	*LOW SPEED LIMIT SETTING PREVENTS CRUISE CONTROL ENGAGEMENTS BELOW THE SPECIFIED SPEED AND IS NOT ADJUSTABLE
RB	25-30 MPH	
RX	35-40 MPH	

Transducer usage and identification chart — 1982–83 Firenza, Omega and Ciera

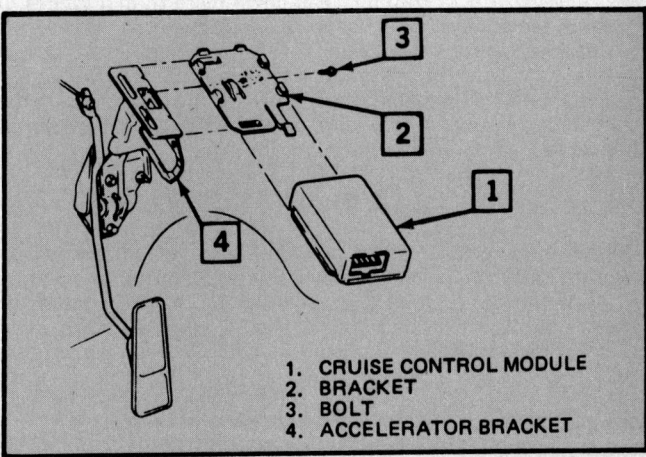

1. CRUISE CONTROL MODULE
2. BRACKET
3. BOLT
4. ACCELERATOR BRACKET

Electronic cruise control module — typical location

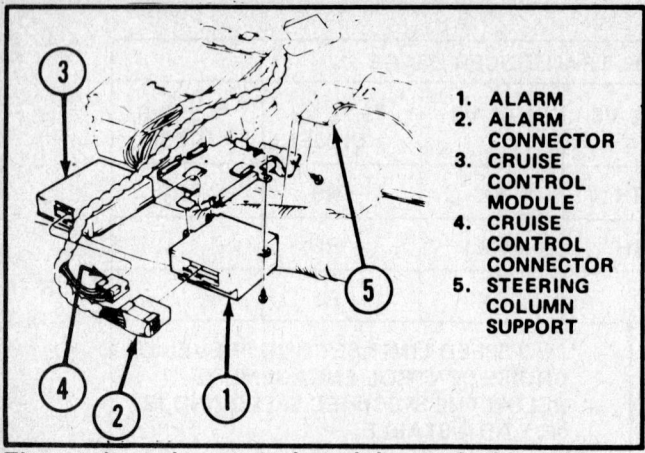

1. ALARM
2. ALARM CONNECTOR
3. CRUISE CONTROL MODULE
4. CRUISE CONTROL CONNECTOR
5. STEERING COLUMN SUPPORT

Electronic cruise control module — typical location

P.M. Generator Speed Signal

The P.M. generator speed signal is a device that supplies vehicle speed input to the electronic controller. Vehicle speed information is provided to the electronic controller by a permanent magnet generator driven by the vehicle transmission. The output frequency of the permanent magnet generator is than routed to a buffer, which in turn will amplify and condition the signal to the electronic controller.

Pontiac

VISUAL INSPECTION

Before performing any tests make a visual inspection of the cruise control system. Check all items in the system for abnormal conditions such as bare broken or disconnected wires and damage to the vacuum hoses. Be sure that the speedometer cables are attached and properly routed. All vacuum hoses must be properly routed and must not have any kinks or bends. Be sure that all electrical connections are complete and tight. The wiring harness must be routed properly.

SERVO TEST (1982–83)

To determine the condition of the servo diaphragm, remove the vacuum hose from the servo assembly. Apply 14 inches of vacuum to the tube opening and hold in in place for about one minute. The vacuum should not leak down more than 5 inches. If vacuum leaks, replace the servo assembly.

Another test consists of removing the vacuum hose attached to the servo assembly, than push the diaphragm in, hold your finger over the nipple and the diaphragm should remain in the pushed in position. If the servo assembly does not perform as indicated it should be replaced.

VACUUM LEAK TEST (1982–83)

The vacuum release valves, the resume valve and all the connecting hoses can be checked by applying 15 inches of vacuum to each component and then sealing off the component for about one minute. The vacuum should not leak down more than 5 inches. Repair or replace defective components as required.

ELECTRICAL SYSTEM TEST (1982–83)

1. Check the cruise control fuse and electrical connector.

2. Check all electrical connections. Disconnect and reconnect after checking for bent, broken or dirty mating tabs.
3. Check the electrical release switch as follows. Unplug the connector at the switch. Connect an ohmmeter to the two terminals on the switch assembly.
4. Depress the brake or clutch pedal. The ohmmeter should not indicate continuity.
5. Release the pedal, the ohmmeter should indicate continunity.

CONTROL LEVER SWITCH TEST (1982–83)

1. Disconnect the electrical connector at the cruise control engagement switch.
2. Connect an ohmmeter to the brown and blue wires.
3. Slide the resume switch to the on position. The ohmmeter should indicate continuity. Push the engage button all the way in and and open circuit should be indicated.
4. Connect an ohmmeter to the brown and black wires, with the resume switch still in the on position. An open circuit should be indicated.
5. Depress the engage button and release it half way. Continuity should exist.
6. Connect an ohmmeter to the blue and black wires with the resume switch still in the on position. With the engaged button released, no continunity should be present.
7. With the engaged button depressed and half way released continunity should exist.

HARNESS AND TRANSDUCER ELECTRICAL TEST (1982–83)

1. Using an ohmmeter engage, with the engagement switch connector disconnected, check the resistance of the dark green wire in the wiring harness. If the transducer is grounded properly, the ohmmeter should indicate between 29 and 36 ohms.
2. If resistance is above or below specification, disconnect the connector at the transducer and at the resume solenoid.
3. Measure the resistance of the dark green wire. It should indicate a resistance reading of 23 ohms, plus or minus one ohm. If the reading is not as indicated the wiring harness should be replaced.
4. With the connectors of the transducer disconnected, measure the resistance of the solenoid coil by connecting the ohmmeter to the hold terminal and ground. A reading of 5 to 6 ohms should be indicated.
5. If a reading of 4 ohms or less is obtained there is excessive resistance in the circuit. If a reading of 6 ohms or more is indicated the transducer should be checked.

TRANSDUCER TEST (1982–83)

The only test that is possible to check the transducer assembly is the transducer orifice tube adjustment. Before adjusting the transducer assembly be sure that all vacuum hoses are in good condition. Be sure that all electrical connections are correct. Be sure that the electrical and vacuum release valves are working properly.

VACUUM REGULATOR TEST (1982–83)

If the vehicle is equipped with a diesel engine a vacuum regulator valve is used. This vacuum regulator valve regulates the vacuum from the engine mounted vacuum pump. To test the regulator use a vacuum pump. The vacuum level should be about 6 in. hg. or slightly higher if cold. If the valve does not perform as indicated it must be replaced.

DIAGNOSIS AND TESTING PROCEDURES

PRELIMINARY CHECKS

1. Check Servo Chain or rod adjustment. Must have minimum slack.
2. Check vacuum hoses. Must be in good condition - no restrictions or leaks.
3. Check drive cable routings. No kinks or sharp bends.
4. Check throttle linkage or cable for binding.
5. Check adjustment of electrical release switch and vacuum release valve.
6. Check engagement switch operation.
7. If steps 1 through 6 do not solve the problem, continue with diagnosis.

CRUISE CONTROL INOPERATIVE

1. Check radio fuse. If blown, check wiring for short circuit and repair. A shorted resume solenoid diode could also cause blow fuse.
2. If fuse and preliminary checks ok, resume solenoid must be checked. Start engine and check source vacuum at resume solenoid (refer to picture at right). Disconnect the two wire connector at resume solenoid. Use jumper wire to ground terminal which had black wire connected to it. Apply 12 volts to terminal which had tan wire connected to it. Disconnect outlet vacuum hose (going to B fitting on transducer). Vacuum should be present. If not, replace resume solenoid. Applying voltage incorrectly to resume solenoid could damage diode. If above checks ok, stop engine and reconnect electrical and vacuum connections.
3. To make test below, turn ignition to RUN position and off/on/resume switch to ON. Disconnect the two wire connector at transducer (Engage-Hold Terminals).
4. Connect 12 volt test light to ground and to engage wire in connector. Push engage/coast button in part way to engage position.
5. Repeat test on hold wire in connector.

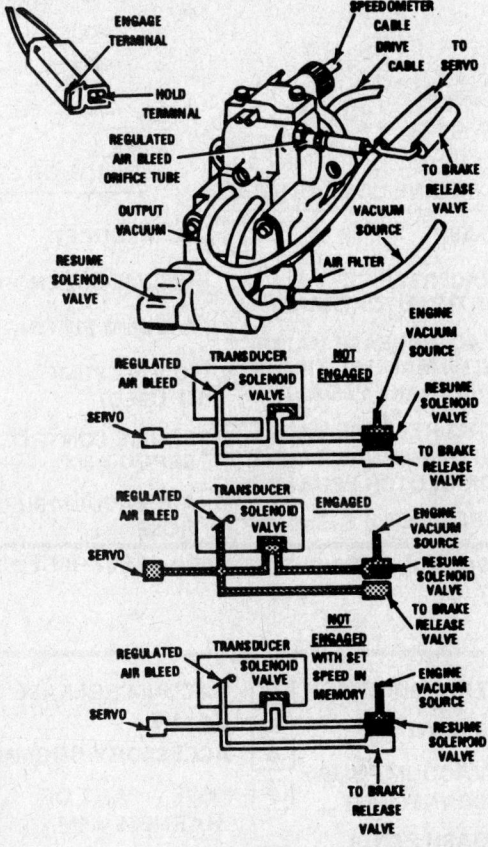

TEST LIGHT OFF AT ONE WIRE ONLY	TEST LIGHT ON AT BOTH WIRES (MAY BE DIM ON HOLD WIRE)	TEST LIGHT OFF AT BOTH WIRES
Test engagement switch. (See test procedure) Check for open circuit in wire if test light did not light. Repair or replace part that checks bad.	Check for poor ground at transducer. If ok, remove transducer for repair.	Check for open circuit in brown/white wire from fuse panel to off/on/resume switch. If circuit ok, check engagement switch operation and replace if necessary.

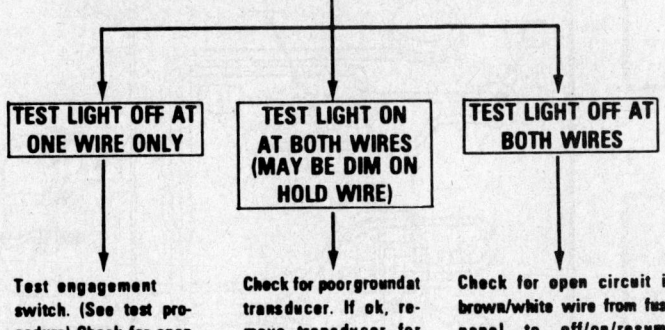

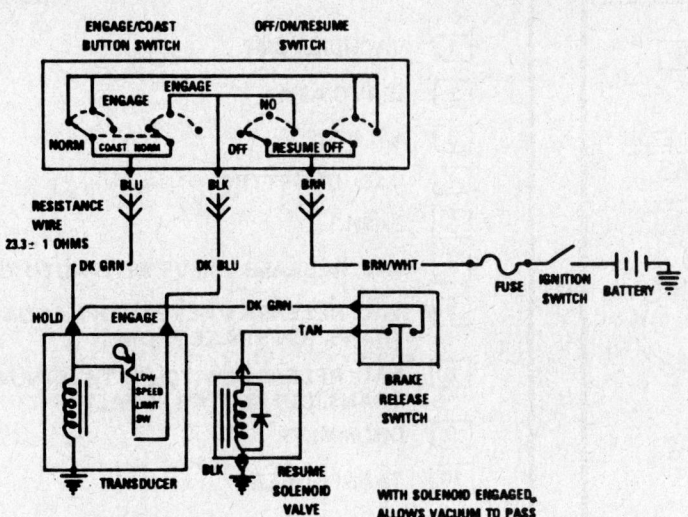

ENGAGEMENT SWITCH TEST PROCEDURE

USE A SELF POWERED TEST LIGHT. LIGHT WILL BE ON FOR EACH TEST IF SWITCH IS GOOD. CONNECTOR TERMINALS AND COLOR 1 — BROWN, 2 — BLUE, 3 — BLACK

SWITCH POSITIONS		TERMINALS		
ENGAGE BUTTON	RESUME SWITCH	1 to 2	1 to 3	2 to 3
Released	on	closed	open	open
Fully Depressed	on	open	open	closed
Partially Released	on	closed	closed	closed
Released	resume	closed	closed	closed
Released	off	open	open	open

Cruise control diagnosis—1982–83 Pontiac

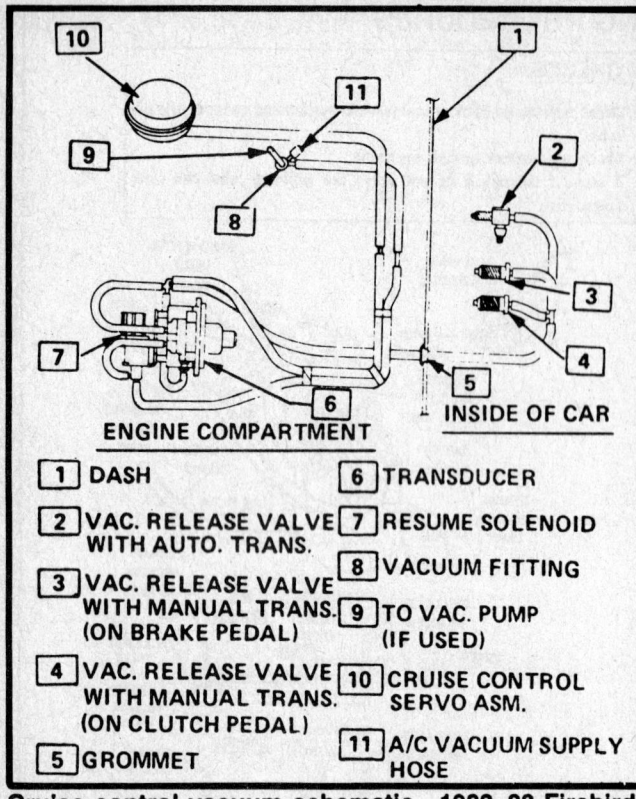

1 DASH	**6** TRANSDUCER
2 VAC. RELEASE VALVE WITH AUTO. TRANS.	**7** RESUME SOLENOID
3 VAC. RELEASE VALVE WITH MANUAL TRANS. (ON BRAKE PEDAL)	**8** VACUUM FITTING
	9 TO VAC. PUMP (IF USED)
4 VAC. RELEASE VALVE WITH MANUAL TRANS. (ON CLUTCH PEDAL)	**10** CRUISE CONTROL SERVO ASM.
5 GROMMET	**11** A/C VACUUM SUPPLY HOSE

Cruise control vacuum schematic – 1982–83 Firebird (typical)

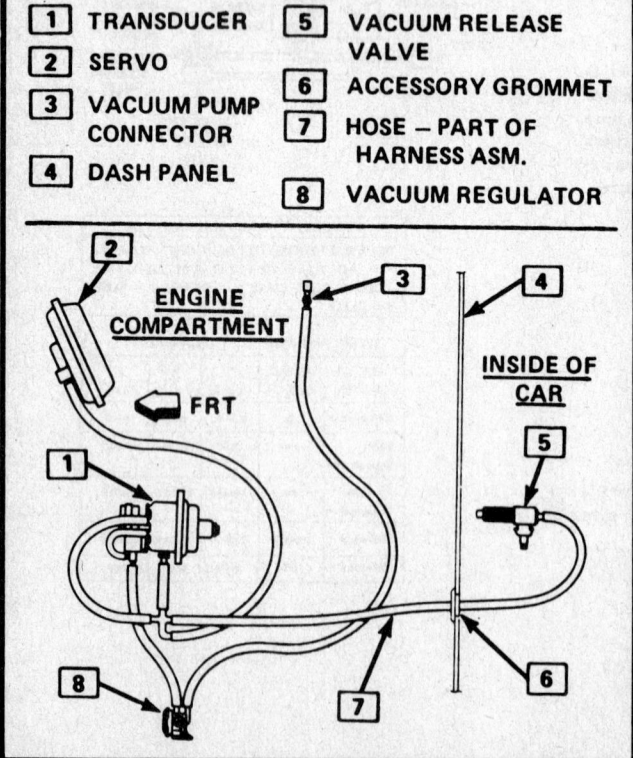

1 TRANSDUCER	**5** VACUUM RELEASE VALVE
2 SERVO	**6** ACCESSORY GROMMET
3 VACUUM PUMP CONNECTOR	**7** HOSE – PART OF HARNESS ASM.
4 DASH PANEL	**8** VACUUM REGULATOR

Cruise control vacuum schematic – Bonneville, Grand Prix and Parisienne with V8 diesel engine

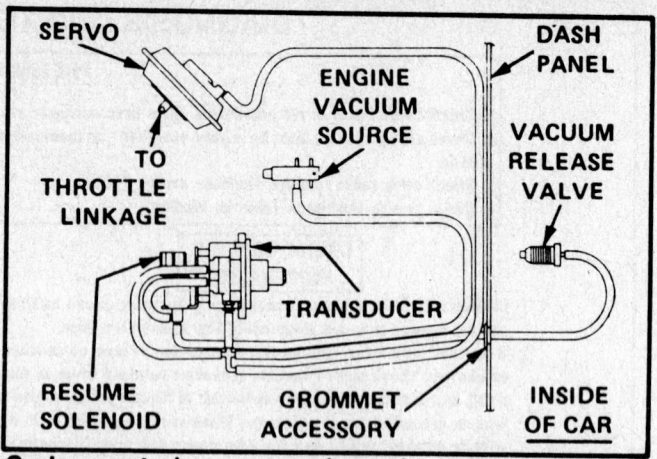

Cruise control vacuum schematic – 1982–83 Bonneville, Grand Prix and Parisienne with 3.8 liter and 4.1 liter engine

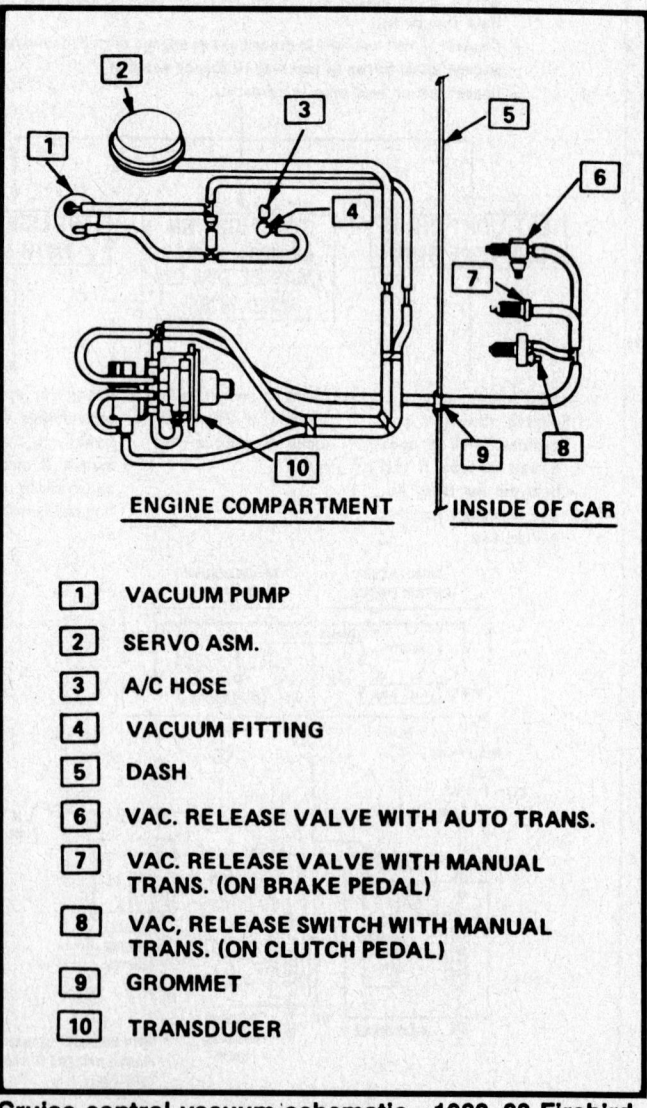

1 VACUUM PUMP

2 SERVO ASM.

3 A/C HOSE

4 VACUUM FITTING

5 DASH

6 VAC. RELEASE VALVE WITH AUTO TRANS.

7 VAC. RELEASE VALVE WITH MANUAL TRANS. (ON BRAKE PEDAL)

8 VAC. RELEASE SWITCH WITH MANUAL TRANS. (ON CLUTCH PEDAL)

9 GROMMET

10 TRANSDUCER

Cruise control vacuum schematic – 1982–83 Firebird 2.5 liter engine

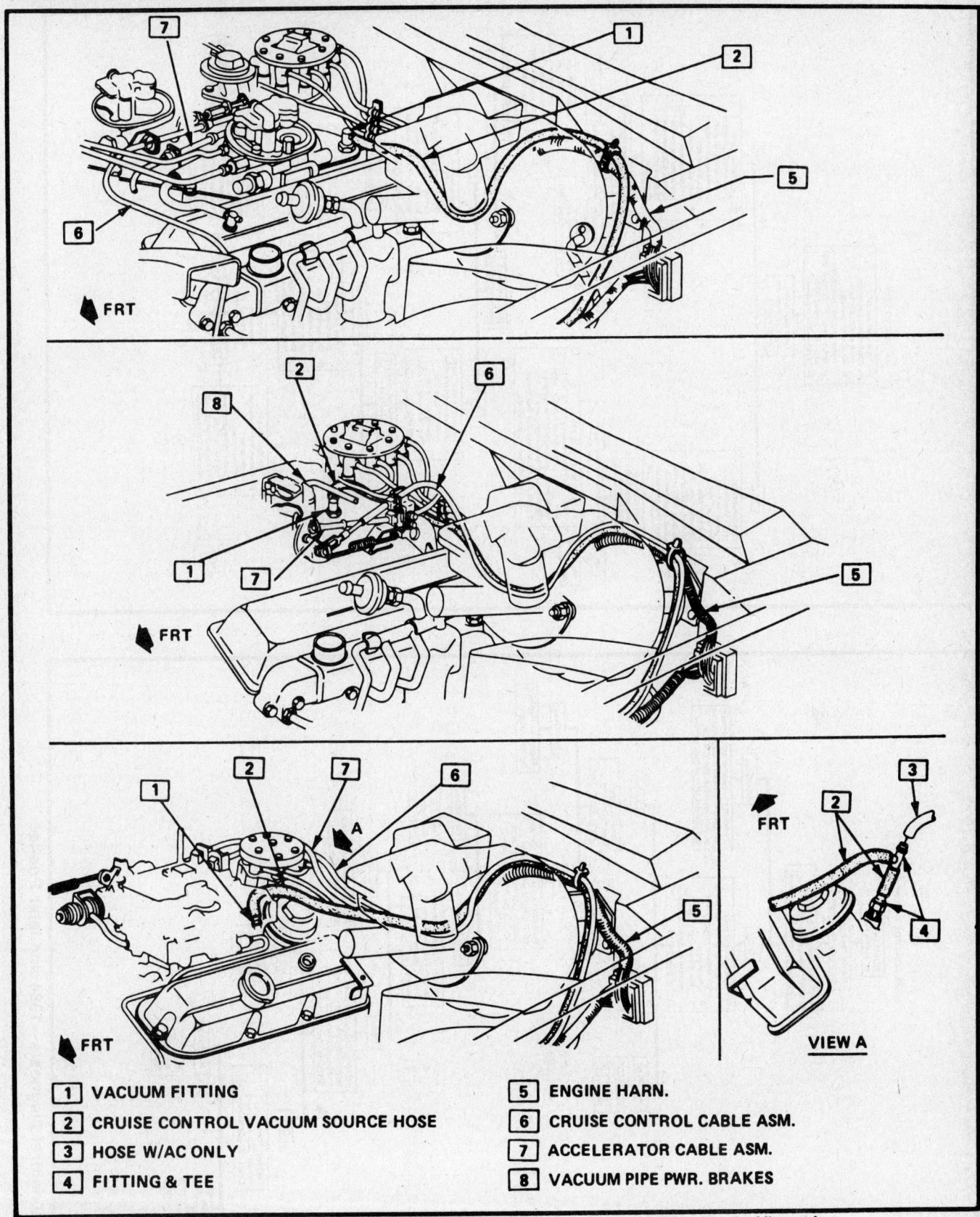

1. VACUUM FITTING
2. CRUISE CONTROL VACUUM SOURCE HOSE
3. HOSE W/AC ONLY
4. FITTING & TEE
5. ENGINE HARN.
6. CRUISE CONTROL CABLE ASM.
7. ACCELERATOR CABLE ASM.
8. VACUUM PIPE PWR. BRAKES

Cruise control vacuum schematic — 1982-83 Firebird with 2.8 liter and 5.0 liter (code H) engine

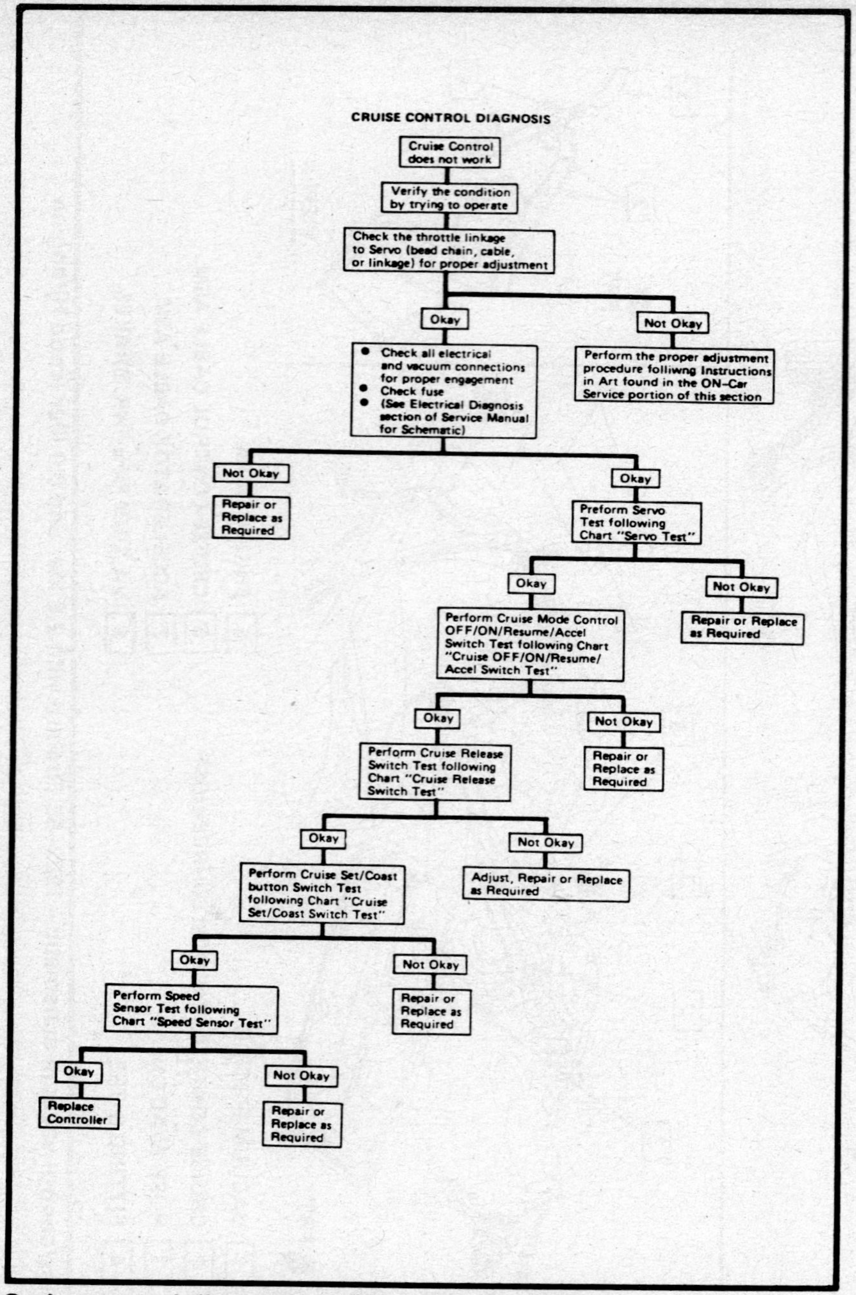

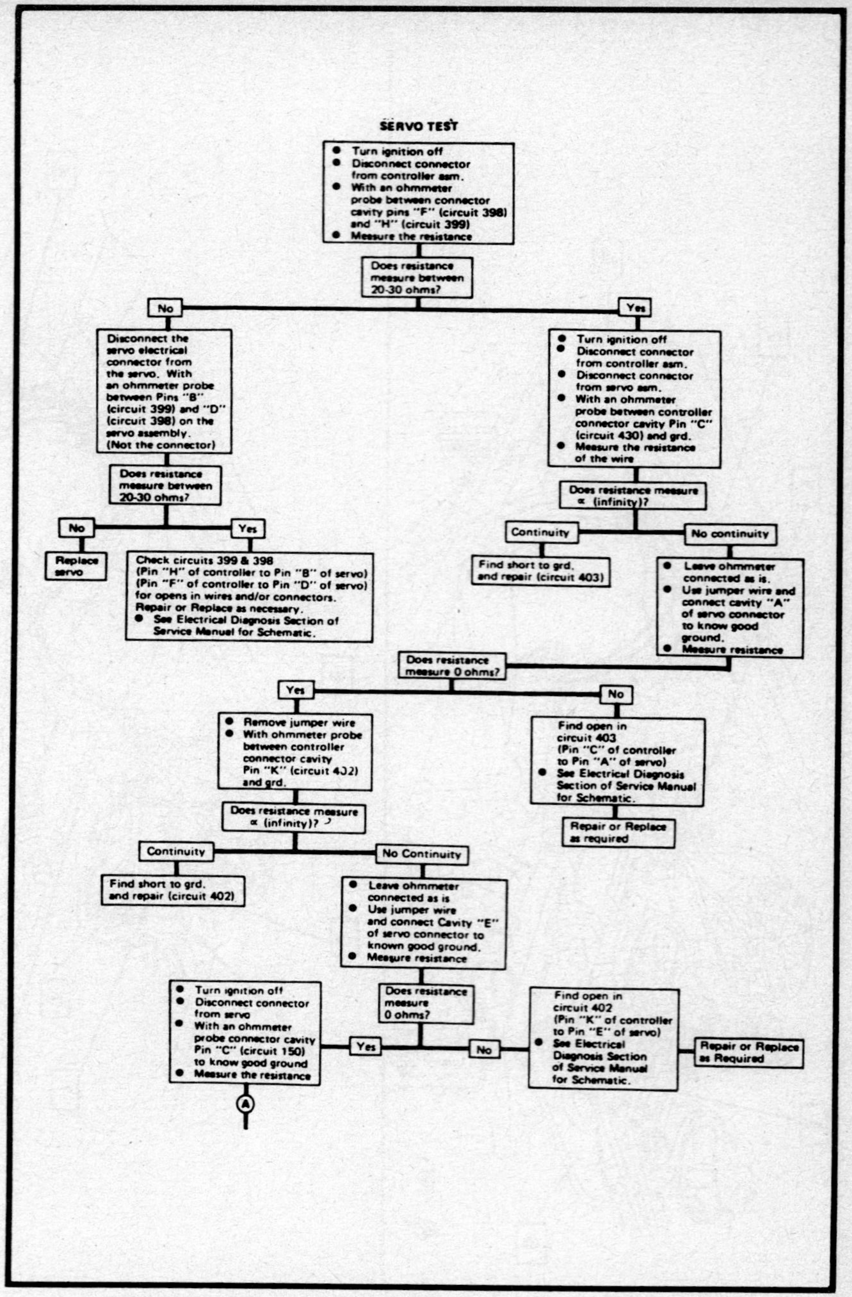

SERVO TEST

Turn ignition off
- Turn ignition off
- Disconnect connector from controller asm.
- With an ohmmeter probe between connector cavity Pin "F" (circuit 398) and "H" (circuit 399)
- Measure the resistance

Does resistance measure between 20-30 ohms?

Yes →
- Turn ignition off
- Disconnect connector from controller asm.
- Disconnect connector from servo asm.
- With an ohmmeter probe between controller connector cavity Pin "C" (circuit 430) and grd.
- Measure the resistance of the wire

Does resistance measure ∞ (infinity)?

No continuity →
- Leave ohmmeter connected as is.
- Use jumper wire and connect cavity "A" of servo connector to know good ground.
- Measure resistance

Continuity → Find short to grd. and repair (circuit 403)

No → Find open in circuit 403 (Pin "C" of controller to Pin "A" of servo) See Electrical Diagnosis Section of Service Manual for Schematic.
Repair or Replace as required

No →
- Disconnect the servo electrical connector from the servo. With an ohmmeter probe between Pins "B" (circuit 399) and "D" (circuit 398) on the servo assembly. (Not the connector.)

Does resistance measure between 20-30 ohms?

Yes → Check circuits 399 & 398 (Pin "H" of controller to Pin "B" of servo) (Pin "F" of controller to Pin "D" of servo) for opens in wires and/or connectors. Repair or Replace as necessary. See Electrical Diagnosis Section of Service Manual for Schematic.

No → Replace servo

Does resistance measure 0 ohm?

Yes →
- Remove jumper wire
- With ohmmeter probe between controller connector cavity Pin "K" (circuit 432) and grd.

Does resistance measure ∞ (infinity)?

No Continuity →
- Leave ohmmeter connected as is
- Use jumper wire and connect Cavity "E" of servo connector to known good ground
- Measure resistance

Continuity → Find short to grd. and repair (circuit 402)

Does resistance measure 0 ohm?

No → Find open in circuit 402 (Pin "K" of controller to Pin "E" of servo) See Electrical Diagnosis Section of Service Manual for Schematic.

Yes →
- Turn ignition off
- Disconnect connector from servo
- With an ohmmeter probe between connector cavity Pin "C" (circuit 150) to known good ground
- Measure the resistance
Ⓐ

Repair or Replace as Required

CRUISE CONTROL DIAGNOSIS

Cruise Control does not work

Verify the condition by trying to operate

Check the throttle linkage to Servo (bead chain, cable, or linkage) for proper adjustment

Not Okay → Perform the proper adjustment procedure following instructions in Art found in the ON-Car Service portion of this section

Okay →
- Check all electrical and vacuum connections for proper engagement
- Check fuse
(See Electrical Diagnosis section of Service Manual for Schematic)

Not Okay → Repair or Replace as Required

Okay → Perform Servo Test following Chart "Servo Test"

Not Okay → Repair or Replace as Required

Okay → Perform Cruise Mode Control OFF/ON/Resume/Accel Switch Test following Chart "Cruise OFF/ON/Resume/Accel Switch Test"

Not Okay → Repair or Replace as Required

Okay → Perform Cruise Release Switch Test following Chart "Cruise Release Switch Test"

Not Okay → Adjust, Repair or Replace as Required

Okay → Perform Cruise Set/Coast button Switch Test following Chart "Cruise Set/Coast Switch Test"

Not Okay → Repair or Replace as Required

Okay → Perform Speed Sensor Test following Chart "Speed Sensor Test"

Not Okay → Repair or Replace as Required

Okay → Replace Controller

Cruise control diagnosis — 1984 and later Pontiac

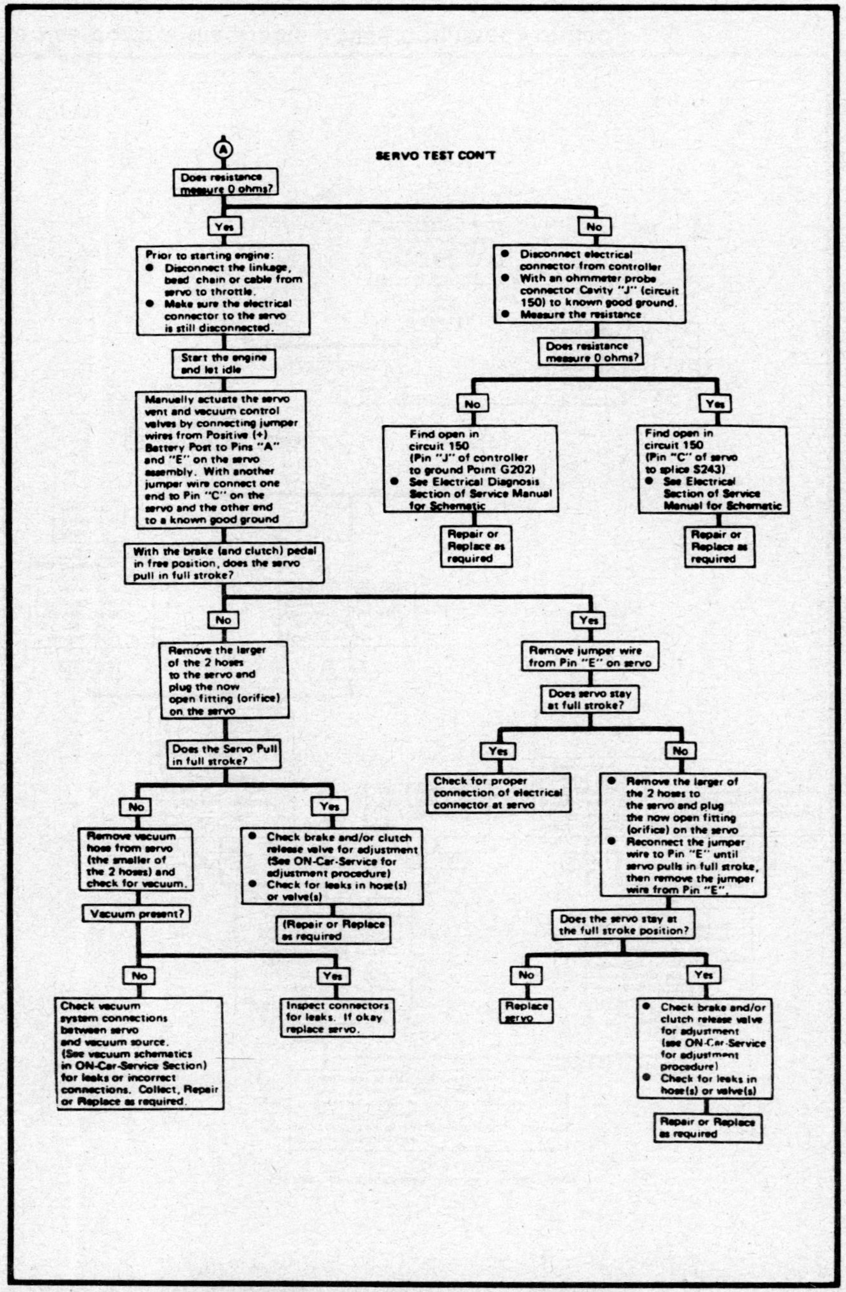

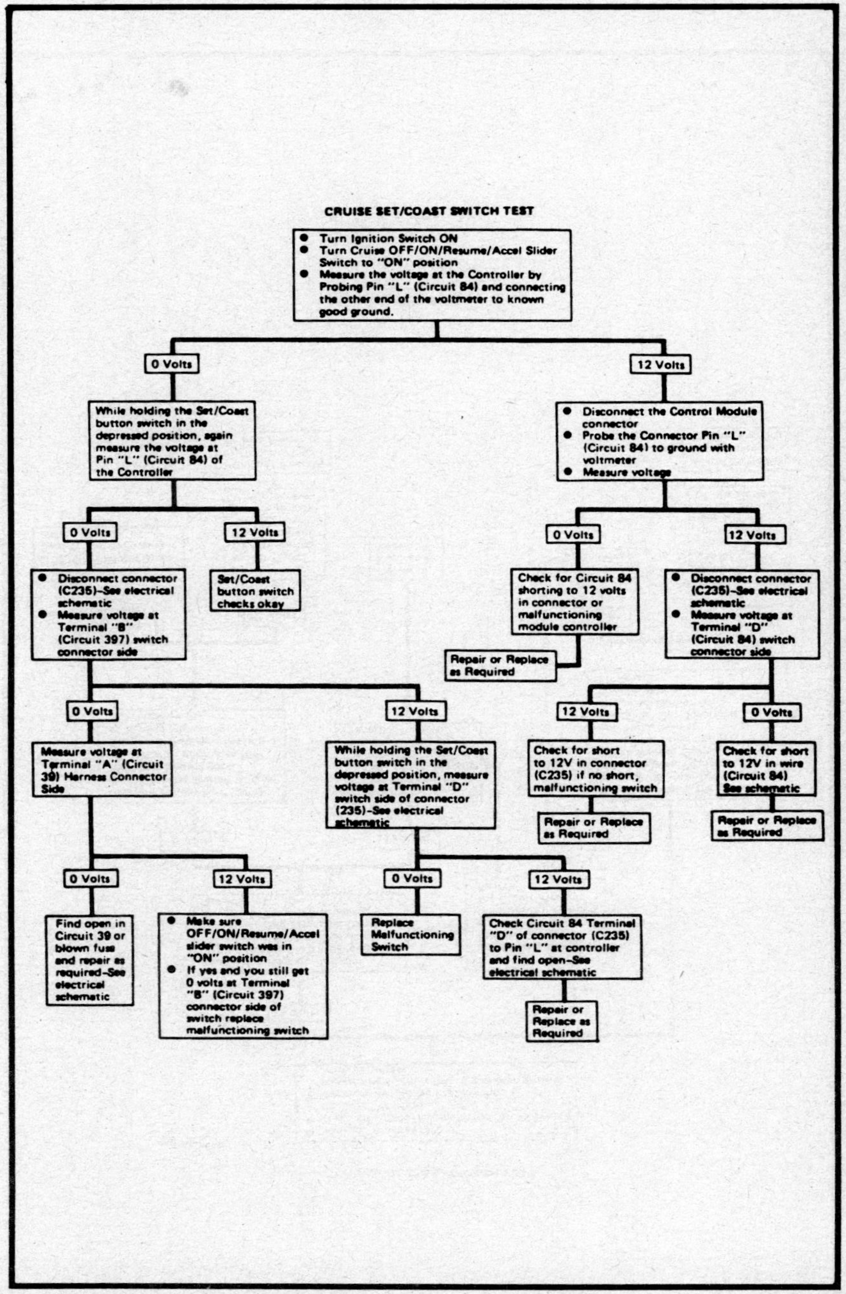

CRUISE SET/COAST SWITCH TEST

- Turn Ignition Switch ON
- Turn Cruise OFF/ON/Resume/Accel Slider Switch to "ON" position
- Measure the voltage at the Controller by Probing Pin "L" (Circuit 84) and connecting the other end of the voltmeter to known good ground.

12 Volts

- Disconnect the Control Module connector
- Probe the Connector Pin "L" (Circuit 84) to ground with voltmeter
- Measure voltage

12 Volts

- Disconnect connector (C235)—See electrical schematic
- Measure voltage at Terminal "D" (Circuit 84) switch connector side

0 Volts → Check for short to 12V in wire (Circuit 84) See schematic → Repair or Replace as Required

0 Volts → Check for Circuit 84 shorting to 12 volts in connector or malfunctioning module controller → Repair or Replace as Required

12 Volts → Check for short to 12V in connector (C235) if no short, malfunctioning switch → Repair or Replace as Required

12 Volts → Check Circuit 84 Terminal "D" of connector (C235) to Pin "L" at controller and find open—See electrical schematic → Repair or Replace as Required

12 Volts → While holding the Set/Coast button switch in the depressed position, measure voltage at Terminal "D" switch side of connector (235)—See electrical schematic

0 Volts → Replace Malfunctioning Switch

0 Volts

While holding the Set/Coast button switch in the depressed position, again measure the voltage at Pin "L" (Circuit 84) of the Controller

12 Volts → Set/Coast button switch checks okay

0 Volts

- Disconnect connector (C235)—See electrical schematic
- Measure voltage at Terminal "B" (Circuit 397) switch connector side

12 Volts → Make sure OFF/ON/Resume/Accel slider switch was in "ON" position, if yes and you still get 0 volts at Terminal "B" (Circuit 397) switch replace malfunctioning switch

0 Volts → Measure voltage at Terminal "A" (Circuit 39) Harness Connector Side

0 Volts → Find open in Circuit 39 or blown fuse and repair as required—See electrical schematic

---

SERVO TEST CONT'D

Ⓐ

Does resistance measure 0 ohms?

No

- Disconnect electrical connector from controller
- With an ohmmeter probe connector Cavity "J" (circuit 150) to known good ground.
- Measure the resistance

Does resistance measure 0 ohm?

Yes → Find open in circuit 150 (Pin "C" of servo to splice S243)
- See Electrical Section of Service Manual for Schematic → Repair or Replace as required

No → Find open in circuit 150 (Pin "J" of controller to ground Point G202)
- See Electrical Diagnosis Section of Service Manual for Schematic → Repair or Replace as required

Yes

Prior to starting engine:
- Disconnect the linkage, bead chain or cable from servo to throttle.
- Make sure the electrical connector to the servo is still disconnected.

Start the engine and set idle

Manually actuate the servo vent and vacuum control valves by inserting jumper wire from Positive (+) Battery Post to Pins "A" and "E" on the servo assembly. With another jumper wire connect one end to Pin "C" on the servo and the other end to a known good ground.

With the brake (and clutch) pedal in free position, does the servo pull in full stroke?

Yes → Remove jumper wire from Pin "E" on servo

Does servo stay at full stroke?

Yes → Check for proper connection of electrical connector at servo

No → Remove the larger of the 2 hoses to the now open fitting (orifice) on the servo. Reconnect the jumper wire to Pin "E" until servo pulls in full stroke, then remove the jumper wire from Pin "E"

Does the servo stay at the full stroke position?

Yes → Check brake and/or clutch release valve for adjustment (See On-Car Service for adjustment procedure) Check for leaks in hose(s) or valve(s) → Repair or Replace as required

No → Replace servo

No → Remove the larger of the 2 hoses to the now open plug the now open fitting (orifice) on the servo

Does the Servo Pull in full stroke?

Yes → Check brake and/or clutch release valve for adjustment (See On-Car Service for adjustment procedure) Check for leaks in hose(s) or valve(s) → (Repair or Replace as required) → Inspect connectors for leaks. If okay replace servo

No → Remove vacuum hose from servo (the smaller of the 2 hoses) and check for vacuum

Vacuum present?

No → Check vacuum system connections and vacuum source (See On-Car and vacuum schematics in On-Car Service Section) for leaks or incorrect connections. Collect, Repair or Replace as required

---

Cruise control diagnosis—1984 and later Pontiac

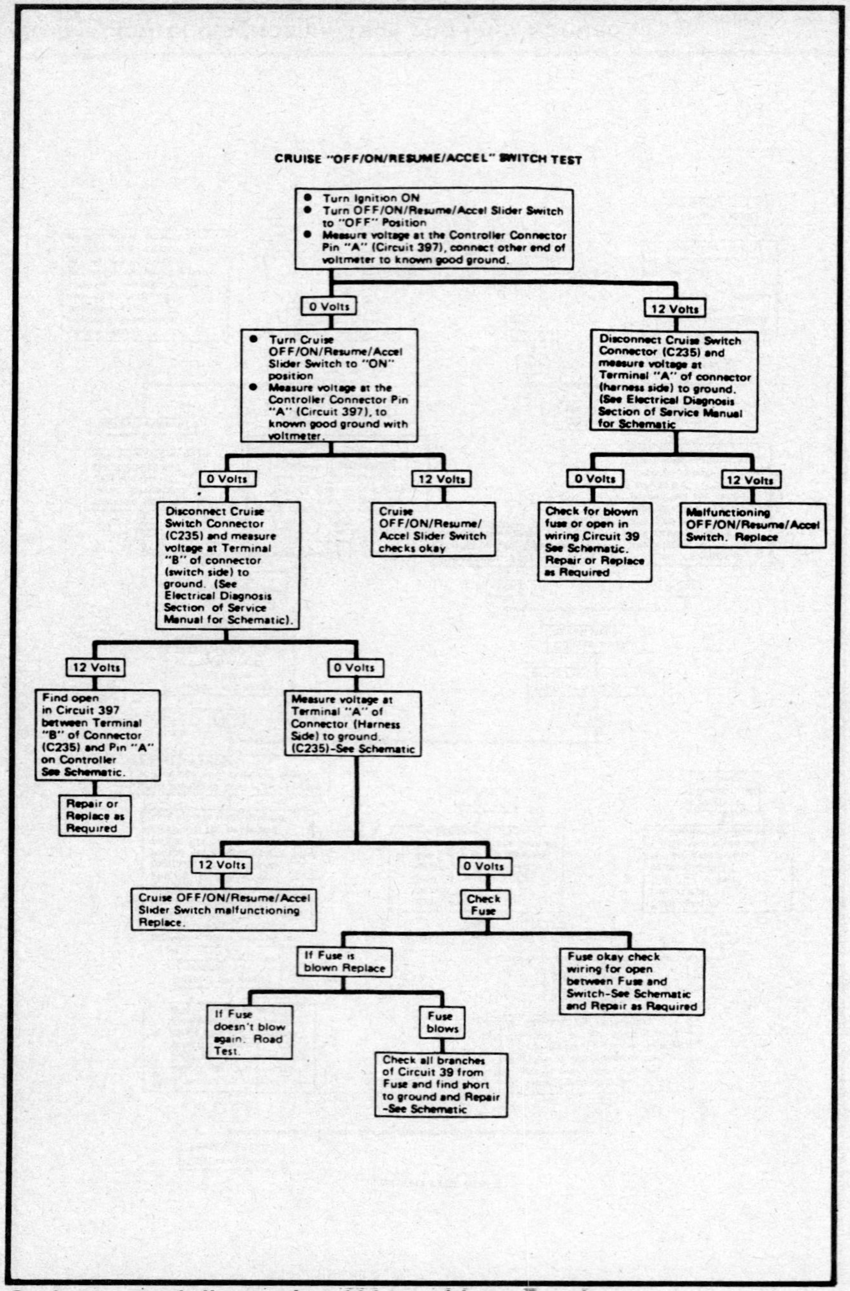

CRUISE RELEASE SWITCH TEST

- Ignition must be ON
- Turn OFF/ON/Resume/Accel Slider Switch to "ON" Position
- Measure voltage by Probing Pin "G" on Controller (Circuit 86) to a known ground with voltmeter.

12 Volts →
Measure voltage by Probing Brake Release Switch (Circuit 86) to a known good ground with voltmeter. (See Electrical Diagnosis Section of Service Manual for Schematic)

If car is equipped with Manual Transaxle make sure there is continuity through the Clutch Release Switch

12 Volts →
While depressing the Brake Pedal, measure the voltage by Probing Brake Release Switch (Circuit 86) to a known good ground with voltmeter. (See Electrical Diagnosis Section of Service Manual for Schematic)

12 Volts → Check Brake and/or Clutch Release Switch for adjustment (See ON-Car-Service portion of this section)

0 Volts → Brake Release Switch okay

→ Adjust or Replace malfunctioning Release Switch(s)

0 Volts →
Measure voltage by Probing Brake Release Switch (Circuit 397) to a known good ground with voltmeter. (See Electrical Diagnosis Section of Service Manual for Schematic)

12 Volts →
Find open in Circuit 86 between Cruise Control Module Connector (Pin "G") and Brake Release Switch Connector.
→ Repair or Replace as Required

0 Volts →

12 Volts →
Measure voltage by Probing Brake Release Switch (Circuit 397) to a known good ground with voltmeter. (See Electrical Diagnosis Section of Service Manual for Schematic)

12 Volts → Check Brake and/or Clutch Release Switch for adjustment (See ON-Car-Service portion of this section)
→ Adjust or Replace malfunctioning Release Switch(s)

0 Volts → Perform Cruise OFF/ON/Resume/Accel Switch Test following chart.

CRUISE "OFF/ON/RESUME/ACCEL" SWITCH TEST

- Turn Ignition ON
- Turn OFF/ON/Resume/Accel Slider Switch to "OFF" Position
- Measure voltage at the Controller Connector Pin "A" (Circuit 397), connect other end of voltmeter to known good ground.

12 Volts →
Disconnect Cruise Switch Connector (C235) and measure voltage at Terminal "A" of connector (Harness side) to ground. (See Electrical Diagnosis Section of Service Manual for Schematic)

12 Volts → Malfunctioning OFF/ON/Resume/Accel Switch, Replace.

0 Volts → Check for blown fuse or open in wiring Circuit 39 See Schematic. Repair or Replace as Required

0 Volts →
- Turn Cruise OFF/ON/Resume/Accel Slider Switch to "ON" position
- Measure voltage at the Controller Connector Pin "A" (Circuit 397), to known good ground with voltmeter.

12 Volts → Cruise OFF/ON/Resume/Accel Slider Switch checks okay

0 Volts →
Disconnect Cruise Switch Connector (C235) and measure voltage at Terminal "B" of connector (switch side) to ground. (See Electrical Diagnosis Section of Service Manual for Schematic).

12 Volts → Find open in Circuit 397 between Terminal "B" of connector (C235) and Pin "A" on Controller. See Schematic.
→ Repair or Replace as Required

0 Volts →
Measure voltage at Terminal "A" of Connector (Harness Side) to Ground (C235)—See Schematic.

0 Volts →

12 Volts → Cruise OFF/ON/Resume/Accel Slider Switch malfunctioning Replace.

0 Volts → Check Fuse

Fuse okay check wiring for open between Fuse and Switch—See Schematic and Repair as Required

If Fuse is blown Replace

If Fuse doesn't blow again, Road Test.

Fuse blows

Check all branches of Circuit 39 from Fuse and find short to ground and Repair —See Schematic.

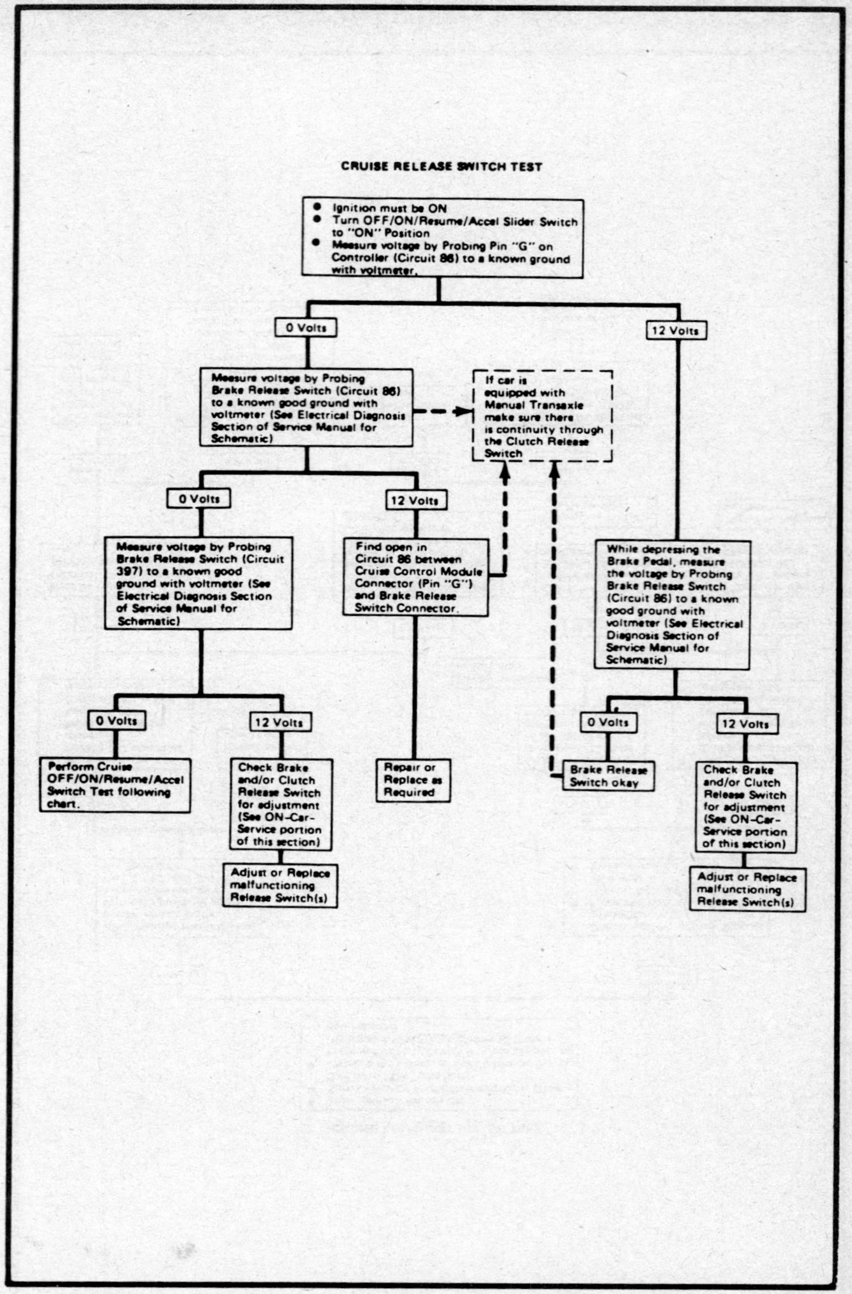

Cruise control diagnosis—1984 and later Pontiac

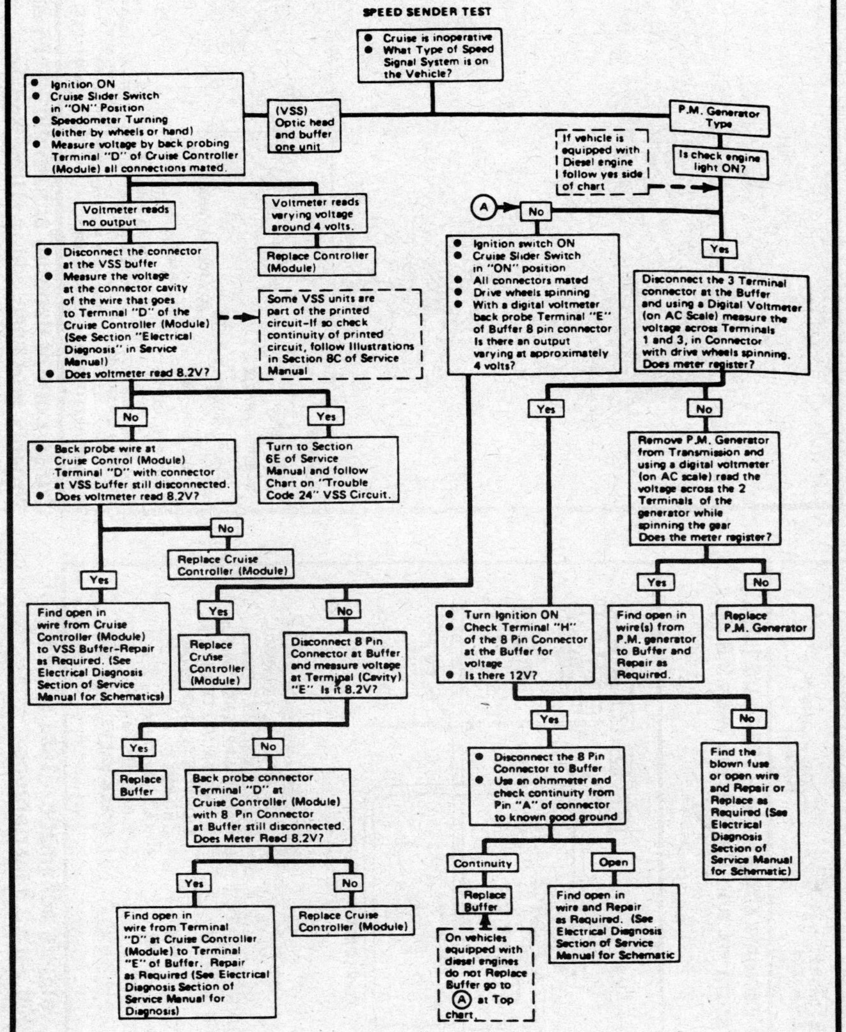
SPEED SENDER TEST
● Cruise is inoperative
● What Type of Speed Signal System is on the Vehicle?
(VSS) Optic head and buffer one unit
P.M. Generator Type
● Ignition ON
● Cruise Slider Switch in "ON" Position
● Speedometer Turning (either by wheels or hand)
● Measure voltage by back probing Terminal "D" of Cruise Controller (Module) all connections mated.
Voltmeter reads no output
Voltmeter reads varying voltage around 4 volts.
Replace Controller (Module)
● Disconnect the connector at the VSS buffer
● Measure the voltage at the connector cavity of the wire that goes to Terminal "D" of the Cruise Controller (Module) (See Section "Electrical Diagnosis" in Service Manual)
● Does voltmeter read 8.2V?
Some VSS units are part of the printed circuit–If so check continuity of printed circuit, follow Illustrations in Section 8C of Service Manual
No
Yes
● Back probe wire at Cruise Control (Module) Terminal "D" with connector at VSS buffer still disconnected.
● Does voltmeter read 8.2V?
Turn to Section 6E of Service Manual and follow Chart on "Trouble Code 24" VSS Circuit.
No
Replace Cruise Controller (Module)
Yes
Find open in wire from Cruise Controller (Module) to VSS Buffer–Repair as Required. (See Electrical Diagnosis Section of Service Manual for Schematics)
If vehicle is equipped with Diesel engine follow yes side of chart
Is check engine light ON?
A
No
Yes
● Ignition switch ON
● Cruise Slider Switch in "ON" position
● All connectors mated
● Drive wheels spinning
● With a digital voltmeter back probe Terminal "E" of Buffer 8 pin connector Is there an output varying at approximately 4 volts?
Disconnect the 3 Terminal connector at the Buffer and using a Digital Voltmeter (on AC Scale) measure the voltage across Terminals 1 and 3, in Connector with drive wheels spinning. Does meter register?
Yes
No
Remove P.M. Generator from Transmission and using a digital voltmeter (on AC scale) read the voltage across the 2 Terminals of the generator while spinning the gear Does the meter register?
Yes
No
Find open in wire(s) from P.M. generator to Buffer and Repair as Required.
Replace P.M. Generator
Yes
No
Replace Cruise Controller (Module)
Disconnect 8 Pin Connector at Buffer and measure voltage at Terminal (Cavity) "E" Is it 8.2V?
Yes
No
Replace Buffer
Back probe connector Terminal "D" at Cruise Controller (Module) with 8 Pin Connector at Buffer still disconnected. Does Meter Read 8.2V?
Yes
No
Find open in wire from Terminal "D" at Cruise Controller (Module) to Terminal "E" of Buffer. Repair as Required (See Electrical Diagnosis Section of Service Manual for Diagnosis)
Replace Cruise Controller (Module)
● Turn Ignition ON
● Check Terminal "H" of the 8 Pin Connector at the Buffer for voltage
● Is there 12V?
Yes
No
● Disconnect the 8 Pin Connector to Buffer
● Use an ohmmeter and check continuity from Pin "A" of connector to known good ground
Continuity
Open
Replace Buffer
On vehicles equipped with diesel engines do not Replace Buffer go to A at Top chart
Find open in wire and Repair as Required. (See Electrical Diagnosis Section of Service Manual for Schematic
Find the blown fuse or open wire and Repair or Replace as Required (See Electrical Diagnosis Section of Service Manual for Schematic)

Cruise control diagnosis—1984 and later Pontiac

CONTROL SWITCH CONTINUITY CHECK

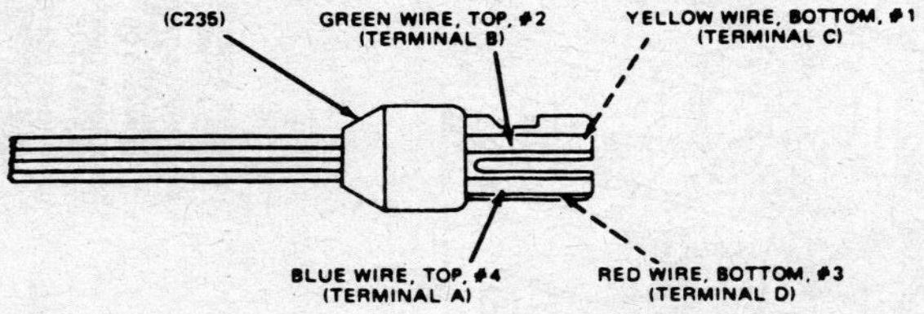
(C235)
GREEN WIRE, TOP, #2 (TERMINAL B)
YELLOW WIRE, BOTTOM, #1 (TERMINAL C)
BLUE WIRE, TOP, #4 (TERMINAL A)
RED WIRE, BOTTOM, #3 (TERMINAL D)

C–CLOSED
O–OPEN

SET/COAST (S/C) SW	POSITION SLIDER	1-2	1-3	1-4	2-3	2-4	3-4
NORMAL	OFF	O	O	O	O	O	O
NORMAL	ON	O	O	O	O	C	O
NORMAL	R/A	C	O	C	O	C	O
DEPRESSED	OFF	O	O	O	C	O	O
DEPRESSED	ON	O	O	O	C	C	C
DEPRESSED	R/A	C	C	C	C	C	C

CRUISE CONTROLLER (MODULE) CHECKS AT CONNECTOR
• IGNITION ON
• CONTROLLER DISCONNECTED

PIN	FUNCTION	VOLTAGE TO GND	RESISTANCE	CONDITIONS
G	BRAKE INPUT	12 V 0 V	– –	BRAKE (AND CLUTCH) NOT DEPRESSED BRAKE (AND/OR CLUTCH) DEPRESSED
L	SET/COAST INPUT	12 V 0 V 0 V	– – –	SLIDER SWITCH "ON" – SET/COAST DEPRESSED SLIDER SWITCH "ON" – SET/COAST NORMAL SLIDER SWITCH "OFF" – SET/COAST NORMAL
M	RESUME/ ACCEL. INPUT	12 V 0 V 0 V	– – –	SLIDER SWITCH "R/A" POSITION SLIDER SWITCH "ON" – SET/COAST DEPRESSED OR NORMAL SLIDER SWITCH "OFF" – SET/COAST DEPRESSED OR NORMAL
J	GROUND	–	0 Ω	MEASURED TO VEHICLE GROUND
A	ON/OFF INPUT	12 V 0 V	– –	SLIDER SWITCH "ON" SLIDER SWITCH "OFF" – SET/COAST DEPRESSED OR NORMAL
B	INDICATOR LAMP	12 V	–	CRUISE ARMED
F H	SPS HIGH SPS LOW	– –	20-30 Ω 0 Ω	MEASURED BETWEEN PINS F & H – SERVO CONNECTED MEASURED BETWEEN PINS F & H – SERVO DISCONNECTED
D	SPEED SIGNAL	→	→	SEE CHART (DIAGNOSTIC) ON SPEED SENDER TEST
K	VACUUM VALVE CONTROL	– –	30-50 Ω ∞ Ω	MEASURED TO GROUND – SERVO CONNECTED MEASURED TO GROUND – SERVO NOT CONNECTED
C	VENT VALVE CONTROL	– –	30-50 Ω ∞ Ω	MEASURED TO GROUND – SERVO CONNECTED MEASURED TO GROUND – SERVO NOT CONNECTED

SERVO CHECKS
• SERVO CONNECTOR DISCONNECTED
• MEASURE AT SERVO PINS

PIN	FUNCTION	RESISTANCE	CONDITIONS
D B	SPS HIGH SPS LOW	20-30 Ω	MEASURED BETWEEN PINS D AND B (IF MEASURED RESISTANCE IS NOT STATED VALVE, REPLACE SERVO)
A	VENT VALVE	30-50 Ω	MEASURED BETWEEN PINS A AND C (IF MEASURED RESISTANCE IS NOT STATED VALVE, REPLACE SERVO)
E	VACUUM VALVE	30-50 Ω	MEASURED BETWEEN PINS E AND C (IF MEASURED RESISTANCE IS NOT STATED VALVE, REPLACE SERVO)

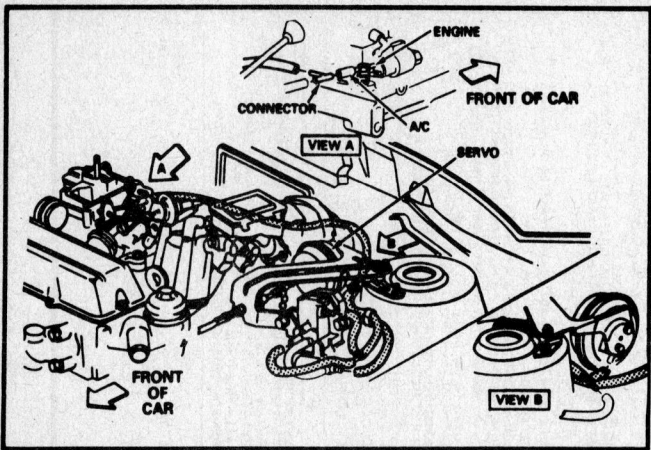

Cruise control vacuum schematic—1982–83 J2000 with 1.8 liter engine

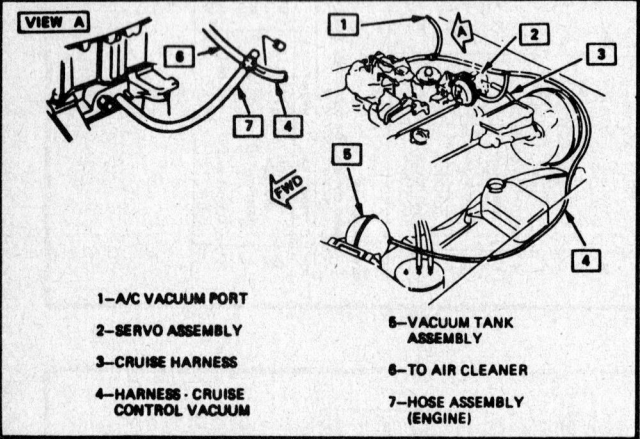

1—A/C VACUUM PORT

2—SERVO ASSEMBLY

3—CRUISE HARNESS

4—HARNESS - CRUISE CONTROL VACUUM

5—VACUUM TANK ASSEMBLY

6—TO AIR CLEANER

7—HOSE ASSEMBLY (ENGINE)

Cruise control vacuum schematic—1984 and later Bonneville, Grand Prix and Parisienne with 3.8 liter engine

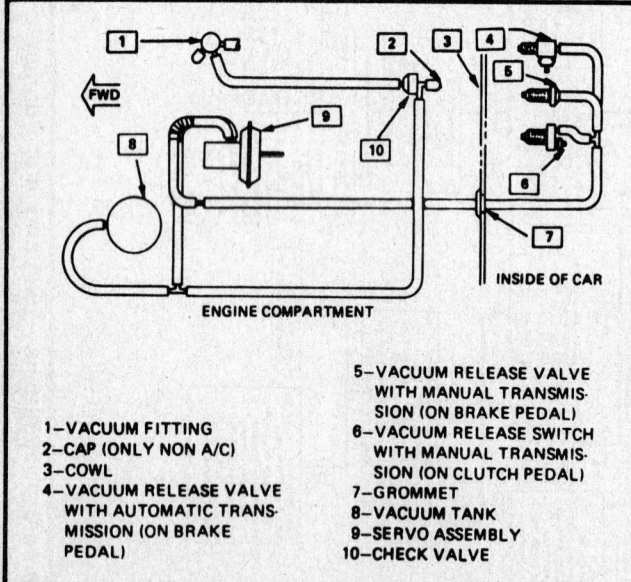

1—VACUUM FITTING
2—CAP (ONLY NON A/C)
3—COWL
4—VACUUM RELEASE VALVE WITH AUTOMATIC TRANS-MISSION (ON BRAKE PEDAL)

5—VACUUM RELEASE VALVE WITH MANUAL TRANSMIS-SION (ON BRAKE PEDAL)
6—VACUUM RELEASE SWITCH WITH MANUAL TRANSMIS-SION (ON CLUTCH PEDAL)
7—GROMMET
8—VACUUM TANK
9—SERVO ASSEMBLY
10—CHECK VALVE

Cruise control vacuum schematic—1984 and later Phoenix and 6000 with 2.5 liter engine

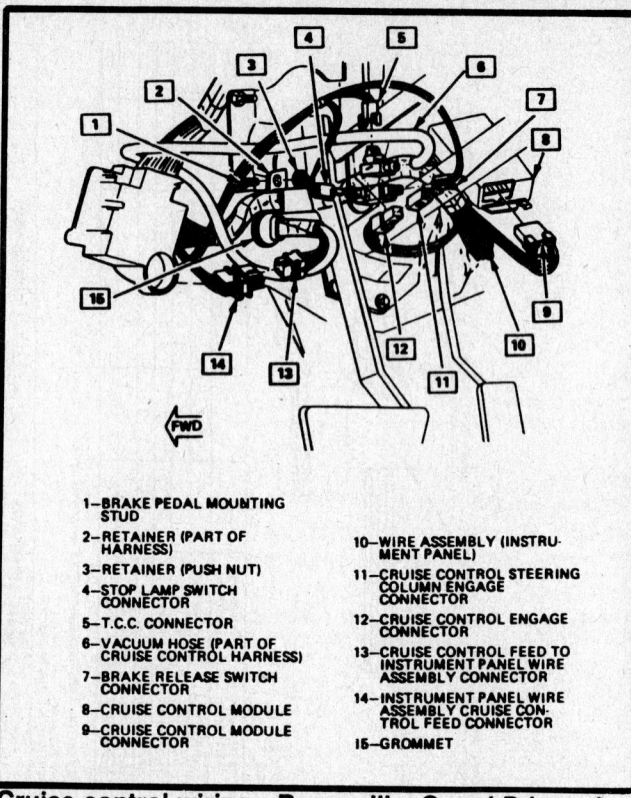

1—BRAKE PEDAL MOUNTING STUD
2—RETAINER (PART OF HARNESS)
3—RETAINER (PUSH NUT)
4—STOP LAMP SWITCH CONNECTOR
5—T.C.C. CONNECTOR
6—VACUUM HOSE (PART OF CRUISE CONTROL HARNESS)
7—BRAKE RELEASE SWITCH CONNECTOR
8—CRUISE CONTROL MODULE
9—CRUISE CONTROL MODULE CONNECTOR

10—WIRE ASSEMBLY (INSTRU-MENT PANEL)
11—CRUISE CONTROL STEERING COLUMN ENGAGE CONNECTOR
12—CRUISE CONTROL ENGAGE CONNECTOR
13—CRUISE CONTROL FEED TO INSTRUMENT PANEL WIRE ASSEMBLY CONNECTOR
14—INSTRUMENT PANEL WIRE ASSEMBLY CRUISE CON-TROL FEED CONNECTOR
15—GROMMET

Cruise control wiring—Bonneville, Grand Prix and Parisienne

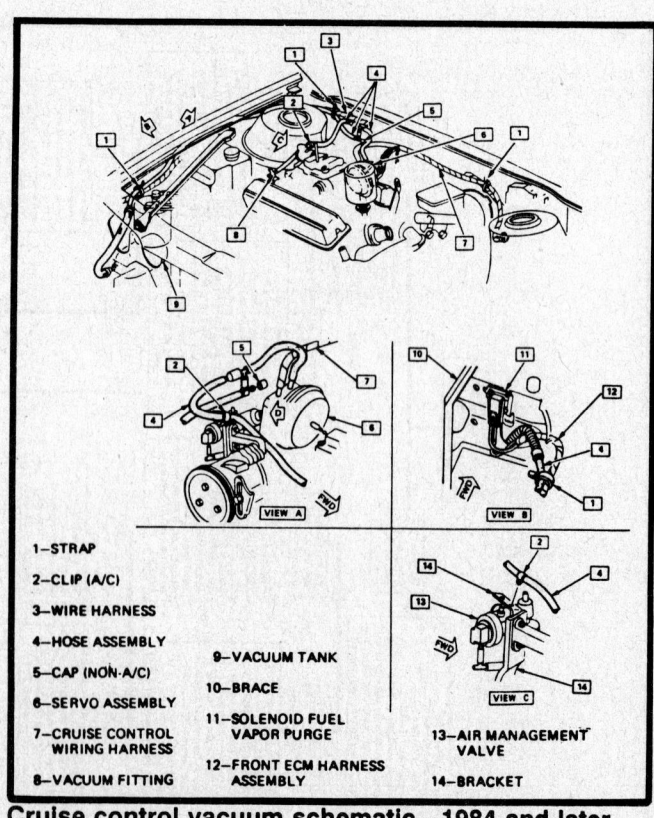

1—STRAP
2—CLIP (A/C)
3—WIRE HARNESS
4—HOSE ASSEMBLY
5—CAP (NON-A/C)
6—SERVO ASSEMBLY
7—CRUISE CONTROL WIRING HARNESS
8—VACUUM FITTING

9—VACUUM TANK
10—BRACE
11—SOLENOID FUEL VAPOR PURGE
12—FRONT ECM HARNESS ASSEMBLY

13—AIR MANAGEMENT VALVE
14—BRACKET

Cruise control vacuum schematic—1984 and later Phoenix and 6000 with 2.8 liter engine

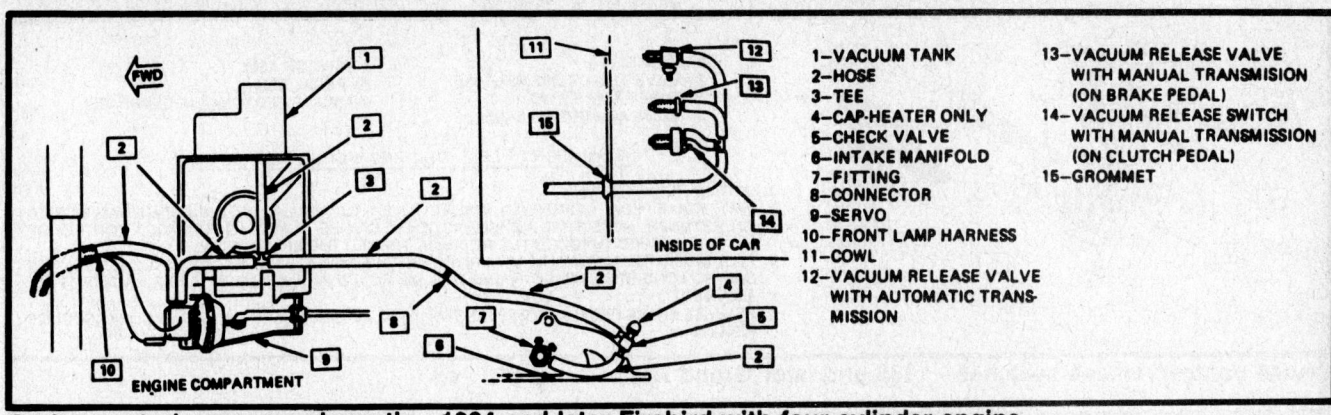

1—VACUUM TANK
2—HOSE
3—TEE
4—CAP-HEATER ONLY
5—CHECK VALVE
6—INTAKE MANIFOLD
7—FITTING
8—CONNECTOR
9—SERVO
10—FRONT LAMP HARNESS
11—COWL
12—VACUUM RELEASE VALVE WITH AUTOMATIC TRANSMISSION
13—VACUUM RELEASE VALVE WITH MANUAL TRANSMISSION (ON BRAKE PEDAL)
14—VACUUM RELEASE SWITCH WITH MANUAL TRANSMISSION (ON CLUTCH PEDAL)
15—GROMMET

Cruise control vacuum schematic—1984 and later Firebird with four cylinder engine

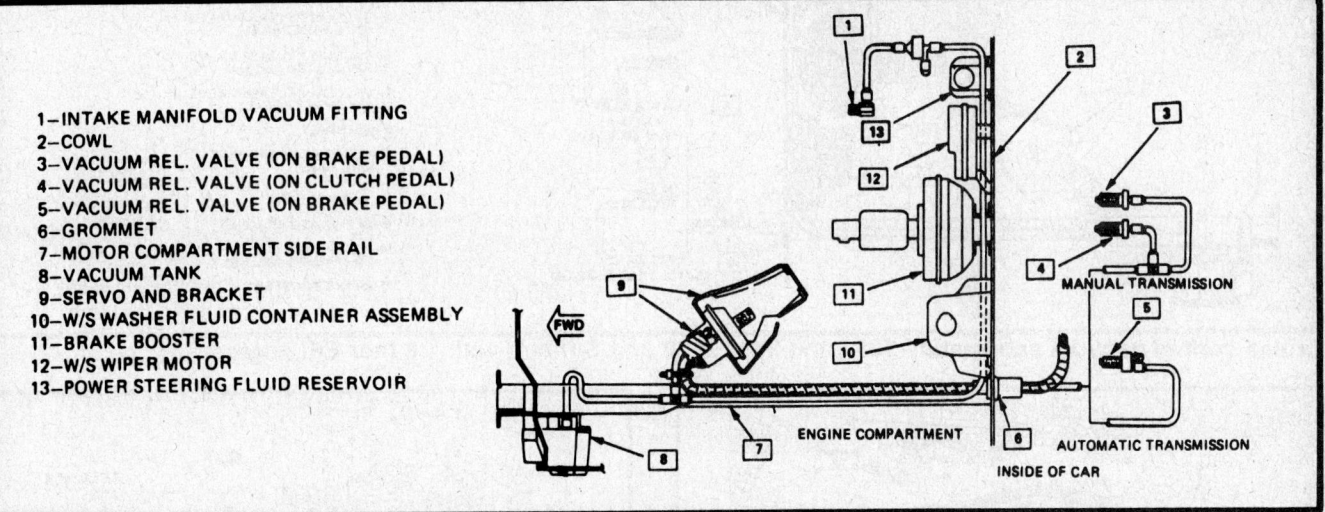

1—INTAKE MANIFOLD VACUUM FITTING
2—COWL
3—VACUUM REL. VALVE (ON BRAKE PEDAL)
4—VACUUM REL. VALVE (ON CLUTCH PEDAL)
5—VACUUM REL. VALVE (ON BRAKE PEDAL)
6—GROMMET
7—MOTOR COMPARTMENT SIDE RAIL
8—VACUUM TANK
9—SERVO AND BRACKET
10—W/S WASHER FLUID CONTAINER ASSEMBLY
11—BRAKE BOOSTER
12—W/S WIPER MOTOR
13—POWER STEERING FLUID RESERVOIR

Cruise control vacuum schematic—1984 and later 2000 and Sunbird with 1.8 liter turbo engine

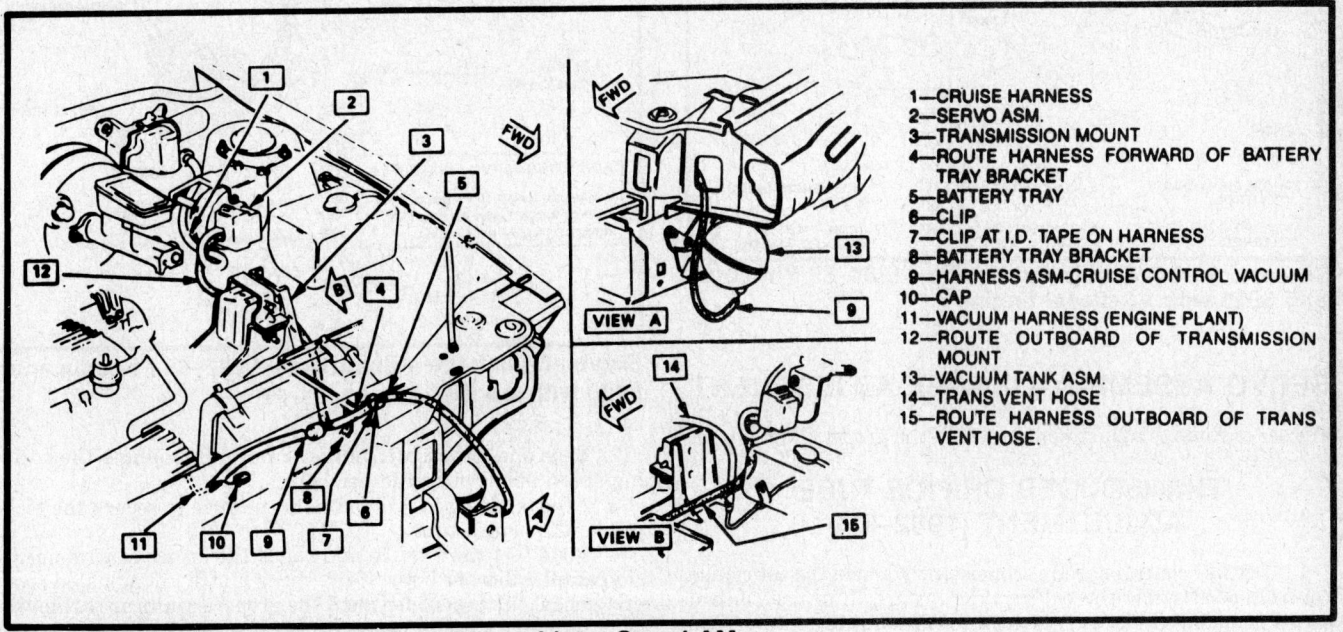

1—CRUISE HARNESS
2—SERVO ASM.
3—TRANSMISSION MOUNT
4—ROUTE HARNESS FORWARD OF BATTERY TRAY BRACKET
5—BATTERY TRAY
6—CLIP
7—CLIP AT I.D. TAPE ON HARNESS
8—BATTERY TRAY BRACKET
9—HARNESS ASM-CRUISE CONTROL VACUUM
10—CAP
11—VACUUM HARNESS (ENGINE PLANT)
12—ROUTE OUTBOARD OF TRANSMISSION MOUNT
13—VACUUM TANK ASM.
14—TRANS VENT HOSE
15—ROUTE HARNESS OUTBOARD OF TRANS VENT HOSE.

Cruise control vacuum schematic—1985 and later Grand AM

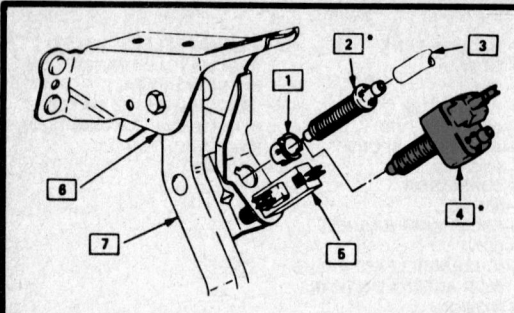

1—RETAINER
2—VALVE ASM-CRUISE RELEASE
3—TUBE FROM SERVO
4—VALVE ASM-VAC RELEASE

5—SWITCH ASM.
6—PEDAL ASM.
7—BRAKE PEDAL MOUNTING BRACKET

* INSTALLATION OF SELF-ADJUSTING VACUUM RELEASE VALVE

1. INSTALL RETAINER.
2. WITH BRAKE PEDAL DEPRESSED, INSERT VALVE INTO TUBULAR RETAINER UNTIL VALVE SEATS ON RETAINER. NOTE THAT AUDIBLE "CLICKS" CAN BE HEARD AS THREADED PORTION OF VALVE IS PUSHED THROUGH THE RETAINER TOWARD THE BRAKE PEDAL.
3. PULL BRAKE PEDAL FULLY REARWARD AGAINST PEDAL STOP UNTIL AUDIBLE "CLICK" SOUNDS CAN NO LONGER BE HEARD. VALVE WILL BE MOVED IN TUBULAR RETAINER PROVIDING ADJUSTMENT
4. RELEASE BRAKE PEDAL AND REPEAT STEP (3) TO ASSURE THAT NO AUDIBLE "CLICK" SOUNDS REMAIN.

Cruise control release switches—1985 and later Grand AM

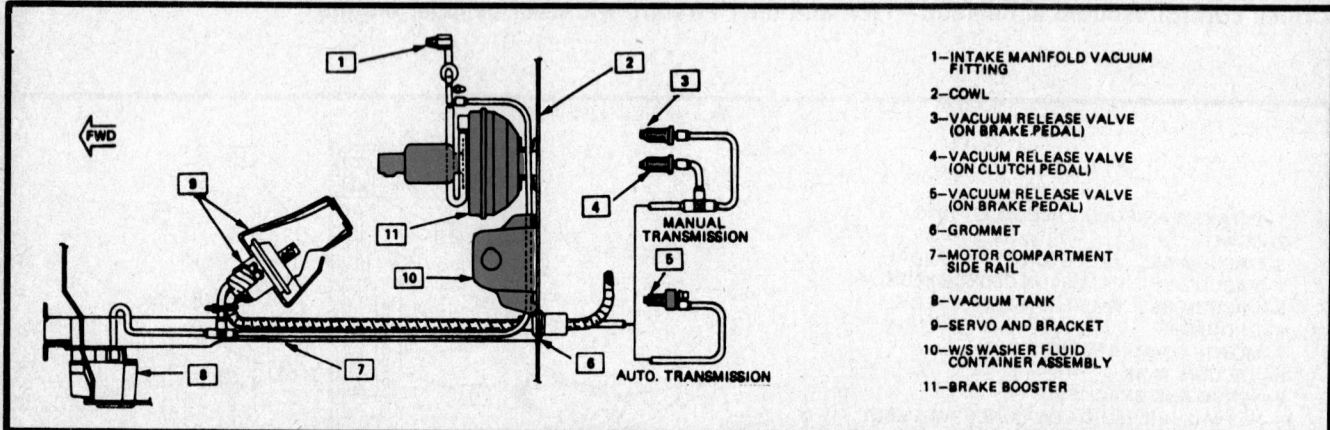

1—INTAKE MANIFOLD VACUUM FITTING
2—COWL
3—VACUUM RELEASE VALVE (ON BRAKE PEDAL)
4—VACUUM RELEASE VALVE (ON CLUTCH PEDAL)
5—VACUUM RELEASE VALVE (ON BRAKE PEDAL)
6—GROMMET
7—MOTOR COMPARTMENT SIDE RAIL
8—VACUUM TANK
9—SERVO AND BRACKET
10—W/S WASHER FLUID CONTAINER ASSEMBLY
11—BRAKE BOOSTER

Cruise control vacuum schematic—1984 and later 2000 and Sunbird with 1.8 liter EFI engine

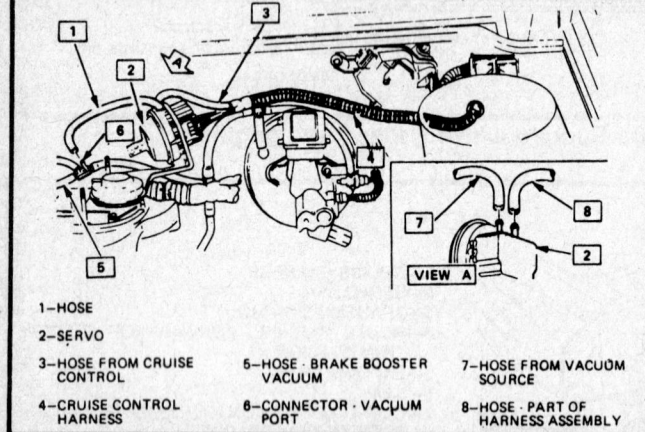

1—HOSE
2—SERVO
3—HOSE FROM CRUISE CONTROL
4—CRUISE CONTROL HARNESS
5—HOSE · BRAKE BOOSTER VACUUM
6—CONNECTOR · VACUUM PORT
7—HOSE FROM VACUUM SOURCE
8—HOSE · PART OF HARNESS ASSEMBLY

Cruise control vacuum schematic—1984–85 Phoenix and 6000 with V6 diesel engine

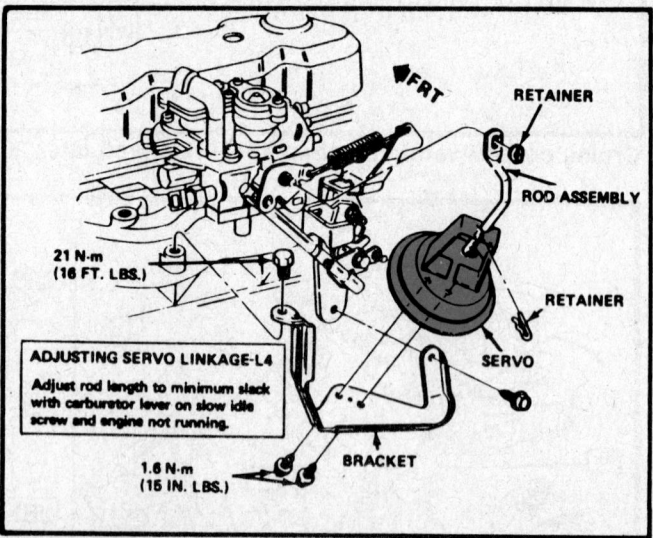

ADJUSTING SERVO LINKAGE-L4
Adjust rod length to minimum slack with carburetor lever on slow idle screw and engine not running.

21 N·m (16 FT. LBS.)

1.6 N·m (15 IN. LBS.)

Servo and linkage adjustment—1982–83 Phoenix and 6000 with 2.5 liter engine

SERVO ASSEMBLY LINKAGE ADJUSTMENT

For servo linkage adjustments refer to the proper illustration.

TRANSDUCER ORIFICE TUBE ADJUSTMENT (1982–83)

1. If cruise control speed is consistently above the set cruise control speed screw the orifice tube inward. If cruise control speed is below the set cruise control speed screw the orifice tube outward.

2. Each one-fourth turn of the orifice tube changes the cruising speed about one mile per hour.

3. After making the adjustment, be sure to secure the locknut to the orifice tube.

4. Road test the vehicle and check the cruise control operation at 50 miles per hour. If the speed is still not adjusted properly repeat the procedure until the proper results are achieved.

5. If unable to achieve the proper test results the cruise control transducer should be serviced.

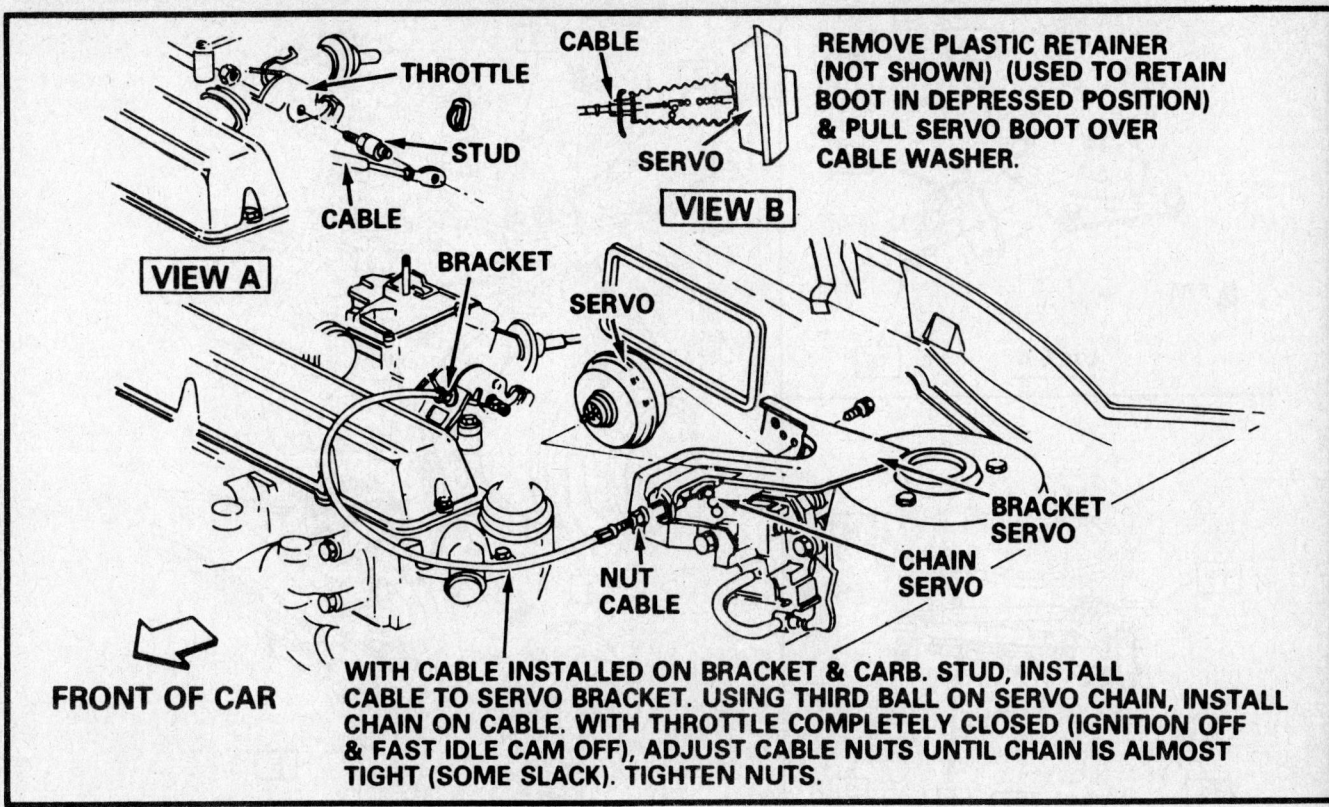

THROTTLE

STUD

CABLE

VIEW A

CABLE

SERVO

VIEW B

REMOVE PLASTIC RETAINER (NOT SHOWN) (USED TO RETAIN BOOT IN DEPRESSED POSITION) & PULL SERVO BOOT OVER CABLE WASHER.

BRACKET

SERVO

BRACKET SERVO

NUT CABLE

CHAIN SERVO

FRONT OF CAR

WITH CABLE INSTALLED ON BRACKET & CARB. STUD, INSTALL CABLE TO SERVO BRACKET. USING THIRD BALL ON SERVO CHAIN, INSTALL CHAIN ON CABLE. WITH THROTTLE COMPLETELY CLOSED (IGNITION OFF & FAST IDLE CAM OFF), ADJUST CABLE NUTS UNTIL CHAIN IS ALMOST TIGHT (SOME SLACK). TIGHTEN NUTS.

Servo and linkage adjustment – 1982–83 J2000

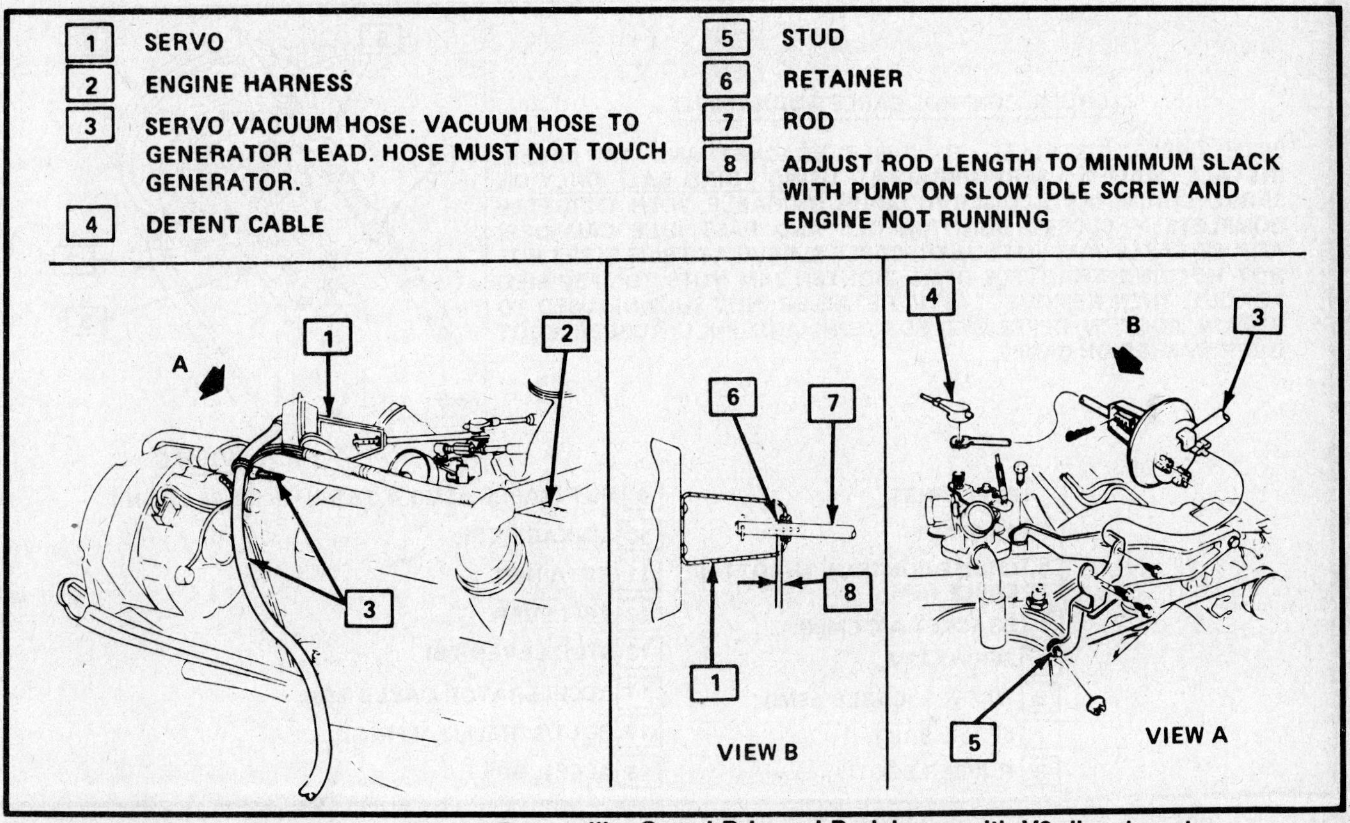

1	SERVO	5	STUD
2	ENGINE HARNESS	6	RETAINER
3	SERVO VACUUM HOSE. VACUUM HOSE TO GENERATOR LEAD. HOSE MUST NOT TOUCH GENERATOR.	7	ROD
4	DETENT CABLE	8	ADJUST ROD LENGTH TO MINIMUM SLACK WITH PUMP ON SLOW IDLE SCREW AND ENGINE NOT RUNNING

VIEW B

VIEW A

Servo and linkage adjustment – 1982–83 Bonneville, Grand Prix and Parisienne with V8 diesel engine

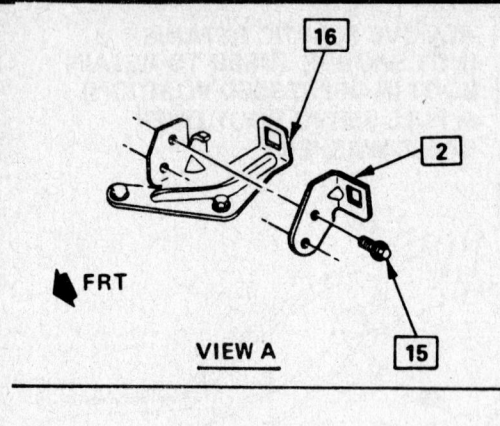

FRT

VIEW A

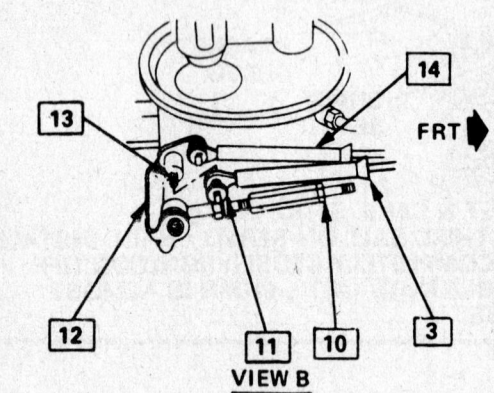

FRT

VIEW B

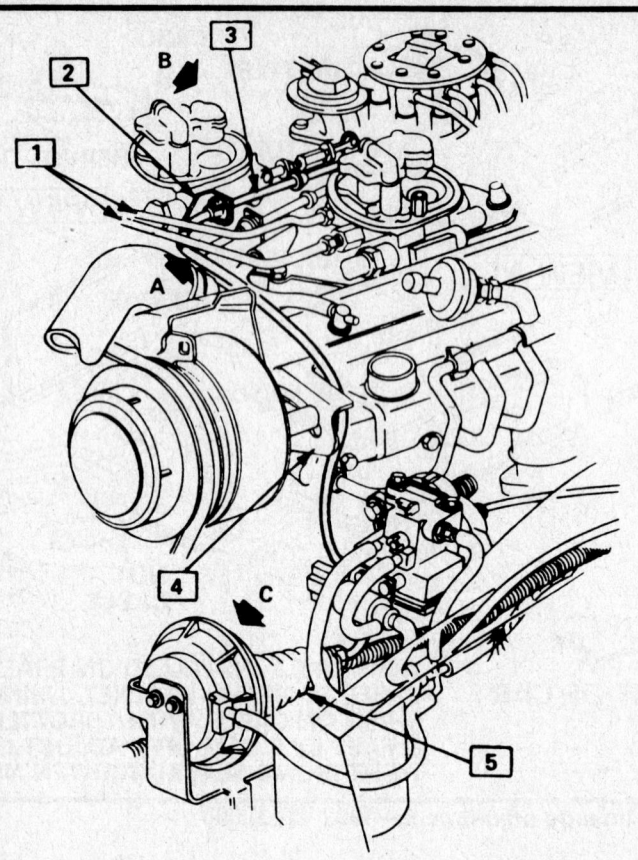

VIEW C

CRUISE CONTROL CABLE ADJUSTMENT

WITH CABLE INSTALLED TO CABLE BRACKET AND TBI LEVER, INSTALL CABLE TO SERVO BRACKET. USING THIRD BALL ONLY ON SERVO CHAIN, INSTALL SERVO CHAIN ON CABLE. WITH THROTTLE COMPLETELY CLOSED (IGNITION OFF AND FAST IDLE CAM OFF) ADJUST CABLE JAM NUTS UNTIL CABLE SLEEVE AT TBI IS TIGHT BUT NOT HOLDING THROTTLE OPEN. TIGHTEN JAM NUTS TO SPECIFIED TORQUE. THEN REMOVE PLASTIC RETAINER (NOT SHOWN) (USED TO RETAIN BOOT IN DEPRESSED POSITION) AND PULL RUBBER BOOT OVER WASHER ON CABLE.

1 FUEL LINES	9 NUT (CABLE ASM.) 4.0-5.5 N•m (35-48 LB. IN.)
2 BRACKET	10 LINKAGE TBI
3 CRUISE CONTROL THROTTLE CABLE ASM.	11 RETAINER
4 BRACKET A/C CMPR.	12 TBI LEVER
5 SERVO ASM.	13 STUD LEVER TBI
6 WASHER (CABLE ASM.)	14 ACCELERATOR CABLE ASM.
7 SERVO BRKT.	15 BOLT/SCREW (TAPPING)
8 RUBBER BOOT	16 ACCEL. BRKT.

Servo and linkage adjustment—1982–83 Firebird with 5.0 liter engine (vin code 7)

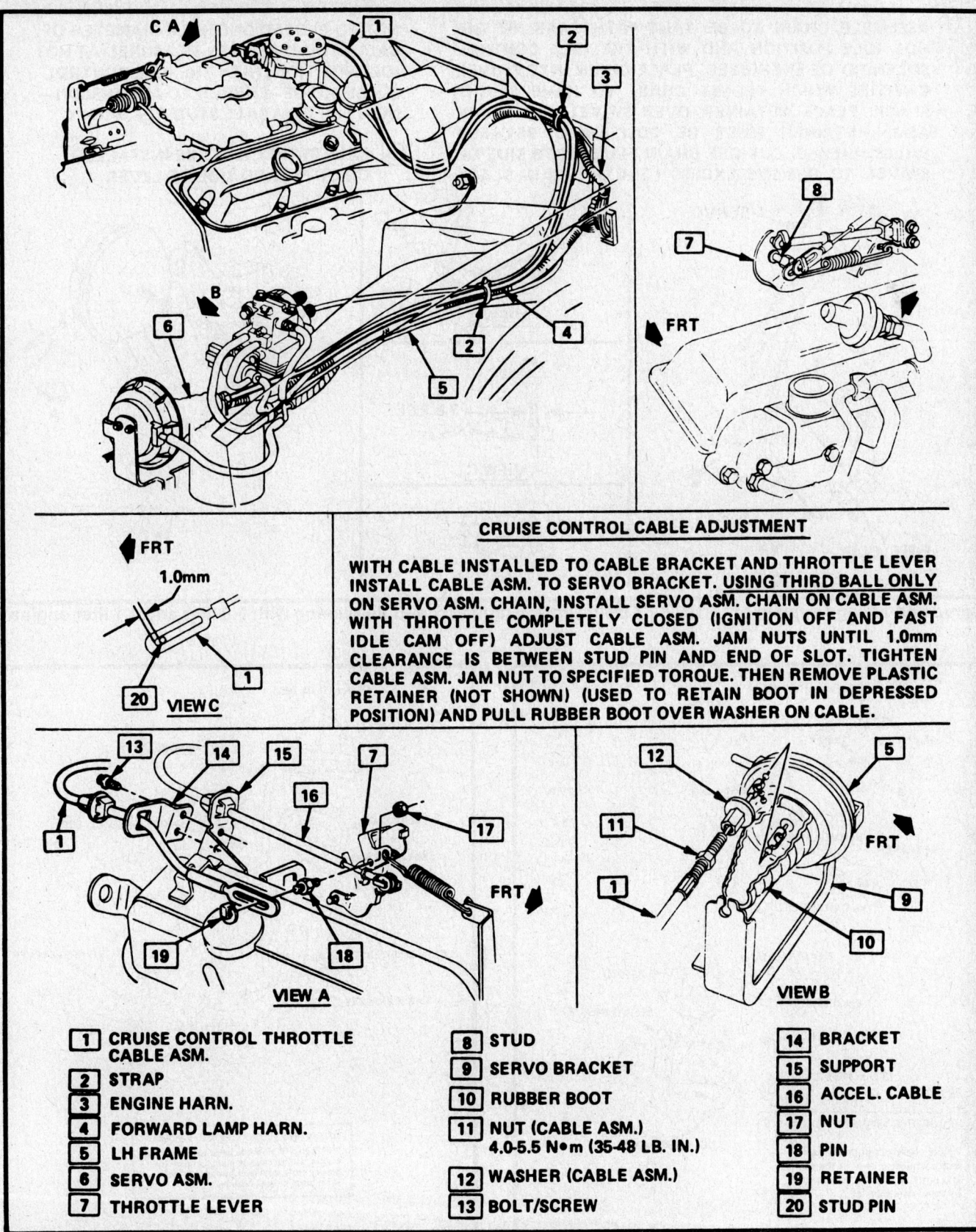

CRUISE CONTROL CABLE ADJUSTMENT

WITH CABLE INSTALLED TO CABLE BRACKET AND THROTTLE LEVER INSTALL CABLE ASM. TO SERVO BRACKET. USING THIRD BALL ONLY ON SERVO ASM. CHAIN, INSTALL SERVO ASM. CHAIN ON CABLE ASM. WITH THROTTLE COMPLETELY CLOSED (IGNITION OFF AND FAST IDLE CAM OFF) ADJUST CABLE ASM. JAM NUTS UNTIL 1.0mm CLEARANCE IS BETWEEN STUD PIN AND END OF SLOT. TIGHTEN CABLE ASM. JAM NUT TO SPECIFIED TORQUE. THEN REMOVE PLASTIC RETAINER (NOT SHOWN) (USED TO RETAIN BOOT IN DEPRESSED POSITION) AND PULL RUBBER BOOT OVER WASHER ON CABLE.

VIEW A

VIEW B

1 CRUISE CONTROL THROTTLE CABLE ASM.	8 STUD	14 BRACKET
2 STRAP	9 SERVO BRACKET	15 SUPPORT
3 ENGINE HARN.	10 RUBBER BOOT	16 ACCEL. CABLE
4 FORWARD LAMP HARN.	11 NUT (CABLE ASM.) 4.0-5.5 N•m (35-48 LB. IN.)	17 NUT
5 LH FRAME	12 WASHER (CABLE ASM.)	18 PIN
6 SERVO ASM.	13 BOLT/SCREW	19 RETAINER
7 THROTTLE LEVER		20 STUD PIN

Servo and linkage adjustment — 1982–83 Firebird with 2.8 liter and 5.0 liter engine (vin code H)

A ASSEMBLE CHAIN TO BE TAUT WITH CARB. IN THE HOT IDLE POSITION AND WITH THE IDLE CONTROL SOLENOID DE-ENERGIZED. PLACE CHAIN INTO SWIVEL CAVITIES WHICH PERMIT CHAIN TO HAVE SLIGHT SLACK. PLACE RETAINER OVER SWIVEL AND CHAIN ASM. RETAINER MUST BE POSITIONED BETWEEN BALLS: VIEW D. CUT OFF CHAIN FLUSH WITH SIDE OF SWIVEL TO REMOVE EXCESS LENGTH. CHAIN SLACK

NOT TO EXCEED ONE HALF DIAMETER OF BALL STUD (3.8) WHEN MEASURED AT HOT IDLE POSITION, WITH THE IDLE CONTROL SOLENOID DE-ENERGIZED AND DISCON-NECTED FROM BALL STUD REF. VIEW C

B BALL SWIVEL MUST BE INSTALLED ON OUTBOARD SIDE OF LEVER.

SERVO

VIEW B

D

3.8 REF.

VIEW C

VIEW D

C

B

A

E.F.E. CLIP

VIEW A

Servo and linkage adjustment – 1982–83 Bonneville, Grand Prix and Parisienne with 3.8 liter and 4.1 liter engine

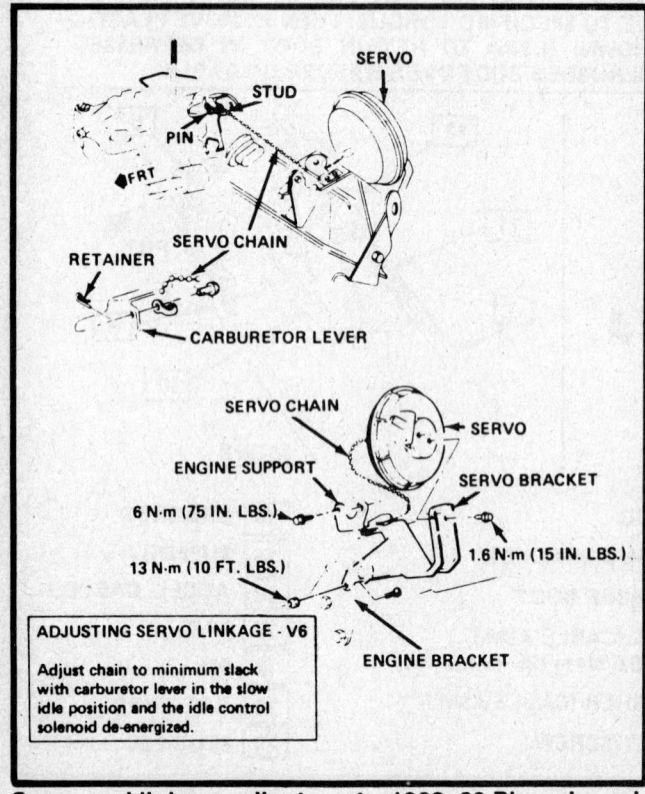

STUD

PIN

FRT

SERVO

RETAINER

SERVO CHAIN

CARBURETOR LEVER

SERVO CHAIN

SERVO

ENGINE SUPPORT

SERVO BRACKET

6 N·m (75 IN. LBS.)

13 N·m (10 FT. LBS.)

1.6 N·m (15 IN. LBS.)

ENGINE BRACKET

ADJUSTING SERVO LINKAGE - V6

Adjust chain to minimum slack with carburetor lever in the slow idle position and the idle control solenoid de-energized.

Servo and linkage adjustment – 1982–83 Phoenix and 6000 with V6 gas engine

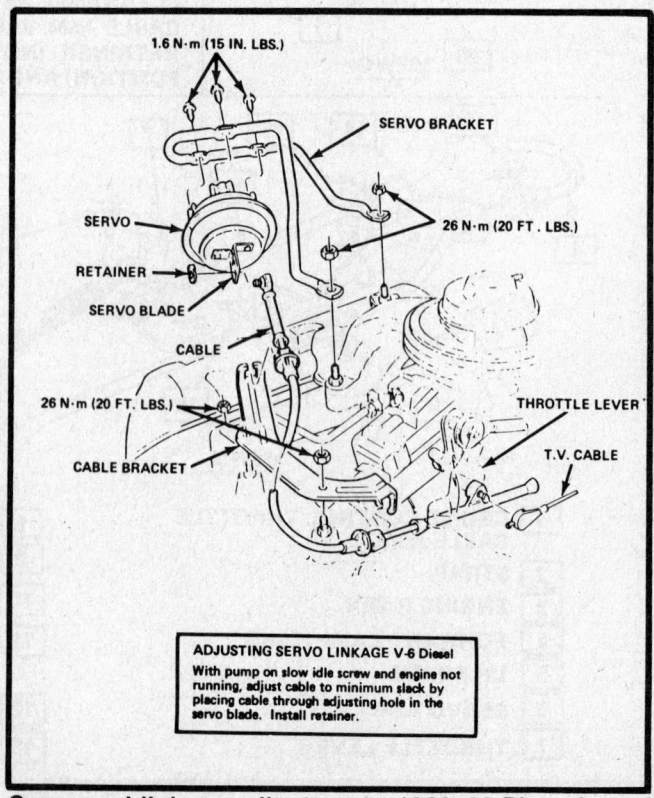

1.6 N·m (15 IN. LBS.)

SERVO BRACKET

SERVO

26 N·m (20 FT. LBS.)

RETAINER

SERVO BLADE

CABLE

26 N·m (20 FT. LBS.)

CABLE BRACKET

THROTTLE LEVER

T.V. CABLE

ADJUSTING SERVO LINKAGE V-6 Diesel

With pump on slow idle screw and engine not running, adjust cable to minimum slack by placing cable through adjusting hole in the servo blade. Install retainer.

Servo and linkage adjustment – 1982–83 Phoenix and 6000 with V6 diesel engine

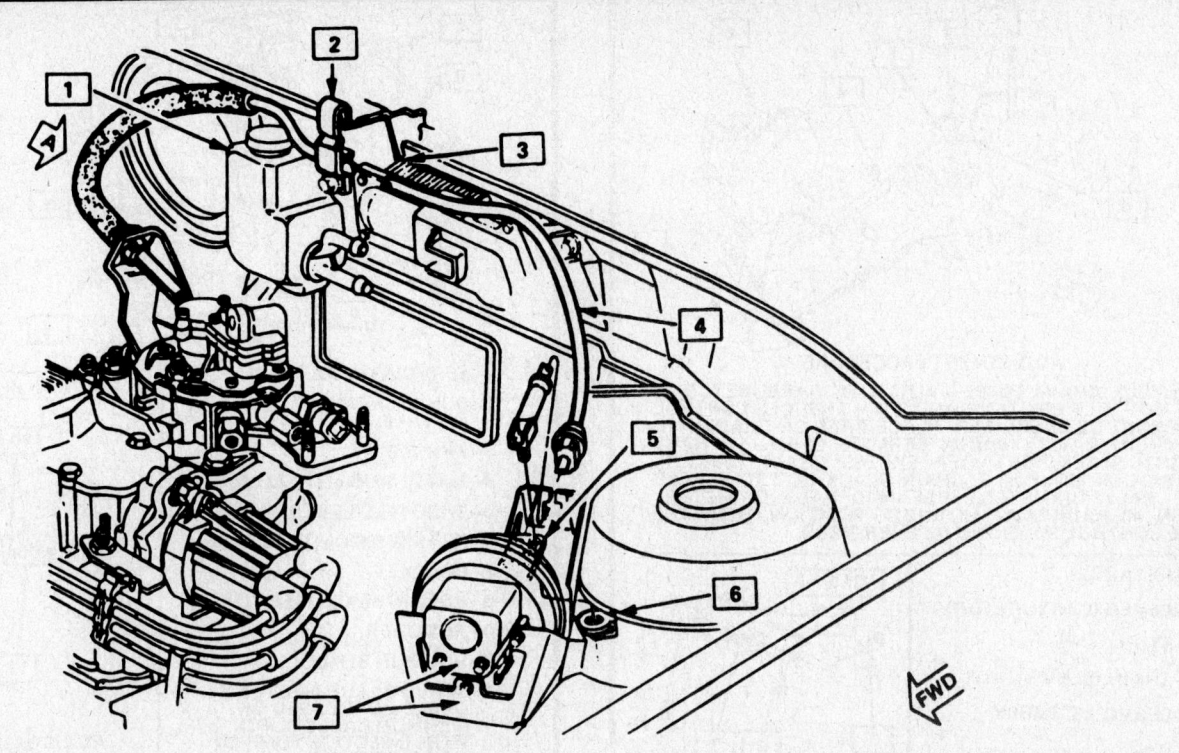

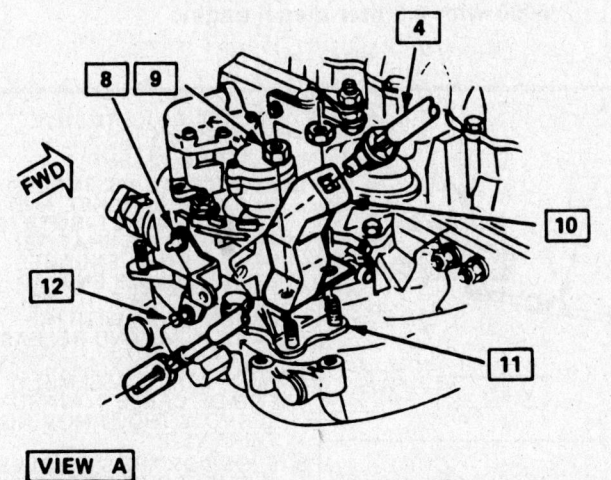

VIEW A

1—POWER STEERING FLUID RESERVOIR

2—CLIP

3—WINDSHIELD WIPER MOTOR

4—CABLE ASSEMBLY

5—SEE ADJUSTMENT PROCEDURE FOR PROPER HOLE

6—RETAINER

7—SERVO ASSEMBLY AND BRACKET

8—TBI ASSEMBLY LEVER

9—NUT

10—BRACKET

11—ADAPTER ASSEMBLY

12—STUD

CABLE ADJUSTMENT PROCEDURE AT SERVO ASSEMBLY

1. WITH CABLE INSTALLED IN BRACKET ON ADAPTER, INSTALL CABLE END (KEY HOLE SLOT) OVER STUD ON TBI LEVER BY ROTATING TBI LEVER UP SO STUD ENGAGES SLOT ON CABLE END. THEN RELEASE TBI LEVER.

2. PULL SERVO ASSEMBLY END OF CABLE TOWARD SERVO WITHOUT MOVING TBI LEVER.

3. IF ONE OF THE SIX HOLES IN THE SERVO ASSEMBLY TAB LINES UP WITH CABLE PIN, CONNECT PIN TO TAB WITH RETAINER.

4. IF A TAB HOLE DOES NOT LINE UP WITH THE PIN, MOVE THE CABLE AWAY FROM THE SERVO ASSEMBLY UNTIL THE NEXT CLOSEST TAB HOLE LINES UP AND CONNECT PIN TO TAB WITH RETAINER.

DO NOT STRETCH CABLE SO AS TO MAKE A PARTICULAR TAB HOLE CONNECT TO PIN, THIS WILL PREVENT ENGINE FROM RETURNING TO IDLE.

Servo and linkage adjustment—1984 and later 2000 and Sunbird with 1.8 liter engine

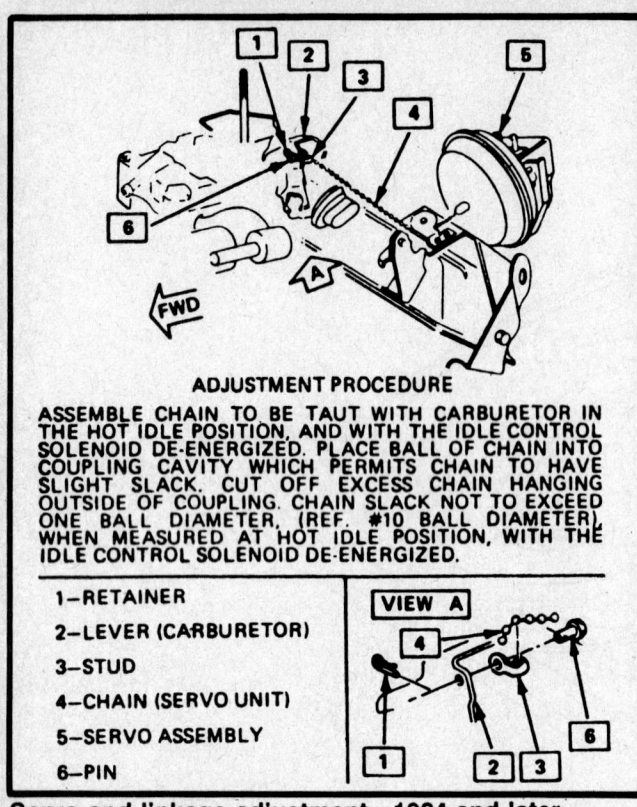

ADJUSTMENT PROCEDURE

ASSEMBLE CHAIN TO BE TAUT WITH CARBURETOR IN THE HOT IDLE POSITION, AND WITH THE IDLE CONTROL SOLENOID DE-ENERGIZED. PLACE BALL OF CHAIN INTO COUPLING CAVITY WHICH PERMITS CHAIN TO HAVE SLIGHT SLACK. CUT OFF EXCESS CHAIN HANGING OUTSIDE OF COUPLING. CHAIN SLACK NOT TO EXCEED ONE BALL DIAMETER, (REF. #10 BALL DIAMETER) WHEN MEASURED AT HOT IDLE POSITION, WITH THE IDLE CONTROL SOLENOID DE-ENERGIZED.

1—RETAINER

2—LEVER (CARBURETOR)

3—STUD

4—CHAIN (SERVO UNIT)

5—SERVO ASSEMBLY

6—PIN

VIEW A

Servo and linkage adjustment—1984 and later Phoenix and 6000 with 2.8 liter and 4.3 liter engine

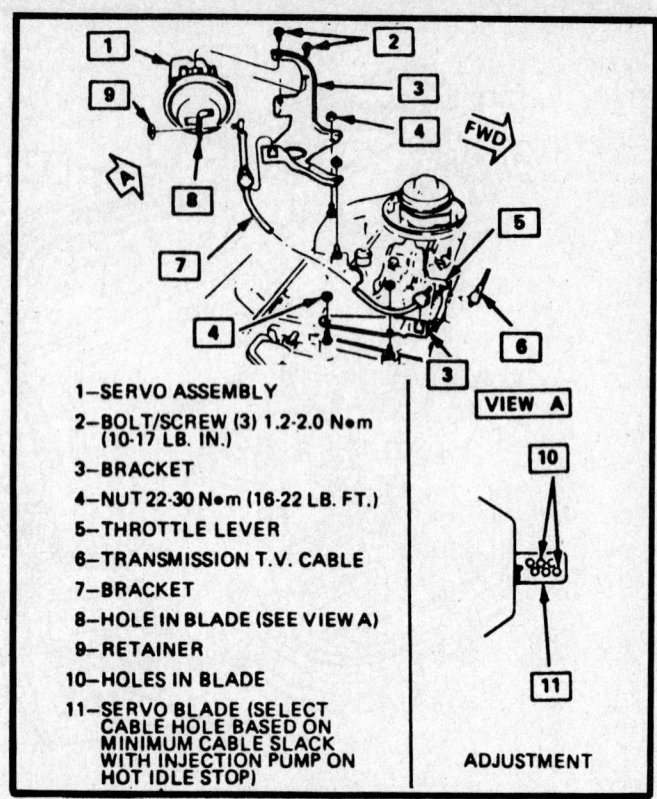

1—SERVO ASSEMBLY

2—BOLT/SCREW (3) 1.2-2.0 N•m (10-17 LB. IN.)

3—BRACKET

4—NUT 22-30 N•m (16-22 LB. FT.)

5—THROTTLE LEVER

6—TRANSMISSION T.V. CABLE

7—BRACKET

8—HOLE IN BLADE (SEE VIEW A)

9—RETAINER

10—HOLES IN BLADE

11—SERVO BLADE (SELECT CABLE HOLE BASED ON MINIMUM CABLE SLACK WITH INJECTION PUMP ON HOT IDLE STOP)

VIEW A

ADJUSTMENT

Servo and linkage adjustment—1984–85 Phoenix and 6000 with 4.3 liter diesel engine

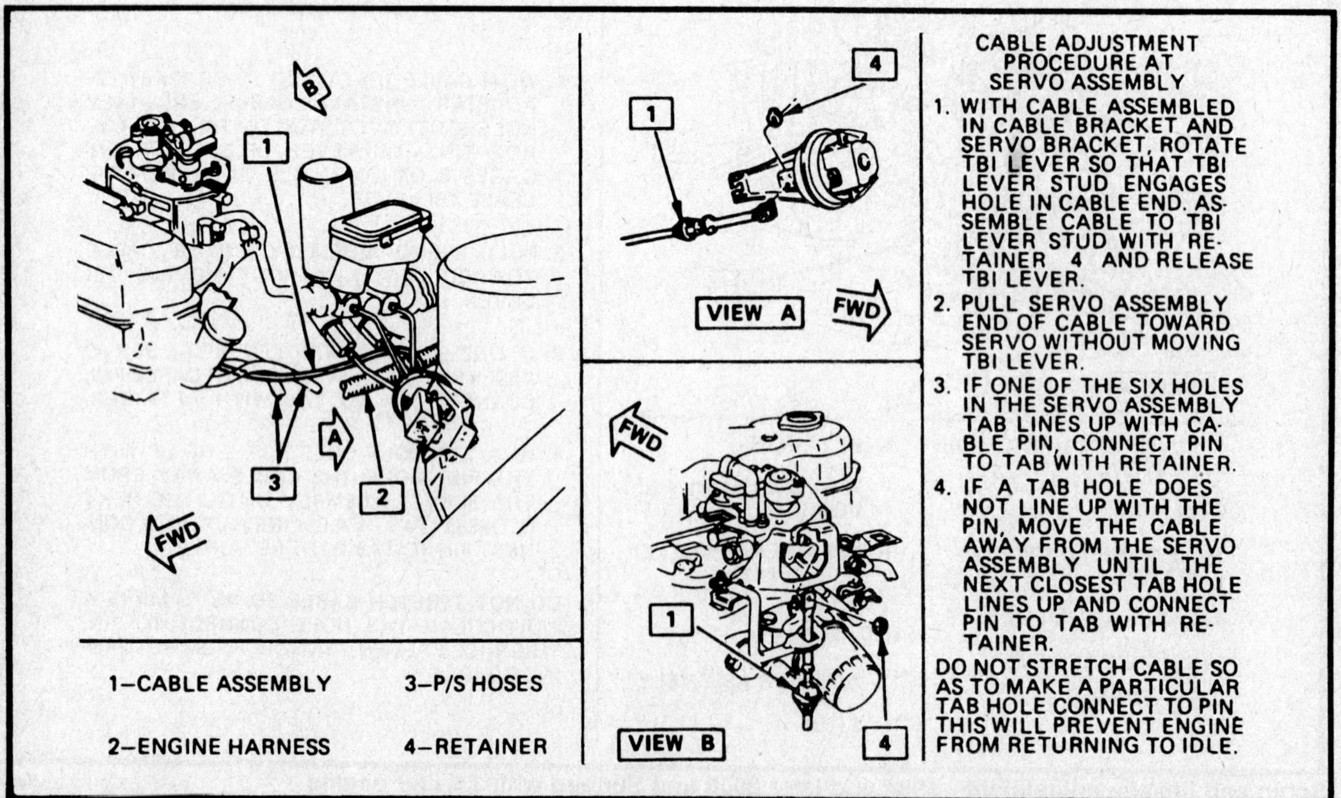

CABLE ADJUSTMENT PROCEDURE AT SERVO ASSEMBLY

1. WITH CABLE ASSEMBLED IN CABLE BRACKET AND SERVO BRACKET, ROTATE TBI LEVER SO THAT TBI LEVER STUD ENGAGES HOLE IN CABLE END. ASSEMBLE CABLE TO TBI LEVER STUD WITH RETAINER 4 AND RELEASE TBI LEVER.

2. PULL SERVO ASSEMBLY END OF CABLE TOWARD SERVO WITHOUT MOVING TBI LEVER.

3. IF ONE OF THE SIX HOLES IN THE SERVO ASSEMBLY TAB LINES UP WITH CABLE PIN, CONNECT PIN TO TAB WITH RETAINER.

4. IF A TAB HOLE DOES NOT LINE UP WITH THE PIN, MOVE THE CABLE AWAY FROM THE SERVO ASSEMBLY UNTIL THE NEXT CLOSEST TAB HOLE LINES UP AND CONNECT PIN TO TAB WITH RETAINER.

DO NOT STRETCH CABLE SO AS TO MAKE A PARTICULAR TAB HOLE CONNECT TO PIN THIS WILL PREVENT ENGINE FROM RETURNING TO IDLE.

VIEW A

VIEW B

1—CABLE ASSEMBLY

2—ENGINE HARNESS

3—P/S HOSES

4—RETAINER

Servo and linkage adjustment—1984 and later Phoenix and 6000 with 2.5 liter engine

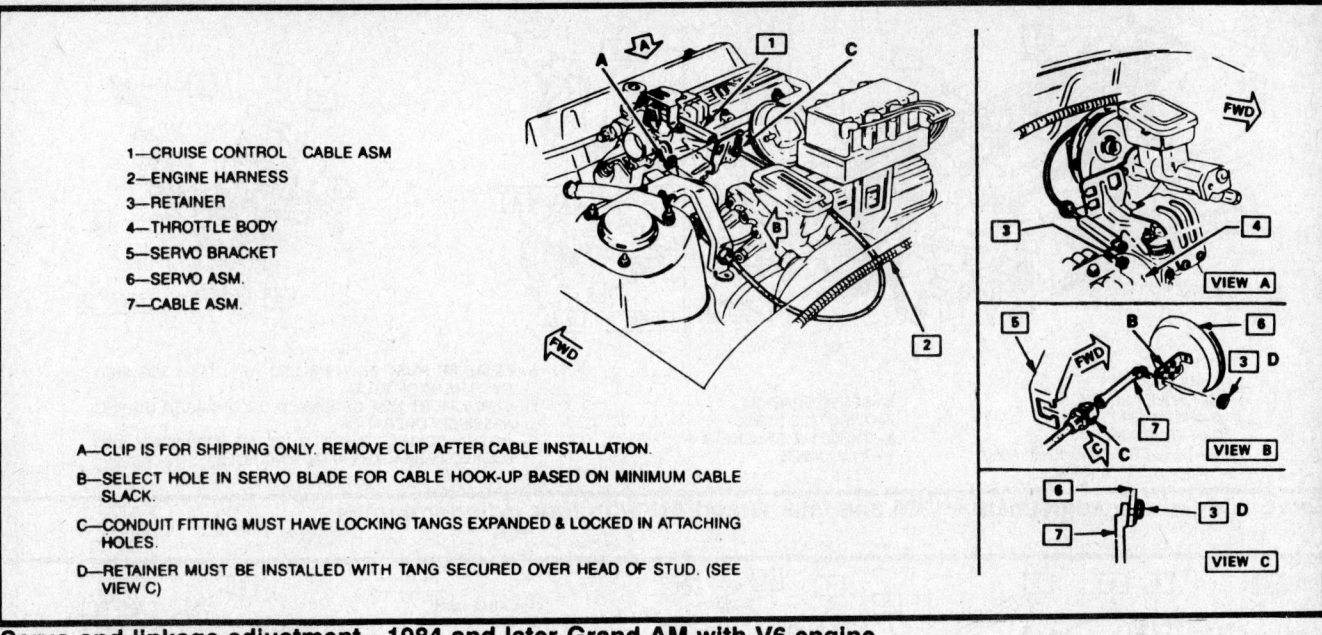

1—CRUISE CONTROL CABLE ASM
2—ENGINE HARNESS
3—RETAINER
4—THROTTLE BODY
5—SERVO BRACKET
6—SERVO ASM.
7—CABLE ASM.

A—CLIP IS FOR SHIPPING ONLY. REMOVE CLIP AFTER CABLE INSTALLATION.

B—SELECT HOLE IN SERVO BLADE FOR CABLE HOOK-UP BASED ON MINIMUM CABLE SLACK.

C—CONDUIT FITTING MUST HAVE LOCKING TANGS EXPANDED & LOCKED IN ATTACHING HOLES.

D—RETAINER MUST BE INSTALLED WITH TANG SECURED OVER HEAD OF STUD. (SEE VIEW C)

Servo and linkage adjustment—1984 and later Grand AM with V6 engine

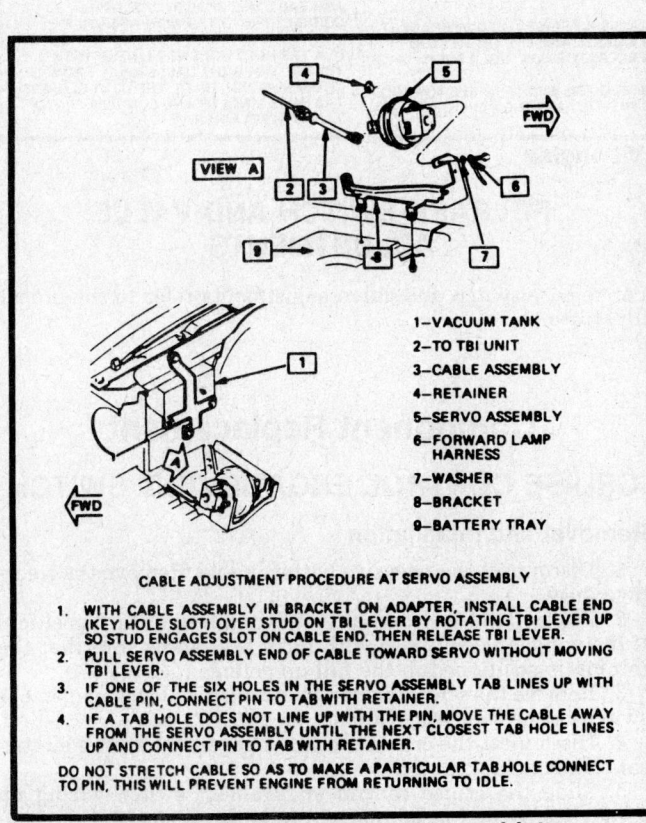

1—VACUUM TANK
2—TO TBI UNIT
3—CABLE ASSEMBLY
4—RETAINER
5—SERVO ASSEMBLY
6—FORWARD LAMP HARNESS
7—WASHER
8—BRACKET
9—BATTERY TRAY

CABLE ADJUSTMENT PROCEDURE AT SERVO ASSEMBLY

1. WITH CABLE ASSEMBLY IN BRACKET ON ADAPTER, INSTALL CABLE END (KEY HOLE SLOT) OVER STUD ON TBI LEVER BY ROTATING TBI LEVER UP SO STUD ENGAGES SLOT ON CABLE END. THEN RELEASE TBI LEVER.
2. PULL SERVO ASSEMBLY END OF CABLE TOWARD SERVO WITHOUT MOVING TBI LEVER.
3. IF ONE OF THE SIX HOLES IN THE SERVO ASSEMBLY TAB LINES UP WITH CABLE PIN, CONNECT PIN TO TAB WITH RETAINER.
4. IF A TAB HOLE DOES NOT LINE UP WITH THE PIN, MOVE THE CABLE AWAY FROM THE SERVO ASSEMBLY UNTIL THE NEXT CLOSEST TAB HOLE LINES UP AND CONNECT PIN TO TAB WITH RETAINER.

DO NOT STRETCH CABLE SO AS TO MAKE A PARTICULAR TAB HOLE CONNECT TO PIN, THIS WILL PREVENT ENGINE FROM RETURNING TO IDLE.

Servo and linkage adjustment—1984 and later Firebird with 2.5 liter engine

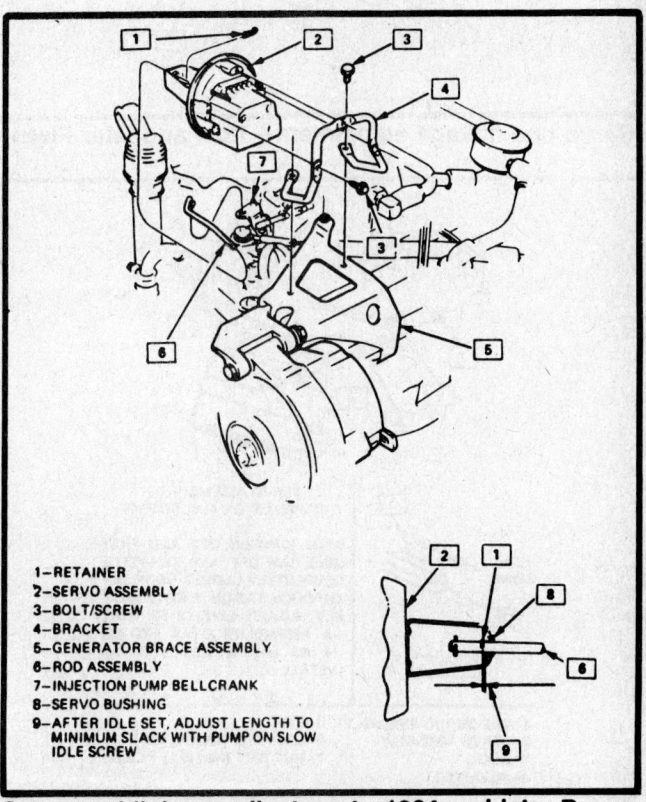

1—RETAINER
2—SERVO ASSEMBLY
3—BOLT/SCREW
4—BRACKET
5—GENERATOR BRACE ASSEMBLY
6—ROD ASSEMBLY
7—INJECTION PUMP BELLCRANK
8—SERVO BUSHING
9—AFTER IDLE SET, ADJUST LENGTH TO MINIMUM SLACK WITH PUMP ON SLOW IDLE SCREW

Servo and linkage adjustment—1984 and later Bonneville, Grand Prix and Parisienne with V8 diesel engine

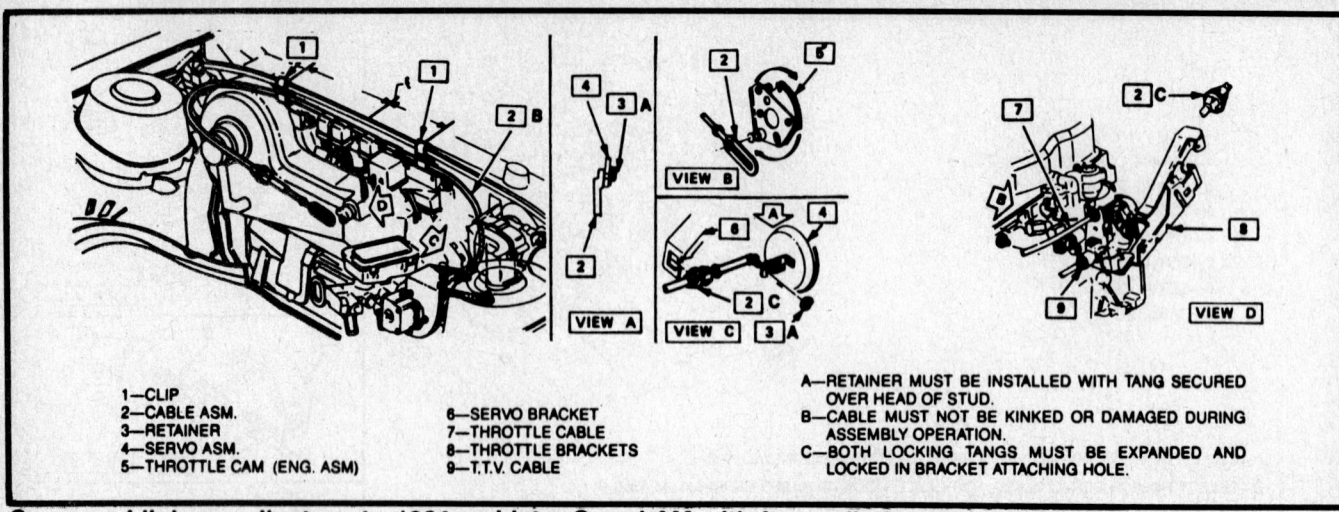

1—CLIP
2—CABLE ASM.
3—RETAINER
4—SERVO ASM.
5—THROTTLE CAM (ENG. ASM)
6—SERVO BRACKET
7—THROTTLE CABLE
8—THROTTLE BRACKETS
9—T.T.V. CABLE

A—RETAINER MUST BE INSTALLED WITH TANG SECURED OVER HEAD OF STUD.
B—CABLE MUST NOT BE KINKED OR DAMAGED DURING ASSEMBLY OPERATION.
C—BOTH LOCKING TANGS MUST BE EXPANDED AND LOCKED IN BRACKET ATTACHING HOLE.

Servo and linkage adjustment—1984 and later Grand AM with four cylinder engine

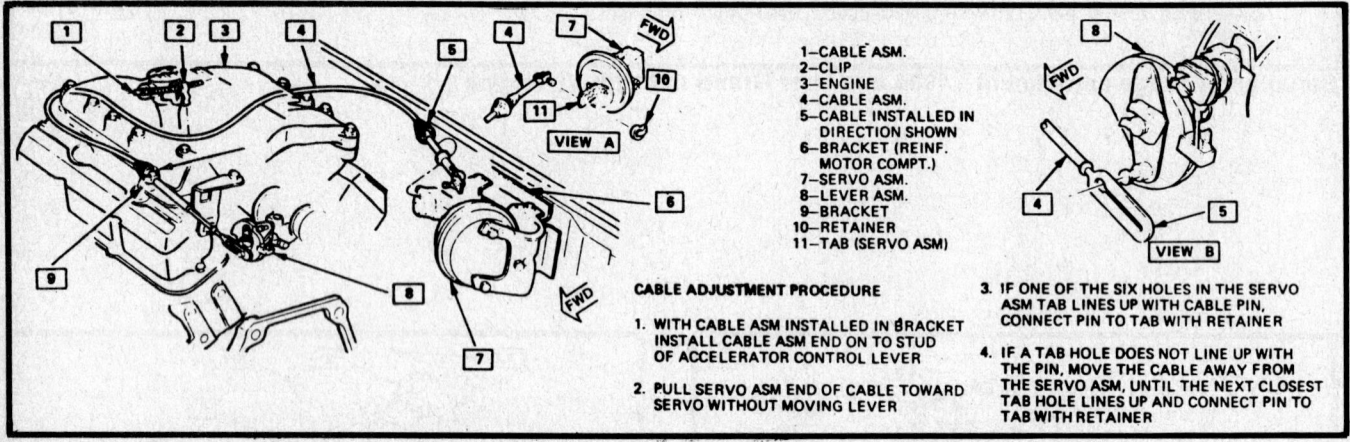

1—CABLE ASM.
2—CLIP
3—ENGINE
4—CABLE ASM.
5—CABLE INSTALLED IN DIRECTION SHOWN
6—BRACKET (REINF. MOTOR COMPT.)
7—SERVO ASM.
8—LEVER ASM.
9—BRACKET
10—RETAINER
11—TAB (SERVO ASM)

CABLE ADJUSTMENT PROCEDURE

1. WITH CABLE ASM INSTALLED IN BRACKET INSTALL CABLE ASM END ON TO STUD OF ACCELERATOR CONTROL LEVER
2. PULL SERVO ASM END OF CABLE TOWARD SERVO WITHOUT MOVING LEVER
3. IF ONE OF THE SIX HOLES IN THE SERVO ASM TAB LINES UP WITH CABLE PIN, CONNECT PIN TO TAB WITH RETAINER
4. IF A TAB HOLE DOES NOT LINE UP WITH THE PIN, MOVE THE CABLE AWAY FROM THE SERVO ASM, UNTIL THE NEXT CLOSEST TAB HOLE LINES UP AND CONNECT PIN TO TAB WITH RETAINER

Servo and linkage adjustment—1984 and later Fiero with V6 engine

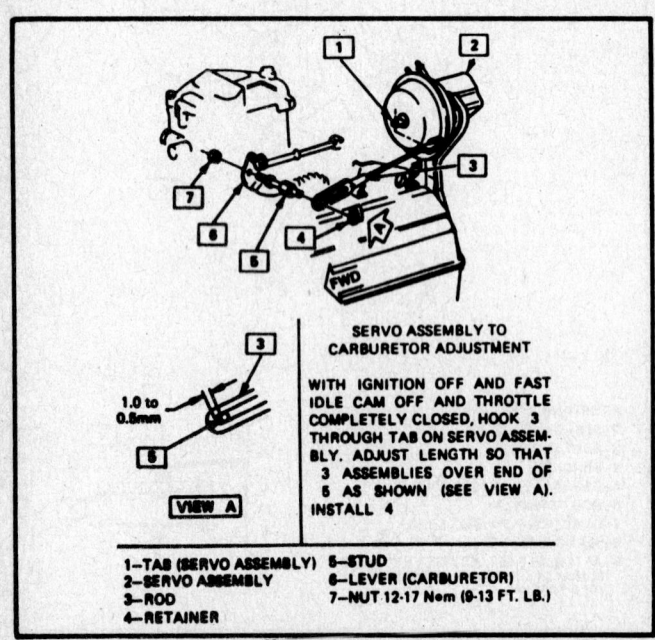

SERVO ASSEMBLY TO CARBURETOR ADJUSTMENT

WITH IGNITION OFF AND FAST IDLE CAM OFF AND THROTTLE COMPLETELY CLOSED, HOOK 3 THROUGH TAB ON SERVO ASSEMBLY. ADJUST LENGTH SO THAT 3 ASSEMBLIES OVER END OF 5 AS SHOWN (SEE VIEW A). INSTALL 4

1.0 to 0.8mm

1—TAB (SERVO ASSEMBLY)
2—SERVO ASSEMBLY
3—ROD
4—RETAINER
5—STUD
6—LEVER (CARBURETOR)
7—NUT 12-17 Nom (9-13 FT. LB.)

Servo and linkage adjustment—1984 and later Bonneville, Grand Prix and Parisienne with 5.0 liter engine

RELEASE SWITCH AND VALVE ADJUSTMENTS

For release switch and valve adjustments refer to the proper illustration.

Component Replacement

CRUISE CONTROL ENGAGEMENT SWITCH

Removal and Installation

1. Disconnect the negative battery cable. Remove the steering wheel.
2. Position the turn signal switch in the right turn position. If the vehicle is equipped with a tilt column be sure that the column is positioned in the full up detent.
3. Remove the screw securing the cruise control engagement switch to the steering column.
4. Disconnect the cruise control engagement switch electrical connection.
5. Slide the cruise control engagement switch wiring up through the steering column carefully. Remove the cruise control engagement switch from the vehicle.
6. Installation is the reverse of the removal procedure.

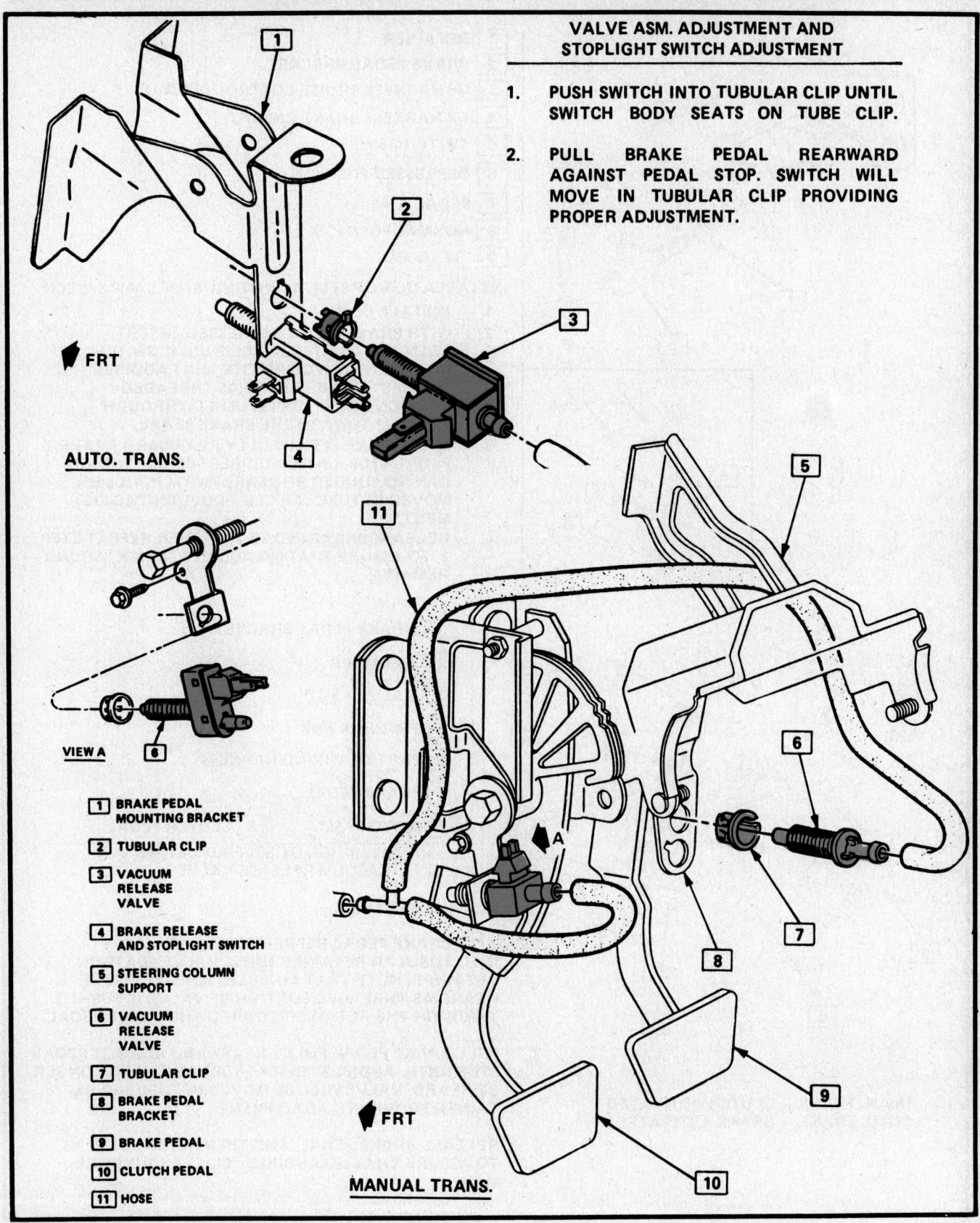

VALVE ASM. ADJUSTMENT AND STOPLIGHT SWITCH ADJUSTMENT

1. PUSH SWITCH INTO TUBULAR CLIP UNTIL SWITCH BODY SEATS ON TUBE CLIP.

2. PULL BRAKE PEDAL REARWARD AGAINST PEDAL STOP. SWITCH WILL MOVE IN TUBULAR CLIP PROVIDING PROPER ADJUSTMENT.

FRT

AUTO. TRANS.

VIEW A

1. BRAKE PEDAL MOUNTING BRACKET
2. TUBULAR CLIP
3. VACUUM RELEASE VALVE
4. BRAKE RELEASE AND STOPLIGHT SWITCH
5. STEERING COLUMN SUPPORT
6. VACUUM RELEASE VALVE
7. TUBULAR CLIP
8. BRAKE PEDAL BRACKET
9. BRAKE PEDAL
10. CLUTCH PEDAL
11. HOSE

FRT

MANUAL TRANS.

Cruise control release switches — Phoenix and 6000

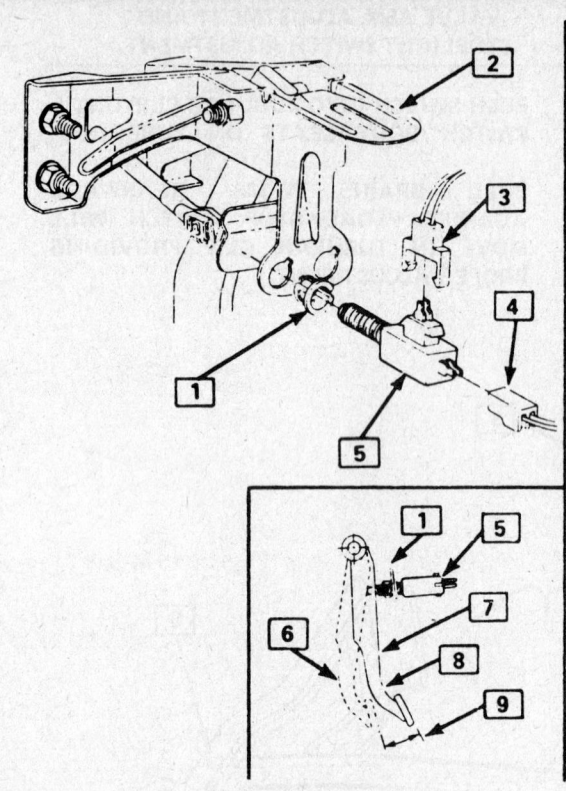

1	RETAINER
2	BRAKE PEDAL BRACKET
3	I/P HARNESS CRUISE CONTROL CIRCUIT
4	I/P HARNESS BRAKE CIRCUIT
5	SWITCH ASM.
6	DEPRESSED POSITION
7	PEDAL ASM.
8	NORMAL POSITION
9	.38 TO .64

INSTALLATION OF SELF ADJUSTING STOP LAMP SWITCH

1. INSTALL CLIP.
2. WITH BRAKE PEDAL DEPRESSED, INSERT SWITCH INTO TUBULAR CLIP UNTIL SWITCH BODY SEATS ON CLIP. NOTE THAT AUDIBLE "CLICKS" CAN BE HEARD AS THREADED PORTION OF SWITCH IS PUSHED THROUGH THE CLIP TOWARD THE BRAKE PEDAL.
3. PULL BRAKE PEDAL FULLY REARWARD AGAINST PEDAL STOP, UNTIL AUDIBLE "CLICK" SOUNDS CAN NO LONGER BE HEARD. SWITCH WILL BE MOVED IN TUBULAR CLIP PROVIDING ADJUSTMENT.
4. RELEASE BRAKE PEDAL, AND THEN REPEAT STEP 3, TO ASSURE THAT NO AUDIBLE "CLICK" SOUND REMAINS.

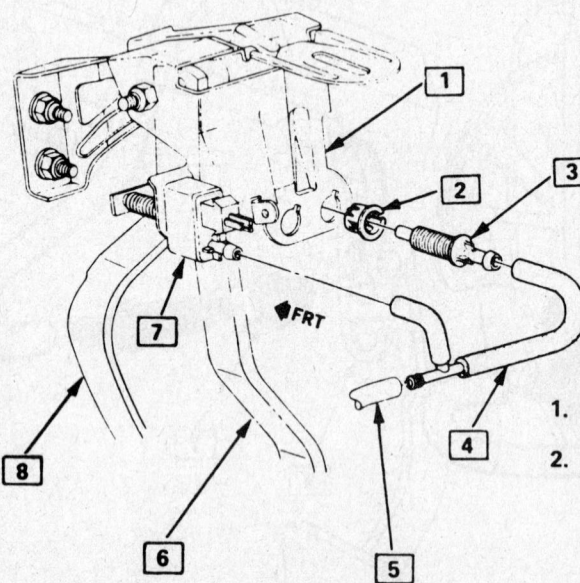

1	BRAKE PEDAL BRACKET
2	RETAINER
3	VALVE ASM.
4	HARNESS ASM.
5	PART OF WIRING HARNESS
6	BRAKE PEDAL
7	SWITCH ASM.*	8	CLUTCH PEDAL

INSTALLATION OF SELF-ADJUSTING VACUUM RELEASE VALVE

1. INSTALL RETAINER
2. WITH BRAKE PEDAL DEPRESSED, INSERT VALVE INTO TUBULAR RETAINER UNTIL VALVE SEATS ON RETAINER. NOTE THAT AUDIBLE "CLICKS" CAN BE HEARD AS THREADED PORTION OF VALVE IS PUSHED THROUGH THE RETAINER TOWARD THE BRAKE PEDAL.
3. PULL BRAKE PEDAL FULLY REARWARD AGAINST PEDAL STOP UNTIL AUDIBLE "CLICK" SOUNDS CAN NO LONGER BE HEARD. VALVE WILL BE MOVED IN TUBULAR RETAINER PROVIDING ADJUSTMENT.
4. RELEASE BRAKE PEDAL, AND THEN REPEAT STEP #3, TO ASSURE THAT NO AUDIBLE "CLICK" SOUNDS REMAIN.

*MAN. TRANS. — CLUTCH ACTIVATED
AUTO. TRANS. — BRAKE ACTIVATED

Cruise control release switches—Firebird

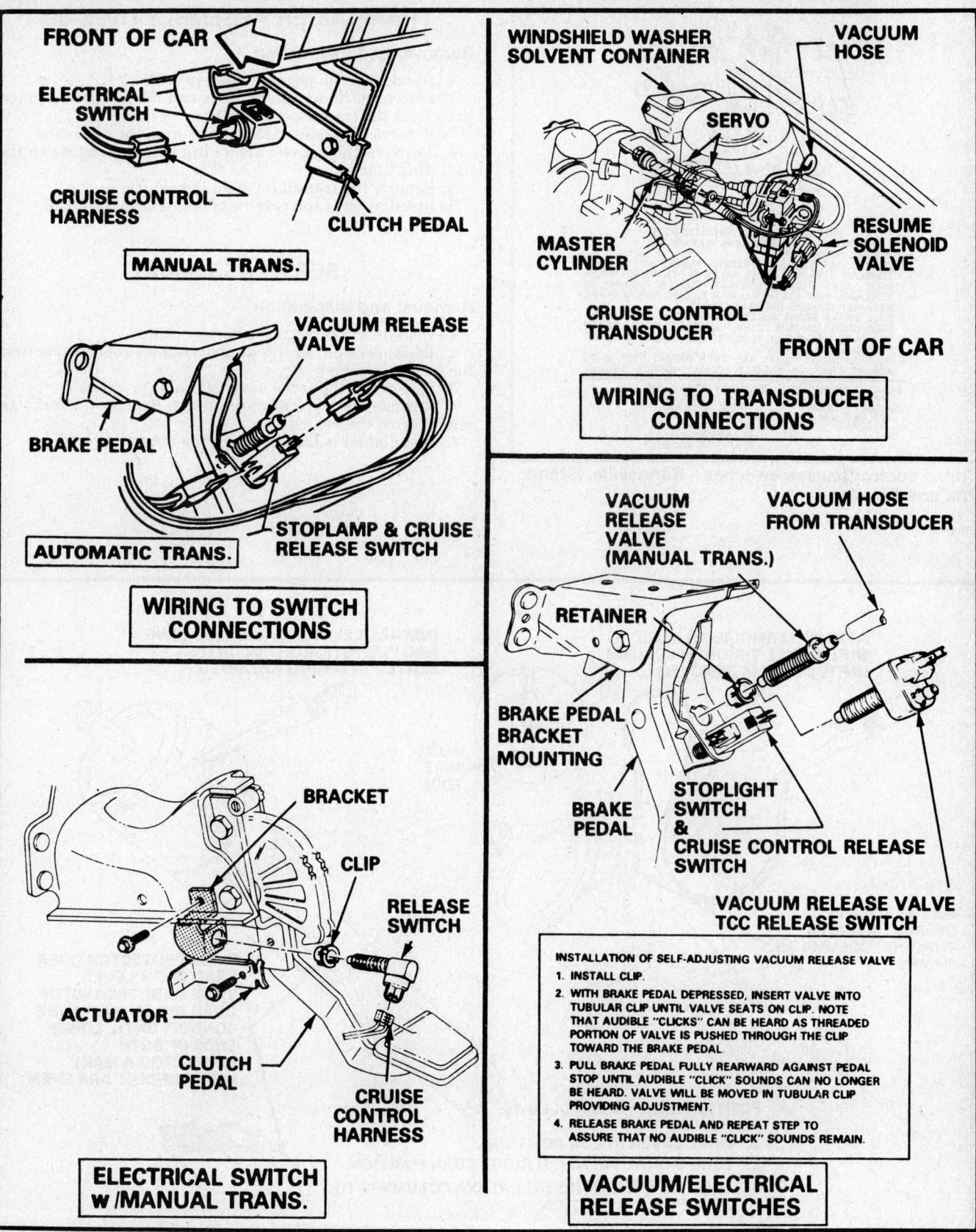

FRONT OF CAR

ELECTRICAL SWITCH

CRUISE CONTROL HARNESS

CLUTCH PEDAL

MANUAL TRANS.

VACUUM RELEASE VALVE

BRAKE PEDAL

STOPLAMP & CRUISE RELEASE SWITCH

AUTOMATIC TRANS.

WIRING TO SWITCH CONNECTIONS

WINDSHIELD WASHER SOLVENT CONTAINER

VACUUM HOSE

SERVO

MASTER CYLINDER

RESUME SOLENOID VALVE

CRUISE CONTROL TRANSDUCER

FRONT OF CAR

WIRING TO TRANSDUCER CONNECTIONS

VACUUM RELEASE VALVE (MANUAL TRANS.)

VACUUM HOSE FROM TRANSDUCER

RETAINER

BRAKE PEDAL BRACKET MOUNTING

BRAKE PEDAL

STOPLIGHT SWITCH & CRUISE CONTROL RELEASE SWITCH

VACUUM RELEASE VALVE TCC RELEASE SWITCH

INSTALLATION OF SELF-ADJUSTING VACUUM RELEASE VALVE

1. INSTALL CLIP.

2. WITH BRAKE PEDAL DEPRESSED, INSERT VALVE INTO TUBULAR CLIP UNTIL VALVE SEATS ON CLIP. NOTE THAT AUDIBLE "CLICKS" CAN BE HEARD AS THREADED PORTION OF VALVE IS PUSHED THROUGH THE CLIP TOWARD THE BRAKE PEDAL.

3. PULL BRAKE PEDAL FULLY REARWARD AGAINST PEDAL STOP UNTIL AUDIBLE "CLICK" SOUNDS CAN NO LONGER BE HEARD. VALVE WILL BE MOVED IN TUBULAR CLIP PROVIDING ADJUSTMENT.

4. RELEASE BRAKE PEDAL AND REPEAT STEP TO ASSURE THAT NO AUDIBLE "CLICK" SOUNDS REMAIN.

BRACKET

CLIP

RELEASE SWITCH

ACTUATOR

CLUTCH PEDAL

CRUISE CONTROL HARNESS

ELECTRICAL SWITCH w/MANUAL TRANS.

VACUUM/ELECTRICAL RELEASE SWITCHES

Cruise control release switches—J2000 and Sunbird

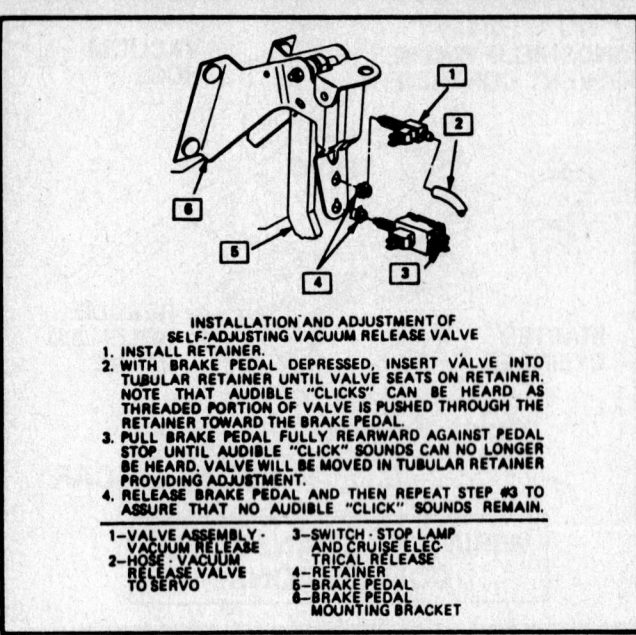

INSTALLATION AND ADJUSTMENT OF
SELF-ADJUSTING VACUUM RELEASE VALVE

1. INSTALL RETAINER.
2. WITH BRAKE PEDAL DEPRESSED, INSERT VALVE INTO TUBULAR RETAINER UNTIL VALVE SEATS ON RETAINER. NOTE THAT AUDIBLE "CLICKS" CAN BE HEARD AS THREADED PORTION OF VALVE IS PUSHED THROUGH THE RETAINER TOWARD THE BRAKE PEDAL.
3. PULL BRAKE PEDAL FULLY REARWARD AGAINST PEDAL STOP UNTIL AUDIBLE "CLICK" SOUNDS CAN NO LONGER BE HEARD. VALVE WILL BE MOVED IN TUBULAR RETAINER PROVIDING ADJUSTMENT.
4. RELEASE BRAKE PEDAL AND THEN REPEAT STEP #3 TO ASSURE THAT NO AUDIBLE "CLICK" SOUNDS REMAIN.

1—VALVE ASSEMBLY - VACUUM RELEASE
2—HOSE - VACUUM RELEASE VALVE TO SERVO
3—SWITCH - STOP LAMP AND CRUISE ELECTRICAL RELEASE
4—RETAINER
5—BRAKE PEDAL
6—BRAKE PEDAL MOUNTING BRACKET

Cruise control release switches—Bonneville, Grand Prix and Parisienne

TRANSDUCER ASSEMBLY (1982–83)

Removal and Installation

1. Disconnect the negative battery cable.
2. Disconnect the vacuum hoses and the electrical connections from the transducer assembly.
3. Remove the speedometer cables from the assembly.
4. Remove the screws attaching the transducer to the mounting bracket.
5. Remove the transducer from the vehicle.
6. Installation is the reverse of the removal procedure.

SERVO ASSEMBLY

Removal and Installation

1. Disconnect the negative battery cable.
2. Disconnect all electrical and vacuum connections from the servo assembly.
3. Disconnect the servo assembly cable or chain.
4. Remove the servo mounting bolts. Remove the servo assembly from the vehicle.
5. Installation is the reverse of the removal procedure.

ATTACH TERMINAL TO MUSIC WIRE & PULL THROUGH COLUMN UNTIL SLACK IS REMOVED

INSTALL LEVER BY ALIGNING TANG AND PUSH STRAIGHT IN UNTIL SEATED IN SPRING RETAINER

MUSIC WIRE TOOL

INSERT TOOL INTO OPENING & ROUTE THROUGH COLUMN AS SHOWN

SLIDE PROTECTOR OVER LEAD FROM LEVER, THEN SLIDE PROTECTOR OVER RIB ON MAIN WIRE CONDUIT UNTIL LOWER ENDS OF BOTH PROTECTOR & MAIN WIRE CONDUIT ARE EVEN

POSITION COLUMN AS FOLLOWS:

1. SHIFT LEVER IN LOW POSITION
2. TURN SIGNAL SWITCH IN RIGHT TURN POSITION
3. FOR TILT COLUMN INSTALLATION, COLUMN IS TO BE IN FULL UP POSITION

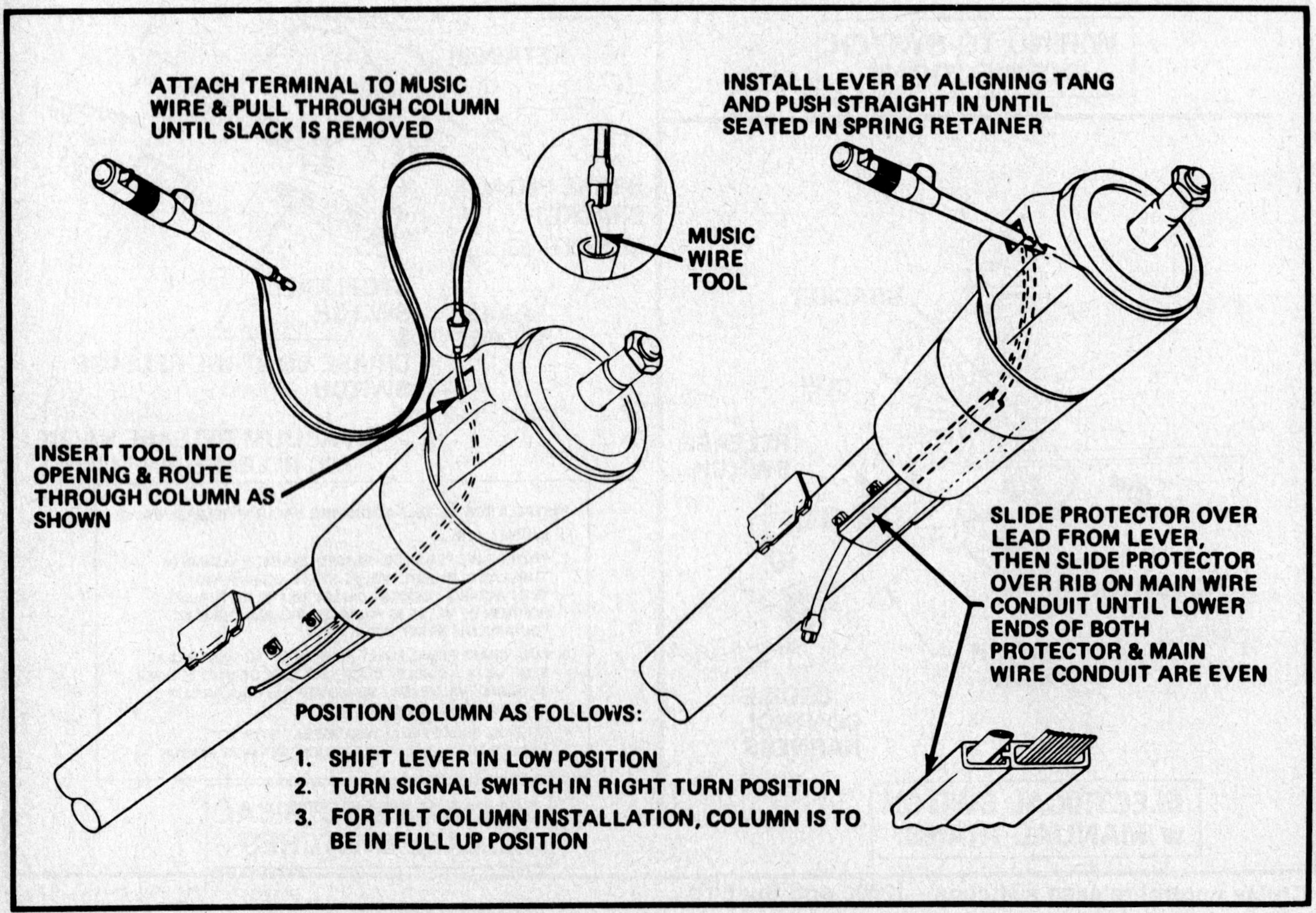

Cruise control engagement switch installation procedure

ELECTRIC BRAKE RELEASE SWITCH AND VACUUM RELEASE VALVE

Removal and installation

1. Disconnect the negative battery cable.
2. Remove the switch electrical and vacuum connectors.
3. Remove the switch from its mounting above the brake pedal.
4. Installation is the reverse of the removal procedure.

Adjustment

1. The switch assembly and the valve assembly cannot be adjusted until after the brake booster push rod is assembled to the brake pedal assembly.
2. To adjust the switch depress the brake pedal and insert the switch assembly and valve assembly into their proper retaining clips until fully seated.
3. Pull the pedal back to its fully retracted position. The switch assembly and the valve assembly will move within the retainers of their adjusted position.
4. The switch assembly contacts must open at 3.5mm to 12.5mm of brake pedal travel. Nominal actuation of the brake light switch is 4.5mm.
5. The vacuum release valve assembly must open at 27.0mm to 33.0mm of brake pedal travel.

ELECTRONIC CRUISE CONTROL CONTROL MODULE

Removal and Installation

Note: The electronic cruise control module is normally mounted on or near the accelerator pedal bracket. Location may vary depending upon vehicle model.

1. Disconnect the negative battery cable.
2. Remove the lower steering column filler panel as required. Remove vehicle carpet as required.
3. Disconnect the electrical connectors from the control module.
4. Remove the control module mounting screws. Remove the control module from the vehicle.
6. Installation is the reverse of the removal procedure.

SPEED SENSORS

VSS Buffer Amplifier

The VSS buffer amplifier is a device that supplies vehicle speed input to the electronic controller. The optic head portion of the assembly is located in the speedometer head frame. A reflec-

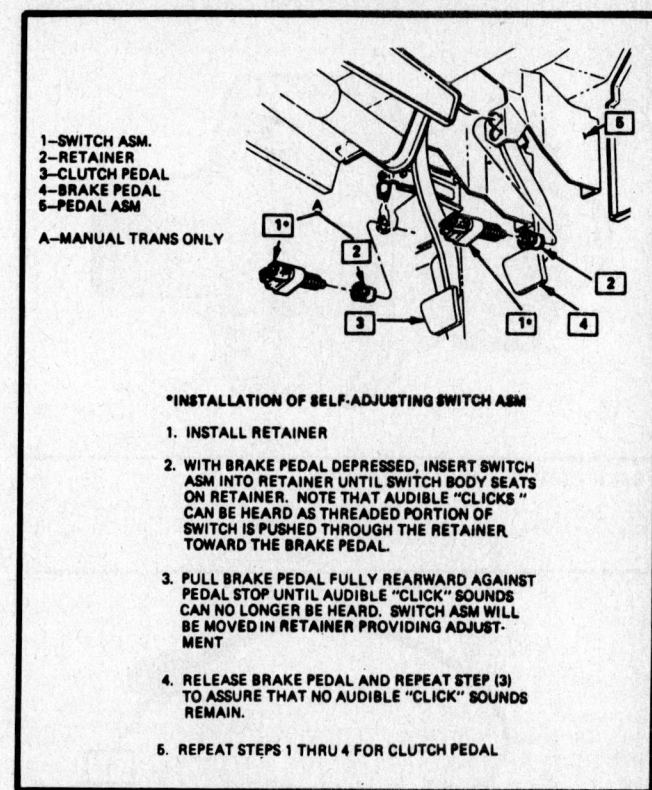

1—SWITCH ASM.
2—RETAINER
3—CLUTCH PEDAL
4—BRAKE PEDAL
5—PEDAL ASM.

A—MANUAL TRANS ONLY

*INSTALLATION OF SELF-ADJUSTING SWITCH ASM

1. INSTALL RETAINER

2. WITH BRAKE PEDAL DEPRESSED, INSERT SWITCH ASM INTO RETAINER UNTIL SWITCH BODY SEATS ON RETAINER. NOTE THAT AUDIBLE "CLICKS" CAN BE HEARD AS THREADED PORTION OF SWITCH IS PUSHED THROUGH THE RETAINER TOWARD THE BRAKE PEDAL.

3. PULL BRAKE PEDAL FULLY REARWARD AGAINST PEDAL STOP UNTIL AUDIBLE "CLICK" SOUNDS CAN NO LONGER BE HEARD. SWITCH ASM WILL BE MOVED IN RETAINER PROVIDING ADJUSTMENT

4. RELEASE BRAKE PEDAL AND REPEAT STEP (3) TO ASSURE THAT NO AUDIBLE "CLICK" SOUNDS REMAIN.

5. REPEAT STEPS 1 THRU 4 FOR CLUTCH PEDAL

Cruise control release switches—Fiero

tive blade is attached to the speedometer head/cable assembly. The blade spins like a propeller with its blades passing through a light beam from a L.E.D. refractor in the optic head. As each blade enters the light beam, light is reflected back to a photocell that is located in the optic head. This in turn causes a power signal to be sent to a buffer for amplification and signal conditioning. This signal is then sent to the controller for processing and calculation of vehicle speed.

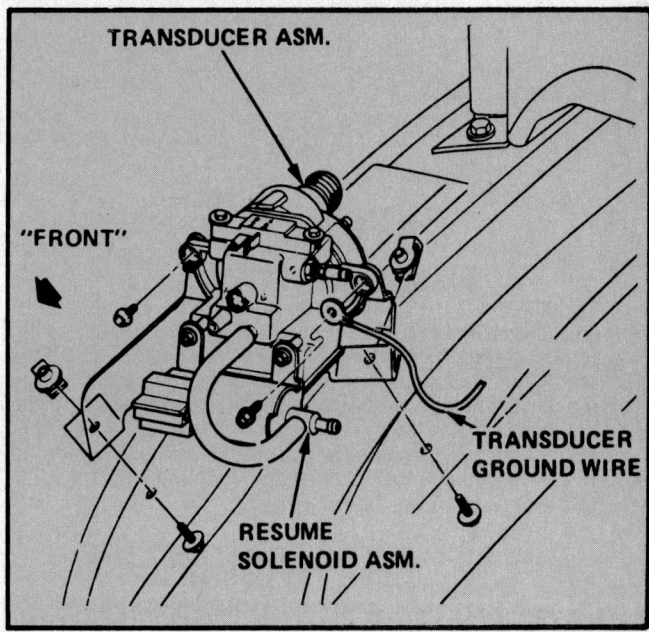

TRANSDUCER ASM.

"FRONT"

TRANSDUCER GROUND WIRE

RESUME SOLENOID ASM.

Typical transducer and mounting bracket assembly

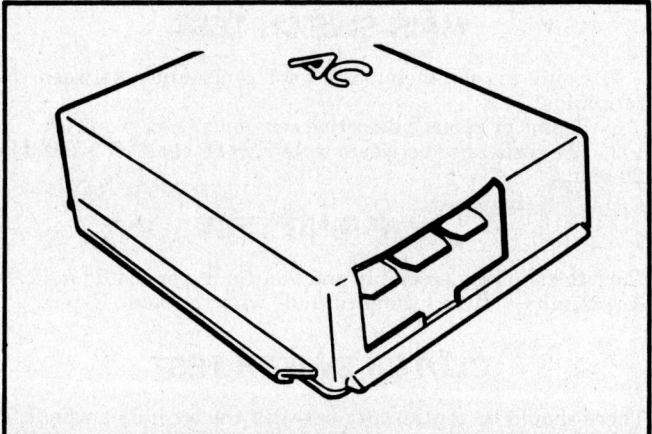

Typical electronic cruise control module

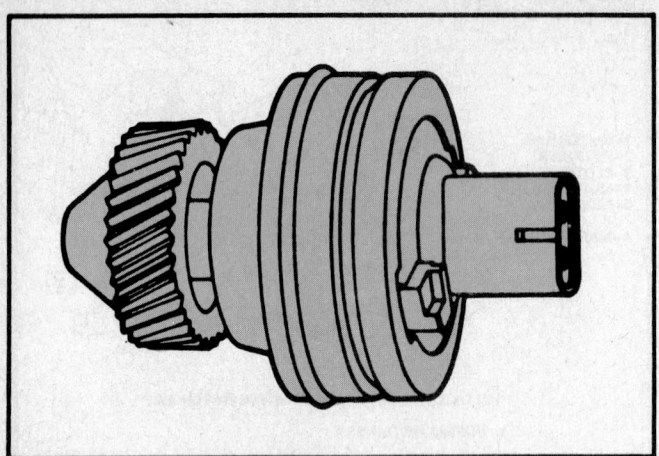

Permanant magnet generator

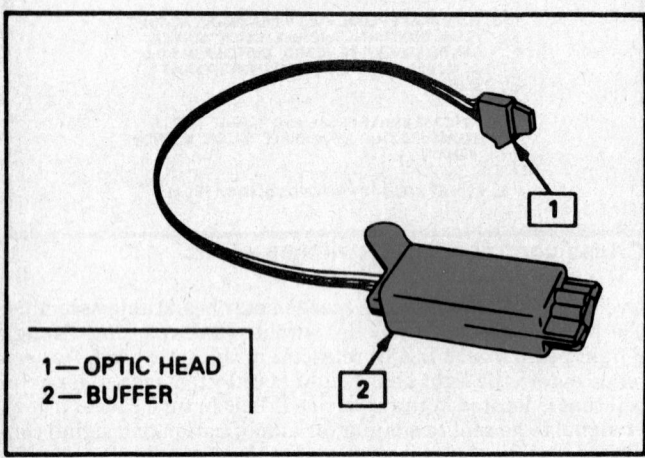

1—OPTIC HEAD
2—BUFFER

Vehicle speed sensor

P.M. Generator Speed Signal

The P.M. generator speed signal is a device that supplies vehicle speed input to the electronic controller. Vehicle speed information is provided to the electronic controller by a permanent magnet generator driven by the vehicle transmission. The output frequency of the permanent magnet generator is than routed to a buffer, which in turn will amplify and condition the signal to the electronic controller.

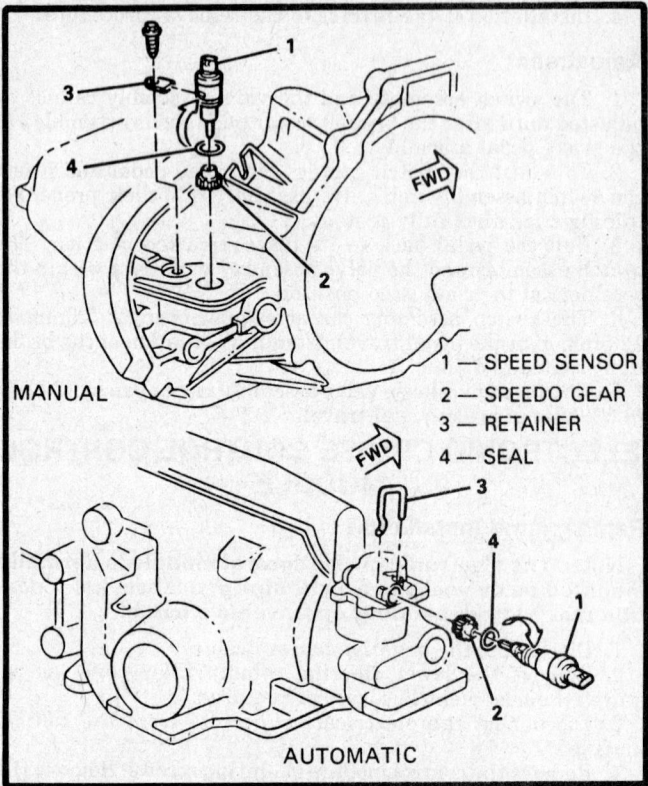

1 — SPEED SENSOR
2 — SPEEDO GEAR
3 — RETAINER
4 — SEAL

Typical PM generator location—Fiero shown

HONDA

Prelude

VISUAL INSPECTION

Before performing any tests make a visual inspection of the cruise control system. Check all items in the system for abnormal conditions such as bare broken or disconnected wires and damage to the vacuum hoses. Be sure that the speedometer cables are attached and properly routed. All vacuum hoses must be properly routed and must not have any kinks or bends. Be sure that all electrical connections are complete and tight. The wiring harness must be routed properly.

CRUISE CONTROL SWITCH TEST

1. Using a test light check for continuity between the terminals.
2. Repair or replace defective components as required.

MAIN SWITCH TEST

1. Using an ohmmeter check for continunity between the terminals.
2. Repair or replace defective components as required.
3. The resistance betweem terminals "C" and "E" should be 20 ohms.

SLIP RING TEST

Turn the slip ring assembly and the ohmmeter should indicate continuity between the terminals with the same letters.

CLUTCH SWITCH TEST

There should be continuity between the terminals when the rod is pushed in. There should be no continuity when the rod is out.

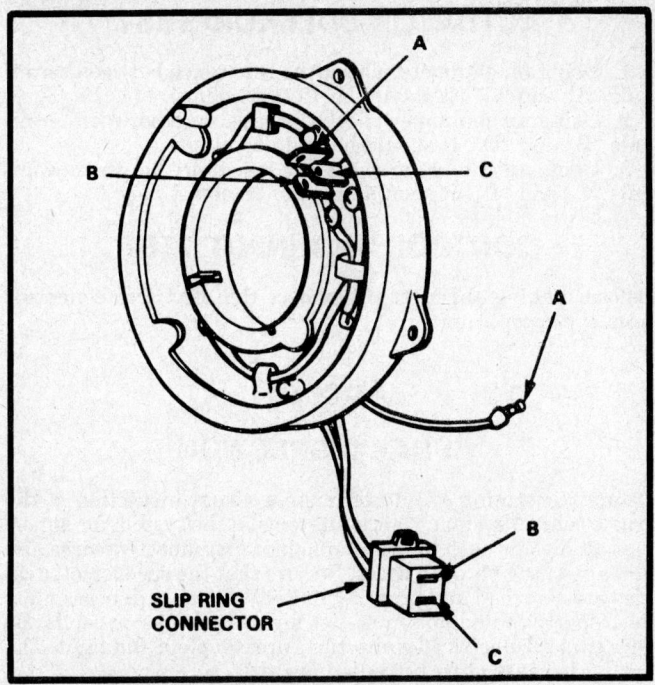

Slip ring test point locations—Prelude

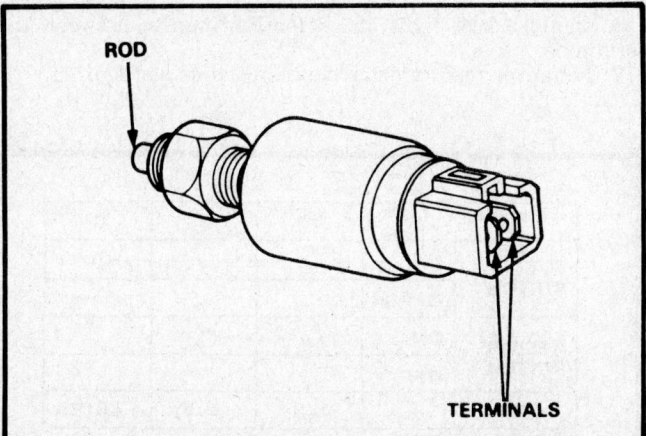

Clutch start switch test point locations—Prelude

NEUTRAL/BACK UP LIGHT SWITCH TEST

1. With the selector lever in the D4, D3, and 2 position there should be continuity between terminal "A" and terminal "B".
2. With the selector lever in the Park, Reverse and Neutral positions there should be no continuity.

BRAKE LIGHT SWITCH TEST

1. There should be continuity between terminal "A" and "D" and there should not be continuity between terminal "B" and "C" when the rod is pushed in.
2. There should not be continuity between terminal "A" and terminal "D" and there should be continuity between terminal "B" and "C" when the switch is free.

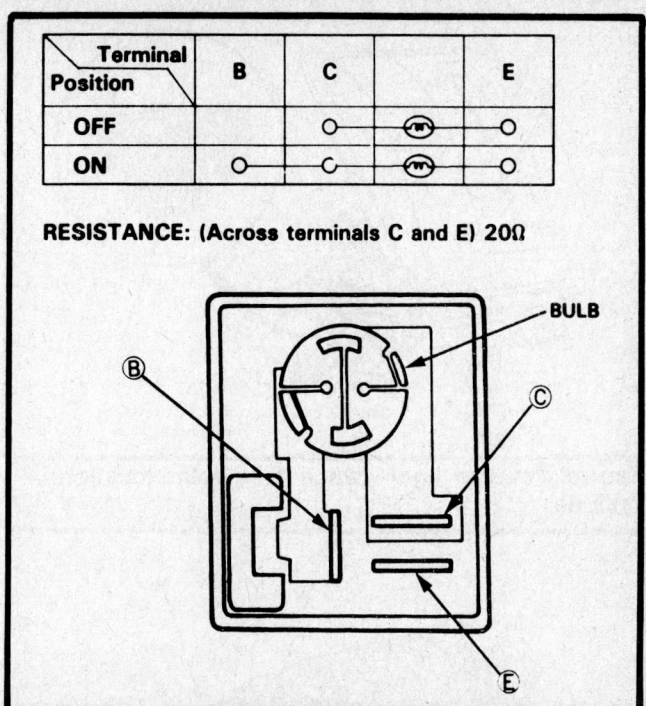

Terminal Position	B	C		E
OFF		○	⊗	○
ON	○	○	⊗	○

RESISTANCE: (Across terminals C and E) 20Ω

Main switch specifications and test point locations—Prelude

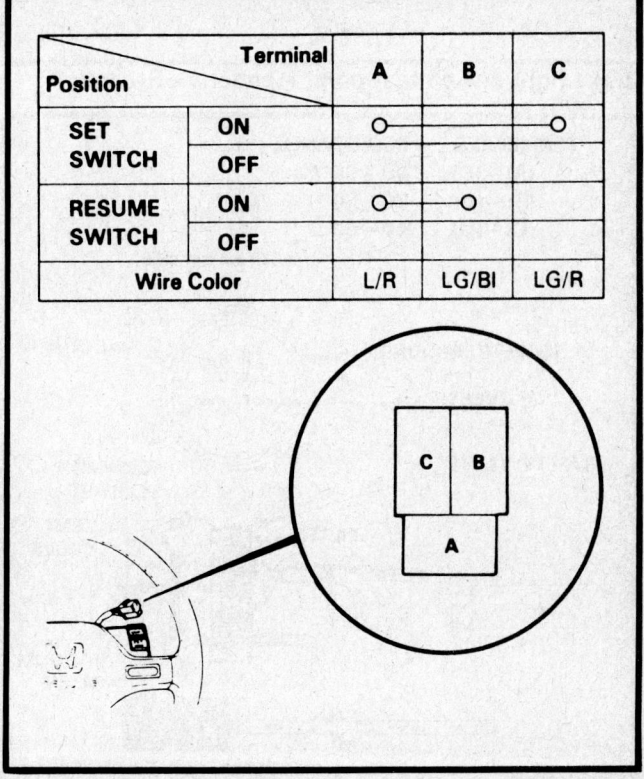

Position	Terminal	A	B	C
SET SWITCH	ON	○		○
	OFF			
RESUME SWITCH	ON	○	○	
	OFF			
Wire Color		L/R	LG/Bl	LG/R

Control switch specifications and test point locations—Prelude

953

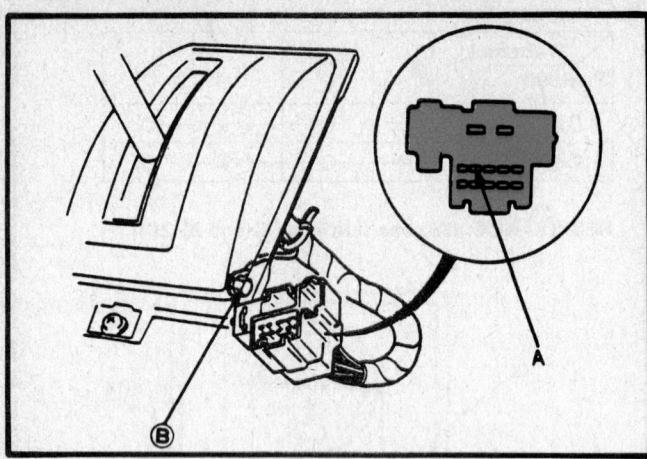

Neutral/Reverse light switch test point locations—
Prelude

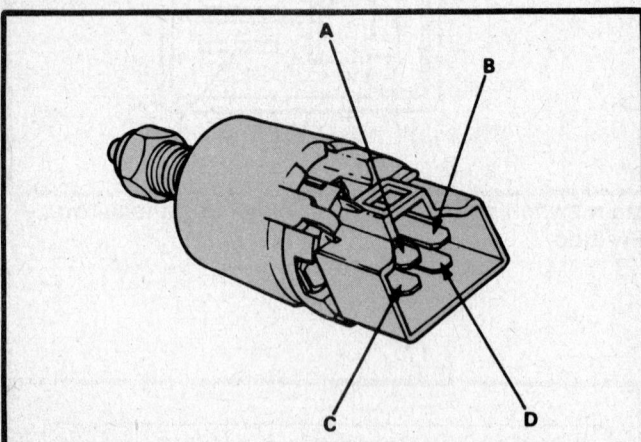

Brake light switch test point locations—Prelude

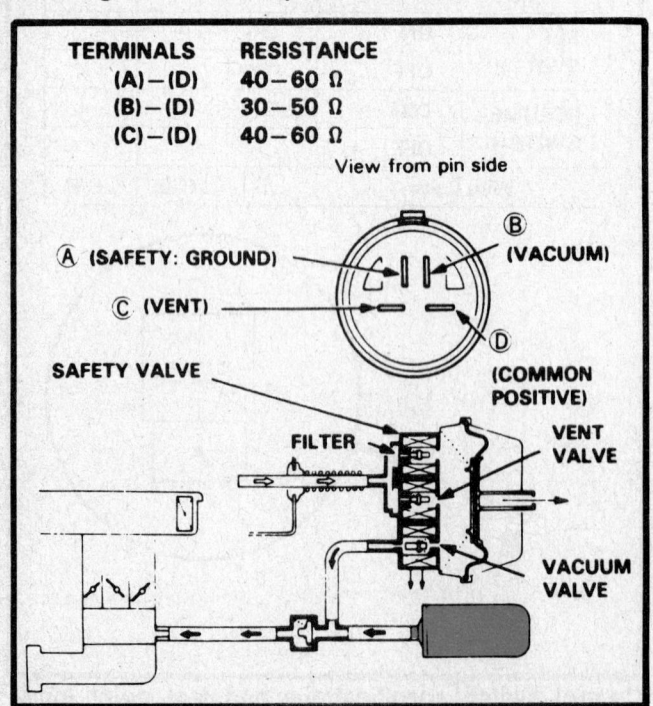

TERMINALS	RESISTANCE
(A)—(D)	40–60 Ω
(B)—(D)	30–50 Ω
(C)—(D)	40–60 Ω

View from pin side

Ⓐ (SAFETY: GROUND)   Ⓑ (VACUUM)
Ⓒ (VENT)   Ⓓ (COMMON POSITIVE)

SAFETY VALVE
FILTER
VENT VALVE
VACUUM VALVE

Actuator assembly and test point locations—Prelude

ACTUATOR SOLENOID TEST

1. Using an ohmmeter check the resistance between terminals "A" and "D". It should be 40 to 60 ohms.
2. Using an ohmmeter check the resistance between terminals "B" and "D". It should be 30 to 50 ohms.
3. Using an ohmmeter check the resistance between terminals "C" and "D". It should be 40 to 60 ohms.

CONTROL UNIT INPUT TEST

Before making this test disconnect the electrical connector from the control unit.

Accord

VISUAL INSPECTION

Before performing any tests make a visual inspection of the cruise control system. Check all items in the system for abnormal conditions such as bare broken or disconnected wires and damage to the vacuum hoses. Be sure that the speedometer cables are attached and properly routed. All vacuum hoses must be properly routed and must not have any kinks or bends. Be sure that all electrical connections are complete and tight. The wiring harness must be routed properly.

CRUISE CONTROL SWITCH TEST

1. Using a test light check for continuity between the terminals.
2. Repair or replace defective components as required.

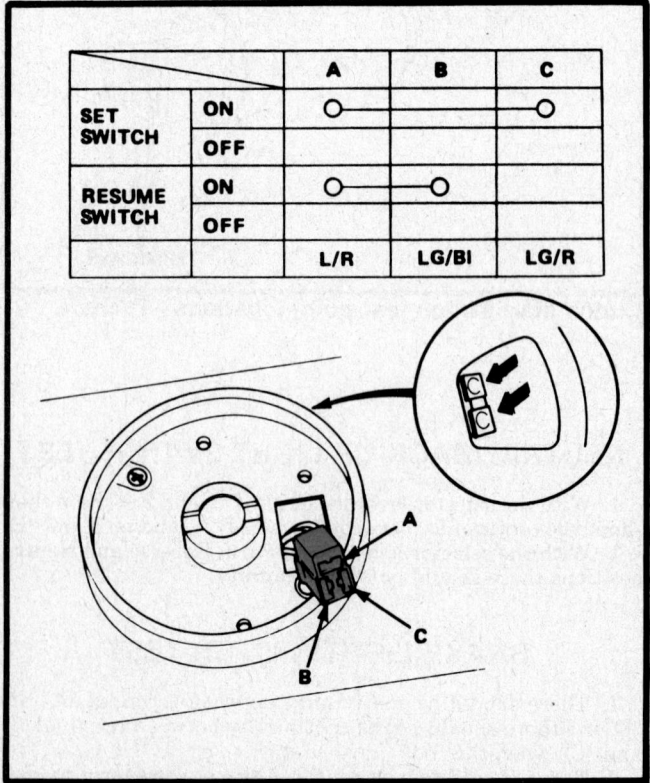

		A	B	C
SET SWITCH	ON	O—————————O		O
	OFF			
RESUME SWITCH	ON	O————O		
	OFF			
		L/R	LG/Bl	LG/R

Control switch specifications and test point locations—1982–85 Accord

DIAGNOSIS AND TESTING PROCEDURES

No.	Wire	Test condition	Test: desired result	Possible cause
1	Black	Ignition switch OFF	Check for resistance to ground: should be 0 ohm.	Poor ground. An open in the Bl wire.
2	Brown/White	Ignition switch OFF	Check for resistance to Brown wire: should have 40–60 ohms.	An open or short in wire. Faulty actuator.
3	Brown/White	Ignition switch OFF	Check for resistance to Black wire: should have 40–60 ohms.	An open or short in wire. Faulty actuator.
4	Brown/White	Ignition switch OFF	Check for resistance to Brown/Black wire: should have 30–50 ohms.	An open or short in wire. Faulty actuator.
5	Light Green	Ignition switch ON and control main switch ON	Check for voltage to ground: should have 12 volts.	An open in the wire. Faulty main switch.
6	Gray	Ignition switch ON, main switch ON and brake pedal released.	Check for voltage to Light Green: should have 12 volts.	An open in the wire. Misadjusted brake switch. Faulty brake switch.
7	Green/White	Brake pedal pushed.	Check for voltage to ground: should have 12 volts.	Poor ground. An open in the wire. Misadjusted brake switch or fauty brake switch.
8	Light Green/Red	Set switch pushed.	Check for voltage to ground: should have 12 volts.	An open in the wire. Faulty set switch. Faulty slip ring.
9	Light Green/Black	Resume switch pushed	Check for voltage to ground: should have 12 volts	An open in the wire. Faulty resume switch. Faulty slip ring.
10	Pink	Clutch released (M/T) or selector in D3, D4 or 2 (A/T)	Check for resistance to ground: there should be 0 ohm.	An open in the wire. Poor ground. Clutch switch misadjusted.
11	Red	Ignition switch ON and ground the red wire	Check the pilot light: the pilot light should go on.	Faulty bulb. An open in the wire.
12	Blue	Start the engine	Check for voltage to ground: there should be system voltage.	Faulty ignition system. An open in the wire.
13	Yellow/Red	Turn speedometer cable by rotating one wheel, Ignition switch ON.	"Confirm 12 V and 0 V is alternately repeated on the voltmeter at the connection described in the figure below."	An open or short in the wire. Faulty speedometer.

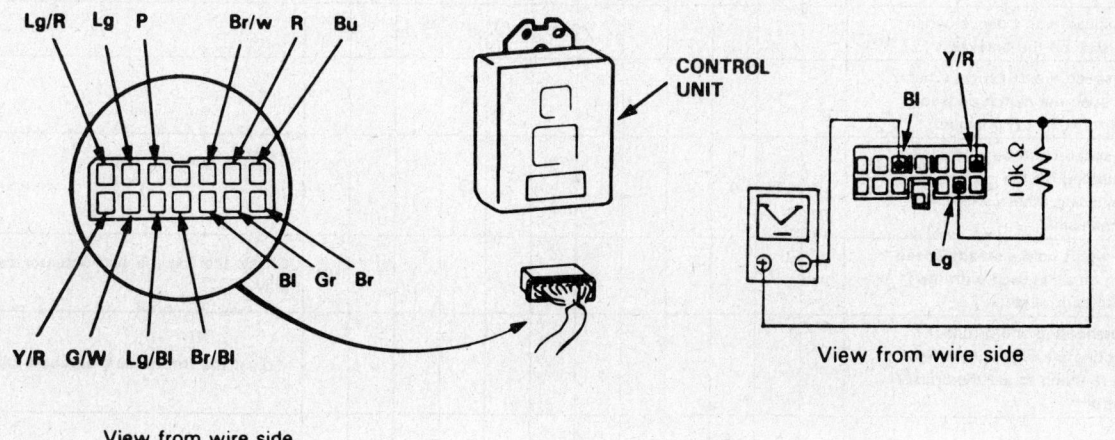

Control unit data and test point locations—Prelude

NOTE: Before you try to diagnose or repair the problem, check:
- Throttle cable free play.

- Actuator cable free play.
- Throttle linkage operation.
- Wire harness connectors.
- Vacuum lines.

If all possible sources of malfunction check OK, replace the control unit.

Possible Cause of Malfunction
NOTE: Check in the order numbered, if more than one possibility.

Symptom	Fuse	Wire Harness	Main Switch	Set Switch	Resume Switch	Ignition Pulse	Brake Switch	Clutch Switch (M/T)	Neutral/Back-Up Switch (A/T)	Cruise Control Pilot Light	Speed Pulser	Actuator	Other
Cruise control can't be set.	2	1	4	3	9	10	5	11	6		8	7	
Cruise control can be set, but the pilot light doesn't go on.	3	2								1			
Cruise control can be set, but, after overriding the system, it won't return to set speed when you push the resume switch.		1			2								
Cruise control can be set, but you can't reduce the car's speed by pushing the set switch.													
Cruise can be set, but the car won't accelerate when you hold the resume switch.													
Set speed won't cancel when you step on the breaks.		1					2						
Set speed won't cancel when you push the clutch pedal or shift to N, P or R position.		1						2	3				
Set speed can't be cancelled by turning off the main switch, or by using other cancelling mechanisms.		1	4					2	3				
Car won't hold a steady speed even on a flat road with the cruise control set.												O	Check the throttle and actuator cables for free play.
Overshooting and/or undershooting are excessive when you're trying to set the cruise control													Adjust the throttle and actuator cable free play.
Won't hold set speed.												O	Replace or repair the vacuum line and clean the actuator filter and tube.

Cruise control trouble shooting chart—Prelude

Position \ Terminal	Lg/Bl	Bu/R	Lg/R
OFF			
SET (ON)	○——○		
RESUME (ON)		○——○	

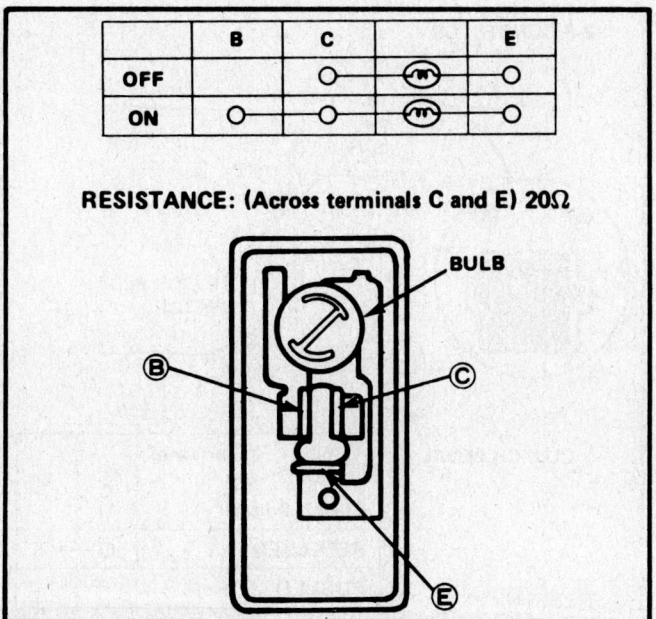

Control switch specifications and test point locations—1986 and later Accord

MAIN SWITCH TEST

1. Using an ohmmeter check for continunity between the terminals.
2. Repair or replace defective components as required.

SLIP RING TEST

1982–85

Turn the slip ring assembly and the ohmmeter should indicate continunity between the terminals with the same letters.

	B	C	E
OFF	○	○——(M)——○	
ON	○	○——(M)——○	

RESISTANCE: (Across terminals C and E) 20Ω

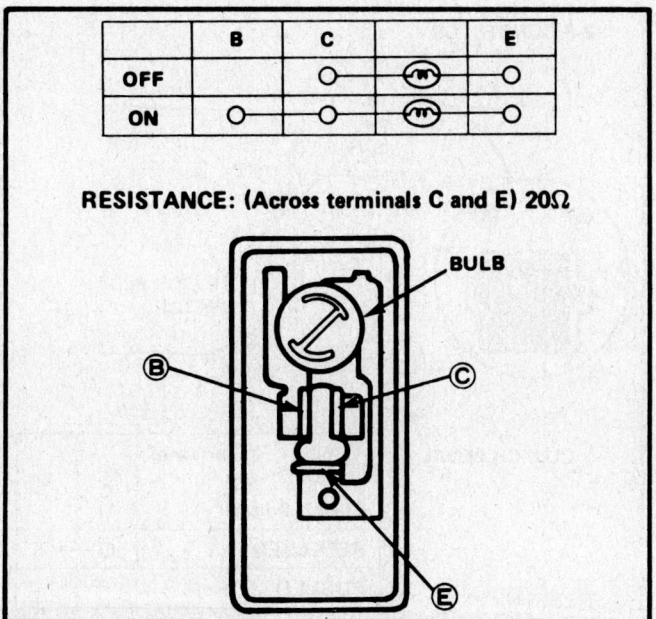

Main switch specifications and test point locations— 1983–85 Accord

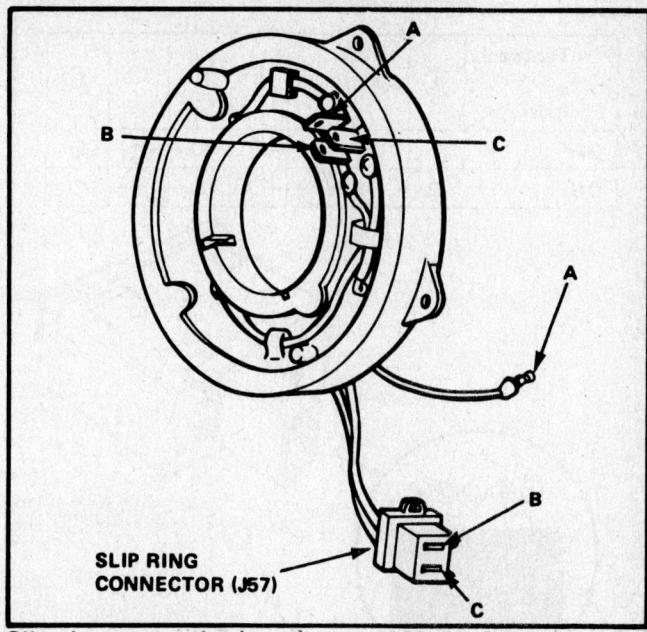

Slip ring test point locations—1982–85 Accord

1986 and Later

1. Remove the steering column cover. Disconnect the two prong connector and the brown/red wire.
2. There should be continuity between the brown/red wire and terminal "A". The light red wire and terminal "B" and the light blue wire and terminal "C" should also have continuity as you turn the slip ring.

CLUTCH SWITCH TEST

There should be continunity between the terminals when the rod is pushed in. There should be no continunity when the rod is out.

	A	B	C
ON	○—⟋⟍⟋—○		○
OFF	○—⟋⟍⟋—○		○

RESISTANCE: (Across terminals A and B) 20Ω

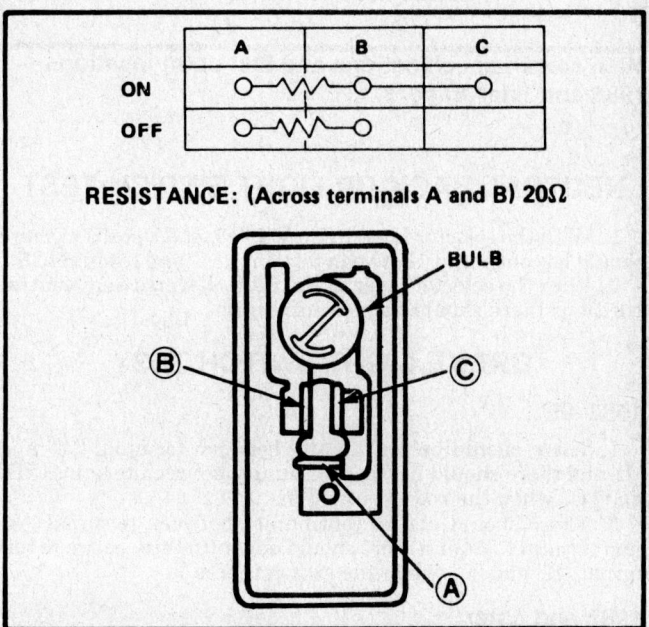

Main switch specifications and test point locations— 1982 Accord

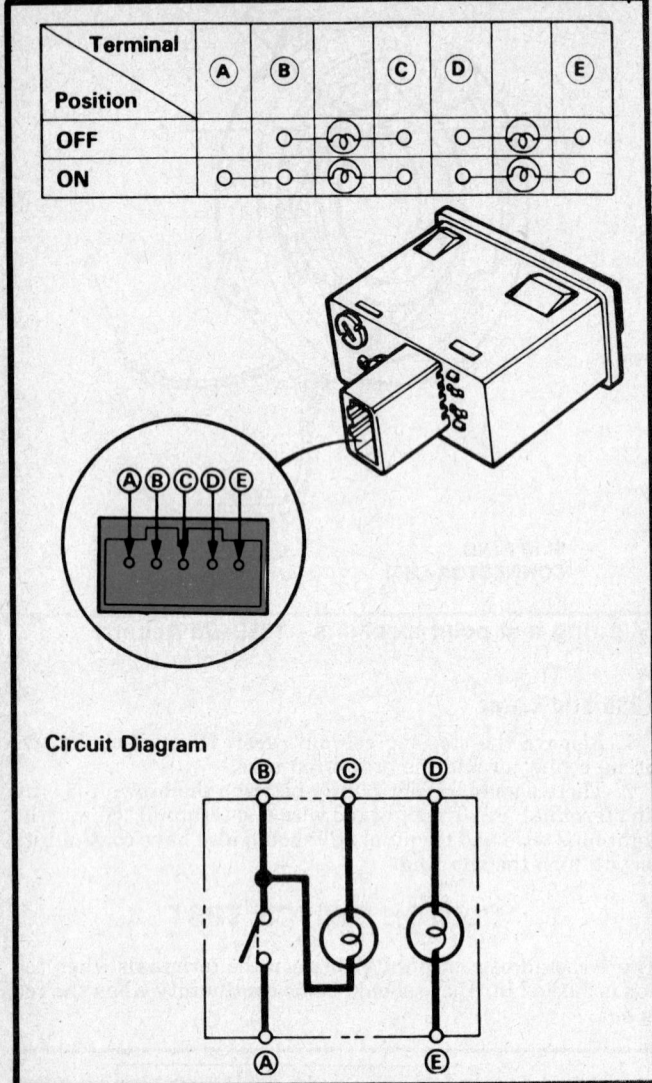

Terminal Position	(A)	(B)		(C)	(D)		(E)
OFF	○	○	○—Ⓣ—○	○	○	○—Ⓣ—○	○
ON	○—○	○	○—Ⓣ—○	○	○—○	○—Ⓣ—○	○

Circuit Diagram

Main switch specifications and test point locations—1986 and later Accord

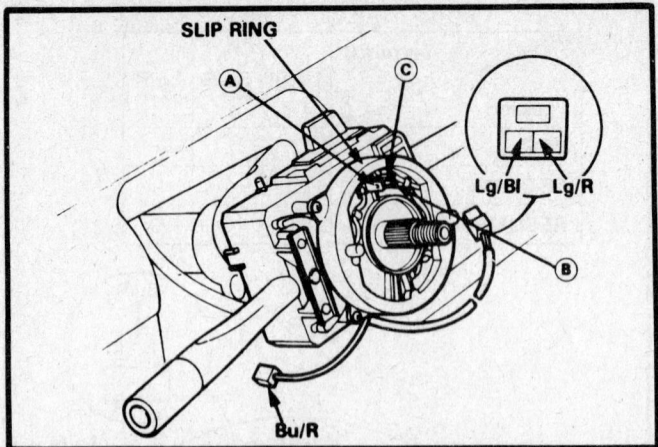

Slip ring test point locations—1986 and later Accord

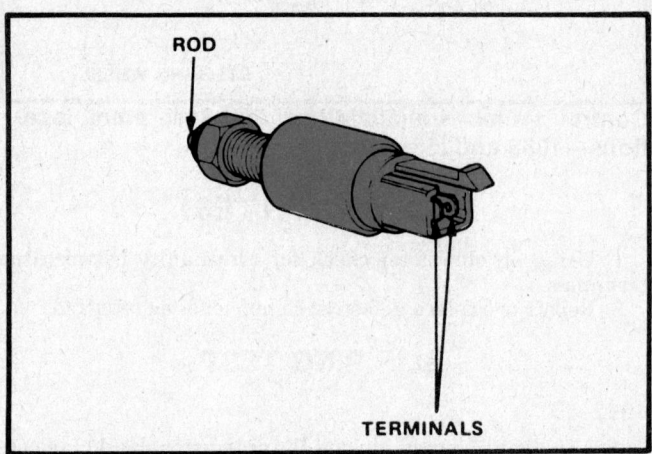

Clutch start switch test point locations—1982–85 Accord

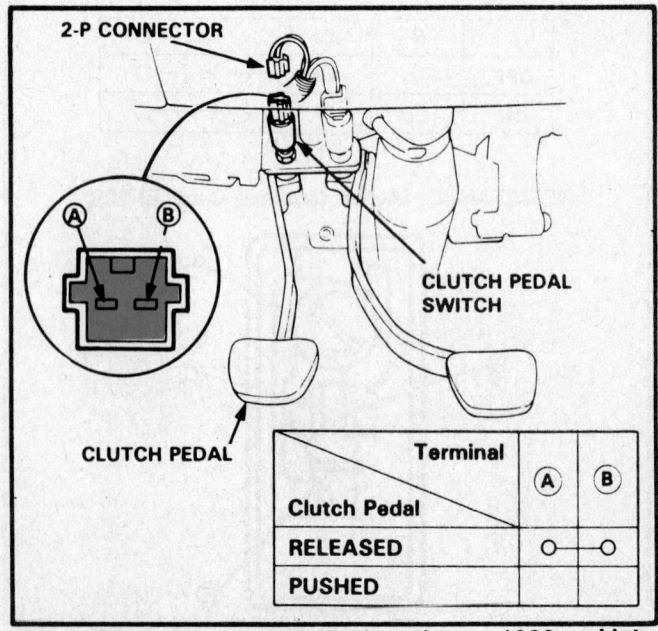

Terminal Clutch Pedal	(A)	(B)
RELEASED	○—○	
PUSHED		

Clutch start switch test point locations—1986 and later Accord

NEUTRAL/BACK UP LIGHT SWITCH TEST

1. With the selector lever in the D4, D3, and 2 position there should be continuity between terminal "A" and terminal "B".
2. With the selector lever in the Park, Reverse and Neutral positions there should be no continuity.

BRAKE LIGHT SWITCH TEST

1982–85

1. There should be continuity between terminal "A" and "D" and there should not be continuity between terminal "B" and "C" when the rod is pushed in.
2. There should not be continuity between terminal "A" and terminal "D" and there should be continuity between terminal "B" and "C" when the switch is free.

1986 and Later

1. Disconnect the four prong connector from the switch assembly.

2. Ckeck for continuity between the terminals.

3. Repair or replace the switch as required.

ACTUATOR SOLENOID TEST

1982–85

1. Using an ohmmeter check the resistance between terminals "A" and "D". It should be 40 to 60 ohms.

2. Using an ohmmeter check the resistance between terminals "B" and "D". It should be 30 to 50 ohms.

3. Using an ohmmeter check the resistance between terminals "C" and "D". It should be 40 to 60 ohms.

4. Disconnect the actuator cable from the actuator. Disconnect the actuator electrical connector. Disconnect the control unit electrical connector.

5. Connect a lead from the battery positive terminal to test terminal "D" and another lead from the negative battery cable to test terminal "A" than to "B" and than to "C".

6. Connect a vacuum pump to the actuator and draw vacuum. The actuator rod should pull in, if not repair or replace defective components as required.

7. With voltage and vacuum still applied to the actuator, try to pull the rod out by hand. If it can be pulled out, replace the actuator.

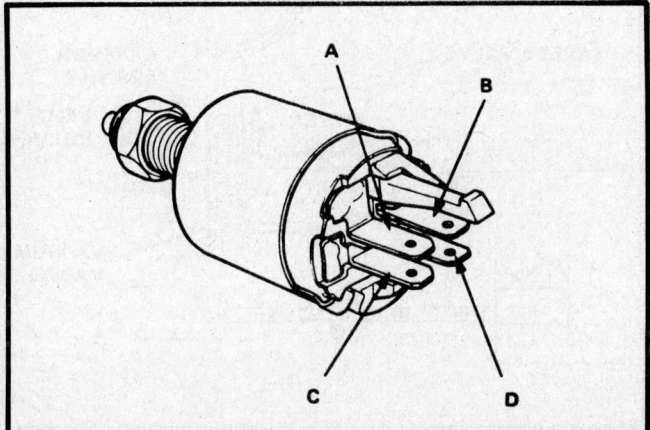

Brake light switch test point locations—1982–85 Accord

Neutral/Reverse light switch test point locations—1982–85 Accord

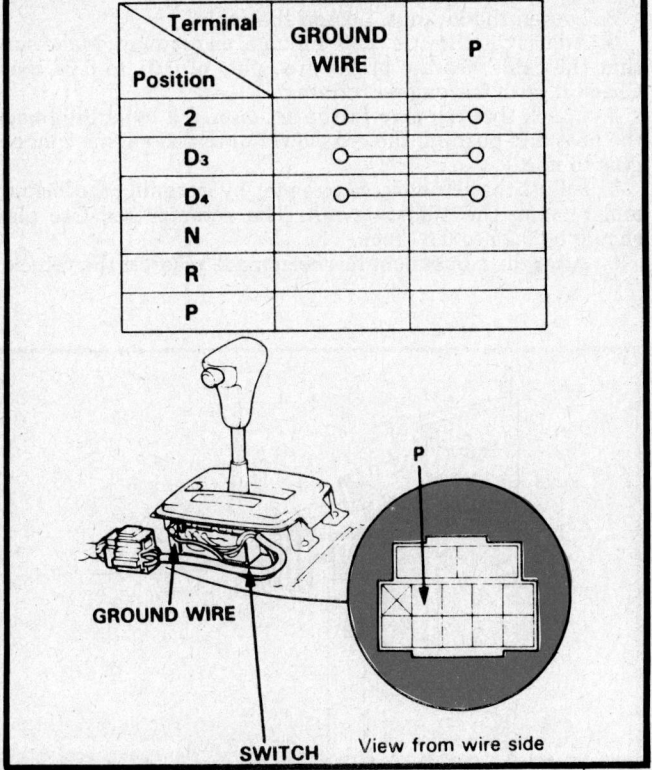

Terminal / Position	GROUND WIRE	P
2	o	o
D₃	o	o
D₄	o	o
N		
R		
P		

Neutral/Reverse light switch test point locations—1986 and later Accord

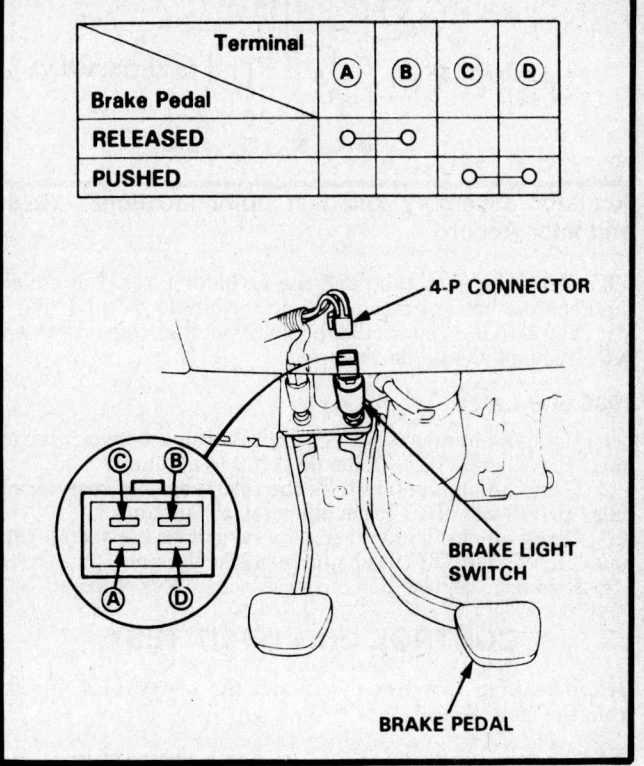

Terminal / Brake Pedal	Ⓐ	Ⓑ	Ⓒ	Ⓓ
RELEASED	o	o		
PUSHED			o	o

Brake light switch test point locations—1986 and later Accord

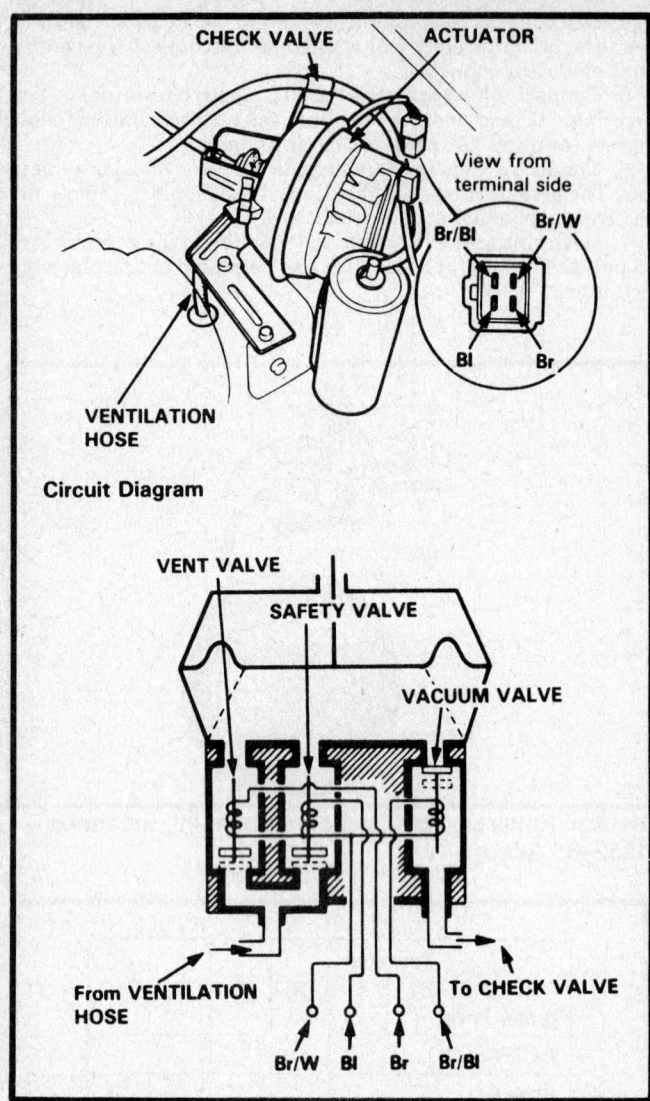

Actuator assembly and test point locations—1986 and later Accord

8. Clean the vent tube and the actuator filter. Disconnect the negative battery terminal from terminals "A" and "B".

9. The actuator rod should return. If not the solenoid valve is defective and should be replaced.

1986 and Later

1. Using an ohmmeter check the resistance between terminals "Br/W" and "BL". It should be 30 to 50 ohms.

2. Using an ohmmeter check the resistance between terminals "Br/W" and "Br". It should be 40 to 60 ohms.

3. Using an ohmmeter check the resistance between terminals "Br/W" and "Bl". It should be 40 to 60 ohms.

4. Repair or replace defective components as required.

CONTROL UNIT INPUT TEST

Before making this test disconnect the electrical connector from the control unit.

ACTUATOR CABLE ADJUSTMENT

1. Run the engine until operating temperature is reached.

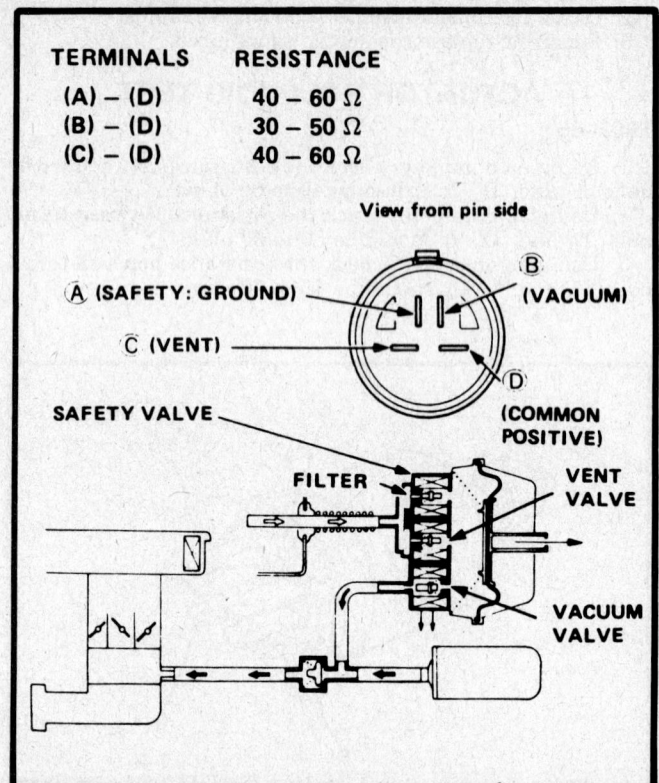

TERMINALS	RESISTANCE
(A) – (D)	40 – 60 Ω
(B) – (D)	30 – 50 Ω
(C) – (D)	40 – 60 Ω

Actuator assembly and test point locations—1982–85 Accord

2. Loosen the locknut. Loosen the cable.

3. Adjust the throttle cable linkage, as required. Make sure that the cable has the proper free play of 0.01 to 0.04 inch. Check it with the engine running.

4. Check the free play in the actuator rod by pulling back the boot and pushing the rod slowly until the engine rpm begins to rise.

5. Adjust the actuator rod free play by loosening the locknut and turning the adjusting nut. The actuator rod free play should be 0.25 to 0.37 inch.

6. After the adjustment has been made roadtest the vehicle.

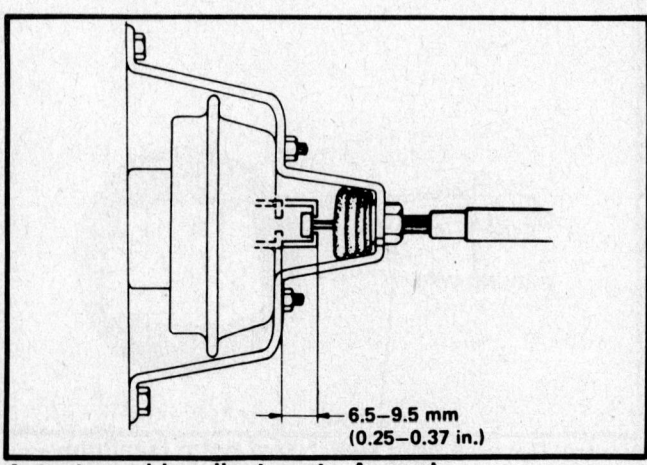

Actuator cable adjustment—Accord

No.	Wire	Test condition	Test: desired result	Possible cause
1	Black	Ignition switch OFF	Check for resistance to ground: should be 0 ohm.	Poor ground. An open in the Bl wire.
2	Brown/White	Ignition switch OFF	Check for resistance to Brown wire: should have 40—60 ohms.	An open or short in wire. Faulty actuator.
3	Brown/White	Ignition switch OFF	Check for resistance to Black wire: should have 40—60 ohms.	An open or short in wire. Faulty actuator.
4	Brown/White	Ignition switch OFF	Check for resistance to Brown/Black wire: should have 30—50 ohms.	An open or short in wire. Faulty actuator.
5	Light Green	Ignition switch ON and control main switch ON	Check for voltage to ground: should have 12 volts.	An open in the wire. Faulty main switch.
6	Gray	Ignition switch ON and main switch ON	Check for voltage to Light Green: should have 12 volts.	An open in the wire. Misadjusted brake switch. Faulty brake switch.
7	Green/White	Ignition switch ON and brake pedal pushed.	Check for voltage to ground: should have 12 volts.	Poor ground. An open in the wire. Misadjusted brake switch or faulty brake switch.
8	Light Green/Red	Ignition switch ON and set switch pushed.	Check for voltage to ground: should have 12 volts.	An open in the wire. Faulty set switch. Faulty slip ring.
9	Light Green/Black	Ignition switch ON and resume switch ON	Check for voltage to ground: should have 12 volts	An open in the wire. Faulty resume switch. Faulty slip ring.
10	Yellow/Red	Turn speedometer cable by rotating one wheel	Check for continuity to ground: there should be 2—3 indications of continuity per one turn.	An open or short in the wire. Faulty speedometer.
11	Pink	Clutch released (M/T) or selector in D3, D4 or 2 (A/T).	Check for resistance to ground: there should be 0 ohm.	An open in the wire. Poor ground. Clutch switch misadjusted.
12	Red	Ignition switch ON and ground the red wire	Check the pilot light: the pilot light should go on.	Faulty bulb. An open in the wire.
13	Blue	Start the engine	Check for voltage to ground: there should be system voltage.	Faulty ignition system. An open in the wire.

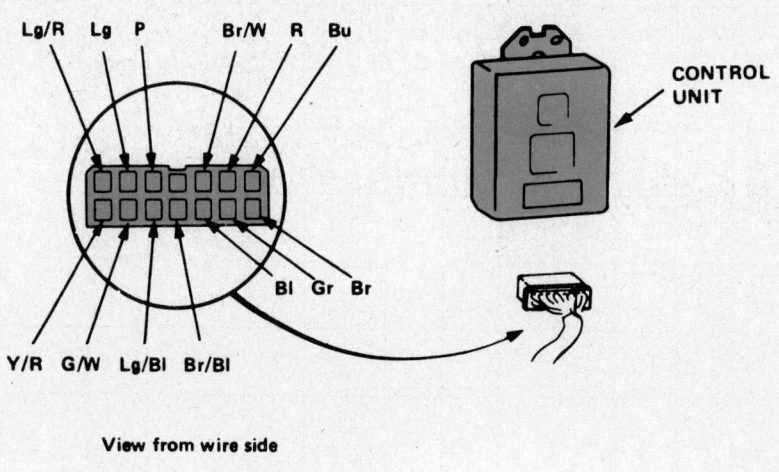

CONTROL UNIT

View from wire side

Control unit data and test point locations—Accord

DIAGNOSIS AND TESTING PROCEDURES

NOTE:
- The numbers in the table show the troubleshooting sequence.
- Before troubleshooting:
  - Check the No.2 (10A) and No.4 (7.5A) fuses in the fuse box, and the No.4 (20A) fuse in the relay box.
  - Check that the horns sound.
  - Check the tachometer for proper operation.

Symptom / Item to be inspected	Main switch	SET/RESUME switch	Brake light switch and mounting	Clutch switch and mounting (M/T)	Shift lever position switch (A/T)	Speedometer pulser or cable (page 25-71)	Dimming circuit in gauges (page 25-71)	Actuator	Disconnected, clogged or restricted vacuum lines/stuck check valve/leaky vacuum reservoir	Control unit	Poor ground	Open circuit in wires or loose or disconnected terminals
Cruise control can't be set	2	3	4	5					6	1	GND-7 GND-8 GND-12	Bu/R, Lg/R, Bu, Bl/R, Lg, Gr, Y/R, Br, Br/Bl, Br/W or P
Cruise control can be set, but indicator light does not go on							2			1	GND-12	Y or R
Cruise speed noticeably higher or lower than what was set						1		2		3		
Excessive overshooting and/or undershooting when trying to set speed						2		1		3		
Steady speed not held even on a flat road with cruise control set						1		2	3	4		
Car does not decelerate or accelerate accordingly when SET or RESUME button is pushed		1								2		Lg/Bl
Set speed not cancelled when clutch pedal is pushed (M/T)				1						2		
Set speed not cancelled when shift lever is moved to N (A/T)					1					2		
Set speed not cancelled when brake pedal is pushed			1							2		
Set speed not cancelled when main switch is pushed OFF	1									2		
Set speed not resumed when RESUME button is pushed (with main switch on, but set speed temporarily cancelled)		1								2		Lg/Bl

Cruise control trouble shooting chart—1986 and later Accord

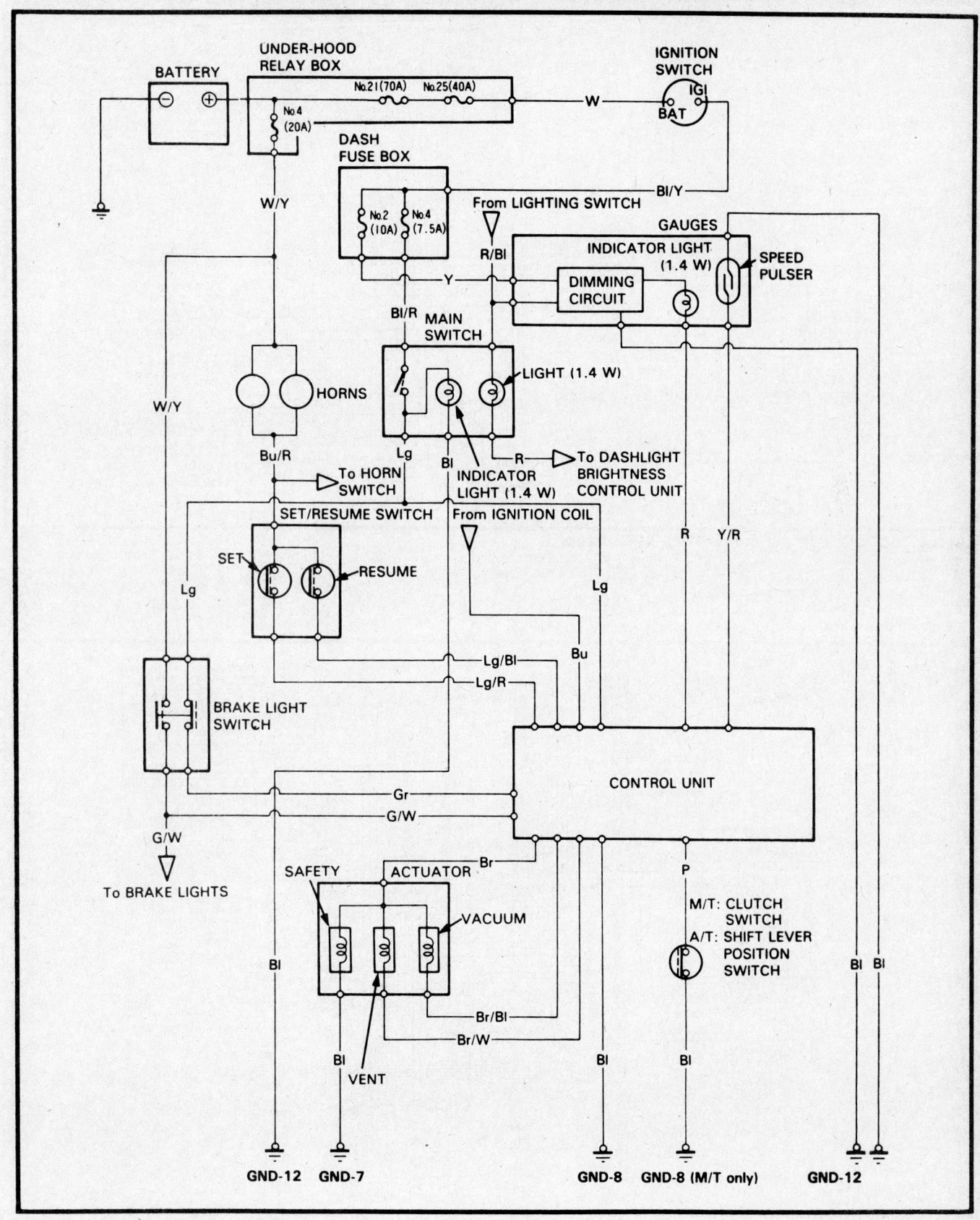

Cruise control electrical schematic—1986 and later Accord

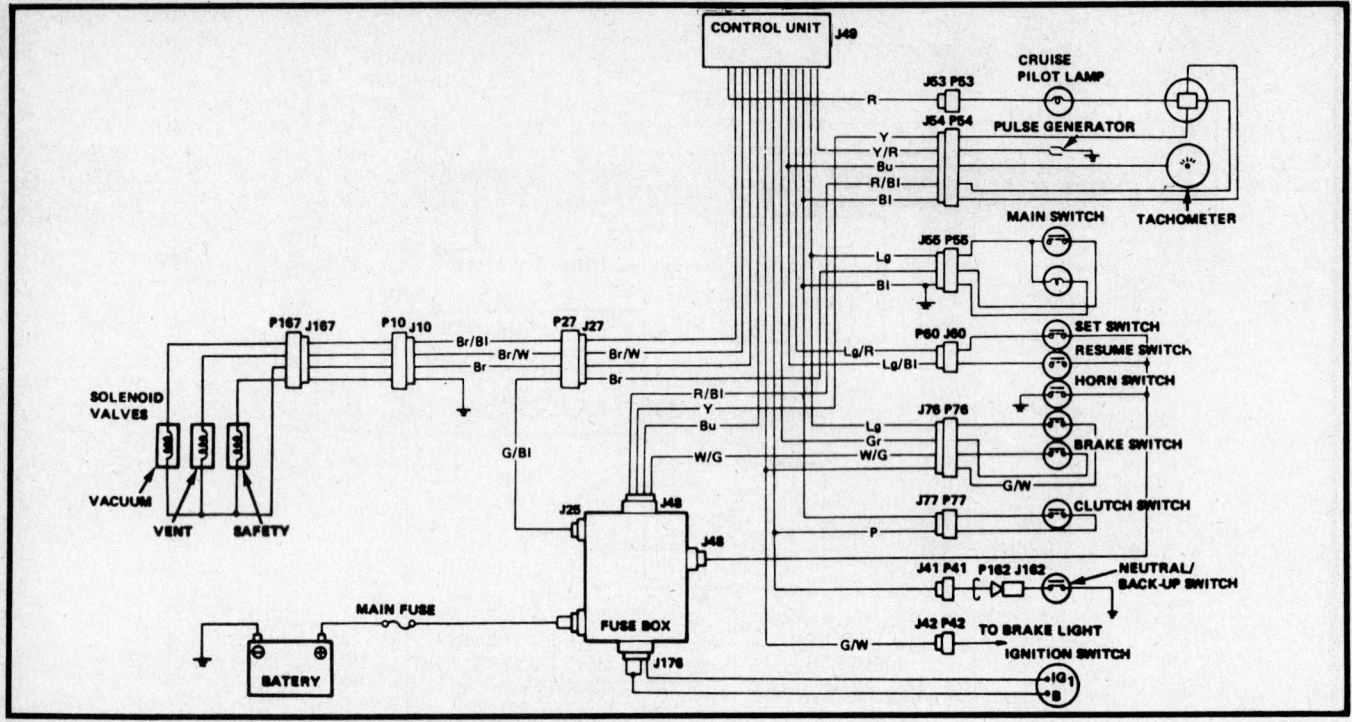

Cruise control electrical schematic – 1982 Accord

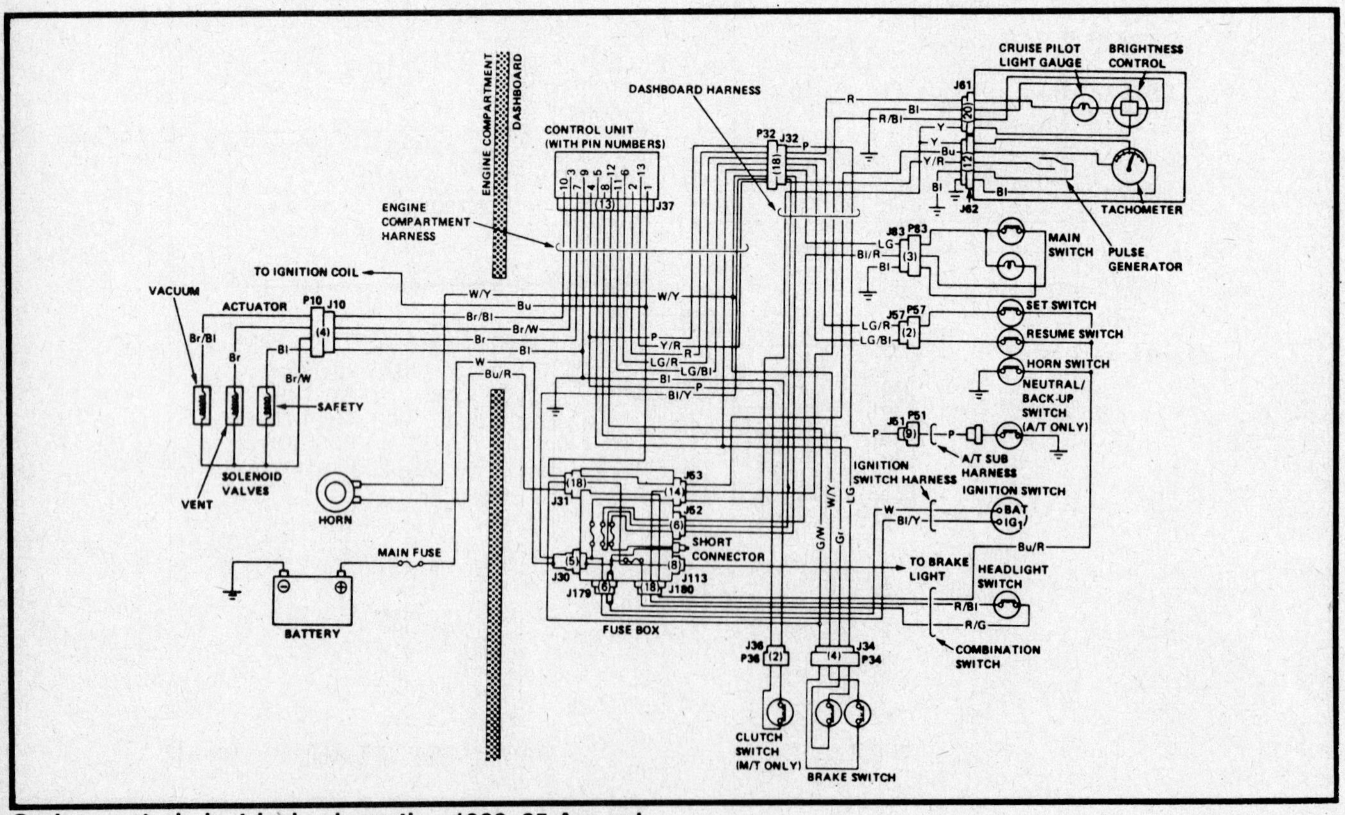

Cruise control electrical schematic – 1983–85 Accord

NOTE: Before you try to diagnose or repair the problem, check:
- Throttle cable free play.
- Actuator cable free play.
- Throttle linkage operation.
- Wire harness connectors.
- Vacuum lines.
- For a full-system check, based on control unit inputs,

Possible Cause of Malfunction
NOTE: Check in the order numbered, if more than one possibility.

Symptom	Fuse	Wire Harness	Main Switch	Set Switch	Resume Switch	Ignition Pulse	Brake Switch	Clutch Switch (M/T)	Neutral/Back-Up Switch (A/T)	Cruise Control Pilot Light	Speed Pulser	Actuator	Other	
Cruise control can't be set.	2	1	4	3	9	10	5	11	6		8	7		If they are OK, replace the control unit.
Cruise control can be set, but the pilot light doesn't go on.	3	2								1				If they are OK, replace the control unit.
Cruise control can be set, but, after overriding the system, it won't return to set speed when you push the resume switch.		1			2									If they are OK, replace the control unit.
Cruise control can be set, but you can't reduce the car's speed by pushing the set switch.														Replace the control unit.
Cruise can be set, but the car won't accelerate when you hold the resume switch.														Replace the control unit.
Set speed won't cancel when you step on the breakes.		1					2							If they are OK, replace the control unit.
Set speed won't cancel when you push the clutch pedal or shift to N, P or R position.		1						2	3					If they are OK, replace the control unit.
Set speed can't be cancelled by turning off the main switch, or by using other cancelling mechanisms.		1	4					2	3					If they are OK, replace the control unit.
Car won't hold a steady speed even on a flat road with the cruise control set.												O	Check the throttle and actuator cables for free play.	If they are OK, replace the control unit.
Overshooting and/or undershooting are excessive when you're trying to set the cruise control.													Adjust the throttle and actuator cable free play.	
Won't hold set speed.												O	Replace or repair the vacuum line and clean the actuator filter and tube.	

Cruise control trouble shooting chart—1985

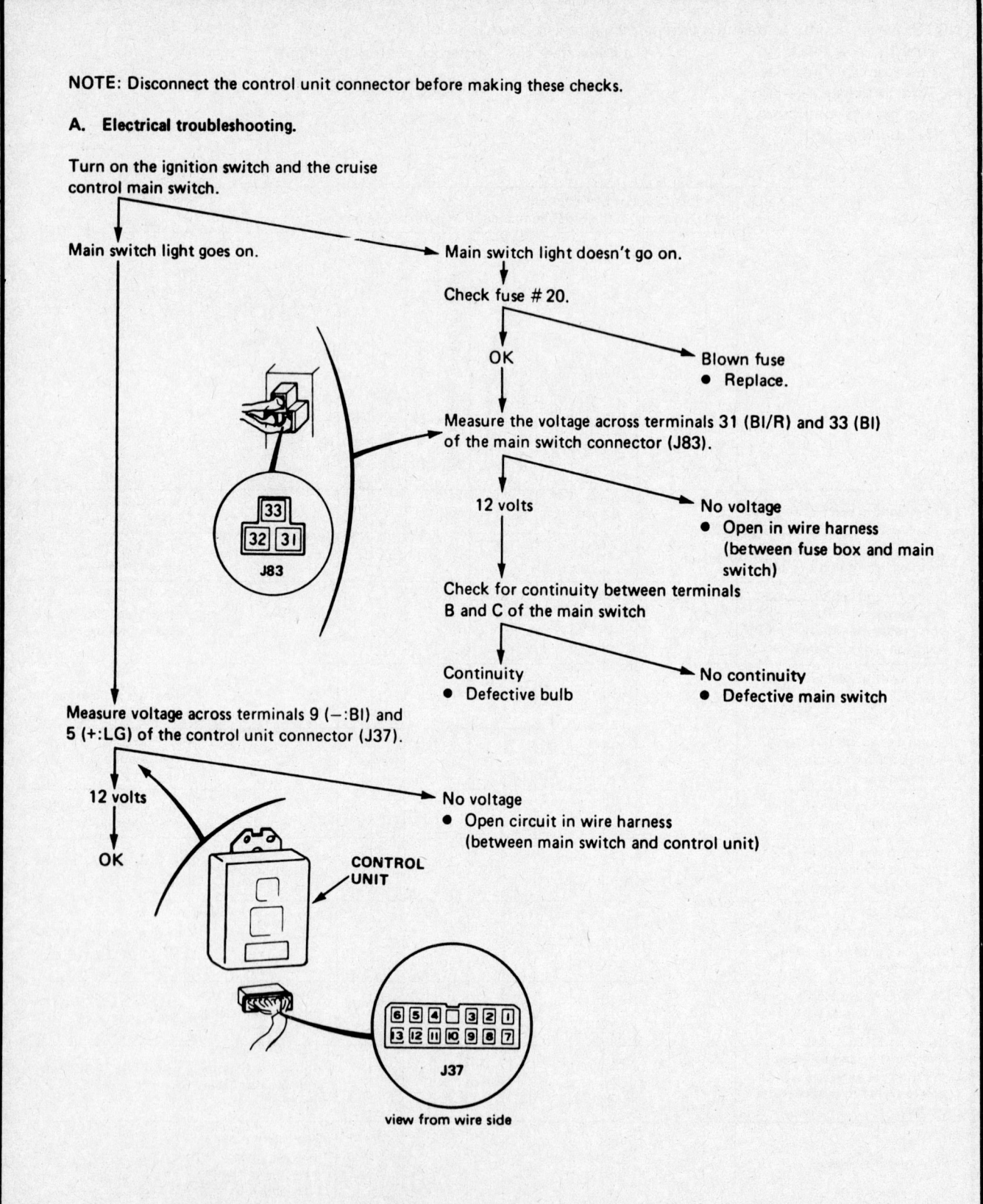

NOTE: Disconnect the control unit connector before making these checks.

A. Electrical troubleshooting.

Turn on the ignition switch and the cruise control main switch.

Main switch light goes on.

Main switch light doesn't go on.

Check fuse # 20.

OK

Blown fuse
- Replace.

Measure the voltage across terminals 31 (Bl/R) and 33 (Bl) of the main switch connector (J83).

33
32 31
J83

12 volts

No voltage
- Open in wire harness (between fuse box and main switch)

Check for continuity between terminals B and C of the main switch

Continuity
- Defective bulb

No continuity
- Defective main switch

Measure voltage across terminals 9 (−:Bl) and 5 (+:LG) of the control unit connector (J37).

12 volts

No voltage
- Open circuit in wire harness (between main switch and control unit)

OK

CONTROL UNIT

6 5 4 3 2 1
13 12 11 10 9 8 7
J37

view from wire side

Cruise control diagnostic chart—1982–85 Accord

B. Set/Resume switch troubleshooting

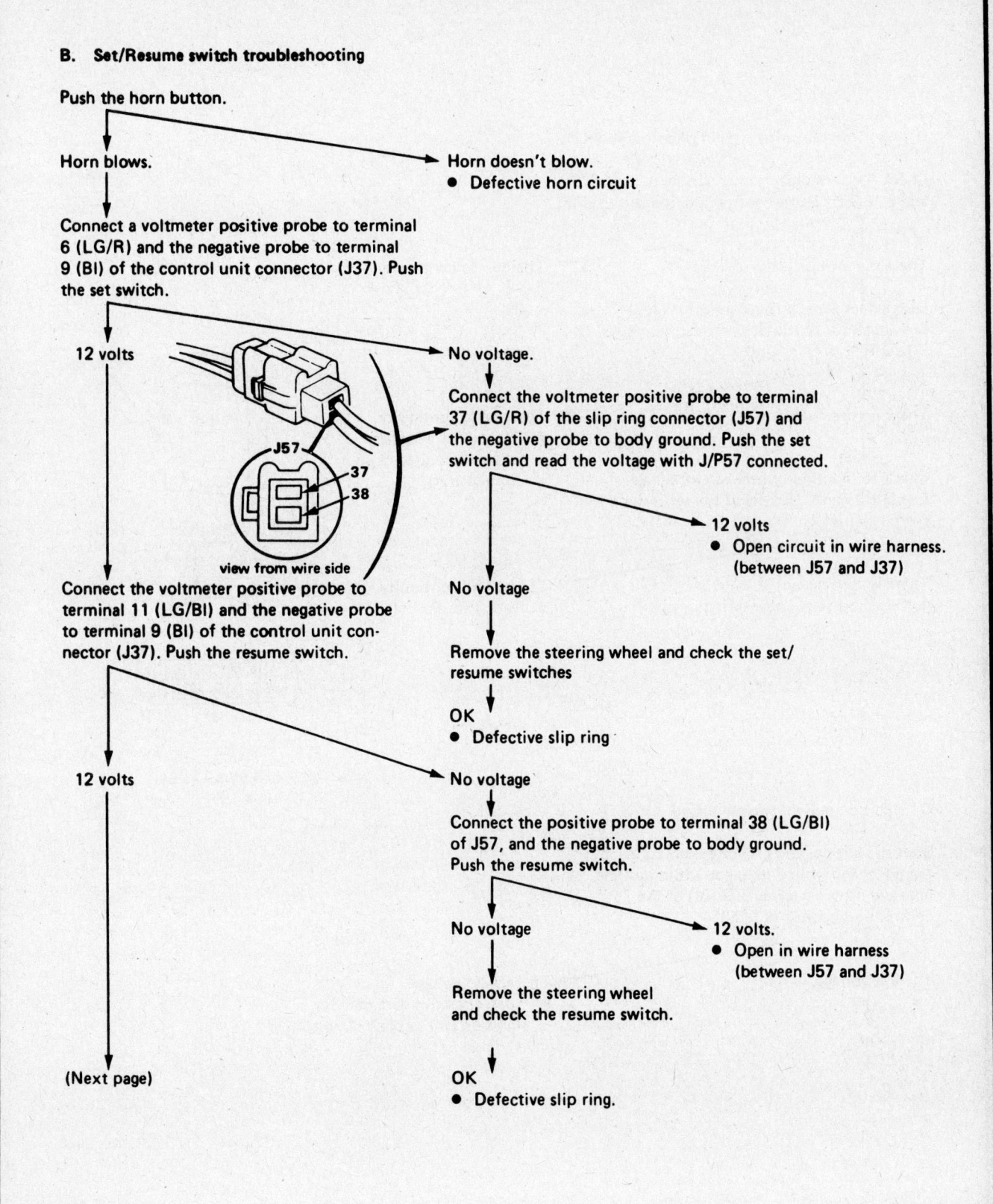

Push the horn button.

Horn blows.

Horn doesn't blow.
- Defective horn circuit

Connect a voltmeter positive probe to terminal 6 (LG/R) and the negative probe to terminal 9 (BI) of the control unit connector (J37). Push the set switch.

12 volts

No voltage.

J57

37
38

view from wire side

Connect the voltmeter positive probe to terminal 37 (LG/R) of the slip ring connector (J57) and the negative probe to body ground. Push the set switch and read the voltage with J/P57 connected.

12 volts
- Open circuit in wire harness. (between J57 and J37)

Connect the voltmeter positive probe to terminal 11 (LG/BI) and the negative probe to terminal 9 (BI) of the control unit connector (J37). Push the resume switch.

No voltage

Remove the steering wheel and check the set/resume switches

OK
- Defective slip ring

12 volts

No voltage

Connect the positive probe to terminal 38 (LG/BI) of J57, and the negative probe to body ground. Push the resume switch.

No voltage

12 volts.
- Open in wire harness (between J57 and J37)

Remove the steering wheel and check the resume switch.

(Next page)

OK
- Defective slip ring.

Cruise control diagnostic chart—1982–85 Accord

POWER ACCESSORIES
CRUISE CONTROL SYSTEMS

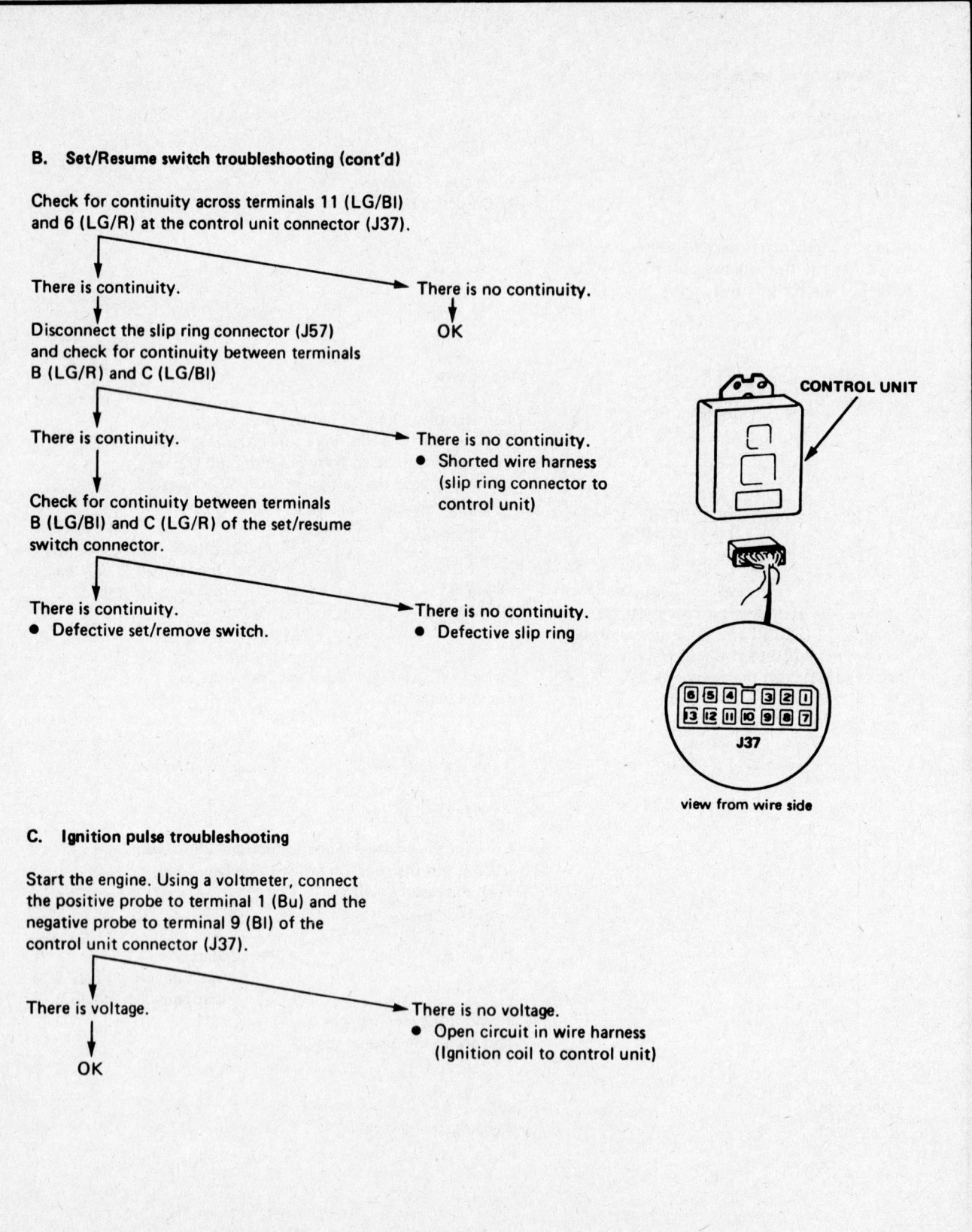

B. Set/Resume switch troubleshooting (cont'd)

Check for continuity across terminals 11 (LG/Bl) and 6 (LG/R) at the control unit connector (J37).

There is continuity. → There is no continuity.
OK

Disconnect the slip ring connector (J57) and check for continuity between terminals B (LG/R) and C (LG/Bl)

There is continuity. → There is no continuity.
• Shorted wire harness (slip ring connector to control unit)

Check for continuity between terminals B (LG/Bl) and C (LG/R) of the set/resume switch connector.

There is continuity. → There is no continuity.
• Defective set/remove switch. • Defective slip ring

CONTROL UNIT

J37

view from wire side

C. Ignition pulse troubleshooting

Start the engine. Using a voltmeter, connect the positive probe to terminal 1 (Bu) and the negative probe to terminal 9 (Bl) of the control unit connector (J37).

There is voltage. → There is no voltage.
• Open circuit in wire harness (Ignition coil to control unit)
OK

Cruise control diagnostic chart—1982–85 Accord

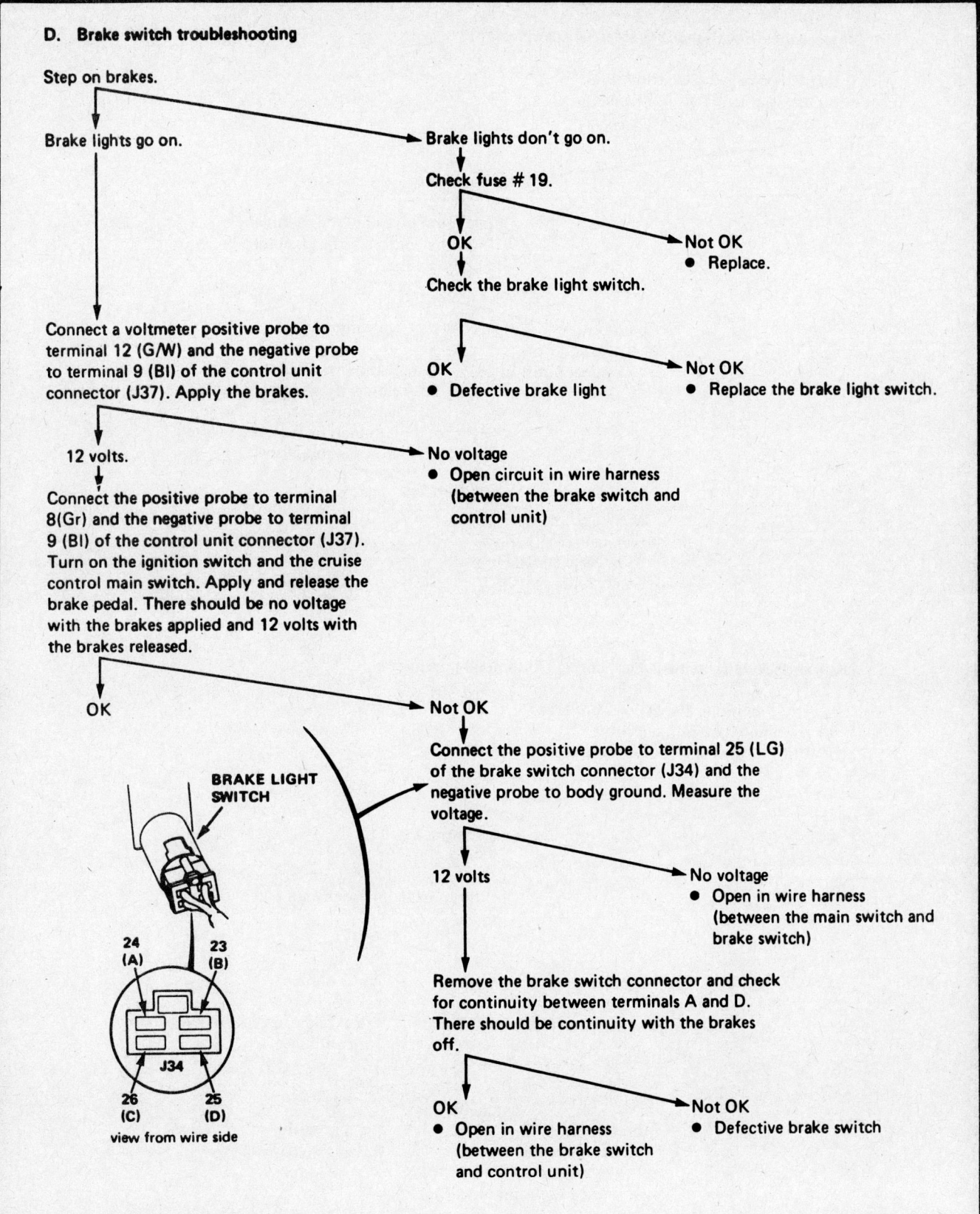

D. Brake switch troubleshooting

Step on brakes.

Brake lights go on. → Brake lights don't go on.

Check fuse # 19.

OK — Not OK
• Replace.

Check the brake light switch.

OK — Not OK
• Defective brake light — • Replace the brake light switch.

Connect a voltmeter positive probe to terminal 12 (G/W) and the negative probe to terminal 9 (Bl) of the control unit connector (J37). Apply the brakes.

12 volts. — No voltage
• Open circuit in wire harness (between the brake switch and control unit)

Connect the positive probe to terminal 8(Gr) and the negative probe to terminal 9 (Bl) of the control unit connector (J37). Turn on the ignition switch and the cruise control main switch. Apply and release the brake pedal. There should be no voltage with the brakes applied and 12 volts with the brakes released.

OK — Not OK

Connect the positive probe to terminal 25 (LG) of the brake switch connector (J34) and the negative probe to body ground. Measure the voltage.

12 volts — No voltage
• Open in wire harness (between the main switch and brake switch)

Remove the brake switch connector and check for continuity between terminals A and D. There should be continuity with the brakes off.

OK — Not OK
• Open in wire harness (between the brake switch and control unit) — • Defective brake switch

BRAKE LIGHT SWITCH

24 (A)   23 (B)
J34
26 (C)   25 (D)
view from wire side

Cruise control diagnostic chart—1982–85 Accord

E. **Clutch switch troubleshooting (Manual transmission)**

With the clutch pedal released, check the
continuity between terminals 4 (P) and
9 (BI) of the control unit connector (J37).

Continuity

No continuity

OK

Check continuity between terminal
4 (P) of the control unit connector
and body ground.

Continuity
- Bad ground:
  Terminal 9 (BI) of J37

No continuity

Remove the clutch switch
connector and check for
continuity between the
terminals of the clutch switch
with the rod pushed.

Continuity.
- Open in wire harness.
  (between control unit
  and clutch switch)

No continuity.
- Defective clutch switch

E. **Neutral/Back-up switch troubleshooting (Automatic transmission)**

With the shift lever in the D4, D3 or 2 position,
check the continuity between terminals
4 (P) and 9 (BI) of the control unit connector
(J37).

Continuity

No continuity

OK

Check continuity between terminal 4 (P)
of the control unit connector and body
ground.

Continuity
- Bad ground:
  Terminal 9 (BI) of J37

No continuity

Check the neutral/back-up switch
for continuity.

Continuity
- Open in wire harness
  (between the control unit
  and neutral/back-up switch)

No continuity
- Defective switch

Cruise control diagnostic chart—1982–85 Accord

F.   Pilot light troubleshooting

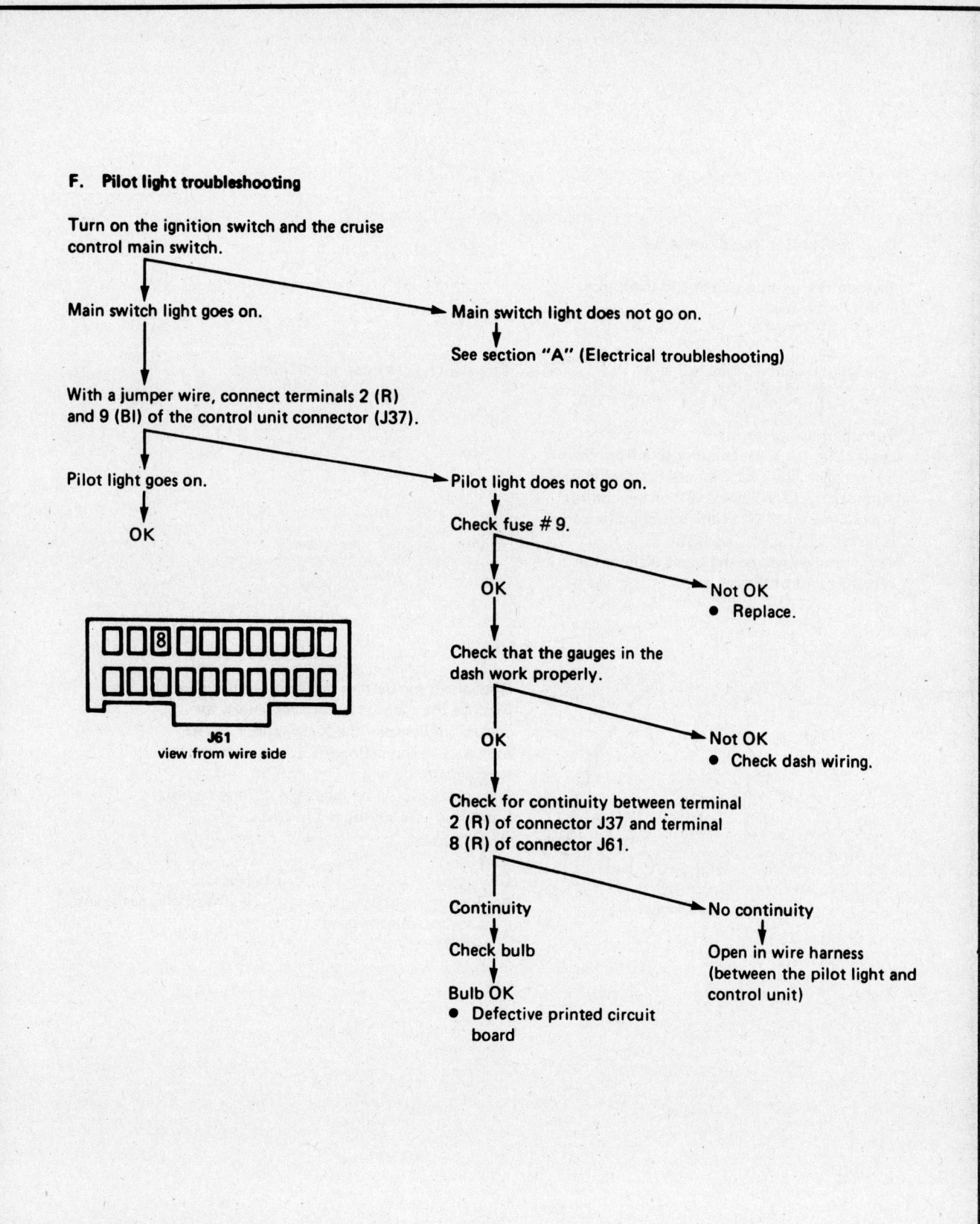

Cruise control diagnostic chart — 1982–85 Accord

G. Speed sensor troubleshooting

Turn on the ignition switch and the cruise control main switch.

Main switch light illuminates. ⟶ Main switch light does not illuminate.

Turn ignition switch off.
Disconnect the speedometer cable from the transmission and check for continuity between terminals 13 (Y/R) and 9 (Bl) of the control unit connector (J37) as the speedometer cable is turned very slowly, by hand.
Continuity should be indicated 4 times for each full turn of the cable.

OK ⟶ Not OK

Disconnect the battery negative (−) terminal.
Remove the gauge assembly and check for continuity between the X (Bl) and Y (Y/R) terminals of connector J62 as you turn the speedometer drive.
Continuity should be indicated 4 times for each full turn of the speedometer drive.

Ⓧ
Ⓨ

view from wire side

OK ⟶ Not OK
● Open in wire harness (Control unit to speed sensor) ● Defective speed sensor

Cruise control diagnostic chart—1982–85 Accord

H. Actuator troubleshooting

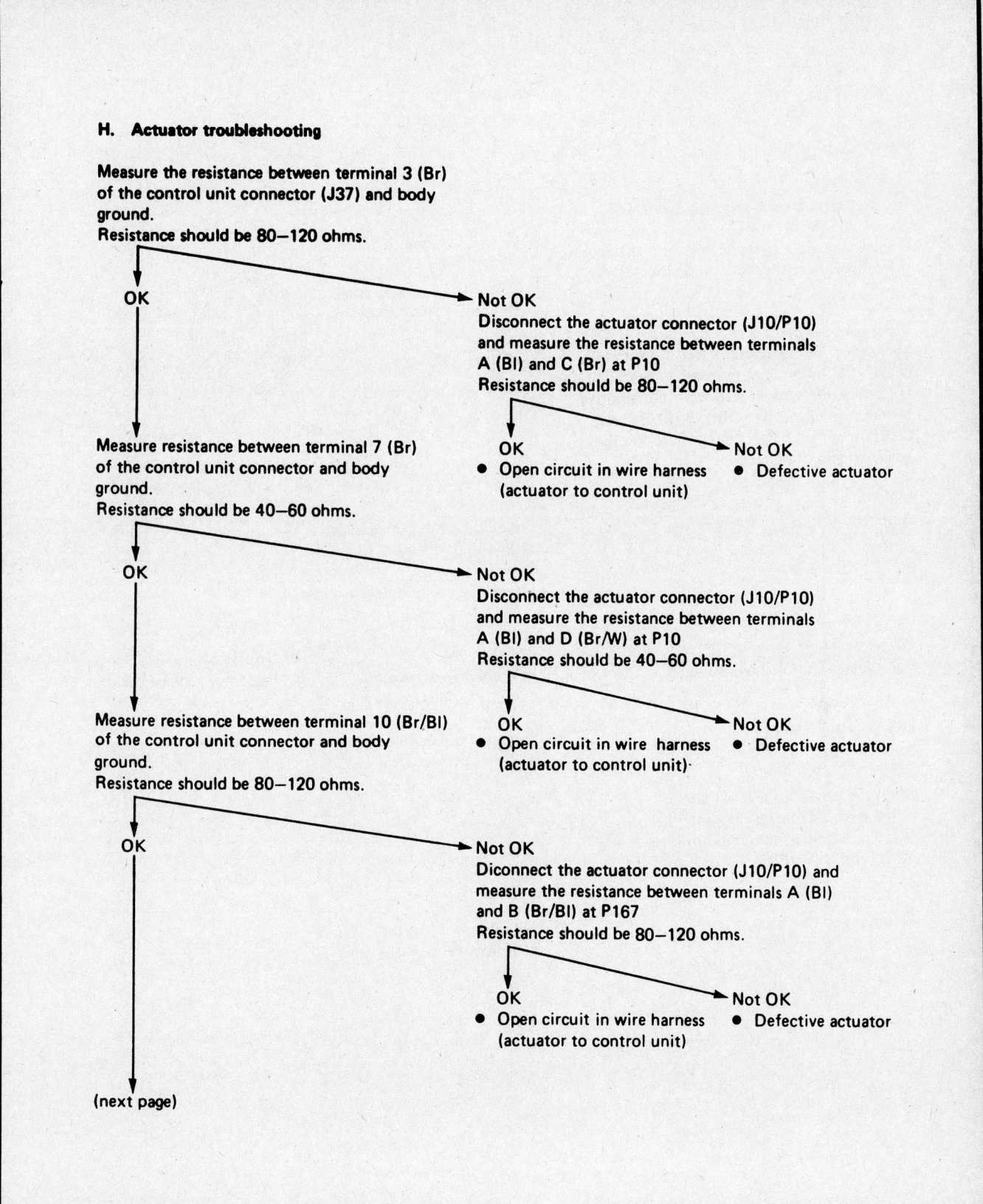

Measure the resistance between terminal 3 (Br)
of the control unit connector (J37) and body
ground.
Resistance should be 80—120 ohms.

OK

Not OK
Disconnect the actuator connector (J10/P10)
and measure the resistance between terminals
A (Bl) and C (Br) at P10
Resistance should be 80—120 ohms.

OK
● Open circuit in wire harness
  (actuator to control unit)

Not OK
● Defective actuator

Measure resistance between terminal 7 (Br)
of the control unit connector and body
ground.
Resistance should be 40—60 ohms.

OK

Not OK
Disconnect the actuator connector (J10/P10)
and measure the resistance between terminals
A (Bl) and D (Br/W) at P10
Resistance should be 40—60 ohms.

OK
● Open circuit in wire harness
  (actuator to control unit)·

Not OK
● Defective actuator

Measure resistance between terminal 10 (Br/Bl)
of the control unit connector and body
ground.
Resistance should be 80—120 ohms.

OK

Not OK
Diconnect the actuator connector (J10/P10) and
measure the resistance between terminals A (Bl)
and B (Br/Bl) at P167
Resistance should be 80—120 ohms.

OK
● Open circuit in wire harness
  (actuator to control unit)

Not OK
● Defective actuator

(next page)

Cruise control diagnostic chart – 1982–85 Accord

H. Actuator troubleshooting (cont'd)

Disconnect the actuator cable from the actuator, then disconnect the actuator connector.

↓

Make sure the control unit connector is disconnected. Then connect a lead from the battery (12V) positive terminal to terminal D (Br/W) and another lead from the negative terminal to terminals A (Bl), B (Br/Bl) and C (Br). Connect hand vacuum pump to the actuated and draw vacuum.

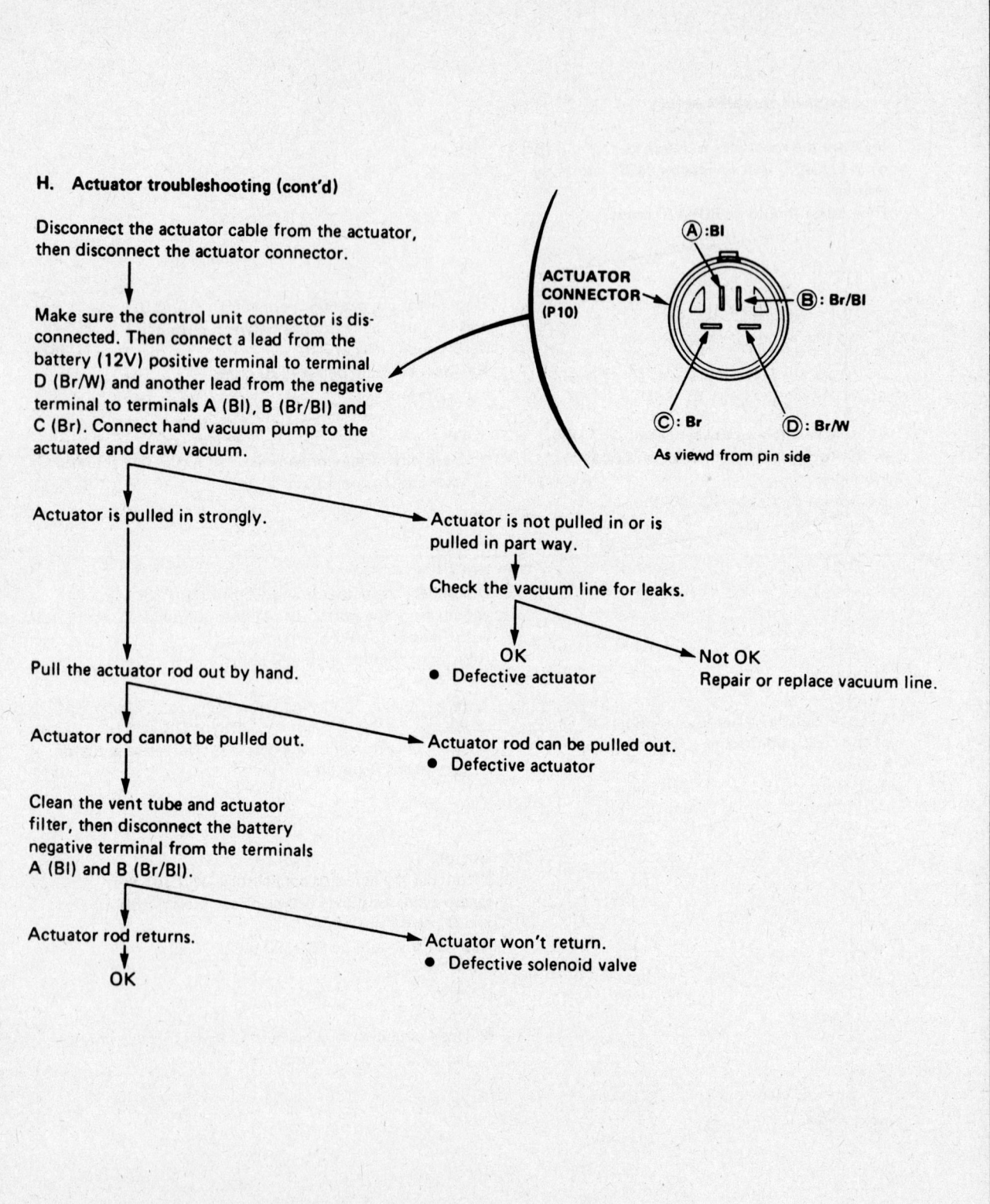

ACTUATOR CONNECTOR (P10)

Ⓐ : Bl
Ⓑ : Br/Bl
Ⓒ : Br
Ⓓ : Br/W

As viewd from pin side

Actuator is pulled in strongly. → Actuator is not pulled in or is pulled in part way.

Check the vacuum line for leaks.

OK
● Defective actuator

Not OK
Repair or replace vacuum line.

↓

Pull the actuator rod out by hand.

↓

Actuator rod cannot be pulled out. → Actuator rod can be pulled out.
● Defective actuator

↓

Clean the vent tube and actuator filter, then disconnect the battery negative terminal from the terminals A (Bl) and B (Br/Bl).

↓

Actuator rod returns. → Actuator won't return.
● Defective solenoid valve

OK

Cruise control diagnostic chart – 1982–85 Accord

Component Replacement

CRUISE CONTROL SWITCH

Removal and Installation

1. Disconnect the negative battery cable.
2. Remove the steering wheel.
3. Separate the horn cover from the body cover.
4. Remove the screws and the set/resume switch from the steering wheel.
5. If necessary, remove the upper and lower steering column covers then remove the screws and the slip ring assembly.
6. Installation is the reverse of the removal procedure.

ACTUATOR CABLE

Removal and Installation

1. Pull back the boot and loosen the locknut. Disconnect the cable from the actuator bracket.
2. Disconnect the end cable from the actuator rod.
3. Disconnect the actuator cable from the cruise control center arm.
4. Turn the grommet, which is located on the firewall, about ninety degrees. Remove the actuator cable from the vehicle.
5. Installation is the reverse of the removal procedure. Adjust the actuator cable as required.

ACTUATOR

Removal and Installation

1. Pull back the boot and loosen the locknut. Disconnect the cable from the actuator bracket.
2. Disconnect the end cable from the actuator rod.
3. Disconnect the actuator cable from the cruise control center arm.
4. Turn the grommet, which is located on the firewall, about ninety degrees. Remove the actuator cable from the vehicle.

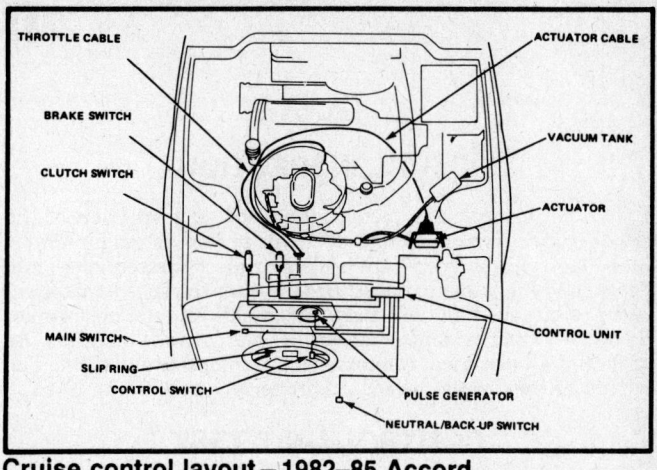

Cruise control layout—1982–85 Accord

5. Disconnect the wire connector from the actuator. Disconnect the vacuum hose from the actuator.
6. Remove the bolts holding the actuator to the mounting bracket. Remove the actuator from the vehicle.
7. Installation is the reverse of the removal procedure. Adjust the actuator cable as required.

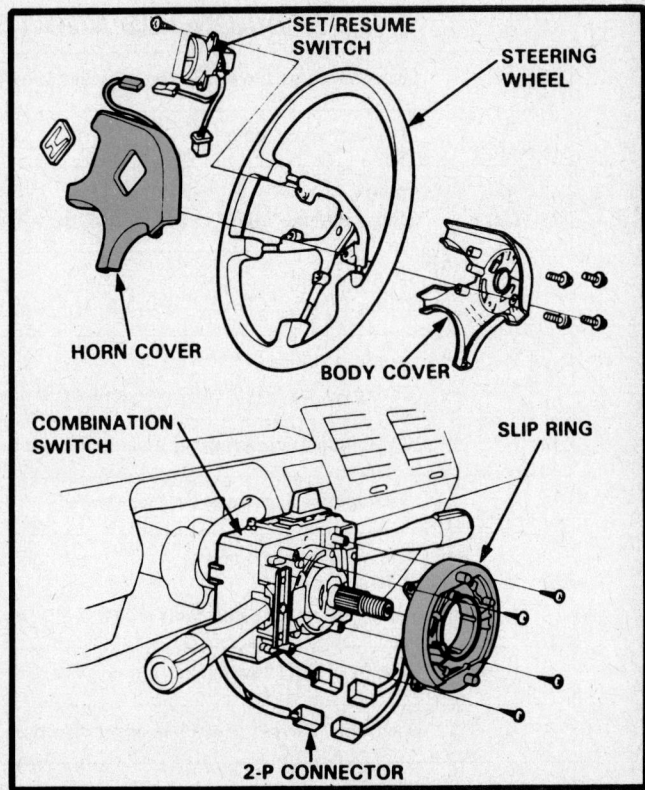

Control switch assembly—1986 and later Accord

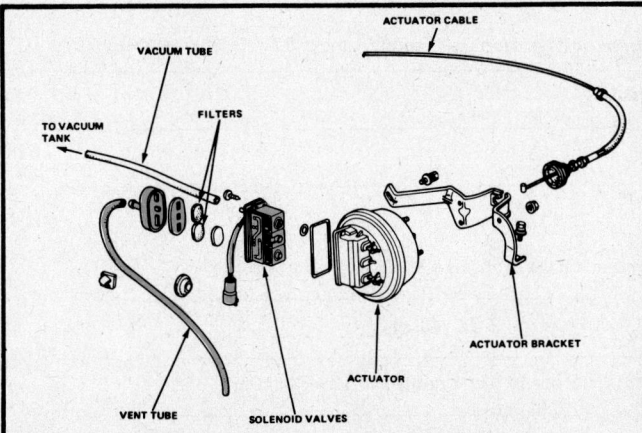

Actuator cable assembly—1982–85 Accord

MAZDA

GLC

VISUAL INSPECTION

Before performing any tests make a visual inspection of the cruise control system. Check all items in the system for abnormal conditions such as bare broken or disconnected wires and damage to the vacuum hoses. Be sure that the speedometer cables are attached and properly routed. All vacuum hoses must be properly routed and must not have any kinks or bends. Be sure that all electrical connections are complete and tight. The wiring harness must be routed properly.

CONTROL UNIT TEST

1. Raise and support the vehicle safely.
2. Turn the ignition switch on.
3. With the above test conditions and using a voltmeter, connect the negative lead of the voltmeter to terminal "M" of the control unit. Connect the positive lead to terminal "D" and "N" of the control unit.
4. Observe the troubleshooting chart.
5. Start the engine. Turn the cruise control main switch to the on position.

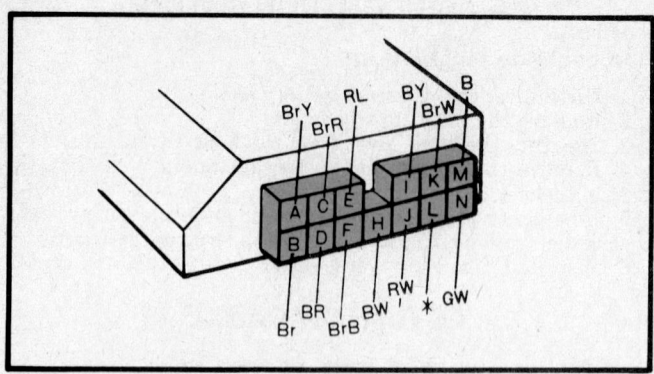

Control unit test point locations—GLC

6. Increase the vehicle speed to about 30 mph and then push the cruise control set switch button.
7. With the above test conditions and using a voltmeter, check the "A", "B" and "C" terminal. Connect the negative lead of the voltmeter to terminal "M" of the control unit. Connect the positive lead to terminal "A", "B" and "C" of the control unit.
8. Observe the troubleshooting chart.

DIAGNOSIS AND TESTING PROCEDURES

Terminal	The voltage exists to each terminal under the following condition.
F (BrB)	12 voltage at any time
I (BY)	Approx. 12 volt (During pushing "SET" switch button, the voltage drops to 0 and returns to 12 volt when releasing it.)
J (RW)	Approx. 12 volt (During turning "COAST" switch to arrow direction, the voltage drops to 0 and returns to 12 volt when releasing it.)
K (BrW)	Approx. 12Volt (During turning "RESUME" switch to arrow direction, the voltage drops to 0 and returns to 12 volt when releasing it.)
E (RL)	12 volt during depressing the brake pedal or clutch pedal
N (GW)	12 volt during depressing the brake pedal
D (BR)	Automatic transaxle only 12 volt (During shifting the shift lever to "P" or "N" position, the voltage drops to 0.)
B (Br)	When push "SET" switch button, the voltage drops to 0 and returns to 12 volt again.
A (BrY)	When turn "COAST" switch to arrow direction, the voltage drops to 0 and returns to 12 volt again.
C (BrR)	When depress clutch pedal, the voltage drops to 0 and returns to 12 volt again.
H (BW)	Perform the followings. 1) Stop the engine. 2) Remove the speedometer cable from the transaxle and turn the ignition switch ON. 3) Rotate the inner cable by hand. 4) The needle of voltmeter moves between 12 to 0 volt.

Cruise control trouble diagnosis chart—GLC

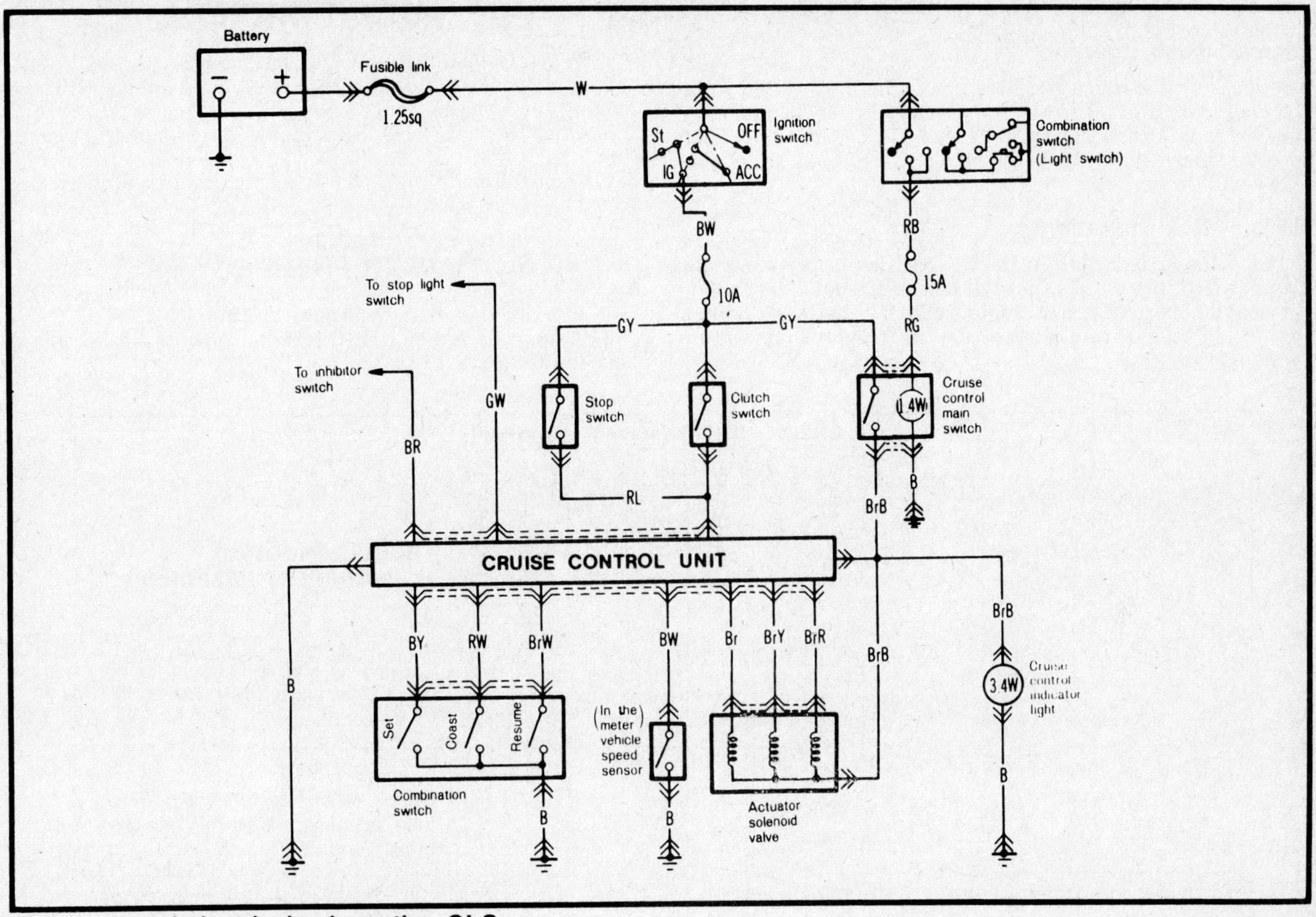

Cruise control electrical schematic — GLC

323

VISUAL INSPECTION

Before performing any tests make a visual inspection of the cruise control system. Check all items in the system for abnormal conditions such as bare broken or disconnected wires and damage to the vacuum hoses. Be sure that the speedometer cables are attached and properly routed. All vacuum hoses must be properly routed and must not have any kinks or bends. Be sure that all electrical connections are complete and tight. The wiring harness must be routed properly.

NOTE: In order to properly diagnosis problems with the cruise control system used in the Mazda 323 a special cruise control diagnostic tool, the ACC checker (tool number 49–9200–010) or equivalent will be needed.

ACC CHECKER TOOL FUNCTIONS

Check Lights

Each component is verified by a check light which is located on the ACC checker tool.

Tool Installation

1. Depress the lock hook of the harness connector.
2. Remove the connector from the control unit after the ignition switch and the main switch are turned off.

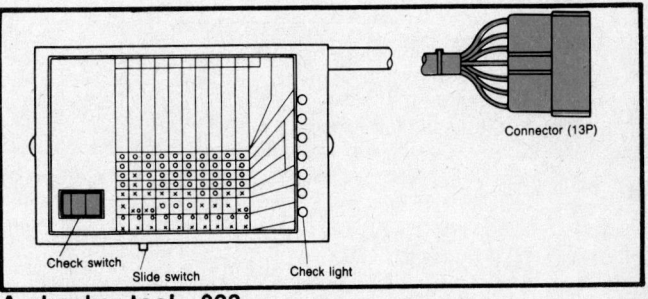

Connector (13P)

A checker tool — 323

Check light	Check Items
MAIN SW.	Ignition switch, fuse, main switch and associated wiring harness terminals and connectors.
ACTUATOR—VAC	VAC coil continuity in the actuator and associated harness.
ACTUATOR— VENT 2	VENT 2 coil continuity in the actuator and associated harness.
ACTUATOR-VENT 1	VENT 1 coil continuity in the actuator and associated harness.
CLUTCH/BRAKE SW.	Clutch switch, brake switch and associated harness.
COMBINATION SW.	"SET", "COAST" and "RESUME" position in the combination switch, and associated harness.
GENERATOR	Speed sensor output and associated harness.

A checker tool data — 323

3. Connect the harness connector to the ACC checker tool.

Check Switch Operation

The check switch is used to check the actuator operation while the engine is running. When the check switch is held on after the engine is started, the engine speed will increase from 2000 to 3000 rpms. When the check switch is released the engine speed will drop to idle.

Slide Switch Operation

Position the slide switch in the "L" position before using the check switch. The engine rpm will increase about 2000 to 3000 rpms, and hold steady. If the engine does not reach and remain in the 2000 to 3000 rpm range adjust the freeplay in the actuator cable.

ACTUATOR TEST

1. Properly install the ACC checker tool.
2. Remove the orifice from the actuator assembly, by first removing the vacuum line.
3. Once the orifice has been removed reinstall the vacuum line.
4. Once the actuator has been evaualted reinstall the orifice.

ACTUATOR FREEPLAY TEST

1. Remove the actuator retaining clip.
2. Adjust the nut so that the actuator control cable play is between 0.04 to 0.12 inch.

CHECK ITEMS AND CONDITIONS	CHECK LIGHTS (correct response)							TROUBLESHOOTING (INCORRECT RESPONSE) O: Light OFF X: Light ON
	MAIN SW.	ACTUATOR			CLUTCH/BRAKE SW.	COMBINATION/INH. SW.	GENERATOR	
		VAC	VENT 2	VENT 1				
1. MAIN SW. CONTINUITY: • Ignition switch ON • Main switch ON	O	O	O	O	X	X	O or X	ALL LIGHTS OFF: Check ignition switch, main switch, fuse, and associated harness terminals and connectors.
2. BRAKE SW. CONTINUITY: • Ignition switch ON • Main switch ON • Depress brake pedal	O	O	O	O	X	X	O or X	CLUTCH/BRAKE SW. LIGHT OFF: Check brake switch and associated harness.
3. CLUTCH SW. CONTINUITY: • Ignition switch ON • Main switch ON • Depress clutch pedal	O	O	O	O	X	X	O or X	CLUTCH/BRAKE SW. LIGHT OFF: Check clutch switch and associated harness.
4. "SET" POSITION OF COMBINATION SWITCH: • Ignition switch ON • Main switch ON • Push to "SET" position of combination switch	O	O	O	O	X	X	O or X	COMBINATION/SW. LIGHT OFF Check "SET" position of combination switch and associated harness.
5. "COAST" POSITION OF COMBINATION SWITCH: • Ignition switch ON • Main switch ON • Turn to "COAST" position of combination switch	O	O	O	O	X	X	O or X	COMBINATION/SW. LIGHT OFF: Check "COAST" position in combination switch and associated harness.
6. "RESUME" POSITION OF COMBINATION SWITCH: • Ignition switch ON • Main switch ON • Turn to "RESUME" position of combination switch	O	O	O	O	X	X	O or OX	COMBINATION/SW. LIGHT OFF: Check "RESUME" position of combination switch and associated harness.

A checker tool data—323

CHECK ITEMS AND CONDITIONS	MAIN SW.	ACTUATOR			CLUTCH/BRAKE SW.	COMBINATION/INH. SW.	GENERATOR	TROUBLESHOOTING (INCORRECT RESPONSE)
		VAC	VENT 2	VENT 1				
7. START THE ENGINE • Shift lever in "N" position	O	O	O	O	X	X	O or X	
8. ACTUATOR OPERATION: • After engine is started, set the slide switch "L". Then turn "ON" check to switch, and keep in "ON" position **Note:** **Make sure engine speed increases. If over 4,000 rpm release the switch immediately.**	O	X O	X	X	X	X	O or X	If engine speed does not reach and remain in the 2,000 to 3,000 rpm range, fault may be in actuator and associated harness.
9. SPEED SENSOR OUTPUT Jack up rear of vehicle and support with stands. Let engine idle in 1st gear.	O	O	O	O	X	X	O X	If GENERATOR LIGHT does not flash, fault may be in speed sensor and associated harness.

A checker tool data—323

ACTUATOR SOLENOID TEST

1. Using an ohmmeter check for continunity between the terminals.
2. Repair or replace defective components as required.

CONTROL UNIT

If there is a problem with the cruise control system and no abnormal condition is found when the ACC checker tool is used, the control unit could be at fault and should be replaced.

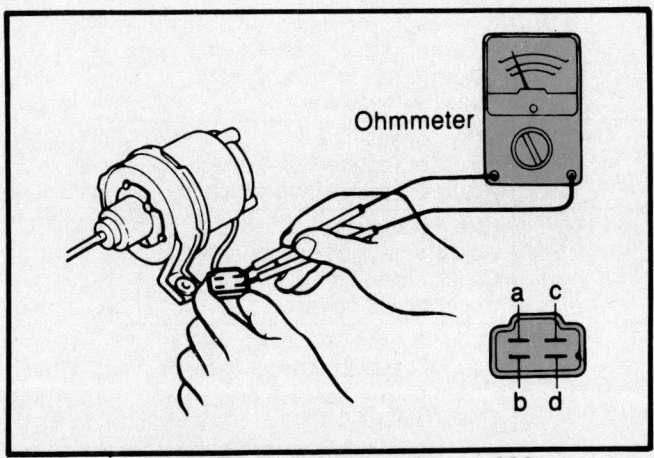

Actuator solenoid test point locations—323

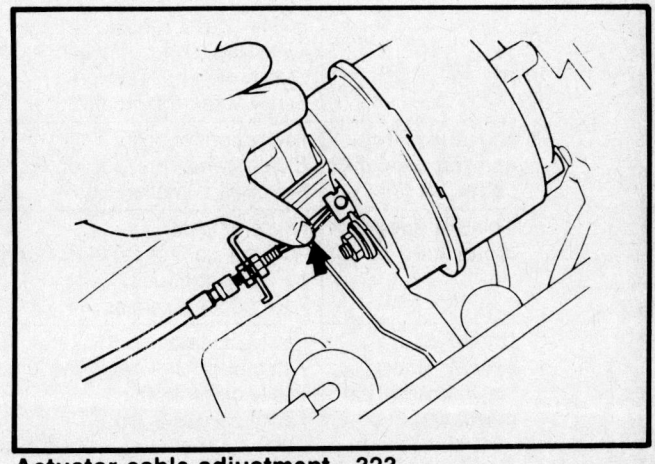

Actuator cable adjustment—323

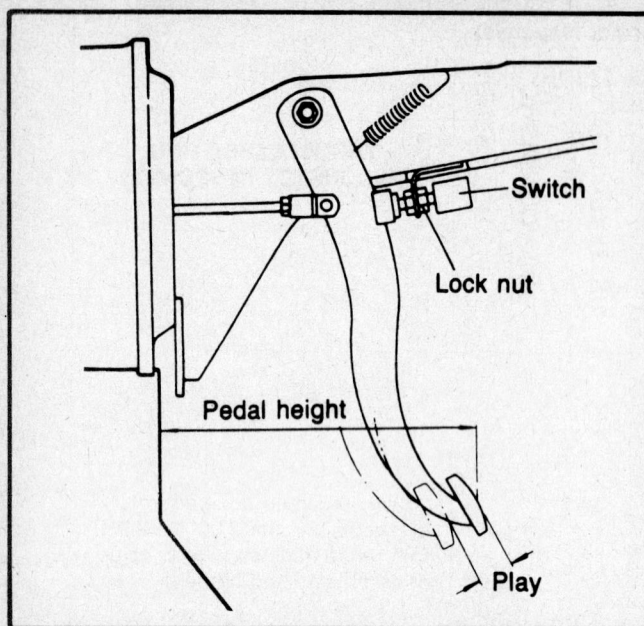

Clutch start switch and brake light switch adjustment – 323

Check terminals	Resistance
a—b	
a—c	Approx. 25 to 35 ohms
a—d	

Actuator solenoid specifications – 323

CLUTCH SWITCH ADJUSTMENT

Adjust the clutch switch so that the pedal height is between 8.34 and 8.62 inches.

BRAKE SWITCH ADJUSTMENT

Adjust the brake switch so that the pedal height is between 8.34 and 8.62 inches.

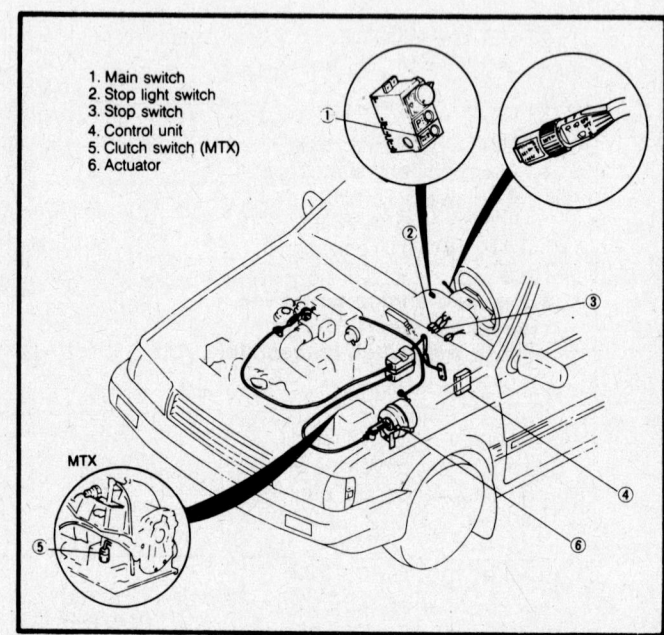

1. Main switch
2. Stop light switch
3. Stop switch
4. Control unit
5. Clutch switch (MTX)
6. Actuator

Cruise control layout – GLC

DIAGNOSIS AND TESTING PROCEDURES

Problem	Possible Cause	Remedy
Cruise control system does not work	Meter circuit board open circuit Faulty main switch Faulty control unit Faulty actuator Faulty control switch Faulty speed sensor Clutch switch malfunction Stop switch malfunction Faulty wiring or ground	Replace fuse and check for short Check main switch Check control unit Check actuator Check control switch Check speed sensor Adjust or replace clutch switch Adjust or replace stop switch Repair as necessary
Speed setting can not be cancelled	Faulty control unit Clutch switch malfunction Stop switch malfunction	Check control unit Adjust or replace clutch switch Adjust or replace stop switch
The set speed is not held	Faulty actuator Actuator control cable malfunction Faulty control unit Faulty speed sensor	Check actuator Adjust or replace control cable Check control unit Check speed sensor
Cruise control system does not function immediately	Faulty actuator Actuator control cable malfunction Faulty control switch Faulty control unit	Check actuator Adjust or replace control cable Check control switch Check control unit

Cruise control trouble diagnosis chart – 323

626

VISUAL INSPECTION

Before performing any tests make a visual inspection of the cruise control system. Check all items in the system for abnormal conditions such as bare broken or disconnected wires and damage to the vacuum hoses. Be sure that the speedometer cables are attached and properly routed. All vacuum hoses must be properly routed and must not have any kinks or bends. Be sure that all electrical connections are complete and tight. The wiring harness must be routed properly.

CONTROL UNIT TEST (1982–84)

1. Disconnect the control unit electrical connector.
2. Turn the ignition switch to the on position. Turn the cruise control main switch on.
3. Using a voltmeter, connect the negative test lead to the black terminal of the control unit and the positive test lead to each terminal that is to be checked.

CONTROL UNIT HARNESS CONNECTOR (1982–84)

1. Disconnect the control unit electrical connector.
2. Turn the ignition switch to the on position. Turn the cruise control main switch on.

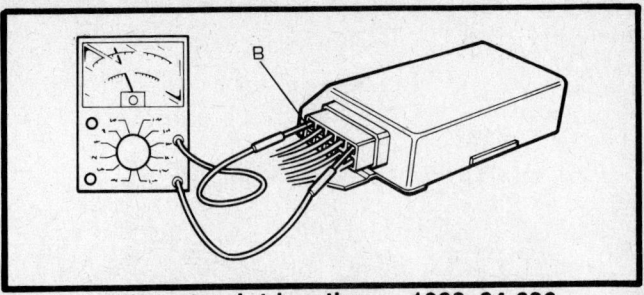

Control unit test point locations – 1982–84 626

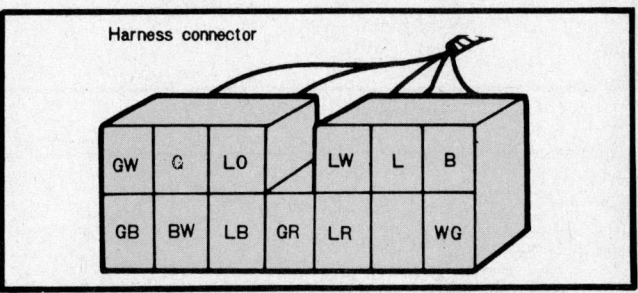

Wire harness test point locations – 1982–84 626

Terminal	Voltage	Problem between control unit and:
Green/white	Continuous 12 V	Actuator or main switch
Green/black	Continuous 12 V	Actuator or main switch
Green	Continuous 12 V	Actuator or main switch
Blue/orange	With clutch or brake depressed, 12 V; without clutch or brake depressed, 0 V	Clutch or stop switch
Blue/black	Continuous 12 V	Main switch
White/green	With brake depressed, 12 V; without brake depressed, 0 V	Stop switch
Black	Body ground	

Wire harness specifications – 1982–84 626

Terminal	Voltage	Problem point
Black/white	(MTX models) Continuous 12 V (ATX models) Except at "P" or "N", 12 V; at "P" or "N", approx. 1 V or less	Control unit or inhibitor switch
Blue/orange	With clutch or brake depressed, 12 V; without clutch or brake depressed, 0 V	Stop or clutch switch, or control unit
Blue/black	Continuous 12 V	Fuse or main switch
Blue/white	With SET switch OFF, 12 V; with SET switch ON, 0 V	Operation switch or control unit
Blue/red	With COAST switch OFF, 12 V; with COAST switch ON, 0 V	Operation switch or control unit
Blue	With RESUME switch OFF, 12 V; with RESUME switch ON, 0 V	Operation switch or control unit
White/green	With brake depressed, 12 V; with brake not depressed, 0 V	Stop switch or control unit
Black	Body ground	

Control unit specifications – 1982–84 626

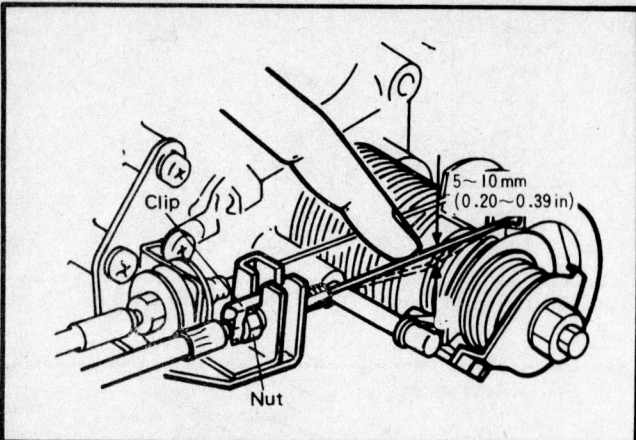

Actuator cable adjustments—626

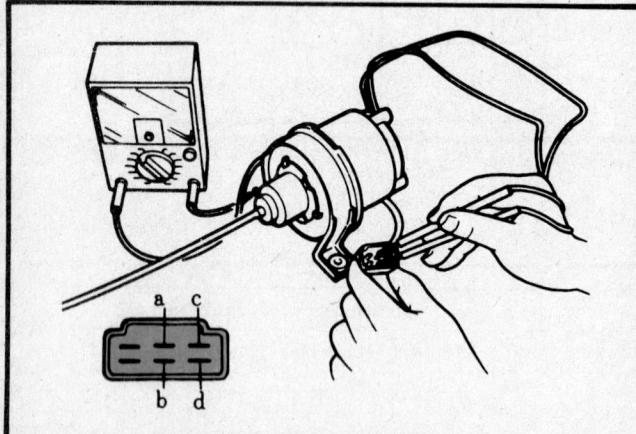

Actuator solenoid test point locations—626 without turbocharger

Terminal condition				Operating condition of control cable
a	b	c	d	
Ground	Power	Power	Ground	Pull
Ground	—	Power	—	Stop
Ground	Ground	Power	Power	Extend
—	—	—	—	Release

Actuator solenoid control cable specifications—1985 and later 626 with turbocharger

Check terminals	Resistance
a − b	
a − c	Approx. 25 to 35 ohms
a − d	

Actuator solenoid specifications—626 without turbocharger

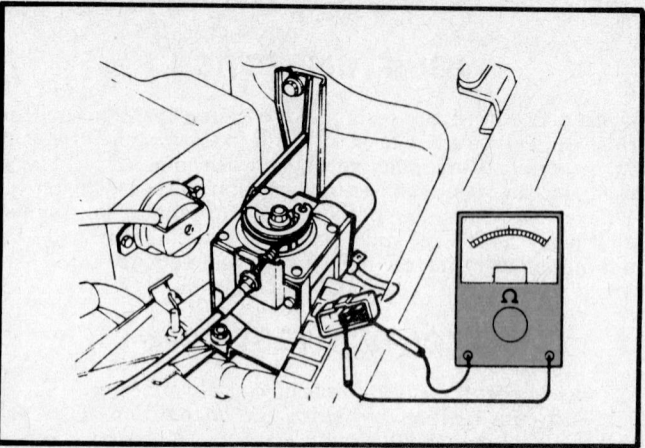

Actuator solenoid test point locations—1985 and later 626 with turbocharger

3. Using a voltmeter, connect the negative test lead to the black terminal of the control unit harness connector and the positive test lead to each terminal that is to be checked.

ACTUATOR FREEPLAY TEST

1. Remove the actuator retaining clip.
2. Adjust the nut so that the actuator control cable play is between 0.04 to 0.12 inch for 1982–84 vehicles.
3. On 1985 vehicles without turbochargers adjust the cable between 0.20 to 0.39 inch and 0.24 to 0.43 inch for vehicles with turbochargers.
3. On 1986 and later vehicles adjust the cable freeplay between 0.039 to 0.118 inch.

ACTUATOR SOLENOID TEST

Except Turbocharged Vehicles

1. Using an ohmmeter check for continuinity between the terminals.
2. Repair or replace defective components as required.

Turbocharged Vehicles

1. Using an ohmmeter check for continuity between the terminals.
2. Connect battery power and ground and check the operation of the control cable using the data in the chart.
3. Repair or replace defective components as required.

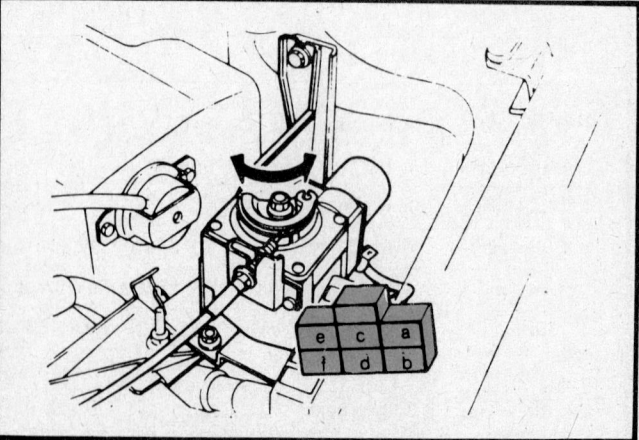

Actuator solenoid control cable test point locations— 1985 and later 626 with turbocharger

Check terminal	Resistance
c – a	Approx. 20 ohms

Actuator solenoid specifications—1985 and later 626 with turbocharger

CLUTCH SWITCH ADJUSTMENT

Adjust the clutch switch so that the pedal height is 8.42 inches.

BRAKE SWITCH ADJUSTMENT

Adjust the brake switch so that the pedal height is 8.42 inches.

CONTROL UNIT (1985 and Later)

If there is a problem with the cruise control system and no abnormal condition is found when the ACC checker tool is used, the control unit could be at fault and should be replaced.

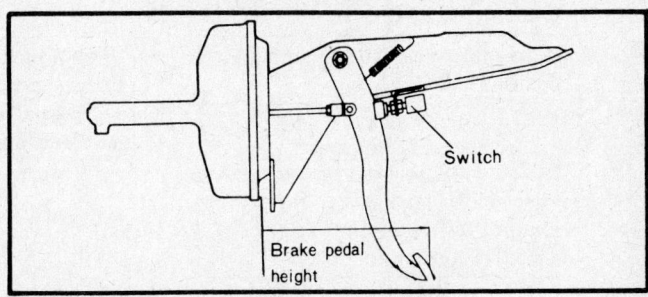

Brake pedal switch adjustment—626

DIAGNOSIS AND TESTING PROCEDURES

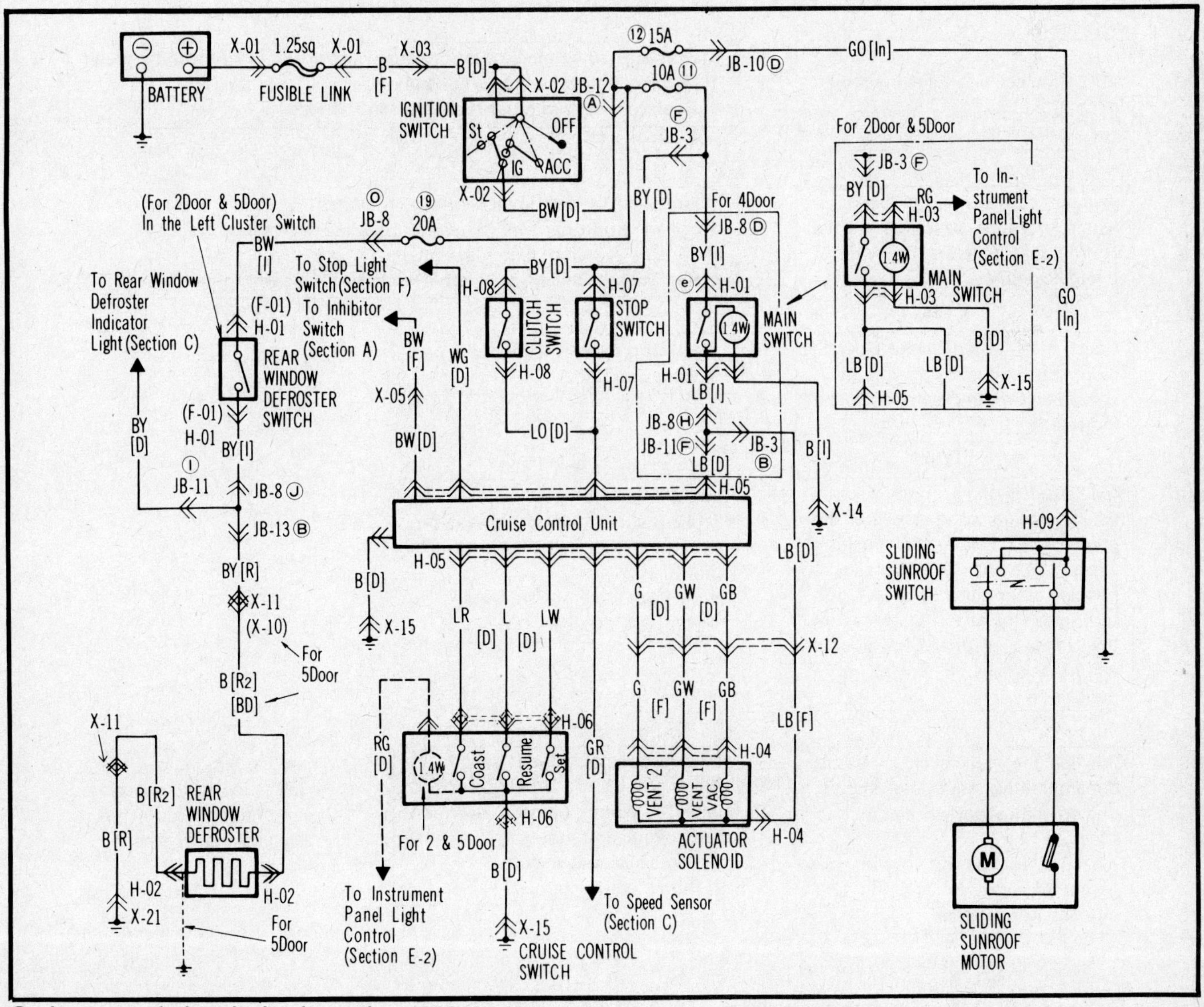

Cruise control electrical schematic—1982–84 626

983

CU ... CRUISE·CONTROL·UNIT
JB ... JOINT·BOX

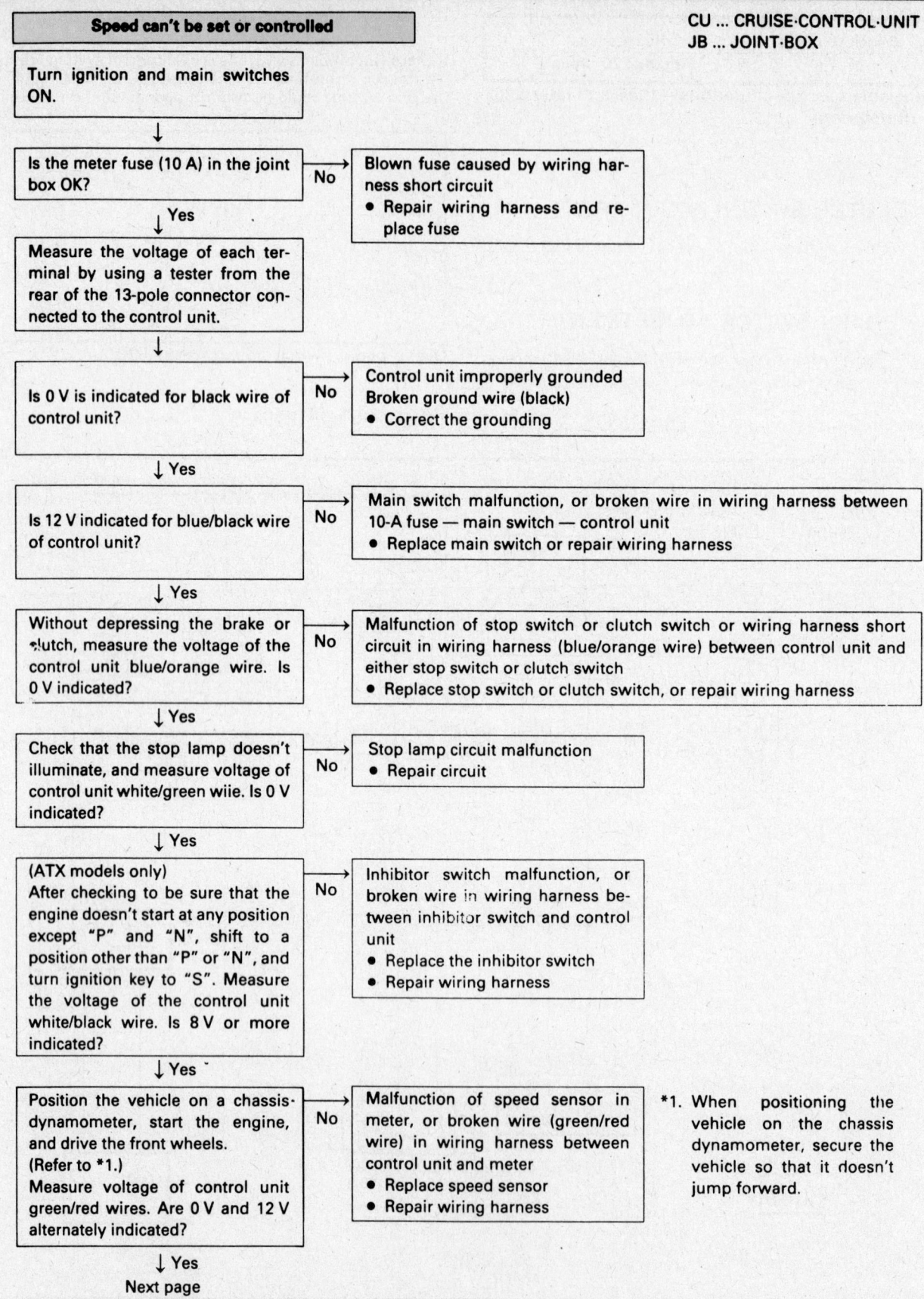

Speed can't be set or controlled

Turn ignition and main switches ON.

↓

Is the meter fuse (10 A) in the joint box OK? → **No** → Blown fuse caused by wiring harness short circuit
● Repair wiring harness and replace fuse

↓ Yes

Measure the voltage of each terminal by using a tester from the rear of the 13-pole connector connected to the control unit.

↓

Is 0 V is indicated for black wire of control unit? → **No** → Control unit improperly grounded
Broken ground wire (black)
● Correct the grounding

↓ Yes

Is 12 V indicated for blue/black wire of control unit? → **No** → Main switch malfunction, or broken wire in wiring harness between 10-A fuse — main switch — control unit
● Replace main switch or repair wiring harness

↓ Yes

Without depressing the brake or clutch, measure the voltage of the control unit blue/orange wire. Is 0 V indicated? → **No** → Malfunction of stop switch or clutch switch or wiring harness short circuit in wiring harness (blue/orange wire) between control unit and either stop switch or clutch switch
● Replace stop switch or clutch switch, or repair wiring harness

↓ Yes

Check that the stop lamp doesn't illuminate, and measure voltage of control unit white/green wire. Is 0 V indicated? → **No** → Stop lamp circuit malfunction
● Repair circuit

↓ Yes

(ATX models only)
After checking to be sure that the engine doesn't start at any position except "P" and "N", shift to a position other than "P" or "N", and turn ignition key to "S". Measure the voltage of the control unit white/black wire. Is 8 V or more indicated? → **No** → Inhibitor switch malfunction, or broken wire in wiring harness between inhibitor switch and control unit
● Replace the inhibitor switch
● Repair wiring harness

↓ Yes

Position the vehicle on a chassis-dynamometer, start the engine, and drive the front wheels. (Refer to *1.) Measure voltage of control unit green/red wires. Are 0 V and 12 V alternately indicated? → **No** → Malfunction of speed sensor in meter, or broken wire (green/red wire) in wiring harness between control unit and meter
● Replace speed sensor
● Repair wiring harness

*1. When positioning the vehicle on the chassis dynamometer, secure the vehicle so that it doesn't jump forward.

↓ Yes

Next page

Cruise control trouble diagnosis chart – 1982–84 626

↓ Yes

Measure voltage of blue/white, blue/red, and blue terminals of control unit while operating the SET, COAST, and RESUME switches. Is 0 V indicated when ON? Is approx. 8 V indicated when OFF?	No →	Malfunction of combination switch (SET, COAST, RESUME); or broken wire (blue/white, blue/red, or blue) in wiring harness between control unit and combination switch Combination switch improperly grounded • Replace combination switch, or repair wiring harness

↓ Yes

Measure actuator solenoid power line and blue/black wire voltage. Is 12 V indicated?	No →	Broken wire (blue/black wire) in wiring harness between main switch and actuator • Repair wiring harness

↓ Yes

Position the vehicle on a chassis dynamometer, start the engine, and set speed to 50 km/h (31 mph). (Refer to *1.) Measure voltage of green/black wire of control unit when SET switch is switched ON. Is 0 V indicated? Measure voltage of green/white wire of control unit when COAST switch is switched ON. Is 12 V indicated? Measure voltage of green wire when clutch or brake is depressed. Is 12 V indicated? • Make the above checks at a speed of 50 km/h (31 mph).	No →	Actuator solenoid malfunction; control unit malfunction; ground short circuit or broken wire in wiring harness between actuator and control unit • Replace actuator, repair wiring harness, or replace control unit • Before deciding on a malfunction of the control unit, carefully check for an actuator malfunction and a broken wire in the wiring harness between the actuator and the control unit.

↓ Yes

Malfunction of actuator vacuum or link
• Repair vacuum or link

Override system doesn't function

Turn ignition and main switch ON

↓

With brake pedal depressed, measure voltage of control unit's blue/orange wire and white/green wire. Is 12 V indicated?	No →	Stop switch or stop light switch malfunction; or broken wire in wiring harness between stop switch and 10-A fuse, or between stop light switch and 15-A fuse. • Replace stop switch or stop light switch; or repair wiring harness

↓ Yes

(MTX models only) With clutch depressed, measure voltage of control unit's blue/orange wire. Is 12 V indicated?	No →	Clutch switch malfunction Broken wire (blue/orange wire) in wiring harness between 10-A fuse ~ clutch switch ~ control unit • Replace clutch switch, or repair wiring harness

↓ Yes

(ATX models only) When select lever is shifted to "P" or "N" with ignition switch at "S", measure the voltage of control unit's black/white wire. Is approx. 1 V indicated?	No →	Faulty inhibitor switch, or broken wire (black/white) in wiring harness between control unit and inhibitor switch • Replace inhibitor switch, or repair wiring harness

↓ Yes **Next page**

Cruise control trouble diagnosis chart — 1982–84 626

Override system doesn't function

| With RESUME switch OFF, measure voltage of control unit's blue wire. Is approx. 8 V indicated? | **No** →| Combination switch malfunction (RESUME switch malfunction); or broken wire in wiring harness between control unit and combination switch (RESUME switch)
• Replace combination or inhibitor switch, or repair wiring harness |

↓ Yes

| Position vehicle on chassis dynamometer, raise the speed to under 50 km/h (31 mph), and then set it. Set the "SET" switch ON, override system by depressing clutch or brake, and measure voltage of control unit's green wire. Is 12 V indicated? | **No** →| Actuator solenoid malfunction, ground shortcircuit of wiring harness (green wire) between actuator and control unit, or control unit malfunction
Replace the actuator, repair wiring harness, or replace control unit |

↓ Yes

Malfunction of actuator vacuum system or link system
• Repair actuator vacuum system or link system

• Before determining that it is a control unit malfunction, first carefully check the actuator solenoid and the wiring harness.

Cruise control trouble diagnosis chart—1982–84 626

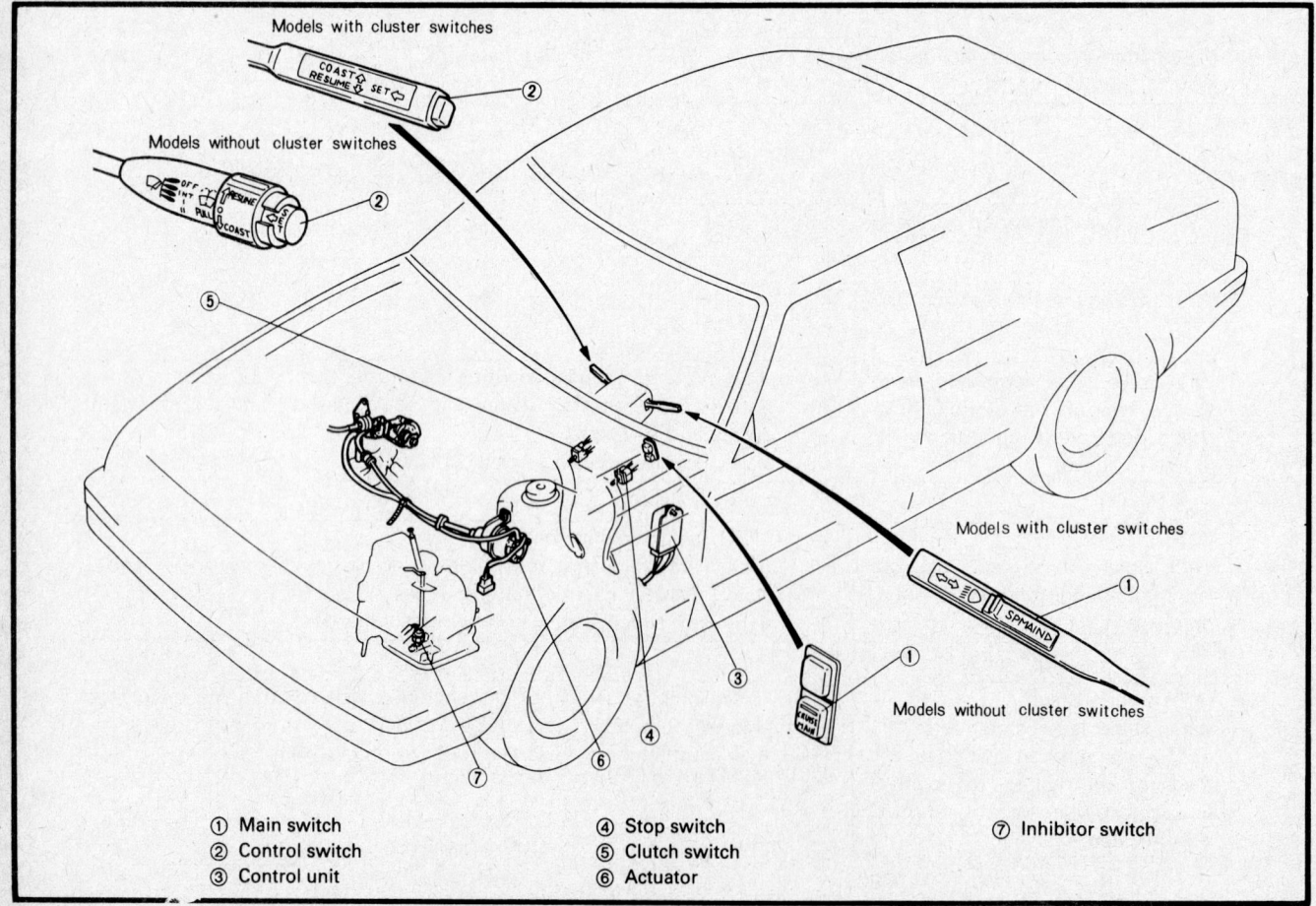

① Main switch   ④ Stop switch   ⑦ Inhibitor switch
② Control switch   ⑤ Clutch switch
③ Control unit   ⑥ Actuator

Cruise control componret layout—1982–84 626

Cruise control component layout – 1985 and later 626

1 Main switch
2 Control switch
3 Control unit
4 Stop switch
5 Clutch switch
6 Actuator
7 Inhibitor switch

(Turbo model)

(Non-turbo model)

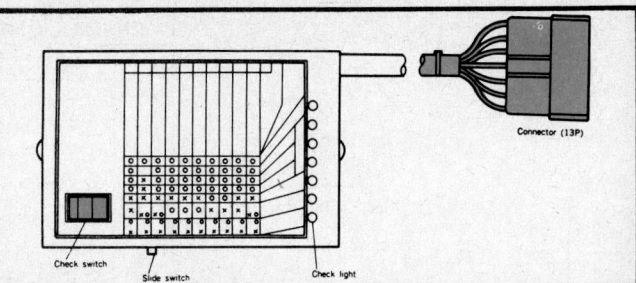

Check switch   Slide switch   Check light

Connector (13P)

A checker tool – 626

CRUISE CONTROL SYSTEM DIAGNOSIS– 1985 AND LATER

NOTE: In order to properly diagnosis problems with the cruise control system used in the 1985 and later Mazda 626 a special cruise control diagnostic tool, the ACC checker (tool number 49–9200–010) or equivalent will be needed. This tool cannot be used on vehicles that are equipped with a turbocharger.

ACC CHECKER TOOL FUNCTIONS

Check Lights

Each component is verified by a check light which is located on the ACC checker tool.

Tool Installation

1. Depress the lock hook of the harness connector.
2. Remove the connector from the control unit after the ignition switch and the main switch are turned off.
3. Connect the harness connector to the ACC checker tool.

Check Switch Operation

The check switch is used to check the actuator operation while the engine is running. When the check switch is held on after the engine is started, the engine speed will increase from 2000 to 3000 rpms. When the check switch is released the engine speed will drop to idle.

Slide Switch Operation

Position the slide switch in the "L" position before using the check switch. Use the check switch to increase engine rpm. The engine rpm will increase about 2000 to 3000 rpms, and hold steady. If the engine does not reach and remain in the 2000 to 3000 rpm range position the slide switch to the "H" position. If there is still no increase in engine rpm, adjust the freeplay in the actuator cable.

Check light	Check items
MAIN SW.	Ignition switch, fuse, main switch and associated wiring harness terminals and connectors.
ACTUATOR—VAC	VAC coil continuity in the actuator and associated harness.
ACTUATOR—VENT 2	VENT 2 coil continuity in the actuator and associated harness.
ACTUATOR—VENT 1	VENT 1 coil continuity in the actuator and associated harness.
CLUTCH/BRAKE SW.	Clutch switch (M/T vehicles only), brake switch and associated harness.
COMBINATION/INH. SW.	"SET", "COAST" and "RESUME" positions in the combination switch, inhibitor switch (A/T vehicles only), and associated harness.
GENERATOR	Speed sensor output and associated harness.

A checker tool data – 626

CHECK ITEMS AND CONDITIONS	CHECK LIGHTS (correct response)							TROUBLESHOOTING (INCORRECT RESPONSE)
	ACTUATOR				CLUTCH/BRAKE SW.	COMBINATION/INH. SW.	GENERATOR	O: Represents: Light ON
	MAIN SW.	VAC	VENT 2	VENT 1				X: Represents: Light OFF
1. MAIN SW. CONTINUITY: • Ignition switch ON • Main switch ON	O	O	O	O	X	A/T O M/T X	O or X	ALL LIGHTS OFF: Check ignition switch, main switch, fuse, and associated harness terminals and connectors
2. INHIBITOR SW. CONTINUITY: • Ignition and main switch ON. • Shift lever to "D" (A/T) • Depress brake pedal	O	O	O	O	X	X	O or X	COMBINATION/INH. SW. LIGHT ON: Check inhibitor switch and associated harness.
3. BRAKE SW. CONTINUITY: • Ignition and main switch ON • Shift lever to "D" (A/T) • Depress brake pedal	O	O	O	O	O	X	O or X	CLUTCH/BRAKE SW. LIGHT OFF: Check brake switch and associated harness.
4. CLUTCH SW. CONTINUITY: • Ignition switch ON • Main switch ON • Depress clutch pedal	O	O	O	O	O	X	O or X	CLUTCH/BRAKE SW. LIGHT OFF: Check clutch switch and associated harness.
5. "SET" POSITION OF COMBINATION SWITCH: • Ignition switch ON • Main switch ON • Shift lever to "D" (A/T) • Push to "SET" position of combination switch	O	O	O	O	X	O	O or X	COMBINATION/INH. SW. LIGHT OFF: Check "SET" position of combination switch and associated harness.
6. "COAST" POSITION OF COMBINATION SWITCH • Ignition switch ON • Main switch ON • Shift lever to "D" (A/T) • Turn to "COAST" position of combination switch	O	O	O	O	X	O	O or X	COMBINATION/INH. SW. LIGHT OFF: Check "COAST" position in combination switch and associated harness.
7. "RESUME" POSITION OF COMBINATION SWITCH • Ignition switch ON • Main switch ON • Shift lever to "D" (A/T) • Turn to "RESUME" position of combination switch	O	O	O	O	X	O	O or X	COMBINATION/INH. SW. LIGHT OFF: Check "RESUME" position of combination switch and associated harness.

A checker tool data—626

CHECK ITEMS AND CONDITIONS	CHECK LIGHTS (correct response)							TROUBLESHOOTING (INCORRECT RESPONSE)
		ACTUATOR						
	MAIN SW	VAC	VENT 2	VENT 1	CLUTCH/BRAKE SW	CONMINATION/INH. SW	GENERATOR	
8. START THE ENGINE • Shift lever to "N" position (A/T)	○	○	○	○	X	A/T ○ M/T X	○ or X	—
9. ACTUATOR OPERATION: (EGI model only) • After engine is started, set the slide switch "L" or "H". Then turn on check switch (keep in "D" position) Note: Engine speed should increase to 2,000–3,000 rpm. If over 4,000 rpm release the switch immediately.	○	X ↓ ○	X	X	X	A/T ○ M/T X	○ or X	If engine revolution does not come up to and remain in the 2,000 to 3,000 rpm range, check the actuator and associated harness.
10 SPEED SENSOR OUTPUT keeping idling condition, drive vehicle slowly.	○	○	○	○	X	X	○ ↕ X	If GENERATOR LIGHT does not flash, trouble may be with speed sensor and associated harness.

A checker tool data—626

RX-7

VISUAL INSPECTION

Before performing any tests make a visual inspection of the cruise control system. Check all items in the system for abnormal conditions such as bare broken or disconnected wires and damage to the vacuum hoses. Be sure that the speedometer cables are attached and properly routed. All vacuum hoses must be properly routed and must not have any kinks or bends. Be sure that all electrical connections are complete and tight. The wiring harness must be routed properly.

CONTROL UNIT TEST (1982–83)

1. Raise and support the vehicle safely.
2. Turn the ignition switch on.

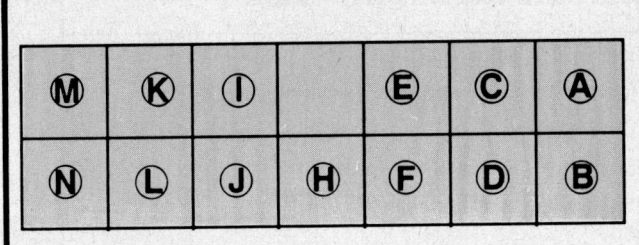

Control unit test point locations—1982–83 RX-7

Position	Terminal Switch	SE	RE	CO	E
SET	ON	●———			———●
RESUME	ON		●———	———●	
COAST	ON			●———	———●

Control switch specifications—1984 and later RX–7

3. With the above test conditions and using a voltmeter, connect the negative lead of the voltmeter to terminal "M" of the control unit. Connect the positive lead to terminal "D" and "N" of the control unit.
4. Observe the troubleshooting chart.
5. Start the engine. Turn the cruise control main switch to the on position.
6. Increase the vehicle speed to about 30 mph and then push the cruise control set switch button.
7. With the above test conditions and using a voltmeter, check the "A", "B" and "C" terminal. Connect the negative lead of the voltmeter to terminal "M" of the control unit. Connect the positive lead to terminal "A", "B" and "C" of the control unit.
8. Observe the troubleshooting chart.

CONTROL SWITCH TEST

1. Check for continunity between the terminals of the switch assembly.
2. Repair or replace defective components as required.

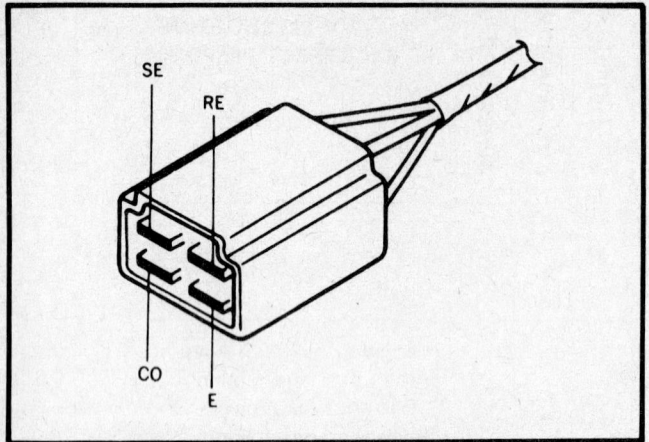

Control switch test point locations—1984 and later RX–7

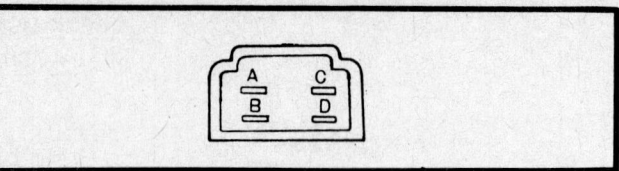

Control switch test point locations—1982–83 RX–7

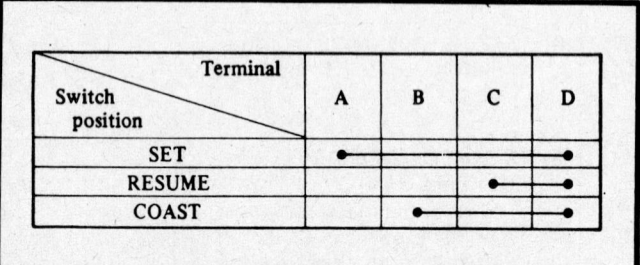

	Terminal	A	B	C	D
Switch position					
SET		●			●
RESUME				●	●
COAST			●	●	●

Control switch specifications—1982–83 RX–7

DIAGNOSIS AND TESTING PROCEDURES

Terminal	The voltage exists to each terminal under the following condition.
F	12 voltage at any time
I	Approx. 12 volt (During pushing "SET" switch button, the voltage drops to 0 and returns to 8 volt when releasing it.)
J	Approx. 12 volt (During turning "COAST" switch to arrow direction, the voltage dorps to 0 and returns to 8 volt when releasing it.)
K	Approx. 12 volt (During turning "RESUME" switch to arrow direction, the voltage drops to 0 and returns to 8 volt when releasing it.)
E	12 volt during depressing the brake pedal or clutch pedal
N	12 volt during depressing the brake pedal
D	Automatic transmission only 12 volt (During shifting the shift lever to "P" or "N" position, the voltage drops to 0.)
B	When push "SET" switch button, the voltage drops to 0 and returns to 12 volt again.
A	When turn "COAST" switch to arrow direction, the voltage drops to 0 and returns to 12 volt again.
C	When depress clutch pedal, the voltage drops to 0 and returns to 12 volt again.
H	Perform the followings. 1) Stop the engine. 2) Remove the speedometer cable from the transmission and turn the ignition switch ON. 3) Rotate the inner cable by hand. 4) The needle of voltmeter moves between 9 to 0 volt.

Cruise control trouble diagnosis chart—1982–83 RX–7

Ploblem	Possible Cause	Remedy
Cruise control system does not work	METER, BACK fuse blown Faulty main switch Faulty control unit Faulty actuator Faulty control switch Faulty speed sensor Clutch switch malfunction (M/T vehicle only) Stop switch malfunction Inhibitor switch malfunction (A/T vehicle only) Faulty wiring or ground	Replace fuse and check for short Check main switch Check control unit Check actuator Check control switch Check speed sensor Adjust or replace clutch switch Adjust or replace stop switch Adjust or replace inhibitor switch Repair as necessary
Speed setting can not be cancelled	Faulty control unit Clutch switch malfunction (M/T vehicle only) Stop switch malfunction Inhibitor switch malfunction (A/T vehicle only)	Check control unit Adjust or replace clutch switch Adjust or replace stop switch Adjust or replace inhibitor switch
The set speed is not held	Faulty actuator Acutator control cable malfunction Faulty control unit Faulty speed sensor	Check actuator Adjust or replace control cable Check control unit Check speed sensor
Cruise control system does not function immediately	Faulty actuator Acutator control cable malfunction Faulty control switch Faulty control unit	Check actuator Adjust or replace control cable Check control switch Check control unit

Cruise control trouble diagnosis chart—1984 and later RX–7

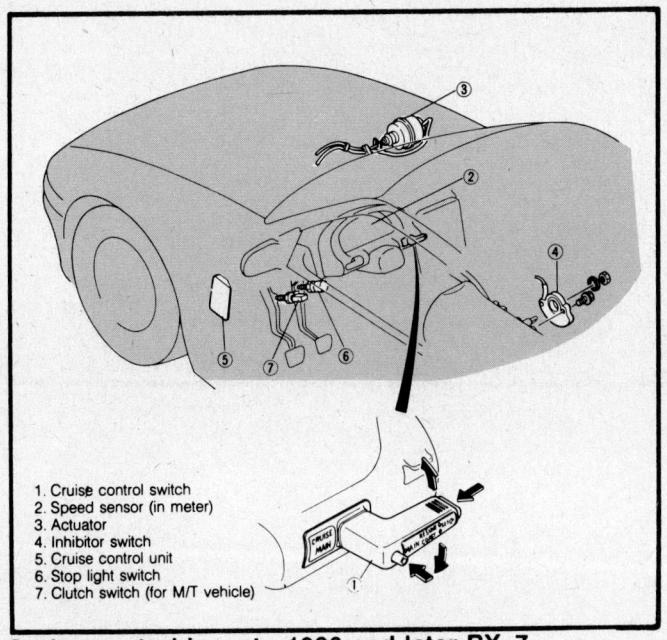

1. Cruise control switch
2. Speed sensor (in meter)
3. Actuator
4. Inhibitor switch
5. Cruise control unit
6. Stop light switch
7. Clutch switch (for M/T vehicle)

Cruise control layout—1986 and later RX–7

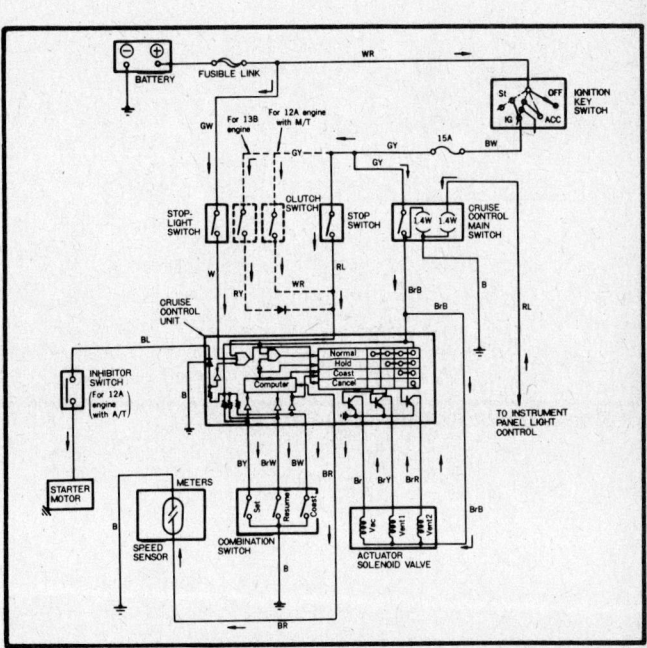

Cruise control electrical acchematic—1984–85 RX–7

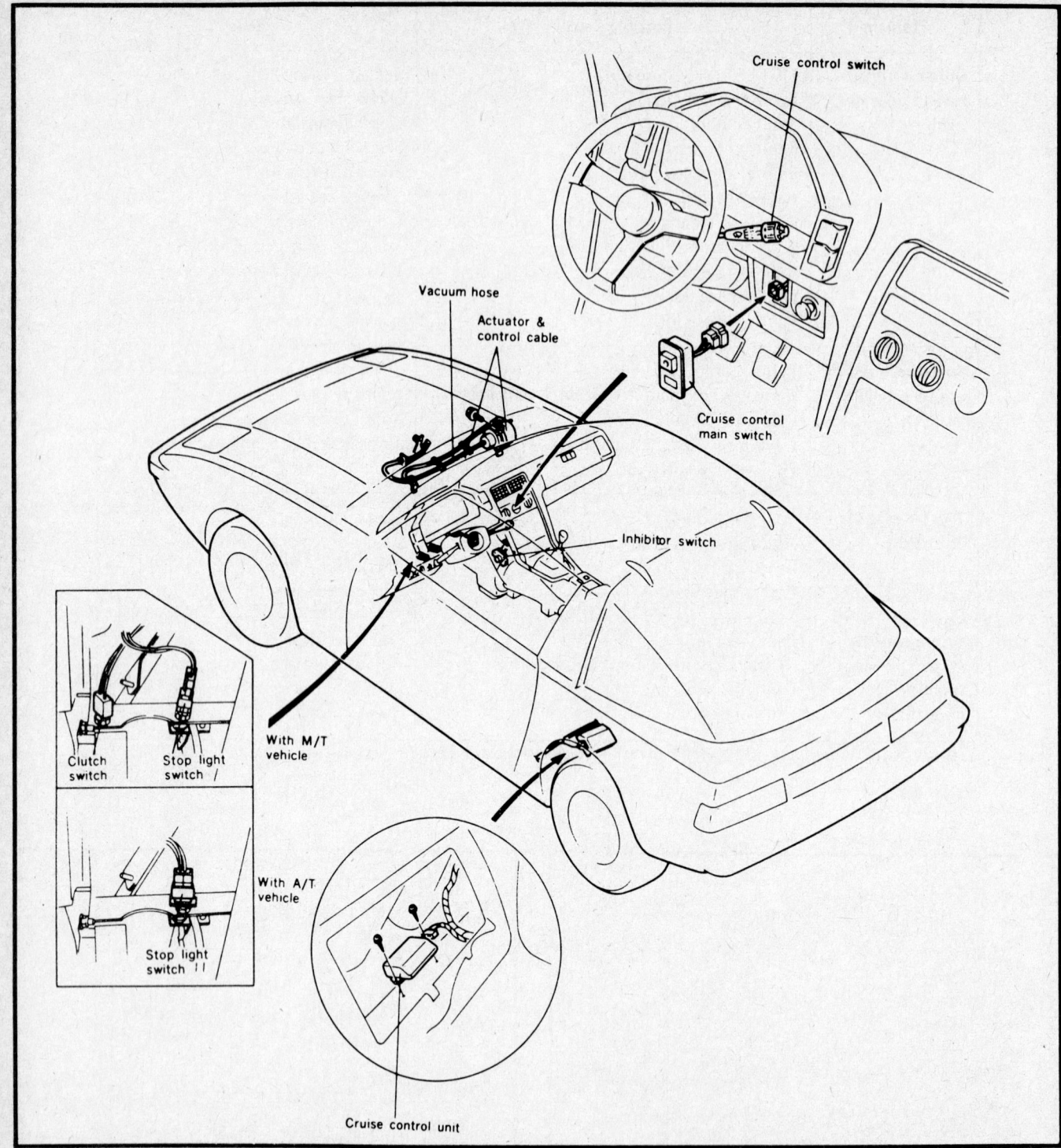

Cruise control layout—1984–85 RX–7

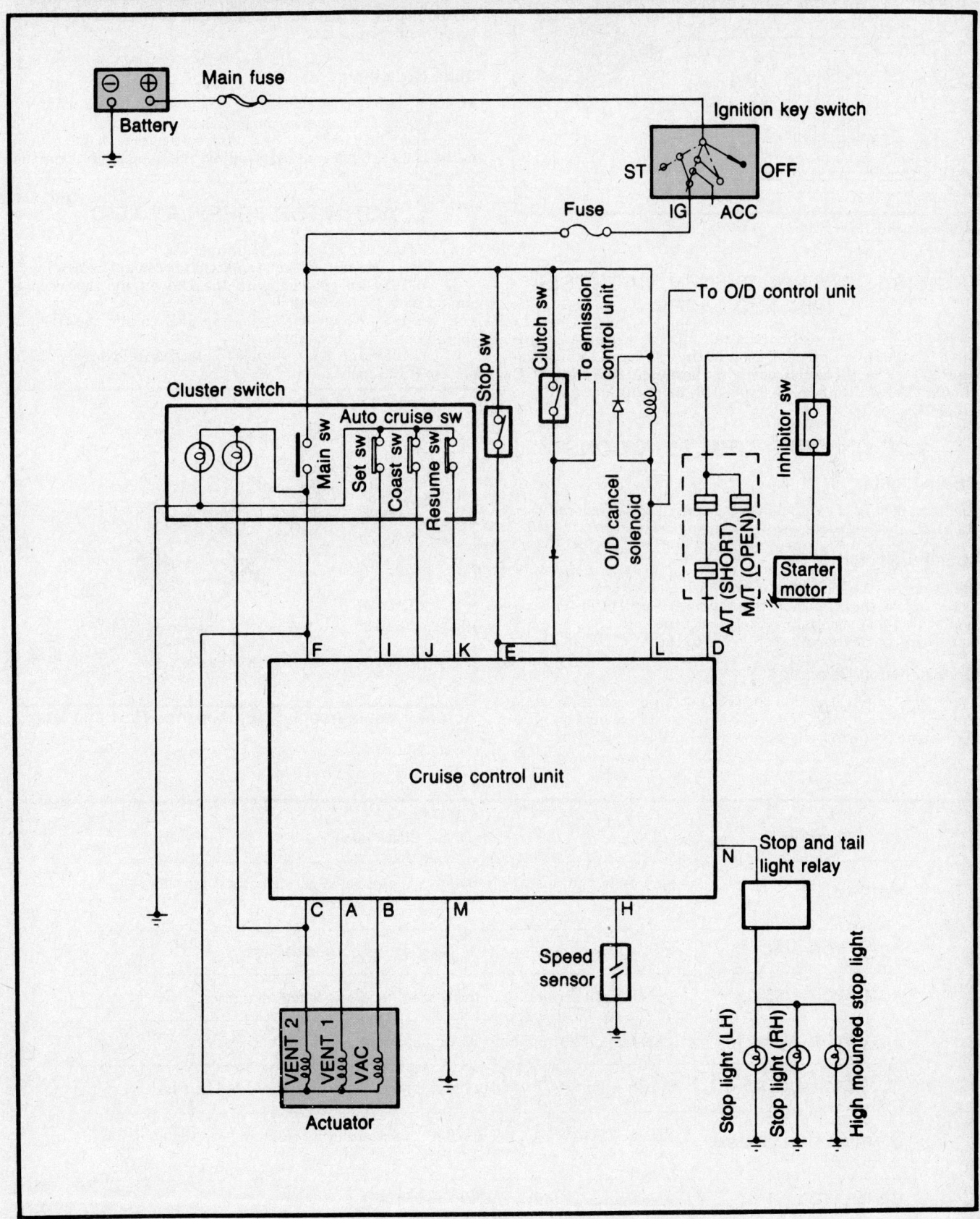

Cruise control electrical schematic—1986 and later RX–7

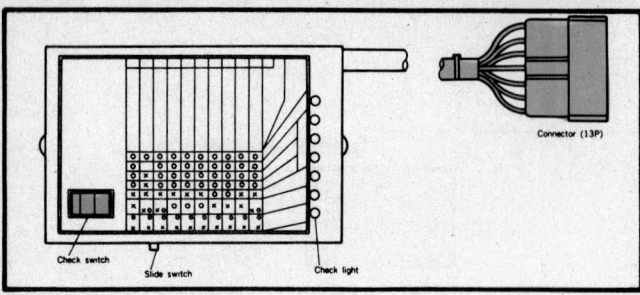

A checker tool—RX-7

CRUISE CONTROL SYSTEM DIAGNOSIS-1984 AND LATER

NOTE: In order to properly diagnosis problems with the cruise control system used in the 1984 and later Mazda RX-7 a special cruise control diagnostic tool, the ACC checker (tool number 49-9200-010) or equivalent will be needed.

ACC CHECKER TOOL FUNCTIONS

Check Lights

Each component is verified by a check light which is located on the ACC checker tool.

Tool Installation

1. Depress the lock hook of the harness connector.
2. Remove the connector from the control unit after the ignition switch and the main switch are turned off.
3. Connect the harness connector to the ACC checker tool.

Check Switch Operation

The check switch is used to check the actuator operation while the engine is running. When the check switch is held on after the engine is started, the engine speed will increase from 2000 to 3000 rpms. When the check switch is released the engine speed will drop to idle.

Slide Switch Operation

Position the slide switch in the "H" position before using the check switch. The engine rpm will increase about 2000 to 3000 rpms, and hold steady. If the engine does not reach and remain in the 2000 to 3000 rpm range adjust the freeplay in the actuator cable.

ACTUATOR FREEPLAY TEST

1. Remove the actuator retaining clip.
2. Adjust the nut so that the actuator control cable play.
3. On 1984–85 vehicles with the 12A engine the freeplay should be 0.28 to 0.51 inch.
4. On 1984–85 vehicles with the 13B engine the freeplay should be 0.24 to 0.43 inch.
5. On 1986 and later vehicles with the freeplay should be 0.39 to 0.118 inch.

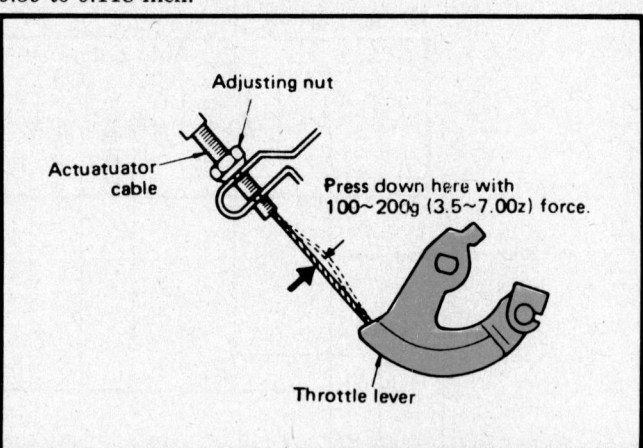

Actuator cable freeplay adjustment—1984 and later RX-7

Check light	Check items
MAIN SW.	Ignition switch, fuse, main switch and associated wiring harness terminals and connectors.
ACTUATOR—VAC	VAC coil continuity in the actuator and associated harness.
ACTUATOR—VENT 2	VENT 2 coil continuity in the actuator and associated harness.
ACTUATOR—VENT 1	VENT 1 coil continuity in the actuator and associated harness.
CLUTCH/BRAKE SW.	Clutch switch (M/T vehicles only), brake switch and associated harness.
COMBINATION/INH. SW.	"SET", "COAST" and "RESUME" positions in the combination switch, inhibitor switch (A/T vehicles only), and associated harness.
GENERATOR	Speed sensor output and associated harness.

A checker tool data—RX-7

CHECK ITEMS AND CONDITIONS	CHECK LIGHTS (correct response)							TROUBLESHOOTING (INCORRECT RESPONSE) O : Represents : Light ON X : Represents : Light OFF
	MAIN SW.	ACTUATOR			CLUTCH/BRAKE SW.	COMBINATION/INH. SW.	GENERATOR	
		VAC	VENT 2	VENT 1				
1. MAIN SW. CONTINUITY: • Ignition switch ON • Main switch ON	O	O	O	O	X	A/T O M/T X	O or X	ALL LIGHTS OFF: Check ignition switch, main switch, fuse, and associated harness terminals and connectors
2. INHIBITOR SW. CONTINUITY: • Ignition and main switch ON. • Shift lever to "D" (A/T) • Depress brake pedal	O	O	O	O	X	X	O or X	COMBINATION/INH. SW. LIGHT ON: Check inhibitor switch and associated harness.
3. BRAKE SW. CONTINUITY: • Ignition and main switch ON • Shift lever to "D" (A/T) • Depress brake pedal	O	O	O	O	O	X	O or X	CLUTCH/BRAKE SW. LIGHT OFF: Check brake switch and associated harness.
4. CLUTCH SW. CONTINUITY • Ignition swith ON • Main switch ON • Depress clutch pedal	O	O	O	O	O	X	O or X	CLUTCH/BRAKE SW. LIGHT OFF: Check clutch switch and associated harness.
5. "SET" POSITION OF COMBINATION SWITCH: • Ignition switch ON • Main switch ON • Shift lever to "D" (A/T) • Push to "SET" position of combination switch	O	O	O	O	X	O	O or X	COMBINATION/INH. SW. LIGHT OFF: Check "SET" position of combination switch and assocaited harness.
6. "COAST" POSITION OF COMBINATION SWITCH • Ignition switch ON • Main switch ON • Shift lever to "D" (A/T) • Turn to "COAST" position of combination switch	O	O	O	O	X	O	O or X	COMBINATION/INH. SW. LIGHT OFF: Check "COAST" position in combination switch and associated harness.
7. "RESUME" POSITION OF COMBINATION SWITCH • Ignition switch ON • Main switch ON • Shift clever to "D" (A/T) • Turn to "RESUME" position of combination switch	O	O	O	O	X	O	O or X	COMBINATION/INH. SW. LIGHT OFF: Check "RESUME" position of combination switch and associated harness.

A checker tool data — RX-7

CHECK ITEMS AND CONDITIONS	CHECK LIGHTS (correct response)							TROUBLESHOOTING (INCORRECT RESPONSE)
	MAIN SW.	ACTUATOR			CLUTCH/BRAKE SW.	COMBINATION/INH. SW.	GENERATOR	
		VAC	VENT 2	VENT 1				
8. START THE ENGINE • Shift lever to "N" position (A/T)	O	O	O	O	X	A/T O M/T X	O or X	————
9. ACTUATOR OPERATION: • After engine is started, set the slide switch "H". Then turn to "ON" check switch and keep "ON" position **Note: Make sure to increase engine speed. If over 4,000 rpm "release the switch" immediately.**	O	X ↓ O	X	X	X	A/T O M/T X	O or X	If engine revolution does not come up, and remain in the 2,000 to 3,000 rpm range, trouble may be with actuator and associated harness.
10. SPEED SENSOR OUTPUT keeping idling condition, drive vehicle slowly.	O	O	O	O	X	X	O X	If GENERATOR LIGHT does not flash, trouble may be with speed sensor and associated harness.

A checker tool data — RX-7

ACTUATOR SOLENOID TEST

1. Using an ohmmeter check for continunity between the terminals.
2. Repair or replace defective components as required.

CONTROL UNIT

If there is a problem with the cruise control system and no abnormal condition is found when the ACC checker tool is used, the control unit could be at fault and should be replaced.

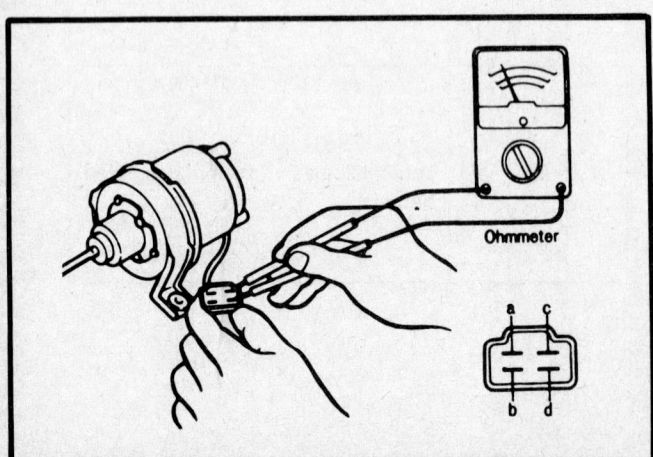

Actuator solenoid test point locations — 1984 and later RX-7

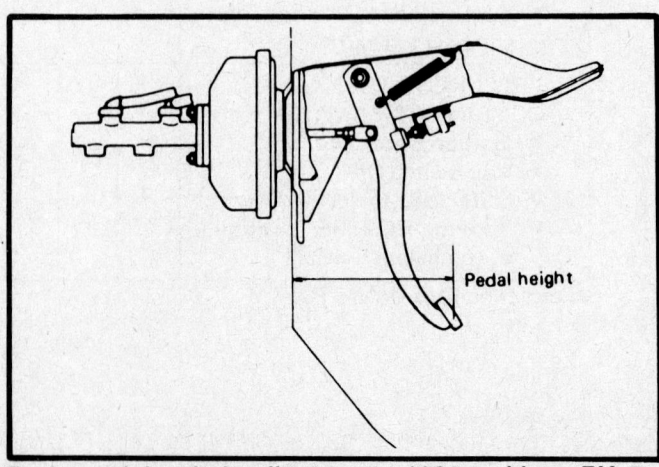

Brake pedal switch adjustment — 1984 and later RX-7

CLUTCH SWITCH ADJUSTMENT

Adjust the clutch switch so that the pedal height is between 7.48 and 7.68 inches for 1984–85 vehicles and between 8.61 and 8.85 inches for 1986 and later vehicles.

BRAKE SWITCH ADJUSTMENT

Adjust the brake switch so that the pedal height is between 7.48 and 7.68 inches for 1984–85 vehicles and between 8.07 and 8.27 inches for 1986 and later vehicles.

Check terminals	Resistance
a – b	
a – c	Approx. 25 to 35 ohms
a – d	

Actuator solenoid specifications — 1984 and later RX–7

MITSUBISHI

Cordia/Tredia

VISUAL INSPECTION

Before performing any tests make a visual inspection of the cruise control system. Check all items in the system for abnormal conditions such as bare broken or disconnected wires and damage to the vacuum hoses. Be sure that the speedometer cables are attached and properly routed. All vacuum hoses must be properly routed and must not have any kinks or bends. Be sure that all electrical connections are complete and tight. The wiring harness must be routed properly.

ACTUATOR TEST

Non Turbocharged Vehicles

1. Using a test light, check the continunity between terminal one and the other terminals.
2. If continunity does not exist repair or replace defective components as required.

Turbocharged Vehicles

1. The resistor between terminal one and terminal two should indicate 30 ohms.
2. Disconnect the accelerator cable from the actuator.
3. When battery voltage is applied to terminal three and terminal four the lever should move.

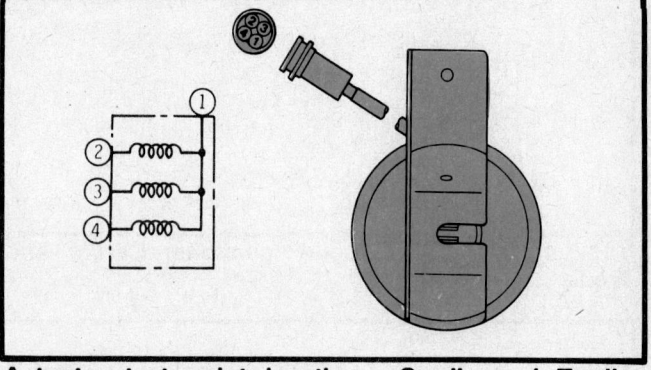

Actuator test point locations—Cordia and Tredia without turbocharged engine

4. When the power supply is connected reversely, the lever should move in the opposite direction.
5. Repair or replace defective components as required.

VACUUM PUMP TEST

1. Using a test light check the continunity between the terminals. If continunity is present the motor is good.
2. Connect terminal one directly to the battery. Ground terminal two. Check the vacuum at inlet "A".
3. Repair or replace the vacuum pump as required.

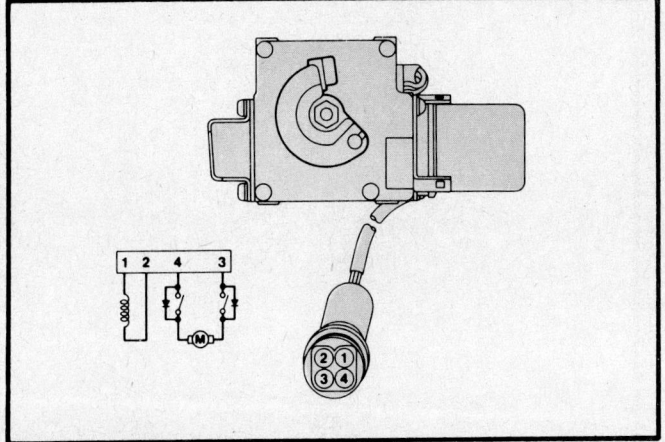

Actuator test point locations—Cordia and Tredia with turbocharged engine

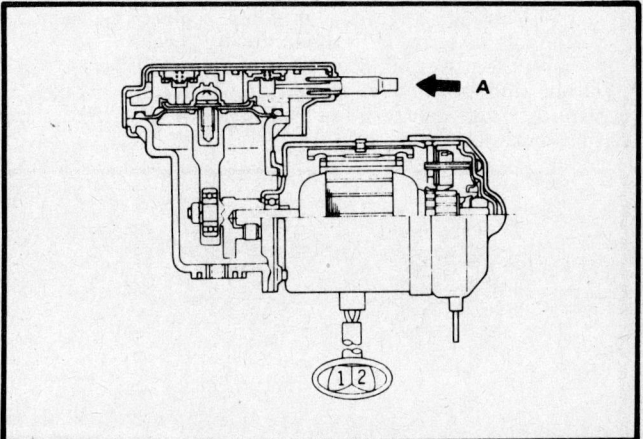

Vacuum pump assembly and test point locations—Cordia and Tredia

VACUUM SWITCH TEST

1. Using a test light check the continunity between the terminals.

2. Apply about 6.2 to 7.8 in. Hg. of vacuum to port "A" of the assembly.

3. Check to be sure that there is no continunity between the terminals.

4. Apply about 8.9 in. Hg. of vacuum to port "A" of the assembly, than reduce the vacuum amount gradually. Check that there is no continunity between the terminals when the vacuum reaches 5.6 to 6.4 in. Hg.

5. Repair or replace defective components as required.

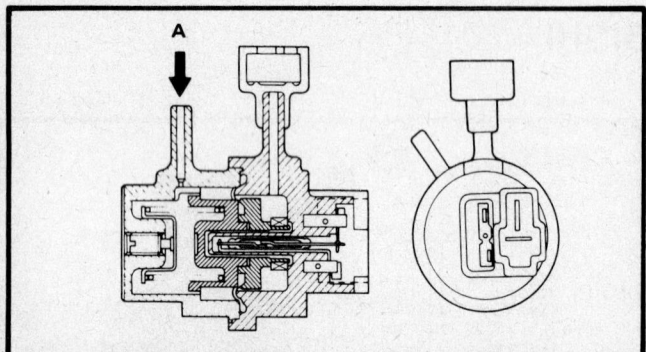

Vacuum switch test point locations—Cordia and Tredia

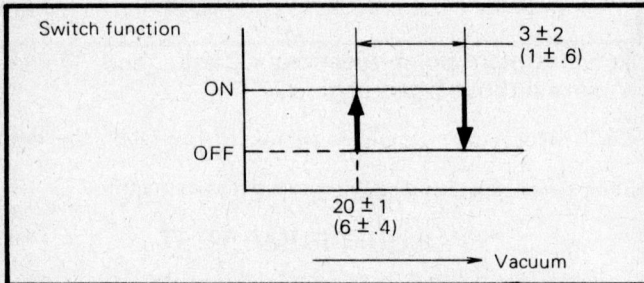

Vacuum switch test results—Cordia and Tredia

VACUUM PUMP RELAY TEST

1. Check and repair the switches, sensors and wire harness that is connected to the control unit.

2. If this fails to correct the problem, replace the speed sensor assembly after making the following checks.

3. With the power off, check the continunity between terminals one and two. There should be continunity. Check the continunity between terminals three and four. There should not be continunity.

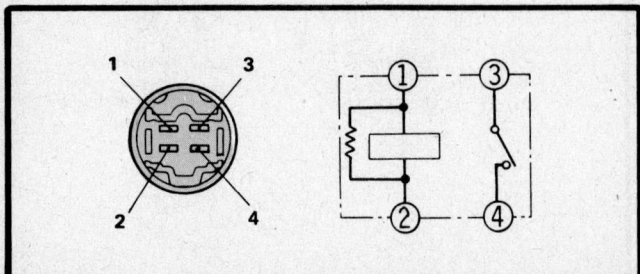

Vacuum pump relay test point locations—Cordia and Tredia

4. With the power on, check the continunity between terminals three and four. There should be continunity.

STOP LIGHT SWITCH TEST

1. Using a test light check for continunity between the terminals.

2. Repair or replace defective components as required.

CRUISE CONTROL SWITCH TEST

1. Using a test light check for continunity between the terminals.

2. Repair or replace defective components as required.

CRUISE CONTROL UNIT TEST

1. Check and repair the switches, sensors and wire harness that is connected to the control unit.

2. If this fails to correct the problem, replace the control unit assembly.

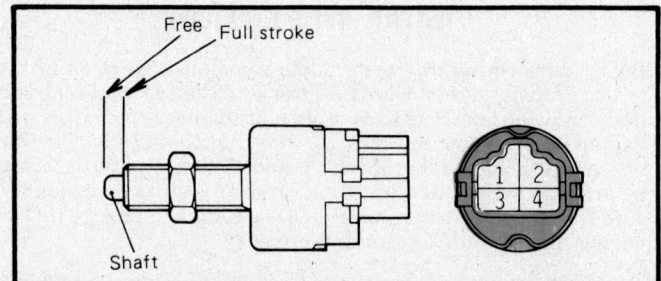

Stoplight switch test point locations—Cordia and Tredia

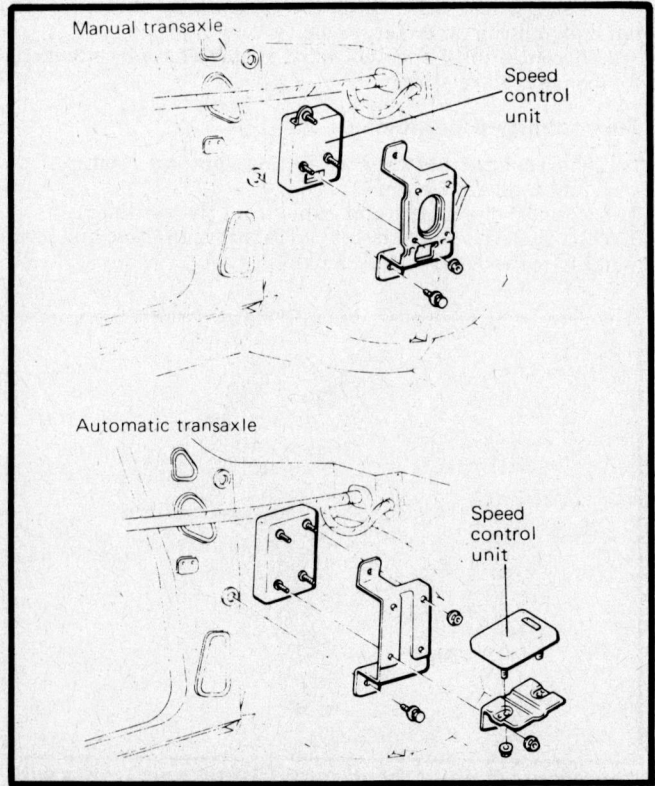

Cruise control unit locations—Cordia and Tredia

Switch / Position	Terminal	1	2	3	4	5
Push switch	OFF					
	SET	o—	—o			
Rotary switch	OFF					
	ON				o—	—o
	RESUME	o—o			o—	—o

Cruise control switch specifications—Cordia and tredia

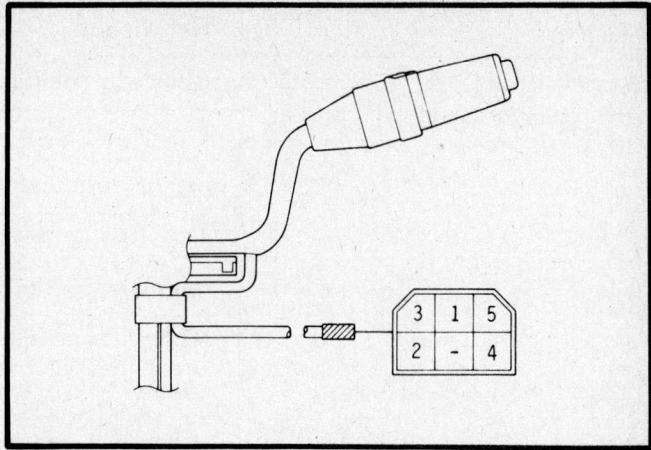

Cruise control switch test point locations—Cordia and tredia

DIAGNOSIS AND TESTING PROCEDURES

Symptom	Probable cause	Remedy
Speed control cannot be set	Clogged actuator filter	Replace actuator
	Dust or dirty water in actuator	Replace actuator
	Improper adjustment of the accelerator cable	Adjust cable free play
	Damaged or twisted vacuum hose	Correct and replace as required
	Improper adjustment of the position of the stop lamp switch	Readjust switch position
	Improper adjustment of the position of the clutch pedal switch	Readjust switch position
	Malfunction of the speed control unit	Replace control unit
	Malfunction of the speed sensor	Replace speedometer
	Broken or shorted wire in the harness	Correct and replace as required
	Burnt-out fuse	Replace fuse and isolate cause
Set vehicle speed cannot be cancelled	Clogged actuator filter	Replace actuator
	Actuator valve seal defective	Replace actuator
	Actuator diaphragm defective	Replace actuator
	Malfunction of the speed sensor	Replace speedometer
	Broken or shorted wire in the harness	Correct and replace as required
	Malfunction of the speed control unit	Replace control unit

Cruise control trouble diagnosis chart—Cordia and tredia

Symptom	Probable cause	Remedy
Large set error for set vehicle speed Hunting occurs during cruising at a set vehicle speed	Clogged actuator filter	Replace actuator
	Dust or dirty water in actuator	Replace actuator
	Improper adjustment of the accelerator cable	Adjust cable free play
	Air enters into vacuum lines	Correct and replace as required
	Malfunction of the speed sensor	Replace speedometer
	Malfunction of the speed control unit	Replace control unit
Vacuum pump does not operate	Malfunction of the vacuum pump	Replace vacuum pump
	Malfunction of the vacuum pump relay	Replace vacuum pump relay
	Malfunction of the vacuum check valve	Replace vacuum check valve
	Broken or shorted wire in the harness	Correct and replace as required
	Malfunction of the vacuum pump switch	Replace vacuum pump switch

Component Replacement

ACTUATOR

Removal and Installation

NOTE: If the vehicle is equipped with a turbocharger the actuator assembly is located on the dash panel.

1. Disconnect the negative battery cable.
2. Disconnect all connectors, lines and cables from the actuator assembly.
3. Remove the retaining bolts holding the actuator assembly to its mounting.
4. Remove the actuator from the vehicle.
5. Installation is the reverse of the removal procedure.

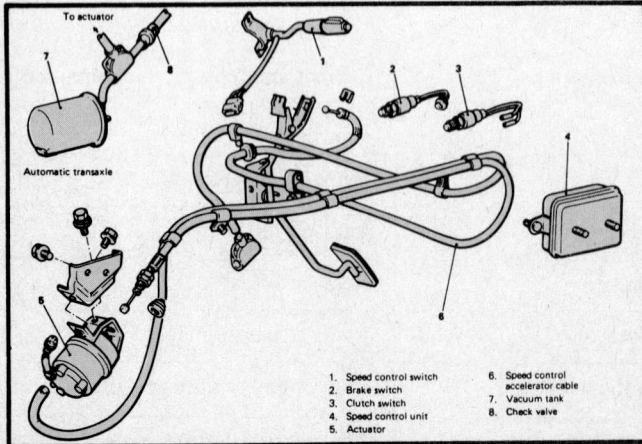

1. Speed control switch
2. Brake switch
3. Clutch switch
4. Speed control unit
5. Actuator
6. Speed control accelerator cable
7. Vacuum tank
8. Check valve

Cruise control system and related components – 1983 Cordia and Tredia

VACUUM PUMP

Removal and Installation

1. Disconnect the negative battery cable. Disconnect all electrical connectors and hoses from the assembly.
2. Remove the vacuum switch. Remove the vacuum pump relay.
3. Remove the bracket installation nuts from the front side left hand member.
4. Remove the vacuum pump assembly from the vehicle.
5. Installation is the reverse of the removal procedure.

VACUUM SWITCH

Removal and Installation

1. Disconnect the negative battery cable.
2. Disconnect the vacuum hose from the vacuum switch.
3. Remove the vacuum switch from the bracket.
4. Installation is the reverse of the removal procedure.

VACUUM PUMP RELAY

Removal and Installation

1. Disconnect the negative battery cable. Disconnect all electrical connectors and hoses from the assembly.
2. Remove the bracket installation nuts from the front side left hand member.
4. Remove the vacuum pump relay from the vehicle.
5. Installation is the reverse of the removal procedure.

CRUISE CONTROL SWITCH

Removal and Installation

1. Disconnect the negative battery cable.
2. Remove the steering wheel and steering column lever.
3. Disconnect the switch electrical connectors. Disconnect the switch retaining bolts.

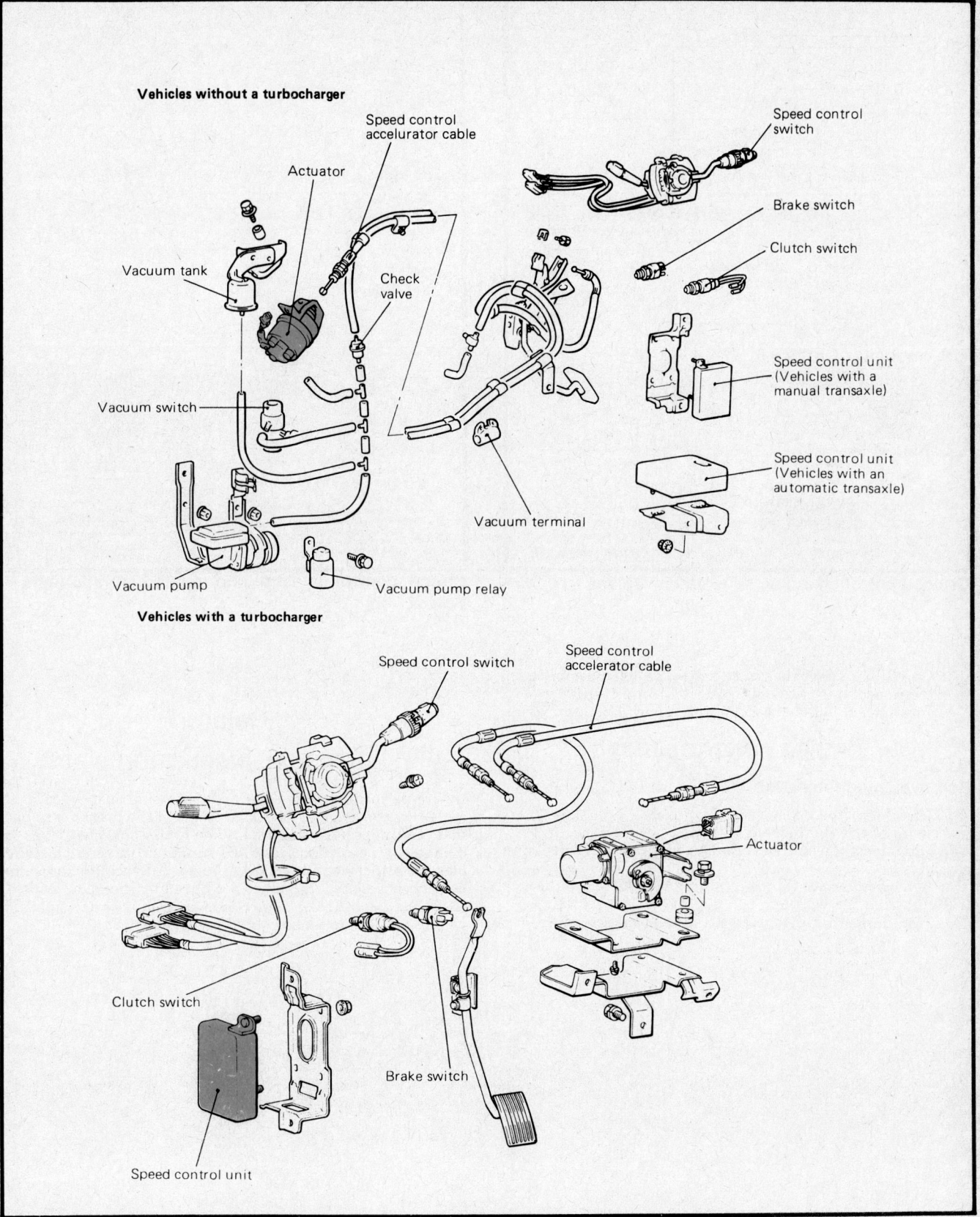

Vehicles without a turbocharger

Speed control accelurator cable

Actuator

Speed control switch

Vacuum tank

Brake switch

Clutch switch

Check valve

Vacuum switch

Speed control unit (Vehicles with a manual transaxle)

Speed control unit (Vehicles with an automatic transaxle)

Vacuum terminal

Vacuum pump

Vacuum pump relay

Vehicles with a turbocharger

Speed control switch

Speed control accelerator cable

Actuator

Clutch switch

Brake switch

Speed control unit

Cruise control system and related components—1984 and later Cordia and Tredia

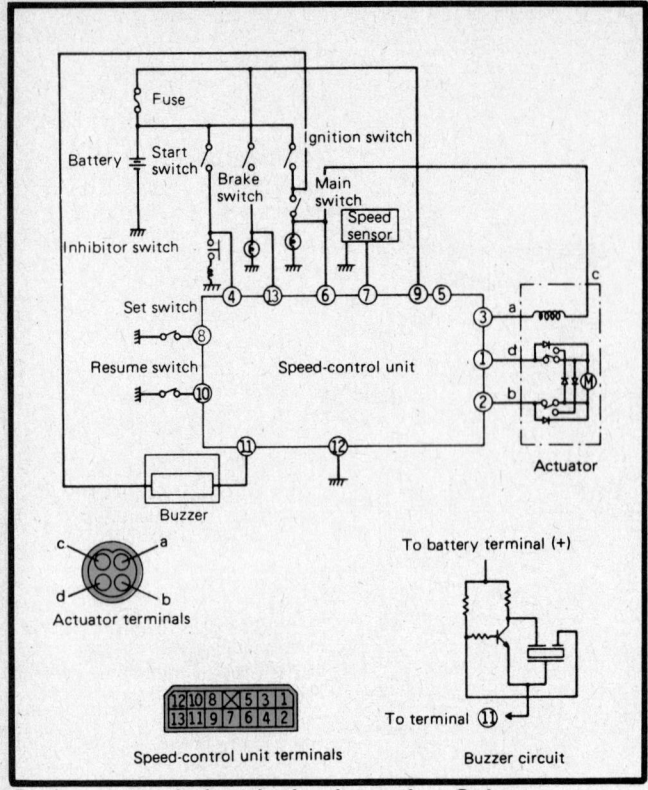

Cruise control electrical schematic—Galant

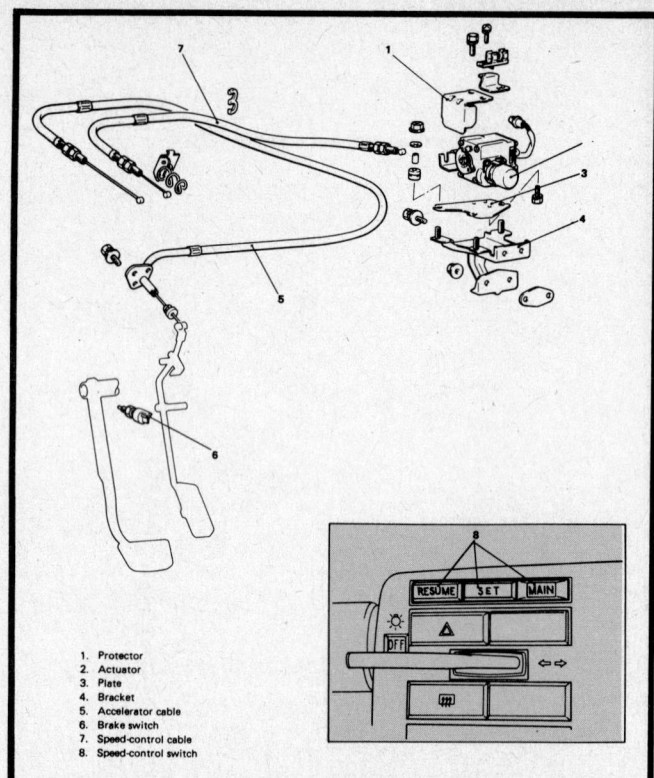

Cruise control system and related components—
Galant

1. Protector
2. Actuator
3. Plate
4. Bracket
5. Accelerator cable
6. Brake switch
7. Speed-control cable
8. Speed-control switch

4. Carefully remove the cruise control switch assembly from the steering column assembly.
5. Installation is the reverse of the removal procedure.

CRUISE CONTROL UNIT

Removal and Installation

1. Disconnect the negative battery cable.
2. Remove the right side cowl trim.
3. Disconnect the electrical connectors from the control unit assembly.
4. Remove the control unit retaining bolts. Remove the control unit from the vehicle.
5. Installation is the reverse of the removal procedure.

Galant

VISUAL INSPECTION

Before performing any tests make a visual inspection of the cruise control system. Check all items in the system for abnormal conditions such as bare broken or disconnected wires and damage to the vacuum hoses. Be sure that the speedometer cables are attached and properly routed. All vacuum hoses must be properly routed and must not have any kinks or bends. Be sure that all electrical connections are complete and tight. The wiring harness must be routed properly.

DIAGNOSIS AND TESTING PROCEDURES

SPEED-CONTROL SYSTEM

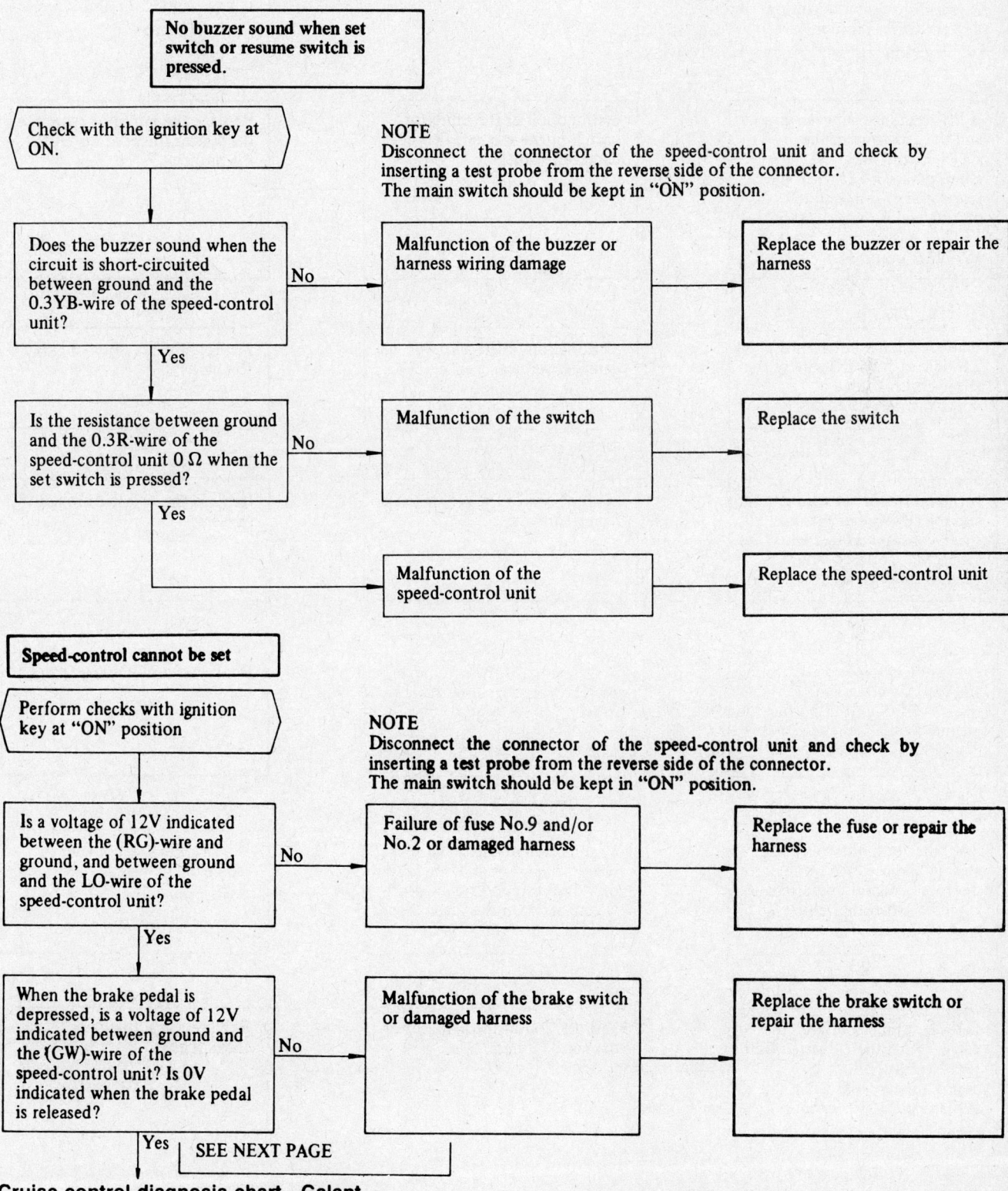

No buzzer sound when set switch or resume switch is pressed.

Check with the ignition key at ON.

NOTE
Disconnect the connector of the speed-control unit and check by inserting a test probe from the reverse side of the connector.
The main switch should be kept in "ON" position.

Does the buzzer sound when the circuit is short-circuited between ground and the 0.3YB-wire of the speed-control unit? — No → Malfunction of the buzzer or harness wiring damage → Replace the buzzer or repair the harness

Yes ↓

Is the resistance between ground and the 0.3R-wire of the speed-control unit 0 Ω when the set switch is pressed? — No → Malfunction of the switch → Replace the switch

Yes ↓

Malfunction of the speed-control unit → Replace the speed-control unit

---

Speed-control cannot be set

Perform checks with ignition key at "ON" position

NOTE
Disconnect the connector of the speed-control unit and check by inserting a test probe from the reverse side of the connector.
The main switch should be kept in "ON" position.

Is a voltage of 12V indicated between the (RG)-wire and ground, and between ground and the LO-wire of the speed-control unit? — No → Failure of fuse No.9 and/or No.2 or damaged harness → Replace the fuse or repair the harness

Yes ↓

When the brake pedal is depressed, is a voltage of 12V indicated between ground and the (GW)-wire of the speed-control unit? Is 0V indicated when the brake pedal is released? — No → Malfunction of the brake switch or damaged harness → Replace the brake switch or repair the harness

Yes → SEE NEXT PAGE

Cruise control diagnosis chart — Galant

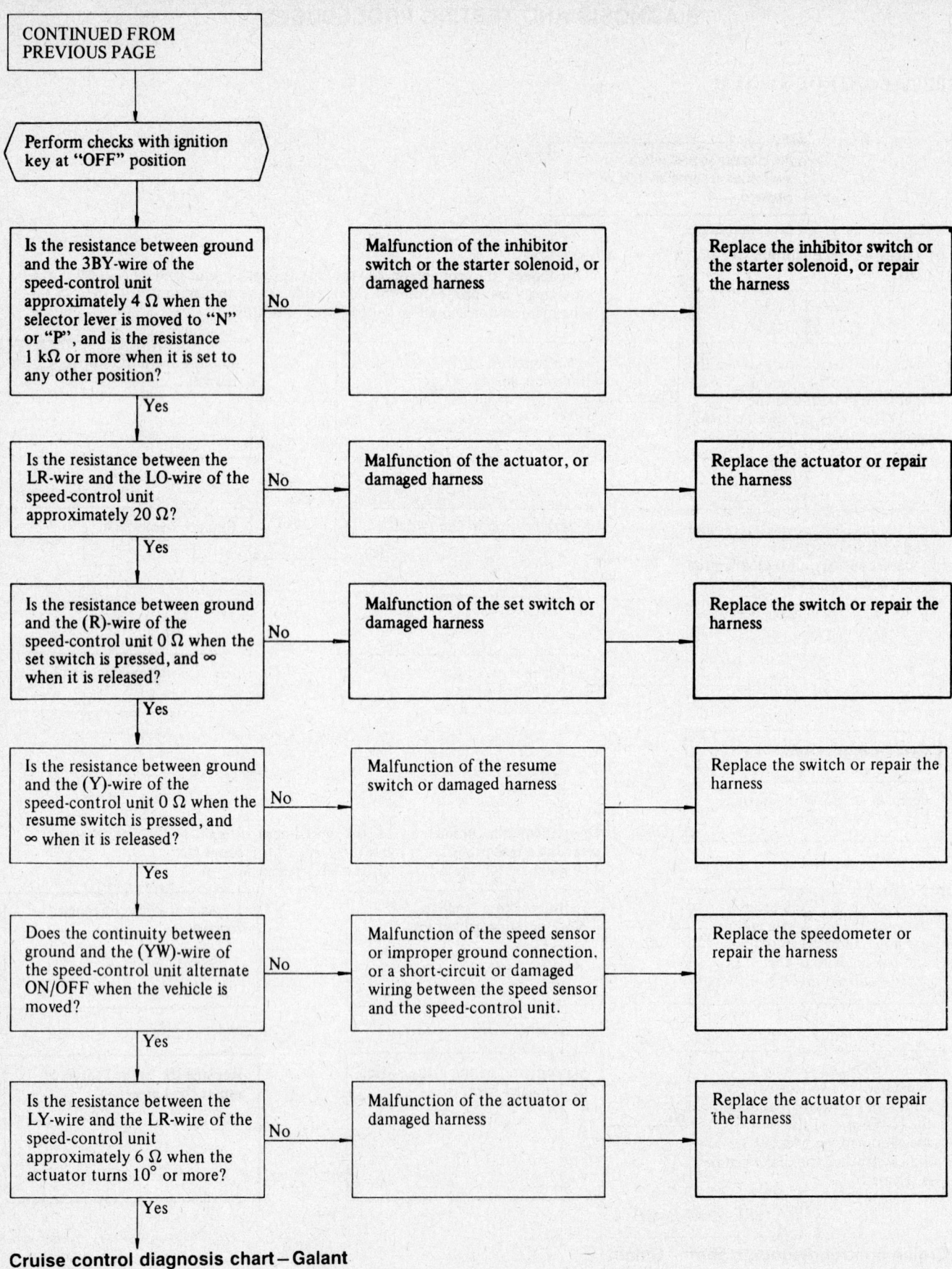

CONTINUED FROM PREVIOUS PAGE

Perform checks with ignition key at "OFF" position

Is the resistance between ground and the 3BY-wire of the speed-control unit approximately 4 Ω when the selector lever is moved to "N" or "P", and is the resistance 1 kΩ or more when it is set to any other position?

— No → Malfunction of the inhibitor switch or the starter solenoid, or damaged harness → Replace the inhibitor switch or the starter solenoid, or repair the harness

Yes ↓

Is the resistance between the LR-wire and the LO-wire of the speed-control unit approximately 20 Ω?

— No → Malfunction of the actuator, or damaged harness → Replace the actuator or repair the harness

Yes ↓

Is the resistance between ground and the (R)-wire of the speed-control unit 0 Ω when the set switch is pressed, and ∞ when it is released?

— No → Malfunction of the set switch or damaged harness → Replace the switch or repair the harness

Yes ↓

Is the resistance between ground and the (Y)-wire of the speed-control unit 0 Ω when the resume switch is pressed, and ∞ when it is released?

— No → Malfunction of the resume switch or damaged harness → Replace the switch or repair the harness

Yes ↓

Does the continuity between ground and the (YW)-wire of the speed-control unit alternate ON/OFF when the vehicle is moved?

— No → Malfunction of the speed sensor or improper ground connection, or a short-circuit or damaged wiring between the speed sensor and the speed-control unit. → Replace the speedometer or repair the harness

Yes ↓

Is the resistance between the LY-wire and the LR-wire of the speed-control unit approximately 6 Ω when the actuator turns 10° or more?

— No → Malfunction of the actuator or damaged harness → Replace the actuator or repair the harness

Yes ↓

Cruise control diagnosis chart—Galant

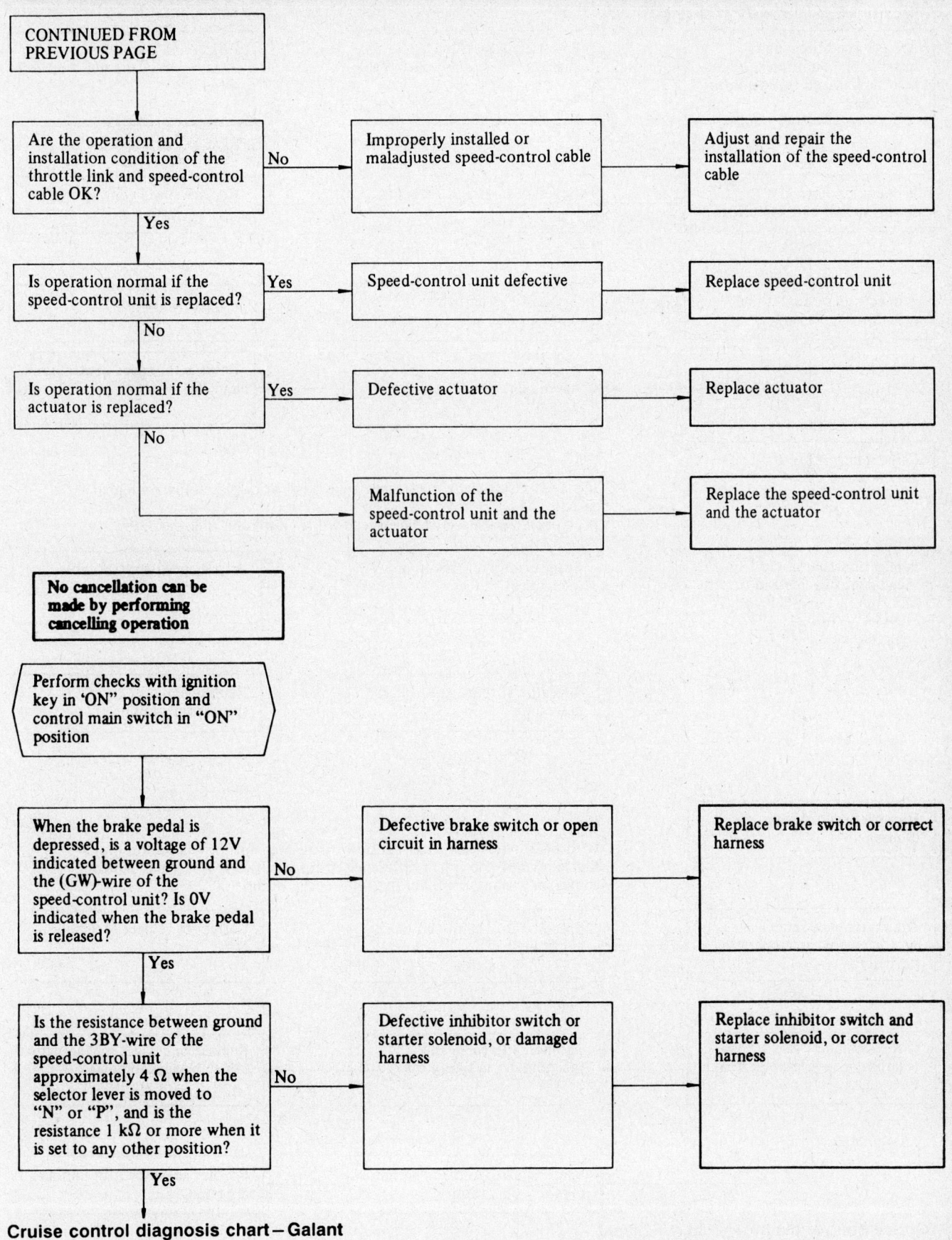

CONTINUED FROM
PREVIOUS PAGE

Are the operation and installation condition of the throttle link and speed-control cable OK? — No → Improperly installed or maladjusted speed-control cable → Adjust and repair the installation of the speed-control cable

Yes

Is operation normal if the speed-control unit is replaced? — Yes → Speed-control unit defective → Replace speed-control unit

No

Is operation normal if the actuator is replaced? — Yes → Defective actuator → Replace actuator

No

Malfunction of the speed-control unit and the actuator → Replace the speed-control unit and the actuator

No cancellation can be made by performing cancelling operation

Perform checks with ignition key in 'ON" position and control main switch in "ON" position

When the brake pedal is depressed, is a voltage of 12V indicated between ground and the (GW)-wire of the speed-control unit? Is 0V indicated when the brake pedal is released? — No → Defective brake switch or open circuit in harness → Replace brake switch or correct harness

Yes

Is the resistance between ground and the 3BY-wire of the speed-control unit approximately 4 Ω when the selector lever is moved to "N" or "P", and is the resistance 1 kΩ or more when it is set to any other position? — No → Defective inhibitor switch or starter solenoid, or damaged harness → Replace inhibitor switch and starter solenoid, or correct harness

Yes

Cruise control diagnosis chart – Galant

CONTINUED FROM PREVIOUS PAGE

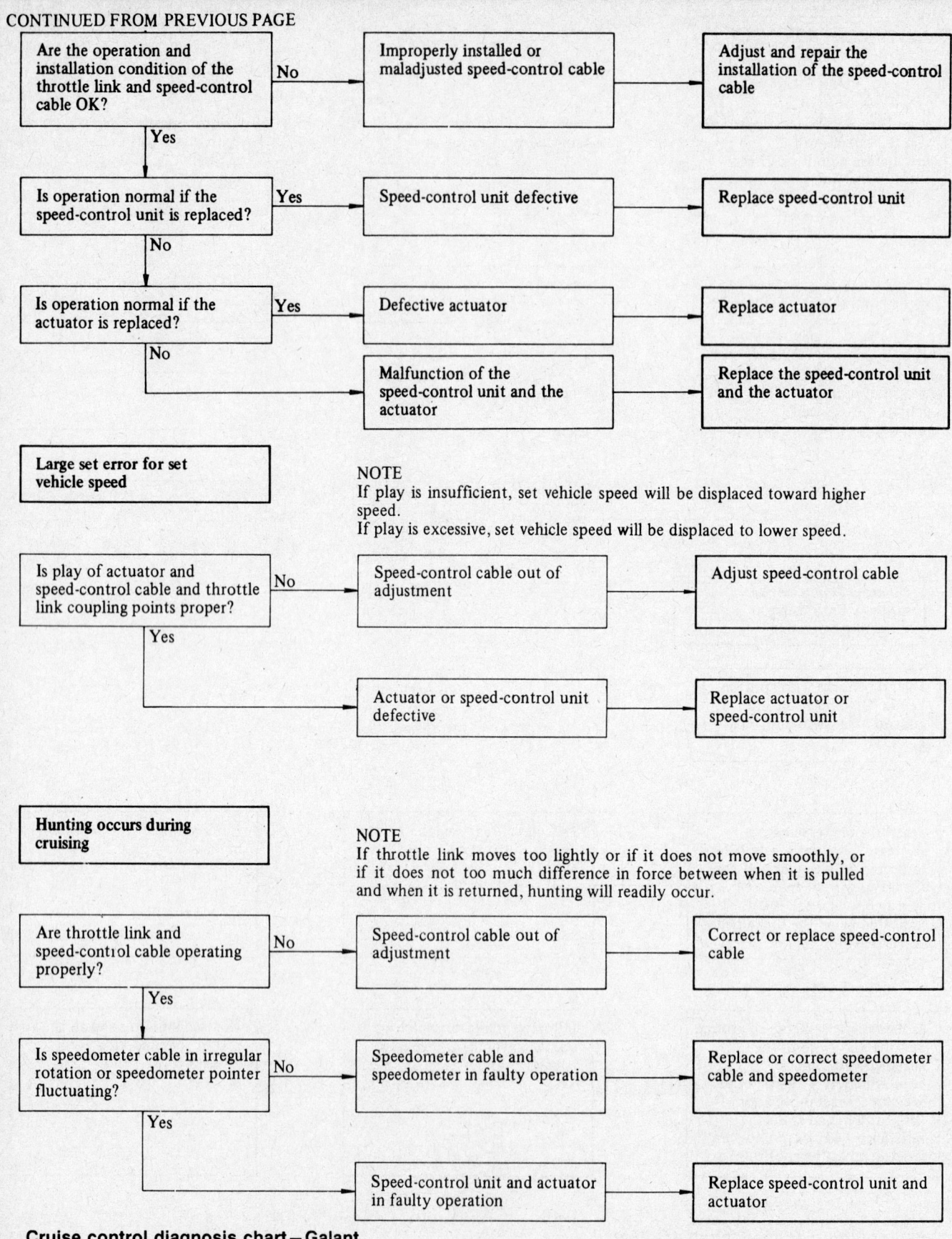

Are the operation and installation condition of the throttle link and speed-control cable OK?	**No** → Improperly installed or maladjusted speed-control cable	→ Adjust and repair the installation of the speed-control cable
↓ **Yes**		
Is operation normal if the speed-control unit is replaced?	**Yes** → Speed-control unit defective	→ Replace speed-control unit
↓ **No**		
Is operation normal if the actuator is replaced?	**Yes** → Defective actuator	→ Replace actuator
↓ **No**	Malfunction of the speed-control unit and the actuator	→ Replace the speed-control unit and the actuator

Large set error for set vehicle speed

NOTE
If play is insufficient, set vehicle speed will be displaced toward higher speed.
If play is excessive, set vehicle speed will be displaced to lower speed.

Is play of actuator and speed-control cable and throttle link coupling points proper?	**No** → Speed-control cable out of adjustment	→ Adjust speed-control cable
↓ **Yes**	Actuator or speed-control unit defective	→ Replace actuator or speed-control unit

Hunting occurs during cruising

NOTE
If throttle link moves too lightly or if it does not move smoothly, or if it does not too much difference in force between when it is pulled and when it is returned, hunting will readily occur.

Are throttle link and speed-control cable operating properly?	**No** → Speed-control cable out of adjustment	→ Correct or replace speed-control cable
↓ **Yes**		
Is speedometer cable in irregular rotation or speedometer pointer fluctuating?	**No** → Speedometer cable and speedometer in faulty operation	→ Replace or correct speedometer cable and speedometer
↓ **Yes**	Speed-control unit and actuator in faulty operation	→ Replace speed-control unit and actuator

Cruise control diagnosis chart—Galant

Component Replacement

ACTUATOR

Removal and Installation

1. Disconnect the negative battery cable.
2. Remove the actuator protective cover.
3. Disconnect the connector for the cruise control cable.
4. Disconnect the actuator electrical connector.
5. Remove the actuator retaining bolts.
6. Remove the actuator from the vehicle.
7. Installation is the reverse of the removal procedure.

CRUISE CONTROL SWITCH

Removal and Installation

1. Disconnect the negative battery cable.
2. Remove the steering wheel and steering column lever.
3. Disconnect the switch electrical connectors. Disconnect the switch retaining bolts.
4. Carefully remove the cruise control switch assembly from the steering column assembly.
5. Installation is the reverse of the removal procedure.

CRUISE CONTROL UNIT

Removal and Installation

1. Disconnect the negative battery cable.
2. Remove the right side cowl trim.
3. Disconnect the electrical connectors from the control unit assembly.
4. Remove the control unit retaining bolts. Remove the control unit from the vehicle.
5. Installation is the reverse of the removal procedure.

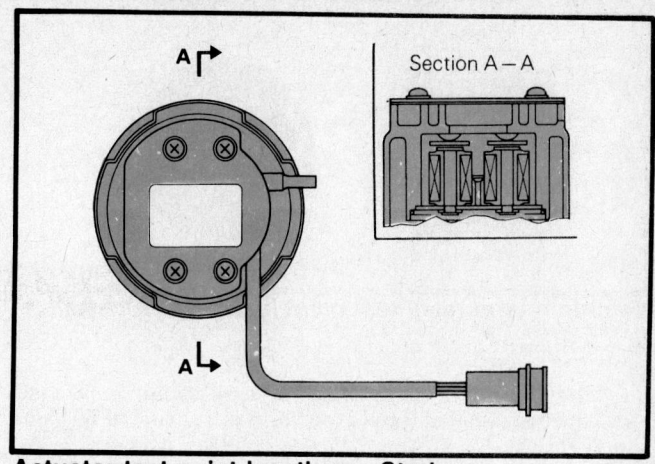

Actuator test point locations – Starion

Starion

VISUAL INSPECTION

Before performing any tests make a visual inspection of the cruise control system. Check all items in the system for abnormal conditions such as bare broken or disconnected wires and damage to the vacuum hoses. Be sure that the speedometer cables are attached and properly routed. All vacuum hoses must be properly routed and must not have any kinks or bends. Be sure that all electrical connections are complete and tight. The wiring harness must be routed properly.

ACTUATOR TEST

1. Measure the resistance values of the release valve coil and the control valve coil.

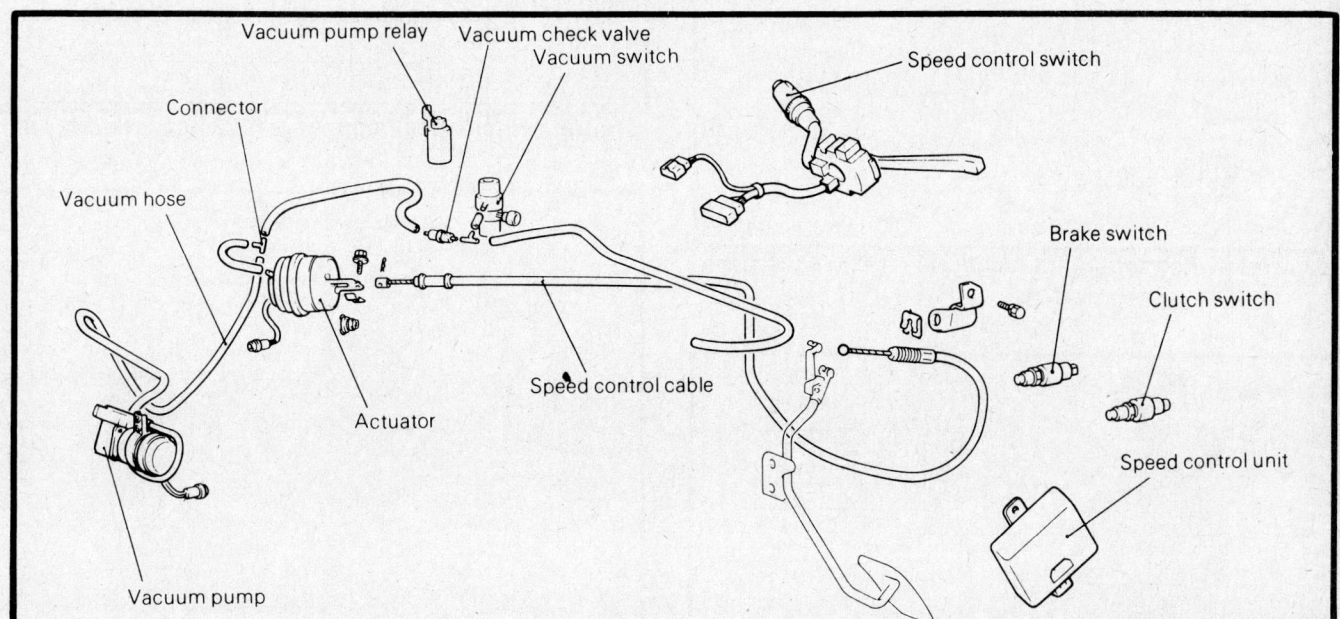

Cruise control system and related components – Starion

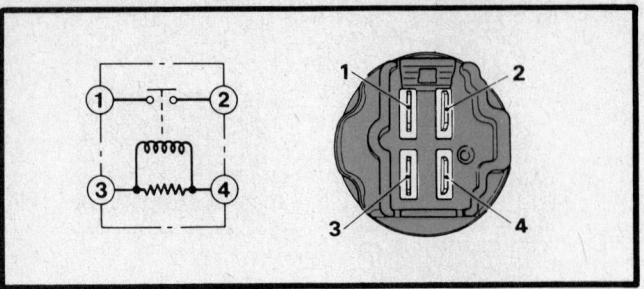

Vacuum pump relay test point locations — Starion

2. The resistance of the release valve coil should be 68 ohms.
3. The resistance of the control valve coil should be 30 ohms.

VACUUM PUMP RELAY TEST

1. Check and repair the switches, sensors and wire harness that is connected to the control unit.
2. If this fails to correct the problem, replace the speed sensor assembly after making the following checks.
3. With the power off, check the continuity between terminals one and two. There should not be continuity. Check the continuity between terminals three and four. There should be continuity.
4. With the power on, check the continuity between terminals three and four. There should be continuity. Check the continuity between terminals one and two. There should not be continuity.

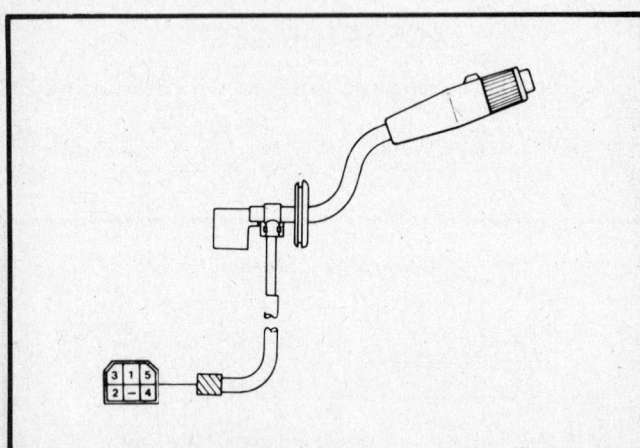

Control switch test point locations — 1983–85 Starion

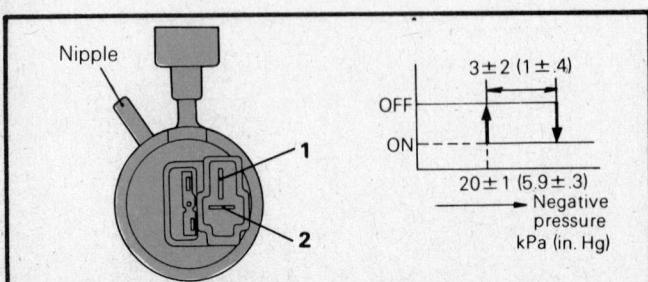

Vacuum switch test point locations — Starion

VACUUM SWITCH TEST

1. With negative pressure applied to the nipple, check the continuity between terminals one and two as follows.
2. Without negative pressure applied, check to see if there is continunity between terminals one and two.
3. With a negative pressure of about 5.9 to 8.0 in. Hg. of vacuum applied, check to see if continunity is lost.
4. From the above condition, increase the negative pressure to about 8.9 in. Hg. of vacuum and then slowly decrease it to 5.8 in. Hg of vacuum.
5. Check to see if continunity exists.

CRUISE CONTROL SWITCH TEST

1. Using a test light check for continuity between the terminals.
2. Repair or replace defective components as required.

Switch	Position	1	2	3	4	5
Push switch	Off					
	SET on	○——————○				
Rotary switch	OFF					
	ON					
	RESUME	○———○			○———○	

Control switch specifications — 1983–85 Starion

Switch	Position	2	5	1	7	3
Push switch	Off					
	SET on	○—————○				
Rotary switch	OFF					
	ON					
	RESUME	○———○			○———○	

Control switch specifications — 1986 and later Starion

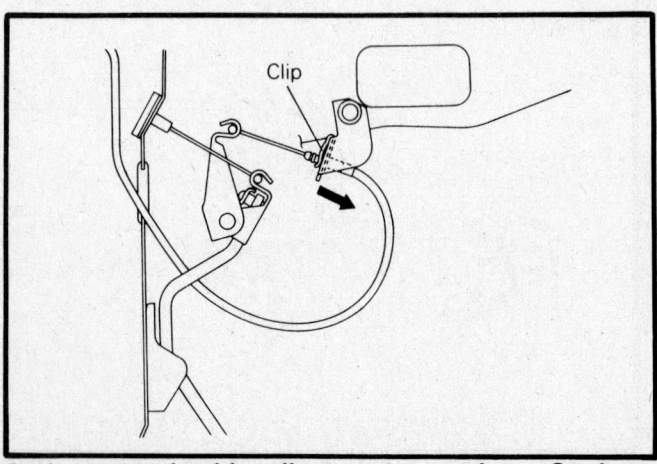

Cruise control cable adjustment procedure — Starion

CRUISE CONTROL CABLE ADJUSTMENT

1. Adjust the accelerator cable.
2. Slide the cruise control cable out up to a point just before the accelerator cable begins to move.
3. Secure the cruise control cable by inserting a retaining clip.
4. Check to be sure that the cable is within the proper specification of 0 to 0.1 inch.

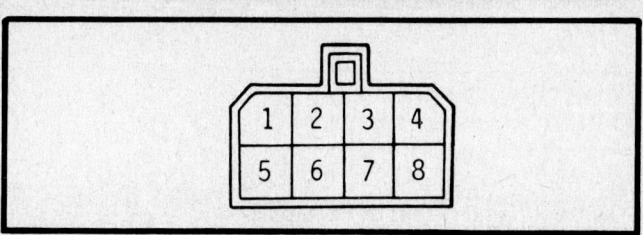

Control switch test point locations—1986 and later Starion

DIAGNOSIS AND TESTING PROCEDURES

SPEED CONTROL SYSTEM

NOTE
Disconnect the connector of the speed control unit and check by inserting a test bar from the reverse side of the connector.
The main switch should be kept in "OFF" position.

Speed control cannot be set

Perform checks with ignition key at "ON" position

Are fuse No. 2 and 14 good?	No →	Short circuit in harness	→	Correct harness or replace fuse

Yes ↓

Does continuity between 0.3YW-wire of speed control unit and ground repeat ON-OFF states when vehicle is operated?	No →	Speed sensor defective or improperly grounded, open or short circuit in harness between speed control unit and speed sensor	→	Replace speedometer or correct harness

Yes ↓

Is there continuity between GW-wire of speed control unit and ground?	No →	Stop light bulb defective or open circuit in harness between GW-wire of speed control unit and stop light switch	→	Replace stop light or correct harness

Yes ↓

Check voltage between G-wire of speed control unit and ground. Is 12V indicated?	No →	Open circuit in harness between speed control unit and fuse block	→	Correct harness

Yes ↓

Is there continuity between 2B-wire of speed control unit and ground when clutch pedal is depressed?	No →	Clutch switch defective or open circuit in harness between speed control unit and clutch switch	→	Replace clutch switch or correct harness

Yes ↓

SEE NEXT PAGE

Cruise control diagnosis chart—Starion

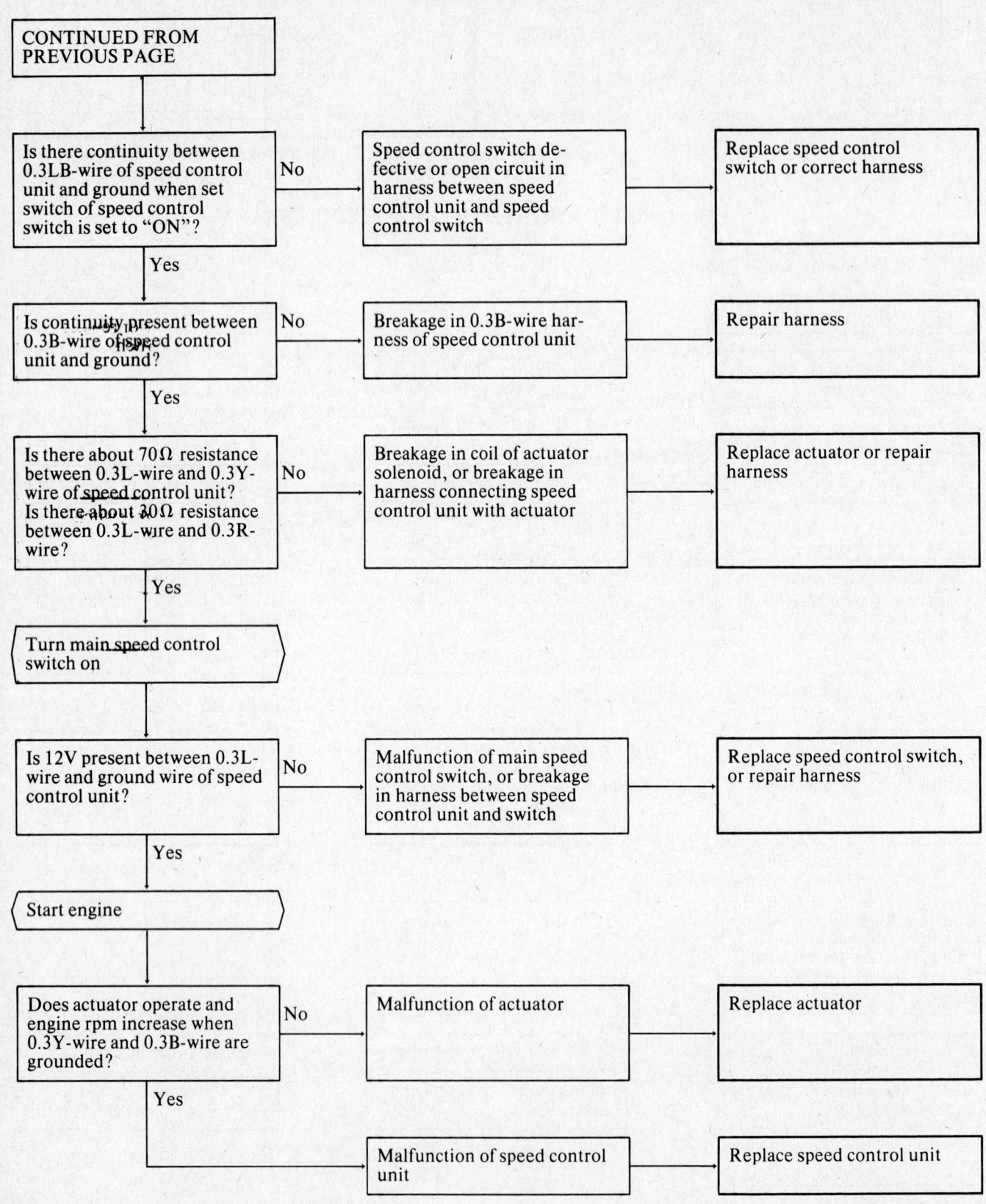

CONTINUED FROM PREVIOUS PAGE

Is there continuity between 0.3LB-wire of speed control unit and ground when set switch of speed control switch is set to "ON"? —No→ Speed control switch defective or open circuit in harness between speed control unit and speed control switch —→ Replace speed control switch or correct harness

↓ Yes

Is continuity present between 0.3B-wire of speed control unit and ground? —No→ Breakage in 0.3B-wire harness of speed control unit —→ Repair harness

↓ Yes

Is there about 70Ω resistance between 0.3L-wire and 0.3Y-wire of speed control unit? Is there about 30Ω resistance between 0.3L-wire and 0.3R-wire? —No→ Breakage in coil of actuator solenoid, or breakage in harness connecting speed control unit with actuator —→ Replace actuator or repair harness

↓ Yes

Turn main speed control switch on

↓

Is 12V present between 0.3L-wire and ground wire of speed control unit? —No→ Malfunction of main speed control switch, or breakage in harness between speed control unit and switch —→ Replace speed control switch, or repair harness

↓ Yes

Start engine

↓

Does actuator operate and engine rpm increase when 0.3Y-wire and 0.3B-wire are grounded? —No→ Malfunction of actuator —→ Replace actuator

↓ Yes

Malfunction of speed control unit —→ Replace speed control unit

Cruise control diagnosis chart—Starion

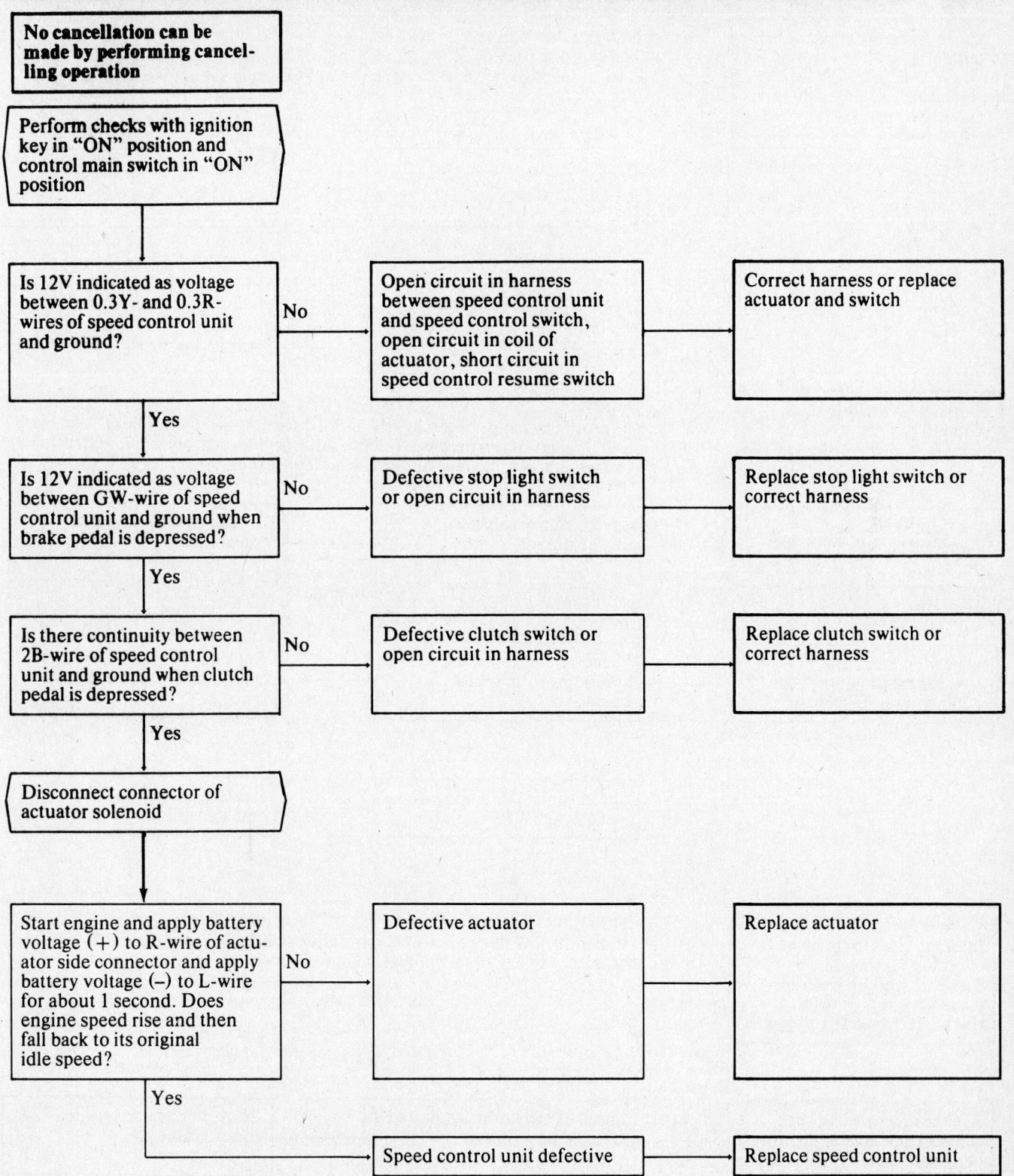

Cruise control diagnosis chart — Starion

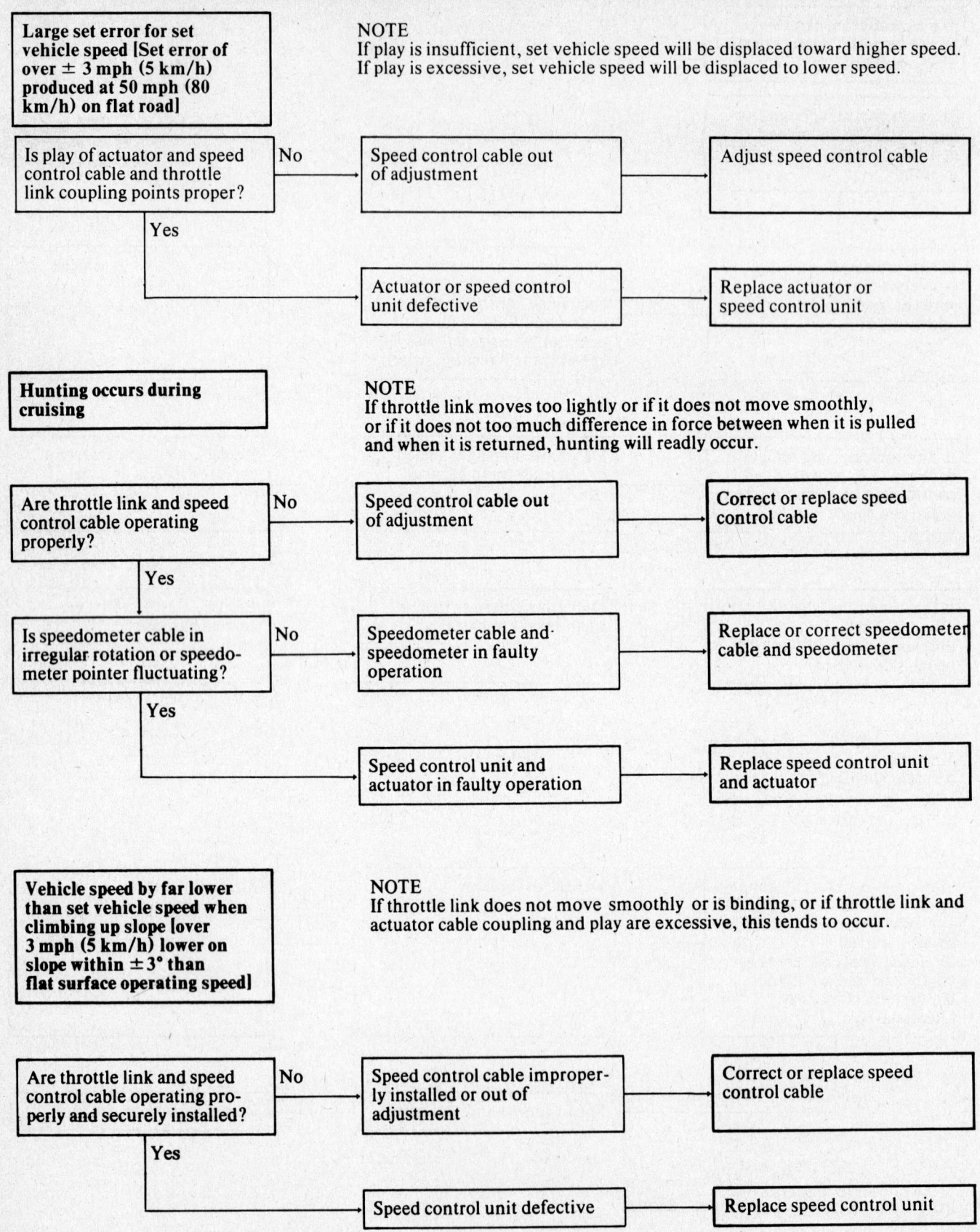

Large set error for set vehicle speed [Set error of over ± 3 mph (5 km/h) produced at 50 mph (80 km/h) on flat road]

NOTE
If play is insufficient, set vehicle speed will be displaced toward higher speed. If play is excessive, set vehicle speed will be displaced to lower speed.

Is play of actuator and speed control cable and throttle link coupling points proper? → No → Speed control cable out of adjustment → Adjust speed control cable

↓ Yes

Actuator or speed control unit defective → Replace actuator or speed control unit

Hunting occurs during cruising

NOTE
If throttle link moves too lightly or if it does not move smoothly, or if it does not too much difference in force between when it is pulled and when it is returned, hunting will readly occur.

Are throttle link and speed control cable operating properly? → No → Speed control cable out of adjustment → Correct or replace speed control cable

↓ Yes

Is speedometer cable in irregular rotation or speedometer pointer fluctuating? → No → Speedometer cable and speedometer in faulty operation → Replace or correct speedometer cable and speedometer

↓ Yes

Speed control unit and actuator in faulty operation → Replace speed control unit and actuator

Vehicle speed by far lower than set vehicle speed when climbing up slope [over 3 mph (5 km/h) lower on slope within ± 3° than flat surface operating speed]

NOTE
If throttle link does not move smoothly or is binding, or if throttle link and actuator cable coupling and play are excessive, this tends to occur.

Are throttle link and speed control cable operating properly and securely installed? → No → Speed control cable improperly installed or out of adjustment → Correct or replace speed control cable

↓ Yes

Speed control unit defective → Replace speed control unit

Cruise control diagnosis chart — Starion

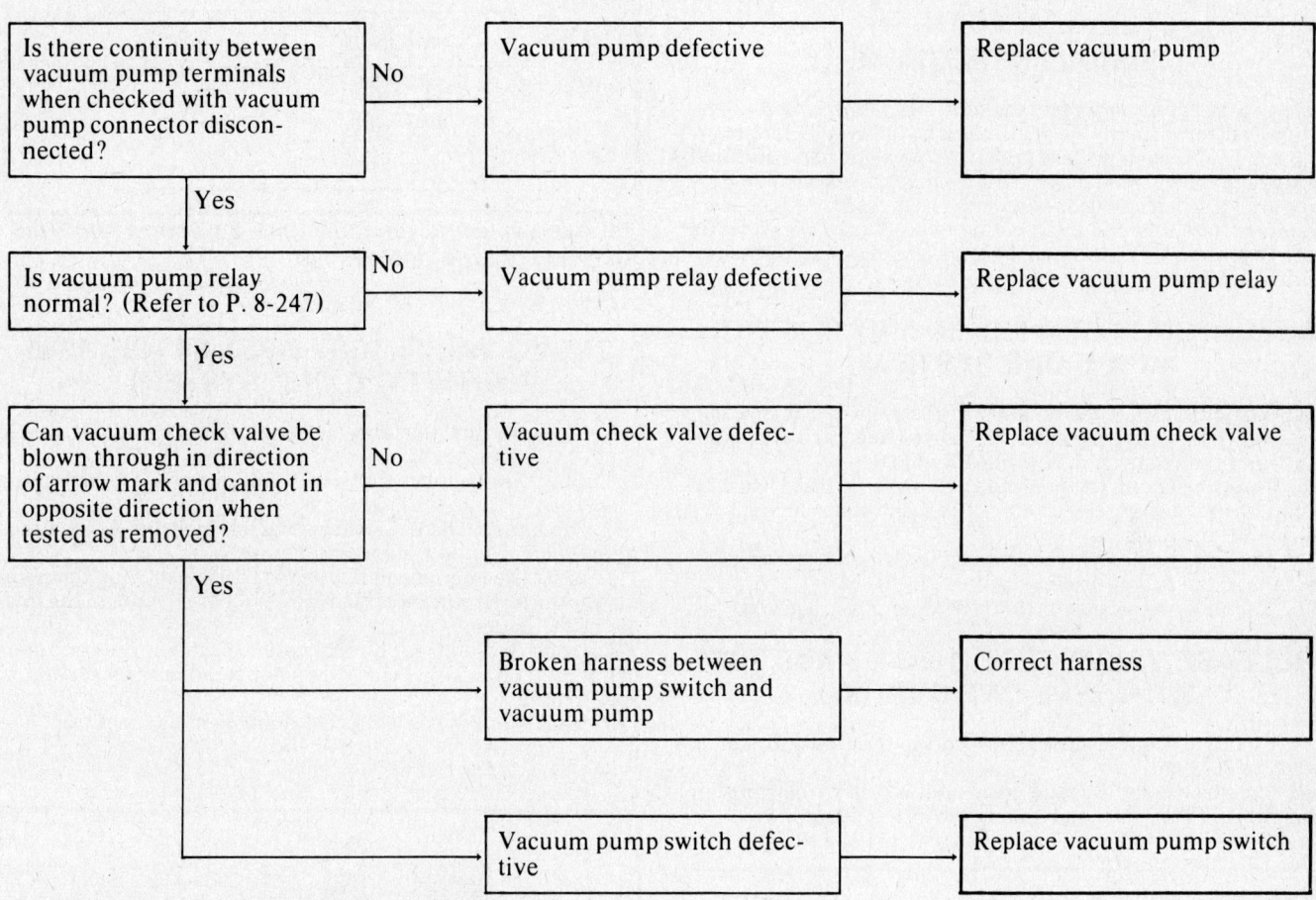

Cruise control diagnosis chart — Starion

The flowchart contains the following boxes:

| Vacuum pump does not run |

| Is there continuity between vacuum pump terminals when checked with vacuum pump connector disconnected? | → No → | Vacuum pump defective | → | Replace vacuum pump |

Yes ↓

| Is vacuum pump relay normal? (Refer to P. 8-247) | → No → | Vacuum pump relay defective | → | Replace vacuum pump relay |

Yes ↓

| Can vacuum check valve be blown through in direction of arrow mark and cannot in opposite direction when tested as removed? | → No → | Vacuum check valve defective | → | Replace vacuum check valve |

Yes ↓

| Broken harness between vacuum pump switch and vacuum pump | → | Correct harness |

| Vacuum pump switch defective | → | Replace vacuum pump switch |

Component Replacement
ACTUATOR

Removal and Installation

1. Disconnect the negative battery cable.
2. Disconnect all connectors, lines and cables from the actuator assembly.
3. Remove the retaining bolts holding the actuator assembly to its mounting.
4. Remove the actuator from the vehicle.
5. Installation is the reverse of the removal procedure.

CRUISE CONTROL SWITCH

Removal and Installation

1. Disconnect the negative battery cable.
2. Remove the steering wheel and steering column lever.

3. Disconnect the switch electrical connectors. Disconnect the switch retaining bolts.
4. Carefully remove the cruise control switch assembly from the steering column assembly.
5. Installation is the reverse of the removal procedure.

CRUISE CONTROL UNIT

Removal and Installation

1. Disconnect the negative battery cable.
2. Remove the quater trim panel.
3. Disconnect the electrical connectors from the control unit assembly.
4. Remove the control unit retaining bolts. Remove the control unit from the vehicle.
5. Installation is the reverse of the removal procedure.

NISSAN/DATSUN

Stanza

VISUAL INSPECTION

Before performing any tests make a visual inspection of the cruise control system. Check all items in the system for abnormal conditions such as bare broken or disconnected wires and damage to the vacuum hoses. Be sure that the speedometer cables are attached and properly routed. All vacuum hoses must be properly routed and must not have any kinks or bends. Be sure that all electrical connections are complete and tight. The wiring harness must be routed properly.

ACTUATOR TEST (1983–84 AND 1985 WITH TYPE ONE SYSTEM)

1. Visually inspect the actuator for damage or deformation.
2. Make sure that the assembly moves freely without binding when the diaphragm is pushed by hand.
3. Apply vacuum to the actuator, using a hand vacuum pump. Do not use engine vacuum. The diaphragm should move to the full up position.
4. Plug the hose with vacuum applied, the actuator should remain in the full position.
5. Repair or replace defective components as required.

RELEASE VALVE TEST (1983–84 AND 1985 WITH TYPE ONE SYSTEM)

1. Measure the resistance between the terminals. It should be 25 to 30 ohms.
2. Be sure that the valve opens and closes by blowing air through the port on the actuator side of the assembly.
3. Repair or replace defective components as required.

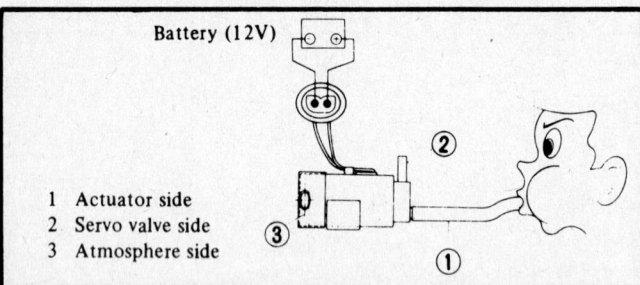

1 Actuator side
2 Servo valve side
3 Atmosphere side

Release valve test point locations—1983–84 Stanza and 1985 Stanza with type one system

Check ports	Air flow
① - ②	Yes
① - ③	No
② - ③	No

Release valve test results—1983–84 Stanza and 1985 Stanza with type one system

Check ports	Air flow
① - ②	
① - ③	Yes
② - ③	

Release valve test results—1983–84 Stanza and 1985 Stanza with type one system

SERVO VALVE TEST (1983–84 AND 1985 WITH TYPE ONE SYSTEM)

1. Measure the resistance between the terminals. It should be 25 to 30 ohms.
2. Check to be sure that the vacuum valve is performing properly.
3. Disconnect the solenoid valve side vacuum hose at the servo valve. Connect a vacuum gauge.
4. Start the engine and allow it to reach operating temperature or until the water temperature indicator points to the middle of the gauge.
5. Apply 0.3 amps of direct current between the terminals using a 20 ohm 5W variable resistor to adjust the current to specification.
6. Repair or replace defective components as required.

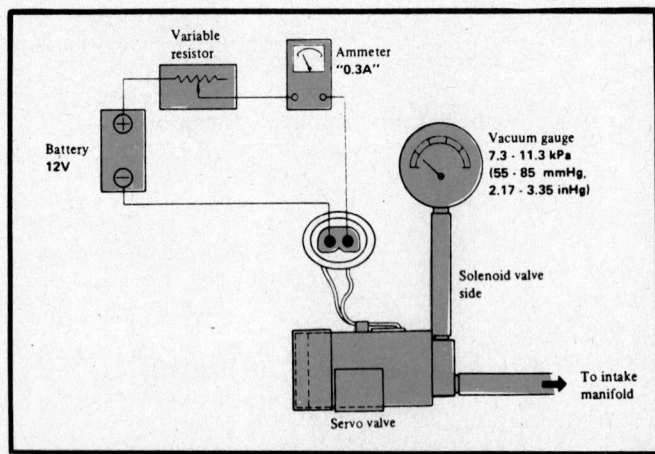

Servo valve test point locations—1983–84 Stanza and 1985 Stanza with type one system

SPEED SENSOR TEST (1983–84 AND 1985 WITH TYPE ONE SYSTEM)

The speed sensor is built into the rear of the speedometer. Inspection of the speed sensor must be made with the speed sensor installed in the speedometer assembly. Turn the speedometer slowly by hand two complete turns. If continuity exists than the sensor is good.

MAIN SWITCH TEST (1983–84 AND 1985 WITH TYPE ONE SYSTEM)

1. Test the continuity of the main switch assembly using and ohmmeter.
2. Repair or replace defective components as required.

STOP LIGHT SWITCH TEST (1983–84 AND 1985 WITH TYPE ONE SYSTEM)

1. Test the continunity of the main switch assembly using and ohmmeter.
2. Repair or replace defective components as required.

ASCD RELAY TEST (1983–84 AND 1985 WITH TYPE ONE SYSTEM)

The ASCD relay is located on the fuse block assembly. Using an ohmmeter check the component for the proper continuity.

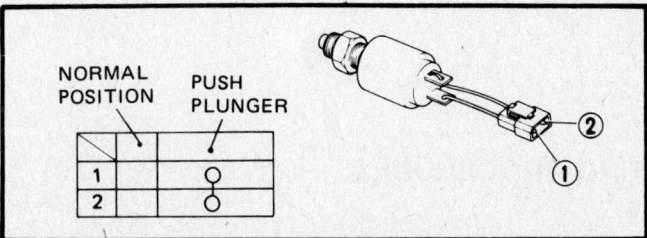

Stoplight switch test point locations – 1983–84 Stanza and 1985 Stanza with type one system

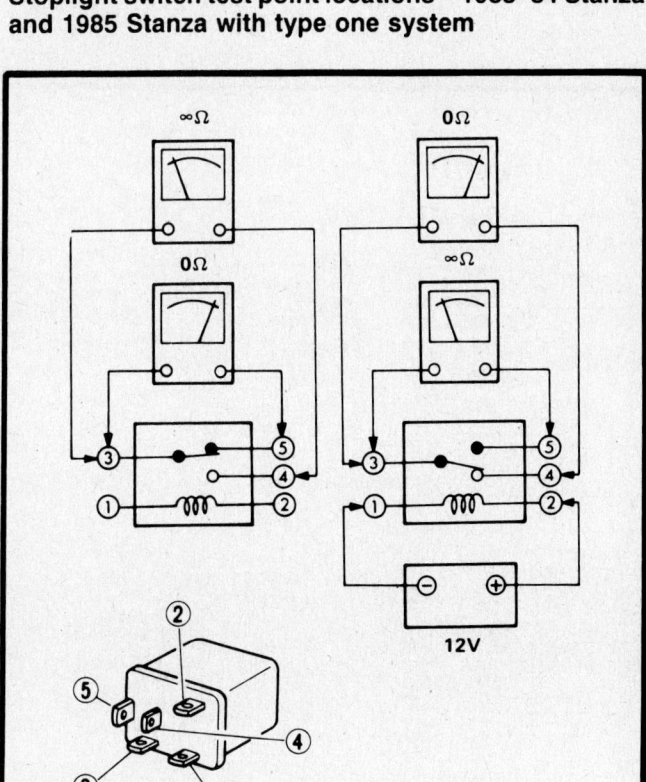

ASCD relay and test point locations – 1983–84 Stanza and 1985 Stanza with type one system

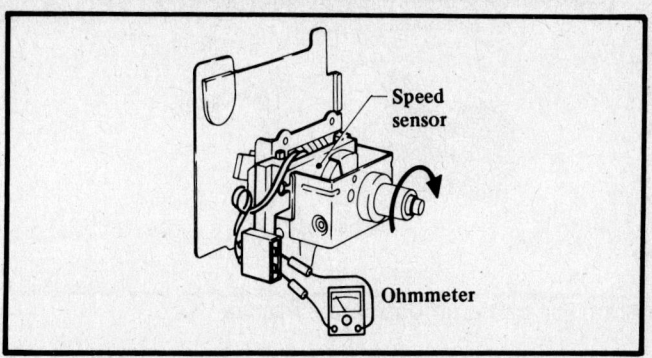

Speed sensor test point locations – 1983–84 Stanza and 1985 Stanza with type one system

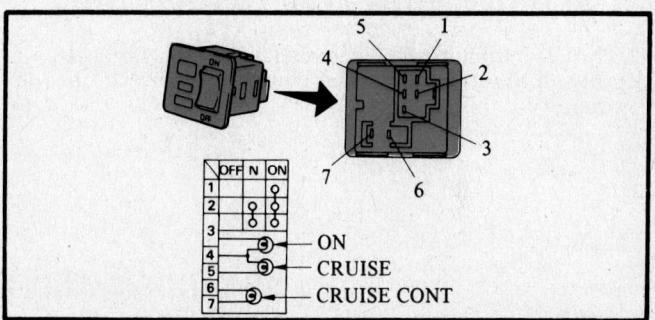

Main switch switch test point locations – 1983–84 Stanza and 1985 Stanza with type one system

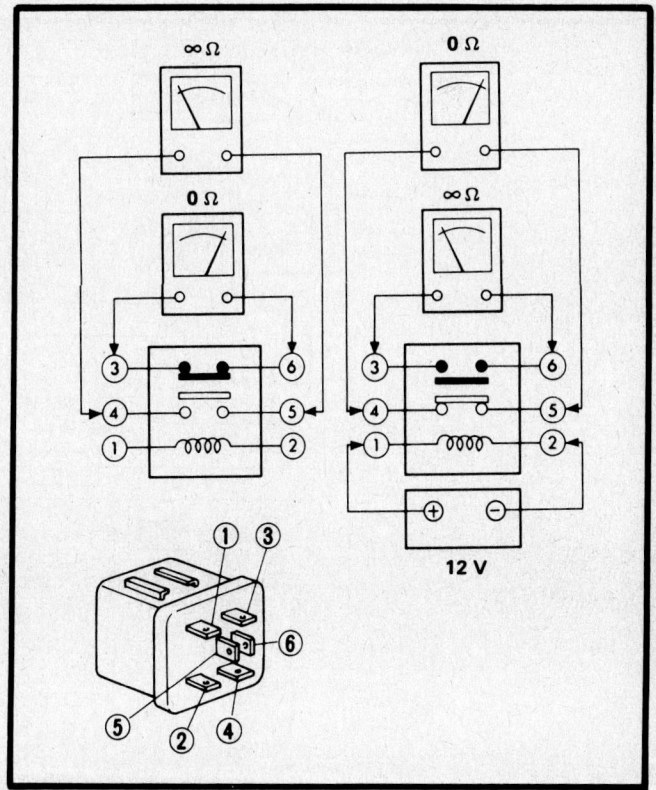

ASCD inhibitor relay and test point locations – 1983–84 Stanza and 1985 Stanza with type one system

1015

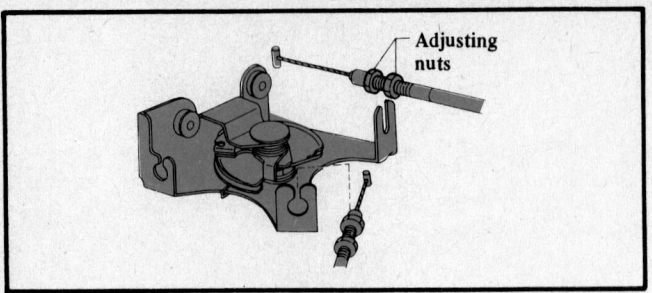

Actuator cable adjustment—Stanza

ASCD CONTROLLER TEST (1983–84 AND 1985 WITH TYPE ONE SYSTEM)

The ASCD controller is located on the left side of the dash panel. This component must be checked as a single part. When checking this component do not touch the test probe to any terminal other than the ones used to check the component as damage to the controller could result. Keep the controller away from electric noise to prevent the ASCD system from malfunctioning and the IC circuit from being destroyed.

ASCD INHIBITOR RELAY TEST (1983–84 AND 1985 WITH TYPE ONE SYSTEM)

The ASCD inhibitor relay is located on the relay bracket. Using an ohmmeter check the component for the proper continunity.

ACTUATOR ADJUSTMENT

1. Without depressing the accelerator, adjust the adjusting nuts until all freeplay is removed.
2. Return the adjusting nuts ½ to 1 turn to gain the proper cable free play.
3. Do not increase the cable tension excessively, as this can cause cable damage.

DIAGNOSIS AND TESTING PROCEDURES

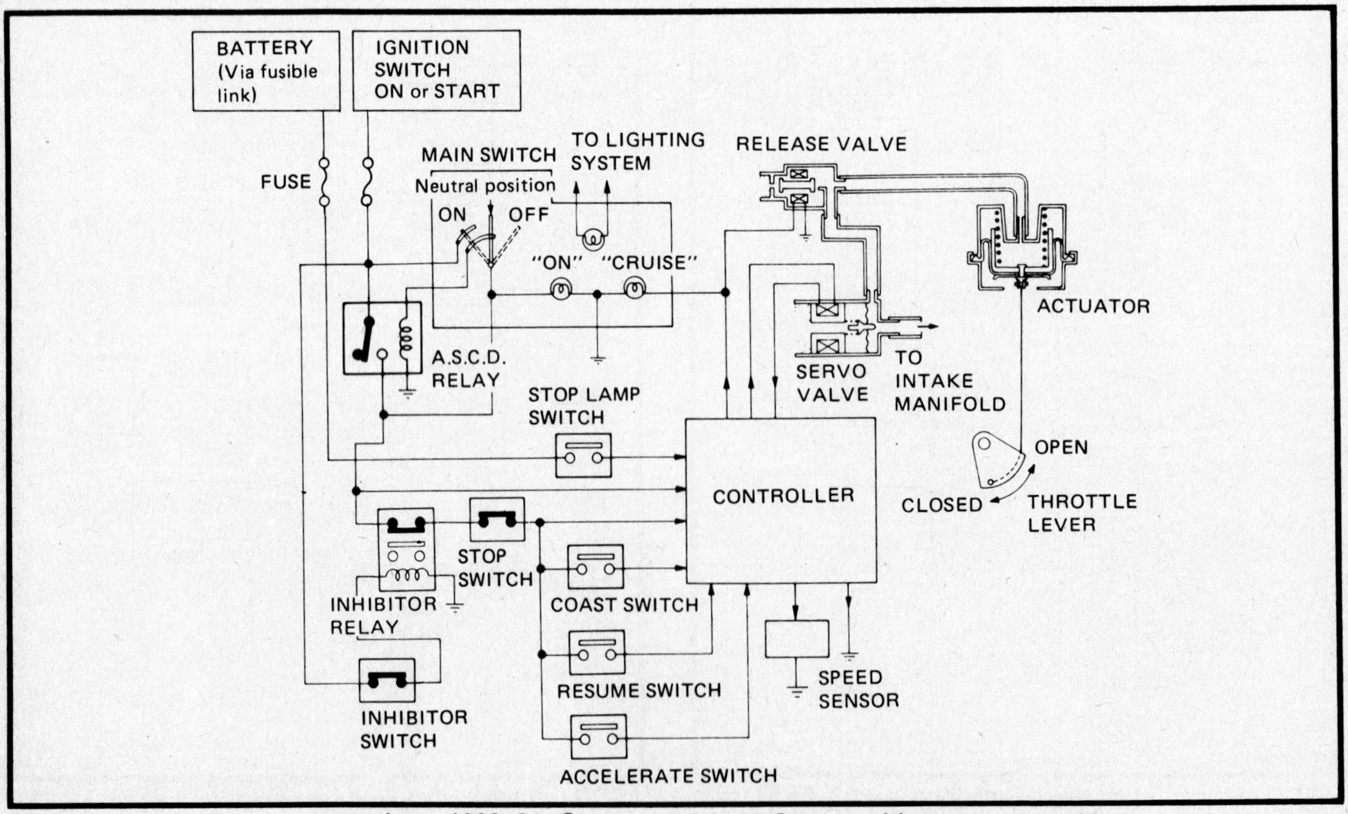

Cruise control system operation—1983–84 Stanza and 1985 Stanza with type one system

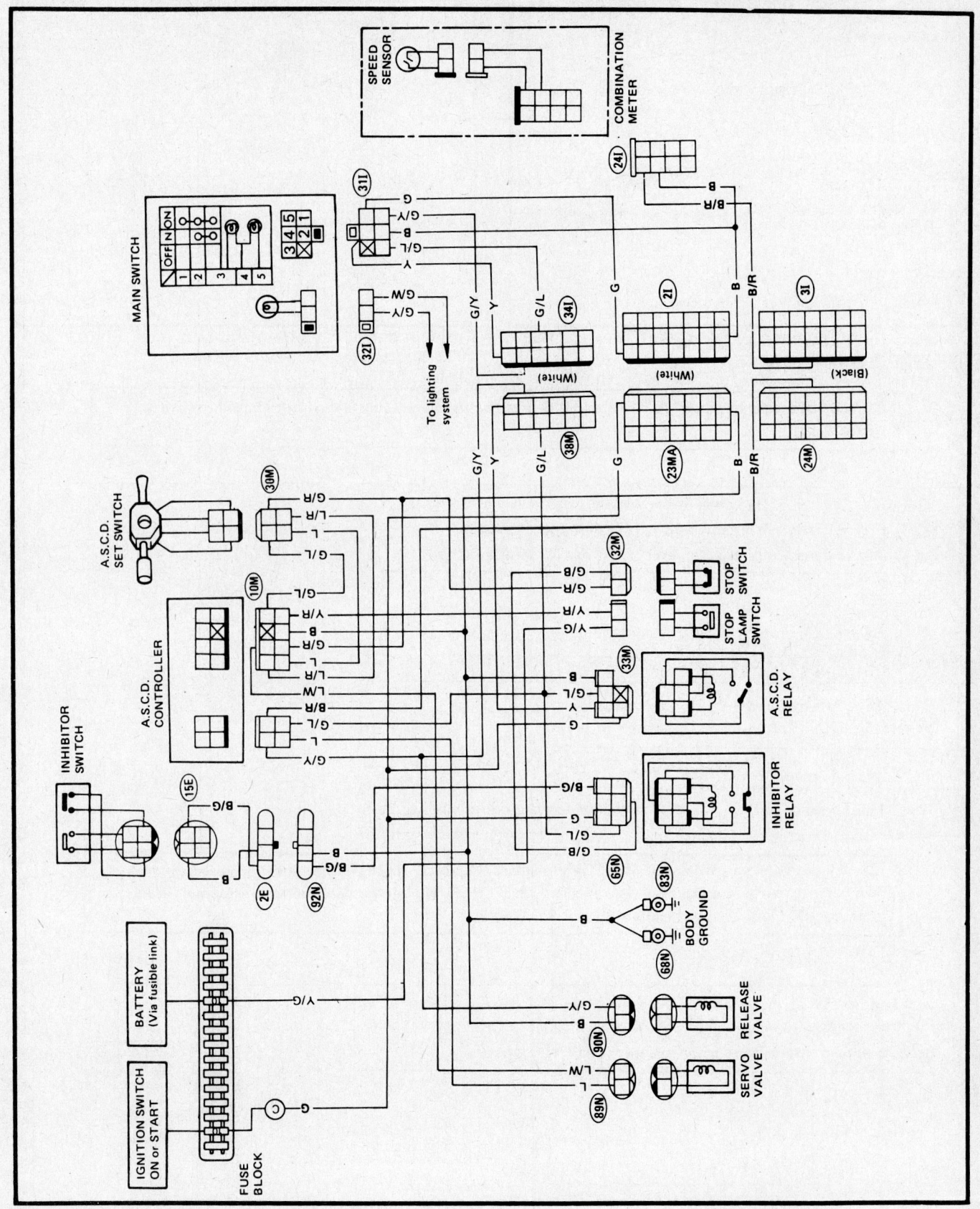

Cruise control electrical schematic—1983–84 Stanza and 1985 Stanza with type one system

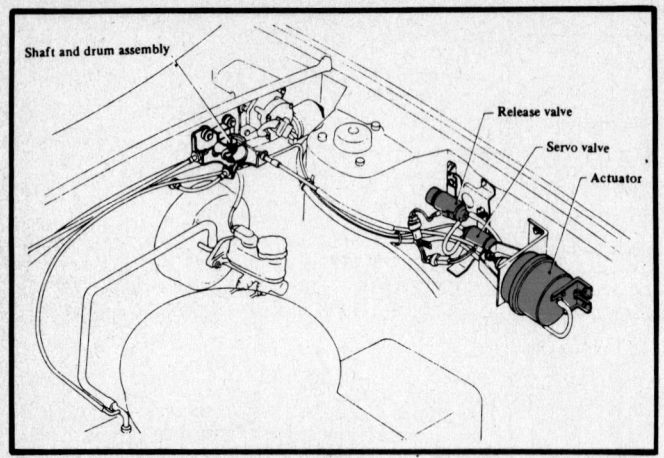

Cruise control layout—1983–84 Stanza and 1985 Stanza with type one system

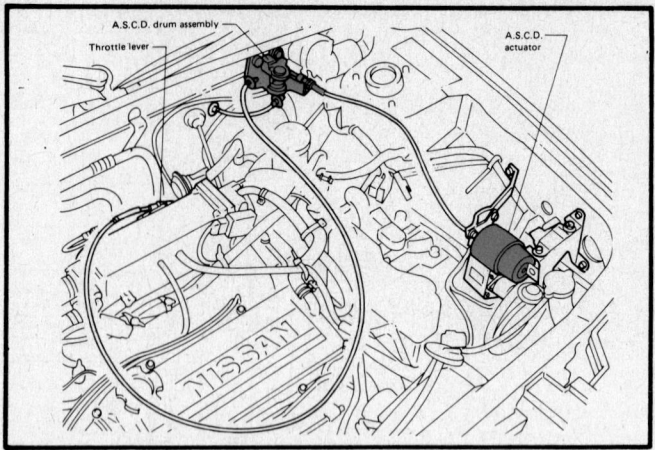

Cruise control layout—1986 and later Stanza and 1985 Stanza with type two system

---

Car will not accelerate when "ACCEL" end is depressed. (However, constant car speed can be maintained by A.S.C.D.)

With ignition switch, main switch and accelerate switch ON, battery voltage (12V) is present between terminals ⑫ and ⑦ of harness connector.
Set automatic transmission selector lever at "P" or "N" position.

YES   NO

NO → Faulty accelerate & resume switch.

When only "ACCEL" end is "OFF", voltage across terminals ⑫ and ⑦ will be zero.

YES   NO

Faulty controller.   Faulty accelerate & resume switch.

12V

Car will not decelerate when "RESUME" end remains ON, or car speed will not return to speed at which it was being driven before set speed was cancelled when "RESUME" end is depressed momentarily. (However, constant speed can be maintained by A.S.C.D.)

With ignition switch, main switch and resume switch ON, battery voltage (12V) is present between terminals ⑪ and ⑦ of harness connector.
Set automatic transmission selector lever at "P" or "N" position.

YES   NO

NO → Faulty accelerate & resume switch.

12V

SEE NEXT PAGE

Cruise control trouble diagnosis chart—1983–84 Stanza and 1985 with type one system

CONTINUED FROM
PREVIOUS PAGE

When only "RESUME" end is "OFF", voltage across terminals ⑪ and ⑦ will be zero.

YES

NO

Faulty controller.

Faulty accelerate & resume switch.

Cruise lamp will not glow, even if set switch is depressed and released at proper car speed, with main switch ON. (Speed not set in system.)

With ignition switch and main switch ON, battery voltage (12V) is present between terminals ③ and ⑦, ⑩ and ⑦ of harness connector.
Set automatic transmission selector lever at any position other than "P" and "N" position.

YES

NO

Open circuit.

Faulty or improperly adjusted stop switch.

Faulty inhibitor switch or inhibitor relay.

When set switch is depressed with ignition switch and main switch ON, battery voltage (12V) is present between terminals ② and ⑦ of harness connector.

YES

NO

Faulty set switch.

With ignition switch and main switch ON, manually rotate meter cable slowly to see if voltages across harness connector terminals ⑧ and ⑦ alternately change from 0 to 7 and vice versa.

YES

NO

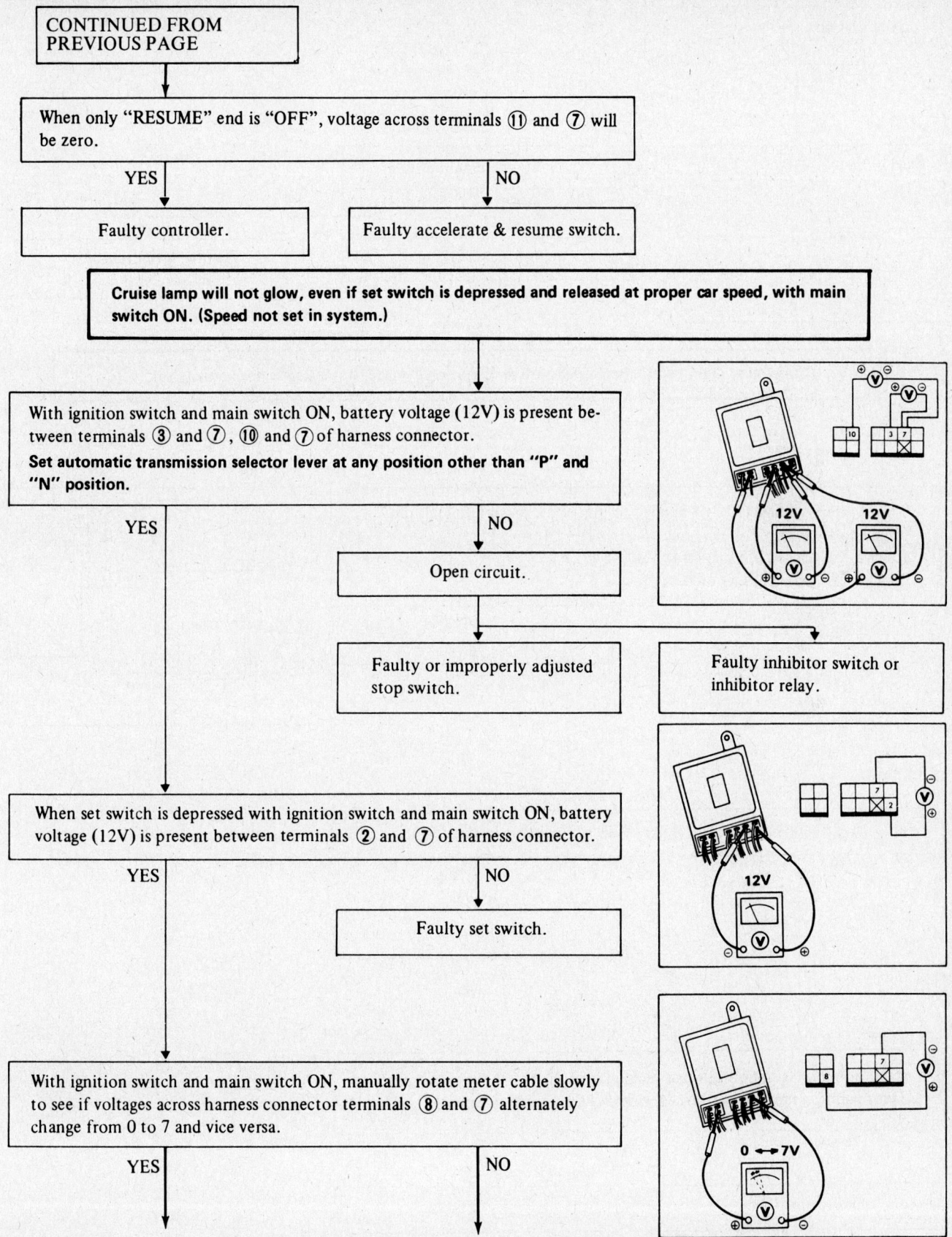

Cruise control trouble diagnosis chart – 1983–84 Stanza and 1985 Stanza with type one system

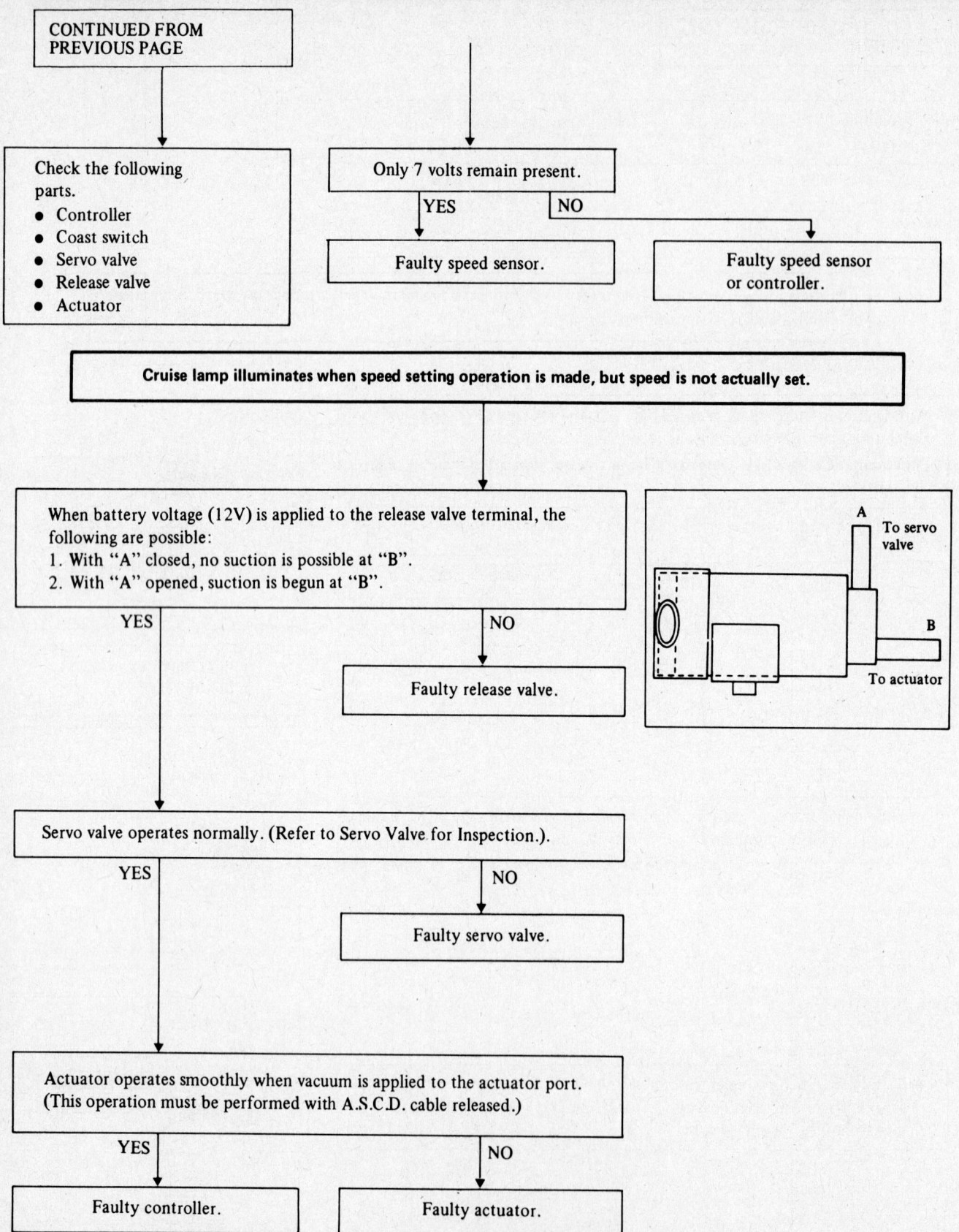

CONTINUED FROM PREVIOUS PAGE

Check the following parts.
- Controller
- Coast switch
- Servo valve
- Release valve
- Actuator

Only 7 volts remain present.

YES → Faulty speed sensor.

NO → Faulty speed sensor or controller.

Cruise lamp illuminates when speed setting operation is made, but speed is not actually set.

When battery voltage (12V) is applied to the release valve terminal, the following are possible:
1. With "A" closed, no suction is possible at "B".
2. With "A" opened, suction is begun at "B".

YES

NO → Faulty release valve.

A — To servo valve
B — To actuator

Servo valve operates normally. (Refer to Servo Valve for Inspection.).

YES

NO → Faulty servo valve.

Actuator operates smoothly when vacuum is applied to the actuator port. (This operation must be performed with A.S.C.D. cable released.)

YES → Faulty controller.

NO → Faulty actuator.

Cruise control trouble diagnosis chart – 1983–84 Stanza and 1985 Stanza with type one system

Condition	Probable cause	Corrective action
Set speed is cancelled.	• Bent meter cable (excessive meter needle deflection.). • Faulty controller.	• Check and repair meter cable, or renew cable. • Renew.
Pulsation of set speed.	• Excessive play or binding of A.S.C.D. cable. • Leakage or clogging in vacuum hose. • Binding in actuator. • Faulty servo valve. • Faulty controller.	• Adjust. • Check and repair piping route, or renew hose. • Renew actuator. • Renew servo valve. • Renew controller.
Excessive setting error.	• Excessive play or binding in A.S.C.D. cable. • Leakage or clogging in vacuum hose. • Faulty actuator. • Faulty servo valve. • Faulty controller. • Faulty speed sensor.	• Readjust. • Check and repair piping route, or renew hose. • Renew actuator. • Renew servo valve. • Renew controller. • Renew speed sensor.
Speed drops immediately after setting.	• Excessive play in A.S.C.D. cable. • Leakage or clogging in vacuum hose. • Faulty release valve. • Faulty servo valve. • Faulty controller.	• Readjust. • Check and repair piping route, or renew hose. • Renew release valve. • Renew servo valve. • Renew controller.
Cancel circuit inoperative.	• Faulty controller.	• Renew controller.

Cruise control trouble diagnosis chart — Stanza

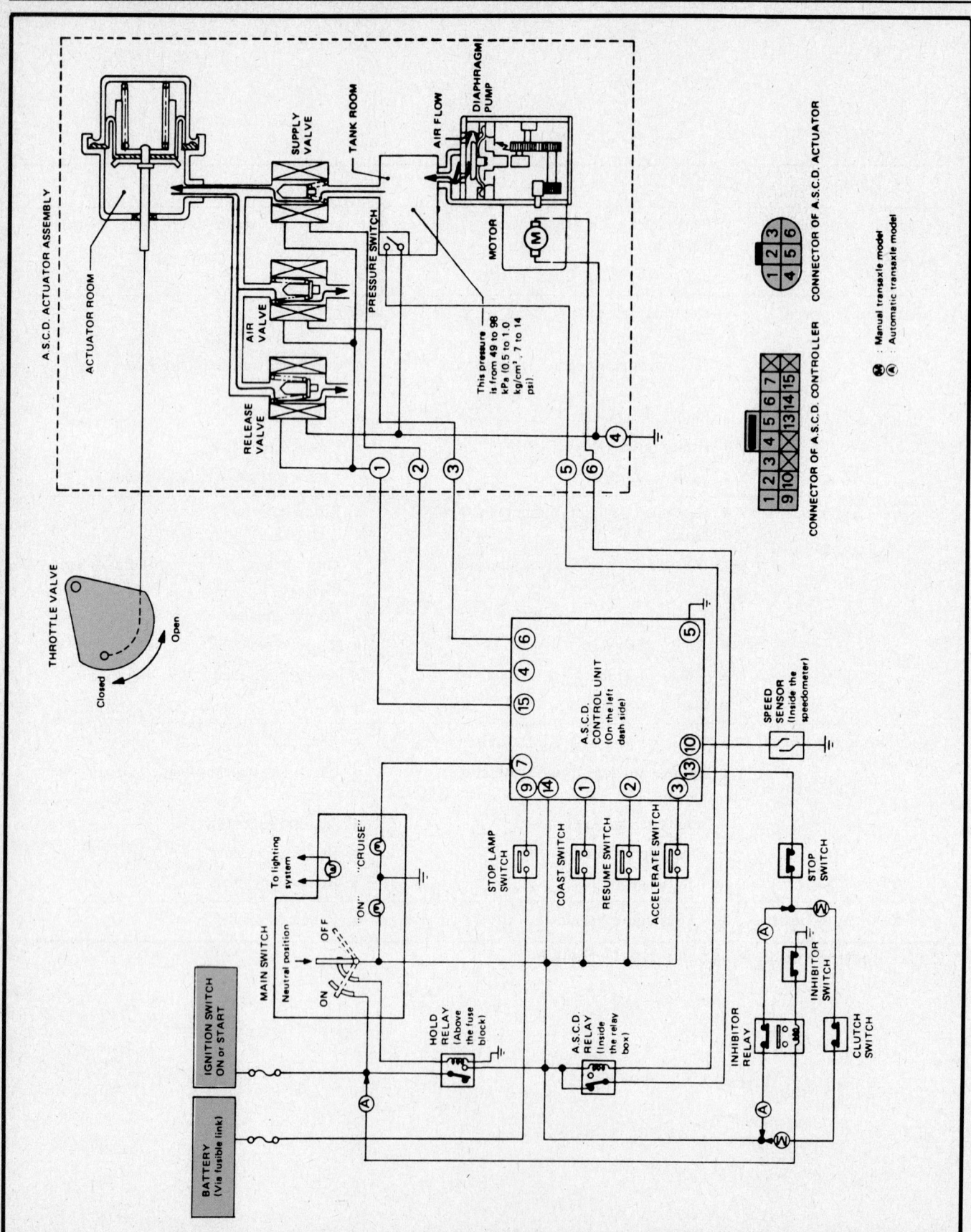

Cruise control vacuum schematic—1986 and later Stanza except station wagon and 1985 Stanza with type two system

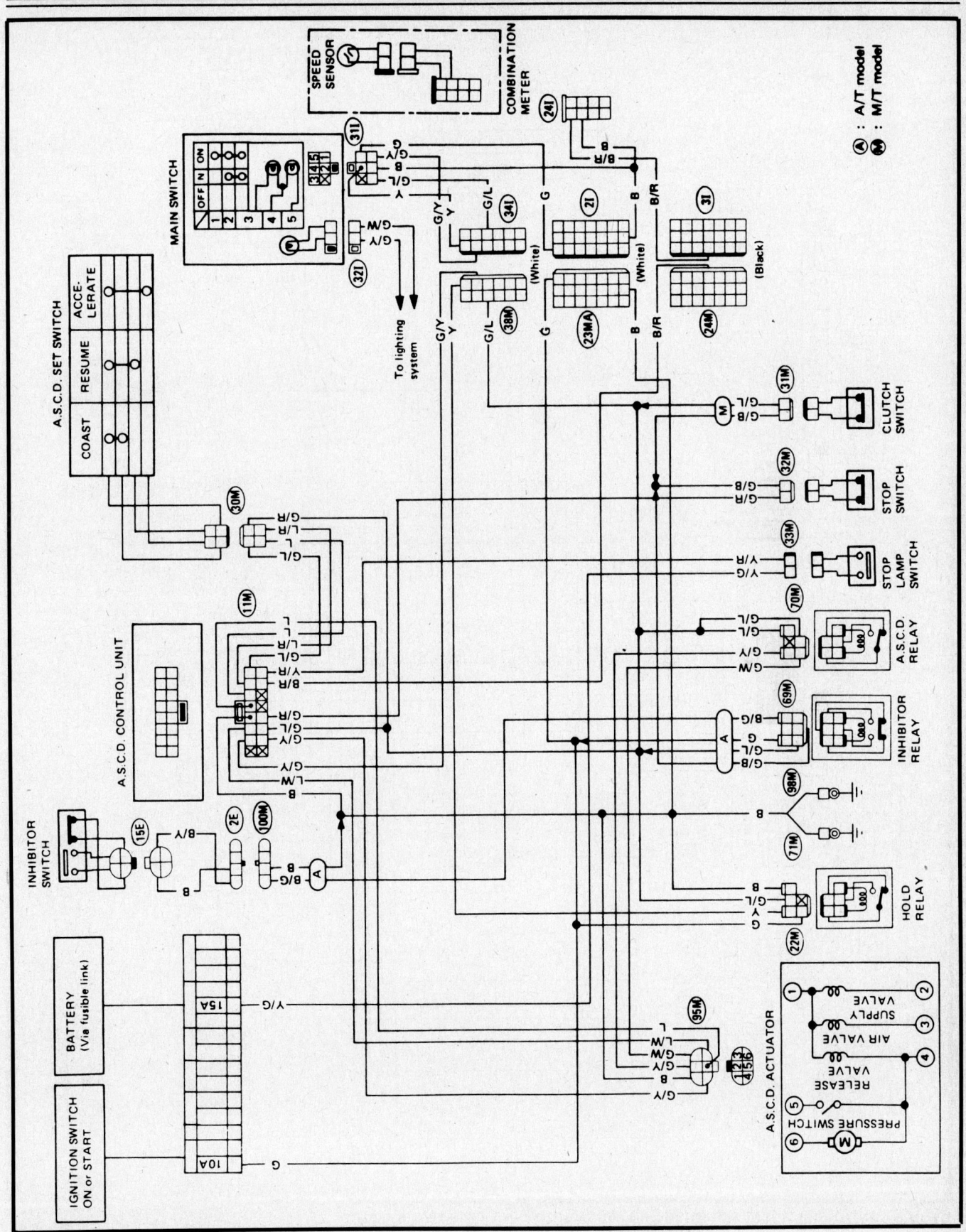

Cruise control electrical schematic—1986 and later Stanza except station wagon

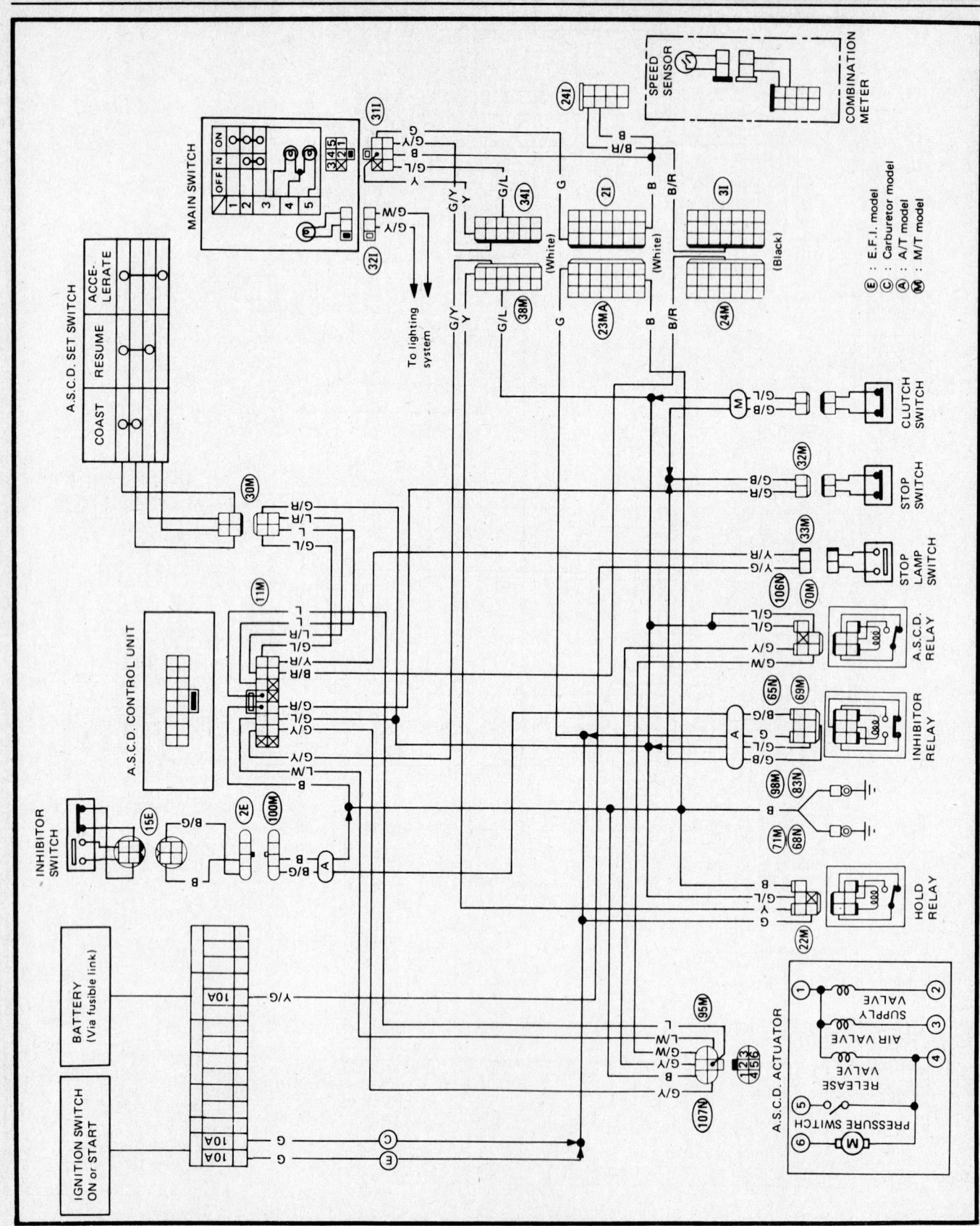

Cruise control electrical schematic—1985 Stanza with type two system

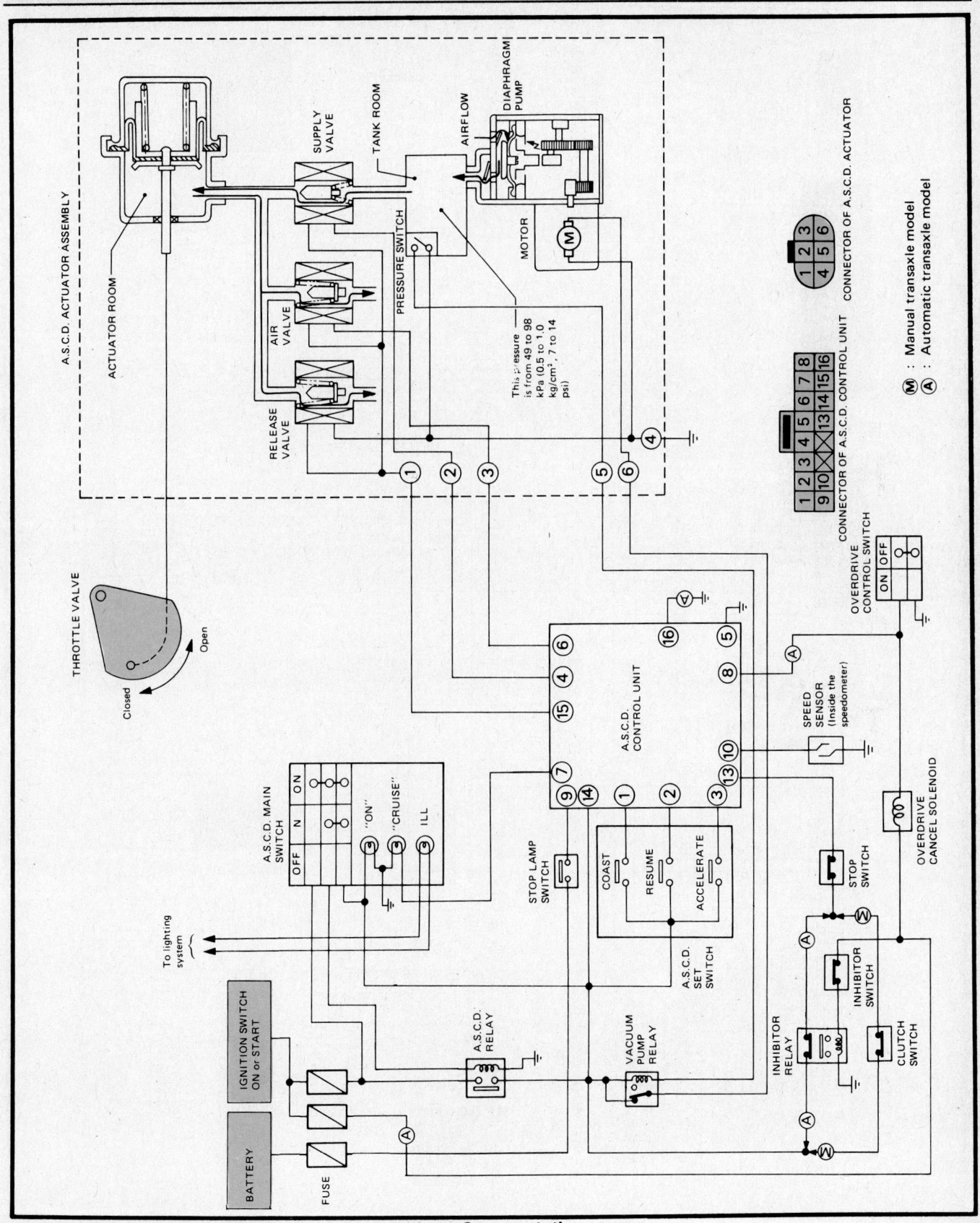

Cruise control vacuum schematict – 1986 and later Stanza station wagon

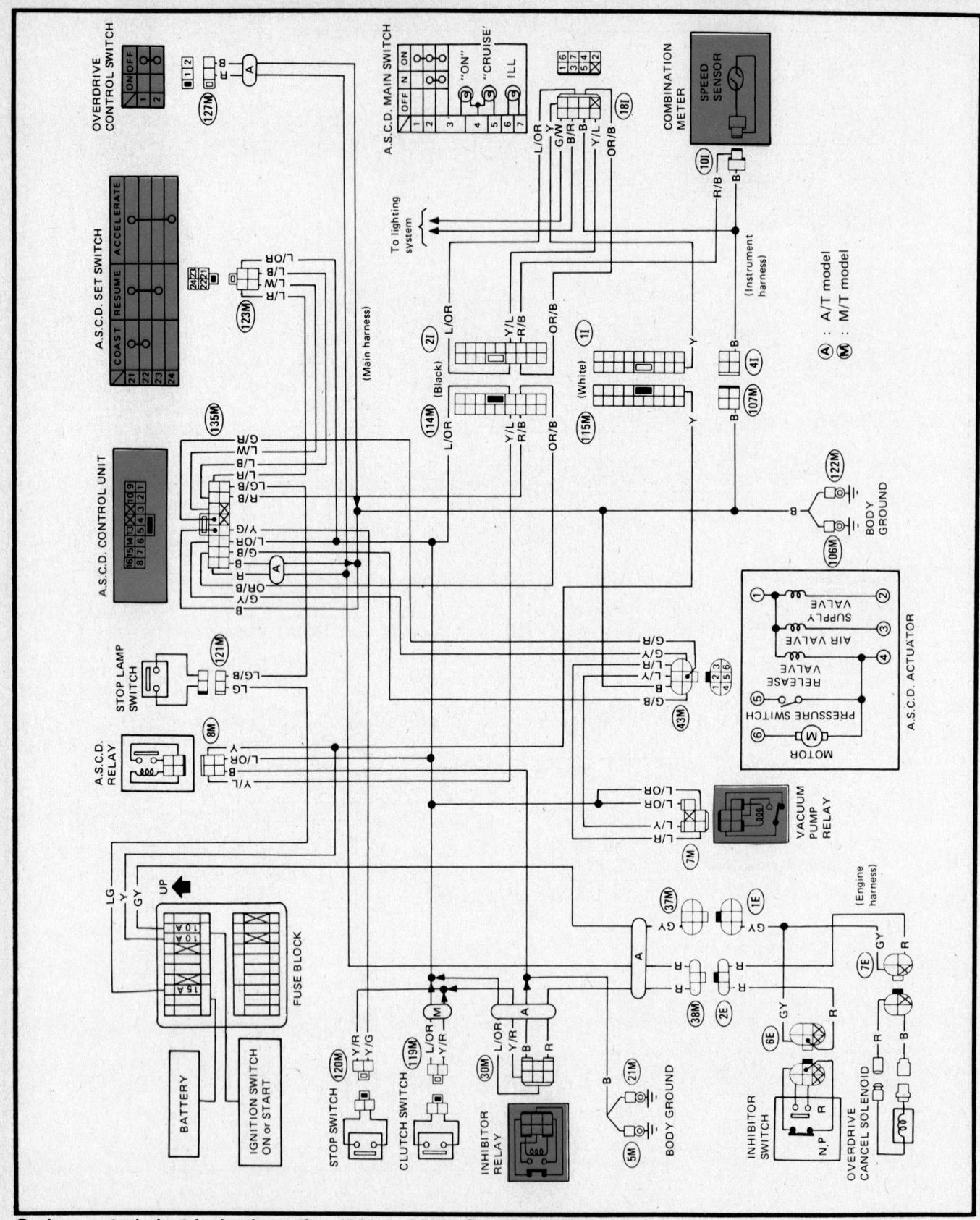

Cruise control electrical schematic—1986 and later Stanza station wagon

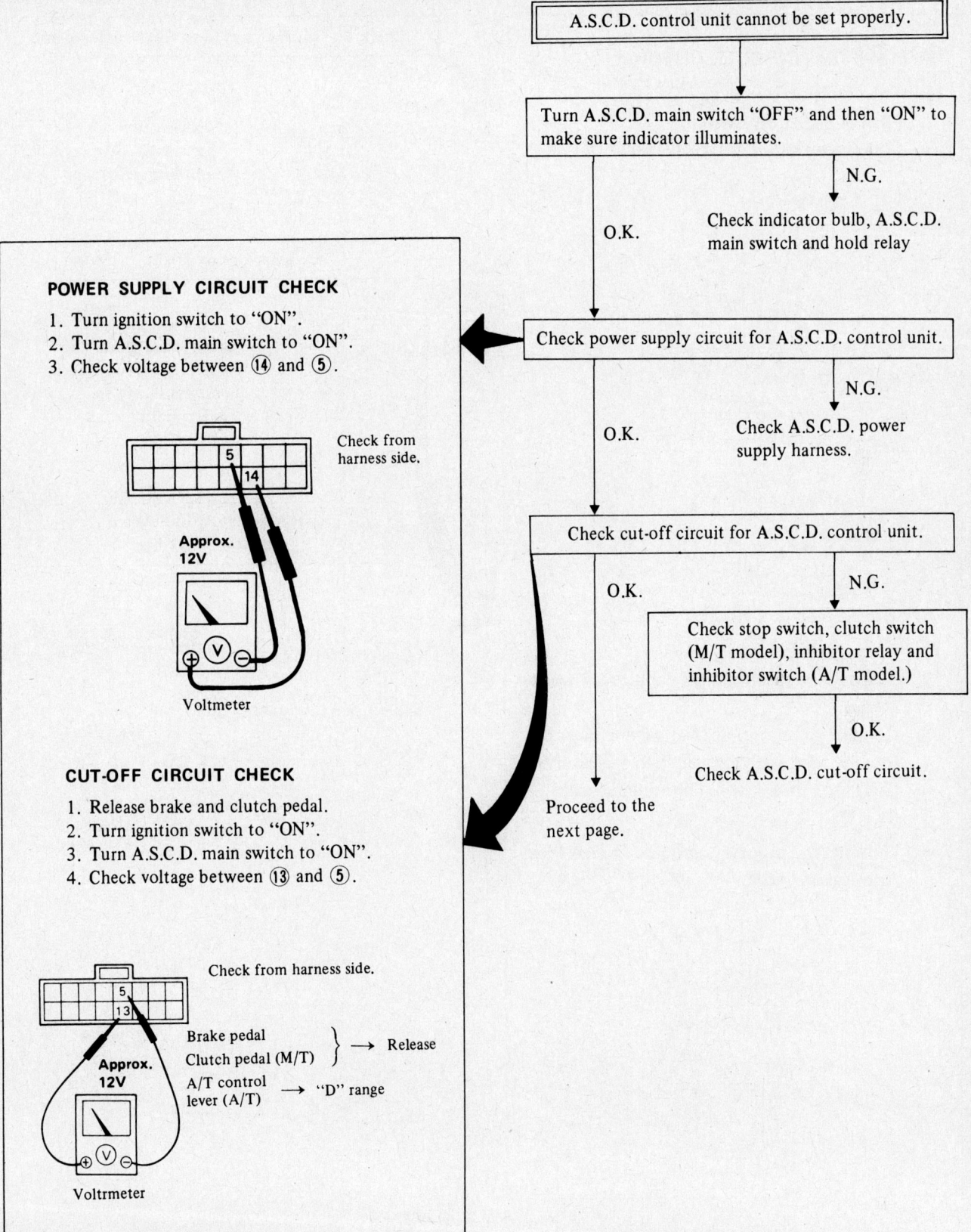

Cruise control trouble diagnosis chart—1986 and later Stanza and 1985 Stanza with type two system

SET SWITCH CIRCUIT CHECK

1. Turn ignition switch to "OFF".
2. Push A.S.C.D. set switch.
3. Check continuity between ⑭ and ①.

Check from harness side.

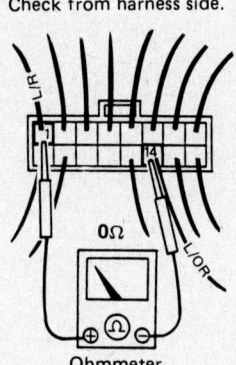

Ohmmeter

SPEED SENSOR CIRCUIT CHECK

1. Turn ignition switch to "OFF".
2. Disconnect speedometer cable from transmission.
3. Connect an ohmmeter between ⑩ and ⑤.
4. Slowly turn speedometer cable pinion by hand to make sure ohmmeter pointer deflects.

- **Ohmmeter pointer deflects twice per rotation of pinion.**

Check from harness side

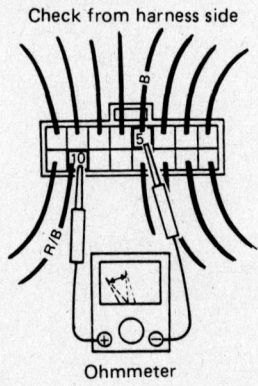

Ohmmeter

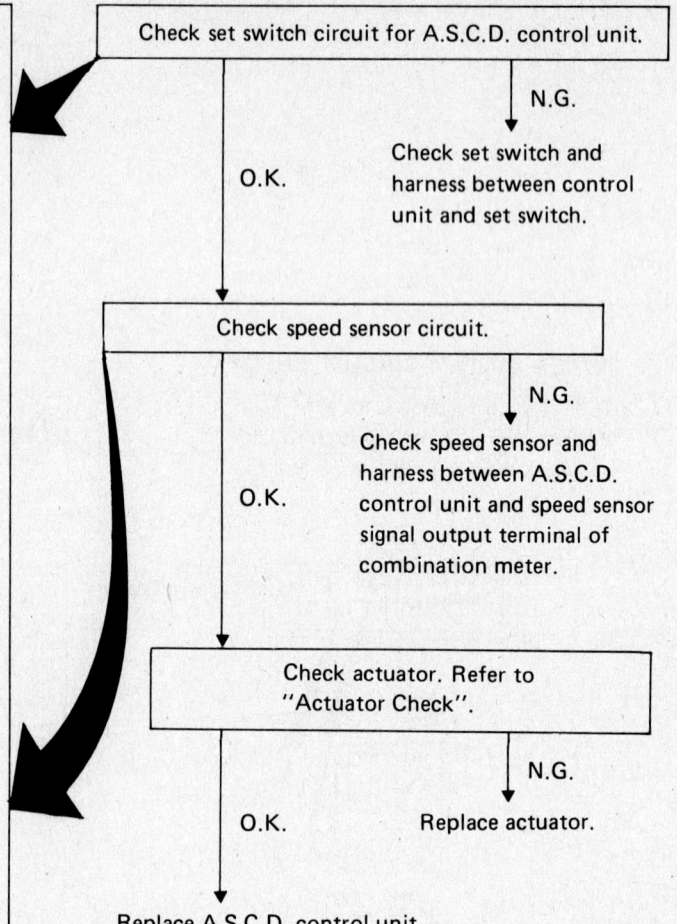

Check set switch circuit for A.S.C.D. control unit.

→ N.G. → Check set switch and harness between control unit and set switch.

O.K.

Check speed sensor circuit.

→ N.G. → Check speed sensor and harness between A.S.C.D. control unit and speed sensor signal output terminal of combination meter.

O.K.

Check actuator. Refer to "Actuator Check".

→ N.G. → Replace actuator.

O.K.

Replace A.S.C.D. control unit.

Cruise control trouble diagnosis chart — 1986 and later Stanza and 1985 Stanza with type two system

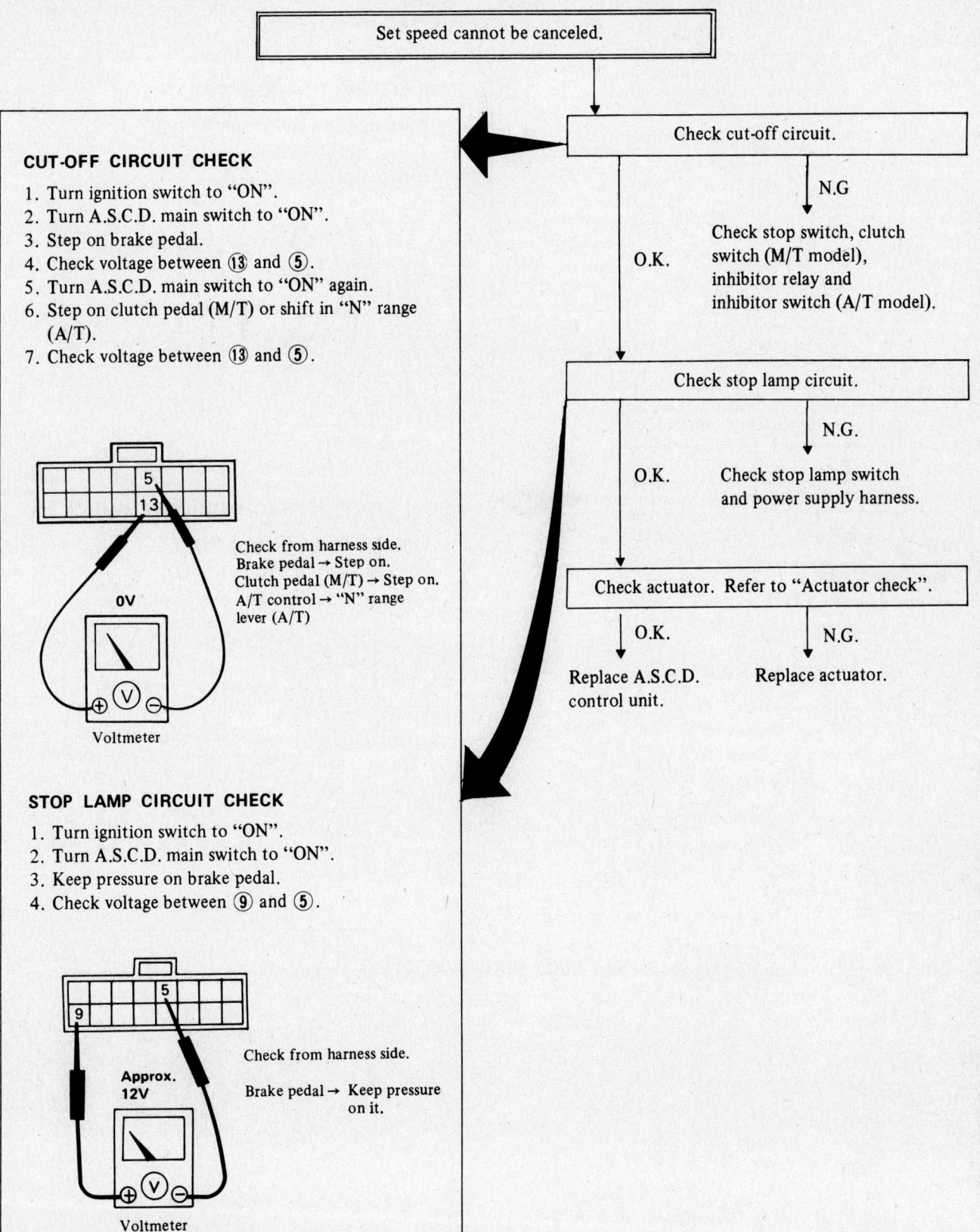

Cruise control trouble diagnosis chart – 1986 and later Stanza and 1985 Stanza with type two system

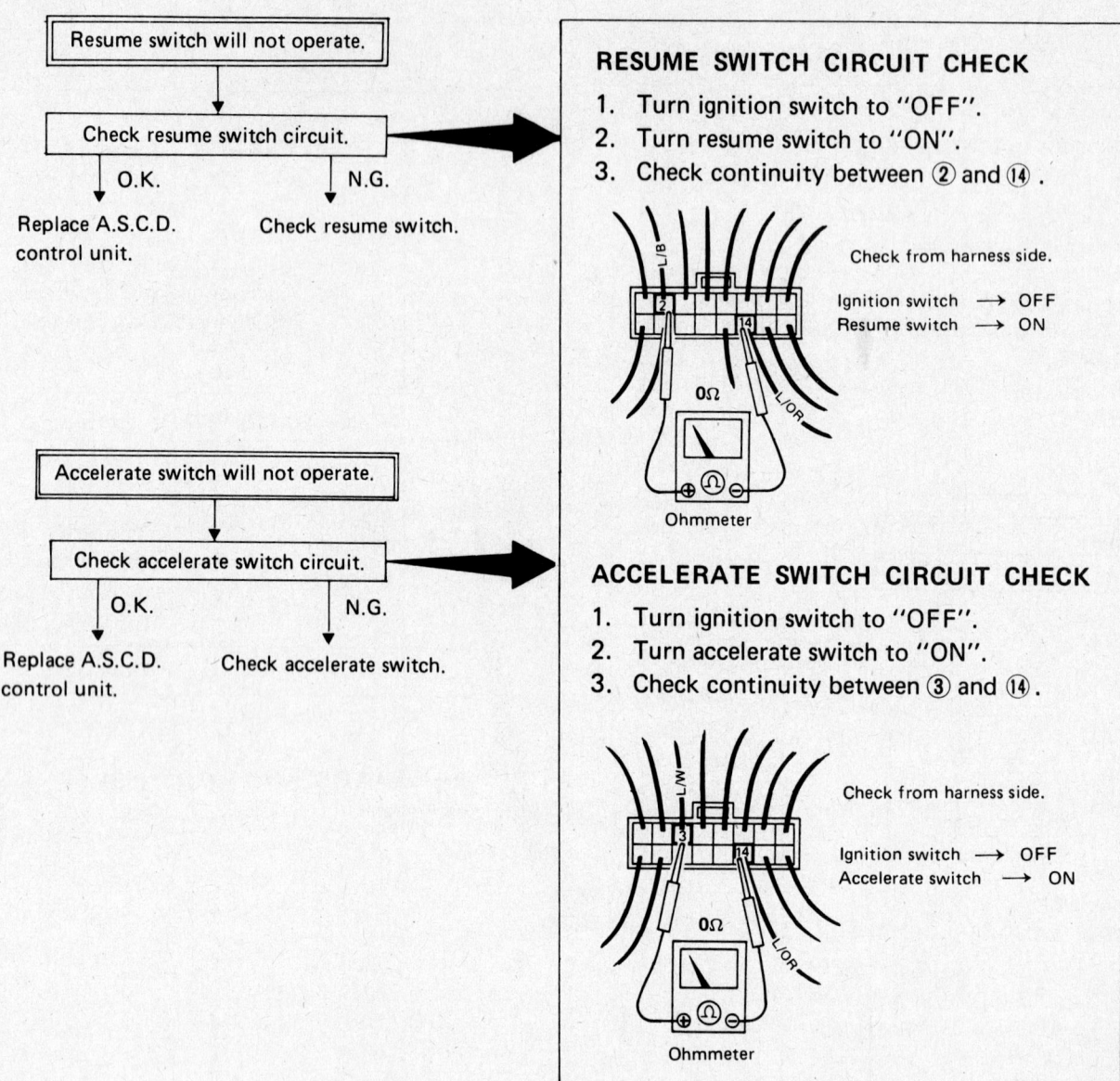

Resume switch will not operate.

↓

Check resume switch circuit.

O.K. → Replace A.S.C.D. control unit.

N.G. → Check resume switch.

RESUME SWITCH CIRCUIT CHECK

1. Turn ignition switch to "OFF".
2. Turn resume switch to "ON".
3. Check continuity between ② and ⑭.

Check from harness side.

Ignition switch ⟶ OFF
Resume switch ⟶ ON

L/B

2   14

0Ω   L/OR

Ohmmeter

Accelerate switch will not operate.

↓

Check accelerate switch circuit.

O.K. → Replace A.S.C.D. control unit.

N.G. → Check accelerate switch.

ACCELERATE SWITCH CIRCUIT CHECK

1. Turn ignition switch to "OFF".
2. Turn accelerate switch to "ON".
3. Check continuity between ③ and ⑭.

Check from harness side.

Ignition switch ⟶ OFF
Accelerate switch ⟶ ON

L/W

3   14

0Ω   L/OR

Ohmmeter

Cruise control trouble diagnosis chart — 1986 and later Stanza and 1985 Stanza with type two system

ACTUATOR CHECK

1. Disconnect the connector of actuator from main harness.
2. Check actuator operations as shown below.

A.S.C.D. actuator assembly

1 2 3
4 5 6

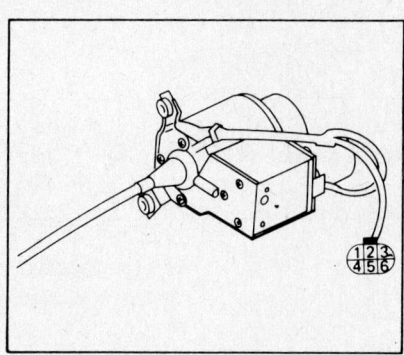

Check actuator.

↓

Check to see if motor starts when 12V D.C. is applied across ⑥ and ④.

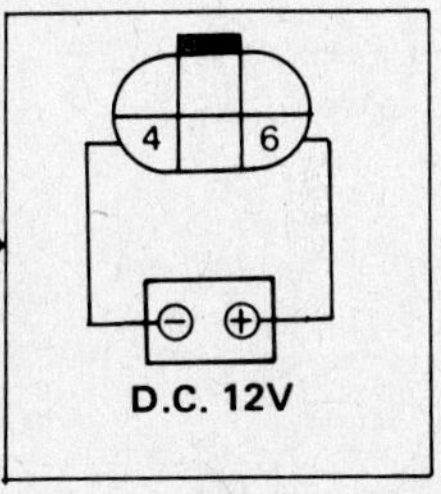

4
6
D.C. 12V

N.G. → Replace actuator.

O.K. ↓

Measure resistance between ④ and ⑤.
Proper reading: 0Ω

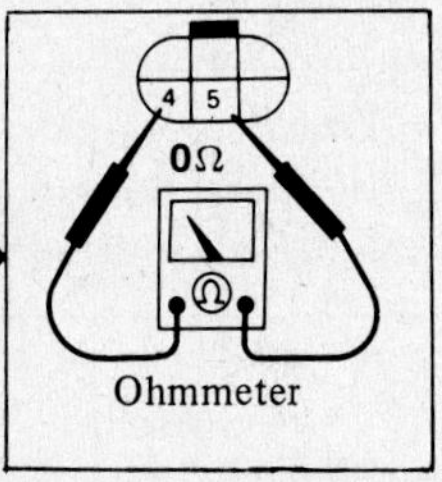

4 5
0Ω
Ohmmeter

O.K. ↓

Apply 12V D.C. across ① and ② and measure resistance between ④ and ⑤.
Proper reading: ∞ Ω

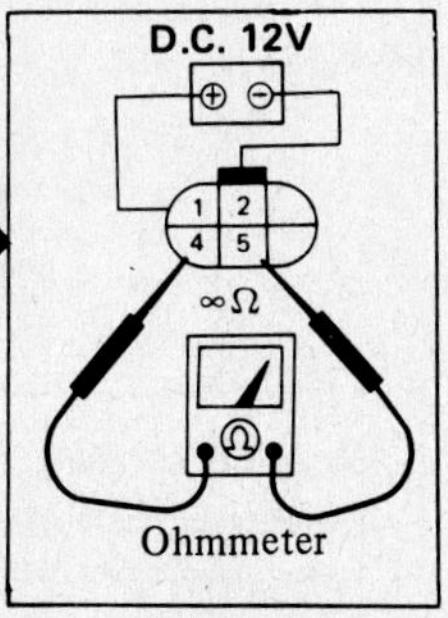

D.C. 12V
1 2
4 5
∞Ω
Ohmmeter

N.G. → Replace actuator.

O.K. ↓

Apply 12V D.C. across ⑥ and ④ to start motor. Measure resistance between ④ and ⑤ after motor has operated for approx. 30 seconds.
Proper reading: 0Ω

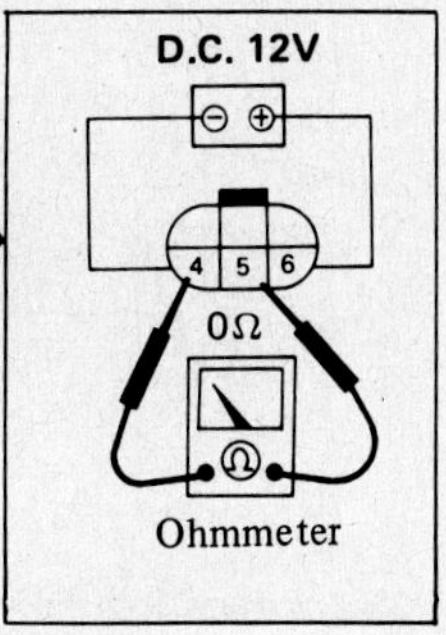

D.C. 12V
4 5 6
0Ω
Ohmmeter

N.G. → Replace actuator

O.K. ↓ Ⓐ

Cruise control trouble diagnosis chart—1986 and later Stanza and 1985 Stanza with type two system

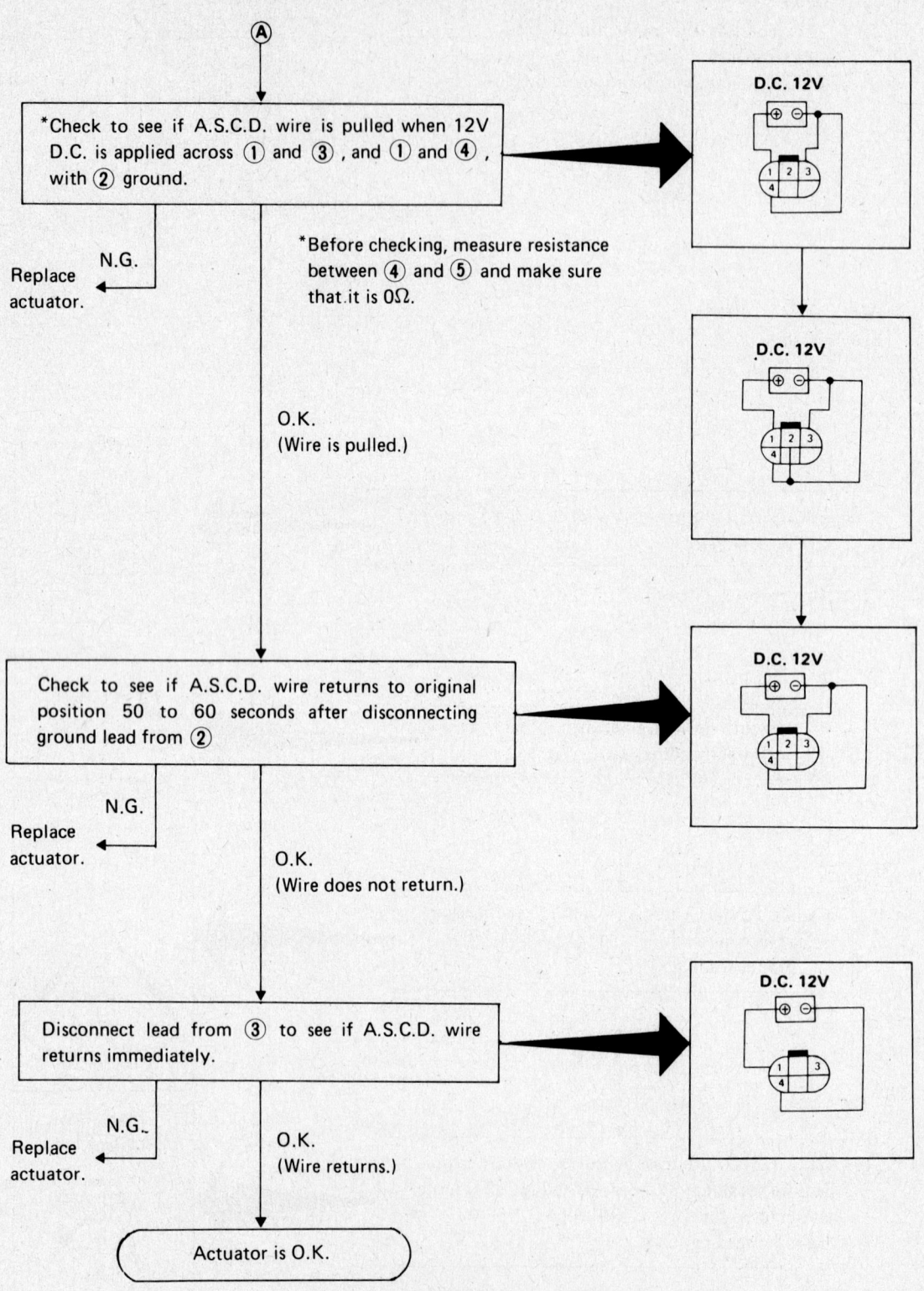

Cruise control trouble diagnosis chart – 1986 and later Stanza and 1985 Stanza with type two system

Component Replacement

ACTUATOR CABLE (1983–84 AND 1985 WITH TYPE ONE SYSTEM)

Removal and Installation

1. Disconnect the actuator cable from the actuator assembly.
2. Loosen the locknut at the actuator.
3. Remove the rubber boots.
4. Loosen the adjusting nuts at the shaft and drum assembly.
5. Remove the cable from the actuator.
6. Installation is the reverse of the removal procedure. Adjust the cable as required.

ACTUATOR (1983–84 AND 1985 WITH TYPE ONE SYSTEM)

Removal and Installation

1. Disconnect the negative battery cable.
2. Disconnect the cable from the actuator assembly.
3. Disconnect the vacuum hose. Disconnect the electrical connector.
4. Remove the actuator retaining bolt.
5. Remove the actuator from the vehicle.
6. Installation is the reverse of the removal procedure.

200SX

VISUAL INSPECTION

Before performing any tests make a visual inspection of the cruise control system. Check all items in the system for abnormal conditions such as bare broken or disconnected wires and damage to the vacuum hoses. Be sure that the speedometer cables are attached and properly routed. All vacuum hoses must be properly routed and must not have any kinks or bends. Be sure that all electrical connections are complete and tight. The wiring harness must be routed properly.

ACTUATOR TEST (1982–83)

1. Visually inspect the actuator for damage or deformation.
2. Make sure that the assembly moves freely without binding when the diaphragm is pushed by hand.
3. Apply vacuum to the actuator, using a hand vacuum pump. Do not use engine vacuum. The diaphragm should move to the full up position.
4. Plug the hose with vacuum applied, the actuator should remain in the full position.
5. Repair or replace defective components as required.

SERVO VALVE TEST (1982–83)

1. Measure the resistance between the terminals. It should be 25 to 30 ohms.
2. Be sure that the valve opens and closes by blowing air through the port on the actuator side of the assembly.
3. Repair or replace defective components as required.

SOLENOID VALVE TEST (1982–83)

1. Measure the resistance between the terminals. It should be 25 to 30 ohms.
2. Check to be sure that the vacuum valve is performing properly.

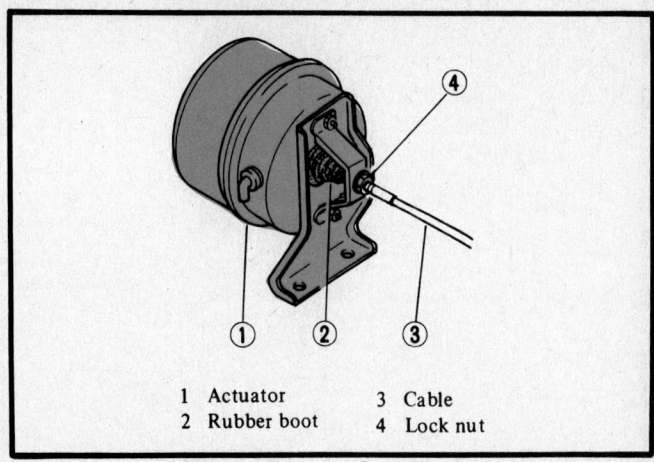

1 Actuator   3 Cable
2 Rubber boot   4 Lock nut

Actuator assembly—1983–84 Stanza and 1985 Stanza with type one system

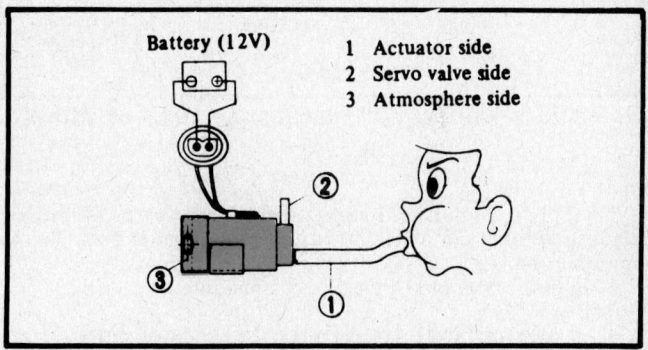

Battery (12V)   1 Actuator side
2 Servo valve side
3 Atmosphere side

Servo valve test point locations—1982–83 200SX

Check ports	Air flow
① - ②	Yes
① - ③	No
② - ③	

Servo valve test results—1982–83 200SX

Check ports	Air flow
① - ②	
① - ③	Yes
② - ③	

Servo valve test results—1982–83 200SX

3. Disconnect the solenoid valve side vacuum hose at the servo valve. Connect a vacuum gauge.
4. Start the engine and allow it to reach operating temperature or until the water temperature indicator points to the middle of the gauge.

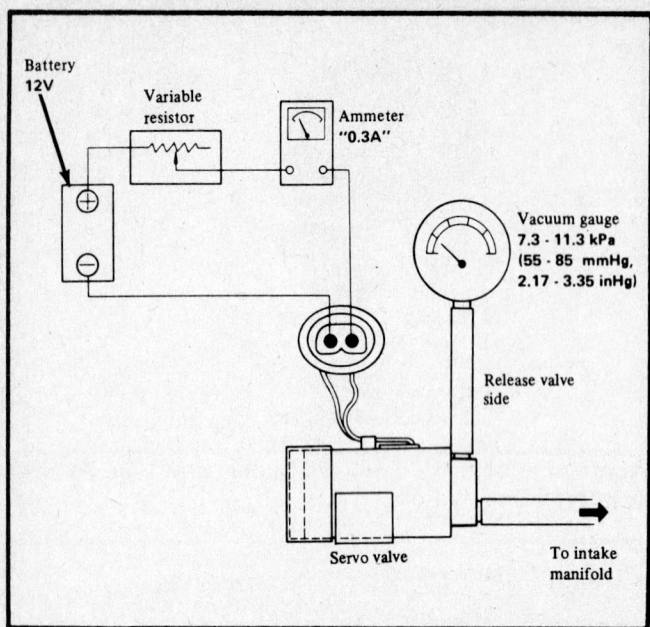

Solenoid valve test point locations – 1982–83 200SX

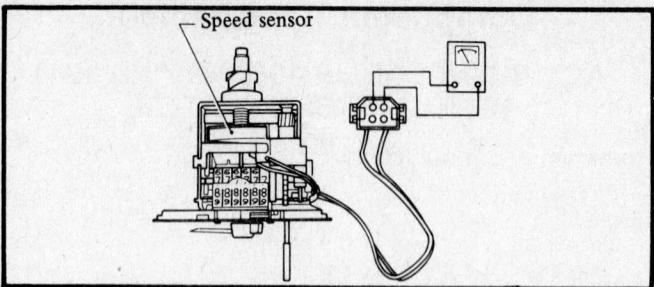

Speed sensor test point locations – 1982–83 200SX

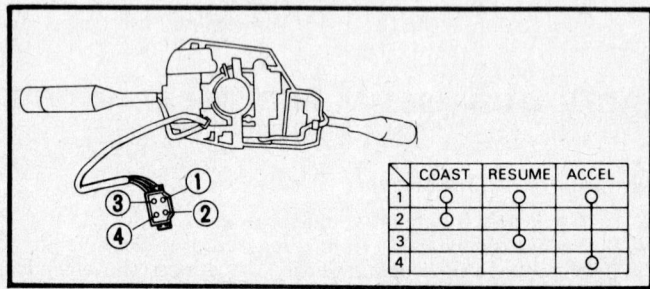

Control switch test point locations – 1982–83 200SX

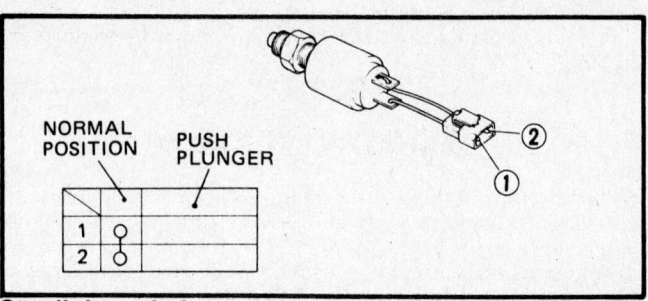

Stoplight switch test point locations – 1982–83 200SX

5. Apply 0.3 amps of direct current between the terminals using a 20 ohm 5W variable resistor to adjust the current to specification.

6. Repair or replace defective components as required.

SPEED SENSOR TEST (1982–83)

The speed sensor is built into the rear of the speedometer. Inspection of the speed sensor must be made with the speed sensor installed in the speedometer assembly. Turn the speedometer slowly by hand two complete turns. If continuity exists than the sensor is good.

MAIN SWITCH TEST (1982–83)

1. Test the continuity of the main switch assembly using and ohmmeter.

2. Repair or replace defective components as required.

CONTROL SWITCH TEST (1982–83)

1. Test the continuity of the main switch assembly using and ohmmeter.

2. Repair or replace defective components as required.

STOP LIGHT SWITCH TEST (1982–83)

1. Test the continunity of the main switch assembly using and ohmmeter.

2. Repair or replace defective components as required.

Switch position Check terminal	Normal	ON	OFF
① - ②	No	Yes	No
① - ⑥	No	Yes	No
② - ⑥	Yes	Yes	No
③ - ④	Yes	–	–
⑤ - ⑦	Yes	–	–
⑥ - ⑦	Yes	–	–

Yes: Continuity should exist.
No: Continuity should not exist.

Main switch specifications – 1982–83 200SX

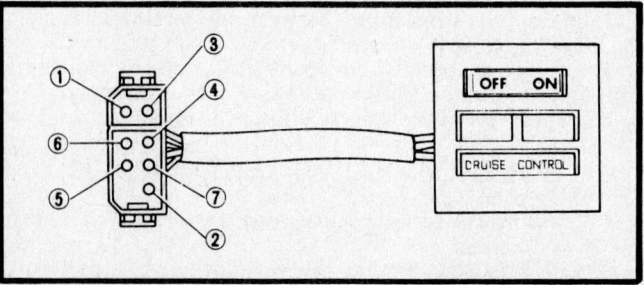

Main switch test point locations – 1982–83 200SX

ASCD RELAY TEST (1982–83)

The ASCD relay is located on the left relay bracket. Using an ohmmeter check the component for the proper continuity.

ASCD INHIBITOR RELAY TEST (1982–83)

The ASCD inhibitor relay is located on the relay bracket. Using an ohmmeter check the component for the proper continuity.

ASCD CONTROLLER TEST (1982–83)

The ASCD controller is located on the left side of the dash panel. This component must be checked as a single part. When checking this component do not touch the test probe to any terminal other than the ones used to check the component as damage to the controller could result. Keep the controller away from electric noise to prevent the ASCD system from malfunctioning and the IC circuit from being destroyed.

VACUUM PUMP TEST (1984 AND LATER)

1. Disconnect the harness connector from the vacuum pump assembly.
2. Check the continunity between the terminals at the connector.
3. If continunity exists than the pump is functioning properly.

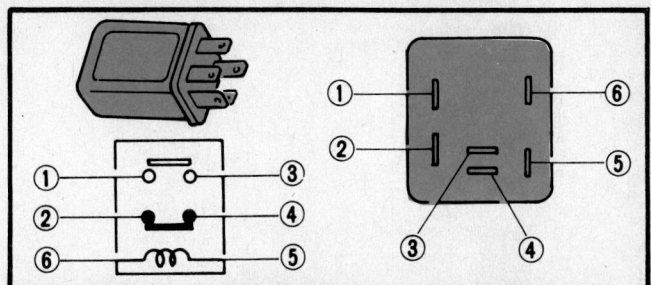

ASCD relay test point locations – 1982–83 200SX

Check terminals	Normal condition	12V direct current is applied between terminals ⑤ and ⑥
⑤ - ⑥	Yes	–
② - ④	Yes	No
① - ③	No	Yes

Yes: Continuity should exist.
No: Continuity should not exist.

ASCD relay test data – 1982–83 200SX

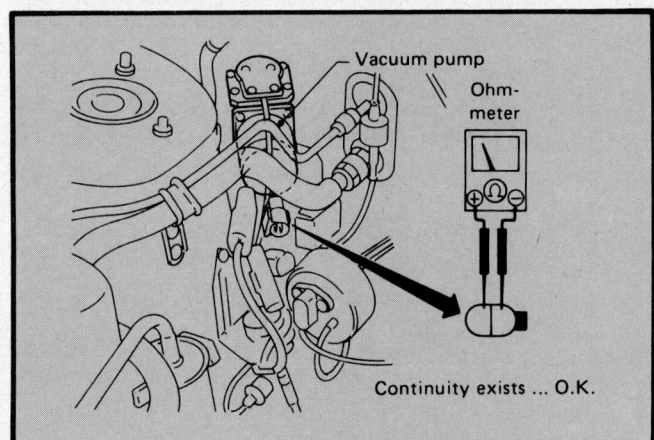

Vacuum pump test point locations – 1984 and later 200SX

VACUUM PRESSURE SWITCH TEST (1984 AND LATER)

1. Disconnect the harness connector from the vacuum tank.
2. Disconnect the vacuum hose between the vacuum pump and the vacuum tank from the vacuum pump.
3. Connect a hand vacuum pump to the vacuum hose. Check the vacuum pressure.
4. Repair or replace defective components as required.

ACTUATOR ADJUSTMENT

1982–83

1. Without depressing the accelerator, adjust the adjusting nuts until all freeplay is removed.

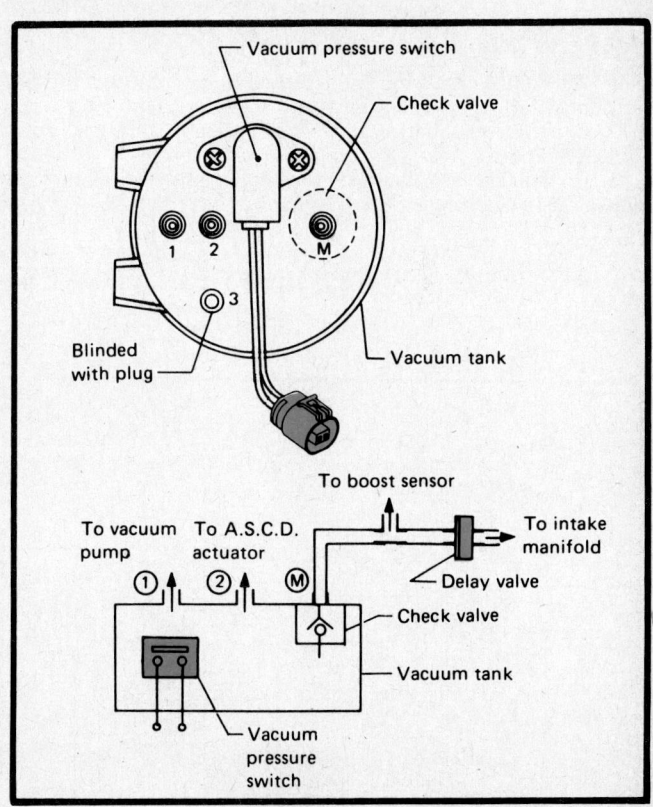

Vacuum tank and related components – 1984 and later 200SX

2. Return the adjusting nuts until 0.08 to 0.12 inch of freeplay is obtained.
3. Do not increase the cable tension excessively, as this can cause cable damage.

1035

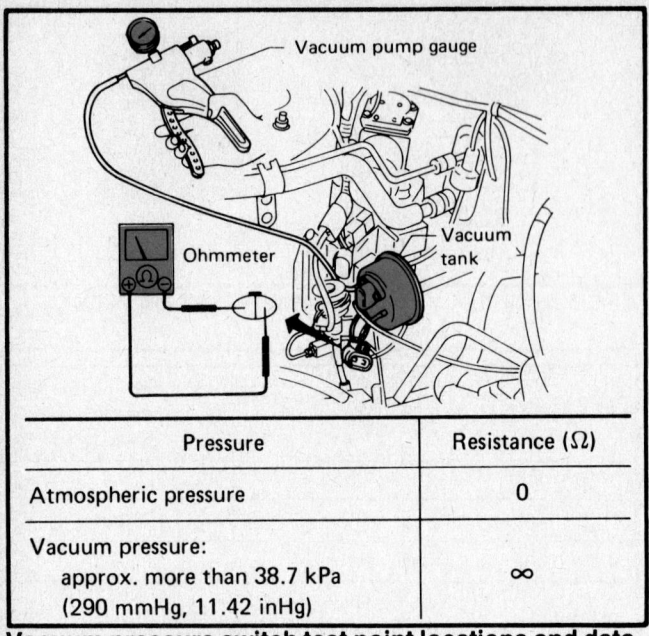

Pressure	Resistance (Ω)
Atmospheric pressure	0
Vacuum pressure: approx. more than 38.7 kPa (290 mmHg, 11.42 inHg)	∞

Vacuum pressure switch test point locations and data 1984 and later 200SX

1984 and Later

1. Without depressing the accelerator, adjust the adjusting nuts until all freeplay is removed.
2. Return the adjusting nuts ½ to 1 turn to gain the proper cable free play.
3. Do not increase the cable tension excessively, as this can cause cable damage.

DIAGNOSIS AND TESTING PROCEDURES

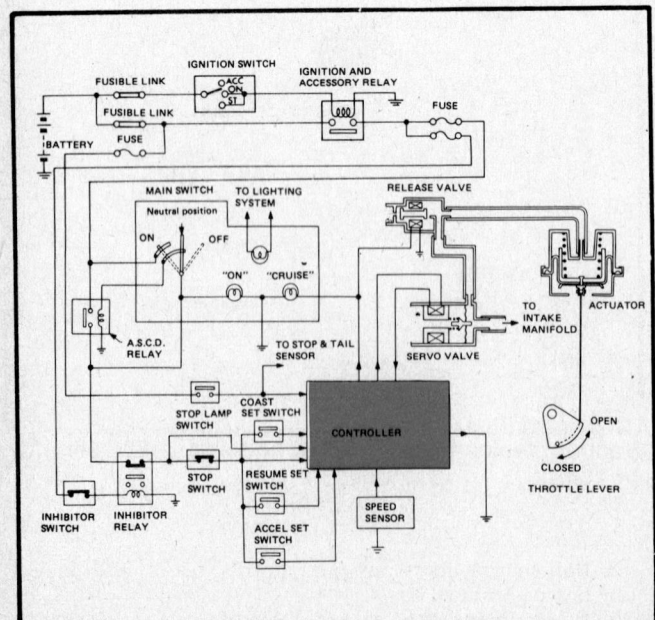

Cruise control layout – 1982–83 200SX

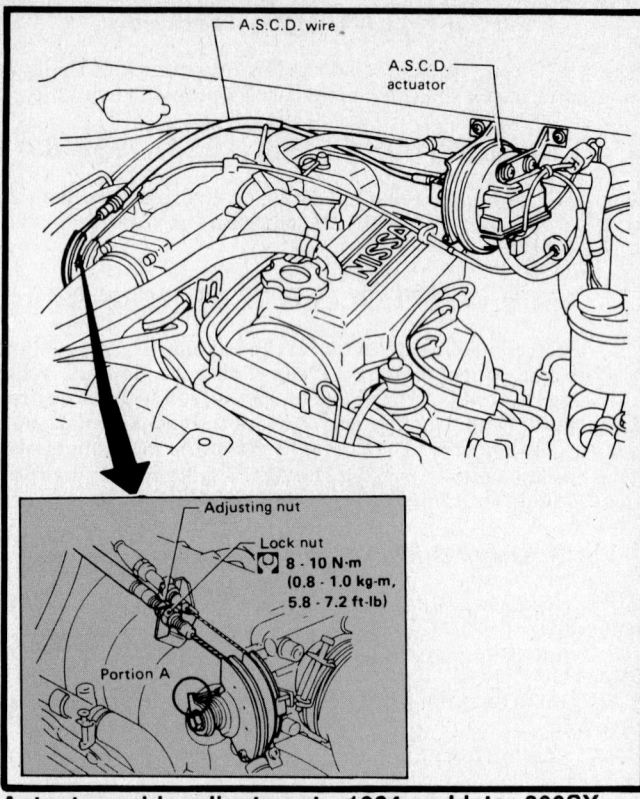

Actuator cable adjustment – 1984 and later 200SX

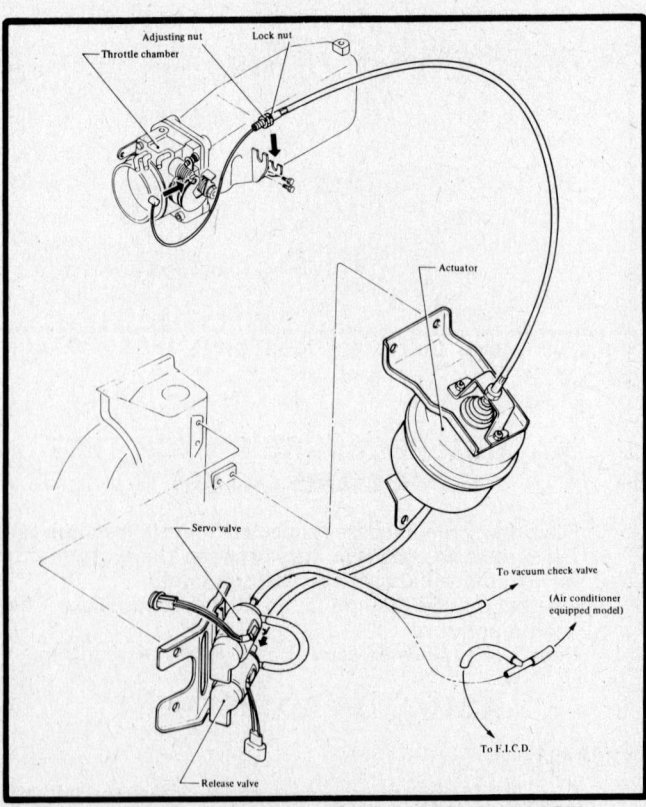

Cruise control vacuum routing – 1982–83 200SX

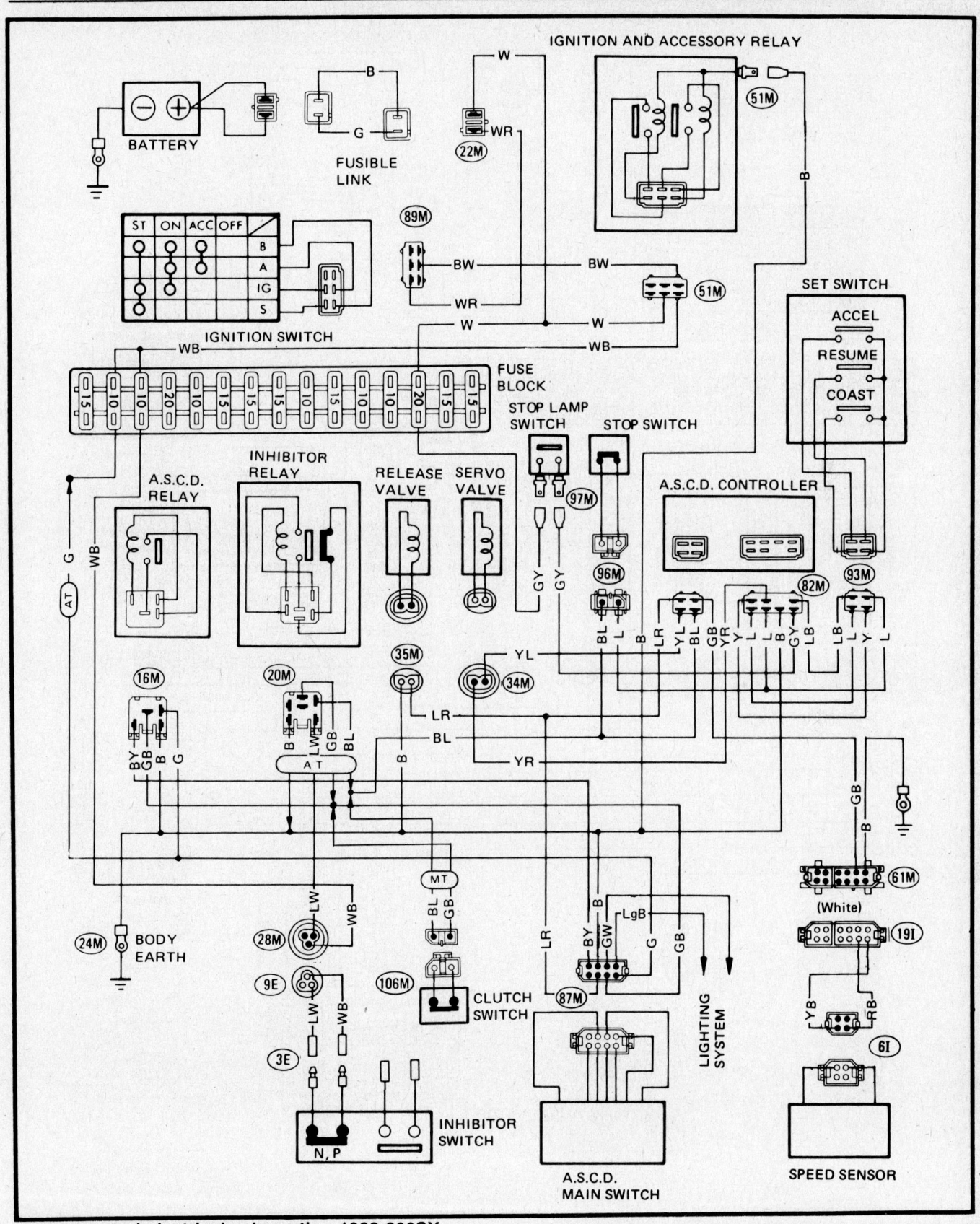

Cruise control electrical schematic – 1982 200SX

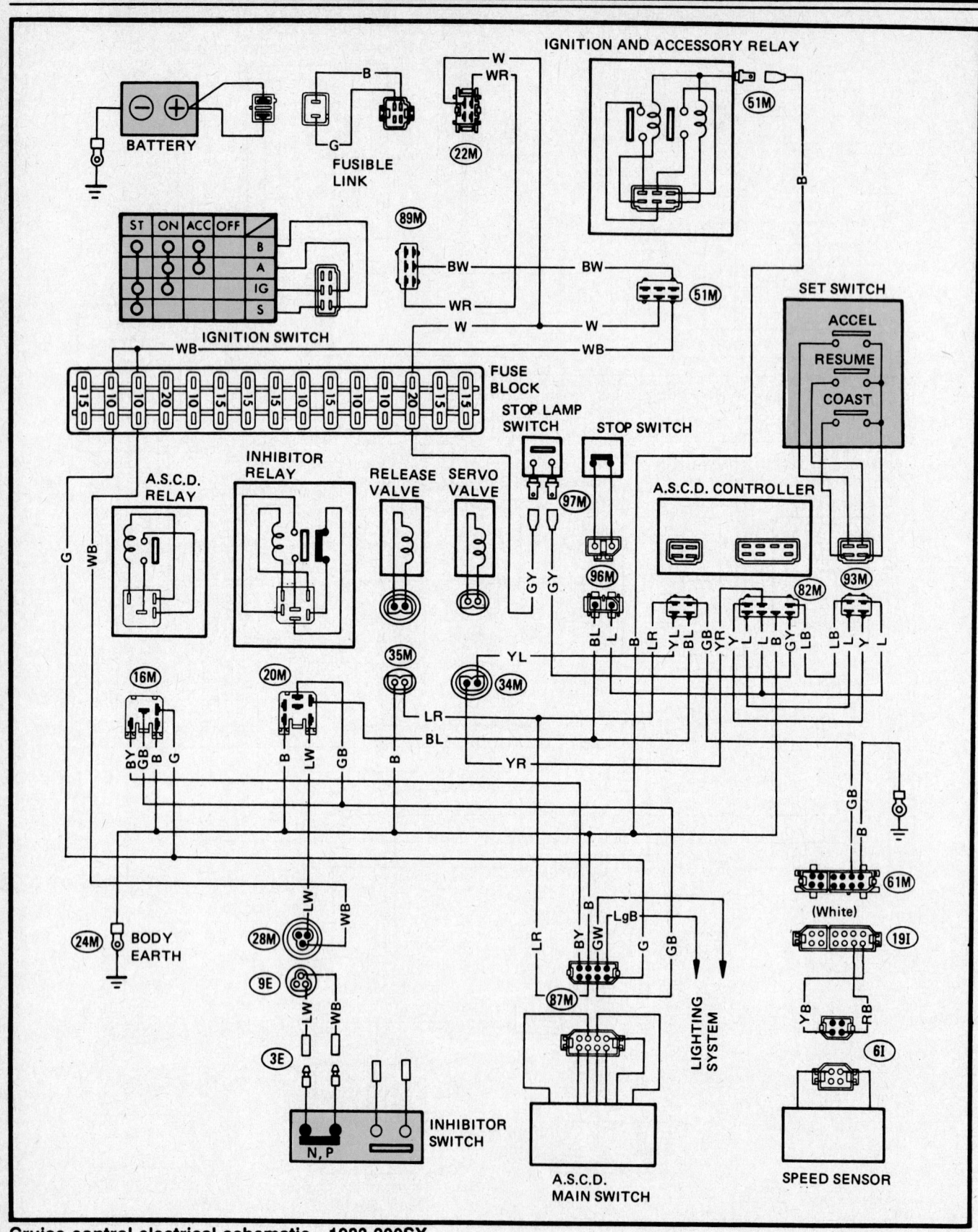

Cruise control electrical schematic — 1983 200SX

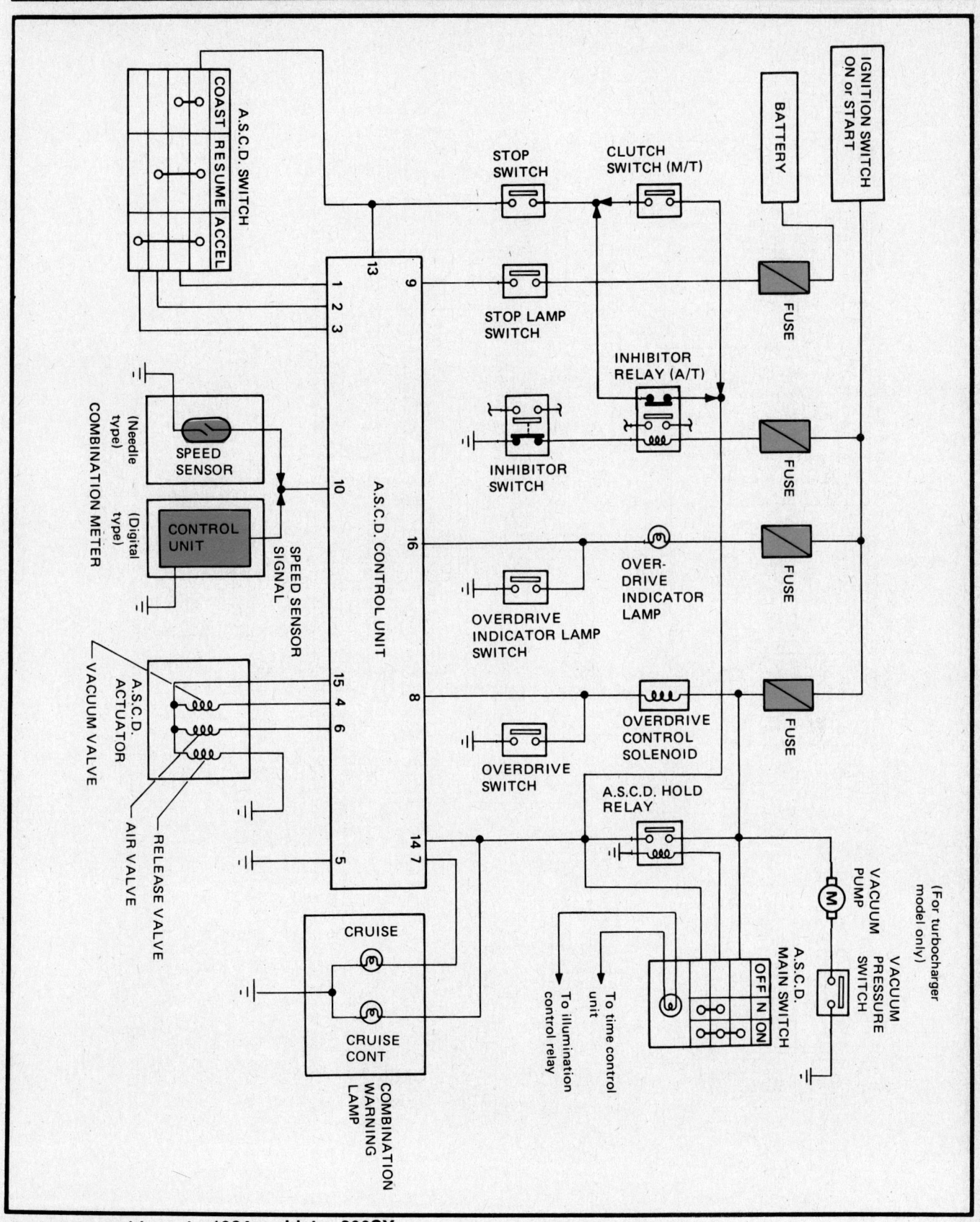

Cruise control layout—1984 and later 200SX

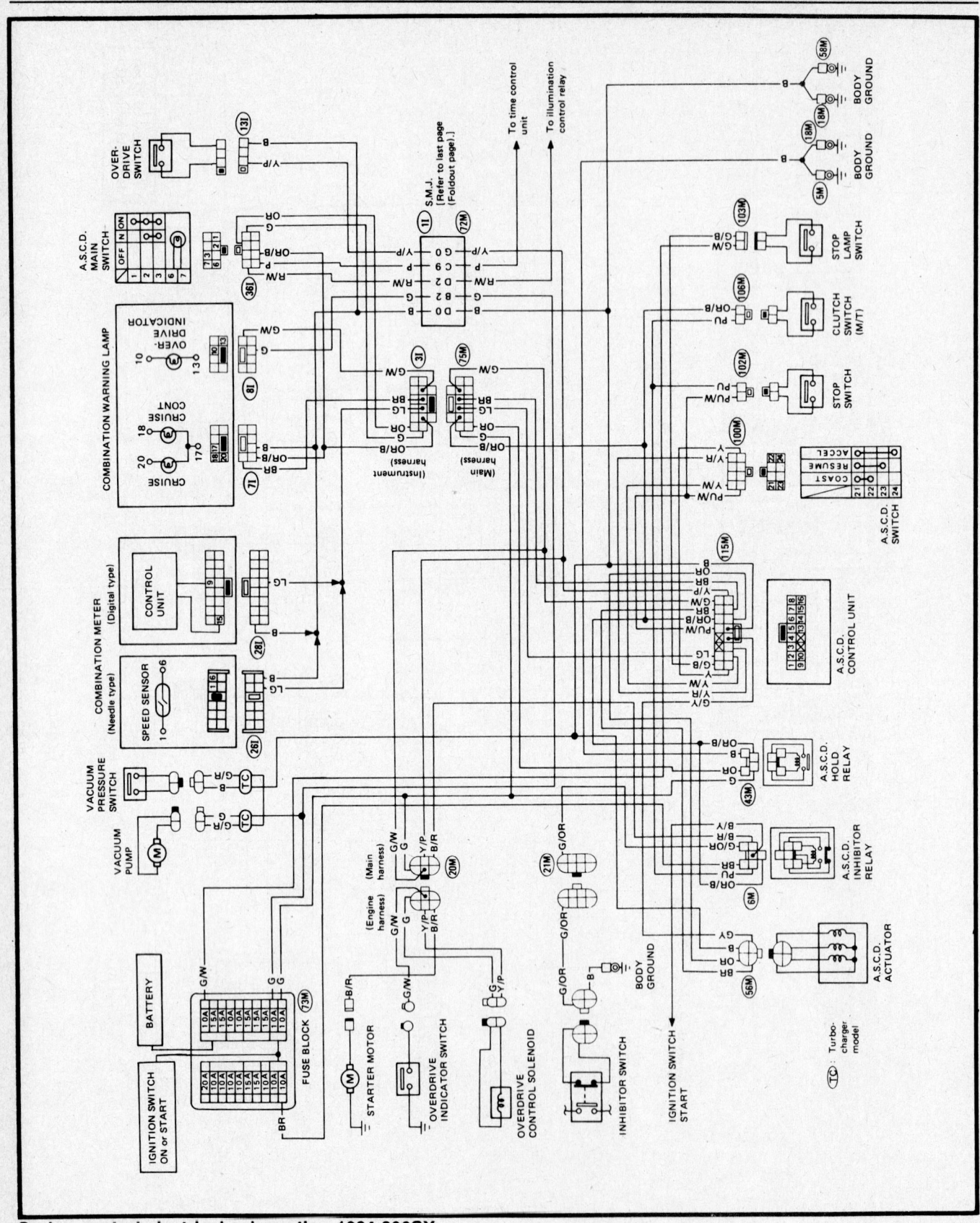

Cruise control electrical schematic — 1984 200SX

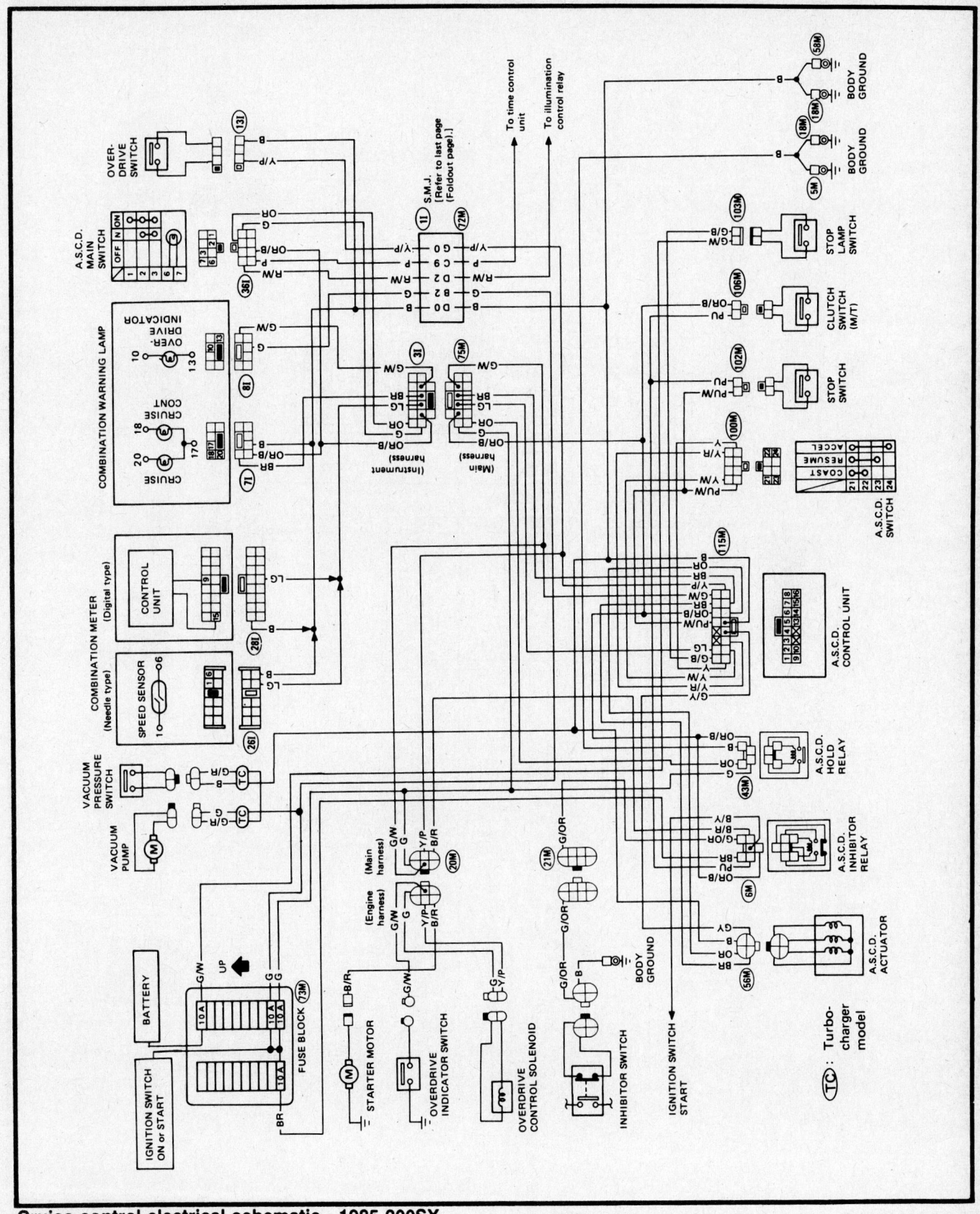

Cruise control electrical schematic – 1985 200SX

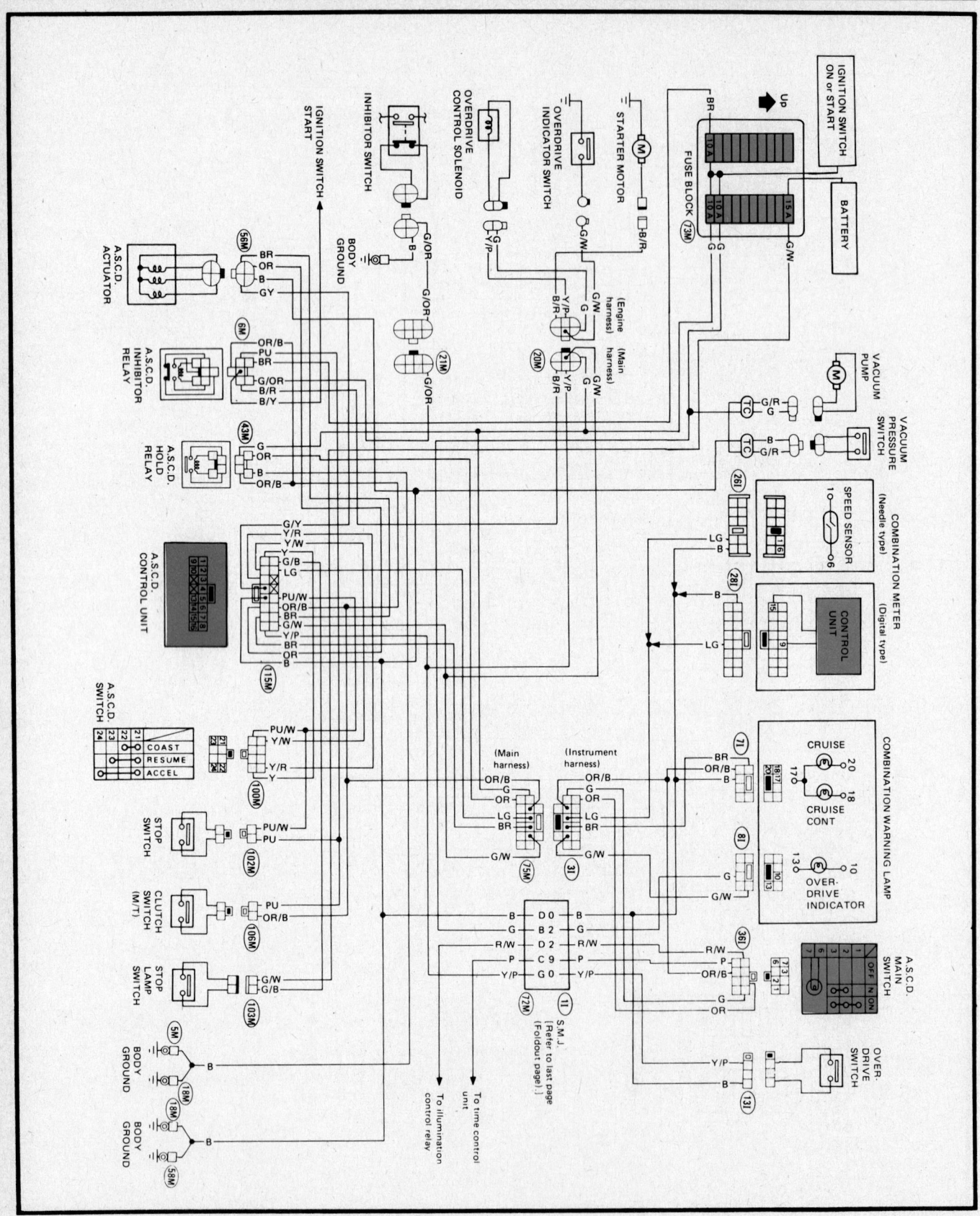

Cruise control electrical schematic – 1986 200SX

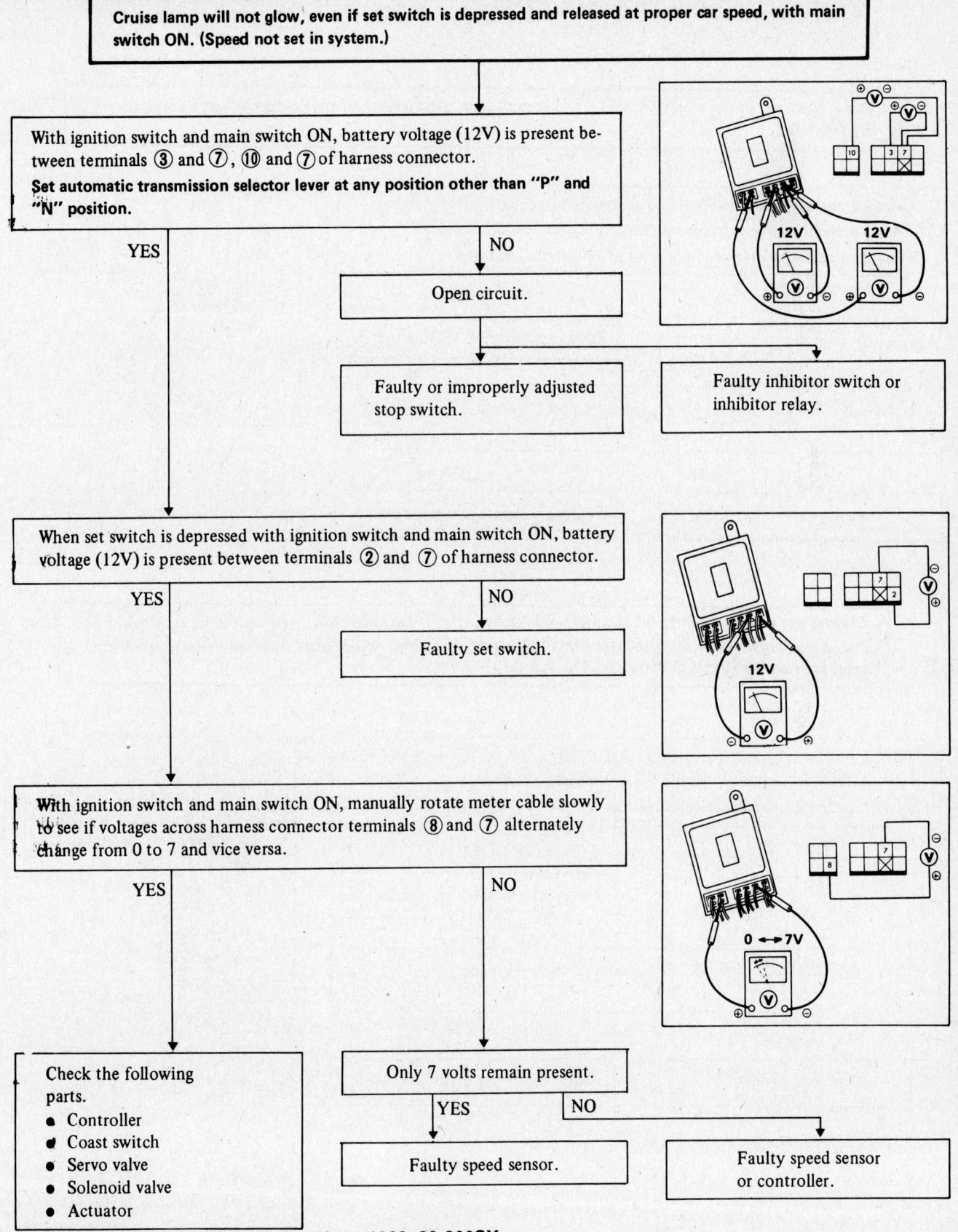

Cruise lamp will not glow, even if set switch is depressed and released at proper car speed, with main switch ON. (Speed not set in system.)

With ignition switch and main switch ON, battery voltage (12V) is present between terminals ③ and ⑦, ⑩ and ⑦ of harness connector.

Set automatic transmission selector lever at any position other than "P" and "N" position.

YES ↓   NO →

Open circuit.

Faulty or improperly adjusted stop switch.

Faulty inhibitor switch or inhibitor relay.

When set switch is depressed with ignition switch and main switch ON, battery voltage (12V) is present between terminals ② and ⑦ of harness connector.

YES ↓   NO →

Faulty set switch.

With ignition switch and main switch ON, manually rotate meter cable slowly to see if voltages across harness connector terminals ⑧ and ⑦ alternately change from 0 to 7 and vice versa.

YES ↓   NO →

Check the following parts.
- Controller
- Coast switch
- Servo valve
- Solenoid valve
- Actuator

Only 7 volts remain present.

YES ↓   NO →

Faulty speed sensor.

Faulty speed sensor or controller.

Cruise control trouble diagnosis cahrt – 1982–83 200SX

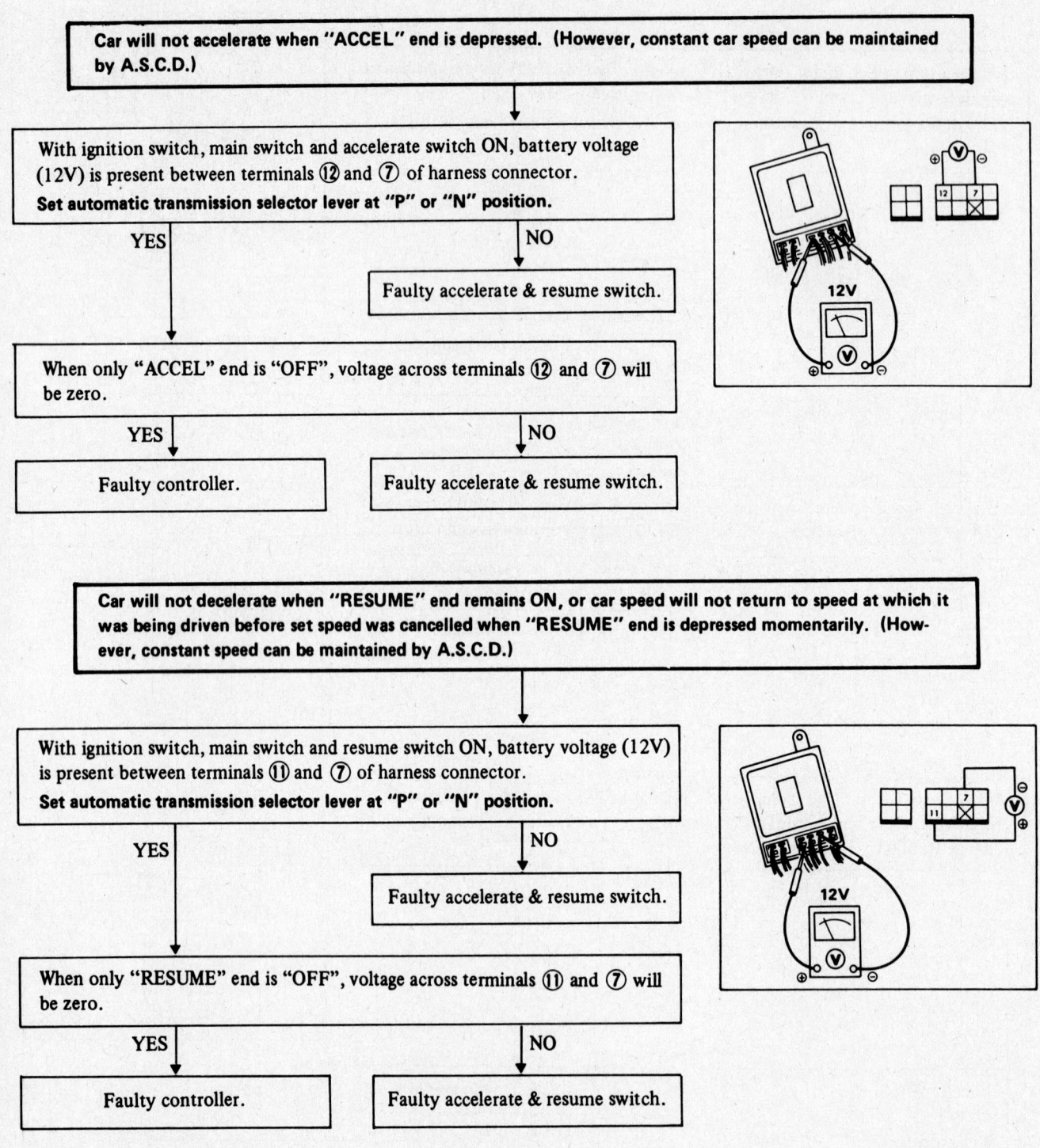

Car will not accelerate when "ACCEL" end is depressed. (However, constant car speed can be maintained by A.S.C.D.)

With ignition switch, main switch and accelerate switch ON, battery voltage (12V) is present between terminals ⑫ and ⑦ of harness connector.
Set automatic transmission selector lever at "P" or "N" position.

YES

NO

Faulty accelerate & resume switch.

When only "ACCEL" end is "OFF", voltage across terminals ⑫ and ⑦ will be zero.

YES

NO

Faulty controller.

Faulty accelerate & resume switch.

Car will not decelerate when "RESUME" end remains ON, or car speed will not return to speed at which it was being driven before set speed was cancelled when "RESUME" end is depressed momentarily. (However, constant speed can be maintained by A.S.C.D.)

With ignition switch, main switch and resume switch ON, battery voltage (12V) is present between terminals ⑪ and ⑦ of harness connector.
Set automatic transmission selector lever at "P" or "N" position.

YES

NO

Faulty accelerate & resume switch.

When only "RESUME" end is "OFF", voltage across terminals ⑪ and ⑦ will be zero.

YES

NO

Faulty controller.

Faulty accelerate & resume switch.

Cruise control trouble diagnosis cahrt – 1982–83 200SX

1044

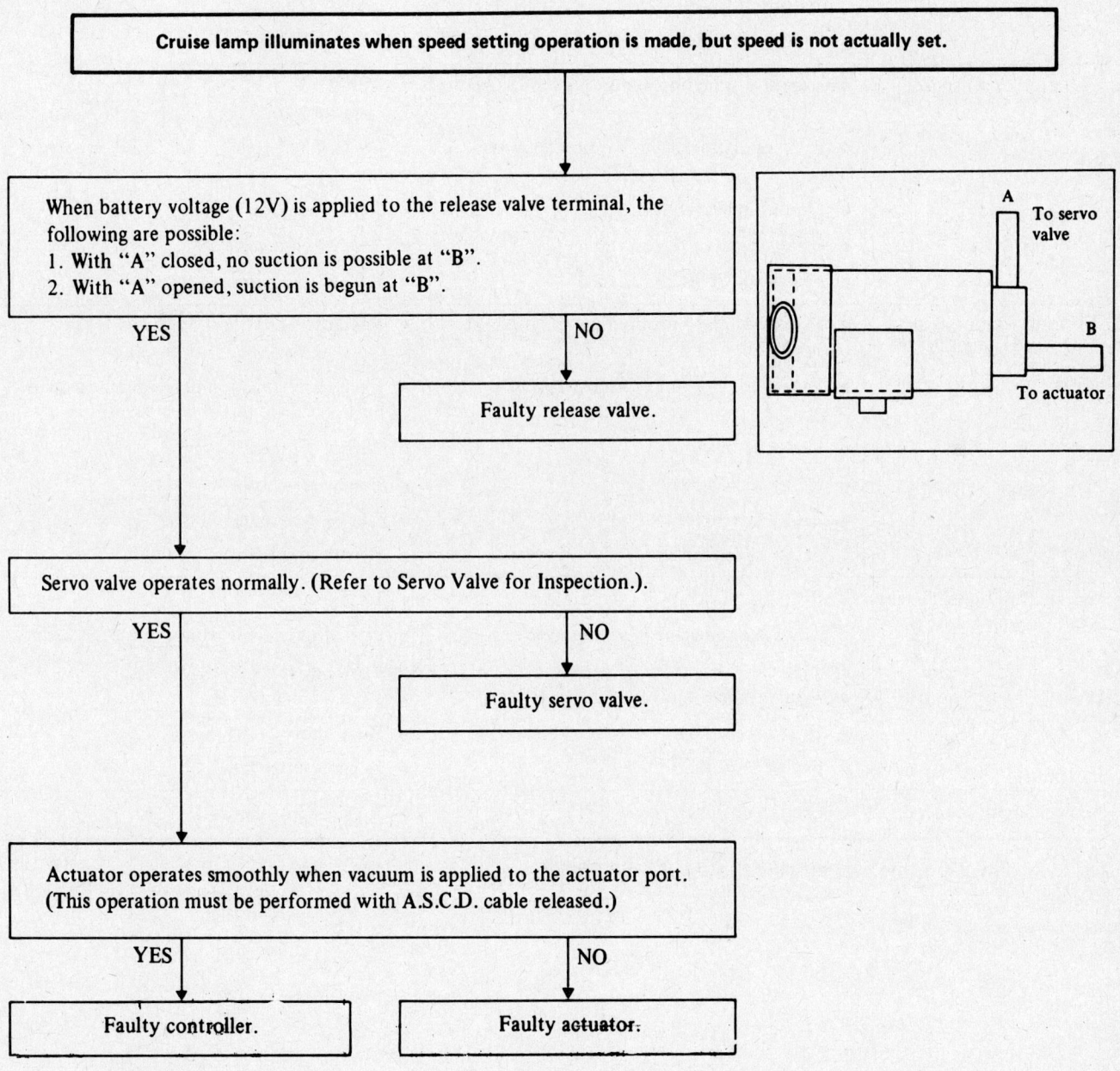

Cruise lamp illuminates when speed setting operation is made, but speed is not actually set.

When battery voltage (12V) is applied to the release valve terminal, the following are possible:
1. With "A" closed, no suction is possible at "B".
2. With "A" opened, suction is begun at "B".

YES

NO

Faulty release valve.

A — To servo valve

B — To actuator

Servo valve operates normally. (Refer to Servo Valve for Inspection.).

YES

NO

Faulty servo valve.

Actuator operates smoothly when vacuum is applied to the actuator port. (This operation must be performed with A.S.C.D. cable released.)

YES

NO

Faulty controller.

Faulty actuator.

Cruise control trouble diagnosis cahrt — 1982–83 200SX

Condition	Probable cause	Corrective action
Set speed is cancelled.	● Bent meter cable (excessive meter needle deflection.). ● Faulty controller.	● Check and repair meter cable, or renew cable. ● Renew.
Pulsation of set speed.	● Excessive play or binding of A.S.C.D. cable. ● Leakage or clogging in vacuum hose. ● Binding in actuator. ● Faulty servo valve. ● Faulty controller.	● Adjust. ● Check and repair piping route, or renew hose. ● Renew actuator. ● Renew servo valve. ● Renew controller.
Excessive setting error.	● Excessive play or binding in A.S.C.D. cable. ● Leakage or clogging in vacuum hose. ● Faulty actuator. ● Faulty servo valve. ● Faulty controller. ● Faulty speed sensor.	● Readjust. ● Check and repair piping route, or renew hose. ● Renew actuator. ● Renew servo valve. ● Renew controller. ● Renew speed sensor.
Speed drops immediately after setting.	● Excessive play in A.S.C.D. cable. ● Leakage or clogging in vacuum hose. ● Faulty solenoid valve. ● Faulty servo valve. ● Faulty controller.	● Readjust. ● Check and repair piping route, or renew hose. ● Renew solenoid valve. ● Renew servo valve. ● Renew controller.
Cancel circuit inoperative.	● Faulty controller.	● Renew controller.

Cruise control trouble diagnosis cahrt – 1982–83 200SX

- Remove A.S.C.D. control unit with harness connected.

Check from harness side.

Dash side L.H.

POWER SUPPLY CIRCUIT CHECK

1. Release brake and clutch pedals.
2. Turn ignition switch to "ON".
3. Turn A.S.C.D. main switch to "ON".
4. Check voltage between ⑬ and ⑤.

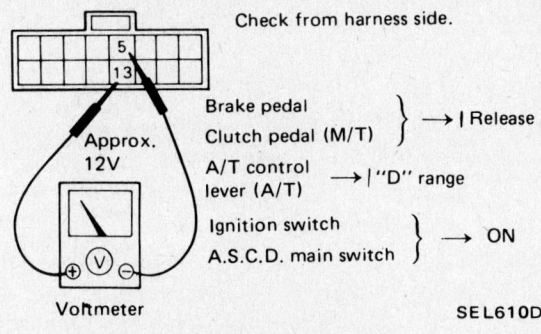

Check from harness side.

Brake pedal
Clutch pedal (M/T) } → | Release

A/T control lever (A/T) → | "D" range

Ignition switch
A.S.C.D. main switch } → ON

Approx. 12V

Voltmeter

SEL610D

SET SWITCH CIRCUIT CHECK

1. Turn ignition switch to "OFF".
2. Push A.S.C.D. set switch.
3. Check continuity between ① and ⑬.

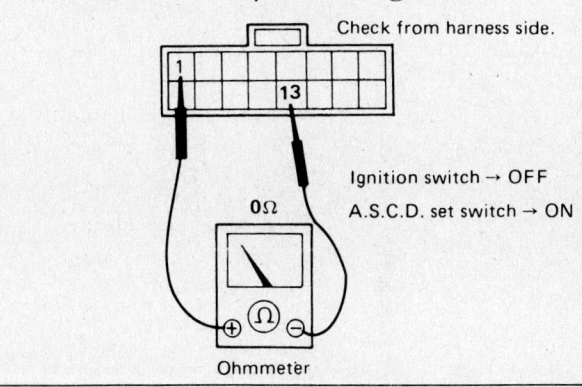

Check from harness side.

0Ω

Ignition switch → OFF
A.S.C.D. set switch → ON

Ohmmeter

Cruise control troubleshooting chart—1984 and later 200SX

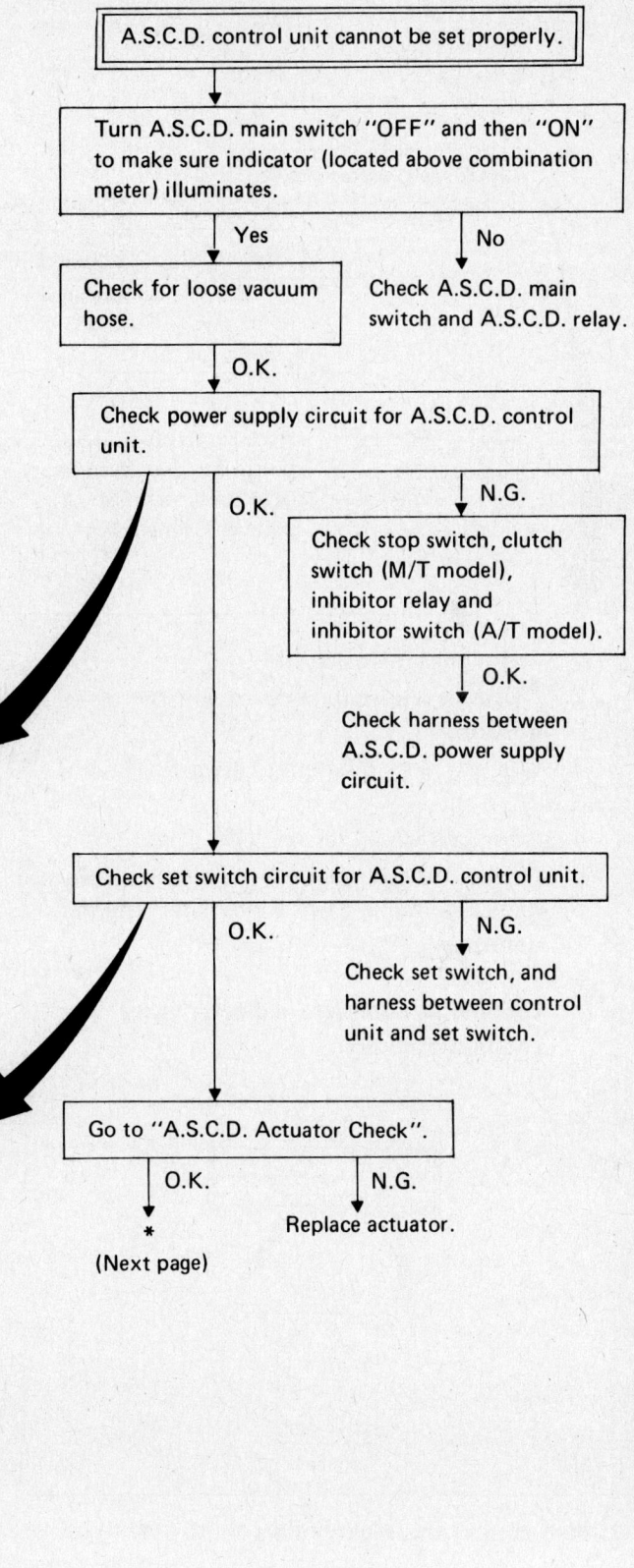

A.S.C.D. control unit cannot be set properly.

↓

Turn A.S.C.D. main switch "OFF" and then "ON" to make sure indicator (located above combination meter) illuminates.

Yes → Check for loose vacuum hose.

No → Check A.S.C.D. main switch and A.S.C.D. relay.

O.K. ↓

Check power supply circuit for A.S.C.D. control unit.

O.K. ↓

N.G. → Check stop switch, clutch switch (M/T model), inhibitor relay and inhibitor switch (A/T model).

O.K. ↓

Check harness between A.S.C.D. power supply circuit.

↓

Check set switch circuit for A.S.C.D. control unit.

O.K. ↓

N.G. → Check set switch, and harness between control unit and set switch.

↓

Go to "A.S.C.D. Actuator Check".

O.K. → *
(Next page)

N.G. → Replace actuator.

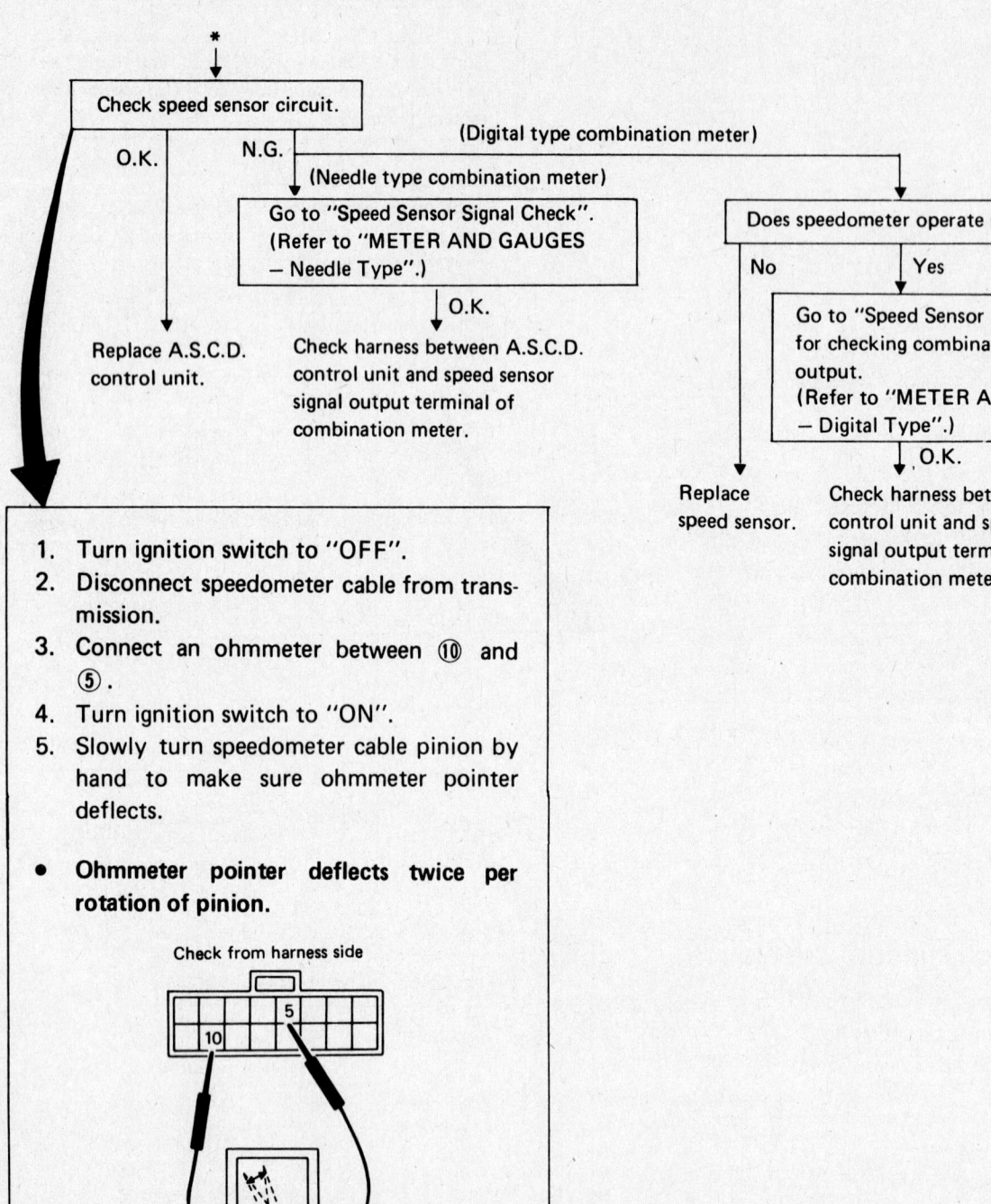

*

Check speed sensor circuit.

O.K.   N.G.   (Digital type combination meter)

(Needle type combination meter)

Go to "Speed Sensor Signal Check".
(Refer to "METER AND GAUGES
— Needle Type".)

Does speedometer operate properly?

No   Yes

O.K.

Replace A.S.C.D.
control unit.

Check harness between A.S.C.D.
control unit and speed sensor
signal output terminal of
combination meter.

Go to "Speed Sensor Signal Check"
for checking combination meter
output.
(Refer to "METER AND GAUGES
— Digital Type".)

O.K.

Replace
speed sensor.

Check harness between A.S.C.D.
control unit and speed sensor
signal output terminal of
combination meter.

1. Turn ignition switch to "OFF".
2. Disconnect speedometer cable from transmission.
3. Connect an ohmmeter between ⑩ and
   ⑤.
4. Turn ignition switch to "ON".
5. Slowly turn speedometer cable pinion by
   hand to make sure ohmmeter pointer
   deflects.

- **Ohmmeter pointer deflects twice per
  rotation of pinion.**

Check from harness side

5

10

Ohmmeter

Cruise control troubleshooting chart—1984 and later 200SX

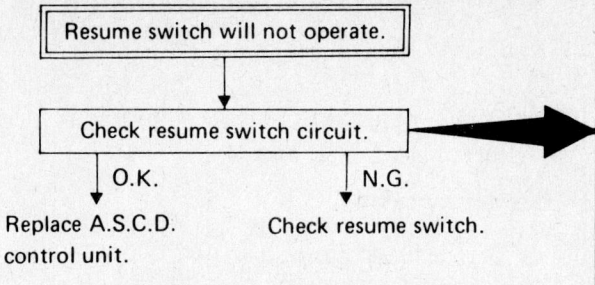

Resume switch will not operate.

↓

Check resume switch circuit.

O.K. → Replace A.S.C.D. control unit.

N.G. → Check resume switch.

RESUME SWITCH CIRCUIT CHECK

1. Turn ignition switch to "OFF".
2. Turn resume switch to "ON".
3. Check continuity between ② and ⑬.

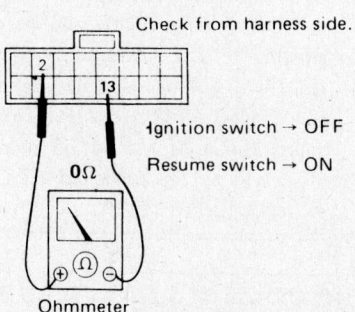

Check from harness side.

Ignition switch → OFF
Resume switch → ON

0Ω

Ohmmeter

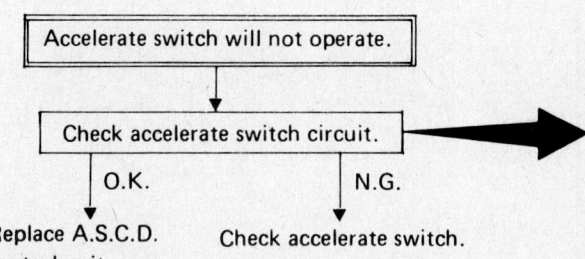

Accelerate switch will not operate.

↓

Check accelerate switch circuit.

O.K. → Replace A.S.C.D. control unit.

N.G. → Check accelerate switch.

ACCELERATE SWITCH CIRCUIT CHECK

1. Turn ignition switch to "OFF".
2. Turn accelerate switch to "ON".
3. Check continuity between ③ and ⑬.

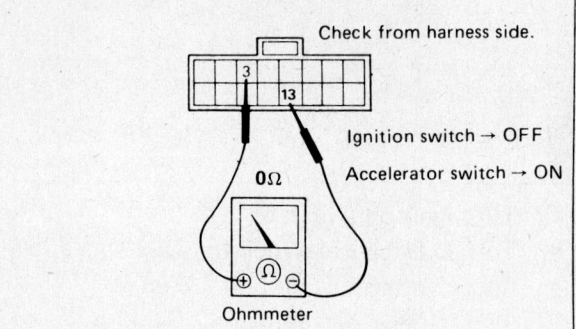

Check from harness side.

Ignition switch → OFF
Accelerator switch → ON

0Ω

Ohmmeter

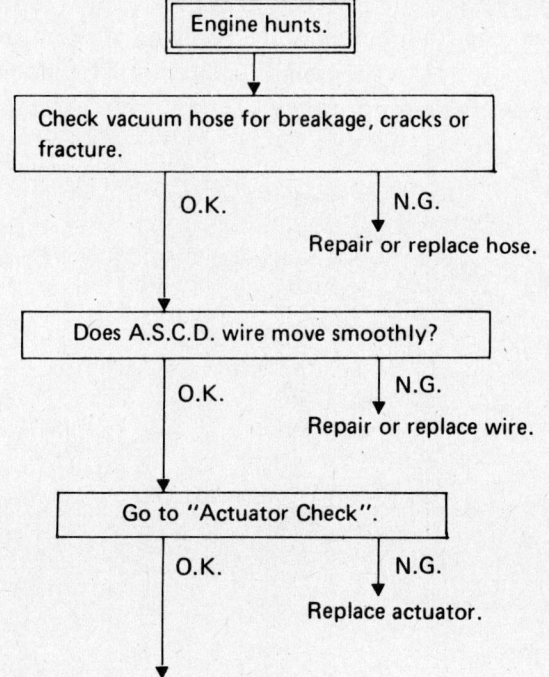

Engine hunts.

↓

Check vacuum hose for breakage, cracks or fracture.

O.K.

N.G. → Repair or replace hose.

↓

Does A.S.C.D. wire move smoothly?

O.K.

N.G. → Repair or replace wire.

↓

Go to "Actuator Check".

O.K.

N.G. → Replace actuator.

↓

Replace A.S.C.D. control unit.

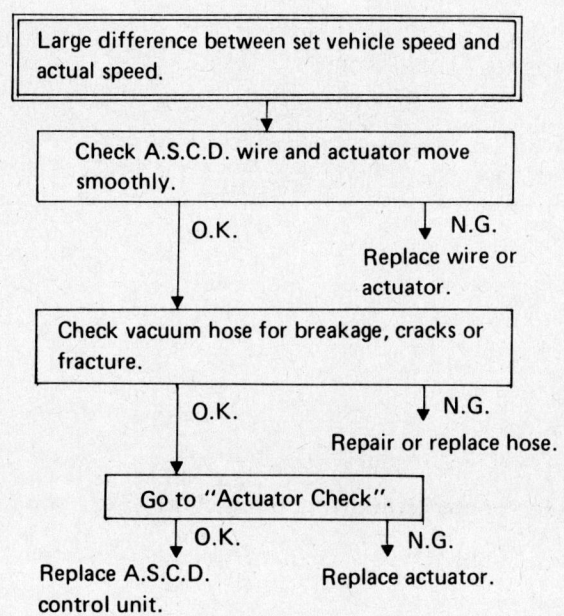

Large difference between set vehicle speed and actual speed.

↓

Check A.S.C.D. wire and actuator move smoothly.

O.K.

N.G. → Replace wire or actuator.

↓

Check vacuum hose for breakage, cracks or fracture.

O.K.

N.G. → Repair or replace hose.

↓

Go to "Actuator Check".

O.K. → Replace A.S.C.D. control unit.

N.G. → Replace actuator.

Cruise control troubleshooting chart—1984 and later 200SX

A/T model only:
- When A.S.C.D. is set while vehicle is operating in "O.D." range, O.D. will be cancelled and shifting to O.D. cannot be made thereafter.
- O.D. will not be cancelled even if actual car speed is 6 km/h (4 MPH) lower than set speed. (Set speed cannot be maintained.)
- O.D. will not be cancelled even if accelerator switch is turned "ON".

↓

Check O.D. cancel circuit for A.S.C.D. control unit.

O.K.	N.G.
Replace A.S.C.D. control unit.	Check harness between O.D. cancel solenoid, O.D. cancel switch and A.S.C.D. control unit.

- Turn ignition switch to "ON".
- Turn O.D. cancel switch to "OFF".
- Check voltage ⑧ - ⑤ and ⑯ - ⑤.

Check from harness side

Ignition switch → ON
O.D. cancel switch → OFF

Approx. 12V

Voltmeter

1. Check continuity between terminal ① and terminals ②, ③ and ④.

Continuity exist ... O.K.

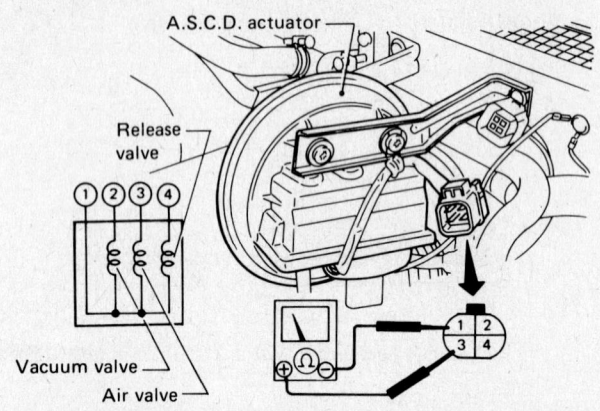

A.S.C.D. actuator

Release valve

Vacuum valve

Air valve

CAUTION:
Do not attempt to remove valves from actuator.

2. Connect battery (approx. 12V) to harness connector of actuator as shown below, and apply vacuum to actuator.
   If diaphragm moves smoothly, actuator is O.K.

CAUTION:
When checking actuator by applying vacuum, do not apply engine vacuum directly as it is too strong to check actuator properly.

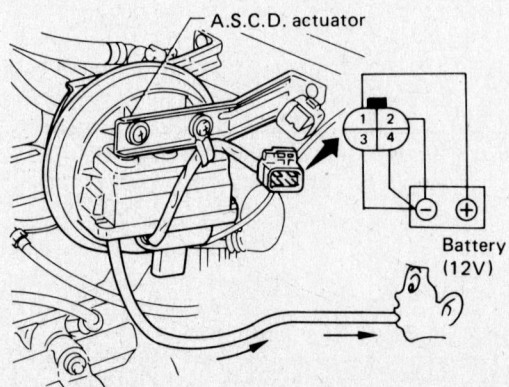

A.S.C.D. actuator

Battery (12V)

Cruise control troubleshooting chart — 1984 and later 200SX

Component Replacement

ACTUATOR CABLE (1982–83)

Removal and Installation

1. Disconnect the actuator cable from the actuator assembly.
2. Loosen the locknut at the actuator.
3. Remove the rubber boots.
4. Loosen the adjusting nuts at the shaft and drum assembly.
5. Remove the cable from the actuator.
6. Installation is the reverse of the removal procedure. Adjust the cable as required.

ACTUATOR (1982–83)

Removal and Installation

1. Disconnect the negative battery cable.
2. Disconnect the cable from the actuator assembly.
3. Disconnect the vacuum hose. Disconnect the electrical connector.
4. Remove the actuator retaining bolt.
5. Remove the actuator from the vehicle.
6. Installation is the reverse of the removal procedure.

Maxima

VISUAL INSPECTION

Before performing any tests make a visual inspection of the cruise control system. Check all items in the system for abnormal conditions such as bare broken or disconnected wires and damage to the vacuum hoses. Be sure that the speedometer cables are attached and properly routed. All vacuum hoses must be properly routed and must not have any kinks or bends. Be sure that all electrical connections are complete and tight. The wiring harness must be routed properly.

ACTUATOR TEST (1982–84)

1. Visually inspect the actuator for damage or deformation.
2. Make sure that the assembly moves freely without binding when the diaphragm is pushed by hand.
3. Apply vacuum to the actuator, using a hand vacuum pump. Do not use engine vacuum. The diaphragm should move to the full up position.
4. Plug the hose with vacuum applied, the actuator should remain in the full position.
5. Repair or replace defective components as required.

SERVO VALVE TEST (1982–84)

1. Measure the resistance between the terminals. It should be 25 to 30 ohms.
2. Be sure that the valve opens and closes by blowing air through the port on the actuator side of the assembly.
3. Repair or replace defective components as required.

RELEASE VALVE TEST (1982–84)

1. Measure the resistance between the terminals. It should be 25 to 30 ohms.
2. Check to be sure that the vacuum valve is performing properly.
3. Disconnect the solenoid valve side vacuum hose at the servo valve. Connect a vacuum gauge.

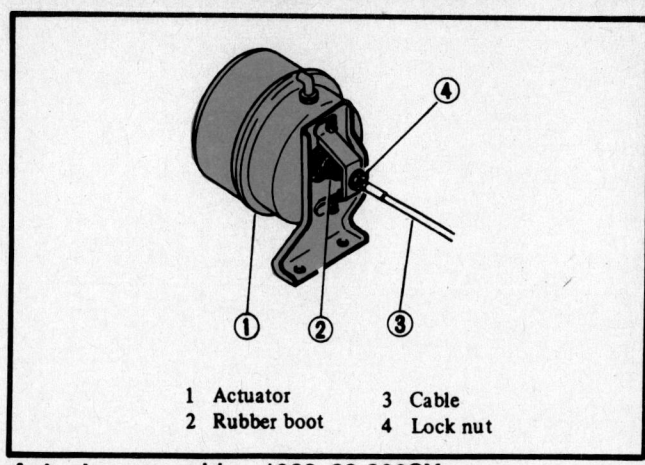

| 1 Actuator | 3 Cable |
| 2 Rubber boot | 4 Lock nut |

Actuator assembly – 1982–83 200SX

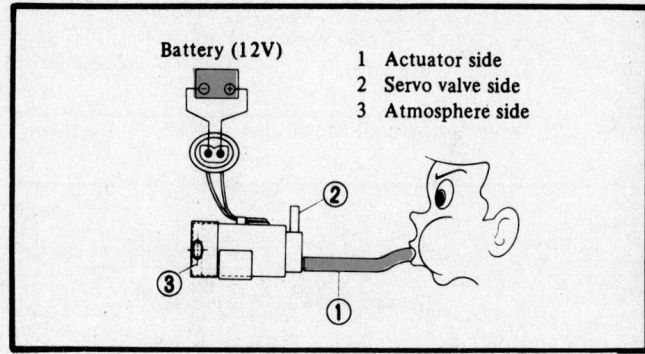

Battery (12V)

1 Actuator side
2 Servo valve side
3 Atmosphere side

Servo valve test point locations – 1982–84 Maxima

Check ports	Air flow
① - ②	
① - ③	Yes
② - ③	

Servo valve test results – 1982–84 Maxima

Check ports	Air flow
① - ②	Yes
① - ③	No
② - ③	

Servo valve test results – 1982–84 Maxima

4. Start the engine and allow it to reach operating temperature or until the water temperature indicator points to the middle of the gauge.
5. Apply 0.3 amps of direct current between the terminals using a 20 ohm 5W variable resistor to adjust the current to specification.
6. Repair or replace defective components as required.

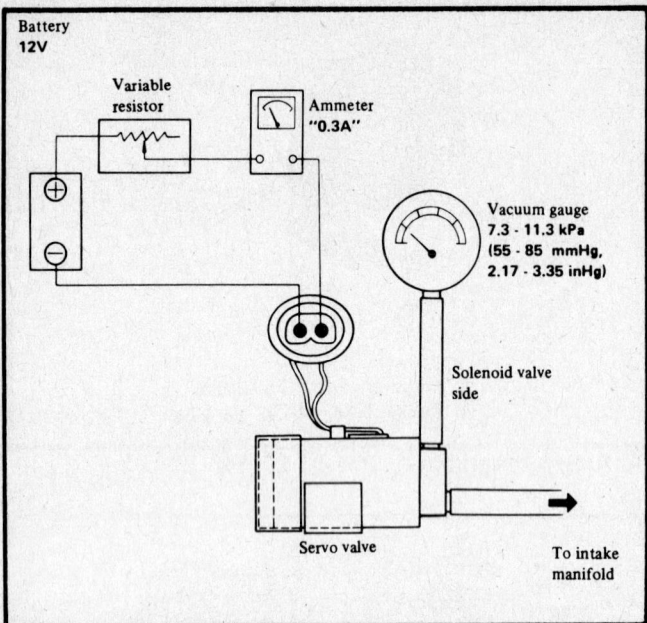

Solenoid valve test point locations—1982–84 Maxima

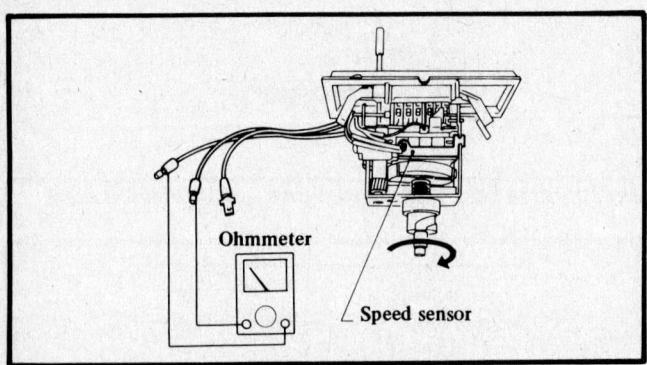

Speed sensor test point locations—1982–84 Maxima

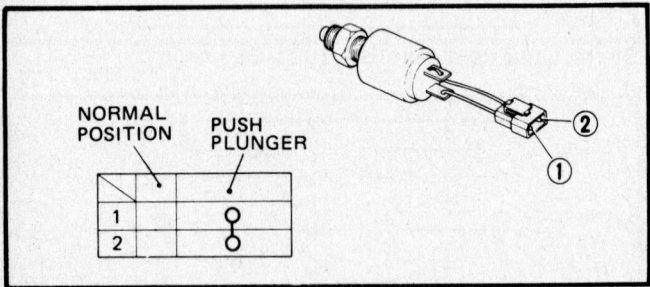

Stoplight switch test point locations—1982–84 Maxima

SPEED SENSOR TEST (1982–84)

The speed sensor is built into the rear of the speedometer. Inspection of the speed sensor must be made with the speed sensor installed in the speedometer assembly. Turn the speedometer slowly by hand two complete turns. If continuity exists than the sensor is good.

Switch position Check terminal	Normal	ON	OFF
① - ②	No	Yes	No
① - ⑥	No	Yes	No
② - ⑥	Yes	Yes	No
③ - ④	Yes	—	—
⑤ - ⑦	Yes	—	—
⑥ - ⑦	Yes	—	—

Yes: Continuity should exist.
No: Continuity should not exist.

Main switch specifications—1982–84 Maxima

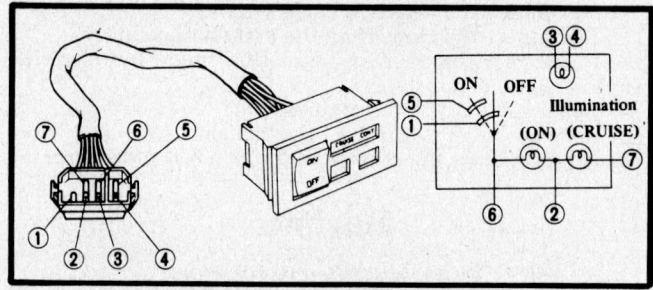

Main switch test point locations—1982–84 Maxima

MAIN SWITCH TEST (1982–84)

1. Test the continuity of the main switch assembly using and ohmmeter.
2. Repair or replace defective components as required.

CONTROL SWITCH TEST (1982–84)

1. Test the continuity of the main switch assembly using and ohmmeter.
2. Repair or replace defective components as required.

STOP LIGHT SWITCH TEST (1982–84)

1. Test the continuity of the main switch assembly using and ohmmeter.
2. Repair or replace defective components as required.

ASCD RELAY TEST (1982–84)

The ASCD relay is located on the left relay bracket. Using an ohmmeter check the component for the proper continuity.

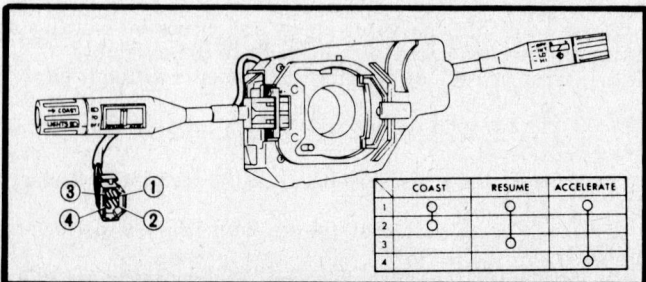

Control switch test point locations—1982–84 Maxima

ASCD INHIBITOR RELAY TEST (1982–84)

The ASCD inhibitor relay is located on the left relay bracket. Using an ohmmeter check the component for the proper continunity.

ASCD CONTROLLER TEST (1982–84)

The ASCD controller is located on the left side of the dash panel. This component must be checked as a single part. When checking this component do not touch the test probe to any terminal other than the ones used to check the component as damage to the controller could result. Keep the controller away from electric noise to prevent the ASCD system from malfunctioning and the IC circuit from being destroyed.

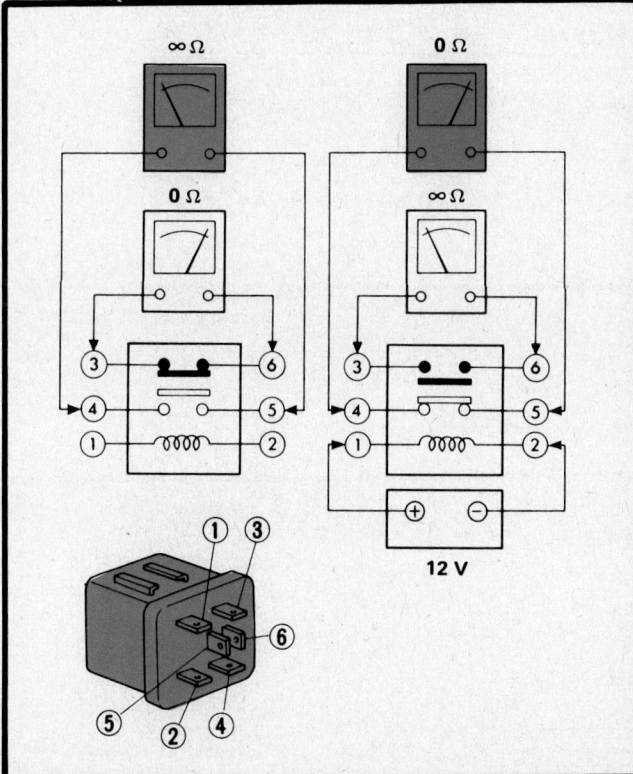

ASCD inhibitor relay test point locations – 1982–84 Maxima

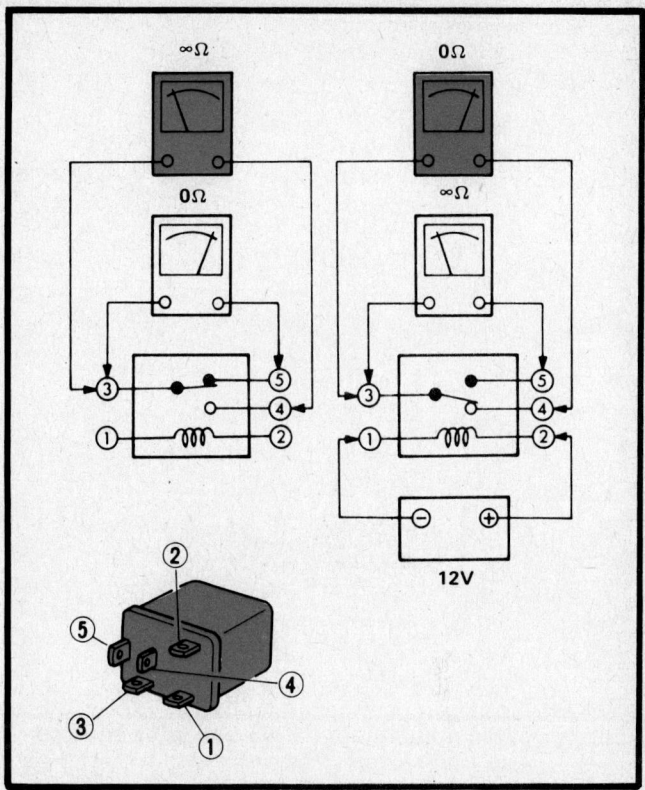

ASCD relay test point locations – 1982–84 Maxima

ACTUATOR ADJUSTMENT

1982–84

1. Without depressing the accelerator, adjust the adjusting nuts until all freeplay is removed.
2. Return the adjusting nuts until 0.08 to 0.12 inch of freeplay is obtained.
3. Do not increase the cable tension excessively, as this can cause cable damage.

1985 and Later

1. Without depressing the accelerator, adjust the adjusting nuts until all freeplay is removed.
2. Return the adjusting nuts ½ to 1 turn to gain the proper cable free play.
3. Do not increase the cable tension excessively, as this can cause cable damage.

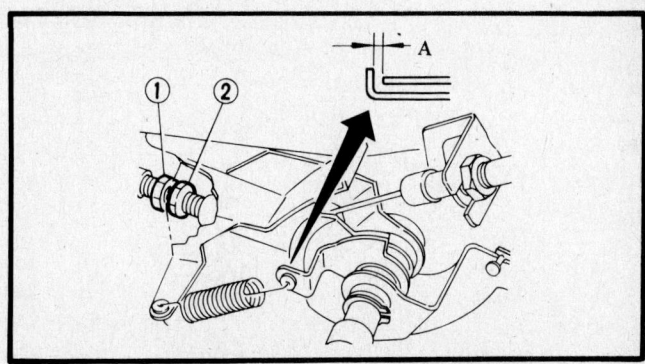

Actuator cable adjustment – 1982–84 Maxima

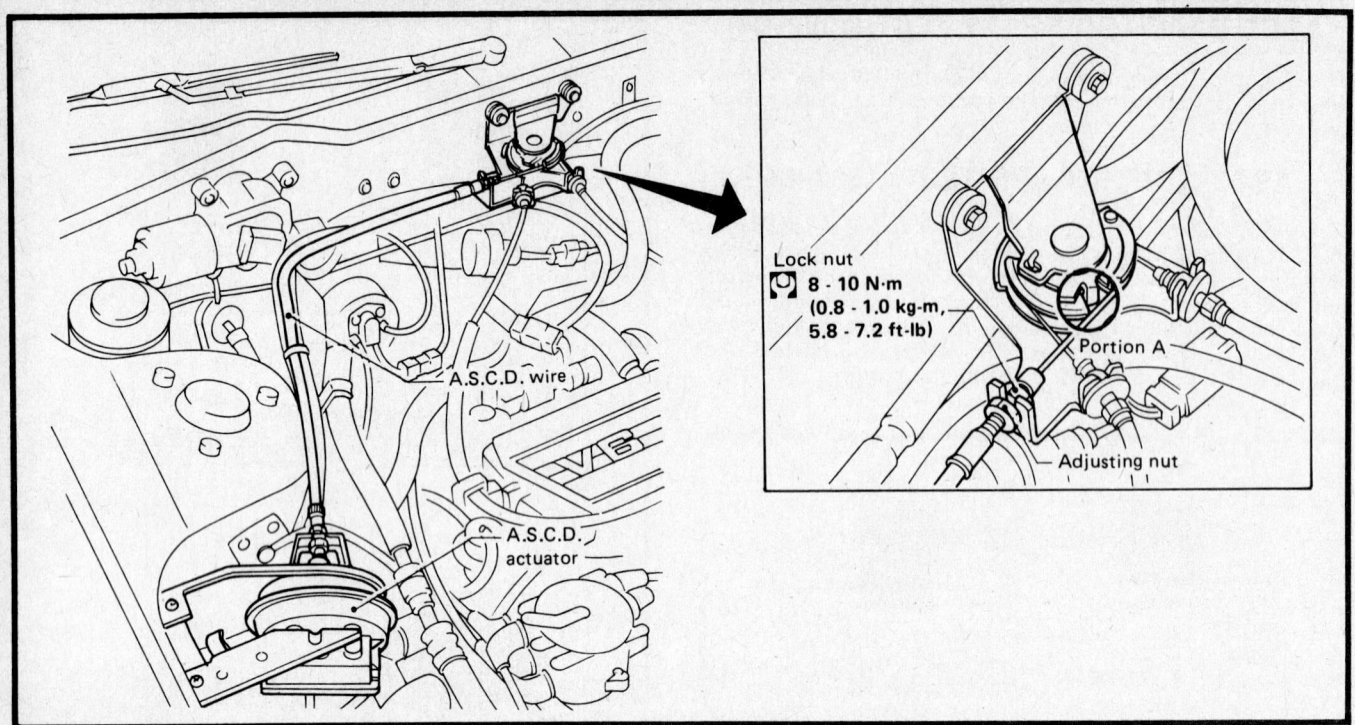

Lock nut
8 - 10 N·m
(0.8 - 1.0 kg-m,
5.8 - 7.2 ft-lb)

Portion A

Adjusting nut

A.S.C.D. wire

A.S.C.D. actuator

Actuator cable adjustment—1985 and later Maxima

DIAGNOSIS AND TESTING PROCEDURES

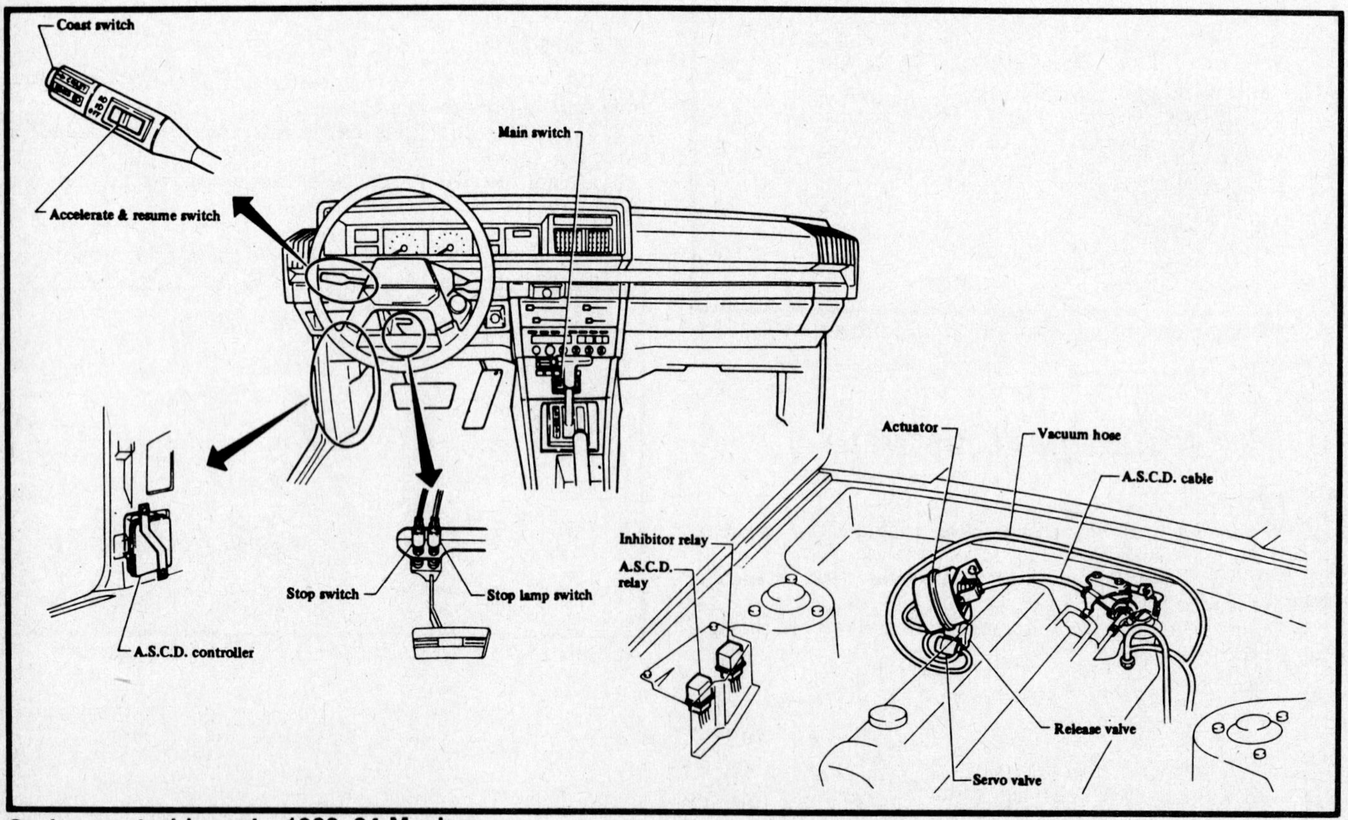

Coast switch

Accelerate & resume switch

Main switch

Stop switch

Stop lamp switch

Inhibitor relay

A.S.C.D. relay

A.S.C.D. controller

Actuator

Vacuum hose

A.S.C.D. cable

Release valve

Servo valve

Cruise control layout—1982-84 Maxima

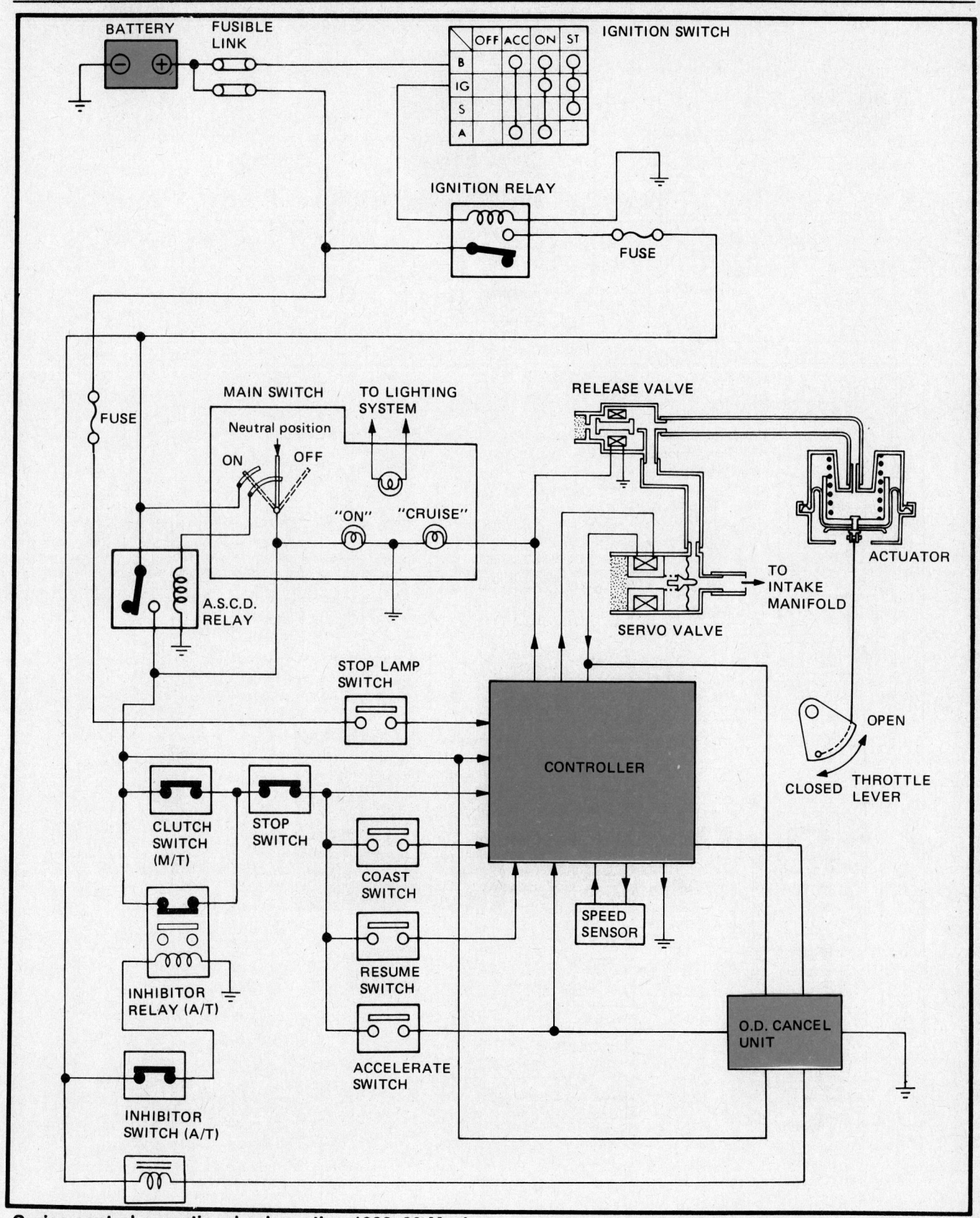

Cruise control operational schematic — 1982–83 Maxima

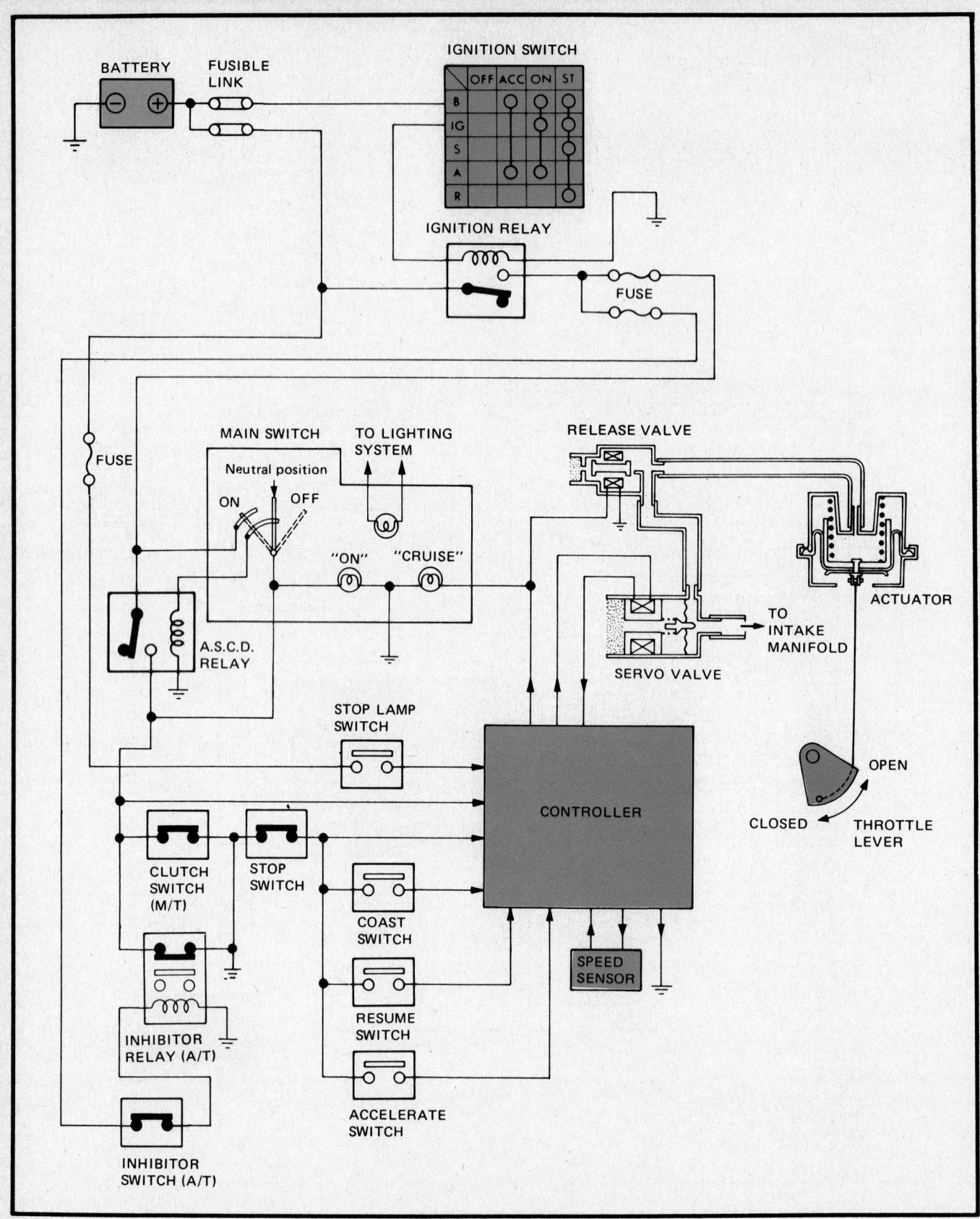

Cruise control operational schematic—1984 Maxima

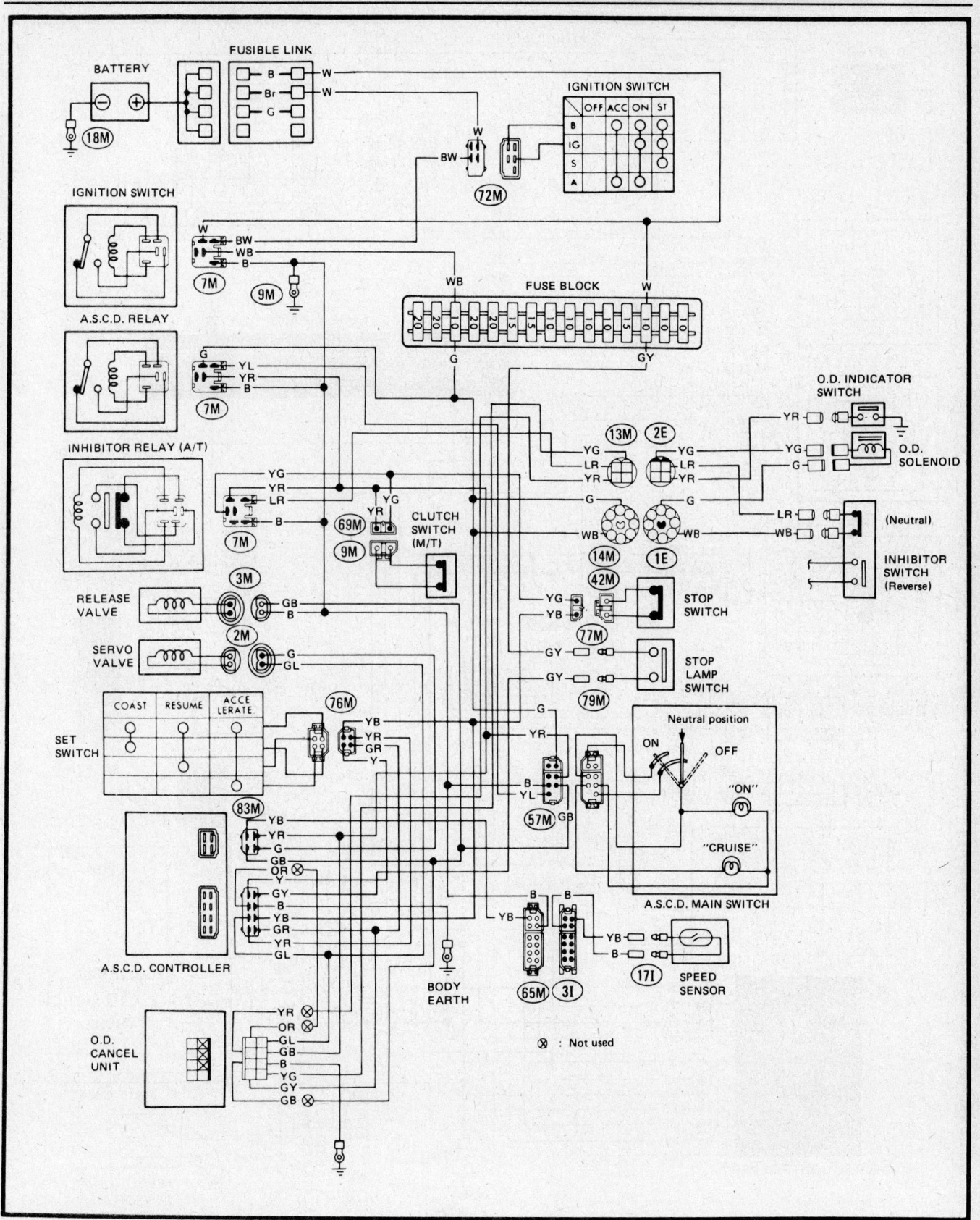

Cruise control electrical schematic – 1982–83 Maxima

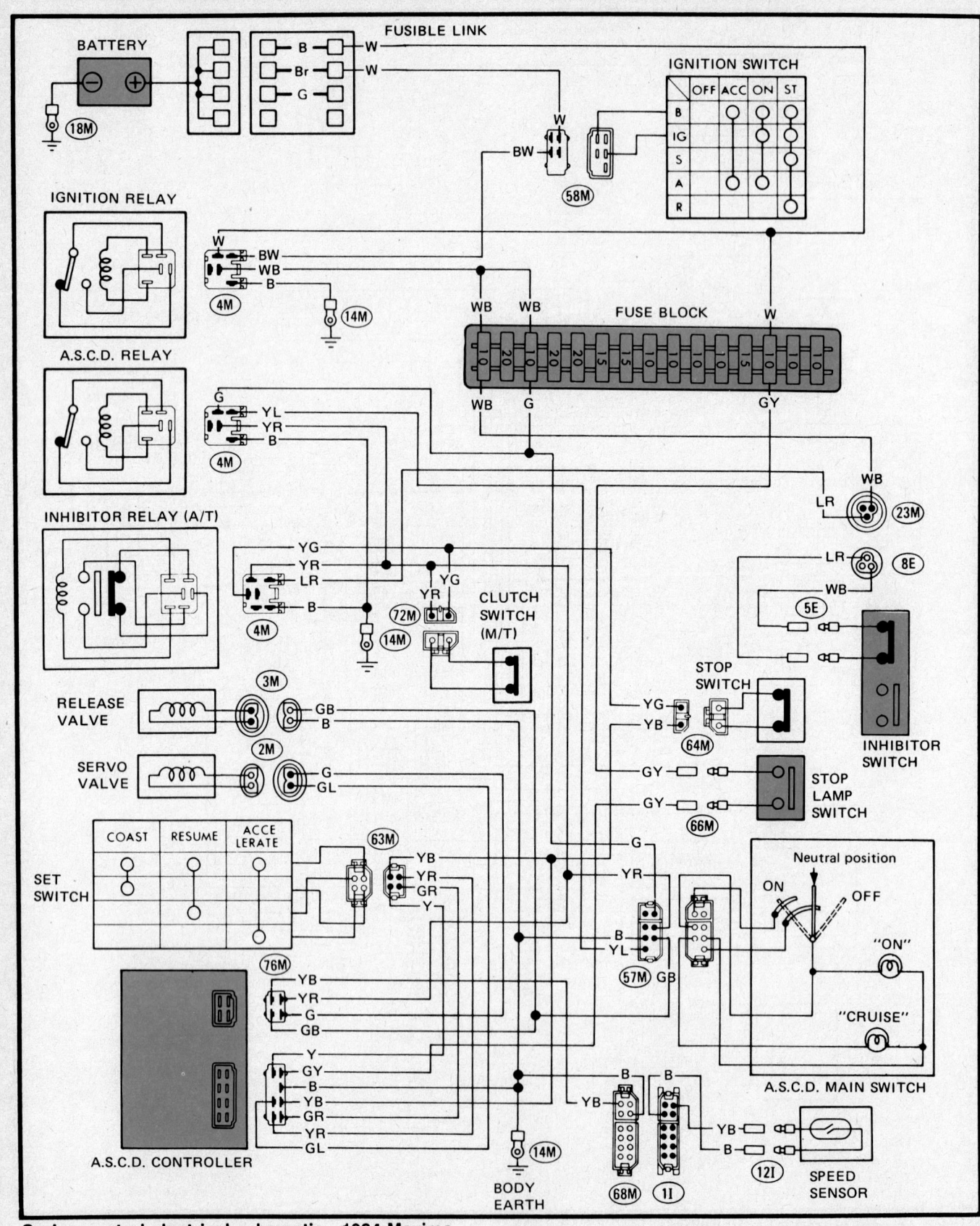

Cruise control electrical schematic—1984 Maxima

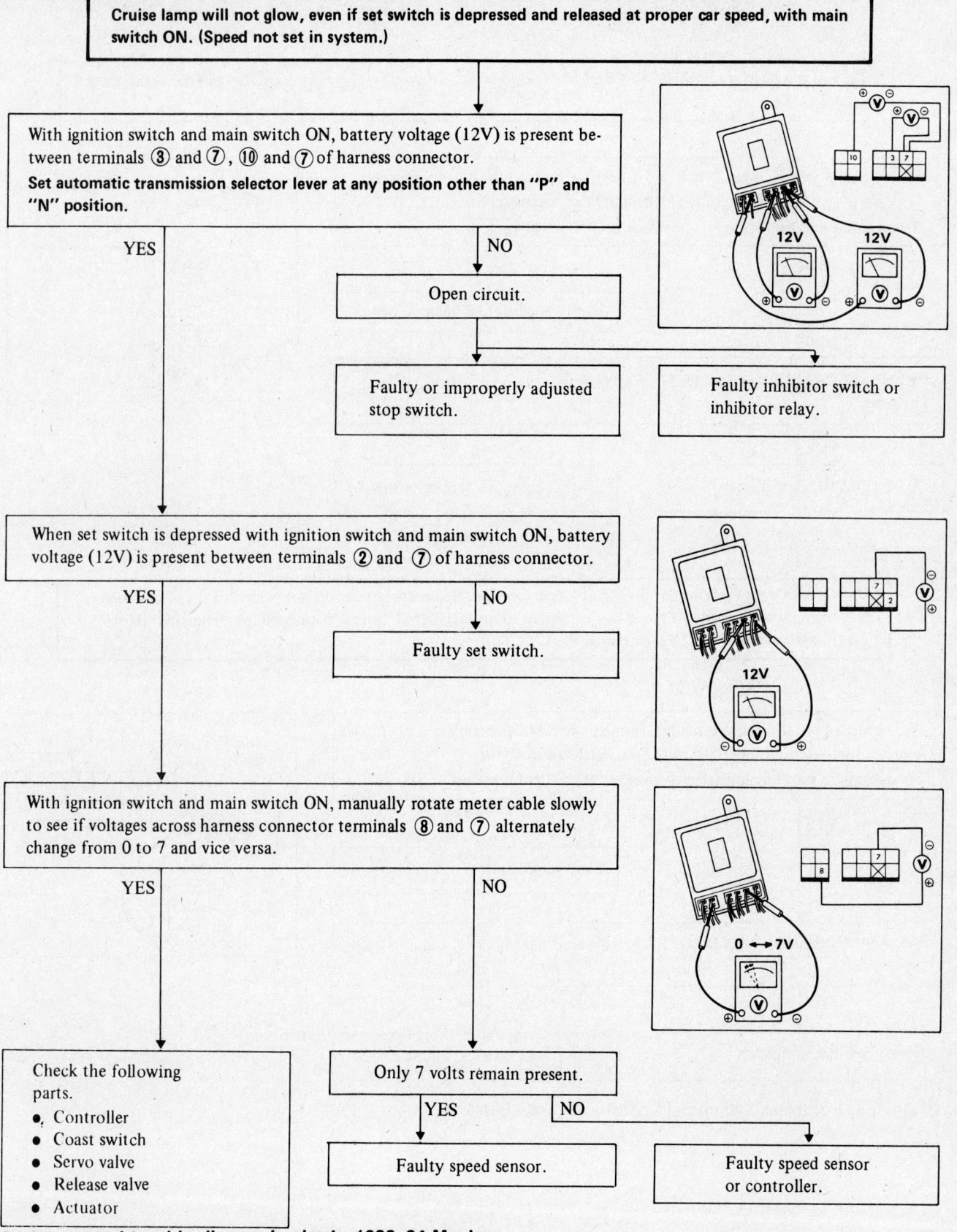

Cruise lamp will not glow, even if set switch is depressed and released at proper car speed, with main switch ON. (Speed not set in system.)

With ignition switch and main switch ON, battery voltage (12V) is present between terminals ③ and ⑦, ⑩ and ⑦ of harness connector.

Set automatic transmission selector lever at any position other than "P" and "N" position.

YES / NO

Open circuit.

Faulty or improperly adjusted stop switch.

Faulty inhibitor switch or inhibitor relay.

When set switch is depressed with ignition switch and main switch ON, battery voltage (12V) is present between terminals ② and ⑦ of harness connector.

YES / NO

Faulty set switch.

With ignition switch and main switch ON, manually rotate meter cable slowly to see if voltages across harness connector terminals ⑧ and ⑦ alternately change from 0 to 7 and vice versa.

YES / NO

Check the following parts.
- Controller
- Coast switch
- Servo valve
- Release valve
- Actuator

Only 7 volts remain present.

YES / NO

Faulty speed sensor.

Faulty speed sensor or controller.

Cruise control trouble diagnosis chart – 1982–84 Maxima

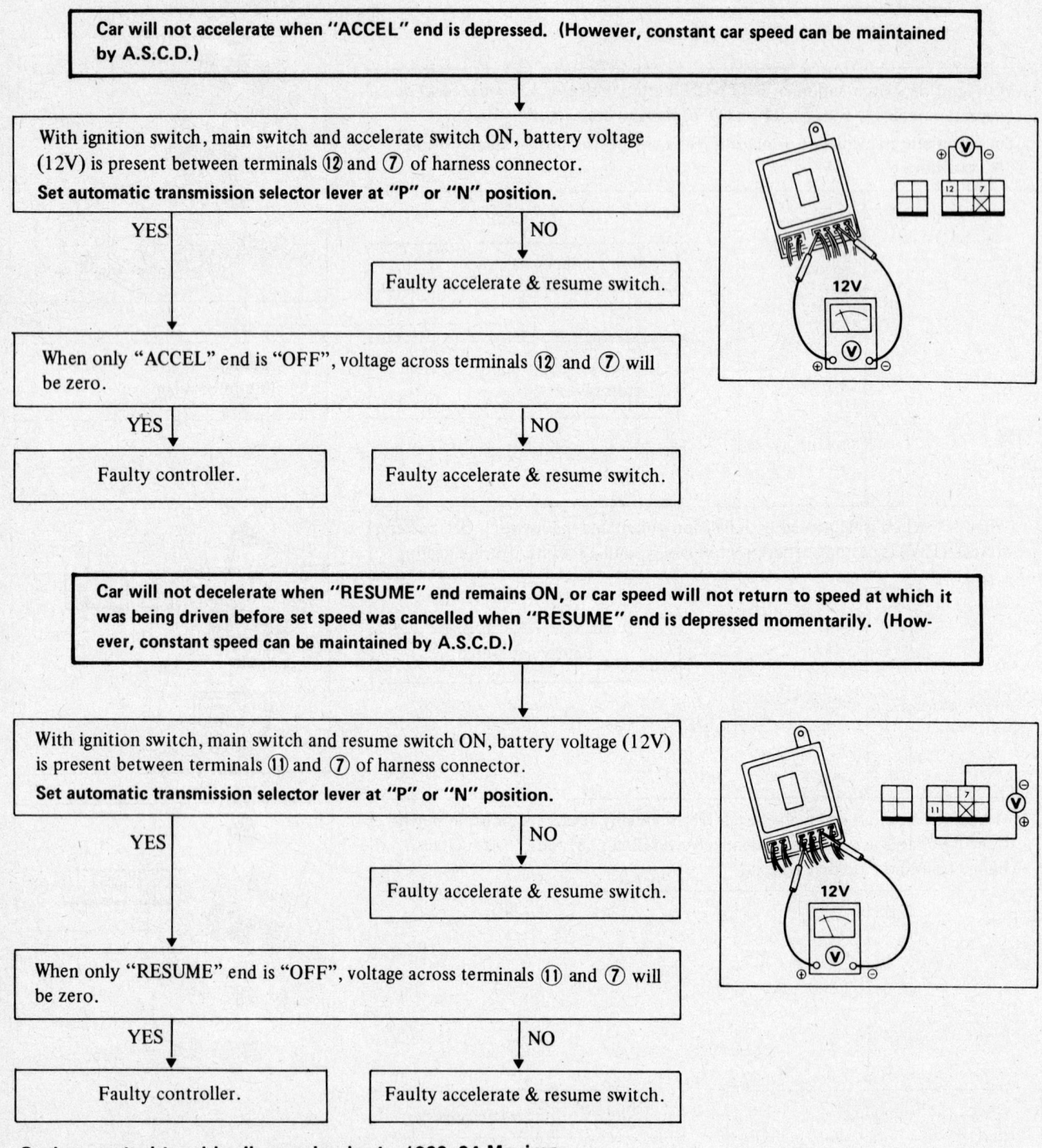

Car will not accelerate when "ACCEL" end is depressed. (However, constant car speed can be maintained by A.S.C.D.)

With ignition switch, main switch and accelerate switch ON, battery voltage (12V) is present between terminals ⑫ and ⑦ of harness connector.
Set automatic transmission selector lever at "P" or "N" position.

YES

NO

Faulty accelerate & resume switch.

When only "ACCEL" end is "OFF", voltage across terminals ⑫ and ⑦ will be zero.

YES

NO

Faulty controller.

Faulty accelerate & resume switch.

Car will not decelerate when "RESUME" end remains ON, or car speed will not return to speed at which it was being driven before set speed was cancelled when "RESUME" end is depressed momentarily. (However, constant speed can be maintained by A.S.C.D.)

With ignition switch, main switch and resume switch ON, battery voltage (12V) is present between terminals ⑪ and ⑦ of harness connector.
Set automatic transmission selector lever at "P" or "N" position.

YES

NO

Faulty accelerate & resume switch.

When only "RESUME" end is "OFF", voltage across terminals ⑪ and ⑦ will be zero.

YES

NO

Faulty controller.

Faulty accelerate & resume switch.

Cruise control trouble diagnosis chart—1982–84 Maxima

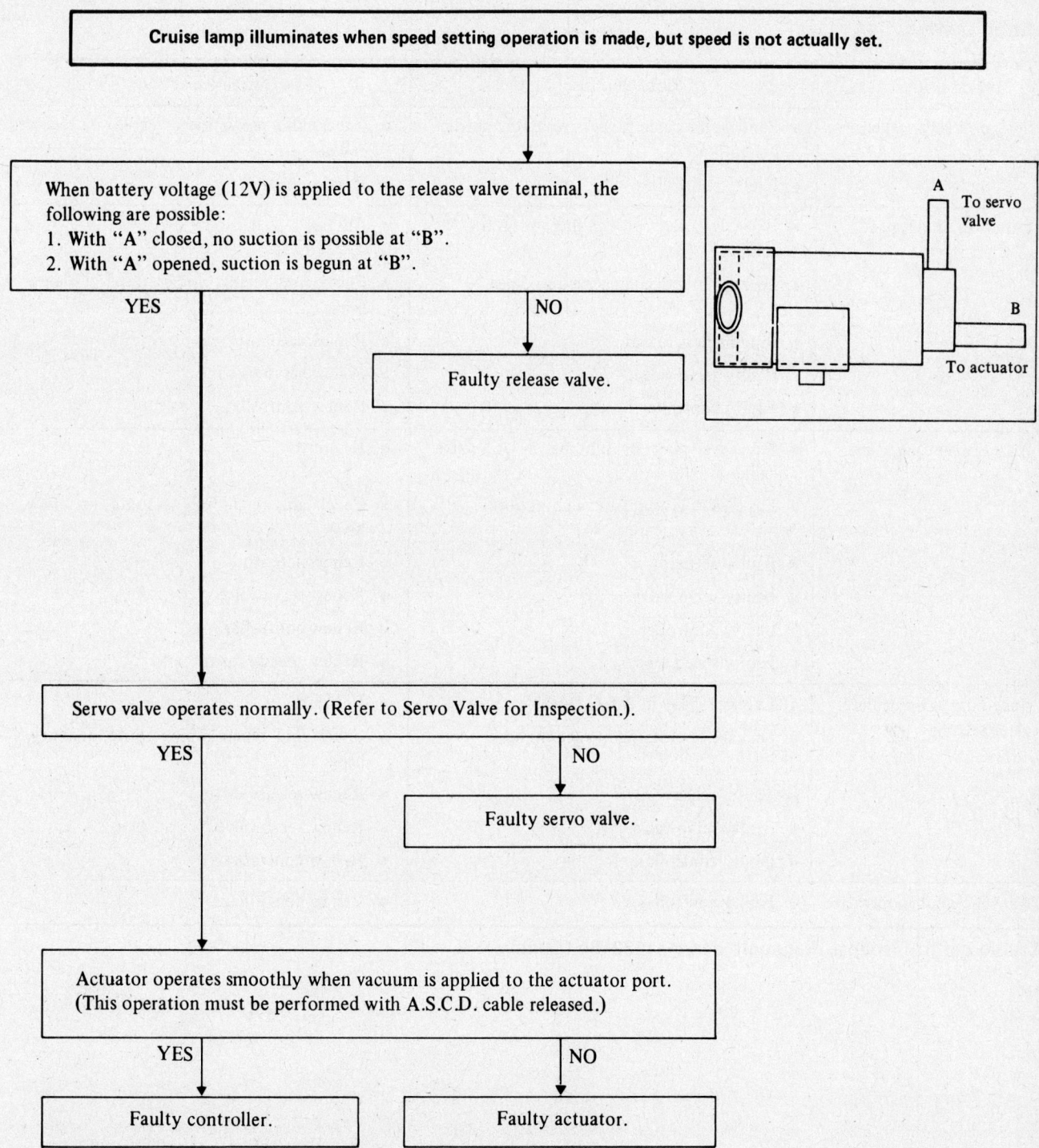

Cruise lamp illuminates when speed setting operation is made, but speed is not actually set.

When battery voltage (12V) is applied to the release valve terminal, the following are possible:
1. With "A" closed, no suction is possible at "B".
2. With "A" opened, suction is begun at "B".

A — To servo valve

B — To actuator

YES | NO

Faulty release valve.

Servo valve operates normally. (Refer to Servo Valve for Inspection.).

YES | NO

Faulty servo valve.

Actuator operates smoothly when vacuum is applied to the actuator port. (This operation must be performed with A.S.C.D. cable released.)

YES | NO

Faulty controller. | Faulty actuator.

Cruise control trouble diagnosis chart – 1982–84 Maxima

Other malfunction

Condition	Probable cause	Corrective action
Set speed is cancelled.	• Bent meter cable (excessive meter needle deflection.). • Faulty controller.	• Check and repair meter cable, or renew cable. • Renew.
Pulsation of set speed.	• Excessive play or binding of A.S.C.D. cable. • Leakage or clogging in vacuum hose. • Binding in actuator. • Faulty servo valve. • Faulty controller.	• Adjust. • Check and repair piping route, or renew hose. • Renew actuator. • Renew servo valve. • Renew controller.
Excessive setting error.	• Excessive play or binding in A.S.C.D. cable. • Leakage or clogging in vacuum hose. • Faulty actuator. • Faulty servo valve. • Faulty controller. • Faulty speed sensor.	• Readjust. • Check and repair piping route, or renew hose. • Renew actuator. • Renew servo valve. • Renew controller. • Renew speed sensor.
Speed drops immediately after setting.	• Excessive play in A.S.C.D. cable. • Leakage or clogging in vacuum hose. • Faulty release valve. • Faulty servo valve. • Faulty controller.	• Readjust. • Check and repair piping route, or renew hose. • Renew release valve. • Renew servo valve. • Renew controller.
Cancel circuit inoperative.	• Faulty controller.	• Renew controller.

Cruise control trouble diagnosis chart – 1982–84 Maxima

A/T model only:

- When A.S.C.D. is set while vehicle is operating in "O.D." range, O.D. will be cancelled and shifting to O.D. cannot be made thereafter.
- O.D. will not be cancelled even if actual car speed is 6 km/h (4 MPH) lower than set speed. (Set speed cannot be maintained.)
- O.D. will not be cancelled even if accelerator switch is turned "ON".

Check O.D. cancel circuit for A.S.C.D. control unit.

O.K.

Replace A.S.C.D. control unit.

N.G.

Check harness between O.D. cancel solenoid, O.D. control switch and A.S.C.D. control unit.

O.D. CANCEL CIRCUIT CHECK FOR A.S.C.D. CONTROL UNIT

- Turn ignition switch to "ON".
- Turn O.D. control switch to "ON"
- Check voltage ⑧ - ⑤.

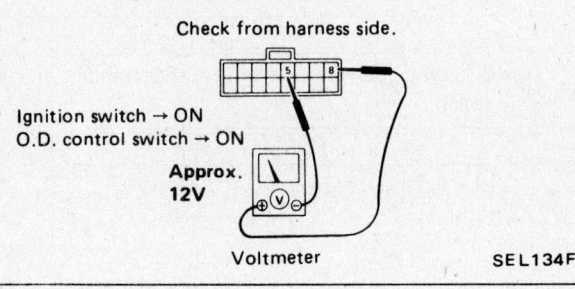

Check from harness side.

Ignition switch → ON
O.D. control switch → ON

Approx. 12V

Voltmeter   SEL134F

1. Check continuity between terminal ① and terminals ②, ③ and ④.

Continuity exist ... O.K.

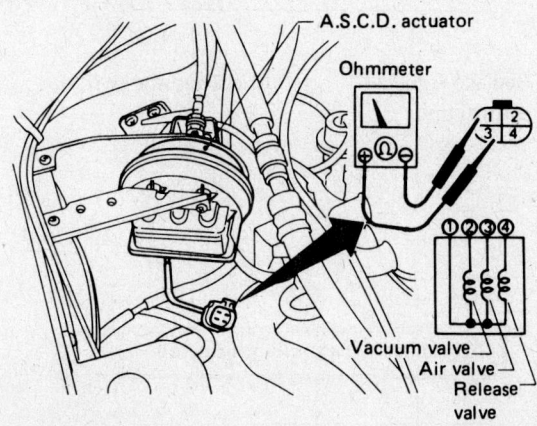

— A.S.C.D. actuator

Ohmmeter

Vacuum valve
Air valve
Release valve

CAUTION:

Do not attempt to remove valves from actuator.

2. Connect battery (approx. 12V) to harness connector of actuator as shown below, and apply vacuum to actuator.
   If diaphragm moves smoothly, actuator is O.K.

CAUTION:

When checking actuator by applying vacuum, do not apply engine vacuum directly as it is too strong to check actuator properly.

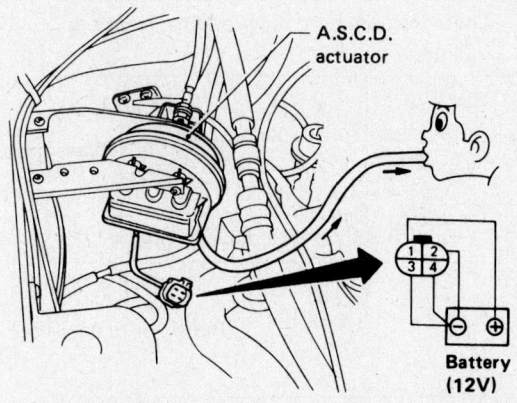

— A.S.C.D. actuator

Battery (12V)

Cruise control trouble diagnosis chart—1985 and later maxima

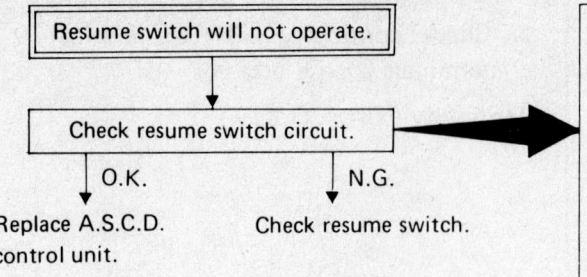

Resume switch will not operate.

↓

Check resume switch circuit.

O.K. → Replace A.S.C.D. control unit.

N.G. → Check resume switch.

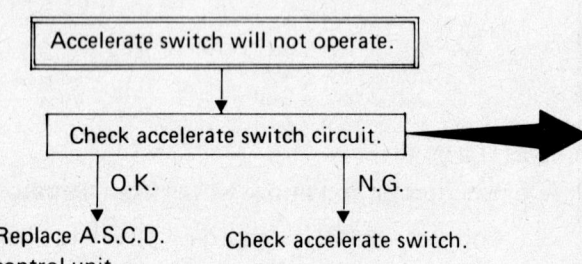

Accelerate switch will not operate.

↓

Check accelerate switch circuit.

O.K. → Replace A.S.C.D. control unit.

N.G. → Check accelerate switch.

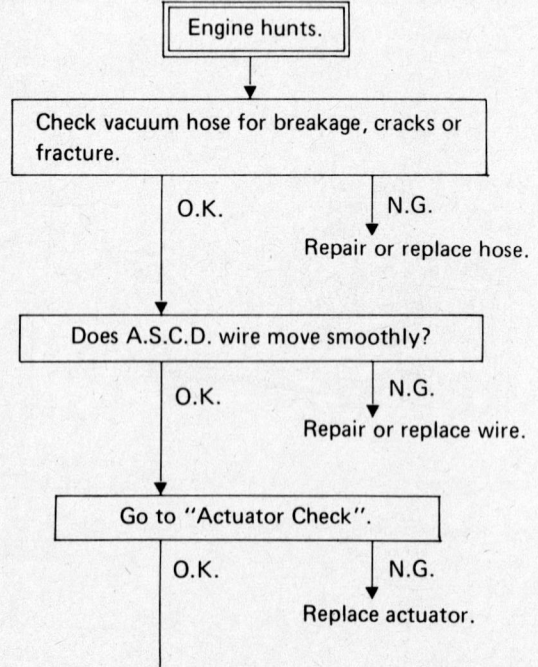

Engine hunts.

↓

Check vacuum hose for breakage, cracks or fracture.

O.K. ↓   N.G. → Repair or replace hose.

Does A.S.C.D. wire move smoothly?

O.K. ↓   N.G. → Repair or replace wire.

Go to "Actuator Check".

O.K. ↓   N.G. → Replace actuator.

Replace A.S.C.D. control unit.

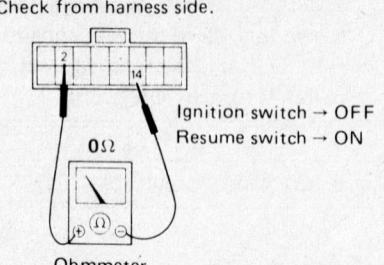

RESUME SWITCH CIRCUIT CHECK

1. Turn ignition switch to "OFF".
2. Turn resume switch to "ON".
3. Check continuity between ② and ⑭.

Check from harness side.

Ignition switch → OFF
Resume switch → ON

0 Ω

Ohmmeter

ACCELERATE SWITCH CIRCUIT CHECK

1. Turn ignition switch to "OFF".
2. Turn accelerate switch to "ON".
3. Check continuity between ③ and ⑭.

Check from harness side.

Ignition switch → OFF
Accelerator switch → ON

0 Ω

Ohmmeter

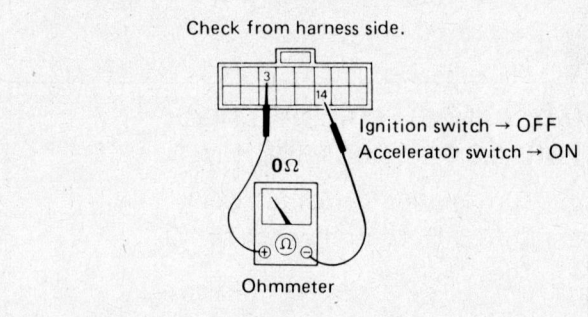

Large difference between set vehicle speed and actual speed.

↓

Check A.S.C.D. wire and actuator move smoothly.

O.K. ↓   N.G. → Replace wire or actuator.

Check vacuum hose for breakage, cracks or fracture.

O.K. ↓   N.G. → Repair or replace hose.

Go to "Actuator Check".

O.K. → Replace A.S.C.D. control unit.

N.G. → Replace actuator.

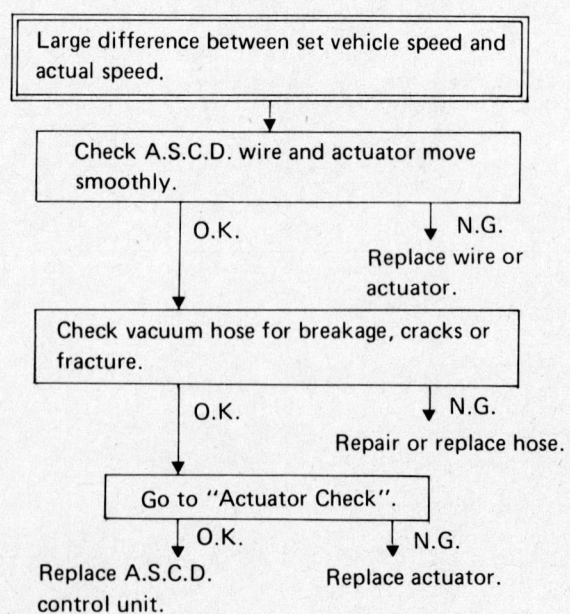

Cruise control trouble diagnosis chart—1985 and later maxima

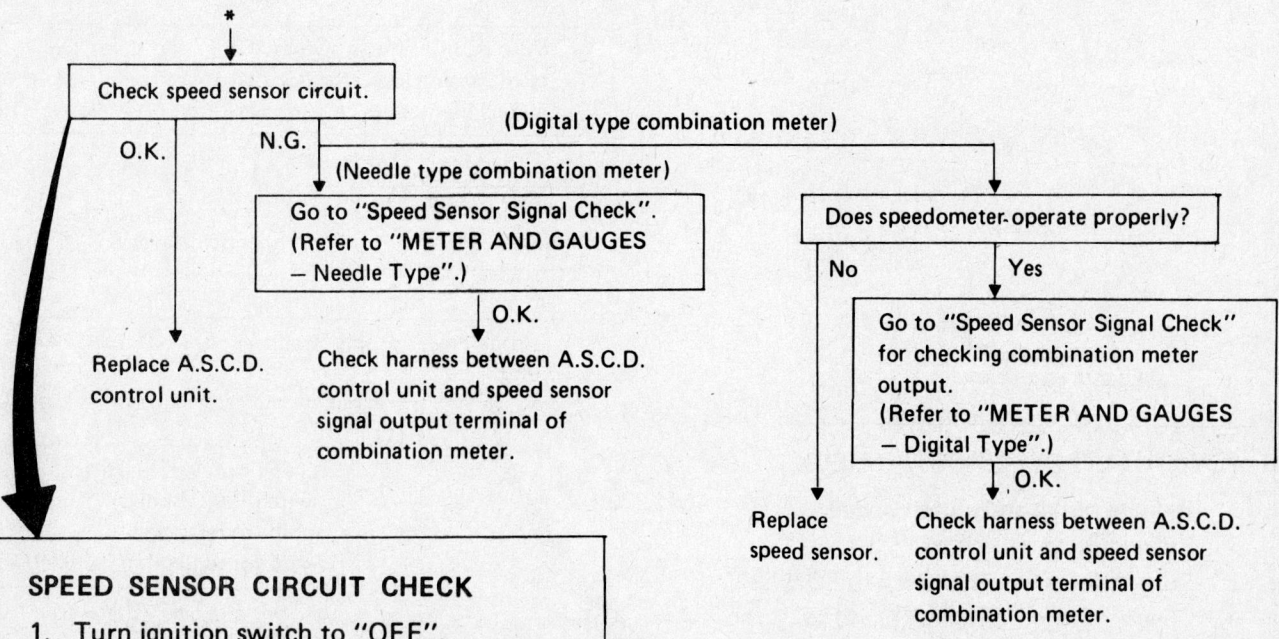

*

Check speed sensor circuit.

O.K.   N.G.   (Digital type combination meter)

(Needle type combination meter)

Go to "Speed Sensor Signal Check".
(Refer to "METER AND GAUGES
— Needle Type".)

Does speedometer operate properly?

No   Yes

O.K.

Replace A.S.C.D.
control unit.

Check harness between A.S.C.D.
control unit and speed sensor
signal output terminal of
combination meter.

Go to "Speed Sensor Signal Check"
for checking combination meter
output.
(Refer to "METER AND GAUGES
— Digital Type".)

O.K.

Replace
speed sensor.

Check harness between A.S.C.D.
control unit and speed sensor
signal output terminal of
combination meter.

SPEED SENSOR CIRCUIT CHECK

1. Turn ignition switch to "OFF".
2. Disconnect speedometer cable from transmission.
3. Connect an ohmmeter between ⑩ and
   ⑤.
4. Slowly turn speedometer cable pinion by
   hand to make sure ohmmeter pointer
   deflects.

- **Ohmmeter pointer deflects twice per
  rotation of pinion.**

Check from harness side

5

10

Ohmmeter

Cruise control trouble diagnosis chart—1985 and later maxima

● Remove A.S.C.D. control unit with harness connected.

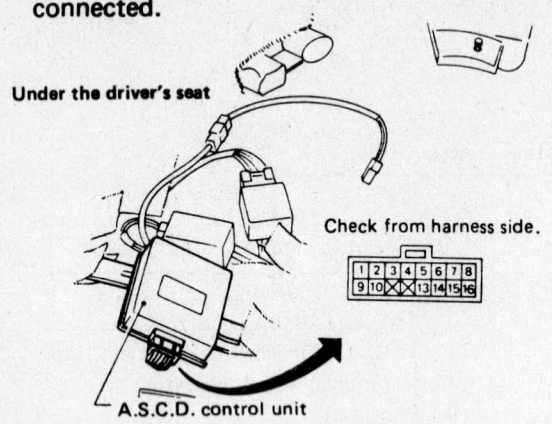

Under the driver's seat

Check from harness side.

A.S.C.D. control unit

A.S.C.D. control unit cannot be set properly.

↓

Turn A.S.C.D. main switch "OFF" and then "ON" to make sure indicator (located above combination meter) illuminates.

Yes ← → No

Yes	No
Check for loose vacuum hose.	Check A.S.C.D. main switch and A.S.C.D. relay.

O.K. ↓

Check power supply circuit for A.S.C.D. control unit.

O.K. ← → N.G.

N.G.: Check stop switch, clutch switch (M/T model), inhibitor relay and inhibitor switch (A/T model).

O.K. ↓

Check harness between A.S.C.D. power supply circuit.

↓

Check set switch circuit for A.S.C.D. control unit.

O.K. ← → N.G.

N.G.: Check set switch, and harness between control unit and set switch.

↓

Go to "A.S.C.D. Actuator Check".

O.K. ← → N.G.

O.K.: ✱ (Next page)

N.G.: Replace actuator.

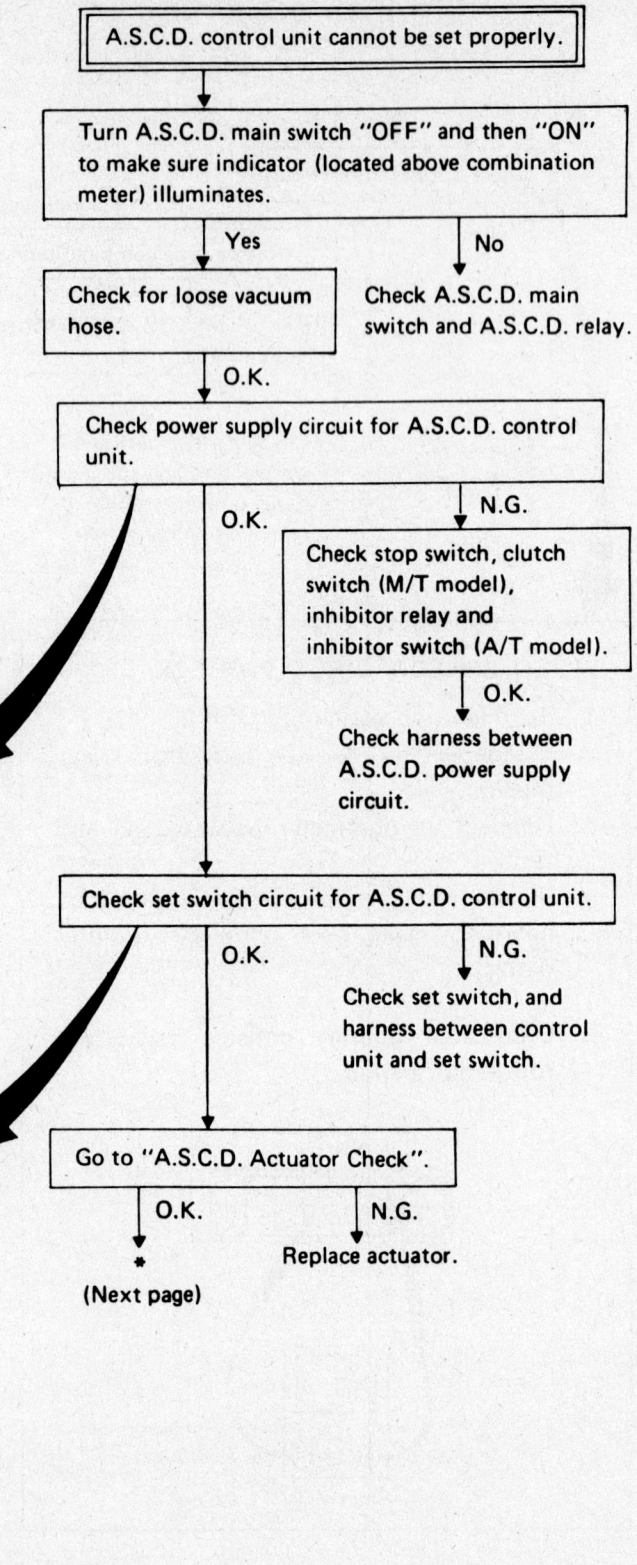

POWER SUPPLY CIRCUIT CHECK

1. Release brake and clutch pedals.
2. Turn ignition switch to "ON".
3. Turn A.S.C.D. main switch to "ON".
4. Check voltage between ⑬ and ⑤.

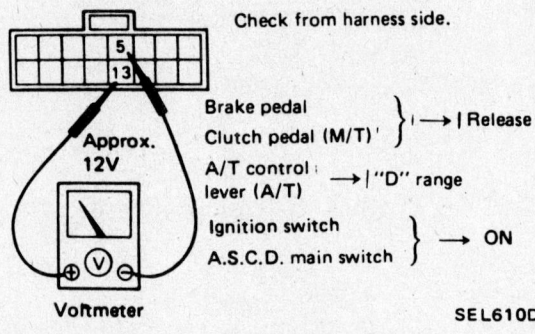

Check from harness side.

Approx. 12V

Brake pedal
Clutch pedal (M/T) } → | Release

A/T control lever (A/T) → | "D" range

Ignition switch
A.S.C.D. main switch } → ON

Voltmeter

SEL610D

SET SWITCH CIRCUIT CHECK

1. Turn ignition switch to "OFF".
2. Push A.S.C.D. set switch.
3. Check continuity between ① and ⑬.

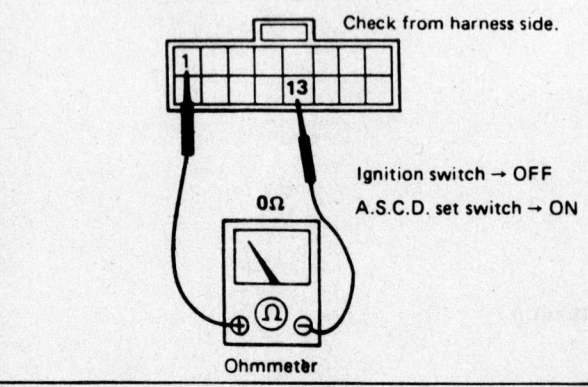

Check from harness side.

0Ω

Ignition switch → OFF
A.S.C.D. set switch → ON

Ohmmeter

Cruise control trouble diagnosis chart—1985 and later maxima

Component Replacement

ACTUATOR CABLE (1982–84)

Removal and Installation

1. Disconnect the actuator cable from the actuator assembly.
2. Loosen the locknut at the actuator.
3. Remove the rubber boots.
4. Loosen the adjusting nuts at the shaft and drum assembly.
5. Remove the cable from the actuator.
6. Installation is the reverse of the removal procedure. Adjust the cable as required.

ACTUATOR (1982–84)

Removal and Installation

1. Disconnect the negative battery cable.
2. Disconnect the cable from the actuator assembly.
3. Disconnect the vacuum hose. Disconnect the electrical connector.
4. Remove the actuator retaining bolt.
5. Remove the actuator from the vehicle.
6. Installation is the reverse of the removal procedure.

280ZX

VISUAL INSPECTION

Before performing any tests make a visual inspection of the cruise control system. Check all items in the system for abnormal conditions such as bare broken or disconnected wires and damage to the vacuum hoses. Be sure that the speedometer cables are attached and properly routed. All vacuum hoses must be properly routed and must not have any kinks or bends. Be sure that all electrical connections are complete and tight. The wiring harness must be routed properly.

ACTUATOR TEST

1. Visually inspect the actuator for damage or deformation.
2. Make sure that the assembly moves freely without binding when the diaphragm is pushed by hand.
3. Apply vacuum to the actuator, using a hand vacuum pump. Do not use engine vacuum. The diaphragm should move to the full up position.
4. Plug the hose with vacuum applied, the actuator should remain in the full position.
5. Repair or replace defective components as required.

SERVO VALVE TEST

1. Measure the resistance between the terminals. It should be 25 to 30 ohms.
2. Be sure that the valve opens and closes by blowing air through the port on the actuator side of the assembly.
3. Repair or replace defective components as required.

SOLENOID VALVE TEST

1. Measure the resistance between the terminals. It should be 25 to 30 ohms.
2. Check to be sure that the vacuum valve is performing properly.
3. Disconnect the solenoid valve side vacuum hose at the servo valve. Connect a vacuum gauge.
4. Start the engine and allow it to reach operating temperature or until the water temperature indicator points to the middle of the gauge.
5. Apply 0.3 amps of direct current between the terminals using a 20 ohm 5W variable resistor to adjust the current to specification.
6. If the vacuum gauge reads 2.17 to 3.35 in. Hg, than the component is good.
7. Repair or replace defective components as required.

SPEED SENSOR TEST

The speed sensor is built into the rear of the speedometer. Inspection of the speed sensor must be made with the speed sensor installed in the speedometer assembly. Turn the speedometer slowly by hand two complete turns. If continuity exists than the sensor is good.

MAIN SWITCH TEST

1. Test the continuity of the main switch assembly using and ohmmeter.
2. Repair or replace defective components as required.

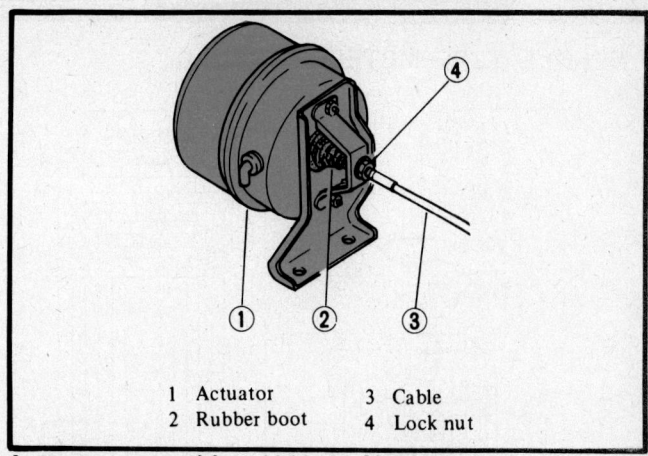

1 Actuator   3 Cable
2 Rubber boot   4 Lock nut

Actuator assembly – 1982–84 Maxima

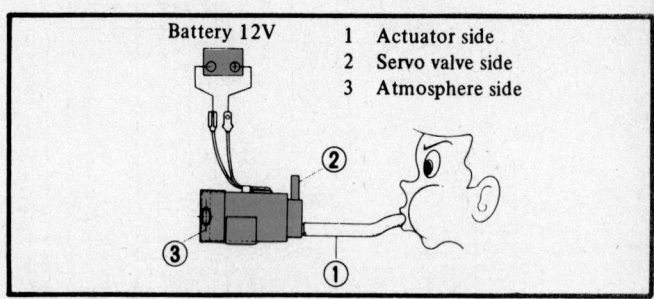

Battery 12V   1 Actuator side
2 Servo valve side
3 Atmosphere side

Servo valve test point locations – 280ZX

	Normal condition	12V direct current is applied between terminals
Normal condition	Yes	Yes
Plug port at servo valve side with a finger.	Yes	No

Yes: Air flow should exist.
No: Air flow should not exist.

Servo valve specifications – 280ZX

NEEDLE TYPE METER MODEL

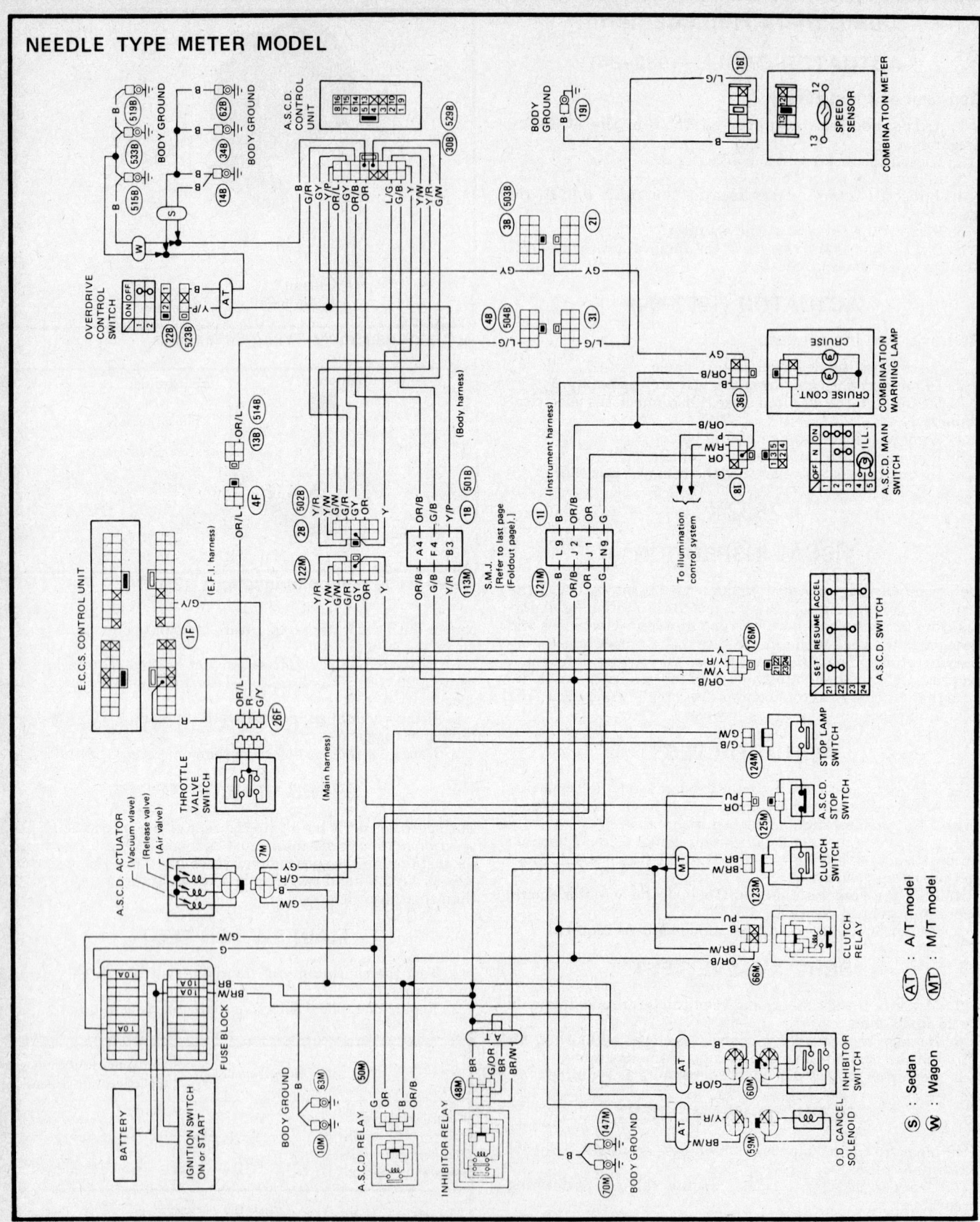

Cruise control electrical schematic—1985 Maxima

NEEDLE TYPE METER MODEL

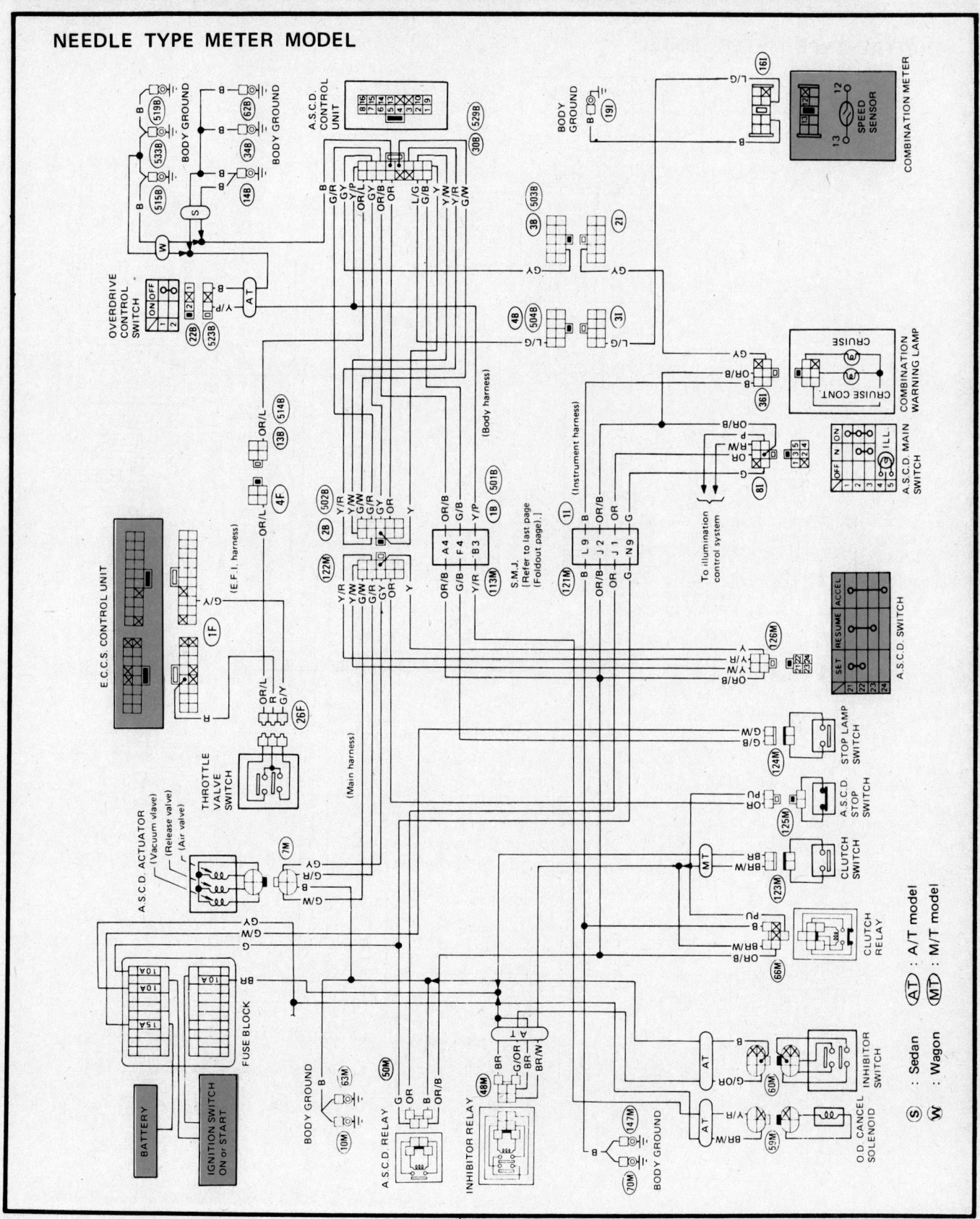

Cruise control electrical schematic—1986 Maxima

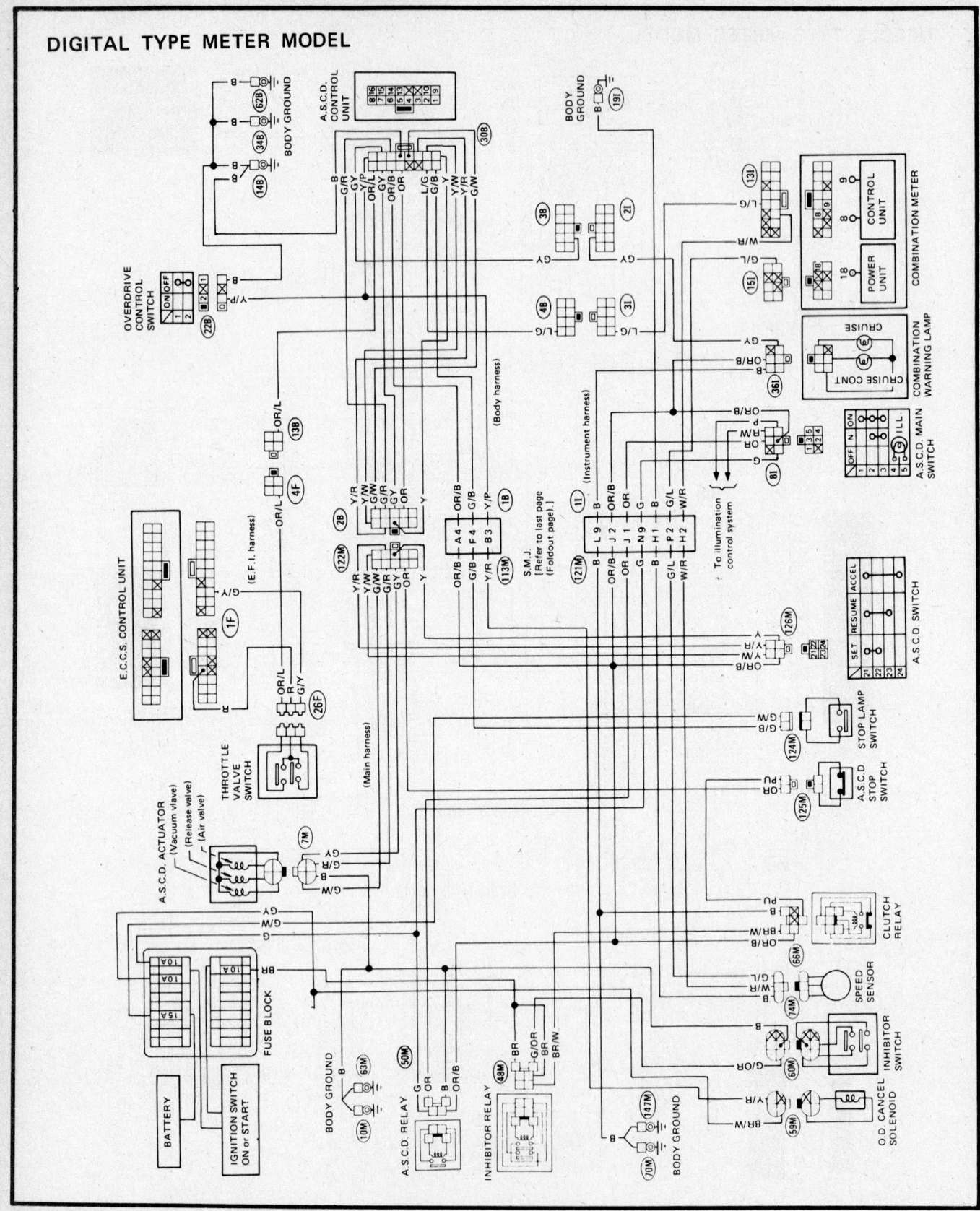

DIGITAL TYPE METER MODEL

Cruise control electrical schematic – 1986 Maxima

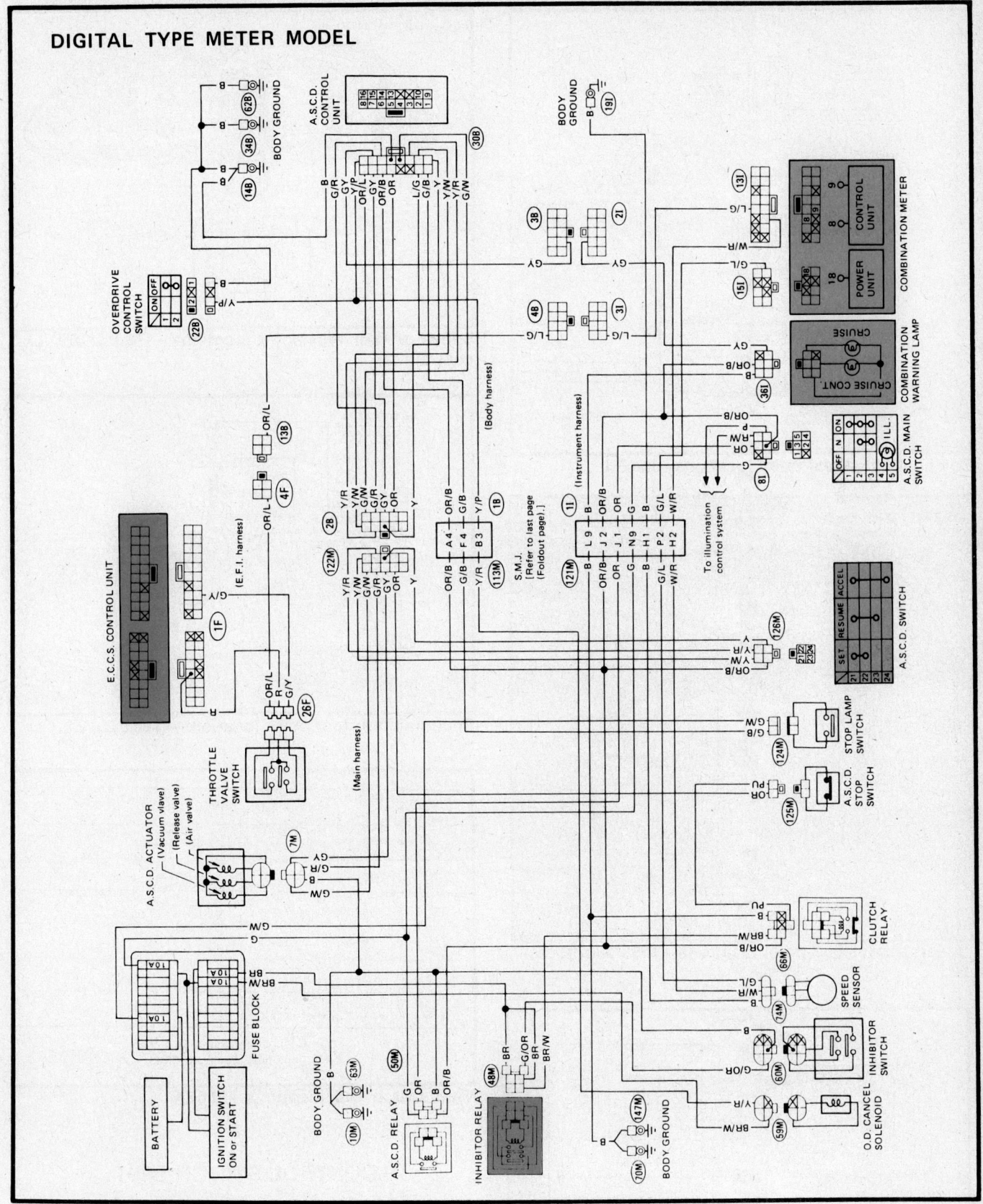

DIGITAL TYPE METER MODEL

Cruise control electrical schematic – 1985 Maxima

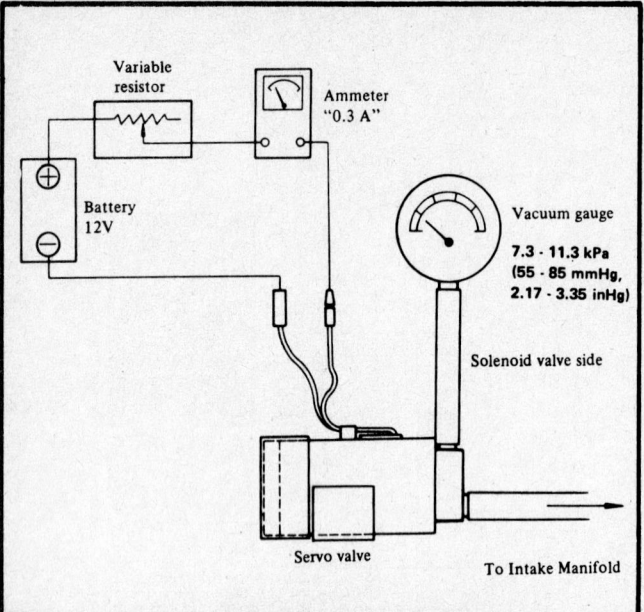

Variable resistor

Ammeter "0.3 A"

Battery 12V

Vacuum gauge
7.3 - 11.3 kPa
(55 - 85 mmHg,
2.17 - 3.35 inHg)

Solenoid valve side

Servo valve

To Intake Manifold

Solenoid valve test point locations — 280ZX

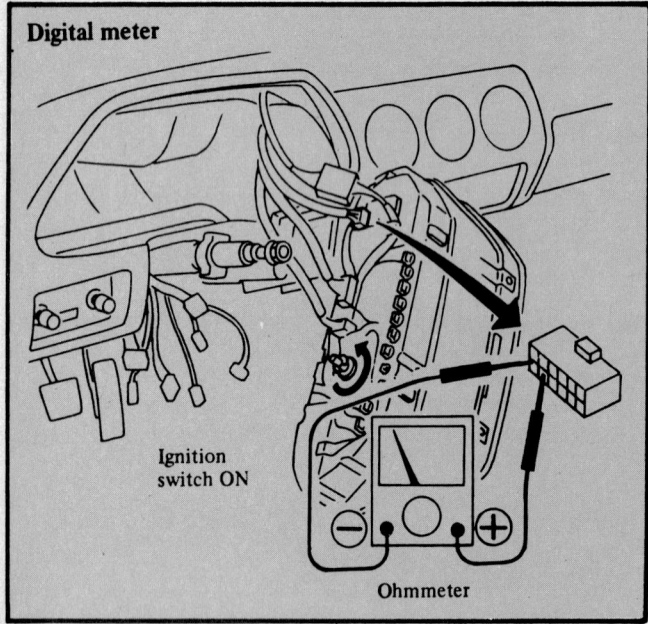

Digital meter

Ignition switch ON

Ohmmeter

Speed sensor test point locations — 1983 280ZX digital

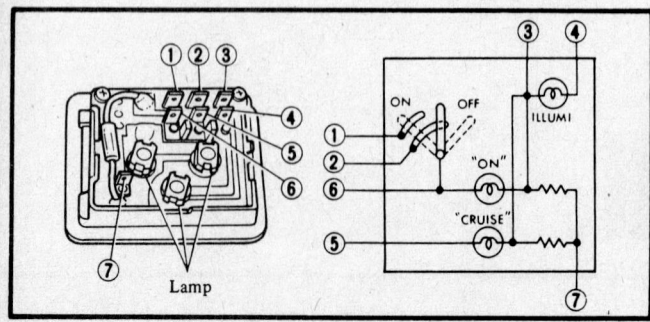

ON OFF

ILLUMI

"ON"

"CRUISE"

Lamp

Main switch test point locations — 280ZX

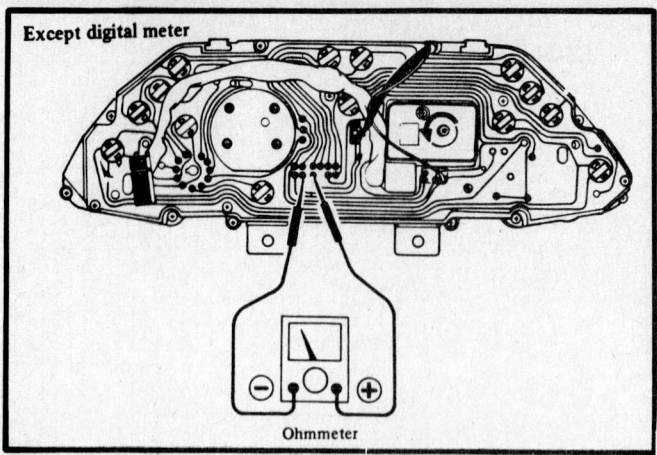

Except digital meter

Ohmmeter

Speed sensor test point locations — 1983 280ZX except digital

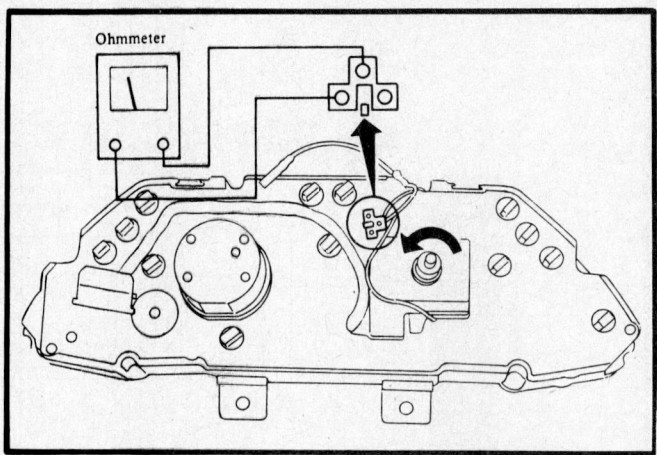

Ohmmeter

Speed sensor test point locations — 1982 280ZX

Switch position / Check terminal	Normal	ON	OFF
① – ②	No	Yes	No
① – ⑥	No	Yes	No
② – ⑥	Yes	Yes	No
③ – ④	Yes	–	–
⑤ – ⑦	Yes	–	–
⑥ – ⑦	Yes	–	–

Yes: Continuity should exist.
No: Continuity should not exist.

Main switch specifications — 280ZX

CONTROL SWITCH TEST

1. Test the continuity of the main switch assembly using and ohmmeter.
2. Repair or replace defective components as required.

STOP LIGHT SWITCH TEST

1. Test the continunity of the main switch assembly using and ohmmeter.
2. Repair or replace defective components as required.

ASCD RELAY TEST

Using an ohmmeter check the component for the proper continunity.

ASCD INHIBITOR RELAY TEST

Using an ohmmeter check the component for the proper continunity.

ASCD CONTROLLER TEST

This component must be checked as a single part. When checking this component do not touch the test probe to any terminal other than the ones used to check the component as damage to the controller could result. Keep the controller away from electric noise to prevent the ASCD system from malfunctioning and the IC circuit from being destroyed.

ACTUATOR ADJUSTMENT

1. Without depressing the accelerator, adjust the adjusting nuts until all freeplay is removed.
2. Return the adjusting nuts until 0.08 to 0.12 inch of freeplay is obtained.
3. Do not increase the cable tension excessively, as this can cause cable damage.

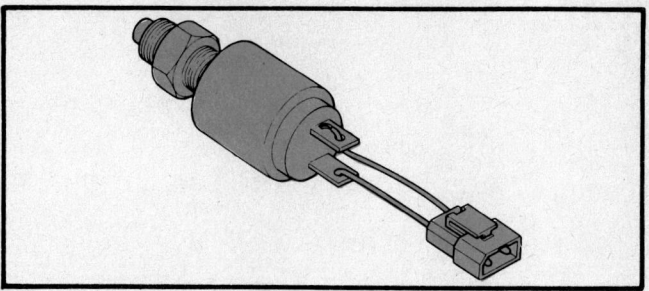

Stoplight switch – 280ZX

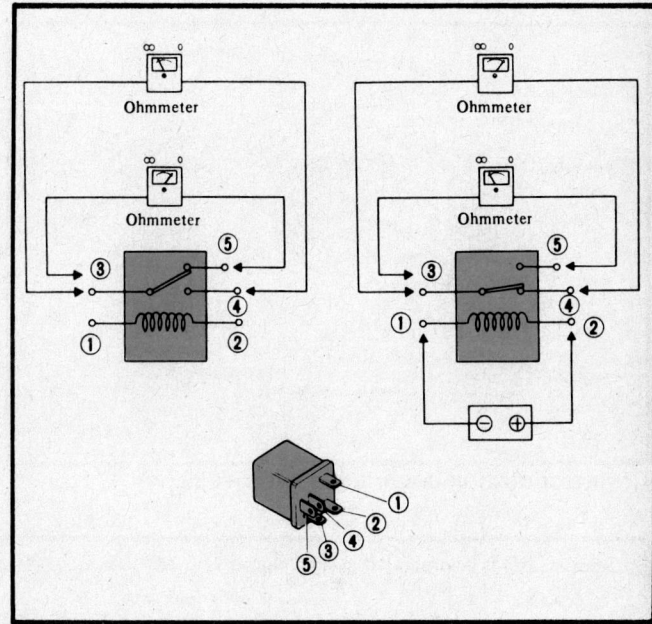

ASCD relay test point locations – 280ZX

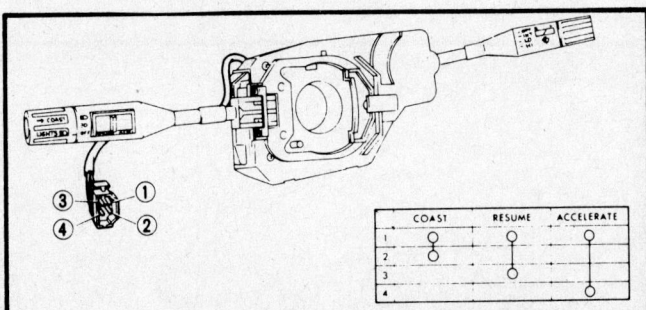

Control switch test point locations – 280ZX

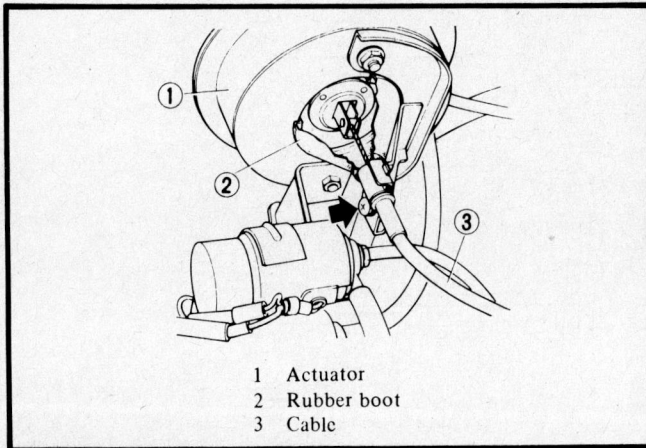

1   Actuator
2   Rubber boot
3   Cable

Actuator assembly – 280ZX

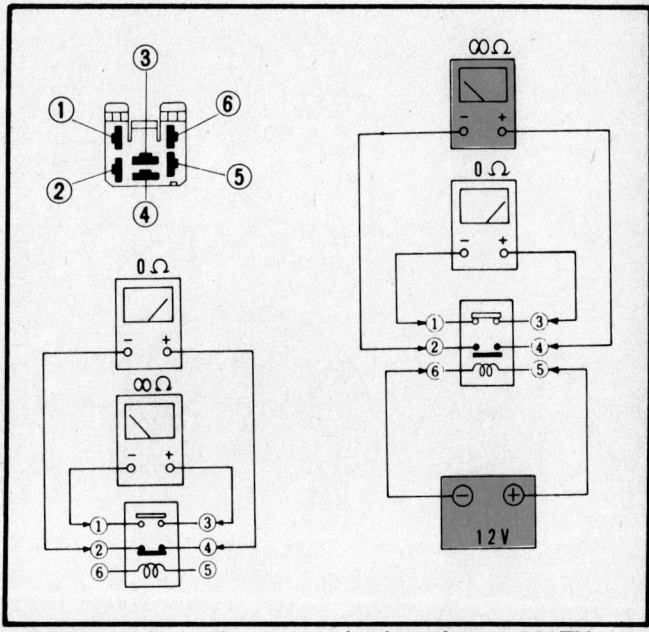

ASCD inhibitor relay test point locations – 280ZX

A
②
①

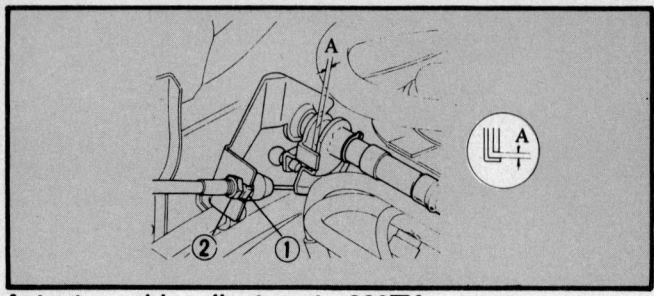

Actuator cable adjustment—280ZX

DIAGNOSIS AND TESTING PROCEDURES

Servo valve
Solenoid valve
Actuator
A.S.C.D. cable
Vacuum pump relay (Ⓟ)
Inhibitor relay (A/T only)
Vacuum tank (Ⓟ)
Vacuum switch (Ⓟ)
Vacuum hose
Vacuum pump (Ⓟ)
Ⓟ: Turbocharger models

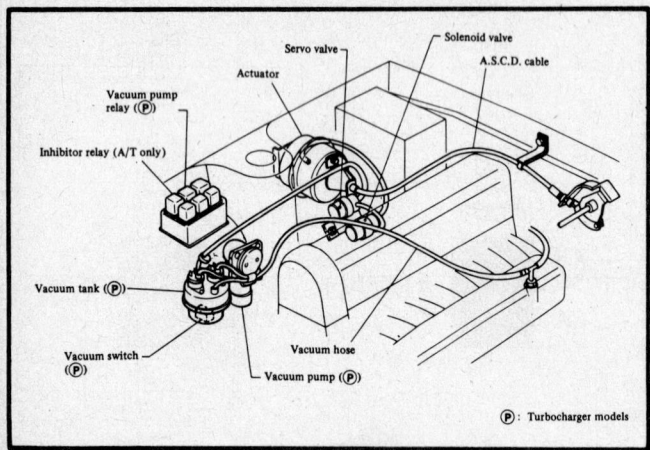

Cruise control vacuum schematic—280ZX

BATTERY
MAIN SWITCH
IGNITION SWITCH
ON
OFF
"ON"
"CRUISE"
SOLENOID VALVE
ACTUATOR
A.S.C.D. RELAY
SERVO VALVE
TO INTAKE MANIFOLD
VACUUM PUMP RELAY
VACUUM TANK
VACUUM PUMP
TO BATTERY
STOP LAMP SWITCH
SET SWITCH
VACUUM SWITCH
RESUME SWITCH
CLUTCH SWITCH (M/T)
STOP SWITCH
SPEED SENSOR
CONTROLLER
ACCELERATE SWITCH
ACCELERATOR TORSION SHAFT
OPEN
CLOSED
INHIBITOR RELAY (A/T)
INHIBITOR SWITCH (A/T)

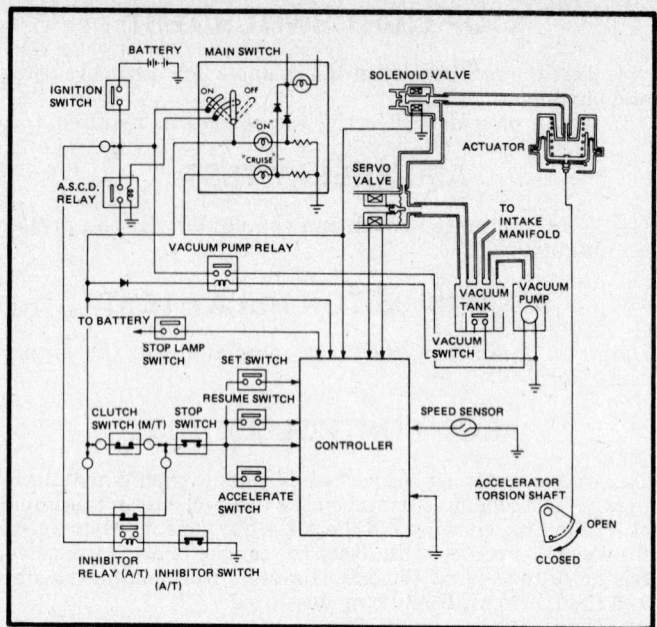

Cruise control system and related components—280ZX

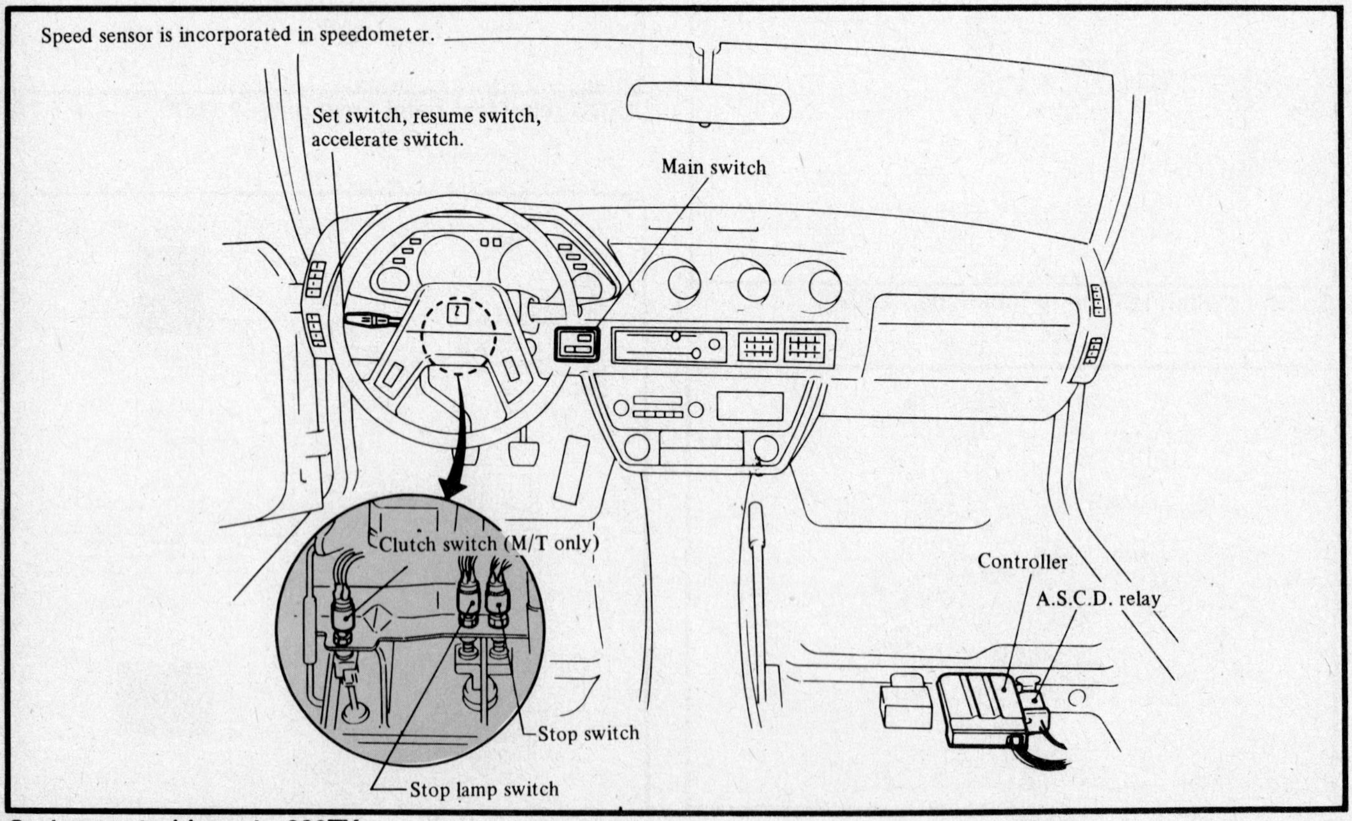

Speed sensor is incorporated in speedometer.
Set switch, resume switch, accelerate switch.
Main switch
Clutch switch (M/T only)
Controller
A.S.C.D. relay
Stop switch
Stop lamp switch

Cruise control layout—280ZX

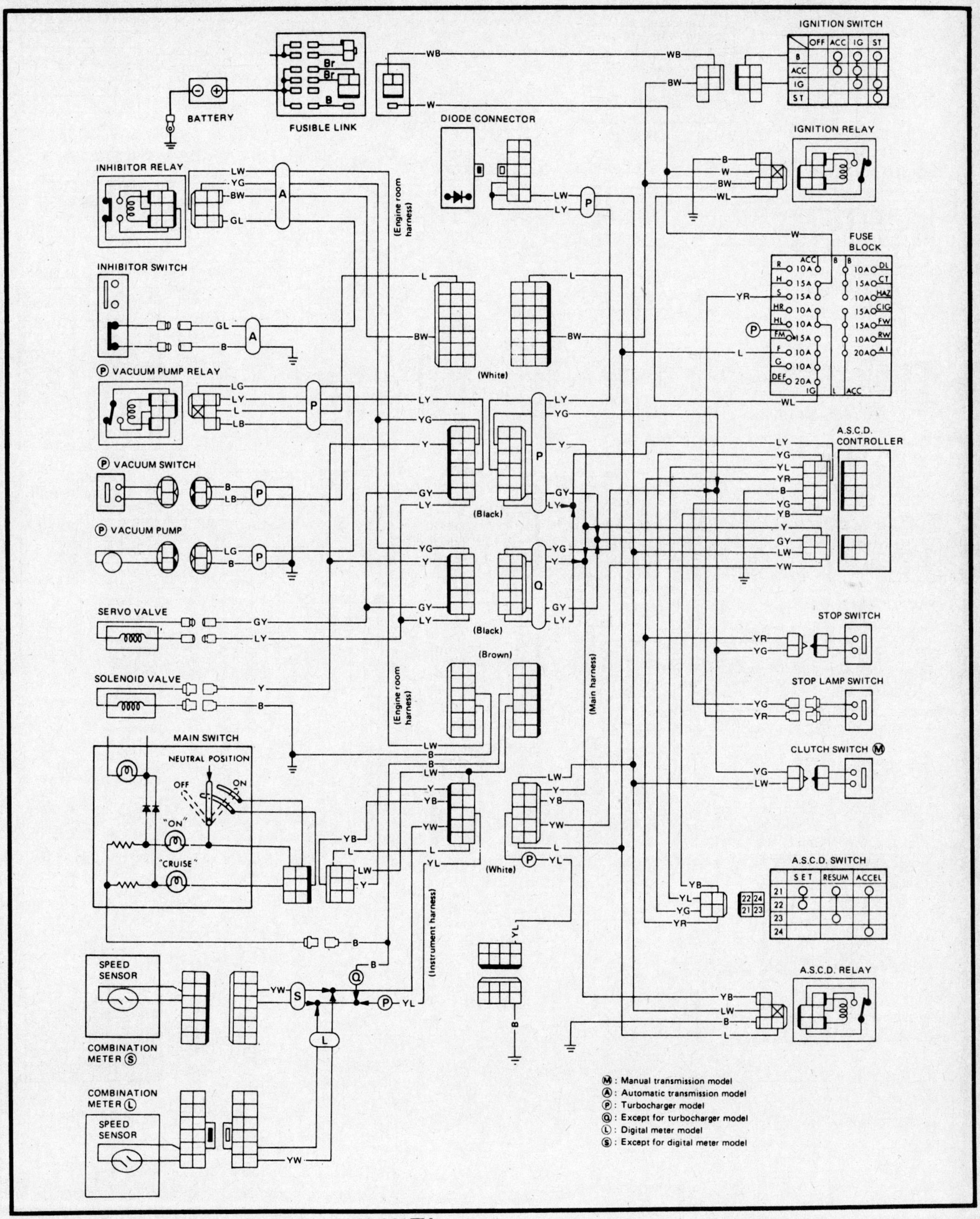

Cruise control electrical schematic – 1982 280ZX

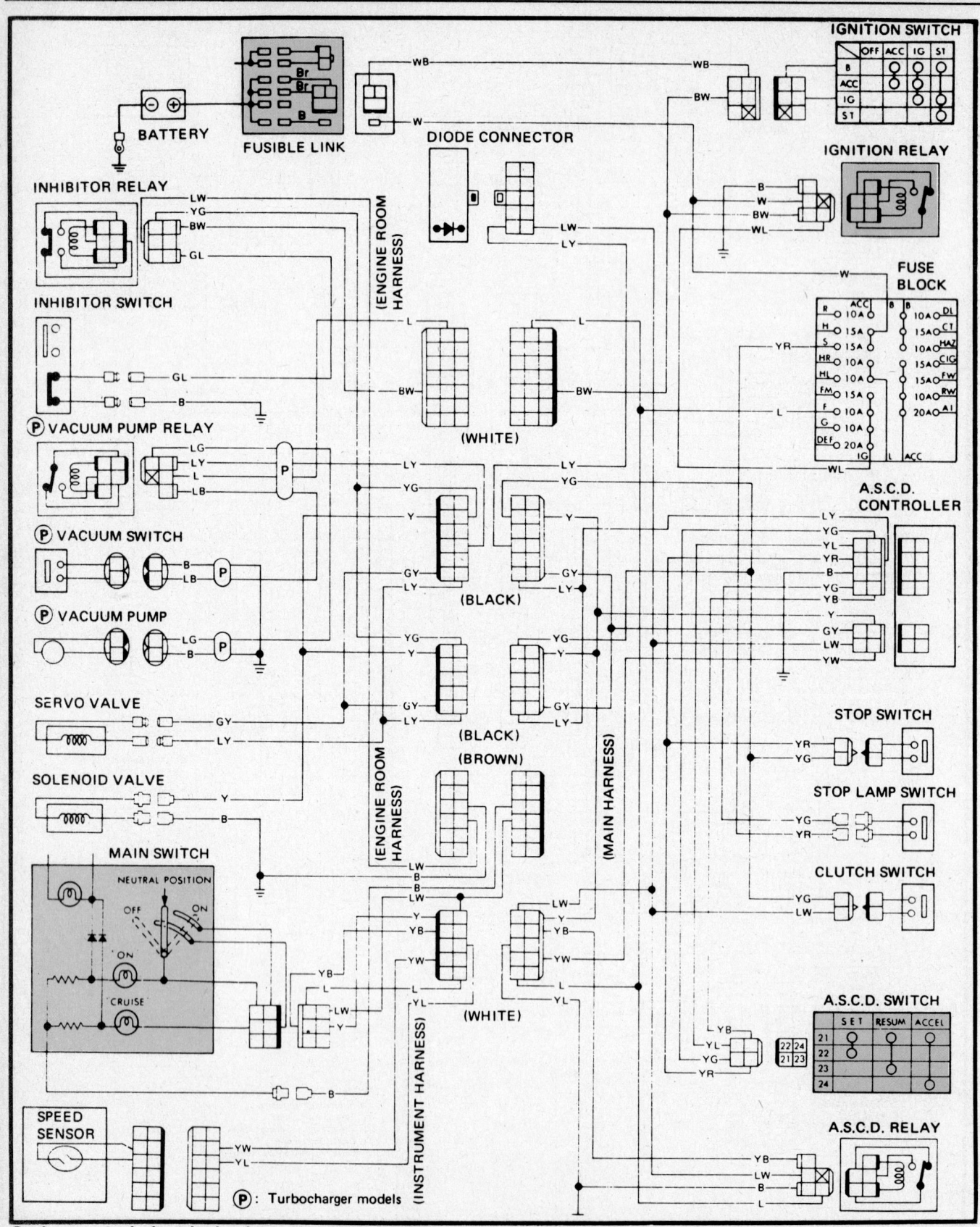

Cruise control electrical schematic – 1983 280ZX

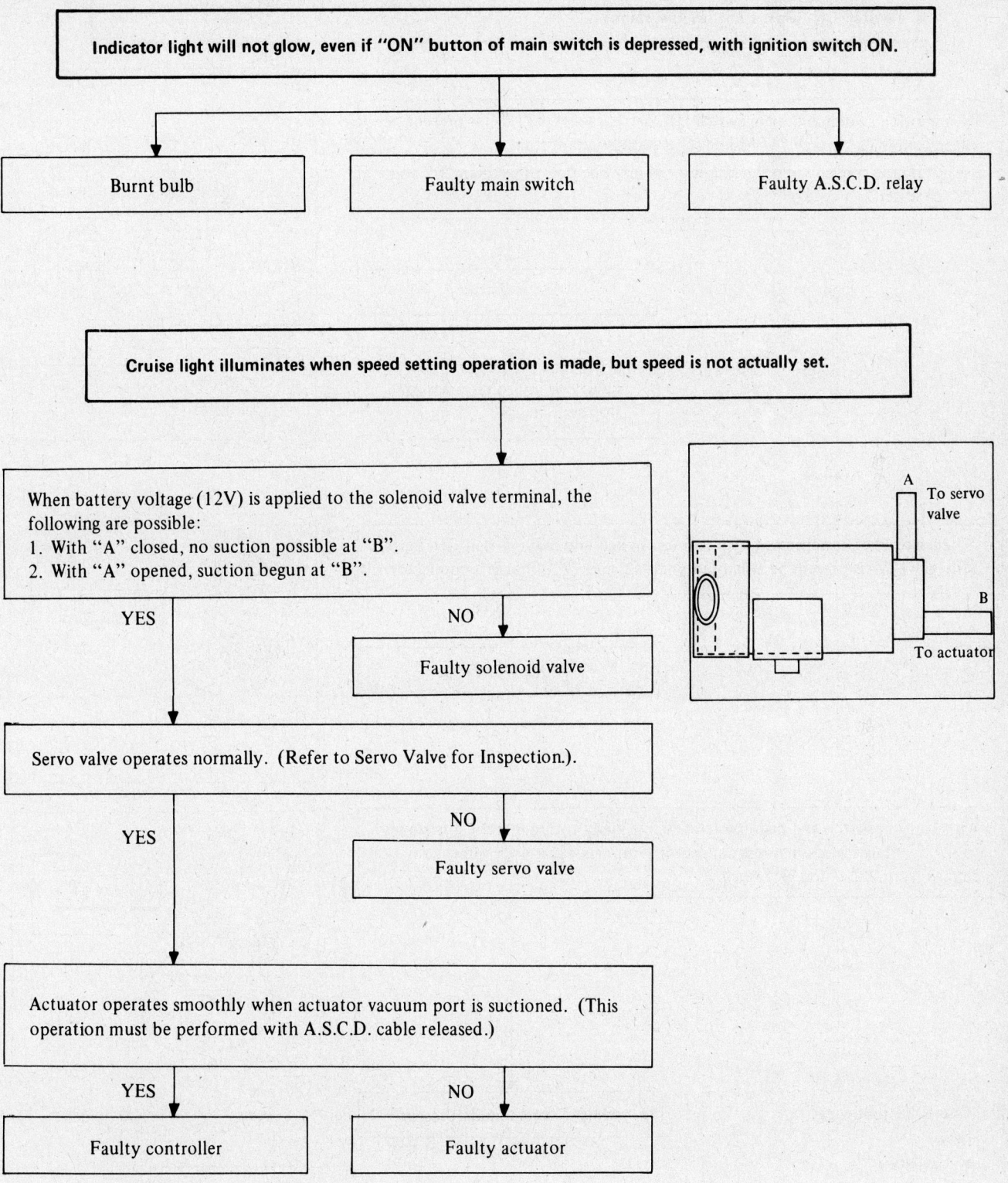

Indicator light will not glow, even if "ON" button of main switch is depressed, with ignition switch ON.

| Burnt bulb | Faulty main switch | Faulty A.S.C.D. relay |

Cruise light illuminates when speed setting operation is made, but speed is not actually set.

When battery voltage (12V) is applied to the solenoid valve terminal, the following are possible:
1. With "A" closed, no suction possible at "B".
2. With "A" opened, suction begun at "B".

YES

NO
Faulty solenoid valve

A — To servo valve
B — To actuator

Servo valve operates normally. (Refer to Servo Valve for Inspection.).

YES

NO
Faulty servo valve

Actuator operates smoothly when actuator vacuum port is suctioned. (This operation must be performed with A.S.C.D. cable released.)

YES
Faulty controller

NO
Faulty actuator

Cruise control trouble diagnosis chart—280ZX

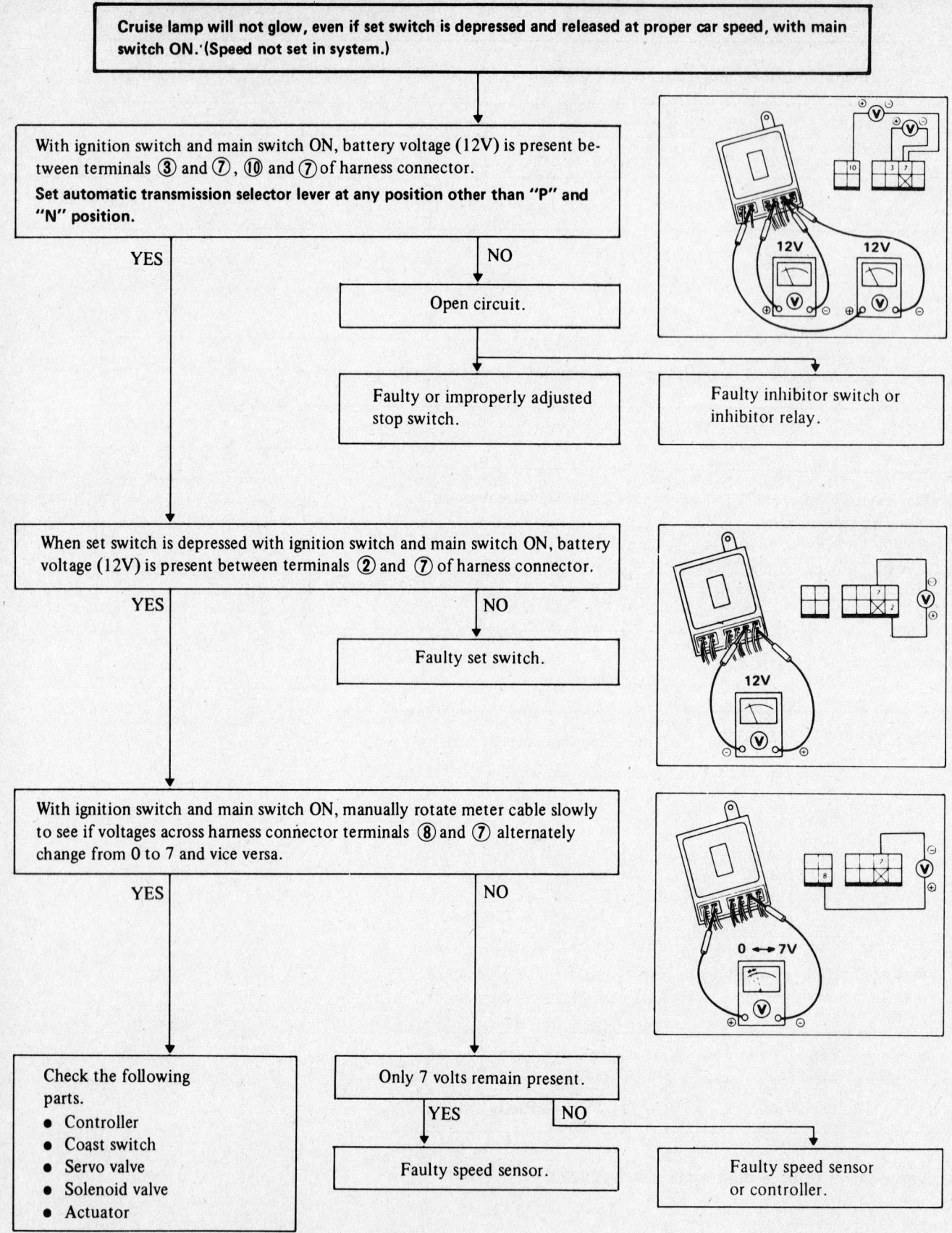

Cruise lamp will not glow, even if set switch is depressed and released at proper car speed, with main switch ON. (Speed not set in system.)

With ignition switch and main switch ON, battery voltage (12V) is present between terminals ③ and ⑦, ⑩ and ⑦ of harness connector.

Set automatic transmission selector lever at any position other than "P" and "N" position.

YES → NO

Open circuit.

Faulty or improperly adjusted stop switch.

Faulty inhibitor switch or inhibitor relay.

When set switch is depressed with ignition switch and main switch ON, battery voltage (12V) is present between terminals ② and ⑦ of harness connector.

YES → NO

Faulty set switch.

With ignition switch and main switch ON, manually rotate meter cable slowly to see if voltages across harness connector terminals ⑧ and ⑦ alternately change from 0 to 7 and vice versa.

YES → NO

Check the following parts.
- Controller
- Coast switch
- Servo valve
- Solenoid valve
- Actuator

Only 7 volts remain present.

YES → NO

Faulty speed sensor.

Faulty speed sensor or controller.

Cruise control trouble diagnosis chart—280ZX

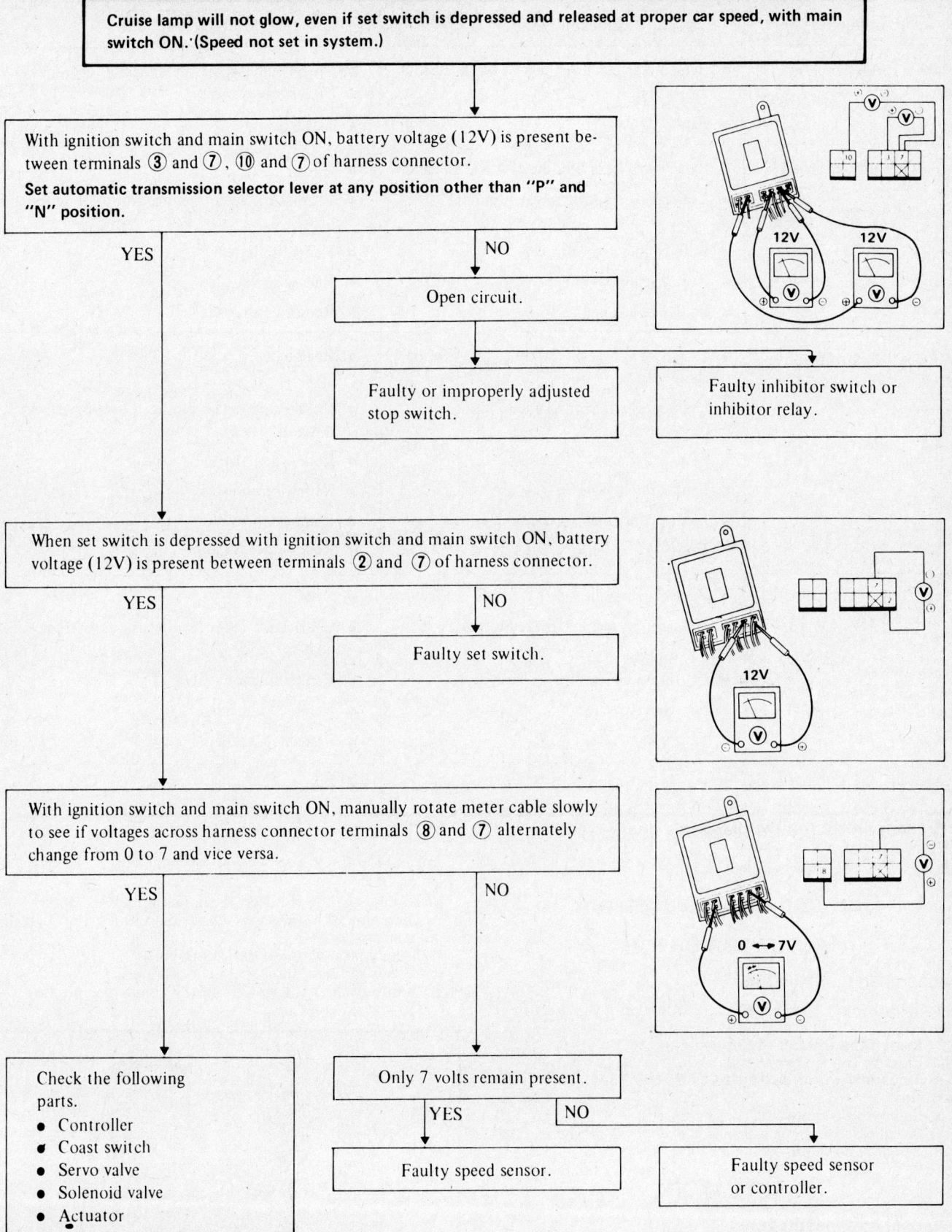

Cruise lamp will not glow, even if set switch is depressed and released at proper car speed, with main switch ON. (Speed not set in system.)

With ignition switch and main switch ON, battery voltage (12V) is present between terminals ③ and ⑦, ⑩ and ⑦ of harness connector.
Set automatic transmission selector lever at any position other than "P" and "N" position.

YES — NO

Open circuit.

Faulty or improperly adjusted stop switch.

Faulty inhibitor switch or inhibitor relay.

When set switch is depressed with ignition switch and main switch ON, battery voltage (12V) is present between terminals ② and ⑦ of harness connector.

YES — NO

Faulty set switch.

With ignition switch and main switch ON, manually rotate meter cable slowly to see if voltages across harness connector terminals ⑧ and ⑦ alternately change from 0 to 7 and vice versa.

YES — NO

Check the following parts.
- Controller
- Coast switch
- Servo valve
- Solenoid valve
- Actuator

Only 7 volts remain present.

YES — NO

Faulty speed sensor.

Faulty speed sensor or controller.

Cruise control trouble diagnosis chart – 280ZX

Condition	Probable cause	Corrective action
Set speed is cancelled.	• Bent meter cable (excessive meter needle deflection.) • Faulty controller	• Check and repair meter cable, or renew cable. • Renew.
Pulsation of set speed	• Excessive play or binding of A.S.C.D. cable • Leakage or clogging in vacuum hose • Binding in actuator • Faulty servo valve • Faulty controller	• Adjust. • Check and repair piping route, or renew hose. • Renew actuator. • Renew servo valve. • Renew controller.
Excessive setting error	• Excessive play or binding in A.S.C.D. cable • Leakage or clogging in vacuum hose • Faulty actuator • Faulty servo valve • Faulty controller • Faulty speed sensor	• Readjust. • Check and repair piping route, or renew hose. • Renew actuator. • Renew servo valve. • Renew controller. • Renew speedometer
Speed drops immediately after setting	• Excessive play in A.S.C.D. cable • Leakage or clogging in vacuum hose • Faulty solenoid valve • Faulty servo valve • Faulty controller	• Readjust. • Check and repair piping route, or renew hose. • Renew solenoid valve. • Renew servo valve. • Renew controller.
Cancel circuit inoperative	• Faulty controller	• Renew controller.

Cruise control trouble diagnosis chart—280ZX

Component Replacement

ACTUATOR CABLE

Removal and Installation

1. Disconnect the actuator cable from the actuator assembly.
2. Loosen the locknut at the actuator.
3. Remove the rubber boots.
4. Loosen the adjusting nuts at the shaft and drum assembly.
5. Remove the cable from the actuator.
6. Installation is the reverse of the removal procedure. Adjust the cable as required.

ACTUATOR

Removal and Installation

1. Disconnect the negative battery cable.

2. Disconnect the cable from the actuator assembly.
3. Disconnect the vacuum hose. Disconnect the electrical connector.
4. Remove the actuator retaining bolt.
5. Remove the actuator from the vehicle.
6. Installation is the reverse of the removal procedure.

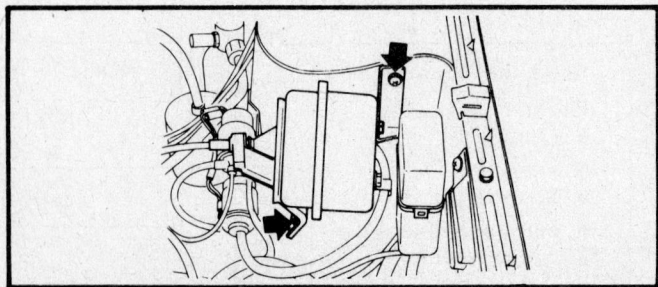

Actuator mounting and related components—280ZX

SOLENOID AND SERVO VALVE

Removal and installation

1. Disconnect the negative battery cable.
2. Disconnect the electrical harness connector. Remove the valve.
3. Installation is the reverse of the removal procedure.

SPEED SENSOR

Removal and Installation

The speed sensor is installed in the speedometer head. In order to remove the speed sensor the speedometer must first be removed from the vehicle.

MAIN SWITCH

Removal and Installation

1. Disconnect the negative battery cable.
2. Push the switch assembly out from behind the instrument panel.
3. Remove the switch electrical connector. Remove the switch from the vehicle.
4. Installation is the reverse of the removal procedure.

ASCD RELAY AND CONTROLLER

Removal and Installation

1. Disconnect the negative battery cable.
2. Remove the passenger seat.
3. Disconnect the electrical connectors from the component to be removed.
4. Remove the component retaining screws. Remove the component.
5. Installation is the reverse of the removal procedure.

INHIBITOR RELAY AND VACUUM PUMP RELAY

Removal and Installation

1. Disconnect the negative battery cable.
2. Remove the relay cover.
3. Remove the relay assembly from its mounting.
4. Installation is the reverse of the removal procedure.

300ZX

VISUAL INSPECTION

Before performing any tests make a visual inspection of the cruise control system. Check all items in the system for abnormal conditions such as bare broken or disconnected wires and damage to the vacuum hoses. Be sure that the speedometer cables are attached and properly routed. All vacuum hoses must be properly routed and must not have any kinks or bends. Be sure that all electrical connections are complete and tight. The wiring harness must be routed properly.

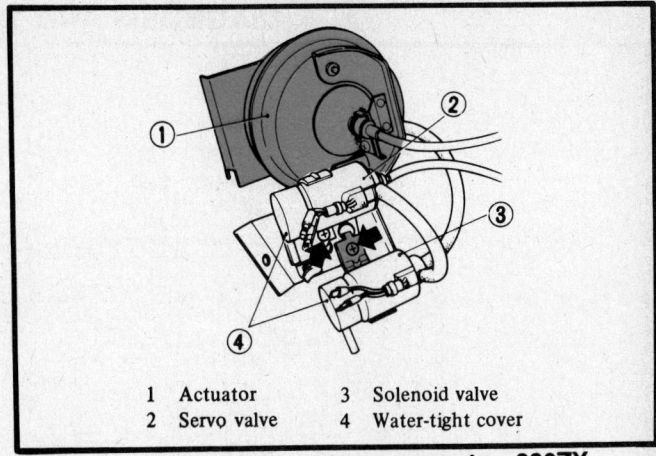

| 1 | Actuator | 3 | Solenoid valve |
| 2 | Servo valve | 4 | Water-tight cover |

Solenoid valve and related components—280ZX

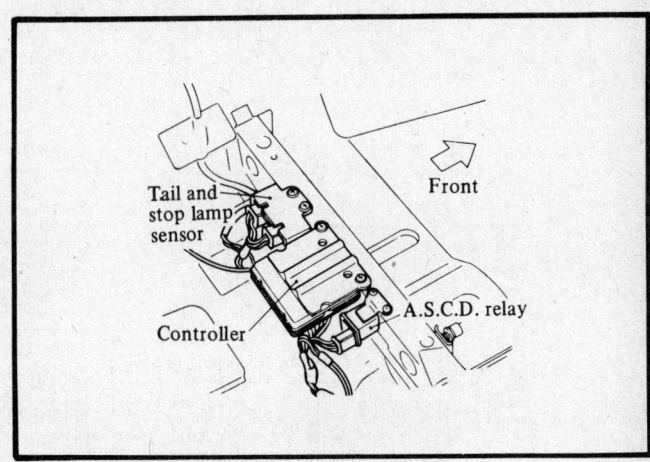

Controller and relay location—280ZX

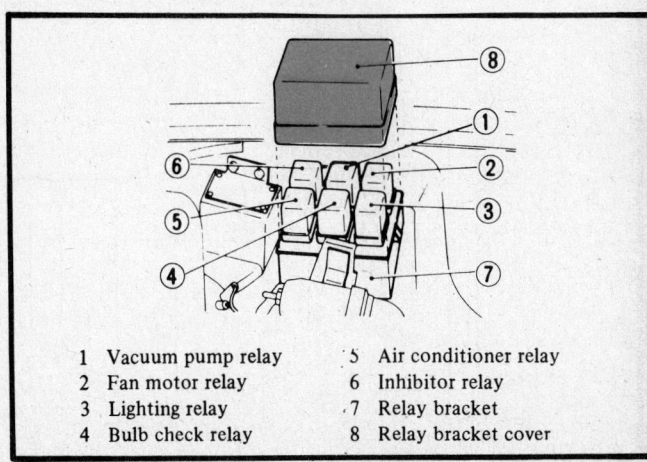

1	Vacuum pump relay	5	Air conditioner relay
2	Fan motor relay	6	Inhibitor relay
3	Lighting relay	7	Relay bracket
4	Bulb check relay	8	Relay bracket cover

Vacuum pump relay and related components—280ZX

DIAGNOSIS AND TESTING PROCEDURES

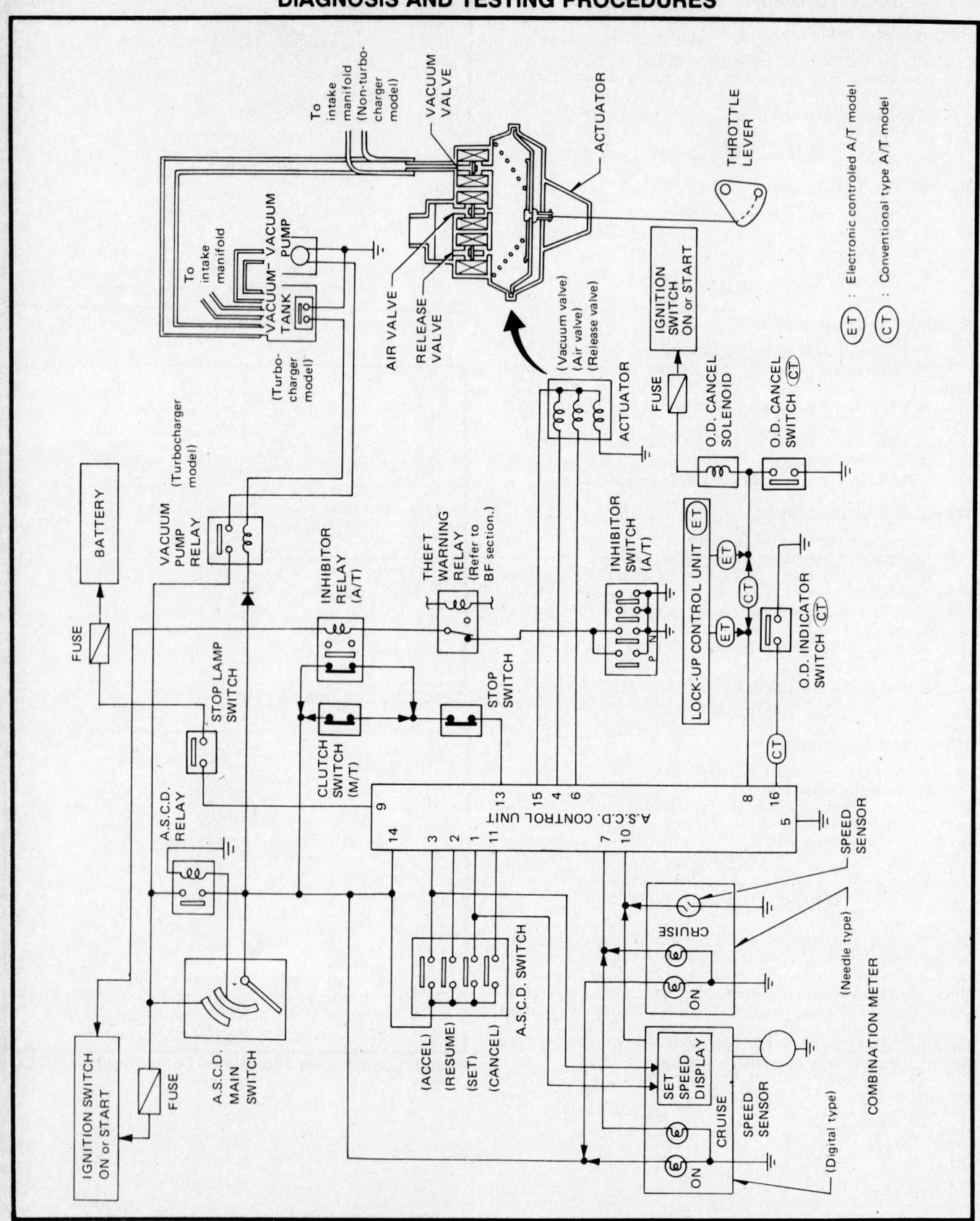

Cruise control operational achematic—1984 300ZX

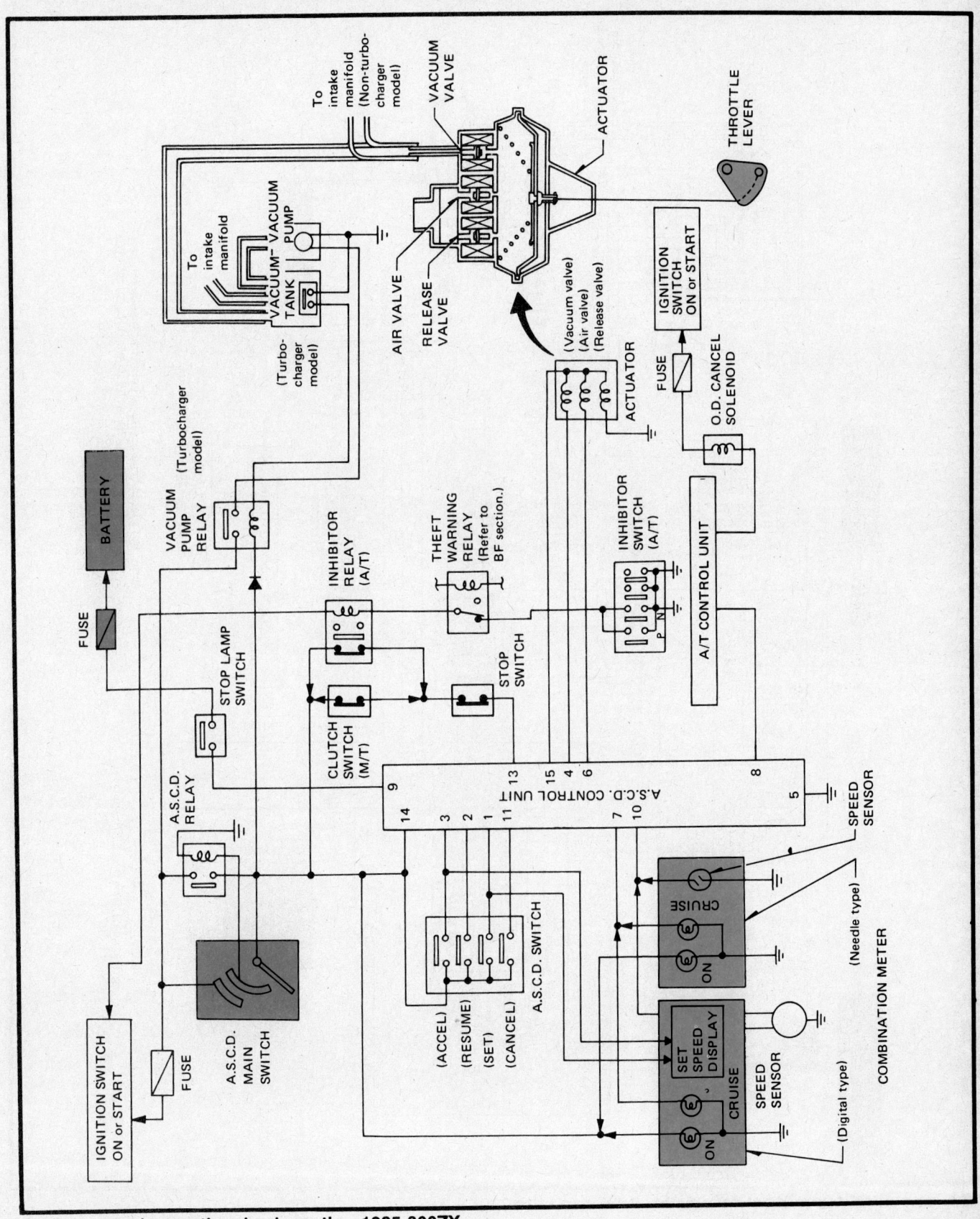

Cruise control operational schematic — 1985 300ZX

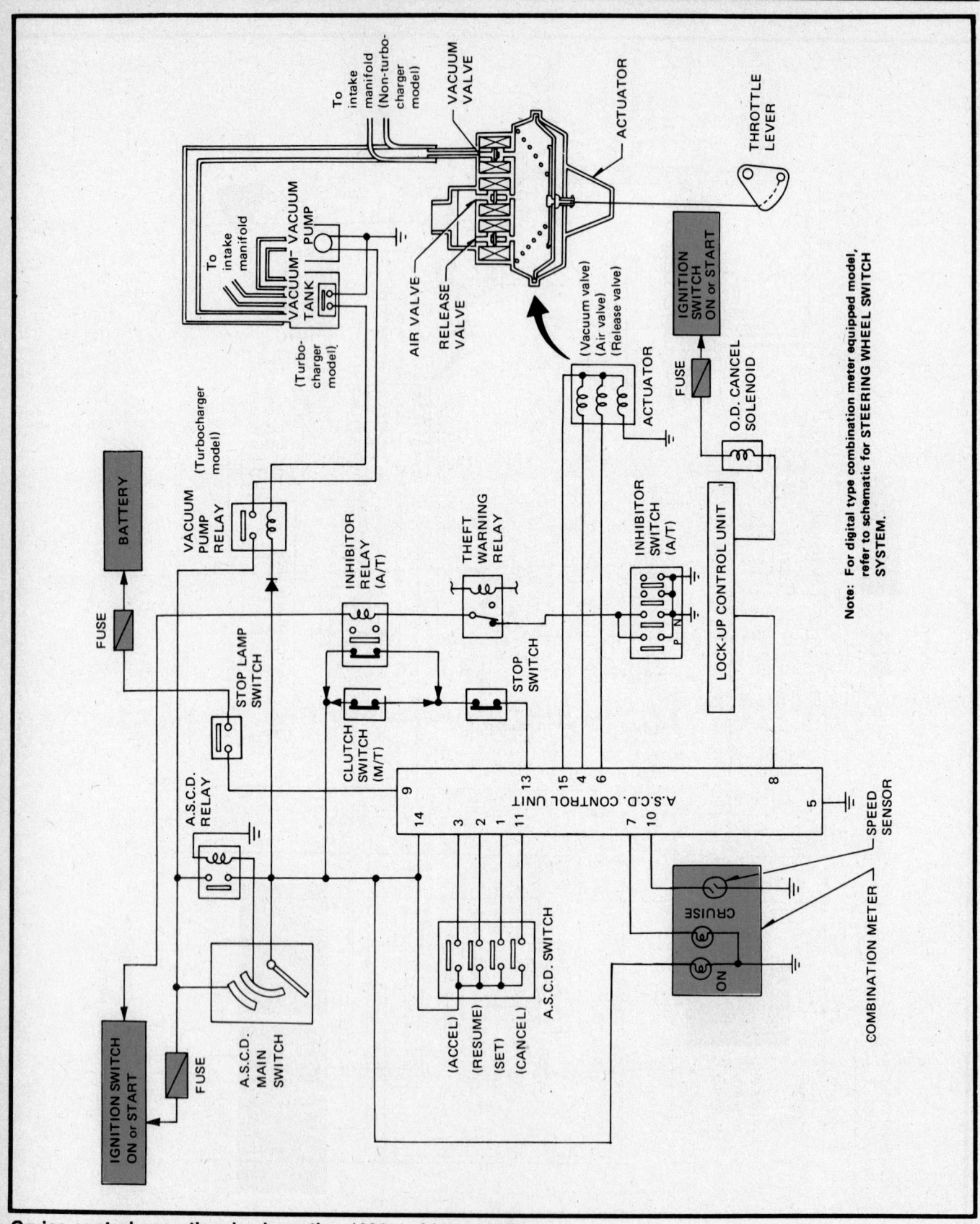

Cruise control operational schematic — 1986 and later 300ZX

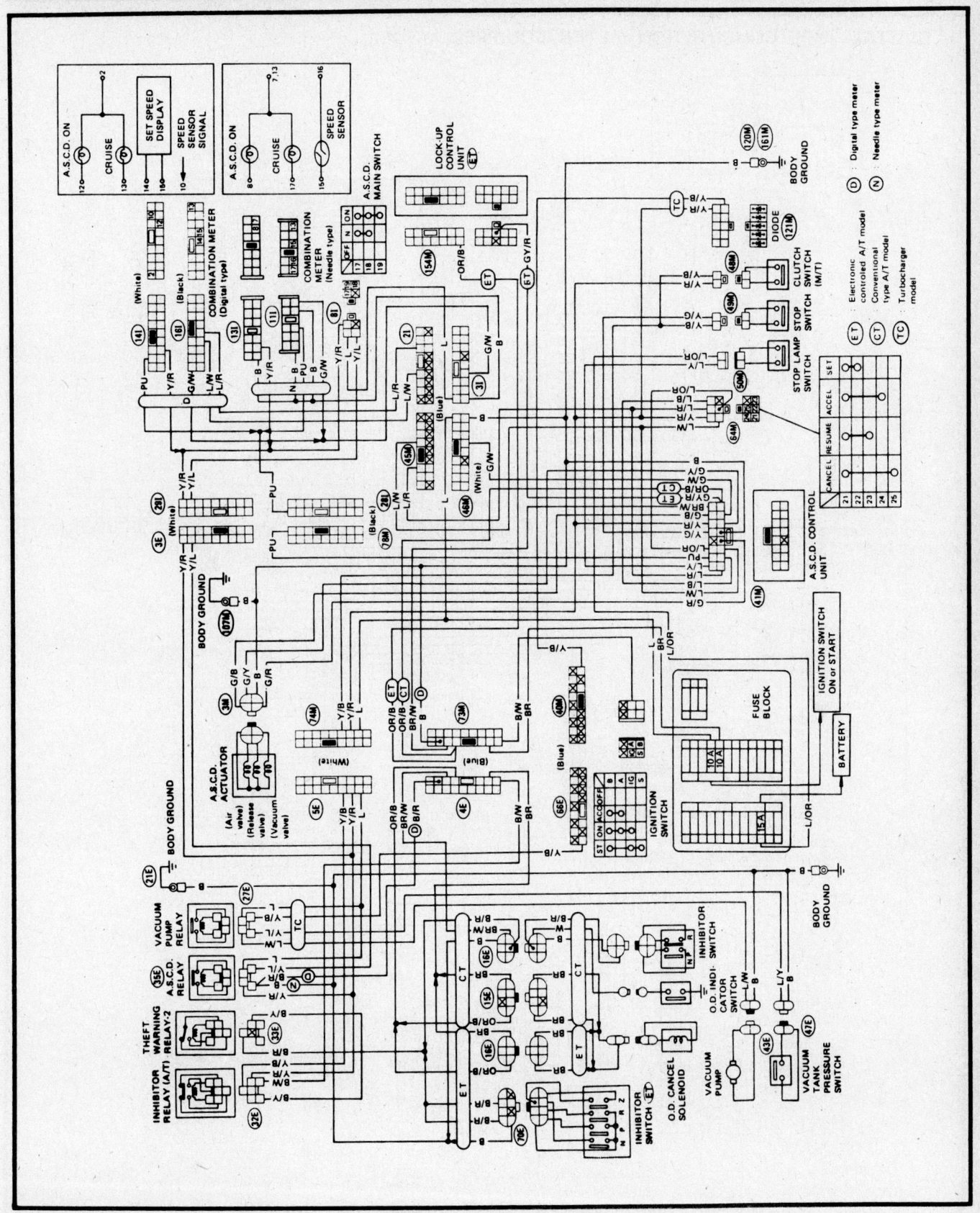

Cruise control electrical schematic—1984 300ZX

DIGITAL TYPE COMBINATION METER EQUIPPED MODEL

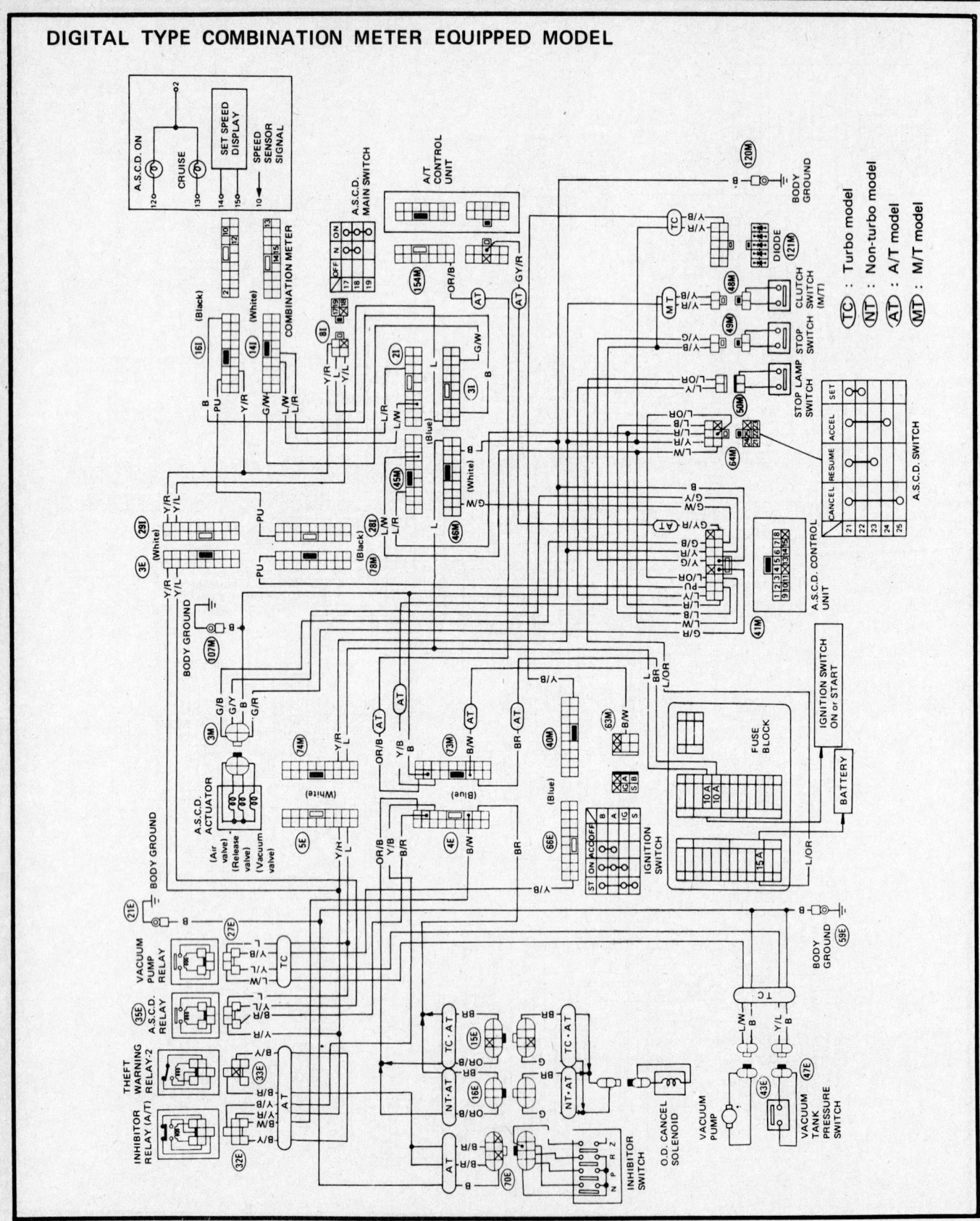

Cruise control electrical schematic—1985 300ZX

NEEDLE TYPE COMBINATION METER EQUIPPED MODEL

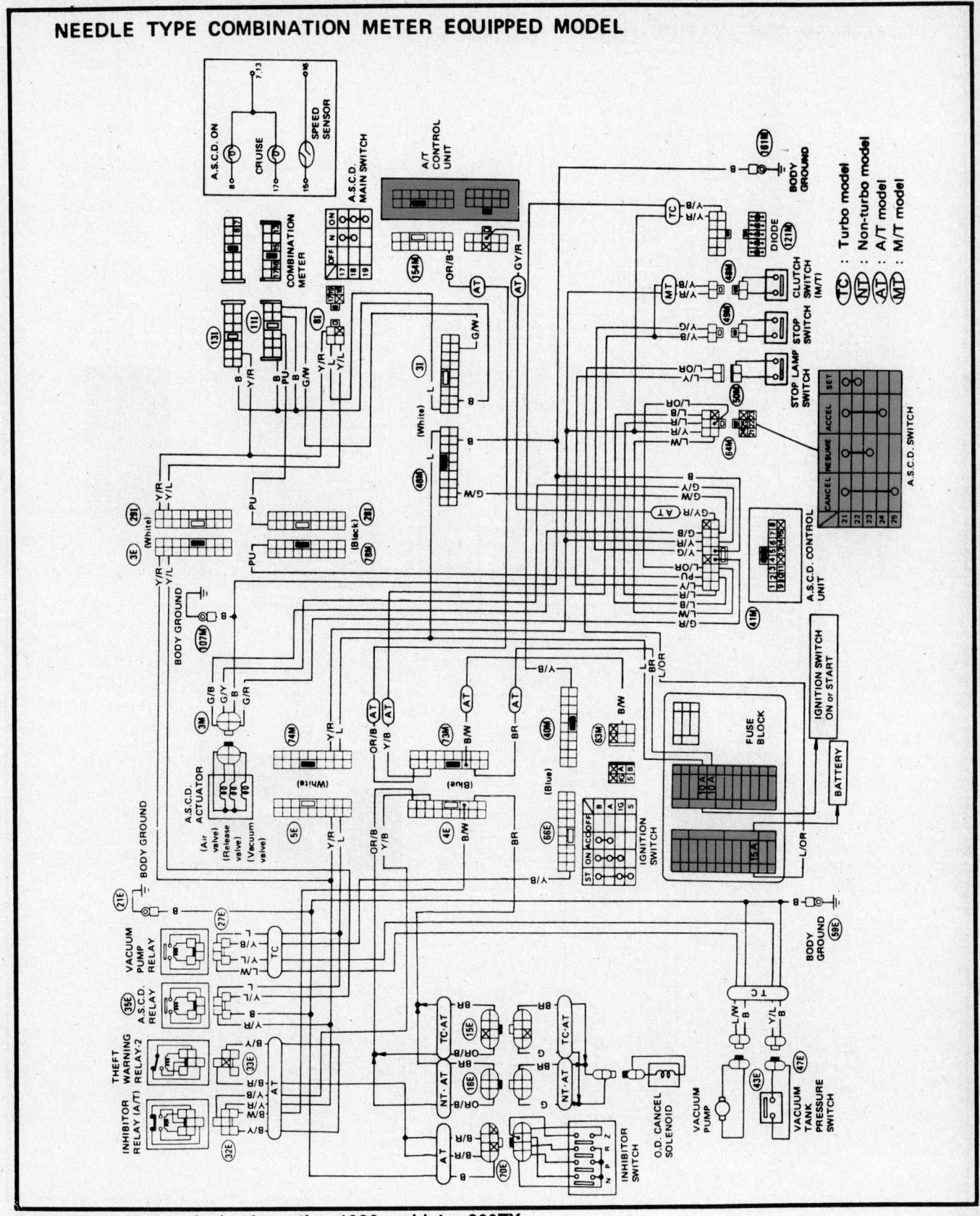

Cruise control electrical schematic—1986 and later 300ZX

NEEDLE TYPE COMBINATION METER EQUIPPED MODEL

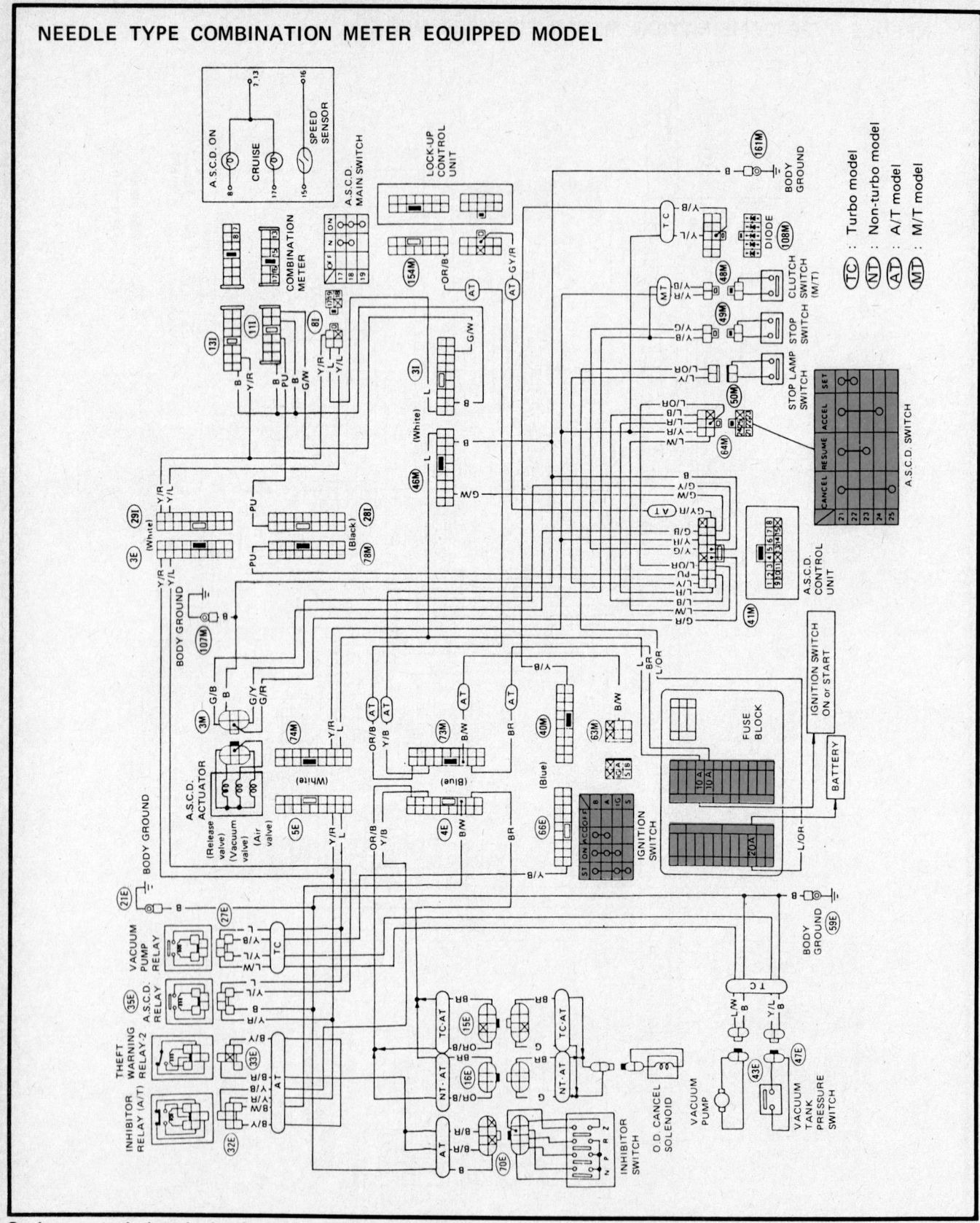

Cruise control electrical schematic — 1986 and 300ZX

Remove A.S.C.D. control unit with harness connected.

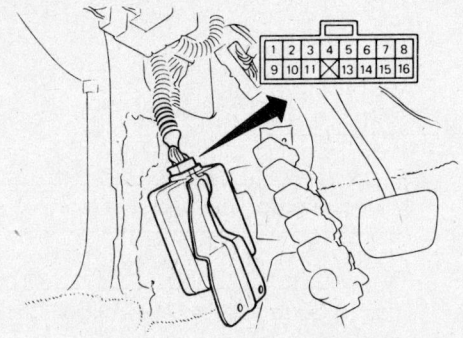

POWER SUPPLY CIRCUIT CHECK

1. Release brake and clutch pedals.
2. Turn ignition switch to "ON".
3. Turn A.S.C.D. main switch to "ON".
4. Check voltage between ⑬ and ⑤.

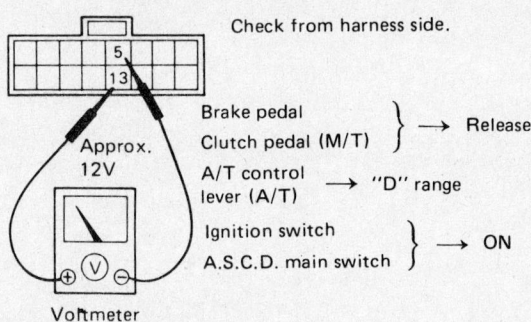

Check from harness side.

Brake pedal
Clutch pedal (M/T) } → Release
A/T control lever (A/T) → "D" range
Ignition switch
A.S.C.D. main switch } → ON

Approx. 12V

Voltmeter

SET SWITCH CIRCUIT CHECK

1. Turn ignition switch to "OFF".
2. Push A.S.C.D. set switch.
3. Check continuity between ① and ⑭.

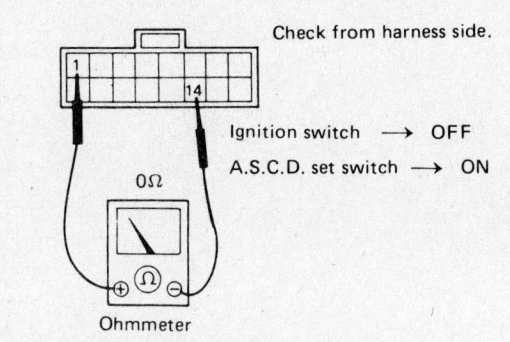

Check from harness side.

Ignition switch → OFF
A.S.C.D. set switch → ON

0Ω

Ohmmeter

Cruise control trouble diagnosis chart — 1984 and later 300ZX

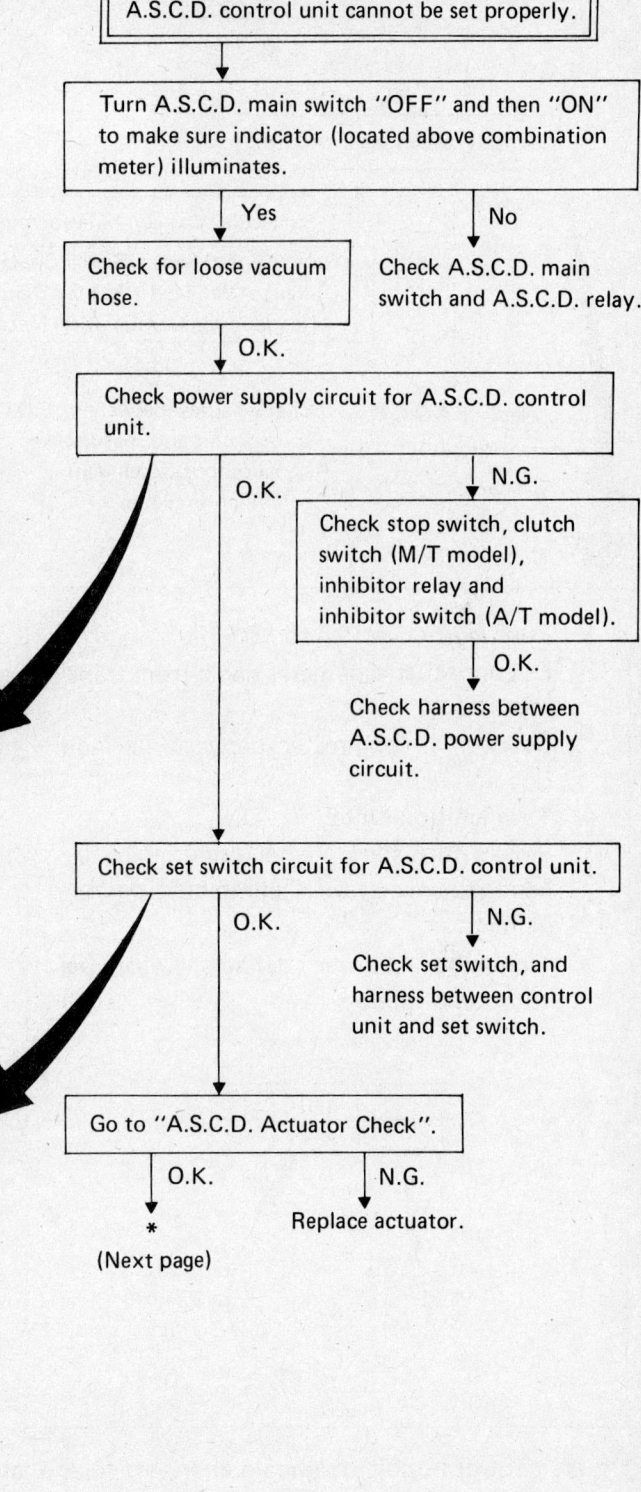

A.S.C.D. control unit cannot be set properly.

↓

Turn A.S.C.D. main switch "OFF" and then "ON" to make sure indicator (located above combination meter) illuminates.

Yes → Check for loose vacuum hose. → O.K.

No → Check A.S.C.D. main switch and A.S.C.D. relay.

Check power supply circuit for A.S.C.D. control unit.

O.K. / N.G.

N.G. → Check stop switch, clutch switch (M/T model), inhibitor relay and inhibitor switch (A/T model). → O.K. → Check harness between A.S.C.D. power supply circuit.

Check set switch circuit for A.S.C.D. control unit.

O.K. / N.G.

N.G. → Check set switch, and harness between control unit and set switch.

Go to "A.S.C.D. Actuator Check".

O.K. → * (Next page)

N.G. → Replace actuator.

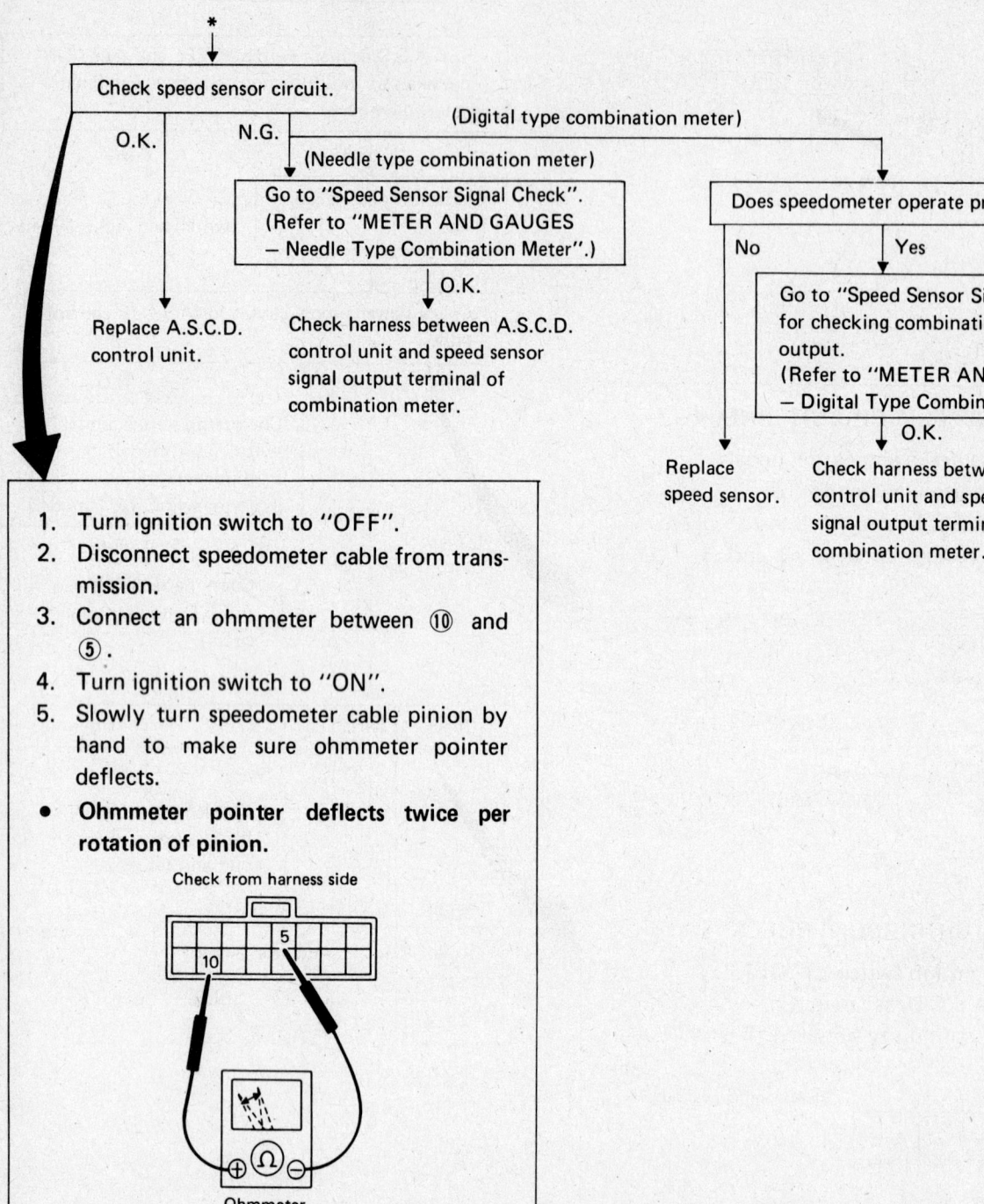

*

Check speed sensor circuit.

O.K.　N.G.

(Digital type combination meter)

(Needle type combination meter)

Go to "Speed Sensor Signal Check".
(Refer to "METER AND GAUGES
— Needle Type Combination Meter".)

Does speedometer operate properly?

No　　Yes

Go to "Speed Sensor Signal Check"
for checking combination meter
output.
(Refer to "METER AND GAUGES
— Digital Type Combination Meter".)

Replace A.S.C.D.
control unit.

O.K.

Check harness between A.S.C.D.
control unit and speed sensor
signal output terminal of
combination meter.

O.K.

Replace
speed sensor.

Check harness between A.S.C.D.
control unit and speed sensor
signal output terminal of
combination meter.

1. Turn ignition switch to "OFF".
2. Disconnect speedometer cable from transmission.
3. Connect an ohmmeter between ⑩ and
   ⑤.
4. Turn ignition switch to "ON".
5. Slowly turn speedometer cable pinion by
   hand to make sure ohmmeter pointer
   deflects.

- **Ohmmeter pointer deflects twice per
  rotation of pinion.**

Check from harness side

5

10

Ohmmeter

Cruise control trouble diagnosis chart—1984 and later 300ZX

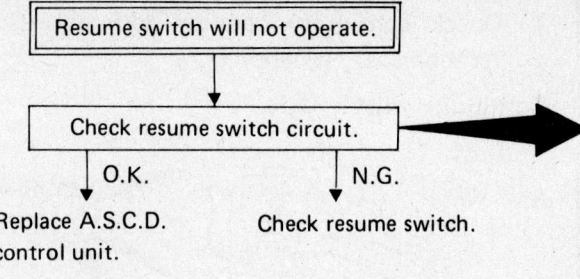

Resume switch will not operate.

↓

Check resume switch circuit.

O.K. → Replace A.S.C.D. control unit.

N.G. → Check resume switch.

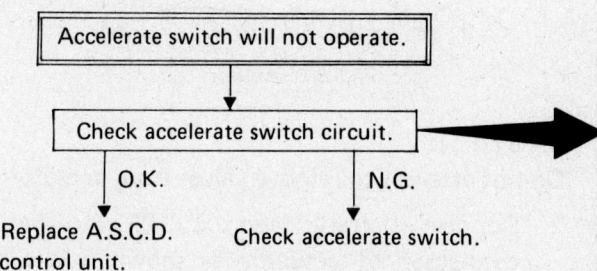

Accelerate switch will not operate.

↓

Check accelerate switch circuit.

O.K. → Replace A.S.C.D. control unit.

N.G. → Check accelerate switch.

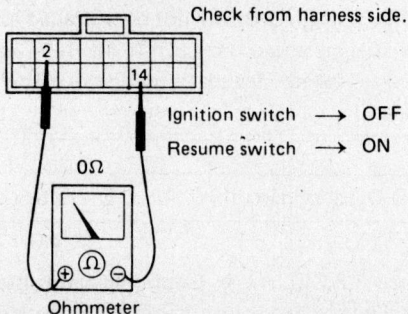

RESUME SWITCH CIRCUIT CHECK

1. Turn ignition switch to "OFF".
2. Turn resume switch to "ON".
3. Check continuity between ② and ⑭

Check from harness side.

Ignition switch → OFF
Resume switch → ON

0Ω

Ohmmeter

ACCELERATE SWITCH CIRCUIT CHECK

1. Turn ignition switch to "OFF".
2. Turn accelerate switch to "ON".
3. Check continuity between ③ and ⑭

Check from harness side.

Ignition switch → OFF
Accelerator switch → ON

0Ω

Ohmmeter

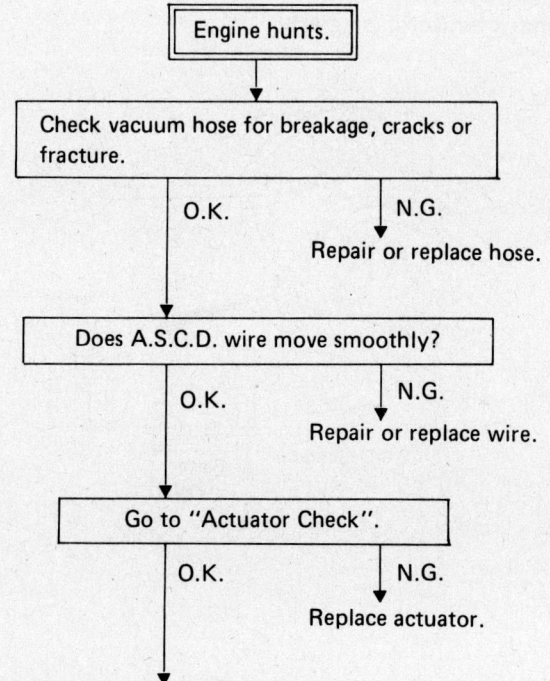

Engine hunts.

↓

Check vacuum hose for breakage, cracks or fracture.

O.K. ↓   N.G. → Repair or replace hose.

Does A.S.C.D. wire move smoothly?

O.K. ↓   N.G. → Repair or replace wire.

Go to "Actuator Check".

O.K. ↓   N.G. → Replace actuator.

Replace A.S.C.D. control unit.

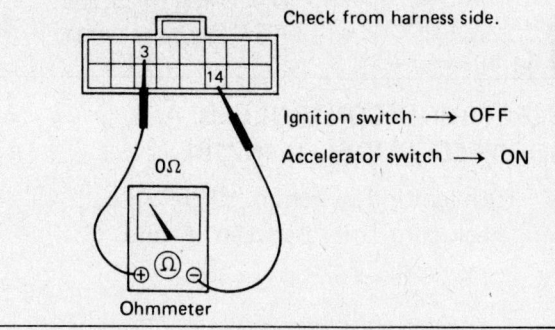

Large difference between set vehicle speed and actual speed.

↓

Check A.S.C.D. wire and actuator move smoothly.

O.K. ↓   N.G. → Replace wire or actuator.

Check vacuum hose for breakage, cracks or fracture.

O.K. ↓   N.G. → Repair or replace hose.

Go to "Actuator Check".

O.K. → Replace A.S.C.D. control unit.

N.G. → Replace actuator.

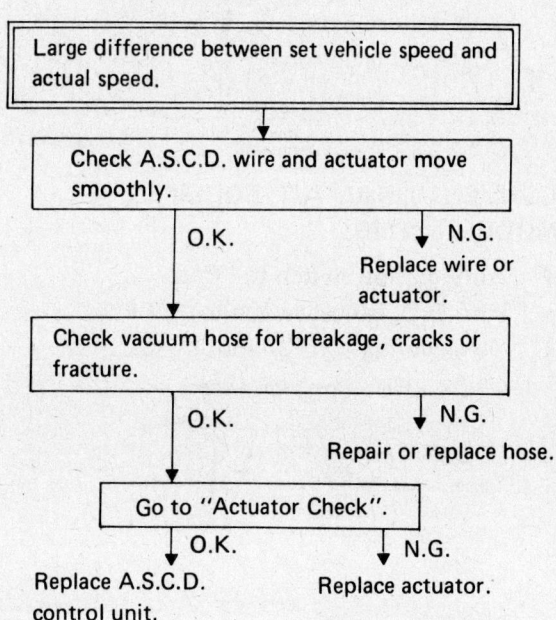

Cruise control trouble diagnosis chart—1984 and later 300ZX

A/T model only:
- When A.S.C.D. is set while vehicle is operating in "O.D." range, O.D. will be cancelled and shifting to O.D. cannot be made thereafter.
- While vehicle is being driven using A.S.C.D. in "O.D." range, O.D. will not be cancelled even if actual car speed is 6 km/h (4 MPH) lower than set speed. (Set speed cannot be maintained.)

↓

Check O.D. cancel circuit for A.S.C.D. control unit.

↓ O.K.   ↓ N.G.

Replace A.S.C.D. control unit.

- **Electronic-controlled A/T**
  Check harness between lock-up control unit and A.S.C.D. control unit.
- **Conventional A/T**
  Check harness between O.D. cancel solenoid, O.D. cancel switch and A.S.C.D. control unit.

ELECTRONIC-CONTROLLED A/T EQUIPPED MODEL (E4N71B)

- Turn ignition switch to "OFF".
- Check continuity between ⑧ and ⑤.

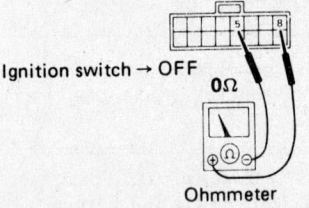

Check from harness side

Ignition switch → OFF

$0\,\Omega$

Ohmmeter

SEL737D

CONVENTIONAL A/T EQUIPPED MODEL (4N71B)

- Turn ignition switch to "ON".
- Turn O.D. cancel switch to "OFF".
- Check voltage ⑧ - ⑤ and ⑯ - ⑤.

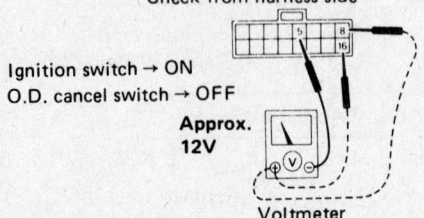

Check from harness side

Ignition switch → ON
O.D. cancel switch → OFF

Approx. 12V

Voltmeter

Cruise control trouble diagnosis chart — 1984 and later 300ZX

1. Check continuity between terminal ① and terminals ②, ③ and ④.

Continuity exist ... O.K.

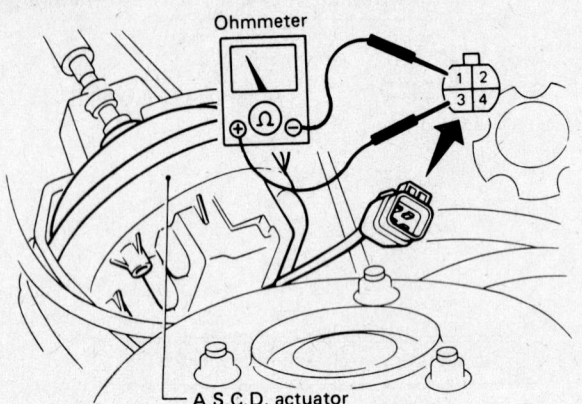

Ohmmeter

A.S.C.D. actuator

CAUTION:
Do not attempt to remove valves from actuator.

2. Connect battery (approx. 12V) to harness connector of actuator as shown below, and apply vacuum to actuator.
   If diaphragm moves smoothly, actuator is O.K.

CAUTION:
When checking actuator by applying vacuum, do not apply engine vacuum directly as it is too strong to check actuator properly.

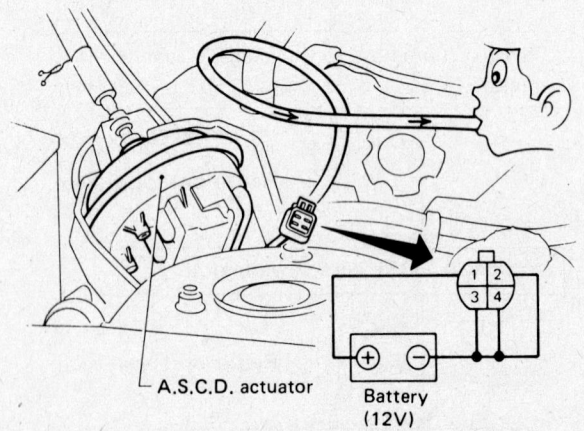

A.S.C.D. actuator

Battery (12V)

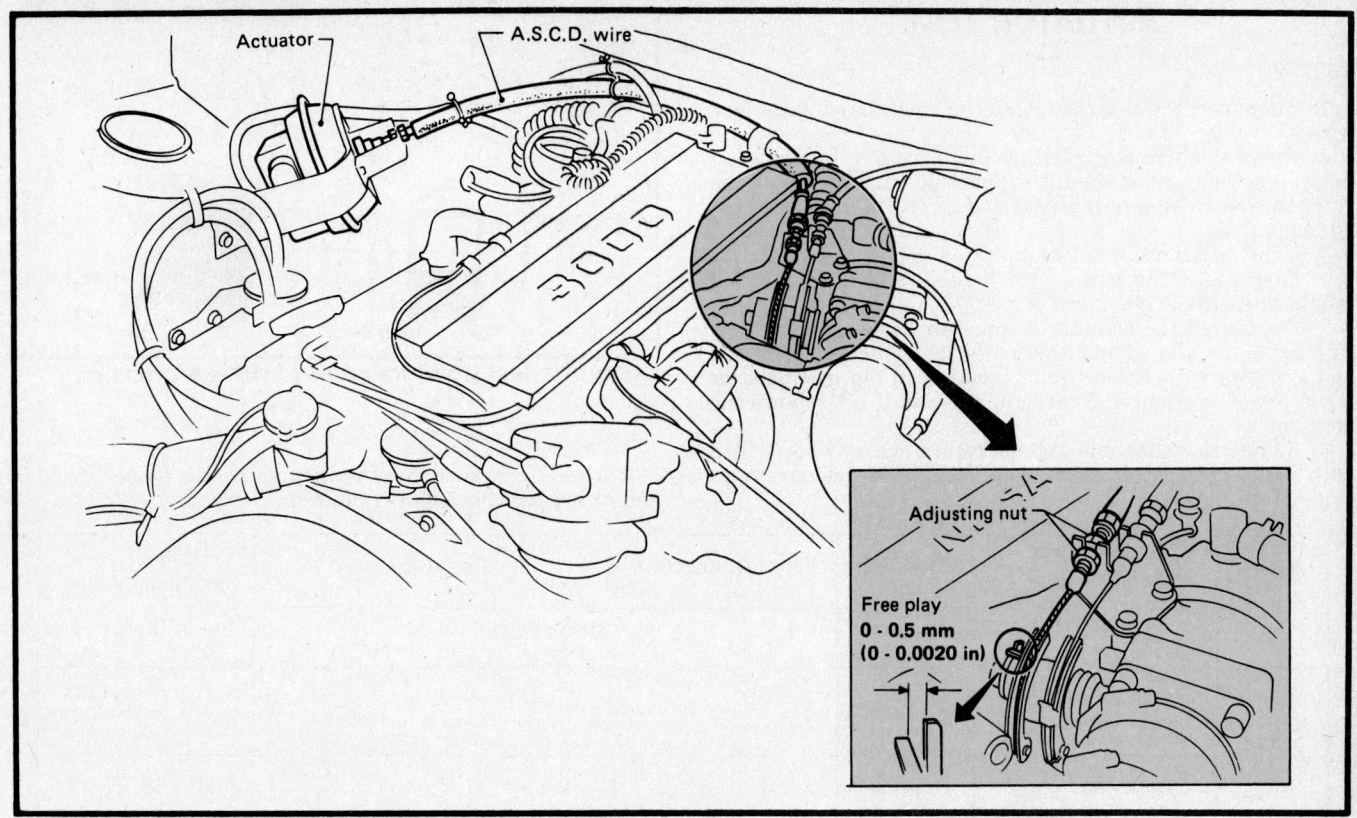

Actuator cable adjustment procedure—1984 and later 300ZX

TOYOTA

Cressida

VISUAL INSPECTION

Before performing any tests make a visual inspection of the cruise control system. Check all items in the system for abnormal conditions such as bare broken or disconnected wires and damage to the vacuum hoses. Be sure that the speedometer cables are attached and properly routed. All vacuum hoses must be properly routed and must not have any kinks or bends. Be sure that all electrical connections are complete and tight. The wiring harness must be routed properly.

COMPUTER AND SENSOR TEST (1982–83)

1. Remove the right side kick panel. Unplug the wiring harness from the computer.
2. Turn the ignition switch to the on position. Using a voltmeter measure the voltage between terminal seven and ground with the main switch in the on position.
3. Battery voltage should be present. If battery voltage is not present, check the control switch.
4. Using the voltmeter measure the voltage between terminal twelve and ground. When the parking brake lever is pulled the voltage should be zero. When the lever is returned the voltage should be 12 volts.
5. Turn the ignition switch off. Using the voltmeter measure the voltage between terminal nine and ground.

6. Battery voltage should be present. If battery voltage is not present, check the stop light switch.
7. Using the voltmeter measure the voltage between terminal eight and ground. When the parking brake lever is pulled the voltage should be 12 volts. When the lever is returned the voltage should be zero. If the voltage is incorrect check the brake pedal switch.
8. Turn the ignition switch to the accessory position. Using an ohmmeter check for continuity between terminal eleven and ground.
9. If equipped with manual transmission depress the clutch pedal (automatic transmission in neutral), if continuity does not exist between the terminals check the clutch or neutral safety switch.
10. Using an ohmmeter measure the resistance between terminals one and ten. The resistance should be about 68 ohms. Measure the resistance between terminals three and ten. The resistance should be about 30 ohms. If the readings are not correct check the actuator.
11. Using an ohmmeter check the continuity between terminal four and ground when the set switch is in the on position. If there is no continuity between the terminals check the control switch.
12. Using an ohmmeter check the continuity between terminal thirteen and ground when the set switch is in the on position. If there is no continuity between the terminals check the control switch.
13. Using an ohmmeter check the continuity between terminal six and ground when the vehicle is slightly pushed. At this time the needle on the ohmmeter should move repeatedly from on to off. If not check the speed sensor.

ACTUATOR TEST

1982–83

1. Disconnect the electrical connector from the actuator lead wire.

2. Using an ohmmeter measure the resistance between terminals one and two. It should be about 30 ohms. Measure the resistance between terminals one and three. It should be about 70 ohms.

3. If the resistance is not as indicated, replace the actuator.

4. Disconnect the carburetor throttle rod from the bell crank. Start the engine.

5. Check that the actuator diaphragm makes a smooth reciprocating motion when either power is applied to terminals one and two with the actuator terminal three grounded or when power is removed from terminal two. If not replace the actuator.

6. Be sure that the cable does not return to easy when pulled with about 4 to 7 lbs. of force. Repair or replace defective components as required.

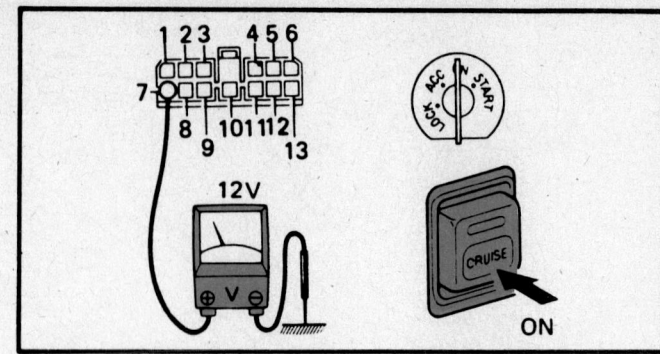

Computer test point location – 1982–83 Cressida

7. Check to be sure that the vacuum hose is properly routed and connected. Correct as required.

Terminal	Connection or Measure Item	Check Item	Tester Connection	Condition	Voltage or Resistance Value
1	Stop Light Switch and Release Valve	Resistance	1 – 2	Brake pedal returned	About 30 Ω
2	Release Valve and Control Valve	–	–	–	–
3	Control Valve	Resistance	3 – 2	–	About 68 Ω
4	Control Switch (Set/Coast)	Continuity	4 – Body Ground	Turn set/coast switch on Turn set/coast switch off	Continuity No continuity
5	OD Relay	–	–	–	–
6	Speed Sensor	–	–	–	–
7	Main Switch	Voltage	7 – Body Ground	Turn ignition switch and main switch on Turn ignition switch and main switch off	Battery voltage No voltage
8	Stop Light Switch	Voltage	8 – Body Ground	Brake pedal depressed Brake pedal returned	Battery voltage No voltage
9	STOP Fuse	Voltage	9 – Body Ground		Battery voltage
10	Body Ground	Continuity	10 – Body Ground	–	Continuity
11	Clutch Switch Neutral Switch	Continuity	11 – Body Ground	Clutch pedal depressed or shift into "N" range Clutch pedal returned or shift into except "N" range	Continuity No continuity
12	Parking Brake Switch	Voltage	12 – Body Ground	Parking brake pulled Parking brake returned	No voltage Battery voltage
13	Control Switch (Accel/Resume)	Continuity	13 – Body Ground	Turn accel/resume switch on Turn accel/resume switch off	Continuity No continuity

Cruise control computer circuit inspection chart – 1984 Cressida

Terminal	Connection or Measure Item	Check Item	Tester Connection	Condition	Voltage or Resistance Value
1	Vacuum Pump	Resistance	1—Body Ground	—	About 80 Ω
2	Stop Light Switch and Release Valve	Resistance	2—14	Brake pedal returned.	About 68 Ω
3	Main Switch	Voltage	3—Body Ground	Turn ignition switch and main switch on.	Battery voltage
				Turn ignition switch and/or main switch off.	No voltage
4	Control Valve	Resistance	4—14	—	About 30 Ω
5	Control Switch (Set/coast)	Continuity	5—Body Ground	Turn set/coast switch on.	Continuity
				Turn set/coast switch off.	No continuity
6	ECT or OD relay	—	—	—	—
7	Speed Sensor (Analog meter)	Continuity	7—Body Ground	Vehicle moving slowly.	1 pulse each 40 cm (15.75 in.)
	Speed Sensor (Digital meter)	Voltage	7—Body Ground	Turn ignition switch on and vehicle moving slowly.	About 2 V pulse each 40 cm (15.75 in.)
9	Vacuum Switch	Continuity	9—Body Ground	Apply vacuum about 170 mmHg (6.69 in.Hg, 22.7 kPa).	No continuity
				No vacuum.	Continuity
10	Main Switch	Voltage	10—Body Ground	Turn ignition switch and main switch on.	Battery voltage
				Turn ignition switch and/or main switch off.	No voltage
11	Clutch Switch Neutral Start Switch	Continuity	11—Body Ground	Clutch pedal depressed or shifted into "N" range.	Continuity
				Clutch pedal returned or shifted into any range except "N" range.	No continuity
12	Parking Brake Switch	Continuity	12—Body Ground	Parking brake pulled.	No continuity
				Parking brake returned and engine running.	Continuity
13	Body Ground	Continuity	13—Body Ground	—	Continuity
14	Release Valve and Control Valve	—	—	—	—
15	Stop Light Switch	Voltage	15—Body Ground	Brake pedal depressed.	Battery voltage
				Brake pedal returned.	No voltage
16	STOP Fuse	Voltage	16—Body Ground	—	Battery voltage
17	Control Switch (Accel/resume)	Continuity	17—Body Ground	Turn accel/resume switch on.	Continuity
				Turn accel/resume switch off.	No continuity

Cruise control computer circuit inspection chart—1985 and later Cressida

1098 of 1540

POWER ACCESSORIES
CRUISE CONTROL SYSTEMS

Actuator test point location—Cressida

1984 and Later

1. Inspect and check the actuator cable. Freeplay should be less than 0.039 inch. Adjust or replace as required.
2. Disconnect the electrical connector from the actuator lead wire.
3. Using an ohmmeter measure the resistance between terminals one and two. It should be about 30 ohms. Measure the resistance between terminals one and three. It should be about 68 ohms.
4. If the resistance is not as indicated, replace the actuator.
5. Connect a positive lead from the positive terminal of the battery to terminals two and three. Connect a negative lead from the negative terminal of the battery to terminal one.
6. Slowly apply 0 to 11.8 in. hg. of vacuum. Check to be sure that the control cable can be pulled smoothly.
7. When the vacuum has stabilized check the control cable and be sure that it does not return.
8. Disconnect terminal two or three and check that the control cable returns to its original position and that the vacuum goes to zero.

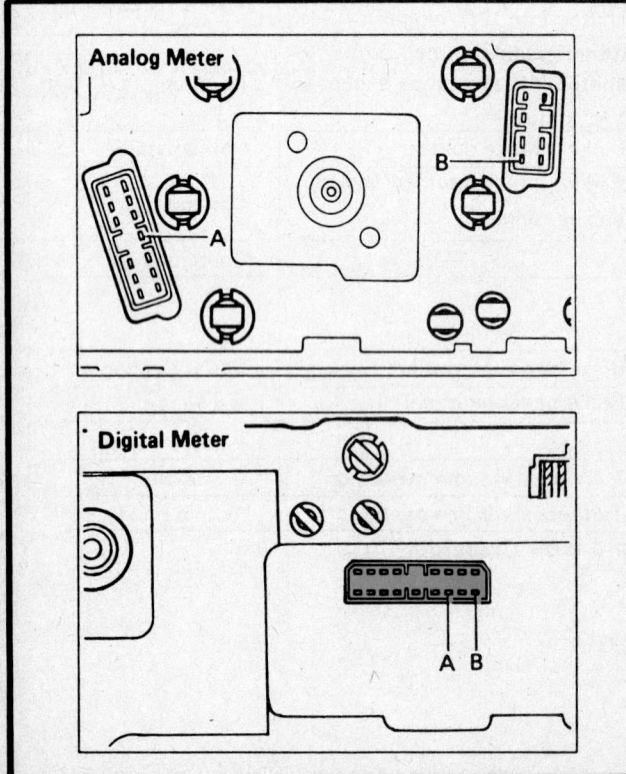

Speed Sensor test point location—1982-84 Cressida

9. If the system does not perform as indicated replace the actuator.

SPEED SENSOR TEST

1982–84

1. Using an ohmmeter, check to see that there is continuity between terminals A and B. It should be four times per revolution of the magnet shaft.
2. If continunity does not exist replace the speed sensor.

1985 and Later
REGULAR SPEEDOMETER

1. Using an ohmmeter, check to see that there is continuity between terminals 7 and 9. It should be four times per revolution of the magnet shaft.
2. If continunity does not exist replace the speed sensor.

DIGITAL SPEEDOMETER

1. Using an ohmmeter, check to see that there is continuity between terminals 9 and 11. It should be four times per revolution of the magnet shaft.
2. If continunity does not exist replace the speed sensor.

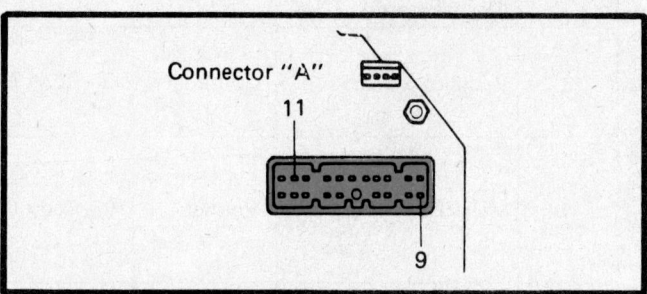

Speed sensor test point location—1985 and later Cressida with digital speedometer

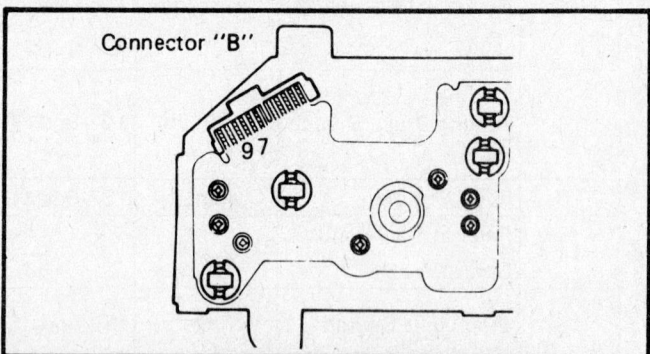

Speed sensor test point location—1985 and later Cressida with regular speedometer

CONTROL SWITCH TEST

1. Using an ohmmeter check for continuity of the terminals for each switch position.
2. If continunity between the terminals is not as specified, replace the switch.

MAIN SWITCH TEST

1984

1. Using an ohmmeter check for continuity of the terminals for each switch position.

2. If continuity between the terminals is not as specified, replace the switch.

1985 and Later

1. Connect a positive lead from the positive terminal of the battery to terminal two. Connect a negative lead from the negative terminal of the battery to terminal four.
2. Check to be sure that continuity exists between terminals two and five with the main switch turned on.
3. Check that there is no continuity between terminals two and five with the main switch off.
4. If the above results are not achieved, replace the switch.

CLUTCH SWITCH TEST (1984 AND LATER)

1. Check to be sure that there is continuity between terminals two and three with the clutch pedal depressed.
2. Check to be sure that there is continuity between terminals two and three with the clutch pedal returned.
3. If continuity is not as indicated, replace the clutch switch.

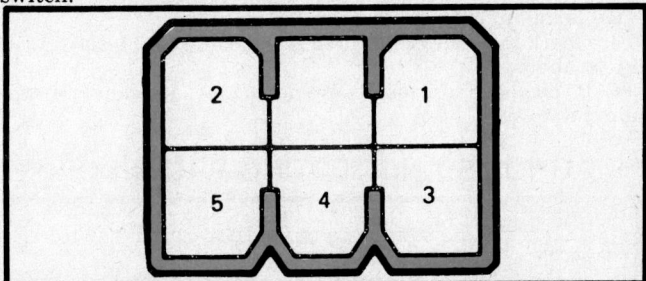

Main switch test point locations 1984 Cressida

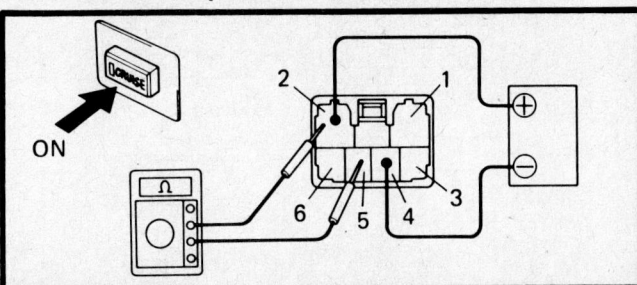

Main switch test point locations 1985 and later Cressida

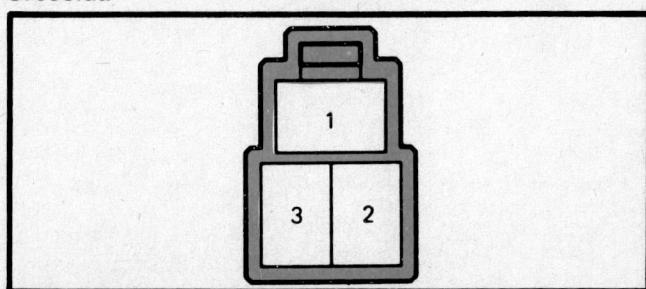

Clutch switch test point locations 1984 and later Cressida

STOP LIGHT SWITCH TEST (1984 AND LATER)

1. Using an ohmmeter check for continuity of the terminals for each switch position.
2. If continuity between the terminals is not as specified, replace the switch.

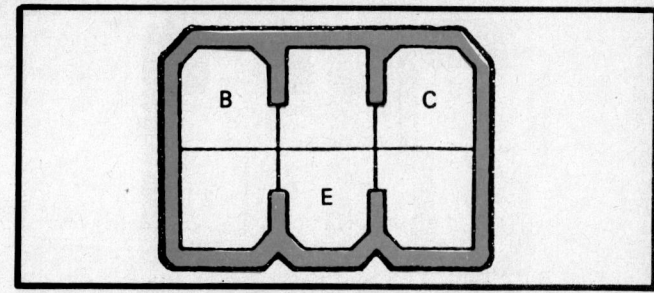

Control switch test point location – 1982–83 Cressida

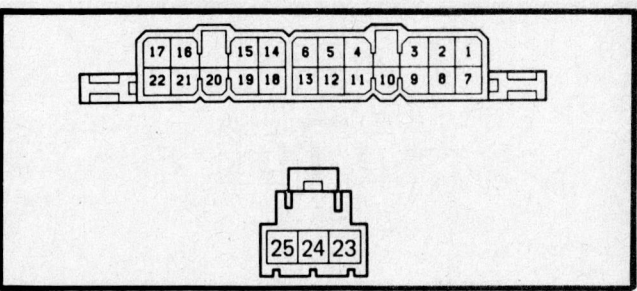

Control switch test point location – 1985 and later Cressida

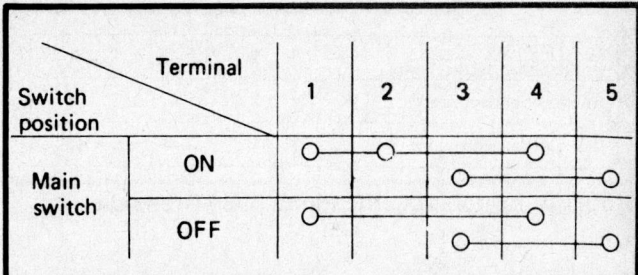

Control switch specifications – 1982–83 later Cressida

Terminal Switch position	14	23	25
ACCEL/RESUME	○—○		
OFF			
SET/COAST	○———————○		

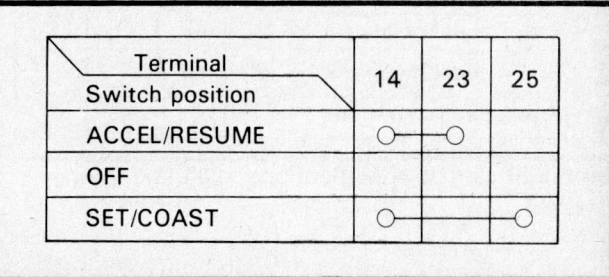

Control switch test point location – 1985 and later Cressida

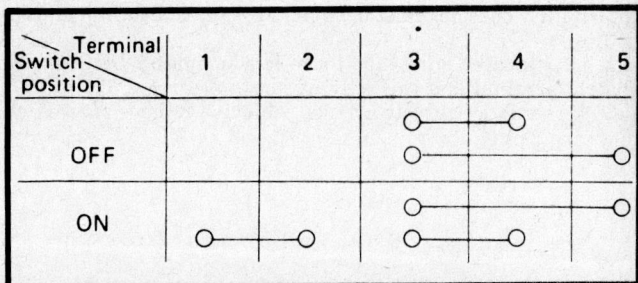

Main switch specifications 1984 Cressida

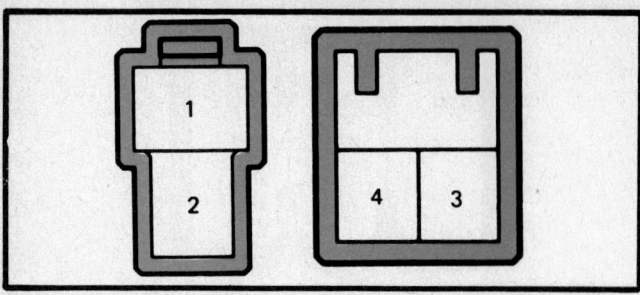

Stoplight switch test point locations 1984 Cressida

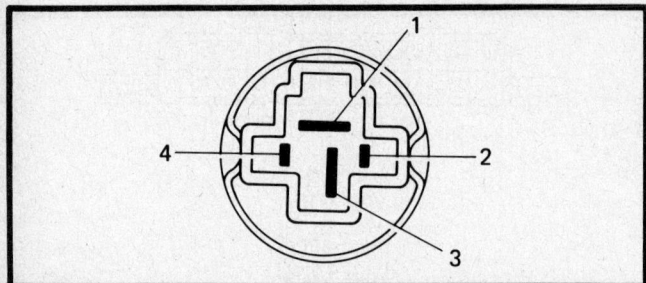

Stoplight switch test point locations 1985 and later Cressida

Terminal Brake pedal position	1	2	3	4
Brake pedal depressed	●	●		
Brake pedal returned			●	●

Stoplight switch specifications 1984 Cressida

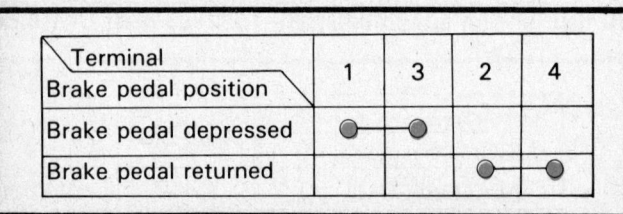

Terminal Brake pedal position	1	3	2	4
Brake pedal depressed	●	●		
Brake pedal returned			●	●

Stoplight switch specifications 1985 and later Cressida

VACUUM SWITCH TEST (1985 AND LATER)

1. With a vacuum of 22.7 in. hg. or higher check that continuity does not exist between the switch terminal and the body.

2. Check to be sure that there is continuity between the switch terminal and the body without vacuum.

3. If the above results are not achieved, replace the switch.

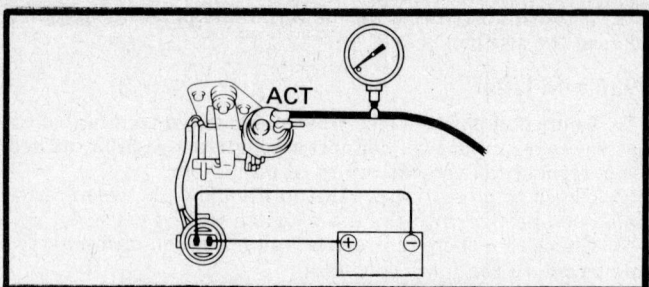

Vacuum pump switch test point locations 1985 and later Cressida

VACUUM PUMP TEST (1985 AND LATER)

1. Connect a vacuum pump to the ACT side of the vacuum pump.

2. Connect a positive lead from the positive terminal of the battery to terminal one. Connect a negative lead from the negative terminal of the battery to terminal two.

3. Check to be sure that there is a vacuum of at least 7.87 in. hg. or above.

4. If the above test results are not achieved, replace the vacuum pump.

DIAGNOSIS AND TESTING PROCEDURES

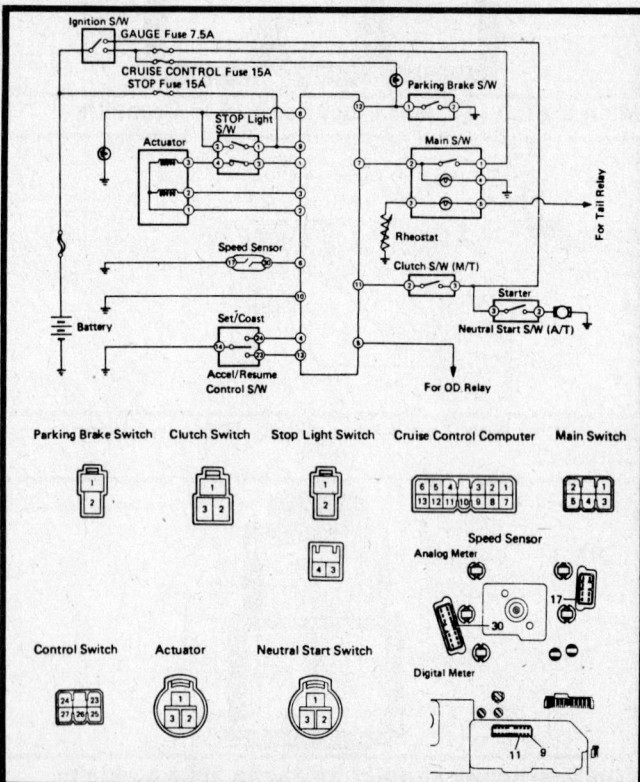

Cruise control electrical schematic — 1984 Cressida

Problem	Inspection Item	No.
Cruise control does not operate.	Inspection of power source circuit	A
Vehicle speed does not reduce when coast switch turned on.	Inspection of control switch and circuit.	B
Vehicle does not accelerate when accel switch turned on.		
Vehicle speed does not return to memorized speed when resume switch turned on.		
Set speed deviates on high side.	Inspection of actuator and circuit	C
Set speed deviates on low side.		
Vehicle speed does not fluctuate when set switch turned on.	Inspection of actuator and circuit Inspection of speed sensor and circuit	C H
Setting speed does not cancel when brake pedal depressed.	Inspection of stop light switch and circuit	D
Setting speed does not cancel when parking brake pulled.	Inspection of parking brake switch and circuit	E
Setting speed does not cancel when clutch pedal depressed (M/T only).	Inspection of clutch switch and circuit	F
Setting speed does not cancel when shifted to "N" range (A/T only).	Inspection of neutral start switch and circuit	G
Speed can be set below 20 km/h.	Inspection of speed sensor and circuit	H
Cruise control will not disengage even below 20 km/h.		

Cruise control troubleshooting data sheet—1984 Cressida

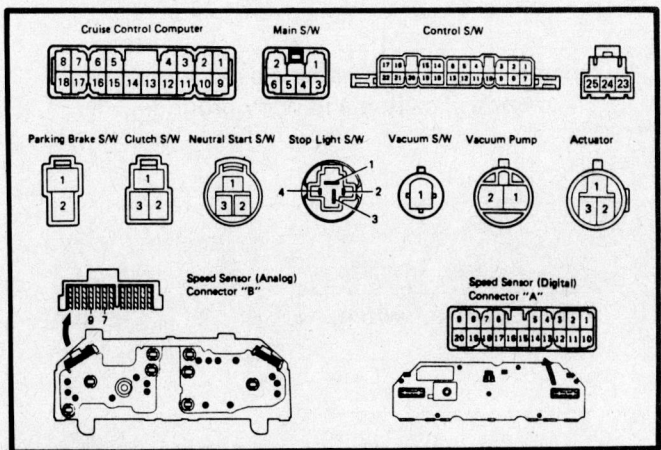

Cruise control electrical connectors—1985 and later Cressida

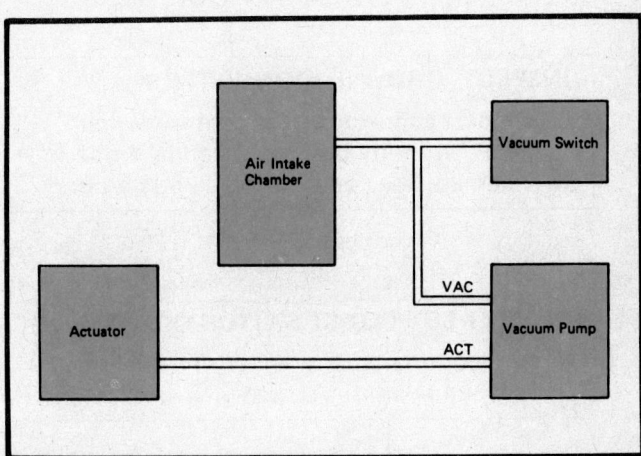

Cruise control vacuum schematic—1985 and later Cressida

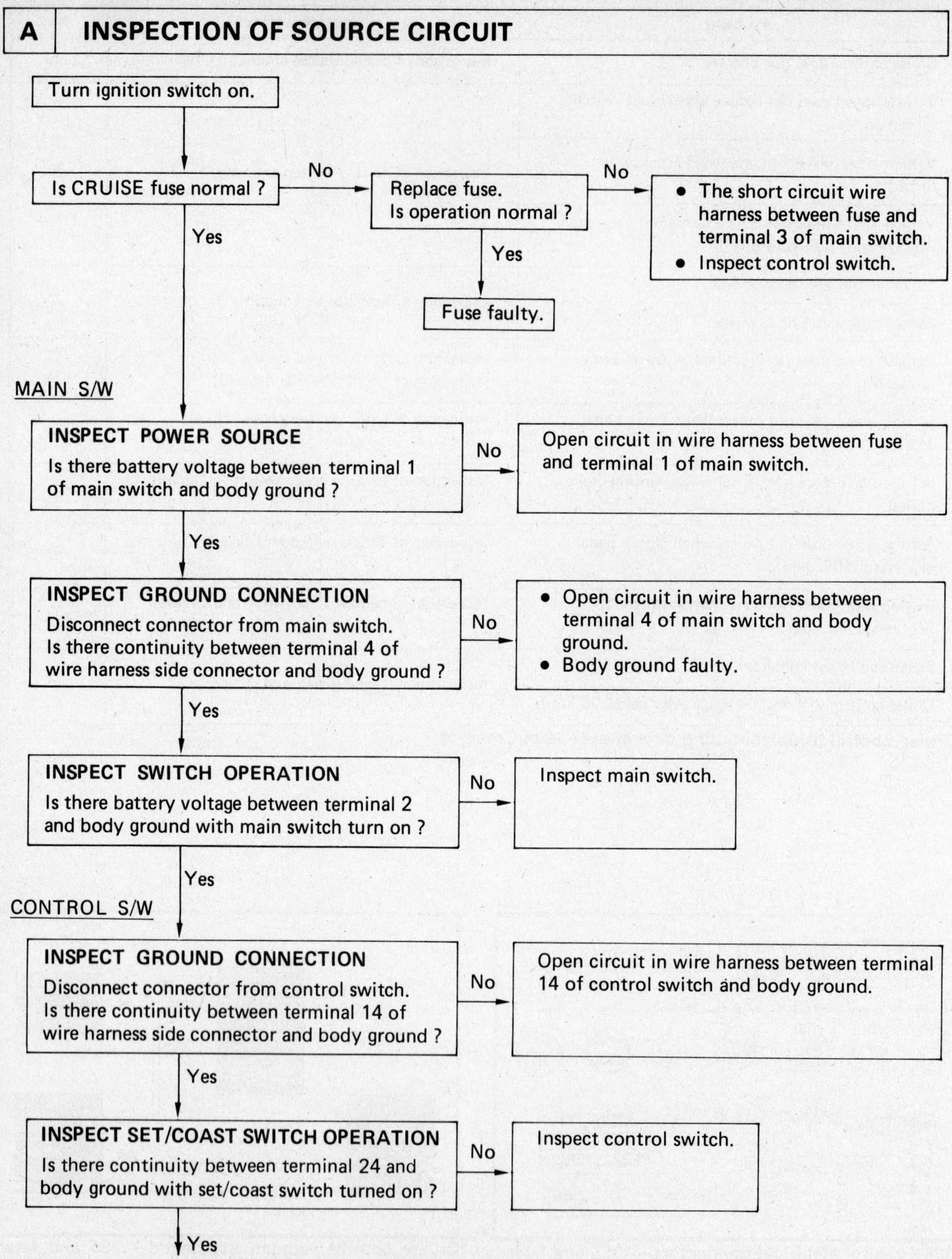

| A | **INSPECTION OF SOURCE CIRCUIT** |

Turn ignition switch on.

Is CRUISE fuse normal ? — No → Replace fuse. Is operation normal ? — No →
- The short circuit wire harness between fuse and terminal 3 of main switch.
- Inspect control switch.

Yes ↓ (from fuse) / Replace fuse: Yes → Fuse faulty.

MAIN S/W

INSPECT POWER SOURCE
Is there battery voltage between terminal 1 of main switch and body ground ? — No → Open circuit in wire harness between fuse and terminal 1 of main switch.

Yes ↓

INSPECT GROUND CONNECTION
Disconnect connector from main switch. Is there continuity between terminal 4 of wire harness side connector and body ground ? — No →
- Open circuit in wire harness between terminal 4 of main switch and body ground.
- Body ground faulty.

Yes ↓

INSPECT SWITCH OPERATION
Is there battery voltage between terminal 2 and body ground with main switch turn on ? — No → Inspect main switch.

Yes ↓

CONTROL S/W

INSPECT GROUND CONNECTION
Disconnect connector from control switch. Is there continuity between terminal 14 of wire harness side connector and body ground ? — No → Open circuit in wire harness between terminal 14 of control switch and body ground.

Yes ↓

INSPECT SET/COAST SWITCH OPERATION
Is there continuity between terminal 24 and body ground with set/coast switch turned on ? — No → Inspect control switch.

↓ Yes

Cruise control trouble diagnosis chart – 1984 Cressida

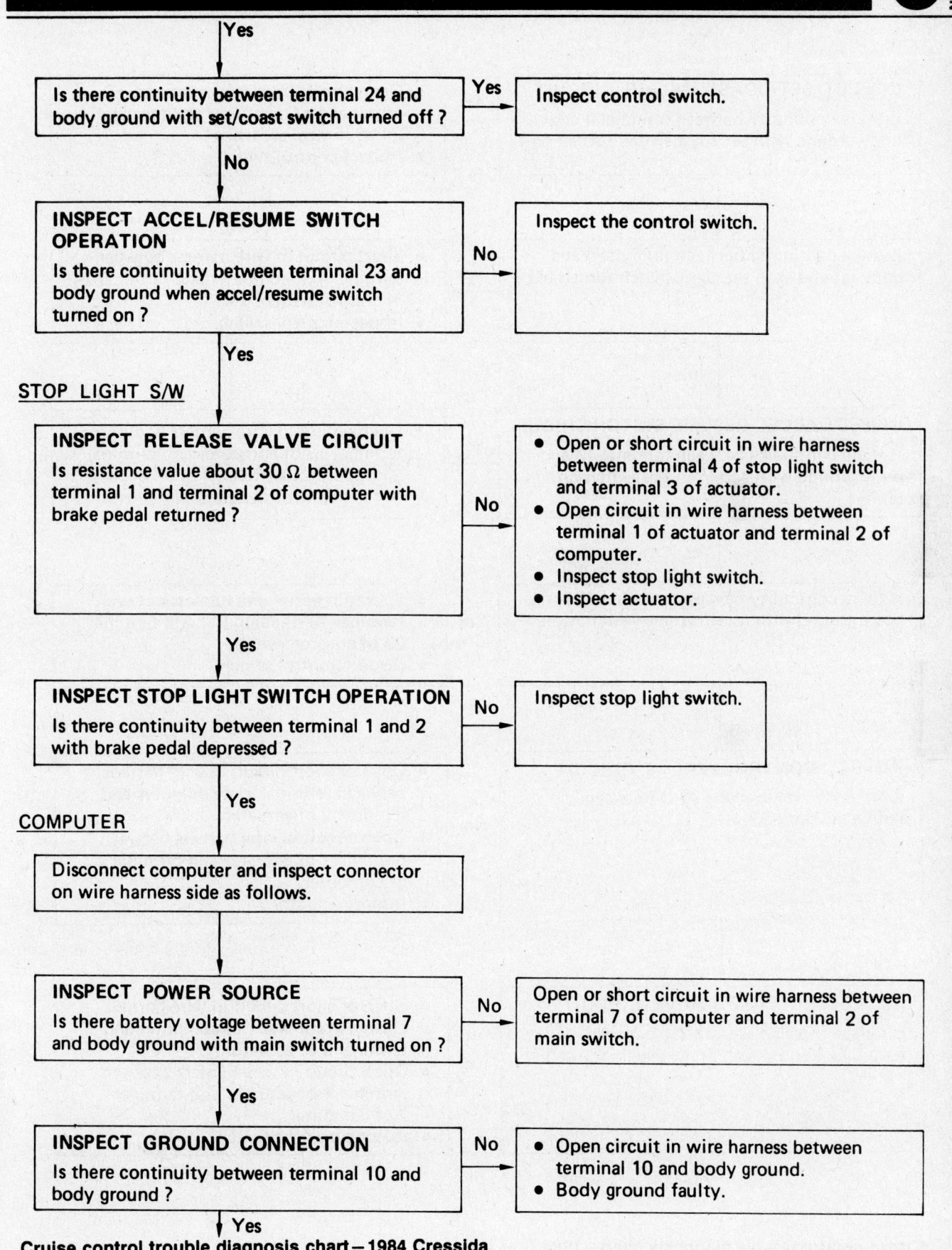

Yes

Is there continuity between terminal 24 and body ground with set/coast switch turned off ? →**Yes**→ Inspect control switch.

↓**No**

INSPECT ACCEL/RESUME SWITCH OPERATION

Is there continuity between terminal 23 and body ground when accel/resume switch turned on ? →**No**→ Inspect the control switch.

↓**Yes**

STOP LIGHT S/W

INSPECT RELEASE VALVE CIRCUIT

Is resistance value about 30 Ω between terminal 1 and terminal 2 of computer with brake pedal returned ? →**No**→
- Open or short circuit in wire harness between terminal 4 of stop light switch and terminal 3 of actuator.
- Open circuit in wire harness between terminal 1 of actuator and terminal 2 of computer.
- Inspect stop light switch.
- Inspect actuator.

↓**Yes**

INSPECT STOP LIGHT SWITCH OPERATION

Is there continuity between terminal 1 and 2 with brake pedal depressed ? →**No**→ Inspect stop light switch.

↓**Yes**

COMPUTER

Disconnect computer and inspect connector on wire harness side as follows.

↓

INSPECT POWER SOURCE

Is there battery voltage between terminal 7 and body ground with main switch turned on ? →**No**→ Open or short circuit in wire harness between terminal 7 of computer and terminal 2 of main switch.

↓**Yes**

INSPECT GROUND CONNECTION

Is there continuity between terminal 10 and body ground ? →**No**→
- Open circuit in wire harness between terminal 10 and body ground.
- Body ground faulty.

↓**Yes**

Cruise control trouble diagnosis chart—1984 Cressida

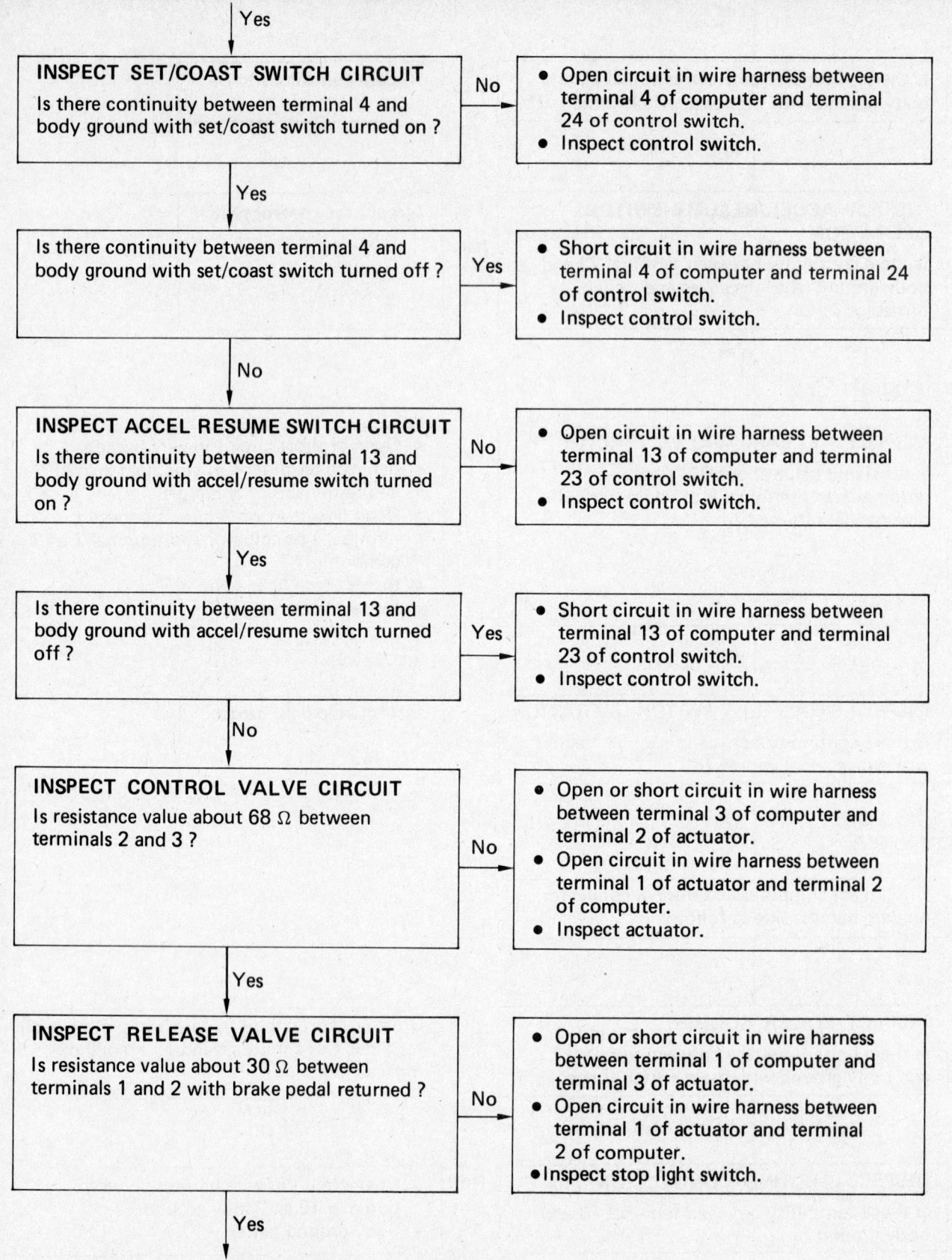

Yes ↓

INSPECT SET/COAST SWITCH CIRCUIT

Is there continuity between terminal 4 and body ground with set/coast switch turned on ?

No →
- Open circuit in wire harness between terminal 4 of computer and terminal 24 of control switch.
- Inspect control switch.

Yes ↓

Is there continuity between terminal 4 and body ground with set/coast switch turned off ?

Yes →
- Short circuit in wire harness between terminal 4 of computer and terminal 24 of control switch.
- Inspect control switch.

No ↓

INSPECT ACCEL RESUME SWITCH CIRCUIT

Is there continuity between terminal 13 and body ground with accel/resume switch turned on ?

No →
- Open circuit in wire harness between terminal 13 of computer and terminal 23 of control switch.
- Inspect control switch.

Yes ↓

Is there continuity between terminal 13 and body ground with accel/resume switch turned off ?

Yes →
- Short circuit in wire harness between terminal 13 of computer and terminal 23 of control switch.
- Inspect control switch.

No ↓

INSPECT CONTROL VALVE CIRCUIT

Is resistance value about 68 Ω between terminals 2 and 3 ?

No →
- Open or short circuit in wire harness between terminal 3 of computer and terminal 2 of actuator.
- Open circuit in wire harness between terminal 1 of actuator and terminal 2 of computer.
- Inspect actuator.

Yes ↓

INSPECT RELEASE VALVE CIRCUIT

Is resistance value about 30 Ω between terminals 1 and 2 with brake pedal returned ?

No →
- Open or short circuit in wire harness between terminal 1 of computer and terminal 3 of actuator.
- Open circuit in wire harness between terminal 1 of actuator and terminal 2 of computer.
- Inspect stop light switch.

Yes ↓

Cruise control trouble diagnosis chart – 1984 Cressida

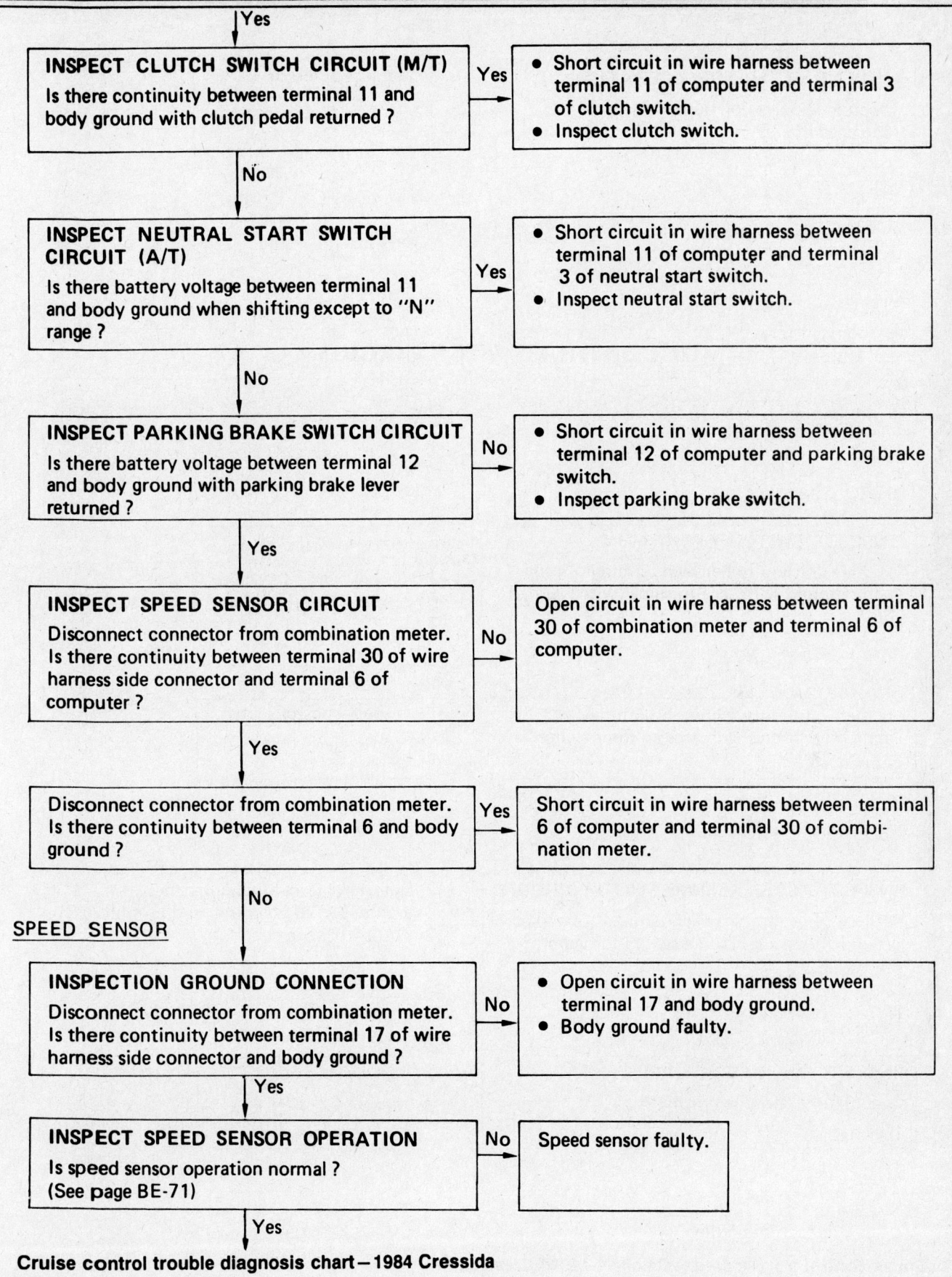

Yes ↓

INSPECT CLUTCH SWITCH CIRCUIT (M/T)

Is there continuity between terminal 11 and body ground with clutch pedal returned ?

→ **Yes** →
- Short circuit in wire harness between terminal 11 of computer and terminal 3 of clutch switch.
- Inspect clutch switch.

↓ **No**

INSPECT NEUTRAL START SWITCH CIRCUIT (A/T)

Is there battery voltage between terminal 11 and body ground when shifting except to "N" range ?

→ **Yes** →
- Short circuit in wire harness between terminal 11 of computer and terminal 3 of neutral start switch.
- Inspect neutral start switch.

↓ **No**

INSPECT PARKING BRAKE SWITCH CIRCUIT

Is there battery voltage between terminal 12 and body ground with parking brake lever returned ?

→ **No** →
- Short circuit in wire harness between terminal 12 of computer and parking brake switch.
- Inspect parking brake switch.

↓ **Yes**

INSPECT SPEED SENSOR CIRCUIT

Disconnect connector from combination meter. Is there continuity between terminal 30 of wire harness side connector and terminal 6 of computer ?

→ **No** →
Open circuit in wire harness between terminal 30 of combination meter and terminal 6 of computer.

↓ **Yes**

Disconnect connector from combination meter. Is there continuity between terminal 6 and body ground ?

→ **Yes** →
Short circuit in wire harness between terminal 6 of computer and terminal 30 of combination meter.

↓ **No**

SPEED SENSOR

INSPECTION GROUND CONNECTION

Disconnect connector from combination meter. Is there continuity between terminal 17 of wire harness side connector and body ground ?

→ **No** →
- Open circuit in wire harness between terminal 17 and body ground.
- Body ground faulty.

↓ **Yes**

INSPECT SPEED SENSOR OPERATION

Is speed sensor operation normal ? (See page BE-71)

→ **No** →
Speed sensor faulty.

↓ **Yes**

Cruise control trouble diagnosis chart – 1984 Cressida

ACTUATOR | Yes

INSPECT ACTUATOR OPERATION

Is actuator operation normal ?
(See page BE-72)

→ No → Replace actuator.

| Yes

Replace computer.

| **B** | **INSPECTION OF CONTROL SWITCH CIRCUIT** |

Turn ignition switch off.

CONTROL S/W

INSPECT SWITCH OPERATION

Is there continuity between terminal 23 and
body ground with accel/resume switch turned
on ?

→ No → Inspect control switch.

| Yes

Is there continuity between terminal 23
and body ground with accel/resume switch
turned off ?

→ Yes → Inspect control switch.

COMPUTER | No

INSPECT ACCEL RESUME SWITCH CIRCUIT

Is there continuity between terminal 13 and body
ground with accel/resume switch turned on ?

→ No → Open circuit in wire harness between
terminal 13 of computer and terminal 23
of control switch.

ACTUATOR | Yes

INSPECT ACTUATOR OPERATION

Is actuator operation normal ?
(See page BE-72)

→ No → Replace actuator.

| Yes

Replace computer.

Cruise control trouble diagnosis chart — 1984 Cressida

C	**INSPECTION OF ACTUATOR CIRCUIT**

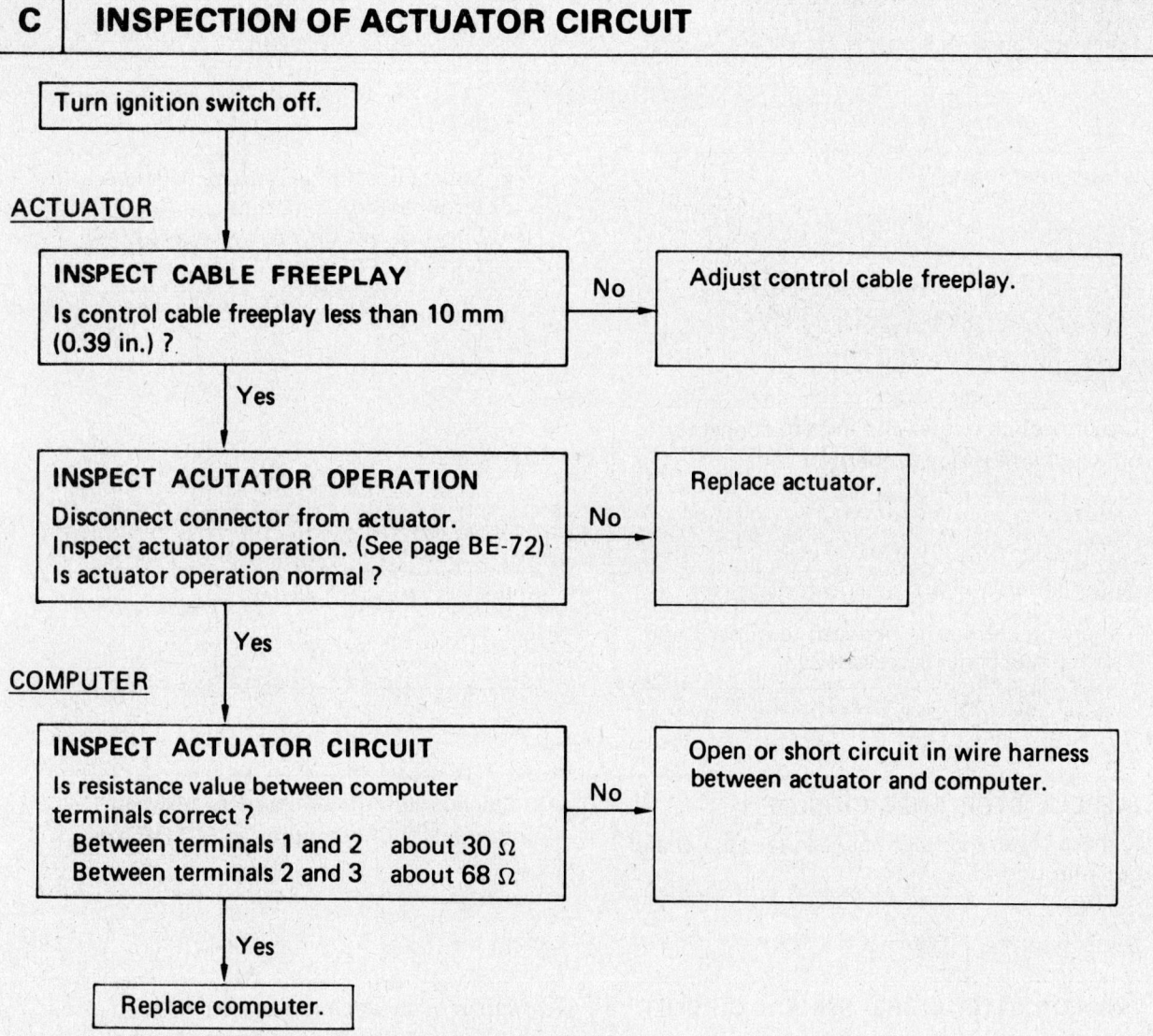

Turn ignition switch off.

ACTUATOR

INSPECT CABLE FREEPLAY
Is control cable freeplay less than 10 mm (0.39 in.) ?

No → Adjust control cable freeplay.

Yes

INSPECT ACUTATOR OPERATION
Disconnect connector from actuator.
Inspect actuator operation. (See page BE-72)
Is actuator operation normal ?

No → Replace actuator.

Yes

COMPUTER

INSPECT ACTUATOR CIRCUIT
Is resistance value between computer terminals correct ?
  Between terminals 1 and 2   about 30 Ω
  Between terminals 2 and 3   about 68 Ω

No → Open or short circuit in wire harness between actuator and computer.

Yes

Replace computer.

Cruise control trouble diagnosis chart — 1984 Cressida

D | INSPECTION OF STOP LIGHT SWITCH CIRCUIT

Turn ignition switch on.

Is stop fuse normal ?

No →
- Short circuit in wire harness between terminal 8 of computer and fuse.
- Short circuit in wire harness between terminal 9 of computer and fuse.

Yes

COMPUTER

Disconnect computer and inspect connector on wire harness side as follows.

INSPECT RELEASE VALVE CIRCUIT
Is there no continuity between terminal 1 and 2 with brake pedal depressed ?

Yes → Inspect stop light switch.

No

INSPECT STOP FUSE CIRCUIT
Is there battery voltage between terminal 9 and body ground ?

No → Open circuit in wire harness between terminal 9 of computer and STOP fuse.

Yes

INSPECT STOP LIGHT SWITCH CIRCUIT
Is there battery voltage between terminal 8 and body ground with brake pedal depressed ?

No → Open or short circuit in wire harness between terminal 8 of computer and terminal 2 of stop light switch.

Yes

Replace computer.

Cruise control trouble diagnosis chart – 1984 Cressida

E	INSPECTION OF PARKING BRAKE SWITCH

Turn ignition switch on.

COMPUTER

INSPECT PARKING BRAKE SWITCH CIRCUIT

Disconnect connector from computer.
Is there battery voltage between terminal 12 of wire harness side connector and body ground ?

→ No →
- Open circuit in wire harness between terminal 12 of computer and terminal 1 of parking brake switch.
- Inspect parking brake switch.

↓ Yes

Replace computer.

F	INSPECTION OF CLUTCH SWITCH CIRCUIT

Turn ignition switch on.

CLUTCH S/W

INSPECT GROUND CONNECTION

Is there continuity between terminal 3 and body ground ?

→ No →
Open circuit in wire harness between terminal 3 and body ground.

↓ Yes

COMPUTER

INSPECT CLUTCH SWITCH CIRCUIT

Disconnect connector from computer.
Is there continuity between terminal 1 of wire harness side connector and body ground with clutch pedal depressed ?

→ No →
- Open circuit in wire harness between terminal 11 of computer and terminal 2 of clutch switch.
- Inspect clutch switch.

↓ Yes

Replace computer.

Cruise control trouble diagnosis chart – 1984 Cressida

G	INSPECTION OF NEUTRAL START SWITCH CIRCUIT

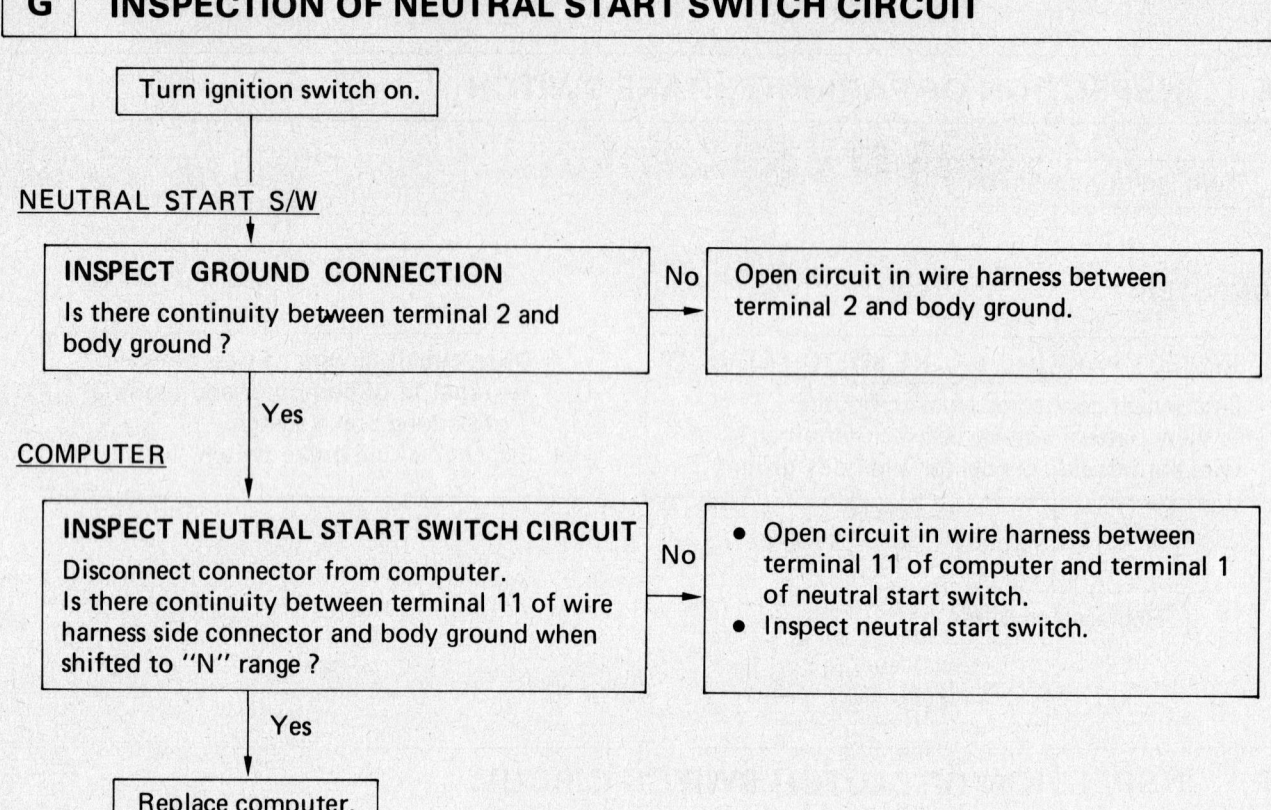

Cruise control trouble diagnosis chart—1984 Cressida

No.	Conditions	Indication Code		Diagnosis
1	Set/coast switch on	ON OFF	0.25S ⊣⊢ ⊢ ⊢ ⊢ 0.25S 1.0S	Set/coast switch circuit is normal.
2	Accel/resume switch on	ON OFF	⊓⊓⊓⊓ ⊓⊓⊓	Accel/resume switch circuit is normal.
3	Vacuum switch on	ON OFF	⊓⊓⊓⊓⊓	Vacuum switch circuit is normal.
4	Each cancel switch on (Stop light switch, Parking brake switch, Clutch switch, Neutral start switch)	ON OFF		Each cancel switch circuit is normal.
5	Drive 30 km/h (19 mph) or over	ON OFF	⊓⊓⊓⊓⊓⊓	Speed sensor circuit is normal.
6	Drive 30 km/h (19 mph) or below	ON OFF		Speed sensor circuit is normal.

Type "A" diagnostic information—1985 and later Cressida

H	INSPECTION OF SPEED SENSOR CIRCUIT

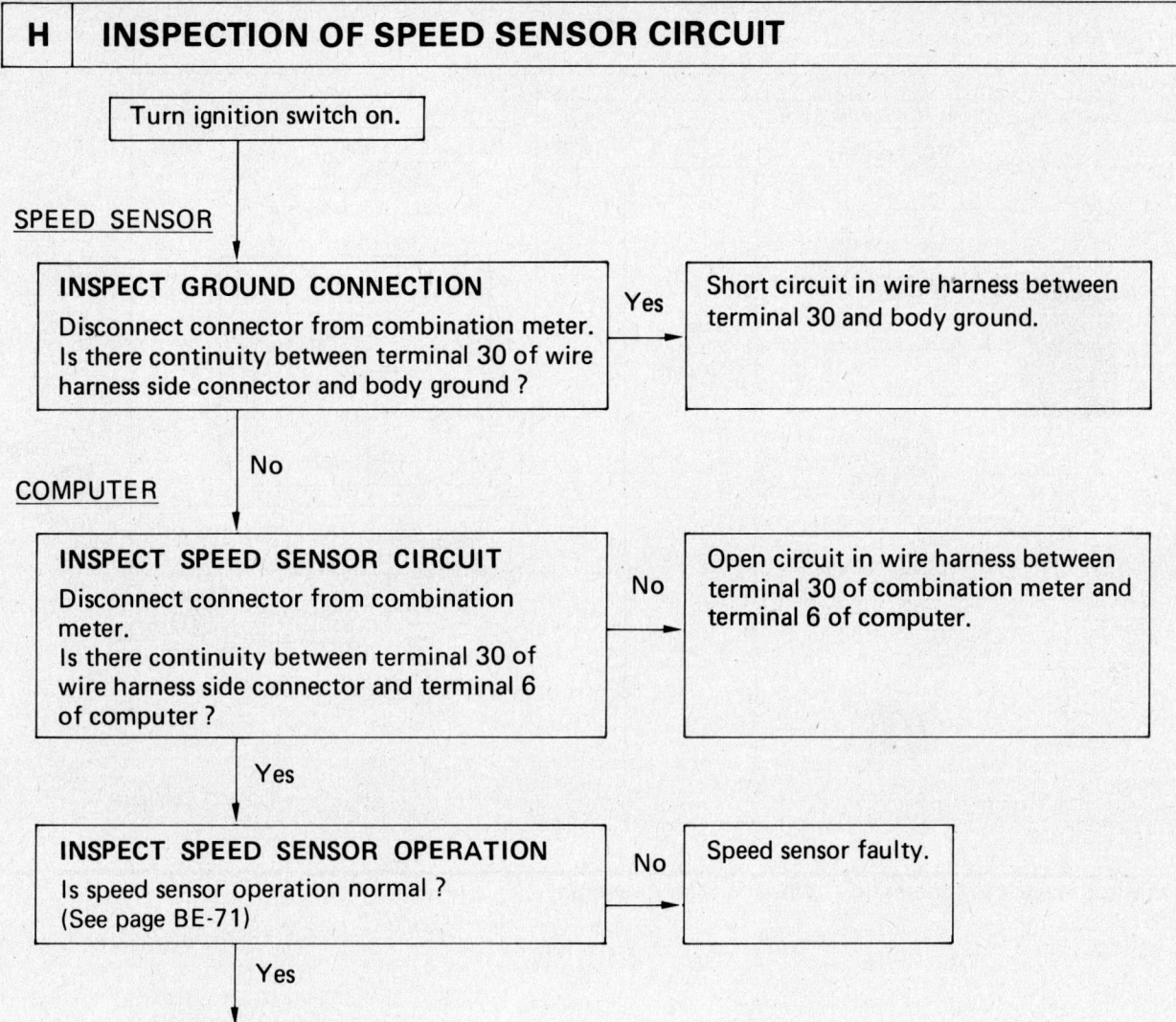

Cruise control trouble diagnosis chart—1984 Cressida

CRUISE CONTROL SYSTEM DIAGNOSIS— 1985 AND LATER

Output of Diagnosis Codes

TYPE A CODE

1. Turn the ignition switch to the on position.
2. Turn the set/coast switch on. Turn the main switch on.
3. Read the diagnosis code on the main switch indicator.
4. Checking the number four code must be done with the vehicle safely supported.
5. Results are as follows.

TYPE B CODE

1. Do not turn the ignition switch off. Do not turn the main switch off.
2. Turn the set/coast switch on three times within two seconds.

3. Read the diagnosis code on the main switch indicator.
4. Indication codes appear with priority from number eleven. Normal codes continue twenty seconds and abnormal codes are repeated three times.
5. Indication is stopped when vehicle speed is over 10 miles per hour or the main switch is turned off.
6. This type of code can be displayed with the super monitor system.
7. Results are as follows.

TYPE B CODE WITH SUPER MONITOR

1. Do not turn the ignition switch off. Do not turn the main switch off.
2. Disconnect the connector from the fuel pump with the engine idling.
3. Connect the connector to the fuel pump with the engine stopped.
4. Simultaneously push and hold in the select and input (M)

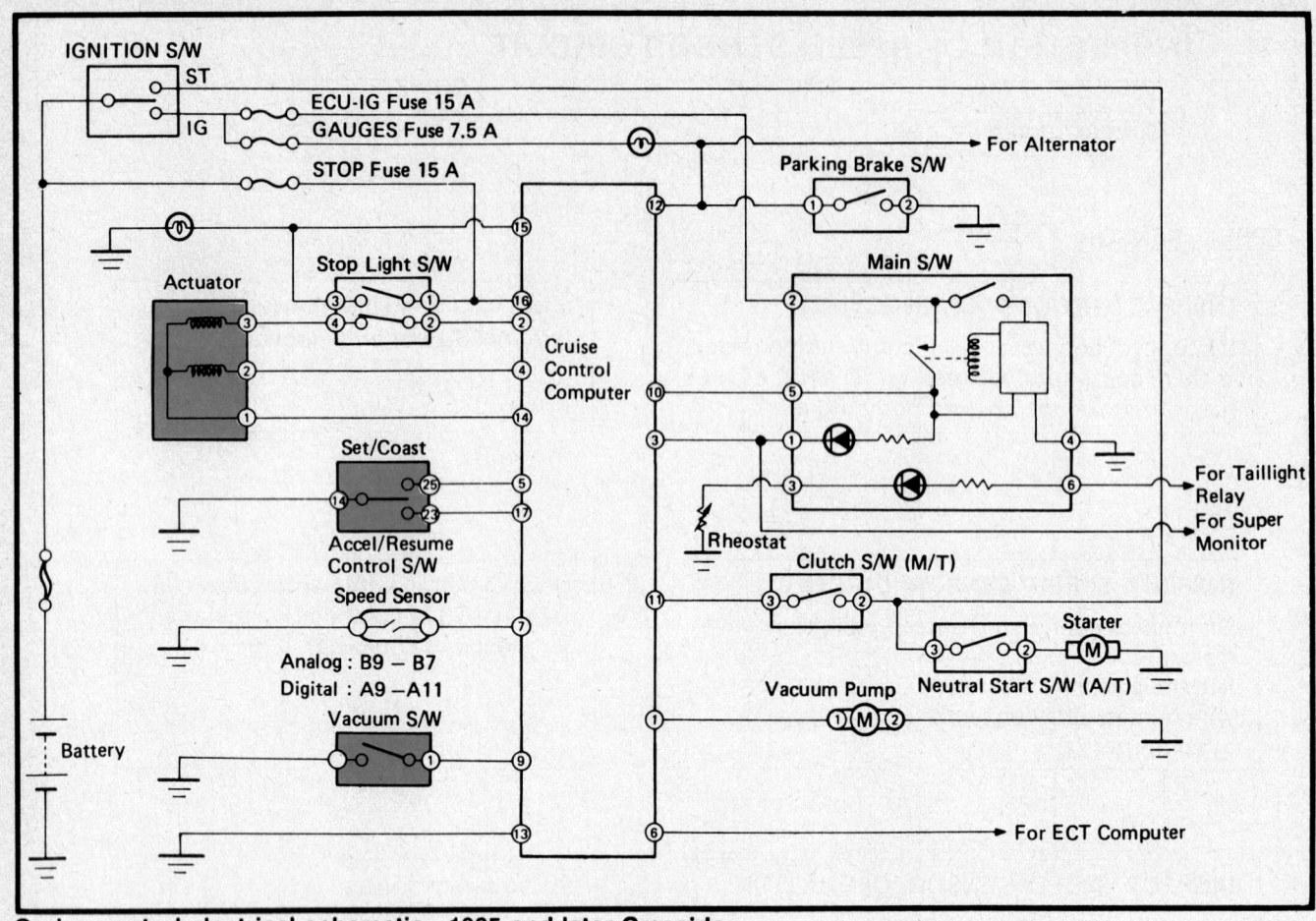

Cruise control electrical schematic – 1985 and later Cressida

No.	Indication Code	Diagnosis
	ON / OFF — 0.25S, 0.25S	Normal.
11	ON / OFF — 0.5S, 1.5S, 4S	Actuator circuit is abnormal.
21	ON / OFF — 0.5S, 1.5S	Speed sensor signal circuit is abnormal.
23	ON / OFF	Speed sensor signal circuit is abnormal.
31	ON / OFF	Accel/resume switch circuit is abnormal.
33	ON / OFF	Accel/resume switch and set/coast switch circuit is abnormal.

Type "B" diagnostic information – 1985 and later Cressida

keys for at least three seconds. The letters DIAG will appear on the screen.

5. After a short pause, hold the set key in for about three seconds. The letters E/G will appear on the screen.

6. Turn the set/coast switch on three times within two seconds when the letters C/C appear. Read the diagnosis code.

7. If the system is normal C/C OK will appear on the screen. If the harness between the cruise control computer and the super monitor are open, C/C OO will appear on the screen.

8. Correct as required.

TROUBLESHOOTING

Symptom	Inspection Area		Section
Cruise control cannot be set.	(a) Inspect type A codes.	No. 1 NO	A
		No. 2 NO	B
		No. 3 NO	C
		No. 4 NO	D
		No. 5 NO	E
		No. 6 NO	E
	(b) Inspect type B codes.	11	F
		21	E
		23	G
		31	B
		33	A and B
	(c) All codes are normal.		Replace computer.
Vehicle speed does not reduce when coast switch turned on.	Inspect No. 1 of type A code.	OK	G
		NO	A
Vehicle does not accelerate when accel switch turned on.	Inspect No. 2 of type A code.	OK	G
		NO	B
Vehicle speed does not return to memorized speed when resume switch turned on.	Inspect No. 2 of type A code.	OK	G
		NO	B
Set speed deviates on high side.	Inspect No. 1 of type A code.	OK	G
		NO	A
Set speed deviates on low side.	Inspect No. 3 of type A code.	OK	G
		NO	C
Vehicle speed fluctuates when set switch turned on.	Inspect No. 1 of type A code.	OK	G
		NO	A
	Inspect No. 3 of type A code.	OK	G
		NO	C
Setting speed does not cancel when brake pedal depressed.	Inspect No. 4 of type A code.	OK	G
		NO	D
Setting speed does not cancel when parking brake pulled.	Inspect No. 4 of type A code.	OK	G
		NO	D
Setting speed does not cancel when clutch pedal depressed. (M/T only)	Inspect No. 4 of type A code.	OK	G
		NO	D
Setting speed does not cancel when shifted to ''N'' range. (A/T only)	Inspect No. 4 of type A code.	OK	G
		NO	D
Speed can be set below 30 km/h (19 mph).	Inspect No. 5 of type A code.	OK	G
		NO	E
Cruise control will not disengage even below 30 km/h (19 mph).	Inspect No. 6 of type A code.	OK	G
		NO	E

Cruise control troubleshooting data sheet—1985 and later Cressida

A | **INSPECTION OF SET/COAST SWITCH CIRCUIT**

COMPUTER

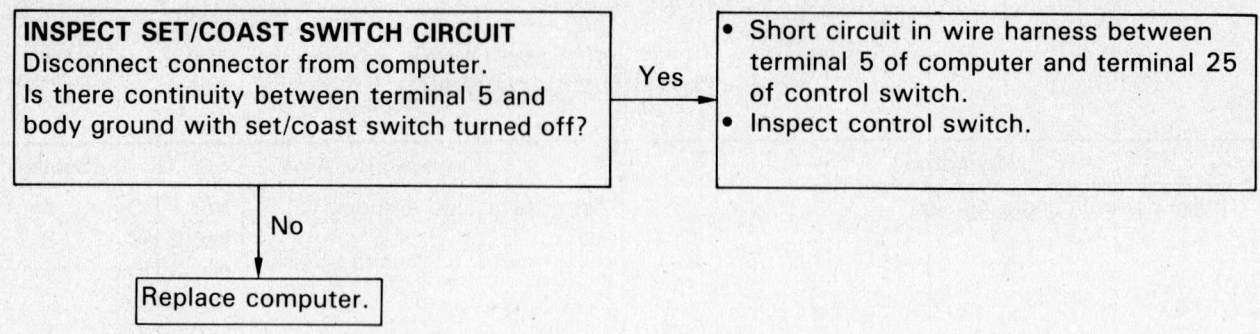

INSPECT SET/COAST SWITCH CIRCUIT
Disconnect connector from computer.
Is there continuity between terminal 5 and
body ground with set/coast switch turned off?

→ Yes →
- Short circuit in wire harness between terminal 5 of computer and terminal 25 of control switch.
- Inspect control switch.

↓ No

Replace computer.

B | **INSPECTION OF ACCEL/RESUME SWITCH CIRCUIT**

CONTROL S/W

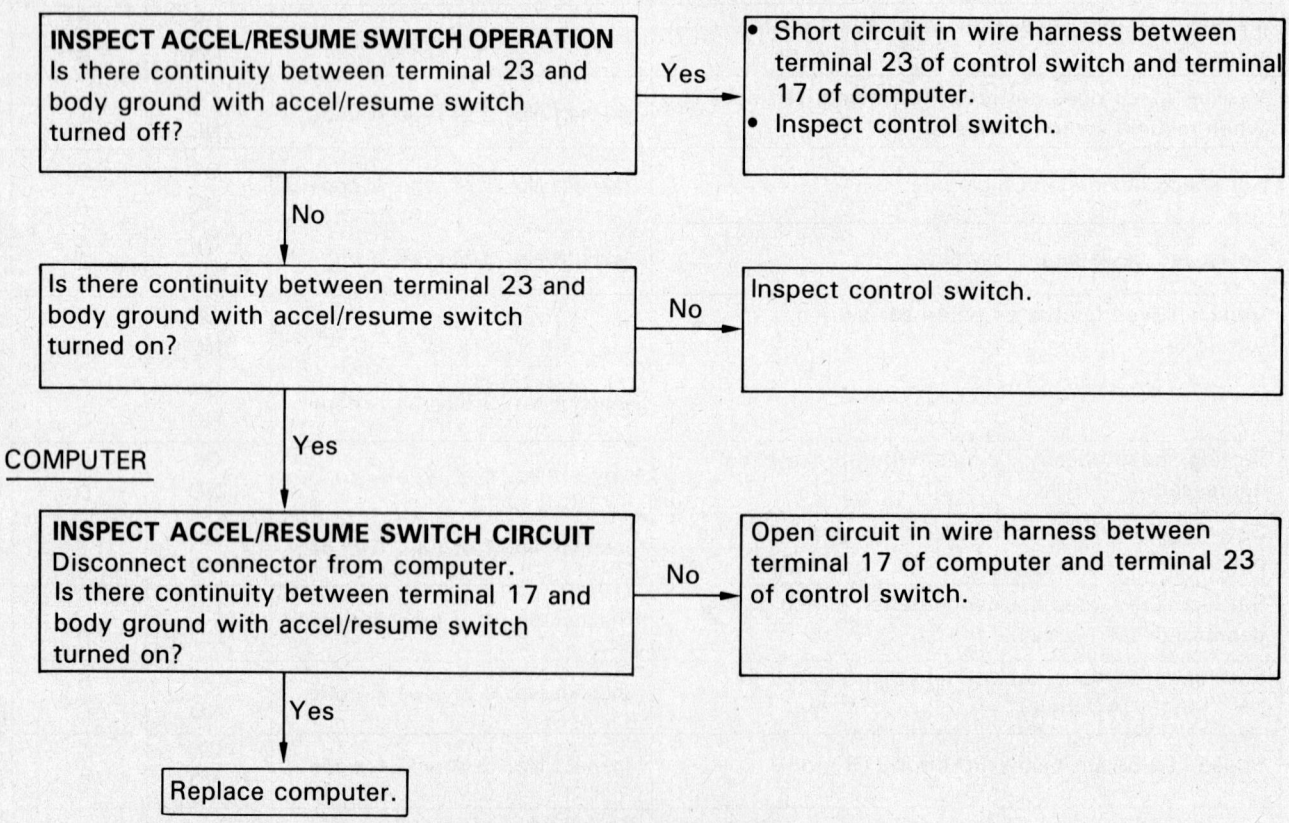

INSPECT ACCEL/RESUME SWITCH OPERATION
Is there continuity between terminal 23 and
body ground with accel/resume switch
turned off?

→ Yes →
- Short circuit in wire harness between terminal 23 of control switch and terminal 17 of computer.
- Inspect control switch.

↓ No

Is there continuity between terminal 23 and
body ground with accel/resume switch
turned on?

→ No → Inspect control switch.

↓ Yes

COMPUTER

INSPECT ACCEL/RESUME SWITCH CIRCUIT
Disconnect connector from computer.
Is there continuity between terminal 17 and
body ground with accel/resume switch
turned on?

→ No → Open circuit in wire harness between terminal 17 of computer and terminal 23 of control switch.

↓ Yes

Replace computer.

Cruise control trouble diagnosis chart—1985 and later Cressida

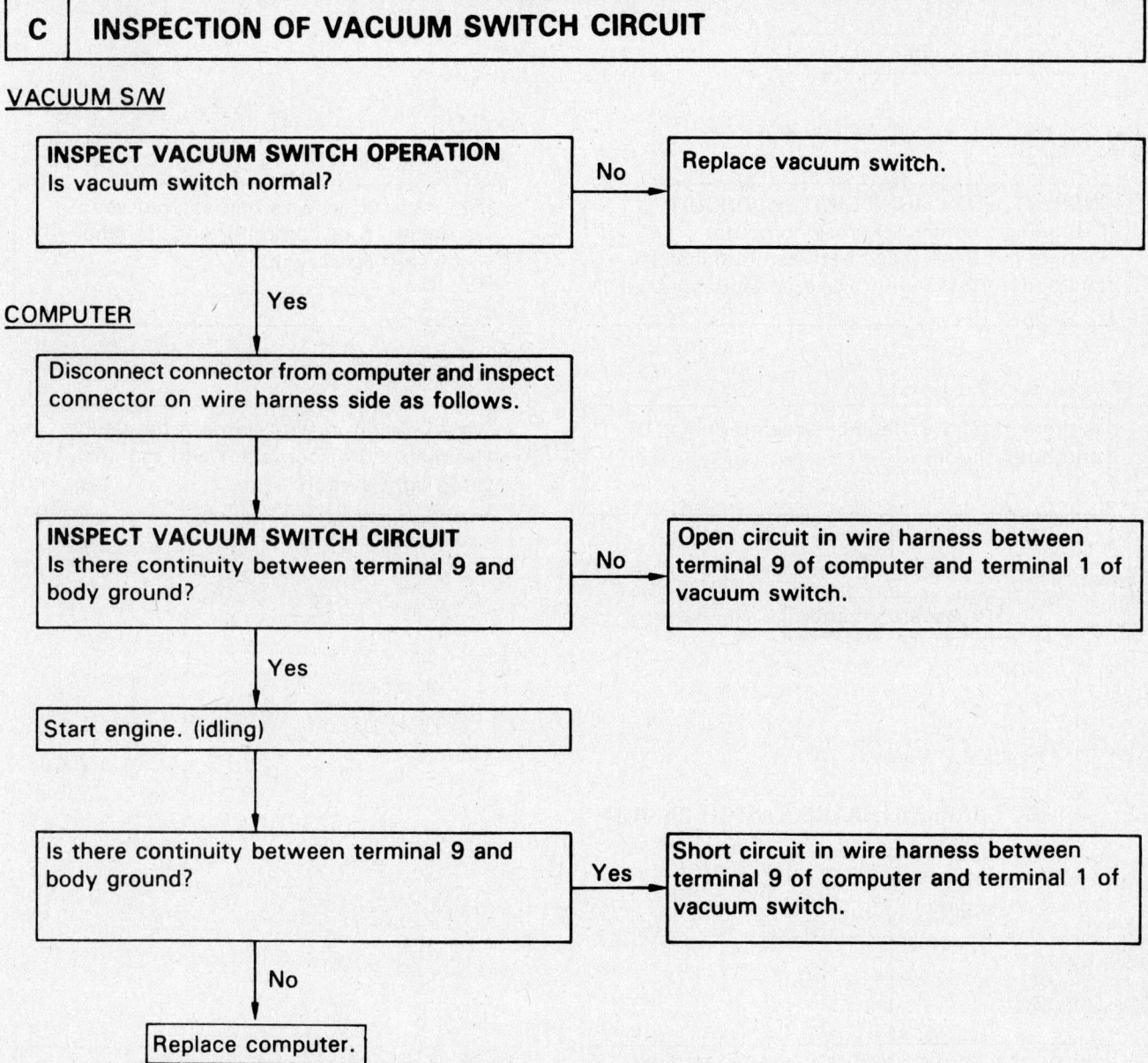

| C | **INSPECTION OF VACUUM SWITCH CIRCUIT** |

VACUUM S/W

INSPECT VACUUM SWITCH OPERATION
Is vacuum switch normal? → No → Replace vacuum switch.

Yes

COMPUTER

Disconnect connector from computer and inspect connector on wire harness side as follows.

INSPECT VACUUM SWITCH CIRCUIT
Is there continuity between terminal 9 and body ground? → No → Open circuit in wire harness between terminal 9 of computer and terminal 1 of vacuum switch.

Yes

Start engine. (idling)

Is there continuity between terminal 9 and body ground? → Yes → Short circuit in wire harness between terminal 9 of computer and terminal 1 of vacuum switch.

No

Replace computer.

Cruise control trouble diagnosis chart — 1985 and later Cressida

| D | INSPECTION CANCEL SWITCH CIRCUIT |

1. INSPECT STOP LIGHT SWITCH CIRCUIT

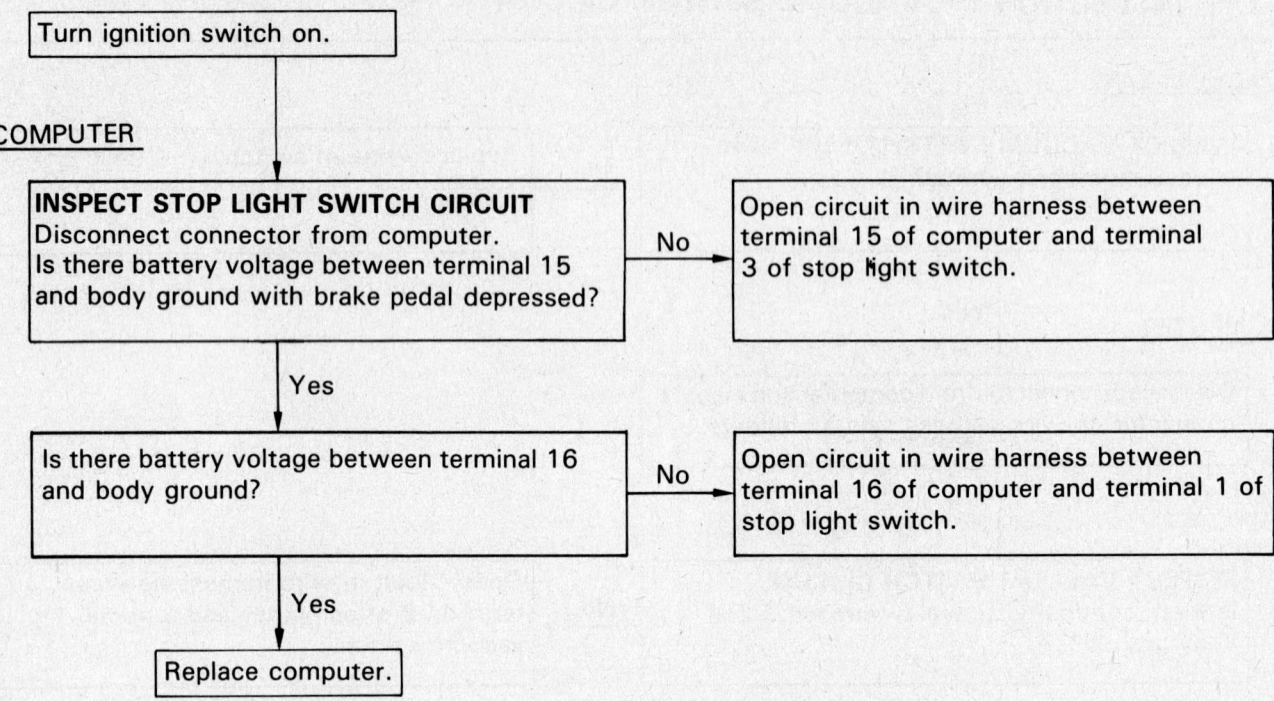

Turn ignition switch on.

COMPUTER

INSPECT STOP LIGHT SWITCH CIRCUIT
Disconnect connector from computer.
Is there battery voltage between terminal 15 and body ground with brake pedal depressed?

— No → Open circuit in wire harness between terminal 15 of computer and terminal 3 of stop light switch.

↓ Yes

Is there battery voltage between terminal 16 and body ground?

— No → Open circuit in wire harness between terminal 16 of computer and terminal 1 of stop light switch.

↓ Yes

Replace computer.

2. INSPECT PARKING BRAKE SWITCH CIRCUIT

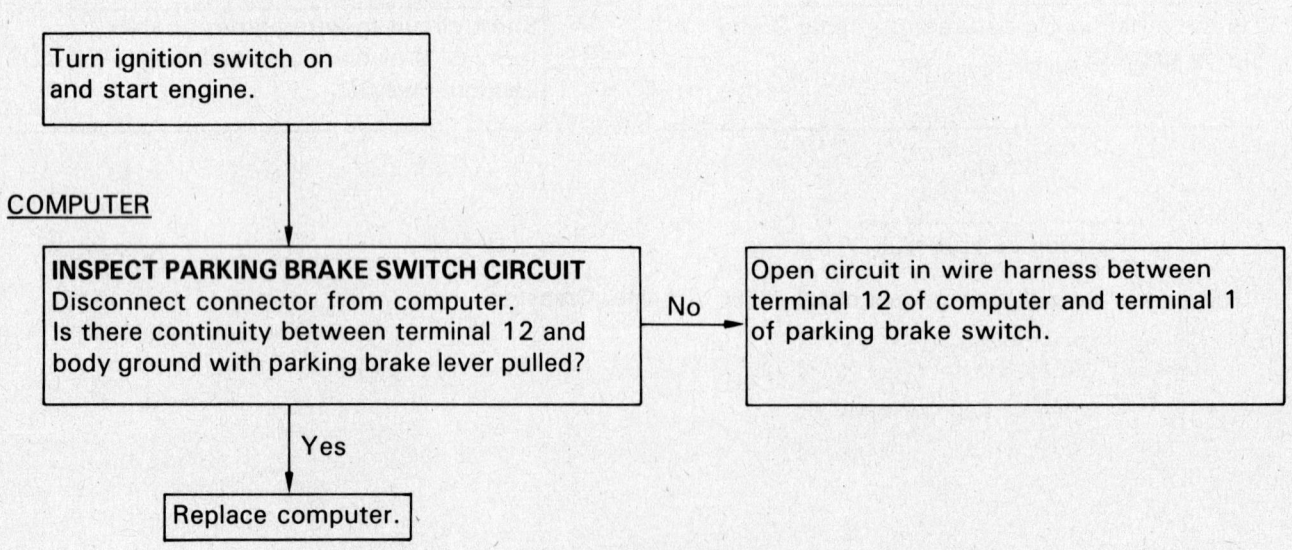

Turn ignition switch on and start engine.

COMPUTER

INSPECT PARKING BRAKE SWITCH CIRCUIT
Disconnect connector from computer.
Is there continuity between terminal 12 and body ground with parking brake lever pulled?

— No → Open circuit in wire harness between terminal 12 of computer and terminal 1 of parking brake switch.

↓ Yes

Replace computer.

Cruise control trouble diagnosis chart — 1985 and later Cressida

3. INSPECT CLUTCH SWITCH CIRCUIT (M/T)

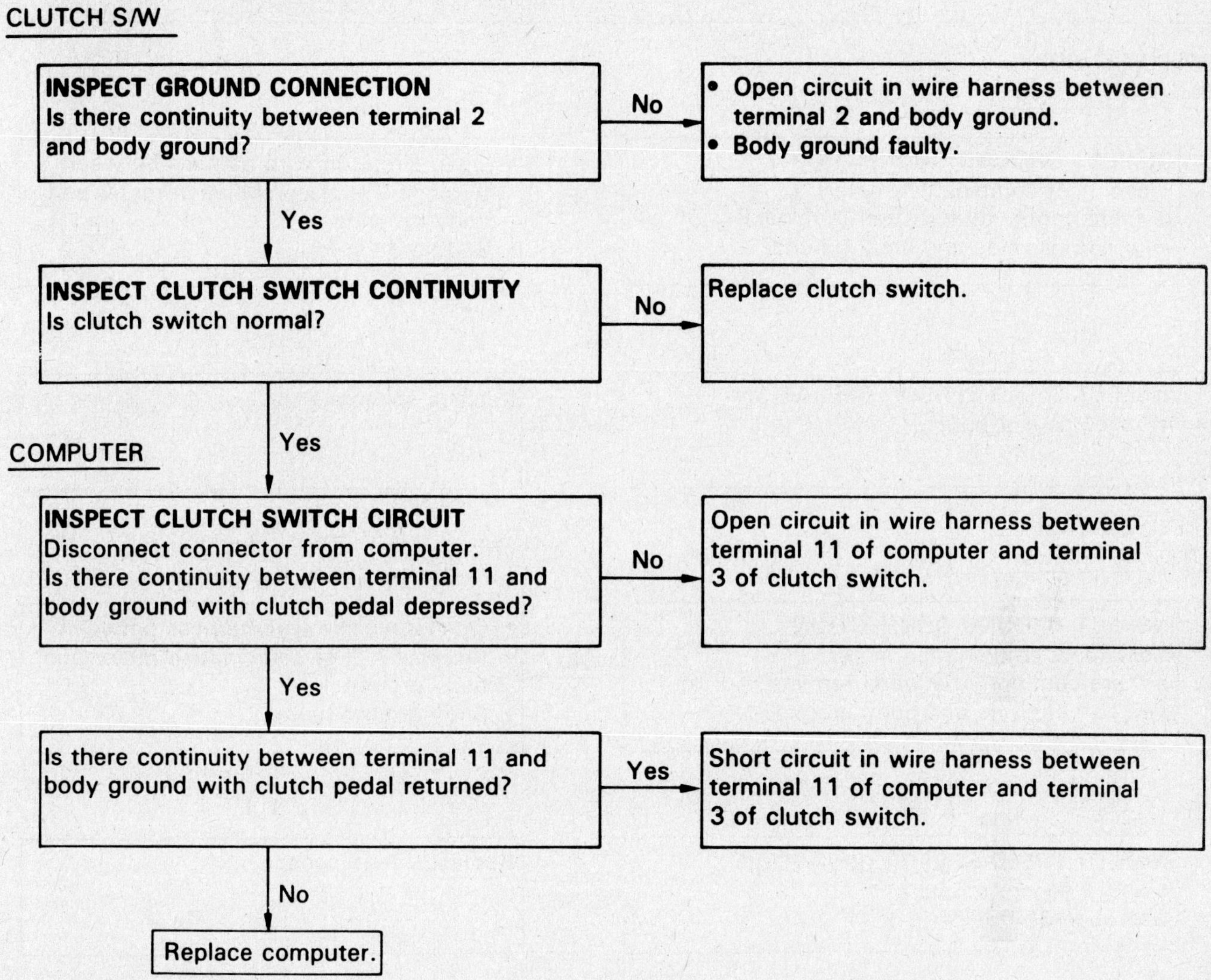

CLUTCH S/W

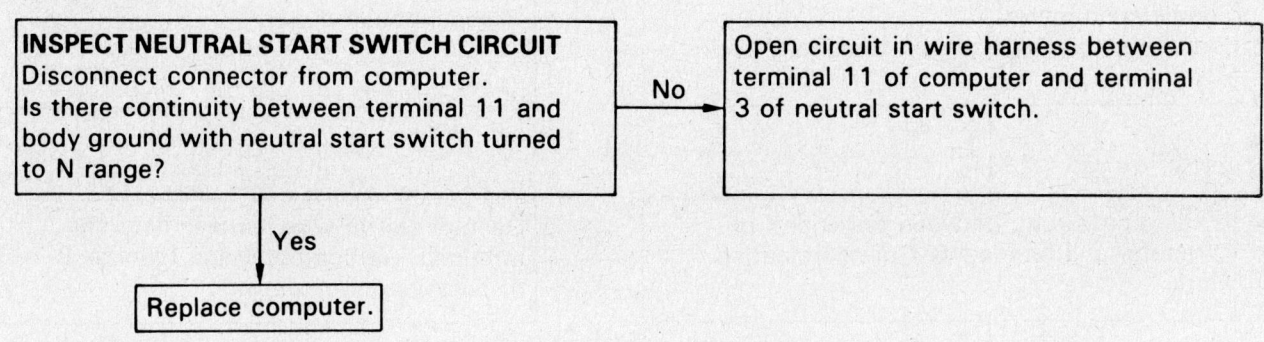

| INSPECT GROUND CONNECTION
Is there continuity between terminal 2 and body ground? | No → | • Open circuit in wire harness between terminal 2 and body ground.
• Body ground faulty. |

Yes ↓

| INSPECT CLUTCH SWITCH CONTINUITY
Is clutch switch normal? | No → | Replace clutch switch. |

COMPUTER

Yes ↓

| INSPECT CLUTCH SWITCH CIRCUIT
Disconnect connector from computer.
Is there continuity between terminal 11 and body ground with clutch pedal depressed? | No → | Open circuit in wire harness between terminal 11 of computer and terminal 3 of clutch switch. |

Yes ↓

| Is there continuity between terminal 11 and body ground with clutch pedal returned? | Yes → | Short circuit in wire harness between terminal 11 of computer and terminal 3 of clutch switch. |

No ↓

Replace computer.

4. INSPECT NEUTRAL START SWITCH CIRCUIT (A/T)

COMPUTER

| INSPECT NEUTRAL START SWITCH CIRCUIT
Disconnect connector from computer.
Is there continuity between terminal 11 and body ground with neutral start switch turned to N range? | No → | Open circuit in wire harness between terminal 11 of computer and terminal 3 of neutral start switch. |

Yes ↓

Replace computer.

Cruise control trouble diagnosis chart – 1985 and later Cressida

E	INSPECTION OF SPEED SENSOR CIRCUIT

SPEED SENSOR
(ANALOG METER)

INSPECT GROUND CONNECTION
Disconnect combination meter.
Is there continuity between terminal B-9 of wire harness side and body ground?

→ No →

- Open circuit in wire harness between terminal B-9 of combination meter and body ground.
- Body ground faulty.

↓ Yes

INSPECT SPEED SENSOR OPERATION
Is speed sensor normal?

→ No → Replace speed sensor.

SPEED SENSOR
(DIGITAL METER)

↓ Yes

INSPECT GROUND CONNECTION
Disconnect combination meter.
Is there continuity between terminal A-9 of wire harness side and body ground?

→ No →

- Open circuit in wire harness between terminal A-9 of combination meter and body ground.
- Body ground faulty.

↓ Yes

INSPECT SPEED SENSOR OPERATION
Is speed sensor normal?
(See page BE-95)

→ No → Replace speed sensor.

COMPUTER
(ANALOG METER)

↓ Yes

INSPECT SPEED SENSOR CIRCUIT
Disconnect connector from computer and combination meter.
Is there continuity between terminal 7 and body ground?

→ Yes → Short circuit in wire harness between terminal 7 of computer and terminal B-7 of combination meter.

↓ No

Is there continuity between terminal 7 of computer and terminal B-7 of combination meter?

→ No → Open circuit in wire harness between terminal 7 of computer and terminal B-7 of combination meter.

↓ Yes

Cruise control trouble diagnosis chart—1985 and later Cressida

COMPUTER
(DIGITAL METER)   Yes

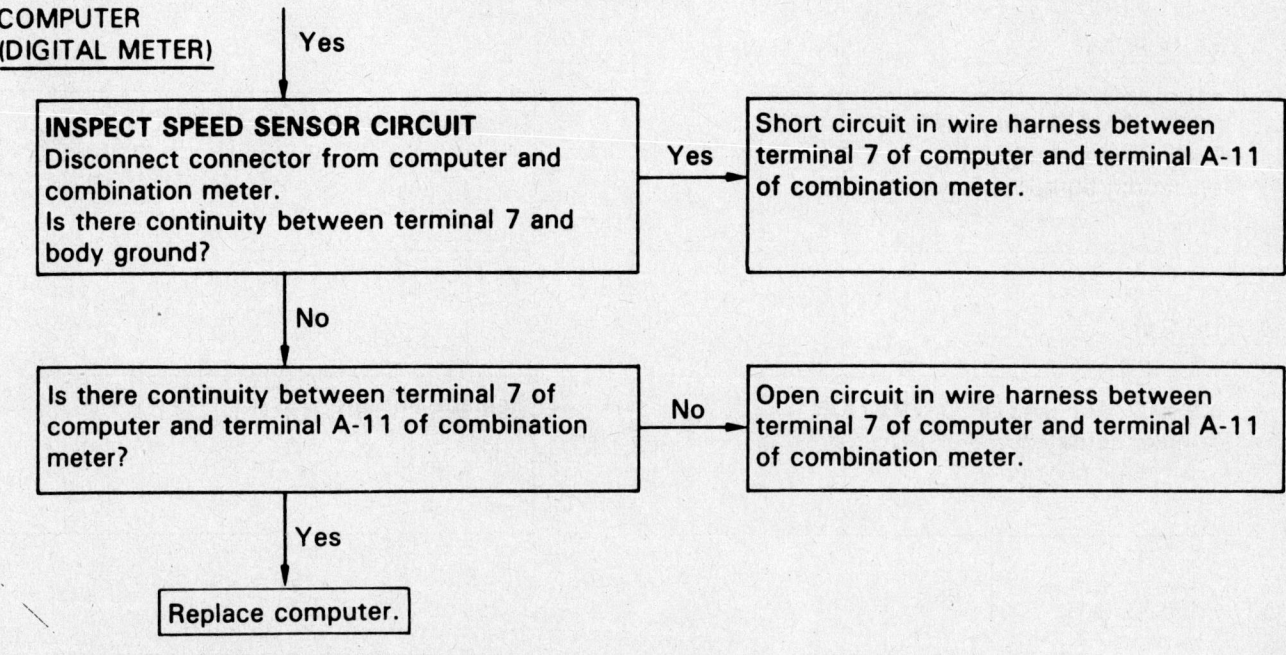

INSPECT SPEED SENSOR CIRCUIT
Disconnect connector from computer and combination meter.
Is there continuity between terminal 7 and body ground?

Yes → Short circuit in wire harness between terminal 7 of computer and terminal A-11 of combination meter.

No

Is there continuity between terminal 7 of computer and terminal A-11 of combination meter?

No → Open circuit in wire harness between terminal 7 of computer and terminal A-11 of combination meter.

Yes

Replace computer.

| F | **INSPECTION OF ACTUATOR OPERATION** |

ACTUATOR

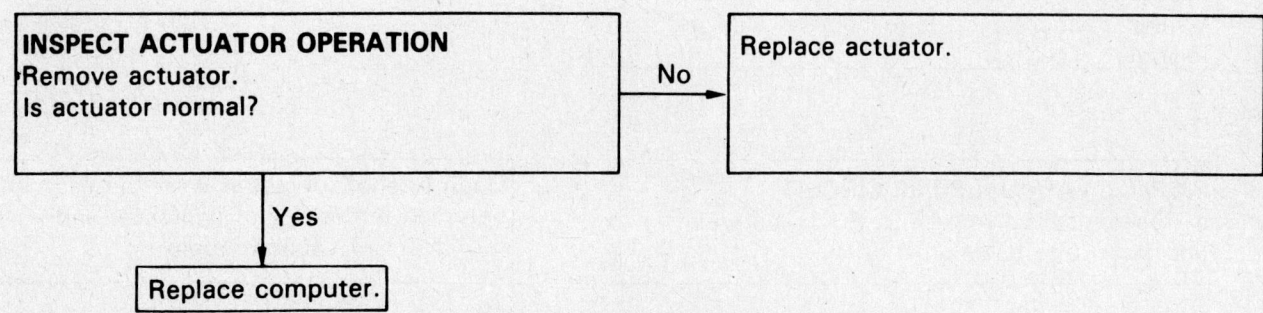

INSPECT ACTUATOR OPERATION
Remove actuator.
Is actuator normal?

No → Replace actuator.

Yes

Replace computer.

Cruise control trouble diagnosis chart—1985 and later Cressida

G	INSPECTION OF ACTUATOR CIRCUIT

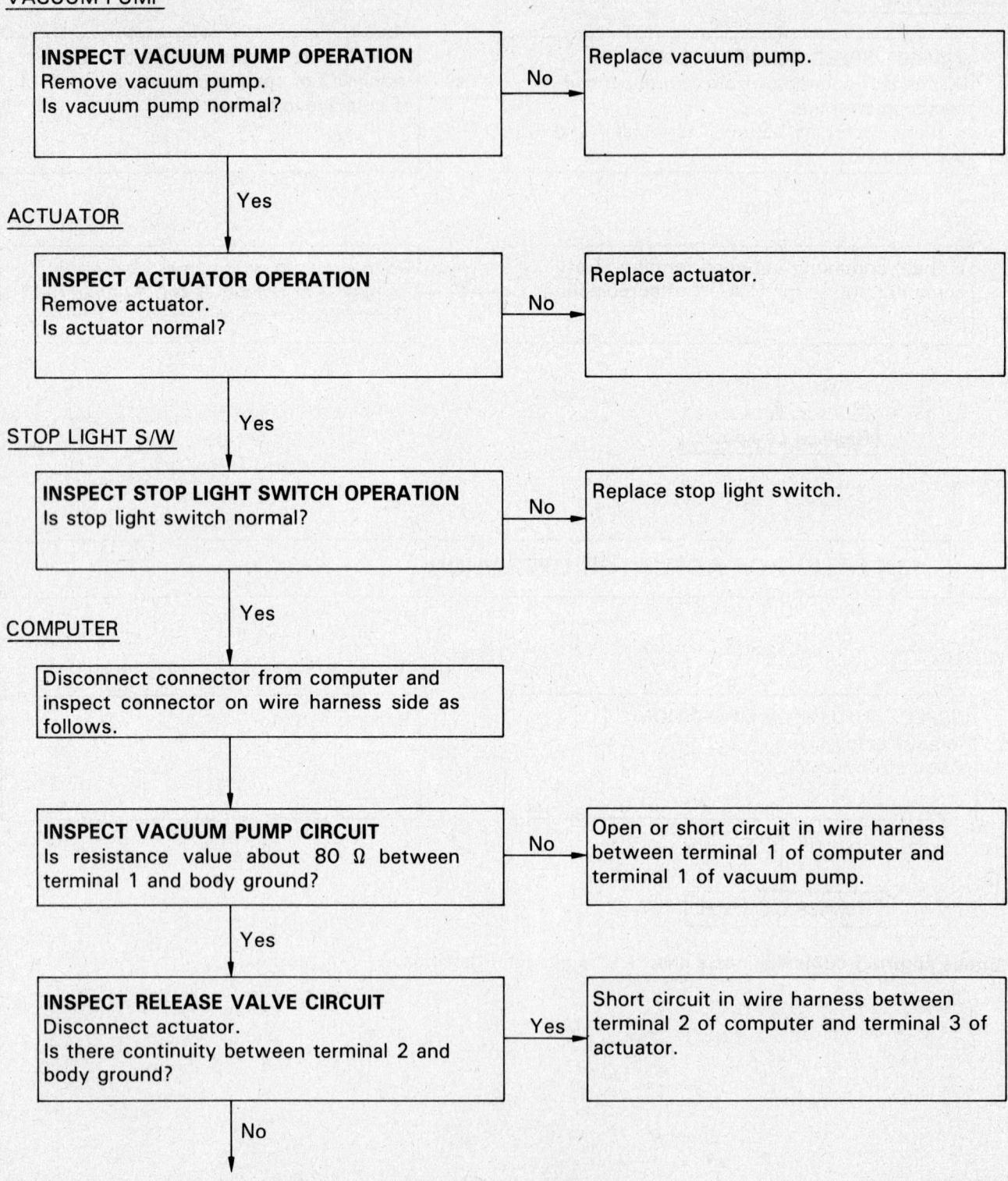

VACUUM PUMP

INSPECT VACUUM PUMP OPERATION
Remove vacuum pump.
Is vacuum pump normal? → No → Replace vacuum pump.

↓ Yes

ACTUATOR

INSPECT ACTUATOR OPERATION
Remove actuator.
Is actuator normal? → No → Replace actuator.

↓ Yes

STOP LIGHT S/W

INSPECT STOP LIGHT SWITCH OPERATION
Is stop light switch normal? → No → Replace stop light switch.

↓ Yes

COMPUTER

Disconnect connector from computer and inspect connector on wire harness side as follows.

↓

INSPECT VACUUM PUMP CIRCUIT
Is resistance value about 80 Ω between terminal 1 and body ground? → No → Open or short circuit in wire harness between terminal 1 of computer and terminal 1 of vacuum pump.

↓ Yes

INSPECT RELEASE VALVE CIRCUIT
Disconnect actuator.
Is there continuity between terminal 2 and body ground? → Yes → Short circuit in wire harness between terminal 2 of computer and terminal 3 of actuator.

↓ No

Cruise control trouble diagnosis chart—1985 and later Cressida

1118

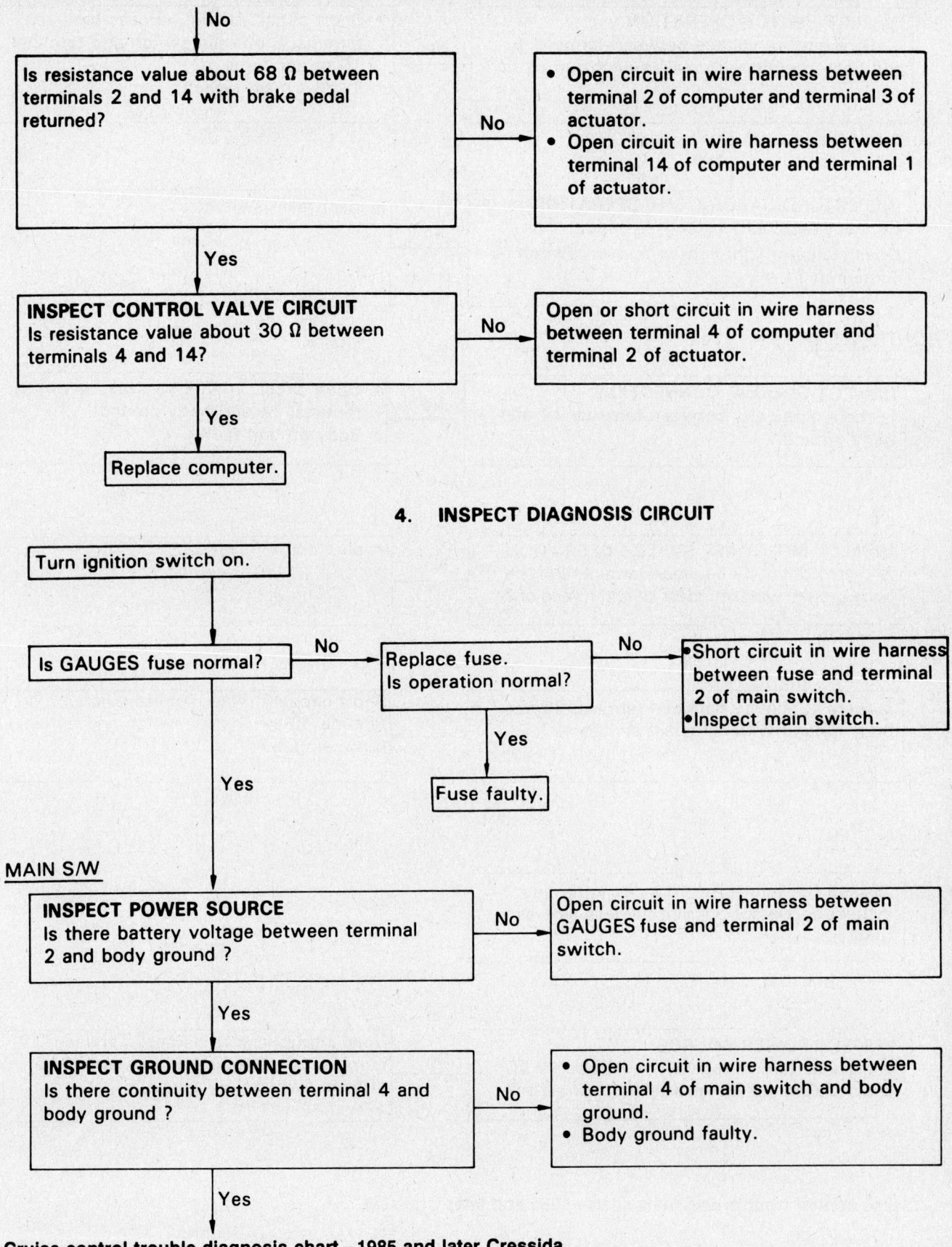

No

Is resistance value about 68 Ω between terminals 2 and 14 with brake pedal returned?

→ No →
- Open circuit in wire harness between terminal 2 of computer and terminal 3 of actuator.
- Open circuit in wire harness between terminal 14 of computer and terminal 1 of actuator.

Yes

INSPECT CONTROL VALVE CIRCUIT
Is resistance value about 30 Ω between terminals 4 and 14?

→ No →
Open or short circuit in wire harness between terminal 4 of computer and terminal 2 of actuator.

Yes

Replace computer.

4. INSPECT DIAGNOSIS CIRCUIT

Turn ignition switch on.

Is GAUGES fuse normal?

→ No →
Replace fuse.
Is operation normal?

→ No →
- Short circuit in wire harness between fuse and terminal 2 of main switch.
- Inspect main switch.

Yes

Fuse faulty.

Yes

MAIN S/W

INSPECT POWER SOURCE
Is there battery voltage between terminal 2 and body ground ?

→ No →
Open circuit in wire harness between GAUGES fuse and terminal 2 of main switch.

Yes

INSPECT GROUND CONNECTION
Is there continuity between terminal 4 and body ground ?

→ No →
- Open circuit in wire harness between terminal 4 of main switch and body ground.
- Body ground faulty.

Yes

Cruise control trouble diagnosis chart—1985 and later Cressida

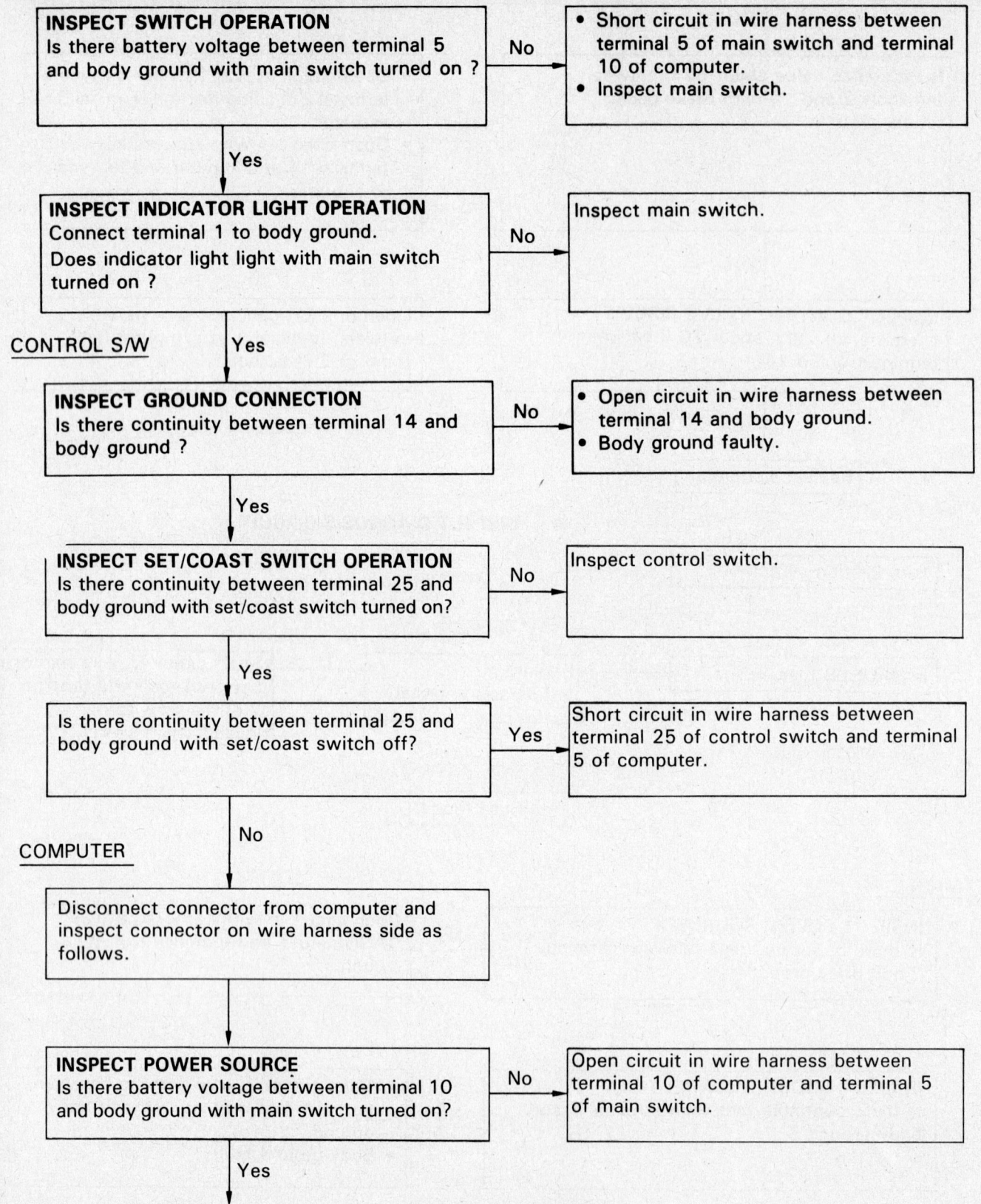

INSPECT SWITCH OPERATION
Is there battery voltage between terminal 5 and body ground with main switch turned on ?

→ No →
- Short circuit in wire harness between terminal 5 of main switch and terminal 10 of computer.
- Inspect main switch.

↓ Yes

INSPECT INDICATOR LIGHT OPERATION
Connect terminal 1 to body ground.
Does indicator light light with main switch turned on ?

→ No →
Inspect main switch.

CONTROL S/W   ↓ Yes

INSPECT GROUND CONNECTION
Is there continuity between terminal 14 and body ground ?

→ No →
- Open circuit in wire harness between terminal 14 and body ground.
- Body ground faulty.

↓ Yes

INSPECT SET/COAST SWITCH OPERATION
Is there continuity between terminal 25 and body ground with set/coast switch turned on?

→ No →
Inspect control switch.

↓ Yes

Is there continuity between terminal 25 and body ground with set/coast switch off?

→ Yes →
Short circuit in wire harness between terminal 25 of control switch and terminal 5 of computer.

COMPUTER   ↓ No

Disconnect connector from computer and inspect connector on wire harness side as follows.

↓

INSPECT POWER SOURCE
Is there battery voltage between terminal 10 and body ground with main switch turned on?

→ No →
Open circuit in wire harness between terminal 10 of computer and terminal 5 of main switch.

↓ Yes

Cruise control trouble diagnosis chart — 1985 and later Cressida

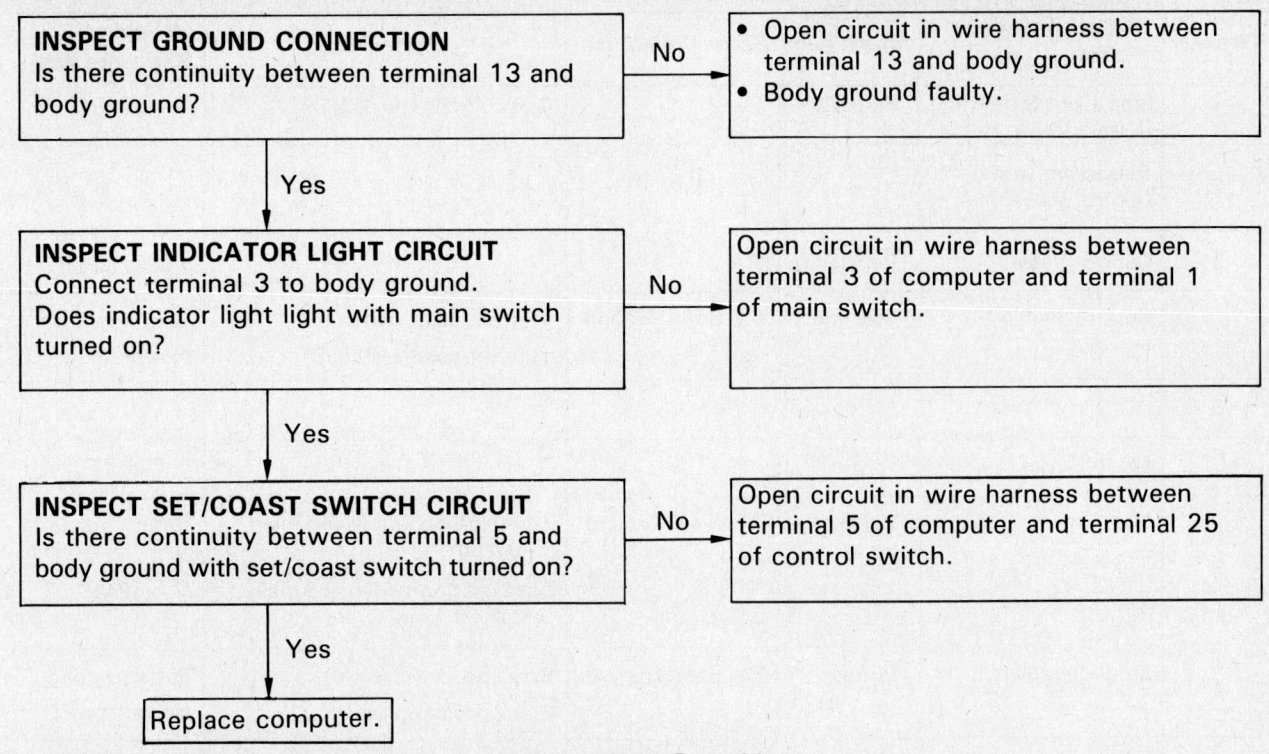

INSPECT GROUND CONNECTION Is there continuity between terminal 13 and body ground?	No →	• Open circuit in wire harness between terminal 13 and body ground. • Body ground faulty.

Yes ↓

INSPECT INDICATOR LIGHT CIRCUIT Connect terminal 3 to body ground. Does indicator light light with main switch turned on?	No →	Open circuit in wire harness between terminal 3 of computer and terminal 1 of main switch.

Yes ↓

INSPECT SET/COAST SWITCH CIRCUIT Is there continuity between terminal 5 and body ground with set/coast switch turned on?	No →	Open circuit in wire harness between terminal 5 of computer and terminal 25 of control switch.

Yes ↓

Replace computer.

Cruise control trouble diagnosis chart—1985 and later Cressida

Supra

VISUAL INSPECTION

Before performing any tests make a visual inspection of the cruise control system. Check all items in the system for abnormal conditions such as bare broken or disconnected wires and damage to the vacuum hoses. Be sure that the speedometer cables are attached and properly routed. All vacuum hoses must be properly routed and must not have any kinks or bends. Be sure that all electrical connections are complete and tight. The wiring harness must be routed properly.

COMPUTER AND SENSOR TEST (1982–83)

1. Remove the right side kick panel. Unplug the wiring harness from the computer.
2. Turn the ignition switch to the on position. Using a voltmeter measure the voltage between terminal thirteen and ground with the main switch in the on position.
3. Battery voltage should be present. If battery voltage is not present, check the control switch.
4. Using the voltmeter measure the voltage between terminal eight and ground. When the parking brake lever is pulled the voltage should be zero. When the lever is returned the voltage should be 12 volts.
5. Turn the ignition switch off. Using the voltmeter measure the voltage between terminal eleven and ground.
6. Battery voltage should be present. If battery voltage is not present, check the stop light switch.
7. Using the voltmeter measure the voltage between terminal twelve and ground. When the parking brake lever is pulled the voltage should be 12 volts. When the lever is returned the voltage should be zero. If the voltage is incorrect check the brake pedal switch.

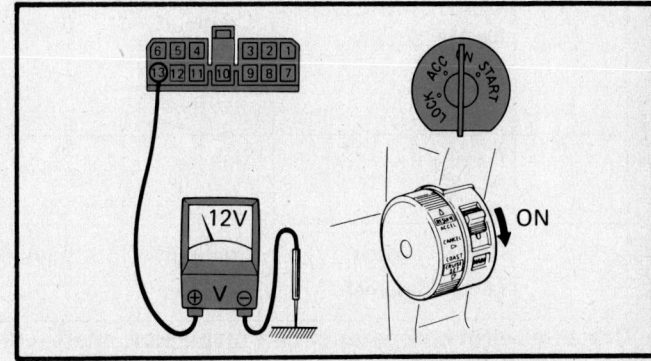

Computer test point locations—1982–83 Supra

8. Turn the ignition switch to the accessory position. Using an ohmmeter check for continuity between terminal nine and ground.
9. If equipped with manual transmission depress the clutch pedal (automatic transmission in neutral), if continuity does not exist between the terminals check the clutch or neutral safety switch.
10. Using an ohmmeter measure the resistance between terminals six and ten. The resistance should be about 68 ohms. Measure the resistance between terminals four and ten. The resistance should be about 30 ohms. If the readings are not correct check the actuator.
11. Using an ohmmeter check the continunity between terminal three and ground when the set switch is in the on position. If there is no continunity between the terminals check the control switch.
12. Using an ohmmeter check the continunity between terminal seven and ground when the set switch is in the on position.

Terminal	Connection or Measure Item	Check Item	Tester Connection	Condition	Voltage or Resistance Value
1	Stop Light Switch and Release Valve	Resistance	1 – 2	Brake pedal returned	About 68 Ω
2	Release Valve and Control Valve	–	–	–	–
3	Control Valve	Resistance	3 – 2	–	About 30 Ω
4	Control Switch (Set/Coast)	Continuity	4 – Body Ground	Turn set/coast switch on Turn set/coast switch off	Continuity No continuity
5	OD Relay	–	–	–	–
6	Speed Sensor	–	–	–	–
7	Main Switch	Voltage	7 – Body Ground	Turn ignition switch and main switch on Turn ignition switch and main switch off	Battery voltage No voltage
8	Stop Light Switch	Voltage	8 – Body Ground	Brake pedal depressed Brake pedal returned	Battery voltage No voltage
9	STOP Fuse	Voltage	9 – Body Ground	–	Battery voltage
10	Body Ground	Continuity	10 – Body Ground	–	Continuity
11	Clutch Switch Neutral Switch	Continuity	11 – Body Ground	Clutch pedal depressed or shift into "N" range Clutch pedal returned or shift into except "N" range	Continuity No continuity
12	Parking Brake Switch	Voltage	12 – Body Ground	Parking brake pulled Parking brake returned	No voltage Battery voltage
13	Control Switch (Accel/Resume)	Continuity	13 – Body Ground	Turn accel/resume switch on Turn accel/resume switch off	Continuity No continuity

Cruise control computer circuit inspection chart – 1984–86 Supra

If there is no continuity between the terminals check the control switch.

13. Using an ohmmeter check the continuity between terminal five and ground when the cancel switch is pushed on.

14. Using an ohmmeter check the continuity between terminal one and ground when the vehicle is slightly pushed. At this time the needle on the ohmmeter should move repeatedly from on to off. If not check the speed sensor.

ACTUATOR TEST

1982–83

1. Disconnect the electrical connector from the actuator lead wire.

2. Using an ohmmeter measure the resistance between terminals one and two. It should be about 30 ohms. Measure the resistance between terminals one and three. It should be about 70 ohms.

3. If the resistance is not as indicated, replace the actuator.

4. Disconnect the carburetor throttle rod from the bell crank. Start the engine.

5. Check that the actuator diaphragm makes a smooth reciprocating motion when either power is applied to terminals two and three with the actuator terminal one grounded or

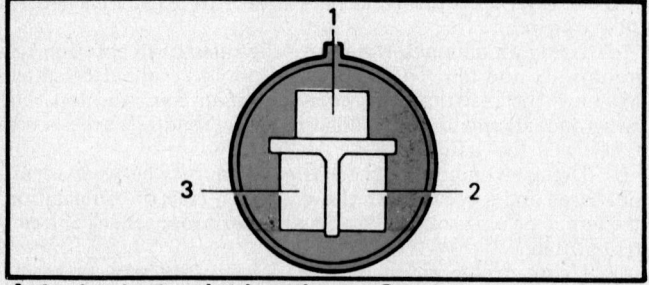

Actuator test point locations – Supra

Connection or Measure item	Check Item	Tester Connection	Condition	Voltage or Resistance Value
Stop Light Switch and Release Valve	Resistance	2 — 14	Brake pedal returned	About 68 ohm
Main Switch	Voltage	3 — Body ground	Turn ignition switch and main switch on	Battery voltage
			Turn ignition switch and/or main switch off	No voltage
Control Valve	Resistance	4 — 14	—	About 30 ohm
Control Switch (set/coast)	Resistance	17 — Body ground	See page BE-64	—
Control Switch (resume/accel)	Resistance	17 — Body ground	See page BE-64	—
Control Switch (cancel)	Resistance	17 — Body ground	See page BE-64	—
Speed Sensor	Continuity	7 — Body ground	Vehicle moving slowly	1 pulse each 40 cm (15.75 in.)
Main Switch	Voltage	10 — Body ground	Turn ignition switch and main switch on	Battery voltage
			Turn ignition switch and/or main switch off	No voltage
Clutch Switch (M/T) or Neutral Start Switch (A/T)	Continuity	11 — Body ground	Clutch pedal depressed or shifted into "N" range	Continuity
			Clutch pedal returned or shifted into only range except "N" range	No continuity
Parking Brake Switch	Continuity	12 — Body ground	Parking brake pulled	Continuity
			Parking brake returned	No continuity
Body Ground	Continuity	13 — Body ground	—	Continuity
Stop Light Switch	Voltage	15 — Body ground	Brake pedal depressed	Battery voltage
			Brake pedal returned	No voltage
STOP Fuse	Voltage	16 — Body ground	—	Battery voltage

Cruise control computer circuit inspection chart—1987 and later Supra

when power is removed from terminal two. If not replace the actuator.

6. Be sure that the cable does not return to easy when pulled with about 4 to 7 lbs. of force. Repair or replace defective components as required.

7. Check to be sure that the vacuum hose is properly routed and connected. Correct as required.

1984 and Later

1. Inspect and check the actuator cable. Freeplay should be less than 0.039 inch. Adjust or replace as required.

2. Disconnect the electrical connector from the actuator lead wire.

3. Using an ohmmeter measure the resistance between terminals one and two. It should be about 30 ohms. Measure the

resistance between terminals one and three. It should be about 68 ohms.

4. If the resistance is not as indicated, replace the actuator.

5. Connect a positive lead from the positive terminal of the battery to terminals two and three. Connect a negative lead from the negative terminal of the battery to terminal one.

6. Slowly apply 0 to 11.8 in. hg. of vacuum. Check to be sure that the control cable can be pulled smoothly.

7. When the vacuum has stabilized check the control cable and be sure that it does not return.

8. Disconnect terminal two or three and check that the control cable returns to its original position and that the vacuum goes to zero.

9. If the system does not perform as indicated replace the actuator.

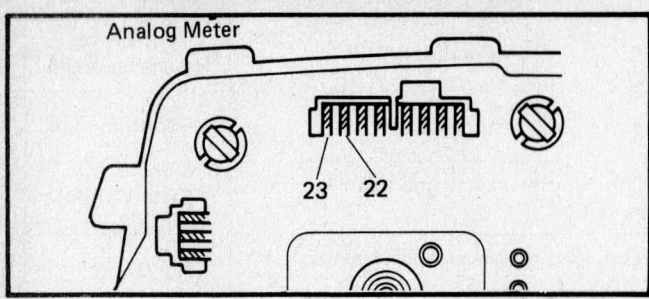

Speed sensor test point locations—1982–83 Supra

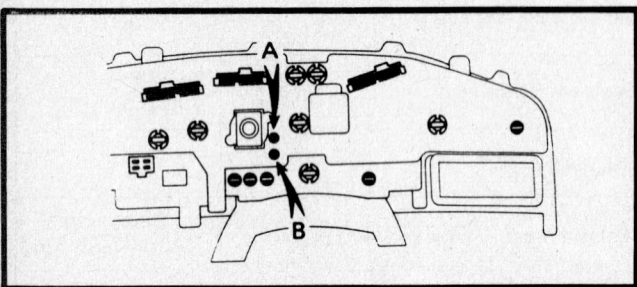

Speed sensor test point locations—1987 and later Supra

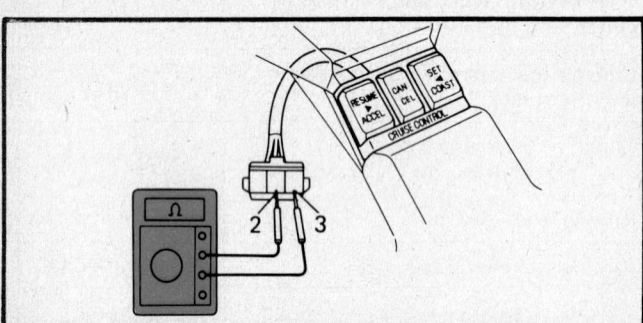

Control switch test point locations—1987 and later Supra

SPEED SENSOR TEST

1982–83

1. Using an ohmmeter, check to see that there is continuity between terminals 23 and 22. It should be four times per revolution of the magnet shaft.
2. If continunity does not exist replace the speed sensor.

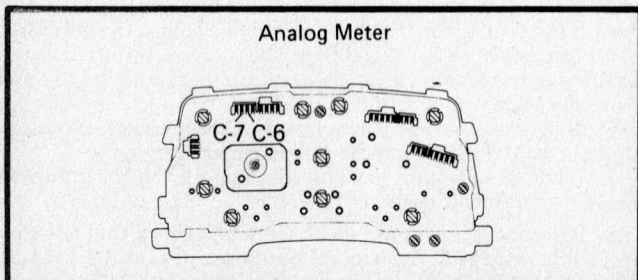

Speed sensor test point locations—1984–86 Supra with regular speedometer

1984–86

REGULAR SPEEDOMETER

1. Using an ohmmeter, check to see that there is continuity between terminals C6 and C7. It should be four times per revolution of the magnet shaft.
2. If continunity does not exist replace the speed sensor.

DIGITAL SPEEDOMETER

1. Using an ohmmeter, check to see that there is continuity between terminals A10 and A12. It should be four times per revolution of the magnet shaft.
2. If continunity does not exist replace the speed sensor.

1987 and Later

1. Using an ohmmeter, check to see that there is continuity between terminals A and B. It should be four times per revolution of the magnet shaft.
2. If continunity does not exist replace the speed sensor.

CONTROL SWITCH TEST

1. Using an ohmmeter check for continuity of the terminals for each switch position.
2. If continunity between the terminals is not as specified, replace the switch.

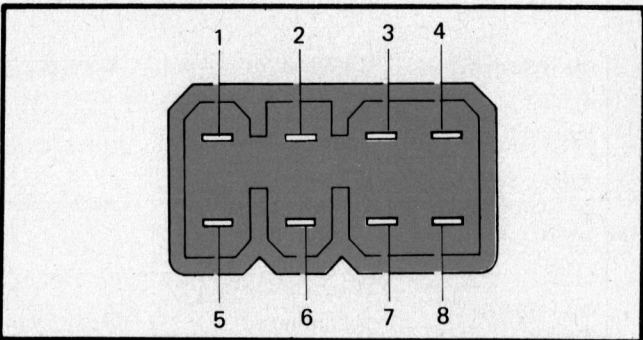

Control switch test point locations—1982–83 Supra

Terminal Switch position		1	2	3	4	5	6	7	8
Main Switch	ON	O—				—O			
	OFF								
Control Switch	SET							O—	—O
	OFF								
	RESUME			O—				—O	
Cancel Switch	ON		O—						—O
	OFF								

Control switch specifications—1982–83 Supra

Switch position	Terminal	28 SR	30 Ss	14 Ew
SET/COAST			●	●
OFF				
ACCEL/RESUME		●		●

Control switch test specifications—1984–86 Supra

MAIN SWITCH TEST

1984–86

1. Using an ohmmeter check for continunity of the terminals for each switch position.
2. If continunity between the terminals is not as specified, replace the switch.

1987 and Later

1. Connect a positive lead from the positive terminal of the battery to terminal two. Connect a negative lead from the negative terminal of the battery to terminal three.
2. Check to be sure that continuity exists between terminals two and six with the main switch turned on.
3. Check that there is no continuity between terminals two and six with the main switch off.
4. If the above results are not achieved, replace the switch.

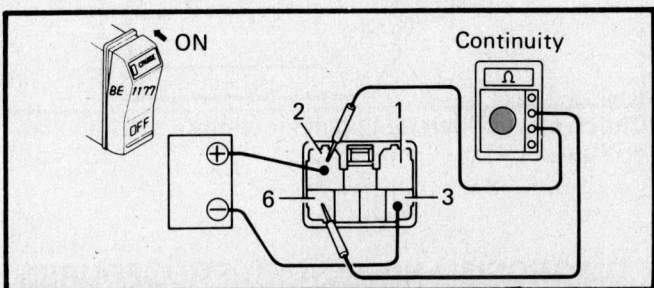

Main switch test point locations—1987 and later Supra

Main switch test point locations—1985–86 Supra

Main switch test point locations—1984 Supra

CLUTCH SWITCH TEST (1984 AND LATER)

1. Check to be sure that there is continuity between terminals two and three with the clutch pedal depressed.
2. Check to be sure that there is continuity between terminals two and three with the clutch pedal returned.
3. If continuity is not as indicated, replace the clutch switch.

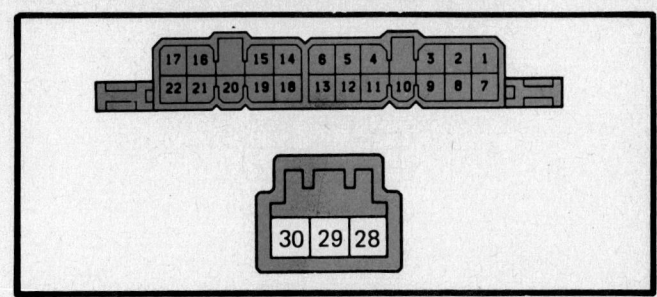

Control switch test point locations—1984–86 Supra

Switch position	Resistance value (Ω)
RESUME/ACCEL	68
SET/COAST	198
CANCEL	418

Control switch specifications—1987 and later Supra

Switch position \ Terminal	1	2	3	4	5
OFF			○———	———○	
ON	○———	———○	○———	———○	

Main switch specifications—1984 Supra

Switch position \ Terminal	1	2	3	4	5
OFF			○———	———○	
ON	○———	———○	○———	———○	

Main switch specifications—1985–86 Supra

STOP LIGHT SWITCH TEST (1984 AND LATER)

1. Using an ohmmeter check for continuity of the terminals for each switch position.
2. If continunity between the terminals is not as specified, replace the switch.

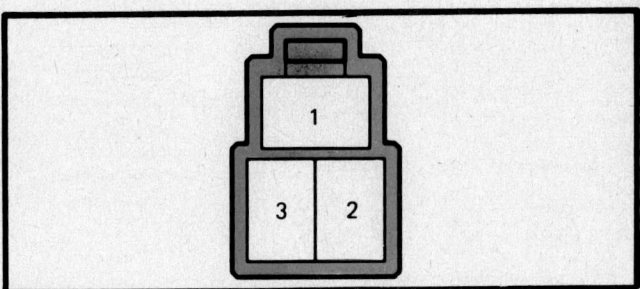

Clutch start switch test point locations—1984–86 Supra

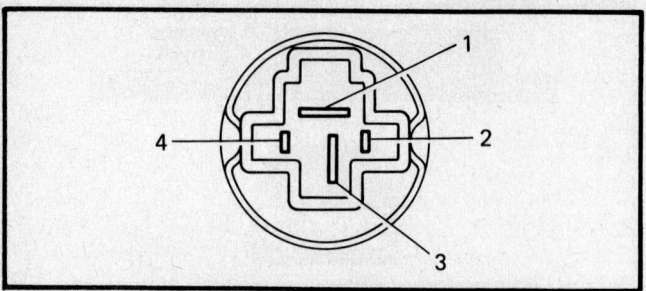

Stoplight switch locations—1987 and later Supra

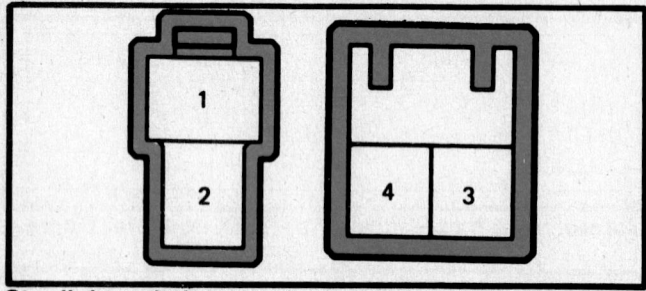

Stoplight switch test point locations—1984–86 Supra

Terminal Brake pedal position	1	2	3	4
Brake pedal depressed	O—	—O		
Brake pedal returned			O—	—O

Stoplight switch specifications—1984–86 Supra

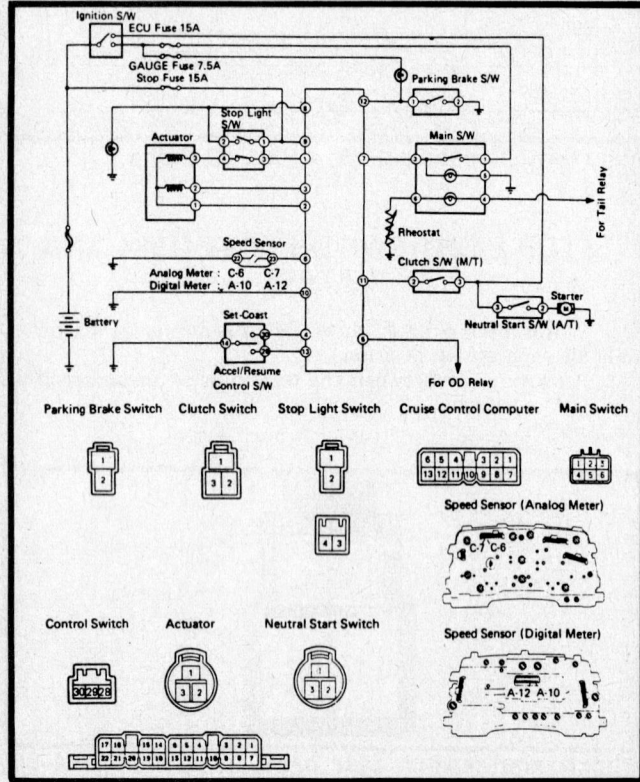

Cruise control electrical schematic—1984–86 Supra

Terminal Brake pedal position	1	3	2	4
Brake pedal depressed	O—	—O		
Brake pedal returned			O—	—O

Stoplight switch specifications—1987 and later Supra

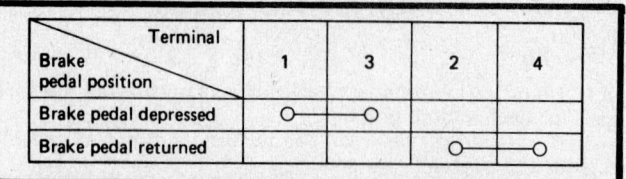

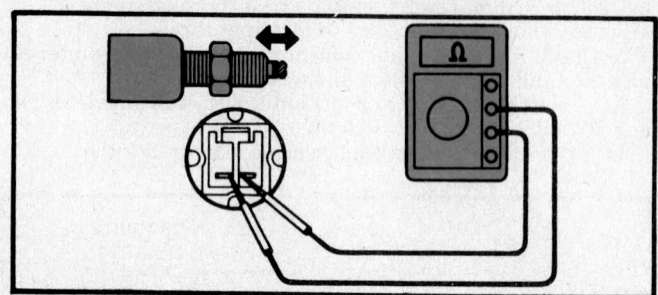

Clutch start switch test point locations—1987 and later Supra

DIAGNOSIS AND TESTING PROCEDURES

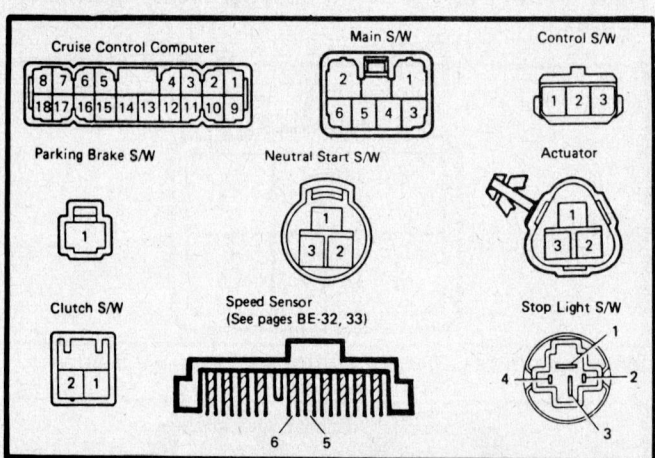

Cruise control electrical connectors—1987 and later Supra

CRUISE CONTROL SYSTEM DIAGNOSIS—1987 AND LATER

Output of Diagnosis Codes

TYPE A CODE

1. Turn the ignition switch to the on position.
2. Turn the set/coast switch on. Turn the main switch on.
3. Read the diagnosis code on the main switch indicator.
4. Checking the number three code must be done with the vehicle safely supported.
5. Results are as follows.

TYPE B CODE

1. Do not turn the ignition switch off. Do not turn the main switch off.

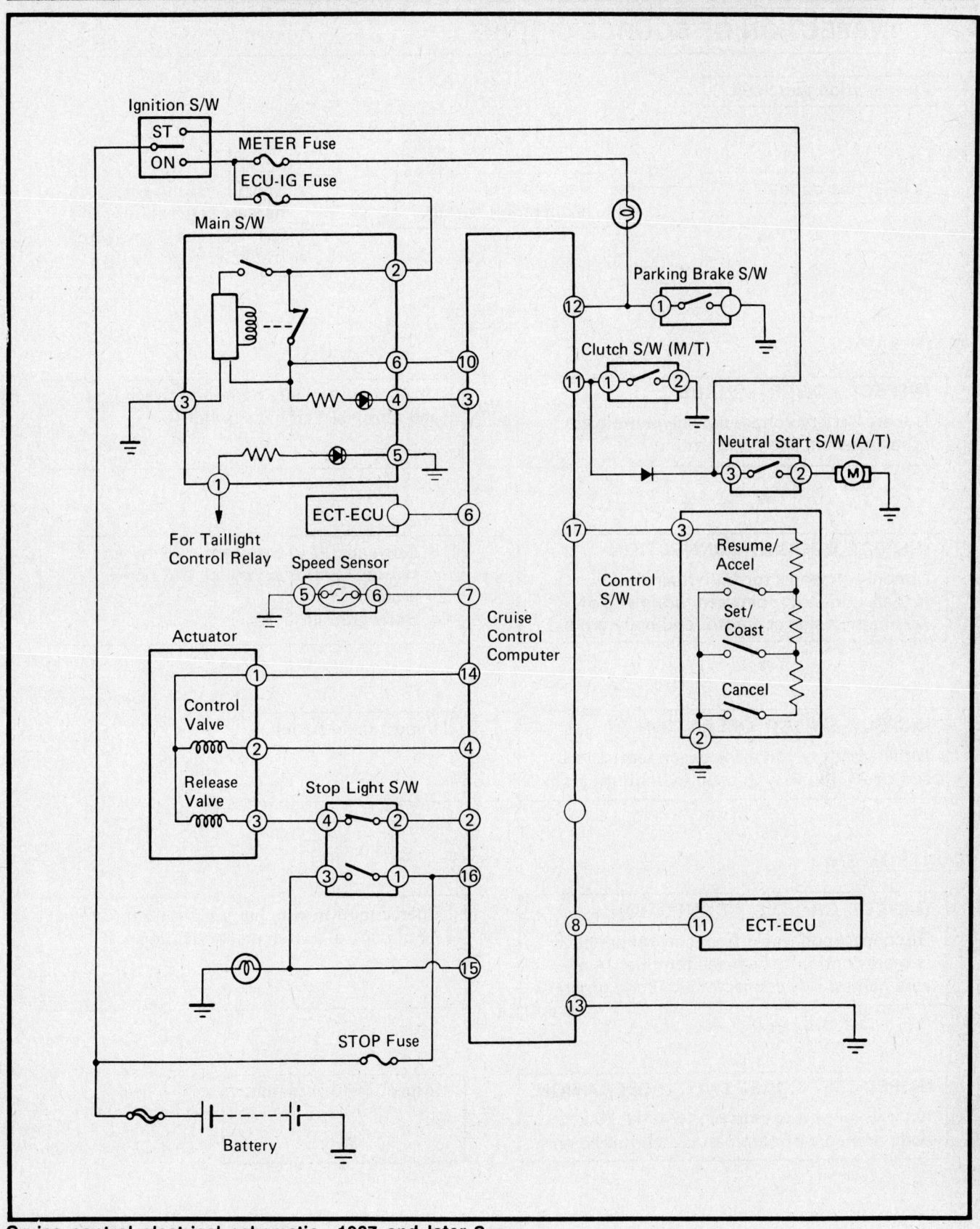

Cruise control electrical schematic – 1987 and later Supra

A | INSPECTION OF SOURCE CIRCUIT

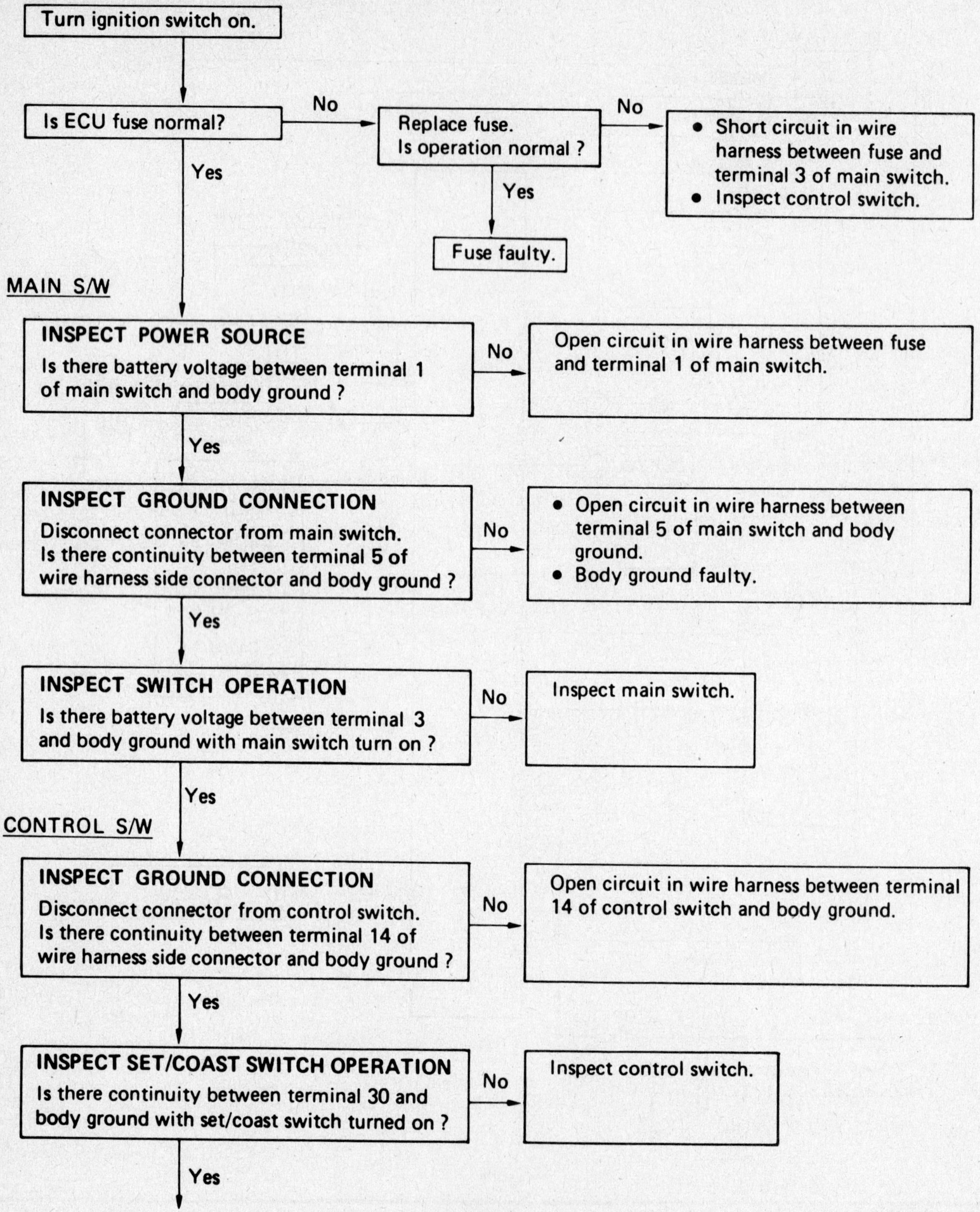

Turn ignition switch on.

Is ECU fuse normal? — **No** → Replace fuse. Is operation normal? — **No** → • Short circuit in wire harness between fuse and terminal 3 of main switch.
• Inspect control switch.

Is ECU fuse normal? — **Yes** ↓

Replace fuse. Is operation normal? — **Yes** → Fuse faulty.

MAIN S/W

INSPECT POWER SOURCE
Is there battery voltage between terminal 1 of main switch and body ground ? — **No** → Open circuit in wire harness between fuse and terminal 1 of main switch.

Yes ↓

INSPECT GROUND CONNECTION
Disconnect connector from main switch. Is there continuity between terminal 5 of wire harness side connector and body ground ? — **No** → • Open circuit in wire harness between terminal 5 of main switch and body ground.
• Body ground faulty.

Yes ↓

INSPECT SWITCH OPERATION
Is there battery voltage between terminal 3 and body ground with main switch turn on ? — **No** → Inspect main switch.

Yes ↓

CONTROL S/W

INSPECT GROUND CONNECTION
Disconnect connector from control switch. Is there continuity between terminal 14 of wire harness side connector and body ground ? — **No** → Open circuit in wire harness between terminal 14 of control switch and body ground.

Yes ↓

INSPECT SET/COAST SWITCH OPERATION
Is there continuity between terminal 30 and body ground with set/coast switch turned on ? — **No** → Inspect control switch.

Yes ↓

Cruise control trouble diagnosis chart—1984–86 Supra

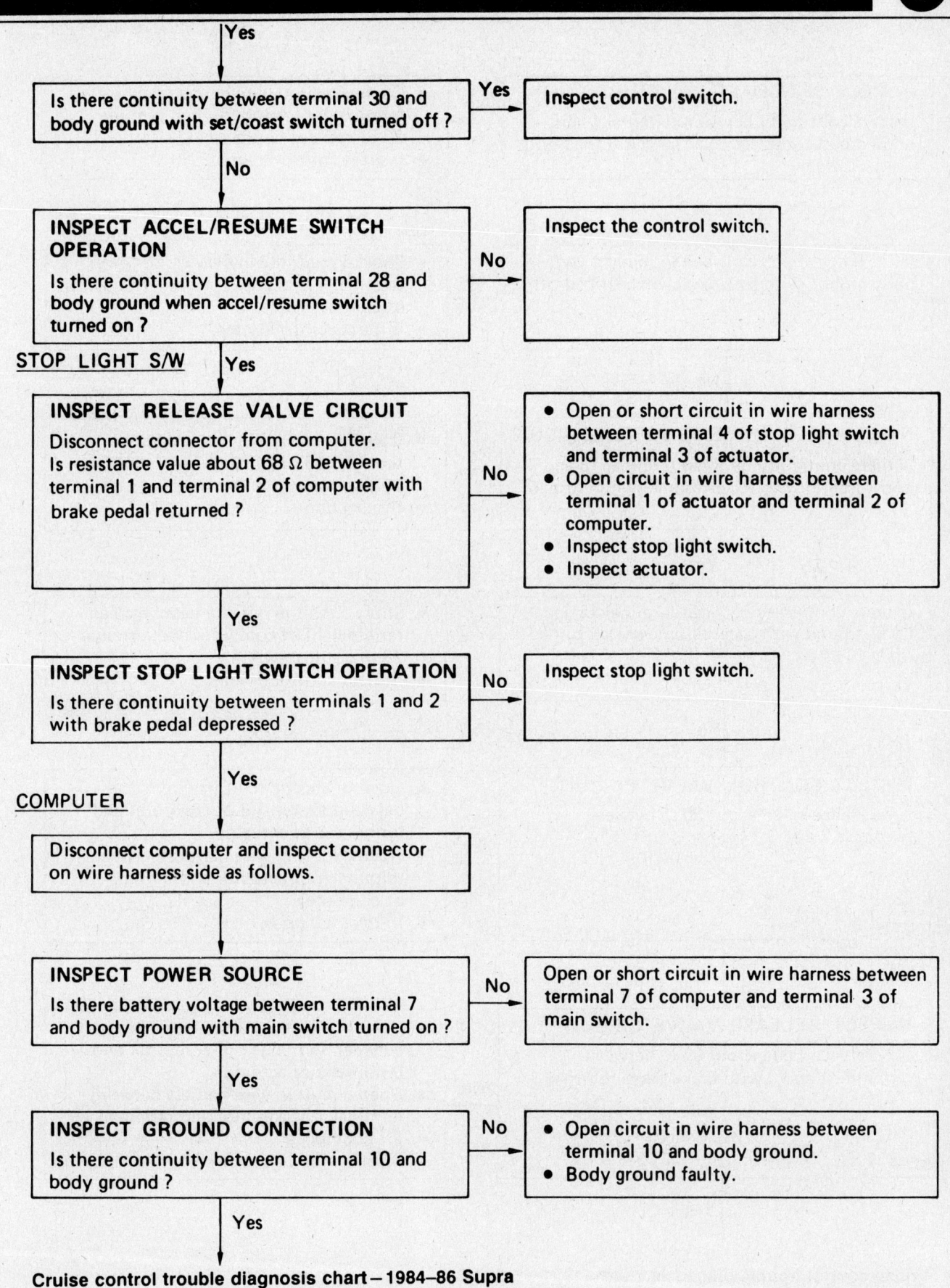

Cruise control trouble diagnosis chart – 1984–86 Supra

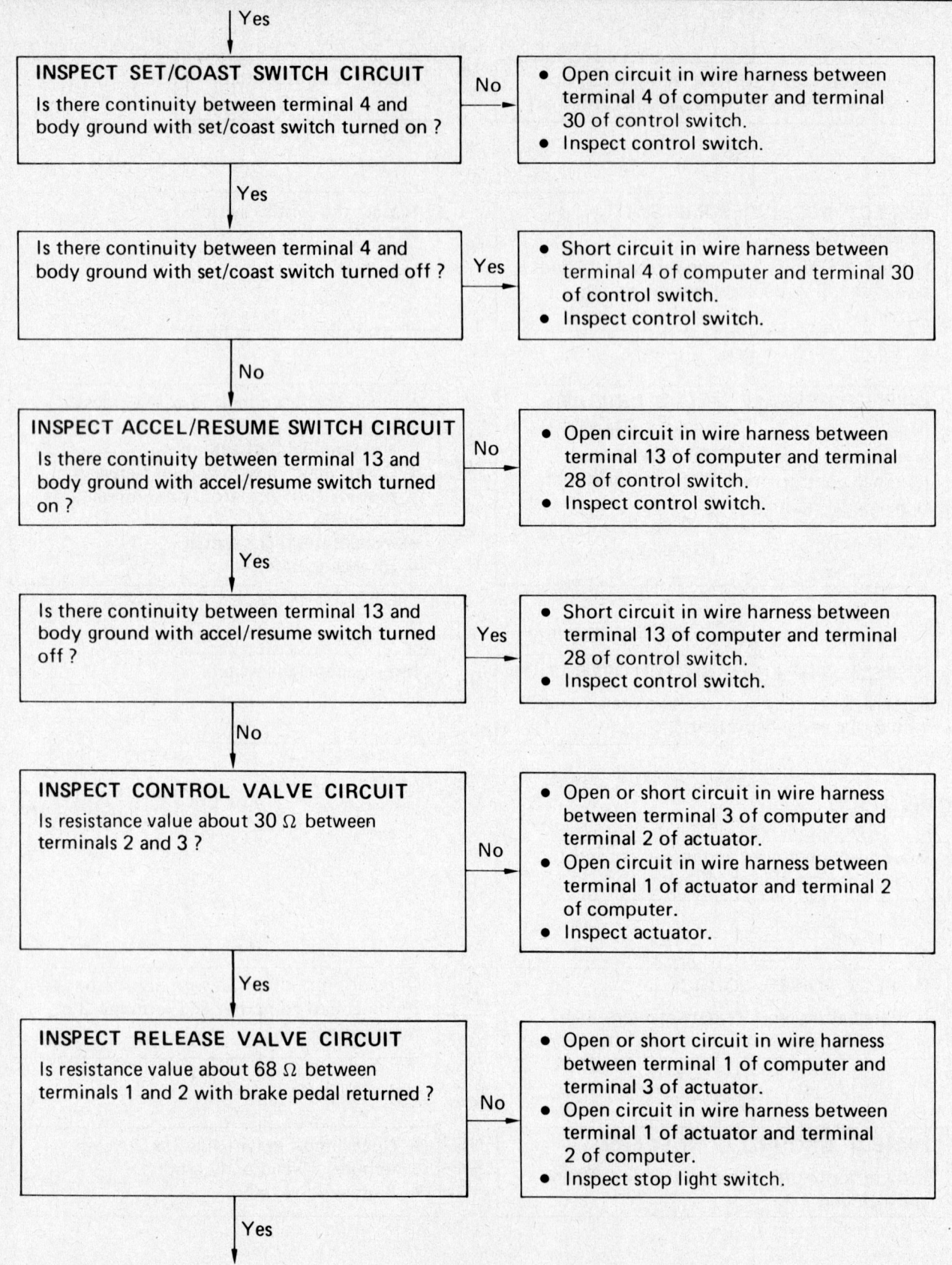

Yes

INSPECT SET/COAST SWITCH CIRCUIT
Is there continuity between terminal 4 and body ground with set/coast switch turned on ?

No →
- Open circuit in wire harness between terminal 4 of computer and terminal 30 of control switch.
- Inspect control switch.

Yes ↓

Is there continuity between terminal 4 and body ground with set/coast switch turned off ?

Yes →
- Short circuit in wire harness between terminal 4 of computer and terminal 30 of control switch.
- Inspect control switch.

No ↓

INSPECT ACCEL/RESUME SWITCH CIRCUIT
Is there continuity between terminal 13 and body ground with accel/resume switch turned on ?

No →
- Open circuit in wire harness between terminal 13 of computer and terminal 28 of control switch.
- Inspect control switch.

Yes ↓

Is there continuity between terminal 13 and body ground with accel/resume switch turned off ?

Yes →
- Short circuit in wire harness between terminal 13 of computer and terminal 28 of control switch.
- Inspect control switch.

No ↓

INSPECT CONTROL VALVE CIRCUIT
Is resistance value about 30 Ω between terminals 2 and 3 ?

No →
- Open or short circuit in wire harness between terminal 3 of computer and terminal 2 of actuator.
- Open circuit in wire harness between terminal 1 of actuator and terminal 2 of computer.
- Inspect actuator.

Yes ↓

INSPECT RELEASE VALVE CIRCUIT
Is resistance value about 68 Ω between terminals 1 and 2 with brake pedal returned ?

No →
- Open or short circuit in wire harness between terminal 1 of computer and terminal 3 of actuator.
- Open circuit in wire harness between terminal 1 of actuator and terminal 2 of computer.
- Inspect stop light switch.

Yes ↓

Cruise control trouble diagnosis chart—1984–86 Supra

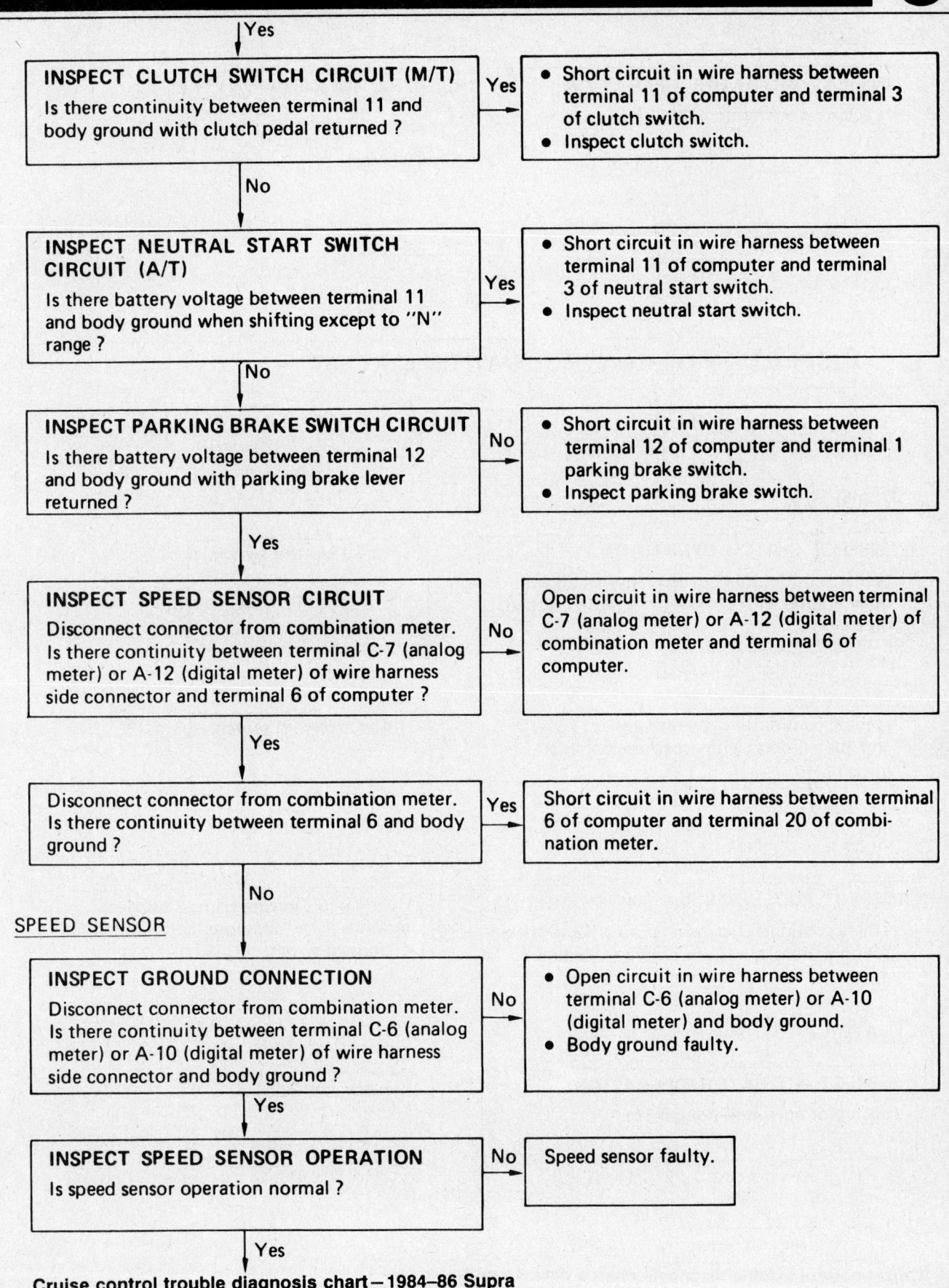

Yes ↓

| INSPECT CLUTCH SWITCH CIRCUIT (M/T)
Is there continuity between terminal 11 and body ground with clutch pedal returned ? | Yes → | • Short circuit in wire harness between terminal 11 of computer and terminal 3 of clutch switch.
• Inspect clutch switch. |

No ↓

| INSPECT NEUTRAL START SWITCH CIRCUIT (A/T)
Is there battery voltage between terminal 11 and body ground when shifting except to "N" range ? | Yes → | • Short circuit in wire harness between terminal 11 of computer and terminal 3 of neutral start switch.
• Inspect neutral start switch. |

No ↓

| INSPECT PARKING BRAKE SWITCH CIRCUIT
Is there battery voltage between terminal 12 and body ground with parking brake lever returned ? | No → | • Short circuit in wire harness between terminal 12 of computer and terminal 1 parking brake switch.
• Inspect parking brake switch. |

Yes ↓

| INSPECT SPEED SENSOR CIRCUIT
Disconnect connector from combination meter. Is there continuity between terminal C-7 (analog meter) or A-12 (digital meter) of wire harness side connector and terminal 6 of computer ? | No → | Open circuit in wire harness between terminal C-7 (analog meter) or A-12 (digital meter) of combination meter and terminal 6 of computer. |

Yes ↓

| Disconnect connector from combination meter. Is there continuity between terminal 6 and body ground ? | Yes → | Short circuit in wire harness between terminal 6 of computer and terminal 20 of combination meter. |

No ↓

SPEED SENSOR

| INSPECT GROUND CONNECTION
Disconnect connector from combination meter. Is there continuity between terminal C-6 (analog meter) or A-10 (digital meter) of wire harness side connector and body ground ? | No → | • Open circuit in wire harness between terminal C-6 (analog meter) or A-10 (digital meter) and body ground.
• Body ground faulty. |

Yes ↓

| INSPECT SPEED SENSOR OPERATION
Is speed sensor operation normal ? | No → | Speed sensor faulty. |

Yes ↓

Cruise control trouble diagnosis chart — 1984–86 Supra

<u>ACTUATOR</u>

| Yes

INSPECT ACTUATOR OPERATION
Is actuator operation normal ? → No → Replace actuator.

| Yes

Replace computer.

| **B** | **INSPECTION OF CONTROL SWITCH CIRCUIT** |

Turn ignition switch off.

<u>CONTROL S/W</u>

INSPECT SWITCH OPERATION
Is there continuity between terminal 28 and body ground with accel/resume switch turned on ? → No → Inspect control switch.

| Yes

Is there continuity between terminal 28 and body ground with accel/resume switch turned off ? → Yes → Inspect control switch.

<u>COMPUTER</u> | No

INSPECT ACCEL/RESUME SWITCH CIRCUIT
Is there continuity between terminal 13 and body ground with accel/resume switch turned on ? → No → Open circuit in wire harness between terminal 13 of computer and terminal 28 of control switch.

<u>ACTUATOR</u> | Yes

INSPECT ACTUATOR OPERATION
Is actuator operation normal ? → No → Replace actuator.

| Yes

Replace computer.

Cruise control trouble diagnosis chart—1984–86 Supra

C | INSPECTION OF ACTUATOR CIRCUIT

Turn ignition switch off.

ACTUATOR

INSPECT CABLE FREEPLAY

Is control cable freeplay less than 10 mm (0.39 in.) ?

→ No → Adjust control cable freeplay.

↓ Yes

INSPECT ACUTATOR OPERATION

Disconnect connector from actuator.
Inspect actuator operation. (See page BE-84)
Is actuator operation normal ?

→ No → Replace actuator.

↓ Yes

COMPUTER

INSPECT ACTUATOR CIRCUIT

Is resistance value between computer terminals correct ?
  Between terminals 1 and 2   about 68 Ω
  Between terminals 2 and 3   about 30 Ω

→ No → Open or short circuit in wire harness between actuator and computer.

↓ Yes

Replace computer.

D | INSPECTION OF STOP LIGHT SWITCH CIRCUIT

Turn ignition switch on.

Is stop fuse normal ?

→ No →
- Short circuit in wire harness between terminal 8 of computer and fuse.
- Short circuit in wire harness between terminal 9 of computer and fuse.

↓ Yes

Cruise control trouble diagnosis chart – 1984–86 Supra

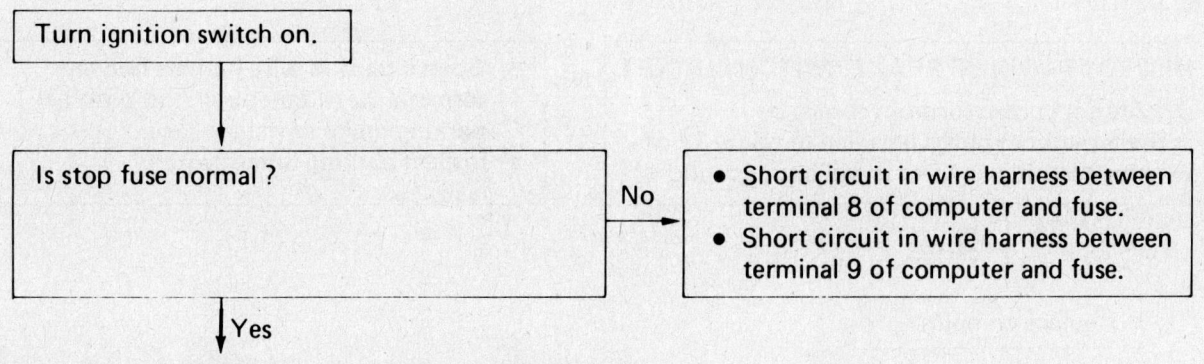

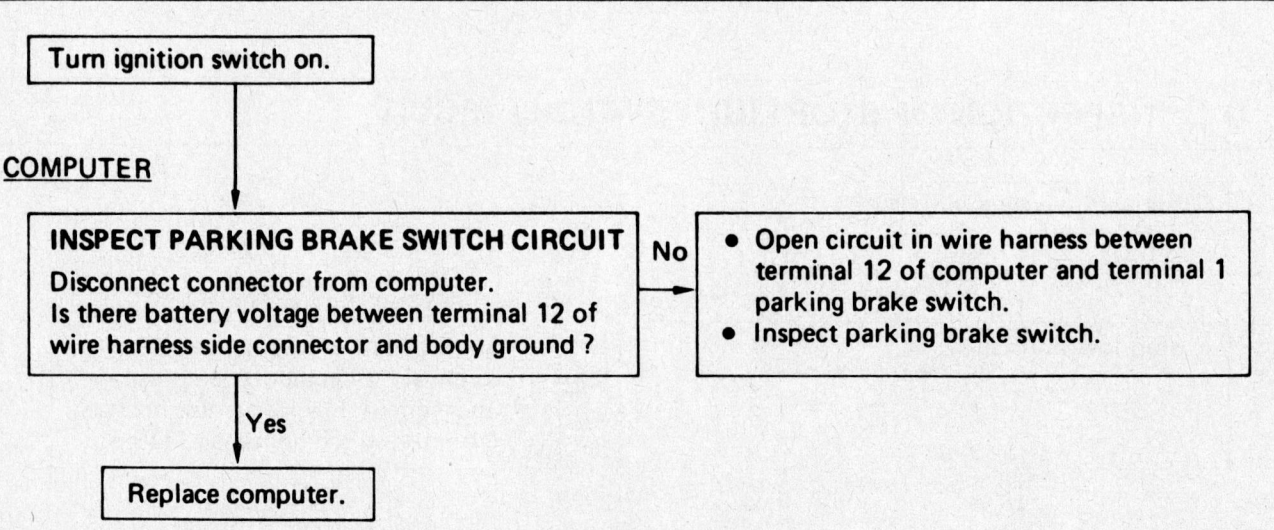

COMPUTER

Disconnect computer and inspect connector on wire harness side as follows.

INSPECT RELEASE VALVE CIRCUIT
Is there continuity between terminal 1 and 2 with brake pedal depressed ?

Yes → Inspect stop light switch.

No ↓

INSPECT STOP FUSE CIRCUIT
Is there battery voltage between terminal 9 and body ground ?

No → Open circuit in wire harness between terminal 9 of computer and STOP fuse.

Yes ↓

INSPECT STOP LIGHT SWITCH CIRCUIT
Is there battery voltage between terminal 8 and body ground with brake pedal depressed ?

No → Open or short circuit in wire harness between terminal 8 of computer and terminal 2 of stop light switch.

Yes ↓

Replace computer.

E | INSPECTION OF PARKING BRAKE SWITCH

Turn ignition switch on.

COMPUTER

INSPECT PARKING BRAKE SWITCH CIRCUIT
Disconnect connector from computer.
Is there battery voltage between terminal 12 of wire harness side connector and body ground ?

No →
- Open circuit in wire harness between terminal 12 of computer and terminal 1 parking brake switch.
- Inspect parking brake switch.

Yes ↓

Replace computer.

Cruise control trouble diagnosis chart – 1984–86 Supra

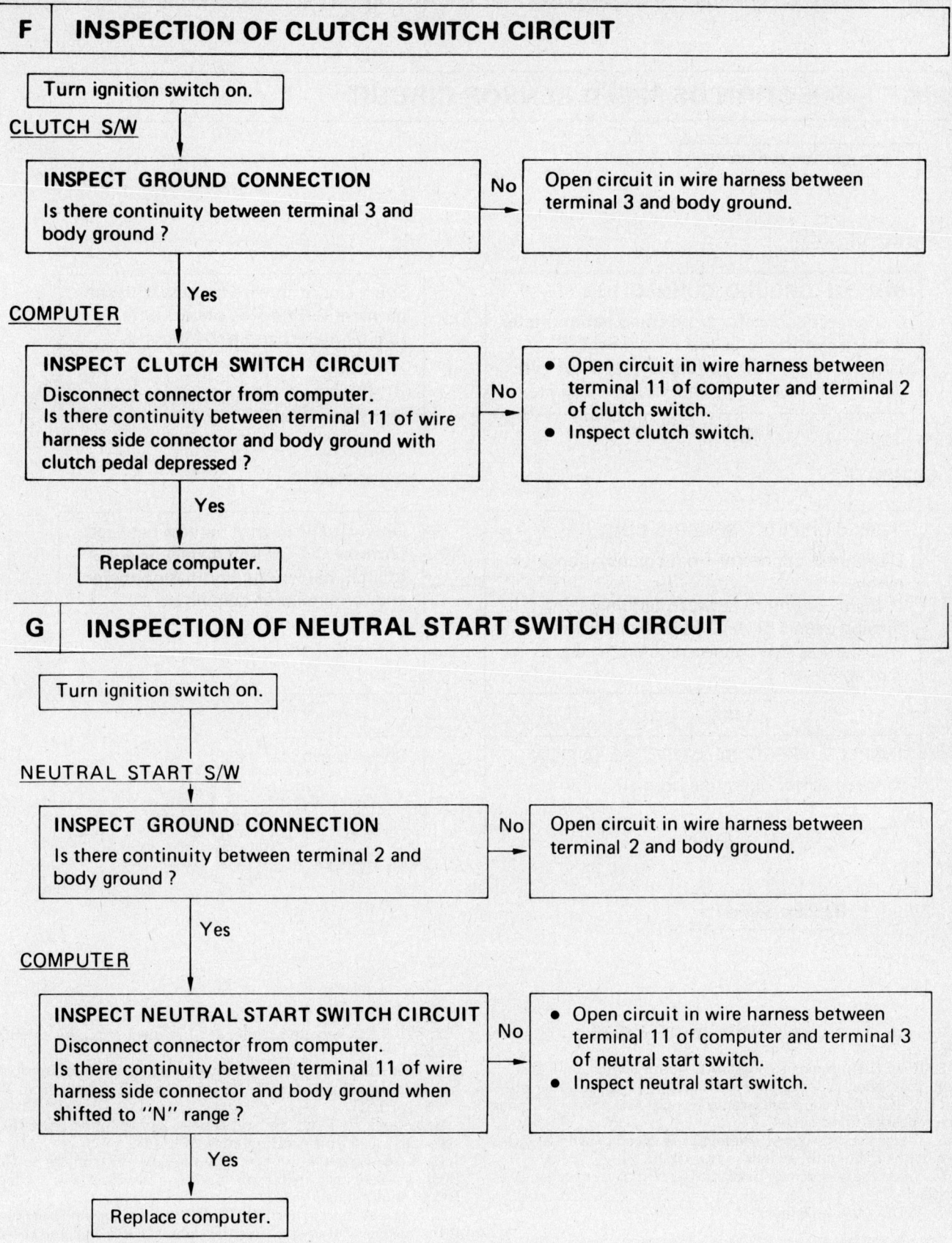

| F | INSPECTION OF CLUTCH SWITCH CIRCUIT |

Turn ignition switch on.

CLUTCH S/W

INSPECT GROUND CONNECTION
Is there continuity between terminal 3 and body ground ?

No → Open circuit in wire harness between terminal 3 and body ground.

Yes

COMPUTER

INSPECT CLUTCH SWITCH CIRCUIT
Disconnect connector from computer.
Is there continuity between terminal 11 of wire harness side connector and body ground with clutch pedal depressed ?

No →
- Open circuit in wire harness between terminal 11 of computer and terminal 2 of clutch switch.
- Inspect clutch switch.

Yes

Replace computer.

| G | INSPECTION OF NEUTRAL START SWITCH CIRCUIT |

Turn ignition switch on.

NEUTRAL START S/W

INSPECT GROUND CONNECTION
Is there continuity between terminal 2 and body ground ?

No → Open circuit in wire harness between terminal 2 and body ground.

Yes

COMPUTER

INSPECT NEUTRAL START SWITCH CIRCUIT
Disconnect connector from computer.
Is there continuity between terminal 11 of wire harness side connector and body ground when shifted to "N" range ?

No →
- Open circuit in wire harness between terminal 11 of computer and terminal 3 of neutral start switch.
- Inspect neutral start switch.

Yes

Replace computer.

Cruise control trouble diagnosis chart – 1984–86 Supra

H	INSPECTION OF SPEED SENSOR CIRCUIT

```
Turn ignition switch on.
```

SPEED SENSOR

INSPECT GROUND CONNECTION
Disconnect connector from combination meter.
Is there continuity between terminal C-6 (analog meter) or A-10 (digital meter) of wire harness side connector and body ground ?

→ Yes → Short circuit in wire harness between terminal C-6 (analog meter) or A-10 (digital meter) and body ground.

↓ No

COMPUTER

INSPECT SPEED SENSOR CIRCUIT
Disconnect connector from combination meter.
Is there continuity between terminal C-7 (analog meter) or A-12 (digital meter) of wire harness side connector and terminal 6 of computer ?

→ No → Open circuit in wire harness between terminal C-7 (analog meter) or A-12 (digital meter) of combination meter and terminal 6 of computer.

↓ Yes

INSPECT SPEED SENSOR OPERATION
Is speed sensor operation normal?

→ No → Speed sensor faulty.

↓ Yes

```
Replace computer.
```

2. Turn the set/coast switch on three times within two seconds.

3. Read the diagnosis code on the main switch indicator.

4. Indication codes appear with priority from number eleven. Normal codes continue twenty seconds and abnormal codes are repeated three times.

5. Indication is stopped when vehicle speed is over 10 miles per hour or the main switch is turned off.

6. This type of code can be displayed with the super monitor system.

7. Results are as follows.

TYPE B CODE WITH SUPER MONITOR

1. Test drive the vehicle.

2. With the vehicle at idle, set the display to the calendar mode.

3. Simultaneously push and hold in the select and input (M) key for about three seconds. The display will change from ERROR to DIAG.

4. After a short pause hold the set key in for at least three seconds. The display will change to ECT.

5. Push the set key once. The display will change to C/C. Push the set/coast switch on three times within two seconds. Read the diagnosis code.

6. If the system is normal C/C OK will appear on the screen. If the harness between the cruise control computer and the super monitor are open, C/C OO will appear on the screen.

8. Correct as required.

Problem	Inspection Item	No.
Cruise control does not operate.	Inspection of power source circuit	A
Vehicle speed does not reduce when coast switch turned on.	Inspection of control switch and circuit.	B
Vehicle does not accelerate when accel switch turned on.		
Vehicle speed does not return to memorized speed when resume switch turned on.		
Set speed deviates on high side.	Inspection of actuator and circuit	C
Set speed deviates on low side.		
Vehicle speed does not fluctuate when set switch turned on.	Inspection of actuator and circuit Inspection of speed sensor and circuit	C H
Setting speed does not cancel when brake pedal depressed.	Inspection of stop light switch and circuit	D
Setting speed does not cancel when parking brake pulled.	Inspection of parking brake switch and circuit	E
Setting speed does not cancel when clutch pedal depressed (M/T only).	Inspection of clutch switch and circuit	F
Setting speed does not cancel when shifted to "N" range (A/T only).	Inspection of neutral start switch and circuit	G
Speed can be set below 20 km/h (12 mph).	Inspection of speed sensor and circuit	H
Cruise control will not disengage even below 20 km/h (12 mph).		

Cruise control troubleshooting data sheet—1984–86 Supra

No.	Conditions	Indication Code	Diagnosis
1	Set/coast switch on	ON / OFF 0.25S — 1.0S — 0.25S	Set/coast switch circuit is normal.
2	Accel/resume switch on	ON / OFF	Accel/resume switch circuit is normal.
3	Each cancel switch on (Stop light switch, Parking brake switch, Clutch switch, Neutral start switch, Cancel switch)	ON / OFF	Each cancel switch circuit is normal.
4	Drive 40 km/h (25 mph) or over	ON / OFF	Speed sensor circuit is normal.
5	Drive 40 km/h (25 mph) or below	ON / OFF	Speed sensor circuit is normal.

Type "A" diagnostic information—1987 and later Supra

Problem	Inspection Item		No.
Cruise control does not operate.	(a) Inspect type A codes.	No. 1 NO	C
		No. 2 NO	C
		No. 3 NO	C to H
		No. 4 NO	I
		No. 5 NO	I
	(b) Inspect type B codes.	11	D
		21	I
		23	D
		31	C
	(c) All codes are normal.		Replace computer.
Vehicle speed does not reduce when coast switch turned on.	Inspection of control switch circuit		C
Vehicle speed does not accelerate when accel switch turned on.			
Vehicle speed does not return to memorized speed when resume switch turned on.			
Setting speed deviates on high side.	Inspection of actuator circuit		D
Setting speed deviates on low side.			
Vehicle speed fluctuates when set switch turned on.	Inspection of actuator circuit		D
	Inspection of speed sensor circuit		I
Setting speed does not cancel when brake pedal depressed.	Inspection of stop light switch circuit		E
Setting speed does not cancel when parking brake pulled.	Inspection of parking brake switch circuit		F
Setting speed does not cancel when clutch pedal depressed (M/T only).	Inspection of clutch switch circuit		G
Setting speed does not cancel when shifted to "N" range (A/T only).	Inspection of neutral start switch circuit		H
Speed can be set below about 40 km/h (25 mph).	Inspection of speed sensor circuit		I
Cruise control will not disengage even below about 40 km/h (25 mph).			
A short period after the O/D cut, (Approx. within 14 seconds) the O/D will resume.	Inspection of ECT solenoid circuit		J

Cruise control troubleshooting data sheet — 1987 and later Supra

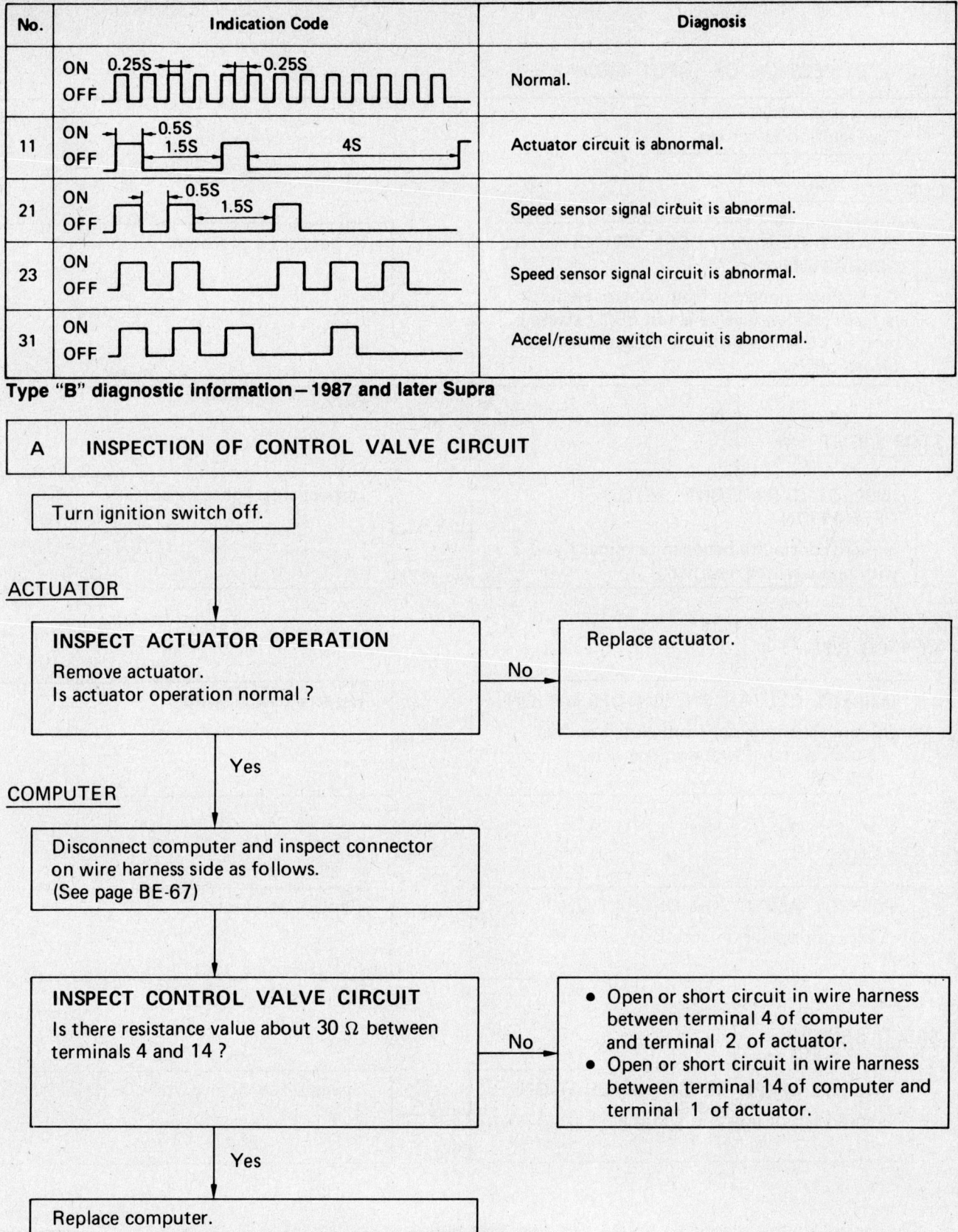

No.	Indication Code	Diagnosis
	ON 0.25S 0.25S OFF	Normal.
11	ON 0.5S 1.5S 4S OFF	Actuator circuit is abnormal.
21	ON 0.5S 1.5S OFF	Speed sensor signal circuit is abnormal.
23	ON OFF	Speed sensor signal circuit is abnormal.
31	ON OFF	Accel/resume switch circuit is abnormal.

Type "B" diagnostic information — 1987 and later Supra

A	INSPECTION OF CONTROL VALVE CIRCUIT

Turn ignition switch off.

ACTUATOR

INSPECT ACTUATOR OPERATION
Remove actuator.
Is actuator operation normal ?

→ No → Replace actuator.

↓ Yes

COMPUTER

Disconnect computer and inspect connector
on wire harness side as follows.
(See page BE-67)

INSPECT CONTROL VALVE CIRCUIT
Is there resistance value about 30 Ω between
terminals 4 and 14 ?

→ No →
- Open or short circuit in wire harness between terminal 4 of computer and terminal 2 of actuator.
- Open or short circuit in wire harness between terminal 14 of computer and terminal 1 of actuator.

↓ Yes

Replace computer.

Cruise control trouble diagnosis chart — 1987 and later Supra

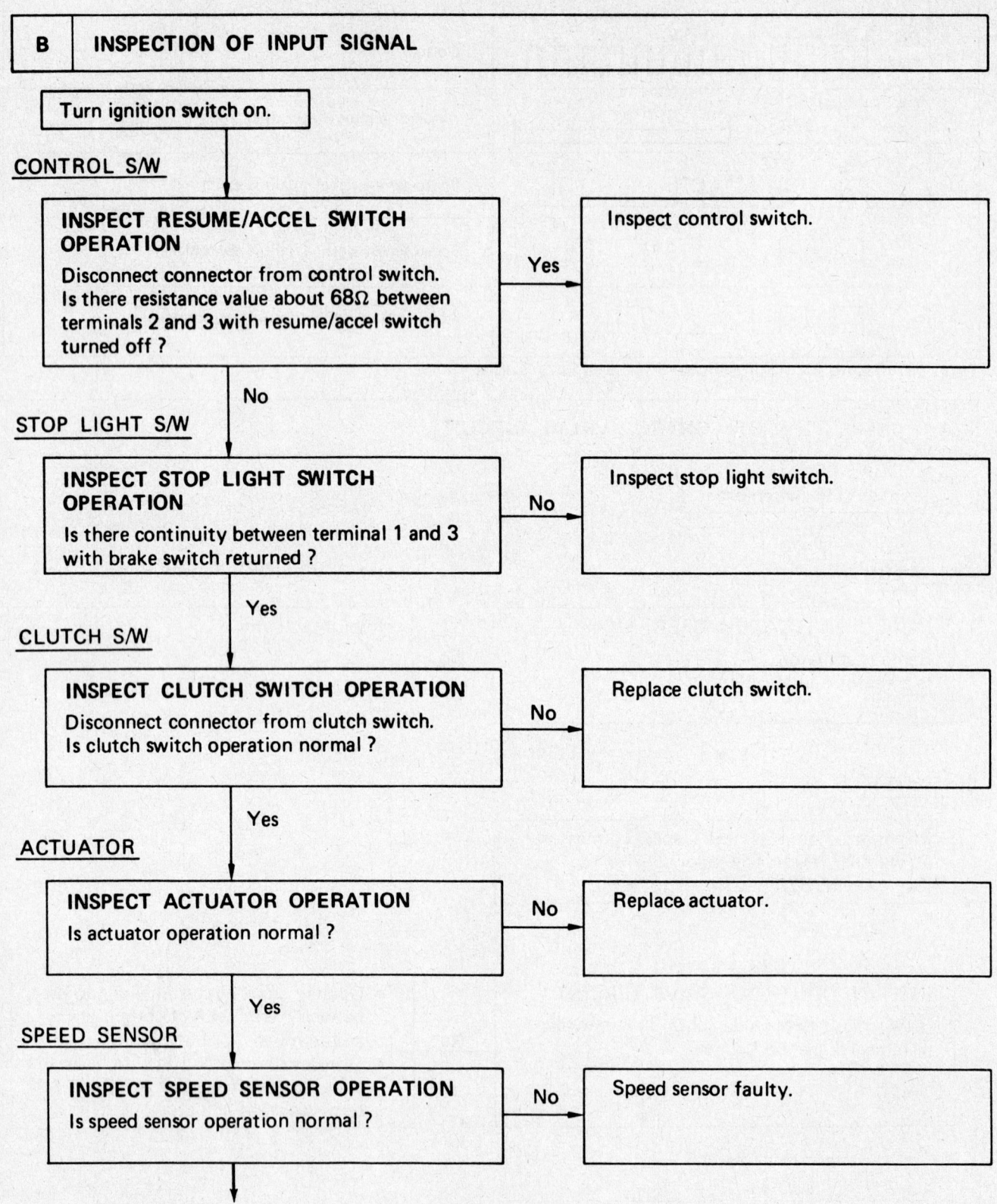

B	INSPECTION OF INPUT SIGNAL

Turn ignition switch on.

CONTROL S/W

INSPECT RESUME/ACCEL SWITCH OPERATION

Disconnect connector from control switch. Is there resistance value about 68Ω between terminals 2 and 3 with resume/accel switch turned off ?

→ Yes → Inspect control switch.

↓ No

STOP LIGHT S/W

INSPECT STOP LIGHT SWITCH OPERATION

Is there continuity between terminal 1 and 3 with brake switch returned ?

→ No → Inspect stop light switch.

↓ Yes

CLUTCH S/W

INSPECT CLUTCH SWITCH OPERATION

Disconnect connector from clutch switch. Is clutch switch operation normal ?

→ No → Replace clutch switch.

↓ Yes

ACTUATOR

INSPECT ACTUATOR OPERATION

Is actuator operation normal ?

→ No → Replace actuator.

↓ Yes

SPEED SENSOR

INSPECT SPEED SENSOR OPERATION

Is speed sensor operation normal ?

→ No → Speed sensor faulty.

Cruise control trouble diagnosis chart — 1987 and later Supra

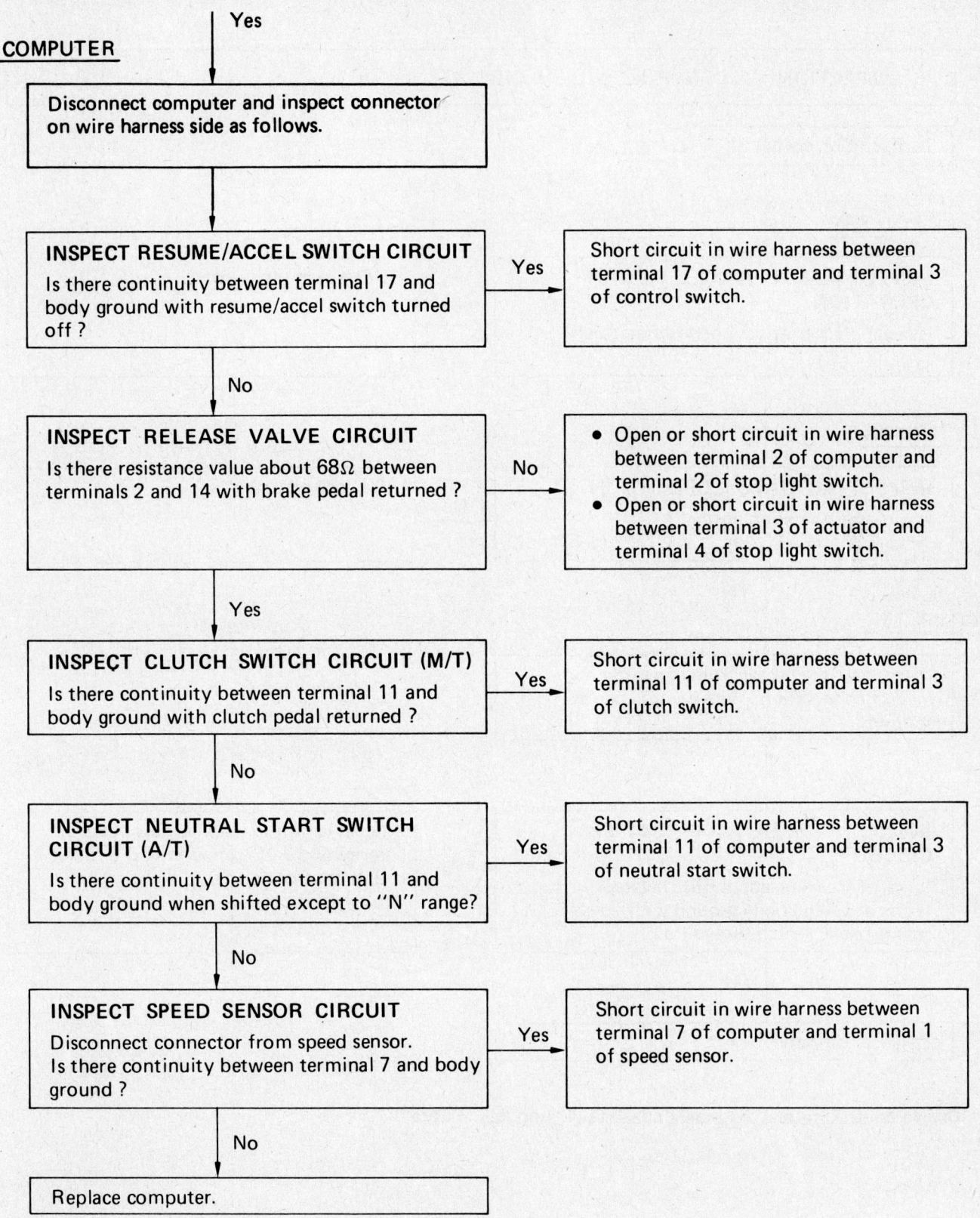

COMPUTER

Yes →

Disconnect computer and inspect connector on wire harness side as follows.

↓

INSPECT RESUME/ACCEL SWITCH CIRCUIT
Is there continuity between terminal 17 and body ground with resume/accel switch turned off ?

Yes → Short circuit in wire harness between terminal 17 of computer and terminal 3 of control switch.

↓ **No**

INSPECT RELEASE VALVE CIRCUIT
Is there resistance value about 68Ω between terminals 2 and 14 with brake pedal returned ?

No →
- Open or short circuit in wire harness between terminal 2 of computer and terminal 2 of stop light switch.
- Open or short circuit in wire harness between terminal 3 of actuator and terminal 4 of stop light switch.

↓ **Yes**

INSPECT CLUTCH SWITCH CIRCUIT (M/T)
Is there continuity between terminal 11 and body ground with clutch pedal returned ?

Yes → Short circuit in wire harness between terminal 11 of computer and terminal 3 of clutch switch.

↓ **No**

INSPECT NEUTRAL START SWITCH CIRCUIT (A/T)
Is there continuity between terminal 11 and body ground when shifted except to "N" range?

Yes → Short circuit in wire harness between terminal 11 of computer and terminal 3 of neutral start switch.

↓ **No**

INSPECT SPEED SENSOR CIRCUIT
Disconnect connector from speed sensor.
Is there continuity between terminal 7 and body ground ?

Yes → Short circuit in wire harness between terminal 7 of computer and terminal 1 of speed sensor.

↓ **No**

Replace computer.

Cruise control trouble diagnosis chart — 1987 and later Supra

C	INSPECTION OF CONTROL SWITCH CIRCUIT

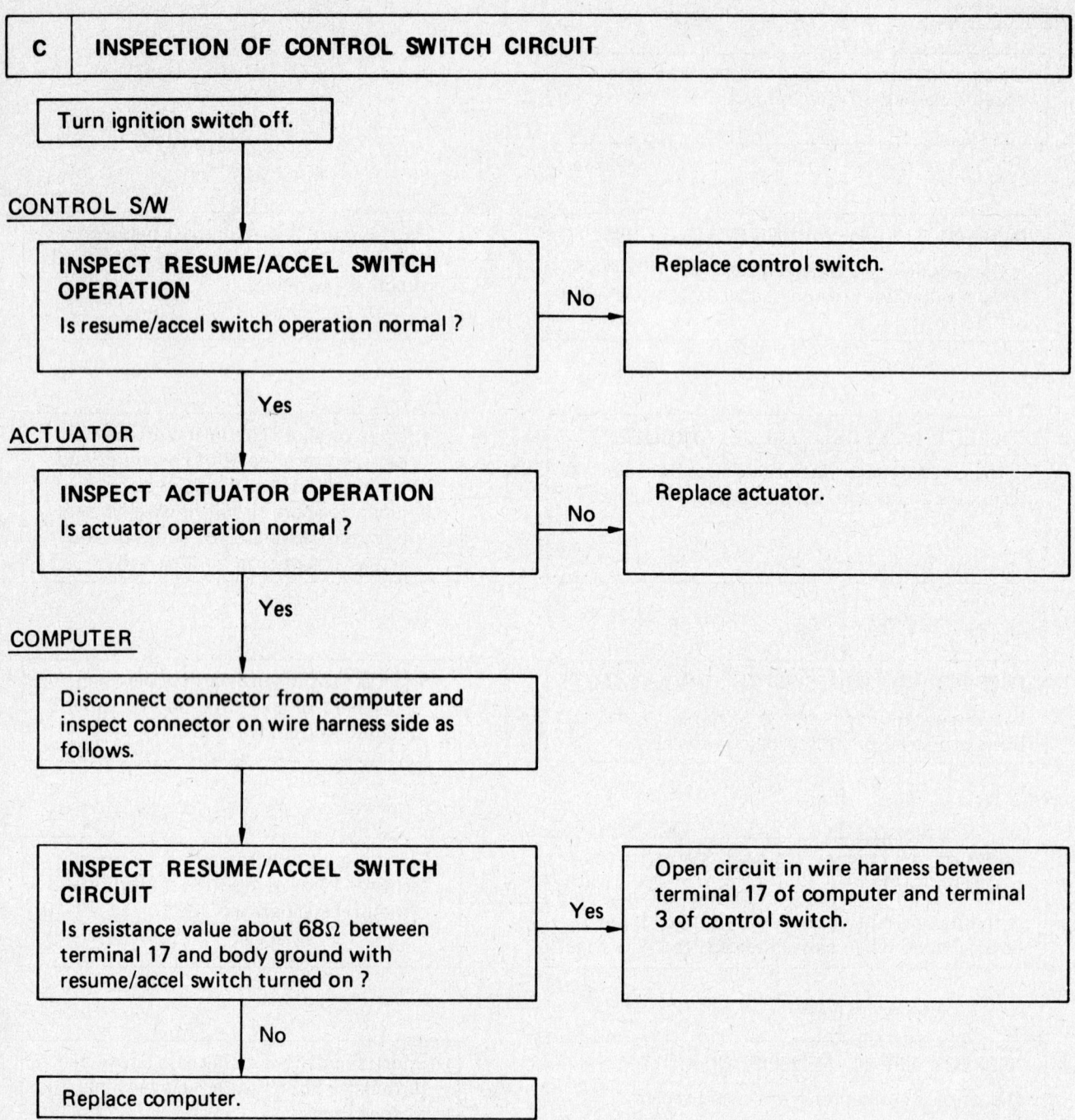

Cruise control trouble diagnosis chart—1987 and later Supra

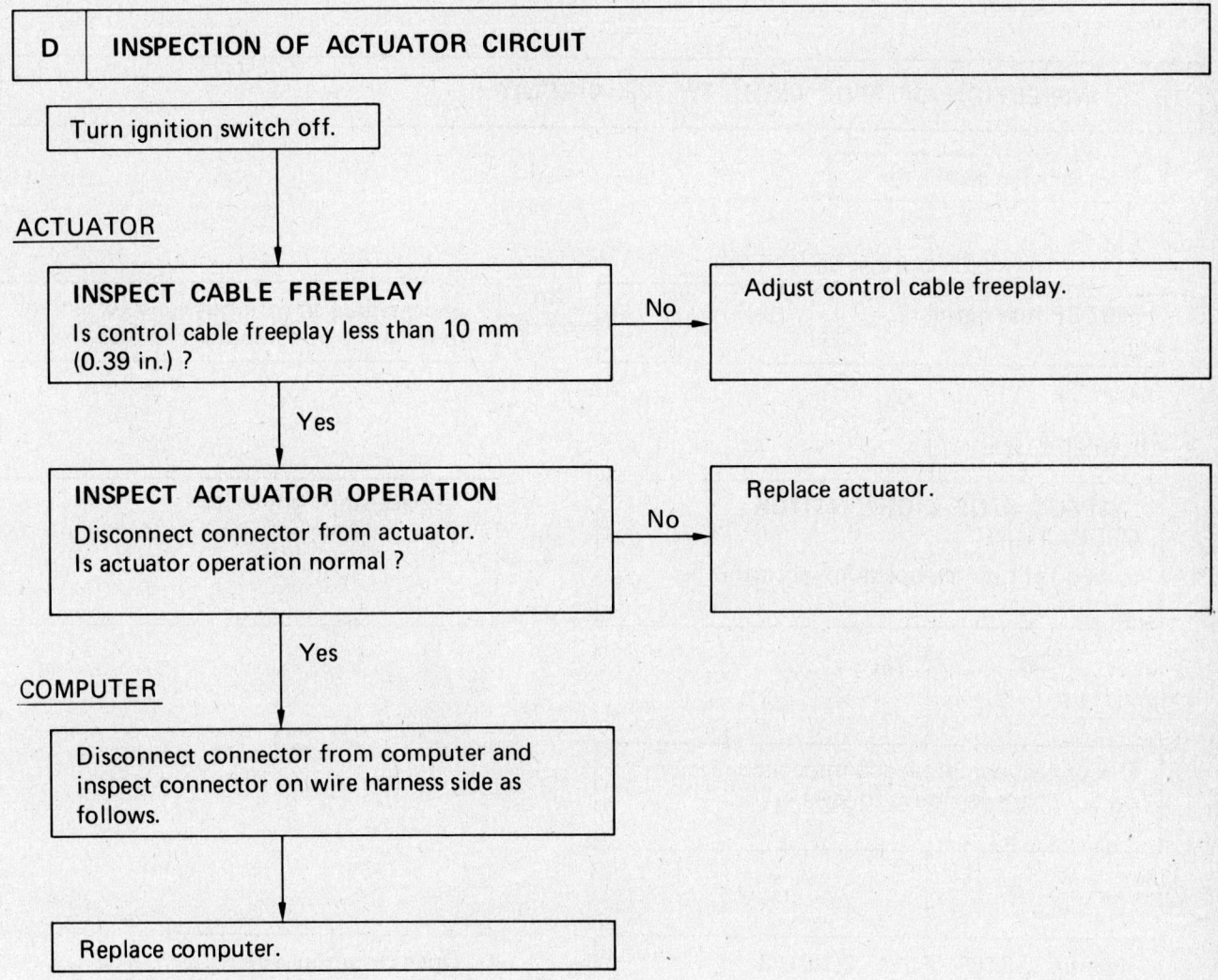

| D | INSPECTION OF ACTUATOR CIRCUIT |

Turn ignition switch off.

ACTUATOR

INSPECT CABLE FREEPLAY
Is control cable freeplay less than 10 mm (0.39 in.) ?

— No → Adjust control cable freeplay.

Yes

INSPECT ACTUATOR OPERATION
Disconnect connector from actuator.
Is actuator operation normal ?

— No → Replace actuator.

Yes

COMPUTER

Disconnect connector from computer and inspect connector on wire harness side as follows.

Replace computer.

Cruise control trouble diagnosis chart – 1987 and later Supra

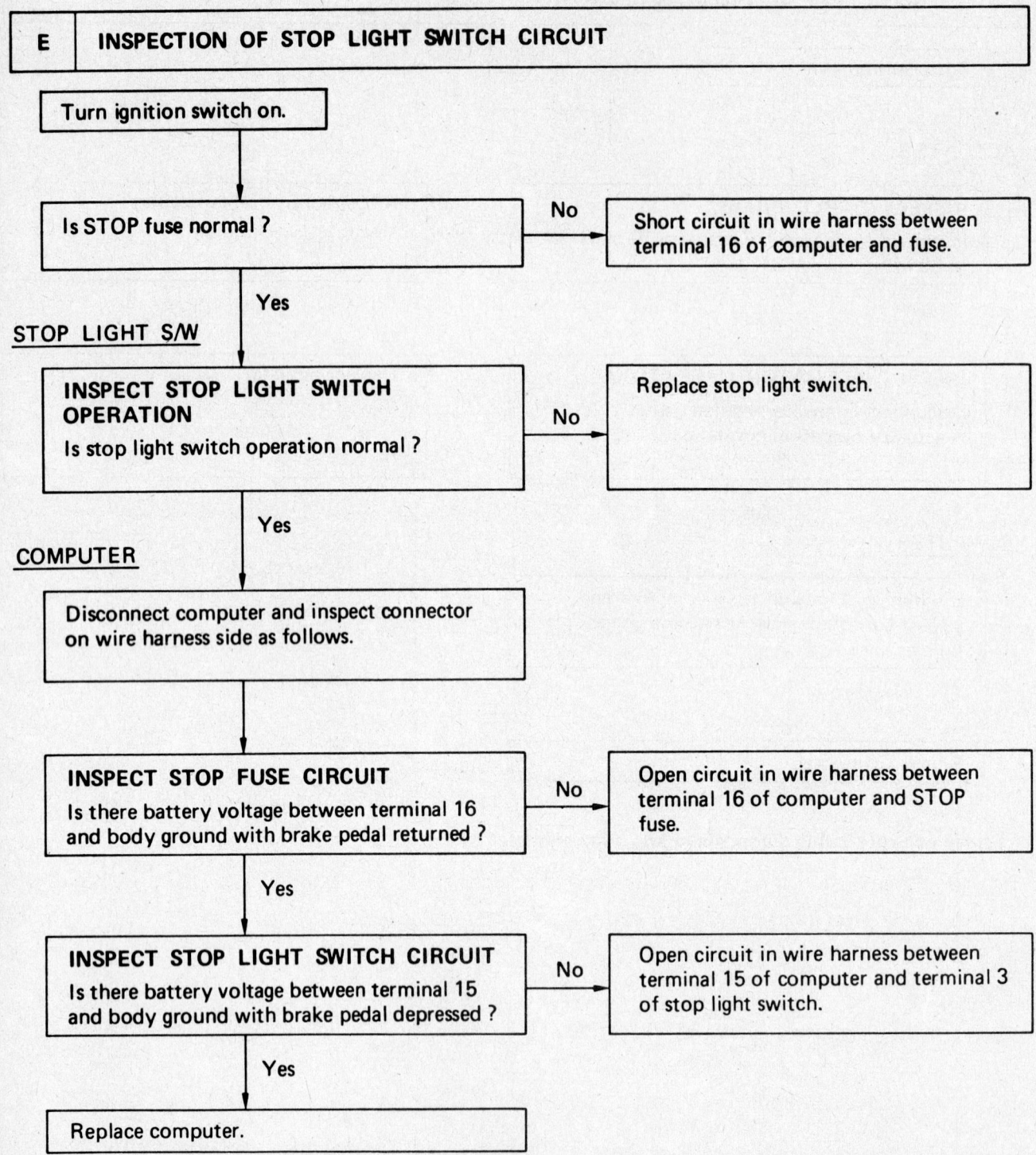

| E | INSPECTION OF STOP LIGHT SWITCH CIRCUIT |

Turn ignition switch on.

↓

Is STOP fuse normal ? —— No → Short circuit in wire harness between terminal 16 of computer and fuse.

↓ Yes

STOP LIGHT S/W

INSPECT STOP LIGHT SWITCH OPERATION
Is stop light switch operation normal ? —— No → Replace stop light switch.

↓ Yes

COMPUTER

Disconnect computer and inspect connector on wire harness side as follows.

↓

INSPECT STOP FUSE CIRCUIT
Is there battery voltage between terminal 16 and body ground with brake pedal returned ? —— No → Open circuit in wire harness between terminal 16 of computer and STOP fuse.

↓ Yes

INSPECT STOP LIGHT SWITCH CIRCUIT
Is there battery voltage between terminal 15 and body ground with brake pedal depressed ? —— No → Open circuit in wire harness between terminal 15 of computer and terminal 3 of stop light switch.

↓ Yes

Replace computer.

Cruise control trouble diagnosis chart — 1987 and later Supra

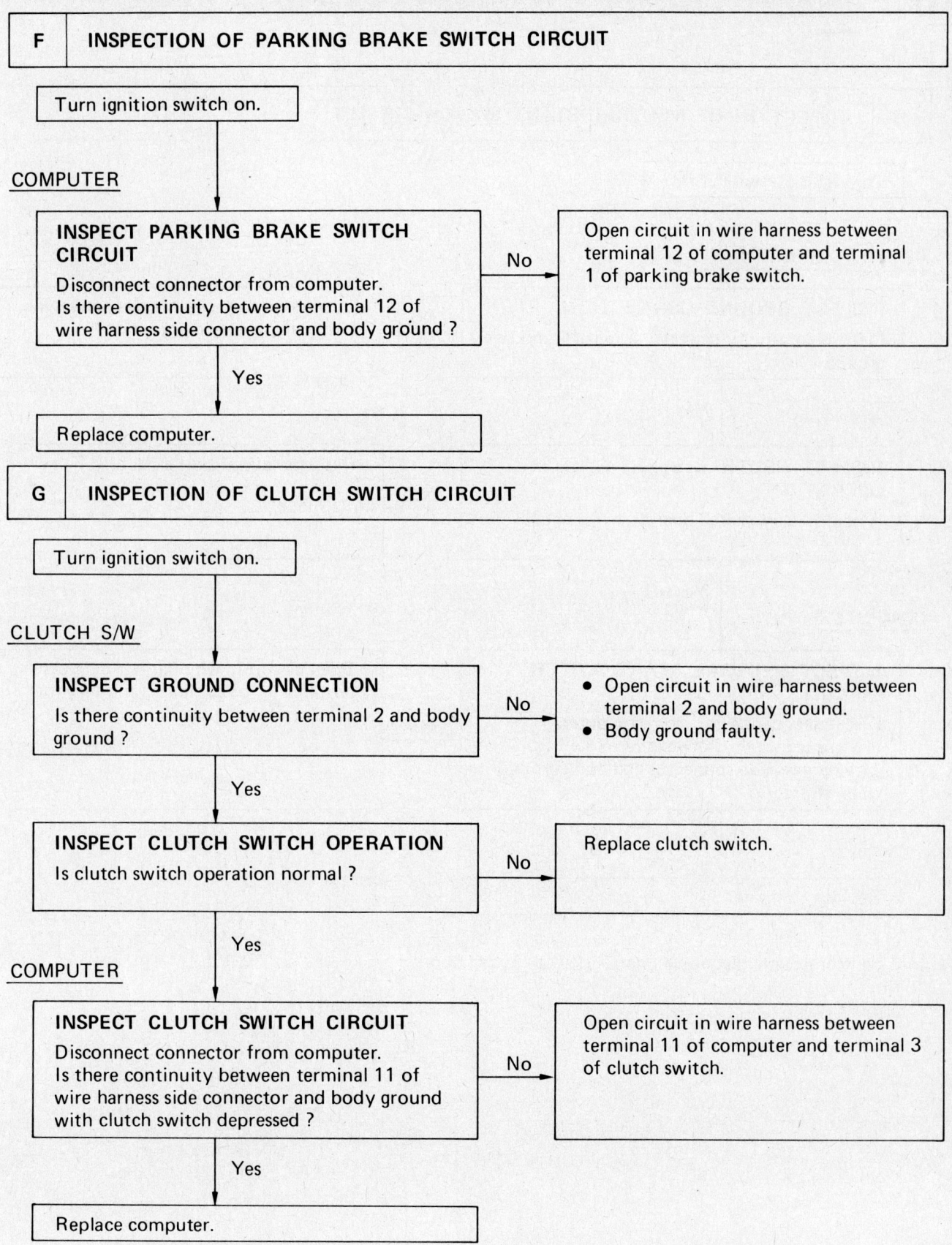

Cruise control trouble diagnosis chart—1987 and later Supra

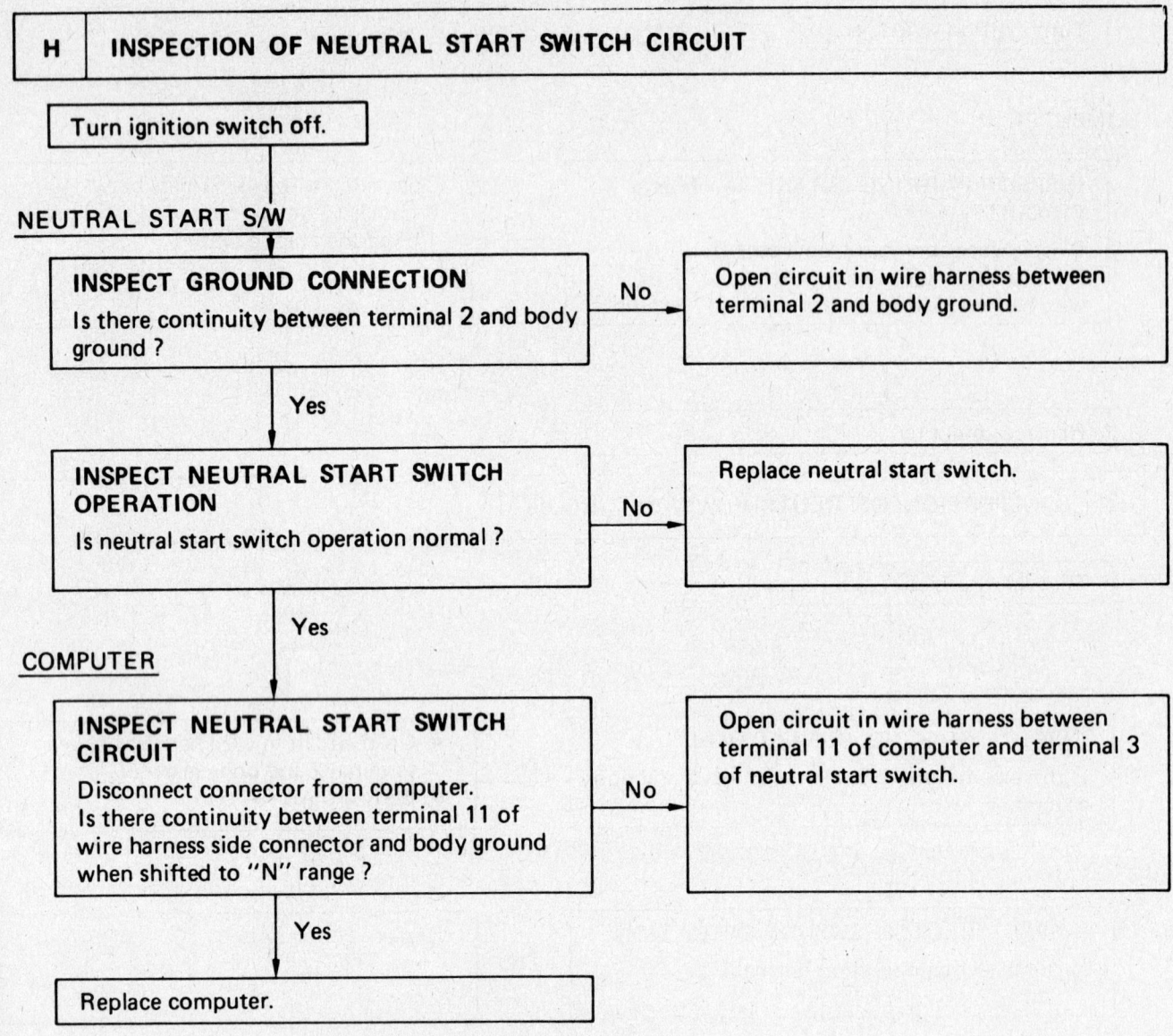

| H | INSPECTION OF NEUTRAL START SWITCH CIRCUIT |

Turn ignition switch off.

NEUTRAL START S/W

INSPECT GROUND CONNECTION
Is there continuity between terminal 2 and body ground ?

No → Open circuit in wire harness between terminal 2 and body ground.

Yes ↓

INSPECT NEUTRAL START SWITCH OPERATION
Is neutral start switch operation normal ?

No → Replace neutral start switch.

Yes ↓

COMPUTER

INSPECT NEUTRAL START SWITCH CIRCUIT
Disconnect connector from computer.
Is there continuity between terminal 11 of wire harness side connector and body ground when shifted to "N" range ?

No → Open circuit in wire harness between terminal 11 of computer and terminal 3 of neutral start switch.

Yes ↓

Replace computer.

Cruise control trouble diagnosis chart – 1987 and later Supra

1146

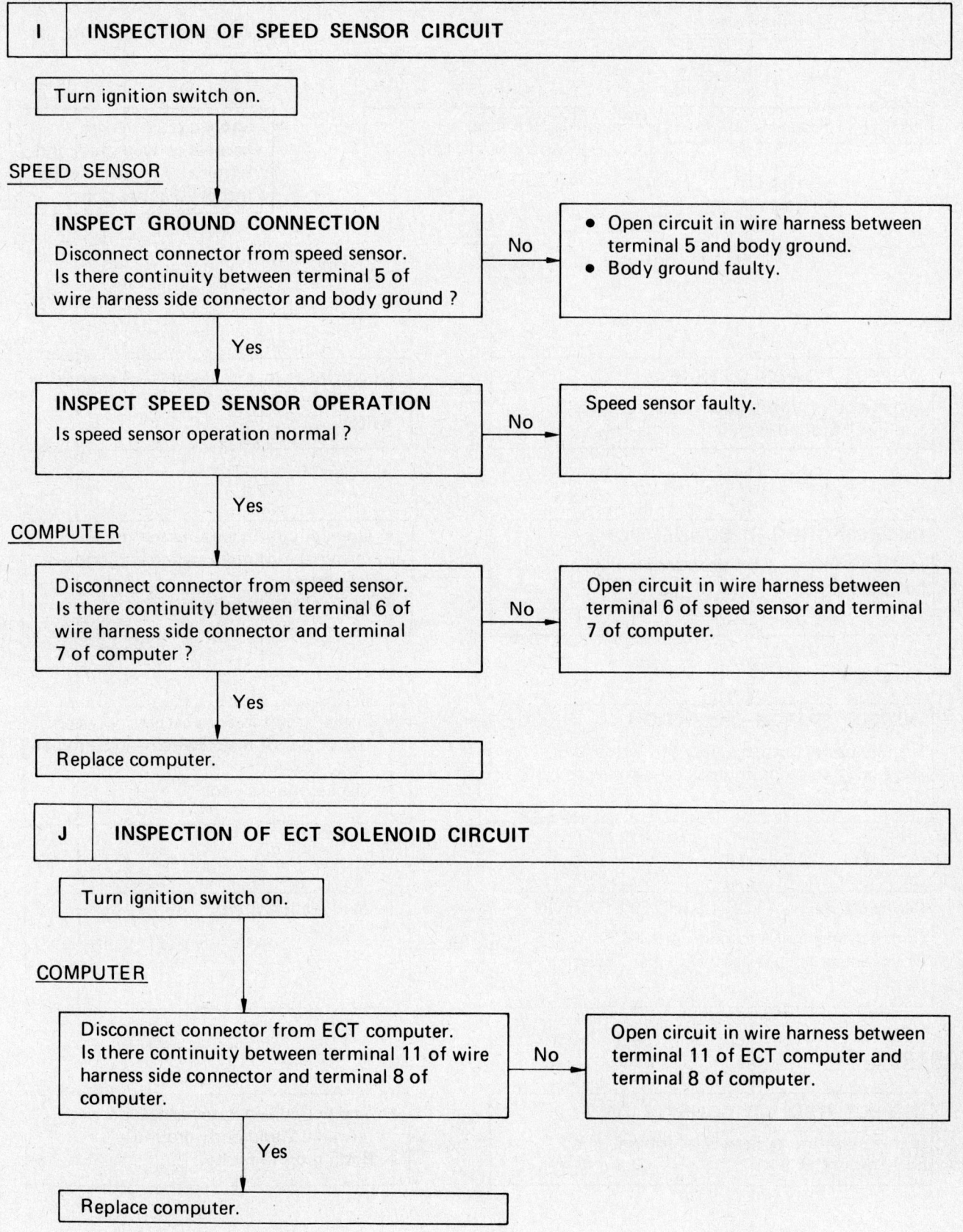

Cruise control trouble diagnosis chart – 1987 and later Supra

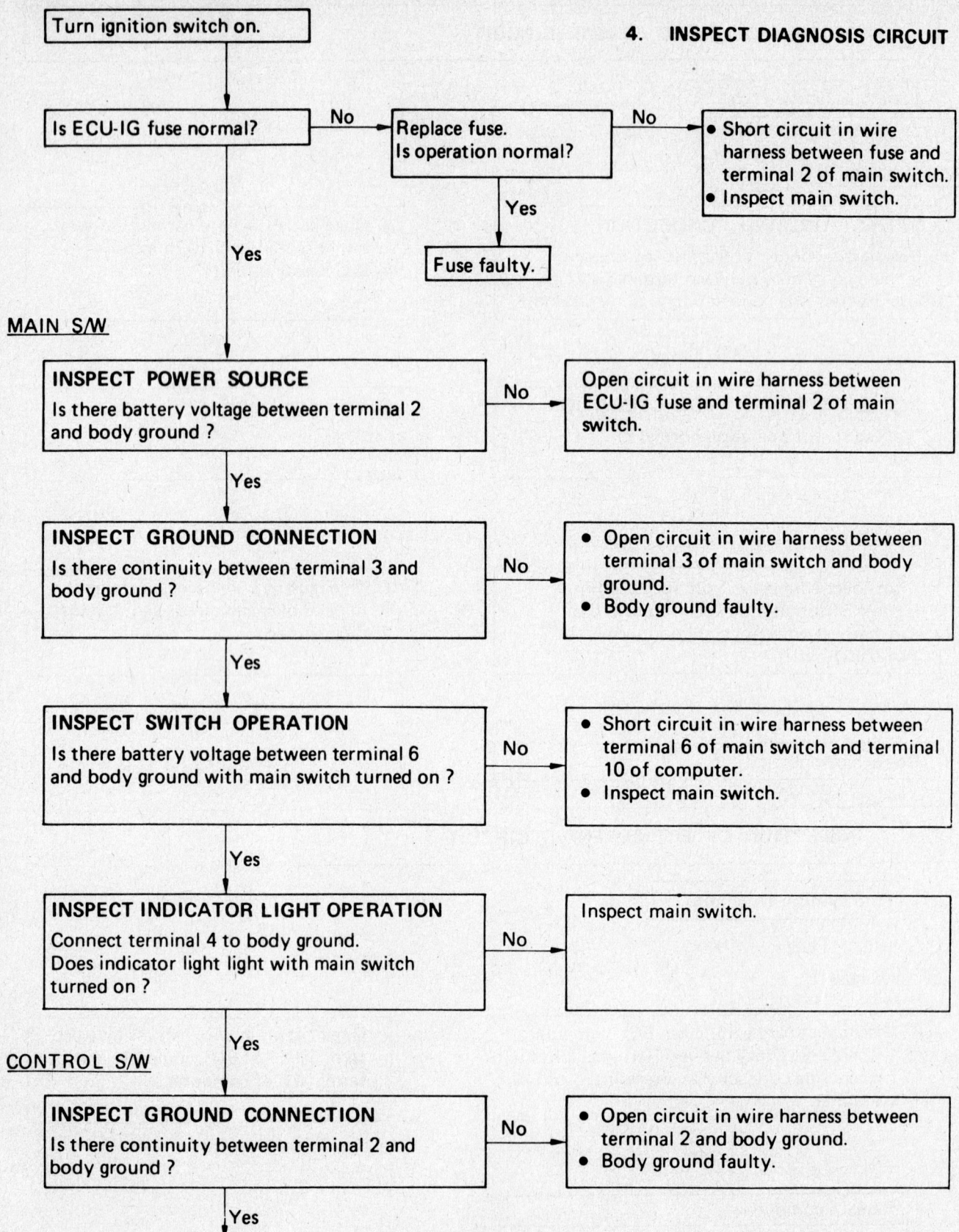

4. INSPECT DIAGNOSIS CIRCUIT

Cruise control trouble diagnosis chart — 1987 and later Supra

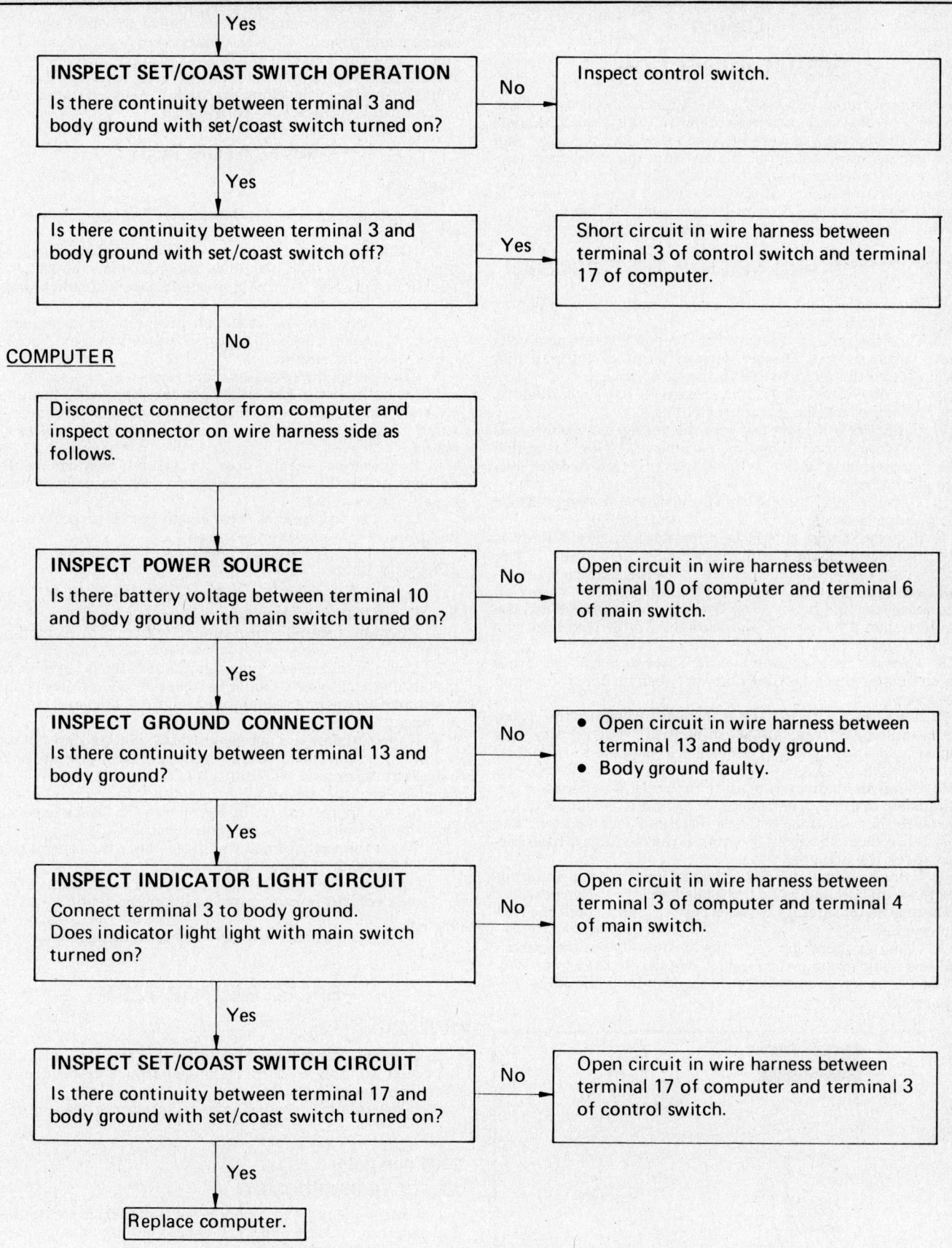

Cruise control trouble diagnosis chart — 1987 and later Supra

The chart contains the following flow:

INSPECT SET/COAST SWITCH OPERATION
Is there continuity between terminal 3 and body ground with set/coast switch turned on?
— No → Inspect control switch.
— Yes ↓

Is there continuity between terminal 3 and body ground with set/coast switch off?
— Yes → Short circuit in wire harness between terminal 3 of control switch and terminal 17 of computer.
— No ↓

COMPUTER

Disconnect connector from computer and inspect connector on wire harness side as follows.
↓

INSPECT POWER SOURCE
Is there battery voltage between terminal 10 and body ground with main switch turned on?
— No → Open circuit in wire harness between terminal 10 of computer and terminal 6 of main switch.
— Yes ↓

INSPECT GROUND CONNECTION
Is there continuity between terminal 13 and body ground?
— No → • Open circuit in wire harness between terminal 13 and body ground.
• Body ground faulty.
— Yes ↓

INSPECT INDICATOR LIGHT CIRCUIT
Connect terminal 3 to body ground.
Does indicator light light with main switch turned on?
— No → Open circuit in wire harness between terminal 3 of computer and terminal 4 of main switch.
— Yes ↓

INSPECT SET/COAST SWITCH CIRCUIT
Is there continuity between terminal 17 and body ground with set/coast switch turned on?
— No → Open circuit in wire harness between terminal 17 of computer and terminal 3 of control switch.
— Yes ↓

Replace computer.

Celica

VISUAL INSPECTION

Before performing any tests make a visual inspection of the cruise control system. Check all items in the system for abnormal conditions such as bare broken or disconnected wires and damage to the vacuum hoses. Be sure that the speedometer cables are attached and properly routed. All vacuum hoses must be properly routed and must not have any kinks or bends. Be sure that all electrical connections are complete and tight. The wiring harness must be routed properly.

COMPUTER AND SENSOR TEST (1982–83)

1. Remove the right side kick panel. Unplug the wiring harness from the computer.
2. Turn the ignition switch to the on position. Using a voltmeter measure the voltage between terminal thirteen and ground with the main switch in the on position.
3. Battery voltage should be present. If battery voltage is not present, check the control switch.
4. Using the voltmeter measure the voltage between terminal eight and ground. When the parking brake lever is pulled the voltage should be zero. When the lever is returned the voltage should be 12 volts.
5. Turn the ignition switch off. Using the voltmeter measure the voltage between terminal eleven and ground.
6. Battery voltage should be present. If battery voltage is not present, check the stop light switch.
7. Using the voltmeter measure the voltage between terminal twelve and ground. When the parking brake lever is pulled the voltage should be 12 volts. When the lever is returned the voltage should be zero. If the voltage is incorrect check the brake pedal switch.
8. Turn the ignition switch to the accessory position. Using an ohmmeter check for continuity between terminal nine and ground.
9. If equipped with manual transmission depress the clutch pedal (automatic transmission in neutral), if continuity does not exist between the terminals check the clutch or neutral safety switch.
10. Using an ohmmeter measure the resistance between terminals six and ten. The resistance should be about 68 ohms. Measure the resistance between terminals four and ten. The resistance should be about 30 ohms. If the readings are not correct check the actuator.
11. Using an ohmmeter check the continuity between terminal three and ground when the set switch is in the on position. If there is no continuity between the terminals check the control switch.
12. Using an ohmmeter check the continuity between terminal seven and ground when the set switch is in the on position. If there is no continuity between the terminals check the control switch.

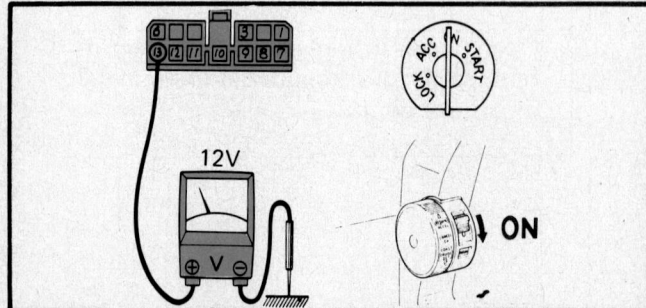

Computer test point locations – 1982–83 Celica

13. Using an ohmmeter check the continuity between terminal five and ground when the cancel switch is pushed on.
14. Using an ohmmeter check the continuity between terminal one and ground when the vehicle is slightly pushed. At this time the needle on the ohmmeter should move repeatedly from on to off. If not check the speed sensor.

ACTUATOR TEST

1982–83

1. Disconnect the electrical connector from the actuator lead wire.
2. Using an ohmmeter measure the resistance between terminals one and two. It should be about 30 ohms. Measure the resistance between terminals one and three. It should be about 70 ohms.
3. If the resistance is not as indicated, replace the actuator.
4. Disconnect the carburetor throttle rod from the bell crank. Start the engine.
5. Check that the actuator diaphragm makes a smooth reciprocating motion when either power is applied to terminals two and three with the actuator terminal one grounded or when power is removed from terminal two. If not replace the actuator.
6. Be sure that the cable does not return to easy when pulled with about 4 to 7 lbs. of force. Repair or replace defective components as required.
7. Check to be sure that the vacuum hose is properly routed and connected. Correct as required.

1984 and Later

1. Inspect and check the actuator cable. Freeplay should be less than 0.039 inch. Adjust or replace as required.
2. Disconnect the electrical connector from the actuator lead wire.
3. Using an ohmmeter measure the resistance between terminals one and two. It should be about 30 ohms. Measure the resistance between terminals one and three. It should be about 68 ohms.
4. If the resistance is not as indicated, replace the actuator.
5. Connect a positive lead from the positive terminal of the battery to terminals two and three. Connect a negative lead from the negative terminal of the battery to terminal one.
6. Slowly apply 0 to 11.8 in. hg. of vacuum. Check to be sure that the control cable can be pulled smoothly.
7. When the vacuum has stabilized check the control cable and be sure that it does not return.
8. Disconnect terminal two or three and check that the control cable returns to its original position and that the vacuum goes to zero.
9. If the system does not perform as indicated replace the actuator.

SPEED SENSOR TEST

1982–83

1. Using an ohmmeter, check to see that there is continuity between terminals A and B. It should be four times per revolution of the magnet shaft.
2. If continuity does not exist replace the speed sensor.

1984 and Later
REGULAR SPEEDOMETER

1. Using an ohmmeter, check to see that there is continuity between terminals C6 and C7. It should be four times per revolution of the magnet shaft.
2. If continuity does not exist replace the speed sensor.

Terminal	Connection or Measure Item	Check Item	Tester Connection	Condition	Voltage or Resistance Value
2	Stop Light Switch and Release Valve	Resistance	2 – 14	Brake pedal returned	About 68 Ω
4	Control Valve	Resistance	4 – 14		About 30 Ω
5	Control Switch (Set/coast S/W)	Continuity	5 – Body ground	Turn set/coast switch on	Continuity
5				Turn set/coast switch off	No continuity
6	OD Relay				
7	Speed Sensor	Continuity	7 – Body ground	Vehicle moving slowly	See page BE-80
10	Main Switch	Voltage	10 – Body ground	Turn ignition switch and main switch on	Battery voltage
10				Turn ignition switch and/or main switch off	No voltage
11	Clutch Switch or Neutral Start Switch	Continuity	11 – Body ground	Clutch pedal depressed or if shifted into "N" range	Continuity
11				Clutch pedal returned or if shifted into any range except "N" range	No continuity
12	Parking Brake Switch	Voltage	12 – Body ground	Parking brake lever pulled	No voltage
12				Parking brake lever returned	Battery voltage
13	Body Ground	Continuity	13 – Body ground		Continuity
14	Release Valve and Control Valve				
15	Stop Light Switch	Voltage	15 – Body ground	Brake pedal depressed	Battery voltage
15				Brake pedal returned	No voltage
16	STOP Fuse	Voltage	16 – Body ground		Battery voltage
17	Control Switch (Accel/resume S/W)	Continuity	17 – Body ground	Turn accel/resume switch on	Continuity
17				Turn accel/resume switch off	No continuity

Cruise control computer circuit inspection chart—1984 and later Celica

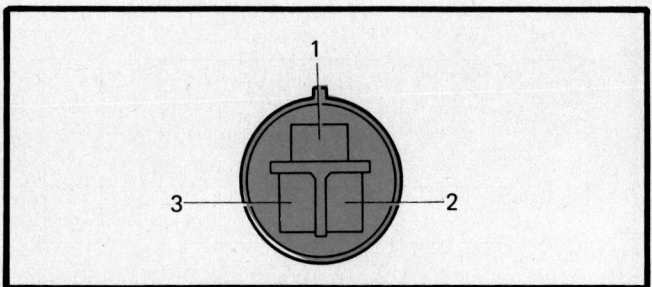

Actuator test point locations—Celica

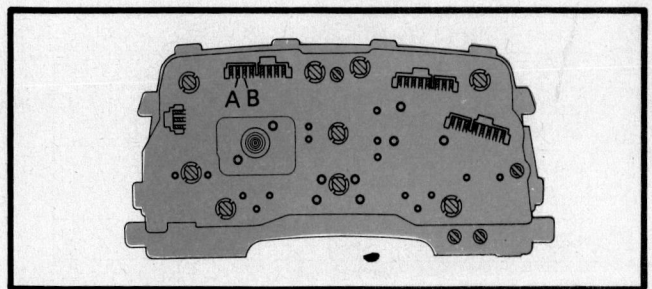

Speed sensor test point locations—1982–83 Celica

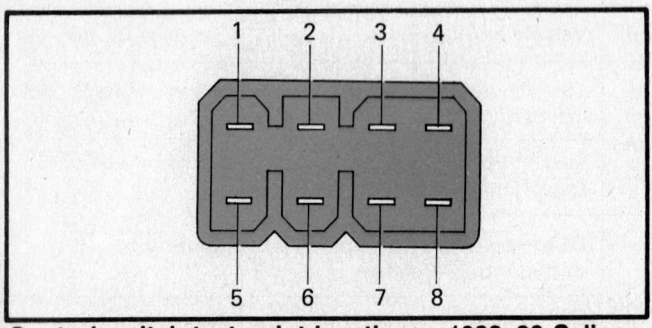

Terminal Switch position		1	2	3	4	5	6	7	8
Main Switch	ON	◯				◯			
	OFF								
Control Switch	SET							◯—◯	
	OFF								
	RESUME			◯—◯					◯
Cancel Switch	ON		◯—◯						◯
	OFF								

Control switch specifications—1982–83 Celica

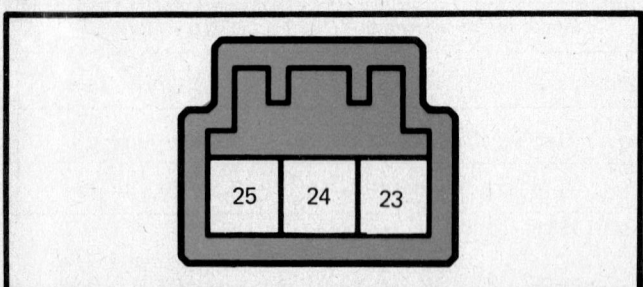

Control switch test point locations—1982–83 Celica

DIGITAL SPEEDOMETER

1. Using an ohmmeter, check to see that there is continuity between terminals A10 and A12. It should be four times per revolution of the magnet shaft.
2. If continuity does not exist replace the speed sensor.

CONTROL SWITCH TEST

1. Using an ohmmeter check for continuity of the terminals for each switch position.
2. If continuity between the terminals is not as specified, replace the switch.

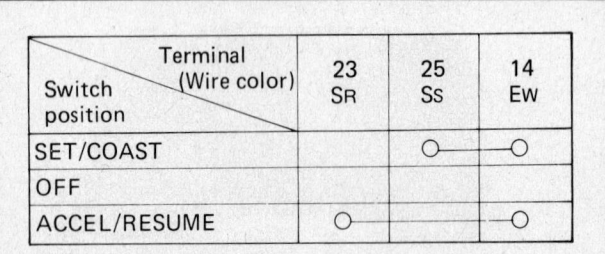

Control switch test point locations—1984–85 Celica

Terminal (Wire color) Switch position	23 SR	25 Ss	14 EW
SET/COAST		◯—◯	
OFF			
ACCEL/RESUME	◯—		—◯

Control switch specifications—1984–85 Celica

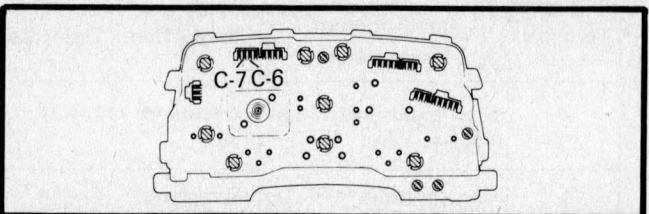

Speed sensor test point locations—1984–85 Celica with regular speedometer

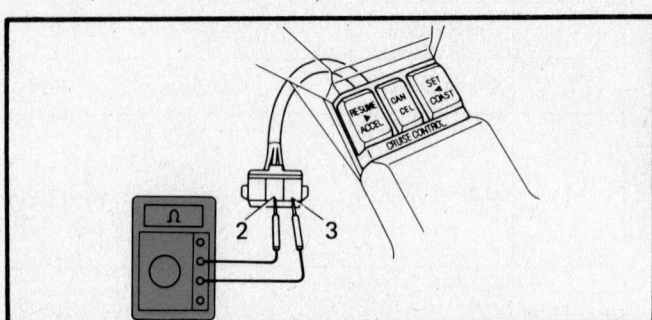

Control switch test point locations—1986 and later Celica

Switch position	Resistance value (Ω)
RESUME/ACCEL	68
SET/COAST	198
CANCEL	418

Control switch specifications—1986 and later Celica

MAIN SWITCH TEST (1984 AND LATER)

1. Using an ohmmeter check for continunity of the terminals for each switch position.
2. If continuity between the terminals is not as specified, replace the switch.

CLUTCH SWITCH TEST (1984 AND LATER)

1. Check to be sure that there is continuity between terminals two and three with the clutch pedal depressed.
2. Check to be sure that there is continunity between terminals two and three with the clutch pedal returned.
3. If continunity is not as indicated, replace the clutch switch.

Terminal Switch position	1	2	3	4	5	6
OFF			◯—	—◯		
				◯—		—◯
ON			◯—	—◯		
	◯—				◯—	—◯

Main switch specifications—1984–85 Celica

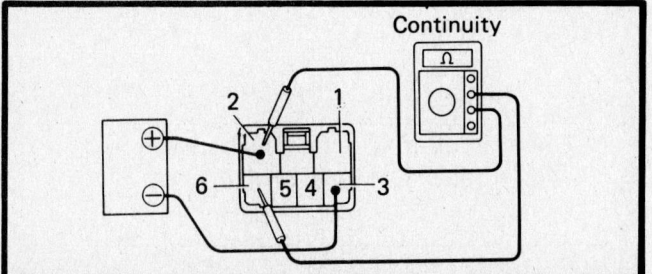

Terminal / Brake pedal position	1	2	3	4
Brake pedal depressed	o———o			
Brake pedal returned			o———o	

Stoplight specifications — 1984–85 Celica

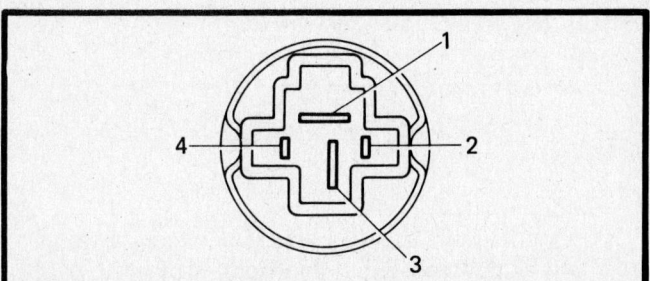

Terminal / Brake pedal position	1	3	2	4
Brake pedal depressed	o———o			
Brake pedal returned			o———o	

Stoplight switch specifications — 1986 and later Celica

Main switch test point locations — 1986 and later Celica

Stoplight switch test point locations — 1986 and later Celica

Main switch test point locations — 1984–85 Celica

Clutch start switch test point locations — 1984–85 Celica

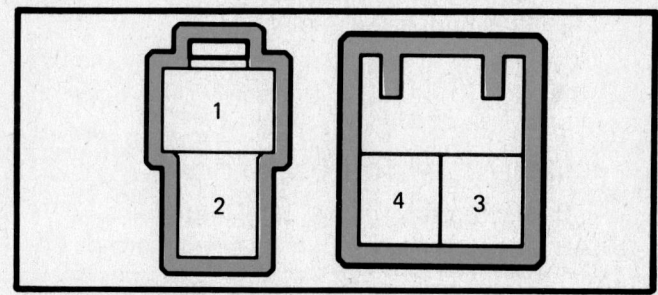

Stoplight switch test point locations — 1984–85 Celica

STOP LIGHT SWITCH TEST (1984 AND LATER)

1. Using an ohmmeter check for continuity of the terminals for each switch position.
2. If continuity between the terminals is not as specified, replace the switch.

DIAGNOSIS AND TESTING PROCEDURES

A | **INSPECTION OF SOURCE CIRCUIT**

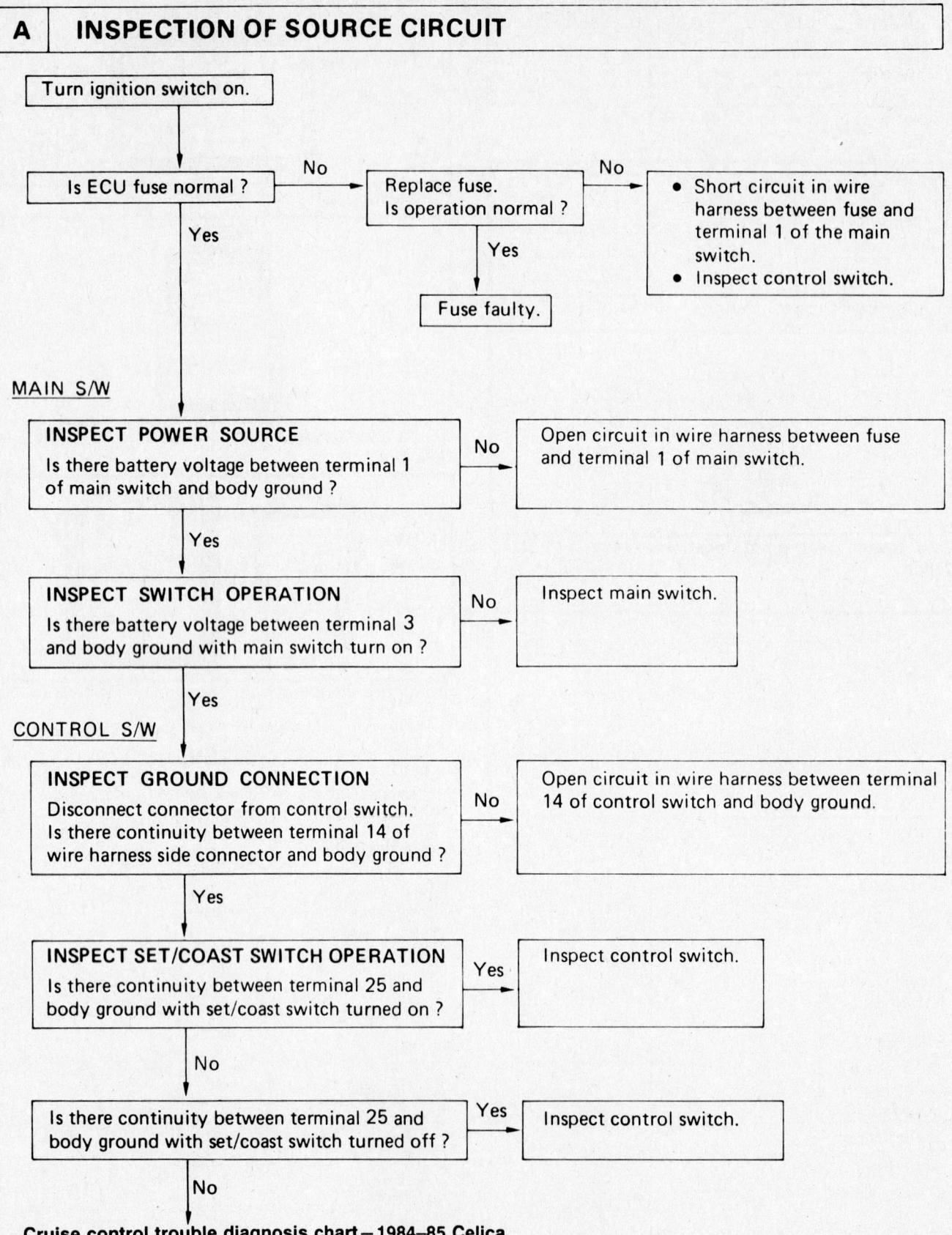

Cruise control trouble diagnosis chart – 1984–85 Celica

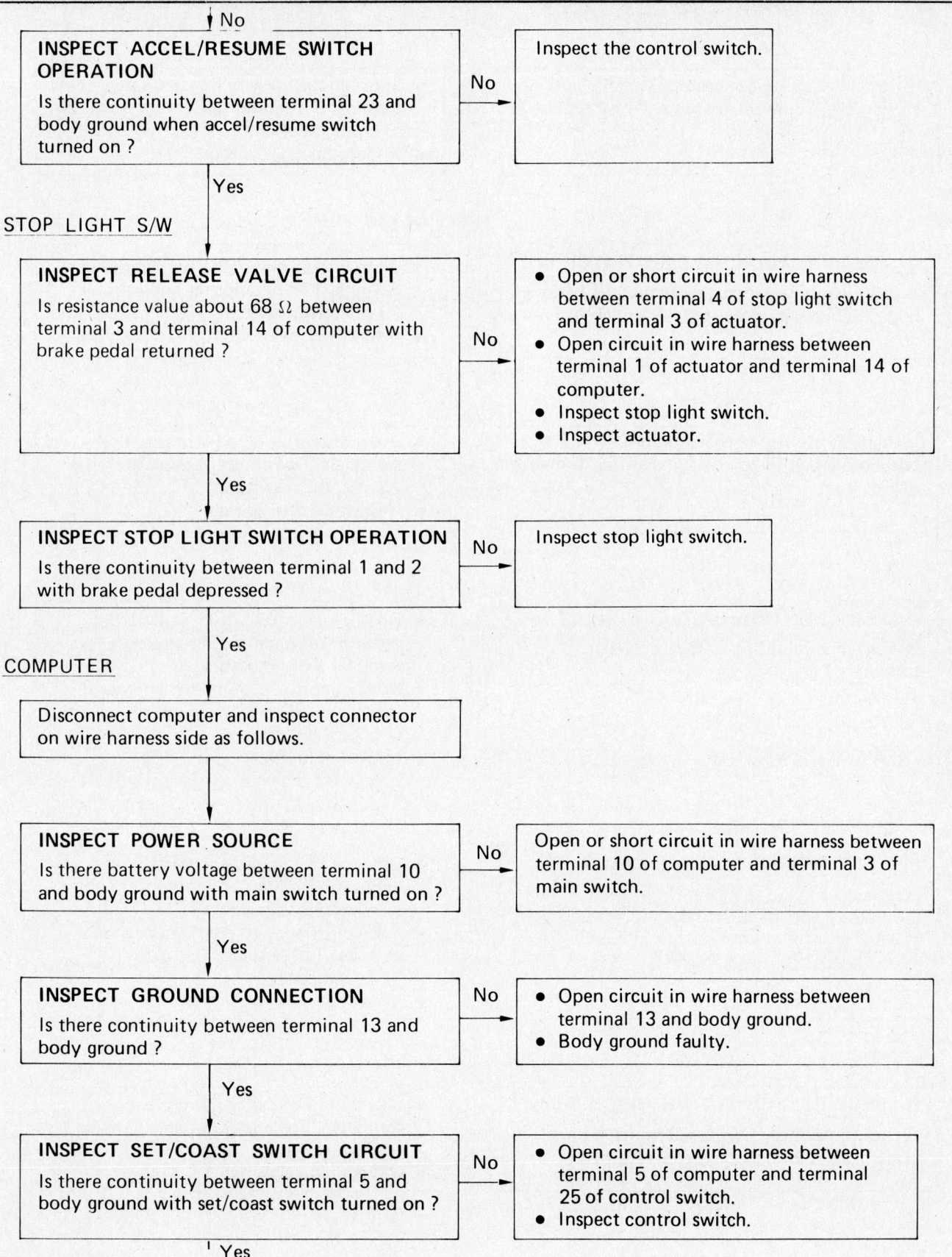

No

INSPECT ACCEL/RESUME SWITCH OPERATION
Is there continuity between terminal 23 and body ground when accel/resume switch turned on ?

No → Inspect the control switch.

Yes

STOP LIGHT S/W

INSPECT RELEASE VALVE CIRCUIT
Is resistance value about 68 Ω between terminal 3 and terminal 14 of computer with brake pedal returned ?

No →
- Open or short circuit in wire harness between terminal 4 of stop light switch and terminal 3 of actuator.
- Open circuit in wire harness between terminal 1 of actuator and terminal 14 of computer.
- Inspect stop light switch.
- Inspect actuator.

Yes

INSPECT STOP LIGHT SWITCH OPERATION
Is there continuity between terminal 1 and 2 with brake pedal depressed ?

No → Inspect stop light switch.

Yes

COMPUTER

Disconnect computer and inspect connector on wire harness side as follows.

INSPECT POWER SOURCE
Is there battery voltage between terminal 10 and body ground with main switch turned on ?

No → Open or short circuit in wire harness between terminal 10 of computer and terminal 3 of main switch.

Yes

INSPECT GROUND CONNECTION
Is there continuity between terminal 13 and body ground ?

No →
- Open circuit in wire harness between terminal 13 and body ground.
- Body ground faulty.

Yes

INSPECT SET/COAST SWITCH CIRCUIT
Is there continuity between terminal 5 and body ground with set/coast switch turned on ?

No →
- Open circuit in wire harness between terminal 5 of computer and terminal 25 of control switch.
- Inspect control switch.

Yes

Cruise control trouble diagnosis chart—1984–85 Celica

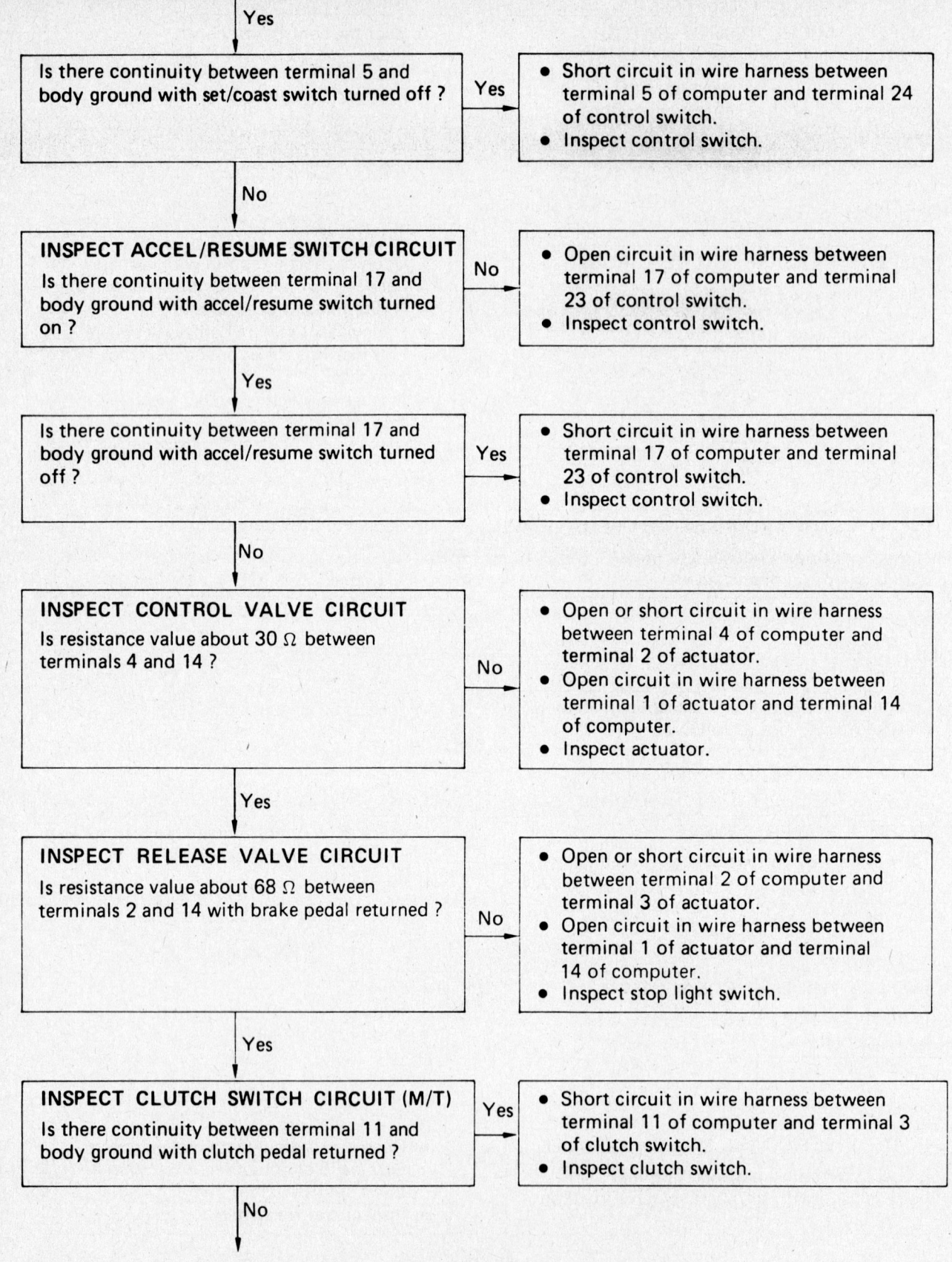

Yes

| Is there continuity between terminal 5 and body ground with set/coast switch turned off ? | Yes | • Short circuit in wire harness between terminal 5 of computer and terminal 24 of control switch.
• Inspect control switch. |

No

| **INSPECT ACCEL/RESUME SWITCH CIRCUIT**
Is there continuity between terminal 17 and body ground with accel/resume switch turned on ? | No | • Open circuit in wire harness between terminal 17 of computer and terminal 23 of control switch.
• Inspect control switch. |

Yes

| Is there continuity between terminal 17 and body ground with accel/resume switch turned off ? | Yes | • Short circuit in wire harness between terminal 17 of computer and terminal 23 of control switch.
• Inspect control switch. |

No

| **INSPECT CONTROL VALVE CIRCUIT**
Is resistance value about 30 Ω between terminals 4 and 14 ? | No | • Open or short circuit in wire harness between terminal 4 of computer and terminal 2 of actuator.
• Open circuit in wire harness between terminal 1 of actuator and terminal 14 of computer.
• Inspect actuator. |

Yes

| **INSPECT RELEASE VALVE CIRCUIT**
Is resistance value about 68 Ω between terminals 2 and 14 with brake pedal returned ? | No | • Open or short circuit in wire harness between terminal 2 of computer and terminal 3 of actuator.
• Open circuit in wire harness between terminal 1 of actuator and terminal 14 of computer.
• Inspect stop light switch. |

Yes

| **INSPECT CLUTCH SWITCH CIRCUIT (M/T)**
Is there continuity between terminal 11 and body ground with clutch pedal returned ? | Yes | • Short circuit in wire harness between terminal 11 of computer and terminal 3 of clutch switch.
• Inspect clutch switch. |

No

Cruise control trouble diagnosis chart — 1984–85 Celica

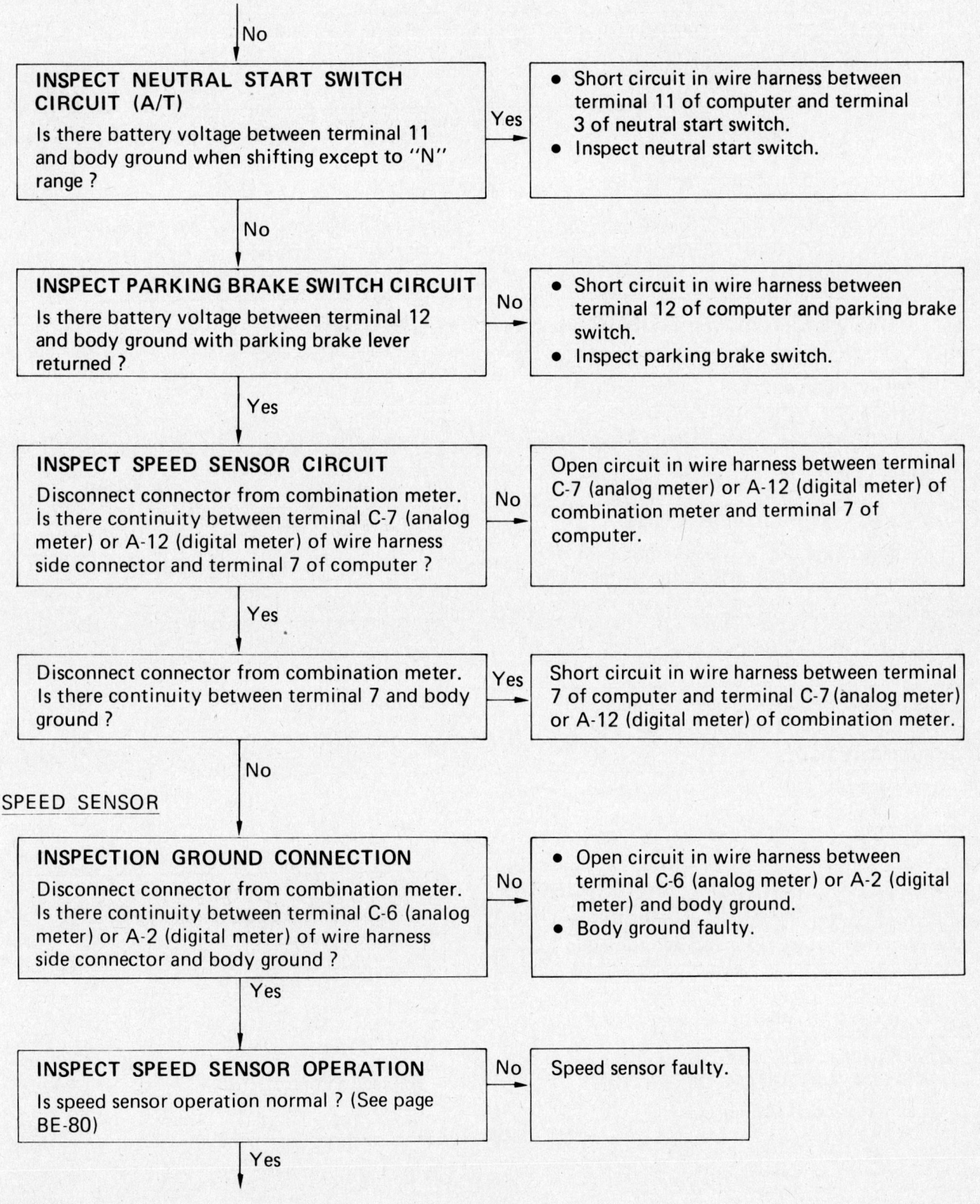

No

INSPECT NEUTRAL START SWITCH CIRCUIT (A/T)

Is there battery voltage between terminal 11 and body ground when shifting except to "N" range ?

Yes →
- Short circuit in wire harness between terminal 11 of computer and terminal 3 of neutral start switch.
- Inspect neutral start switch.

No ↓

INSPECT PARKING BRAKE SWITCH CIRCUIT

Is there battery voltage between terminal 12 and body ground with parking brake lever returned ?

No →
- Short circuit in wire harness between terminal 12 of computer and parking brake switch.
- Inspect parking brake switch.

Yes ↓

INSPECT SPEED SENSOR CIRCUIT

Disconnect connector from combination meter. Is there continuity between terminal C-7 (analog meter) or A-12 (digital meter) of wire harness side connector and terminal 7 of computer ?

No →
Open circuit in wire harness between terminal C-7 (analog meter) or A-12 (digital meter) of combination meter and terminal 7 of computer.

Yes ↓

Disconnect connector from combination meter. Is there continuity between terminal 7 and body ground ?

Yes →
Short circuit in wire harness between terminal 7 of computer and terminal C-7 (analog meter) or A-12 (digital meter) of combination meter.

No ↓

SPEED SENSOR

INSPECTION GROUND CONNECTION

Disconnect connector from combination meter. Is there continuity between terminal C-6 (analog meter) or A-2 (digital meter) of wire harness side connector and body ground ?

No →
- Open circuit in wire harness between terminal C-6 (analog meter) or A-2 (digital meter) and body ground.
- Body ground faulty.

Yes ↓

INSPECT SPEED SENSOR OPERATION

Is speed sensor operation normal ? (See page BE-80)

No →
Speed sensor faulty.

Yes ↓

Cruise control trouble diagnosis chart — 1984–85 Celica

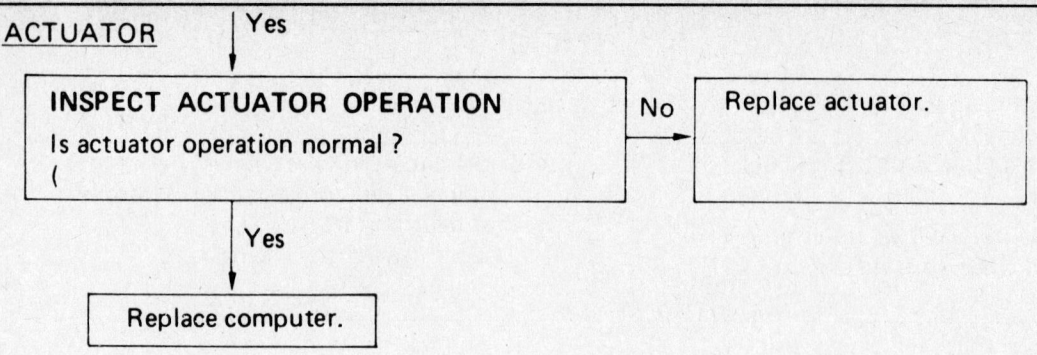

ACTUATOR   Yes

INSPECT ACTUATOR OPERATION	No →	Replace actuator.
Is actuator operation normal ? (		

Yes ↓

Replace computer.

B   INSPECTION OF CONTROL SWITCH CIRCUIT

Turn ignition switch off.

CONTROL S/W

INSPECT SWITCH OPERATION	No →	Inspect control switch.
Is there continuity between terminal 23 and body ground with accel/resume switch turned on ?		

Yes ↓

Is there continuity between terminal 23 and body ground with accel/resume switch turned off ?	Yes →	Inspect control switch.

COMPUTER   No ↓

INSPECT ACCEL/RESUME SWITCH CIRCUIT	No →	Open circuit in wire harness between terminal 17 of computer and terminal 23 of control switch.
Is there continuity between terminal 17 and body ground with accel/resume switch turned on?		

ACTUATOR   Yes ↓

INSPECT ACTUATOR OPERATION	No →	Replace actuator.
Is actuator operation normal ?		

Yes ↓

Replace computer.

Cruise control trouble diagnosis chart – 1984–85 Celica

C | INSPECTION OF ACTUATOR CIRCUIT

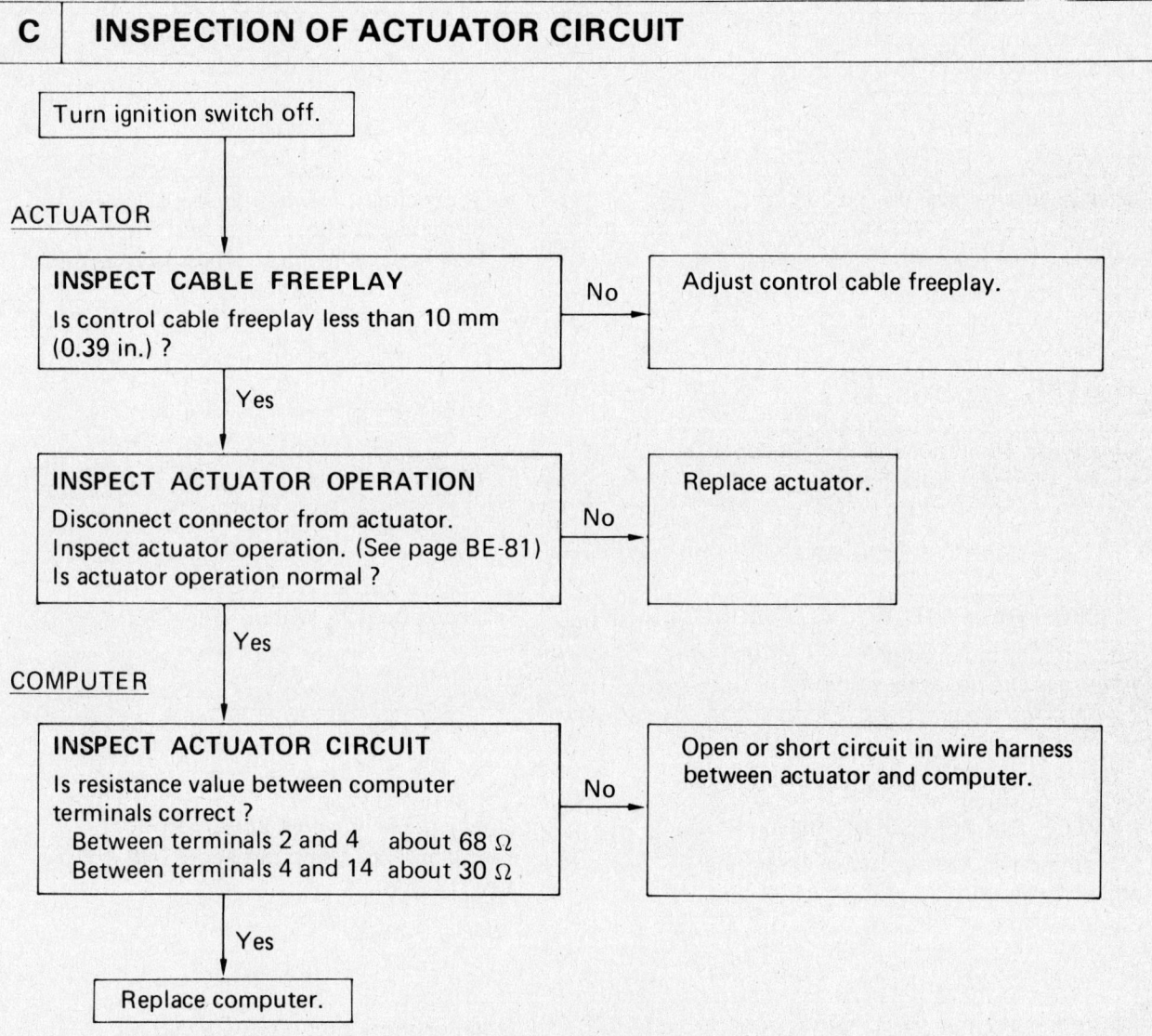

Turn ignition switch off.

ACTUATOR

INSPECT CABLE FREEPLAY
Is control cable freeplay less than 10 mm (0.39 in.) ?

No → Adjust control cable freeplay.

Yes

INSPECT ACTUATOR OPERATION
Disconnect connector from actuator.
Inspect actuator operation. (See page BE-81)
Is actuator operation normal ?

No → Replace actuator.

Yes

COMPUTER

INSPECT ACTUATOR CIRCUIT
Is resistance value between computer terminals correct ?
  Between terminals 2 and 4   about 68 Ω
  Between terminals 4 and 14   about 30 Ω

No → Open or short circuit in wire harness between actuator and computer.

Yes

Replace computer.

Cruise control trouble diagnosis chart — 1984—85 Celica

D | INSPECTION OF STOP LIGHT SWITCH CIRCUIT

Turn ignition switch on.

↓

Is STOP fuse normal ? — **No** →
- Short circuit in wire harness between terminal 15 of computer and fuse.
- Short circuit in wire harness between terminal 16 of computer and fuse.

Yes ↓

COMPUTER

Disconnect computer and inspect connector on wire harness side as follows.

↓

INSPECT RELEASE VALVE CIRCUIT
Is there continuity between terminals 2 and 14 with brake pedal depressed ? — **Yes** → Inspect stop light switch.

No ↓

INSPECT STOP FUSE CIRCUIT
Is there battery voltage between terminal 16 and body ground ? — **No** → Open circuit in wire harness between terminal 16 of computer and STOP fuse.

Yes ↓

INSPECT STOP LIGHT SWITCH CIRCUIT
Is there battery voltage between terminal 15 and body ground with brake pedal depressed ? — **No** → Open or short circuit in wire harness between terminal 15 of computer and terminal 2 of stop light switch.

Yes ↓

Replace computer.

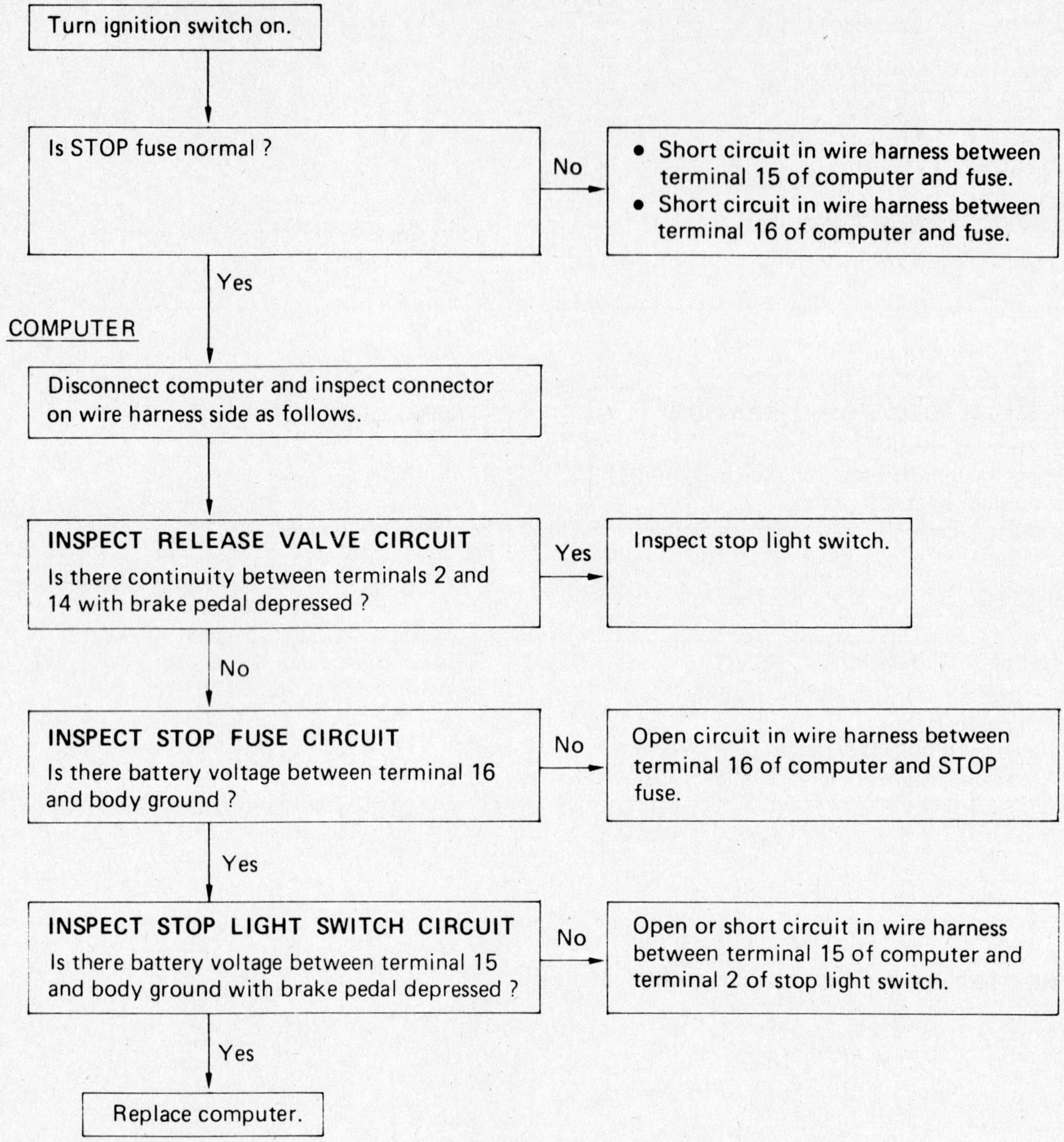

Cruise control trouble diagnosis chart – 1984–85 Celica

E	INSPECTION OF PARKING BRAKE SWITCH

Turn ignition switch on.

COMPUTER

INSPECT PARKING BRAKE SWITCH CIRCUIT

Disconnect connector from computer.
Is there battery voltage between terminal 12 of
wire harness side connector and body ground ?

No →
- Open circuit in wire harness between terminal 12 of computer and parking brake switch.
- Inspect parking brake switch.

Yes

Replace computer.

F	INSPECTION OF CLUTCH SWITCH CIRCUIT

Turn ignition switch off.

CLUTCH S/W

INSPECT GROUND CONNECTION

Is there continuity between terminal 3 and
body ground ?

No →
Open circuit in wire harness between terminal 3 and body ground.

Yes

COMPUTER

INSPECT CLUTCH SWITCH CIRCUIT

Disconnect connector from computer.
Is there continuity between terminal 11 of wire
harness side connector and body ground with
clutch pedal depressed ?

No →
- Open circuit in wire harness between terminal 11 of computer and terminal 2 of clutch switch.
- Inspect clutch switch.

Yes

Replace computer.

Cruise control trouble diagnosis chart – 1984–85 Celica

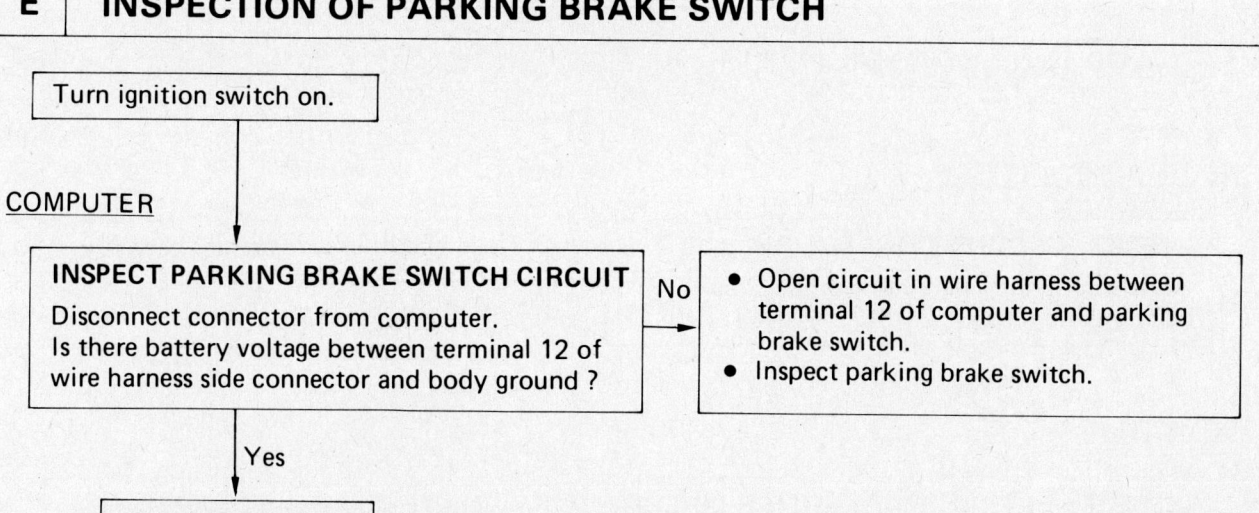

G	INSPECTION OF NEUTRAL START SWITCH CIRCUIT

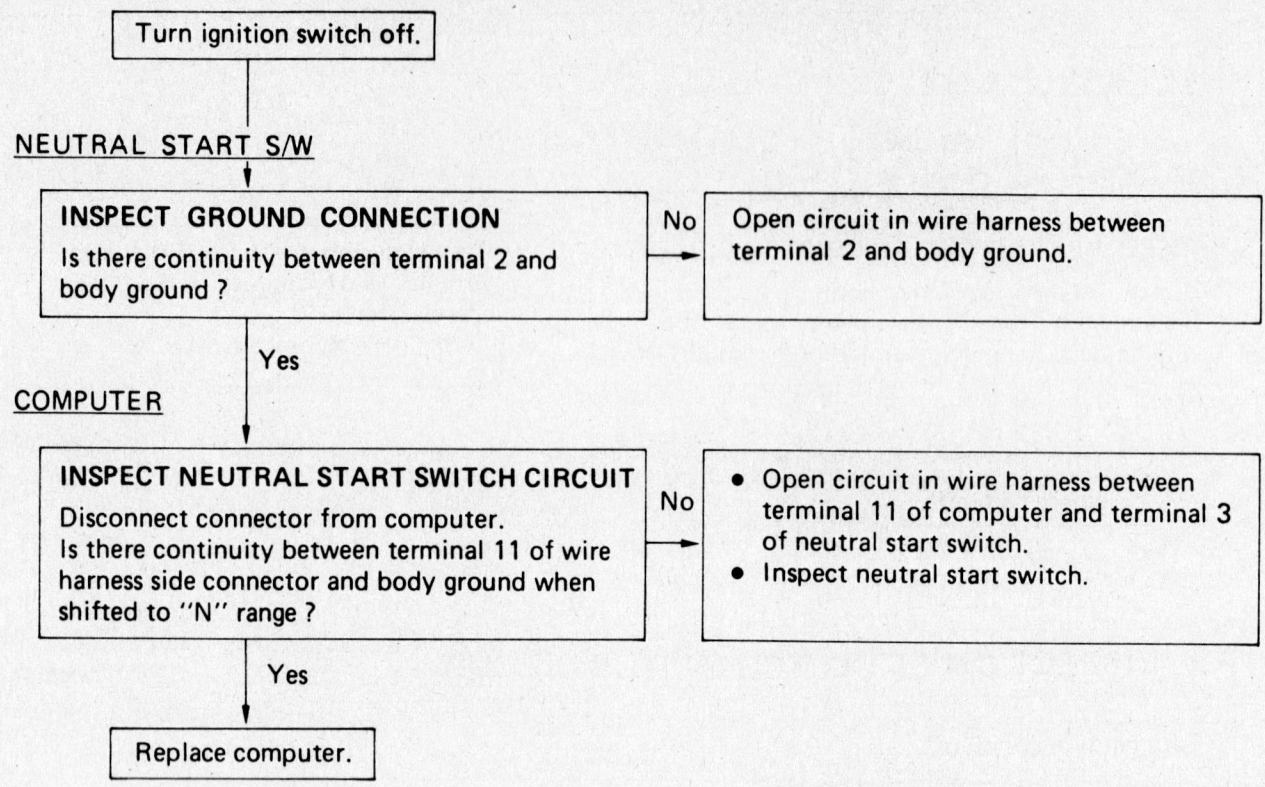

Turn ignition switch off.

NEUTRAL START S/W

INSPECT GROUND CONNECTION
Is there continuity between terminal 2 and body ground ?

No → Open circuit in wire harness between terminal 2 and body ground.

Yes

COMPUTER

INSPECT NEUTRAL START SWITCH CIRCUIT
Disconnect connector from computer.
Is there continuity between terminal 11 of wire harness side connector and body ground when shifted to "N" range ?

No →
- Open circuit in wire harness between terminal 11 of computer and terminal 3 of neutral start switch.
- Inspect neutral start switch.

Yes

Replace computer.

H	INSPECTION OF SPEED SENSOR CIRCUIT

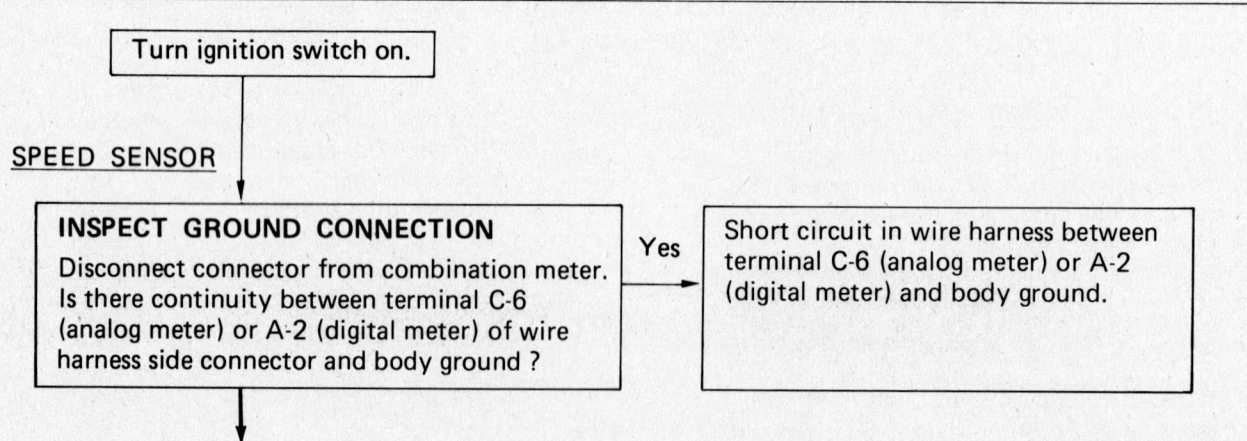

Turn ignition switch on.

SPEED SENSOR

INSPECT GROUND CONNECTION
Disconnect connector from combination meter.
Is there continuity between terminal C-6 (analog meter) or A-2 (digital meter) of wire harness side connector and body ground ?

Yes → Short circuit in wire harness between terminal C-6 (analog meter) or A-2 (digital meter) and body ground.

Cruise control trouble diagnosis chart – 1984–85 Celica

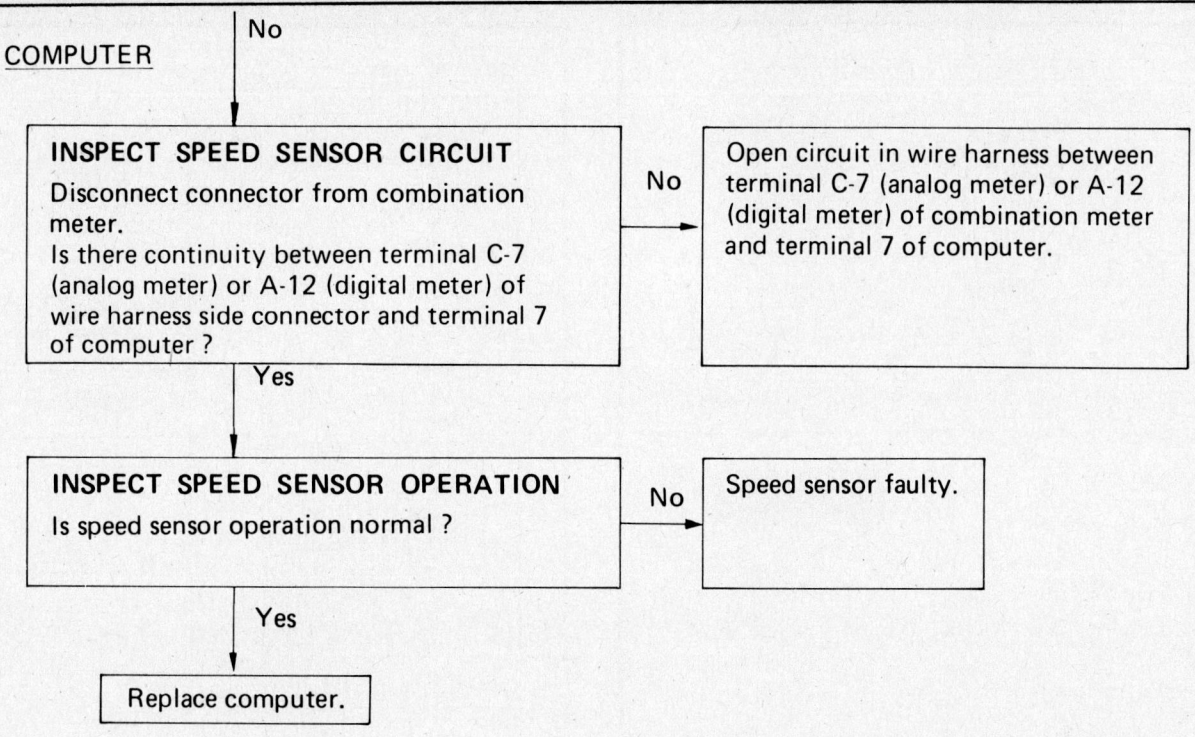

COMPUTER

Problem	Inspection Item	Section
Cruise control does not operate.	Inspection of power source circuit	A
Vehicle speed does not reduce when coast switch turned on.	Inspection of control switch and circuit.	B
Vehicle does not accelerate when accel switch turned on.		
Vehicle speed does not return to memorized speed when resume switch turned on.		
Set speed deviates on high side.	Inspection of actuator and circuit	C
Set speed deviates on low side.		
Vehicle speed does not fluctuate when set switch turned on.	Inspection of actuator and circuit Inspection of speed sensor and circuit	C H
Setting speed does not cancel when brake pedal depressed.	Inspection of stop light switch and circuit	D
Setting speed does not cancel when parking brake pulled.	Inspection of parking brake switch and circuit	E
Setting speed does not cancel when clutch pedal depressed (M/T only).	Inspection of clutch switch and circuit	F
Setting speed does not cancel when shifted to "N" range (A/T only).	Inspection of neutral start switch and circuit	G
Speed can be set below 20 km/h.	Inspection of speed sensor and circuit	H
Cruise control will not disengage even below 20 km/h.		

Cruise control troubleshooting data sheet—1984–85 Celica

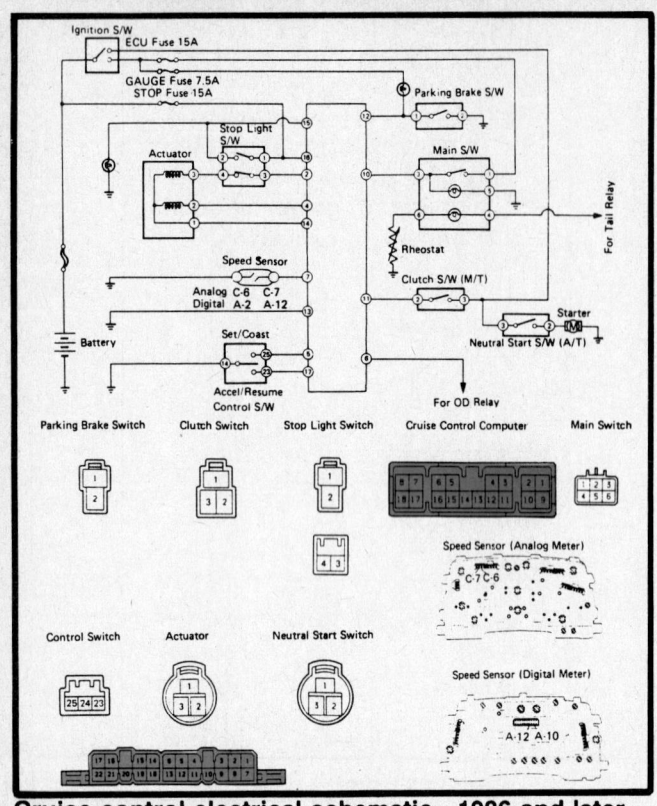

Cruise control electrical schematic—1986 and later Celica

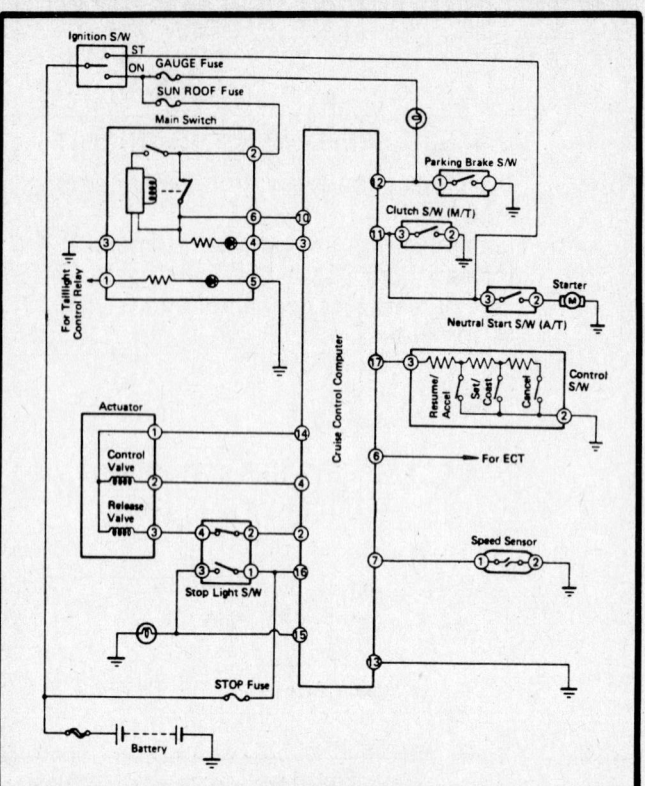

Cruise control electrical schematic—1986 and later Celica

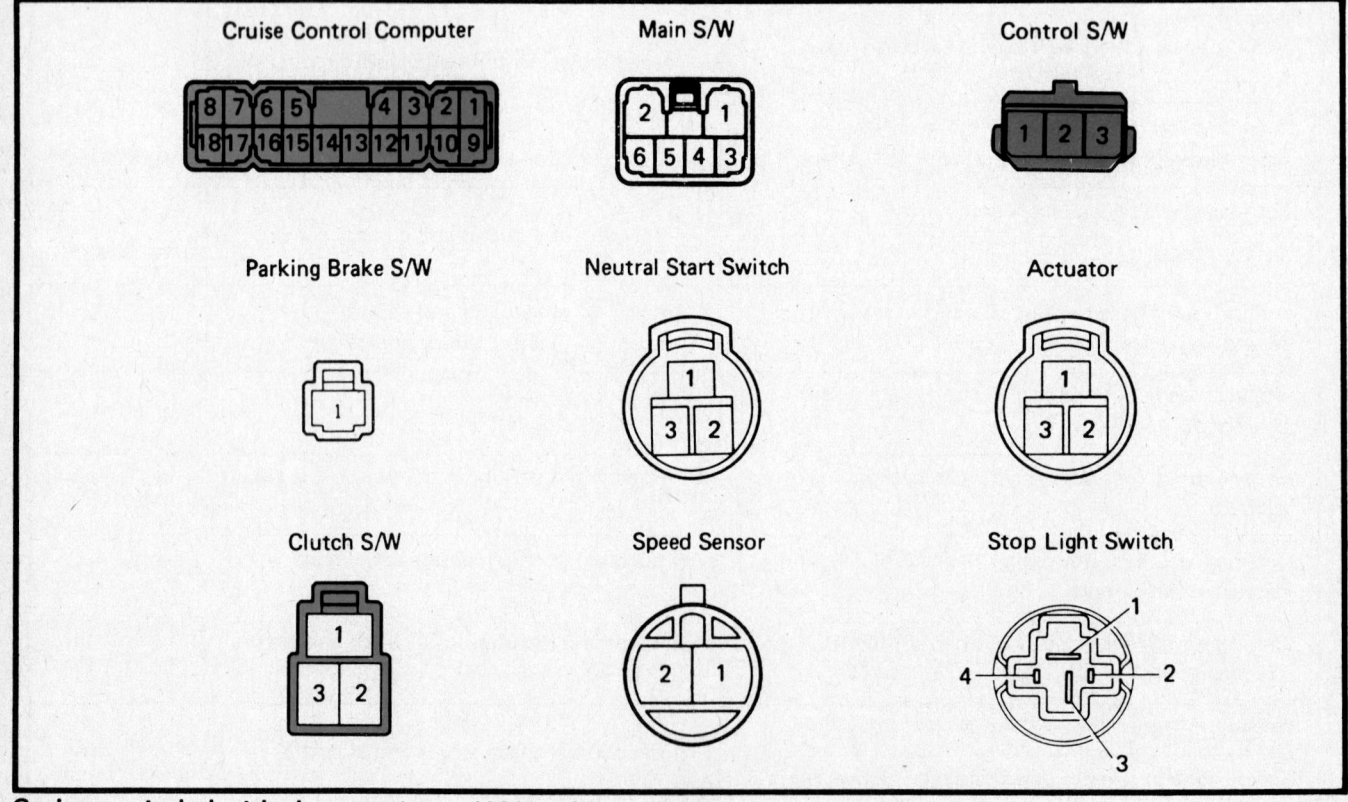

Cruise control electrical connectors—1986 and later Celica

CRUISE CONTROL SYSTEM DIAGNOSIS— 1986 AND LATER

Output of Diagnosis Codes

1. Do not turn the ignition switch off. Do not turn the main switch off.
2. Turn the set/coast switch on three times within two seconds.

3. Read the diagnosis code on the main switch indicator.
4. Indication codes appear with priority from number eleven. Normal codes continue twenty seconds and abnormal codes are repeated three times.
5. Indication is stopped when vehicle speed is over 10 miles per hour or the main switch is turned off.
6. Results are as follows.

No.	Indicator Code	Diagnosis
	ON / OFF	Normal.
11	ON / OFF	Actuator circuit is abnormal.
21	ON / OFF	Speed sensor signal circuit is abnormal.

Diagnostic information—1986 and later Celica

Problem	Inspection Item	No.
Cruise control does not operate.	Inspect diagnosis code Indication Code No.11	A
	No.21	I
	Diagnosis code normal	B
Vehicle speed does not reduce when coast switch turned on.	Inspection of control switch circuit	C
Vehicle speed does not accelerate when accel switch turned on.		
Vehicle speed does not return to memorized speed when resume switch turned on.		
Setting speed deviates on high side.	Inspection of actuator circuit	D
Setting speed deviates on low side.		
Vehicle speed fluctuates when set switch turned on.	Inspection of actuator circuit / Inspection of speed sensor circuit	D / I
Setting speed does not cancel when brake pedal depressed.	Inspection of stop light switch circuit	E
Setting speed does not cancel when parking brake pulled.	Inspection of parking brake switch circuit	F
Setting speed does not cancel when clutch pedal depressed (M/T only).	Inspection of clutch switch circuit	G
Setting speed does not cancel when shifted to "N" range (A/T only).	Inspection of neutral start switch circuit	H
Speed can be set below about 40 km/h (25 mph).	Inspection of speed sensor circuit	I
Cruise control will not disengage even below about 40 km/h (25 mph).		

Cruise control troubleshooting data sheet—1986 and later Celica

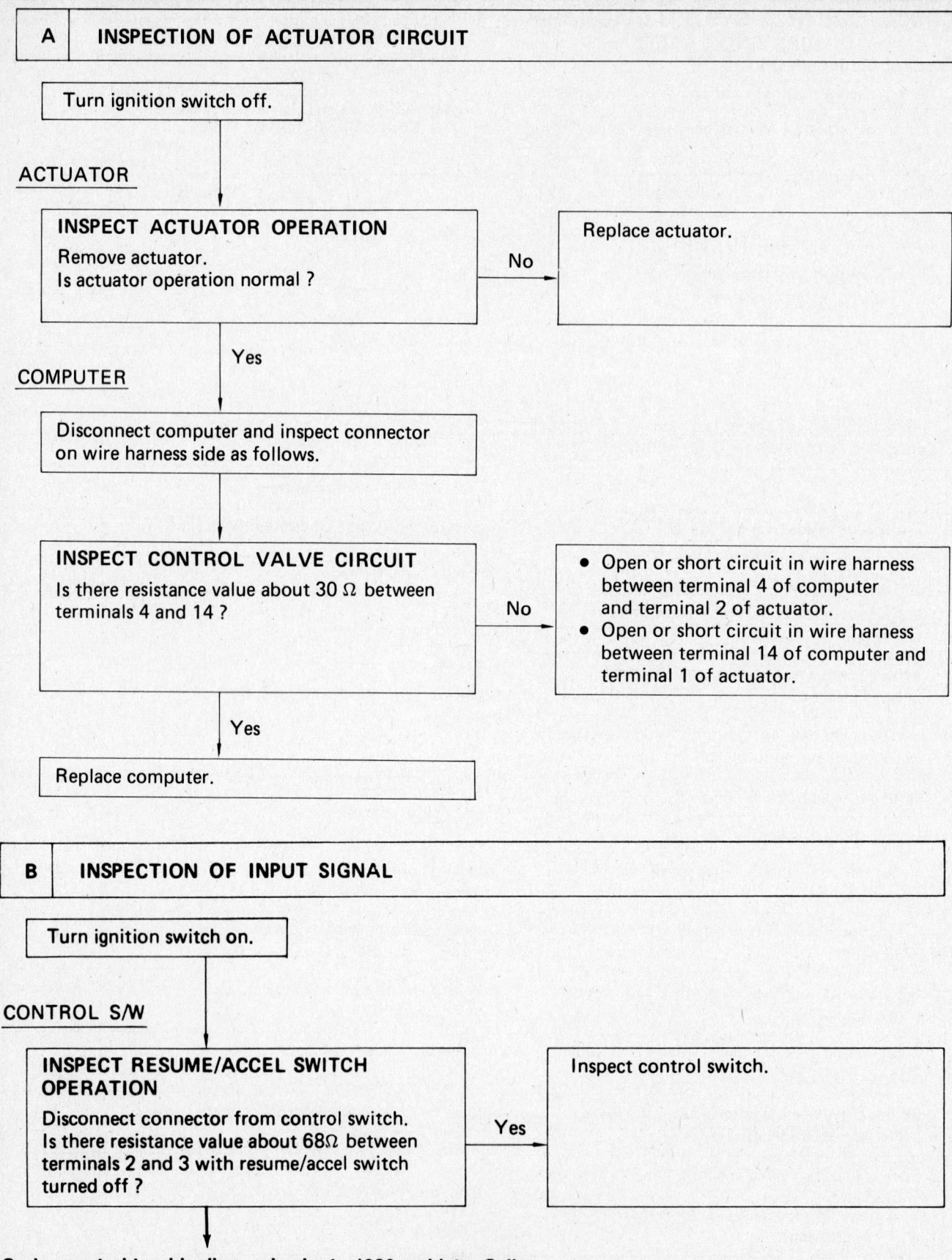

| A | INSPECTION OF ACTUATOR CIRCUIT |

Turn ignition switch off.

ACTUATOR

INSPECT ACTUATOR OPERATION
Remove actuator.
Is actuator operation normal ?

No → Replace actuator.

Yes

COMPUTER

Disconnect computer and inspect connector on wire harness side as follows.

INSPECT CONTROL VALVE CIRCUIT
Is there resistance value about 30 Ω between terminals 4 and 14 ?

No →
- Open or short circuit in wire harness between terminal 4 of computer and terminal 2 of actuator.
- Open or short circuit in wire harness between terminal 14 of computer and terminal 1 of actuator.

Yes

Replace computer.

| B | INSPECTION OF INPUT SIGNAL |

Turn ignition switch on.

CONTROL S/W

INSPECT RESUME/ACCEL SWITCH OPERATION
Disconnect connector from control switch.
Is there resistance value about 68Ω between terminals 2 and 3 with resume/accel switch turned off ?

Yes → Inspect control switch.

Cruise control trouble diagnosis chart – 1986 and later Celica

1166

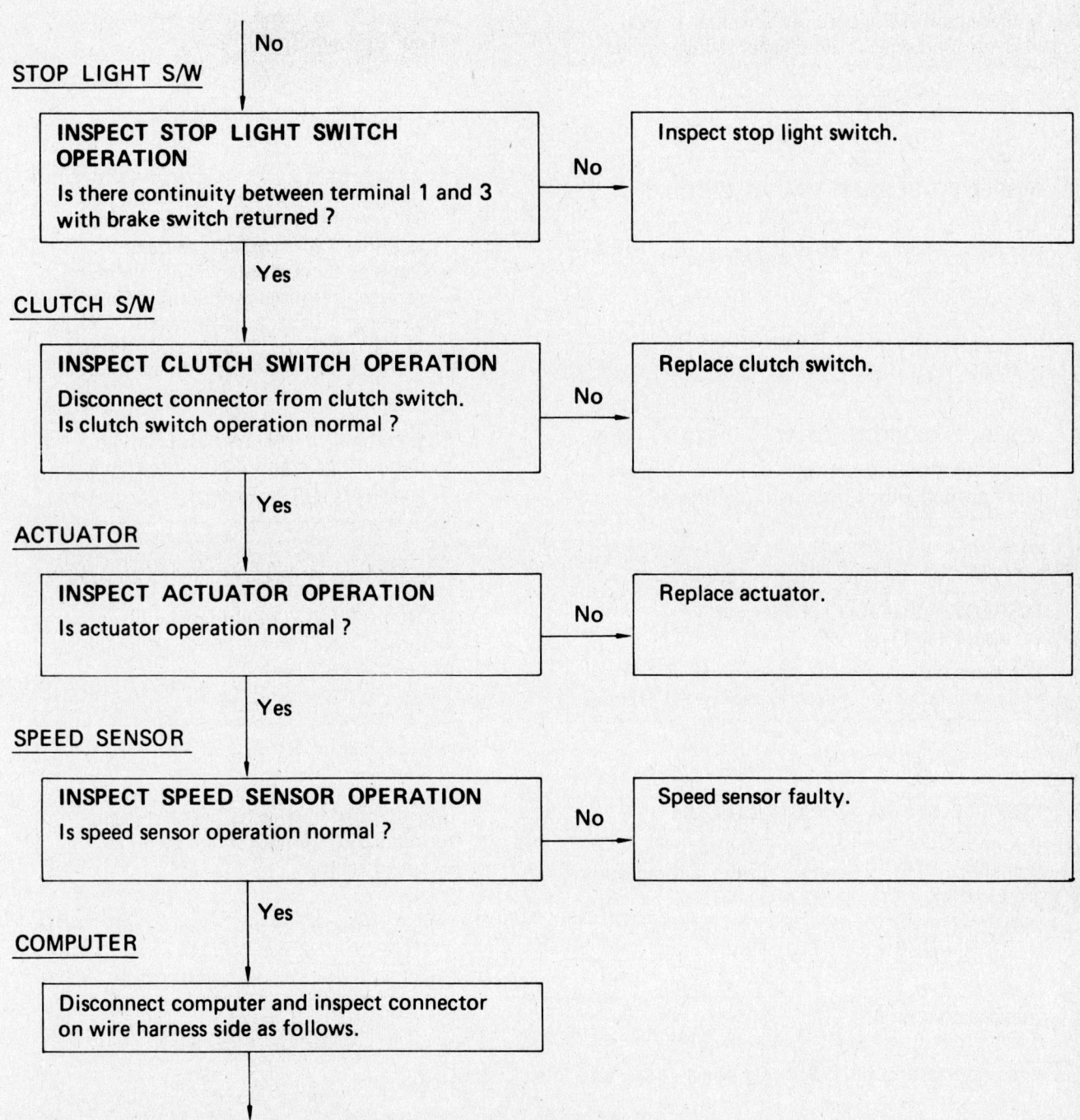

STOP LIGHT S/W

No

| **INSPECT STOP LIGHT SWITCH OPERATION** Is there continuity between terminal 1 and 3 with brake switch returned ? | No → | Inspect stop light switch. |

Yes

CLUTCH S/W

| **INSPECT CLUTCH SWITCH OPERATION** Disconnect connector from clutch switch. Is clutch switch operation normal ? | No → | Replace clutch switch. |

Yes

ACTUATOR

| **INSPECT ACTUATOR OPERATION** Is actuator operation normal ? | No → | Replace actuator. |

Yes

SPEED SENSOR

| **INSPECT SPEED SENSOR OPERATION** Is speed sensor operation normal ? | No → | Speed sensor faulty. |

Yes

COMPUTER

Disconnect computer and inspect connector on wire harness side as follows.

Cruise control trouble diagnosis chart — 1986 and later Celica

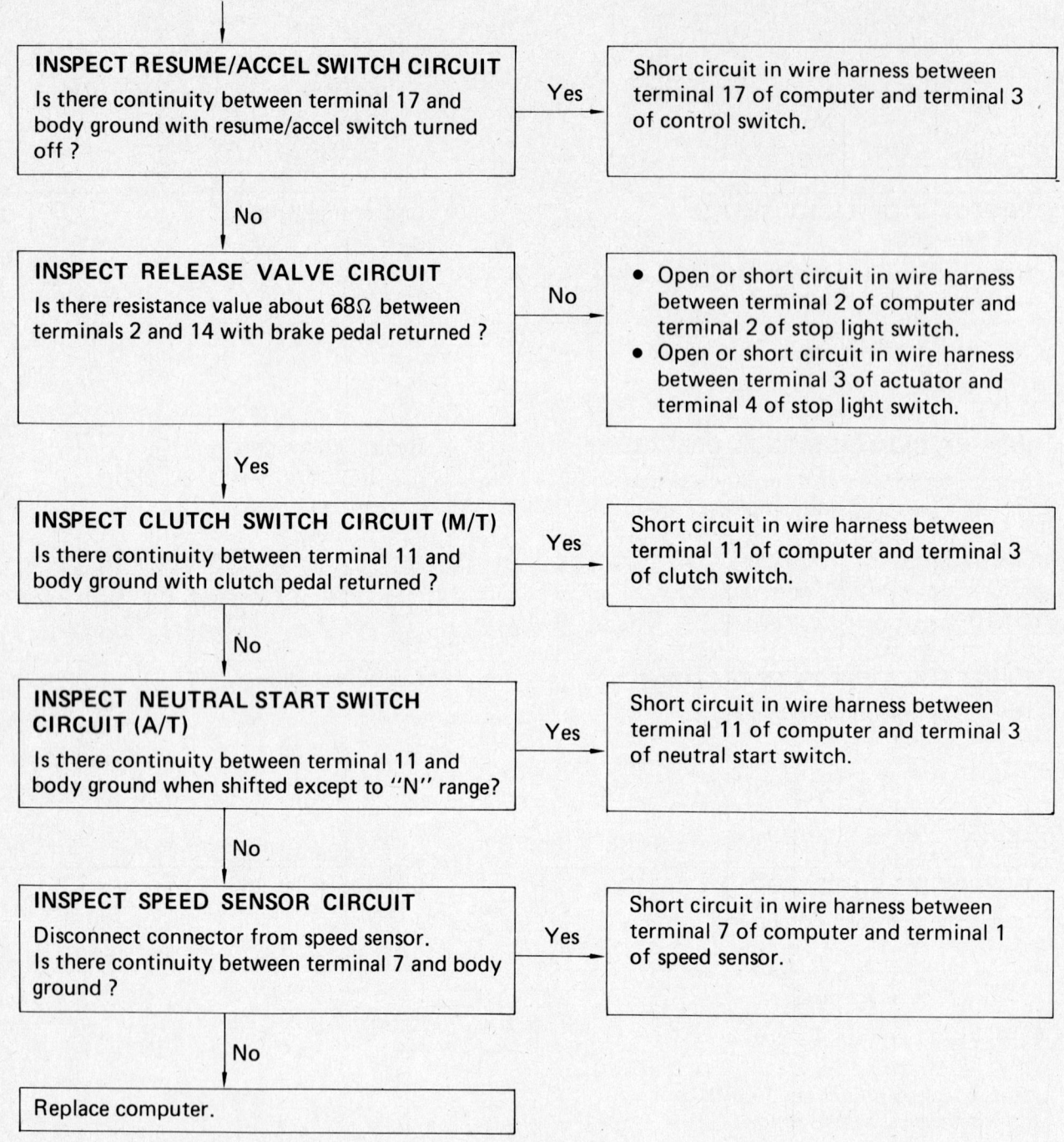

INSPECT RESUME/ACCEL SWITCH CIRCUIT

Is there continuity between terminal 17 and body ground with resume/accel switch turned off?

→ Yes → Short circuit in wire harness between terminal 17 of computer and terminal 3 of control switch.

↓ No

INSPECT RELEASE VALVE CIRCUIT

Is there resistance value about 68Ω between terminals 2 and 14 with brake pedal returned?

→ No →
- Open or short circuit in wire harness between terminal 2 of computer and terminal 2 of stop light switch.
- Open or short circuit in wire harness between terminal 3 of actuator and terminal 4 of stop light switch.

↓ Yes

INSPECT CLUTCH SWITCH CIRCUIT (M/T)

Is there continuity between terminal 11 and body ground with clutch pedal returned?

→ Yes → Short circuit in wire harness between terminal 11 of computer and terminal 3 of clutch switch.

↓ No

INSPECT NEUTRAL START SWITCH CIRCUIT (A/T)

Is there continuity between terminal 11 and body ground when shifted except to "N" range?

→ Yes → Short circuit in wire harness between terminal 11 of computer and terminal 3 of neutral start switch.

↓ No

INSPECT SPEED SENSOR CIRCUIT

Disconnect connector from speed sensor. Is there continuity between terminal 7 and body ground?

→ Yes → Short circuit in wire harness between terminal 7 of computer and terminal 1 of speed sensor.

↓ No

Replace computer.

Cruise control trouble diagnosis chart — 1986 and later Celica

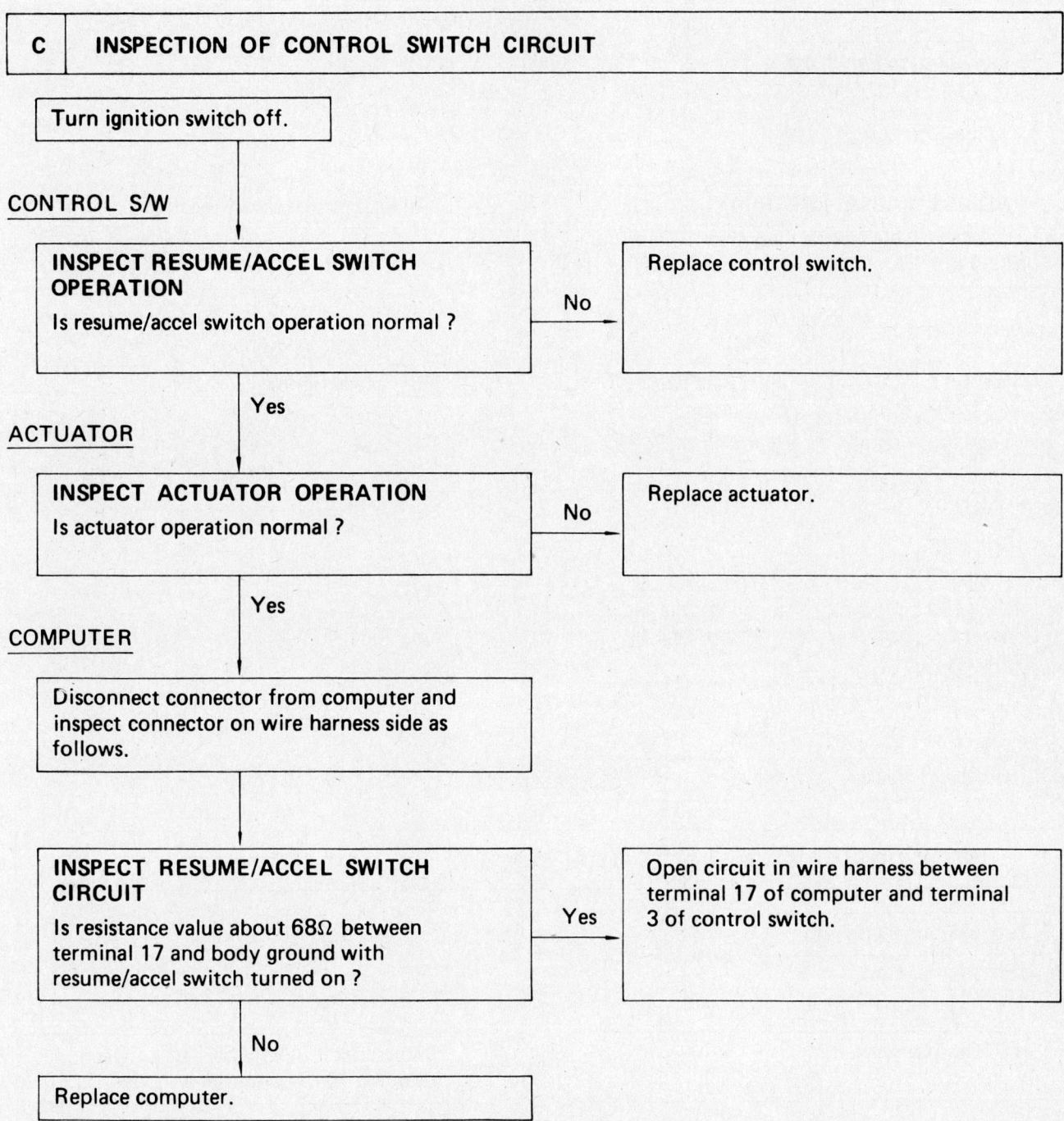

C	INSPECTION OF CONTROL SWITCH CIRCUIT

Turn ignition switch off.

CONTROL S/W

INSPECT RESUME/ACCEL SWITCH OPERATION

Is resume/accel switch operation normal ?

No → Replace control switch.

Yes

ACTUATOR

INSPECT ACTUATOR OPERATION

Is actuator operation normal ?

No → Replace actuator.

Yes

COMPUTER

Disconnect connector from computer and inspect connector on wire harness side as follows.

INSPECT RESUME/ACCEL SWITCH CIRCUIT

Is resistance value about 68Ω between terminal 17 and body ground with resume/accel switch turned on ?

Yes → Open circuit in wire harness between terminal 17 of computer and terminal 3 of control switch.

No

Replace computer.

Cruise control trouble diagnosis chart — 1986 and later Celica

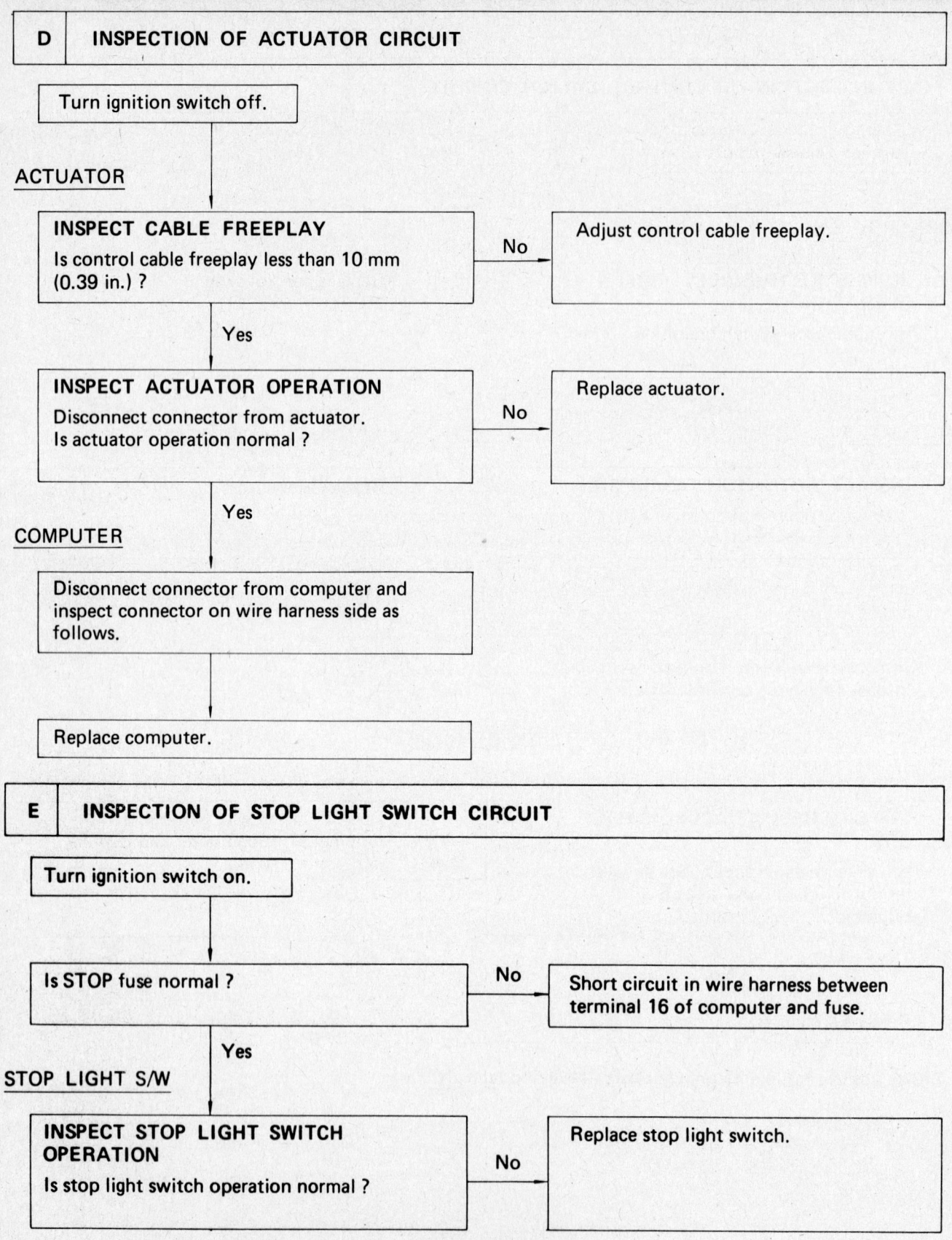

D	INSPECTION OF ACTUATOR CIRCUIT

Turn ignition switch off.

ACTUATOR

INSPECT CABLE FREEPLAY

Is control cable freeplay less than 10 mm (0.39 in.) ?

→ No → Adjust control cable freeplay.

↓ Yes

INSPECT ACTUATOR OPERATION

Disconnect connector from actuator.
Is actuator operation normal ?

→ No → Replace actuator.

↓ Yes

COMPUTER

Disconnect connector from computer and inspect connector on wire harness side as follows.

Replace computer.

E	INSPECTION OF STOP LIGHT SWITCH CIRCUIT

Turn ignition switch on.

Is STOP fuse normal ?

→ No → Short circuit in wire harness between terminal 16 of computer and fuse.

↓ Yes

STOP LIGHT S/W

INSPECT STOP LIGHT SWITCH OPERATION

Is stop light switch operation normal ?

→ No → Replace stop light switch.

Cruise control trouble diagnosis chart—1986 and later Celica

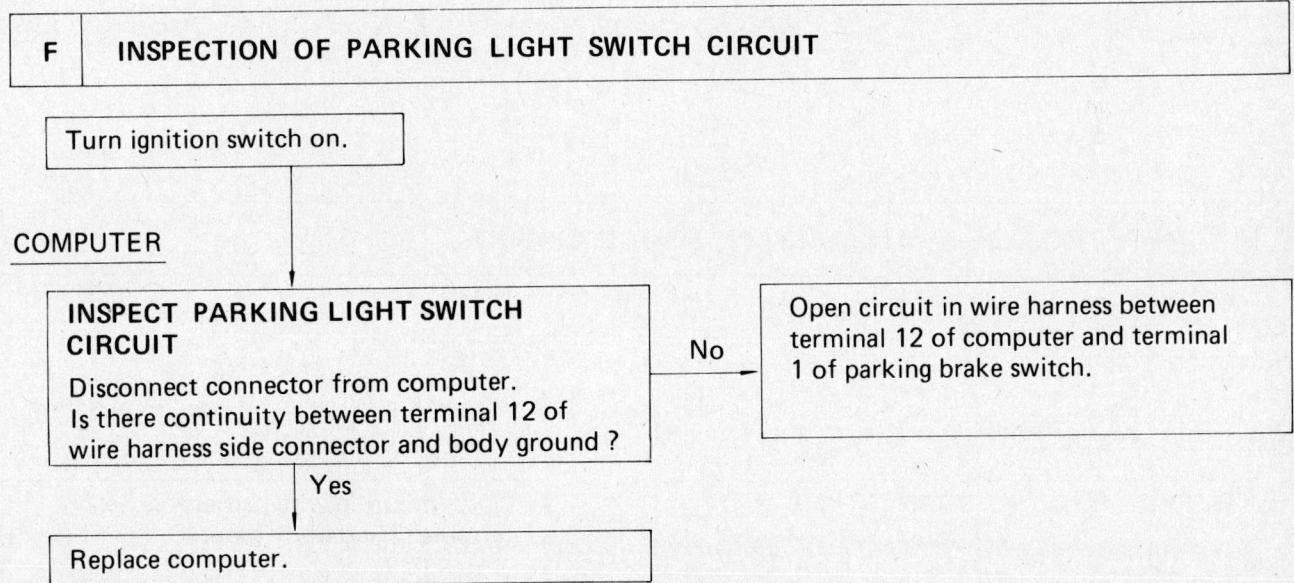

Yes

COMPUTER

Disconnect computer and inspect connector on wire harness side as follows.

INSPECT STOP FUSE CIRCUIT
Is there battery voltage between terminal 16 and body ground with brake pedal returned ?

No → Open circuit in wire harness between terminal 16 of computer and STOP fuse.

Yes

INSPECT STOP LIGHT SWITCH CIRCUIT
Is there battery voltage between terminal 15 and body ground with brake pedal depressed ?

No → Open circuit in wire harness between terminal 15 of computer and terminal 3 of stop light switch.

Yes

Replace computer.

F	INSPECTION OF PARKING LIGHT SWITCH CIRCUIT

Turn ignition switch on.

COMPUTER

INSPECT PARKING LIGHT SWITCH CIRCUIT
Disconnect connector from computer.
Is there continuity between terminal 12 of wire harness side connector and body ground ?

No → Open circuit in wire harness between terminal 12 of computer and terminal 1 of parking brake switch.

Yes

Replace computer.

Cruise control trouble diagnosis chart—1986 and later Celica

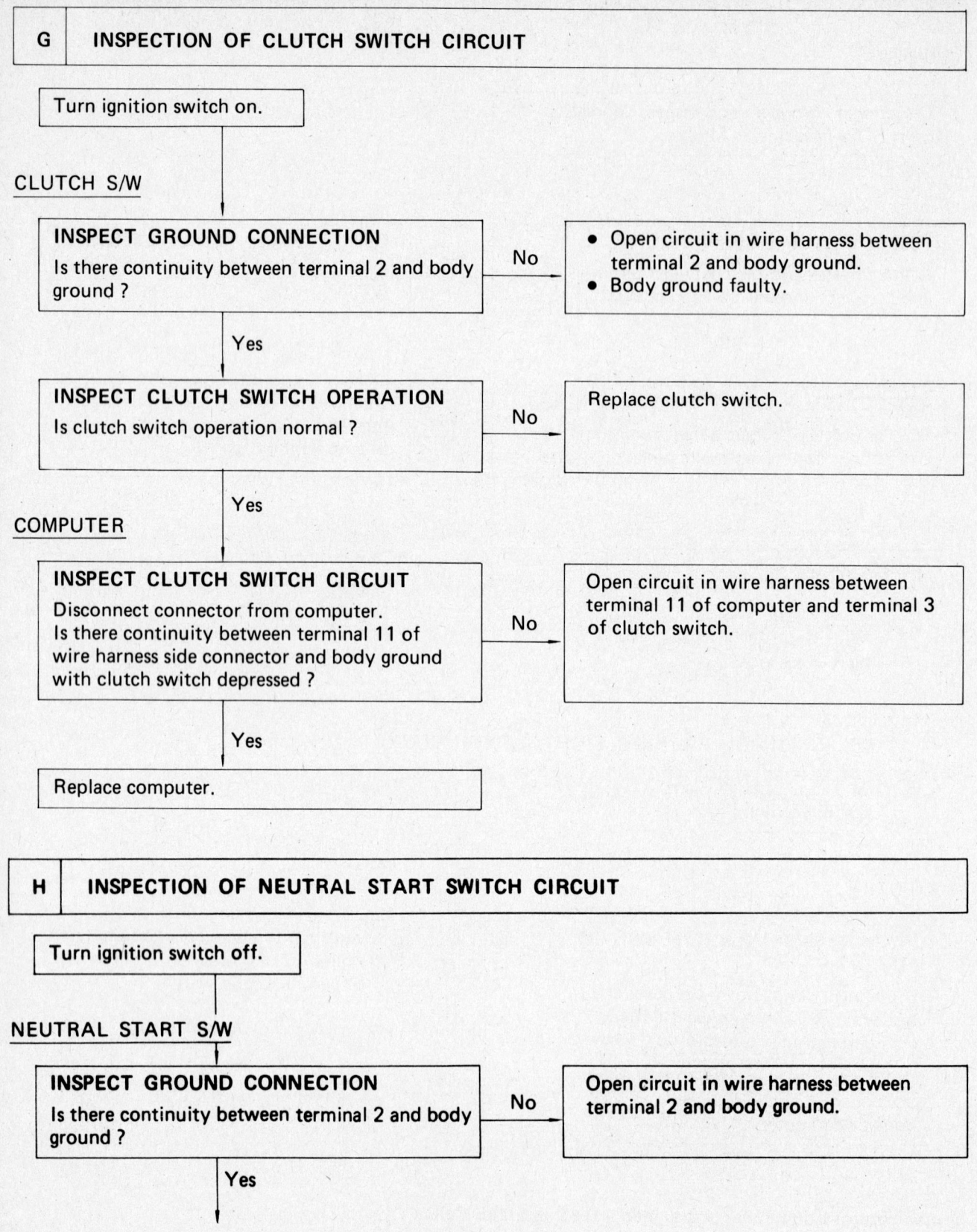

| G | INSPECTION OF CLUTCH SWITCH CIRCUIT |

Turn ignition switch on.

CLUTCH S/W

INSPECT GROUND CONNECTION
Is there continuity between terminal 2 and body ground ?

→ No →
- Open circuit in wire harness between terminal 2 and body ground.
- Body ground faulty.

Yes

INSPECT CLUTCH SWITCH OPERATION
Is clutch switch operation normal ?

→ No → Replace clutch switch.

Yes

COMPUTER

INSPECT CLUTCH SWITCH CIRCUIT
Disconnect connector from computer.
Is there continuity between terminal 11 of wire harness side connector and body ground with clutch switch depressed ?

→ No → Open circuit in wire harness between terminal 11 of computer and terminal 3 of clutch switch.

Yes

Replace computer.

| H | INSPECTION OF NEUTRAL START SWITCH CIRCUIT |

Turn ignition switch off.

NEUTRAL START S/W

INSPECT GROUND CONNECTION
Is there continuity between terminal 2 and body ground ?

→ No → Open circuit in wire harness between terminal 2 and body ground.

Yes

Cruise control trouble diagnosis chart – 1986 and later Celica

---

INSPECT NEUTRAL START SWITCH OPERATION

Is neutral start switch operation normal ?

No → Replace neutral start switch.

Yes ↓

COMPUTER

INSPECT NEUTRAL START SWITCH CIRCUIT

Disconnect connector from computer.
Is there continuity between terminal 11 of wire harness side connector and body ground when shifted to "N" range ?

No → Open circuit in wire harness between terminal 11 of computer and terminal 3 of neutral start switch.

Yes ↓

Replace computer.

I	INSPECTION OF SPEED SENSOR CIRCUIT

Turn ignition switch on.

SPEED SENSOR

INSPECT GROUND CONNECTION

Disconnect connector from speed sensor.
Is there continuity between terminal 2 of wire harness side connector and body ground ?

No →
- Open circuit in wire harness between terminal 2 and body ground.
- Body ground faulty.

Yes ↓

INSPECT SPEED SENSOR OPERATION

Is speed sensor operation normal ?

No → Speed sensor faulty.

Yes ↓

COMPUTER

Disconnect connector from speed sensor.
Is there continuity between terminal 1 of wire harness side connector and terminal 7 of computer ?

No → Open circuit in wire harness between terminal 1 of speed sensor and terminal 7 of computer.

Yes ↓

Replace computer.

Cruise control trouble diagnosis chart—1986 and later Celica

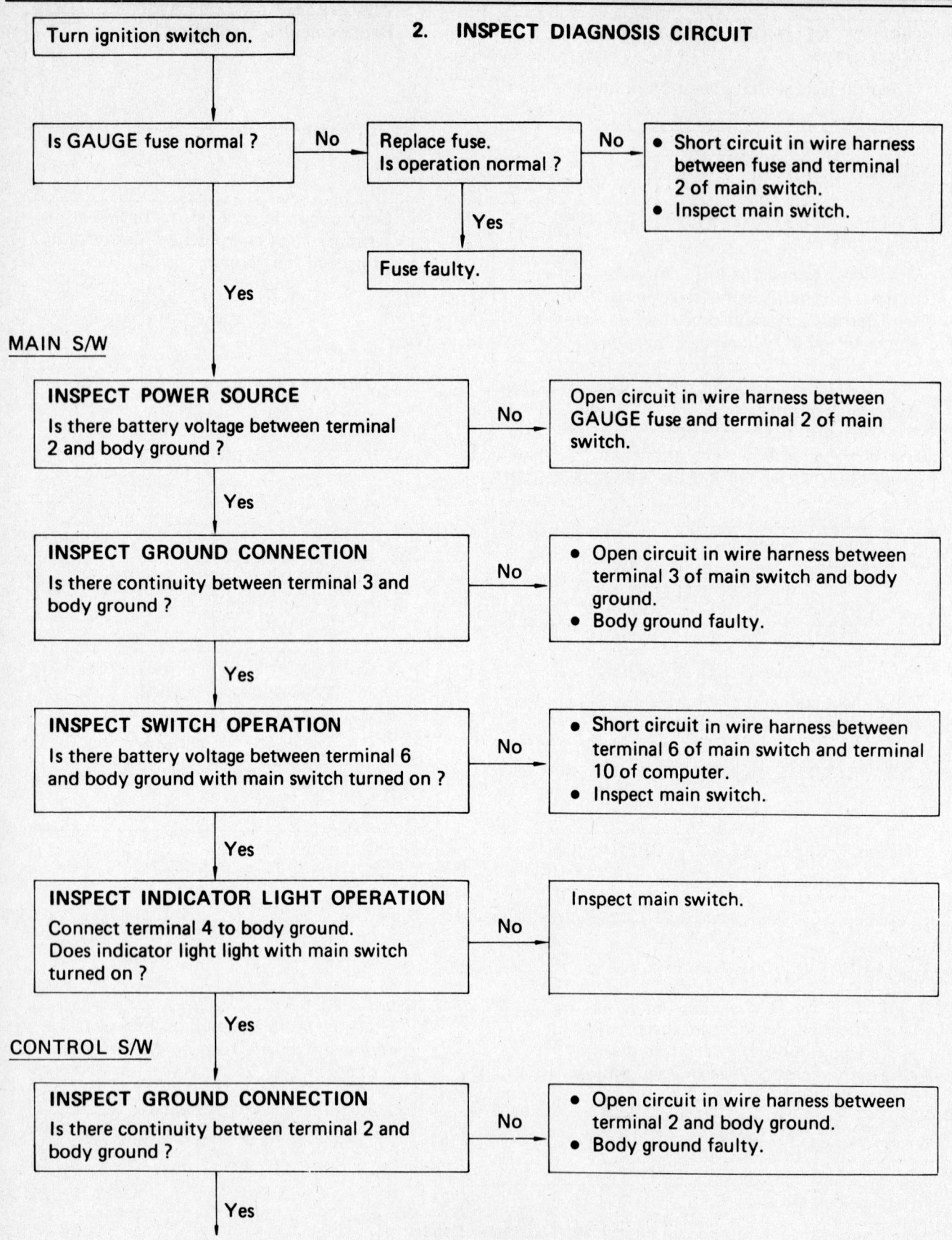

2. INSPECT DIAGNOSIS CIRCUIT

Turn ignition switch on.

Is GAUGE fuse normal ? — **No** → Replace fuse. Is operation normal ? — **No** → • Short circuit in wire harness between fuse and terminal 2 of main switch. • Inspect main switch.

↓ **Yes** → Fuse faulty.

Yes

MAIN S/W

INSPECT POWER SOURCE
Is there battery voltage between terminal 2 and body ground ? — **No** → Open circuit in wire harness between GAUGE fuse and terminal 2 of main switch.

Yes

INSPECT GROUND CONNECTION
Is there continuity between terminal 3 and body ground ? — **No** → • Open circuit in wire harness between terminal 3 of main switch and body ground. • Body ground faulty.

Yes

INSPECT SWITCH OPERATION
Is there battery voltage between terminal 6 and body ground with main switch turned on ? — **No** → • Short circuit in wire harness between terminal 6 of main switch and terminal 10 of computer. • Inspect main switch.

Yes

INSPECT INDICATOR LIGHT OPERATION
Connect terminal 4 to body ground. Does indicator light light with main switch turned on ? — **No** → Inspect main switch.

Yes

CONTROL S/W

INSPECT GROUND CONNECTION
Is there continuity between terminal 2 and body ground ? — **No** → • Open circuit in wire harness between terminal 2 and body ground. • Body ground faulty.

Yes

Cruise control trouble diagnosis chart – 1986 and later Celica

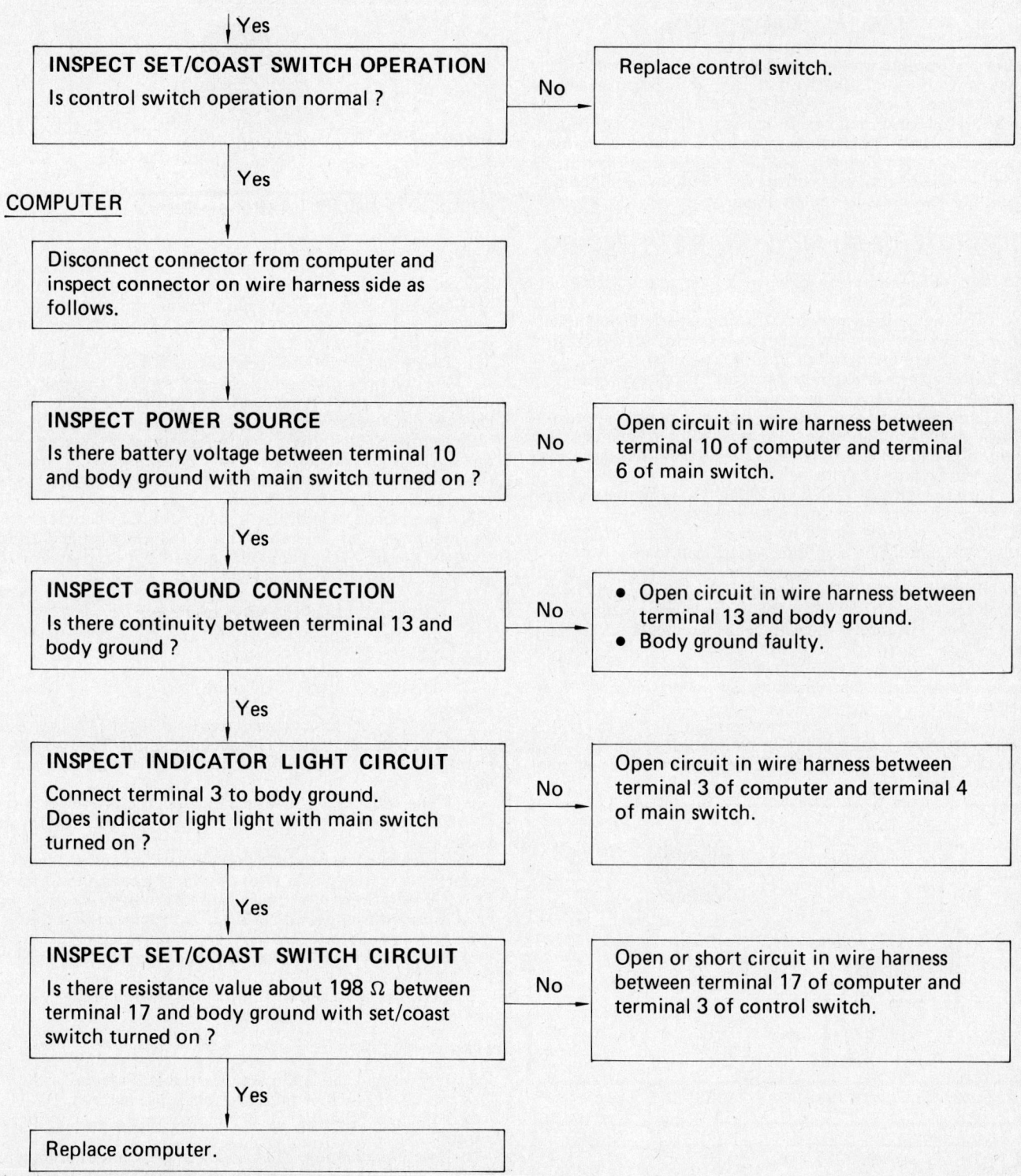

Yes

INSPECT SET/COAST SWITCH OPERATION
Is control switch operation normal ?
→ No → Replace control switch.

Yes

COMPUTER

Disconnect connector from computer and inspect connector on wire harness side as follows.

INSPECT POWER SOURCE
Is there battery voltage between terminal 10 and body ground with main switch turned on ?
→ No → Open circuit in wire harness between terminal 10 of computer and terminal 6 of main switch.

Yes

INSPECT GROUND CONNECTION
Is there continuity between terminal 13 and body ground ?
→ No →
- Open circuit in wire harness between terminal 13 and body ground.
- Body ground faulty.

Yes

INSPECT INDICATOR LIGHT CIRCUIT
Connect terminal 3 to body ground.
Does indicator light light with main switch turned on ?
→ No → Open circuit in wire harness between terminal 3 of computer and terminal 4 of main switch.

Yes

INSPECT SET/COAST SWITCH CIRCUIT
Is there resistance value about 198 Ω between terminal 17 and body ground with set/coast switch turned on ?
→ No → Open or short circuit in wire harness between terminal 17 of computer and terminal 3 of control switch.

Yes

Replace computer.

Cruise control trouble diagnosis chart – 1986 and later Celica

Camry

VISUAL INSPECTION

Before performing any tests make a visual inspection of the cruise control system. Check all items in the system for abnormal conditions such as bare broken or disconnected wires and damage to the vacuum hoses. Be sure that the speedometer cables are attached and properly routed. All vacuum hoses must be properly routed and must not have any kinks or bends. Be sure that all electrical connections are complete and tight. The wiring harness must be routed properly.

COMPUTER AND SENSOR TEST (1983–84)

1. Remove the right side kick panel. Unplug the wiring harness from the computer.
2. Turn the ignition switch to the on position. Using a voltmeter measure the voltage between terminal seven and ground with the main switch in the on position.
3. Battery voltage should be present. If battery voltage is not present, check the main switch.
4. Using the voltmeter measure the voltage between terminal twelve and ground. When the parking brake lever is pulled the voltage should be zero. When the lever is returned the voltage should be 0 to 14 volts.
5. Turn the ignition switch off. Using the voltmeter measure the voltage between terminal nine and ground.
6. Battery voltage should be present. If battery voltage is not present, check the stop light switch and fuse.
7. Using the voltmeter measure the voltage between terminal eight and ground. When the parking brake lever is pulled the voltage should be 12 volts. When the lever is returned the voltage should be zero. If the voltage is incorrect check the stop light switch.
8. Turn the ignition switch to the accessory position. Using an ohmmeter check for continuity between terminal eleven and ground.
9. If equipped with manual transmission depress the clutch pedal (automatic transmission in neutral), if continuity does not exist between the terminals check the clutch or neutral safety switch.

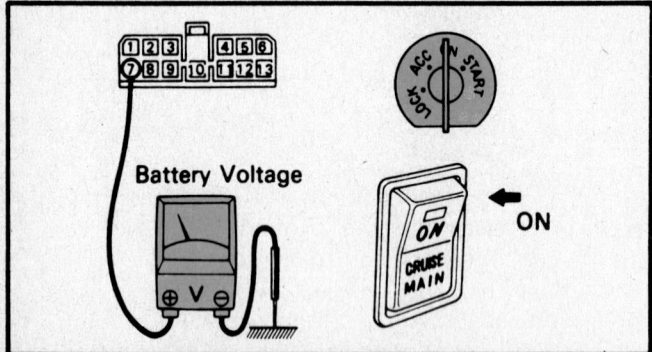

Computer test point locations – 1983–84 Camry

Switch position \ Terminal	1	2	3	4	5
ACCEL (RESUME)	○—○		○—○		
CRUISE	○—○				
COAST (SET)	○—○			○—○	

Control switch specifications – 1983–84 Camry

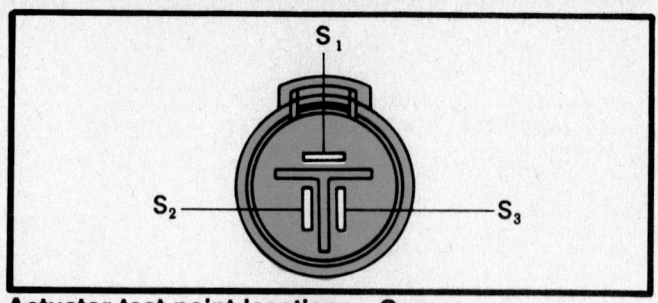

Actuator test point locations – Camry

10. Using an ohmmeter measure the resistance between terminals one and two. The resistance should be about 68 ohms. Measure the resistance between terminals two and three. The resistance should be about 30 ohms. If the readings are not correct check the actuator.
11. Using an ohmmeter check the continuity between terminal four and ground when the control switch is pushed to the set position. If there is no continuity between the terminals check the control switch.
12. Using an ohmmeter check the continuity between terminal thirteen and ground when the control switch is pushed to the resume position. If there is no continuity between the terminals check the control switch.
13. Using an ohmmeter check the continuity between terminal six and ground when the vehicle is slightly pushed. At this time the needle on the ohmmeter should move repeatedly from on to off. If not check the speed sensor.

ACTUATOR TEST

1983–84

1. Disconnect the electrical connector from the actuator lead wire.
2. Using an ohmmeter measure the resistance between terminals S1 and S2. It should be about 68 ohms. Measure the resistance between terminals S1 and S3. It should be about 30 ohms.
3. If the resistance is not as indicated, replace the actuator.
4. Disconnect the carburetor throttle rod from the throttle body.
5. Check that the actuator diaphragm makes a smooth reciprocating motion when either power is applied to terminals S1 or S2 with the actuator terminal S3 grounded or when power is removed from terminal S2. If not replace the actuator.
6. Be sure that the cable does not return to easy when pulled with about 4 to 7 lbs. of force. Repair or replace defective components as required.
7. Check to be sure that the vacuum hose is properly routed and connected. Correct as required.

1985 and Later

1. Inspect and check the actuator cable. Freeplay should be less than 0.039 inch. Adjust or replace as required.
2. Disconnect the electrical connector from the actuator lead wire.
3. Using an ohmmeter measure the resistance between terminals one and two. It should be about 30 ohms. Measure the resistance between terminals one and three. It should be about 68 ohms.
4. If the resistance is not as indicated, replace the actuator.
5. Connect a positive lead from the positive terminal of the battery to terminals two and three. Connect a negative lead from the negative terminal of the battery to terminal one.
6. Slowly apply 0 to 11.8 in. hg. of vacuum. Check to be sure that the control cable can be pulled smoothly.

Terminal	Connection or Measure Item	Check Item	Tester Connection	Condition	Voltage or Resistance Value
2	Stop Light Switch and Release Valve	Resistance	2–14	Brake pedal returned	About 68 Ω
3	Main Switch	Voltage	3–Body Ground	Turn ignition switch and/or main switch on	Battery voltage
				Turn ignition switch and main switch off	No voltage
4	Control Valve	Resistance	4–14	—	About 30 Ω
5	Control Switch (Set/Coast)	Continuity	5–Body Ground	Turn set/coast switch on	Continuity
				Turn set/coast switch off	No continuity
6	ECT Computer or OD Main Switch	—	—		—
7	Speed Sensor (Analog Meter)	Continuity	7–Body Ground	Vehicle moving slowly	1 pulse each 40 cm (15.75 in.)
	Speed Sensor (Digital Meter)	Voltage	7–Body Ground	Turn ignition switch on and vehicle moving slowly	More than 4V pluse each 40 cm (15.75 in.)
10	Main Switch	Voltage	10–Body Ground	Turn ignition switch and main switch on	Battery voltage
				Turn ignition switch and/or main switch off	No voltage
11	Clutch Switch (M/T) Neutral start switch (A/T)	Continuity	11–Body Ground	Clutch pedal depressed or shift into "N" range	Continuity
				Clutch pedal returned or shift into except "N" range	No continuity
12	Parking Brake Switch	Continuity	12–Body Ground	Parking brake pulled	Continuity
				Parking brake returned	No continuity
13	Body Ground	Continuity	13–Body Ground	—	Continuity
14	Release Valve and Control Valve	—	—	—	—
15	Stop Light Switch	Voltage	15–Body Ground	Brake pedal depressed	Battery voltage
				Brake pedal returned	No voltage
16	STOP Fuse	Voltage	16–Body Ground	—	Battery voltage
17	Control Switch (Accel/Resume)	Continuity	17–Body Ground	Turn accel/resume switch on	Continuity
				Turn accel/resume switch off	No continuity

Cruise control computer circuit inspection chart — 1985 and later Camry

7. When the vacuum has stabilized check the control cable and be sure that it does not return.

8. Disconnect terminal two or three and check that the control cable returns to its original position and that the vacuum goes to zero.

9. If the system does not perform as indicated replace the actuator.

SPEED SENSOR TEST

1. Using an ohmmeter, check to see that there is continuity between terminals A and B. It should be four times per revolution of the magnet shaft.

2. If continuity does not exist replace the speed sensor.

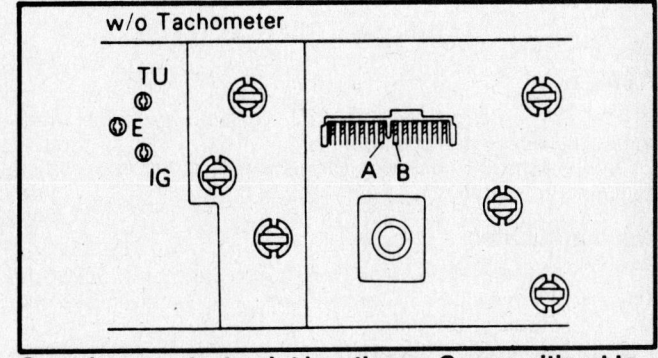

Speed sensor test point locations — Camry without tachometer and with regular speedometer

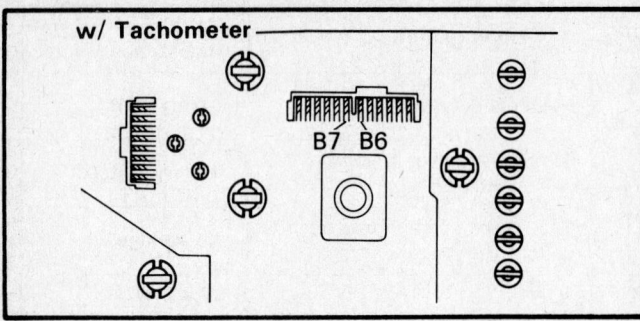

Speed sensor test point locations—Camry with tachometer and digital speedometer

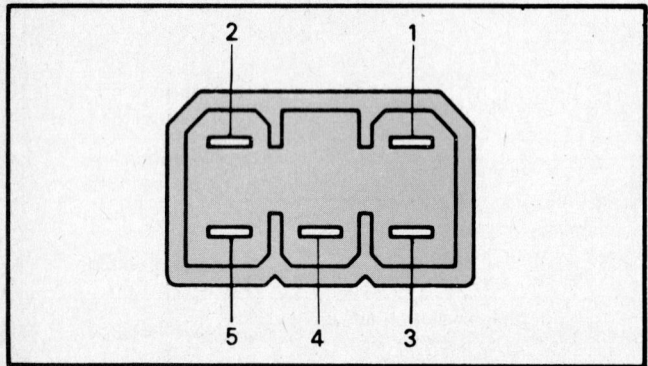

Main switch test point locations—1983–84 Camry

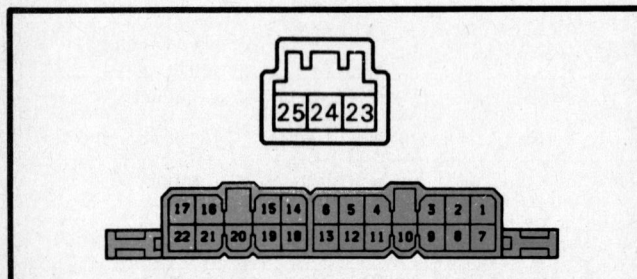

Control switch test point locations—1985 and later Camry

CONTROL SWITCH TEST

1. Using an ohmmeter check for continuity of the terminals for each switch position.
2. If continuity between the terminals is not as specified, replace the switch.

MAIN SWITCH TEST

1983–84

1. Using an ohmmeter check for continuity of the terminals for each switch position.
2. If continuity between the terminals is not as specified, replace the switch.

1985 and Later

1. Connect a positive lead from the positive terminal of the battery to terminal two. Connect a negative lead from the negative terminal of the battery to terminal three.
2. Check to be sure that continuity exists between terminals two and six with the main switch turned on.

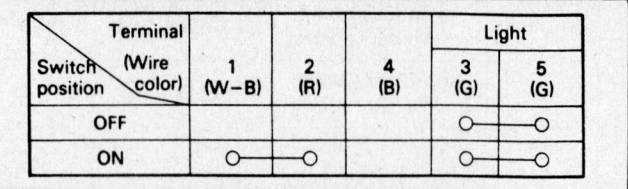

Switch position	Terminal (Wire color)	1 (W–B)	2 (R)	4 (B)	Light 3 (G)	Light 5 (G)
OFF					○———	———○
ON		○———	———○		○———	———○

Main switch specifications—1983–84 Camry

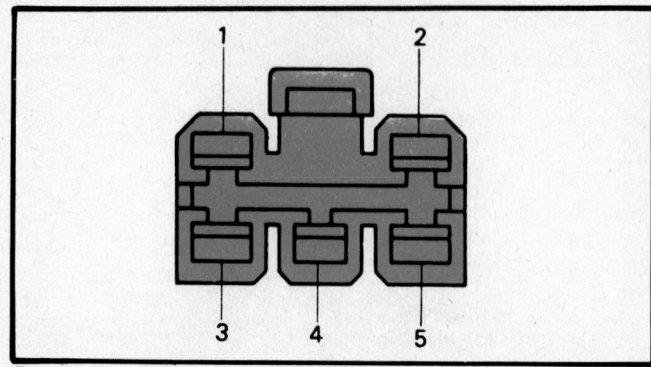

Control switch test point locations—1983–84 Camry

Switch position	Terminal	14	23	25
ACCEL/RESUME		○———	———○	
OFF				
SET/COAST		○———		———○

Control switch specifications—1985 and later Camry

3. Check that there is no continuity between terminals two and six with the main switch off.
4. If the above results are not achieved, replace the switch.

CLUTCH SWITCH TEST (1985 AND LATER)

1. Check to be sure that there is continuity between terminals two and three with the clutch pedal depressed.
2. Check to be sure that there is continuity between terminals two and three with the clutch pedal returned.
3. If continuity is not as indicated, replace the clutch switch.

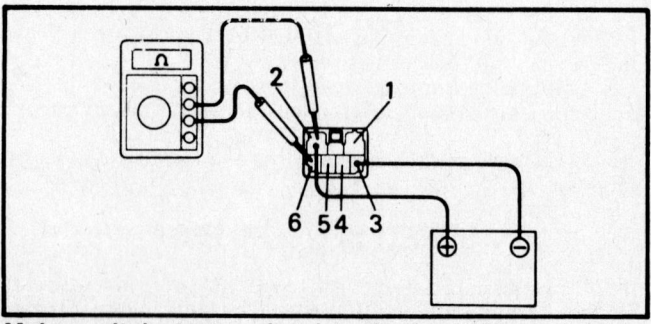

Main switch test point locations—1985 and later Camry

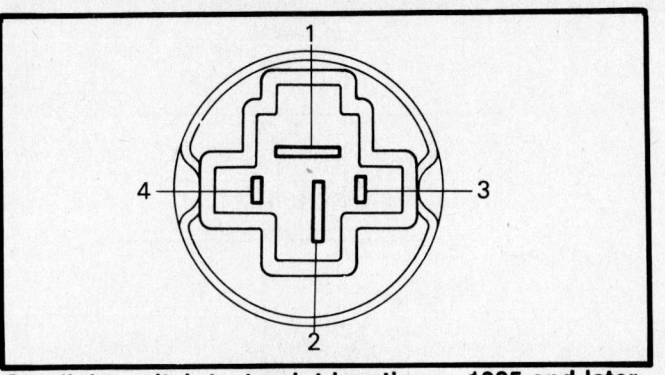

Stoplight switch test point locations – 1985 and later Camry

Clutch start switch test point locations – 1985 and later Camry

STOP LIGHT SWITCH TEST (1985 AND LATER)

1. Using an ohmmeter check for continunity of the terminals for each switch position.
2. If continuity between the terminals is not as specified, replace the switch.

Terminal Brake pedal position	1	2	3	4
Brake pedal depressed	○	○		
Brake pedal returned			○	○

Stoplight specifications – 1985 and later Camry

DIAGNOSIS AND TESTING PROCEDURES

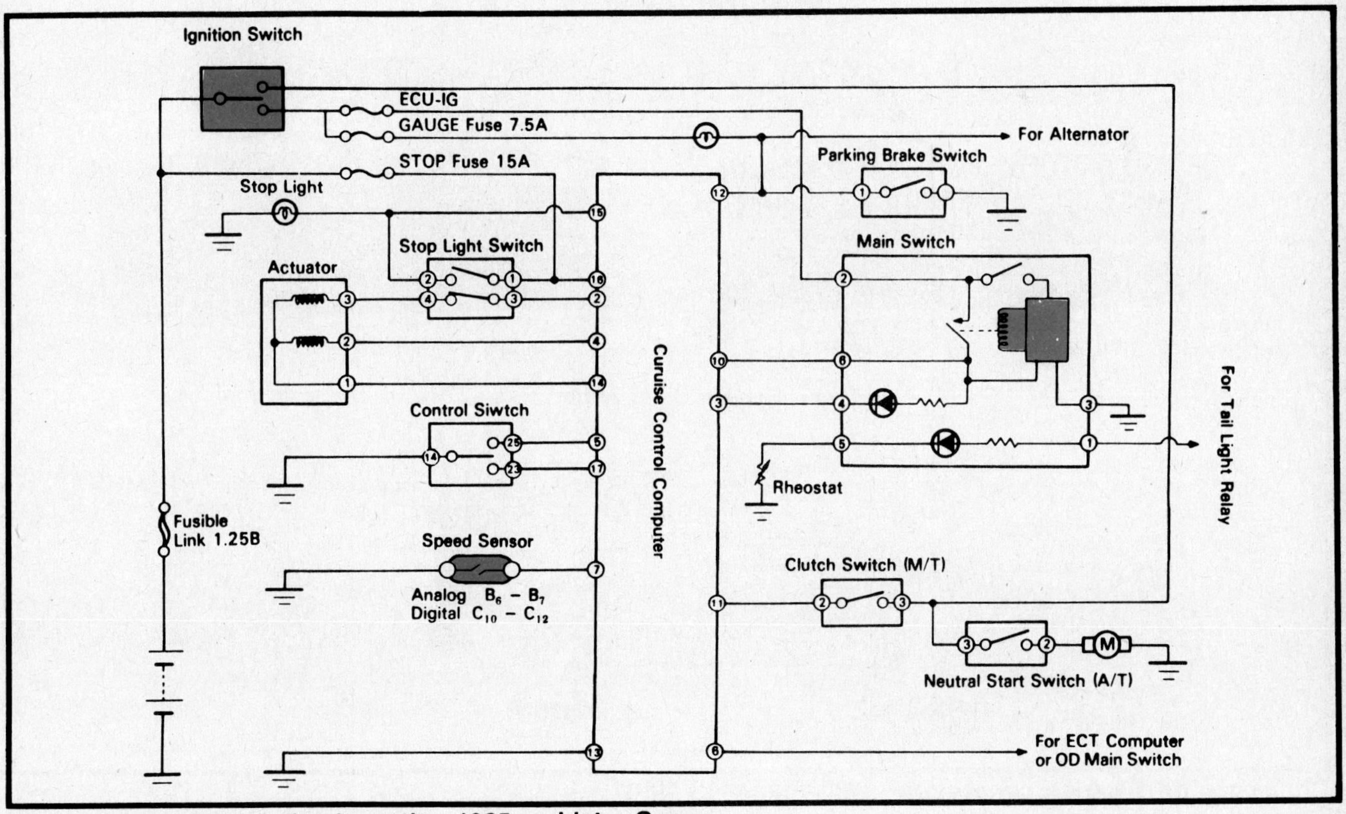

Cruise control electrical schematic – 1985 and later Camry

1179

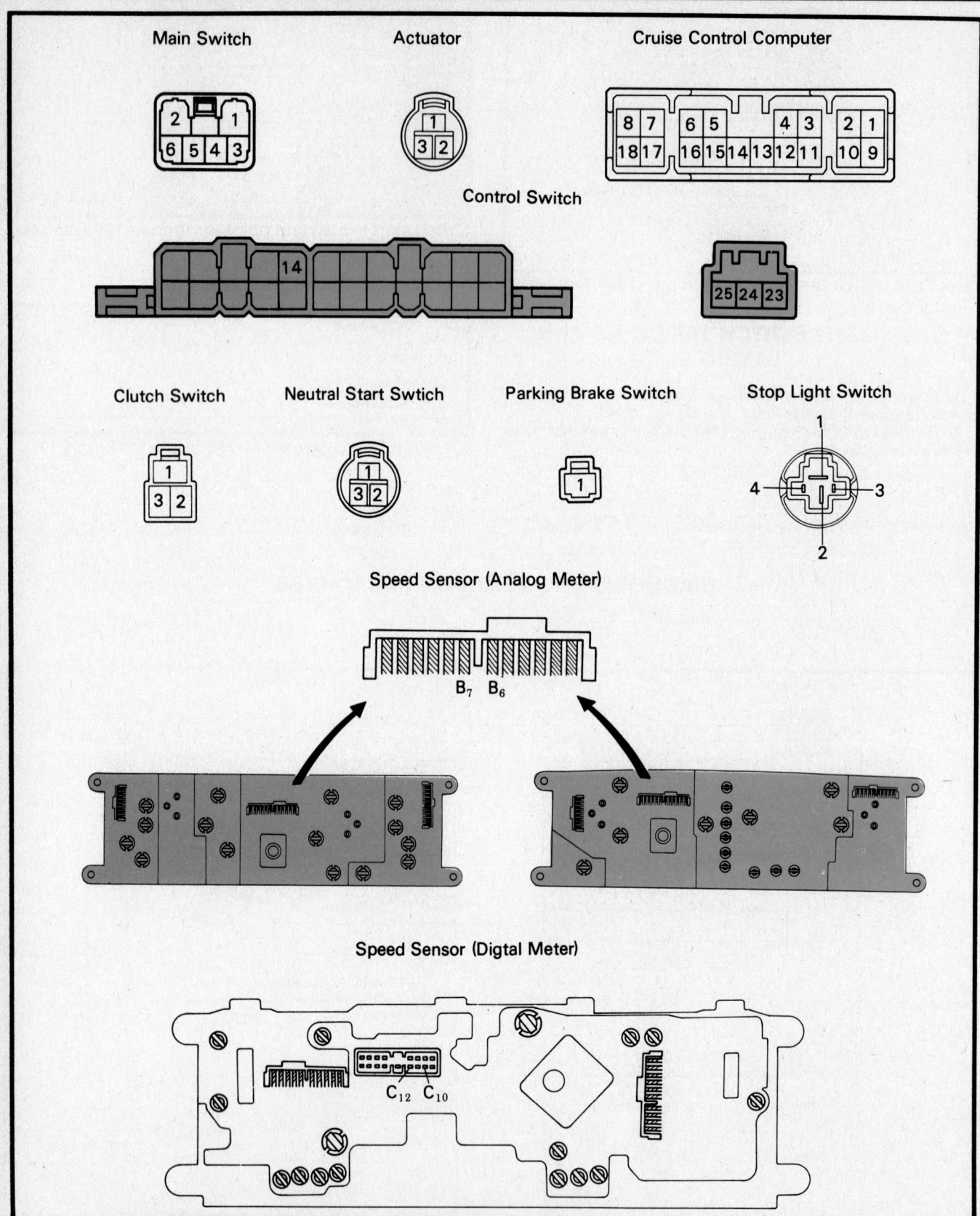

Cruise control electrical connectors—1985 and later Camry

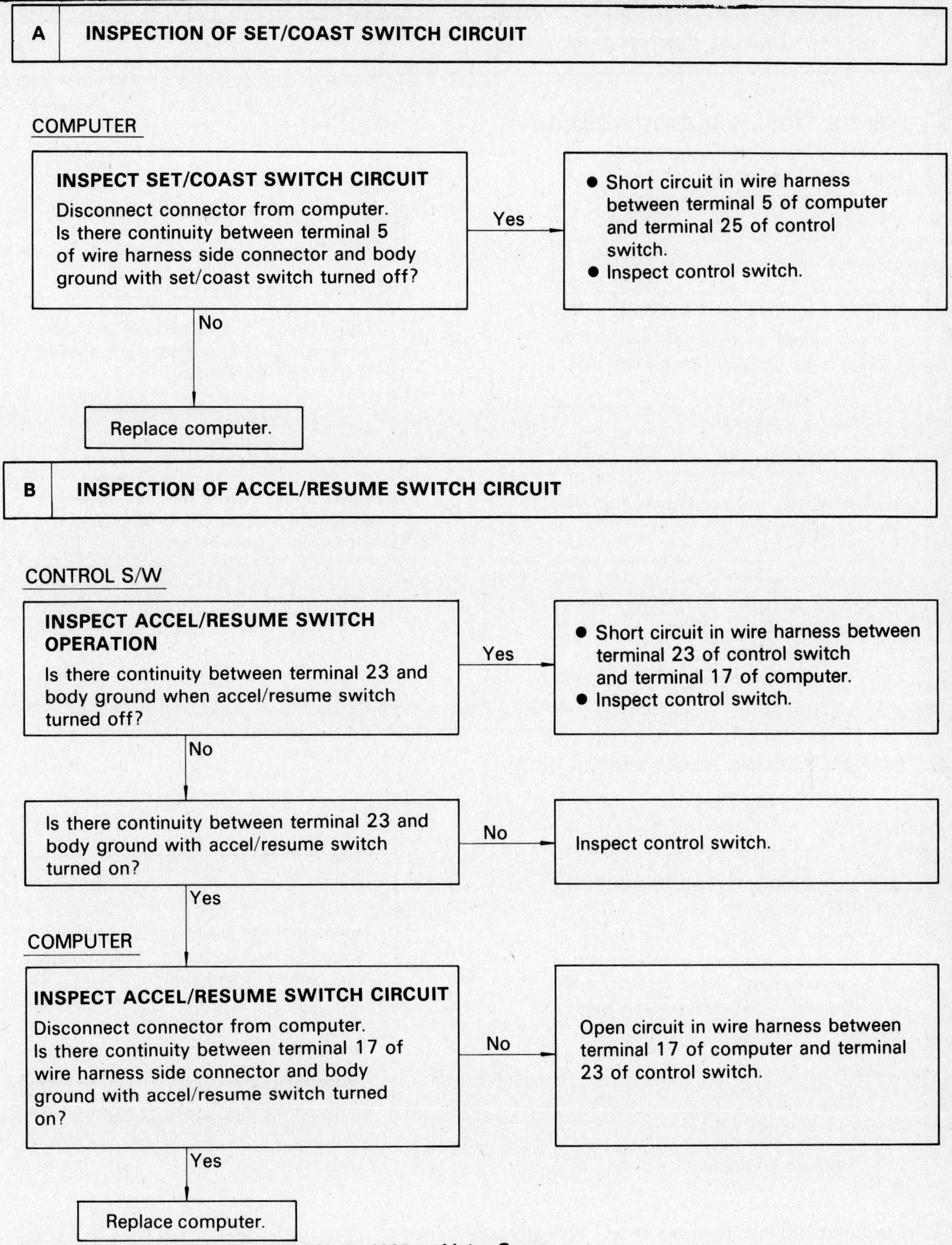

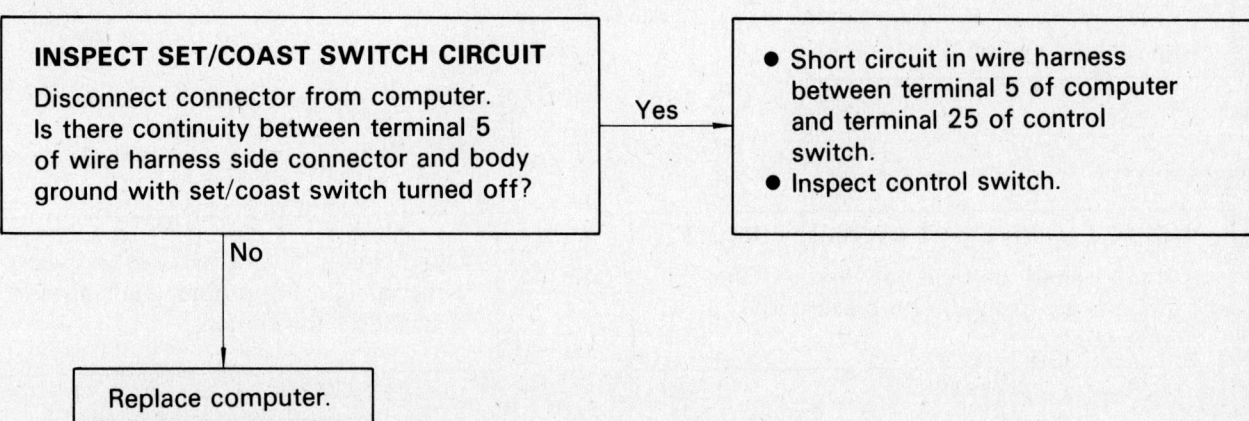

A | **INSPECTION OF SET/COAST SWITCH CIRCUIT**

COMPUTER

INSPECT SET/COAST SWITCH CIRCUIT
Disconnect connector from computer.
Is there continuity between terminal 5
of wire harness side connector and body
ground with set/coast switch turned off?

Yes →

- Short circuit in wire harness
  between terminal 5 of computer
  and terminal 25 of control
  switch.
- Inspect control switch.

No ↓

Replace computer.

B | **INSPECTION OF ACCEL/RESUME SWITCH CIRCUIT**

CONTROL S/W

**INSPECT ACCEL/RESUME SWITCH
OPERATION**
Is there continuity between terminal 23 and
body ground when accel/resume switch
turned off?

Yes →

- Short circuit in wire harness between
  terminal 23 of control switch
  and terminal 17 of computer.
- Inspect control switch.

No ↓

Is there continuity between terminal 23 and
body ground with accel/resume switch
turned on?

No → Inspect control switch.

Yes ↓

COMPUTER

INSPECT ACCEL/RESUME SWITCH CIRCUIT
Disconnect connector from computer.
Is there continuity between terminal 17 of
wire harness side connector and body
ground with accel/resume switch turned
on?

No →

Open circuit in wire harness between
terminal 17 of computer and terminal
23 of control switch.

Yes ↓

Replace computer.

Cruise control trouble diagnosis chart — 1985 and later Camry

1181

C	INSPECT CANCEL SWITCH CIRCUIT

1. INSPECT STOP LIGHT SWITCH CIRCUIT

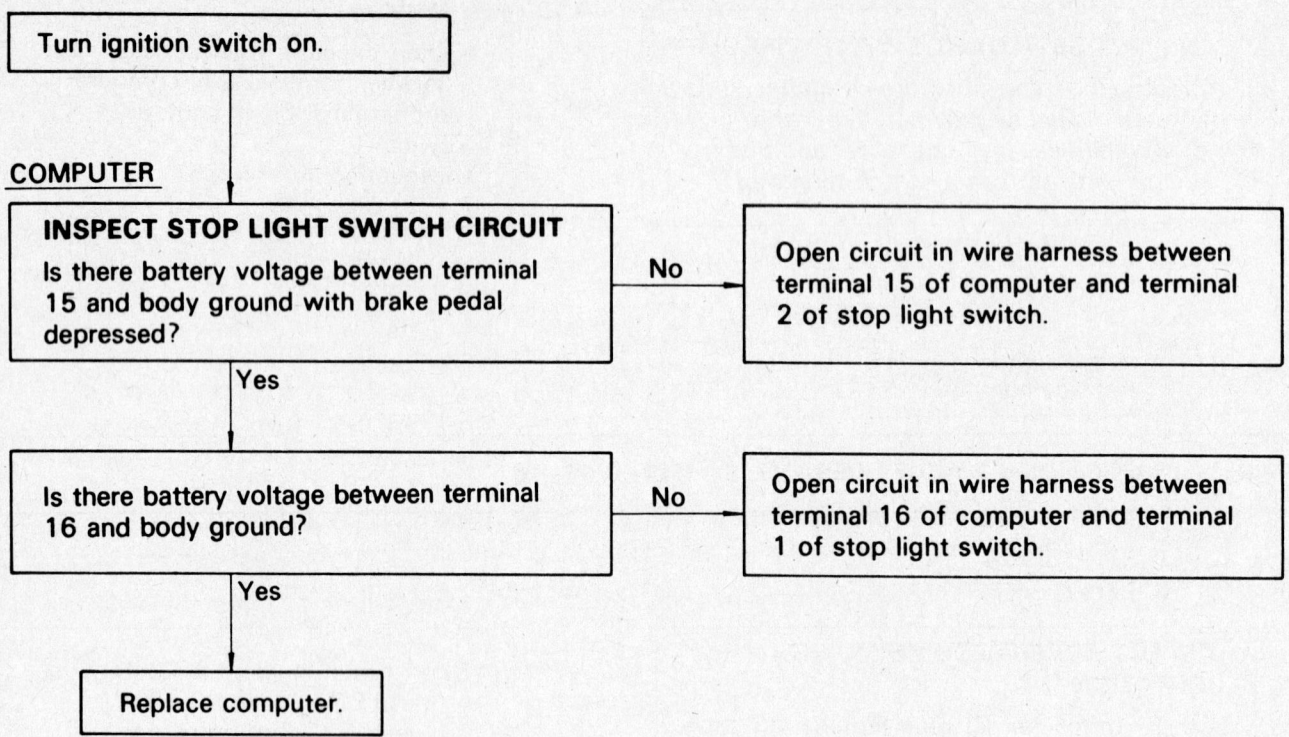

Turn ignition switch on.

COMPUTER

INSPECT STOP LIGHT SWITCH CIRCUIT

Is there battery voltage between terminal 15 and body ground with brake pedal depressed?

No → Open circuit in wire harness between terminal 15 of computer and terminal 2 of stop light switch.

Yes

Is there battery voltage between terminal 16 and body ground?

No → Open circuit in wire harness between terminal 16 of computer and terminal 1 of stop light switch.

Yes

Replace computer.

2. INSPECT PARKING BRAKE SWITCH CIRCUIT

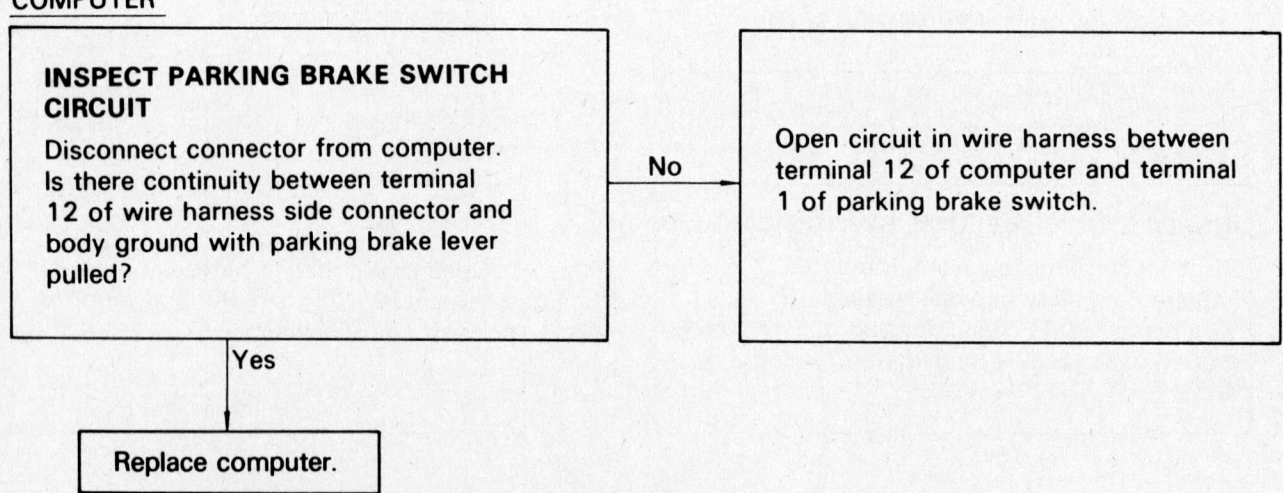

COMPUTER

INSPECT PARKING BRAKE SWITCH CIRCUIT

Disconnect connector from computer. Is there continuity between terminal 12 of wire harness side connector and body ground with parking brake lever pulled?

No → Open circuit in wire harness between terminal 12 of computer and terminal 1 of parking brake switch.

Yes

Replace computer.

Cruise control trouble diagnosis chart—1985 and later Camry

3. INSPECT CLUTCH SWITCH CIRCUIT (M/T)

CLUTCH S/W

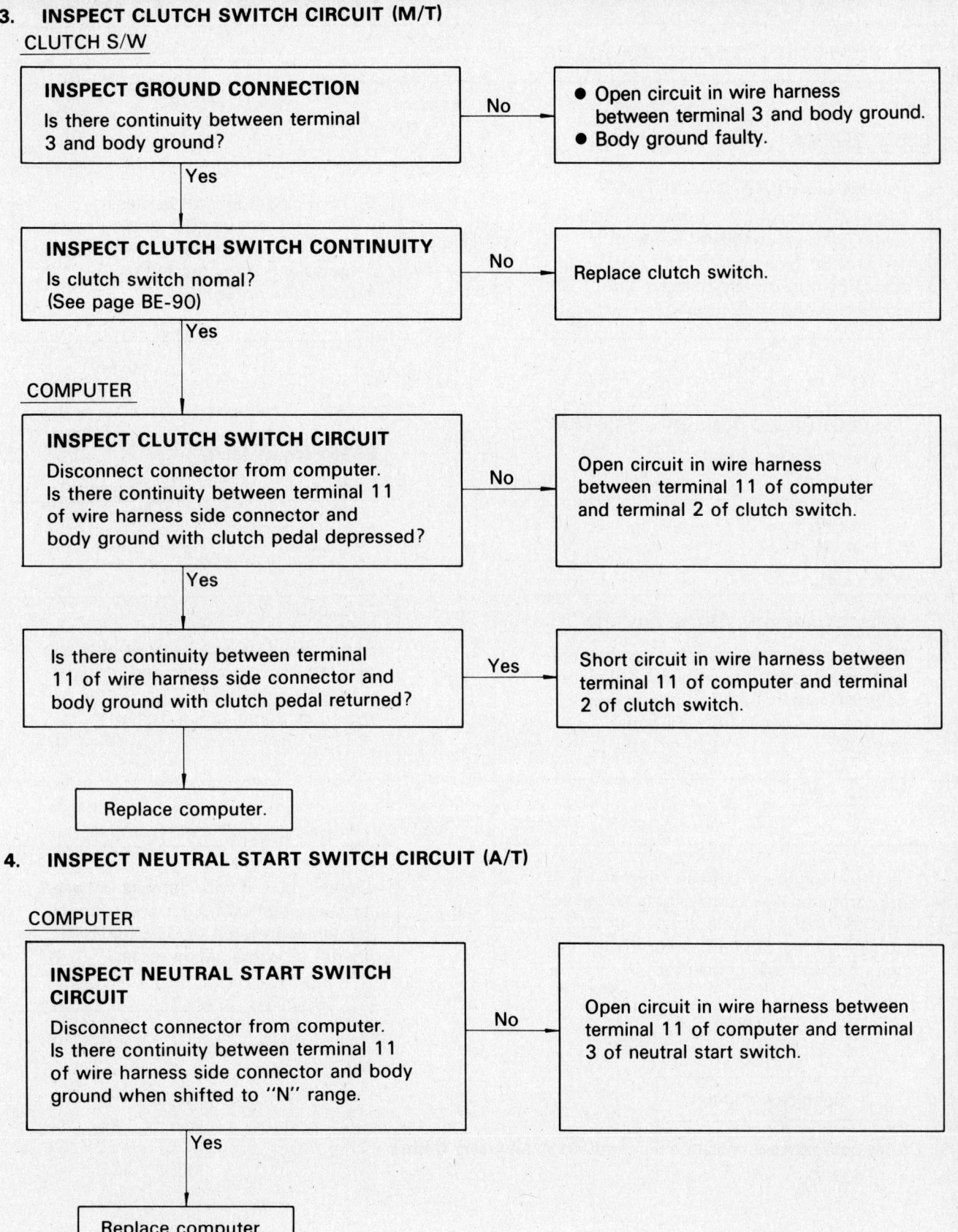

INSPECT GROUND CONNECTION

Is there continuity between terminal 3 and body ground?

No →
- Open circuit in wire harness between terminal 3 and body ground.
- Body ground faulty.

Yes ↓

INSPECT CLUTCH SWITCH CONTINUITY

Is clutch switch nomal?
(See page BE-90)

No → Replace clutch switch.

Yes ↓

COMPUTER

INSPECT CLUTCH SWITCH CIRCUIT

Disconnect connector from computer.
Is there continuity between terminal 11 of wire harness side connector and body ground with clutch pedal depressed?

No → Open circuit in wire harness between terminal 11 of computer and terminal 2 of clutch switch.

Yes ↓

Is there continuity between terminal 11 of wire harness side connector and body ground with clutch pedal returned?

Yes → Short circuit in wire harness between terminal 11 of computer and terminal 2 of clutch switch.

Replace computer.

4. INSPECT NEUTRAL START SWITCH CIRCUIT (A/T)

COMPUTER

INSPECT NEUTRAL START SWITCH CIRCUIT

Disconnect connector from computer.
Is there continuity between terminal 11 of wire harness side connector and body ground when shifted to "N" range.

No → Open circuit in wire harness between terminal 11 of computer and terminal 3 of neutral start switch.

Yes ↓

Replace computer.

Cruise control trouble diagnosis chart – 1985 and later Camry

D	INSPECTION OF SPEED SENSOR CIRCUIT

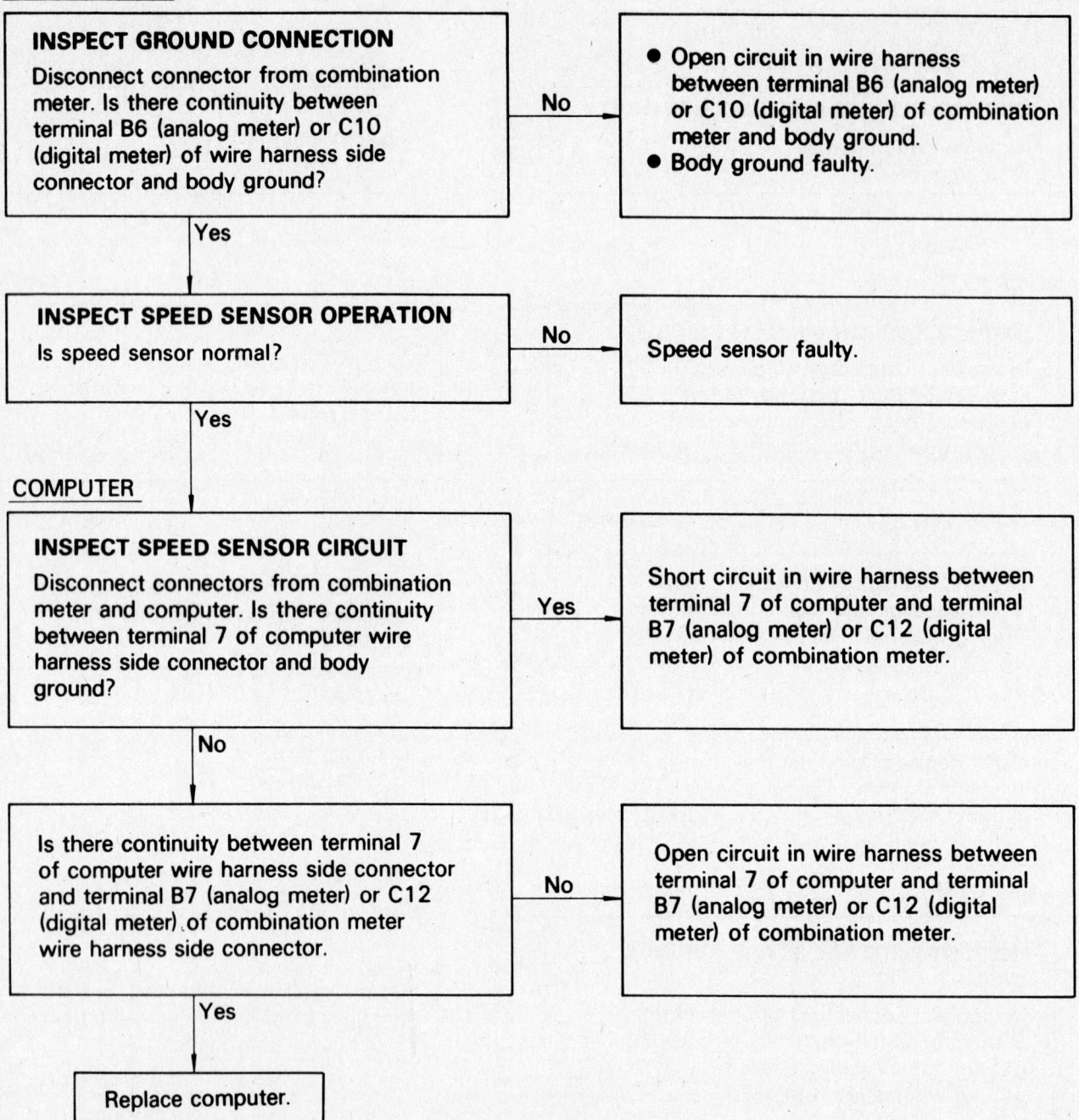

SPEED SENSOR

INSPECT GROUND CONNECTION
Disconnect connector from combination meter. Is there continuity between terminal B6 (analog meter) or C10 (digital meter) of wire harness side connector and body ground?

No →
- Open circuit in wire harness between terminal B6 (analog meter) or C10 (digital meter) of combination meter and body ground.
- Body ground faulty.

Yes ↓

INSPECT SPEED SENSOR OPERATION
Is speed sensor normal?

No → Speed sensor faulty.

Yes ↓

COMPUTER

INSPECT SPEED SENSOR CIRCUIT
Disconnect connectors from combination meter and computer. Is there continuity between terminal 7 of computer wire harness side connector and body ground?

Yes → Short circuit in wire harness between terminal 7 of computer and terminal B7 (analog meter) or C12 (digital meter) of combination meter.

No ↓

Is there continuity between terminal 7 of computer wire harness side connector and terminal B7 (analog meter) or C12 (digital meter) of combination meter wire harness side connector.

No → Open circuit in wire harness between terminal 7 of computer and terminal B7 (analog meter) or C12 (digital meter) of combination meter.

Yes ↓

Replace computer.

Cruise control trouble diagnosis chart — 1985 and later Camry

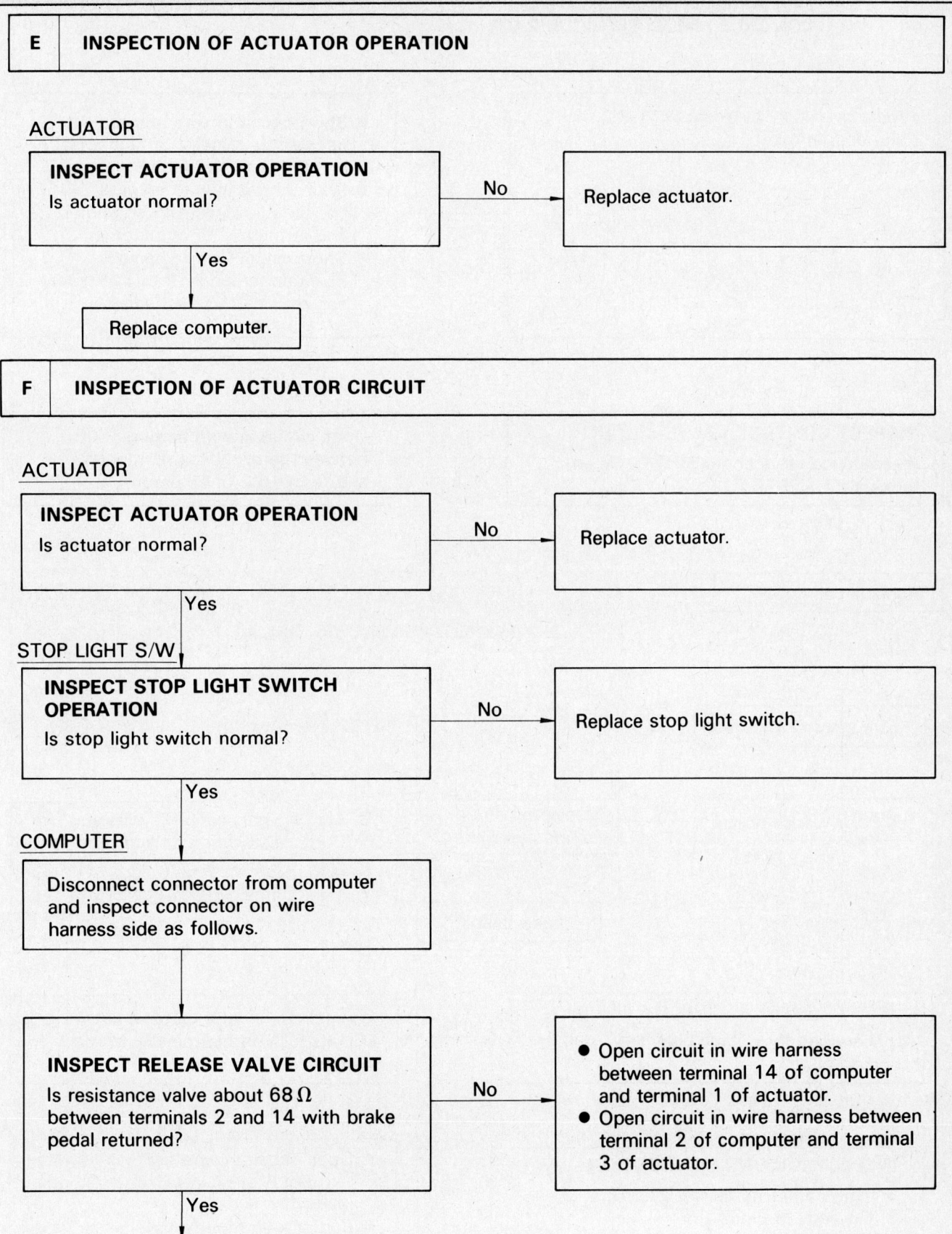

| E | INSPECTION OF ACTUATOR OPERATION |

ACTUATOR

INSPECT ACTUATOR OPERATION
Is actuator normal? — No → Replace actuator.

↓ Yes

Replace computer.

| F | INSPECTION OF ACTUATOR CIRCUIT |

ACTUATOR

INSPECT ACTUATOR OPERATION
Is actuator normal? — No → Replace actuator.

↓ Yes

STOP LIGHT S/W

INSPECT STOP LIGHT SWITCH OPERATION
Is stop light switch normal? — No → Replace stop light switch.

↓ Yes

COMPUTER

Disconnect connector from computer and inspect connector on wire harness side as follows.

↓

INSPECT RELEASE VALVE CIRCUIT
Is resistance valve about 68 Ω between terminals 2 and 14 with brake pedal returned? — No →

- Open circuit in wire harness between terminal 14 of computer and terminal 1 of actuator.
- Open circuit in wire harness between terminal 2 of computer and terminal 3 of actuator.

↓ Yes

Cruise control trouble diagnosis chart — 1985 and later Camry

1185

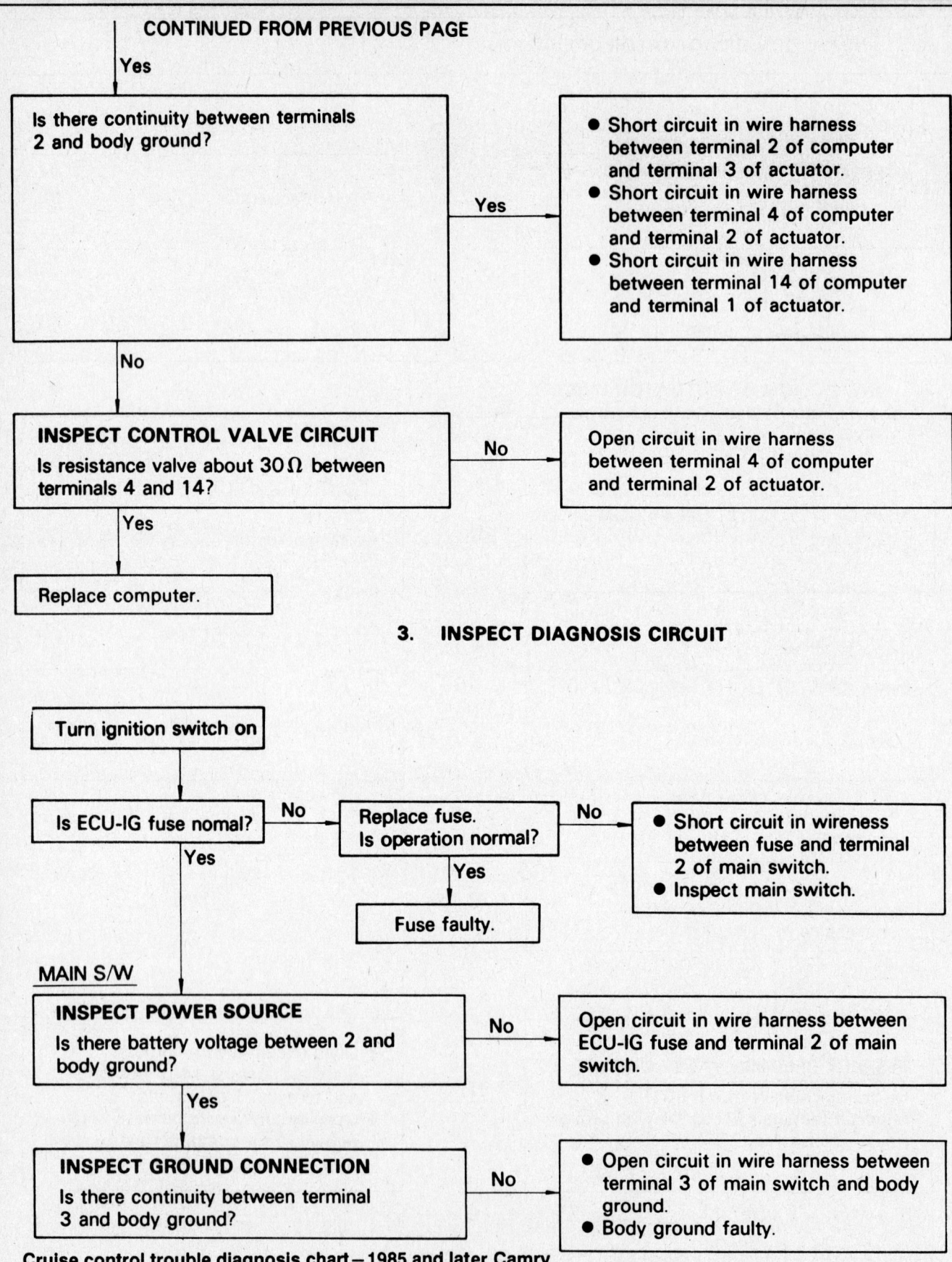

CONTINUED FROM PREVIOUS PAGE

Yes

Is there continuity between terminals 2 and body ground?

Yes →
- Short circuit in wire harness between terminal 2 of computer and terminal 3 of actuator.
- Short circuit in wire harness between terminal 4 of computer and terminal 2 of actuator.
- Short circuit in wire harness between terminal 14 of computer and terminal 1 of actuator.

No

INSPECT CONTROL VALVE CIRCUIT
Is resistance valve about 30 Ω between terminals 4 and 14?

No → Open circuit in wire harness between terminal 4 of computer and terminal 2 of actuator.

Yes

Replace computer.

3. INSPECT DIAGNOSIS CIRCUIT

Turn ignition switch on

Is ECU-IG fuse nomal?

No → Replace fuse. Is operation normal?

No →
- Short circuit in wireness between fuse and terminal 2 of main switch.
- Inspect main switch.

Yes

Fuse faulty.

MAIN S/W

INSPECT POWER SOURCE
Is there battery voltage between 2 and body ground?

No → Open circuit in wire harness between ECU-IG fuse and terminal 2 of main switch.

Yes

INSPECT GROUND CONNECTION
Is there continuity between terminal 3 and body ground?

No →
- Open circuit in wire harness between terminal 3 of main switch and body ground.
- Body ground faulty.

Cruise control trouble diagnosis chart — 1985 and later Camry

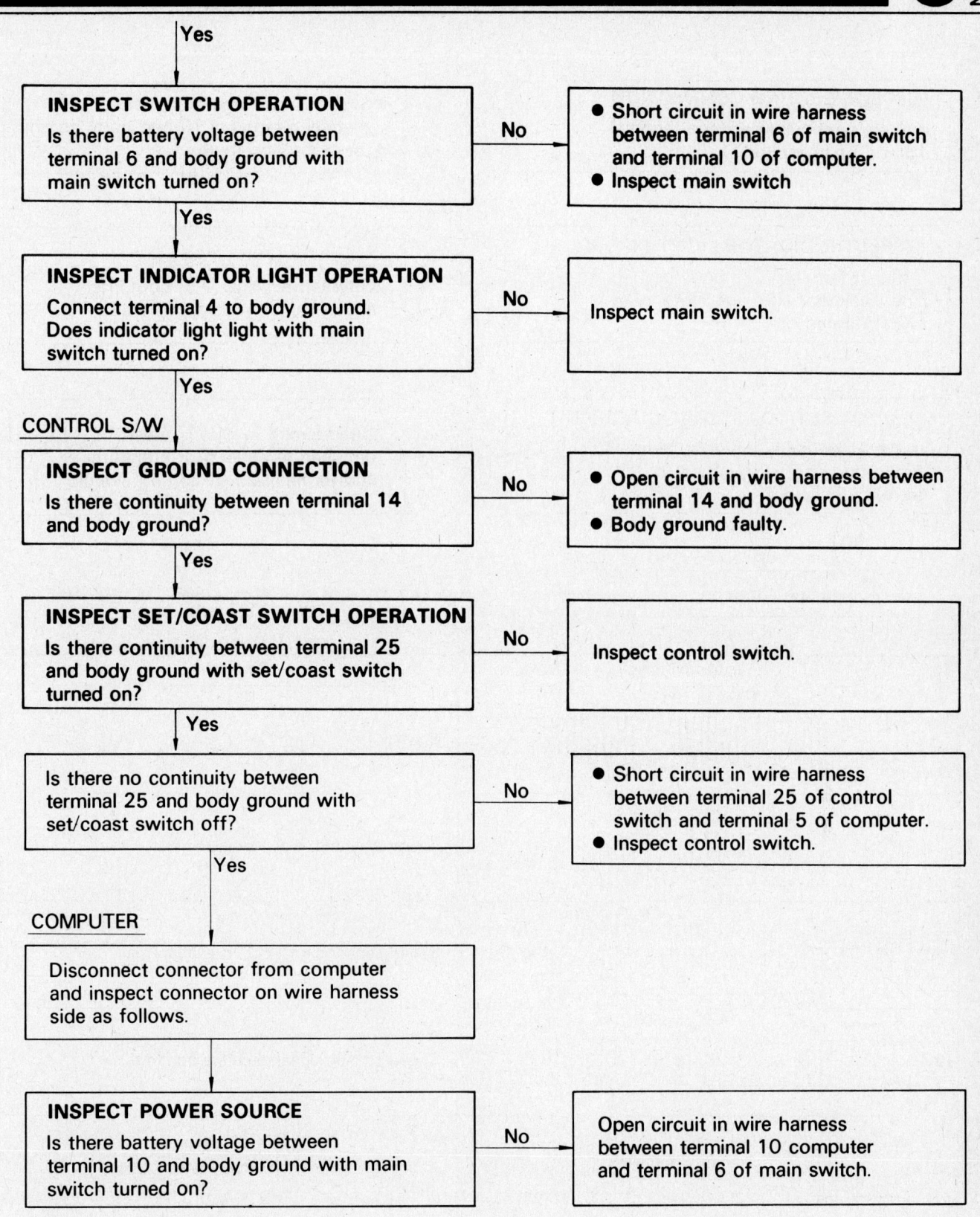

Yes

INSPECT SWITCH OPERATION

Is there battery voltage between terminal 6 and body ground with main switch turned on?

No →
- Short circuit in wire harness between terminal 6 of main switch and terminal 10 of computer.
- Inspect main switch

Yes

INSPECT INDICATOR LIGHT OPERATION

Connect terminal 4 to body ground. Does indicator light light with main switch turned on?

No → Inspect main switch.

Yes

CONTROL S/W

INSPECT GROUND CONNECTION

Is there continuity between terminal 14 and body ground?

No →
- Open circuit in wire harness between terminal 14 and body ground.
- Body ground faulty.

Yes

INSPECT SET/COAST SWITCH OPERATION

Is there continuity between terminal 25 and body ground with set/coast switch turned on?

No → Inspect control switch.

Yes

Is there no continuity between terminal 25 and body ground with set/coast switch off?

No →
- Short circuit in wire harness between terminal 25 of control switch and terminal 5 of computer.
- Inspect control switch.

Yes

COMPUTER

Disconnect connector from computer and inspect connector on wire harness side as follows.

INSPECT POWER SOURCE

Is there battery voltage between terminal 10 and body ground with main switch turned on?

No → Open circuit in wire harness between terminal 10 computer and terminal 6 of main switch.

Cruise control trouble diagnosis chart—1985 and later Camry

POWER ACCESSORIES
CRUISE CONTROL SYSTEMS

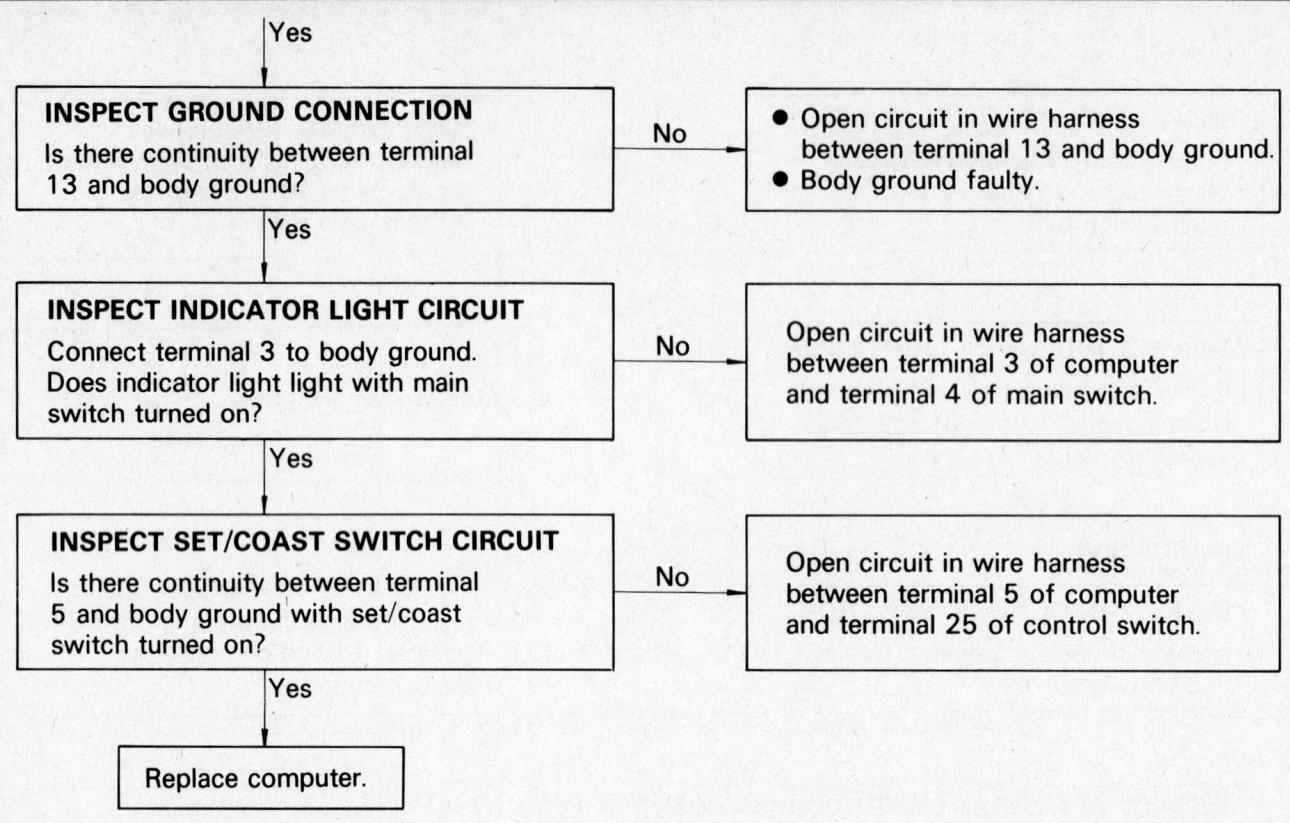

Yes

INSPECT GROUND CONNECTION

Is there continuity between terminal 13 and body ground?

No →
- Open circuit in wire harness between terminal 13 and body ground.
- Body ground faulty.

Yes

INSPECT INDICATOR LIGHT CIRCUIT

Connect terminal 3 to body ground. Does indicator light light with main switch turned on?

No → Open circuit in wire harness between terminal 3 of computer and terminal 4 of main switch.

Yes

INSPECT SET/COAST SWITCH CIRCUIT

Is there continuity between terminal 5 and body ground with set/coast switch turned on?

No → Open circuit in wire harness between terminal 5 of computer and terminal 25 of control switch.

Yes

Replace computer.

No.	Indicator code	Diagnosis
–	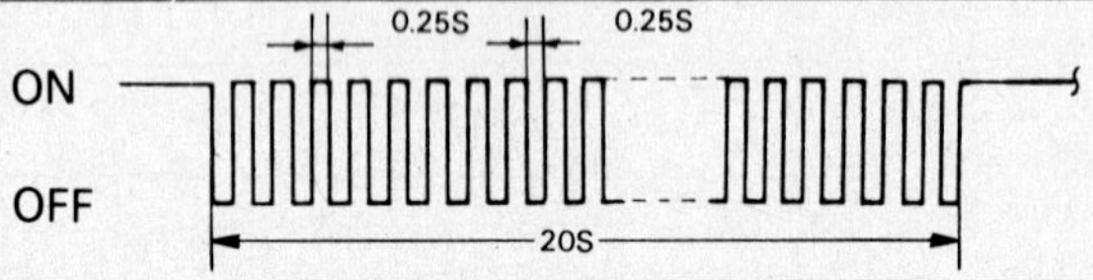 ON / OFF — 0.25S / 0.25S — 20S	Normal
11	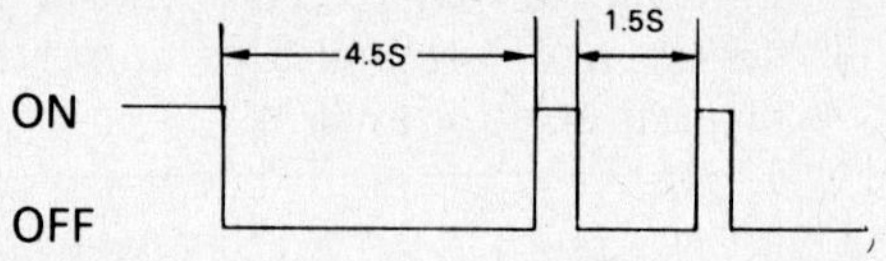 ON / OFF — 4.5S / 1.5S	Actuator circuit is abnormal
21	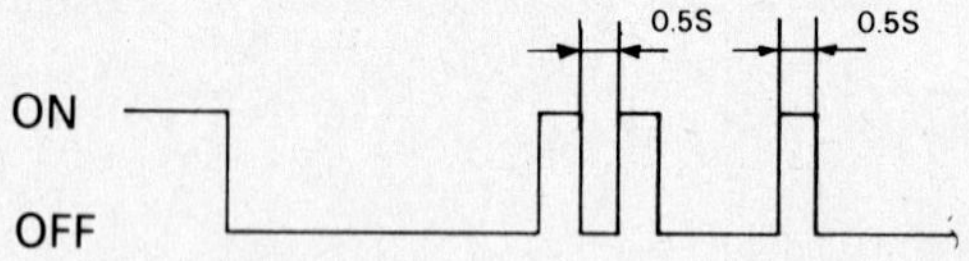 ON / OFF — 0.5S / 0.5S	Speed sensor signal circuit is abnormal
23	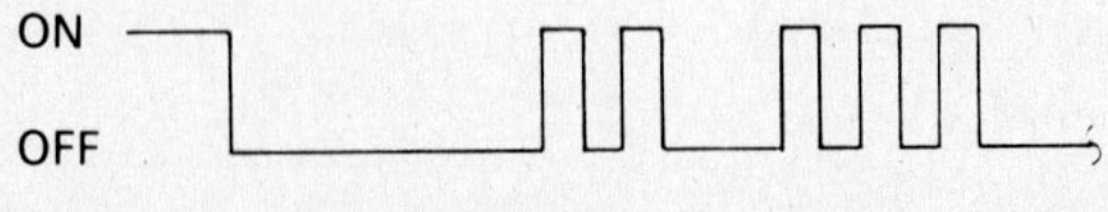 ON / OFF	Speed sensor signal circuit is abnormal
31	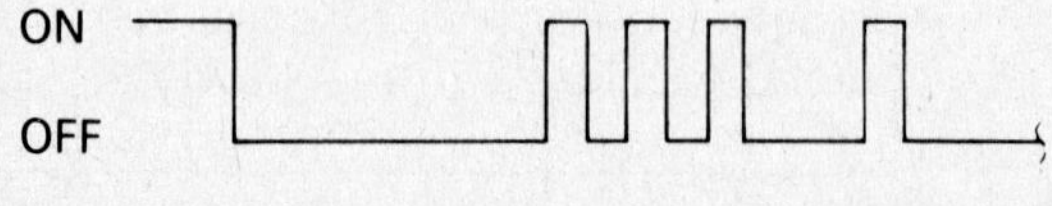 ON / OFF	Accel/resume switch circuit is abnormal
33	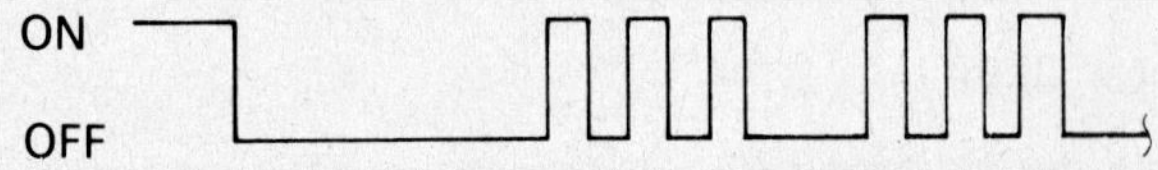 ON / OFF	Accel/resume switch and set/coast switch circuit is abnormal

Type "B" diagnostic information—1985 and later Camry

Symptom	Inspection Area			Section
Cruise control cannot be set.	(a)	Inspect type A codes.	No. 1 NO	A
			No. 2 NO	B
			No. 3 NO	C
			No. 4 NO	D
			No. 5 NO	D
	(b)	Inspect type B codes.	11	E
			21	D
			23	F
			31	B
			33	A and B
	(c)	All codes is normal.		Replace computer
Vehicle speed does not reduce when coast switch turned on.	Inspect No. 1 of type A code.		OK	F
			NO	A
Vehicle does not accelerate when accel switch turned on.	Inspect No. 2 of type A code.		OK	F
			NO	B
Vehicle speed does not return to memorized speed when resume switch turned on.	Inspect No. 2 of type A code.		OK	F
			NO	B
Set speed deviates on high side.	Inspect No. 1 of type A code.		OK	F
Set speed deviates on low side.			NO	A
Vehicle speed does fluctuate when set switch turned on.	Inspect No. 1 of type A code.		OK	F
			NO	A
Setting speed does not cancel when brake pedal depressed.	Inspect No. 3 of type A code.		OK	F
			NO	C
Setting speed does not cancel when parking brake pulled.	Inspect No. 3 of type A code.		OK	F
			NO	C
Setting speed does not cancel when clutch pedal depressed (M/T only).	Inspect No. 3 of type A code.		OK	F
			NO	C
Setting speed does not cancel when shifed to "N" range (A/T only).	Inspect No. 3 of type A code.		OK	F
			NO	C
Speed can be set below 16 km/h (10 mph).	Inspect No. 4 of type A code.		OK	F
			NO	D
Cruise control will not disengage even below 16 km/h (10 mph).	Inspect No. 5 of type A code.		OK	F
			NO	D

Cruise control troubleshooting data sheet — 1985 and later Camry

CRUISE CONTROL SYSTEM DIAGNOSIS — 1985 AND LATER

Output of Diagnosis Codes

TYPE A CODE

1. Turn the ignition switch to the on position.
2. Turn the set/coast switch on. Turn the main switch on.
3. Read the diagnosis code on the main switch indicator.
4. Checking the number four code must be done with the vehicle safely supported.
5. Results are as follows.

TYPE B CODE

1. Do not turn the ignition switch off. Do not turn the main switch off.
2. Turn the set/coast switch on three times within two seconds.
3. Read the diagnosis code on the main switch indicator.
4. Indication codes appear with priority from number eleven. Normal codes continue twenty seconds and abnormal codes are repeated three times.
5. Indication is stopped when vehicle speed is over 10 miles per hour or the main switch is turned off.
6. Results are as follows.

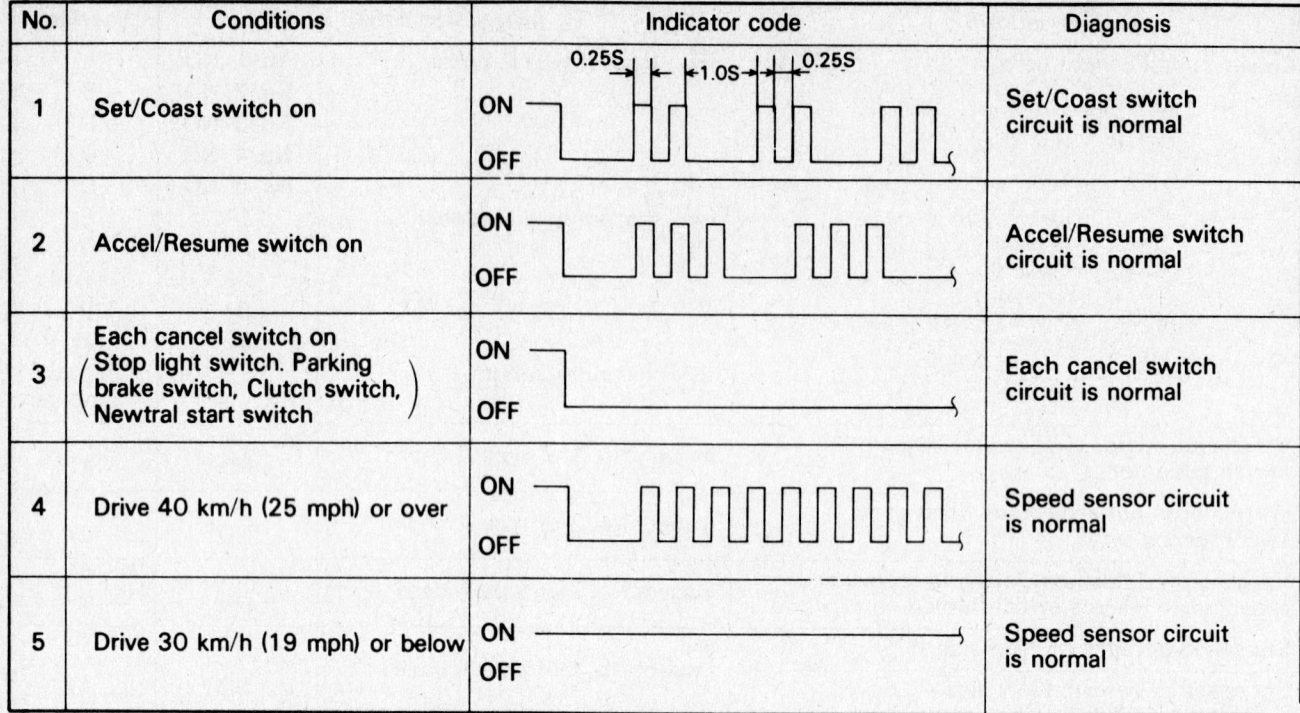

No.	Conditions	Indicator code		Diagnosis
1	Set/Coast switch on	ON / OFF	0.25S ⟶ 1.0S ⟶ 0.25S	Set/Coast switch circuit is normal
2	Accel/Resume switch on	ON / OFF		Accel/Resume switch circuit is normal
3	Each cancel switch on (Stop light switch. Parking brake switch, Clutch switch, Newtral start switch)	ON / OFF		Each cancel switch circuit is normal
4	Drive 40 km/h (25 mph) or over	ON / OFF		Speed sensor circuit is normal
5	Drive 30 km/h (19 mph) or below	ON / OFF		Speed sensor circuit is normal

Type "A" diagnostic information — 1985 and later Camry

MR2

VISUAL INSPECTION

Before performing any tests make a visual inspection of the cruise control system. Check all items in the system for abnormal conditions such as bare broken or disconnected wires and damage to the vacuum hoses. Be sure that the speedometer cables are attached and properly routed. All vacuum hoses must be properly routed and must not have any kinks or bends. Be sure that all electrical connections are complete and tight. The wiring harness must be routed properly.

ACTUATOR TEST

1. Inspect and check the actuator cable. Freeplay should be less than 0.039 inch. Adjust or replace as required.
2. Disconnect the electrical connector from the actuator lead wire.
3. Using an ohmmeter measure the resistance between terminals one and two. It should be about 30 ohms. Measure the resistance between terminals one and three. It should be about 68 ohms.
4. If the resistance is not as indicated, replace the actuator.
5. Connect a positive lead from the positive terminal of the battery to terminals two and three. Connect a negative lead from the negative terminal of the battery to terminal one.
6. Slowly apply 0 to 11.8 in. hg. of vacuum. Check to be sure that the control cable can be pulled smoothly.
7. When the vacuum has stabilized check the control cable and be sure that it does not return.
8. Disconnect terminal two or three and check that the control cable returns to its original position and that the vacuum goes to zero.
9. If the system does not perform as indicated replace the actuator.

Actuator test point locations — MR2

SPEED SENSOR TEST

1. Using an ohmmeter, check to see that there is continuity between terminals B4 and B6. It should be four times per revolution of the magnet shaft.
2. If continuity does not exist replace the speed sensor.

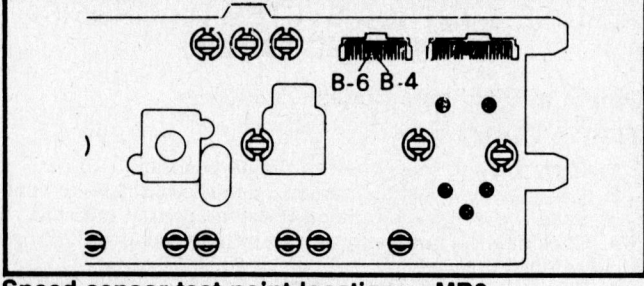

Speed sensor test point locations — MR2

Terminal	Connection or Measure Item	Check Item	Tester Connection	Condition	Voltage or Resistance Value
2	Stop Light Switch and Release Valve	Resistance	2 – 14	Brake pedal returned	About 68Ω
4	Control Valve	Resistance	4 – 14	—	About 30Ω
5	Control Switch (Set/coast S/W)	Continuity	5 – Body ground	Turn set/coast switch on	Continuity
5				Turn set/coast switch off	No continuity
7	Speed Sensor	Continuity	7 – Body ground	Vehicle moving slowly	1 pulse each 40 cm (15.75 in.)
10	Control Switch (Main S/W)	Voltage	10 – Body ground	Turn ignition switch and main switch on.	Battery voltage
10				Turn ignition switch and main switch off.	No voltage
11	Clutch Switch (M/T) or Neutral Start Switch (A/T)	Continuity	11 – Body ground	Clutch pedal depressed or shifted into "N" range	Continuity
11				Clutch pedal returned or shifted into only range except "N" range	No continuity
12	Parking Brake Switch	Voltage	12 – Body ground	Parking brake pulled	No voltage
12				Parking brake returned	Battery voltage
13	Body Ground	Continuity	13 – Body ground	—	Continuity
14	Release Valve and Control Valve	—	—	—	—
16	Stop Fuse	Voltage	16 – Body ground	—	Battery voltage
17	Control Switch (Resume/accel switch)	Continuity	17 – Body ground	Turn resume/accel switch on	Continuity
17				Turn resume/accel switch off	No continuity

Cruise control computer circuit inspection chart—MR2

CONTROL SWITCH TEST

1. Using an ohmmeter check for continunity of the terminals for each switch position.
2. If continunity between the terminals is not as specified, replace the switch.
3. Connect a positive lead from the positive terminal of the battery to terminal sixteen. Connect a negative lead from the negative terminal of the battery to terminal twenty.
4. Check to be sure that continuity exists between terminals sixteen and twenty-one with the main switch turned on.
5. Check that there is no continuity between terminals sixteen and twenty-one with the main switch off.
4. If the above results are not achieved, replace the switch.

CLUTCH SWITCH TEST

1. Check to be sure that there is continuity between terminals two and three with the clutch pedal depressed.
2. Check to be sure that there is continuity between terminals two and three with the clutch pedal returned.
3. If continuity is not as indicated, replace the clutch switch.

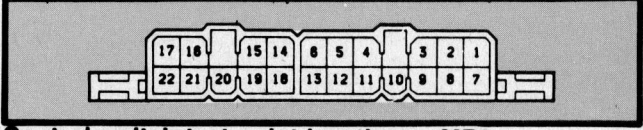

Control switch test point locations—MR2

Switch position \ Terminal (Wire color)	14 (BR)	15 (W)	16 (R)	18 (O)	19 (L)	20 (B)	21 (Y)
OFF							
Main S/W ON			o			o——o	
Set/coast S/W ON	o					o——o	
Accel/resume S/W ON		o				o——o	

Control switch specifications—MR2

Stoplight test point locations—MR2

Terminal / Brake pedal position	1	2	3	4
Brake pedal depressed	○———	———○		
Brake pedal returned			○———	———○

Stoplight switch specfications—MR2

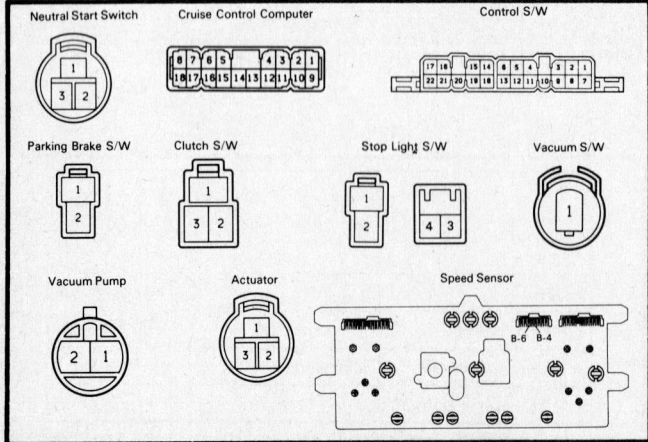

Clutch start switch test point locations—MR2

STOP LIGHT SWITCH TEST

1. Using an ohmmeter check for continunity of the terminals for each switch position.
2. If continunity between the terminals is not as specified, replace the switch.

VACUUM SWITCH TEST

1. With a vacuum of 22.7 in. hg. or higher check that continunity does not exist between the switch terminal and the body.
2. Check to be sure that there is continunity between the switch terminal and the body without vacuum.
3. If the above results are not achieved, replace the switch.

VACUUM PUMP TEST

1. Connect a vacuum pump to the ACT side of the vacuum pump.
2. Connect a positive lead from the positive terminal of the battery to terminal one. Connect a negative lead from the negative terminal of the battery to terminal two.
3. Check to be sure that there is a vacuum of at least 7.87 in. hg. or above.
4. If the above test results are not achieved, replace the vacuum pump.

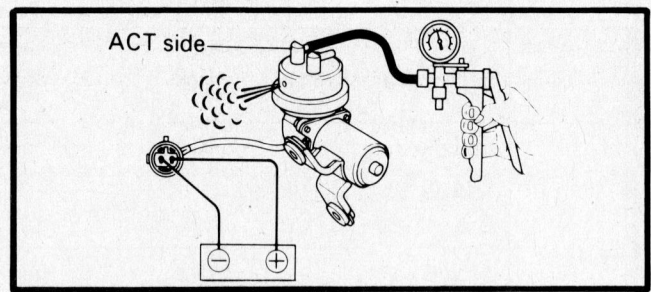

Vacuum pump test point locations—MR2

DIAGNOSIS AND TESTING PROCEDURES

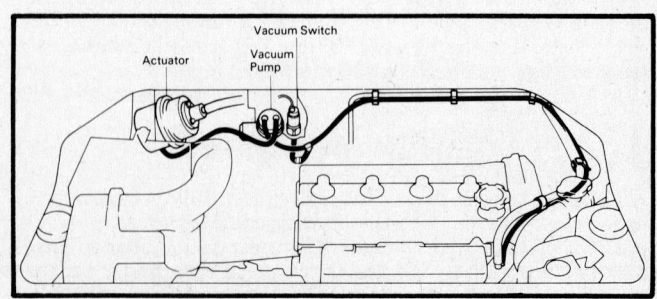

Cruise control electrical connectors—MR2

Cruise control vacuum schematic—MR2

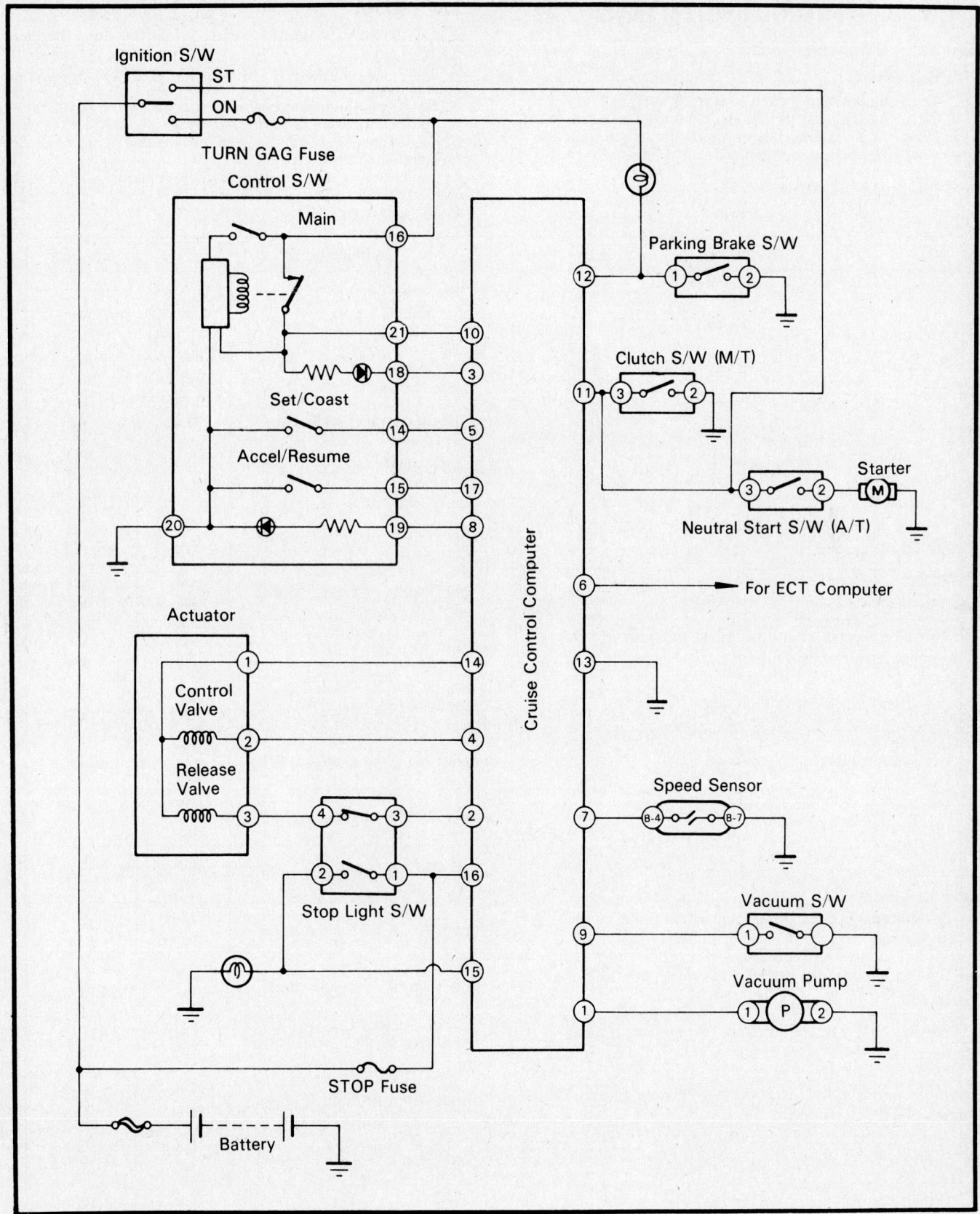

Cruise control electrical schematic—MR2

CRUISE CONTROL SYSTEM DIAGNOSIS

Output of Diagnosis Codes

TYPE A CODE

1. Turn the ignition switch to the on position.
2. Turn the set/coast switch on. Turn the main switch on.
3. Read the diagnosis code on the main switch indicator.
4. Checking the number four code must be done with the engine idling.
5. Results are as follows.

TYPE B CODE

1. Do not turn the ignition switch off. Do not turn the main switch off.
2. Turn the set/coast switch on three times within two seconds.
3. Read the diagnosis code on the main switch indicator.
4. Indication codes appear with priority from number eleven. Normal codes continue twenty seconds and abnormal codes are repeated three times.
5. Indication is stopped when vehicle speed is over 10 miles per hour or the main switch is turned off.
6. Results are as follows.

Symptom	Inspection Area		Section
Cruise control cannot be set.	(a) Inspect type A codes.	No. 1 NO	A
		No. 2 NO	B
		No. 3 NO	C
		No. 4 NO	D
		No. 5 NO	E
		No. 6 NO	E
	(b) Inspect type B codes.	11	F
		21	E
	(c) All codes are normal.		Replace computer.
Vehicle speed does not reduce when coast switch turned on.	Inspect No. 1 of type A code.	OK	G
		NO	A
Vehicle does not accelerate when accel switch turned on.	Inspect No. 2 of type A code.	OK	G
		NO	B
Vehicle speed does not return to memorized speed when resume switch turned on.	Inspect No. 2 of type A code.	OK	G
		NO	B
Set speed deviates on high side.	Inspect No. 1 of type A code.	OK	G
		NO	A
Set speed deviates on low side.	Inspect No. 3 of type A code.	OK	G
		NO	C
Vehicle speed fluctuates when set switch turned on.	Inspect No. 1 of type A code.	OK	G
		NO	A
	Inspect No. 3 of type A code.	OK	G
		NO	C
Setting speed does not cancel when brake pedal depressed.	Inspect No. 4 of type A code.	OK	G
		NO	D
Setting speed does not cancel when parking brake pulled.	Inspect No. 4 of type A code.	OK	G
		NO	D
Setting speed does not cancel when clutch pedal depressed (M/T only).	Inspect No. 4 of type A code.	OK	G
		NO	D
Setting speed does not cancel when shifted to "N" range (A/T only).	Inspect No. 4 of type A code.	OK	G
		NO	D
Speed can be set below about 35 km/h (22 mph).	Inspect No. 5 of type A code.	OK	G
		NO	E
Cruise control will not disengage even below about 35 km/h (22 mph).	Inspect No. 6 of type A code.	OK	G
		NO	E

Cruise control troubleshooting data sheet – MR2

No.	Conditions	Indication Code	Diagnosis
1	Set/coast switch on	ON / OFF — 0.25S ⊓⊔⊓⊔ 1.0S 0.25S	Set/coast switch circuit is normal.
2	Accel/resume switch on	ON / OFF ⊓⊔⊓⊔⊓⊔	Accel/resume switch circuit is normal.
3	Vacuum switch on	ON / OFF ⊓⊔⊓⊔⊓	Vacuum switch circuit is normal.
4	Each cancel switch on (Stop light switch, Parking brake switch, Clutch switch, Neutral start switch)	ON / OFF ————	Each cancel switch circuit is normal.
5	Drive 35 km/h (22 mph) or over	ON / OFF ⊓⊔⊓⊔⊓⊔	Speed sensor circuit is normal.
6	Drive 35 km/h (22 mph) or below	ON / OFF ————	Speed sensor circuit is normal.

Type "A" diagnostic information—MR2

No.	Indicator Code	Diagnosis
	ON / OFF 0.25S 0.25S ⊓⊔⊓⊔	Normal.
11	ON / OFF 0.5S 4S 1.5S 4S	Actuator circuit is abnormal.
21	ON / OFF 4S 0.5S 1.5S	Speed sensor signal circuit is abnormal.

Type "B" diagnostic information—MR2

A | INSPECTION OF SET/COAST SWITCH CIRCUIT

CONTROL S/W

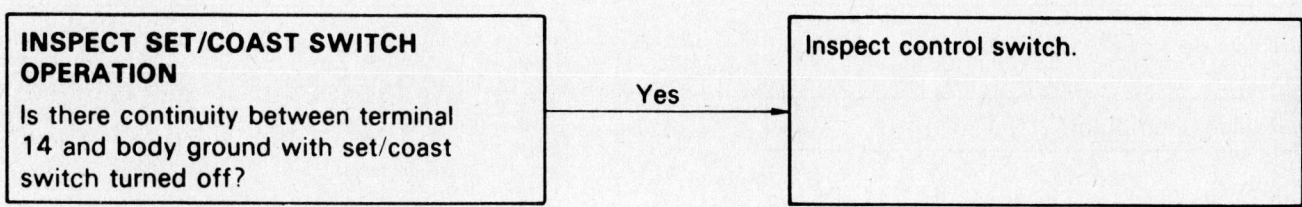

INSPECT SET/COAST SWITCH OPERATION
Is there continuity between terminal 14 and body ground with set/coast switch turned off? —Yes→ Inspect control switch.

Cruise control trouble diagnosis chart—MR2

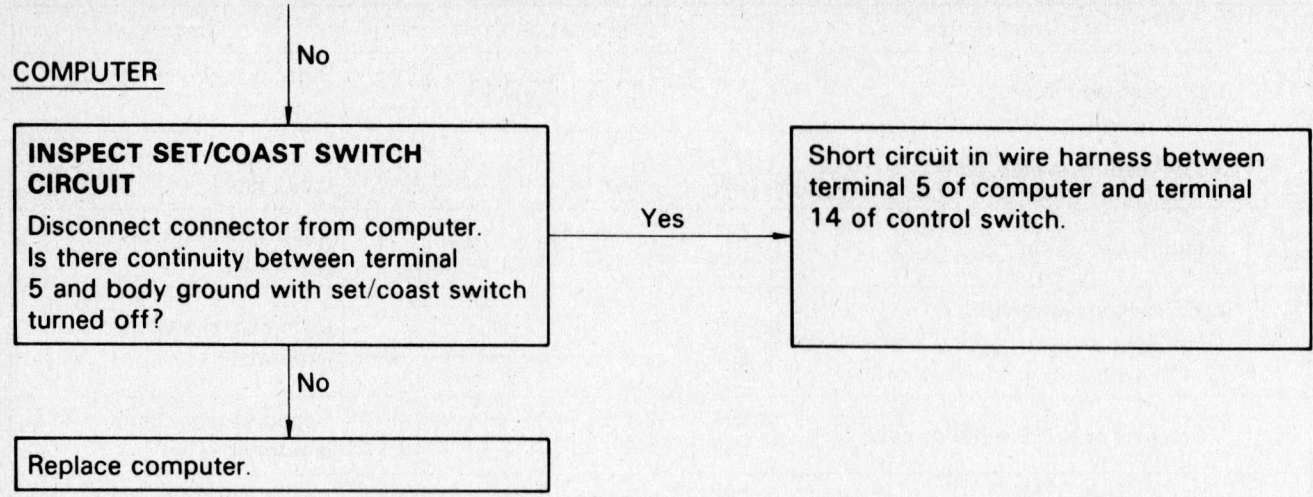

COMPUTER

INSPECT SET/COAST SWITCH CIRCUIT

Disconnect connector from computer. Is there continuity between terminal 5 and body ground with set/coast switch turned off?

→ Yes → Short circuit in wire harness between terminal 5 of computer and terminal 14 of control switch.

↓ No

Replace computer.

| **B** | **INSPECTION OF RESUME/ACCEL SWITCH CIRCUIT** |

CONTROL S/W

INSPECT RESUME/ACCEL SWITCH OPERATION

Is there continuity between terminal 15 and body ground with resume/accel switch turned off?

→ Yes →
- Short circuit in wire harness between terminal 15 of control switch and terminal 17 of computer.
- Inspect control switch.

↓ No

Is there continuity between terminal 15 and body ground with resume/accel switch turned on?

→ No → Inspect control switch.

↓ Yes

COMPUTER

INSPECT RESUME/ACCEL SWITCH CIRCUIT

Is there continuity between terminal 17 and body ground with resume/accel switch turned on?

→ No → Open circuit in wire harness between terminal 17 of computer and terminal 15 of control switch.

↓ Yes

Replace computer.

Cruise control trouble diagnosis chart — MR2

C	INSPECTION OF VACUUM SWITCH CIRCUIT

VACUUM S/W

INSPECT GROUND CONNECTION
Is there continuity between terminal 2 and body ground?

→ No →
- Open circuit in wire harness between terminal 2 and body ground.
- Body ground faulty.

↓ Yes

INSPECT VACUUM SWITCH OPERATION
Is vacuum switch normal?

→ No → Replace vacuum switch.

↓ Yes

COMPUTER

Disconnect connector from computer and inspect connector on wire harness side as follows.

↓

INSPECT VACUUM SWITCH CIRCUIT
Is there continuity between terminal 9 and body ground?

→ No → Open circuit in wire harness between terminal 9 of computer and terminal 1 of vacuum switch.

↓ Yes

Start engine. (idling)

↓

Is there continuity between terminal 9 and body ground?

→ Yes → Short circuit in wire harness between terminal 9 of computer and terminal 1 of vacuum switch.

↓ No

Replace computer.

Cruise control trouble diagnosis chart — MR2

D	INSPECT CANCEL SWITCH CIRCUIT

1. INSPECT STOP LIGHT SWITCH CIRCUIT

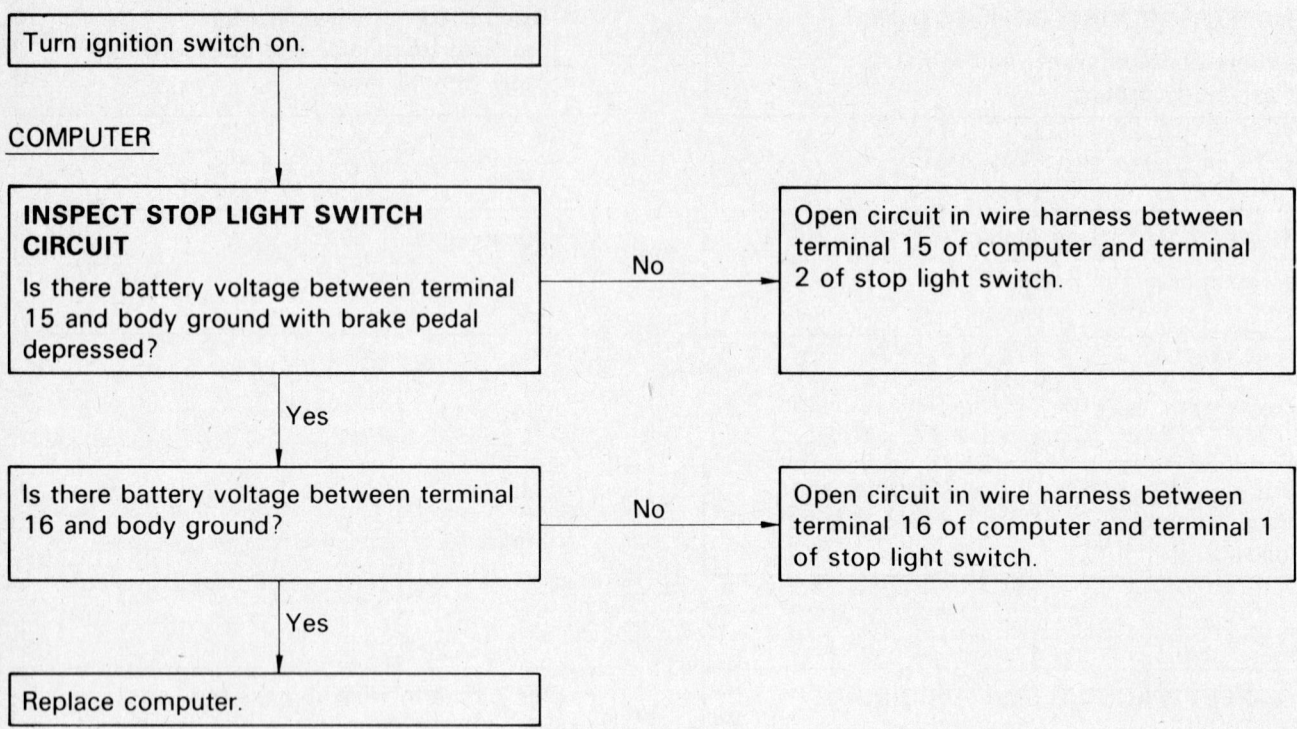

Turn ignition switch on.

COMPUTER

INSPECT STOP LIGHT SWITCH CIRCUIT

Is there battery voltage between terminal 15 and body ground with brake pedal depressed?

No → Open circuit in wire harness between terminal 15 of computer and terminal 2 of stop light switch.

Yes

Is there battery voltage between terminal 16 and body ground?

No → Open circuit in wire harness between terminal 16 of computer and terminal 1 of stop light switch.

Yes

Replace computer.

2. INSPECT PARKING BRAKE SWITCH CIRCUIT

COMPUTER

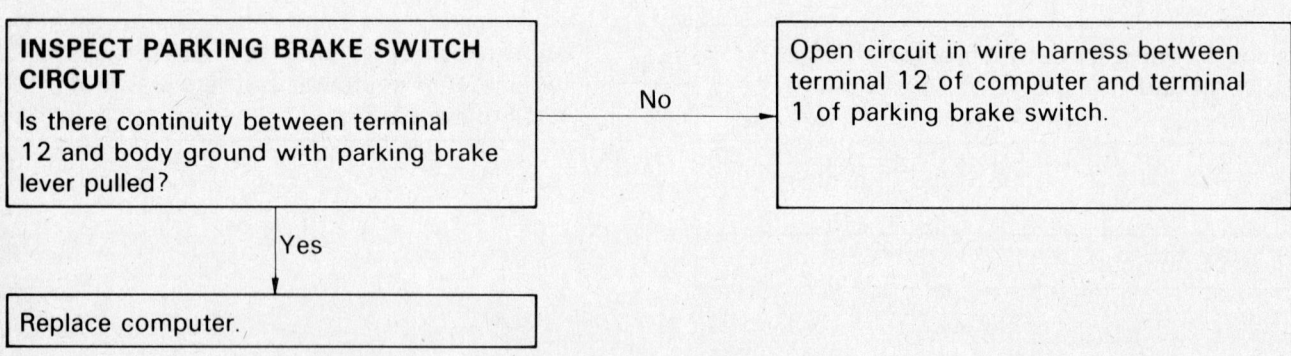

INSPECT PARKING BRAKE SWITCH CIRCUIT

Is there continuity between terminal 12 and body ground with parking brake lever pulled?

No → Open circuit in wire harness between terminal 12 of computer and terminal 1 of parking brake switch.

Yes

Replace computer.

Cruise control trouble diagnosis chart — MR2

3. INSPECT CLUTCH SWITCH CIRCUIT (M/T)

<u>CLUTCH S/W</u>

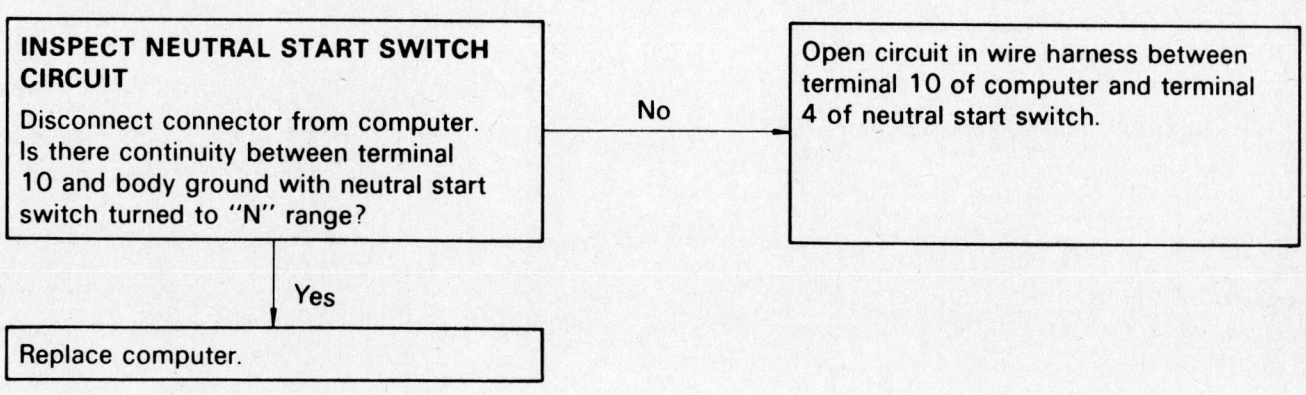

INSPECT GROUND CONNECTION

Is there continuity between terminal 2 and body ground?

— No →
- Open circuit in wire harness between terminal 2 and body ground.
- Body ground faulty.

↓ Yes

INSPECT CLUTCH SWITCH CONTINUITY

Is clutch switch normal?

— No → Replace clutch switch.

↓ Yes

<u>COMPUTER</u>

INSPECT CLUTCH SWITCH CIRCUIT

Is there continuity between terminal 11 and body ground with clutch pedal depressed?

— No → Open circuit in wire harness between terminal 11 of computer and terminal 2 of clutch switch.

↓ Yes

Is there continuity between terminal 11 and body ground with clutch pedal returned?

— Yes → Short circuit in wire harness between terminal 11 of computer and terminal 2 of clutch switch.

↓ No

Replace actuator.

4. INSPECT NEUTRAL START SWITCH CIRCUIT (A/T)

<u>COMPUTER</u>

INSPECT NEUTRAL START SWITCH CIRCUIT

Disconnect connector from computer. Is there continuity between terminal 10 and body ground with neutral start switch turned to "N" range?

— No → Open circuit in wire harness between terminal 10 of computer and terminal 4 of neutral start switch.

↓ Yes

Replace computer.

Cruise control trouble diagnosis chart—MR2

E	INSPECTION OF SPEED SENSOR CIRCUIT

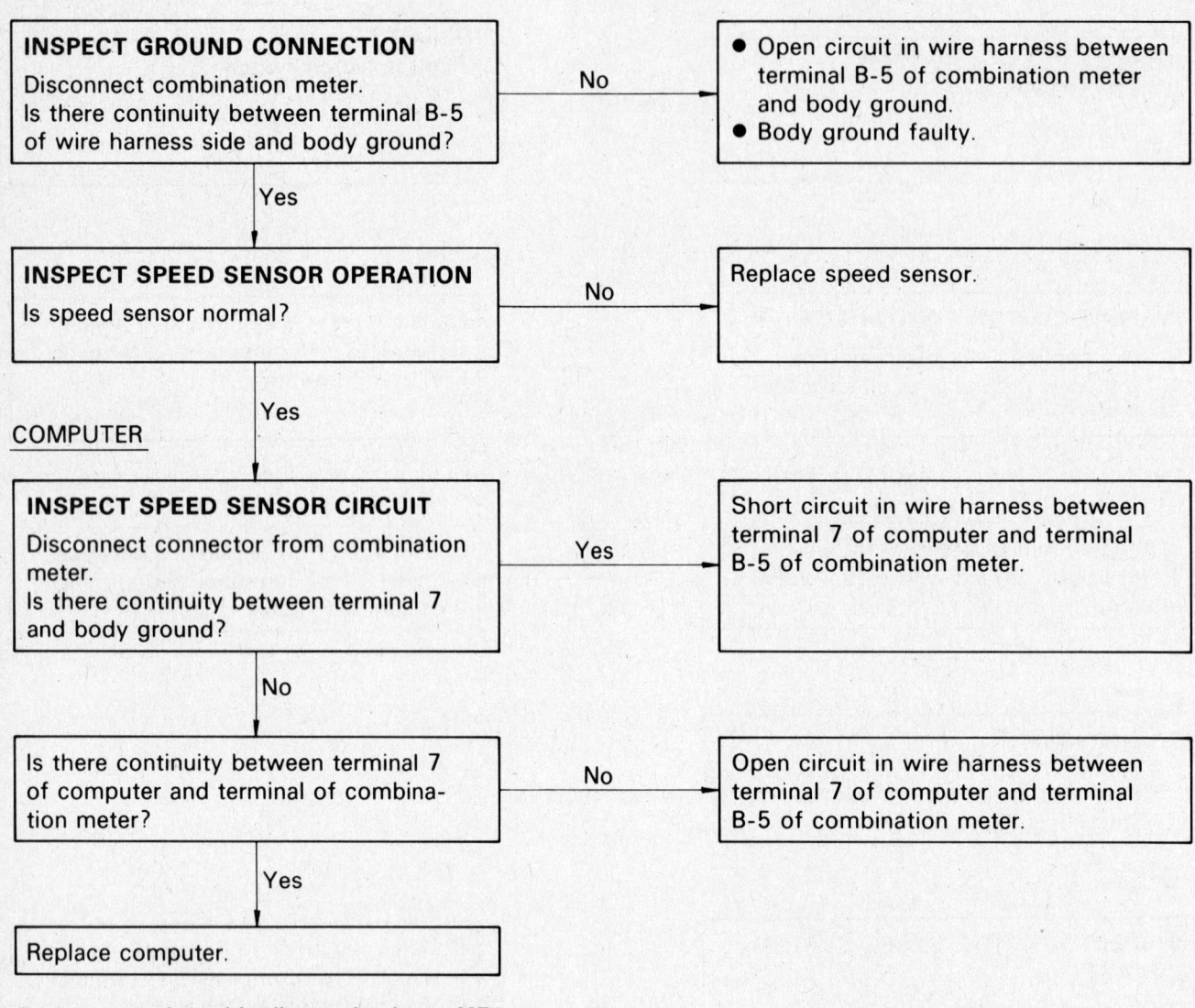

SPEED SENSOR

INSPECT GROUND CONNECTION
Disconnect combination meter.
Is there continuity between terminal B-5
of wire harness side and body ground?

→ No →

- Open circuit in wire harness between terminal B-5 of combination meter and body ground.
- Body ground faulty.

↓ Yes

INSPECT SPEED SENSOR OPERATION
Is speed sensor normal?

→ No →

Replace speed sensor.

↓ Yes

COMPUTER

INSPECT SPEED SENSOR CIRCUIT
Disconnect connector from combination
meter.
Is there continuity between terminal 7
and body ground?

→ Yes →

Short circuit in wire harness between terminal 7 of computer and terminal B-5 of combination meter.

↓ No

Is there continuity between terminal 7
of computer and terminal of combination meter?

→ No →

Open circuit in wire harness between terminal 7 of computer and terminal B-5 of combination meter.

↓ Yes

Replace computer.

Cruise control trouble diagnosis chart – MR2

F INSPECTION OF ACTUATOR OPERATION

ACTUATOR

INSPECT ACTUATOR OPERATION
Remove actuator.
Is actuator normal?

No → Replace actuator.

Yes → Replace computer.

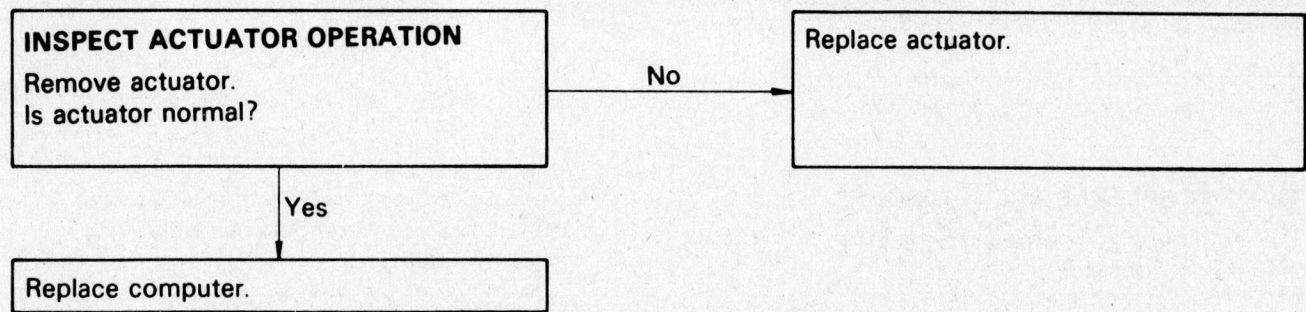

G INSPECTION OF ACTUATOR CIRCUIT

VACUUM PUMP

INSPECT VACUUM PUMP OPERATION
Remove vacuum pump.
Is vacuum pump normal?

No → Replace vacuum pump.

Yes ↓

ACTUATOR

INSPECT ACTUATOR OPERATION
Remove actuator.
Is actuator normal?

No → Replace actuator.

Yes ↓

STOP LIGHT S/W

INSPECT STOP LIGHT SWITCH OPERATION
Is stop light switch normal?

No → Replace stop light switch.

Yes ↓

Cruise control trouble diagnosis chart—MR2

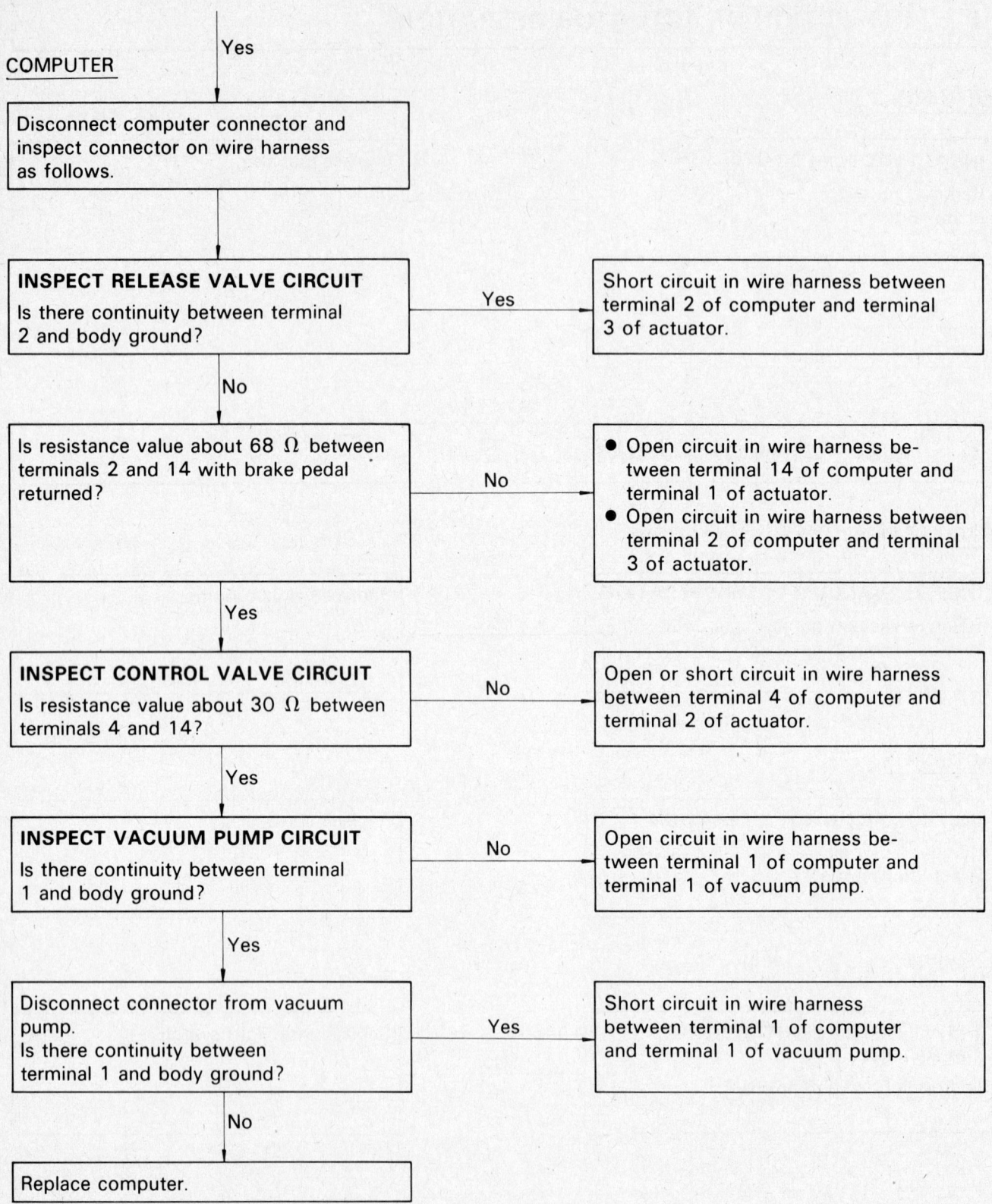

COMPUTER

Yes

Disconnect computer connector and
inspect connector on wire harness
as follows.

INSPECT RELEASE VALVE CIRCUIT
Is there continuity between terminal
2 and body ground?

Yes → Short circuit in wire harness between
terminal 2 of computer and terminal
3 of actuator.

No

Is resistance value about 68 Ω between
terminals 2 and 14 with brake pedal
returned?

No →
- Open circuit in wire harness between terminal 14 of computer and
  terminal 1 of actuator.
- Open circuit in wire harness between
  terminal 2 of computer and terminal
  3 of actuator.

Yes

INSPECT CONTROL VALVE CIRCUIT
Is resistance value about 30 Ω between
terminals 4 and 14?

No → Open or short circuit in wire harness
between terminal 4 of computer and
terminal 2 of actuator.

Yes

INSPECT VACUUM PUMP CIRCUIT
Is there continuity between terminal
1 and body ground?

No → Open circuit in wire harness between terminal 1 of computer and
terminal 1 of vacuum pump.

Yes

Disconnect connector from vacuum
pump.
Is there continuity between
terminal 1 and body ground?

Yes → Short circuit in wire harness
between terminal 1 of computer
and terminal 1 of vacuum pump.

No

Replace computer.

Cruise control trouble diagnosis chart — MR2

3. INSPECT DIAGNOSIS CIRCUIT

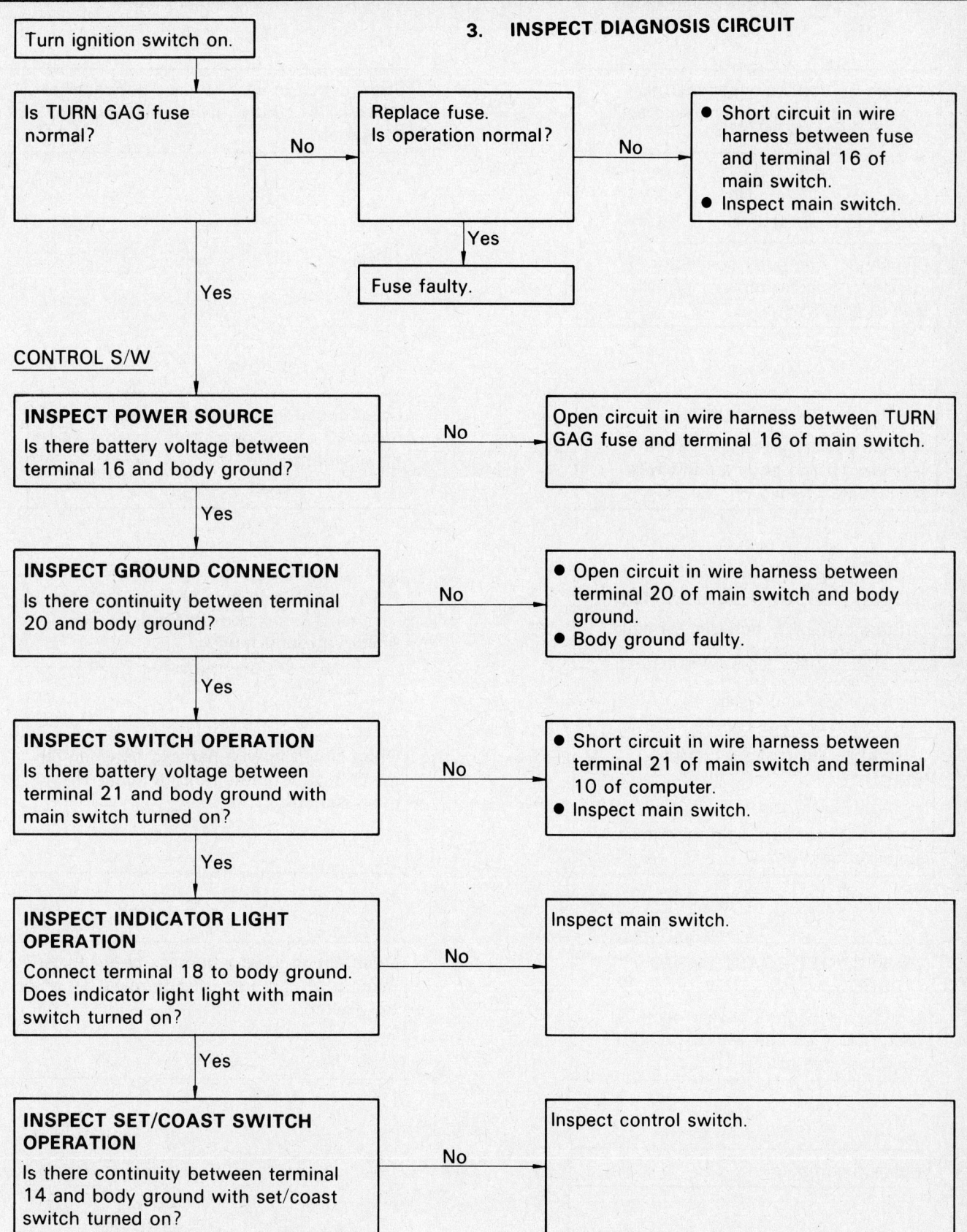

Turn ignition switch on.

Is TURN GAG fuse normal? — No → Replace fuse. Is operation normal? — No → • Short circuit in wire harness between fuse and terminal 16 of main switch. • Inspect main switch.

Replace fuse. Is operation normal? — Yes → Fuse faulty.

Is TURN GAG fuse normal? — Yes ↓

CONTROL S/W

INSPECT POWER SOURCE
Is there battery voltage between terminal 16 and body ground? — No → Open circuit in wire harness between TURN GAG fuse and terminal 16 of main switch.

Yes ↓

INSPECT GROUND CONNECTION
Is there continuity between terminal 20 and body ground? — No → • Open circuit in wire harness between terminal 20 of main switch and body ground. • Body ground faulty.

Yes ↓

INSPECT SWITCH OPERATION
Is there battery voltage between terminal 21 and body ground with main switch turned on? — No → • Short circuit in wire harness between terminal 21 of main switch and terminal 10 of computer. • Inspect main switch.

Yes ↓

INSPECT INDICATOR LIGHT OPERATION
Connect terminal 18 to body ground. Does indicator light light with main switch turned on? — No → Inspect main switch.

Yes ↓

INSPECT SET/COAST SWITCH OPERATION
Is there continuity between terminal 14 and body ground with set/coast switch turned on? — No → Inspect control switch.

Cruise control trouble diagnosis chart — MR2

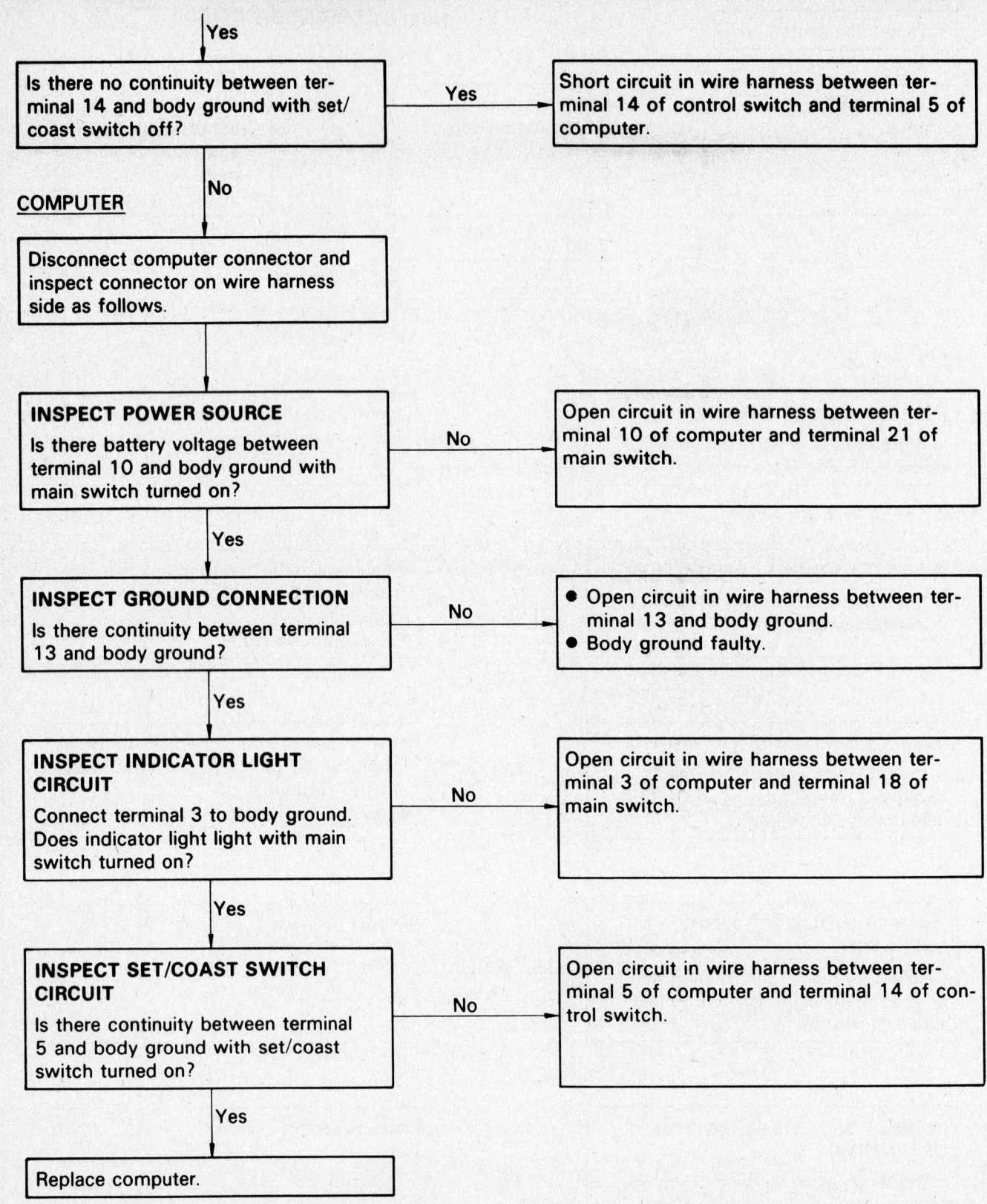

Yes

| Is there no continuity between terminal 14 and body ground with set/coast switch off? | → Yes → | Short circuit in wire harness between terminal 14 of control switch and terminal 5 of computer. |

No

COMPUTER

Disconnect computer connector and inspect connector on wire harness side as follows.

| **INSPECT POWER SOURCE** Is there battery voltage between terminal 10 and body ground with main switch turned on? | → No → | Open circuit in wire harness between terminal 10 of computer and terminal 21 of main switch. |

Yes

| **INSPECT GROUND CONNECTION** Is there continuity between terminal 13 and body ground? | → No → | ● Open circuit in wire harness between terminal 13 and body ground. ● Body ground faulty. |

Yes

| **INSPECT INDICATOR LIGHT CIRCUIT** Connect terminal 3 to body ground. Does indicator light light with main switch turned on? | → No → | Open circuit in wire harness between terminal 3 of computer and terminal 18 of main switch. |

Yes

| **INSPECT SET/COAST SWITCH CIRCUIT** Is there continuity between terminal 5 and body ground with set/coast switch turned on? | → No → | Open circuit in wire harness between terminal 5 of computer and terminal 14 of control switch. |

Yes

Replace computer.

Cruise control trouble diagnosis chart — MR2

Tercel

VISUAL INSPECTION

Before performing any tests make a visual inspection of the cruise control system. Check all items in the system for abnormal conditions such as bare broken or disconnected wires and damage to the vacuum hoses. Be sure that the speedometer cables are attached and properly routed. All vacuum hoses must be properly routed and must not have any kinks or bends. Be sure that all electrical connections are complete and tight. The wiring harness must be routed properly.

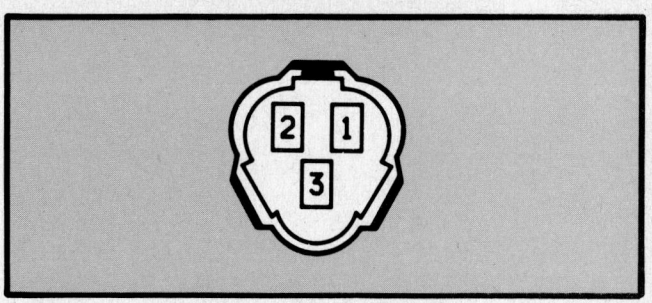

Actuator test point locations – Tercel

ACTUATOR TEST

1. Inspect and check the actuator cable. Freeplay should be less than 0.039 inch. Adjust or replace as required.
2. Disconnect the electrical connector from the actuator lead wire.
3. Using an ohmmeter measure the resistance between terminals two and three. It should be about 30 ohms. Measure the resistance between terminals one and three. It should be about 68 ohms.

4. If the resistance is not as indicated, replace the actuator.
5. Connect a positive lead from the positive terminal of the battery to terminals one and two. Connect a negative lead from the negative terminal of the battery to terminal one.
6. Slowly apply 0 to 11.8 in. hg. of vacuum. Check to be sure that the control cable can be pulled smoothly.
7. When the vacuum has stabilized check the control cable and be sure that it does not return.

Terminal	Connection or Measure Item	Check Item	Tester Connection	Condition	Voltage or Resistance value
2	Stop Light Switch and Release Valve	Resistance	2–14	Brake pedal returned	About 30Ω
4	Control Valve	Resistance	4–14		About 68Ω
5	Control Switch (Set/coast S/W)	Continuity	5–Body ground	Turn set/coast switch on	Continuity
				Turn set/coast switch off	No continuity
7	Speed Sensor	Continuity	7–Body ground	Vehicle moving slowly	1 pulse each 40 cm (15.75 in.)
10	Main Switch	Voltage	10–Body ground	Turn ignition switch and main switch on	Battery voltage
				Turn ignition switch and/or main switch off	No voltage
11	Clutch Switch or Neutral start switch	Continuity	11–Body ground	Clutch pedal depressed or if shifted into "N" range	Continuity
				Clutch pedal returned or if shifted into any range except "N" range	No continuity
12	Parking Brake Switch	Voltage	12–Body ground	Parking brake lever pulled	No voltage
				Parking brake lever returned	Battery voltage
13	Body Ground	Continuity	13–Body ground		Continuity
14	Release Valve and Control Valve				
15	Stop Light Switch	Voltage	15–Body ground	Brake pedal depressed	Battery voltage
				Brake pedal returned	No voltage
16	STOP Fuse	Voltage	16–Body ground		Battery voltage
17	Control Switch (Resume/accel S/W)	Continuity	17–Body ground	Turn resume/accel switch on	Continuity
				Turn resume/accel switch off	No continuity

Cruise control computer circuit inspection chart – Tercel

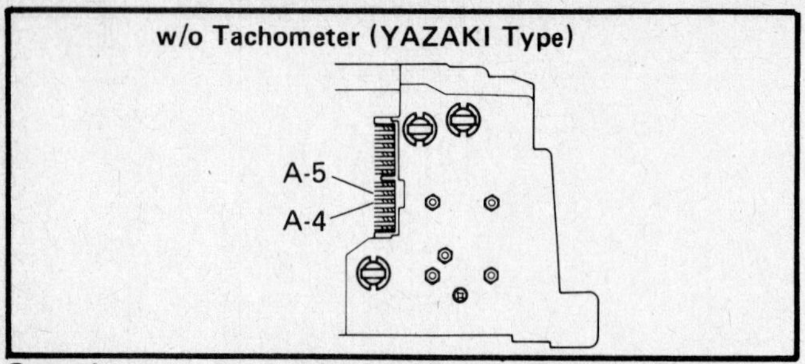

Speed sensor test point locations – Tercel without tachometer

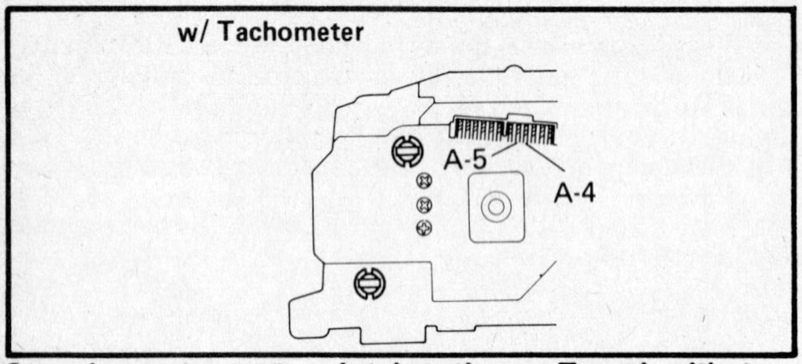

Speed sensor test point locations – Tercel with tachometer

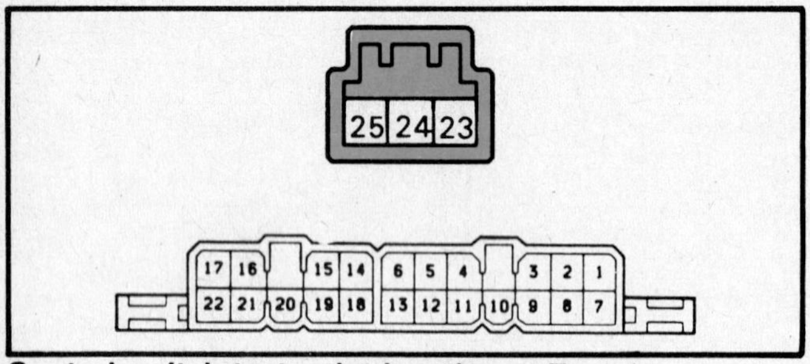

Control switch test point locations – Tercel

Switch position \ Terminal	14	23	25
RESUME/ACCEL	○	○	
OFF			
SET/COAST	○		○

Control switch specifications – Tercel

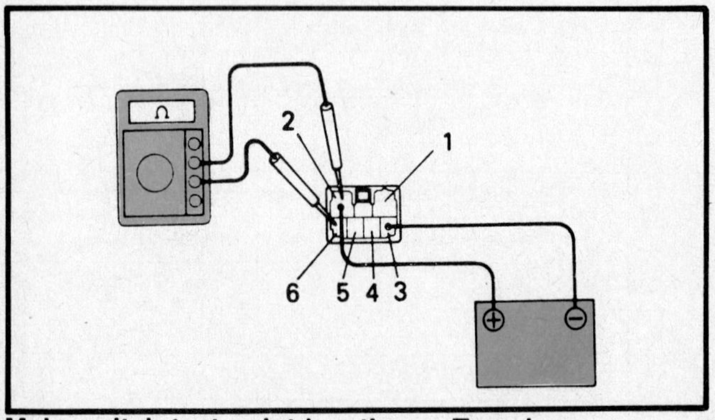

Main switch test point locations – Tercel

8. Disconnect terminal one or two and check that the control cable returns to its original position and that the vacuum goes to zero.

9. If the system does not perform as indicated replace the actuator.

SPEED SENSOR TEST

1. Using an ohmmeter, check to see that there is continuity between terminals A4 and A5. It should be four times per revolution of the magnet shaft.

2. If continuity does not exist replace the speed sensor.

CONTROL SWITCH TEST

1. Using an ohmmeter check for continuity of the terminals for each switch position.

2. If continuity between the terminals is not as specified, replace the switch.

MAIN SWITCH TEST

1. Connect a positive lead from the positive terminal of the battery to terminal two. Connect a negative lead from the negative terminal of the battery to terminal three.

4. Check to be sure that continuity exists between terminals two and six with the main switch turned on.

5. Check that there is no continuity between terminals two and six with the main switch off.

4. If the above results are not achieved, replace the switch.

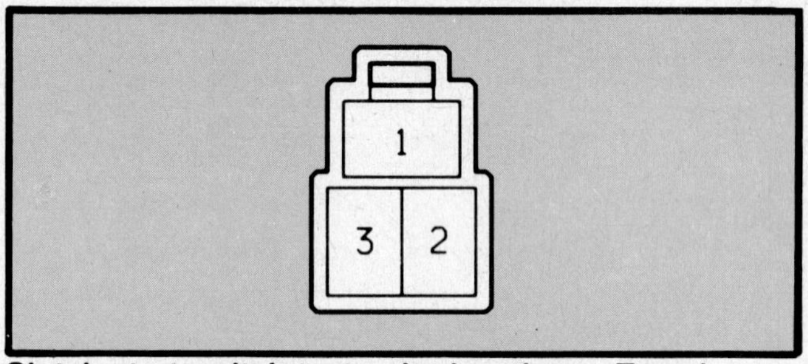

Clutch start switch test point locations – Tercel

CLUTCH SWITCH TEST

1. Check to be sure that there is continuity between terminals two and three with the clutch pedal depressed.

2. Check to be sure that there is continuity between terminals two and three with the clutch pedal returned.

3. If continuity is not as indicated, replace the clutch switch.

STOP LIGHT SWITCH TEST

1. Using an ohmmeter check for continuity of the terminals for each switch position.

2. If continuity between the terminals is not as specified, replace the switch.

Brake pedal position \ Terminal	1	2	3	4
Brake pedal depressed	○	○		
Brake pedal returned			○	○

Stoplight switch specifications – Tercel

DIAGNOSIS AND TESTING PROCEDURES

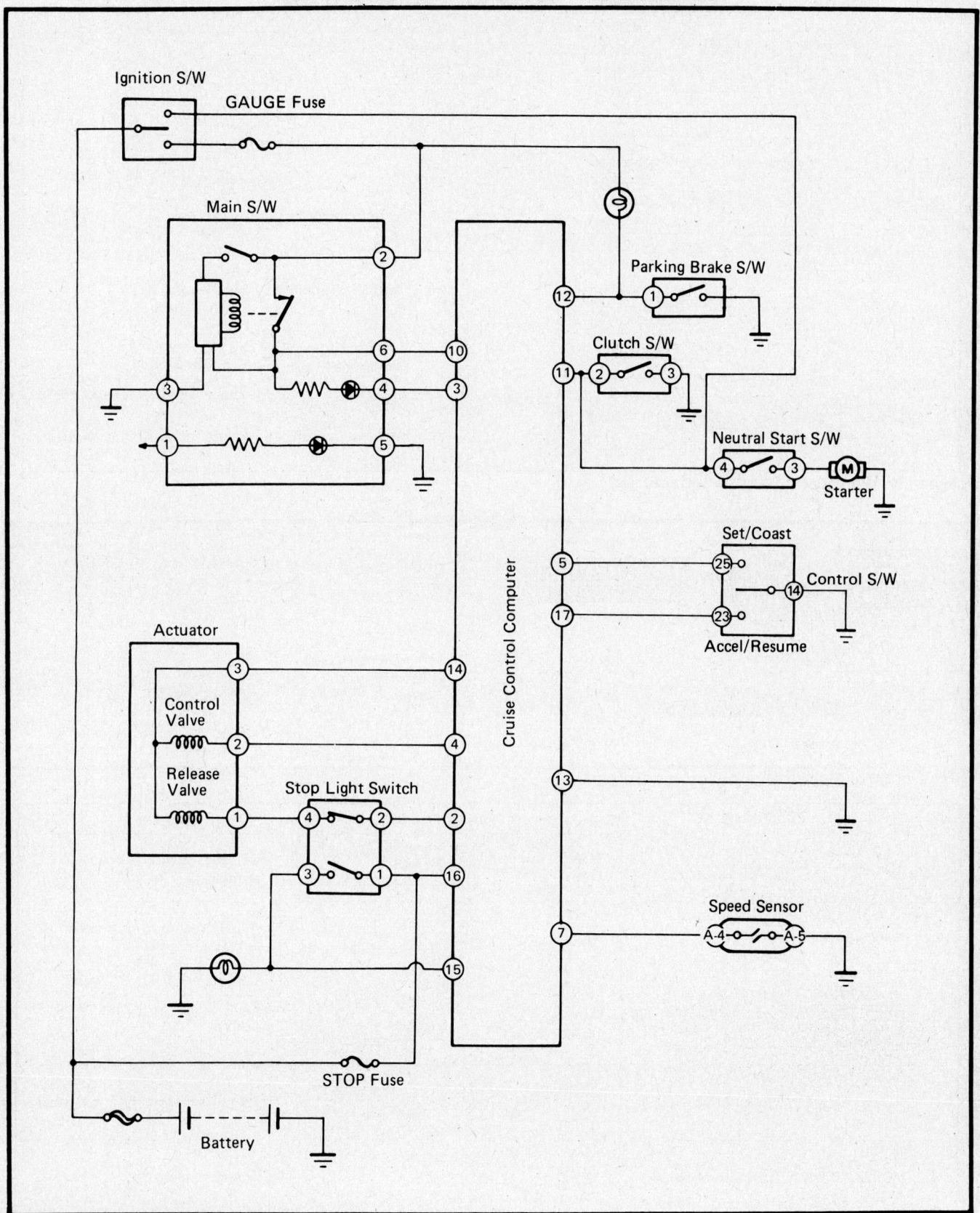

Cruise control electrical schematic—Tercel

No.	Indicator code	Diagnosis
	ON 0.25S 0.25S OFF	Normal
11	ON 0.5S OFF 1.5S 4S	Actuator circuit is abnormal.
21	ON 0.5S OFF 1.5S	Speed sensor signal circuit is abnormal.
23	ON OFF	Speed sensor signal circuit is abnormal.
31	ON OFF	Accel/resume switch circuit is abnormal.
33	ON OFF	Accel/resume switch and set/coast switch is abnormal.

Type "B" diagnostic information—Tercel

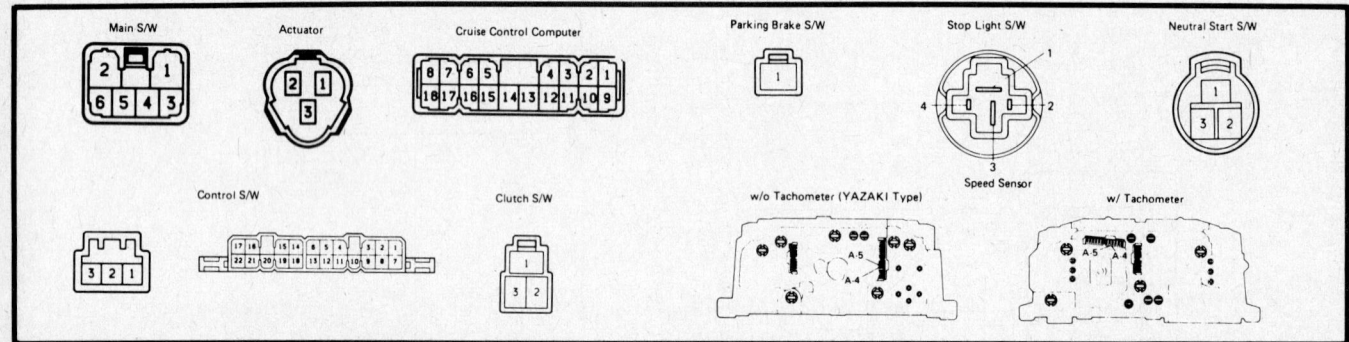

Cruise control electrical connectors—Tercel

No.	Conditions	Indicator code	Diagnosis
1	Set/coast switch on	ON 0.25S 0.25S OFF 1.0S	Set/coast switch circuit is normal.
2	Accel/resume switch on	ON OFF	Accel/resume switch circuit is circuit is normal.
3	Each cancel switch on (Stop light switch, Parking brake switch, Clutch switch, Neutral start switch)	ON OFF	Each cancel switch circuit is normal.
4	Drive 40 km/h (25 mph) or over	ON OFF	Speed sensor circuit is normal.
5	Drive 40 km/h (25 mph) or below	ON OFF	Speed sensor circuit is normal.

Type "A" diagnostic information—Tercel

CRUISE CONTROL SYSTEM DIAGNOSIS

Output of Diagnosis Codes

TYPE A CODE

1. Turn the ignition switch to the on position.
2. Turn the set/coast switch on. Turn the main switch on.
3. Read the diagnosis code on the main switch indicator.
4. Indicator codes appear in order from number one.
5. Results are as follows.

TYPE B CODE

1. Do not turn the ignition switch off. Do not turn the main switch off.
2. Turn the set/coast switch on three times within two seconds.
3. Read the diagnosis code on the main switch indicator.
4. Indication codes appear with priority from number eleven. Normal codes continue twenty seconds and abnormal codes are repeated three times.
5. Indication is stopped when vehicle speed is over 10 miles per hour or the main switch is turned off.
6. Results are as follows.

Troubleshooting

Symptom	Inspection Area		Section
Cruise control cannot be set.	(a) Inspect type A code	No. 1 NO	A
		No. 2 NO	B
		No. 3 NO	C
		No. 4 NO	D
		No. 5 NO	D
	(b) Inspect type B code	11	E
		21	D
		23	F
		31	B
		33	A and B
	(c) All codes are normal.		Replace computer
Vehicle speed does not reduce when coast switch turned on.	Inspect No. 1 of type A code.	OK	F
		NO	A
Vehicle does not accelerate when accel switch turned on.	Inspect No. 2 of type A code.	OK	F
		NO	B
Vehicle speed does not return to memorized speed when resume switch turned on.	Inspect No. 2 of type A code.	OK	F
		NO	B
Set speed deviates on high side.	Inspect No. 1 of type A code.	OK	F
Set speed deviates on low side.		NO	A
Vehicle speed fluctuates when set switch turned on.	Inspect No. 1 of type A code.	OK	F
		NO	A
Setting speed does not cancel when brake pedal depressed.	Inspect No. 3 of type A code.	OK	F
		NO	C
Setting speed does not cancel when parking brake pulled.	Inspect No. 3 of type A code.	OK	F
		NO	C
Setting speed does not cancel when clutch pedal depressed (M/T only).	Inspect No. 3 of type A code.	OK	F
		NO	C
Setting speed does not cancel when shifted to "N" range (A/T only).	Inspect No. 3 of type A code.	OK	F
		NO	C
Speed can be set below about 40 km/h (25 mph).	Inspect No. 4 of type A code.	OK	F
		NO	D
Cruise control will not disengage even below about 40 km/h (25 mph).	Inspect No. 5 of type A code.	OK	F
		NO	D

Cruise control troubleshooting data sheet—Tercel

A | INSPECTION OF SET/COAST SWITCH CIRCUIT

CONTROL S/W

INSPECT SET/COAST SWITCH OPERATION
Is there continuity between terminal 25 and body ground with set/coast switch turned off?

— Yes → Inspect control switch.

No ↓

COMPUTER

INSPECT SET/COAST SWITCH CIRCUIT
Disconnect connector from computer.
Is there continuity between terminal 5 and body ground with set/coast switch turned off?

— Yes → Short circuit in wire harness between terminal 5 of computer and terminal 25 of control switch.

No ↓

Replace computer.

B | INSPECTION OF RESUME/ACCEL SWITCH CIRCUIT

CONTROL S/W

INSPECT RESUME/ACCEL SWITCH OPERATION
Is there continuity between terminal 23 and body ground with resume/accel switch turned off?

— Yes → ● Short circuit in wire harness between terminal 23 of control switch and terminal 17 of computer.
● Inspect control switch.

No ↓

Is there continuity between terminal 23 and body ground with resume/accel switch turned on?

— No → Inspect control switch.

Yes ↓

COMPUTER

INSPECT RESUME/ACCEL SWITCH CIRCUIT
Is there continuity between terminal 17 and body ground with resume/accel switch turned on?

— No → Open circuit in wire harness between terminal 17 of computer and terminal 23 of control switch.

Yes ↓

Replace computer.

Cruise control trouble diagnosis chart – Tercel

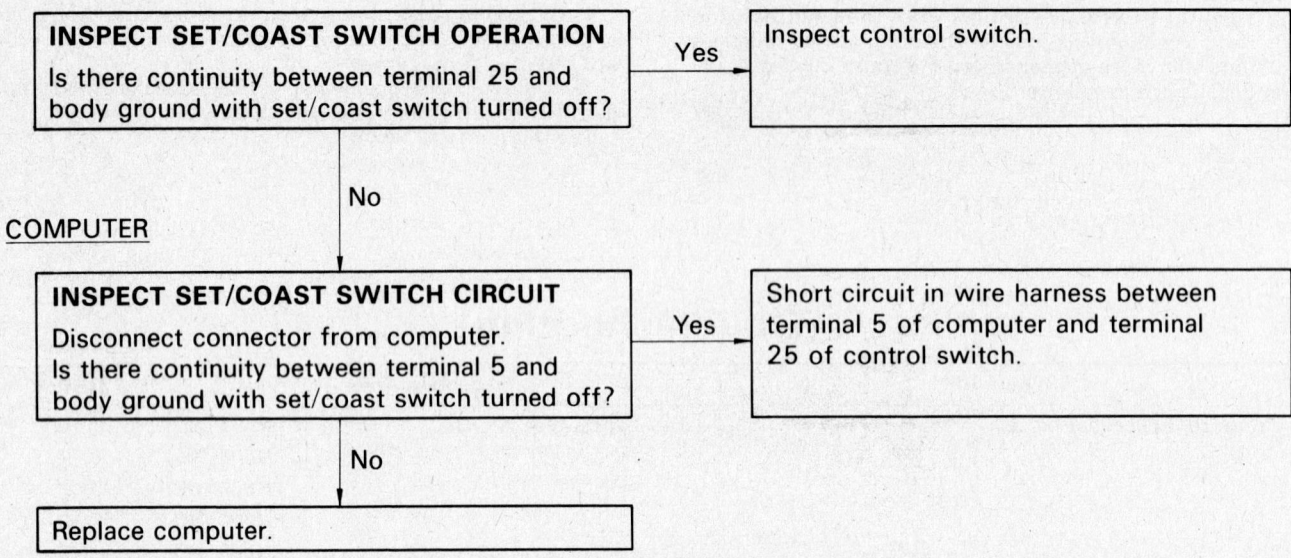

C | INSPECT CANCEL SWITCH CIRCUIT

1. INSPECT STOP LIGHT SWITCH CIRCUIT

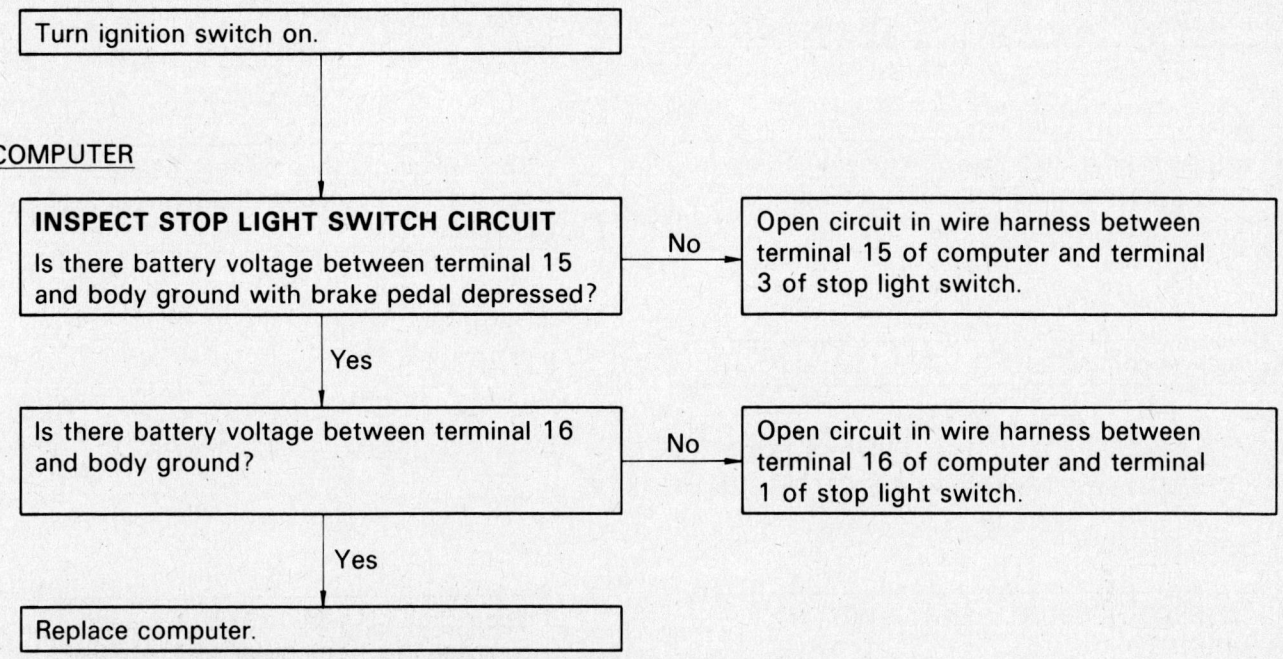

Turn ignition switch on.

COMPUTER

INSPECT STOP LIGHT SWITCH CIRCUIT
Is there battery voltage between terminal 15 and body ground with brake pedal depressed?

— No → Open circuit in wire harness between terminal 15 of computer and terminal 3 of stop light switch.

↓ Yes

Is there battery voltage between terminal 16 and body ground?

— No → Open circuit in wire harness between terminal 16 of computer and terminal 1 of stop light switch.

↓ Yes

Replace computer.

2. INSPECT PARKING BRAKE SWITCH CIRCUIT

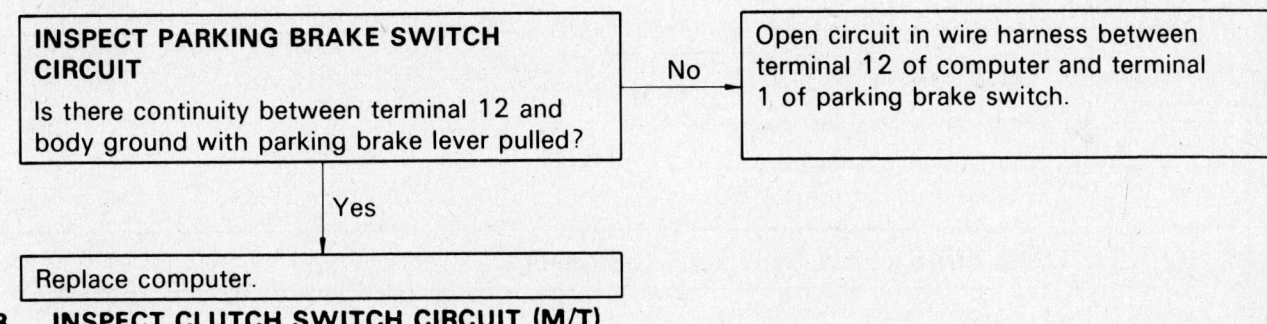

COMPUTER

INSPECT PARKING BRAKE SWITCH CIRCUIT
Is there continuity between terminal 12 and body ground with parking brake lever pulled?

— No → Open circuit in wire harness between terminal 12 of computer and terminal 1 of parking brake switch.

↓ Yes

Replace computer.

3. INSPECT CLUTCH SWITCH CIRCUIT (M/T)

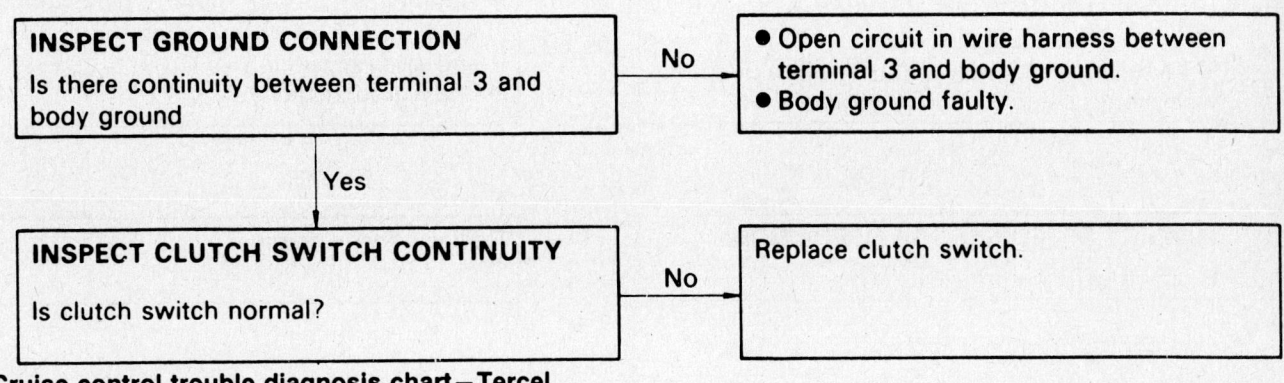

CLUTCH S/W

INSPECT GROUND CONNECTION
Is there continuity between terminal 3 and body ground

— No →
- Open circuit in wire harness between terminal 3 and body ground.
- Body ground faulty.

↓ Yes

INSPECT CLUTCH SWITCH CONTINUITY
Is clutch switch normal?

— No → Replace clutch switch.

Cruise control trouble diagnosis chart — Tercel

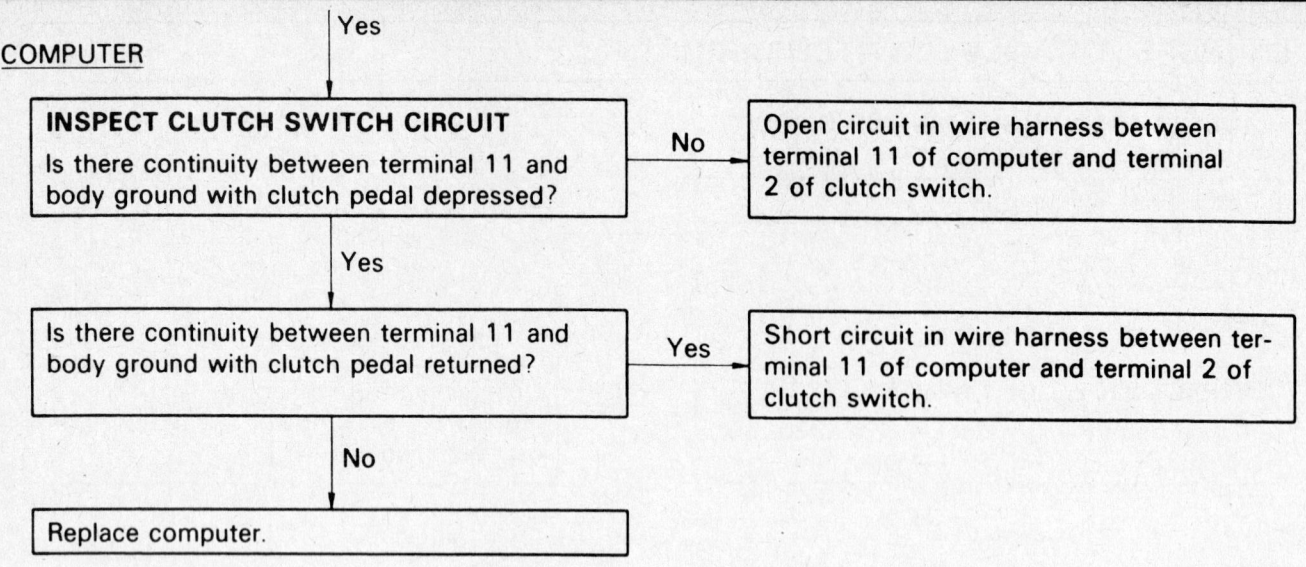

COMPUTER

Yes

INSPECT CLUTCH SWITCH CIRCUIT

Is there continuity between terminal 11 and body ground with clutch pedal depressed?

No → Open circuit in wire harness between terminal 11 of computer and terminal 2 of clutch switch.

Yes

Is there continuity between terminal 11 and body ground with clutch pedal returned?

Yes → Short circuit in wire harness between terminal 11 of computer and terminal 2 of clutch switch.

No

Replace computer.

4. INSPECT NEUTRAL START SWITCH CIRCUIT (A/T)

COMPUTER

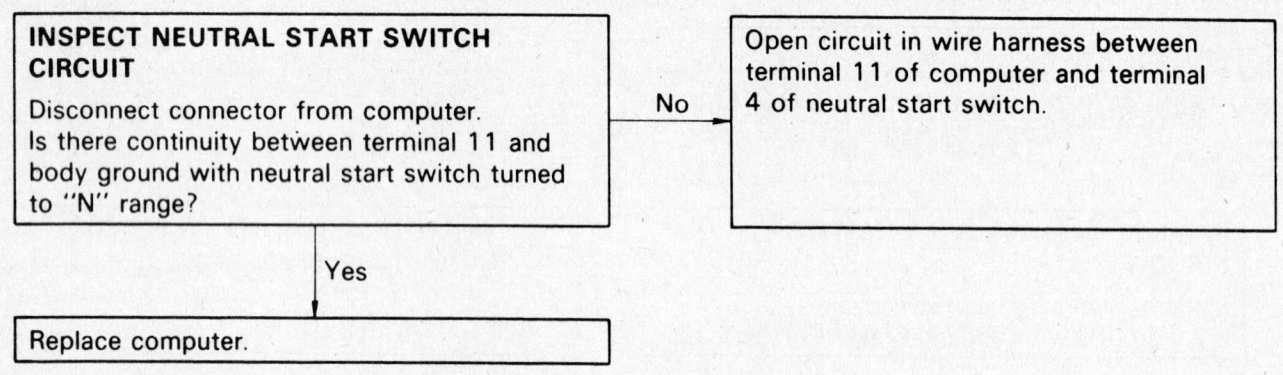

INSPECT NEUTRAL START SWITCH CIRCUIT

Disconnect connector from computer.
Is there continuity between terminal 11 and body ground with neutral start switch turned to "N" range?

No → Open circuit in wire harness between terminal 11 of computer and terminal 4 of neutral start switch.

Yes

Replace computer.

D | INSPECTION OF SPEED SENSOR CIRCUIT

SPEED SENSOR

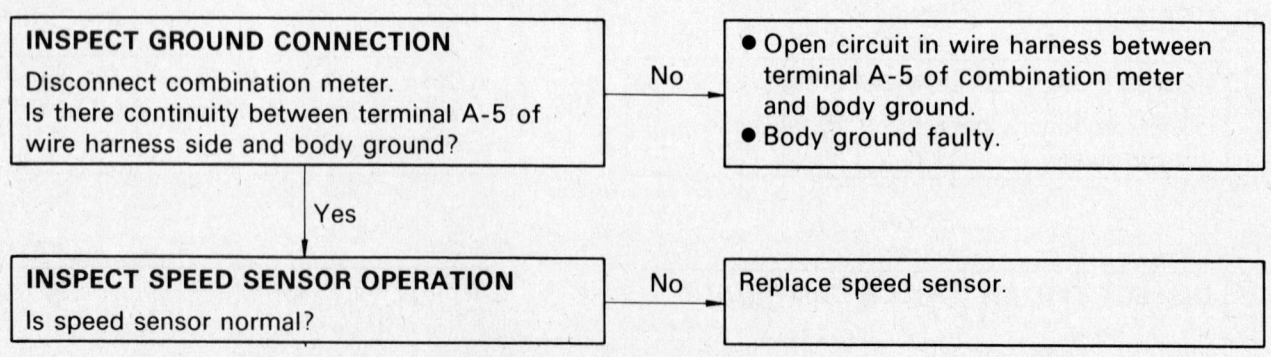

INSPECT GROUND CONNECTION

Disconnect combination meter.
Is there continuity between terminal A-5 of wire harness side and body ground?

No → • Open circuit in wire harness between terminal A-5 of combination meter and body ground.
• Body ground faulty.

Yes

INSPECT SPEED SENSOR OPERATION

Is speed sensor normal?

No → Replace speed sensor.

Cruise control trouble diagnosis chart—Tercel

Yes

COMPUTER

INSPECT SPEED SENSOR CIRCUIT

Disconnect connector from combination meter.
Is there continuity between terminal 7 and
body ground? → Yes → Short circuit in wire harness between terminal 7 of computer and terminal A-4 of combination meter.

No

Is there continuity between terminal 7 of computer and terminal A-4 of combination meter? → No → Open circuit in wire harness between terminal 7 of computer and terminal A-4 of combination meter.

Yes

Replace computer.

E │ INSPECTION OF ACTUATOR OPERATION

ACTUATOR

INSPECT ACTUATOR OPERATION

Remove actuator.
Is actuator normal? → No → Replace actuator.

Yes

Replace computer.

F │ INSPECTION OF ACTUATOR CIRCUIT

ACTUATOR

INSPECT ACTUATOR OPERATION

Remove actuator.
Is actuator normal? → No → Replace actuator.

Yes

STOP LIGHT S/W

INSPECT STOP LIGHT SWITCH OPERATION

Is stop light switch normal? → No → Replace stop light switch.

Cruise control trouble diagnosis chart — Tercel

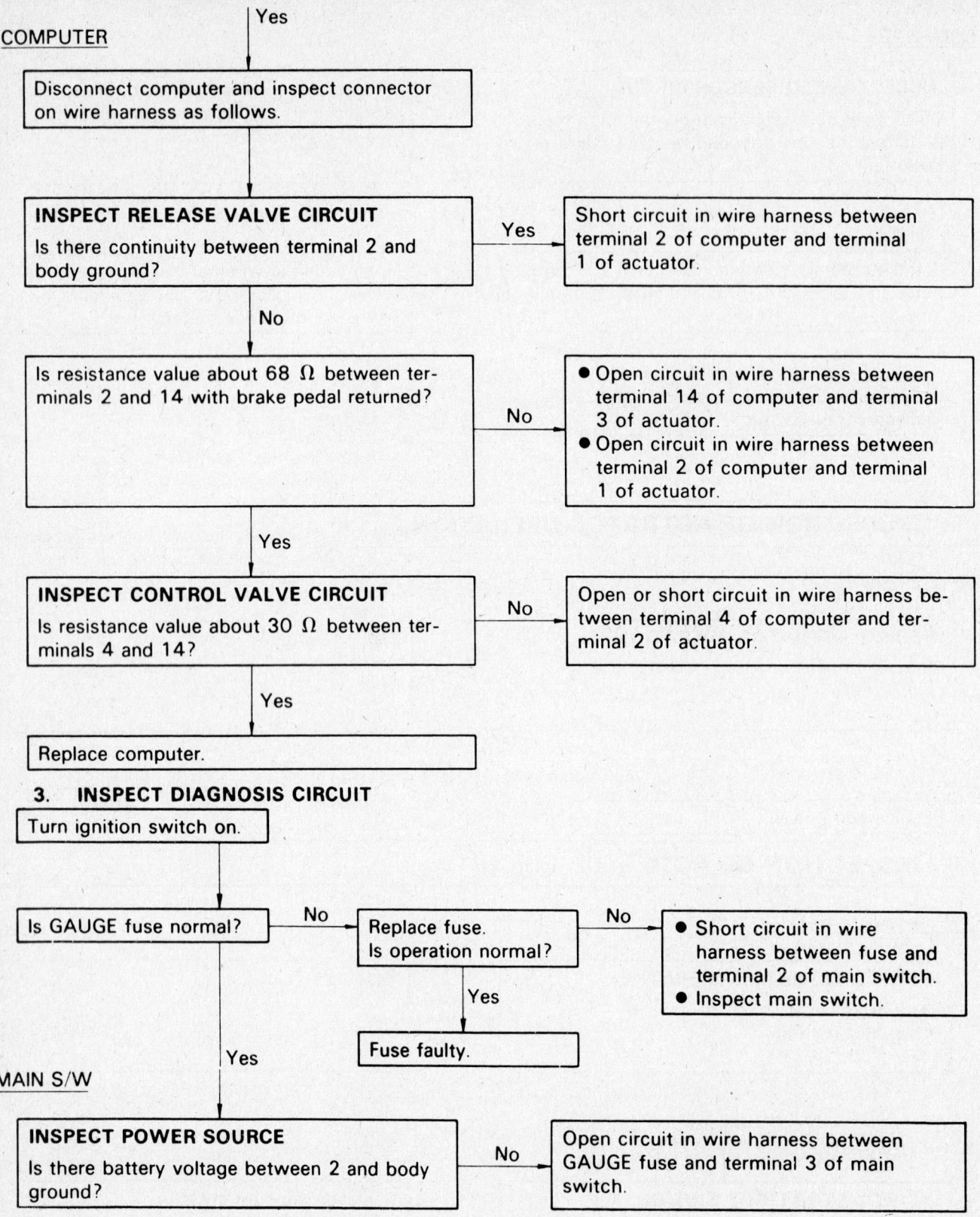

COMPUTER

Yes

Disconnect computer and inspect connector on wire harness as follows.

INSPECT RELEASE VALVE CIRCUIT

Is there continuity between terminal 2 and body ground?

Yes → Short circuit in wire harness between terminal 2 of computer and terminal 1 of actuator.

No

Is resistance value about 68 Ω between terminals 2 and 14 with brake pedal returned?

No →
- Open circuit in wire harness between terminal 14 of computer and terminal 3 of actuator.
- Open circuit in wire harness between terminal 2 of computer and terminal 1 of actuator.

Yes

INSPECT CONTROL VALVE CIRCUIT

Is resistance value about 30 Ω between terminals 4 and 14?

No → Open or short circuit in wire harness between terminal 4 of computer and terminal 2 of actuator.

Yes

Replace computer.

3. INSPECT DIAGNOSIS CIRCUIT

Turn ignition switch on.

Is GAUGE fuse normal?

No → Replace fuse. Is operation normal?

No →
- Short circuit in wire harness between fuse and terminal 2 of main switch.
- Inspect main switch.

Yes → Fuse faulty.

Yes

MAIN S/W

INSPECT POWER SOURCE

Is there battery voltage between 2 and body ground?

No → Open circuit in wire harness between GAUGE fuse and terminal 3 of main switch.

Cruise control trouble diagnosis chart—Tercel

1214

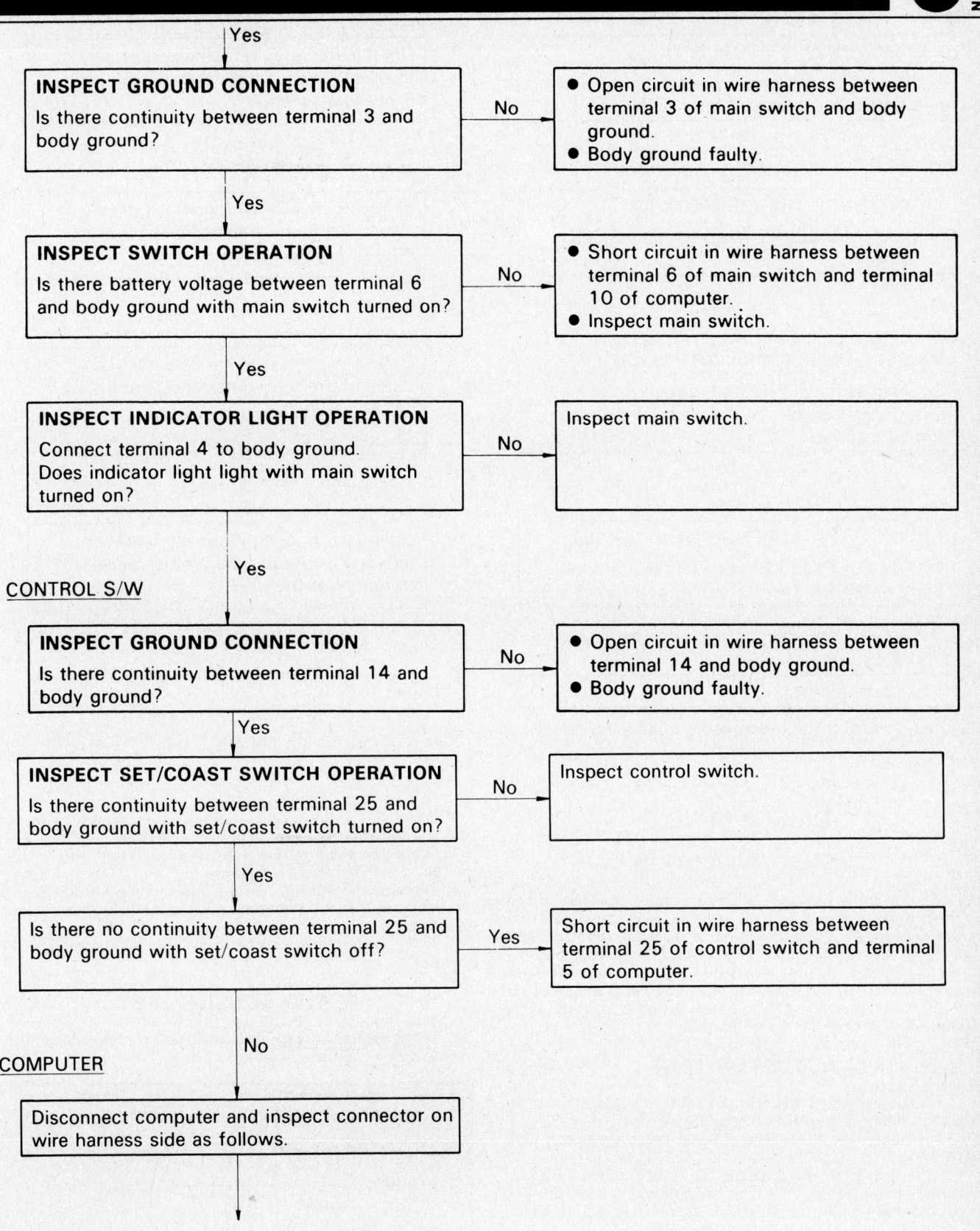

Yes

INSPECT GROUND CONNECTION

Is there continuity between terminal 3 and body ground?

No →
- Open circuit in wire harness between terminal 3 of main switch and body ground.
- Body ground faulty.

Yes

INSPECT SWITCH OPERATION

Is there battery voltage between terminal 6 and body ground with main switch turned on?

No →
- Short circuit in wire harness between terminal 6 of main switch and terminal 10 of computer.
- Inspect main switch.

Yes

INSPECT INDICATOR LIGHT OPERATION

Connect terminal 4 to body ground.
Does indicator light light with main switch turned on?

No →
Inspect main switch.

Yes

CONTROL S/W

INSPECT GROUND CONNECTION

Is there continuity between terminal 14 and body ground?

No →
- Open circuit in wire harness between terminal 14 and body ground.
- Body ground faulty.

Yes

INSPECT SET/COAST SWITCH OPERATION

Is there continuity between terminal 25 and body ground with set/coast switch turned on?

No →
Inspect control switch.

Yes

Is there no continuity between terminal 25 and body ground with set/coast switch off?

Yes →
Short circuit in wire harness between terminal 25 of control switch and terminal 5 of computer.

No

COMPUTER

Disconnect computer and inspect connector on wire harness side as follows.

Cruise control trouble diagnosis chart—Tercel

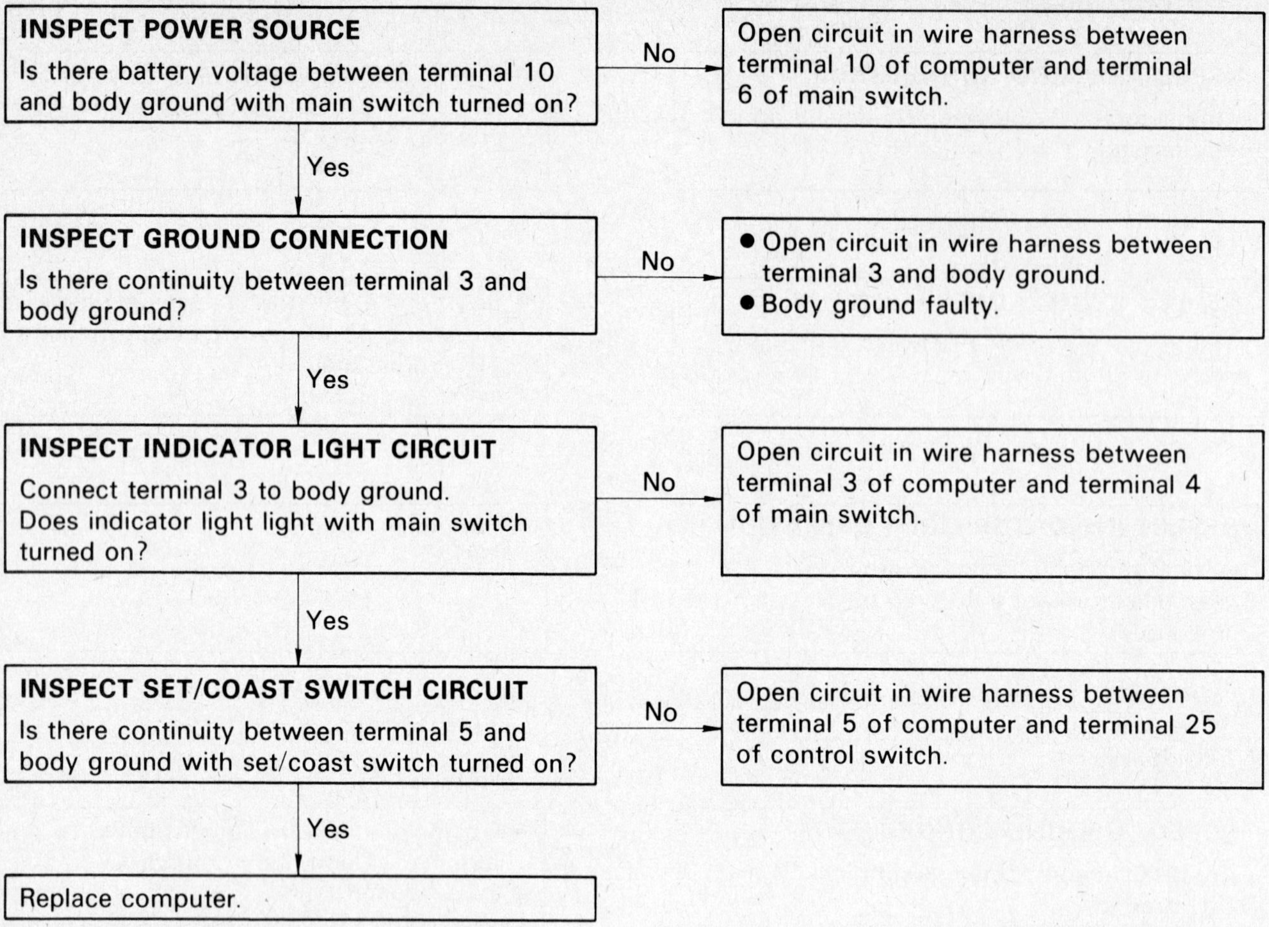

INSPECT POWER SOURCE

Is there battery voltage between terminal 10 and body ground with main switch turned on?

— No → Open circuit in wire harness between terminal 10 of computer and terminal 6 of main switch.

↓ Yes

INSPECT GROUND CONNECTION

Is there continuity between terminal 3 and body ground?

— No → • Open circuit in wire harness between terminal 3 and body ground.
• Body ground faulty.

↓ Yes

INSPECT INDICATOR LIGHT CIRCUIT

Connect terminal 3 to body ground. Does indicator light light with main switch turned on?

— No → Open circuit in wire harness between terminal 3 of computer and terminal 4 of main switch.

↓ Yes

INSPECT SET/COAST SWITCH CIRCUIT

Is there continuity between terminal 5 and body ground with set/coast switch turned on?

— No → Open circuit in wire harness between terminal 5 of computer and terminal 25 of control switch.

↓ Yes

Replace computer.

Cruise control trouble diagnosis chart — Tercel

Corolla (RWD)

VISUAL INSPECTION

Before performing any tests make a visual inspection of the cruise control system. Check all items in the system for abnormal conditions such as bare broken or disconnected wires and damage to the vacuum hoses. Be sure that the speedometer cables are attached and properly routed. All vacuum hoses must be properly routed and must not have any kinks or bends. Be sure that all electrical connections are complete and tight. The wiring harness must be routed properly.

ACTUATOR TEST

1. Inspect and check the actuator cable. Freeplay should be less than 0.039 inch. Adjust or replace as required.
2. Disconnect the electrical connector from the actuator lead wire.
3. Using an ohmmeter measure the resistance between terminals one and two. It should be about 68 ohms. Measure the resistance between terminals one and three. It should be about 30 ohms.
4. If the resistance is not as indicated, replace the actuator.
5. Connect a positive lead from the positive terminal of the battery to terminals two and three. Connect a negative lead from the negative terminal of the battery to terminal one.

6. Slowly apply 0 to 11.8 in. hg. of vacuum. Check to be sure that the control cable can be pulled smoothly.
7. When the vacuum has stabilized check the control cable and be sure that it does not return.
8. Disconnect terminal two or three and check that the control cable returns to its original position and that the vacuum goes to zero.
9. If the system does not perform as indicated replace the actuator.

SPEED SENSOR TEST

1. Using an ohmmeter, check to see that there is continunity

Actuator test point locations — Corolla (RWD)

Terminal	Connection or Measure Item	Check Item	Tester Connection	Condition	Voltage or Resistance Value
1	Stop Light Switch and Release Valve	Resistance	1 – 2	Brake pedal returned	about 30 Ω
2	Release Valve and Control Valve				
3	Control Valve	Resistance	3 – 2		about 68 Ω
4	Control Switch (Set/Coast)	Continuity	4 – Body Ground	Turn set/coast switch on Turn set/coast switch off	continuity no continuity
5	OD Relay				
6	Speed Sensor	Continuity	6 – Body Ground	Vehicle moving slowly	1 pulse each 40 cm (15.75 in.)
7	Control Switch (Main)	Voltage	7 – Body Ground	Turn ignition switch and main switch on. Turn ignition switch and main switch off.	battery voltage no voltage
8	Stop Light Switch	Voltage	8 – Body Ground	Brake pedal depressed Brake pedal returned	battery voltage no voltage
9	STOP Fuse	Voltage	9 – Body Ground		battery voltage
10	Body Ground	Continuity	10 – Body Ground		continuity
11	Clutch Switch Neutral Switch	Continuity	11 – Body Ground	Clutch pedal depressed or shift into "N" range Clutch pedal returned or shift into any range except "N"	continuity no continuity
12	Parking Brake Switch	Voltage	12 – Body Ground	Parking brake pulled Parking brake returned	no voltage battery voltage
13	Control Switch (Accel/Resume)	Continuity	13 – Body Ground	Turn accel/resume switch on Turn accel/resume switch off	continuity no continuity

Cruise control computer circuit inspection chart—1984 Corolla (RWD)

between terminals 18 and 19. It should be four times per revolution of the magnet shaft.

2. If continunity does not exist replace the speed sensor.

CONTROL SWITCH TEST

1. Using an ohmmeter check for continuity of the terminals for each switch position.

2. If continunity between the terminals is not as specified, replace the switch.

CLUTCH SWITCH TEST

1. Check to be sure that there is continunity between terminals two and three with the clutch pedal depressed.

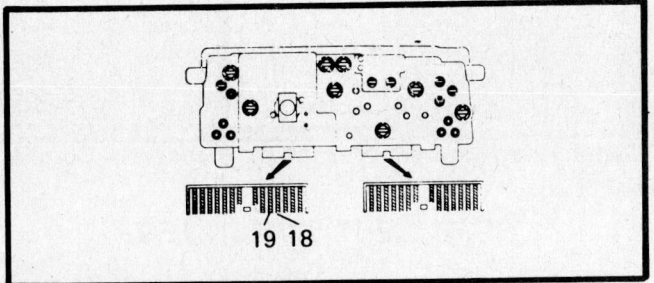

Speed sensor test point locations—Corolla (RWD)

Control switch test point locations—1984 Corolla (RWD)

Terminal	Connection or Measure Item	Check Item	Tester Connection	Condition	Voltage or Resistance Value
2	Stop Light Switch and Release Valve	Resistance	2 – 14	Brake pedal returned	About 30
4	Control Valve	Resistance	4 – 14		About 68
5	Control Switch (Set/coast S/W)	Continuity	5 – Body ground	Turn set/coast switch on	Continuity
				Turn set/coast switch off	Continuity
6	OD Relay				
7	Speed Sensor	Continuity	7 – Body ground	Vehicle moving slowly	1 pulse each 40 cm (15.75 in.)
10	Control Switch (Main S/W)	Voltage	10 – Body ground	Turn ignition switch and main switch on.	Battery voltage
				Turn ignition switch and main switch off.	No voltage
11	Clutch Switch or Neutral Start Switch	Continuity	11 – Body ground	Clutch pedal depressed or if shifted into "N" range	Continuity
				Clutch pedal returned or if shifted into any range except "N" range.	No continuity
12	Parking Brake Switch	Voltage	12 – Body ground	Parking brake pulled	No voltage
				Parking brake returned	Battery voltage
13	Body Ground	Continuity	13 – Body ground		Continuity
14	Release Valve and Control Valve				
15	Stop Fuse	Voltage	15 – Body ground		Battery voltage
17	Control Switch (Accel/resume S/W)	Continuity	17 – Body ground	Turn accel/resume switch on	Continuity
				Turn accel/resume switch off	No continuity

Cruise control computer circuit inspection chart—1985 and later Corolla (RWD)

2. Check to be sure that there is continuity between terminals two and three with the clutch pedal returned.

3. If continuity is not as indicated, replace the clutch switch.

Switch position \ Terminal	1	2	3	4	5	6	7
OFF							
Main S/W ON			O				O
SET/COAST S/W ON				O	O		
ACCEL/RESUME S/W ON		O		O			

Control switch specifications—1984 Corolla (RWD)

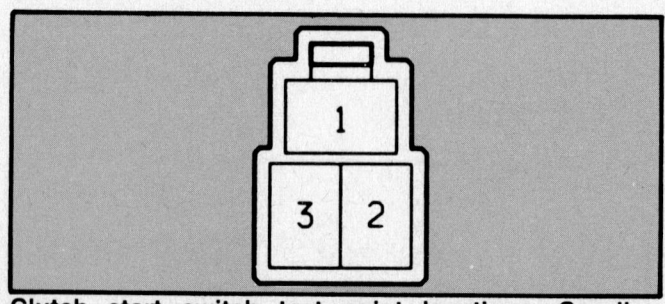

Clutch start switch test point locations—Corolla (RWD)

STOP LIGHT SWITCH TEST

1. Using an ohmmeter check for continuity of the terminals for each switch position.

2. If continuity between the terminals is not as specified, replace the switch.

VACUUM PUMP TEST (1986 AND LATER)

1. Connect a vacuum pump to the ACT side of the vacuum pump.

2. Connect a positive lead from the positive terminal of the battery to terminal one. Connect a negative lead from the negative terminal of the battery to terminal two.

3. Check to be sure that there is a vacuum of at least 7.87 in. hg. or above.

4. If the above test results are not achieved, replace the vacuum pump.

Stoplight switch test point locations – 1984–85 Corolla (RWD)

Terminal / Brake pedal position	1	2	3	4
Brake pedal depressed	O—————O			
Brake pedal returned			O—————O	

Stoplight switch specifications – Corolla (RWD)

Switch Position \ Terminal (Wire color)	14	15	16	18	19	20	21
OFF							
Main S/W ON							
Set/coast S/W ON	O					O	
Accel/resume S/W ON		O				O	

Control switch specifications – 1985 and later Corolla (RWD)

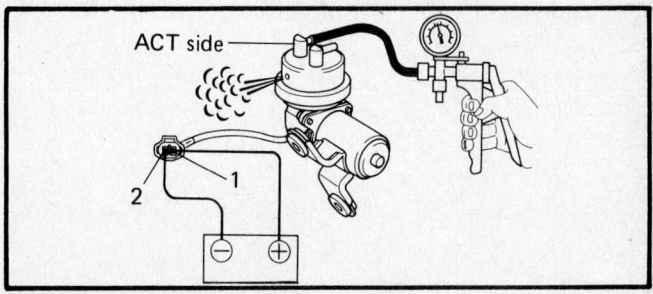

Vacuum pump test point locations – 1986 and later

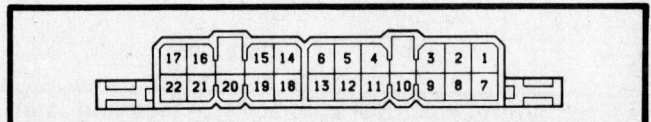

Cotrol switch test point locations – 1985 and later Corolla (RWD)

DIAGNOSIS AND TESTING PROCEDURES

No.	Conditions	Indicator Code	Diagnosis
1	Set/coast switch on	0.25S / 1.0S / 0.25S — ON/OFF pulse waveform	Set/coast switch circuit is normal
2	Accel/resume switch on	ON/OFF pulse waveform	Accel/resume switch circuit is normal
3	Each cancel switch on (Stop light switch, Parking brake switch, Clutch switch, Neutral start switch)	ON then OFF step	Each cancel switch circuit is normal
4	Drive 40 km/h (25 mph) or over	ON/OFF pulse waveform	Speed sensor circuit is normal
5	Drive 40 km/h (25 mph) or below	ON (flat line) / OFF	Speed sensor circuit is normal

Type "A" diagnostic information – 1985 Corolla (RWD)

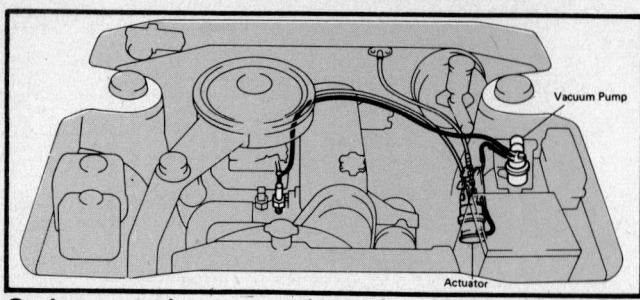

Cruise control vacuum schematic — 1986 and later Corolla (RWD)

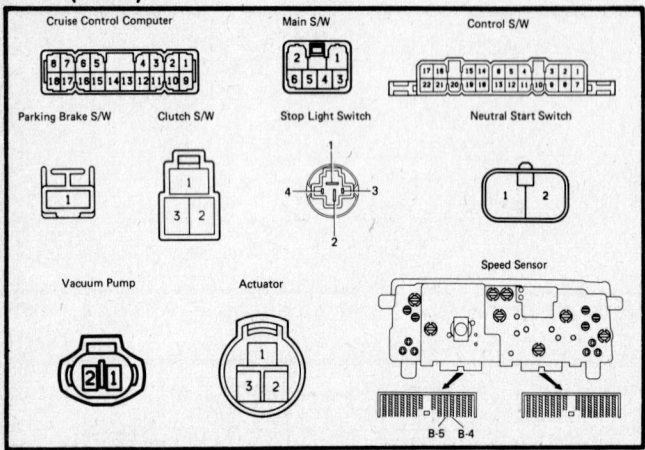

Cruise control electrical connectors — 1986 and later Corolla (RWD)

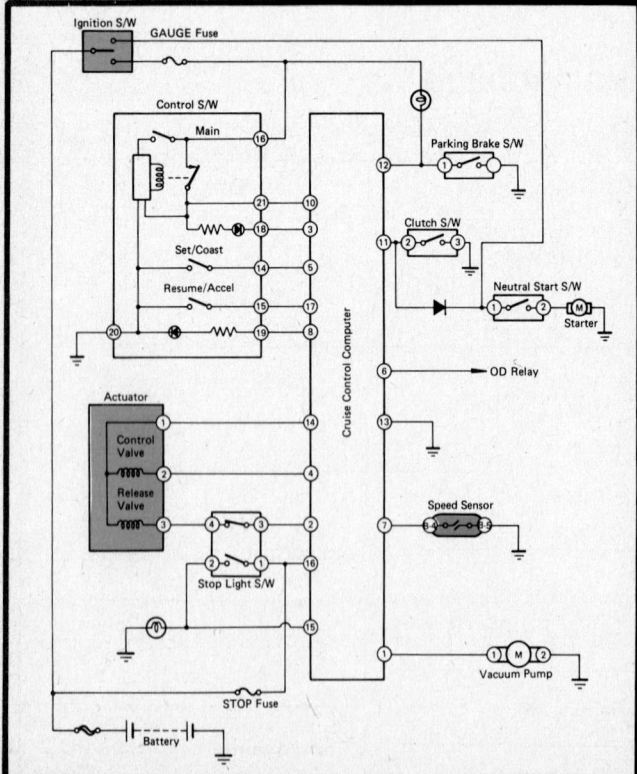

Cruise control electrical schematic — 1986 and later Corolla (RWD)

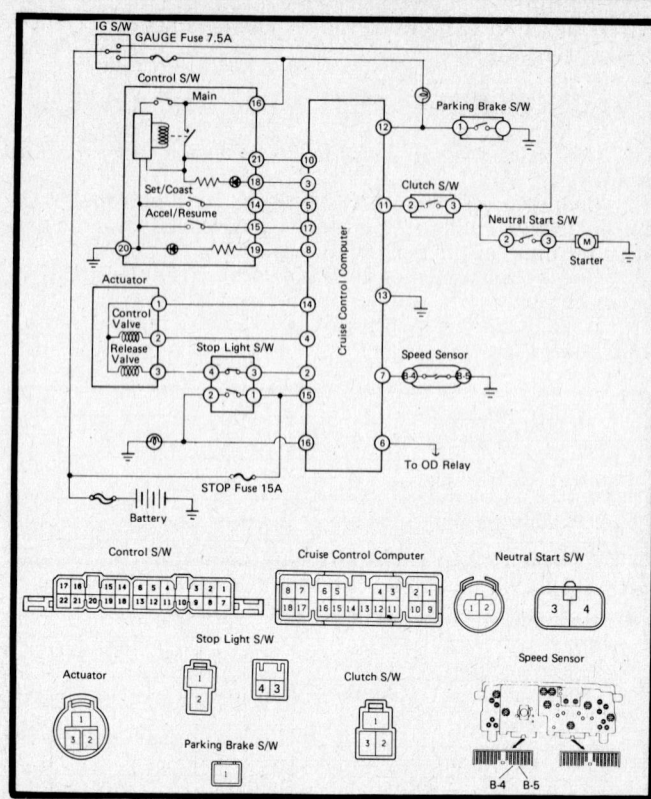

Cruise control electrical schematic — 1985 Corolla (RWD)

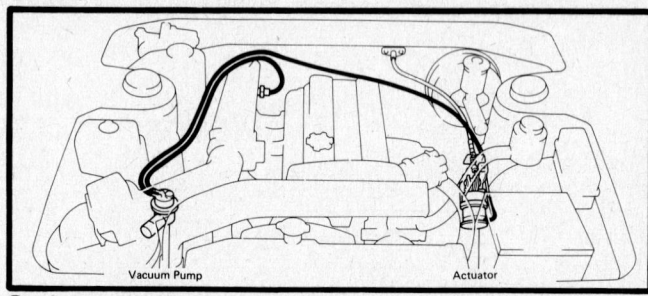

Cruise control vacuum schematic — 1986 and later Corolla (RWD)

CRUISE CONTROL SYSTEM DIAGNOSIS — 1985 AND LATER

Output of Diagnosis Codes

TYPE A CODE (1985 ONLY)

1. Turn the ignition switch to the on position.
2. Turn the set/coast switch on. Turn the main switch on.
3. Read the diagnosis code on the main switch indicator.
4. Results are as follows.

TYPE B CODE

1. Do not turn the ignition switch off. Do not turn the main switch off.
2. Turn the set/coast switch on three times within two seconds.
3. Read the diagnosis code on the main switch indicator.
4. Indication codes appear with priority from number eleven. Normal codes continue twenty seconds and abnormal codes are repeated three times.
5. Indication is stopped when vehicle speed is over 10 miles per hour or the main switch is turned off.
6. Results are as follows.

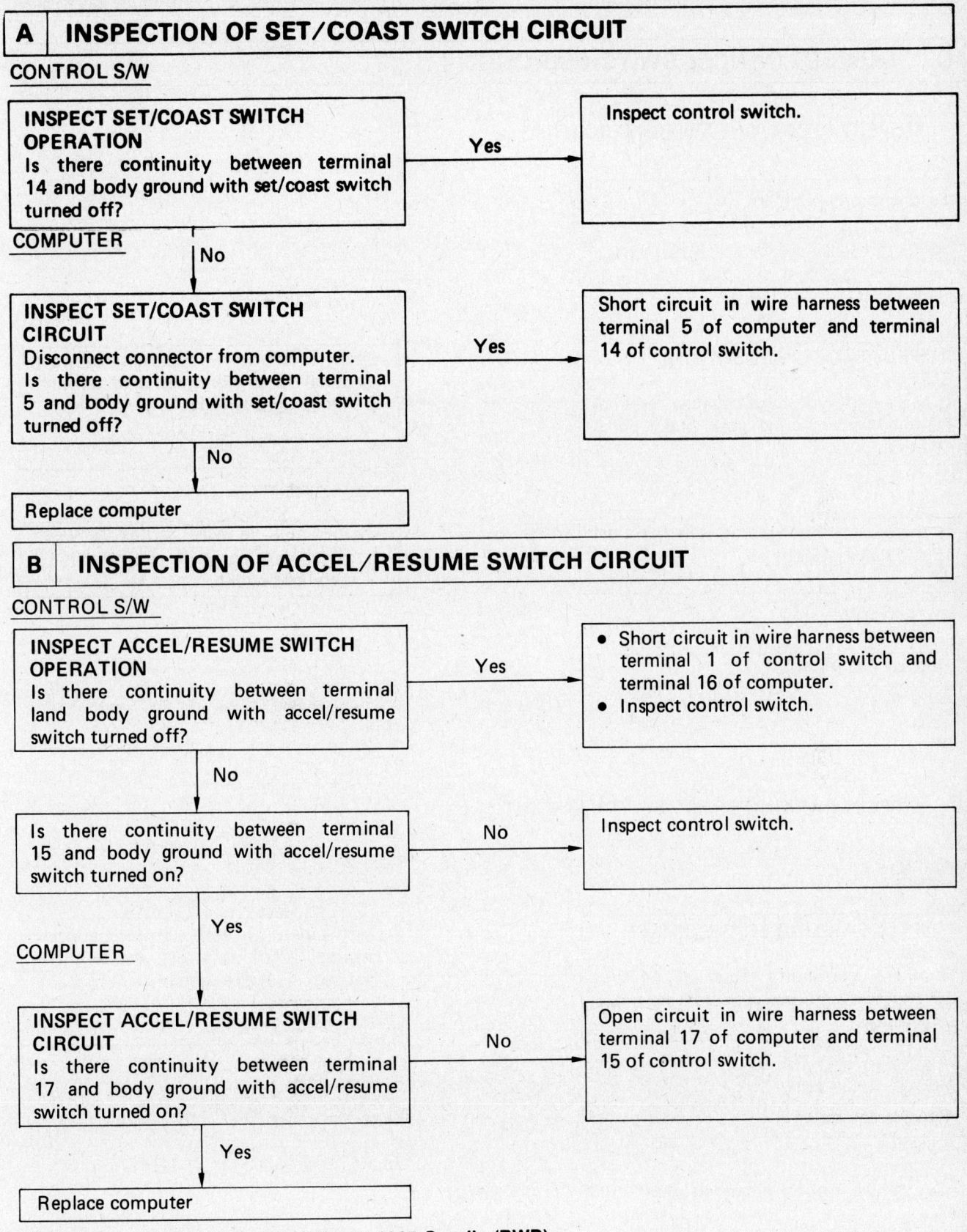

A | INSPECTION OF SET/COAST SWITCH CIRCUIT

CONTROL S/W

INSPECT SET/COAST SWITCH OPERATION
Is there continuity between terminal 14 and body ground with set/coast switch turned off?
— Yes → Inspect control switch.

COMPUTER

| No ↓

INSPECT SET/COAST SWITCH CIRCUIT
Disconnect connector from computer.
Is there continuity between terminal 5 and body ground with set/coast switch turned off?
— Yes → Short circuit in wire harness between terminal 5 of computer and terminal 14 of control switch.

| No ↓

Replace computer

B | INSPECTION OF ACCEL/RESUME SWITCH CIRCUIT

CONTROL S/W

INSPECT ACCEL/RESUME SWITCH OPERATION
Is there continuity between terminal land body ground with accel/resume switch turned off?
— Yes →
- Short circuit in wire harness between terminal 1 of control switch and terminal 16 of computer.
- Inspect control switch.

| No ↓

Is there continuity between terminal 15 and body ground with accel/resume switch turned on?
— No → Inspect control switch.

| Yes ↓

COMPUTER

INSPECT ACCEL/RESUME SWITCH CIRCUIT
Is there continuity between terminal 17 and body ground with accel/resume switch turned on?
— No → Open circuit in wire harness between terminal 17 of computer and terminal 15 of control switch.

| Yes ↓

Replace computer

Cruise control trouble diagnosis chart—1985 Corolla (RWD)

C	INSPECT CANCEL SWITCH CIRCUIT

1. INSPECT STOP LIGHT SWITCH CIRCUIT

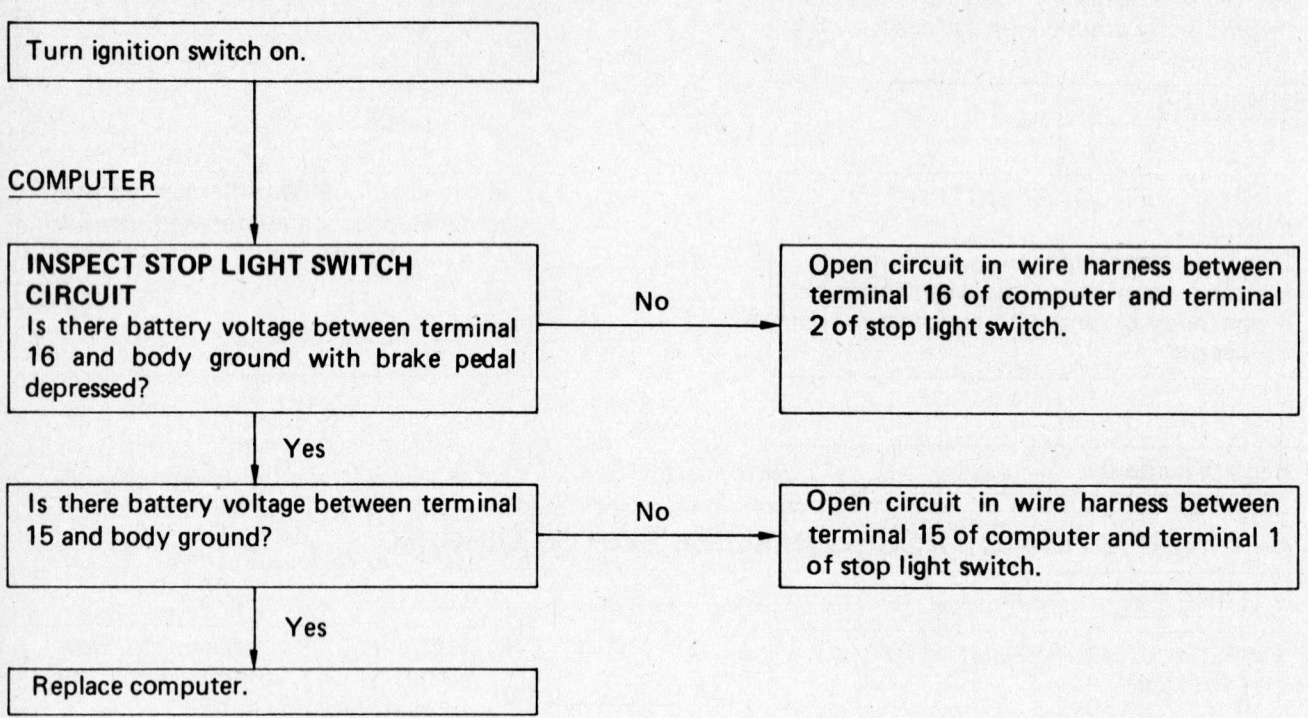

COMPUTER

Turn ignition switch on.

INSPECT STOP LIGHT SWITCH CIRCUIT
Is there battery voltage between terminal 16 and body ground with brake pedal depressed?

— No → Open circuit in wire harness between terminal 16 of computer and terminal 2 of stop light switch.

Yes

Is there battery voltage between terminal 15 and body ground?

— No → Open circuit in wire harness between terminal 15 of computer and terminal 1 of stop light switch.

Yes

Replace computer.

2. INSPECT PARKING BRAKE SWITCH CIRCUIT

COMPUTER

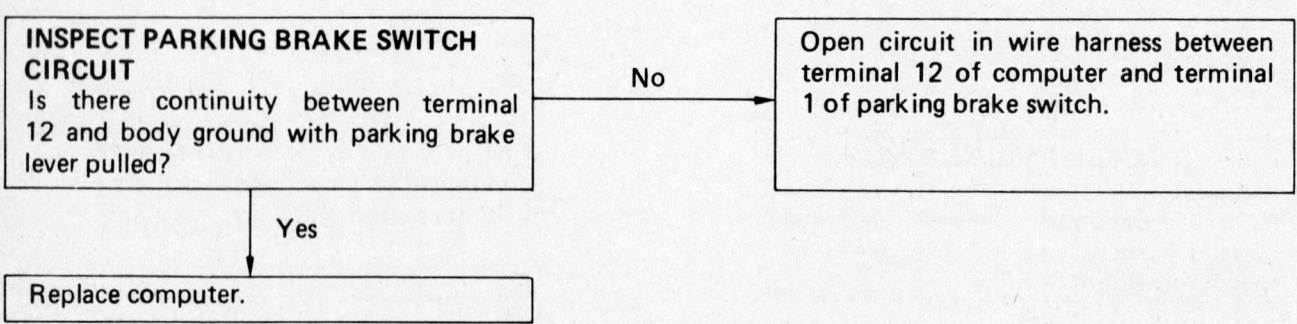

INSPECT PARKING BRAKE SWITCH CIRCUIT
Is there continuity between terminal 12 and body ground with parking brake lever pulled?

— No → Open circuit in wire harness between terminal 12 of computer and terminal 1 of parking brake switch.

Yes

Replace computer.

Cruise control trouble diagnosis chart—1985 Corolla (RWD)

3. INSPECT CLUTCH SWITCH CIRCUIT (M/T)

CLUTCH S/W

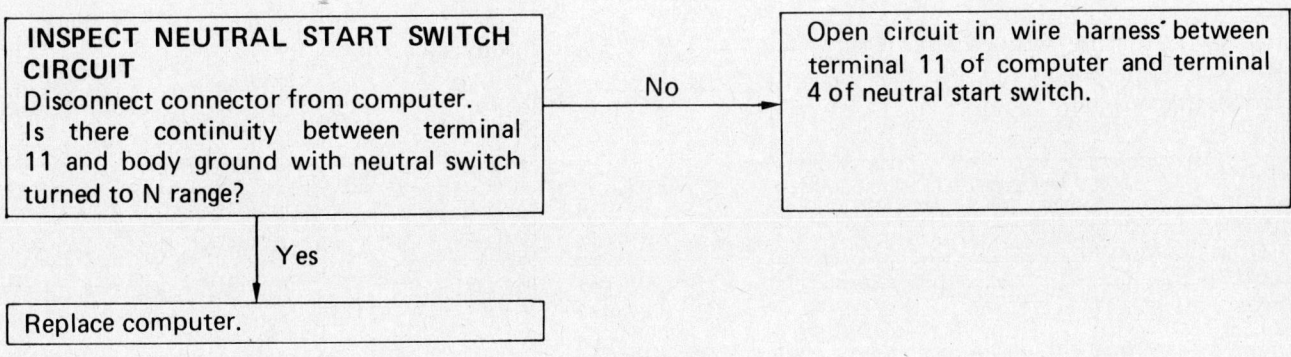

| INSPECT GROUND CONNECTION
Is there continuity between terminal 3 and body ground? | → No → | • Open circuit in wire harness between terminal 3 and body ground.
• Body ground faulty. |

↓ Yes

| INSPECT CLUTCH SWITCH CONTINUITY
Is clutch switch normal?
(See page BE-49) | → No → | Replace clutch switch. |

↓ Yes

COMPUTER

| INSPECT CLUTCH SWITCH CIRCUIT
Is there continuity between terminal 11 and body ground with clutch pedal depressed? | → No → | Open circuit in wire harness between terminal 11 of computer and terminal 2 of clutch switch. |

↓ Yes

| Is there continuity between terminal 11 and body ground with clutch pedal returned? | → Yes → | Short circuit in wire harness between terminal 11 of computer and terminal 2 of clutch switch. |

↓ No

Replace actuator.

4. INSPECT NEUTRAL START SWITCH CIRCUIT (A/T)

COMPUTER

| INSPECT NEUTRAL START SWITCH CIRCUIT
Disconnect connector from computer.
Is there continuity between terminal 11 and body ground with neutral switch turned to N range? | → No → | Open circuit in wire harness between terminal 11 of computer and terminal 4 of neutral start switch. |

↓ Yes

Replace computer.

Cruise control trouble diagnosis chart — 1985 Corolla (RWD)

D | INSPECTION OF SPEED SENSOR CIRCUIT

SPEED SENSOR

INSPECT GROUND CONNECTION
Disconnect combination meter.
Is there continuity between terminal B-5 of wire harness side and body ground?

→ No →
- Open circuit in wire harness between terminal B-5 of combination meter and body ground.
- Body ground faulty.

↓ Yes

INSPECT SPEED SENSOR OPERATION
Is speed sensor normal?

→ No →
Replace speed sensor.

COMPUTER

↓ Yes

INSPECT SPEED SENSOR CIRCUIT
Disconnect connector from combination meter.
Is there continuity between terminal 7 and body ground?

→ Yes →
Short circuit in wire harness between terminal 7 of computer and terminal B-5 of combination meter.

↓ No

Is there continuity between terminal 7 of computer and terminal of combination meter?

→ No →
Open circuit in wire harness between terminal 7 of computer and terminal B-5 of combination meter.

↓ Yes

Replace computer.

E | INSPECTION OF ACTUATOR OPERATION

ACTUATOR

INSPECT ACTUATOR OPERATION
Remove actuator.
Is actuator normal?

→ No →
Replace actuator.

↓ Yes

Replace computer.

Cruise control trouble diagnosis chart—1985 Corolla (RWD)

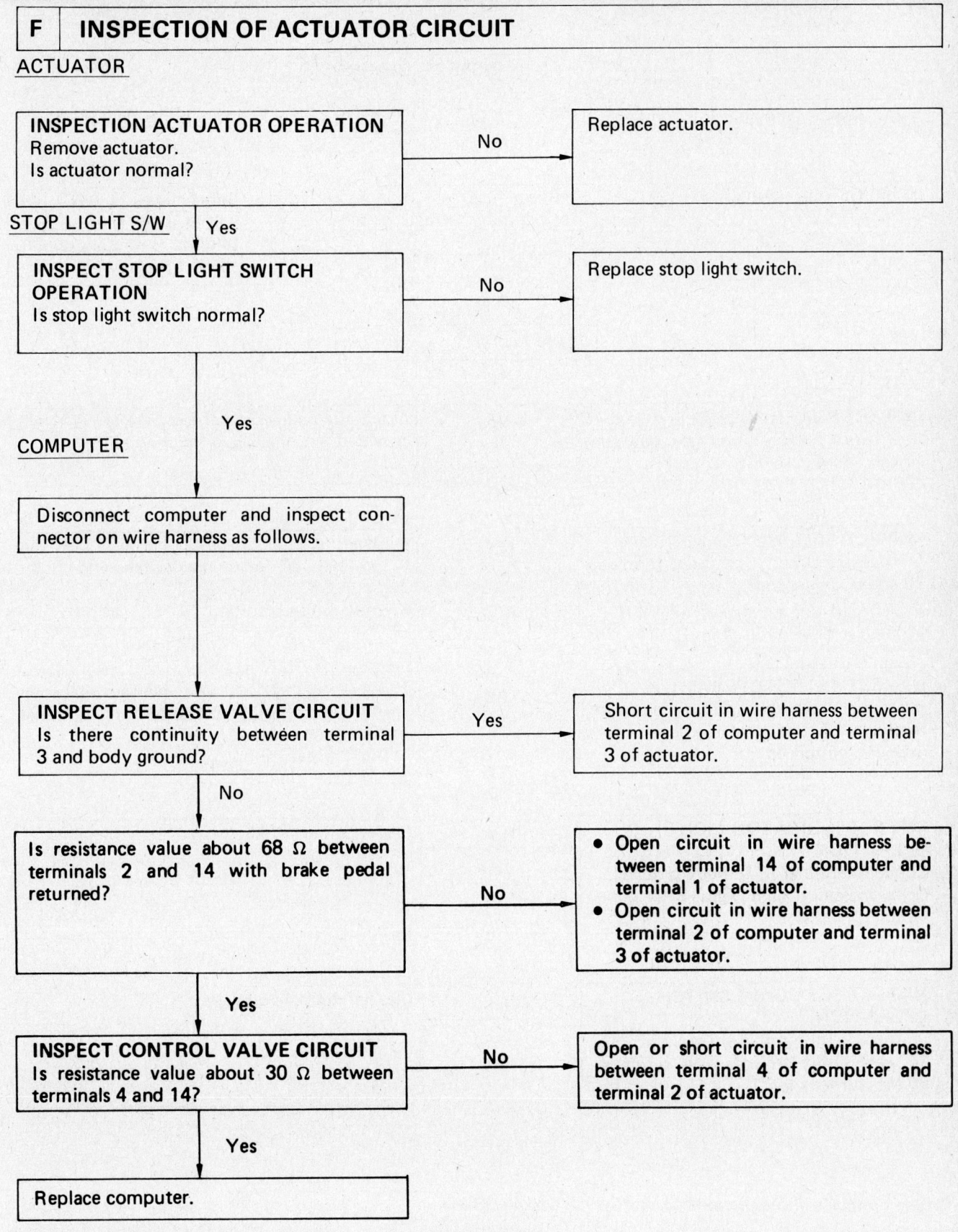

F | INSPECTION OF ACTUATOR CIRCUIT

ACTUATOR

INSPECTION ACTUATOR OPERATION
Remove actuator.
Is actuator normal?

→ No → Replace actuator.

STOP LIGHT S/W | Yes

INSPECT STOP LIGHT SWITCH OPERATION
Is stop light switch normal?

→ No → Replace stop light switch.

Yes

COMPUTER

Disconnect computer and inspect connector on wire harness as follows.

INSPECT RELEASE VALVE CIRCUIT
Is there continuity between terminal 3 and body ground?

→ Yes → Short circuit in wire harness between terminal 2 of computer and terminal 3 of actuator.

No

Is resistance value about 68 Ω between terminals 2 and 14 with brake pedal returned?

→ No →
- Open circuit in wire harness between terminal 14 of computer and terminal 1 of actuator.
- Open circuit in wire harness between terminal 2 of computer and terminal 3 of actuator.

Yes

INSPECT CONTROL VALVE CIRCUIT
Is resistance value about 30 Ω between terminals 4 and 14?

→ No → Open or short circuit in wire harness between terminal 4 of computer and terminal 2 of actuator.

Yes

Replace computer.

Cruise control trouble diagnosis chart—1985 Corolla (RWD)

1225

3. INSPECT DIAGNOSIS CIRCUIT

Turn ignition switch on.

↓

Is GAUGE fuse normal? —**No**→ Replace fuse. Is operation normal? —**No**→
- Short circuit in wire harness between fuse and terminal 3 of main switch.
- Inspect main switch.

Yes ↓ (from Replace fuse)

Fuse faulty.

Yes ↓

CONTROL S/W

INSPECT POWER SOURCE
Is there battery voltage between 16 and body ground? —**No**→ Open circuit in wire harness between GAUGE fuse and terminal 16 of main switch.

Yes ↓

INSPECT GROUND CONNECTION
Is there continuity between terminal 20 and body ground? —**No**→
- Open circuit in wire harness between terminal 20 of main switch and body ground.
- Body ground faulty.

Yes ↓

INSPECT SWITCH OPERATION
Is there battery voltage between terminal 21 and body ground with main switch turned on? —**No**→
- Short circuit in wire harness between terminal 21 of main switch and terminal 10 of computer.
- Inspect main switch.

Yes ↓

INSPECT INDICATOR LIGHT OPERATION
Connect terminal 18 to body ground. Does indicator light light with main switch turned on? —**No**→ Inspect main switch.

Yes ↓

INSPECT SET/COAST SWITCH OPERATION
Is there continuity between terminal 14 and body ground with set/coast switch, turned on? —**No**→ Inspect control switch.

Yes ↓

Cruise control trouble diagnosis chart – 1985 Corolla (RWD)

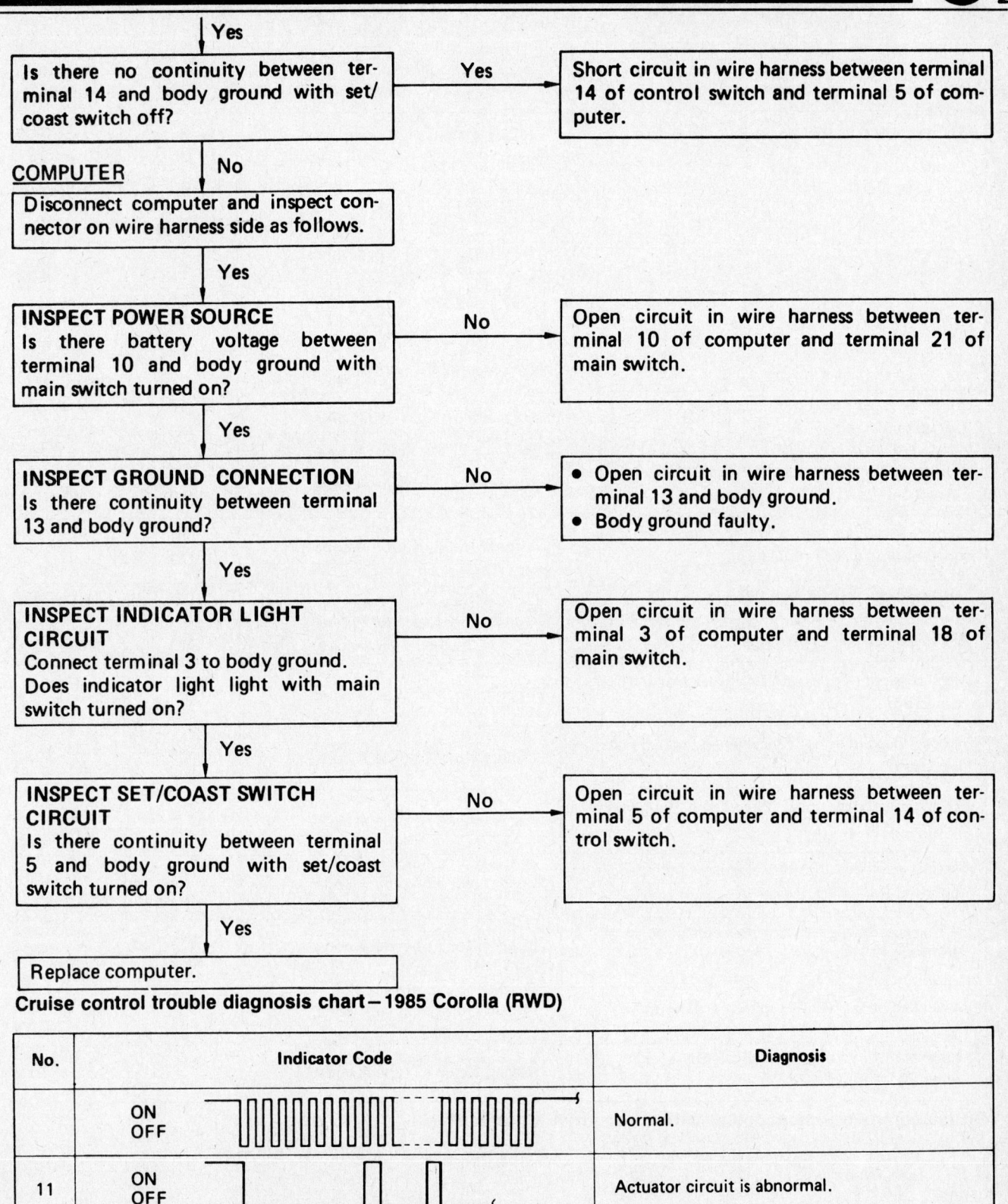

Yes

| Is there no continuity between terminal 14 and body ground with set/coast switch off? | → Yes → | Short circuit in wire harness between terminal 14 of control switch and terminal 5 of computer. |

COMPUTER

No

Disconnect computer and inspect connector on wire harness side as follows.

Yes

| **INSPECT POWER SOURCE** Is there battery voltage between terminal 10 and body ground with main switch turned on? | → No → | Open circuit in wire harness between terminal 10 of computer and terminal 21 of main switch. |

Yes

| **INSPECT GROUND CONNECTION** Is there continuity between terminal 13 and body ground? | → No → | • Open circuit in wire harness between terminal 13 and body ground. • Body ground faulty. |

Yes

| **INSPECT INDICATOR LIGHT CIRCUIT** Connect terminal 3 to body ground. Does indicator light light with main switch turned on? | → No → | Open circuit in wire harness between terminal 3 of computer and terminal 18 of main switch. |

Yes

| **INSPECT SET/COAST SWITCH CIRCUIT** Is there continuity between terminal 5 and body ground with set/coast switch turned on? | → No → | Open circuit in wire harness between terminal 5 of computer and terminal 14 of control switch. |

Yes

Replace computer.

Cruise control trouble diagnosis chart—1985 Corolla (RWD)

No.	Indicator Code		Diagnosis
	ON OFF	⊓⊔⊓⊔⊓⊔⊓⊔⊓⊔⊓⊔	Normal.
11	ON OFF		Actuator circuit is abnormal.
21	ON OFF		Speed sensor signal circuit is abnormal.

Type "B" diagnostic information—1986 and later Corolla (RWD)

Symptom	Inspection Area		Section
Cruise control cannot be set.	(a) Inspect type A codes.	No. 1 NO No. 2 NO No. 3 NO No. 4 NO No. 5 NO	A B C D D
	(b) Inspect type B codes.	11 21 23 31 33	E D F B A and B
	(c) All codes is normal.		Replace computer
Vehicles speed does not reduce when coast switch turned on.	Inspect No. 1 of type A code.	OK NO	F A
Vehicles does not accelerate when accel switch turned on.	Inspect No. 2 of type A code.	OK NO	F B
Vehicle speed does not return to memorized speed when resume switch turned on.	Inspect No. 2 of type A code.	OK NO	F B
Set speed deviates on high side.	Inspect No. 1 of type A code.	OK	F
Set speed deviates on low side.		NO	A
Vehicle speed does fluctuate when set switch turned on.	Inspect No. 1 of type A code.	OK NO	F A
Setting speed does not cancel when brake pedal depressed.	Insepct No. 3 of type A code.	OK NO	F C
Setting speed does not cancel when parking brake pulled.	Inspect No. 3 of type A code.	OK NO	F C
Setting speed does not cancel when clutch pedal depressed (M/T only).	Insepct No. 3 of type A code.	OK NO	F C
Setting speed does not cancel when shifted to "N" range (A/T only).	Inspect No. 3 of type A code.	OK NO	F C
Speed can be set below 20 km/h (12 mph).	Inspect No. 4 of type A code.	OK NO	F D
Cruise control will not disengage even below 20 km/h (12 mph).	Inspect No. 5 of type A code.	OK NO	F D

Cruise control troubleshooting data sheet—1985 Corolla (RWD)

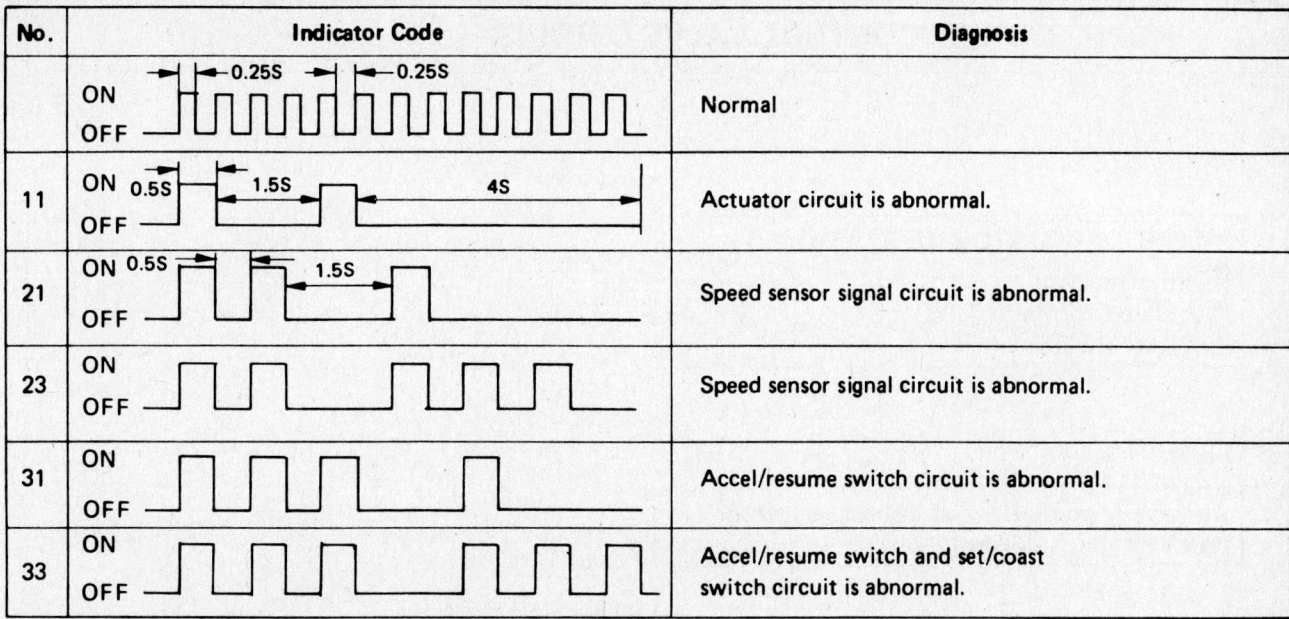

No.	Indicator Code	Diagnosis
	ON / OFF (0.25S, 0.25S)	Normal
11	ON / OFF (0.5S, 1.5S, 4S)	Actuator circuit is abnormal.
21	ON / OFF (0.5S, 1.5S)	Speed sensor signal circuit is abnormal.
23	ON / OFF	Speed sensor signal circuit is abnormal.
31	ON / OFF	Accel/resume switch circuit is abnormal.
33	ON / OFF	Accel/resume switch and set/coast switch circuit is abnormal.

Type "B" diagnostic information — 1985 Corolla (RWD)

Problem	Inspection Item	No.
Cruise control does not operate.	Inspect diagnosis code Indication Code No.11 No.21 Diagnosis code normal	A I B
Vehicle speed does not reduce when coast switch turned on.		
Vehicle does not accelerate when accel switch turned on.	Inspection of control switch circuit	C
Vehicle speed does not return to memorized speed when resume switch turned on.		
Set speed deviates on high side.	Inspection of actuator circuit	D
Set speed deviates on low side.		
Vehicle speed fluctuates when set switch turned on.	Inspection of actuator circuit Inspection of speed sensor circuit	D I
Setting speed does not cancel when brake pedal depressed.	Inspection of stop light switch circuit	E
Setting speed does not cancel when parking brake pulled.	Inspection of parking brake switch circuit	F
Setting speed does not cancel when clutch pedal depressed (M/T only).	Inspection of clutch switch circuit	G
Setting speed does not cancel when shifted to "N" range (A/T only).	Inspection of neutral start switch circuit	H
Speed can be set below about 40 km/h (25 mph).	Inspection of speed sensor circuit	I
Cruise control will not disengage even below about 40 km/h (25 mph).		

Cruise control troubleshooting data sheet — 1986 and later Corolla (RWD)

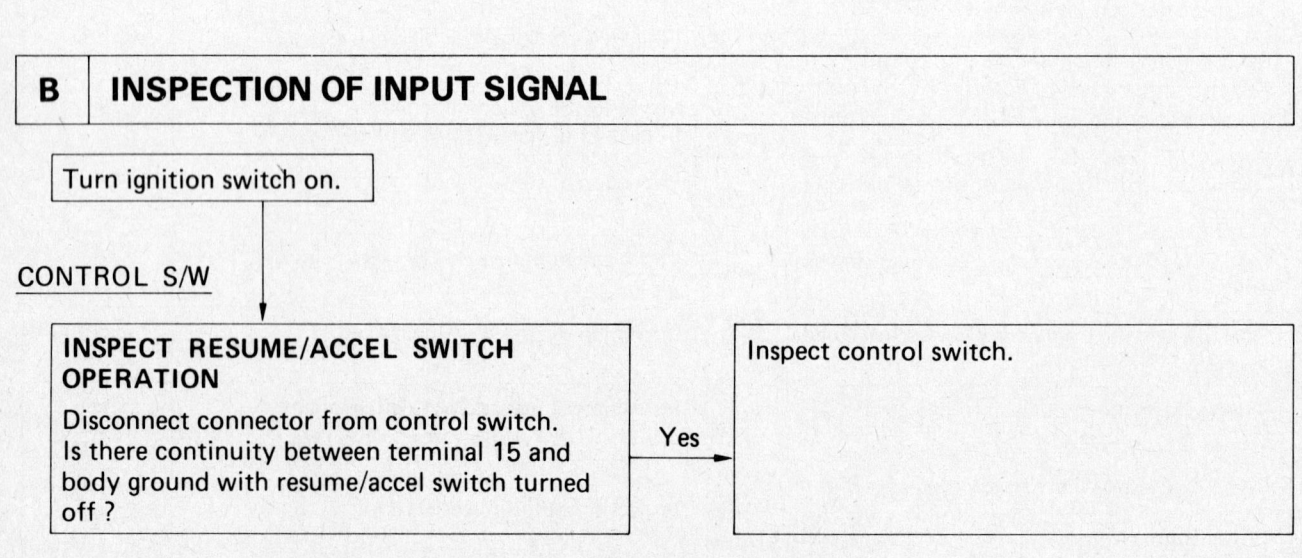

| A | INSPECTION OF CONTROL VALVE CIRCUIT |

Turn ignition switch off.

ACTUATOR

INSPECT ACTUATOR OPERATION
Remove actuator.
Is actuator normal ?
(See page BE-59)

→ No → Replace actuator.

↓ Yes

COMPUTER

Disconnect computer and inspect connector on wire harness side as follows.

↓

INSPECT CONTROL VALVE CIRCUIT
Is resistance value about 30 Ω between terminals 4 and 14 ?

→ No →
- Open or short circuit in wire harness between terminal 4 of computer and terminal 2 of actuator.
- Open or short circuit in wire harness between terminal 14 of computer and terminal 1 of actuator.

↓ Yes

Replace computer.

| B | INSPECTION OF INPUT SIGNAL |

Turn ignition switch on.

CONTROL S/W

INSPECT RESUME/ACCEL SWITCH OPERATION
Disconnect connector from control switch.
Is there continuity between terminal 15 and body ground with resume/accel switch turned off ?

→ Yes → Inspect control switch.

Cruise control trouble diagnosis chart – 1986 and later Corolla (RWD)

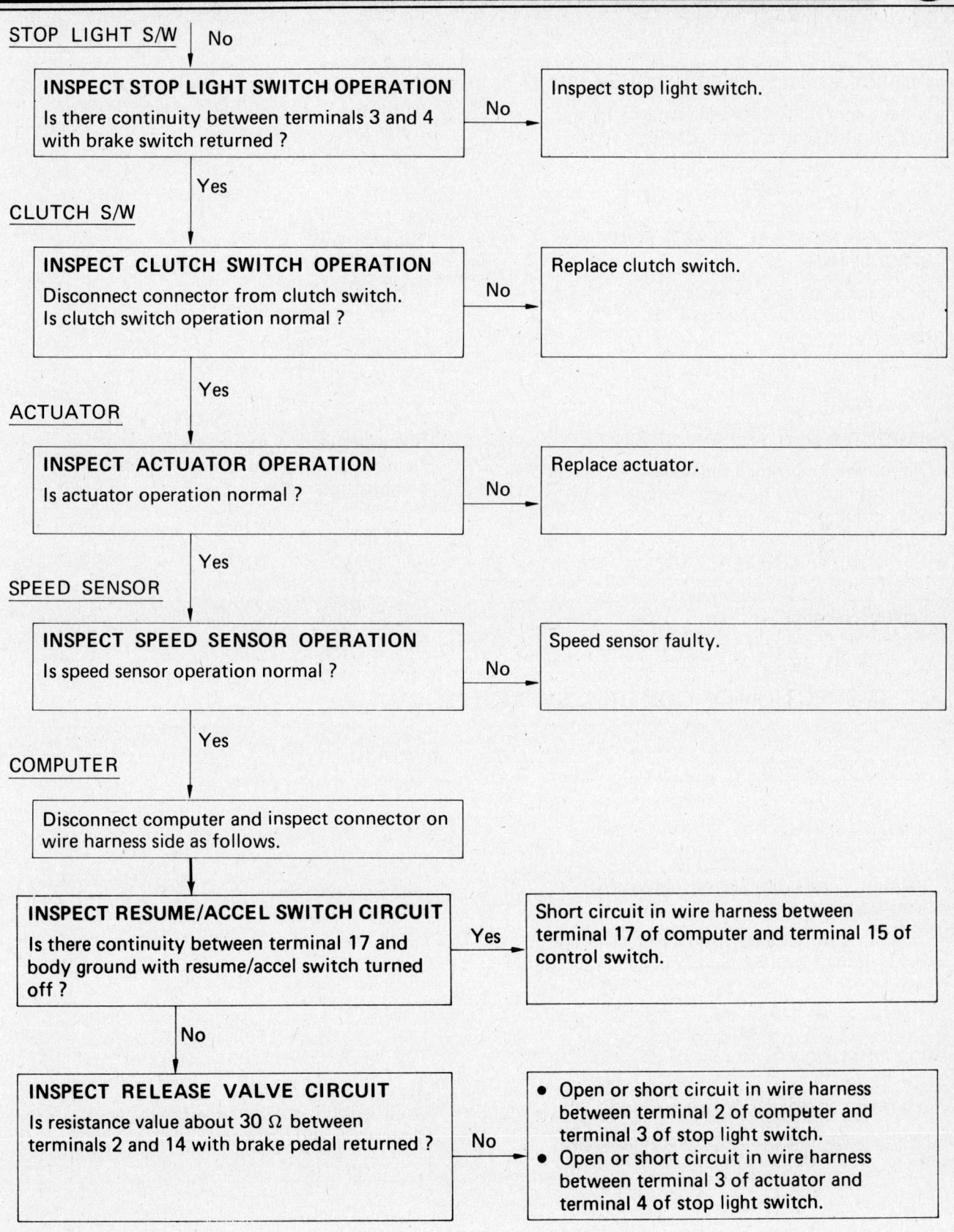

STOP LIGHT S/W | No

INSPECT STOP LIGHT SWITCH OPERATION
Is there continuity between terminals 3 and 4 with brake switch returned ?

→ No → Inspect stop light switch.

Yes

CLUTCH S/W

INSPECT CLUTCH SWITCH OPERATION
Disconnect connector from clutch switch.
Is clutch switch operation normal ?

→ No → Replace clutch switch.

Yes

ACTUATOR

INSPECT ACTUATOR OPERATION
Is actuator operation normal ?

→ No → Replace actuator.

Yes

SPEED SENSOR

INSPECT SPEED SENSOR OPERATION
Is speed sensor operation normal ?

→ No → Speed sensor faulty.

Yes

COMPUTER

Disconnect computer and inspect connector on wire harness side as follows.

INSPECT RESUME/ACCEL SWITCH CIRCUIT
Is there continuity between terminal 17 and body ground with resume/accel switch turned off ?

→ Yes → Short circuit in wire harness between terminal 17 of computer and terminal 15 of control switch.

No

INSPECT RELEASE VALVE CIRCUIT
Is resistance value about 30 Ω between terminals 2 and 14 with brake pedal returned ?

→ No →
- Open or short circuit in wire harness between terminal 2 of computer and terminal 3 of stop light switch.
- Open or short circuit in wire harness between terminal 3 of actuator and terminal 4 of stop light switch.

Cruise control trouble diagnosis chart — 1986 and later Corolla (RWD)

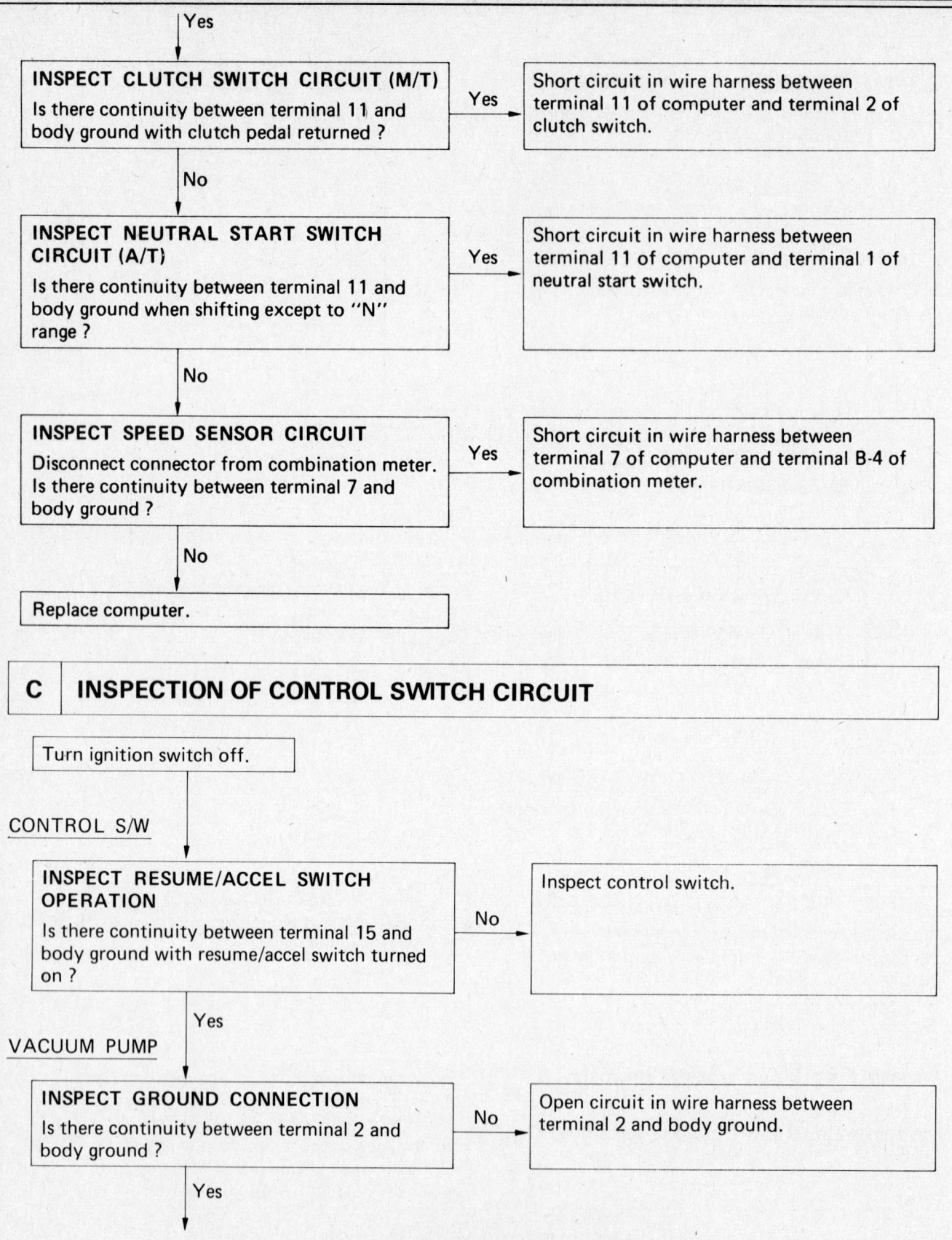

Yes

INSPECT CLUTCH SWITCH CIRCUIT (M/T)

Is there continuity between terminal 11 and body ground with clutch pedal returned ?

→ Yes → Short circuit in wire harness between terminal 11 of computer and terminal 2 of clutch switch.

No ↓

INSPECT NEUTRAL START SWITCH CIRCUIT (A/T)

Is there continuity between terminal 11 and body ground when shifting except to "N" range ?

→ Yes → Short circuit in wire harness between terminal 11 of computer and terminal 1 of neutral start switch.

No ↓

INSPECT SPEED SENSOR CIRCUIT

Disconnect connector from combination meter. Is there continuity between terminal 7 and body ground ?

→ Yes → Short circuit in wire harness between terminal 7 of computer and terminal B-4 of combination meter.

No ↓

Replace computer.

C | **INSPECTION OF CONTROL SWITCH CIRCUIT**

Turn ignition switch off.

CONTROL S/W

INSPECT RESUME/ACCEL SWITCH OPERATION

Is there continuity between terminal 15 and body ground with resume/accel switch turned on ?

→ No → Inspect control switch.

Yes ↓

VACUUM PUMP

INSPECT GROUND CONNECTION

Is there continuity between terminal 2 and body ground ?

→ No → Open circuit in wire harness between terminal 2 and body ground.

Yes ↓

Cruise control trouble diagnosis chart—1986 and later Corolla (RWD)

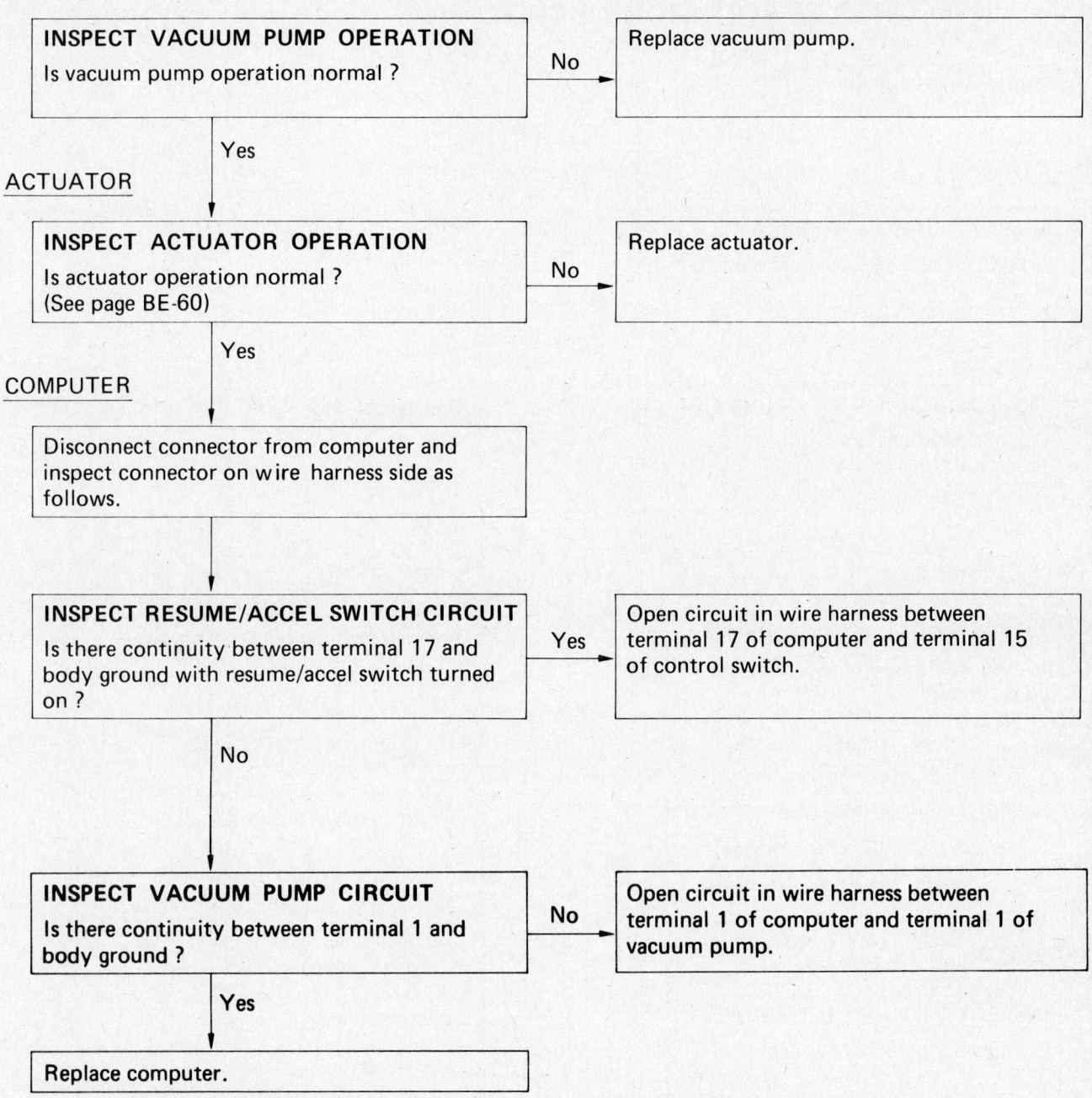

Cruise control trouble diagnosis chart—1986 and later Corolla (RWD)

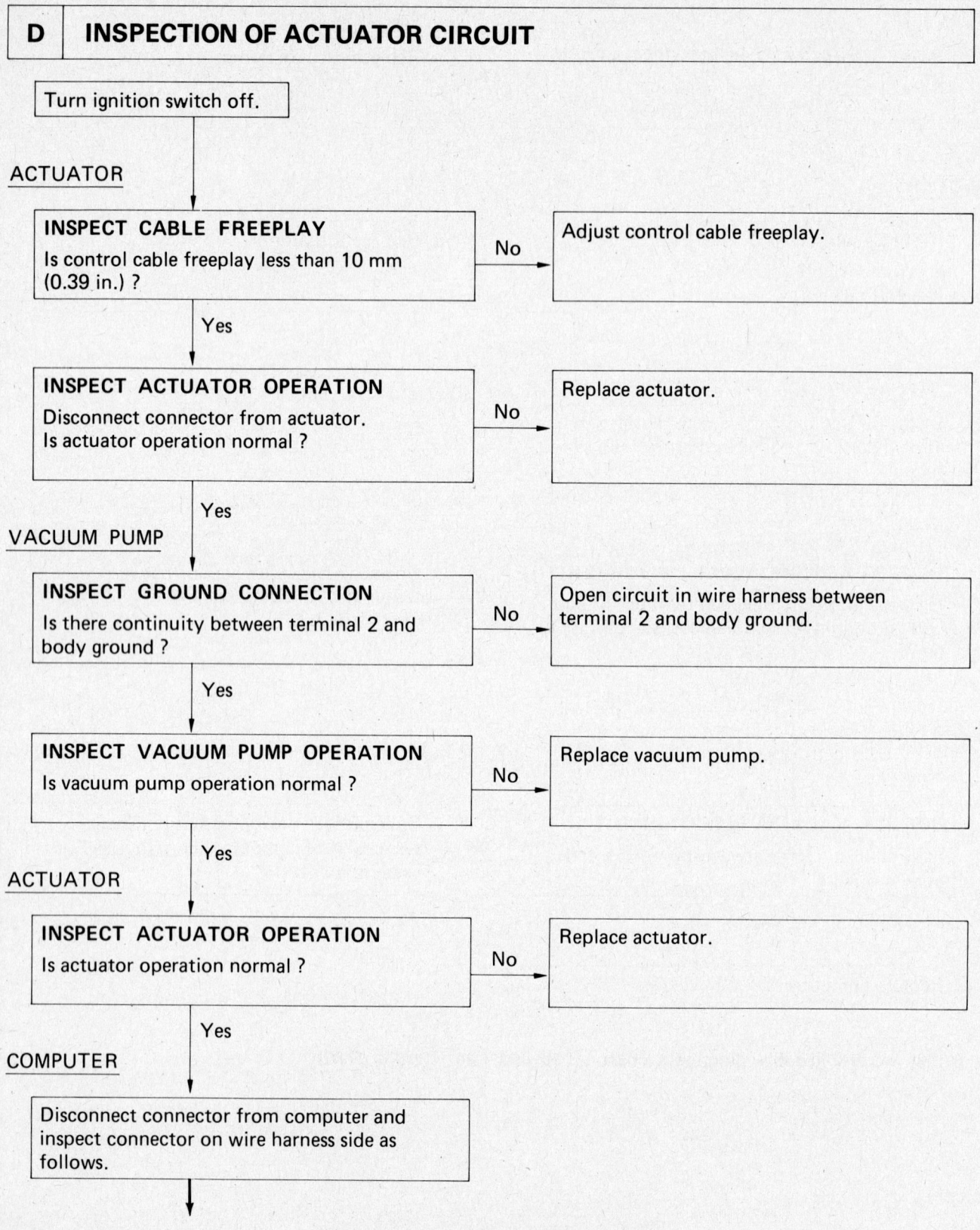

| D | INSPECTION OF ACTUATOR CIRCUIT |

Cruise control trouble diagnosis chart—1986 and later Corolla (RWD)

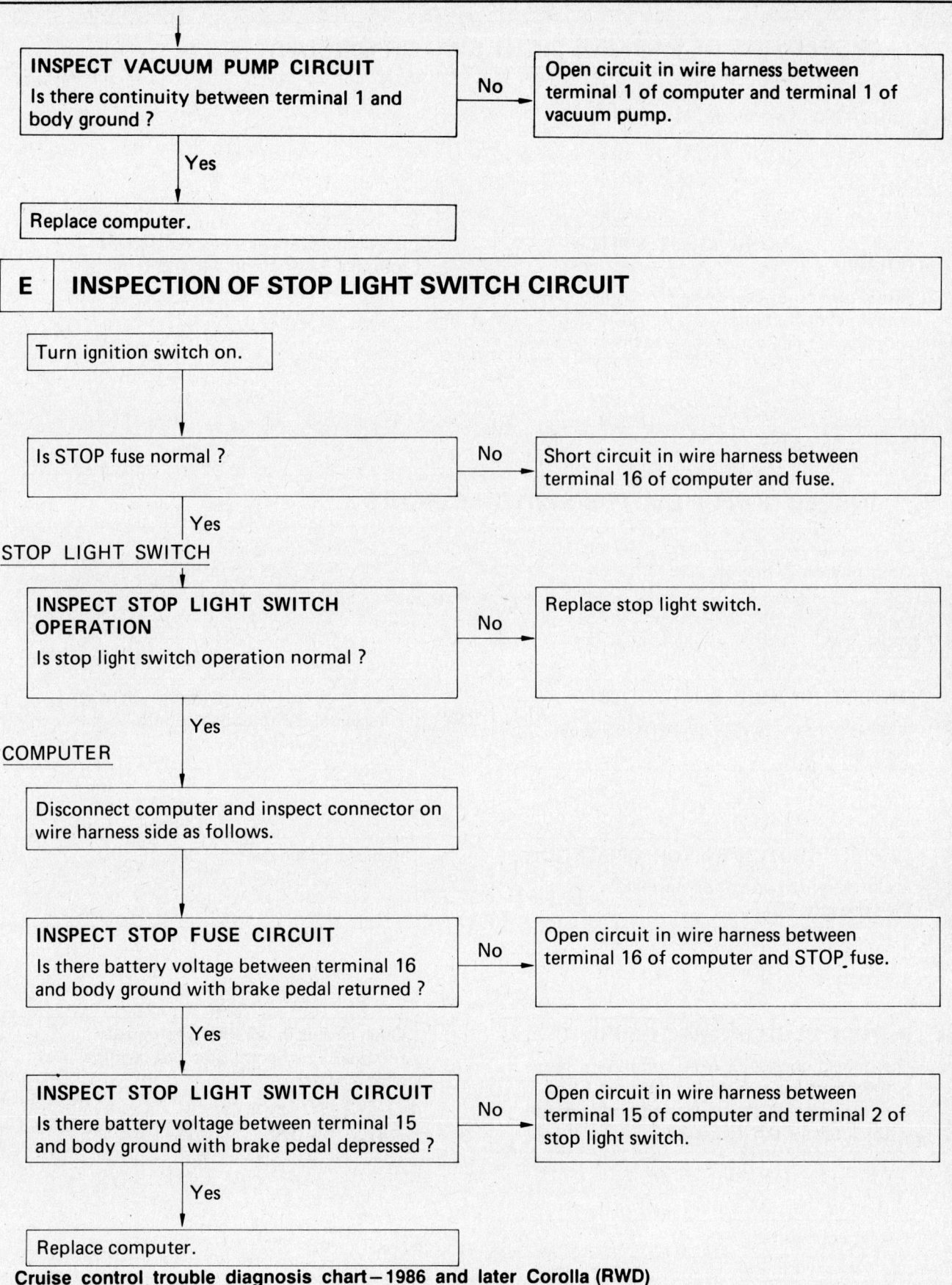

INSPECT VACUUM PUMP CIRCUIT

Is there continuity between terminal 1 and body ground ?

No → Open circuit in wire harness between terminal 1 of computer and terminal 1 of vacuum pump.

Yes ↓

Replace computer.

| E | **INSPECTION OF STOP LIGHT SWITCH CIRCUIT** |

Turn ignition switch on.

↓

Is STOP fuse normal ?

No → Short circuit in wire harness between terminal 16 of computer and fuse.

Yes ↓

STOP LIGHT SWITCH

INSPECT STOP LIGHT SWITCH OPERATION

Is stop light switch operation normal ?

No → Replace stop light switch.

Yes ↓

COMPUTER

Disconnect computer and inspect connector on wire harness side as follows.

↓

INSPECT STOP FUSE CIRCUIT

Is there battery voltage between terminal 16 and body ground with brake pedal returned ?

No → Open circuit in wire harness between terminal 16 of computer and STOP fuse.

Yes ↓

INSPECT STOP LIGHT SWITCH CIRCUIT

Is there battery voltage between terminal 15 and body ground with brake pedal depressed ?

No → Open circuit in wire harness between terminal 15 of computer and terminal 2 of stop light switch.

Yes ↓

Replace computer.

Cruise control trouble diagnosis chart—1986 and later Corolla (RWD)

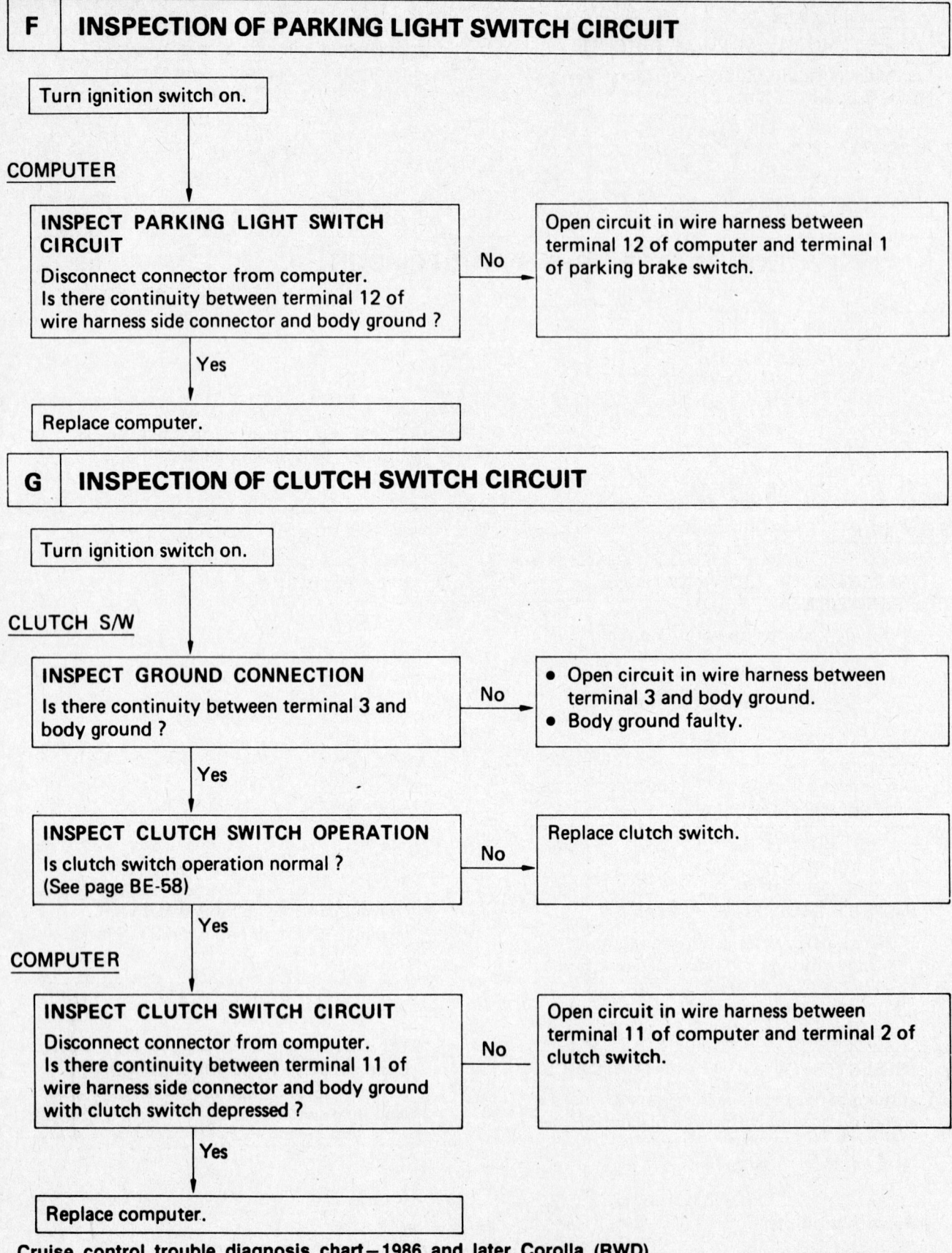

F | **INSPECTION OF PARKING LIGHT SWITCH CIRCUIT**

Turn ignition switch on.

COMPUTER

INSPECT PARKING LIGHT SWITCH CIRCUIT

Disconnect connector from computer.
Is there continuity between terminal 12 of
wire harness side connector and body ground ?

→ No → Open circuit in wire harness between terminal 12 of computer and terminal 1 of parking brake switch.

↓ Yes

Replace computer.

G | **INSPECTION OF CLUTCH SWITCH CIRCUIT**

Turn ignition switch on.

CLUTCH S/W

INSPECT GROUND CONNECTION

Is there continuity between terminal 3 and
body ground ?

→ No → • Open circuit in wire harness between terminal 3 and body ground.
• Body ground faulty.

↓ Yes

INSPECT CLUTCH SWITCH OPERATION

Is clutch switch operation normal ?
(See page BE-58)

→ No → Replace clutch switch.

↓ Yes

COMPUTER

INSPECT CLUTCH SWITCH CIRCUIT

Disconnect connector from computer.
Is there continuity between terminal 11 of
wire harness side connector and body ground
with clutch switch depressed ?

→ No → Open circuit in wire harness between terminal 11 of computer and terminal 2 of clutch switch.

↓ Yes

Replace computer.

Cruise control trouble diagnosis chart – 1986 and later Corolla (RWD)

H INSPECTION OF NEUTRAL START SWITCH CIRCUIT

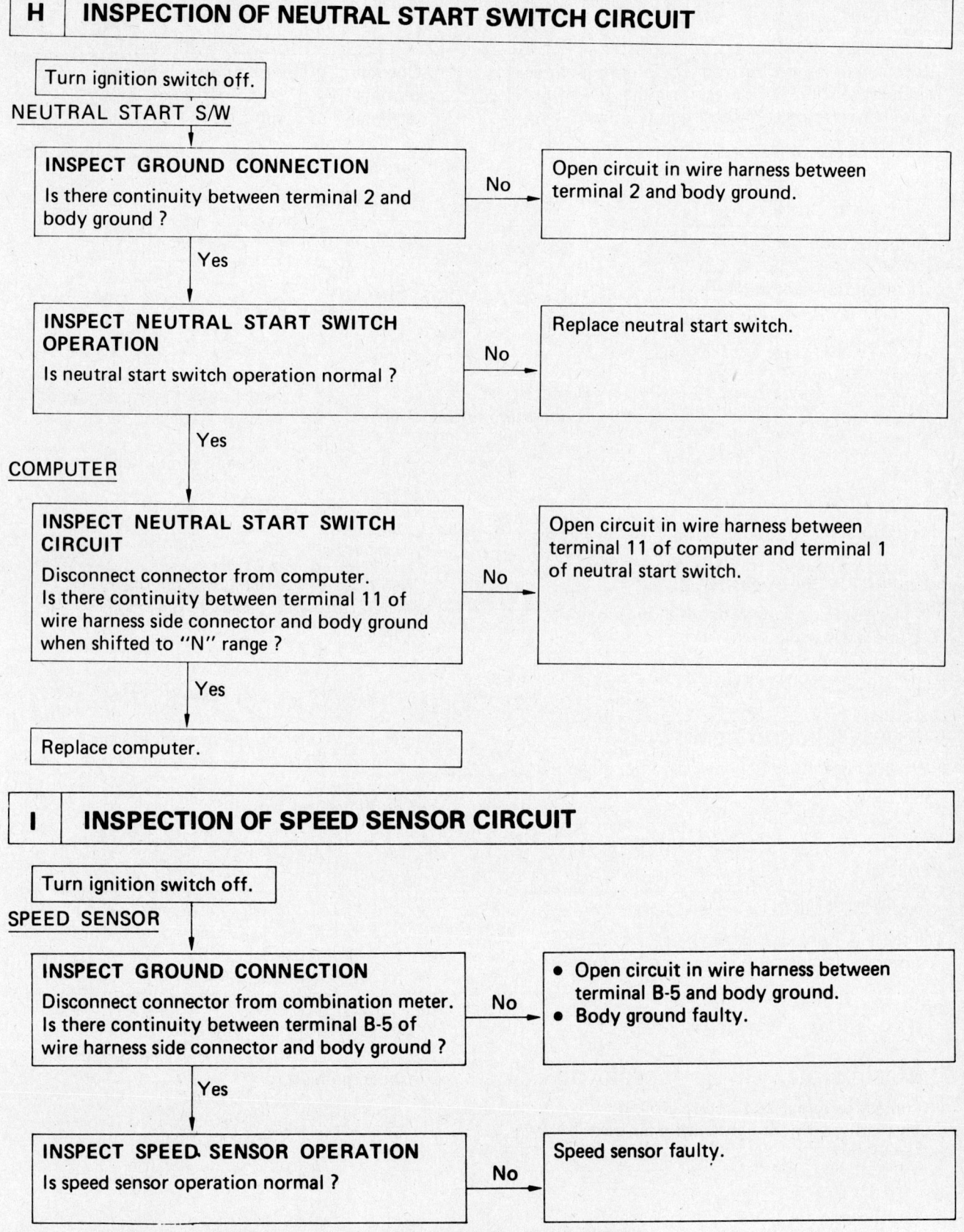

Turn ignition switch off.

NEUTRAL START S/W

INSPECT GROUND CONNECTION

Is there continuity between terminal 2 and body ground ?

— No → Open circuit in wire harness between terminal 2 and body ground.

Yes

INSPECT NEUTRAL START SWITCH OPERATION

Is neutral start switch operation normal ?

— No → Replace neutral start switch.

Yes

COMPUTER

INSPECT NEUTRAL START SWITCH CIRCUIT

Disconnect connector from computer.
Is there continuity between terminal 11 of wire harness side connector and body ground when shifted to "N" range ?

— No → Open circuit in wire harness between terminal 11 of computer and terminal 1 of neutral start switch.

Yes

Replace computer.

I INSPECTION OF SPEED SENSOR CIRCUIT

Turn ignition switch off.

SPEED SENSOR

INSPECT GROUND CONNECTION

Disconnect connector from combination meter.
Is there continuity between terminal B-5 of wire harness side connector and body ground ?

— No → • Open circuit in wire harness between terminal B-5 and body ground.
• Body ground faulty.

Yes

INSPECT SPEED SENSOR OPERATION

Is speed sensor operation normal ?

— No → Speed sensor faulty.

Cruise control trouble diagnosis chart—1986 and later Corolla (RWD)

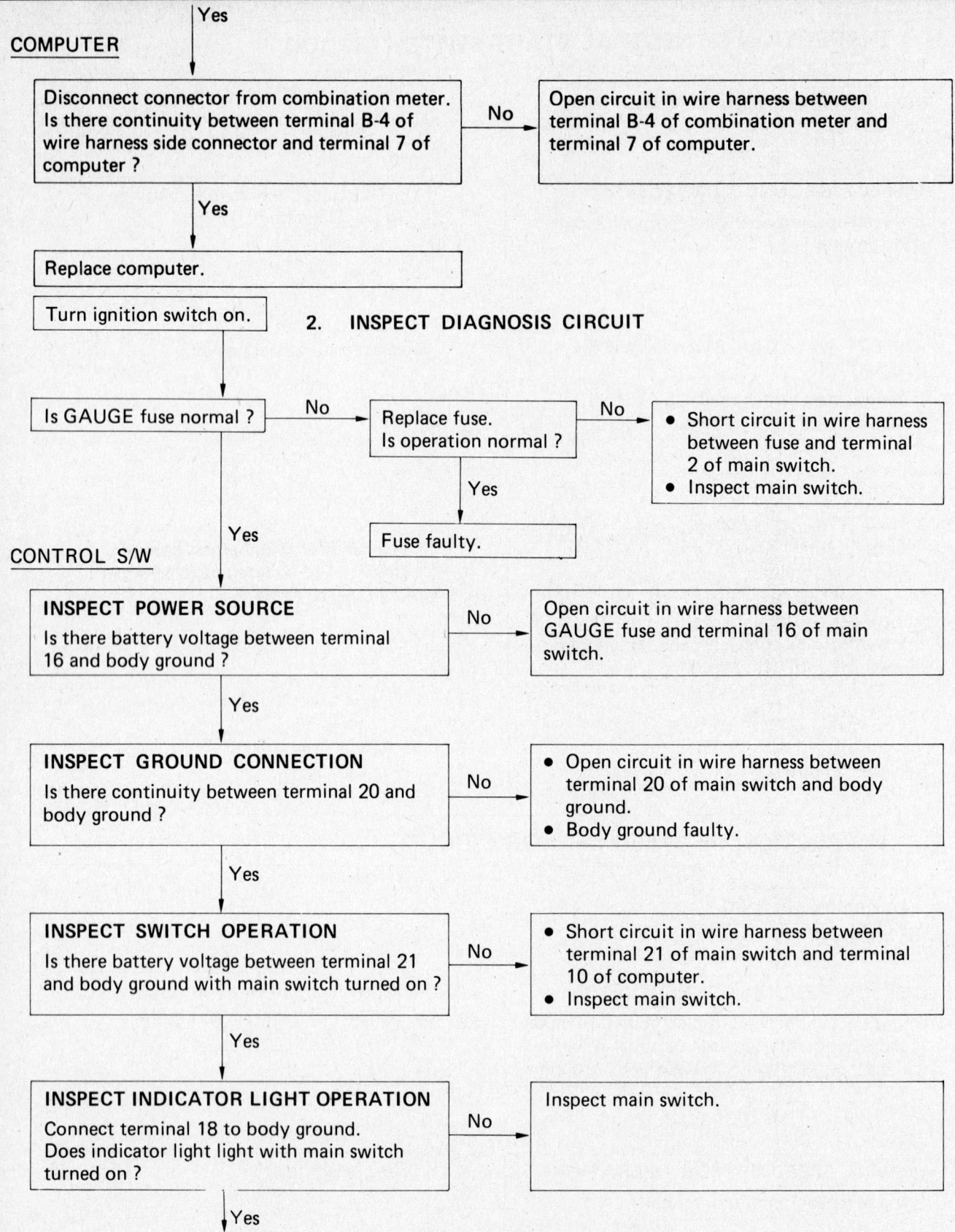

Cruise control trouble diagnosis chart—1986 and later Corolla (RWD)

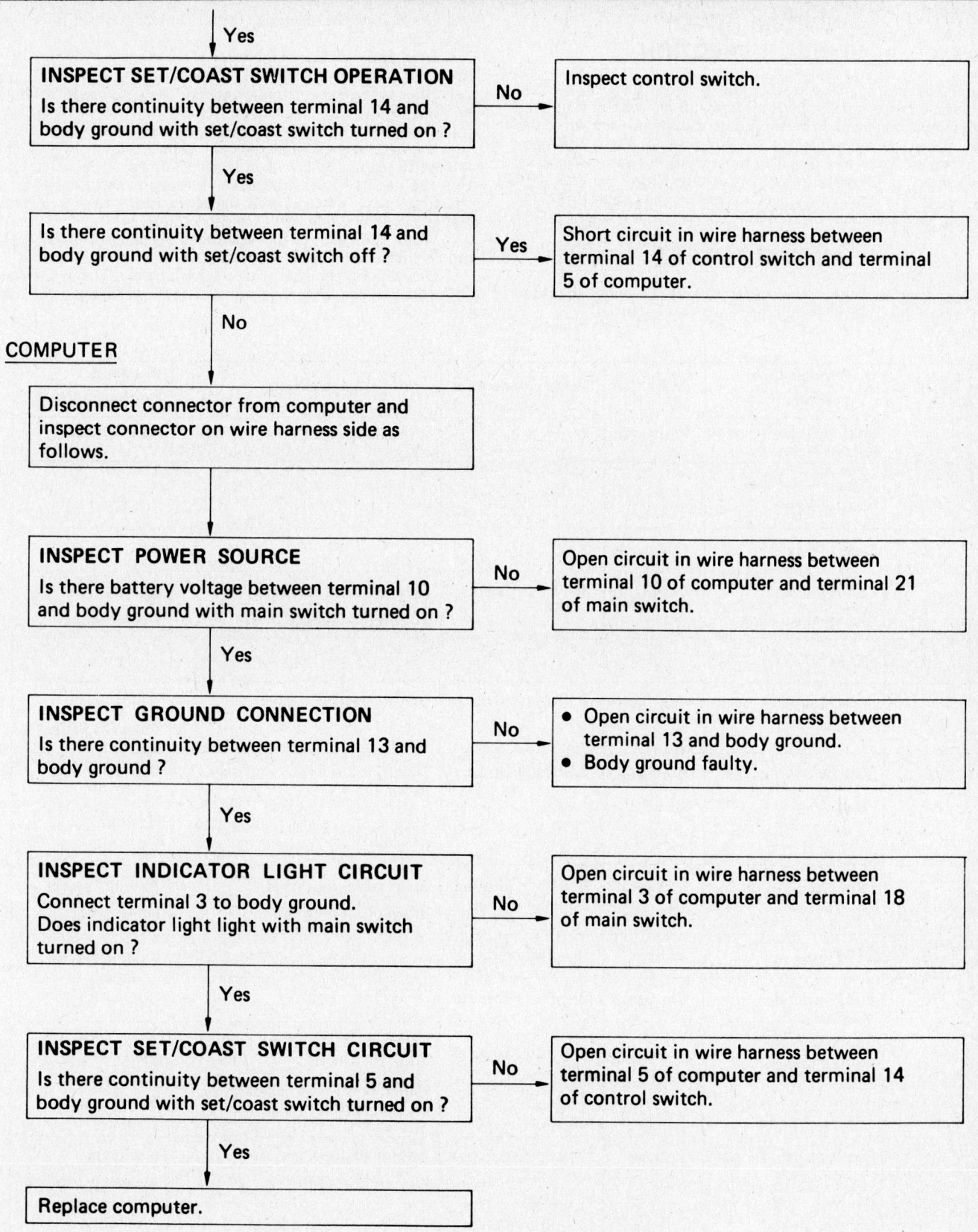

INSPECT SET/COAST SWITCH OPERATION

Is there continuity between terminal 14 and body ground with set/coast switch turned on ?

→ No → Inspect control switch.

↓ Yes

Is there continuity between terminal 14 and body ground with set/coast switch off ?

→ Yes → Short circuit in wire harness between terminal 14 of control switch and terminal 5 of computer.

↓ No

COMPUTER

Disconnect connector from computer and inspect connector on wire harness side as follows.

INSPECT POWER SOURCE

Is there battery voltage between terminal 10 and body ground with main switch turned on ?

→ No → Open circuit in wire harness between terminal 10 of computer and terminal 21 of main switch.

↓ Yes

INSPECT GROUND CONNECTION

Is there continuity between terminal 13 and body ground ?

→ No →
- Open circuit in wire harness between terminal 13 and body ground.
- Body ground faulty.

↓ Yes

INSPECT INDICATOR LIGHT CIRCUIT

Connect terminal 3 to body ground.
Does indicator light light with main switch turned on ?

→ No → Open circuit in wire harness between terminal 3 of computer and terminal 18 of main switch.

↓ Yes

INSPECT SET/COAST SWITCH CIRCUIT

Is there continuity between terminal 5 and body ground with set/coast switch turned on ?

→ No → Open circuit in wire harness between terminal 5 of computer and terminal 14 of control switch.

↓ Yes

Replace computer.

Cruise control trouble diagnosis chart—1986 and later Corolla (RWD)

Corolla (FWD)
VISUAL INSPECTION

Before performing any tests make a visual inspection of the cruise control system. Check all items in the system for abnormal conditions such as bare broken or disconnected wires and damage to the vacuum hoses. Be sure that the speedometer cables are attached and properly routed. All vacuum hoses must be properly routed and must not have any kinks or bends. Be sure that all electrical connections are complete and tight. The wiring harness must be routed properly.

ACTUATOR TEST

1. Inspect and check the actuator cable. Freeplay should be less than 0.039 inch. Adjust or replace as required.

2. Disconnect the electrical connector from the actuator lead wire.

3. Using an ohmmeter measure the resistance between terminals one and two. It should be about 68 ohms. Measure the resistance between terminals one and three. It should be about 30 ohms.

4. If the resistance is not as indicated, replace the actuator.

5. Connect a positive lead from the positive terminal of the battery to terminals two and three. Connect a negative lead from the negative terminal of the battery to terminal one.

6. Slowly apply 0 to 11.8 in. hg. of vacuum. Check to be sure that the control cable can be pulled smoothly.

7. When the vacuum has stabilized check the control cable and be sure that it does not return.

8. Disconnect terminal two or three and check that the control cable returns to its original position and that the vacuum goes to zero.

Terminal	Connection or Measure Item	Check Item	Tester Connection	Condition	Voltage or Resistance Value
1	Stop Light Switch and Release Valve	Resistance	1 – 2	Brake pedal returned	About 30 Ω
2	Release Valve and Control Valve	–	–	–	–
3	Control Valve	Resistance	3 – 2	–	About 68 Ω
4	Control Switch (Set/Coast)	Continuity	4 – Body Ground	Turn set/coast switch on / Turn set/coast switch off	Continuity / No continuity
5	OD Relay	–	–	–	–
6	Speed Sensor	Continuity	6 – Body Ground	Vehicle moving slowly	1 pulse each 40 cm (1.58 in.)
7	Main Switch	Voltage	7 – Body Ground	Turn ignition switch and main switch on / Turn ignition switch and main switch off	Battery voltage / No voltage
8	Stop Light Switch	Voltage	8 – Body Ground	Brake pedal depressed / Brake pedal returned	Battery voltage / No voltage
9	STOP Fuse	Voltage	9 – Body Ground	–	Battery voltage
10	Body Ground	Continuity	10 – Body Ground	–	Continuity
11	Clutch Switch Neutral Switch	Continuity	11 – Body Ground	Clutch pedal depressed or shift into "N" range / Clutch pedal returned or shift into except "N" range	Continuity / No continuity
12	Parking Brake Switch	Voltage	12 – Body Ground	Parking brake pulled / Parking brake returned	No voltage / Battery voltage
13	Control Switch (Accel/Resume)	Continuity	13 – Body Ground	Turn accel/resume switch on / Turn accel/resume switch off	Continuity / No continuity

Cruise control computer circuit inspection chart—1984 Corolla (FWD)

9. If the system does not perform as indicated replace the actuator.

SPEED SENSOR TEST

1984

1. Using an ohmmeter, check to see that there is continuinity between terminals 8 and 20. It should be four times per revolution of the magnet shaft.
2. If continuinity does not exist replace the speed sensor.

1985 and Later

1. Using an ohmmeter, check to see that there is continuinity between terminals B6 and A8. It should be four times per revolution of the magnet shaft.
2. If continuinity does not exist replace the speed sensor.

CONTROL SWITCH TEST (1985 AND LATER)

1. Using an ohmmeter check for continuinity of the terminals for each switch position.
2. If continuinity between the terminals is not as specified, replace the switch.

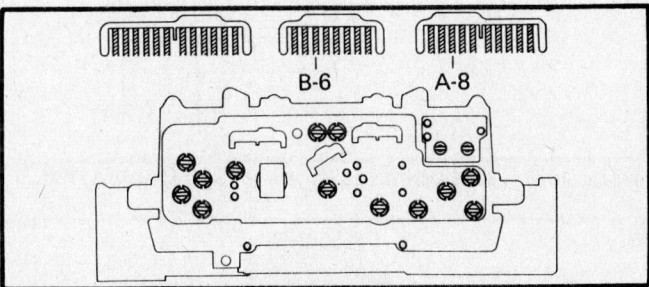

Speed sensor test point locations—1985 Corolla (FWD)

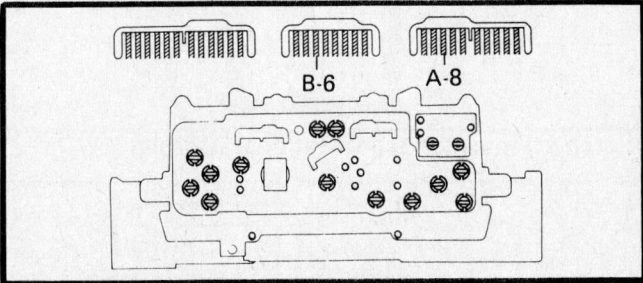

Speed sensor test point locations—1986 and later Corolla (FWD) without tachometer

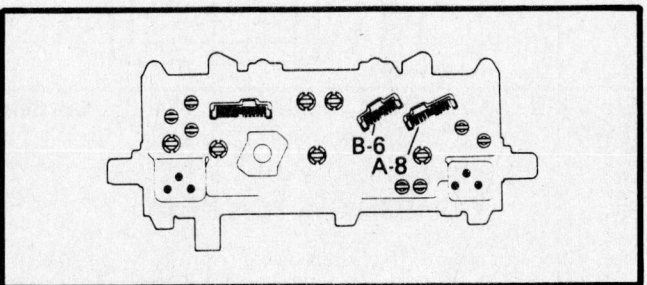

Speed sensor test point locations—1986 and later Corolla (FWD) with tachometer

Actuator test point locations—Corolla (FWD)

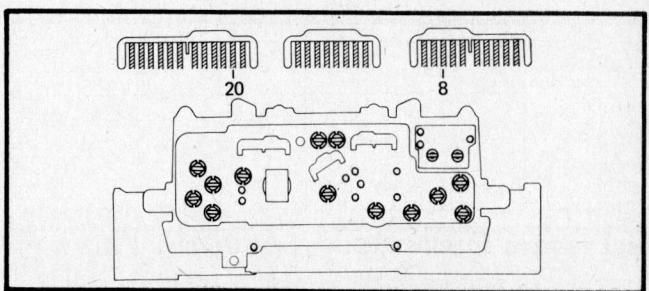

Speed sensor test locations—1984 Corolla (FWD)

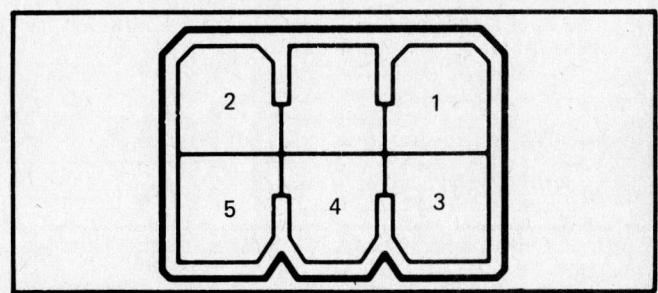

Main switch test locations—1984 Corolla (FWD)

Switch position	Terminal 23	25	17
SET/COAST		○———	———○
OFF			
ACCEL/RESUME	○———		———○

Control switch specifications—1985 Corolla (FWD)

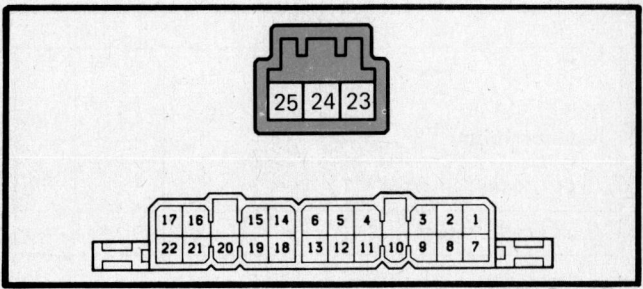

Control switch test point locations—1985 Corolla (FWD)

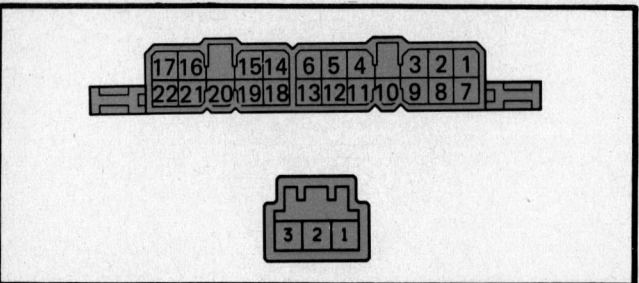

Control switch test point locations—1986 and later Corolla (FWD)

Switch position \ Terminal	1	2	3	4	5
OFF			○—○		○
ON	○—○		○—○		○

Main switch specifications—1984 Corolla (FWD)

Switch position \ Terminal	14	23	25
RESUME/ACCEL	○—○		
OFF			
SET/COAST	○—		—○

Control switch specifications—1986 and later Corolla (FWD)

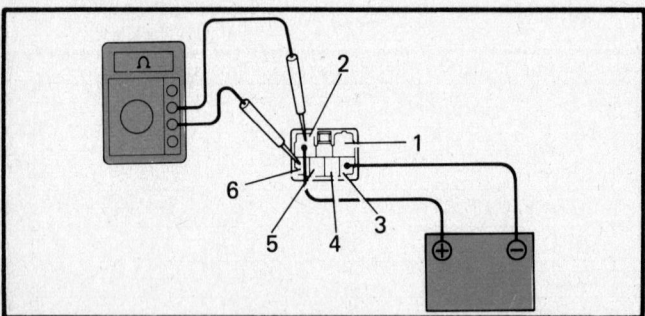

Main switch test point locations—1986 and later Corolla (FWD)

Brake pedal position \ Terminal	1	3	2	4
Brake pedal depressed	○——	—○		
Brake pedal returned			○——	—○

Stoplight switch specifications—1986 and later Corolla (FWD)

MAIN SWITCH TEST

1984

1. Using an ohmmeter check for continuity of the terminals for each switch position.
2. If continuity between the terminals is not as specified, replace the switch.

1985 and Later

1. Connect a positive lead from the positive terminal of the battery to terminal two (terminal three 1985 vehicles). Connect a negative lead from the negative terminal of the battery to terminal three (terminal number five 1985 vehicles).
4. Check to be sure that continuity exists between terminals two and six (terminals one and three 1985 vehicles) with the main switch turned on.
5. Check that there is no continuity between terminals two and six (terminals one and three 1985 vehicles) with the main switch off.
4. If the above results are not achieved, replace the switch.

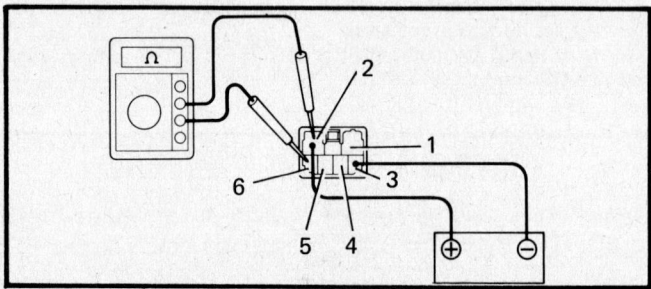

Main switch test point locations—1985 Corolla (FWD)

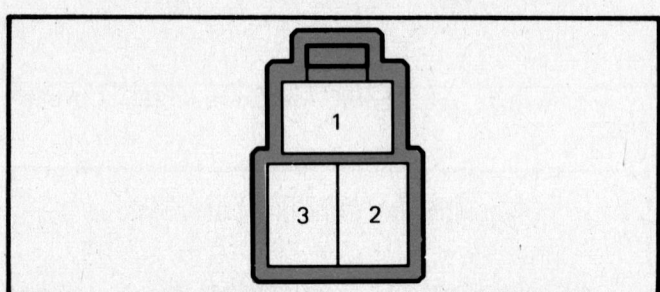

Clutch start switch test locations—Corolla (FWD)

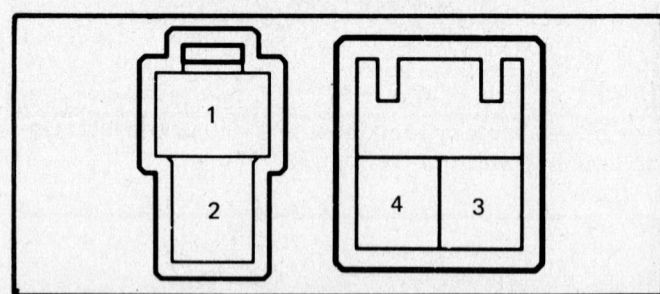

Stoplight switch test locations—1984–85 Corolla (FWD)

CLUTCH SWITCH TEST

1. Check to be sure that there is continuity between terminals two and three with the clutch pedal depressed.
2. Check to be sure that there is continuity between terminals two and three with the clutch pedal returned.

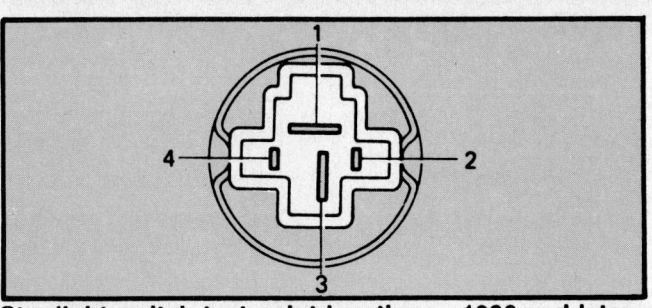

Stoplight switch test point locations—1986 and later Corolla (FWD)

Terminal Brake pedal position	1	2	3	4
Brake pedal depressed	○—————○			
Brake pedal returned			○—————○	

Stoplight switch specifications—1984–85 Corolla (FWD)

3. If continuity is not as indicated, replace the clutch switch.

STOP LIGHT SWITCH TEST

1. Using an ohmmeter check for continunity of the terminals for each switch position.
2. If continuity between the terminals is not as specified, replace the switch.

VACUUM PUMP TEST (1986 and Later)

1. Connect a vacuum pump to the ACT side of the vacuum pump.
2. Connect a positive lead from the positive terminal of the battery to terminal one. Connect a negative lead from the negative terminal of the battery to terminal two.

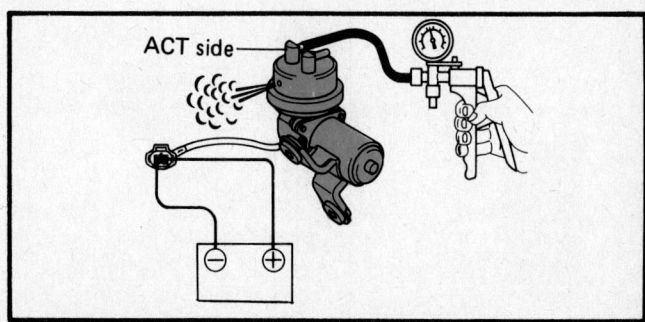

Vacuum pump test point locations—1986 and later Corolla (FWD)

3. Check to be sure that there is a vacuum of at least 7.87 in. hg. or above.
4. If the above test results are not achieved, replace the vacuum pump.

DIAGNOSIS AND TESTING PROCEDURES

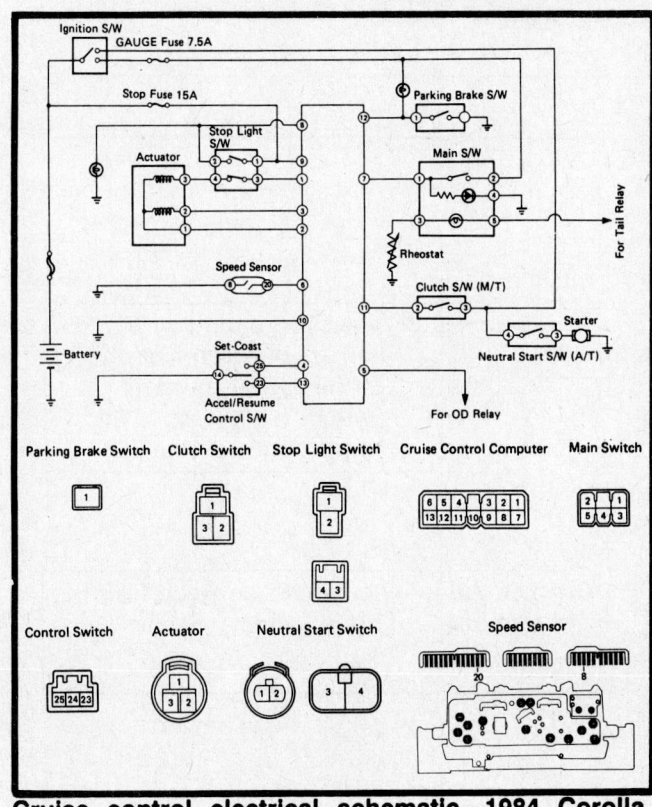

Cruise control electrical schematic—1984 Corolla (FWD)

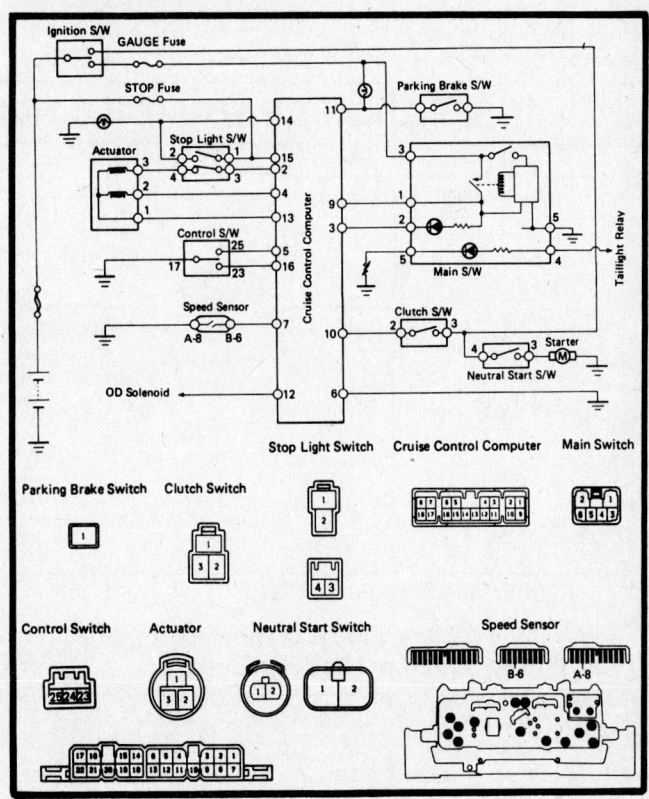

Cruise control electrical schematic—1985 Corolla (FWD)

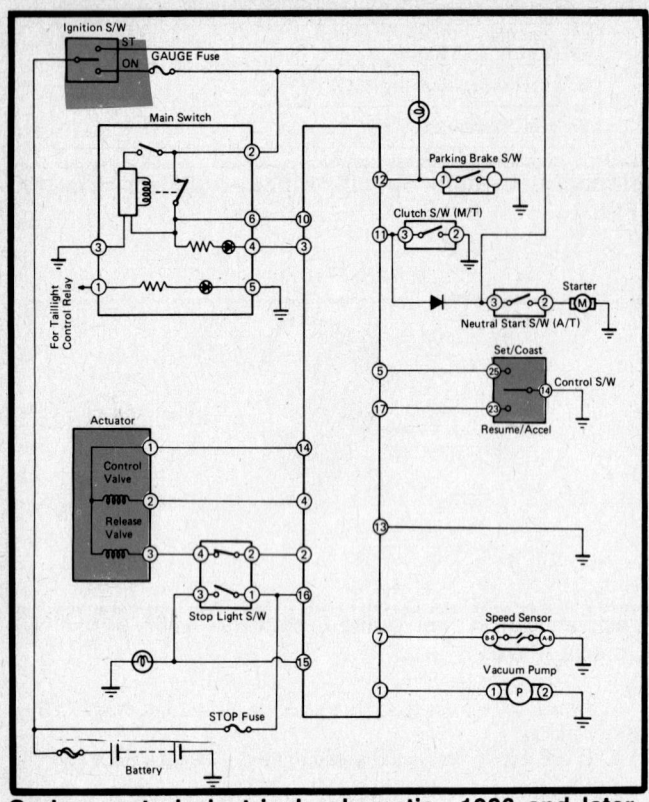

Cruise control electrical schematic—1986 and later Corolla (FWD)

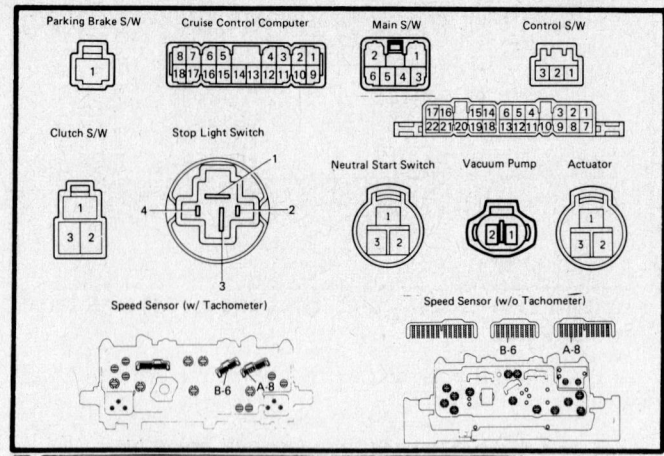

Cruise control electrical connectors—1986 and later Corolla (FWD)

Cruise control vacuum schematic—1986 and later Corolla (FWD)

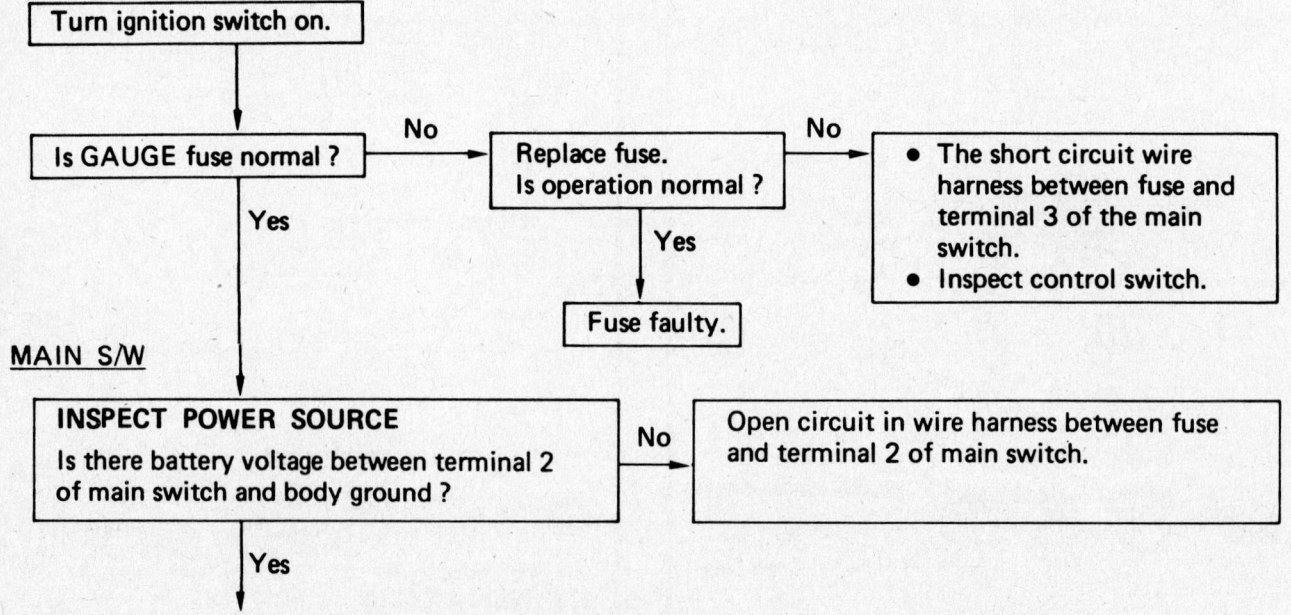

| A | INSPECTION OF SOURCE CIRCUIT |

Cruise control trouble diagnosis chart—1984 Corolla (RWD)

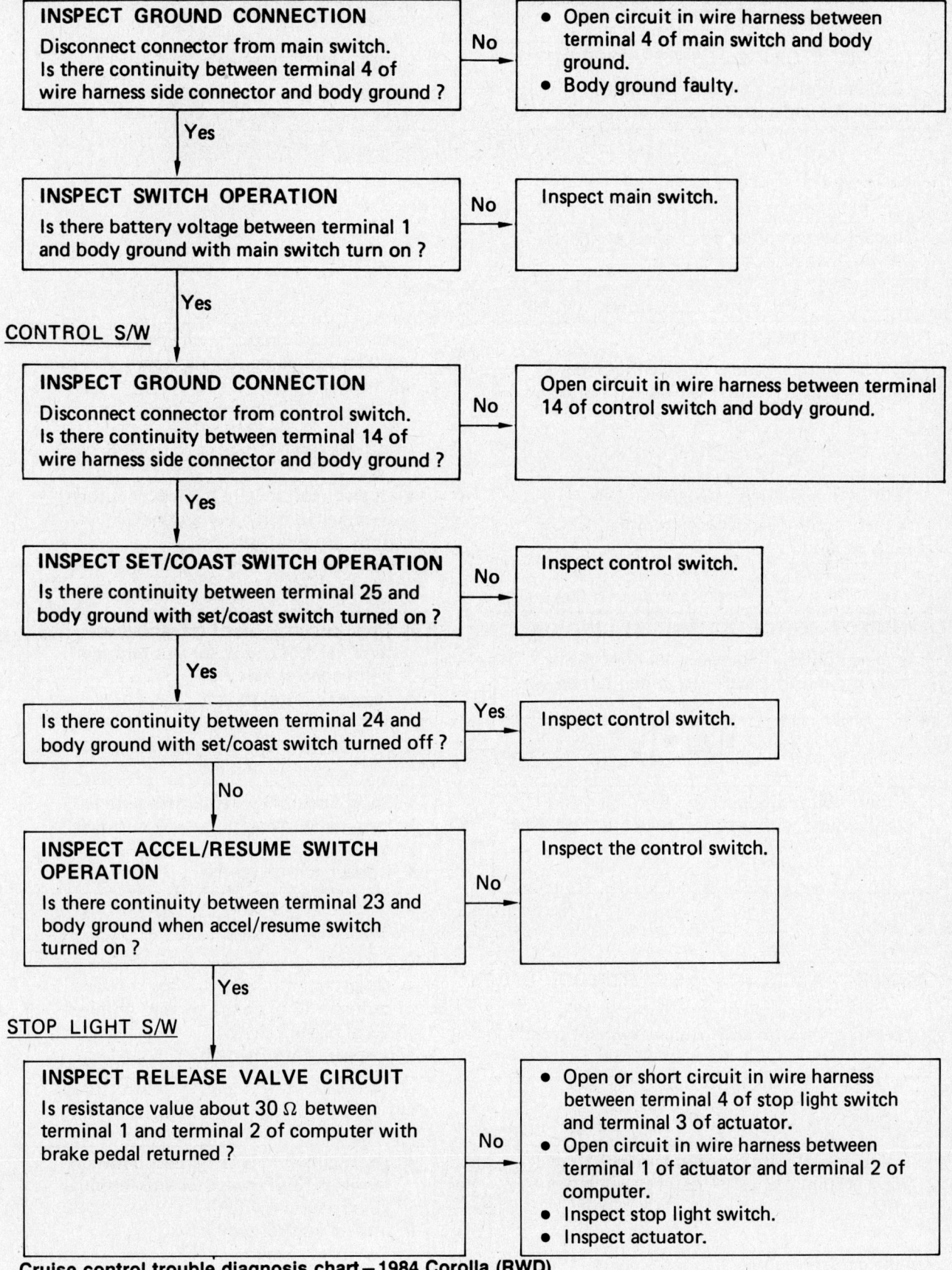

INSPECT GROUND CONNECTION

Disconnect connector from main switch.
Is there continuity between terminal 4 of
wire harness side connector and body ground ?

→ No →
- Open circuit in wire harness between terminal 4 of main switch and body ground.
- Body ground faulty.

↓ Yes

INSPECT SWITCH OPERATION

Is there battery voltage between terminal 1
and body ground with main switch turn on ?

→ No → Inspect main switch.

↓ Yes

CONTROL S/W

INSPECT GROUND CONNECTION

Disconnect connector from control switch.
Is there continuity between terminal 14 of
wire harness side connector and body ground ?

→ No → Open circuit in wire harness between terminal 14 of control switch and body ground.

↓ Yes

INSPECT SET/COAST SWITCH OPERATION

Is there continuity between terminal 25 and
body ground with set/coast switch turned on ?

→ No → Inspect control switch.

↓ Yes

Is there continuity between terminal 24 and
body ground with set/coast switch turned off ?

→ Yes → Inspect control switch.

↓ No

INSPECT ACCEL/RESUME SWITCH OPERATION

Is there continuity between terminal 23 and
body ground when accel/resume switch
turned on ?

→ No → Inspect the control switch.

↓ Yes

STOP LIGHT S/W

INSPECT RELEASE VALVE CIRCUIT

Is resistance value about 30 Ω between
terminal 1 and terminal 2 of computer with
brake pedal returned ?

→ No →
- Open or short circuit in wire harness between terminal 4 of stop light switch and terminal 3 of actuator.
- Open circuit in wire harness between terminal 1 of actuator and terminal 2 of computer.
- Inspect stop light switch.
- Inspect actuator.

Cruise control trouble diagnosis chart — 1984 Corolla (RWD)

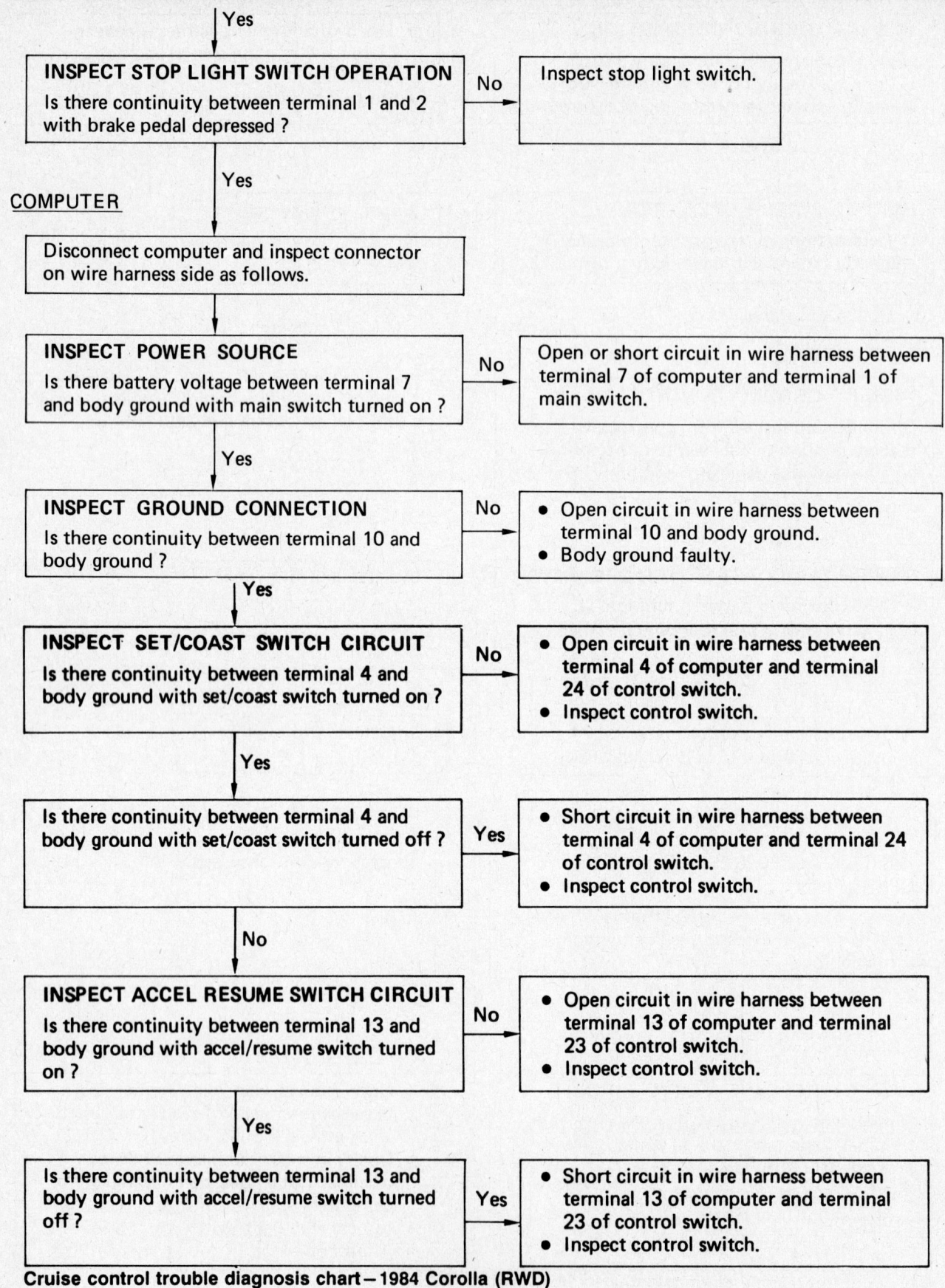

Cruise control trouble diagnosis chart — 1984 Corolla (RWD)

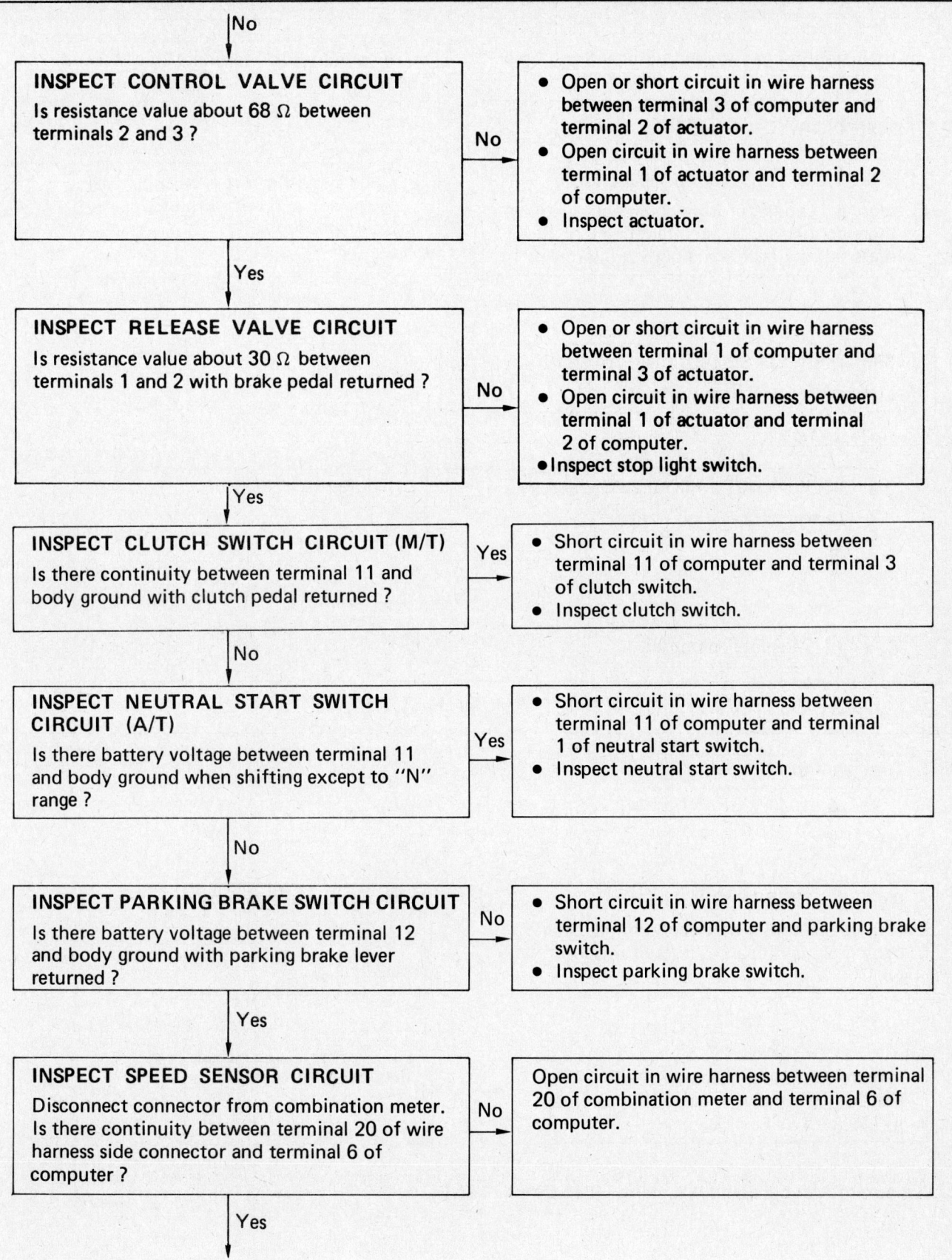

↓ No

INSPECT CONTROL VALVE CIRCUIT
Is resistance value about 68 Ω between terminals 2 and 3 ?

→ No
- Open or short circuit in wire harness between terminal 3 of computer and terminal 2 of actuator.
- Open circuit in wire harness between terminal 1 of actuator and terminal 2 of computer.
- Inspect actuator.

↓ Yes

INSPECT RELEASE VALVE CIRCUIT
Is resistance value about 30 Ω between terminals 1 and 2 with brake pedal returned ?

→ No
- Open or short circuit in wire harness between terminal 1 of computer and terminal 3 of actuator.
- Open circuit in wire harness between terminal 1 of actuator and terminal 2 of computer.
- Inspect stop light switch.

↓ Yes

INSPECT CLUTCH SWITCH CIRCUIT (M/T)
Is there continuity between terminal 11 and body ground with clutch pedal returned ?

→ Yes
- Short circuit in wire harness between terminal 11 of computer and terminal 3 of clutch switch.
- Inspect clutch switch.

↓ No

INSPECT NEUTRAL START SWITCH CIRCUIT (A/T)
Is there battery voltage between terminal 11 and body ground when shifting except to "N" range ?

→ Yes
- Short circuit in wire harness between terminal 11 of computer and terminal 1 of neutral start switch.
- Inspect neutral start switch.

↓ No

INSPECT PARKING BRAKE SWITCH CIRCUIT
Is there battery voltage between terminal 12 and body ground with parking brake lever returned ?

→ No
- Short circuit in wire harness between terminal 12 of computer and parking brake switch.
- Inspect parking brake switch.

↓ Yes

INSPECT SPEED SENSOR CIRCUIT
Disconnect connector from combination meter. Is there continuity between terminal 20 of wire harness side connector and terminal 6 of computer ?

→ No
Open circuit in wire harness between terminal 20 of combination meter and terminal 6 of computer.

↓ Yes

Cruise control trouble diagnosis chart—1984 Corolla (RWD)

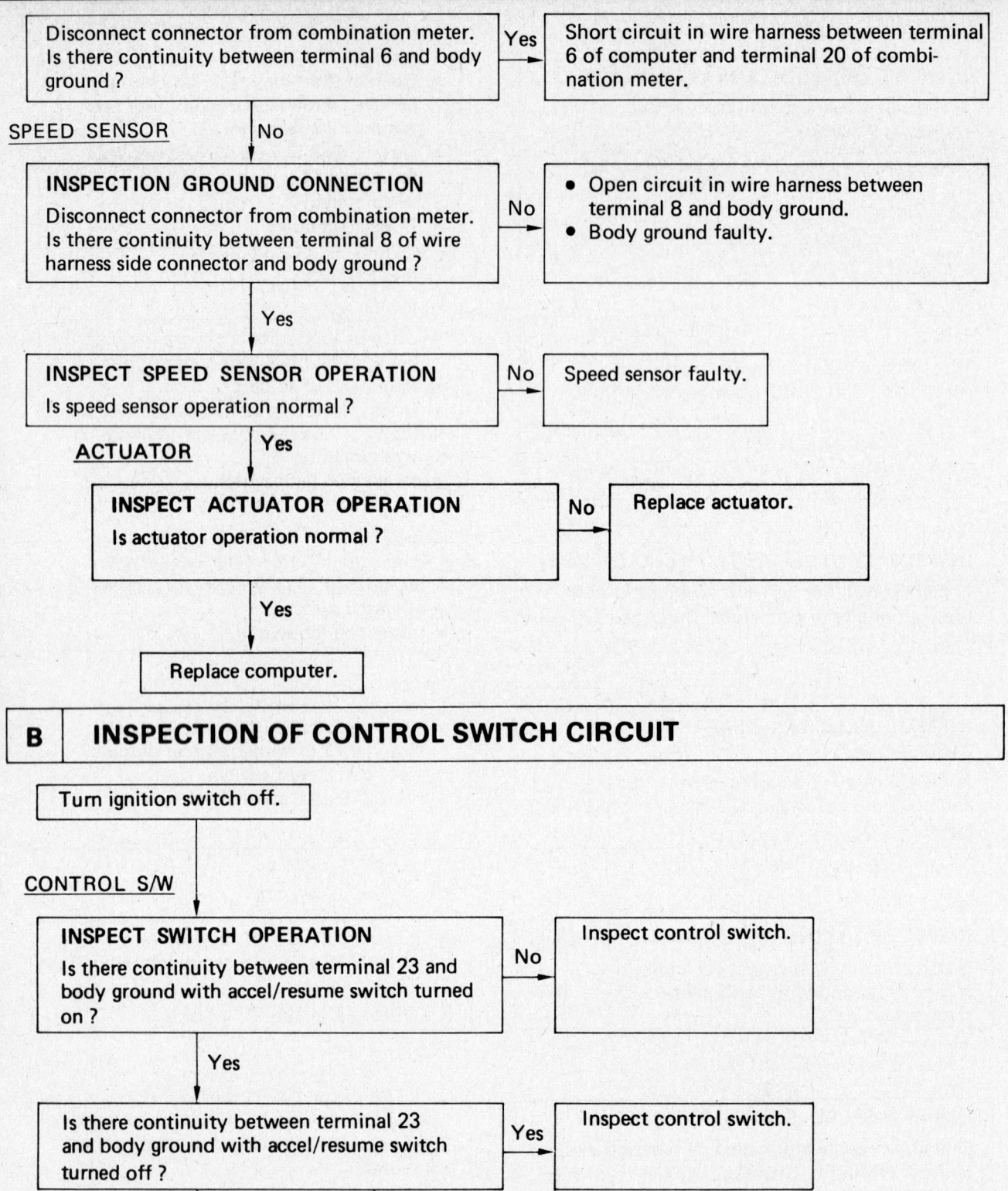

Disconnect connector from combination meter. Is there continuity between terminal 6 and body ground ?
→ Yes → Short circuit in wire harness between terminal 6 of computer and terminal 20 of combination meter.

↓ No

SPEED SENSOR

INSPECTION GROUND CONNECTION
Disconnect connector from combination meter. Is there continuity between terminal 8 of wire harness side connector and body ground ?
→ No →
- Open circuit in wire harness between terminal 8 and body ground.
- Body ground faulty.

↓ Yes

INSPECT SPEED SENSOR OPERATION
Is speed sensor operation normal ?
→ No → Speed sensor faulty.

ACTUATOR ↓ Yes

INSPECT ACTUATOR OPERATION
Is actuator operation normal ?
→ No → Replace actuator.

↓ Yes

Replace computer.

| B | **INSPECTION OF CONTROL SWITCH CIRCUIT** |

Turn ignition switch off.

CONTROL S/W

INSPECT SWITCH OPERATION
Is there continuity between terminal 23 and body ground with accel/resume switch turned on ?
→ No → Inspect control switch.

↓ Yes

Is there continuity between terminal 23 and body ground with accel/resume switch turned off ?
→ Yes → Inspect control switch.

Cruise control trouble diagnosis chart — 1984 Corolla (RWD)

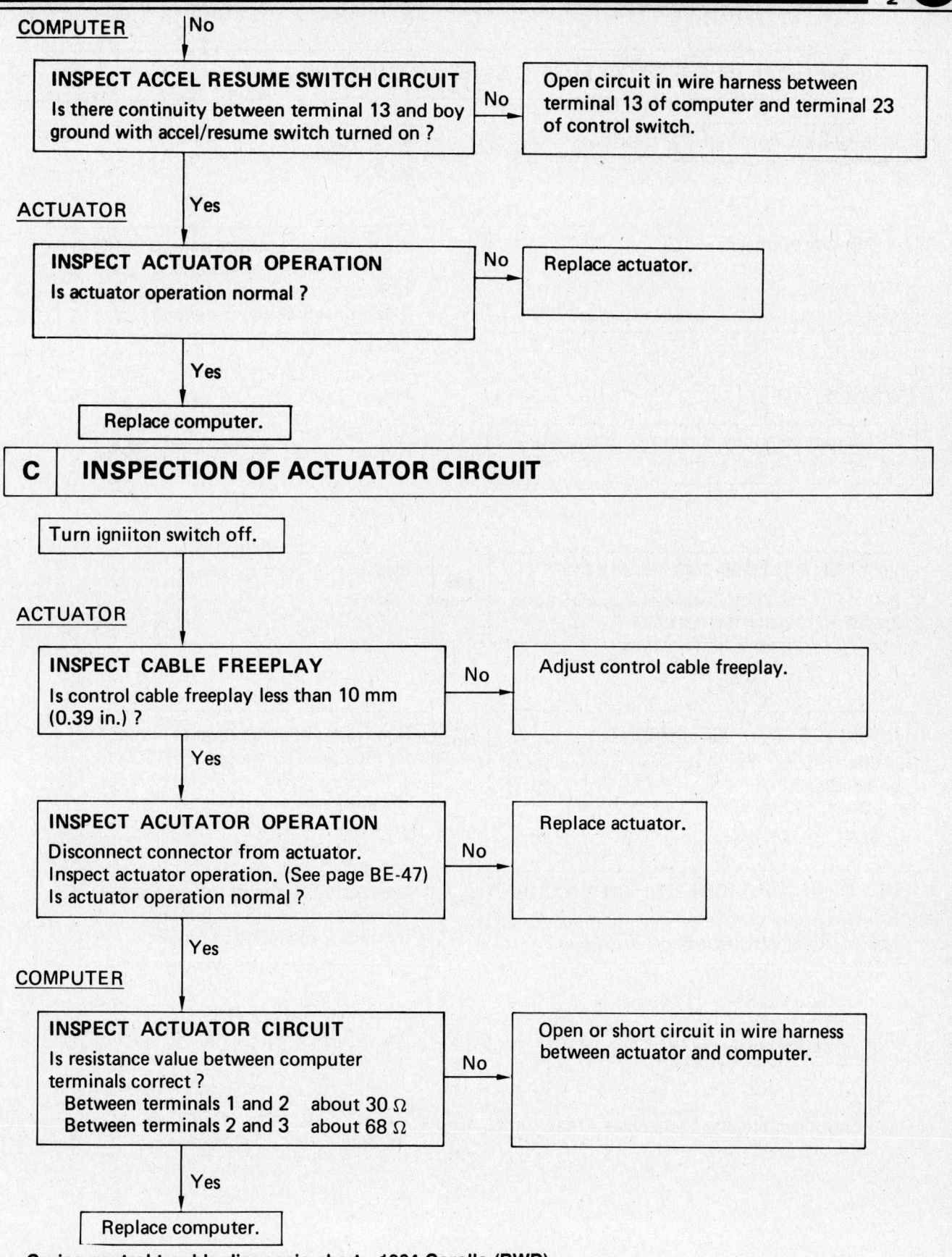

COMPUTER | No

INSPECT ACCEL RESUME SWITCH CIRCUIT
Is there continuity between terminal 13 and boy ground with accel/resume switch turned on ?

→ No → Open circuit in wire harness between terminal 13 of computer and terminal 23 of control switch.

ACTUATOR | Yes

INSPECT ACTUATOR OPERATION
Is actuator operation normal ?

→ No → Replace actuator.

Yes

Replace computer.

C | **INSPECTION OF ACTUATOR CIRCUIT**

Turn igniiton switch off.

ACTUATOR

INSPECT CABLE FREEPLAY
Is control cable freeplay less than 10 mm (0.39 in.) ?

→ No → Adjust control cable freeplay.

Yes

INSPECT ACUTATOR OPERATION
Disconnect connector from actuator.
Inspect actuator operation. (See page BE-47)
Is actuator operation normal ?

→ No → Replace actuator.

Yes

COMPUTER

INSPECT ACTUATOR CIRCUIT
Is resistance value between computer terminals correct ?
 Between terminals 1 and 2 about 30 Ω
 Between terminals 2 and 3 about 68 Ω

→ No → Open or short circuit in wire harness between actuator and computer.

Yes

Replace computer.

Cruise control trouble diagnosis chart – 1984 Corolla (RWD)

| D | **INSPECTION OF STOP LIGHT SWITCH CIRCUIT** |

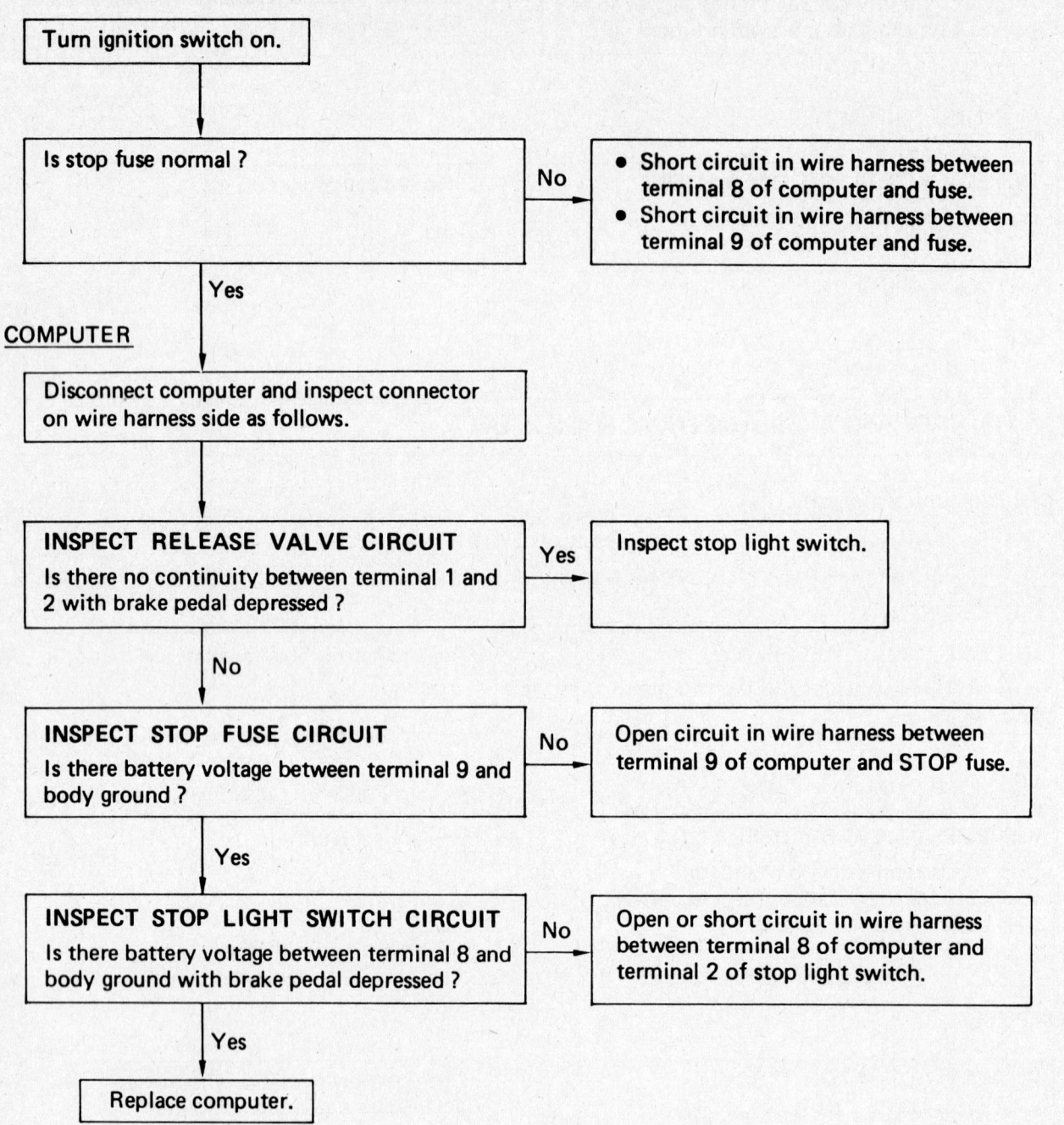

Cruise control trouble diagnosis chart — 1984 Corolla (RWD)

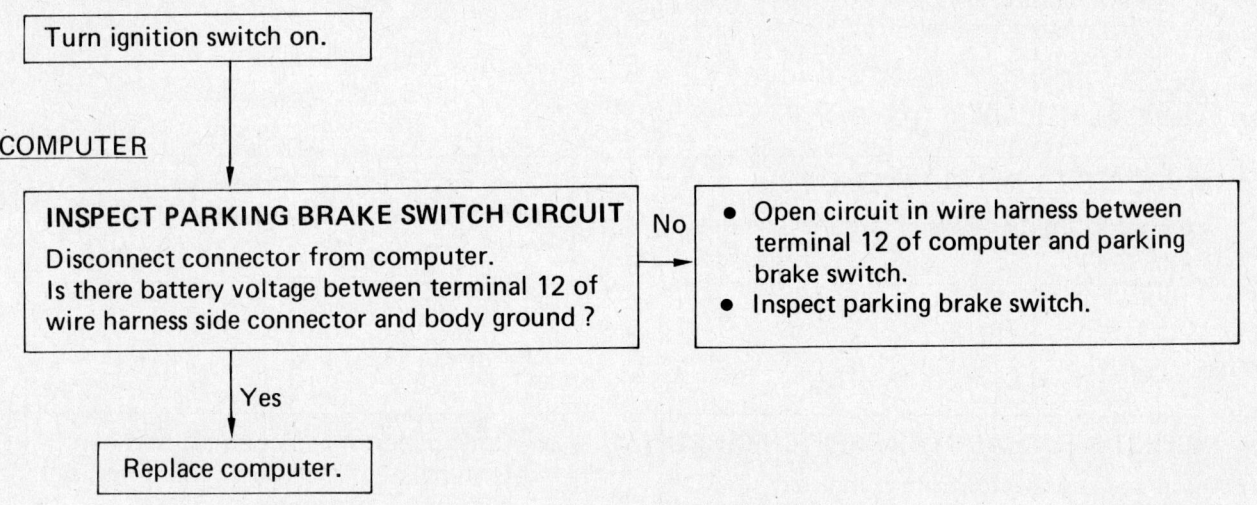

| E | INSPECTION OF PARKING BRAKE SWITCH |

Turn ignition switch on.

COMPUTER

INSPECT PARKING BRAKE SWITCH CIRCUIT
Disconnect connector from computer.
Is there battery voltage between terminal 12 of
wire harness side connector and body ground ?

No →
- Open circuit in wire harness between terminal 12 of computer and parking brake switch.
- Inspect parking brake switch.

Yes

Replace computer.

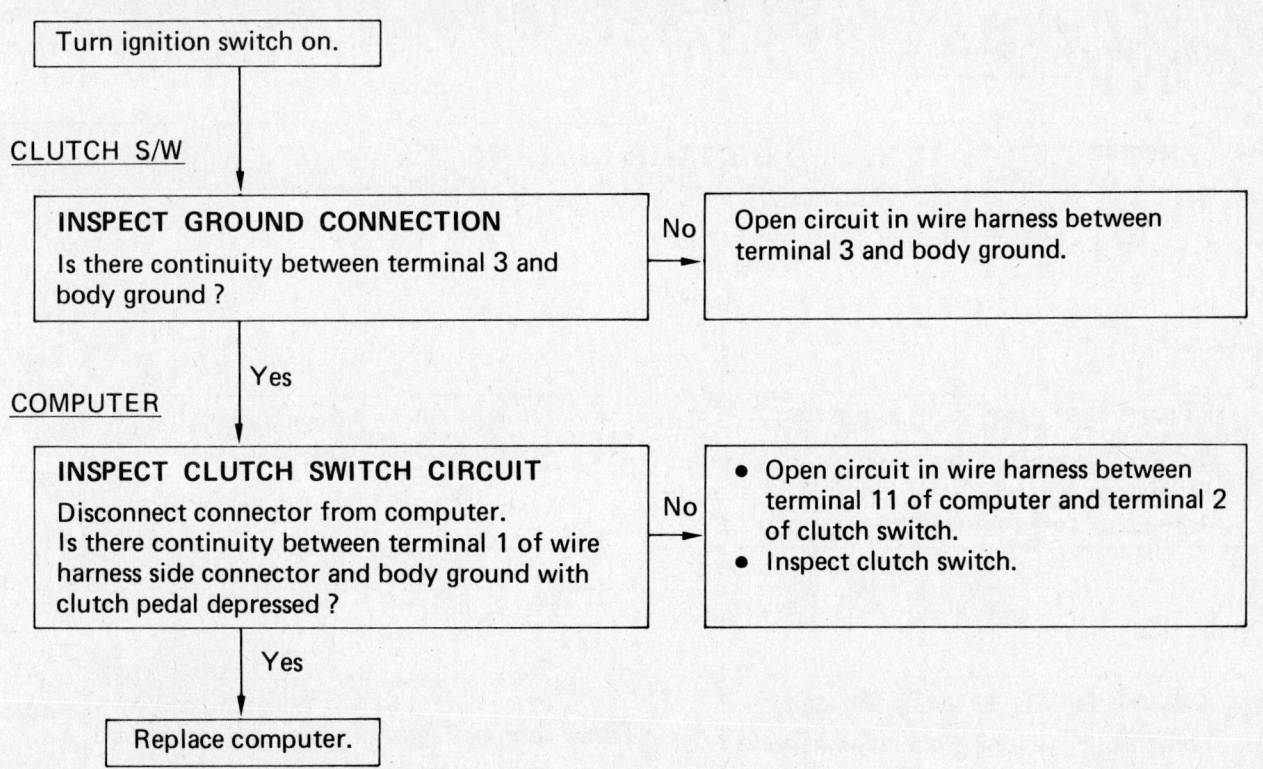

| F | INSPECTION OF CLUTCH SWITCH CIRCUIT |

Turn ignition switch on.

CLUTCH S/W

INSPECT GROUND CONNECTION
Is there continuity between terminal 3 and
body ground ?

No →
Open circuit in wire harness between
terminal 3 and body ground.

Yes

COMPUTER

INSPECT CLUTCH SWITCH CIRCUIT
Disconnect connector from computer.
Is there continuity between terminal 1 of wire
harness side connector and body ground with
clutch pedal depressed ?

No →
- Open circuit in wire harness between terminal 11 of computer and terminal 2 of clutch switch.
- Inspect clutch switch.

Yes

Replace computer.

Cruise control trouble diagnosis chart — 1984 Corolla (RWD)

| G | **INSPECTION OF NEUTRAL START SWITCH CIRCUIT** |

Turn ignition switch on.

NEUTRAL START S/W

INSPECT GROUND CONNECTION
Is there continuity between terminal 2 and body ground ?

No → Open circuit in wire harness between terminal 2 and body ground.

Yes

COMPUTER

INSPECT NEUTRAL START SWITCH CIRCUIT
Disconnect connector from computer.
Is there continuity between terminal 11 of wire harness side connector and body ground when shifted to "N" range ?

No →
- Open circuit in wire harness between terminal 11 of computer and terminal 1 of neutral start switch.
- Inspect neutral start switch.

Yes

Replace computer.

| H | **INSPECTION OF SPEED SENSOR CIRCUIT** |

Turn ignition switch on.

SPEED SENSOR

INSPECT GROUND CONNECTION
Disconnect connector from combination meter.
Is there continuity between terminal 20 of wire harness side connector and body ground ?

Yes → Short circuit in wire harness between terminal 20 and body ground.

No

COMPUTER

INSPECT SPEED SENSOR CIRCUIT
Disconnect connector from combination meter.
Is there continuity between terminal 20 of wire harness side connector and terminal 6 of computer ?

No → Open circuit in wire harness between terminal 20 of combination meter and terminal 6 of computer.

Cruise control trouble diagnosis chart—1984 Corolla (RWD)

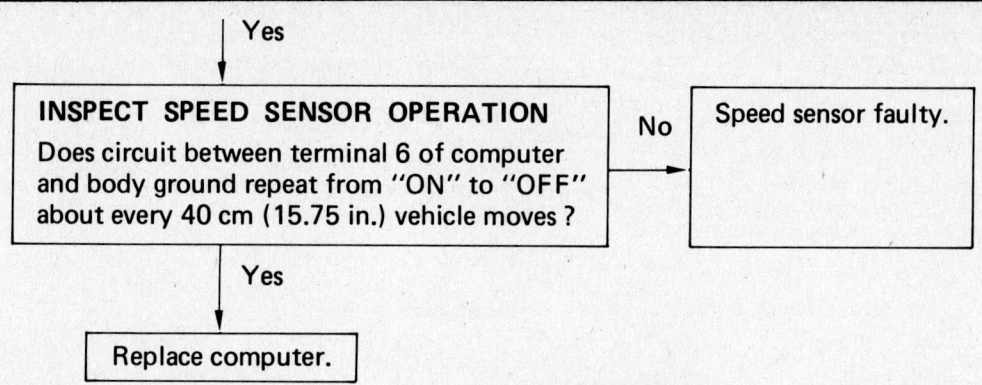

Cruise control trouble diagnosis chart—1984 Corolla (RWD)

Problem	Inspection Item	No.
Cruise control does not operate.	Inspection of power source circuit	A
Vehicle speed does not reduce when coast switch turned on.	Inspection of control switch and circuit.	B
Vehicle does not accelerate when accel switch turned on.		
Vehicle speed does not return to memorized speed when resume switch turned on.		
Set speed deviates on high side.	Inspection of actuator and circuit	C
Set speed deviates on low side.		
Vehicle speed does not fluctuate when set switch turned on.	Inspection of actuator and circuit Inspection of speed sensor and circuit	C H
Setting speed does not cancel when brake pedal depressed.	Inspection of stop light switch and circuit	D
Setting speed does not cancel when parking brake pulled.	Inspection of parking brake switch and circuit	E
Setting speed does not cancel when clutch pedal depressed (M/T only).	Inspection of clutch switch and circuit	F
Setting speed does not cancel when shifted to "N" range (A/T only).	Inspection of neutral start switch and circuit	G
Speed can be set below 20 km/h.	Inspection of speed sensor and circuit	H
Cruise control will not disengage even below 20 km/h.		

Cruise control troubleshooting data sheet—1984 Corolla (RWD)

CRUISE CONTROL SYSTEM DIAGNOSIS- 1985 AND LATER

Output of Diagnosis Codes

TYPE A CODE (1985 ONLY)

1. Turn the ignition switch to the on position.
2. Turn the set/coast switch on. Turn the main switch on.
3. Read the diagnosis code on the main switch indicator.
4. Results are as follows.

TYPE B CODE

1. Do not turn the ignition switch off. Do not turn the main switch off.
2. Turn the set/coast switch on three times within two seconds.
3. Read the diagnosis code on the main switch indicator.
4. Indication codes appear with priority from number eleven. Normal codes continue twenty seconds and abnormal codes are repeated three times.
5. Indication is stopped when vehicle speed is over 10 miles per hour or the main switch is turned off.
6. Results are as follows.

No.	Conditions	Indicator Code	Diagnosis
1	Set/coast switch on	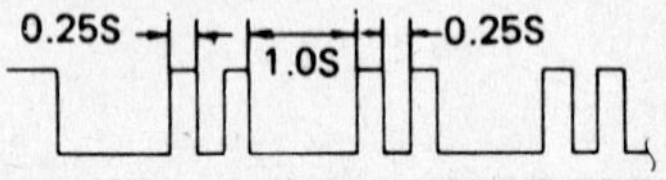	Set/coast switch circuit is normal.
2	Accel/resume switch on	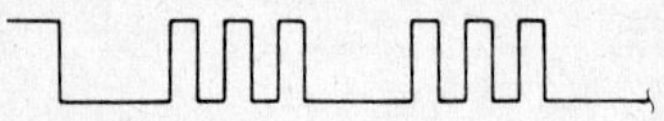	Accel/resume switch circuit is normal.
3	Each cancel switch on (Stop light switch. Parking brake switch, Clutch switch, Neutral start switch)	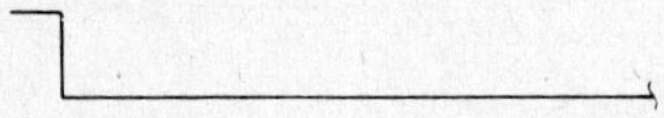	Each cancel switch circuit is normal.
4	Drive 40 km/h (25 mph) or over	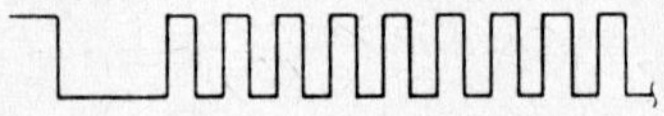	Speed sensor circuit is normal.
5	Drive 40 km/h (25 mph) or below	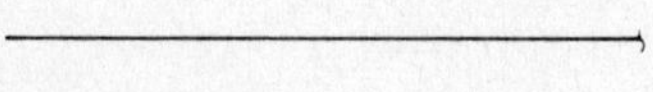	Speed sensor circuit is normal.

Type "A" diagnostic information—1985 Corolla (FWD)

No.	Indicator code	Diagnosis
	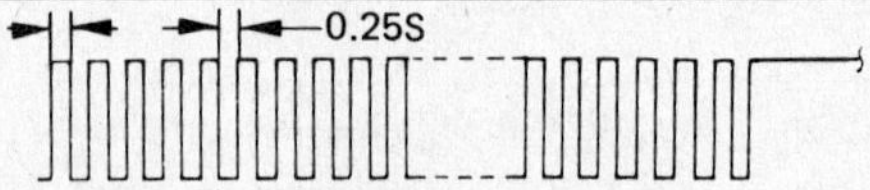	Normal
11	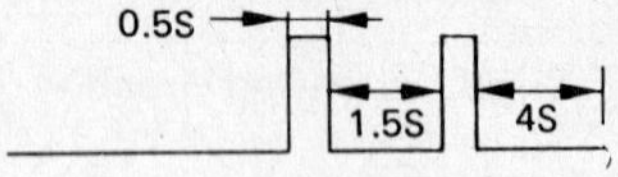	Actuator circuit is abnormal.
21	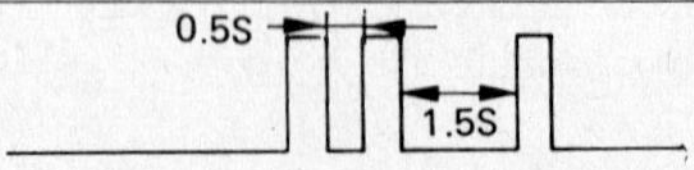	Speed sensor signal circuit is abnormal.
23	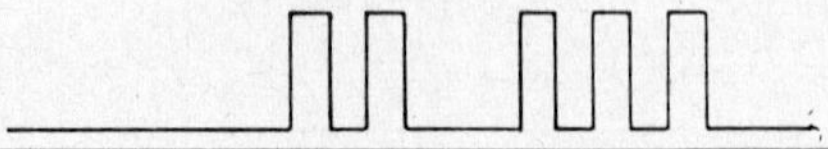	Speed sensor signal circuit is abnormal.
31	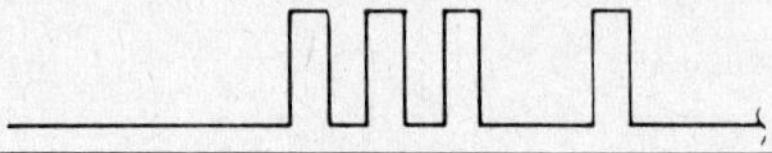	Accel/resume switch circuit is abnormal.
33	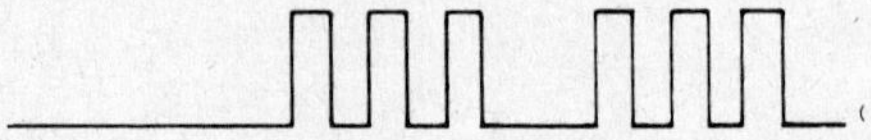	Accel/resume switch and set/coast switch is abnormal.

Type "B" diagnostic information—1985 Corolla (FWD)

Symptom	Inspection Area			Section
Cruise control cannot be set.	(a) Inspect type A code.	No. 1	NO	A
		No. 2	NO	B
		No. 3	NO	C
		No. 4	NO	D
		No. 5	NO	D
	(b) Inspect type B code.		11	E
			21	D
			23	F
			31	B
			33	A and B
	(c) All codes are normal.			Replace computer
Vehicle speed does not reduce when coast switch turned on.	Inspect No. 1 of type A code.		OK	F
			NO	A
Vehicle does not accelerate when accel switch turned on.	Inspect No. 2 of type A code.		OK	F
			NO	B
Vehicle speed does not return to memorized speed when resume switch turned on.	Inspect No. 2 of type A code.		OK	F
			NO	B
Set speed deviates on high side.	Inspect No. 1 of type A code.		OK	F
Set speed deviates on low side.			NO	A
Vehicle speed fluctuates when set switch turned on.	Inspect No. 1 of type A code.		OK	F
			NO	A
Setting speed does not cancel when brake pedal depressed.	Inspect No. 3 of type A code.		OK	F
			NO	C
Setting speed does not cancel when parking brake pulled.	Inspect No. 3 of type A code.		OK	F
			NO	C
Setting speed does not cancel when clutch pedal depressed (M/T only).	Inspect No. 3 of type A code.		OK	F
			NO	C
Setting speed does not cancel when shifted to "N" range (A/T only).	Inspect No. 3 of type A code.		OK	F
			NO	C
Speed can be set below 20 km/h.	Inspect No. 4 of type A code.		OK	F
			NO	D
Cruise control will not disengage even below 20 km/h.	Inspect No. 5 of type A code.		OK	F
			NO	D

Cruise control troubleshooting data sheet – 1985 Corolla (FWD)

No.	Indicator Code	Diagnosis
	ON OFF	Normal.
11	ON OFF	Actuator circuit is abnormal.
21	ON OFF	Speed sensor signal circuit is abnormal.

Type "A" diagnostic information – 1986 and later Corolla (FWD)

Problem	Inspection Item	No.
Cruise control does not operate.	Inspect diagnosis code Indication Code No.11 No.21 Diagnosis code normal	A I B
Vehicle speed does not reduce when coast switch turned on.	Inspection of control switch circuit	C
Vehicle does not accelerate when accel switch turned on.		
Vehicle speed does not return to memorized speed when resume switch turned on.		
Set speed deviates on high side.	Inspection of actuator circuit	D
Set speed deviates on low side.		
Vehicle speed does not fluctuate when set switch turned on.	Inspection of actuator circuit Inspection of speed sensor circuit	D I
Setting speed does not cancel when brake pedal depressed.	Inspection of stop light switch circuit	E
Setting speed does not cancel when parking brake pulled.	Inspection of parking brake switch circuit	F
Setting speed does not cancel when clutch pedal depressed (M/T only).	Inspection of clutch switch circuit	G
Setting speed does not cancel when shifted to "N" range (A/T only).	Inspection of neutral start switch circuit	H
Speed can be set below about 40 km/h (25 mph).	Inspection of speed sensor circuit	I
Cruise control will not disengage even below about 40 km/h (25 mph).		

Cruise control troubleshooting data sheet – 1986 and later Corolla (FWD)

A	INSPECTION OF SET/COAST SWITCH CIRCUIT

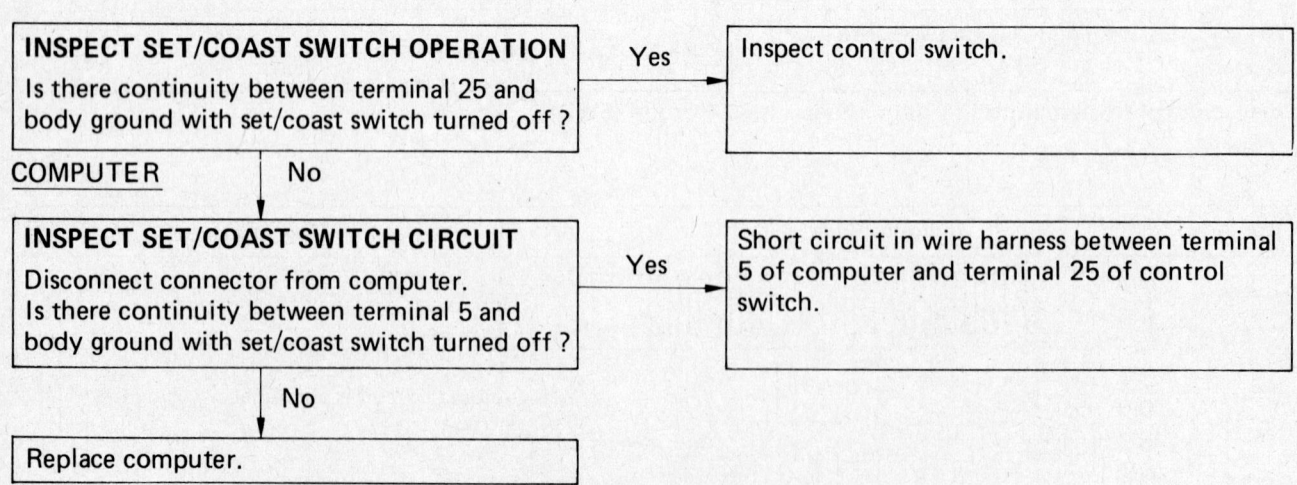

Cruise control trouble diagnosis chart – 1985 Corolla (FWD)

| B | **INSPECTION OF ACCEL/RESUME SWITCH CIRCUIT** |

CONTROL S/W

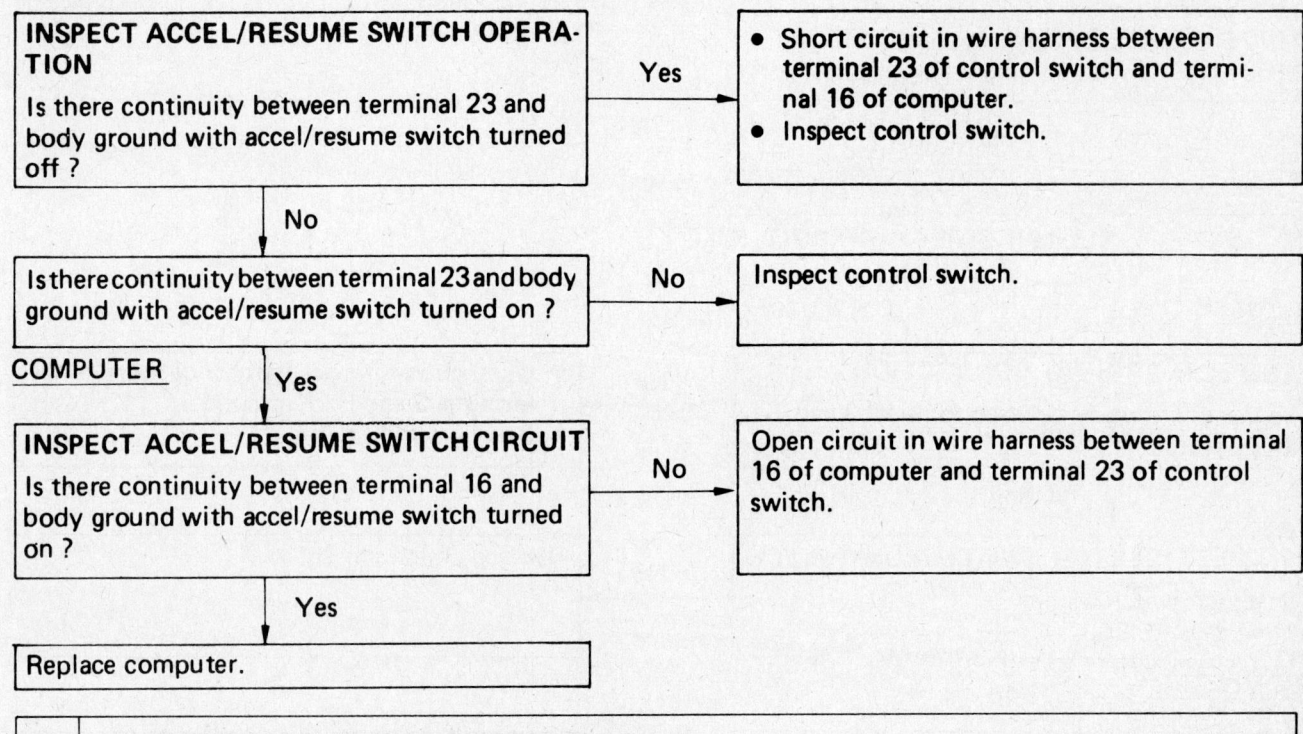

| C | **INSPECT CANCEL SWITCH CIRCUIT** |

1. INSPECT STOP LIGHT SWITCH CIRCUIT

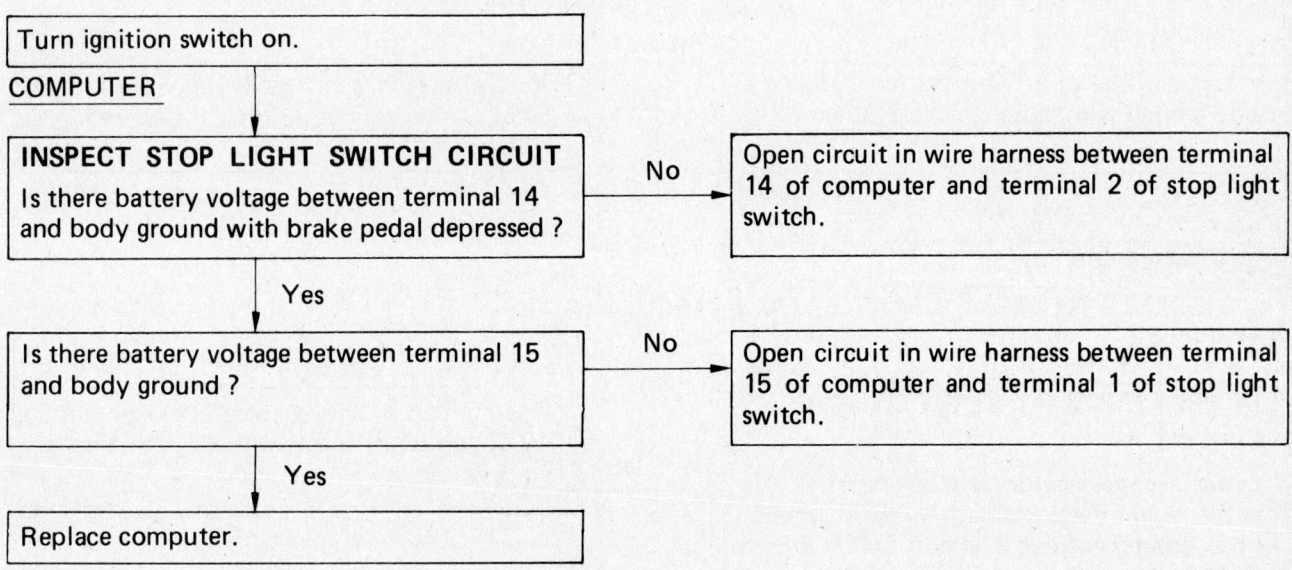

Cruise control trouble diagnosis chart — 1985 Corolla (FWD)

2.   INSPECT PARKING BRAKE SWITCH CIRCUIT

COMPUTER

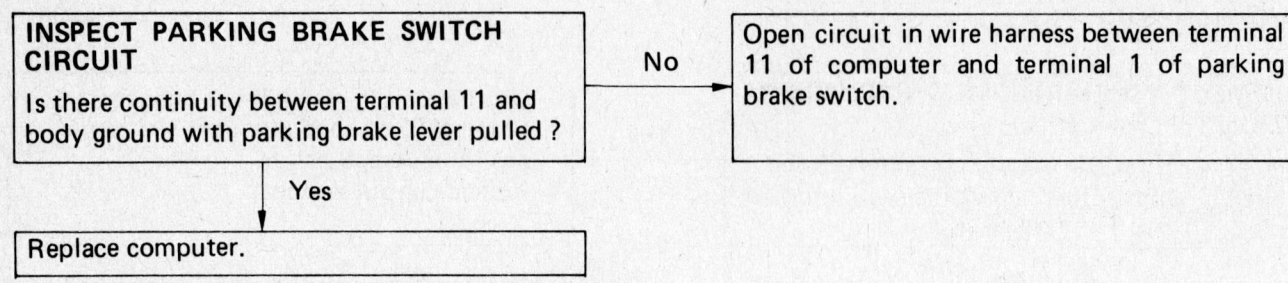

INSPECT PARKING BRAKE SWITCH CIRCUIT		
Is there continuity between terminal 11 and body ground with parking brake lever pulled ?	→ No →	Open circuit in wire harness between terminal 11 of computer and terminal 1 of parking brake switch.

↓ Yes

Replace computer.

3.   INSPECT CLUTCH SWITCH CIRCUIT (M/T)

CLUTCH S/W

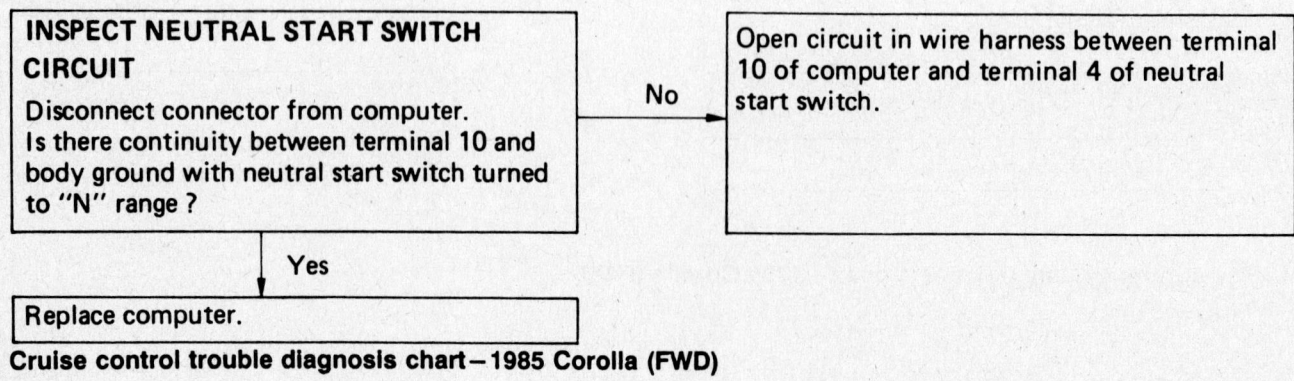

INSPECT GROUND CONNECTION

Is there continuity between terminal 3 and body ground ?

→ No →
- Open circuit in wire harness between terminal 3 and body ground.
- Body ground faulty.

↓ Yes

INSPECT CLUTCH SWITCH CONTINUITY

Is clutch switch normal ?
(See page BE-50)

→ No → Replace clutch switch.

COMPUTER   ↓ Yes

INSPECT CLUTCH SWITCH CIRCUIT

Is there continuity between terminal 10 and body ground with clutch pedal depressed ?

→ No → Open circuit in wire harness between terminal 10 of computer and terminal 2 of clutch switch.

↓ Yes

Is there continuity between terminal 10 and body ground with clutch pedal returned ?

→ Yes → Short circuit in wire harness between terminal 10 of computer and terminal 2 of clutch switch.

↓ No

Replace computer.

4.   INSPECT NEUTRAL START SWITCH CIRCUIT (A/T)
COMPUTER

INSPECT NEUTRAL START SWITCH CIRCUIT

Disconnect connector from computer.
Is there continuity between terminal 10 and body ground with neutral start switch turned to "N" range ?

→ No → Open circuit in wire harness between terminal 10 of computer and terminal 4 of neutral start switch.

↓ Yes

Replace computer.

Cruise control trouble diagnosis chart—1985 Corolla (FWD)

D	**INSPECTION OF SPEED SENSOR CIRCUIT**

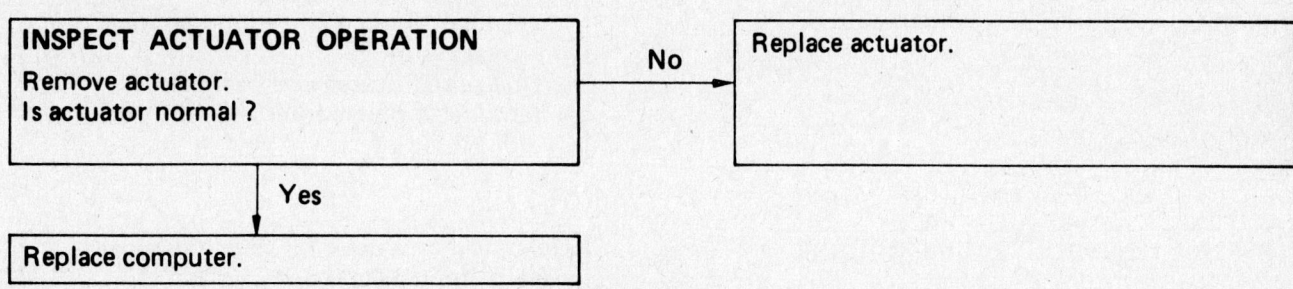

SPEED SENSOR

INSPECT GROUND CONNECTION
Disconnect combination meter.
Is there continuity between terminal of wire harness side and body ground ?

→ No →
- Open circuit in wire harness between terminal of combination meter and body ground.
- Body ground faulty.

↓ Yes

INSPECT SPEED SENSOR OPERATION
Is speed sensor normal ?

→ No → Replace speed sensor.

COMPUTER ↓ Yes

INSPECT SPEED SENSOR CIRCUIT
Disconnect connector from combination meter.
Is there continuity between terminal 7 and body ground ?

→ Yes → Short circuit in wire harness between terminal 7 of computer and terminal of combination meter.

↓ No

Is there continuity between terminal 7 of computer and terminal of combination meter ?

→ No → Open circuit in wire harness between terminal 7 of computer and terminal of combination meter.

↓ Yes

Replace computer.

E	**INSPECTION OF ACTUATOR OPERATION**

ACTUATOR

INSPECT ACTUATOR OPERATION
Remove actuator.
Is actuator normal ?

→ No → Replace actuator.

↓ Yes

Replace computer.

Cruise control trouble diagnosis chart – 1985 Corolla (FWD)

| F | **INSPECTION OF ACTUATOR CIRCUIT** |

ACTUATOR

INSPECT ACTUATOR OPERATION
Remove actuator.
Is actuator normal ?

→ No → Replace actuator.

↓ Yes

STOP LIGHT S/W

INSPECT STOP LIGHT SWITCH OPERATION
Is stop light switch normal ?

→ No → Replace stop light switch.

↓ Yes

COMPUTER

Disconnect computer and inspect connector on wire harness as follows.

↓

INSPECT RELEASE VALVE CIRCUIT
Is there continuity between terminal 2 and body ground ?

→ Yes → Short circuit in wire harness between terminal 2 of computer and terminal 3 of actuator.

↓ No

Is resistance value about 68 Ω between terminals 2 and 13 with brake pedal returned ?

→ No →
- Open circuit in wire harness between terminal 13 of computer and terminal 1 of actuator.
- Open circuit in wire harness between terminal 2 of computer and terminal 3 of actuator.

↓ Yes

INSPECT CONTROL VALVE CIRCUIT
Is resistance value about 30 Ω between terminals 4 and 13 ?

→ No → Open or short circuit in wire harness between terminal 4 of computer and terminal 2 of actuator.

↓ Yes

Replace computer.

Cruise control trouble diagnosis chart—1985 Corolla (FWD)

Terminal	Connection or Measure item	Check item tester connection		Condition	Voltage or Resistance value
2	Stop Light Switch and Release Valve	Resistance	2 – 13	Brake pedal returned	About 30
4	Control Valve	Resistance	4 – 13		About 68
5	Control Switch (Set/coast S/W)	Continuity	5 – Body ground	Turn set/coast switch on	Continuity
				Turn set/coast switch off	Continuity
6	OD Relay				
7	Speed Sensor	Continuity	7 – Body ground	Vehicle moving slowly	1 pulse each 40 cm (15.75 in.)
9	Main Switch	Voltage	9 – Body ground	Turn ignition switch and main switch on	Battery voltage
				Turn ignition switch and/or main switch off	No voltage
10	Clutch Switch or Neutral Start Switch	Continuity	10 – Body ground	Clutch pedal depressed or if shifted into "N" range	Continuity
				Clutch pedal returned or if shifted into any range except "N" range	No continuity
11	Parking Brake Switch	Voltage	11 – Body ground	Parking brake lever pulled	No voltage
				Parking brake lever returned	Battery voltage
12	Body Ground	Continuity	12 – Body ground		Continuity
13	Release Valve and Control Valve				
14	Stop Light Switch	Voltage	14 – Body ground	Brake pedal depressed	Battery voltage
				Brake pedal returned	No voltage
15	STOP Fuse	Voltage	15 – Body ground		Battery voltage
16	Control Switch (Accel/resume S/W)	Continuity	17 – Body ground	Turn accel/resume switch on	Continuity
				Turn accel/resume switch off	No continuity

Cruise control trouble diagnosis chart – 1985 Corolla (FWD)

3. INSPECT DIAGNOSIS CIRCUIT

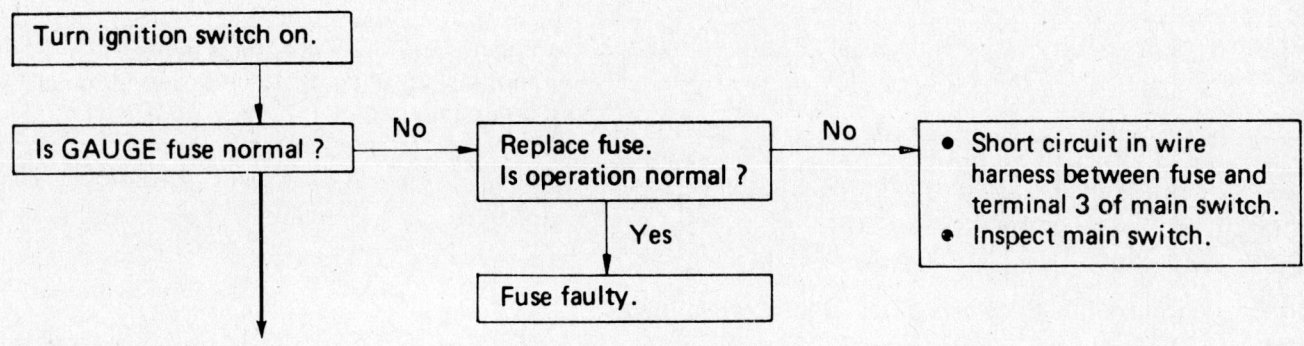

Cruise control trouble diagnosis chart – 1985 Corolla (FWD)

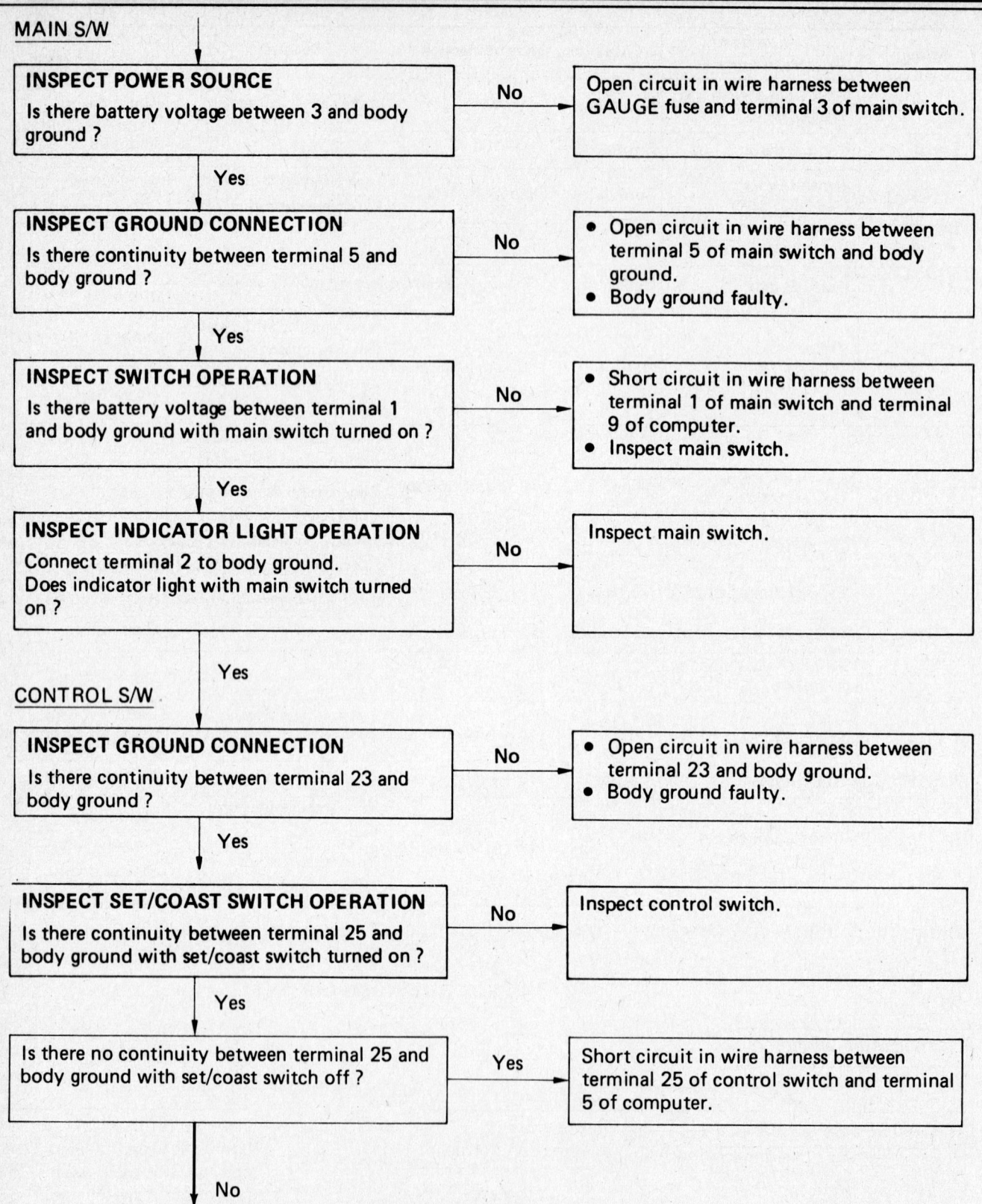

MAIN S/W

| INSPECT POWER SOURCE — Is there battery voltage between 3 and body ground ? | No → | Open circuit in wire harness between GAUGE fuse and terminal 3 of main switch. |

↓ Yes

| INSPECT GROUND CONNECTION — Is there continuity between terminal 5 and body ground ? | No → | • Open circuit in wire harness between terminal 5 of main switch and body ground.
• Body ground faulty. |

↓ Yes

| INSPECT SWITCH OPERATION — Is there battery voltage between terminal 1 and body ground with main switch turned on ? | No → | • Short circuit in wire harness between terminal 1 of main switch and terminal 9 of computer.
• Inspect main switch. |

↓ Yes

| INSPECT INDICATOR LIGHT OPERATION — Connect terminal 2 to body ground. Does indicator light with main switch turned on ? | No → | Inspect main switch. |

↓ Yes

CONTROL S/W

| INSPECT GROUND CONNECTION — Is there continuity between terminal 23 and body ground ? | No → | • Open circuit in wire harness between terminal 23 and body ground.
• Body ground faulty. |

↓ Yes

| INSPECT SET/COAST SWITCH OPERATION — Is there continuity between terminal 25 and body ground with set/coast switch turned on ? | No → | Inspect control switch. |

↓ Yes

| Is there no continuity between terminal 25 and body ground with set/coast switch off ? | Yes → | Short circuit in wire harness between terminal 25 of control switch and terminal 5 of computer. |

↓ No

Cruise control trouble diagnosis chart – 1985 Corolla (FWD)

COMPUTER

Disconnect computer and inspect connector on wire harness side as follows.

Yes

INSPECT POWER SOURCE		
Is there battery voltage between terminal 9 and body ground with main switch turned on ?	No →	Open circuit in wire harness between terminal 9 of computer and terminal 1 of main switch.

Yes

INSPECT GROUND CONNECTION		
Is there continuity between terminal 12 and body ground ?	No →	• Open circuit in wire harness between terminal 12 and body ground. • Body ground faulty.

Yes

INSPECT INDICATOR LIGHT CIRCUIT		
Connect terminal 3 to body ground. Does indicator light with main switch turned on ?	No →	Open circuit in wire harness between terminal 3 of computer and terminal 2 of main switch.

Yes

INSPECT SET/COAST SWITCH CIRCUIT		
Is there continuity between terminal 5 and body ground with set/coast switch turned on ?	No →	Open circuit in wire harness between terminal 5 of computer and terminal 25 of control switch.

Yes

Replace computer.

Cruise control trouble diagnosis chart — 1985 Corolla (FWD)

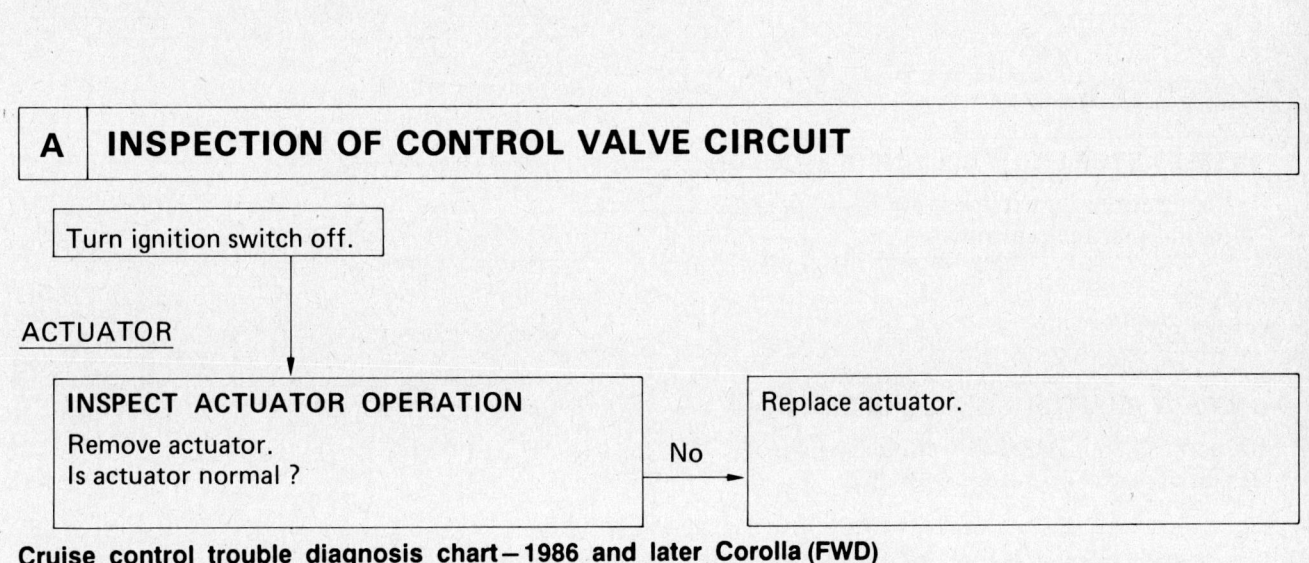

A	INSPECTION OF CONTROL VALVE CIRCUIT

Turn ignition switch off.

ACTUATOR

INSPECT ACTUATOR OPERATION		
Remove actuator. Is actuator normal ?	No →	Replace actuator.

Cruise control trouble diagnosis chart — 1986 and later Corolla (FWD)

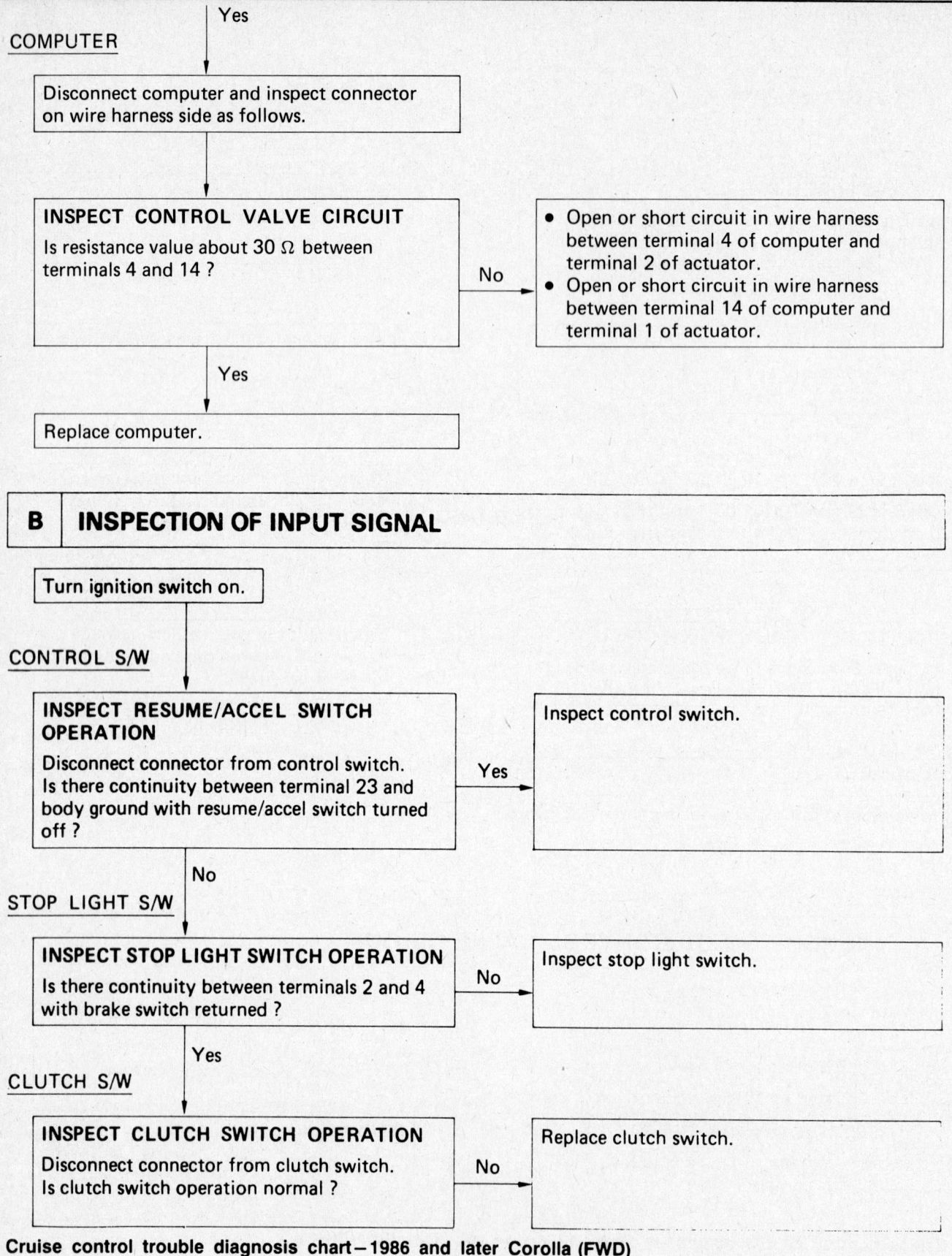

COMPUTER

Disconnect computer and inspect connector on wire harness side as follows.

INSPECT CONTROL VALVE CIRCUIT

Is resistance value about 30 Ω between terminals 4 and 14 ?

No →
- Open or short circuit in wire harness between terminal 4 of computer and terminal 2 of actuator.
- Open or short circuit in wire harness between terminal 14 of computer and terminal 1 of actuator.

Yes ↓

Replace computer.

B   INSPECTION OF INPUT SIGNAL

Turn ignition switch on.

CONTROL S/W

INSPECT RESUME/ACCEL SWITCH OPERATION

Disconnect connector from control switch.
Is there continuity between terminal 23 and body ground with resume/accel switch turned off ?

Yes → Inspect control switch.

No ↓

STOP LIGHT S/W

INSPECT STOP LIGHT SWITCH OPERATION

Is there continuity between terminals 2 and 4 with brake switch returned ?

No → Inspect stop light switch.

Yes ↓

CLUTCH S/W

INSPECT CLUTCH SWITCH OPERATION

Disconnect connector from clutch switch.
Is clutch switch operation normal ?

No → Replace clutch switch.

Cruise control trouble diagnosis chart—1986 and later Corolla (FWD)

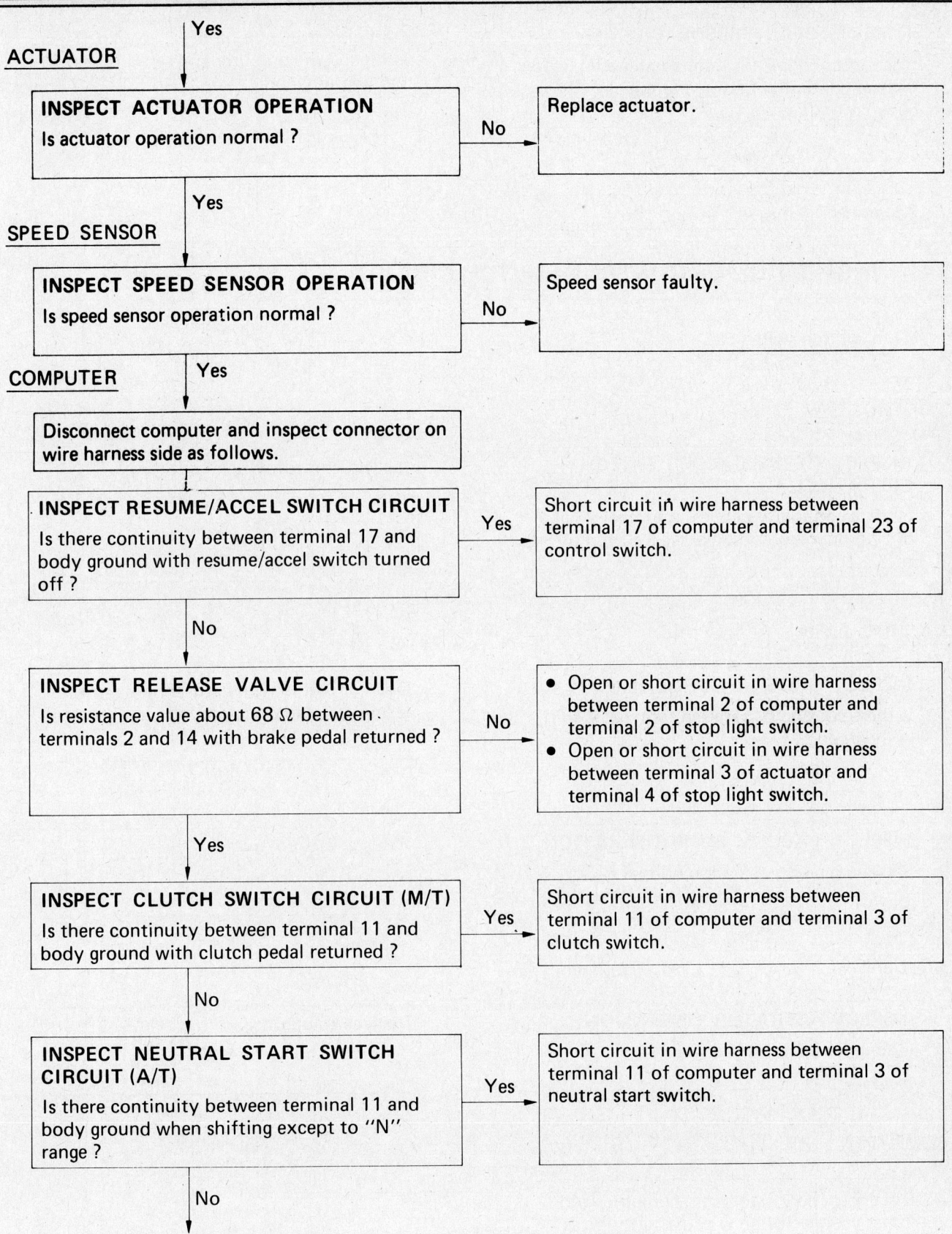

ACTUATOR

INSPECT ACTUATOR OPERATION

Is actuator operation normal ?

No → Replace actuator.

Yes

SPEED SENSOR

INSPECT SPEED SENSOR OPERATION

Is speed sensor operation normal ?

No → Speed sensor faulty.

Yes

COMPUTER

Disconnect computer and inspect connector on wire harness side as follows.

INSPECT RESUME/ACCEL SWITCH CIRCUIT

Is there continuity between terminal 17 and body ground with resume/accel switch turned off ?

Yes → Short circuit in wire harness between terminal 17 of computer and terminal 23 of control switch.

No

INSPECT RELEASE VALVE CIRCUIT

Is resistance value about 68 Ω between terminals 2 and 14 with brake pedal returned ?

No →
- Open or short circuit in wire harness between terminal 2 of computer and terminal 2 of stop light switch.
- Open or short circuit in wire harness between terminal 3 of actuator and terminal 4 of stop light switch.

Yes

INSPECT CLUTCH SWITCH CIRCUIT (M/T)

Is there continuity between terminal 11 and body ground with clutch pedal returned ?

Yes → Short circuit in wire harness between terminal 11 of computer and terminal 3 of clutch switch.

No

INSPECT NEUTRAL START SWITCH CIRCUIT (A/T)

Is there continuity between terminal 11 and body ground when shifting except to "N" range ?

Yes → Short circuit in wire harness between terminal 11 of computer and terminal 3 of neutral start switch.

No

Cruise control troubleshooting data sheet — 1986 and later Corolla (FWD)

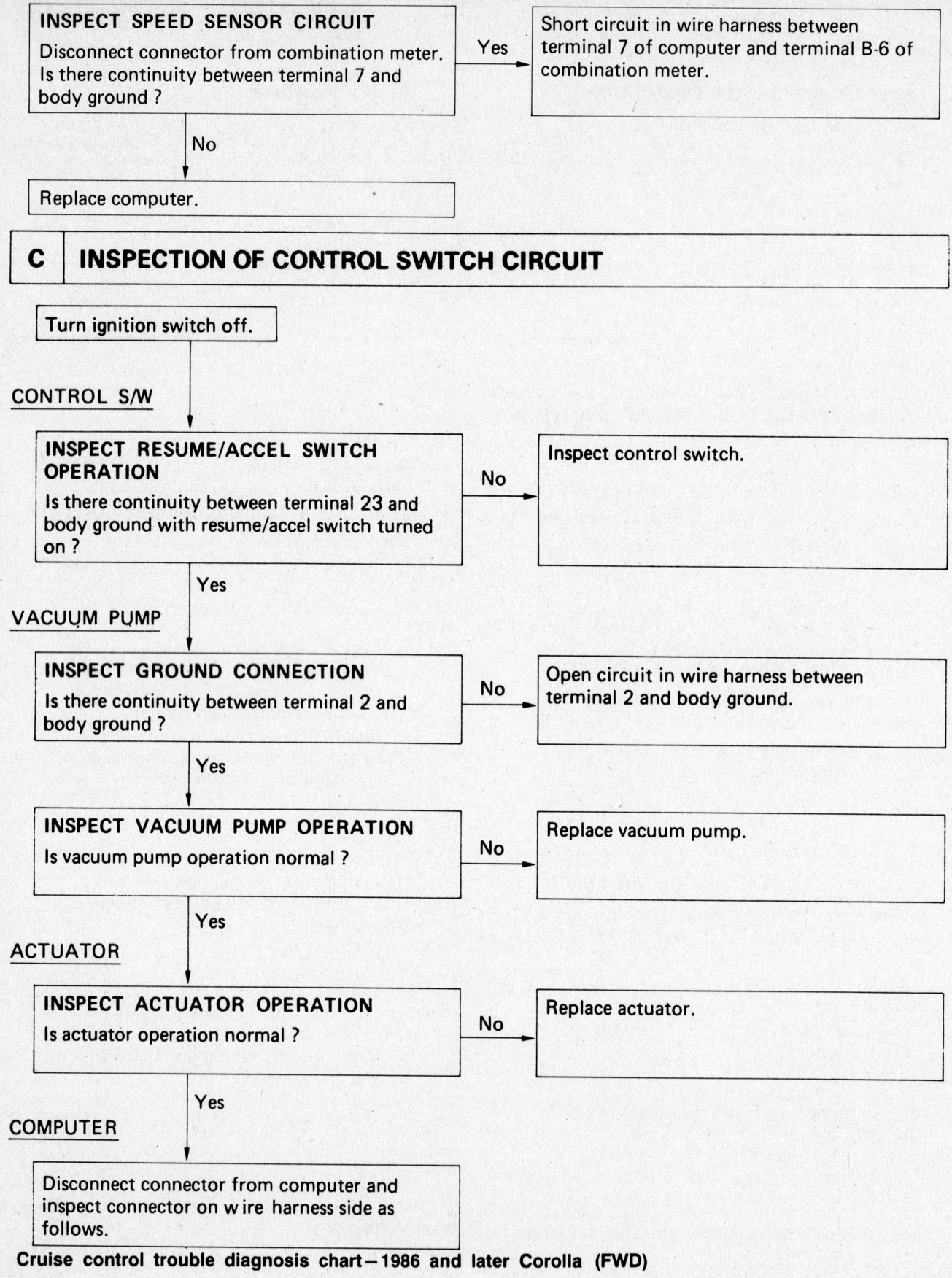

INSPECT SPEED SENSOR CIRCUIT

Disconnect connector from combination meter. Is there continuity between terminal 7 and body ground ?

→ Yes → Short circuit in wire harness between terminal 7 of computer and terminal B-6 of combination meter.

↓ No

Replace computer.

C | **INSPECTION OF CONTROL SWITCH CIRCUIT**

Turn ignition switch off.

CONTROL S/W

INSPECT RESUME/ACCEL SWITCH OPERATION

Is there continuity between terminal 23 and body ground with resume/accel switch turned on ?

→ No → Inspect control switch.

↓ Yes

VACUUM PUMP

INSPECT GROUND CONNECTION

Is there continuity between terminal 2 and body ground ?

→ No → Open circuit in wire harness between terminal 2 and body ground.

↓ Yes

INSPECT VACUUM PUMP OPERATION

Is vacuum pump operation normal ?

→ No → Replace vacuum pump.

↓ Yes

ACTUATOR

INSPECT ACTUATOR OPERATION

Is actuator operation normal ?

→ No → Replace actuator.

↓ Yes

COMPUTER

Disconnect connector from computer and inspect connector on wire harness side as follows.

Cruise control trouble diagnosis chart—1986 and later Corolla (FWD)

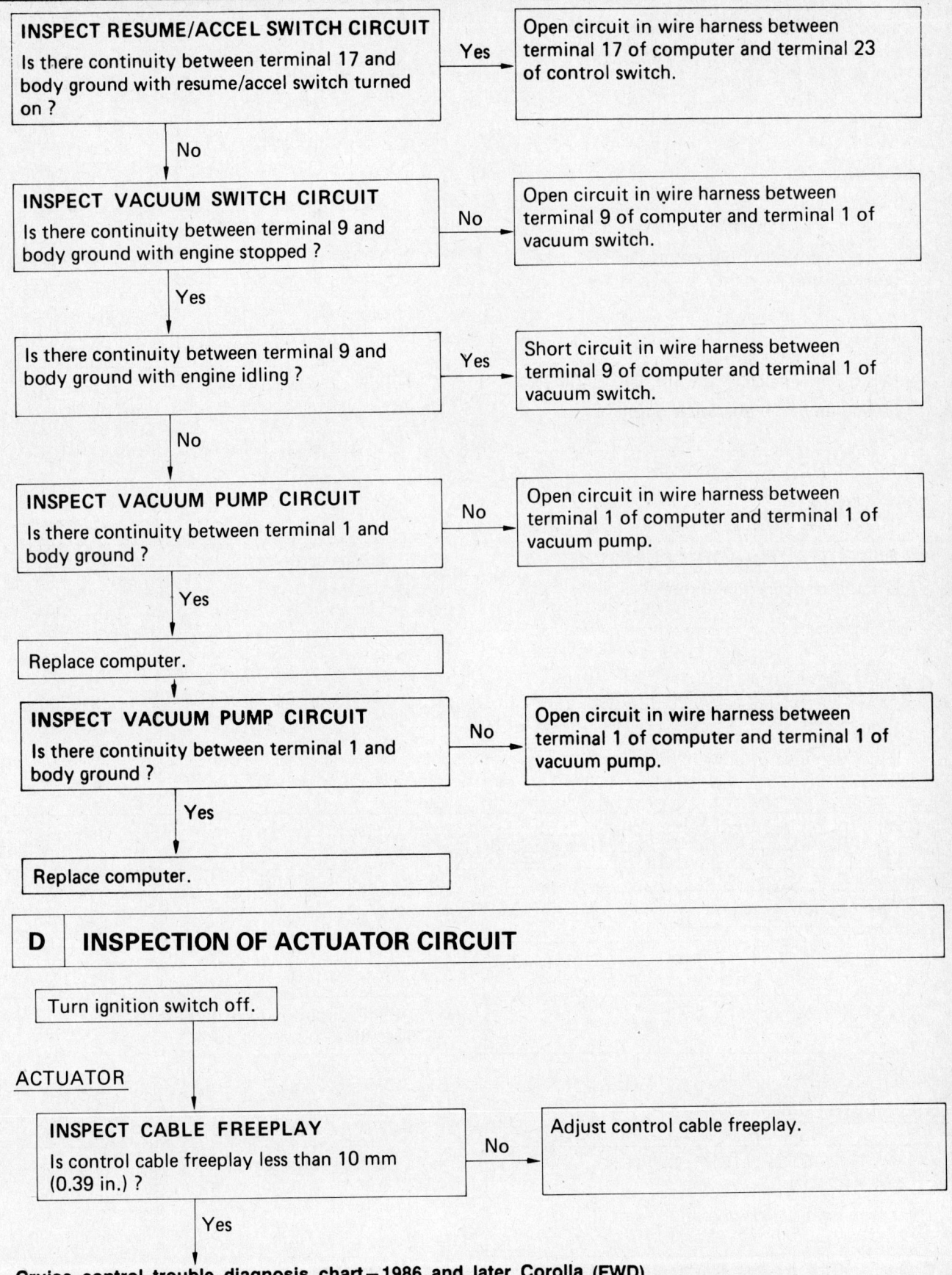

INSPECT RESUME/ACCEL SWITCH CIRCUIT

Is there continuity between terminal 17 and body ground with resume/accel switch turned on ?

→ Yes → Open circuit in wire harness between terminal 17 of computer and terminal 23 of control switch.

↓ No

INSPECT VACUUM SWITCH CIRCUIT

Is there continuity between terminal 9 and body ground with engine stopped ?

→ No → Open circuit in wire harness between terminal 9 of computer and terminal 1 of vacuum switch.

↓ Yes

Is there continuity between terminal 9 and body ground with engine idling ?

→ Yes → Short circuit in wire harness between terminal 9 of computer and terminal 1 of vacuum switch.

↓ No

INSPECT VACUUM PUMP CIRCUIT

Is there continuity between terminal 1 and body ground ?

→ No → Open circuit in wire harness between terminal 1 of computer and terminal 1 of vacuum pump.

↓ Yes

Replace computer.

↓

INSPECT VACUUM PUMP CIRCUIT

Is there continuity between terminal 1 and body ground ?

→ No → Open circuit in wire harness between terminal 1 of computer and terminal 1 of vacuum pump.

↓ Yes

Replace computer.

D   INSPECTION OF ACTUATOR CIRCUIT

Turn ignition switch off.

ACTUATOR

↓

INSPECT CABLE FREEPLAY

Is control cable freeplay less than 10 mm (0.39 in.) ?

→ No → Adjust control cable freeplay.

↓ Yes

Cruise control trouble diagnosis chart — 1986 and later Corolla (FWD)

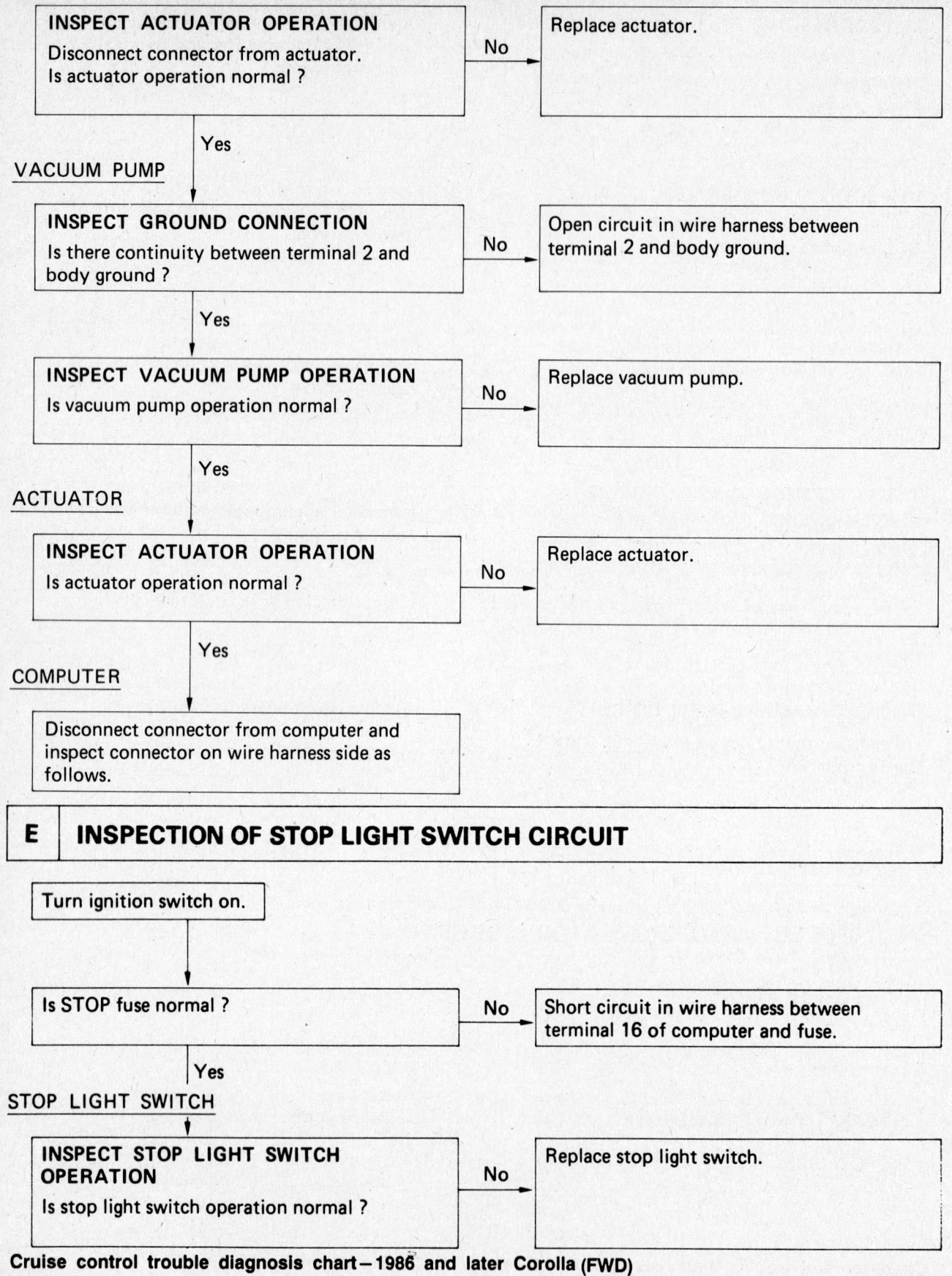

INSPECT ACTUATOR OPERATION

Disconnect connector from actuator.
Is actuator operation normal ?

→ No → Replace actuator.

↓ Yes

VACUUM PUMP

INSPECT GROUND CONNECTION

Is there continuity between terminal 2 and body ground ?

→ No → Open circuit in wire harness between terminal 2 and body ground.

↓ Yes

INSPECT VACUUM PUMP OPERATION

Is vacuum pump operation normal ?

→ No → Replace vacuum pump.

↓ Yes

ACTUATOR

INSPECT ACTUATOR OPERATION

Is actuator operation normal ?

→ No → Replace actuator.

↓ Yes

COMPUTER

Disconnect connector from computer and inspect connector on wire harness side as follows.

E   INSPECTION OF STOP LIGHT SWITCH CIRCUIT

Turn ignition switch on.

↓

Is STOP fuse normal ?

→ No → Short circuit in wire harness between terminal 16 of computer and fuse.

↓ Yes

STOP LIGHT SWITCH

INSPECT STOP LIGHT SWITCH OPERATION

Is stop light switch operation normal ?

→ No → Replace stop light switch.

Cruise control trouble diagnosis chart—1986 and later Corolla (FWD)

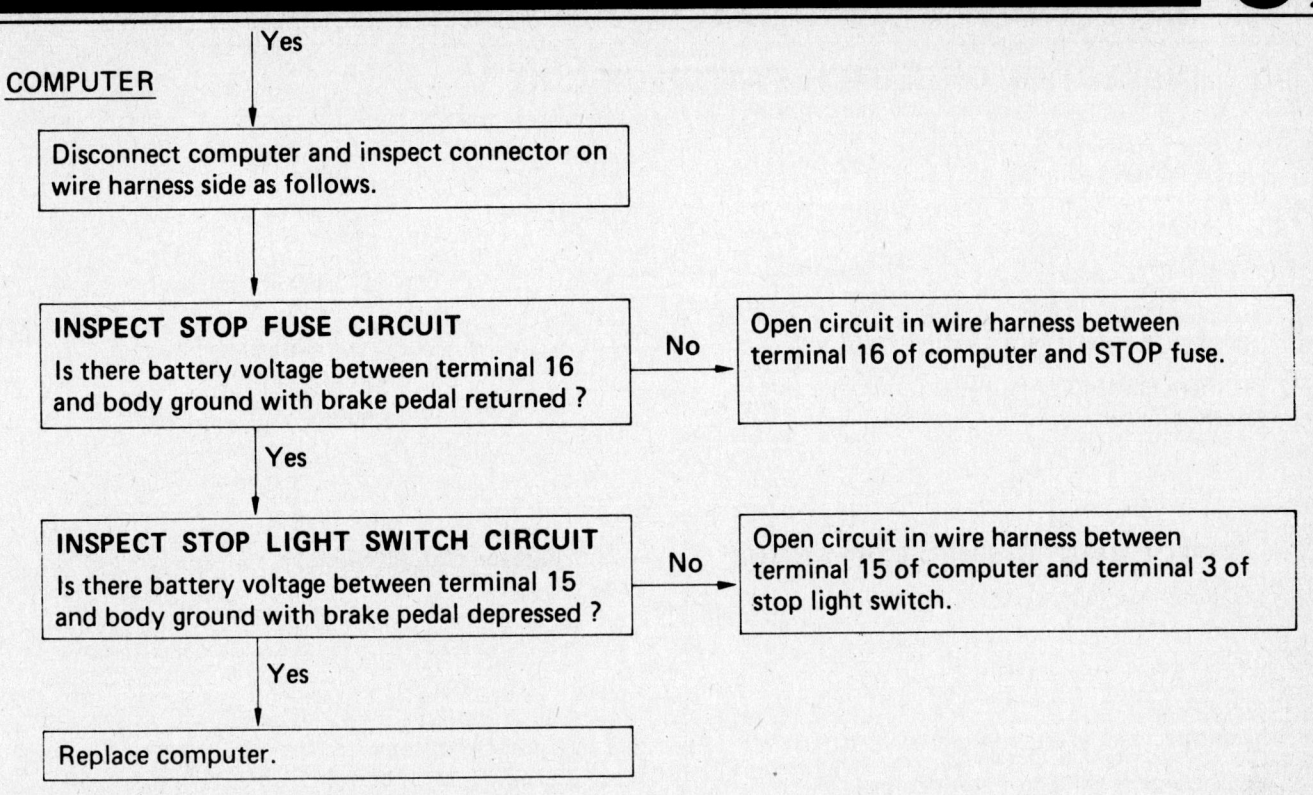

COMPUTER

Yes

Disconnect computer and inspect connector on wire harness side as follows.

INSPECT STOP FUSE CIRCUIT
Is there battery voltage between terminal 16 and body ground with brake pedal returned ?

No → Open circuit in wire harness between terminal 16 of computer and STOP fuse.

Yes

INSPECT STOP LIGHT SWITCH CIRCUIT
Is there battery voltage between terminal 15 and body ground with brake pedal depressed ?

No → Open circuit in wire harness between terminal 15 of computer and terminal 3 of stop light switch.

Yes

Replace computer.

F   INSPECTION OF PARKING LIGHT SWITCH CIRCUIT

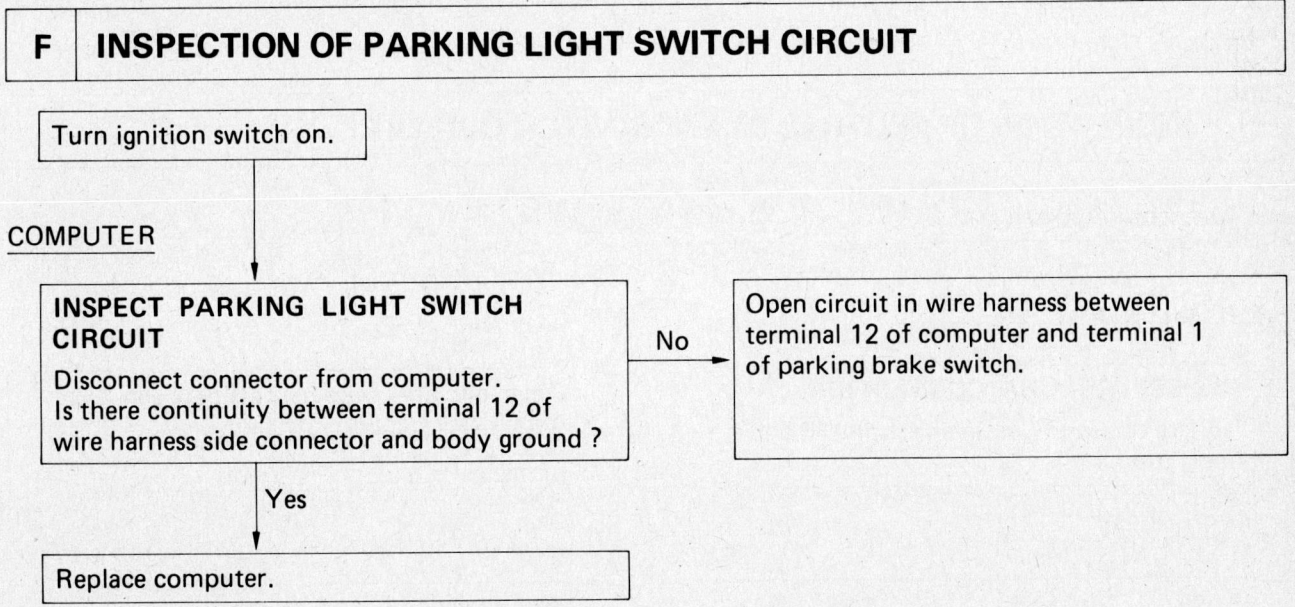

Turn ignition switch on.

COMPUTER

INSPECT PARKING LIGHT SWITCH CIRCUIT
Disconnect connector from computer.
Is there continuity between terminal 12 of wire harness side connector and body ground ?

No → Open circuit in wire harness between terminal 12 of computer and terminal 1 of parking brake switch.

Yes

Replace computer.

Cruise control trouble diagnosis chart – 1986 and later Corolla (FWD)

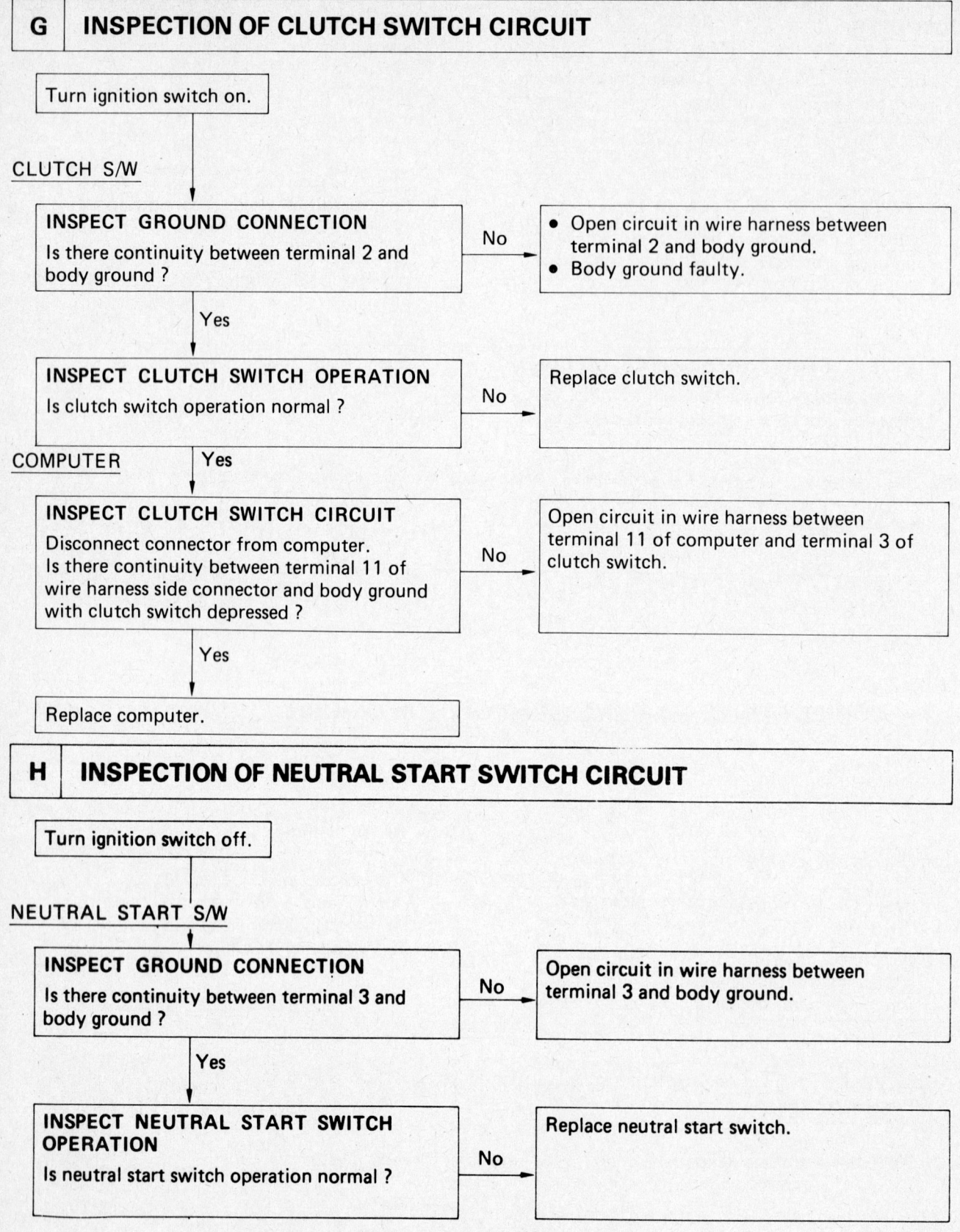

G | INSPECTION OF CLUTCH SWITCH CIRCUIT

Turn ignition switch on.

CLUTCH S/W

INSPECT GROUND CONNECTION

Is there continuity between terminal 2 and body ground ?

No →
- Open circuit in wire harness between terminal 2 and body ground.
- Body ground faulty.

Yes ↓

INSPECT CLUTCH SWITCH OPERATION

Is clutch switch operation normal ?

No → Replace clutch switch.

COMPUTER   Yes ↓

INSPECT CLUTCH SWITCH CIRCUIT

Disconnect connector from computer.
Is there continuity between terminal 11 of wire harness side connector and body ground with clutch switch depressed ?

No → Open circuit in wire harness between terminal 11 of computer and terminal 3 of clutch switch.

Yes ↓

Replace computer.

H | INSPECTION OF NEUTRAL START SWITCH CIRCUIT

Turn ignition switch off.

NEUTRAL START S/W

INSPECT GROUND CONNECTION

Is there continuity between terminal 3 and body ground ?

No → Open circuit in wire harness between terminal 3 and body ground.

Yes ↓

INSPECT NEUTRAL START SWITCH OPERATION

Is neutral start switch operation normal ?

No → Replace neutral start switch.

Cruise control trouble diagnosis chart—1986 and later Corolla (FWD)

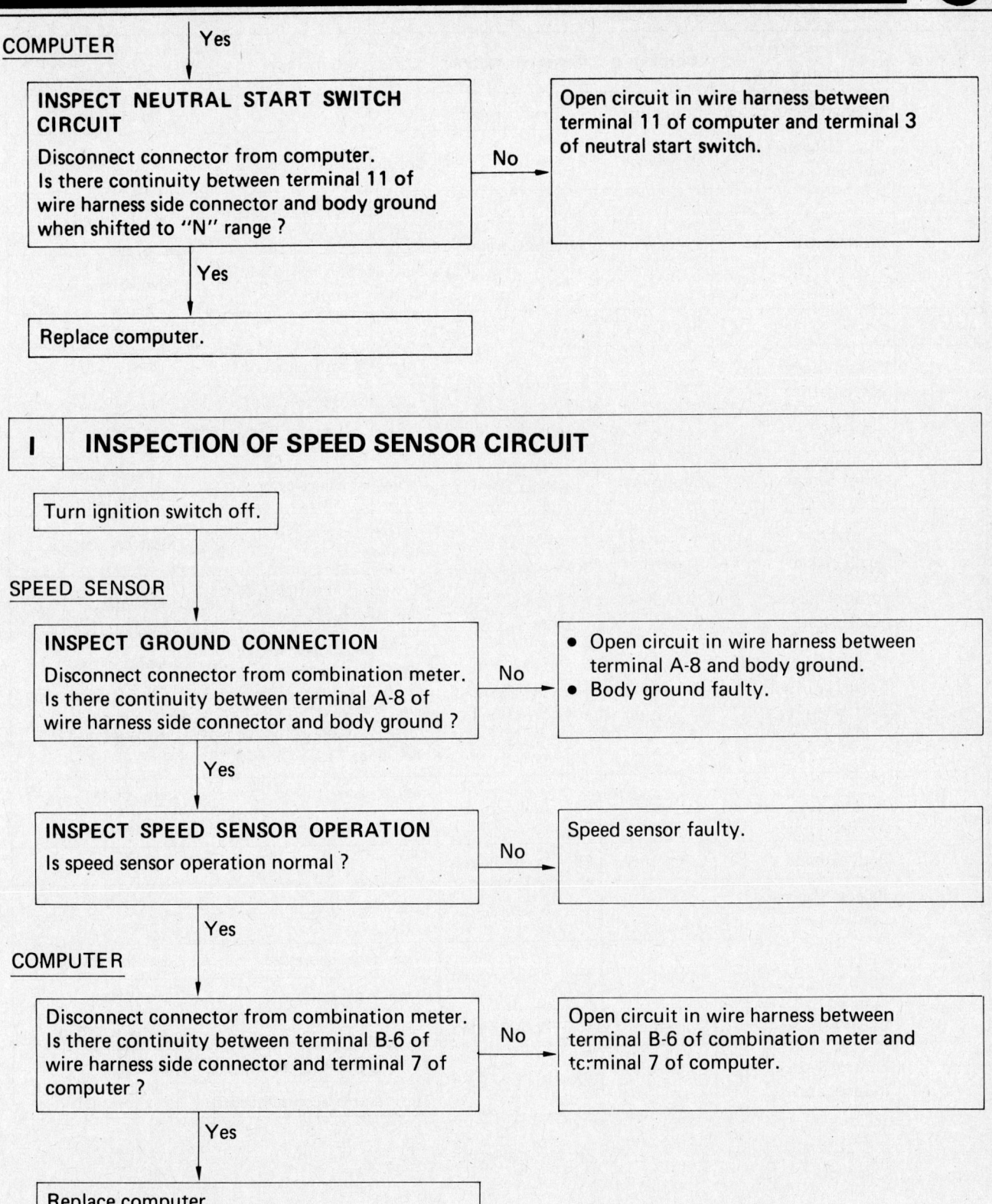

COMPUTER

INSPECT NEUTRAL START SWITCH CIRCUIT

Disconnect connector from computer.
Is there continuity between terminal 11 of wire harness side connector and body ground when shifted to "N" range ?

— No → Open circuit in wire harness between terminal 11 of computer and terminal 3 of neutral start switch.

↓ Yes

Replace computer.

I   INSPECTION OF SPEED SENSOR CIRCUIT

Turn ignition switch off.

SPEED SENSOR

INSPECT GROUND CONNECTION

Disconnect connector from combination meter.
Is there continuity between terminal A-8 of wire harness side connector and body ground ?

— No →
- Open circuit in wire harness between terminal A-8 and body ground.
- Body ground faulty.

↓ Yes

INSPECT SPEED SENSOR OPERATION

Is speed sensor operation normal ?

— No → Speed sensor faulty.

↓ Yes

COMPUTER

Disconnect connector from combination meter.
Is there continuity between terminal B-6 of wire harness side connector and terminal 7 of computer ?

— No → Open circuit in wire harness between terminal B-6 of combination meter and terminal 7 of computer.

↓ Yes

Replace computer.

Cruise control trouble diagnosis chart—1986 and later Corolla (FWD)

Terminal	Connection or Measure item	Check item	Tester connection	Condition	Voltage or Resistance value
1	Vacuum Pump	Continuity	1 — Body ground	—	Continuity
2	Stop Light Switch and Release Valve	Resistance	2 — 14	Brake pedal returned	About 68 Ω
3	Main Switch	Voltage	3 — Body ground	Turn ignition switch and main switch on	Battery voltage
				Turn ignition switch and/or main switch off	No voltage
4	Control Valve	Resistance	4 — 14	—	About 30 Ω
5	Control Switch (set/coast)	Continuity	5 — Body ground	Turn set/coast switch on	Continuity
				Turn set/coast switch off	No continuity
6	OD relay	—	—	—	—
7	Speed Sensor	Continuity	7 — Body ground	Vehicle moving slowly	1 pulse each 40 cm (15.75 in.)
10	Main Switch	Voltage	10 — Body ground	Turn ignition switch and main switch on	Battery voltage
				Turn ignition switch and/or main switch off	No voltage
11	Clutch Switch (M/T) or Neutral Start Switch (A/T)	Continuity	11 — Body ground	Clutch pedal depressed or shifted into "N" range	Continuity
				Clutch pedal returned or shifted into only range except "N" range	No continuity
12	Parking Brake Switch	Voltage	12 — Body ground	Parking brake pulled	No voltage
				Parking brake returned	Battery voltage
13	Body Ground	Continuity	13 — Body ground	—	Continuity
14	Release Valve and Control Valve	—	—	—	—
15	Stop Light Switch	Voltage	15 — Body ground	Brake pedal depressed	Battery voltage
				Brake pedal returned	No voltage
16	STOP Fuse	Voltage	16 — Body ground	—	Battery voltage
17	Control Switch (resume/accel)	Continuity	17 — Body ground	Turn resume/accel switch on	Continuity
				Turn resume/accel switch off	No continuity

-2.   INSPECT DIAGNOSIS CIRCUIT

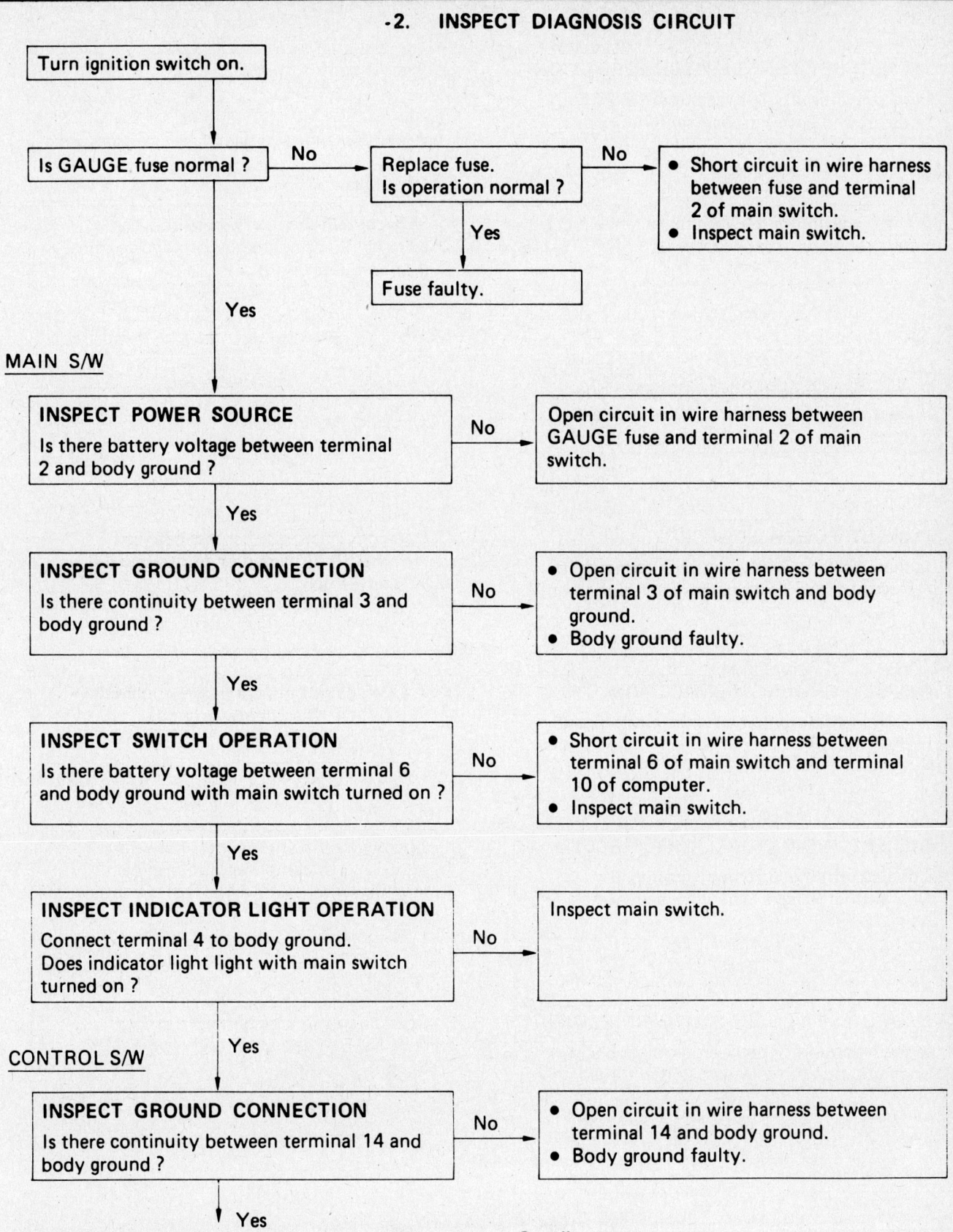

Cruise control trouble diagnosis chart — 1986 and later Corolla (FWD)

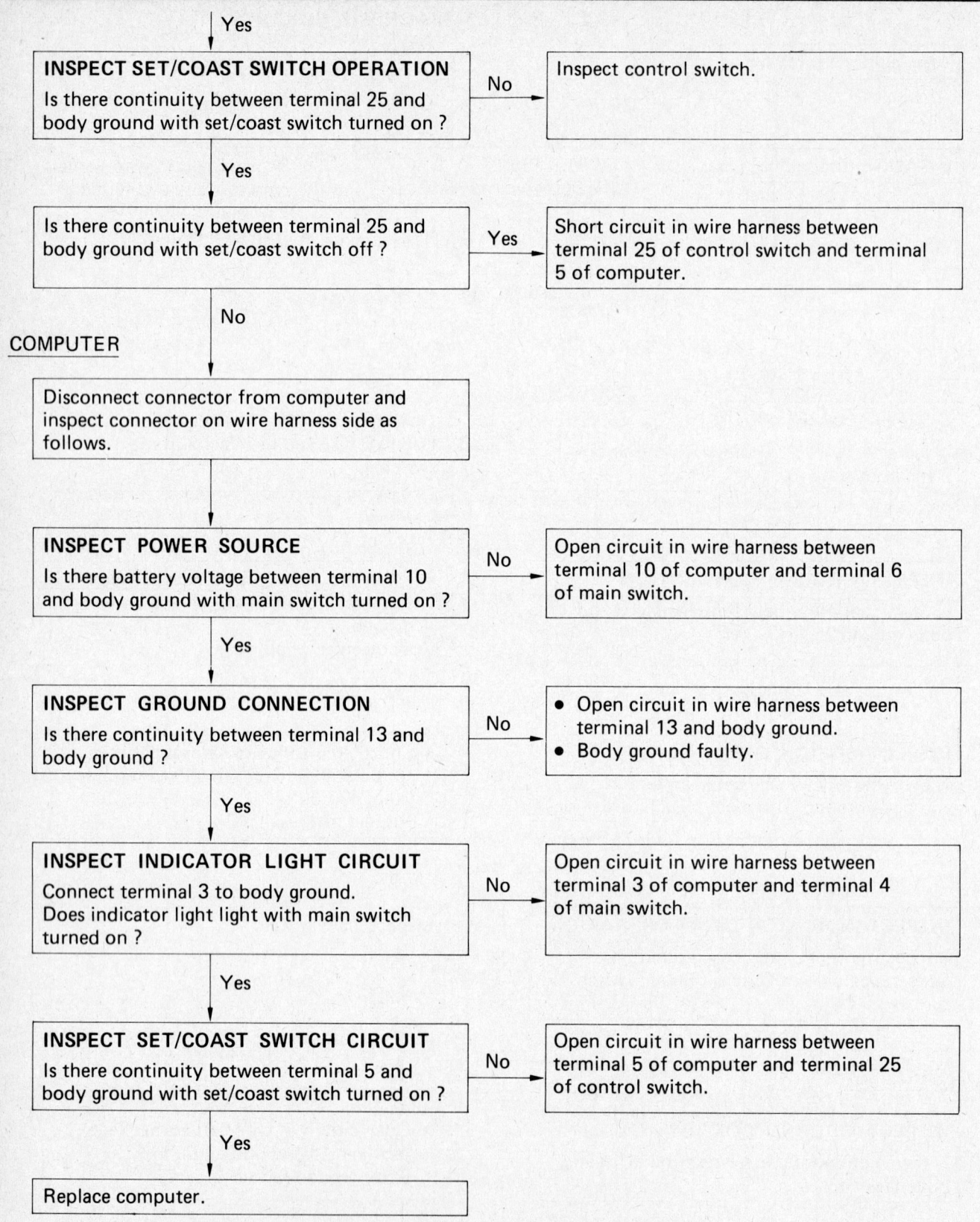

Yes

INSPECT SET/COAST SWITCH OPERATION

Is there continuity between terminal 25 and body ground with set/coast switch turned on ?

No → Inspect control switch.

Yes

Is there continuity between terminal 25 and body ground with set/coast switch off ?

Yes → Short circuit in wire harness between terminal 25 of control switch and terminal 5 of computer.

No

COMPUTER

Disconnect connector from computer and inspect connector on wire harness side as follows.

INSPECT POWER SOURCE

Is there battery voltage between terminal 10 and body ground with main switch turned on ?

No → Open circuit in wire harness between terminal 10 of computer and terminal 6 of main switch.

Yes

INSPECT GROUND CONNECTION

Is there continuity between terminal 13 and body ground ?

No →
- Open circuit in wire harness between terminal 13 and body ground.
- Body ground faulty.

Yes

INSPECT INDICATOR LIGHT CIRCUIT

Connect terminal 3 to body ground.
Does indicator light light with main switch turned on ?

No → Open circuit in wire harness between terminal 3 of computer and terminal 4 of main switch.

Yes

INSPECT SET/COAST SWITCH CIRCUIT

Is there continuity between terminal 5 and body ground with set/coast switch turned on ?

No → Open circuit in wire harness between terminal 5 of computer and terminal 25 of control switch.

Yes

Replace computer.

Cruise control trouble diagnosis chart—1986 and later Corolla (FWD)

GENERAL INFORMATION

The power seat has six different positions. Forward, back, up, down and the front and rear of the seat can be moved up or down to give it a forward or rearward tilt. Some vehicles may be equipped with both driver and passenger power seat assemblies.

In most cases a single wire comes from the power source to a circuit breaker, which is usually located in or near the fuse panel. Power is then supplied to the control switch.

Some vehicles may be equipped with a seat memory, which allows the seat to be automatically positioned in two preset seat positions.

Some vehicles are equipped with both driver and passenger power seat recliners, which enable the driver or the passenger to recline the seat rearward about twenty degrees.

AMC

DIAGNOSIS AND TESTING PROCEDURES

Before any testing is attempted be sure that the battery is fully charged and all connections and terminals cleaned and tightened. This should be done to insure proper continuity and grounds.

Checking Power Seat Switch

With vehicle dome light on, apply the power seat switch in the direction of seat failure. If the dome light dims, the seat may be jamming. Check for seat binding and correct as required. If the light does not dim, proceed as follows.

Disconnect the wiring harness at the switch connector. Connect a test lamp between the red and black wire in the female switch connector on the harness. If the test lamp lights, the harness to the switch connector is good. If the test lamp does not light check for current at the fuse panel circuit breaker, Check for continuity in the red wire between the fuse panel and the harness connector under the seat, and check for continuity in the black wire and proper connection to ground. If continuity exists remove the switch assembly from the seat harness and replace or repair it as required.

Checking Front Up/Down Motor

Connect a jumper wire between the red terminal in the center section of the power seat switch connector and the orange terminal in the front section of the switch connector.

Connect another jumper wire between the black terminal in the center section of the power seat switch connector and the light blue terminal in the front section of the switch connector. The power seat should move up. If the motor is in the full up position it will not operate.

Reverse the jumper wires on the front section of the switch connector. The seat should now move down.

If the motor does not operate in either direction, the harness or the complete three motor assembly is defective. Repair or replace defective components as required.

If the motor runs but the seat does not move check for a broken or disconnected drive cable.

Checking Rear Up/Down Motor

Connect a jumper wire between the red terminal in the center section of the power seat switch connector and the light green terminal in the rear section of the switch connector.

Connect another jumper wire between the black terminal in the center section of the power seat switch connector and the yellow terminal in the rear section of the switch connector. The power seat should move upward. If the motor is in the full upward position it will not operate.

Reverse the jumper wires on the rear section of the switch connector. The seat should now move downward.

If the motor does not operate in either direction, the harness or the complete three motor assembly is defective. Repair or replace defective components as required.

If the motor runs but the seat does not move check for a broken or disconnected drive cable.

Checking Forward/Horizontal Motor

Connect a jumper wire between the red terminal in the center section of the power seat switch connector and the tan terminal in the center section of the switch connector.

Connect another jumper wire between the black terminal in the center section of the power seat switch connector and the white terminal in the center section of the switch connector. The power seat should move forward. If the motor is in the full forward position it will not operate.

Reverse the white and tan wires and the motor should move rearward.

If the motor does not operate in either direction, the harness or the complete three motor assembly is defective. Repair or replace defective components as required.

If the motor runs but the seat does not move check for a broken or disconnected drive cable.

Component Replacement

POWER SEAT SWITCH

Removal and Installation
SEAT MOUNTED SWITCH

1. Disconnect the negative battery cable.
2. Remove the power seat switch retaining screws.
3. Pull the switch from its mounting. Disconnect the electrical connector from the back of the switch assembly.
4. Remove the power seat switch from the vehicle.
5. Installation is the reverse of the removal procedure.

SEAT TRACKS

Removal and Installation

1. Remove the retaining bolts that hold the seat assembly to the floorpan. It may be necessary to move the seat forward and backward in order to gain access to the retaining bolts.
2. Disconnect the negative battery cable.
3. Tilt the seat back and disconnect the wiring harness.
4. Remove the seat belt retaining bolts, as required. Remove the seat assembly from the vehicle.
5. Remove the bolts that attach the seat track to the seat frame. Remove tie straps, as required, that may be holding the cable housing to the seat assembly.
6. Installation is the reverse of the removal procedure.

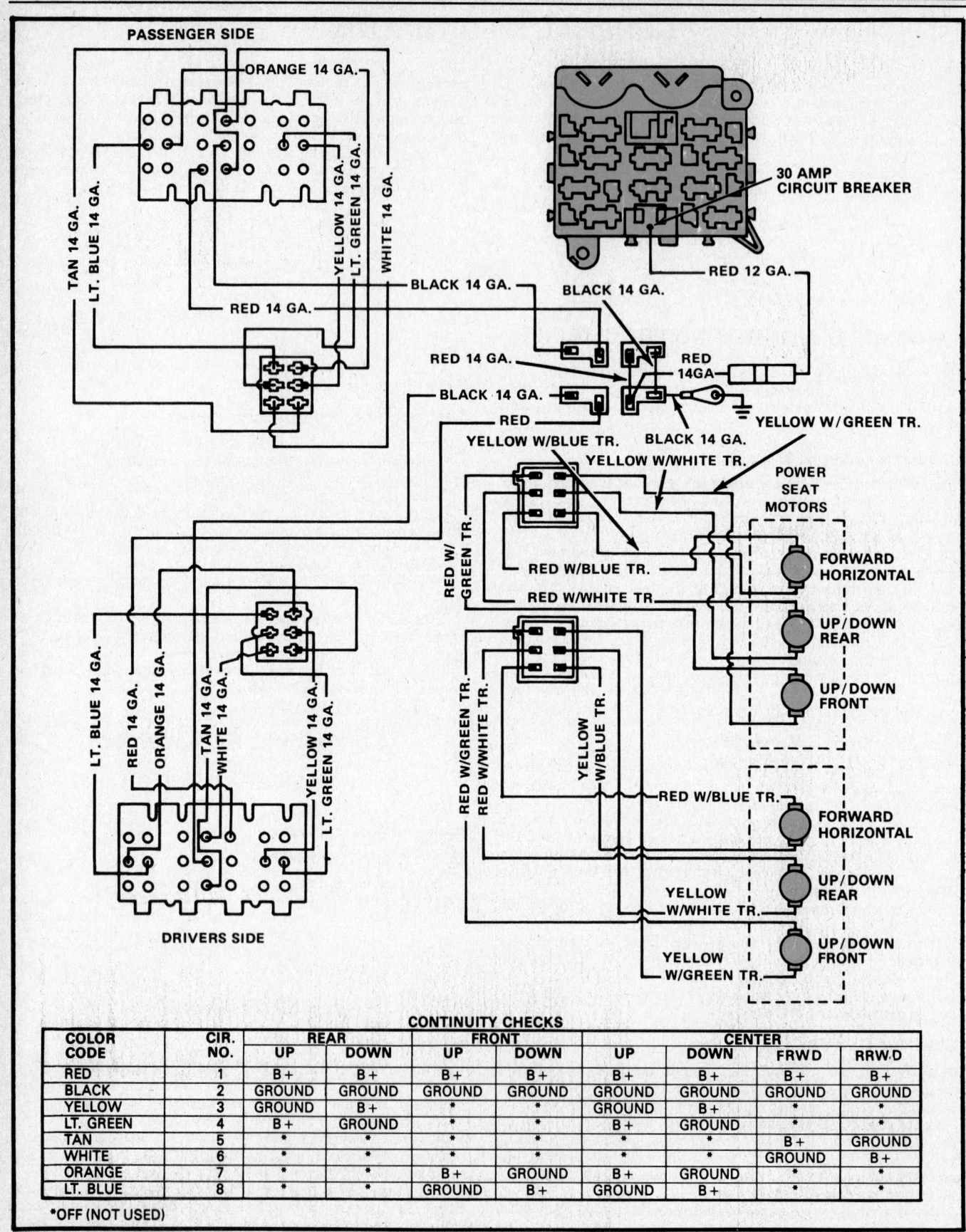

CONTINUITY CHECKS

COLOR CODE	CIR. NO.	REAR UP	REAR DOWN	FRONT UP	FRONT DOWN	CENTER UP	CENTER DOWN	CENTER FRWD	CENTER RRW.D
RED	1	B+	B+	B+	B+	B+	B+	B+	B+
BLACK	2	GROUND	GROUND	GROUND	GROUND	GROUND	GROUND	GROUND	GROUND
YELLOW	3	GROUND	B+	*	*	GROUND	B+	*	*
LT. GREEN	4	B+	GROUND	*	*	B+	GROUND	*	*
TAN	5	*	*	*	*	*	*	B+	GROUND
WHITE	6	*	*	*	*	*	*	GROUND	B+
ORANGE	7	*	*	B+	GROUND	B+	GROUND	*	*
LT. BLUE	8	*	*	GROUND	B+	GROUND	B+	*	*

*OFF (NOT USED)

AMC power seat system

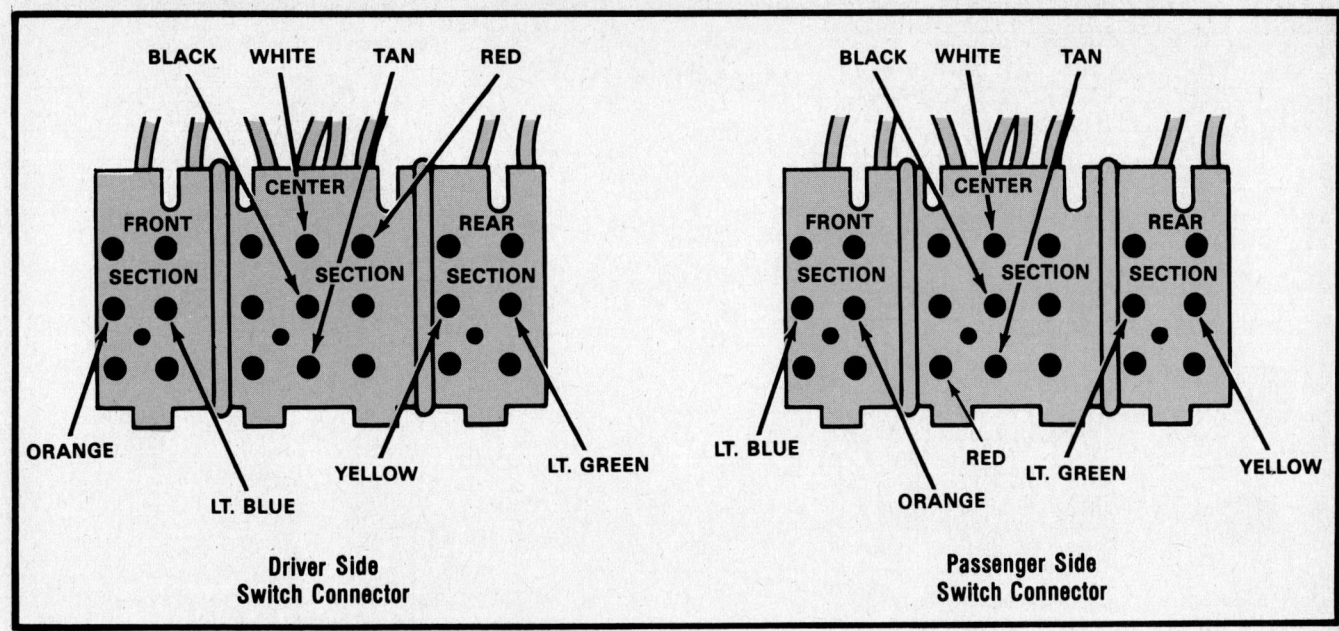

AMC power seat electrical test location points

SEAT MOTOR AND CABLES

Removal and Installation

NOTE: It is recommended that when a cable is to be replaced, the power seat motor should be removed in order to ease the replacement of the defective cable.

1. Disconnect the negative battery cable.
2. Remove the seat assembly from the vehicle.
3. Remove the motor retaining bolts from the seat mounting.
4. Disconnect the housings and the cables from the motor.
5. Remove the motor assembly from its mounting.
6. Installation is the reverse of the removal procedure.

VERTICAL AND HORIZONTAL ACTUATORS

Removal and Installation

The actuators are not removable and no maintenance is required. If the actuator is defective, replace the entire seat assembly.

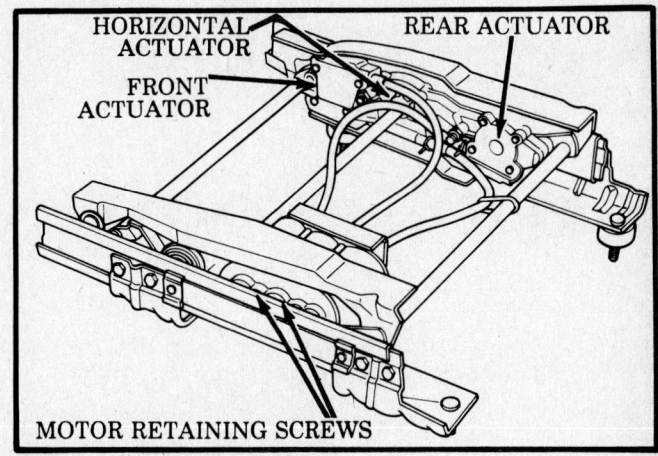

AMC power seat assembly

CHRYSLER CORPORATION

DIAGNOSIS AND TESTING PROCEDURES

Before any testing is attempted be sure that the battery is fully charged and all connections and terminals cleaned and tightened. This should be done to insure proper continuity and grounds.

Checking Power Seat Switch

With vehicle dome light on, apply the power seat switch in the direction of seat failure. If the dome light dims, the seat may be jamming. Check for seat binding and correct as required. If the light does not dim, proceed as follows.

Disconnect the wire from the instrument panel feed at the fuse block side cowl circuit breaker. Connect a test lamp between the instrument panel feed and a good ground. If the test lamp lights, feed in wire is good. Remove the test lamp and connect it to the circuit breaker. Disconnect the wiring from the other side of the circuit breaker. Connect the test lamp in series with the circuit breaker and a good ground. If the test lamp lights the circuit breaker is good. Remove the test light and connect the wiring harness.

Disconnect the wiring harness at the connector under the seat. Connect the test lamp between the red and black wire in the female connector on the wiring harness. If the test lamp lights the wiring harness to the seat is good. If not remove and repair or replace the power seat switch as required.

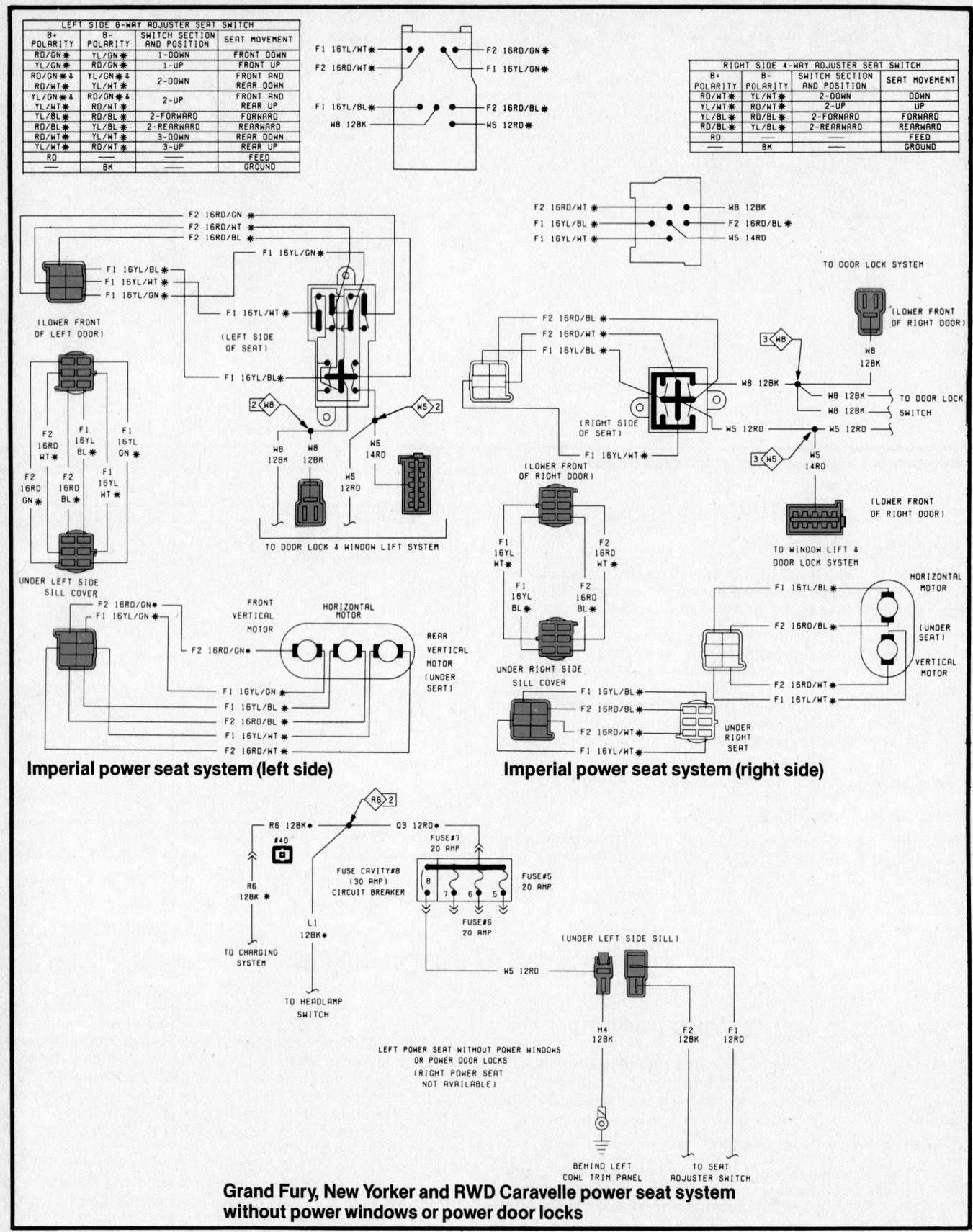

LEFT SIDE 6-WAY ADJUSTER SEAT SWITCH			
B+ POLARITY	B- POLARITY	SWITCH SECTION AND POSITION	SEAT MOVEMENT
RD/GN ✱	YL/GN ✱	1-DOWN	FRONT DOWN
YL/GN ✱	RD/GN ✱	1-UP	FRONT UP
RD/GN ✱ & RD/WT ✱	YL/GN ✱ & YL/WT ✱	2-DOWN	FRONT AND REAR DOWN
YL/GN ✱ & YL/WT ✱	RD/GN ✱ & RD/WT ✱	2-UP	FRONT AND REAR UP
YL/BL ✱	RD/BL ✱	2-FORWARD	FORWARD
RD/BL ✱	YL/BL ✱	2-REARWARD	REARWARD
RD/WT ✱	YL/WT ✱	3-DOWN	REAR DOWN
YL/WT ✱	RD/WT ✱	3-UP	REAR UP
RD	—	—	FEED
—	BK	—	GROUND

RIGHT SIDE 4-WAY ADJUSTER SEAT SWITCH			
B+ POLARITY	B- POLARITY	SWITCH SECTION AND POSITION	SEAT MOVEMENT
RD/WT ✱	YL/WT ✱	2-DOWN	DOWN
YL/WT ✱	RD/WT ✱	2-UP	UP
YL/BL ✱	RD/BL ✱	2-FORWARD	FORWARD
RD/BL ✱	YL/BL ✱	2-REARWARD	REARWARD
RD	—	—	FEED
—	BK	—	GROUND

Imperial power seat system (left side)

Imperial power seat system (right side)

**Grand Fury, New Yorker and RWD Caravelle power seat system
without power windows or power door locks**

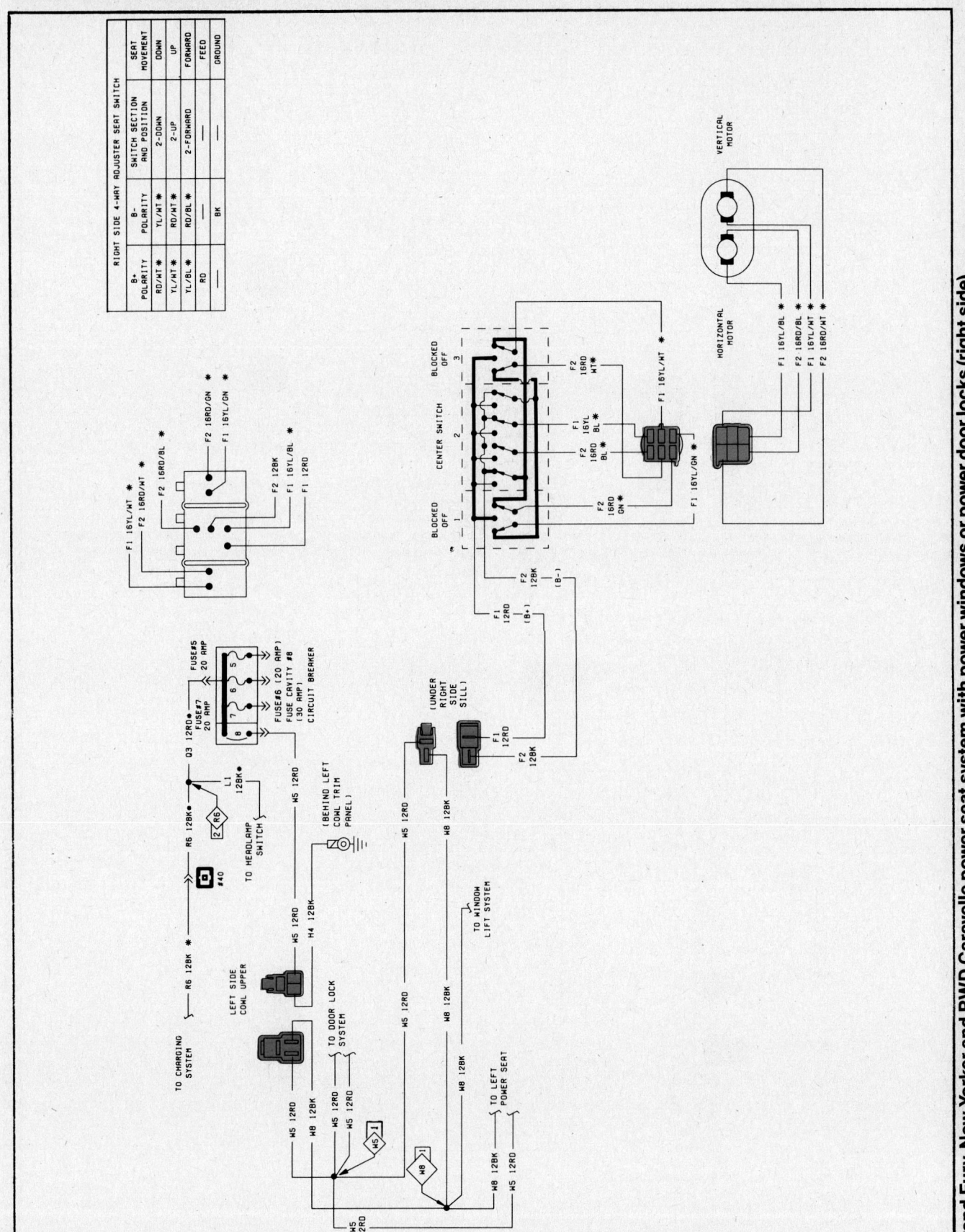

RIGHT SIDE 4-WAY ADJUSTER SEAT SWITCH

B+ POLARITY	B- POLARITY	SWITCH SECTION AND POSITION	SEAT MOVEMENT
RD/WT *	YL/WT *	2-DOWN	DOWN
YL/WT *	RD/WT *	2-UP	UP
YL/BL *	RD/BL *	2-FORWARD	FORWARD
RD			FEED
	BK		GROUND

Grand Fury, New Yorker and RWD Caravelle power seat system with power windows or power door locks (right side)

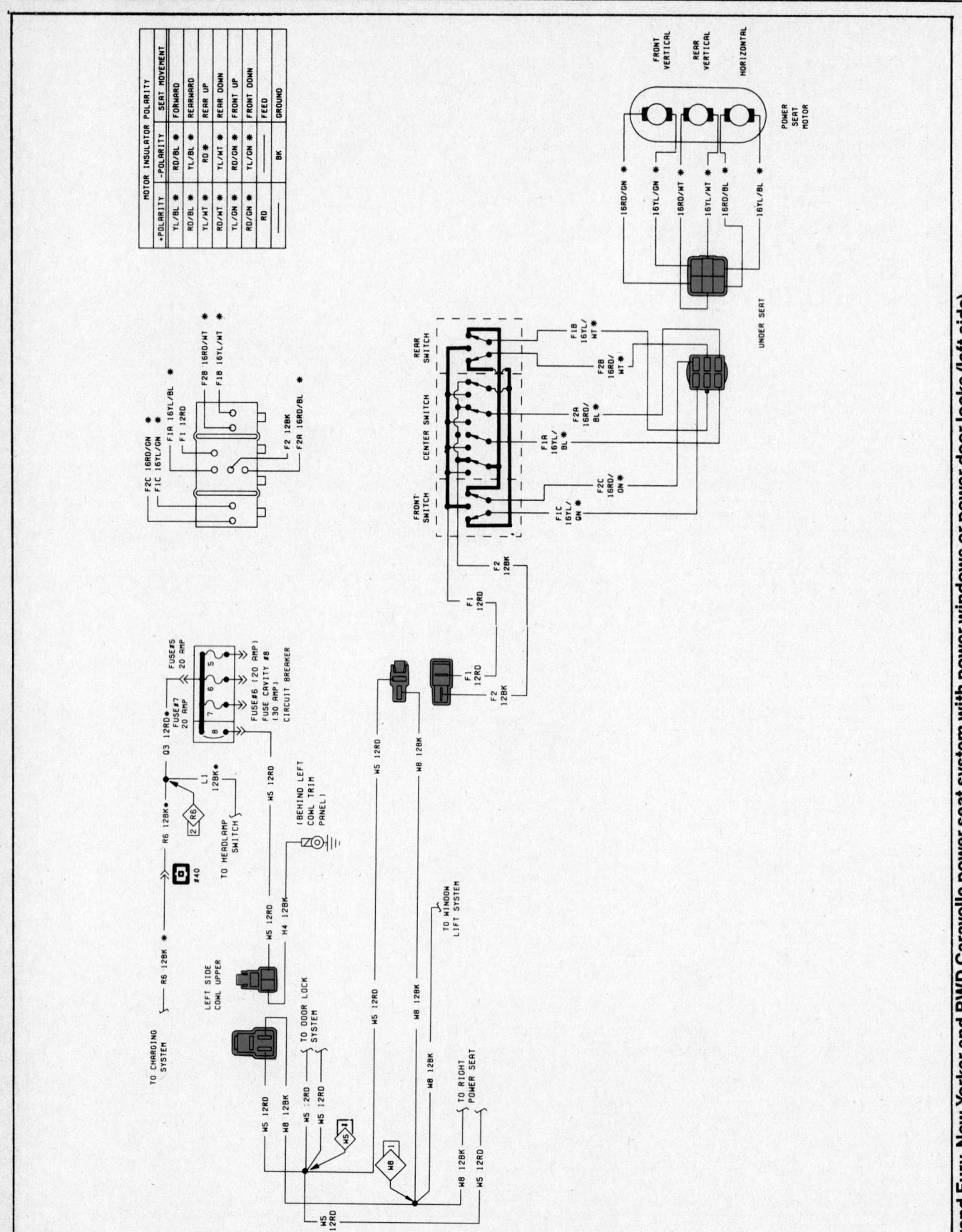

Grand Fury, New Yorker and RWD Caravelle power seat system with power windows or power door locks (left side)

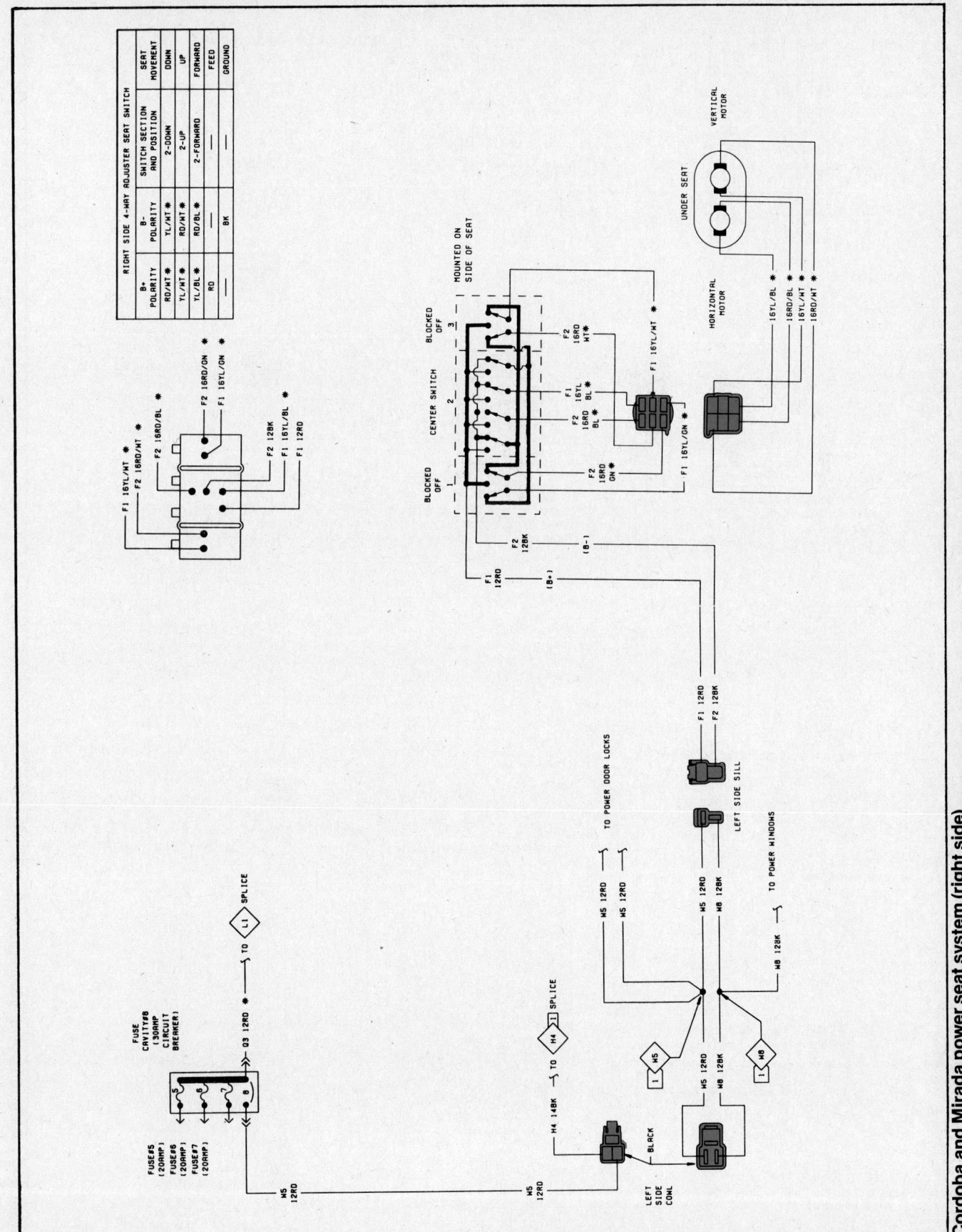

Cordoba and Mirada power seat system (right side)

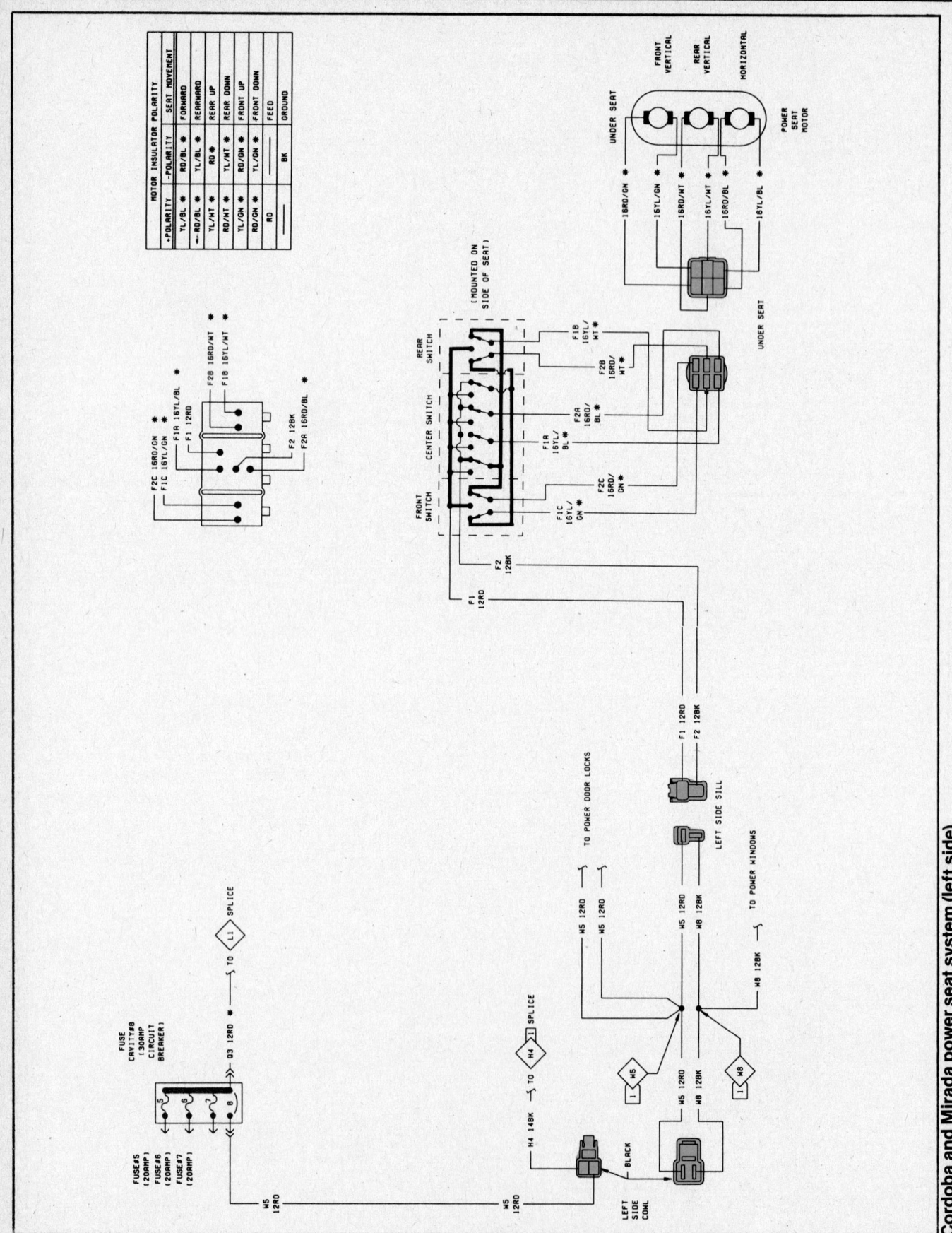

MOTOR INSULATOR POLARITY		SEAT MOVEMENT
+POLARITY	-POLARITY	
YL/BL *	RD/BL *	FORWARD
→RD/BL *	YL/BL *	REARWARD
RD *	YL/WT *	REAR UP
RD/WT *	RD *	REAR DOWN
YL/GN *	RD/GN *	FRONT UP
RD/GN *	YL/GN *	FRONT DOWN
RD		FEED
BK		GROUND

Cordoba and Mirada power seat system (left side)

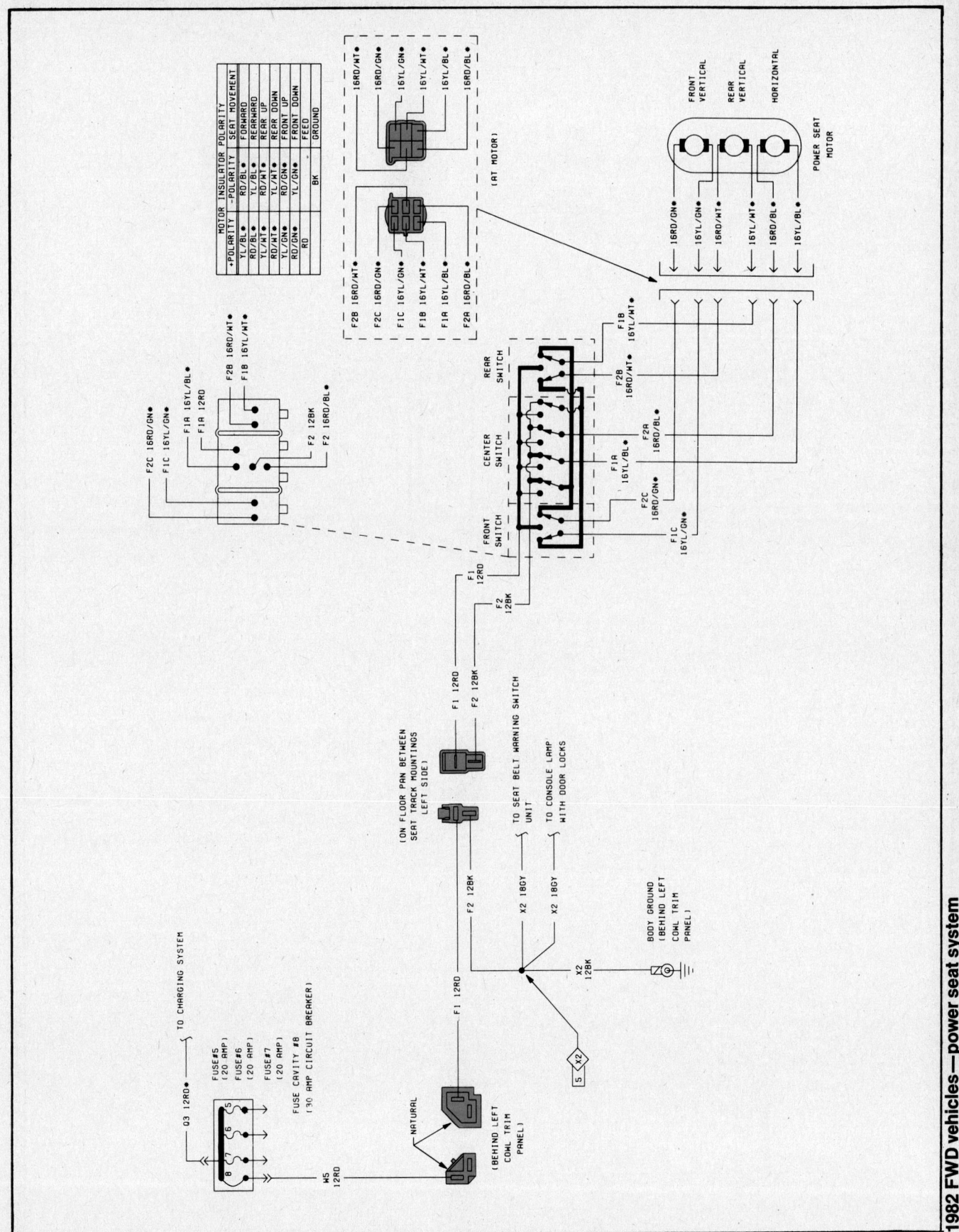

MOTOR INSULATOR POLARITY		SEAT MOVEMENT
+POLARITY	-POLARITY	
YL/BL●	RD/BL●	FORWARD
RD/BL●	YL/BL●	REARWARD
YL/WT●	RD/WT●	REAR UP
RD/WT●	YL/WT●	REAR DOWN
RD/GN●	YL/GN●	FRONT UP
YL/GN●	RD/GN●	FRONT DOWN
RD●		FEED
BK		GROUND

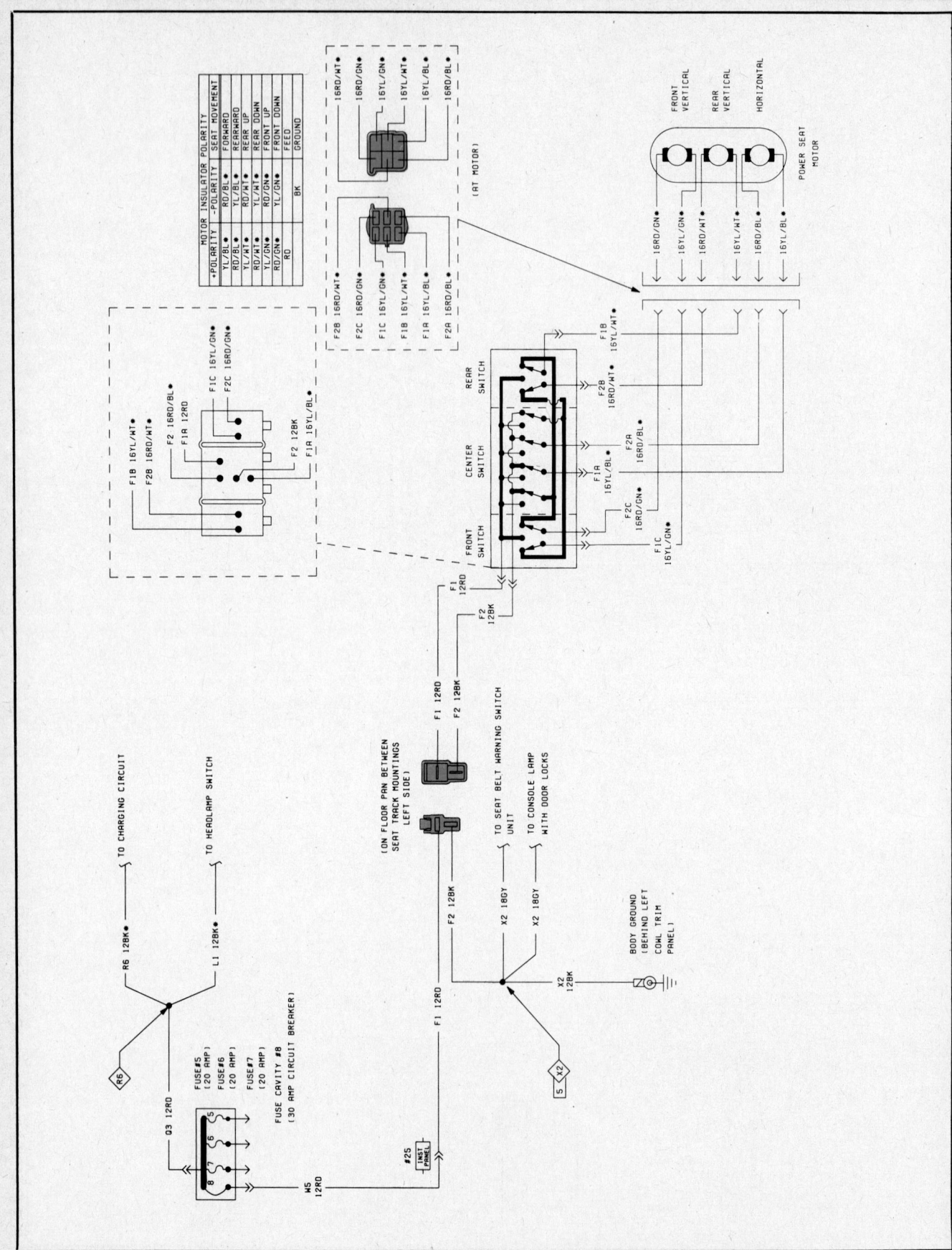

MOTOR INSULATOR POLARITY		SEAT MOVEMENT
+POLARITY	-POLARITY	
YL/BL*	RD/BL*	FORWARD
RD/BL*	YL/BL*	REARWARD
YL/WT*	RD/WT*	REAR UP
RD/WT*	YL/WT*	REAR DOWN
YL/GN*	RD/GN*	FRONT UP
RD/GN*	YL/GN*	FRONT DOWN
RD	BK	FEED
	BK	GROUND

1983 and later FWD vehicles—with bench and left bucket power seat

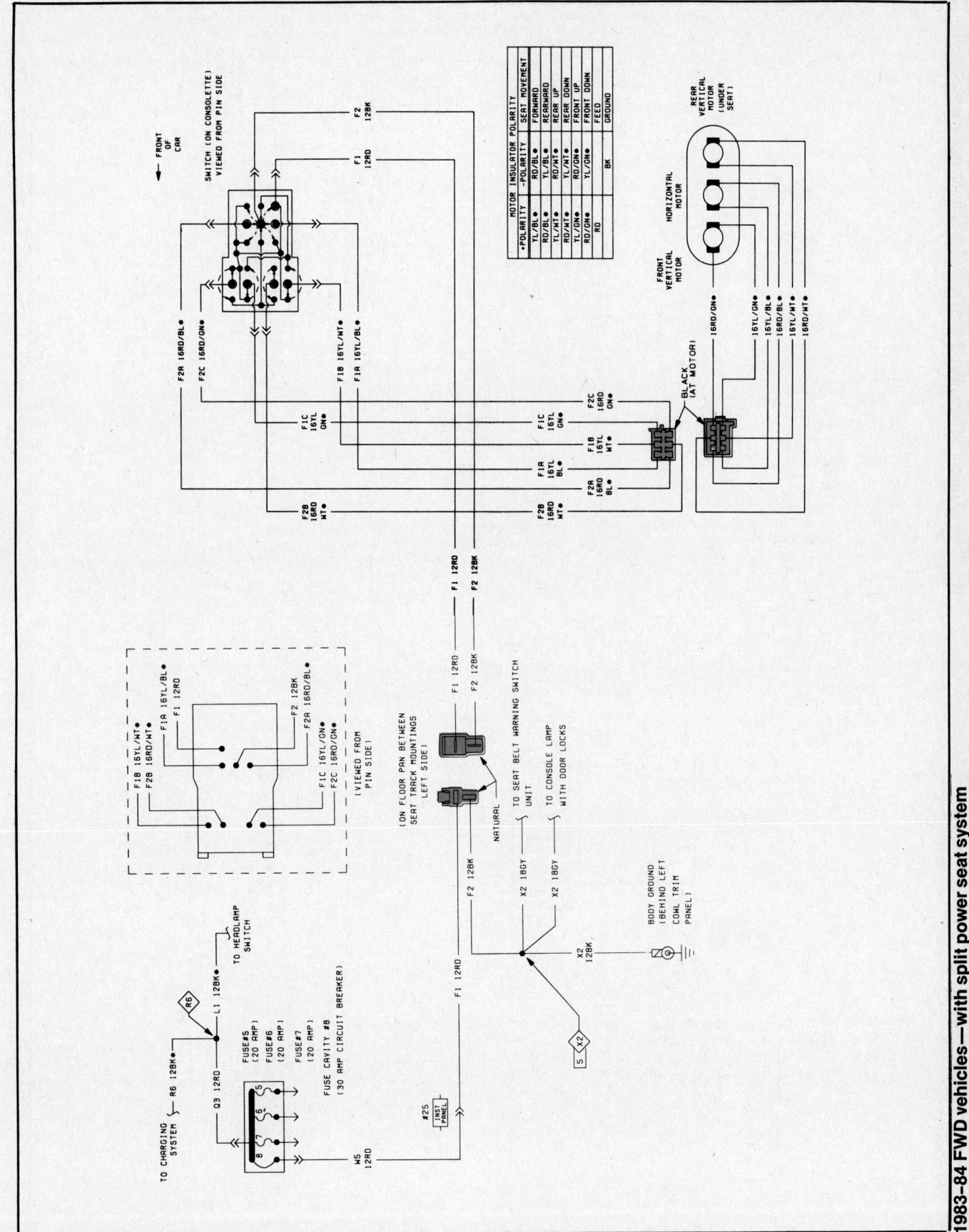

1983–84 FWD vehicles—with split power seat system

MOTOR	INSULATOR POLARITY	SEAT MOVEMENT
+POLARITY	−POLARITY	
YL/BL●	RD/BL●	FORWARD
RD/BL●	YL/BL●	REARWARD
YL/WT●	RD/WT●	REAR UP
RD/WT●	YL/WT●	REAR DOWN
YL/GN●	RD/GN●	FRONT UP
RD/GN●	YL/GN●	FRONT DOWN
RD		FEED
	BK	GROUND

1985 and later FWD vehicles—with split power seat system

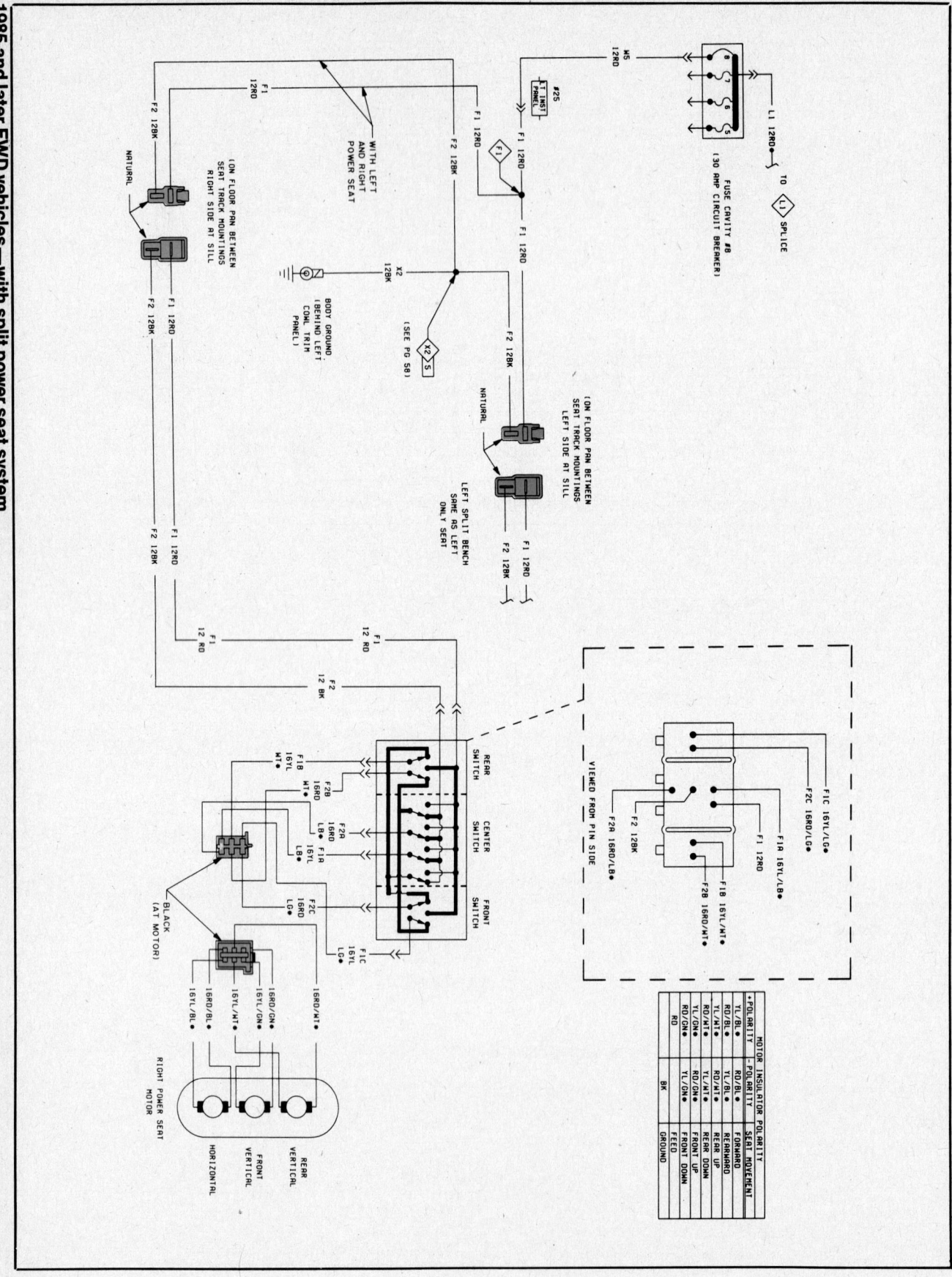

Checking Front Up/Down Motor

Connect a jumper wire between the red terminal in the center section of the power seat switch connector and either the red with green tracer or the yellow with green tracer connection in the front section of the switch connector.

Connect another jumper wire between the black terminal in the center section of the power seat switch connector and the open connection in the front section of the switch connector. The power seat should move up. If the motor does not operate reverse the jumper wire in the front section. If the motor still does not operate either the wiring harness or the motor may be defective.

If the motor runs but the seat does not move check for a broken or disconnected drive cable.

Checking Rear Up/Down Motor

Connect a jumper wire between the red terminal in the center section of the power seat switch connector and either the red with white tracer or the yellow with white tracer connection in the rear section of the switch connector.

Connect another jumper wire between the black terminal in the center section of the power seat switch connector and the open connection in the rear section of the switch connector. The power seat should move up. If the motor does not operate reverse the jumper wire in the front section. If the motor still does not operate either the wiring harness or the motor may be defective.

If the motor runs but the seat does not move check for a broken or disconnected drive cable.

Checking Center Motor

Connect a jumper wire between the red terminal in the center section of the power seat switch connector and either the red with blue tracer or the yellow with blue tracer connection in the center section of the switch connector.

Connect another jumper wire between the black terminal in the center section of the power seat switch connector and the open connection in the center section of the switch connector. If the motor does not operate reverse the jumper wire in the front section. If the motor still does not operate either the wiring harness or the motor may be defective.

If the motor runs but the seat does not move check for a broken or disconnected drive cable.

Component Replacement

POWER SEAT SWITCH

Removal and Installation
DOOR MOUNTED SWITCH

1. Disconnect the negative battery cable.
2. Remove the necessary trim in order to gain access to the power seat switch retaining screws.

3. Remove the switch retaining screws. Pull the switch from its mounting. Disconnect the electrical connections from the switch.
4. Remove the power seat switch from the vehicle.
5. Installation is the reverse of the removal procedure.

SEAT MOUNTED SWITCH

1. Disconnect the negative battery cable.
2. Remove the power seat switch retaining screws.
3. Pull the switch from its mounting. Disconnect the electrical connector from the back of the switch assembly.
4. Remove the power seat switch from the vehicle.
5. Installation is the reverse of the removal procedure.

SEAT TRACKS

Removal and Installation

NOTE: If the vehicle is equipped with a passenger side power seat assembly, the adjuster must be positioned in the full forward position before removal.

1. Remove the retaining bolts that hold the seat assembly to the floorpan. It may be necessary to move the seat forward and backward in order to gain access to the retaining bolts.
2. Disconnect the negative battery cable.
3. Tilt the seat back and disconnect the wiring harness.
4. Remove the seat belt retaining bolts, as required. Remove the seat assembly from the vehicle.
5. Remove the bolts that attach the seat track to the seat frame. Remove tie straps, as required, that may be holding the cable housing to the seat assembly.
6. Installation is the reverse of the removal procedure.

SEAT MOTOR AND CABLES

Removal and Installation

NOTE: It is recommended that when a cable is to be replaced, the power seat motor should be removed in order to ease the replacement of the defective cable.

1. Disconnect the negative battery cable.
2. Remove the seat assembly from the vehicle.
3. Remove the motor retaining bolts from the seat mounting.
4. Disconnect the housings and the cables from the motor.
5. Remove the motor assembly from its mounting.
6. Installation is the reverse of the removal procedure.

VERTICAL AND HORIZONTAL ACTUATORS

Removal and Installation

The actuators are not removable and no maintenance is required. If the actuator is defective, replace the entire seat assembly.

FORD MOTOR COMPANY

DIAGNOSIS AND TESTING PROCEDURES

Before attempting to repair the power seat assembly the following diagnostic test procedures should be followed.

Component Replacement- Tempo and Topaz

POWER SEAT SWITCH

Removal and Installation

SEAT MOUNTED SWITCH

1. Disconnect the negative battery cable.
2. Remove the power seat switch retaining screws.
3. Pull the switch from its mounting. Disconnect the electrical connector from the back of the switch assembly.
4. Remove the power seat switch from the vehicle.
5. Installation is the reverse of the removal procedure.

SEAT TRACKS

Removal and Installation

1. Remove the retaining bolts that hold the seat assembly to the floorpan. It may be necessary to move the seat forward and backward in order to gain access to the retaining bolts.
2. Disconnect the negative battery cable.
3. Tilt the seat back and disconnect the wiring harness.
4. Remove the seat belt retaining bolts, as required. Remove the seat assembly from the vehicle.
5. Remove the bolts that attach the seat track to the seat frame. Remove tie straps, as required, that may be holding the cable housing to the seat assembly. Separate the seat track assembly from the seat.
6. Installation is the reverse of the removal procedure.

SEAT MOTOR AND CABLES

Removal and Installation

NOTE: It is recommended that when a cable is to be replaced, the power seat motor should be removed in order to ease the replacement of the defective cable.

1. Disconnect the negative battery cable.
2. Remove the seat assembly from the vehicle.
3. Remove the motor retaining bolts from the seat mounting.
4. Disconnect the housings and the cables from the motor.
5. Remove the motor assembly from its mounting.
6. Installation is the reverse of the removal procedure.

	TEST STEP	RESULT ▶	ACTION TO TAKE
E1	CHECK MOTOR OPERATION		
	• Disconnect leads from motor.	(OK) ▶	GO to **E2**.
	• Connect jumper wires from battery positive and negative to motor terminals.		
	• Motor should operate in one direction.	(⊘OK) ▶	REPLACE motor.
E2	REVERSE JUMPER WIRES		
	• Reverse jumper wires to motor.	(OK) ▶	Motor OK. Problem is elsewhere in systems.
	• Motor should operate in opposite direction.	(⊘OK) ▶	REPLACE motor.

Ford Motor Company—power seat motor diagnosis

	TEST STEP	RESULT ▶	ACTION TO TAKE
C0	VERIFY CONDITION		
	• Operate power seat and verify that seat mechanism does not make full travel.	(OK) ▶	Power seat OK.
		(⊘OK) ▶	GO to **A1**.
C1	TRACK OBSTRUCTION		
	• Check for an obstruction in track mechanism.	(OK) ▶	Power seat OK.
		(⊘OK) ▶	GO to **D0** diagnosis chart.

Ford Motor Company—power seat does not make full travel

TEST STEP		RESULT ▶	ACTION TO TAKE
D0	VERIFY CONDITION		
	• Operate power seat and verify condition.	(OK) ▶	Power seat OK.
		(OK̸) ▶	GO to **D1**.
D1	CHECK CABLE DEFLECTION		
	• Check power seat track drive cables for deflection when the switch is activated.	Cables deflect ▶	GO to **D2**.
		Cables do not deflect ▶	GO to **D3**.
D2	CABLE ROTATION CHECK		
	• Remove cable attachments from transmission and check that flex cables in the tubes are free to rotate and slide.	(OK) ▶	REMOVE and REPLACE transmission and bar assembly. REPEAT Step **D0**.
		(OK̸) ▶	REMOVE and REPLACE flex cable and tube assembly. REPEAT Step **D0**.
D3	POWER CHECK		
	• Disconnect motor leads frcm harness. Check for voltage at power seat harness when switch is activated.	Voltage present ▶	REMOVE and REPLACE motor assembly. REPEAT Step **D0**.
		No voltage present ▶	GO to **D4**.
D4	TEST POWER SEAT SWITCH		
	• Test power seat switch.	Switch OK ▶	GO to **D5**.
		Switch Not OK ▶	REPLACE switch assembly. REPEAT Step **D0**.
D5	CHECK MOTOR GROUND CONNECTIONS		
	• Check power seat motor for tight ground connections.	(OK) ▶	CHECK for damaged connectors, shorts or open circuit. SERVICE as necessary. REPEAT Step **D0**.
		(OK̸) ▶	TIGHTEN ground connection. REPEAT Step **D0**.

Ford Motor Company—track does not move horizontally and/or vertically

TEST STEP		RESULT ▶	ACTION TO TAKE
B0	VERIFY CONDITION		
	• Operate power seat and check for looseness.	(OK) ▶	Power seat OK.
		(OK̸) ▶	RETIGHTEN all attachment hardware. GO to **B1**.

Ford Motor Company—power seat moves but is loose

TEST STEP		RESULT	▶	ACTION TO TAKE
B1	CHECK SEAT OPERATION			
	• Check if loose condition has been corrected.	OK ▶		Power seat OK.
		⊘OK ▶		REPLACE track assembly.

TEST STEP		RESULT	▶	ACTION TO TAKE
A0	VERIFY CONDITION			
	• Operate power seat and listen for noise.	OK ▶		Power seat OK.
		Noisy operation ▶		GO to A1.
A1	ISOLATE NOISE			
	• Determine if noise is from motor, transmission or cable.	Motor noise ▶		REPLACE motor. REPEAT Step A0.
		Transmission noise ▶		REPLACE transmission. REPEAT Step A0.
		Cable noise ▶		REMOVE and LUBRICATE cables. REINSTALL cables and GO to A2.
A2	CABLE NOISE			
	• Operate seat to verify that noisy condition has been corrected.	OK ▶		Power seat OK.
		⊘OK ▶		REPLACE cables. REPEAT Step A0.

Ford Motor Company—power seat moves but is noisy

VERTICAL AND HORIZONTAL ACTUATORS

Removal and Installation

1. Remove the seat assembly from the vehicle.
2. Remove the motor mount bracket mounting bolts from the motor mount bracket to the motor. Disconnect the clamps from the drive input shafts.
3. Manually position the seat track in the full up and mid horizontal position. This is done by inserting the square end of a drive cable into one of the vertical drives and manually turning the drive unit until it is in the full up position. Using the horizontal drive unit, insert the cable drive and manually turn it to the mid horizontal position.
4. Remove the spring pins from the pivot pins on the secondary track.
5. Remove the base and carriage from the secondary track by driving the pinion gear through the carriage rack.
6. Remove the bolts and nuts from the primary track and retain the drive assembly to the carriage.
7. Replace the defective drive assembly, as required.
8. Assembly is the reverse of the disassembly procedure.

Component Replacement—Taurus and Sable

POWER SEAT SWITCH

Testing

1. With all switch controls in the neutral position there should be continuity between terminals 1, 3, 4,5, 6, 7 and 8. Terminal 2 should be disconnected from all of the others.
2. With stud knob A depressed there should be continuity between terminals 1, 3, 4, 6, 7 and 8 and terminals 2 and 7.
3. With switch knob B depressed there should be continuity between terminals 1, 3, 4, 6, 7 and 8 and terminals 2 and 5.
4. With switch knob C pushed up there should be continuity between terminals 1, 2 and 7 and terminals 3, 4, 5, 6 and 8.
5. With switch knob C pushed down there should be continuity between terminals 1, 3, 4, 7 and 8 and terminals 2, 5 and 6.

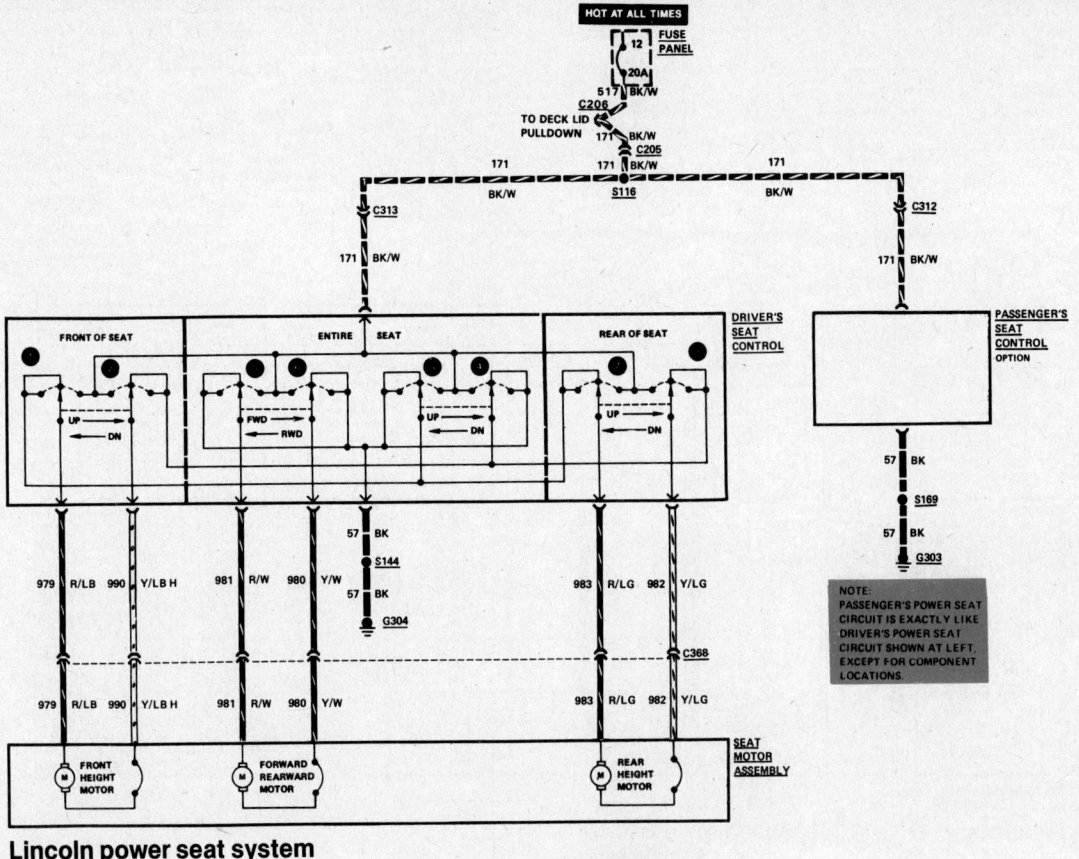

Lincoln power seat system

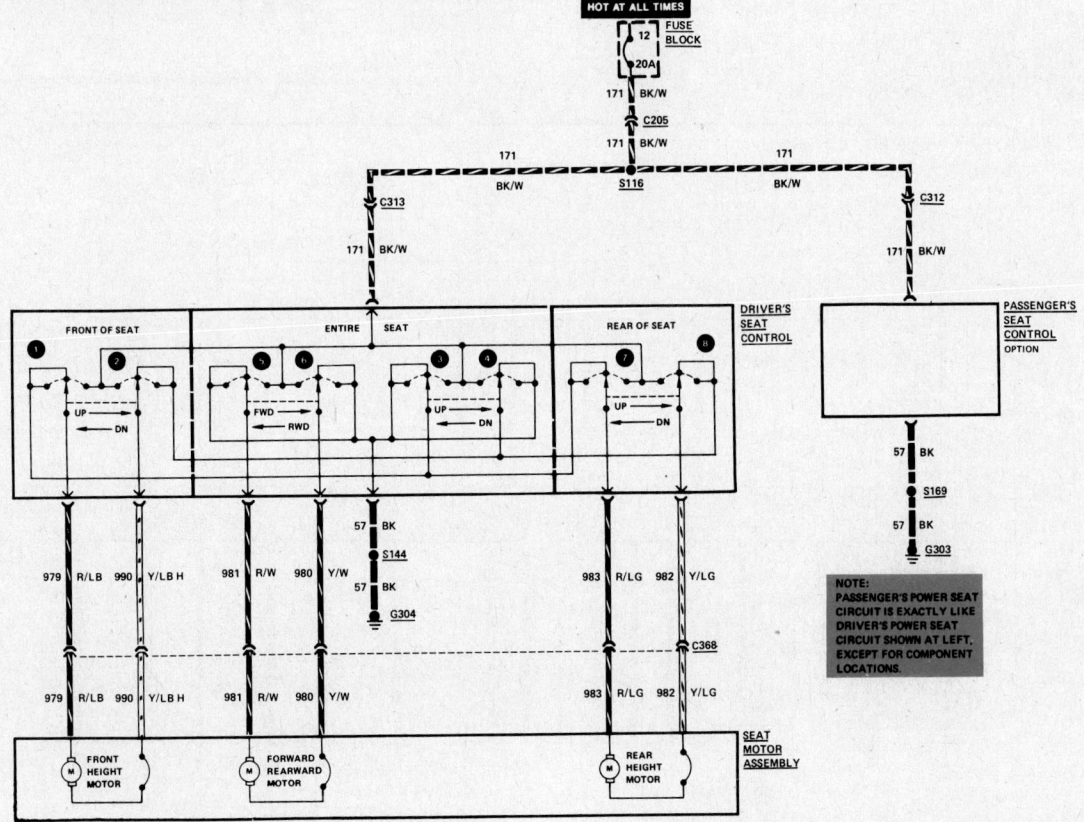

Town Car and Mark VI power seat system

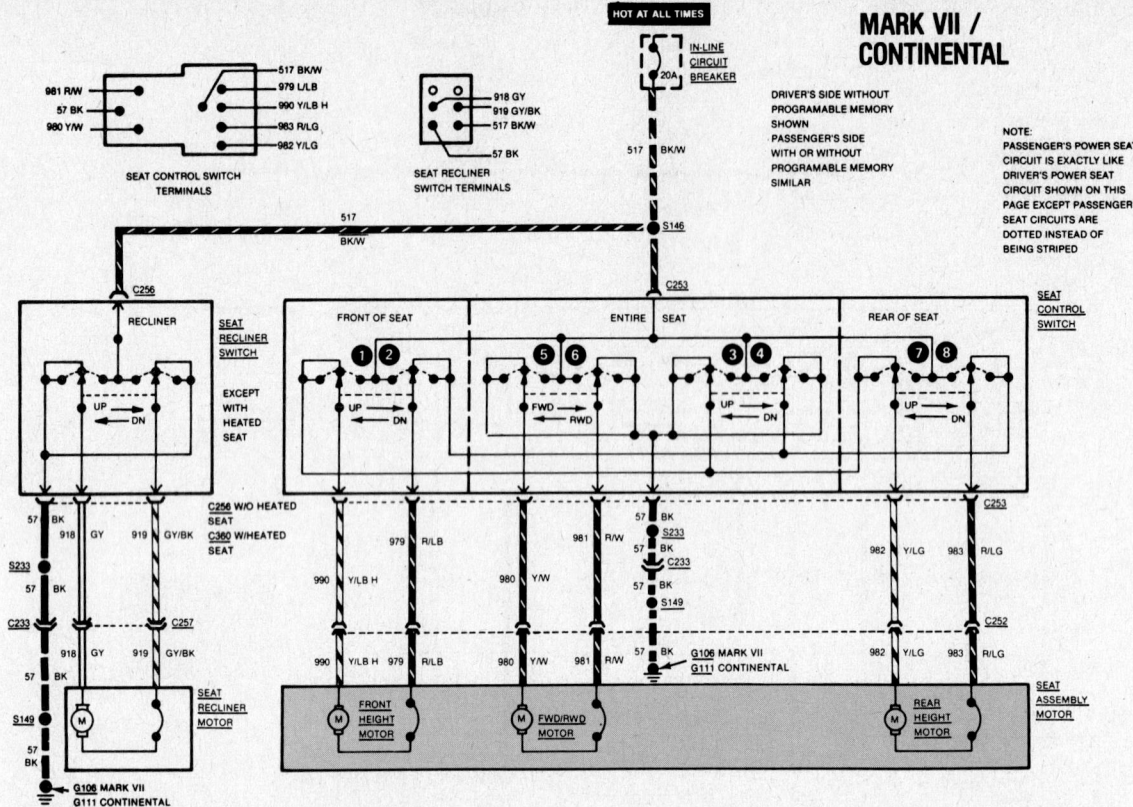

Continental and Mark VII power seat system

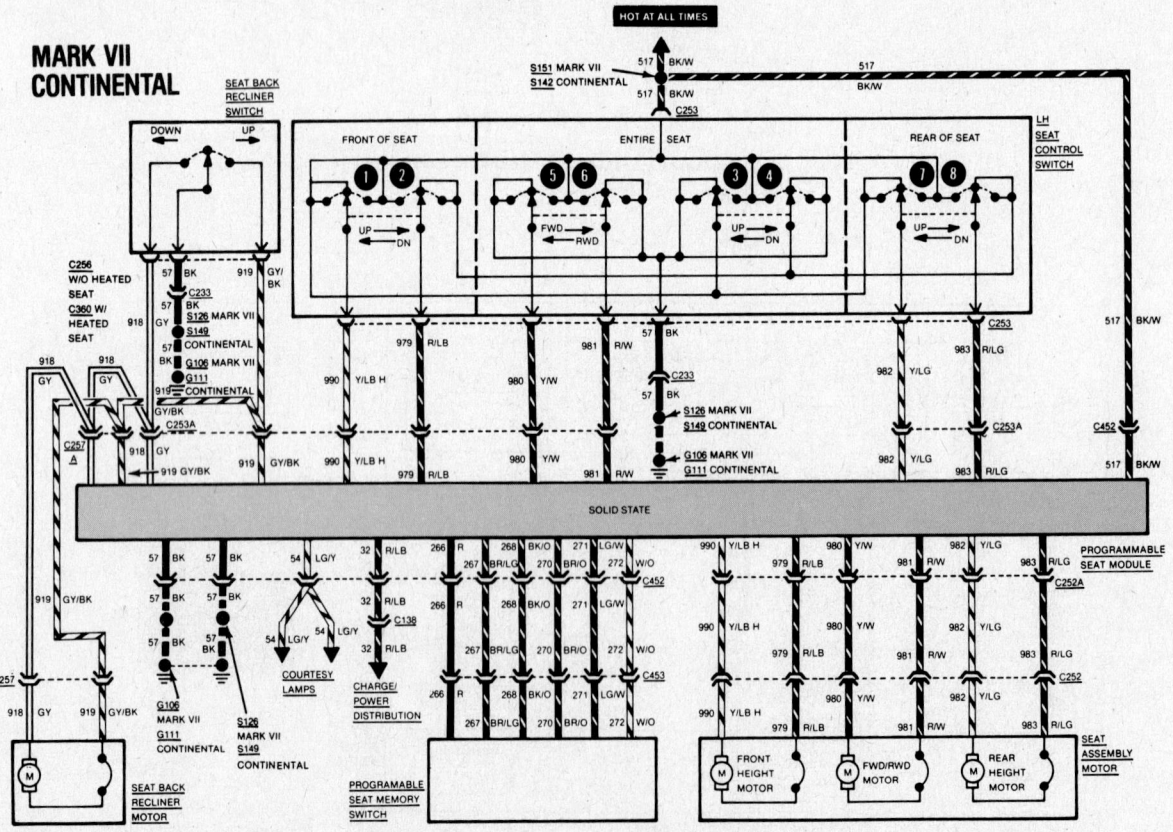

Continental and Mark VII programmable power seat system

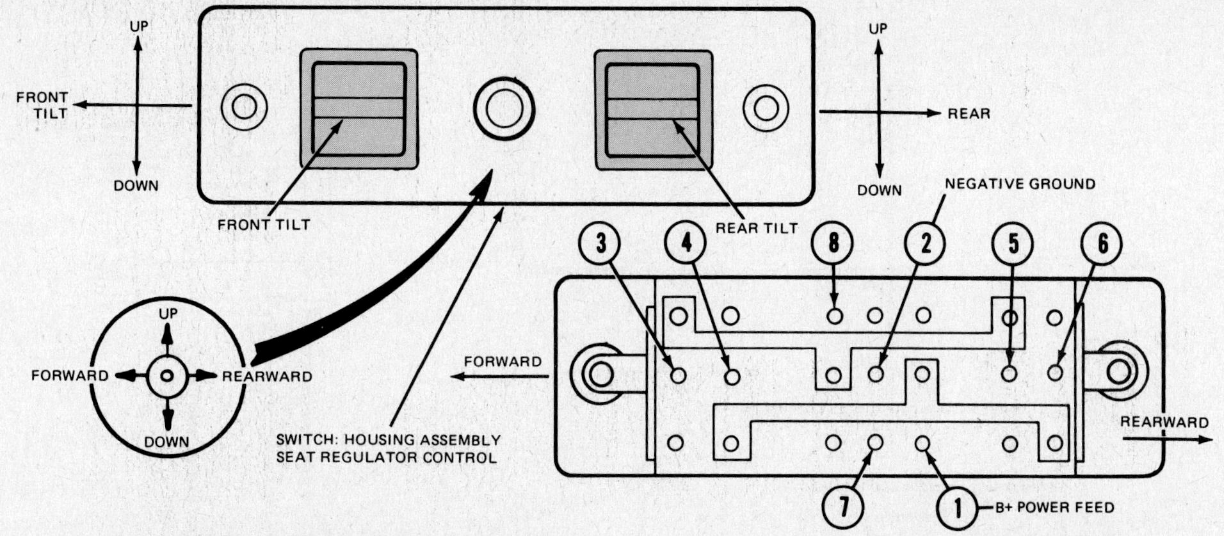

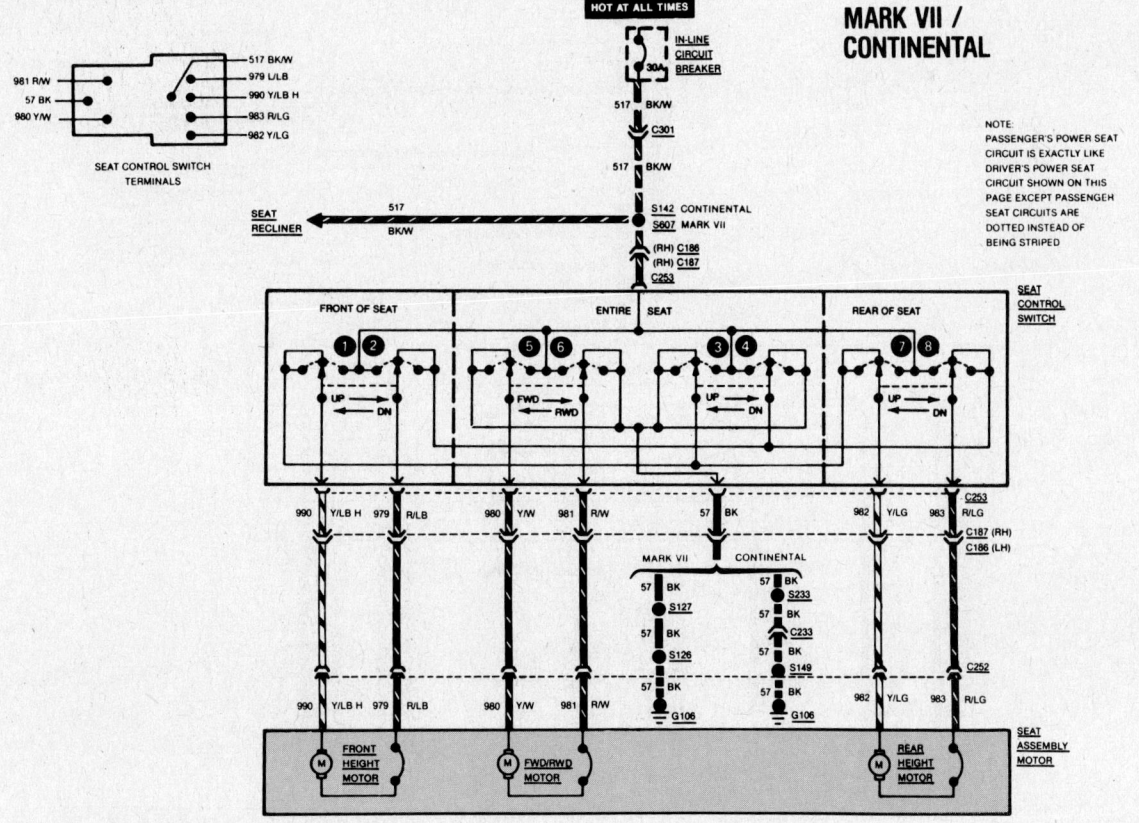

UP
FRONT TILT
DOWN

FRONT TILT

REAR TILT

UP
REAR
DOWN

NEGATIVE GROUND

③ ④ ⑧ ② ⑤ ⑥

UP
FORWARD — ○ — REARWARD
DOWN

FORWARD

REARWARD

SWITCH: HOUSING ASSEMBLY
SEAT REGULATOR CONTROL

⑦ ① — B+ POWER FEED

TEST SWITCH WITH SELF POWERED TEST LIGHT OR OHMMETER
WHEN SWITCH IS DISCONNECTED FROM WIRING

SWITCH POSITION

4-WAY KNOB	REAR TILT	FRONT TILT	CONTINUITY
NEUT. (DEAD)	NEUT. (DEAD)	NEUT. (DEAD)	2-3-4-5-6-7-8, 1 ISOLATED
FORWARD	NEUT. (DEAD)	NEUT. (DEAD)	1-7, 2-3-4-5-6-8
REARWARD	NEUT. (DEAD)	NEUT. (DEAD)	1-8, 2-3-4-5-6-7
UP	NEUT. (DEAD)	NEUT. (DEAD)	1-4-6, 2-3-5-7-8
DOWN	NEUT. (DEAD)	NEUT. (DEAD)	1-3-5, 2-4-6-7-8
NEUT. (DEAD)	UP	NEUT. (DEAD)	1-6, 2-3-4-5-7-8
NEUT. (DEAD)	DOWN	NEUT. (DEAD)	1-5, 2-3-4-6-7-8
NEUT. (DEAD)	NEUT. (DEAD)	UP	1-4, 2-3-5-6-7-8
NEUT. (DEAD)	NEUT. (DEAD)	DOWN	1-3, 2-4-5-6-7-8

Tempo and Topaz power seat switch test points

HOT AT ALL TIMES

**MARK VII /
CONTINENTAL**

IN-LINE
CIRCUIT
BREAKER
30A

517 BK/W

C301

517 BK/W

981 R/W — 517 BK/W
57 BK — 979 L/LB
980 Y/W — 990 Y/LB H
— 983 R/LG
— 982 Y/LG

SEAT CONTROL SWITCH
TERMINALS

SEAT
RECLINER

517
BK/W

S142 CONTINENTAL
S607 MARK VII

(RH) C186
(RH) C187

C253

NOTE:
PASSENGER'S POWER SEAT
CIRCUIT IS EXACTLY LIKE
DRIVER'S POWER SEAT
CIRCUIT SHOWN ON THIS
PAGE EXCEPT PASSENGER
SEAT CIRCUITS ARE
DOTTED INSTEAD OF
BEING STRIPED

SEAT
CONTROL
SWITCH

FRONT OF SEAT	ENTIRE SEAT		REAR OF SEAT
① ②	⑤ ⑥	③ ④	⑦ ⑧

UP / DN   FWD / RWD   UP / DN   UP / DN

C253

990 Y/LB H   979 R/LB   980 Y/W   981 R/W   57 BK   982 Y/LG   983 R/LG

C187 (RH)
C186 (LH)

MARK VII   CONTINENTAL
57 BK   57 BK
S127   S233
57 BK   57 BK
           C233
57 BK   57 BK
S126   S149
57 BK   57 BK
G106   G106

C252

990 Y/LB H   979 R/LB   980 Y/W   981 R/W   57 BK   982 Y/LG   983 R/LG

SEAT
ASSEMBLY
MOTOR

(M) FRONT
HEIGHT
MOTOR

(M) FWD/RWD
MOTOR

(M) REAR
HEIGHT
MOTOR

Continental and Mark VII power seat system

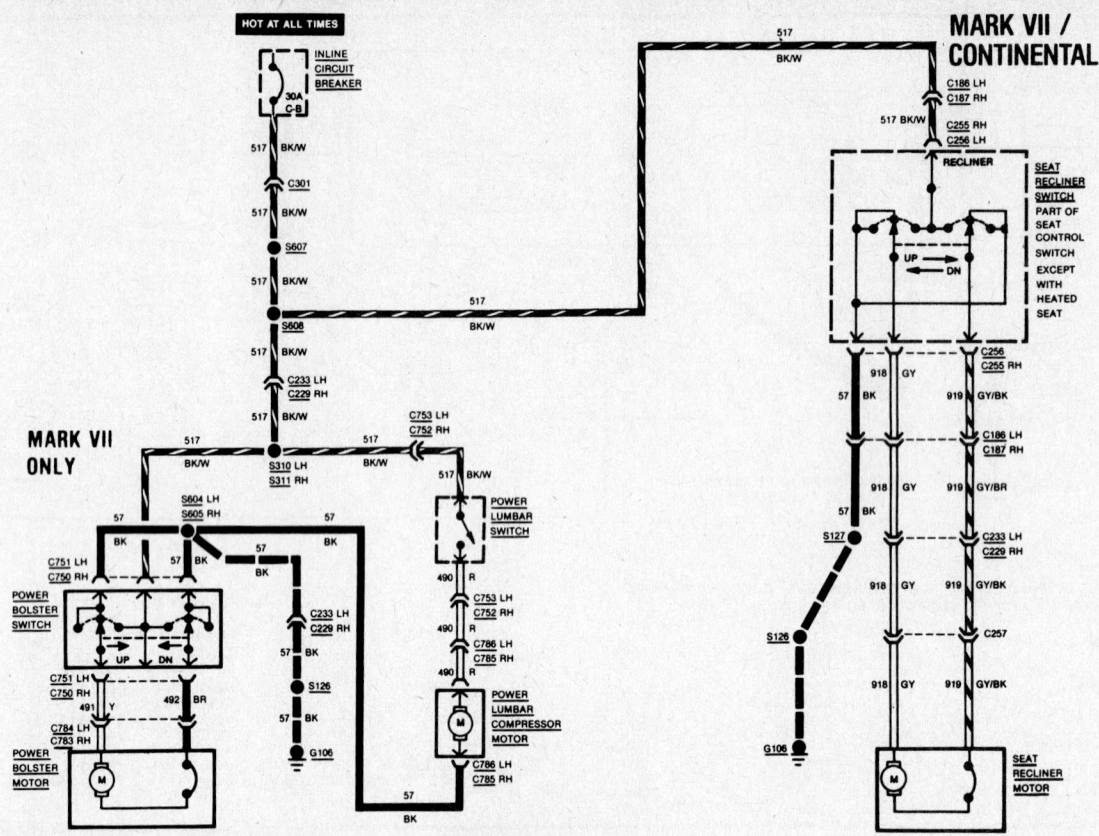

Continental and Mark VII bolster, lumbar and recliner system

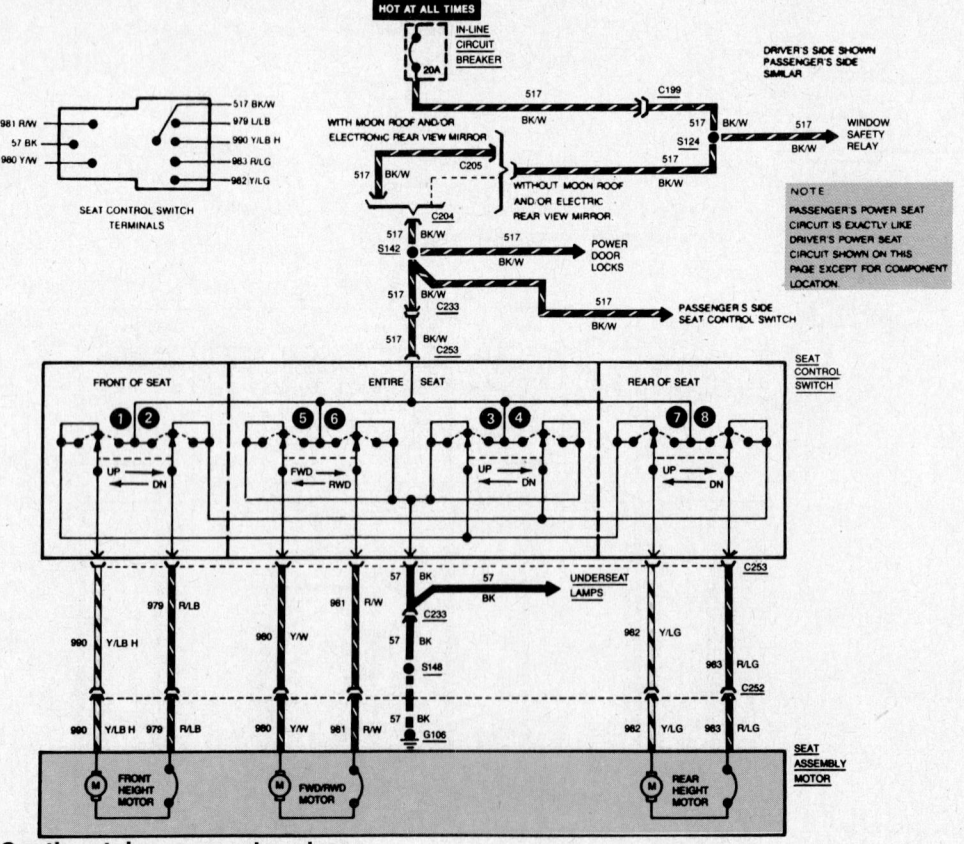

Continental power seat system

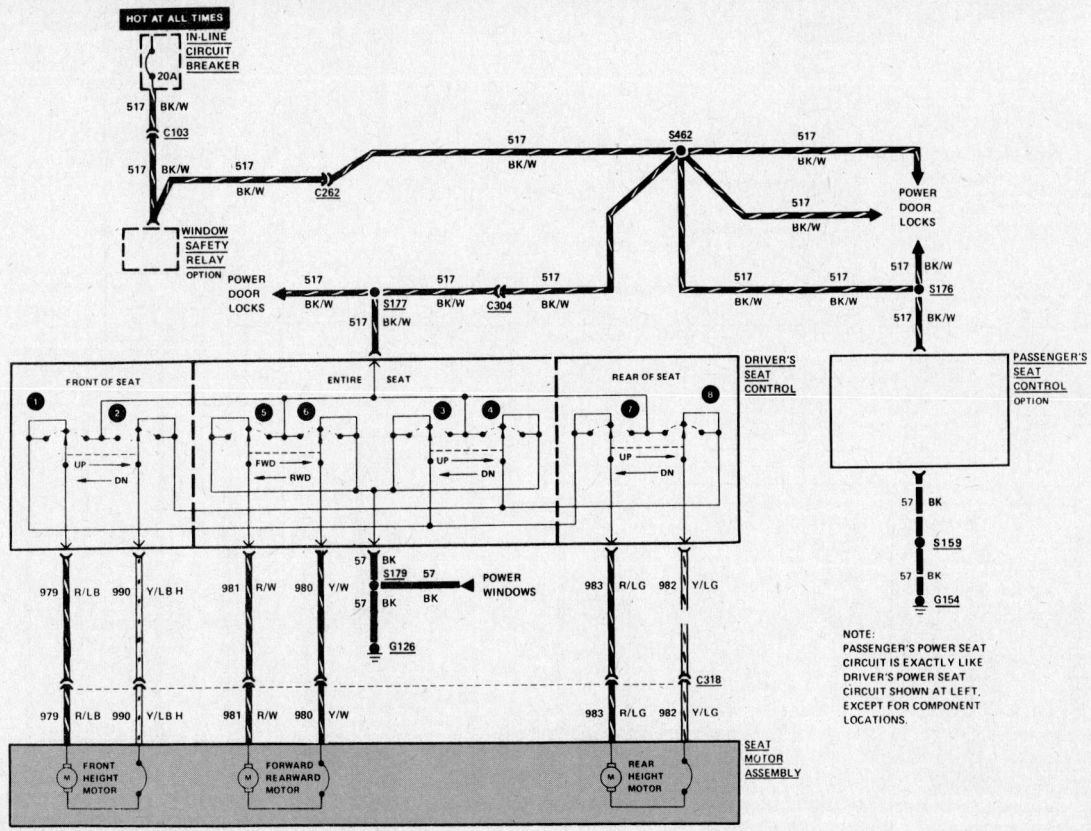

LTD and Marquis power seat system

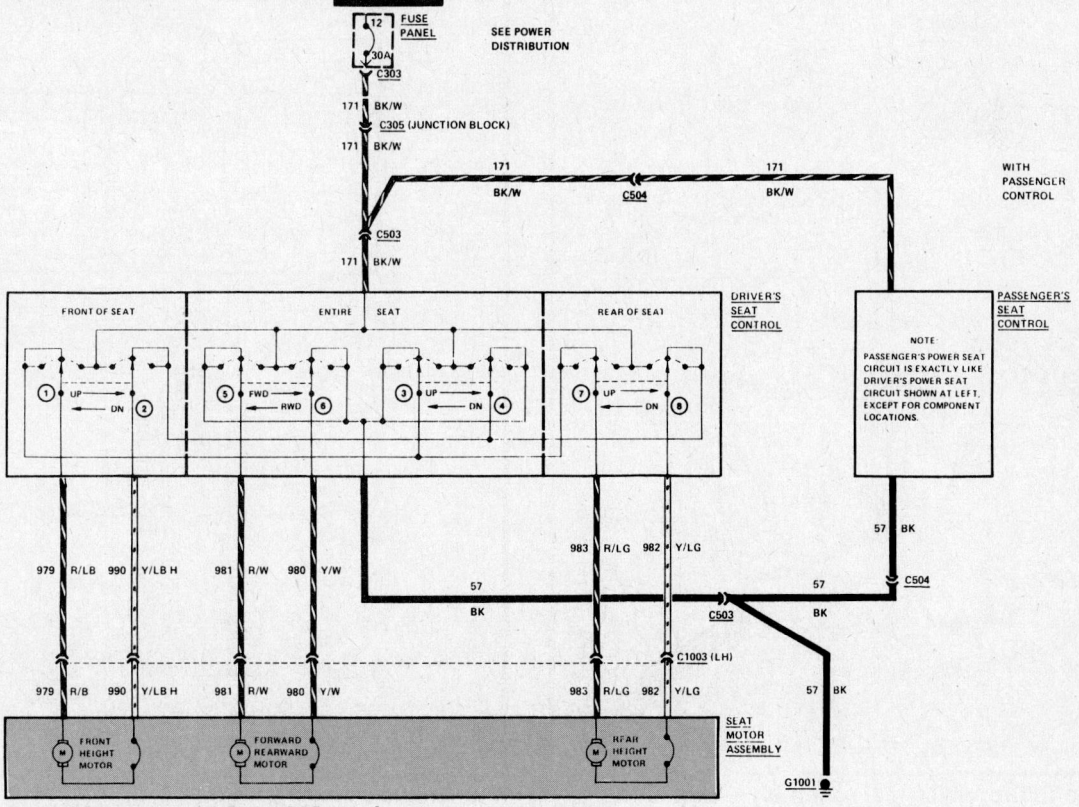

Ford, Mercury and Grand Marquis power seat system

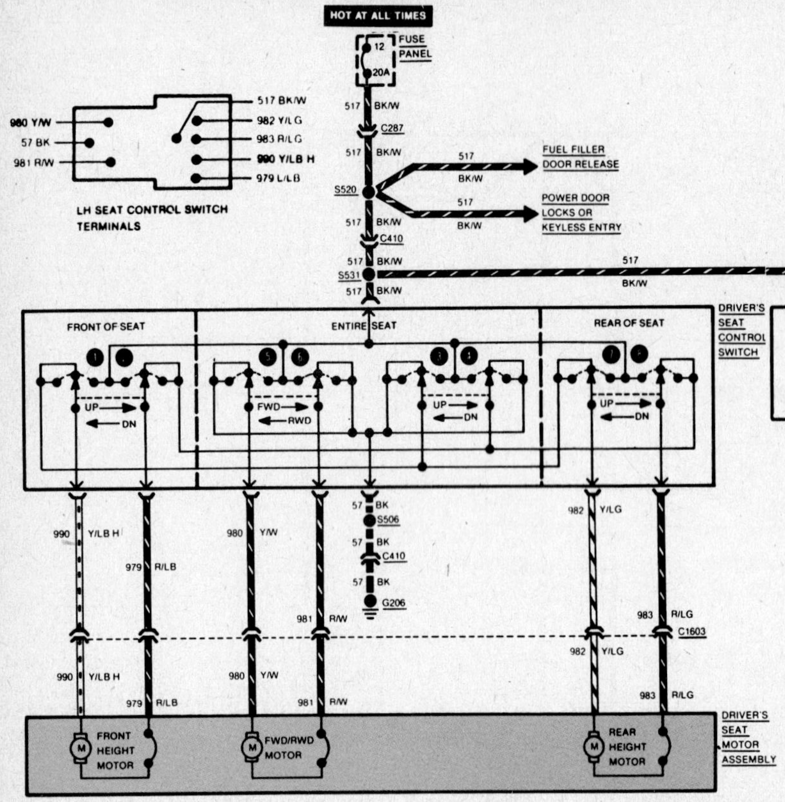

HOT AT ALL TIMES

12 FUSE PANEL
20A

980 Y/W — 517 BK/W
982 Y/LG
57 BK — 983 R/LG
981 R/W — 990 Y/LB H
979 L/LB

517 BK/W

C287

517 BK/W

FUEL FILLER
DOOR RELEASE

S520 517 BK/W

POWER DOOR
LOCKS OR
KEYLESS ENTRY

517 BK/W C410

S531 517 BK/W 517 BK/W

517 BK/W

LH SEAT CONTROL SWITCH TERMINALS

PASSENGER'S SEAT CONTROL SWITCH

FRONT OF SEAT | ENTIRE SEAT | REAR OF SEAT

DRIVER'S SEAT CONTROL SWITCH

UP DN | FWD RWD | UP DN | UP DN

57 BK
S506
57 BK
C410
57 BK
G206

990 Y/LB H | 979 R/LB | 980 Y/W | 981 R/W | 982 Y/LG | 983 R/LG

57 BK
S506
57 BK
C410
57 BK
G206

57 BK
S506
57 BK
C410
57 BK
G206

C1603

990 Y/LB H | 979 R/LB | 980 Y/W | 981 R/W | 982 Y/LG | 983 R/LG

FRONT HEIGHT MOTOR | FWD/RWD MOTOR | REAR HEIGHT MOTOR

DRIVER'S SEAT MOTOR ASSEMBLY

NOTE:
PASSENGER'S POWER SEAT CIRCUIT IS EXACTLY LIKE DRIVER'S POWER SEAT CIRCUIT SHOWN AT LEFT, EXCEPT FOR COMPONENT LOCATIONS.

Thunderbird and Cougar power seat system

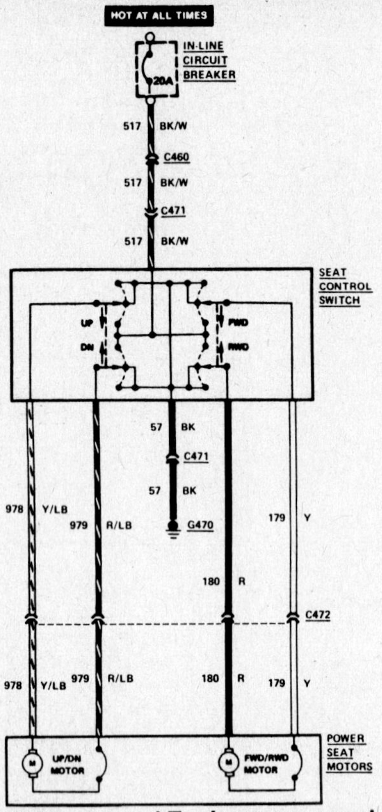

HOT AT ALL TIMES

IN-LINE CIRCUIT BREAKER
20A

517 BK/W
C460
517 BK/W
C471
517 BK/W

SEAT CONTROL SWITCH

UP DN | FWD RWD

57 BK
C471
57 BK
G470

978 Y/LB | 979 R/LB | 180 R | 179 Y

C472

978 Y/LB | 979 R/LB | 180 R | 179 Y

UP/DN MOTOR | FWD/RWD MOTOR

POWER SEAT MOTORS

Fairmont and Zephyr power seat system

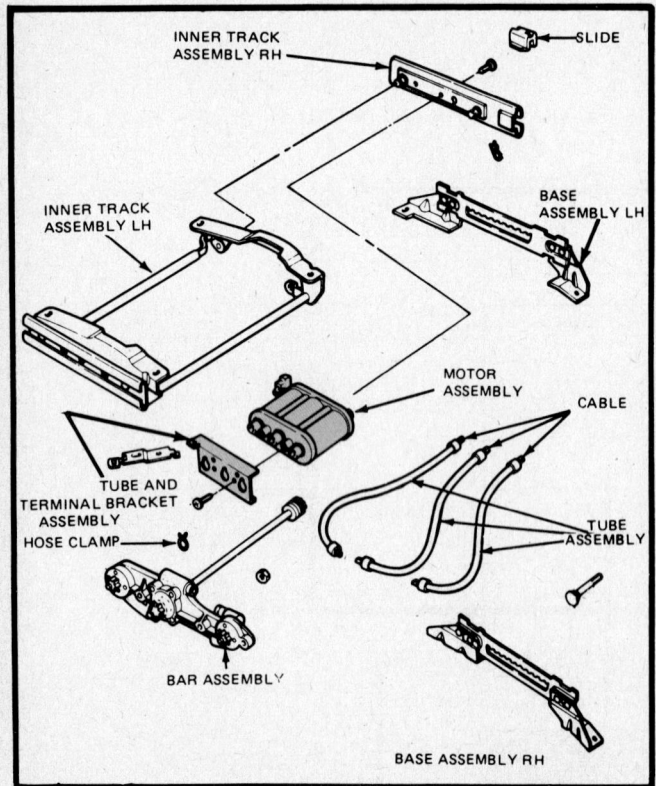

Tempo and Topaz power seat assembly—exploded view

INNER TRACK ASSEMBLY RH
SLIDE
INNER TRACK ASSEMBLY LH
BASE ASSEMBLY LH
MOTOR ASSEMBLY
CABLE
TUBE AND TERMINAL BRACKET ASSEMBLY
HOSE CLAMP
TUBE ASSEMBLY
BAR ASSEMBLY
BASE ASSEMBLY RH

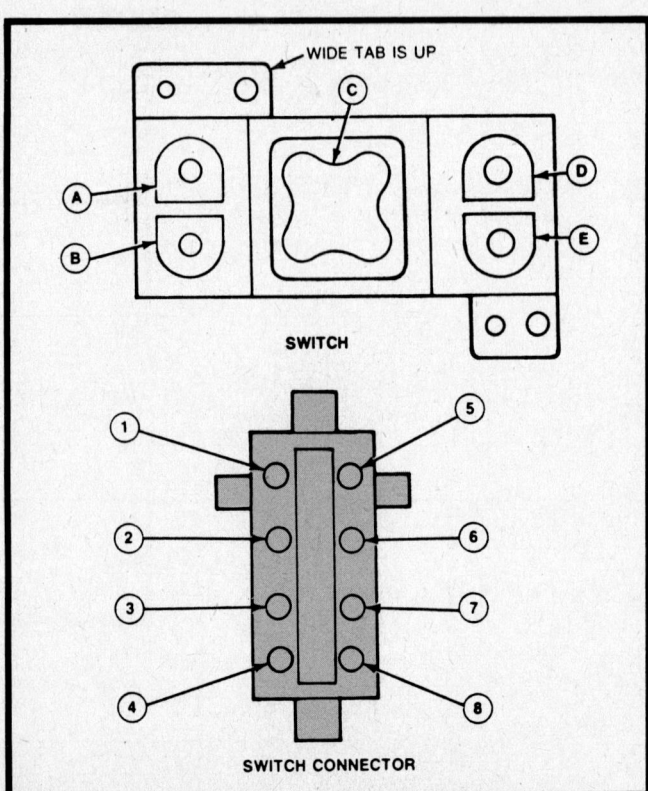

Taurus and Sable—power seat switch test points

WIDE TAB IS UP
A
B
C
D
E
SWITCH

1 | 5
2 | 6
3 | 7
4 | 8
SWITCH CONNECTOR

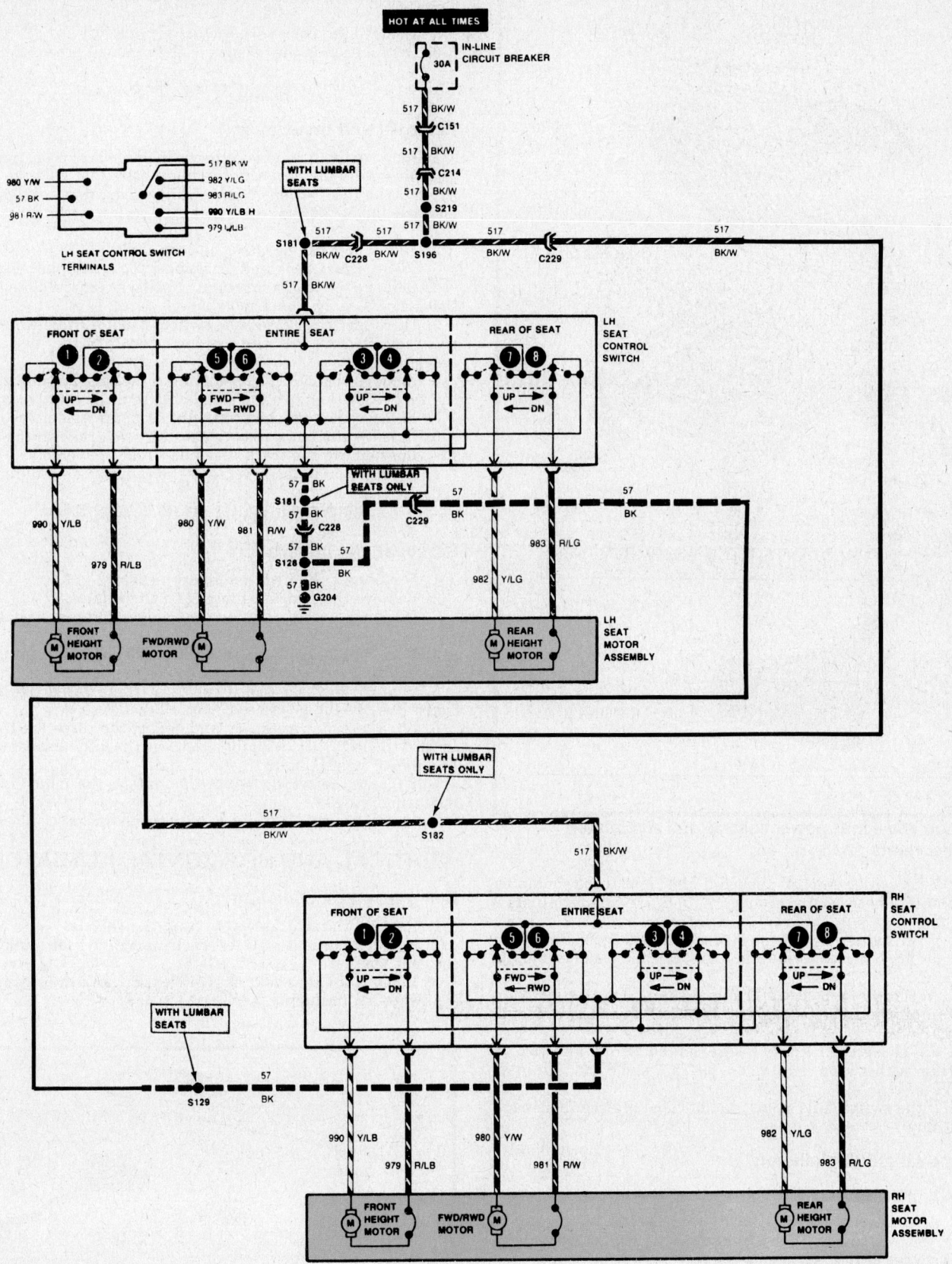

Taurus and Sable power seat system

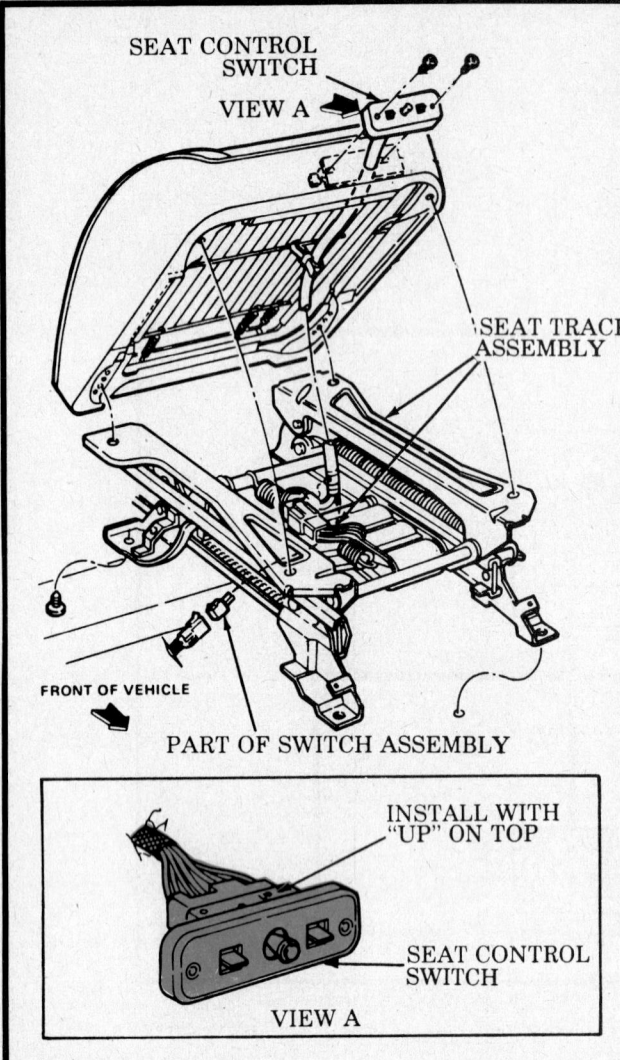

Tempo and Topaz power seat control and related components

6. With switch knob C pushed to the right there should be continuity between terminals 1, 4, 5, 6, 7, 8 and terminals 2 and 3.

7. With switch knob C pushed to the left there should be continuity between terminals 1, 3, 4, 5, 6 and 7 and terminals 2 and 8.

8. With switch knob D depressed there should be continuity between terminals 1 and 2 and terminals 3, 4, 5, 6, 7 and 8.

9. With switch knob E depressed there should be continuity between terminals 1, 3, 4, 5, 7 and 8 and terminals 2 and 6.

10. If the switch fails to test as indicated replace the switch assembly.

Removal and Installation

SEAT MOUNTED SWITCH

1. Disconnect the engative battery cable.

2. Remove the screws retaining the seat cushion side shield. Remove the seat cushion side shield.

3. Remove the screws securing the power seat switch to the seat shield.

4. Disconnect the electrical connectors from the switch assembly.

5. Remove the power seat switch assembly.

6. Installation is the reverse of the removal procedure.

SEAT TRACKS

Removal and Installation

1. Remove the heat shield covers in order to expose the seat retaining bolts. Remove the retaining bolts that hold the seat assembly to the floorpan. It may be necessary to move the seat forward and backward in order to gain access to the retaining bolts.

2. Disconnect the negative battery cable.

3. Tilt the seat back and disconnect the wiring harness.

4. Remove the seat belt retaining bolts, as required. Remove the seat assembly from the vehicle.

5. Disconnect the power seat switch to motor wire harness, if equipped. Remove the side cushion cover from the seat track assembly.

6. Remove the bolts that retain the recliner mechanism to the seat track. Remove the seat back from the seat track.

7. Remove the outboard occupant seat belt assembly.

8. Remove the bolts that retain the seat track to the seat cushion. Remove the track assembly from the vehicle.

9. Installation is the reverse of the removal procedure.

SEAT MOTOR AND CABLES

Removal and Installation

1. Disconnect the negative battery cable.

2. Remove the seat assembly from the vehicle.

3. Remove the seat recliner mechanism and seat back from the seat track.

4. Remove the seat belt, as required. Remove the seat track from the seat cushion.

5. Identify the seat motor cables at there respective locations. Remove the power seat motor bracket screw.

6. Lift the motor assembly and deflect the three left cables toward the left track assembly. Remove the left hand cable assemblies from the motor.

7. Remove the two locknuts that retain the motor to the mounting bracket.

8. Installation is the reverse of the removal procedure.

VERTICAL AND HORIZONTAL ACTUATORS

Removal and Installation

1. Remove the seat assembly from the vehicle.

2. Remove the seat recliner mechanism and seat back from the seat track.

3. Remove the seat belt, as required. Remove the seat track from the seat cushion.

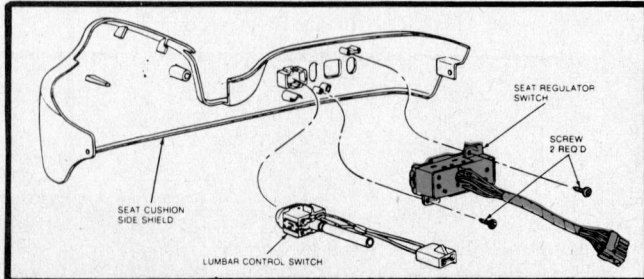

Taurus and Sable—power seat control and related components

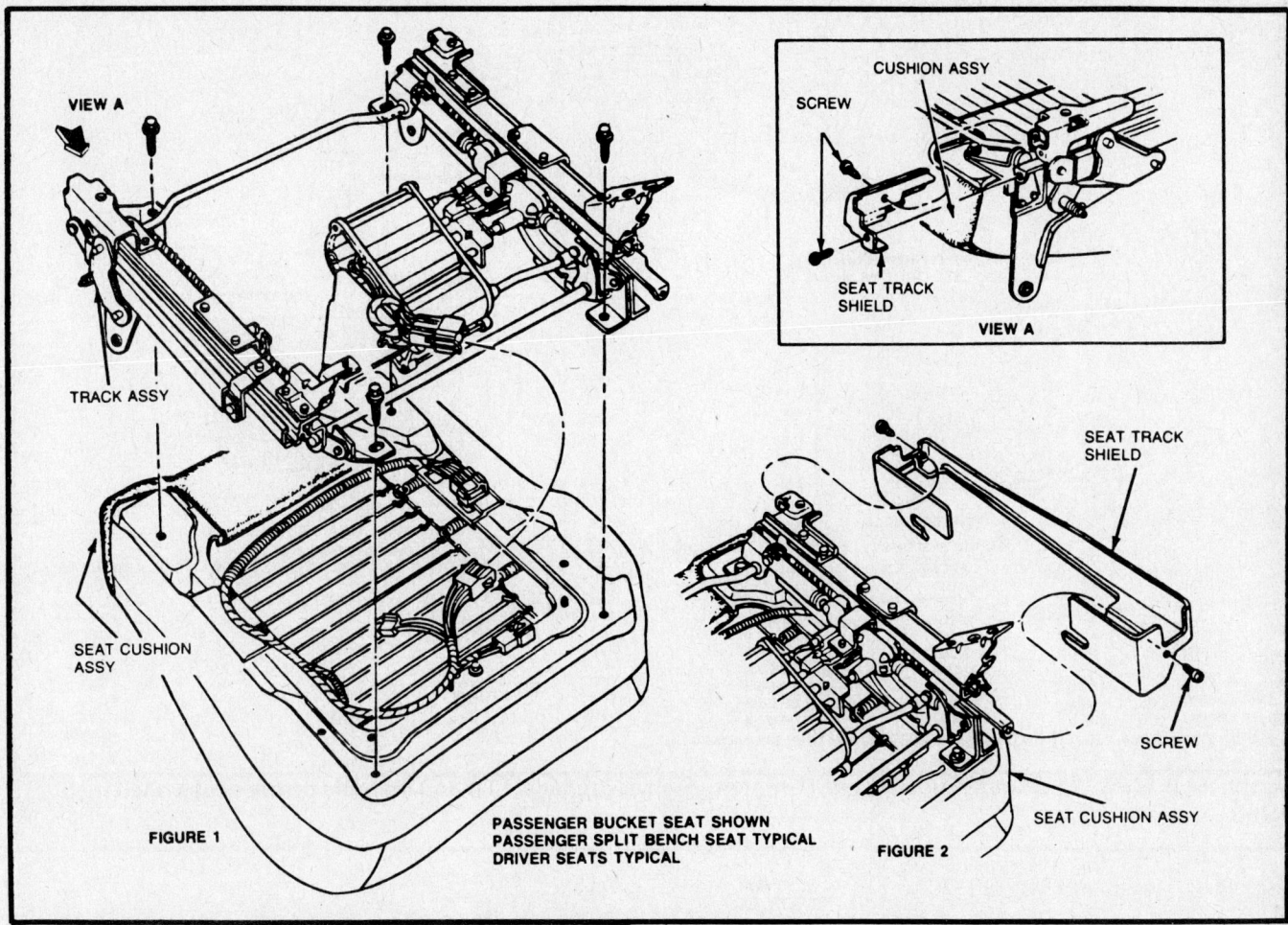

VIEW A

TRACK ASSY

SEAT CUSHION ASSY

FIGURE 1

PASSENGER BUCKET SEAT SHOWN
PASSENGER SPLIT BENCH SEAT TYPICAL
DRIVER SEATS TYPICAL

CUSHION ASSY

SCREW

SEAT TRACK SHIELD

VIEW A

SEAT TRACK SHIELD

SCREW

SEAT CUSHION ASSY

FIGURE 2

Taurus and Sable power seat assembly—exploded view

NOTE: When servicing the seat track assembly, position the seat track assembly about ¼ inch from the full up position, if possible.

4. Remove the power seat motor assembly.

5. Remove the screw from the vertical transmission bracket. Remove the four retaining clips.

6. Slide the right hand track assembly off of the upper support assembly. Then, rotate the right hand track assembly to allow disengagement of the stabilizer rod.

7. Remove the E-ring and the clevis pin used to retain the vertical transmission drive nuts to the upper support rod.

8. Slide the left hand track assembly off of the upper support assembly. Remove the upper support assembly.

9. Installation is the reverse of the removal procedure.

Component Replacement—Continental, Mark VII, Thunderbird, Cougar, Fairmont, Zephyr, Granada, LTD and Marquis

POWER SEAT SWITCH

Removal and Installation
CONSOLE MOUNTED SWITCH

1. Disconnect the negative battery cable.

2. Remove the console trim finish panel. On some vehicles it will be necessary to insert a small suitable tool in the notch at the rear of the switch plate and carefully pry upward, than tilt the switch up and pull back in order to disengage the tab on the front end of the plate from the console.

3. Remove the screws from the bottom side of the connector. Remove the switch and the connector from the trim finish panel.

4. The power seat switch is held in place on the connector by the switch terminals. Using a suitable tool pry the power seat switch from the connector.

5. Installation is the reverse of the removal procedure.

CONSOLE MOUNTED 60/40 SEAT SWITCH

1. Disconnect the negative battery cable.

2. Remove the console finish trim panel.

3. Remove the screws from the bottom side of the connector. Remove the switch and the connector from the trim finish panel.

4. The power seat switch is held in place on the connector by the switch terminals. Using a suitable tool pry the power seat switch from the connector.

5. Installation is the reverse of the removal procedure.

CONSOLETTE MOUNTED SWITCH

1. Disconnect the negative battery cable.

2. Using a suitable tool, pry the rear of the switch housing up and pull it rearward in order to disengage the front clip on the housing from the consolette.

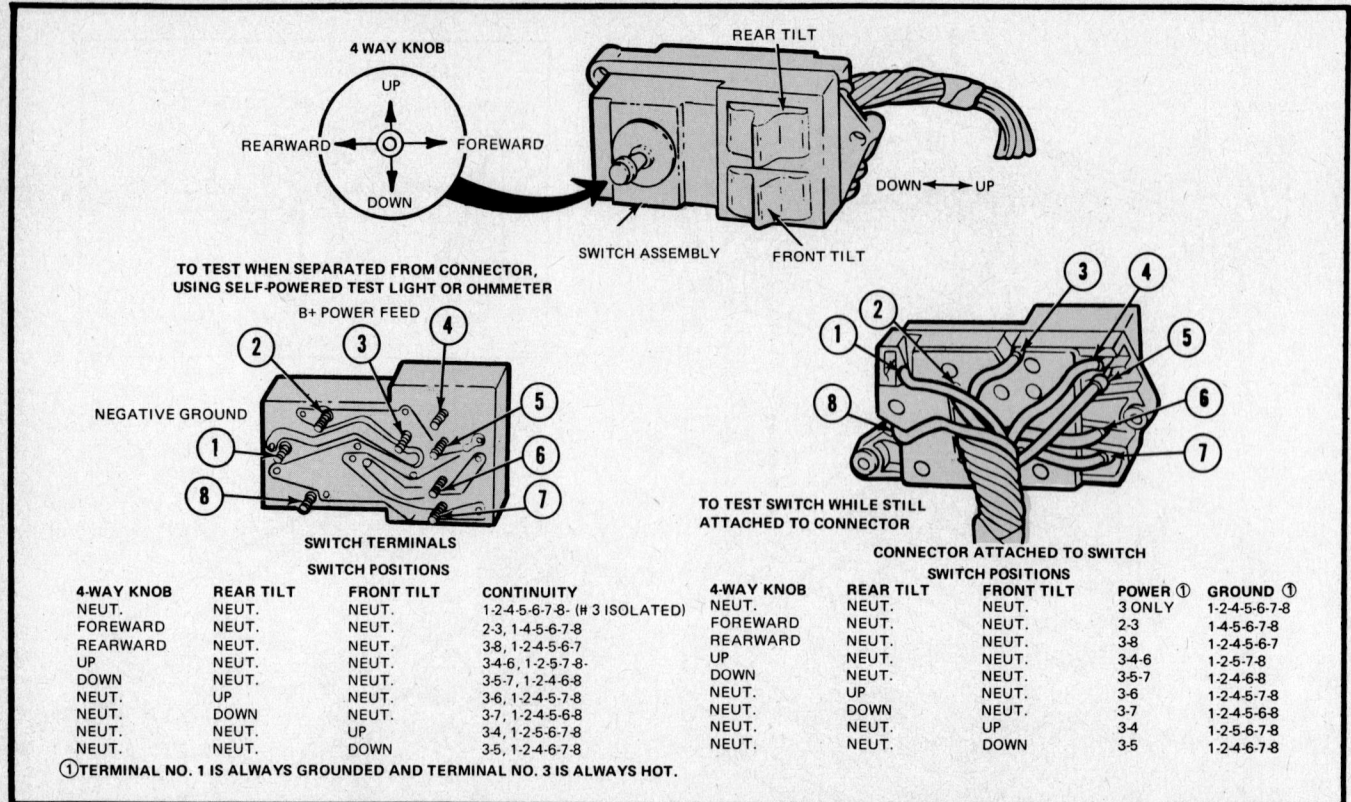

4-WAY KNOB	REAR TILT	FRONT TILT	CONTINUITY
NEUT.	NEUT.	NEUT.	1-2-4-5-6-7-8- (# 3 ISOLATED)
FOREWARD	NEUT.	NEUT.	2-3, 1-4-5-6-7-8
REARWARD	NEUT.	NEUT.	3-8, 1-2-4-5-6-7
UP	NEUT.	NEUT.	3-4-6, 1-2-5-7-8-
DOWN	NEUT.	NEUT.	3-5-7, 1-2-4-6-8
NEUT.	UP	NEUT.	3-6, 1-2-4-5-7-8
NEUT.	DOWN	NEUT.	3-7, 1-2-4-5-6-8
NEUT.	NEUT.	UP	3-4, 1-2-5-6-7-8
NEUT.	NEUT.	DOWN	3-5, 1-2-4-6-7-8

①TERMINAL NO. 1 IS ALWAYS GROUNDED AND TERMINAL NO. 3 IS ALWAYS HOT.

4-WAY KNOB	REAR TILT	FRONT TILT	POWER ①	GROUND ①
NEUT.	NEUT.	NEUT.	3 ONLY	1-2-4-5-6-7-8
FOREWARD	NEUT.	NEUT.	2-3	1-4-5-6-7-8
REARWARD	NEUT.	NEUT.	3-8	1-2-4-5-6-7
UP	NEUT.	NEUT.	3-4-6	1-2-5-7-8
DOWN	NEUT.	NEUT.	3-5-7	1-2-4-6-8
NEUT.	UP	NEUT.	3-6	1-2-4-5-7-8
NEUT.	DOWN	NEUT.	3-7	1-2-4-5-6-8
NEUT.	NEUT.	UP	3-4	1-2-5-6-7-8
NEUT.	NEUT.	DOWN	3-5	1-2-4-6-7-8

Continental, Mark VII, Thunderbird, Cougar, Fairmont, Zephyr, Granada, LTD and Marquis power seat switch test points—six way system

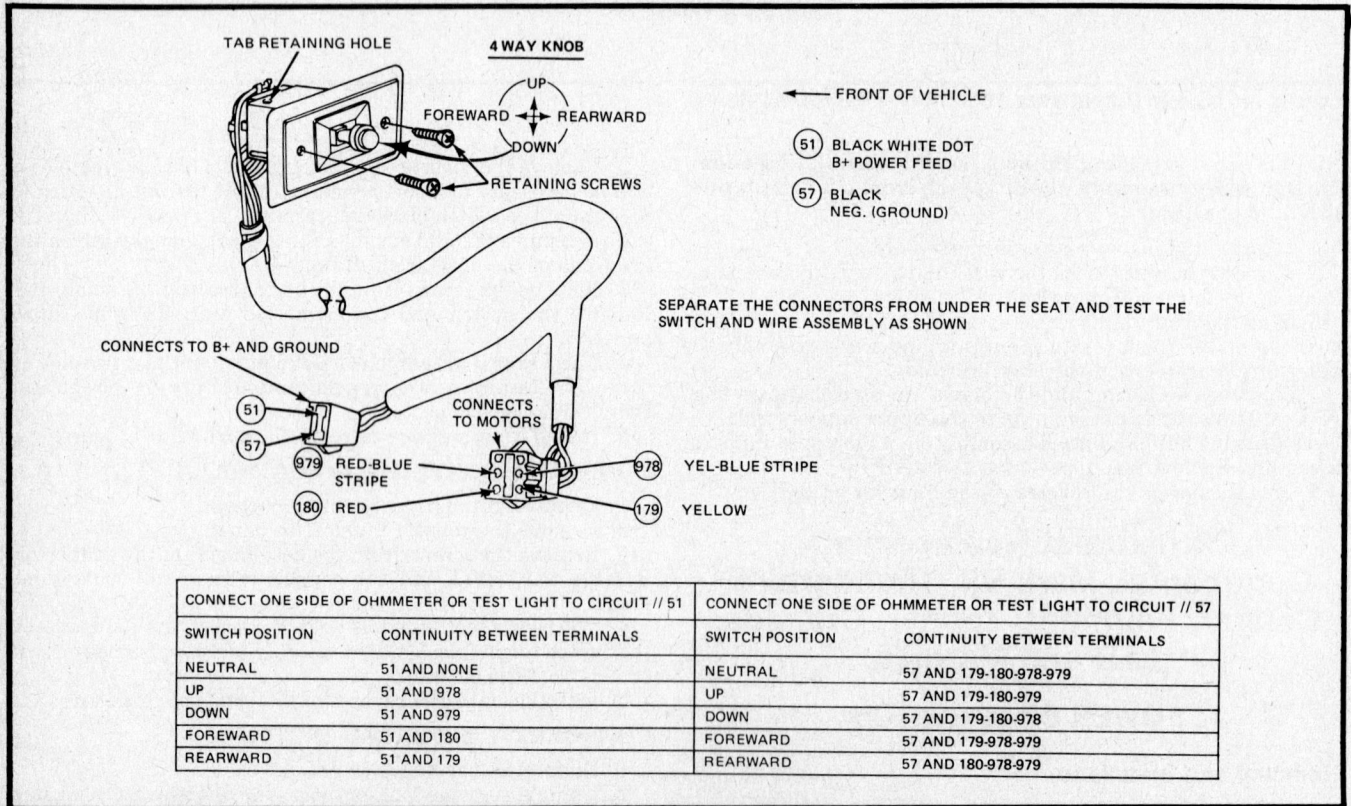

CONNECT ONE SIDE OF OHMMETER OR TEST LIGHT TO CIRCUIT // 51		CONNECT ONE SIDE OF OHMMETER OR TEST LIGHT TO CIRCUIT // 57	
SWITCH POSITION	CONTINUITY BETWEEN TERMINALS	SWITCH POSITION	CONTINUITY BETWEEN TERMINALS
NEUTRAL	51 AND NONE	NEUTRAL	57 AND 179-180-978-979
UP	51 AND 978	UP	57 AND 179-180-979
DOWN	51 AND 979	DOWN	57 AND 179-180-978
FOREWARD	51 AND 180	FOREWARD	57 AND 179-978-979
REARWARD	51 AND 179	REARWARD	57 AND 180-978-979

Fairmont, Zephyr, Granada, and Cougar power seat test points—four way system

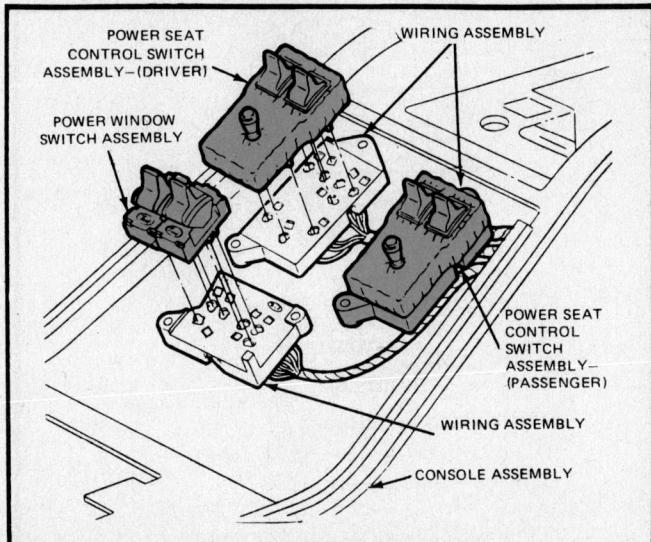

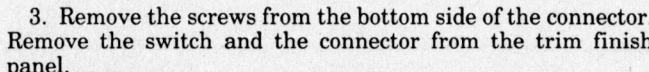

Power seat control—console mounted (type two)

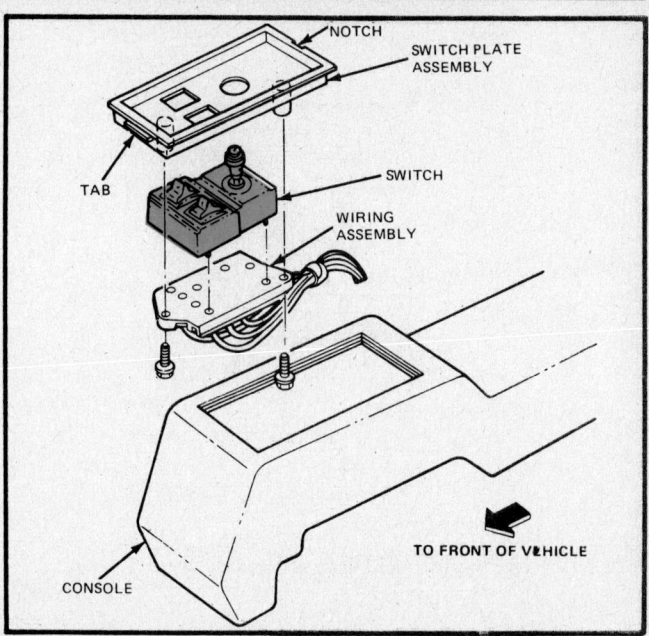

Power seat control—console mounted (type one)

3. Remove the screws from the bottom side of the connector. Remove the switch and the connector from the trim finish panel.
4. The power seat switch is held in place on the connector by the switch terminals. Using a suitable tool pry the power seat switch from the connector.
5. Installation is the reverse of the removal procedure.

DOOR MOUNTED SWITCH

1. Disconnect the negative battery cable.

2. Remove the door trim moulding assembly by carefully prying it away from the door trim panel.
3. Remove the fire door trim panel retaining screws and remove the panel.
4. Remove the power seat switch retaining screws. Pry the switch wiring and connector from the finish panel.

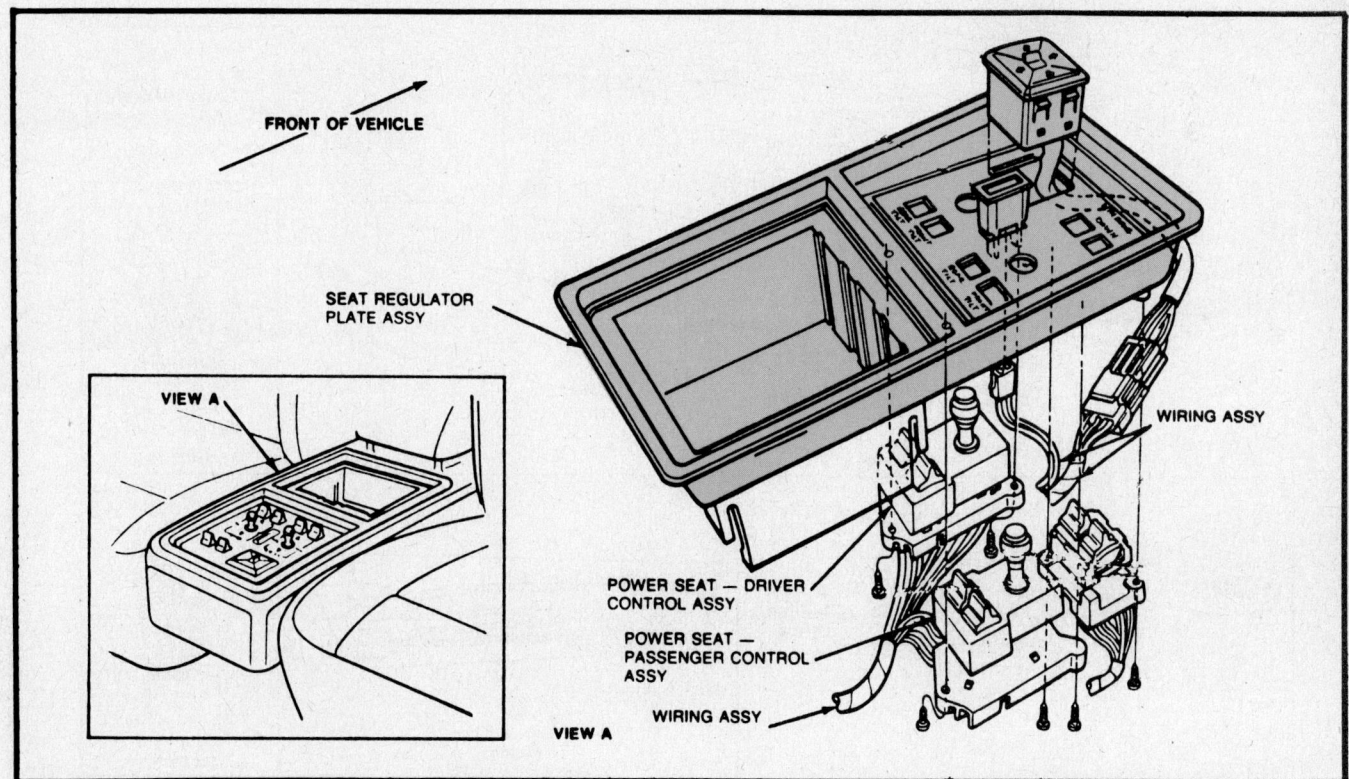

Power seat control—console mounted 60/40 seat

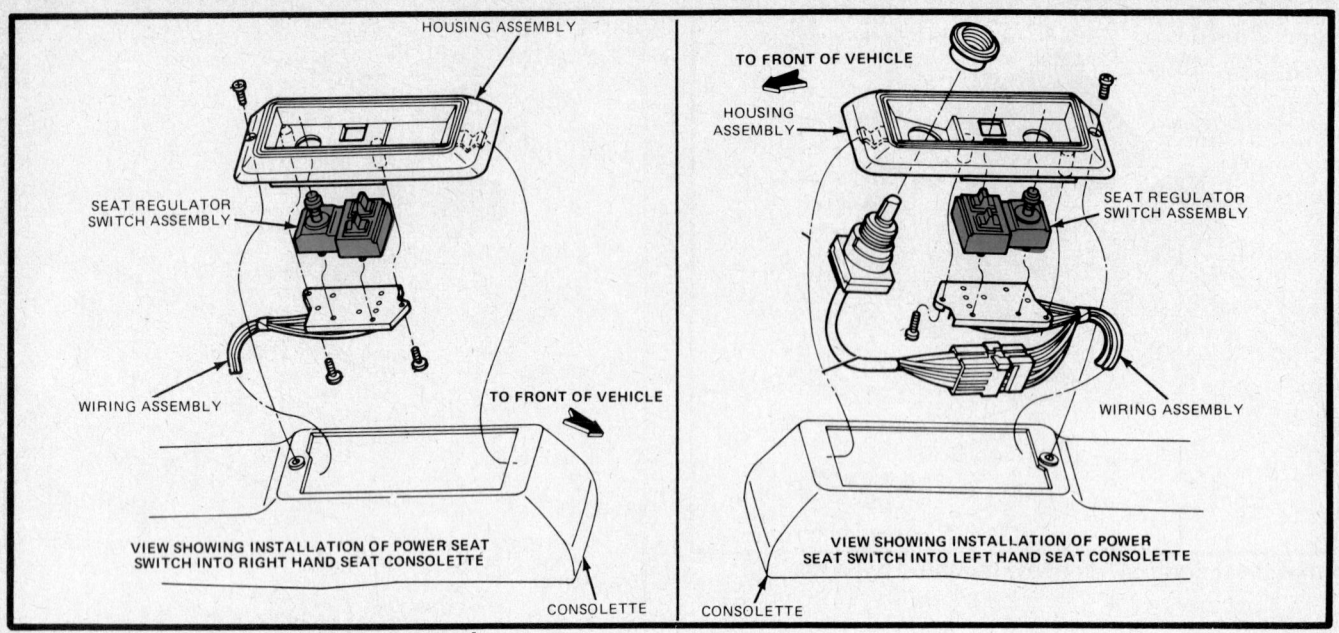

Power seat control—consolette mounted

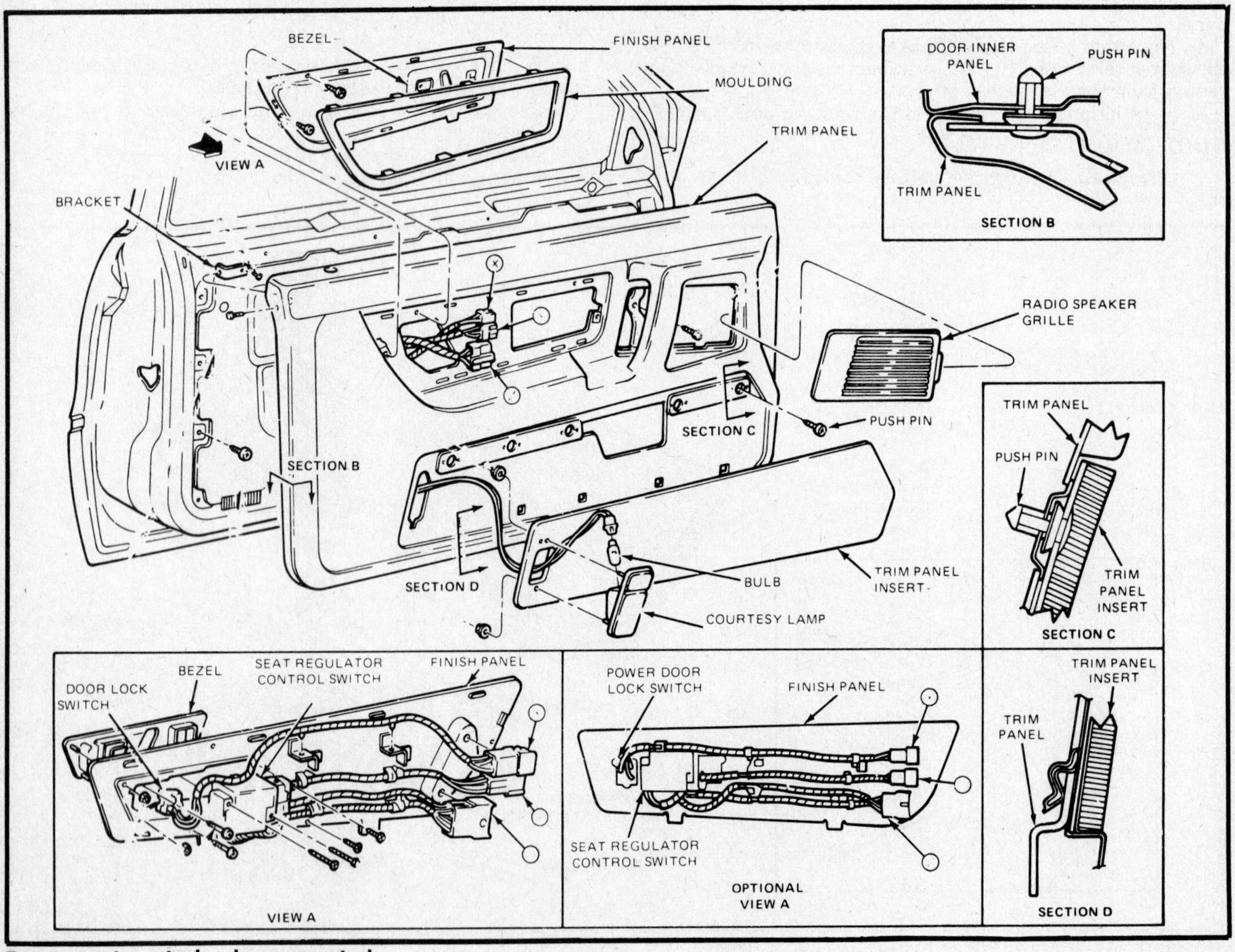

Power seat control—door mounted

5. Disconnect the switch connector and remove the power seat switch.

6. Installation is the reverse of the removal procedure.

DOOR ARMREST MOUNTED SWITCH

1. Disconnect the negative battery cable.

2. Insert a suitable tool under the power seat switch housing assembly and carefully pry away from the armrest.

3. Remove the screws from the bottom side of the connector. Remove the switch and the connector from the trim finish panel.

4. The power seat switch is held in place on the connector by the switch terminals. Using a suitable tool pry the power seat switch from the connector.

5. Installation is the reverse of the removal procedure.

SEAT MOUNTED SWITCH

1. Disconnect the negative battery cable.

2. Remove the power seat switch retaining screws.

3. Pull the switch from its mounting. Disconnect the electrical connector from the back of the switch assembly.

4. Remove the power seat switch from the vehicle.

5. Installation is the reverse of the removal procedure.

SEAT TRACKS

Removal and Installation

1. If equipped, remove the heat shields plugs in order to expose the seat assembly retaining bolts. Remove the retaining bolts that hold the seat assembly to the floorpan. It may be necessary to move the seat forward and backward in order to gain access to the retaining bolts.

2. Disconnect the negative battery cable.

3. Tilt the seat back and disconnect the wiring harness.

4. Remove the seat belt retaining bolts, as required. Remove the seat assembly from the vehicle.

5. Remove the bolts that attach the seat track to the seat frame. Remove tie straps, as required, that may be holding the cable housing to the seat assembly. Separate the seat track assembly from the seat.

6. Installation is the reverse of the removal procedure.

SEAT MOTOR AND CABLES

Removal and Installation

NOTE: It is recommended that when a cable is to be replaced, the power seat motor should be removed in order to ease the replacement of the defective cable.

RACK AND PINION TYPE

1. Disconnect the negative battery cable.

2. Remove the seat assembly from the vehicle.

3. Remove the motor retaining bolts from the seat mounting.

4. Disconnect the housings and the cables from the motor.

5. Remove the motor assembly from its mounting.

6. Installation is the reverse of the removal procedure.

SCREW DRIVE TYPE

1. Disconnect the negative battery cable. Remove the seat assembly from the vehicle. Remove the seat track assembly from the cushion.

2. Identify the drive cables and their respective locations. Remove the nut from the stabilizer rod. Remove the motor and the bracket screw.

3. Lift the motor and deflect the three left cables toward the left track assembly. Remove the three left hand cable assemblies from the motor.

4. Move the motor along the stabilizer rod to the right, disengaging the right hand cables.

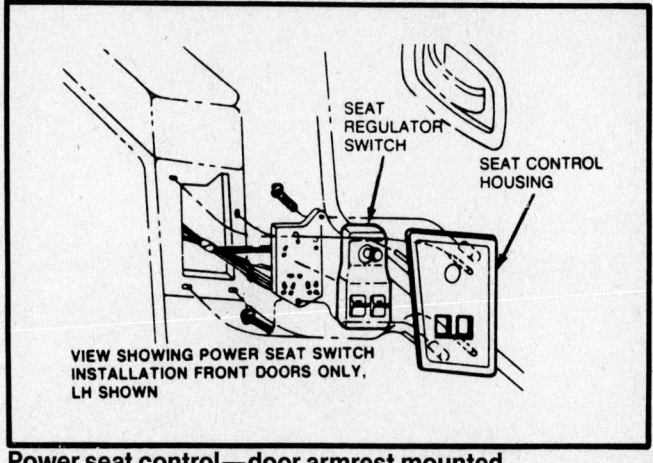

VIEW SHOWING POWER SEAT SWITCH
INSTALLATION FRONT DOORS ONLY,
LH SHOWN

Power seat control—door armrest mounted

5. Lift and slide the motor off of the stabilizer rod. Remove the two lock nuts retaining the motor to the mounting bracket. Remove the motor assembly.

6. Installation is the reverse of the removal procedure.

VERTICAL AND HORIZONTAL ACTUATORS- RACK AND PINION DRIVE SYSTEM

Removal and Installation

1. Remove the seat assembly from the vehicle.

2. Remove the motor mount bracket mounting bolts from

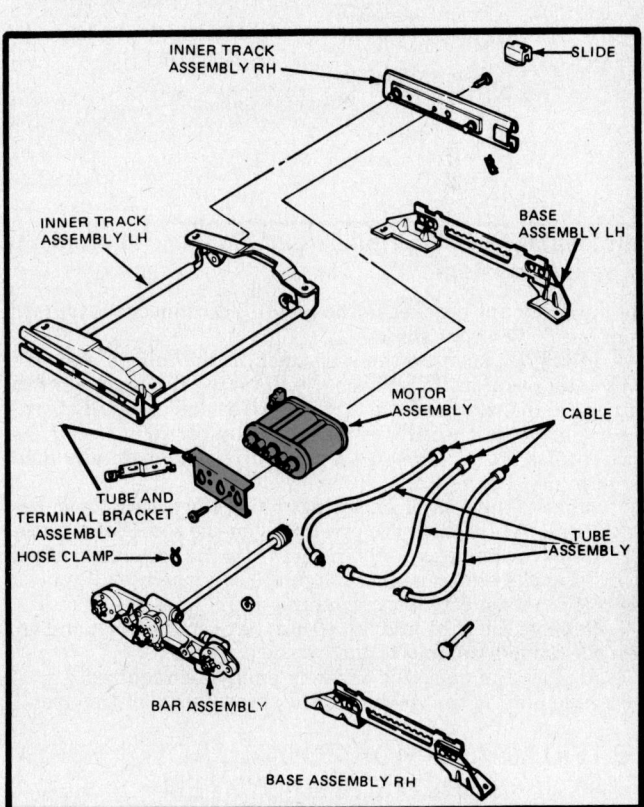

Continental, Mark VII, Thunderbird, Cougar, Fairmont, Zephyr, Granada, LTD and Marquis power seat assembly—rack and pinion drive system

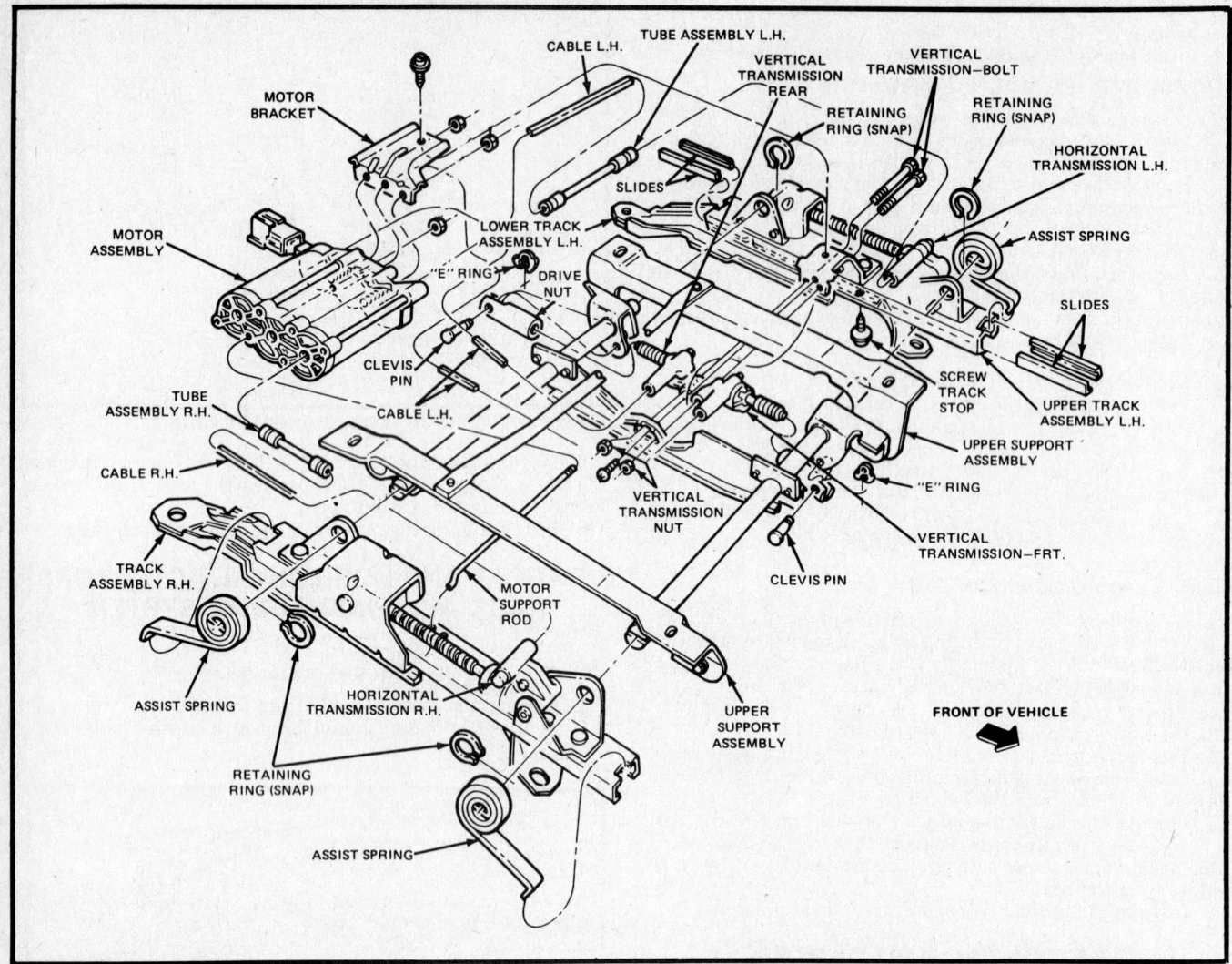

Continental, Mark VII, Thunderbird, Cougar, Fairmont, Zephyr, Granada, LTD and Marquis power seat assembly—screw drive system

the motor mount bracket to the motor. Disconnect the clamps from the drive input shafts.

3. Manually position the seat track in the full up and mid horizontal position. This is done by inserting the square end of a drive cable into one of the vertical drives and manually turning the drive unit until it is in the full up position. Using the horizontal drive unit, insert the cable drive and manually turn it to the mid horizontal position.

4. Remove the rear clock springs using the proper tools. Remove the roll pins from the pivot pins on the secondary track.

5. Remove the base and carriage from the secondary track by driving the pinion gear through the carriage rack. Remove the roll pin from the drive side pinion.

6. Remove the bolts and nuts from the primary track and retain the drive assembly to the carriage.

7. Replace the defective drive assembly, as required.

8. Assembly is the reverse of the disassembly procedure.

VERTICAL AND HORIZONTAL ACTUATORS- SCREW DRIVE SYSTEM

Removal and Installation

VERTICAL DRIVE TRANSMISSIONS

1. Disconnect the negative battery cable. Remove the seat

assembly from the vehicle. Remove the seat track assembly from the cushion.

2. Remove the power seat motor from the seat track.

3. Remove the seat track stop screw from the underside of the left hand track assembly.

4. Using one of the adjusting cables, insert it into the horizontal transmission and rotate the cable counterclockwise this will cause the lead screw to back out of the nylon drive block.

5. Slide the lower half of the left hand drive assembly rearward far enough to allow the lead screw to be lifted high enough to gain access to the vertical transmission retaining bolts. Remove the bolt.

NOTE: Be careful when separating the upper and lower left hand seat track assembly in order to prevent the loss of the plastic slides.

6. Remove the transmission from the seat assembly.

7. Installation is the reverse of the removal procedure. Do not tighten the transmission retaining bolts more than 22 inch lbs.

8. For proper seat track installation the left horizontal drive screw and the right horizontal drive screw must be synchronized.

UPPER SUPPORT ASSEMBLY

1. Disconnect the negative battery cable. Remove the seat assembly from the vehicle.

2. Remove the seat track from the cushion. When servicing the seat track assembly position it about $\frac{1}{4}$ inch from the full up seat position.

3. Before removing the clock springs identify them to aid in reinstallation. To prevent injury cover the springs with a cloth before removal.

4. Remove the power seat motor from the seat track.

5. Remove the screw from the vertical transmission bracket. Remove the four retaining clips.

6. Slide the right hand track assembly off of the upper slide support assembly, then rotate the right hand track assembly to allow the disengagement of the stabilizer rod.

7. Remove the E-ring and the clevis pin used to retain the vertical transmission drive nuts to the upper support assembly.

8. Slide the left hand track assembly off of the upper support assembly. Remove the upper support assembly.

9. Installation is the reverse of the removal procedure.

ASSIST SPRINGS

1. Disconnect the negative battery cable. Remove the seat assembly from the vehicle. Remove the seat track assembly from the cushion.

2. With the seat track assembly clamped firmly to the work station, position the clock spring to the seat track assembly. Use a pair of channel locks to clamp the spring to the seat track assembly.

3. Position a cloth over the springs before removal. With the aid of an assistant and using a pair of vise grips clamp the end of the clock spring. Rotate the spring end clockwise and position the spring end in the retaining notch in the seat track.

POWER RECLINER

Some vehicles are equipped with a power recliner assembly which provides tilt adjustment of the seat back. By pressing the power recliner seat switch the seat back will move forward or rearward until the power recliner seat switch is released.

Power Recliner Motor and Transmission

Removal and Installation

1. Disconnect the negative battery cable.

2. Remove the seat from the vehicle.

3. Disengage the cushion trim cover, as required, to gain access to the seat back to seat cushion retaining screws. Remove the retaining screws.

4. Disengage the seat back trim cover, as required, to gain access to the screws securing the latch/recliner assembly to the seat back. Remove the retaining screws.

5. If equipped, remove the plastic cover from the recliner assembly.

6. Secure the latch/recliner assembly in a vise.

NOTE: Copper inserts must be installed in the vise in order to prevent damage to the latch/recliner assembly.

7. On some latch/recliner assemblies it may be necessary to clamp a vise grip on the lower portion of the assembly, butted against the upper portion of the latch.

NOTE: Due to the force exerted on the two portions of the recliner assembly by the clock spring, the recliner assembly must be secured in the vise properly. Failure to do so could result in damage and injury.

8. Remove the retaining screws attaching the cover plate to the motor and transmission. Remove the cover plate.

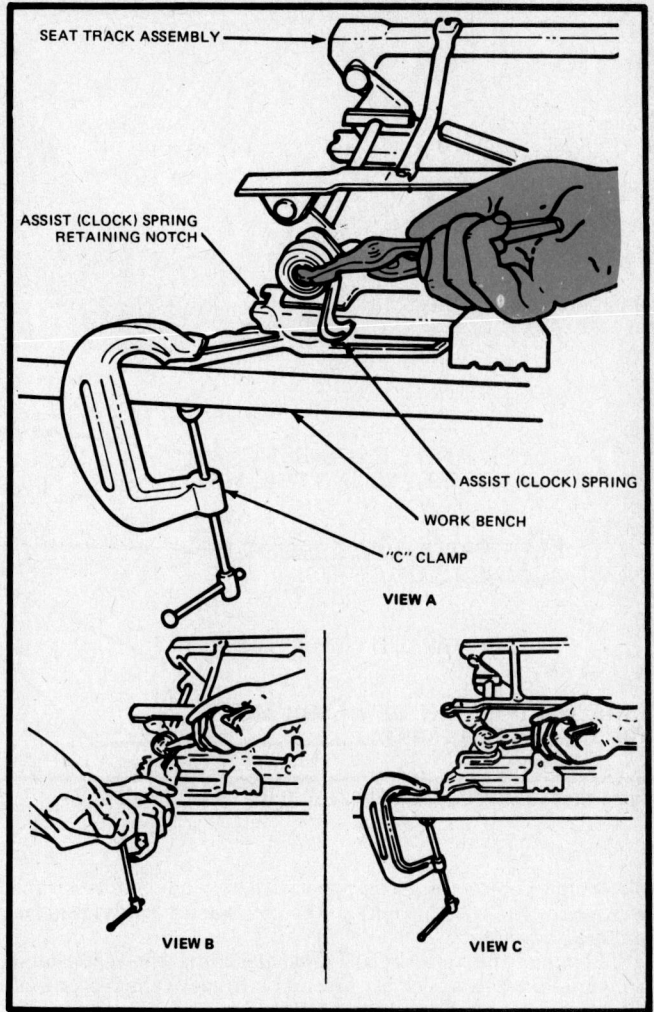

Screw drive system—spring assist removal

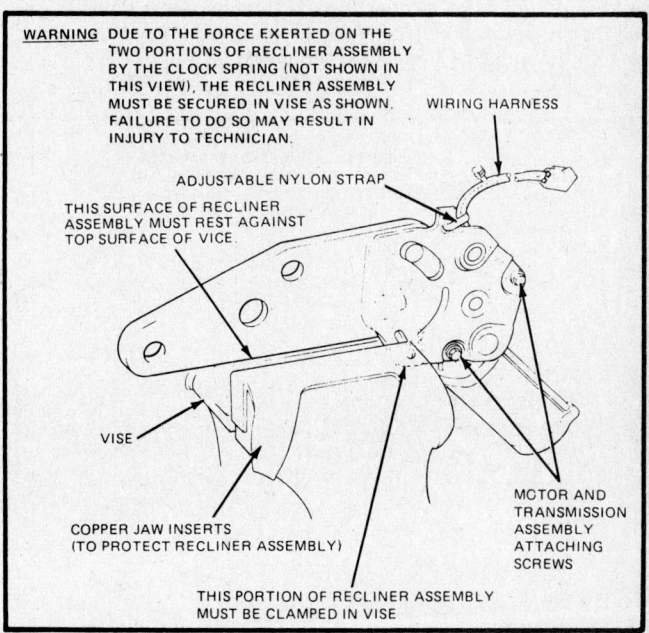

Type two latch/recliner assembly installed in vise

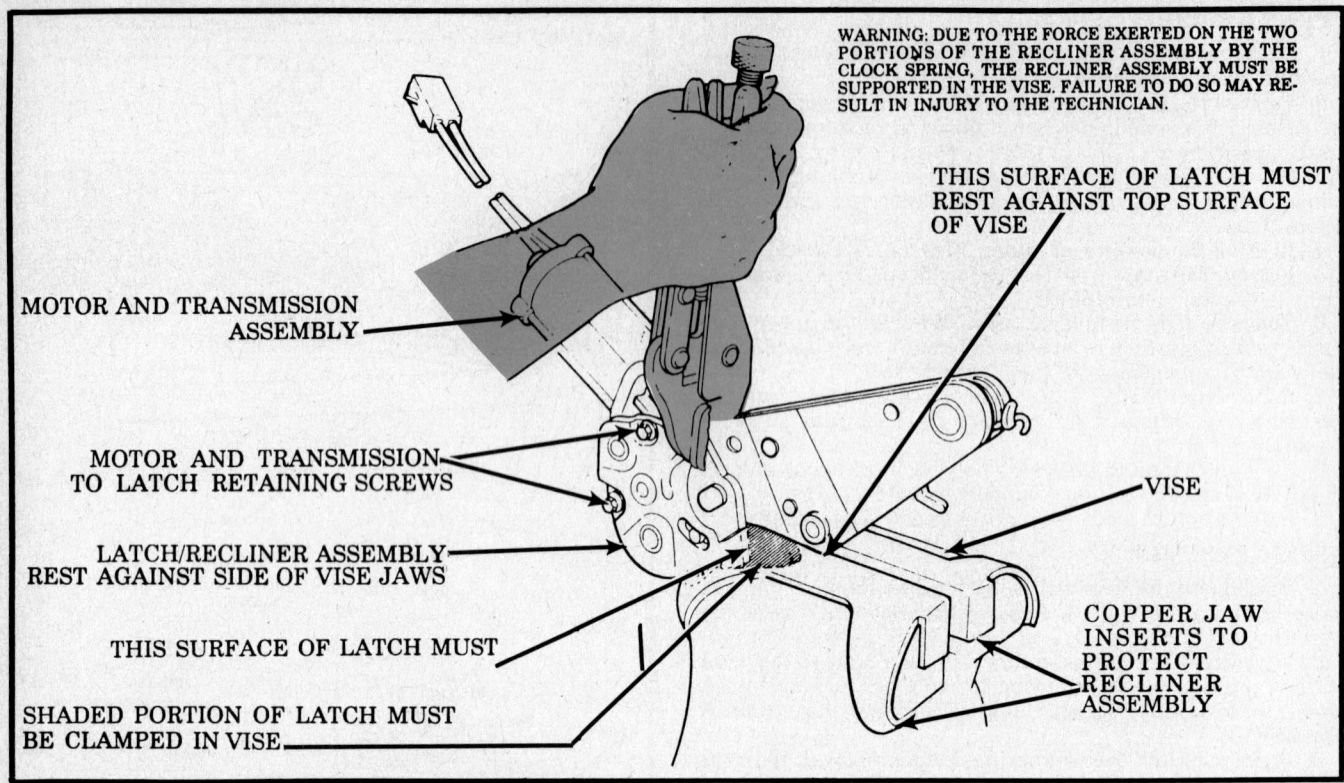

Type one latch/recliner assembly installed in vise

9. Some vehicles are equipped with two adjustable straps that secure the wire harness to the recliner assembly, remove and discard them.

10. Remove the retaining screws attaching the motor and transmission to the recliner assembly. Remove the motor and transmission from the recliner assembly.

11. Installation is the reverse of the removal procedure.

12. If the threaded holes in the motor and transmission assembly do not align properly with the clearance holes in the recliner assembly, or the gears do not mesh, it will be necessary to momentarily energize the motor.

Component Replacement- Lincoln Town Car, MarkVI, Crown Victoria and Grand Marquis

POWER SEAT SWITCH
Removal and Installation
DOOR MOUNTED SWITCH

1. Disconnect the negative battery cable.

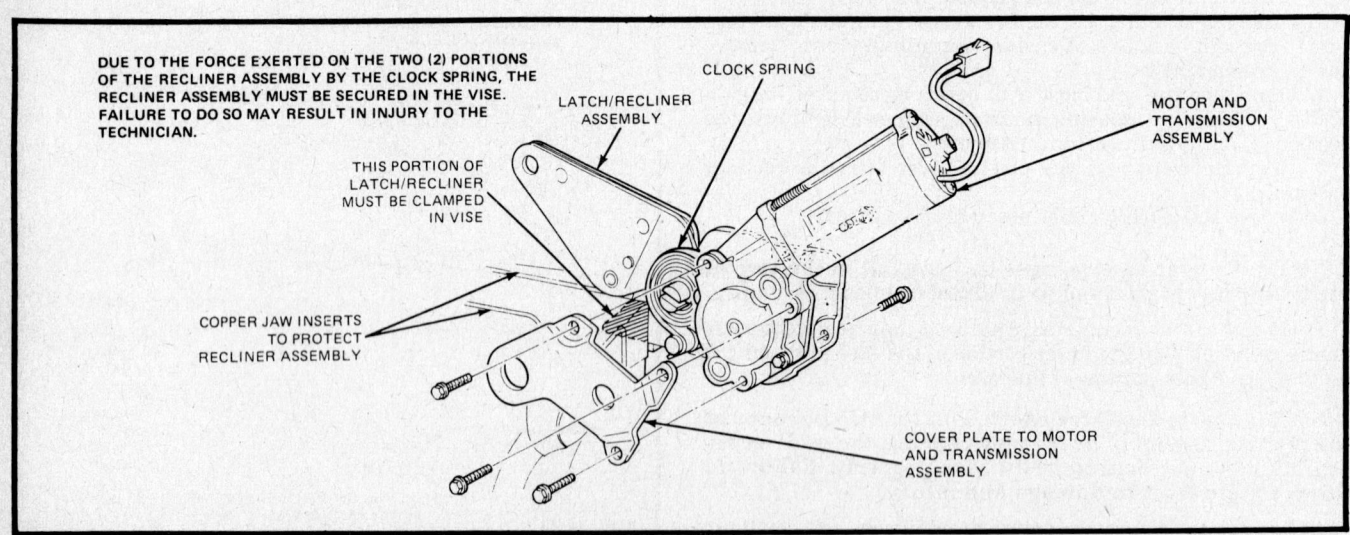

Recliner and motor transmission with related components

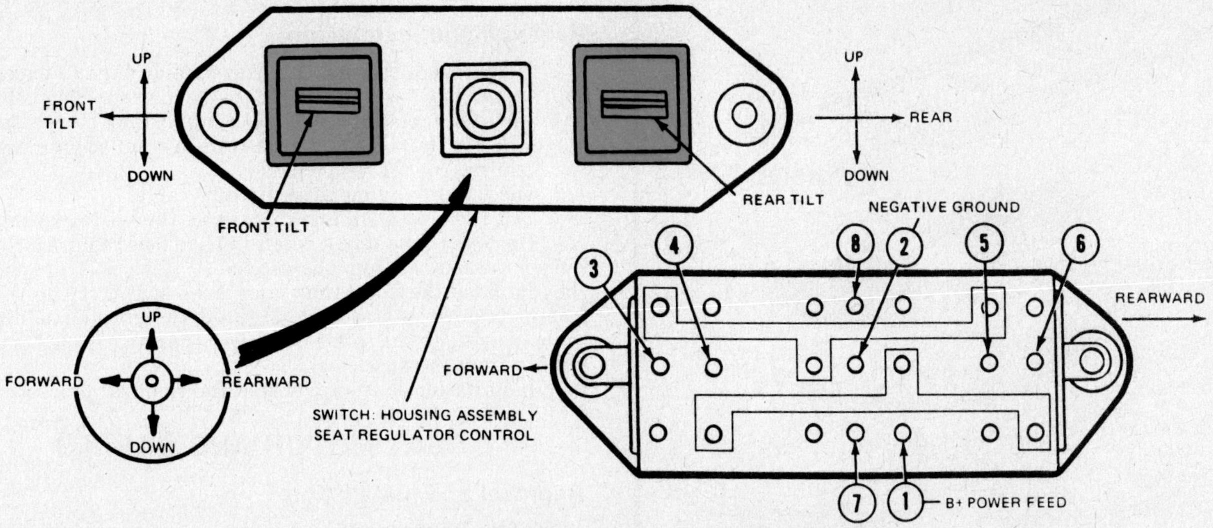

4-WAY KNOB	REAR TILT	FRONT TILT	CONTINUITY
NEUT. (DEAD)	NEUT. (DEAD)	NEUT. (DEAD)	2-3-4-5-6-7-8, 1 ISOLATED
FORWARD	NEUT. (DEAD)	NEUT. (DEAD)	1-7, 2-3-4-5-6-8
REARWARD	NEUT. (DEAD)	NEUT. (DEAD)	1-8, 2-3-4-5-6-7
UP	NEUT. (DEAD)	NEUT. (DEAD)	1-4-6, 2-3-5-7-8
DOWN	NEUT. (DEAD)	NEUT. (DEAD)	1-3-5, 2-4-6-7-8
NEUT. (DEAD)	UP	NEUT. (DEAD)	1-6, 2-3-4-5-7-8
NEUT. (DEAD)	DOWN	NEUT. (DEAD)	1-5, 2-3-4-6-7-8
NEUT. (DEAD)	NEUT. (DEAD)	UP	1-4, 2-3-5-6-7-8
NEUT. (DEAD)	NEUT. (DEAD)	DOWN	1-3, 2-4-5-6-7-8

SWITCH POSITION

TEST SWITCH WITH SELF POWERED TEST LIGHT OR OHMMETER WHEN SWITCH IS DISCONNECTED FROM WIRING

Lincoln Town Car, Mark VI, Crown Victoria and Grand Marquis power seat switch test points—seat mounted switch

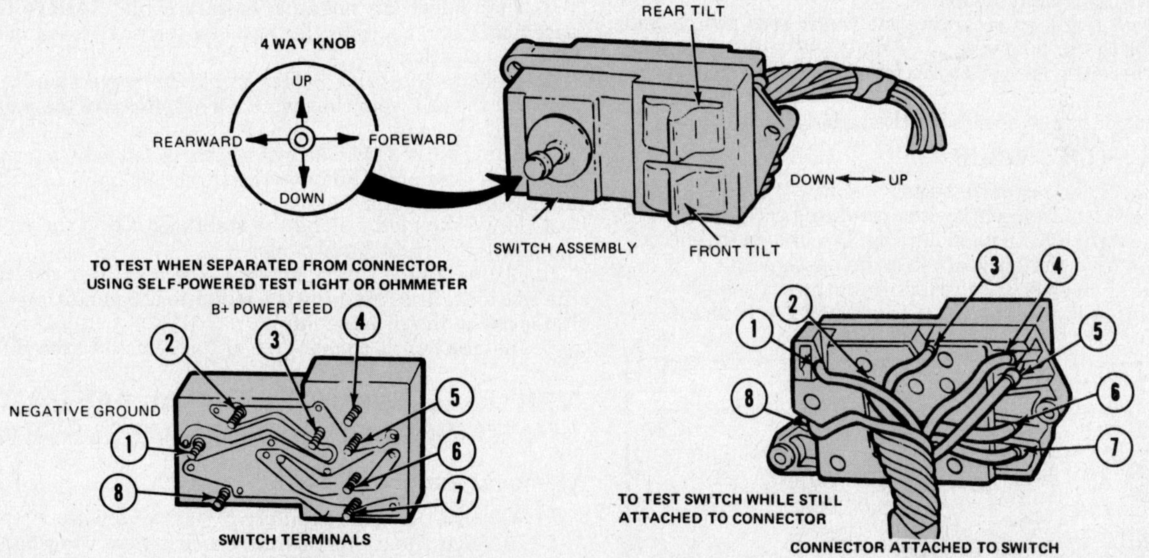

SWITCH TERMINALS

SWITCH POSITIONS

4-WAY KNOB	REAR TILT	FRONT TILT	CONTINUITY
NEUT.	NEUT.	NEUT.	1-2-4-5-6-7-8- (# 3 ISOLATED)
FOREWARD	NEUT.	NEUT.	2-3, 1-4-5-6-7-8
REARWARD	NEUT.	NEUT.	3-8, 1-2-4-5-6-7
UP	NEUT.	NEUT.	3-4-6, 1-2-5-7-8-
DOWN	NEUT.	NEUT.	3-5-7, 1-2-4-6-8
NEUT.	UP	NEUT.	3-6, 1-2-4-5-7-8
NEUT.	DOWN	NEUT.	3-7, 1-2-4-5-6-8
NEUT.	NEUT.	UP	3-4, 1-2-5-6-7-8
NEUT.	NEUT.	DOWN	3-5, 1-2-4-6-7-8

TO TEST WHEN SEPARATED FROM CONNECTOR, USING SELF-POWERED TEST LIGHT OR OHMMETER

CONNECTOR ATTACHED TO SWITCH

SWITCH POSITIONS

4-WAY KNOB	REAR TILT	FRONT TILT	POWER ①	GROUND ①
NEUT.	NEUT.	NEUT.	3 ONLY	1-2-4-5-6-7-8
FOREWARD	NEUT.	NEUT.	2-3	1-4-5-6-7-8
REARWARD	NEUT.	NEUT.	3-8	1-2-4-5-6-7
UP	NEUT.	NEUT.	3-4-6	1-2-5-7-8
DOWN	NEUT.	NEUT.	3-5-7	1-2-4-6-8
NEUT.	UP	NEUT.	3-6	1-2-4-5-7-8
NEUT.	DOWN	NEUT.	3-7	1-2-4-5-6-8
NEUT.	NEUT.	UP	3-4	1-2-5-6-7-8
NEUT.	NEUT.	DOWN	3-5	1-2-4-6-7-8

TO TEST SWITCH WHILE STILL ATTACHED TO CONNECTOR

① TERMINAL NO. 1 IS ALWAYS GROUNDED AND TERMINAL NO. 3 IS ALWAYS HOT.

Lincoln Town Car, Mark VI, Crown Victoria and Grand Marquis power seat switch test points—door mounted switch

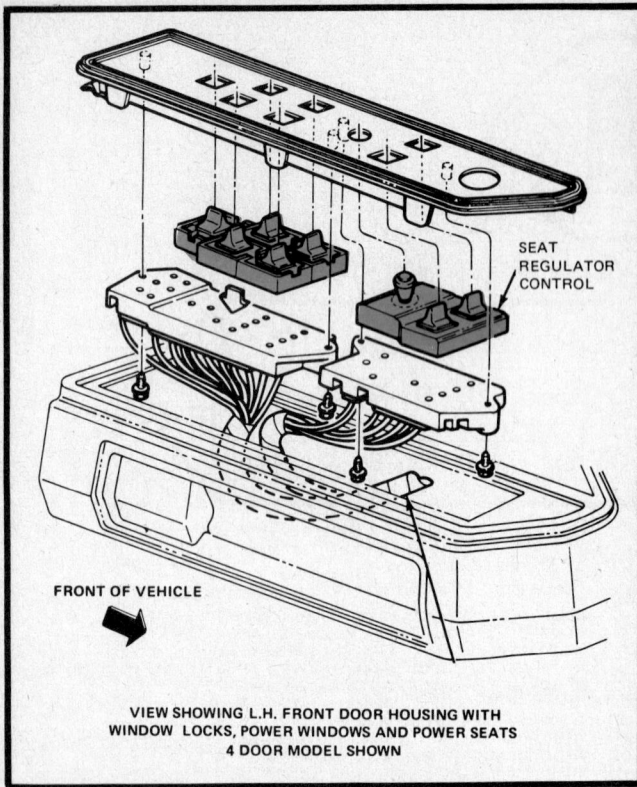

Power seat control—door mounted switch

2. Remove the remote mirror control retaining bezel. Remove the switch housing snaps.

3. Remove the screws retaining the power seat switch and the connector to the housing.

4. Disconnect the switch connector and remove the power seat switch.

5. Installation is the reverse of the removal procedure.

SEAT MOUNTED SWITCH

1. Disconnect the negative battery cable.

2. Remove the power seat switch retaining screws.

3. Pull the switch from its mounting. Disconnect the electrical connector from the back of the switch assembly.

4. Remove the power seat switch from the vehicle.

5. Installation is the reverse of the removal procedure.

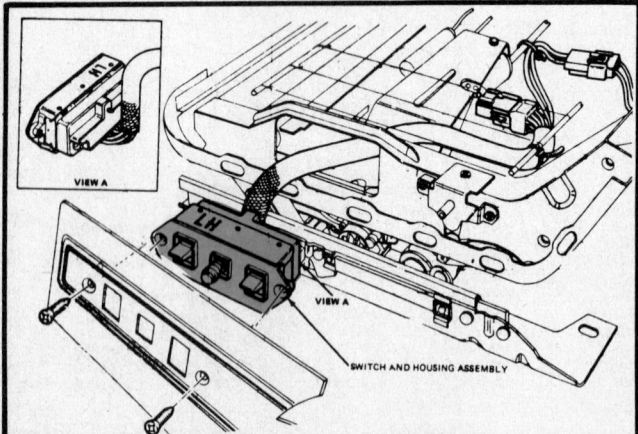

Power seat control—seat mounted switch

SEAT TRACKS

Removal and Installation

1. If equipped, remove the heat shield plugs to expose the seat assembly retaining bolts. Remove the retaining bolts that hold the seat assembly to the floorpan. It may be necessary to move the seat forward and backward in order to gain access to the retaining bolts.

2. Disconnect the negative battery cable.

3. Tilt the seat back and disconnect the wiring harness.

4. Remove the seat belt retaining bolts, as required. Remove the seat assembly from the vehicle.

5. Remove the bolts that attach the seat track to the seat frame. Remove tie straps, as required, that may be holding the cable housing to the seat assembly. Separate the seat track assembly from the seat.

6. Installation is the reverse of the removal procedure.

SEAT MOTOR AND CABLES

Removal and Installation

NOTE: It is recommended that when a cable is to be replaced, the power seat motor should be removed in order to ease the replacement of the defective cable.

RACK AND PINION TYPE

1. Disconnect the negative battery cable.

2. Remove the seat assembly from the vehicle.

3. Remove the motor retaining bolts from the seat mounting.

4. Disconnect the housings and the cables from the motor.

5. Remove the motor assembly from its mounting.

6. Installation is the reverse of the removal procedure.

SCREW DRIVE TYPE

1. Disconnect the negative battery cable. Remove the seat assembly from the vehicle. Remove the seat track assembly from the cushion.

2. Identify the drive cables and their respective locations. Remove the nut from the stabilizer rod. Remove the motor and the bracket screw.

3. Lift the motor and deflect the three left cables toward the left track assembly. Remove the three left hand cable assemblies from the motor.

4. Move the motor along the stabilizer rod to the right, disengaging the right hand cables.

5. Lift and slide the motor off of the stabilizer rod. Remove the two lock nuts retaining the motor to the mounting bracket. Remove the motor assembly.

6. Installation is the reverse of the removal procedure.

VERTICAL AND HORIZONTAL ACTUATORS- RACK AND PINION DRIVE SYSTEM

Removal and Installation

1. Remove the seat assembly from the vehicle.

2. Remove the motor mount bracket mounting bolts from the motor mount bracket to the motor. Disconnect the clamps from the drive input shafts.

3. Manually position the seat track in the full up and mid horizontal position. This is done by inserting the square end of a drive cable into one of the vertical drives and manually turning the drive unit until it is in the full up position. Using the horizontal drive unit, insert the cable drive and manually turn it to the mid horizontal position.

4. Remove the rear clock springs using the proper tools. Remove the roll pins from the pivot pins on the secondary track.

5. Remove the base and carriage from the secondary track by driving the pinion gear through the carriage rack. Remove

the roll pin from the drive side pinion.

6. Remove the bolts and nuts from the primary track and retain the drive assembly to the carriage.

7. Replace the defective drive assembly, as required.

8. Assembly is the reverse of the disassembly procedure.

VERTICAL AND HORIZONTAL ACTUATORS-SCREW DRIVE SYSTEM

Removal and Installation

VERTICAL DRIVE TRANSMISSIONS

1. Disconnect the negative battery cable. Remove the seat assembly from the vehicle. Remove the seat track assembly from the cushion.

2. Remove the power seat motor from the seat track.

3. Remove the seat track stop screw from the underside of the left hand track assembly.

4. Using one of the adjusting cables, insert it into the horizontal transmission and rotate the cable counterclockwise this will cause the lead screw to back out of the nylon drive block.

5. Slide the lower half of the left hand drive assembly rearward far enough to allow the lead screw to be lifted high enough to gain access to the vertical transmission retaining bolts. Remove the bolt.

NOTE: Be careful when separating the upper and lower left hand seat track assembly in order to prevent the loss of the plastic slides.

6. Remove the transmission from the seat assembly.

7. Installation is the reverse of the removal procedure. Do not tighten the transmission retaining bolts more than 22 inch lbs.

8. For proper seat track installation the left horizontal drive screw and the right horizontal drive screw must be synchronized.

UPPER SUPPORT ASSEMBLY

1. Disconnect the negative battery cable. Remove the seat assembly from the vehicle.

2. Remove the seat track from the cushion. When servicing the seat track assembly position it about ¼ inch from the full up seat position.

3. Before removing the clock springs identify them to aid in reinstallation. To prevent injury cover the springs with a cloth before removal.

4. Remove the power seat motor from the seat track.

5. Remove the screw from the vertical transmission bracket. Remove the four retaining clips.

6. Slide the right hand track assembly off of the upper slide support assembly, then rotate the right hand track assembly to allow the disengagement of the stabilizer rod.

7. Remove the E-ring and the clevis pin used to retain the vertical transmission drive nuts to the upper support assembly.

8. Slide the left hand track assembly off of the upper support assembly. Remove the upper support assembly.

9. Installation is the reverse of the removal procedure.

ASSIST SPRINGS

1. Disconnect the negative battery cable. Remove the seat assembly from the vehicle. Remove the seat track assembly from the cushion.

2. With the seat track assembly clamped firmly to the work station, position the clock spring to the seat track assembly. Use a pair of channel locks to clamp the spring to the seat track assembly.

3. Position a cloth over the springs before removal. With the aid of an assistant and using a pair of vise grips clamp the end of the clock spring. Rotate the spring end clockwise and position the spring end in the retaining notch in the seat track.

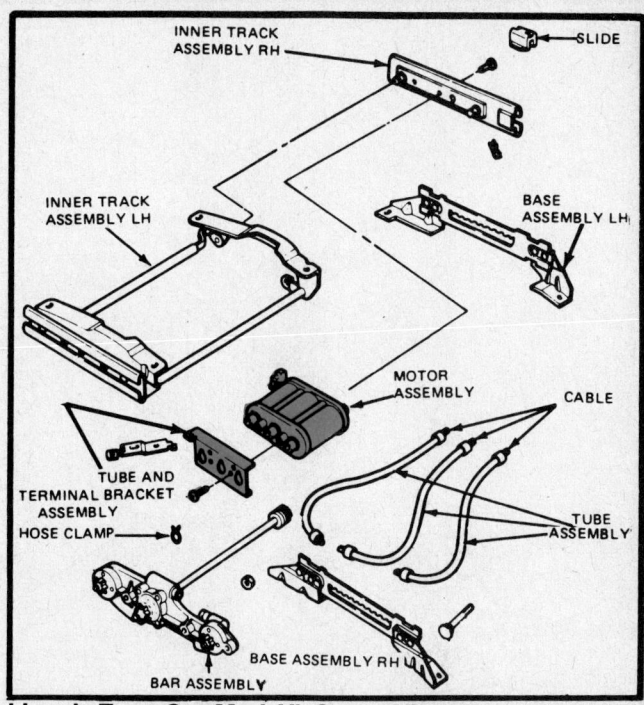

Lincoln Town Car, Mark VI, Crown Victoria and Grand Marquis power seat assembly—rack and pinion system

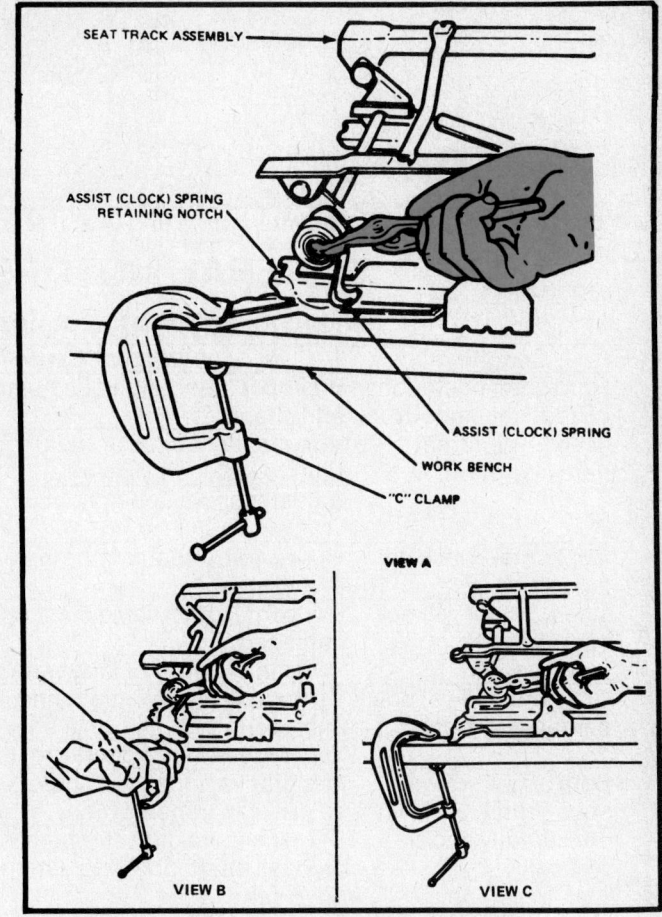

Screw drive system—spring assist removal

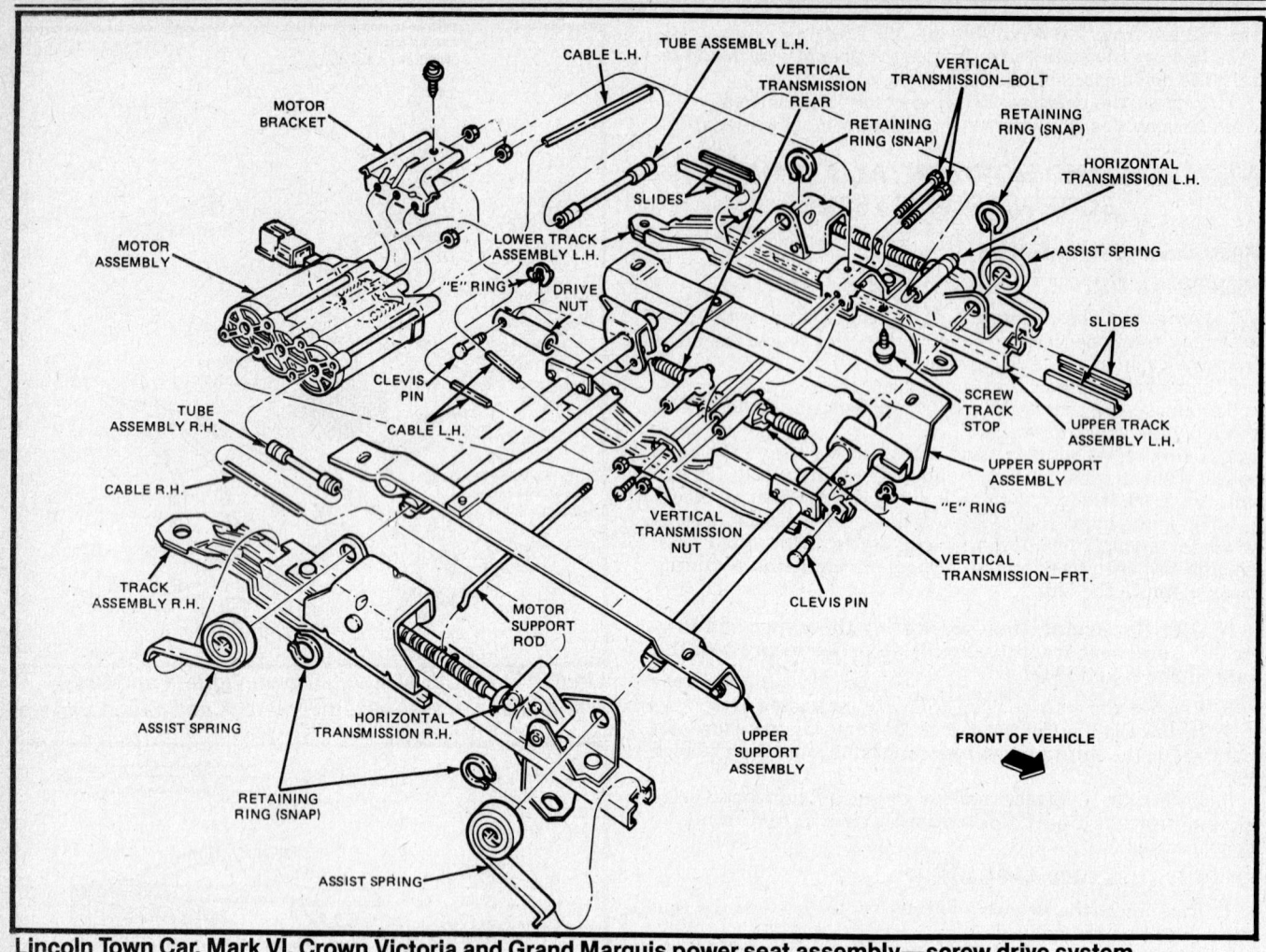

Lincoln Town Car, Mark VI, Crown Victoria and Grand Marquis power seat assembly—screw drive system

GENERAL MOTORS CORPORATION

GENERAL MOTORS—POWER SEAT DIAGNOSTIC CHART

Condition	Apparent Cause	Correction
Horizontal operation of seat not smooth (jerky)—apparent hard operation.	Improper lubrication of adjuster shoes and channels.	Lubricate adjuster upper channel and plastic shoes.
	Adjuster horizontal actuator gear too tight to rack gear.	Adjust horizontal actuator.
	Adjuster shoes too tight in upper channel.	Install new shoes on adjuster lower channel.
Horizontal chuck or looseness	Horizontal actuator improperly adjusted to rack gear.	Adjust horizontal actuator.
One adjuster will not operate horizontally.	Horizontal drive cable disconnected or damaged.	Check horizontal drive cables, replace if damaged.
	Horizontal actuator inoperative	Replace horizontal actuator assembly.
One adjuster will not operate vertically.	Vertical drive cable disconnected or damaged.	Check vertical drive cables, replace if damaged.
	Vertical gearnut inoperative.	Replace vertical actuator assembly.
Both adjusters will not operate horizontally and/or vertically.	Inoperative horizontal and/or vertical solenoid in transmission.	Replace damaged, broken or inoperable solenoid part with new part.
	Damaged, broken or inoperable solenoid plunger, shaft, dog, dog spring, gear or drive gear.	
Vertical chuck or looseness	Excessive clearance at vertical gearnut tension spring.	Grind down top of vertical gearnut shoulder nut 0.40 to 1.19mm (1/64 to 3/64 in.) max.

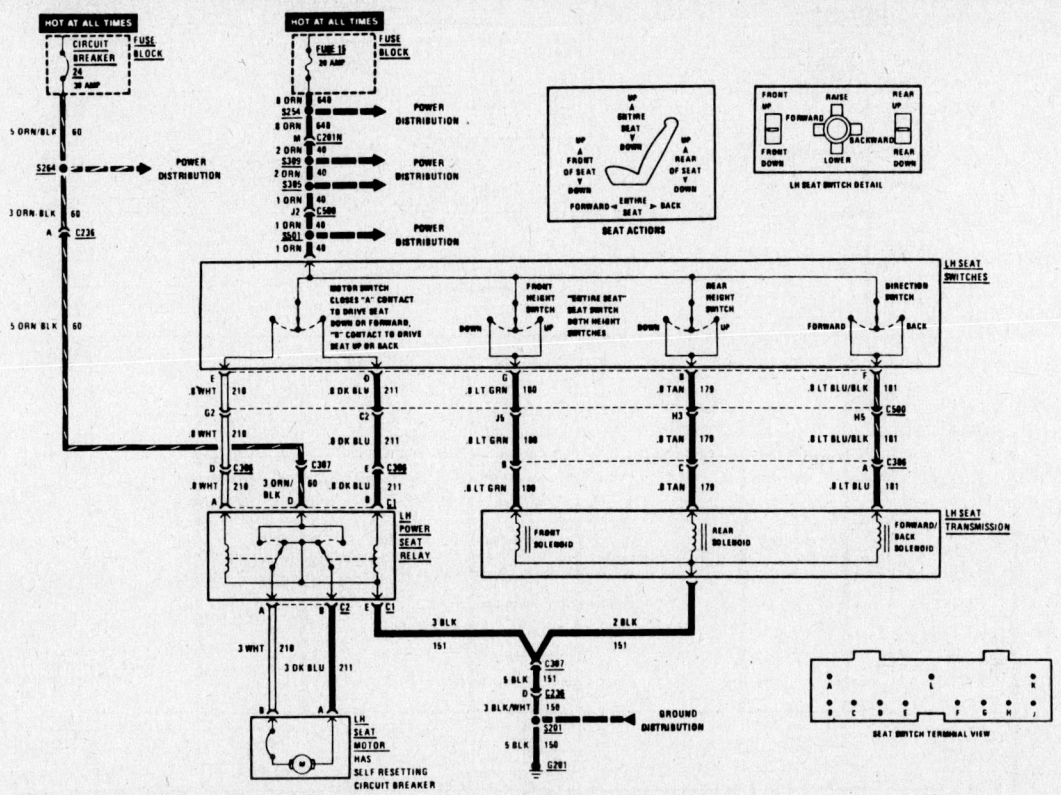

1985 and later Electra, Regency and DeVille—typical power seat system—left side (type one)

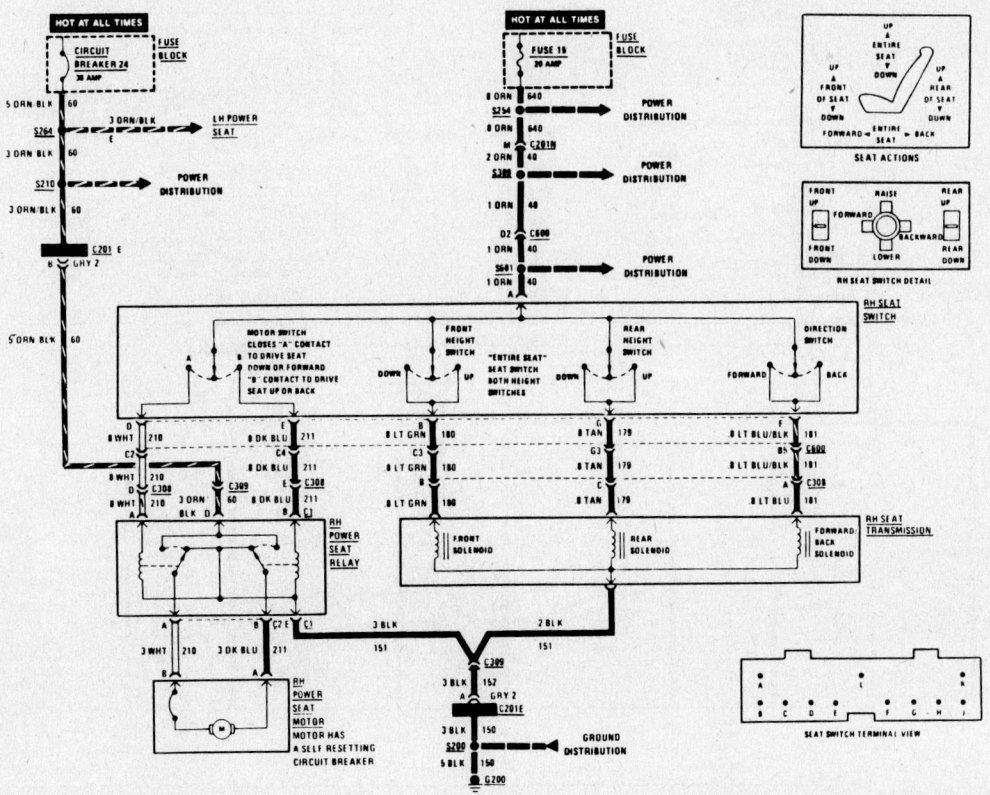

1985 and later Electra, Regency and DeVille—typical power seat system—right side (type one)

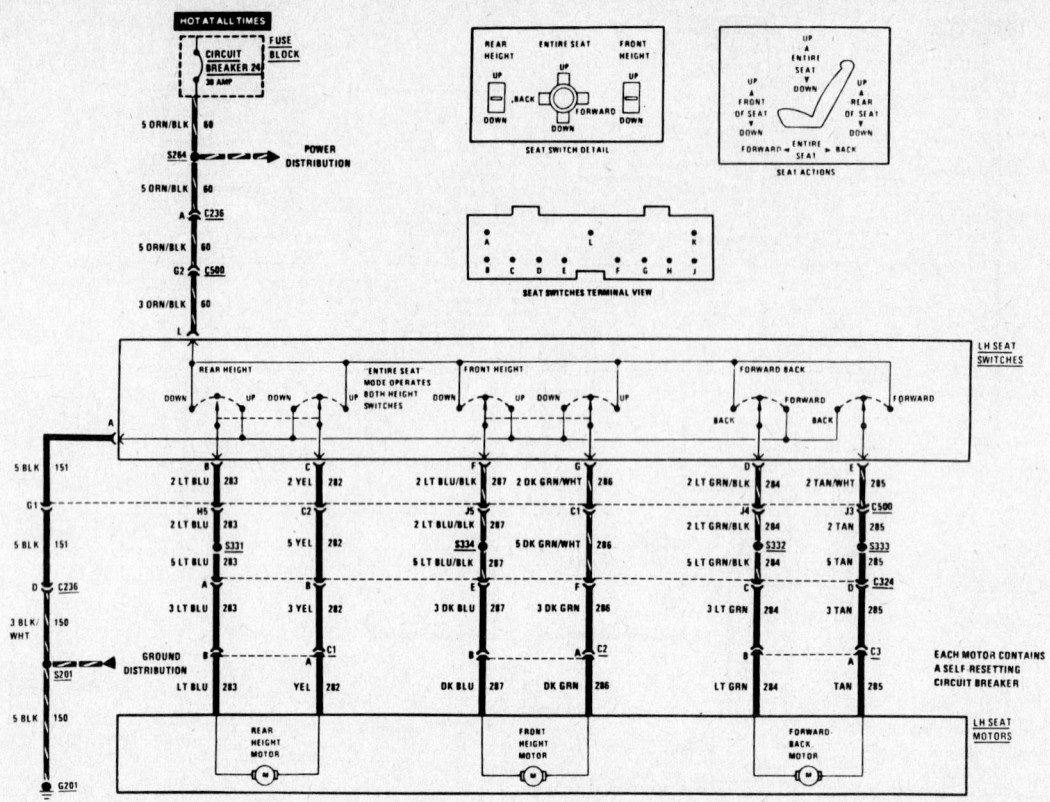

1985 and later Electra, Regency and DeVille—typical power seat system—left side (type two)

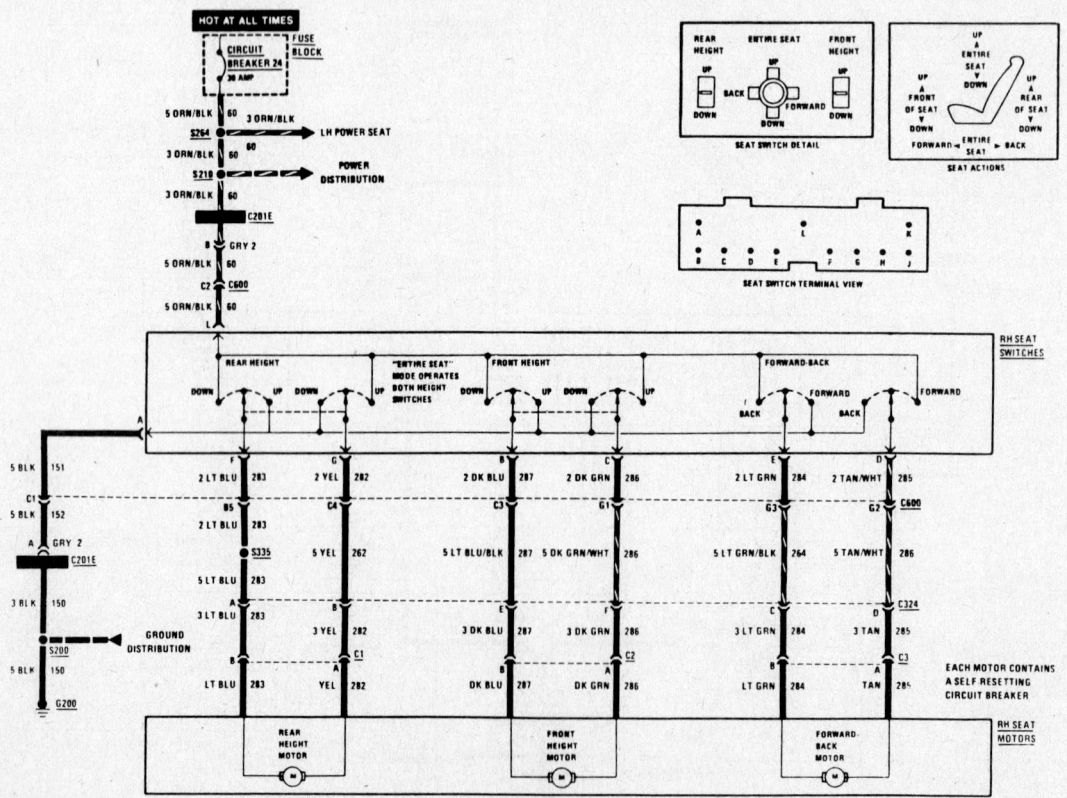

1985 and later Electra, Regency and DeVille—typical power seat system—right side (type two)

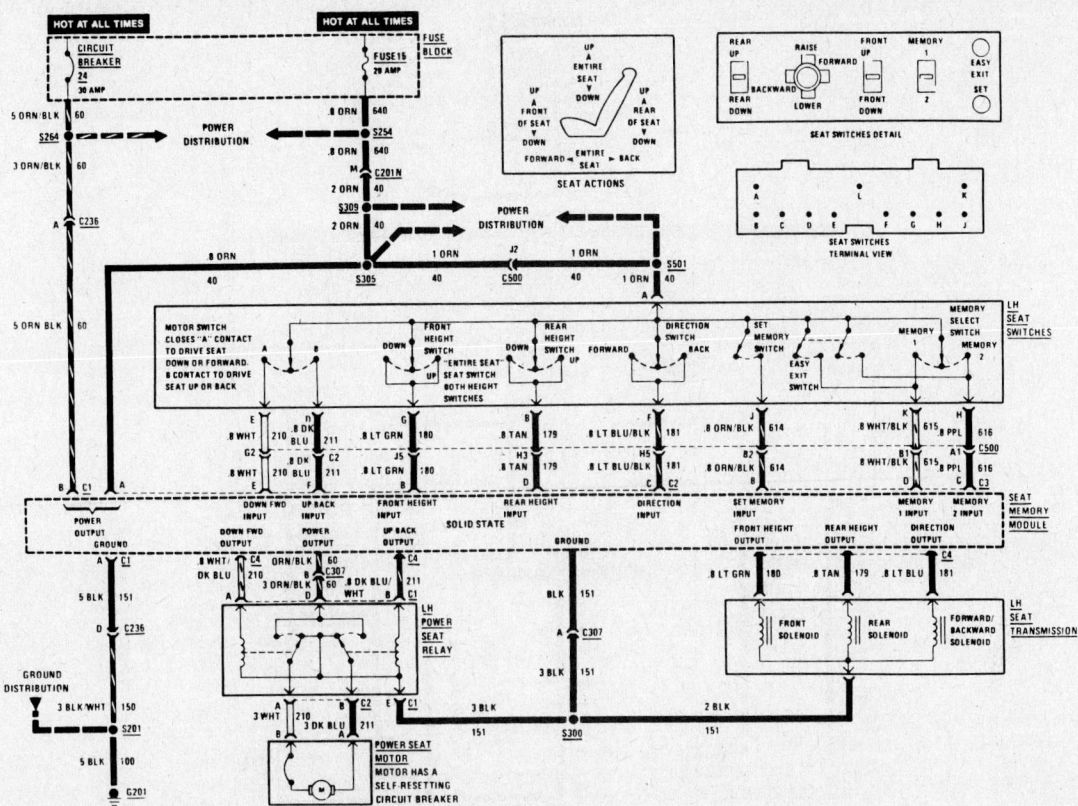

1985 and later Electra, Regency and DeVille—typical memory seat system—seat wiring schematic

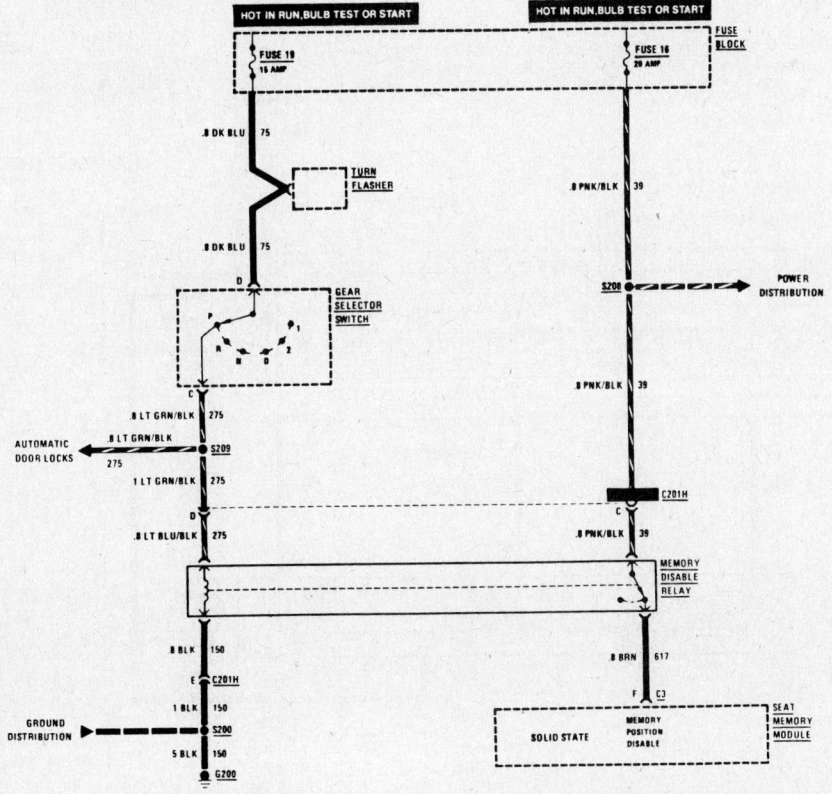

1985 and later Electra, Regency and DeVille—typical memory seat system—wiring schematic

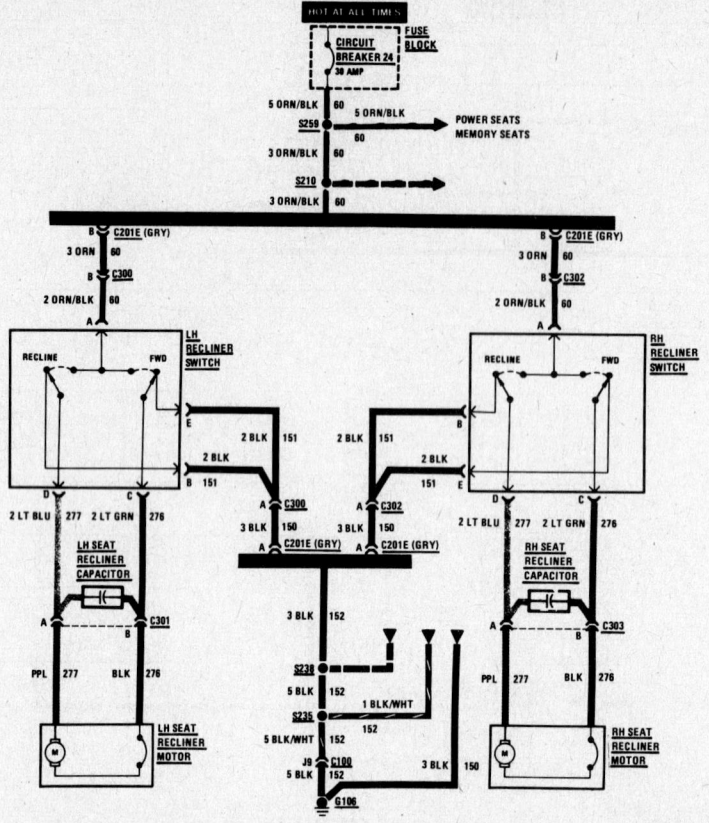

1985 and later Electra, Regency and DeVille—typical power seat recliner system

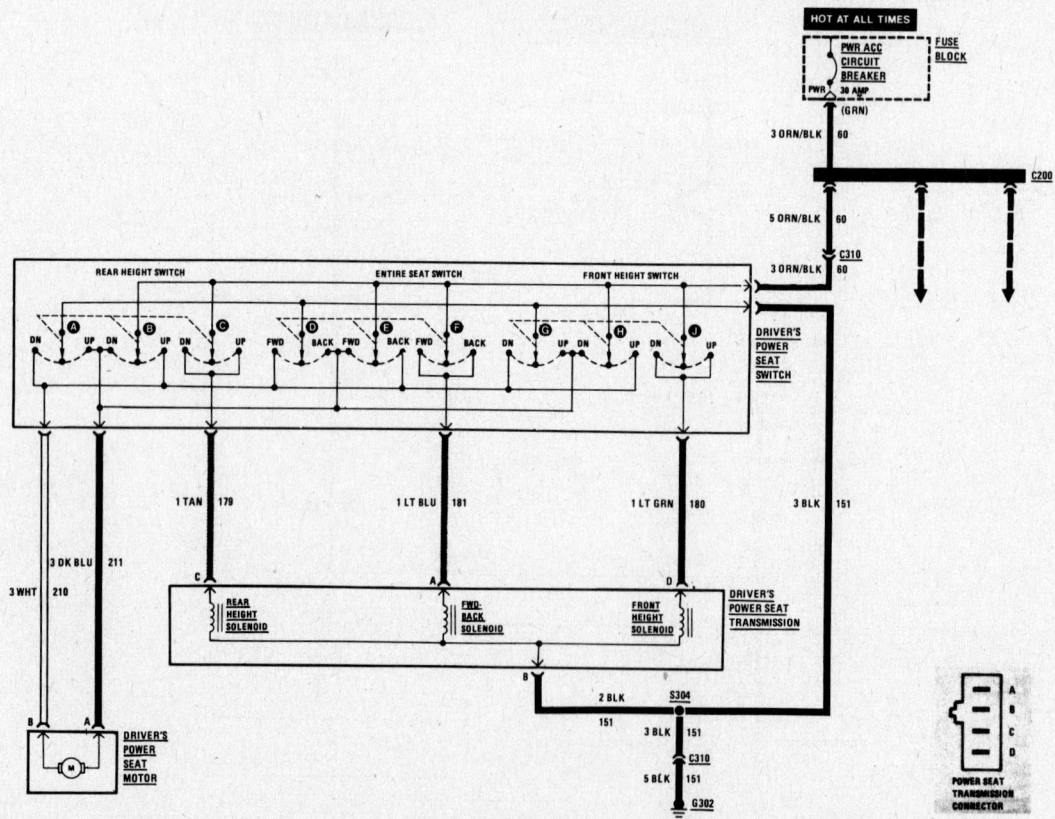

Skylark ('82-'85), Citation, Phoenix and Omega—typical power seat system

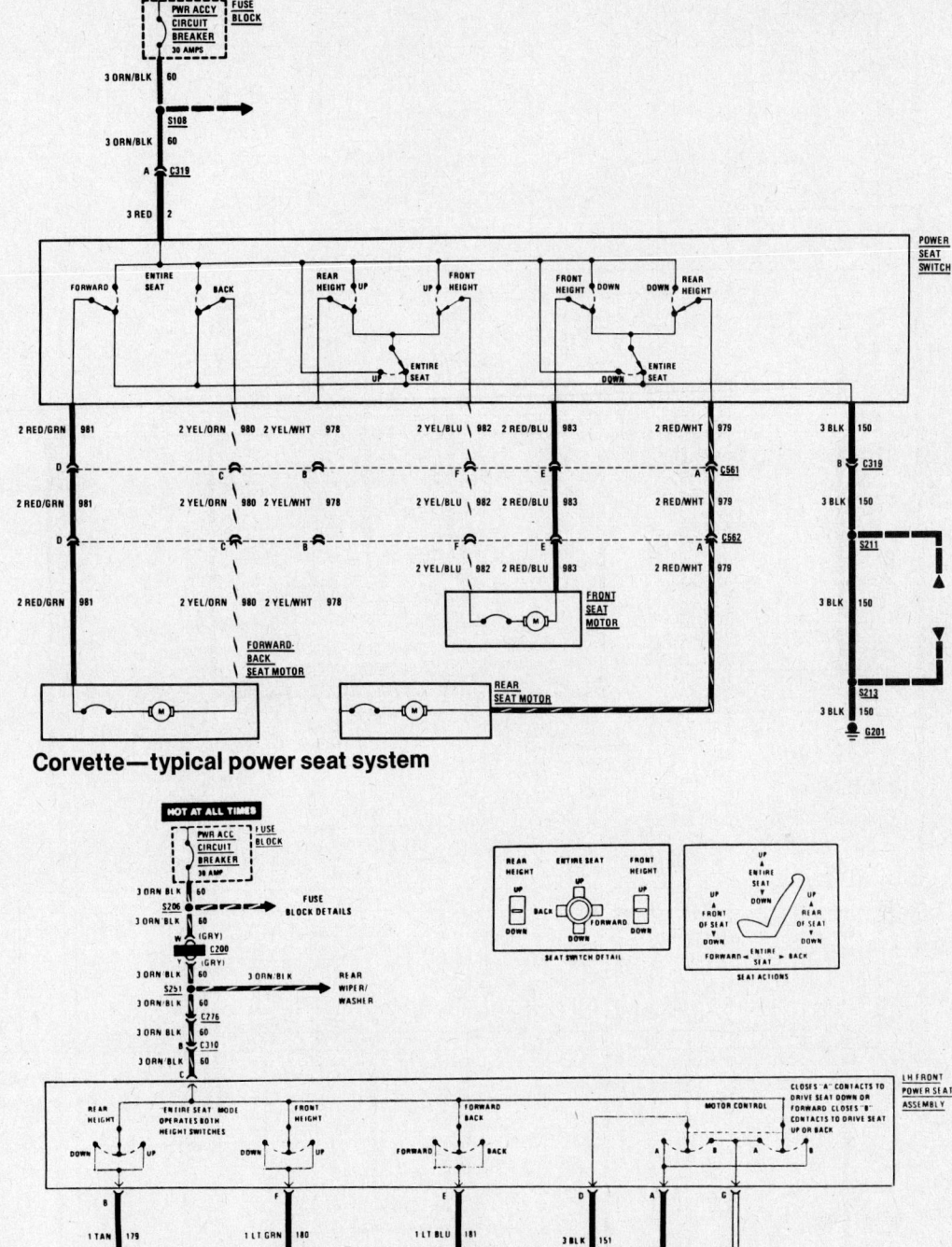

Corvette—typical power seat system

Celebrity, Ciera, Century and 6000—typical power seat system (type one)

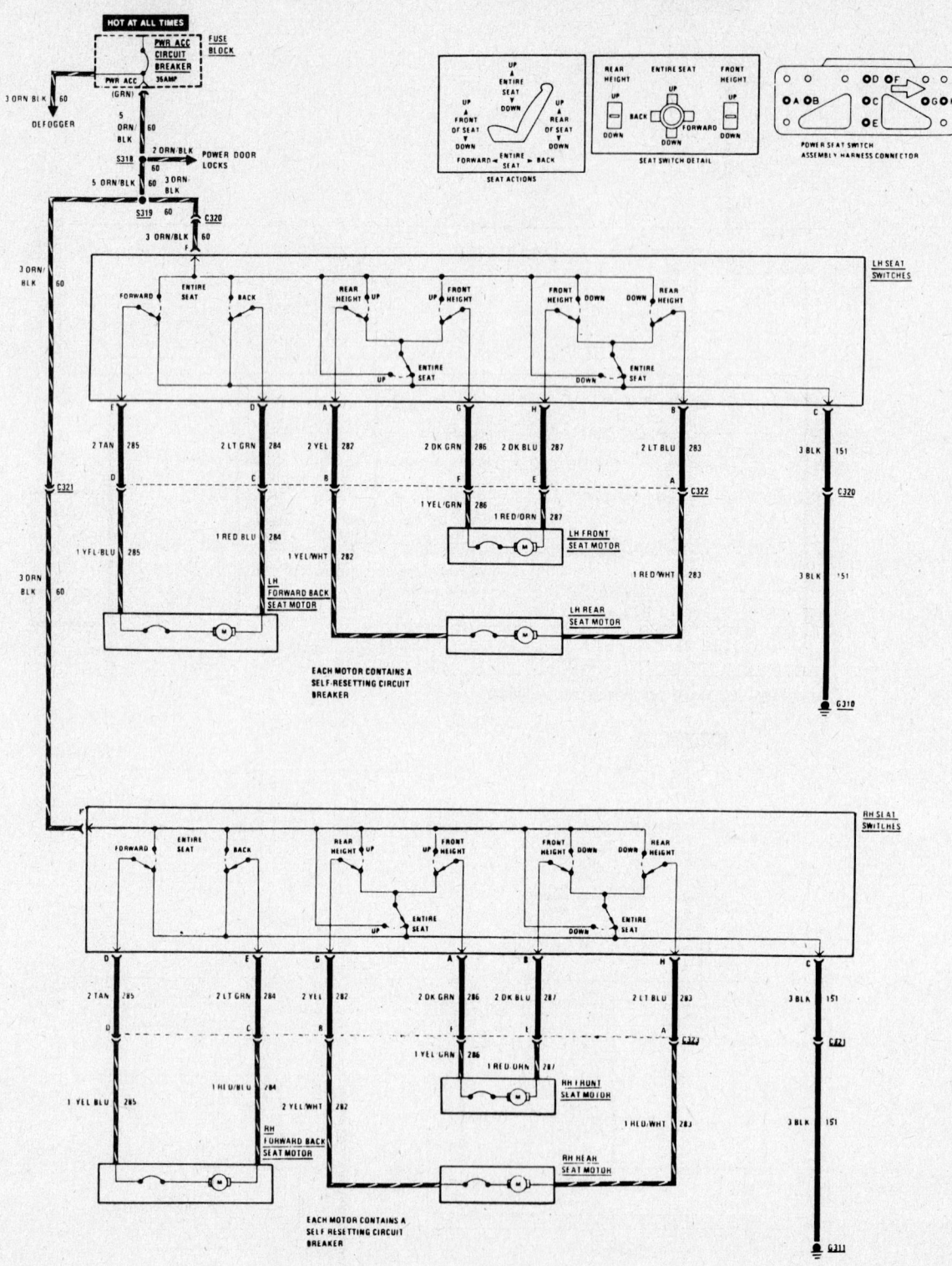

Cavalier, Firenza, Skyhawk, 2000/Sunbird and Cimarron—typical power seat system

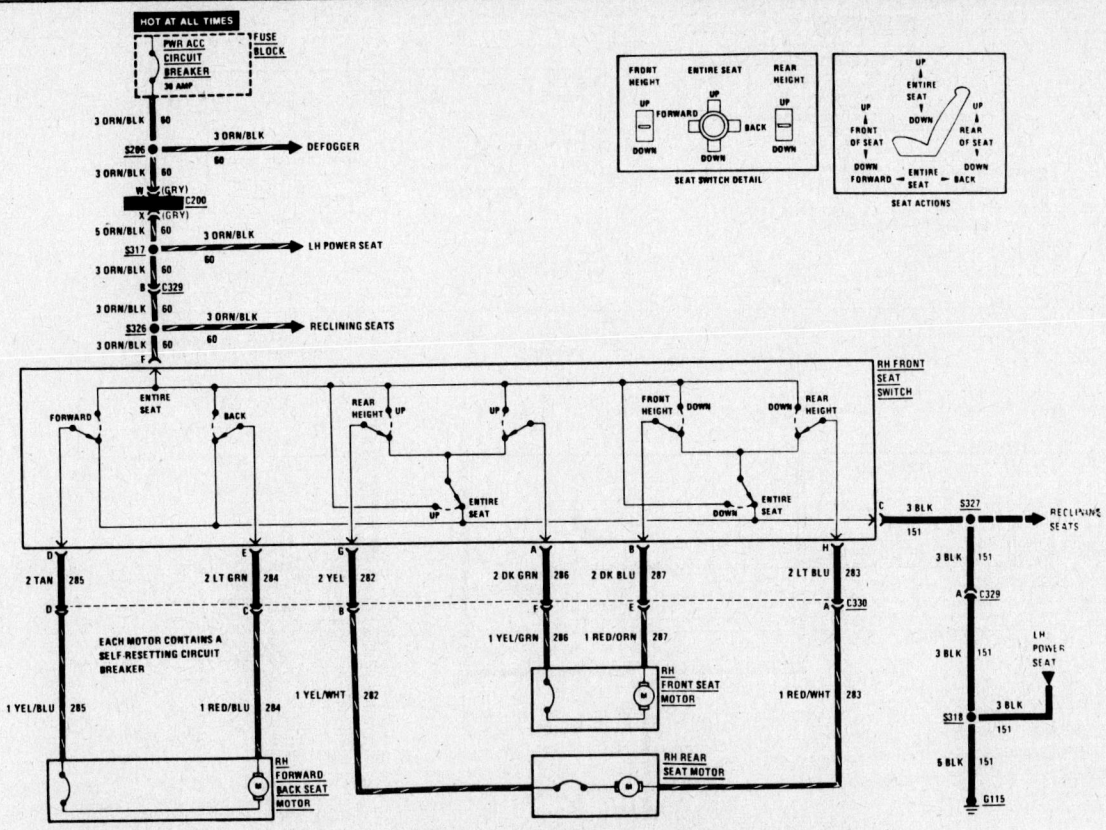

Celebrity, Ciera, Century and 6000—typical power seat system (type two)

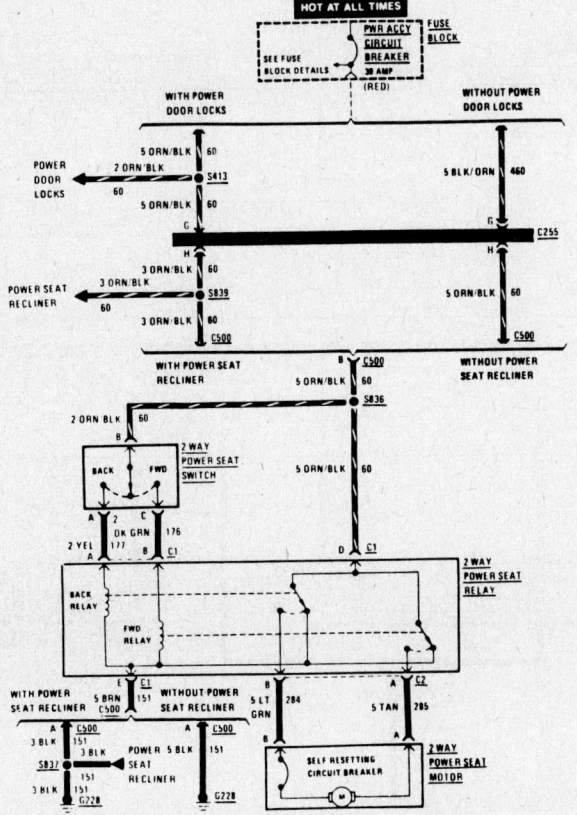

Custom Cruiser, Estate Wagon, Safari Wagon and Caprice Classic—typical power seat system (two way seat)

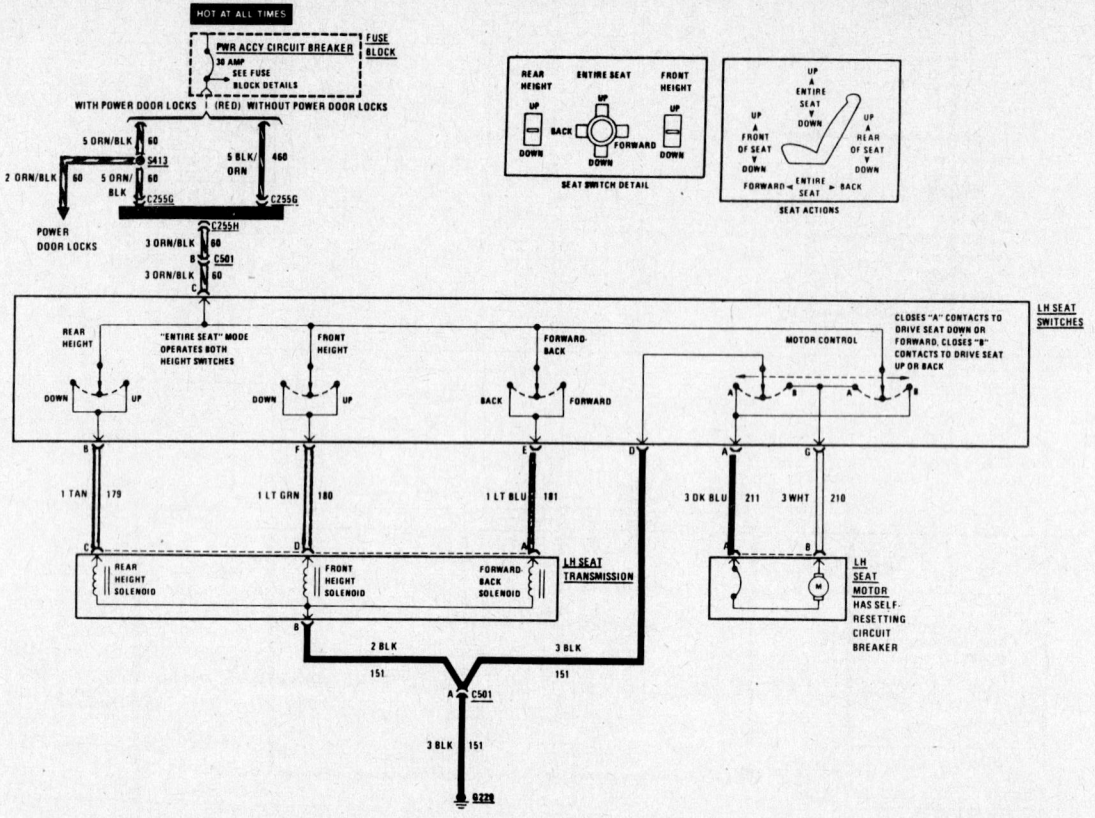

Custom Cruiser, Estate Wagon, Safari Wagon and Caprice Classic—typical power seat system—left side (six way seat)

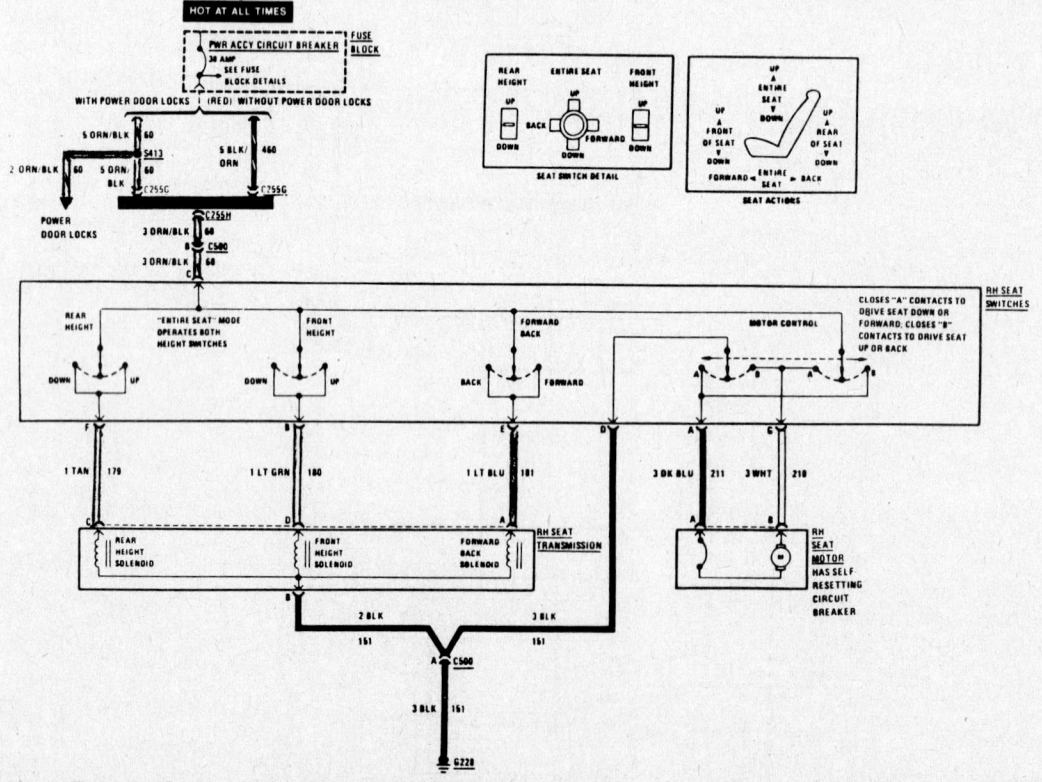

Custom Cruiser, Estate Wagon, Safari Wagon and Caprice Classic—typical power seat system—right side (six way seat)

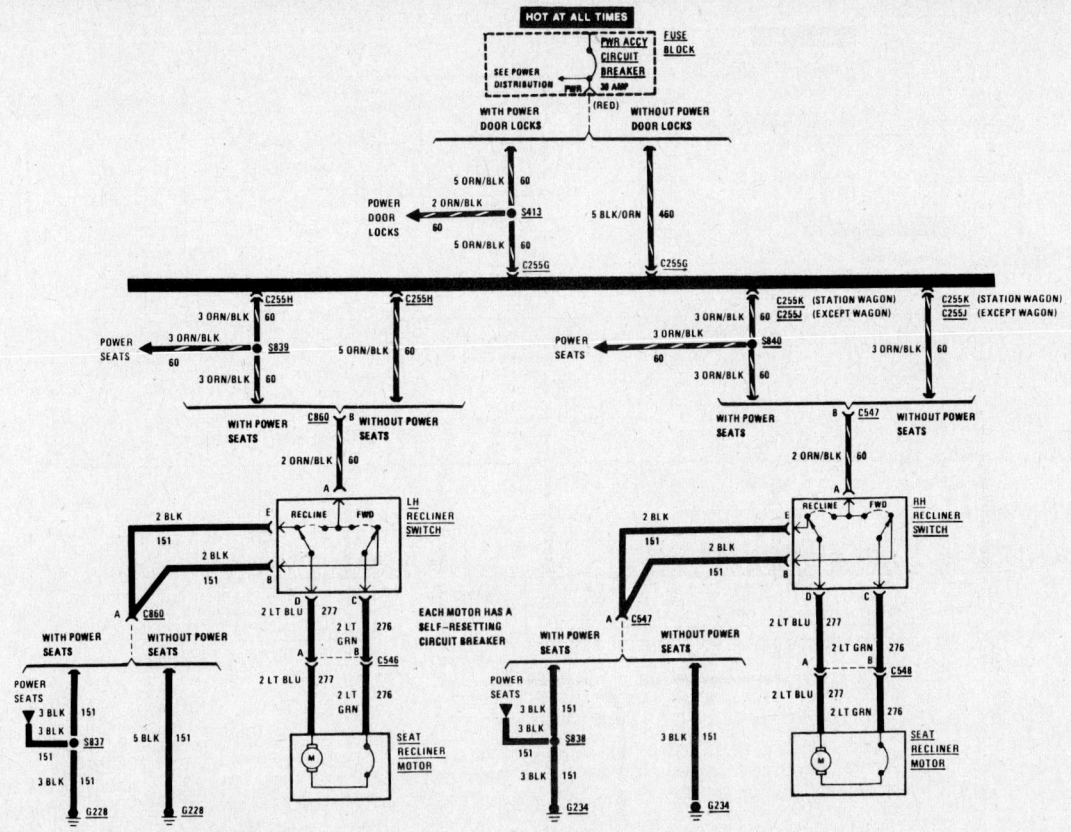

Custom Cruiser, Estate Wagon, Safari Wagon and Caprice Classic—typical power recliner system

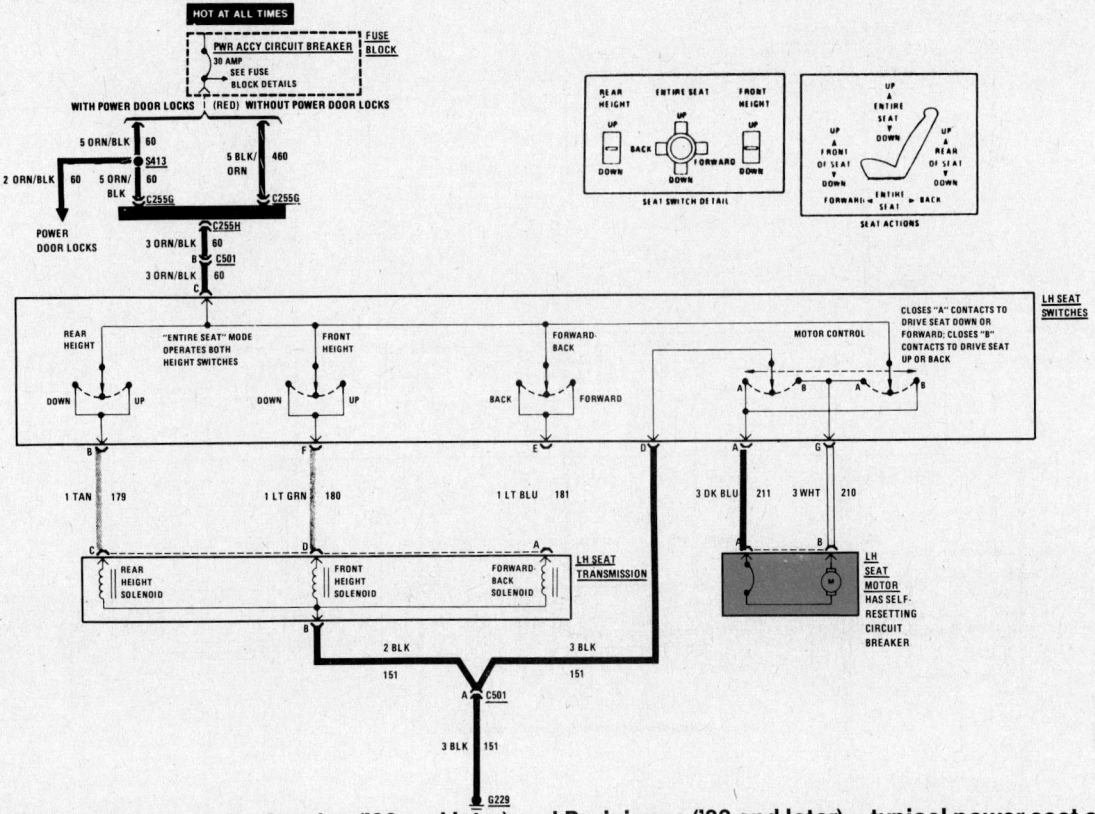

1982-85 LeSabre, Delta, Impala, Caprice ('82 and later) and Parisienne ('83 and later)—typical power seat system—left side

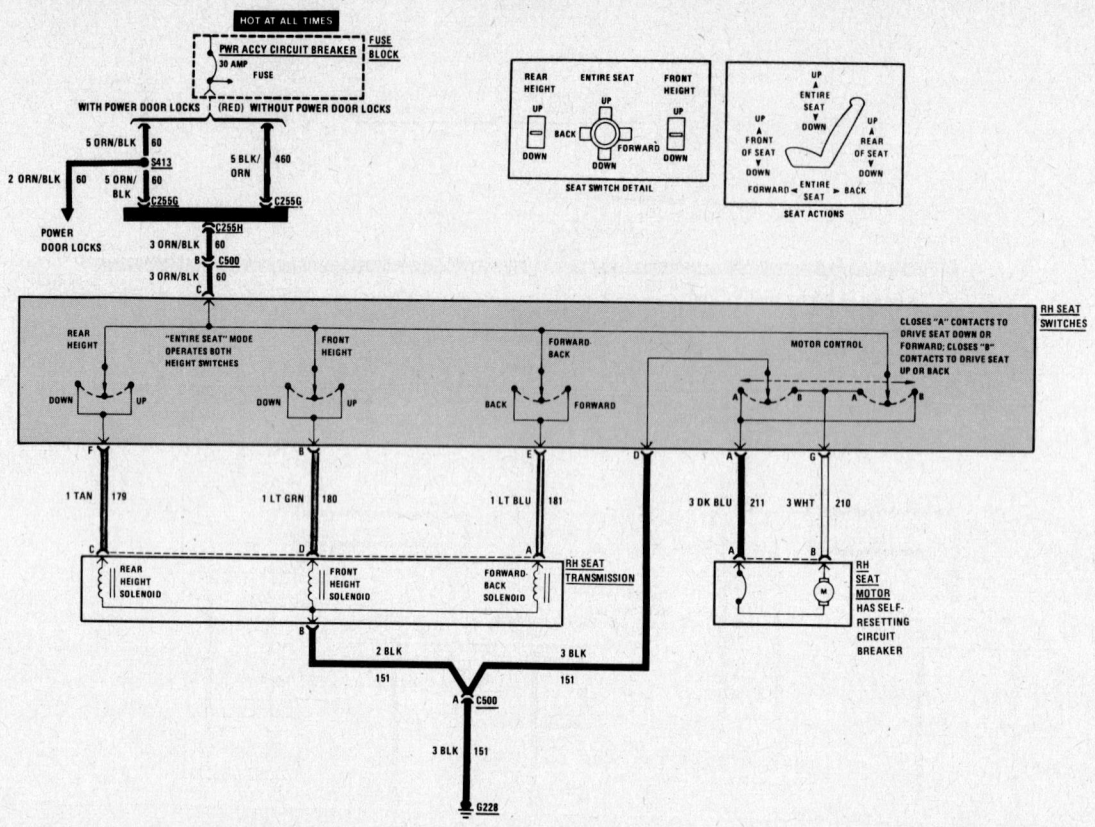

1982–85 LeSabre, Delta, Impala, Caprice ('82 and later) and Parisienne ('83 and later)—typical power seat system—right side

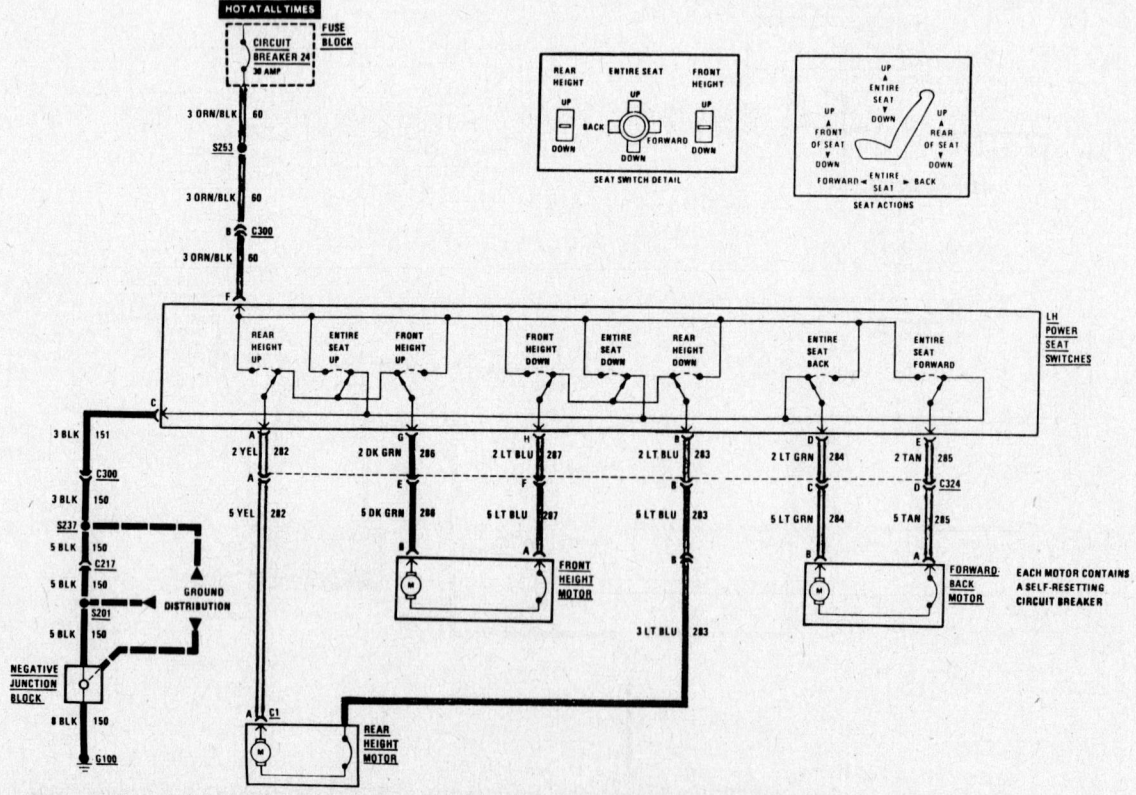

1986 and later Delta and LeSabre—typical power seat system—left side

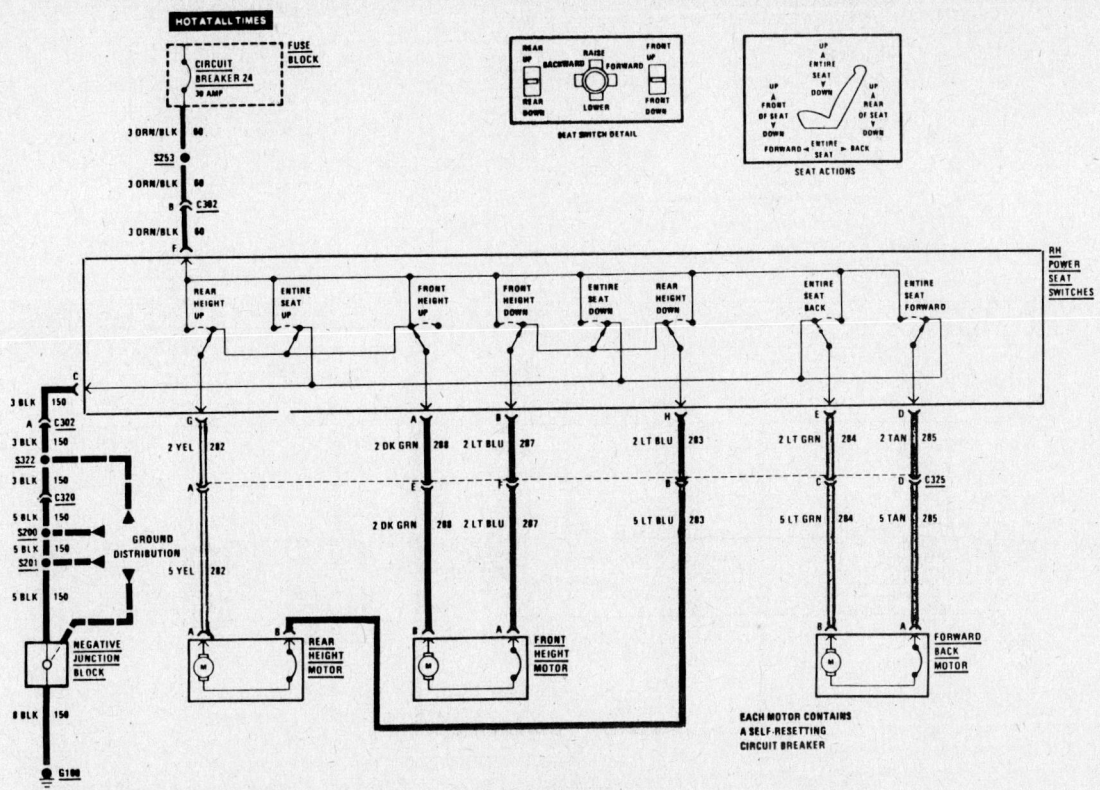

1986 and later Delta and LeSabre—typical power seat system—right side

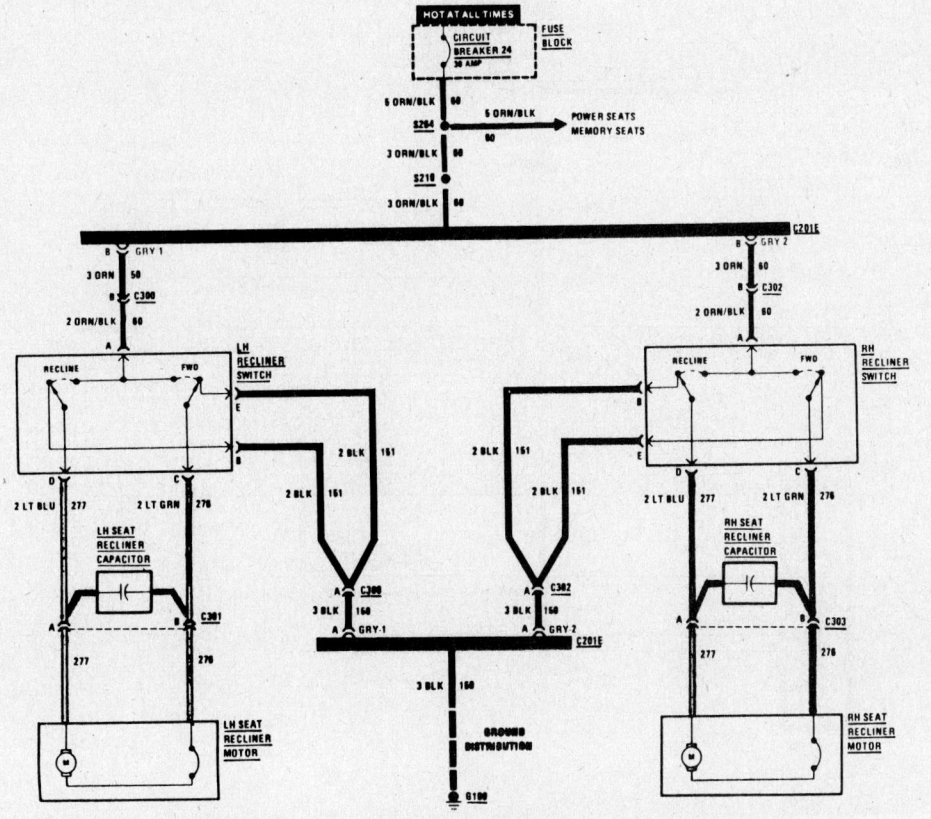

1986 and later Delta and LeSabre—typical power recliner system

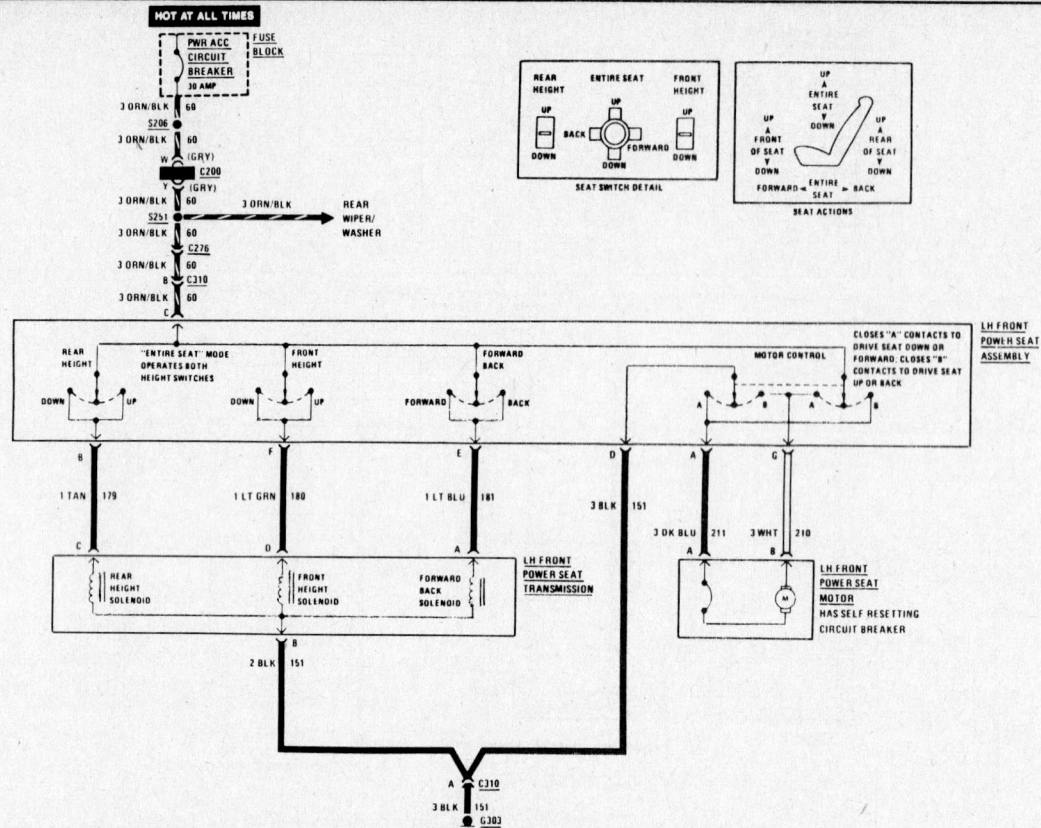

Somerset, Skylark ('86 and later), Calis and Grand AM—typical power seat system

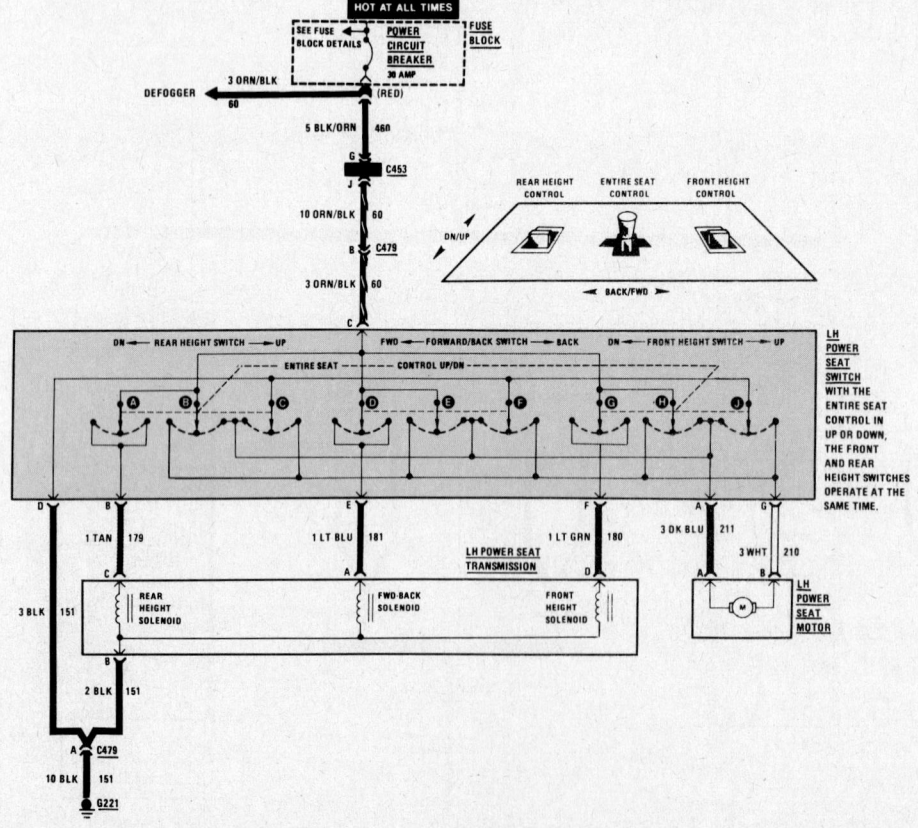

Monte Carlo, Malibu, Cutlass, Regal and Bonneville—typical power seat system

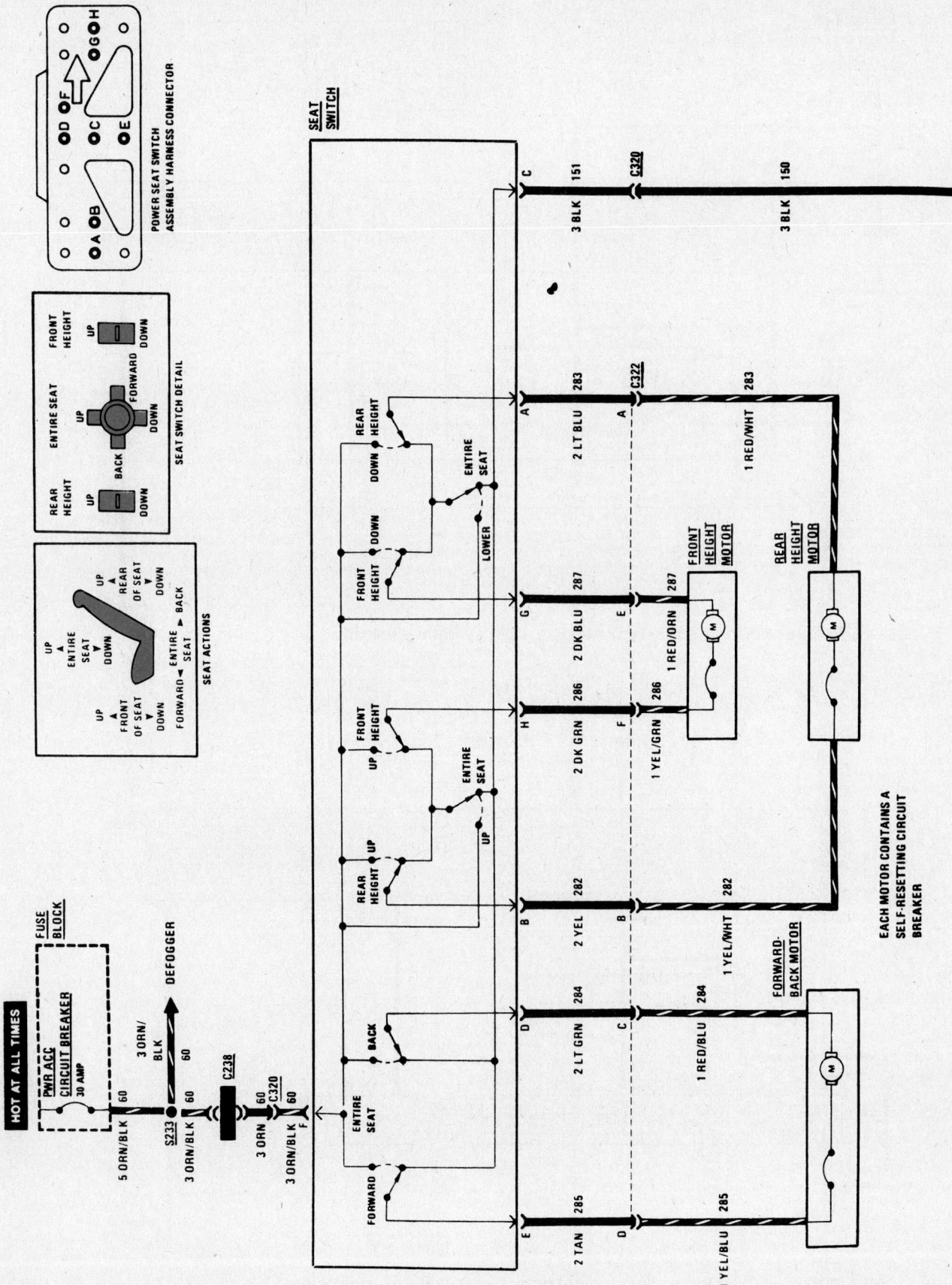

Camaro and Firebird—typical power seat system

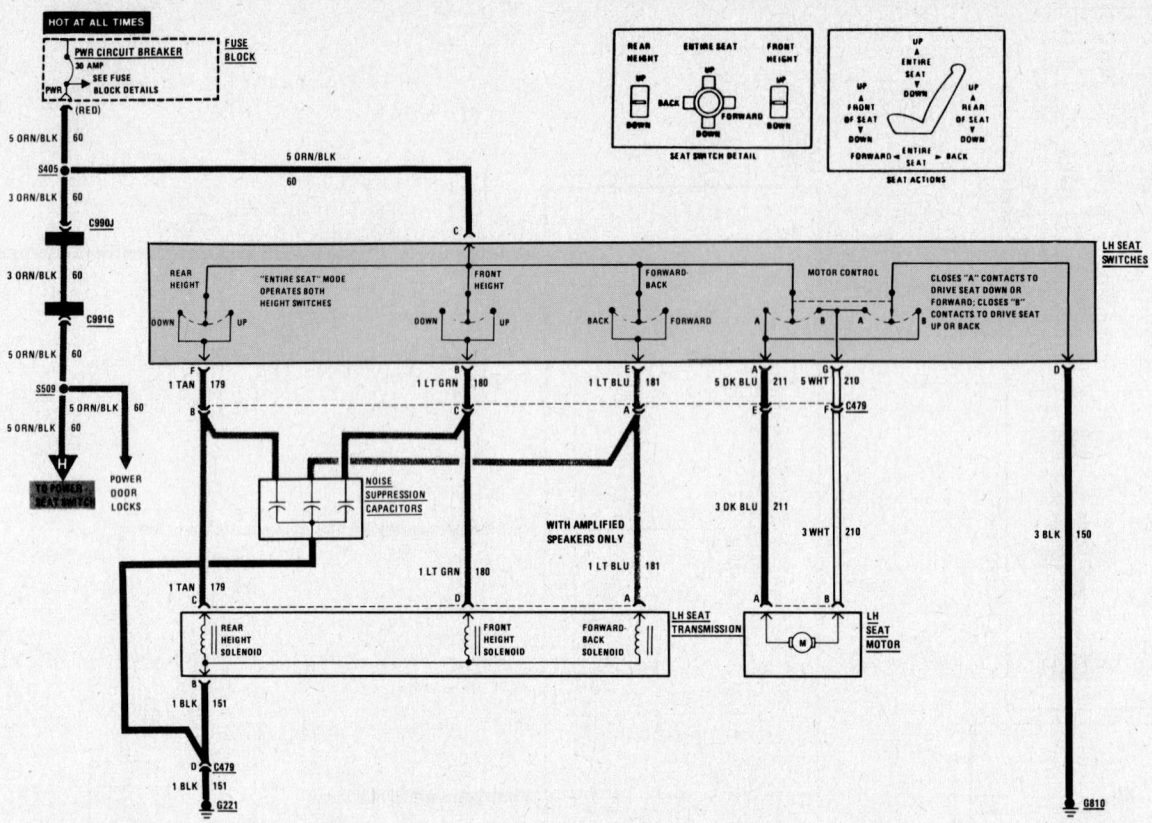

1982–85 Riviera and Toronado—typical power seat system—left side

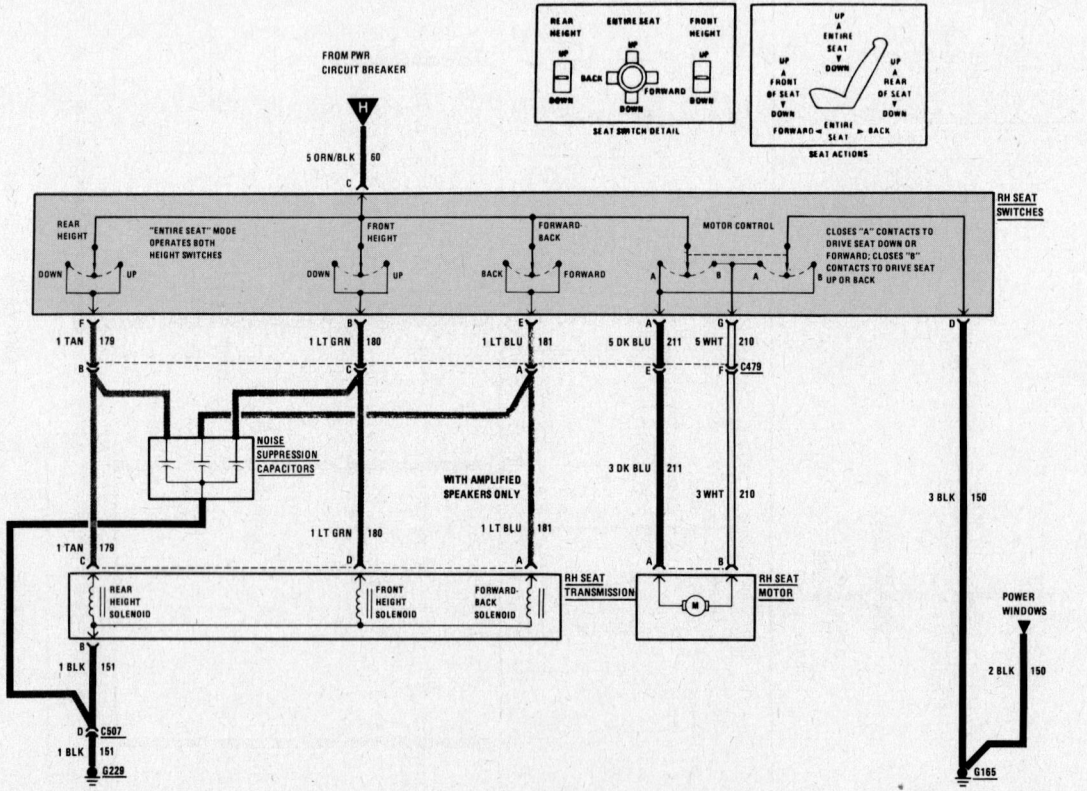

1982–85 Riviera and Toronado—typical power seat system—right side

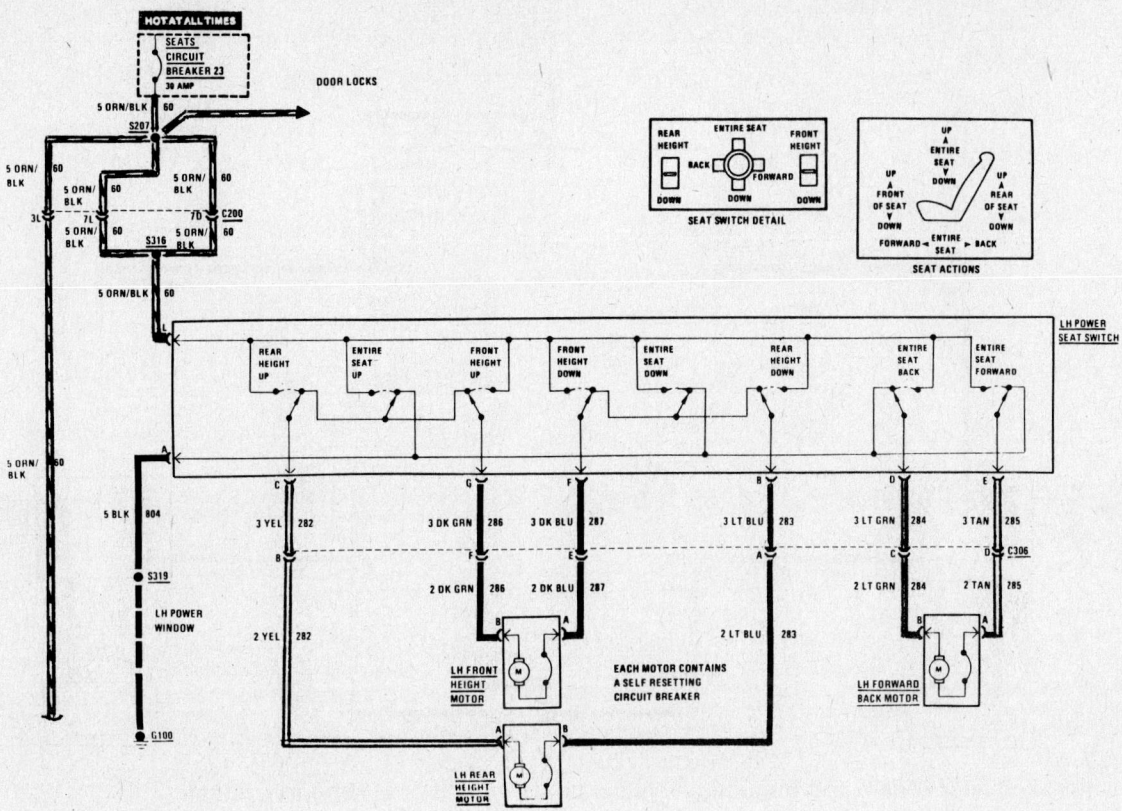

1986 and later Riviera and Toronado—typical power seat system—left side

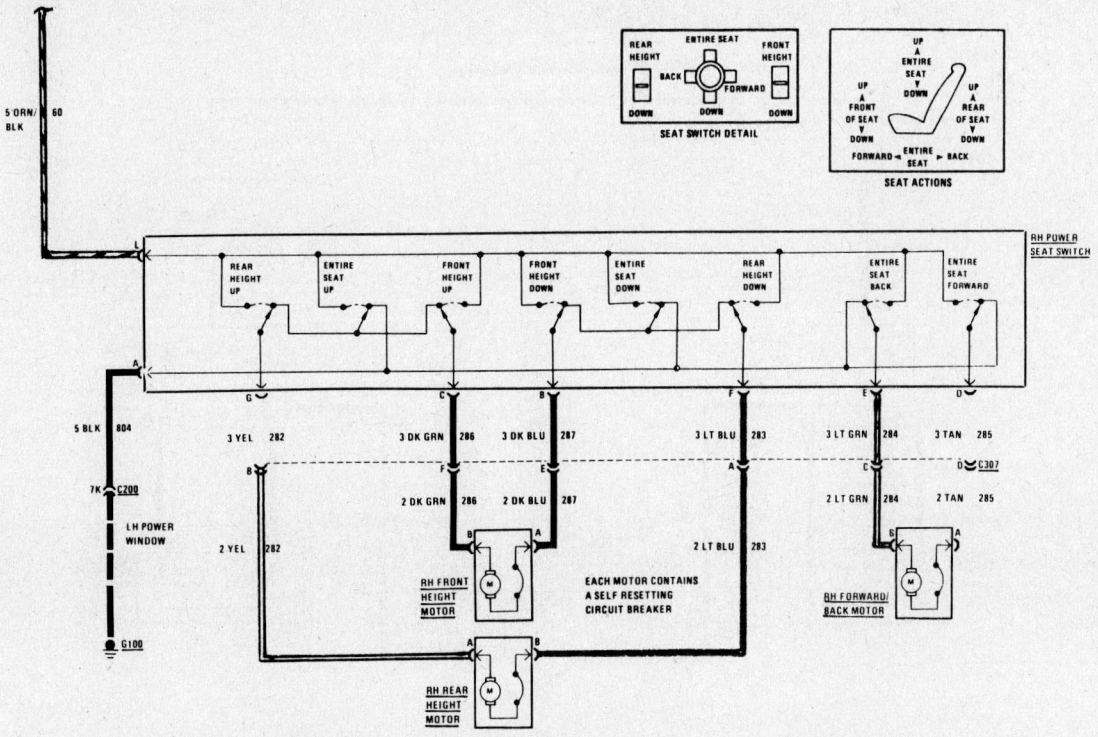

1986 and later Riviera and Toronado—typical power seat system—right side

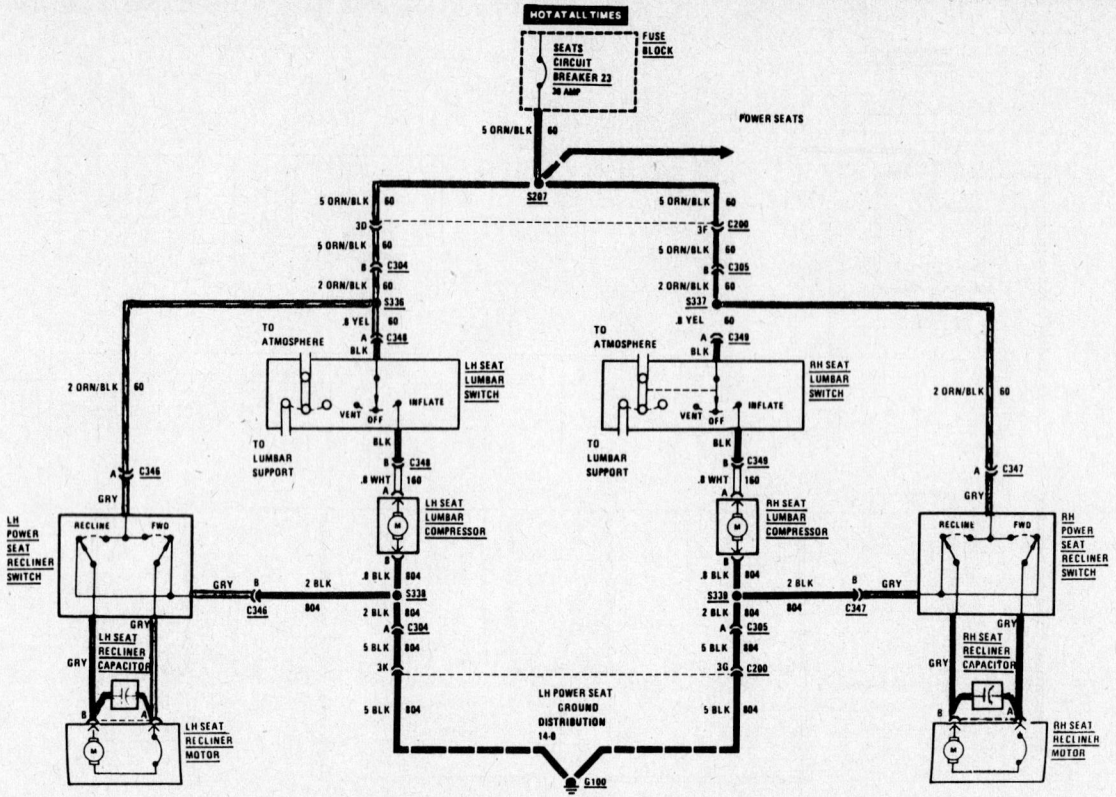

1986 and later Riviera and Toronado—typical power seat lumbar support system

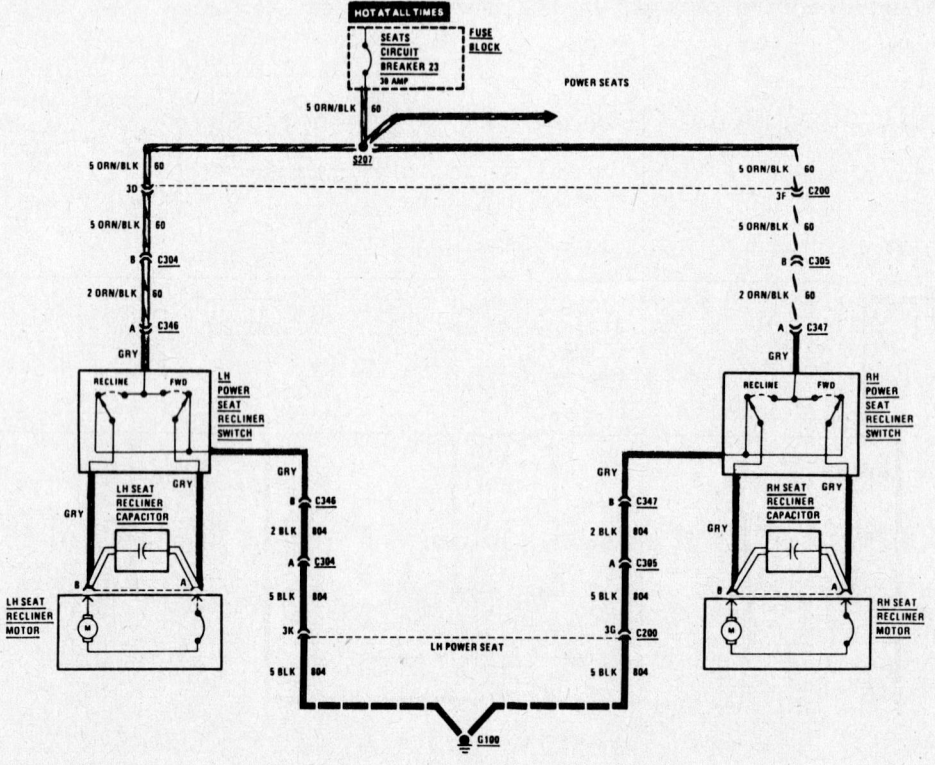

1986 and later Riviera and Toronado—typical power recliner system

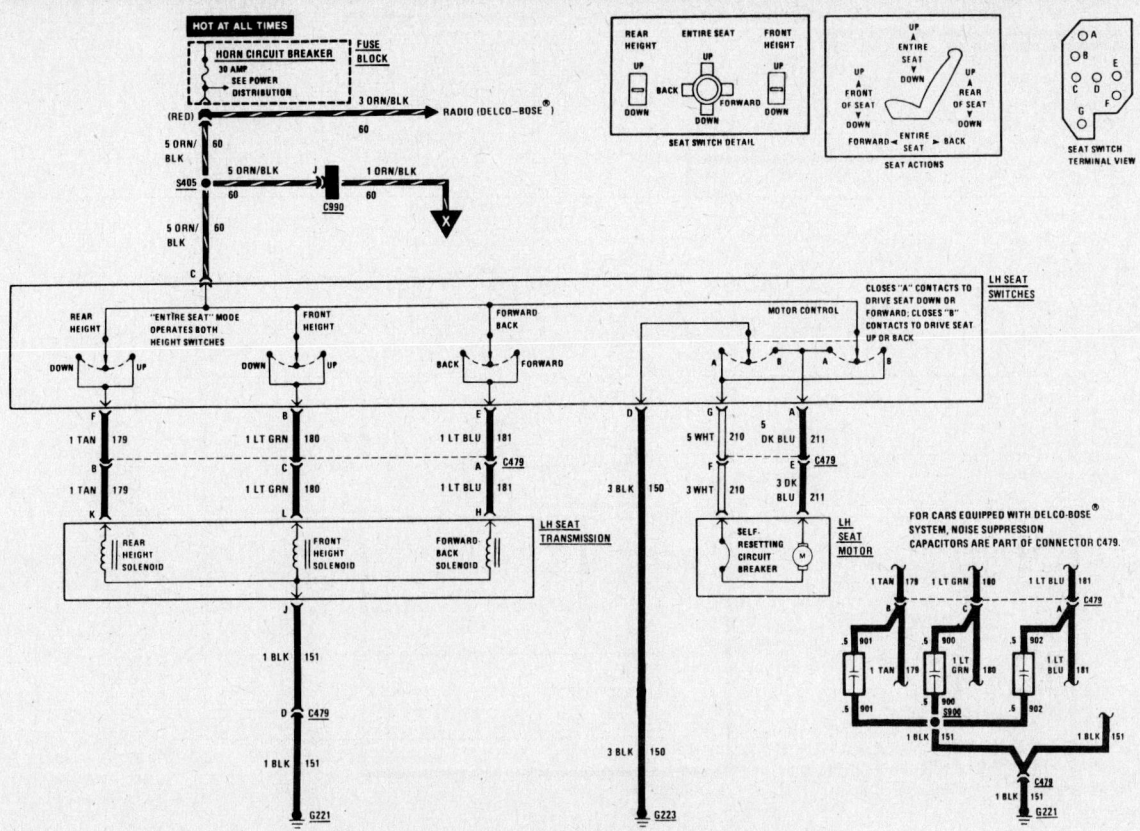

1982–85 Eldorado—typical power seat system—left side (type one)

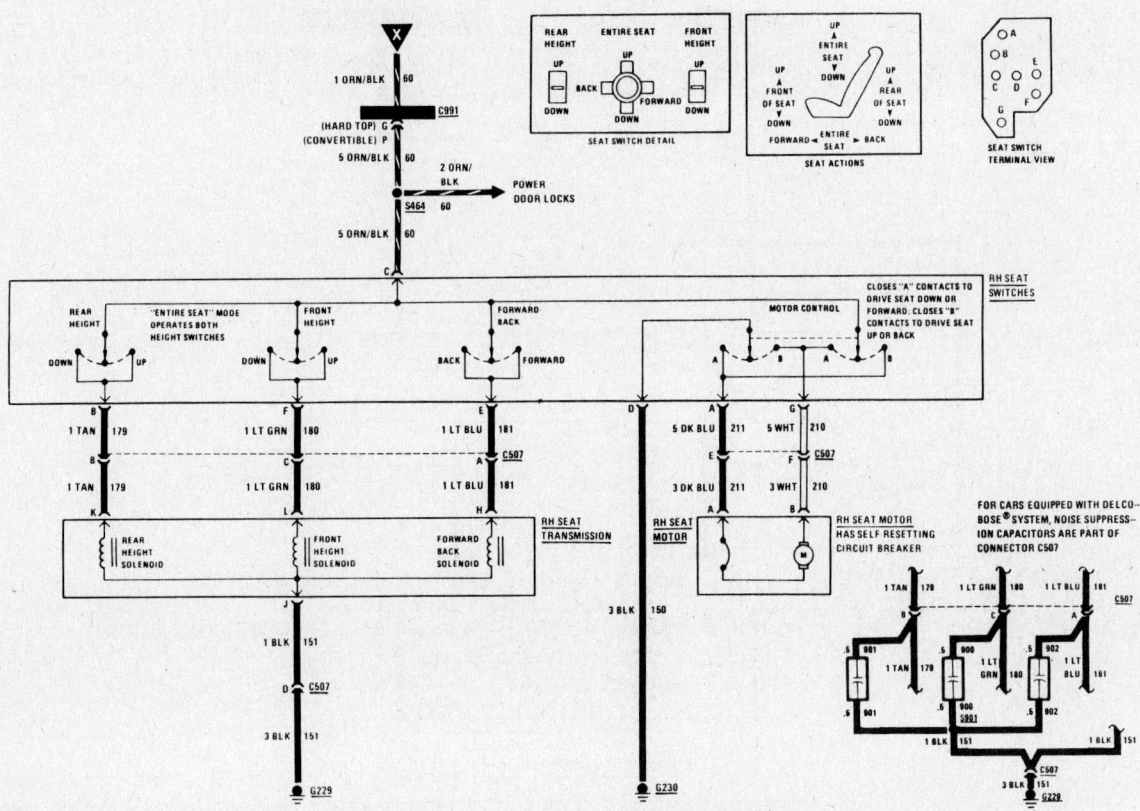

1982–85 Eldorado—typical power seat system—right side (type one)

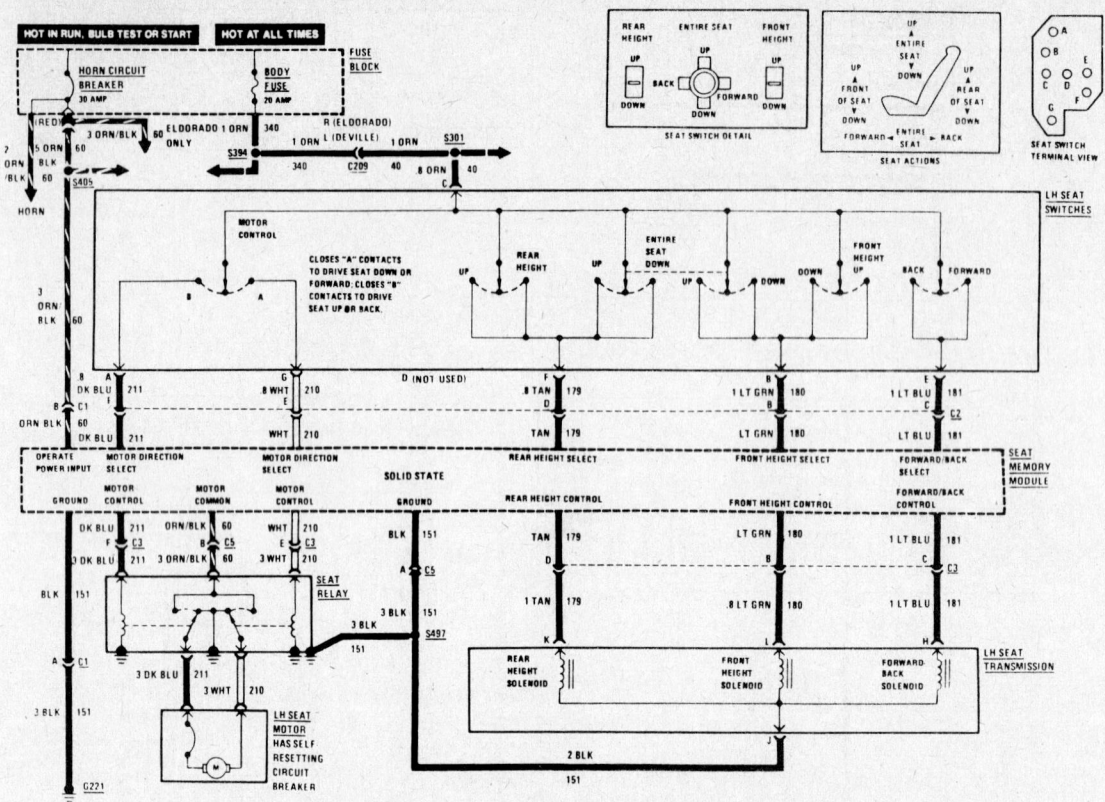

1982-85 Eldorado—typical memory seat system—seat wiring schematic (type one)

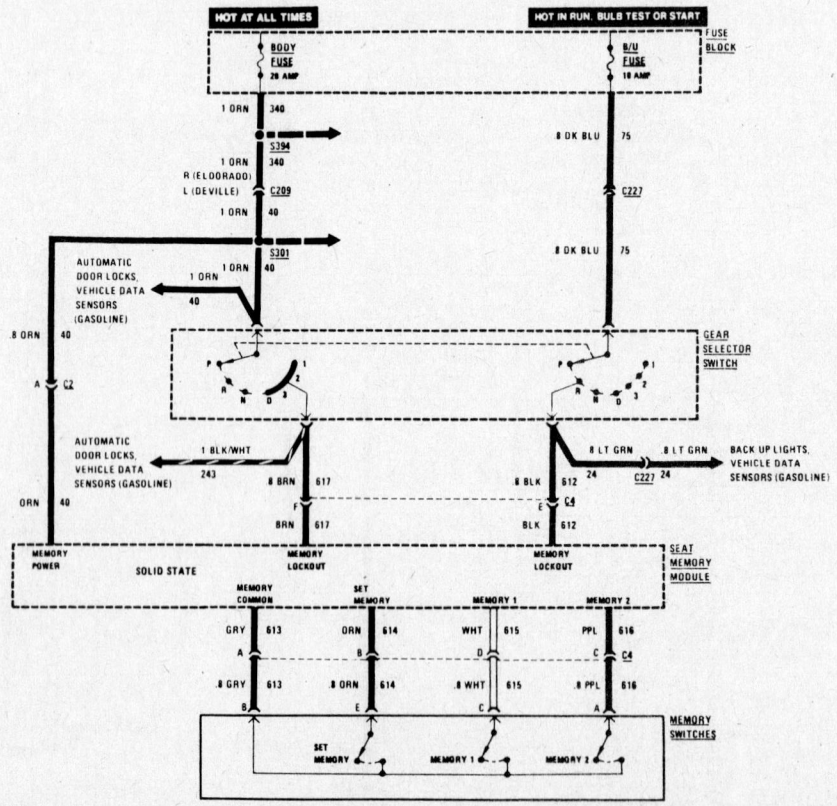

1982-85 Eldorado—typical memory seat system—wiring schematic (type one)

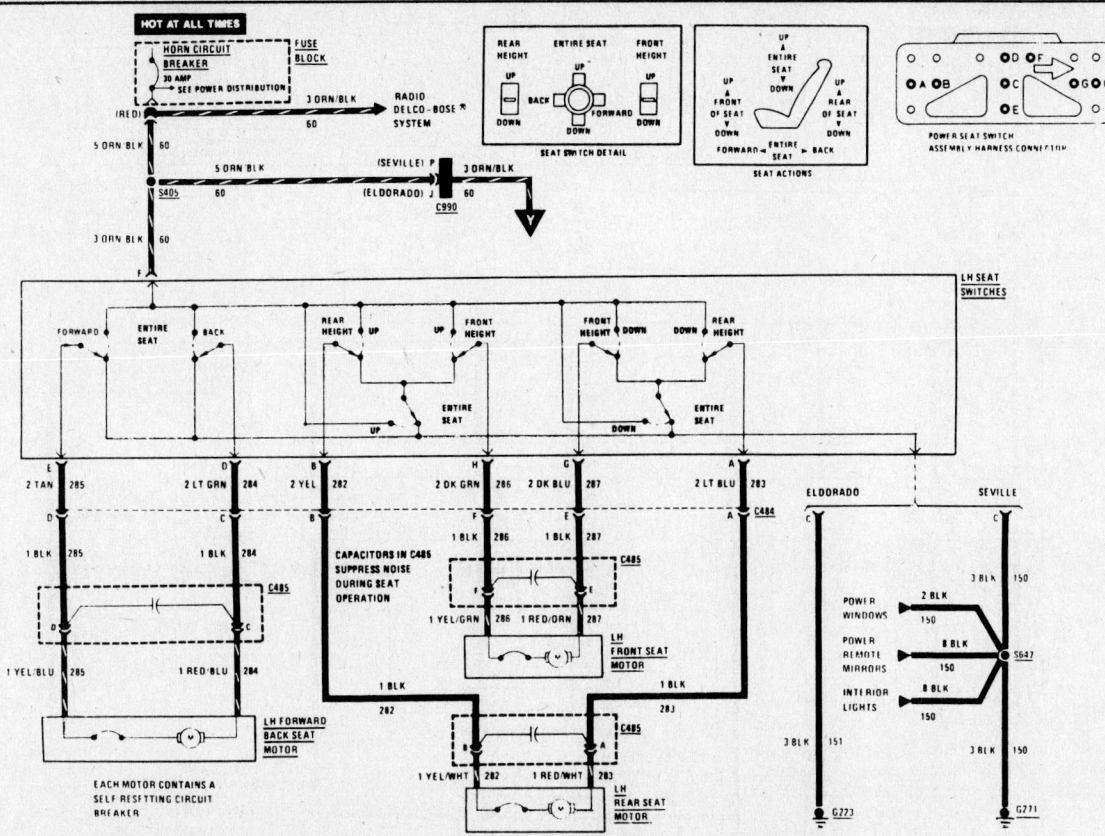

1982-85 Eldorado and Seville—typical power seat system—left side (type two)

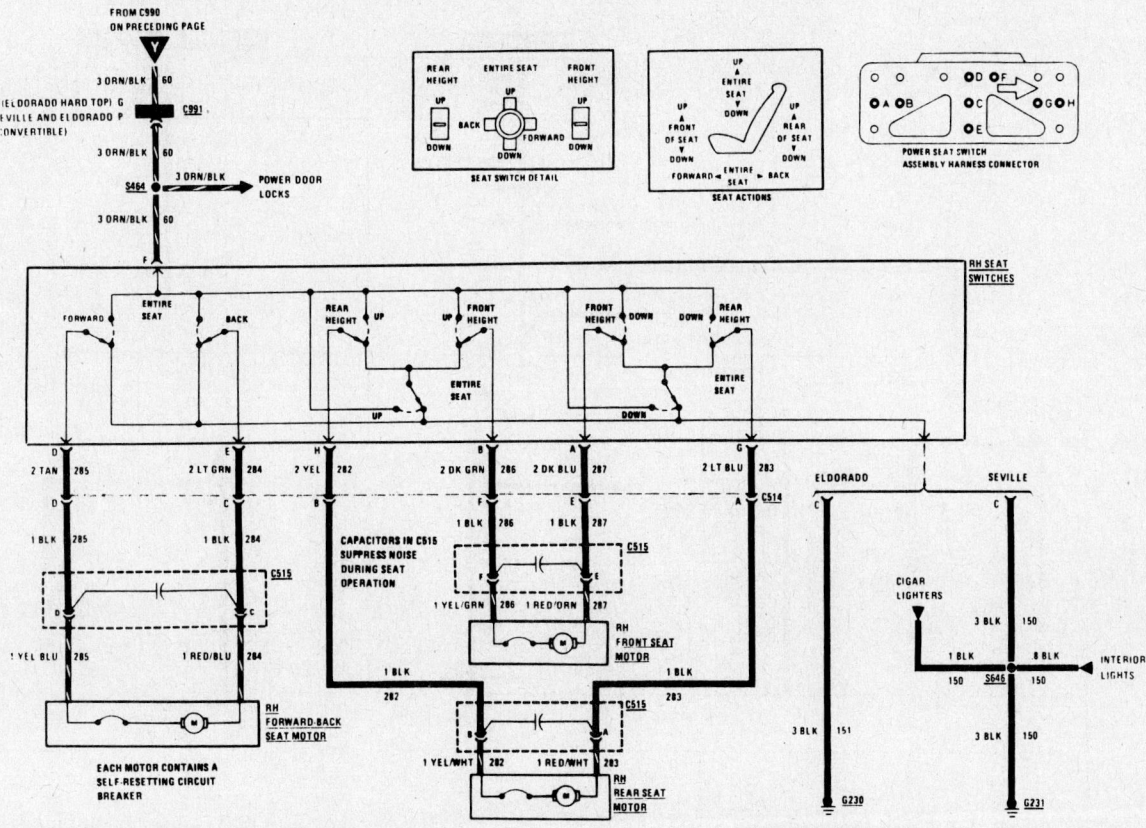

1982-85 Eldorado and Seville—typical power seat system—right side (type two)

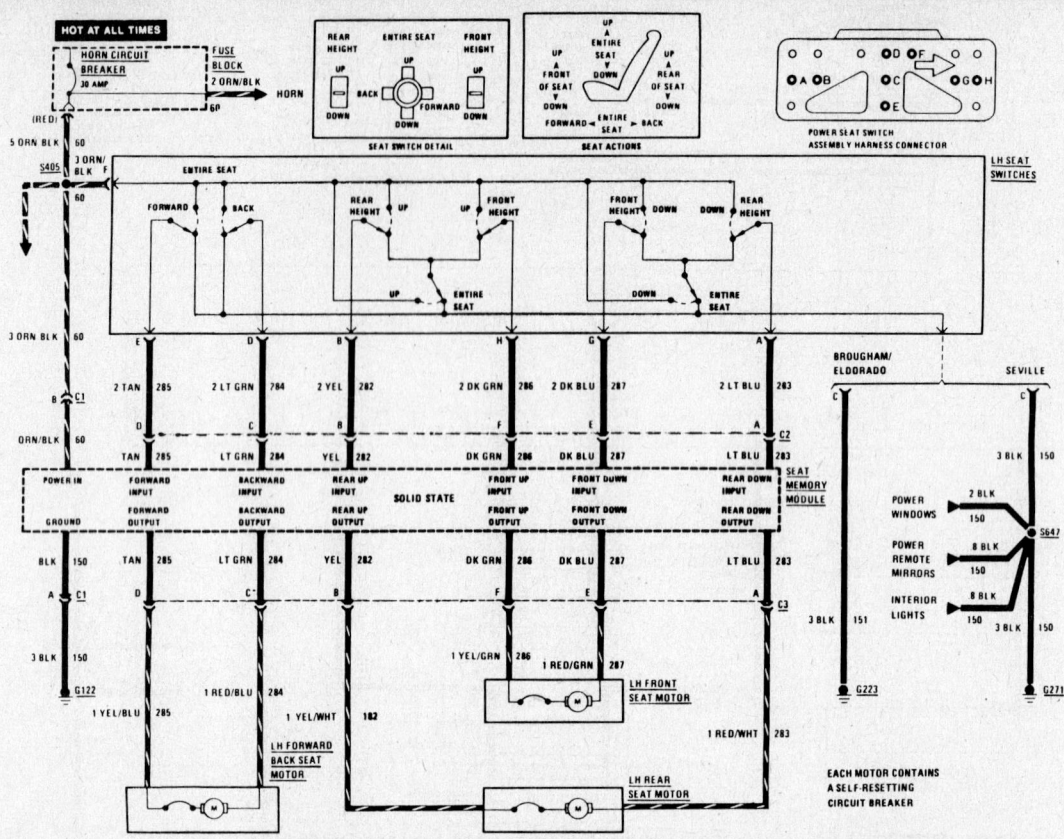

1982-85 Brougham, Eldorado and Seville—typical memory seat system—seat wiring schematic (type two)

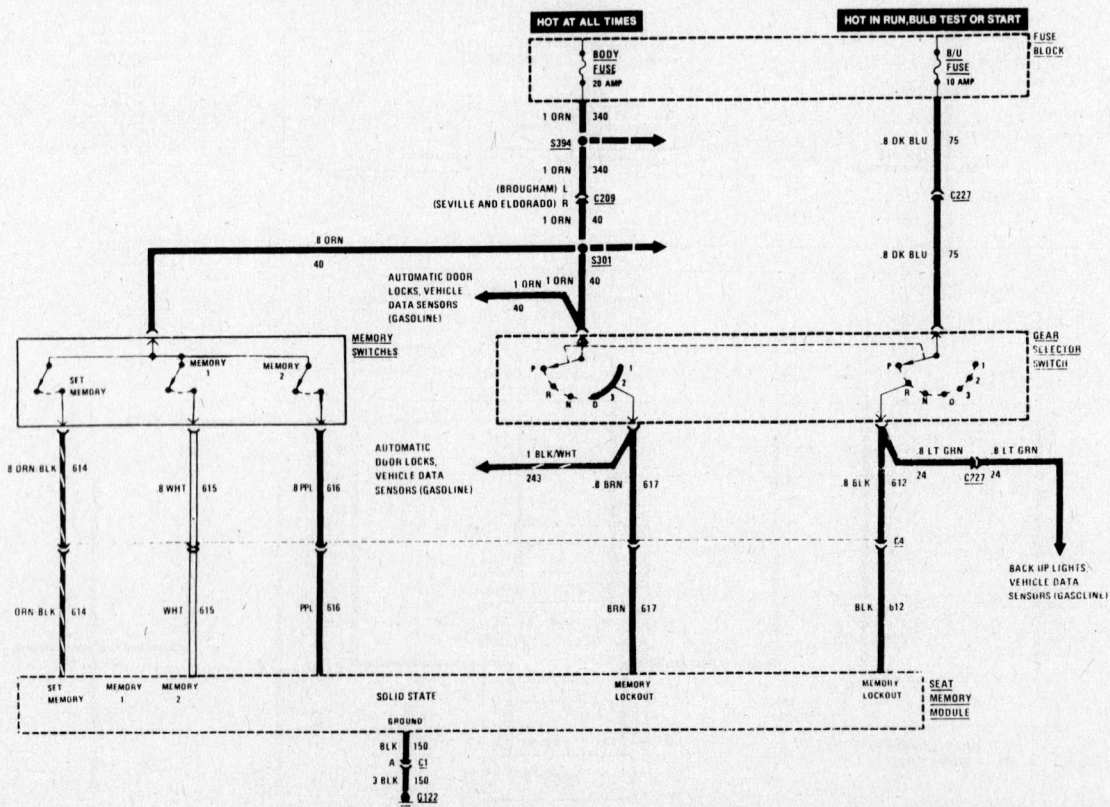

1982-85 Brougham, Elcdorado and Seville—typical memory seat system—wiring schematic (type two)

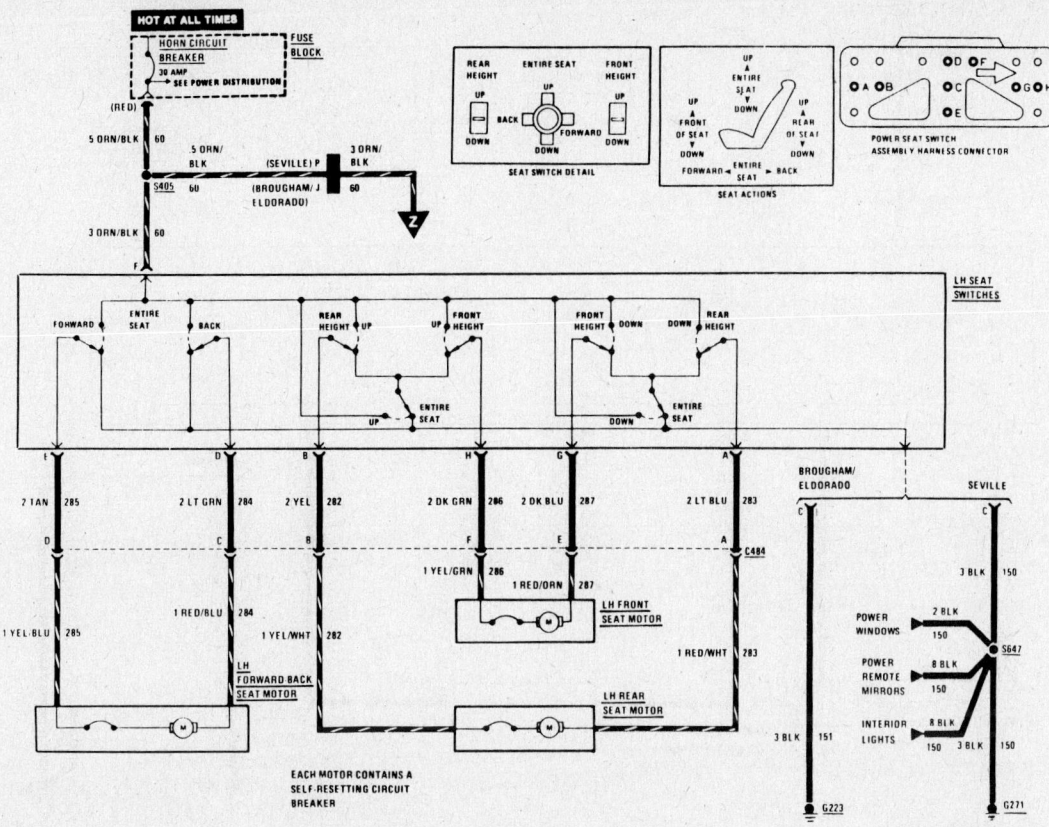

1982-85 Brougham, Eldorado and Seville—typical power seat system—left side (type two)

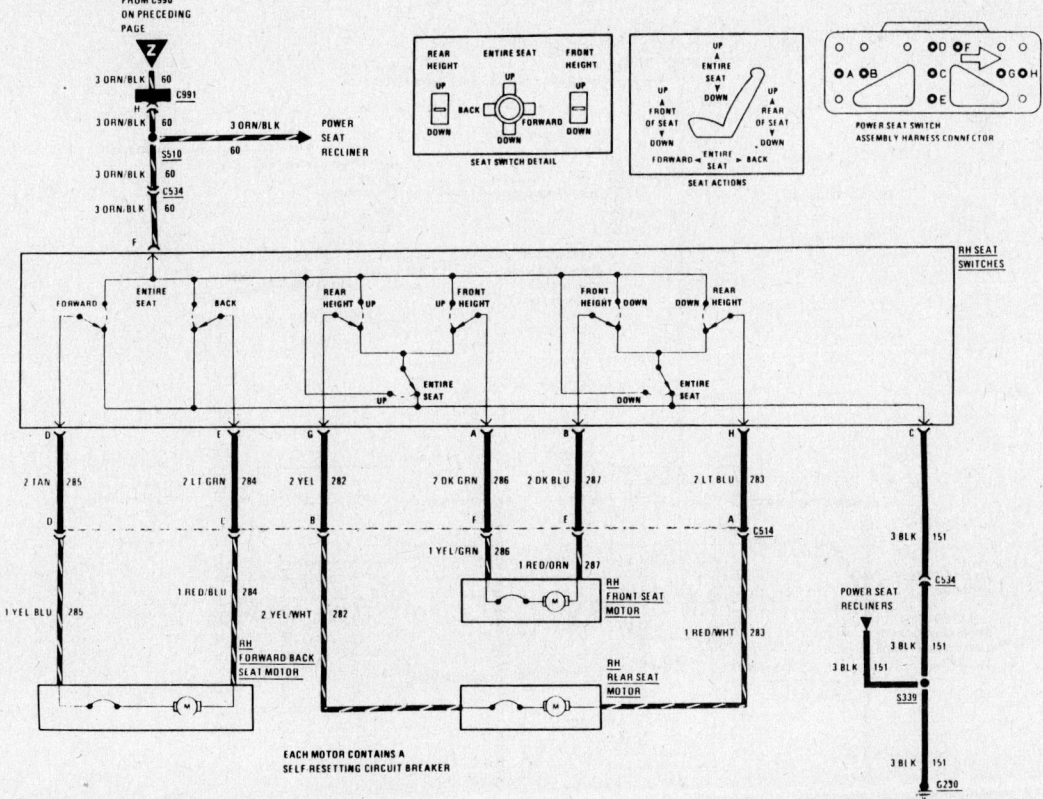

1982-85 Brougham, Eldorado and Seville—typical power seat system—right side (type one)

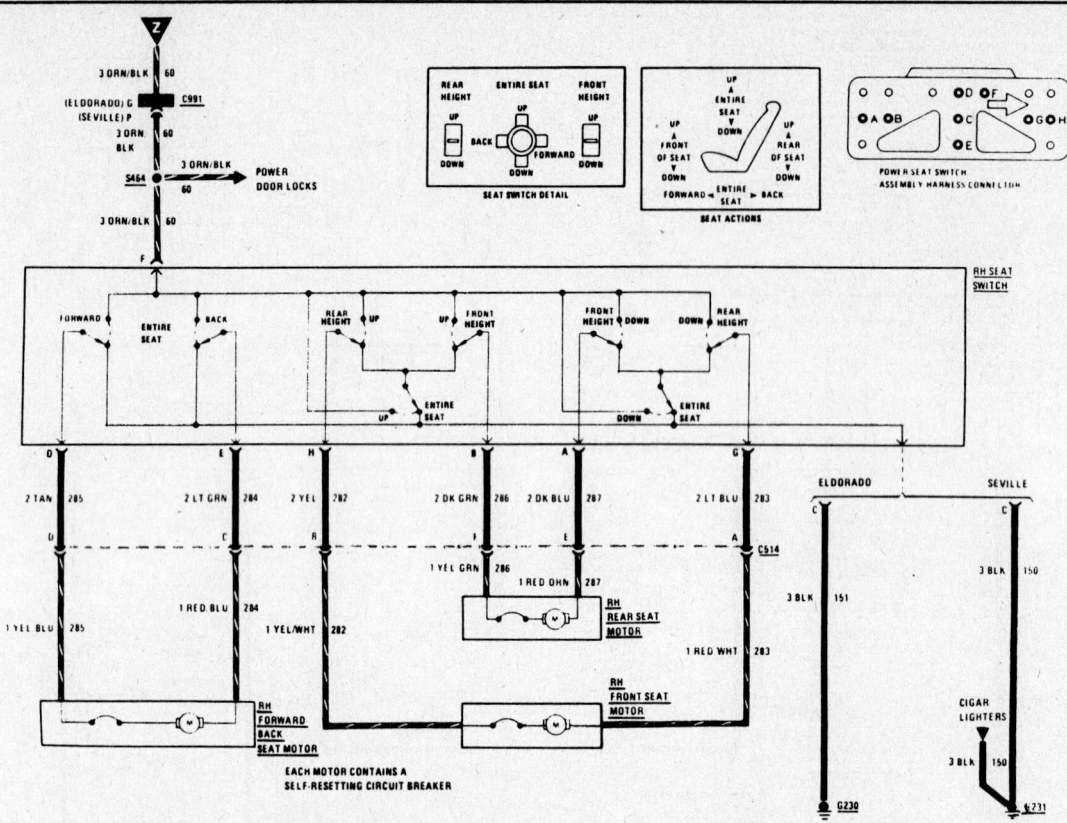

1982-85 Eldorado and Seville—typical power seat system—right side (type two)

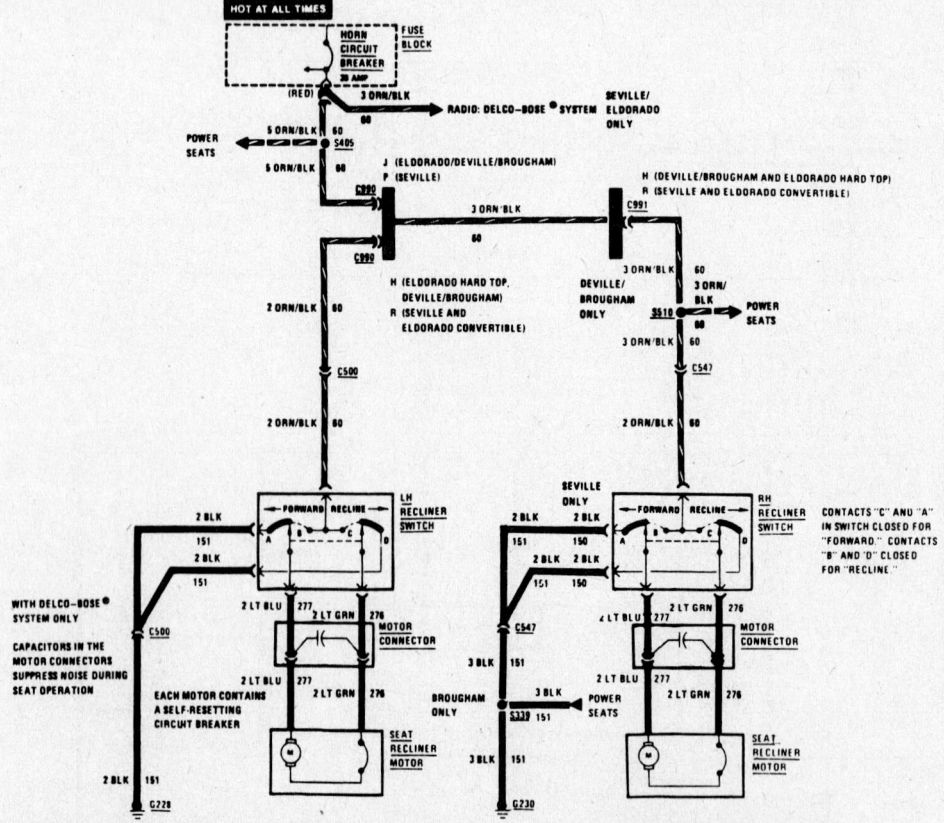

1982-85 Brougham, Eldorado and Seville—typical power recliner system

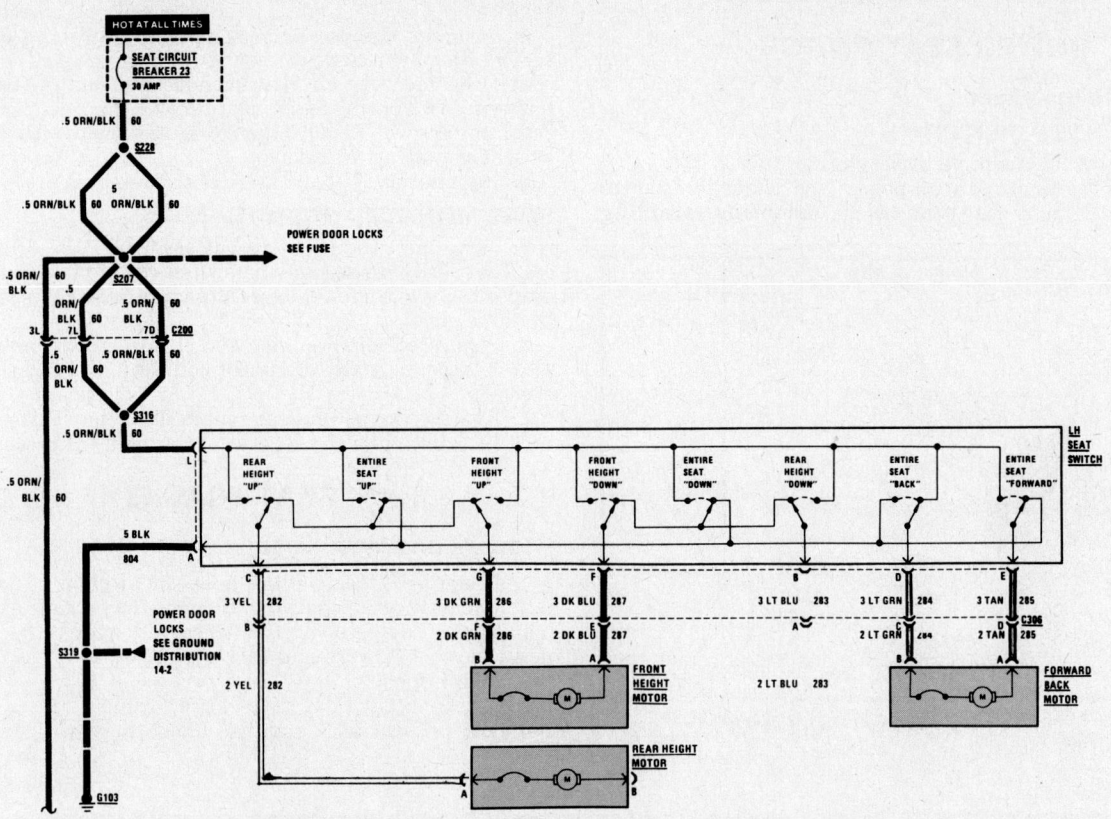

1986 and later Eldorado and Seville—typical power seat system—left side

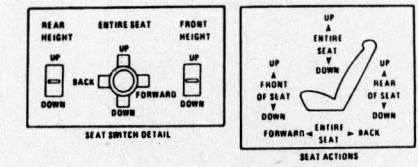

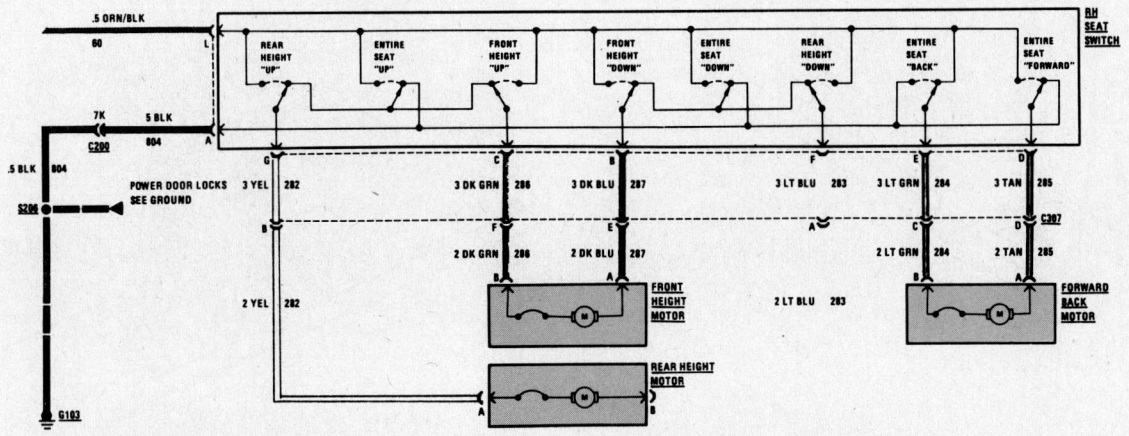

1986 and later Eldorado and Seville—typical power seat system—right side

1333

Component Replacement

POWER SEAT SWITCH

Removal and Installation
DOOR MOUNTED SWITCH

1. Disconnect the negative battery cable.
2. Remove the required trim panels and plates in order to gain access to the power seat switch mounting retaining

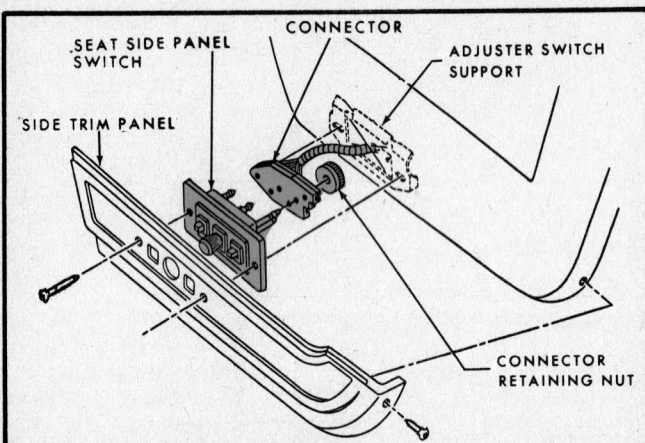

Typical General Motors power seat control—seat mounted switch

screws. Remove the remote control mirror trim plate, as required.
3. Remove the power seat switch mounting retaining screws. Remove the power seat switch mounting.
4. Disconnect the electrical connectors from the back of the power seat mounting assembly. Remove the power seat switch retaining screws. Remove the power seat switch from the power seat mounting assembly.
5. Installation is the reverse of the removal procedure.

SEAT MOUNTED SWITCH

1. Disconnect the negative battery cable.
2. Carefully disengage the switch cover plate using a flat bladed tool. On some vehicles the switch cover plate is retained by three screws.
3. Separate the power seat switch assembly from the cover plate. Disconnect the electrical connections from the switch assembly.
4. Remove the power seat switch from the vehicle.
5. Installation is the reverse of the removal procedure.

SEAT TRACKS

Removal and Installation

1. If equipped, remove the heat shield plugs to expose the seat assembly retaining bolts. Remove the retaining bolts that hold the seat assembly to the floorpan. It may be necessary to move the seat forward and backward in order to gain access to the retaining bolts.
2. Disconnect the negative battery cable.
3. Tilt the seat back and disconnect the wiring harness.

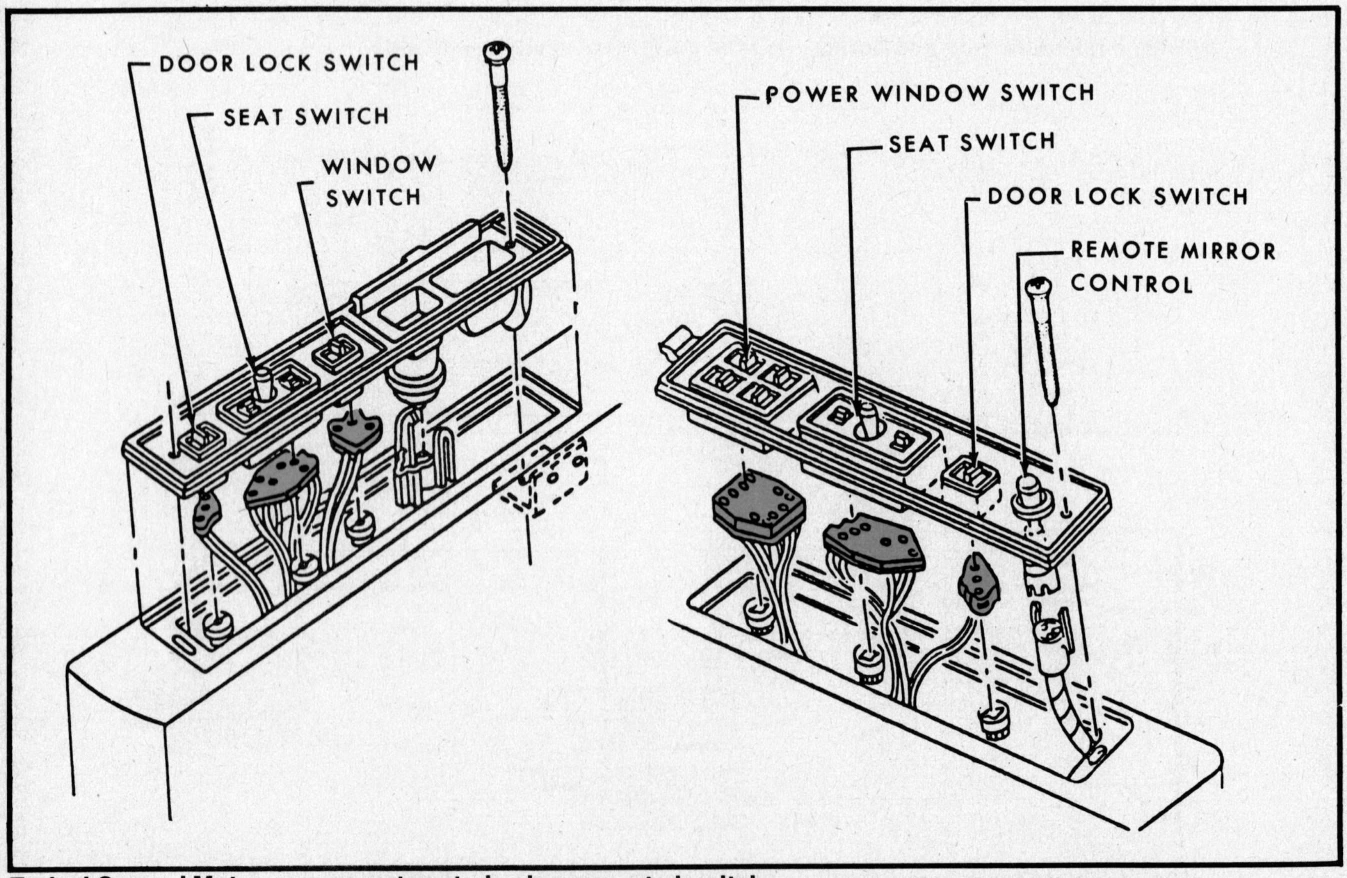

Typical General Motors power seat control—door mounted switch

4. Remove the seat belt retaining bolts, as required. Remove the seat assembly from the vehicle.

5. Remove the bolts that attach the seat track to the seat frame. Disconnect the drive cables as required. Remove tie straps that may be holding the cable housing to the seat assembly. Separate the seat track assembly from the seat.

6. Installation is the reverse of the removal procedure. Be sure that both seat tracks are in adjustment with one another.

7. To adjust the horizontal travel operate the seat control switch until one adjuster reaches the full forward position. Remove the horizontal drive cable from the adjuster that has reached the full forward position. Operate the seat until the other adjuster reaches the full forward position, then reconnect the horizontal drive cable. Check for proper operation.

8. To adjust the front or rear vertical travel, operate the seat control until one adjuster has reached the fully raised position at both front and rear vertical travel. Disconnect both vertical drive cables. Operate the control switch until the other adjuster has reached the fully raised position, then reconnect the vertical drive cables. Check for proper operation.

SEAT MOTOR AND CABLES

Removal and Installation
TWO WAY SEAT

1. If the seat is operable, position it in the midway position.
2. Disconnect the negative battery cable.
3. Remove the seat assembly floor to seat retaining nuts and tilt the seat rearward.
4. If the vehicle is equipped with the full bench seat, disconnect both power drive cables from the power seat motor.
5. Disconnect the feed harness from the actuator motor.
6. Remove the screws that secure the power seat motor support to the bottom of the frame. Remove the power seat motor with the motor attached to the frame support.
7. Installation is the reverse of the removal procedure.

SIX WAY SEAT (TRANSMISSION MOTOR TYPE)

1. Disconnect the negative battery cable. Remove the front seat assembly from the vehicle.

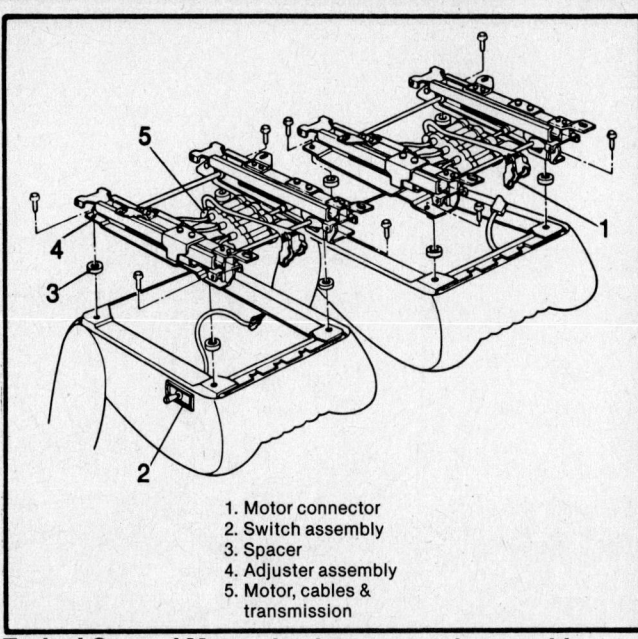

1. Motor connector
2. Switch assembly
3. Spacer
4. Adjuster assembly
5. Motor, cables & transmission

Typical General Motors bucket seat track assembly

NOTE: If the drive cables are to be replaced, remove the seat track assembly from the seat. If removing the short front or horizontal cables on the right side of the seat assembly remove the right seat adjuster. Remove the screws securing the horizontal and vertical cable end plate on the side of the transmission unit, then disengage the cables from the end plate.

2. Disconnect the power seat motor feed wires from the power seat motor control relay.
3. Remove the power seat motor support retaining screws. Remove the retaining screws that attach the transmission to the power seat motor.

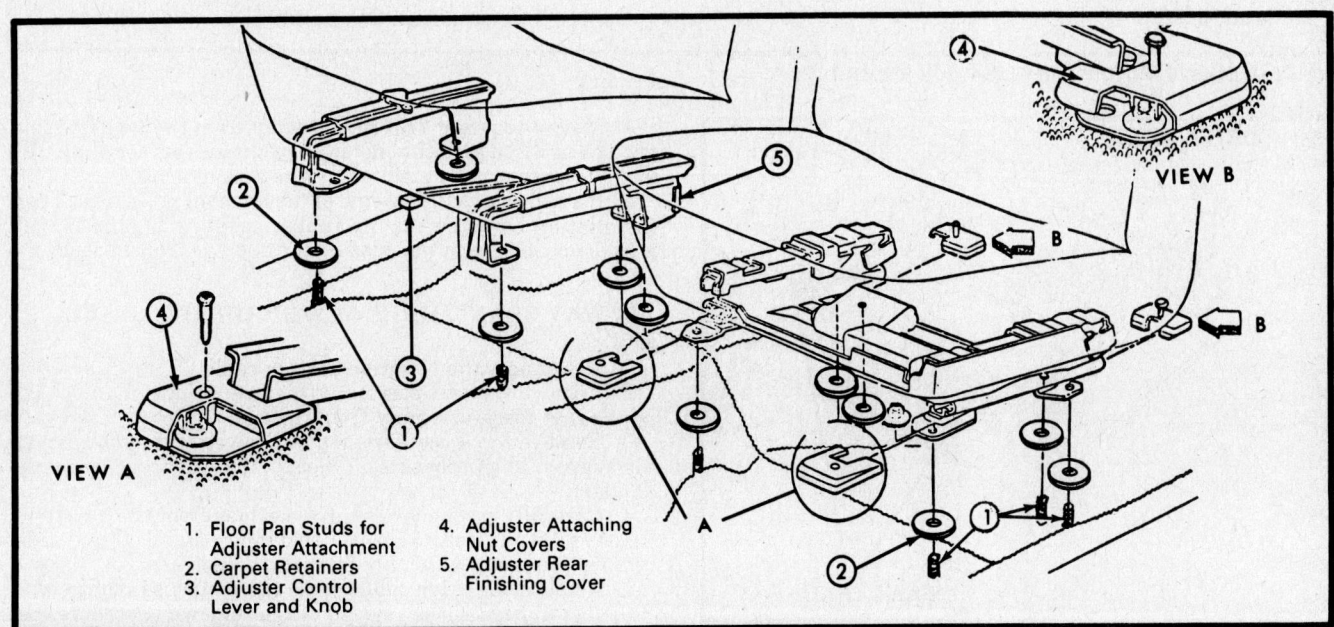

1. Floor Pan Studs for Adjuster Attachment
2. Carpet Retainers
3. Adjuster Control Lever and Knob
4. Adjuster Attaching Nut Covers
5. Adjuster Rear Finishing Cover

Typical General Motors split seat track assembly

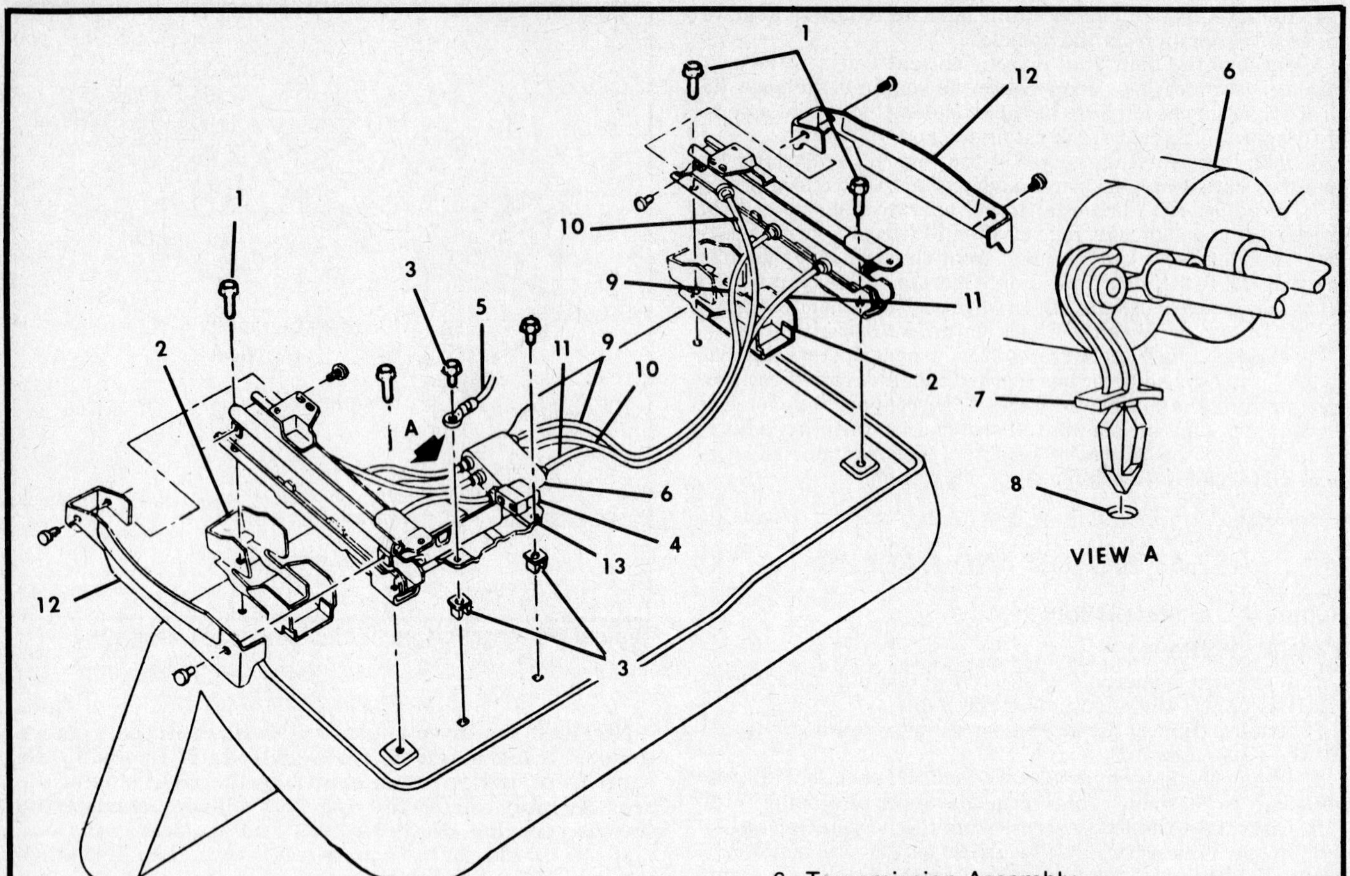

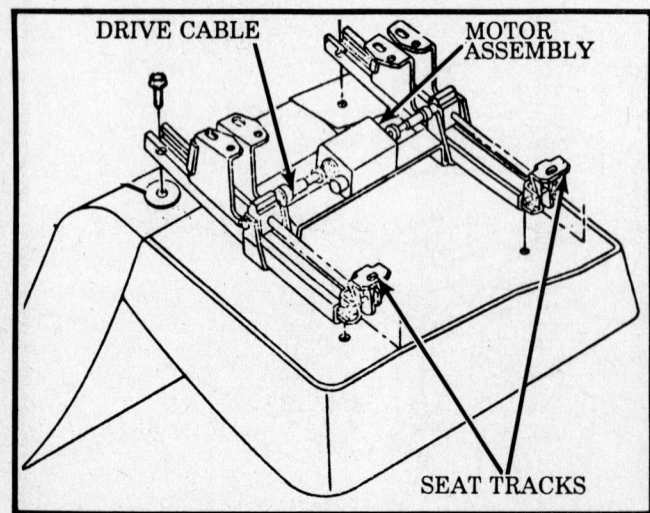

6. Transmission Assembly
7. Transmission Stabilizer Support
8. Hole In Seat Frame For Stabilizer Support
9. Horizontal Drive Cable (Blue)
10. Rear Vertical Drive Cable (Blue)
11. Front Vertical Drive Cable (Blue)
12. Adjuster Track Lower Cover
13. Transmission Support

1. Adjuster-To-Seat Frame Attaching Bolts
2. Adjuster Track Upper Cover
3. Transmission And Motor Support Attaching Screws And Push-In Nuts
4. Motor Relay
5. Ground Wire

VIEW A

Typical General Motors full seat track assembly

Seat motor and related components—two way seat

DRIVE CABLE

MOTOR ASSEMBLY

SEAT TRACKS

4. Move the power seat motor away from the transmission enough to disengage the motor from the rubber coupling. Remove the power seat motor from the seat assembly.

5. Installation is the reverse of the removal procedure. Upon installation be sure that the rubber coupling is properly engaged at both the power seat motor and the transmission.

SIX WAY SEAT (THREE MOTOR DIRECT DRIVE TYPE)

1. Disconnect the negative battery cable.

2. Remove the seat assembly from the vehicle. Remove the power seat track assembly from the seat.

3. Remove the screw securing the power seat motor assembly support to the power seat motor mounting bracket on the adjuster.

4. Carefully disengage the drive cables from the adjusters. Remove the nut from the power seat motor stabilizer rod, then remove the motor assembly from the adjusters.

5. Remove the drive cables from the motor, as required.

6. Installation is the reverse of the removal procedure. Before installing the power seat motor be sure that the drive cables are installed in the same position as they were removed.

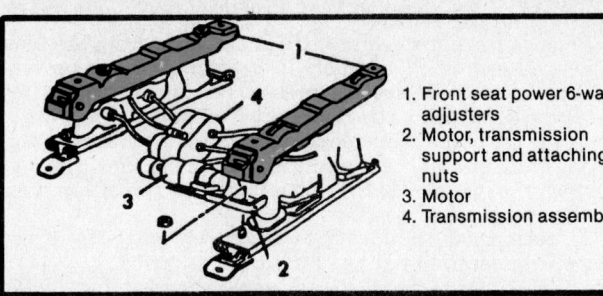

Seat motor and related components—split six way seat (transmission motor type)

1. Front seat power 6-way adjusters
2. Motor, transmission support and attaching nuts
3. Motor
4. Transmission assembly

SIX WAY SEAT (THREE MOTOR LOW PROFILE DIRECT DRIVE TYPE)

1. Disconnect the negative battery cable.
2. Remove the seat from the vehicle.

NOTE: The drive cables can be removed without removing the power seat motor from the seat assembly. Proceed as follows. Remove the power seat drive cables by squeezing the oblong connectors and then removing the cable. When removing the cable connector at the power seat motor for the inboard (passenger side) or outboard (drivers side) the rear vertical gearnut that attaches the nut to the motor support bracket must first be removed in order to gain access to the cable connector at the power seat motor.

3. Disconnect the power seat motor feed wires from the motor.
4. Remove the nut retaining the front of the power seat motor support bracket to the inboard adjuster and remove the assembly from the adjuster and the gearnut drives.

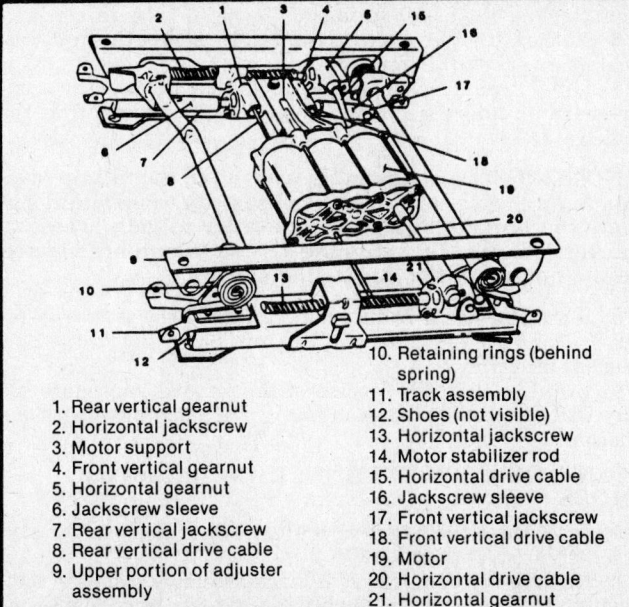

1. Rear vertical gearnut
2. Horizontal jackscrew
3. Motor support
4. Front vertical gearnut
5. Horizontal gearnut
6. Jackscrew sleeve
7. Rear vertical jackscrew
8. Rear vertical drive cable
9. Upper portion of adjuster assembly
10. Retaining rings (behind spring)
11. Track assembly
12. Shoes (not visible)
13. Horizontal jackscrew
14. Motor stabilizer rod
15. Horizontal drive cable
16. Jackscrew sleeve
17. Front vertical jackscrew
18. Front vertical drive cable
19. Motor
20. Horizontal drive cable
21. Horizontal gearnut

Seat motor and related components—six way seat (three motor direct drive type)

5. Disconnect the drive cables from the motor. Remove the power seat motor with the motor support attached.
6. Grind off the peened over ends of the grommet assembly that secures the power seat motor to the motor support. Separate the components as needed.
7. Installation is the reverse of the removal procedure.

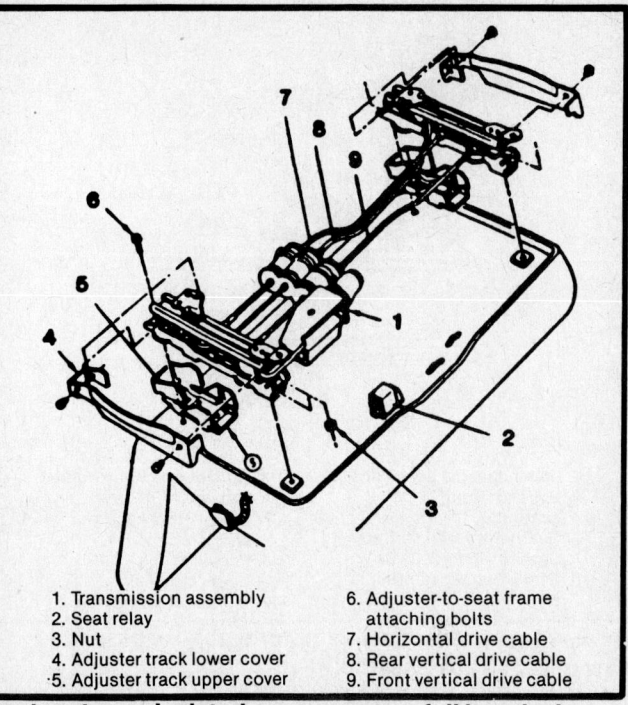

1. Transmission assembly
2. Seat relay
3. Nut
4. Adjuster track lower cover
5. Adjuster track upper cover
6. Adjuster-to-seat frame attaching bolts
7. Horizontal drive cable
8. Rear vertical drive cable
9. Front vertical drive cable

Seat motor and related components—full bench six way seat (transmission motor type)

When assembling the power seat motor to the support bracket, drill out the top end of the grommet assembly using a ⅜ inch drill then use a rivet to hold the two assemblies in place.

TWO WAY SEAT

Removal and Installation
HORIZONTAL JACKSCREW/GEARNUT ASSEMBLY

1. Disconnect the negative battery cable. Remove the seat assembly from the vehicle.

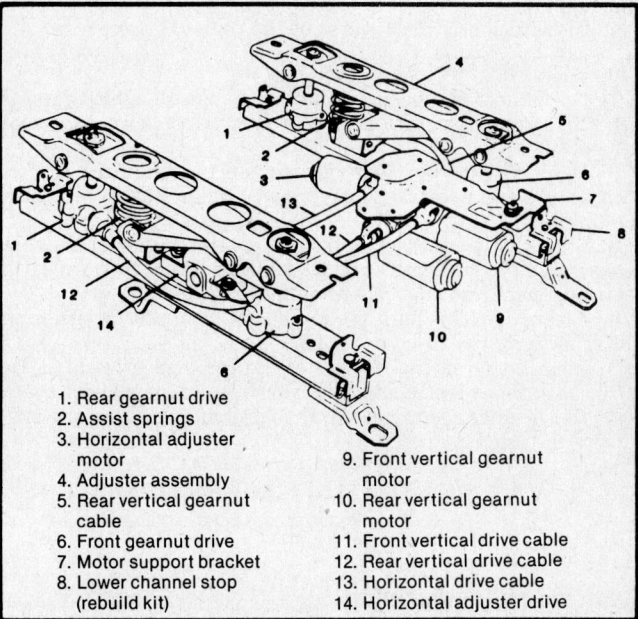

1. Rear gearnut drive
2. Assist springs
3. Horizontal adjuster motor
4. Adjuster assembly
5. Rear vertical gearnut cable
6. Front gearnut drive
7. Motor support bracket
8. Lower channel stop (rebuild kit)
9. Front vertical gearnut motor
10. Rear vertical gearnut motor
11. Front vertical drive cable
12. Rear vertical drive cable
13. Horizontal drive cable
14. Horizontal adjuster drive

Seat motor and related components—six way seat (three motor low profile direct drive type)

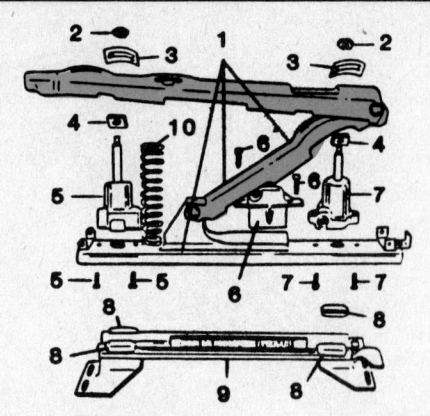

1. Upper channel assembly
2. Upper channel to gearnuts
3. Gearnut tension springs
4. Gearnut shoulder nuts
5. Rear vertical gearnut and screws
6. Horizontal actuator and screws
7. Front vertical gearnut and screws
8. Plastic shoes
9. Lower channel
10. Vertical assist spring

Six way seat (transmission motor type)—exploded view of seat track assembly

2. The adjusters should be in a rearward position. If the adjuster from which the jackscrew or gearnut is being removed is not in a rearward position, operate the gearnut manually with a suitable tool to position the component properly.

3. Remove the power drive cable from the gearnut, that is to be removed.

4. Remove the retainer securing the jackscrew front support crosspin to the adjuster front pedestal. Remove the crosspin.

5. With the adjuster upper channel in the rearward position, slide the upper channel forward until the jackscrew front support is out from between the adjuster front pedestals. Unscrew the jackscrew out of the gearnut assembly.

6. Remove the gearnut by removing the two shoulder screws securing the gearnut to the support. Remove the gearnut from the support.

7. Installation is the reverse of the removal procedure.

PLASTIC SHOES

1. Disconnect the negative battery cable. Remove the seat assembly from the vehicle. Remove the seat track from the seat assembly.

2. Using the proper tool remove the two shoulder screws that secure the gearnut to the upper channel and seat track assembly.

3. Slide the lower track and support base section of the seat track, with the jackscrew and gearnut attached, forward until it disengages from the upper channel assembly.

4. Disengage the four plastic shoes from the positioning slots on the lower track assembly.

5. Installation is the reverse of the removal procedure. Be sure that groove in the plastic shoe slips onto the lower track with the thinner section of the shoe protruding above the surface of the track.

SIX WAY SEAT (TRANSMISSION MOTOR TYPE)

Removal and Installation
HORIZONTAL ACTUATOR

1. Disconnect the negative battery cable. Remove the seat assembly from the vehicle.

2. Remove the damaged seat track assembly from the seat. Position the seat track assembly in a vise in order to prevent accidental ejection of the compressed vertical assist spring when the rear gearnut attaching nut is removed.

3. At the top of the seat track assembly remove the rear vertical gearnut retaining nut and the tension spring.

4. Open the vise slowly to relieve the assist spring compression. Remove the assist spring.

5. At the top of the seat track assembly remove the front vertical gearnut retaining nut.

6. Lift the front of the seat track upper channel upward. Remove the screws securing the horizontal actuator to the seat track upper channel assembly. Remove the actuator from the seat track assembly.

7. Installation is the reverse of the removal procedure.

8. When installing the horizontal actuator be sure that the actuator drive gear is fully engaged with the teeth on the lower channel and rack gear.

9. With the actuator retaining screws tight there should be no free motion between the upper and lower adjusting channels. Adjust the actuator as required to remove excessive free play.

10. Be sure that the seat track assemblies are in adjustment with one another.

FRONT AND REAR VERTICAL GEARNUT

1. Position the seat assembly in the full forward position.

2. Disconnect the negative battery cable. Remove the seat assembly from the vehicle.

3. Remove the damaged seat track assembly from the seat. Position the seat track assembly in a vise in order to prevent accidental ejection of the compressed vertical assist spring when the rear gearnut attaching nut is removed.

4. At the top of the seat track assembly remove the rear vertical gearnut retaining nut and the tension spring.

5. Open the vise slowly to relieve the assist spring compression. Remove the assist spring.

6. At the top of the seat track assembly remove the front vertical gearnut retaining nut.

7. Lay the seat track assembly on its side. Remove the vertical gearnut retaining screws and remove the gearnut from the seat track.

NOTE: If the seat assembly was not in the full up position before removal, it may be necessary to manually operate the horizontal actuator in order to gain access to the vertical gearnut retaining screws which are located on the bottom of the lower channel.

8. If the gearnut is being replaced with a new one, transfer the gearnut shoulder nut and the tension spring to the new gearnut assembly.

9. Installation is the reverse of the removal procedure. Be sure that the seat track assemblies are in adjustment with one another.

LOWER OR UPPER CHANNEL AND PLASTIC SHOES

1. Disconnect the negative battery cable. Remove the seat assembly from the vehicle.

2. Remove the damaged seat track assembly from the seat. Position the seat track assembly in a vise in order to prevent accidental ejection of the compressed vertical assist spring when the rear gearnut attaching nut is removed.

3. Remove the vertical gearnut retaining nuts, tension and assist springs. Lift the seat track upper channel upward. Remove the horizontal actuator retaining screws, then remove the actuator from the seat track assembly.

4. Slide the lower channel until it is completely disengaged from the upper channel. Remove the plastic shoes from the lower channel, as required.

5. Installation is the reverse of the removal procedure.

6. When installing the horizontal actuator be sure that the actuator drive gear is fully engaged with the teeth on the lower channel and rack gear.

7. With the actuator retaining screws tight there should be no free motion between the upper and lower adjusting channels. Adjust the actuator as required to remove excessive free play.

8. Be sure that the seat track assemblies are in adjustment with one another.

TRANSMISSION UNIT

1. Disconnect the negative battery cable. Remove the seat from the vehicle.

2. On split and bucket seats remove the right seat track assembly. On full width seat detach the transmission stabilizer support from the transmission assembly.

3. Remove the transmission to support retaining screws that secure the cable end plate on both ends of the transmission. Disengage the transmission from the motor drive coupling and cables. Remove the transmission from the seat assembly.

4. Installation is the reverse of the removal procedure.

SIX WAY SEAT (THREE MOTOR DIRECT DRIVE TYPE)

Removal and Installation
VERTICAL JACKSCREW AND GEARNUT

1. Disconnect the negative battery cable. Remove the seat from the vehicle. Remove the seat track assembly from the seat.

2. With the seat track assembly in the full rearward position remove the jackscrew retaining nut. It may be necessary to exert light pressure on the horizontal jackscrew for clearance to the bolt. Slide the bolt out to disengage the vertical gearnut from the seat track assembly.

3. Disengage the vertical drive cable from the motor assembly. Remove the jackscrews from the assembly.

4. To remove the jackscrew sleeve, remove the retaining pin and c-clip then disengage the sleeve from the jackscrew.

5. Installation is the reverse of the removal procedure.

VERTICAL TORQUE TUBE SPRINGS

1. Disconnect the negative battery cable. Remove the seat from the vehicle. Remove the seat track assembly from the seat.

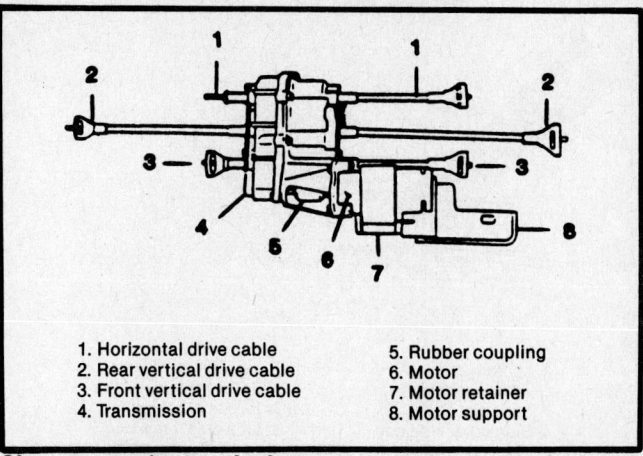

1. Horizontal drive cable
2. Rear vertical drive cable
3. Front vertical drive cable
4. Transmission
5. Rubber coupling
6. Motor
7. Motor retainer
8. Motor support

Six way seat (transmission motor type)—transmission, motor and cable assemblies

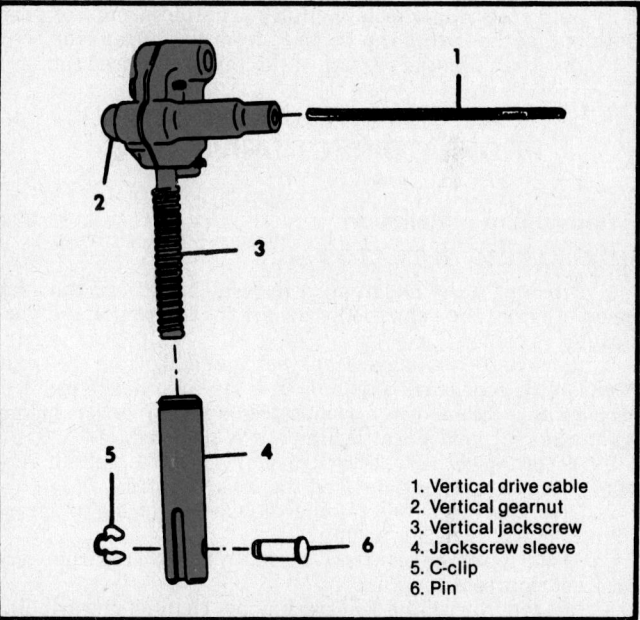

1. Vertical drive cable
2. Vertical gearnut
3. Vertical jackscrew
4. Jackscrew sleeve
5. C-clip
6. Pin

Six way seat (three motor direct drive type)—vertical jackscrew and gearnut assembly

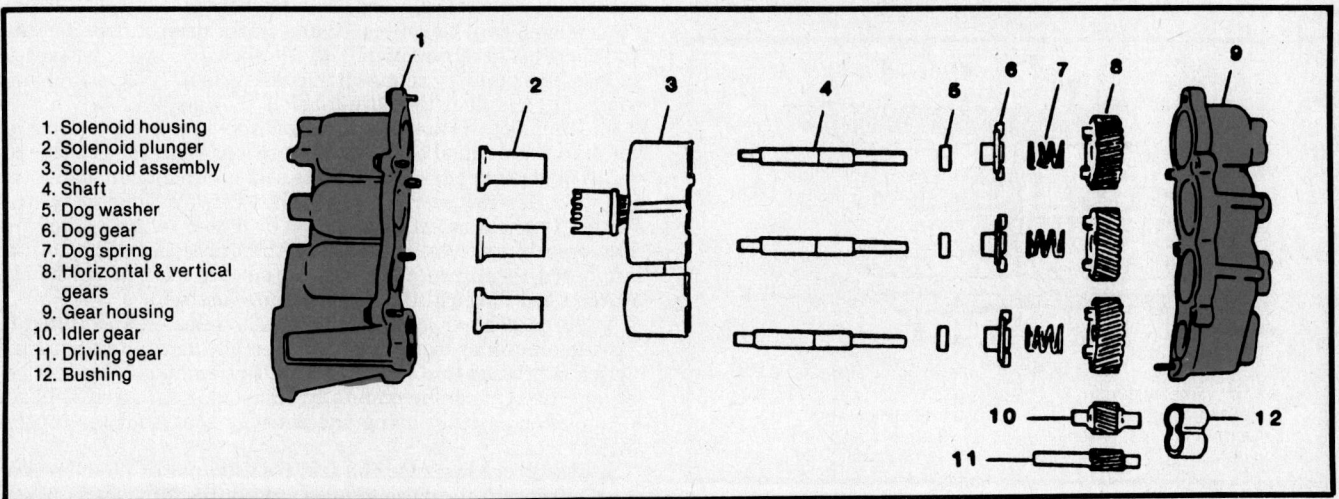

1. Solenoid housing
2. Solenoid plunger
3. Solenoid assembly
4. Shaft
5. Dog washer
6. Dog gear
7. Dog spring
8. Horizontal & vertical gears
9. Gear housing
10. Idler gear
11. Driving gear
12. Bushing

Six way seat (transmission motor type)—exploded view of transmission unit

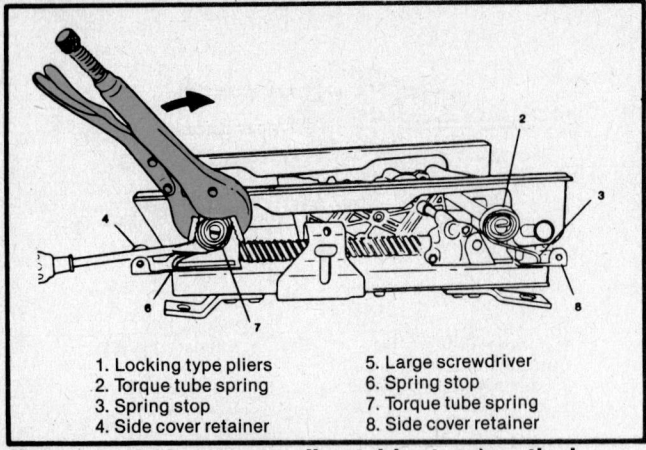

1. Locking type pliers
2. Torque tube spring
3. Spring stop
4. Side cover retainer
5. Large screwdriver
6. Spring stop
7. Torque tube spring
8. Side cover retainer

Six way seat (three motor direct drive type) vertical torque tube spring removal

2. Using the proper tools carefully turn the spring until the hook end of the spring can be pried from the spring stop.

3. Installation is the reverse of the removal procedure.

SIX WAY SEAT (THREE MOTOR LOW PROFILE DIRECT DRIVE TYPE)

Removal and Installation
HORIZONTAL ACTUATOR

1. Disconnect the negative battery cable. Remove the seat assembly from the vehicle. Disconnect the horizontal and vertical drive cables.

2. Remove the damaged seat track assembly from the seat. Position the seat track assembly in a vise in order to prevent accidental ejection of the compressed vertical assist spring when the rear gearnut attaching nut is removed.

3. At the top of the seat track assembly remove the rear vertical gearnut retaining nut and the tension spring.

4. Open the vise slowly to relieve the assist spring compression. Remove the assist spring.

5. At the top of the seat track assembly remove the front vertical gearnut retaining nut.

6. Lift the front of the seat track upper channel upward. Remove the screws securing the horizontal actuator to the seat track upper channel assembly. Remove the actuator from the seat track assembly.

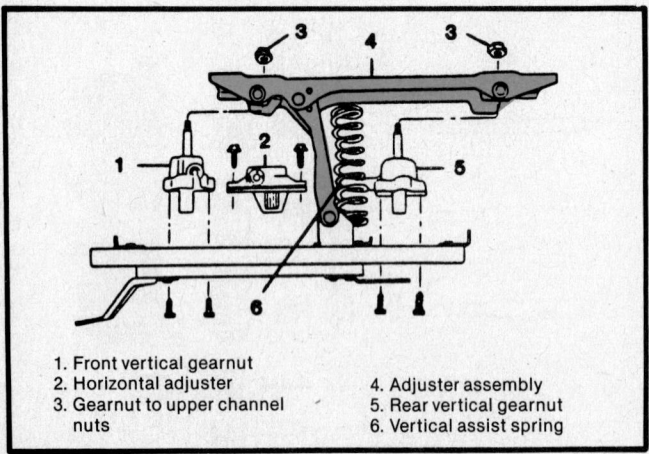

1. Front vertical gearnut
2. Horizontal adjuster
3. Gearnut to upper channel nuts
4. Adjuster assembly
5. Rear vertical gearnut
6. Vertical assist spring

Six way seat (three motor low profile direct drive type)—seat track and major components

7. Installation is the reverse of the removal procedure.

8. When installing the horizontal actuator be sure that the actuator drive gear is fully engaged with the teeth on the lower channel and rack gear.

9. With the actuator retaining screws tight there should be no free motion between the upper and lower adjusting channels. Adjust the actuator as required to remove excessive free play.

10. Be sure that the seat track assemblies are in adjustment with one another.

FRONT AND REAR VERTICAL GEARNUT

1. Position the seat assembly in the full forward position.

2. Disconnect the negative battery cable. Remove the seat assembly from the vehicle. Disconnect the horizontal and vertical drive cables.

3. Remove the damaged seat track assembly from the seat. Position the seat track assembly in a vise in order to prevent accidental ejection of the compressed vertical assist spring when the rear gearnut attaching nut is removed.

4. At the top of the seat track assembly remove the rear vertical gearnut retaining nut and the tension spring.

5. Open the vise slowly to relieve the assist spring compression. Remove the assist spring.

6. At the top of the seat track assembly remove the front vertical gearnut retaining nut.

7. Lay the seat track assembly on its side. Remove the vertical gearnut retaining screws and remove the gearnut from the seat track.

NOTE: If the seat assembly was not in the full up position before removal, it may be necessary to manually operate the horizontal actuator in order to gain access to the vertical gearnut retaining screws which are located on the bottom of the lower channel.

8. If the gearnut is being replaced with a new one, transfer the gearnut shoulder nut and the tension spring to the new gearnut assembly.

9. Installation is the reverse of the removal procedure. Be sure that the seat track assemblies are in adjustment with one another.

TWO POSITION POWER MEMORY SEAT

Some vehicles are equipped with power memory seats. There two types of power memory seats available, type one is a one motor design six way power memory seat system and type two is a three motor design six way power memory seat system. The memory seat control is located on the drivers door armrest and operates in conjunction with the six way power seat control switch. The memory seat switch consists of a "SET" switch and two recall switches that are labeled "1" and "2".

The memory system will function only when the selector lever is in the neutral or the park position. With the selector lever in neutral or park, the drivers seat occupant can adjust the seat to a desired position using the six way adjuster control switch. The seat selection can then be placed in the memory by first pressing the set switch and then pressing either of the numbered recall switches. This numbered switch will be the switch used to recall the seat position just set.

A second drivers seat position can be selected and stored in the same manner except that the remaining numbered recall switch is pressed to store and recall the second drivers seat position. The seat can be manually adjusted in any gear shift selector lever position using the six way seat adjuster control switch.

Service procedures for the two position power memory seat are no different than the service procedures for six way power seat assemblies.

POWER RECLINER

Some vehicles are equipped with a power recliner assembly which provides tilt adjustment of the seat back. By pressing the power recliner seat switch the seat back will move forward or rearward until the power recliner seat switch is released.

Removal and Installation

POWER RECLINER SWITCH

1. Disconnect the negative battery cable.
2. Remove the seat side panel retaining screws. Pull the seat side panel outward in order to expose the seat side trim panel moulding retaining nuts.
3. Remove the trim panel retaining nuts. Remove the trim panel from the seat side panel.
4. Disconnect the recliner switch from the electrical connector and remove the switch from its mounting.
5. Installation is the reverse of the removal procedure.

POWER RECLINER MOTOR ASSEMBLY

1. Disconnect the negative battery cable.
2. Remove the seat assembly retaining bolts. Tilt the seat assembly rearward in order to gain access to the recliner motor retaining bolts.
3. Disconnect the recliner motor electrical connection. Remove the recliner motor attaching nuts. Detach the drive cable to motor coulping. Remove the recliner motor from its mounting.
4. Installation is the reverse of the removal procedure.

POWER RECLINER ACTUATOR (TYPE ONE)

1. Disconnect the negative battery cable. Remove the seat assembly from the vehicle.
2. Detach the outboard side of the cushion trim enough to gain access to the reclining actuator retaining screws and the acutator coupling.
3. Unscrew the reclining drive cable from the reclining actuator. Detach the drive cable from the actuator.

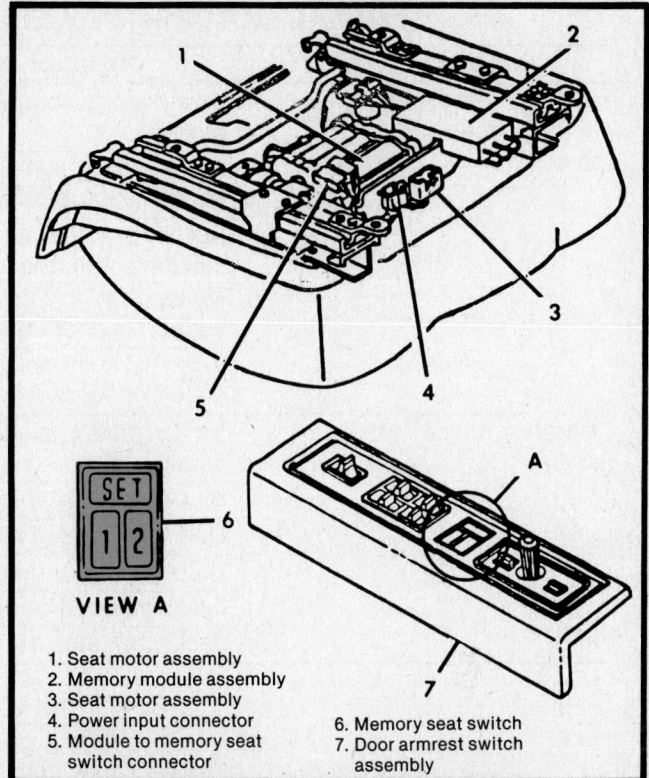

1. Seat motor assembly
2. Memory module assembly
3. Seat motor assembly
4. Power input connector
5. Module to memory seat switch connector
6. Memory seat switch
7. Door armrest switch assembly

Two position power memory seat and related components (type one)

4. Remove the pin retainer. Remove the pin securing the reclining actuator coupling to the seatback hindge arm.
5. Remove the actuator to seat cushion frame retaining

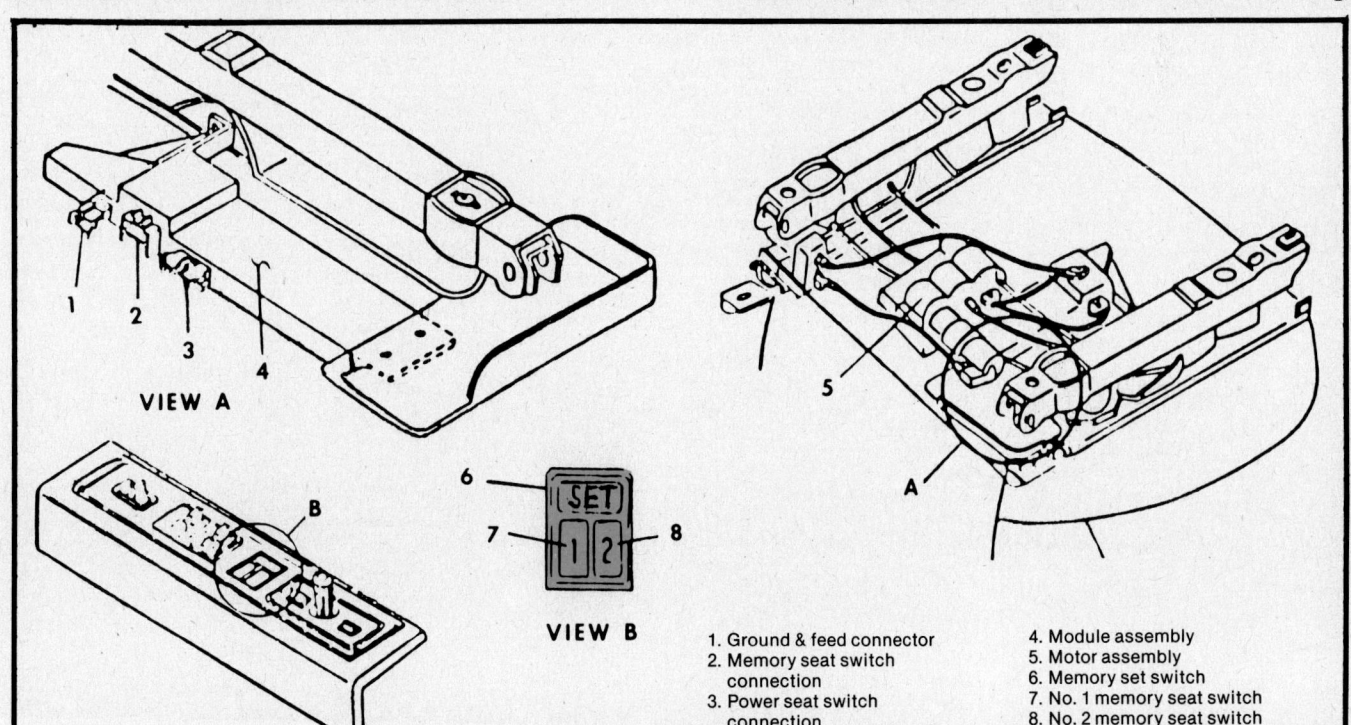

1. Ground & feed connector
2. Memory seat switch connection
3. Power seat switch connection
4. Module assembly
5. Motor assembly
6. Memory set switch
7. No. 1 memory seat switch
8. No. 2 memory seat switch

Two position power memory seat and related components (type two)

GENERAL MOTORS—POWER RECLINER DIAGNOSTIC CHART

Condition	Apparent Cause	Correction
Motor operates but seatback does not move.	Drive cable disconnected or broken.	Check drive cable and correct, replace if broken.
	Damaged, broken or inoperable reclining actuator gearnut.	Check reclining actuator gearnut, replace if damaged.
	Reclining actuator disconnected from arm of seatback lock (2-door styles) or support (4-door styles).	Check reclining actuator.
	Incorrect seatback lock (2-door styles) or support (4-door styles).	Replace lock.
Operation not smooth (jerky).	Kink in drive cable or damaged cable.	Check items described; where required, eliminate binds and lubricate. Replace any damaged parts.
	Bind in reclining hinge arms.	
	Damaged or bent jackscrew.	
	Damaged actuator gearnut.	
	Jackscrew not lubricated.	
	Jackscrew stop nut loose.	

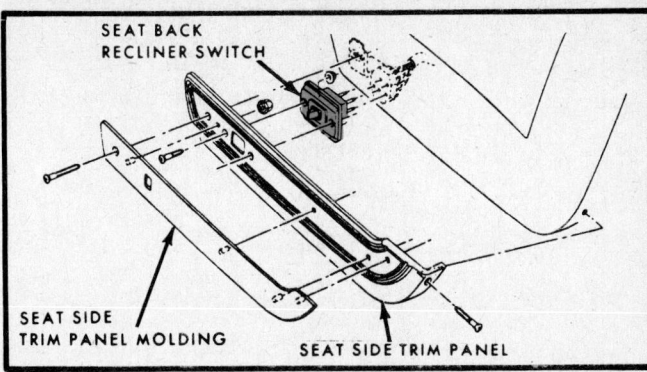

Power recliner control switch and related components

bolts. Remove the actuator assembly from its mounting on the seat.

6. Installation is the reverse of the removal procedure.

POWER RECLINER ACTUATOR (TYPE TWO)

1. Disconnect the negative battery cable. Remove the seat assembly from the vehicle.

2. Detach the outboard side of the cushion trim enough to gain access to the reclining actuator front and rear attachments.

3. Detach the actuator drive cable coupling from the actuator gearnut. Remove the bolt securing the reclining actuator coupling to the seatback hindge arm.

4. Remove the actuator to seat cushion frame retaining bolts. Remove the actuator assembly from the seat.

5. Installation is the reverse of the removal procedure.

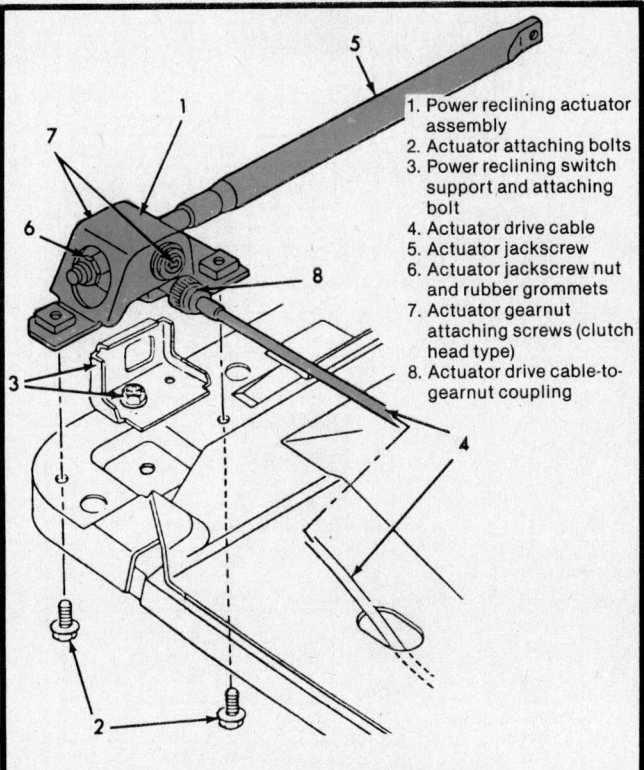

Power recliner actuator and related components (type two)

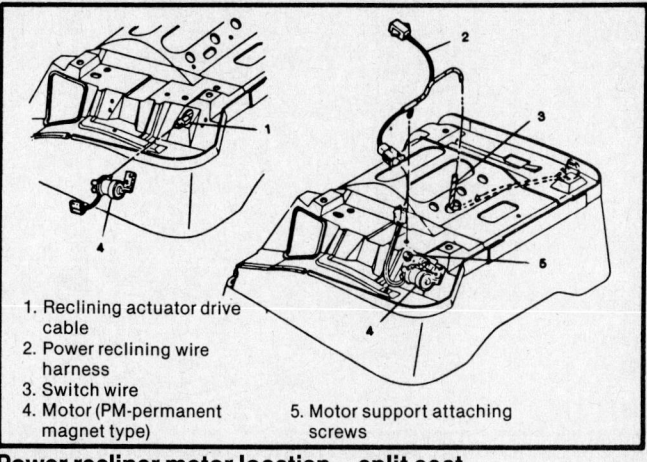

1. Reclining actuator drive cable
2. Power reclining wire harness
3. Switch wire
4. Motor (PM-permanent magnet type)
5. Motor support attaching screws

Power recliner motor location—split seat

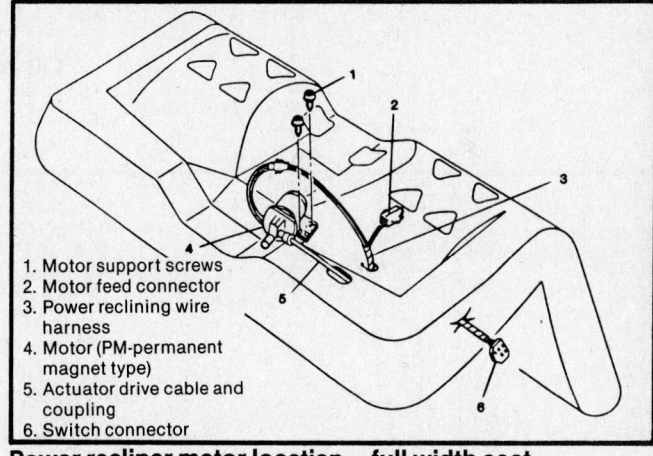

1. Motor support screws
2. Motor feed connector
3. Power reclining wire harness
4. Motor (PM-permanent magnet type)
5. Actuator drive cable and coupling
6. Switch connector

Power recliner motor location—full width seat

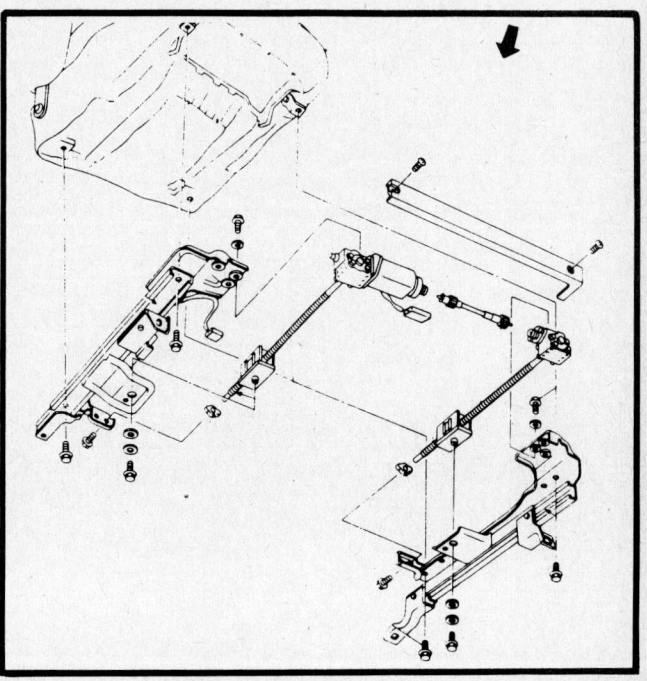

Power seat assembly—Maxima

The actuator and related components diagram (type two) includes the following legend:

1. Power reclining actuator assembly
2. Actuator attaching bolts
3. Power reclining switch support and attaching bolt
4. Actuator drive cable
5. Actuator jackscrew
6. Actuator jackscrew nut and rubber grommets
7. Actuator gearnut attaching screws (clutch head type)
8. Actuator drive cable-to-gearnut coupling

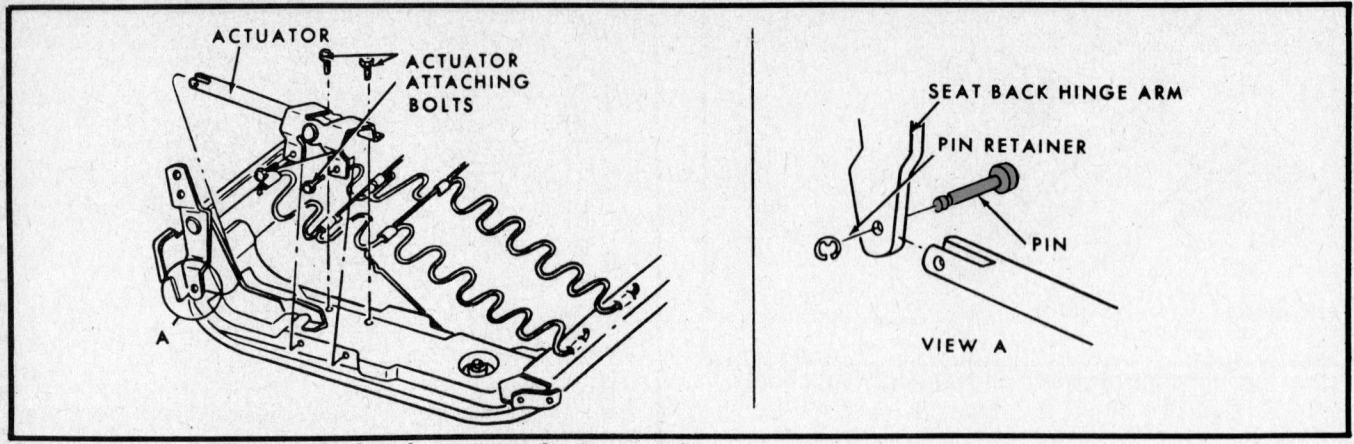

Power recliner actuator and related components (type one)

NISSAN

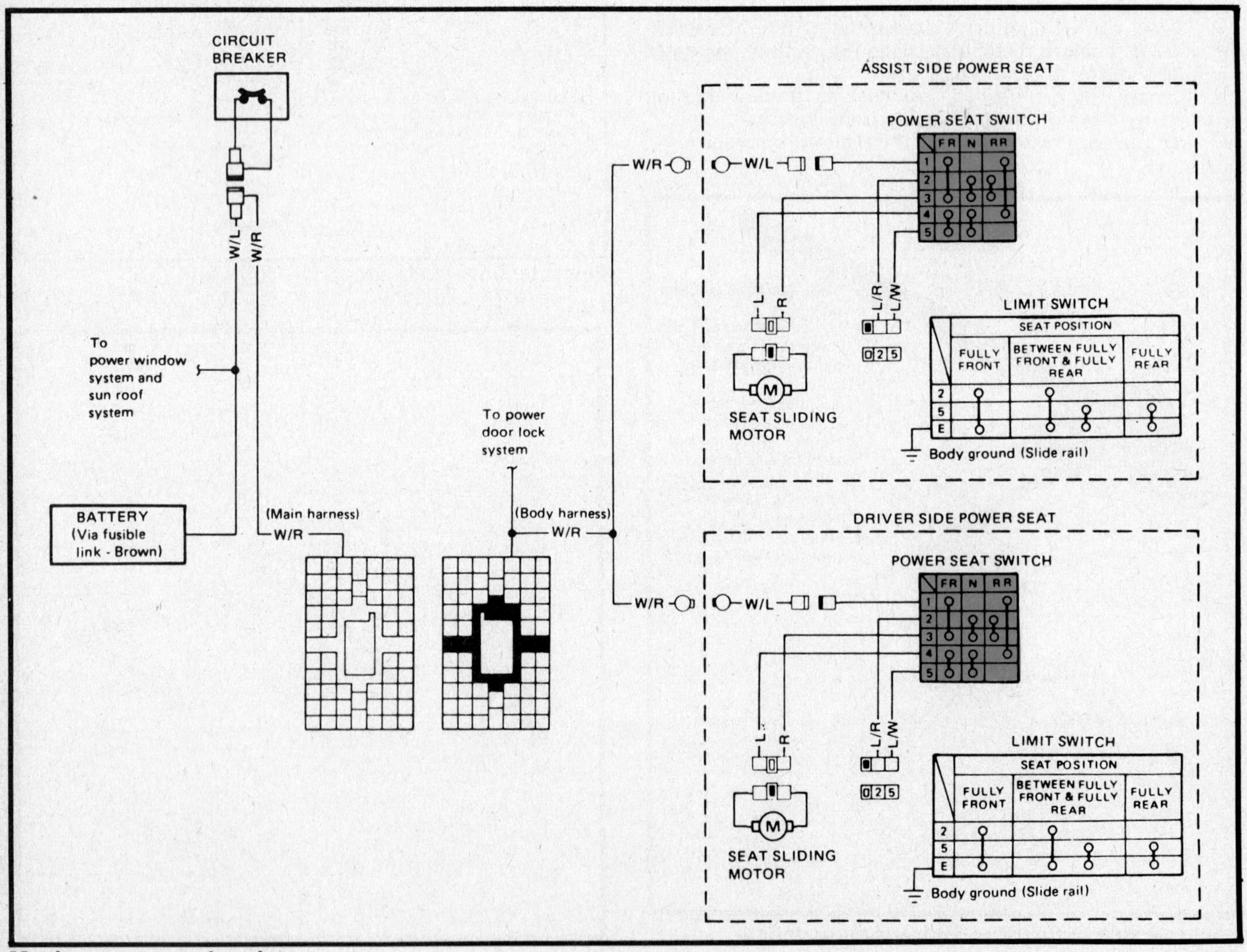

Maxima power seat system

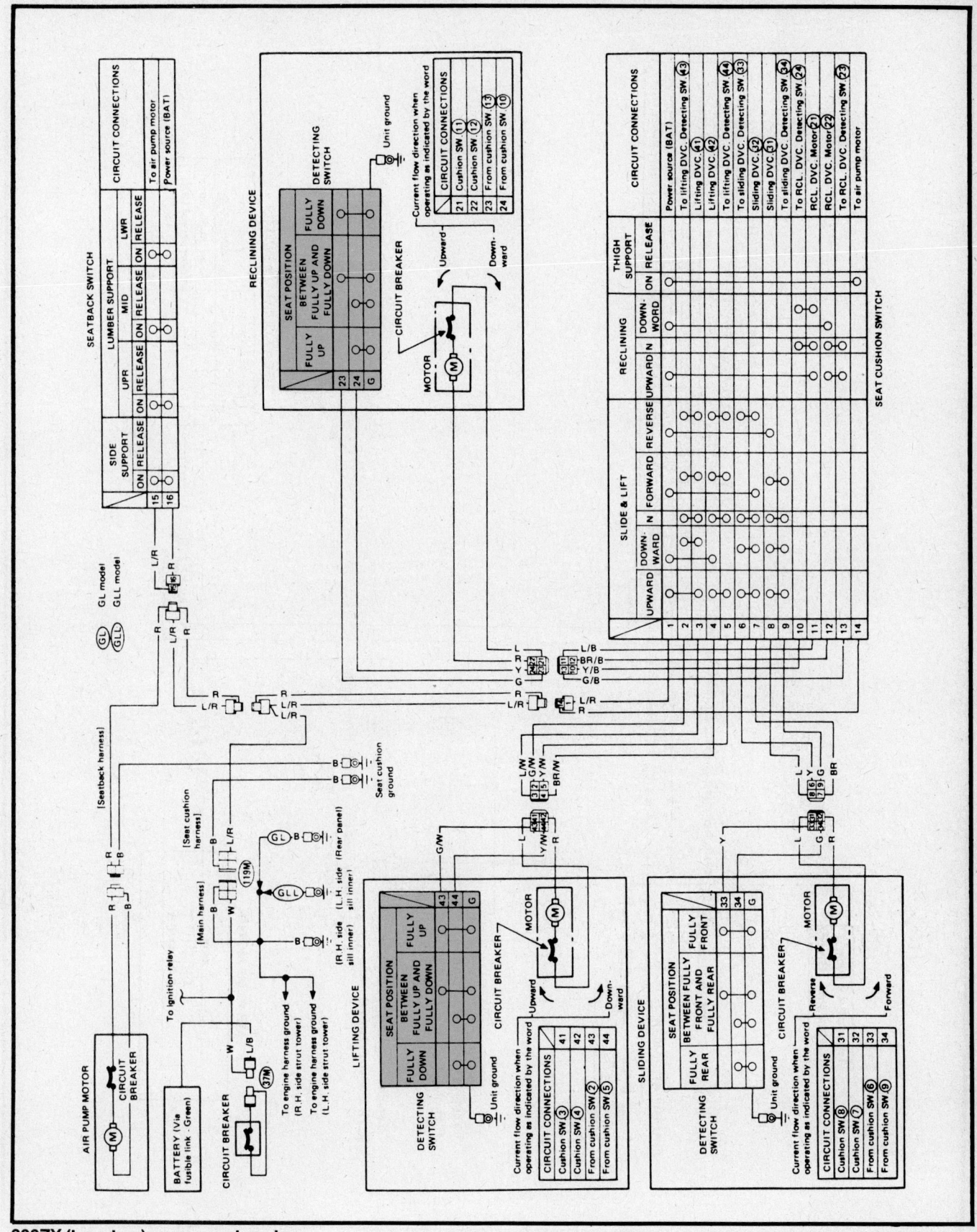

300ZX (type two) power seat system

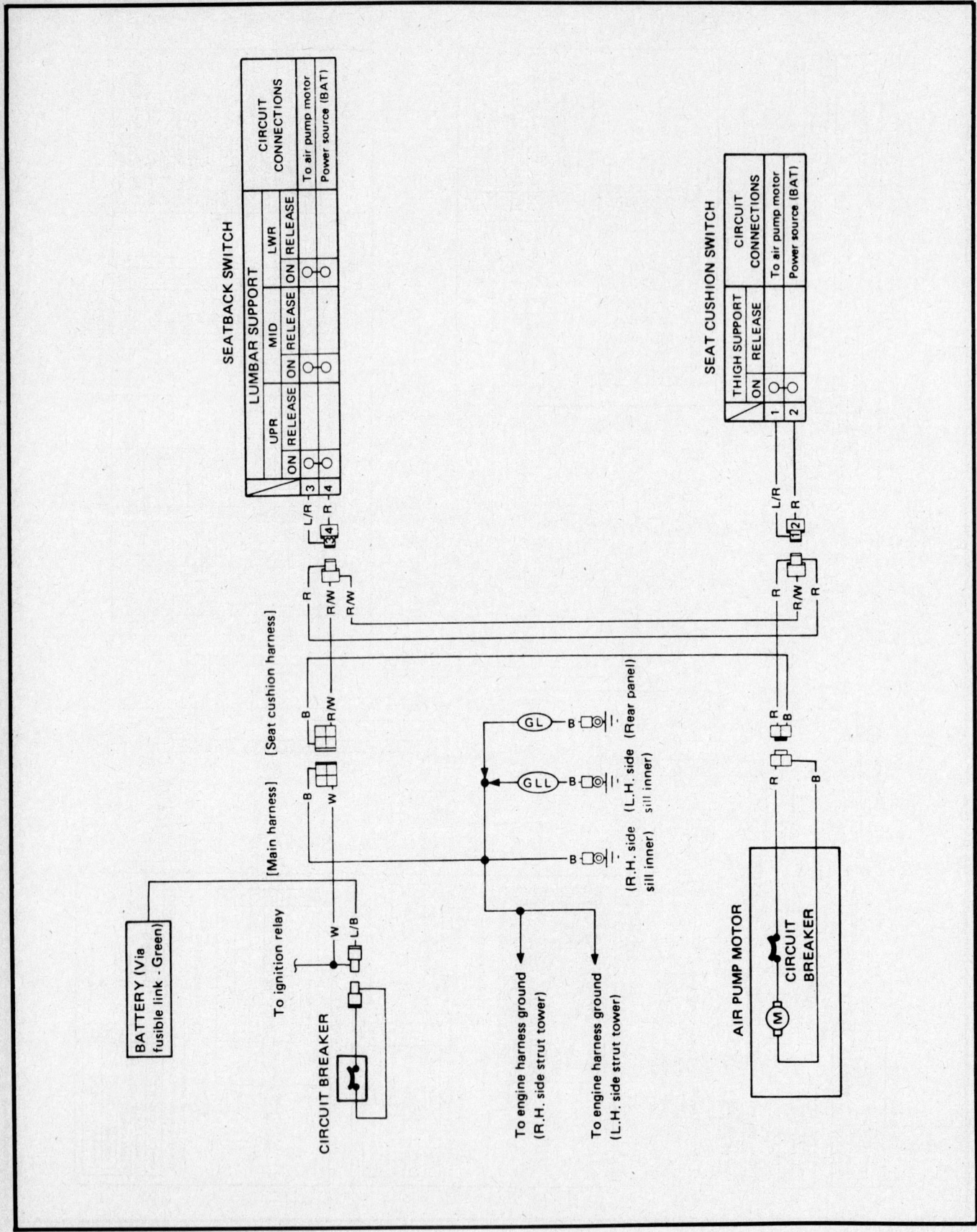

300ZX (type one) power seat system

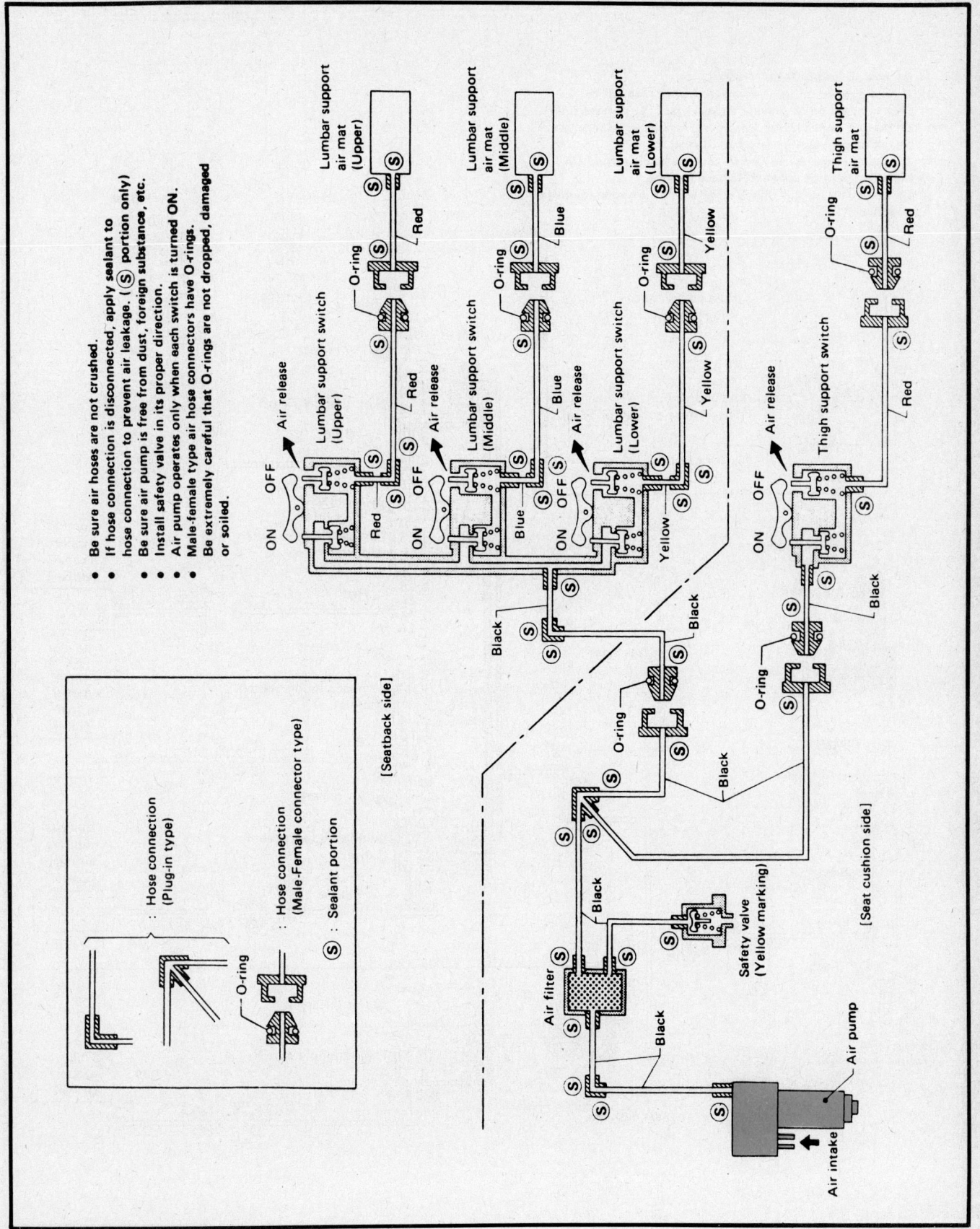

300ZX (type one) lumbar support air schematic

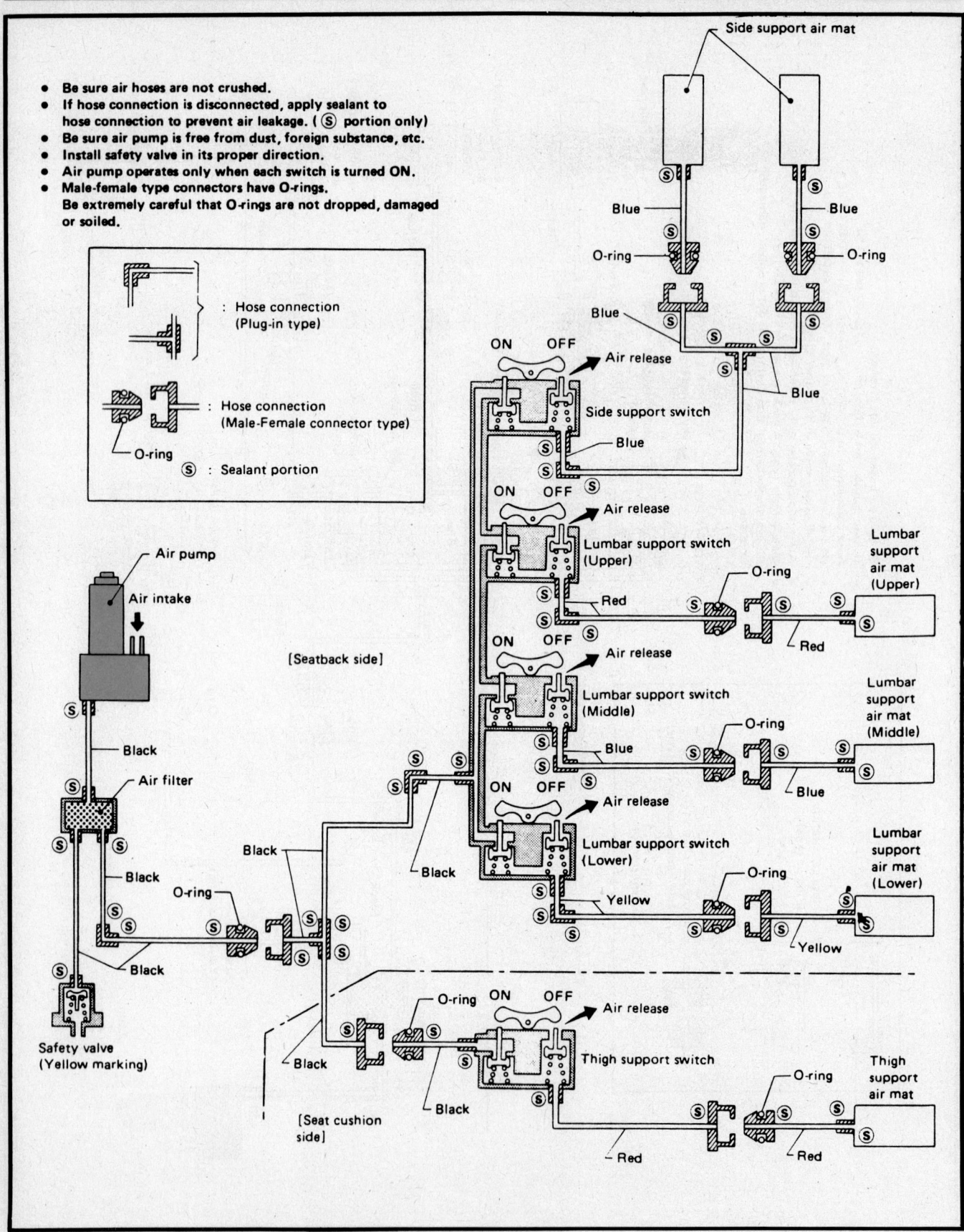

- Be sure air hoses are not crushed.
- If hose connection is disconnected, apply sealant to hose connection to prevent air leakage. (Ⓢ portion only)
- Be sure air pump is free from dust, foreign substance, etc.
- Install safety valve in its proper direction.
- Air pump operates only when each switch is turned ON.
- Male-female type connectors have O-rings.
  Be extremely careful that O-rings are not dropped, damaged or soiled.

: Hose connection (Plug-in type)

: Hose connection (Male-Female connector type)

O-ring

Ⓢ : Sealant portion

Side support air mat

Blue — Blue

O-ring — O-ring

Blue

ON   OFF

Air release

Side support switch

Blue

ON   OFF

Air release

Lumbar support switch (Upper)

O-ring

Red

Red

Lumbar support air mat (Upper)

ON   OFF

Air release

Lumbar support switch (Middle)

Blue

O-ring

Blue

Lumbar support air mat (Middle)

ON   OFF

Air release

Lumbar support switch (Lower)

Yellow

O-ring

Yellow

Lumbar support air mat (Lower)

Air pump

Air intake

[Seatback side]

Black

Air filter

Black

O-ring

Black

Black

Black

Safety valve (Yellow marking)

O-ring   ON   OFF

Air release

Thigh support switch

O-ring

Red   Red

Thigh support air mat

Black

[Seat cushion side]

Black

300ZX (type two) lumbar support air schematic

Component Replacement

POWER SEAT SWITCH

Removal and Installation

SEAT MOUNTED SWITCH

1. Disconnect the negative battery cable. Remove the seat trim plate, as required.
2. Remove the power seat switch retaining screws.
3. Pull the switch from its mounting. Disconnect the electrical connector from the back of the switch assembly.
4. Remove the power seat switch from the vehicle.
5. Installation is the reverse of the removal procedure.

SEAT TRACKS

Removal and Installation

1. Remove the retaining bolts that hold the seat assembly to the floorpan. It may be necessary to move the seat forward and backward in order to gain access to the retaining bolts.
2. Disconnect the negative battery cable.
3. Tilt the seat back and disconnect the wiring harness.
4. Remove the seat belt retaining bolts, as required. Remove the seat assembly from the vehicle.

5. Remove the bolts that attach the seat track to the seat frame. Remove tie straps, as required, that may be holding the cable housing to the seat assembly.
6. Installation is the reverse of the removal procedure.

SEAT MOTOR AND CABLES

Removal and Installation

1. Disconnect the negative battery cable.
2. Remove the seat assembly from the vehicle.
3. Remove the motor retaining bolts from the seat mounting.
4. Disconnect the housings and the drive cable from the motor.
5. Remove the motor assembly from its mounting.
6. Installation is the reverse of the removal procedure.

VERTICAL AND HORIZONTAL ACTUATORS

Removal and Installation

1. Disconnect the negative battery cable.
2. Remove the seat assembly from the vehicle. Remove the seat tracks from the seat assembly.
3. Remove the seat sliding mechanism retaining bolts. Remove the seat sliding mechanism from its mounting on the seat track assembly.
4. Installation is the reverse of the removal procedure.

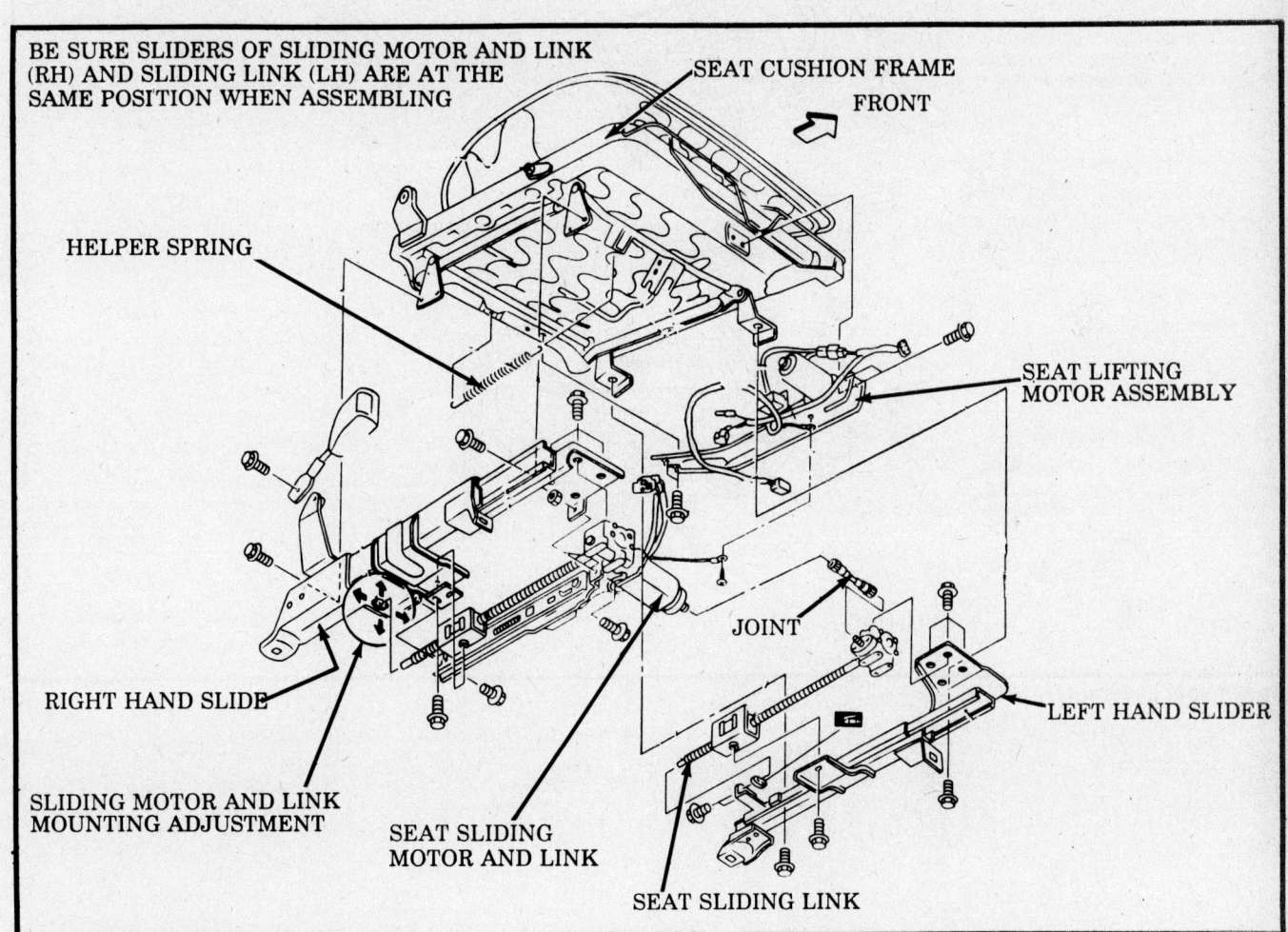

BE SURE SLIDERS OF SLIDING MOTOR AND LINK (RH) AND SLIDING LINK (LH) ARE AT THE SAME POSITION WHEN ASSEMBLING

SEAT CUSHION FRAME

FRONT

HELPER SPRING

SEAT LIFTING MOTOR ASSEMBLY

JOINT

RIGHT HAND SLIDE

LEFT HAND SLIDER

SLIDING MOTOR AND LINK MOUNTING ADJUSTMENT

SEAT SLIDING MOTOR AND LINK

SEAT SLIDING LINK

Power seat assembly—300ZX (type two)

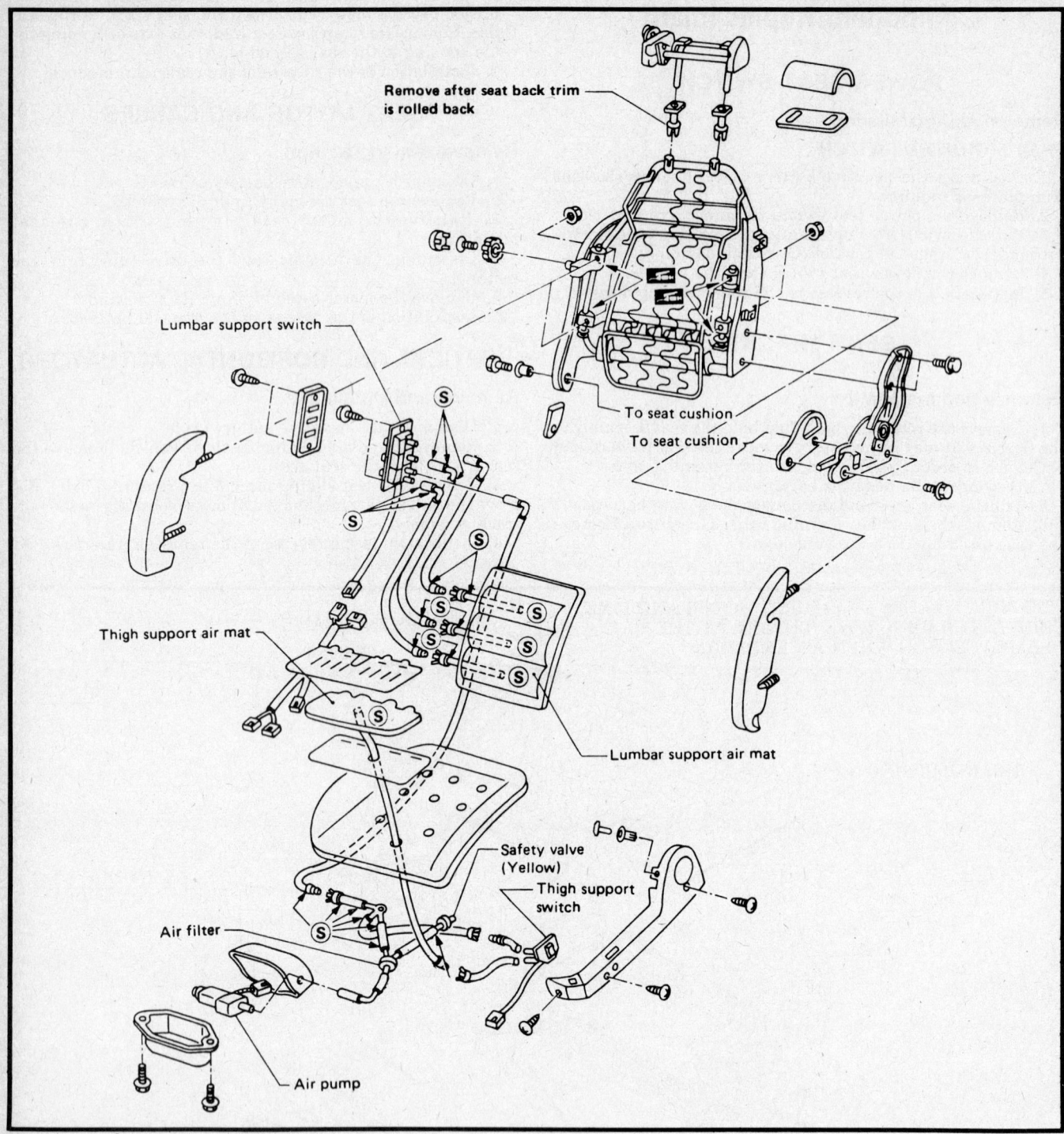

Remove after seat back trim
is rolled back

Lumbar support switch

To seat cushion

To seat cushion

Thigh support air mat

Lumbar support air mat

Safety valve
(Yellow)

Thigh support
switch

Air filter

Air pump

Power seat assembly—300ZX

DIAGNOSIS AND TESTING

All power window units covered in this section are basically similar in operation.

Failure of the window to operate satisfactorily, or at all, is either mechanical or electrical in nature.

Mechanical problems are apparent once the door trim panel is removed, and the components inspected in place or removed for inspection.

The most common mechanical problems are jamming of the regulator or a failure of the lift belt or guides.

Electrical failures are traceable to a fault in the switch, wiring or motor. Each component must be removed to be tested and the switches and wiring are tested in the conventional way for continuity and resistance.

To test the motor, connect it to a 12 volt source with an ammeter in series on the negative side.

Operate the motor and observe the current draw. The no-load current should not exceed the rating stamped on the motor, and should not fluctuate.

The motors are not repairable and are serviced by replacement only.

AMERICAN MOTORS

Electric Window Motor

REMOVAL AND INSTALLATION

Linkage Type Lift Mechanism

1. Position the window about halfway up.
2. Disconnect the battery ground.
3. Remove the door trim panel and weather sheet.
4. Hold the window in place with masking tape.
5. Remove the regulator arm retaining clip and remove the arm from the bottom window channel.

6. Disconnect the motor wiring.
7. Unbolt and remove the regulator and motor.
8. Installation is the reverse of removal.

Belt Type Lift Mechanism

1. Position the window about halfway up.
2. Disconnect the battery ground.
3. Remove the door trim panel and weather sheet.
4. Remove the speaker.
5. Remove the glass-to-belt drive retaining pin from the window channel by rotating it 90°, so that it is parallel with the window channel.

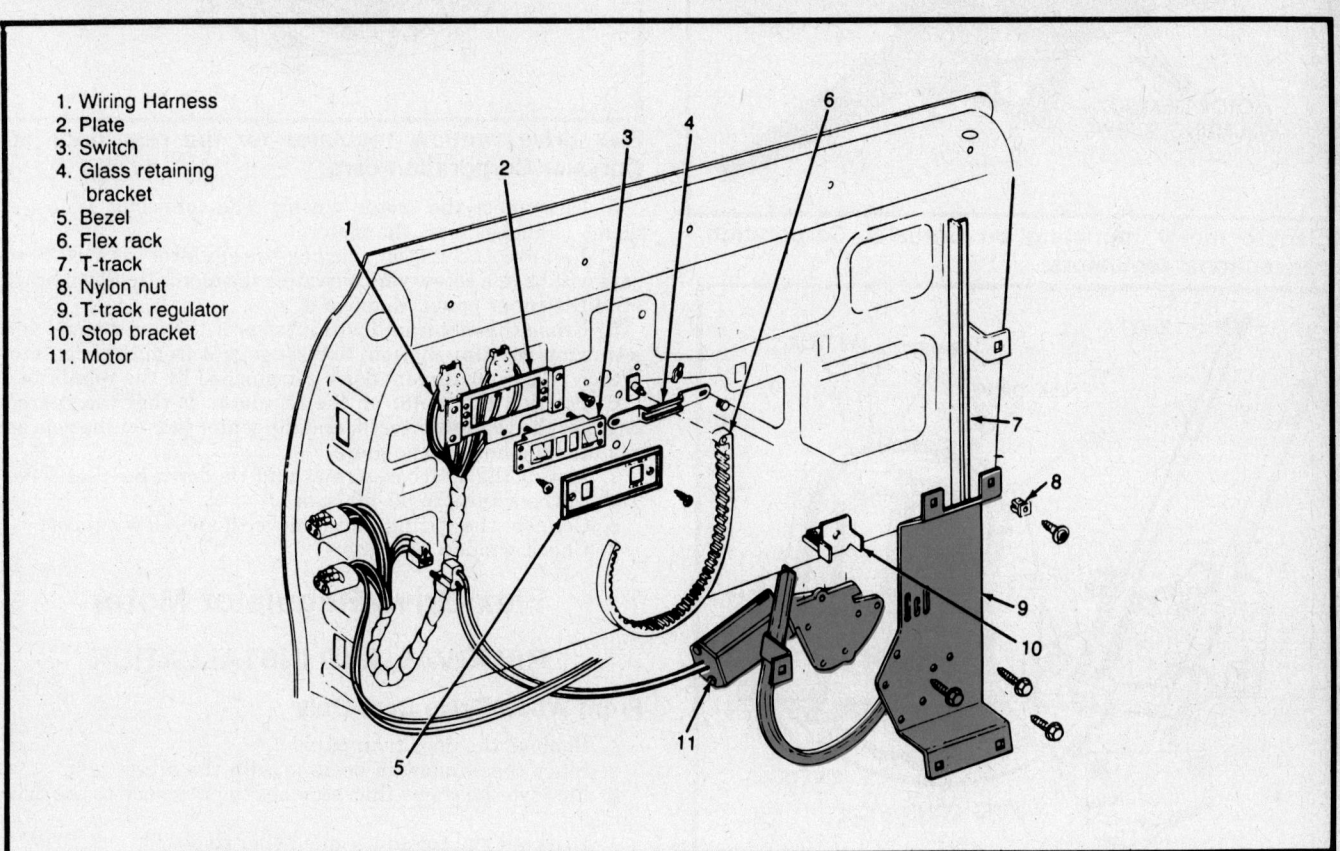

1. Wiring Harness
2. Plate
3. Switch
4. Glass retaining bracket
5. Bezel
6. Flex rack
7. T-track
8. Nylon nut
9. T-track regulator
10. Stop bracket
11. Motor

AMC belt drive power window system

6. Carefully pull the retaining pin through the window channel slot and push the window glass to the fully raised position. Hold it in place with masking tape.

7. Remove the window drive belt track retaining screws.

8. Disconnect the motor wiring.

9. Remove the track and motor assembly through the access hole in the bottom of the door.

10. Installation is the reverse of removal.

CHRYSLER CORPORATION

Sector Gear Type Lift Motor

REMOVAL AND INSTALLATION

All Cars

1. Remove the door trim panel.

2. Place the window in the full up position and hold it there with a block when removing and installing the motor.

———— CAUTION ————

If the window is in any position other than the full up position, and the motor is separated from the regulator, the regulator counterbalance spring will tend to propel the window upwards!

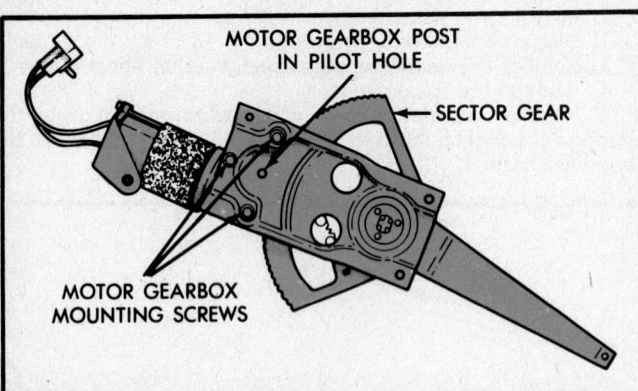

Electric motor mounting on Chrysler Corporation conventional regulators

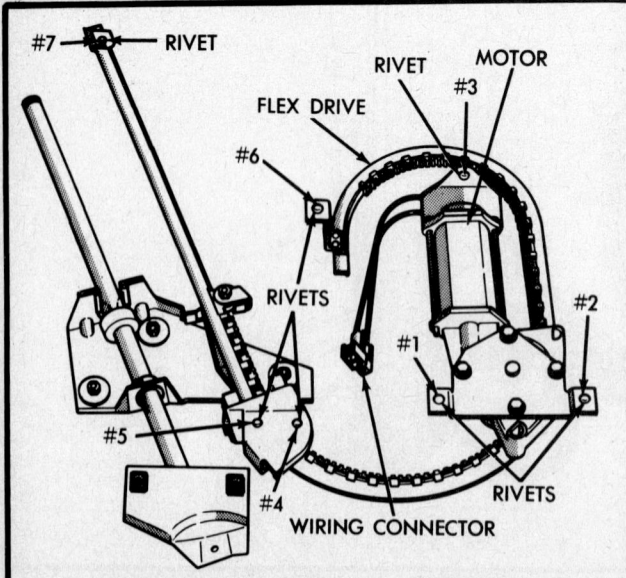

Flex drive window regulator for the front door of Chrysler Corporation cars

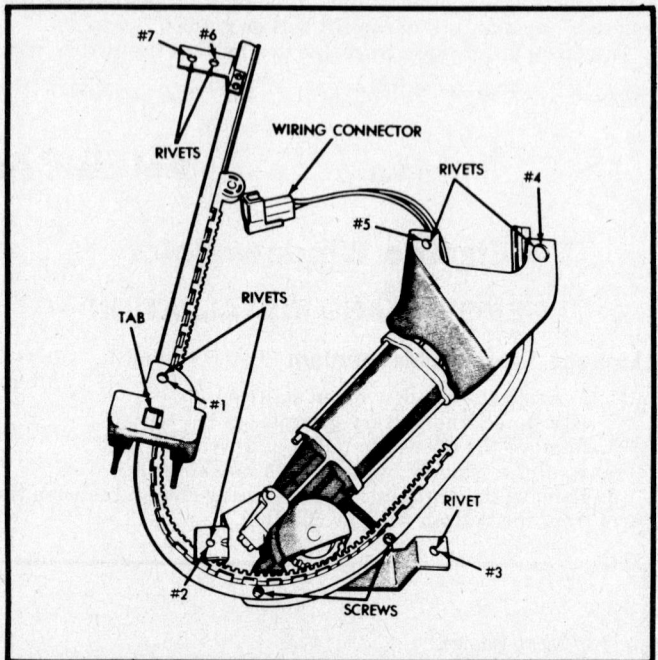

Flex drive window regulator for the rear door of Chrysler Corporation cars

3. Disconnect the motor wiring. The connector is located about 11 inches from the motor.

4. Remove the motor gearbox-to-regulator screws. Some cars will have a screw which secures the motor tie-down bracket to the inner panel. Remove it.

5. Grasp the motor and pull it towards the outer panel with a turning twisting motion, to disengage it from the regulator. Watch that your fingers don't get pinched by the regulator.

6. Position the motor on the regulator so that the gearbox engages the regulator teeth, and the center post on the gearbox fits into the hole in the plate.

7. Install the gearbox screws and tie-down bracket screw. Torque the screws to 50–60 in.lb.

8. Connect the wiring and remove the window support

9. Check window operation.

Flex Drive Regulator Motor

REMOVAL AND INSTALLATION

Front Wheel Drive Cars Only

1. Remove the door trim panel.

2. Place the window in position with the access hole.

3. Remove the screw that attaches the flex rack to the drive arm.

4. Drill out the regulator mounting rivets.

5. Manuever the motor end of the flex drive regulator outboard of the large inside panel access hole and rotate it out of the door.

NOTE: If the window is stuck so that the regulator cannot be removed through the access hole, it will be necessary, after rivet removal, to manually lift the window into position, an, if necessary, remove the T-track-to-motor screws.

6. Install the motor to the T-track and torque the screws to 40 in.lb.
7. Feed the top of the T-track into the access hole and rotate it towards the hinge pillar until the motor is about horizontal. Then, rotate it in the opposite direction about ¼ turn and line up the bracket tab with the inner panel slot.
8. Install the rivets in the sequence shown in the accompanying illustration.
9. Actuate the motor until the flex rack is visible within the access slot and attach the window and drive arm assembly to the flex rack.
10. Install the trim panel.

FORD MOTOR COMPANY

Window Lift Motor

REMOVAL AND INSTALLATION

Lincoln Town Car
Crown Victoria
Grand Marquis
FRONT DOOR

1. Raise the window to the full up position.
2. Disconnect the battery ground.
3. Remove the door trim panel.
4. Disconnect the motor wiring and move it well aside.
5. Drill three ½ inch diameter holes in the inner door panel, using the preformed dimples.

— **CAUTION** —

Make certain that the window is blocked in the full up position and that the regulator arm is in a fixed position to prevent sudden counterbalance spring unwinding when the motor is removed.

6. Remove the three window motor mounting bolts.
7. Push the motor towards the outer door panel to disengage it from the regulator.
8. Remove the motor from the door.

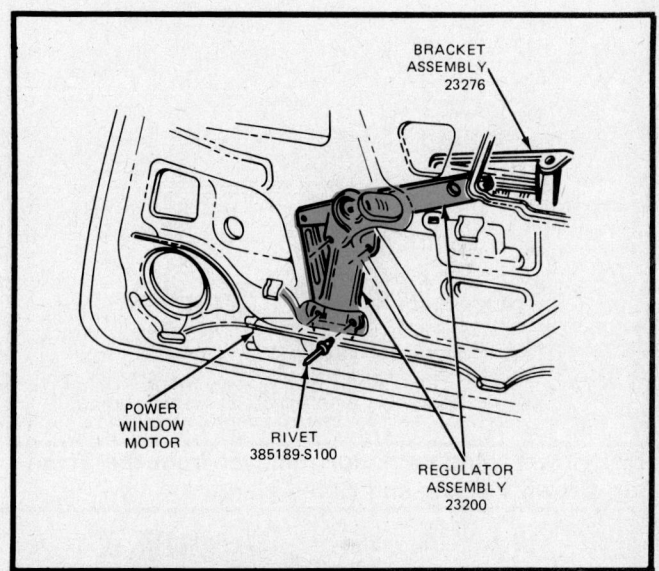

Front window power regulator on the Town Car, Crown Victoria and Grand Marquis

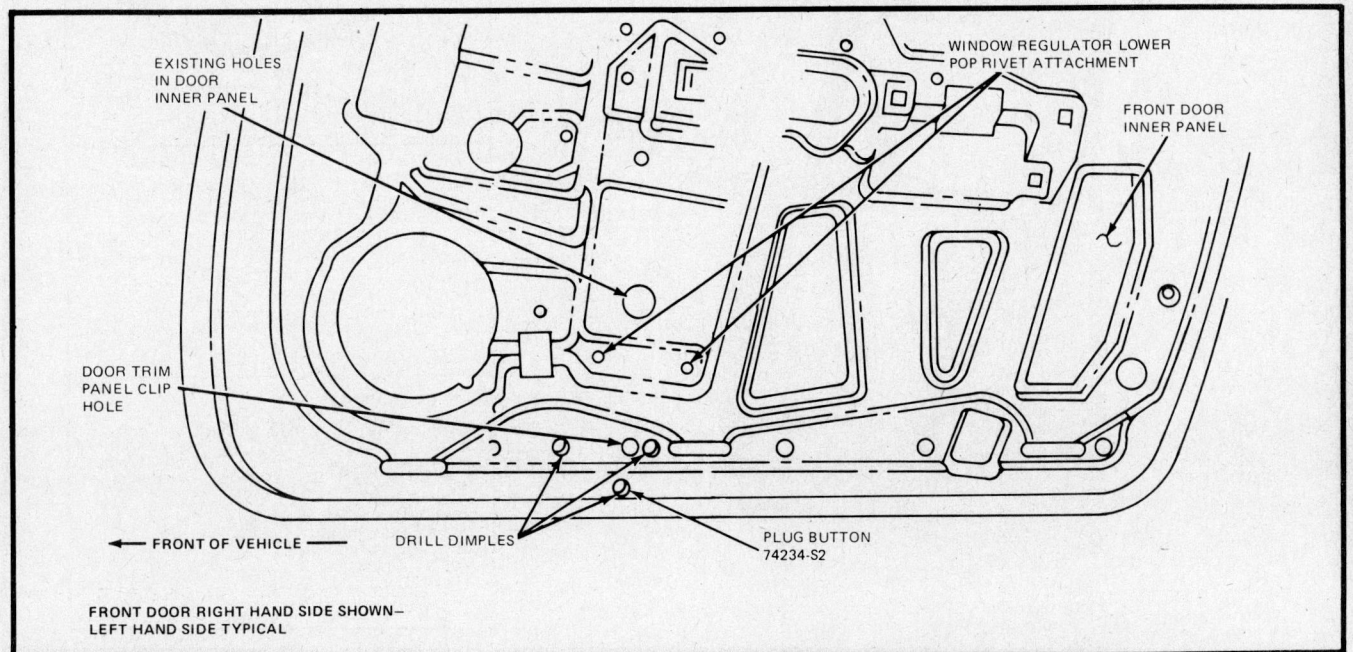

Front power window motor removal from the Town Car, Crown Victoria and Grand Marquis

9. When installing the motor, engage the regulator gears with the motor drive and torque the mounting bolts to 50–85 in.lb. Install plug button 74234-5 in the lower access hole that you drilled and paint it to match the sheet metal. This hole is not covered by the trim panel. Seal the other two access holes with waterproof tape.

10. Connect the wiring and test the window operation.

11. Install the trim panel.

REAR DOOR

1. Raise the window to the full up position.
2. Disconnect the battery ground.
3. Remove the door trim panel.
4. Disconnect the motor wiring and move it well aside.

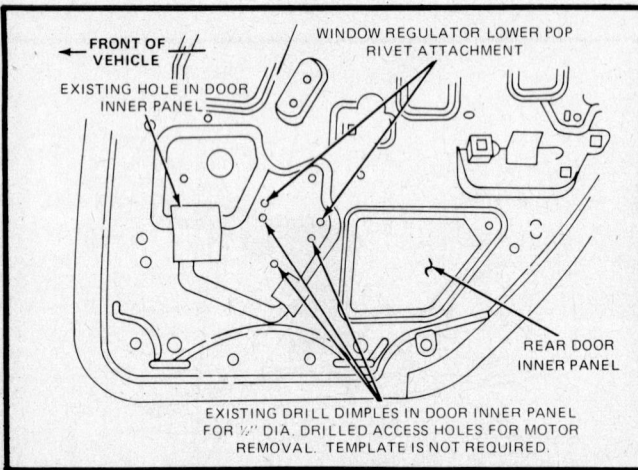

Rear power window motor removal from the Town Car, Crown Victoria and Grand Marquis

5. Using a ¾" hole saw with a ¼" pilot, drill three holes in the inner door panel, using the preformed dimples.

CAUTION

Make certain that the window is blocked in the full up position and that the regulator arm is in a fixed position to prevent sudden counterbalance spring unwinding when the motor is removed.

6. Remove the three window motor mounting bolts.
7. Push the motor towards the outer door panel to disengage it from the regulator.
8. Remove the motor from the door.
9. When installing the motor, engage the regulator gears with the motor drive and torque the mounting bolts to 50–85 in.lb. Seal the access holes with waterproof tape.
10. Connect the wiring and test the window operation.
11. Install the trim panel.

Continental
Mark VII
Thunderbird
Cougar
Granada
LTD
Marquis
Mustang
Capri

1. Raise the window to the full up position.
2. Disconnect the battery ground.
3. Remove the door trim panel.
4. Disconnect the motor wiring and move it well aside.
5. On the Mark VII, Thunderbird, Cougar, LTD and Marquis, using a ¾" hole saw with a ¼" pilot, drill three holes in the inner door panel, using the preformed dimples.

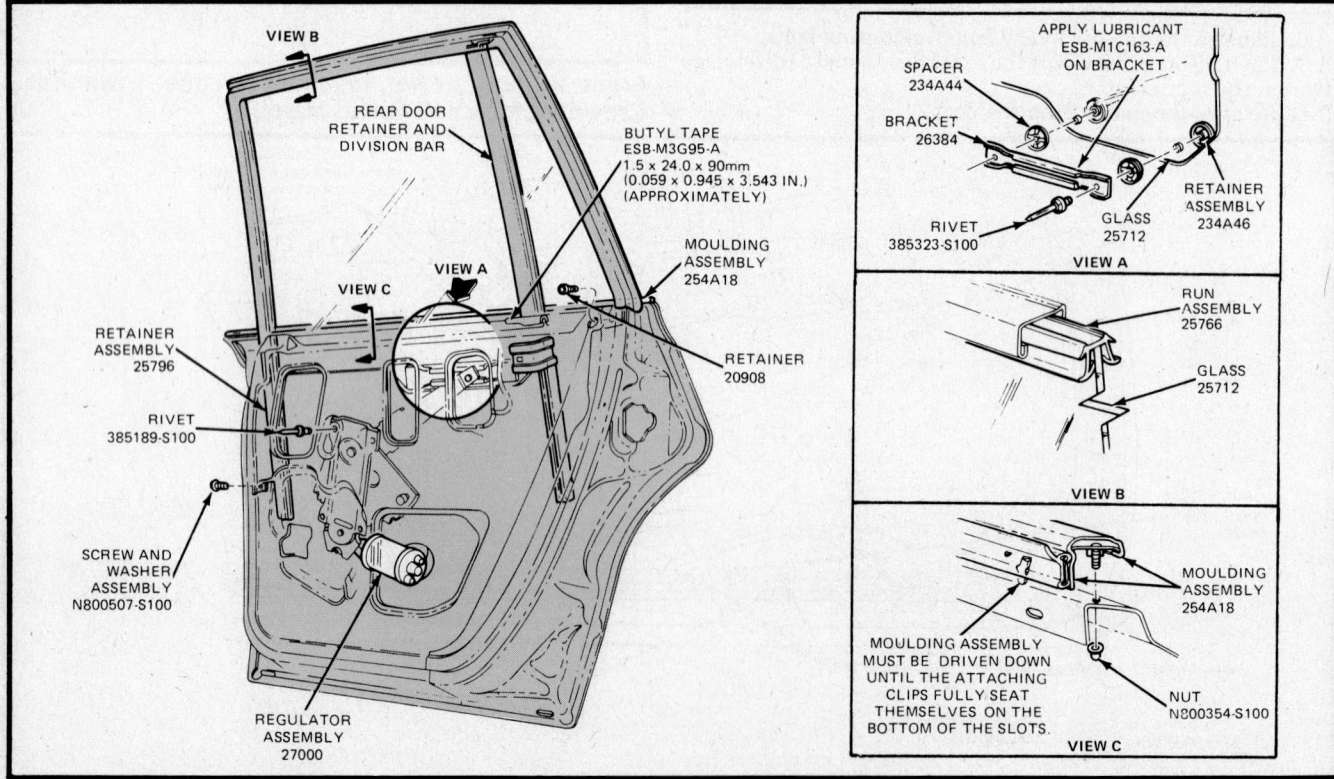

Window mechanism for the rear door of the Town Car

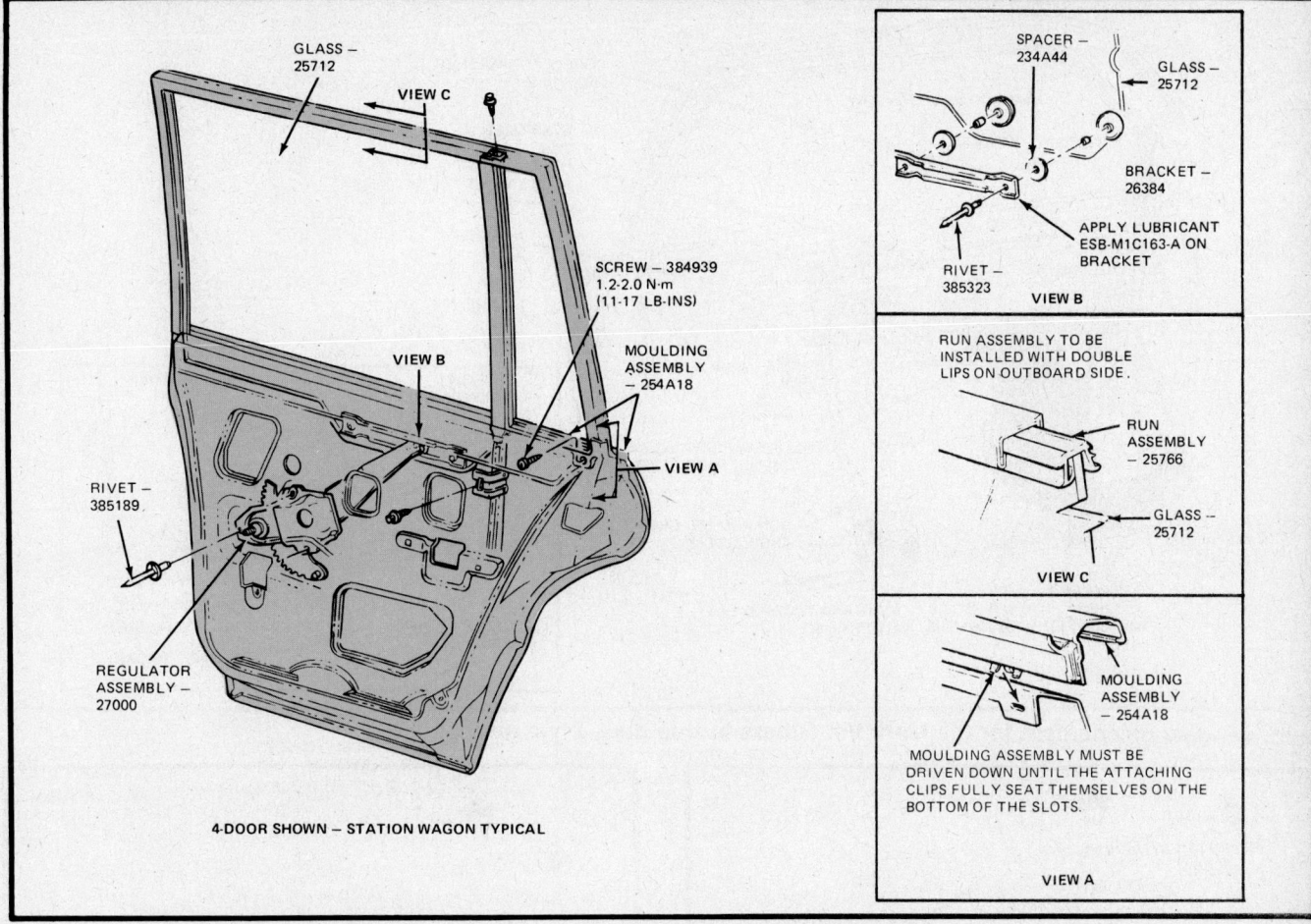

GLASS –
25712

VIEW C

SCREW – 384939
1.2-2.0 N·m
(11-17 LB-INS)

VIEW B

MOULDING
ASSEMBLY
– 254A18

VIEW A

RIVET –
385189

REGULATOR
ASSEMBLY –
27000

4-DOOR SHOWN – STATION WAGON TYPICAL

SPACER –
234A44

GLASS –
25712

BRACKET –
26384

APPLY LUBRICANT
ESB-M1C163-A ON
BRACKET

RIVET –
385323

VIEW B

RUN ASSEMBLY TO BE
INSTALLED WITH DOUBLE
LIPS ON OUTBOARD SIDE.

RUN
ASSEMBLY
– 25766

GLASS –
25712

VIEW C

MOULDING
ASSEMBLY
– 254A18

MOULDING ASSEMBLY MUST BE
DRIVEN DOWN UNTIL THE ATTACHING
CLIPS FULLY SEAT THEMSELVES ON THE
BOTTOM OF THE SLOTS.

VIEW A

Window mechanism for the rear door of the Crown Victoria and Grand Marquis

---

CAUTION

Make certain that the window is blocked in the full up position and that the regulator arm is in a fixed position to prevent sudden counterbalance spring unwinding when the motor is removed.

6. Remove the three window motor mounting bolts.
7. Push the motor towards the outer door panel to disengage it from the regulator.
8. Remove the motor from the door.
9. When installing the motor, engage the regulator gears with the motor drive and torque the mounting bolts to 50–85 in.lb. Install plug button 74234-5 in the lower access hole that you drilled and paint it to match the sheet metal. This hole is not covered by the trim panel. Seal the other two access holes with waterproof tape.
10. Connect the wiring and test the window operation.
11. Install the trim panel.

Tempo and Topaz

2-DOOR

1. Raise the window to the full up position.
2. Disconnect the battery ground.
3. Remove the door trim panel.
4. Disconnect the motor wiring and move it well aside.
5. Using a ¾″ hole saw with a ¼″ pilot, drill two holes in the inner door panel, using the preformed dimples.

CAUTION

Make certain that the window is blocked in the full up position and that the regulator arm is in a fixed position to prevent sudden counterbalance spring unwinding when the motor is removed.

6. Remove the three window motor mounting bolts.
7. Push the motor towards the outer door panel to disengage it from the regulator.
8. Remove the motor from the door.
9. When installing the motor, engage the regulator gears with the motor drive and torque the mounting bolts to 50–85 in.lb. Seal the two access holes with waterproof tape.
10. Connect the wiring and test the window operation.
11. Install the trim panel.

4-DOOR, FRONT DOOR

1. Raise the window to the full up position.
2. Disconnect the battery ground.
3. Remove the door trim panel.
4. Disconnect the motor wiring and move it well aside.
5. Using a ¾″ hole saw with a ¼″ pilot, drill a hole in the inner door panel, adjacent to the speaker opening, using the preformed dimple. At the upper mounting screw, sheet metal interference can be removed by grinding.

CAUTION

Make certain that the window is blocked in the full up position and that the regulator arm is in a fixed position to prevent sudden counterbalance spring unwinding when the motor is removed.

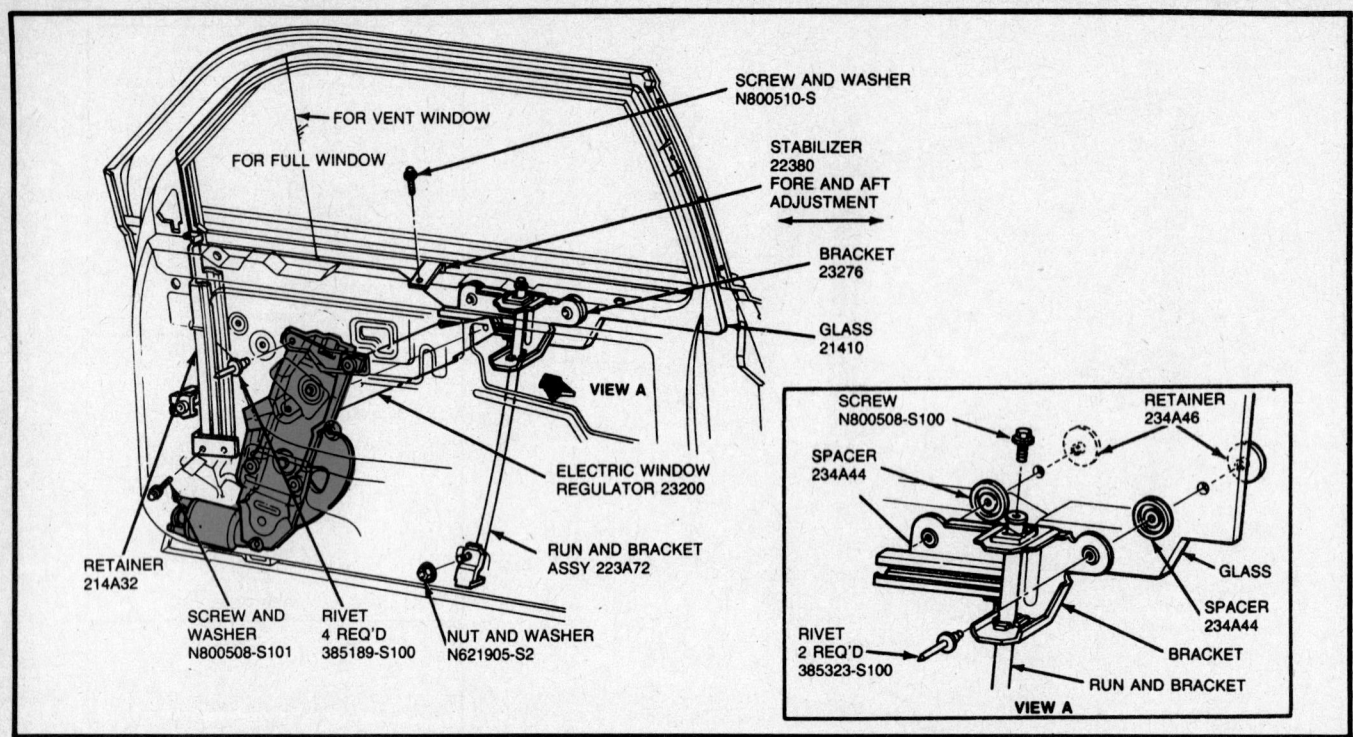

Door window mechanism for the Mark VII. Others in this body style are similar

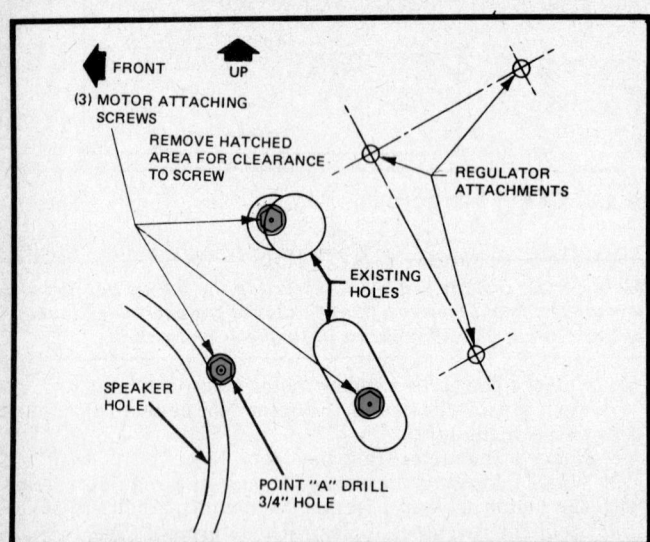

Power window motor removal from the front door of a 4-door Escort, Lynx, Tempo and Topaz

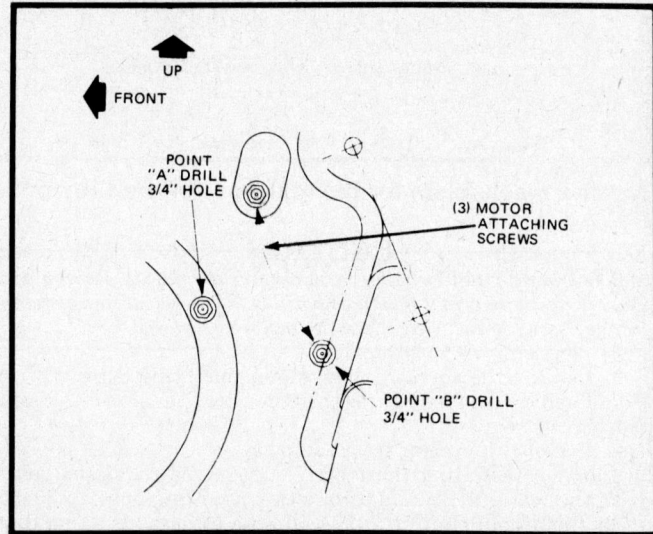

Power window motor removal from the 2-door Escort, Lynx, Tempo and Topaz

6. Remove the three window motor mounting bolts.
7. Push the motor towards the outer door panel to disengage it from the regulator.
8. Remove the motor from the door.
9. When installing the motor, engage the regulator gears with the motor drive and torque the mounting bolts to 50–85 in.lb. Seal the access hole with waterproof tape.
10. Connect the wiring and test the window operation.
11. Install the trim panel.

4-DOOR, REAR DOOR

1. Raise the window to the full up position.
2. Disconnect the battery ground.

3. Remove the door trim panel.
4. Disconnect the motor wiring and move it well aside.
5. Using a ¾" hole saw with a ¼" pilot, drill three holes in the inner door panel, using the preformed dimples.

CAUTION

Make certain that the window is blocked in the full up position and that the regulator arm is in a fixed position to prevent sudden counterbalance spring unwinding when the motor is removed.

6. Remove the three window motor mounting bolts.
7. Push the motor towards the outer door panel to disengage it from the regulator.

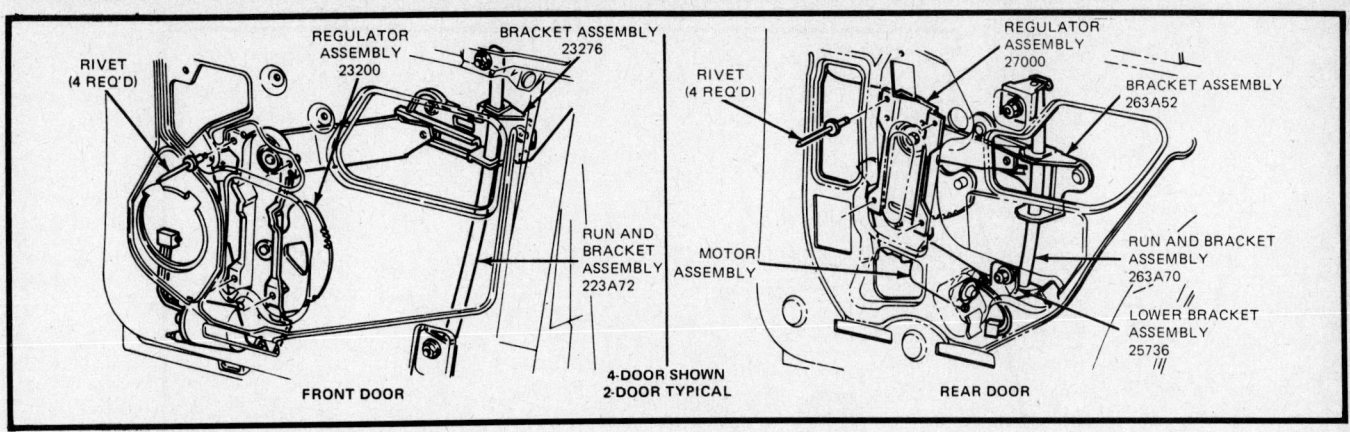

Window regulator used in the Escort, Lynx, Tempo and Topaz

8. Remove the motor from the door.

9. When installing the motor, engage the regulator gears with the motor drive and torque the mounting bolts to 50–85 in.lb. Seal the access holes with waterproof tape.

10. Connect the wiring and test the window operation.

11. Install the trim panel.

Fairmont
Zephyr

4-DOOR, FRONT DOOR AND STATION WAGONS

1. Raise the window to the full up position.

2. Disconnect the battery ground.

3. Remove the door trim panel.

4. Disconnect the motor wiring and move it well aside.

5. Using a ¾″ hole saw with a ¼″ pilot, drill a hole in the inner door panel, adjacent to the speaker opening, using the preformed dimple. At the upper mounting screw, sheet metal interference can be removed by grinding.

— CAUTION —

Make certain that the window is blocked in the full up position and that the regulator arm is in a fixed position to prevent sudden counterbalance spring unwinding when the motor is removed.

6. Remove the three window motor mounting bolts.

7. Push the motor towards the outer door panel to disengage it from the regulator.

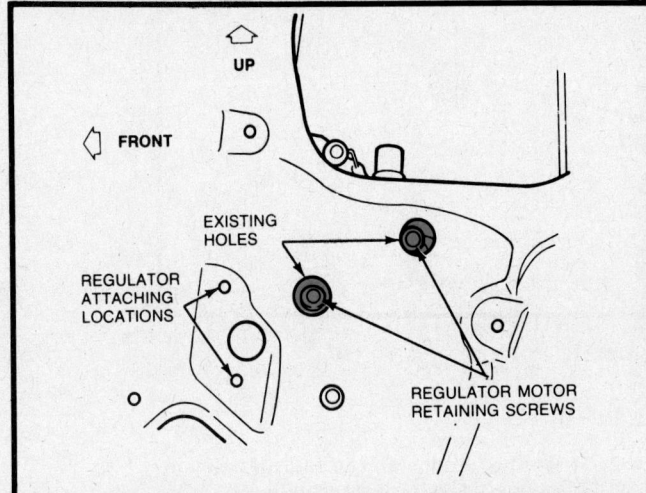

Regulator attaching bolts on the Taurus and Sable

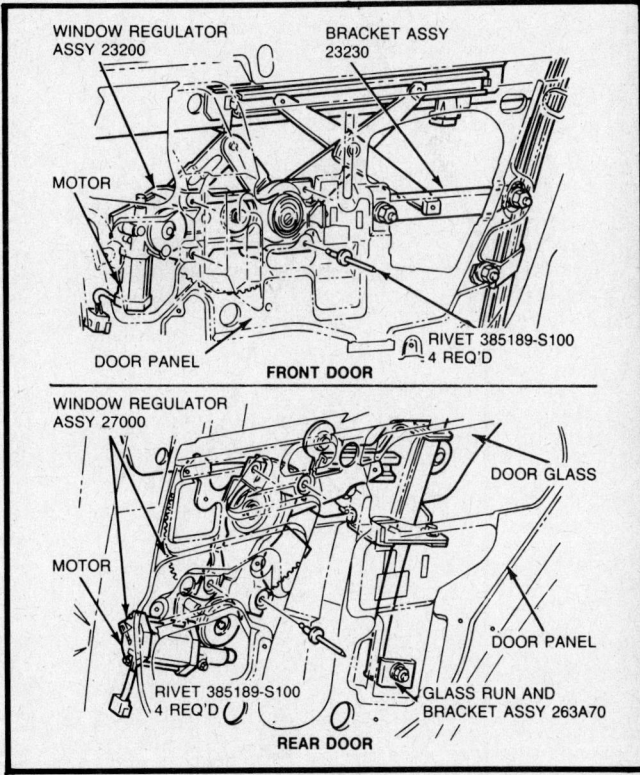

Taurus and Sable power window mechanisms

8. Remove the motor from the door.

9. When installing the motor, engage the regulator gears with the motor drive and torque the mounting bolts to 50–85 in.lb. Seal the access hole with waterproof tape.

10. Connect the wiring and test the window operation.

11. Install the trim panel.

4-DOOR, REAR DOOR

1. Raise the window to the full up position.

2. Disconnect the battery ground.

3. Remove the door trim panel.

4. Disconnect the motor wiring and move it well aside.

5. Using a ¾″ hole saw with a ¼″ pilot, drill three holes in the inner door panel, using the preformed dimples.

6. Remove the three window motor mounting bolts.

7. Push the motor towards the outer door panel to disengage it from the regulator.

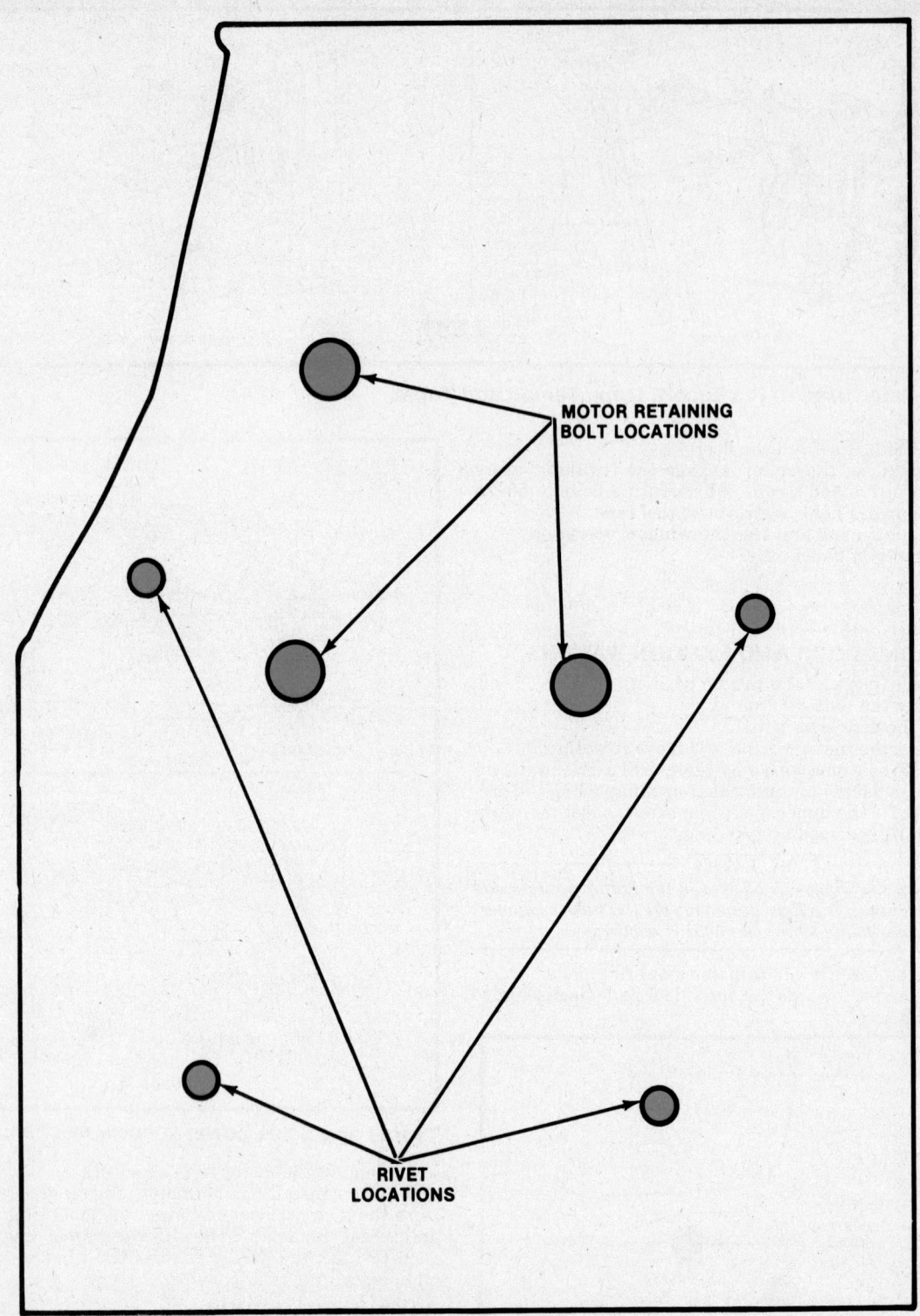

**MOTOR RETAINING
BOLT LOCATIONS**

**RIVET
LOCATIONS**

Taurus/Sable template

8. Remove the motor from the door.
9. When installing the motor, engage the regulator gears with the motor drive and torque the mounting bolts to 50–85 in.lb. Seal the access holes with waterproof tape.
10. Connect the wiring and test the window operation.
11. Install the trim panel.

2-DOOR

1. Raise the window to the full up position.
2. Disconnect the battery ground.
3. Remove the door trim panel.
4. Disconnect the motor wiring and move it well aside.

5. Drill out the regulator mounting rivets.

6. Slide the regulator square slide out of the glass bracket C-channel and suuport the glass in the up position.

7. Move the regulator base to the large access hole in the door panel so that the counterbalance spring is within reach for removal. Using a C-clamp, clamp the regulator base to the door panel.

CAUTION

Make certain that the window is blocked in the full up position and that the regulator arm is in a fixed position to prevent sudden counterbalance spring unwinding when the motor is removed.

8. Fabricate a tool, such as the one illustrated, and release the tension from the spring.

9. Remove the C-clamp and move the regulator to expose the three motor and drive mounting screws.

10. Reclamp the base and remove the screws.

11. Remove the clamp and disengage the motor and drive from the regulator.

12. When installing the motor, torque the screws to 50–85 in.lb. Move the regulator to the large access hole and clamp it

to the panel when installing the counterbalance spring. The spring must be installed in the same position as when it was removed. Replace the rivets, or use ¼"-20 x ½" bolts with nuts.

13. Connect the wiring and check the window operation.

14. Install the trim panel.

Taurus and Sable

1. Raise the window to the full up position.

2. Disconnect the battery ground.

3. Remove the door trim panel and watershield.

4. Support the glass in the up position. Unplug the motor wiring connector.

5. Copy the template shown here and position it over the rivets on the door panel.

6. Mark the motor attaching bolt locations with a punch and drill out three access holes using a ¾" hole saw with a ¼" pilot.

7. Remove the motor attaching bolts.

8. Push the motor towards the outer door panel and disengage the motor drive from the drive gear.

9. Remove the motor from the door.

10. Installation is the reverse of removal.

GENERAL MOTORS

Motor and Regulator

REMOVAL AND INSTALLATION

Impala
Caprice
Parisienne
Delta 88
Custom Cruiser
98 Regency RWD
LeSabre RWD
Electra RWD
Fleetwood RWD
DeVille RWD

1. Remove the door trim panel and watershield.
2. Raise the glass to the full up position and support it.
3. Remove the lower sash channel bolts.

Power window motor used on almost all General Motors cars

4. Drill out the regulator mounting rivets with a ¼" drill bit.

5. Unplug the motor connector and remove the motor and regulator through an access hole.

CAUTION

If the motor and regulator are to be separated, the sector gear MUST be locked in position. The counterbalance spring could unwind and cause personal injury, otherwise.

8. Drill a hole through the regulator sector gear and backplate, and install a bolt and nut to lock the gear.

9. Installation is the reverse of removal. Replace the rivets with ¼" x ½" aluminum peel type rivets.

El Camino
Monte Carlo
Grand Prix
Bonneville
Cutlass
Regal
1982–84 Riviera
1982–84 Toronado
1982–84 Eldorado

COUPE

1. Remove the door trim panel and watershield.

2. Support the window in the half up position, or remove the glass all together.

3. Matchmark the inner panel cam and remove the attaching screws and cam.

4. Matchmark the vertical guide and remove the attaching screws and guide.

5. Unplug the regulator motor wiring connector.

6. Drill out the regulator attaching rivets with a ¼" drill bit.

7. Remove the lower sash channel-to- glass rear attaching nut.

8. Slide the regulator and motor rearward to disengage the regulator rollers from the lower sash channel cam.

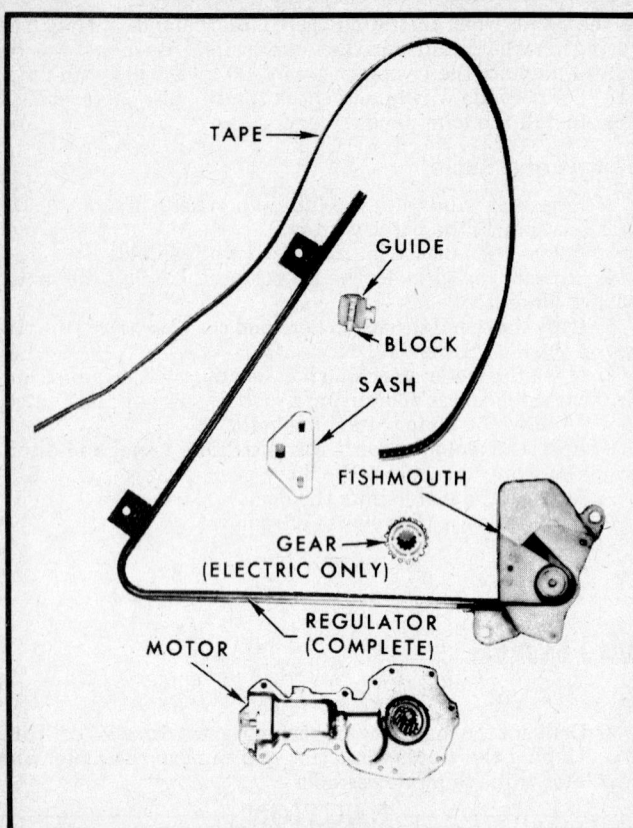

Typical GM tape drive regulator

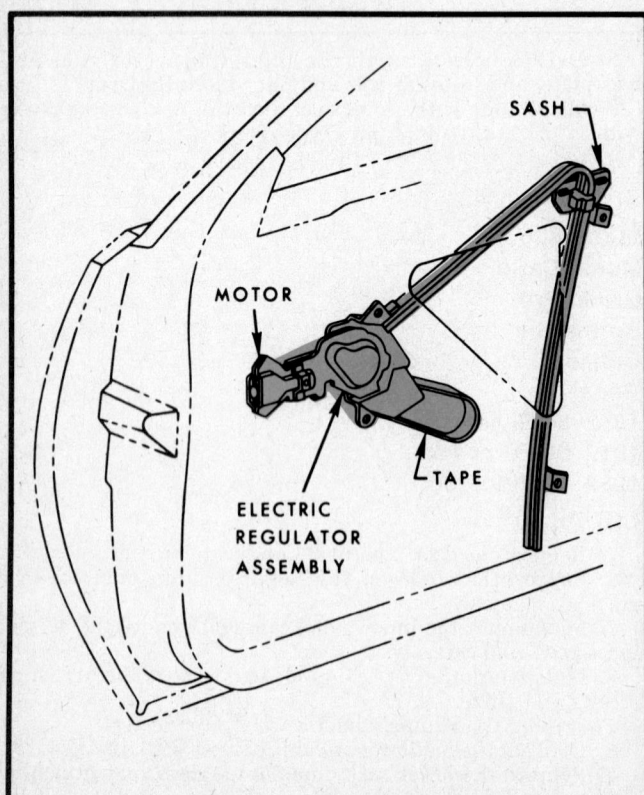

Front door regulator and motor on the Century, Celebrity, Ciera, 6000, Citation, Skylark, Phoenix and Omega

9. Remove the regulator and motor through the access hole.

———— **CAUTION** ————

If the motor and regulator are to be separated, the sector gear MUST be locked in position. The counterbalance spring could unwind and cause personal injury, otherwise.

10. Drill a hole through the regulator sector gear and backplate, and install a bolt and nut to lock the gear.
11. Installation is the reverse of removal. Replace the rivets with ¼"-20 x ½" bolts and nuts. Torque them to 10 ft.lb.

SEDAN

1. Remove the door trim panel and watershield.
2. Raise the glass to the full up position and support it.
3. Matchmark the inner panel cam and remove the attaching screws and cam.
4. Unplug the wiring at the motor.
5. Drill out the regulator attaching rivets with a ¼" drill bit.
6. Slide the regulator and motor rearward to disengage the regulator rollers from the lower sash channel cam.
7. Remove the regulator and motor through the access hole.

———— **CAUTION** ————

If the motor and regulator are to be separated, the sector gear MUST be locked in position. The counterbalance spring could unwind and cause personal injury, otherwise.

8. Drill a hole through the regulator sector gear and backplate, and install a bolt and nut to lock the gear.
9. Installation is the reverse of removal. Replace the rivets with ¼"-20 x ½" bolts and nuts. Torque them to 10 ft.lb.

Century
Celebrity
Ciera
6000
Citation
Skylark
Phoenix
Omega

1. Remove the door trim panel and watershield.
2. Raise the glass to the full up position and support it there.
3. Remove the lower sash bolts.
4. Drill out the regulator attaching rivets with a ¼" drill bit.
5. Move the assembly rearward and unplug the electrical connector.

———— **CAUTION** ————

If the motor and regulator are to be separated, the sector gear MUST be locked in position. The counterbalance spring could unwind and cause personal injury, otherwise.

6. Drill a hole through the regulator sector gear and backplate, and install a bolt and nut to lock the gear.
7. With the regulator still in the door, drill out the regulator-to-motor rivets and remove the motor.
8. Installation is the reverse of removal. Replace the rivets with 3/16" bolts and nuts.

Seville

FRONT DOOR

1. Remove the door trim panel.
2. Remove the watershield.
3. Lower the glass until the sash attaching nuts are accessible in the inner panel access hole.
4. Loosen the glass stabilizer attaching bolts at the belt line.
5. Remove the glass-to-sash attaching bolts and pull the

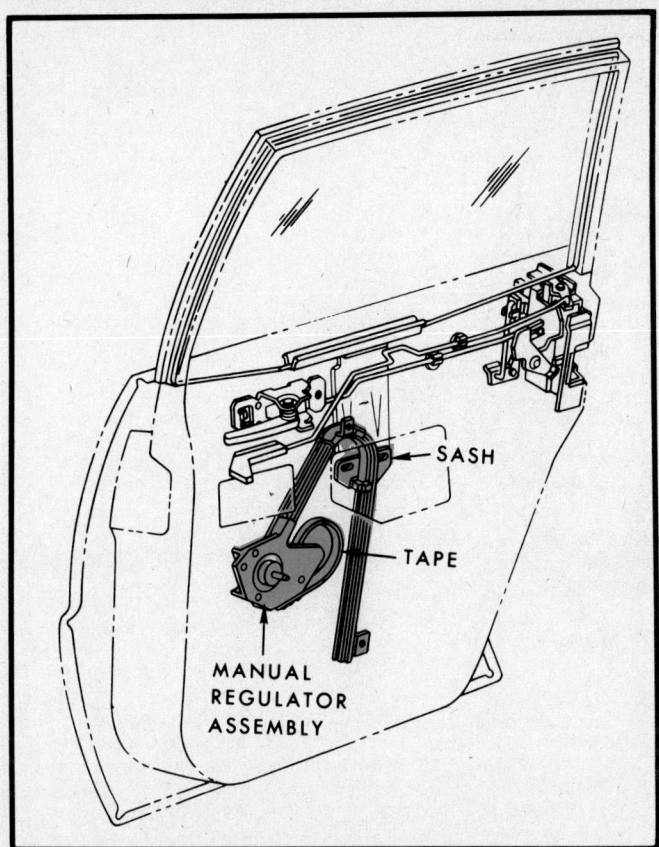

SASH

TAPE

MANUAL
REGULATOR
ASSEMBLY

Rear door regulator and motor on the Century, Celebrity, Ciera, 6000, Citation, Skylark, Phoenix and Omega

glass up and out of the door. The front up-stop is attached to the glass and must be guided out of the door.

6. Remove the guide assembly attaching bolts and lift the guide from the door.

7. Drill out the regulator-to-door frame rivets.

8. Remove the upper and lower regulator attaching bolts.

9. Unplug the electrical connector at the motor.

10. Manuever the regulator and motor assembly from the door.

─────── **CAUTION** ───────

If the motor and regulator are to be separated, the sector gear MUST be locked in position. The counterbalance spring could unwind and cause personal injury, otherwise.

11. Drill a hole through the regulator sector gear and backplate, and install a bolt and nut to lock the gear.

12. Installation is the reverse of removal. Tighten all attaching bolts to 125 in.lb. (10–11 ft.lb.). Replace the rivets using ¼" x 0.500" aluminum peel type rivets.

REAR DOOR

1. Remove the door trim panel.
2. Remove the watershield.
3. Remove the door lock linkage rods.
4. Lower the glass until the sash attaching nuts are accessible in the inner panel access hole.
5. Remove the glass-to-sash attaching bolts and pull the glass up and out of the door. The front up-stop is attached to the glass and must be guided out of the door.
6. Drill out the regulator-to-door frame rivets.
7. Remove the regulator lower support screw and the adjusting bolt.
8. Remove the rear up-stop.

9. Remove the regulator upper attaching nuts.

10. Rotate the regulator so that the harness is accessible and unplug the connector.

11. Position the regulator in its normal position.

12. Rotate the upper portion of the regulator toward the upper front corner of the door.

13. Pull the lower guide tube out through the access hole.

14. Rotate the regulator rearward, working the sash plate and upper part of the regulator out through the access hole.

15. Slide the regulator rearward and out of the door.

─────── **CAUTION** ───────

If the motor and regulator are to be separated, the sector gear MUST be locked in position. The counterbalance spring could unwind and cause personal injury, otherwise.

16. Drill a hole through the regulator sector gear and backplate, and install a bolt and nut to lock the gear.

17. Installation is the reverse of removal. Torque all fasteners to 125 in.lb. (10–11 ft.lb.). Lubricate the regulator with chassis lube. Replace the rivets using ¼" x 0.500" aluminum peel type rivets.

Firebird and Camaro

1. Remove the door trim panel and watershield.
2. Support the window in the half up position, or remove the glass all together.
3. Matchmark the inner panel cam and remove the attaching screws and cam.
4. Matchmark the vertical guide and remove the attaching screws and guide.
5. Unplug the regulator motor wiring connector.
6. Drill out the regulator attaching rivets with a ¼" drill bit.
7. Slide the regulator and motor rearward to disengage the regulator rollers from the lower sash channel cam.
8. Remove the regulator and motor through the access hole.

─────── **CAUTION** ───────

If the motor and regulator are to be separated, the sector gear MUST be locked in position. The counterbalance spring could unwind and cause personal injury, otherwise.

9. Drill a hole through the regulator sector gear and backplate, and install a bolt and nut to lock the gear.

10. Drill out the motor-to-regulator rivets with a ³⁄₁₆" drill bit.

11. For installation, replace the motor-to-regulator rivets with ³⁄₁₆" bolts and nuts.

12. Remove the bolt and nut used to lock the sector gear.

13. Place the regulator and motor assembly in the door panel and connect the wiring.

14. Place the lift arm roller in the sash channel.

15. Attach the regulator assembly to the door panel with ¼" x ½" aluminum peel type rivets.

16. The remainder of installation is the reverse of removal.

Cavalier
Skyhawk
Cimaron
Sunbird
2000
Firenza

1. Remove the door trim panel and watershield.
2. Raise the glass to the full up position and support it.
3. Unplug the wiring at the motor.
4. Drill out the regulator attaching rivets with a ¼" drill bit.
5. Slide the regulator and motor rearward to disengage the regulator roller from the lower sash channel.
6. Remove the regulator and motor through the access hole.

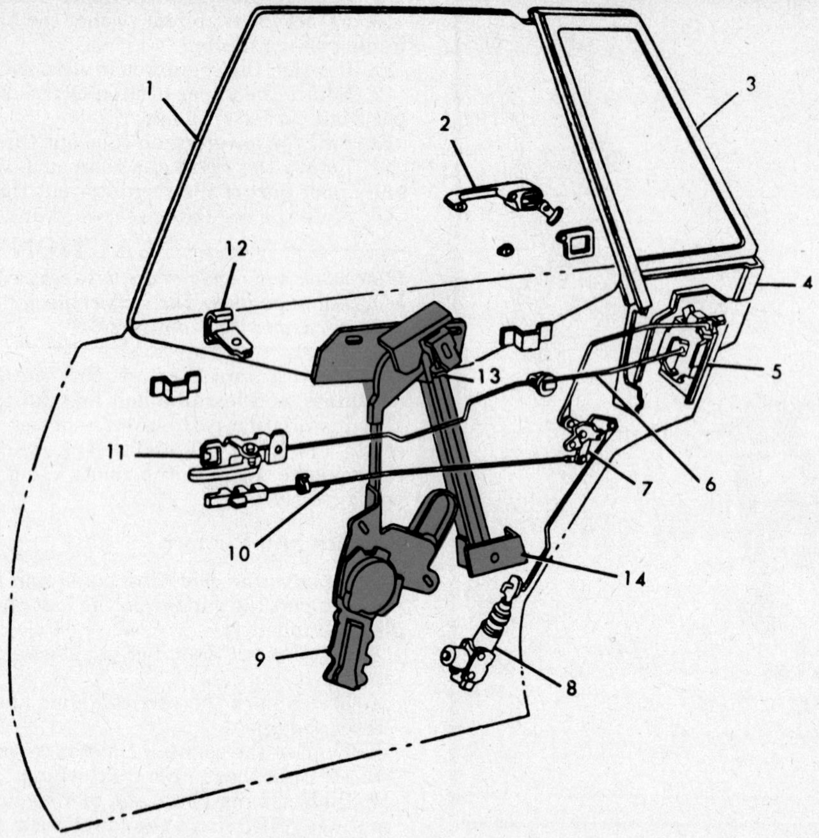

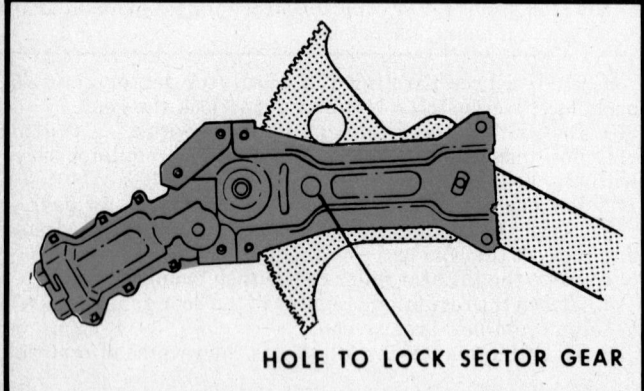

Seville rear door power window system

1. Door glass
2. Outside door handle
3. Stationary vent window
4. Vent window support
5. Door lock
6. Inside handle connecting rod
7. Locking rod bell crank
8. Power door lock actuator
9. Power regulator assembly
10. Inside locking rod
11. Inside remote handle
12. Glass stabilizer
13. Rear up stop
14. Regulator lower support

HOLE TO LOCK SECTOR GEAR

Firebird and Camaro reulator and motor assembly

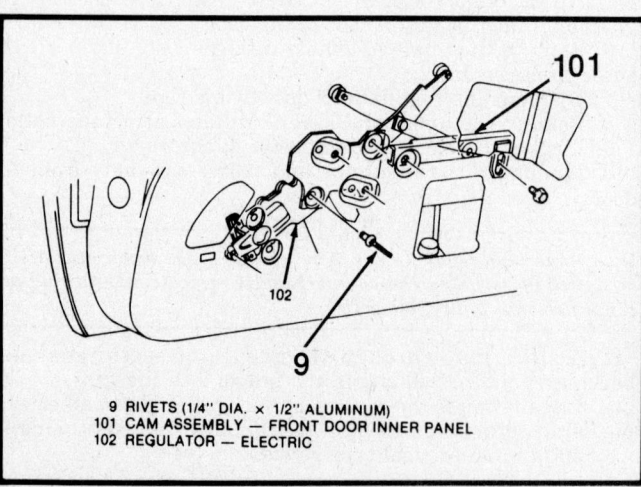

9 RIVETS (1/4" DIA. × 1/2" ALUMINUM)
101 CAM ASSEMBLY — FRONT DOOR INNER PANEL
102 REGULATOR — ELECTRIC

Firebird and Camaro regulator installation

CAUTION

If the motor and regulator are to be separated, the sector gear MUST be locked in position. The counterbalance spring could unwind and cause personal injury, otherwise.

7. Drill a hole through the regulator sector gear and backplate, and install a bolt and nut to lock the gear.

8. Installation is the reverse of removal. Replace the rivets with ¼"-20 x ½" bolts and nuts. Torque them to 10 ft.lb.

Grand Am FWD
Calais FWD

Somerset FWD
98 Regency FWD
Electra FWD
Park Avenue FWD
Fleetwood Brougham FWD
DeVille FWD

The doors incorporate a lightweight tape drive regulator design. The tape length is $40\frac{13}{16}$ in. (1037mm) for N-Body cars;

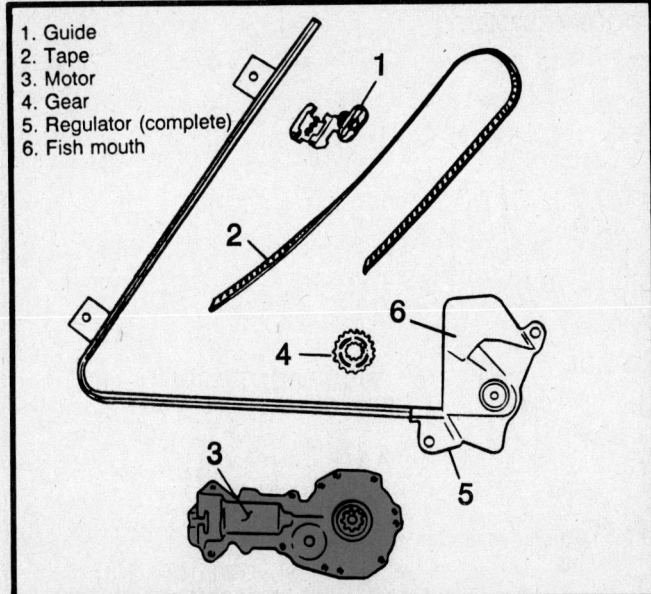

1. Guide
2. Tape
3. Motor
4. Gear
5. Regulator (complete)
6. Fish mouth

Tape drive regulator used on front wheel drive Grand Am, Calais, Somerset, 98 Regency, Electra, Park Avenue, Fleetwood Brougham, deVille

41¾ in. for C-Body door; 38½ in. for C-Body sedan front door; 27¾ for C-Body sedan rear door. The service tape is 54½ in. (1385mm) and must be cut to the specified length when replacing the tape.

1. Remove the inner belt sealing strip.
2. Remove the door panel.
3. Remove the armrest support brackets.
4. Remove the water deflector.
5. Block the window glass in the full up position.
6. Remove the rivets using a ¼ in. drill bit.
7. Disconnect the electrical connector.
8. Remove the regulator by moving it until the guide is disengaged from the sash channel on the glass, then lifting the regulator out throught the access hole in the door inner panel.
9. If the electric window motor is being replaced, remove it from the regulator on the bench by drilling out the rivets.

────────── **CAUTION** ──────────

If the motor and regulator are to be separated, the sector gear MUST be locked in position. The counterbalance spring could unwind and cause personal injury, otherwise.

10. Drill a hole through the regulator sector gear and backplate, and install a bolt and nut to lock the gear.
11. Installation is the reverse of removal.

Nova

1. Remove the inside handle bezel.
2. Remove the armrest.
3. Remove the outside rear view mirror (front doors only).
4. Pry the trim panel from the front door.
5. Remove the water deflector.
6. Remove the wire harness at the power door lock switch (if so equipped).
7. Remove the sash channel mounting bolts.
8. Remove the door window assembly.
9. Remove the window regulator mounting bolts, unplug the wiring connector and remove the regulator.
10. Installation is the reverse of removal. Adjust the equalizer arm up or down to level the window in the opening.

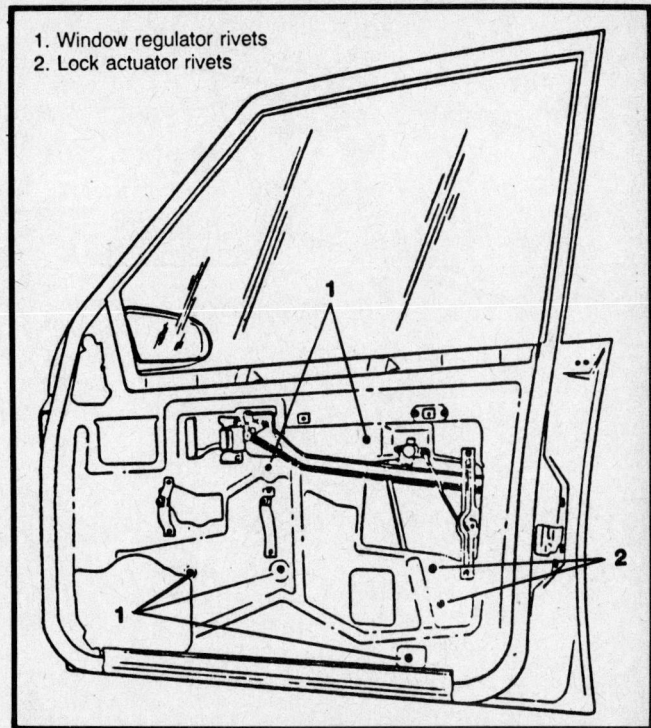

1. Window regulator rivets
2. Lock actuator rivets

1982 Corvette power window mechanism

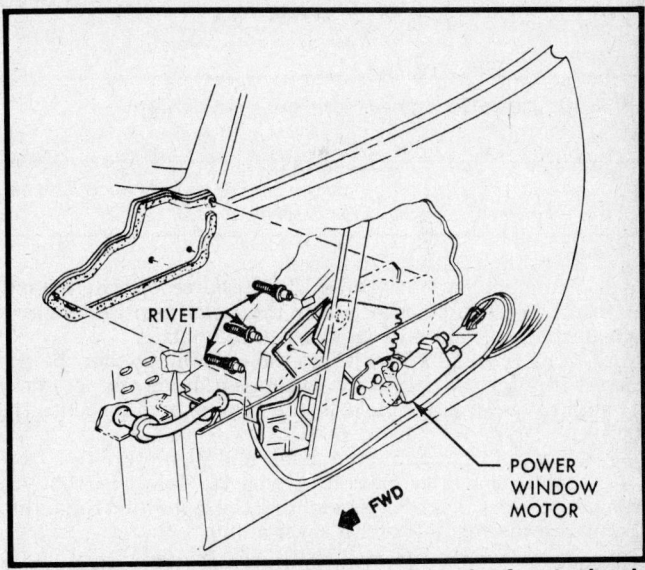

RIVET

POWER WINDOW MOTOR

FWD

Front door window regulator used on the front wheel drive Grand Am, Calais, Somerset, 98 Regency, Electra, Park Avenue, Fleetwood Brougham, deVille

Corvette
1982

1. Remove the door trim panel.
2. Remove the watershield.
3. Raise the window and prop it in position with cloth tape applied over the door frame.
4. Unplug the wiring harness at the motor.
5. Remove the inner panel cam.
6. Drill out the regulator mounting rivets.
7. Disengage the regulator rollers from the sash channel cam and remove the regulator from the door.

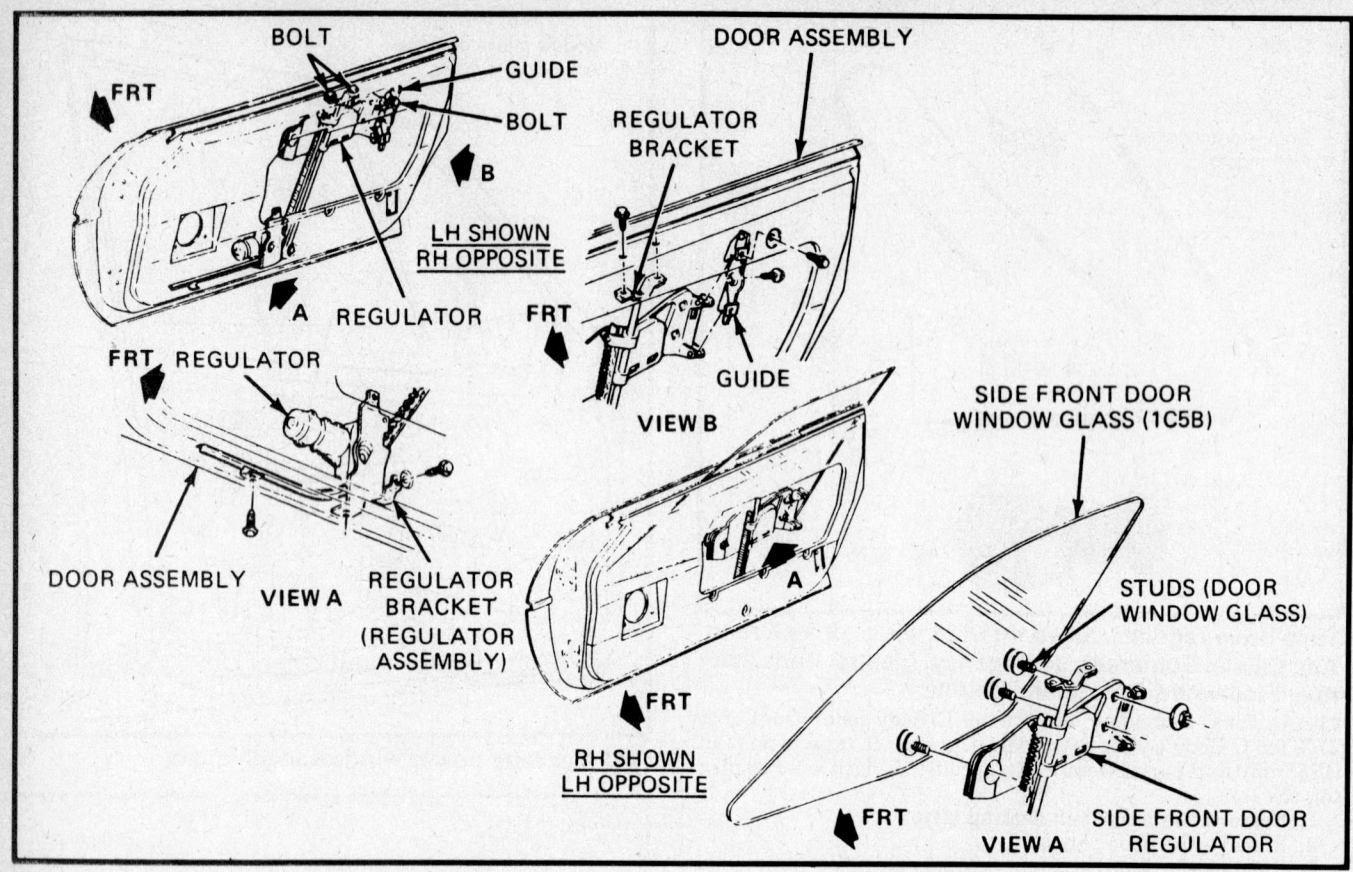

1984-86 Corvette power window mechanism

— CAUTION —

Don't attempt to separate the motor and regulator until Steps 8, 9, and 10 are performed. The regulator is spring-loaded!

8. Place the regulator in a vise.

9. Using jumper leads and a 12 volt source, operate the motor until the semi-circular hole in the sector gear centers over one of the two weld nuts on the mounting plate.

10. Screw a ¼"-20 x 1" bolt into the weld nut so that the end passes through the hole in the sector gear. It may be necessary to slightly enlarge the hole in the gear to accommodate the bolt.

11. Unbolt and separate the motor and regulator.

12. Installation is the reverse of removal. Make sure that you remove the lock bolt *after* assembling the motor and regulator. Lubricate the regulator with chassis lube.

1984-86

1. Lower the glass slightly.
2. Disconnect the battery ground.
3. Remove the door trim panel.
4. Remove the watershield.
5. Unplug the wiring harness connectors at the rear edge of the inner mounting plate.
6. Remove the eight inner mounting plate-to-door frame bolts. Mark the position of the guide bolts.
7. Remove the inner mounting plate-to-motor bolt.
8. Remove the guide-to-inner plate bolt.
9. Remove the guide-to-door frame bolt.
10. Remove the guide.
11. Disconnect the lock linkage rods at the control and actuator. Push the inner plate downward and pull the top out to gain access to the lock linkage rod clip and plastic guide.

12. Unplug the wiring connector at the motor.

13. Pull the plate out of the door and let it hang by the linkage rod.

14. Remove the two weatherstripping screws at the window opening.

15. Matchmark its position and remove the glass stop bracket.

16. Loosen the three anti-rattle pads and move them to facilitate removal of the glass.

17. Remove the regulator-to-glass attaching nuts and pull the glass out of the door.

18. Unbolt the regulator and motor assembly and remove it from the door.

19. Drill out the motor-to-regulator rivets and separate the two.

20. Installation is the reverse of removal.

Fiero

1. Put the glass in the full up position.
2. Disconnect the battery ground.
3. Remove the door trim panel.
4. Remove the watershield.
5. Block the window in place.
6. Remove the regulator cam assembly.
7. Disconnect the bellcrank and bracket assembly.
8. Drill out the regulator-to-door frame rivets.
9. Remove the regulator and motor assembly through the access hole in the door panel.
10. Disconnect the wiring harness from the motor.
11. Installation is the reverse of removal.

CHRYSLER/MITSUBISHI

Lift Motor

REMOVAL AND INSTALLATION

Galant

1. Remove the door trim panel and watershield.
2. Remove the glass channel-to-regulator bolts.
3. Using a shielded screwdriver, pry off the weatherstripping at the top of the door channel.
4. Remove the glass by lifting it out.
5. Remove the 6 regulator mounting bolts.
6. Unplug the wiring connector and remove the regulator and motor assembly from the door.

CAUTION

When loosening the regulator-to-motor bolts, take great care to avoid sudden spring windup. The regulator spring is under considerable tension. It's best to first remove the spring.

7. Installation is the reverse of removal.

Starion/Conquest

1. Remove the door trim panel and watershield.
2. Raise the window to the full up position.
3. Remove the glass stabilizer.
4. Remove the glass mounting nuts.
5. Pull the glass up and out of the door.
6. Remove the glass guide.
7. Unplug the motor wiring connector.
8. Remove the regulator mounting bolts and remove the regulator and motor assembly from the door.

CAUTION

When loosening the regulator-to-motor bolts, take great care to avoid sudden spring windup. The regulator spring is under considerable tension. It's best to first remove the spring.

9. Installation is the reverse of removal.

Vista

1. Remove the door trim panel and watershield.
2. Remove the glass channel-to-regulator bolts.
3. Using a shielded screwdriver, pry off the weatherstripping at the top of the door channel.
4. Remove the glass by lifting it out.
5. Remove the 5 regulator mounting bolts.
6. Unplug the wiring connector and remove the regulator and motor assembly from the door.

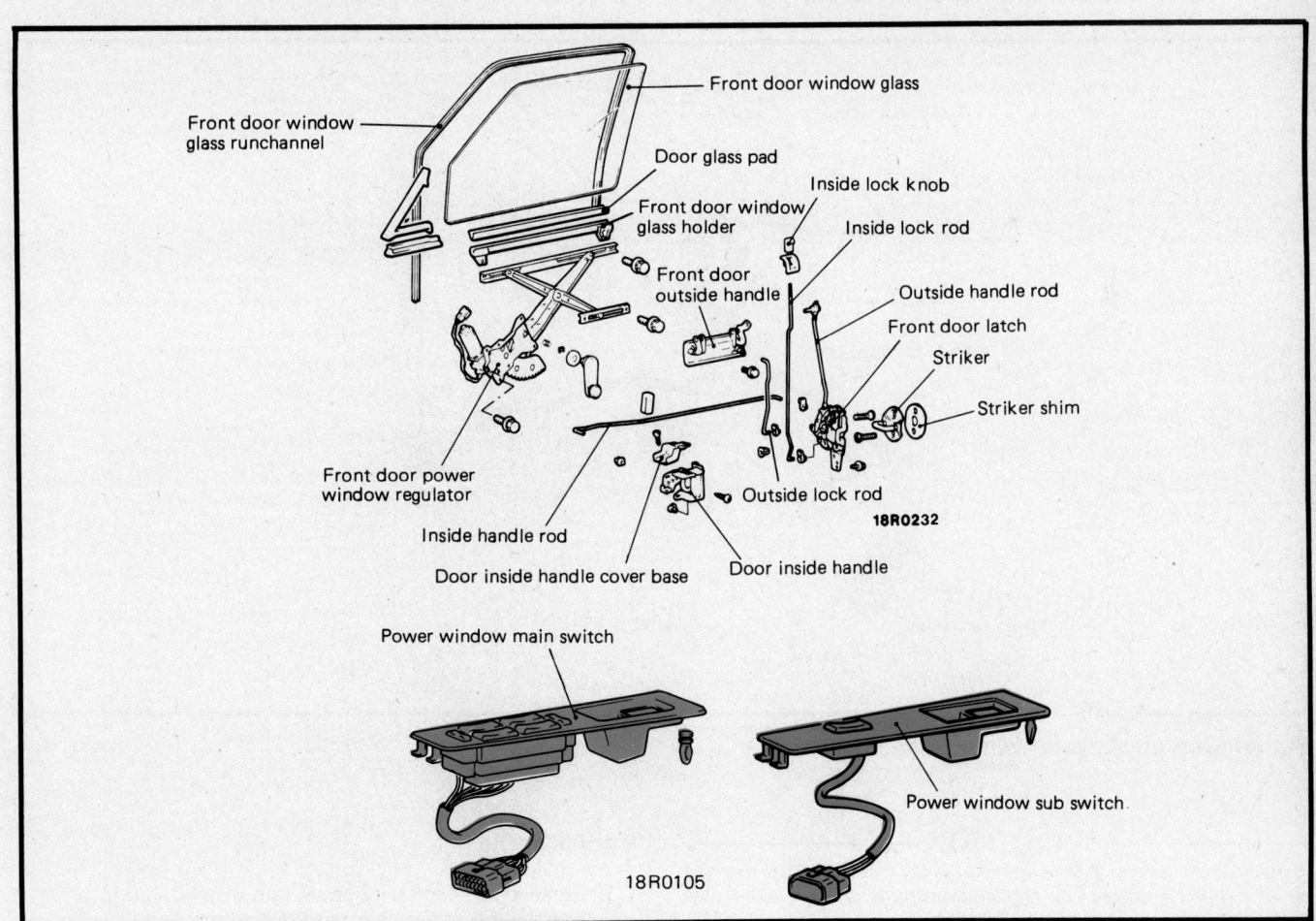

Galant front door power window mechanism

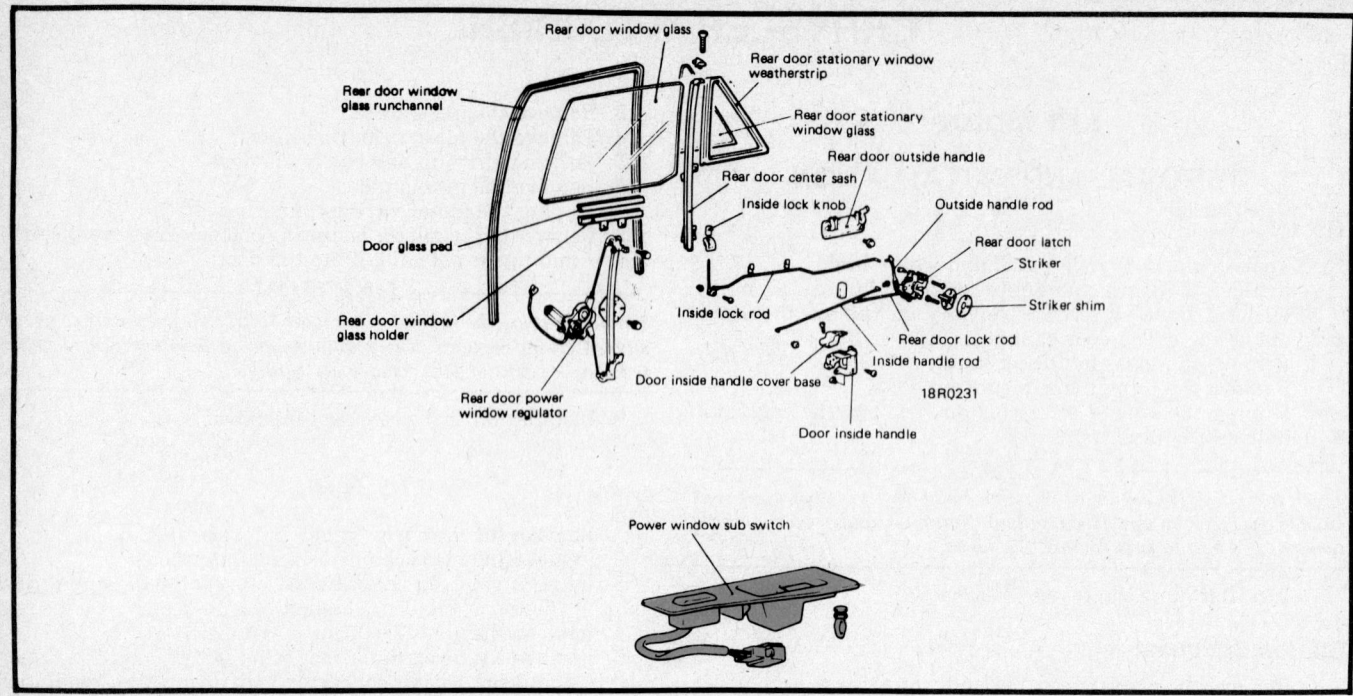

Galant rear door power window mechanism

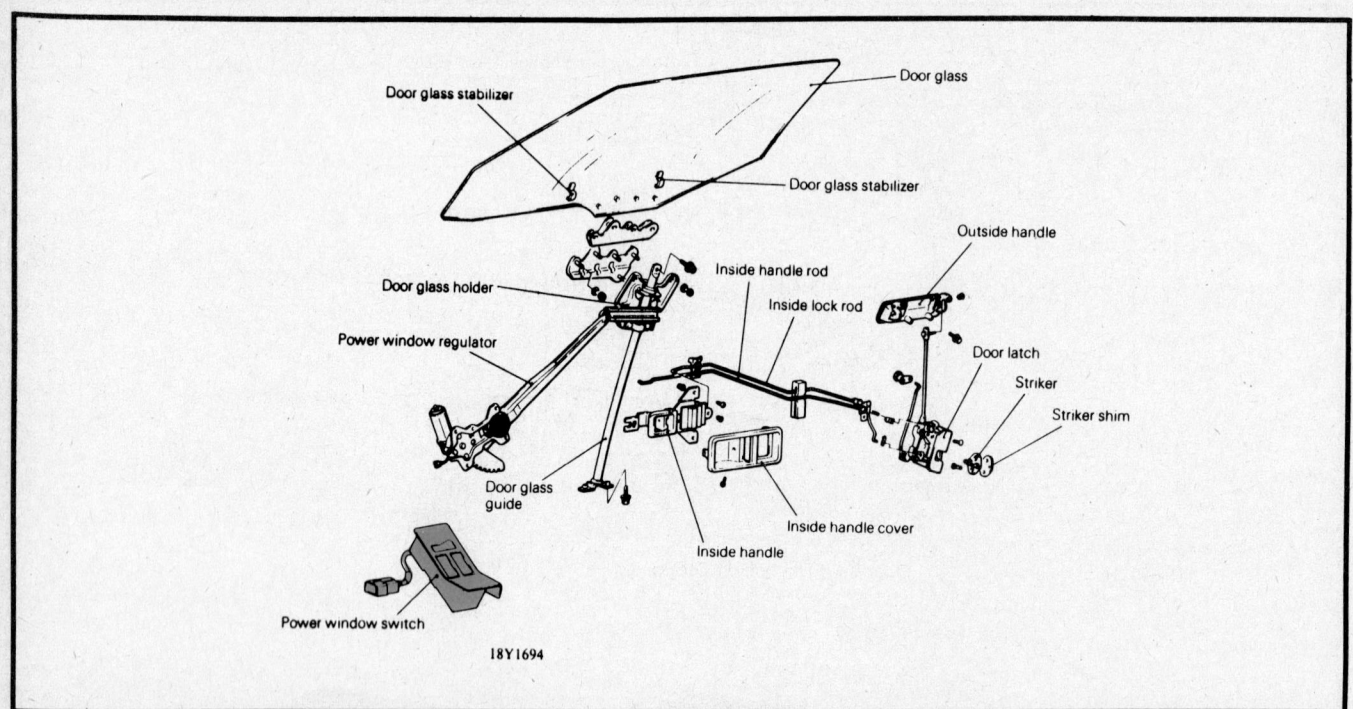

Starion/Conquest power window mechanism

─────────── **CAUTION** ───────────

When loosening the regulator-to-motor bolts, take great care to avoid sudden spring windup. The regulator spring is under considerable tension. It's best to first remove the spring.

7. Installation is the reverse of removal.

Cordia/Tredia

1. Remove the door trim panel and watershield.
2. Remove the glass channel-to-regulator bolts.
3. Using a shielded screwdriver, pry off the weatherstripping at the top of the door channel.

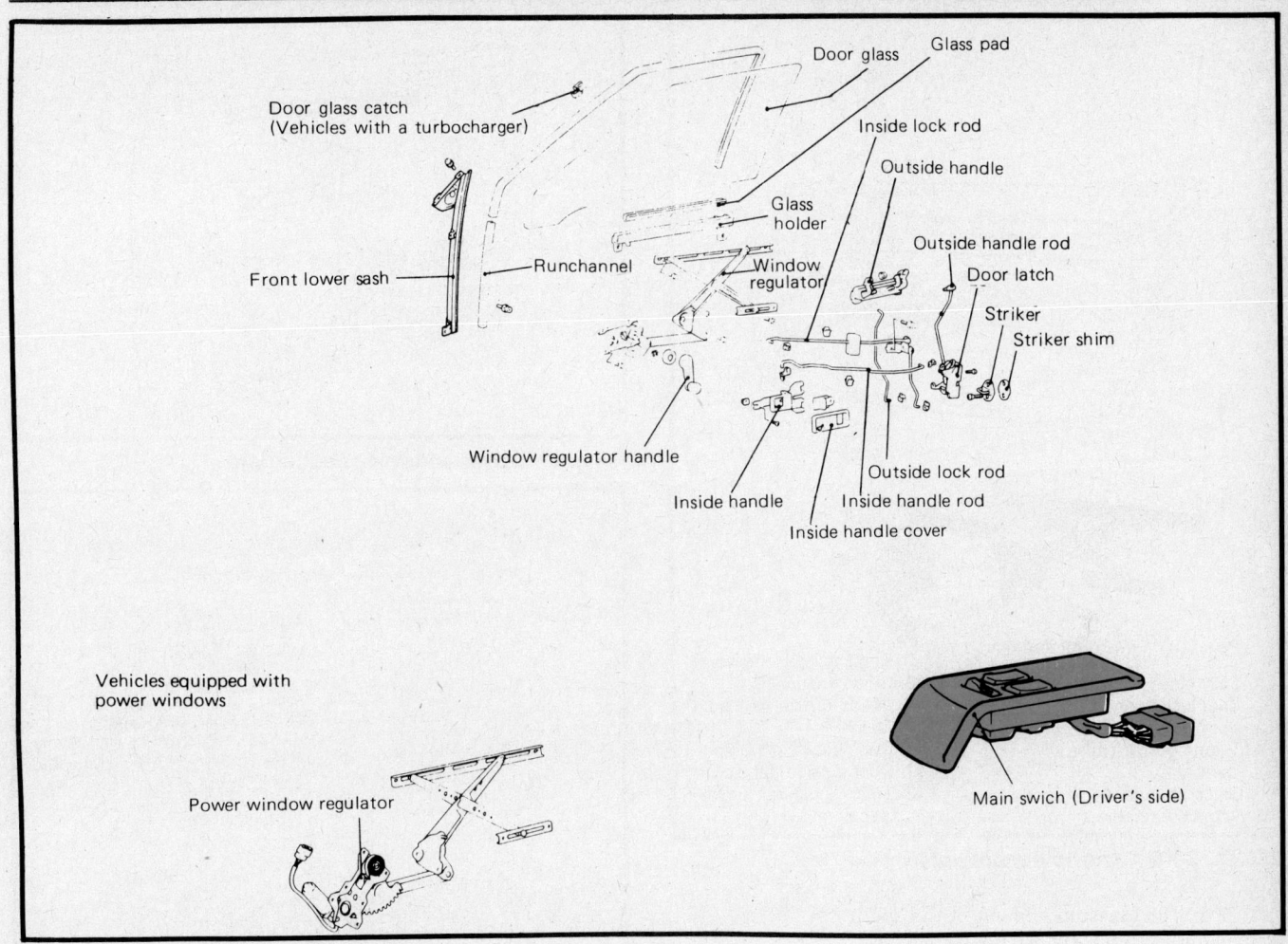

Cordia power window mechanism. The Tredia is similar

4. Remove the glass by lifting it out.
5. Remove the regulator mounting bolts. Tredia has 6 bolts; Cordia has 8 bolts and 1 nut.
6. Unplug the wiring connector and remove the regulator and motor assembly from the door.

— CAUTION —
When loosening the regulator-to-motor bolts, take great care to avoid sudden spring windup. The regulator spring is under considerable tension. It's best to first remove the spring.

7. Installation is the reverse of removal.

NISSAN

Regulator and Lift Motor

REMOVAL AND INSTALLATION

280ZX, 300ZX

1. Remove the door trim panel and watershield.
2. Lower the window as far as possible.
3. Remove the molding clips and molding.
4. Raise the glass until the glass attaching screws are accessible. Remove them.
5. Remove the front and rear stopper bolts.
6. Raise the glass to the full up position and pull it out of the door.

7. Remove the front glass rail.
8. Unplug the motor connector and remove the regulator and motor assembly through the large access hole.
9. Installation is the reverse of removal.

Maxima
200SX
Pulsar
Stanza

1. Lower the glass fully.
2. Remove the door trim panel.
3. Remove the window-to-guide channel bolts.
4. Remove the lower sash.

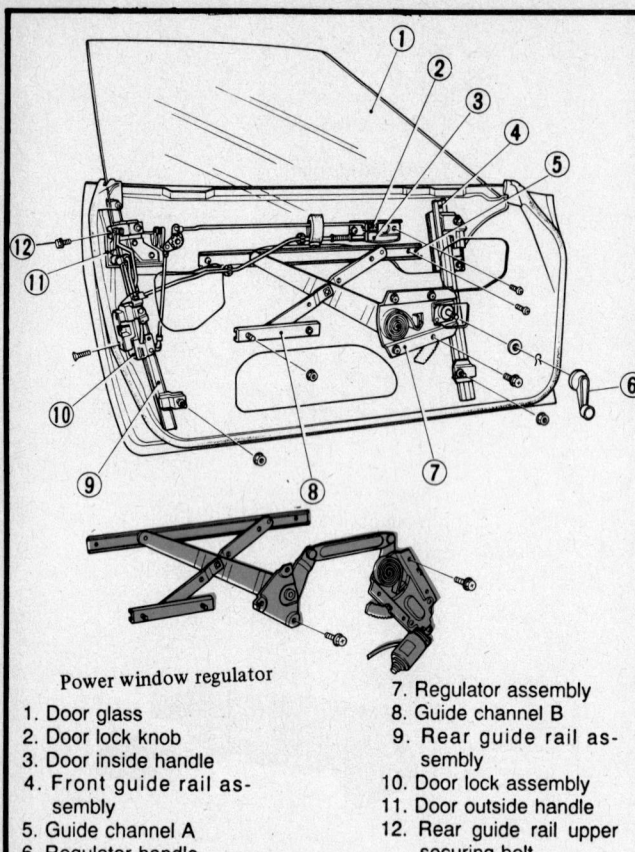

Power window regulator

1. Door glass
2. Door lock knob
3. Door inside handle
4. Front guide rail assembly
5. Guide channel A
6. Regulator handle
7. Regulator assembly
8. Guide channel B
9. Rear guide rail assembly
10. Door lock assembly
11. Door outside handle
12. Rear guide rail upper securing bolt

280ZX, 300ZX window mechanism

5. Pull the glass up and out of the door.
6. Unplug the motor wiring connector.
7. Remove the regulator/motor assembly attaching bolts.
8. Pull the regulator out through the large access hole.
9. Installation is the reverse of removal. Torque the regulator attaching bolts to 35 in.lb.

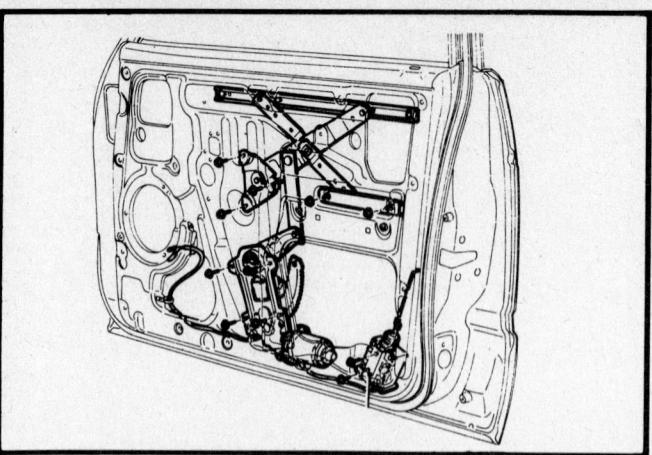

Maxima power window mechanism

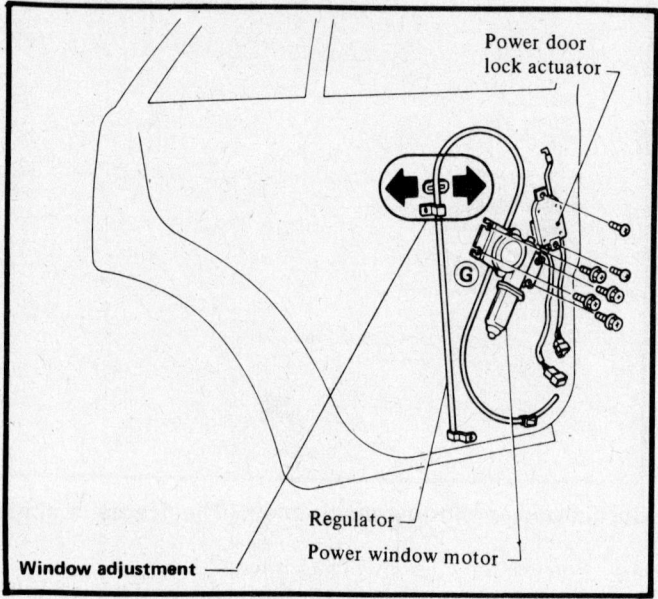

Stanza power window mechanism

MAZDA

Regulator and Lift Motor

REMOVAL AND INSTALLATION

1982-85

1. Remove the trim panel from the door.
2. Remove the window frame assembly from from the door by removing the seven attaching screws.
3. Lower the door glass.
4. Disengage the regulator roller and arm from the glass.
5. Tilt the glass slightly and slide it up and out of the door.
6. Remove and discard the tape from the door glass channel.
7. Unplug the wiring connector. Unbolt and remove the regulator and motor assembly.

8. Installation is the reverse of removal. Use new tape in the channel. Use waterproof sealer on the window frame screws.

1986

1. Remove the door panel.
2. Remove the weatherscreening carefully, so that it can be reused.
3. Remove the door glass mounting screws.
4. Remove the inner and outer weatherstripping around the frame.
5. Remove the glass guide mounting bolt.
6. Pull the glass up and out of the door.
7. Unplug the wiring connector. Remove the mounting bolts and pull the regulator assembly from the access hole.
8. Installation is the reverse of removal. Adjust the door glass so that it closes properly.

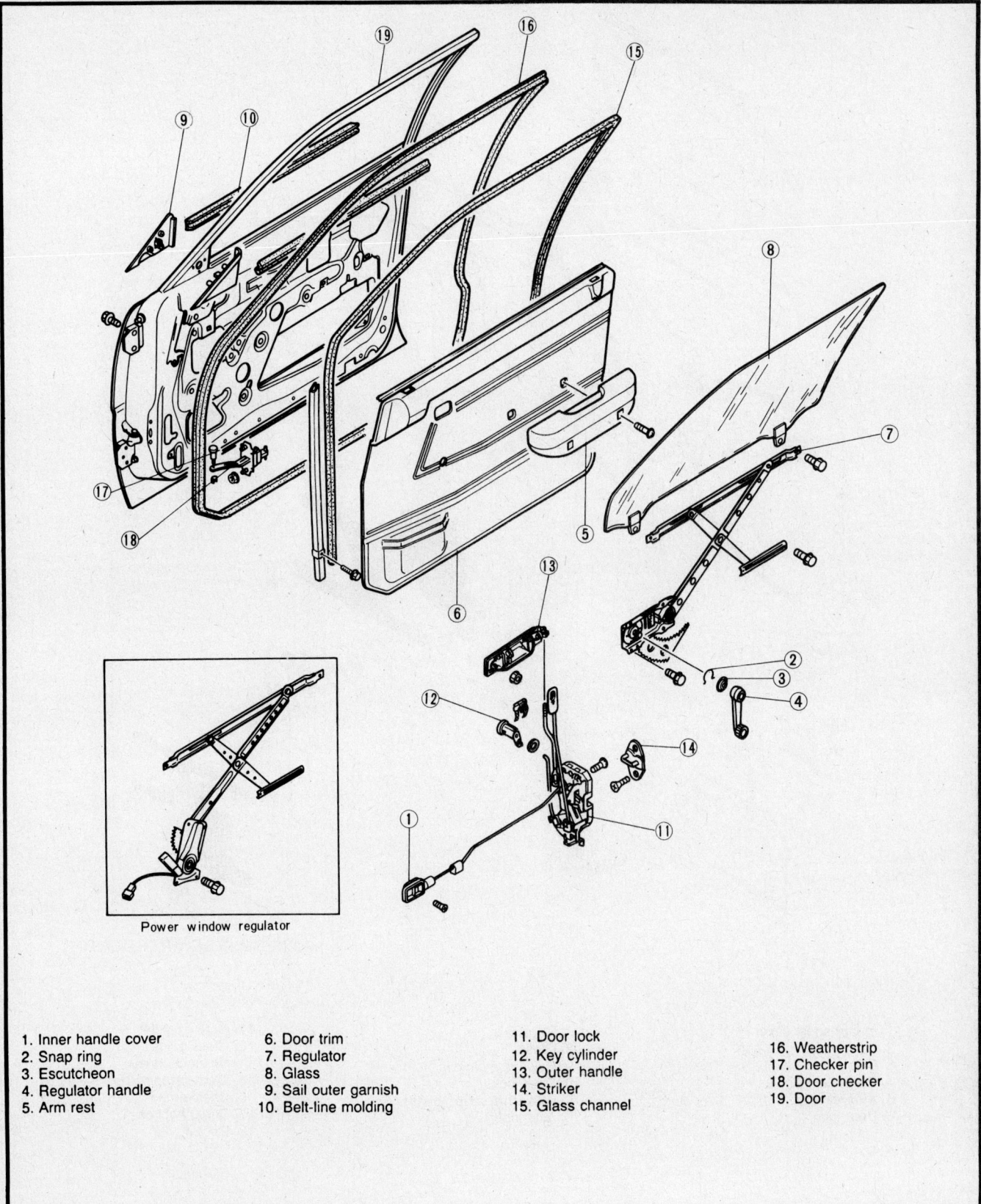

1. Inner handle cover
2. Snap ring
3. Escutcheon
4. Regulator handle
5. Arm rest
6. Door trim
7. Regulator
8. Glass
9. Sail outer garnish
10. Belt-line molding
11. Door lock
12. Key cylinder
13. Outer handle
14. Striker
15. Glass channel
16. Weatherstrip
17. Checker pin
18. Door checker
19. Door

Power window regulator

Mazda 626 front door power window mechanism

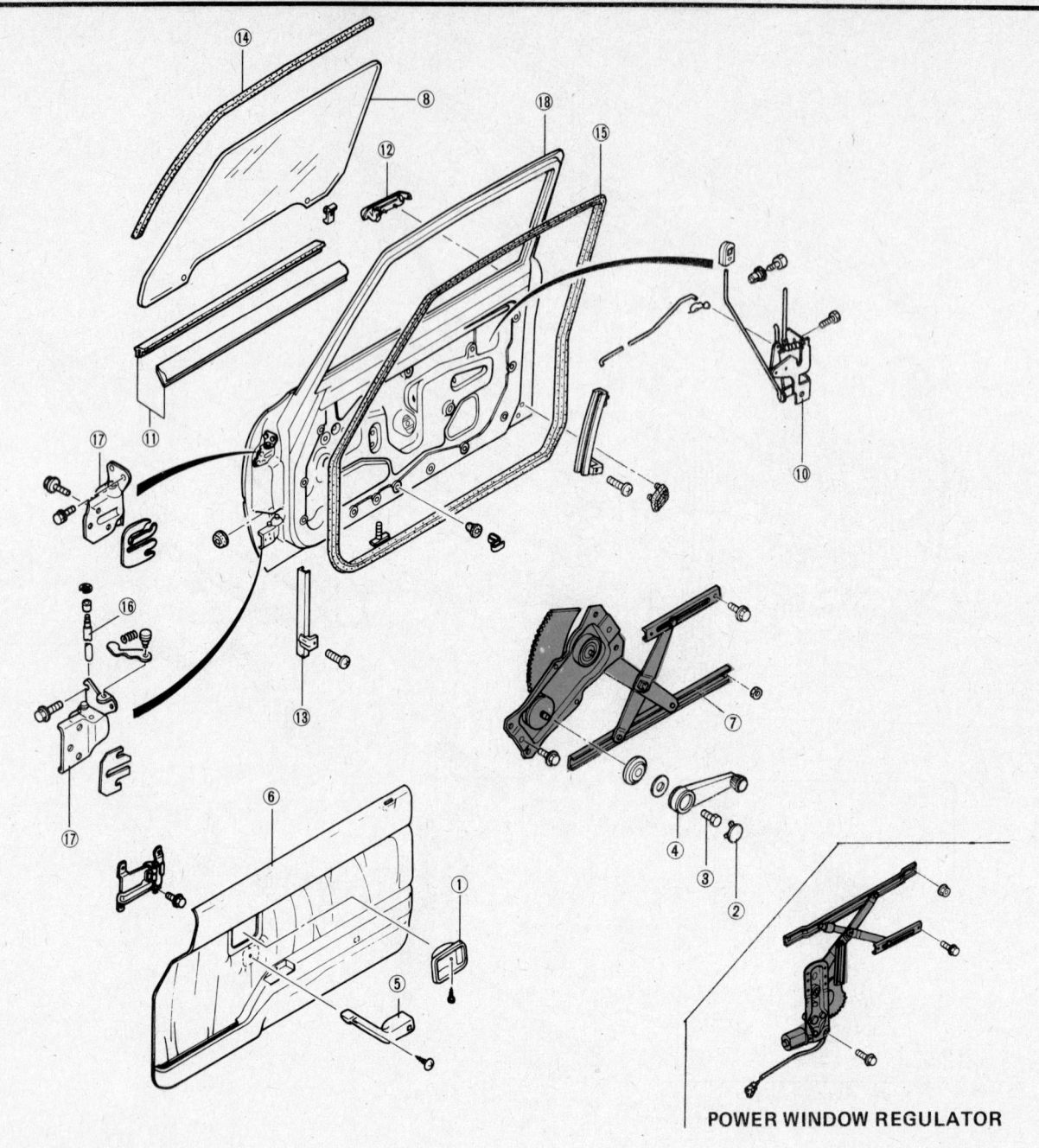

1. Inner handle cover
2. Regulator handle cap
3. Bolt
4. Regulator handle
5. Arm rest
6. Door trim
7. Regulator
8. Glass
9. Belt-line moldiong
10. Door lock
11. Weatherstrip (outer and inner)
12. Outer handle
13. Glass guide
14. Glass channel
15. Wetherstrip
16. Checker pin
17. Door checker
18. Door

POWER WINDOW REGULATOR

1982-85 RX-7 window mechanism

REAR DOOR

STRUCTURAL VIEW

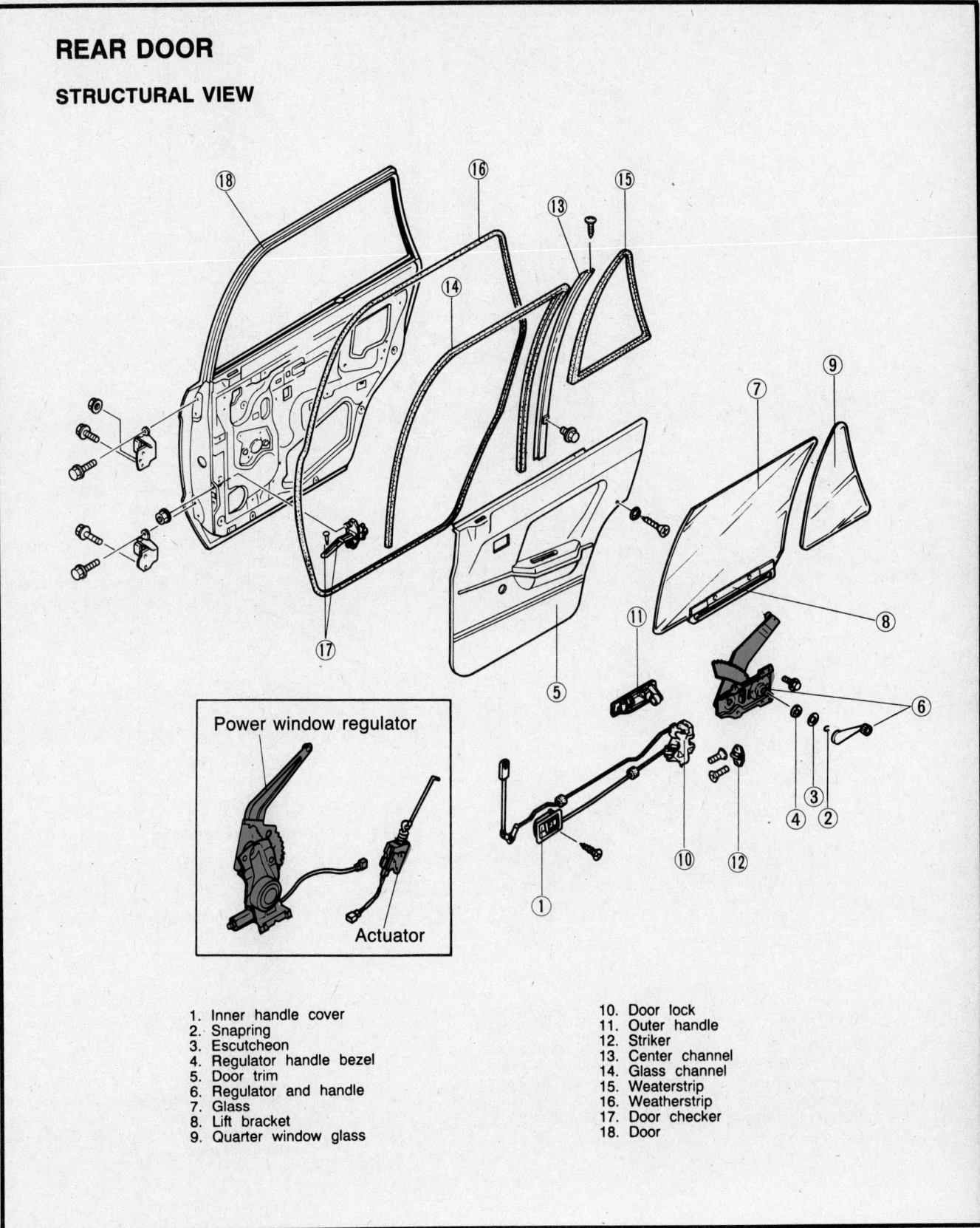

Power window regulator

Actuator

1. Inner handle cover
2. Snapring
3. Escutcheon
4. Regulator handle bezel
5. Door trim
6. Regulator and handle
7. Glass
8. Lift bracket
9. Quarter window glass
10. Door lock
11. Outer handle
12. Striker
13. Center channel
14. Glass channel
15. Weaterstrip
16. Weatherstrip
17. Door checker
18. Door

Mazda 626 rear door power window mechanism

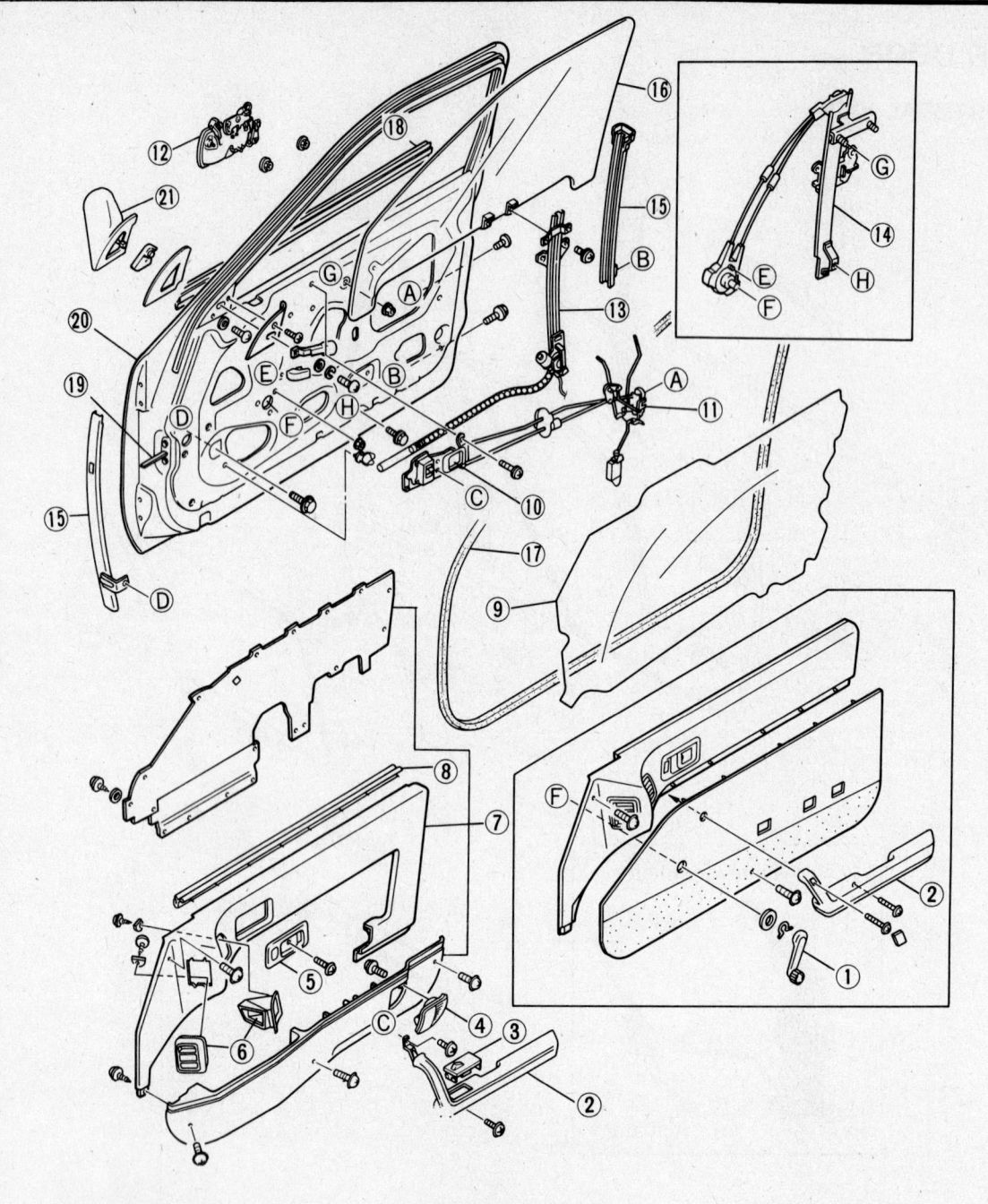

1. Regulator handle
   (manual type)
2. Arm rest
3. Power window switch
4. Courtesy light lens
5. Inner handle cover
6. Door ventillation grill
7. Door trim

8. Weatherstrip (inner)
9. Watersheild
10. Inner handle
11. Door lock
12. Outer handle
13. Regulator (power
    type)

14. Regulator (manual
    type)
15. Glass guide
16. Glass
17. Weatherstrip
18. Weatherstrip (outer)
19. Door checker
20. Door
21. Door mirror

1986 RX-7 window mechanism

1. Inner handle cover
2. Snap ring
3. Escutcheon
4. Regulator
5. Arm rest
6. Door trim
7. Belt-line molding
8. Center channel
9. Lift bracket
10. Glass
11. Weatherstrip (quarter window)
12. Glass (quarter window)
13. Door lock
14. Outer handle
15. Striker
16. Glass channel
17. Weatherstrip
18. Checker pin
19. Door checker
20. Door

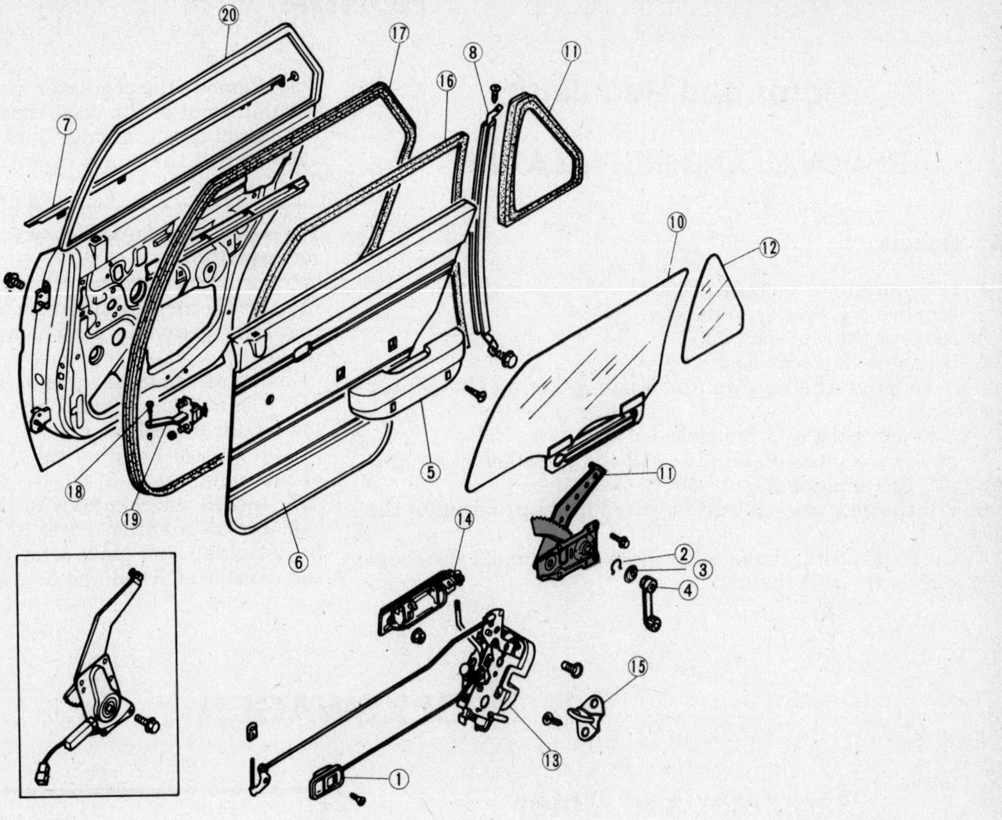

Mazda 626 rear door power window mechanism

SUBARU

Door Glass and Regulator

REMOVAL AND INSTALLATION

1. Remove the trim panel.
2. Remove the remote assembly (if so equipped).
3. Remove the sealing cover.
4. Remove the rearview mirror from the door.
5. Remove the outer weatherstrip.
6. Remove the inner stabilizer.
7. Loosen the upper stopper bolt from the front of door and glass stoppers, and move the door glass. Then, remove the upper stopper from the rear of the door. Remove the two bolts which hold the glass holder to the regulator slider.

NOTE: When removing bolts on the regulator slider, move the glass to a position where the bolts can be seen through the service hole. Mark the position and tightening allowance of upper stopper bolts before removal. This will make adjustment after installation easy.

8. Open the door, hold the door glass with both hands and pull it straight up from the door panel.
9. Remove the wire clip (manual type only).
10. Remove the regulator base plate and rail.
11. Remove the regulator assembly through the service hole in the underside of the door.
12. Disconnect the electrical connectors to the window motor. Unbolt the motor and remove it through the lower service hole in the underside of the door.
13. Replace any worn or broken parts. Lubricate all sliding parts and reinstall.
14. Installation is the reverse of removal. Tighten the base plate mounting bolts 4–7 ft.lb. and the rail mounting nut 7–13 ft.lb..

HONDA

Motor and Regulator

REMOVAL AND INSTALLATION

All Models

1. Disconnect the battery ground.
2. Remove the door trim panel.
3. Remove the watershield.
4. On the sedan rear door:
   a. Remove the screws and bolts securing the center channel.
   b. Remove the quarter glass.
5. Lower the glass manually until the glass holder mounting bolts are accessible and remove them.
6. Tilt the door glass inward as you pull it up and out of the door.
7. On front doors, remove the glass run channel fasteners and remove the run channel.

8. Remove the regulator mounting bolts and maneuver the regulator out of the door, through the access hole.
9. Unplug the wiring connector from the motor.
10. Unbolt the motor from the regulator.

—————————— CAUTION ——————————
The regulator spring will move suddenly when the motor is removed. Be careful!
————————————————————————————

11. When attaching the motor to the regulator, engage the regulator gear and pinion motor while moving the gear by hand.
12. Install the collar and attaching bolt.
13. Connect the wiring harness and lower the regulator to allow easier installation.
14. Route the breather tube through the two clips on the back of the regulator.
15. Install the regulator in the door
16. Install all other parts in reverse order of removal. Don't fully tighten any glass attaching parts until the operation of the glass is checked and adjusted.

VOLKSWAGEN

Regulator and Motor

REMOVAL AND INSTALLATION

All Models

1. Lower the window fully.
2. Disconnect the battery ground.
3. Remove the door trim panel.
4. Remove the watershield.
5. Unbolt the window assembly from the regulator and lower it into the door.
6. Unplug the electrical connector from the motor.
7. Remove the two motor-to-door frame mounting bolts.
8. Remove the three guide rail-to-door frame bolts.
9. Remove the regulator, motor, cables and guide rail through the access hole in the door frame.
10. Installation is the reverse of removal.

NOTE: During installation, position the upper cable below the guide rail mounting bracket.

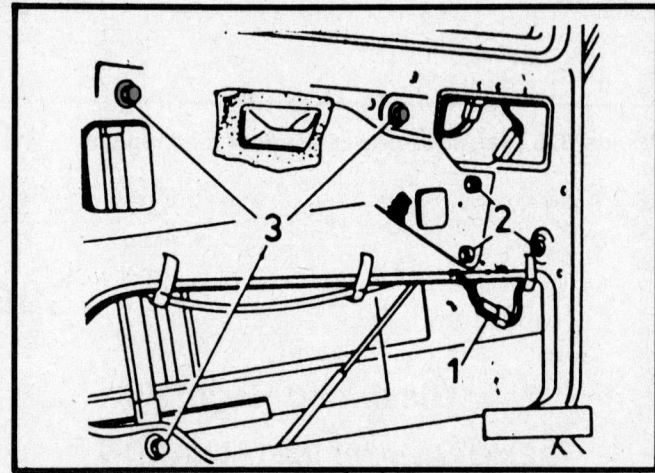

Volkswagen power window attachment points: 1 is the connector; 2 are the motor mounting bolts; 3 are the guide rail bolts

DIAGNOSIS AND TESTING

All door locks covered in this section are electrically actuated, with the exception of those used in Volkswagen cars.

Those used in Volkswagens are pneumatically operated.

No component in either type system is repairable. Service is by replacement only.

Failure of the electrically operated types can be traced to either a mechanical or electrical fault.

Mechanical faults are rare, and involve bending or jamming of the linkage.

Mechanical problems are confined to the switches, wiring and actuators. To test these components, each must be removed. The switches and wiring are tested in the conventional manner for continuity and resistance.

To test the actuator, remove it and connect it to a 12 volt source. Observe its operation. If it operates sluggishly, incompletely or not at all, replace it.

For testing of the Volkswagen system, see the Volkswagen procedures at the end of this section.

AMERICAN MOTORS

Power Door Locks

REMOVAL AND INSTALLATION

Switch

1. Disconnect the battery ground.
2. Remove the door trim panel and watershield.
3. Remove the switch housing from the inner door panel.
4. Disconnect the wiring and pry up the switch retaining clips. Remove the switch.

5. Installation is the reverse of removal.

Actuator Motor

1. Disconnect the battery ground.
2. Remove the door trim panel and watershield.
3. Using a ¼″ drill bit, drill out the motor mounting rivets.
4. Disconnect the motor actuator rod from the bellcrank.
5. Disconnect the wires from the motor and lift the motor from the door.
6. Installation is the reverse of removal. Use ¼″-20 x ½″ bolts and locknuts in place of the rivets.

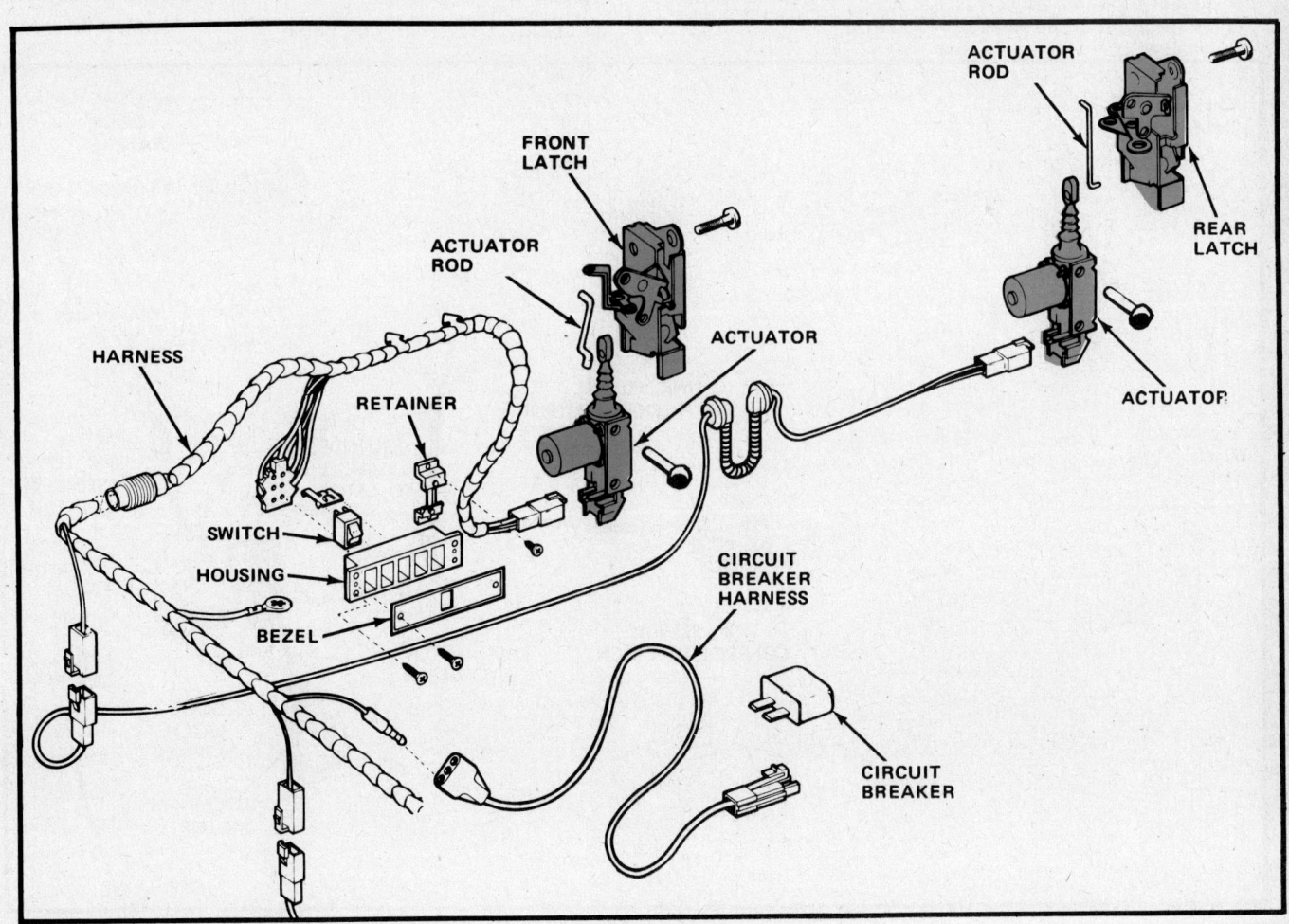

AMC power door lock system

CHRYSLER CORPORATION

Door Lock Motor

REMOVAL AND INSTALLATION

All Front and Rear Wheel Drive Cars

1. Remove the inside door handle, the window regulator handle and the door trim panel.

2. Roll the door watershield away from the lower rear corner of the door to uncover the panel access opening.
3. Remove the motor link at the door latch.
4. Disconnect the motor lead wires.
5. Drill out the motor mounting rivets and remove the motor.
6. Install the motor using pop rivets.
7. Install the door trim panel and handles.

FORD MOTOR COMPANY

Door Lock Motor

REMOVAL AND INSTALLATION

All Models, Except Taurus and Sable

1. Remove the door trim panel and watershield.
2. Drill out the rivet attaching the motor to the door panel.
3. Disconnect the wiring.
4. Disconnect the actuator motor link from the door latch.
5. Remove the motor.
6. Installation is the reverse of removal.

— CAUTION —

Make certain that the actuator boot is not twisted during installation. The pop rivet must be installed with the bracket base tightly against the door panel.

7. Install the watershield and trim panel.

Central Locking Solenoid
REMOVAL AND INSTALLATION

Taurus and Sable

1. Remove the door trim panel.

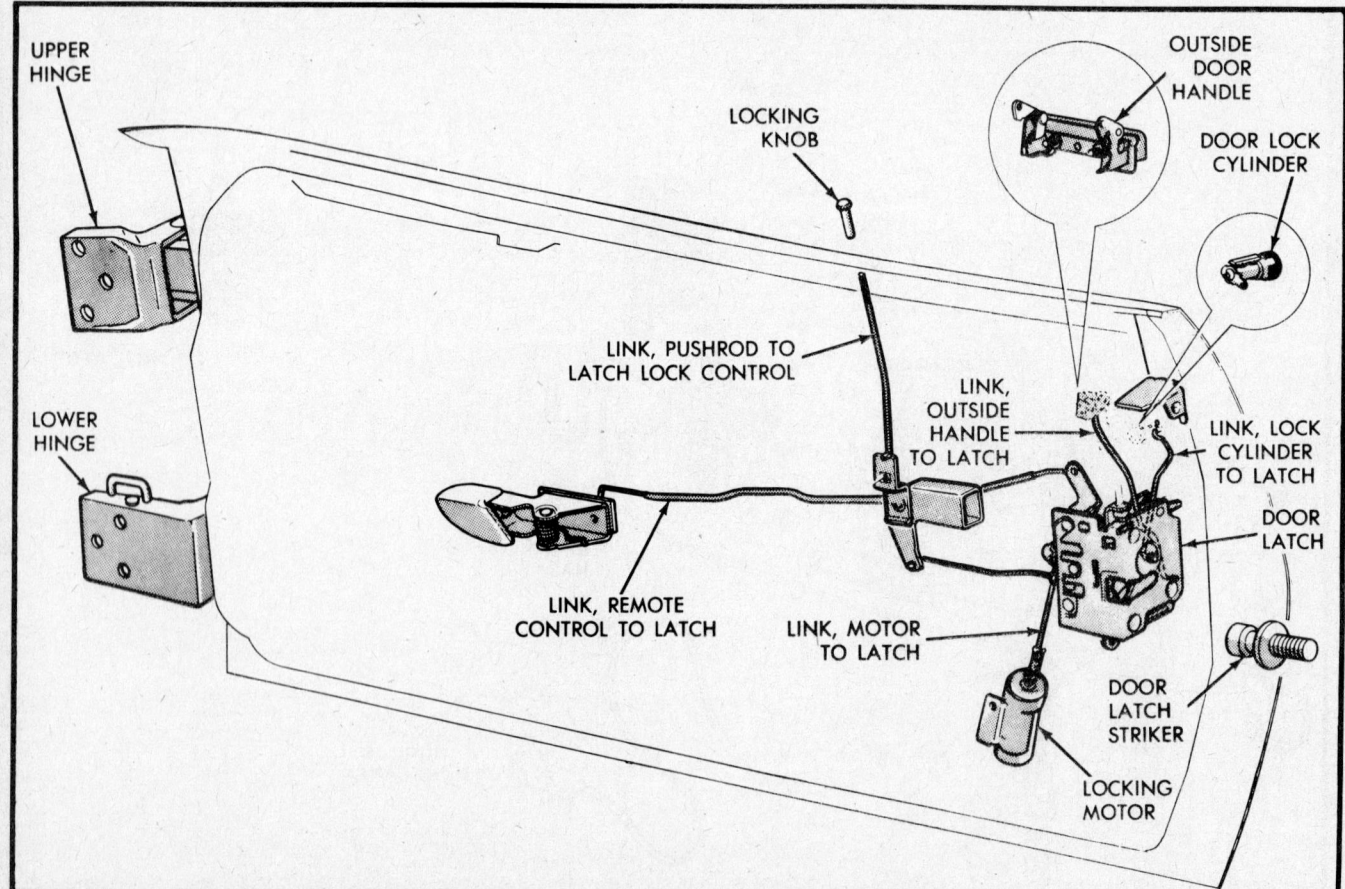

UPPER HINGE

LOWER HINGE

LOCKING KNOB

OUTSIDE DOOR HANDLE

DOOR LOCK CYLINDER

LINK, PUSHROD TO LATCH LOCK CONTROL

LINK, OUTSIDE HANDLE TO LATCH

LINK, LOCK CYLINDER TO LATCH

DOOR LATCH

LINK, REMOTE CONTROL TO LATCH

LINK, MOTOR TO LATCH

DOOR LATCH STRIKER

LOCKING MOTOR

Power door lock system used on rear wheel drive Chrysler Corporation cars

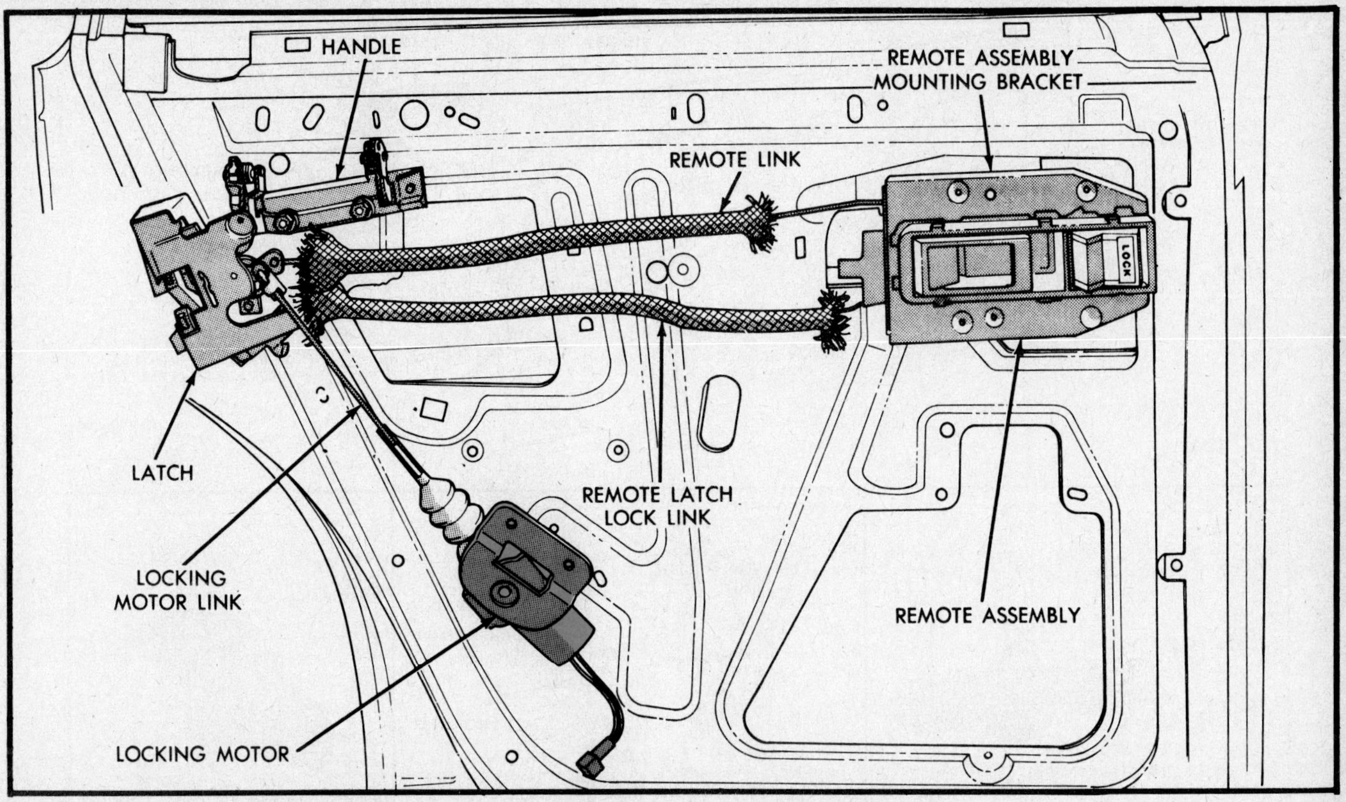

Power door lock system used on front wheel drive Chrysler Corporation cars

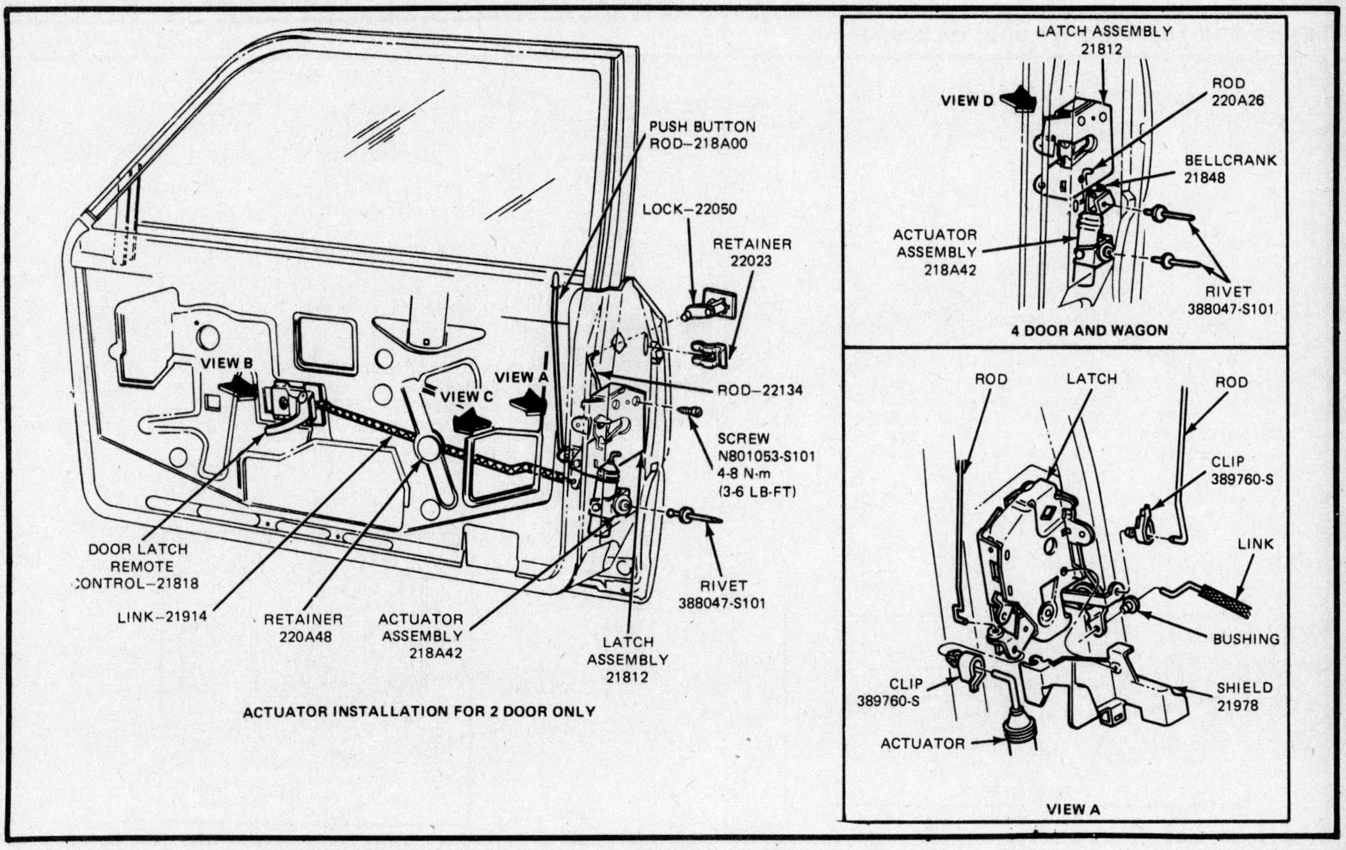

ACTUATOR INSTALLATION FOR 2 DOOR ONLY

4 DOOR AND WAGON

VIEW A

Power door lock system used on Escort, Lynx and EXP models

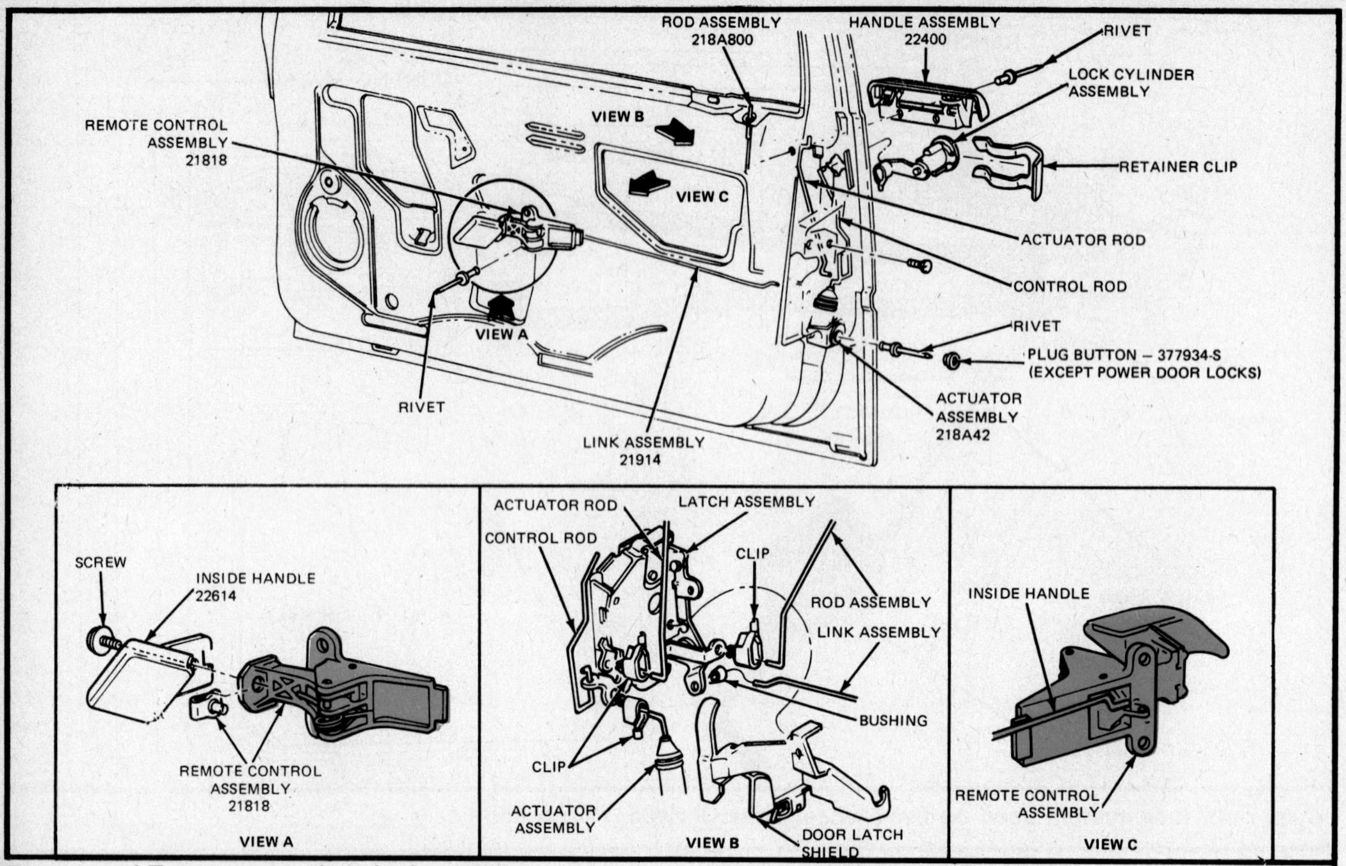

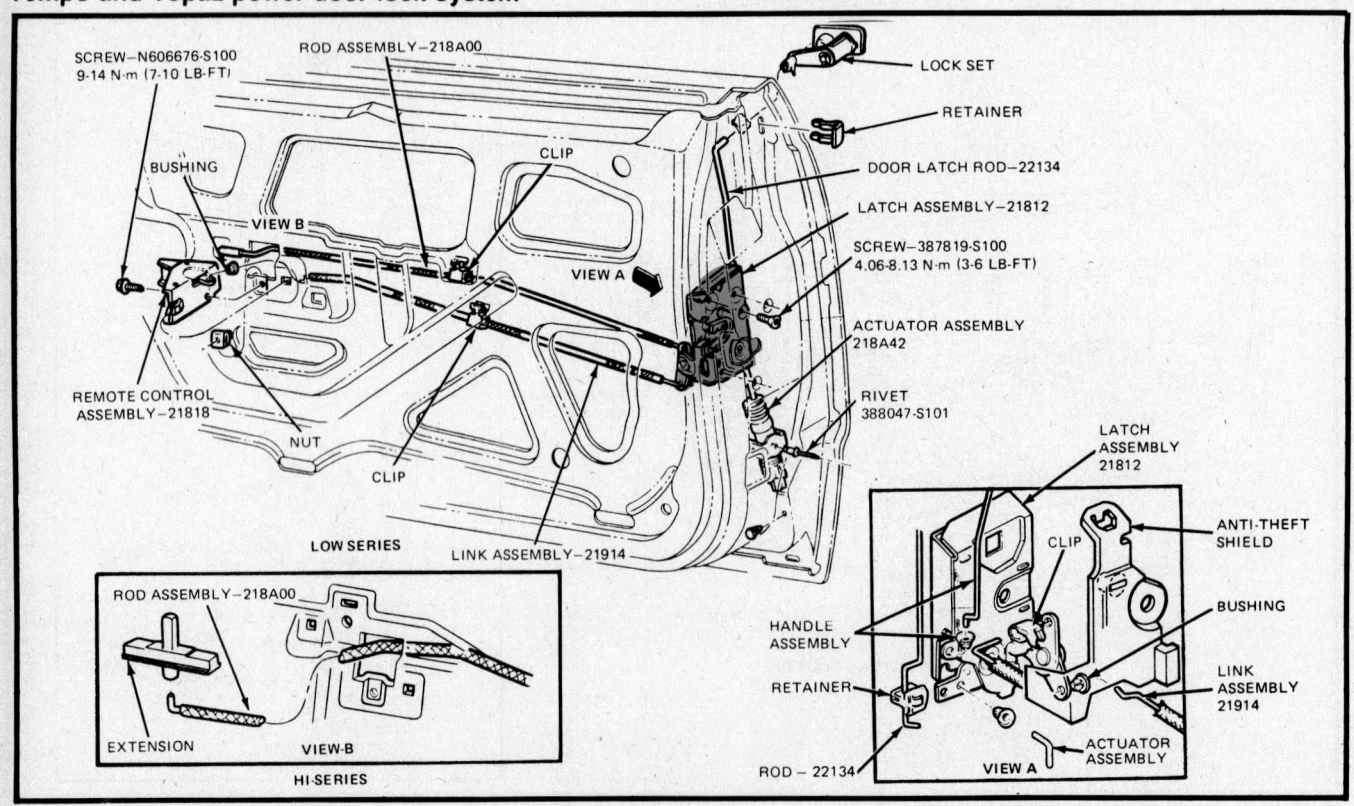

ROD ASSEMBLY 218A800
HANDLE ASSEMBLY 22400
RIVET
LOCK CYLINDER ASSEMBLY
RETAINER CLIP
ACTUATOR ROD
CONTROL ROD
RIVET
PLUG BUTTON – 377934-S (EXCEPT POWER DOOR LOCKS)
ACTUATOR ASSEMBLY 218A42

REMOTE CONTROL ASSEMBLY 21818
VIEW B
VIEW C
VIEW A
RIVET
LINK ASSEMBLY 21914

SCREW
INSIDE HANDLE 22614
REMOTE CONTROL ASSEMBLY 21818
VIEW A

ACTUATOR ROD
CONTROL ROD
LATCH ASSEMBLY
CLIP
ROD ASSEMBLY
LINK ASSEMBLY
BUSHING
CLIP
ACTUATOR ASSEMBLY
DOOR LATCH SHIELD
VIEW B

INSIDE HANDLE
REMOTE CONTROL ASSEMBLY
VIEW C

Tempo and Topaz power door lock system

SCREW–N606676-S100 9-14 N·m (7-10 LB-FT)
ROD ASSEMBLY–218A00
LOCK SET
RETAINER
BUSHING
DOOR LATCH ROD–22134
LATCH ASSEMBLY–21812
CLIP
VIEW B
VIEW A
SCREW–387819-S100 4.06-8.13 N·m (3-6 LB-FT)
ACTUATOR ASSEMBLY 218A42
RIVET 388047-S101
REMOTE CONTROL ASSEMBLY–21818
NUT
CLIP
LOW SERIES
LINK ASSEMBLY–21914

LATCH ASSEMBLY 21812
ANTI-THEFT SHIELD
CLIP
HANDLE ASSEMBLY
BUSHING
LINK ASSEMBLY 21914
RETAINER
ROD – 22134
ACTUATOR ASSEMBLY
VIEW A

ROD ASSEMBLY–218A00
EXTENSION
VIEW-B
HI-SERIES

Crown Victoria/Grand Marquis 2-door power lock system

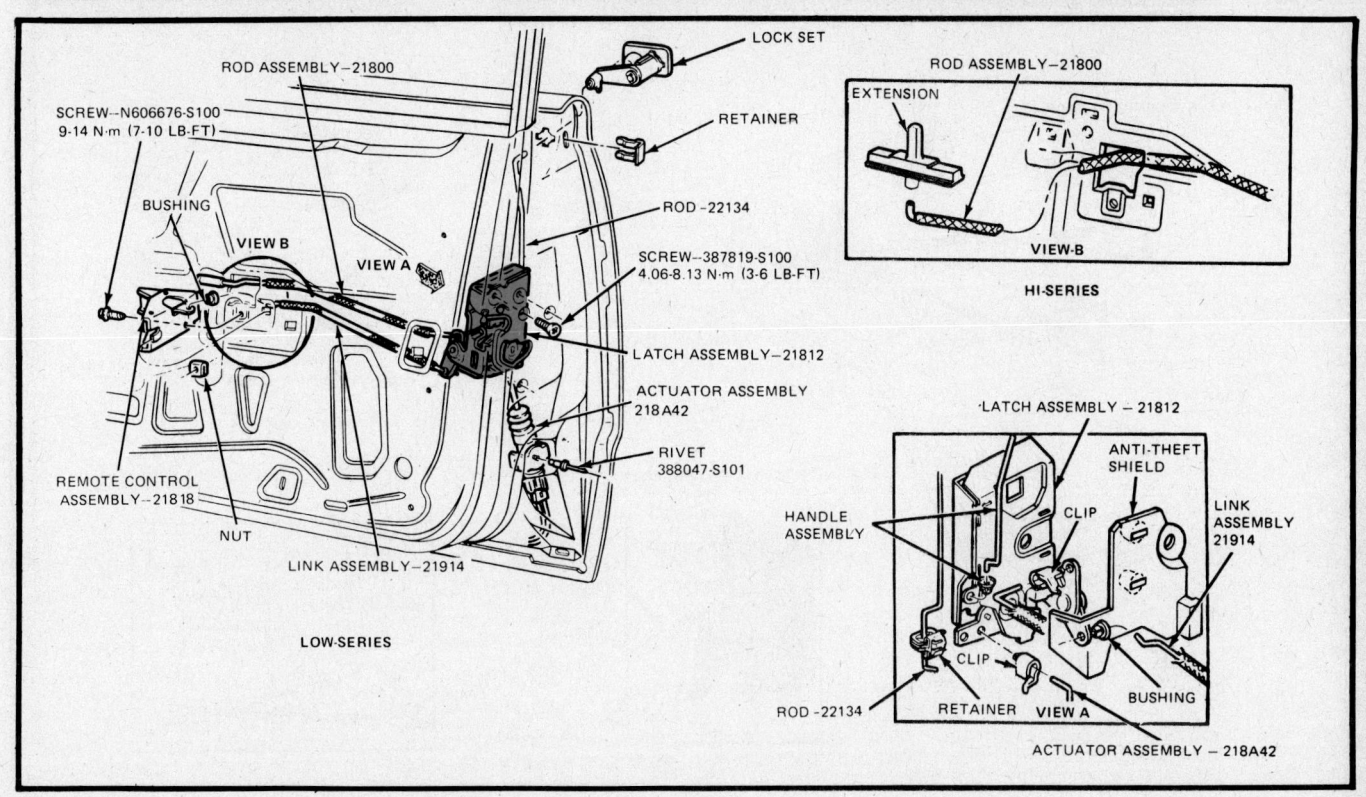

Crown Victoria/Grand Marquis 4-door power lock system, front door

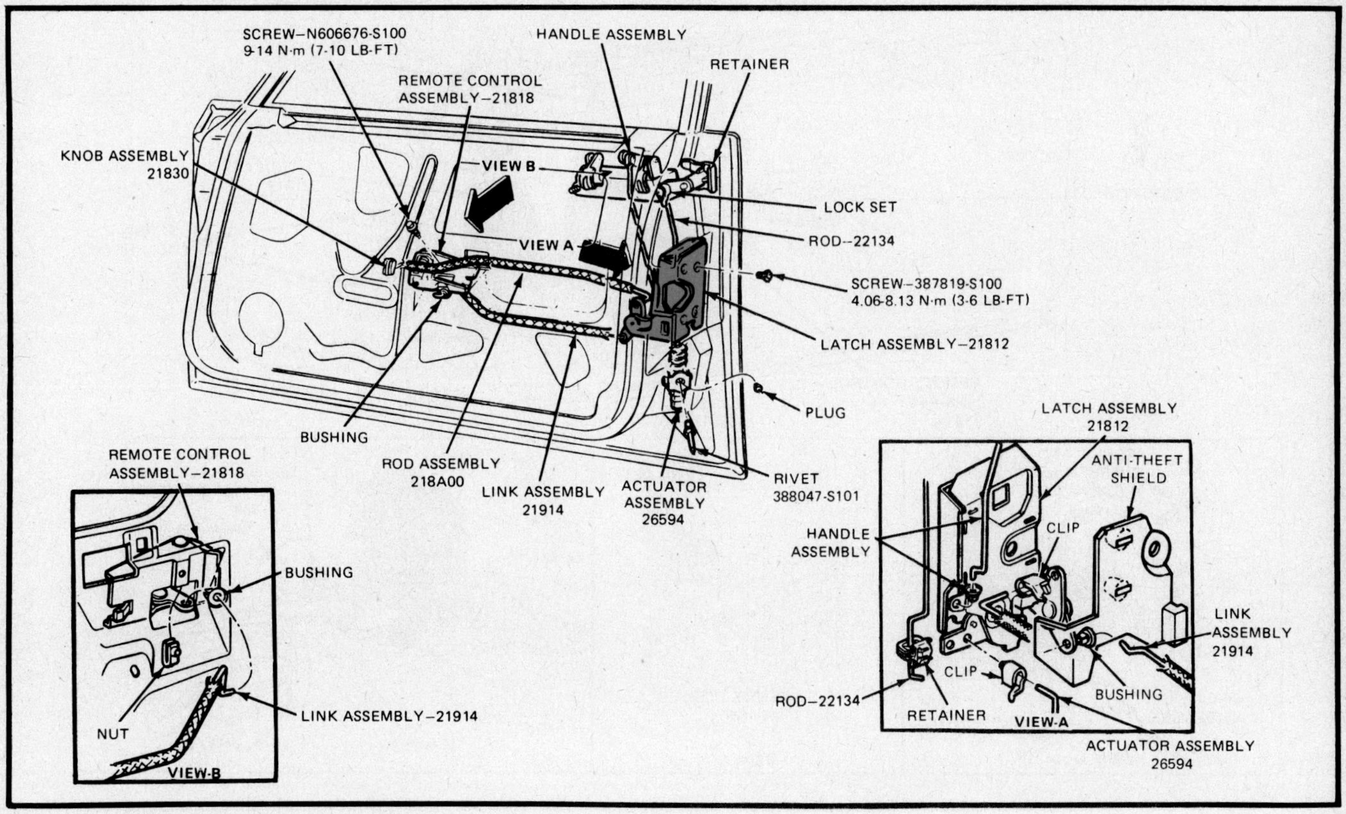

Lincoln Town Car front door system

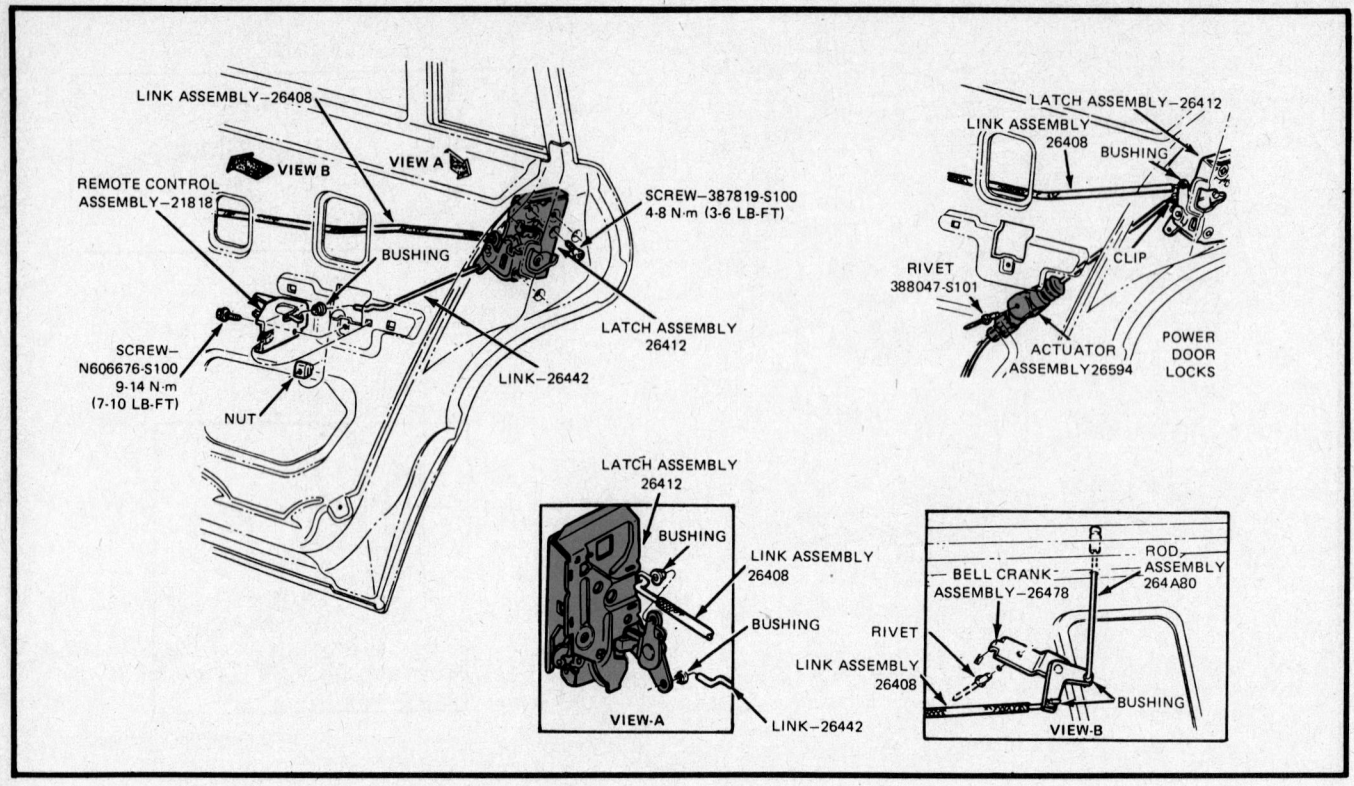

LINK ASSEMBLY—26408

VIEW B

VIEW A

LATCH ASSEMBLY—26412

LINK ASSEMBLY
26408

BUSHING

REMOTE CONTROL
ASSEMBLY—21818

BUSHING

SCREW—387819-S100
4-8 N·m (3-6 LB-FT)

LATCH ASSEMBLY
26412

RIVET
388047-S101

CLIP

ACTUATOR
ASSEMBLY 26594

POWER
DOOR
LOCKS

SCREW—
N606676-S100
9-14 N·m
(7-10 LB-FT)

NUT

LINK—26442

LATCH ASSEMBLY
26412

BUSHING

LINK ASSEMBLY
26408

BUSHING

LINK ASSEMBLY
26408

VIEW-A

LINK—26442

BELL CRANK
ASSEMBLY—26478

RIVET

ROD
ASSEMBLY
264 A80

BUSHING

VIEW-B

Crown Victoria/Grand Marquis 4-door power lock system, rear door

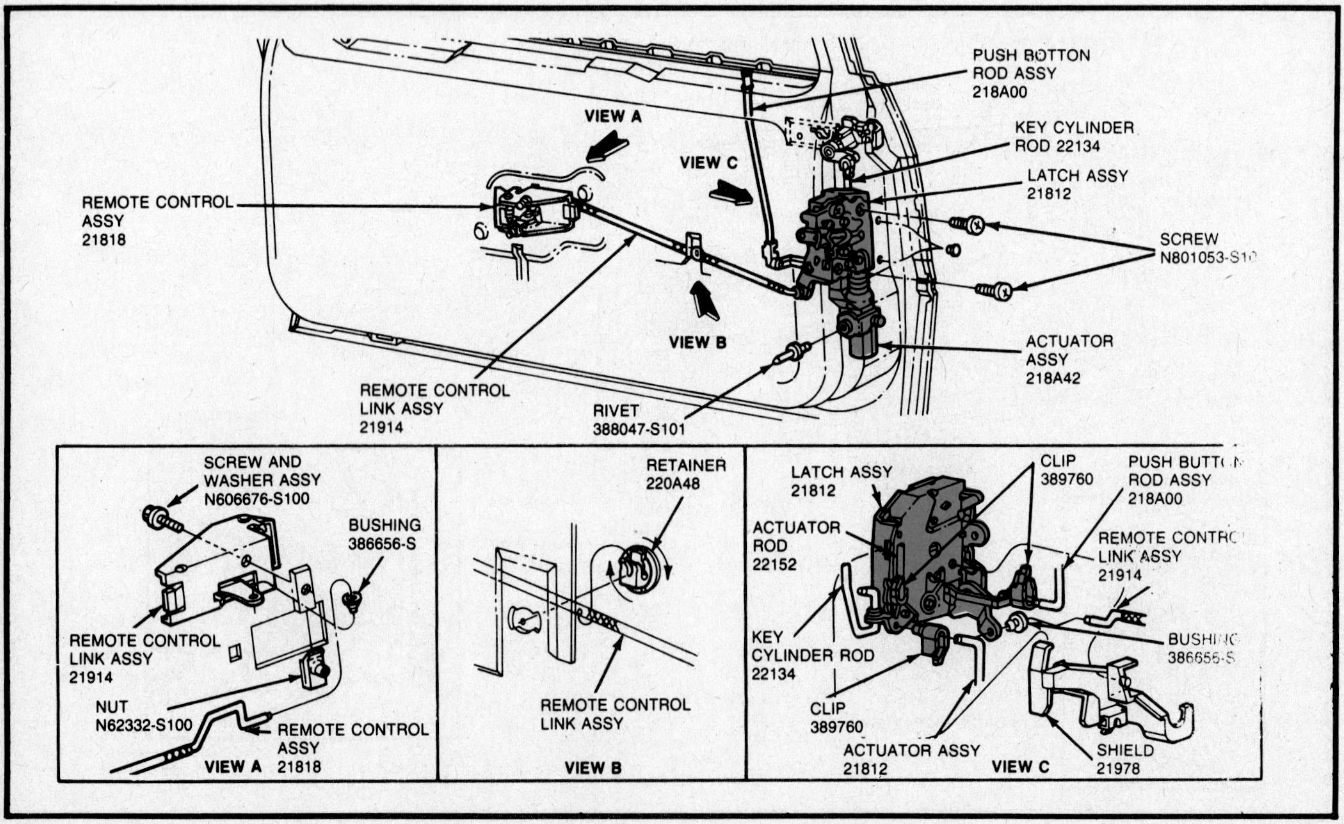

PUSH BUTTON
ROD ASSY
218A00

VIEW A

VIEW C

KEY CYLINDER
ROD 22134

LATCH ASSY
21812

REMOTE CONTROL
ASSY
21818

SCREW
N801053-S10

ACTUATOR
ASSY
218A42

VIEW B

REMOTE CONTROL
LINK ASSY
21914

RIVET
388047-S101

SCREW AND
WASHER ASSY
N606676-S100

BUSHING
386656-S

RETAINER
220A48

LATCH ASSY
21812

CLIP
389760

PUSH BUTTON
ROD ASSY
218A00

REMOTE CONTROL
LINK ASSY
21914

ACTUATOR
ROD
22152

REMOTE CONTROL
LINK ASSY
21914

NUT
N62332-S100

REMOTE CONTROL
ASSY 21818

VIEW A

REMOTE CONTROL
LINK ASSY

VIEW B

KEY
CYLINDER ROD
22134

CLIP
389760

ACTUATOR ASSY
21812

BUSHING
386656-S

SHIELD
21978

VIEW C

Mark VII, Thunderbird and Cougar actuator assembly

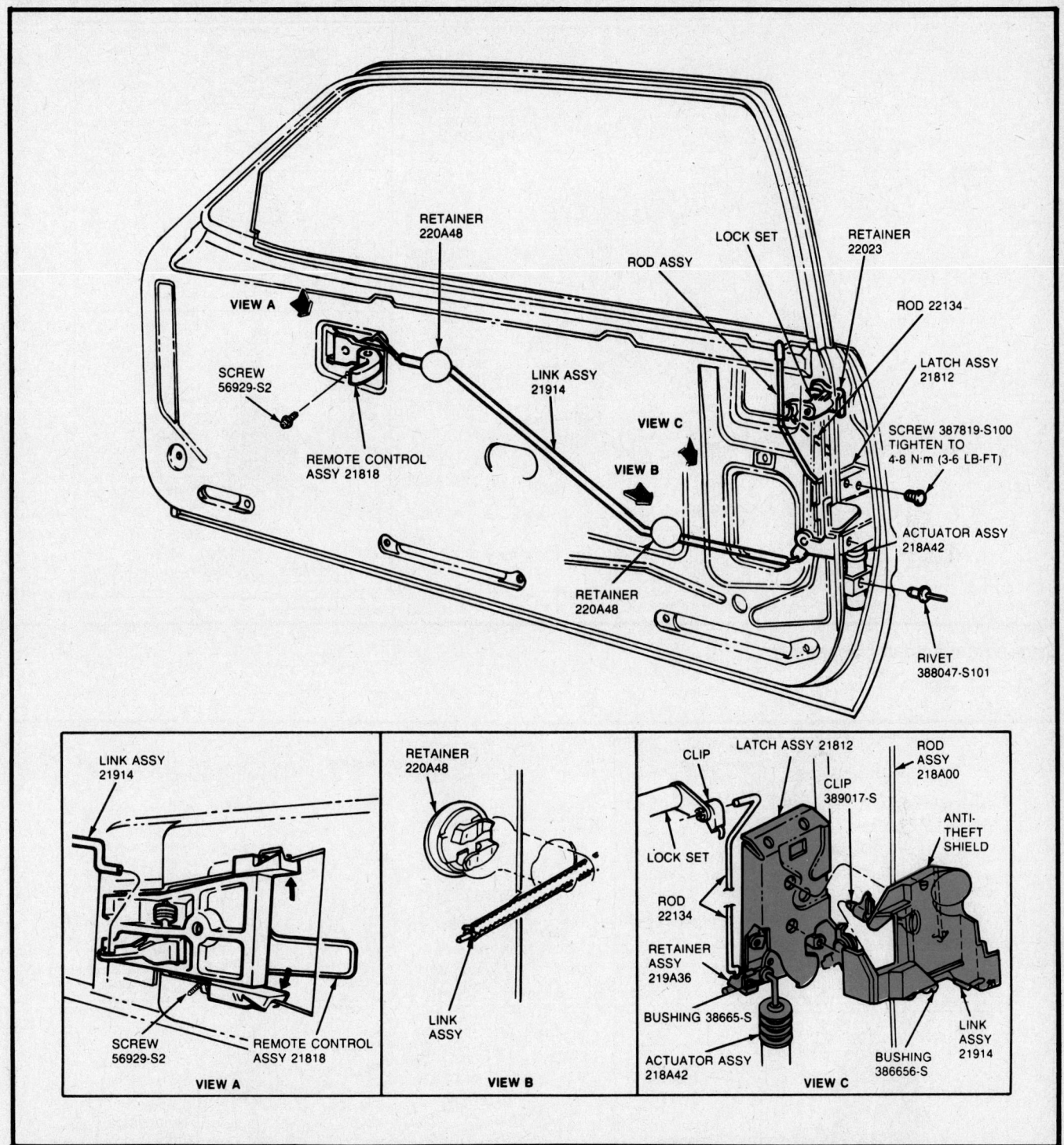

Mustang/Capri actuator assembly

2. Disconnect the lock cylinder rod at the latch.
3. Remove the lock cylinder retainer and remove the cylinder from the door.

4. Remove the two Phillips screws attaching the solenoid to the lock.
5. Unplug the wiring connector and remove the lock solenoid.
6. Installation is the reverse of removal.

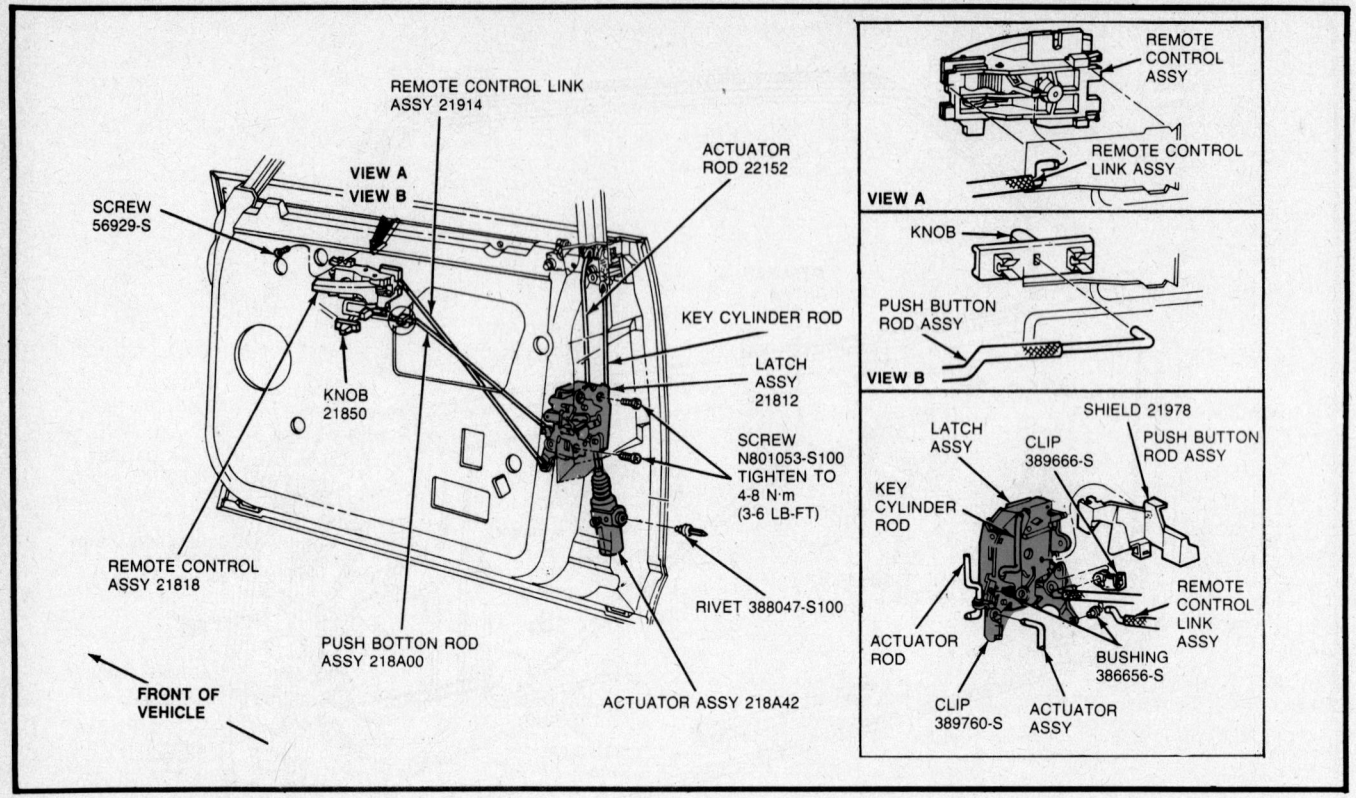

Continental actuator assembly

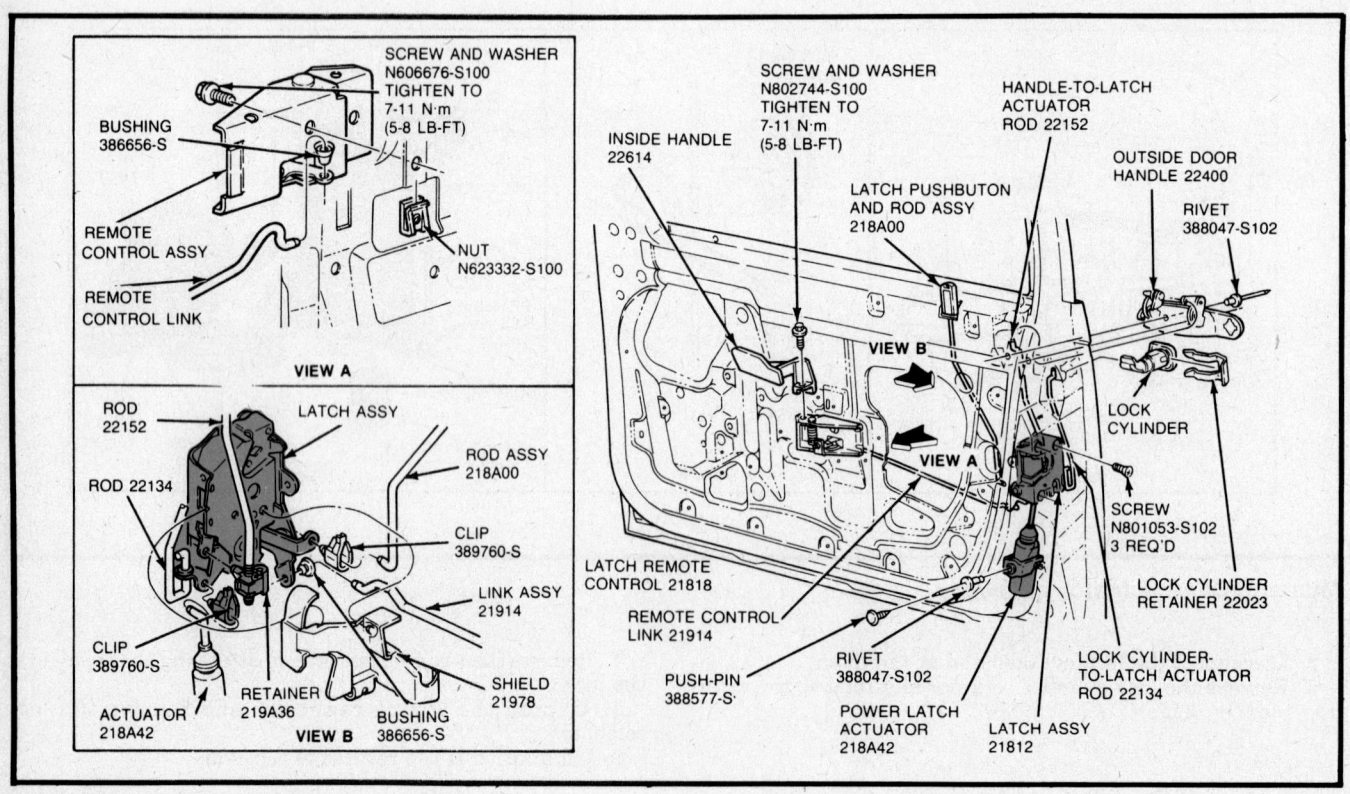

Taurus/Sable front door lock system

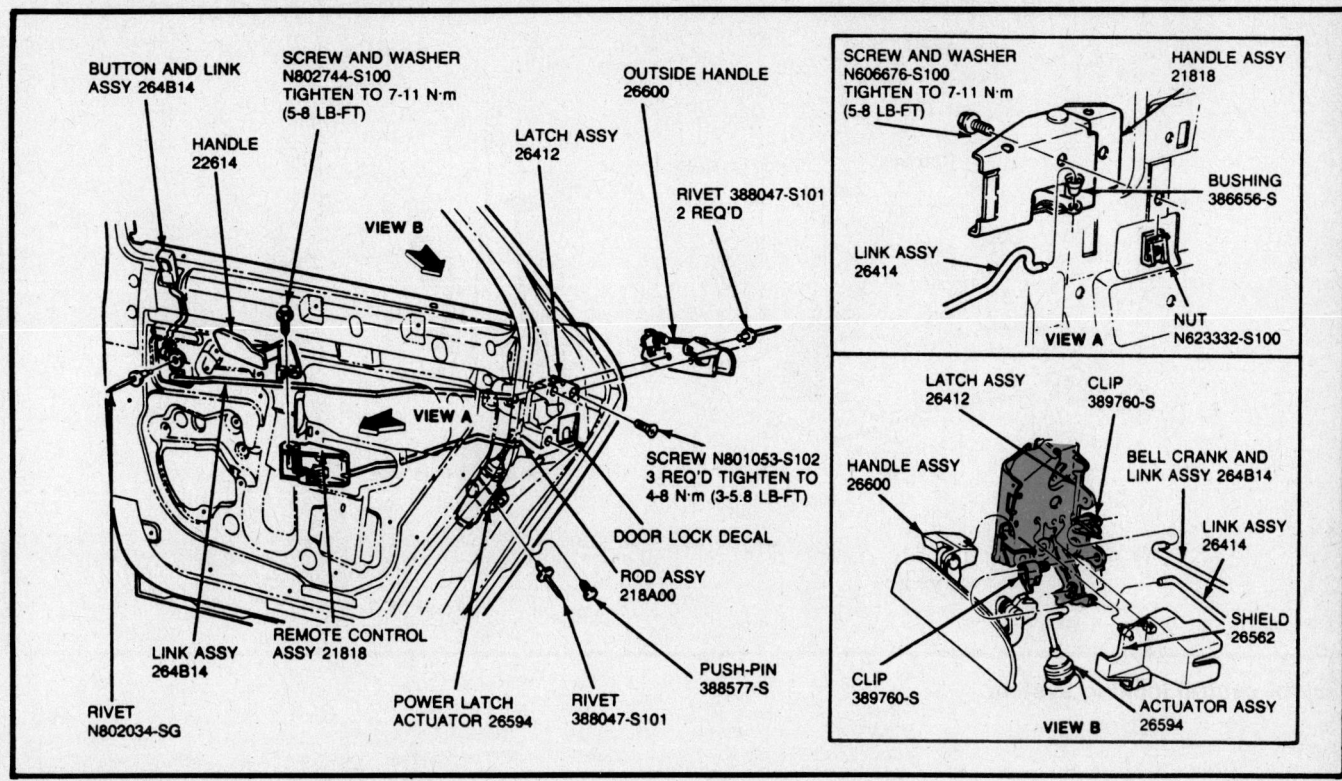

Taurus/Sable rear door lock system

GENERAL MOTORS

Actuator Motor

REMOVAL AND INSTALLATION

All Car Lines

1. Raise the window and remove the door trim panel and watershield.
2. Drill out the actuator motor attaching rivets.
3. Disconnect the actuator rod, unplug the wiring connector and lift out the motor.
4. Installation is the reverse of removal. If you are using replacement rivets, use ¼" x ½" aluminum peel type rivets. If not, use ¼"-20 bolts and self-locking nuts. Tighten the bolts to 10 ft.lb.

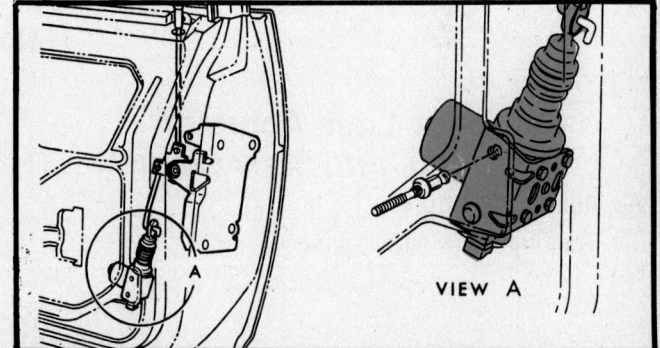

Typical General Motors power door lock actuator mounting

CHRYSLER/MITSUBISHI

Door Lock Actuator

REMOVAL AND INSTALLATION

Galant

FRONT DOOR

1. Remove the door trim panel and watershield.

2. Remove the door latch attaching bolts and lift out the latch assembly.
3. Disconnect the actuator rod from the connector and latch and remove the actuator.
4. Installation is the reverse of removal. The lock lever and actuator rod should be in the LOCK position for installation.

REAR DOOR

1. Remove the door trim panel and watershield.

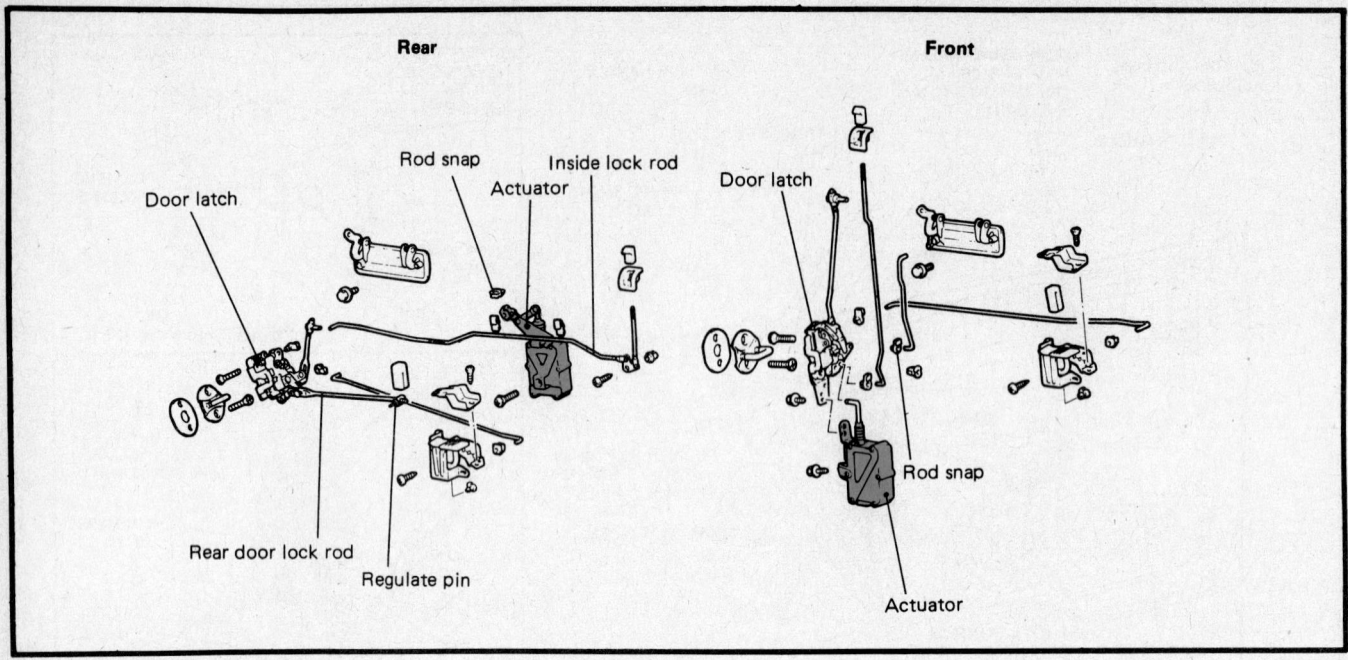

Rear   Front

Door latch   Rod snap   Inside lock rod
Actuator

Door latch

Rod snap

Rear door lock rod   Actuator

Regulate pin

Galant central locking system

2. Remove the actuator attaching screws and disconnect the linkage.

3. Lift out the actuator.

4. Attach the connecting rod to the actuator and secure the actuator to the door panel with the screws.

5. Move the inside lock rod to the UNLOCK position.

6. Move the actuator rod to the UNLOCK position and make the connection.

7. Align the regulator pin on the lock rod with the center of the actuator clip and install the lock rod.

HONDA

Door Lock Actuator
REMOVAL AND INSTALLATION

All Models/All Doors

1. Disconnect the battery ground.

2. Remove the door trim panel.

3. Remove the watershield.

4. Remove the two screws securing the actuator.

5. Disconnect the linkage rod at the actuator.

6. Unplug the wiring connector from the actuator.

7. Installation is the reverse of removal.

NISSAN

Door Lock Actuator

REMOVAL AND INSTALLATION

280ZX, 300ZX

1. Remove the door trim panel and watershield.

2. Unplug the wiring connector and unbolt the actuator motor, found at the lower rear corner of the door.

3. Swivel the actuator outward to disengage it from the linkage and remove it.

4. Installation is the reverse of removal.

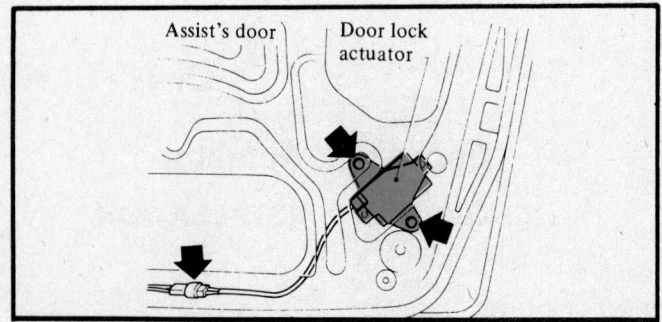

Assist's door   Door lock actuator

280ZX, 300ZX power lock actuator

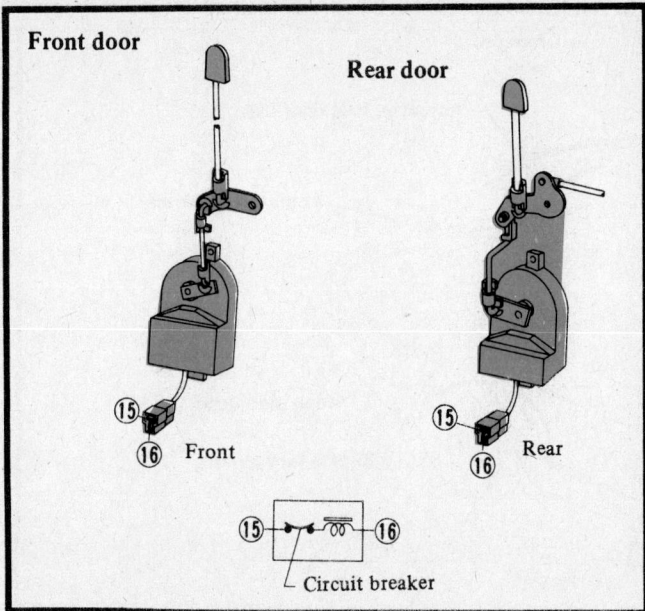

Stanza lock actuator

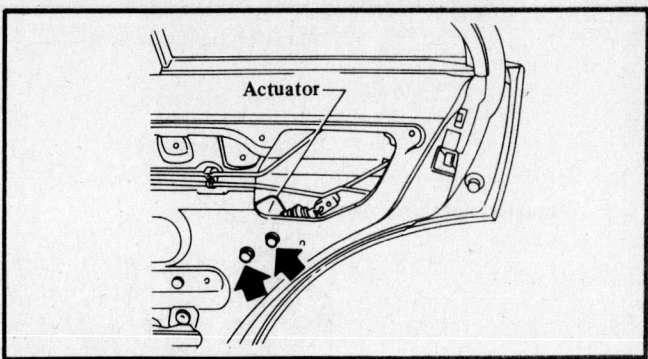

Maxima actuator bolts

Maxima
200SX
Pulsar
Stanza

1. Remove the door trim panel and watershield.
2. Disconnect the linkage at the lock knob and actuator.
3. Remove the actuator attaching screws and lift out the actuator.
4. Installation is the reverse of removal.

SUBARU

Door Lock Actuator

REMOVAL AND INSTALLATION

All Models/All Doors

1. Remove the door trim panel.
2. Remove the watershield.
3. Raise the glass completely.
4. Remove the two screws securing the switch to the door frame.
5. Disconnect the linkage from the actuator.
6. Unplug the harness connector from the actuator.
7. Remove the actuator from the door.
5. Installation is the reverse of removal.

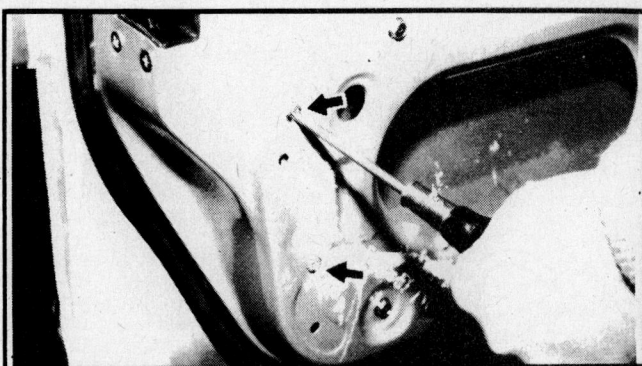

Removing the door lock actuator screws, typical of all Subaru models

VOLKSWAGEN

Diagnosis and Testing

The system has two aspects: an electrically operated pump and a vacuum operating system.

Each system must be verified as working, before the other can be tested.

Testing the Pump

1. Remove the left trunk trim panel.

2. Position the left front door lock button in the OPEN position.
3. Unplug the electrical connector at the pump.
4. Connect a test light between the center and right terminals of the plug connector.
5. If the lamp does not light, the left front door valve is defective or the wiring has an open or short.
6. If the lamp lights, push the door button to the CLOSED position. Connect the test light between the center and left terminals of the plug connector. If the lamp does not light, the door valve is defective. If the lamp lights, the pump is defective.

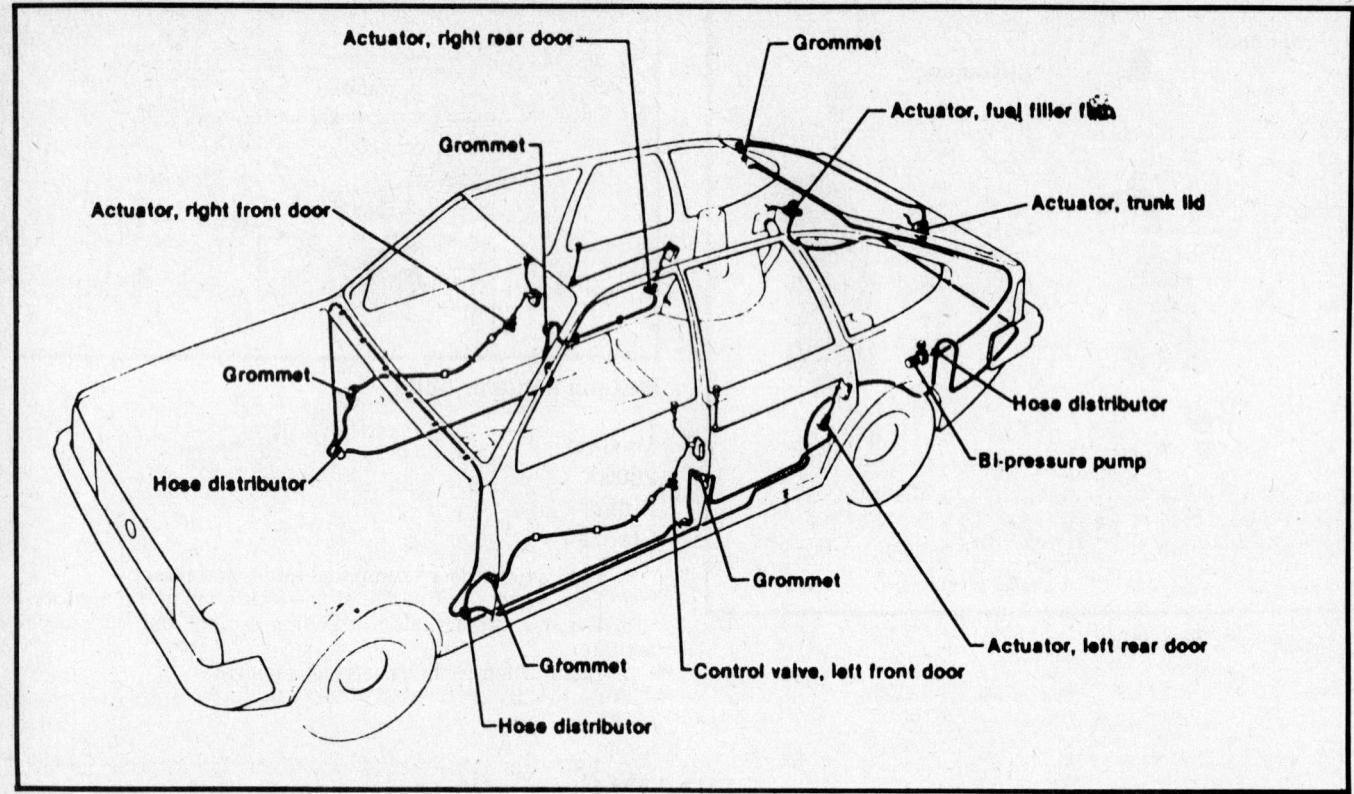

Volkswagen power door lock schematic

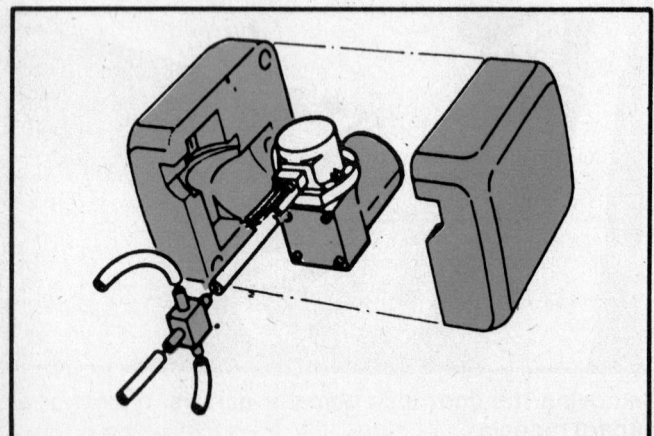

Bi-pressure pump used to power the Volkswagen locking system

TESTING THE PNUEMATIC SYSTEM

All locks should close within 2 seconds. If the pump runs for more than 5 seconds, the system is leaking. The pump should automatically stop after 35 seconds.

To test the pump, remove the outlet hose from the distributor and clamp it. Operate the pump, if the pump runs for more than 5 seconds, it is defective.

Test each door's lines by isolating the line and operating the pump.

Actuator

REMOVAL AND INSTALLATION

Left or Right Rear Door
Right Front Door

1. Remove the door trim panel.
2. Remove the watershield.
3. Remove the actuator attaching screw.
4. Disconnect the hose from the actuator.
5. Unhook the linkage rod and remove the actuator.
6. Installation is the reverse of removal.

Left Front Door

1. Remove the door trim panel.
2. Remove the watershield.
3. Remove the actuator attaching screw.
4. Disconnect the hose from the actuator.
5. Unhook the linkage rod.
6. Unplug the electrical connector from the actuator.
7. Remove the actuator.
8. Installation is the reverse of removal.

AMERICAN MOTORS

Power Mirrors

The power mirrors are controlled by a dual control switch located on the left front door. The left and right control switch is used for directing the current to the desired motor. The horizontal and vertical switch directs the current to the mirror assembly which moves the mirror as desired.

There is a safety or overrun feature designed into the mirror to prevent damage to the motor when the mirror is moved by hand or when running the mirror to the maximum limit.

POWER MIRROR ELECTRIC MOTOR

Test

1. Using a suitable test light, check for current in the orange input wire to the power mirror switch. If there is no current present, check the following:

a. Check for a broken ground (black) wire or the (orange) feed wire between the switch and the fuse panel.

b. If the orange wire checks out good, check the power mirror switch output.

NOTE: When checking the yellow and white wire the control switches must be activated before checking for current.

2. Using the same test light check for current at the (yellow) horizontal wire and the (white) vertical wire.

3. If there is no current found in both the yellow and white wire, replace the switch, if there is current found in both the yellow and white wire, replace the mirror.

NOTE: Before replacing the right side mirror, check for current input at the motor.

POWER MIRROR SWITCH

Removal and Installation

1. Disconnect the negative battery cable. Remove the set screw from the power mirror switch.

2. Remove the door trim panel and remove the insulator paper. Disconnect the wiring harness from the mirror and door harness and remove the switch.

3. Installation is the reverse order of the removal procedure.

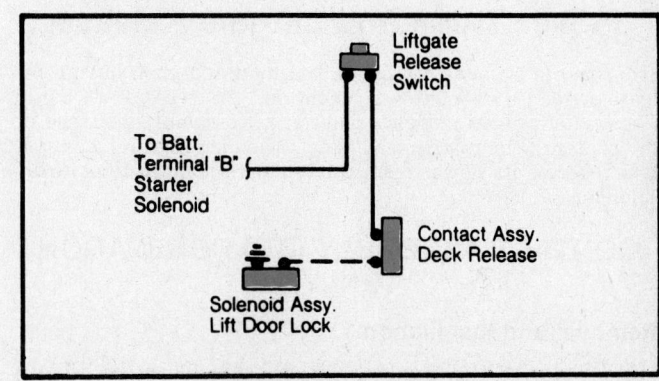

Liftgate/Trunk release electrical schematic—Eagle

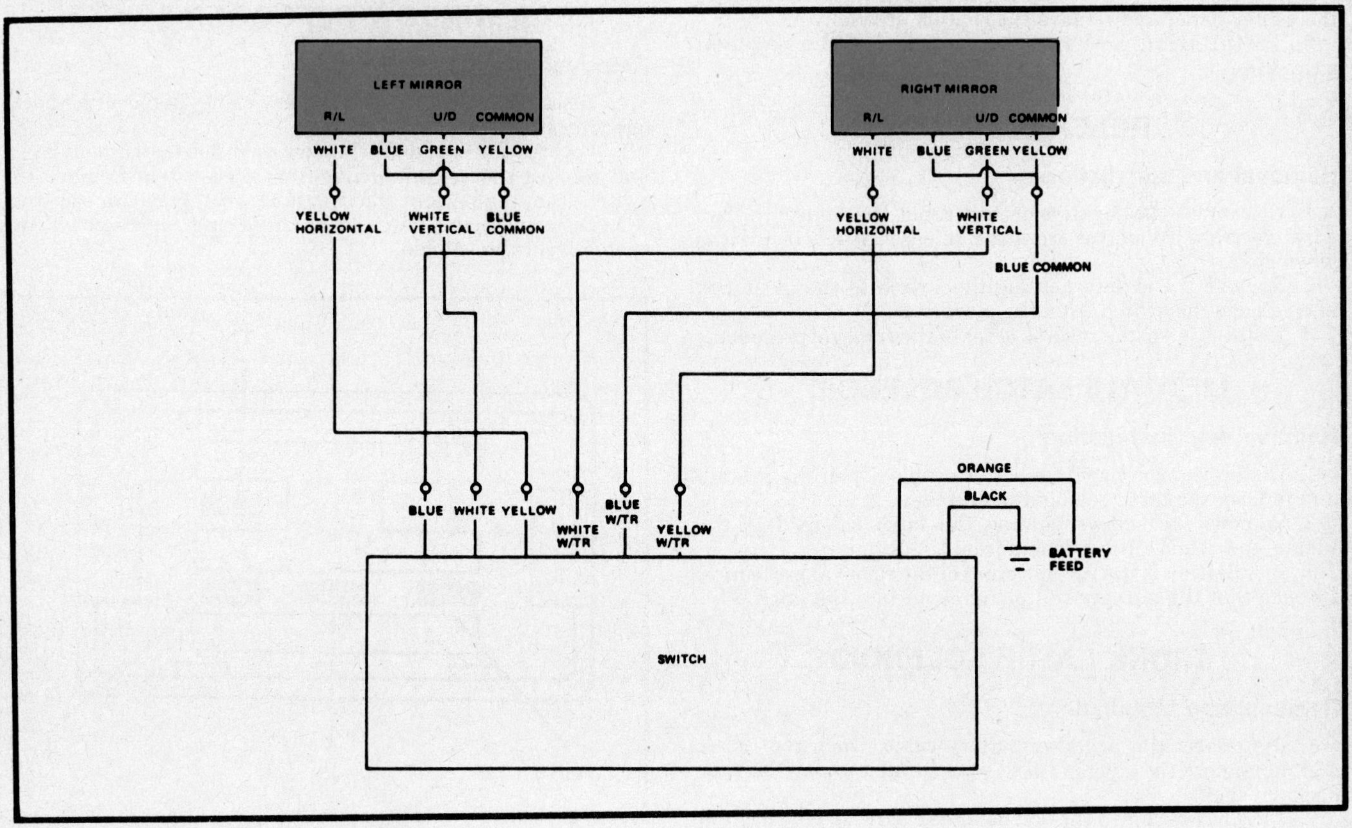

Power mirror electrical schematic

POWER MIRROR

Removal and Installation

1. Disconnect the negative battery cable. Remove the set screw from the power mirror switch plate and remove the plate.

2. Remove the door trim panel and remove the insulator paper. Disconnect the door wiring harness from the mirror harness.

3. Remove the tape holding the the mirror harness to the inner door panel. Remove the mirror retaining screws, mirror and gasket from the outer door panel.

4. Pull the mirror harness out of the door along with the gasket.

5. Installation is the reverse order of the removal procedure.

Power Trunk and Liftgate Release

This system consists of a glove box mounted push button release switch, a door latch solenoid and the necessary wiring. The station wagon models use a contact assembly mounted in the center of the instrument panel. The electrical release system receives its power from the hot wire lead on the starter solenoid.

CONTACT ASSEMBLY (STATION WAGON ONLY)

Removal and Installation

1. Disconnect the negative battery cable. Open the liftgate and remove the trim panel from the lower center panel.

2. Disconnect the electrical terminal connector from the switch. Remove the screw holding the the contact assembly to the center panel and remove the contact assembly.

3. Installation is thew reverse order of the removal procedure.

RELEASE SWITCH

Removal and Installation

1. Disconnect the negative battery cable. Disconnect the two wire electrical connector from the release switch inside the glove box.

2. Remove the screws holding the switch to the glove box and remove the switch from the glove box.

3. Installation is the reverse order of the removal procedure.

LIFTGATE LATCH SOLENOID

Removal and Installation

1. Disconnect the negative battery cable. Open the liftgate and remove the latch solenoid trim cover.

2. Remove the screws holding the latch solenoid to the lifgate and remove the solenoid from the liftgate.

3. Installation is the reverse order of the removal procedure. Be sure that the plunger roll pin engages into the latch.

TRUNK LATCH SOLENOID

Removal and Installation

1. Disconnect the negative battery cable. Open the trunk and disconnect the solenoid feed wire located under the rear package shelf.

2. Attach a string to the solenoid feed wire, make sure the string is long enough to have access to both ends of the solenoid when pulled through the deck lid.

3. Remove the screws holding the latch solenoid to the deck lid. Remove the solenoid and wire from the deck lid.

4. Installation is the reverse order of the removal procedure. Be sure the roll pin engages into the latch. Close the trunk and check the latch solenoid for proper operation.

Rear Window Defogger

This system consists of two vertical bus bars and horizontal rows of heating elements of a silver bearing, ceramic enamel compound fused to the inside of the glass.

The control switch assembly also houses the pilot lamp and the timer relay. The current feed wire is incorporated into the body wiring harness and is routed along the left side of the vehicle.

REAR DEFOGGER SYSTEM

Test

1. Using a suitable test light check for current at the red wire at the fuse block. If there is current present and the fuse id good, turn the ignition switch to the "ON" position and check the current at the following terminals:

a. Check for current at the number one and two terminals. If there is current, check the circuits and repair them as necessary.

b. Make sure the switch has a good ground through the wire connected to the number three terminal on the switch.

c. With a good ground circuit established and the igniton switch in the "ON" position, there should be current at the number four terminal. If there is no current present, replace the switch.

REAR WINDOW DEFOGGER SWITCH

Removal and Installation

1. Disconnect the negative battery cable. Remove the package tray if so equipped.

2. Located the rear defroster switch on the instrument panel and remove the retaining nut from the switch. Remove the switch from the back of the instrument panel center housing.

3. Disconnect the wires from the switch and remove the switch from the vehicle.

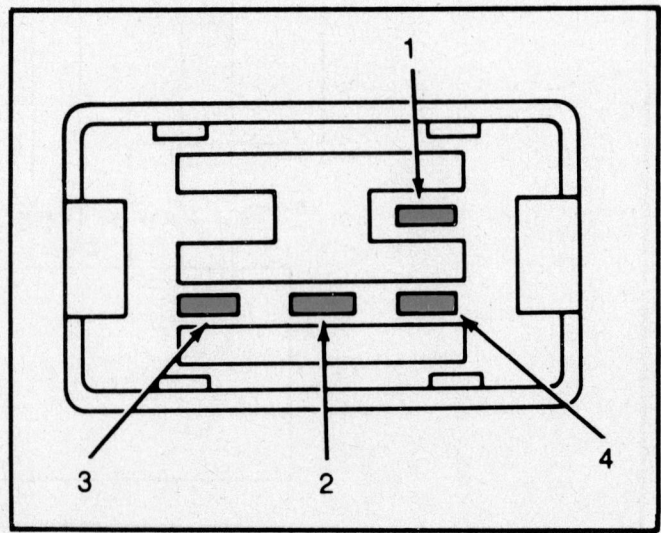

Rear window defogger switch terminal locations

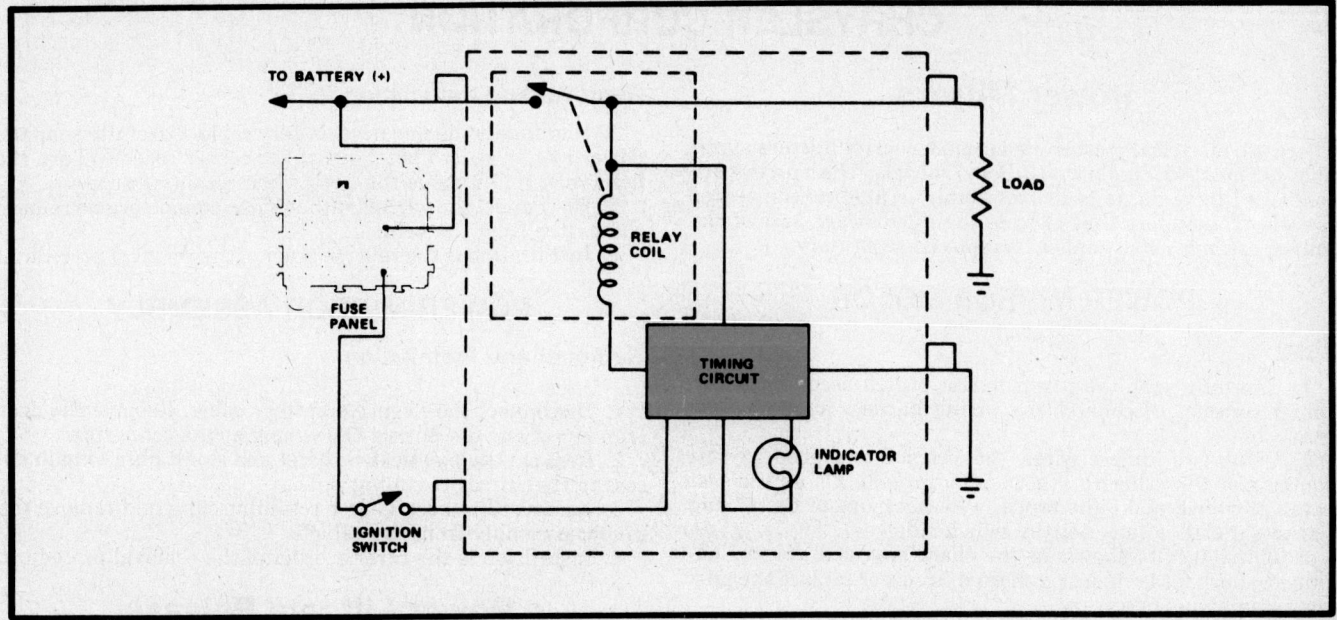

Rear window defogger electrical schematic

4. Installation is the reverse order of the removal procedure. Be sure to align the anti-rotation pin when installing the switch.

REAR DEFOGGER GRID

Test Procedure

When a grid is inoperable due to an open circuit, the area of glass normally cleared by that grid will remained fogged or iced until cleared by the adjacent grids. Use the following procedure to located a broken grid.

Note: The feed wire is connected to the driver's side of the window and the ground connection is located on the right side of the window.

1. With the engine running at idle, place the rear defogger switch in the "ON" position. The pilot lamp is the switch lever should light up indicating the defogger is operating.

2. Using a 12 volt voltmeter, connect the positive lead of the voltmeter to the hot side of the vertical bus element on the inside surface of the glass.

3. Connect the negative lead of the voltmeter to the ground side of the bus element. The voltage drop indicated on the meter should be 11 to 13 volts. Connect the negative lead of the voltmeter to a good ground, the meter reading should stay constant.

4. Keep the negative lead connected to the ground and carefully use the positive lead to contact each grid at the approxi-

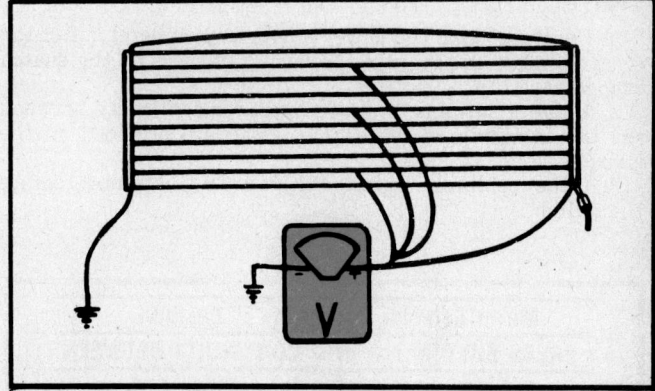

Using a voltmeter to locate a broken grid

mate centerline of the window. A voltage drop of approximately 6 volts. indicates a good grid or a closed circuit.

5. No voltage indicated a broken grid wire. To located the exact location of the break, move the voltmeter lead along the grid wire. The voltage should decrease gradually. if the voltage drops suddenly, there is a break at that location.

NOTE: Grid repair kits are available from the manufacturer and the enclosed manufactures instruction should be followed for a proper grid repair.

CHRYSLER CORPORATION

Power Mirrors

There are electrically controlled remote control mirrors available in the 1987 Sundance (P-Body) models. The mirrors are controlled by a single switch assembly located on the center console. The motors that operate the mirrors are part of the mirror assembly and cannot be replaced separately.

POWER MIRROR MOTOR

Test

1. Carefully snap the power mirror switch bezel out of the center console. Disconnect the wiring harness at the switch connector.
2. Using two jumper wires, connect one to a good 12 volt source and the other to a good body ground. Using the test chart provided, make the proper wire hook ups at the wiring harness (harness side, not the switch side).
3. If the results shown in the chart provided are not obtained, check for broken or a shorted circuit or replace the mirror assembly as necessary.

POWER MIRROR SWITCH

Test

1. Carefully snap the power mirror switch bezel out of the center console. Disconnect the wiring harness at the switch connector.
2. Using a suitable ohmmeter test for continuity between the the terminals of the switch which are provided on the chart.
3. If the results shown in the chart are not obtained, replace the switch.

Mirror Selector Rocker in "L" Position	
PRESS BUTTON	**CONTINUITY BETWEEN**
▲	PK and YL BK and DG
▶	PK and DG BK and DB
▼	PK and DG BK and YL
◀	PK and DB BK and DG
Mirror Selector Rocker in "R" Position	
PRESS BUTTON	**CONTINUITY BETWEEN**
▲	PK and YL/RD BK and DG
▶	PK and DG BK and RD/DB
▼	PK and DG BK and YL/RD
◀	PK and RD/DB BK and DG

Power mirror switch continuity chart

Removal and Installation

1. Disconnect the negative battery cable. Carefully snap the power mirror switch bezel out of the center console. Turn the bezel over and remove the two switch retaining screws.
2. Disconnect the wiring at the switch connector and remove the switch from the vehicle.
3. Installation is the reverse order of the removal procedure.

POWER MIRROR ASSEMBLY

Removal and Installation

1. Disconnect the negative battery cable. Remove the door trim panel and disconnect the wiring at the connector.
2. Remove the plastic door bezel and small plug to gain access to the mirror retaining nuts.
3. Remove the three mirror retaining nuts and remove the mirror assembly from the vehicle.
4. Installtion is the reverse order of the removal procedure.

Power Liftgate Release

The power liftgate release system consists of a release button (usually found in the glove box or on the dash panel), a 6 amp circuit breaker, a relay and a solenoid.

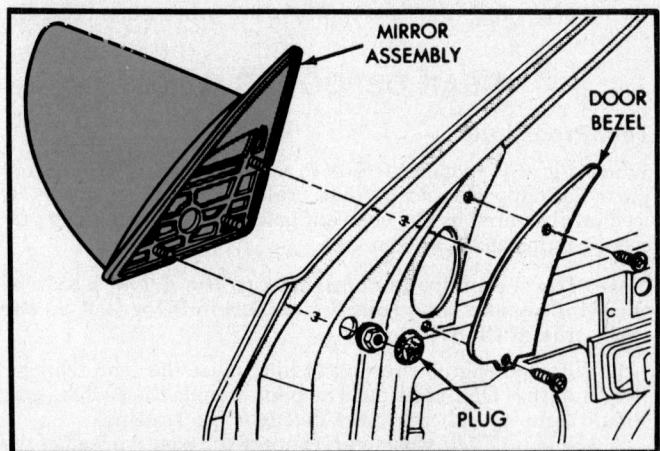

Power mirror removal and installation

12 Volts	Ground	MIRROR REACTION	
		Right	**Left**
YL/RD	DG/WT	UP	
YL	DG/WT		UP
DG/WT	YL/RD	DOWN	
DG/WT	YL		DOWN
DG/WT	DB/RD	RIGHT	
DG/WT	DB		RIGHT
DB/RD	DG/WT	LEFT	
DB	DG/WT		LEFT

Power mirror test chart

Power Liftgate Release Test

1. With the battery fully charged and the ignition switch in the "ON" or "ACC" position the liftgate should unlock when the button is pressed.
2. If the liftgate does not unlock, open the liftgate manually and disconnect the electrical connector at the solenoid.
3. Connect a suitable voltmeter between the solenoid connector and a good ground. When the liftgate button is pressed in, there should be at least 10 volts at the connector.
4. If there is not 10 volts present at the connector, check the power lead and wiring, if there is voltage indicated, check the solenoid ground connection.
5. Remove the solenoid from the lift gate. Check the plunger and plunger spring for proper operation (free movement of at least $\frac{5}{8}$ in. Reinstall the solenoid and adjust the solenoid plunger until the liftgate release system operates properly.

NOTE: Adjust the liftgate latch and striker so that the liftgate lid latches with a moderate slam. Should the latch fail to lock, replace the latch assembly.

Rear Window Defogger

All vehicles equipped with an electrically heated rear windows, use a 65 amp alternator. The rear window defogger system consists of a rear window with two vertical bus bars and a series of electrically connected grid lines baked on the inside surface. A control switch and a timer relay combined into a single assembly is used on all models.

All circuit protection is provided by a fusible link, located in the charging circuit, for the heater grid circuit and by a fuse for the relay control circuit.

NOTE: Since the grid lines can be damaged or scraped off with sharp instruments, caution should be used when cleaning the glass or removing foreign materials, decals or stickers. Normal glass cleaning solvents or hot water used with rags or toweling is recommended.

REAR WINDOW DEFOGGER SYSTEM

Test

The rear window defogger system operation can be checked in the vehicle using the following test procedure.
1. Turn the ignition switch to the "ON" position, also turn the rear window defogger control switch to the "ON" position.
2. Monitor the vehicle voltmeter (ammeter on the RWD vehicles). with the control switch in the "ON" position, a distinct needle deflection should be noted.

NOTE: If the vehicle is not equipped with a voltmeter or a ammeter, the rear window defogger operation can be checked by feeling the glass in the rear windshield. A distinct difference in temperature between the grid lines and adjacent clear glass can be detected in three to four minutes of operation.

3. Using a suitable DC voltmeter connect terminal "B" with the negative lead and terminal "I" with the positive lead. The voltmeter should rear 10 to 14 volts.
4. Only Steps 1, 2 and 3 will confirm the system is operational. The indicator or pilot light illumination means that there is power available at the output of the relay only and does not necessarily prove the system is operational.
5. If the rear window defogger system does not operate properly, the problem should be isolated as outlined in the following procedure:
   a. Check to be sure the ignition switch is in the "ON" position. Be sure that the rear defogger feed (HOT) wire is connected to the terminal or pigtail and that the ground wire is indeed grouned.
   b. Be sure the fusible link and control circuit fuse is operational and all electrical connections are secure. When all of these things have been completely checked out, one of the following is defective; the control switch/timer relay module or the rear window defogger grid lines.
   c. If the grid lines were to blame, either all the grid lines would have to be broken, or one of the feed (HOT) wires are not connected for the system to be inoperative.
6. If the turning the control switch procedures give severe voltmeter (ammeter) deflections, check the system for a shorting condition. If the systems check out but the indicator bulb does not light, replace the control switch/timer relay on the RWD vehicles and check or replace the bulb on the FWD vehicles.

REAR WINDOW DEFOGGER GRID

Test

1. Turn the ignition switch and the control switch to the "ON" position. The indicator or pilot light should come on (this lamp is incorporated in the switch knob).
2. Using a suitable DC voltmeter with a range of 0 to 15 volts, connect terminal "B" with the negative lead of the voltmeter. With the positive lead of the voltmeter connected to terminal "A". The voltmeter reading should be 10 to 14 volts. A lower voltage reading indicated a poor ground connection.
3. Connect the negative lead of the voltmeter to a good body ground. The voltage reading should not change.
4. On the RWD vehicles, connect the negative lead of the voltmeter to terminal "A" and touch midpoint "C" of the grid lines with the positive lead of the voltmeter. If the grid line id good it will have a voltage reading of approximately 6 volts.
5. A voltage reading of 0 usually indicated a break between midpoint "C" and terminal "B". A voltage reading of 10 to 14 volts will indicated a break between the midpoint "C" and terminal "A". Slowly move the positive lead of the voltmeter toward the break in the grid and the voltage will change as soon as the break is reached.
6. On the FWD vehicles, connect the negative lead of the voltmeter to terminal "B" and touch the positive lead of the voltmeter to midpoint "C" of the grid lines. A good grid line will be indicated with a voltage reading of approximately 6 volts.
7. A voltage reading of 0 usually indicated a break between midpoint "C" and terminal "A". A voltage reading of 10 to 14 volts will indicated a break between the midpoint "C" and terminal "B". Slowly move the positive lead of the voltmeter toward the break in the grid and the voltage will change as soon as the break is reached.

NOTE: The repair of the grid lines or the terminal is possible by using the Mopar repair kit number 4267922 or equivalent.

CONTROL SWITCH/TIMER RELAY MODULE

Test

1. Remove the switch by reaching behind the instrument panel and depressing the lock tabs at the top and bottom of the switch case while pushing the switch towards the front of the instrument panel.
2. Turn the ignition switch to the "ON" position. Using a suitable DC voltmeter, with a range of 0 to 15 volts, check the voltage at terminals B, I and L. Terminals B and I should show a voltage reading of 10 to 14 volts to ground. Terminal L should show 0 volts to ground.
3. When terminals B and I show no voltage, trace the circuit

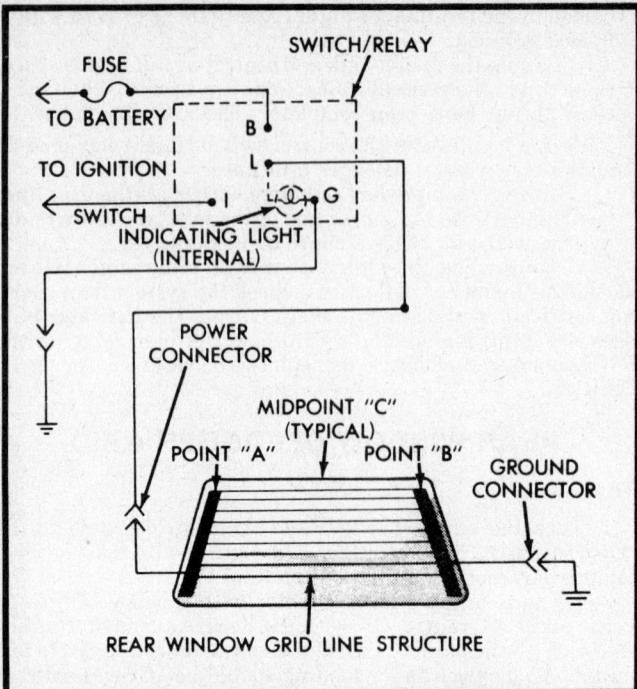

Rear window defogger grid wiring schematic

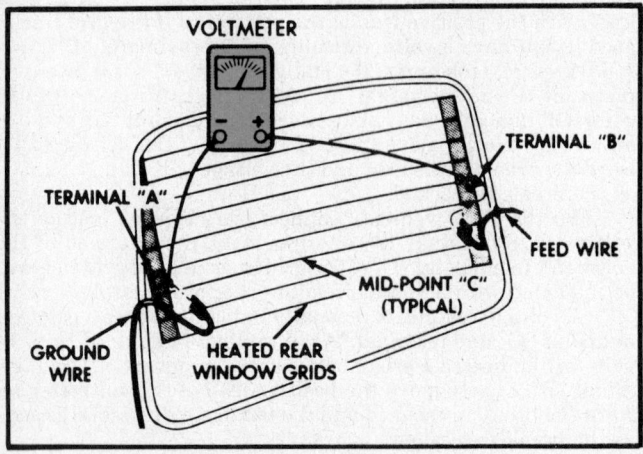

Rear window defogger broken grid test

NOTE: Bench checking the relay may be accomplished by following this procedure except for step two. Using a suitable DC power supply, apply 12 volts to terminal B and I and ground terminal G.

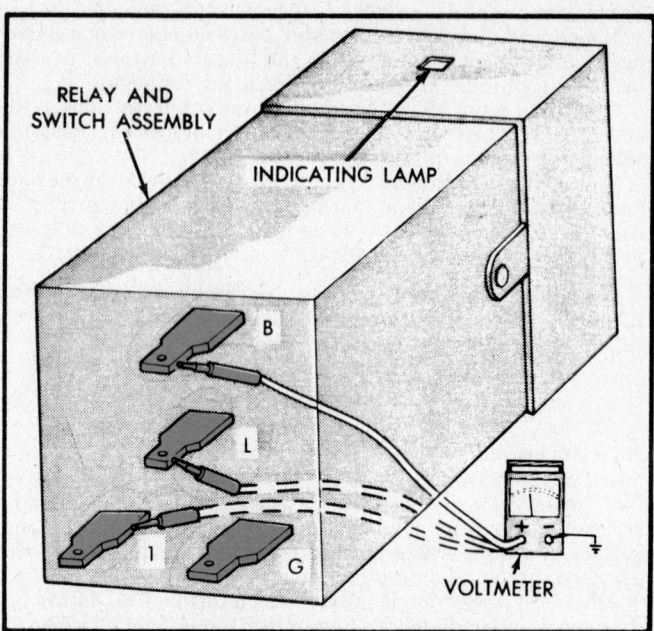

Typical control switch/timer relay

ISOLATION DIODES (RWD)

Test

1. Connect a suitable self-powered test light to the test points indicated for the A/C isolation diode and refer to the A/C isolation diode chart for the proper response of the test light and polarity.

2. If the diode is installed backwards or has failed in the shorted mode, this condition will cause the A/C clutch to energize when the electric backlight isolation diode is turned on. This could effect the long term operation of the clutch.

3. Should both diodes be shorted, the stop idle solenoid could also be shorted, resulting in damage to the electric backlight isolation diode overlay wiring, damage stop idle solenoid wiring or an open fuse on fuse cavity 16 of the fuse block.

upstream of the switch/relay module for the problem (wiring cut, fusible link or circuit braker inoperative, bulkhead connector inoperative.

4. If terminal L indicates voltage, place the switch knob in the "OFF" positionand allow the knob to return to its normal position. If the voltage at terminal L is still indicated or the indicator lamp remains on, the switch/relay module should be replaced.

5. If the relay checks out to this point, momentarily operate the switch knob to the "ON" position. The indicator lamp should come on and remain on for approximately ten minutes. Terminal L should indicated voltage.

6. If the indicator lamp fails to come on or voltage at terminal L is not indicated, the switch/relay module should be replaced.

EBL ISOLATION DIODE CHART*			
+	−	Diode Good	Diode Bad
1	2	No Light	Light
2	1	Light	No Light
*Diode must be checked both ways			

A/C ISOLATION DIODE CHART*			
+	−	Diode Good	Diode Bad
3	4	Light	No Light
4	3	No Light	Light
*Diode must be checked both ways			

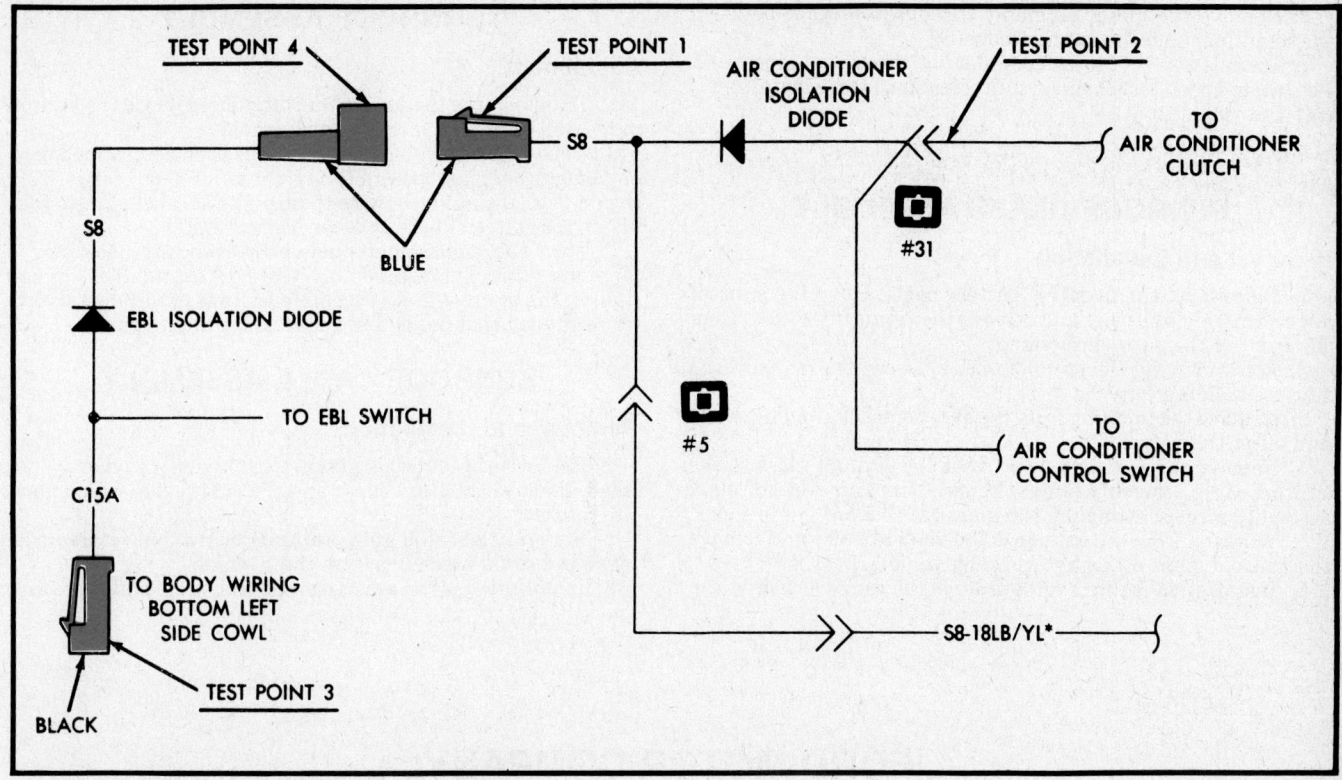

Isolation diodes test point locations (RWD)

4. If this is the case, repair or replace the shorted stop idle solenoid and other damaged parts.

Electric Sunroofs

The sunroof is operated by a switch in the headliner. The system is consists of the sunroof switch, motor drive cables and 15 amp circuit breaker. The sunroof can be closed manually, (should it be necessary) by removing the headliner plug, insert the handle and turn the gear to close the sunroof.

NOTE: The sunroof assembly is equipped with water drain tubes, it is important to keep these drain tubes open. So it is recommended to blow compressed air through the drain tubes at regular intervals, in order to keep the drain tubes clear.

CONTROL SWITCH

Removal and Installation

1. Disconnect the negative battery cable. Carefully pull the toggle switch from the headliner while holding the toggle switch bezel.
2. Disconnect the control switch electrical connector. Be sure to take notice to the position of the connectors during the removal for ease at installation.
3. Installation is the reverse order of the removal procedure. Check to see if the switch is operating properly.

SUNROOF MOTOR

Removal and Installation

1. Disconnect the negative battery cable. Remove the tack welt from surface of the sunroof opening.

2. Pull the headliner down far enough to allow access to the drive assembly retainer bolts. Be careful not to bend or damage the headliner during this procedure. Remove the motor retaining bolts.

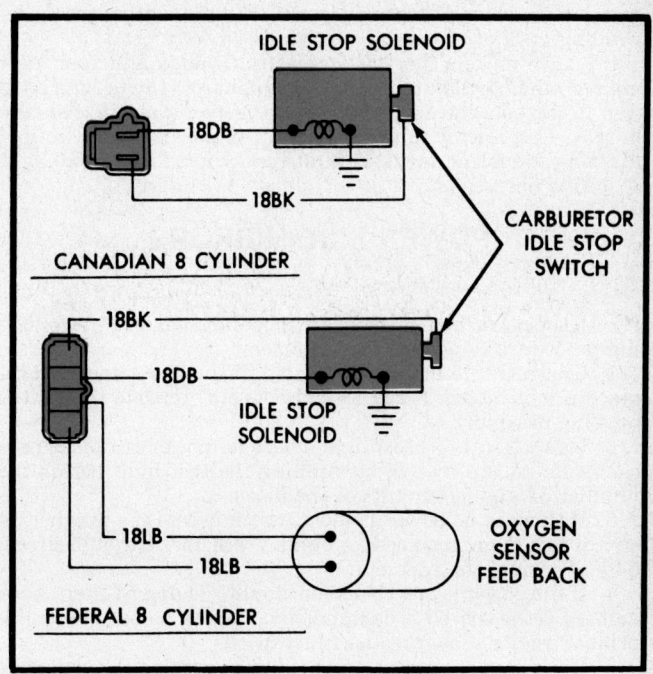

Idle stop solenoid wiring schematic

3. Remove the motor assembly through the space between the headliner and the sunroof housing.

4. Installation is the reverse order of the removal procedure. Be sure to bench test the new sunroof motor before installing it into the vehicle.

SUNROOF GLASS ASSEMBLY

Removal and Installation

1. Disconnect the negative battery cable. Open the sunroof approximately half-way and remove the retaining screws from the front of the sunroof molding.

2. While moving the sunroof to the closed position, pull the sunroof molding forward.

3. Remove the molding from the sunroof tracks and lift it out and off of the vehicle.

4. Remove the four bolts that hold the sunroof glass to the sunroof cable assembly plates. Remove the four sunroof glass assembly screws, attaching the glass to the front guide shoes.

5. Working from the outside of the vehicle, raise and remove the sunroof glass assembly from the vehicle.

6. Installation is the reverse order of the removal procedure.

SUNROOF ASSEMBLY

Adjustment

1. To determine the area of misalignment, close the sunroof panel and carefully survey the situation.

2. Once the area of misalignment has been determined, loosen the sunroof glass assembly to front guide shoe screws. Turn the adjustment nut clockwise to raise the sunroof glass assembly or counterclockwise to lower the assembly.

3. Turn the adjustment nut which ever way necessary to align the sunroof glass assembly. Once the assembly is aligned, tighten the sunroof glass assembly to front guide shoe screws. Close the sunroof panel and recheck the alignment.

SUNROOF CABLE ASSEMBLY

Removal and Installation

1. Remove the sunroof glass assembly as previously outlined. Remove the front cover and the side covers which house the cables.

2. Remove the cable guide retainer screw and retainer. Remove the cable assembly from the sunroof.

3. Installation is the reverse order of the removal procedure.

FORD MOTOR COMPANY

Power Mirror

A right hand and left hand electrically powered outside rear view mirror is available. The servo motor is part of the mirror head assembly and cannot be serviced separately on the Continental. The servo can be serviced separately on the other models. The switch for controlling the the mirror adjustments is located on the driver's door trim panel or in the center console depending on the vehicle.

On some models there is an electronic day/night rear view mirror, which will automatically change from the normal position to the non-glare position when the ever glare reaches the mirror. This mirror functions only at night and has a limited function at dusk or dawn. This mirror is controlled by two light sensitive photocells.

POWER SIDE MIRRORS

Test

If both the power side mirrors are inoperational, use the following procedure to pinpoint the problem.

1. Check the 15 amp fuse, located in the fuse panel and replace if it is blown. If the fuse checks out, remove the switch housing assembly.

2. Using a suitable test light, check for power at the harness connector to the switch, by running the test light across the number 54 and 57 circuits of the harness.

3. If there is no power present, check across the number 54 circuit to a know good body ground. Trace back through circuit 54 and correct the problem.

4. If the power is good between circuits 54 and 57 then check and see if the switch is damaged by jumping across the appropriate circuits shown in the illustrations.

5. If the mirrors can be operated by bypassing the switch as described in Step 4, then replace the damaged switch and reinstall the switch housing assembly.

Either Left Hand or Right Hand Mirror Does Not Operate

1. Remove the door trim panel and verify that the harness is connected to the mirror. Using at a suitable test light check continuity of the circuits in the harness connector to the mirror by operating the switch.

2. If the circuit check does not show continuity, trace the circuit to the connector in the seat consolette.

3. If the circuit continuity and logic is correct replace the mirror assembly.

Either Left Hand or Right Hand Mirror Does Not Operate or Operate at Variance With System Logic

1. Remove the front door trim panel on the vehicle side experiencing the malfunction.

2. Using a suitable test light verify circuit logic at the harness connector to the mirror with switch operation.

3. If this checks out, replace the mirror. If this does not check out, check to see if the circuit logic is good at the switch connector.

4. If the switch checks out, trace along the harness to determine where the cross circuitry took place and correct.

ELECTRONIC DAY/NIGHT MIRROR

The following procedure must be performed with the shift lever in the Park position and the ignition switch in the run position with the mirror switch in the Auto position.

Check the mirror operation by covering up the photocell on the back side of the mirror case with a dark cloth and shining a light on the photocell window of the lower half of the the mirror control panel.

The mirror should cycle from the normal position to the non-glare position. When the light is removed from the photocell

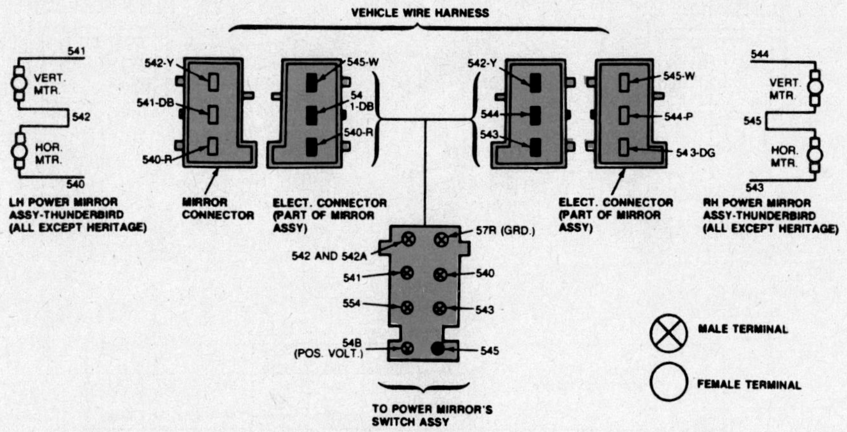

VEHICLE WIRE HARNESS

541
VERT. MTR.
542
HOR. MTR.
540

LH POWER MIRROR ASSY-THUNDERBIRD (ALL EXCEPT HERITAGE)

542-Y
541-DB
540-R

MIRROR CONNECTOR

545-W
541-DB
540-R

ELECT. CONNECTOR (PART OF MIRROR ASSY)

542-Y
544
543

ELECT. CONNECTOR (PART OF MIRROR ASSY)

545-W
544-P
543-DG

544
VERT. MTR.
545
HOR. MTR.
543

RH POWER MIRROR ASSY-THUNDERBIRD (ALL EXCEPT HERITAGE)

57R (GRD.)
542 AND 542A
541
554
54B (POS. VOLT.)

540
543
545

TO POWER MIRROR'S SWITCH ASSY

⊗ MALE TERMINAL

○ FEMALE TERMINAL

POWER MIRROR LOGIC TABLE

MIRROR OPERATIONAL MODE	DIRECTIONAL MOVEMENT	LH MIRROR			
		POS. VOLTAGE (+)	GRD. (-)	POS. VOLTAGE (+)	GRD. (-)
VERTICAL	UP	541	542	544	542A
VERTICAL	DOWN	542	541	542A	544
HORIZONTAL	LEFT	540	542	543	542A
HORIZONTAL	RIGHT	542	540	542A	543

Power mirror wiring schematic—Taurus/Sable, Thunderbird/Cougar, LTD/Marquis, Escort/Lynx, Tempo/Topaz

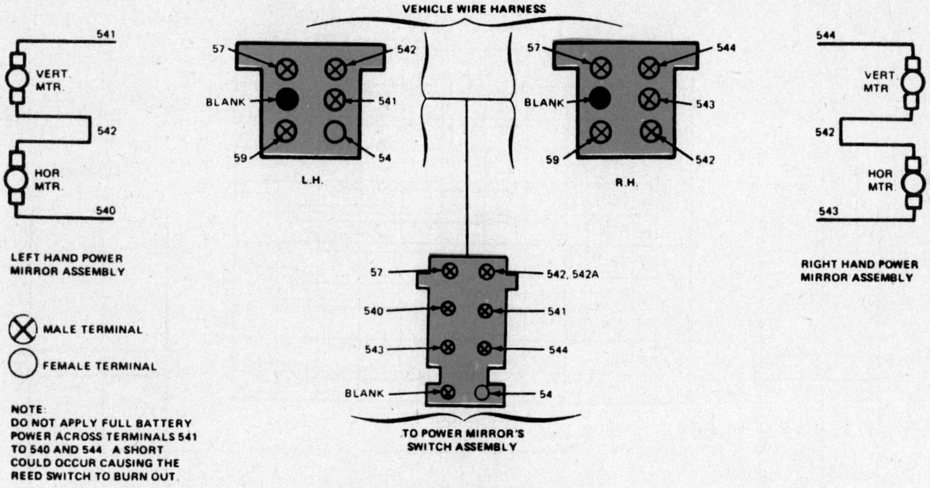

VEHICLE WIRE HARNESS

541
VERT. MTR.
542
HOR. MTR.
540

LEFT HAND POWER MIRROR ASSEMBLY

57
BLANK
59

542
541
54

L.H.

57
BLANK
59

544
543
542

R.H.

544
VERT. MTR.
542
HOR. MTR.
543

RIGHT HAND POWER MIRROR ASSEMBLY

⊗ MALE TERMINAL

○ FEMALE TERMINAL

NOTE:
DO NOT APPLY FULL BATTERY POWER ACROSS TERMINALS 541 TO 540 AND 544. A SHORT COULD OCCUR CAUSING THE REED SWITCH TO BURN OUT.

57
540
543
BLANK

542, 542A
541
544
54

TO POWER MIRROR'S SWITCH ASSEMBLY

POWER MIRROR LOGIC TABLE

MIRROR OPERATIONAL MODE	DIRECTIONAL MOVEMENT	LEFT HAND MIRROR		RIGHT HAND MIRROR	
		POS. VOLTAGE (+)	GRD. (-)	POS. VOLTAGE (+)	GRD. (-)
VERTICAL	UP	541	542	544	542A
VERTICAL	DOWN	542	541	542A	544
HORIZONTAL	LEFT	540	542	543	542A
HORIZONTAL	RIGHT	542	540	542A	543

Power mirror wiring schematic—Continental, MARK VII

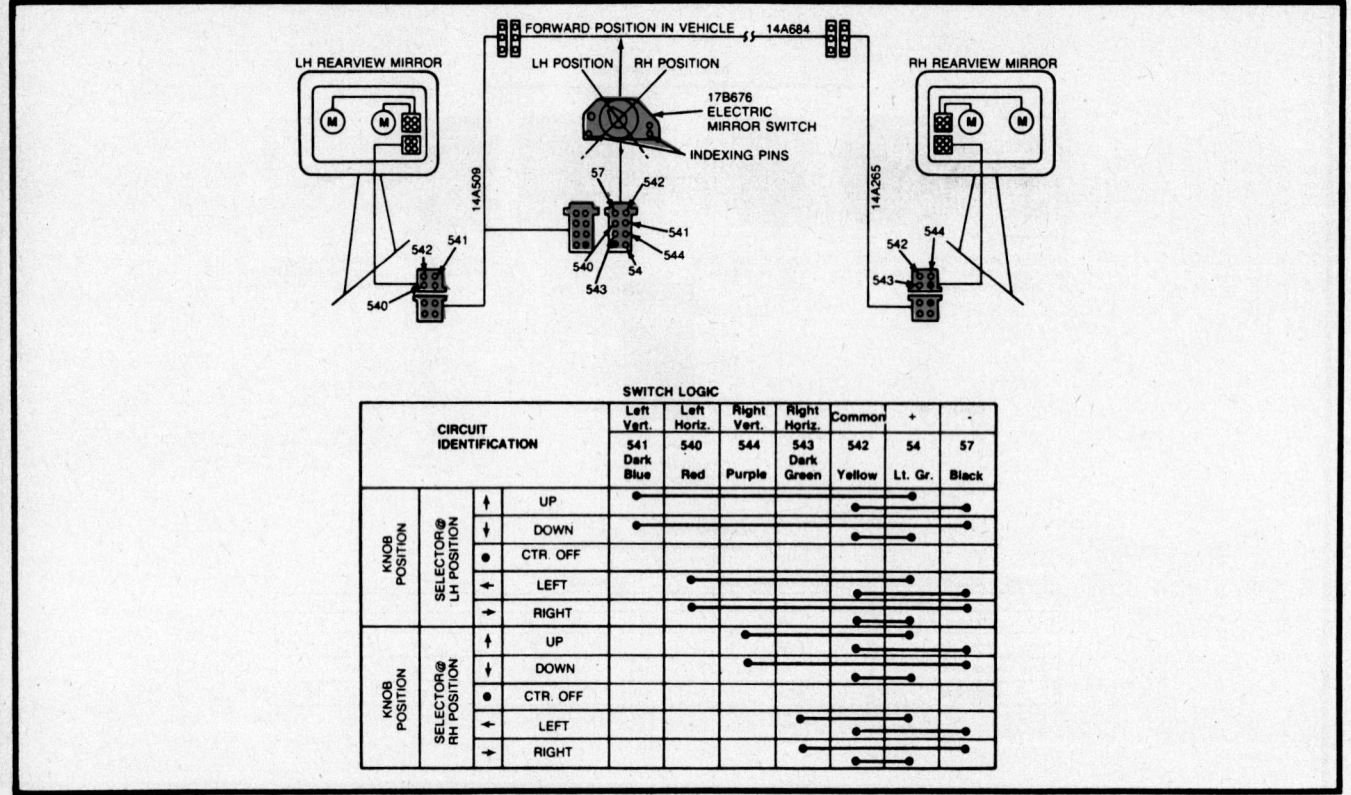

SWITCH LOGIC — Town Car

	CIRCUIT IDENTIFICATION			Left Vert.	Left Horiz.	Right Vert.	Right Horiz.	Common	+	-
				541 Dark Blue	540 Red	544 Purple	543 Dark Green	542 Yellow	54 Lt. Gr.	57 Black
KNOB POSITION	SELECTOR @ LH POSITION	↑	UP	●				●	●	●
		↓	DOWN	●				●	●	●
		●	CTR. OFF							
		←	LEFT		●			●	●	●
		→	RIGHT		●			●	●	●
KNOB POSITION	SELECTOR @ RH POSITION	↑	UP			●		●	●	●
		↓	DOWN			●		●	●	●
		●	CTR. OFF							
		←	LEFT				●	●	●	●
		→	RIGHT				●	●	●	●

Power mirror wiring schematic — Town Car

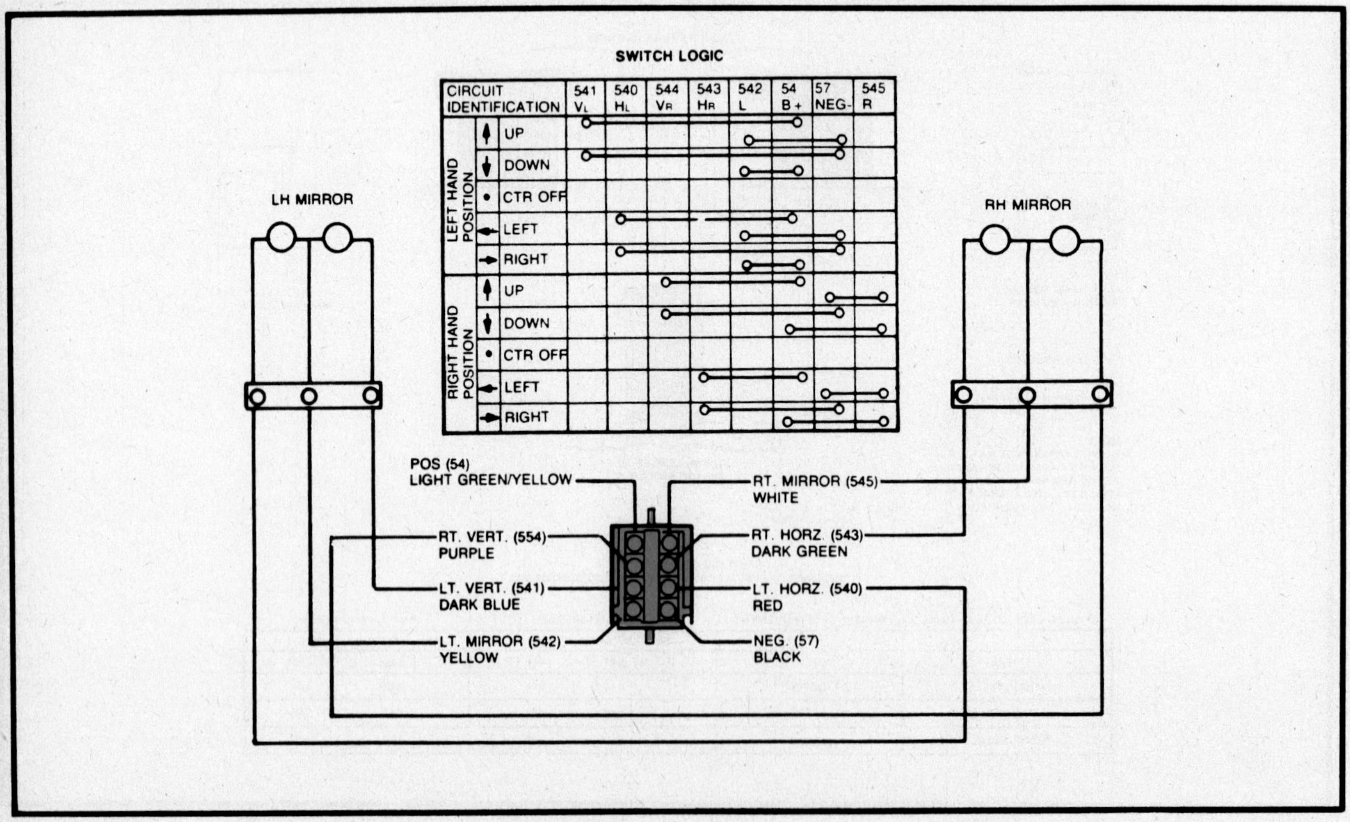

SWITCH LOGIC — Crown Victoria/Grand Marquis

	CIRCUIT IDENTIFICATION			541 VL	540 HL	544 VR	543 HR	542 L	54 B+	57 NEG-	545 R
LEFT HAND POSITION		↑	UP	○				○	○		
		↓	DOWN					○	○		
		●	CTR OFF								
		←	LEFT	○					○		
		→	RIGHT	○					○		
RIGHT HAND POSITION		↑	UP			○		○	○		
		↓	DOWN			○		○	○		
		●	CTR OFF								
		←	LEFT			○			○		
		→	RIGHT				○		○		

POS (54) LIGHT GREEN/YELLOW

RT. MIRROR (545) WHITE

RT. VERT. (554) PURPLE

RT. HORZ. (543) DARK GREEN

LT. VERT. (541) DARK BLUE

LT. HORZ. (540) RED

LT. MIRROR (542) YELLOW

NEG. (57) BLACK

Power mirror wiring schematic — Crown Victoria/Grand Marquis

and the cloth is removed, the mirror should return to the normal position after a time delay of fifteen minutes. If the mirror does not operate properly perform the following test.

NOTE: If the back-up light switch is damaged or stuck in the closed position (lights on), the mirror will not function.

1. Check for a blown fuse. If the fuse is bad replace it and re-test the mirror.
2. If the fuse is good, pull the connector out from the rear of the mirror. Using a suitable test light, see if there is voltage between the bottom red/yellow terminal (#640) and the middle black terminal (#57) at the harness connector.
3. If there is no voltage present, check across the bottom terminal to a known good ground to determine which circuit is open and repair as necessary.
4. If there is voltage present, replace the mirror.

ELECTRONIC DAY/NIGHT MIRROR

Removal and Installation

1. Disconnect the negative battery cable. Disconnect the wiring connectors at the mirror and the auto dimmer sensor, if so equipped.
2. Loosen the mirror assembly to the mounting bracket set screw. Remove the mirror assembly by sliding upward and away from the mounting bracket.
3. Installation is the reverse order of the removal procedure.

POWER MIRROR ASSEMBLY

Removal and Installation

Because of the varied applications of power mirrors, a general power mirror removal and installation procedure is outlined. The removal steps can be altered as required by the technician.
1. Disconnect the negative battey cable. Remove the door trim panel.
2. Disconnect the mirror assembly wiring connector and remove the necessary wiring guides.
3. Remove the two mirror retaining nuts and remove the mirror slowly, make to guide the wiring and connector through the hole in the door.
4. Installation is the reverse order of the removal procedure.

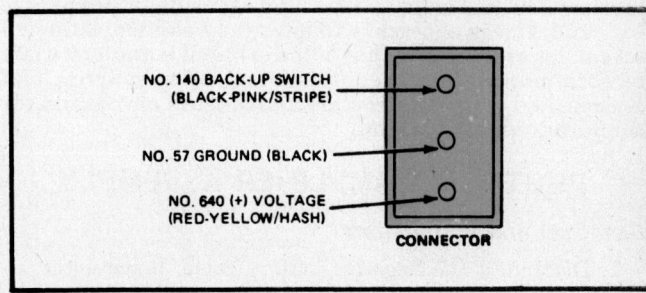

Electronic day/night mirror—harness connection

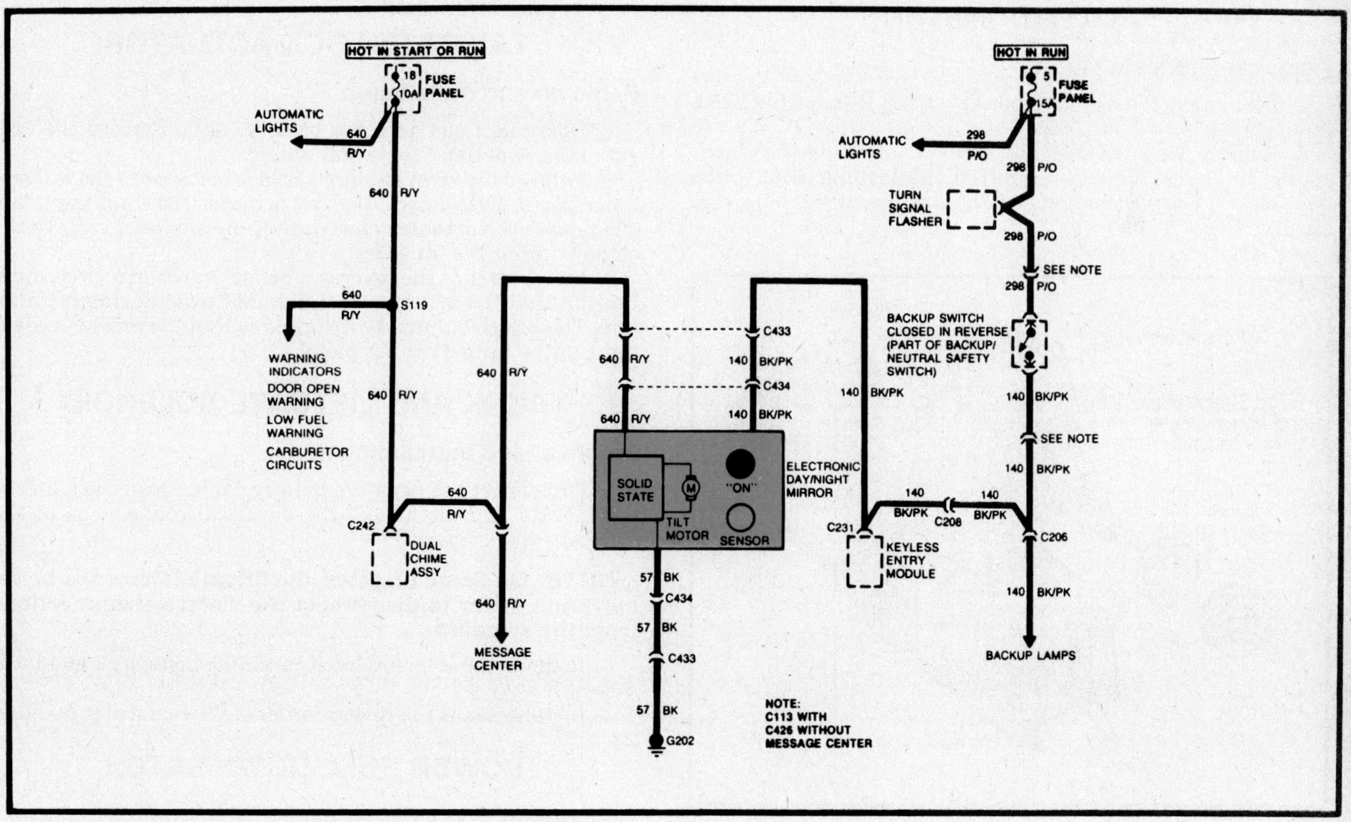

Electronic day/night mirror—wiring schematic

Headlamp Delay System - Autolamp

The autolamp system provides light sensitive automatic on and off control of the exterior lamps normally controlled by the regular headlamp switch. This system also provides for increased visibility for occupants when leaving the vehicle.

The auto lamp system keeps the lamps on for preselected period of time after the ignition has been shut off. This preselected time laspe can be adjusted by the operator from 4 to 12 minutes. The system consists of a light sensitive photocell/amplifier assembly, a headlamp control relay and a time delay control which includes an on/off switch.

NOTE: There are two different appearing photocell/ amplifier assemblies that are used. The difference in the two units is the early/later turn-on adjustment procedure for each. If it is necessary to have the headlamps turned on earlier or later that that of the original manufacturer's calibration, both units contain an adjustment screw and are marked with the direction and amount of rotation for the required adjustment.

PHOTOCELL/AMPLIFIER ASSEMBLY

Removal and Installation

1. Disconnect the negative battery cable. Remove the instrument panel pad.
2. Unscrew the two screws holding the photocell/amplifier assembly to the upper instrument panel.
3. Remove the connector from the photocell/amplifier assembly and remove the assembly from the vehicle.
4. Installation is the reverse order of the removal procedure.

HEADLAMP SWITCH WITH POTENTIOMETER

Removal and Installation

1. Disconnect the negative battery cable. Remove the headlamp switch.
2. Remove the knob and shaft assembly. Remove the plastic spacer at the rear of the potentiometer by pushing it out with a suitable screwdriver and remove the strap securing the wiring harness to the switch.

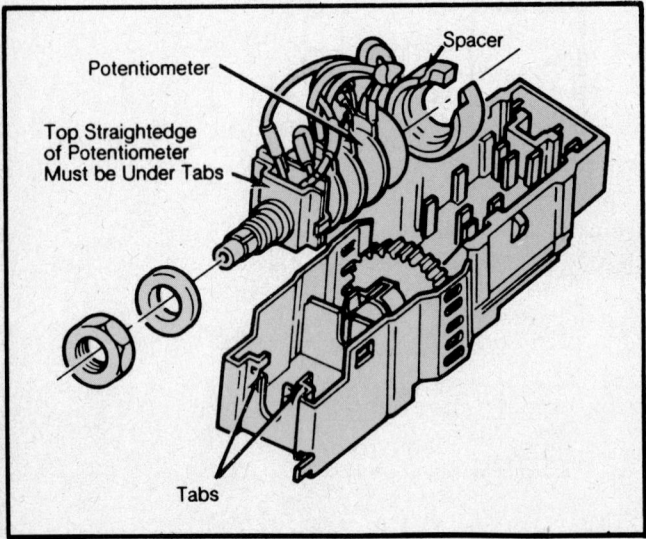

Exploded view of headlamp switch with potentiometer

3. Loosen the potentiometer retaining nut and washer and slide it out of the headlamp switch.
4. Installation is the reverse order of the removal procedure.

HEADLAMP DELAY SYSTEM

Quick Checks

1. Make sure the photocell lens of the photo amplifier unit is clean and not obstructed.
2. Make sure there is a clean, tight ground connection for circuit 57 from the potentiometer control unit at the headlamp switch. Make sure the headlamps operate normally from the manual headlamp switch.
3. Remember that it is normal to have a slight delay between turning the switch on and off (or covering or uncovering the photo unit lens) and the response of the headlamps.
4. Make sure that the autolamp relay connector is properly attached to the relay.

Trunk, Tailgate and Liftgate Release

The releases in this system are operated by a solenoid which is incorporated into the latch. To engage the solenoid there is push button usually located in the glove box or on the dash panel. The station wagon models use a tailgate lock actuator which is operated by a toggle switch in the dash panel.

Some models are equipped with a electrical trunk pull-down latch that will automatically close the trunk once it is lowered. There is a permanent magnet reversible motor that pulls the strike down, which in turn locks the trunk lid in the fully lock position. When the release mechanism is energized it reverses the motor, which allow the trunk lid to rise up to the open position.

TAILGATE LOCK ACTUATOR

Removal and Installation

1. Disconnect the negative battery cable. Remove the tailgate trim panel and the water shield.
2. Remove the rivet holding the lock actuator to the tailgate inner panel. Disconnect the lock actuator rod from the latch. Disconnect the actuator electrical connection and remove the actuator from the tailgate.
3. Installation is the reverse order of the removal procedure. Be sure that the actuator boot does not twist during installation. The pop rivet must be installed so that the bracket base is tight to the tailgate inner panel.

TRUNK AND LIFTGATE SOLENOID

Removal and Installation

1. Disconnect the negative battery cable. Open the trunk or the liftgate and disconnect the electrical connections at the solenoid.

NOTE: On Some liftgates, the liftgate latch must be removed in order to disconnect the electrical connections from the solenoid.

2. Remove the solenoid latch retaining bolts, lock and latch assembly.
3. Installation is the reverse order of the removal procedure.

POWER PULL-DOWN LATCH

Adjustment

1. Open the trunk lid. loosen the latch attaching screws.

AUTOLAMP CONNECTOR (ON/OFF DELAY SYSTEM)

CIRCUIT NUMBERS

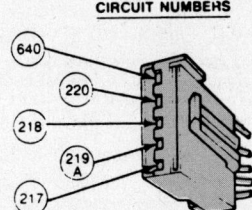

CIRCUIT	WIRE COLOR CODE
640	RED/YELLOW HASH (IGNITION)
220	PURPLE/ORANGE DOT (AUTOLAMP SENSOR AMPLIFIER TO CONTROL SWITCH)
218	WHITE PURPLE HASH (AUTOLAMP SENSOR AMPLIFIER TO RELAY)
219A	DARK/GREEN. YELLOW DOT (HEADLAMP SWITCH TO AUTOLAMP SENSOR AMPLIFIER)
217	DARK/BLUE. ORANGE DOT (AUTOLAMP SENSOR AMPLIFIER TO RHEOSTAT)

AUTOLAMP RELAY CONNECTOR

CIRCUIT NUMBERS

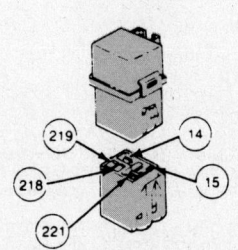

CIRCUIT	WIRE COLOR CODE
221	ORANGE/WHITE HASH (HEADLAMP SWITCH TO RELAY)
219	DARK/GREEN. YELLOW DOT (HEADLAMP SWITCH TO RELAY)
15	RED/YELLOW STRIPE (RELAY TO HEADLAMPS AND HEADLAMP SWITCH)
14	BROWN (RELAY TO REAR LAMPS)
218	WHITE/PURPLE HASH (AUTOLAMP SENSOR AMPLIFIER TO RELAY)

(AUTOLAMP (ON/OFF DELAY SYSTEM)

TAILLAMP CIRCUIT

CONNECT A 12 VOLT TEST LAMP BETWEEN CIRCUIT (14) AND A GOOD GROUND

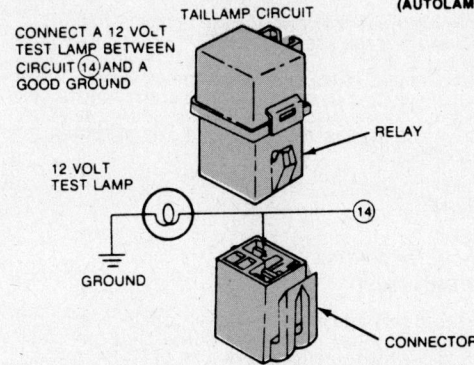

TEST AND RESULT

WITH MANUAL HEADLAMP SWITCH IN "PARK" OR FULL "ON" POSITION. VOLTAGE SHOULD BE MEASURED AT AUTOLAMP RELAY CONNECTOR (CIRCUIT 14). THIS CHECKS FOR CORRECT WIRING TO TAILLAMP CIRCUIT.

IF NOT OK, CHECK CONTINUITY OF THE NO. 14 BROWN WIRE BETWEEN THE AUTOLAMP RELAY CONNECT. OR AND THE COMMON POINT WITH THE REAR LAMP CIRCUIT.

HEADLAMP CIRCUIT

CONNECT A 12 VOLT TEST LAMP BETWEEN CIRCUIT (15) AND A GOOD GROUND

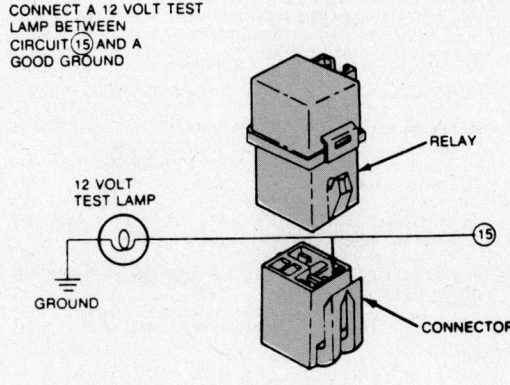

TEST AND RESULT

WITH MANUAL HEADLAMP SWITCH IN FULL ON POSITION. VOLTAGE SHOULD BE MEASURED AT AUTOLAMP RELAY CONNECTOR. THIS CHECKS FOR CORRECT WIRING TO HEADLAMP CIRCUIT (CIRCUIT 15).

IF NOT OK, CHECK CONTINUITY OF CIRCUIT 15 — RED AND YELLOW WIRE — BETWEEN THE HEADLAMP SWITCH CONNECTOR AND THE AUTOLAMP RELAY CONNECTOR.

Headlamp delay system—autolamp—test procedures

ON-OFF CONTROL SWITCH

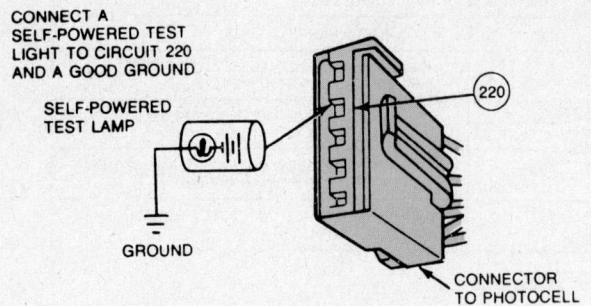

CONNECT A
SELF-POWERED TEST
LIGHT TO CIRCUIT 220
AND A GOOD GROUND

SELF-POWERED
TEST LAMP

GROUND

220

CONNECTOR
TO PHOTOCELL

TEST AND RESULT

CHECK FOR SYSTEM GROUND THROUGH DRIVER'S DELAY
CONTROL SWITCH. GROUND SHOULD BE MEASURED WITH
AUTOLAMP SWITCH IN "ON" POSITION. CIRCUIT IS OPEN WITH
SWITCH IN "OFF" POSITION.

IF NOT OK, PERFORM STEPS 1 AND 2 OF THE POTENTIOMETER
TEST.

IF POTENTIOMETER TESTS OK, CHECK CIRCUIT 220 —
PURPLE WIRE WITH ORANGE DOTS — BETWEEN THE
POTENTIOMETER CONNECTOR AND AUTOLAMP AMPLIFIER
CONNECTOR.

DELAY CONTROL POTENTIOMETER

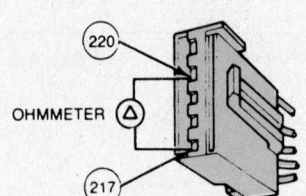

CONNECT AN OHMMETER BETWEEN
CIRCUITS 217 AND 220.

220

OHMMETER

217

TEST AND RESULT

TEST FOR CONTINUITY TO DRIVER DELAY CONTROL WITH
CONTROL IN "MAXIMUM" DELAY POSITION READING
SHOULD BE APPROXIMATELY 200,000 OHMS.

IF NOT OK, PERFORM STEP 3 OF THE POTENTIOMETER
TEST. IF POTENTIOMETER TEST OK, CHECK CIRCUIT 227 —
DARK BLUE WIRE WITH ORANGE DOTS — BETWEEN THE
POTENTIOMETER CONNECTOR AND AUTOLAMP AMPLIFIER
CONNECTOR.

IF POTENTIOMETER TEST NOT OK, REPLACE THE
POTENTIOMETER ASSEMBLY.

IF ALL OF THE PRECEDING TESTS CHECK OUT OK, AND THE
AUTOLAMP (ON/OFF DELAY) SYSTEM IS MALFUNCTIONING,
THE AUTOLAMP AMPLIFIER IS THE CAUSE OF THE PROBLEM
IT WILL BE NECESSARY TO REPLACE THE AMPLIFIER
ASSEMBLY.

HEADLAMP SWITCH POTENTIOMETER CONTROL

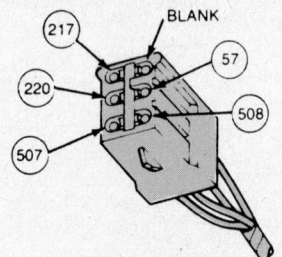

BLANK
217
57
220
508
507

LINCOLN TOWN CAR

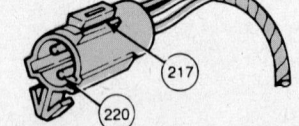

217
220

FORD CROWN VICTORIA/MERCURY GRAND MARQUIS

TEST AND RESULT

1. USING A SELF-POWERED TEST LAMP, CHECK THE CIRCUIT
   CONTINUITY FROM THE WIRE IN CONNECTOR FOR CIRCUIT
   57 TO THE SWITCH BRACKET. IF NOT, REPLACE POTEN-
   TIOMETER ASSEMBLY

2. USING EITHER A SELF-POWERED TEST LAMP OR AN OHM-
   METER, CHECK THE AUTOLAMP "ON-OFF" SWITCH FUNC-
   TION BY ROTATING THE "AUTOLAMP" CONTROL KNOB
   FROM "OFF" TO "ON" IT IS NECESSARY TO GO JUST PAST
   THE DETENT POSITION WITH THE CONTROL SWITCH IN THE
   "ON" POSITION. THE CONTINUITY CHECK IS PERFORMED
   BETWEEN CIRCUITS 220 AND 57

3. USING AN OHMMETER, CHECK THE RESISTANCE VALVE AS
   THE AUTOLAMP CONTROL IS ROTATED FROM OFF TO THE
   MAXIMUM TIME DELAY THE RESISTANCE SHOULD GRADUAL-
   LY INCREASE FROM 2,500/4,500 OHMS AT THE OFF POSITION
   TO 140/260K OHMS. THIS CHECK IS PERFORMED BETWEEN
   CIRCUITS 217 AND 57.

4. ON LINCOLN TOWN CAR, CIRCUITS 507 AND 508 ARE FOR
   AUTOMATIC HEADLAMP DIMMER OPERATION

5. IF ANY OF THE ABOVE TESTS ARE NOT OK, REPLACE THE
   POTENTIOMETER ASSEMBLY.

Headlamp delay system — autolamp — test procedures (cont.)

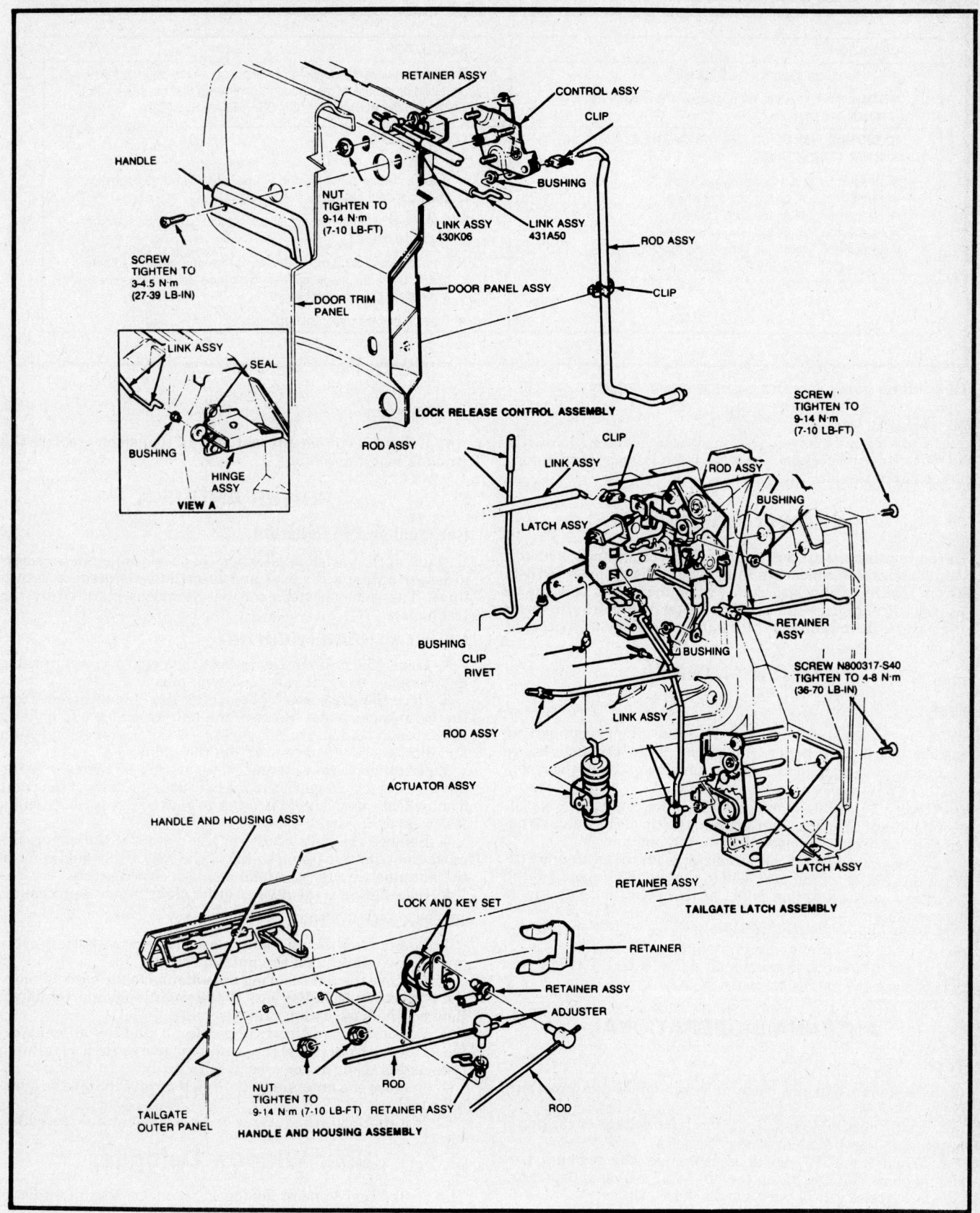

RETAINER ASSY

CONTROL ASSY

CLIP

HANDLE

BUSHING

NUT TIGHTEN TO 9-14 N·m (7-10 LB-FT)

LINK ASSY 430K06

LINK ASSY 431A50

ROD ASSY

SCREW TIGHTEN TO 3-4.5 N·m (27-39 LB-IN)

DOOR PANEL ASSY

CLIP

DOOR TRIM PANEL

LINK ASSY

SEAL

BUSHING

HINGE ASSY

VIEW A

LOCK RELEASE CONTROL ASSEMBLY

ROD ASSY

CLIP

LINK ASSY

ROD ASSY

SCREW TIGHTEN TO 9-14 N·m (7-10 LB-FT)

BUSHING

LATCH ASSY

BUSHING CLIP RIVET

RETAINER ASSY

SCREW N800317-S40 TIGHTEN TO 4-8 N·m (36-70 LB-IN)

ROD ASSY

BUSHING

LINK ASSY

ACTUATOR ASSY

LATCH ASSY

RETAINER ASSY

TAILGATE LATCH ASSEMBLY

HANDLE AND HOUSING ASSY

LOCK AND KEY SET

RETAINER

RETAINER ASSY

ADJUSTER

NUT TIGHTEN TO 9-14 N·m (7-10 LB-FT)

ROD

RETAINER ASSY

ROD

TAILGATE OUTER PANEL

HANDLE AND HOUSING ASSEMBLY

Tailgate actuator motor assembly—typical

CONDITION	RESOLUTION
• The autolamp system will not operate. • The autolamp system will not delay long enough after the vehicle has been shut down.	Problems resulting from Operator Error are caused by failure to follow operating procedure or sequence requirements that have been designed into the AUTOLAMP (ON/OFF DELAY SYSTEM).
SYMPTOMS AND QUICK CHECKS OF THE ELECTRICAL SYSTEM CONDITIONS: • Headlamps do not turn on when it gets dark outside. • Headlamps turn on too late at evening. • Headlamps turn on too early at evening. • Headlamps turn off too late in the morning. • Headlamps turn off too early in the morning.	**QUICK CHECKS:** • Place autolamp control in the Off position. Turn on headlamps using standard headlamp switch control. • If headlamps do not operate, check out and correct the standard headlamp circuit. • If headlamp operation is OK using the standard headlamp switch, check the autolamp fuse. If the fuse is OK, proceed with a complete checkout procedure. • Refer to autolamp amplifier adjustment.

Headlamp delay system—quick check chart

2. Move the latch as required so as to enter the striker without deflecting the deck lid. Once the latch is in the proper position, tighten the latch screws.

Power Antenna

The power antenna system is made up of the antenna, a motor, switch and on some models a relay. The system is operated by a switch located on the dash panel, when the switch is in the on position, it energizes the antenna motor which inturn raises and lowers the antenna to the height selected by the operator.

POWER ANTENNA

Test

If the the radio is starting to fade or the reception keeps getting weaker, check the antenna connections. If the connections are connected properly and tall connection s are good but the reception is still weak, replace the antenna.

1. Using a suitable ohmmeter, check for continuity by connecting one of the ohmmeter leads to the tip of the antenna cable and the other ohmmeter lead to the antenna.
2. Now connect one of the ohmmeter leads to the antenna cable and the other ohmmeter lead to the ground located behind the sheath of the antenna cable. At this point there should be no continuity.
3. If the ohmmeter readings do not agree with Steps one and two, replace the antenna and antenna cable assembly.
4. If the ohmmeter readings do agree with Steps one and two, replace the extension cable.

ANTENNA INOPERATIONAL

Test

If the antenna will not raise or lower follow the procedure below.

1. Using a suitable test light, check for voltage at the power antenna motor electrical connector.
2. When the "UP" switch is depressed, the red/pink wire should show voltage. When the "DOWN" switch is depressed, the dark green/yellow wire should show voltage.
3. If the voltage is not present as described in Step one, in one or both of the connectors, check the fuse and antenna switch wiring.

4. If there is voltage present at both connectors, replace the antenna motor assembly.

POWER ANTENNA

Removal and Installation

Because of the varied applications of power antennas, a general power antenna removal and installation procedure is outlined. The removal steps can be altered as required by the technician.

FRONT FENDER MOUNTED

1. Lower the antena. Disconnect the negative battery cable and remove the right side cowl trim panel.
2. Drop the glove box by detaching the holding straps from the instrument panel. Remove the antenna cable clip holding the antenna lead and motor wiring the the heater-A/C plenum and disconnect the antenna from the radio.
3. Disconnect the antenna motor wiring at the rear of the antenna switch. Remove the rear attaching screws of the right front wheel splash shield in order to gain access to the antenna lower attaching bolt.
4. Remove the bolt located at the bottom of the motor. Remove the trim nut from the top of the motor tube and remove the antenna through the fender/splash shield access.
5. Installation is the reverse order of the removal procedure.

TRUNK MOUNTED

1. Lower the antenna. Disconnect the negative battery cable and remove the cap on the antenna base.
2. Remove the nut securing the antenna to the base. Remove the two screws from the base to the right hand quarter panel. Remove the base and gasket assembly.
3. Disconnect the electrical connector and the antenna cable. Working from inside the trunk, remove the bolt reataining tube and bracket motor assembly to trunk.
4. Remove the antenna by pulling it down through the quarter panel.
5. Installation is the reverse order of the removal procedure.

Rear Window Defogger

The heated rear window defogger system consists of a control assembly (which is mounted to the climate control head), a series of grid lines baked on the inside surface of the rear window and system wiring. The grid lines consist of two layers.

REAR WINDOW CONTROL ASSEMBLY

Test

The control switch/timer relay is mounted to the climate control head on all models except for the Escort/Lynx, Continental and Mark VII. On these models the control switch/timer relay is located on the instrument cluster trim. The numbers or the letters used for terminal identification in the following procedure are to used according the the type of control assembly being used on the vehicle in questioned.

1. Remove the control assembly electrical harness. Ground the bottom right terminal (G or 2) and connect a jumper wire between the upper left and right terminals (I or 3 and B or 4). Using a suitable test light, connect the test light between the bottom left terminal (L or 1) and a known good ground.

2. Apply power to the upper right terminal (B or 4). The test light should not light up. On the Taurus/Sable, Continental/Mark VII and Escort/Lynx, apply the power to lower left terminal (S). The rear window defogger symbol on the switch knob should light up.

3. Momentarily actuate the lever to the on position. The test light should come on and stay on after the lever returns to its normal position.

4. The test light should go off under any one or more of the following conditions:

 a. If the lever is moved to the "OFF" position.

 b. The jumper wire between terminals I or 3 and B or 4 is removed.

 c. Approximately ten minutes has gone past.

5. If all the test results are positive, reconnect the harness to the control assembly.

REAR WINDOW DEFOGGER GRID

Test

1. Working from inside the vehicle, shine a high powered light on the windshield and visually check the wire grid from the outside. A broken grid will appear as a brown spot.

2. Run the engine idle at idle speed. Set the rear defigger control switch to on. The indicator lamp should come on.

3. Working from inside the vehicle, use a suitable 12−volt DC voltmeter, contact the broad red-brown strips on the rear window (positive lead to the battery side and the negative lead to the ground side. The volt meter should show a reading of 10 to 13 volts. A lower voltage reading indicates a a loose ground wire (pigtail) connection at the ground side of the glass.

4. Contact a good ground point with the negative lead of the meter. The voltage reading should not change.

5. With the negative lead of the meter grounded, touch each grid line of the rear window defogger at its midpoint with the positive lead.

6. A reading of approximately 6 volts that grid line is good. A reading of 0 volts indicates that the grid line is broken between the mid-point and B+ side of the gridline.

7. A reading of 12 volts indicates that a circuit is broken between the mid-point of the grid line and the ground. Any break in a grid line longer than one inch, cannot be repaired. The rear window must be replaced. For breaks less than a inch long there is a repair kit available.

NOTE: If the first layer of the rear window grid (brown color) is damaged or missing, it will be necessary to apply brown acrylic lacquer touch-up paint AL81-5477-B (ESR-M2P100-B) or equivalent on the glass prior to applying the silver Grid Repair Compound D8AZ-19562-A (ESB-M4J58-A) or equivalent.

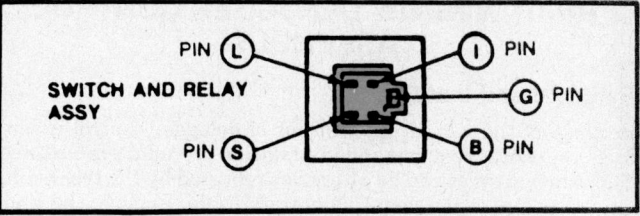

Control switch/timer relay terminal locations— Taurus/Sable, Escort/Lynx, Continental/MarkVII

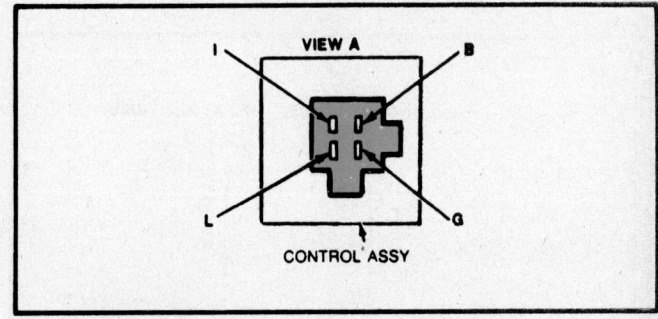

Control switch/timer relay terminal locations— Mustang/Capri

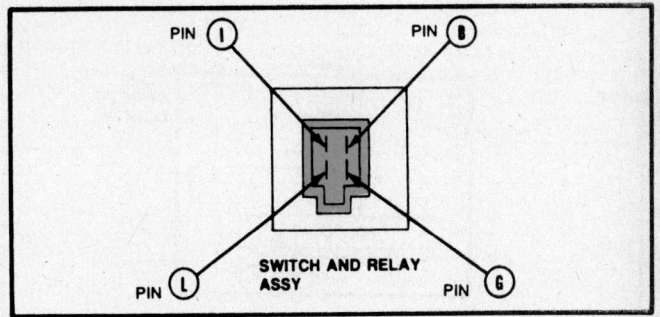

Control switch/timer relay terminal locations— Tempo/Topaz

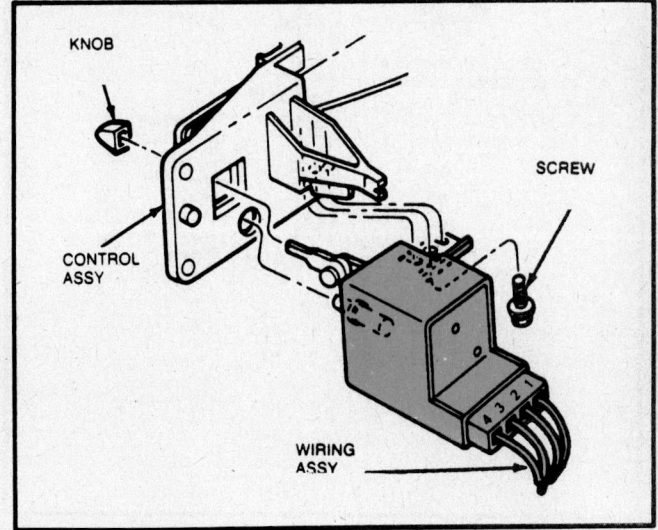

Control switch/timer relay terminal locations— all other models

REAR WINDOW DEFOGGER CONTROL ASSEMBLY

Removal and Installation

Because of the varied applications of defogger control assemblies, a general removal and installation procedure is outlined. The removal steps can be altered as required by the technician

1. Disconnect the negative battery cable. Remove the knob from the control lever. Remove the lens cover and or the trim panel if so equipped.

2. Remove the screws retaining the climate control head to the instrument panel and remove the climate control head.

3. Remove the control assembly from the climate control head assembly.

4. Installation is the reverse order of the removal procedure.

Electric Sunroof/Moonroof

The sunroof is electrically operated and can be closed by manual operation in case of electrical failure. When the control switch is moved to the open position, the sliding roof panel moves into a storage space between the headlining and the stationary roof panel exposing a opening over the front seat.

To close the the sunroof manually, remove the motor drive

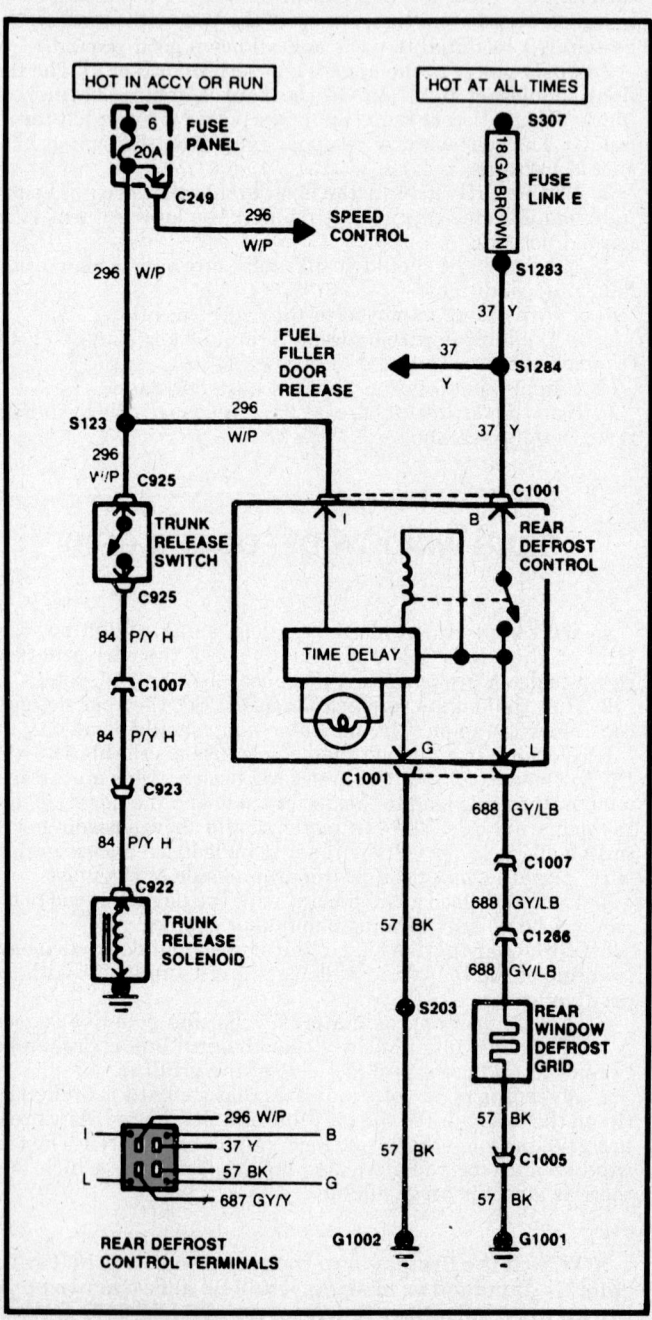

Rear window defogger electrical schematic — Taurus/ Sable, Escort/Lynx, Continental/MarkVII

Rear window defogger electrical schematic — all other models

crank cover by pulling it downward . The cover is a one inch plug located behind the interior dome lamp of the roof interior panel. Using the handcrank supplied with the vehicle, attach it to the auxiliary socket drive and crank the sunroof closed. After performing this operation, remove the crank and replace the motor drive cover.

SUNROOF/MOONROOF SWITCH

Test

MARK VII, THUNDERBIRD/COUGAR AND TAURUS/SABLE

1. Place the switch in the neutral position, check for continuity between terminals two and four.
2. Once the switch is pushed rearward, there should be no continuity between terminals one and two and three and four.
3. Now push the switch forward , there should be no continuity between terminals two and three and one and four. Terminal number one should be disconnect from the other terminal.
4. If the switch does not test out the way the procedure describes, replace the switch.

TOWN CAR AND CONTINENTAL

1. Place the sunroof switch in neutral position. Connect a suitable ohmmeter or a self powered test lamp between the terminals number one and three, two and five or four and six. There should be no continuity present between these terminals.
2. Push the switch downward, there should be no continuity between terminals two and four, two and five or one and three. Terminal number six should be disconnected from the other terminal.
3. With the switch pushed upward, there should be no continuity between terminals two and three, two and five or number four and six. Terminal number one should be disconnected from the other terminal.
4. If the switch does not test out the way the procedure describes, replace the switch.

SUNROOF/MOONROOF GLASS PANEL ASSEMBLY

Removal and Installation

TAURUS AND SABLE

1. Open the glass panel and sunshade fully. Disconnect the negative battery cable.
2. Disconnect the air deflector arms by pulling up on on the rear arm to disengage from the track retainer and rotating arm to remove the air deflector.
3. Using a ³/₈ in. drill stop, drill out the ten rivets. Be sure to use a suitable shield so that the headliner is not damaged while the rivets are being drilled out.
3. Close the glass panel. Remove the roof console so as to expose the motor and the mounting bracket. Disconnect the electrical connections.
4. Remove the two attaching screws while holding the motor in place, then remove the motor.
5. Remove the two screws retaining the sunroof frame to the roof panel. Lift and slide the sunroof module assembly out of the vehicle. Be sure to protect the roof's painted surface and make sure the halo trough will clear the roof's edge.
6. Installation is the reverse order of the removal procedure. Be sure to align the lifter arm and guidance ramp.

MARK VII AND THUNDERBIRD/COUGAR

1. To remove the glass panel, remove three halo front retaining screws. Slide halo and sunshade full rearward to expose six glass retaining screws (there is three on each side).

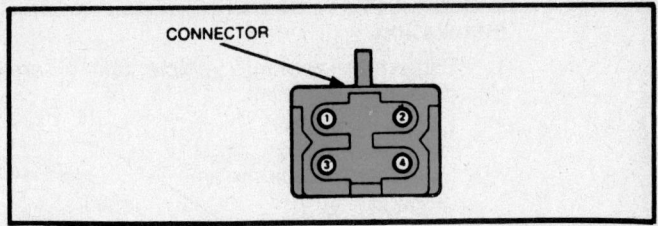

Switch connector terminal locations—Continental/Mark VII, Taurus/Sable

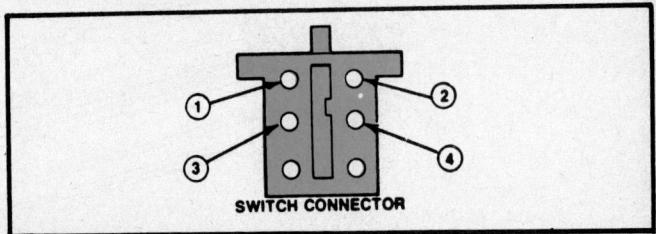

Switch connector terminal locations—Thunderbird/Cougar

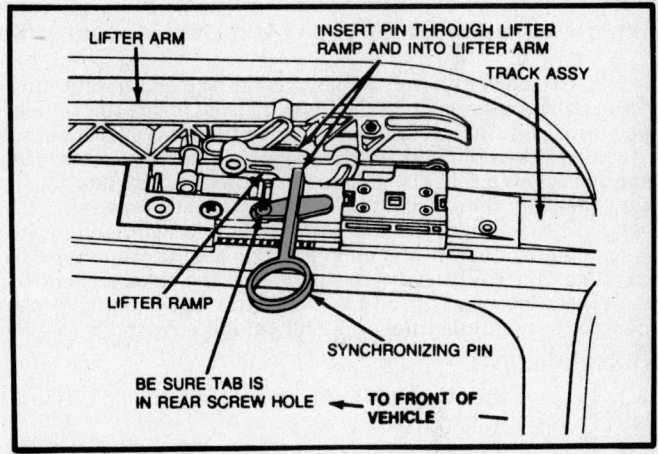

Aligning the lifter arm and guide bracket—Taurus/Sable, Thunderbird/Cougar

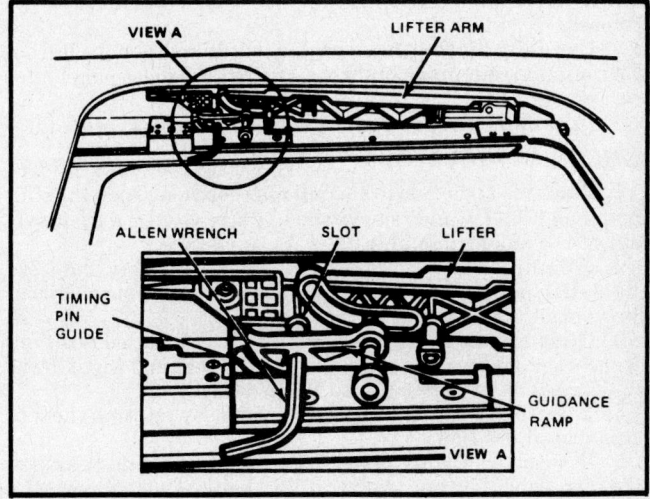

Aligning the lifter arm and guide bracket—Mark VII

Installation

1. Slide moon roof into vehicle, taking care not to damage roof finish.

SEDAN SHOWN
WAGON SIMILAR

Sunroof/moonroof removal and installation — Taurus/Sable (Sedan)

2. To remove the sunshade, remove the glass retaining screws and washers. Push the glass up from inside the vehicle and remove it. Be careful not to scratch the glass or roof paint.

3. Slide the halo and sunshade forward halfway across the sunroof opening. Lift the halo to clear the sunshade tabs. Push the halo fully rearward and slide the sunshade forward.

4. Lift the front of the sunshade, slide it forward and rotate it to remove. Remove the magnets that hold the sunshade to the halo (Mark VII), squeeze the tabs on the sides magnet.

5. Installation is the reverse order of the removal procedure. Be sure to align the lifter arm and guidance ramp.

CONTINENTAL

1. Position the moon roof to the closed position and manually open the sunshade.

2. Remove the four screws that secure the sight shields to the glass panel and remove the sight shields. Remove the front adjusting bolts that hold the glass panel to the front guide bracket.

3. Pull out the guide pins (use caution due to the spring load on the guide pins) and turn the pins so that the head points forward.

4. Carefully lift the glass panel upwards and remove it from the front and rear guide brackets. Remove the glass panel from the vehicle.

5. Installation is the reverse order of the removal procedure.

LINCOLN TOWN CAR

1. Place the sunshade in the full rear position. Open the sliding panel halfway and remove the five screws on the front surface of the shield assembly.

2. Carefully lower the edge of the shield assembly and close the sliding panel. Turn the shield sideways and remove it from the vehicle. Remove the sunshade.

3. Cycle the sliding glass panel to the full closed position. Detach the sliding panel from both the left and right front guide assemblies (there are two bolts on each side).

4. Release the rear slide tension springs by rotating them to the inboard position.

5. Detach the sliding panel from the two rear slide assemblies by removing the two retaining bolts. Then remove the mounting bracket to panel retainers from the tabs in the panel and remove the glass panel.

6. Installation is the reverse order of the removal procedure. If the sliding panel is to be replaced, the rear weatherstrip assembly may be transferred to the new panel.

Motor Synchronization

1. Firmly hold the motor in hand with the gears facing upward. Using the hand held crank (provided supplied with the vehicle), rotate the gears until the centerline of the cam and the hole in the cam are aligned with the centerline of the gear.

2. Place the glass panel in the fully closed position. Remove the hand held crank .

3. Make sure the lifter arm and guide bracket are aligned and install the motor.

Anti-Theft Protection System

This system is designed to provide the vehicle with protection from a forced entry into the passenger or luggage compartment . If triggered, the system provides both audio and visual alarm signals as well as disabling the vehicle starter circuit.

The system is controlled by an electronic controller. The electronic controller is a digital device which acts on a sequence of inputs to arm, disarm, activate or deactivate the alarm system.

The alarm is tripped by opening switches strategically located in the door jambs, the door lock cylinders and the trunk lock cylinder. When a door lock cylinder or trunk lock cylinder is violated by rotating it or moving it in or out, or if any door is opened without using the key, the alarm will be actuated by the electronic controller. The anti-theft protection system is made up of the following components:

a. Anti-Theft Controller --- this is a electronic controlled module the controls the anti-theft protection system. This controller is located in the luggage compartment under the package tray.

b. Alarm Relay --- this relay is turned on and off by the control module to flash the vehicle lamps and sound the horn. This relay is located in the luggage compartment under the package tray.

c. Starter Interrupt Relay --- this relay is turned on and off by the control module and will open the vehicle starter circuit to prevent the vehicle from being started. This relay is located

CONDITION	POSSIBLE SOURCE	ACTION
● Water leaks	● Glass panel not properly aligned or fitted to roof.	● Align glass panel to specifications.
	● Glass panel not fully closing.	● Adjust to specifications.
	● Drain tubes not properly connected and/or blocked.	● Connected properly and/or fix or replace drain tubes as required.
	● Cracks in housing.	● Service as required.
	● Glass assembly seal not properly in place and/or attached securely.	● Install seal properly and/or attach correctly.
● Windnoise	● Glass panel not properly fitted or aligned.	● Align and/or fit glass panel to specifications.
	● Glass panel not fully closing.	● Adjust to specifications.
	● Glass assembly seal not properly in place and/or not attached securely.	● Install seal properly and/or attach correctly.
● Moon Roof does not function and/or perform properly	● Glass panel not properly aligned or fitted to roof.	● Align and/or fit glass panel to specifications.
	● Glass assembly seal not properly in place and/or not attached securely.	● Install seal properly and/or attach correctly.
	● Obstructions or foreign objects in tracks or troughs.	● Remove obstructions or foreign objects as required.
	● Rear guide pin not properly engaged in cam slot of lifter assembly.	● Engage rear guide pin properly. Add retaining clip as required.
	● Rear lifter assemblies not properly connected to glass module.	● Properly connect lifter assemblies to glass module.
	● Front guides not properly installed and/or secured.	● Install and/or secure front guides as required.
	● Adequate voltage not being supplied to the motor (12.6 volts).	● Check voltage and correct if voltage not adequate.
	● Tracks not securely attached to housing.	● Attach track securely to housing.
	● Rear guide cables not properly synchronized.	● Synchronize cables and motor.
	● Rear drive cable or guide broken.	● Replace or service as required.
	● Sunshade not properly installed.	● Check and install sunshade properly as required.
	● Amperage range for glass running not adequate (3-5 Amps).	● Check for proper amperage and correct if required.

Electric sunroof/moonroof troubleshooting chart

CONDITION	POSSIBLE SOURCE	ACTION
• Noisy Operation	• Glass panel not fitted properly to housing.	• Fit glass panel to specification.
	• Glass assembly seal not properly in place and/or secured.	• Properly fit and/or secure glass assembly seal.
	• Rear guide pins not properly engaged in cam slot of lifter assembly.	• Engage rear guide pins properly and add retaining clip as required.
	• Rear lifter assemblies not properly attached to glass module.	• Properly attach lifter assembly to glass module.
	• Front guides not properly installed and/or secured.	• Properly install or service as required.
	• Track assembly not properly secured to housing.	• Secure track assembly to housing.
	• Rear drive cables not properly synchronized.	• Synchronize cables and motor.
	• Sunshade not installed properly.	• Check and install sunshade properly as required.
	• Amperage range for glass running not adequate.	• Check for proper amperage and correct if required.
• Rattles	• Glass panel not properly aligned or fitted to roof.	• Align glass panel to specification. Band glass attaching tabs inboard 1.5 mm.
	• Glass panel not fully closing.	• Adjust to specification.
	• Drain tubes not properly connected and/or blocked.	• Connect properly and/or fix to replace drain tubes as required.
	• Glass assembly seals not properly in place and/or not attached securely.	• Install seals properly and/or attach correctly.
	• Obstructions or foreign objects in tracks or troughs.	• Remove obstructions or foreign objects as required.
	• Rear guide pin not properly engaged in cam slot of lifter assembly.	• Engage rear guide pin properly. Add retaining clip as required.
	• Rear lifter assemblies not properly connected to glass module.	• Properly connect lifter assemblies to glass module.
	• Front guides not properly installed and/or secured.	• Install and/or secure front guides.
	• Tracks not attached to housing securely.	• Attach tracks securely to housing.
	• Sunshade not installed properly.	• Check and install sunshade properly as required.
	• Sunshade magnets rattle.	• Replace sunshade magnets as required.
• Glass Broken or Scratched	• Glass panel not fitted or aligned properly.	• Align or fit to specification.
	• Obstructions or foreign objects in tracks or troughs.	• Remove foreign objects and/or obstructions as required.
	• Clearances to underside of roof panel and reinforcement ring not adequate.	• Adjust clearance as required to obtain adequate clearance.

Electric sunroof/moonroof troubleshooting chart (cont.)

under the instrument panel to the right side of the steering column.

d. Anti-Theft Warning Lamp --- The lamp is located in the instrument panel on the Continental and in the console on the Mark VII and Thunderbird/Cougar. This lamp is used for indication of the alarm system standby and arming condition status.

e. Door Key Unlock Switches --- these switches are located in the driver and front passenger door locks. The switches provide a ground signal to the control module to disarm or deactivate the alarm system.

f. Courtesy Lamp Inverter Relay --- this relay is energized when a vehicle door is opened. The relay sends a ground signal to the control module. The relay is located in the luggage compartment under the package tray.

g. Luggage Compartment Lock Cylinder Tamper Switch --- this switch provides a ground signal to the control module when ever an attempt to remove the lock cylinder is made.

h. Disarm Relay --- this relay provides a disarm signal to the anti-theft controller upon actuation of the electric door locks using a keyless entry. The relay is located in the luggage compartment under the package tray.

The other components already exist in the vehicle and are also incorporated into the anti-theft protection system. The components are the electric door lock and unlock switches, ignition switch, vehicle horns, vehicle lights and a optional keyless entry system. There are also three in-line fuses located inside the luggage compartment leading from the alarm relay.

The system is armed when the ignition switch is turned off and the doors are locked. The system is activated when ever a door is opened without a key or when the trunk lock cylinder is removed. When the system has been activated, the alarm warning system will go off and cause the horn to blow intermittently and the exterior lights to flash on and off.

The starter interrupt relay will open the vehicle starter circuit and prevent the vehicle from being started. The system can be disarmed by unlocking either front door with a key. This system will also disarm the anti-theft protection system automatically within a two to four minute time period after the alarm has been activated and then automatically return the system to the alarm state.

Removal and Installation

CONTROL MODULE

1. Disconnect the negative battery cable. Open the trunk lid.
2. Remove the two screws attaching the module to the package tray. Remove the control module from the package tray, disconnect the electrical connectors from the control module and remove the module from the vehicle.

3. Installation is the reverse order of the removal procedure.

ALARM RELAY

1. Disconnect the negative battery cable. Open the trunk lid.
2. Disconnect the wiring connector from the alarm relay. Remove the two nuts attaching the alarm relay to the package tray and remove the relay.
3. Installation is the reverse order of the removal procedure.

DISARM RELAY

1. Disconnect the negative battery cable. Open the trunk lid.
2. Disconnect the electrical connector from the disarm relay and remove the relay by pulling it away from the brace.
3. Installation is the reverse order of the removal procedure.

INVERTER RELAY

1. Disconnect the negative battery cable. Open the trunk lid.
2. Disconnect the electrical connector to the inverter relay and remove the relay by pulling it away from the package tray brace.
3. Installation is the reverse order of the removal procedure.

STARTER INTERRUPT RELAY

1. Disconnect the negative battery cable. Locate the starter interrupt relay under the right side of the instrument panel, near the steering column.
2. Disconnect the electrical connector to the starter interrupt relay and remove the relay by pulling it away from the brace.
3. Installation is the reverse order of the removal procedure.

Testing

DOOR LOCK SWITCH

1. Using a suitable ohmmeter measure the resistance with the key removed from the door lock. The resistance should be more than 25,000 ohms. If the resistance is less than 25,000 ohms, replace the door lock switch.
2. Measure the switch resistance with the key fully rotated to the end of travel in the unlock direction.
3. The resistance should be less than 200 ohms. If the resistance is higher than 200 ohms, replace the door lock switch.

DECK LID LOCK TAMPER SWITCH

1. Using a suitable ohmmeter measure the installed switch resistance. The resistance should be more than 25,000 ohms.
2. If the resistance is less than 25,000 ohms, replace the deck lid lock tamper switch.

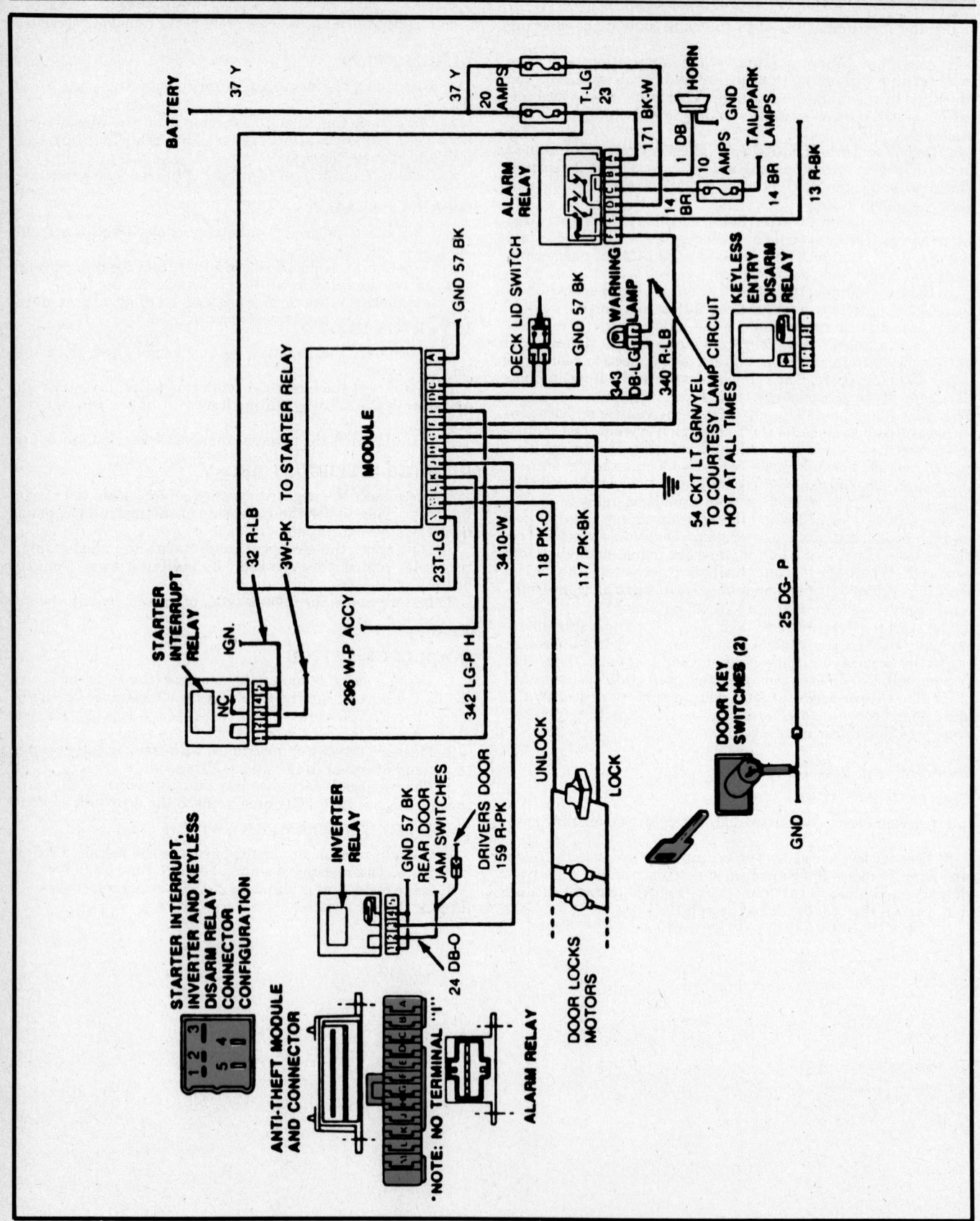

Anti-theft protection system wiring schematic

TEST A
VERIFICATION OF ALARM ARMING SEQUENCE

TEST STEP	RESULT ▶	ACTION TO TAKE
A0 START VEHICLE THEN TURN IGN. SWITCH OFF	Assures alarm system is reset ▶	GO to **A1**.
A1 • Close all vehicle doors. • Verify warning lamp is off.	Off? (OK) ▶ Blinking? (not OK) ▶ On steady? (not OK) ▶	GO to **A2**. GO to **A5**. GO to **A10**.
A2 • Open a vehicle door. • Verify warning lamp blinks.	Blinks? (OK) ▶ No blinking (not OK) ▶	GO to **A3**. GO to **A6**.
A3 • Activate the Electric door lock switch. (Or press buttons 7 and 9 of the keyless entry.) • Verify the warning lamp glows continuously.	Yes (OK) ▶ No (not OK) ▶	GO to **A4**. GO to **A8**.
A4 • Close the vehicle door. • Verify the warning lamp turns off after 32 seconds.	Yes (OK) ▶ No (not OK) ▶	STOP. Arming sequence verified. REPLACE control module.
A5 • Verify Circuit 341 O-W at terminal. • Terminal J of the module greater than 9 V.	Greater than 9V (OK) ▶ Less than 2V (not OK) ▶	Damaged module. REPLACE. RETEST system. Courtesy lamp door switch contacts may be shorted to B+ or inverter relay contacts are shorted to ground or relay is damaged.

TEST A
VERIFICATION OF ALARM ARMING SEQUENCE — Continued

TEST STEP	RESULT	▶	ACTION TO TAKE
A6			
● Courtesy lamps on?	Yes	(OK) ▶	GO to **A7**.
	No	(ØK) ▶	SERVICE door courtesy lamp switch or Circuit 24 DB/O or Circuit 159 R/PK. RETEST system.
A7			
● Measure the voltage at terminal J of the control module. Check if it is less than 2 V.	Less than 2 V	(OK) ▶	Damaged module. REPLACE. RETEST system.
	2 V or more	(ØK) ▶	Verify that the courtesy lamp inverter relay turns On and the relay contacts close when the doors close. SERVICE as required. RETEST system.
A8			
● Did the doors lock?		(OK) ▶	GO to **A9**.
	Doors did not lock	(ØK) ▶	SERVICE as required. RETEST system.
A9			
● Verify terminal M (Circuit 118 PK/O) door unlock of the module is less than 2 V and a momentary B+ signal is applied to terminal G (Circuit 117 PK/BK) when the door lock switch is activated.		(OK) ▶	Damaged module. REPLACE. RETEST system.
		(ØK) ▶	SERVICE Circuit 117 PK/BK or Circuit 118 PK/O. (Note Circuit 117 PK/BK should be at B+ voltage level only momentarily when the lock switch is activated. RETEST system.
A10			
● Disconnect the harness connector from the control module.	Lamp still on	▶	SERVICE Circuit 343 DB/LG for short. RETEST system.
	Lamp goes off	▶	REPLACE control module. RETEST system.

TEST B
VERIFICATION OF ALARM DISARMING MODES

TEST STEP	RESULT ▶	ACTION TO TAKE
B1 DOOR KEY DISARM ● Arm the alarm system. ● Insert door key and turn to the unlock position. ● Open a vehicle door.	Lamp blinks (OK) ▶ Alarm sounds (O̸K̸) ▶	REFER to arming procedures given in this section. Door key input OK. GO to **B3**. Try other door key or Keyless Entry Code or DISCONNECT battery to stop alarm. GO to **B2**.
B2 ● Verify terminal H (Circuit 25 DG/P) of the control module is less than 1 V when the door key is in the unlocked position.	(OK) ▶ (O̸K̸) ▶	Damaged module. REPLACE, RETEST system. SERVICE door key switch or Circuit 25 DG/P for open Circuit.
B3 KEYLESS ENTRY DISARM ● Arm the alarm system. ● Activate Keyless Entry door unlock code. ● Open a vehicle door.	Lamp blinks (OK) ▶ Alarm sounds (O̸K̸) ▶	Input OK. GO to **B4**. Use door key to stop alarm. SERVICE Keyless entry alarm disarm relay, Circuit 25 DG/P for open Circuit RETEST system after repair.

TEST B
VERIFICATION OF ALARM DISARMING MODES — Continued

TEST STEP	RESULT ▶	ACTION TO TAKE
B4 ELECTRIC DOOR UNLOCK • Open vehicle door and activated electric lock switch. • Activate electric door unlock switch. Alarm lamp blinks.	Lamp glows steadily (OK) ▶ Lamp blinks (ǑK) ▶	STOP. Alarm disarm OK. GO to **B5**.
B5 • Verify a momentary B+ signal is applied to terminal M (Circuit 118 PK/O) when unlock switch is activated.	(OK) ▶ (ǑK) ▶	Damaged module. REPLACE. RETEST system. SERVICE and/or REPLACE Circuit 118 PK/O. RETEST system.
B6 IGNITION KEY DISARM • Arm the Alarm system from inside the vehicle. • Insert ignition key and turn to ACC or RUN. • Open vehicle door.	Alarm lamp blinks (OK) ▶ Alarm sounds (ǑK) ▶	Ignition input OK. STOP. Use door key to stop alarm. GO to **B7**.
B7 • Verify terminal K (Circuit 296 W/P) of control module is greater than 9 V with ignition key in RUN, ACC.	(OK) ▶ (ǑK) ▶	DAMAGED module. REPLACE. RETEST system. SERVICE ignition switch or Circuit 296 W/P for open circuit. RETEST system.

TEST C
VERIFICATION OF ALARM ACTIVATION

TEST STEP	RESULT	▶	ACTION TO TAKE
C1 • Arm the alarm system with a window down. • Unlock a door from the inside of the vehicle. • Open a vehicle door.	Alarm turns on and off.	(OK) ▶	GO to **C2**.
	Alarm does not turn on.	(ØK) ▶	GO to **C7**.
	Alarm turns on continuous.	(ØK) ▶	REPLACE damaged module. RETEST system.
C2 ALARM VERIFICATION • Horns should turn off and on.		(OK) ▶	GO to **C3**.
		(ØK) ▶	SERVICE alarm relay contact and/or Circuit 1 DB (Horn). RETEST.
C3 • Tail and parking lamps should turn off and on.		(OK) ▶	GO to **C4**.
		(ØK) ▶	SERVICE alarm relay contact and/or Circuit 14 BR. RETEST system.
C4 • Low beam headlamps should turn off and on.		(OK) ▶	System OK. STOP.
		(ØK) ▶	SERVICE alarm relay contact and/or Circuit 13 R/BK. RETEST system.
C5 • Attempt to start the vehicle.	Will not start	(OK) ▶	System OK. STOP test.
	Vehicle starts	(ØK) ▶	GO to **C6**.
C6 • Measure the voltage at terminal E (Circuit 342 LG/P) of the control module. • Verify that it is less than two volts.	Less than 2 V?	(OK) ▶	SERVICE malfunctioning starter interrupt relay or open in Circuit 33 W/PK.
	Greater than 2 V?	(ØK) ▶	REPLACE damaged module. RETEST system.

TEST C
VERIFICATION OF ALARM ACTIVATION — Continued

TEST STEP	RESULT	▶	ACTION TO TAKE
C7			
• Measure the voltage at terminal F of the control module. • Voltage switches between B+ and less than 2 V? • Voltage reads a steady B+ valve? • Voltage reads below 2 V.	Module output (OK) ▶		SERVICE damaged alarm relay. RETEST system.
	Module output (ⓄⓀ̸) ▶		REPLACE damaged module.
	(ⓄⓀ̸) ▶		SERVICE open in Circuit 23 T/LG. RETEST system.
C8			
• Arm the alarm system. • Open the luggage compartment. • Remove luggage compartment lock cylinder.	Alarm activates (OK) ▶		System OK. STOP test. INSERT door key to stop alarm.
	Alarm does not activate (ⓄⓀ̸) ▶		GO to **C9**.
C9			
• Measure the voltage at terminal C (Circuit 486 BR/W). • Verify the voltage is less than 2 V.	Less than 2 V (OK) ▶		Module damaged. REPLACE. RETEST system.
	Greater than 2 volts (ⓄⓀ̸) ▶		SERVICE Circuit 486 BR/W and/or trunk lock cylinder switch. RETEST system.

TEST D
VERIFICATION OF ALARM DEACTIVATION

TEST STEP	RESULT	▶	ACTION TO TAKE
D1 • Arm the alarm system with a window down. • Unlock a door from the inside. • Open the door. • Insert the door key and turn to the unlock position.	Alarm activates Alarm turns Off (OK) ▶ Alarm continuous (OK̸) ▶		System OK. GO to **D3**. GO to **D2**.
D2 • Verify terminal H of the control module reads less than 1 V with key in unlock position.	(OK) ▶ (O̸K̸) ▶		REPLACE damaged module. RETEST system. SERVICE door key switch or Circuit 25 DG/ P for open. RETEST system.
D3 KEYLESS ENTRY CHECK • Arm and activate alarm as in step D1. • Activate the Keyless Entry door unlock code.	Alarm turns Off (OK) ▶ Alarm continuous (O̸K̸) ▶		System OK. GO to **D5**. GO to **D4**.
D4 • Verify the following when the unlock code is pressed. B+ is applied momentarily to Circuit 163 R/O which turns the Keyless Entry alarm disarm relay on which provides a ground to Circuit 25 DG P.		▶	SERVICE the relay, or Circuit 25 DG/P, 163 R/ O, and 118 PK/O as required. RETEST system.
D5 • Arm the alarm system with a window down. • Unlock the door from the inside then open. • Wait 4 minutes.	Alarm activates (OK) ▶ Alarm shuts Off Alarm continues (O̸K̸) ▶		System OK. STOP. REPLACE damaged module. RETEST system.

TEST E
VEHICLE WILL NOT START

TEST STEP		RESULT	▶	ACTION TO TAKE
E0	ENSURE ALARM SYSTEM IS DISARMED			
			▶	INSERT door key and TURN to the unlock position. GO to **E1**.
E1	CHECK START INTERRUPT RELAY CONTACTS			
	• Short terminals 3 and 5 of the relay with a jumper wire. • Start the vehicle.	Vehicle starts? (OK)	▶	GO to **E2**.
		Vehicle will not start	▶	Alarm system OK. REFER to Powertrain manual, Section 28-02.
E2				
	• Measure terminal 1 C of the relay or terminal E (Circuit 342 LG/P) of the control module. • Verify the voltage is greater than 2 V.	Greater than 2 V (OK)	▶	REPLACE damaged relay. RETEST system.
		Less than 2 V	▶	REPLACE damaged module. RETEST system.

TEST F
ALARM LAMP IS ON ALL THE TIME

TEST STEP		RESULT	▶	ACTION TO TAKE
F0	ENSURE ALARM SYSTEM IS DISARMED			
		Lamp is still on	▶	INSERT door key and TURN to the unlock position.
F1	DISCONNECT MODULE CONNECTOR			
		Lamp turns off	▶	REPLACE damaged module. RETEST system.
		Lamp remains on	▶	SERVICE Circuit 343 DB/LG for short circuit. RETEST system.

TEST G
ALARM LAMP DOES NOT WORK

	TEST STEP	RESULT ▶		ACTION TO TAKE
G0	TURN IGNITION SWITCH TO OFF			
G1	CHECK LAMP AND CIRCUIT 343 DB/LG			
	• With a jumper wire, short terminal D (Circuit 343 DB/LG) of the control module to ground.	Lamp turns On	▶	GO to **G2**.
		Lamp remains Off	▶	SERVICE warning lamp or Circuit 343 DB/LG for open circuit. RETEST system.
G2	CHECK MODULE B +			
	• Measure terminal N (Circuit 23 T/LG) of the module for greater than 9 V.	Greater than 9 V	(OK) ▶	GO to **G3**.
		Less than 9 V	(ØK) ▶	SERVICE fuse and/or Circuit 23 T/LG and 37 Y. RETEST system.
G3	CHECK MODULE IGNITION INPUT			
	• Measure terminal K (Circuit 296 W/P) of the module for less than 9 V.	Less than 9 V	(OK) ▶	GO to **G4**.
		Greater than 9 V	(ØK) ▶	SERVICE Circuit 296 W/P for short. RETEST.
G4	CHECK MODULE OPERATION			
	• Open a vehicle door. • Activate the electric door lock switch.	Lamp glows	(OK) ▶	STOP System OK.
		Lamp does not glow	(ØK) ▶	REPLACE damaged module. RETEST system.

TEST H
HORN, HEADLAMPS, TAILLAMPS ARE ON ALL THE TIME

	TEST STEP	RESULT ▶		ACTION TO TAKE
H1	REMOVE MODULE CONNECTOR			
		They remain on	▶	REPLACE the alarm relay. RETEST system.
		They turn off	▶	REPLACE damaged control module. RETEST system.

POWER ACCESSORIES
CONVENIENCE OPTIONS

GENERAL MOTORS

Power Mirrors

The power remote mirrors are adjusted from the interior of the car by moving the outside mirror switch in the desired position. Each mirror has two reversible motors. One to adjust the mirror view up and the other to adjust the mirror view right and left.

The driver operates the Up-Down and Left-Right switch that controls the polarity of the voltage to the motors. The mirror select switch directs these control voltages to either the right or left outside mirror.

The Corvette and Cadillac models incorporate a heating system in the power mirror. This heating system for the power mirrors is tied in with the rear window defogger. When the rear window defogger switch is energized, the base of the power mirror heats up through a ground lead soldered which is soldered to the mirror base. A thermistor in the wiring circuit interrupts the current flow when the mirror base reaches 158°F.

On some models there is an Automatic Day/Night mirror that will automatically change from the normal day position to the non-glare position when the rear headlamp glare reaches the mirror at night . When the glare is nor present, the mirror will automatically return to the normal position. This Automatic Day/Night mirror is a non-repairable item as must be replaced as an assembly.

HEATED MIRROR

System Check

CORVETTE AND CADILLAC

1. With the ignition switch in the "RUN" position, turn on the rear window defogger.
2. The rear window defogger and the face of the heated mirror should be warm to the touch. If they are not warm make the following system checks:
   a. Check the rear window defogger fuse, and replace if blown.
   b. Check the stop-hazard fuse by operating the hazard flasher.
   c. Check the A/C fuse by operating the air conditioning system.
   d. Make sure all the ground and connectors are clean and tight.

Mirror Defogger Will Not Operate

CADILLAC

1. Disconnect connector C651 or C652 (defogger control connector). Connect a suitable test light between the PPL wire and the black wire.
2. Turn the defroster on, if the test light does not light up, check the defogger in-line fuse and the PPL (192) wire and Black (192) wire for a short.
3. If the test light does light, repair or replace the mirror assembly as necessary.

CORVETTE

1. Remove the connector from the defogger control and measure the voltage to the ground terminal B (orange) and E (pink and black). Place the ignition switch in the "RUN" position. The reading at these terminals should be 12 volts.
2. If the voltage readings are correct go on to the next step. If the voltage readings are incorrect, at any of the terminals, check the circuit attaches to the terminal in question.
3. With the connector still disconnected from the defogger control unit and the negative battery cable disconnected, mea-

sure the resistance to the ground at the D (PPL) wire. The resistance should be 1 ohm or less.

POWER MIRROR ASSEMBLY

Removal and Installation

ALL MODELS EXCEPT SOMERSET, GRAND AM AND CALAIS

1. Disconnect the negative battery cable. Remove the door trim panel and disconnect the wiring harness at the connector.
2. In order to gain access to the wire harness, it will be necessary to pull back the insulator pad and water deflector. Remove the wire harness from any retaining tabs in the door.
3. Remove the mirror retaining nuts from the bottom of the mirror. Remove the mirror and wire harness from the door.
4. Installation is the reverse order of the removal procedure.

SOMERSET, GRAND AM AND CALAIS

1. Disconnect the negative battery cable. Remove the inner belt sealing strip and door trim panel.
2. Remove the mirror switch trim panel. remove the mirror assembly retaining screw.
3. Remove the wiring harness, nuts, mirror assembly and mirror assembly gasket.
4. Installation is the reverse order of the removal procedure.

POWER MIRROR GLASS AND MOTOR ASSEMBLY

Removal and Installation

ALL MODELS EXCEPT FIERO, SOMERSET, GRAND AM AND CALAIS

NOTE: Before attempting this procedure a new mirror glass must be available. The old mirror glass will be broken in order to gain access to the mirror motor. When breaking the mirror glass, cover the painted surface of the door to avoid any damage from the broken glass.

─────────── **CAUTION** ───────────
To minimize the chance of personal injury during this procedure, gloves and safety glasses should be worn when removing broken glass.
────────────────────────────────

1. Disconnect the negative battery cable. Remove the mirror face by tapping the glass and breaking the mirror. Remove the broken glass.
2. Remove the mirror frame attaching screw and remove the frame from the housing.
3. Remove the motor attaching screws. Lift the motor assembly out of the housing and disconnect the wiring harness. The motor assembly contains no serviceable parts, the assembly has to be replaced.
4. Installation is the reverse order of the removal procedure. Remove the paper backing from the service mirror face and center the mirror in the mirror frame. Press firmly to ensure adhesion of the mirror glass to the mirror frame.

FIERO

1. Disconnect the negative battery cable. Grasp the inboard and outboard edges of the glass with fingers and pull rearward to disengage the mirror glass from the pivot.
2. Remove the door trim panel. Remove the front filler weatherstrip.
3. Remove the mirror assembly retaining nuts. Disconnect the electrical connector and remove the mirror housing.

MIRROR DOES NOT AUTOMATICALLY OPERATE

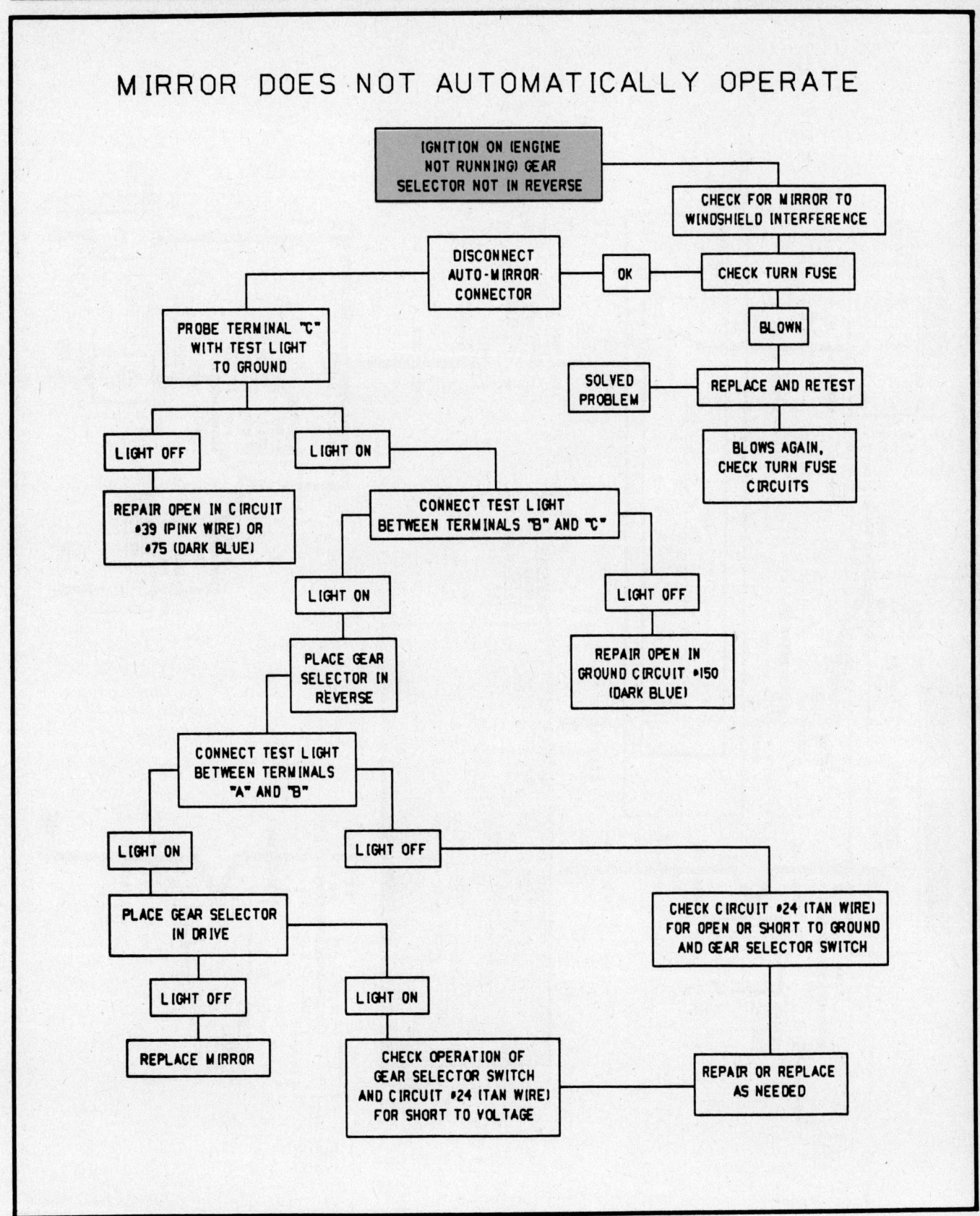

Automatic day/night mirror diagnosis chart

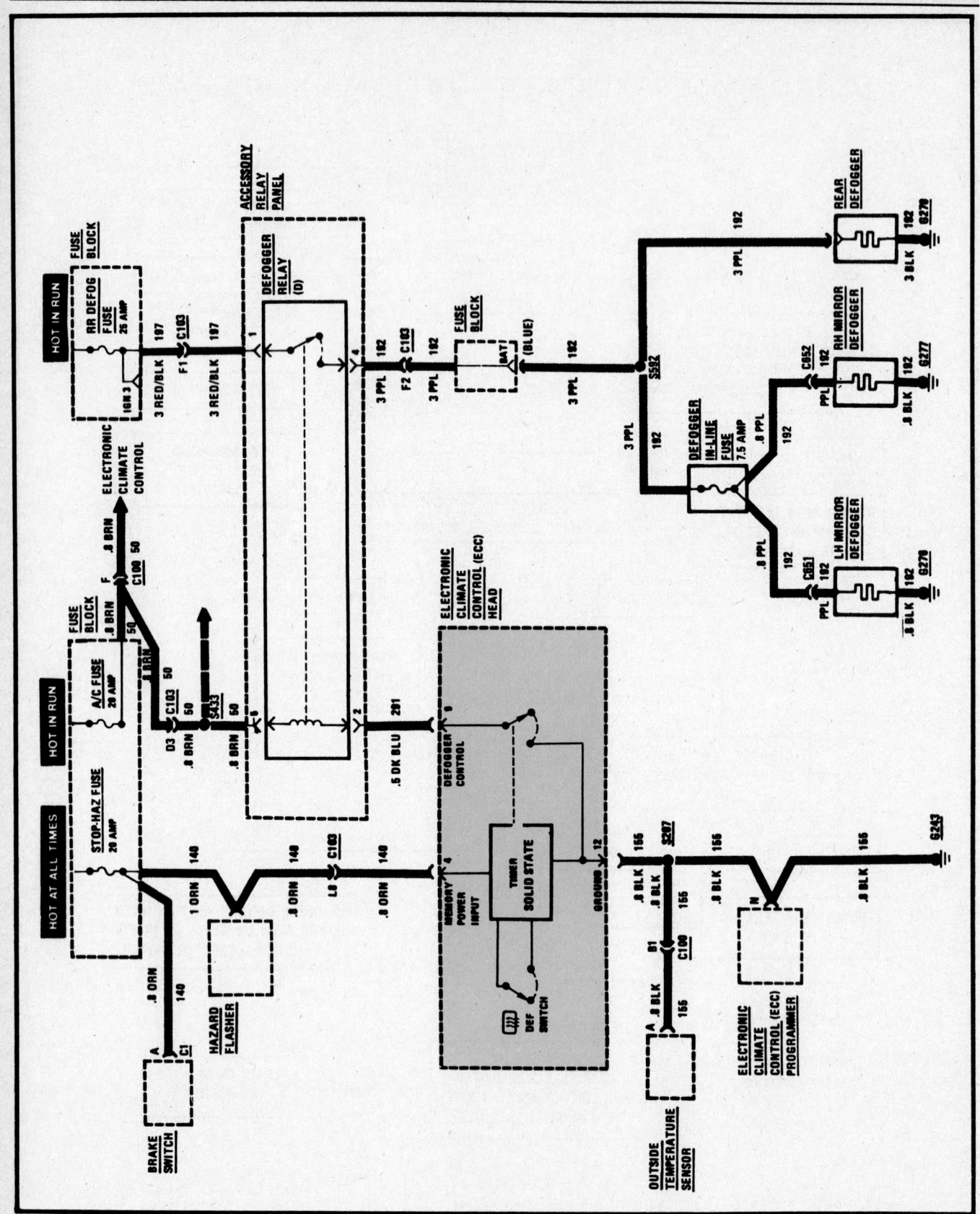

39 Rear window defogger and heated mirror wiring schematic—Cadillac

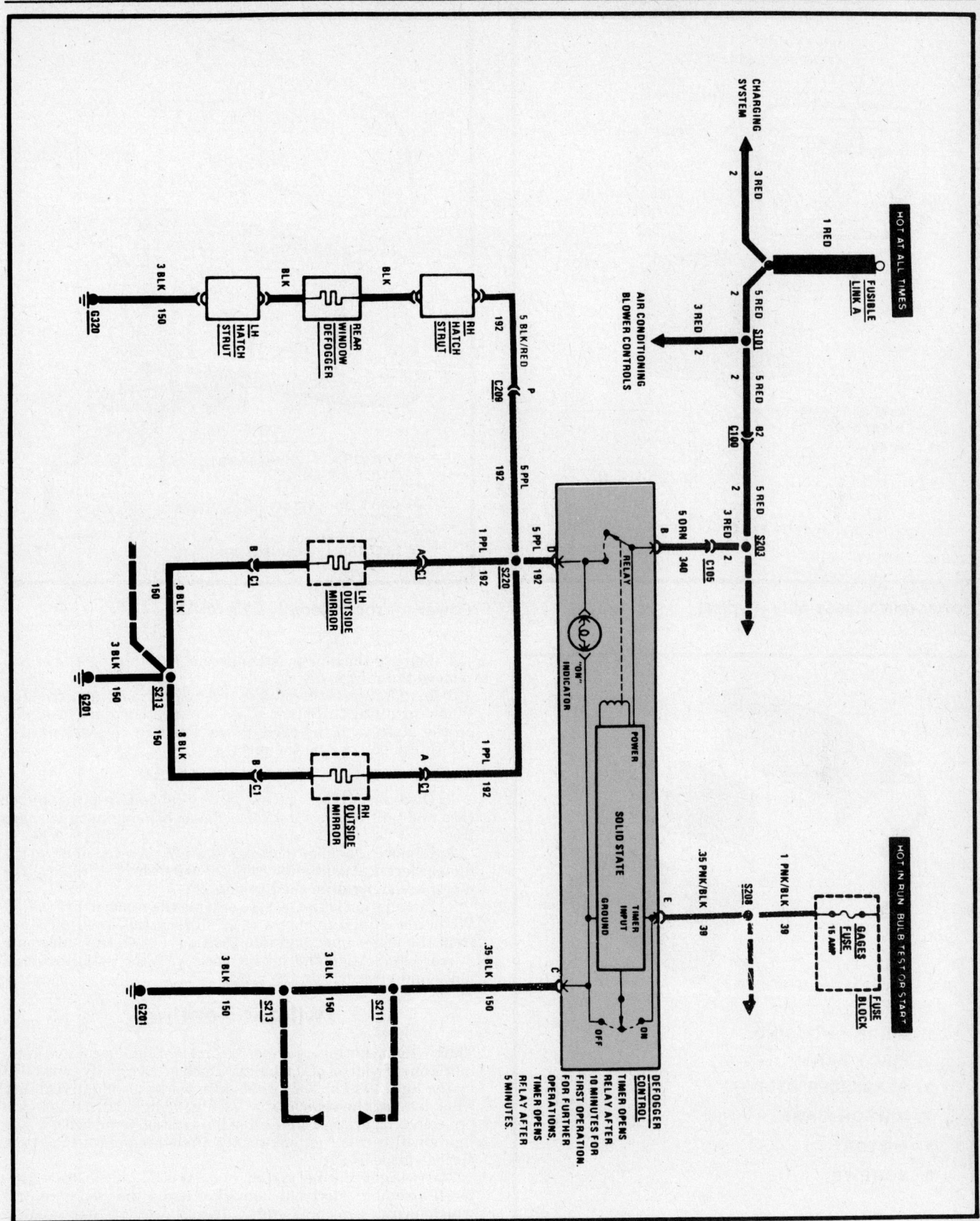

Rear window defogger and heated mirror wiring schematic—Corvette

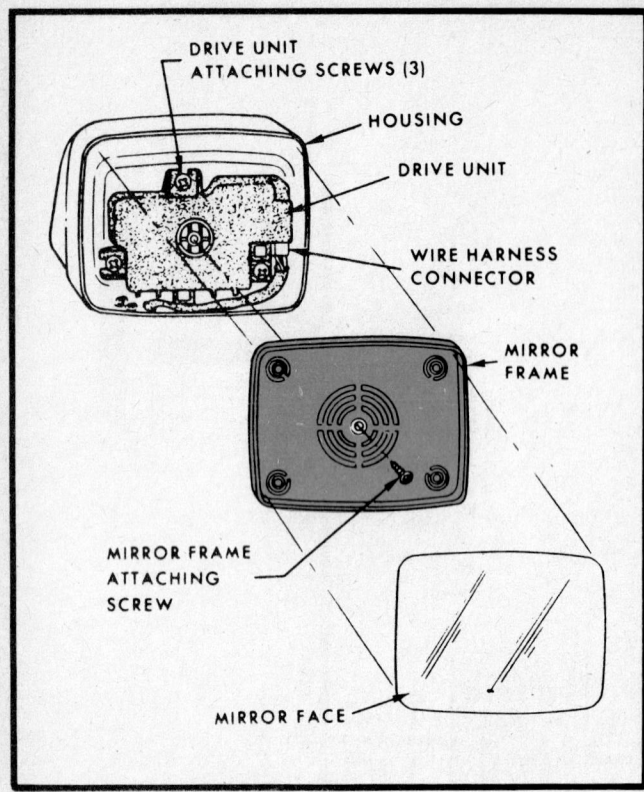

Power mirror assembly—typical

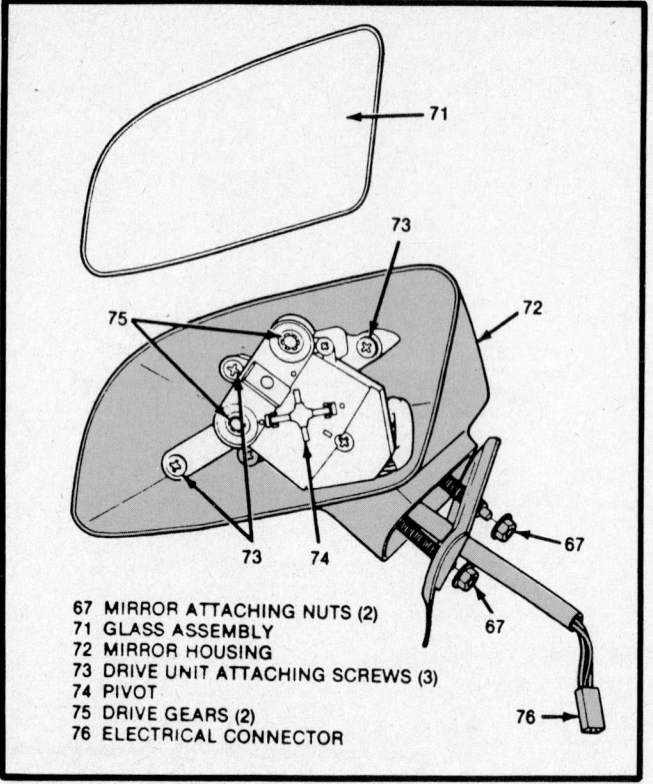

67 MIRROR ATTACHING NUTS (2)
71 GLASS ASSEMBLY
72 MIRROR HOUSING
73 DRIVE UNIT ATTACHING SCREWS (3)
74 PIVOT
75 DRIVE GEARS (2)
76 ELECTRICAL CONNECTOR

Power mirror assembly—Fiero AM

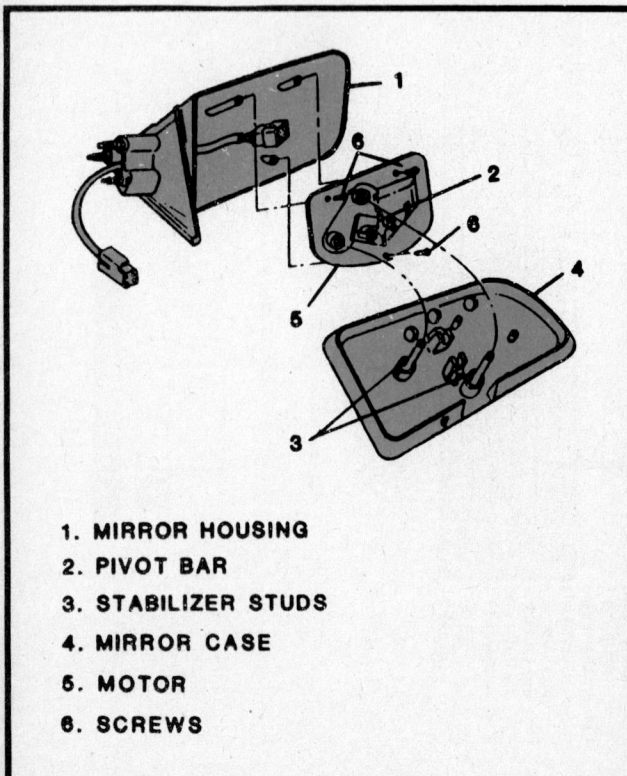

1. MIRROR HOUSING
2. PIVOT BAR
3. STABILIZER STUDS
4. MIRROR CASE
5. MOTOR
6. SCREWS

Power mirror assembly—Grand AM

4. Remove the mirror motor assembly retaining screws and remove the mirror motor.

5. Installation is the reverse order of the removal procedure. When installing the mirror glass, align both worm gear shafts on the glass with the drive gears. Press in on glass until it snaps into position on the pivot.

SOMERSET, GRAND AM AND CALAIS

1. Disconnect the negative battery cable. Grasp the mirror case and pull it away from the mirror housing until it snaps free.

2. Remove the motor housing retaining screws. Remove the motor electrical connector from the wire harness. remove the motor assembly from the housing.

3. Installation is the reverse order of the removal procedure. When installing the mirror case, pull out the stabilizer studs from the motor and snap into position. Install the studs onto mirror case. Align the mirror case with the stabilizer stud holes and pivot bar on the motor.

Twilight Sentinel

The twilight sentinel provides an ambient light sensitive automatic on-off control of the lights, which are normally controlled by the light switch. The system also works for night visibility when leaving the vehicle, it will keep the lights turned on for a pre-selected period of time after the ignition is turned off. The lights will turn off automatically after this pre-selected time period elaspes.

The twilight sentinel system consists of a light sensitive photocell assembly, electronic amplifier and a time delay control which includes an on-off switch. The connections to the vehicle lights parallel the regular light switch connections, therefore requiring the light switch to be turned off to obtain the automatic control.

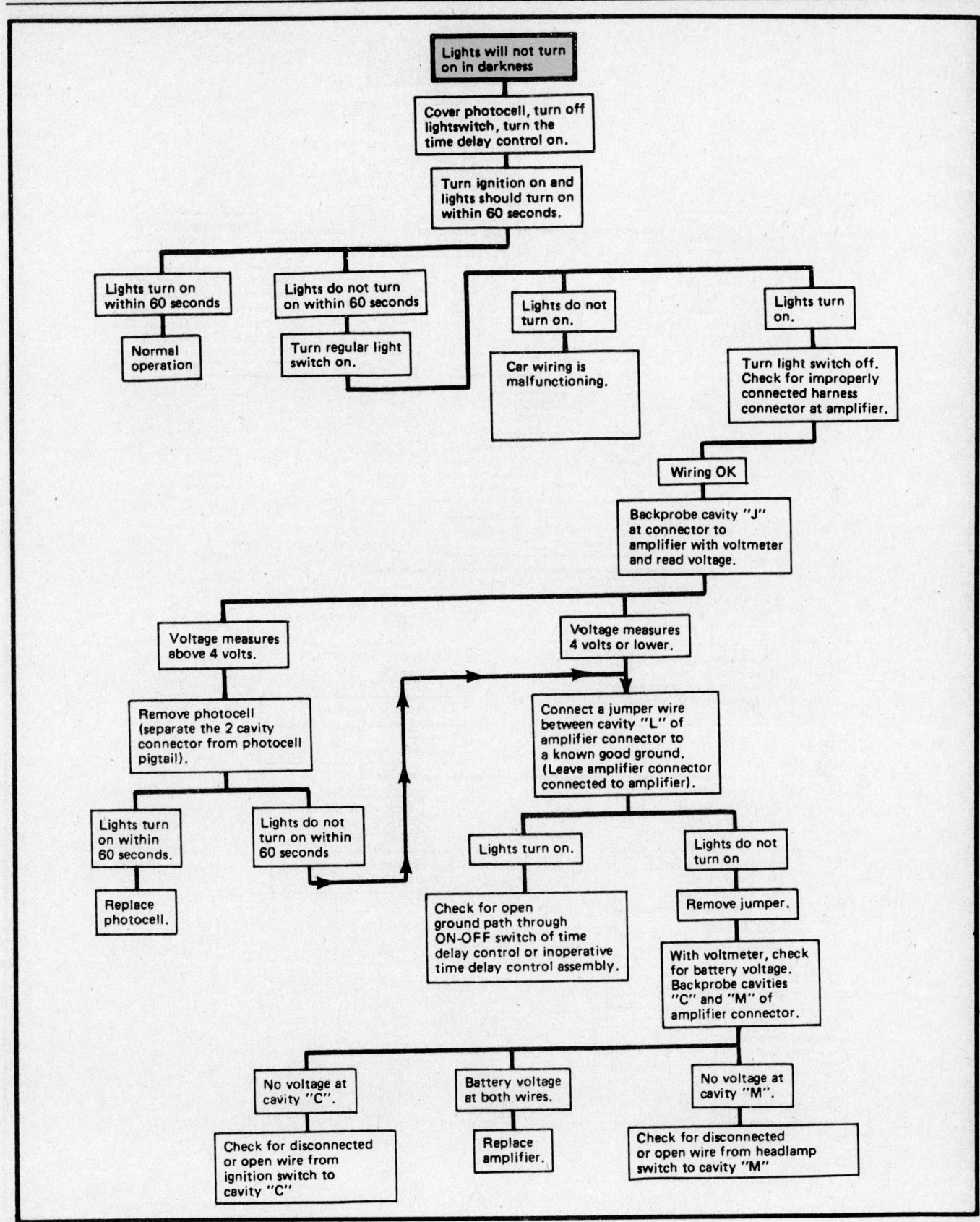

Diagnosis chart for the twilight sentinel

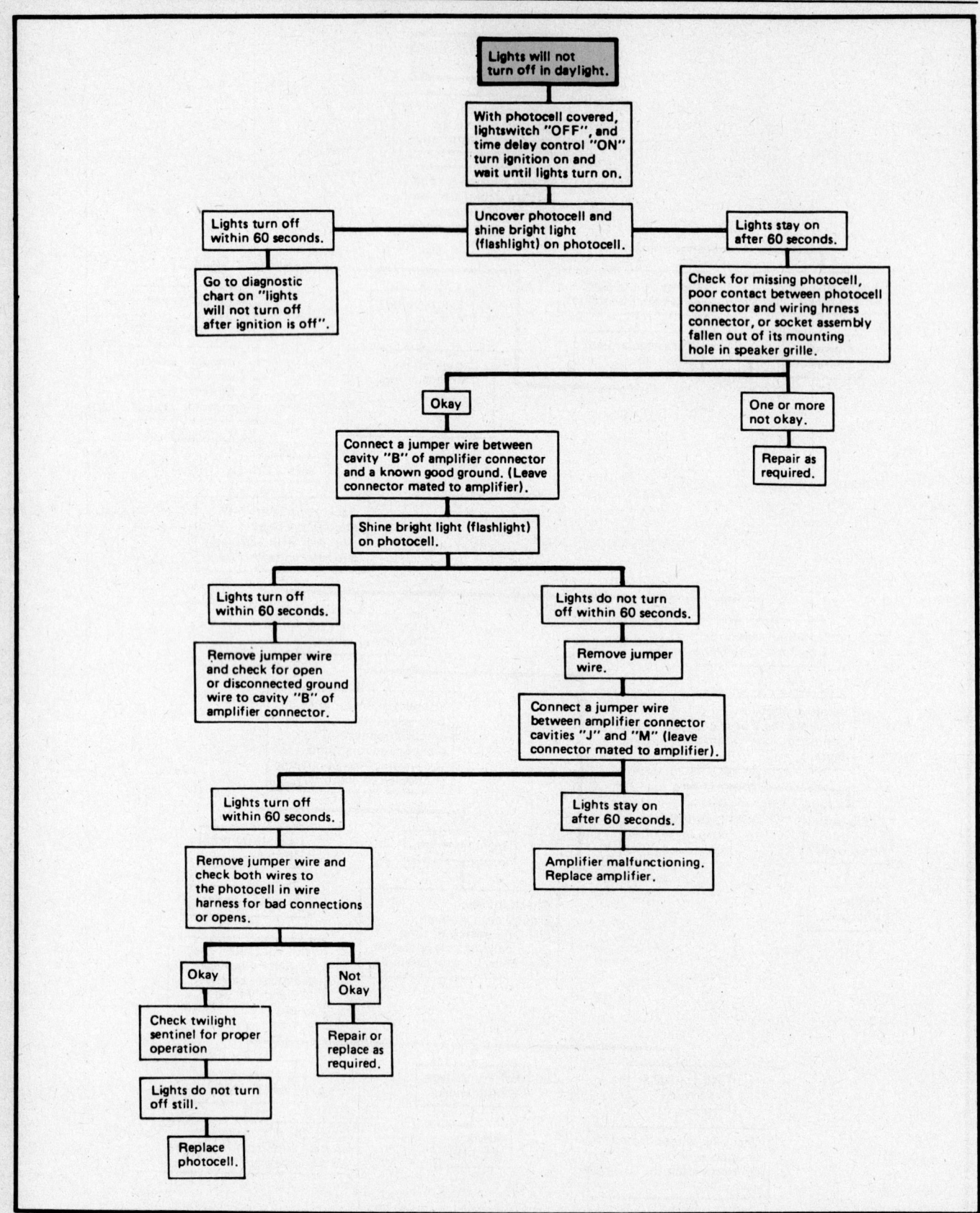

Lights will not turn off in daylight.

With photocell covered, lightswitch "OFF", and time delay control "ON" turn ignition on and wait until lights turn on.

Uncover photocell and shine bright light (flashlight) on photocell.

Lights turn off within 60 seconds.
→ Go to diagnostic chart on "lights will not turn off after ignition is off".

Lights stay on after 60 seconds.
→ Check for missing photocell, poor contact between photocell connector and wiring hrness connector, or socket assembly fallen out of its mounting hole in speaker grille.

Okay
→ Connect a jumper wire between cavity "B" of amplifier connector and a known good ground. (Leave connector mated to amplifier).

Shine bright light (flashlight) on photocell.

One or more not okay.
→ Repair as required.

Lights turn off within 60 seconds.
→ Remove jumper wire and check for open or disconnected ground wire to cavity "B" of amplifier connector.

Lights do not turn off within 60 seconds.
→ Remove jumper wire.

Connect a jumper wire between amplifier connector cavities "J" and "M" (leave connector mated to amplifier).

Lights turn off within 60 seconds.
→ Remove jumper wire and check both wires to the photocell in wire harness for bad connections or opens.

Lights stay on after 60 seconds.
→ Amplifier malfunctioning. Replace amplifier.

Okay
→ Check twilight sentinel for proper operation

Lights do not turn off still.
→ Replace photocell.

Not Okay
→ Repair or replace as required.

Diagnosis chart for the twilight sentinel (cont.)

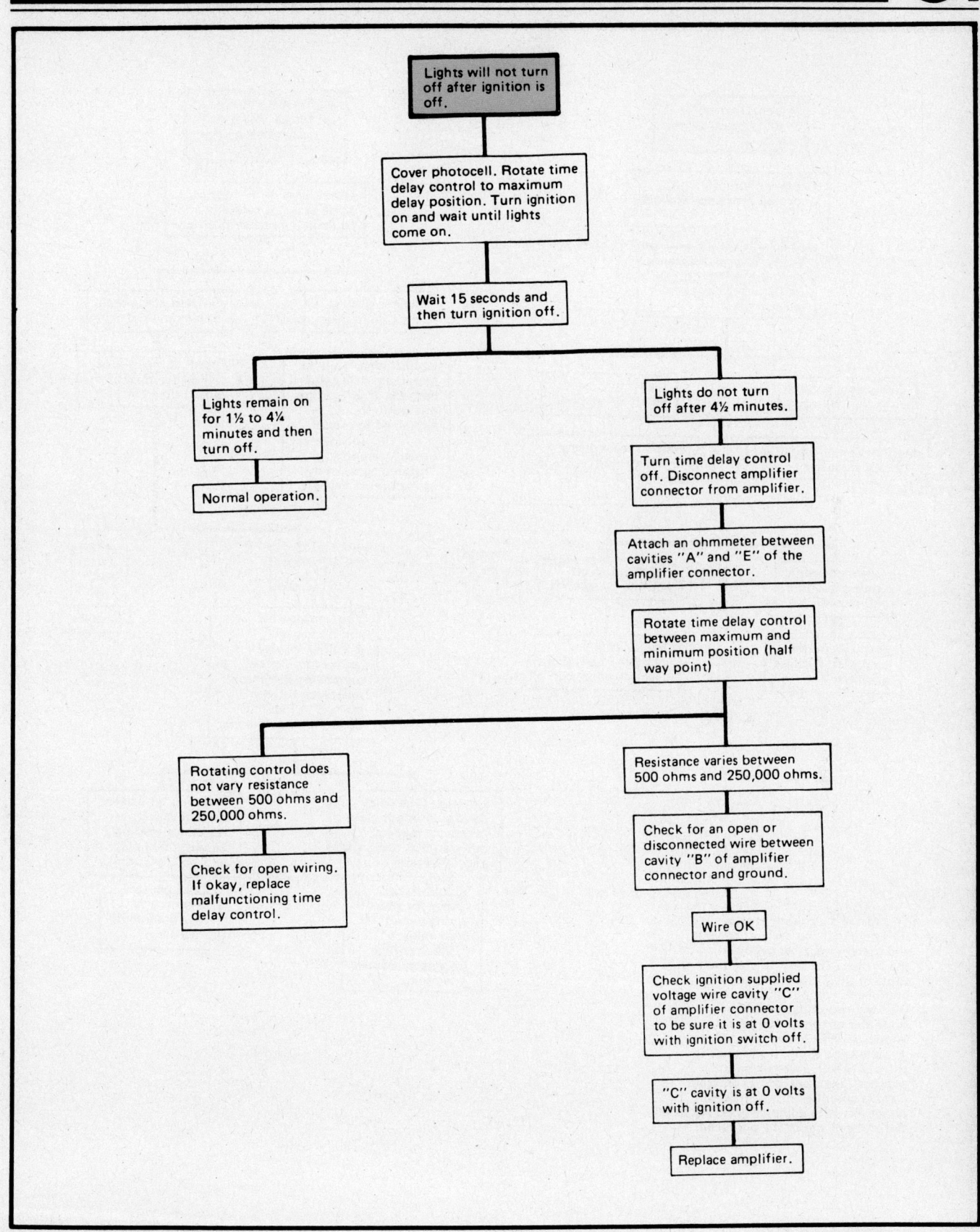

Diagnosis chart for the twilight sentinel (cont.)

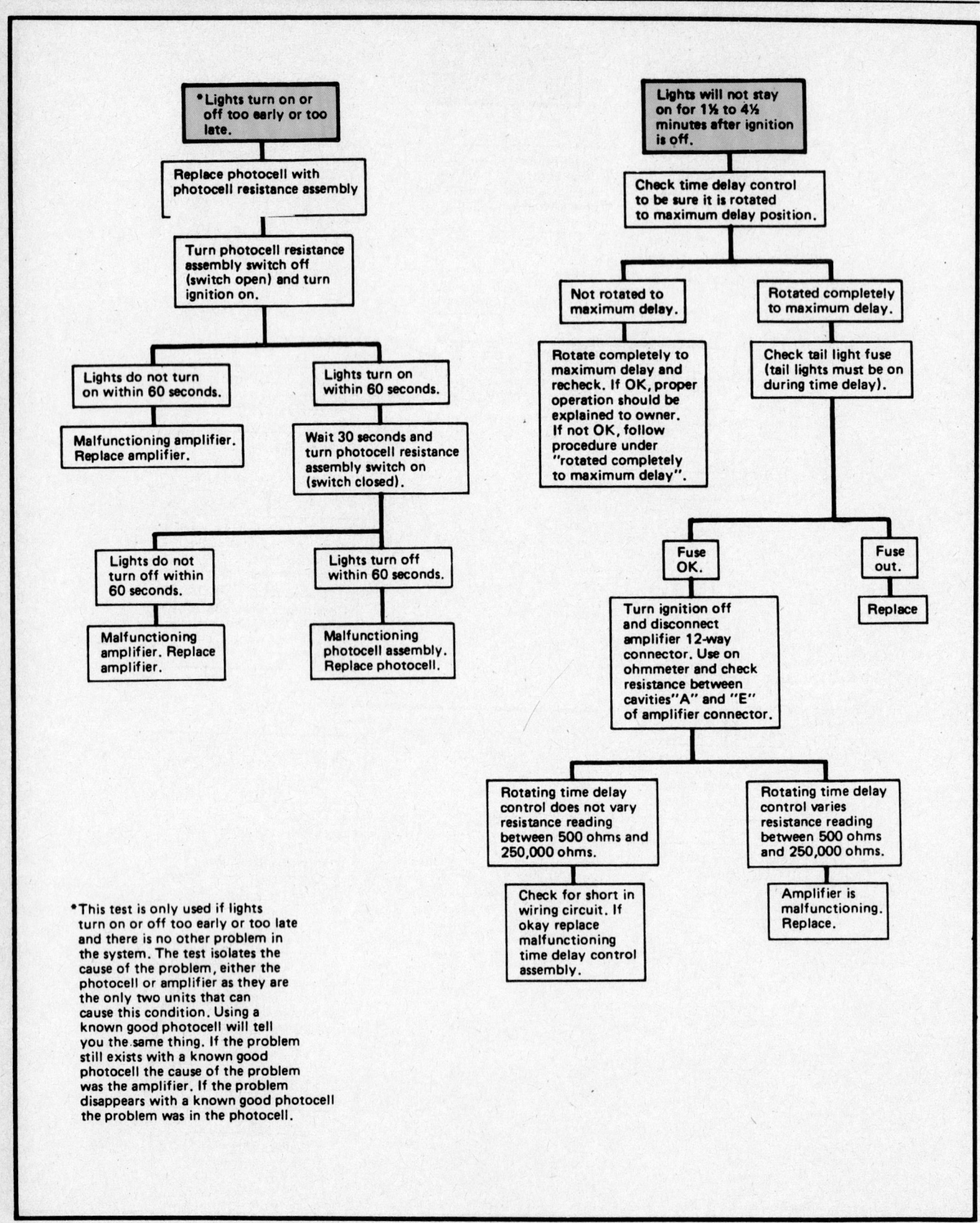

*Lights turn on or off too early or too late.

Replace photocell with photocell resistance assembly

Turn photocell resistance assembly switch off (switch open) and turn ignition on.

Lights do not turn on within 60 seconds.

Malfunctioning amplifier. Replace amplifier.

Lights turn on within 60 seconds.

Wait 30 seconds and turn photocell resistance assembly switch on (switch closed).

Lights do not turn off within 60 seconds.

Malfunctioning amplifier. Replace amplifier.

Lights turn off within 60 seconds.

Malfunctioning photocell assembly. Replace photocell.

*This test is only used if lights turn on or off too early or too late and there is no other problem in the system. The test isolates the cause of the problem, either the photocell or amplifier as they are the only two units that can cause this condition. Using a known good photocell will tell you the same thing. If the problem still exists with a known good photocell the cause of the problem was the amplifier. If the problem disappears with a known good photocell the problem was in the photocell.

Lights will not stay on for 1½ to 4½ minutes after ignition is off.

Check time delay control to be sure it is rotated to maximum delay position.

Not rotated to maximum delay.

Rotate completely to maximum delay and recheck. If OK, proper operation should be explained to owner. If not OK, follow procedure under "rotated completely to maximum delay".

Rotated completely to maximum delay.

Check tail light fuse (tail lights must be on during time delay).

Fuse OK.

Fuse out.

Replace

Turn ignition off and disconnect amplifier 12-way connector. Use on ohmmeter and check resistance between cavities "A" and "E" of amplifier connector.

Rotating time delay control does not vary resistance reading between 500 ohms and 250,000 ohms.

Check for short in wiring circuit. If okay replace malfunctioning time delay control assembly.

Rotating time delay control varies resistance reading between 500 ohms and 250,000 ohms.

Amplifier is malfunctioning. Replace.

Diagnosis chart for the twilight sentinel (cont.)

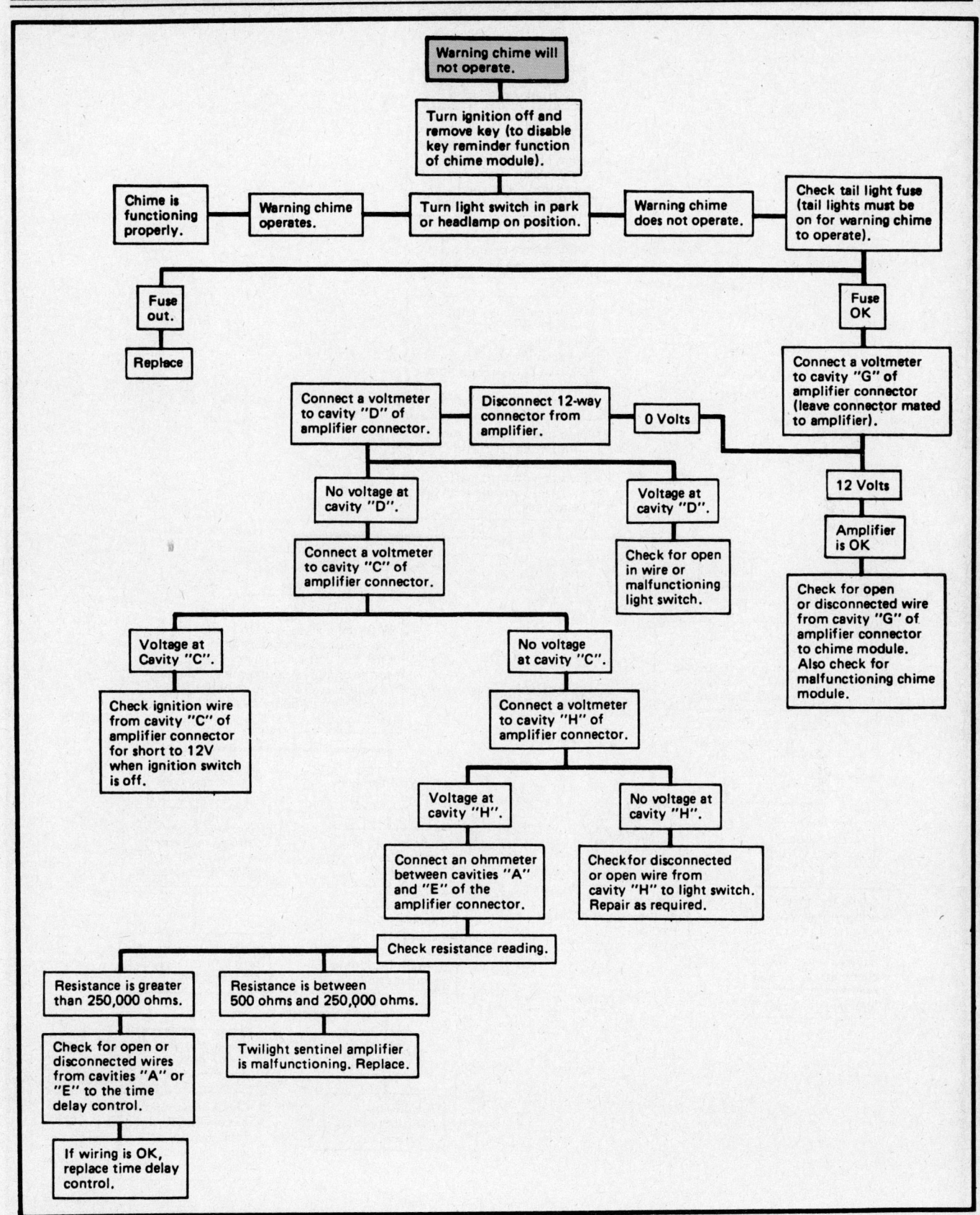

Diagnosis chart for the twilight sentinel (cont.)

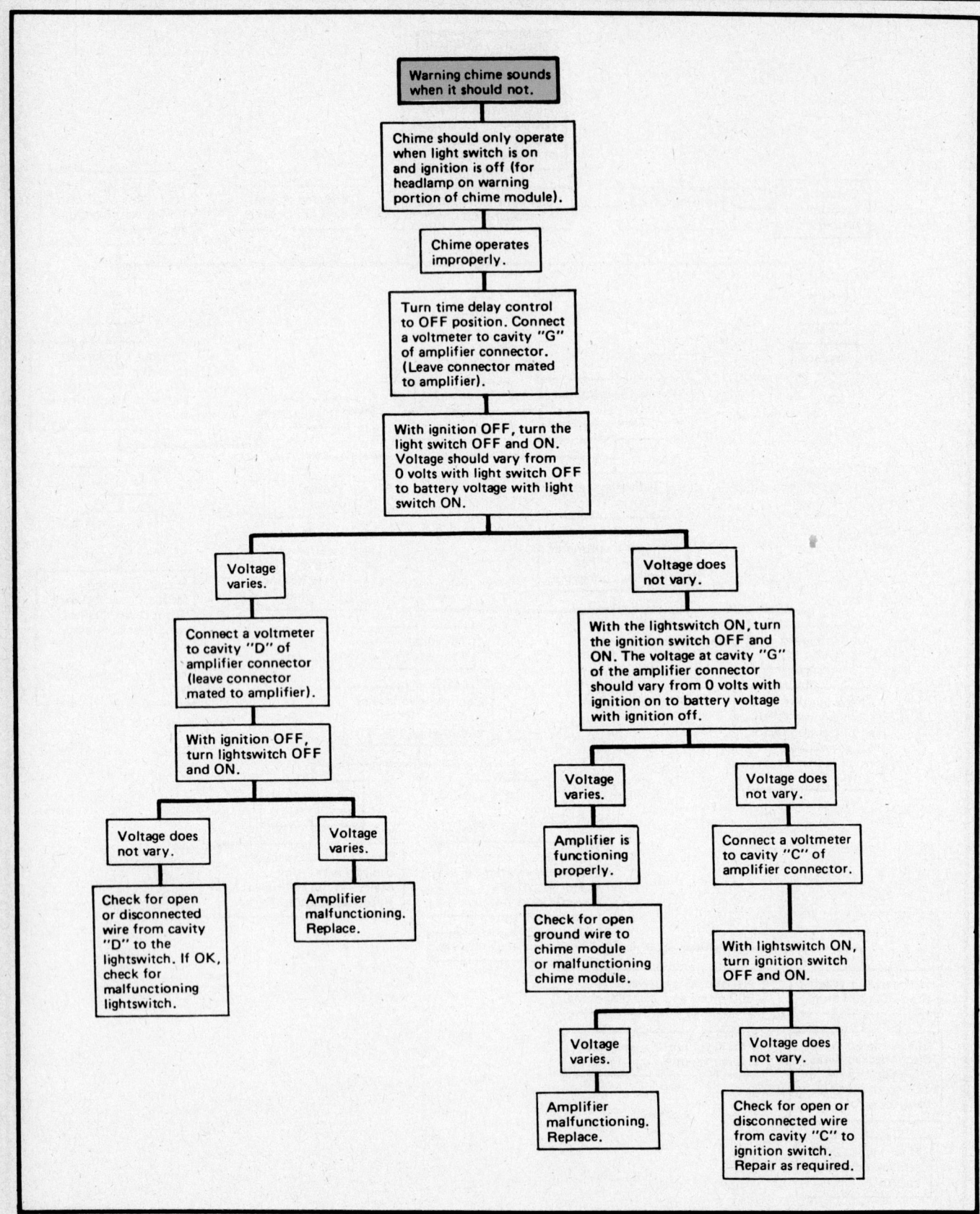

Diagnosis chart for the twilight sentinel (cont.)

TWILIGHT SENTINEL SYSTEM

Functional Test

1. With the twilight sentinel system in the "OFF" position check for normal operation of the park, tail and headlamps using the light switch.

2. With the lights in the manual "ON" position and the ignition off. The chimer should sound if the car is equipped with a chime package.

3. Turn the light switch to the "OFF" position and turn the twilight sentinel to the "ON" position. Cover the photocell and turn the ignition switch to the "ON" position. The lights should come on within ten seconds.

4. Remove the cover from the photocell and apply a bright light. The lights should turn "OFF" after ten seconds and before sixty seconds.

5. Cover the photocell and wait for the lights to turn "ON". Wait fifteen seconds and turn the ignition switch to the "OFF" position. The lights should turn off after a time delay, a few seconds with the control rotated to the minimum delay position and one and half to four and a half minutes with the control rotated to the maximum delay position.

Headlights Turn On In The Daylight When The Ignition Is Turned On

Some vechiles equipped with the twilight sentinel may experience a condition where the headlights turn on in the daylight when the ignition is turned on. Whenever this happens, the most likely cause is a disconnected or a short in the photocell leads.

The problem could also be that the photocell itself has dropped from its mounting hole and is laying somewhere in darkness under the instrument panel top cover (this will cause the lights to go on in the day time). There is no adjustment on the amplifier for later/earlier turn-on or turn-off for lights.

Headlights Turn On Too Late Or Too Early In The Evening

Make the complete functional test to make sure that the twilight sentinel operates properly, then use the diagnosis chart to determine if there is a problem in the amplifier or the photocell with the evening turn-on or morning turn-off of the lights.

Lights Turn Off Only When The On-Off Switch Of The Time Delay Control Is Off

If this situation occurs, the most likely cause is a disconnected or short in the black wire to terminal B of the 12 way amplifier connector. This wire provides a ground path to the amplifier.

If the black wire is reconnected or repaired, the functional test should be performed to make sure the amplifier is functioning properly.

PHOTOCELL AND AMPLIFIER

Test

To determined whether the amplifier or photocell assembly is the cause of a twilight sentinel malfunction, a resistance simulator can be assembled and used as follows.

1. Using two suitable alligator clips and a 120 K ohm resistor in parrallel with a 56 K ohm resistor and a switch can be used to simulate the photocells reaction to varying light conditions.

2. By replacing the photocell with the simulator it can be determined if the photocell or amplifier is the cause of the malfunction.

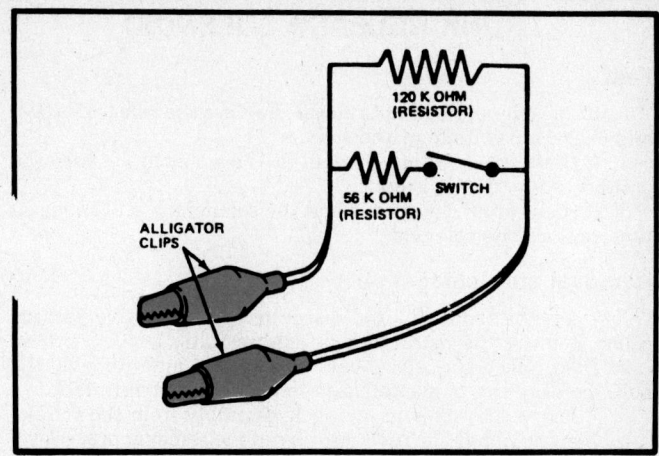

Photocell replacement (simulated) resistance assembly

Sensitivity Adjustment

TORONADO

NOTE: This adjustment is only possible on the Toronado models.

1. Using a suitable tool, go through the hole in the right side of the amplifier. Each mark around the hole will portray approximately five minutes of daylight.

2. In order to make the lights turn on earlier, turn the screw clockwise. To make the lights turn on later or when it is darker, turn the screw counterclockwise.

3. Test the photocell by measuring the voltage to ground with a digital voltmeter at the white wire on the photocell.

4. The voltmeter reading should vary less then two volts with the cell covered to more then nine volts in bright light.

Power Trunk and Tailgate Release

The power trunk release system has a release button in the glove box, a release solenoid in the trunk and an ignition switch controlled by the power connection. The station wagon models have an power tailgate release.

Some models are equipped with a electrical trunk pull-down motor that will automatically close the trunk once it is lowered. There is a permanent magnet reversible motor that pulls the strike down, which in turn locks the trunk lid in the fully lock position. When the release mechanism is energized it reverses the motor, which allow the trunk lid to rise up to the open position.

TRUNK RELEASE SWITCH

Removal and Installation

Because of the varied applications of power trunk switches, a general power trunk switch removal and installation procedure is outlined. The removal steps can be altered as required by the technician.

1. Disconnect the negative battery cable. Remove the glove box liner.

2. Depress the spring clip on the rear of the switch and push the switch out through the passenger side of the panel.

3. Disconnect the electrical connector from the trunk release switch and remove the switch from the vehicle.

4. Installation is the reverse order of the removal procedure.

TRUNK RELEASE SOLENOID

Test

1. If the solenoid will not release, depress the release button and check for voltage at the solenoid.
2. If there is no voltage present at the solenoid, be sure the ground connection is good.
3. If the ground checks out and the solenoid is still inoperative, replace the solenoid.

Removal and Installation

1. Open the trunk lid and disconnect the negative battery cable. Remove the trunk lock attaching bolts.
2. Disconnect the electrical connections and remove the bolts holding the trunk release solenoid to the trunk lock.
3. Remove the solenoid and lock assembly from the trunk.
4. Installation is the reverse order of the removal procedure.

ELECTRICAL TRUNK PULL—DOWN MOTOR

Removal and Installation

1. Open the trunk lid and disconnect the negative battery cable.
2. Remove the pull-down motor trim panel. Disconnect the electrical connections and remove the pull-down motor from the trunk.
3. Installation is the reverse order of the removal procedure.

Trunk Lock Assembly Adjustment

1. Be for starting the adjustment procedure, be sure that the trunk lid is properly aligned.
2. Loosen the lock assembly bolts on the trunk lid and place the lock in the desired position.
3. Holding the lock in this position, tighten the lock assembly bolts and close the trunk lid. Be sure that the trunk lock is now operating properly.

Power Antenna

The power antenna automatically raises the antenna mast to its full height whenever the radio and ignition are tuned on. The antenna retracts into the fender when either the ignition or the radio is turned off.

The power antenna drive unit is housed in a two-piece plastic housing attached to the mast and tube assembly. A permanent magnet motor with the worm drive moves the antenna mast up and down with a plastic cable attached to the top mast section. There is no clutch used in this unit. A circuit breaker is used to protect the motor armature from overheating.

There are two types of power antennas being used, the AM/FM type and the AM-FM/CB (tri-band) type. Which antenna is used depends upon what radio is being used.

POWER ANTENNA TROUBLESHOOTING

Many of the antenna problems can be prevented by cleaning and lightly oiling the antenna rod at periodic intervals. If the vehicle has been undercoated make sure the drain holes have not been plugged.

Antenna Motor Electrical Noise

Excessive antenna motor electrical noise is often caused by the antenna lead-in cable ferrule at the antenna mast not being installed properly. This condition can be corrected by removing (cleaning if necessary) and properly reconnecting the antenna lead-in cable and tightening both retaining bolts.

Antenna Will Not Raise Or Lower

This condition can be due to a blown fuse, a loose electrical connection on the receiver unit or the antenna motor, a bent antenna mast or a malfunctioning relay. If all of these conditions check out and the antenna still will not raise or lower, remove the antenna assembly, disassemble the antenna assembly and replace any inoperative parts.

Antenna Trimmer Adjustment

This trimmer adjustment matches the antenna coil in the radio to the car antenna. Only AM radios, or the AM part of the AM/FM radios, need the adjustment. Electronic Tuned Radios (ETR) do not have trim adjustments.

1. Tune the radio to a weak AM station near 1400 KHz. Turn the volume all the way up. You should barely be able to hear the station. The fender mounted antennas should be fully extended.
2. Remove the right inner and outer radio knobs. Using a suitable tool, reach in a turn the trimmer screw until the loudest or clearest volume is obtained.

POWER ANTENNA REMOVAL

Because of the varied applications of power antennas, a general power antenna removal and installation procedure is outlined. The removal steps can be altered as required by the technician.

1. Disconnect the negative battery cable. Turn the steering wheel to the maximum right or left stop, depending on which front fender the antenna is attached to.
2. Remove the inner splash shield from the fender. Remove the instrument panel sound asorber pad.
3. Disconnect the antenna lead wires from the radio and antenna relay. Remove the retainers holding the antenna to the fender.
3. Remove the tire and wheel assembly if it is necessary to gain access under the fender. Remove the inner fender support brackets.
4. Remove the antenna bracket bolts and or the lower antenna attaching screws. Disconnect any other antenna electrical connections and guide the wire and antenna through the fender opening.
5. On the RWD Cadillac models, hook a four-foot wire to the top of the antenna to aid in guiding the antenna mast section out of the housing.
6. Installation is the reverse order of the removal procedure.

DIAGNOSIS PROCEDURES

STEP 1   Try operating antenna independently of car wiring as shown and observe current draw.

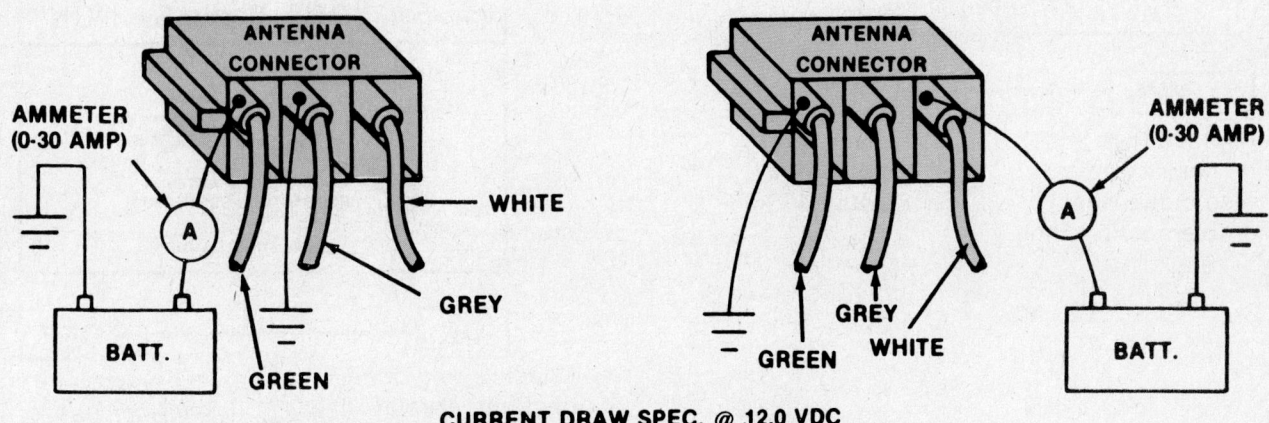

EXTEND-UP CYCLE

RETRACT-DOWN CYCLE

ANTENNA CONNECTOR

AMMETER (0-30 AMP)

AMMETER (0-30 AMP)

WHITE

GREY

BATT.

GREEN

GREEN

GREY

WHITE

BATT.

CURRENT DRAW SPEC. @ 12.0 VDC
                                              AMPS
(1) MAST EXTENDING OR RETRACTING   3.0
(2) STALL CURRENT   10.5 (COLD) MAX.

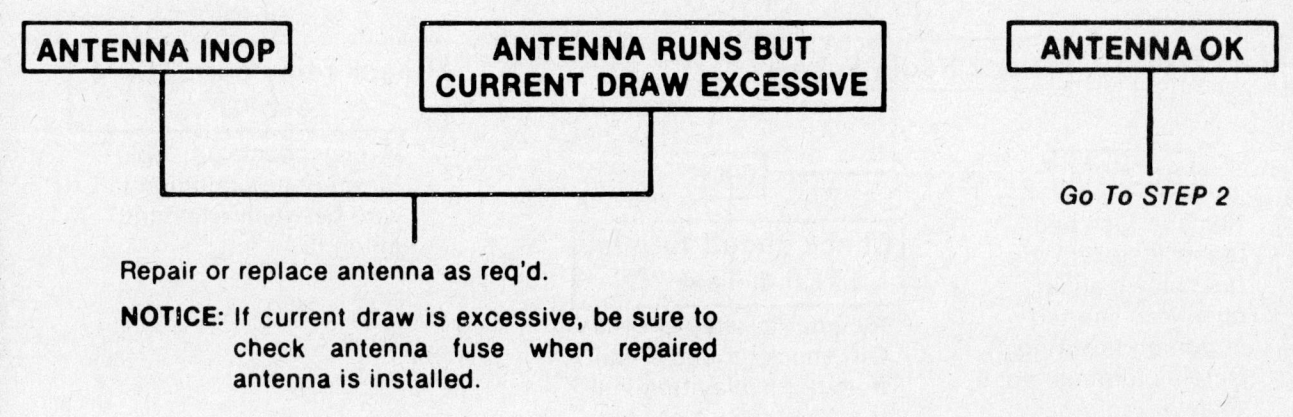

ANTENNA INOP

ANTENNA RUNS BUT CURRENT DRAW EXCESSIVE

ANTENNA OK

Go To STEP 2

Repair or replace antenna as req'd.

NOTICE: If current draw is excessive, be sure to check antenna fuse when repaired antenna is installed.

Power antenna diagnosis chart — antenna inoperative

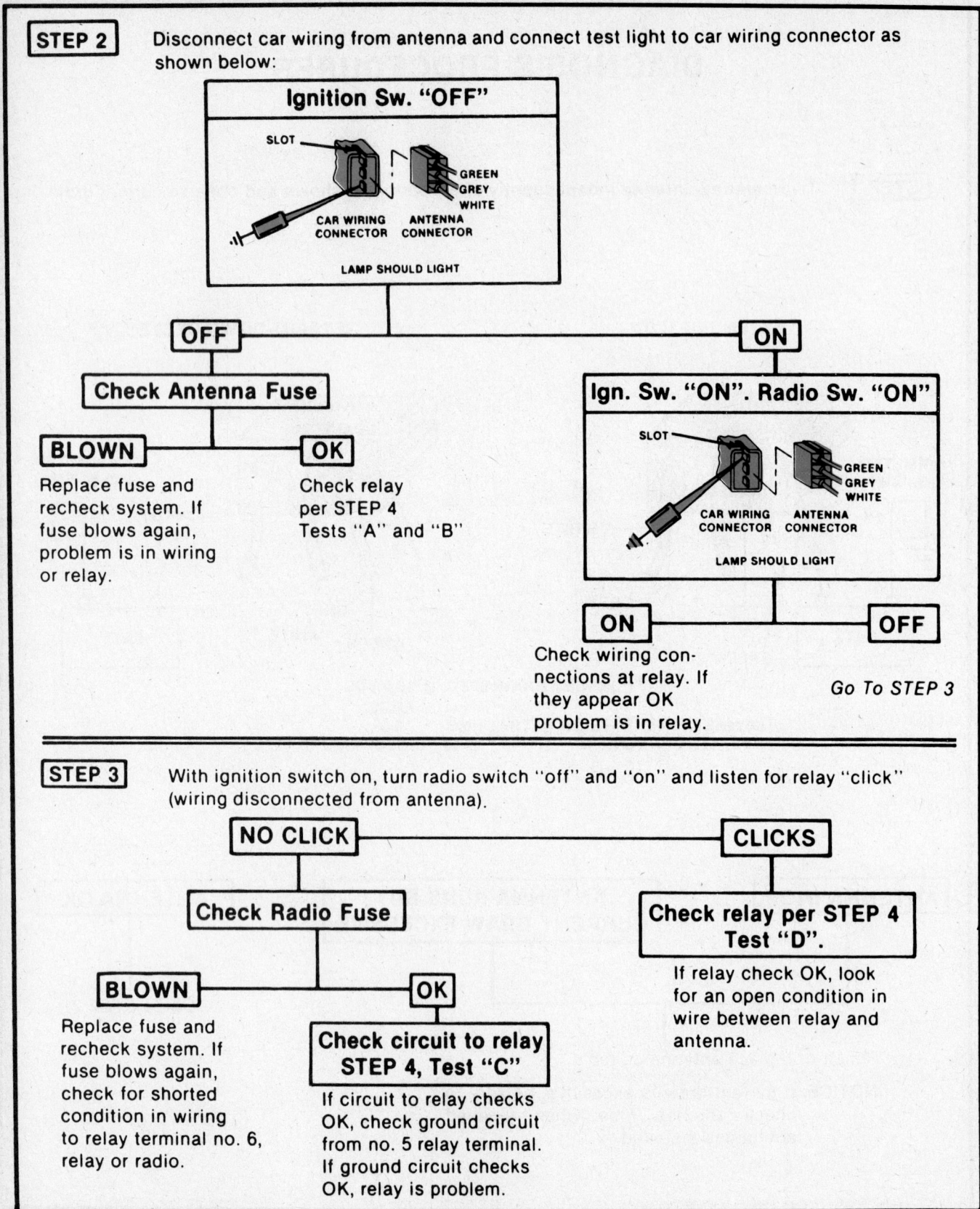

STEP 2 — Disconnect car wiring from antenna and connect test light to car wiring connector as shown below:

Ignition Sw. "OFF"

SLOT
CAR WIRING CONNECTOR
ANTENNA CONNECTOR
GREEN
GREY
WHITE
LAMP SHOULD LIGHT

OFF ─────────────── ON

Check Antenna Fuse

BLOWN — Replace fuse and recheck system. If fuse blows again, problem is in wiring or relay.

OK — Check relay per STEP 4 Tests "A" and "B"

Ign. Sw. "ON". Radio Sw. "ON"

SLOT
CAR WIRING CONNECTOR
ANTENNA CONNECTOR
GREEN
GREY
WHITE
LAMP SHOULD LIGHT

ON ─────────────── OFF

Check wiring connections at relay. If they appear OK problem is in relay.

Go To STEP 3

STEP 3 — With ignition switch on, turn radio switch "off" and "on" and listen for relay "click" (wiring disconnected from antenna).

NO CLICK ─────────────── CLICKS

Check Radio Fuse

Check relay per STEP 4 Test "D".

If relay check OK, look for an open condition in wire between relay and antenna.

BLOWN — Replace fuse and recheck system. If fuse blows again, check for shorted condition in wiring to relay terminal no. 6, relay or radio.

OK

Check circuit to relay STEP 4, Test "C"

If circuit to relay checks OK, check ground circuit from no. 5 relay terminal. If ground circuit checks OK, relay is problem.

Power antenna diagnosis chart—antenna inoperative (cont.)

STEP 4   **Checking Relay Circuits: (Antenna Disconnected)**

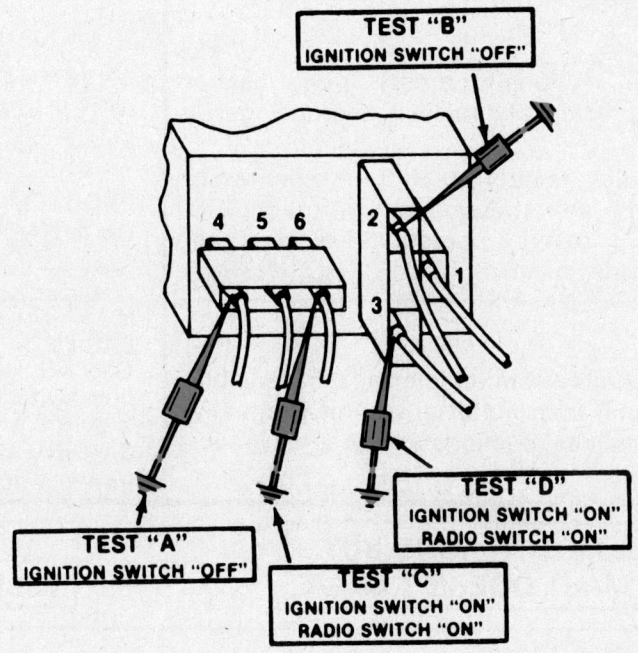

TEST "B"
IGNITION SWITCH "OFF"

TEST "A"
IGNITION SWITCH "OFF"

TEST "C"
IGNITION SWITCH "ON"
RADIO SWITCH "ON"

TEST "D"
IGNITION SWITCH "ON"
RADIO SWITCH "ON"

TEST	TEST LIGHT	ANALYSIS
A	ON OFF	— 12V circuit from antenna fuse to relay OK. — Fuse blown or wire open to relay terminal 4.
B	ON OFF	— Circuit thru relay OK. — Replace relay.
C	ON OFF	— 12V circuit via radio fuse and radio sw to relay OK. — Radio fuse blown; radio switch open; wiring open.
D	ON OFF	— Circuit thru relay OK. — Replace relay.

Power antenna diagnosis chart—antenna inoperative (cont.)

ANTENNA MOVES UP AND DOWN BUT DOES NOT EXTEND TO FULL UP POSITION AND/OR RETRACT TO FULL DOWN POSITION

PROCEDURE	RESULT
STEP 1 Inspect antenna mast sections for a dirty or bent condition. Make necessary repairs and recheck antenna operation. **NOTICE:** If antenna mast is dirty, clean it first then wipe off mast with a cloth dampened with light oil. May require several operations of antenna before it comes clean.	**ANTENNA OPERATES CORRECTLY AFTER REPAIRS** End of test. **PROBLEM NOT CORRECTED.** *Go to STEP 2.*
STEP 2 Remove antenna assembly from vehicle and disassemble mast and support tube from motor drive unit. Manually extend and retract the mast sections and observe if sections move freely.	**MAST SECTIONS EXTEND AND RETRACT EASILY.** Check for correct wiring connections to gear box switch. Replace switch as req'd. See Figure 2. **BINDING CONDITION IN MAST.** Replace mast assembly.

ANTENNA MOTOR RUNS BUT ANTENNA MAST DOESN'T MOVE   OR   ANTENNA MOTOR WILL NOT SHUT OFF

PROCEDURE	RESULTS
STEP 1 Manually try to move the top section of the mast up or down.	**TOP SECTION MOVES UP AND DOWN.** Replace mast and tube assy. **TOP SECTION DOESN'T MOVE.** Disassemble motor/gear box. Check mast assy for a jammed condition. If no jammed condition exists, repair motor/drive unit.

RADIO RECEPTION POOR OR NONE AT ALL (ANTENNA EXTENDS AND RETRACTS OK)

CHECK THE FOLLOWING:

1) RF cable connections at radio and antenna unit. (Note: Chevrolet has a 3rd connection.)

2) Antenna *mast* is not grounded. (Telescoping rod sections)

3) Check continuity between antenna R.F. pin and mast.

4) Antenna support tube is securely grounded.

5) Antenna mast for a dirty condition.

Power antenna diagnosis chart—antenna inoperative (cont.)

ANTENNA NOISE
(Fixed or Power Mast)

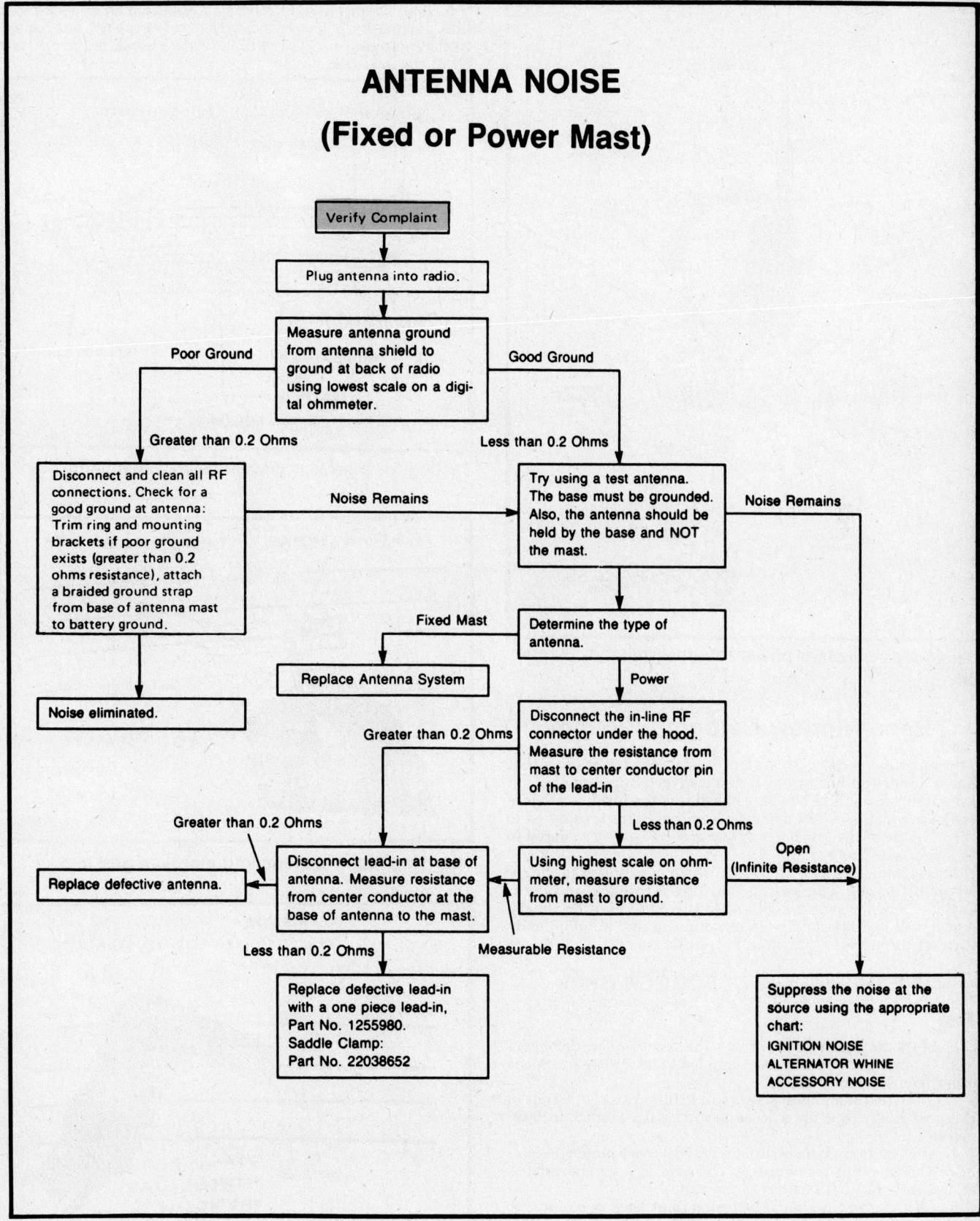

Verify Complaint

Plug antenna into radio.

Measure antenna ground from antenna shield to ground at back of radio using lowest scale on a digital ohmmeter.

Poor Ground — Greater than 0.2 Ohms

Good Ground — Less than 0.2 Ohms

Disconnect and clean all RF connections. Check for a good ground at antenna: Trim ring and mounting brackets if poor ground exists (greater than 0.2 ohms resistance), attach a braided ground strap from base of antenna mast to battery ground.

Noise Remains

Try using a test antenna. The base must be grounded. Also, the antenna should be held by the base and NOT the mast.

Noise Remains

Determine the type of antenna.

Fixed Mast

Replace Antenna System

Noise eliminated.

Power

Disconnect the in-line RF connector under the hood. Measure the resistance from mast to center conductor pin of the lead-in

Greater than 0.2 Ohms

Less than 0.2 Ohms

Greater than 0.2 Ohms

Replace defective antenna.

Disconnect lead-in at base of antenna. Measure resistance from center conductor at the base of antenna to the mast.

Using highest scale on ohmmeter, measure resistance from mast to ground.

Open (Infinite Resistance)

Measurable Resistance

Less than 0.2 Ohms

Replace defective lead-in with a one piece lead-in, Part No. 1255980. Saddle Clamp: Part No. 22038652

Suppress the noise at the source using the appropriate chart:
IGNITION NOISE
ALTERNATOR WHINE
ACCESSORY NOISE

Power antenna diagnosis chart—antenna inoperative (cont.)

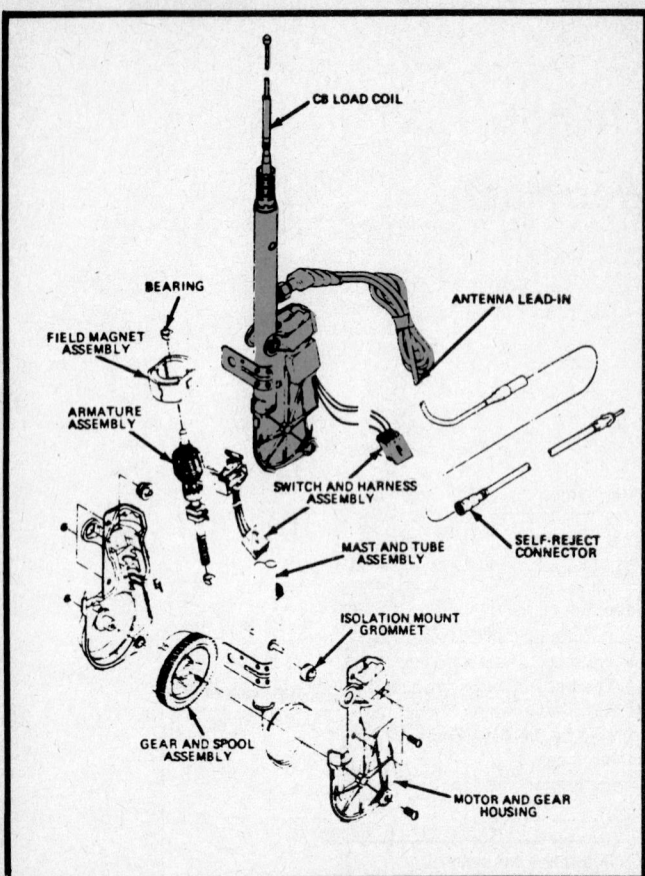

Exploded view of the power antenna (tri-band) assembly

Rear Window Defogger System

The rear window defogger system consists of a tinted glass that has a number of horizontal ceramic silver compound element lines and two vertical bus bars baked into the inside surface of the rear winshield. The defogger lead (hot) wire is soldered to the left side of the bus bar and the ground wire is soldered to the right side bus bar.

The system uses a on-off switch which is mounted to the instrument panel. The switch contains a integral indicator switch. Once the switch is placed in the "ON" position the defogger will operate for five to ten minutes and automatically turn off through the use of an automatic timer.

REAR WINDOW DEFOGGER GRID

Test

1. Start the engine and turn on the rear window defogger.
2. Ground one end of a test lamp lead and lightly touch the other lead to each grid line.
3. If the test lamp bulb shows full brilliance at both ends of the grid line check for a loose ground wire contact to body metal.
4. The test lamp bulb brilliance will decrease proportionately to the increase resistance in the grid line as the prod is moved from the left bus bar to the right.
5. All the grid lines must be tested in at least two places to eliminate the possibility of bridging a break. For best results, contact each grid line a few inches either side of the glass centerline.

6. If an abnormal light reading is apparent on a specific grid line, place test the lamp prod on the grid at the left bus bar until the light goes out. This will indicate a break in the continuity of the grid line.

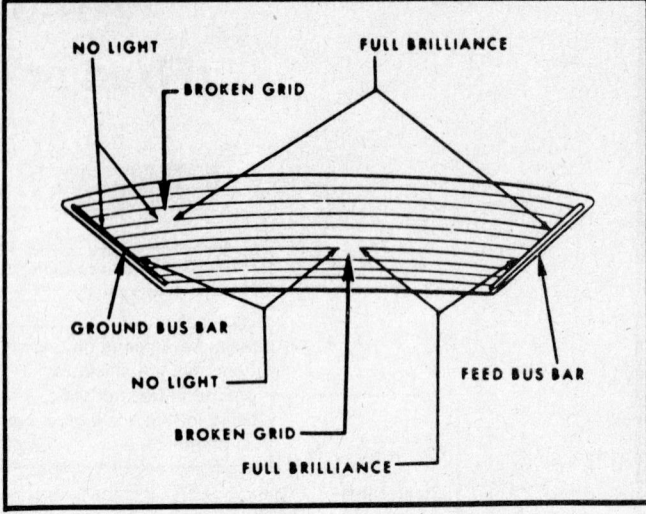

Testing for a broken grid line with a test lamp

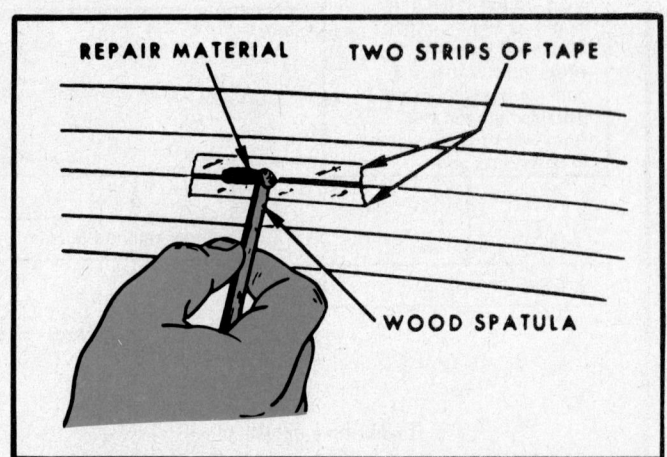

Applying repair materials to a broken grid line

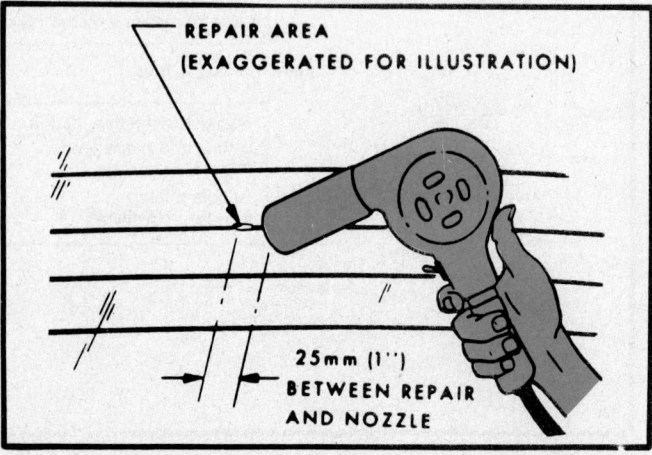

Using the heat gun to apply heat to a repaired grid line

NOTE: To repair a broken grid line there is a Rear Window Defogger Kit (#1052858) available from the manufacturer and the enclosed manufactures instruction should be followed for a proper grid repair. A heat gun capable of 500°F, will also be needed during the grid line repairs.

Rear Window Defogger Troubleshooting

1. Check the rear window defogger fuse, and replace if blown.

2. Check the stop-hazard fuse by operating the hazard flasher, Cadillac only.

3. Check the A/C fuse by operating the air conditioning system, Cadillac only.

4. Make sure all the ground and connectors are clean and tight.

5. If the symptom involves only the time that the defogger operates, replace the defogger control.

6. If the resistance is incorrect, troubleshoot the defogger grid.

7. If all measurementa are correct for both the voltage and the resistance, replace the defogger control with a new one.

Rear Window Defogger System Check

1. Turn the defogger control switch on and check to see that the indicator lamp comes on and that the rear window defogger grid gets hot (check to see that the RH and LH ouside mirrors become warm, if the vehicle is equipped with heated mirrors).

2. Wait approximately ten minutes and the indicator lamp should go off. Turn the defogger control switch on again and check to see if the indicator lamp goes off after five minutes.

3. Again turn on the defogger control switch, check to see that the indicator lamp comes on and as soon as it comes off turn the switch off. The indicator lamp should go off and the rear window defogger grid should cool down.

Braided Lead Wire Repair

The rear window defogger bus bar lead wire or terminal can be reattached by resoldering using a solder containing three percent silver and rosin flux paste.

1. Before soldering the bus bar, prepair the area in question by buffing it with a fine steel wool pad. This will remove the oxide coating formed during the glass manufacture.

2. Apply a paste type rosin flux in small amounts to the wire lead and bus bar repair area using a flux brush.

3. The soldering iron tip should be coated with the soldered beforehand. Use only enough heat to melt the solder and only enough solder to ensure a complete repair.

4. Do not over heat the wire when resoldering it to the bus bar.

Power Sunroof/Moonroof

The electrically operated sunroof is controlled by a two-position switch mounted in the windshield header area of the headlining on some models and in the sunshade lamp reatainer assembly on other models.

During the opening cycle, the sunroof sliding panel retracts on guide channels into the storage area of the sunroof housing. During the closing cycle as the sunroof panel moves forward and nears the end of its forward travel, the rear portion initially moves upward on ramps located on the inboard side of the guide channels.

The panel continues to move forward until the front support rollers contact the front stops. The motor driven cables continue forward until the front support rollers are located on top of the front cable ramps and the rear lifter links of the cable assemblies are vertical.

The sunroof assembly is equipped with water drain tubes, it is important to keep these drain tubes open. So it is recommended to blow compressed air through the drain tubes at regular intervals, in order to keep the drain tubes clear.

Vertical Adjustments At The Front Of The Panel

For easy access to the adjustment provisions, slide the sunroof panel rearward into the sunroof housing.

1. To obtain a flush fit with the roof, insert tool J-28652, BT-7919 or equivalent under the guide 3 inches rearward of screws and loosen the two screws on the front guide with a T-25 star-shaped recess driver enough to disengage serrations provided on a guide rail and guide plate.

2. To raise the panel upward, insert toll J-28652, BT-7919 or equivalent between the housing and the guide, loosen the two screws and rotate the tool sideways to the cam rail upward. Hold the guide assembly in position with the tool until the screws are tightened, thus engaging serrations.

3. After the proper alignment is obtained, tighten the screws to the proper torque specification. For proper adjustment use the following procedure.

    a. The lifter links located at the rear cable supports must be vertical or the top of the link slightly rearward of vertical.

    b. The sliding panel front support rollers must be positioned on top of the cable guide ramps.

4. Adjust the opposite front guide in the same manner if necessary. If an additional adjustment is necessary, a stack of washers not to exceed $\frac{1}{16}$ in. thick can be added over the panel adjusting studs before the supports are installed.

Vertical Adjustments At The Rear Of The Panel

1. To obtain a flush fit with the roof, insert tool J-28652, BT-

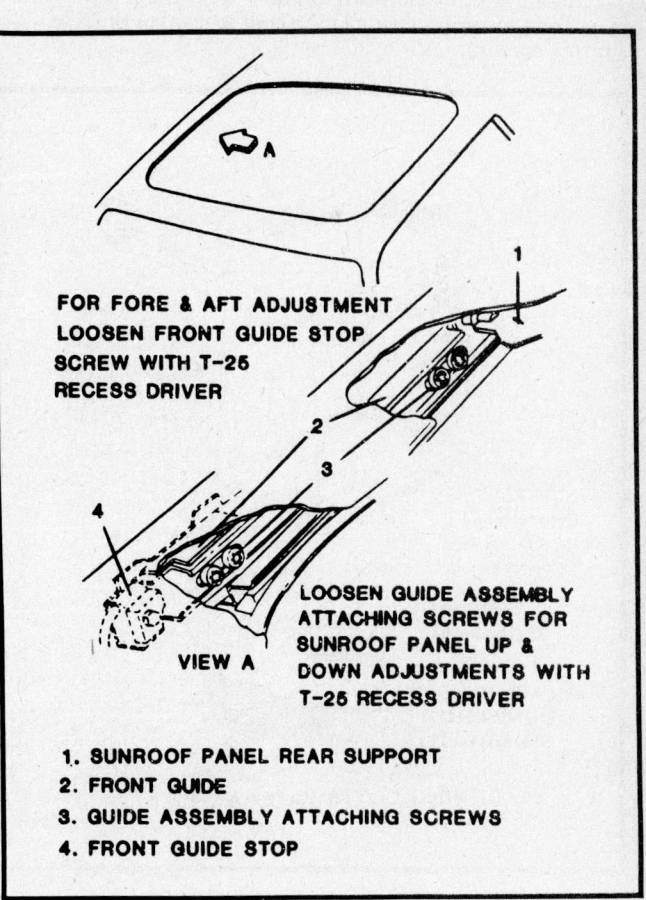

FOR FORE & AFT ADJUSTMENT LOOSEN FRONT GUIDE STOP SCREW WITH T-25 RECESS DRIVER

LOOSEN GUIDE ASSEMBLY ATTACHING SCREWS FOR SUNROOF PANEL UP & DOWN ADJUSTMENTS WITH T-25 RECESS DRIVER

VIEW A

1. SUNROOF PANEL REAR SUPPORT
2. FRONT GUIDE
3. GUIDE ASSEMBLY ATTACHING SCREWS
4. FRONT GUIDE STOP

Sunroof panel adjustment procedure

7919 or equivalent under the guide 3 inches forward of the rear adjustment screws.

2. Loosen the two screws at the rear corners of the guide assembly. Follow Steps 2, 3 and 4 of the front panel adjustment procedure.

3. Adjust the opposite rear guide in the same manner, if necessary.

Sunroof Panel Alignment

1. Close the roof panel to find which side of the panel jams. With the roof closed, remove the actuator.

2. Align the panel within the opening to desired position, assuring constant margins.

3. Reinstall the actuator.

Horizontal Adjustment Of The Sliding Panel

1. To obtain the porper fit in the center of the roof opening, place the sliding panel in the open position. Loosen the front quide stops, slide the stops forward or rearward, tighten the guide screws and close the sliding panel.

2. The addtional adjustment can be achieved by loosening all eight support to sliding panel nuts (with the sliding panel in the closed position). Move the sliding panel either fore or aft and tighten the nuts.

SUNROOF HEADLINER RETAINER

Removal and Installation

1. Remove the headlining close-out lace. Remove the headlining material from the headlining retainer.

2. Remove the headlining retainer from the housing flange by pulling inward starting at the ends located at the rear of the sunroof opening.

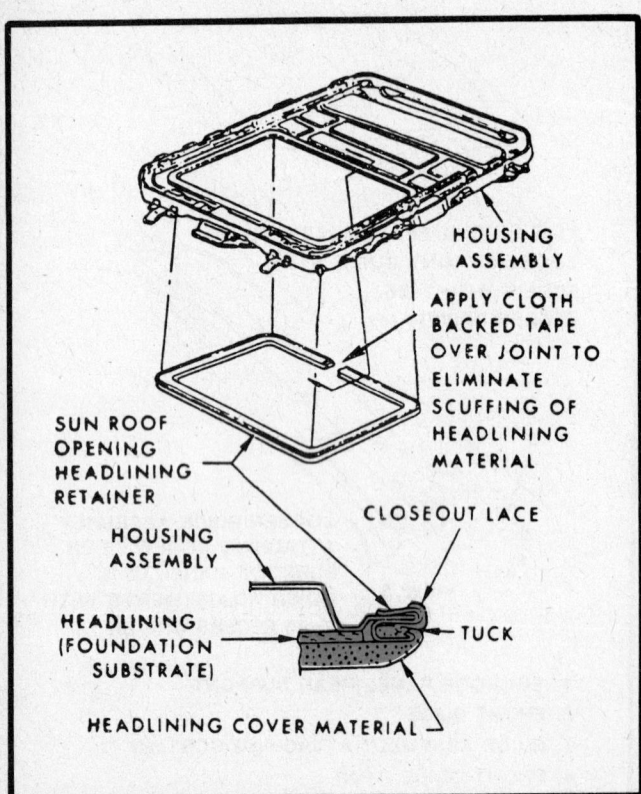

Headlining retainer and close-out lace—removal and installation

3. Install the headlining reatainer, place the ends of the retainer at the center of the rear line of the sunroof housing opening.

4. Tap the retainer onto the housing around the entire perimeter of the opening, corners must be fully installed.

SUNROOF ACTUATOR

The actuator is protected against any stall force imposed upon it by a slip clutch contained within the gearbox.

1. Place the sunroof sliding panel in the full rearward position. Remove the sunroof headlining close-out lace.

2. Remove the headlining material from the headlining retainer. Pull downward carefully on the front edge of hard headlining and remove the two actuator attaching screws.

3. Disengage the wire harness from the actuator. Remove the actuator assembly.

4. Insert the edge of the headlining into opening in the headliner retainer, using a headliner installer tool J-2772 or equivalent. Insert the headlining close-out lace starting at the left side center of the housing opening.

SUNROOF SLIDING PANEL SUNSHADE

Removal and Installation

1. Remove the sliding glass finishing cover with a downward and forward motion. Move the sliding glass panel to the full-rearward position.

2. Remove the guide retaining clips from studs located on the right hand side only , of the housing.

3. Remove the right side headlining guide. Remove the handle from the sunshade by removing the retaining screws.

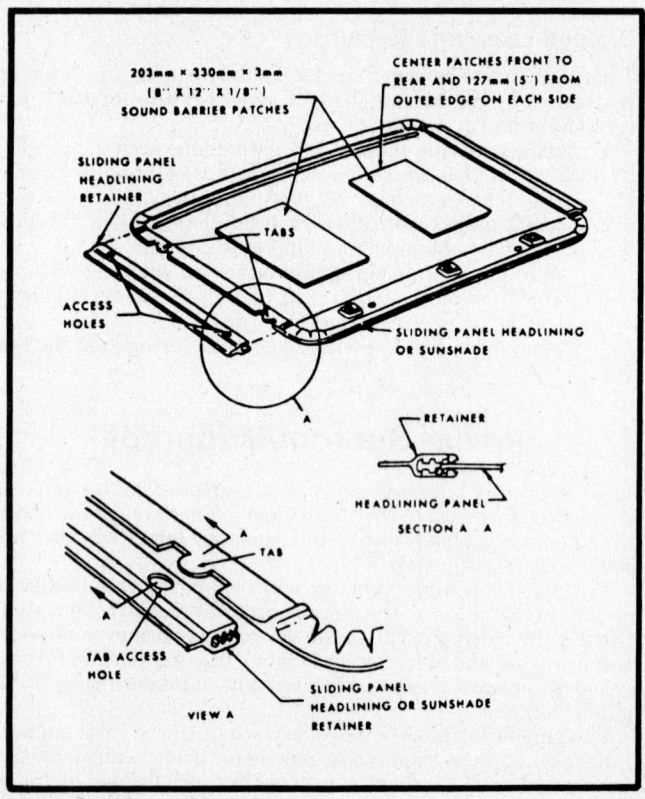

Sliding panel sunshade and side retainer—removal and installation

4. Disengage the sunshade from the housing. lifting upward and outward on the right side front corner of the sunshade. Remove the sunshade through the sunroof sliding panel opening.

5. Installation is the reverse order of the removal procedure. Make sure, when installing the right-hand side sunshade retainer, that the tab on the forward end of the rear sunshade retainer is over the rear end of the front sunshade retainer.

SUNROOF CONTROL SWITCH

This procedure is for the switch mounted in the windshield header area of the headlining.

Removal and Installation

1. Place the sunroof sliding panel in the full rearward position. Remove the sunroof opening headlining close-out lace.

2. Remove the headlining material from the headlining retainer along the front of the sunroof opening. Pull down hard the headlining enough to insert hand between the headlining and the actuator at the switch.

3. Compress the spring retainers. Carefully grip the switch toggle bezel with fingers and pull downward to remove the switch from the retainer in the headlining.

4. Be careful when removing the switch so as not to lose the switch retainer in the front roof cavity. Pull the electrical connector through the opening and disconnect. Remove the switch from the vehicle.

5. Installation is the reverse order of the removal procedure.

SWITCH MOUNTED IN THE SUNSHADE LAMP RETAINER ASSEMBLY

1. Remove both retainer lenses by inserting a thin-bladed tool between the lens and retainer, then snap the lens from the retainer.

2. Remove the screws from the retainer and lower the retainer to gain access for the switch.

3. Disconnect the switch wire harness and remove the switch from the retainer.

4. Installation is the reverse order of the removal procedure.

MAP LIGHT SUPPORT

Removal and Installation

1. Remove the sunshade rod and map light retainer. Remove the map light support attaching screws and remove the support.

2. Installation is the reverse order of the removal procedure.

SUNROOF SLIDING PANEL SUNSHADE SIDE RETAINER

Removal and Installation

1. Remove the sunroof sliding panel sunshade. Remove the retainer by first depressing the retaining tabs through a small access holes near the ends of the retainer.

2. Pull the outboard and disengage the retainer from the panel.

3. Installation is the reverse order of the removal procedure.

SUNROOF HOUSING ASSEMBLY

Removal and Installation

1. Place the sunshade in the stowed position . Move the sliding panel rearward until the front rollers on the sliding panel contact the bottom of the cable guide ramp.

2. Remove the garnish moldings, coat hooks, map light retainer and dome light. Remove the sunroof opening headlining close-out lace.

3. Remove the headlining material from the headlining retainer. Disengage the lower headheadlining.

4. Disconnect the wire harness from the switch and dome light, remove the headlining. Remove the dome light retaining studs and remove the hoses from the housing.

5. Remove the screws from each of the rear most side supports. Remove the screws holding the housing to the front header.

6. Support the sunroof housing and remove the nuts from the side front screws that retain the housing to the roof supports. Lower and remove the sunroof housing.

7. Installation is the reverse order of the removal procedure. Torque the nuts at the side front locations to 7 to 10 ft.lbs.

SUNROOF OPENING TRIM RETAINER

Removal and Installation

1. Remove the sunroof housing. Using a 1/8 in. drill with a drill stop set at 3/8 in. depth, drill out the retaining rivets.

2. Remove the retainer. Apply, as necessar, saturated urethane foam strip around the inner edge of the retainer.

3. Install the retainer and rivet it into position. Install the sunroof housing.

SUNROOF SLIDING GLASS PANEL

Removal and Installation

1. Remove the right or left side garnish moldings. Remove the sunshade, windshield side garnish molding and disengage headlining from the side garnish area for access to the housing attaching nuts and screws.

2. Remove the sliding glass finishing cover. Activate the sunroof sliding panel slightly to lower the sliding panel until the front rollers on the sliding panel make contact with the bottom surface of the cable guide ramp.

3. Position the sliding glass panel sunshade in the stowed position. Remove the attaching nuts from front and rear sliding panel supports. Move the cable fully rearward to remove the contact of the cable supports with the sliding panel.

4. Pull downward on one of the headlining to remove the double end screw attaching nuts and rear support rail retaining screws and lower the housing.

5. Tape the front edge of the roof opening to eliminate damage to the roof vinyl top or painted surface. Rotate and remove the sliding panel upward throught the roof opening.

6. Installation is the reverse order of the removal procedure.

SUNROOF CABLE AND CABLE CONDUIT

Removal and Installation

If one cable assembly is defective, replace both to assure the parallel travel of the sunroof.

1. Remove the plastic finishing cover around the glass. Remove the four front and four rear sliding panel support attaching nuts and slide the panel rearward into the module.

2. Remove the finishing lace, reatainer and headliner material across the front of the sunroof opening. Remove the black rubber filler located at the front opening between the sunroof housing and the roof.

3. Remove the map light assembly , if so equipped. Loosen the sunroof drive motor. Remove the center guide.

4. Remove the two upper and lower conduit attaching nuts and two front guide attaching nuts. Use a six-lobed socket head driver to remove the right and left guide stops.

5. Remove the screws holding the housing to the front header. Remove the side front nuts and screws that retain the housing to the roof support and partially lower the housing.

6. Raise the conduit assembly to clear the two outboard at-

CONDITION	POSSIBLE CAUSE	CORRECTION
1. Sunroof fails to rise or close completely.	1. Weak battery.	a. Start car motor to get proper battery voltage and activate system.
	2. Panel mispositioned in opening.	a. Loosen 8 nuts (with panel in closed position) and position panel. b. Loosen front guide stop and adjust fore or aft.
	3. Panel not flush to roof surface	a. Loosen guide assembly and adjust guide up or down. (Cable lifter links must be vertical for proper sealing.)
	4. Cable front guides and front guide stop(s) misaligned.	a. Loosen cable guide adjusting screws and raise or lower guide. b. Loosen front guide stop and adjust fore or aft.
	5. Cable assembly lifter link not positioned identically (right to left), out of synchronization.	a. Loosen sliding panel front support(s) and pivot support(s) forward or rearward and retighten. b. Remove actuator and adjust cable cams by sliding cables forward or rearward. (Cams must be in same position on each side.)
	6. Actuator slippage. Motor buzzing with no cable movement.	a. Tighten bolt in bottom of actuator. b. Replace actuator.
	7. Cable slippage, clicking or ratcheting sound.	a. Remove actuator and center guide and replace guide or actuator gear if damaged. b. Check cable at center guide area for wear or stripping; replace cable if damaged.
	8. Wrong sliding panel weatherstrip	a. Replace weatherstrip
2. Sunroof panel jammed in roof opening.	1. Broken or stripped cable.	a. Replace cable.
	2. Foreign material in guide.	a. Remove foreign material from guide.
	3. Cable jammed in conduit.	a. Replace cable and conduit.
	4. Side guide(s) out of adjustment.	a. Adjust guide(s).
3. Sunroof actuator inoperative (ignition switch on).	1. Short or open within sunroof wiring.	
	2. Faulty switch.	a. Replace switch.
	3. Defective actuator.	a. Replace actuator
4. Sunroof panel snaps or clicks when closing.	1. Rear cable support(s) mispositioned to panel.	a. Loosen support(s) and adjust.

Sunroof diagnosis chart

taching studs. Remove the loose ends of each cable out of the left and right conduit.

7. Remove the right and left side conduits and remove the right and left drive cables.

8. Installation is the reverse order of the removal procedure.

Theft Deterrent System

This system is designed to provide a warning in the event of a forced entry throught the driver and passenger doors and trunk. When a forced entry is attempted, the alarm warning system will be tripped off. This will set the horns off and the exterior light to flash in unison for three to seven minutes. The starter interlock feature prevents the engine from starting if the warning system is tripped.

The alarm is tripped by opening switches strategically located in the door jambs, the door lock cylinders and the trunk lock cyclinder. When a door lock cylinder or trunk lock cylinder is violated by rotating it or moving it in or out, or if any door is opened without using the key, the alarm will be actuated by the controller.

The controller is linked to the required circuitry with just two connectors. One is a 13 way connector and the other is a 6 way connector. The controller and alarm relay is serviced only as a unit. When all circuits external to the controller are found to be operating normally and the system does not operate properly, the controller and the relay must be repaired.

There is a 25 amp in-line fuse in the feed line to the horns which also supplies the main power to the controller . There also a 25 amp in-line fuse which feeds power to the low beam and parking lamps.

Arming The System

1. Close all the windows, place the shift lever in the park position. Turn the ignition to the lock position and remove the key.

2. Open any door, lock the doors with the electrical switch, or manually if equipped with the manual system. Close the doors.

3. The system is now armed to sound the alarm if any of the door jamb or tamper switches are activated or tripped.

NOTE: The system can also be armed with the windows open. The alarm will be disarmed only when a door is opened with a key.

4. When the doors are opened during the arming procedure, the security system warning light located in the dash panel will flash intermittently to remind the driver to lock the doors and arm the system.

5. The light will glow steadily after the doors are locked and go on and off within 6 seconds after the doors have been closed.

Disarming The System

1. To disarm the system, once the security light glows steadily and the doors are still open, the electric door switch to the unlock position.

2. To disarm it, once the doors have been closed, unlock the door with a key from the outside or turn the ignition switch to the on position from inside the car.

3. To deactivate the alarm once it is in operation (that is actually sounding) unlock one of the front doors with a key.

Troubleshooting

Mechanical and corrosion factors on both types of cylinder tamper switches can cause the system to activate for no apparent reason. If this condition occurs, check the lock cylinder for looseness. Any movement of the cylinders equipped with a tamper switch could cause the switch to activated the alarm.

One possible cause for this problem may be a retainer that does not lock firmly to the cylinder. This proble can be corrected, by replacing the old retainer with a new retainer.

Loose, corroded or poorly adjusted jamb switches can also cause the system to activate without reason, Check the jamb switches for corrosion and replace as necessary. Check the jamb switches for corrosion and replace as necessary. Check and adjust the switches to ensure that they remain in the off position when the doors are fully closed.

The door jamb switches can be adjusted by turning the adjustment nut located at the base of the switch. With either lock cylinder or jamb switches, check the ground wires for corrosion and repair or replace as necessary.

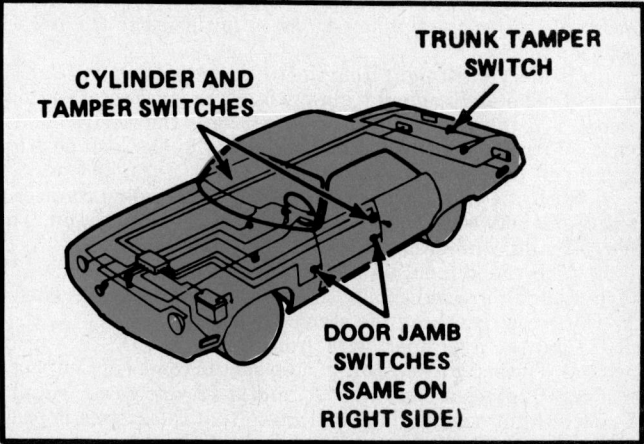

Cylinder, tamper and door jam switches—location

Diode Test

The diode is located under the instrument panel in the light blue wire from the terminal J of the controller to the driver's front door jamb switch. Use the following procedure to check for the proper operation of the diode.

1. Unplug the connector at the diode. Attach one probe of a suitable ohmmeter to each side of the diode and see if there is continuity present.

2. Reverse the ohmmeter probes, and check for continuity.
   a. The diode is working properly when there is continuity present with the probed attached in one position only.
   b. The diode is not working properly when the ohmmeter shows continuity with the probes ends in both positions or does not show continuity with the probe ends in either position.

3. Replace the diode as necessary.

DIAGNOSING THE THEFT DETERRENT ELECTRICAL SYSTEM

To check the electrical system, a test light and a jumper wire will be needed. All the switches are to be in the off position unless other wise specified. All test are to made with the 13 and 6 way connectors disconnected. If they are left connected, the wrong test results could be obtained.

Controller Test (With Controller Harness Disconnected)

1. Connect one test light to the "N" terminal at the connector and a suitable ground. The test light should glow, which will indicate a power supply to the horns and controller.

2. Connect a test light between the "M" terminal and a suitable ground. The light should glow only when the electrical door lock switch in the armrest is moved to the unlock position.

3. Connect the test light between terminal "B" and a 12 volt power supply. The light should glow at its full brightness only if the doors are locked. If any door is unlocked, the light should not glow

4. Connect the test light between terminal "K" and a good ground. The test light should glow only when the ignition switch is turned on. If not check for a bad fuse in the fuse block.

5. Connect a test light between terminal "J" and a 12 volt power supply. The light should glow to its full brightness only if a door is opened. If the test light glows when the doors are closed, a door or trunk lock cylinder may have been tampered with.

6. Connect the test light between the "H" terminal and a 12 volt power supply. The test light should glow at its full brightness only when the outside door key is turned to the unlock position.

7. Connect a test light from the "G" terminal and a suitablee ground. The light should glow while the electric door lock switch is being used, indicating the power to the electrical door lock switches. The test light should light in the lock position and go off in the unlock position.

8. With the relay harness installed to the relay, connect a test light between the "F" terminal and a good ground. The horn should sound and the lights should come on.

9. With the key on, a test light connected between the "E" terminal and ground should make the relay open, preventing 12 volts from reaching the starter.

10. Connect a jumper wire from terminal "D" to a good ground. The security warning lamp should come on. Connect a test light between terminal "A" and a 12 volt power supply. The test light should glow, indicating that the system is properly grounded. Use a jumper wire to check the circuits in the 6-way harness connector to the relay.

Relay Test (With The Relay Harness Disconnected)

1. Connect a jumper wire between the "A" terminal and the "B" terminal connectors. The horns should sound indicating power to the horns and complete a horn circuit to ground.

2. Connect a jumper wire between the "D" and "C" terminal connectors. The park, tail and side marker lights should come on. Connect a jumper wire between the "D" and "E" terminal connectors. The low beam headlights should come on.

3. With the relay harness connected, place a jumper wire from terminal "F" to the ground. The relay should click (close) and activate the lights and horn circuits.

4. Checking each of the circuits in this manner with the nor-mal results should indicate that all circuits are complete. If any of these test fail, check the components, fuses or circuit breakers affecting the particular circuit.

5. Repair or replace the component or wiring to complete the circuit. If all circuits external to the controller are complete and trouble-free, the controller and alarm relay should be repaired or replaced.

THEFT DETERRENT CONTROLLER AND RELAY

Removal and Installation
CADILLAC BROUGHAM

1. Unlock the door with the key. Disconnect the negative battery cable.

2. Remove the left-hand sound insulator. Remove the two screws securing controller and relay to the bracket. The bracket is attached to the brake pedal support bracket.

3. Disconnect the electrical connectors from the controller and relay. Cut the strap holding the relay to the controller and separate.

4. Installation is the reverse order of the removal procedure. Check for proper operation of the theft deterrent system.

ELDORADO AND SEVILLE

1. Unlock the door with the key. Disconnect the negative battery cable.

2. Remove the left-hand sound insulator. Remove the two screws securing theft deterrent bracket to the accelerator ped-al lever plate.

3. Disconnect the electrical connectors from the controller assembly. Cut the strap holding the relay to the controller and separate.

4. Installation is the reverse order of the removal procedure. Check for proper operation of the theft deterrent system.

ALL OTHER MODELS

1. Unlock the door with the key. Disconnect the negative battery cable.

2. Disconnect the 13-way and 6-way connectors at the con-troller. Remove the two mounting screws holding the control-ler to the bracket and remove the controller assembly.

3. Installation is the reverse order of the removal procedure. Check for proper operation of the theft deterrent system.

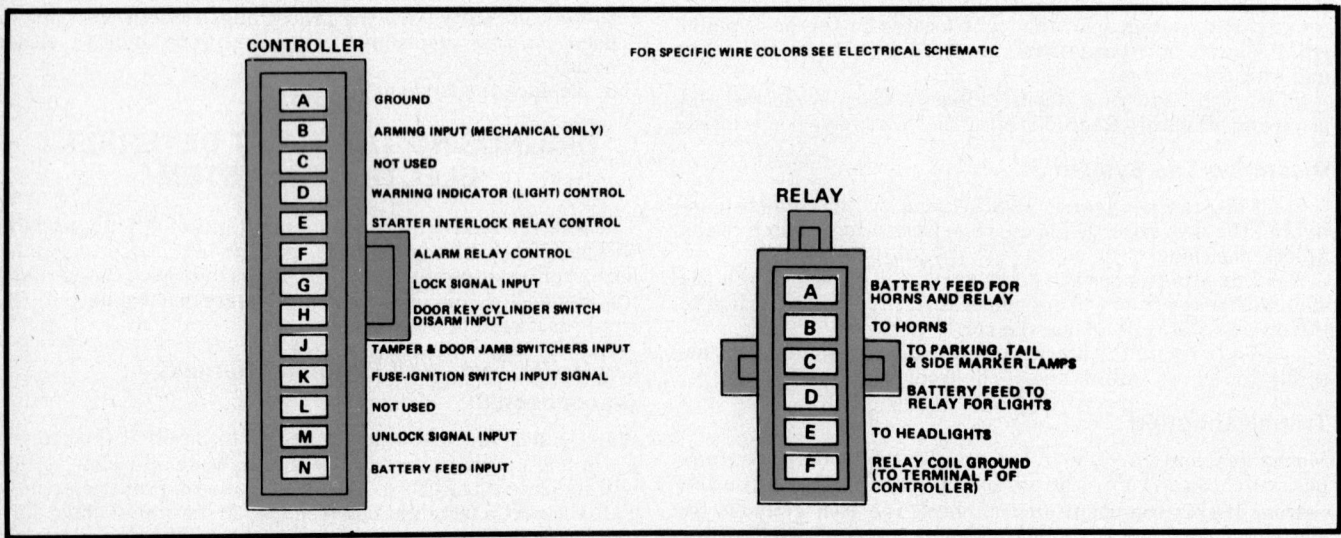

Controller and relay harness connectors

COMPREHENSIVE TROUBLESHOOTING GUIDE

System Won't Disarm

- CHECK LOCK CYLINDER SWITCHES FOR LOOSENESS.
- TRY TO DISARM THE SYSTEM USING A KEY IN THE PASSENGER DOOR LOCK CYLINDER. (THIS WILL TELL IF THERE IS A PROBLEM ON THE DRIVER'S SIDE.)
- IF SYSTEM DISARMS, CHECK FOR AN OPEN IN THE LIGHT-GREEN WIRE LEADING TO THE LOCK CYLINDER IN THE DRIVER'S SIDE DOOR.
- IF NO OPEN IN THE WIRE, REPLACE THE LOCK CYLINDER SWITCH ASSEMBLY.

System Won't Disarm from Either Door

- HOLD THE LOCK CYLINDER IN THE UNLOCK POSITION WITH THE DOOR KEY.
- CHECK FOR AN OPEN IN THE LIGHT-GREEN WIRE COMING FROM THE CONTROLLER, TERMINAL H.

System Goes Off by Itself

- CHECK THE DIODE (LOCATED UNDER THE DASH IN THE LT. BLUE WIRE FROM TERMINAL J OF CONTROLLER TO DRIVER'S FRONT DOOR JAMB SWITCH).
- ON CARS EQUIPPED WITH AUTOMATIC DOOR LOCKS (ADL), CHECK FOR DIODE IN YELLOW WIRE FROM DOOR UNLOCK RELAY TO DRIVER'S DOOR LOCK CYLINDER SWITCH.
- CHECK JAMB SWITCHES AND GROUND WIRES FOR CORROSION AND CLEAN OR REPLACE AS NECESSARY.
- CHECK LOCK CYLINDERS, TAMPER SWITCHES, AND THE DOOR JAMB SWITCH WIRE FOR LOOSENESS.

Security Light Inoperative

- CHECK 20 AMP FUSES (SEE ELECTRICAL DIAGNOSIS SECTION).
- CHECK SECURITY LIGHT BULB.
- CHECK FOR A BREAK IN THE ORANGE WIRE LEADING TO THE BULB.
- CHECK THE DIODE (LOCATED UNDER THE DASH IN THE LT. BLUE WIRE FROM TERMINAL J OF CONTROLLER TO DRIVER'S FRONT DOOR JAMB SWITCH).

Security Light Glows But System Won't Disarm

- CHECK TO SEE IF EITHER DOOR OR TRUNK CYLINDER SWITCHES HAVE BEEN TAMPERED WITH.
- CHECK TAMPER SWITCHES FOR LOOSENESS.
- CHECK FOR FRAYS OR PINCHED WIRES TO THE CYLINDER AND JAMB SWITCHES.
- CHECK JAMB SWITCHES FOR PROPER ADJUSTMENT.
- CHECK CIRCUITS EXTERNAL TO THE CONTROLLER. (PLEASE SEE WIRING DIAGRAMS.)
- IF ALL CIRCUITS EXTERNAL TO THE CONTROLLER ARE COMPLETE, SEND THE CONTROLLER AND RELAY TO AN AUTHORIZED REPAIR STATION FOR SERVICE.

Security Light Blinks On and Off

- CHECK FOR LOOSE TAMPER SWITCHES.
- CHECK WIRE BETWEEN DOOR JAMB SWITCH AND CONTROLLER FOR PINCH OR FRAY.
- CHECK WIRE LEADING TO TAMPER SWITCHES.
- CHECK TO SEE THAT LIGHT BLUE WIRE IS PROTECTED BY PLASTIC CONDUIT.
- CHECK DOOR LOCKED SWITCHES AND WIRING.

Theft deterrent system troubleshooting chart

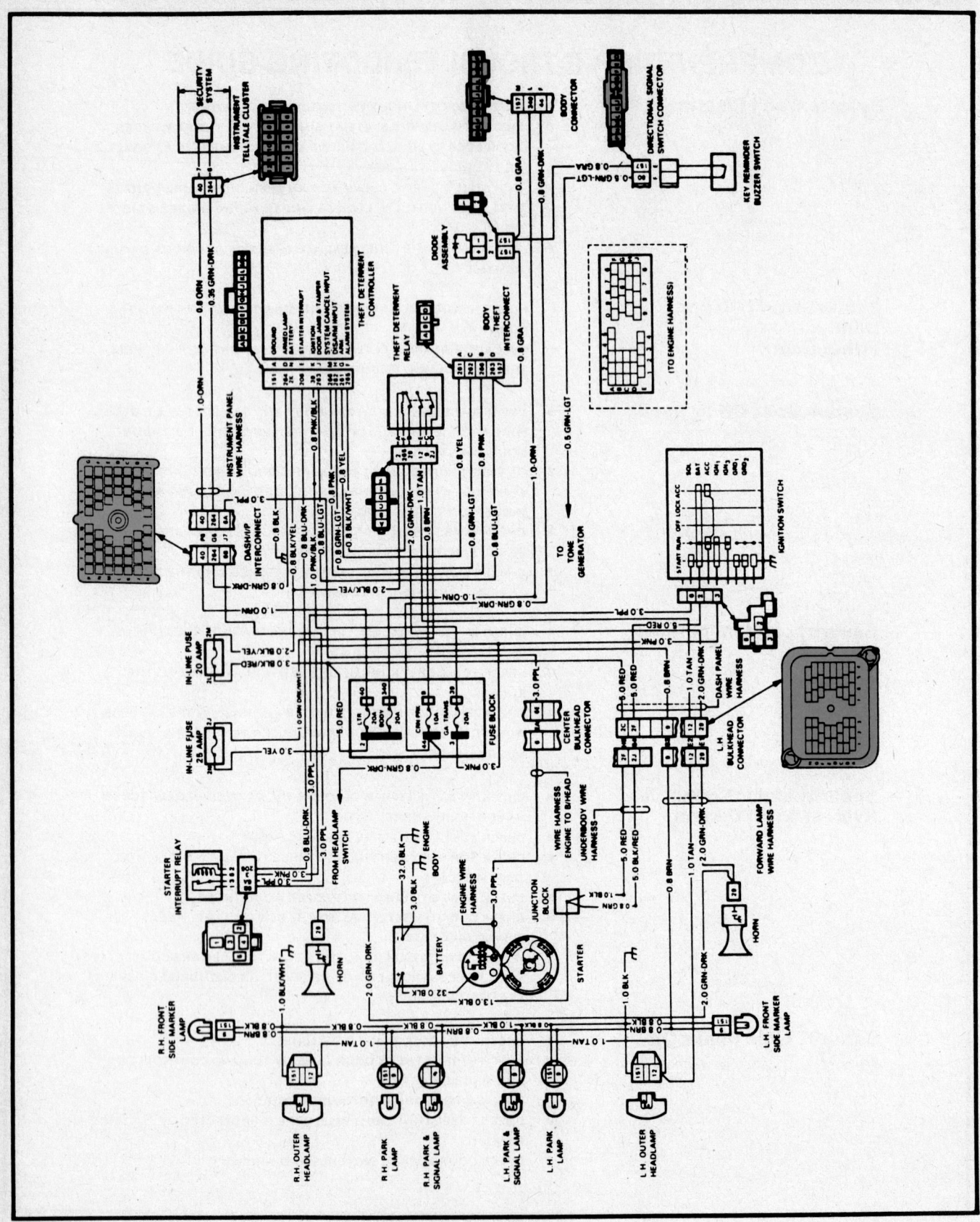

Theft deterrent system wiring schematic—Cadillac Brougham

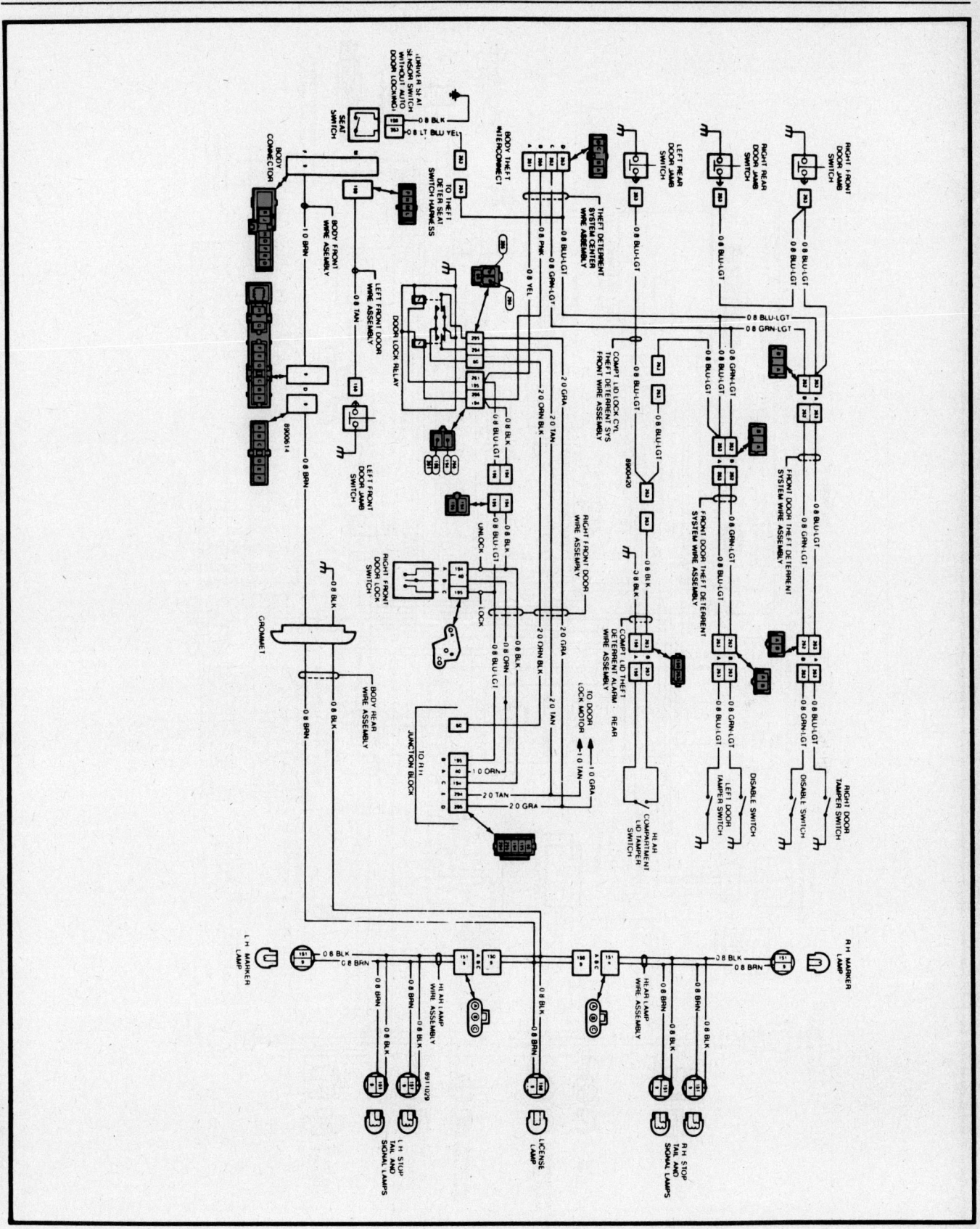

Theft deterrent system wiring schematic—Cadillac Brougham (cont.)

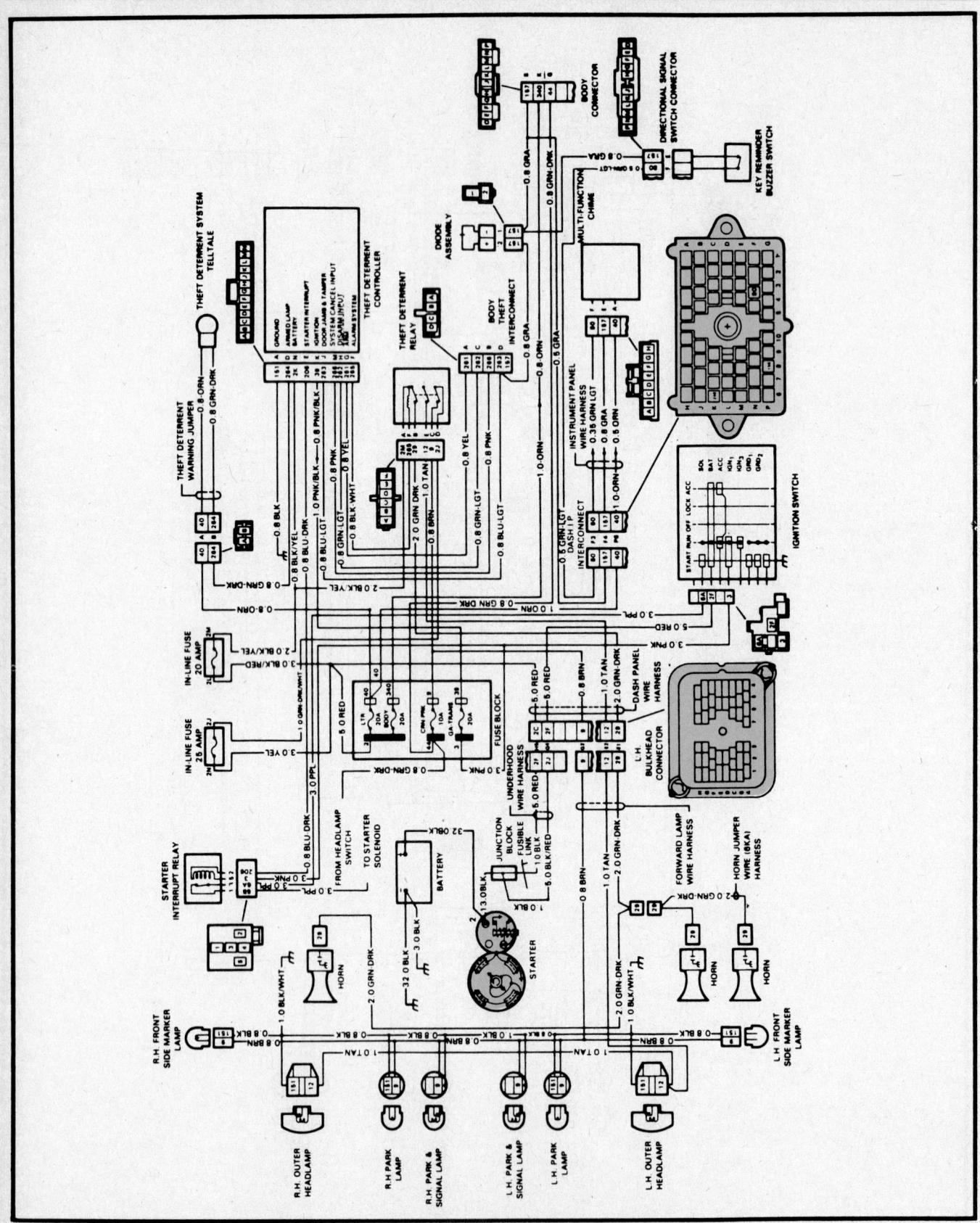

Theft deterrent system wiring schematic—Eldorado/Seville

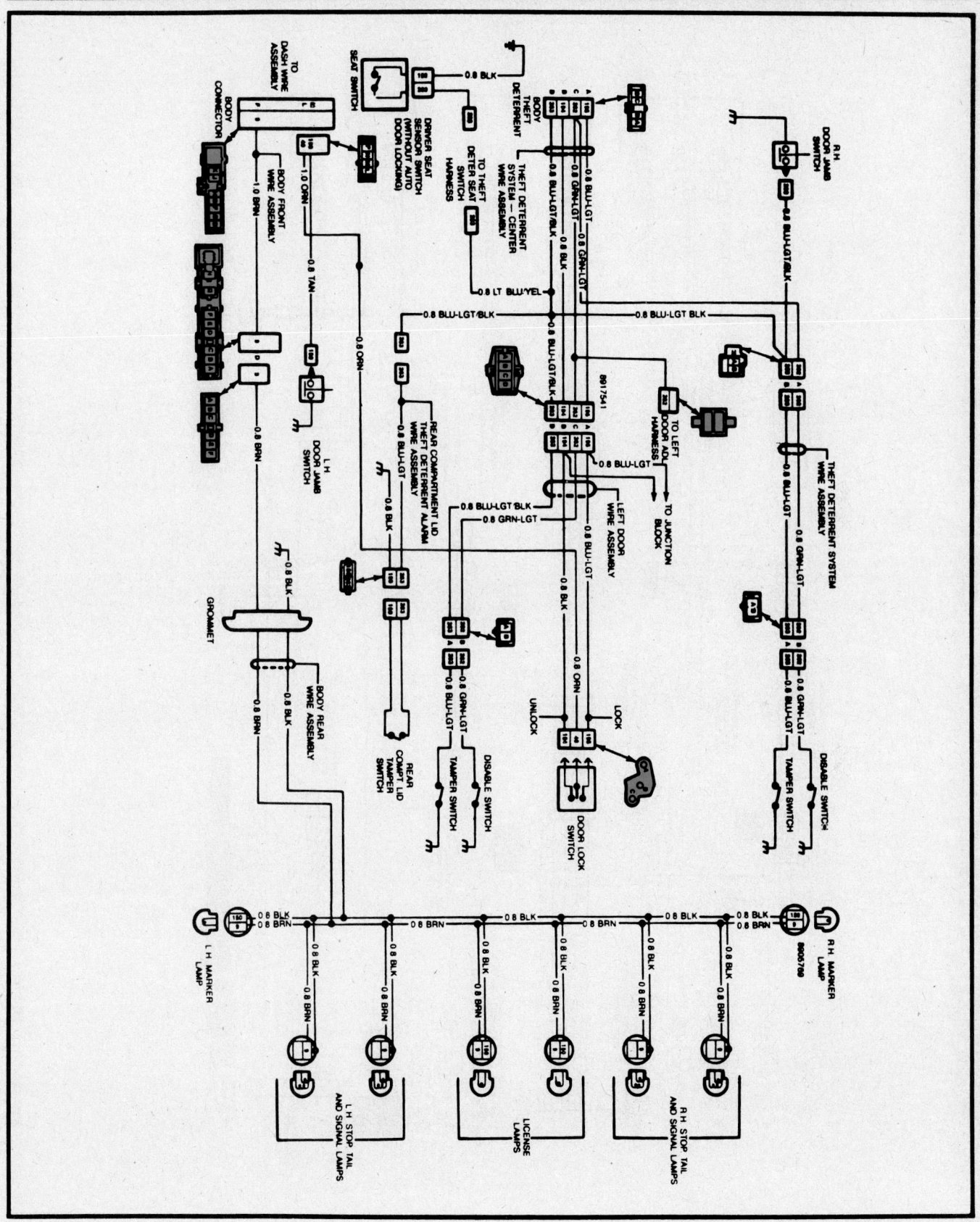

Theft deterrent system wiring schematic—Eldorado (cont.)

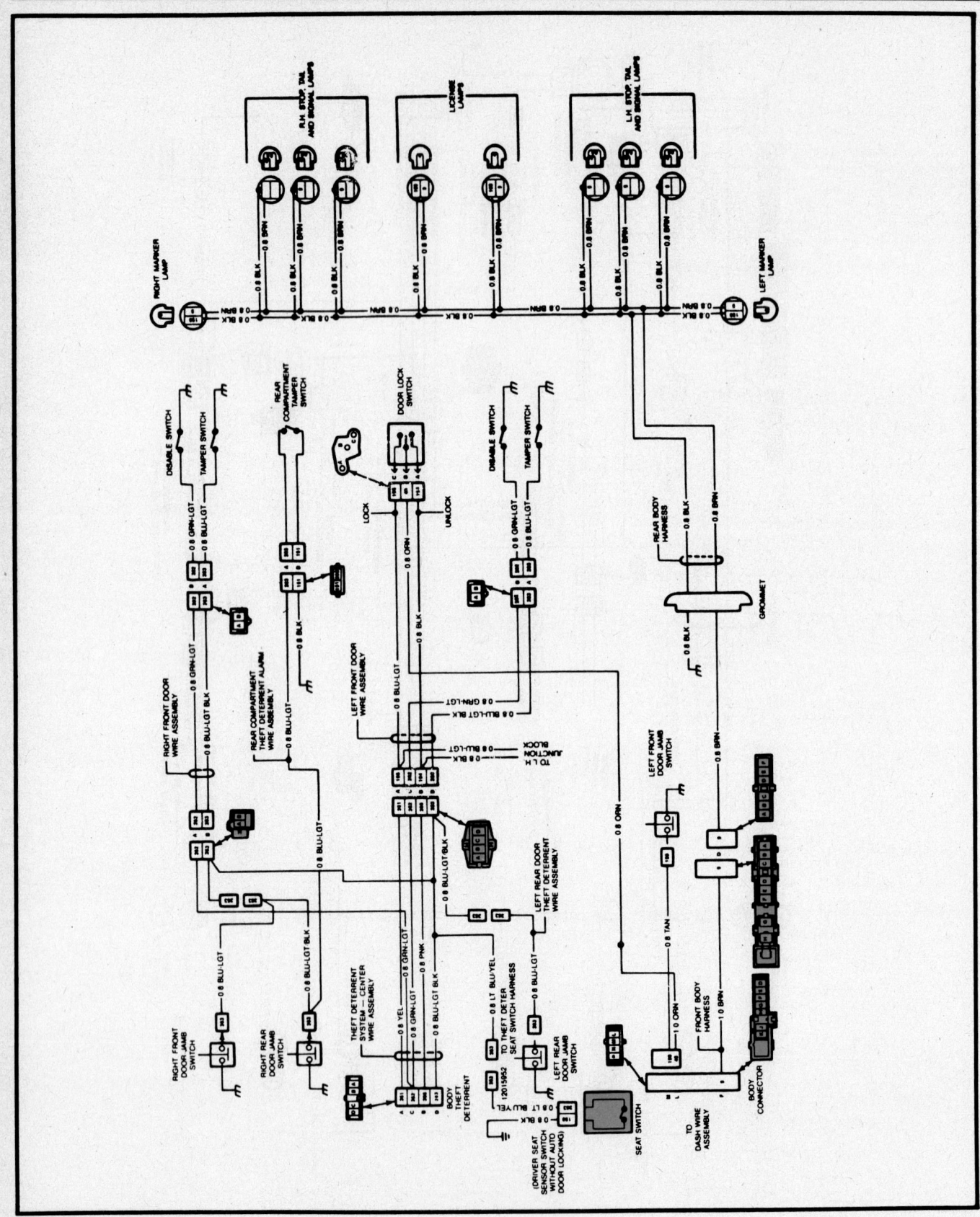

Theft deterrent system wiring schematic—Seville (cont.)

CHRYSLER IMPORTS

Power Mirrors

The mirrors are controlled by a single switch assembly located on the center console on some models and in the dash panel next to the steering column on other models. The motor that operates the mirror is part of the mirror assembly and cannot be replaced separately.

POWER MIRROR SWITCH

Removal and Installation

1982-84 CHAMP AND COLT

1. Disconnect the negative battery cable. Remove the floor console box mounting screws.
2. Remove the remote control switch wire harness and remove the switch from the console box.
3. Installation is the reverse order of the removal procedure.

1985 AND LATER

1. Disconnect the negative battery cable. Remove the parking brake cover.
2. Depress the claws on the power mirror switch and disconnect the electrical connector. Remove the switch.
3. Installation is the reverse order of the removal procedure.

COLT VISTA

1. Disconnect the negative battery cable. Remove the driver's side cover and remove the lap heater duct (2) retaining screws. Remove the lap duct from under the dash panel.
2. Remove the side bracket at the left hand side of the instrument panel.
3. Disconnect the power mirror switch connector. Remove the mirror switch retaining screws and remove the switch from the vehicle.
4. Installation is the reverse order of the removal procedure.

CONQUEST

1. Disconnect the negative battery cable. Remove the inner box from the rear console box.
2. Lift the front portion of the mirror switch assembly and remove the mirror switch assembly from the rear console box.
3. Disconnect the harness connector at the switch and remove the mirror switch assembly from the console.
4. Installation is the reverse order of the removal procedure.

SAPPORO/CHALLENGER

1. Disconnect the negative battery cable. Remove the inner box from the accessory box (on the console).
2. Remove the mirror switch out of the asccessory box by pressing the catch on the switch.
3. Disconnect the electrical connector and remove the switch from the console.
4. Installation is the reverse order of the removal procedure.

POWER MIRROR ASSEMBLY

Removal and Installation

CHAMP, COLT AND COLT VISTA

1. Remove the power mirror cover by pulling it inward.
2. Remove the power mirror mounting nuts, disconnect the electrical connections and remove the power mirror from the door.
3. Installation is the reverse order of the removal procedure.

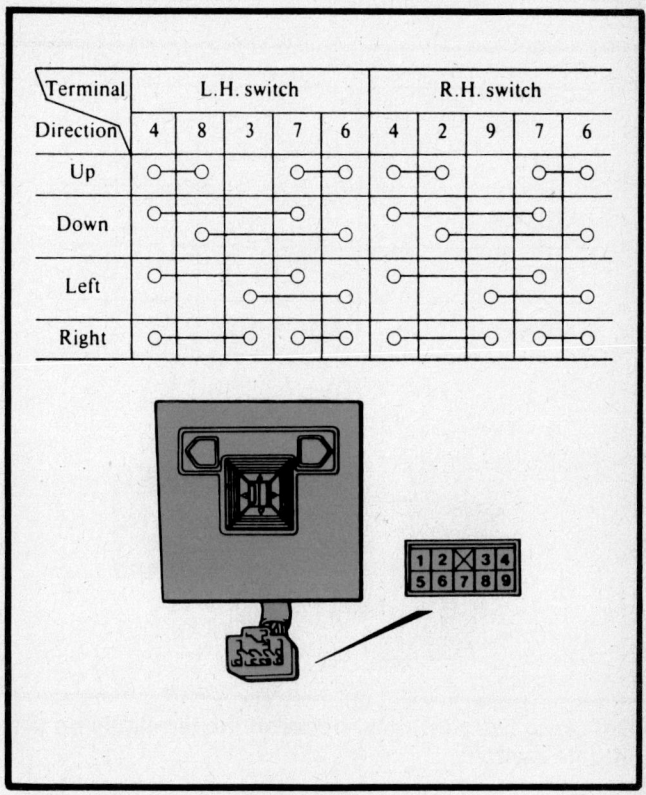

Terminal / Direction	L.H. switch					R.H. switch				
	4	8	3	7	6	4	2	9	7	6
Up	○—○			○—○		○—○			○—○	
Down	○	○		○—○		○	○		○—○	
Left	○		○			○		○		
Right	○—○		○		○	○—○		○		○

Checking for continuity between various terminals on the power mirror switch—conquest

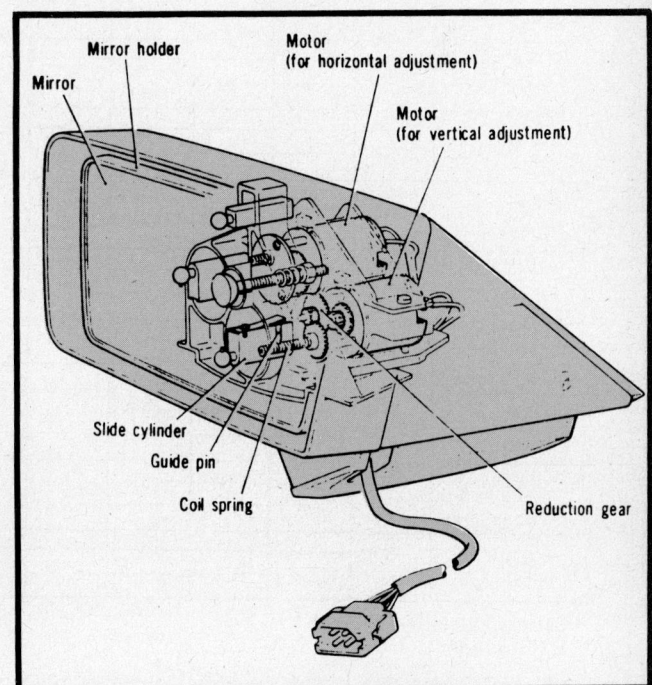

Labels: Mirror holder · Mirror · Motor (for horizontal adjustment) · Motor (for vertical adjustment) · Slide cylinder · Guide pin · Coil spring · Reduction gear

Typical Chrysler power mirror assembly

CONQUEST

1. Remove the door corner trim panel with a suitable trim stick. Remove the power mirror mounting nut.

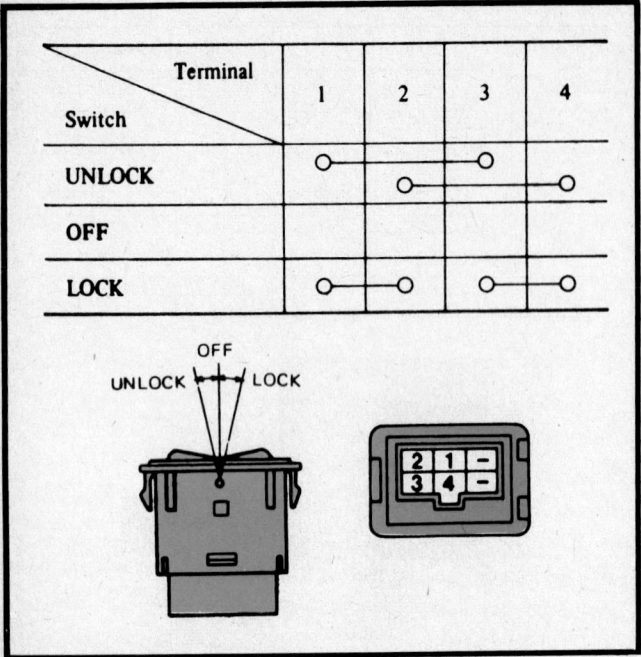

Checking the continuity between the terminals on the liftgate switch

2. Remove the boot and remove the door mirror mounting screws. Disconnect the the electrical connector and remove the power mirror from the door.

3. Installation is the reverse order of the removal procedure.

CHALLENGER/SAPPORO

1. Disconnect the negative battery cable. Remove the mirror retaining screw protective cap from the base of the mirror.

2. Remove the mirror retaining screws. Remove the mirror assembly from the bracket and disconnect the electrical connector. Remove the mirror from the door.

3. Installation is the reverse order of the removal procedure.

Power Liftgate Locking System

The power liftgate release system consists of a release switch (usually found on the left side of the dash panel), a wiring harness, lock actuator and linkage rods.

POWER LIFTGATE LOCKING SWITCH

Removal and Installation

1. Disconnect the negative battery cable. Using a suitable tool, slip the tool behind the liftgate switch far enough to depress the locking tab. Repeat this procedure for the opposite side of the switch. Be careful not to damage the instrument panel.

2. Disconnect the electrical connector and remove the switch from the dash panel.

3. Installation is the reverse order of the removal procedure.

Liftgate Switch Inspection

Move the liftgate locking switch to the on and off positions and check for continuity between the terminals.

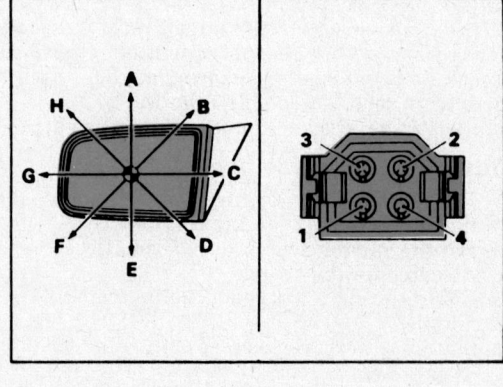

* Battery (Electrical source)
** E (Ground)

Checking for continuity between various terminals on the power mirror – conquest

LIFTGATE LOCK ACTUATOR

Removal and Installation

1. Disconnect the negative battery cable. Remove the liftgate trim and waterproof film.
2. Remove the actuator mounting bolts and then disconnect the tailgate lock wiring harness.
3. Disconnect the rod from the liftgate link and remove the actuator from the liftgate.
4. Installation is the reverse order of the removal procedure. Once installation is completed check the locking and unlocking operation. If the lock does not operate properly, adjust it by moving the the link assembly.

Power Antenna

The power antenna automatically raises the antenna mast to its full height whenever the radio and ignition are tuned on. The antenna retracts into the rear fender when either the ignition or the radio is turned off. The antenna relay is located on the rear trunk panel, to the left of the license plate.

POWER ANTENNA ASSEMBLY

Removal and Installation

Be sure the antenna mast is retracted before operation. Disconnect the antenna relay before removing the high floor side panel.

1. Disconnect the negative battery cable. Remove the trunk room side trim panel and high floor side panel.
2. Disconnect the harness connector, ground wire and antenna lead wire and the drain hose.

3. Remove the antenna assembly mounting nuts and take out the antenna assembly from the trunk room side.
4. Installation is the reverse order of the removal procedure.

Pole Assembly With Cable Replacement

1. Remove the antenna asembly. Remove the gear cover from the antenna motor.
2. Pull out the drive mechanism sub-assembly from the inside of the gear housing.
3. Remove the drum from the drive mechanism sub-assembly. Cut the cable and remove the drum and the rod sub-assembly.

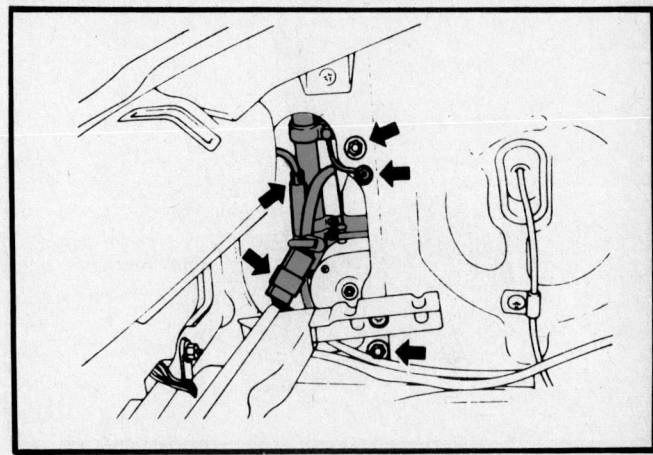

Power antenna assembly removal and installation

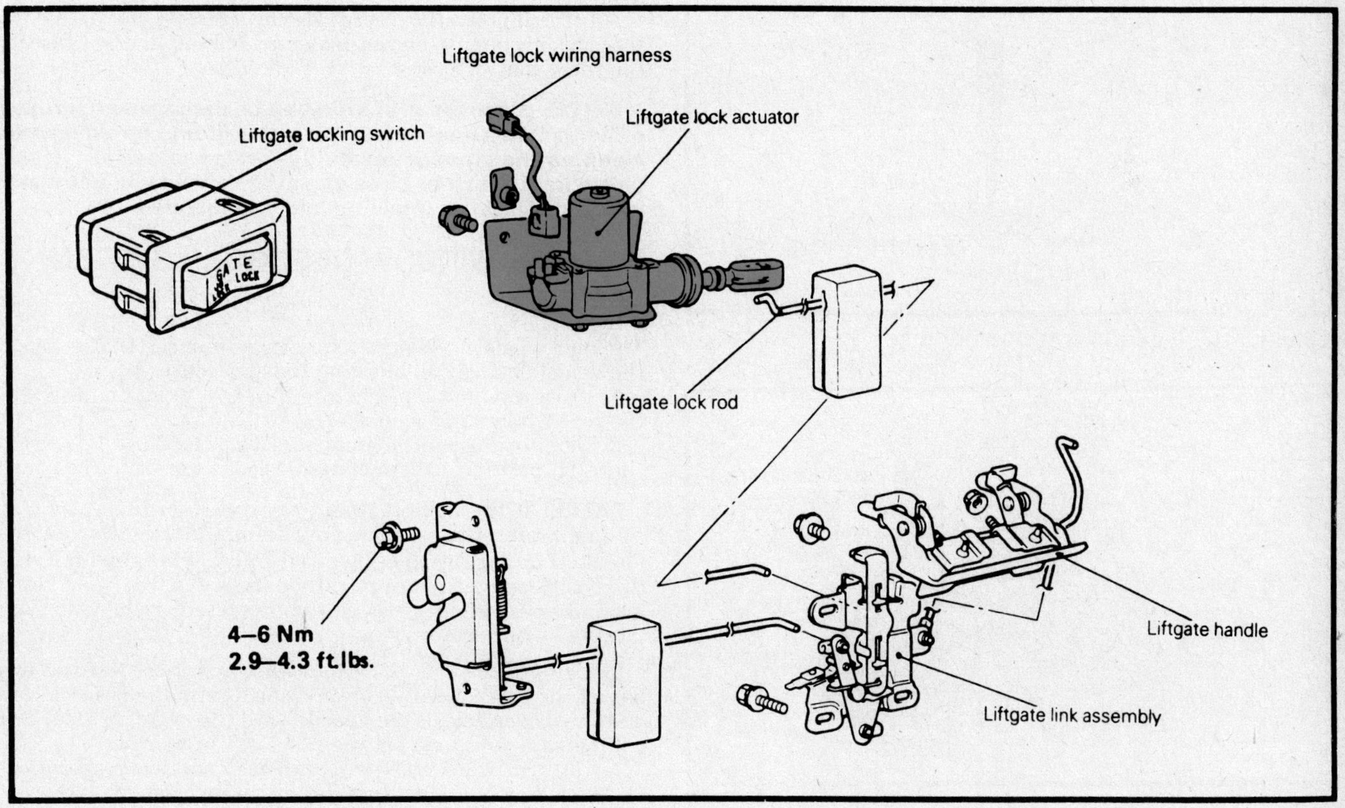

Exploded view of the power liftgate switch assembly

4. Pass the new cable through the gear housing before it is put into the drum. Using a suitable tool stake the cable at two positions. Install the drum to the drive mechanism sub-assembly.

5. With the antenna fully extended, install the drive mechanism sub-assembly. Install the two plate washers on the drive mechanism sub-assembly (be sure that the washers are not bound to the shaft).

6. Locate the projection of count lever so that it may engage with the recess in the limiter plate on the gear cover side, then install the counter lever. Check for proper operation before installing the assembly into the vehicle.

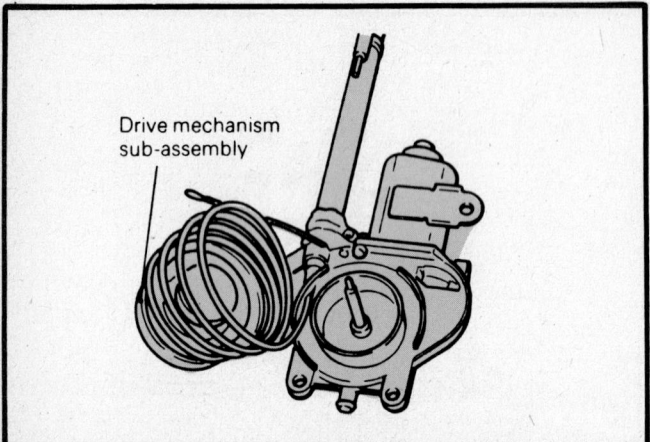

Removing the drive mechanism sub-assembly

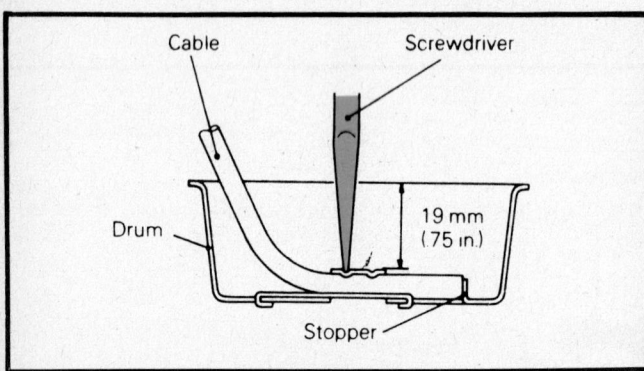

Staking the cable in two positions

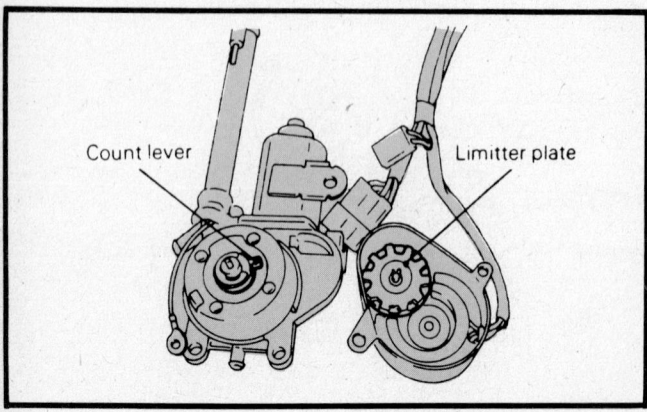

Location of the count lever and limitter plate

Power Antenna Relay Test

1. With the harness connector connected and the antenna mast extending and retracting, use a suitable voltmeter and check the voltage readings.

2. With the antenna mast extending, there should be -1 to +1 volts at the top left corner (1) terminal. There should be 10 to 13 volts at the upper right corner (4) terminal.

3. With the antenna mast retracting, there should be 10 to 13 volts at the top left corner (1) terminal. There should be -1 to +1 volts at the upper right corner (4) terminal.

4. If the voltage readings do not agree with those in this procedure, replace the relay.

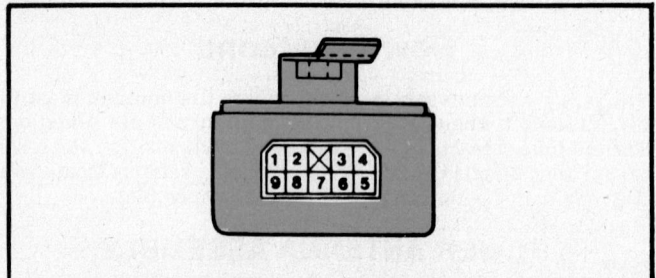

Power antenna relay terminal locations

Rear Window Defogger System

The rear window defogger system consists of a rear window with two vertical bus bars and a series of electrically connected grid lines baked on the inside surface. A control switch and a timer relay combined into a single assembly is used on all models.

All circuit protection is provided by a fusible link, located in the charging circuit, for the heater grid circuit and by a fuse for the relay control circuit.

NOTE: Since the grid lines can be damaged or scraped off with sharp instruments, caution should be used when cleaning the glass or removing foreign materials, decals or stickers. Normal glass cleaning solvents or hot water used with rags or toweling is recommended.

REAR WINDOW DEFOGGER SYSTEM

Test

The rear window defogger system operation can be checked in the vehicle using the following test procedure.

1. Turn the ignition switch to the "ON" position, also turn the rear window defogger control switch to the "ON" position.

2. Monitor the vehicle ammeter. With the control switch in the "ON" position, a distinct needle deflection should be noted.

NOTE: If the vehicle is not equipped with a voltmeter or a ammeter, the rear window defogger operation can be checked by feeling the glass in the rear windshield. A distinct difference in temperature between the grid lines and adjacent clear glass can be detected in three to four minutes of operation.

3. Using a suitable DC voltmeter connect the vertical bus bar on the passenger side of the vehicle with the positive lead and the driver side of the vehicle with the negative lead. The voltmeter should read between 10 to 14 volts.

4. Only Steps 1, 2 and 3 will confirm the system is operational. The indicator or pilot light illumination means that there is power available at the output of the relay only and does not necessarily prove the system is operational.

5. If the rear window defogger system does not operate properly, the problem should be isolated as outlined in the following procedure:

a. Check to be sure the ignition switch is in the "ON" position. Be sure that the rear defogger feed (HOT) wire is connected to the terminal or pigtail and that the ground wire is indeed grouned.

b. Be sure the fusible link and control circuit fuse is operational and all electrical connections are secure. When all of these things have been completely checked out, one of the following is defective; the control switch/timer relay module or the rear window defogger grid lines.

c. If the grid lines were to blame, either all the grid lines would have to be broken, or one of the feed (HOT) wires are not connected for the system to be inoperative.

6. If turning the control switch procedures give severe voltmeter (ammeter) defelctions, check the system for a shorting condition. If the systems check out but the indicator bulb does not light, check and or replace the bulb.

REAR WINDOW DEFOGGER GRID

Test

When a grid is inoperable due to an open circuit, the area of glass normally cleared by that grid will remained fogged or iced until cleared by the adjacent grids. Use the following procedure to located a broken grid.

Note: The ground wire is connected to the driver's side of the window and the feed wire connection is located on the right side of the window.

1. With the engine running at idle, place the rear defogger switch in the "ON" position. The pilot lamp is the switch lever should light up indicating the defogger is operating.

2. Using a 12 volt voltmeter, connect the positive lead of the voltmeter to the hot side of the vertical bus element on the inside surface of the glass.

3. Connect the negative lead of the voltmeter to the ground side of the bus element. The voltage drop indicated on the meter should be 11 to 13 volts. Connect the negative lead of the voltmeter to a good ground, the meter reading should stay constant.

4. Keep the negative lead connected to the ground and carefully use the positive lead to contact each grid at the approximate centerline of the window. A voltage drop of approximately 6 volts. indicates a good grid or a closed circuit.

5. No voltage indicated a broken grid wire. To located the exact location of the break, move the voltmeter lead along the

grid wire. The voltage should decrease gradually. if the voltage drops suddenly, there is a break at that location.

NOTE: A Grid repair kit (Mopar # 4106356) is available from the manufacturer and the enclosed manufactures instruction should be followed for a proper grid repair.

Grid Resistance Test

1. Turn the defogger switch off. Use a ohmmeter (with a scale ranging from 0 to 100 ohms) to measure the resistance at each grid line between the center and the end , left and right separately.

2. The section involving a broken grid line indicates resistance twice that in other sections.

3. Once in the affected area, move the tester bar for a position where the resistance sharply changes. Mark the broken grid line and repair as necessary.

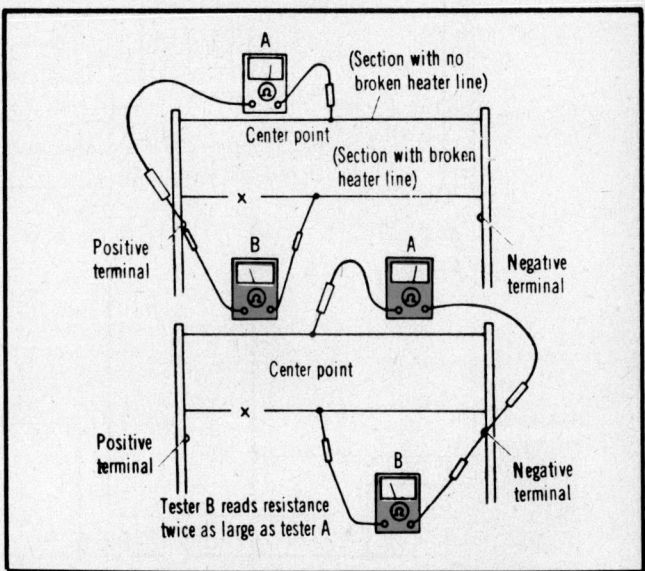

Performing the resistance test on the grid lines

REAR DEFOGGER SWITCH

Removal and Installation

1982-84 COLT AND CHAMP
< 59 >

1.
Disconnect the negative battery cable. Remove the instrument cluster hood mounting screws.

2.Remove the instrument panel trim plate. Remove the defogger switch harness and remove the switch by pressing the claw on the top of the switch.

3.Installation is the reverse order of the removal procedure.

1984 AND LATER COLT AND COLT VISTA

1. Disconnect the negative battery cable. Using a suitable tool, slip the tool behind the liftgate switch far enough to depress the locking tab. Repeat this procedure foɪ the opposite side of the switch. Be careful not to damage the instrument panel.

2. Disconnect the electrical connector and remove the switch from the dash panel.

3. Installation is the reverse order of the removal procedure.

CONQUEST

1. Disconnect the negative battery cable. Remove the dimmer control knob.

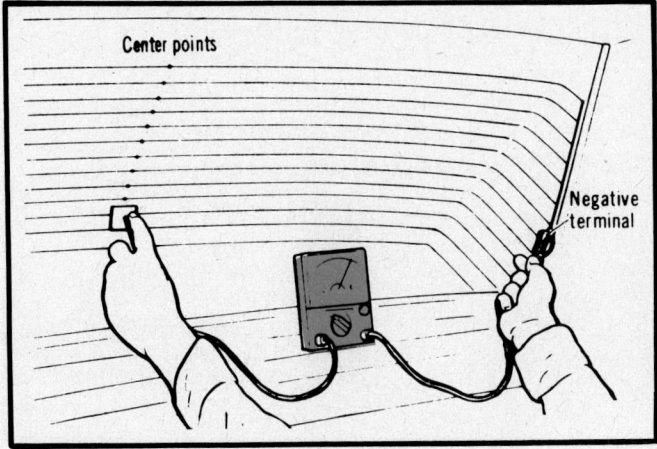

Performing the voltage test on the grid lines

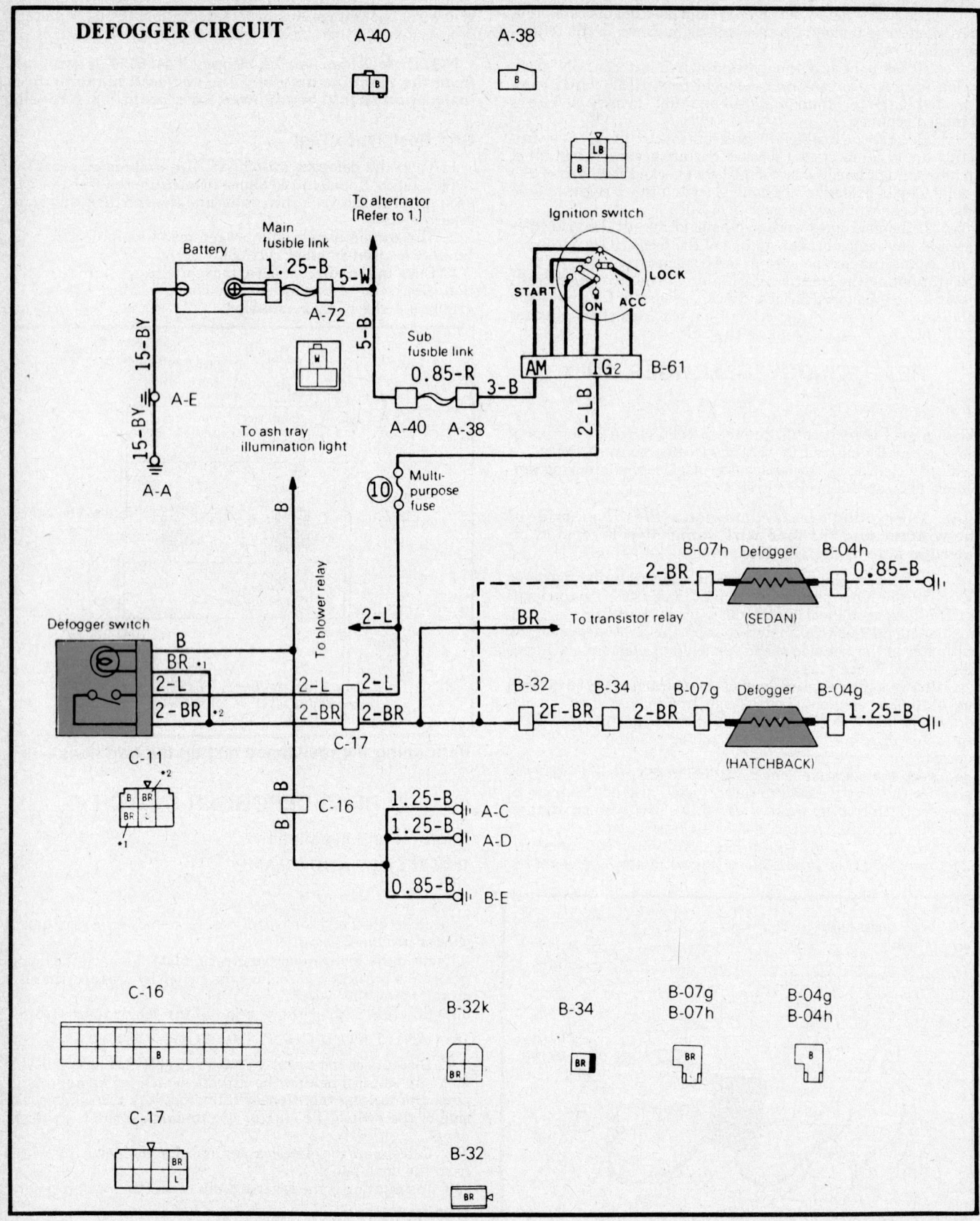

Typical rear window defogger schematic

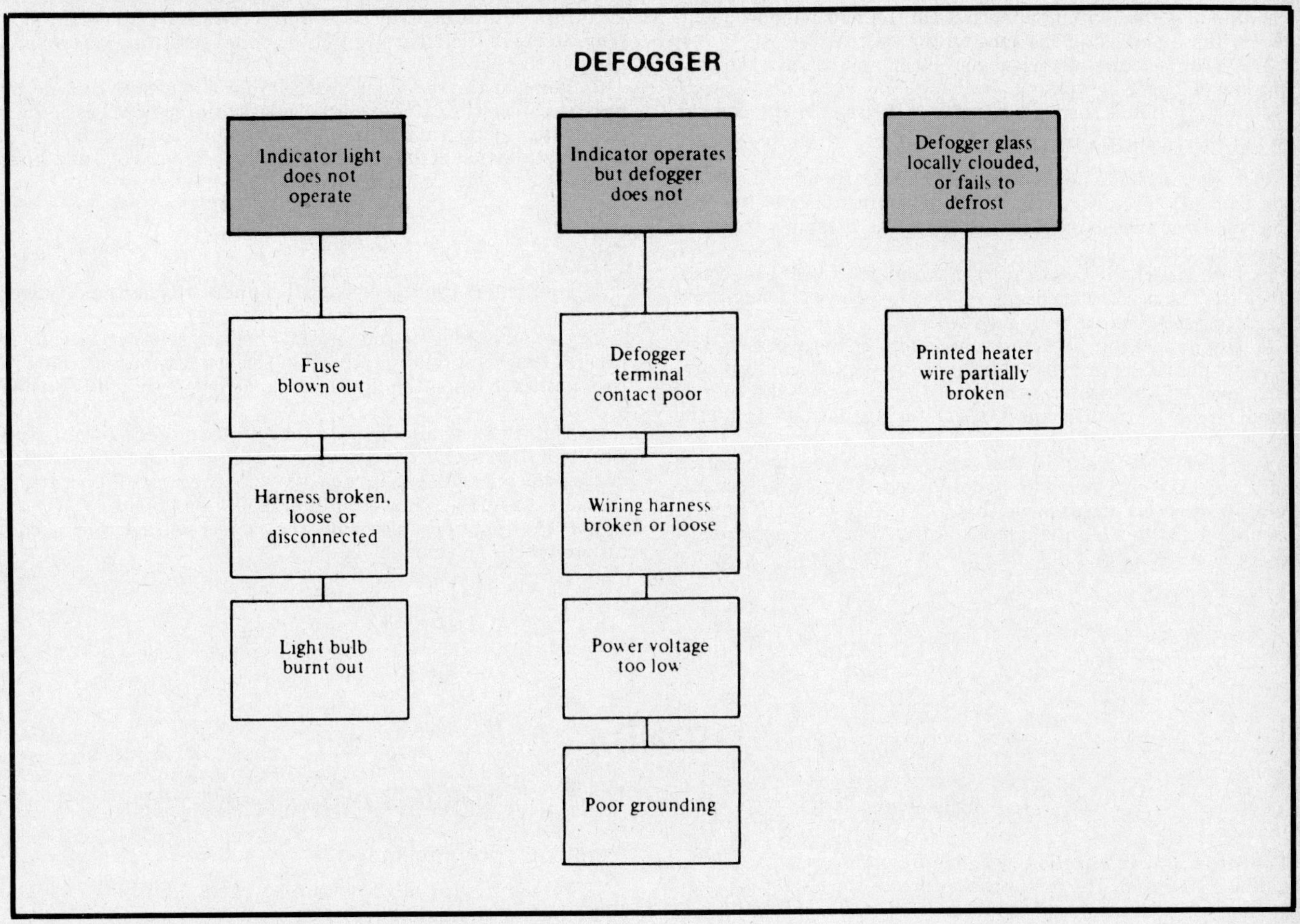

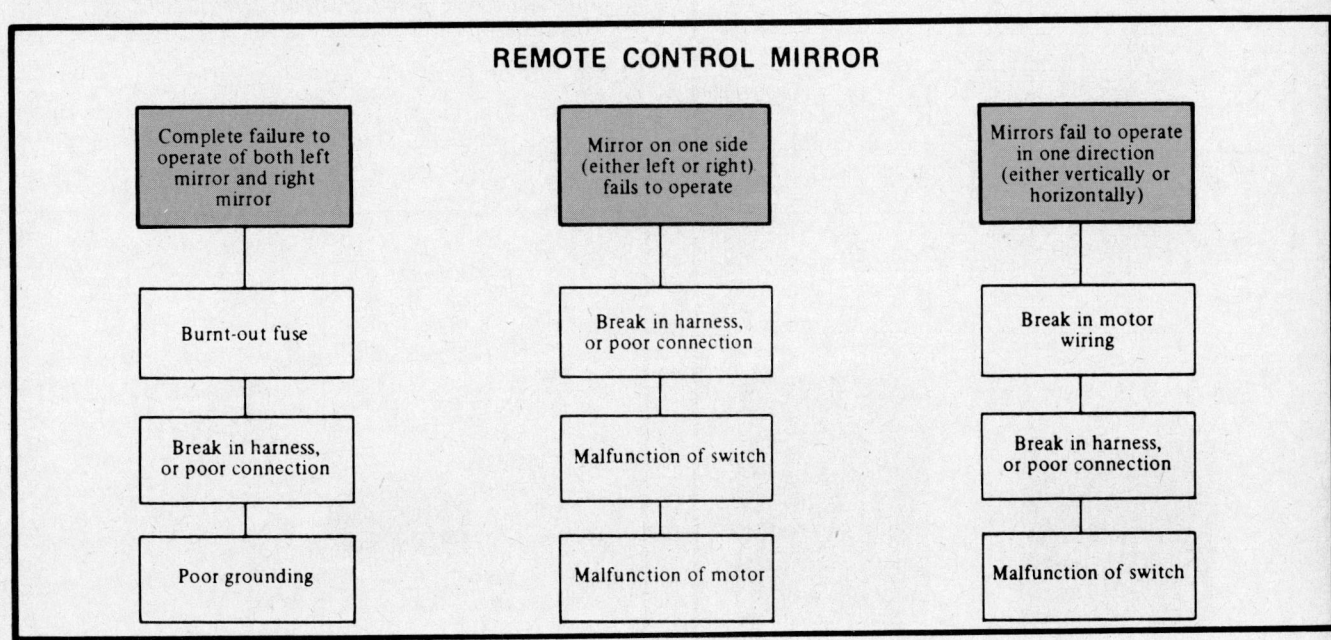

DEFOGGER

| Indicator light does not operate | Indicator operates but defogger does not | Defogger glass locally clouded, or fails to defrost |

- Fuse blown out
- Harness broken, loose or disconnected
- Light bulb burnt out

- Defogger terminal contact poor
- Wiring harness broken or loose
- Power voltage too low
- Poor grounding

- Printed heater wire partially broken

Rear window defogger troubleshooting chart

REMOTE CONTROL MIRROR

| Complete failure to operate of both left mirror and right mirror | Mirror on one side (either left or right) fails to operate | Mirrors fail to operate in one direction (either vertically or horizontally) |

- Burnt-out fuse
- Break in harness, or poor connection
- Poor grounding

- Break in harness, or poor connection
- Malfunction of switch
- Malfunction of motor

- Break in motor wiring
- Break in harness, or poor connection
- Malfunction of switch

Power mirror troubleshooting chart

2. Remove the switch panel. Detach the rear window defogger switch by pressing the tabs on the switch.

3. Disconnect the electrical connector and remove the rear window defogger switch.

4. Installation is the reverse order of the removal procedure.

CHALLENGER/SAPPORO

1. Disconnect the negative battery cable. Remove the inner box from the accessory box and by pressing the catch of the power mirror switch assembly, remove the assembly from the accessory box.

2. Disconnect the power mirror switch electrical connector. Once the the accessory case is removed, remove the front and rear accessory box retaining screws.

3. Disconnect the electrical connections of the accessory box wire harness and remove the the accessory box assembly. Carefully pull off the heat control knobs and remove the control panel, be sure to disconnect the lighting harness from the panel.

4. Pull off the radio knobs, remove the radio installation nuts and take out the radio panel. Remove the center console retaining screws and remove the center console. If the vehicle is equipped with a manual transmission, remove the gear-shift knob.

5. Pull out the ashtray retaining screws and remove the ashtray. Remove the cigarette lighter panel retaining screws and remove the panel.

6. Remove the defogger switch from the center console by pressing in on the catches on the sides of the switch. Disconnect the switch electrical connector and remove the switch.

7. Installation is the reverse order of the removal procedure.

DEFOGGER TIMER

Test

1. Disconnect the the electrical connector from the defogger timer.

2. Use a suitable voltmeter and check to see that 12 volts is present at the middle terminal on the top row of terminals in the connector when the ignition and defogger switch is turned on.

3. The timer should operate for approximately eleven minutes and ten stop. If the defogger switch is pressed once again or the ignition switch is turned off while the timer is operating, the voltage at the same terminal should be 0 volts.

4. If the timer does not show the correct voltage during this test, replace the timer.

HONDA

Power Mirrors

The mirrors are controlled by a single switch assembly located on the door panel. The motor that operates the mirror is part of the mirror assembly and cannot be replaced separately.

Terminal Position		B	E	C	LH	L	RH	R
L	UP	o		o	o			
	DOWN	o	o	o		o		
	LEFT	o			o	o		
	RIGHT	o		o		o		
R	UP	o	o				o	o
	DOWN	o	o	o				o
	LEFT	o		o				o
	RIGHT	o		o			o	o

RH LH C R L B E

Checking the continuity on the power mirror switch

POWER MIRROR SWITCH

Removal and Installation

1. Disconnect the negative battery cable. Lift the front of the switch using a suitable tool.

2. Clear the tab of the switch rear end from the door panel. Pull up on the switch and disconnect the switch electrical connector. Remove the switch from the door panel.

3. Installation is the reverse order of the removal procedure.

Power Mirror Test

1. Connect the battery to the right hand or left hand and and the R or L terminals. The mirror is operating properly if it moves smoothly.

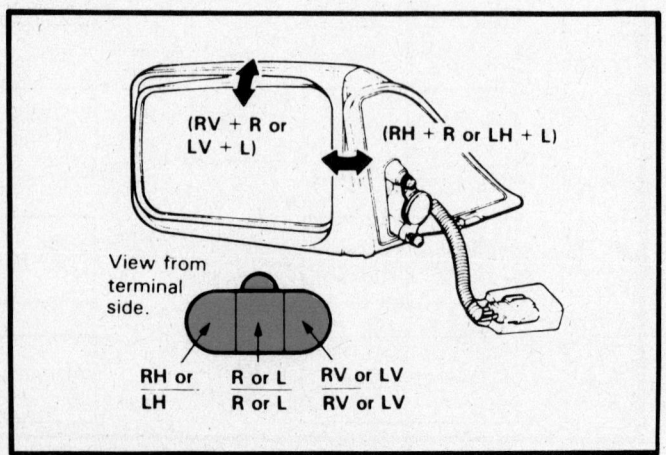

(RV + R or LV + L)   (RH + R or LH + L)

View from terminal side.

| RH or LH | R or L
R or L | RV or LV
RV or LV |

Performing the power mirror test

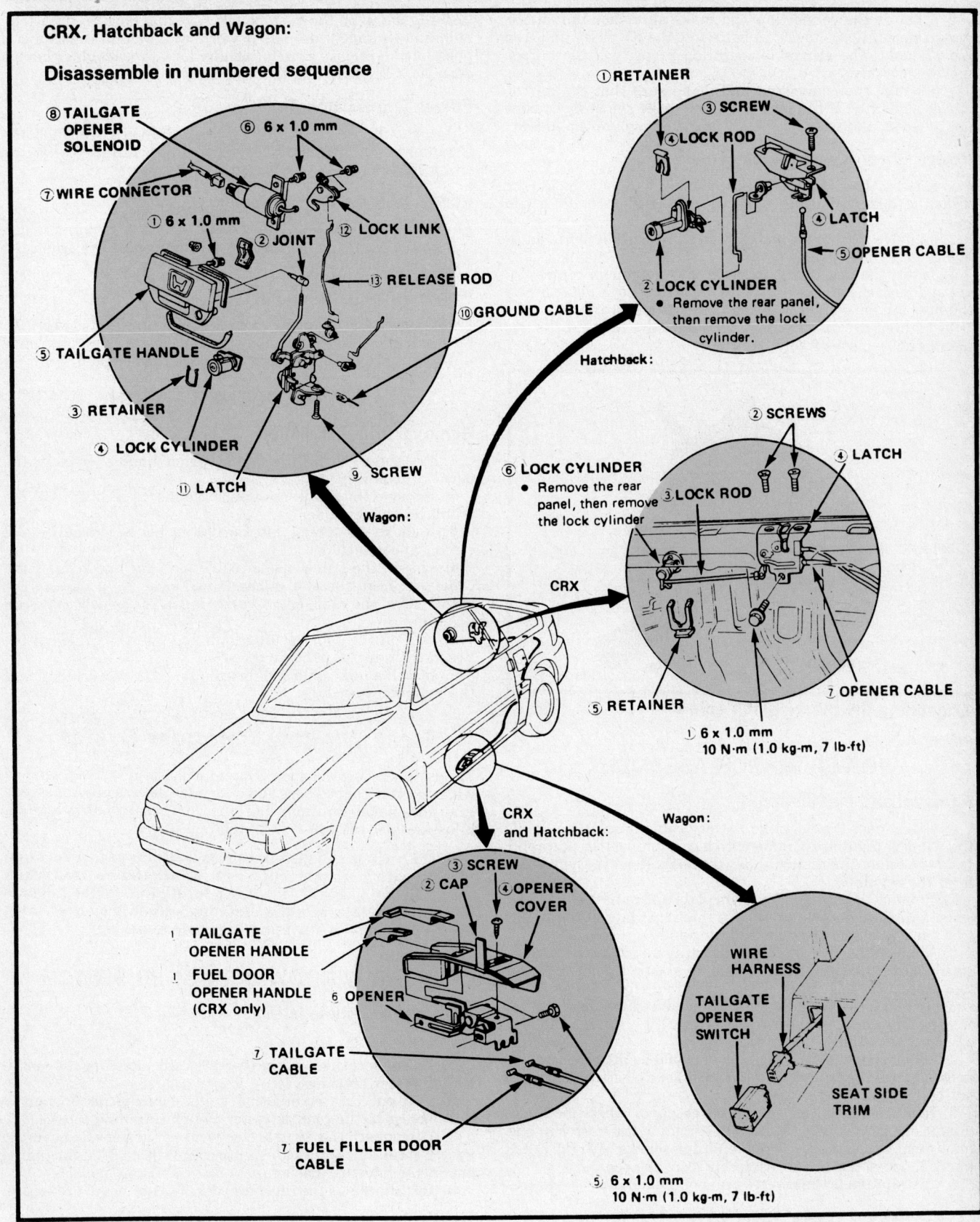

CRX, Hatchback and Wagon:

Disassemble in numbered sequence

⑧ TAILGATE OPENER SOLENOID

⑦ WIRE CONNECTOR

① 6 x 1.0 mm

⑥ 6 x 1.0 mm

② JOINT

⑤ TAILGATE HANDLE

③ RETAINER

④ LOCK CYLINDER

⑪ LATCH

⑨ SCREW

⑫ LOCK LINK

⑬ RELEASE ROD

⑩ GROUND CABLE

① RETAINER

③ SCREW

④ LOCK ROD

④ LATCH

⑤ OPENER CABLE

② LOCK CYLINDER
- Remove the rear panel, then remove the lock cylinder.

Hatchback:

Wagon:

CRX

⑥ LOCK CYLINDER
- Remove the rear panel, then remove the lock cylinder

② SCREWS

④ LATCH

③ LOCK ROD

⑤ RETAINER

⑦ OPENER CABLE

① 6 x 1.0 mm
10 N·m (1.0 kg-m, 7 lb-ft)

CRX and Hatchback:

Wagon:

③ SCREW

② CAP

④ OPENER COVER

① TAILGATE OPENER HANDLE

① FUEL DOOR OPENER HANDLE (CRX only)

⑥ OPENER

⑦ TAILGATE CABLE

⑦ FUEL FILLER DOOR CABLE

⑤ 6 x 1.0 mm
10 N·m (1.0 kg-m, 7 lb-ft)

WIRE HARNESS

TAILGATE OPENER SWITCH

SEAT SIDE TRIM

Power tailgate and latch removal and installation

2. Change the connection and make sure that the mirror moves smoothly. Connect the battery to the RV or LV and R or L terminals. The mirror is operating properly if the mirror moves smoothly.

3. Change the connection and make sure that the mirror moves smoothly. If the mirror fails to move smoothly or does not move at all during this test, repair or replace the mirror.

Power Mirror (Glass) Replacement

1. Loosen the mirror joint pinch screw. Pull out the mirror from the mirror housing until the joint separates from the mirror.

2. Remove the mirror and discard it. Be careful not to damage the mirror housing.

3. Insert the new mirror grooves onto the mirror control lever and push the mirror into place. Be careful so as not to brake the new mirror while installing it into the mirror housing.

4. Tighten the pinch screw and make sure the that the adjusting lever moves freely.

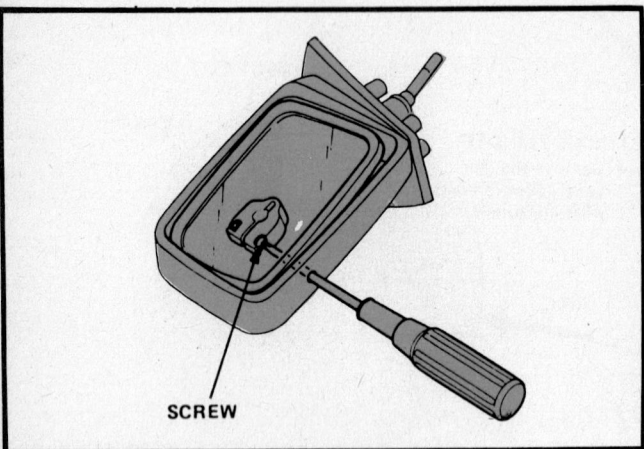

SCREW

Loosening the mirror pinch screw

POWER MIRROR ASSEMBLY

Removal and Installation

1. Disconnect the negative battery cable. Push the clip off the window regulator handle with a suitable tool, or pull it off from the other direction with a wire hook. Remove the handle from the regulator.

2. Remove the cap from the trim plate and remove the screw. Then pull the handle and remove the trim plate. Remove the front and rear screws from the door panel.

3. Remove the door panel by inserting a stiff putty knife or equivalent between the panel and the plastic shield, slide the tool around the edge until it hits a retainer clip, then pry it up sharply to remove the clip. Repeat this procedure on all the retaining clips, once the door panel is free, lift it straight up and off the window sill.

4. When removing the panel try to bend as little as possible to avoid creasing or breaking it. Peel off the plastic shield without tearing it.

5. Remove the power mirror cover panel. Disconnect the mirror electrical connections. While holding the mirror in one hand remove the three mirror retaining screws with the other hand. Remove the mirror assembly from the door.

6. Installation is the reverse order of the removal procedure.

Power Trunk and Liftgate System

The power liftgate release system consists of a release switch

(usually found on the dash panel), a wiring harness, lock solenoid and linkage rods. The power trunk system consists of a push button release switch (usually found in the glove box), a door latch solenoid and the necessary wiring.

Power Trunk Latch Test

There should be continuity between the G/Bl lead and the ground when the trunk lid is open and no continuity when the trunk lid is closed.

Power Tailgate Switch Test

There should be continuity between the switch terminals when the switch is in the on position and no continuity when the switch is in the off position.

Power Tailgate Solenoid Test

Using a suitable ohmmeter, check for continuity between the terminal and the solenoid body ground. There should be continuity, if there is no continuity, replace the solenoid.

TRUNK OPENER LATCH

Removal and Installation

1. Pry the cover off the trunk opener handle. Remove the door sill molding.

3. Remove the trunk opener. Disconnect the link from the trunk lid lock cylinder.

3. Remove the trunk latch molding bolts. Disconnect all electrical connections.

4. Loosen the trunk opener cable lock nut and remove the cable end from the slot in the trunk lock. Tie a wire to the trunk end of the cable before removing it, so the new cable can be pulled in.

5. Pull off the door opening trim and pull the cable out between the quarter panel and body.

6. Install a new cable and installation is the reverse order of the removal procedure.

Rear Window Defogger System

The rear window defogger system consists of a rear window with two vertical bus bars and a series of electrically connected grid lines baked on the inside surface. A control switch and a relay are also used in this system.

NOTE: Since the grid lines can be damaged or scraped off with sharp instruments, caution should be used when cleaning the glass or removing foreign materials, decals or stickers. Normal glass cleaning solvents or hot water used with rags or toweling is recommended.

REAR WINDOW DEFOGGER SWITCH

Removal and Installation

ACCORD

1. Disconnect the negative battery cable. Remove the combination meter housing.

2. Pull out the combination meter housing far enough to gain access to the rear defroster switch retaining screws.

3. Disconnect the switch electrical connector. Remove the switch retaining screws and remove the switch from the rear of the meter housing (dash panel on the Prelude models).

4. Installation is the reverse order of the removal procedure.

CIVIC

1. Disconnect the negative battery cable and remove the lower dashboard panel (except for the wagon models).

2. Disconnect the wire harness from behind the console. Depress the switch locking pawls and remove the switch from the front of the dash panel.

3. Installation is the reverse order of the removal procedure.

PRELUDE

1. Disconnect the negative battery cable. Lower the steering column and remove the lower dashboard panel.

2. Remove the four instrument panel retaining screws. Pull the instrument panel out and disconnect the wire connectors.

3. Remove the instrument panel. Remove the two rear defroster switch retaining screws and pull the switch out of the instrument panel.

4. Installation is the reverse order of the removal procedure.

Rear Defroster Relay Test

1. Using a suitable ohmmeter there should be continuity between top left (A) terminal and the bottom left (B) terminal, when applying 12 volts to upper right (C) terminal and the lower right (D) terminals.

2. Once the 12 volts is removed from the C and D terminals there should be no continuity in the relay. If the relay fails this test replace it. The relays are located in the following areas:

    a. Accord --- the defrost relay is located under the left side of the dash panel.

    b. Civic --- the defrost relay is located on a relay brace under the left side of the dash panel.

    c. Prelude --- the defrost relay is located in the fuse/relay junction block under the left side of the dash panel next the left side kick panel.

NOTE: There is no defrost grid test procedures available at the time of this publication.

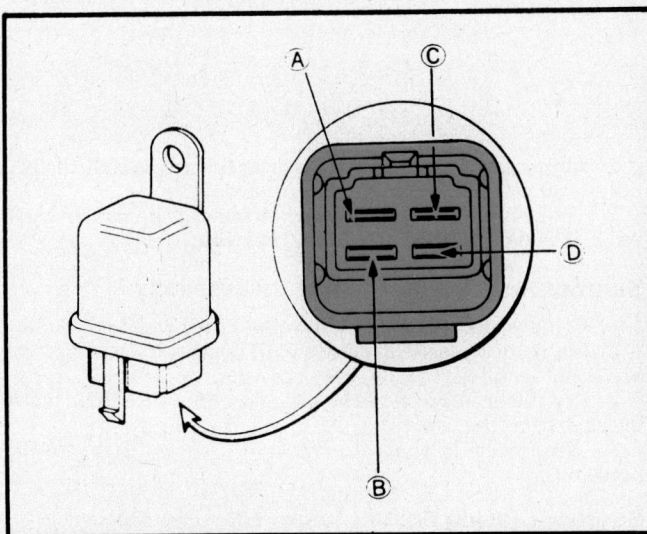

Testing the defrost relay

Electric Sunroofs

The sunroof is operated by a switch which is usually located on the left side of the instrument panel. The system is consists of the sunroof switch, motor drive cables and two relays (open and close) which are located in a fuse/relay junction block in the engine compartment.

A 35 amp fuse which is located in a fuse/relay junction block in the engine compartment, is used to power/protect the sys-

tem. The sunroof can be closed manually, (should it be necessary) by removing the headliner plug, insert the handle and turn the gear to close the sunroof.

NOTE: The sunroof assembly is equipped with water drain tubes, it is important to keep these drain tubes open. So it is recommended to blow compressed air through the drain tubes at regular intervals, in order to keep the drain tubes clear.

SUNROOF GLASS AND SUNSHADE REPLACEMENT

Removal and Installation

1. Slide the sunshade all the way back. Pry the plug out of each mount bracket cover, remove the screw, then slide the cover off to the rear.

2. Close the glass fully. Remove the nuts from the front and rear mounts on both sides.

3. Remove the glass by lifting it up and pulling it towards the front of the vehicle. Once the glass is removed , pull the sunshade out. When removing the sunshade it is alright to bend the sunshade slightly to aid in the removal.

4. Installation is the reverse order of the removal procedure.

SUNROOF MOTOR, DRAIN TUBE AND FRAME

Removal and Installation

1. Remove the headliner from inside of the vehicle.

2. Remove the sunroof motor by removing two bolts and three nuts from the bottom of the motor mount plate. Disconnect the motor wire harness at the connector and remove the motor.

3. Slide back the drain tube clamps and remove the drain tubes. Remove the eleven mounting bolts from the sunroof frame and remove the frame from the vehicle.

4. To install, insert the frame's rear pins into the body holes, then install the rest of the assembly in the reverse order of the removal procedure.

NOTE: Before installing the sunroof motor, measure the effort required to close the sliding panel using a suitable spring scale. If the load is over 22 lbs., check the side clearance and the glass height adjustment. Be sure when using the spring scale to protect the leading edge of the sunroof with a shop rag.

Sunroof Cable Replacement

With the sun roof out of the vehicle, remove the guide rail mounting nuts, lift off the guide rails and remove the cables with the rear mounts attached. Be sure to fill the groove in each grommet with a suitable sealant and apply a suitable grease to the inner cable.

SUNROOF GLASS

Height Adjustment

The roof molding should be even with the glass weather strip, to within 0.04 ± 0.06 in. all the way around. If it is not, slide the sunshade back and follow this procedure.

1. Pry the plug out of the glass mount bracket cover, remove the screw, then slide the cover off to the rear.

2. Loosen the mount bracket nuts and install shims between the glass frame and bracket. Repeat this on the other side if necessary.

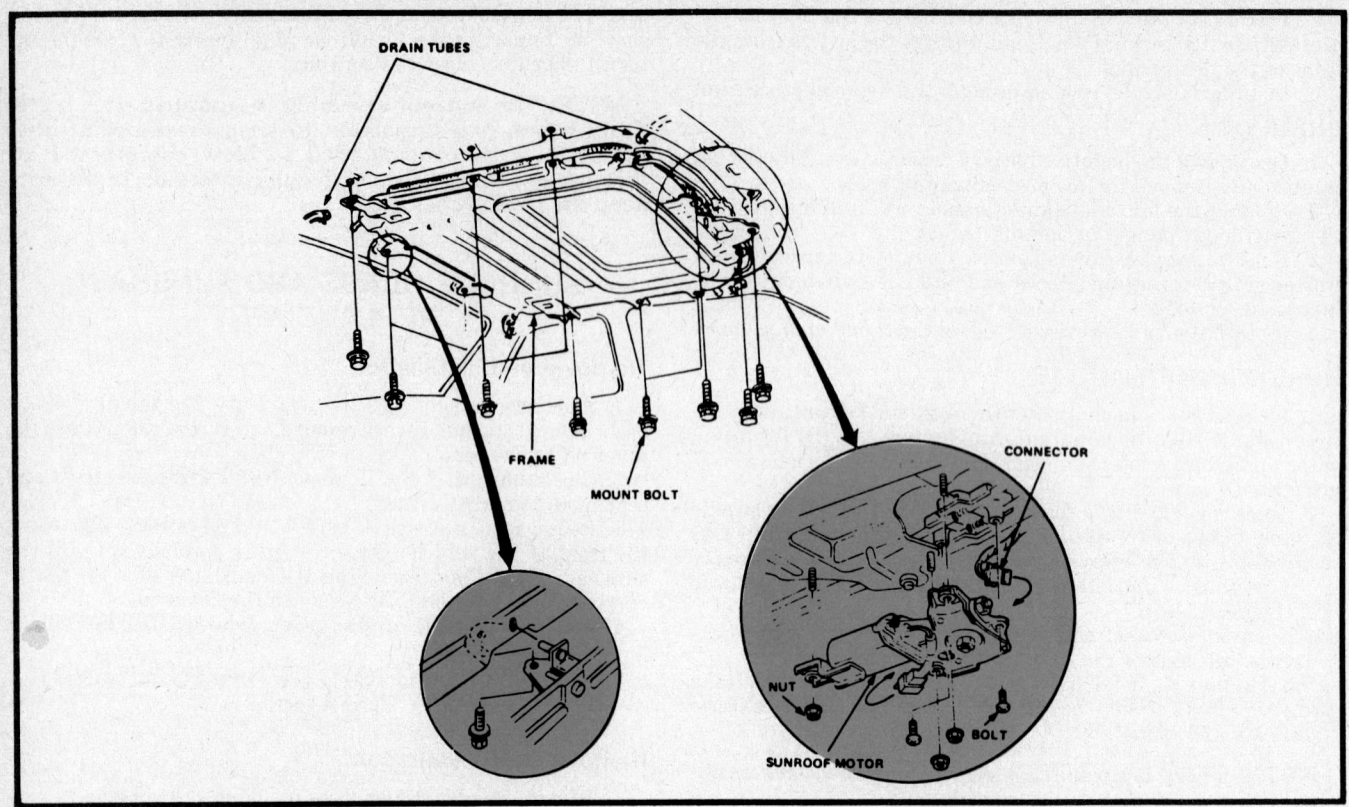

Sunroof motor and frame assembly

Side Clearance Adjustment

If the glass weather strip fits too tight against the roof molding on one side when closed, slide the sunshade back and follow this procedure.

1. Pry the plug out of each mount bracket cover, remove the screw, then slide the cover off to the rear.
2. Loosen all eight mount bracket nuts. Move the glass right or left as necessary and tighten the mount bracket nuts.

Rear Edge Closing Adjustment

Open the glass approximately one foot then close it to check where the rear edge begins to rise. If it rises too soon and seat too tight against the roof molding or too late and does not seat tight enough adjust as follows.

1. Open the glass fully. Remove the rail covers from both sides and loosen the lift-up guide screws.
2. Move the guide forward or backward, then tighten the screws and recheck the roof closing. The guides have notches 0.06 in. each and can be adjusted two notches forward or backward.

Wind Deflector Adjustment

A gap between the deflector seal and roof molding will cause wind noise when driving at high speed with the roof opening.

1. Open the sunroof and pry the rail covers off of both sides. Loosen the deflector mounting nuts. The wind deflector can be adjusted 0.08 in. forward or backward.

2. Adjust the deflector forward or backward so that the edge of its seal touches the roof molding evenly.
3. The height of the deflector when opened can not be adjusted. If it is damaged or deformed, replace it.

Sunroof Rear Mount Bracket Disassembly

1. Remove the side guides from the rear mount brackets. It is available to replace the guides with new ones whenever they are disassembled.
2. Pry the "E" clip off of the pin and remove the rear mount bracket from the cable.
3. Assembly is the reverse order of the disassembly procedure.

Sunroof Closing Force Check (With The Motor Installed)

1. After installing all removed parts, using a second person, have them hold the switch to close the sunroof while measuring the force required to stop the sunroof with a suitable spring scale.
2. Read the force on the scale as soon as the glass stops moving, then immediately release the switch and spring scale. The closing force should be 44-56 lbs.
3. If the force required to stop the sunroof is not within specifications, adjust it, by turning the sunroof motor clutch adjusting nut. Turn the clockwise to increase the force and counterclockwise to decrease the force.
4. After the proper adjustment has been made, install a new lockwasher and bend it against the flat on the adjusting nut.

Symptom	Probable Causes
Water leak	1. Gap between glass weatherstrip and roof panel. 2. Deflective or improperly installed glass weatherstrip. 3. Clogged drain tube. 4. Gap between glass weatherstrip and body.
Wind noise	1. Excessive clearance between glass weatherstrip and roof panel.
Deflector noise	1. Improper clearance between deflector blade and roof panel. 2. Insufficient deflector extension. 3. Deformed deflector.
Motor noise	1. Loose motor. 2. Worn gear or bearing. 3. Outer cable deformed.
Sunroof does not move, but motor turns	1. Foreign matter stuck between guide rail and sliding panel. 2. Interference between parts. 3. Outer cable loose. 4. Outer cable not attached properly. 5. Clutch out of adjustment.
Sunroof does not move and motor does not turn (Sliding panel can be moved with sunroof wrench)	1. Blown fuse. 2. Faulty switch. 3. Battery run down. 4. Defective motor.

Sunroof troubleshooting chart

MAZDA

Power Mirrors

The mirrors are controlled by a single switch assembly located on the door panel on some models and on the center console on other models. The motor that operates the mirror is part of the mirror assembly and cannot be replaced separately.

POWER MIRROR ASSEMBLY

Removal and Installation

1. Disconnect the negative battery cable. Remove the power mirror retaining screw cover from inside the vehicle.
2. Remove the three power mirror retaining screws, disconnect the mirror electrical connector and remove the mirror.
3. Installation is the reverse order of the removal procedure.

Power Mirror Test

Using a suitable ohmmeter check each of the terminals of the mirror connector for continuity. There should be continuity at terminals A and B, and terminals C and D. There should be no continuity at terminals A and C and terminals B and D. If the mirror fails the continuity test, repair or replace it.

Power Mirror Switch

Using a suitable ohmmeter check each of the terminals of the mirror switch connector. If the continuity is not as specified, replace the switch.

Power Antenna

The power antenna automatically raises the antenna mast to its full height whenever the radio and ignition are tuned on. The antenna retracts into the fender when either the ignition or the radio is turned off. The antenna relay is located on the antenna motor housing on the 626 and in the rear trunk panel on the RX-7.

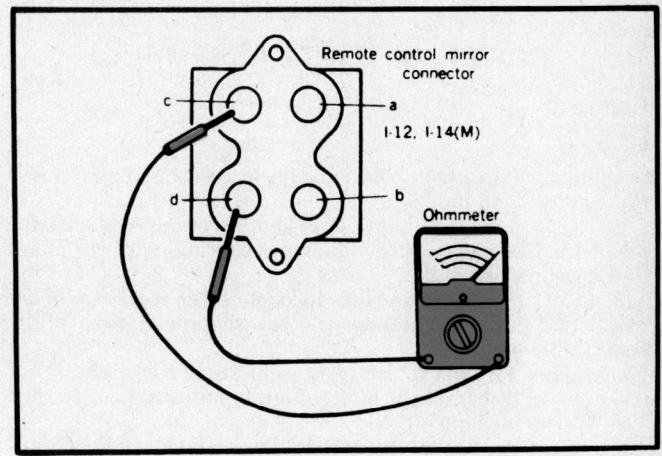

Testing the power mirror assembly connector

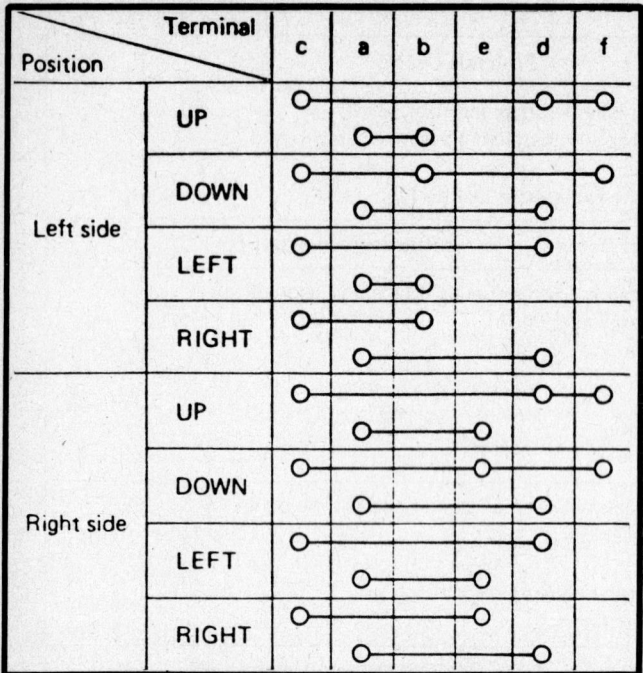

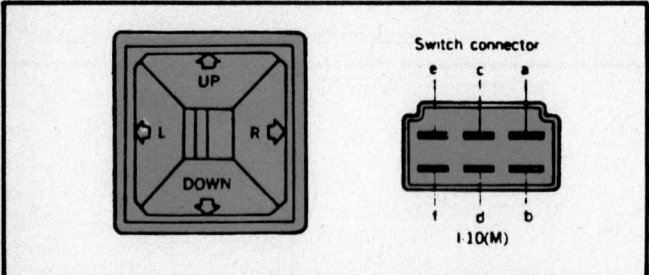

Power mirror switch test specifications

Power mirror switch connector terminal locations

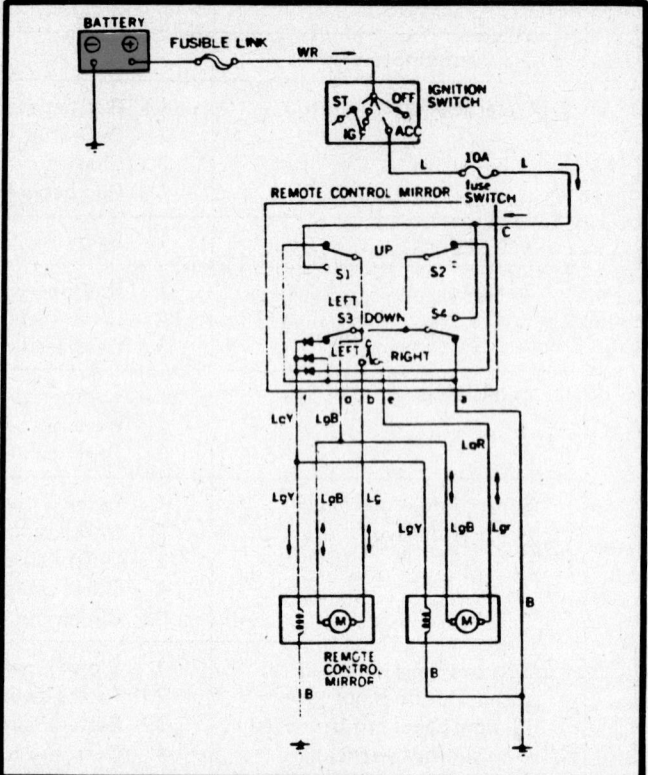

Power mirror wiring schematic

If the power antenna fails to raise or lower, check the radio and antenna fuse. If that checks out, check the power antenna connector for voltage. If that checks out, Check the continuity of the terminals in the power antenna relay. If the problem stiil occurs after checking into these areas, the problem could be in the wiring harness or the radio.

POWER ANTENNA ASSEMBLY

Removal

626

1. Remove the under board and glove compartment. Remove the air duct and blower unit.
2. Remove the side trim panel and disconnect the antenna feed wire. Remove the antenna motor bracket (with the motor and antenna pole).
3. insert a suitable tool into the slot on the connector of the motor and pull the antenna pole out abpproximatey 0.39 in. from the motor.
4. Supply 12 volts to the two terminals in the connector of the motor and operate the motor. Lightly pull out the rack rope from the motor housing.
5. Loosen the two screws in the pillar and remove the antenna pole. Remove the any antenna assembly retaining screws and brackets and remove the assembly from the vehicle.

Installation

1. Install the new antenna pole and connect the antenna feed wire. Face the tooth side of the rack rope with the motor clutch.
2. Insert the rack rope into the motor and hold in this position. Supply 12 volts to the two terminals in the connector of the motor and entwine the rack rope into the motor.
3. Push the antenna pole into the motor housing until it lock throughly. Install the antenna motor bracket and antenna pole (with the motor and antenna pole), and any reataining screws.
4. Make sure that the power antenna operates properly. The slack of the rack rope can be adjusted by operating the motor for several times. Then the antenna wil extend to its fullest.

RX-7

1. Remove the left rear trunk side trim panel. Disconnect the antenna feed wire and connector.
2. Remove the attaching nuts and bolts and remove the power antenna assembly.
3. Remove the power antenna bracket. Remove the drive mechanism cover. Remove the rod insulator and the rod assembly.
3. Insert the new rod assembly into the mast assembly. Roll the cable into the case and place the case into position.
4. Insert the rod insulator into the mast assembly. Install the drive mechanism. Attach the power antenna assembly to the vehicle and connect the feed wire and connector.
5. Check the operation of the power antenna and install the left rear trunk side trim panel.

Rear Window Defogger System

The rear window defogger system consists of a rear window

with two vertical bus bars and a series of electrically connected grid lines baked on the inside surface. A control switch and a relay are also used in this system.

REAR WINDOW DEFOGGER GRID

Test

1. Turn on the rear window defroster switch. Connect the positive lead of a voltmeter to the center of each filament and connect the negative lead to the body of the vehicle.

2. The standard voltage at the center of the filament is six volts. If the meter indications is higher than six volts, the problem exists in the ground side of the filament.

3. If the indication is low or zero the problem is between the center and the power side. Isolate the problem grid line and mark the break in the grid wire.

Defogger Grid Repair

1. Clean the faulty portion of the grid line with a thinner or eythyl alcohol.

2. Apply tape to either side of the faulty portion, leaving the broken grid wire exposed.

3. Use a small paint brush or drafting pen to apply silver paint # 2835-77-600 or equivalent.

4. Completely dry the repaired section by letting it stand (at a temperature of 68°F) for 24 hours. The drying process can be 30 minutes if a hot air gun (at a temperature of 140°F) is used.

—————— CAUTION ——————

Do not use the rear window defogger until the repaired section is completely dried. Do not use gasoline or other cleaning solvents to clean the damaged section of the grid line.

Electric Sunroof

The sunroof is operated by a switch which is usually located on the top of the headliner. The system is consists of the sunroof switch, motor drive cables and a relay which are located in a fuse/relay junction block in the engine compartment.

SUNROOF ASSEMBLY

Removal

RX-7

1. Open the outer panel approximately 4 in. Remove the ceiling opening seaming welt.

2. Pull the front of the inner trim panel down the at the front and forward. Remove the trim by lifting trim panel by lifting it up and out of the vehicle.

3. Remove the top ceiling and disconnect the drain hose. Close the sunroof with the emergencey handle and disconnect the the wire connectors.

4. Remove the outer panel by removing the outer panel retaining nuts. If the outer panel is to be removed without removing the top ceiling, fully open the outer panel and remove the rear reataining nuts from the outside of the vehicle.

5. Remove the motor bracket attaching bolts and remove the rear header attaching bolts.

6. Remove the set bracket attaching bolts. Support the lower unit and remove the four height adjusting nuts. Remove the lower unit.

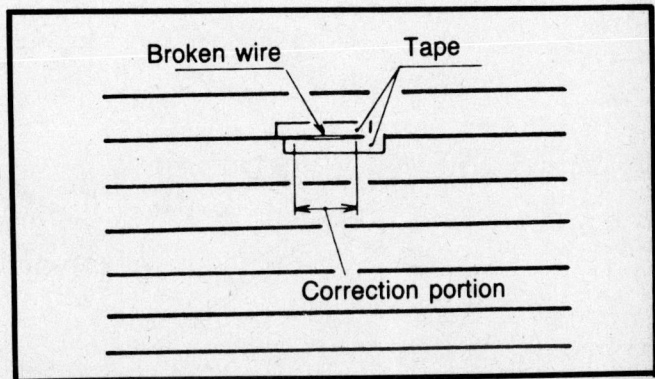

Repairing a broken section of the grid line

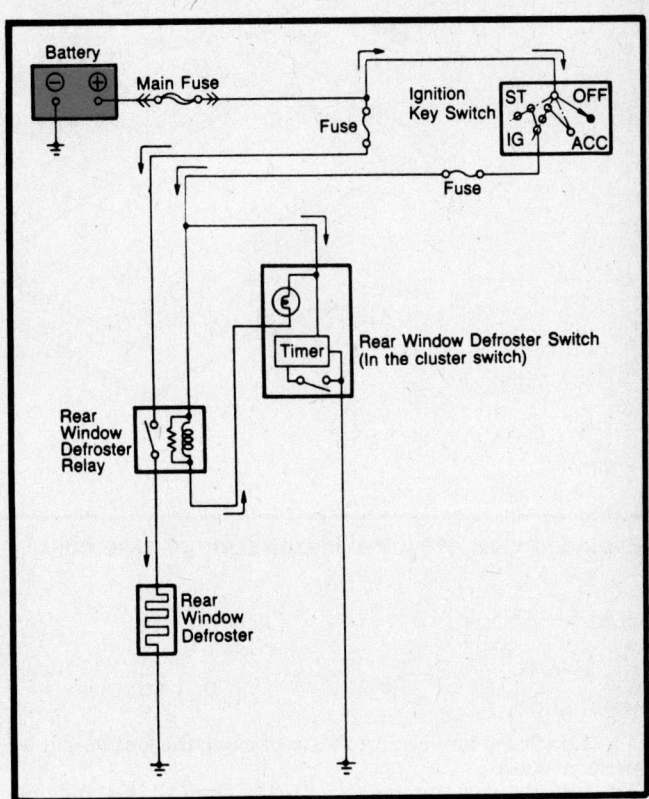

Typical rear defroster wiring schematic

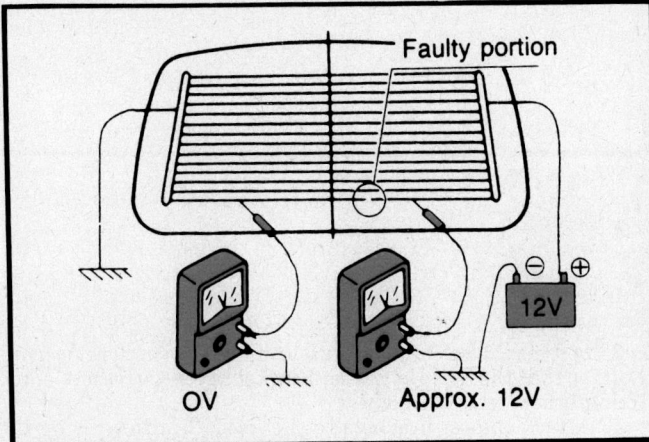

Testing the defroster grid for a broken grid line

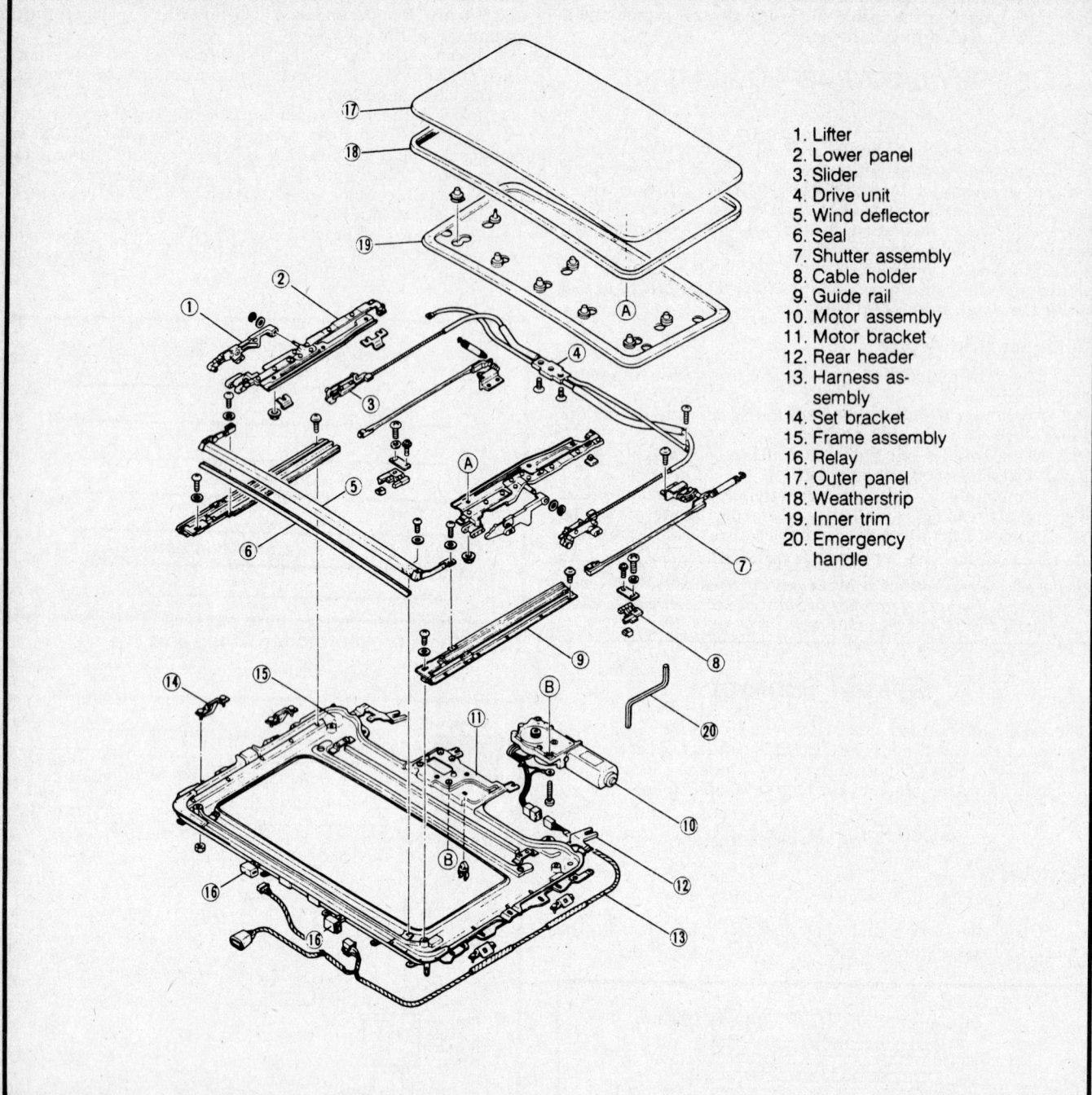

1. Lifter
2. Lower panel
3. Slider
4. Drive unit
5. Wind deflector
6. Seal
7. Shutter assembly
8. Cable holder
9. Guide rail
10. Motor assembly
11. Motor bracket
12. Rear header
13. Harness assembly
14. Set bracket
15. Frame assembly
16. Relay
17. Outer panel
18. Weatherstrip
19. Inner trim
20. Emergency handle

Exploded view of typical Mazda sunroof assembly

Installation

1. Attach the lower unit to the roof using the four height adjustment nuts.

2. Install the outer panel with the front shims and rear shims between the lower and outer panel. Adjust the sunroof height by using the height adjusting nuts. The height difference limit around the circumference is 0.06 in.

3. Loosen the set bracket nuts. Adjust the set bracket positions so that the holes of the set bracket agree with those of the fixing brackets of the body.

4. Attach the set brackets to the fixing brackets using the set bracket attaching bolts. Tighten the set bracket nuts.

5. Tighten the rear header attaching bolts and the motor bracket attaching bolts. Install the wire connectors, drain

hose, top ceiling, inner tim panel, seaming welt. Finish the installation by reversing the removal procedure.

323 AND 626

1. Open the sunshade all the way. Completely close the sliding panel. Before removing the lower panel cover, protect the glass with tape or a cloth and remove the lower panel cover by prying it out with a suitable tool.

2. Remove the sliding panel and lower panel retaining nuts. Remove the sliding panel by pushing it upward from inside the vehicle. Completely open the sliding panel.

3. Disconnect the deflector links from the connectors and remove the deflector. Be sure to hold the deflector down while disconnecting the deflector links.

4. Remove the screws and set plate. Remove the screw and remove the guide rail cover. Remove the screws and bracket assembly, remove the screws from the drip rail link and then remove the lower panel by lifting it upward.

5. Remove the interior mirror, overhead console and seaming welt. Remove the screws and disconnect the electrical connector at the motor and remove the motor .

6. Remove the guide bracket assembly from the rail and then pull the driving cable out.

Installation

1. Insert the driving cable into the tube assembly. Apply a small amount of grease to the driving cable and insert the cable through the end of the assembly. Apply a small amount of grease on the sliding surface of the cam and guide shoe.

2. Properly adjust the left and right positions of the driving cable. Insert the guide rail into its bracket and insert the rear end of the bracket into the notch at the rear of the rail.

3. Check that the limit switches of the motor are at the off position (it may be necessary to move the cam, to position the switches in the off position). Install the motor and connect the motor and switch electrical connectors.

4. Install the lower panel to guide bracket assembly screws. Pull out the drip rail from the rear and tighten the link. Use the handle to turn the motor and open the slide panel fully.

5. Install the guide rail cover and set plate. Install the deflector and connect the deflector links. Use the motor and check the sliding operation of the sunroof, also check the tilt up and tilt down operations. Install the sliding panel.

6. Adjust the sunroof height by using the height adjusting nuts. The height difference limit around the circumference is 0.06 in.

7. Complete the installation by reversing the order of the removal procedure.

SUNROOF MOTOR

Removal and Installation

RX-7

1. Tilt the sunroof up. Remove the motor bracket attaching bolts and remove the motor assembly.

2. Set the timing gear of the new motor assembly in the tilt-up position. Install the motor assembly and check the sunroof for proper operations.

3. The position of the timing gear can be checked through the check hole of the motor assembly. If the position of the timing gear is not in the tilt-up position, adjust the gear position by using the emergency handle.

Sunroof Closing Force Check (With The Motor Installed)

1. After installing all removed parts, using a second person, have them hold the switch to close the sunroof while measuring the force required to stop the sunroof with a suitable spring scale.

2. Read the force on the scale as soon as the glass stops moving, then immediately release the switch and spring scale. The closing force should be 33-58 lbs.

3. If the force required to stop the sunroof is not withi specifications, adjust it, by turning the sunroof motor clutch adjusting nut. Turn the nut clockwise to increase the force and counterclockwise to decrease the force.

4. After the proper adjustment has been made, install a new lockwasher and bend it against the flat on the adjusting nut.

Theft Deterrent System

This system is designed to provide a warning in the event of a forced entry through the driver and passenger doors and trunk. When a forced entry is attempted, the alarm warning system will be tripped off. This will set the horns off and the exterior light to flash in unison for three to seven minutes. The starter interlock feature prevents the engine from starting if the warning system is tripped.

The alarm is tripped by opening switches strategically located in the door jambs, the door lock cylinders and the trunk lock cylinder. When a door lock cylinder or trunk lock cylinder is violated by rotating it or moving it in or out, or if any door is opened without using the key, the alarm will be actuated by the controller.

Group	Condition	Phase	Code
Security light	Will not flash (Remain out)	Pre arming phase	SEC1
	Remain flashing	Dead, Initial phase	SEC2
	Will not come on	Arming phase	SEC3
	Remains ON	Dead, Initial, pre arming phase	SEC4
Armed	Is set	Dead, Initial, pre arming phase	ARM1
Alarm	Is given without cause	Armed phase	ALR1
	Will not operate	Alarm phase	ALR2
	Will not stop	Alarm phase 1	ALR3
	Sounds continuously, not intermittently	Alarm phase 1	ALR4
Starter	Will not operate	Except alarm phase	ST1
	Will operate	Alarm phase 1-2	ST2

Theft deterrent system—troubleshooting chart

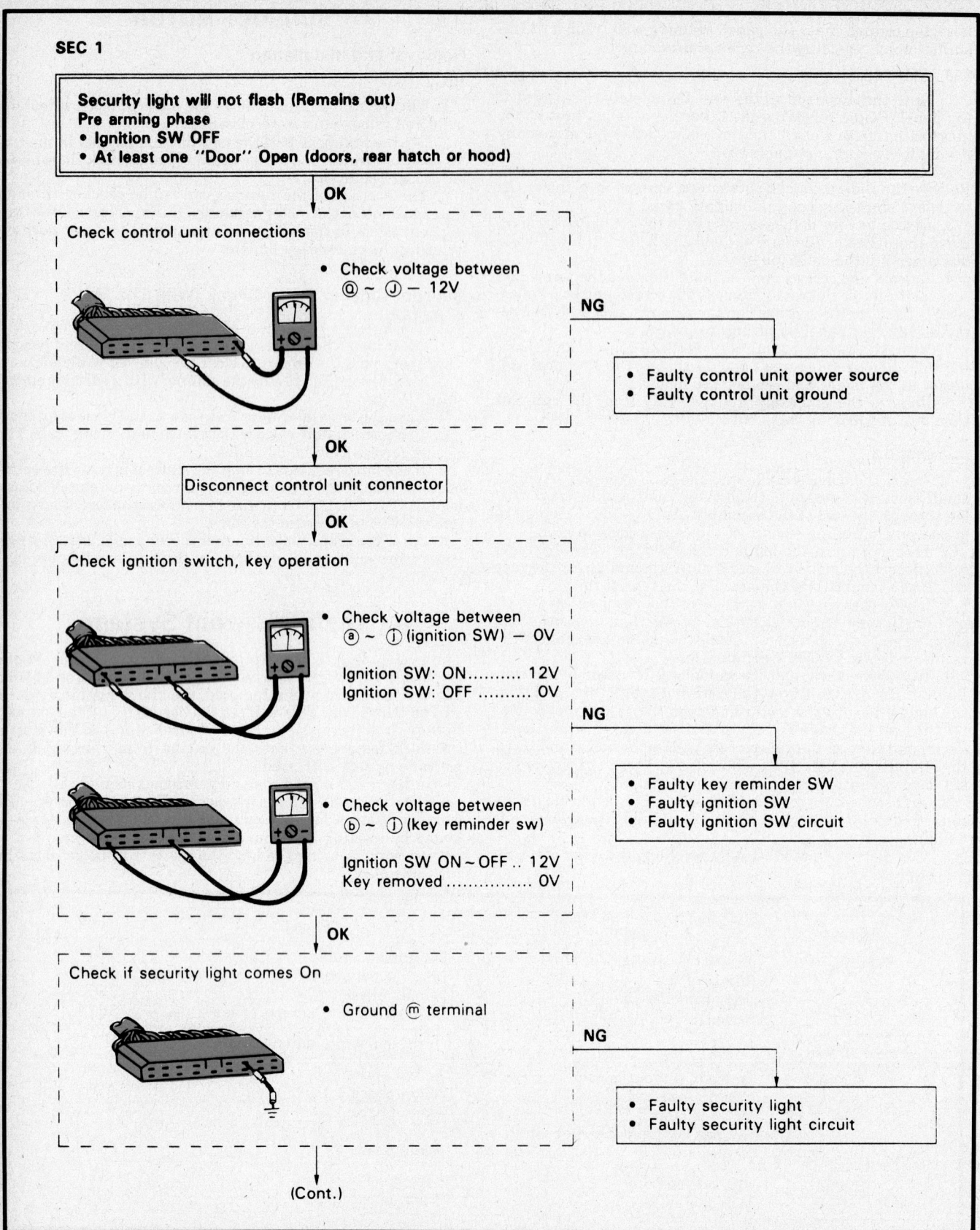

SEC 1

Security light will not flash (Remains out)
Pre arming phase
• Ignition SW OFF
• At least one "Door" Open (doors, rear hatch or hood)

OK

Check control unit connections

• Check voltage between
ⓐ ~ ⓙ — 12V

NG

• Faulty control unit power source
• Faulty control unit ground

OK

Disconnect control unit connector

OK

Check ignition switch, key operation

• Check voltage between
ⓐ ~ ⓙ (ignition SW) — 0V

Ignition SW: ON.......... 12V
Ignition SW: OFF 0V

NG

• Faulty key reminder SW
• Faulty ignition SW
• Faulty ignition SW circuit

• Check voltage between
ⓑ ~ ⓙ (key reminder sw)

Ignition SW ON ~ OFF .. 12V
Key removed 0V

OK

Check if security light comes On

• Ground ⓜ terminal

NG

• Faulty security light
• Faulty security light circuit

(Cont.)

Theft deterrent system – troubleshooting chart (cont.)

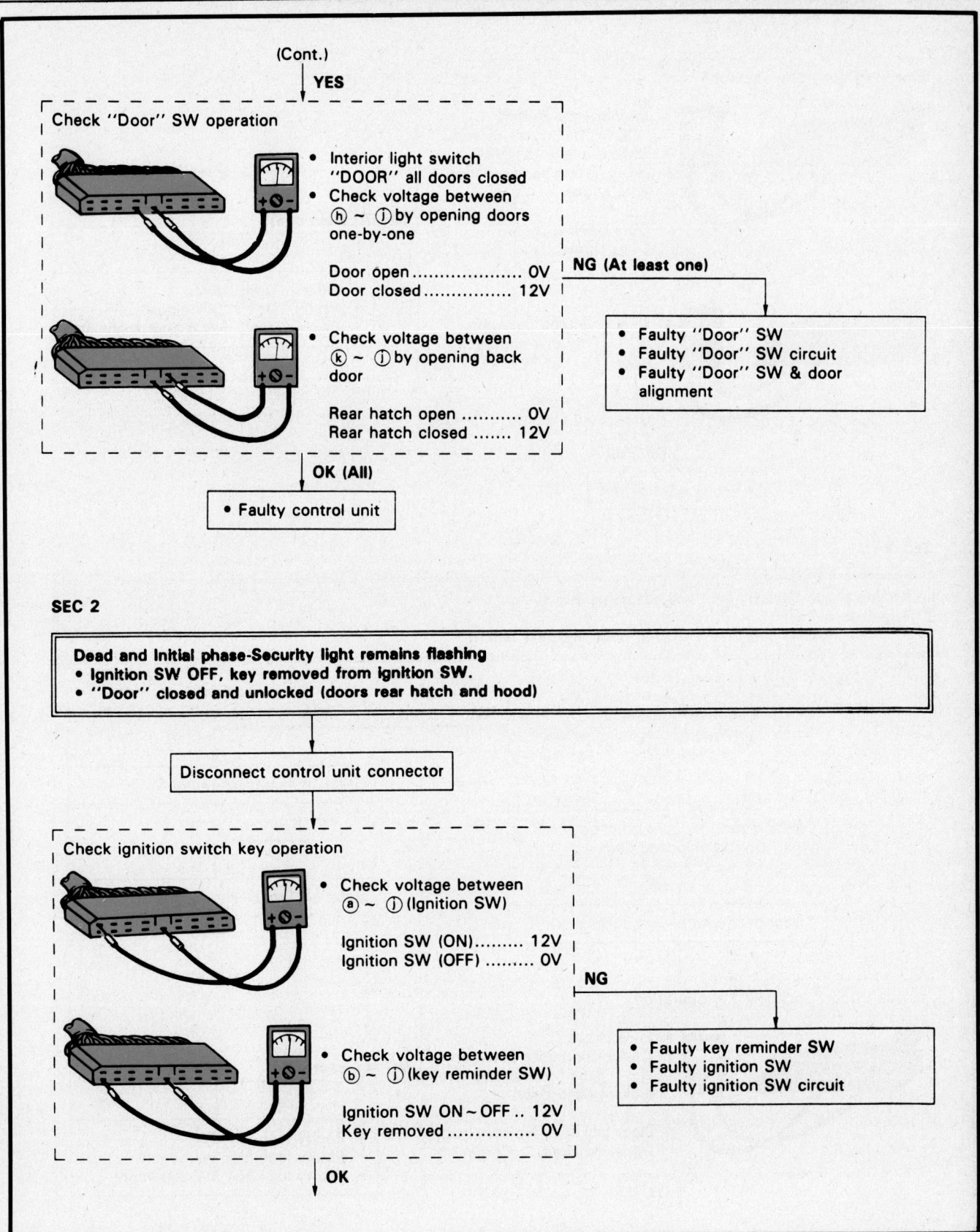

(Cont.)

YES

Check "Door" SW operation

- Interior light switch "DOOR" all doors closed
- Check voltage between ⓗ ~ ⓙ by opening doors one-by-one

Door open 0V
Door closed 12V

NG (At least one)

- Check voltage between ⓚ ~ ⓙ by opening back door

Rear hatch open 0V
Rear hatch closed 12V

- Faulty "Door" SW
- Faulty "Door" SW circuit
- Faulty "Door" SW & door alignment

OK (All)

- Faulty control unit

SEC 2

Dead and Initial phase-Security light remains flashing
- **Ignition SW OFF, key removed from ignition SW.**
- **"Door" closed and unlocked (doors rear hatch and hood)**

Disconnect control unit connector

Check ignition switch key operation

- Check voltage between ⓐ ~ ⓙ (Ignition SW)

Ignition SW (ON) 12V
Ignition SW (OFF) 0V

NG

- Check voltage between ⓑ ~ ⓙ (key reminder SW)

Ignition SW ON ~ OFF .. 12V
Key removed 0V

- Faulty key reminder SW
- Faulty ignition SW
- Faulty ignition SW circuit

OK

Theft deterrent system — troubleshooting chart (cont.)

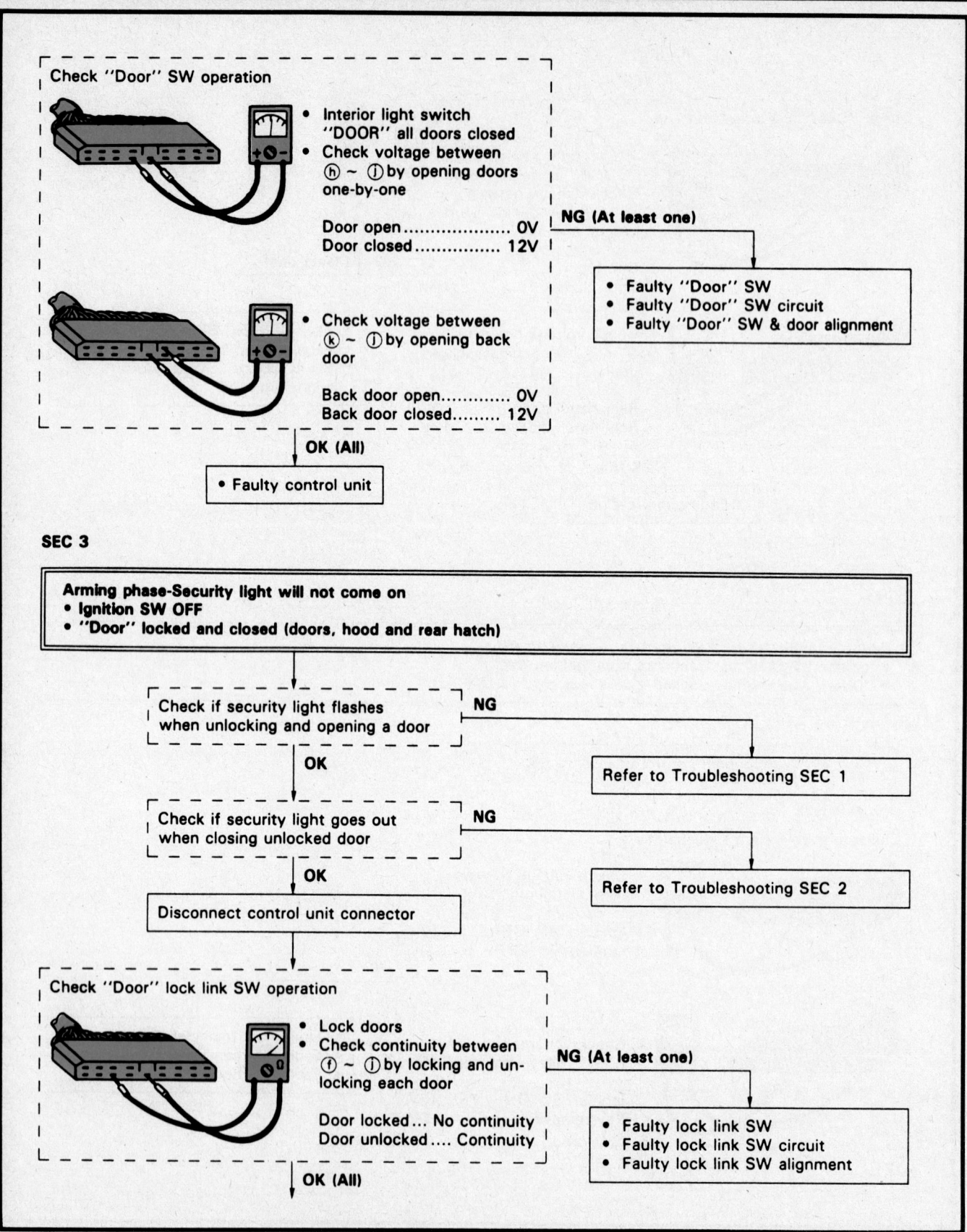

Check "Door" SW operation

- Interior light switch "DOOR" all doors closed
- Check voltage between ⓗ ~ ⓘ by opening doors one-by-one

Door open 0V
Door closed 12V

- Check voltage between ⓚ ~ ⓘ by opening back door

Back door open 0V
Back door closed 12V

NG (At least one)
- Faulty "Door" SW
- Faulty "Door" SW circuit
- Faulty "Door" SW & door alignment

OK (All)
- Faulty control unit

SEC 3

Arming phase-Security light will not come on
- Ignition SW OFF
- "Door" locked and closed (doors, hood and rear hatch)

Check if security light flashes when unlocking and opening a door

NG → Refer to Troubleshooting SEC 1

OK

Check if security light goes out when closing unlocked door

NG → Refer to Troubleshooting SEC 2

OK

Disconnect control unit connector

Check "Door" lock link SW operation

- Lock doors
- Check continuity between ⓕ ~ ⓘ by locking and unlocking each door

Door locked... No continuity
Door unlocked.... Continuity

NG (At least one)
- Faulty lock link SW
- Faulty lock link SW circuit
- Faulty lock link SW alignment

OK (All)

Theft deterrent system – troubleshooting chart (cont.)

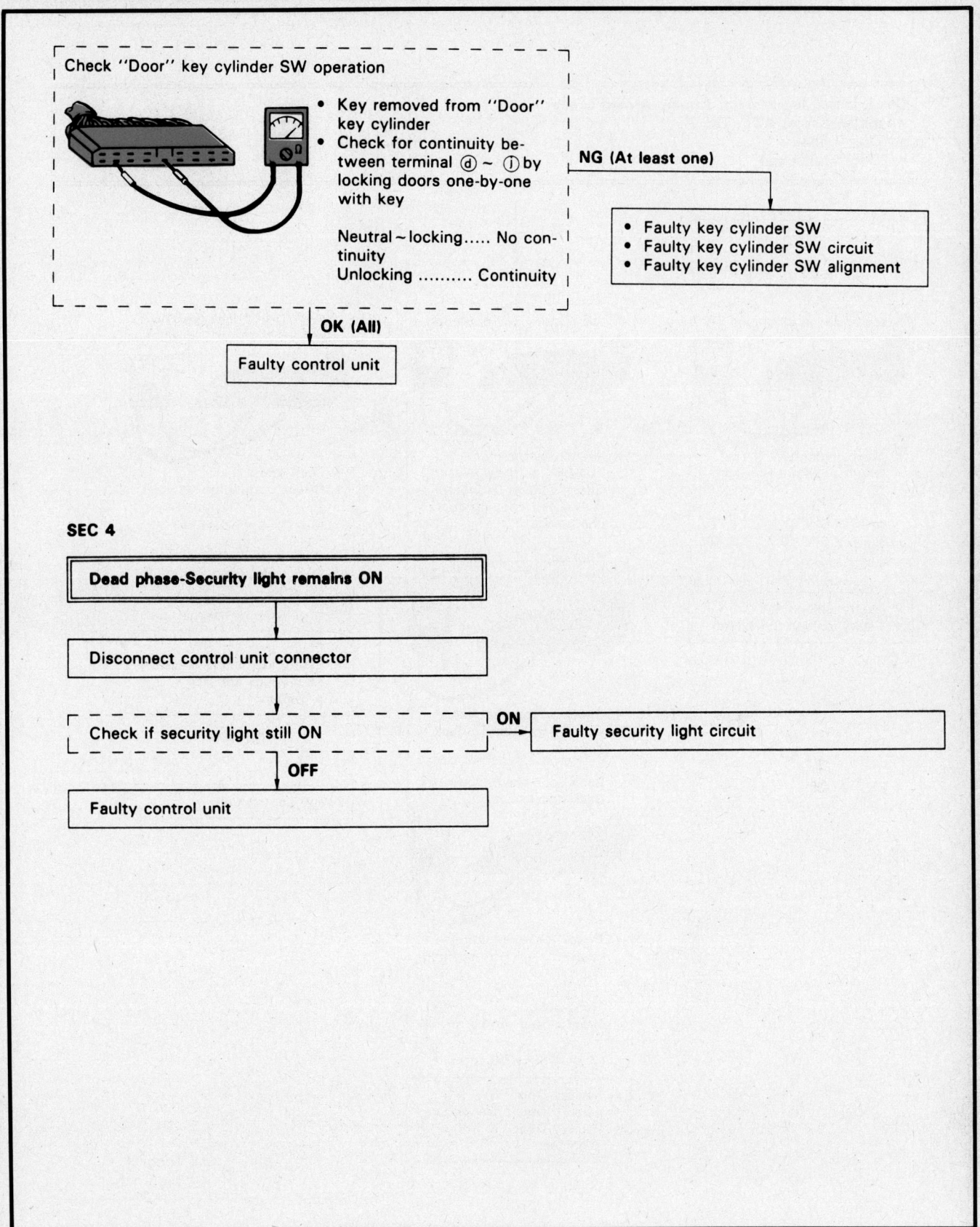

Check "Door" key cylinder SW operation

- Key removed from "Door" key cylinder
- Check for continuity between terminal ⓓ ~ ① by locking doors one-by-one with key

  Neutral~locking..... No continuity
  Unlocking .... Continuity

NG (At least one)
- Faulty key cylinder SW
- Faulty key cylinder SW circuit
- Faulty key cylinder SW alignment

OK (All)
Faulty control unit

SEC 4

Dead phase-Security light remains ON

Disconnect control unit connector

Check if security light still ON

ON → Faulty security light circuit

OFF
Faulty control unit

Theft deterrent system — troubleshooting chart (cont.)

ARM 1

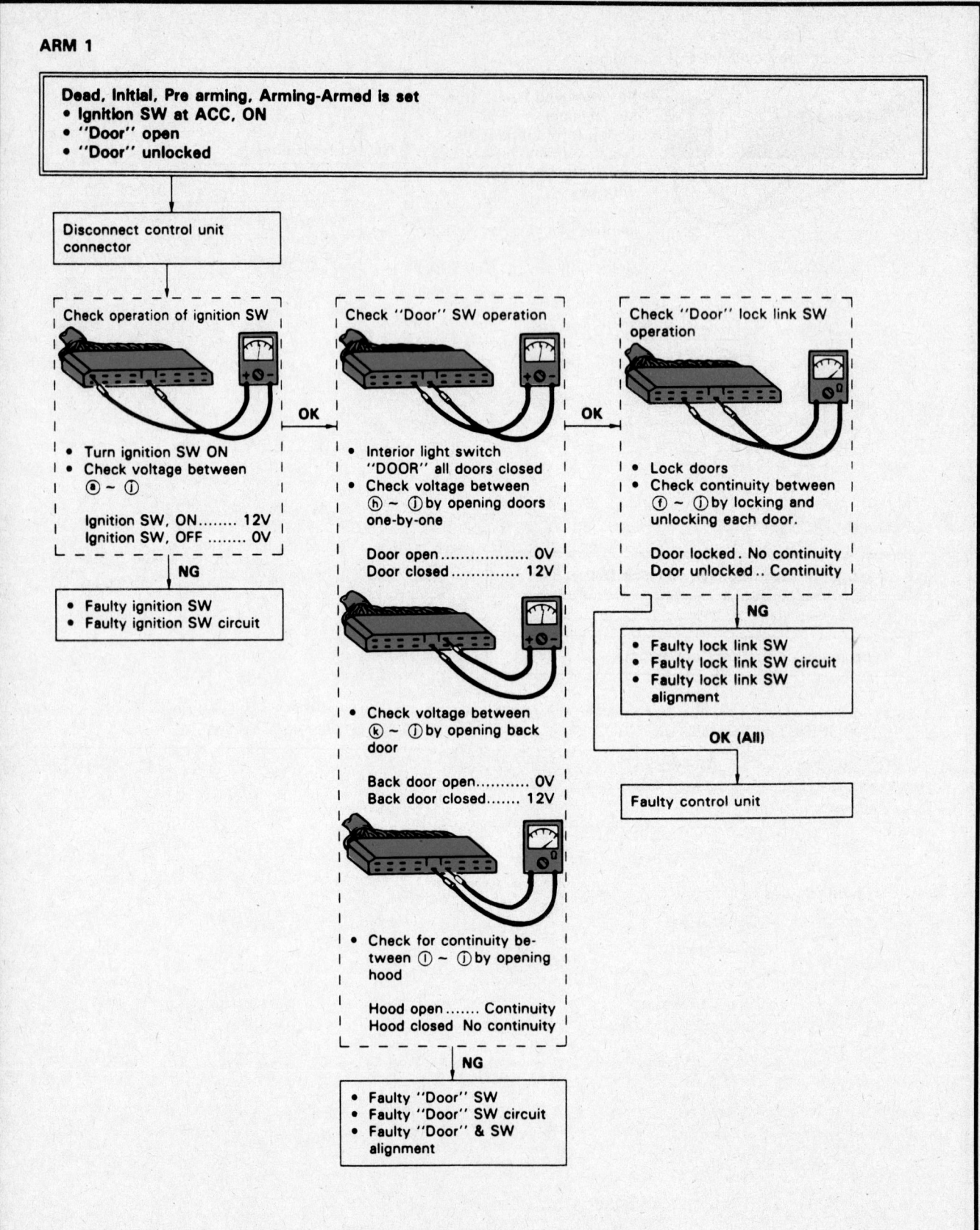

Dead, Initial, Pre arming, Arming-Armed is set
- Ignition SW at ACC, ON
- "Door" open
- "Door" unlocked

↓

Disconnect control unit connector

↓

Check operation of ignition SW

- Turn ignition SW ON
- Check voltage between
  ⓐ ~ ⓙ

  Ignition SW, ON........ 12V
  Ignition SW, OFF 0V

OK →

NG ↓

- Faulty ignition SW
- Faulty ignition SW circuit

Check "Door" SW operation

- Interior light switch "DOOR" all doors closed
- Check voltage between ⓗ ~ ⓙ by opening doors one-by-one

  Door open 0V
  Door closed 12V

- Check voltage between ⓚ ~ ⓙ by opening back door

  Back door open 0V
  Back door closed 12V

- Check for continuity between ⓘ ~ ⓙ by opening hood

  Hood open .... Continuity
  Hood closed No continuity

OK →

NG ↓

- Faulty "Door" SW
- Faulty "Door" SW circuit
- Faulty "Door" & SW alignment

Check "Door" lock link SW operation

- Lock doors
- Check continuity between ⓕ ~ ⓙ by locking and unlocking each door.

  Door locked . No continuity
  Door unlocked .. Continuity

NG ↓

- Faulty lock link SW
- Faulty lock link SW circuit
- Faulty lock link SW alignment

OK (All) ↓

Faulty control unit

Theft deterrent system – troubleshooting chart (cont.)

ALR 1

Armed Phase-Alarm is given without causes
- **Ignition SW OFF**
- **"Door" locked and closed (door, back door and hood)**
- **Arming Phase period finished**

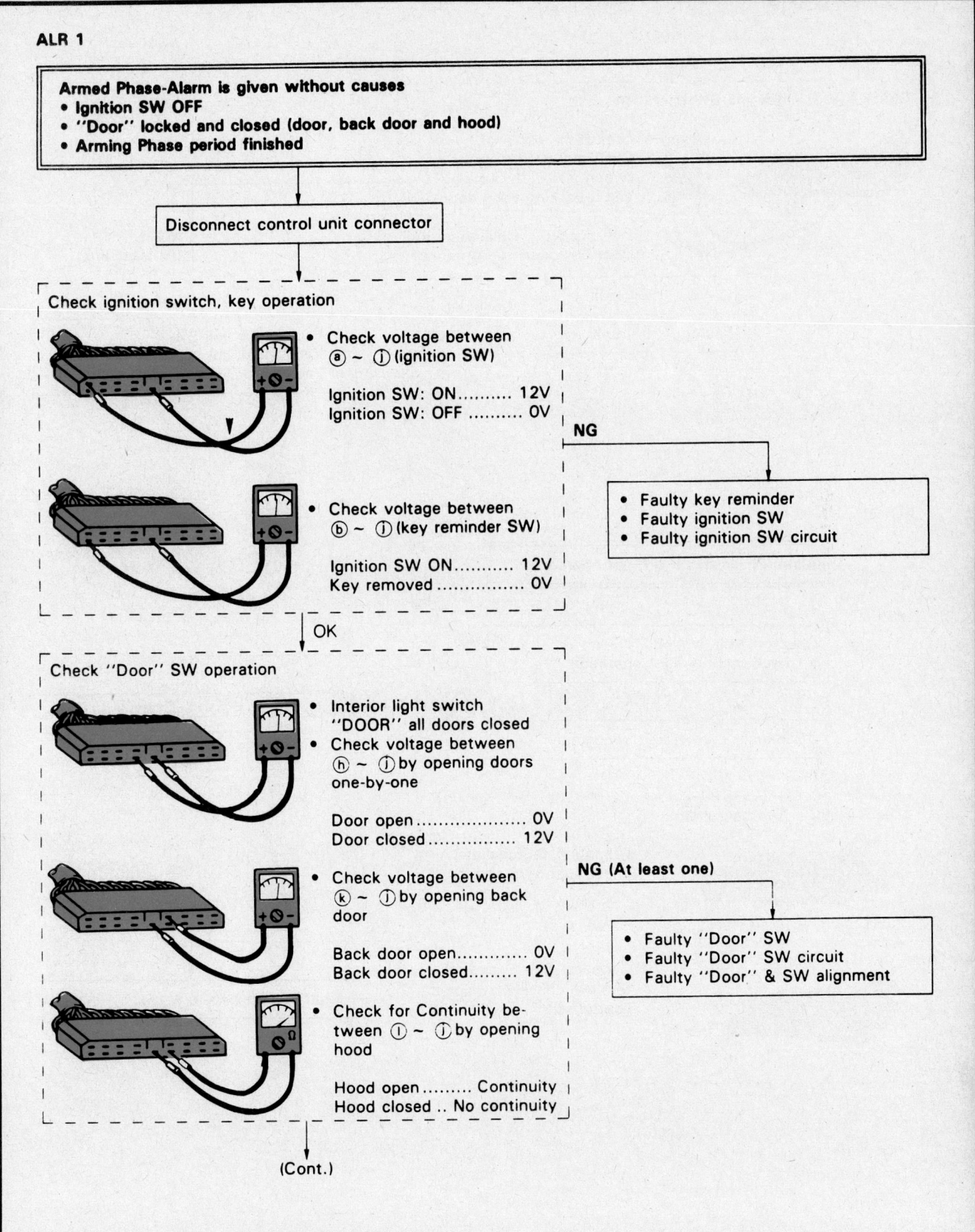

Disconnect control unit connector

Check ignition switch, key operation

- Check voltage between
  (a) ~ (j) (ignition SW)

  Ignition SW: ON.......... 12V
  Ignition SW: OFF 0V

- Check voltage between
  (b) ~ (j) (key reminder SW)

  Ignition SW ON........... 12V
  Key removed 0V

NG

- Faulty key reminder
- Faulty ignition SW
- Faulty ignition SW circuit

OK

Check "Door" SW operation

- Interior light switch "DOOR" all doors closed
- Check voltage between
  (h) ~ (j) by opening doors one-by-one

  Door open 0V
  Door closed 12V

- Check voltage between
  (k) ~ (j) by opening back door

  Back door open............. 0V
  Back door closed......... 12V

NG (At least one)

- Faulty "Door" SW
- Faulty "Door" SW circuit
- Faulty "Door" & SW alignment

- Check for Continuity between (i) ~ (j) by opening hood

  Hood open .... Continuity
  Hood closed .. No continuity

(Cont.)

Theft deterrent system — troubleshooting chart (cont.)

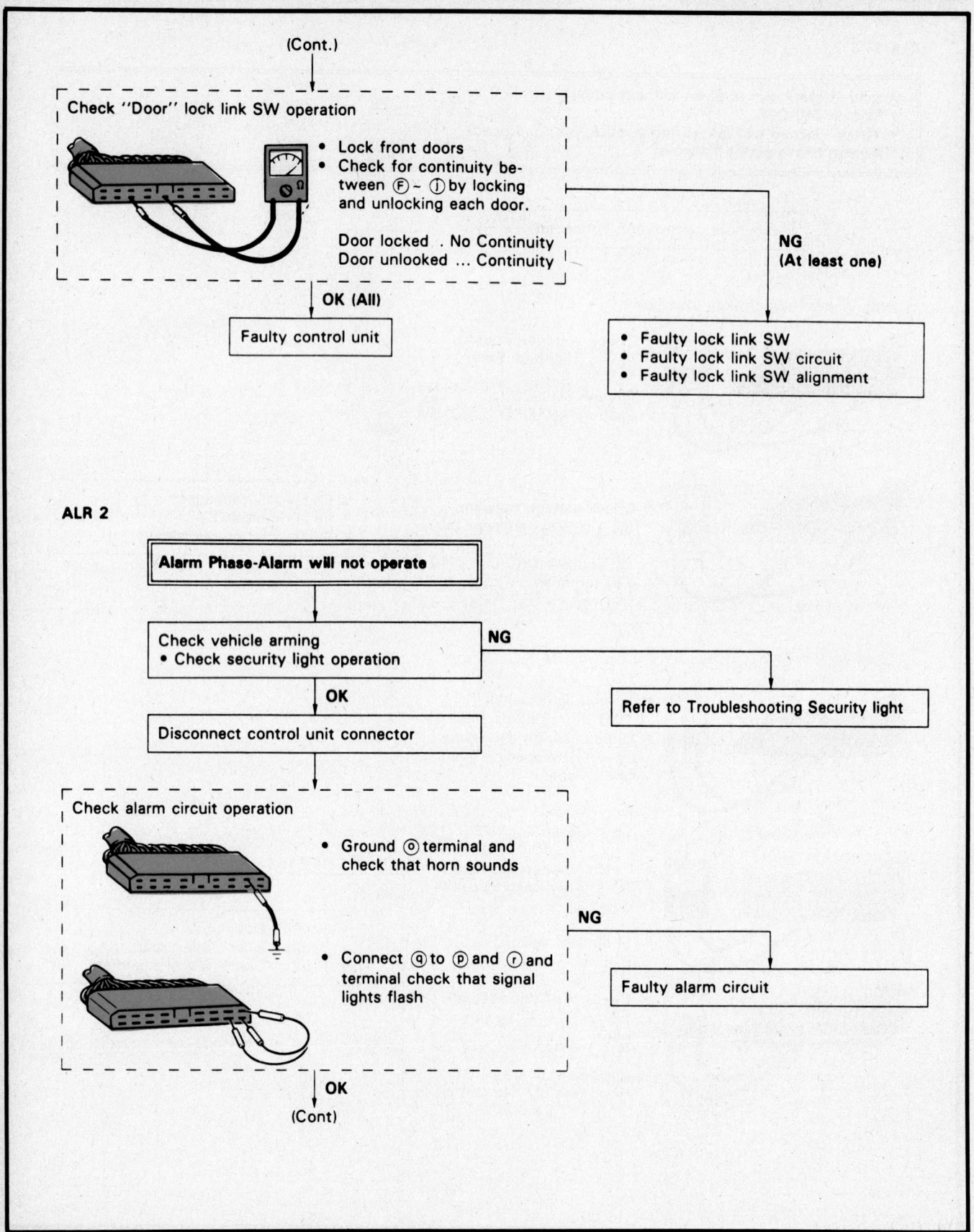

(Cont.)

Check "Door" lock link SW operation

- Lock front doors
- Check for continuity between ⒡ - ⒥ by locking and unlocking each door.

  Door locked . No Continuity
  Door unlooked ... Continuity

OK (All)

Faulty control unit

NG
(At least one)

- Faulty lock link SW
- Faulty lock link SW circuit
- Faulty lock link SW alignment

ALR 2

Alarm Phase-Alarm will not operate

Check vehicle arming
• Check security light operation

NG

OK

Disconnect control unit connector

Refer to Troubleshooting Security light

Check alarm circuit operation

- Ground ⓞ terminal and check that horn sounds

- Connect ⓠ to ⓟ and ⓡ and terminal check that signal lights flash

NG

Faulty alarm circuit

OK

(Cont)

Theft deterrent system – troubleshooting chart (cont.)

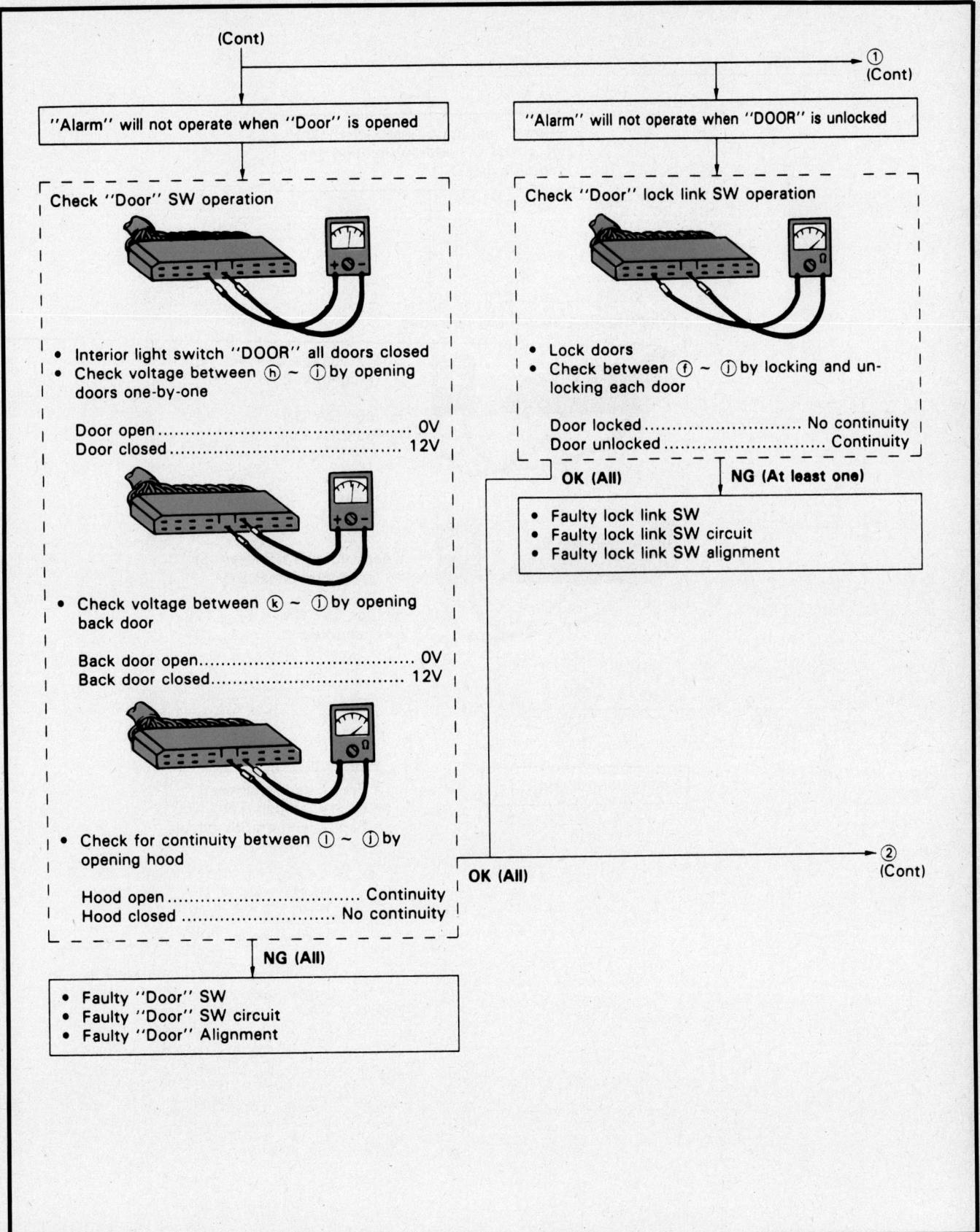

(Cont)

① (Cont)

"Alarm" will not operate when "Door" is opened

"Alarm" will not operate when "DOOR" is unlocked

Check "Door" SW operation

- Interior light switch "DOOR" all doors closed
- Check voltage between ⓗ ~ ① by opening doors one-by-one

  Door open 0V
  Door closed 12V

- Check voltage between ⓚ ~ ① by opening back door

  Back door open... 0V
  Back door closed.................................... 12V

- Check for continuity between ① ~ ① by opening hood

  Hood open .... Continuity
  Hood closed .... No continuity

Check "Door" lock link SW operation

- Lock doors
- Check between ⓕ ~ ① by locking and unlocking each door

  Door locked .... No continuity
  Door unlocked .... Continuity

OK (All)　　　　NG (At least one)

- Faulty lock link SW
- Faulty lock link SW circuit
- Faulty lock link SW alignment

OK (All)

② (Cont)

NG (All)

- Faulty "Door" SW
- Faulty "Door" SW circuit
- Faulty "Door" Alignment

Theft deterrent system — troubleshooting chart (cont.)

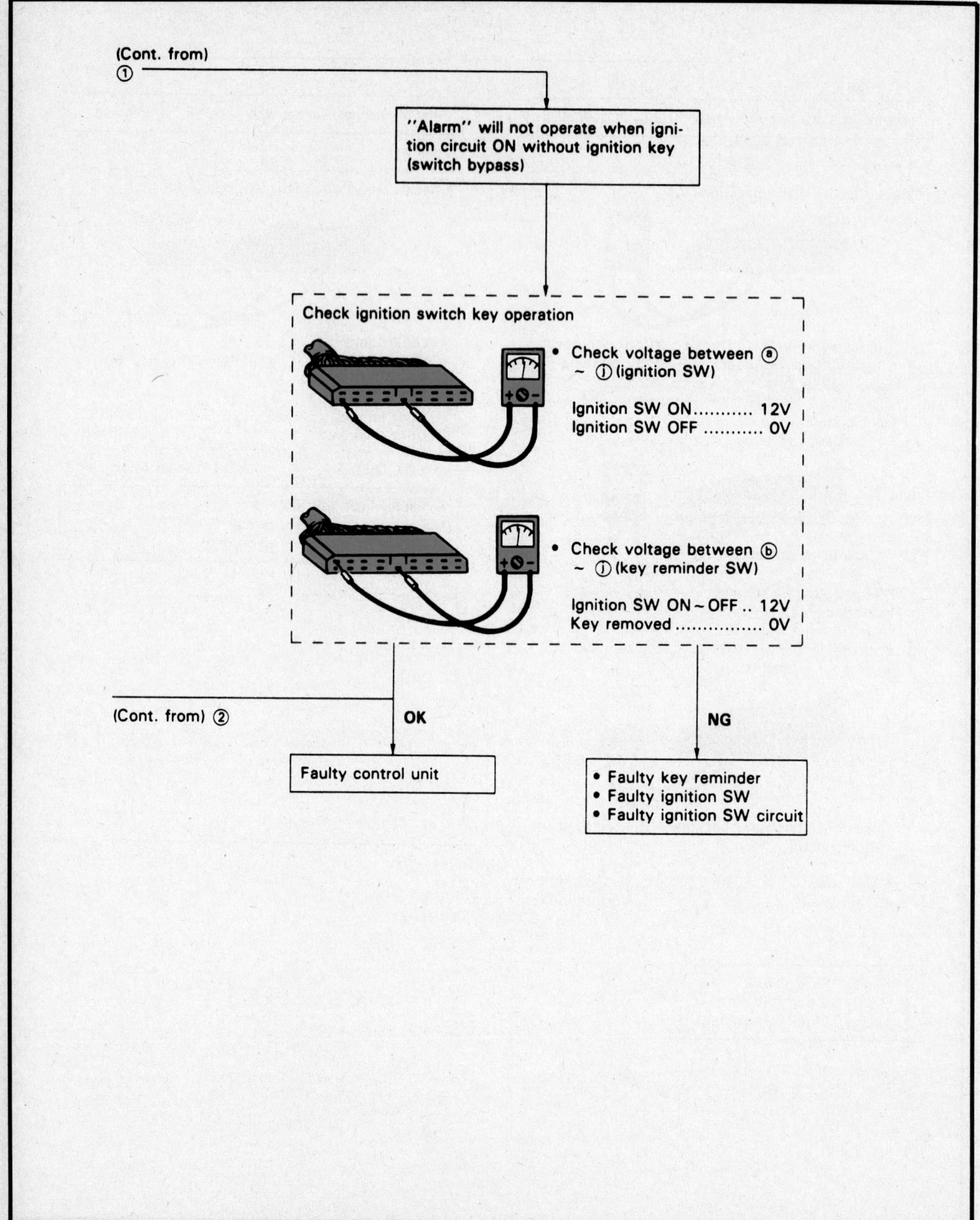

(Cont. from)
①

"Alarm" will not operate when ignition circuit ON without ignition key (switch bypass)

Check ignition switch key operation

- Check voltage between ⓐ ~ ① (ignition SW)

  Ignition SW ON........... 12V
  Ignition SW OFF 0V

- Check voltage between ⓑ ~ ① (key reminder SW)

  Ignition SW ON ~ OFF .. 12V
  Key removed 0V

(Cont. from) ②   **OK**   **NG**

Faulty control unit

- Faulty key reminder
- Faulty ignition SW
- Faulty ignition SW circuit

Theft deterrent system — troubleshooting chart (cont.)

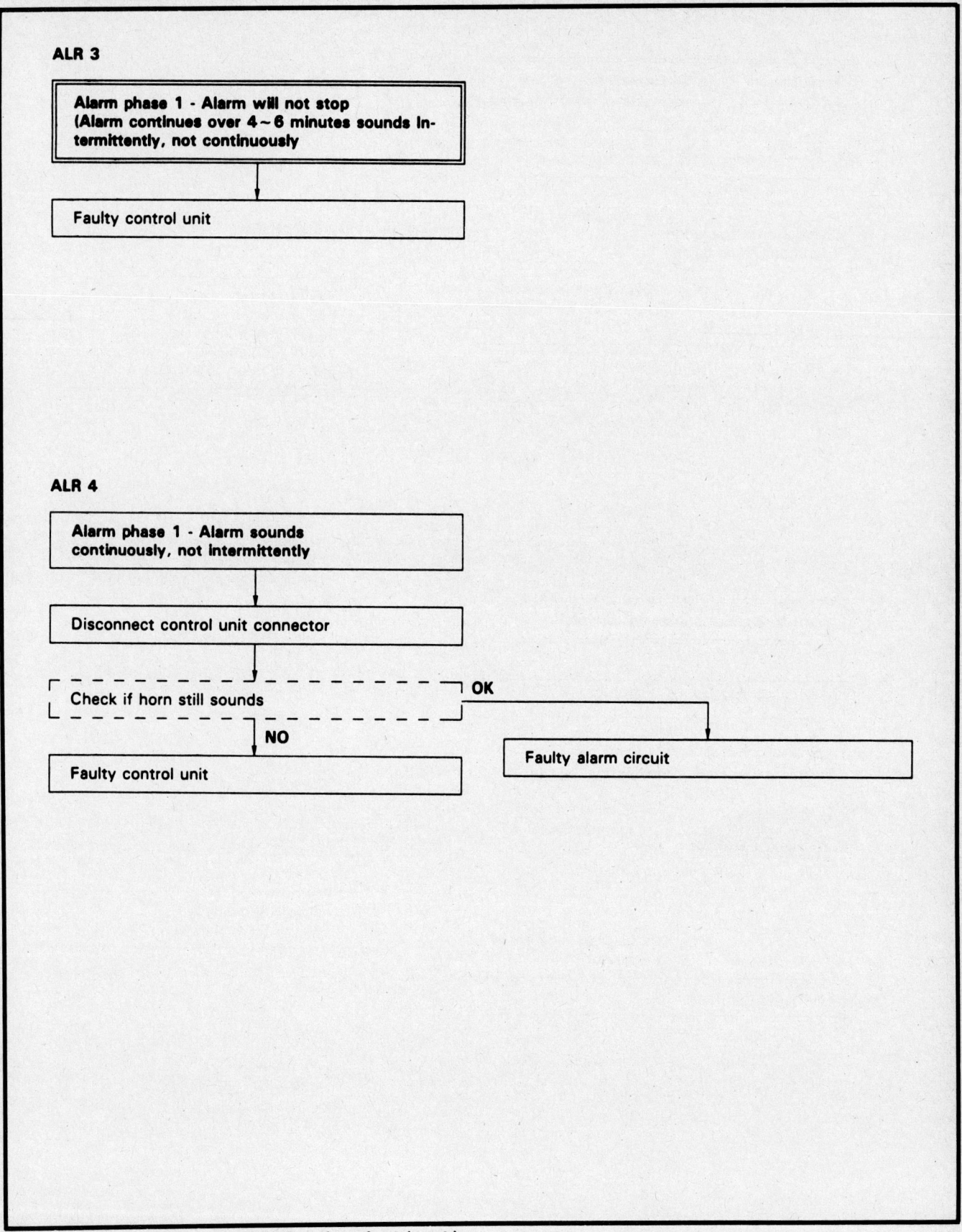

ALR 3

Alarm phase 1 - Alarm will not stop
(Alarm continues over 4~6 minutes sounds intermittently, not continuously

↓

Faulty control unit

ALR 4

Alarm phase 1 - Alarm sounds
continuously, not intermittently

↓

Disconnect control unit connector

↓

Check if horn still sounds ─────────── OK

│ NO   ↓

Faulty control unit   Faulty alarm circuit

Theft deterrent system — troubleshooting chart (cont.)

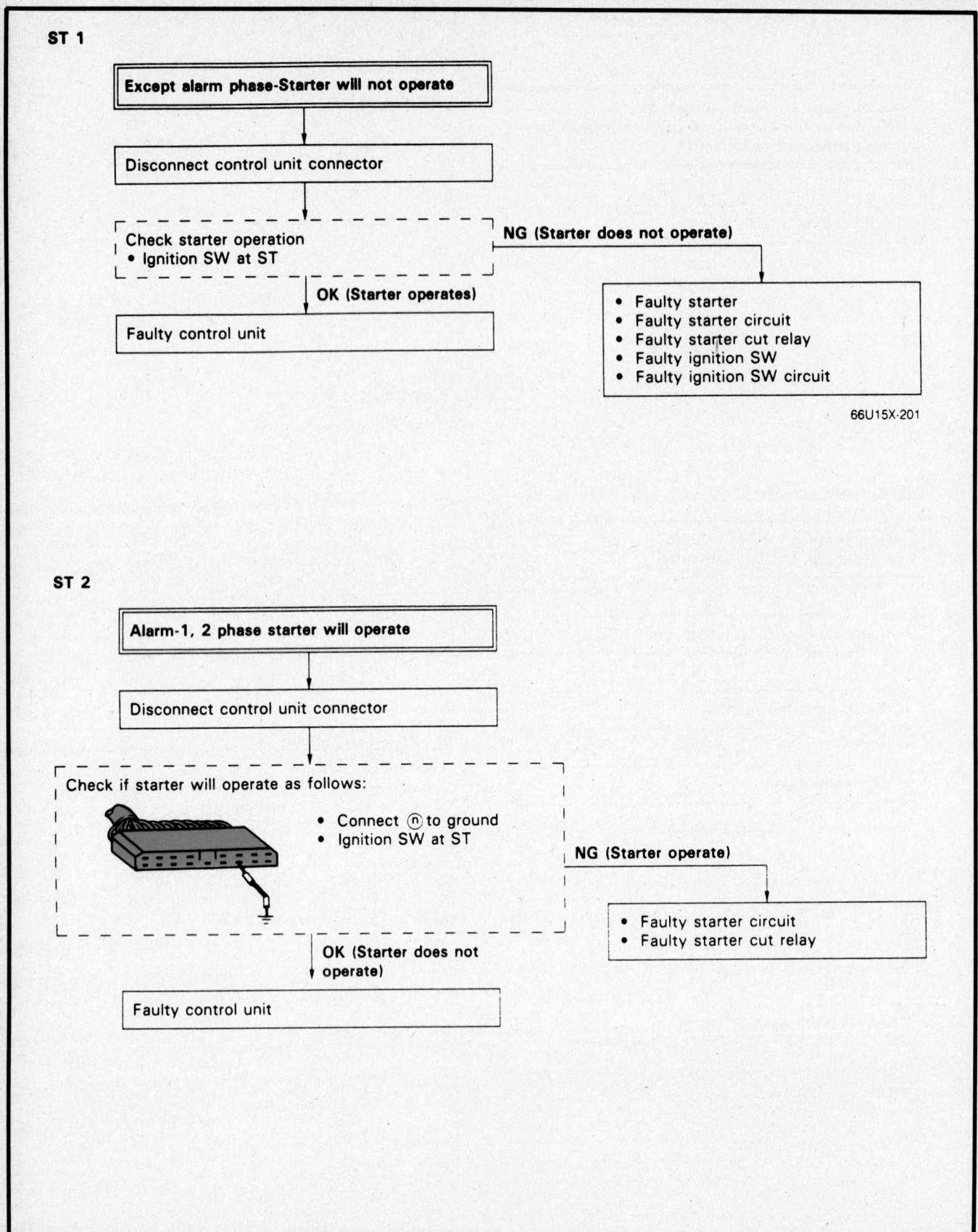

ST 1

Except alarm phase-Starter will not operate

↓

Disconnect control unit connector

↓

Check starter operation
• Ignition SW at ST

→ **NG (Starter does not operate)**

OK (Starter operates) ↓

Faulty control unit

- Faulty starter
- Faulty starter circuit
- Faulty starter cut relay
- Faulty ignition SW
- Faulty ignition SW circuit

66U15X-201

ST 2

Alarm-1, 2 phase starter will operate

↓

Disconnect control unit connector

↓

Check if starter will operate as follows:

• Connect ⓝ to ground
• Ignition SW at ST

→ **NG (Starter operate)**

OK (Starter does not operate) ↓

Faulty control unit

- Faulty starter circuit
- Faulty starter cut relay

Theft deterrent system — troubleshooting chart (cont.)

MITSUBISHI

Power Mirrors

The mirrors are controlled by a single switch assembly located on the door panel on some models and on the center console (or instrument panel) on other models. The motor that operates the mirror is part of the mirror assembly and cannot be replaced separately.

POWER MIRROR ASSEMBLY

Removal and Installation

1. Remove the power mirror cover by pulling it inward.
2. Remove the power mirror mounting nuts, disconnect the electrical connections and remove the power mirror from the door.
3. Installation is the reverse order of the removal procedure.

POWER MIRROR SWITCH

Removal and Installation

STARION

1. Disconnect the negative battery cable. Remove the inner box from the rear console box.
2. Lift the front portion of the mirror switch assembly and remove the mirror switch assembly from the rear console box.
3. Disconnect the harness connector at the switch and remove the mirror switch assembly from the console.
4. Installation is the reverse order of the removal procedure.

GALANT

1. Disconnect the negative battery cable. Remove the blank cover at the front portion of the mirror switch.
2. Remove the mirror switch out of the accessory box by pressing the catch on the switch.
3. Disconnect the electrical connector and remove the switch from the console.
4. Installation is the reverse order of the removal procedure.

TREDIA

1. Disconnect the negative battery cable. Remove the side ventilator knob.
2. Using a suitable tool pry up the left side of the switch panel and pull the panel outward.
3. Disconnect the mirror switch connector and remove the mirror switch together with the switch panel. Remove the mirror switch from the panel.
4. Installation is the reverse order of the removal procedure.

CORDIA

1. Disconnect the negative battery cable . Remove the steering wheel.
2. Remove the instrument panel under cover. Remove the lap duct heater. Remove the glove box.
3. Remove the defroster duct and the three heater control wires. Remove the meter hood mounting screws disconnect the the connectors for the rear window wiper/washer and rear window defogger and remove the meter hood.
4. Disconnect the speedometer cable from the back of the meter case. Remove the meter case mounting screws and withdraw the case slightly inward.
5. Disconnect all the connectors and remove the meter case from the instrument panel. Remove the defroster garnish.
6. Remove the left and right instrument panel side covers. Remove the fuse block from the instrument panel. Disconnect the connectors connecting the instrument panel wiring harness and main wiring harness at the rear of the fuse block.

7. Disconnect the connector at the lower end of the blower case. Remove the floor console audio bracket upper mounting screws. Remove the steering column assembly from the pedal support member.
8. Remove the antenna feed wire. Remove the instrument panel mounting bolts and nuts. Remove the instrument panel assembly.
9. Remove the power mirror switch from the instrument panel.
10. Installation is the reverse order of the removal procedure.

Power Antenna

The power antenna automatically raises the antenna mast to its full height whenever the radio and ignition are tuned on. The antenna retracts into the rear fender when either the ignition or the radio is turned off.

POWER ANTENNA ASSEMBLY

Removal and Installation

Be sure the antenna mast is retracted before operation. Disconnect the antenna relay before removing the high floor side panel.

1. Disconnect the negative battery cable. Remove the trunk room side trim panel and high floor side panel.
2. Disconnect the harness connector, ground wire and antenna lead wire and the drain hose.
3. Remove the antenna assembly mounting nuts and take out the antenna assembly from the trunk room side.
4. Installation is the reverse order of the removal procedure.

Pole Assembly With Cable Replacement

1. Remove the antenna asembly. Remove the gear cover from the antenna motor.
2. Pull out the drive mechanism sub-assembly from the inside of the gear housing.
3. Remove the drum from the drive mechanism sub-assembly. Cut the cable and remove the drum and the rod sub-assembly.
4. Pass the new cable through the gear housing before it is put into the drum. Using a suitable tool stake the cable at two positions. Install the drum to the drive mechanism sub-assembly.
5. With the antenna fully extended, install the drive mechanism sub-assembly. Install the two plate washers on the drive mechanism sub-assembly (be sure that the washers are not bound to the shaft.
6. Locate the projection of count lever so that it may engage with the recess in the limiter plate on the gear cover side, then install the counter lever. Check for proper operation before installing the assembly into the vehicle.

Power Antenna Relay Test

1. With the harness connector connected and the antenna mast extending and retracting, use a suitable voltmeter and check the voltage readings.
2. With the antenna mast extending, there should be -1 to + 1 volts at the top left corner (1) terminal. There should be 10 to 13 volts at the upper right corner (4) terminal.
3. With the antenna mast retracting, there should be 10 to 13 volts at the top left corner (1) terminal. There should be -1 to + 1 volts at the upper right corner (4) terminal.
4. If the voltage readings do not agree with those in this procedure, replace the relay.

Rear Window Defogger System

The rear window defogger system consists of a rear window with two vertical bus bars and a series of electrically connected grid lines baked on the inside surface. A control switch and a timer relay combined into a single assembly is used on all models.

All circuit protection is provided by a fusible link, located in the charging circuit, for the heater grid circuit and by a fuse for the relay control circuit.

NOTE: Since the grid lines can be damaged or scraped off with sharp instruments, caution should be used when cleaning the glass or removing foreign materials, decals or stickers. Normal glass cleaning solvents or hot water used with rags or toweling is recommended.

REAR WINDOW DEFOGGER SYSTEM

Test

The rear window defogger system operation can be checked in the vehicle using the following test procedure.

1. Turn the ignition switch to the "ON" position, also turn the rear window defogger control switch to the "ON" position.
2. Monitor the vehicle ammeter. With the control switch in the "ON" position, a distinct needle deflection should be noted.

NOTE: If the vehicle is not equipped with a voltmeter or a ammeter, the rear window defogger operation can be checked by feeling the glass in the rear windshield. A distinct difference in temperature between the grid lines and adjacent clear glass can be detected in three to four minutes of operation.

3. Using a suitable DC voltmeter connect the vertical bus bar on the passenger side of the vehicle with the positive lead and the driver side of the vehicle with the negative lead. The voltmeter should read between 10 to 14 volts.
4. Only Steps 1, 2 and 3 will confirm the system is operational. The indicator or pilot light illumination means that there is power available at the output of the relay only and does not necessarily prove the system is operational.
5. If the rear window defogger system does not operate properly, the problem should be isolated as outlined in the following procedure:
   a. Check to be sure the ignition switch is in the "ON" position. Be sure that the rear defogger feed (HOT) wire is connected to the terminal or pigtail and that the ground wire is indeed grouned.
   b. Be sure the fusible link and control circuit fuse is operational and all electrical connections are secure. When all of these things have been completely checked out, one of the following is defective; the control switch/timer relay module or the rear window defogger grid lines.
   c. If the grid lines were to blame, either all the grid lines would have to be broken, or one of the feed (HOT) wires are not connected for the system to be inoperative.
6. If turning the control switch procedures give severe voltmeter (ammeter) deflections, check the system for a shorting condition. If the systems check out but the indicator bulb does not light, check and or replace the bulb.

REAR WINDOW DEFOGGER GRID

Test

When a grid is inoperable due to an open circuit, the area of glass normally cleared by that grid will remained fogged or iced until cleared by the adjacent grids. Use the following procedure to located a broken grid.

1. With the engine running at idle, place the rear defogger switch in the "ON" position. The pilot lamp is the switch lever should light up indicating the defogger is operating.
2. Using a 12 volt voltmeter, connect the positive lead of the voltmeter to the hot side of the vertical bus element on the inside surface of the glass.
3. Connect the negative lead of the voltmeter to the ground side of the bus element. The voltage drop indicated on the meter should be 11 to 13 volts. Connect the negative lead of the voltmeter to a good ground, the meter reading should stay constant.
4. Keep the negative lead connected to the ground and carefully use the positive lead to contact each grid at the approximate centerline of the window. A voltage drop of approixmately 6 volts. indicates a good grid or a closed circuit.
5. No voltage indicated a broken grid wire. To located the exact location of the break, move the voltmeter lead along the grid wire. The voltage should decrease gradually. if the voltage drops suddenly, there is a break at that location.

NOTE: A Grid repair kit is available from the manufacturer and the enclosed manufactures instruction should be followed for a proper grid repair.

Grid Resistance Test

1. Turn the defogger switch off. Use a ohmmeter (with a scale ranging from 0 to 100 ohms) to measure the resistance at each grid line between the center and the end , left and right separately.
2. The section involving a broken grid line indicates resistance twice that in other sections.
3. Once in the affected area, move the tester bar for a position where the resistance sharply changes. Mark the broken grid line and repair as necessary.

REAR DEFOGGER SWITCH

Removal and Installation
STARION

1. Disconnect the negative battery cable. Remove the dimmer control knob.
2. Remove the switch panel. Detach the rear window defogger switch by pressing the tabs on the switch.
3. Disconnect the electrical connector and remove the rear window defogger switch.
4. Installation is the reverse order of the removal procedure.

MIRAGE

1. Disconnect the negative battery cable. Using a suitable tool, slip the tool behind the defogger switch far enough to depress the locking tab. Repeat this procedure for the opposite side of the switch. Be careful not to damage the instrument panel.
2. Disconnect the electrical connector and remove the switch from the dash panel.
3. Installation is the reverse order of the removal procedure.

GALANT

1. Disconnect the negative battery cable. Remove the turn signal switch.
2. Remove the lighting switch and the two-level unit. Remove the dimmer and passing switch.
3. Remove the light panel retaining screws and remove the light panel. Remove the retaining screws for defogger switch and remove the switch.
4. Installation is the reverse order of the removal procedure.

CORDIA

1. Disconnect the negative battery cable. Remove the steering wheel.

2. Remove the instrument panel under cover. Remove the lap duct heater. Remove the glove box.

3. Remove the defroster duct and the three heater control wires. Remove the meter hood mounting screws disconnect the connectors for the rear window wiper/washer and rear window defogger and remove the meter hood.

4. Depress the locking tabs on the defroster switch and remove the switch from the back of the meter hood.

5. Installation is the reverse order of the removal procedure.

TREDIA

1. Disconnect the negative battery cable. Detach the switch panel.

2. Detach the defogger switch and pull it forward. Disconnect the electrical connectors at the rear of the defogger switch and remove the switch.

3. Installation is the reverse order of the removal procedure.

Electric Sunroofs

The sunroof is operated by a switch in the headliner. The system is consists of the sunroof switch, motor drive cables and 15 amp circuit breaker. The sunroof can be closed manually, (should it be necessary) by removing the headliner plug, insert the handle and turn the gear to close the sunroof.

NOTE: The sunroof assembly is equipped with water drain tubes, it is important to keep these drain tubes open. So it is recommended to blow compressed air through the drain tubes at regular intervals, in order to keep the drain tubes clear.

SUNROOF ASSEMBLY

Removal and Installation

1. Fully close the sunroof glass and fully open the sunshade.

2. Remove the rear view mirror, sun visor(s), assist grip, front pillar, front headlining trim, rear headlining trim, rear pillar trim, headlining and roof rail trim.

3. Remove the dome light cover, retaining screws and remove the dome light from the panel.

4. Remove the motor mounting screws, disconnect the electrical connectors and remove the motor from the roof panel.

5. Remove the sunroof glass retaining bolts and remove the sunroof glass assembly from the vehicle.

6. Remove the Sunroof deflector retaining screws and remove the deflector from the sunroof.

7. Remove the front and rear drain tubes from the housing assembly. Remove the sunroof assembly to roof panel attaching bolts and nuts and remove the sunroof assembly. Be sure to remove the left and right drain tubes and nuts.

8. Remove the set bracket from the body. Remove the set plate and the guide rail cover.

9. Remove the drive tube from the guide rail and remove the rear guide from the drive tube. Remove the drive tube from the housing assembly. Remove the sun shade from the guide rail and remove the guide rail from the housing assembly.

10. Installation is the reverse order of the removal procedure. Be sure to apply a thin coat of grease to the rear guide cable before it is mounted in the drive tube. Wherever seal tape was removed, replace it with new seal tape. When the weather stripe is mounted to the sunroof, be sure that it is positioned at the center toward the the front of the vehicle.

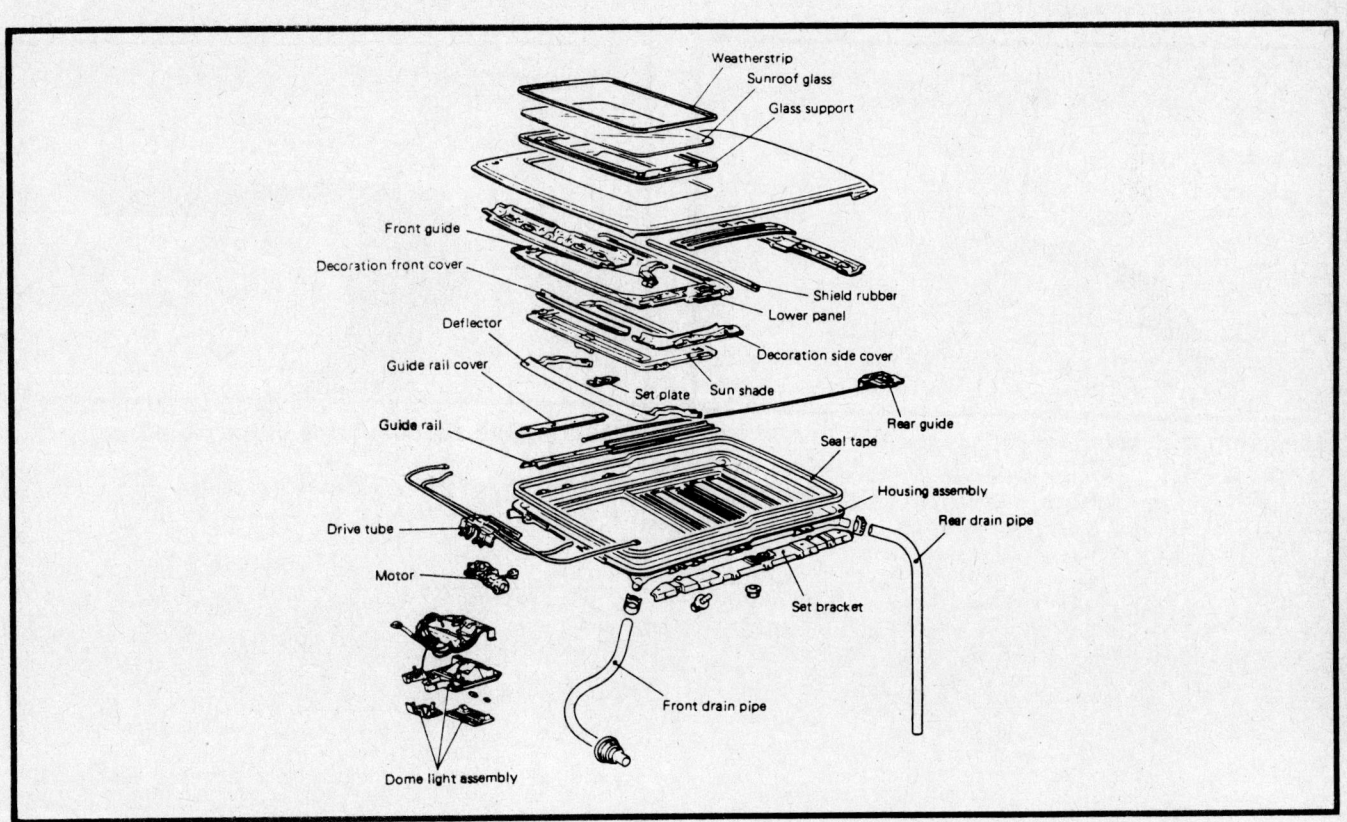

Exploded view of the Mitsubishi sunroof

Sunroof Height Adjustment

Be sure to loosen the attaching screws of the front and rear guides before adjustment.

1. Fully close the roof lid and fully open the sun shade. Remove the decoration cover.

2. Adjust the roof and roof lid to the same height with the front and rear guide screws at the the bottom of the adjustment slot.

3. If the roof and roof lid are not parallel, adjust by removing the motor and changing the engagement of the cable and gear.

4. Adjust the stopper so that when the roof lid is fully closed, the front roller guide of the rear guide will be placed in the between the middle of the rear guide and front roller guide.

Sliding Resistance Force Test

1. Remove the deflector and the decoration cover. Remove the dome light bezel, dome light and motor.

2. Remove the sunroof lid glass attaching nuts (on the rear corners) and install a strong string to stud bolts.

3. Install a suitable spring scale to the string and measure the sliding force by pulling on the scale. The force should be 26 lbs. or less.

NOTE: When the sliding resistance force is measured, pull the roof lid in the direction that the roof lid closes.

4. If the measured sliding resistance force exceeds the standard specification, check for foreign substances which might have been caught in the drive tube. Be sure that the front and rear guides move in parallel with the guide rail without binding.

Slipping Force Of Clutch Test

This is a test to ensure that the clutch slipping force of the sunroof motor is within specifications.

1. Insert one end of the sunroof wrench (which is provided in the tool bag that is incorported with the vehicle) into the motor gear hole.

2. Hook a suitable spring scale to the other end of this wrench and pull the spring scale in a direction at right angles to the wrench.

3. Measure the force when the clutch starts to slip (this is when the sunroof wrench begins to turn). The scale should rear 6 to 7 lbs.

NOTE: If a wrench other than the one provided in the tool bag (by the manufacturer) is used, the measured value may not conincide with the standard value.

4. If the slipping force of the clutch is out of specifications, adjust the force by turning the adjusting nut on the motor. Turn the nut clockwise to increase the force and counterclockwise to decrease the force. Be sure to tighten the adjusting nut after a proper adjustment has been made.

Sunroof Motor Test

1. Remove the motor as previously outlined. Connect the motor terminals directly to the battery and check to see if the motor operates smoothly.

2. Now reverse the polarity and check that the motor operates smoothly in the reverse direction.

3. Check the circuit breaker incorporated in the motor by using the following procedure:

   a. Depress the switch to close the roof lid fully. Keep the switch depressed for ten seconds.

   b. Release the switch and simultaneously depress the open switch. If the roof lid starts to open with in sixty seconds, the circuit breaker is in working condition.

4. Reinstall the sunroof motor.

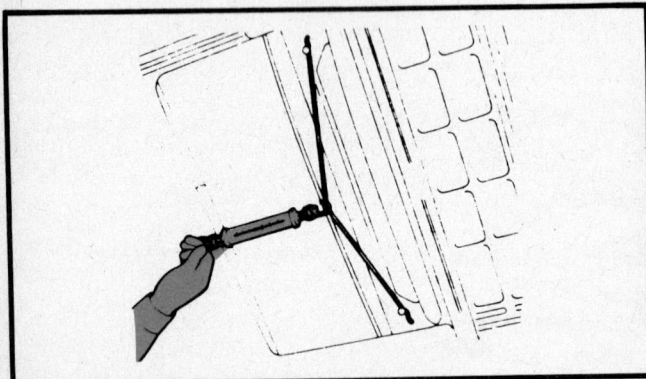

Measuring the sliding resistance force

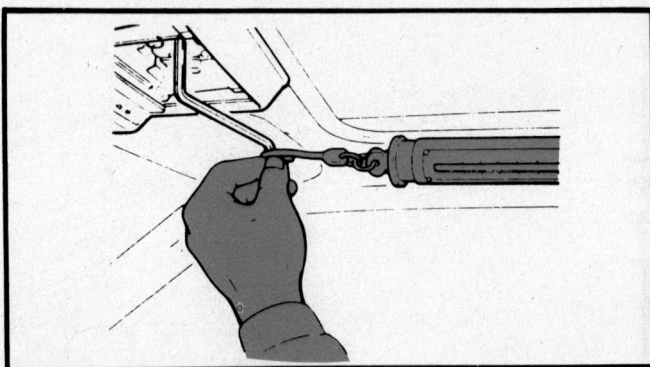

Measuring the slipping force of the clutch

NISSAN

Power Mirrors

The mirrors are controlled by a single switch assembly located on the door panel on some models and on the center console (or instrument panel) on other models. The motor that operates the mirror is part of the mirror assembly and cannot be replaced separately.

POWER MIRROR ASSEMBLY

Removal and Installation

280ZX

1. Disconnect the negative battery cable. Remove the inner door finishing panel and sealing screen.
2. Disconnect the mirror electrical connectors. Remove the mirror retaining nuts and remove the mirror assembly from the door.
3. Installation is the reverse order of the removal procedure.

200SX, 300ZX AND MAXIMA

1. Disconnect the negative battery cable. Working from inside the of the vehicle, remove the power mirror finish trim panel.

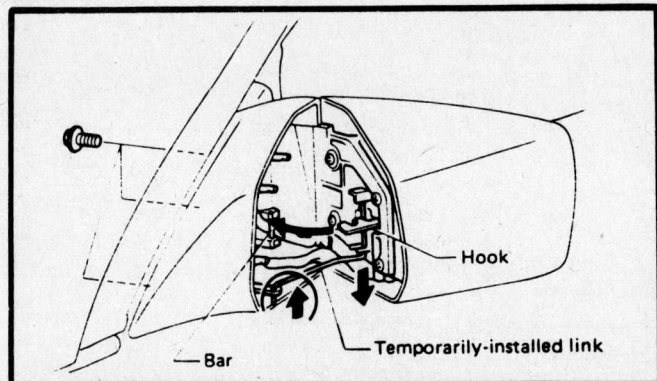

Power mirror removal and installation – 200SX, 300ZX and Maxima

2. While holding the mirror with on hand, remove the three mirror retaining screws with the other. Remove the mirror assembly from the door.
3. After installing the mirror base to the door and remove the bottom hooked portion of the temporarily installed link.
4. Hook the linkage bar into its proper position in the mirror head. Tilt the mirror head backward and while holding the mirror remove the temporarily installed link.

NOTE:On some of the earlier models it may be necessary to remove the inner door panel to gain access to the power mirror retaining screws and electrical connections.

MIRROR CONTROL SWITCH

Removal and Installation

280ZX

1. Disconnect the negative battery cable. loosen the screws retaining the console box and disconnect the electrical connections.
2. Remove the ring nuts retaining the mirror switch to the console box. Remove the mirror switch from behind the console box.
3. Installation is the reverse order of the removal procedure.

DASH MOUNTED SWITCHES

1. Disconnect the negative battery cable. Using a suitable tool, slip the tool behind the mirror switch far enough to depress the locking tab. Repeat this procedure for the opposite side of the switch. Be careful not to damage the instrument panel.
2. Disconnect the electrical connector and remove the switch from the dash panel.
3. Installation is the reverse order of the removal procedure.

NOTE: There is not a a specific mirror switch removal procedure available for the 200SX, 300ZX and Maxima (at the time of this publication). So the switch should be looked at very carefully to decide its removal procedure. If the switch does have locking tabs, then use the dash mounted removal procedure already outlined.

Condition	Probable cause	Corrective action
Either of the mirrors does not move up, down and to right and left sides.	Loose connection or open circuit.	Check wiring and/or repair connection.
One side mirror does not move up, down and to right and left sides.	Loose connection or open circuit. Faulty mirror switch. Faulty mirror motor.	Check wiring and/or repair connection. Replace. Replace.
Mirror does not move to one direction.	Faulty mirror motor. Faulty mirror switch.	Replace. Replace.

Power mirror troubleshooting chart

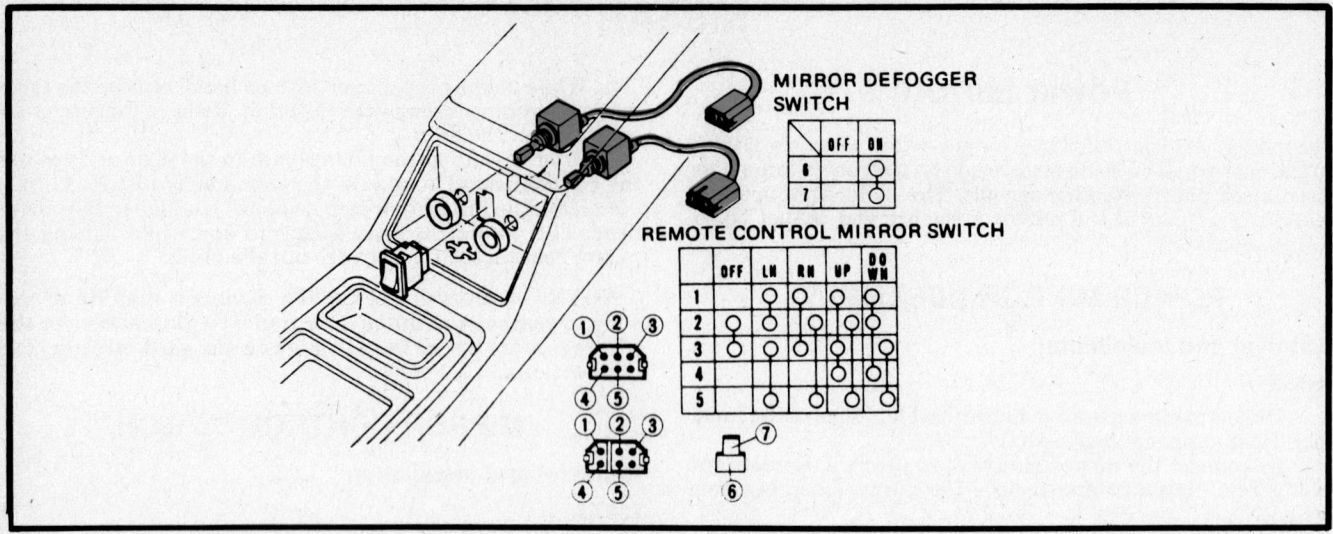

Power mirror switch removal and test procedure—280ZX

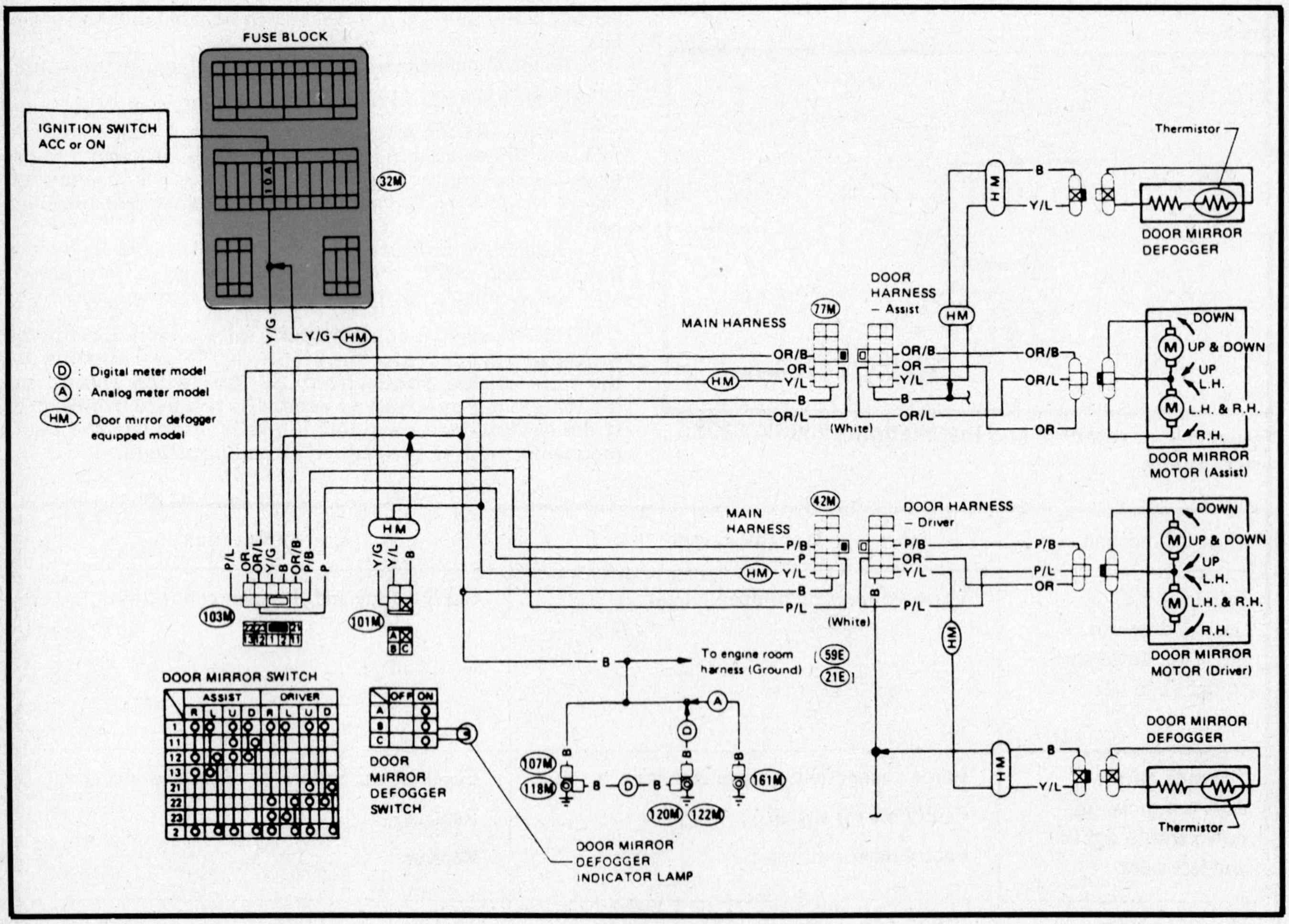

Power mirror wiring schematic—300ZX

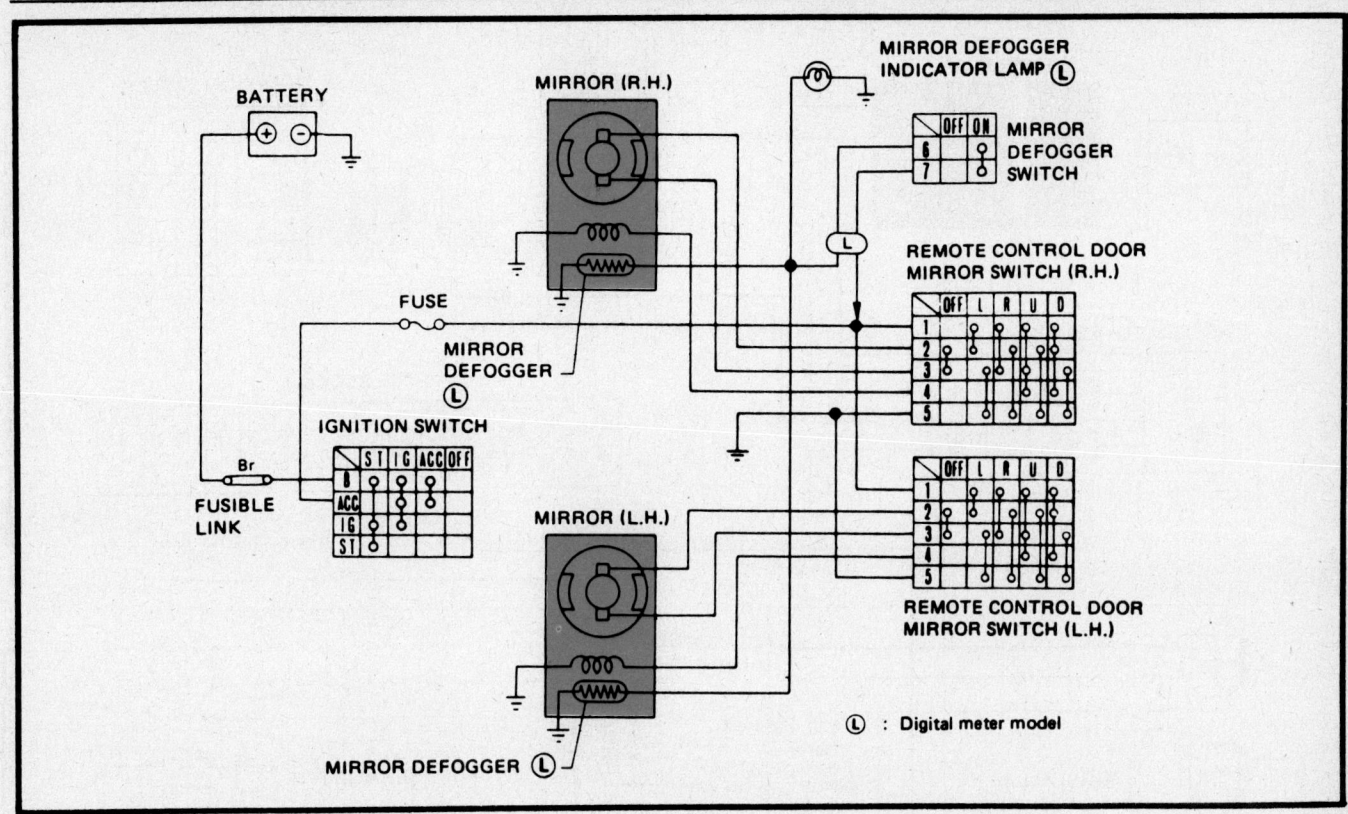

Power mirror wiring schematic—280ZX

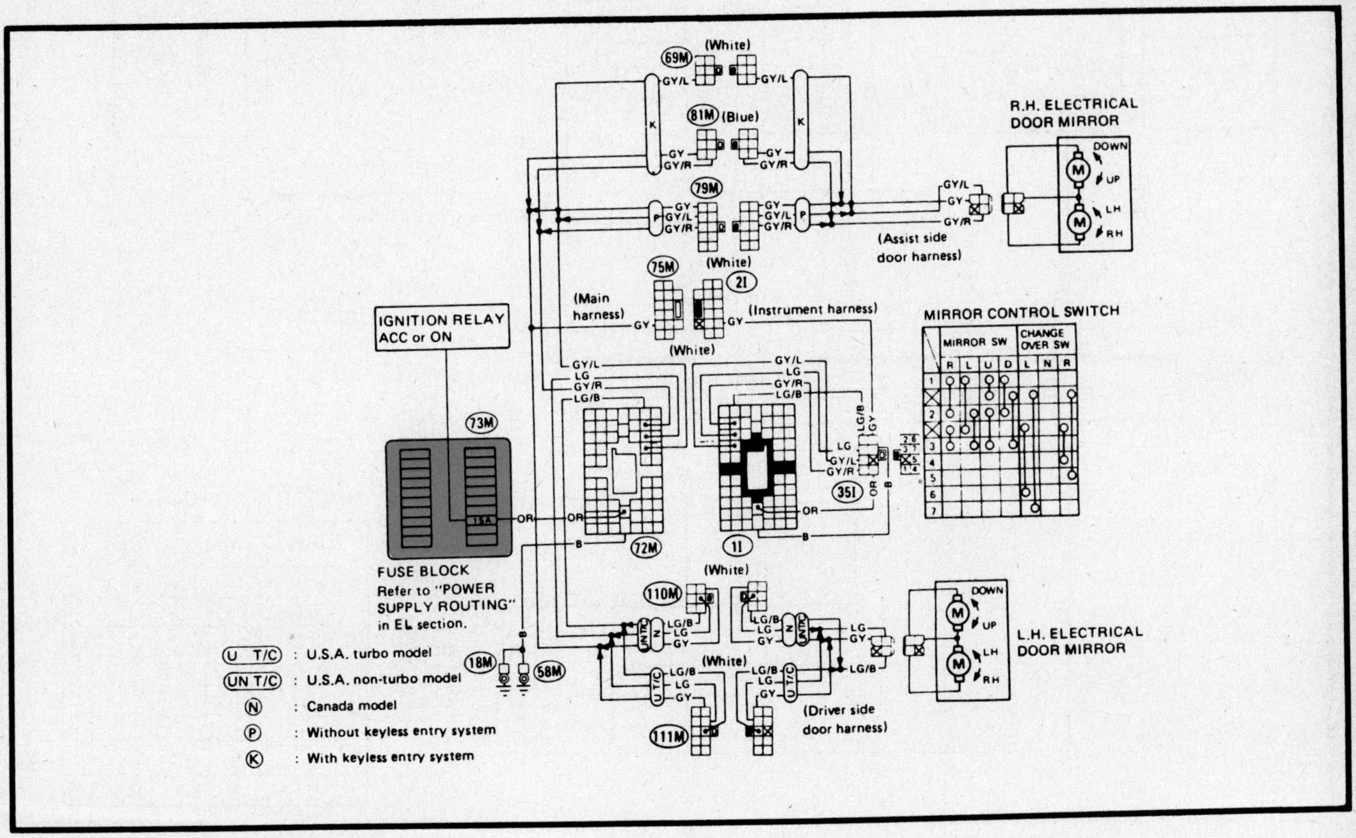

Power mirror wiring schematic—200SX

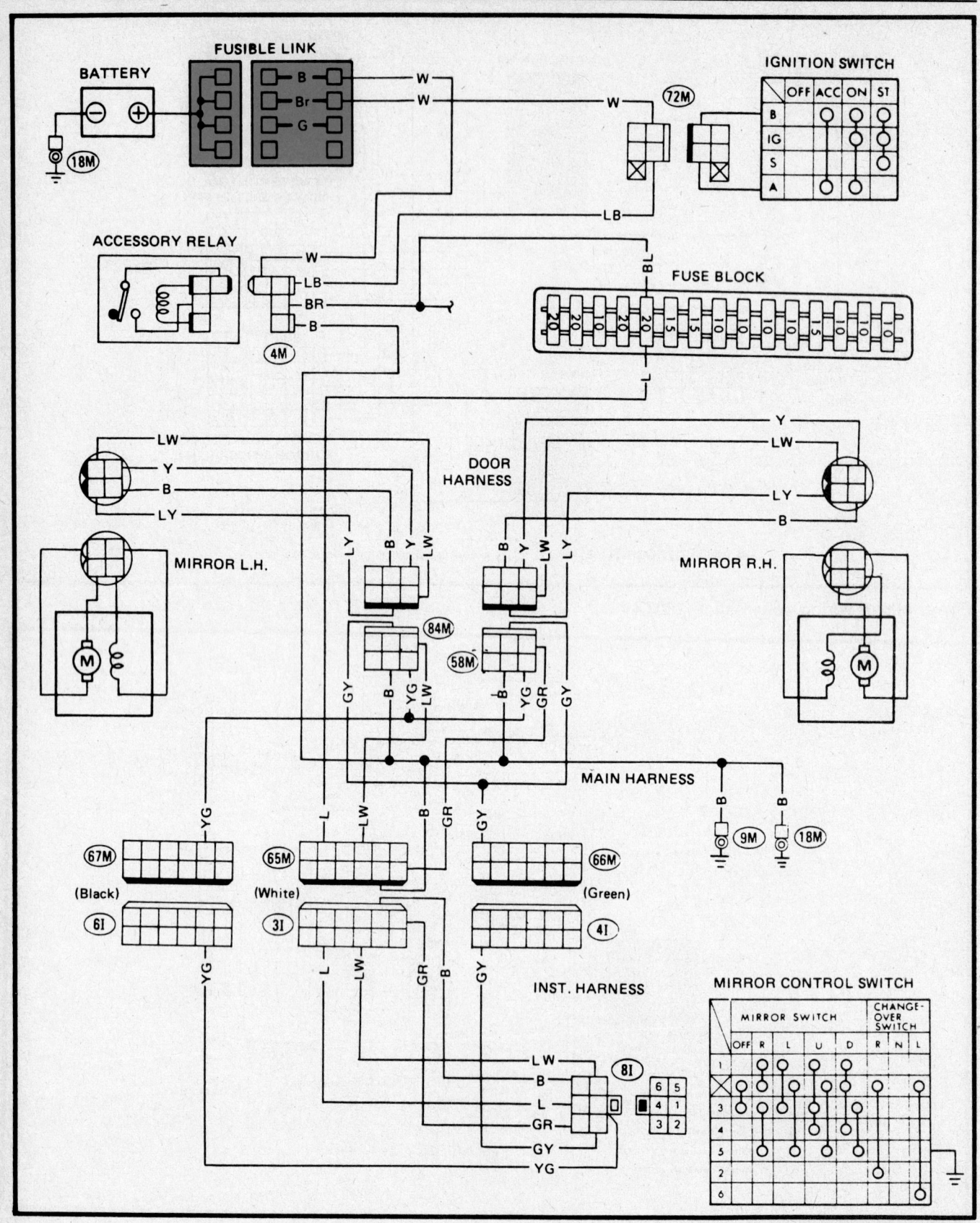

Power mirror wiring schematic—Maxima

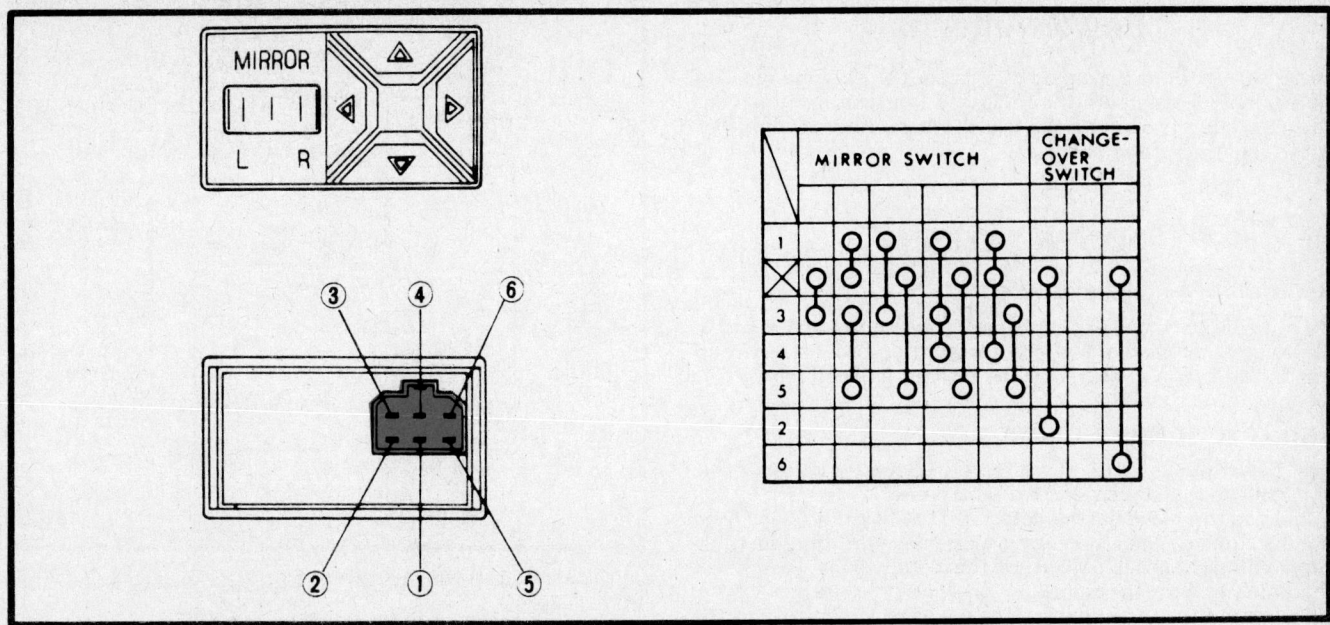

Power mirror switch test procedure — all other models

Condition	Probable cause	Corrective action
Power antenna motor does not rotate.	Burnt fuse.	Correct cause and replace fuse.
	Burnt fusible link.	Correct cause and replace fusible link.
	Faulty power antenna motor.	Replace.
	Faulty power antenna timer.	Replace.
	Faulty power antenna switch.	Replace.
	Faulty radio.	Replace.
	Loose connection or open circuit.	Check wiring and/or repair connection.
Antenna does not extend or retract fully.	Faulty power antenna timer.	Replace.
	Faulty power antenna motor.	Replace.
	Antenna rod is stuck.	Repair or replace.
Switchover between fully extended height and half extended height cannot be made.	Faulty power antenna switch.	Replace.
	Faulty power antenna motor.	Replace.
Antenna does not retract if ignition switch or radio power switch is turned to OFF.	Faulty power antenna motor.	Replace.
	Faulty power antenna timer.	Replace.
	Antenna rod is stuck.	Repair or replace.
Antenna operates when radio power switch is ON and ignition switch is in the ST position.	Burnt fuse.	Correct cause and replace fuse.
	Faulty power antenna timer.	Replace.

Power antenna troubleshooting chart

Power Antenna

The power antenna automatically raises the antenna mast to its full height whenever the radio and ignition are tuned on. The antenna retracts into the fender when either the ignition or the radio is turned off.

POWER ANTENNA

Removal and Installation

Because of the varied applications of power antennas, a general power antenna removal and installation procedure is outlined. The removal steps can be altered as required by the technician.

FRONT FENDER MOUNTED

1. Lower the antenna. Disconnect the negative battery cable and remove the right side cowl trim panel.
2. Drop the glove box by detaching the holding straps from the instrument panel (if necessary). Remove the antenna cable clip holding the antenna lead and the motor wiring. Disconnect the antenna from the radio.
3. Disconnect the antenna motor wiring at the rear of the antenna switch. Remove the rear attaching screws of the right front wheel splash shield in order to gain access to the antenna lower attaching bolt.
4. Remove the antenna motor retaining bolts. Remove the trim nut from the top of the motor tube and remove the antenna through the fender/splash shield access.
5. Installation is the reverse order of the removal procedure.

TRUNK MOUNTED

1. Lower the antenna. Disconnect the negative battery cable and remove the cap on the antenna base.
2. Remove the nut securing the antenna to the base. Remove the two screws from the base to the right hand quarter panel. Remove the base and gasket assembly.
3. Disconnect the electrical connector and the antenna cable. Working from inside the trunk, remove the bolt retaining tube and bracket motor assembly to trunk.
4. Remove the antenna by pulling it down through the quarter panel.
5. Installation is the reverse order of the removal procedure.

Power Antenna Motor Test

1. Disconnect, at the connector, the harness between the power antenna unit and antenna timer.
2. Apply 12 volts across the first two terminals (starting from the left) to make sure the antenna rod extends and retracts.

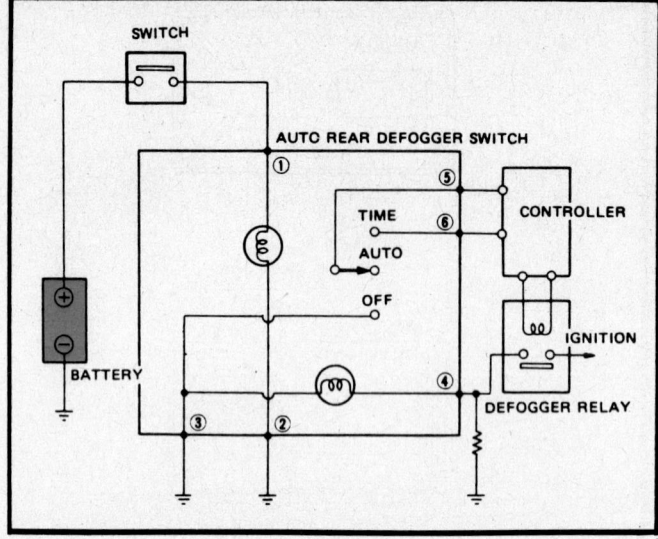

Typical Nissan rear window defogger wiring schematic

3. Connect a suitable voltmeter across the last terminal and the ground terminal of the battery.
4. Check to determine if the voltmeter varies between 0 to 12 volts in relation to movement of the antenna rod when 12 volts is applied across the first two terminals (starting from the left).
5. If the test results are not satisfactory, replace the antenna motor.

Rear Window Defogger System

The rear window defogger system consists of a rear window with two vertical bus bars and a series of electrically connected grid lines baked on the inside surface. A control switch and a timer relay combined into a single assembly is used on all models.

REAR DEFOGGER GRID

Test

When a grid is inoperable due to an open circuit, the area of glass normally cleared by that grid will remained fogged or iced until cleared by the adjacent grids. Use the follwing procedure to located a broken grid.

1. With the engine running at idle, place the rear defogger switch in the "ON" position. The pilot lamp is the switch lever should light up indicating the defogger is operating.

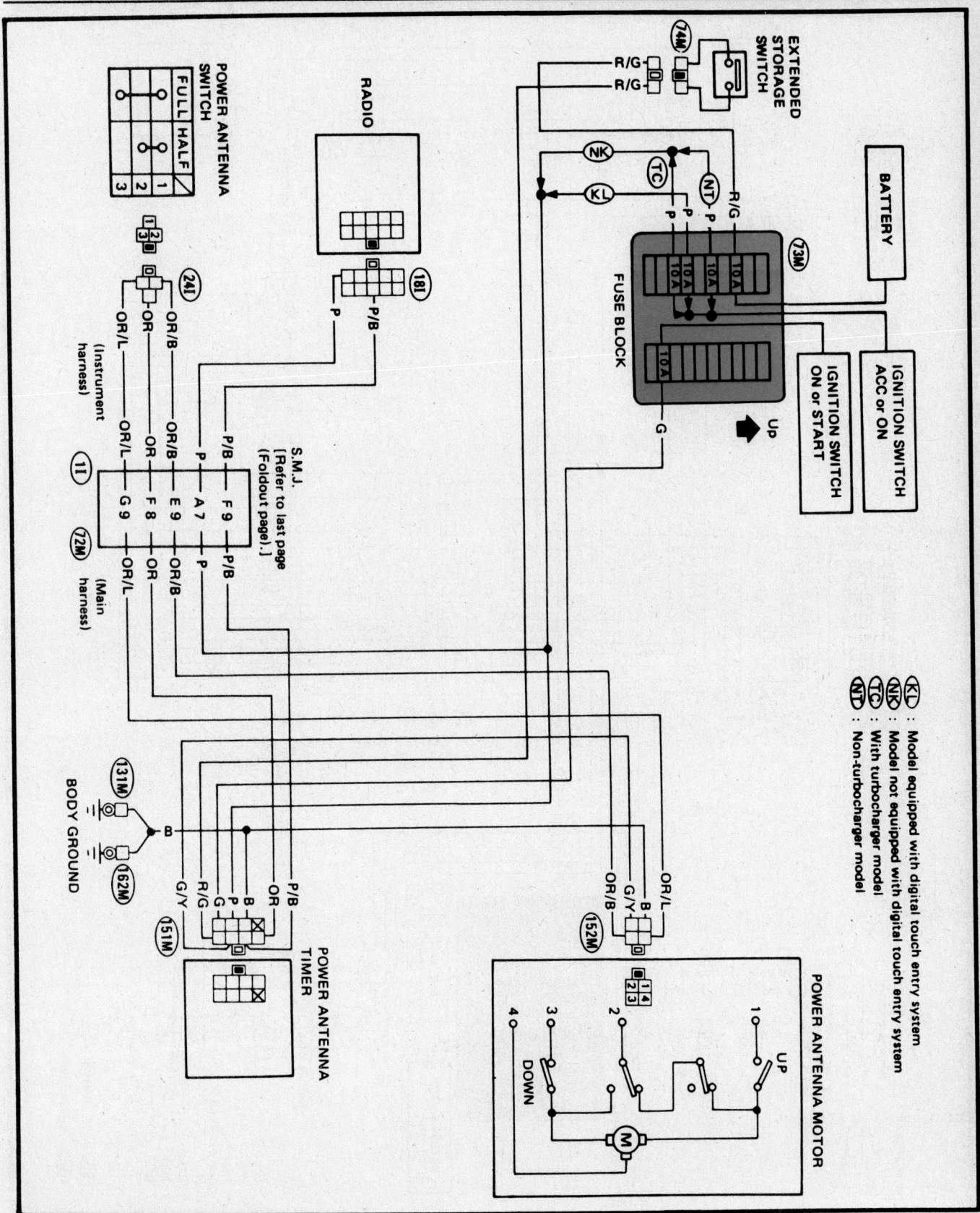

Power antenna wiring schematic — 200SX

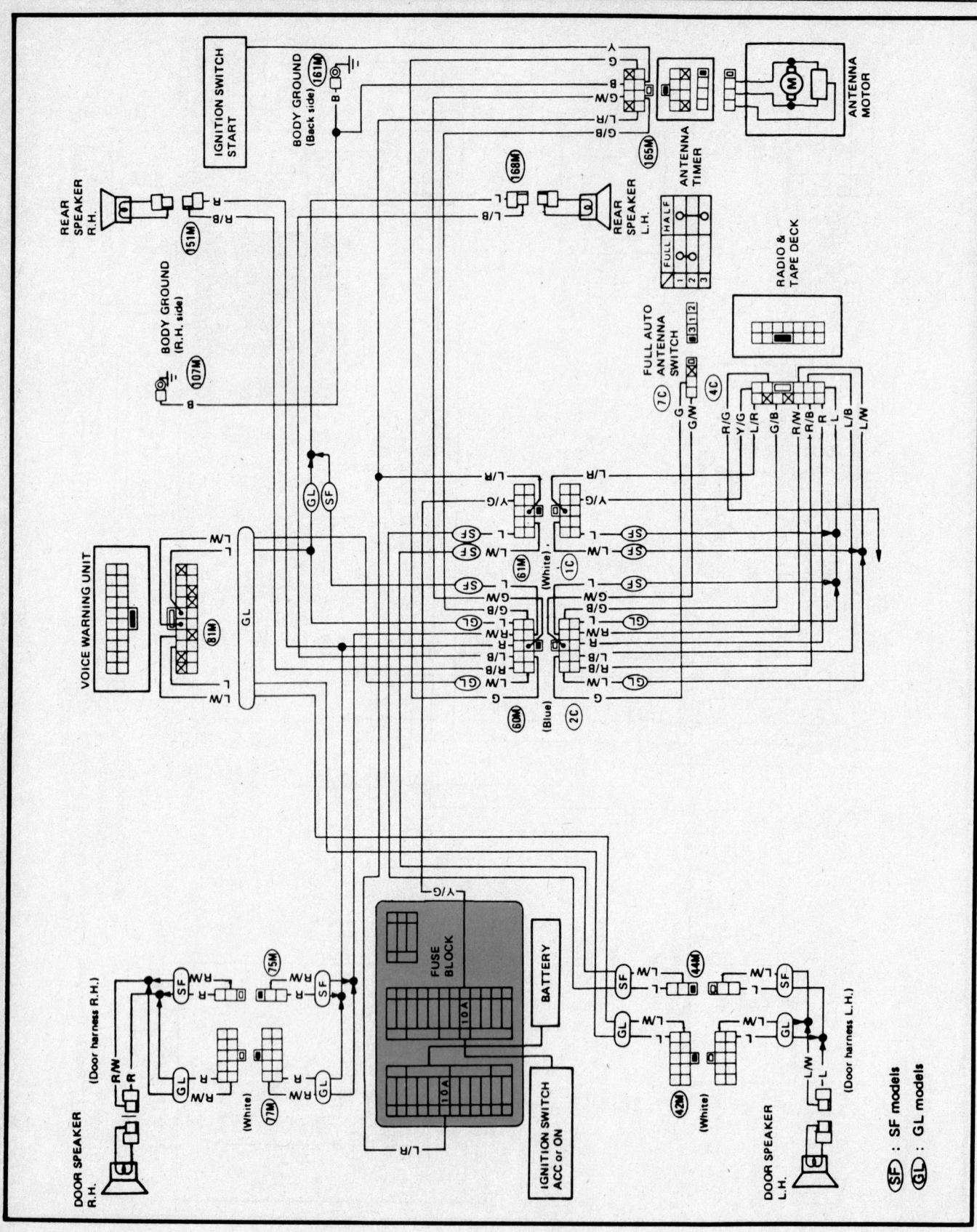

Power antenna wiring schematic – 300SX

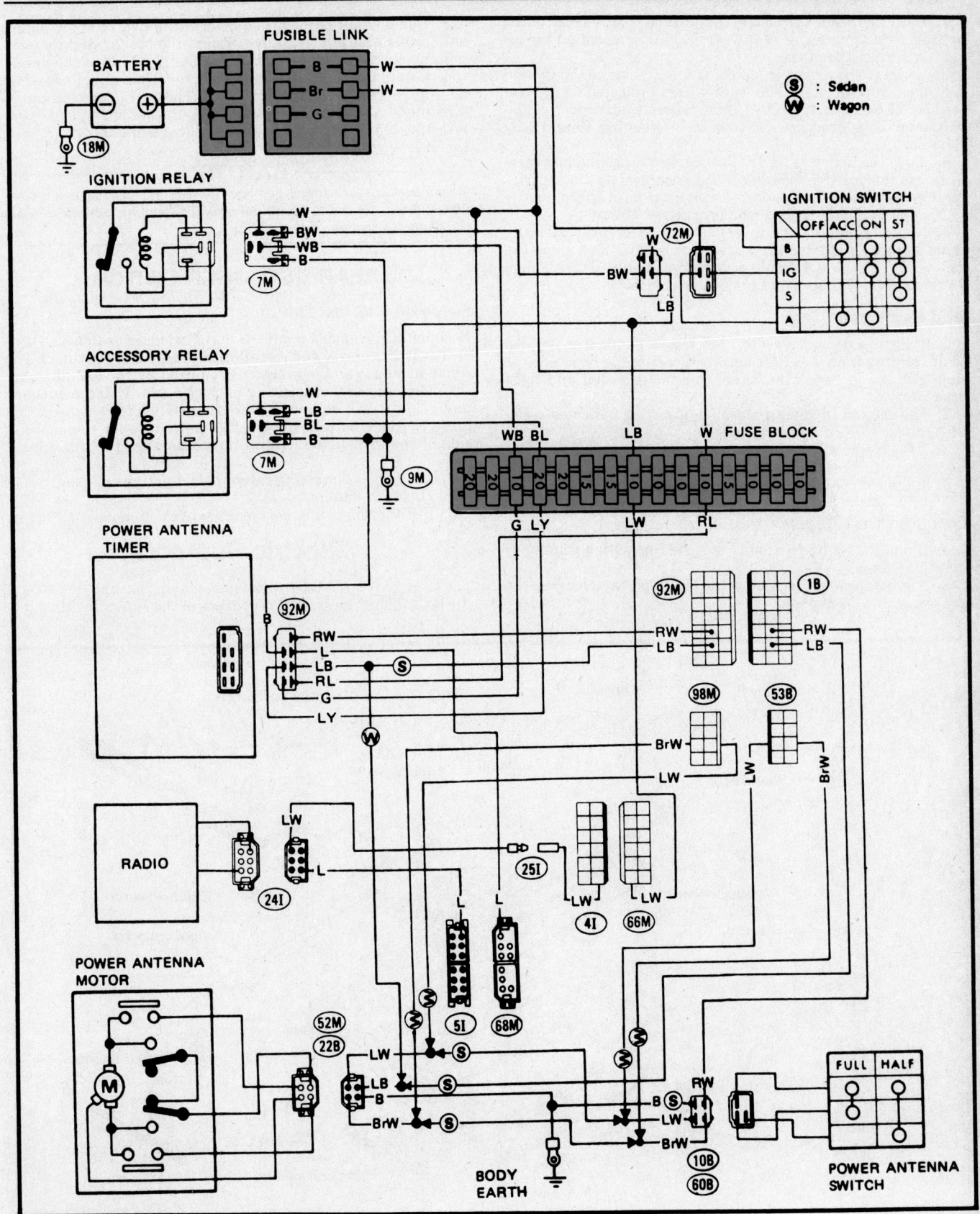

Power antenna wiring schematic—Maxima

2. Using a 12 volt voltmeter, connect the positive lead of the voltmeter to the hot side of the vertical bus element on the inside surface of the glass.

3. Connect the negative lead of the voltmeter to the ground side of the bus element. The voltage drop indicated on the meter should be 11 to 13 volts. Connect the negative lead of the voltmeter to a good ground, the meter reading should stay constant.

4. Keep the negative lead connected to the ground and carefully use the positive lead to contact each grid at the approximate centerline of the window. A voltage drop of approximately 6 volts. indicates a good grid or a closed circuit.

5. No voltage indicated a broken grid wire. To located the exact location of the break, move the voltmeter lead along the grid wire. The voltage should decrease gradually. if the voltage drops suddenly, there is a break at that location.

Grid Resistance Test

1. Turn the defogger switch off. Use a ohmmeter (with a scale ranging from 0 to 100 ohms) to measure the resistance at each grid line between the center and the end , left and right separately.

2. The section involving a broken grid line indicates resistance twice that in other sections.

3. Once in the affected area, move the tester bar for a position where the resistance sharply changes. Mark the broken grid line and repair as necessary.

Defogger Grid Repair

1. Clean the faulty portion of the grid line with a thinner or eythyl alcohol.

2. Apply tape to either side of the faulty portion, leaving the broken grid wire exposed.

3. Use a small paint brush or drafting pen to apply a suitable conductive silver composition to the break, slightly overlap the existing grid wire on both sides (0.20 in.) of the break.

4. Completely dry the repaired section by letting it stand (at a temperature of 68°F) for 24 hours. The drying process can be 30 minutes if a hot air gun (at a temperature of 140°F) is used. If the heat gun is used it should be held at a distance of 1.2 in. of the grid wire.

CAUTION
Do not use the rear window defogger until the repaired section is completely dried. Do not use gasoline or other cleaning solvents to clean the damaged section of the grid line.

REAR DEFOGGER SWITCH

Removal and Installation

Because of the varied applications of defogger switches, a general switch removal and installation procedure is outlined. The removal steps can be altered as required by the technician.

1. Disconnect the negative battery cable. Using a suitable tool, slip the tool behind the defogger switch far enough to depress the locking tab. Repeat this procedure for the opposite side of the switch. Be careful not to damage the instrument panel.

2. Disconnect the electrical connector and remove the switch from the dash panel.

3. Installation is the reverse order of the removal procedure.

Electric Sunroofs

The sunroof is operated by a switch, which is usually located in the headliner. The system is consists of the sunroof switch, mo-

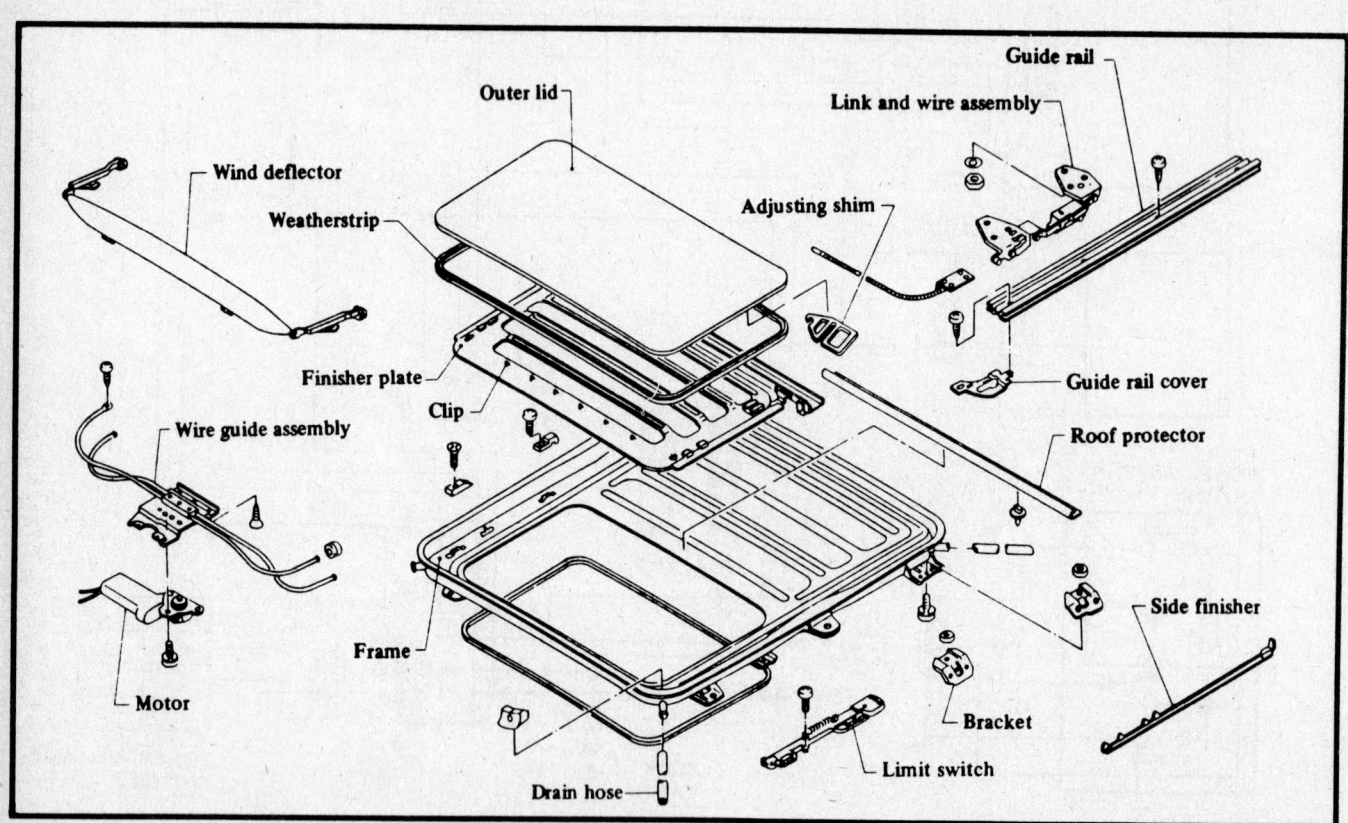

Exploded view of a typical Nissan sunroof assembly

tor drive cables and circuit breaker and two relays. The sunroof can be closed manually, (should it be necessary) by removing the headliner plug, insert the handle and turn the gear to close the sunroof.

NOTE: The sunroof assembly is equipped with water drain tubes, it is important to keep these drain tubes open. So it is recommended to blow compressed air through the drain tubes at regular intervals, in order to keep the drain tubes clear.

SUNROOF OUTER LID AND FINISHER PLATE

Removal and Installation

1. Open the outer lid until it is approximately 4 inches from the fully closed position.
2. Remove the trim clip located in the front of the finisher plate from the outer lid. Push the finisher plate rearward.
3. Close the outer lid completely and remove the outer lid retaining screws from both sides of the outer lid.
4. Remove the outer lid from the vehicle. Be sure to take note of the shims that are placed between the outer lid and the link assembly.
5. Draw the finisher plate out through the guide rail cutout portion. Remove the finisher pate by pulling diagonally upward.

Installation and Adjustment

1. Insert the finisher plate into the guide rail through the guide rail cutout portion. Set the link and wire assembly in the fully closed position.
2. Position the outer lid so that the lid to roof clearances are equal at all points.
3. Temporarily tighten outer lid to link and wire assembly. Adjust the frame wedge so that the rollers attached to the link are in contact with the upper face of the frame rear wedge when the roof is fully closed.
4. On wagon models, adjust the position of the lid stopper bracket by reducing or adding shims on both sides of the bracket so that the stopper tip tightly touches the roof.
5. Tighten the bolts securely. Pull the finisher plate forward. Attach the clip located at the forward portion of the finisher plate to the outer lid.
6. Slide the outer lid to determined whether it moves smoothly.

SUNROOF WIND DEFLECTOR

Removal and Installation

1. Place the sunroof to the have open position. Remove the screws from the rear of the link.
2. Slide the link out of the frame outside the vehicle and remove the screws from the front link. Remove the wind deflector.
3. Installation is the reverse order of the removal procedure.

SUNROOF MOTOR

Removal and Installation

1. Remove the rear view mirror, sun visor and front pillar garnish. Detach the front portion of the headlining.
2. Remove the motor cover and motor retaining screws. disconnect the motor wiring harness and remove the motor.
3. Installation is the reverse order of the removal procedure.

SUNROOF LIMIT SWITCH

Removal and Installation

1. Remove the rear view mirror, sun visor, front pillar garnish, left seat belt (at the anchor) and left pillar garnish. Detach the front portion of the headlining.
2. Remove the limit switch and wire guide retaining screws, disconnect the wire harness. Remove the limit switch by pulling it toward the rear of the vehicle.
3. Installation is the reverse order of the removal procedure.

SUNROOF FRAME, LINK AND WIRE ASSEMBLY

Removal and Installation

1. Remove the outer lid as previously outlined. Remove the headlining, beginning with the front section.
2. Remove the listing wire from the clip of the frame. Remove the harness terminal from the right of the sunroof.
3. Remove the wire guide bracket retaining screws. Disconnect the drain tube from the frame. Remove the frame assembly retaining bolts and detach the frame assembly.
4. Remove the guide rail cover. Remove the guide rail retaining screws from the frame assembly and slide the finisher plate and rain rail out of the rear frame assembly.
5. Remove the link and wire assembly together with the guide rails. Detach the guide rails from the link and wire assembly.
6. Remove the limit switch, wind deflector and wire guide assembly from the frame.

Installation

1. Attach the wire guide assembly wind deflector and limit switch to the frame. Be sure to fit the tip of the wire guide between the upper and lower grooves on the limit switch and tighten the limit switch securely.
2. Attach the rain rail to the finisher plate and insert them as a unit into the rear of the rail grove.
3. Attach the guide rail to the link and wire assembly, fit the wire in the wire guide and attach the guide rail to the frame. Be sure to apply a suitable sealing compound to the guide rail of the frame side.
4. Install the guide rail covers, connect the sunroof harness. Set the link and wire assembly in the fully closed position.
5. Install the motor. Install the outer lid and slide switch on the frame. Install the frame assembly. Connect the drain hose and wiring connectors.
6. Install the insulators and headlining and adjust the outer lid and finisher plate. Check the operation of the sunroof.

Theft Warning System

This system is designed to provide a warning in the event of a forced entry through the driver and passenger doors and trunk. When a forced entry is attempted, the alarm warning system will be tripped off. This will set the horns off and the exterior light to flash in unison for three to seven minutes. The starter interlock feature prevents the engine from starting if the warning system is tripped.

The alarm is tripped by opening switches strategically located in the door jambs, the door lock cylinders and the trunk lock cylinder. When a door lock cylinder or trunk lock cylinder is violated by rotating it or moving it in or out, or if any door is opened without using the key, the alarm will be actuated by the controller.

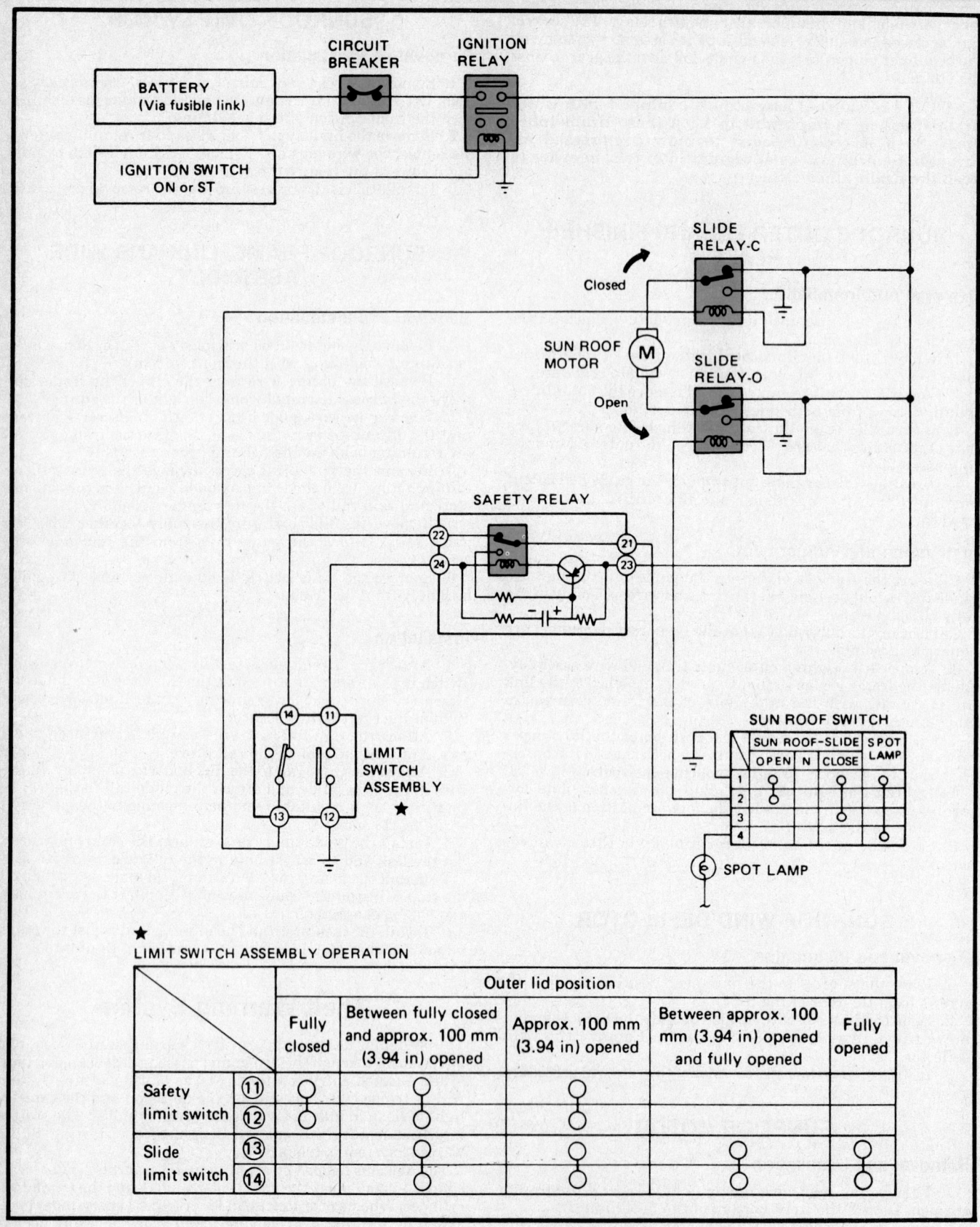

Typical Nissan sunroof wiring schematic

The following text labels appear within the schematic:

BATTERY (Via fusible link)

IGNITION SWITCH ON or ST

CIRCUIT BREAKER

IGNITION RELAY

SLIDE RELAY-C

Closed

SUN ROOF MOTOR

SLIDE RELAY-O

Open

SAFETY RELAY

LIMIT SWITCH ASSEMBLY ★

SUN ROOF SWITCH

SPOT LAMP

	SUN ROOF–SLIDE			SPOT LAMP
	OPEN	N	CLOSE	
1	○		○	○
2	○			
3			○	
4				○

★

LIMIT SWITCH ASSEMBLY OPERATION

		Outer lid position				
		Fully closed	Between fully closed and approx. 100 mm (3.94 in) opened	Approx. 100 mm (3.94 in) opened	Between approx. 100 mm (3.94 in) opened and fully opened	Fully opened
Safety limit switch	⑪	○	○	○		
	⑫	○	○	○		
Slide limit switch	⑬		○	○	○	○
	⑭		○	○	○	○

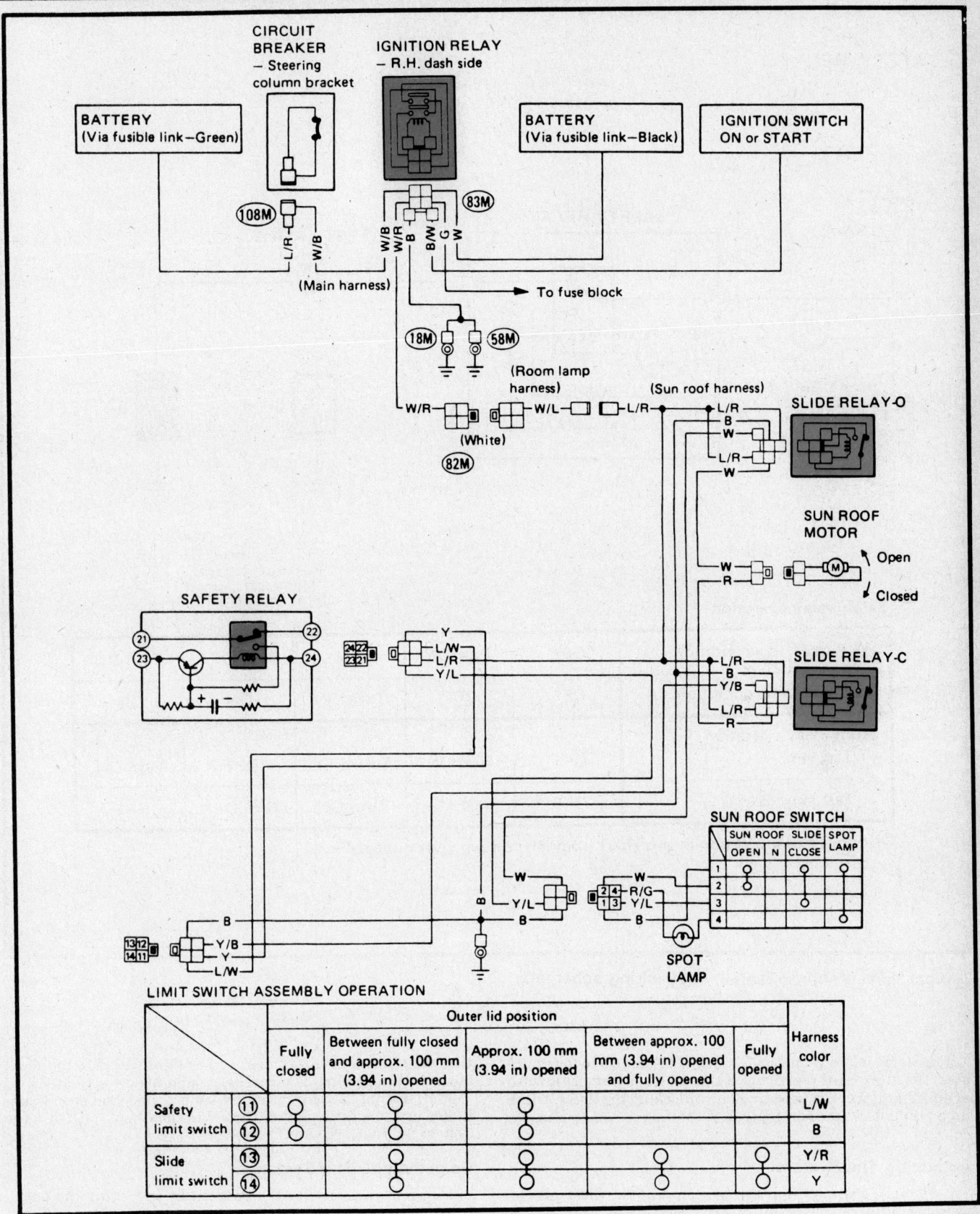

Typical Nissan sunroof wiring schematic (cont.)

Within the figure:

CIRCUIT BREAKER – Steering column bracket

IGNITION RELAY – R.H. dash side

BATTERY (Via fusible link—Green)

BATTERY (Via fusible link—Black)

IGNITION SWITCH ON or START

(108M)

(83M)

W/B W/R B B/W G W

L/R W/B

(Main harness)

To fuse block

(18M) (58M)

(Room lamp harness)

W/R W/L L/R L/R SLIDE RELAY-O

B
W
L/R
W

(White)

(82M)

SUN ROOF MOTOR

W →Open
R →Closed

SAFETY RELAY

21 22
23 24

24 22
23 21

Y
L/W
L/R
Y/L

L/R SLIDE RELAY-C
B
Y/B
L/R
R

SUN ROOF SWITCH

		SUN ROOF	SLIDE	SPOT LAMP
		OPEN	N	CLOSE	
	1				
	2	○			○
	3			○	
	4				

W Y/L

B

2 4 R/G
1 3 Y/L

W
R/G
Y/L
B

SPOT LAMP

13 12
14 11

B
Y/B
Y
L/W

LIMIT SWITCH ASSEMBLY OPERATION

		Outer lid position					Harness color
		Fully closed	Between fully closed and approx. 100 mm (3.94 in) opened	Approx. 100 mm (3.94 in) opened	Between approx. 100 mm (3.94 in) opened and fully opened	Fully opened	
Safety limit switch	⑪	○	○	○			L/W
	⑫	○	○	○			B
Slide limit switch	⑬		○	○	○	○	Y/R
	⑭		○	○	○	○	Y

SAFETY RELAY

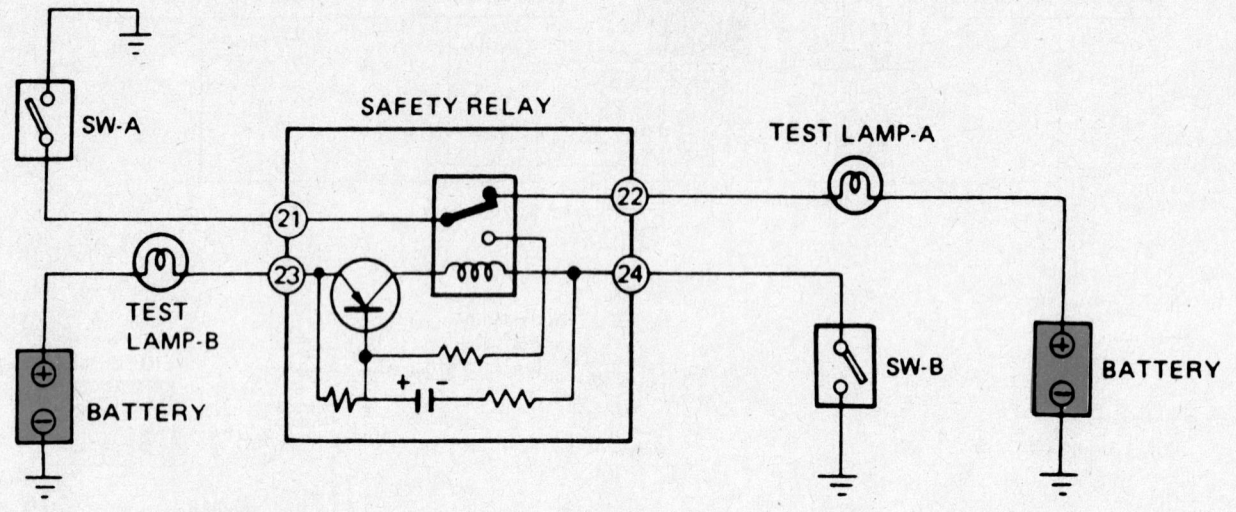

Safety relay operation

	OFF	Turn ON	ON	Turn OFF	Turn ON
SW-A operating condition	OFF	Turn ON	ON	Turn OFF	Turn ON
SW-B operating condition	OFF	OFF	Turn ON	ON	ON
Safety relay operation Test lamp-A	OFF	Turn ON	Turn OFF	OFF	Turn ON
Test lamp-B	OFF	OFF	Turn ON	Turn OFF	OFF

Carry out this inspection in this chart from left to right continuously.

Typical Nissan sunroof safety relay wiring schematic

The alarm will automatically turn off after two to four minutes, the alarm will reactivate if the vehicle is tampered with again. The alarm can be shut off by unlocking the doors, trunk lid or tailgate with the proper key.

Activating The System

1. Remove the key from the ignition switch. Close all the windows, close and lock all of the doors, hood, trunk lid or tailgate.
2. The door can be locked with or without the key. Confirm that the indicator light comes on. The light will glow for about 30 seconds and then go out. The system is now activated.
3. If, during the thirty second time period, the door is unlocked or the ignition key is turned to the "ACC" or "ON", the system will not activate.

De-activating The System

The system can only be de-activated by unlocking the doors, trunk lid or tailgate with the proper key. The alarm will not stop even if the ignition key is switched to the "ACC" or "ON" position.

Terminal arrangement of connector for theft warning
sub-control unit (View from harness side)

Check table of connector terminals for sub-control unit. (Disconnect connector at sub-control unit)

Terminal	Function	From	Normal operation	If N.G., check
A	System source	Fuse box	Battery voltage should come between [A] and body ground	10A fuse, Harness
B	Security lamp operating control	Fuse box (Through extended storage switch)	Ground [B], security lamp should come on.	10A fuse, Harness, Bulb of security lamp Extended storage switch
C	System cancel signal	Fuse box	Battery voltage should come between [C] and body ground when key is in A CC or ON.	10A fuse, Harness
D	Starter kill	(Through interrupt relay)	Ground [D] starter should not operate.	Theft interrupt relay, Harness
F	Door switch trigger and tamper switch trigger for passenger's side	Passenger's door switch and tamper switch	Battery voltage should come between [F] and body ground when passenger's door is closed. Zero voltage between [F] and body ground when passenger's door is open. Battery voltage between [F] and body ground when passenger's tamper switch is installed to key cylinder when passenger's door is closed.	Door switch, Tamper switch, Harness
E	Door switch trigger and tamper switch trigger of driver's side.	Driver's door switch and tamper switch.	Battery voltage should come between [E] and body ground when driver's door is closed. Zero voltage between [E] and body ground when driver's door is open. Battery voltage should come between [E] and body ground when driver's door tamper switches is installed to key cylinders (when driver's door is closed).	Door switch, Tamper switch, Harness
G	Arm signal	Door lock switches.	Continuity exists between [G] and body ground when key stops between neutral and full stroke of lock.	Door lock switch, Harness

Theft warning system troubleshooting and terminal check chart

Terminal	Function	From	Normal operation	If N.G., check
I	Driver's and passenger's door unlock sensor signal	Door unlock sensor	Continuity exists between [I] and body ground when at least one of driver's and passenger's doors is unlocked. No continuity between [I] and body ground when driver's and passenger's doors are locked.	Door unlock sensor, Harness
J	Disarm signal Back door	Back door unlock switch	Continuity exists between [J] and body ground when key stops between neutral and full stroke of unlock.	Unlock switch, Harness
K	Disarm signal (Driver's and passenger's doors)	Door unlock switches	Continuity exists between [K] and body ground when key stops between neutral and full stroke of unlock.	Unlock switch, Harness
L	Alarm signal	Fuse box (Through horn relay)	Ground [L], horn should sound.	Horn relay, 10A fuse, Harness
M	Rise up headlamps	Retract control relay	Connect [A] and [M] with jumper cable. Headlamps should rise up.	Retract control relay, Harness, Headlamp retract circuit
N	Back door switch trigger	Back door switch	Battery voltage should come between [N] and body ground when back door is closed. Zero voltage between [N] and body ground when back door is open.	Back door switch, Harness
O	Hood switch trigger	Hood switch	No continuity between [O] and body ground when hood is closed. Continuity exists between [O] and body ground when hood is open.	Hood switch, Harness
P	System ground	Body ground	Continuity exists between [P] and body ground.	Body ground terminal, Harness

Connect connector to sub-control unit

Terminal	Function	From	Normal operation	If N.G., check
L	Alarm signal	Fuse box (Through horn relay) Fuse box (Through retract relay-up)	Connect voltmeter between [A] and [L]. Pointer deflection should come intermittently under alarm phase.	Sub-control unit, Main control unit, Adapter harness

Theft warning system troubleshooting and terminal check chart (cont.)

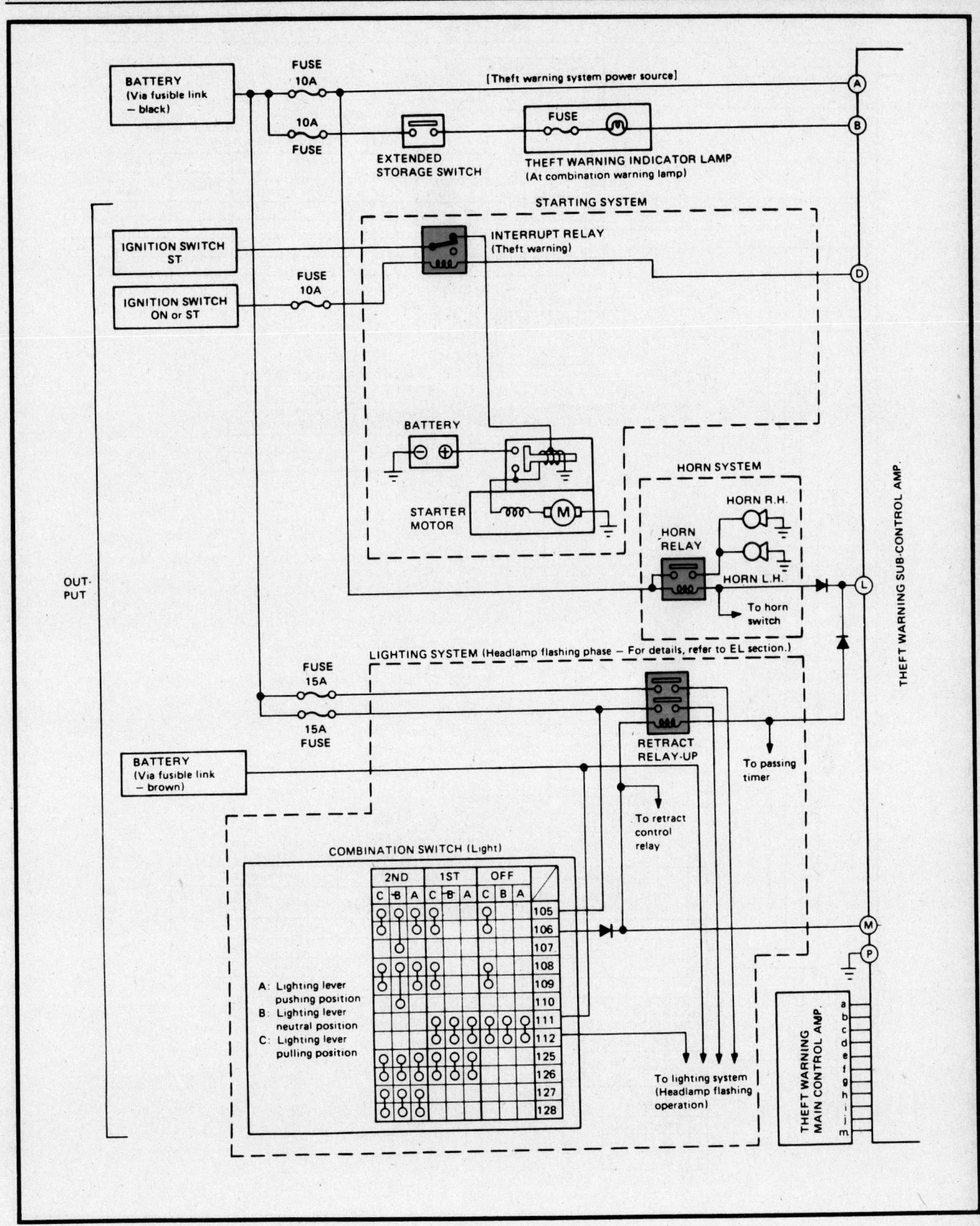

Theft warning system schematic — 200SX

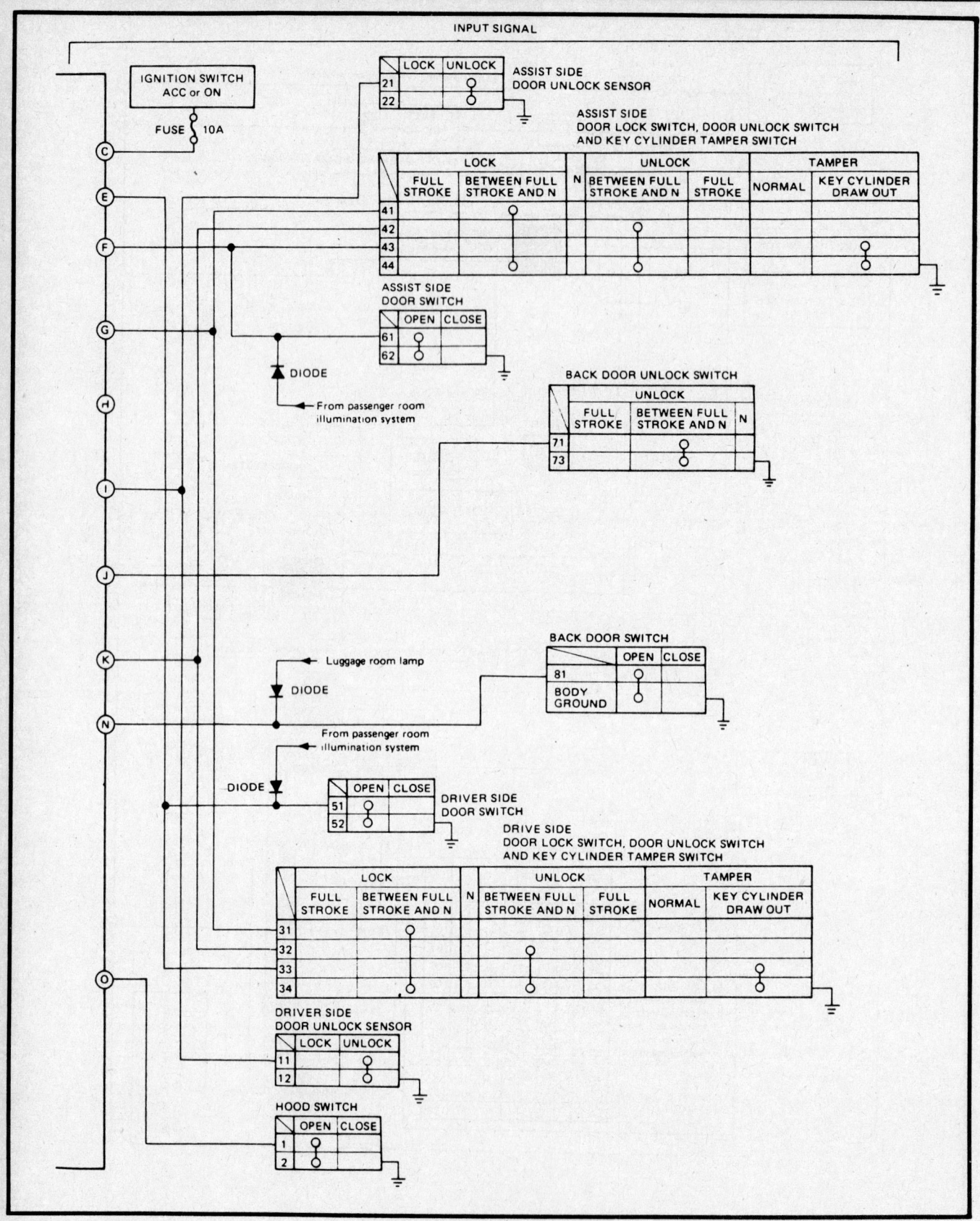

Theft warning system schematic—200SX (cont.)

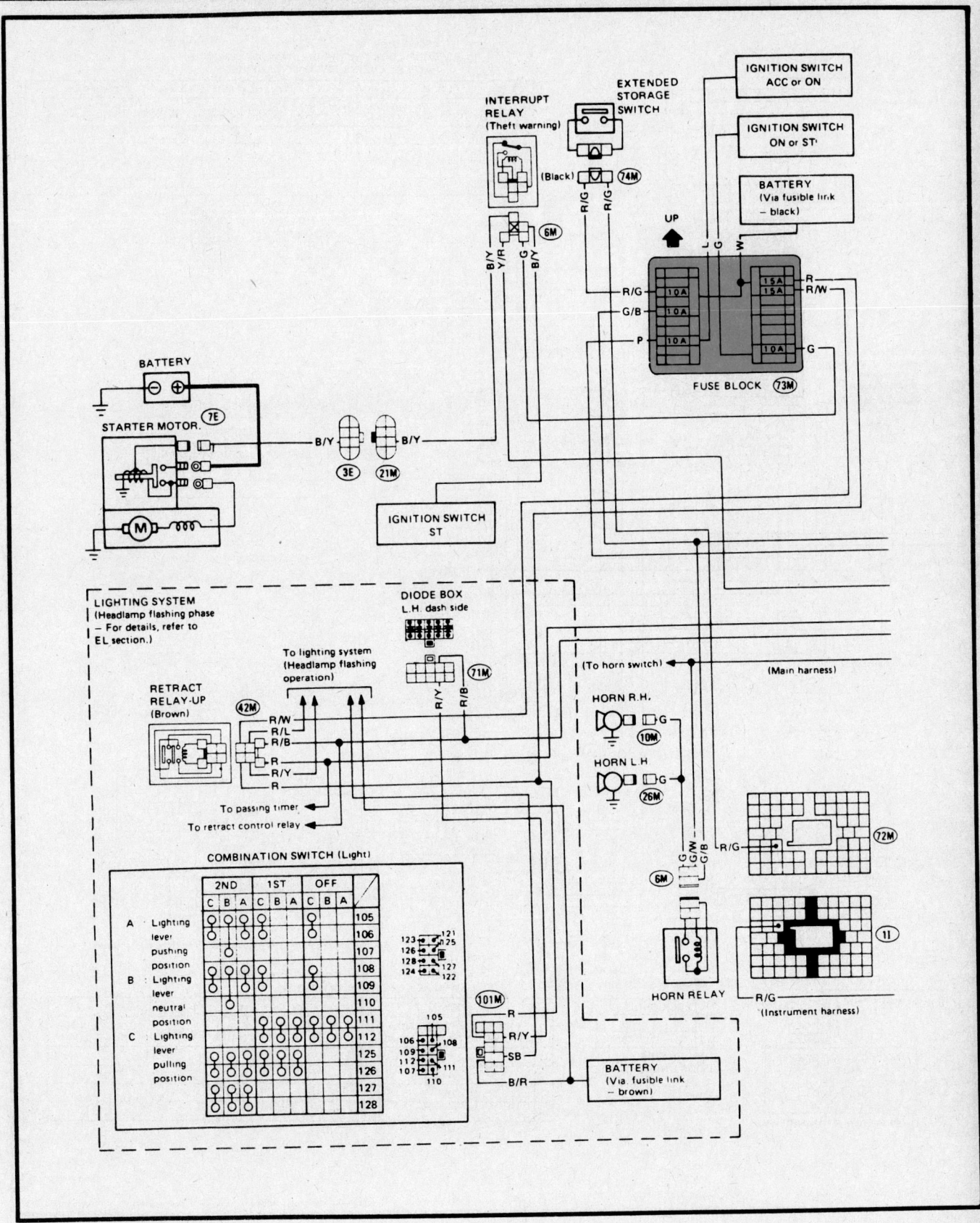

Theft warning system wiring diagram – 200SX

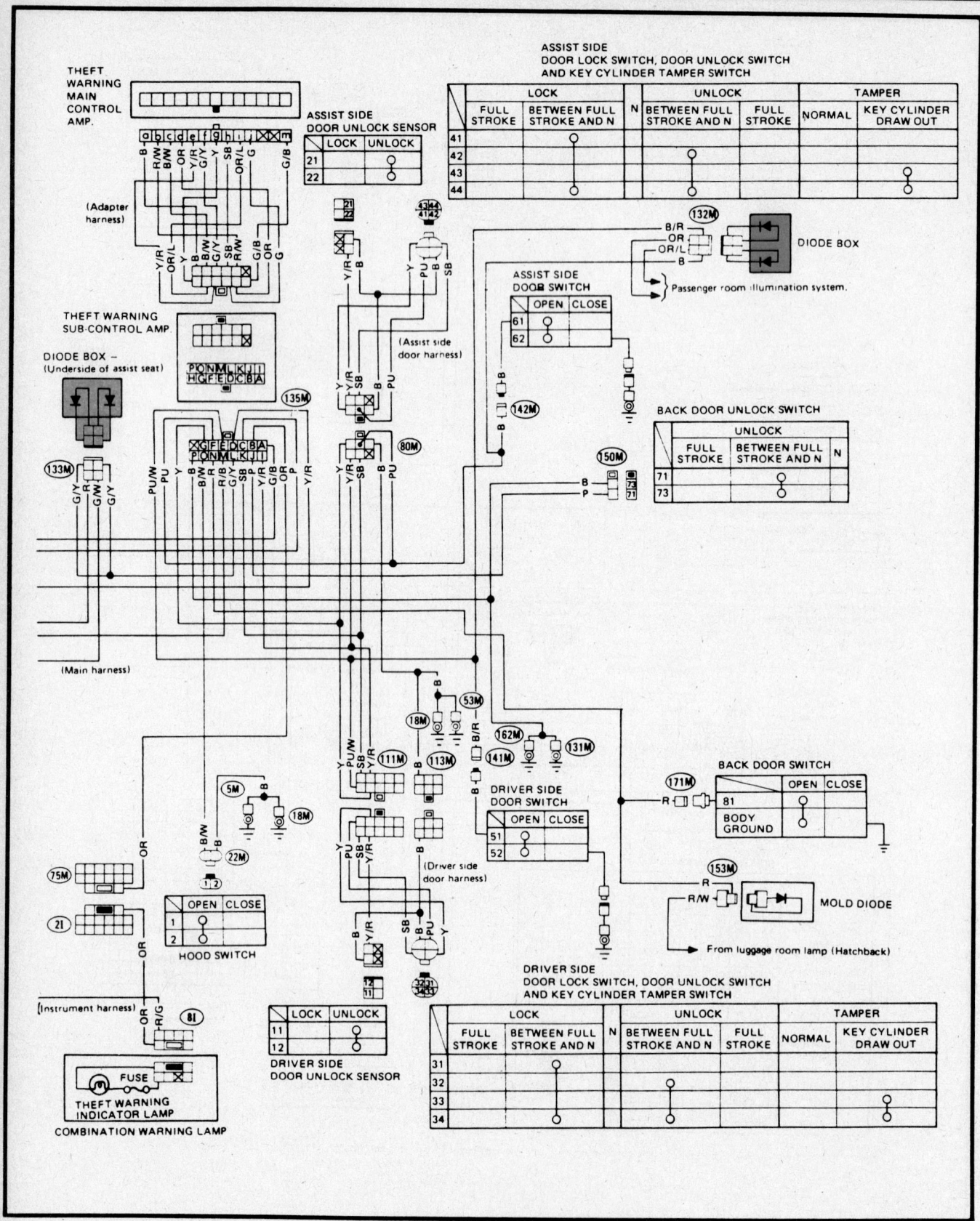

Theft warning system wiring diagram—200SX (cont.)

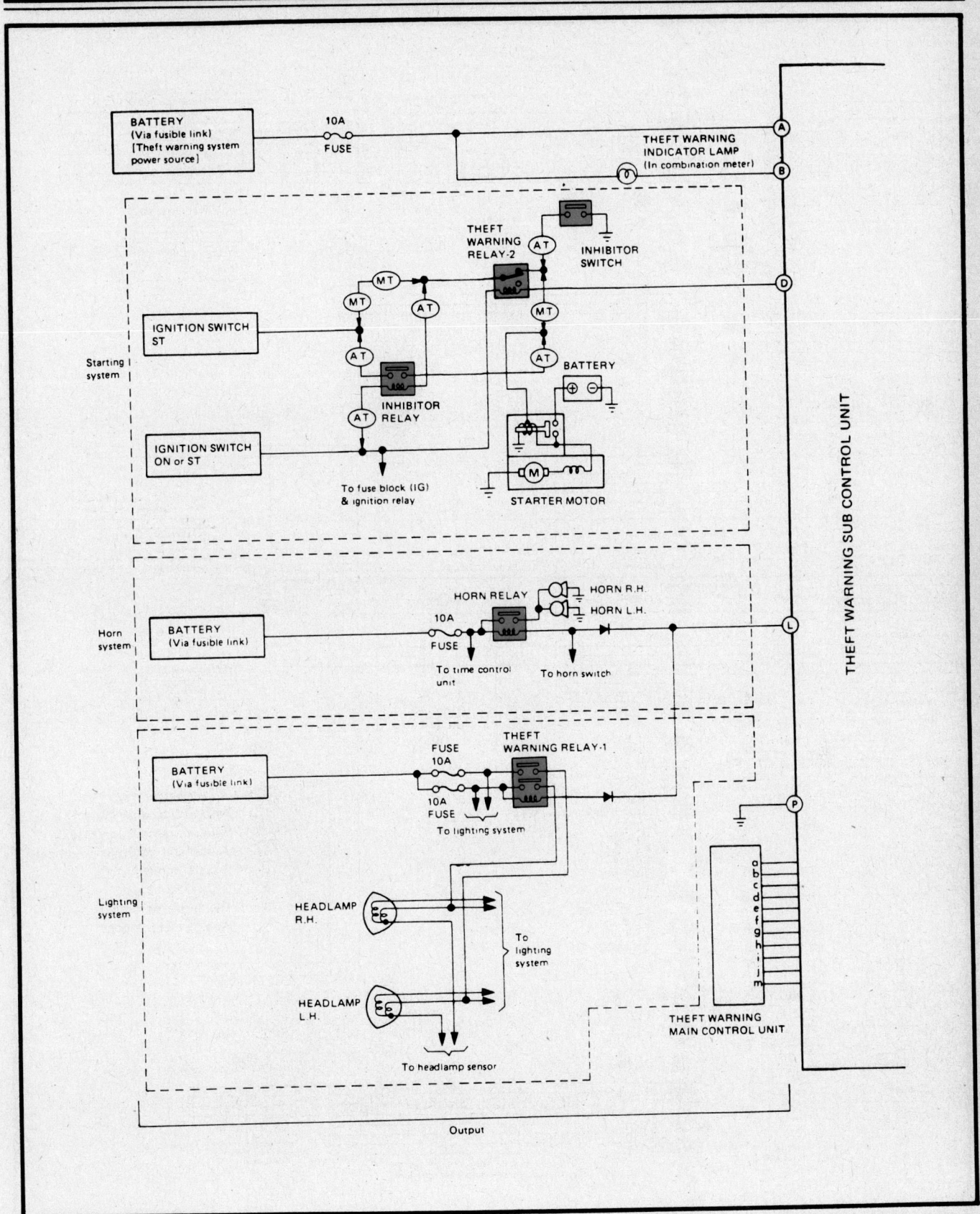

Theft warning system schematic – 300ZX

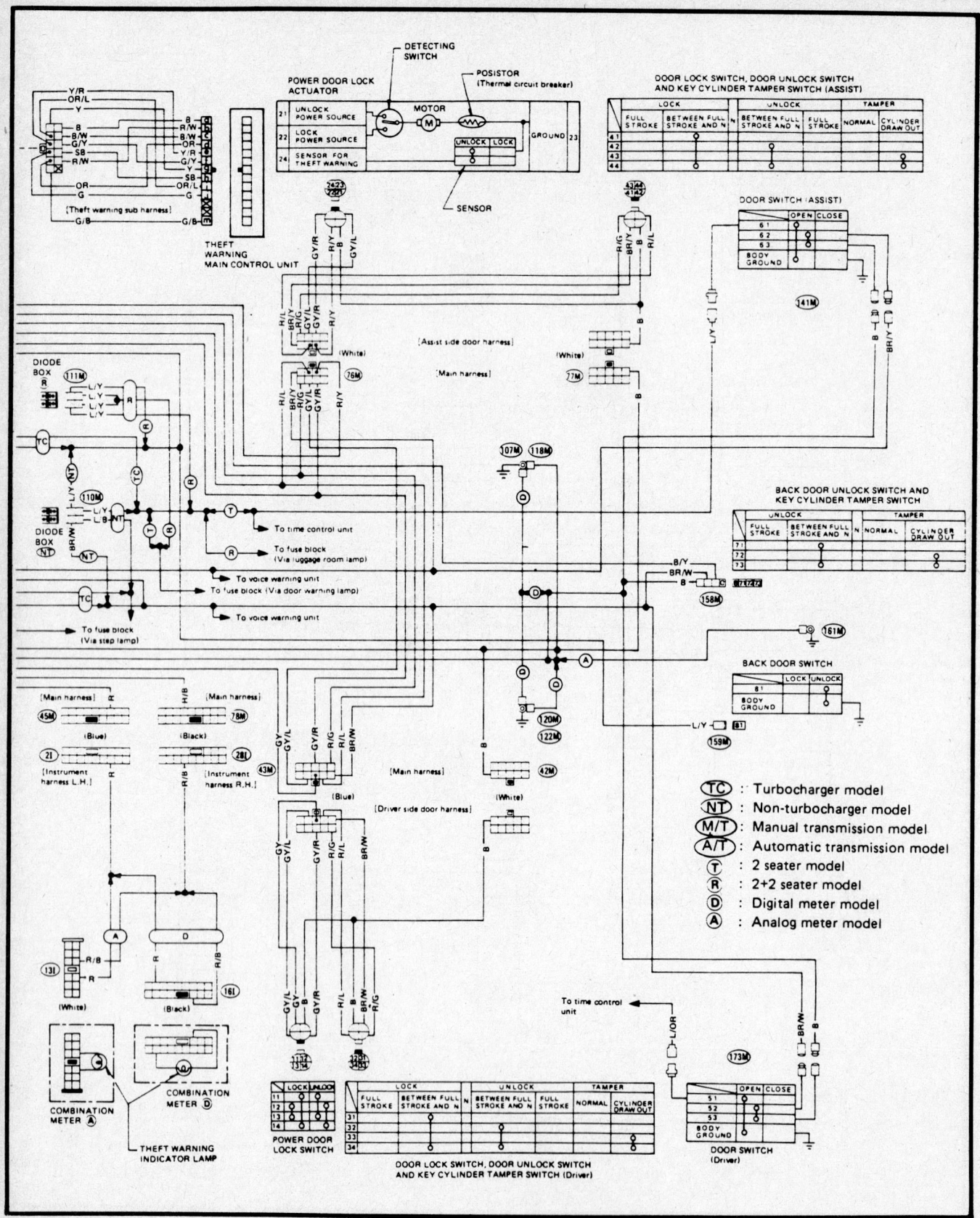

Theft warning system schematic—300ZX (cont.)

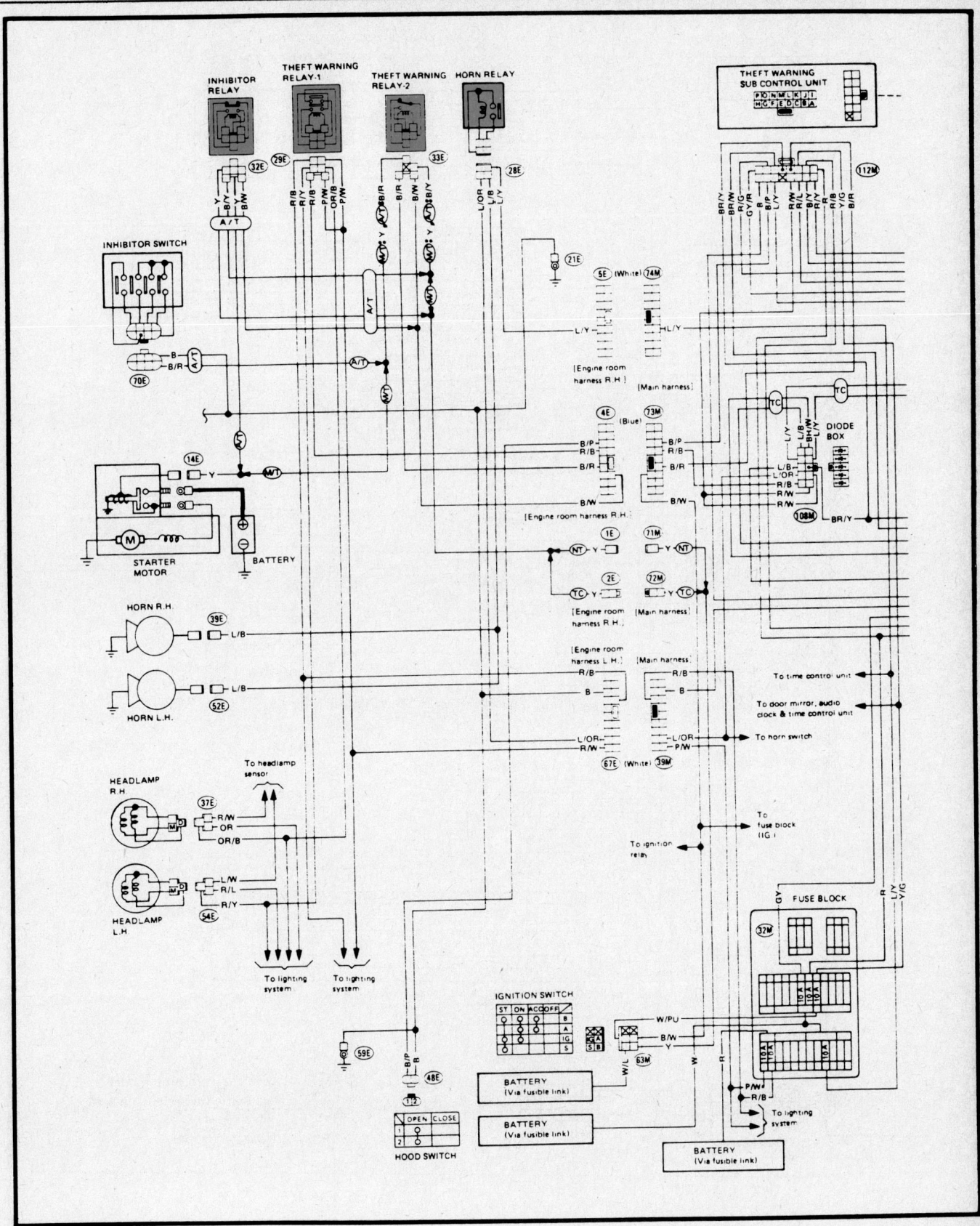

Theft warning system wiring diagram—300ZX

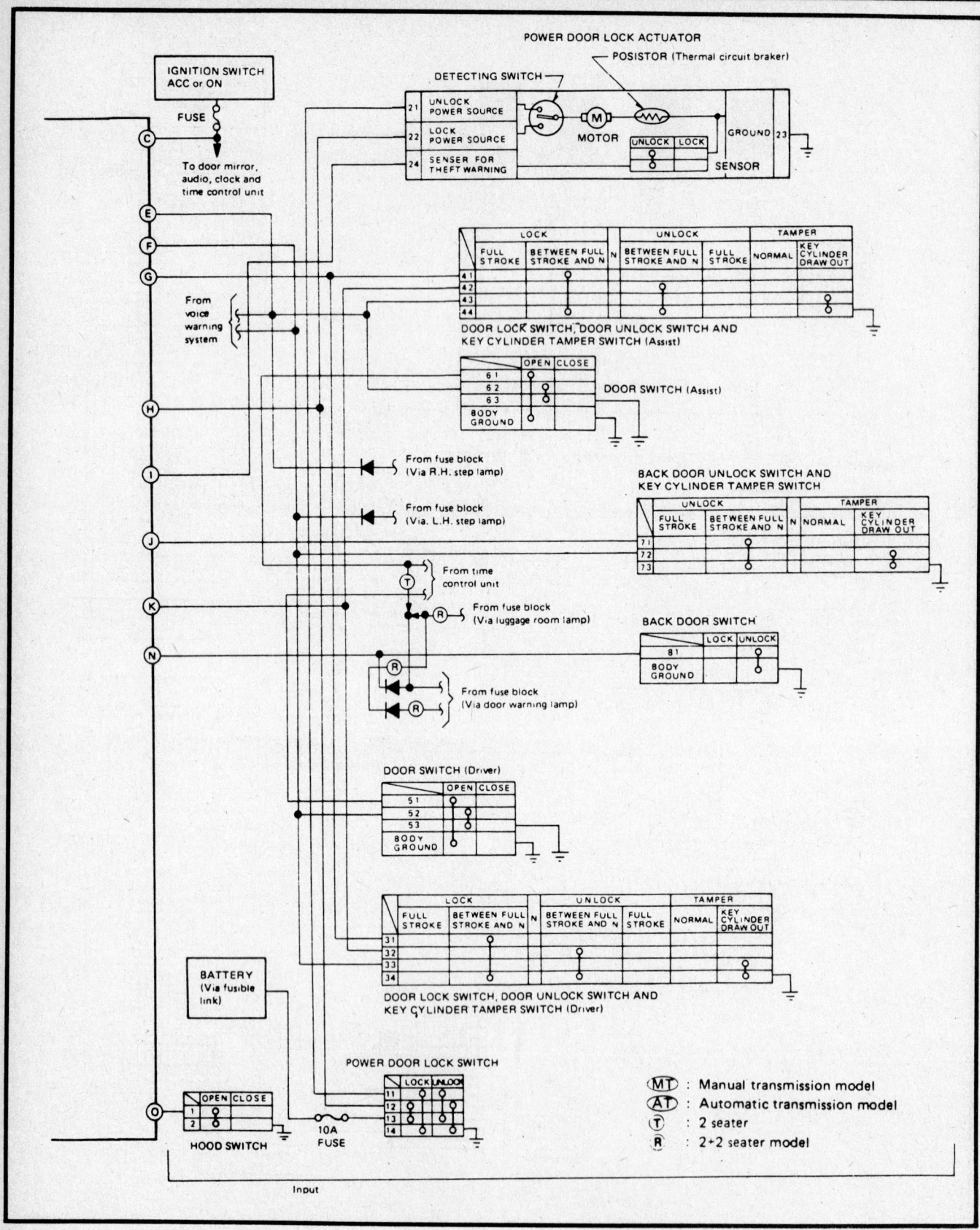

Theft warning system wiring diagram – 300ZX (cont.)

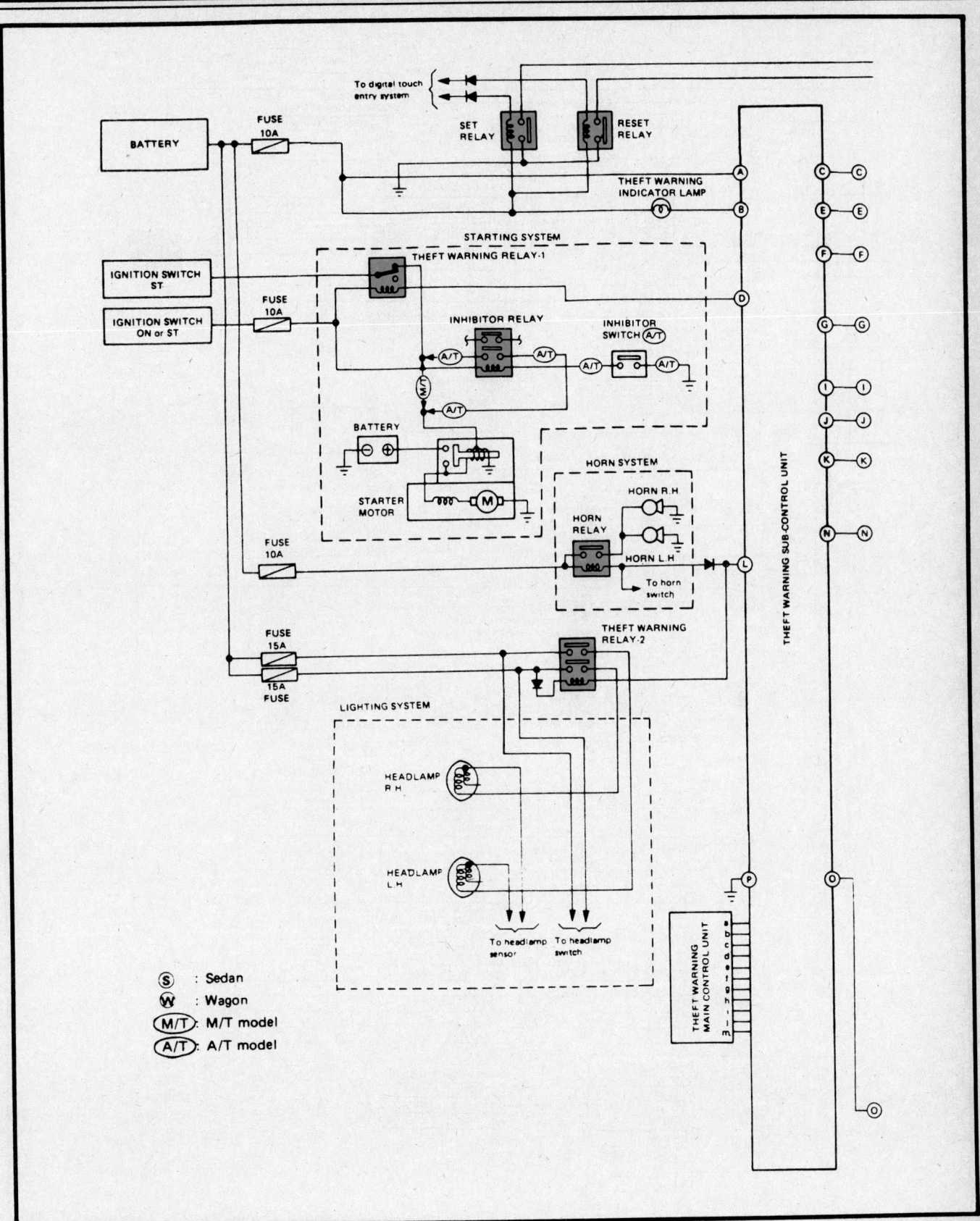

Theft warning system schematic – Maxima

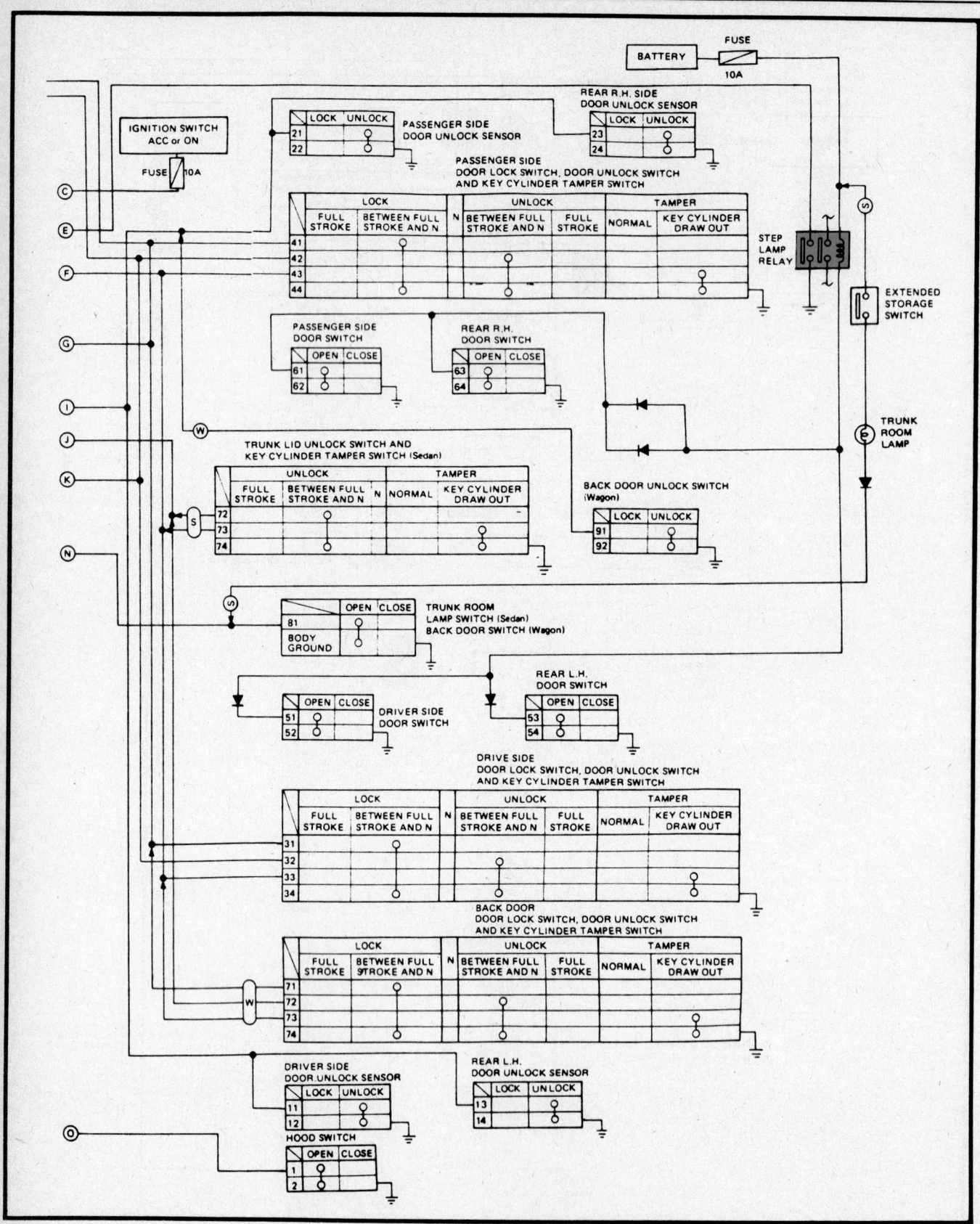

Theft warning system schematic — Maxima (cont.)

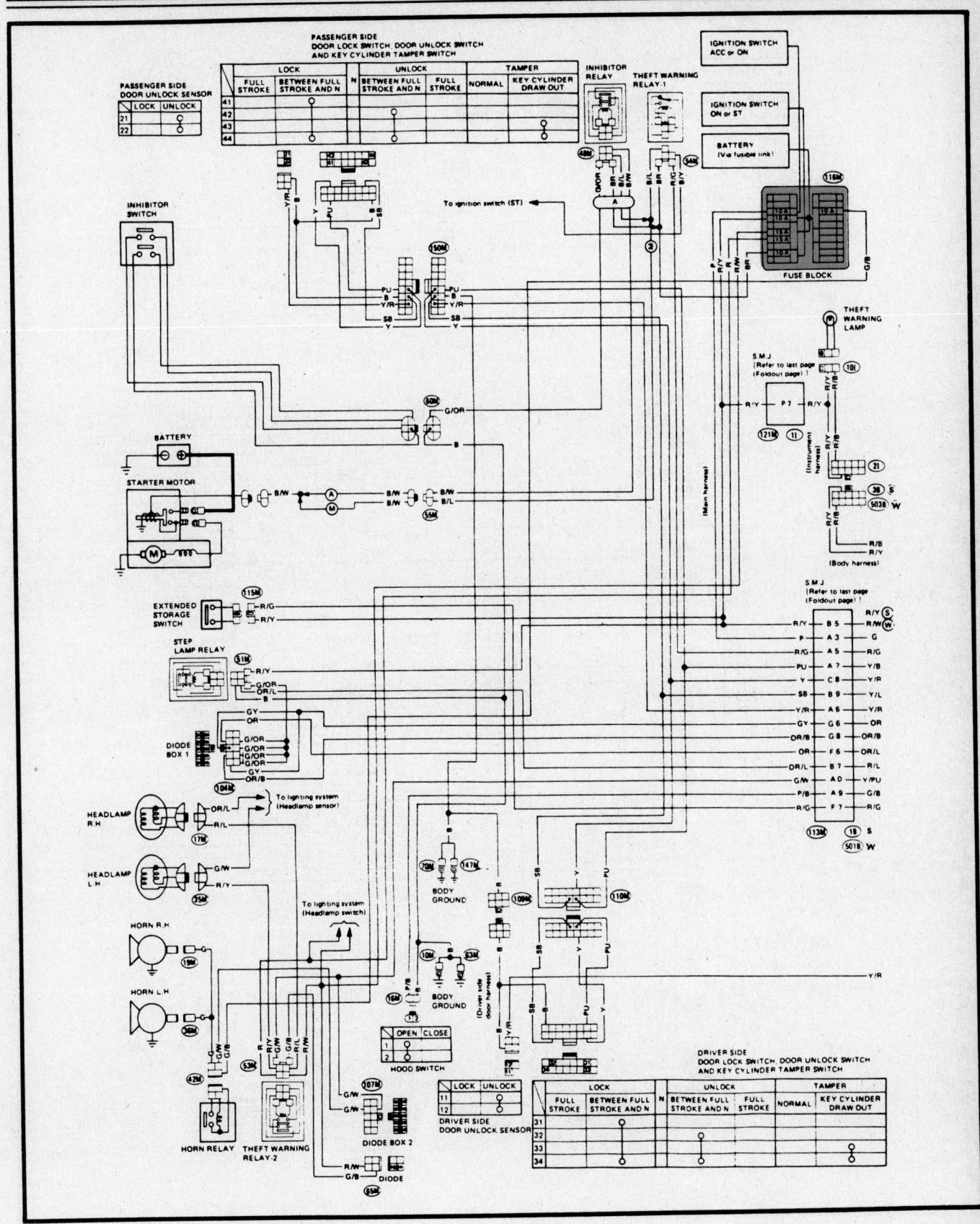

Theft warning system wiring diagram—Maxima

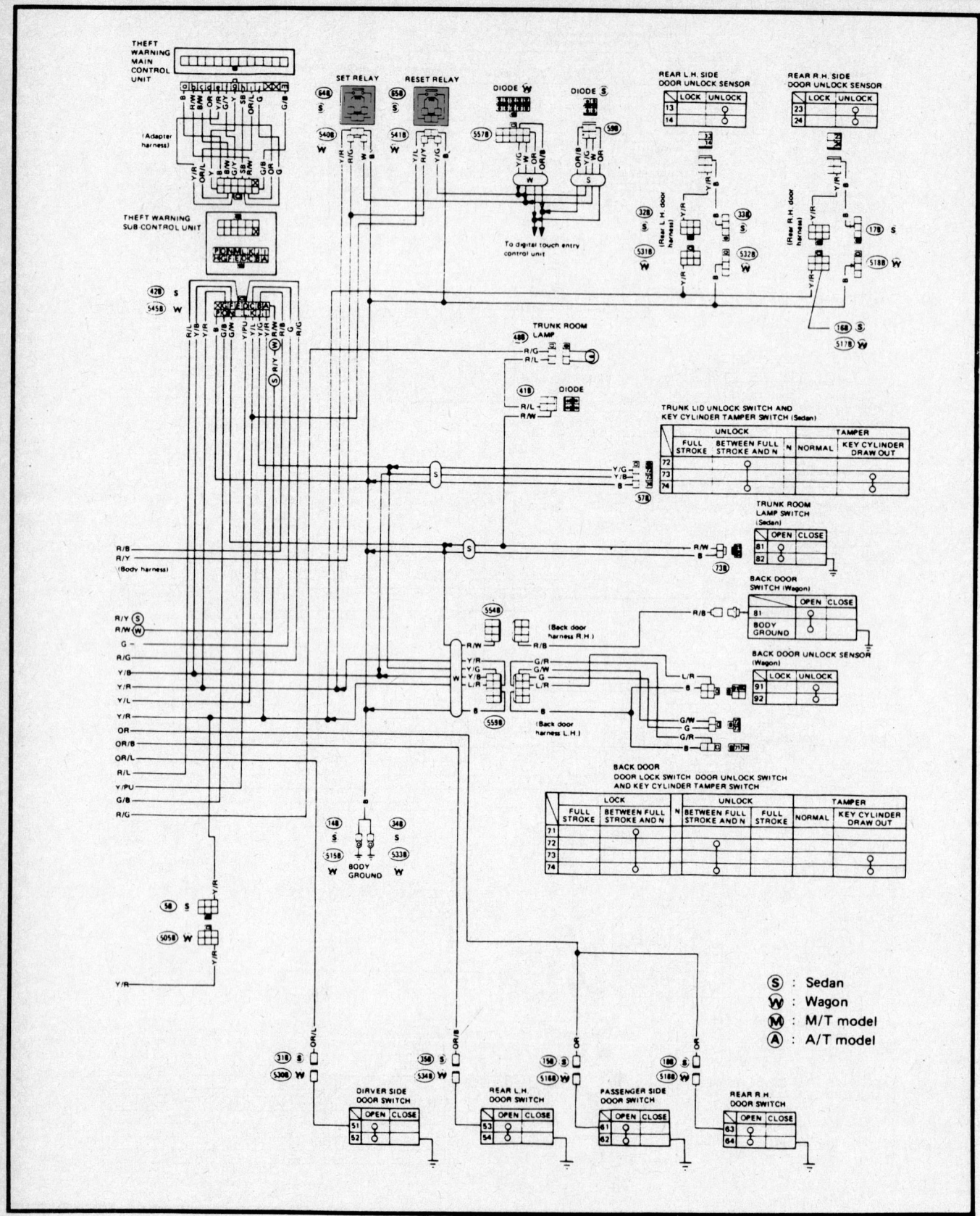

Theft warning system wiring diagram—Maxima (cont.)

SUBARU

Power Mirror

The mirrors are controlled by a single switch assembly usually located on the center console. The motor that operates the mirror is part of the mirror assembly and cannot be replaced separately.

The mirror switch consists of a left-right changeover select knob and control knobs. The switch is ready to function only when the ignition switch is in the "ACC" or "ON" position. Movement of the mirror is accomplished by the motor located in the mirror housing.

POWER MIRROR ASSEMBLY

Removal and Installation

1982-84

1. Disconnect the negative battery cable. Remove the inner door trim panel. Remove the sealing cover.
2. Disconnect the power mirror wire connectors. Remove the mirror retaining screws and remove the mirror assembly from the door.
3. Installation is the reverse order of the removal procedure.

1985 AND LATER

1. Disconnect the negative battery cable. Working from inside the of the vehicle, remove the power mirror finish trim panel.
2. While holding the mirror with on hand, remove the three mirror retaining screws with the other. Remove the mirror assembly from the door.
3. Installation is the reverse order of the removal procedure.

POWER MIRROR GLASS

Removal and Installation

4-DOOR SEDAN AND STATION WAGON

NOTE: Before attempting this procedure a new mirror glass must be available. The old mirror glass will be broken in order to gain access to the mirror motor. When breaking the mirror glass, cover the painted surface of the mirror assembly to avoid any damage from the broken glass.

─── CAUTION ───

To minimize the chance of personal injury during this procedure, gloves and safety glasses should be worn when removing broken glass.

1. Disconnect the negative battery cable. Remove the mirror assembly. Remove the mirror face by tapping the glass and breaking the mirror. Remove the broken glass.
2. Remove the mirror holder retaining screws and remove the mirror holder. Clean the mirror holder of all foreign material.
3. Fill a washbowl with hot water (158 to 176°F) and place the mirror holder in the water for at least three minutes.

NOTE: The following steps must be completed within two minutes or the mirror holder will shrink as it cools and the mirror glass will not fit.

4. Remove the mirror holder from the bowl and wipe off all the moisture. Affix a double-faced adhesive tape to the mirror holder.
5. Install the mirror holder. Remove the protective paper of the double-faced adhesive tape.

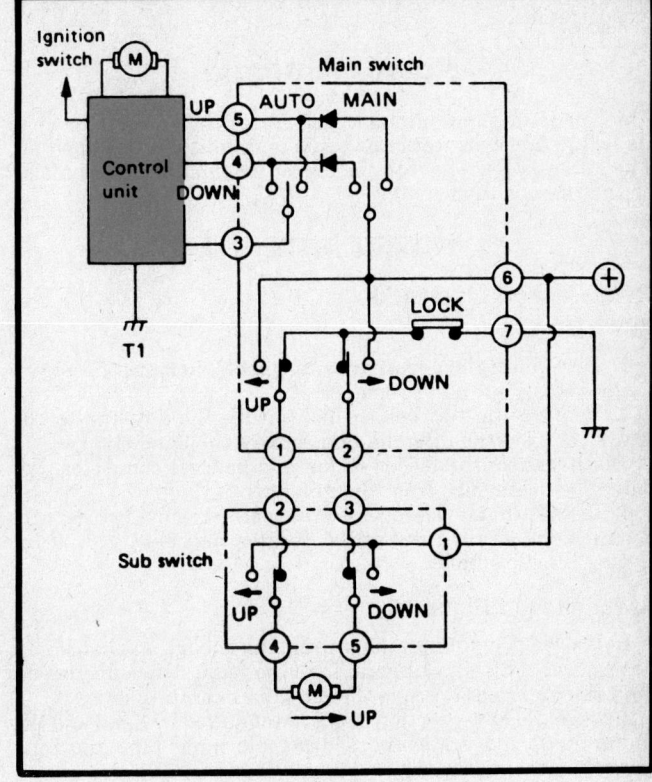

Power mirror wiring schematic—Subaru

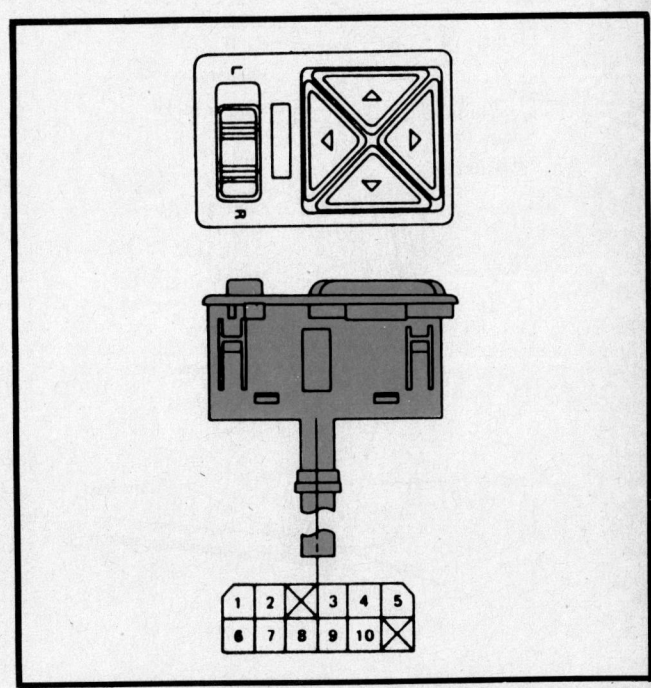

Exploded view of the power mirro switch and switch connector—Subaru

6. Fit the mirror into the mirror holder, by placing one side in the mirror holder first and then press in the remaining portions of the mirror.

7. Install the mirror assembly and check the mirror for proper operations.

Power Antenna

The power antenna automatically raises the antenna mast to its full height whenever the radio and ignition are tuned on. The antenna retracts into the fender when either the ignition or the radio is turned off.

POWER ANTENNA

Removal and Installation
XT COUPE

1. Disconnect the negative battery cable. Remove the antenna mounting nut and supporter.
2. Remove the two bolts which secure the antenna to the trunk. Extract the antenna and remove the band clip.
3. Disconnect the feeder socket and harness connector. Remove the drain tube from the grommet.
4. Installation is the reverse order of the removal procedure. Be sure the drain tube protrudes approximately 0.79 in. through the grommet.

Antenna Rod Removal

1. Loosen the antenna mounting nut enough so that it can be removed with your fingers. Turn the radio switch on and extend the antenna. Remove the antenna mounting nut.
2. Hold the lower section of the antenna rod by hand and lift the antenna rod vertically. Extract the inner pipe and rope from the antenna housing.

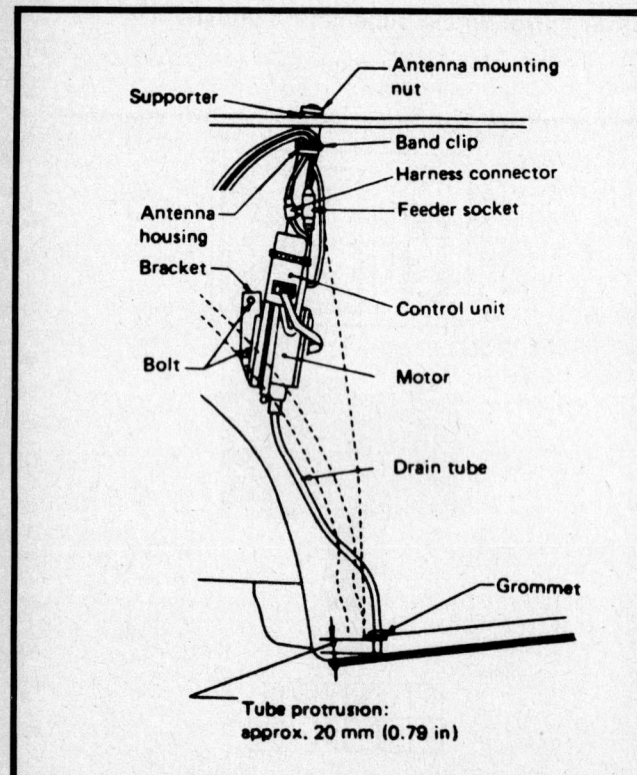

Exploded view of the power antenna assembly

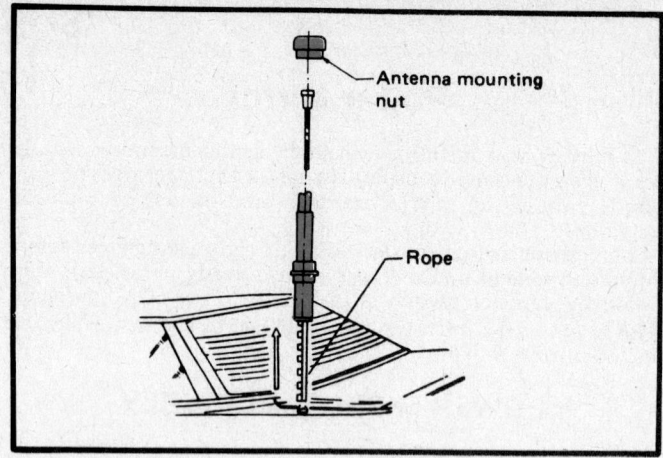

Antenna rod removal and installation

Installation

1. Insert the center pipe (supplied with the new antenna rod) into the antenna housing until it bottoms out.
2. Insert the antenna rod rope into the antenna housing through the centering pipe with the rack facing outward; at the same time turn the radio switch off.
3. Be sure the antenna rod is vertical to the antenna housing. This prevents the rack from sustaining damage and makes it easy to insert the rope. Remove the centering pipe from the antenna housing and detach it from the rope.
4. Face the inner pipe spring toward the center of the car and insert the inner pipe into the antenna housing. Temporarily tighten the antenna mounting nut.
5. Turn the radio switch On and Off to ensure the antenna rod extends and retracts properly. Tighten to secure the antenna mounting nut.

Rear Window Defogger System

The rear window defogger system consists of a rear window with two vertical bus bars and a series of electrically connected grid lines baked on the inside surface. A control switch and a timer relay combined into a single assembly is used on all models.

REAR DEFOGGER GRID

Test

When a grid is inoperable due to an open circuit, the area of glass normally cleared by that grid will remained fogged or iced until cleared by the adjacent grids. Use the following procedure to located a broken grid.
1. With the engine running at idle, place the rear defogger switch in the "ON" position. The pilot lamp is the switch lever should light up indicating the defogger is operating.
2. Using a 12 volt voltmeter, connect the positive lead of the voltmeter to the hot side of the vertical bus element on the inside surface of the glass.
3. Connect the negative lead of the voltmeter to the ground side of the bus element. The voltage drop indicated on the meter should be 11 to 13 volts. Connect the negative lead of the voltmeter to a good ground, the meter reading should stay constant.
4. Keep the negative lead connected to the ground and carefully use the positive lead to contact each grid at the approximate centerline of the window. A voltage drop of approximately 6 volts. indicates a good grid or a closed circuit.

5. No voltage indicated a broken grid wire. To located the exact location of the break, move the voltmeter lead along the grid wire. The voltage should decrease gradually. if the voltage drops suddenly, there is a break at that location.

Defogger Grid Repair

1. Clean the faulty portion of the grid line with a thinner or eythyl alcohol.
2. Apply tape to either side of the faulty portion, leaving the broken grid wire exposed.
3. Use a small paint brush or drafting pen to apply a suitable conductive silver composition to the break, slightly overlap the existing grid wire on both sides (0.20 in.) of the break.
4. Completely dry the repaired section by letting it stand (at a temperature of 68°F) for 24 hours. The drying process can be 30 minutes if a hot air gun (at a temperature of 140°F) is used. If the heat gun is used it should be held at a distance of 1.2 in. of the grid wire.

--- **CAUTION** ---

Do not use the rear window defogger until the repaired section is completely dried. Do not use gasoline or other cleaning solvents to clean the damaged section of the grid line.

REAR DEFOGGER SWITCH

Removal and Installation

1982-84 MODELS

1. Disconnect the negative battery cable. Take out the heater and ventilator control panel after pulling down console box by removing the retaining screws.
2. Disconnect the electrical connectors from the switch. Remove the defogger switch retaining screw and remove the switch.
3. Installation is the reverse order of the removal procedure.

ALL 1985 AND LATER MODELS (EXCEPT THE XT COUPE)

1. Disconnect the negative battery cable. Using a suitable tool, remove the all the knobs from the switch panel on the right side of the dash panel.
2. Remove the four switch panel retaining screws. Disconnect the electrical connectors and remove the switch panel.
3. Installation is the reverse order of the removal procedure.

1985 AND LATER XT COUPE

1. Disconnect the negative battery cable. Using a stub phillips head screwdriver, remove the left control wing retaining screws.

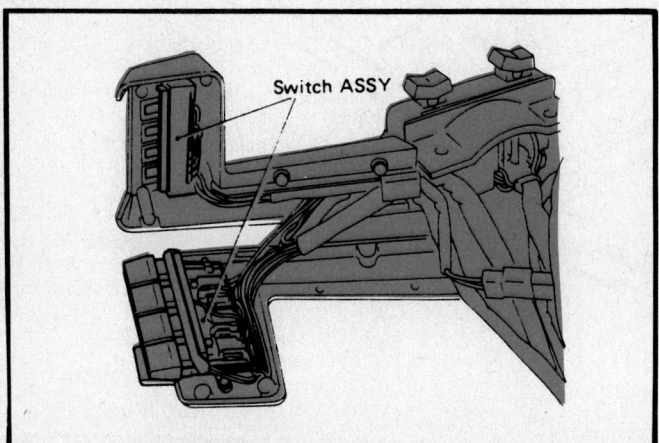

Switch ASSY

Left control wing assembly—XT coupe

2. Pull the front part of the control wing down and remove the switch assembly. Disconnect the switch assembly wiring harness and remove the switch.
3. Installation is the reverse order of the removal procedure.

Electric Sunroofs

The sunroof is operated by a switch, which is usually located in the headliner. The system is consists of the sunroof switch, motor drive cables and circuit breaker and a relay. The sunroof can be closed manually, (should it be necessary) by removing the headliner plug, insert the handle and turn the gear to close the sunroof.

NOTE: The sunroof assembly is equipped with water drain tubes, it is important to keep these drain tubes open. So it is recommended to blow compressed air through the drain tubes at regular intervals, in order to keep the drain tubes clear.

SUNROOF ASSEMBLY

Removal and Installation

1. Remove the roof trim. Disconnect the drain tubes and disconnect the motor harness connector.
2. Remove the six bolts from the sunroof frame bracket, starting from the front and moving to the rear.
3. Hold the front and rear side of the sunroof (a second person will be needed) and slide the sunroof assembly off by moving it to the rear.
4. Installation is the reverse order of the removal procedure.

SUNROOF LID ASSEMBLY

Removal and Installation

1. Completely close the sunroof glass. Completely open the sunshade. Remove the bracket cap and screws and detach the bracket cover.
2. Completely close the sunroof lid assembly and lift it up. Remove the eight nuts from the left and right ring bracket.
3. Working from inside the vehicle, slightly raise the sunroof lid assembly until it is disengaged from the link bracket. Hold both ends of the lid assembly and remove it at an angle.

Height Adjustment

1. Place shim(s) between the link bracket and the lid assembly to align the sunroof with the roof panel.
2. The difference in the height between the roof and the main seal should be adjusted to within the 0.051 ± 0.039 in. range.

Horizontal Adjustment

1. Loosen the eight nuts which hold the sunroof lid assembly.
2. Move the sunnroof lid assembly to either side, along the oblong hole at the stay location, until proper adjustment is reached. Then tighten the nuts.
3. Check to see if the deflector is positioned at a proper height. The height of the deflector cannot be adjusted. Repair or replace the deflector if it is deformed or damaged.

Sunshade Removal

1. Unhook the sunshade hooks. Move the sunroof lid assembly rearward.
2. Set the sunshade to the forward position and remove the retaining nuts from both sides of the sunshade.
3. Installation is the reverse order of the removal procedure.

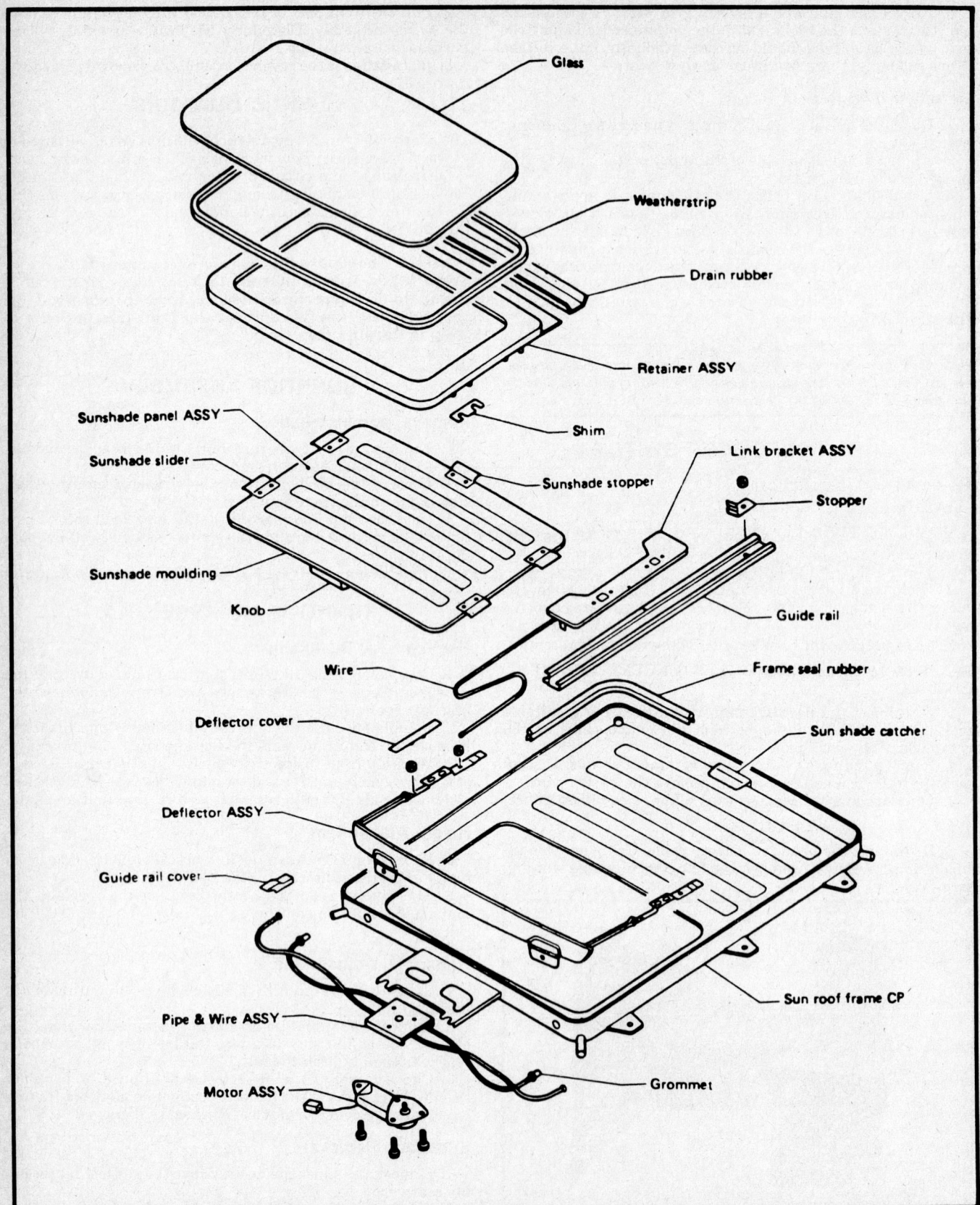

Glass

Weatherstrip

Drain rubber

Retainer ASSY

Shim

Sunshade panel ASSY

Sunshade slider

Sunshade stopper

Link bracket ASSY

Stopper

Sunshade moulding

Knob

Guide rail

Wire

Frame seal rubber

Deflector cover

Sun shade catcher

Deflector ASSY

Guide rail cover

Sun roof frame CP

Pipe & Wire ASSY

Grommet

Motor ASSY

Exploded view of typical Subaru sunroof

Trouble	Point to check
Water leaks in compartment.	1. Improper clearance between roof and weatherstrip. 2. Rubber drain for proper fit. 3. Drain tube for obstruction. 4. Roof sealing for breakage. 5. Any clearance between sunroof frame seal and car body.
Wind noise.	1. Improper clearance between sunroof and weatherstrip. 2. Sunshade and roof trim for unseated section.
Wind noise at deflector.	1. Improper lift of deflector. 2. Deflector for deformity.
Unusual motor noise.	1. Loose motor mounting bolt. 2. Worn gear or bearing. 3. Worn cable. 4. Deformed pipe.
Failure of sunroof to operate. (motor runs)	1. Foreign matter caught in guide rail. 2. Interference with adjacent parts. 3. Improper caulking at cable slider location. 4. Incorrect connection of cable. 5. Improper tightening of clutch adjustment nut.
Failure of sunroof motor to operate. (Sunroof can operate when sunroof wrench is used.)	1. Burned fuse. 2. Switch function. 3. Motor's terminal voltage. 4. Relay operation.

Sunroof troubleshooting chart

Sunroof Frame Removal

1. Remove the sunroof trim. Disconnect the front and rear drain tubes.
2. Remove the six bolts which hold the sunroof frame and detach the sunroof frame.
3. Installation is the reverse order of the removal procedure.

Sunroof Motor

1. Disconnect the negative battery cable. Remove the roof trim.
2. Remove the sunroof motor nut and harness coupler and remove the sunroof motor.
3. Before installing the motor, wrap a shop towel around the main seal of the sunroof lid. Then connect a suitable spring scale, pull the sunroof lid out using the spring scale.
4. The sunroof lid pull should be 22 lbs. maximum. If the sunroof exceeds the specified amount, check the condition of the guard rail and interference of the main seal with the guard rail.

5. Installation of the motor is the reverse order of the removal procedure.

Sunroof Closing Force Check (With The Motor Installed)

1. After installing all removed parts, using a second person, have them hold the switch to close the sunroof while measuring the force required to stop the sunroof with a suitable spring scale.
2. Read the force on the scale as soon as the glass stops moving, then immediately release the switch and spring scale. The closing force should be 44-55 lbs.
3. If the force required to stop the sunroof is not within specifications, adjust it, by turning the sunroof motor clutch adjusting nut (using the handle furnished by the manufacturer). Turn the nut clockwise to increase the force and counterclockwise to decrease the force.
4. After the proper adjustment has been made, install a new lockwasher and bend it against the flat of the adjusting nut.

TOYOTA

Power Mirrors

The power remote mirrors are adjusted from the interior of the car by moving the outside mirror switch in the desired position. Each mirror has two reversible motors. One to adjust the mirror view up and the other to adjust the mirror view right and left.

The driver operates the Up-Down and Left-Right switch that controls the polarity of the voltage to the motors. The mirror select switch directs these control voltages to either the right or left outside mirror.

The Celica, Celica Supra and the Cressida models incorporate a heating system in the power mirror. This heating system for the power mirrors is tied in with the rear window defogger.

When the rear window defogger switch is energized, the base of the power mirror heats up through a ground lead soldered which is soldered to the mirror base. A thermistor in the wiring circuit interrupts the current flow when the mirror base reaches a certain temperature.

POWER MIRROR ASSEMBLY

Removal and Installation

1. Disconnect the negative battery cable. Working from inside the of the vehicle, remove the power mirror finish trim panel.

2. While holding the mirror with on hand, remove the three mirror retaining screws with the other. Remove the mirror assembly from the door.

3. Installation is the reverse order of the removal procedure.

NOTE On some of the older models it may be necessary to remove the inner door trim panel in order to gain access to the power mirror retaining nuts.

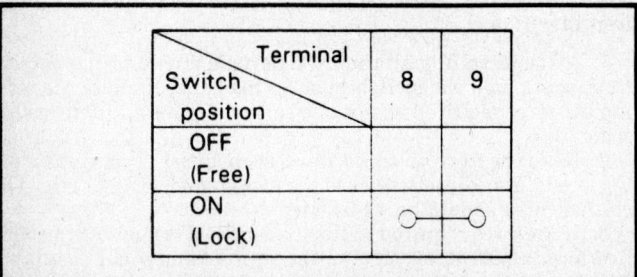

Mirror Terminal / Switch position	Left Mirror (Slide switch to left)					Right Mirror (Slide switch to right)			
	7	6	2	1	3	1	2	5	4
UP									
DOWN									
LEFT									
RIGHT									

Power mirror switch continuity switch

Terminal / Switch position	8	9
OFF (Free)		
ON (Lock)	o—o	

Heated power mirror switch continuity

Heated Mirror Test

1. Disconnect the harness connector at the heated mirror. Measure the resistance between the last two (right side) terminals.

2. The resistance should be 5 to 30 ohms. If the resistance measured does not fall into specifications, replace the mirror assembly. The resistance value will increase as the temperature rises.

Power Antenna

The power antenna automatically raises the antenna mast to its full height whenever the radio and ignition are tuned on. The antenna retracts into the fender when either the ignition or the radio is turned off.

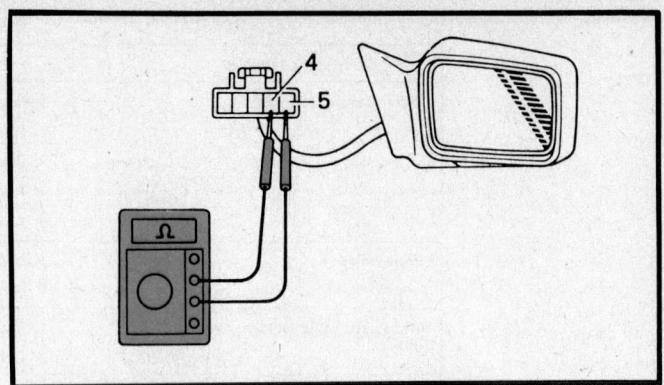

Testing the heated mirror

POWER ANTENNA MOTOR CONTROL RELAY

Test With The Antenna Up

1. Connect the positive lead of a suitable voltmeter to number one terminal of the relay connector and the negative lead of the voltmeter to the number four terminal.

2. Connect the positive lead from the battery to terminals six, seven and eight. Connect the negative lead to terminal number three.

3. Check to see if there is battery voltage. Measure the voltage within seven seconds after connecting the positive lead battery lead to terminal number eight.

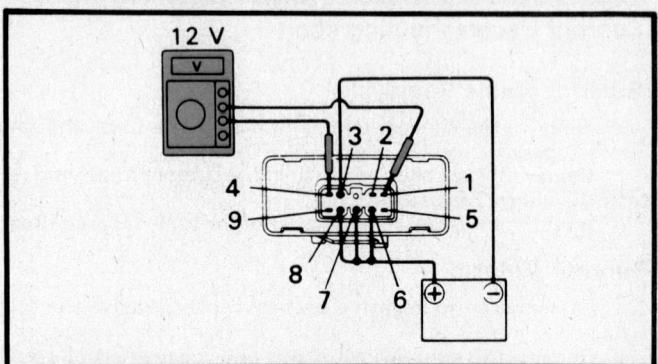

Inspecting the power antenna motor relay

Test With The Antenna Down

1. Connect the voltmeter positive lead to terminal number four and the negative lead to terminal number one.

2. Connect the positive lead from the battery to terminal six and seven. Connect the negative lead battery lead to terminal number two.

3. Disconnect the positive battery lead from terminal number six. Check to see that there is battery voltage.

4. Measure the voltage within seven seconds after connecting the positive lead battery lead to terminal number six.

Test With The Antenna Stop

1. Connect the voltmeter positive lead to terminal number one and the negative bleed to terminal number four.

2. Connect the positive lead from the battery to terminals seven and nine. Connect the negative lead from the battery to terminal number two. Check to see that there is battery voltage.

3. If the relay fails any of these test, replace it.

POWER ANTENNA MOTOR

Test

1. Test the motor by removing the wire connector and applying battery voltage between terminals seven and ten.
2. Next check the limit switch operation as follows.
   a. If the motor stops with the antenna up, check that there is no continuity between terminals two and nine.
   b. If the motor stops with the antenna down, check that there is no continuity between terminals two and eight.
3. If the limit switch fails any of these checks, replace it.

NOTE: There is no power antenna assembly removal and installation procedure available at the time of this publication.

Power antenna motor wiring connector — terminal identification

Rear Window Defogger

The rear window defogger system consists of a rear window with two vertical bus bars and a series of electrically connected grid lines baked on the inside surface. A control switch and a timer relay combined into a single assembly is used on all models.

REAR DEFOGGER GRID

Test

When a grid is inoperable due to an open circuit, the area of glass normally cleared by that grid will remained fogged or iced until cleared by the adjacent grids. Use the following procedure to located a broken grid.

1. With the engine running at idle, place the rear defogger switch in the "ON" position. The pilot lamp is the switch lever should light up indicating the defogger is operating (if so equipped).
2. Using a 12 volt voltmeter, connect the positive lead of the voltmeter to the hot side of the vertical bus element on the inside surface of the glass.
3. Connect the negative lead of the voltmeter to the ground side of the bus element. The voltage drop indicated on the meter should be 10 volts. Connect the negative lead of the voltmeter to a good ground, the meter reading should stay constant.
4. Keep the negative lead connected to the ground and carefully use the positive lead to contact each grid at the approximate centerline of the window. A voltage drop of approximately 5 volts, indicates a good grid or a closed circuit.
5. No voltage indicated a broken grid wire. To located the

exact location of the break, move the voltmeter lead along the grid wire. The voltage should decrease gradually. if the voltage drops suddenly, there is a break at that location.

Defogger Grid Repair

1. Clean the faulty portion of the grid line with a thinner or eythyl alcohol.
2. Apply tape to either side of the faulty portion, leaving the broken grid wire exposed.
3. Use a small paint brush or drafting pen to apply a suitable conductive silver composition to the break, slightly overlap the existing grid wire on both sides (0.20 in.) of the break.
4. Completely dry the repaired section by letting it stand (at a temperature of 68°F) for 24 hours. The drying process can be 30 minutes if a hot air gun (at a temperature of 140°F) is used. If the heat gun is used it should be held at a distance of 1.2 in. of the grid wire.

--- **CAUTION** ---

Do not use the rear window defogger until the repaired section is completely dried. Do not use gasoline or other cleaning solvents to clean the damaged section of the grid line.

REAR WINDOW DEFOGGER RELAY

Continuity Test

1. Using a suitable ohmmeter, check that there is continuity between terminals one and three.
2. Check that there is continuity between terminals two and four.
3. If the relay fails the continuity test, replace it.

Operational Test

1. Using a suitable jumper wire, apply 12 volts across terminals one and three. Now with a suitable ohmmeter, check for continuity at terminals two and four.
2. If the realy fails this test replace it.

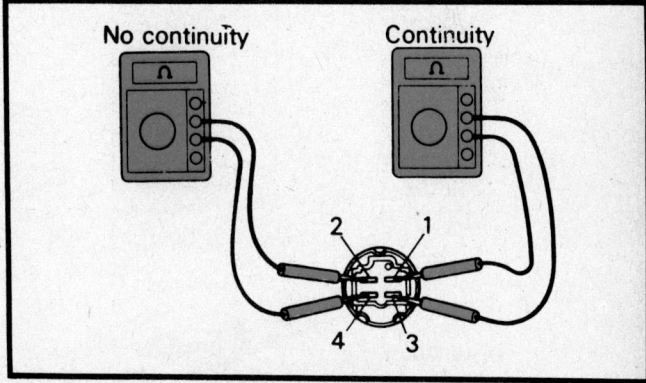

Testing the rear window defogger relay

Sunroof

The sunroof is operated by a switch, which is usually located in the headliner. The system is consists of the sunroof switch, motor drive cables and circuit breaker and two relays. The sunroof can be closed manually, (should it be necessary) by removing the headliner plug, insert the handle and turn the gear to close the sunroof.

NOTE: The sunroof assembly is equipped with water drip panels, it is important to keep these drip panels

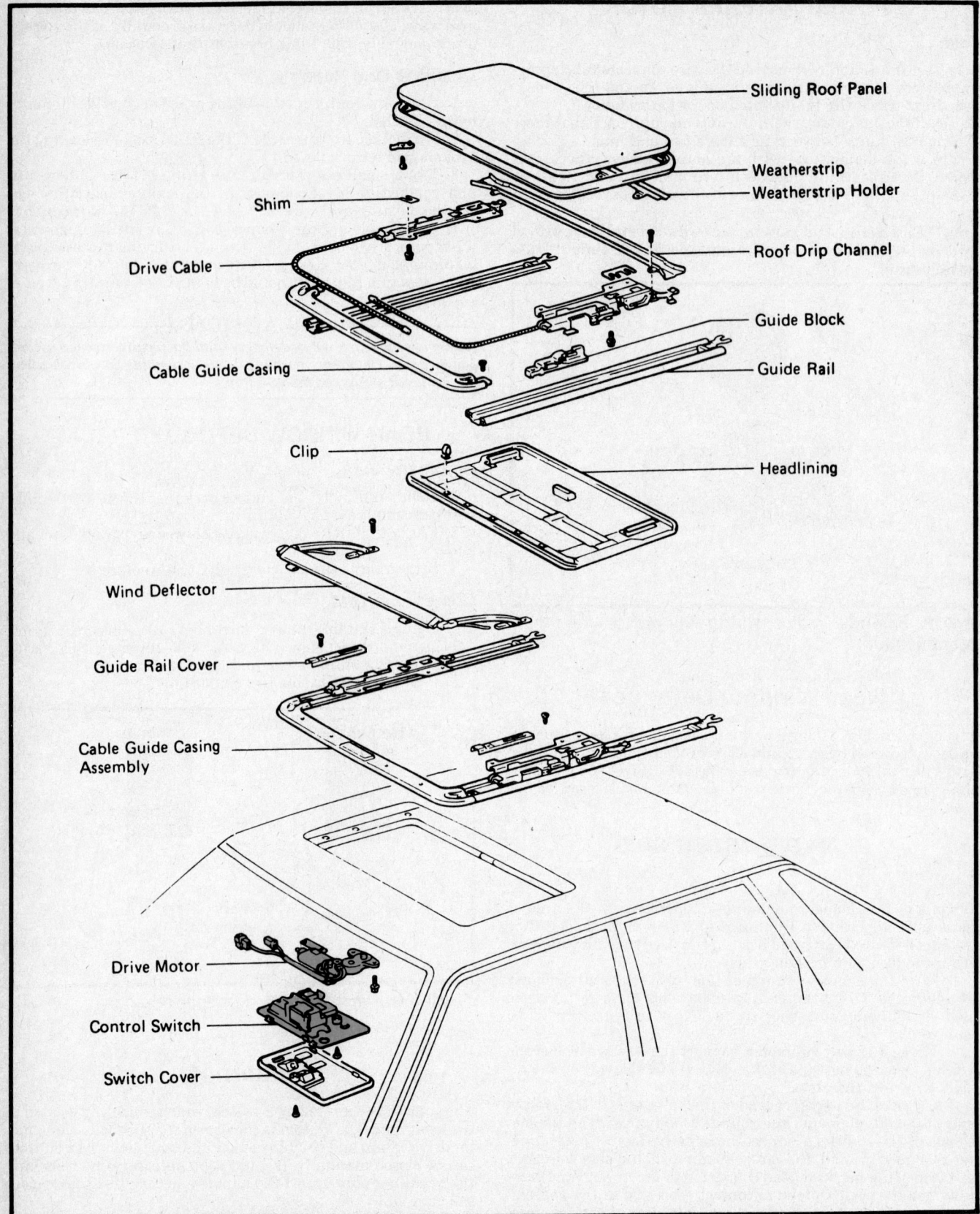

- Sliding Roof Panel
- Weatherstrip
- Weatherstrip Holder
- Roof Drip Channel
- Guide Block
- Guide Rail
- Shim
- Drive Cable
- Cable Guide Casing
- Clip
- Headlining
- Wind Deflector
- Guide Rail Cover
- Cable Guide Casing Assembly
- Drive Motor
- Control Switch
- Switch Cover

Exploded view of a typical Toyota sunroof

open. So it is recommended to blow compressed air through the drip panels at regular intervals, in order to keep the them clear.

SUNROOF ASSEMBLY

Removal and Installtion

1. Remove the headlining. Using the sunroof switch, tilt the sunroof position down fully.
2. Disconnect the negative battery cable. Remove the front portion of the switch cover nut, disengage the the two switch tabs and remove the switch.
3. Remove the roof headlining and drive motor retaining bolts. Disconnect the motor wiring harness and remove the motor.
4. Apply adhesive tape to protect the body. Remove the six sliding roof retaining bolts and remove the sliding roof. Be sure to take note of the number and position of any shims at this time.
5. Remove the roof drip channel by removing the two set screws and pulling it forward. Slide the drive cable rearward and remove the wind deflector. Remove the two guide rails covers.
6. Slide the drive cable forward and remove the six set screws. Apply adhesive tape to protect the body. While pushing down on the center of the casing, pull the cable guide casing assembly off in an upward direction.

Disassembly

1. Remove the two cable guide casing set screws and pull the cable guide casing forward to remove.
2. Remove the cable guide block from the guide rail and pull the drive cable from the guide rail.

Assembly

1. Apply a suitable multi-purpose grease to the drive cable. Place the drive cables into the guide rail.
2. Install the cable guide block to the guide rail. Insert the drive cable into the casing and align it with the guide rail. Install the guide rail and guide casing with screws.
3. Use a butyl tape to cover the cut portion of the weatherstripe at the connection between the guide casing and the guide rail.

Installation

1. Install the cable guide casing assembly by, inserting a pin or equivalent into the base hole, align it with the link position and set the roof in the tilt fully closed position.
2. While pushing down on the center of the casing, insert the cable guide casing assembly from the front of the roof and install the six set screws.
3. Install the roof drip panel. Install the sliding roof panel, be sure to install only the same number of shims that were disassembled.
4. Be sure when installing the drive motor, when operating the drive gear, use the control switch and be sure the cam is set at the closed position. Install the drive motor to the roof and install the control switch and switch cover.
5. Reconnect the battery cable, using the sunroof switch, fully open the sliding roof. Install the guide rail covers with the set screws.
6. Install the wind deflector and adjust the sliding roof.
7. Using the sunroof switch, fully tilt up the sliding roof. Insert the headling from the upper portion of the roof and then insert the sun shade lock spring case into the shoe link.
8. Open the sliding roof halfway and tap the headlining clips into the sliding roof panel.

NOTE: After the installation procedure is complete, start the engine and check the operation of the sunroof (approximately 10 seconds). Fully open and close the sunroof and check that the motor stops after operation. If the motor does not stop, add another shim to the sunroof motor screws.

Sliding Roof Adjustment

1. Open the sliding roof halfway. Remove the clips on the front part of the headlining.
2. Using the switch, fully tilt up the sliding roof. Pull the headling rear-ward and remove it.
3. Adjust the level difference by increasing or decreasing the number of shims. If the front of the sliding roof is too high, it will not close completely.
4. To adjust it forward or rearward adjust it by loosening the sliding roof retaining bolts and move the sliding roof to the forward and rearward. With the sliding roof closed, insert a pin or equivalent into the base hole to insure alignment of the holes.
5. To adjust it left or right, loosen the sliding roof installation bolts and move the sliding roof to the right or left.

Theft Warning System

This system is designed to provide a warning in the event of a forced entry throught the driver and passenger doors and trunk. When a forced entry is attempted, the alarm warning system will be tripped off. This will set the horns off and the exterior light to flash in unison for three to seven minutes. The starter interlock feature prevents the engine from starting if the warning system is tripped.

The alarm is tripped by opening switches strategically located in the door jambs, the door lock cylinders and the trunk lock cylinder. When a door lock cylinder or trunk lock cylinder is violated by rotating it in or moving it in or out, or if any door is opened without using the key, the alarm will be actuated by the controller.

The alarm will automatically turn off after two to four minutes, the alarm will reactivate if the vehicle is tampered with again. The alarm can be shut off by unlocking the doors, trunk lid or tailgate with the proper key.

Activating The System

1. Remove the key from the ignition switch. Close all the windows, close and lock all of the doors, hood, trunk lid or tailgate.
2. The door can be locked with or without the key. Confirm that the indicator light comes on. The light will glow for about 30 seconds and then go out. The system is now activated.
3. If, during the thirty second time period, the door is unlocked or the ignition key is turned to the "ACC" or "ON", the system will not activate.

De-activating The System

The system can only be de-activated by unlocking the doors, trunk lid or tailgate with the proper key. The alarm will not stop even if the ignition key is switched to the "ACC" or "ON" position.

Testing the System

1. Open all the windows. Set the system as previously outlined, be sure to wait until the indicator light starts flashing.
2. Unlock one of the doors from the inside. The system should set off the alarm. Cancel the system by unlocking either front door with the key.
3. Repeat this operation for the other doors, trunk and hood. If system does not work properly, the system will have to be checked and repaired.

Problem	Section
Theft deterrent system can not be set.	A
Theft deterrent system does not operate when LH door opened.	B
Theft deterrent system does not operate when RH door opened.	C
Theft deterrent system does not cancel when ignition switch turned on or ACC position.	D
Theft deterrent system does not cancel when LH door unlocked with key.	E
Theft deterrent system does not cancel when RH door unlocked with key.	F
Horn does not blow even if theft deterrent system operated.	G
Headlights and taillights do not flash even if theft deterrent system operated.	H

Troubleshooting the theft deterrent system

A	INSPECTION OF SOURCE CIRCUIT

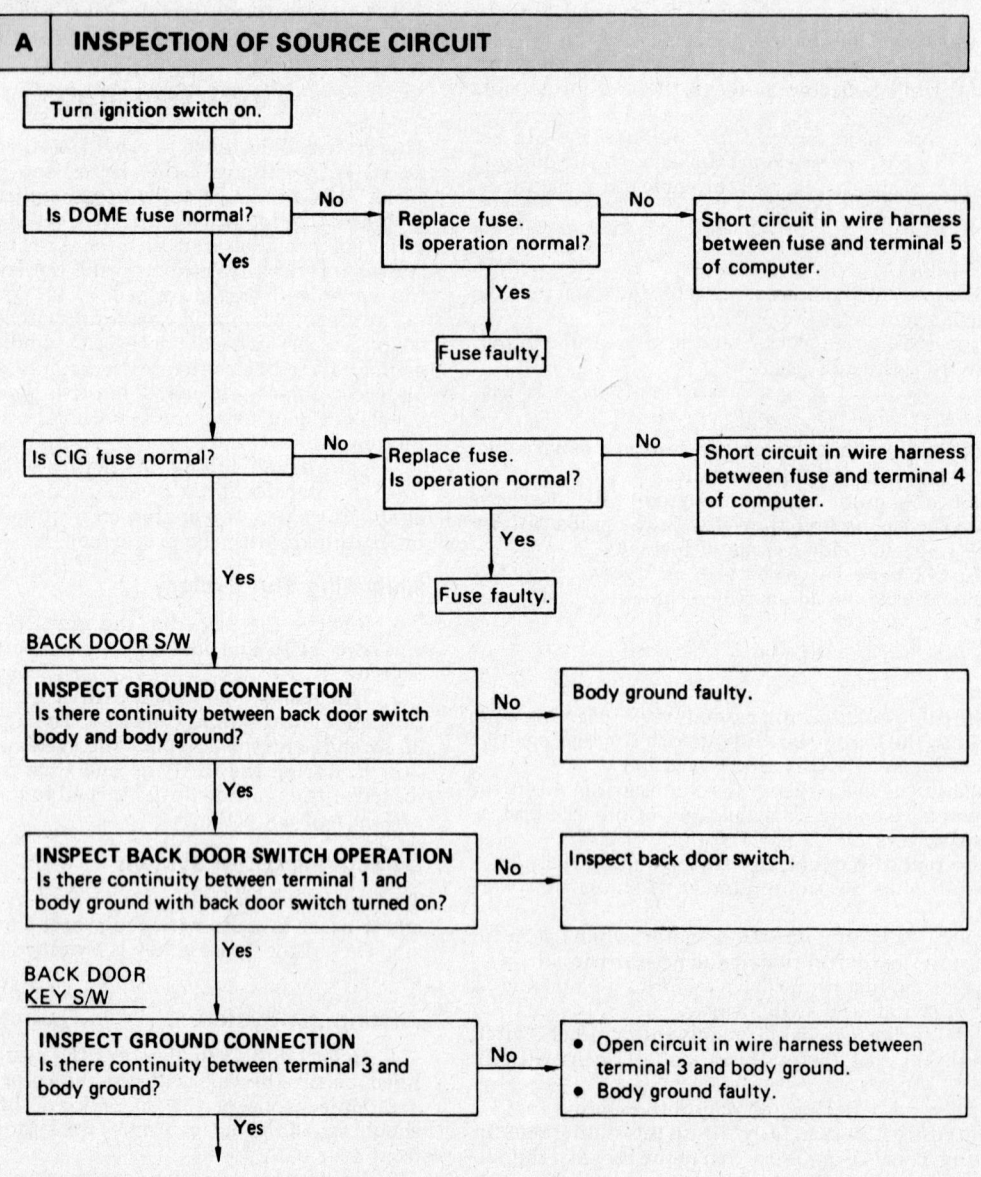

Turn ignition switch on.

Is DOME fuse normal? — No → Replace fuse. Is operation normal? — No → Short circuit in wire harness between fuse and terminal 5 of computer.

Yes (DOME) ; Yes (Replace) → Fuse faulty.

Is CIG fuse normal? — No → Replace fuse. Is operation normal? — No → Short circuit in wire harness between fuse and terminal 4 of computer.

Yes (CIG) ; Yes (Replace) → Fuse faulty.

BACK DOOR S/W

INSPECT GROUND CONNECTION
Is there continuity between back door switch body and body ground? — No → Body ground faulty.

Yes

INSPECT BACK DOOR SWITCH OPERATION
Is there continuity between terminal 1 and body ground with back door switch turned on? — No → Inspect back door switch.

Yes

BACK DOOR KEY S/W

INSPECT GROUND CONNECTION
Is there continuity between terminal 3 and body ground? — No →
- Open circuit in wire harness between terminal 3 and body ground.
- Body ground faulty.

Yes

Troubleshooting the theft deterrent system (cont.)

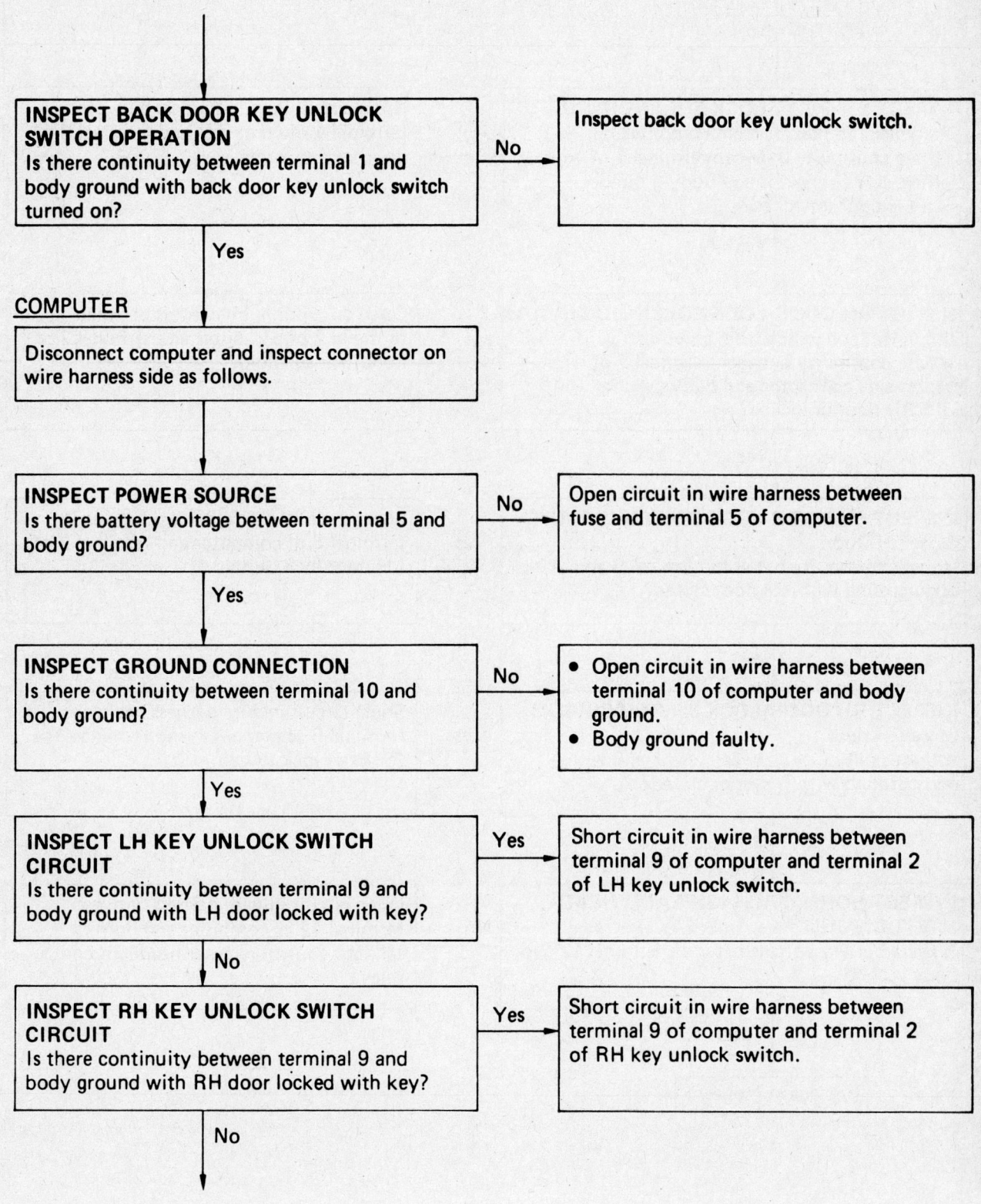

INSPECT BACK DOOR KEY UNLOCK SWITCH OPERATION
Is there continuity between terminal 1 and body ground with back door key unlock switch turned on?

No → Inspect back door key unlock switch.

Yes

COMPUTER

Disconnect computer and inspect connector on wire harness side as follows.

INSPECT POWER SOURCE
Is there battery voltage between terminal 5 and body ground?

No → Open circuit in wire harness between fuse and terminal 5 of computer.

Yes

INSPECT GROUND CONNECTION
Is there continuity between terminal 10 and body ground?

No →
- Open circuit in wire harness between terminal 10 of computer and body ground.
- Body ground faulty.

Yes

INSPECT LH KEY UNLOCK SWITCH CIRCUIT
Is there continuity between terminal 9 and body ground with LH door locked with key?

Yes → Short circuit in wire harness between terminal 9 of computer and terminal 2 of LH key unlock switch.

No

INSPECT RH KEY UNLOCK SWITCH CIRCUIT
Is there continuity between terminal 9 and body ground with RH door locked with key?

Yes → Short circuit in wire harness between terminal 9 of computer and terminal 2 of RH key unlock switch.

No

Troubleshooting the theft deterrent system (cont.)

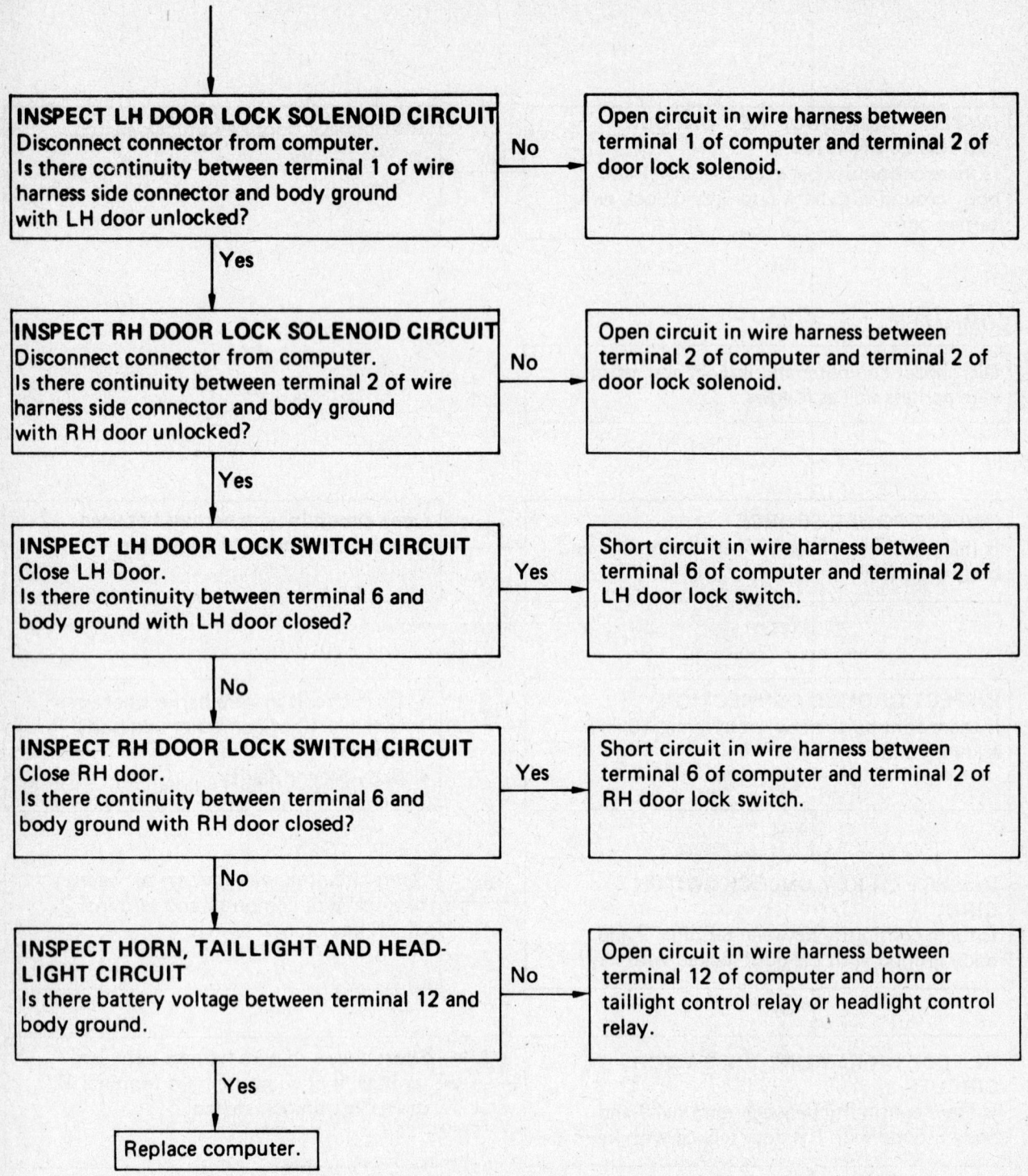

INSPECT LH DOOR LOCK SOLENOID CIRCUIT Disconnect connector from computer. Is there continuity between terminal 1 of wire harness side connector and body ground with LH door unlocked?	**No** → Open circuit in wire harness between terminal 1 of computer and terminal 2 of door lock solenoid.

Yes ↓

INSPECT RH DOOR LOCK SOLENOID CIRCUIT Disconnect connector from computer. Is there continuity between terminal 2 of wire harness side connector and body ground with RH door unlocked?	**No** → Open circuit in wire harness between terminal 2 of computer and terminal 2 of door lock solenoid.

Yes ↓

INSPECT LH DOOR LOCK SWITCH CIRCUIT Close LH Door. Is there continuity between terminal 6 and body ground with LH door closed?	**Yes** → Short circuit in wire harness between terminal 6 of computer and terminal 2 of LH door lock switch.

No ↓

INSPECT RH DOOR LOCK SWITCH CIRCUIT Close RH door. Is there continuity between terminal 6 and body ground with RH door closed?	**Yes** → Short circuit in wire harness between terminal 6 of computer and terminal 2 of RH door lock switch.

No ↓

INSPECT HORN, TAILLIGHT AND HEAD-LIGHT CIRCUIT Is there battery voltage between terminal 12 and body ground.	**No** → Open circuit in wire harness between terminal 12 of computer and horn or taillight control relay or headlight control relay.

Yes ↓

Replace computer.

Troubleshooting the theft deterrent system (cont.)

B INSPECTION OF LH DOOR UNLOCK CIRCUIT

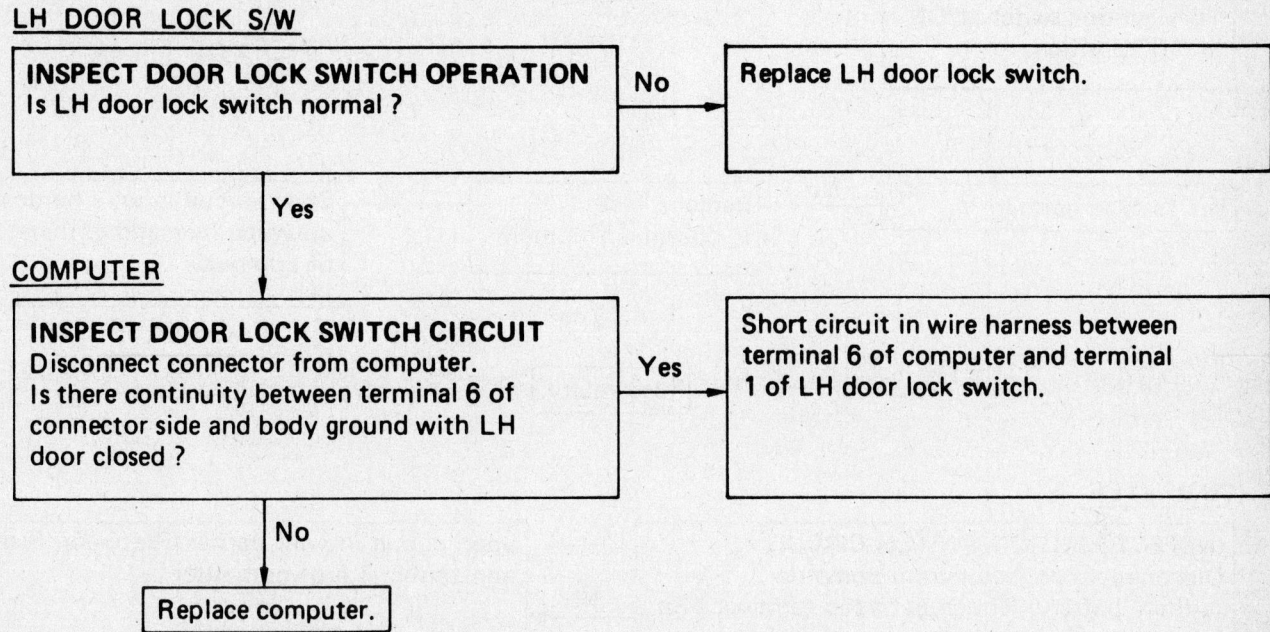

LH DOOR LOCK S/W

INSPECT DOOR LOCK SWITCH OPERATION
Is LH door lock switch normal ?

— No → Replace LH door lock switch.

↓ Yes

COMPUTER

INSPECT DOOR LOCK SWITCH CIRCUIT
Disconnect connector from computer.
Is there continuity between terminal 6 of connector side and body ground with LH door closed ?

— Yes → Short circuit in wire harness between terminal 6 of computer and terminal 1 of LH door lock switch.

↓ No

Replace computer.

C INSPECTION OF RH DOOR UNLOCK CIRCUIT

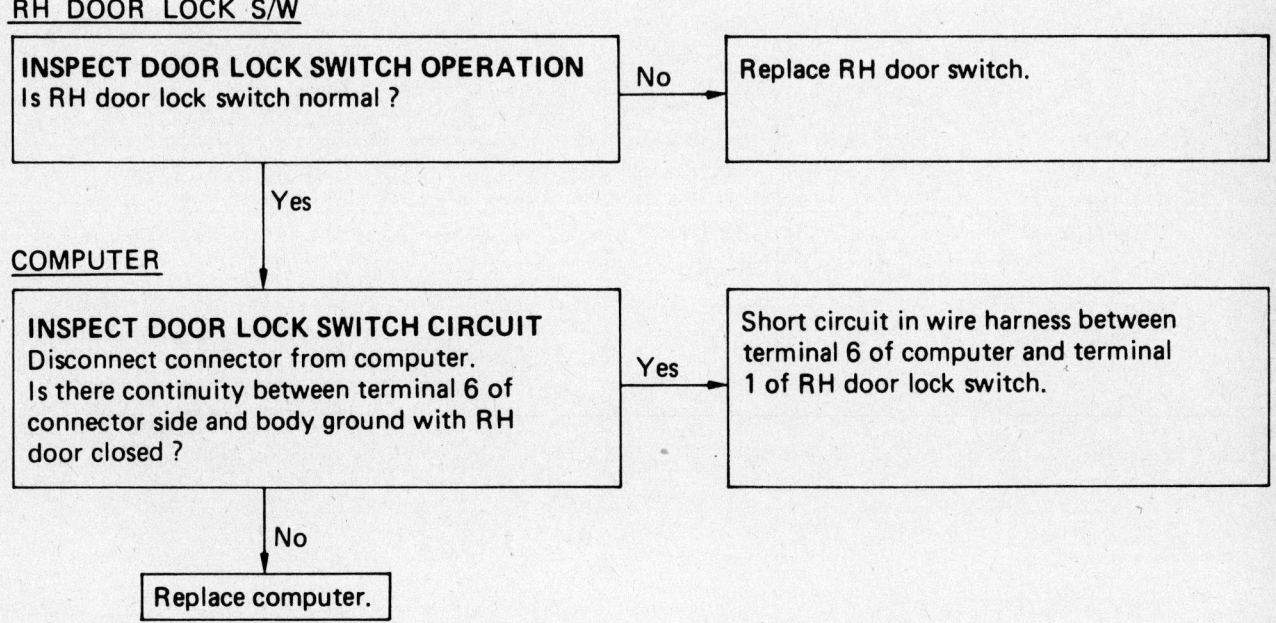

RH DOOR LOCK S/W

INSPECT DOOR LOCK SWITCH OPERATION
Is RH door lock switch normal ?

— No → Replace RH door switch.

↓ Yes

COMPUTER

INSPECT DOOR LOCK SWITCH CIRCUIT
Disconnect connector from computer.
Is there continuity between terminal 6 of connector side and body ground with RH door closed ?

— Yes → Short circuit in wire harness between terminal 6 of computer and terminal 1 of RH door lock switch.

↓ No

Replace computer.

Troubleshooting the theft deterrent system (cont.)

D | **INSPECTION OF IGNITION SWITCH CIRCUIT**

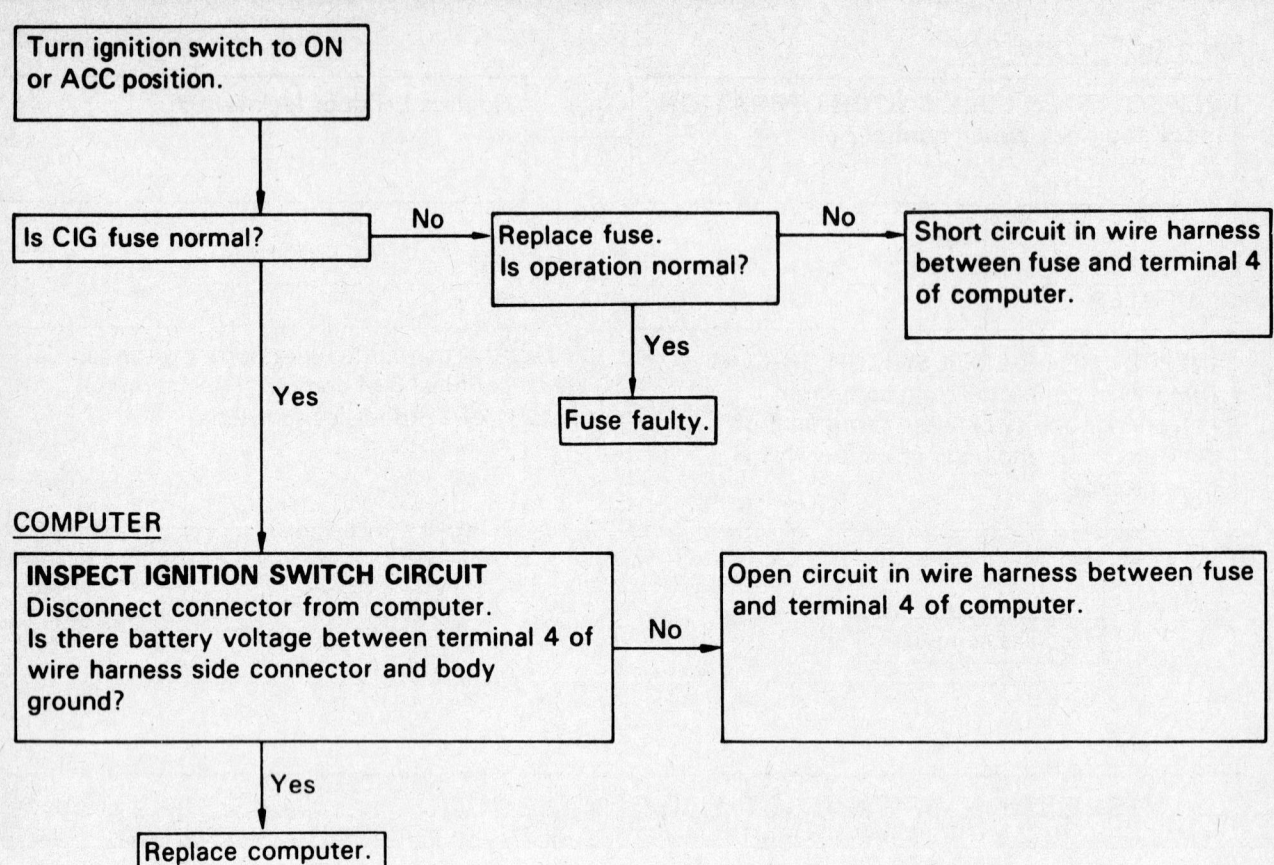

COMPUTER

E	INSPECTION OF LH KEY UNLOCK SWITCH CIRCUIT

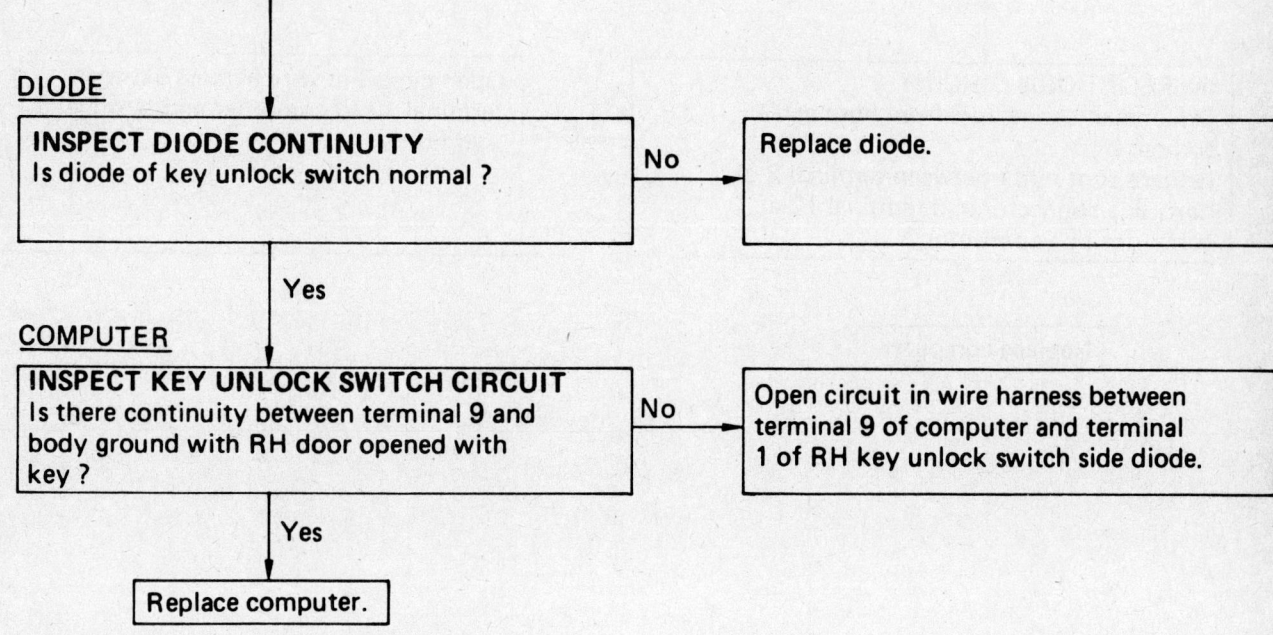

Turn ignition switch off.

DIODE

INSPECT DIODE CONTINUITY
Is diode of key unlock switch normal ?

→ No → Replace diode.

↓ Yes

COMPUTER

INSPECT KEY UNLOCK SWITCH CIRCUIT
Is there continuity between terminal 9 and
body ground with LH door opened with key ?

→ No → Open circuit in wire harness between
terminal 9 of computer and terminal
1 of LH key unlock switch side diode.

↓ Yes

Replace computer.

F	INSPECTION OF RH KEY UNLOCK SWITCH CIRCUIT

Turn ignition switch off.

DIODE

INSPECT DIODE CONTINUITY
Is diode of key unlock switch normal ?

→ No → Replace diode.

↓ Yes

COMPUTER

INSPECT KEY UNLOCK SWITCH CIRCUIT
Is there continuity between terminal 9 and
body ground with RH door opened with
key ?

→ No → Open circuit in wire harness between
terminal 9 of computer and terminal
1 of RH key unlock switch side diode.

↓ Yes

Replace computer.

Troubleshooting the theft deterrent system (cont.)

| G | **INSPECTION OF THEFT DETERRENT HORN CIRCUIT** |

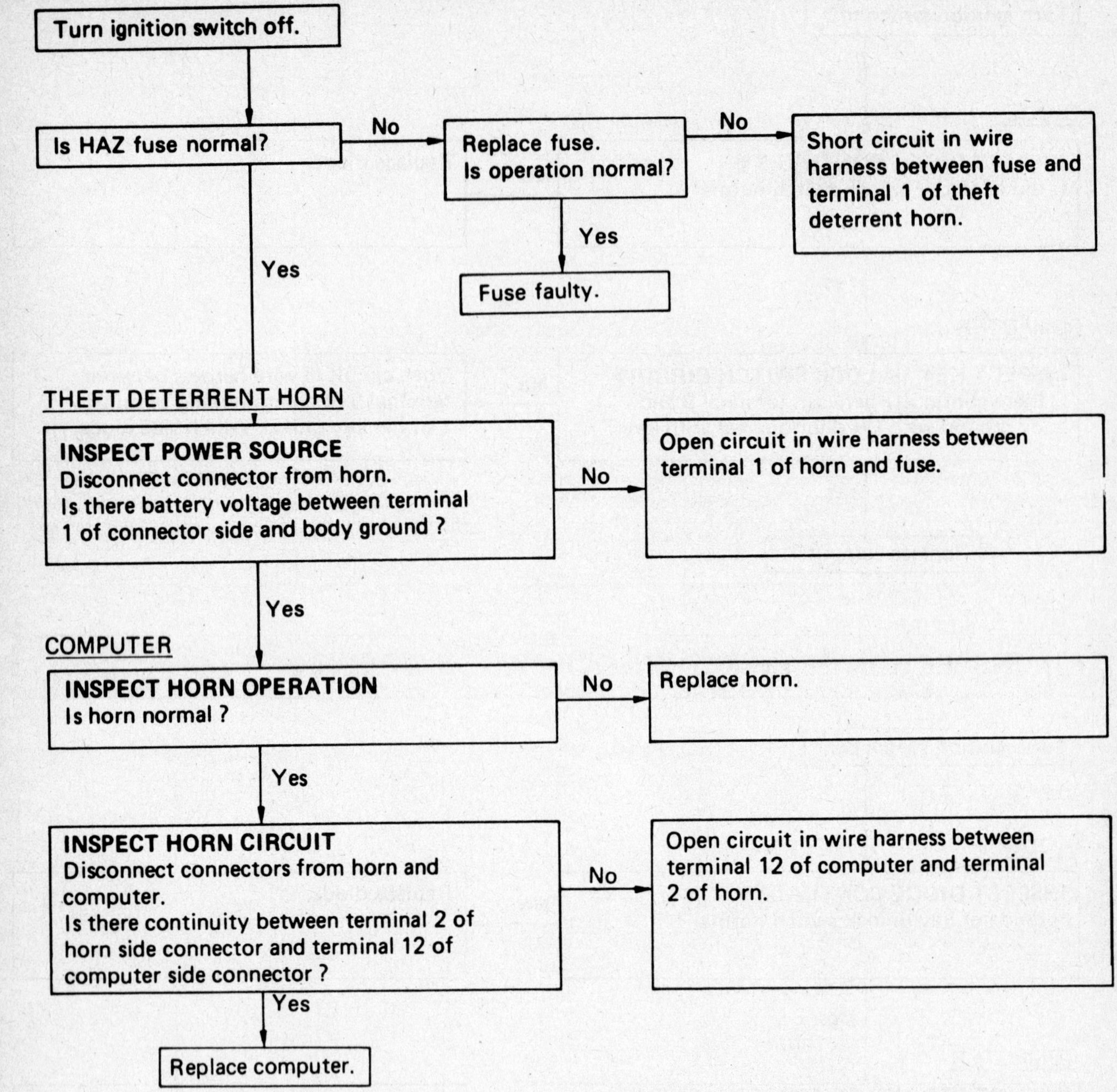

Turn ignition switch off.

Is HAZ fuse normal? —No→ Replace fuse. Is operation normal? —No→ Short circuit in wire harness between fuse and terminal 1 of theft deterrent horn.

Yes↓ (from Replace fuse) → Fuse faulty.

Yes

THEFT DETERRENT HORN

INSPECT POWER SOURCE
Disconnect connector from horn.
Is there battery voltage between terminal 1 of connector side and body ground ? —No→ Open circuit in wire harness between terminal 1 of horn and fuse.

Yes

COMPUTER

INSPECT HORN OPERATION
Is horn normal ? —No→ Replace horn.

Yes

INSPECT HORN CIRCUIT
Disconnect connectors from horn and computer.
Is there continuity between terminal 2 of horn side connector and terminal 12 of computer side connector ? —No→ Open circuit in wire harness between terminal 12 of computer and terminal 2 of horn.

Yes

Replace computer.

Troubleshooting the theft deterrent system (cont.)

1526

| H | **INSPECTION OF LIGHT CONTROL RELAY CIRCUIT** |

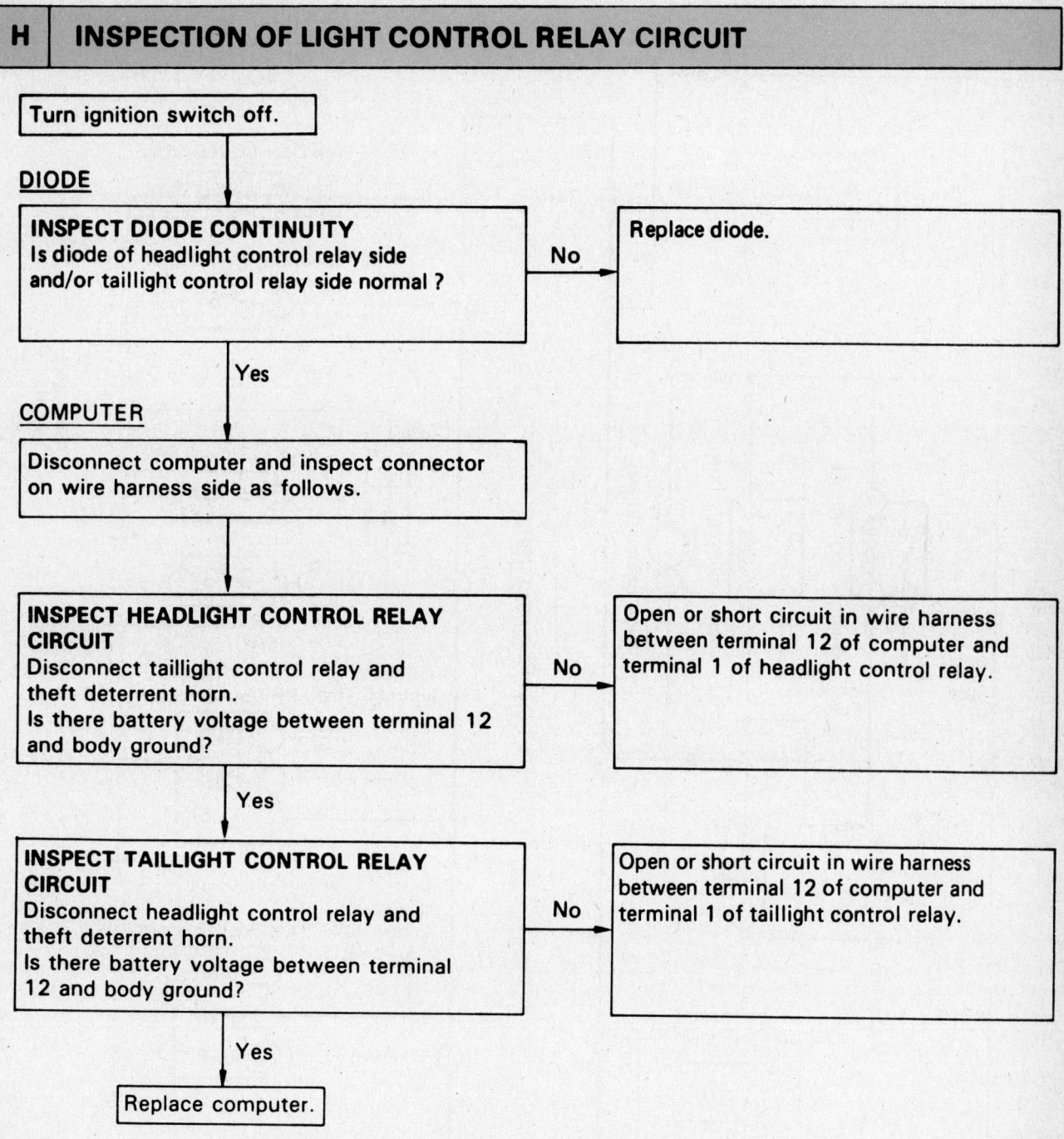

Turn ignition switch off.

DIODE

INSPECT DIODE CONTINUITY
Is diode of headlight control relay side and/or taillight control relay side normal ? — No → Replace diode.

↓ Yes

COMPUTER

Disconnect computer and inspect connector on wire harness side as follows.

↓

INSPECT HEADLIGHT CONTROL RELAY CIRCUIT
Disconnect taillight control relay and theft deterrent horn.
Is there battery voltage between terminal 12 and body ground? — No → Open or short circuit in wire harness between terminal 12 of computer and terminal 1 of headlight control relay.

↓ Yes

INSPECT TAILLIGHT CONTROL RELAY CIRCUIT
Disconnect headlight control relay and theft deterrent horn.
Is there battery voltage between terminal 12 and body ground? — No → Open or short circuit in wire harness between terminal 12 of computer and terminal 1 of taillight control relay.

↓ Yes

Replace computer.

Troubleshooting the theft deterrent system (cont.)

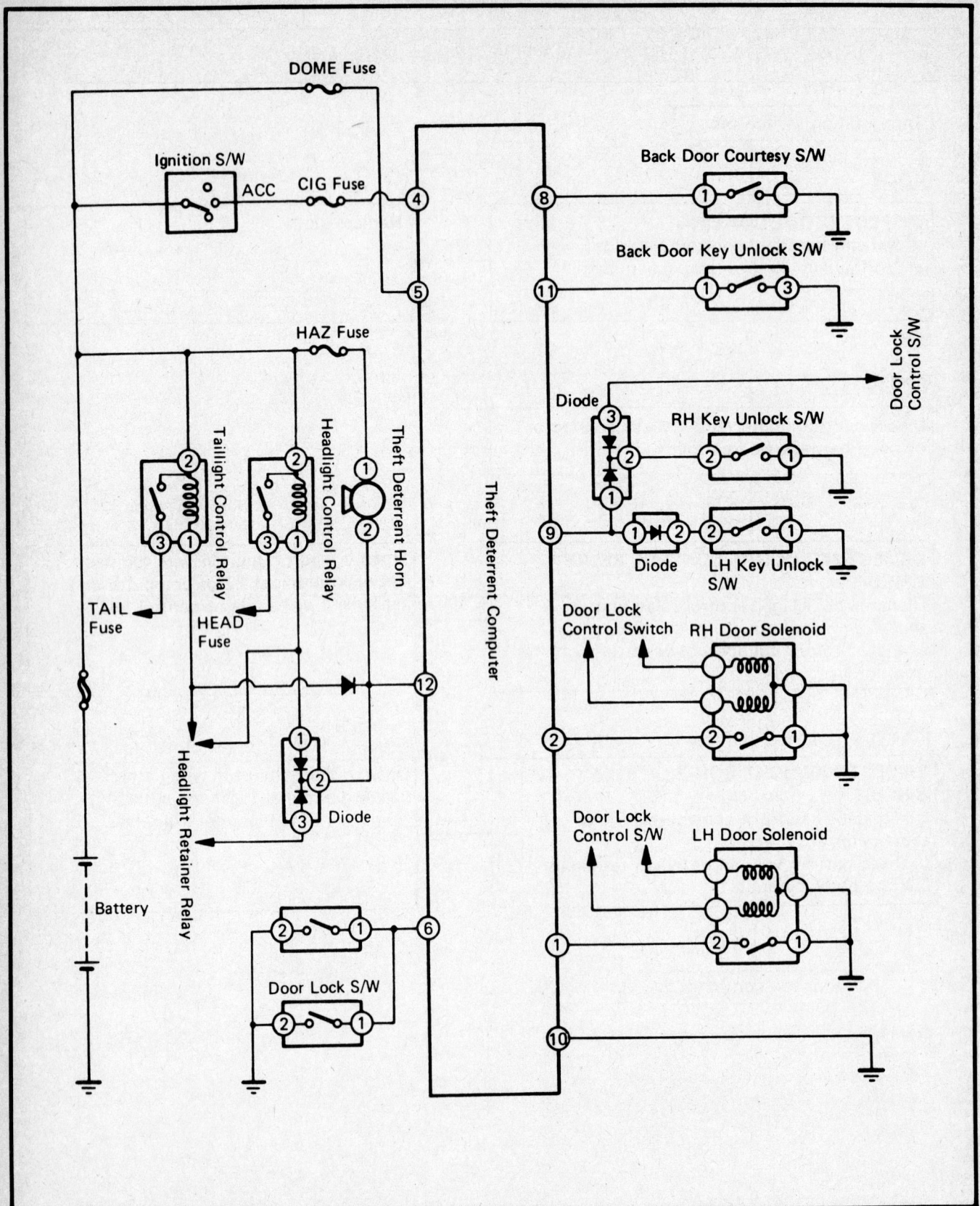

Theft deterrent wiring diagram—Celica Supra

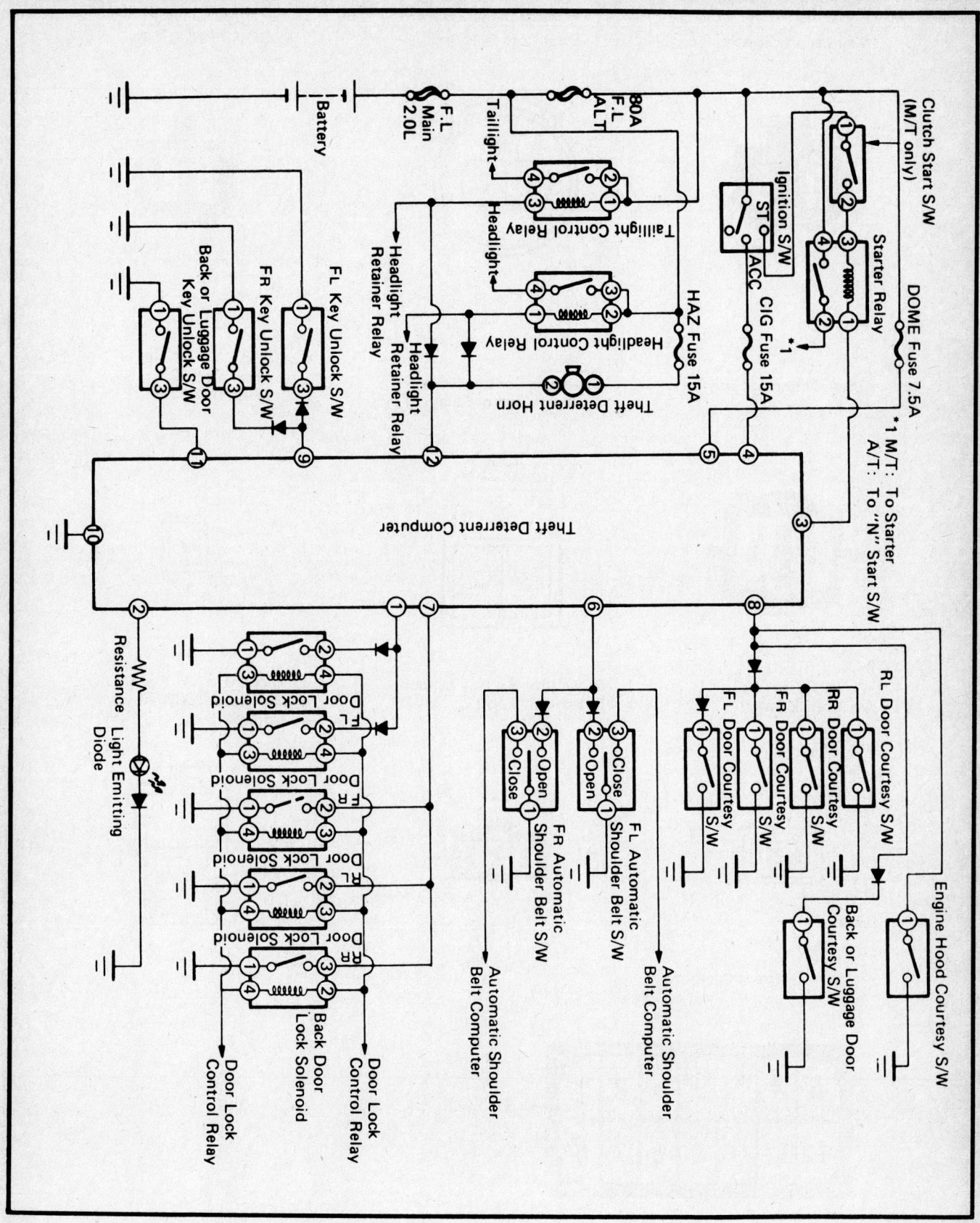

Theft deterrent wiring diagram—Cressida

Key Unlock Switch

Door Lock Solenoid

Door Lock Switch

Theft Deterrent Horn

Headlight Control Relay
Taillight Control Relay

Back Door Courtesy
Switch

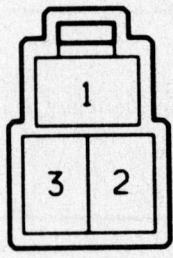

Back Door Key
Unlock Switch

Diode (For RH Key Unlock
Switch and Horn)

Diode (For LH Key Unlock
Switch and Taillight
Control Relay)

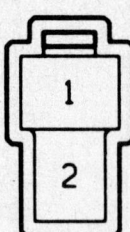

Theft Deterrent Computer

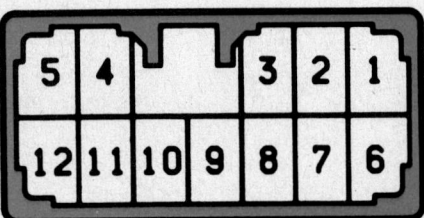

Theft deterrent connectors and terminal identification—Celica Supra

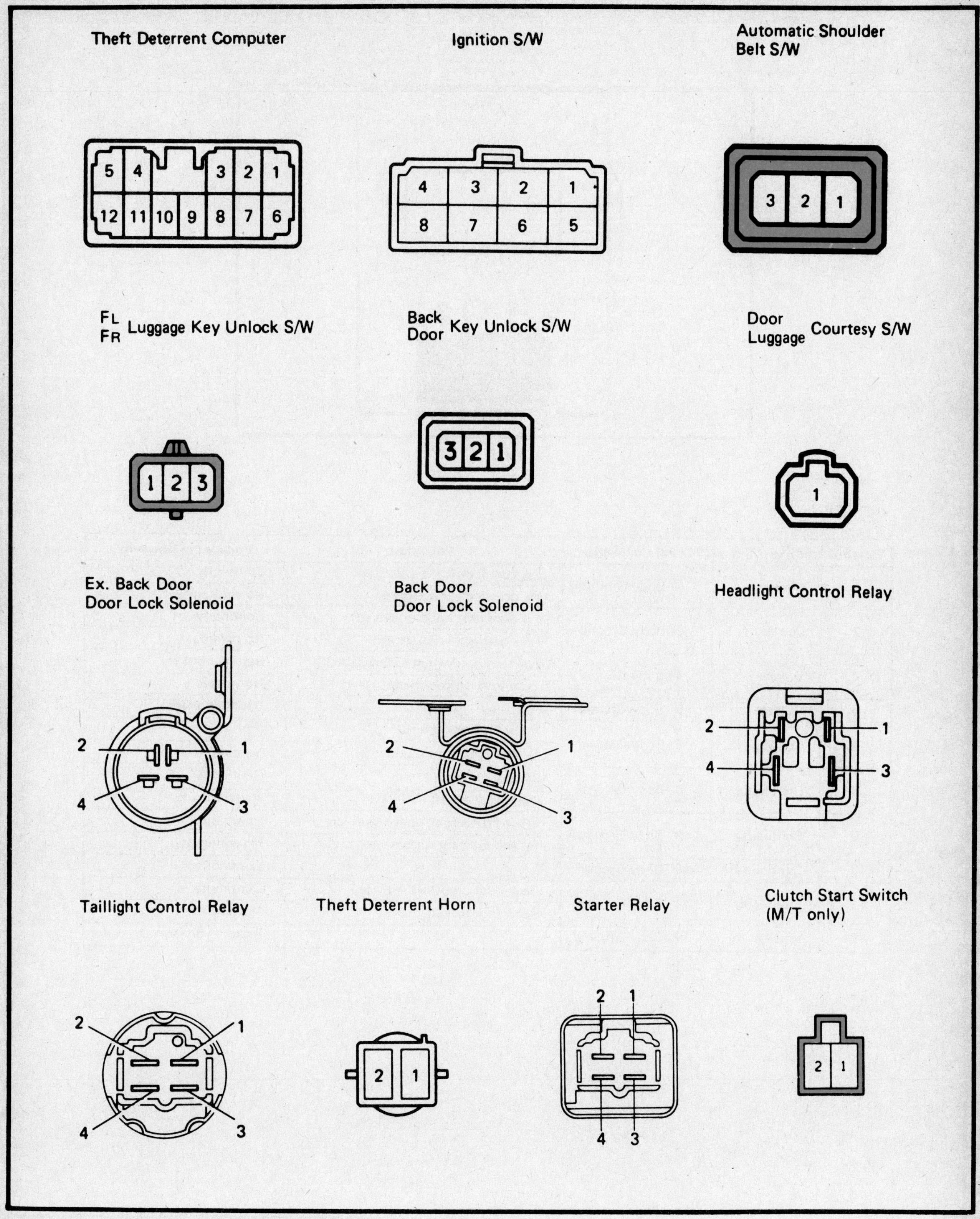

Theft Deterrent Computer
5 4 3 2 1
12 11 10 9 8 7 6
Ignition S/W
4 3 2 1
8 7 6 5
Automatic Shoulder Belt S/W
3 2 1
FL FR Luggage Key Unlock S/W
1 2 3
Back Door Key Unlock S/W
3 2 1
Door Luggage Courtesy S/W
1
Ex. Back Door Door Lock Solenoid
2 1 4 3
Back Door Door Lock Solenoid
2 1 4 3
Headlight Control Relay
2 1 4 3
Taillight Control Relay
2 1 4 3
Theft Deterrent Horn
2 1
Starter Relay
2 1 4 3
Clutch Start Switch (M/T only)
2 1

Theft deterrent connectors and terminal identification—Cressida

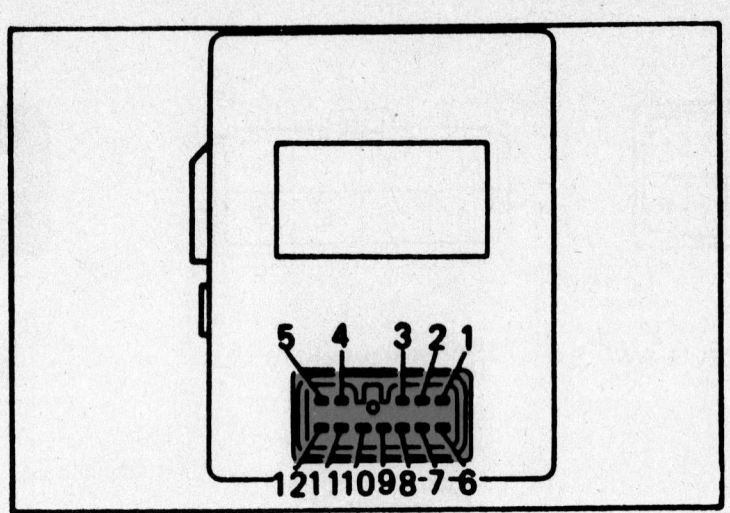

Terminal	Check Item	Tester Connection	Condition	Voltage or Continuity
1	Continuity	1 – Body Ground	F_L door lock knob unlocked	Continuity
			F_L door lock knob locked	No continuity
2	Continuity	2 – Body Ground	F_R door lock knob unlocked	Continuity
			F_R door lock knob locked	No continuity
4	Voltage	4 – Body Ground	Turn ignition switch to ON or ACC	Battery voltage
			Turn ignition switch off	No voltage
5	Voltage	5 – Body Ground	–	Battery voltage
6	Continuity	6 – Body Ground	F_L or F_R door opened	Continuity
			F_L and F_R door closed	No continuity
8	Continuity	8 – Body Ground	Back door opened	Continuity
			Back door closed	No continuity
9	Continuity	9 – Body Ground	F_L or F_R door unlocked with key	Continuity
			F_L and F_R door locked with key	No continuity
10	Continuity	10 – Body Ground	–	Continuity
11	Continuity	11 – Body Ground	Back door unlocked with key	Continuity
			Back door locked	No continuity
12	Voltage	12 – Body Ground	–	Battery voltage

Testing the theft deterrent computer

VOLKSWAGEN

Power Mirror

The power remote mirrors are adjusted from the interior of the car by moving the outside mirror switch in the desired position. Each mirror has two reversible motors. One to adjust the mirror view up and the other to adjust the mirror view right and left.

The driver operates the Up-Down and Left-Right switch that controls the polarity of the voltage to the motors. The mirror select switch directs these control voltages to either the right or left outside mirror.

Some models incorporate a heating system in the power mirror. This heating system for the power mirrors is tied in with the rear window defogger. When the rear window defogger switch is energized, the base of the power mirror heats up through a ground lead soldered which is soldered to the mirror base.

POWER MIRROR ASSEMBLY

Removal and Installation

1. Disconnect the negative battery cable. Remove the power mirror switch from the door trim panel.
2. Remove the door trim panel and loosen the plastic liner in the area of the electrical connectors.
3. Pull the two power mirror wiring harness clips off and remove the power mirror retaining bolt finish cover.
4. Remove the three mirror retaining screws and remove the power mirror assembly from the door.
5. Installation is the reverse order of the removal procedure.

POWER HEATED MIRROR ASSEMBLY

Removal and Installation

1. Disconnect the negative battery cable. Located the mirror detent adjustment hole in the mirror housing. Insert a suitable tool turn the detent counterclockwise.
2. Remove the mirror lens and electrical wires. Remove the four retaining screws in the middle of the mirror housing.
3. Remove the mirror adjustment motor and disconnect the electrical wires. Carefully pull the mirror switch out of the door panel.
3. Unplug the switch electrical connector. Remove the door trim panel and then remove the protective plastic cover from the door near the mirror wire connectors.
4. Disconnect all electrical connection and remove all mirror retaining screws, remove the mirror assembly from the door.
5. Installation is the reverse order of the removal procedure.

POWER MIRROR MOTOR ASSEMBLY

Removal and Installation

1. Located the slot on the underside of the mirror housing. Press inward at the bottom of the mirror lens. Insert a suitable tool through the slot and into the notch in the plastic lock ring behind the glass lens.
2. Hold the mirror and turn the lock ring counterclockwise, unplug the electrical leads and rome the mirror lens from the housing.
3. Remove the four motor clutch assembly retaining screws and remove the motor assembly from the mirror housing.
4. Installation is the reverse order of the removal procedure.

Vanagon

POWER SLIDING DOOR LOCK MOTOR

Starting in March of 1986 power door locks are available for the Vanagon vehicles.

Removal and Installation

1. Disconnect the negative battery cable. Remove the sliding door inner trim panel.
2. Pull off the plastic moisture barrier as necessary. Disconnect the electrical connectors from the power lock motor.
3. Remove the two power lock motor retaining screws and remove the power lock motor assembly.
4. Installation is the reverse order of the removal procedure.

REAR LID DOOR LOCK MOTOR

1. Disconnect the negative battery cable. Remove the rear lid door inner trim panel.
2. Pull off the plastic moisture barrier as necessary. Disconnect the electrical connectors from the power lock motor.
3. Remove the sheet metal retaining screws from the motor assembly. Remove the motor assembly from the door.
4. Installation is the reverse order of the removal procedure.

Rear Window Defogger

The rear window defogger system consists of a rear window with two vertical bus bars and a series of electrically connected grid lines baked on the inside surface. A control switch and a timer relay combined into a single assembly is used on all models.

REAR DEFOGGER GRID

Test

When a grid is inoperable due to an open circuit, the area of glass normally cleared by that grid will remained fogged or iced until cleared by the adjacent grids. Use the following procedure to located a broken grid.

1. With the engine running at idle, place the rear defogger switch in the "ON" position. The pilot lamp is the switch lever should light up indicating the defogger is operating (if so equipped).
2. Using a 12 volt voltmeter, connect the positive lead of the voltmeter to the hot side of the vertical bus element on the inside surface of the glass.
3. Connect the negative lead of the voltmeter to the ground side of the bus element. The voltage drop indicated on the meter should be 10 volts. Connect the negative lead of the voltmeter to a good ground, the meter reading should stay constant.
4. Keep the negative lead connected to the ground and carefully use the positive lead to contact each grid at the approximate centerline of the window. A voltage drop of approximately 5 volts, indicates a good grid or a closed circuit.
5. No voltage indicated a broken grid wire. To located the exact location of the break, move the voltmeter lead along the grid wire. The voltage should decrease gradually. if the voltage drops suddenly, there is a break at that location.

Defogger Grid Repair

1. Clean the faulty portion of the grid line with a thinner or eythyl alcohol.

2. Apply tape to either side of the faulty portion, leaving the broken grid wire exposed.

3. Use a small paint brush or drafting pen to apply a suitable conductive silver composition to the break, slightly overlap the existing grid wire on both sides (0.20 in.) of the break.

4. Completely dry the repaired section by letting it stand (at a temperature of 68°F) for 24 hours. The drying process can be 30 minutes if a hot air gun (at a temperature of 140°F) is used.

If the heat gun is used it should be held at a distance of 1.2 in. of the grid wire.

――――――― **CAUTION** ―――――――
Do not use the rear window defogger until the repaired section is completely dried. Do not use gasoline or other cleaning solvents to clean the damaged section of the grid line.

629.28 CHI

Chilton's chassis
 electronics service manual